THE ENCYCLOPAEDIA OF ISLAM

THE ENCYCLOPAEDIA OF ISLAM

NEW EDITION

PREPARED BY A NUMBER OF
LEADING ORIENTALISTS

EDITED BY

.E. BOSWORTH, E. VAN DONZEL, W.P. HEINRICHS AND G. LECOMTE

ASSISTED BY P.J. BEARMAN AND MME S. NURIT

UNDER THE PATRONAGE OF
THE INTERNATIONAL UNION OF ACADEMIES

VOLUME VIII

NED — SAM

LEIDEN
E.J. BRILL
1995

The preparation of this volume of the Encyclopaedia of Islam was made possible in part through grants from the Research Tools Program of the National Endowment for the Humanities, an independent Federal Agency of the United States Government; the British Academy; the Oriental Institute, Leiden; Académie des Inscriptions et Belles-Lettres; and the Royal Netherlands Academy of Sciences.

The articles in this volume were published in double fascicules of 128 pages, the dates of publication being:

1993: Fascs. 131-136, pp. 1-384

1994: Fascs. 137-142, pp. 385-768

1995: Fascs. 143-146, pp. 769-1056

ISBN 90 04 09834 8

PRINTED IN THE NETHERLANDS

AUTHORS OF ARTICLES IN THIS VOLUME

For the benefit of readers who may wish to follow up an individual contributor's articles, the Editors have decided to list after each contributor's name the pages on which his signature appears. Academic but not other addresses are given (for a retired scholar, the place of his last known academic appointment).

In this list, names in square brackets are those of authors of articles reprinted or revised from the first edition of this Encyclopaedia or from the *Shorter Encyclopaedia of Islam*. An asterisk after the name of the author in the text denotes an article reprinted from the first edition which has been brought up to date by the Editorial Committee; where an article has been revised by a second author his name appears within square brackets after the name of the original author.

Feroz Ahmad, University of Massachusetts. 511
Hamid Algar, University of California, Berkeley. 48, 117, 136, 704
[J. Allan, London]. 239, 267, 288, 289, 726
R. Amitai-Preiss, Hebrew University, Jerusalem. 759
Barbara Watson Andaya, University of Hawaii at Manoa. 295
P.A. Andrews, University of Cologne. 270
Ghaus Ansari, University of Vienna. 32
Sarah Ansari, University of London. 244
A. Arazi, Hebrew University, Jerusalem. 539, 885
[A.J. Arberry, Cambridge]. 14
A. Arioli, University of Rome. 389
R. Arnaldez, University of Paris. 25, 588, 667
M. Athar Ali, Aligarh Muslim University. 371, 573, 751
[A.S. Atiya, Salt Lake City]. 36, 325, 351
A. Ayalon, Tel Aviv University. 813
Ramzi Baalbaki, American University of Beirut. 821
[F. Babinger, Munich]. 1, 3, 8, 9, 36, 43, 62, 65, 110, 172, 190, 296, 308, 317, 391, 393, 419, 422
T. Bachrouch, University of Tunis. 764
Roswitha Badry, University of Freiburg. 333
[T.G. Bailey]. 23
[F. Bajraktarević]. 85, 279, 285, 322
Mohammad al-Bakhit, Al al-Bayt University, Amman. 385, 883, 1000
Çiğdem Balim, University of Manchester. 168, 170, 175, 177, 179, 484, 670, 818, 838, 1044
R.B. Barnett, University of Virginia, Charlottesville. 793
[Th. Bauer]. 1042
A.F.L. Beeston, University of Oxford. 665
M.A.J. Beg, University of Brunei. 672, 871, 892
Doris Behrens-Abouseif, University of Freiburg/Breisgau. 344, 683
[A. Bel]. 654
Afif Ben Abdesselem, University of Tunis. 738
Omar Bencheikh, Centre National de la Recherche Scientifique, Paris. 15
M. Bencheneb, Algiers. 693
R. Bencheneb, Paris. 127
H. Ben-Shammay, Hebrew University, Jerusalem. 539
[E. Berthels]. 44, 48, 68, 81, 478
Th. Bianquis, University of Lyons. 396, 654
J. Bisson, University of Tours. 850
W. Björkman, Uppsala. 481
J.R. Blackburn, University of Toronto. 185, 236, 521
Sheila S. Blair, Richmond, New Hampshire. 383
F.C. de Blois, Royal Asiatic Society, London. 445, 586, 675, 683, 972
[Tj. de Boer, Amsterdam]. 123
H. Boeschoten, University of Tilburg. 893
P.N. Boratav, Centre National de la Recherche Scientifique, Paris. 179, 232, 271
C.E. Bosworth, University of Manchester. 12, 24, 64, 67, 73, 76, 82, 110, 127, 149, 154, 155, 161, 163, 174, 175, 178, 191, 231, 235, 236, 237, 239, 245, 259, 278, 288, 300, 303, 306, 309, 312, 313, 373, 381, 385, 386, 393, 403, 404, 417, 450, 453, 460, 463, 469, 470, 473, 519, 526, 568, 586, 587, 591, 595, 598, 606, 607, 618, 630, 636, 652, 661, 670, 679, 694, 695, 701, 746, 749, 794, 798, 807, 808, 809, 811, 830, 842, 853, 860, 869, 879, 895, 918, 924, 959, 973, 979, 997, 999, 1029, 1034, 1041, 1043, 1050
G. Böwering, Yale University, New Haven, Conn. 841
Mary Boyce, University of London. 343
Jean Boyd, Penrith, Cumbria. 35
F. Braemer, Centre National de la Recherche Scientifique, Paris. 757
Barbara Brend, London. 453
J.T.P. de Bruijn, University of Leiden. 84, 134, 272, 423, 532, 637, 685, 777, 1012
Kathleen Burrill, Columbia University, NJ. 490
J. Burton, University of St. Andrews. 362
J. Burton-Page, Church Knowle, Dorset. 48, 64, 121, 252
Y. Callot, University of Tours. 481, 838, 847
J. Calmard, Centre National de la Recherche Scientifique, Paris. 748, 750, 756
Sheila R. Canby, British Museum, London. 510, 514
J. Carswell, Sotheby's, London. 226
M.G. Carter, New York University. 668, 836
J. Chabbi, University of Paris. 506
C. Chaline, University of Paris. 548
H. Chaouch, University of Tunis. 858
Mounira Chapoutot-Remadi, Institut français d'Etudes arabes, Damas. 160, 1001
E. Chaumont, University of Aix-Marseille. 900
the late J. Chelhod, Paris. 362, 654
P. Chelkowski, New York University. 81, 465
M. Chenoufi, University of Tunis. 402
W.C. Chittick, State University of New York, Stony Brook. 755, 861, 1024
M. Chodkiewicz, Ecole des Hautes Etudes en Sciences Sociales, Paris. 594
Y.M. Choueiri, University of Exeter. 49
V. Christides, University of Ioannina, Athens. 90
J. Couland, University of Paris. 26
Stephanie Cronin, London. 1051
Yolande Crowe, London. 1031, 1038
F. Dachraoui, University of Tunis. 118
F. Daftary, Institute of Ismaili Studies, London. 134, 443, 599, 923
H. Daiber, Free University, Amsterdam. 649, 660
M. van Damme, University of Utrecht. 350
J. Danecki, University of Warsaw. 573
R.E. Darley-Doran, Winchester. 231, 793, 974, 978
G. Dávid, Budapest. 292, 302
[C.C. Davies, Oxford]. 125, 245, 254, 258, 271, 368, 383, 426
R. Davis, Ohio State University, Columbus. 723

R. Deladrière, University of Lyons. 547
F.M. Denny, University of Colorado, Boulder. 299
W.B. Denny, University of Massachusetts, Amherst. 224
Sylvie Denoix, University of Aix-en-Provence. 861
[J. Deny, Paris]. 281, 282, 371, 483, 529, 531, 566
A. Dietrich, University of Göttingen. 37, 112, 687, 693, 707, 732, 1043
S. Digby, Rozel, Jersey. 1050
Christine Dobbin, Australian National University, Canberra. 238
G. Doerfer, University of Göttingen. 583
E. van Donzel, Leiden. 830, 850
H.J. Drossaart Lulofs, University of Amsterdam. 37
J. During, University of Strasbourg. 1019
H. Eisenstein, University of Vienna. 4, 1024
D.S. El Alami, Leicester. 708
Nadia El Cheikh, American University of Beirut. 602
N. Elisséeff, University of Lyons. 133, 817
W. Ende, University of Freiburg im Breisgau. 448, 909
G. Endress, University of Bochum. 859
C. Ernst, University of North Carolina, Chapel Hill. 652
T. Fahd, University of Strasbourg. 52, 65, 97, 108, 155, 350, 381, 562, 601, 647, 678, 705, 706, 728, 734, 830, 889
[H.G. Farmer, Glasgow]. 348
Suraiya Faroqhi, University of Munich. 12, 210, 406, 489, 567, 593, 1054
P.-B. Fenton, University of Strasbourg. 662
Halima Ferhat, University of Rabat. 691, 899
Maribel Fierro, C.S.I.C., Madrid. 480, 574, 636, 708, 819
H.J. Fisher, University of London. 17
J. Flanagan, Somerville, Mass. 615
J. Fontaine, Institut des Belles Lettres Arabes, Tunis. 471, 693
M. Forcada, University of Barcelona. 527
C.H. de Fouchecour, University of Paris. 580
G.S.P. Freeman-Grenville, Sheriff Hutton, York. 287, 292, 564, 857
M. Gaborieau, Centre National de la Recherche Scientifique, Paris. 6
J.C. Garcin, University of Aix-en-Provence. 866
Teresa Garulo, University of Madrid. 407, 633
G.J.H. van Gelder, University of Groningen. 997
A. Ghédira, University of Lyons. 835
[H.A.R. Gibb, Harvard]. 83
A. Giladi, University of Haifa. 827
D. Gimaret, Ecole Pratique des Hautes Etudes, Paris. 363, 399, 649, 881, 918
M. Glünz, University of Washington, Seattle. 998
F. Müge Göçek, University of Michigan. 3
P.B. Golden, Rutgers University, Newark, New Jersey. 291, 629, 878, 898
L.E. Goodman, Vanderbilt University, Nashville. 477
G. Goodwin, London. 223
A.H. de Groot, University of Leiden. 124, 288, 480, 994
M. Guettat, Institut Supérieur de Musique, Tunis. 449
P. Guichard, University of Lyons. 834, 881
J.G.J. ter Haar, University of Leiden. 596
U. Haarmann, University of Kiel. 895
C.-P. Haase, University of Kiel. 631
[T.W. Haig, London]. 833, 925
W. Hale, University of London. 168, 174
Margaret Hall, London. 742
H. Halm, University of Tübingen. 148, 438, 468, 683, 998, 1047
Talat Said Halman, New York University. 172
G.R.G. Hambly, University of Texas, Dallas. 514
W.L. Hanaway, University of Pennsylvania, Philadelphia. 801, 885
S. Nomanul Haq, Cambridge, Mass. 597
[W. Hartner, Frankfurt]. 122
L.P. Harvey, University of London. 272
A. Havemann, Free University, Berlin. 403
G.R. Hawting, University of London. 466, 697
J.A. Haywood, Lewes, East Sussex. 154, 334
P. Heath, Washington University, St. Louis. 921
A. Heinen, Pontifical Istituto Orientale, Rome. 1018
W.P. Heinrichs, Harvard University. 370, 379, 383, 428, 578, 668, 734, 748, 805, 819, 831, 856, 894, 990, 1008
[B. Heller, Budapest]. 109, 397
G. Herrmann, University of Göttingen. 277
[M. Hidayet Hosain]. 67, 124
the late D.R. Hill, Great Brookham, Surrey. 656
[S. Hillelson]. 89
Carole Hillenbrand, University of Edinburgh. 133, 440, 461, 705
R. Hillenbrand, University of Edinburgh. 964
J.R. Hinnells, University of London. 275
the late M. Hiskett, London. 23, 357
M.C. Hoadley, Lund University. 284
Birgit Hoffmann, University of Bamberg. 343
P.M. Holt, Oxford. 171
[E. Honigmann]. 112, 114, 424, 435, 528, 671
M.B. Hooker, Australian National University, Canberra. 483
Virginia Matheson Hooker, Australian National University, Canberra. 286, 491, 668, 1042
D. Hopwood, University of Oxford. 718
J. Huehnergard, Harvard University. 1011
F.R. Hunter, Tulane University. 93
J.O. Hunwick, Northwestern University, Evanston, Illinois. 719
C.H. Imber, University of Manchester. 182, 831
Halil İnalcik, Bilkent University, Ankara. 487, 611, 612
M. Ipşirli, University of Istanbul. 843
Riazul Islam, University of Karachi. 1048
Mawil Y. Izzi Dien, University of Wales, Lampeter. 667, 718, 818, 842
S.A. Jackson, Indiana University, Bloomington, Indiana. 991
Renate Jacobi, University of the Saar, Saarbrücken. 398, 467, 919
[B. Joel]. 756
G.H.A. Juynboll, The Hague. 385, 421, 519, 820, 836, 857, 984
O. Kahl, Frankfurt am Main. 417, 694
Kemal Karpat, University of Wisconsin, Madison. 138, 144
A.S. Kaye, California State University, Fullerton. 92
B. Kellner-Heinkele, Free University, Berlin. 833
H. Kennedy, University of St. Andrews. 985
J. Kenny, University of Ibadan. 232
[R.A. Kern, Leiden]. 279, 333, 433
R.G. Khoury, University of Heidelberg. 265, 409, 478
M. Kiel, University of Munich. 11, 168, 170, 188, 312, 320, 341
[H. Kindermann, Cologne]. 354
D.A. King, University of Frankfurt. 575, 650, 872, 1056
G.R.D. King, University of London. 85, 436, 437, 577, 614
M.J. Kister, Hebrew University, Jerusalem. 375

A. Rouaud, Centre National de la Recherche Scientifique, Paris. 162, 178, 438
E.K. Rowson, University of Pennsylvania, Philadelphia. 390
U. Rubin, Tel Aviv University. 125, 657
[J. Ruska, Heidelberg]. 149
P.C. Sadgrove, University of Manchester. 920, 993
T. Saguchi, Kanazawa. 51, 924
R.M. Savory, University of Toronto. 753, 774, 801
A. Savvides, Centre for Byzantine Studies, Athens. 266, 335
Ayman F. Sayyid, The Egyptian National Library, Cairo. 832, 1031
[J. Schacht, New York]. 29, 400, 493
Annemarie Schimmel, Bonn. 140, 416, 663
Barbara von Schlegell, University of California, Berkeley. 732
J. Schmidt, University of Manchester. 509
[C. Schoy]. 842
R. Schulze, University of Bamberg. 361, 701
O. Schumann, University of Hamburg. 245
R. Sellheim, University of Frankfurt. 739, 740, 1020, 1025
C. Shackle, University of London. 257
[Moḥammad Shafīʿ, Lahore]. 386, 459
R. Shaham, Hebrew University, Jerusalem. 32
Ahmed al-Shahi, University of Newcastle-upon-Tyne. 93
Irfan Shahîd, Georgetown University, Washington, D.C. 120, 982
Audrey C. Shalinsky, University of Wyoming. 234
P. Shinar, Hebrew University, Jerusalem. 671, 765, 795, 906
M.Y. Siddiq, Islamic University Kushtia, Bangladesh. 594
Elizabeth M. Sirriyeh, University of Leeds. 439, 669
P. Sluglett, University of Utah. 143, 446
G.R. Smith, University of Manchester. 97, 454, 457, 566, 636, 706, 914, 1002
Priscilla P. Soucek, New York University. 183, 887
S. Soucek, Princeton, New Jersey. 173, 183, 236, 309, 403, 571, 892
M. Souissi, University of Tunis. 728
J.-F. Staszak, University of Paris. 87
K.A. Steenbrink, University of Leiden. 295
J. Stewart-Robinson, University of Michigan, Ann Arbor. 991
A.J. Stockwell, University of London. 276
W. Stoetzer, University of Leiden. 421, 585
[M. Streck]. 51
Jacqueline Sublet, Centre National de la Recherche Scientifique, Paris. 56
Viviane Sukanda-Tessier, Ecole français d'Extrême Orient, Djakarta. 154
M. Talbi, University of Tunis. 466, 640, 688, 689, 845

I. Talbot, Coventry Polytechnic. 255
Gönül Alpay Tekin, Harvard University. 214, 3
544, 549
D. Thomas, Selly Oaks Colleges, Birmingham. 9
J. Tolan, Stanford University. 302
Tevfik Rüştü Topuzoğlu, University of Istanbul
R. Traini, University of Rome. 613
J.-L. Triaud, Ecole des Hautes Etudes en Scien Sociales, Paris. 1049
J.F. Troin, University of Tours. 508
G. Troupeau, Ecole Pratique des Hautes Etud Paris. 121, 344, 349, 384, 696
C.P. Turner, University of Edinburgh. 751
M. Ullmann, University of Tübingen. 378, 589
[V. Vacca, Rome]. 739
I. Vásáry, Ankara. 86
Odile Verberkmoes, Wijk bij Duurstede. 407
R. Vernet, Centre National de la Recherche Scie tifique, Paris. 848
Chantal de La Véronne, Institut National Langues et Civilisations Orientales, Paris. 726, 9
J. Vignet-Zunz, Centre National de la Recherc Scientifique, Aix-en-Provence. 523
M.J. Viguera, University of Madrid. 814
F. Viré, Centre National de la Recherche Scienti que, Paris. 50, 111, 1007, 1023
F.E. Vogel, Harvard University. 936
D. Waines, University of Lancaster. 653, 1048
[J. Walker]. 139
D.J. Wasserstein, Tel Aviv University. 479
W. Montgomery Watt, University of Edinburg 595, 697, 698
O. Weintritt, University of Freiburg. 465
R. Weipert, University of Munich. 401
A. Welch, University of Victoria. 789
[A.J. Wensinck, Leiden]. 67, 397, 455, 459, 68 765, 1056
[E. Wiedemann, Erlangen]. 842
J.C. Wilkinson, University of Oxford. 993
A. Wink, University of Wisconsin, Madison. 28 301, 342, 572
J.J. Witkam, University of Leiden. 153, 410
[F. Wittek, London]. 16
R. Wixman, University of Oregon, Eugene. 643
M. Woidich, University of Amsterdam. 867
Christine Woodhead, University of Durham. 7, 164, 291, 441, 594, 641, 652
O. Wright, University of London. 853
M.E. Yapp, University of London. 283
[G. Yver, Algiers]. 685
E.A. Zachariadou, University of Crete. 177, 195
Mohsen Zakeri, University of Frankfurt. 840, 985
[K.V. Zetterstéen, Uppsala]. 119, 239, 356, 368 716
E.J. Zürcher, University of Nijmegen. 66, 486, 669 726
A. Zysow, University of Washington, Seattle. 425 716

ABBREVIATED TITLES OF SOME OF THE MOST OFTEN QUOTED WORKS

bu'l-Fidā', *Taḳwīm* = *Taḳwīm al-buldān*, ed. J.-T. Reinaud and M. de Slane, Paris 1840

bu'l-Fidā', *Taḳwīm*, tr. = *Géographie d'Aboulféda, traduite de l'arabe en français*; vol. i, ii/1 by Reinaud, Paris 1848; vol. ii/2 by St. Guyard, 1883

ghānī[1] or [2] or [3] = Abu'l-Faradj al-Iṣfahānī, *al-Aghānī*; [1]Būlāḳ 1285; [2]Cairo 1323; [3]Cairo 1345-

ghānī, Tables = *Tables alphabétiques du Kitāb al-aghānī*, rédigées par I. Guidi, Leiden 1900

ghānī, Brünnow = *The XXIst vol. of the Kitāb al-Aghānī*, ed. R.E. Brünnow, Leiden 1883

lī Djewād = *Memālik-i ʿOthmāniyyenin̄ taʾrīkh we djughrāfiyā lughāti*, Istanbul 1313-17/1895-9

lī Mubārak, *Khiṭaṭ* = ʿAlī Mubārak, *al-Khiṭaṭ al-tawfīḳiyya al-djadīda li-Miṣr al-Ḳāhira wa-mudunihā wa-bilādihā 'l-ḳadīma wa-'l-shahīra*, 20 vols., Būlāḳ 1304-6

nbārī, *Nuzha* = *Nuzhat al-alibbāʾ fī ṭabaḳāt al-udabāʾ*, [1]Cairo 1294; [2]Stockholm, etc. 1963

wfī, *Lubāb* = *Lubāb al-albāb*, ed. E.G. Browne, London-Leiden 1903-6

abinger, *GOW* = F. Babinger, *Die Geschichtsschreiber der Osmanen und ihre Werke*, 1st ed., Leiden 1927

aghdādī, *Farḳ* = *al-Farḳ bayn al-firaḳ*, ed. Muḥammad Badr, Cairo 1328/1910

alādhurī, *Futūḥ* = *Futūḥ al-buldān*, ed. M.J. de Goeje, Leiden 1866

alādhurī, *Ansāb* = Balādhurī, *Ansāb al-ashrāf*, i, ed. M. Hamid Allāh, Cairo 1960; iii, ed. ʿAbd al-ʿAzīz al-Dūri, Beirut 1978; iv A. ed. Iḥsān ʿAbbās, Beirut 1979; iv B, v. ed. M. Schlössinger and S.D.F. Goitein, Jerusalem 1936-39

arkan, *Kanunlar* = Ömer Lûtfi Barkan, *XV vc XVI inci asırlarda Osmanlı Imparatorluğunda ziraî ekonominin hukukí ve malí esasları, I. Kanunlar*, Istanbul 1943

arthold, *Four studies* = V.V. Barthold, *Four studies on the history of Central Asia*, tr. by V. and T. Minorsky, 3 vols., Leyden 1956-63

arthold, *Turkestan* = W. Barthold, *Turkestan down to the Mongol invasion*, London 1928 (GMS, N.S. V)

arthold, *Turkestan*[2] = *ibid.*, revised edition, London 1958

arthold, *Turkestan*[3] = *ibid.*, revised and enlarged ed., London 1968

achère, *HLA* = R. Blachère, *Histoire de la littérature arabe*, 3 vols., Paris 1952-64

Blois, *Persian literature* = F. de Blois, *Persian literature, a bio-bibliographical survey, begun by the late C.A. Storey*, vol. v, London 1992-

rockelmann, I, II = C. Brockelmann, *Geschichte der arabischen Literatur*, zweite den Supplementbänden angepasste Auflage, Leiden 1943-49

rockelmann, S I, II, III = *G. d. a. L.*, Erster (zweiter, dritter) Supplementband, Leiden 1937- 42

rowne, *LHP* = E.G. Browne, *A literary history of Persia*, 4 vols., London and Cambridge 1902-24

rowne, ii = *A literary history of Persia, from Firdawsi to Saʿdi*, London 1908

rowne, iii = *A history of Persian literature under Tartar Dominion*, Cambridge 1920

rowne, iv = *A history of Persian literature in modern times*, Cambridge 1924

aetani, *Annali* = L. Caetani, *Annali dell'Islam*, Milan 1905-26

Camb. hist. Iran = *The Cambridge history of Iran*, 7 vols., Cambridge 1968-91

Camb. hist. Ar. lit = *The Cambridge history of Arabic literature*, ed. A.F.L. Beeston *et alii*, 4 vols., Cambridge 1983-92

Chauvin, *Bibliographie* = V. Chauvin, *Bibliographie des ouvrages arabes et relatifs aux Arabes*, Lille 1892

Clauson, *Etymological dictionary* = Sir Gerard Clauson, *An etymological dictionary of pre-thirteenth century Turkish*, Oxford 1972

Creswell, *Bibliography* = K.A.C. Creswell, *A bibliography of the architecture, arts and crafts of Islam to 1st Jan. 1960*, Cairo 1961

Ḍabbī = *Bughyat al-multamis fī taʾrīkh ridjāl ahl al-Andalus*, ed. F. Codera and J. Ribera, Madrid 1885 (BAH III)

Damīrī = *Ḥayāt al-ḥayawān* (quoted according to titles of articles)

Dawlatshāh = *Tadhkirat al-shuʿarāʾ*, ed. E.G. Browne, London-Leiden 1901

Dhahabī, *Ḥuffāẓ* = al-Dhahabī, *Tadhkirat al-ḥuffāẓ*, 4 vols., Hyderabad 1315 H.

Dictionnaire arabe-français-anglais = *Dictionnaire arabe-français-anglais (langue classique et moderne)*, Paris 1963-

Djuwaynī = *Taʾrīkh-i Djihān-gushā*, ed. Muḥammad Ḳazwīnī, Leiden 1906-37 (GMS XVI)

Djuwaynī-Boyle = *The history of the Worldconqueror*, by ʿAṭā-Malik Djuwaynī, trans. J.A. Boyle, 2 vols., Manchester 1958

Doerfer, *Elemente* = G. Doerfer, *Türkische und mongolische Elemente im Neupersischen*, Wiesbaden 1963-

Dozy, *Notices* = R. Dozy, *Notices sur quelques manuscrits arabes*, Leiden 1847-51

Dozy, *Recherches*[3] = *Recherches sur l'histoire et la littérature de l'Espagne pendant le moyen-âge, third edition, Paris-Leiden 1881*

Dozy, Suppl. = R. Dozy, *Supplément aux dictionnaires arabes*, Leiden 1881 (anastatic reprint Leiden-Paris 1927)

EMA[1] = K.A.C. Creswell, *Early Muslim architecture*, 2 vols., Oxford 1932-40

EMA[2] = K.A.C. Creswell, *Early Muslim architecture*, 2nd ed., London 1969-

Fagnan, *Extraits* = E. Fagnan, *Extraits inédits relatifs au Maghreb*, Alger 1924

Farhang = Razmārā and Nawtāsh, *Farhang-i djughrāfiyā-yi Īrān*, Tehran 1949-1953

Firishta = Muḥammad Ḳāsim Firishta, *Gulshan-i Ibrāhīmi*, lith. Bombay 1832

Gesch. des Qor. = Th. Nöldeke, *Geschichte des Qorāns*, new edition by F. Schwally, G. Bergsträsser and O. Pretzl, 3 vols., Leipzig 1909-38

Gibb, *HOP* = E.J.W. Gibb, *A history of Ottoman poetry*, 7 vols., London 1900-9

Gibb-Bowen = H.A.R. Gibb and Harold Bowen, *Islamic society and the West*, London 1950-1957

Goldziher, *Muh. St.* = I. Goldziher, *Muhammedanische Studien*, 2 vols., Halle 1888-90

Goldziher, *Vorlesungen* = I. Goldziher, *Vorlesungen über den Islam*, Heidelberg 1910

Goldziher, *Vorlesungen*[2] = 2nd ed., Heidelberg 1925

Goldziher, *Dogme* = *Le dogme et la loi de l'Islam*, tr. F. Arin, Paris 1920

Gövsa, *Türk meshurları* = Ibrahim Alaettin Gövsa, *Türk meşhurları ansiklopedisi*, Istanbul 1946

Ḥādjdjī Khalīfa, *Djihān-nümā* = Istanbul 1145/1732

Ḥādjdjī Khalīfa = *Kashf al-ẓunūn*, ed. Ş. Yaltkaya and Kilisli Rifat Bilge, Istanbul 1941-43
Ḥādjdjī Khalīfa, ed. Flügel = *K. al-ẓ.*, Leipzig 1835-58
Ḥamd Allāh Mustawfī, *Nuzha* = *Nuzhat al-ḳulūb*, ed. G. Le Strange, Leiden 1913-19 (GMS XXIII)
Hamdānī = *Ṣifat Djazīrat al-ʿArab*, ed. D.H. Müller, Leiden 1884-91
Hammer-Purgstall, *GOR* = J. von Hammer(-Purgstall), *Geschichte des Osmanischen Reiches*, Pest 1828-35
Hammer-Purgstall, *GOR*² = the same, 2nd ed. Pest 1840
Hammer-Purgstall, *Histoire* = the same, trans. by J.J. Hellert, 18 vols., Bellizard [etc.], Paris [etc.], 1835-43
Hammer-Purgstall, *Staatsverfassung* = J. von Hammer, *Des Osmanischen Reichs Staatsverfassung und Staatsverwaltung*, 2 vols., Vienna 1815 (repr. 1963)
Houtsma, *Recueil* = M.Th. Houtsma, *Recueil des textes relatifs à l'histoire des Seldjoucides*, Leiden 1886-1902
*Ḥudūd al-ʿālam*¹ = *Ḥudūd al-ʿālam. The regions of the world*, translated by V. Minorsky, London 1937 (GMS, N.S. XI)
*Ḥudūd al-ʿālam*² = *ibid.*, 2nd revised and enlarged ed., London 1970
Ibn al-Abbār = *K. Takmilat al-Ṣila*, ed. F. Codera, Madrid 1887-89 (BHA V-VI)
Ibn al-Athīr, ed. Tornberg = Ibn al-Athīr, *al-Kāmil fi 'l-tawārīkh*, ed. C.J. Tornberg, 12 vols., Leiden 1851-76
Ibn al-Athīr, ed. Beirut = *ibid.*, Beirut, 13 vols., 1385-7/ 1965-7
Ibn al-Athīr, trad. Fagnan = *Annales du Maghreb et de l'Espagne*, tr. E. Fagnan, Algiers 1901
Ibn Bashkuwāl = *K. al-Ṣila fī akhbār aʾimmat al-Andalus*, ed. F. Codera, Madrid 1883 (BHA II)
Ibn Baṭṭūṭa = *Voyages d'Ibn Batouta*. Arabic text, ed. with Fr. tr. by C. Defrémery and B.R. Sanguinetti, 4 vols., Paris 1853-58
Ibn Baṭṭūṭa, tr. Gibb = *The travels of Ibn Battuta*, Eng. tr. H.A.R. Gibb, 3 vols., Cambridge 1958-71
Ibn al-Faḳīh = *Mukhtaṣar K. al-Buldān*, ed. M.J. De Goeje, Leiden 1886 (BGA V)
Ibn Ḥawḳal = *K. Ṣūrat al-arḍ*, ed. J.H. Kramers, Leiden 1938-39 (BGA II, 2nd edition)
Ibn Ḥawḳal-Kramers-Wiet = Ibn Hauqal, *Configuration de la terre*, trans. J.H. Kramers and G. Wiet, Beirut 1964, 2 vols.
Ibn Hishām = *Sira*, ed. F. Wüstenfeld, Göttingen 1859-60
Ibn ʿIdhārī = *K. al-Bayān al-mughrib*, ed. G.S. Colin and E. Lévi-Provençal, Leiden 1948-51; vol. iii, ed. E. Lévi-Provençal, Paris 1930
Ibn al-ʿImād, *Shadharāt* = *Shadharāt al-dhahab fī akhbār man dhahab*, Cairo 1350-51 (quoted according to years of obituaries)
Ibn Isḥāḳ, tr. Guillaume = *The life of Muhammad, a translation of Isḥāq's (sic)* Sīrat Rasūl Allāh, tr. A. Guillaume, Oxford 1955
Ibn Khaldūn, *ʿIbar* = *K. al-ʿIbar wa-dīwān al-mubtadaʾ wa 'l-khabar etc.*, Būlāḳ 1284
Ibn Khaldūn, *Muḳaddima* = *Prolégomènes d'Ebn Khaldoun*, ed. E. Quatremère, Paris 1858-68 (*Notices et Extraits* XVI-XVIII)
Ibn Khaldūn-Rosenthal = *The Muqaddimah*, trans. from the Arabic by Franz Rosenthal, 3 vols., London 1958
Ibn Khaldūn-de Slane = *Les prolégomènes d'Ibn Khaldoun*, traduits en français et commentés par M de Slane, Paris 1863-68 (anastatic repri 1934-38)
Ibn Khallikān = *Wafayāt al-aʿyān wa-anbāʾ abnāʾ zamān*, ed. F. Wüstenfeld, Göttingen 1835- (quoted after the numbers of biographies)
Ibn Khallikān, ed. ʿAbbās = *ibid.*, ed. Iḥsān ʿAbbā 8 vols., Beirut 1968-72
Ibn Khallikān, Būlāḳ = *ibid.*, ed. Būlāḳ 1275
Ibn Khallikān-de Slane = *Kitāb Wafayāt al-aʿyā* trans. by Baron MacGuckin de Slane, 4 vol Paris 1842-1871
Ibn Khurradādhbih = *al-Masālik wa 'l-mamālik*, e M.J. De Goeje, Leiden 1889 (BGA VI)
Ibn Ḳutayba, *al-Shiʿr* = Ibn Ḳutayba, *Kitāb al-Sh wa 'l-shuʿarā*, ed. De Goeje, Leiden 1900
Ibn al-Nadīm, *Fihrist* = Ibn al-Nadīm, *K. al-Fihri* ed. G. Flügel, 2 vols., Leipzig 1871-2
Ibn al-Nadīm, tr. Dodge = *The Fihrist of al-Nadīm*, t B. Dodge, 2 vols., New York and London 19
Ibn Rusta = *al-Aʿlāḳ al-nafīsa*, ed. M.J. De Goej Leiden 1892 (BGA VII)
Ibn Rusta-Wiet = *Les Atours précieux*, traduction de (Wiet, Cairo 1955
Ibn Saʿd = *al-Ṭabaḳāt al-kubrā*, ed. H. Sachau ar others, Leiden 1905-40
Ibn Taghrībirdī = *al-Nudjūm al-zāhira fī mulūk M wa-l-Ḳāhira*, ed. W. Popper, Berkeley-Leid 1908-1936
Ibn Taghrībirdī, Cairo = the same, ed. Cai 1348 ff.
Idrīsī, *Maghrib* = *Description de l'Afrique et de l'Espagn* ed. R. Dozy and M.J. De Goeje, Leiden 18(
Idrīsī-Jaubert = *Géographie d'Édrisi*, trad. de l'aral en français par P. Amédée Jaubert, 2 vols Paris 1836-40
Iṣṭakhrī = *al-Masālik wa 'l-mamālik*, ed. M.J. I Goeje, Leiden 1870 (BGA I) (and reprint 192
Justi, *Namenbuch* = F. Justi, *Iranisches Namenbuc* Marburg 1895
Juynboll, *Handbuch* = Th.W. Juynboll, *Handbuch d islāmischen Gesetzes*, Leiden 1910
Kaḥḥāla, *Nisāʾ* = ʿUmar Riḍā Kaḥḥāla, *Aʿlām a nisāʾ fī ʿālamay al-ʿArab wa 'l-Islām*, 5 vols Damascus 1379/1959
Khʷāndamīr = *Ḥabīb al-siyar*, Tehran 1271
Kutubī, *Fawāt*, ed. Būlāḳ = Ibn Shākir al-Kutub *Fawāt al-wafayāt*, Būlāḳ 1299/1882, 2 vols.
Kutubī, *Fawāt*, ed. ʿAbbās = *ibid.*, ed. Iḥsān ʿAbbā 5 vols., Beirut 1973-4
LA = *Lisān al-ʿArab* (quoted according to the root)
Lambton, *Landlord and peasant* = A.K.S. Lambto *Landlord and peasant in Persia, a study of land tenu and revenue administration*, London 1953
Lane = E.W. Lane, *An Arabic-English lexicon*, Londo 1863-93 (reprint New York 1955-6)
Lane-Poole, *Cat.* = S. Lane-Poole, *Catalogue of orient coins in the British Museum*, 1877-90
Lavoix, *Cat.* = H. Lavoix, *Catalogue des monnai musulmanes de la Bibliothèque Nationale*, Par 1887-96
Le Strange = G. Le Strange, *The lands of the Easte Caliphate*, 2nd ed., Cambridge 1930
Le Strange, *Baghdad*, = G. Le Strange, *Baghdad durir the Abbasid Caliphate*, Oxford 1924
Le Strange, *Palestine* = G. Le Strange, *Palestine una the Moslems*, London 1890
Lévi-Provençal, *Hist.Esp.Mus.* = E. Lévi-Provença *Histoire de l'Espagne musulmane*, new ed., Leide Paris 1950-53, 3 vols.
Lévi-Provençal, *Chorfa* = E. Lévi-Provençal, *L historiens des Chorfa*, Paris 1922

E = K.A.C. Creswell, *The Muslim architecture of Egypt*, 2 vols., Oxford 1952-9
ḳḳarī, *Analectes* = *Nafḥ al-ṭīb fī ghuṣn al-Andalus al-raṭīb (Analectes sur l'histoire et la littérature des Arabes de l'Espagne)*, Leiden 1855-61
ḳḳarī, Būlāḳ = *ibid.*, ed. Būlāḳ 1279/1862
rquart, *Ērānšahr* = J. Marquart, *Ērānšahr nach der Geographie des Ps. Moses Xorenacʿi*, Berlin 1901
rquart, *Streifzüge* = J. Marquart, *Osteuropäische und ostasiatische Streifzüge. Ethnologische und historisch-topographische Studien zur Geschichte des 9. und 10. Jahrhunderts (c. 840-940)*, Leipzig 1903
spero-Wiet, *Matériaux* = J. Maspéro et G. Wiet, *Matériaux pour servir à la géographie de l'Egypte*, Le Caire 1914 (MIFAO XXXVI)
sʿūdī, *Murūdj* = *Murūdj al-dhahab*, ed. C. Barbier de Meynard and Pavet de Courteille, 9 vols., Paris 1861-77; ed. and tr. Ch. Pellat, *Les prairies d'or*, 7 vols. text and 4 vols. translation, Paris-Beirut 1962-89 (cited according to paragraph)
sʿūdī, *Tanbīh* = *K. al-Tanbīh wa 'l-ishrāf*, ed. M.J. De Goeje, Leiden 1894 (BGA VIII)
yer, *Architects* = L.A. Mayer, *Islamic architects and their works*, Geneva 1956
yer, *Astrolabists* = L.A. Mayer, *Islamic astrolabists and their works*, Geneva 1958
yer, *Metalworkers* = L.A. Mayer, *Islamic metalworkers and their works*, Geneva 1959
yer, *Woodcarvers* = L.A. Mayer, *Islamic woodcarvers and their works*, Geneva 1958
z, *Renaissance* = A. Mez, *Die Renaissance des Islams*, Heidelberg 1922
z, *Renaissance*, Eng. tr. = *The renaissance of Islam*, translated into English by Salahuddin Khuda Bukhsh and D.S. Margoliouth, London 1937
z, *Renaissance*, Spanish trans. = *El renacimiento del Islam*, translated into Spanish by S. Vila, Madrid-Granada 1936
quel, *Géographie humaine* = A. Miquel, *La géographie humaine du monde musulman jusqu'au milieu du 11ᵉ siècle*, 4 vols., Paris-The Hague 1973-88
rkhʷānd = *Rawḍat al-ṣafā*, Bombay 1266/1849
skawayh, in *Eclipse of the ʿAbbasid caliphate* = Miskawayh, *Tadjārib al-umam*, in *The eclipse of the ʿAbbasid caliphate*, ed. and tr. H.F. Amedroz and D.S. Margoliouth, 7 vols., Oxford 1920-21
ıḳaddasī = *Aḥsan al-taḳāsīm fī maʿrifat al-aḳālīm*, ed. M.J. De Goeje, Leiden 1877 (BGA III)
ınadjdjim Bashi = *Ṣaḥāʾif al-akhbār*, Istanbul 1285
llino, *Scritti* = C.A. Nallino, *Raccolta di scritti editi e inediti*, Roma 1939-48
hmānlī Müʾellifleri = Bursalī Meḥmed Ṭābir, *ʿOthmānlī müʾellifleri*, Istanbul 1333
ıalın = Mehmet Zeki Pakalın, *Osmanlı tarih deyimleri ve terimleri sözlüğü*, 3 vols., Istanbul 1946 ff.
ıly-Wissowa = *Realenzyklopaedie des klassischen Altertums*
ırson = J.D. Pearson, *Index Islamicus*, Cambridge 1958; S I = *Supplement, 1956-60*
ns Boigues = *Ensayo bio-bibliográfico sobre los historiadores y geógrafos arábigo-españoles*, Madrid 1898
'F = *Fundamenta philologiae turcica*, ed. J. Deny *et alii*, 2 vols., Wiesbaden 1959-64
'pka, *Hist. of Iranian literature* = J. Rypka *et alii*, *History of Iranian literature*, Dordrecht 1968
fadī = *al-Wāfī bi 'l-wafayāt. Das biographische Lexikon des Ṣalāḥaddīn Ḫalīl ibn Aibak aṣ-Ṣafadī*, ed. H. Ritter, S. Dedering *et alii*, 22 vols., Wiesbaden-Beirut-Damascus 1962-
mʿānī, *Ansāb*, facs. = *K. al-Ansāb*, facsimile edition by D.S. Margoliouth, Leiden 1912 (GMS, XX)
Samʿānī, ed. Ḥaydarābād = *ibid.*, ed. M. ʿAbd al-Muʿīd Khān *et alii*, 13 vols., Ḥaydarābād 1382-1402/1962-82
Santillana, *Istituzioni* = D. Santillana, *Istituzioni di diritto musulmano malichita*, Roma 1926-38
Sarkīs = Sarkīs, *Muʿdjam al-maṭbūʿāt al-ʿarabiyya*, Cairo 1346/1928
Schwarz, *Iran* = P. Schwarz, *Iran im Mittelalter nach den arabischen Geographen*, Leipzig 1896-
Sezgin, *GAS* = F. Sezgin, *Geschichte des arabischen Schrifttums*, 9 vols., Leiden 1967-84
Shahrastānī = *al-Milal wa 'l-niḥal*, ed. W. Cureton, London 1846
Sidjill-i ʿOthmānī = Meḥmed Thüreyyā, *Sidjill-i ʿOthmānī*, Istanbul 1308-1316
Snouck Hurgronje, *Verspr. Geschr.* = C. Snouck Hurgronje, *Verspreide Geschriften*, Bonn-Leipzig-Leiden 1923-27
Sources inédites = Comte Henry de Castries, *Les sources inédites de l'histoire du Maroc*, Première Série, Paris [etc.] 1905 —, Deuxième Série, Paris 1922 —
Spuler, *Horde*[1] = B. Spuler, *Die Goldene Horde, die Mongolen in Russland*, 1st ed., Leipzig 1943
Spuler, *Horde*[2] = *ibid.*, 2nd ed., Wiesbaden 1965
Spuler, *Iran* = B. Spuler, *Iran in früh-islamischer Zeit*, Wiesbaden 1952
Spuler, *Mongolen*[1] = B. Spuler, *Die Mongolen in Iran*, 1st ed., Leipzig 1939
Spuler, *Mongolen*[2] = *ibid.*, 2nd ed., Berlin 1955
Spuler, *Mongolen*[3] = *ibid.*, 3rd ed., Berlin 1968
Storey = C.A. Storey, *Persian literature: a bio-bibliographical survey*, London 1927-
Survey of Persian Art = ed. by A.U. Pope, Oxford 1938
Suter = H. Suter, *Die Mathematiker und Astronomen der Araber und ihre Werke*, Leipzig 1900
Suyūṭī, *Bughya* = *Bughyat al-wuʿāt*, Cairo 1326
TA = Muḥammad Murtaḍā b. Muḥammad al-Zabīdī, *Tādj al-ʿarūs* (quoted according to the root)
Ṭabarī = *Taʾrīkh al-rusul wa 'l-mulūk*, ed. M.J. De Goeje and others, Leiden 1879-1901
Taeschner, *Wegenetz* = Franz Taeschner, *Das anatolische Wegenetz nach osmanischen Quellen*, 2 vols., Leipzig 1924-6
Taʾrīkh Baghdād = al-Khaṭīb al-Baghdādī, *Taʾrīkh Baghdād*, 14 vols., Cairo 1349/1931
Taʾrīkh Dimashk = Ibn ʿAsākir, *Taʾrīkh Dimashk*, 7 vols., Damascus 1329-51/1911-31
Taʾrīkh-i Guzīda = Ḥamd Allāh Mustawfī al-Ḳazwīnī, *Taʾrīkh-i guzīda*, ed. in facsimile by E.G. Browne, Leiden-London 1910
TAVO = Tübinger Atlas des Vorderen Orients, Wiesbaden
Thaʿālibī, *Yatīma*, ed. Damascus = Thaʿālibī, *Yatīmat al-dahr fī maḥāsin ahl al-ʿaṣr*, 4 vols., Damascus 1304/1886-7
Thaʿālibī, *Yatīma*, ed. Cairo = *ibid.*, ed. Muḥammad Muḥyī al-Dīn ʿAbd al-Ḥamīd, 4 vols., Cairo 1375-7/1956-8
Tomaschek = W. Tomaschek, *Zur historischen Topographie von Kleinasien im Mittelalter*, Vienna 1891
Weil, *Chalifen* = G. Weil, *Geschichte der Chalifen*, Mannheim-Stuttgart 1846-82
Wensinck, *Handbook* = A.J. Wensinck, *A handbook of early Muhammadan Tradition*, Leiden 1927
Wensinck, *Concordances* = A.J. Wensinck *et alii*, *Concordances et indices de la tradition musulmane*, 7 vols., Leiden 1936-79

WKAS = *Wörterbuch der klassischen arabischen Sprache*, Wiesbaden 1957-
Yaʿḳūbī = *Taʾrīkh*, ed. M.Th. Houtsma, Leiden 1883
Yaʿḳūbī, *Buldān* = ed. M.J. De Goeje, Leiden 1892 (BGA VII)
Yaʿḳūbī-Wiet = *Yaʿḳūbī. Les pays*, trad. par Gaston Wiet, Cairo 1937
Yāḳūt, ed. Wüstenfeld = *Muʿdjam al-buldān*, ed. F. Wüstenfeld, 5 vols., Leipzig 1866-3
Yāḳūt, ed. Beirut = *ibid.*, 5 vols., Beirut 1374-6/1955-7
Yāḳūt, *Udabāʾ* = *Irshād al-arīb ilā maʿrifat al-adīb*, ed. D.S. Margoliouth, Leiden 1907-31 (GMS
Zambaur = E. de Zambaur, *Manuel de généalogie chronologie pour l'histoire de l'Islam*, Hanover (anastatic reprint Bad Pyrmont 1955)
Zinkeisen = J. Zinkeisen, *Geschichte des osmani Reiches in Europa*, Gotha 1840-83
Ziriklī, *Aʿlām* = Khayr al-Dīn al-Ziriklī, *al-Aʿ ḳāmūs tarādjim li-ashhar al-ridjāl wa 'l-nisāʾ al-ʿArab wa 'l-mustaʿribīn wa 'l-mustashriḳīn* vols., Damascus 1373-8/1954-9
Zubayrī, *Nasab* = Muṣʿab al-Zubayrī, *Nasab Ḳur* ed. E. Lévi-Provençal, Cairo 1953

ABBREVIATIONS FOR PERIODICALS ETC.

1RP = *Art and Archaeology Research Papers*
bh. A. W. Gött. = *Abhandlungen der Gesellschaft der Wissenschaften zu Göttingen.*
bh. K. M. = *Abhandlungen für die Kunde des Morgenlandes.*
bh. Pr. Ak. W. = *Abhandlungen der preussischen Akademie der Wissenschaften.*
r. Fr. = *Bulletin du Comité de l'Afrique française.*
I = *Annales Islamologiques*
EO Alger = *Annales de l'Institut d'Études Orientales de l'Université d'Alger* (N.S. from 1964).
UON = *Annali dell' Istituto Universitario Orientale di Napoli.*
nz. Wien = *Anzeiger der* [*kaiserlichen*] *Akademie der Wissenschaften, Wien. Philosophisch-historische Klasse.*
O = *Acta Orientalia.*
O Hung. = *Acta Orientalia* (*Academiae Scientiarum Hungaricae*).
rO = *Archiv Orientální.*
RW = *Archiv für Religionswissenschaft.*
SI = *Archaeological Survey of India.*
SI, NIS = *ditto*, New Imperial Series.
SI, AR = *ditto*, Annual Reports.
ÜDTCFD = *Ankara Üniversitesi Dil ve Tarih-Coğrafya Fakültesi Dergisi.*
AH = *Bibliotheca Arabico-Hispana.*
ASOR = *Bulletin of the American Schools of Oriental Research.*
lleten = *Belleten* (of *Türk Tarih Kurumu*)
Fac. Ar. = *Bulletin of the Faculty of Arts of the Egyptian University.*
Ét. Or. = *Bulletin d'Études Orientales de l'Institut Français de Damas.*
GA = *Bibliotheca geographorum arabicorum.*
Or = *Bibliotheca Orientalis*
IE = *Bulletin de l'Institut d'Égypte.*
IFAO = *Bulletin de l'Institut Français d'Archéologie Orientale du Caire.*
RAH = *Boletín de la Real Academia de la Historia de España.*
SE = *Bol'shaya Sovetskaya Éntsiklopediya* (Large Soviet Encyclopaedia) 1st ed.
*SE*² = the same, 2nd ed.
SL[P] = *Bulletin de la Société de Linguistique de Paris.*
SO[A]S = *Bulletin of the School of Oriental* [*and African*] *Studies.*
TLV = *Bijdragen tot de Taal-, Land- en Volkenkunde* [*van Nederlandsch-Indië*].
Z = *Byzantinische Zeitschrift.*
AJ = *Central Asiatic Journal*
OC = *Cahiers de l'Orient contemporain.*
T = *Cahiers de Tunisie.*
*I*¹ = *Encyclopaedia of Islam*, 1st edition.
IM = *Epigraphia Indo-Moslemica.*
RE = *Encyclopaedia of Religions and Ethics.*
W = *East and West*
GA = *Göttingische Gelehrte Anzeigen.*
J = *Geographical Journal*
MS = *Gibb Memorial Series.*
r. I. Ph. = *Grundriss der Iranischen Philologie.*
db d. Or. = *Handbuch der Orientalistik*
A = *Islâm Ansiklopedisi.*
BLA = *Revue de l'Institut des Belles Lettres Arabes*, Tunis.
C = *Islamic Culture.*
FD = *Ilahiyat Fakültesi Dergisi.*
HQ = *Indian Historical Quarterly.*
IMES = *International Journal of Middle Eastern Studies*
IOS = *Israel Oriental Studies*
IQ = *The Islamic Quarterly.*
Iran JBIPS = *Iran, Journal of the British Institute of Persian Studies*
Isl. = *Der Islam.*
JA = *Journal Asiatique.*
JAfr. S = *Journal of the African Society.*
JAL = *Journal of Arabic Literature*
JAnthr. I = *Journal of the Anthropological Institute.*
JAOS = *Journal of the American Oriental Society*
JARCE = *Journal of the American Research Center in Egypt*
JASB = *Journal of the Asiatic Society of Bengal*
JBBRAS = *Journal of the Bombay Branch of the Royal Asiatic Society.*
JE = *Jewish Encyclopaedia.*
JESHO = *Journal of the Economic and Social History of the Orient.*
JIS = *Journal of Islamic Studies*
J[R]Num. S. = *Journal of the* [*Royal*] *Numismatic Society.*
JNES = *Journal of Near Eastern Studies.*
JPak.HS = *Journal of the Pakistan Historical Society.*
JPHS = *Journal of the Punjab Historical Society.*
JQR = *Jewish Quarterly Review.*
JRAS = *Journal of the Royal Asiatic Society.*
J[R]ASB = *Journal and Proceedings of the* [*Royal*] *Asiatic Society of Bengal.*
JRGeog. S. = *Journal of the Royal Geographical Society.*
JSAI = *Jerusalem Studies in Arabic and Islam*
JSFO = *Journal de la Société Finno-ougrienne.*
JSS = *Journal of Semitic Studies.*
KCA = *Körösi Csoma Archivum.*
KS = *Keleti Szemle* (Oriental Review).
KSIE = *Kratkie Soobshčeniya Instituta Étnografiy* (Short communications of the Institute of Ethnography).
LE = *Literaturnaya Éntsiklopediya* (Literary Encyclopaedia).
MDOG = *Mitteilungen der Deutschen Orient-Gesellschaft.*
MDPV = *Mitteilungen und Nachrichten des Deutschen Palästina-Vereins.*
MEA = *Middle Eastern Affairs.*
MEJ = *Middle East Journal.*
Méms. DAFA = *Mémoires de la Délégation Française en Afghanistan*
MES = *Middle East Studies*
MFOB = *Mélanges de la Faculté Orientale de l'Université St. Joseph de Beyrouth.*
MGMN = *Mitteilungen zur Geschichte der Medizin und Naturwissenschaften.*
MGWJ = *Monatsschrift für die Geschichte und Wissenschaft des Judentums.*
MIDEO = *Mélanges de l'Institut Dominicain d'Études Orientales du Caire.*
MIE = *Mémoires de l'Institut d'Égypte.*
MIFAO = *Mémoires publiés par les membres de l'Institut Français d'Archéologie Orientale du Caire.*
MMAF = *Mémoires de la Mission Archéologique Française au Caire.*
MME = *Manuscripts of the Middle East*
MMIA = *Madjallat al-Madjma' al-'Ilmī al-'Arabī*, Damascus.
MO = *Le Monde oriental.*
MOG = *Mitteilungen zur osmanischen Geschichte.*
MSE = *Malaya Sovetskaya Éntsiklopediya* (Small Soviet Encyclopaedia).
MSFO = *Mémoires de la Société Finno-ougrienne.*
MSL[P] = *Mémoires de la Société Linguistique de Paris.*
MSOS Afr. = *Mitteilungen des Seminars für Orientalische Sprachen, Afrikanische Studien.*

MSOS As. = *Mitteilungen des Seminars für Orientalische Sprachen, Westasiatische Studien.*
MTM = *Millī Tetebbüᶜler Medjmūᶜasī.*
MW = *The Muslim World.*
NC = *Numismatic Chronicle.*
Nak. W. Gött. = *Nachrichten von der Gesellschaft der Wissenschaften zu Göttingen.*
NZ = *Numismatische Zeitschrift*
OC = *Oriens Christianus.*
OLZ = *Orientalistische Literaturzeitung.*
OM = *Oriente Moderno.*
PEFQS = *Palestine Exploration Fund. Quarterly Statement.*
Pet. Mitt. = *Petermanns Mitteilungen.*
PTF = *Philologiae Tvrcicae Fundamenta*, Wiesbaden 1959-
QDAP = *Quarterly Statement of the Department of Antiquities of Palestine.*
RAfr. = *Revue Africaine.*
RCEA = *Répertoire chronologique d'Épigraphie arabe.*
REJ = *Revue des Études Juives.*
Rend. Lin. = *Rendiconti della Reale Accademia dei Lincei, Classe di scienze morali, storiche e filologiche.*
REI = *Revue des Études Islamiques.*
RHR = *Revue de l'Histoire des Religions.*
RIMA = *Revue de l'Institut des Manuscrits Arabes.*
RMM = *Revue du Monde Musulman.*
RN = *Revue Numismatique*
RO = *Rocznik Orientalistyczny.*
ROC = *Revue de l'Orient Chrétien.*
ROL = *Revue de l'Orient Latin.*
RSO = *Rivista degli studi orientali.*
RT = *Revue Tunisienne.*
SB Ak. Heid. = *Sitzungsberichte der Heidelberger Akademie der Wissenschaften.*
SB Ak. Wien = *Sitzungsberichte der Akademie der Wissenschaften zu Wien.*
SBBayer. Ak. = *Sitzungsberichte der Bayerischen Akademie der Wissenschaften.*
SBPMS Erlg. = *Sitzungsberichte der Physikalisch-medizinischen Sozietät in Erlangen.*
SBPr. Ak. W. = *Sitzungsberichte der Preussischen Akade[mie] der Wissenschaften zu Berlin.*
SE = *Sovetskaya Étnografiya* (Soviet Ethnography).
SO = *Sovetskoe Vostokovedenie* (Soviet Orientalism).
Stud. Ir. = *Studia Iranica*
Stud. Isl. = *Studia Islamica.*
S.Ya. = *Sovetskoe Yazïkoznanie* (Soviet Linguistics)
TBG = *Tijdschrift van het Bataviaasch Genootschap [voor] Kunsten en Wetenschappen.*
TD = *Tarih Dergisi.*
TIE = *Trudï instituta Étnografiy* (Works of the Instit[ute] of Ethnography).
TM = *Türkiyat Mecmuası.*
TOEM/TTEM = *Taʾrīkh-i ᶜOthmānī* (*Türk Taʾrīkh*) *Endjümeni medjmūᶜasī.*
UAJb = *Ural-altäische Jahrbücher*
Verh. Ak. Amst. = *Verhandelingen der Koninklijke A[ka]demie van Wetenschappen te Amsterdam.*
Versl. Med. Ak. Amst. = *Verslagen en Mededeelingen [der] Koninklijke Akademie van Wetenschappen [te] Amsterdam.*
VI = *Voprosï Istoriy* (Historical Problems).
WI = *Die Welt des Islams.*
WI, n.s. = the same, new series.
Wiss. Veröff. DOG = *Wissenschaftliche Veröffentlichun[gen] der Deutschen Orient-Gesellschaft.*
WO = *Welt des Orients*
WZKM = *Wiener Zeitschrift für die Kunde des Morg[en]landes.*
ZA = *Zeitschrift für Assyriologie.*
ZAL = *Zeitschrift für Arabische Linguistik*
ZATW = *Zeitschrift für die alttestamentliche Wissensch[aft]*
ZDMG = *Zeitschrift der Deutschen Morgenländisc[hen] Gesellschaft.*
ZDPV = *Zeitschrift des Deutschen Palästinavereins.*
ZfN = *Zeitschrift für Numismatik*
ZGAIW = *Zeitschrift für Geschichte der Arabis[ch-] Islamischen Wissenschaften*
ZGErdk. Birl. = *Zeitschrift der Gesellschaft für Erdkund[e zu] Berlin.*
ZS = *Zeitschrift für Semitistik.*

LIST OF TRANSLITERATIONS

SYSTEM OF TRANSLITERATION OF ARABIC CHARACTERS:

Consonants						*Long Vowels*		*Diphthongs*	
ء	ʾ (except when initial)	ز	z	ق	ḳ	ا ى	ā	ـَوْ	aw
ب	b	س	s	ك	k	و	ū	ـَيْ	ay
ت	t	ش	sh	ل	l	ي	ī		
ث	th	ص	ṣ	م	m			ـِيّ	iyy (final form ī)
ج	dj	ض	ḍ	ن	n	*Short Vowels*		ـُوّ	uww (final form ū)
ح	ḥ	ط	ṭ	ه	h	ـَ	a		
خ	kh	ظ	ẓ	و	w	ـُ	u		
د	d	ع	ʿ	ي	y	ـِ	i		
ذ	dh	غ	gh						
ر	r	ف	f						

ة a; at (construct state)

ال (article), al- and 'l- (even before the antero-palatals)

PERSIAN, TURKISH AND URDU ADDITIONS TO THE ARABIC ALPHABET:

پ	p	ژ	zh	ٹ	ṭ́	ڑ	ŕ
چ	č	ك or گ	g (sometimes ñ in Turkish)	ڈ	ḍ́	ں	ṇ

Additional vowels:

a) Turkish: e, ı, o, ö, ü. Diacritical signs proper to Arabic are, in principle, not used in words of Turkish etymology.

b) Urdu: ē, ō.

For modern Turkish, the official orthography adopted by the Turkish Republic in 1928 is used. The following letters may be noted:

c = dj	ğ = gh	j = zh	k = k and ḳ	t = t and ṭ
ç = č	h = h, ḥ and kh	ş = sh	s = s, ṣ and th	z = z, ẓ, ḍ and dh

SYSTEM OF TRANSLITERATION OF THE RUSSIAN ALPHABET:

а	a	е	e	к	k	п	p	ф	f	щ	shč	ю	yu
б	b	ж	ž	л	l	р	r	х	kh	ы	ı	я	ya
в	v	з	z	м	m	с	s	ц	ts	ь	ʾ	ѣ	ě
г	g	и	i	н	n	т	t	ч	č	ъ	ʿ		
д	d	й	y	о	o	у	u	ш	sh	э	é		

ADDENDA AND CORRIGENDA

VOLUME II

P. 862b, **FĀṬIMIDS**, *add to Bibl.*: H. Halm, *Das Reich des Mahdi. Der Aufsteig der Fatimiden (875-973)*, Munich 1991.

VOLUME III

P. 736b, **IBN BAṬṬŪṬA**, *add to Bibl.*: H.A.R. Gibb (tr.), *The travels*, iii, Cambridge 1971; R.E. Dunn, *The adventures of Ibn Battuta, a Muslim traveller of the 14th century*, Berkeley and Los Angeles 1986.

VOLUME V, p. 88b, **ḲIBLA**, and VOLUME VI, p. 187a, **MAKKA**. 4, *add to Bibliography*: See the addenda and corrigenda to the reprints thereof in King, *Astronomy in the service of Islam*, Aldershot 1993, and add R.P. Lorch, *The Qibla table attributed to al-Khāzinī*, in *Journal for the History of Arabic Science*, iv, (1980), 259-64; J.L. Berggren, *A comparison of four analemmas for determining the azimuth of the Qibla*, in *ibid.*, 69-80, and idem, *The origins of al-Bīrūnī's "Method of the Zījes" in the theory of sundials*, in *Centaurus*, xxviii (1985), 1-16; J. Carandell, *An analemma for the determination of the azimuth of the Qibla in the* Risāla fī ʿilm al-ẓilāl *of Ibn al-Raqqām*, in *ZGAIW*, i (1984), 61-72; Takanori Suzuki, *A solution of the Qibla-problem by Abu 'l-Qāsim Aḥmad ibn Muḥammad al-Ghandajānī*, in *ibid.*, iv (1987-8), 139-48; King, *The earliest Islamic methods and tables for finding the direction of Mecca*, in *ibid.*, iii (1986), 82-146, repr. in idem, *Astronomy in the service of Islam* (see above), no. XIV; J. Samsó and H. Mielgo, *Ibn Isḥāq al-Tūnisī and Ibn Muʿādh al-Jayyānī on the Qibla*, in Samsó, *Islamic astronomy and Medieval Spain*, Aldershot 1994, no. VI; J.P. Hogendijk, *The Qibla-table in the* Ashrafī Zīj, in Anton von Gotstedter (ed.), *Ad radices - Festband zum 50jährigen Bestehen des Instituts für Geschichte der Naturwissenschaften Frankfurt am Main*, Stuttgart 1994; and Ahmed Dallal, *Ibn al-Haytham's universal solution for finding the direction of the Qibla*, in *Arabic Science and Philosophy*, forthcoming.

P. 231b, **KITĀBĀT**. 9. Iran and Transoxania, *add to Bibl.*: Sheila S. Blair, *The monumental inscriptions from early Islamic Iran and Transoxania* (Studies in Islamic art and architecture, supplements to *Muqarnas*, v), Leiden 1992.

P. 807a, **LUGHZ**, *add to Bibliography*, Shams Anwari-Alhosseyni, *Loġaz und Moʿammā. Eine Quellenstudie zur Kunstform des persischen Rätsels*, Berlin 1986.

VOLUME VI

P. 750a, **MASRAḤ**. 1. In the Arab East, *add to Bibl.*: S. Moreh, *Live theatre and dramatic literature in the medieval Arabic world*, Edinburgh 1992.

VOLUME VII

P. 793a, **MUʿTAZILA**, l. 28, *omit* and is in the form of a simple outline of what the author expects to develop, and eventually correct, in his *Geschichte der frühen islamischen Theologie*.

P. 816b, AL-**MUẒAFFAR**, l. 20, *for* 292-4, 309-30, *read* 202-4, 209-30.

P. 913a, **NAḤW**, ll. 3-4, *for* which has become the technical term used to denote "grammar", *read* which has become the technical term used to denote "grammar" in general (to be contrasted with *lugha* "lexical studies"), and more specifically, "syntax" (which is the counterpart of *ṣarf* or *taṣrīf* "morphology" (so that for "grammar" one also finds the phrase *naḥw wa-ṣarf*).

P. 913b, l. 16, *for* relativeness, *read* relativity (i.e. subordination of clauses)
l. 43, *for* Greek grammar and logic, *read* Greek grammar and logic, and, especially, rhetorical education.

P. 914a, l. 31, *for* flexional, *read* inflectional.
l. 22 from below, *for* in the ʿAbbāsid capital, *read* in the ʿAbbāsid capital, which remained the dominant theory ever after.

P. 914b, l. 11, *for* philology, *read* lexicology
ll. 17-18, *replace* the Persian...*al-miʾa*, *by* the Persian al-Djurdjānī (d. 471/1078, [*q.v.* in Suppl.]), author, among other works, of the *K. al ʿAwāmil al-miʾa*

P. 915a, *add to Bibl.*: G. Bohas, J.-P. Guillaume, D.E. Kouloughli, *The Arabic linguistic tradition*, London and New York 1990; M. Carter, *Arab linguistics. An introductory classical text with translation and notes*, Amsterdam 1981 (ed. and tr. of Muḥammad al-Shirbīnī al-Khaṭīb, *Nūr al-sadjiya fī ḥall alfāẓ al-Ādjurrūmiyya*); G. Bohas and J.-P. Guillaume, *Étude des théories des grammairiens arabes. I. Morphologie et phonologie*, Damascus 1984; J. Owens, *The foundations of grammar. An introduction to medieval Arabic grammatical theory*, Amsterdam and Philadelphia 1988; idem, *Early Arabic grammatical theory: heterogeneity and standardization*, Amsterdam and Philadelphia 1990. See also special issues of the following journals: *Arabica*, xxviii (1981) (*Études de linguistique arabe*); *Historiographia Linguistica*, viii (1981) (*The History of Linguistics in the Near East*). For the proceedings of the Symposia on the History of Arabic Grammar, see; *Zeitschrift für Arabische Linguistik*, xv (1985) (*Proceedings of the First Symposium on the History of Arabic Grammar, held at Nijmegen, 16-19 April 1984*); K. Versteegh and M. Carter (eds.), *Studies in the history of Arabic grammar. II. Proceedings of the 2nd Symposium on the History of Arabic Grammar, Nijmegen, 27 April-1 May 1987*, Amsterdam 1990; *The Arabist. Budapest Studies in Arabic*, 3-4 (1991) (*Proceedings of the Colloquium on Arabic Grammar, Budapest, 1-7 September 1991*). On basic terms and methods, see G. Weil, *Zum Verständnis der Methode der moslemischen Grammatiker*, in *Festschrift Eduard Sachau*, Berlin 1915, 380-92; C.H.M. Versteegh, *The Arabic terminology of syntactic position*, in *Arabica*, xxv (1978), 261-81; idem, *The origin of the term "qiyās" in Arabic grammar*, in *ZAL*, iv (1980), 7-30. For a bibliographical survey, see Werner Diem, *Sekundärliteratur zur einheimischen arabischen Grammatikschreibung*, in *Historiographia Linguistica*, viii (1981), 431-86, continued by Versteegh in *ZAL*, x (1983), xi (1983), xii (1984), xiv (1985), and xvi (1987).

P. 920b, AL-NAḲB, *add to Bibl.*: al-Ṭabarī, *Taʾrīkh al-uman wa ʾl-mulūk*, Cairo 1326/1908.

P. 963b, **NARDJIS**, *add to first paragraph*: Note also that in the Arab West *nardjis* refers to the "daffodil", while *bahār* is the term for "narcissus" (see H. Pérès, *La Poésie andalouse en arabe classique*, Paris 1953, 170-3).

P. 964a, *add to Bibl.*: W. Heinrichs, *Rose versus narcissus. Observations on an Arabic literary debate*, in *Dispute poems and dialogues in the ancient and mediaeval Near East*, ed. G.J. Reinink and H.L.J. Vanstiphout, Leuven 1991, 179-98.

P. 977a, **NASHWĀN B. SAʿĪD**, *add to Bibl.*: Ismāʿīl b. ʿAlī al-Akwaʿ, *Naschwān Ibn Saʿīd al-Ḥimyarī und die geistigen, religiösen und politischen Auseinandersetzungen seines Epoche*, in Werner Daum (ed.), *Jemen*, Innsbruck and Frankfurt/Main 1987, 205-16 (English ed. 1988).

P. 996b, **AL-NĀṢIR LI-DĪN ALLĀH**, Aḥmad Abu l'-Ḥasan, *add to Bibl.*: W. Madelung, *Der Imam al-Qāsim ibn Ibrāhīm und die Glaubenslehre der Zaiditen*, Berlin 1965 (on al-Nāṣir li-Dīn Allāh's life and teachings); his theological work published by idem, *Kitāb al-Najāt. Streitschrift des Zaiditenimams Aḥmad an-Nāṣir wider die ibaditische Prädestinationslehre*, Wiesbaden, 1985; and his biography published by idem, *The* Sīra *of Imām Aḥmad b. Yaḥyā al-Nāṣir li-Dīn Allāh from Musallam al-Lahjī's* Kitāb Akhbār al-Zaydiyya bi l-Yaman, Exeter 1990. See also for al-Nāṣir's father, AL-HĀDĪ ILĀ 'L-ḤAḲḲ in Suppl.

P. 1027, **NAṢRIDS**, in genealogical table, *for* the date of Muḥammad XI (*el Chiquito*), *read* (1451-2/1453-5).

P. 1027a, l. 7 from below, *for* 949/1533-4, *read* 940/1533-4.

VOLUME VIII

P. 81a, **NIẒĀMĪ GANDJAWĪ**, *add to Bibl.*: J.C. Bürgel, *Die Geschichte von König Bahram Gor und seinem Sklavenmädchen*, in *Bustan*, viii/2 (1967), 26-35; idem, *Nizami über Sprache und Dichtung*, in *Islamwissenschaftliche Studien Fritz Meier zum sechzigsten Geburtstag*, ed. R. Gramlich, Wiesbaden 1974, 9-28; G. Krotkoff, *Colour and number in the Haft Paykar*, in R.M. Savory and D. Agius (eds.), *Logos islamikos, studia islamica in honorem Georgii Michaelis Wickens*, Toronto 1984, 97-118; J.S. Meisami, *Medieval Persian court poetry*, Princeton 1987, chs. iii-v, vii; eadem, *Allegorical gardens in the Persian poetical tradition: Nezami, Rumi, Hafez*, in *IJMES*, xvii (1985), 229-60; eadem, *Kings and lovers: the ethical dimension of Persian courtly romance*, in *Edebiyat*, N.S. i (1987), 1-27; eadem, *The Grand Design: medieval Persian poetic microcosms*, in *Procs. 12th Internat. Comparative Lit. Assoc. Congress, Munich 1988*, Munich 1990, iii, 438-63; eadem, *Fitnah or azadah? Nizami's ethical poetic*, in *Edebiyat*, N.S. i/2 (1988), 41-75; eadem, *The theme of the journey in Nizami's Haft Paikar.*, forthcoming in *Festschrift for Prof. George Krotkoff*, 1994.

P. 84a, **NIZĀRĪ ḲUHISTĀNĪ**, *add to Bibl.*: M. Muṣaffā (ed.), *Dīwān*, i, Tehran 1371 sh./1992 (contains also the *Dastūr-nāma*); Č. Gh. Bayburdī, *Zindagī wa āthār-i Nizārī*, transl. by M. Ṣadrī, Tehran 1370 sh./1991.

P. 172a, **ÖMER SEYFEDDIN**, *add to Bibl.*: Kemal H. Karpat, *The reflection of the Young Turk era (1908-1918)*, in *The literary work of Ömer Seyfeddin (1884-1920)*, in C.E. Bosworth *et al.* (eds.), *The Islamic world. Essays in honor of Bernard Lewis*, Princeton 1989, 551-75.

P. 378b, **RADJAZ**, Section 4, *instead of the headline* As a term of non-metrical poetry *read* As a term denoting line structure.

P. 422a, **RAMAL**, l. 8 should read: the alternative form of (3/2) ♩♩♩ which was con-.

P. 428a, **RAMZ**, l. 23, *for* allegories, *read* allegoreses.
l. 57, *for* signal, *read* sigla.

P. 461b, **AL-RĀWANDIYYA**, l. 12, *for* the imāmate was no longer believed to have started with ʿAlī rather than with al-ʿAbbās, *read* the imāmate was no longer believed to have started with ʿAlī but rather with al-ʿAbbas, ...

P. 683b, **SABK-I HINDĪ**. Delete comma in heading.

SUPPLEMENT

P. 150a, **BÖLÜKBASHI**, RIḌĀ TEWFĪḲ, *add to Bibl.*: Tahir Alangu, *100 ünlü Türk eseri*, Istanbul 1960; Seyit Kemal Karaalioğlu, *Türk edebiyatı tarihi*, iii, Istanbul 1985; Yusuf Ziya Ortaç, *Bir varmış bir bir yokmuş portreler*, Istanbul 1960; Mahir Ünlü and Ömer Özcan, *20. yüzyıl Türk edebiyatı*, Istanbul 1987.

N

CONTINUATION

NEDĪM, Aḥmed, an Ottoman poet, born in Istanbul, the son of a judge named Meḥmed Bey who had come from Merzifun. His grandfather (according to Gibb, *HOP*, iv, 30) was a military judge named Muṣṭafā. Aḥmed Refīḳ mentions as his great-grandfather Ḳara-Čelebi-zāde [*q.v.*] Maḥmūd Efendi, who also was a military judge. The genealogy given by Aḥmed Refīḳ is, however, wrong because he confuses Ḳaramānī Meḥmed Pas̲h̲a [*q.v.*] with Rūm Meḥmed Pas̲h̲a. The statement that Aḥmed Nedīm is descended from D̲j̲elāl al-Dīn is therefore simply the result of confusion. Little is known of his life. He was a *müderris*, later on intimate terms with Aḥmed III and his grand vizier Dāmād Ibrāhīm Pas̲h̲a [see al-dāmād]. He probably got his *laḳab* Nedīm from this friendship. Latterly he held the office of librarian in the library founded by his patron Dāmād Ibrāhīm Pas̲h̲a. On hearing of the end of Ibrāhīm Pas̲h̲a and the deposition of the sultan, Nadīm lost his life at the beginning of Rabīʿ I 1143/October 1730 in a horrible way; while escaping from the mob leaving the grand-vizier's palace he fell from the roof and was killed. He was buried in Ayās Pas̲h̲a in Pera beside the historian Fi̊ndi̊ḳli̊li̊ Silāḥdār Meḥmed Agha [*q.v.*].

Aḥmed Nedīm is regarded as one of the greatest of Ottoman poets, one who is still appreciated for his pure language, free from foreign additions. Many literary historians have discussed his merits as a poet (cf. the specimens collected by Gibb, *HOP*, iv, 30 ff.). His collected poems (*Dīwān*; printed Būlāḳ, n.d.; a critical edition with introductions by Aḥmed Refīḳ Bey and Meḥmed Fuʾād Bey appeared in 1338-40 in Istanbul; the most recent critical edition is that of Abdülbâki Gölpınarlı, *Nedim divanı*, Istanbul 1951, 2nd ed. Istanbul 1972; there are manuscripts of the *Dīwān* in Europe in Munich, London and Vienna) enjoys great popularity. Nedīm translated into Turkish the history of Müned̲j̲d̲j̲im-bas̲h̲i̊ [*q.v.*] Aḥmed Efendi (cf. F. Babinger, *GOW*, 234-5; cf. thereon *JA* ser. 7, xiii, 272); he was also one of the Turkish translators of ʿAynī's history (cf. Babinger, *GOW*, 259 ff.; the edict relating to this in Aḥmed Refīḳ, *Hicri on ikinci asırda İstanbul hayatı, 1100-1200*, Istanbul 1930, 85-5) but the manuscript seems to be lost.

Bibliography: Aḥmed Refīḳ's preface to his edition of the *Dīwān*; *Sid̲j̲ill-i ʿot̲h̲mānī*, iv, 549 (very superficial; here his grandfather is said to have been a certain *Ṣadr* Muṣliḥ al-Dīn and his father the judge Meḥmed); Bursali̊ Meḥmed Ṭāhir, *ʿOt̲h̲mānli̊ müʾellifleri*, ii, 453-4; J. von Hammer-Purgstall, *GOD*, iv, 310 ff. (who does not appreciate him highly); Gibb, *HOP*, iv, 30; A. Bombaci, *Storia della letteratura turca*, Milan 1956, 385-8; *PTF*, ii, Wiesbaden 1964, 448; Fahir İz, *Eski türk edebiyatında nazım*, Istanbul 1966-7, i, 92-107, 400-5, 442, 467-8, 521, ii, 530; W.G. Andrews, *Introduction to Ottoman poetry*, Minneapolis 1976, index; idem, *Poetry's voice, society's song, Ottoman lyric poetry*, Seattle 1985, index; L. Miller, *Ottoman Turkish writers, a bibliographical dictionary of significant figures in pre-Republican Turkish literature*, New York etc. 1988, 105-7 (lists many relevant works in Turkish); Ahmet Evin, *Nedim, poet of the Tulip Age*, University Microfilms, Ann Arbor, Mich. 1988; *IA* art. *Nedîm, Aḥmed* (Fevziye Abdullah Tansel).

(F. Babinger*)

NED̲J̲ĀTĪ BEY, properly ʿĪsā (Nūḥ, also given, is not certain), the first great Turkish lyric poet of the pre-classical period, one of the founders of the classical Ottoman poetry. Born in Edirne (Amasia and Ḳasṭamūnī are also given), the son of a slave, obviously a Christian prisoner of war for which reason he is called ʿAbd Allāh, the name given to converts, he was adopted by a well-to-do lady of Edirne, received a good education and was trained by the poet Sāʾilī. In spite of the fact that his non-Turkish origin was generally known, he was regarded as their equal in every way by the Turks in keeping with their democratic ideas. He came to Ḳasṭamūnī early and there began his poetic career, soon gaining a great reputation. His poems are said here and there to bear traces of the Ḳasṭamūnī dialect. Coming to Istanbul, he at once gained the favour of Sultan Meḥemmed II by a *ḳaṣīda* on winter; in 886/1481 he celebrated the accession of Bāyezīd II in a *ḳaṣīda* and was rewarded by an appointment as secretary in the *Dīwān*. He gained such favour with the Sultan that he was appointed secretary to his eldest son ʿAbd Allāh and was given the title of *bey* when the prince went to Ḳaramān as governor (*müteṣarrif*). After the prince's early death (888/1483), Ned̲j̲ātī returned to the capital with an elegy on the death of the prince which showed deep emotion. After a long interval in which he wrote a great deal but was in continual need, through the influence of Muʾayyad-zāde [*q.v.*] he became *nis̲h̲ānd̲j̲i̊* [*q.v.*] to Bāyezīd's younger son Maḥmūd when the latter went to Ṣārūk̲h̲ān in 910/1504. Ned̲j̲ātī wrote his finest verse while on the staff of this prince; this was the happiest period of his life. Maḥmūd also died prematurely in 913/1507 in Manisa, the capital of Ṣārūk̲h̲ān, and Ned̲j̲ātī again lost his patron. He returned with a beautiful elegy to Istanbul and finally retired from the service of the court on a modest pension. He took a house on the Wefā Meydāni̊, where many friends gathered round him, especially his pupils, the poet and *tedhkered̲j̲i* Edirneli Sehī and the poet Ṣunʿī. Ned̲j̲ātī died on 25 D̲h̲u 'l-Ḳaʿda 914/17

March 1509. He was buried near his own house, at the monastery of Sheykh Wefā and a tombstone was put up by Sehī for him.

He left a *Dīwān* which he had collected on the advice of Muʾayyad-zāde and dedicated to prince Maḥmūd. There is also attributed to him a *methnewī*, which is not otherwise known, entitled *Münāẓara-yi Gül u Khosrew*, also quoted as *Layla u Medjnūn* and *Mihr u Māh*. Even more uncertain seems to be the existence of the *methnewī* mentioned by Sehī, *Gül u Ṣabā*. Nedjātī is also mentioned as a translator of Persian works, but his pupil Sehī says nothing of this. He is said to have translated for prince Maḥmūd the *Kīmiyā-yi seʿādet* of al-Ghazālī (the Persian version of the Arabic *Iḥyāʾ*) and the *Djāmiʿ al-ḥikāyāt* (properly *Djawāmiʿ al-ḥikāyāt wa-lawāmiʿ al-riwāyāt*) from the Persian of Djamāl al-Dīn al-ʿAwfī.

His *Dīwān*, of which there are 21 mss. in Istanbul libraries has been edited by Ali Nihad Tarlan, *Necati Bey divanı*, Istanbul 1963, and gives Nedjātī a very prominent place in Ottoman literature; the *Dīwān* was regarded as a model for all Ottoman poets. Nedjātī, whom Idrīs Bidlīsī in his *Hasht bihisht* calls *Khosrew-i Shuʿarāʾ-i Rūm* and others *Malik al-Shuʿarāʾ* and *Ṭūsī-yi Rūm* (i.e. the Firdawsī of Anatolia), was regarded as the best poet of Rūm. He does not, it is true, reach the heights of Nesīmī, but he surpasses all his predecessors, of whom Aḥmed Pasha and Dhātī were the greatest, in originality and creative power. Only Bāḳī and Fuḍūlī have surpassed him. The problem to be solved by Aḥmed Pasha, Nedjātī and Dhātī was to incorporate completely into Turkish the matter borrowed and translated from Persian literature, which was still felt to be foreign, to adapt Turkish to Perso-Arabic metres and to domesticate fully the Arabic and Persian vocabulary. This was a great achievement for the time. Nedjātī brought about a great change in the literature as regards outlook, feeling and language. In him the age of Sultan Bāyezīd is most clearly reflected. Although he is not to be claimed as a very great poet, he was the king of the gild of poets of his time, who started a great literary movement. Nedjātī combined a thorough knowledge of Persian with a masterly command of Turkish. In the number of his *ghazels* he far surpasses Bāḳī. His work as a poet of *ḳaṣīdas* was original and stimulating. He was specially celebrated for his skill in the use of the proverb.

Bibliography: Ḥādjdjī Khalīfa, ed. Flügel, ii, 511, iii, 317, v, 285, 347; Laṭīfī, *Tedhkere*, Istanbul 1314, 325-30; Sehī, *Hesht bihisht*, 1325, 75-7; *Sidjill-i ʿothmānī*, iv, 541; Bursalî Meḥmed Ṭāhir, *ʿOthmānlî müʾellifleri*, ii, 435; F. Reshād, *Taʾrīkh-i Edebiyyāt-i ʿothmāniyye*, i, 188-200; idem, *Terādjim-i aḥwāl-i meshāhīr*, Istanbul 1313, 3-16; Ibrāhīm Nedjmī, *Taʾrīkh-i edebiyyāt dersleri*, Istanbul 1338, i, 69-73; Shihāb al-Dīn Süleymān, *Taʾrīkh-i edebiyyāt-i ʿothmāniyye*, 1328, 52-8; Köprülüzāde Meḥmed Fuʾād and Shihāb al-Dīn Süleymān, *ʿOthmānlî taʾrīkh-i edebiyyātî*, 1332, 243-47; Muʿallim Nādjī, *Esāmī*, 1308, 317; Von Hammer, *GOD*, i, 162-78; Gibb, *HOP*, ii, 93-122; Smirnov, *Očerk istorii Turtskoi literaturî*, St. Petersburg 1891, 476; idem, *Obrazotsovîya proizvedeniya Osmanskoi literaturî*, St. Petersburg 1903, 445-8; Rieu, *Catalogue*, London 1888, 171a; Flügel, *Katalog*, i, 624; Basmadjian, *Essai sur l'histoire de la littérature turque*, Constantinople 1910, 44-5; *PTF*, ii, Wiesbaden 1964, 429-30; A. Bombaci, *La letteratura turca*, Florence 1969, 325-8; M. Çavuşoğlu, *Necatî divanı'nın tahlili*, Istanbul 1971; W.G. Andrews, *Poetry's voice, society's song*, Seattle and London 1985, 84-5; *İA*, art. *Necatî Bey* (Fevzıye Abdullah Tansel). (Th. Menzel*)

NEFES (T., from Ar. *nafas* "breath"), the name given to the Turkish folk religious poetry of the Bektāshī Ṣūfī order and other ʿAlawī, Shīʿī or Shīʿī-tinged groups, often performed with a certain *maḳām* [*q.v.*] or melodic musical line.

Legends on the origin of the *nefes* connect Ḥādjdjī Bektāsh [see BEKTĀSHIYYA] with the early 8th/14th century popular mystical poet Yūnus Emre [*q.v.*], recounting that the reluctant Yūnus eventually received the *nefes* or inspiration of the saint, and poured forth hymns on the theme of divine love which themselves became known as *nefesler* "breaths". The *nefes* also expresses strongly love for the Prophet Muḥammad, for ʿAlī and for the Ahl al-Bayt [*q.v.*] in general, and it came to be particularly, though not exclusively, identified with the Bektāshī order. It (and the similar *ilāhī* "divine [hymn]", which had slightly less of a folk character) was often performed to the accompaniment of the *sāz*, a stringed instrument, by the so-called *sāz shāʿirleri* or *ʿāshiḳlar* [see ʿĀSHIḲ].

Only a few *nefesler* were composed in the classical *ʿarūḍ* [*q.v.*] metre, and the vast majority are in *hedje* or syllabic metre, usually of 11 syllables divided 6-5 with one caesura or of 7 or 5 syllables with no caesura. They thus form part of the general body of Turkish folk poetry called *ḳoshma* [*q.v.*] or *türkü*, often sung to a free musical accompaniment.

Most of the writers of the considerable corpus of *nefesler* which has come down to us are anonymous, probably reflecting the secrecy with which the Bektāshīs veiled their rituals; the words of a *nefes* might be written down but not generally made public, and almost none of the musical accompaniments was ever recorded in any kind of notation. We do, however, have some poems after Yūnus Emre's time associated with such famous figures as Ḳayghusuz Abdāl (d. 818/1415 [*q.v.*]), and the *nefesler* of Khatāʾī (i.e. the Ṣafawid Shāh Ismāʿīl [*q.v.*]) are still sung by the Bektāshīs today; and by the 19th century, the names of several Bektāshī *sāz shāʿirleri* are known, such as Seyrānī (d. 1866), Turābī (d. 1868), Dertli (d. 1874), Mirʾātī (*flor.* in the 19th century) and Ḥilmī Dede Baba (d. 1907). The famous poet and philosopher Riḍā Tewfīḳ (d. 1949) [see BÖLÜKBASHÎ RIḌĀ TEWFĪḲ, in Suppl.] also wrote several highly valued poems in the genre.

Bibliography: F.W. Hasluck, *Bektaşilik tetkikleri*, tr. Rağib Hulûsi, Istanbul 1928; Yusuf Ziya, *Anadoluda Alevi itikadları*, in *Hayat Mecmuası*, no. 58 (Istanbul 1928), 105-6; Hasluck, *Christianity and Islam under the sultans*, Oxford 1929, i, 139-66; S.N. Ergun, *Bektaşi şairleri*, Istanbul 1930; *Türk musikisi klasiklerinden Bektaşî nefesleri*, in *İstanbul Belediye Konservatuarı neşriyatı*, iv-v (Istanbul 1933); J.K. Birge, *The Bektashi order of dervishes*, London-Hartford 1937, 53-5, 81, 89 ff., 93-5, 150-241; V.L. Salcı, *Gizli Türk musikisi ve Türk musikisinde armoni meseleleri*, Istanbul 1940; idem, *Kızılbaş şairleri I-X*, in *Halk Bilgisi Haberleri*, nos. 102-7 (Istanbul 1940-1); idem, *Gizli Türk dini oyunları*, Istanbul 1941; M.E. Beşe, *Anadolu Bektaşi köylerinde muharrem ayini*, in *Halk Bilgisi Haberleri*, no. 115 (Istanbul 1941), 158-60; Ergun, *Türk musikisi antolojisi*, Istanbul 1942; H.B. Yönetken, *Bektaşilerde müzik ve oyun*, in *Ülkü Gazetesi* (December, Sivas 1945), 4; Salcı, *Gizli halk musikisi*, in *Ülkü Halkevleri ve Halk Odaları Dergisi*, xi (Ankara, April 1948), 113-23; Ergun, *Bektaşi şairleri ve nefesleri I-II* [up to the 19th century], Ankara 1955; idem, *Bektaşi-Kızılbaş-Alevî şairleri ve nefesleri III* [since the19th century], Ankara 1956; T. Oytan, *Bektaşiligin içyüzü*, Istanbul 1962; Yönetken, *Sirac ve nalcı Alevîlerinde samah*, in *Türk Folklor Araştır-*

maları, vii (Istanbul 1962), 2909-11; A. Gölpınarlı, *Alevi-Bektaşi nefesleri*, Istanbul 1963; B. Noyan, *Bektaşilikte musiki*, in *Musiki ve nota*, Istanbul 1970-1; Gölpınarlı, *Türk tasavvuf şiiri antolojisi*, Milliyet Yayinları, Istanbul 1972; P.N. Boratav, in *PTF*, ii, 29-47, 92; C. Sunar, *Melâmîlik ve Bektaşilik*, Ankara 1975; N. Birdoğan, *Samahlar*, in *Folklor ve Etnografya Araştırmaları Yıllığı* (Istanbul 1984), 31-51; T. Koca and Z. Onaran, *Güldeste, nefesler-ezgiler*, Ankara 1987; N. Özcan, *Bektaşî mûsikisi*, in *Türkiye Diyanet Ansiklopedisi*, v, Istanbul 1992, 371-2; A.Y. Ocak, *Bektaşilik*, in *ibid.*, 373-9.

(Tevfik Rüştü Topuzoğlu)

NEFʿĪ (980-1044/1572-1635), the greatest satirist of the Ottomans. ʿÖmer Efendi, whose nom-de-plume (*makhlaṣ*) was Nefʿī, came from the village of Ḥasan Ḳalʿa near Erzerūm (eastern Anatolia). Not much is known of his early life. He spent his early years in Erzerūm where the historian ʿĀlī [*q.v.*], who was a *defterdār* there, became acquainted with him. During the reign of Aḥmed I, fate brought him to the capital Istanbul where he worked for a time as a book-keeper. He failed in an attempt to gain the sultan's favour or that of his son, the unfortunate ʿOthmān II, with some brilliant *ḳaṣīdas*. It was not till the reign of Murād IV that he gained the imperial favour, but his malicious, sarcastic and indecent poems soon brought him into disgrace. He was appointed to the office concerned with the levying and collection of the *djizya* [*q.v.*], and later again became a member of the sultan's circle. His irresistible impulse to make all the notables of the empire the butt of his mockery made him a host of enemies. A satire on Bayrām Pasha, the sultan's brother-in-law and vizier, who had succeeded in being recalled from banishment and again attaining influence, cost him his life. The *muftī* gave his sanction to the execution of the great poet. With the sultan's consent he was shut up in the wood-cellar of the Imperial Palace, then strangled and his body thrown into the sea. The year of his death was Shaʿbān 1044/February 1635, not 1045 as Ḥādjdjī Khalīfa, *Fedhleke*, ii, 183, wrongly says (cf. on the other hand his *Kashf al-ẓunūn*, iii, 318, 631, where the correct date is given).

Nefʿī wrote Turkish and Persian with equal ease. His mastery of technique and natural poetical talent make him one of the greatest Ottoman poets; he is also undoubtedly one of the greatest, although hitherto little-known satirists. The reason why he is so little known is that a scholarly edition with full annotations of his Turkish *Dīwān* entitled "Arrows of Fate", *Sihām-i ḳaḍāʾ*, has so far never been undertaken, so that at the present day hardly any one is able to understand the countless allusions to particular circumstances and the veiled attacks on the individuals dealt with. The publication of his poems demands a knowledge of the conditions of his period, and particularly of life at court, which it is hardly possible to attain and which it would be very difficult to gather from the existing sources. Many of his flashes of wit and allusions are very difficult to understand. Many of his poems are distinguished by an obscenity which can hardly be surpassed and, however great may be their importance for the social history of his time, they are of little value as evidence of his poetic gifts. The "Arrows of Fate" are directed against almost every one prominent in politics and society in his time. In *GOD*, iii, 241, J. von Hammer has compiled a list of them. Some of his poems which pillory existing institutions, like the popular saints, the Ḳalender dervishes [see ḲALANDARIYYA] etc., are of value for social history. Hardly one important contemporary was able to escape his scorn and ridicule. They were all made targets for his "Arrows of Fate" without mercy. He attacked the theologians (*ʿulemāʾ*) particularly unsparingly. Nefʿī's Turkish *Dīwān* has been several times printed: two parts at Būlāḳ in 1253, and in 1269 at Istanbul. Selections (with ample evidence of ʿAbd al-Ḥamīd's censorship!) were published by Abu 'l-Ḍiyāʾ Tewfīḳ in 1311 at Istanbul. There are mss. in European collections in London, Leiden and Vienna. A short *Sāḳī-nāme* by Nefʿī is mentioned in the catalogue of mss. of the Leipzig council library by H.L. Fleischer (p. 547b). His Persian *dīwān*, not yet printed in its entirety, exists in several mss.; a Turkish translation, based on four mss. has been made by Ali Nihad Tarlan, *Nef'i'nin farsça divânı tercümesi*, Istanbul 1944. A collection of *münsheʾāt* is attributed to him, though it is dubious whether this was ever an independent collection.

On the circumstances of his death, see al-Muḥibbī, *Khulāṣat al-athar*, Cairo 1284/1867-8, iii, 228-9; Farāʾiḍī-zāda, *Taʾrīkh-i gülshen-i maʿārif*, i, Istanbul 1252, 668; and Naʿīmā, *Taʾrīkh*, ii, 489.

Bibliography: In addition to the sources mentioned, see also Gibb, *Ottoman poems*, 208, and *HOP*, iii, 252 ff.; the history of Naʿīmā, i, 586, and Bursalī Meḥmed Ṭāhir, *ʿOthmānlī müʾellifleri*, ii, 441 (according to which parts of his Persian *Dīwān* were published in the *Khazīne-yi Fünūn*); A. Karahan, *Nefʾi*, Istanbul 1954; A. Bombaci, *La letteratura turca*, Florence 1969, 370-3; Karahan, *Nefʾi divanında seçmeler*, Ankara 1985, ²Istanbul 1986; M. Çavuşoğlu, *Ölümünün üçyüzellinci yılında Nefʾi*, Ankara 1987; *İA*, art. s.v. (Abdülkadir Karahan). Examples of Nefʿī's poems are given in Fahir İz, *Eski türk edebiyatında nazım*, Istanbul 1966-7, i, 17-19, 70-86, 120-4, 519, 528-9. (F. Babinger)

NEFĪR (A.), a term alluding in Ottoman usage to a musical instrument similar to a horn that comprised a part of the Ottoman band [see MEHTER]. The person playing the instrument was referred to as *nefīrī*, and, according to the 1755 and 1776 Ottoman salary registers, there were twelve such players in the sultan's band of approximately sixty members. This band, and similar ones like it belonging to high-level Ottoman officials, travelled with their owners wherever they went, and normally played during the day before three prayers, sc. the afternoon one, the one two hours after sunset, and then the one in the morning. They also performed during ceremonial events such as upon a sultan's accession, or during celebrations such as upon the arrival of the news of an Ottoman campaign victory.

The term, in its military usage, alludes to a body of men assembled for a common purpose. The Ottoman practice of the recruitment of volunteers by a general call to arms, referred to as *nefīr-i ʿāmm*, was resorted to on the declaration of war against Russia in 1769 by Muṣṭafā III. He took such a measure because of his reluctance to rely on the ill-trained and financially demanding Janissaries. *Nefīr-i khāṣṣ*, on the other hand, referred to the mobilisation of only a certain well-defined group of people.

Bibliography: For the musical usage, see Rāshid Meḥmed Pasha, *Tārīkh-i Rāshid*, Istanbul 1865, iii, 70, 82; M. D'Ohsson *Tableau général de l'Empire ottoman*, Paris 1791, vii, part 6; I.H. Uzunçarşılı, *Osmanlı devletinin saray teşkilatı*, Ankara 1984, 150, 273, 275, 277, 449; idem, *Osmanlı devletinin merkez ve bahriye teşkilatı*, Ankara 1984, 208. For the military usage: Gibb-Bowen, i/1, 194; Baron de Tott, *Mémoires sur les Turcs et les Tatares*, Amsterdam 1784, iii, 4-5; M. Zeki Pakalın, *Osmanlı tarih deyimleri ve terimleri sözlüğü*, Istanbul 1953, 672.

(F. Müge Göçek)

NEGEV [see AL-NAḲB].

NEMČE (NEMSE; A. *al-Nimsā*), a term (meaning "mute") borrowed from the Slavonic used by the Ottomans to indicate the Germans. In a broader sense, they also used it for the territory of the Holy Roman Empire, which lasted until 1806, and in a restricted sense for the territories under Habsburg rule within the boundaries of modern Austria.

In more recent Arabic sources, Germany is indicated by two terms which occur simultaneously: *Almāniyā* and *Djarmāeniya*. In Ottoman sources *Al(a)mān*, and occasionally *Djermāniya*, also occur next to *Nemče*, without further differentiation. It was only after the foundation of the Austrian Empire in 1804 that the Ottomans, in the course of the 19th century, adopted *Almanya* and *Awusturya* (*Aghusturya* being the older form) as different concepts. In Arabic, on the other hand, *al-Nimsā* was accepted as indicating Austria.

1. In Arabic sources.

Already in the 10th century, al-Masʿūdī (*Murūdj*, iii, 63 = § 906) mentions the Nāmdjīn as a tribe of the Slavs. Amongst the travellers and merchants who travelled through their territory (Germany), al-Masʿūdī's contemporary Ibrāhīm b. Yaʿḳūb [*q.v.*] deserves particular mention, although the name of the territory cannot be established from his account. The most comprehensive mediaeval source in Arabic concerning Austria is al-Idrīsī's *Nuzhat al-mushtāḳ* where information about Austrian toponyms is found in the various climes and sections. The name *al-Nimsā*, however, does not appear. The only Austrian region named specifically is Carinthia (*Ḳaranṭāra*), whose territory stretches out over wide parts of Austria, Hungary and other adjoining states. Cities in Styria, like Graz (*Ikrīzā*), and in Carinthia, like Villach (*Bilāḥ*), are described in greater detail, but Vienna (*Wiyāna*) appears only in an itinerary. The rivers Danube (*Nahr Danū*) and Drau (*Nahr D-r-wa*) are given as boundaries of Carinthia, while the Alps (*Munt Dj-w-z* – Mont [Mons] Jovis) are also attributed to other territories. Al-Idrīsī's criterion for including Austrian cities in his *Geography* apparently was their significance as trading places. He may have been informed by merchants.

Endeavours to identify an Austrian (Styrian) city from Abu 'l-Fidā's *Taḳwīm al-buldān* (Reinaud, *Géographie d'Aboulféda*, ii/1, 311, quoted after Ibn Saʿīd al-Maghribī, cf. *Kitāb al-Djughrāfiyā*, ed. al-ʿArabī 1970, 194) have been unsuccessful.

Bibliography: P. Engels, *Der Reisebericht des Ibrāhīm b. Yaʿqūb*, in *Kaiserin Theophanu*, ed. A. von Euw and P. Schreiner, i, Cologne 1991; H. Eisenstein, *Kärnten in al-Idrīsī's Geographie (1154)* in *WZKM*, lxxxiii (1993). (H. EISENSTEIN)

2. In Ottoman sources and in Ottoman-Habsburg relations.

The hereditary provinces of the Habsburgs had their first contacts with the Ottomans when Carniola, Styria and Carinthia were repeatedly attacked by Ottoman incursions. Sultan Bāyezīd II [*q.v.*] and the Emperor Maximilian I having sounded out diplomatic relations in 1497, 1504 and 1510-11, Ottomans and Habsburgs were brought into continuous, immediate and hostile contact through the political situation in Hungary after the battle of Mohács [*q.v.*] in 1526. Sultan Süleymān I [*q.v.*] undertook two campaigns against Habsburg territory, in 1529 against Vienna and in 1532 across southern Lower Austria, Styria and Carniola. After part of Hungary had been put under direct Ottoman rule in 1541, it was only in 1547 that Ferdinand I succeeded in concluding a treaty, which compelled him to pay to the sultan a yearly tribute of 30,000 golden ducats. This liability of the Habsburgs to paying tribute, interrupted only by war, lasted until the treaty of Zsitvatorok in 1606. At the beginning, the open state of war was interrupted by truce treaties, which were fixed for several years and repeatedly renewed and extended. Only in 1747 did Habsburg diplomacy succeed in concluding an unrestricted treaty (... *mesāgh-i sherʿī oldughī vedjhile müddet-i memdūde* ...). The wars of the 16th and 17th centuries found their origin in the conflict of interests about political power in Hungary. The unsuccessful attack against Vienna in 1683 of Ḳara Muṣṭafā Pasha [*q.v.*] was for the Ottomans the climax of a protracted war, marked by great losses, which led to losing Hungary to the Habsburgs. In the 18th century the latter, due to their alliances with Venice and Russia, and to their political ambitions on the Balkan Peninsula, became involved in three further wars with the Ottoman Empire.

After 1547 the Habsburgs continuously kept ambassadors at the Porte and, during the period of tribute—but only in times of peace—missions were sent yearly to deliver the tribute. After 1606 important embassies used to be sent on specific occasions like the ratification of a treaty or the access to the throne of a new sultan. At first, the Ottomans sent to Vienna *čāʾūsh*s [*q.v.*], dragomans [see TARDJUMĀN] and the like in emergency cases only; in the 17th century they also began to send important missions but only for specific purposes. A permanent diplomatic representation of the Ottoman Empire in Vienna began only in 1797 (with a vacancy between 1823 and 1832).

The Treaties of Vienna of 1615 and of Karlowitz [see ḲARLOFČA] of 1699 already contained articles on reciprocal trade. In 1718 a separate commercial treaty was concluded at Passarowitz (Požarevac) [see PASAROFČA], in which it was permitted for Habsburg subjects freely to establish consulates in the ports and on the islands of the Mediterranean, and to organise free shipping on the Danube (the Black Sea excepted). In the twenties of the 18th century, commercial and navigation treaties were also concluded with local leaders of the Barbarian states which were part of the Ottoman Empire. An agreement of 1783 with the Ottomans aimed at protecting Habsburg subjects from piracy and settling questions of compensation. In the commercial treaty of 1784 Habsburg subjects were granted the privilege of free commercial navigation on the Black Sea, a right given to Russia already a year earlier.

Next to the Habsburg Emperors, the Dutch Republic and the Kings of Prussia were the only powers within the Holy Roman Empire to maintain independent diplomatic relations with the Ottomans before the 19th century. During the last war between the Ottomans and the Habsburgs (1788-91), Prussia, in the Convention of Reichenbach of 1790, forced the Emperor Leopold II to renounce any conquest of Ottoman territory.

Apart from the detailed description of the campaigns of Sultan Süleymān I in 1529 and 1532, of the siege of Vienna by Ḳara Muṣṭafā Pasha in 1683, and of the warfare in Hungary and later on in the Balkan Peninsula, Ottoman historiography contains, from the middle of the 17th century onwards, references to the political events in Europe, including the Holy Roman Empire. The data, at first sparse and sporadic (for instance in Kātib Čelebi, Münedjdjim-Bashī Aḥmed, Muṣṭafā Naʿīmā, Silāḥdār Fīndīḳlīlī Meḥmed [*q.vv.*]), became increasingly extensive and accurate in the course of the 18th century because diplomatic contacts intensified and interest in information grew. From the second half of the 17th century onwards, the official embassy reports (*sefāret-nāme*), the travel accounts of those who accompanied the important diplomatic missions, and individual treatises provided the Ottomans with a detailed and differentiated picture of the political situation in Europe. Among the travel accounts, a particular place is taken up by Ewliyā Čelebi's description of his journey to Vienna while in the train of the Ottoman embassy of 1665. Further information undoubtedly came from Ottoman prisoners of war: Ḥasan Esīrī left a description of the campaign of 1683 against Vienna, and ʿO<u>th</u>mān A<u>gh</u>a of Temesvár provides us with information about his stay in Styria and in Vienna during his captivity.

Samples of the German language are given by Ewliyā Čelebi, who put together a highly imaginative etymology of the term *Nemče* (= *nem Čeh*/Hungarian *nem Cseh* "not Czech").

Bibliography: See the general works on the history of the Ottoman Empire by von Hammer, Zinkeisen, Iorga, Uzunçarşılı, Shaw, etc.; Z. Abrahamowicz-V. Kopčan-M. Kunt-E. Marosi-N. Močanin-C. Serban-K. Teply, *Die Türkenkriege in der historischen Forschung*, Vienna 1983; *Die Autobiographie des Dolmetschers ʿOs̱mān Aġa aus Temeschwar*, ed. R.F. Kreutel, Cambridge 1980; K. Beydilli, *Büyük Friedrich ve Osmanlılar*, Istanbul 1985; idem, *1790 Osmanlı-Prusya ittifâkı*, Istanbul 1984; L. Bittner, *Chronologisches Verzeichnis der österreichischen Staatsverträge*, i-iv, Vienna 1903-17; Ewliyā Čelebi, *Seyāḥat-nāme*, vii, German tr. of the relevant section by R.F. Kreutel, *Im Reiche des Goldenen Apfels* ..., ed. E. Prokosch and K. Teply, Graz-Vienna-Cologne 1987; *Habsburgisch-osmanische Beziehungen/Relations Habsbourg-ottomanes* ..., ed. A. Tietze, Vienna 1985; M. Köhbach, *Die diplomatischen Beziehungen zwischen Österreich und dem Osmanischen Reich*, in *Osmanlı Araştırmaları*, iv (1984); B. Lewis, *The Muslim discovery of Europe*, New York-London 1982; E.D. Petritsch, *Regesten der osmanischen Dokumente im Österreichischen Staatsarchiv. 1 (1480-1574)*, Vienna 1991; A.C. Schaendlinger. *Die osmanisch-habsburgischen Beziehungen in der ersten Hälfte des 16. Jhs.*, in *Osmanlı Araştırmaları*, iv (1984); A.C. Schaendlinger-C. Römer, *Die Schreiben Süleymāns des Prächtigen an Karl V., Ferdinand I. und Maximilian I. aus dem Haus-, Hof- und Staatsarchiv zu Wien*, Vienna 1983; K. Teply, *Türkische Sagen und Legenden um die Kaiserstadt Wien*, Vienna-Cologne-Graz 1980; F.R. Unat, *Osmanlı sefirleri ve sefaretnâmeleri*, Ankara 1968; A.H. de Groot, *The Ottoman Empire and the Dutch Republic*, Leiden-Istanbul 1978. (M. Köhbach)

NEPAL, a Hindu kingdom with an area of 147,000 km² (80°-88° 15′E, 26° 20′-30° 10′N) rising up on the southern edge of the Himalayas between the Ganges plain (India) and Tibet (China). The southern plain and the central mountains, with a sub-tropical climate suitable for rice culture, nourish a dense population of Indian origin and who speak Indo-Aryan languages: the Hindus of the plain speak Hindi, and the Indo-Nepalese of the mountains speak the official language, Nepali, a branch of Pahāṛī; they dominate tribes speaking Muṇḍā and Tibeto-Burmese languages [see hind. iii. Languages.]. The high valleys shelter a thinly-scattered population of Tibetans. The total population was 19,360,000 according to the 1991 census. It is almost 90% Hindu, and Hinduism is the official religion. The main religious minorities, whose numbers fluctuate from one census to another, are the Buddhists (between 5 and 10%) and the Muslims (*ca.* 3%).

The toponym Nēpāl, with no known etymology (written *Naypāl* or *Nīpāl*, نيپال), is attested from the 4th century AD in Sanskrit epigraphy, and was known to the Muslims of the 5th/11th century through al-Bīrūnī's India (Eng. tr. Sachau, *Alberuni's India*, London 1910, i, 98); it designated solely the valley of Katmandu (Kāṭhmāṇḍū). Hindu kings ruled there over an ethnically Tibeto-Burmese population, the Newār (largely Hindu with a strong Buddhist minority) which prospered thanks to trade with India, Tibet and China. The valley recognised the suzerainty of the Dihlī sultan ʿAlāʾ al-Dīn <u>Kh</u>al<u>dj</u>ī (695-715/1296-1316 [see <u>kh</u>al<u>dj</u>īs]); it was raided by the Bengal sultan <u>Sh</u>ams al-Dīn Ilyās (746-59/1345-58) in 750/1349 (L. Petech, *Medieval Nepal*, Rome 1958, 103-4, 118-22, 177; *Hommage à Sylvain Lévi*, Paris 1964, 23). According to the chronicles, the first Muslim merchants coming from Ka<u>sh</u>mīr established themselves at Kāṭhmāṇḍū under Ratna Malla (1482-1512); their presence is attested from the 17th century onwards by the Catholic missionaries then established in Tibet and Nepal, and, from 1738 onwards by official Nepali documents. The remainder of what is now modern Nepal was shared out amongst some fifty kingdoms; the land of the plain cultivated by the petty rulers of the mountains came, in the 14th century, under the control of the Dihlī Sultans, those of Bengal and then the Mu<u>gh</u>al emperors; these petty rulers, like the kings of the Kāṭhmāṇḍū valley, paid tribute to them in the form of elephants. The population of the Nepal plain thus included some Muslims from that time; some of these, makers of glass bracelets above all, became established in the mountains during the 17th century.

With the decline of the Mu<u>gh</u>als, whilst the English East India Co. secured a foothold in northern India, the present Indo-Nepalese dynasty of Gorkha created the modern state of Nepal. Prithwī Narāyań (1742-74) conquered the Kāṭhmāṇḍū valley in 1768-9 (despite armed intervention by the Nawwāb of Bengal and the British) and subdued the eastern districts, including Sikkim; his successors continued the policy of expansion towards the west until, in 1814, their lands became contiguous with those of the Sikhs. Prithwī Narāyań secured British recognition and that of the puppet Mu<u>gh</u>al emperor <u>Sh</u>āh ʿĀlam II (1759-1806) in a *farmān* of 1184/1771 (B. Āčārya, *<u>Sh</u>rī 5 bařā-mahārā<u>dj</u>ādhirā<u>dj</u> Prithwī Narāyań <u>Sh</u>āh-ko sankśipta <u>dj</u>īwanī*, Katmandu 1967, iv, 713-18). Tribute was paid from that time onwards to the British until the Anglo-Nepalese War of 1814-16 and the treaty of 1818 which blocked Gorkha expansion and set up the frontier between Nepalese and British territories. The Rāńās, mayors of the palace who directed affairs in the country from 1846 to 1951, put relations with Britain on a normal footing; they helped them in 1857-8 to recover Lucknow, but gave refuge to some <u>Sh</u>īʿī nobles from that city. The independence of Nepal was recognised in a treaty of 1923.

The evidence of travellers like Francis Hamilton and the British Residents in Nepal like Brian H. Hodgson, confirmed by the archives and by legal texts, has brought out the religious policy of the new dynasty. It strengthened the Hindu character of the kingdom. Faithful to the tradition already set forth by al-Bīrūnī (*op. cit.*, i, 19-20), it insisted on the impurity of Muslims; they were considered as "barbarians" (*mleččha*) and severely punished if they caused the pollution of Hindus of pure caste. It introduced new measures in forbidding them to proselytise (allowed until then), as also were forbidden Christian missionaries, who were definitively expelled, together with their converts. The Muslims were nevertheless (apart from a temporary expulsion of Kashmīrī traders at the end of the 18th century) able to stay, to engage in commerce and to enjoy freedom to practise their religion. They did not have any personal law of their own; in regard to marriage (except for prohibited degrees), divorce, inheritance and the administration of pious foundations, they were always subject to Hindu law and answerable to Hindu judges. The discriminatory clauses regarding them were enshrined in the legal codes of 1854 and 1935; they remained in force until the Code of 1963. This last abolished the penalties to which Muslims were liable for breakages of the caste rules; but despite the suppression of the principle of religious discrimination in the 1962 Constitution, it retained the prohibition of proselytism, and this last was even inserted in the Constitution of 1990.

Meanwhile, with the fall of the Rāṅās in 1951, the land was opened up to modernisation. Censuses and ethnological fieldwork allow us to construct an ethnology of the Muslims of Nepal. Amounting to some 570,000 persons, they are almost all living on the plain, where they make up an average of 10% of the population there. They are petty traders, artisans and peasants; also, some 2,000 petty traders (Kashmīrīs and Hindūstānīs) live in the Kāthmāndū valley, whilst the 10-15,000 manufacturers of bracelets in the mountains to the west of Kāthmāndū live by agriculture and the peddling of ornaments. All of these originate from the Ganges plain and speak dialects of Hindi; stemming mainly from Hindus converted to Islam, they form a very hierachical society, an Islamic version of the Hindu caste system. They are almost all Ḥanafī Sunnīs, with a few Twelver Shīʿīs attested in the plain. The religious life has an Indian character and is heavily impregnated with Ṣūfism and the cult of saints [see HIND. ii. Ethnography]. This fidelity to the cult of saints, current in the highest classes, amongst the Kashmīrīs of Kāthmāndū in particular, is under fire in the more popular circles from the reform doctrines (called "Wahhābism" by their opponents) of the Deoband [*q.v.*] and of the Ahl-i Ḥadīth [*q.v.*] schools introduced as far as the mountains by migrant workers who come back from the towns of India bearing cheap, edifying literature in Urdu; mosques and village Ḳurʾān schools have multiplied, and a few scores of Nepalis make the *ḥadjdj* each year.

The firm and constant policy of the monarchy has been to forbid all violence against religious minorities, so that, despite the legal discrimination under which they live, the Muslims have always felt themselves more secure in Nepal than in India. Facing an internal opposition more and more active since 1979, the monarchy has since then cultivated its Muslim subjects, whose vote is a valuable support.

Bibliography: For a general survey of Nepal, see M. Gaborieau, *Le Népal et ses populations*, Brussels-Paris 1978. On the history and position of the Muslims there, there are two outstandingly important pieces of evidence: F. Hamilton, *An account of the kingdom of Nepal*, Edinburgh 1819, repr. Delhi 1971; and B.H. Hodgson, *Some account of the system of law and police as recognized in the State of Nepal*, in *JRAS*, i/2 (1834), 258-79. The general body of sources (to be completed by the references given in the text of the article) are gathered together, and often edited for the first time, in Gaborieau, *Récit d'un voyageur musulman au Tibet*, Paris 1973; idem, *Minorités musulmans dans le royaume hindou du Népal*, Paris 1977. For the ethnology and political evolution of these minorites, see also Gaborieau, *Muslim minorities in Nepal*, in R. Israeli (ed.), *The crescent in the East Islam in Asia Major*, London 1982, 79-101; idem, *Ni Brahmanes, ni Ancêtres: colporteurs musulmans du Népal*, Paris 1992. (M. GABORIEAU)

NERGISĪ, NERGISĪ-ZĀDE MEḤMED EFENDI (d. 1044/1635), pre-eminent Ottoman prose stylist.

He was born in Sarajevo, probably around 994/1586, son of the *ḳāḍī* Nergis Aḥmed Efendi, and completed his education in Istanbul, becoming a protégé of Ḳāf-zāde Fayḍ Allāh Efendi (d. 1020/1611), from whom (and not, as in some accounts, from his son Kāf-zāde ʿAbd al-Ḥayy Fāʾiḍī Efendi) he received his *mülāzemet* [*q.v.*]. He may have served briefly as a *müderris*, but his principal employment was as *ḳāḍī* in various posts in Rūmeli, mainly in Bosnia. Following early appointments (during the period *ca.* 1022-27/*ca.* 1613-18) to Gabela and Čayniče, he was invited by Ḳāf-zāde Fāʾiḍī, then *ḳāḍī* of Salonica, to act as his *nāʾib* (early 1028/1619). On Ḳāf-zāde's dismissal in early 1029/1620, Nergisī again sought a *ḳāḍīlīḳ*, and was appointed, successively but with intervals, to Mostar (1030/1620-1) and shortly afterwards to Yeñi Pazar, to Elbasan (1034/1624-5), Banjaluka (1038/1628-9), and Monastir (1042/1632). In 1044/1634-5 he was appointed by Murād IV as *waḳʿa-nüwīs* for the Revan campaign, but died at its outset, near Gebze on the Gulf of Izmit, as the result of a fall from his horse (9 Shewwāl 1044/28 March 1635). (On Nergisī's career, see Ö.F. Akün, *Nergisī*, in *İA*, ix, 194-6.)

Though a minor figure as a *ḳāḍī*, Nergisī was recognised as one of the leading prose writers of his day, aided by his friendship with the Ḳāf-zādes and with fellow littérateurs such as Weysī and Sheykh al-Islām Yaḥyā among others. His principal works fall into three groups:

1. *Khamse*, printed Būlāḳ 1255/1839 (once in *taʿlīḳ* script, once in *neskh*), and Istanbul 1285/1868-9. In chronological order of composition, these five works are: (i) *Ghazawāt-i Mesleme* (1030/1620-1), a brief account (attributed to Ibn al-ʿArabī, Muḥyi l'-Dīn [*q.v.*], but generally considered spurious) of the campaign of the Umayyad general Maslama b. ʿAbd al-Malik [*q.v.*] against the Byzantines and his five sieges of Istanbul. The work was translated into French in 1741 (E. Blochet, *Catalogue des manuscrits turcs*, Paris, 1933 ii, 38). (ii) *Ḳānūn al-reshād*, written 1033/1623-4 as an accession gift for Murād IV. Initially a translation of a 16th-century Persian "mirror for princes" written for Shāh Muḥammad Khudābanda [*q.v.*], the work was considerably expanded with Nergisī's own observations on Ottoman history. (iii) *Meshāḳḳ al-ʿushshāḳ* (1034/1624-5), originally a collection of ten love stories, of contemporary origin and significance, apart from two tales taken from the *tedhkire* of ʿĀshīḳ Čelebi [*q.v.*]. Nergisī later re-used six of the stories in the *Nihālistān*. (iv) *Iksīr-i seʿāda* (or *Iksīr-i dewlet*, 1041/1632), a translation of part of al-Ghazālī's [*q.v.*] *Kīmiyāʾ al-saʿāda* on ethics. Nergisī's text became a popular Ottoman version and was separately printed several times. (v) *Nihālistān*, (1042/1632-3, his last work). Containing 25 stories arranged in five sections (*nihāl* = "offshoots"), this was compiled as a collection of ethical, exemplary and cautionary tales intended as an Ottoman literary and cultural *naẓīre* to Saʿdī's *Gülistān* and the *Bahāristān* of Djāmi [*q.vv.*]. Like *Meshāḳḳ al-ʿushshāḳ*, it too is significant for the use of contemporary allusions.

2. *Münsheʾāt*. Nergisī's autograph collection of his

own letters (finally totalling 38) was first made for presentation to Sheykh al-Islām Yaḥyā during the latter's first *meshīkhat* (1031/1622-3) and later expanded to include letters down to 1036/1626-7 (published in J.R. Walsh, *The* Esālībü 'l-mekātīb (Münşe'āt) *of Meḥmed Nergisī Efendi*, in *Archivum Ottomanicum*, i [1969], 213-302). Manuscripts of a later collection, probably made by Shaykh Meḥmed b. Meḥmed Sheykhī, contain over 50 letters.

3. *al-Waṣf al-kāmil fī aḥwāl al-wazīr al-ʿādil* (1038/1628), an account of the exemplary character and deeds of Murtaḍā Pasha as governor of Buda 1626-8. (On the various mss. of this unpublished work, see A.S. Levend, *Gazavāt-nāmeler ve Mihaloğlu Ali Bey'in gazavāt-nāmesi*, Ankara 1956, 105-6.)

Nergisī was also an accomplished poet, and renowned as a calligrapher both for his skill in the *taʿlīḳ* script, and for his speed of copying.

For two centuries after his death, Nergisī was honoured as master of the mature Ottoman *inshā'* prose, and his style was widely imitated. However, with the rising popularity of a simpler, more direct literary style in the *Tanẓīmāt* era and later, he was reviled for promoting what was considered a stilted and unnaturally affected style, a florid elegance which was held to have completely sacrificed sense to sound in a bombastic, overladen language. In the wake of this extreme critical reaction, his works have become largely neglected. It is nonetheless accepted that his influence upon the development of the Ottoman *inshā'* style was profound.

Bibliography: The scanty details on Nergisī's career are found mainly in his own works listed above; for entries (not always reliable) in Ottoman *tedhkire* and other biographical works, see the bibl. to Ö.F. Akün's essential article s.v. in *İA*, ix, 194-7.

(Christine Woodhead)

NESH'ET Khōdja Süleymān, an Ottoman poet. He was born in Edirne in 1148/1735, the son of the poet Aḥmed Rafīʿ Efendi, then in exile; the latter is known as *Muṣāḥib-i Shahriyārī*. With his father, who had regained the sultan's favour by writing a *sharḳī* which met with general approval, he came to Istanbul. He also accompanied his father on a journey to the Ḥidjāz, and the young *Ḥādjdjī*, on his way back, joined the Mewlewī order in Ḳonya. After his father's death, he devoted himself to study, especially Persian, in order to understand the *Methnewī*. In Persian, which he came to love passionately, he attained a high degree of perfection, with the result that he had more pupils than an ordinary school in his house in Mollā Gūrānī, where he taught Persian and expounded the *Methnewī* (*Methnewī-khwānlīḳ*). He enjoyed great prestige among the people. Later he attached himself to the Naḳshbandī Sheykh Bursawī Emīn Efendi. He held a fief, and therefore took part in 1182/1768 in the Russian campaign. He could use the sword as well as the pen. Nesh'et died in 1222/1807 and was buried outside the Top Ḳapu.

He received the nom-de-plume of Nesh'et from Djūdī. Nesh'et was a moderate poet but an admirable teacher. No-one would say an unkind word about him, and they winked at his smoking the *čibuḳ*, which was otherwise forbidden. He wrote poetry in Turkish and in Persian. Many of his pupils far surpassed him, such as Ghālib Dede [*q.v.*]. He left a *Dīwān*, collected together in 1200/1785 by his pupil Pertew Efendi, which was printed in two parts in Būlāḳ (1252/1836). His *Makhlaṣ-nāmes* (about 20 in the *Dīwān*) are distinctive in character; these are poems in which he bestowed epithets upon gifted pupils. In addition, he left writings on the Naḳshbandiyye: *Ṭūfān-i maʿrifet; Tardjamat al-ʿishḳ; Maslak al-anwār wa-manbaʿ al-asrār*. His *Terdjeme-i sharḥ-i dū-ʿbayt-i Mollā Djāmī* was printed at Istanbul in 1263. A biography of him by Pertew Efendi which was continued by Emīn Efendi is said to exist.

Bibliography: Bursalï Meḥmed Ṭāhir, *ʿOthmānlï müʾellifleri*, ii, 461; Muʿallim Nādjī, in *Medjmūʿa*, no. 8, 74-6; idem, *ʿOthmānlï shāʿirleri*, 64-70; *Khazīne-yi funūn*, Istanbul 1312, ii, 230 (*Eslāf*); Thüreyyā, *Sidjill-i ʿothmānī*, iv, 552; Sāmī, *Ḳāmūs al-aʿlām*, vi, 4576; Meḥmed Djelāl, *ʿOthmānlï edebiyyātï nümüneleri*, Istanbul 1312, 263; Flügel, *Die arabischen ... Hss. ... zu Wien*, i, 686; *İA*, art. *Neş'et* (Fevziye Abdullah Tansel). Two of his *ghazels* are given in Fahir İz, *Eski türk edebiyatında nazım*, Istanbul 1966-7, i, 435-6.

(Th. Menzel)

NESHRĪ (d. before 926/1520), Ottoman historian.

Neshrī's one, partially-surviving, historical work, the *Djihān-nümā*, marks a pivotal point in both the development and the study of Ottoman historiography. However, very little is known with certainty about its author, aside from his *makhlaṣ* Neshrī, which occurs at the end of the history in a *ḳaṣīda* addressed to the reigning sultan Bāyezīd II [*q.v.*]. From scanty and largely unreliable references by later Ottoman writers such as Laṭīfī, ʿĀshïḳ Čelebi, ʿĀlī and Kātib Čelebi [*q.vv.*], it was long thought that his given name was Meḥmed and that he lived mainly in Bursa, for some time as *müderris* at the Sulṭāniyye *medrese*. References in the *Djihān-nümā* implying a personal knowledge of Bursa support the assumption of his residence there, and the style of his history suggests that he was a member of the *ʿulemā'*. Otherwise, there is nothing in the history or in other known contemporary sources to confirm either his name or his profession. A certain Neshrī Ḥüseyn b. Eyne Beg mentioned in a Bursa court register of 884/1479 may or may not be identical with the historian. The only explicitly personal information in the *Djihān-nümā* establishes that Neshrī was present in the Ottoman camp at the time of Meḥemmed II's death in 886/1481, and that his account of the subsequent Janissary riots in Istanbul is based on personal observation. The date of his death is also uncertain, though it is possible that, as stated by Laṭīfī, he lived into the reign of Selīm I (for biographical discussion, see F. Taeschner, *Ǵihānnümā. Die altosmanische Chronik des Mevlānā Meḥemmed Neschrī*, Leipzig, i, 1951, 9-14; M.C. Şehabeddin Tekindağ, *Neşrî*, in *İA*, ix, 214-15; V.L. Ménage, *Neshrī's History of the Ottomans: the sources and development of the text*, London 1964, 1-5).

Neshrī's *Djihān-nümā* was originally conceived as a universal history in six parts, but only the last section is known to be extant. This consists of an introduction, and three *ṭabaḳas* covering respectively the Oghuz Turks, the Saldjūḳs of Rūm and the Ottomans; it chronicles events down to 890/1485 (Bāyezīd II's conquest of Akkerman), and concludes with a list of the principal viziers and holy men of the Ottoman period, followed by the dedication to Bāyezīd II. The style is a relatively straightforward Ottoman prose. The work was probably completed between 892/1487 and Rabīʿ II 898/February 1493 (Ménage, *Neshrī's History*, 9). Neshrī's sources are not named in the text, but for the Ottoman period appear to have been principally ʿĀshïḳ-pasha-zāde's history, a chronological list, *taḳwīm*, of the mid-15th century, and an anonymous chronicle of the late 15th century (P. Wittek, *Zum Quellenproblem der ältesten osmanischen Chroniken (mit Auszügen aus Neśrī)*, in *MOG*, i [1921-2], 77-150; Ménage, *op. cit.*, 10-19). The *Djihān-nümā* thus amalgamates the three principal Ottoman historiographical traditions then existing (H. İnalcık, *The rise of Ottoman historiography*, in B. Lewis and P.M. Holt (eds.), *Historians of the Middle East*, London 1962, 152-67; Ménage, *The beginnings of Ottoman historiography*, in Lewis and Holt (eds.), *op. cit.*, 168-79). The *Djihān-nümā* became a principal source for many later Ottoman historians (e.g. Idrīs Bidlīsī, Saᶜd al-Dīn, ᶜĀlī, Solaḳ-zāde and Münedjdjim-bashî [*q.vv.*]), and thus had a major influence upon subsequent interpretations of early Ottoman history. It was also one of the main sources used in Leunclavius's *Historiae Musulmanae Turcorum ... libri xviii*, Frankfurt 1591, and so entered into European writing on the Ottomans (Ménage, *Neshrī's History*, 31-40, on the "Codex Hanivaldus").

The *Djihān-nümā* has been published twice, once in facsimile (F. Taeschner, *Ğihānnümā* ..., i [Codex Menzel], 1951, ii [Codex Manisa], 1955), and once as an edition with modern Turkish transcription (F.R. Unat and M.A. Köymen (eds.), *Mehmed Neşrî: Kitâb-i Cihân-nümâ, Neşrî tarihi*, i, Ankara 1949, ii, Ankara 1957).

Bibliography: In addition to works mentioned above, see F. Babinger, *GOW*, 38-9; F. Arık, *Onbeşinci asır tarihçilerinden Neşrî'nin hayatı ve eserleri* Istanbul 1936; F. Taeschner, *Neşri tarihi elyazıları üzerine araştırmalar*, in *Belleten*, xv (1951), 497-505.

(Christine Woodhead)

NESĪMĪ, Seyyid ᶜImād al-Dīn, known as Nesīmī, an early Ottoman poet and mystic, believed to have come from Nesīm near Baghdād, whence his name. As a place of this name no longer exists, it is not certain whether the *laḳab* should not be derived simply from *nasīm* "zephyr, breath of wind". That Nesīmī was of Turkoman origin seems to be fairly certain, although the "Seyyid" before his name also points to Arab blood. Turkish was as familiar to him as Persian, for he wrote in both languages. Arabic poems are also ascribed to him. Little is known of his life; part of it fell in the reign of Murād I (761-91/1360-89), as his biographers tell us. He was at first a member of the school of Shaykh Shiblī (247-334/861-945), but about 804/1401 he became an enthusiastic follower of Faḍl Allāh Ḥurūfī [*q.v.*], with whom he was undoubtedly personally acquainted. He championed the views of his master with ardour and at the risk of his life. The poet Refīᶜī, author (811/1408) of the *Beshāret-nāme* (copies in London, cf. Rieu, *Cat.*, 164-5, and Vienna, cf. Flügel, *Katal.*, 461, 462, two mss.; the second more complete), and presumably a *Gendj-nāme* (in Vienna, cf. Flügel, *Kat.*, i, 720) was his pupil. A certain Shāh Khandān who was a dervish mystic is mentioned as his full brother. Nesīmī met a cruel death in 820/1417-18 at Aleppo, where he was flayed for his heretical poems, on a *fetwā* of the extremely fanatical *muftī*. He is considered the greatest poet and preacher of the Ḥurūfī sect.

His work consists of two collections of poems, one of which, the rarer, is in Persian and the other in Turkish. The Turkish *Dīwān* consists of 250-300 *ghazels* and about 150 quatrains, but the existing mss. differ considerably from the printed edition (Istanbul 1298/1881). No scholarly edition has so far been undertaken, but a study of his vocabulary is given by Jahangir Gahramanov, *Nasimi divanynyn leksikasy*, Baku 1970. The Persian *Dīwān* has been edited by Muḥammad Riḍā Marᶜashī, *Khurshīd-i Darband. Dīwān-i ᶜImād al-Dīn Nasīmī*, Tehran 1370 *Sh.*/1991. Nesīmī's spiritual influence on the dervish system of the earlier Ottoman empire was considerable. The pro-ᶜAlid guilds, in particular, honour Nesīmī as one of their masters, testimony to whose far-reaching influence is found even in the earlier European travellers like Giov. Antonio Menavino (*ca.* 1540; cf. F. Babinger, in *Isl.*, xi. 19, n. 1, from which it is evident that Nicolas de Nicolay copied him and therefore cannot be regarded as an independent source, as Gibb, *HOP*, i, 356-7, thought) and Sir Paul Ricaut (17th century; cf. Gibb, *HOP*, i, 357 ff.). Nesīmī's importance as a poet and mystic can only be estimated and realised in connection with a thorough study of the older Ḥurūfī texts, among which a most important one is that mentioned but not recognised by W. Pertsch, *Pers. Handschr. Berlin*, 264-5, no. 221, by Sayyid ᶜAlī al-Aᶜlā (d. 822/1419) because it might show the connection of the Ḥurūfiyya with the Bektashiyya. Nesīmī's poems were made popular in earlier times, especially by the wandering Ḳalendar dervishes [see ḲALANDARIYYA] and were known to everyone.

Bibliography: Gibb, *HOP*, i, 343 ff.; J. von Hammer, *GOD*, i, 124-5; Abdülbâki Gölpınarlı, *Nesimi-Usuli-Ruhi*, Istanbul 1953; Kathleen Burrill, *The quatrains of Nesimî*, The Hague 1972. *İA*, art. s.v. (Gölpınarlı); also the Ottoman biographers of poets who, however, contribute practically nothing to the life history of Nesīmī. Some examples of his work are given in Fahır İz, *Eski türk edebiyatında nazım*, Istanbul 1966-7, i, 154-6, 522-6.

(F. Babinger*)

NEWᶜĪ, Yaḥyā b. Pīr ᶜAlī b. Naṣūḥ, an Ottoman theologian and poet, with the nom de plume (*makhlaṣ*) of Newᶜī, was born in Malghara [see MALḲARA] (Rumelia), the son of Shaykh Pīr ᶜAlī, in 940/1533. Up to his tenth year he was taught by his learned father and then became a pupil of Ḳaramānī-zāde Meḥmed Efendi. His fellow pupils were the poet Bāḳī [*q.v.*] and Saᶜd al-Dīn, the famous historian [*q.v.*]. He was an intimate friend of the former. He joined the *ᶜulamā*ʾ, became *müderris* of Gallipoli in 973/1565 and after filling several other offices became a teacher in the Medrese of Mihr u Māh Sulṭān [*q.v.*]. In 998/1598 he was appointed *Ḳāḍī* of Baghdād, but before he could take up office, Sultan Murād III appointed him tutor to his son Muṣṭafā and to the princes Bāyezīd, ᶜOthmān and ᶜAbd Allāh. When after Murād III's death (1003/1595) the usual slaughter of the princes deprived him of all his charges, he retired completely from public life and lived on a pension granted him by the new sultan. He died at Istanbul in Dhu 'l-Ḳaᶜda 1007/June 1599 and was buried in the court of the Sheykh Wefāʾ mosque. His son was Newᶜī-zāde ᶜAṭāʾī [*q.v.*].

Newᶜī was a man of great learning, and his encyclopædic knowledge was most clearly revealed in the best-known of his works, the *Natāʾidj al-funūn wa-maḥāsin al-mutūn*, in which he surveyed the twelve most important branches of learning; on it see [J. von Hammer] *Encyklopädische Übersicht der Wissenschaften des Orients*, part i, Leipzig 1804, 22 ff., and the German translation of the story of Shādān and Beshīr, *ibid.*, 24 ff., which forms the concluding section of this work. Bursalî Meḥmed Ṭāhir gives a list of other prose works in his *ᶜOthmānlî müʾellifleri*, iii, 437-8, with references to the libraries in which they are. In poetry, Newᶜī imitated the style of his contemporary Bāḳī without however reaching his level. His poems which were collected in a scarce *Dīwān* (ms. in Istanbul, Ḥamīdiyye library), lack ease and betray too readily the learned author who frequently makes his work difficult to understand with unusual words and obscure allusions. He tried his skill in different forms of verse, the *ḳaṣīda*, *ghazel* and *methnewī*, without however attaining popularity in any one of them. His fame as a poet was completely overshadowed by that of his contemporary and friend Bāḳī. Newᶜī's high position as an author he owes to his learned work, particularly the already-mentioned encyclopædia, which was very popular, as is evident from the numerous mss. still in existence in European collections (e.g. Berlin, Bologna, Dresden, Leiden, London [3 copies], Uppsala, Vienna). A *Süleymān-nāme* by him (Paris, *Bib. Nat.*, cod. reg. 44, Cat. no. 308 und F. Babinger, *GOW*, 76) does not seem to be mentioned by his biographers. His son Newᶜī-zāde ᶜAṭāʾī wrote a very full life of him (418-27 of the *dhayl* to Ṭashköprüzāde's work), mentioning that he wrote over 30 *risāle*s on *kalām, fiḳh, ᶜaḳāʾid, manṭiḳ, taṣawwuf*, etc.

Bibliography: Meḥmed Thüreyyā, *Sidjill-i ᶜothmānī*, iv, 634; Von Hammer, *GOD*, iii, 108; Gibb, *HOP*, iii, 171 ff.; Ḥādjdjī Khalīfa, *Fedhleke*, i, 120 ff., also the biographies of poets by Ḳïnalï-zāde and ᶜAhdī; Brockelmann, II², 587-8, S II, 658; *İA* s.v. (Abdülkadir Karahan). (F. Babinger)

NEWᶜĪ-ZĀDE [see ᶜAṬĀʾĪ].

NEWRES, the names of two Ottoman poets.

1. ᶜAbd al-Razzāḳ, known as Newres, or more accurately, Newres-i Ḳadīm, "Newres the Elder", to distinguish him from ᶜOthmān Newres [see below], came from Kirkūk in northern ᶜIrāḳ and was probably of Kurdish origin. He seems, however, to have come to Istanbul at an early age to prosecute his studies. Here he became a *müderris* but in the year 1159/1746 entered upon a legal career. According to the *Sidjill-i ᶜothmānī*, he held the office of *ḳāḍī* in Sarajevo and Kütahya. His sharp tongue, which found particular expression in daring and malicious chronograms (*tawārīkh*), earned him banishment to Rethymno (Crete) along with the poet Hashmet and then to Bursa; he was later, according to Wāṣif (*Taʾrīkh*, 211), sent back to Kütahya. In any case, he died in Bursa in Shawwāl 1175/May 1762 and was buried in the cemetery opposite the entrance to the mosque of Pīr Uftāde Meḥmed, the founder of the order of the Djalwatiyya. ᶜAbd al-Razzāḳ Newres composed a *Dīwān* in Persian and Turkish (printed Istanbul 1290 and probably 1304), and also a history of the war with Nādir Shāh in 1143/1730 in which he took part on the staff of Ḥekīm-Oghlu ᶜAlī Pasha. The little book called *Tebrīziyye-i Ḥekīm-Oghlu ᶜAlī Pasha* is written in ornate language and is of no historical value. The fair copy in the author's hand is preserved in the Berlin Staatsbibliothek (Cod. Or. 8°, 2186). Newres also enjoyed the reputation of being a distinguished *munshiʾ*. Excerpts from his *inshāʾ* are given by J. von Hammer in his *GOR*, ix, 643-4. His *Dīwān* is called *Mabāligh al-ḥikam*, which gives the year 1172/1758 for its completion (cf., however, a similarly titled work in Vienna: Flügel, *Cat.*, iii, 486, no. 1991).

Bibliography: See F. Babinger, *GOW*, 294-5, with further references; von Hammer, *GOD*, iv, 321-7; Gibb, *HOP*, iv, 133-9, vi, 287-90; *İA* art s.v. (Ömer Faruk Akın).

2. ᶜOthmān, called Newres or, to distinguish him from his older namesake, Newres-i Djedīd, came from Chios. He held several military posts in the capital and died there in 1293/1876 in retirement. He is buried in the Ḳaradja Aḥmed cemetery in Üsküdār. His collected poems have been twice printed at Istanbul in 1257 and in 1290 (by Yūsuf Kāmil Pasha) (*Dīwān-i ᶜOthmān Newres*). In 1302 there was published at the suggestion of ᶜAbd al-Karīm Nādir Pasha in Istanbul under the title *Ether-i nādir* specimens of his prose and verse. A Turkish translation of the *Gulistān* of Saᶜdī [*q.v.*] by him exists in ms. ᶜOthmān Newres had a very thorough command of the three languages of Islam and wrote poetry in all three.

Bibliography: Bursalï Meḥmed Ṭāhir, *ᶜOthmānlï müʾellifleri*, iii, 465-6; *İA*, art. s.v. (Fevziye Abdullah Tansel). (F. Babinger)

NEWROKOP, Nevrokop, a town in south-western Bulgaria, in Ottoman times (*ca.* 1380-1912) *chef-lieu* of a *ḳāḍīlïḳ* of the *sandjaḳ* of Siroz (Serres) and a centre of Islamic life of considerable importance. Nevrokop is situated in a wide plain (30 × 10 km) between the Rhodopes and Pirin Mountains, at an altitude of 565 m, 20 km to the north of the present Greco-Bulgarian frontier. The river Mesta (Kara Su), whose valley constitutes the only traffic artery of any importance, passes the town a few kilometres to the east.

Nevrokop is the indirect successor of the ancient town of Nicopolis ad Mestum, whose ruins are situated 9 km to the east of the town, opposite the river. The *Notitiae Episcopatuum* mention this town as the seat of an archbishopric until the 11th century. Near the present town of Nevrokop, the ruins of a 9th-10th century castle and a settlement have been found, which are the more direct forerunner of the present town. The district in which Nevrokop is situated must have been conquered by the Ottomans between 1374 and 1383 (capture of the nearby key-fortresses of Drama and Serres; see SIROZ). With the capture of the Nevrokop valley and that of Razlog more to the north-west, connection could be made with the Thracian plain around Filibe (Plovdiv), by following the upper course of the Mesta and then across a low pass to the valley of Čepino, which is in direct communication with Thrace, which was in Ottoman hands since the late 1360s. The town is first mentioned with its present name in the Ottoman *Taḥrīr defter* Mal. no. 525 from 1445, in which it is described as a large Christian village numbering 137 households. With *ca.* 600 inhabitants, it was by far and wide the largest settlement in the area. After this date, Nevrokop was to develop rapidly and in a century changed into a predominantly Muslim town. The *Taḥrīr* T.D. 3 from 1453-4 has Nevrokop with 265 Christian and twelve Muslim households, or roughly 1250 inhabitants. Great changes occured in the interval 1454-1517, when Muslim civilians came to settle in the town, and Yürüks from Anatolia by way of the Aegean plains settled in or next to many formerly entirely Christian Bulgarian villages. The *Taḥrīr* T.D. 70, of which the actual census was taken in 1517, mentions Nevrokop as a town, containing 167 Muslim households and 319 households of Christians, or *ca.* 2070 inhabitants. The settlement, which in 1454 was only 4% Muslim now had 34% Muslims. Further rapid expansion is shown by the register T.D. 167 from 1529. By then the Muslims had gone up to 281 households and the Christians to 385. This gives a town of almost 4000 inhabitants, of which 42% was Muslim. The *Taḥrīr* of 1569/79 (KuK 194, Ankara) shows a different pattern. In the 40 years after 1529, the positions are reversed. The Muslims had grown slowly, to 318 households whilst the Christians had declined sharply, to 186 households. In the interval, some Islamisation of the local population must have taken place. The 1569-70 register shows that 14% of the Muslim households were of convert origin. This suggest that besides conversion, immigration must have played an important role. The outcome of these movements was that the population of the town was now composed of 63% Muslims. The number of *maḥalle*s also show the reversal of the pattern: in 1529 5 Muslim *maḥalle*s and 13 Christian *maḥalle*s, in 1569 13 Muslim *maḥalle*s and

6 of Christians. The transformation of Nevrokop from a Christian village into a predominantly Muslim town was stimulated by the erection of a monumental domed mosque and a school by Meḥmed Bey, son of the *Beylerbey* of Rumeli, Dayî Ḳarača Pas̲h̲a. The latter died in 1456 before Belgrade. His son Meḥmed must have erected his buildings in Nevrokop in the 1480s or 1490s, to which the stylistic features point. Shortly before his death in 1512, the favourite of Sultan Bāyezīd II, Ḳod̲j̲a Muṣṭafā Pas̲h̲a, founded another important mosque in Nevrokop, as well as a school and a *ḥammām*. The 1529 *Taḥrīr* mentions both buildings, as well as the fact that their founders were dead (*merḥūm*), and adds a *mesd̲j̲id* of Dāwūdlî. The register also mentions that Meḥmed Bey had constructed a bridge over the Kara Su and had allotted the yearly rent of 10 watermills in Nevrokop and Drama, 50 shops and rooms in Selānik and some important urban property in Filibe, totalling 57,000 *aḳčes*, for the upkeep of his foundations. The buildings of Ḳod̲j̲a Muṣṭafā Pas̲h̲a in Nevrokop were financed by his enormous *ewḳāf* in many places in Rumeli. These included also five villages in the *ḳaḍā*ʾ of Nevrokop. An order in the *Mühimme defter* 6 from S̲h̲ewwāl 972/May 1565 discusses the problems of erecting a mosque and a *muṣallā* on orders of Sultan Süleymān for the memory of his son S̲h̲ehzāde Meḥmed . The *Taḥrīr* of 1569-70 gives other information on the growing importance of Nevrokop as an Islamic centre. In that year there were three Friday mosques and seven *mesd̲j̲ids*. The register mentions 12 imāms in the town and 14 muezzins besides four school teachers and a large number of craftsman, both Muslim and Christian (hatters, tanners, shoemakers, soapmakers, carpenters, blacksmiths, quiltmakers, goldsmiths).

In the villages of the *ḳaḍā*ʾ of Nevrokop a similar process of slow Islamisation can be observed. According to the 1445 *Taḥrīr*, the entire district numbered not a single Muslim. An isolated few are mentioned in 1453-4, but by 1529, 13% of the rural population was Muslim and some 28% in 1569-70. This process had the same two aspects as in the town: settlement of a substantial number of Turkish (*Yürük*) settlers after 1517, secondly a creeping process of Islamisation of a part of the rural, Bulgarian-speaking population. By 1900 the entire *ḳaḍā*ʾ of Nevrokop, with 123 villages, numbered 12,500 Turkish-speaking Muslims, 26,960 Bulgarian-speaking Muslims (Pomaks) and 35,310 Bulgarian Christians, the latter including some Greek-orientated Vlachs. These numbers show that Islam in the western Rhodope resulted from a slow process of colonisation and an even slower process of Islamisation, instead of being the result of one violent, government-ordered, campaign of mass Islamisation, which is supposed to have taken place in the second half of the 11th/17th century under the Köprülü administration. This last-mentioned viewpoint is usually taken in the Bulgarian historiography.

A 16th century list of bishoprics belonging to the Greek Orthodox Patriarchate of Constantinople mentions a "see of Nikopolis, that is Nevrokop", but names of bishops of Nevrokop are only known since 1622.

In the 17th century the expansion of the town must have slowed down. Kātib Čelebi mentions Nevrokop as the seat of a *ḳāḍīlīḳ* and noted the presence of rich iron mines near the town. The official list of *ḳāḍīlīḳs* of 1078/1667-8 has Nevrokop in the fourth rank of the twelve ranks of *ḳāḍīlīḳs* of Rumeli, which illustrates its importance. The most detailed description of Ottoman Nevrokop is given in vol. viii of the *Seyāḥat-nāme* of Ewliyā Čelebi, although the town appears under the wrong name of Vetrine (modern Neon Petritsi in Greece), which is historically and geographically impossible, since it never was a *ḳaḍā*ʾ centre. Ewliyā called the town large and fine, with many mosques, dervish *tekkes*, *k̲h̲āns*, *ḥammāms*, schools and very beautiful houses and the seat of an elaborate provincial administration. In the 18th century, the town must have grown slowly. In 1847 the traveller Viquesnel saw a thousand houses (in 1569, 500), inhabited by Turks and a few Greeks and Bulgarians. He saw 12 minarets and a fairly large bazaar with many *k̲h̲āns* and coffee shops. In 1809-11 the Christian community of Nevrokop had constructed the small church of the Archangels Michael and Gabriel. In 1833-41 they built the large and monumental church of the Holy Virgin, expression of the changed conditions under the *Tanẓīmāt*. In the 1820s, the last great domed mosque of the town was built, of which only old photographs remain. The *Sālnāme* of the *wilāyet* of Selānik of 1324/1906-7 mentions that the town had 20 *maḥalles* with 1,432 houses, 598 shops, 12 Friday mosques, four *mesd̲j̲ids*, two churches and no less than eight *tekkes*, pointing to a well-developed Islamic life. Besides this, there were seven schools for Muslims and two for Christians. A Greek source from 1908 mentions that the town had 5,900 inhabitants: 3,865 Turks, 490 Muslim Gipsies, 595 Christians belonging to the Greek Orthodox church and 900 Christians belonging to the Bulgarian Exarchate. The same source mentions that the population of the *ḳaḍā*ʾ of Nevrokop was in majority Muslim, sc. 51,000 of the 83,000 inhabitants (=61%). The *Sālnāme* of 1303/1885-6) gives slightly lower numbers but has the same percentage of Muslims. The statistics of Verković and Kănčev give 55% and 53% respectively, with slightly varying numbers.

The Bulgarian conquest of 1912, during the Balkan Wars, led to a mass exodus of the Muslim population of the town and, to a lesser extent, of the villages. Their place was immediately taken by Bulgarian refugees from the *ḳaḍā*ʾs of Drama and Serres, which had been conquered by the Greek army and were to remain part of the enlarged Greek state. The Bulgarian census of 1926 shows these changes clearly. By then the town numbered 1,057 Muslim inhabitants, but the number of Bulgarians stood as high as 5,882. The 1934 census show that the new trend continued: 824 Muslim and 7,726 Christian inhabitants. After 1912 the mosques, *tekkes* and *ḥammāms* disappeared one after the other. The oldest mosque of the town, that of Meḥmed Bey ben Ḳarača Pas̲h̲a, was the last to be given up. It still stands as a ruin (1990). Apart from a few Muslim Gypsy families, Islam has disappeared from Nevrokop, which after 1912 was rebuilt in a new fashion. In the late 1960s, culminating in the events of 1973, the Pomak population of the mountain villages of the Nevrokop district was put under heavy pressure when the Communist government tried to "lead them back into the Bulgarian nation" with help of the army units using poison gas. After the opposition had been broken, large sections of the Pomaks were deported to northern Bulgaria, given other names and scattered among purely Christian Bulgarian villages. After the end of Communist rule, many returned to their native homes, reverting to their simple Islamic community life. After their ordeal, they decided to identify completely with Turkish Islam, learning to speak Turkish instead of Bulgarian and identifying themselves as descendants of the Bulgarised Pečeneg and Kuman settlers in the Rhodope to which the 12th-13th century

Mosque of Meḥmed Bey ibn Karadja Pasha, *ca.* 1490. Only surviving Ottoman building in Nevrokop.
(Photo: Arch. Julii Fărkov, 1992)

Byzantine sources refer. This process is now in full swing. The restoration of Islamic life to the Nevrokop villages has been seen in the large-scale rebuilding during 1991-2 of the mosques of the district destroyed in the assimilation campaign of 1985.

Nevrokop, which in 1978 rose to 17,805 inhabitants, saw its name changed to Goce Delčev (in 1950). Ottoman Nevrokop was the native town of some Ottoman men of letters. Among them is the very learned poet Raᶜna Muṣṭafā Efendi, a Naḳs̲h̲bendī dervish and for long in the service of Muḥammad ᶜAlī of Egypt. He died in 1248/1832-3 in his native Nevrokop. It was very probably this man who constructed the last domed mosque in the town, showing close similarity with the buildings of Muḥammed ᶜAlī in Kavalla (erected 1818-1821). Of more importance is Zührī Aḥmed Efendi, the founder of the Zühriyye branch of the K̲h̲alwetiyye order. Zühri Efendi died in Selānik/Thessaloniki in 1165/1751-2 and was buried in the tekke which he had himself founded in that city.

Bibliography: M. Sokoloski, Nevrokop i Nevrokopsko vo XV i XVI vek, in Prilozi, Mak. Akad. Naukite i Umetnost, ii, Skopje 1975, 5-31; Ewliyā Čelebi, Seyāḥat-nāme, viii, 761-2 (1928 ed.); A. Stojanovski, La population dans les villes Macédoniennes aux XVe et XVIe siècles, in Les Macédoniens dans le passé, Skopje 1970, 119-34; Str. Dimitrov, Demografski otnošenija i pronikvane na Isljama v zapadnite Rodopi i dolinata na Mesta prez XV-XVII v., in Rodopski Sbornik, i, Sofia 1965, 63-114 (argues for a slow process of Islamisation instead of violent mass conversion); Cvetana Dremsizova-Nelčinova, Arheologičeski pametnitsi Blagoevgradski Okrăg, Sofia 1987; Kănčev, Makedonija, etnografija i statistika, Sofia 1900; B. Laourdas, I Metropolis Neurokopiou 1900-1907, Thessaloniki 1961; A. Viquesnel, Voyage dans la Turquie d'Europe, Paris 1868 (travelled in 1847-8); Žečo Čankov, Geografski rečnik na Bălgarija, Sofia 1900. There is no satisfying local history of Nevrokop. The Ottoman sources noted in the text are unpublished. (M. Kiel)

NEWS̲H̲EHIR, modern Turkish Nevşehir, a town of central Anatolia in the Cappadocia of classical antiquity. It lies 60 km/40 miles to the west of Kayseri [see ḲAYṢARIYYA] and 13 km/9 miles south of the Kızıl Irmak river [q.v.] at an altitude of approx. 1,180 m/3,600 feet (lat. 38° 38′ N., long. 34° 43′ E.). It is now the chef-lieu of an il or province of the same name; in 1970 the town had a population of 57,556 and the il one of 231,873.

The News̲h̲ehir region was in the 6th to 9th centuries AD known for its monastic caves, and became a frontier region during the Arab invasions. The inhabitants protected themselves by digging underground refuges into the soft tuff; these consisted of several floors, with tables and benches, water supply and cooking hearths. Often special arrangements prevented the smoke from escaping in times of danger, and thus betraying the hiding place. Most of these "underground cities" were discovered only in the 1950s, and little is known about them from written sources. The largest such shelters are located in Kaymaklı and Derinkuyu (Melegübü in 10th/16th century Ottoman sources), within the modern province of Nevşehir.

Until the Grand Vizierate of Ibrāhīm Pas̲h̲a Newṣ̲h̲ehirli (killed in 1143/1730 [q.v.]), the settlement called Nevşehir today was known as the village of Mus̲h̲ḳara, located in the judicial district (ḳaḍā) of Ürgüb. The latter ḳaḍā was sometimes included in the sandjaḳ of Niğde and at other times in that of Kayseri. Ibrāhīm Pas̲h̲a, who was born in Mus̲h̲ḳara, elevated

it to the status of a town and renamed it News̲h̲ehir. He established a foundation, consisting of a mosque, library, medrese, and ᶜimāret, and associated with it were shops and an official residence for the foundation administrator. Ibrāhīm Pas̲h̲a also had the small Saldjūḳ fortress on the hilltop overlooking the settlement restored. The foundation inscriptions were composed by the major Istanbul poets of the time, among whom Ibrāhīm Pas̲h̲a organised a competition explicitly for this purpose. Seyyid Wehbī's, Nedīm's and ᶜĀṣim's inscriptions have been published (by Aḥmed Refīḳ, 1340/1921-22). These texts emphasise that the Grand Vizier owed everything to his master the Sultan (Aḥmed III [q.v.]), but also glorify the founder: one of them even contains his elaborate curriculum vitae.

Among the architects of the külliyye, we know a Sargis K̲h̲alfa, who supervised the construction process. Ibrāhīm Pas̲h̲a also involved the Chief Architect Meḥmed Ag̲h̲a, ordering him to send some of his junior colleagues to visit the Muṣṭafā Pas̲h̲a mosque in Gebze and other important vizierial mosques of western Anatolia. The architects were enjoined to study the aesthetic appearance of the buildings and also construction details, bringing back drawings for the Grand Vizier's inspection. The latter apparently reserved for himself the ultimate decision, and, taking an eclectic approach, consciously modelled his foundation on the buildings put up by 10th/16th century Grand Viziers.

As 12th/18th century Anatolia was only sparsely inhabited, many of the measures designed to further News̲h̲ehir were to the detriment of nearby Ürgüb. The seat of the district ḳāḍī was moved from Ürgüb to News̲h̲ehir, and so was the market; in spite of the distances involved, Ürgüb residents were ordered to henceforth conduct their business in News̲h̲ehir. Wealthy people recently settled in Kayseri were ordered to move to News̲h̲ehir, and to ensure a stable urban population, well-to-do residents of the new town were forbidden to move their families to Istanbul; 800 families of central Anatolian nomads were also to settle in News̲h̲ehir. Scrub land was assigned to the townsmen which they could convert into gardens and vineyards, and they were also granted the land of certain abandoned villages for farming and pasture. In the early 12th/18th century, the urban population must have been a few thousands.

In the 13th/19th century, News̲h̲ehir was a small town in the sandjaḳ of Niğde, in majority inhabited by Muslims, but with an active community of Turcophone Orthodox Christians. Out of 17,660 townsmen in 1316-17/1899, 10,972 were Muslims and 6,080 Orthodox. Grape cultivation and winemaking constituted one of the region's principal economic activities. The exchange of populations which followed the war between Greece and Turkey (1923) resulted in a decline of the vineyards, as the new settlers from Thrace were not familiar with viticulture. However as natural conditions (low rainfall, frosts in spring and fall) limited agricultural options, raisin and wine production soon resumed.

Down to the present day, the News̲h̲ehir district has remained an agricultural region. In 1978, 78.6% of the economically-active population was employed in agriculture (1965: 86.2%, 1955: 87.6%). The productivity of many agricultural enterprises is low, due to limited investment in erosion control, irrigation and seed selection. The employment of tractors and the cultivation of sugar beet and potatoes on irrigated land have, however, become sufficiently widespread to push down the demand for family labour. This decrease particularly affects women; while in 1965, 46% of the labour force consisted of women, by 1975 this percentage had dropped to 41%. Since opportunities in manufacturing (cotton textiles, wine-production, food processing) are also limited, out-migration is widespread. In spite of a high birthrate, the district's population has recently declined.

From the 1960s onwards, tourism has become a significant source of gain, as both Turkish holiday-makers and foreign tourists have visited the cave churches of Göreme, the "underground cities" of Derinkuyu and Kaymaklı and the extraordinary tuff formations of this volcanic landscape. In 1982, the district recorded 50,000 Turkish and 82,000 foreign visitors, who have given a boost to retail trade, transportation and the manufacture of *objets d'art* from locally available agate. However, to date this injection of capital has had only a limited impact upon the region, as the owners usually prefer to invest in other parts of the country.

In the cultural life of the region, the former main lodge (*zāwiye*) of the Bektās̲h̲ī order of dervishes once again has a role to play. The complex (located in the town of Hacıbektaş, *il* of Nevşehir) contains the mausolea of Ḥād̲j̲d̲j̲ī Bektās̲h̲ and Balîm Sulṭān, constructed in the 9th/15th and 10th/16th centuries, as well as a meeting room and an elaborate domed kitchen. In the latter there is a large kettle, which an inscription identifies as a Janissary gift. A silver door was donated by an 11th/17th century governor of Ḳîrs̲h̲ehir [*q.v.*]. After the abolition of all dervish orders in 1925, the complex was allowed to deteriorate; but once a museum had been established, largely through community efforts, the building was restored and local residents voluntarily returned many former possessions of the lodge. Now the town of Hacıbektaş hosts an annual cultural festival. It is attended by a large number of Alevî families, who combine a visit to the shrine with attendance at concerts and recitals of a more secular nature.

Bibliography: Aḥmed Refīḳ, *Dāmād Ibrāhīm Pas̲h̲a zamanînda Ürgüb we News̲h̲ehir*, in *TTEM*, xiv/3 (no. 80) (1340/1921-2), 156-85; Remzi Gürses, *Hacıbektaş rehberi*, Istanbul n.d. [*ca.* 1970]; S. Kostof, *Caves of God: the monastic environment of Byzantine Cappadocia*, Cambridge, Mass. 1972; art. *Nevşehir*, in *Yurt Ansiklopedisi, Türkiye İl: dünü, bugünü, yarını*, Istanbul 1982-3; R. Jennings, *The population, society and economy of the region of Erciyes dağı in the 16th century*, in *Contributions a l'histoire économique et sociale de l'Empire ottoman*, ed. J.L. Bacqué-Grammont and P. Dumont, Istanbul-Paris 1983, 149-250.

(Suraiya Faroqhi)

NICOBARS, the name of a group of nineteen islands in the Indian Ocean, to the south of the Bay of Bengal and lying between lats. 6°40′ and 9°20′ N.; the largest southernmost of them, Great Nicobar, is 190 km/120 miles to the northwest of the northern tip of Sumatra. Their area is 1,953 km²/627 sq. miles. The Arabic geographers place them at 15 days' voyage from Sarandīb (= Ceylon) and 6 days' voyage from Kalah [*q.v.*] (= probably in the Malacca peninsula or, less probably, at Kedah).

The Nicobar Islands appear in Arabic travel and geographical literature as early as the *Ak̲h̲bār al-Ṣīn wa 'l-Hind* (237/851), ed. and tr. J. Sauvaget, *Relation de la Chine et de l'Inde*, Paris 1948, § 7, text and tr. 5, comm. 38-9 (*Land̲j̲abālūs*, linked here with *Andāmān*, i.e. the Andaman Islands to the north, whose inhabitants are described as dark-skinned and cannibals); Ibn K̲h̲urradād̲h̲bih, 66 (*Alankabālūs*); al-Masʿūdī, *Murūd̲j̲ al-d̲h̲ahab*, i, 338-9 = § 372 (*Land̲j̲abālūs*); Buzurg b. S̲h̲ahriyār, *K. ʿAd̲j̲āʾib al-Hind* (first half of the 4th/10th century), tr. G.S.P. Freeman-Grenville. *The book of the wonders of India*, London 1981, § 81, pp. 74-5 (*Lad̲j̲bālūs*). The forms *Lankabālūs*/*Land̲j̲abālūs*, etc., became the standard renderings for the Islands, appearing e.g. some two centuries later in al-Idrīsī's text and on his map, with the distances mentioned above for the Nicobars' distance from Ceylon and the Malay peninsula (tr. S. Maqbul Ahmad, *India and the neighbouring territories in the* Kitāb Nuzhat al-mus̲h̲tāq ..., §§ 42-5, 48, tr. 32-3, 34, comm. 117-18). As characteristics of the islands' people are mentioned their unintelligible language (in fact, the Nicobarese languages are of the Austro-Asiatic family, either a branch of the Mon-Khmer group or a separate branch, in any case demonstrating older ethnic connections with South-East Asia and Indonesia); their white skins and nakedness; their hospitableness; and their trading of ambergris and coconuts for iron by means of dumb barter with the voyagers who called there en route from Ceylon to China; their diet of coconuts, freshly-caught fish, bananas, etc. (see the above references, plus *Ḥudūd al-ʿālam*, tr. Minorsky, § 4.10, p. 57, comm. 188; Minorsky, *Sharaf al-Zamān b. Ṭāhir Marvazī on China, the Turks and India*, London 1942, ch. xv, § 10, tr. 57-8, comm. 158-9).

Various explanations have been proffered for the name of the islands. Sauvaget, *op. cit.*, comm. 38, cited a Chinese phrase *lang-pʾo-lu-seu*, denoting western Sumatra, as the original of the Arabic form, though this seems less likely. Minorsky cited an etymology from *laṅkā* "island" + *Bālūs* = Baros on the southwestern coast of Sumatra, cf. *Ḥudūd al-ʿālam,* § 4.8, p. 57, comm. 187, but as more probable *al-Nankabār* or *Nakavvar*>Nicobar "the naked" (*Sharaf al-Zamān Ṭāhir Marvazī*, comm. 158-9). Certainly, on the Catalan Map of 1375 we have the *Insulae Nudorum.*

Marco Polo briefly mentions the island which he calls Necuvaran as being about 150 miles north of Sumatra (Sir Henry Yule, *The Book of Ser Marco Polo the Venetian*, London 1871, ii, 248-50), but there is much more detail on the island of Nicoveran in the account of the voyages of Friar Odoric of Pordenone (1316-30), who travelled from the Coromandel coast to Sumatra en route for China (Yule and H. Cordier, *Cathay and the way thither*, Cambridge 1915, ii, 248-50, describing the inhabitants as having dogs' faces (*Cinocofuli*), a detail more often attached to the Andaman islanders).

In more recent times, the Nicobars were probably visited by Portuguese missionaries, but in 1756 Denmark took them over as a colony affiliated to their trading factory at Tranquebar on the Coromandel coast. In 1848 the Danes formally relinquished sovereignty, and in 1869 Britain took formal possession of them. After an occupation by the Japanese 1942-5, the Nicobars passed in 1947 to India and are now part of the Union Territory of the Andaman and Nicobar Islands, with the seat of the Lieutenant-Governor at Port Blair in the Andamans. The population of the Nicobars (1961 census) is 14,563.

Bibliography (in addition to references given in the article): E. Balfour, *The cyclopaedia of India and of eastern and southern Asia, commercial, industrial and scientific*³, London 1885, ii, 1094; *Imperial gazetteer of India*², xix, 59-84; E.H. Man, *The Nicobar Islands and their people*, London 1933.

(C.E. Bosworth)

NIFFAR, Nuffar, a ruined site, ancient Nippur, in southern ʿIrāḳ, situated in lat. 32°7′ N. and long. 45°10′ E., now in the *liwā* or province of al-Ḳādisiyya; close by lies the K̲h̲ōr al-ʿAfak.

The site is very extensive. Rising 20 m above the

plain, it has proved to be one of the earliest cities to have developed in the region. Even before neighbouring Uruk and Akkad became political centres in the last centuries of the third millennium Nippur seems to have been a religious centre for the independent communities, no doubt because, according to the Sumerian version of the Flood Story, man was first created at Nippur. So it was here that Ur-Nammu, king of Ur built the temple for Enlil, the god of storms, with its great ziggurat. The associated library is one of the richest sources for Sumerian literature even though so many of the original documents have been lost; much of what remains was preserved accidentally since the clay documents were used as fill for the walls of later houses. A beautifully decorated chlorite vessel with a cat-like figure in conflict with a snake has been described as a representation of Inanna (Ishtar). When Layard visited the site in 1854 he was overcome by its appearance, and from 1889-1900 an American excavation under the supervision of J.P. Peters (University of Pennsylvania) carried out the first thorough study of the site. More recent excavations have been conducted by McGown (University of Chicago). It was being built on up to the Parthian period. But what Peters described as "Parthian columns" still standing when he was at the site had disappeared by 1948 when the Chicago team were there. The site is particularly suited to new historical assessments, as evidenced by the work of Stone, who integrates linguistic, archaeological and anthropological material in her study. In an unusual Akkadian satirical poem a poor man from Nippur, who has been oppressed by the mayor of his town, is able by his guile to humiliate his oppressor; this may well reflect the attitude of contemporary society to the place, for Nippur is often mentioned in lists of places that are excused the taxation burdens imposed on other towns.

Nippur was also an inhabited place in Muslim times; for example, we find it mentioned in 38 /659 on the occasion of a rising against the caliph ʿAlī (al-Ṭabarī, i, 3423, 3424) as well as during the Khāridjī troubles (*op. cit.*, ii, 929, $_7$); cf. also Yāḳūt, iv, 275, 798, and Ibn al-Faḳīh, 210. In the later Middle Ages we find Niffar mentioned as a Nestorian bishopric in the chronicles of the Patriarchs (*Akhbār Faṭārika kursī al-Mashriḳ*, ed. Gismondi, Rome 1897-9), of ʿAmr b. Mattā (83, 95,) and of Marī b. Sulaymān, in the period 900-1058 A.D. (cf. also Sachau, in *Abh. Pr. Ak. W.* [1909], no. 1, p. 31). When the town was abandoned by its inhabitants and became completely desolate we do not know. It was probably the result of one of the Turco-Mongol invasions, that under Hülegü or that under Tīmūr, which dealt their death-blow to so many flourishing places in Mesopotamia.

According to the cuneiform inscriptions, Nippur must have in ancient times lain on the Euphrates itself or at least in its immediate vicinity (cf. e.g. *OLZ*, xx, 142, n. 1); this fact forces us to the assumption that this river in the Babylonian period must have taken a much more easterly course below Babylon than in the middle ages and present day. The inner city is divided into two parts by a canal now dry but once navigable, which the natives call Shaṭṭ al-Nīl. This was an important watercourse which, according to Hilprecht, was in many places at one time 20-25 feet deep and 150-190 feet broad and which the modern inhabitants rightly describe not as a mere *nahr* (stream, canal) but as *shaṭṭ* (river).

According to the mediaeval Arab geographers, Nahr al-Nīl was the name of one of the canals leading off from the Euphrates to the Tigris. It still survives in its entirety; as in the Middle Ages, it starts from Babylon and flows a little above lat. 32°30′ N. in an almost straight line eastwards. The geographer Suhrāb or Ibn Sarābiyūn [*q.v.*], writing in the 4th/10th century, observes that this canal bears the name Nahr al-Nīl only after passing the town of al-Nīl (the modern ruins Nīliyye). At the present day, it is called only Shaṭṭ al-Nīl throughout its course. Somewhat east of Nīliyye a side-canal, now dry, branches off to the south for which, not only in its lower part where it flows by the ruins of Niffar but along its whole extent, the name Shaṭṭ al-Nīl, the same as that of the main canal, was and is usual. Yāḳūt, however, says (iv, 77, 798) that Niffar lay not on the Nahr al-Nīl but on the bank of the Nahr al-Nars, a canal dug, it is said, by the Sāsānid king Narsē b. Bahrām (293-303 A.D.) which leaves the Euphrates at al-Ḥilla a little below the Nahr al-Nīl and turns southeastward. It was presumably connected by a branch with the southern small canal of the same name which branches off from the Nahr al-Nīl, so that the occurrence of the two names Nahr al-Nīl and Nahr al-Nars for the river in Niffar is explained. It should be noted also that the nomenclature of the Babylonian canals changed several times already in the Middle Ages. On the Nahr al-Nīl or Shaṭṭ al-Nīl and Nahr al-Nars, see W.K. Loftus, *Travels and researches in Chaldaea and Susiana*, London 1857, 238; G. Le Strange, in *JRAS* (1895), 256, 260-1, and idem, *The lands of the eastern caliphate*, Cambridge 1905, 72-4; Streck, *Babylonien nach den arab. Geographen*, i, Leiden 1900, 30-1; Herzfeld, in Sarre-Herzfeld, *Archäolog. Reise im Euphrat- und Tigrisgebiet*, i, Berlin 1911, 134-5; Hāshim al-Saʿdī, *Djughrāfiyyat al-ʿIrāḳ al-ḥadītha*², Baghdād 1927, 34, 35.

Bibliography: J.P. Peters, *Nippur, or explorations and adventures on the Euphrates*, New York 1897; H.V. Hilprecht, *Die Ausgrabungen der Universität von Pennsylvania in Bel Tempel zu Nippur*, Leipzig 1903; D.E. McGown and R.C. Haines, *Nippur I. Temple of Enlil, scribal quarter and soundings, II. The north temple and sounding* E. Chicago 1967-78; Elizabeth C. Stone, *Nippur neighborhoods*, Chicago 1987.

(M. STRECK-[M.E.J. RICHARDSON])

AL-**NIFFARĪ**, MUḤAMMAD B. ʿABD AL-DJABBĀR, Ṣūfī mystic, whom the principal Ṣūfī biographers fail to mention, and who flourished in the 4th/10th century, and, according to Ḥādjdjī Khalīfa, died in the year 354/965, but more probably in *ca.* 366/976-7. His *nisba* refers to the town of Niffar [*q.v.*] in ʿIrāḳ, and one ms. of his works asserts that it was during his residence at Niffar and Nīl that he committed his thoughts to writing. Al-Niffarī's literary reliquiae consist of two books, the *Mawāḳif* and the *Mukhāṭabāt* (ed. A.J. Arberry, London 1935), together with a number of fragments. It is improbable that Niffarī himself was responsible for the editing of his writings; according to his principal commentator, ʿAfīf al-Dīn al-Tilimsānī (d. 690/1291), either his son or his grandson collected his scattered writings and published them according to his own ordering. The *Mawāḳif* consists of 77 sections of varying length, made up for the most part of brief apothegms touching on the main aspects of Ṣūfī teaching, and purporting to be inspired and dictated by God; the *Mukhāṭabāt* is similar in content, and is divided into 56 sections. Al-Niffarī's most characteristic contribution to mysticism is his doctrine of *waḳfa*. This term, which would appear to be used by him in a peculiarly technical sense, implies a condition in the mystic which is accompanied by direct divine audition, and perhaps even automatic script. *Mawḳif* is the name given to the state of the mystic in which *waḳfa* is classed higher than *maʿrifa*, and *maʿrifa* is above *ʿilm*. The *wāḳif* is nearer to God than any other thing, and almost transcends the condition of *bas̲h̲ariyya*, being alone separated from all limitation. Al-Niffarī definitely maintains the possibility of seeing God in this world; for he says that vision (*ruʾya*) in this world is a preparation for vision in the world to come. In several places, al-Niffarī distinctly touches on the theory of the Mahdī [*q.v.*], and indeed appears to identify himself with the Mahdī, if these passages are genuine; and this claim is seemingly in the mind of al-Zabīdī, when he describes al-Niffarī as *ṣāḥib al-daʿāwā wa 'l-ḍalāl*. Al-Tilimsānī, however, interprets these passages in an esoteric and highly mystical sense; and it does not accord with the general character of the author that he should make for himself such extravagant claims. Al-Niffarī shows himself in his writings to be a fearless and original thinker. While undoubtedly influenced by his great predecessor al-Ḥallād̲j̲ [*q.v.*], he acknowledges no obligations and has a thorough conviction of the reality of his own mission.

Bibliography: D.S. Margoliouth, *Early development of Muhammedanism*, 186-98; R.A. Nicholson, *The mystics of Islam, passim;* Arberry, *The Mawāqif of al-Niffarī*, in *JRAS* (1930), 404-6; P. Nwyia, *Trois œuvres inédits de mystiques musulmans: Šaqīq al-Balḫī, Ibn ʿAṭaʾ, Niffarī*, Beirut 1973; A. Schimmel, *Mystical dimensions of Islam*, Chapel Hill 1975, index; Ziriklī, *Aʿlām*, vii, 55-6; Brockelmann, I², 217, S I, 358; Sezgin, *GAS*, i, 528, 661-2.

(A.J. ARBERRY)

NIFṬAWAYH, ABŪ ʿABD ALLĀH IBRĀHĪM b. MUḤAMMAD b. ʿArafa b. Sulaymān b. al-Mug̲h̲īra b. al-Muhallab b. Abī Ṣufra al-ʿAtakī al-Azdī, grammarian, lexicographer, *ak̲h̲bārī*, leading expert in poetry, Ḳurʾānic readings and well-authenticated *muḥaddit̲h̲*, who owed his nickname, derived from the term *nifaṭ* (naphtha) to his dark complexion; this name is formed according to the same pattern as that of Sībawayh, whom he admired, whose grammatical methods he followed and on whose *Kitāb* he composed a commentary. Born at Wāsiṭ in 244/858, he lived and studied in Bag̲h̲dād where he died on 12 Rabīʿ I 323/20 February 935.

He studied grammar and *lug̲h̲a* with the eminent scholars al-Mubarrad (d. 285/898), T̲h̲aʿlab (d. 291/904) and Muḥammad b. al-D̲j̲ahm (d. 277/891). Among his masters in *ḥadīth*, his biographers mention numerous traditionists including Isḥāk b. Wahb b. Ziyād al-ʿAllāf (d. after 255/869 according to Ibn Ḥad̲j̲ar, *Tahd̲h̲īb al-Tahd̲h̲īb*, i, 259) and ʿAbbās b. Muḥammad b. Wāḳid al-Dūrī (d. 271/885). He studied the Ḳurʾān with, in particular, Ibn al-D̲j̲ahm and S̲h̲uʿayb b. Ayyūb al-Ṣarīfīnī (d. 261/875), collected *ak̲h̲bār*, took an interest in *fiḳh* and in history and learned by heart a considerable quantity of poems, including the entire *dīwāns* of D̲j̲arīr, of al-Farazdaḳ and of D̲h̲u 'l-Rumma. He himself composed some short pieces, mostly in the *g̲h̲azal* genre of amorous poetry, numerous fragments of which have been preserved by Yāḳūt (*ʿUdabāʾ*, i, 257-71) and al-ʿĀmilī (*Aʿyān*, ii, 222-3).

His erudition and his reputation as an upright and rigorous scholar were recognised during his lifetime, and attracted to him a number of pupils, notably including the *faḳīh* and *adīb* al-Nahrawānī (d. 390/1000), the *muḥaddit̲h̲* Ibn S̲h̲ād̲h̲ān (d. 383/993), the biographer and *adīb* al-Marzubānī (d. 384/994), the grammarian Ibn K̲h̲ālawayh (d. 370/980), the lexicographer al-Azharī (d. 370/980), the exegete al-Naḥḥās (d. 338/950), the *lug̲h̲awī* Abu 'l-Ḥasan al-ʿAskarī (d. 382/993), al-Masʿūdī (d. 345/956), Abu 'l-Farad̲j̲ al-Iṣbahānī (d. 356/967) and the philologist Abū ʿAlī al-Ḳālī (d. 356/967). The last-named is noted for having cited in his *Amālī* (ed. Dār al-Kutub n.d., i, 23, 30, 47 ff., ii, 83, 110, 191, 199 ff.), hundreds of verses which he had read in Nifṭawayh's presence or had heard recited, with critical comments, by him.

Of the various titles given him by his biographers, it is that of *naḥwī* which is most prominent. The majority of them, with the exception of al-Zubaydī (*Ṭabaḳāt*, 154), credited him, besides his mastery of the linguistic sciences and his integrity in the transmission of *ḥadīt̲h̲s* and in readings of the Ḳurʾān, with an outstanding grammatical ability which earned him admission to the prestigious *ṭabaḳa* which included among other grammarians of renown Ibn Kaysān (d. 299/911), al-Zad̲j̲d̲j̲ād̲j̲ (d. 311/923) and Abū Bakr al-Anbārī (d. 328/940) (see al-Azharī, *Tahd̲h̲īb*, i, 28; al-Suyūṭī, *Muzhir*, Cairo n.d., iii, 455). Furthermore, they stress that he was neither Baṣran nor Kūfan, but rather an eclectic who blended the two schools (*k̲h̲alaṭa al-mad̲h̲habayn*: *Fihrist*, 121). On the other hand, opinions differed regarding the school of *fiḳh* to which he belonged. Ibn Ḥad̲j̲ar (*Lisān*, i, 109) and al-ʿĀmilī (*Aʿyān*, ii, 220) classed him among the S̲h̲īʿīs. Al-Farg̲h̲ānī (d. 398/1007), quoted by Yāḳūt (i, 270), relates that he adopted the point of view of the Ḥanbalīs who maintain that the noun is the thing named (*al-ism huwa al-musammā*). For others, more numerous, he was a *ẓāhirī* partisan of the Dāwūdiyya and was regarded as a master of it (*raʾasa fī-hi*; al-Ṣafadī, *Wāfī*, vi, 130; Ibn Ḥad̲j̲ar, *loc. cit.*).

It is highly probable that Nifṭawayh was, in *fiḳh* as in *naḥw*, an eclectic who stood aside from partisan controversies. His close friendship with the eminent Ẓāhirī jurist Ibn Dāwūd (d. 294/907) does not necessarily signify that he was exclusively Ẓāhirī, nor does the fact that the Ḥanbalī al-Barbahārī (d. 329/941) recited the funeral prayers at his burial indicate that he was a master of Ḥanbalism. Regarding other questions, this versatility of mind was superseded by fixed and frankly polemical opinions. Thus he categorically rejected the principle of derivation (*is̲h̲tiḳāḳ*) among the Arabs and accused one of its proponents, the illustrious Ibn Durayd (d. 321/933), of having composed his dictionary (*al-D̲j̲amhara*) by altering (*g̲h̲ayyara*) the *Kitab al-ʿAyn* of al-K̲h̲alīl (d. 175/791). Regarding the origin of the language, he declared that Arabic was a natural (*ṭabīʿiyya = tawḳīfiyya*), not a conventional (*taʿlīmiyya = iṣṭilāḥiyya*) language, and he refuted the Muʿtazilī notion according to which the Ḳurʾān is created.

Ibn al-Nadīm (*Fihrist*, 121) lists fourteen of his works: 1. *K. al-Taʾrīk̲h̲*; 2. *K. al-Iḳtiṣārāt*; 3. *K. G̲h̲arīb al-Ḳurʾān* (a very large book, according to al-Bag̲h̲dādī, *Taʾrīk̲h̲*, vi, 159); 4. *K. al-Muḳniʿ fi 'l-naḥw*; 5. *K. al-Istit̲h̲nāʾ wa'l-s̲h̲urūṭ fi 'l-ḳirāʾāt* (var. *Wāfī*, vi, 132, ... *wa 'l-s̲h̲arṭ fi 'l-Ḳurʾān*; al-Ḳifṭī, *Inbāh*, i, 215: *al-Istīfāʾ fi 'l-s̲h̲urūṭ*); 6. *K. al-Ḳawāfī*; 7. *K. al-Radd ʿalā man ḳāla bi-k̲h̲alḳ al-Ḳurʾān*; 8. *K. al-Mulaḥ*; 9. *K. al-Amt̲h̲āl*; 10. *K. al-S̲h̲ahādāt*; 11. *K. al-Maṣādir*; 12. *K. al-Radd ʿalā man zaʿama anna 'l-ʿArab tas̲h̲taḳḳu 'l-kalām baʿḍahu min baʿḍ*; 13. *K. al-Radd ʿalā 'l-Mufaḍḍal fī naḳḍih ʿalā 'l-K̲h̲alīl*; 14. *Fī anna 'l-ʿArab tatakallamu ṭabʿan lā taʿalluman*.

Yāḳūt revised the list of the *Fihrist* and added three titles to it: *K. al-Amt̲h̲āl fi 'l-Ḳurʾān, K. al-Wuzarāʾ* and *K. al-Bāriʿ*. Ibn K̲h̲ayr (*Fahrasa*, 372, 376, 407) mentioned three other titles: *K. Aṭrag̲h̲as̲h̲s̲h̲a* (= "to recover, regain strength", cf. *LA*, root *ṭ-r-g̲h̲-s̲h̲*) *fi 'l-lug̲h̲a, Masʾalat subḥān* and *K. al-Amālī*. Finally, Ismāʿil Pas̲h̲a (*Hadiyya*, i, 5) adds a *Ḳaṣīda fī g̲h̲arīb al-lug̲h̲a*.

With the exception of the brief survey (8 folios) *Masʾalat subḥān*, and a work entitled *al-Maḳṣūr wa ʾl-mamdūd* which is attributed to him but is mentioned in none of the biographies, all the other works have been lost. The *Masʾala* has been edited by Y. Muḥ. al-Sawwās, in *RAAD*, lxiv/3 (1989), 361-91, on the basis of the Ẓāhiriyya ms., *madjmūʿa* 79. In it Nifṭawayh examines 32 Ḳurʾānic verses containing the words *subḥān* or *tasbīḥ* and comments on them from a linguistic viewpoint, with the support of numerous examples drawn from ancient poetry, *ḥadīth* and Ḳurʾānic exegesis. As for *al-Maḳṣūr wa ʾl-mamdūd*, Ḥ. Sh. Farhūd believes it to be the work of Nifṭawayh and as such has published it in *Madjallat Kulliyyat al-Ādāb, Djāmiʿat al-Riyāḍ*, iv (1973) (cf. U. Haarman, in *Studia Arabica et Islamica, Festschr. for I. ʿAbbās*, Beirut 1981, 169 n. 31).

The majority of the lost works were known, however, either by the title or by the quotations drawn from them. A.Ḍ. al-ʿUmarī (*Nifṭawayh wa-dawruh fi ʾl-kitāba wa ʾl-taʾrīkh*, in *Madjallat Kulliyyat al-Ādāb*, Baghdād, xv [1972], 71-102) gives a list of the quotations which are to be found in literature, without any indication of title (cf. F. Sezgin, *GAS*, viii, 149). Certain of these works feature among the sources for *al-Amālī* of al-Ḳālī, for the *Iʿrāb al-Ḳurʾān* of al-Naḥḥās (ed. Ghāzī Zāhid, introd., 15, 48), for the *K. al-Murūdj* of al-Masʿūdī (§§ 11, 2889, 3391), for the *Siyar aʿlām al-nubalāʾ* of al-Dhahabī (vi, 69, vii, 55, x, 281, 302 ff.) and for *al-Khizāna* of ʿAbd al-Ḳādir al-Baghdādī (ed. ʿA. Muḥ. Hārūn, vi, 458, ix, 146, xiii, 26). Of his numerous recensions, it seems that only two have survived. In one, he edits the *dīwān* of Suḥaym ʿAbd Banī ʾl-Ḥasḥās (ed. Maymanī, introd., 7) and in the other, that of al-Samawʾal (ed. L. Cheikho, Beirut 1910).

The disappearance of almost all of his literary works cannot fail to raise questions. For, while it is generally accepted that the loss of a great many Arabic books is most often due to the natural or human scourges which have ravaged the Islamic metropolises, it is remarkable that all the works of a writer of Nifṭawayh's versatility should have suffered the same fate. It may be suspected that the loss of his work is to be accounted for, to a certain extent, by the eclecticism of this author in questions of *fiḳh*, his intransigence in questions of language (concerning *ishtiḳāḳ* and the nature of language), his polemics against the Muʿtazila or the absence of one or more disciples dedicated to passing on his teaching.

Furthermore, a point made by Ibn Khayr (*Fahrasa*, 395-6) may provide a partial explanation of the cause of this loss. In effect, he states that al-Ḳālī brought with him from Baghdād to Spain (in 220/942) a large quantity of the recensions and works of al-Nifṭawayh, in addition to those which he had left behind and which had been taken from him in Ḳayrawān.

Bibliography (in addition to the works cited in the text): Masʿūdī, *Murūdj*, Arabic index, vi, 85; Azharī, *Tahdhīb*, Cairo 1964, i, 27-8; Zubaydī, *Ṭabaḳat al-naḥwiyyīn wa ʾl-lughawiyyīn*, Cairo 1954, 154; Ibn al-Nadīm, *Fihrist*, Beirut 1978, 121; Khaṭīb Baghdādī, *Taʾrīkh Baghdād*, Cairo 1931, vi, 159-62; Ibn Khayr, *Fahrasa*, Saragossa 1893, 395-6, 398 ff; Ḳifṭī, *Inbāh al-ruwāt*, Cairo 1950, i, 176-82; Yāḳūt, *Muʿdjam al-udabāʾ*, Cairo 1936, i, 254-72; Ibn al-Athīr, *Kāmil*, Cairo 1953, vi, 250; Ibn Khallikān, *Wafayāt*, Cairo 1948, i, 30-1; Dhahabī, *Siyar aʿlām al-nubalāʾ*, Beirut 1986, xv, 75; Ṣafadī, *Wāfī*, vi, 129-33; Subkī, *Ṭabaḳāt al-Shāfiʿiyya*, Cairo 1965, iii, 64, 269 ff.; Ibn Kathīr, *Bidāya*, Beirut 1985, xi, 195; Ibn Taghrībirdī, *Nudjūm*, Cairo 1932, iii, 250; Ibn Ḥadjar, *Lisān al-Mīzān*, Ḥaydarābād 1329, i, 109; Suyūṭī, *Bughya*, Cairo 1326, 187; Ibn al-ʿImād, *Shadharāt al-dhahab*, Cairo n.d., ii, 299; G. Flügel, *Gramm. Schulen der Araber*, Leipzig 1862, 213-15; Brockelmann, S I, 184; Ismāʿīl Pasha, *Hadiyyat al-ʿārifīn*, Istanbul 1951, i, 5; Muḥsin al-ʿĀmilī, *Aʿyān al-Shīʿa*, Beirut 1983, ii, 220-3; Ziriklī, *Aʿlām*, i, 57; Kaḥḥāla, *Muʾallifīn*, i, 102; Sezgin, *GAS*, ii, index, viii, 149-51.

(Omar Bencheikh)

NĪGDE, modern Turkish form Niğde, a town of south-central Anatolia in a fertile trough between mountainous regions, hence important in earlier times as a station on the trade route connecting Cilicia with the interior of Anatolia and with Sinope on the Black Sea coast. It lies in lat. 37° 58' N. and long. 34° 42' E. at an altitude of 1,250 m/4,100 feet.

The town is first mentioned in the Turkish period; previously, the chief town of the district was Tyana (Ar. Ṭuwāna), but it is probable that the striking hill which commands the important road from Cilicia across the Taurus to Ḳaysāriyye at its entrance to a pass over the mountains had a fortified settlement upon it in the pre-Turkish period. The old place-name may be the origin of the modern one, an older form of which was Nekīde (Yāḳūt, iv, 811, Nakīdā; Ibn Bībī and others, also in inscriptions down to the 10th/16th century, Nakīda; the modern form Nīgde is already found in Ḥamd Allāh Mustawfī, *Nuzhat al-ḳulūb*, 99). In this particular district, some villages have retained their ancient names (Andaval-Andabalis, Melegop-Malakopaia), and considerable numbers of descendants of the original Christian inhabitants survived until the early 20th century (R.M. Dawkins, *Modern Greek in Asia Minor*, Cambridge 1916, 16 ff.).

Nīgde is first mentioned in connection with the partition of Saldjūḳ territory among the sons of Ḳïlïdj Arslān II (685/1189), when it was allotted as an independent lordship to Arslān Shāh (Ibn Bībī, ed. Houtsma, in *Rec.*, iv, 11). Nīgde had perhaps previously belonged to the Danishmendids [*q.v.*], but Ewliyā Čelebi, iii, 189, cannot be taken as evidence of this. Kay Kāwūs I granted Nīgde to the Amīr-i Ākhūr Zayn al-Dīn Bashāra (Ibn Bībī, 44), who shortly before his death built the important mosque of ʿAlāʾ al-Dīn here (620/1223). In the 7th/13th century Nīgde was the headquarters (*sar-i lashkarī*) of one of the great military districts of the Ṣaldjūḳs. Under Ḳïlïdj Arslān IV, Ibn al-Khaṭīr Masʿūd held this office. At first an ally of the all-powerful Muʿīn al-Dīn Parwāne [*q.v.*], with whom he killed the sultan in 662/1264, he endeavoured to remove the young Kay Khusraw III out of the Parwāne's influence and brought him to Nīgde (674/1276). But the help for which he had appealed to Egypt came too late, and he succumbed to the Parwāne, who was supported by the Mongols (Ibn Bībī; Weil, *Gesch. d. Chalifen*, iv, 80-1). He built a well in Nīgde opposite the ʿAlāʾ al-Dīn mosque (666/1268). Under the Īlkhāns, there ruled in their name, or in the name of their Anatolian governor Eretna, Sunḳur Agha, who is known only from inscriptions and is, it is remarkable to note, not mentioned by Ibn Baṭṭūṭa, who visited Nīgde about 1333 (ii, 286-7, tr. Gibb, ii, 433); he made himself independent after the death of sultan Abū Saʿīd. He gave the town a large mosque, on the wall of which facing the Bezistān is a Persian inscription, in which he grants Christian foreigners exemption from *djizya* and *kharādj* (736/1335). The Saldjūk princess Khudāwand Khātūn, buried in 732/1332 in her splendid *türbe* built in 712/1312, on the other hand, probably did not rule in Nīgde although she resided there. She was, if the lady buried beside her in 745/1344 was her daughter, the wife of the *amīr* Shudjāʿ al-Dīn, who is mentioned as the father of the lady on her sarcophagus; he ruled, according to al-ʿUmarī (ed. Taeschner, 31), in the Bulghardagh, where a *wilāyet* called Shudjāʿ al-Dīn is still mentioned in Saʿd al-Dīn (i, 517, following Idrīs) and where lies Uluḳi̊shla, which, according to Ḥādjdjī Khalīfa (*Djihān-numā*, 617), was also called Shudjāʿ al-Dīn. After the period of Sunḳur's rule, Nīgde probably passed directly to the Ḳaramānoghlu, who held it against the attacks of the Eretnid ʿAlāʾ al-Dīn ʿAlī (*ca.* 781/1379) (ʿAzīz b. Ardashīr, *Bezm u rezm*, 141 ff.). In 792/1390 Nīgde surrendered with other Ḳaramānid towns to the Ottomans, but was restored to the Ḳaramānids, who defended it successfully against Ḳāḍī Burhān al-Dīn, lord of Ḳaysāriyye and Siwās (*Bezm u rezm*, 424, 523). After Tīmūr's invasion, the power of the Ḳaramānids extended northwards as far as Deweli Ḳaraḥiṣār, which previously belonged to Ḳaysāriyye itself. Nīgde then ceased to be a frontier town. Apart from a temporary occupation by Mamlūk Egyptian troops in 822/1419 (Weil, v, 146 ff.), it enjoyed peace and prosperity and the special care of the Ḳaramānids, who had one of the bulwarks of their power there till the end of the dynasty. A series of buildings, the first of which not only in time but also in size and quality is the Aḳ Medrese of the year 812/1409, is evidence of their interest in the town. Nīgde surrendered in 875/1470 to the Ottoman general Isḥāḳ Pasha, who had the defences of the town restored. In 878/1473 the Ottoman *sandjaḳ-bey* of Nīgde, Koči Bey, forced Deweli Ḳaraḥiṣār, which still belonged to the Ḳaramānoghlu, to surrender to prince Muṣṭafā. The latter died on the way back at Nīgde (Saʿd al-Dīn, i, 517, 550).

The *sandjaḳ* of Nīgde belonging to the *beylerbeylik* of Ḳaramān, contained the *ḳaḍāʾ*s of Ürgüb, Bor, Dewelu, Deweli Ḳaraḥisār and Uluḳi̊shla. In about 1132/1720 the grand vizier Ibrāhīm Pasha transformed his birthplace of Mushkara in the *ḳaḍāʾ* of Ürgüb into the imposing town of Newshehir [*q.v.*], and the fiefs for the garrisons of the decayed fortresses of Nīgde and Deweli Ḳaraḥisār were transferred to the new foundation (von Hammer, *GOR*², iv, 250-1). At the end of the Ottoman period, the *sandjaḳ* of Nīgde, to which the *ḳaḍāʾ* of Aḳ Saray also belonged, contained 148,700 Muslims and 49,551 Christians, the latter mainly natives and mostly speaking Turkish. Nīgde was the residence of the metropolitan of Konya. The town numbered at this time 11,526 inhabitants, but in 1927 (after the exchange of populations with Greece) only 9,463.

Nīgde (now on the Kayseri-Ulukışla railway) consists of an upper town running north and south, now largely uninhabited (Tepe Wirāne), at the highest point of which in the north stands the imposing citadel, and the lower town (Shehr altï) which was also once surrounded by a wall. In the upper town is the ʿAlāʾ al-Dīn mosque, one of the oldest mosques in Anatolia, with an architect's inscription in Persian. Before the gate of the upper town at its south end is the Gothic-influenced mosque of Sunḳur (*ca.* 1330), showing influences from Little Armenia and Cyprus, and the bazaar. West of and below it is the Ḳaramānid Aḳ Medrese of 812/1409. A little apart to the west of the town, separated by a broad road, running north and south is the modern quarter of Ḳayabashï with a few remains of the old cemetery and a group of *türbe*s, among which that of Khudāwand Khātūn from the year 712/1312 is prominent.

Modern Niğde is also the chef-lieu of an *il* or province of the same name; in 1970 the town had a population of 84,427 and the *il*, which has good agricultural land where it can be irrigated, one of 408,684.

Bibliography: Cuinet, *Turquie d'Asie*, i, 839 ff.; *Türkiyyenin̄ ṣiḥḥī we-idjtimāʿī djoghrafiyasï medjmūʿasï*, no. 2, *Nīgde* (1922); A. Gabriel, *Monuments turcs d'Anatolie*, i, 1931, 105 (historical and Muslim monuments of Nīgde, Bor and Uluḳi̊shla). — Inscriptions: Khalīl Edhem, in *TOEM*, ii, 747 ff., iii, 821 ff., 873 ff., and A. Tewḥīd, in Gabriel, *op. cit.* — On the Christian monuments of the region see Rott, *Kleinasiatische Denkmäler*, 1908; and De Jerphanion, *Eglises rupestres de Cappadocie*, 1925. See also Admiralty handbooks, *Turkey*, London 1942-3, ii, 575-6; *İA* art. s.v. (Besim Darkot).

(P. Wittek*)

NIGER, the great river of West Africa, with its source in the southeastern Fūta Djallon [*q.v.*] at an altitude of 800 m/2,624 ft. It runs northeastwards to the Sahara Desert, and then it turns southeastwards before descending southwards and ending in its delta on the Gulf of Guinea, in present-day Nigeria [*q.v.*].

Under the name of al-Nīl, the Niger river appears early in Muslim geographical writing, perhaps first in Ibn al-Faḳīh [*q.v.*], whose *Kitāb al-Buldān* was completed after 290/903. For many centuries, however, Muslim geographical analysis of the river was straitjacketed by widespread deference to the Ptolemaic model linking the Niger to the Nile. The early geographers seem frequently also to have regarded the Niger and Senegal rivers as one and the same. It was the northernmost part of the Niger, the so-called Niger bend (*boucle* in French), flowing eastwards through the desert, which first became known to the outside world in some detail.

Two major centres of trade, political centralisation, and religious change here first attracted Muslim attention, Ghāna [*q.v.*] some distance west of the bend but with its sphere of influence extending to the river, and Gao [*q.v.*] (variously Kūkū, Kawkaw, KRKR, Kāghū, etc.) lying on the river after it has turned south at the eastern tip of the bend. Ghāna and Gao were known in the first half of the 3rd/9th century, even before the Niger. Al-Muhallabī [*q.v.*], who died in 380/990, was perhaps the first to associate Gao with the river; his own work is lost, but Yāḳūt quotes the following passage:

> Kūkū, the name of a people and a country of the Sūdān .... Their king pretends before his subjects to be a Muslim (*yuẓāhir bi 'l-islām*) and most of them pretend to be Muslim too. He has a town on the Nile, on the eastern bank, which is called Sarnāh, where there are markets and trading houses (*matādjir*) and to which there is continuous traffic from all parts. He has another town to the west of the Nile where he and his men and those who have his confidence live. There is a mosque there where he prays but the communal prayer-ground (*muṣallā* [*q.v.*]) is between the two towns. In his own town he has a palace which nobody inhabits with him or has resort to except a eunuch slave (*khādim maḳṭūʿ*). They are all Muslims ...

It seems unclear exactly how much of this is from al-Muhallabī; there is an internal inconsistency concerning the extent of local Islam. The passage, nonetheless, is interesting. The river here is a meeting-point, with markets and trading houses nearby, implying considerable trans-shipment between land and water transport. A religious meeting-point too: the reference to a pretended Islam may indicate "mixed" religion, with Muslim and traditional elements commingled; isolation within the royal palace may echo an earlier (and still surviving?)

divine kingship. The river is at the same time a barrier: Sarnāh, the trading town, is east of the Niger, outside the bend; in another town, on the western, inner bank, the king lives with his own people, with those in whom he has confidence—suggesting that there were some traders and other visitors whom the king mistrusted.

As well as a meeting-point, and a dividing line, the Niger was also a channel of communication. Abū ʿUbayd al-Bakrī [*q.v.*], writing in or before 460/1068, well described the route from Ghāna to Kawkaw, mentioning markets, agriculture, routes into the desert, and locating pagan Sūdān south of the river, Muslim Berbers to its north. Al-Bakrī places the town of Kawkaw inside the bend, curiously not mentioning any settlement on the opposite bank here. Journeying north and west along the Niger, from Gao back towards Ghāna, al-Bakrī has the traveller encounter the cannibalistic Damdam, whose local religion is described; whether these details are correct or not, they do suggest that the traveller is inside the bend, while the described route from Ghāna to Gao follows the northern, desert bank. Al-Bakrī vividly pictures Gao, comprising two towns, one Muslim, the other the royal residence. During the royal meals, a drum is beaten, women dance, and all business in the town ceases; leftovers are then thrown into the Niger with the courtiers boisterously shouting, the whole clearly indicating pre-Islamic ritual intimately associated with the river. The king is Muslim, "for they entrust the kingship only to Muslims".

The celebrated geographer, al-Idrīsī [*q.v.*], in the mid-6th/12th century, refers often to the Niger, but his double conviction that a branch of the Nile flowed westward across Africa, and that as all civilised life in Egypt depended upon the Nile, so in western Africa all cities must be riverain, makes his account less reliable than al-Bakrī's.

Because of its length (approx. 4,000 km/2,486 miles), difficulties of crossing, occasional rapids obstructing navigation, islands and inundation, and the different climate zones through which it flows, the Niger could also be a refuge. In 1591, with Moroccan invaders threatening the Songhay empire, then the major power on the Niger bend, the clerics of Timbuktu proposed evacuating the city southwards across the river—sound advice turned down because men of religion were judged unfit for counsels of war. An estimated 2,000 boats were available to evacuate Gao, but again no full-scale withdrawal occurred. The Moroccans, having occupied Timbuktu, and desperate for boats, cut down every tree, even stripping houses of their doors. A branch of the legitimate *askiya* dynasty retreated downstream from Gao, to the Dendi region, where, protected by rapids, forest, and the river barrier, an independent Songhay presence successfully survived. Comparable patterns of raiding and sanctuary-seeking, depopulation and repopulation, communication and conflict, recur at divers times and places: Samuel Crowther's 1854 journal, for example, of travel on the lower Niger and the Benue, gives many instances in the aftermath of the Sokoto *djihād*.

The liminal experience of river crossing figures in many accounts of pilgrimage, *djihād*, etc. Abdullahi dan Fodio's *Tazyīn al-waraḳāt* mentions several cases, one of special interest. Describing a raid across the Niger early in the Sokoto *djihād*, the prose version recounts the plucky, and lucky, finding of a practicable ford. The verse recension, coloured by the Ḳurʾān (VII, 160, XX, 77-80, XXVI, 63), elaborates:

When we came to the river it obeyed, parting
To the staff of (divine) assistance, all its creatures obedient,
Its water creatures were turned on their backs,
Their teeth and their fangs broken;
They became for us as food offered to a guest; like game animals they became tractable, and its water
Became like quails and manna—a limpid cup,
Until we returned...

Bibliography: ʿAbd Allāh b. Muḥammad, *Tazyīn al-waraḳāt*, ed. and tr. M. Hiskett, Ibadan 1963 (the quotation is at 77/126); E.W. Bovill, *The Niger explored*, London 1968; S. Crowther, *Journal of an expedition up the Niger and Tshadda rivers ... in 1854*, 1st ed. London 1855, 2nd ed. London 1970; N. Levtzion and J.F. Hopkins, *Corpus of early Arabic sources for West African history*, Cambridge 1981 (the quotation from al-Muhallabī *apud* Yāḳūt is on p. 174); Elias N. Saad, *Social history of Timbuktu: the role of Muslim scholars and notables 1400-1900*, Cambridge 1983; M. Tymowsky, *Le Niger, voie de communication des grands états du Soudan occidental jusqu'à la fin du XVI*[e] *siècle*, in *Africana Bulletin*, vi (1967), 73-95.

(H.J. Fisher)

NIGER (The Republic of Niger, La République du Niger, Djumhūriyyat al-Naydjar), a modern state of West Africa, formerly the French colony of that name.

The Niger Republic is, to quote Djibo Mallam Hamani (though specifically of the Ayar Massif, which fills the north of it), a "carrefour du Soudan et de la Berbérie". Its geographical position on the map, and the multi-ethnic character of its societies, has had a profound effect on the Islamic life of the *Nigériens* throughout their history.

1. Geography and peoples

The Niger Republic covers an area of some 1,267,000 km². However, 800,000 of these are within the Sahara, much of which is uninhabited or is uninhabitable. The bulk of the remainder of the country is Sahel. It is only along the banks of the Niger river [*q.v.*] (where Niamey, the capital, is located) that there is any intensive cultivation and continuous settlement. Within the Sahara area are found the mountains of Ayar (Aïr [*q.v.*] or Azbin). This massif extends approximately 480 km from north to south and about 240 km from east to west. Within it there is a region of lush vegetation. Its capital is the important city of Agadès (Agadez) and this whole northerly massif contains some 600,000 inhabitants. Niger borders upon Libya and Algeria to the north, Chad to the east, Nigeria to the south and Mali and Burkina Faso, formerly Haute Volta, to the west. The total population of Niger is estimated to number upwards of 6,500,000 people; 97% of them are nominally Muslim, though this has not prevented ethnic tensions. All of them are Sunnīs and are Mālikī in *madhhab*. Some 45% of these are Hausaphone. The remainder are very mixed; Songhai and Zerma comprise 21.2%; Fulanis 13.8%; Tuareg (Tamashegh-speakers), who are largely nomadic, 11.2%; and Kanuri (who border on Lake Chad) 7.5%. Other minorities include Tubu (Teda) in the region of Kawār and Agadem, Gourmantche and Arabophone Awlād Sulaymān, Kunta and Tādjakānt. The wealth of the country is principally in agriculture, in trans-Saharan trade, cattle herding and pastoral nomadism, and in the past, its salt caravans. Recent droughts have devastated the herds. The discovery of uranium at Arlit (in 1965) now makes Niger the world's fifth-largest producer.

2. Islam in Niger

Next to Mauritania [see MŪRĪTĀNIYĀ], Niger is, by repute, the most Islamised of the territories of former

French West Africa. Even so, pockets of paganism survive. For example, the Wodaabe Fulani are still pagan in many of their beliefs and in their practices (see Carol Beckwith and Marion Van Offelen, *Nomads of Niger*, London 1984, and A. Maliki Bonfigliori, *Dudal*, Cambridge-Paris 1988), though belief in magic, in charms, in *djinn* and demonic forces is to be found amongst all the *nigérien* communities (see, for example, the *kel esuf* among the Ayar Tuareg, in D. Casajus, *La tente dans la solitude*, Cambridge-Paris 1987). Throughout its Islamic history, Niger has witnessed the growth of Ṣūfī [see TAṢAWWUF] movements of a kind and of a diversity unmatched elsewhere in the Sahelian countries. It has also been sensitive to puritan reformist movements inspired by the works of ʿAbd al-Karīm al-Maghīlī [*q.v.*], by the teaching of Shaykh ʿUmar Djibrīl, by the Sokoto *djihād* of Shehu ʿUthmān dan (b.) Fodio (Fūdī) [*q.v.*] and by reformers inspired by the Wahhābiyya [*q.v.*]. The Tuareg scholar community (*inesleman*) has played a major rôle in composing literary works in Arabic, or in religious verse in Arabic and Tamashegh, out of all proportion to their meagre numbers (see below).

When Niger became independent in 1960, it was established as a secular republic. In the 1970s it sought closer ties with the Arab World. On August 15 1974, steps were taken to constitute a Niger Islamic association and plans were pursued to found an Islamic university. This has now been established at Say, south of Niamey. Students from all over Muslim West Africa are taught there. *Nigérien* students have been sent to study in the Arab East, and there is constant encouragement to teach classical Arabic at all levels. According to J.-L. Triaud, *Islam and state in the Republic of Niger (1974-81)*, in *Islam and the state in the world today*, ed. O. Carré, New Delhi 1987, 253, "The new regime has drawn from this Arabized group to fill high level posts in the Islamic structure. The students have in general received a solid grounding in Arabic and religious studies. They embody a position which could be termed 'moderate reformism', based on openness to the outside world, refusal of superstition and unsophisticated practices and opposition to simplistic or fanatical formulations. The creation of the Islamic Association is in many ways an alliance between the central power and these reformist leaders against little local Marabouts or against the activism of certain fundamentalist tendencies".

3. An outline of the important phases of Islamic history in Niger

Islam has become integrated into the life of the *nigériens* over the centuries through a gradual process of Islamisation. It has produced a number of Arabic scholars and poets worthy of a place beside those from Timbuctoo in Mali, or from several towns in Mauritania. The following periods, religious leaders, regions, cities and events, have played a key part in determining that Islamisation:

(a) The earliest encounters between the Arabs, led by the Companion, and commander 'Uḳba b. Nāfiʿ [*q.v.*] and the inhabitants of the oases of Kawār, on the Fazzān border. This was followed by commercial contacts between the communities of the Ibāḍiyya [*q.v.*] in the Fazzān and towards the region of Ayar (see, in particular, K. Vikør, *The Oasis of Salt, the history of Kawar, a Saharan centre of salt production*, Bergen 1979, 97-111). Vikør furnishes a useful selection of passages from important Arab geographers (159-76 together with English translation) including Ibn ʿAbd al-Ḥakam (d. 258/871-2), al-Yaʿḳūbī (wrote 278/891), al-Bakrī (wrote 460/1067-8), al-Idrīsī (wrote 548-1154), Yāḳūt (wrote 621/1224), Ibn al-Athīr (d. 630/1233), Ibn Saʿīd (wrote 638/1240) and al-Ḥarrānī (wrote *ca.* 1330). (See also T. Lewicki, *Etudes maghrébines et soudanaises*, i, Warsaw 1976, 59-60.)

(b) The establishment of Berber Massūfa Ṣanhādja (who originated in Mauritania and Mali) centres in the vicinity of Takaddā (Teggidan Tesemt/Azelik), and later within the Ayar massif itself. The area was visited by Ibn Baṭṭūṭa [*q.v.*], in 754/1353, who mentions the names of two *ḳāḍīs*. Two noted scholars from Takaddā and its satellite Anū Ṣamman were al-ʿĀḳib b. ʿAbd Allāh, d. after 955/1548-9, and al-Nadjīb b. Muḥammad, d. after 1004/1595-6. Both of them wrote substantial works on the *Mukhtaṣar* of al-Khalīl and left other religious compositions (see J.O. Hunwick, *The Central Sūdān before 1800, biographies and bibliographies*, in *Arabic literature in Africa*, no. 1, Northwestern University, Evanston 1985, 23-41). The great Algerian reformer ʿAbd al-Karīm al-Maghīlī [*q.v.*] allegedly visited this area for a while on his way to Gao.

(c) The religious significance of the foundation of the Agadès sultanate, recognised by the caliphate, in the 15th century, its supplanting of Takaddā, its temporal subordination to the Askias and to Borno, its rôle as a clearing house for trans-Saharan commerce and its growth as a focus and haven for scholars who were in touch with Djalāl al-Dīn al-Suyūṭī [*q.v.*] by correspondence, and who visited the Arab East. Each and all made an impact on more southerly areas of Niger.

(d) The establishment of Ḳādiriyya lodges in Ayar, for example, at Agalal and in Agadès city. Other Ṣūfī orders followed. Prominent amongst them was the Shādhiliyya. Evidence of a Shādhilī presence in the city of Agadès in the mid-17th century may be found in the biography of Shaykh ʿUthmān b. al-Shaykh ʿAlī al-Ḥuḍayrī whose compositions are cited in a manuscript (now being edited in Libya), of a work attributed to Aḥmad al-Dardīr al-Ḥuḍayrī. It contains the biographies of leading Fazzānī scholars. A specifically Tuareg and Fulani order that was founded by a little-known Oriental darwīsh, Sīdī Maḥmūd al-Baghdādī, martyred in the early 16th century, has become the focal point of Ayar Ṣūfism in general. He would appear to have been an eclectic divine (the only Maḥmūdiyya found elsewhere is a sub-order of the Nuḳṭawiyya dating from about the same period, though it is to be doubted whether there can be any connection). Later, both the local Suhrawardiyya and the Khalwatiyya adopted, adapted and possibly "sanitised" many of the teachings and practices (*ādāb*) that were handed down in the Maḥmūdiyya.

Ṣūfism spread from Ayar into adjacent Azawagh, and at a later date into the Imanan canton, in Zerma country, and to a Ṣūfī *zāwiya* established, under Borno's aegis, at Kalumbardo, near Lake Chad, though within Niger's existing borders. In Agadès city, the sultanate attracted scholars and sustained a number of *ʿulamāʾ* and *fuḳahāʾ* who were revered amongst the city's mixed population.

(e) The reform movement of the Agadès-born Djibrīl b. ʿUmar (died after 1198/1784). He visited Egypt and Mecca and his pupils included Shaykh ʿUthmān b. Fūdī. The latter at a later date criticised his master's view that one who commits a grave sin (*kabīra*) becomes an unbeliever, a view that was akin to that used by earlier petty Tuareg *mudjāhidūn* from the Iborkarayan and Aït Awari in the region, in order to justify their razing of Ṣūfī centres in villages of Azawagh and Ayar.

(f) The Sokoto *djihād* itself, during which the

Islamic movement embraced large Hausa areas of Southern Niger, especially Gobir, the Agadès sultanate, the Aït Awari (where Muḥammad al-Djaylānī their leader tried to settle his followers) and other Tuareg groups such as the Kel Geres. The Hausa and Zarma river areas were subject to inroads from the Iwillimmeden Tuareg whose "chaplains", the Kelessuk, were often adepts of the Kunta Ḳādiriyya and who habitually fabricated charms and potions and who issued *fatwās* and composed sermons.

(g) Sanūsī [*q.v.*] penetration into northern Niger from 1870 onwards. The revolt and struggle of Kaoussen against the French in Agadès and Ayar, were backed by German-Turkish military sponsors based in the Fazzān. The consequences of the French expedition, mounted from Zinder in 1906, and which achieved the defeat of Kaoussen's *mudjāhidūn* in 1916, was to lead to a mass emigration of population from Ayar and major destruction of its Muslim centres (see F.R. Rodd, *People of the veil*, London 1926, A. Salifou, *Kaoussan ou la révolte sennoussiste*, in *Etudes Nigériennes*, no. 33, Niamey 1973, and F. Fuglestad, *A history of Niger, 1850-1960*, Cambridge 1983).

(h) The current Islamic revival; this has included a Khalwatiyya headquarters in Ayar at Egandawel (accompanied by an agricultural settlement at Tabellot-Akririb) inspired by a revivalist, Mūsā Abatūl, a resurgence of Islamic practice in Agadès (see Aboubacar Adamou, *Agadez et sa région*, in *Etudes Nigériennes*, no. 44, 318-21), and growth of the Niassist Tidjāniyya amongst Hausa and Zerma, led by Shaykh al-Ḥādjdj Abū Bakar, from Kiota, near Dosso, who married a daughter of the master, from Kaolack in Senegal. The Niassists, the *madrasa* at Say, neo-Wahhābīsm, fundamentalism, and the Niger Islamic Association, and the reformist movement, strong around Maradi, aiming at an increase of wealth, and the building of *madrasas*, known as *izāla* (*djamā*ʿ*at izālat al-bid*ʿ*a wa-iḳāmat al-sunna*) to name the most important centres of power, all make a significant contribution or compete for the souls of the Muslims in Niger today.

Bibliography: Besides the works already mentioned, see P. Bataillon, *L'Islam et l'organisation politique des Touaregs du Niger (Mémoires du CHEAM, 937)*, Paris 1946; E. Bernus, *Colporteurs de charmes magiques, les Ikadammatan*, in *Journal des Africanistes*, lv/1-2 (1985), 16-27; idem, *Histoires parallèles et croisées. Nobles et religieux chez les Touaregs Kel Denneg*, in *L'Homme*, no. 115, vol. xxx/3, July-September, 1990), 31-47; A.D.H. Bivar, and M. Hiskett, *The Arabic literature of Nigeria to 1804; a provisional account*, in *BSOAS*, xxv (1962), 104-48; Nicole Echard, *Histoire et histoires. Conception du passé chez les Hausa et les Twareg Kel Gress de l'Adar (République du Niger)*, in *Cahiers d'Etudes Africaines*, nos. 61-2, vol. xvi (1976), 237-96; D. Casajus, *Islam et noblesse chez les Touaregs*, in *L'Homme*, no. 115, vol. xxx/3 (July-September 1990), 7-30; Echard, *L'expérience du passé; histoire de la société paysanne Hausa de l'Adar*, in *Etudes Nigériennes*, no. 36, Niamey 1975; J. Godrie, *Le Niassisme au Niger-Est, Mémoire du CHEAM*, no. 3441, Paris 1961; H. Guillaume, *Les Nomades interrompus. Introduction à l'étude du canton Twareg de l'Imanan*, in *Etudes Nigériennes*, no. 35, Niamey 1974; Djibo Mallam Hamani, *Au carrefour du Soudan et de la Berbérie; le Sultanat Touareg de l'Ayar*, in *Etudes Nigériennes*, no. 55, Niamey 1989 (contains an extremely full bibliography); E. Hodgkin, *Social and political relations on the Niger bend in the seventeenth century*, Ph.D. thesis, Univ. of Birmingham 1987; J.O. Hunwick, *Notes on a late fifteenth century document concerning "al-Takrūr"*, in C. Allen and R.W. Johnson (eds.), *Africa perspectives: papers in the history, politics and economics of Africa presented to Thomas Hodgkin*, Cambridge 1970, 7-33; idem, *Sharī*ʿ*a in Songhay. The Replies of al-Maghīlī to ten questions of Askia al-Ḥājj Muḥammad*, ed. and tr. with an introduction and commentary, Fontes Historiae Africanae, Series Arabica V, Oxford 1985; M. Last, *The Sokoto Caliphate*, London 1967; J.E. Lavers, *Two Sufi communities in seventeenth and eighteenth century Borno*, paper submitted to the workshop on Ṣūfīsm in Africa in the seventeenth and eighteenth centuries (16th-18th September 1987), School of Oriental and African Studies, University of London; M. Le Cœur, *Les oasis du Kawar, une route, un pays, tome 1, le passé pré-colonial*, in *Etudes Nigériennes*, no. 54, Niamey, 1958; M. Hanspeter, *Die innere und äussere islamische Mission Libyens. Historisch-politischer Kontext, innerer Struktur, regionale Ausprägung am Beispiel Afrikas*, Mainz-Munich 1986; F. Nicolas, *L'Islam et les confréries en pays touareg nigérien*, in *Questions Sahariennes, 99-121, CHEAM 1009*, Paris 1947; idem, *Etude sur l'Islam, les confréries et les centres maraboutiques chez les Twareg du Sud*, in *Contribution à l'étude de l'Aïr*, Paris 1950, 480-91; H.T. Norris, *The Tuaregs, their Islamic legacy and its diffusion in the Sahel*, Warminster 1975; idem, *Ṣūfī mystics of the Niger Desert, Sīdī Maḥmūd and the hermits of Aïr*, Oxford 1990; A. Salifou, *Le Damagaram ou Sultanat de Zinder au XIXᵉ siècle*, in *Etudes Nigériennes*, no. 27, Niamey 1971; J.L. Triaud, *L'Islam et l'état en République du Niger*, in *Le Mois en Afrique*, nos. 192-3 (1981), 9-26; nos. 194-5 (1982), 35-48; idem, *Hommes de religion et confréries islamiques dans une société en crise, l'Aïr aux XIXᵉ et XXᵉ siècles*, in *Cahiers d'Etudes Africaines*, no. 91, vol. xxiii/3 (1983), 239-80; idem, *Les Alhazai de Maradi, Histoire d'un groupe de riches marchands Sahéliens*, ORSTOM, *Collection Travaux de Documents*, no. 187, Paris 1986, 1990. (H.T. Norris)

NIGERIA, the largest of the West African coastal states.

i. Modern Nigeria

Nigeria was put together in 1914 from the former British protectorates of Northern and Southern Nigeria, to become the Colony and Protectorate of Nigeria. It is bounded in the south by the Gulf of Guinea, in the west by Benin, in the north by Niger, in the north-east by Chad [*q.v.* in Suppl.] and in the east by Cameroon. The administrative capital is Abuja. The chief towns include Lagos, Ibadan, Ilorin, Kano and Sokoto. The population as at 1984 was 88,148,000 in an area of 923,768 km²/356,574 sq. mls. This comprises more than 250 tribal groups, of which the largest are the Hausas [see HAUSA], the Fulani [see FULBE] and the Kanuri of Bornū [*q.v.*], in the north; the Yorubas in the south-west; and the Ibos in the east.

The terrain encompasses the sandy shoreline and mango swamps of the coast, behind which lies a belt of tropical rain forest. This gradually gives way to orchard savannah as one moves north, to the area of Zaria. From there on the country becomes progressively drier and more barren until one reaches the thin scrub savannah and the near-desert conditions of the immediate sub-Saharan north.

Nigeria has numerous rivers, of which the Niger [*q.v.*], the Benue and the Gongola have been historically important. The coastal areas have two rainy seasons. The highest annual rainfall exceeds 2,500 mm/100 ins. This decreases the farther north one travels. The northern dry season extends from October to April and is the time of the harmattan, the hot, dust-laden wind from the Sahara.

The main religions of Nigeria are Islam (*ca.* 50%);

Christianity (*ca.* 34%) and a receding African animism.

A.H.M. Kirk-Greene, in his *The linguistic statistics of northern Nigeria: a tentative presentation*, in *African language review*, vi (1967), 75-101, lists some fifty-three "'Other' northern languages" in addition to Hausa, Fulani, Kanuri (of Bornū), Tiv, Nupe and Yoruba that were still spoken in northern Nigeria *ca.* 1952. The total number of languages spoken in the whole of Nigeria has been put at 250. Hausa, Yoruba, Edo and Ibo are now the most widely used indigenous tongues. English is the official language of the present Federal Republic of Nigeria, although there is strong pressure in the north for Hausa to be adopted as the national language. The minor northern vernaculars, some of which are confined to individual villages, are becoming extinct, replaced mainly by Hausa.

On 1 October 1954, the Federation of Nigeria was established under British tutelage. It consisted of an Eastern Region, a Western Region and a Northern Region, together with the Southern Cameroons and the Federal Territory of Lagos. The Federation was granted independence on 1 October 1960, within the British Commonwealth. It consisted of Northern Nigeria, Western Nigeria, Eastern Nigeria and the Federal Territory of Lagos. In 1963 it became the Federal Republic of Nigeria.

Nigeria experienced widespread disturbances, a military coup and then a civil war during the period from 1966 to 1970. During this time the Republic of Biafra was declared in the former Eastern Region. It surrendered to the Federal Republic in 1970, at the end of the civil war. After a further period of military rule, a return to parliamentary government based on democratic elections was cut short by a military coup in 1983, followed by another in 1985. The Federal Republic is at present governed by a President with an Armed Forces Ruling Council, which appoints a Council of Ministers. In 1985 it comprised 19 states and a federal capital district. In 1991 the number of states was increased to 30.

Nigeria had a varied and mainly agricultural economy until oil production began in the late 1950s. This gave rise to an oil boom. It was short-lived. The country later suffered from the drop in world oil prices and sustained a damaging revaluation of its currency.

The recent general history of Nigeria, up to and including the declaration of independence, is most conveniently available in Sir Alan Burn's *History of Nigeria*, eighth revised edition, London 1972.

The following sections of this article will set out briefly the course and extent of the adhesion to Islam of certain non-Hausa peoples of Nigeria; and will consider recent trends in Islam in Nigeria.

ii. The *Banza Bakwai*

The modern Hausas believe they spring from seven traditional Hausa states, the *Hausa Bakwai* [see HAUSA]. They also distinguish seven neighbours—the *Banza Bakwai*, the "Bastard Seven"—not of Hausa stock, who have supposedly adopted the Hausa language and way of life, and with whom their history has been continuously involved. They are the people of Zamfara, Kebbi, Yauri, the Yorubas, the Nupes, the Kwararafas and the Gwaris. These people are now, for the most part, drawn together with the Hausas within modern Nigeria.

The kingdom of Zamfara was located north-west of present Zaria, between Kebbi and Kano. Islam was introduced there, reputedly in the 11th/17th century. It probably came as a consequence of Zamfara's involvement in the trans-Saharan and sub-Saharan trade. The so-called "Fulani" *d̲j̲ihād* overtook Zamfara early in the 13th/19th century. Its trading pre-eminence thereupon declined. It became absorbed into the Islamic empire of Sokoto [*q.v.*].

The ancient kingdom of Kebbi, located north-west of Zamfara, may have come under Islamic influences during the hegemony of the Songhay empire. Its ruling family had accepted Islam by 921/1515. Its inclusion among the *Banza Bakwai* is tenuous. For the Kebbawa appear to have used Hausa only as a trade language; while their claim to Islam is as ancient as that of the Hausas.

Yauri lies south-east of Kebbi, astride the route to the gold-bearing regions of the Volta. By 1025/1616 it seems that Muslim-Hausa traders were settled in the kingdom. Under their influence the Yaurawa were won over to Islam by the end of the 11th/17th century.

The Yorubas dwell south-west of the Niger-Benue confluence. They are yet more doubtful candidates to be regarded as *Banza Bakwai* than even the Kebbawa. They retain their ancestral tongue to this day. They use Hausa only as a *lingua franca.* Their Islam, though incomplete, has ancient roots. It surely stems from the Mandingo empire of Mali [*q.v.*], that reached its Islamic apogee in the 8th/14th century. This is reflected in the Yoruba word for a Muslim—*Imale.* Subsequent Yoruba history has included a tussle between the ancient cult of Oduduwa, centred on Ile-Ife, and an intrusive Islam from the north. A substantial Muslim community had developed among the Yorubas by *ca.* 1078/1667. As a result of political rivalries within the Yoruba empire of Oyo [*q.v.*], an Islamic party revolted against the traditional authority early in the 13th/19th century. Consequently, most Yorubas were drawn into the aftermath of the Islamic *d̲j̲ihād* [*q.v.* and also MUD̲J̲ĀHID] in the north and were formally incorporated into the empire of Sokoto, as the emirate of Ilorin, in 1246/1831. But other Yorubas remained outside the emirate, in Lagos and elsewhere. They have continued to be subject to Islamic influences, none the less.

Islam is less complete among the Yorubas than it is among the northern Hausas and Fulani. Many are Christians, or adhere to the ancestral belief system. It is not uncommon to find Muslims and Christians in the same Yoruba extended family.

The Nupes, located within the northern angle of the Niger-Benue Confluence, resemble the Yorubas in their continuing attachment to an ancestral cult and language. They were in trading contact with the Muslim Hausas as early as the 9th/15th century, and have experienced Islam from that point on. Yet there is no firm evidence of the official adoption of Islam among them until early in the second half of the 12th/18th century. Thereafter, there is evidence of a swing back to the traditional belief system among some Nupes, later in the century. In modern times, Islam has become stronger among them; but not all Nupes are Muslims, even today.

The Kwararafas are a warlike people inhabiting the Gongola and Benue valleys. They have been traditional enemies of the Hausas to their north. A Muslim tradition among them cherishes a fantastic legend of origin in Yemen, which echoes the *Sīra* [*q.v.*] story of the Prophet's letters to erstwhile hostile neighbours, calling them to Islam. It is surely an importation of visiting Muslims. It is as likely to reflect Kwararafa hostility to the Muslim Hausas as any conversions to Islam. It probably arose *ca.* 905/1500, as a result of the establishing of Islam in Zaria at that time. Despite their improbable legend of origin, Islam has until recently made scant impression upon the Kwararafas. Up until *ca.* 1370/1950, they remained substantially committed to polytheism. However, more recent pressures for a uniform, Sunnī, Mālikī Islam throughout northern and riverain Nigeria now impinge upon them.

The Gwaris are scattered in the country of southern Zaria. Their Islam is of uncertain date and tenuous substance. Some venerate an *Allah Bango*, "Allah-of-the-book-boards", surely a reference to the presence of literate Hausa *malams* (Hausa = *ʿulamāʾ*) among them. Another of their deities is "Sheshu" or "Shekohi", probably reflecting Hausa "Shehu" (*shaykh*) ʿUthmān b. Fūdī [*q.v.*]. Yet another is "Mama", alias, no doubt, Muḥammad. While the origin of these Islamic fragments is uncertain, their most likely provenance is the Muslim drive south that followed the 13th/19th-century *djihād* in northern Nigeria. As is frequent among the Muslim Hausas' smaller neighbours, a reformist, Sunnī Islam has recently pushed aside most of what obtained before it. Islamic names and the ubiquitous Hausa *riga*, the Muslim gown, now make most Gwaris—at any rate in the towns and villages—indistinguishable from the surrounding Hausas.

This account, a more detailed version of which will be found in M. Hiskett's *The development of Islam in West Africa*, London and New York 1984, 110-19, covers most of the non-Hausa peoples of present Nigeria. There remain the Fulani [see FULBE], Borné [*q.v.*], the Ibos, *et alii*, of the former Eastern Region and certain smaller, animist groups such as the Dakarkaris and the Plateau people.

iii. Recent trends in Islam in Nigeria

Lugard's amalgamation of Southern and Northern Nigeria resulted in bundling the Ibos, Ibibios and other non-Muslim peoples of what, during the colonial period, was known as the Eastern Region, together with the Muslim northerners , in one federation. These people had remained untouched by Islam—except as potential slaves—up to the colonial occupations. Many had by this time become protégés of Christian missionaries from the Coast. They were mainly Roman Catholics. They continued under missionary tutelage until Nigerian independence, the civil war, the oil boom and a series of military coups, brought about sweeping changes.

During the colonial period these inveterate petty traders from the east flocked north in the train of the British. Because of their missionary education many became minor civil servants. They set up *Sabon Garis* "New Towns", outside the northern Muslim cities. With Nigerian independence approaching, they became the victims of ethnic and religious hostility on the part of the Muslim northerners, which their own posturing prior to the declaration of Biafra did nothing to diminish. Immediately before the outbreak of the civil war, a mass exodus of Ibos from the north, back to the east, took place, against the background of an ugly blood bath.

After the civil war, and in the more congenial atmosphere of the Nigerian oil boom, Ibos and other easterners returned to the north, as traders and in certain professional capacities that ranged from bank clerk to lecturer in the new northern Nigerian universities. However, they faced different conditions from those that had obtained under the British colonial administration. For there was among radical northern Muslims a wide consensus that such returning easterners should subscribe to Islam, as a condition of their new acceptability in the Muslim north. This was not official and was seldom openly expressed. It was, however, the unspoken extension of the policy of "Northernisation" that the old Northern Region had officially adopted during the terminal days of the colonial administration, and continued ever since. While Christian enclaves of eastern and Coastal Nigerians remain in northern townships, there are, nonetheless, an increasing number of "Musas", "Muhammadus", "Aliyus" *et alii* in northern Nigeria who, apart from such names and the Hausa-Muslim *riga*, display all the characteristics of a southern, Coastal Christian mission upbringing. How significant such conversions of convenience may be, is questionable. Nonetheless, they represent a widening of Islamic influence.

Such pressures have a precedent. From *ca.* 1380/1960 to his assassination in 1385/1966, the Sardauna of Sokoto, then Premier of the Northern Region, pursued a policy of "Islamisation", the purpose of which was to persuade—or coerce—all indigenous northern Nigerian peoples to accept Islam. It had the fervour of "Djihād of the Heart" behind it. It also involved some harassment, as well as bribery, of residual animist groups such as the Dakarkaris and the Plateau people. And it convinced, or allowed certain Ibo army officers to claim, that the Sardauna was preparing Holy War against all non-Muslims. This then became part of their justification for declaring an independent Biafra. In the event, the Sardauna's campaign resulted in widespread nominal conversions, in which chiefs, village heads, etc., adopted Islamic names in addition to their traditional ones. This was taken as sufficient to establish the Islam of their people as a whole. Once again, it is questionable how deep such mass "conversions" go. But certainly the Sardauna's essay after the hearts and minds of his non-Muslim countrymen has been a precedent after the renewal of which in a more thoroughgoing fashion, northern Muslim radicals now hanker. They enjoy some support in this among certain Yoruba Muslims.

The period from the end of the Second World War to the granting of northern independence in 1960, is known to the Hausas as *Zamanin siyasa*, "The Time of Politics". It saw the rise of Nigerian political parties, superficially resembling those of the British parliamentary system. In fact, the Northern Peoples' Congress (NPC) was identified with the interests of the aristocratic Fulani emirates and the "Native Authority" (NA) system that sustained them. It advocated a modified Islamic theocracy for independent northern Nigeria. This party was challenged in the north by the Northern Elements Progressive Union (NEPU), ostensibly mimicking the European left but also representing the ancient antagonism of Hausa commoners towards their Fulani overlords; and pursuing a tradition of Islamic dissidence. It was closely associated with the Tidjāniyya [*q.v.*] *ṭarīḳa*, that had, hitherto, reflected this dissidence. Both parties vied with one another in their claims to represent the true Islam, and excoriated the other for betraying that Islam. By and large, the establishmentarian NPC had the better of the radical NEPU, a consequence, no doubt, of the prevailing ethos of Sunnī, Mālikī conservatism at that time. Their tussle produced a plethora of ding-dong Hausa political verse, admirably recorded by Haruna Abdullahi Birniwa (*Conservatism and dissent; a comparative study of NPC/NPN and NEPU/PRP Hausa political verse from circa 1946 to 1983*, PhD thesis, University of Sokoto, Nigeria 1987, unpubl.).

The Nigerian civil war, the oil boom and the military administrations shattered the old Islamic party lineaments and created new interests and alliances. While the People's Redemption Party

(PRP), launched in 1978, continued to reflect certain attitudes of the old NEPU, the National Party of Nigeria (NPN), founded in the same year, had a more Federal base. It represented Christian-Yoruba and other minority-Christian interests, as well as those of the Muslim Hausas. Moreover, it eschewed Islamic theocracy. But the party system was short-lived in Nigeria. Under the military, party politics were banned. What has taken their place is a division between modernists and moderates on the one hand, who favour a democratic, pluralist federation; and on the other, Muslim iconoclasts who want no more truck with democracy and call for the north to return to Islamic theocracy. As the banners of radical-Muslim campus demonstrators put it, on the eve of the fall of the egregious Shagari administration on 31 December 1983, "Democracy is unbelief! We do not want a constitution! We want government by the Koran alone!" It is surely the military administration alone that keeps this tendency at bay.

Some recent scholarly comment has suggested that polygyny in Islam has given way to monogamy, as education and emancipation have their influence upon Muslim women. The assumption is unsafe in the case of Nigeria. Here, undoubtedly, some loosening of purdah has occured. Muslim women in Kano, Sokoto and elsewhere, teach in schools and universities and fulfil other professional roles. But there are unspoken conditions. Virtually all are married. They are expected to deport themselves with exemplary Islamic modesty. They are indeed educated. Some are university graduates. But this greater freedom has led them to see themselves not as victims of the Islamic system but as its articulate defenders. Most of them uphold Islamic polygyny within the strict construction of the Mālikī *madhhab*, and contrast what they regard as the admirable stability of the Muslim extended family with the decline of the Western nuclear family, the growth of the "one-parent family", abortion and the rest, which frankly horrify them.

As for the men, especially the Muslim academics to whom the growth of universities in the north has given considerable influence, many are among the most ardent advocates of polygyny, though once again with due regard for the law. They regard it as essential to defend an Islamic way of life, increasingly threatened by secularism. Whatever may be happening elsewhere in the Islamic *umma*, the decline of polygyny in northern Nigeria is not evident.

Expatriate Europeans have been largely replaced in northern Nigeria by Muslims from Pakistan, Egypt and the Republic of the Sudan, who now work as university lecturers, educationists, agriculturalists and in other roles once filled by Europeans. Some turn out to be tutors in an Islamic radicalism that resembles the popular notion of "fundamentalism". Especially influential have been Egyptian disciples of the *Ikhwān al-muslimīn* [*q.v.*]. Though an older generation of Sunnī, Mālikī *malams* still fights shy of such immoderation, a younger generation of Muslim activists has taken to it fervently. The Hausa Muslim tendency known as the *'Yan Izala* broadly mimics the stance of the Saudi Wahhābiyya.

The Middle East imbroglio, through the rise of Khomeini (al-Khumaynī [*q.v.* in Suppl.]) to the seizure of the Masdjid al-Ḥarām in Mecca in 1400/1979, had its repercussions in northern Nigeria. For, while the conservative Sunnī *malams* were chary of what was a largely Shīʿī enthusiasm, the activists had no such hesitations. In this they received encouragement from certain expatriate Muslims. For in the ardour of the times, these Sunnī radicals were ready to side with Shīʿīs they might otherwise have execrated. Likewise, President Muʿammar al-Ḳadhdhāfī (Gaddafi) became an object of radical Muslim admiration, until his meddling in Chad turned Nigerian sentiment against him. Indeed, many Nigerian Christians joined with their Muslim countrymen in hailing both al-Khumaynī and al-Ḳadhdhāfī. They thus illustrated the way in which so-called Islamic fundamentalism and more generalised third-world sentiment converge at many points.

The most spectacular Nigerian concomitant to the seizure of the Grand Mosque of Mecca and all it represented, was the gruesome Mai Tatsine riots that disturbed northern Nigeria from 1980 to 1984. This eruption, widely misunderstood as just another outbreak of Iranian-style Islamic radicalism, had complex origins. It is best described as a manifestation of traditional Islamic messianism—21 November 1979 marked the beginning of A.H. 1400, a fact that excited many Nigerian Muslims to apocalyptic expectations—mixed with resurgent African animism that was wholly un-Islamic. Thus the protests of outraged Sunnī *malams* that this was not Islam but downright *kafirci* (Hausa "unbelief"). An assessment of these events by M. Hiskett will be found in *The Mai Tatsine riots in Kano, 1980: an assessment*, in *Journal of Religion in Africa*, xvii/3 (1987), 209-23.

By 1985 the lid was still held down firmly on what seemed at that time to be a cauldron of Islamic militancy in Nigeria, by the Military Administration. This Administration's policy of increasing the number of states, which enjoy considerable internal autonomy, is apparently intended to reduce ethnic and religious tensions as far as is possible. It remains to be seen whether it will prove successful in restraining the Islamic radicalism that undoubtedly exists among northern Muslims.

Bibliography: Among printed books and articles, the following are useful: Mahdi Adamu, *The Hausa factor in West African history*, Zaria and Ibadan 1978, is essential for an understanding of Hausa-Muslim influences beyond Hausaland; G.N. Brown and M. Hiskett (eds.), *Conflict and harmony in education in tropical Africa*, London 1975, selected chapters; A. Christelow, *Religious protest and dissent in northern Nigeria: From mahdism to Qurʾānic integralism*, in *Journal Institute of Muslim Minority Affairs*, vi/2 (n.d.), 375-448; idem, *The 'Yan Tatsine disturbances in Kano—a search for perspectives*, in *MW*, lxxv/2 (1985), 69-84; Catherine Coles and Beverly Mack (eds.), *Hausa women in the twentieth century*, Madison, Wisconsin 1991; B.J. Dudley, *Parties and politics in northern Nigeria*, London 1968; H.J. Fisher, *Some reflexions on Islam in independent West Africa*, in *The Clergy Review* (March, 1968), 1-13; T.G.O. Gbadamosi, *The growth of Islam among the Yoruba*, London 1978; Government Printer, Enugu, *The north and constitutional developments in Nigeria: Nigerian crisis 1966*, v, Enugu n.d., gives the Ibo view of the background to the Nigerian civil war; A.H.M. Kirk-Greene, *The genesis of the Nigerian civil war and the theory of fear*, Scandinavian Institute of African Studies Research Report, no. 27, Uppsala 1975; K. Krieger, *Geschichte von Zamfara*, Berlin 1959; V.N. Low, *Three Nigerian emirates*, Illinois 1972, is useful for its account of the Kwararafas; P.M. Lubeck, *Islamic protest under semi-capitalism: 'Yan Tatsine explained*, in J.D.Y. Peel and C.C. Stewart (eds.), *Popular Islam south of the Sahara*, Manchester 1985, 369-89; P. Morton-Williams, *The Fulani penetration into Nupe and Yoruba in the nineteenth century*, A.S.A. Monographs, 7. History and social anthropology,

London and New York 1968; P.J. Ryan, *Imale: Yoruba participation in the Muslim tradition*, Missoula, Montana 1978; N. Skinner and Kabir Galadanci, *Wakar soja—a Hausa poem on the civil war*, in *Spectrum*, iii (1973), 97-125, for a Muslim-Hausa view of the civil war; D. Westermann and M.A. Bryan's *Languages of West Africa*, in *Handbook of African languages*, Part II, London (1952) includes a useful language map of West Africa.

Much of the most valuable work on recent developments in Islam in Nigeria will be found in unpublished MA and PhD dissertations. Birniwa's work, cited above, not only provides primary source material in the form of Hausa verse; it also includes an acute analysis of the history of the northern Nigerian political parties. Muhammad Sani Aliyu's *Shortcomings in Hausa society as seen by representative Hausa Islamic poets*, MA thesis, Bayero University, Kano 1983 unpubl., throws light on the *malam*'s reactions to secularism; Samaila Mohammed's *Some aspects of the culture and institutions of the Dakarkari people examined in the light of their contiguity with the Hausa people*, MA thesis, Bayero University, Kano 1982 unpubl., is an admirable study of contacts between the Muslim Hausas and an animist society; Abdullahi Bayero Yahya's *A critical anthology of the verse of Aljaji Bello Gidawa*, MA thesis, Bayero University, Kano 1983 unpubl., enshrines valuable source material for studying the genesis of NPC. (M. Hiskett)

NIGHT WATCHMAN [see ʿasas].

NIHĀL ČAND LĀHAWRĪ, Indian man of letters, Hindū by religion, was born in Dihlī, but left it in early life and went to Lahore where he lived for a considerable time. Owing to this circumstance he called himself Lāhawrī. Search for a livelihood led him to Calcutta. Here he was introduced to Dr. J.B. Gilchrist, who asked him to translate into *Hindī re*k͟h*ta* the story of Tād͟j al-Mulūk and Bakāwalī. He consented, and thus became one of the famous band of Fort William translators. He made the translation from *Gul-i Bakāwalī*, a Persian rendering by S͟hayk͟h ʿIzzat Allāh, 1772, of an old Hindī story, which has been reproduced in Urdu verse by Dayā S͟hankar Kawl Nasīm [*q.v.*], in his well-known *mat͟hnawī Gulzār-i Nasīm*.

Nihāl Čand called his work *Mad͟hhab-i ʿis͟hḳ*. It is in very good prose mixed with verse. The title gives the date 1217/1802. Apart from the above-mentioned facts, nothing is known about the writer.

Bibliography: M. Yaḥyā Tanhā, *Siyar al-muṣannifīn*, i, 117-19; Garcin de Tassy, *Histoire de la littérature hindouie et hindoustanie*, 2nd ed. Paris 1870, ii, 468-70; T. Grahame Bailey, *A short history of Urdu literature*, Oxford 1931, 82; R.B. Saksena, *Hist. of Urdu literature*, Allahabad 1927, 249.

(T.G. Bailey)

NIHĀWAND, a town in the Zagros Mountains of western Persia, in the mediaeval Islamic province of D͟jibāl [*q.v.*], situated in lat. 34° 13' N. and long. 48° 21' E. and lying at an altitude of 1,786 m/5,860 feet. It is on the branch of the Gāmāsāb which comes from the south-east from the vicinity of Burūd͟jird; the Gāmāsāb then runs westwards to Bisūtūn. Nihāwand lies on the southern road which, coming from Kirmāns͟hāh (Ibn K͟hurradād͟hbih, 198), leads into central Persia (Iṣfahān) avoiding the massif of Alwand ('Ὀροωτης) which rises to the west of Hamad͟hān. Hence the importance of the town in the wars of Persia with her western neighbours.

The French excavations of 1931 (Contenau) showed that the site of Nihāwand was inhabited from prehistoric times. The ceramics ("I-bis style") which have been found there, seem to be older than those of style I and II of Susa. Ptolemy, VI, 2, knows of Νιφαυάνδα and according to Ibn Faḳīh, 258, the town already existed before the Deluge. In the Sāsānid period the district of Nihāwand seems to have formed the fief of the Kārin family (al-Dīnāwarī, 99). There was a fire-temple there. According to Ibn Faḳīh, 259, there could be seen on the mountains near Nihāwand two figures of snow in the form of a bull and a fish (similar talismans are said to have existed at Bitlīs also, cf. the steles of *wis͟hap* ("dragons", protectors of waters) in Armenia west of Lake Sewan which combine these symbols, *Zap.*, xxiii/3 [1916], 409). The same legend is reflected in the name of the river Gāmāsāb (*Gāw-māsī-āb* = "water of the bull and fish"; *māsī* is the Kurdish form of the Persian *māhī*).

Among the products of Nihāwand, the Arab authors mention willow wood which was used for polo-sticks (*ṣawālid͟ja*), aromatic reeds (*ḳaṣabat al-d͟harīra* or *al-ḳumḥa al-ʿirāḳiyya*) which were used like *ḥanūṭ* (a perfume put in coffins) and black clay used as wax for sealing letters. The district of Rūdrāwar [*q.v.*] was under Nihāwand (cf. de Morgan, *Mission*, ii, 136: *Rūdīlāwar*) and was famous for its abundance of saffron (al-Iṣṭak͟hrī, 199). For a list of the places more or less dependent on Nihāwand, cf. Schwarz, *Iran*, 505-9. In the Mongol period, Ḥamd Allāh Mustawfī's *Nuzhat al-ḳulūb* mentions three districts of Nihāwand: Malāyir (now Dawlatābād), Isfīd͟hān (= Isbīd͟hahān, see below) and D͟jahūḳ.

Near Nihāwand was fought the famous battle which decided the fate of the Iranian plateau and in which the Kūfī commander al-Nuʿmān b. Muḳarrin defeated the Sāsānid generals. The commander-in-chief is given different names: D͟hu 'l-Ḥād͟jibayn Mardāns͟hāh (cf. al-Balād͟hurī, 303 n. *e*; Marquart, *Ērānšahr*, 113 identifies him with the *darīkpet* K͟hurrazād) of Fīrūzān (cf. al-Ṭabarī, i, 2608; the latter also gives the names of his generals: Zarduḳ, Bahman D͟jādōya and the commander of the cavalry Anūs͟haḳ). The Arab camp was at Isbīd͟hahān and that of the Persians at Wāyk͟hurd (?). The sources do not agree about the date: Sayf b. ʿUmar (al-Ṭabarī, i, 2615-19) gives the end at the year 18/639 or the beginning of 19/640 (cf. Wellhausen, *Skizzen und Vorarbeiten*, vi, 1899, 97), while Ibn Isḥāḳ, Abū Maʿs͟har and al-Wāḳidī, followed by Caetani, *Annali dell' Islām*, iv, 1911, 474-504, put the battle in 21/642.

The district of Nihāwand (formerly called Māh-Bahrād͟hān or Māh-Dīnār) was finally incorporated in the possessions of the Baṣrans and called Māh Baṣra ("the Media of Baṣra"; al-Balād͟hurī, 306).

Nihāwand is often mentioned in the period of the wars between the Ṣafawids and the Ottomans. In 998/1589 at the beginning of the reign of ʿAbbās I, the Ottoman vizier Čig͟hāle-zāde [*q.v.*] built a fortress at Nihāwand (*ʿĀlam-ārā*, 372). After the death of Murād IV, a rebellion took place among the garrison of Nihāwand; the Ottomans were driven out by the S͟hīʿī inhabitants. As a result, in 1012/1603 war again broke out with Turkey (*ibid.*, 440). In the spring of 1142/1730 Nādir S͟hāh [*q.v.*] took Nihāwand again from the Turks.

In modern Persia, Nihāwand is the chef-lieu (population in 1960, 26,452) of a *s͟hahrastān* of the same name (population 70,000) in the fifth *ustān* or province of Kurdistān.

Bibliography: J. de Morgan, *Mission scientifique en Perse*, ii, *Études géographiques*, 1895, 152 and *passim*, pl. lxvi (view of Nihāwand); Marquart, *Ērānšahr*, index; Le Strange, *Lands of the Eastern*

Caliphate, 196-7; Schwarz, *Iran im Mittelalter*, i, 498-509, index; G. Conteneau and R. Ghirshman, *Rapport préliminaire sur les fouilles de Tépé-Giyān, près de Néhavand, 1931*, in *Syria* (1933), 1-11; Admiralty handbooks, *Persia*, London 1945, 368; Razmārā, *Farhang-i d̲j̲ug̲h̲rāfiyā-yi Īrān*, v, 460-2; A. Noth, *Isfahan-Nihawand, eine quellenkritische Studie zur frühislamischen Historiographie*, in *ZDMG*, cxviii (1968), 274-96; Sylvia A. Matheson, *Persia, an archaeological guide*, London 1972, 115; W. Barthold, *An historical geography of Iran*, Princeton 1984, 180-1, 208. (V. Minorsky)

NIHĀWANDĪ, ʿAbd al-Bāḳī b. Abī Bakr Kurd, Indo-Muslim historian of the Mug̲h̲al period (978-after 1046/1570-after 1637). Of Kurdish origin from D̲j̲ūlak near Nihāwand [*q.v.*], he served the Ṣafawids as a tax official and eventually became a *wazīr* in the administration. But then he fell from grace, and like many Persians of his age, decided to migrate to India, and entered the service of the K̲h̲ān-i K̲h̲ānān [*q.v.*] Mīrzā ʿAbd al-Raḥīm, one of Akbar's generals, subsequently holding official posts in the Deccan and Bihār. The K̲h̲ān-i K̲h̲ānān asked him to write a biography of himself, the *Maʾāt̲h̲ir-i Raḥīmī*, completed by ʿAbd al-Bāḳī in 1025/1616 (ed. Hidāyat Ḥusayn, Bibl. Indica, Calcutta 1910-31) an important source for the period, which also contains a history of Muslim India in his own and previous times, starting with the G̲h̲aznawids [*q.v.*].

Bibliography: Storey, i, 522-3, 1315.

(C.E. Bosworth)

NIHĀYA (a.), a term of Islamic philosophy which (together with its negation *mā lā nihāya lahu*) is entirely governed by its lexical meaning. Ibn Manẓūr, in *LA*, defines it thus: "the extremity (*g̲h̲āya*) and final limit (*āk̲h̲ir*) of a thing; and this is because its final limit prevents it from being prolonged (*yanhā-hu ʿan al-tamādī*), so that it is stopped (*fa-yartadiʾ*)". This definition of *nihāya* is based on its etymology, since the verb *nahā* means "to forbid". The *nihāya* is thus that which forbids access to something beyond a certain limit. Ibn Manẓūr explains the Ḳurʾānic phrase *sidrat al-muntahā* (LIII, 14) by saying that it is the lotus "which one reaches by arriving at it and which one does not go beyond (*wa-lā yutad̲j̲āwaz*)".

This concept of not going beyond can apply to such realities as time, space and the division of bodies. Does time have a limit in the past (an original time) or in the future (a final time), limits before or beyond which there is no more time, or is there an extension of time into infinity, an eternity of time *a parte ante* (*al-lam-yazal*) which has never ceased to exist in the past, and *a parte post* (*al-lā-yazāl*) which will never end in the future? The same question can be put regarding space: does there exist an infinite space, or is all existing space limited? Likewise, is there or is there not a limit to the division of bodies; is a body composed of an infinite number of parts, or is it built up from a finite assemblage of indivisible atoms? But the concept of not going beyond is also applicable to the operations of thought: does it reach as far as definitive conclusions, i.e. can it define final and "completed" truths, without being obliged to to go back incessantly and infinitively in its reasonings, "until there is no *nihāya*", which is, in the eyes of logicians, the sign of a defect in a proof? One can thus discern that the concept of *nihāya* is involved in everything touching such problems as what is finite, the infinite and the undefined.

The question in regard to space and time was treated in the discussions of the opposing views of al-G̲h̲azālī and Ibn Rus̲h̲d in the two *Tahāfut*s. Is there a parallelism between space and time in regard to their limits? Al-G̲h̲azālī, in an eristic form of augumentation against the philosophers, supports it. He remarks that the future and the past are relative to each other, since all future becomes a past, and all past is merely such in as far as it precedes the future. But these are equally relative to the human soul which, in its present form, represents these two dimensions of time thanks to its faculty of imagination (*wahm*, *tawahhum*) which, itself, cannot come to a halt, neither to an initial term nor to a final one. Hence it has no *nihāya*. But the same is true in regard to space; our imagination cannot stop at a higher or lower limit, so that one can conceive of an undefined growth of the world in space (or, contrariwise, an undefined contraction), which raises the question of our knowing whether the world could have been created greater or smaller than it in fact is. Further, one can ask oneself if it could have been created earlier or later. In effect, if spatial dimension accompanies a body, then temporal dimension accompanies movement. If one thus admits, in spite of the imagination, that the body of the world is limited and that it does not exist beyond the created world as it actually is, neither open space nor empty space, as the philosophers, following Aristotle and his theory of place (τόπος, cf. *Physics*, book IV), then they must be compelled to recognise that, beyond the movement of the world, there exists no empty time nor filled time, and, as a result, that the world has a temporal *nihāya* just as it has a spatial one. If the philosophers refuse to grant that the world has a first beginning at which one must stop when one traces back the succession of movements which are characteristic of it, despite being carried away by the imagination, then they are not in conformity with their own beliefs, since they admit a *nihāya* for space but refuse it for time whilst the case of time is identical with that of space.

Ibn Rus̲h̲d replies that, if the future and past are relative to our own imagination, they are not then "things which exist in themselves; they have no existence outside the soul and are only a creation of the soul (*s̲h̲ayʾ tafʿalu 'l-nafs*)". The fact that the imagination goes beyond all spatial limit as much as beyond all temporal limit does not imply that, in reality, the case of time is the same as that of space. Or, to be precise, there exists, from the point of view of real existence, a great difference: this is that every body, as such, forms a whole, an ensemble which can be added up into a totality, which is not the case with movement which, on the contrary, by its very nature flows along and cannot be halted in a total stop. This is why, according to reason, and not this time according to the imagination, one can conceive of a spatial limit to the world, whilst one cannot conceive of a limit to movement and, consequently, to time, since time is made up of a enumerated number of movements, on which it depend. This is the explanation why, when there is a question of a reality which comes into existence (*al-muḥdat̲h̲*) after its non-existence, one must not trace back the anteriority (*ḳabliyya*) of its non-existence to an act of the imagination, since if one does that, one suppresses the reality of what comes into existence (cf. *Tahāfut al-Tahāfut*, ed. Bouyges, Beirut, 72-80).

Another question regarding creation *ab aeterno* also brings in the concept of *nihāya*. The two *Tahāfut*s are clearly opposed on this point. How can one conceive of an eternal creation? asks al-G̲h̲azālī, when the eternity of the world is impossible. In effect, the revolution of the Sun takes place over a year and that of Saturn over 30 years. The Sun's revolution is thus one-thirtieth of the revolution of Saturn, or, putting it another way, for one revolution of Saturn, there are 30 revolutions of the Sun; for two revolutions of Saturn, there will be two times 30 revolutions of the Sun. When one takes a finite number *n* of revolutions of Saturn, one will have a finite number 30*n* revolutions of the Sun. The relationship between the totality of the revolutions of Saturn and the totality of the revolutions of the Sun remains the same in relationship to the parts of these totalities, i.e. 1:30. Ibn Ru<u>sh</u>d replies, however, that if there are an infinite number of revolutions of Saturn and the Sun, this relationship disappears, since there is no conceivable relationship between infinity "once" and "30 times" infinity. Hence infinities of revolutions are impossible, and the world cannot have been created *ab aeterno*. These considerations are already to be found in the *Fiṣal* of Ibn Ḥazm. Furthermore, is the infinite number of these revolutions an even or an odd number, or both at the same time, or is it neither? One must say that it is either one or the other. But if one says that it is an equal number, it will become an odd number by the addition of a unity, and if one says that it is an odd number, it will become an even number by the subtraction of a unity. But how can one conceive adding a unity to or taking a unity away from what is infinite? One can only reply that the infinite number is neither odd nor even, which is contrary to the nature of the concept of number. Finally, Ibn Ru<u>sh</u>d's reply rests on a completely Aristotelian principle: sc. that an infinite number of revolutions is only infinite in potentiality, and that there does not exist any act of any kind such that one can take it as a whole which is defined and genuinely capable of being totalised (cf. *Tahāfut al-Tahāfut*, 12-18).

Another question involving *nihāya* arises in regard to the division of bodies. Ibn Sīnā discusses it, in particular in his *I<u>sh</u>ārāt* (ed. Sulaymān Dunyā, Cairo 1957, ii, 130 ff.). Should one come to a stop at indivisible atoms, in finite number, or not? If division proceeds to the infinite, are the final parts of which bodies are made up bodies themselves or something else? This question raises numerous difficulties. It is a fact that, if one defines a body geometrically as that which has three dimensions in space, sc. length, breadth and depth, it is always possible for the imagination to divide up a line, surface or volume infinitely. But how can one put together again a body from constituents thus arrived at? According to Ibn Sīnā, what makes up a body as such is not three-dimensionality but "corporeity" (*<u>dj</u>ismiyya*), a principle which is not divisible, unlike geometrical dimension. It should be observed that Ibn Sīnā is raising here the important question of the continuous and the discontinuous.

The theologians also tackled this question of the constituting of bodies. Let us merely cite al-Naẓẓām [*q.v.*], a Muʿtazilī of the Baṣran school, who denied the existence of the indivisible part or atom. The division of bodies can go on infinitely, which brings into consideration their continuity and, at the same time, the question of the nature of space and the possibility of movement. He resolved it by his doctrine of the "leap" (*ṭafra*); a moving body which cannot pass by means of an infinite number of positions from A to B "leaps" from one point to another. ʿAbd al-Ḳāhir al-Ba<u>gh</u>dādī, in his *Farḳ bayn al-firaḳ*, remarks that this idea of the possibility of divisibility as far as the infinite brings in the thesis of the simultaneous occupation of bodies of a single space (*tadā<u>kh</u>ul al-a<u>dj</u>sām fī ḥayyiz wāḥid*). In practice, as Ibn Sīnā discerned clearly, one cannot explain the contact of parts thus infinitely divided up in order to take into account the composition of the body, except by considering that they have two distinct extremities (*ṭarafānⁱ*), so that contact with one is different from contact with the other; which is contrary to the hypothesis of division to infinity. Furthermore, one must freely admit that the elements which are supposed to be in contact become completely penetrated within each other, which cannot explain the constituting of the volume of bodies.

These are the main problems which the concept of *nihāya* raises.

Bibliography: Given in the article.

(R. Arnaldez)

NIḲĀBA (a.), a term whose sense has been fixed in the 20th century for "trade union", i.e. association for defending the interests of and promoting the rights of wage and salary earners, can also however denote the liberal professions and even those of employers. The term derives from the corporative function of the *naḳīb*, with the adjective *niḳābī* (in practice applied as a substantive only to wage and salary earners) and the abstract *niḳābiyya* "syndicalism"; there is no verbal form in this sense.

The term's usage became general after the First World War. Trade unionism, free from the theoretical non-differentiation between employers and employees of the guilds, is already attested in those countries in which capitalist enterprise was most advanced. In Algeria (1880 onwards) it referred primarily to the dominant Europeans, with some slight reference to the autochthonous peoples, and utilised the French term *syndicalisme*. In Egypt, where the corporative system was abolished in 1890, the first trade unions (1899 onwards), at first dominated by foreign or Ottoman-minority elements, but later mixed, became known as associations (*<u>dj</u>amʿiyya*). This term prevailed when Egyptian trade unionism was put on a nationalist basis (1908-14). *Niḳāba* came into usage at the same time in the terminology of the Nationalist (*Waṭanī*) Party of Muḥammad Farīd [*q.v.*], from 1908 onwards. It referred to an agricultural co-operative, in the Italian co-operativist sense (*niḳāba zirāʿiyya*) and at the same time to the *Niḳābat al-Ṣanāʾiʿ al-Yadawiyya* (Union of Manual Workers), an educational and co-operative association under the patronage of Nationalist lawyers, with individual and group, interprofessional, membership, including artisans. It did not exclude the *<u>dj</u>amʿiyyāt*. Muḥammad Farīd's projects for labour legislation, inspired by British Labour Party's activity, established *niḳāba* as the equivalent of trade union/syndicat. Henceforth, the Egyptian press used the term to translate the titles of trade unions formed by foreign workers.

In the Ottoman empire, the corporative system, although in decay, remained longer in usage, with mutual insurance societies only permitted to foreigners and to members of the minorities employed in the foreign concessionary companies. The first trade unions arose at the time of the strikes during the 1908 Revolution, which however hardly touched the Arab provinces. Laws were passed (1908-12) to counter and to regulate the movement. Trade unions were forbidden and the old corporations dissolved. They were replaced by professional associations, comprising employers and employed, with representativeness reserved for the former. In the Arab version, for a long time after the War, *niḳāba* denoted corporative groups (*niḳābat al-aṣnāf, n. al-ḥiraf wa 'l-ṣanāʾiʿ*), whilst *<u>dj</u>amʿiyya, pace* the case in Egypt, referred to legal "associations", not trade unions.

After the War, whilst modern Turkey adopted, in order to remove ambiguity, the loan form *sendika, niḳāba* became the predominant term in the Arab-speaking lands.

The history of Arab trade unionism went, briefly speaking, through three phases. Until the 1940s, under colonial domination, it became firmly established in Egypt, spread through the British and French mandates of the Near East and became general in the three countries of French North Africa. In this context, it acquired a strong political tinge, within the framework of the combined stakes of class and nationalism. The first vehicle of diffusion of the form and the term was the current which claimed to belong to the Communist International and the International Red Trade Union Movement, i.e. within the organic link between the Communist Party and trade unionism till the middle of the 1930s. In the Near East, where these organisations were independent of those of the metropolises, the first Egyptian federation (*Ittiḥād Niḳābat al-ʿUmmāl*) was crushed by the Wafdist repression of 1924, and the sole lasting effect of this current was in Lebanon. Trade unionisation was slower in Syria, and more pluralist there. In ʿIrāḳ, it enjoyed periods of expansion and contraction. The tendency of the mandatary or tutelary authorities was to suppress this movement, considered as a prop of nationalism, or at most to oppose to it the Ottoman regulations regarding associations, for long maintained in force. The demands made were as much juridical as economic, and in view of the resistance encountered, nationalist. With its class current broken, Egyptian trade unionism was taken over, through the exertion of political patronage, by the nationalist parties, on reformist lines close to the International Trade Union Federation, connected with the Second Socialist International. But the use of their capability of mobilising on the streets and in strikes served largely for these parties to embarrass their enemy in power. Once the power was taken over, repression began again. The presence of a colonial population in French North Africa allowed the securing of more rights. The lines of cleavage were those of the metropolis, opposing the reformist movement to the current class, until the reunification of the Confédération Générale du Travail (C.G.T.) in 1936. The second current, also anti-colonialist, was aimed, despite prohibitions and repression, at unionising the indigenous peoples and even supported, in Tunisia, a first experience of trade union federation on national class bases (C.G.T.T., 1924: *Djāmiʿat ʿUmūm al-ʿAmala al-Tūnisiyya*). The sole attempt at a take-over by a nationalist party failed (Tunisia, 1937-8). The implanting of Zionist trade unionism in Palestine (from 1920 onwards) did not favour an ethnic mix of workers. The Communist Party envisaged it, but failed. Arab associations or trade unions were formed, but without avoiding the cleavages of the two main nationalist clans.

The second phase, beginning in 1942 during the Second World War, was one of an increase in struggles and the acquisition of legal rights. Class orientations prevailed, but in pluralist structures, either running parallel to or in alliance with a national movement which led up to the first manifestations of political independence. This was also true for Palestine before the partition in 1948. The creation of the World Trade Union Federation (W.F.T.U.) from 1945 onwards favoured the exchange of experiences. Extended coverage was made (Sudan, Libya, Somalia and Aden). The politics of economic development increased the numbers of salaried members. The new governments used, however, the split in the World Trade Union Movement (I.C.F.T.U. after 1949) to install here an official trade unionism, and to forbid there all syndicalist activity. The context favoured the swallowing up of Maghribī trade unionism by the dominant nationalist parties.

The last phase is thus characterised by the permanent introduction of democratic stakes, until then never permanently resolved: liberty to form trade unions, and their autonomy regarding the state and political parties. Under the influence of the nationalist-reformist currents, dominant since the 1950s, an International Confederation of Arab Trade Unions (*al-Ittiḥād al-Duwalī li-Niḳābāt al-ʿUmmāl al-ʿArab* = I.C.A.T.U.), autonomous of the central world organisations but open to co-operation with them, was created in 1956. It assured inter-Arab trade union solidarity with repressed movements, at the same time getting involved politically in regional happenings (Arab-Israeli conflict, oil, etc.). It concerned itself with the harmonisation of Arab legislation on labour, after 1965 in liaison with the Arab Labour Organisation (*Munaẓẓamat al-ʿAmal al-ʿArabiyya* = A.L.O.). But apart from the two Yemens (unified in 1990) and Kuwayt, which had old-established federations, there is strong resistance within the Arab peninsula to expanding the labour legislation on trade union rights. Clandestine trade union structures are severely repressed there.

Bibliography: Further bibliographical references and orientations are to be found in J. Sagnes (ed.), *Histoire du syndicalisme dans le monde des origines à nos jours*, Toulouse 1993 (relevant chs. by C. Coquery-Vidrovitch, J. Couland, R. Gallissot and G. Heuzé). See also J. Berque (dir.) and J. Couland (ed.), *Bibliographie de la culture arabe contemporaine*, Paris 1981. (J. Couland)

NIKĀḤ (a.), marriage (properly, sexual intercourse, but already in the Ḳurʾān used exclusively of the contract of marriage). In the present article, marriage is dealt with as a legal institution; for marriage customs, see ʿURS.

I. In classical Islamic law
II. In the modern Islamic world
1. The Arab, Persian and Turkish lands of the Middle East
2. In Muslim India up to 1930 [see ʿurs]
3. In Muslim India after 1930
4. In Indonesia
5. In East Africa
6. In Nigeria

I. In Classical Islamic Law

1. The essential features of the Muslim law of marriage go back to the customary law of the Arabs which previously existed. In this, although there were differences according to districts and the conditions of the individual cases, the regulations governing marriage were based upon the patriarchal system, which permitted the man very great freedom and still bore traces of an old matriarchal system. It is true that before the coming of Islam, a higher conception of the marriage state had already begun to exist, but the position of the woman was still a very unfavourable one. The marriage contract was made between the suitor and the "guardian" i.e. the father or the nearest male relative of the bride, the latter's consent not being regarded as necessary. But even before Islam it had already become generally usual for the dowry to be given to the woman herself and not to the guardian. In marriage, the woman was under the unrestricted authority of her husband, the only

bounds to which were consideration for her family. Dissolution of the marriage rested entirely on the man's opinion; and even after his death his relatives could enforce claims upon his widow.

2. Islam reformed these old marriage laws in far-reaching fashion, while retaining their essential features; here as in other fields of social legislation Muḥammad's chief aim was the improvement of the woman's position. The regulations regarding marriage which are the most important in principle are laid down in the Ḳurʾān in sūra IV (from the period shortly after the battle of Uḥud): "3. If ye fear that ye cannot act justly to the orphans marry the women whom ye think good (to marry), by twos, threes or fours; but if ye fear (even then) not to be just then marry one only or (the slaves) whom you possess; this will be easier that ye be not unjust. Give the women their dowry freely; but if they voluntarily remit you a part of it, enjoy it and may it prosper you.—26. Marry not the woman whom your fathers have married (except what is already past); for this is shameful and abominable and an evil way. 27. Forbidden to you are your mothers, your daughters, your sisters, your aunts paternal and maternal, the daughters of your brother and sister, your foster-mothers and foster-sisters, the mothers of your wives and the step-daughters who are in your care, born of your wives, with whom ye have had intercourse—but if ye have not had intercourse with them, it is not a sin for you—and the wives of the sons, who are your offspring, also that ye marry two sisters at the same time except what is already past; Allāh is gracious and merciful. 28. Further married women except (slaves) that you possess. This is ordained by Allāh for you. But he has permitted you to procure (wives) outside of these cases with your money in decency and not in fornication. To those of them that ye have enjoined give their reward as their due, but it is no sin to make an agreement between you beyond the legal due. Allāh is all-knowing and wise. 29. If however any one of you has not means sufficient to marry free believing women (let him marry) among your believing slaves, whom you possess; Allāh best knows (to distinguish) your faith. Marry them with the permission of their masters, and give them their dowry in kindness; they should be modest and not unchaste and take no lovers". Also sūra II, 220 (uncertain date), the prohibition of marriage with infidels, male or female (cf. sūra IX, 10), sūra XXXIII, 49 (probably of the year 5), an exception in favour of the Prophet, and sūra V, 7 (of the farewell pilgrimage in the year 10), permission of marriage with the women of the possessors of a scripture. Other passages of the Ḳurʾān which emphasise the moral side of marriage are sūra XXIV, 3, 26, 32, and sūra XXX, 20. In Tradition, various attitudes to marriage find expression; at the same time, the positive enactments regulating it are supplemented in essential points. The most important is the limitation of the number of wives permitted at one time to four; although sūra IV, 3, contains no such precise regulation, this interpretation of it must have predominated very early, as in the traditions it is assumed rather than expressly demanded. The co-operation of the "guardian", the dowry and the consent of the woman is regarded as essential, and competition with a rival, the result of whose suit is still in doubt, is forbidden.

3. The most important provisions of Islamic law (according to the S̲h̲āfiʿī school) are the following. The marriage contract is concluded between the bridegroom and the bride's *walī* (guardian), who must be a free Muslim of age and of good character. The *walī* is in his turn bound to assist in carrying out the contract of marriage demanded by the woman, if the bridegroom fulfils certain legal conditions. The *walī* should be one of the following in this order: 1. the nearest male ascendant in the male line; 2. the nearest male relative in the male line among the descendants of the father; 3. do. among the descendants of the grandfather, etc.; 4. in the case of a freed woman the *mawlā* (manumitter) and (if the case arises) his male relatives in the order of heirs in intestacy [see MĪRĀT̲H̲, 6, *b*]; 5. the representative of the public authority (*ḥākim*) appointed for the purpose; in many countries it is the *ḳaḍī* or his deputy. In place of the *ḥākim* the future husband and wife may agree to choose a *walī* and must do so if there is no authorised *ḥākim* in the place. The *walī* can only give the bride in marriage with her consent, but in the case of a virgin, silent consent is sufficient. The father or grandfather, however, has the right to marry his daughter or granddaughter against her will, so long as she is a virgin (he is therefore called *walī mud̲j̲bir, walī* with power of coercion); the exercise of this power is, however, very strictly regulated in the interests of the bride. As minors are not in a position to make a declaration of their wishes which is valid in law, they can only be married at all by a *walī mud̲j̲bir*. According to the Ḥanafīs, on the other hand, every blood relative acting as *walī* is entitled to give a virgin under age in marriage without her consent; but a woman married in this way by another than her ascendant is entitled on coming of age to demand that her marriage be declared void (*fask̲h̲*) by the *ḳāḍī*. A bridegroom who is a minor may also be married by his *walī mud̲j̲bir*. As a kind of equivalent for the rights which the husband acquires over the wife, he is bound to give her a bridal gift (*mahr, ṣadāḳ*) which is regarded as an essential part of the contract. The contracting parties are free to fix the *mahr*; it may consist of anything that has value in the eyes of the law; if it is not fixed at the conclusion of the contract and if the parties cannot agree upon it, we have a case for the *mahr al-mit̲h̲l*, a bridal gift fixed by the *ḳāḍī* according to the circumstances of the bridegroom. It is not necessary to pay the *mahr* at once; frequently a portion is paid before the consummation of the marriage and the remainder only at the dissolution of the marriage by divorce or death. The wife's claim to the full *mahr* or the full *mahr al-mit̲h̲l* arises only when the marriage has been consummated; if the marriage is previously dissolved by the man, the wife can only claim half the *mahr* or a present (*mutʿa*) fixed arbitrarily by the man; these regulations go back to sūra II, 237-8 (cf. XXXIII, 48). In form, the marriage contract, which is usually prefaced by a solicitation (*k̲h̲iṭba*), follows the usual scheme in Muslim contracts, with offer and acceptance; the *walī* of the bride is further recommended to deliver a pious address (*k̲h̲uṭba*) on the occasion. The marriage must be concluded in the presence of at least two witnesses (*s̲h̲āhid*) who possess the legal qualifications for a witness; their presence is here not simply, as in other contracts, evidence of the marriage but an essential element in its validity. On the other hand, no collaboration by the authorities is prescribed. But since great importance is usually attached to fulfilling the formalities of the marriage contract, upon which the validity of the marriage depends, it is usual not to carry through this important legal matter without the assistance of an experienced lawyer. We therefore everywhere find men whose profession this is and who usually act under the supervision of the *ḳāḍī*. The part which they take is to pronounce the necessary formulae to the parties or even to act as authorised agents

of one of them, usually the *walī* of the bride. The most important impediments to marriage are the following: 1. blood relationship, namely between the man and his female ascendants and descendants, his sisters, the female descendants of his brothers and sisters as well as his aunts and great-aunts; 2. foster-relationship, which, by extension of the Ḳurʾānic law, by tradition is regarded as an impediment to marriage in the same degrees as blood relationship; 3. relationship by marriage, namely, between a man and his mother-in-law, daughter-in law, step-daughter, etc., in the direct line; marriage with two sisters or with an aunt and niece at the same time is also forbidden; 4. the existence of a previous marriage, in the case of a woman without limitation (inclusive of the period of waiting after the dissolution of the marriage, *ʿidda* [*q.v.*]), and in the case of a free man with the provision that he cannot be married to more than four women at once; 5. the existence of a threefold *ṭalāḳ* [*q.v.*] or of a *liʿān* [*q.v.*]; 6. social inequality; the man must not be by birth, profession, etc. below the woman (unless both the woman and *walī* agree); a free Muslim can only marry another's slave girl if he cannot provide the bridal gift for a free woman, and the marriage between a master (or mistress) and his slave (or her slave) is quite impossible (a master is however permitted concubinage with his slave); 7. difference of religion; there is no exception to the prohibition of marriage between a Muslim woman and an infidel, while the permission given in theory for marriage between Muslim men and the women of the possessors of a scripture is, at least by the S̲h̲āfiʿīs, so restricted by conditions as to be prohibited in practice; 8. temporary obstacles, such as the state of *iḥrām* [*q.v.*]. On the other hand, the law knows no minimum age for a legal marriage. If a marriage contract does not fulfil the legal requirements, it is invalid; the Ḥanafīs and especially the Mālikīs, but not the S̲h̲āfiʿīs, distinguish in this case between invalid (*bāṭil*) and incorrect (*fāsid*), according as the error affects an essential or unessential element in the contract; in the former case, there is no marriage at all, in the second, its validity may be attacked but (according to the Mālikīs) consummation removes any defect. Marriage does not produce any community of property between husband and wife, and the woman retains her complete freedom of dealing; but certain laws regarding inheritance come into operation [see MĪRĀT̲H̲, 6, *c*]. The man alone has to bear the expense of maintaining the household and is obliged to support his wife in a style befitting her station (*nafaḳa*); if he should not be in a position to do so, his wife may demand the dissolution of the marriage by *fask̲h̲* [*q.v.*]. The man can demand from his wife readiness for marital intercourse and obedience generally; if she is regularly disobedient, she loses her claim to support and may be chastised by the man. The latter, however, is expressly forbidden to take upon himself vows of continence (*īlāʾ* and *ẓihār*). Children are only regarded as legitimate if they are born at least six months after consummation of the marriage and not more than 4 years (the predominant S̲h̲āfiʿī view) after its dissolution; it is presumed that such children are begotten by the husband himself; the latter has the right to dispute his paternity by *liʿān*. Parentage can also be established by the husband's *iḳrār* [*q.v.*], while both recognition and adoption of illegitimate children are impossible.

4. The laws regarding the rights and duties of husband and wife cannot be modified by the parties at the drawing-up of the contract. This can, however, be effected by the man pronouncing a conditional *ṭalāḳ* [see ṬALĀḲ, vii.] immediately after the conclusion of the marriage contract; this shift to secure the position of the woman is particularly common among Indian Muslims. For the rest, the couple are left to private agreements which need not be mentioned in the marriage contract. The actual position of the woman in marriage is in all Muslim countries entirely dependent on local conditions and on many special circumstances. It is not a contradiction of this to say that the legal prescriptions regarding marriage are most carefully observed as a rule. In spite of certain ascetic tendencies, Islam as a whole has been decidedly in favour of marriage.—In modern Islam, the problem of the woman's position in marriage and polygamy is especially discussed between conservatives and adherents of modern social ideas. For the different views resulting from these conditions, see the works in the *Bibliography* cited below.

5. Alongside of the usual form of the old Arabian marriage, which in spite of its laxity aimed at the foundation of a household and the procreation of children, there existed the temporary marriage in which the pair lived together temporarily for a period previously fixed. Such temporary marriages were entered upon mainly by men who found themselves staying for a time abroad. It is by no means certain that these are referred to in sūra IV, 28, although the Muslim name of this arrangement (*mutʿa* [*q.v.*], "marriage of pleasure") is based on the literal meaning of the verse; it is, however, certain from Tradition that Muḥammad really permitted *mutʿa* to his followers especially on the longer campaigns. But the caliph ʿUmar strictly prohibited *mutʿa* and regarded it as fornication (*zināʾ*) (a group of traditions already ascribes this prohibition to the Prophet). As a result, *mutʿa* is permitted only among the S̲h̲īʿīs but prohibited by the Sunnīs. The latter have, however, practically the same arrangement; those who wish to live contrary to the law as husband and wife for a certain period simply agree to do so without stipulating it in the marriage contract.

Bibliography: For the pre-Islamic Arabs: G.A. Wilken, *Het matriarchaat bij de oude Arabieren*, German tr., *Das Matriarchat bei den alten Arabern*, Leipzig 1884; W. Robertson Smith, *Kinship and marriage in early Arabia*, new ed., London 1903; Wellhausen, *Die Ehe bei den Arabern*, in *Nachrichten der GW Gött.*, Berlin 1893; Lammens, *Le berceau de l'Islam*, 276 ff. Tradition: Wensinck, *A handbook of early Muhammadan tradition*, s.v. Marriage; Gertrude H. Stern, *Marriage in early Islam*, London 1939. On the doctrine of *Fiḳh*: Snouck Hurgronje, *Verspreide Geschriften*, vi, index, s.v. Huwelijk; Juynboll, *Handleiding*³, 174 ff.; Santillana, *Istituzioni*, 150 ff.; J. Lópiz Ortiz, *Derecho musulmán*, 154 ff. On marriage and society: Lammens, *Moʿâwia Ier*, 306 ff.; R. Levy, *The social structure of Islam*, 91-124; Snouck Hurgronje, *Mekka in the latter part of the 19th century*, index, s.v. Marriage; *Verspreide Geschriften*, iv/1, 218 ff.; Polak, *Persien*, i, 194 ff. Modern conditions: Goldziher, *Die Richtungen der islamischen Koranauslegung*, 360 ff.; R. Paret, *Zur Frauenfrage in der arabisch-islamischen Welt*, Stuttgart 1934. On the ethical estimation of marriage: H. Bauer, *Islamische Ethik*, fasc. ii; Mez, *Renaissance des Islâms*, 276-7; Becker, *Islamstudien*, i, 407. See also Hughes, *Dictionary of Islam*, s.v. Marriage; R. Roberts, *The social laws of the Qorân*, London 1925, 7-18; M. Gaudefroy-Demombynes, *Muslim institutions*, London 1950, 128-37; G.-H. Bousquet, *La morale de l'Islam et son ethique sexuelle*, Paris 1953, 79-141; N.J. Coulson, *A history of Islamic law*, Edinburgh 1964, index s.v. Marriage, law of; Schacht, *An introduction to Islamic law*, Oxford 1964, 161-8. Of recent treatises in Arabic, see Muḥammad Abū Zahra, *al-Aḥwāl al-shakhṣiyya*, Cairo 1950; ʿAlī al-Khafīf, *Farḳ al-zawādj fi 'l-madhāhib al-islāmiyya*, Cairo 1958; Amīr ʿAbd al-ʿAzīz, *al-Ankiḥa al-fāsida wa 'l-manhī ʿanhā fi 'l-sharīʿa al-islāmiyya*, ʿAmmān 1983; Kamāl Aḥmad ʿAwn, *al-Talāḳ fi 'l-Islām muḥaddad wa-muḳayyad*, Riyāḍ, 1403/1983. (J. Schacht)

II. In The Modern Islamic World

1. The Arab, Persian and Turkish lands of the Middle East

i. *Impetus for reform*

Increasing dissatisfaction in recent years with traditional marriage law, particularly the discord between legal norms adapted to the patrilineal, patriarchal family, and changing social conditions, has spawned reforms motivated by a desire to adapt *sharʿī* norms to the transition from the extended to the nuclear family, to strengthen the position of women *qua* women and equitably to redefine the rights and duties of spouses.

Juristic basis for the reforms has been provided by a wide gamut of methods: the procedural expedient coupled with denial of judicial relief; the "eclectic" (*takhayyur*) expedient; stipulations in the marriage contract; extension of the court's discretion; penal and legal sanctions; "modernistic" interpretation of textual sources (neo-*idjtihād*); and substantive legislation with no apparent basis in the *sharīʿa* [see MAḤKAMA. 4. xiii, at VI, 40-1].

Relevant legislation: *Egypt*—Law No. 25, 1920; Law No. 56, 1923; Law No. 25, 1929; Code of Procedure No. 78, 1931; Law No. 62, 1976; Presidential Decree No. 44, 1979, repealed and re-enacted by Law No. 100, 1985; *Iran*—Family Protection Act, 1967, replaced by Family Protection Act, 1975 (repealed in 1979); *ʿIrāḳ*—Personal Status Law No. 188, 1959, amended by Act No. 11, 1963; *Israel*—Marriage Age Law, 1950, amended in 1960; Women's Equal Rights Law, 1951; Maintenance (Assurance of Payment) Law, 1972; *Jordan*—Law of Family Rights, No. 92, 1951, replaced by Law of Personal Status, No. 61, 1976; *Kuwait*—Law of Personal Status, 1980; *Lebanon*—[Ottoman] Family Rights Law, 1917 (hereafter referred to as Ottoman Family Law), put into effect by Decree No. 241, 1942 and reasserted in 1962; *North Yemen*—Family Law, 1978; *South Yemen*—Family Law, No. 1, 1974; *The Sudan*—Judicial Circulars: No. 17, 1915; No. 28, 1927; No. 41, 1936; No. 45, 1936; No. 54, 1960; *Syria*—Decree No. 59, 1953, on Personal Status Law, amended by Law No. 34, 1975; *Turkey*—Turkish Civil Code, 1926.

ii. *Impediments to marriage*

Sharʿī impediments to marriage, excepting foster relationship, have been completely abandoned in Turkey. A reform unique to Kuwait to safeguard the family's integrity prohibits a man's marrying a woman he has deliberately and viciously turned against her former husband.

iii. *Marriage guardian*

The marriage guardian's role has been virtually restricted to protecting the interests of wards physically mature but under the statutory age of competence for marriage. Moreover, the court is empowered to permit marriage even against the guardian's will. Under Ottoman family law (still applicable in Lebanon and Israel), as well as in Jordan, Syria, and ʿIrāḳ (all bound by the Ḥanafī school), the marriage guardian's right to contract a valid compulsory (*idjbār*) marriage, even with regard to minors, has almost completely been abolished through innovative changes in the minimun age for marriage (see below, v). In the Sudan (1960), the traditional Mālikī rule that an adult woman must be given in marriage by her guardian still obtains, although the woman's consent is now as a rule essential for its validity.

iv. *Equality in marriage*

Criteria for equality between spouses (*kafāʾa*), as well as the guardian's right to demand annulment of the marriage on grounds of inequality, have been curtailed. Ottoman family law explicitly mentions as criteria only profession and property (out of which the prompt dower can be paid and the wife's maintenance provided). In Jordan the only remaining criterion is property. In Kuwait religious piety is the sole criterion. In Syria equality is a matter of local convention, not law. So far ʿIrāḳ alone totally ignores this institution, implying its complete abandonment. However, a new criterion has emerged: parity in age between the spouses (see below, vi).

v. *Age of marriage*

Restrictions on child-marriage are intended to prevent the harmful social implications of premature marriage. Distinction has been made to this end between an age of competence for marriage and a minimum age below which marriage is never possible, the parties being presumed to be under puberty. Most Middle Eastern countries have followed the precedent set by Ottoman family law in prescribing the age of competence for marriage: eighteen for a boy and seventeen for a girl. Marriage below these ages is permissible, however, on proof of sexual maturity (see below). Simultaneously, traditional *sharʿī* (and Ottoman family law) age limits (nine for girls, twelve for boys), below which no claim of sexual maturity will be heard (in effect, minimum ages for marriage), have been raised: fifteen or sixteen for a boy, and between thirteen and sixteen for a girl. In Egypt (1923, 1931) no distinction is drawn between puberty and competence for marriage. Prescribed ages for marriage are eighteen for a boy and sixteen for a girl. Marriage below these ages is not permissible (nor registered—see below, viii) even on proof of sexual maturity. In the Sudan (1960) a pre-pubescent girl at least ten years old may be given in marriage with the consent of the court where there are grounds for anxiety about her morals.

Adolescents having reached the prescribed ages of puberty but not of competence for marriage may marry in the interim period of two or three years (irrelevant under Ḥanafī law), subject usually to the marriage guardian's consent and always to the court's permission. In Israel the "good defences" (physical maturity and the guardian's consent) against a charge of contravention of age-of-marriage legislation were abrogated (1950), but simultaneously a district judge was empowered to permit the marriage of a girl who was pregnant or had given birth or, since 1960, had reached the age of sixteen.

Ottoman family law concerning marriageable age has directly affected the validity of marriage. Marriage in violation of the provisions pertaining to the age of competence to marry and the conditions concerning permission to marry is deemed irregular (*fāsid*) with no legal effects before consummation. In North Yemen, the marriage of a boy (not a girl) below fifteen is not valid. Laws in other Middle Eastern countries evade this issue. Courts, however, tend to validate such marriages retroactively once the parties reach puberty.

Other devices intended to enforce reformist restrictions on child-marriage are prohibition of registration of any union in which the parties have not reached the legal ages for marriage (Egypt, 1923; Kuwait; Israel, 1950), preclusion of courts from entertaining any matrimonial cause whatsoever in such marriages, i.e. the marriage is valid but not effective (*nāfidh*) (Egypt, 1923, 1931), and rendering the parties liable to statutory penalties (Jordan, Iran, Lebanon, Israel).

vi. *Disparity in age*

Prohibition, by means of registration, of a marriage in which there is a gross disparity in age between the parties (unless there is some genuine benefit in the union) is intended to defend the wife's interests. Jordan was the first to act on this issue: marriage of a woman under eighteen is prohibited if the husband-to-be is more than twenty years her senior, unless it is established in court that she consents of her own free will and that the marriage is in her interest. In Syria disparity in age may lead the court to withhold permission for marriage, taking into account the welfare of the parties. In South Yemen, marriage in which there is a twenty-year disparity in age is prohibited unless the wife has reached thirty-five.

vii. *Stipulations in the marriage contract*

Application of the mechanism of inserting stipulations benefiting the wife into the marriage contract (provided they do not conflict with marriage aims, affect the rights of others, or restrict the liberty of the husband), is intended mainly to improve the position of married women. Anchored in the Ḥanbalī school, this mechanism rests on voluntary agreement between spouses. Non-observance of a stipulation is grounds for dissolving the marriage at the wife's request without prejudice to her financial rights. Ottoman family law first introduced this mechanism. Jordan, Syria, ʿIrāḳ, Iran and Kuwait followed suit. The stipulations pertaining to marriage are (1) that the wife should not be removed from a locality agreed upon between the parties; (2) that the husband should not marry a co-wife (see below, ix); (3) that the wife may work outside the matrimonial home; and (4) that the wife may complete her studies (Kuwait).

viii. *Registration of marriage*

Registration (performed by the *sharīʿa* court or its authorised notary; in Syria, a district judge must review the marriage application), a wholly new departure from the traditional legal system, has become a necessary legal formality in most Muslim countries. Its purpose is to strengthen state control over marriage proceedings and to impose reforms relating to marriageable age and compulsory marriage (see above, iii). Registration is enforced by (1) the *sharīʿa* court's deeming an unregistered marriage (though not invalid under the *sharīʿa*) not effective (*nāfidh*), unless or until pregnancy becomes apparent (South Yemen, Lebanon, Syria); (2) considering the registration certificate as the sole proof of marriage, lacking which the parties will be denied judicial relief (Egypt 1931); and (3) making the solemniser, bridegroom (or both spouses), and witnesses liable to penal sanction (Jordan, ʿIrāḳ, North Yemen).

ix. *Polygamy*

Reforms aimed at consolidating monogamy restrict polygamy to the extent of complete abolition. Polygamy has been totally abolished as yet only in Turkey. In ʿIrāḳ it was first abolished (1959), only to be reduced to prohibition (1963). Complementary measures taken concerning polygamy are:

(1) Stipulation in the marriage contract (see above, vii). Ottoman family law allows a woman to stipulate in her marriage contract that her husband shall not marry another wife and that should he do so, either she or the polygamous wife will be divorced. Jordan followed suit, though the first wife may dissolve only her own marriage, not that of the co-wife.

(2) Prohibition. Polygamy has been prohibited (in Iran this presumably applies to both permanent and temporary marriage) unless permitted by court (district court in South Yemen) on the basis of "good defences": The court must be satisfied that the husband is financially able to properly maintain multiple wives (Syria; Iran, 1967); that the co-wives will be treated with equal justice (ʿIrāḳ, Iran, 1967); and that the first wife consents to the marriage, is unable or unwilling to co-habit, has been sentenced to imprisonment, is addicted to drink, drugs or gambling, has deserted the family or disappeared, or has become barren, insane or afflicted with incurable disease (Iran, 1967, 1975). In South Yemen a medical certificate to this effect is required. In ʿIrāḳ these defences are presumably implied by the phrase "some lawful benefit in the polygamous marriage". In Israel (1951) the defence available to Muslims *qua* Muslims against a charge of polygamy (prohibited by the Mandatary authorities) was abolished and replaced by two defences against such a charge: prolonged absence or mental illness of the spouse.

Prohibition of polygamy, unlike abolition, does not in itself invalidate polygamous marriage, though those failing to obtain the court's permission are liable to penal sanctions.

(3) Divorce. This obtains in circumstances where no stipulation barring co-marriage has been inserted in the marriage contract or where permission for polygamy has been granted by court. A woman finding the position of co-wife intolerable may dissolve her own marriage on grounds (anchored in the Mālikī school) of injury (extended to cover unequal treatment of co-wives), or disputes between the spouses (once again extended to cover cases of unequal treatment), in which case the marriage will be dissolved through the arbitration procedure. With slight variations this remedy obtains in the Sudan (1915), Lebanon and Israel (under Ottoman family law), Jordan, South Yemen, and ʿIrāḳ (1959). In Egypt (1979, 1985) the wife's option to dissolve the marriage lapses one year after the conclusion of the polygamous marriage. The husband and the solemniser must inform the first wife when a co-wife is taken, failing which they are liable to penal sanction. In Iran (before 1979), a wife who had not consented to a polygamous marriage might petition the court on these grounds asking for a certificate of impossibility of reconciliation and subsequent divorce.

x. *Void and irregular marriages*

Modern legislation in this respect aims to mitigate the harsh legal effects of prohibited marriages. Ottoman family law, and in its wake Jordan (1951) and Syria, reduced the category of void (*bāṭil*) marriage, entailing no legal effects whatsoever, solely to marriage of a Muslim woman to a non-Muslim. In Jordan this category applied also to the marriage of a man to a woman related to him within the prohibited degrees (*maḥram*) and (since 1976) to marriage of a Muslim man to an adherent of a non-revealed religion (*ghayr kitābiyya*). All other prohibited marriages are deemed irregular (*fāsid*) which, if consummated, entail some of the legal and financial effects of valid (*ṣaḥīḥ*) marriage.

Syria introduced an innovative reform (with no apparent basis in the *sharīʿa*) entitling the wife to maintenance even in a consummated irregular (*fāsid*) marriage, provided she was not aware of its irregularity. In ʿIrāḳ (1959) it is indicated, though not explicitly, that even in cases of void (*ghayr ṣaḥīḥ*) marriage, the woman is entitled to dower and must observe the waiting period.

The general aim of reformist legislation pertaining

to temporary marriage (*mutᶜa*) is the curtailment of some of its legal effects to the point of complete abolition of the institution. Temporary marriage is no longer valid in ᶜIrāḳ (1959), although a child born of such a liaison is considered legitimate with all attendant consequences. In Iran (before 1979) temporary marriages were valid, though it seems that mutual rights of inheritance between partners might no longer be created. Traditional *mutᶜa* was reintroduced after the 1979 revolution. Under Ottoman family law, and in its wake Jordan, temporary marriage is deemed irregular, not void.

With the abolition of slavery in Saudi Arabia (1962), concubinage, i.e. a man's *sh͟arᶜī* right to have sexual relations with an unlimited number of his female slaves, ceased to exist.

xi. *Dower*

In Ottoman family law, and in its wake Jordan, Syria and ᶜIrāḳ (1959), no mention is made regarding minimum dower, implying abandonment of *sh͟arᶜī* doctrine in this respect. In South Yemen, dower (prompt and deferred combined) must not exceed one hundred dīnārs, contrary to traditional doctrine which does not acknowledge a maximum dower.

Egypt (1929) and the Sudan (1935) introduced, via *tak͟hayyur* with the Ḥanafī school, that where a married couple or their respective heirs dispute the amount of dower stipulated, the burden of proof falls on the wife. Syria, Kuwait, and Jordan (1976) followed suit.

Ottoman family law, and in its wake Jordan but not other countries, followed the view of those jurists within the Ḥanafī school who maintain, unlike others, that the wife must not be compelled to buy the trousseau (*d͟jihāz*) out of her dower.

In Jordan (1976) any agreement that all or part of the dower be deferred shall be recorded in writing, otherwise the whole dower shall be deemed prompt. Non-payment of the prompt dower before consummation has become (since 1951), contrary to the Ḥanafī view, grounds for dissolution [see ṬALĀḲ].

xii. *Maintenance between the spouses*

General trends in this respect favour either one spouse or the other, depending on the circumstances.

(1) Definition of maintenance. In Jordan, and in its wake Syria, ᶜIrāḳ, Egypt (1979, 1985) and Kuwait, the definition of maintenance has been extended to cover medical treatment in addition to traditional components. In Egypt (1979) maintenance also includes "everything that is requisite by custom," "custom" being replaced in 1985 by "*sh͟arīᶜa*".

(2) Criteria for fixing maintenance. Egypt (1929) and the Sudan (1936) and, with some variation, Kuwait, innovated via *tak͟hayyur* that a wife's maintenance shall be calculated by exclusive reference to her husband's means, regardless of her own condition. Jordan, Syria, and Egypt (1979, 1985) followed suit with the proviso that the rate of maintenance must not be below minimum sufficiency.

Though maintenance may be increased or decreased depending on the husband's condition and the cost of living (as in traditional law) no application shall be heard before the expiration of a certain time period (six months in Syria and Jordan, one year in Kuwait, but no time period in ᶜIrāḳ) from the date of the court order, save in exceptional emergencies.

South Yemen introduced an unprecedented innovation—in glaring contradiction to the *sh͟arīᶜa*—according to which spouses bear the expenses of their common life as well as the maintenance of their children according to their respective means and abilities. This reflects a radical concept, anchored in 1974 law, according to which a marriage is a contract between two parties equal in rights and duties.

(3) Arrears of maintenance. Egypt (1920), and ᶜIrāḳ (1959) in its wake, acknowledged via *tak͟hayyur* the principle of arrears of maintenance: maintenance of a wife who has submitted herself, even putatively, to her husband is deemed a debt owed by him from the time when he fails to support her, not (as in Ḥanafī law) from the time when she sues him in court. The Sudan (1927) adopted a less radical approach: arrears of maintenance still lapse on the death of either party unless the wife has been given judicial permission to raise maintenance on credit. In Jordan and Syria, as in Ottoman family law, arrears of maintenance are created solely by mutual agreement or by judicial judgment (in conformity with traditional law), however—contrary to the Ḥanafī school—they lapse only by payment or renouncement, not on the death of either party or on dissolution.

In Egypt (1931), and the Sudan (1936) in its wake, as a precaution against dubious claims for maintenance alleged to have been due over many years, courts were forbidden by the procedural expedient of denial of judicial relief from entertaining claims of arrears of maintenance in regard to any period more than three years (one year in Egypt since 1979) prior to the suit. In Syria the court will not allow the wife more than four months' arrears of maintenance.

(4) Provisional maintenance. In Syria, ᶜIrāḳ, Kuwait and Egypt (1979, 1985) the court may order payment of provisional maintenance before handing down its final decision.

(5) Collection of maintenance. The Sudan (1915), and Egypt (1920) in its wake, decreed that if a husband has property out of which his wife's legally entitled maintenance can be obtained, a decree to this effect will be executed. In Lebanon, Israel (both under Ottoman family law), Jordan, and ᶜIrāḳ, such a judicial decree is possible only if the husband is absent.

In ᶜIrāḳ, where maintenance cannot be collected from the husband and in the absence of any person willing to lend money to the wife who, in her turn, is incapable of earning a living, maintenance shall be provided by the state. Egypt (1976) and Israel (1972) transferred the burden of maintenance payment fixed by judicial decree to governmental authority, which in turn recoups itself from the judgment debtor.

(6) Non-provision of maintenance as grounds for divorce. In Egypt (1920), Jordan, Syria, ᶜIrāḳ, Iran (before 1979), and South Yemen, failure to provide the wife with maintenance due to unwillingness or hardship on the part of the husband (provided, in some of the countries, that he has no property out of which maintenance may be obtained, and that a period of delay has been exhausted) is deemed, via *tak͟hayyur*, legal grounds for judicial divorce [see ṬALĀḲ].

(7) Maintenance of a working wife. Syria, ᶜIrāḳ and Jordan (1976) explicitly deny the right to maintenance to a wife who works away from home without her husband's consent. In Egypt (1979, 1985) and Kuwait, however, the husband's permission for that purpose is not required, provided the wife's exercise of her right to a lawful job is not abused or in conflict with the family's interest, and that she was not forbidden by the husband to attend her work. This, with some variation, applied also in Iran (before 1979).

xiii. *Inheritance rights between the spouses* (see MĪRĀT͟H. 2. In modern Islamic countries, at VII, 111-13).

xiv. *Obedience*

Reform in this respect was aimed at correcting

injustice and abuse of women. In Egypt (1967) and the Sudan (1969), the institution of *bayt al-ṭāʿa* (i.e. police-executed enforced obedience of rebellious wives, which has no apparent basis in the *sharīʿa*) was abolished. In Egypt (1979) a disobedient wife wishing to object to the written request of the husband for her return to the conjugal home may do so, on *sharʿī* grounds, within ten days (30 days since 1985) of the court's request. The court will try to reconcile the parties, failing which it will refer them to arbitration. If arbitration is unsuccessful, judicial dissolution may be granted [see ṬALĀḲ].

Bibliography: J.N.D. Anderson, *Law reform in the Muslim world*, London 1976, with important bibl.; idem, *Islamic law in Africa*, London 1954, 301-21; N.J. Coulson, *A history of Islamic law*, Edinburgh 1964, part iii; Y. Linant de Bellefonds, *Traité de droit musulman comparé*, ii, Paris and the Hague 1965, with important bibl.; J. Schacht, *An introduction to Islamic law*, repr. London 1966, 100-11, with important bibl. on 252 ff.; J.J. Nasir, *The status of women under Islamic law*, London 1990; Carolyn Fluehr-Lobban, *Islamic law and society in the Sudan*, London 1987; Doreen Hinchcliffe, *Polygamy in traditional and contemporary Islamic law*, in *Islam and the modern age*, i (1970), 13-38; A. Layish, *Women and Islamic law in a non-Muslim state*, Jerusalem and New York 1975; idem, *The status of the Sharīʿa in a non-Muslim state*, in *Asian and African Studies* (forthcoming); M. al-Nowaihi, *Changing the law on personal status in Egypt within a liberal interpretation of the Sharīʿa*, in M. Curtis (ed.), *Religion and politics in the Middle East*, Boulder 1981, 109-23; R. Shaham, *Ha-Mishpaḥa ha-muslimit be-Mitzrayim 1900-1955: hemshekhiyut u-temura* ("The Muslim family in Egypt 1900-1955: continuity and change"), Ph.D. diss. Hebrew University, Jerusalem 1991, unpubl.; Muḥammad Abū Zahra, *al-Aḥwāl al-shakhṣiyya*, Cairo 1957; Muḥammad Muṣṭafā Shalabī, *Aḥkām al-usra fi 'l-Islām; dirāsa muḳārina bayna fiḳh al-madhāhib al-sunniyya wa 'l-madhhab al-djaʿfarī wa 'l-ḳānūn*, Beirut 1973; Shahla Haeri, *Law of desire. Temporary marriage in Shiʿi Iran*, Syracuse 1989.

(A. LAYISH and R. SHAHAM)

2. In Muslim India up to 1930 [see ʿURS].

3. In Muslim India after 1930

Marriage in Islam, not being a sacrament but a contract between husband and wife, is literally termed in Indian Islam *ʿaḳd-e-nikāḥ* ("marriage contract"). Among Indian Muslims, however, *nikāḥ* is considered to be the establishment of relationship between the families of the bride and the groom, which is reflected in the formal procedure and series of ceremonies which precede the final *nikāḥ* ceremony.

In spite of the impact of modern education among Indian Muslims, allowing some degree of freedom in expressing preference for selecting marriage partner by both boys and girls, the formal *nikāḥ* proposal (*nikāḥ ka payghām*) is sent—or conveyed—by the elders of the boy to the elder family members of the girl. The ceremonial modesty requires some delay in accepting the proposal (*payghām*). After the formal declaration of engagement (*nisbat*), an auspicious date is fixed for the *nikāḥ*. Generally, the month of Muḥarram and the following thirteen days of Ṣafar are avoided for *nikāḥ* ceremony by both Sunnīs and Shīʿīs in commemoration of martyrdom of Imām Ḥusayn.

On the appointed day, the marriage party (*nikāḥ ki bārāt*), comprising the male relatives and friends of the groom's family, proceeds to the house of the bride, where they are received by the male members of that household. Soon afterwards, the preparations for the main ceremony begin, which includes changing of the groom's clothes into a completely new set prepared and provided by the bride's family. For the *ʿaḳd* ceremony, besides the *ḳāḍī* (usually a Mawlawī or Muslim religious scholar) and a *wakīl* (representing the bride), two witnesses are required. It is the privilege of the bride's family to choose a Mawlawī to act as *ḳāḍī*; whereas the *wakīl* (to be a neutral person in any unforeseen future dispute) is usually the bride's maternal uncle or her paternal or maternal aunt's husband. The two witnesses are selected from among the relatives of the bride. In order to obtain advance consent of the bride, the *wakīl* and the two witnesses proceed to the women's quarter, where the *wakīl* in a loud voice asks the bride three times her consent for her *ʿaḳd-e-nikāḥ* (specifying the name of the groom and the amount of her *mahr*), to which she is expected to respond in her modest and subdued voice. Thereafter, the *wakīl*'s party returns to the male gathering and informs the *ḳāḍī* that the bride's consent has been obtained for her *nikāḥ*. It is followed by a brief religious ceremony in which the *ḳāḍī* loudly recites in Arabic the marriage sermon (*nikāḥ ka khuṭba*), which consists of some Ḳurʾānic verses and a history of successful marriages in an Islamic context, citing those of Adam and Eve, Abraham and Hagar, Muḥammad and his four prominent wives, and ʿAlī and Fāṭima. After this recital, the *ḳāḍī* sits in front of the groom, facing towards him; the *wakīl* and both the witnesses, already sitting close to the groom, lean slightly towards him so that they can hear his consent clearly. The *ḳāḍī*, in a low voice as if maintaining secrecy, asks the groom three times in the following words (in the native language): "I marry you to such-and-such girl, daughter of so-and-so person against so much amount of *mahr*. Do you accept?" Each time the groom is expected to reply in clear voice, "I accept." After the acceptance, the *ḳāḍī* recites in Arabic a long prayer, again in a loud voice, blessing the newly-married couple with a future happiness like those of all the early marriages cited in Islamic history. This brings the *ʿaḳd-e-nikāḥ* to its conclusion, which is followed by a feast prepared by the bride's household. Finally, the *rukhṣati* (departure of the bride) with the groom's party back to the groom's house takes place.

Bibliography: Jafar Sharif, *Qānoon-e-Islām (Manners and customs of the Mussalmans of India)*, 1832, tr. G.A. Herklots, *Islam in India*, Oxford 1921; Tara Chand, *Influence of Islam on Indian culture*, Allahabad 1946; A.A.A. Fyzee, *Outline of Muhammadan law*, 1949, 2nd ed., London 1955; G. Ansari, *Muslim marriage in India*, in *Wiener Völkerkundliche Mitteilungen*, iii/2 (1955), 191-206; idem, *Muslim caste in Uttar Pradesh (a study of culture contact)*, Lucknow 1960.

(GHAUS ANSARI)

4. In Indonesia

In Bahasa Indonesian, the country's national language, there are two words for marriage: *nikah* and *perkawinan*. *Nikah* generally refers to the conclusion of a marriage between Muslims. *Perkawinan* is a broader concept which prevails nowadays in national legislation, in popular use and even in Islamic writings. *Hukum perkawinan*, marriage law, includes the rules concerning polygamy, divorce and alimony (*nafkah*).

The sources of Indonesian marriage law include those of national law, religious law, *adat* law [see ʿĀDA] and colonial law. Over the past forty years, the relevance of colonial law and *adat* law has significantly decreased. Since Independence, efforts have been made to enact a national marriage law for all citizens. This goal was reached with Law no. 1 of 1974 concerning marriage and its executive regulations, which will be referred to as the "national law".

Historically speaking, customary or *adat* law came

first. Within Indonesian society, the relationship between *adat* law and Islamic law has been debated for centuries. The debate carried over to the Dutch when L.W.C. van den Berg claimed in the 1870s that Islamic law should be applied in its integrity to Muslims in Indonesia. Van den Berg was opposed by Snouck Hurgronje, who held the view that Islamic law should only be applied insofar as accepted by society through its customary law. This so-called "reception theory" came to prevail in the colonial government, and it was eventually incorporated in the colonial constitution of 1925. After independence, this theory lost favour in Indonesia. At the same time, the political appeal of *adat* law has considerably weakened. As a result, recent debates on marriage have mainly focussed on national law and Islamic law and the relationship between the two.

Law no. 1 of 1974 says that in order to be valid, a marriage has to be concluded according to religion and belief. For most Indonesians this means Islamic marriage law. Some provisions of the law seem to contain codified Islamic law. However, the wording of the law is not always unequivocal. As differences of interpretation arise, in conservative Muslim circles national law is considered binding upon Muslims but "God's law" provides the final standard: thus interpretations of the national law cannot go against Islamic law. Among liberal Muslims, modernists and nationalists, the supremacy of national law is honoured. The latter groups aim at improvement of the position of women and unification of the law, whereas the former tend to maintain the unfavourable position of women and hold the *umma* above the nation-state.

The marriage contract between Muslims is laid down in an *akta nikah*, which according to national law has to be approved by the Marriage Registrar, an official of the local Religious Office (*Kantor Urusan Agama, K.U.A.*) which is a branch of the Ministry of Religion. In practice, centrally-designed and printed model contracts are commonly used. Procedures are explained to the people with the help of citizens with a specific religious function in village or neighbourhood government. Besides these, however, *adat* ceremonies often take place at the time of the wedding. The national law permits in principle only monogamous marriages, but the religious courts may allow a man to marry more than one wife on certain grounds and conditions, such as the consent of the first spouse. National law has altogether forbidden polygamy between partners who belong to the civil service or the army.

Unilateral divorce, generally called *talak*, has been embedded in a court procedure as well. The judge first has to check whether there is a valid motive as specified by national law in a limitative list of divorce grounds. If this is the case, he functions as an official witness to the *talak*. The old custom of concluding *taklik talak* upon marriage has been continued through the uniform model contract that reiterate the same divorce grounds as those mentioned in national law.

In colonial times, the government had found various types of Islamic courts deciding marriage disputes among Muslims, in what was regarded to often be an unsystematic way. In the 1870s, L.W.C. van den Berg was commissioned to draft a law on Islamic courts. This became the Law on Priest Courts of 1882, which remained the basic law on Islamic jurisdiction until its replacement by Law no. 7 of 1989 concerning religious jurisdiction. This law has made the religious courts competent not only in all marriage and divorce cases between Muslims but also in mat-

ters of inheritance. The decisions of the religious courts, however, can be subject to final appeal to the Supreme Court, the *Mahkamah Agung*.

Religious courts, *K.U.A.*s and institutes of higher Islamic learning (*I.A.I.N.*) where the Islamic law is taught, are all under the jurisdiction of the Ministry of Religion. Interpretations of Sunnī schools other than the S̲h̲āfiʿī one have gained currency, contributing to flexibility of reasoning. In this respect mention has even been made of a fifth *mazhab*, the *mazhab Indonesia*. Nevertheless, Juynboll's *Inleiding* is still held in high esteem among Islamic scholars.

There are indications that the religious courts, the *K.U.A.*s and the local functionaries, do not always apply the law as it appears to have been intended by the national legislator. This happens notably when the national and the s̲h̲arīʿa norms seem to be incongruent. Consequently, the protection of women as intended in the national law can be undermined. Also, marriages between partners of different religions, which have since long been allowed in national law, are becoming increasingly difficult in practice.

Bibliography: H. Mahmud Yunus, *Hukum perkawinan dalam islam*, Jakarta 1956; D.S. Lev, *Islamic courts in Indonesia*, Los Angeles 1972; Hazairin, *Tinjauan mengenai Undang-undang perkawinan nomor 1/1974 dan lampiran Undang-undang nomor 1/1974*, Jakarta, Tinta Mas 1975; K. Wantjik Saleh, *Hukum perkawinan Indonesia*, Jakarta, Ghalia 1980; M.B. Hooker, *Islamic law in Southeast Asia*, Singapore 1984; Departemen Agama RI, *Kompilasi hukum islam tentang, nikah, talak, cerai, rujuk*, i, Jakarta 1985; R. Soetojo Prawirohamidjojo, *Pluralisme dalam perundang-undangan perkawinan di Indonesia*, Soerabaya, Universitas Airlangga 1986; B. Siregar, *Pengembangan hukum islam dan penerapannya dalam hukum nasional*, in *Varia Peradilan*, iii (1988); S. Pompe and J.M. Otto, *Some comments on recent developments in the Indonesian marriage law with particular respect to the rights of women*, in *Verfassung und Recht in Übersee*, iv (1990).

(J.M. Otto and S. Pompe)

5. In East Africa

The number of Muslims in East Africa can only be estimated; it has been given as 20% of the total population, but 10% is more realistic. That is still more than six million persons; of these only a few hundred thousand live in Uganda, more than five million in Tanzania, and over a million in Kenya. They all follow the S̲h̲āfiʿī school, except the Indian Muslims, who are Ḥanafīs, or Ismāʿīlīs, Bohorās [*q.v.*], Twelver S̲h̲īʿīs and a few others. Of the African Muslims, only the Somalis retain their own language, except when they settle in the towns. All other Muslims in East Africa are Swahili-speaking, or adopt Swahili when converting to Islam. Marriage is probably the commonest reason for conversion for either sex.

In many ways, Islam requires few changes for a convert. The proposal for a marriage is made by a senior member of the family, usually but not necessarily, the groom's family. This proposer, the *mposa*, has to make numerous journeys between the two family homes until all the details of presents have been settled. The "bride price" is called *mahari* in many East African languages; it is an ancient custom, although strictly speaking *mahr* [*q.v.*] is not the same as the "bride price" of customary law. Some Swahili scholars insist that *mahari* should be only a token sum, others that it is payment to the bride's father for the trousseau, including furniture. On the Coast, some marriages are uxorilocal: the bridegroom moves in with his wife. Elsewhere, almost always the bride is taken ceremoniously to the bridegroom's home. Traditional songs accompany every stage of the proceedings.

The preferred marriage partners are parallel cousins, in the paternal lineage; since many houses are the family homes of brothers living together, the bride and groom will have known each other since childhood. Since everyone has to obey his father, the latter can and does decide on the choice of partner for both his sons and his daughters.

The Ḳurʾānic impediments are not always enforceable, e.g. in many parts of Africa it is customary for a man in certain circumstances to marry two sisters; often it is obligatory for a man to marry his father's widows, his brother's widows (this is not forbidden in the Ḳurʾān), and even his father's brother's widows, so that he has to marry his aunts to raise seed for the patrilineal clan. In many African villages it is normal for any lactating woman to suckle a baby crying with hunger. A Muslim scholar's objections are shrugged off. As a result, two persons may marry who have sucked the same breast.

In Africa, many women cultivate their own plot of land within the area of land belonging to their husband's clan. They can sell their produce and cook for the family when it is their turn. As a result, they will not be so much affected by their husband's neglect as a townswoman would be. However, the husband is anxious not to neglect his wives because they might take lovers. In Africa, Islam has become diluted with local customs so that numerous forms of syncretism are found. Though most men have only one wife, the chiefs may have more wives than the four permitted by Islam. Since Africans are keen to have surviving children, the type of marriage called *mutʿa* [*q.v.*] is rare. Sailors and traders may have a wife in each of the towns where their business takes them more or less regularly, and have children by all of them. Although slavery was abolished at the beginning of the century, a rich man can still obtain a girl by paying her father *mahari*, which in this case acquires a new meaning. There is no minimum age for girls to marry, but the majority of the men will be in their twenties when marrying. *Kufu*, a husband of equal socio-economic class [see KAFĀʾA], is essential for a girl born of the *ḳabāʾila*, the established clans on the East Coast. If a virgin takes a lover of a lower class, this is considered a scandal that affects the whole family, to the extent that girls are known to have been executed for it.

Bibliography: Al-Amin Bin Aly, *Uwongozi*, Mombasa 1955; Sheikh Ali Hemedi el Buhriy, *Nikahi*, tr. J.W.T. Allen, Dar es Salaam 1959; Sheikh Muhammad Saleh Abdulla Farsy, *Ada za Harusi katika Unguja*, East African Literature Bureau, Dar es Salaam 1956; J. Knappert, *Islam in Mombasa*, in *Acta Orientalia Neerlandica*, ed. by P.W. Pestman, Leiden 1971, 75-81; idem, *Traditional Swahili poetry*, Leiden 1967; idem, *Wedding songs from Mombasa*, in *Africana Marburgensia*, vii/2 (1974), 11-32; idem, *East Africa: Kenya, Tanzania and Uganda*, New Delhi 1987; I.M. Lewis, *Peoples of the Horn of Africa, Somali, Afar and Saho*, London 1955; Mwinyi Haji Mzale, *Ndoa na Faida Nyinginezo*, Zanzibar n.d.; Al-Hakir Mzee Bin Ali Muhammad, *Umuri Swalat Al-Kubra Madhabi ya Imam Shafiy*, Dar es Salaam 1961; A.H.J. Prins, *The Swahili-speaking peoples*, London 1961; E. Sachau, *Muhammedanisches Recht*, Stuttgart and Berlin 1897; F. Schildknecht, *Tanzania*, in J. Kritzeck and W.H. Lewis (eds.), *Islam in Africa*, New York 1969; R.E.S. Tanner, *Cousin marriage in the Afro-Arab community of Mombasa, Kenya*, in *Africa*, xxxiv/2 (April 1964), 127-38; Margaret Strobel, *Muslim women in Mombasa, 1890-1975*, New Haven 1979; C. Velten, *Sitten und Gebräuche der Suaheli*, tr. from *Desturi za Wasuaheli* by Mtoro bin Mwenyi Bakari, both publ. Göttingen 1903, Eng. tr. J.W.T. Allen, ed. N.Q. King, *The customs of the Swahili people*, Berkeley and Los Angeles 1981.

(J. KNAPPERT)

6. In Nigeria

Whereas the Northern Region of Nigeria, as it then was, adopted a new penal and criminal code based on the Sudan code in 1960, the year of independence, personal law and family law have continued to be administered according to the traditional Mālikī *ma<u>dh</u>hab*. In practice, however, this has become much distorted by customary and non-canonical observances at which the strict *malams* (Ar. *ʿulamāʾ*) protest, mostly in vain. An illustrative example of this occurs in the poem *Hakuran zama da iyali* ("Living patiently with the family") by Alhaji Sadisu Lawal Sugogi:

> The useless things that they have to provide (for the bride)
> Place marriage beyond the reach of every husband.
> Even those that wish to add another wife
> Must certainly suffer financially as a result of this.
> Once you enter into the marriage contract
> It is with difficulties that you get out of it.

(Muhammed Sani Aliyu, *Shortcomings in Hausa society as seen by representative poets from ca. 1950 to ca. 1982*, M.A. diss. Bayero University, Kano 1983, unpubl.)

The Sultan of Sokoto, Abubakar III, on realising the extent of the problem, set up a committee in 1967 to examine alcohol and drug abuse and extravagant wedding customs. The committee's findings were largely ignored because it proved impossible to pass legislation to enforce compliance with the suggested regulations, including those relating to wedding gifts. The same fate met the recommendations of a second committee convened in 1969. Undeterred, and prompted by increased concern over drunkenness, prostitution and deviant marriage customs, the Sultan established a third committee, this time under the chairmanship of Alhaji Shehu Shagari, the first executive President of Nigeria from 1979 to 1983. This committee received 1,200 letters and conducted 600 interviews; its findings were summarised in a booklet *Nasiha ga Musulmi kan yaki da shashanci da almubazzaranci* ("Good advice to Muslims about the battle against immorality and extravagance") which was distributed in 1973 by the influential organisation *Jam'atu Nasaril Islam* ("People for the victory of Islam"). The Sultan said he wished *Nasiha ga Musulmi* to be a public record of the endeavours of the *ulama* to stem the tide; its tone was uncompromising. The following is an example:

> There are some customs which give rise to such extravagance that marriage has become a kind of trade in itself. For that reason the custom known as *lefe* is abolished completely. Any dress-lengths of cloth the bridegroom intends to give to the bride should not be handed over to her until she is under his roof, whereupon he can give her as many dress-lengths as he likes and it is entirely his own business. It is expressly forbidden to allow them to be paraded about for inspection.

Some of the recommendations later became bye-laws of the Sokoto Local Authority but proved to be as unenforceable as before, especially in the climate created by the 1970s oil boom when newly-rich entrepreneurs and bureaucrats vied with each other in the marriage market.

In 1981 the Federal Law Reform Commission proposed a bill for the reform of the Marriage Act. It failed to recognise religious and cultural sensibilities and was therefore dropped. However criticisms continued to surface and women's groups, notably FOMWAN (The Federation of Muslim Women's Associations in Nigeria) aroused awareness of the issues through its nationwide organisation which had attracted university-trained Muslim women. In 1991 a four-day seminar, *Better Protection for Women and Children under the Law*, was organised by the Federal Ministry of Justice. Aisha Lemu, a FOMWAN executive member and the wife of the Grand Kadi of Niger State, addressed the seminar on the subject "Muslim women and marriage under the Shari'a". Her remarks on the financial and marital rights of Muslim women echoed some of the earlier views expressed in *Nasiha ga Musulmi*, but went further and blamed the courts for not implementing the law in respect of divorce and the custody of children. She said:

> The main problems faced by Muslim women in Nigeria are caused by pre-Islamic customs. In the North women who are ready to take their cases to the Shari'a courts can sometimes still fail to get their rights in the lower courts because of either ignorance of the Shari'a or corruption. However, if they are patient and persistent enough to appeal to the higher Shari'a courts their rights will be upheld.

In the multi-cultural context of Nigeria, which is a secular state, it is difficult to see how the Federal Law Reform Commission will be able to effect change without causing deep resentment in one section of the country or the other. Gradual shifts in attitude may, however, be engineered by women's pressure groups characterised by FOMWAN and others, notably *The Women's Commission* in Kano, which are backed by Muslim intellectuals predominantly based in Northern Nigerian universities.

Bibliography: A detailed and scholarly account of marriage customs and law in Northern Nigeria has yet to be written. Meanwhile, see A. Phillips and H.F. Moons, *Marriage laws in Africa*, 1971; Edwin Nwogogu, *Nigerian family law*; Awwalu Hamisu Yadudu, *Islamic law and law reform discourse in Nigeria*, diss. Harvard Univ. 1986, unpubl.; Zainab Kabir, *Law and marital problems in Kano State*, in *The Muslim Woman*, i/2 (1990); Beverley Mack and Catherine Coles (eds.), *Hausa women in the 20th century*, Madison 1991.

(Jean Boyd)

NĪKBŪLĪ, Nikbūlī, the most commonly used Ottoman Turkish form of the Byzantine town of Nikopolis, modern Bulgarian Nikopol, a town on the southern bank of the Danube in lat. 43° 43' N. and long. 24° 54' E., famed as the scene of a battle between the Ottomans and the European Crusaders in 1396.

This Nikopolis, founded by Heraclius (*ca.* 575-642), has often been confused, especially in mediæval literature, with Nikopolis *ad Istrum* or *ad Haemum*, founded by Trajan in 101 in commemoration of his victory over the Dacians (ruins excavated near modern Niküp in the upper valley of the D̲j̲antra by Mt. Haemus). The Byzantine Nikopolis is sometimes called Nikopolis Major to distinguish it from Trajan's Nikopolis and Nikopolis Minor on the opposite bank of the Danube near the Rumanian town of Tornu Magurele.

The importance of Nikopolis as a trade centre and military post is due chiefly to the command which it holds over the Osma and the Aluta, the two Danubian arteries reaching into the heart of Bulgaria and Rumania respectively. Situated on a naturally fortified plateau, it dominates the plains to the south, the Danube to the north, and the eastern gorge connecting the interior of Bulgaria with the river. The mediæval double walls and strong towers surrounding Nikopolis were destroyed by the Russians during their occupation of the city in 1810 and 1877.

Nikopolis was first captured from the Bulgarians in 791/1389 by ʿAlī Pas̲h̲a Čandarlî [see ʿAlī Pas̲h̲a Čandarlîzāde]. Seven years later, it was the scene of the famous battle in the Crusade which is called by its name. The acquisition of Bulgaria by the Turks and their continual irruptions north of the Danube into territories claimed by Hungary, together with a state of comparative peace in Western Europe in the last decade of the 14th century, made it both necessary and possible for most Catholic countries to participate in the expedition. An army of about 100,000 Crusaders (according to the most reliable estimates) from France, Burgundy, England, Germany, Italy, Spain, Hungary, Poland, Wallachia and Transylvania marched along the Danube, seized Vidin and Rahova, and finally set siege to Nikopolis while an allied Veneto-Genoese fleet blockaded the city from the river. The siege lasted about fifteen days, during which Bāyezīd I [*q.v.*] abandoned the siege of Constantinople, burnt the siege machinery, and summoned his Asiatic and European contingents to arms. A Turkish army of perhaps 110,000 men met at Adrianople and, marching through the Shipka Pass, descended into the valley of the Osma and pitched their camp on the southern hill commanding the Nikopolis plain.

The battle took place on Monday 21 D̲h̲u 'l-Ḥid̲j̲d̲j̲a 798/25 September 1396, and the Crusaders were completely routed owing to the superiority of Ottoman tactics and the dissensions amongst the leaders of the Christian host. Bāyezīd divided his army into two large sections. The first, consisting of two large bodies of irregular cavalry and of irregular infantry, occupied the slope of the hill. Between the cavalry vanguard and the infantry rearguard of this section, the Turks planted a field of pointed stakes. Beyond the skyline on the other slope of the hill, hidden from their unsuspecting enemy, the second and more important section, consisting of Bāyezīd with his Sipāhīs and Stephen Lazarović with his Serbs, watched for the right moment to advance against the exhausted Christians. These tactics proved to be effective when the Crusaders' vanguard of French and foreign auxiliaries defeated the Turkish irregular cavalry and, after forced dismounting to uproot the stakes, routed the irregular infantry and pursued them uphill to face the new and unseen forces. Meanwhile, a stampede of riderless horses produced confusion in the Crusaders' rear which comprised the Eastern European armies. Mircea and Laczković, who had no sympathy for Sigismund of Hungary, retired with their Wallachian and Transylvanian auxiliaries who constituted the left and right wings of the rearguard. After desperate fighting for the relief of the French and foreign contingents, the Hungarian nobles persuaded their king to board a Venetian galley and escape by way of Byzantium and the Morea to Dalmatia. The rest were either killed or captured, only to be massacred on the following day by Bāyezīd in order to avenge in this way the severe losses which he had sustained. A small number of nobles were, however, saved from the massacre for a ransom of 200,000 gold florins.

The immediate result of the Ottoman victory was the extension of the conquests into Greece and the submission of Wallachia to Ottoman suzerainty. More important, however, was the breathing-space it gave for the consolidation of the Turkish territories in Europe, which enabled the Ottoman empire to survive the critical struggles of the next decades.

In later history, Nikopolis plays only a minor part. During the wars of the 19th century it was thrice captured by Russian armies (September 1810; July 1829; July 1877), and by the Treaty of Berlin (13 July 1878) was included in the tributary principality of Bulgaria. The modern town of Nikopol (estimated population 1970, 5,715) lies in the province (*okrŭg*) of Pleven (Ottoman Turkish Plewne [*q.v.*]).

Bibliography: See the standard histories of the Ottoman Empire. For the Crusade, a full and classified bibliography of the extensive ms. and printed sources, both Eastern and Western, is contained in A.S. Atiya, *The Crusade of Nicopolis*, London 1934. See also the following older monographs: A. Brauner, *Die Schlacht bei Nikopolis, 1396*, Breslau 1876; J. Delaville le Roulx, *La France en Orient au XIVème siècle*, Paris 1886; H. Kiss, *A Nicapolye ulkozet*, Magyar Academiai ertestito, 1896; I. Köhler, *Die Schlachten bei Nikopoli und Warna*, Breslau 1882; F. Šišic, *Die Schlacht bei Nikopolis*, Vienna 1893. Of more recent studies, see *İA*, art. *Niğbolu* (M.C. Şehabeddin Tekindağ); Halil Inalcık, *The Ottoman empire. The classical age 1300-1600*, London 1973, 15-16; H.W. Hazard (ed.), *A history of the Crusades*, iii. *The fourteenth and fifteenth centuries*, Madison 1975, 21-6, 82-5; S.J. Shaw, *History of the Ottoman empire and modern Turkey*, i, Cambridge 1976, 33-4. (A.S. Atiya)

NĪKSĀR, the classical Neo-Caesarea in Bithynia, a town lying on the southern rim of the Pontic mountain chain of Asia Minor (the modern Turkish Kuzey Anadolu Dağları) on the right bank of the Kelkit river. It is situated at an altitude of 350 m/1,150 feet in lat. 40°35′ N. and long. 36°59′ E.

The nucleus of the town is picturesquely situated at the foot of a hill, crowned by the ruins of a mediaeval castle which was erected from the material provided by the numerous buildings of antiquity there. Here in remote antiquity was Cabira and after its decline Diospolis founded by Pompey, later called Sebaste. In Church history Nīksār is famous as the scene of a Council (314 A.D.) and as the birthplace of Gregory the miracle-worker. In the Muslim period it became important under the Saldjūḳs, of whom numerous and important buildings have survived to the present day. It became more important under the Dānishmandids [*q.v.*], whose founder Malik Dānishmand Aḥmad Ghāzī took Nīksār among other places. His grandson Muḥammad successfully resisted a siege by the emperor Manuel in Nīksār. His son Yaghibaṣan (537-62/1142-66), of whom there survives an inscription of the year 552/1157, died in 562/1166, whereupon Nīksār was taken by the Byzantine emperor Manuel (Kinnamos, 296-7, 300) although only for a short time. In 799/1397 Nīksār passed to the Ottomans and gradually lost its former importance. It remained noted for its very prolific orchards, celebrated already in al-Ḳazwīnī's time (*Āthār*, ed. Wüstenfeld, Göttingen 1848) the special produce of which, very large and sweet cherries, pears, figs etc., were famous at all times. Ewliyā Čelebi (cf. *Seyāḥatnāma*, ii, 389, v, 14; *Travels*, ii, 102) who visited Nīksār in 1083/1672, describes the town in his usual extravagant fashion, mentioning 70 schools, 7 monasteries, many mills and waterwheels and 500 shops with a large number of shoe-makers. The pomegranates there, he says, are the size of a man's head and weighed 1 *oḳḳa*. The remains of the Islamic period, so far as they bear inscriptions, have been published by Ismāʿīl Ḥaḳḳī, *Kitābeler* (Istanbul 1345/1927), 58-73. The *türbe*s (sepulchral cupolas) of Malik Ghāzī and of Ḥādjdjī Čiḳrīḳ are worth mentioning; among old dervish monasteries there are the Ishīḳ-tekke and the Ḳolaḳ-tekke. Nīksār has often been visited and described by modern travellers. The population before the First World War (*ca.* 4,000) was one-quarter Christian; they were mainly engaged in the silk and rice trades.

In modern Turkey, Nīksār is the centre of an *ilçe* or district in the *il* or province of Tokat. In *ca.* 1960 it had a population of 10,550.

Bibliography: Ḥādjdjī Khalīfa, *Djihān-numā*, 628; F. Taeschner, *Anatol. Wegenetz*, i, 216 ff., ii, 12 ff.; Gyllius, *Bosph. Thrac.*, 334; J. von Hammer, *GOR*, i, 339, 426; C. Ritter, *Erdkunde von Kleinasien*, i, 221 ff.; J. Morier, *A journey through Persia, Armenia and Asia Minor to Constantinople*, London 1812, 42; R. Ker Porter, *Travels in Georgia, Persia, Armenia*, etc., London 1821, 700; W. Ouseley, *Travels in various countries of the East*, London 1819, 484; J.B. Fraser, *Winter journey*, London 1838, 209; J.E. Alexander, *Travels from India to England*, London 1827, 235; Eli Smith and H.G.O. Dwight, *Missionary researches in Armenia*, London 1834, 46; W.J. Hamilton, *Researches in Asia Minor, Pontus and Armenia*, London 1842, 346; V. Cuinet, *La Turquie d'Asie*, i, 734-5; Admiralty handbooks, *Turkey*, London 1942-3, ii, 576; *İA*, art. Niksar (Besim Darkot); *PW*, xvi/2, cols. 2409-13 (W. Ruge).

(F. Babinger)

NĪḲŪLĀʾŪS, the Arabised form of the name of Nicolaus of Damascus, born 64 B.C., distinguished politician (adviser of King Herod, friend of Emperor Augustus), and scholar of vast erudition and versatility. Greek fragments of his rhetorical, historical and biographical works have survived, but philosophical fragments are scarce. On the other hand, his literary legacy was unknown in the Orient, but Syriac and Arabic translations of his philosophical works have recently come to light.

1. The *Book on Plants*: *K. Arisṭūṭālīs fī 'l-nabāt, tafsīr Nīḳūlāʾūs* is probably an adaptation of Aristotle's lost work Περὶ φυτῶν. The Arabic translation was discovered in 1923, edited by Arberry (1933) and Badawī (1954). See now Drossaart Lulofs and Poortman, *Nicolaus De plantis, five translations*, in *Verh. Ak. Amst.* (1989) (= *DLP*). Because in the Latin version by Alfred of Sareshel (1200 A.D.) the words *tafsīr Nīḳūlāʾūs* were omitted, *De plantis* was attributed to Aristotle himself. Some 160 mss. testify to its popularity in the Middle Ages, and yet it was eclipsed by the Greek retroversion from Alfred's text (13th cent.), which from 1539 onwards figured as an appendix to all Greek editions of Aristotle, but was generally considered spurious. In 1841 Alfred's Latin version was edited by E.H.F. Meyer, who knew the title in Arabic from Ḥādjdjī Khalīfā (ed. Flügel v, 162, no. 10564). In his commentary, Meyer marked off a long digression (§§ 66-*ca.* 130) on the parts of plants that was borrowed from the *History of Plants* by Theophrastus, whose name was not mentioned. Apparently, Nicolaus inserted this detailed account because Aristotle used to maintain that the parts of plants were few and simple. A comparison with Theophrastus' Greek text shows that Nicolaus, in compiling, sometimes left out important words, e.g. restrictive particles, and had the habit of conflating parallel passages. Consequently, the tenor of the original work was often distorted and obscured. Obviously, he did the same to the Aristotelean part. Glossators swamped the text with enigmatic glosses and digressions on alien matters. Hence the rambling character of the book.

In the Orient, many authors have used the *K. al-Nabāt*, and though some of them (e.g. Ibn al-Ṭayyib) had a poor opinion of it, Ibn Rus̲h̲d appears to have written an epitome (*DLP*, 363 ff.). The fragment of a long commentary in Hebrew (Oxford Hunt. 576) is a clever imitation. Ullmann, *Die Natur- und Geheimwissenschaften im Islam*, Leiden 1972, 73 ff., rightly asserts that the book has primarily been one of the few sources for the knowledge of Theophrastean botany among the Arabs. And indeed, Ibn Sīnā and Ibn al-Ṭayyib, for instance, had a strong preference for the relevant part which, of course, they attributed to Aristotle.

2. *On the Philosophy of Aristotle* in at least 13 books. In this extensive compendium of Aristotle's physical treatises, Nicolaus acted as a pioneer; at the time when commentators used to begin with *Logic*, he turned to the philosophy of nature. The remnants in Europe are very scarce, but a curtailed Syriac version in the mutilated Cambridge ms. Syr. Gg. 2.14 was discovered in 1901. Drossaart Lulofs edited the first five books in 1963 (= Nicol. *Philos.*). Owing to the rapidly increasing mutilation of the ms. leaves, the others are less accessible.

Some remarkable features are that: (a) throughout the whole work the same habit of compiling and the same use (and abuse) of conflation is observed as in *De plantis*; (b) a compendium of the *Metaphysics* is added and placed after (!) the *Physics*; (c) Ibn Rus̲h̲d's objections against Nicolaus' peculiar way of adjusting the *Metaphysics* to his purpose, which were discussed from Th. Roeper (1844) onwards, can now be explained (Nicol. *Philos.*, 27-34); and (d) abridged excerpts of *Meteorology*, i-iii, are interspersed with parts of Olympiodorus' *Commentary* in a very bad translation. In the Paris ms. B.N. Syr. 346, some of these comments are collected and wrongly ascribed to Nicolaus. In editing these quotations under Nicolaus' name, F. Nau (in *ROC*, xv [1910]) created confusion. (e) In Nicolaus' book, *Meteor.*, iv, is concerned with mineralogy and deviates from Aristotle because Nicolaus has supplemented Aristotle's own short and unfinished observations on the subject (at the end of *Meteor.*, iii) with quotations from Theophrastus, *De lapidibus*. So, just as in *De plantis*, Nicolaus turned to Theophrastus where Aristotle failed.

Large parts of the compendium have been translated from Syriac into Arabic, and both translations have been used by Oriental authors as a kind of source book of Aristotelian tenets. A case in point is Barhebraeus, who possessed an unabridged copy of Nicolaus in Syriac, of which in the *Candelabrum* and the *Butyrum sapientiae* he often availed himself without mentioning the Damascene (see *DLP*, 17-49). On the other hand, Ibn Rus̲h̲d inserted a lengthy passage from Nicolaus' (unabridged) summary of the *Metaphysics*, where his copy of the Arabic translation of Aristotle's work had a lacuna, see Ibn Rus̲h̲d, *Tafsīr mā baʿd al-ṭabīʿa*, 843.8-850.7 Bouyges = Nicol. *Philos.*, F. 22.

Bibliography: Th. Roeper, *Lectiones abulpharagianae*, Gedani 1844, 35-43, contain the first discussion of Nicolaus' philosophical fragments known at the time. See further the bibl. in H.J. Drossaart Lulofs, *Nicolaus Damascenus on the Philosophy of Aristotle*, Leiden 1969², 6-7; P. Moraux, *Der Aristotelismus bei den Griechen I*, in *Peripatoi*, v (Berlin 1973), 445-514; Drossaart Lulofs, *Aristotle's ΠΕΡΙ ΦΥΤΩΝ*, in *Jnal. of Hellenic Studies*, lxxvii/1 (1957), 75-80; idem, *Aristotle, Barhebraeus and Nicolaus*, in *On nature and living things*, ed. A. Gotthelf, Bristol 1985, 345-357; idem, *Das Prooimion von ΠΕΡΙ ΦΥΤΩΝ*, in *Aristoteles' Werk und Wirkung*, ed. J. Wiesner, ii, Berlin 1987, 1-16.

(H.J. Drossaart Lulofs)

NĪL, also *nīladj̲* (Persian, from Skr. *nīla* "blue") is *Indigo tinctoria* L., *Indigoferae*, the oldest known organic dye. It is the main component of natural indigo, which can be obtained from various kinds of indigofera (*Isatis tinctoria, Cruciferae*) and from the knotweed (*Polygonum tinctorium, Polygonaceae*). For thousands of years indigo has been used in India, China, as well as in Egypt, to paint and dye various fabrics. Classical antiquity knew indigo as a medicine; the Arabs cultivated the plant and produced the dye themselves.

The Arab translators of Dioscurides did not find an equivalent for *isāṭīs*, and so the early Arab authors confused the ἰσάτις of Dioscurides—Pliny's *glastum* (*Nat. Hist.* xxii, 2), *Isatis tinctoria*—with Dioscurides' ἰνδικόν, Pliny's *indicum* (xxxv, 27), Arabic *nīl* = *Indigo tinctoria*. In the Middle Ages, the Arabs used the word *nīl*—actually indigo—to indicate woad. However, they realised the difference: al-Suwaydī, *K. al-Simāt fī asmāʾ al-nabāt* (ms. Paris ar. 3004, fol. 198b, 10), referring to the identification of *isāṭīs* with *nīl*, only remarks that many scholars have a different opinion, but al-G̲h̲āfiḳī (in Ibn al-Bayṭār, *al-Dj̲āmiʿ*, Būlāḳ 1291, iv, 186, 28-30) expresses himself more clearly: Dioscurides' *nīl* (= ἰσάτις) is known in Spain under the name *al-samāʾī* ("the sky-blue"), but it is not much used in the land of the Franks, whereas the *nīl* of the dyers is said to be *al-ʿiẓlim*, the (Indian) *nīl*, whose description applies to indigo. The constant confusion between the two plants led to a series of Arabic synonyms, like *ʿiẓlim, wasma (wāsima), k̲h̲iṭr, nīla, tīn ak̲h̲ḍar*, etc., which were used indifferently for the two plants.

Both isatis and indigo were used as medicines, especially as astringents, by way of compresses, for wounds, tumours and sores. Indigo was an important commercial product, used for colouring fabrics and wool. The main source of exports was always India, Bag̲h̲dād being the intermediate place of transfer. From here the dyeing plant reached mediaeval Europe as "Baghdad indigo" (see W. Heyd, *Histoire du commerce du Levant*, Leipzig 1885-6, repr. Amsterdam 1959, 626-9). Outside India, the indigo plant was also grown on Persian soil, in Kirmān and K̲h̲ūzistān (see P. Schwarz, *Iran im Mittelalter*, 273, 276, 422). In modern times, it is mostly synthetic indigo which comes on the market.

Bibliography: A. Dietrich, *Dioscurides triumphans. Ein anonymer arabischer Kommentar (Ende 12. Jahrh. n. Chr.) zur Materia medica*, Göttingen 1988, 636-7, with references to sources and literature.

(A. Dietrich)

AL-**NĪL**, the river Nile. The Nile is one of the large rivers (length *ca.* 6,648 km./4,132 miles) which from the beginning have belonged to the territory of Islam, and the valleys and deltas of which have favoured the development of an autonomous cultural centre in Islamic civilisation. In the case of the Nile, this centre has influenced at different times the cultural and political events in the Islamic world. Thus the Nile has, during the Islamic period, continued to play the same part as it did during the centuries that preceded the coming of Islam.

The name al-Nīl or, very often, Nīl Miṣr, goes back to the Greek name Νεῖλος and is found already in early Arabic literary sources, though it does not occur in the Ḳurʾān (in sūra XX, 39, the Nile may be meant by *al-yamm*). The Christian habit of calling the river Gēḥōn, after one of the rivers of Paradise, as found in the works of Ephraim Syrus and Jacob of

Edessa and in the Arabic-Christian author Agapius (*Patrologia Orientalis*, v, 596), is not followed by the Muslims who know only the Oxus under this name. Al-Zamakhsharī (*Kitāb al-Amkina*, ed. Salvedra de Grave, 127) mentions as another name al-Fayḍ, no doubt a poetical allusion to the yearly flood. Already in the Middle Ages, the word *baḥr* having come to acquire in Arabic the meaning of "river", the Nile is also called al-Baḥr or Baḥr Miṣr (cf. al-Maḳrīzī, ed. Wiet, i, 218), which is also the case with several separate parts of its river system, such as Baḥr Yūsuf or Baḥr al-Ghazal. In the Delta, the different ramifications of the river are occasionally also called Nile, but where necessary the main stream (*ʿamūd*) is distinguished from the minor branches (*dhirāʿ* or *khalīdj*) and the canals (*turʿa*).

The geography of the Nile is treated here only from a historico-geographical point of view so far as the knowledge of Islamic science is concerned. The geographical knowledge of the Nile among the Muslims, so far as we can learn from their literary sources, is based partly on direct observation, but for the most part on legendary or pseudo-scientific traditions which go back to local beliefs or to classical knowledge. For a long time during the Middle Ages the limit of Islamic territory on the Nile was well fixed; it ended at the first cataract near the island of Bilāḳ (Philae) to the south of Uswān (Assouan); here began, since the treaty (*baḳt* [*q.v.*]) concluded by ʿAbd Allāh b. Abī Sarḥ with the Nubians, the Nubian territory [see NŪBA], where for long centuries Christianity prevailed (al-Balādhurī, 236; Ibn ʿAbd al-Ḥakam, *Futūḥ Miṣr*, ed. Torrey, 188). The first locality on Nubian territory, where tribute was paid, was called al-Ḳaṣr (al-Masʿūdī, *Murūdj*, iii, 40-1 = § 883).

Historical tradition has preserved parts of the alleged correspondence between ʿAmr b. al-ʿĀṣ and the caliph ʿUmar on the subject of Egypt, then newly-conquered; here the Nile is described as a river "whose course is blessed", while the flood and the inundations are praised in poetical terms (ʿUmar b. Muḥammad al-Kindī, *Faḍāʾil Miṣr*, ed. Østrup, 204; al-Dimashḳī, ed. Mehren, 109). The same correspondence reveals the perhaps historical fact that ʿUmar did not wish to see the Arab army established in Alexandria, because there would be then a great river between the army and the caliph (Ibn ʿAbd al-Ḥakam, 91; cf. also what is said on p. 128 about those who went to live in al-Djīza).

The principal towns by which the Nile passed in mediaeval Egypt in Upper Egypt, between Uswān and al-Fusṭāṭ, were Adfū (Edfu, on the left), Isnā (Esne, l.), Armant (l.), Ḳūṣ (r.), al-Aḳṣur (Luxor, r.), Ḳifṭ (r.), Ikhmīm (Akhmīm, r.), Usyūṭ (Asyūṭ, Suyūṭ, l.), al-Ushmūnayn (l.), Anṣina (r. opposite al-Ushmūnayn), Ṭaḥā (l.), al-Ḳays (l.), Dalāṣ (l.), Ahnās (l.) and Iṭfīḥ (Aṭfīḥ, r.). This succession of towns is given for the first time by al-Yaʿḳūbī (331-4), while Ibn Ḥawḳal (ed. de Goeje, 95) is the first to give a table of the distance between these towns, expressed in *barīds*, the entire distance being 21 days' journey (al-Idrīsī, ed. Dozy and de Goeje, 52, gives 25 days' journey for the same distance). Shortly before al-Ushmūnayn, there branched off on the left the canal that conducted the water to al-Fayyūm, which is known to Ibn al-Faḳīh (74) as Nahr al-Lāhūn and to al-Idrīsī (50) as Khalīdj al-Manhī: this canal, which according to unanimous tradition was dug by Joseph, occurs already on the ms. map from the year 479/1086, of Ibn Ḥawḳal in Istanbul, Top Kapu Saray ms. no. 3346 (reproduction on fol. 658 of *Monumenta Africae et Aegypti* by Youssouf Kamāl). It is the Baḥr Yūsuf of our days; on it was situated al-Bahnasā. The banks of the Nile in Upper Egypt are not very completely described by the geographers; one finds repeated everywhere the assertion that the borders were cultivated without interruption between Uswān and al-Fusṭāṭ (cf. al-Iṣṭakhrī, 50), but that the width of the cultivated territory varied during the river's course, dependent on the greater or lesser distance of the two mountain ranges that border the stream. Ibn Ḥawḳal (Istanbul ms., see above) describes two extremely narrow strips, one between Uswān and Atfū (now called Gebelein) and one between Isnā and Armant (now called Gebel Silsile). The curves in the course of the Nile, especially in the upper part of the Ṣaʿīd, are not indicated on the maps of al-Iṣṭakhrī and Ibn Ḥawḳal. The oldest extant Arab map of the Nile, however—which is at the same time the oldest Arab map that we know of—gives clear indications that its sinuous course was a known fact. This map is found in the Strasbourg ms. of the year 428/1037 of al-Khʷārazmī's *Ṣūrat al-arḍ* and has been reproduced in the edition of that text by H. v. Mžik (*BAHUG*, iii, Leipzig 1926). The representation of the Nile here is connected with the classical tradition of astronomical geography; al-Khʷārazmī himself, and after him Suhrāb (Ibn Serapion) and Ibn Yūnus (ms. 143 Gol. of the University Library at Leiden, where on p. 136 a special table is given of the towns lying on the banks of the Nile), give exact indications as to the longitudes and latitudes of the Nile towns, but these indications need many very uncertain corrections to allow of the reconstruction of a map, as von Mžik has tried to do for al-Khʷārazmī in *Denkschr. Ak. Wiss. Wien*, lix, Vienna 1916, and J. Lelewel for Ibn Yūnus in pl. ii of the Atlas annexed to his *Géographie du Moyen-âge*, Paris 1850. But the fact that the course of the Nile runs from south to north was well known to all the Arabic sources, which often repeat the assertion that the Nile is the only river in the world for which this is the case. Only the text of Ibn Ḥawḳal seems to imply that the Nile reached al-Fusṭāṭ from the south-east (96).

The Delta of the Nile begins to the north of al-Fusṭāṭ, where the distance between the two mountain ranges widens, while these hills themselves become lower and pass gradually into the desert. Immediately below al-Fusṭāṭ began the canal that was dug by ʿAmr b. al-ʿĀṣ to link up the Nile with the Red Sea; this canal (Khalīdj Miṣr or Khalīdj Amīr al-Muʾminīn) was made in 23/644 according to Muḥammad b. Yūsuf al-Kindī (cited by al-Maḳrīzī, *Khiṭaṭ*, Būlāḳ, ii, 143; cf. Yāḳūt, ii, 466) and served for the conveyance of provisions to the Ḥidjāz until the reign of ʿUmar b. ʿAbd al-ʿAzīz; afterwards it was neglected and even obstructed by the order of the caliph al-Manṣūr, so that, in the 4th/10th century, it ended at Dhanab al-Timsāḥ in the lakes to the north of al-Ḳulzum (cf. al-Masʿūdī, *Murūdj*, iv, 97 = § 1426).

The two principal arms of the Nile in the Delta began about 12 miles to the north of al-Fusṭāṭ (a little further than nowadays, according to Guest) and had, as now, a great number of ramifications which communicated in many ways and ended for the greater part in the big lakes or lagoons stretching behind the sea coast from west to east; these lakes were called in the Middle Ages: Buḥayrat Maryūṭ (behind Alexandria), B. Idkū, B. al-Burullus or B. al-Bushtīm and the very large B. Tinnīs, which last contained a large number of islands with Tinnīs as the most important. On the land tongue, where the two main arms separated, was situated the town of Shaṭnāf. The western arm went as now to the town of Rashīd (Rosetta), after which it reached the sea; near the town of Shābūr a branch parted from this arm in the direction of Alexandria, ending in the Buḥayrat Maryūṭ; this branch was only filled with water in the time of the flood (see a very complete survey of the different "canals" of Alexandria by P. Kahle, in *Isl.*, xii, 83 ff.). The eastern arm ran, as is still the case, past Dimyāṭ (Damietta) and reached the sea shortly afterwards; it had several branches that went to the Buḥayrat Tinnīs, one of which continued one of the Nile mouths of antiquity. Though many sources, based on a pseudo-historical tradition, repeat after each other that there are seven Nile arms (Ibn ʿAbd al-Ḥakam, 6; further, al-Khʷārazmī, Ḳudāma, Suhrāb, al-Masʿūdī, Ibn Zūlāḳ), the more realistic authors (Ibn Khurradādhbih, al-Yaʿḳūbī, Ibn Rusta, al-Iṣṭakhrī, Ibn Ḥawḳal, al-Idrīsī) only know of the two main arms. These were linked up by a canal system which, in the Middle Ages, differed considerably from the present situation. The chief sources from which we know them are Ibn Ḥawḳal and al-Idrīsī, who give itineraries following the different branches, but as the places named in these itineraries have been identified only in part, an integral reconstruction is not yet possible (on this problem cf. R. Guest, *The Delta in the Middle Ages*, in *JRAS* [1912], 941 ff., and the map annexed to this article). The description in the text of Suhrāb (ed. von Mžik, *BAHUG*, v) has little value as an endeavour to trace back to his time (4th/10th century) the seven legendary arms; among these arms special attention is paid to the "arm of Saradūs", which, according to tradition, was dug by Hāmān (Ibn ʿAbd al-Ḥakam, 6; cf. Guest, *op. cit.*, 944, and Maspéro and Wiet, *Matériaux*, in *MIFAO*, xxxvi, 104). Al-Maḳrīzī has preserved a detailed description of the canal system in the province of al-Buḥayra, to the east of Alexandria, from the *Kitāb al-Minhādj* of Abu 'l-Ḥasan al-Makhzūmī, who wrote in the 6th/12th century (*MIFAO*, xlvi, 167 ff.). It seems possible that a study of the ancient maps (especially the Delta map of the Istanbul ms. of Ibn Ḥawḳal and the maps of al-Idrīsī) may be useful for a more complete reconstruction of the mediaeval situation.

The Nile arms have always been decisive for the administrative division of the Delta, which the sources call by the name of Asfal al-Arḍ or Asfal Arḍ Miṣr. The region to the east of the eastern branch was called al-Ḥawf; the texts of al-Iṣṭakhrī and Ibn Ḥawḳal place al-Ḥawf to the north of the Nile, which may be understood in connection with the view referred to above that the Nile at al-Fusṭāṭ had a direction from S.E. to N.W. The region between the two main arms was called al-Rīf (a name sometimes used for the entire Delta as well) or Baṭn al-Rīf, while the country to the west of the western arm was called al-Buḥayra and later al-Ḥawf al-Gharbī, the original Ḥawf being called then al-Ḥawf al-Sharḳī. The three sections were divided into *kūras*, the limits of which were determined by the more important branches; the bigger administrative units of later times [see MIṢR] depended likewise on the river system. The present geographical aspect of the Delta is the result of the new irrigation works that began in the 19th century under Muḥammad ʿAlī; the most conspicuous new canals are the Maḥmūdiyya canal, dug from Fūwa on the western arm to Alexandria, the Tawfīḳiyya, Manūfiyya and Buḥayriyya canals that were completed in 1890, and the Ismāʿīliyya canal, which links up the Nile with the Suez canal.

As to the knowledge of the course of the Nile to the south of Egypt, the Islamic geographical literature begins rather late to give information based on direct observation. At first, these sources content themselves with saying that the Nile comes from the country of the Nūba; for the rest, there were ancient sources of a different kind that helped to complete the geographical conception of the course of the great river. This conception involved also the origin of the Nile, covered since antiquity by a veil of mystery. The real origin of the Nile always remained unknown to Muslim scholars and travellers. It is a curious fact, however, that the information on this subject which we find uniformly repeated in the Islamic sources from the treatise of al-Khʷārazmī (*ca.* 215/830) onwards gives an idea of the origin of the Nile which does not correspond entirely to the data furnished by the classical sources. This conception makes the Nile emerge from the Mountains of the Moon (Djabal al-Ḳamar) to the south of the equator; from this mountain come ten rivers, of which the first five and the second five reach respectively two lakes lying on the same latitude; from each lake one or more rivers flow to the north where they fall into a third lake and it is from this lake that the Nile of Egypt begins. This conception is largely schematised and corresponds only partly to Ptolemy's description of the Nile sources; Ptolemy knows only of two lakes, not lying on the same latitude and does not speak of a great number of rivers coming from the Mountains of the Moon. The third lake especially is an innovation (cf. von Mžik, in *Denkschr. Ak. Wiss. Wien*, lxxxix, 44); in later authors such as Ibn Saʿīd and al-Dimashḳī this third lake is called Kūrā and may be connected with some notion of Lake Chad (the same authors change the name of Djabal al-Ḳamar into Djabal al-Ḳumr, which pronunciation is commented on by al-Maḳrīzī, ed. Wiet, i, 219), but this is not probable for the time of al-Khʷārazmī; the knowledge of more equatorial lakes, however, may perhaps be traced to the experiences of the two centurions despatched by Nero to explore the Nile and who reached, according to Seneca, a marshy impassable region, which has been identified with the Baḥr al-Ghazal. The system described by al-Khʷārazmī of the origin of the Nile is represented on the map in the Strasbourg ms. and is repeated many times after him (Ibn Khurradādhbih, Ibn al-Faḳīh, Ḳudāma, Suhrāb, al-Idrīsī and later authors). Al-Masʿūdī, in describing a map he has seen, does not speak of the third lake (*Murūdj*, i, 205-6 = § 215) and Ibn Rusta (90) says that the Nile comes from a mountain called B.b.n and also knows only two lakes. Al-Iṣṭakhrī and Ibn Ḥawḳal, on the contrary, frankly admit that the origin of the Nile is unknown, which is also illustrated by their maps. Still the system of al-Khʷārazmī continued to be a geographical dogma and is found as late as al-Suyūṭī. Al-Khʷārazmī also took over from Ptolemy a western tributary of the Nile, which comes from a lake on the equator; this river is called by Ptolemy Astapos and may perhaps be identified with the Atbara. A later development, which connects with the Nile system a river that flows to the east in the Indian Ocean, is found for the first time in al-Masʿūdī (*Murūdj*, i, 205-6, ii, 383-4 = §§ 215, 796); this view is later taken up again by Ibn Saʿīd and al-Dimashḳī.

Another category of notions about the origins of the Nile is connected with the Jewish and Christian traditions which make the Nile come from Paradise. Mediaeval cosmographical theory places Paradise in the extreme East, on the other side of the sea (cf. the maps of Beatus), so that the Nile, like the other rivers of Paradise would have to cross the sea. This state of things is actually described in an old tradition, probably of Jewish origin, of a man who went in search of the sources of the Nile and had to cross the sea, after which he reached Paradise (al-Masʿūdī, *Murūdj*, i, 268-9 = § 288 and *Akhbār al-zamān*, ms. Vienna, fol. 156a-b; al-Muḳaddasī, 21). With this origin in Paradise is perhaps connected the view, which all sources attribute to al-Djāḥiẓ in his lost *Kitāb al-Buldān*, that the Nile and the Mihrān [*q.v.*] (Indus) have the same origin (cf. al-Masʿūdī, *Tanbīh*, 55), a view which is sarcastically criticised by al-Bīrūnī (*India*, 101). To the same origin may go back the idea, often found in Islamic sources, that, when the Nile rises, all the rivers of the earth go down in level.

Thirdly, there is a cycle of geographical conceptions which link up the western part of Africa with the river system of the Nile. Herodotus already had sought a western origin and Pliny quotes the *Lybica* of King Juba of Mauritania, who makes the Nile rise in western Mauritania. Marquart (*Benin-Sammlung*, 125 ff.) explained this view from a corruption of the name of the river Nuhul, which he identifies with the Wādī Nūl and which has its origin in the Mauritanian Atlas. Traces of this western Nile are to be found in Ibn al-Faḳīh (87) who, following an authority of the time of the conquest, places the origin of the Nile in al-Sūs al-Aḳṣā. Al-Bakrī for the first time identifies this western Nile with the river Niger, although we find already in al-Masʿūdī the knowledge of a great river, far to the south of Sidjilmāsa (*Murūdj*, iv, 92-3 = § 1420). Al-Bakrī describes the Nile as passing through the territory of the Sūdān (ed. de Slane, 172) and enumerates a number of Berber and Sūdān tribes and their towns which border the river; the westernmost town is with him Ṣanghāra, followed in an eastern direction by Takrūr, Sillā, Ghāna, Tiraḳḳā and finally the country of Kawkaw. After al-Bakrī, a similar description is given by al-Idrīsī, but this last author goes back to another source than al-Bakrī when he places the mouth of the Nile in the neighbourhood of the salt town Awlīl, thus identifying the lower course of this Nile with the Senegal (Marquart, *op. cit.*, 171). Al-Idrīsī likewise shows himself informed on the course of the Nile to the east of Kawkaw, though he is in doubt whether Kawkaw is situated on the Nile itself or on a side arm (ed. Dozy and de Goeje, 11); he finally derives this western Nile from the third of the big Nile lakes mentioned above, thus connecting the Nile of the Sūdān with the Nile of Egypt in one river system. So long as the complete text of al-Bakrī is not known, we cannot ascertain if this conception goes back already to that author. Al-Idrīsī's Nile course is clearly indicated on his maps of the 1st to the 4th sections of the first climate. After him, it is especially Ibn Saʿīd who described the western Nile in this way and who was followed again by Abu 'l-Fidāʾ. Al-Dimashḳī (ed. Mehren, 89) gives the same representation; this last author even makes the third lake, which he calls like Ibn Saʿīd the lake of Kūrā, give birth to three rivers: the Nile of the Sūdān, the Nile of Egypt, and a third river running in eastern direction towards Maḳdishū [*q.v.*] in the Zandj country on the Indian Ocean. This last river, which was also connected by al-Masʿūdī with the Nile (see above) is probably identical with the Webi river in Somalia.

While the geographical authors constructed in this way the Nile system with a good deal of credulity and imagination, the real knowledge of the Nile south of Egypt advanced but slowly. The southernmost point reached by the Arab conquerers was Dongola [*q.v.*] (al-Kindī, ed. Guest, 12), and it was well-known that this town was situated on the Nile; its latitude and longitude are given by al-Khʷārazmī and Suhrāb. Al-Yaʿḳūbī (*Taʾrīkh*, i, 217) knows that, in the country of the Nūba called ʿAlwa, whose people live behind the Nūba in the region called Muḳurra, the Nile divides into various branches; this same author, however, places Sind behind ʿAlwa. Al-Masʿūdī (*Murūdj*, iii, 31-2 = § 873) knows that the country of the Nūba is divided into two parts by the Nile. Ibn Ḥawḳal (Istanbul ms.) describes two places where there are cataracts (*djanādil*), namely the one above Uswān, which is the "first cataract", and one near Dongola, of which it is not certain whether the "second" or the "third" cataract is meant. About the same time, however, a traveller named Ibn Sulaym al-Uswānī wrote a valuable description of the middle Nile course, which has been preserved in al-Maḳrīzī's *Khiṭaṭ* (ed. Wiet, in *MIFAO*, xlvi, 252 ff.). This Ibn Sulaym, on whom al-Maḳrīzī's *Kitāb al-Muḳaffā* gives some information (cf. Quatremère, *Mémoires sur l'Egypte*, ii), had been sent by the Fāṭimid general Djawhar to the king of the Nūba on a diplomatic errand, and was the author of a *Kitāb Akhbār al-Nūba wa 'l-Muḳurra wa-ʿAlwa wa 'l-Budja wa 'l-Nīl* (Fr. tr. G. Troupeau, in *Arabica*, i/3 [1954], 276-88), in which a detailed description is given of these countries. He says that the region between Uswān and Dunḳula is inhabited in the north by the Marīs [*q.v.*] and more to the south by the Muḳurra [*q.v.*]; the northern part is barren and the great cataracts are correctly described. The country between Dunḳula and ʿAlwa (this last spot is the region of Khartūm [*q.v.*]) is described as highly flourishing; the big winding of the Nile here is perfectly known to Ibn Sulaym. The Nile "is divided" then into seven rivers; from the description it is clear that the northern one of these rivers is the Atbara, coming from the east; further south the "White Nile" and the "Green Nile" join near the capital of ʿAlwa, and the "Green Nile", which comes from the east, is again the result of four rivers, one of which comes, as the author thinks, from the country of the Ḥabasha, and one from the country of the Zandj; this last, incorrect, statement may have been influenced by learned tradition. Between the "White Nile" and the "Green Nile" there stretches a large island (*djazīra*, as it is still called on our maps), which has no limits in the south. This is about the only description in mediaeval Islamic literature that shows how far the knowledge of the middle Nile really went. Only a little of it seems to have reached the systematic geographic treatises; al-Idrīsī, e.g., describes this part of the river in a way which only shows that he did not make good use of the inadequate sources that were at his disposal.

The exploration of the upper Nile and its sources since the end of the 18th century was the work of European travellers. They discovered, or perhaps rediscovered, the really large Nile lakes and identified the Ruwenzori mountain range with the Moon Mountains, the name of which was found again by the explorer Speke in the name of the Unyamwezi country, the "country of the moon". A part of the exploration of the Nile was due, however, also to Egyptian initiative. The well-known military expedition of 1820-2 under Muḥammad ʿAlī's son Ismāʿīl Pasha, during which the city of Khartūm was founded, established Egyptian domination in the Egyptian Sūdān and opened the way for further scientific exploration. In the years 1839-42 three Egyptian expeditions went up the White Nile, and during the reign of Ismāʿīl Pasha b. Ibrāhīm [*q.v.*] the Egyptian government repeatedly tried to cleanse the swamps of the White Nile above Sobat from the masses of vegatation (*sudd*) which hindered navigation.

The yearly flood of the Nile (*ziyāda, fayḍ, fayaḍān*) is the phenomenon to which Egypt has been at all times indebted for its fertility and prosperity, as it provides, in compensation for the almost complete lack of rain in the country, a natural and almost regular irrigation for the lands on its borders and in the delta. It is the foundation of all cultural life and justifies entirely the attribute *mubārak* so often given to the river. On the same account, the Nile is considered, as well as the Euphrates, as a "believing" river (al-Maḳrīzī, ed. Wiet, *MIFAO*, xxx, 218). The flood deeply influences the private and public life of villagers and townsfolk alike, and already the oldest Islamic traditions about Egypt reflect the feelings of wonder and thankfulness that animated the people of Egypt before them (Ibn ʿAbd al-Ḥakam, 109, 205). Having reached its lowest level towards the end of May at Aswan and in the middle of June at Cairo, the Nile begins to rise again, reaching its highest level in the beginning of September at Aswan and in the beginning of October at Cairo. This regularity brings about a similar regularity in the methods of irrigation in the several parts of Egypt, in the times of the sowing and reaping of the different crops and consequently in the modes of levying the land taxes (e.g. al-Maḳrīzī, ed. Būlāḳ, i, 270, which text comes from Ibn Ḥawḳal); all the dates referring to these occupations have always continued to be fixed according to the Coptic solar calendar.

There is much discussion in the literary sources about the causes of the flood. The most ancient belief, which at the same time corresponds best with reality, was that the flood is caused by heavy rainfalls in the countries where the Nile and its tributaries have their origin. This is expressed in a somewhat exaggerated way in a tradition that goes back to ʿAbd Allāh b. ʿAmr b. al-ʿĀṣ, according to which all the rivers of the world contribute, by divine order, with their waters to the flood of the Nile (Ibn ʿAbd al-Ḥakam, *loc. cit.*, and 149). This implies the belief that all other rivers fall while the Nile rises, but, on the other hand, it is sometimes observed that other rivers also show the same phenomenon of rising and falling, especially the Indus, and this again is considered as a proof of the common origin of the two rivers (al-Maḳrīzī, ed. Wiet, *MIFAO*, xxx, 227). There are, however, other views, which attribute the cause of the flood to the movement of the sea, or to the effect of the winds; these views have been inherited from sources of the pre-Islamic period, among others from the treatise on the flood of the Nile attributed to Aristotle, and they are discussed and refuted at length in a special chapter of al-Maḳrīzī's *K͟hiṭaṭ (MIFAO*, xxx, 236 ff.).

Up to the 19th century, the irrigation system of Egypt continued along the same lines. When the flood began, all the outlets on both sides of the main stream and its principal arms in the Delta were closed, to be opened again about the time of the highest flood, when the water level had reached the necessary height according to the different places. The most important of these yearly "openings" was that of the canal (*K͟halīd͟j*) of Cairo, which, until recent times, remained a public festival. In Cairo the flood is complete (*wafāʾ al-Nīl*), when it has reached 16 *d͟hirāʿ*s, generally in the first decade of the Coptic month of Mesore (about the midst of August), and this was proclaimed everywhere in the town (cf. the description by Lane, *Manners and customs*, ch. XXVI, and E. Littmann, *Ein arabischer Text über die Nilschwelle*, in *Festschrift Oppenheim*, Berlin 1933, 66 ff.; cf. for older times, al-Ḳalḳas͟handī, iii, 516).

The height of the level of the Nile has been measured since olden times by the Nilometers [see MIḲYĀS]. Many of these *miḳyās* are recorded by the sources, the southernmost being that of ʿAlwa and the most celebrated the one of al-Fusṭāṭ, constructed by Usāma b. Zayd al-Tanūk͟hī in *ca.* 92/711 and often restored afterwards (a complete survey of all the *miḳyās* is given in Omar Toussoun, *Mémoire sur l'Histoire du Nil*, ii, 265 ff.). These instruments generally were made of stone, with marks upon them, but they were sometimes of other material (e.g. a fig-tree near the monastery of Safanūf in Nubia; cf. Evetts, *Churches*, 262). The level necessary for the operations of irrigation varied in different places; in the capital the average level had to be 16 *d͟hirāʿ*s above the lowest level of the Nile; if the flood surpassed 18 *d͟hirāʿ*s it became dangerous, while a flood not exceeding 12 *d͟hirāʿ*s meant famine (cf. e.g. al-Idrīsī, 145, 146). In the history of Egypt, the years after 444/1052 and especially the year 451/1059 were notorious for the famine and disaster caused by the failure or practical failure of the flood. A historical account of the flood from the years 152-1296/769-1879 is given in Omar Toussoun, *Mémoire sur l'Histoire du Nil*, ii, 454 ff.

The regulation of the main stream and its branches are ascribed to the ancient Egyptian kings (al-Maḳrīzī, on the authority of Ibn Waṣīf S͟hāh), but no real irrigation work of a wider scope existed in the Middle Ages and later except the famous canal system of al-Fayyūm [*q.v.*], which all the sources ascribe to the prophet Yūsuf. In the rest of Egypt the water was allowed to flow freely over the lands after the piercing of the dams, so that large areas were completely inundated for some time; the Arabic sources contain some vivid descriptions of the large stretches of water, above which rose the villages, communication between the villages being only possible by means of boats during that time of the year (al-Masʿūdī, *Murūd͟j*, i, 162-3 = § 778; Ibn ʿAbd al-Ḥakam, 205). From the reign of Muḥammad ʿAlī [*q.v.*] new irrigation works were planned with the aim of making the country more productive, a possibility at which already the mediaeval authors hinted more than once. The first efforts, however, failed. About 1840 was begun the construction of a great barrier across the two arms of the Nile at the apex of the Delta, according to the plans of the French engineer Mouget, but this enterprise began to bear fruit only fifty years later when this barrage project, including the Tawfīḳiyya, Manūfiyya and Buḥayriyya canals, had been completed in 1890. The later great irrigation works were executed higher up the river, such as the great dam and locks at the head of the cataracts near Philae above Aswan in 1902, which was raised again in 1912 and again in 1933. While allowing, on one side, a better regulation of the distribution of Nile water in Egypt, these barrages higher up enabled at the same time a better irrigation of the borders to the south of Egypt. Herewith is connected the enormous barrage of Makwār, near Sennār on the Blue Nile above K͟harṭūm, which permits the irrigation of the region called al-D͟jazīra, between the Blue Nile and the White Nile. This work was finished in 1925 and was completed by a similar barrage on the White Nile (1937), on the Atbara (1964) and on the Blue Nile (1966). In this way, the control of the Nile waters passed to a certain extent out of Egypt itself; it recalls the days of the great famine in 451/1059, when the Egyptians thought that the Nubians were holding up the flood of the Nile. The same problem came up in the 1930s with regard to the new project of constructing a dam on the frontier of the Sūdān and the Belgian Congo, and the question was raised whether this dam would prove a *fāʾida ʿādjila* or a *fāʾida ādjila* for Egypt (cf. the newspaper *al-Balāgh* of 17 March 1934). Since the establishment of the Egyptian Republic in 1953, the most notable change in the Egyptian part of the Nile's course has been the construction (1959-71) of the High Dam (*al-Sadd al-ʿĀlī*) at Aswān, *ca.* 965 km/600 miles upstream from Cairo, with the aim of providing controlled water for irrigation in the lower Nile valley, protection against unusually high floods and the generation of hydroelectric power. The reservation formed behind the barrage, Lake Nasser, stretches 480 km/300 miles upstream well into the Sudan. Whilst there have been great benefits for land reclamation and increased power generation in Egypt, there have on the other hand been indications of some deleterious effects also for the ecology of the Nile valley, such as increased salinisation of the river valley in Lower Egypt and alterations to the water flow in the Sudd region of southern Sudan.

It has already been shown how the flood of the Nile was the occasion of popular festivals such as the opening of the canal of Cairo. But in other respects also, the Nile is connected with traditional customs of a religious character, which are to be traced back through the Greco-Christian period into very ancient times. When the Arabs conquered Egypt, the sacrifice of the "Nile Bride" was still in use; every year a richly apparelled young virgin was thrown into the Nile to obtain a plentiful inundation. According to a tradition first recorded by Ibn ʿAbd al-Ḥakam (150), this custom was abolished by ʿAmr b. al-ʿĀṣ and the Nile resumed its flood after a note of the caliph ʿUmar had been thrown into it requiring the river to rise if the flood was willed by God. In later times, a symbolic offering of a girl called *ʿArūsat al-Nīl* was still practised on the Coptic *ʿĪd al-Ṣalīb* (Norden, *Travels in Egypt and Nubia*, 1757, 63-5); Lane (*Manners and customs*, ch. XXVI) mentions a round pillar of earth, near the dam of the canal of Cairo, which pillar was called *al-ʿArūsa*. Another custom, practised formerly by Christians and Muslims alike, was to bathe in the Nile on the eve of the Epiphany, in memory of the Baptism of Christ (cf. Evetts, *Churches*, 129). Al-Masʿūdī (*Murūdj*, ii, 364-5 = §§ 779-80) describes this festival, which he calls *Laylat al-Ghiṭās*, for the year 330/942. Lane describes the same ceremony, but in his time the Muslims did not take part in it. But bathing in Nile water in general procures *baraka* (cf. W. Blackman, *The Fellāḥīn of Upper Egypt*, 32, with regard to bathing in the Baḥr Yūsuf).

The quality of the Nile water is a matter of discussion in medical treatises. Ibn Sīnā (*al-Ḳānūn fi 'l-ṭibb*, ed. Būlāḳ 1294, i, 98; cited by al-Maḳrīzī) holds that the circumstance that a river flows from south to north has a bad influence on the water, especially when a south wind blows, and on this account he thinks that the abundant praise given to the Nile is exaggerated. The Egyptian physician Ibn Riḍwān (d. 453/1061) says that the Nile water reaches Egypt in a pure state, owing to healthy conditions in the country of the Sūdān, but that the water is spoilt by the impurities that mix with it on Egyptian soil (cited by al-Maḳrīzī, *MIFAO*, xxx, 275 ff.). This same author describes very clearly the turbid condition of the water when the flood begins. He discusses likewise the influence of the Nile on the climate of Egypt and the medicinal properties of its water.

Other authors speak at length of the fauna of the Nile, giving especial attention to the fish. A very long list of fishes is given by al-Idrīsī (16 ff.), with a description of their often curious qualities. The animals most frequently described by the geographers are, however, the crocodiles, and the animal called *saḳanḳūr*, which is said to be the result of a cross between a crocodile and a fish, but which seems to be in reality a kind of skunk.

The possibilities which the Nile afforded for navigation are best seen from the historical sources. Seagoing vessels do not seem ever to have entered its arms, while the traffic on the river was maintained by small craft; various names of Nile boats occur in literature; in the 19th century the vessel called *dhahabiyya* is especially known. In earlier times, the term *zallādj* is used for a Nile boat (al-Kindī, *Kitāb al-Umarāʾ*, ed. Guest, 157; Dozy, *Supplément*, s.v.). The skill of the fishermen in their sailing boats on the lakes in the Delta is often recorded; in shallow places, however, as well as on the inundated lands, boats had to be moved by means of oars or poles. The rapids between Egypt and Nubia were, as nowadays, an insurmountable barrier to river traffic; the loads were conveyed along the shore to the other side of the falls (Ibn Ḥawḳal, ms. Ahmet III, no. 3346, fol. 86).

The cataracts above Aswan for a long time continued to form a barrier to the spread of Islam towards the countries bordering the Nile to the south of Egypt, which forms a curious contrast with the part played by the Nile in the introduction of Christianity into Nubia (cf. J. Kraus, *Die Anfänge des Christentums in Nubien*, diss. Münster 1930). Islam penetrated only slowly into Nubia and became more generally disseminated in the Sūdān only in the 19th century [see NŪBA; SŪDĀN].

Something has been said already about the praises of the Nile and its descriptions in poetical terms, by which this river has contributed to Arabic literature. Al-Maḳrīzī (*loc. cit.*, 270 ff.) cites some fragments of poems in praise of the Nile and its flood; among the poets whom he names are Tamīm b. al-Muʿizz [*q.v.*] (d. 375/985) and Ibn Ḳalāḳis (d. 567/1172). Further, Yāḳūt (i, 592, iv, 865) cites some poems which he attributes to Umaiya b. Abi 'l-Ṣalt; this poet is probably Abu 'l-Ṣalt Umayya b. ʿAbd al-ʿAzīz (d. 528/1134) who wrote a treatise *al-Risāla al-Miṣriyya*, from which also al-Maḳrīzī makes quotations. The earliest Arabic poems on the Nile are probably those found in the *Dīwān* of Ibn Ḳays al-Ruḳayyāt [*q.v.*], the court poet of ʿAbd al-ʿAzīz Ibn Marwān at the beginning of the 8th century. Several treatises have been especially devoted to the Nile. Ibn Zūlāḳ (d. 387/997) says in his *Faḍāʾil Miṣr* ms. arabe no. 1818 of the Bibliothèque Nationale at Paris, fol. 31a) that he has written a book on the importance and the salutary qualities of the Nile, which now seems to be lost. Further, there are a treatise *Tabṣirat al-akhyār fī Nīl Miṣr wa-akhawātihi min al-anhār* (ms. in Algiers; cf. Brockelmann, II², 666), and two short opuscula by Djalāl al-Dīn al-Maḥallī (d. 863/1459) and al-Suyūṭī, which are found together in the ms. Or. 1535 of the British Museum (Rieu, *Suppl.*, no. 1198; Brockelmann, II², 138).

Bibliography: As the aim of the present article is to give only an account of the Nile from the point of view of Islam and its history, it seems superfluous to quote here even the most important modern works and articles belonging to the abundant bibliography of the Nile. The earlier Islamic authors have all been named in the text; the later ones, such as Yāḳūt, ʿAbd al-Laṭīf, Abu 'l-Fidāʾ, al-Ḳalḳashandī, al-Maḳrīzī, al-Suyūṭī (*Ḥusn al-*

muḥāḍara), al-Nuwayrī and others are in most cases a compendium of earlier earlier views and statements. A very important later Islamic source is *al-Khiṭaṭ al-Tawfīḳiyya* by ʿAlī Bāshā Mubārak. The Islamic literary sources have been used in the following works: Else Reitemeyer, *Beschreibung Aegyptens im Mittelalter*, Leipzig 1903, 31-61; J. Maspero and G. Wiet, *Matériaux pour servir à la géographie de l'Egypte*, in *MIFAO*, xxxvi, 215 ff.; and very profusely, Omar Toussoun, *Mémoire sur l'Histoire du Nil*, i, ii, iii, in *Mémoires présentés à l'Institut d'Egypte*, viii, ix, x, Cairo 1925. The last of these three volumes contains a series of cartographical reconstructions. A number of ancient Islamic maps of the Nile are to be found in the *Mappae Arabicae*, ed. K. Miller, Stuttgart 1926-30, and more completely in vol. iii of the *Monumenta cartographica Africae et Aegypti* by Youssouf Kemal; in this same work all the geographical references to the Nile are also to be found in a chronological order.

(J.H. KRAMERS*)

NĪLŪFER KHĀTŪN, wife of the Ottoman sultan Orkhan and mother of Murād I [*q.vv.*], apparently the Greek Nenuphar (i.e. Lotus-flower) (cf. J. von Hammer, *GOR*, i, 59), was the daughter of the lord of Yārḥiṣār (Anatolia, near Bursa; cf. Ḥādjdjī Khalīfa, *Djihān-numā*, 659) and according to one story was betrothed to the lord of Belokoma (Biledjik). ʿOthmān [*q.v.*], the founder of the dynasty which bears his name, is said to have kidnapped and carried her off in 699/1299 and to have destined her to be the wife of his son Orkhan [*q.v.*], then only 12 years old. Idrīs Bitlīsī, and following him Neshrī, tell the story of the rape, but the Byzantine sources make no reference to it. Nīlūfer Khātūn became the mother of Murād I and also of Süleymān Pasha. The river which flows through the plain of Bursa bears the same name, as also does the bridge over it in front of the town and monastery there. The bridge and monastery are said to have been endowed by Nīlūfer Khātūn. Nothing more is known of her life. She was buried beside Orkhan in his *türbe* at Bursa. That Ibn Baṭṭūṭa, ii, 323-4, tr. Gibb, ii, 453-4, really means Nīlūfer Khātūn by Bayalūn Khātūn, which both F. Giese (cf. *ZS*, ii [1924], 263) and F. Taeschner (cf. *Isl.*, xx, 135) think to be obvious, as they take *B.y.lūn* to be a corruption of *N.y.lūf.r*, is, however, by no means proved, because Bayalūn is a name which occurs again in Ibn Baṭṭūṭa for a Byzantine princess (cf. ii, 393-4). Besides, the mention in Ibn Baṭṭūṭa, who paid his respects to the princess at her court in Iznīḳ (*ca.* 740/1339), is very brief. F. Taeschner suggests that Nīlūfer (cf. Pers. *nīlūfar* "water lily" and Greek i.e. λουλούφερον and νούφαρα with the same meaning) has been derived from the Greek. Nīlūfer was and is also popularly known as Lulufer (e.g. in the early Ottoman chronicles) or Ulufer, as in the river Ülfer Čay; cf. F. Taeschner, *op. cit.*, 135-6.

Bibliography: von Hammer, *GOR*, i, 59-60; *Sidjill-i ʿothmānī*, i, 86 (according to Neshrī); F. Taeschner, in *Isl.*, xx, 133-7; *İA*, art. *Nilüfer Hatun* (C.B.). (F. BABINGER)

NĪMĀ YŪSHĪDJ, modern Persian poet, born ʿAlī Isfandiyārī on 11 November 1897 in Yūsh, a village in the Āmul township of Māzandarān, died in 1960. His pen name, Nīmā Yūshīdj, which he later took for himself, and which has come to replace his real name in popular use, described his place affiliation, since Yūshīdj, in the local dialect, means "a native of Yūsh". The poet's father, Ibrāhīm Nūrī, was a farmer and cattleman. Nīmā Yūshīdj's early boyhood was spent in the tribal environment which distinguished the life of his region. He received his initial education in his native village and subsequently went to Tehran where he was enrolled in the Saint Louis High School, an institution operated by Roman Catholic missionaries. From there he graduated on 15 June 1917, acquiring a competent knowledge of the French language. Together with French, he also learned Arabic, which he studied in a separate school. During his school days, he came to know the poet Niẓām Wafā, who was a teacher at the Saint Louis High School, and whose encouragement and guidance initiated Nīmā Yūshīdj into the art of composing poetry.

After his graduation, Nīmā Yūshīdj was in and out of work for several years. The jobs which he held were short-lived, and there were periods when he had no regular employment. His first assignment involved a low-paid job in the Ministry of Finance. Subsequently, he worked as a school teacher, first in Āstārā and afterwards in Tehran. When the journal *Mūsīḳī* came out in early 1939 under the auspices of the Ministry of Education, he was appointed as a member of its editorial board, a position which he held until the journal ceased publication at the end of 1941. To this journal he contributed numerous poems as well as a series of articles dealing with the individual and social basis of creative arts. The articles were later published as a book under the title *Arzish-i aḥsāsāt* ("The value of feelings"). After the suspension of *Mūsīḳī*, Nīmā Yūshīdj remained without work for some years. In 1326/1947-8 he found a job in the printing and publication department of the Ministry of Education. He continued to work in that capacity till the time of his death, which took place in early January 1960.

Nīmā Yūshīdj's writings began to appear in print from 1921. Among the first journals to publish his works were *Naw bahār* and *Ḳarn-i bīstum*. Some of his poems were included in the *Muntakhabāt-i āthār*, a literary anthology published in 1342/1923-4. Until the poet's association with the journal *Mūsīḳī*, his works appeared sporadically. After that, they began to be published on a more regular basis. During the forties and fifties, his poetical works came out in *Payām-i naw, Nāma-yi mardum, Khurūs-i djangī, Andīsha-yi naw, Kawīr*, and several other journals upholding new literary tendencies. A volume of his selected poems appeared in 1955, and a complete edition of his verse was published in 1364/1985-6.

The earliest work of Nīmā Yūshīdj was his long poem *Ḳiṣṣa-yi rang-parīda* ("The pale story"), which was published in 1921. It was composed in the *mathnawī* form, employing the same metre as the one used in Djalāl al-Dīn Rūmī's *Mathnawī*. Its theme was personal, and it showed the poet's involvement with love and its unhappiness, alienation from society, and disgust with city life and its people. In spite of its conventional form and style, the poem represented a departure from the ordinary trend, in that it depicted a new sensibility based upon the Western concept of literary romanticism.

The next important work of Nīmā Yūshīdj, and in fact his masterpiece, was another long poem entitled *Afsāna* ("Myth"). Composed in 1922, it was published partially, soon afterwards, in *Ḳarn-i bīstum*. This poem, which evokes a vague comparison with Alfred de Musset's *Les Nuits*, may be said to have heralded the beginning of modernism in Persian poetry. It contained a dialogue between a lover, dismayed by his experience, and the Myth which consoles him in his sorrow. Besides setting a new example in amatory verse, *Afsāna* was unique for its impressionistic approach to the subject as well as for using an imagery derived from personal observation.

Many of Nīmā Yū<u>sh</u>īdj's poems had a strong social appeal. Notable specimens reflecting this aspect of his verse included *Maḥbas* ("Prison"), *<u>Kh</u>ānwāda-yi sarbāz* ("The soldier's family"), *Āy ādamhā!* ("O you people!"), *Nāḳūs* ("The bell"), *Kār-i <u>sh</u>ab pā* ("The night watchman"), and *Mur<u>gh</u>-i āmīn* ("The amen bird"). Works such as these show a predilection for popular causes, and pro-leftist sympathies could be discerned among them.

Nīmā Yū<u>sh</u>īdj left an unmistakable mark on contemporary trends in Persian poetry. The generation of poets that emerged after the forties recognised him as their leader. One of his most important contributions was his effort to provide Persian poetry with a new formal structure, and he was the first to popularise free verse, which became the major vehicle of expression for future poets.

Bibliography: Nīmā Yū<u>sh</u>īdj, *Madjmūᶜa-yi ā<u>th</u>ār*, i, ed. Sīrūs Ṭāhbāz, Tehran 1364/1985-6; idem, *Nāmahā*, ed. Ṭāhbāz, Tehran 1368/1989-90; idem, *Arzi<u>sh</u>-i aḥsāsāt dar zindigī-yi hunarpī<u>sh</u>agān*, ed. Abu 'l-Ḳāsim Djannatī ᶜAṭāʾī, Tehran 1334/1956; idem, *Nīmā, zindigānī wa ā<u>th</u>ār-i ū*, ed. ᶜAṭāʾī, Tehran 1334/1955; Muḥammad Ḍiyāʾ Ha<u>sh</u>trūdī (ed.), *Munta<u>kh</u>abāt-i ā<u>th</u>ār az nawīsandigān wa <u>sh</u>uᶜarā-yi muᶜāṣirīn*, Tehran 1342/1923-4; *Nu<u>kh</u>ustīn kungra-yi nawīsandigān-i Īrān*, Tehran 1326/1947-8; *Āri<u>sh</u>*, ii (= special issue on Nīmā Yū<u>sh</u>īdj) (Tehran Dī Māh 1340/December 1961-January 1962); Muḥammad Riḍā Lāhūtī (ed.), *Yādmān-i Nīmā Yū<u>sh</u>īdj*, Tehran 1368/1989-90; Munibur Rahman, *Post-revolution Persian verse*, Aligarh 1955; idem, *Nīmā Yū<u>sh</u>ij: founder of the modernist school of Persian poetry*, in *Bulletin of the Institute of Islamic Studies*, iv (Aligarh 1960); F. Machalski, *La littérature de l'Iran contemporain*, ii, Wroclaw-Warszawa-Krakow 1967; J. Rypka *et alii*, *History of Iranian literature*, Dordrecht 1968; H. Pārsā, *Āti<u>sh</u>-i muḳaddas-i Nīmā rā furūzān nigāh dārīm*, in *Payām-i nuwīn*, iii/3 (1339/1960); Yaḥyā Āryānpūr, *Az Ṣabā tā Nīmā*, ii, Tehran 1350/1971; Bahman <u>Sh</u>āriḳ, *Nīmā wa <u>sh</u>iᶜr-i Fārsī*, Tehran 1350/1971; Djalīl Dūst<u>kh</u>ʷāh, *Nīmā Yū<u>sh</u>īdj kīst wa ḥarfa<u>sh</u> čīst*, in *Rāhnamā-yi kitāb*, iv/10 (1340/1961-2); Yad Allāh Ruʾyāʾī, *Siwwumīn sāl-i dargud<u>hasht</u>-i Nīmā Yū<u>sh</u>īdj*, in *Rāhnamā-yi kitāb*, iv/10 (1340/1961-2); ᶜAbd al-ᶜAlī Dast<u>gh</u>ayb, *Nīmā Yū<u>sh</u>īdj (naḳd wa barrasī)*, Tehran 1356/1977; idem, *Nīmā Yu<u>sh</u>idj*, in *Payām-i nuwīn*, iii/6 (1339/1960); Ahmad Karimi-Hakkak, *An anthology of modern Persian poetry*, Boulder, Colo. 1978; Ḥamīd Zarrīnkūb, *Ča<u>sh</u>mandāz-i <u>sh</u>iᶜr-i naw-i Fārsī*, Tehran 1358/1979-80; L. P. Alishan, *Ten poems by Nima Yushij*, in *Literature East and West*, xx (1976), Austin, Texas 1980; Amīr Ḥasan ᶜĀbidī, *Īrān kā bunyād gud<u>h</u>ār-i <u>sh</u>iᶜr-i naw*, in *Hindustānī Fārsī adab*, Delhi 1984; Anwar <u>Kh</u>āmayī, *Čahār čihra*, Tehran 1368/1990.

(Munibur Rahman)

NIᶜMAT ALLĀH b. AḤMAD b. Ḳāḍī Mubārak, known as <u>Kh</u>alīl Ṣūfī, author of a Persian-Turkish dictionary entitled *Lu<u>gh</u>at-i Niᶜmat Allāh*. Born in Sofia, where as an enameller he made a reputation as an artist, he moved to Istanbul and there entered the Naḳ<u>sh</u>bandī order. Association with the Naḳ<u>sh</u>bandī dervishes made him more closely acquainted with literature and especially with Persian poetry. Niᶜmat Allāh decided to make accessible to others the knowledge he had acquired by an ardent study of Persian literature, and thus arose his lexicographical work, which he probably compiled at the instigation and with the assistance of the famous Kemāl Pa<u>sh</u>a-zāde (d. 940/1533 [*q.v.*]). He died in 969/1561-2 and was buried in the court of the monastery at the Edirne gate in Istanbul. His work, which survives in a considerable number of manuscripts, is divided into three parts: verbs, particles and inflection, and nouns. His sources were: 1. *Uḳnūm-i ᶜAdjam* (see Oxford, Bodleian, Uri, 291, no. 108); 2. *Ḳāsima-yi Luṭf Allāh Ḥalīmī* (Ḥādjdjī <u>Kh</u>alīfa, iv, 503); 3. *Wasīla-yi maḳāṣid* (Flügel, *Vienna catalogue*, i, 197); 4. *Lu<u>gh</u>āt-i Ḳarā-Ḥiṣārī* (Rieu, 513a); 5. *Ṣiḥāḥ-i ᶜAdjam* (Ḥādjdjī <u>Kh</u>alīfa, vi, 91 and *Leiden catalogue*, i, 100). Besides making careful use of these sources, Niᶜmat Allāh added much independent material, of which his dialect notes and ethnographical observations are especially valuable. This work is of considerable scientific importance and deserves greater attention than it has so far received.

Bibliography: O. Blau, *Über Niᶜmatullah's persisch-türkisches Wörterbuch*, in *ZDMG*, xxx (1877), 484; Rieu, *Catalogue*, 514b; Ḥādjdjī <u>Kh</u>alīfa, vi, 362. The dictionary was partly used by Golius for the Persian part of Castell's *Lexicon Heptaglotton*. The best mss. are Dorn, *St. Petersburg catalogue*, no. 431 (p. 426) and Fleischer, *Dresden catalogue*, no. 182.

(E. Berthels)

NIᶜMAT ALLĀH b. ḤABĪB ALLĀH HARAWĪ, a Persian historian. His father was for 35 years in the service of the Great Mu<u>gh</u>al Akbar (963-1014/1556-1605) where he was a *<u>kh</u>āliṣa* inspector. Niᶜmat Allāh himself was for 11 years historian to Djahāngīr (1014-37/1605-28), then entered the service of <u>Kh</u>ān-Djahān Lōdī [*q.v.*] whom he accompanied in 1018/1609-10 on the campaign against the Deccan. Soon afterwards he became acquainted with Miyān Haybat <u>Kh</u>ān b. Salīm <u>Kh</u>ān Kākar of Sāmāna, who persuaded him to write a history of the reign of <u>Kh</u>ān-Djahān. Niᶜmat Allāh began his work in Malkāpūr in <u>Dh</u>ū 'l-Ḥidjdja 1020/February 1612 and finished it on 10 <u>Dh</u>u 'l-Ḥidjdja 1021/2 February 1613. The work is dedicated to <u>Kh</u>ān-Djahān, and is entitled *Taʾrī<u>kh</u>-i <u>Kh</u>āndjahānī* and consists of a *muḳaddima*, 7 *bābs* and a *<u>kh</u>ātima*. It deals with the history of the Af<u>gh</u>āns, beginning with their legendary descent from the Banū Ismāᶜīl and treats with special fullness of the history of Bahlūl Lodī, <u>Sh</u>īr <u>Sh</u>āh Sūr and Nawwāb <u>Kh</u>ān-Djahān Lōdī. The last chapters are devoted to the genealogy of the Af<u>gh</u>ān tribes and the reign of Djahāngīr. The *<u>kh</u>ātima* contains biographies of famous Af<u>gh</u>ān *<u>sh</u>ay<u>kh</u>s*. There is also an abbreviated version of the work entitled *Ma<u>kh</u>zan-i Af<u>gh</u>ānī*.

Bibliography: H. Ethé, in *GIPh*, ii, 362-3; Rieu, *Catalogue*, 210a, 212a, 903b; Elliot and Dowson, *History of India*, v, 67-115. The shorter version is translated by B. Dorn, *History of the Afghans: translated from the Persian of Neamet Ullah*, in *Orient. Transl. Fund*, London 1829-36. See also Storey, i, 393-5, 1302; Storey-Bregel, ii, 1209-14.

(E. Berthels)

NIᶜMAT-ALLĀHIYYA, a Persian Ṣūfī order that soon after its inception in the 8th/14th century transferred its loyalties to <u>Sh</u>īᶜī Islam. The Niᶜmat-Allāhiyya first took root in south-eastern Persia where it continued to prosper until the time of <u>Sh</u>āh ᶜAbbās. For the next two centuries it survived only in the Deccani branch that had been established in the 9th/15th century. Reintroduced into Persia with considerable vigour in the early 13th/late 18th century, the Niᶜmat-Allāhiyya became the most widespread Ṣūfī order in the country, a position it has retained until recent times.

1. The founder and the development of his order.

The eponym of the order, <u>Sh</u>āh Niᶜmat Allāh Nūr

al-Dīn b. ᶜAbd Allāh Walī (sometimes designated additionally as Kirmānī, especially in Indian sources) was born in Aleppo, in either 730/1329-30 or 731/1330-1. His father was a *sayyid*, claiming descent from Ismāᶜīl b. Djaᶜfar (which may help to account for the loyalty given the Niᶜmat Allāhī order by several Nizārī *imāms* of the Ḳāsim-Shāhī line), and his mother was descended from the Shabānkāra rulers of Fārs. The stylistic superiority of Niᶜmat Allāh's Persian to his Arabic writings suggests that he must have been brought to a Persian-speaking environment while still a child. In any event, he is recorded to have studied during his early youth in Shīrāz with theologians such as Sayyid Djalāl al-Dīn Khʷārazmī and ᶜAḍud al-Dīn al-Īdjī (d. 756/1355). Niᶜmat Allāh was initiated into Ṣūfism by the well-known Yemeni historian and *muḥaddith*, ᶜAbd Allāh al-Yāfiᶜī (d. 768/1367), whose spiritual lineage went back through three generations to Abū Madyan (d. 590/1194). Niᶜmat Allāh joined al-Yāfiᶜī's circle in Mecca when he was twenty-four years of age, and stayed with him until his death. Most probably it was al-Yāfiᶜī, who frequently described the Ṣūfīs as "kings" in his writings, who bestowed the title of Shāh on Niᶜmat Allāh.

After the death of his master, Niᶜmat Allāh embarked on a long series of travels. These brought him first to Egypt, where he spent a period of retreat in the cave on Mt. Muḳaṭṭam that had been used for the same purpose by the Bektāshī saint Ḳayghūsuz Abdāl [*q.v.*]. He then travelled through Syria and ᶜIrāḳ to Adharbāydjān, meeting in Ardabīl with the progenitor of the Ṣafawids, Shaykh Ṣadr al-Dīn and possibly with Ḳāsim al-Anwār (although the latter can have been little more than an adolescent).

It was in Transoxiana that Niᶜmat Allāh first presented himself as a *murshid* and the propagator of a new order. Conditions there must have appeared propitious, for the Turkic nomads of the area, awaiting Islamisation, offered a vast pool of potential recruits on which other Ṣūfī *shaykhs* were already drawing. It was, however, precisely the extent of Niᶜmat Allāh's success in establishing *khānaḳāhs* in several locations and, more importantly, in recruiting a large number of nomads in the area of Shahr-i Sabz that aroused the suspicion of Tīmūr [*q.v.*] and led to Niᶜmat Allāh's expulsion from Transoxiana. Accounts differ regarding the precise circumstances of his departure; several of them attribute it to the jealousy of Amīr Kulāl (d. 772/1370), the spiritual master of Bahāʾ al-Dīn Naḳshband (J. Aubin, *Matériaux pour la biographie de Shah Niᶜmatullah Wali Kirmani*², 12-15). There is, however, no mention in the sources on Amīr Kulāl of any clash with Niᶜmat Allāh, which could, after all, have been presented in favourable and even triumphant terms. On the other hand, the clearly deliberate omission of Niᶜmat Allāh by the Naḳshbandī ᶜAbd al-Raḥmān Djāmī from his *Nafaḥāt al-uns* may indeed reflect some inherited distaste for the founder of the Niᶜmat-Allāhiyya.

From Transoxiana, Niᶜmat Allāh went first to Ṭūs and then to Harāt, arriving there probably in 774/1372-3. He emerged from a period of seclusion to marry the granddaughter of Amīr Ḥusayn Harawī, a well-known poet, and to engage in agriculture, a pursuit he continued to follow for the rest of his life and to recommend to his disciples as "the true alchemy". At the suggestion of the followers whom he acquired while in Harāt, he moved the following year to Kirmān, an area which may have seemed desirable because of its comparative remoteness from the main centres of power of the day. At first he settled in Kūhbanān, outside the city; it was there that Shāh Khalīl Allāh, his only son, was born. Later he moved to the city itself and then to its suburb of Māhān, leaving the Kirmān area only rarely to visit Yazd, Taft and, in 816/1413-14, Shīrāz, in response to an invitation by Iskandar b. ᶜUmar Shaykh, the Tīmūrid governor of Fārs. Niᶜmat Allāh died in Māhān in 834/1430-1 and was buried in the proximity of the *madrasa* and *khānaḳāh* he had constructed there.

This last period in the life of Niᶜmat Allāh was by far the most fruitful. Apart from his disciples in Kirmān, he had several thousand devotees in Shīrāz, who are said to have included the Ṣūfī poet Shāh Dāᶜī Shīrāzī, the theologian Mīr Sayyid Sharīf Djurdjānī and the gastronome-poet Busḥāḳ-i Aṭᶜima (by contrast, a somewhat later poet, Ḥāfiẓ, is said to have condemned Shāh Niᶜmat Allāh obliquely for his claims to spiritual eminence, in the poem that begins "Might those who transmute the soil with their gaze also glance briefly on us?", *Dīwān*, ed. Ḳazwīnī and Ghanī, Tehran n.d., 132-3).

Shāh Niᶜmat Allāh also wrote profusely; many hundreds of treatises have been attributed to him. Even allowing for exaggeration and misattribution and taking into account the fact that many of the "treatises" are brief notes or communications, the size of Shāh Niᶜmat Allāh's literary corpus remains impressive. His writings include exegetical essays on the Ḳurʾān and the dicta of earlier *shaykhs* and, more importantly, treatises that expound leading themes in the Ṣūfism of Ibn ᶜArabī, especially *waḥdat al-wudjūd*. He also composed a commentary on Ibn ᶜArabī's *Fuṣūṣ al-ḥikam*, claiming that he had been vouchsafed a perfect comprehension of the book by inspiration from the Prophet, just as the author had received the book itself from the same infallible source.

Better known and more widely read than Niᶜmat Allāh's treatises is, perhaps, his *Dīwān*, which consists for the most part of verses expounding *waḥdat al-wudjūd* with a particular emphasis on the impossibility of ontological multiplicity. Despite the manifest influence on Niᶜmat Allāh's poetry of ᶜAṭṭār and Rūmī, his fondness for the technical terminology and conventional symbols of Ṣūfism detracts heavily from the poetic effect of his verse. The most frequently cited poems in his *Dīwān* are those of prophetic or apocalyptic nature which have been interpreted as foretelling events as diverse as the rise of the Ṣafawids, the separation of Bangladesh from Pakistan and the Islamic Revolution in Iran of 1978-9. These verses, the authenticity of at least some of which is open to question, have tended to make of Shāh Niᶜmat Allāh the Persian equivalent of Nostradamus (Browne, *LHP*, iii, 463-73).

There can be little doubt that Niᶜmat Allāh remained a Sunnī throughout his life. His master al-Yāfiᶜī was a Shāfiᶜī, and he himself frequently cited the *ḥadīths* of Abū Hurayra in his works, something unthinkable in a Shīᶜī author. Nonetheless, elements that may have facilitated the later transition of the Niᶜmat-Allāhiyya to Shīᶜism are also to be encountered in his writings. These include a belief in Twelve Poles (*aḳṭāb-i dawāzdah-gāna*) of the spiritual universe and an emphasis on *wilāya* as the inner dimension of prophethood.

Shāh Niᶜmat Allāh Walī was succeeded by his son Shāh Khalīl Allāh, then fifty-nine years of age. Not long after his father's death, he was summoned to the court of the Tīmūrid Shāhrukh in Harāt. According to the hagiographical sources, this invitation was a sign of the monarch's veneration for him, but it is more likely that Shāhrukh sensed a political danger in the strength and number of the Niᶜmat-Allāhīs. That relations between Khalīl Allāh and the ruler were not altogether harmonious is shown by Shāhrukh's refusal to exempt the family lands from taxation. For whatever reason, some time between 836/1432 and 840/1436, Khalīl Allāh decided to leave Persia. Entrusting the shrine at Māhān to one of his sons, Mīr Shams al-Dīn, he departed for the Deccan with his two other sons, Muḥibb al-Dīn Ḥabīb Allāh and Ḥabīb al-Dīn Muḥibb Allāh.

Aḥmad Shāh Bahman, the ruler of the Deccan [see BAHMANIDS], had already sent a delegation to Shāh Niᶜmat Allāh inviting him to settle at Bīdar [*q.v.*] in his kingdom. Formerly a devotee of the Čishtī saint Gīsū darāz, he was searching for a new preceptor, one who might enjoy prestige among the immigrant élite, the so-called Āfāḳīs, on which he was coming increasingly to rely. Shāh Niᶜmat Allāh had refused the invitation, but he sent Aḥmad Shāh a letter of initiation that also granted him the title of *walī*. Some years later, Aḥmad Shāh sent a second delegation to Māhān, this time asking for Khalīl Allāh to be sent to the Deccan. This request, too, was refused, but his grandson Nūr Allāh was sent by way of compensation. Aḥmad Shāh received him with great honour, giving him his daughter in marriage and elevating him over all the indigenous Ṣūfīs by naming him *malik al-mashāyikh*.

Now that Khalīl Allāh had finally come, he and his party were greeted with similar enthusiasm. Although links with Persia were not entirely broken, the leadership of both the Niᶜmat-Allāhī family and order was now to remain in the Deccan for several generations: Khalīl Allāh died in 860/1456, and was succeeded in turn by Ḥabīb al-Dīn; Mīr Shāh Kamāl al-Dīn; Burhān al-Dīn Khalīl Allāh II; Mīr Shāh Shams al-Dīn Muḥammad; Mīr Shāh Ḥabīb al-Dīn Muḥibb Allāh II; Mīr Shāh Shams al-Dīn Muḥammad II; Mīr Shāh Kamāl al-Dīn II; and Mīr Shāh Shams al-Dīn Muḥammad III. The leadership of the Niᶜmat-Allāhī order then passed out of the family to a certain Mīr Maḥmūd Dakkanī. Although the Niᶜmat-Allāhīs retained their influence among the Deccani aristocracy even after the dynasty that had brought them there was replaced by the Ḳuṭb Shāhīs [*q.v.*], they never succeeded in putting down roots among the population at large.

The Niᶜmat-Allāhīs who stayed in Persia initially enjoyed good relations with the Ṣafawids. One of them, Mīr Niẓām al-Dīn ᶜAbd al-Bāḳī, was appointed *ṣadr* by Shāh Ismāᶜīl in 917/1511-12, and subsequently became the *wakīl-i nafs-i humāyūn* (regent). ᶜAbd al-Bāḳī's son mediated between the next Shāh, Ṭahmāsp, and his brother in 956/1549, and the new reign saw several marriages between the Niᶜmat-Allāhī family and the Ṣafawid house. The relationship began to sour in the time of Shāh ᶜAbbās I when one member of the family, Amīr Ghiyāth al-Dīn Mīrmīrān, became involved in an Afshār rebellion in Kirmān. Thereafter, although members of the family continued to hold the posts of *naḳīb* and *kalāntar* in Yazd until at least 1082/1671-2, the Niᶜmat-Allāhiyya seems to have disappeared from Persia as a functioning Ṣūfī order. The only trace left of its existence consisted of the Niᶜmatī gangs that, oblivious to their Ṣūfī origins, waged intermittent warfare with their Ḥaydarī rivals in a number of Persian cities, often with royal encouragement.

The Niᶜmat-Allāhī order was reintroduced into Persia by a certain Maᶜṣūm ᶜAlī Shāh Dakkanī, sent there for the purpose by Riḍā ᶜAlī Shāh Dakkanī (d. 1214/1799), the grandson and second successor of Mīr Maḥmūd Dakkanī. With his ecstatic mode of preaching, Maᶜṣūm ᶜAlī Shāh swiftly gained a large following, particularly in Shīrāz, Iṣfahān, Hamadān, and Kirmān. The resurgent Niᶜmat-Allāhiyya had, however, to confront the hostility of the Shīᶜī *mudjtahids*, newly invigorated by the triumph of the Uṣūlī doctrine which assigned them supreme authority in all religious affairs. Maᶜṣūm ᶜAlī Shāh and several of his followers fell victim to this hostility; he was put to death himself at Kirmānshāh in 1212/1797-8, while *en route* from Nadjaf to Mashhad, by Āḳā Muḥammad ᶜAlī Bihbahānī, a *mudjtahid* popularly known as *ṣūfīkush* ("Ṣūfī killer").

Maᶜṣūm ᶜAlī Shāh's principal companion and disciple was Nūr ᶜAlī Shāh of Iṣfahān, a prolific author in both poetry and prose. His works are replete with theopathic utterances; themes of *ghulāt* Shīᶜism that seem to echo the verse of Shāh Ismāᶜīl; and criticisms of the Shīᶜī *ᶜulamā*ʾ. (The combination of these elements suggests that the renascent Niᶜmat-Allāhiyya of the time had doctrinally little in common with the order as first established by Shāh Niᶜmat Allāh and his immediate descendants.) Particularly provocative of *ᶜulamā*ʾ indignation was, no doubt, Nūr ᶜAlī Shāh's assertion that the Ṣūfī master is the true deputy (*nāʾib*) of the Hidden Imām. Nūr ᶜAlī Shāh accompanied his master on all his journeys except the last, fatal one, dying himself the same year in Mawṣil, allegedly from poison administered by agents of Bihbahānī.

Four years later, Bihbahānī himself died, and the antagonism between the Niᶜmat-Allāhīs and the *ᶜulamā*ʾ began to decline. This development was furthered by the adoption of more circumspect doctrines and attitudes by the Niᶜmat-Allāhīs themselves, which permitted them to establish themselves as a lasting although subordinate element of Persian religious life. No longer seeming subversive, the Niᶜmat-Allāhīs also ceased to arouse the hostility of the Ḳādjār monarchs, one of whom, Muḥammad Shāh, himself became an initiate of the order. The Niᶜmat-Allāhī order was thus able to grow throughout the 13th/19th century. However, as it expanded, it divided into several, often mutually hostile branches, only the more important of which will be mentioned here.

Muḥammad Djaᶜfar Kabūdar-āhangī Madjdhūb ᶜAlī Shāh (d. 1238/1823) was the last leader to exercise undisputed control over the whole order. Three separate claimants to the leadership arose after him: Kawthar ᶜAlī Shāh (d. 1247/1831); Sayyid Ḥusayn Astarābādī; and Zayn al-ᶜĀbidīn Shirwānī Mast ᶜAlī Shāh (d. 1253/1837-8). The first became the eponym of a sub-order known as the Kawthariyya, which has survived down to the present, although with a very small membership; its best-known leader in modern times was Nāṣir ᶜAlī Shāh Malik-niyā (still living in the late 1970s). The line descended from Astarābādī also reached into the 20th century, producing one of the most celebrated Persian Ṣūfīs of recent times, Sayyid Ḥusayn Ḥusaynī Shams al-ᶜUrafāʾ (d. 1353/1935), after whom it is retrospectively known as the Shamsiyya. Its following, too, has generally been very restricted.

The main line of Niᶜmat-Allāhī descent is that which passes through Mast ᶜAlī Shāh. He was the author of several important works refuting the legalistic criticisms that were still being directed against Niᶜmat-Allāhī Sufism (see in particular his *Kashf al-maᶜārif*, Tehran 1350 *Sh.*/1971) and three compendious travelogues, valuable for the detailed information they contain on the Ṣūfīs of diverse affiliations whom Mast ᶜAlī Shāh met in the course of his travels.

After the death in 1278/1861 of Zayn al-ᶜĀbidīn

Raḥmat ᶜAlī Shāh, the successor of Mast ᶜAlī Shāh, a further trifurcation took place, one more serious than the first because it affected the main body of the Niᶜmat-Allāhīs. The first of the three claimants to leadership was Saᶜādat ᶜAlī Shāh Ṭāwūs al-ᶜUrafāᵓ (d. 1293/1876 in Tehran), who is said to have been a Ṣūfī of the traditional ecstatic type, the clarity of whose heart was unclouded by any learning. His successor, Sulṭān ᶜAlī Shāh Gunābādī from Bīdukht in Khurāsān, was a man of quite different type. He studied philosophy with the celebrated Mullā Hādī Sabzawārī before embarking on the Ṣūfī path, and even after beginning to train his own *murīds* he continued to give instruction in the formal religious sciences at his *khānaḳāh* in Bīdukht. He wrote a well-regarded commentary on the Ḳurᵓān of a mystical-philosophical nature, entitled *Bayān al-saᶜāda*. Murdered by an unknown assailant in 1327/1909, he was succeeded by his son, Ḥādjdj Mullā ᶜAlī Gunābādī Nūr ᶜAlī Shāh-i Thānī (d. 1337/1918). This introduction of hereditary succession gave rise to a new sub-order known as the Gunābādī, with reference to the area surrounding Sulṭān ᶜAlī Shāh's place of origin. Ḥādjdj Mullā ᶜAlī was succeeded first by Ṣāliḥ ᶜAlī Shāh (d. 1386/1966) and then by Riḍā ᶜAlī Shāh Tābanda (still living in 1992). Although the Gunābādīs generally eschew the designation Niᶜmat-Allāhī and cannot therefore be regarded as representing the main line of the Niᶜmat-Allāhī order, they have been for several decades the largest single group of Niᶜmat-Allāhī descent in Iran. It is no doubt because of the sober, *sharīᶜa*-oriented nature of their Ṣūfism that they have been able to retain this position even after the establishment of the Islamic Republic.

The Ṣafī-ᶜAlī-Shāhiyya, another offshoot of the Niᶜmat-Allāhī order emerging from the dispute over the succession to Raḥmat ᶜAlī Shāh, developed in a quite different direction. Its eponym, Ḥādjdj Mīrzā Ḥasan Iṣfahānī Ṣafī ᶜAlī Shāh, spent some time in India promoting his father's mercantile interests before returning to Iran and becoming a disciple of Raḥmat ᶜAlī Shāh. On the death of his master, he initially accepted the authority of Munawwar ᶜAlī Shāh, another of Raḥmat ᶜAlī Shāh's disciples, but the following year he declared himself the immediate successor of Raḥmat ᶜAlī Shāh and proclaimed his independence. Like his contemporary and rival, Sulṭān ᶜAlī Shāh Gunābādī, he also wrote a commentary on the Ḳurᵓān, but it was widely criticised, both because of its contents and because it was composed in verse. On Ṣafī ᶜAlī Shāh's death in 1316/1899, the leadership of the order was assumed by Ẓahīr al-Dawla Ṣafā ᶜAlī Shāh, minister of the court and brother-in-law of the ruling monarch, Muẓaffar al-Dīn Shāh; not surprisingly, this gave a somewhat aristocratic complexion to the Ṣafī-ᶜAlī-Shāhiyya. Given the incipient westernising tendencies among the Iranian political élite, it was perhaps natural that a further transformation should also have set in during Ṣafā ᶜAlī Shāh's lifetime. He established a twelve-man committee to supervise the operations of the order which under its new designation *Andjuman-i Ukhuwwat* ("Society of Brotherhood") was effectively transformed into a pseudo-masonic lodge; many of its members were, in fact, also initiates of *Bīdārī-yi Īrān* ("The Awakening of Iran"), the first masonic lodge in Iran affiliated with the French Grand Orient. The society abandoned virtually all the traditional rites of Ṣūfism, but continued to flourish among certain classes until the advent of the Islamic Republic, when its activities were brought to an end, together with those of all other masonic organisations. Its last leader was ᶜAbd Allāh Intiẓām (d. 1982).

It is the line of a third claimant to the succession of Raḥmat ᶜAlī Shāh, Ḥādjdj Muḥammad Āḳā Munawwar ᶜAlī Shāh (d. 1310/1884) that has the best claim to be regarded as the main line of Niᶜmat-Allāhī descent; its adherents continue to designate themselves exclusively as Niᶜmat-Allāhī, although the clarificatory expression "line of Dhu 'l-Riyāsatayn" (an epithet borne by the third successor to Munawwar ᶜAlī Shāh) is sometimes additionally used. Munawwar ᶜAlī Shāh was succeeded in turn by Wafāᵓ ᶜAlī Shāh (d. 1336/1918), Ṣādiḳ ᶜAlī Shāh (d. 1340/1922) and Ḥādjdj Mīrzā ᶜAbd al-Ḥusayn Dhu 'l-Riyāsatayn Muᵓnis ᶜAlī Shāh (d. 1372/1953). A man of wide erudition, Muᵓnis ᶜAlī Shāh enjoyed great respect during the thirty years he directed the order, but its unity could not be maintained on his death. The traditional pattern of discord reasserted itself as thirteen claimants to the succession came forward. The most visibly successful of them was Dr. Djawād Nūrbakhsh, a psychiatrist. He managed to recruit many members of Tehran high society at a time when the profession of a certain type of Ṣūfism was becoming fashionable; to build a whole series of new *khānaḳāhs* around the country; and to publish a large quantity of Niᶜmat-Allāhī literature, including many of his own writings. As the Islamic Revolution of 1978-9 approached victory, Nūrbakhsh left Iran, and he now administers a mixed following of Iranian émigrés and Western converts resident in many cities of Europe and North America.

Bibliography: Nazir Ahmad, *An old Persian treatise of the Bahmani period*, in *IC*, xlvi/3 (July 1972), 209-26; Hamid Algar, *Religion and state in Iran, 1785-1906. The role of the Ulama in the Qajar period*, Berkeley and Los Angeles 1969, 36-40; idem, *Religious forces in eighteenth- and nineteenth-century Iran*, in *Camb. hist. Iran*, vii, 720-4; idem, *The revolt of Agha Khan Mahallati and the transference of the Ismaᶜili Imamate to India*, in *SI*, xxix (1969), 62-5; ᶜA. Anwār, *Anjoman-e Oḳowwat*, in *EIr*; Said Amir Arjomand, *Religious extremism (ghuluww), Sufism and Sunnism in Safavid Iran 1501-1722*, in *Journal of Asian History*, xv (1981), 17-20; J. Aubin, *Matériaux pour la biographie de Shah Niᶜmatullah Wali Kirmani*², Tehran and Paris 1982; ᶜAbd al-Ḥudjdjat Balāghī, *Maḳālāt al-ḥunafāᵓ fī maḳāmāt Shams al-ᶜUrafāᵓ*, 2 vols., n.p., 1369/1950 and 1371/1952; ᶜAṭāᵓ Karīm Barḳ, *Djustudjū dar aḥwāl wa āthār-i Ṣafī ᶜAlī Shāh*, Tehran 1352 *Sh*./1973; Nūr al-Dīn Mudarrisī Čahārdihī, *Sayrī dar taṣawwuf: sharḥ-i haftād tan az mashāyikh wa aḳṭāb-i ṣūfiyya*, Tehran 1359 *Sh*./1980, 13-28, 78-83, 86-101, 124-127; idem, *Sayrī dar taṣawwuf, dar sharḥ-i ḥāl-i mashāyikh wa aḳṭāb*, Tehran 1361 *Sh*./1982, 12-21, 47-63, 132-232, 265-72; idem, *Silsilahā-yi Ṣūfiyya-yi Īrān*, Tehran 1360 *Sh*./1981, 7-63, 140-7, 189-245, 265-307; Farhad Daftary, *The Ismāᶜīlīs: their history and doctrines*, Cambridge 1990, 463, 467, 498, 503-7, 517-18; Ḥamīd Farzām, *Musāfirathā-yi Shāh Niᶜmat-Allāh Walī-yi Kirmānī*, Isfahan 1347 *Sh*./1968; idem, *Shāh Walī wa daᶜwī-yi mahdawīyat*, Isfahan 1348 *Sh*./1969; idem, *Rawābiṭ-i maᶜnawī-yi Shāh Niᶜmat-Allāh Walī bā salāṭīn-i Īrān wa Hind*, Isfahan 1351 *Sh*./1972; idem, *Munāsibāt-i Ḥāfiẓ wa Shāh Walī*, in *Nashriyya-yi Dānishkada-yi Adabiyyāt-i Iṣfahān*, 1345 *Sh*./1966, 1-28; R. Gramlich, *Die schiitischen Derwischorden Persiens, erster Teil: die Affiliationen*, Wiesbaden 1965 (*AKM*, xxxvi/1), 27-69, *zweiter Teil: Glaube und Lehre*, Wiesbaden 1976 (*AKM*, xxxvi/2-4), *passim*, *dritter Teil: Brauchtum und Riten (AKM*, xlv/2), *passim*; idem, *Pol und Scheich im heutigen Derwischtum der Schia*, in *Le Shīᶜisme Imâmite*, ed. Toufic Fahd, Paris 1970, 175-82; Masᶜūd

Humāyūnī, *Tārīkh-i silsilahā-yi ṭarīḳat-i Niᶜmat-Allāhiyya dar Īrān*, 4th ed. London 1992 Sh./1979; idem, *Memoirs of a Sufi Master in Iran*, London 1991; Maᶜṣūm ᶜAlī Shāh, *Ṭarāʾiḳ al-ḥaḳāʾiḳ*, ed. Muḥammad Djaᶜfar Maḥdjūb, Tehran n.d., iii, 1-60, 84-104; W.M. Miller, *Shiᶜa mysticism (the Sufis of Gunābād)*, in *MW*, xiii, 343-63; Mīrzā Ḍiyāʾ al-Dīn Beg, *Aḥwāl wa āthār-i Shāh Niᶜmat-Allāh Walī Kirmānī*, Karachi 1975; M. de Miras, *La méthode spirituelle d'un maître du soufisme iranien*, Paris 1973; Hossein Mirjafari, *The Ḥaydarī-Niᶜmatī conflicts in Iran*, in *Iranian Studies*, xii 3-4 (Summer-Autumn 1979), 135-62; Djawād Nūrbakhsh, *Zindagī wa āthār-i Djanāb-i Shāh Niᶜmat Allāh Walī Kirmānī*, Tehran 1337 Sh./1958; idem, *Masters of the Path: a history of the masters of the Nimatullahi Sufi order*, New York 1980; idem, *The Nimatullāhī*, in *Islamic spirituality: manifestations*, ed. S.H. Nasr, New York 1991, 144-61; Nasrollah Pourjavady and P.L. Wilson, *Kings of Love. The history and poetry of the Niᶜmatullāhī Sufi order of Iran*, Tehran 1978; eidem, *The descendants of Shāh Niᶜmatullāh Walī*, in *IC*, xlviii/1 (January 1974), 49-57; eidem, *Ismāᶜīlīs and Niᶜmatullāhīs*, in *SI*, xli (1974), 113-35; Ismāᶜīl Rāʾīn, *Farāmūshkhānah wa frāmāsūnrī dar Īrān*, Tehran 1357 Sh./1978, iii, 480-505; J. Rypka, *Dans l'intimité d'un mystique iranien*, in *L'Âme de l'Iran*, ed. R. Grousset, H. Massé and L. Massignon, Paris 1951, 181-200; Muhammad Suleman Siddiqi, *The Bahmani Sufis*, New Delhi n.d., 78-85, 155-62; ᶜAbd al-Ḥusayn Zarrīnkūb, *Dunbāla-yi djustudjū dar taṣawwuf-i Īrān*, Tehran 1362 Sh./1983, 189-200, 317-32, 336-47. (Hamid Algar)

2. Niᶜmat Allāh and his family at the Bahmanī court of South India.

When Khalīl Allāh b. Niᶜmat Allāh arrived in the Bahmanī capital Bīdar after his father's death in 834/1431, he established there a *khānḳāh* for his kinsfolk and followers, and his own tomb (*čawkhandī*) became a prominent landmark near the royal tombs, where many of his descendants still live. The Bahmanī sultan Aḥmad Shāh's own tomb is liberally embellished with extracts from the *dīwān* and other writings of Niᶜmat Allāh (the texts are given *in extenso*, with translations, in G. Yazdani, *Bidar, its history and monuments*, Oxford 1947, 115-28, with some illustrations on Pls. LXIX-LXXIV).

The tomb of Niᶜmat Allāh at Māhān, some 20 miles/36 km south-east of Kirmān in eastern Persia, was erected in 840/1437 by Aḥmad Shāh Bahmanī's orders, although the splendid dome dates from the time of the Ṣafawid Shāh ᶜAbbās I and the minarets at the entrance are from the early Ḳādjār period.

Bibliography: See also R.M. Eaton, *The Sufis of Bijapur 1300-1700*, Princeton 1978, 56 ff.; H.K. Sherwani, *The Bahmanis of the Deccan*², Delhi 1985, 133-4. Sherwani's accounts differ slightly from those in Yazdani, *Bidar*, and are based on fuller information. (J. Burton-Page)

NIᶜMAT KHĀN, called ᶜĀLĪ, Mīrzā Nūr al-Dīn Muḥammad, son of Ḥakīm Fatḥ al-Dīn Shīrāzī, a Persian author, was born in India and came of a family several of whom had been distinguished physicians in their ancestral home in Shīrāz. He entered the service of the state under Shāh-Djahān (1037-68/1628-57) and was appointed keeper of the crown jewels with the title of *dārūgha-yi djawāhir-khāna*. He attained his highest honours under Awrangzīb (1069-1118/1659-1707), who gave him the title of Niᶜmat Khān (1104/1692-3), which was later changed to Muḳarrab Khān and then to Dānishmand Khān. He died at Dihlī on 1 Rabīᶜ II 1122/30 May 1710. Niᶜmat Allāh, who wrote under the *takhalluṣ* of ᶜĀlī, was exceedingly prolific and wrote a number of works in prose and verse, of which the following are the most important: 1. *Waḳāʾiᶜ-i Ḥaydarābād*: a description of the siege of Ḥaydarābād by Awrangzīb in 1097/1685-6. This work is characterised by a biting wit and describes the siege in a satirical form, which procured the little book the greatest popularity; 2. *Djang-nāma*, a chronicle which covers the last years of Awrangzīb's reign and the war which broke out after his death among his sons; 3. *Bahādur-Shāh-nāma*, a chronicle of the first two years of the reign of Shāh ᶜĀlam Bahādūr-Shāh (1119-24/1707-12); 4. *Ḥusn u ᶜIshḳ*, also called *Katkhudāyī* or *Munākaḥa-yi Ḥusn u ᶜIshḳ*, an allegorical love story, an imitation of the celebrated *Ḥusn u Dil* of Fattāḥī [*q.v.*]; 5. *Rāḥat al-ḳulūb*, satirical sketches of a number of contemporaries; 6. *Risāla-yi hadjw-i ḥukamāʾ*, anecdotes of physicians and their incompetence; 7. *Khān-i niᶜmat*, a work on cookery; 8. *Ruḳaᶜāt*, letters to Mīrzā Mubārak Allāh Irādat Khān Wāḍiḥ, Mīrzā Muḥammad Saᶜīd, the head of the imperial kitchen, and others, which were very highly thought of as models of a choice style of letter writing; 9. a lyrical *Dīwān*; 10. a short *Mathnawī* without a title, which deals with the usual Ṣūfī ethical themes. This survey shows a great versatility on the part of Niᶜmat Khān, but it must be pointed out that, with the exception of the satirical works which are really original and of great value for the characterisation of his age, none of them rises above the level of pale imitations of classical models.

Bibliography: H. Ethé, in *GIPh*, ii, 334, 336-8; Rieu, *Catalogue*, 268a, 702b, 703a, 738b, 744b, 745a, 796a, 807a, 938b, 1021a, 1049b; *Dīwān*, lith. Lucknow 1881; *Ḥusn u ᶜIshḳ*, Lucknow 1842, 1873, 1878-80, 1899, Dihlī 1844 (almost all editions have a commentary); *Waḳāʾiᶜ-i Ḥaydarābād* or *Waḳāʾiᶜ-i Niᶜmat Khān*, lith. Lucknow 1844, 1848, 1859, Cawnpore 1870, 1878; *Bahādur-Shāh-nāma*, in Elliot and Dowson, *History of India*, vii, 568; *Djang-nāma*, in *ibid.*, vii, 202, English tr., *An English translation of Niamat Khan Ali's Jang Nama. With.... a short sketch of the author's life*, Chandra Lall Gupta and Angra Lall Varma, Agra 1909; *Ruḳaᶜāt wa muḍḥikāt*, Lucknow 1845. A ms. of the *Khān-i Niᶜmat* in Pertsch, *Berlin catalogue*, no. 341. See also Storey, i, 589-92, 600, 1172, 1318. (E. Berthels)

NIMR, Fāris, Syro-Lebanese journalist, scientist and politician, born in Ḥasbayyā, South Lebanon, in 1855 to an Arab Orthodox family, died in 1951. He studied Arabic, English, German and mathematics in Jerusalem, Mount Lebanon and Beirut. In 1870 he entered the Syrian Protestant College (SPC, subsequently renamed the American University of Beirut), and graduated with a Bachelor degree in Arts and Science. In 1874 he was appointed assistant to the American missionary Dr Cornelius Van Dyck (1818-95) in the Astronomical Observatory at SPC, and taught subjects such as Latin, chemistry and astronomy. During the same year, and after his conversion to Protestantism, he joined the Beirut Masonic Lodge, becoming eventually its Master. Together with four other Christians he formed in 1875 a secret society which agitated for Syrian independence within the Ottoman empire by means of posting anonymous placards in Beirut and other Syrian cities.

In 1876 Fāris Nimr and his colleague at the SPC Yaᶜḳūb Ṣarrūf (1852-1927) began to publish, under the patronage of Van Dyck, the famous scientific magazine *al-Muḳtaṭaf*. His adoption of Darwinism under the influence of Dr Edwin R. Lewis (d. 1907), a chemistry teacher at the SPC, seems to have alienated various influential individuals and institutions, including the Board of Trustees of his college. Consequently, in 1885 the SPC terminated his contract and that of his colleague Ṣarrūf. This decision prompted both Nimr and Ṣarrūf to transfer their magazine to Cairo.

Once in Egypt, Nimr was received with open arms by British and Egyptian officials. In 1888 he married the daughter of the British Consul in Alexandria, and one year later he founded a daily evening paper, *al-Muḳaṭṭam*. Subsidised by the British Agency in Cairo, *al-Muḳaṭṭam* accepted the principle of the British occupation of Egypt while criticising at the same time the details of certain policies and attitudes connected with European influence. His editorship of *al-Muḳaṭṭam* and that of *The Sudan Times*, an English and Arabic bi-weekly founded in 1903, consumed much of his time and energy, forcing him to give up his work in *al-Muḳtaṭaf*.

In 1907 Nimr announced the foundation of a new political organisation, the Liberal National Party. Its main aim was to refute the nationalist ideas of the Egyptian leader Muṣṭafā Kāmil (1874-1908 [*q.v.*]), but this was a short-lived and marginal episode in his career. Nimr continued the publication of his newspapers until his death in 1951. The new régime of the Free Officers closed down both *al-Muḳaṭṭam* and *al-Muḳtaṭaf* in 1952.

Bibliography: Nadia Farag, *Al-Muqtataf 1876-1900: a study of the influence of Victorian thought on modern Arabic thought*, PhD thesis, Oxford 1969, unpubl., 42-118; Ph. de Tarrāzī, *Taʾrīkh al-Ṣaḥāfa al-ʿarabiyya*, i, Beirut 1913, 138-42; G. Antonius, *The Arab awakening*, London 1938, 79-89; Z. Zeine, *The emergence of Arab nationalism*, Delmar, N.Y. 1976, 51-4. (Y.M. Choueiri)

NIMRŪD, a ruined site of ancient Assyria, now in northern ʿIrāḳ some 30 km/20 miles south of al-Mawṣil [*q.v.*] in lat. 36°5′N. and long. 43°20′E.

The ruins on the plateau of Nimrūd are those of the ancient Assyrian city of Kalkhū, apparently mentioned in Gen. x. 11-12 as Calah. It is mentioned in Syriac sources, but the mediaeval Islamic geographers mention it only incidentally and under differing names; thus Yāḳūt, i, 119, iii, 113, says that al-Salāmiyya is in the vicinity of the ruins of the town of Athūr, which can only mean the ruins of Kalkhū. The modern name Nimrūd for the site appears first in Niebuhr, who was in al-Mawṣil in 1776, and the name is probably modern, being associated in the popular local mind with the legendary hunter Nimrod first mentioned in Gen. x. 8-9 and connected in Muslim legend, as in the Haggada, with Abraham [see namrūd].

The ziggurat at Nimrūd is one of the most impressive landmarks in northern ʿIrāḳ and the recent discovery (in 1988 and 1989) of more than one thousand items of gold jewellery (earrings, necklaces, brooches, armlets and other items) has revived the flames of popular interest in what was already considered to be one of the most important cities of ancient Assyria. It was first built as an alternative capital to Ashur by the 13th century king Shalmaneser I after he had viciously reasserted his political authority in the land of Urartu (southern Armenia). But sited as it was at the important confluence of the Upper Zāb and the Tigris, it was naturally developed by later Assyrian kings as their main residence. Ashurnasirpal (883-859) moved there from Ashur, providing a water supply from the river and a sewerage system. He settled there people from many different parts of his empire and developed parkland. His successors all contributed to extensions and improvements there. Here lived Sammurammat, the queen of Shalmaneser III (858-824 B.C.) made famous in Greek traditions as Semiramis, and the recently discovered gold belonged to Yabay, the queen of Tiglath-Pileser III (744-727), Banitu, the queen of Shalmaneser V (726-722) and Ataliya, the queen of Sargon II (721-705). Amidst the archives associated with the great temple of Nabu (in Greek Nebo, the god of knowledge) and his consort Tashmetum, which was called Ezida, "the house of truth", there was found the "will of Esarhaddon (680-669), a document in which he decrees that after his death one of his sons should become king of Babylon, and the other, Ashurbanipal, the king of Assyria. In fact, Ashurbanipal was the last king to control Assyria and Nimrūd was overthrown by the revolutionary forces before the final attack on Nineveh brought the Assyrian empire to an end. The two hundred letters found in the archives are an important addition to our knowledge of Assyrian statecraft.

From the ruins excavators have retrieved many marvellous limestone reliefs which decorated the inner walls of the palace rooms most of which, along with those from Khorsābād [*q.v.*] and Nineveh [see nīnawā], have found their way to museums in the West (especially the British Museum). Fragments of beautifully glazed bricks (which presuppose a sophisticated knowledge of industrial chemistry using tin-glaze) dating back to the 9th century have also been found. The site has provided the largest collection of carved ivory which was worked by expatriate Phoenician craftsmen resident (probably obligatorily) in what must have been one of the major artistic centres of the time in the Fertile Crescent. The life-sized female mask exquisitely carved from one piece of ivory is especially famous.

The importance of the site was recognised by the 19th century British excavator Layard, who dug there in 1845-51, but the archaeological work of Mallowan, who followed his footsteps in this century from 1949 to 1958, has been much more thoroughly recorded. Bronze saddlery fittings and Aramaic mason's marks which have been found confirm that there is still much more to be learned about the position of foreign workmen at the site.

Bibliography: M.E.L. Mallowan, *Nimrud and its remains* 2. vols. and suppl., London 1966; Muzahim Mahmud and J. Black, *Recent work at the Nabu temple, Nimrud*, in *Sumer*, xliv (1985-6), 135-55. For older bibl., see M. Streck, *EI*[1] art. s.v.

(M.E.J. Richardson)

NIMS (a.), masculine noun (pl. *numūs*, *numūsa*) denoting the ichneumon or Egyptian mongoose (*Herpestes ichneumon*), a small carnivore of the family Viverridae, native to Africa and common in Egypt, Morocco and Palestine. In Egypt, with the geographical sub-species *pharaonis*, the ichneumon was called "Pharaoh's rat" (*faʾr Firʿawn*) and sometimes "Pharaoh's cat" (*ḳiṭṭ Firʿawn*), since in the time of the Pharaohs it enjoyed a sacred status and was embalmed after its death. In the Maghrib there is the sub-species *numidicus* (Moroccan Berber *sarrū*, Kabyle *izirdi*, Tunisian *zīrda*). In the Aïr district of the Sahara there is the sub-species *phoenicurus saharae* and, in the rest of Africa, the sub-species *albicaudus* (white-tailed). Persia is the home of the sub-species *persicus* or *auropunctatus*, which is given the Arabic name *djuraydī 'l-nakhl* "palm-tree rat" in ʿIrāḳ. Afghānistān and India have the sub-species *griseus* or *mongo* (Indian mongoose) and *edwardsi*.

For the Greeks, Aristotle and Herodotus (*History*,

ii, 67) had already mentioned the ichneumon (ἰχνεύμων "which follows the trail of the crocodile") as a major domestic destroyer of the rodents and reptiles infesting the households of Egypt as well as of the eggs of the crocodile. Aristotle gives details (*History of animals*, Fr. tr. J. Tricot, Paris 1957, ii, 453, 601) of the stratagem used by this mongoose when biting a snake to death; it rolls beforehand in slippery clay so that the reptile cannot take a grip on its body which it tries in vain to enwrap.

On the other hand, al-Djāḥiẓ describes, quoting an anonymous source (*Ḥayawān*, iv, 120) another tactic of the ichneumon which belongs to fable. At the approach of the snake, the wily mongoose huddles itself up, emptying its lungs as far as possible, and plays dead; the reptile wraps itself around its body to choke it and, abruptly, the mongoose takes a deep breath to inflate its rib-cage, which has the effect of breaking the snake into several pieces like an over-tensed spring.

After al-Djāḥiẓ, the few Arab authors who have mentioned the ichneumon confine themselves to repeating these accounts; this is true in the case of Ibn al-Faḳīh al-Hamadhānī (3rd/9th century) (Fr. tr., *Abrégé*, 76, 252), of al-Masʿūdī (4th/10th century) (*Murūdj*, ii, 57 = § 492) and of al-Damīrī (*Ḥayāt*, ii, 365). However, there is no doubt that the ichneumon was useful in Egypt, and because of the ease with which it was tamed it successfully played the role of the domestic cat; tradesmen, watchmen and caretakers could not dispense with this valued ally which rid them of unwanted guests—rodents and reptiles being especially abundant in the humid regions of Lower Egypt. The only precaution to be taken with this mongoose was to deny it any access to chicken coops and dovecotes, for the safety of their occupants and of their eggs.

The extreme vigilance of this small carnivore passed into metaphor and it was said of someone who had sharp eyesight *ʿaynuhu ka-ʿayn al-nims* "he has the eye of an ichneumon". To describe somebody as *nims* was to express admiration for his great perspicacity.

In some parts of the Islamic world such as the Maghrib and Lebanon, the term *nims* has been erroneously applied to the weasel (*Mustela nivalis* [see IBN ʿIRS]). According to fable, both these creatures enter the stomach of the crocodile, when it is sunbathing, to devour its entrails, not being content with stealing its eggs, like those of turtles, snakes and birds. As a result of similar confusion, some Arabic dialects employ *nims* to identify various other members of the sub-family Mustelidae such as the stone-marten (*Martes foina*), the polecat (*Mustela putorius*) and the ferret (*Mustela putorius furo*); the term is even found erroneously applied to that other viverrine, the civet (*Genetta genetta*). As for the two expressions *ḳūr* and *lashak* which Dozy attributes to the ichneumon (*Supplément*, s.vv.), one is found in a manuscript of the Escurial and the other in al-Idrīsī, where the context is the topic of the crocodile; they do not seem to have any connection with the mongoose.

As is the case with every animal studied, al-Damīrī does not fail to list the specific qualities of various organs of the ichneumon. Thus if a dovecote is fumigated with the burning tail of an ichneumon, all the pigeons are put to flight irrevocably. The spleen mixed with the white of an egg is an excellent eyewash, curing conjunctivitis. A *ḳirāṭ* of blood diluted in a woman's milk and poured into the nose of a lunatic restores his reason. A broth made from the animal's penis and taken as a drink cures retention of urine. The right eye wrapped in linen reduces the four-day fever of an invalid; on the other hand, in the same conditions, the left eye causes the recurrence of this fever. An ointment based on mashed brain mixed with horse-radish juice and oil of rose is a violent irritant of the skin, the equal of scabies; only a mixture of the animal's excrement with oil of jasmine can suppress its noxious effect. Finally, the same excrement diluted in water and swallowed plunges the drinker into agony and into terror of demons which he imagines are in pursuit of him.

In botany, the Arabic name of the ichneumon is given to two plants: (a) *al-nims* is, in the Maghrib, Downy koelaria (*Koelaria pubescens*) a graminaceous plant related to Fescue grass (*Festuca*); (b) *biṭṭīkh nims* "ichneumon melon" or *biṭṭīkh ʿayn al-nims* "ichneumon's eye melon" is a nickname given to the watermelon (*Citrullus vulgaris*, of the variety *ennemis*).

Bibliography (by alphabetical order of authors): Damīrī, *Ḥayāt al-ḥayawān al-kubrā*, Cairo 1928-9, s.v.; Djāḥiẓ, *Kitāb al-Ḥayawān*, Cairo 1938-45; E. Ghaleb, *al-Mawsūʿa fī ʿulūm al-ṭabīʿa. Dictionnaire des sciences de la nature*, Beirut 1965, s.v.; Ibn al-Faḳīh al-Hamadhānī, *Abrégé du livre des pays*, tr. H. Massé, Damascus 1973; A. ʿĪsā, *Muʿdjam asmāʾ al-nabāt. Dictionnaire des noms des plantes*, Beirut 1981, 50; A. Lakhdar-Ghazal, J.P. Farouat, M. Thévenot, (Albums didactiques) *Faune du Maroc* (*les mammifères*), Rabat 1975, 43; L. Lavauden, *Les Vertébrés du Sahara*, Tunis 1926, 189; A. al-Maʿlūf, *Muʿdjam al-ḥayawān. An Arabic zoological dictionary*, Cairo 1932, s.v. *Herpestes*; H. Eisenstein, *Einführung in die arabische Zoographie. Das tierkundliche Wissen in der arabisch-islamischen Literatur*, Berlin 1990, index, s.n. Ichneumon-nims.

(F. VIRÉ)

NĪNAWĀ. 1. An extensive area of ruins in northern ʿIrāḳ, on the left bank of the Tigris and opposite the city of al-Mawṣil [*q.v.*]. Where the river Khawsar joins the Tigris was a natural place to build a city and those early settlers of the seventh millennium spawned the greatest metropolis of Ancient ʿIrāḳ. Sedimentation has now moved the main course of the Tigris more than a kilometre westwards. In 1932 R. Campbell Thompson dug a pit 30 m deep from the top of the mound to virgin soil. At the lowest level he found obsidian flints from Southern Armenia (Van) and later pottery can be traced to Southern ʿIrāḳ (Uruk, Halaf and Ur types are represented). It seems always to have been a place where different cultures easily met, so when Sennacherib, who had campaigned far and wide to extend his empire, laid out the walls of his great city containing a "palace with no equal", he was building in a long tradition.

Epigraphic and archaelogical research of the last decades has shown that it must have measured 180 x 190 m and contained 80 rooms, many of which were lined with beautifully carved limestone reliefs depicting and recording his domination of the surrounding nations. To walk all round the walls means a journey of 12 km, and access was through one of fifteen large gates. Tariq Madhloum's excavations of one of them have shown it to be an extremely elaborate construction with an arched ramp crossing two watercourses. Sennacherib had brought water from the hills to the city by constructing an aqueduct at Jerwan 40 km away. Later kings continued to build, but many of their splendid monuments were ruined once and for all when the military alliance led by Babylon smashed and burned their way through the city in 612 B.C. to mark the end of the Assyrian Empire and the beginning of the Babylonian.

It is very easy to reach the site across the river from al-Mawṣil and the visitor will notice two important areas. The first, Ḳoyundjiḳ, was an old Yazīdī village whose inhabitants were massacred in 1836; it has also been known as al-Ḳalʿa "the citadel". Here Layard began his excavations on behalf of the British Museum from 1845-51 and found the rich library of Ashurbanipal; it was shipped to London and still today it represents one of the richest archives we have of Sumerian and Akkadian literature. Because it contained many late copies of important historical, religious and scientific literature it provides special opportunities to study how texts were transmitted in the scribal circles of the ancient Near East. The other important area is Nabī Yūnus where Esarhaddon carried out building works. This place has a rich aetiological tradition with the prophet Yūnus (Jonah), whose mission to convert the terrible Assyrians was accomplished because God brought him there in the "belly of the great fish", and is mentioned in Jewish, Christian and Muslim sources [see YŪNUS]. Hence both a monastery and then a mosque were in turn built on the ancient mound, known as Tall al-Tawba "hill of repentance". The tomb of Nabī Yūnus has long been the most esteemed shrine of northern ʿIrāḳ, much visited by Sunnīs, and the large modern cemetery on the east of the mound continues the old tradition of corpses being brought there for burial. Outside the eastern wall of the former city is the sulphurous thermal spring known as ʿAyn Yūnus and visited by pilgrims for its curative powers; and some local inhabitants perpetuate the tradition that the "great fish" is buried at Ḳoyundjiḳ.

Bibliography: Le Strange, *Lands*, 87-9; R. Campbell Thompson and R.W. Hutchinson, *A century of exploration at Nineveh*, London 1929; T. Jacobsen and Seton Lloyd, *Sennacherib's aqueduct at Jerwan*, Chicago 1935; Government of Iraq, Directorate-General of Antiquities, *Nineveh and Khorsabad, a note on the ruins for visitors*, Baghdād 1943. (M.E.J. RICHARDSON)

2. A place in central ʿIrāḳ, after which a district (*nāḥiya*) was named, to which Karbalāʾ [*q.v.*] belonged (cf. Yāḳūt, iv, 470). Nīnawā is frequently mentioned in the history of the Muslim wars of the first three centuries of the Hidjra: e.g. in connection with the tragedy of Karbalāʾ of 61/680 when al-Ḥusayn met his death (al-Ṭabarī, ii, 287, 307, 309), in 122/739 in connection with the fighting with the ʿAlid Zayd b. ʿAlī ([*q.v.*] and Ṭabarī, ii, 1710), in the account of the subjection of a later ʿAlid rebel in 251/865 (al-Ṭabarī, iii, 1620, 1623; Ibn al-Athīr, vii, 110), and lastly in the history of the Ḳarmaṭian troubles in 287/900 (al-Ṭabarī, iii, 2190). Nīnawā (Ninā, Ni-na-a) is mentioned in old Babylonian inscriptions as a place not very far from Babylon (cf. e.g. *ZA*, xv, 217). It is not to be confused with a place of the same name mentioned in old Babylonian cuneiform inscriptions as a suburb or quarter of the South Babylonian Lagash (the modern ruins of Telloh). On the Nineveh in Babylonia of the cuneiform inscriptions, see Hommel, *Grundriss der Gesch. u. Geogr. des alten Orients*, Munich 1904-26, 392-3 and *passim* (consult the Index, 1083, s.v. Ni-ná-a or Ninua). According to A. Musil, *The Middle Euphrates*, New York 1927, 43, 44, the site of Nīnawā is marked by the mound of ruins called Ishān Nainwa, below the modern town of Musayyib, 2 miles east of the Euphrates and about 20 north-east of Karbalāʾ, in 32°45′N. (see Musil's map).

Bibliography: Given in the article.

(M. STRECK)

NING-HSIA, a Muslim autonomous region in Northwest China under the People's Republic of China.

The province of Ning-hsia was created in 1929 separately from the province of Kansu [*q.v.*] under Republican China. After the PRC was established in 1954, the greater part of Ning-hsia province was incorporated into Inner Mongolia (Nei-Mengku) and the central part was newly-raised to the status of Ning-hsia Hui-tsu Autonomous Region in 1958, with its present boundaries redrawn in 1976. This Region is situated along the middle reaches of the Yellow River and its tributaries, and it borders on Inner Mongolia in the north, on Kansu in the west and southeast, and on Shen-hsi in the east. The capital is at Yin-chʻuan.

Ning-hsia is the most densely-populated region of *Hui-tsu* ("Islamic race") in the PRC. Its population is 3,895,500, of which *Hui-tsu* number 1,235,207, forming about one-third of the total population (1982 statistics). The origin of the Ning-hsia Muslims goes back to 13th century Yüan times, when the Mongol dynasty ruled China and when many Muslims emigrated from West and Central Asia to the Ning-hsia region. They were soon naturalised, as was also the case in other provinces, and consequently, communities of *Hui-min* or *Hui-tsu*, that is Chinese-speaking Muslims, were formed. Historical materials show that there were many Muslims there since early Ming times down to Chʿing times (15th-19th centuries), and they had regional relations with co-religionists of Kansu, Chʻing-hai and Sinkiang. Ning-hsia Muslims are traditionally Sunnīs of the Ḥanafī school, and among them there have always been a number of Ṣūfī groups, such as the Djahriyya (a branch of the Naḳshbandiyya [*q.v.*]), the Khafiyya or Khufiyya, Ḳādiriyya, Ikhwān, etc., and they still prevail among present-day Ning-hsia Muslims. These last have now more than 1,400 *masdjids* (*chʻing-chen ssu*), distributed over the region, and a class of religious leaders including *ahongs*, *khalīfas*, *mullās*, *murshids*, etc. Ning-hsia was the headquarters of Ma Hua-lung's [*q.v.*] Northwest Hui Rebellion (1862-77), and his successors have been leaders of the Djahriyya order of Ning-hsia until the present time; but Ning-hsia Muslims now coexist with the Han Chinese under the PRC régime.

Bibliography: R. Israeli, *Muslims in China. A study in cultural confrontation*, London and Malmö 1980; Mien Wei-lin, *Ning-hsia Issu-lan chiao-pai kai-yao* ("An outline of the Islamic factions of Ning-hsia"), Yin-chʻuan 1981; Li Kʻai-hsün *et alii* (eds.), *Ning-hsia Hui-tsu tzu-chih-chʻü kai-kʻuang* ("An outline of Ning-hsia Hui-tsu Autonomous Region"), Yin-chʻuan 1986; D.C. Gladney, *Muslim Chinese. Ethnic nationalism in the People's Republic*, Cambridge, Mass. and London 1991, 120-2, 160-2. (T. SAGUCHI)

NĪRANDJ (A.), derived from Persian *nayrang, nīrang*, pl. *nīrandjāt, nīrandjiyyāt* (Ibn Sīnā, ms. Paris; Brockelmann, S I, 828), *nārandjiyyāt* (al-Djināʿī, ms. Strasbourg 4212, fol. 102b), designates, in the two languages, the operations of white magic, comprising prestidigitation, fakery and counter-fakery, the creating of illusions and other feats of sleight-of-hand (*ḥiyal*). A certain al-Ḥasan b. Muḥammad al-Iskandarī al-Kūshī al-ʿAbdarī described the whole set of these operations in his work *Fi 'l-ḥiyal al-bābiliyya li 'l-khizāna al-kāmiliyya* (ms. Bursa, Haraççioğlu 1221, ff. 119, 18.5 x 14 cm, *naskhī*, copied in 881/1476 from another ms. of the same *Khizāna* dated 632/1234). Both author and work are virtually unknown, and it seems useful to give here the titles of the chapters, as already given by the present author in *Sources orientales*, vii, Paris 1966, 184-5:

I. The principles of this art; how to get to know it; appreciation of its subtlety and finesse.
II. Tricks involving the air and atmospherical vapours.
III. Lamps and wicks; description of them in seances.
IV. Tricks with fire and the illusions produced in the minds of the spectators.
V. The making of talismans and the trickery involved in the conjuration of spirits.
VI. Bottles; the devices and tricks that can be done with them.
VII. Cups and glasses; the satisfaction which they can bring about.
VIII. Eggs; devices and tricks in their usage.
IX. The sowing of seed, germination and fruits outside their seasons.
X. Wax effigies; their putting together, taking apart and reconstitution.
XI. The taming of animals by means of traps on terra firma, and by fishing in the sea.
XII. The concealment of hidden objects and the ruses used to uncover thefts.
XIII. Enthusiasm for the manual arts and the transformation of colours and dyes.
XIV. Writing, the preparation of the ink well (read *layḳ* and not *līḳ*, the black powder of collyrium), the removal of writing and the colour of the paper.
XV. The natural characteristics and the distinction between drunkenness and sleep.
(Cf. the classification of magic and its branches given by Ḥādjdjī Khalīfa, *Kashf*, i, 34-5 (and vi, 412: definition of the *ᶜilm al-nīrandjāt*), set forth in T. Fahd, *La divination arabe*, 40; see also KIHĀNA.)

According to al-Djāḥiẓ (*Ḥayawān*, iv, 369 ff.), Musaylima al-Kadhdhāb [*q.v.*] practiced *nīrandjāt*; he was the first to get an egg inside a bottle and to stick back on again the wings of birds which had been cut off (cf. Ibn Ḳutayba, *Maᶜārif*, ed. Wüstenfeld, 206, ed. ᶜUkkāsha, 405). Al-Djāḥiẓ adds (cf. G. van Vloten, in *WZKM*, viii [1894], 71-3) that the pseudo-prophet had learnt these tricks in the markets frequented by the Arabs and Persians (Ubulla, Baḳḳa, Anbār and Ḥīra), which would explain the borrowing of the term *nīrandj* from Middle Persian.

But if the name itself comes from the Persian world, the matter which it denotes is found in a literary genre already in vogue since Hellenistic times, in late Antiquity and in the Middle Ages. This involves the literature of *physica* (*khawāṣṣ*), whose great disseminator, if not originator, is said to have been the "Pythagorean Bolus of Mendes (*ca.* 200 B.C.), who, under the pseudonym of the philosopher Democritus, is said to have gathered together everything marvellous and extraordinary which, in the realm of the natural sciences, both popular and learned fantasy, the experience of artisans and cultivators, and the charlatanry of the astrologers and magicians, had found" (P. Kraus, *Jâbir*, ii, 61). It was W. Wellmann who made the work known (see *Die φυσικά des Bolos Demokritos und der Magier Anaxilaos von Larissa*, in *Abh. Pr. Ak. W*, phil.-hist. Kl. (1928), 7; for other works on the subject, see Kraus, *loc. cit.*, n. 1). An apocryphal work in Syriac, attributed to Aristotle and probably dating from the 6th century, the *Ktābā da kᵉyānāyātā* (= *physica*), marks the transition between the Greek literature and the abundant literature of the genre in Arabic, whose obvious representatives are ᶜAlī b. Rabban al-Ṭabarī, Muḥammad b. Zakariyyāʾ al-Rāzī, Ps. al-Madjrīṭī, ᶜUbayd Allāh b. Djibrīl b. Bukhtīshūᶜ, al-Ḳazwīnī, al-Djildakī, Dāwūd al-Anṭākī, the numerous authors of books on agriculture, zoology, pharmacopeias and lapidaries (Kraus, *loc. cit.*). The work which best preserves this ancient heritage is the *K. al-Khawāṣṣ al-kabīr* of Djābir b. Ḥayyān [*q.v.*], set forth by P. Kraus (*op. cit.*, i, 148-52) and summarised by him (ii, 64-95). This work of Djābir's is an important source for numerous popular writings, still in manuscript. Two of them worth mentioning are: *al-Mukhtār fī kashf al-asrār wa-hatk al-asrār* and the *K. al-Ḥalāl fi 'l-alᶜāb al-sīmāwiyya* (= σημεῖα) of 'Abd al-Raḥmān al-Djawbarī, publ. Damascus 1302/1884; these were used by E. Wiedemann in several of his works, notably in his *Über das Goldmachen und die Verfälschung von Perlen nach al Gaubarī*, in *Beiträge zur Kenntnis des Orients*, v (1905-6), 77-96, repr. in E. Wiedemann, *Gesammelte Schr. zur arab.-islam. Wiss.-gesch.*, 1. Bd, Frankfurt 1984, 262-81.

Finally, one should note that in the *Ghāyat al-ḥakīm* of Abū Maslama (and not Abu 'l-Ḳāsim Maslama) Muḥammad al-Madjrīṭī (see Fahd, *Sciences naturelles et magie dans Ghâyat al-ḥakîm du Ps.-Madjrîṭî*, in *Ciencias de la naturaleza en Al Andalus. Textos y estudios*, i, ed. E. García Sanchez, Granada 1990, 11-21), *nīrandj* denotes amulets which have an extraordinary power over men and over natural phenomena, such as the magic ring which brings under its power anyone who looks at it, the amulet which protects against bad weather, that which neutralises the action of arms wielded by an enemy and that which calms the passions and desires of soldiers, who risk bringing about the victory of the enemy. The making of these *nīrandjāt* requires perfect precision and careful precautions against the poisonous materials which they comprise. These last include above all philtres having their effect through absorption or fumigations by means of powders and strange balms and greases (242 ff.).

Also to be classed under this name are the acts done by magicians; in the time of ᶜUthmān's caliphate, a magician entered and left the stomach of a cow (*Aghānī*, iv, 186). Ibn Khaldūn speaks of magicians who had only to point their finger at a piece of clothing or a skin, whilst mumbling certain words, for that object to fall into shreds; with the same gestures, fixing upon sheep, they could instantaneously cleave them. These people were called *baᶜᶜādjūn* "cleavers", a name which already figures in the *Nabataean agriculture*, used by Ibn Khaldūn. A description of their art can be found in a treatise called *al-Khinzīriyya* (*Muḳaddima*, iii, 129/178, and 131-2/181-2); F. Rosenthal, *The Muqaddimah*, iii, 165 n. 781, connects this name with the family of Ibn Abī Khinzīr which furnished some governors of Sicily in the 4th/10th century).

Bibliography: In addition to references in the article, see KHAWĀṢṢ AL-ḲURʾĀN and al-Bāḳillānī, *K. al-Bayān ᶜan al-farḳ bayn al-muᶜdjiza wa 'l-karāmāt wa 'l-ḥiyal wa 'l-kihāna wa 'l-siḥr wa 'l-nārandjāt*, ed. as *Miracle and magic* by R.J. McCarthy, in *Publs. of al-Ḥikma University of Baghdad*, Beirut 1958.

(T. FAHD)

NIRĪZ, a place in Ādharbāydjān on the road from Marāgha [*q.v.*] to Urmiya [*q.v.*] south of the Lake of Urmiya. The stages on this route are still obscure. At about 15 *farsakhs* south of Marāgha was the station of Barza where the road bifurcated; the main road continued southward to Dīnawar, while the northwestern one went from Barza to Tiflīs (2 *farsakhs*), thence to Djābarwān (6 *farsakhs*), thence to Nirīz (4 *farsakhs*), thence to Urmiya (14 *farsakhs*); cf. Ibn Khurradādhbih, 121 (repeated by Ḳudāma with some variations); al-Muḳaddasī, 383.

The distance from Urmiya indicates that Nirīz was in the vicinity of Sulduz [*q.v.*], which would find confirmation in the etymology from *ni-rēz* "flowing". Sulduz lies in the low plain, through which the Gādir flows to the Lake of Urmiya. At the present day the name Nirīz is unknown, but a Kurdish tribe of the region of Sāwdj-bulaḳ [*q.v.*] bears the name of Nirīzhī.

After the Arab conquest, a family of Ṭāʾī Arabs settled in Nirīz. The first of these semi-independent chiefs was Murr b. ʿAlī al-Mawṣilī, who built a town at Nirīz and enlarged the market of Djābarwān (cf. al-Balādhurī and al-Yaʿḳūbī, ii, 466). One of his sons, ʿAlī, was among the rebels of 212/827 whom the governor of Ādharbāydjān Muḥammad b. Ḥamīd al-Ṭūsī deported to Baghdād, but ʿAlī succeeded, it seems, in returning to his lands (cf. Ibn Khurradādhbih, 119). Abū Rudaynī ʿUmar b. ʿAlī, appointed in 260/873 governor of Ādharbāydjān by the caliph, made war on his predecessor ʿAlī b. Aḥmad al-Azdī and killed him (al-Ṭabarī, iii, 1886). He was supported by the Khāridjīs. Cf. the account in Sayyid Aḥmad Kasrawī, *Pādshāhān-i gumnām*, Tehran 1929, ii, 27, 34.

In the 4th/10th century, al-Iṣṭakhrī, 186, and Ibn Ḥawḳal, ed. Kramers, 337, tr. Kramers and Wiet, 329-30, mention the Banū Rudaynī as a dynasty already forgotten which had reigned over Dākharḳān (read Djābarwān), Tabrīz (read Nirīz) and Ushnuh al-Ādhariyya [see USHNŪ].

Bibliography: In addition to references given in the article, see *Ḥudūd al-ʿālam*, comm., 493; Minorsky, *Abū-Dulaf Misʿar ibn Muhalhil's travels in Iran (circa A.D. 950)*, Cairo 1955, tr. 40, comm. 82-3.

(V. MINORSKY)

NĪRĪZ, in Fārs [see NAYRĪZ].

AL-**NĪSĀBŪRĪ**, AL-ḤASAN B. MUḤAMMAD b. Ḥabīb b. Ayyūb, Abu 'l-Ḳāsim, was a famous littérateur and Ḳurʾānic scholar who died in either Dhu 'l-Ḥidjdja or Dhu 'l-Ḳaʿda, 406/1015-16.

One of the most learned men of Nīshāpūr, Abu 'l-Ḳāsim was considered the leader of his time in Ḳurʾānic sciences. He was not only a grammarian but was also knowledgeable in *maghāzī* (the accounts of the expeditions and raids of the Prophet) [*q.v.*], stories, and biography-history. Al-Nīsābūrī was a Karrāmī [see KARRĀMIYYA], who later became a Shāfiʿī. He transmitted *ḥadīths* [*q.v.*] on the authority of, among others, the famous Nīshāpūrī Shāfiʿī traditionist Abu 'l-ʿAbbās al-Aṣamm (d. 346/957-8 [*q.v.*]). For personality, we have but one anecdote. He owned a well and an orchard and obliged guests to pay for his hospitality, the rich with money, the poor with labour. Works attributed to al-Nīsābūrī on the Ḳurʾānic sciences, including exegesis (*tafsīr*), for which Ḥādjdjī Khalīfa cites one work. Sezgin notes the existence of a *Kitāb al-Tanzīl wa-tartībih*, only a few folios in length.

Al-Nīsābūrī is most famous for his *ʿUḳalāʾ al-madjānīn* [see MADJNŪN], a collection on intelligent madmen, a work in the entertaining and informative sub-genre of *adab* [*q.v.*], sc. character literature. In the introduction to the work, al-Nīsābūrī places himself in the *adab* tradition, citing names like the famous al-Djāḥiẓ (d. 255/868-9 [*q.v.*]) and Ibn Abi 'l-Dunyā al-Ḳurashī (d. 281/894 [*q.v.*]). After a standard philological introduction, anecdotes centre on flag-bearers for the character type, like Buhlūl, as well as the famous Madjnūn Laylā [*q.v.*], and a number of anonymous men and women. Most fascinating in these anecdotes is their range, which extends from the silly to the elusively mystical.

Bibliography: Dhahabī, *al-ʿIbar fī khabar man ghabar*, Kuwayt 1961, iii, 93; idem, *Siyar aʿlām al-nubalāʾ*, ed. Sh. al-Arnaʾūṭ, Beirut 1983, vii, 237-8; Ṣafadī, *al-Wāfī bi'l-wafayāt*, xii, ed. R. ʿAbd al-Tawwāb, Wiesbaden 1979, 239-40; Suyūṭī, *Bughya*, i, 519; al-Suyūṭī, *Ṭabaḳāt al-mufassirīn*, ed. ʿU.M. ʿUmar, Cairo 1976, 45-48; al-Dāwūdī, *Ṭabaḳāt al-mufassirīn*, ed. ʿU.M. ʿUmar, Cairo 1972, i, 140-3; Ibn al-ʿImād, *Shadharāt al-dhahab*, Beirut n.d., iii, 181; Ḥādjdjī Khalīfa, i, 460; Kh. al-Ziriklī, *Aʿlām*, Beirut 1980, ii, 213; ʿU.R. Kaḥḥāla, *Muʾallifīn*, Beirut n.d., iii, 278; *ʿUḳalāʾ al-madjānīn*, ed. M. Baḥr al-ʿUlūm, Nadjaf 1968; U. Marzolph, *Der Weise Narr Buhlūl*, Wiesbaden 1983.

(FEDWA MALTI-DOUGLAS)

NĪSĀN, the seventh month in the Syrian calendar. Its name is taken from the first month of the Jewish religious (seventh of the civil) year with the period of which it roughly coincides. It corresponds to April of the Roman year and like it has 30 days. On the 10th and 23rd Nīsān, according to al-Bīrūnī, the two first stations of the moon rise (the numbering of these two as first and second shows that the numbering was established by scholars for whom Nīsān was the first month) and on the 15th and the 16th set. In 1300 of the Seleucid era (989 A.D.), according to al-Bīrūnī, the stars of the 28th and 1st stations of the moon rose and those of the 14th and 15th set, while the rising and setting of the 2nd and 16th stations of the moon took place in Ayyār.

Bibliography: Bīrūnī, *Āthār*, ed. Sachau, 60, 70, 347-9; cf. also the *Bibl.* to TAMMŪZ.

(M. PLESSNER)

NĪSĀNIDS or Banū Nīsān, the name of a family of *ruʾasāʾ* (pl. of *raʾīs* [*q.v.*]), of a fabulous richness, who held power at Āmid [see DIYĀR BAKR] in the 6th/12th century under the nominal suzerainty of the Inālid [*q.v.*] Turcomans. They even placed their name on coins. Their rule came to an end with the conquest of the town by Ṣalāḥ al-Dīn [*q.v.*], who accused them of having cultivated the friendship of, and even to have provided assistance for, the Assassins [see ḤASHĪSHIYYA].

Bibliography: Ibn al-Athīr, xi, 103, 297; Abū Shāma, ii, 39; Cl. Cahen, *Mouvements populaires*, in *Arabica*, v/3 (1958), 20.

(ED.)

NISBA (A.), the adjective of relation formed by the addition to a noun of the suffix *-iyy^{un}* in the masc. sing., *iyyat^{un}* in the fem. sing., *-iyyūna* in the masc. pl. and *-iyyāt^{un}* in the fem. pl. As a result of the increasingly frequent omission of the *tanwīn*, the long syllable of the masc. sing., henceforward in the final position, is abbreviated to **-iy*, and subsequently this diphthong is reduced to the vowel *-ī*, transliterated thus but further abbreviated to *-i* in pronunciation. A different, no longer productive, *nisba* formation is the pattern *faʿāli^{n}*/*al-faʿālī*, fem. *faʿāliya^{tun}*: *yamāni^{n}*, from *al-Yaman*, *shaʾāmi^{n}*, from al-*Shaʾm*, *tahāmi^{n}*, from *Tihāma^{tu}*.

1. In Arabic morphology

In general, the formation of these adjectives is a simple matter, the suffixation taking place directly without modification of the vocalisation or consonantal structure of the nouns to which it is applied: *shams* "sun", *shamsī* "solar"; *ḳamar* "moon", *ḳamarī* "lunar"; *Miṣr* "Egypt", *Miṣrī* "Egyptian", etc. It should be noted, however, that in certain cases alterations occur for which the grammarians have been at pains to codify rules. Only the most frequent modifications will be cited here: omission of the *tāʾ marbūṭa*: *Baṣra*; transformation of the final *-ā* (ا or ى) into *-aw-*: *dunyā* "world", *dunyawī* "material, etc."; *maʿnā* "sense, etc.", *maʿnawī* "semantic, etc.", even after omission of the final *-tāʾ marbūṭa*: *nawāt* "nucleus", *nawawī* "nuclear"; similarly the feminine ending *-ā'u* is transformed into *-āwī*: *ṣaḥrā'* "desert", *ṣaḥrāwī* "belonging to the desert". There is a tendency to amplify short words by reinstating (or adding) a third radical (*w* or *y*): *ab* "father", *abawī* "paternal", *akh* "brother", *akhawī* "fraternal", *dam* "blood", *damawī* "sanguine, etc."; an *h* also appears sometimes: *shafatun* "lip", *shafawī/shafahī* "labial". A *w* is even substituted for *y* in *ḳarawī* (instead of **ḳaryī*) "rustic", from *ḳarya* "village".

The internal vocalisation is modified in a number of *nisba*s formed from proper nouns of the pattern $R^1aR^2īR^3$, $R^1aR^2īR^3a$, $R^1uR^2ayR^3$ and $R^1uR^2ayR^3a$: *Balawī*, from *Balīy*, *Madanī*, from *al-Madīna* (but also *Madīnī*), *Ḳurashī*, from *ḳuraysh*, and *Muzanī*, from *Muzayna*. The two forms with or without *-ī-* > *-a-* also exist as a means of avoiding confusion: *Djazarī*, from al-Djazīra "Mesopotamia", but *djazīrī* "insular", from *djazīra* "island".

Since the Middle Ages, but especially in modern times, the *nisba* in the feminine has served to create a host of abstract nouns, apparently to be formed at will according to requirements: *insān* "man", *insāniyya* "humanity"; *taʿbīr* "expression", *taʿbīriyya* "expressiveness". There is also recourse to the intensive suffix *-ānī*: *nafs* "soul", *nafsī* "psychological", *nafsānī* "psychic", for example. Finally, certain particles and pronouns are used to support relative adjectives and abstract nouns: *kayfa* "how", *kayfī* "qualitative, etc.", *kayfiyya* "modality, etc."; *kam* "how much", *kammī* "quantitative", *kammiyya* "quantity"; *huwa* "he", *huwiyya* "identity"; *anā* "I", *anāniyya* "egotism".

In theory, a relative adjective is never formed from a plural (*lā yunsab ʿalā djamʿ*) but even in the earliest times this rule enunciated by the grammarians was already being circumvented: *Aʿrāb* "Bedouins", *Aʿrābī* "bedouin"; *Baṭā'iḥ* "marshes in the vicinity of Baṣra", *Baṭā'iḥī*, etc. Since mediaeval times, usages of this type have proliferated, especially for the formation of nouns of profession: *kitāb* "book", pl. *kutub, kutubī* "bookseller"; alongside *faraḍī* "specialist in *farā'iḍ*" [*q.v.*], the form *farā'iḍī* is also encountered. In certain cases, the plural appears to be artificial: *makhzan* [*q.v.*] "government of Morocco", has no plural in this sense, but *makhāzinī* > *mkhāzni*, pl. *mkhāzniyya*, denotes a horseman paid by the state; similarly, *kafta* "skewers" (no pl.) gives *kafā'itī* "seller of skewers", etc.

Finally, it should be noted that in names such as Shawḳī, the suffix is not that of the *nisba*, but the personal pronominal affix of the first person.

Bibliography: See the Arab grammarians and the European manuals of Arabic grammar, in particular, W. Wright, *A grammar of the Arabic language*, Cambridge ³1955, i, 149-65 (§§ 249-67). (Ed.)

2. In Arabic nomenclature

In nomenclature, the *nisba* or "noun of relation" is one of the components of the mediaeval Arabic proper name. Its function is to express the relation of the individual to a group, a person, a place, a concept or a thing. It is most often preceded by the definite article *al-*. Numerous *nisba*s are employed in the contemporary period in the function of family names.

In general, the individual who is the subject of a reference in a mediaeval Arabic biographical register possesses among the various elements of his name—along with *ism, kunya, laḳab* [*q.vv.*], professional designations—one or more *nisba*s which testify to inherited or acquired characteristics, to his path through life, geographical as well as intellectual, to his religious opinions and to the links that he has with his contemporaries. Inherited, the *nisba* relates the individual to a group, such as tribe, tribal subdivision, dynasty, family, eponymous ancestor, etc.; to a place, such as a country, region, city, village, quarter, street, etc.; or even to a nickname or a professional designation handed down by his ancestors. Acquired, the *nisba* takes into account the activity of the person: it originates with the names of places in which he has been resident, those of persons with whom he has established favourable links, the ideas which he has defended and his beliefs. Alternatively, the *nisba* may refer to quoted remarks or to a physical peculiarity. The following are examples of *nisba*s which denote the connection to a tribe: *al-Kindī* "of the tribe of Kinda"; to an ancestor: *al-Ḥusaynī* "the descendent of al-Ḥusayn"; to a place: *al-Dimashḳī* "the Damascene"; to a school of thought: *al-Mālikī* "the disciple of the Mālikī legal school"; to an event: *al-Badrī* "he who took part in the battle of Badr". There are also examples of *nisba*s which are rare, if not unique, and are analogous to nicknames; *nisba*s which denote a connection with a text: a person bears the *nisba* al-ʿAntarī because he has copied the *Sīrat ʿAntar* (F. Rosenthal, *A history of Muslim historiography*², Leiden 1968, 47); connection with a poetical work: one who knew by heart the *Maḳāmāt* of al-Ḥarīrī is called al-Maḳāmātī (G. Gabrieli, *Il nome proprio arabo musulmane*, in *Onomasticon arabicum, introduzione e fonti*, Rome 1914, § 205).

*Nisba*s derived from professional designations should be considered separately, in that their termination in *-ī* appears to be optional: the cotton trader is called, apparently arbitrarily, *al-kaṭṭān* or *al-kaṭṭānī*. Other professional designations appear only with the *-ī* termination, such as *al-ṣaydalānī*, the chemist.

Role and limits of the nisba

In the earliest Arabic inscriptions, written in Sabaic script, the term *dhū* "he of ..." was used to signify the relationship of the member of a tribe to his group (see Ch. Robin, *Les plus anciens monuments de la langue arabe, dans l'Arabie antique de Karib'īl à Mahomet. Nouvelles données sur l'histoire des Arabes grâce aux inscriptions*, in *REMM*, lxi, 114-15). Subsequently, the *nisba* had the function of indicating to which tribe an individual belonged, either through his origins (*ṣarīḥan*) or through links of clientage, for example in the capacity of *mawlā* [*q.v.*]. This "tribal" *nisba* implicitly contains the genealogy of the tribe. Having in one's name an element such as al-Kindī signifies belonging to the tribe of the Banū Kinda, with its eponymous ancestor, its achievements, its history and its territory which forms a part of the *dār al-Islām* [*q.v.*].

It is also to the *dār al-Islām* that the *nisba*s refer which are acquired by individuals on the basis of geographical names. It may in fact be stated that the names listed by the biographers do not contains *nisba*s formed on the basis of the names of places which do not belong to the *dār al-Islām*. If an individual changes his abode, like the scholars who are identified by the sources as having travelled in search of knowledge, henceforward his *nisba*s, formed on the basis of the names of places in which he has resided, may be added to his name (a citizen of Damascus who goes to Baghdād will be called al-Baghdādī "the Baghdādī" on his return; while in Baghdād he would be known by the name of al-Dimashḳī, "the Damascene". On his death, a biographer could preserve in the wording of the name of this person both these *nisba*s: al-Dimashḳī (with the added detail: *al-Dimashḳī al-aṣl*, originally from Damascus), al-Baghdādī. But if he leaves the *dār al-Islām*, to travel for example to China (al-Ṣīn), India (Bilād al-Hind) or to Asia Minor (al-Rūm), countries which belong to the *dār al-ḥarb* [*q.v.*], he will not bear the *nisba*s al-Ṣīnī, al-Hindī or al-Rūmī except in cases where these are employed as nicknames (see Ibn al-Athīr, *al-Lubāb*, ii, 64: "he is called *al-Ṣīnī* because he has returned from China and he spends his time copying Chinese characters"). The individuals recorded in the biographical sources with the *nisba*s al-Ṣīnī, al-Hindī or al-Rūmī are natives of these countries; they are not, as a general rule, travellers who have become long-term residents in these countries, for in such cases the biographer would have described them as *nazīl*, followed by the name of the place in question.

In the context of the *dār al-Islām*, two further aspects of the process of formation of *nisba*s should be noted: (a) Within the confines of the *dār al-Islām*, there are some quasi-mythical regions such as Khurāsān, the cradle of Ṣūfism. The *nisba* Khurāsānī is found in the names of scholars who are not natives of this region, who have not even visited it, but who seek to ally themselves with Ṣūfī masters, claiming a spiritual heritage emanating supposedly from Khurāsān (see *Les Cent et une Nuits*, tr. M. Gaudefroy-Demombynes, Paris 1911, 3; J. Sublet, *Le voile*, 169, with a further example: the *nisba* al-Ḳayrawānī, which could represent the Far West).
(b) In the spiritual centre of this *dār al-Islām* are the holy cities of Islam, Mecca and Medina, the names of which can only be used in the form of a *nisba* in specific circumstances. Performing the Pilgrimage does not confer the right to call oneself Makkī or Madanī. One who resides as a guest-scholar in a mosque or an educational establishment is entitled to the epithet *mudjāwir* [*q.v.*] or *djār Allāh*. Only those who are natives or established citizens of these places may use these *nisba*s which, furthermore, have become (without the article, such as Makkī and Madanī) what are known as proper nouns, *ism ᶜalam* [*q.v.*], borne primarily, so it seems, by Sunnīs living in a Shīᶜī milieu who are anxious to affirm their orthodoxy (see Sublet, *Le voile*, 99-102, 170-1). Also worthy of note are *ism*s in the form of a *nisba* without the article, such as Balkhī and Bīrī (cf. Ibn al-Athīr, *al-Lubāb*, i, 140, 161).

In the Mamlūk period, *nisba*s have a specific role in the composition of the names of the Mamlūk slaves who, originally, have only an *ism*. They acquire a *nisba* formed on the basis of the name of the merchant who has imported them (for example, Azdamur al-Mudjīrī, see Ibn al-Dawādārī, *Kanz al-durar* (*Die Chronik des Ibn al-Dawādārī*), ed. Munajjid-Roemer-Haarmann, Cairo 1960 ff., ix, 71). When circumstances require it, the addition of one or more *nisba*s deriving from the name of the master who gives them their freedom is possible (the sultan Baybars I, for example, bore the *nisba*s al-Ṣāliḥī al-Nadjmī, which derived from the name of his master (al-Malik) al-Ṣāliḥ Nadjm (al-Dīn Ayyūb). In Ayalon, *Names, titles and "nisbas" of the Mamluks*, in *IOS*, v (1975), 189-231, there is a list of these *nisba*s which were to be replaced, in the Circassian period, by the expression *min* followed by the name of the master (for example, Ṭūmānbāy min Ḳānṣawḥ).

The feminine nisba

The *nisba*s of women whose names are recorded in the mediaeval biographical sources are masculine or feminine, the two forms being capable of co-existing in the same name, according to whether the biographer considers them as forming part of the patrilineal genealogy or as elements of the woman's name. The order in which he writes the elements of the name, and in particular the *kunya*, seems to have a bearing on the gender of the *nisba* or *nisba*s. For example, where the *kunya* is placed at the beginning of the name, as in Umm al-Khayr *wa-tusammā* Saᶜīda bint Muḥammad b. Ḥasan al-Ṭabarī al-Ḥusaynī al-Makkī, the *nisba*s are in the masculine form, being a part of the patrilineal genealogy. In the alternative formula, the *kunya* is placed after the genealogy and before the *nisba*s, as in Saᶜīda bint Muḥammad b. Ḥasan Umm al-Khayr al-Ṭabariyya al-Ḥusayniyya al-Makkiyya; the *nisba*s placed after the *kunya* composed with Umm are in the feminine (see especially the volume devoted to female biographies by al-Sakhāwī, *al-Ḍawʾ al-lāmiᶜ li-ahl al-ḳarn al-tāsiᶜ*, Cairo 1934, xii). These feminine *nisba*s are seldom likely to supply information regarding the places visited by the women; some women performed the Pilgrimage, but they travelled far less than men, and if they were scholars, men tended to travel to them to receive or convey *ḥadīth*s and to study texts under their supervision.

Children generally inherit the *nisba*s of their father, very rarely those of their mother. If sons or daughters are mentioned in the text of an article devoted to their mother, they are currently designated by their *ism* followed by the *nisba* most often used to designate their father or their father's family; for example: ᶜĀʾisha bint al-Ḥarīrī... *wa-kānat* Umm Aḥmad al-Ḥidjāzī (see Sublet, *Le voile*, 117).

Composite (murakkab) *nisbas*

Derived from composite names, of persons and of places in particular, these *nisba*s can have two forms: (a) A contracted form, e.g. the *nisba* ᶜAbshamī corresponds to the name ᶜAbd Shams, ᶜAbdalī to ᶜAbd Allāh, Marḳasī to Imruʾ al-Ḳays, Dāraḳuṭnī to the place-name Dar al-Ḳuṭn, Bābaṣrī to Bāb al-Baṣra and Rasᶜānī to Raʾs al-ᶜAyn.
(b) A simple form derived from one of the two elements of the name, e.g. the *nisba* Muṭṭalibī corresponds to ᶜAbd al-Muṭṭalib, Bakrī to Abū Bakr, Zubayrī to Ibn al-Zubayr and Fakhrī to Fakhr al-Dīn.

On the other hand, certain *nisba*s are formed on the basis of several names. In the *Muᶜdjam al-buldān*, Beirut 1979, i, 456, Yāḳūt gives the place name Baghdakhzarḳand. This is a fictitious name derived from a composite *nisba*, al-Baghdakhzarḳandī, borne by a single individual whose origin it describes: his father was Baghdādī, his mother Khazariyya and he was born in Samarḳand. Two other examples given by G. Gabrieli, *Il nome proprio*, § 20: al-Ṭabarkhazī is a composite of Ṭabarī (of Ṭabaristān) and Khʷārazmī (of Khʷārazm); Shafᶜanatī is a composite of Shāfiᶜī and Ḥanafī, denoting one who was a Shāfiᶜī and subsequently became a Ḥanafī.

A particular case: the fictitious nisba

Al-Suyūṭī mentions among the ten types of *ansāb* (*nasab* or genealogy and *nisba*) which he describes (*al-Muzhir*, ii, 444-7): *man nusiba ilā 'smihi wa 'smi abīhī*, giving the example of the name Numayr b. Abī Numayr al-Numayrī. The *nasab* is b. Abī Numayr, literally, "son of the father of al-Numayr" and the *nisba* al-Numayrī. This is one of the formulas used to give an identity to a person born of an unknown father (the supposed father is sometimes given the name of monetary units such as Dīnār or Dirham) or to an individual without a genealogy, a slave, for example. The *nisba* al-Numayrī is likewise derived from the *ism*; it appears with the name of the father as a repetition of this *ism*.

The nisba *in the sources*

The average number of *nisba*s borne by an individual (scholar, man of science, soldier or prince) whose biography is recorded in the mediaeval Arab sources is five. But this does not apply to the naming of eminent persons, for whom the biographer supplies only one or two *nisbas*, which often form part of the name by which the individual is best known (Sublet, *Le voile*, 104-7). The fragile distinction between *nisba* and nickname is apparent here, as in the works devoted to *ansāb*. The latter in fact combine not only the *nisbas* (pl. *nisab*) a part of which refers to genealogy (*nasab*, pl. *ansāb*) and to the eponymous ancestor, but also *laḳabs* (nicknames) and professional designations. A specific form of biographical literature is devoted to homographic *ansāb*. The authors experiment with possible readings of the various consonantal patterns with their vocalisations and they determine the identity of those who bear these *nisbas*, these *laḳabs* and these professional designations, with the object of avoiding confusion between individuals, and in certain instances the authors of these erudite works have other objectives in mind, as in the case of Ibn Mākūlā [*q.v.*].

Bibliography: Dictionaries of genealogy include Samʿānī, *al-Ansāb*, 13 vols., Ḥaydarābād 1962 ff.; available also are a facsimile of the complete manuscript, ed. D.S. Margoliouth, Leiden-London 1912, a summary with additions by ʿIzz al-Dīn Ibn al-A̲th̲īr, *al-Lubāb fī tahd̲h̲īb al-Ansāb*, 3 vols., Cairo 1938, and Beirut 1980, and a supplement to Ibn al-A̲th̲īr by Suyūṭī, *Lubb al-lubāb fī taḥrīr al-Ansāb*, ed. P.J. Veth, Leiden 1842, repr. Bag̲h̲dād n.d.; Ḥāzimī Hamdānī Muḥammad b. Abī ʿU̲th̲mān, *Kitāb ʿUd̲j̲ālat al-mubtadiʾ wa-fuḍālat al-muntahī fi 'l-nisab*, Cairo 1965. Dictionaries of homographs include D̲h̲ahabī, *al-Mus̲h̲tabih fi 'l-rid̲j̲āl asmāʾihim wa-ansābihim*, 2 vols., Cairo 1962, and Ibn Ḥad̲j̲ar al-ʿAsḳalānī, *Tabṣīr al-muntabih bi-taḥrīr al-mus̲h̲tabih*, 4 vols., Cairo 1964. On the nomenclature of *ḥadīt̲h̲*, see ʿAbd al-G̲h̲anī al-Azdī, *al-Muʾtalif wa-muk̲h̲talif*, Ḥaydarābād 1909, and Ibn Mākūlā ʿAlī b. Hibat Allāh, *al-Ikmāl fī rafʿ al-irtiyāb ʿan al-muʾtalif wa 'l-muk̲h̲talif min al-asmāʾ wa 'l-kunā wa 'l-ansāb*, 6 vols. Ḥaydarābād 1962, and Ibn al-Ṣābūnī, *Takmilat ikmāl al-Ikmāl fi 'l-ansāb wa 'l-asmāʾ wa 'l-alḳāb*, Bag̲h̲dād 1957; Ibn K̲h̲aṭīb al-Dahs̲h̲a, *Tuḥfat d̲h̲awī 'l-irab fī mus̲h̲kil al-asmāʾ wa 'l-nisab* (... *über Namen und Nisben bei Buḫārī, Muslim, Mālik*), ed. T. Mann, Leiden 1905. On South Arabia, Hamdānī, *al-Iklīl min ak̲h̲bār al-Yaman wa-ansāb Ḥimyar (Südarabische Muštabih)*, ed. Löfgren, Bibliotheka Ekmaniana no. 57, Uppsala-Leiden 1953, 1-54. Comprehensive works include G. Gabrieli, *Il nome proprio* (ref. in the article); J. Sublet, *Le voile du nom. Essai sur le nom propre arabe*, Paris 1991. (Jacqueline Sublet)

3. In Persian and Turkish

In Persian, the suffix *-ī* (MP-*īk*) is used to form relative adjectives, but with *-gī/d̲j̲ī* after the silent *hāʾ* at the end of words: (a) from places, e.g. Iṣfahānī, Dihlawī, Sāwad̲j̲ī; some apparently irregular ones go back to earlier forms of place names, e.g. Rāzī<Rayy, Sagzī<Sid̲j̲istān/Sīstān. (b) from concrete nouns to form adjectives indicating function or craft, e.g. *k̲h̲ānagī* "domestic"<*k̲h̲āna*, *ḳalʿad̲j̲ī* "garrison soldier"<*ḳalʿa*, *s̲h̲ikārī* "hunter, pertaining to hunting"<*s̲h̲ikār*.

In Turkish, the suffix *-li* in its various realisations is used for relative adjectives of place, e.g. Izmirli, Ḳonyalî, Merzifonlu, Üsküblü, and—*d̲j̲i/či* in its various realisations for adjectives denoting functions, professions, crafts, etc., e.g. *eskid̲j̲i* "old clothes dealer", *awd̲j̲î* "hunter", *mumd̲j̲u* "candlemaker", *bakîrd̲j̲î* "coppersmith", *sütd̲j̲ü* "milk seller". Several of these forms have survived in the colloquial Arabic speech of such lands as Egypt and the Levant, former parts of the Ottoman empire, e.g. *postad̲j̲ī* "postman", *boyad̲j̲ī* "shoe-cleaner", *ḳahwad̲j̲ī* "coffee-house proprietor, servant", *sufrad̲j̲ī* "waiter".

Bibliography: D.C. Phillott, *Higher Persian grammar*, Calcutta 1919, 400-1; A.K.S. Lambton, *Persian grammar*, Cambridge 1953, 124; J. Deny, *Grammaire de la langue turque, dialecte osmanli*, Paris 1921, §§ 531-2, 542-4; G.L. Lewis, *Turkish grammar*, Oxford 1975, 60-1. (Ed.)

NIṢF al-NAHĀR (a.) "half of the day", "midday", is used in astronomy in the expression which denotes the "meridian circle" (*dāʾirat niṣf al-nahār*) passing through the two poles of the horizon (*ḳuṭbā 'l-ufuḳ*) of a place, which it cuts at the two cardinal points (*d̲j̲iha, watid*) North and South and through the two poles of the celestial equator (*muʿaddal al-nahār*, etc.). As the demarcation between the East and West of a place, the meridian serves as the determination of the longitude (*ṭūl* [see ḳubbat al-arḍ]) and for fixing the hour of midday prayer [see mīḳāt] by the passage of the Sun (*zawāl*). (Ed.)

NIS̲H̲ (in Serbian, Niš), the second town of Serbia, situated at a height of 214 m/650 feet in a fertile plain surrounded by mountains, on the two banks of the Nišava not far from its junction with the Morava. It forms an important communications centre, for roads and railway lines, on the international routes to Sofia-Istanbul and Salonica-Athens. The most important part of the town lies on the right bank, with the remains of the fortress on the right one.

In antiquity, Nis̲h̲ (Naïssus, Niz, Nissa, etc.) belonged at first to the Roman province of Moesia Superior and later became the capital of Dardania. Nish's greatest claim to fame is that it was the birthplace of Constantine the Great (306-37) and attained great prosperity in ancient times. The Romans had a state munition works here.

In the time of the migrations of the Huns, Nis̲h̲ was taken after a vigorous resistance by Attila (434-53) and destroyed but rebuilt and refortified very soon afterwards by Justinian I (527-65). By the middle of the 6th century, the first forces of the Slavs who had entered the Balkan peninsula in their endeavour to found states at the expense of the Byzantine empire appeared before Nis̲h̲. Nis̲h̲ was thus in the 9th century usually in the hands of the Bulgars and until 1018 it belonged to a Slav state founded in Macedonia in 976 by the emperor Samuel. The Byzantines held it from 1018 to the end of the 12th century, when we find it described as large and prosperous; al-Idrīsī who calls it "Nīsu" (also on his map of 1154, ed. K. Miller) lays special emphasis on the quantity and cheapness of food and the importance of its trade. But even then it did not enjoy peace. In 1072 the Hungarians reached the town on a marauding campaign; in 1096 its inhabitants had to defend themselves in a strenuous battle "at the Bridge" against the Crusaders, in which the latter suffered very heavily, and in 1182 the town was taken by Bela III supported by the Serbian prince Nemanja. A little later Nemanja took Nish and the whole country as far as Serdica (Sofia). The town suffered considerably in these troubled times. The Third Crusade (1189) found it almost empty and practically destroyed. In spite of this, Nemanja was able to receive the emperor Barbarossa in Nis̲h̲ with great ceremony. From this time until the Turkish conquest Nis̲h̲ was generally in Serbian hands.

In the earlier Turkish chronicles (e.g. S̲h̲ükrullāh, Urud̲j̲ b. ʿĀdil, ʿĀs̲h̲îḳpas̲h̲azāde, Nes̲h̲rī (Nöldeke), Anonymous Giese), there is no mention of the taking of Nis̲h̲: Saʿd al-Dīn (i, 92-3), Ḥād̲j̲d̲j̲ī K̲h̲alīfa and Ewliyā Čelebi, then von Hammer (*GOR*², i, 157) and Lane-Poole (*Turkey*⁵, 40) on the other hand, assume that it took place in the reign of Murād I in 777/1375-

6. The Serbian chronicles, however, definitely give 1386, and this year, which Gibbons strongly urged as the correct date (*The foundations of the Ottoman Empire*, Oxford 1916, 161-2), is now generally accepted.

During the Turkish period (1386-1878) Nis̲h̲ had chequered fortunes. In 1443 it was taken by the Christian army under king Vladislav III and John Hunyadi and destroyed. After the fall of Smederevo in 1459 the Serbian despotate became a Turkish province and Nis̲h̲ was even more securely in Turkish hands. For several days after 20 June 1521 a great fire raged in Nis̲h̲ which would have destroyed it completely if the Beglerbeg Aḥmed Pas̲h̲a, who was leading an army against Hungary at the time, had not come at the last moment to its assistance (F. Tauer, *Histoire de la campagne du Sultan Suleyman Ier contre Belgrade en 1521,* Prague 1924, 26 (Persian text), 31 (tr.)).

Western travellers who visited Nis̲h̲ in this period (Dernschwam, Contarini, etc.) were not particularly attracted by it.

Turkish writers give us an idea of the appearance of Nis̲h̲ in the 17th century. Ḥād̲j̲d̲j̲ī K̲h̲alīfa (*ca.* 1648) describes it as a great town and *ḳāḍīlīḳ* in the *sand̲j̲aḳ* of Sofia. The description which Ewliyā Čelebi (*ca.* 1660) gives is much fuller: it is a fortified town in the plain with 2,060 houses, 200 shops, three mosques (1. G̲h̲āzī K̲h̲udāwendigār; 2. Muṣlī Efendi; 3. Ḥusayn Ketk̲h̲udā), 22 schools for children, several *masd̲j̲ids*, dervish *tekke*s, fountains, baths, many vineyards and gardens, etc.

On 23 September 1689, Nis̲h̲ was taken by the Austrians under Lewis of Baden but abandoned the very next year to the Turks (1690). In 1737 Nis̲h̲ was again taken by the Austrians under Seckendorf but left to the Turks again after two months' occupation. It is to this period that the city owes its fortifications.

When in 1804 the Serbians under Karadjerdje rebelled against the Turks, they soon won a number of successes and in 1809 were able to build redoubts against Nis̲h̲, in which Stevan Sindjelić, one of Karadjeordje's voivods, on May 31 blew up himself and the attacking Turks. Nis̲h̲ was nevertheless not relieved and the Turks built the so-called Čele-Kula ("tower of skulls") with the heads of the Serbians killed there, of which A. de Lamartine gave a moving description on his way home in 1833 (cf. *Voyage en Orient*, Paris 1859, 255-6). It was not till 11 January 1878 that Nis̲h̲, hitherto the capital of a Turkish *liwā*, finally passed from the Turks. This induced many Muslims to migrate to Turkey.

Lying on the military road between Istanbul and Vienna and therefore exposed to every campaign, Nis̲h̲ was by no means favourably situated to become a centre for the development of even a modest intellectual life. It appears, at least according to Gibb, that Nis̲h̲ produced no Turkish poets or authors, except perhaps Sünbülzāde Wehbī (end of the 18th century), who celebrated in song his meeting with the young Sara in the Turkish camp at Nis̲h̲ (*HOP*, iv, 259). In Nis̲h̲, however, two Turks worked for a time who later were to become celebrated: 1. Aḥmed Luṭfī (1815-1907), afterwards imperial historiographer, served in Vidin and Nis̲h̲ from April 1845 (*GOW*, 384); 2. the famous statesman and author of the Turkish constitution of 1876, Midḥat Pas̲h̲a [*q.v.*], was appointed governor of Nis̲h̲ and Prizren in 1861. (On the work that he did at Nis̲h̲ between 1861 and 1864, see especially N. Göyünç, *Midhat Paşa'nın Niş valiliği hakkında notlar ve belgeler*, in *IÜEF Tarih Enstitüsü Dergisi*, xii [1981-2], 279-316.)

At the end of the Ottoman period (1878), Nis̲h̲ had 19 mosques, but because of the rapid disappearance of the city's Muslim population, their number speedily diminished; after 1886, there remained only "a few" (cf. *De Paris à Constantinople*, Collection des Guides Joanne, Paris 1886, 92). The next-to-the-last was destroyed in 1896 by a violent flood, and the last one, within the fortress, is still in place. As for the local Muslims, they were already no more than 3.7% of the 35,384 inhabitants of the town in 1931. According to the statistics of December 1933 (established on the basis of the marriage registers of the local imāmate), Nis̲h̲ had at that time 1,982 Muslims spread over 365 households, chiefly Gypsies (the others being Serbo-Croat, Turkish and Albanian speakers). These Gypsies called themselves Muslims, bore Muslim names and married according to Islamic law, etc., but also observed some of the Christian festivals and from time to time prayed in churches. There still existed at this time in Nis̲h̲ a regional *s̲h̲arīʿa* court (set up in October 1929 after the abolition of the former jurisdiction of the local *muftī*, whose authority till then had extended over the whole of the former kingdom of Serbia, cf. *Glasnik Islamske Vjerske Zajednice*, i/11 [Belgrade 1934], 30-1). The new court extended over a part of that of the older jurisdiction (19 districts), whilst the rest were dependent on the *ḳāḍī* of Belgrade. The Muslims of Nis̲h̲ also had a district *waḳf meʿārif* council, a community council (*dzematski medzlis*) and a office for registration (*imāmat*). All these institutions disappeared in the course of the Second World War, and one only finds in Nis̲h̲ now individual Muslims dependent on the *muftī* of Belgrade.

Bibliography (in addition to references in the text): *PW*, s.v. Naissus (for the classical period): A. Cevat Evren, *İA* art. *Niş* (extensive information on the Ottoman period); E.H. Ayverdi, *Yugoslavya'da türk âbideleri*, in *Vakıflar Dergisi*, iii (1956), 151 ff.; idem, *Avrupa'da osmanlı mimari eserleri, III. cild, 3. kitab, Yugoslavya*, Istanbul 1981, 129-35 and photos. 1118-38; *Enciklopedija Jugoslavije*, Zagreb 1965, vi, 295-8 (several arts., on all the periods); C. Jireček, *Die Herrstrasse von Belgrad nach Constantinopel und die Balkanpässe*, Prague 1877, index; idem, *Die Handelstrassen und Bergwerke von Serbien und Bosnien während des Mittelalters*, Prague 1879, index; R. Hajdarović, *Medžmua Mula Mustafe Firakije*, in *Prilozi za Orijentalnu Filologiju*, xxii-xxiii (Sarajevo 1972-3 [1976]), 301-14 (on some unpubl. sources concerning the battle between the Turks and Austrians for the capture of the fortress of Nis̲h̲ [at the opening of the 19th century?]); V. Stojančevič, *Narodno-oslobodilački pokret u niškom kraju 1833 i 1834/35 godine*, in *Istoriski Časopis*, v. (Belgrade 1954-5), 427-35 (anti-Turkish activity in 1833-5); S. Andrejević, *Posledice Istočne Krize na privredni razvitak Juzne Srbije (novih krajeva)*, in *Srbija u završnoj fazi Velike Istočne Krize (1877-1878)*, Belgrade 1980, 225-46 (the purchasing of the large estates belonging to Turks); Ž. Živanovic, *Niš i niške znamenitosti*, Belgrade 1883; B. Lovrić, *Istorija Niša*, Nis̲h̲ 1927 (an illustrated monograph to mark the 50th anniversary of the town's passing out of Turkish hands); S. Anastasijevic, *Istorija Niša*, Nis̲h̲ 1940.

(Fehim Bajraktarević-[A. Popovic])

NIS̲H̲ĀN (P.), means a sign, banner, seal (and hence letter of a prince), or order/decoration. As a loanword in Ottoman Turkish, it basically denoted a sign or mark and also designated the sultan's signature, or *ṭug̲h̲ra* [*q.v.*] and, by extension, a document bearing it (its scribe was a *nis̲h̲ānd̲j̲ī* [*q.v.*]); the standards of the Janissaries or *Yeñi Čeri* [*q.v.*]; the insignia on military, naval and other uniforms; and, later, decorations bestowed by the sultan. In 19th and 20th century literary Arabic, *nis͟hān (also nīs͟hān)*, similarly a loanword, had essentially the same connotations. This entry considers orders/decorations alone. These are to be distinguished from medals (Persian *madāl*, Turkish *madālya*, Arabic *madāliya* or *midāliya*—all from Italian *medaglia*). The former, awarded by a sovereign ruler for extended service (frequently coinciding with promotion or retirement), were richly elaborate; medals, in contrast, designated a specific occasion and were rarely bejewelled. Among Muslims and others, the main intent of both was military (rewarding prowess), administrative (for officials), political (for foreign dignitaries and ambassadors), social (determining status in society) and cultural (encouraging educators and intellectuals).

While other marks of appreciation (e.g. coins or clothes) may have been bestowed by ʿAbbāsid caliphs and Sald͟jūḳ rulers, the practice of granting *nis͟hān*s was institutionalised in Ḳād͟jār Persia, the Ottoman Empire and Afg͟hānistān, visibly patterned on Western European practice in the early 19th century.

1. In the Middle East

Persia. The prevailing pattern was a star of bejewelled sunrays surrounding a central design; *nis͟hān*s were worn on the breast, frequently with a coloured sash. Every new *nis͟hān* was first issued on the basis of a *farmān* [*q.v.*], setting down its classes (*martaba*), subdivided into degrees (*darad͟ja*) and the type and colour of the sash (*ḥamāyil*), as well as the services meriting reward and categories of recipients. The orders, manufactured at the government mint in Tehran, were accompanied by a document and, at times, a gift of money as well. Some orders had to be returned upon the recipient's death. The most noteworthy *nis͟hān*s were the following: the *Nis͟hān-i K͟hūrs͟hīd* (Order of the Sun), instituted by Fatḥ ʿAlī S͟hāh in 1807, who renamed it (in 1810) *Nis͟hān-i S͟hīr ū K͟hūrs͟hīd* (Order of the Lion and Sun) to increase its prestige. For generations, this remained a distinguished honour for notable Persians and foreigners, such as military officers and ambassadors to Tehran. It was an eight-pointed star, richly bejewelled and enamelled (each degree less costly than the one above it), with a central circle exhibiting a crouching lion and a sun rising behind its back. On the *nis͟hān* for military recipients, the lion was standing and holding a sword. Fatḥ ʿAlī also instituted a Red Crescent *nis͟hān*, for foreigners, together with a green sash; and later a *Nis͟hān-i Ẓafar* (Order of Victory), established in Tabrīz in 1243/1827-8, for notables. His successor, Muḥammad S͟hāh, decreed a *farmān* in 1252/1836-7 establishing all details of the *Nis͟hān* of the Lion and Sun, its divisions and artistic characteristics, eligibility criteria and nomination procedures. He also established a *Nis͟hān-i Timt͟hāl-i Humāyūn* (Order of the Royal Portrait—of Muḥammad S͟hāh), first distributed, apparently, to those responsible for law and order in Southern Persia.

Nāṣir al-Dīn S͟hāh's long reign witnessed more activity in this domain. He laid down the formal rules for the *Nis͟hān-i Timt͟hāl-i Humāyūn* in a *farmān* dated 1855: it was to comprise ʿAlī's portrait, to be worn by the S͟hāh alone, or the S͟hāh's portrait, to be bestowed only on the Grand Vizier or distinguished military commanders. A later *farmān* of his, in 1287/1870, introduced three new orders to replace that of the Lion and Sun: the highest was the *Nis͟hān-i Aḳdas* (Most Sacred Order), mostly for foreign rulers, less frequently for prime ministers (local and foreign), local governors and members of Persia's royal family; the *Nis͟hān-i Ḳuds* (Order of Holiness), for ranking ambassadors and Persian governors; finally, the *Nis͟hān-i Muḳaddas* (Sacred Order), for governors and generals. Their allocation was to be determined by a grand master, appointed by the S͟hāh. Yet another *farmān*, dated 1290/1873, established the *Nis͟hān-i Āftāb* (Order of the Sun), intended for queens and royal princesses; one of the first recipients was Queen Victoria. The sun was represented by the full face of a female beauty. During his brief reign, Nāṣir al-Dīn S͟hāh's son, Muẓaffar al-Dīn S͟hāh, instituted a *Nis͟hān-i Timt͟hāl-i Humāyūn*, first bearing his father's likeness, then his own. The succeeding Ḳād͟jārs do not seem to have innovated *nis͟hān*s, although they did insert their own respective likenesses.

The Pahlawīs, as a new dynasty, introduced new *nis͟hān*s, although some borrowed old *motifs*. Their details and awarding were published in the *Gazette d'Iran*. The highest civil order was the *Nis͟hān-i Pahlawī* (Pahlawī Order), whose first class, with a collar, was worn only by the S͟hāh and the Crown Prince; the second, with a sash, and the third, with a riband, were bestowed on foreign heads of state and crown princes. *Nis͟hān-i tād͟j-i Īrān* (Order of the Crown of Īrān), a star with the Persian crown at its centre, was awarded to high civil servants and, in special cases, to high-ranking foreigners. *Nis͟hān-i humāyūn* (Royal Order), for distinguished persons, consisted of a star with an encircled lion and sun at its centre. In 1938, due to religious opposition, it was altered so that no human face appeared on the sun. The highest military *nis͟hān*s were *Nis͟hān-i D͟hu 'l-Faḳār* (Order of D͟hu 'l-Faḳār), introduced in 1922, for gallantry in action, with ʿAlī's figure in the centre; *Nis͟hān-i Liyāḳat* (Order of Merit) and *Nis͟hān-i Iftik͟hār* (Order of Honour) were reserved for officers. Several other *nis͟hān*s and medals were established by Riḍā S͟hāh and continued under Muḥammad Riḍā S͟hāh, as reported annually in the *Iran Almanac and Book of Facts* (Tehran). The Islamic Republic of Iran abolished them all.

Ottoman Empire. *Nis͟hān*s were regarded as signs of sovereignty and the sultans jealously guarded their exclusive prerogative to grant them. In the second half of the 19th century, there were attempts by the Princes of Bulgaria, starting with Alexander von Battenberg, to strike and award their own *nis͟hān*s. One, sent by Prince Alexander to Alfonso XII of Spain, had to be returned by the latter because of Ottoman pressure. Ismāʿīl Pasha [*q.v.*], K͟hedive of Egypt, did not strike his own *nis͟hān*s, but obtained permission from the sultan's court to award Ottoman ones.

From ʿAbd ül-Med͟jīd I's reign, each *nis͟hān* was prepared and distributed according to regulations (*niẓām-nāma*) published in the official *Düstūr*. Struck at the mint or *ḍarb k͟hāna* [*q.v.*], it usually had the form of a star, crescent or sunrays. As in Persia, each was a work of art, made of precious metals and gems, frequently accompanied by a sash (*s͟herīṭ*) or riband. Presented by the Sultan or dispatched via a delegate, it was boxed and awarded with a specially-written *berāt* [*q.v.*], phrased in stylised language, mentioning the name of the recipient, the *nis͟hān* and its class (if any), and the reason for the award. No one was permitted to wear a *nis͟hān* without a suitable *berāt*, for which the recipient had to pay, the price varying with time and degree. Some *nis͟hān*s had only one degree (*rütbe*), others up to five. Above the first degree, even more prestigious *nis͟hān*s were elaborately adorned with diamonds or brilliants and called *muraṣṣaʿ*. These and first-degree *nis͟hān*s were usually worn with a sash across the breast, with a small medal attached to the hip, resembling (but not identical to) the larger and more valuable one worn on the breast. Lower degrees had only one decoration, tied around the neck with a riband or pinned to one's breast. All were of gold or silver (according to their degree), mostly enamelled in the centre and bejewelled. When presented to military personnel, many *nis̲h̲āns* had interlocking swords added at the top. Persons awarded a higher degree were expected to return the lower one. Most *nis̲h̲āns* could be inherited, but not worn by heirs, who were requested to pay a fee to keep them.

Medals predated *nis̲h̲āns* in the Ottoman Empire; Maḥmūd I, ʿOt̲h̲mān III and ʿAbd ül-Ḥamīd I each issued a medal. The first *nis̲h̲ān* dates from the reign of Selīm III. There were still no decorations with which to reward Admiral Nelson following his 1798 destruction of the French navy at Abū Ḳīr in Egypt, but the matter was then accorded initial consideration. In 1216/1801, following the battle of Alexandria, the *Nis̲h̲ān-i̊ Hilāl*, or *Hilāl Nis̲h̲āni̊* (Order of the Crescent), sometimes called that of the *Waḳāʾiʿ-i Miṣriyye* (Order of the Battles of Egypt), was struck to be worn as a pendant around the neck. Made of gold and adorned with diamonds, its central ornaments were an enamelled crescent and the Ottoman arms. Its first recipients were an Ottoman naval officer, Aḥmed, and a British one, Hutchinson; later, it was presented to one of Napoleon I's generals, Sebastiani de la Porta.

During Maḥmūd II's reign, in 1831, the *Nis̲h̲ān-i̊ Iftik̲h̲ār* (Order of Honour) was struck, with a crescent or star (depending on degree) at its centre. With this order, the sultan initiated the practice of distributing *nis̲h̲āns* among military officers, NCOs and administrative officials. The *Taṣwīr-i Hümāyūn Nis̲h̲āni̊* (Order of the Imperial Portrait), struck a year later, comprised Maḥmūd II's portrait, in miniature, on ivory, in a rectangular frame ornamented with brilliants, set among yellow and pink roses, surrounded by blue flowers. Aware of criticism in religious circles for using a human portrait, the sultan presented this *nis̲h̲ān* to the *S̲h̲eyk̲h̲ ül-Islām* himself (1248/1832).

Several *nis̲h̲āns* were issued during ʿAbd ül-Med̲j̲īd's reign. Some were smaller, more modest ones, rewarding the services of various officers, officials, engineering service personnel and others. These awards and many others were all recalled and sent back to the mint. Nonetheless, this remained an era of artistically significant *nis̲h̲āns*, three of which merit special mention: the *Nis̲h̲ān-i̊ Iftik̲h̲ār* differed from the one similarly named under Maḥmūd II. Oval-shaped, it resembled a flat medal. The base was a golden plaque; the flowery *ṭug̲h̲ra* at its centre was silver-plated, surrounded by 32 silver sunrays, and the upper part was of gold. It bore a total of 160 gems. The *Nis̲h̲ān-i̊ Imtiyāz* (Order of Distinction) had only one degree, but its makeup varied with the reward which the sultan thought suitable for services rendered. Thus in 1257/1841, Muṣṭafā Res̲h̲īd Pasha [see RES̲H̲ĪD PAS̲H̲A, MUṢṬAFĀ], Minister for Foreign Affairs, was rewarded for ably solving the problem of Egypt a year earlier with a beautiful ornamented *Nis̲h̲ān-i̊ Imtiyāz*, whose centre bore the *ṭug̲h̲ra* within a red enamel laurel twig surrounded by 35 bejewelled sunrays. The *Med̲j̲īdī Nis̲h̲āni̊* (Order of ʿAbd ül-Med̲j̲īd, popularly known as *Med̲j̲īdiyye*) was struck in 1268/1851. While the number of *nis̲h̲āns* struck for foreigners was not pre-determined, the quantity struck for Ottomans was: 1st degree, 50; 2nd, 150; 3rd, 800; 4th, 3,000; 5th, 6,000. In the centre of seven sections of sunrays, the *ṭug̲h̲ra* appeared as a sun in relief, around which the following terms were inscribed in gold: *ṣadāḳat* (fidelity), *ḥamiyyet* (patriotism) and *g̲h̲ayret* (zeal). This was awarded to the military, civil servants and intellectuals (succeeding sultans continued to award it). Not surprisingly, the regulations governing this Order stipulated that anyone guilty of treason, robbery, murder or corruption would have to return it.

The enamel-on-gold *Nis̲h̲ān-i̊ ʿĀlī Imtiyāz* (Order of High Distinction), struck during ʿAbd ül-Azīz's reign, in 1861, greatly resembled the earlier *Nis̲h̲ān-i̊ Imtiyāz*. The *Nis̲h̲ān-i̊ ʿOt̲h̲mānī* (Ottoman Order), struck in the following year, was presented only to previous recipients of the *Med̲j̲īdī Nis̲h̲āni̊*. Again, the number of pieces produced was strictly limited in advance (although foreigners were excluded from this quota), as well as the payment, by degree, for the accompanying *berāt*. The sultan's *ṭug̲h̲ra* was again the centre-piece, on red enamel and gold, surrounded by 35 sunrays.

During ʿAbd ül-Ḥamīd II's reign, the number of *nis̲h̲āns*, old and new, increased so much that their intrinsic value declined. This was due not only to his long reign, but also to his large-scale distribution of *nis̲h̲āns* among both Ottomans and foreigners as a means of gaining allies and saving the Empire. Even on such occasions as the sinking of the Ottoman frigate *Ertog̲h̲rul*, in a storm off the coast of Japan, *nis̲h̲āns* were sent to the local people who had tried to rescue and tend the shipwrecked. Only the more important orders will be mentioned. The *S̲h̲efḳat Nis̲h̲āni̊* (Order of Compassion) was struck in 1878 for Ottoman women (and, in rare cases, for foreign ones) who had made efforts to help during wars, earthquakes, floods and similar disasters. This first Ottoman *nis̲h̲ān* for women was in gold and silver, in the form of a five-cornered star with a violet-coloured enamel at its centre, bearing ʿAbd ül-Ḥamīd's *ṭug̲h̲ra* and the words *insāniyyet* (humanity), *muʿāwenet* (assistance) and *ḥamiyyet* (patriotism). Like ʿAbd ül-ʿAzīz, ʿAbd ül-Ḥamīd issued his own version of *Nis̲h̲ān-i̊ ʿĀlī Imtiyāz*. Struck in 1878, it was designed for military personnel, administrators and intellectuals—both Ottoman and foreign—who had performed exceptional services for the Empire. Of one degree only (plus the bejewelled, *murassaʿ* one), it looked like a rayed sun with golden laurel twigs at its base. The sultan's *ṭug̲h̲ra* was inscribed on green enamel, surrounded by the inscription *ḥamiyyet* (patriotism), *g̲h̲ayret* (zeal), *s̲h̲ed̲j̲āʿat* (courage) and *ṣadāḳat* (fidelity). The *k̲h̲ānedān-i̊ Āl-i ʿOt̲h̲mān Nis̲h̲āni̊* (Order of the Ottoman Dynasty), struck in 1892, was intended for rulers of foreign states and their families, as well as members of the reigning Ottoman family and Turkish personalities who had excelled in service. Golden, oval-shaped, with the *ṭug̲h̲ra* at its centre, surrounded by a red enamel frame, it was usually worn on a grand formal uniform. The *Ertog̲h̲rul Nis̲h̲āni̊* (Order of Ertog̲h̲rul), named for one of the Sultan's ancestors, was struck in 1901. Shaped like a star with gold enamel at its corners, it was intended for those whom ʿAbd ül-Ḥamīd particularly liked.

In the time of Meḥemmed V Res̲h̲ād and the Young Turks, more *nis̲h̲āns* were struck. The *Maʿārif Nis̲h̲āni̊* (Education Order), issued in 1910, was intended for persons distinguishing themselves publicly in teaching, culture and the arts. Made of gold-plated silver, the *ṭug̲h̲ra* was again in the centre on a red enamel background, surrounded by a white enamel crescent and terminating in a small five-pointed star joined to a green enamel laurel. An inscription set out the *nis̲h̲ān*'s intent: *ʿUlūm we-fünūn we-ṣanāʾiʿ-i nefīse*. Eligible recipients had to have been employed for at least five years (3rd degree), ten (2nd) and another ten (1st). Teachers who had failed at their jobs could be requested to return their *nis̲h̲āns*. Foreigners were equally eligible for this award. The *Meziyyet Nis̲h̲ānī* (Order of Excellence), considered even more prestigious then the *Med̲j̲īdī Nis̲h̲ānī* and the *Nis̲h̲ān-ī ʿOt̲h̲mānī*, was planned in 1910 and intended for both Ottoman and foreign subjects in the highest offices. This *nis̲h̲ān*, however, was never issued. The same is true of the *Zirāʿat Liyāḳat Nis̲h̲ānī* (Order of Capability in Agriculture), planned in 1912 for men particularly successful in agriculture. It was designed with a three-word inscription: *ḥürriyyet* (liberty), *ʿadālet* (justice) and *müsāwāt* (equality)—a common slogan in the Young Turk decade. The *Med̲j̲lis-i Mebʿūt̲h̲ān Aʿḍālarīna Mak̲h̲ṣūṣ Nis̲h̲ānī* (Order for the Members of Parliament) was issued in 1916 to all members in the 1916-19 Parliament. Made up of heptagonal groups of sunrays, its centre was a crescent-and-star in gold on white enamel.

In the successor states of the Ottoman Empire, heads of state variously continued to bestow orders and medals. In Turkey, a law passed in Parliament on 26 November 1934 and published in the *Resmî Gazete* three days later, forbade wearing Ottoman *nis̲h̲āns* (unless won in war) or foreign decorations. Instead, the state provided the *Istiklâl madalyasī* (Independence Medal), approved by Parliament in 1920 and distributed in 1923 to Members of Parliament and later to all those who fought or assisted in the War of Independence. In Egypt, King Fuʾād instituted several orders: the *Ḳalādat Muḥammad ʿAlī* (Muḥammad ʿAlī Collar) for a limited number of kings; the *Ḳalādat Fuʾād* (Fuʾād Collar), for heads of state and eminent Egyptians; the *Nis̲h̲ān Muḥammad ʿAlī* (Order of Muḥammad ʿAlī), sometimes called *al-Wis̲h̲āḥ al-akbar* (The Highest Decoration), for Prime Ministers, both Egyptian and foreign; the *Nis̲h̲ān Ismāʿīl* (Order of Ismāʿīl), for prominent Egyptians and others; the *Wis̲h̲āḥ al-Nīl* (Nile Decoration), for ministers and pashas; and the *Wisām al-Kamāl* (Decoration of Perfection), for women only. King Fārūḳ introduced no new orders, while the Republic did, e.g. the *Wisām al-Nīl* (Nile Decoration), for heads of state, and the *Wisām al-istiḥḳāḳ* (Order of Merit).

Bibliography: Persia: E. Flandin and P. Coste, *Voyage en Perse*, Paris 1851, ii, 331-2; J.E. Polak, *Persien. Das Land und seine Bewohner*, Leipzig 1865, ii, 41-2; E. Collinot and A. de Beaumont, *Ornements de la Perse*, Paris 1883; R.S. Poole, *The coins of the Shahs of Persia*, London 1887, esp. pl. xxiv; C.E. Yate, *Khurasan and Sistan*, Edinburgh 1900, 45; L. Brasier and J.L. Brunet, *Les ordres persans*, Paris 1902; J. Greenfield, *Die Verfassung des persischen Staates*, Berlin 1904, 195-9; H.L. Rabino, *Médailles des Qadjars (= Collection de la RMM*, Paris 1916); idem, *Orders and decorations of H.I.M. Rezā Shāh Pahlavī, of Īrān*, in *Spink and Son's Circular* (Aug.-Sept. 1939), 288-95; *Iran almanac and book of facts*[8], Tehran 1969, 36-7; A.M. Piemontese, *The statutes of the Qājār orders of knighthood*, in *EW*, NS, xix/1-2 (March-June 1969), 431-77; Muḥammad Mus̲h̲īrī, *Nis̲h̲ānhā wa-madālhā-yi Īrān az āg̲h̲āz-i salṭanat-i Ḳād̲j̲āriyya tā imrūz*, in *Barrasīhā-yi Taʾrīk̲h̲ī*, vi/5 (1350 s̲h̲/1971), 185-220, ix/1 (1353 s̲h̲/1974), 177-91 (plus plates) (this was later reissued, with additions, by Mus̲h̲īrī, with the same title, Tehran 1354 s̲h̲/1975); H.L. Rabino di Borgomale, *Coins, medals, and seals of the Shâhs of Îrân, 1500-1941*, n.p. 1945, repr. Dallas 1973; ʿAbd al-Ḥusayn K̲h̲ān Sipihr, *Mirʾāt al-waḳāʾiʿ-i Muẓaffarī wa-yāddās̲h̲t-hā-yi malik al-muwarrik̲h̲īn*, Tehran 1368 s̲h̲, 291-300; Sir Denis Wright, *Sir John Malcolm and the order of the lion and sun*, in *Iran JBIPS*, xvii (1979), 135-41; H.-G. Migeod, *Die persische Gesellschaft unter Nāṣiru'd-Dīn Šāh (1848-1896)*, Berlin 1990, 96-7.

Ottoman Empire. *Nis̲h̲āns* can be found in many museums in Turkey (such as the Topkapı and the military and naval museums in Istanbul) and elsewhere and in many private collections, worldwide. Copies of the *berāts* accompanying them, for 1262-1337/1845-1918, are housed in the Başbakanlık Arşivi, *Hümayun nişan defterleri*, vols. 1-44. Foreign recipients of *nis̲h̲āns* were generally listed in the official *sālnāmes*. Regulations (*niẓāmnāme*) governing the awards were printed in *Düstūr*, e.g. 1st series, suppl. vols. (*d̲h̲eyl-i düstūr*), iv, Istanbul 1302, 2-3. See also Meḥmed Tewfīḳ, *Nis̲h̲ān-ī ittiḥād. Yādigār-ī Mad̲j̲aristān ʿaṣr-ī ʿAbd ül-Ḥamīd K̲h̲ān*, Istanbul 1294; F. von Kraelitz, *Ilk ʿOt̲h̲mānlī pādis̲h̲āhlarīnīñ iṣdār etmis̲h̲ olduḳlarī baʿḍī berātlar*, in *TOEM*, v/28 (1 Oct. 1330/1914), 242-50; Köprülüzade Mehmet Fuat, *Reisülküttaplık ve nişancılık*, in *Türk Hukuk ve Iktisat Tarihi Mecmuası*, i (1931), 198-201; Sermet Muhtar Alus, *Eski rütbeler, elkaplar, nişan ve madalyalar*, in *Resimli Tarih Mecmuası*, iii/33 (Sept. 1952), 1736-9; Hâlûk Y. Şahsuvaroğlu, *Nişan ve madalyalara dair*, in *Cumhuriyet* (1 Dec. 1958), 2; İbrahim Artuk, *Nişanı Osmani*, in *Arkeoloji Müzeleri Yıllığı*, x (1961), 74-6, plus plates; idem and Cevriye Artuk, *The Ottoman orders*, Istanbul 1967; İ. Artuk, *Orta ve yeni çağa ait sikke ve nişanlar*, in *VI. Türk Tarih Kongresi (20-26 Ekim 1961)*, Ankara 1967, 237-53; C. Artuk, *The medallion of glory*, in *Actes du 8ème Congrès International de Numismatique, New York and Washington, Sept. 1973*, Basel 1976, 489-93; eadem, *Şefkat nişanı*, in *I. Milletlerarası Türkoloji Kongresi (İstanbul, 15-20.X.1973). Tebliğler. I. Türk Tarihi*, Istanbul 1979, 7-14; İ. Artuk, *Nişân-ı Osmanî*, in *ibid.*, 15-22; C. Artuk, *İftihar madalyası*, in *Belleten*, xliv/175 (July 1980), 535-7; İsmet Çetinyalçın, *Liyakat madalyası*, in *VIII. Türk Tarih Kongresi (11-15 Ekim 1976)*, Ankara 1983, iii, 1723-32, plus plates; Afif Büyüktuğrul, *Sultan II. Mahmut döneminde rütbe alameti boyun nişanları*, in *Belleten*, xlvii/186 (April 1983) [publ. Ankara 1984], 537-46; *History of the Turkish frigate Ertuğrul*, n.p., n.d., 17, 21-3.

(J.M. Landau)

2. In the Mag̲h̲rib

In North Africa, it was Tunisia which, whilst part of the Ottoman empire, was the first to award decorations. The oldest and most popular one is the *Nis̲h̲ān al-Iftik̲h̲ār* ("Order of Honour"), begun in 1837 by Aḥmad Bey, modified in 1855, then on 29 Muḥarram 1300/10 December 1882 and on 1 D̲h̲u 'l-Ḥid̲j̲d̲j̲a 1304/21 August 1887, before being definitively regulated by a beylical decree of 22 S̲h̲aʿbān 1315/16 January 1898 (apart from a few later modifications relating to the rights of chancellery).

The *Nis̲h̲ān al-Iftik̲h̲ār* had at the outset only one class, whose insignia was a silver, enamelled plaque, oval in shape, on which the name of the Bey was picked out encrusted with diamonds. Later, it became an order arranged hierarchically in five classes. The highest decoration (the Grand Sash) was a silver plaque with carved faces, rounded and raised in its centre, in the form of a star with ten rays radiating outwards intertwined with each other; in the centre of the plate, on a green enamelled field, the name of His Highness the Bey stood out in incised silver letters. This decoration was worn over the left side of the breast, by means of a green silk ribbon with a double red bordering; this ribbon, 85 mm wide, had to be worn cross-wise over the right shoulder; at its ends, a

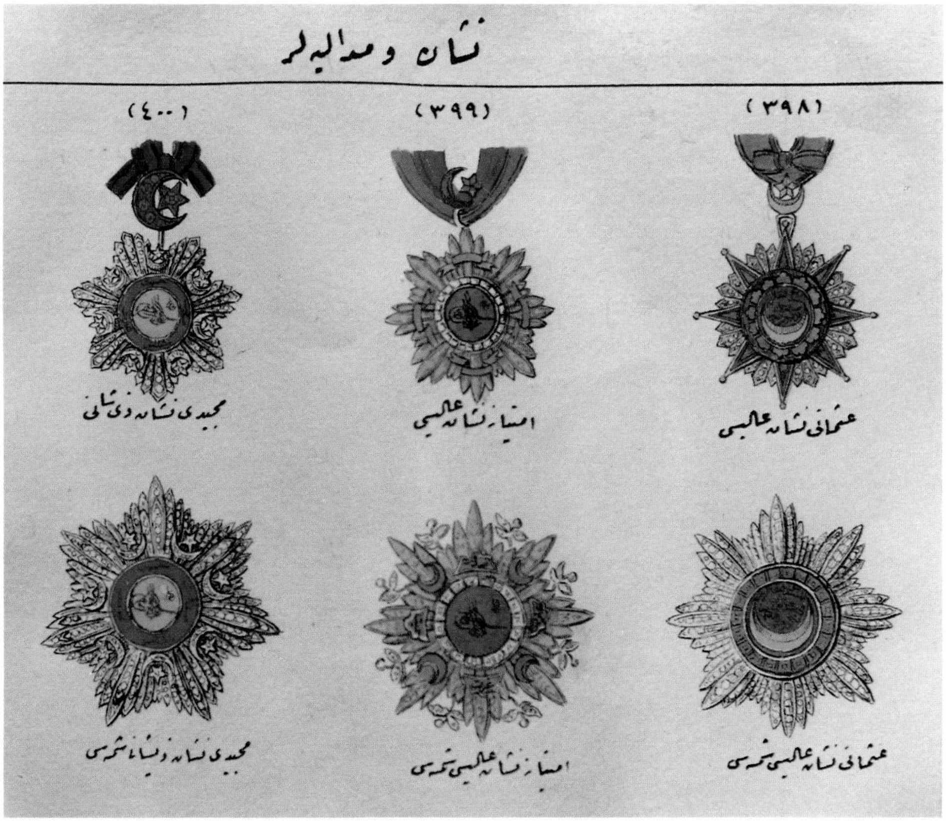

Some *nishāns* of the late Ottoman Empire (above with a riband, below with a pin for the breast). From right to left: *Nishān-i̊ ʿOthmānī*; *Nishān-i̊ ʿālī imtiyāz*; *Medjīdī nishānī*. From Mahmut Shevket's manuscript, *ʿOthmānli̊ ḳi̊yāfet-i ʿaskariyye*, Istanbul University Library, Türkçe Yazma 9393; with the kind permission of Istanbul University Library.

knot supported the plaque of a Commander (see below). The plaque of a Grand Officer was smaller and was worn on the right side of the breast. The plaque of a Commander, smaller still, differed only in detail; a green ribbon four cm wide had a double red bordering which allowed the insignia to be worn below the neck. The decoration of an Officer, smaller still, was supported by a green ribbon with a double edging, with a rosette, which was pinned on the left side of the breast. The decoration of a Knight (first and second classes) was simpler, but the ribbon was the same as for the other classes. The *Nis͟hān al-Iftik͟hār* was awarded on the recommendation of the Prime Minister for Tunisian nationals, and of the Foreign Affairs Minister for other recipients.

In the same year as the *Nis͟hān al-Iftik͟hār* was instituted (1837), the Bey founded the *Nis͟hān al-Dam* ("Order of the Blood") for himself and members of his family, but this decoration was also granted to the Prime Minister and to foreign sovereigns and their families. Its insignia was a rounded plaque of gold, with rings set with diamonds, and it was worn crosswise by means of a green ribbon with two thin red borders. After the promulgation of the Fundamental Pact (*ʿAhd al-Amān* [see DUSTŪR, i]), the Bey Muḥammad al-Ṣādiḳ in 1860 created a special order, the *Nis͟hān ʿAhd al-Amān*, reserved for princes and for Tunisian ministers, but also granted to generals and civilian officials of high rank. The insignia was a plaque in gold, round in shape, with a red enamelled surface and set with emeralds, and it was worn cross-wise by means of a green ribbon with two red borders on each side. In 1874 the same Bey inaugurated the *Nis͟hān ʿAhd al-Amān al-Muraṣṣaʿ*, whose insignia was a golden plaque set (*muraṣṣaʿ*) with diamonds, but this decoration was granted only to a limited number of Tunisian dignitaries and foreign personalities: Marshal Lyautey, General de Gaulle and King Alfonso XIII of Spain. These four orders were thus placed in the following order of importance: *Dam*, *ʿAhd al-Amān al-Muraṣṣaʿ*, *ʿAhd al-Amān* and *Iftik͟hār*. All were abolished in 1957.

Once Tunisia became independent, it acquired three new orders plus a certain number of medals. The *Nis͟hān al-Istiḳlāl* ("Order of Independence") was founded by a decree of 6 September 1956 and reorganised by the law 59-32 of 16 March 1959; it was intended to reward civil or military services from the time of the war of national liberation and has five classes (of Knight with Grand Cross). On the same day, law 59-33 instituted the *Nis͟hān al-D̲j̲umhūriyya al-Tūnisiyya* ("Order of the Tunisian Republic") meant to reward the services of those who had contributed to the establishment of the republic; it also had five classes. Finally, the Order of 7 November 1987 (beginning of the new era) was set up by the law 88-78 of 2 July 1988 to reward the merits of those who had either contributed to the re-establishment of the sovereignty of the people and the strengthening of democracy or had worked for the consolidation of the gains of 7 November; it likewise has five classes. The President of the Republic is the Grand Master of these three orders, which may also be given to foreigners.

Furthermore, the government ministerial departments are able to grant decorations and medals for rewarding services rendered: the Medal of Honour of the State Security Service, of the National Guard, of Civil Defence, of the Prison and Rehabilitation Services, and for the Safety of the Head of State and of official figures, all medals stemming from the Ministry of the Interior. The Ministry of Education and Science has the National Order of Merit for the Universities set up by the law 85-41 of 15 April 1985 and comprising three classes, and the National Order of Merit for Teaching created by the law 79-41 of 15 August 1979, also of three classes; the president of the Republic is the Grand Master of these two orders. The Ministry of Public Health has a medal, whilst that of Agriculture has an Order of Merit for Agricultural Services set up by the law 71-44 of 28 July 1971 and comprising two grades, those of knight and officer. The Ministry of Youth and Children has two medals, for Merit in Sport and Merit of Youth. The Ministry of Social Affairs has the Medal of Social Merit and the Medal of Labour. There was attached to the Ministry of Culture the National Order of Cultural Merit created by the law 66-61 of 5 July 1966, but replaced, by law 69-23 of 27 March 1969, by the Medal of Culture, which also has five classes. Finally, the Ministry of National Defence has the Military Medal, whose holders form an Order, and the Medal commemorating the Battle and the Evacuation of Bizerta set up by the law 63-45 of 12 December 1963.

(This information concerning Tunisia has been kindly communicated by the National Foundation Beit Al-Hikma [*Bayt al-Ḥikma*] which had been given the task of drawing up a report on the Tunisian decorations.)

In Morocco, a dahir (*ẓahīr*) of 1 Ramaḍān 1386/14 December 1966 regulated the kingdom's orders; this document, which followed and summed up earlier ones, was itself modified or completed by the dahirs of 26 Ramaḍān 1388/17 December 1968, of 12 Rabīʿ II 1396/12 April 1976 and of 3 Rabīʿ II 1403/18 January 1983.

In descending hierarchical order, the nine orders designated by the term *wisām*, and not *nis͟hān*, were as follows. (1) *al-Wisām al-Muḥammadī*, reserved for monarchs or heads of foreign states, the royal family and foreign princes. It has three classes. For the outstanding class, a gold plaque whose base in green enamel is surrounded by jewels and which is worn suspended from a collar of gold or of precious stones; for the other two classes, there is only a plaque, without the jewels for the third one. (2) *Wisām al-Istiḳlāl* ("Order of Independence") intended for those who contributed to the achievement of independence. It has three classes also: for the outstanding one, the gold medal forms a star with eight points hung from a red ribbon with black vertical stripes. For the other classes, the medal is in silver or bronze respectively. (3) *Wisām al-Walāʾ* ("Order of Fidelity"), meant for persons who have shown their devotion to the sovereign. It has only one class, and the plaque is a star in gold with five points. (4) *Wisām al-ʿArs͟h* ("Order of the Throne") is meant to reward civil and military officials. It has five classes; the gold medal (silver for the fourth class) is worn hung from a red band, with a green stripe on each side. (5) *al-Wisām al-ʿAskarī* ("Military Medal") is for private soldiers and NCOs in time of war, and also for general officers holding the *Wisām al-ʿArs͟h*. It has only one class; the medal is bronze, oval in shape, with a white and red ribbon. (6) *Wisām al-Istiḥḳāḳ al-ʿAskarī* ("Medal for Military Merit") is for career officers. It has five classes; the outstanding class comprises a gold plaque plus a gold medal with a green ribbon with a red border; the first class, a plaque and medal of silver; the others, only a medal in silver or bronze. (7) *Wisām al-Istiḥḳāḳ al-Waṭanī* ("National Order for Merit"), meant for civil and military officials. It has three classes, a gold medal for the outstanding level, one of silver or bronze for the other two, and red ribbon with wide edges. (8) *al-Wisām al-ʿAlawī*, the celebrated Ouissam Alaouite, which has five classes. The highest (the Grand Sash), has for its insignia a plaque 84 mm in diameter with five clusters of silver rays, surmounted by a golden star 40 mm in diameter with five white enamelled branches, a red cord, held together by a cluster of palm leaves in green enamel with a 16 mm golden circle in its centre, on a red enamelled ground. This plaque is worn on the left side of the breast. Also, a gold star 60 mm in diameter, identical on both sides to that of the plaque, with a circle 25 mm in diameter in its centre; the second side bears a representation of the royal parasol, red in colour, on a golden ground; this star is hung from a ring of golden foliage by a wide ribbon in bright orange, 10 cm wide with, on each side, a white stripe. The Grand Sash is worn over the shoulder from right to left. For the rank of Grand Officer, the plaque is the same as above; it is worn on the right side of the breast, the star of an Officier (see above) on the left side. The Commander wears a star identical with that of the Grand Sash hung from a bright orange neck band 37 mm wide, with a white stripe on each side. The star of an Officer is like that of the Grand Sash with the same measurements as the star of the plaque; the ribbon, bright orange and 37 mm wide, has a white stripe on each side and bears a white-striped rosette. The insignia of a Knight is the same, except that it is hung from a silver (and not gold) ring and has no rosette. (9) *Wisām al-Mukāfaʾa al-Waṭaniyya* (no information about this order). (Ch. Pellat)

NIS̲H̲ĀNDJĪ, secretary of state for the Sultan's *ṭug̲h̲ra*, chancellor, in Ottoman administration.

The Saldjūḳs and Mamlūks already had special officials for drawing the *ṭug̲h̲ra*, the sultan's signature. As their official organisation was inherited in almost all its details by the Ottomans, this post naturally was included. Its holder was called *nis̲h̲āndjī* or *tewḳīʿī*. The *nis̲h̲āndjī* held the same rank as the *defterdārs* [*q.v.*] and indeed even preceded them, for we find *defterdārs* promoted to *nis̲h̲āndjīs* but never a *nis̲h̲āndjī* becoming a *defterdār*. The *nis̲h̲āndjī* was included among the "pillars of the empire" (*erkān-i dewlet*). The part which he played varied in course of time. Besides being secretary of state for the imperial *ṭug̲h̲ra* (*nis̲h̲ān*), he had originally considerable legislative powers and he was called *muftī-yi ḳānūn* (to distinguish him from the *muftī* proper, i.e. the *S̲h̲ayk̲h̲ al-Islām*). In his office, the texts of the laws were prepared under his supervision. Most of the Ottoman codes of law (*ḳānūn*) that have come down to us go back to *nis̲h̲āndjīs*. As they had moreover the right to approve the contents of documents put before them for the imperial *ṭug̲h̲ra*, they had no slight influence on the business of administration. Of their official career we know that, according to the *Ḳānūn-nāme* [*q.v.*] of Meḥemmed II, they had to be chosen from teachers acquainted with law (*müderris*), apparently because they had to display legislative ability, or from the *defterdārs* and *ruʾasāʾ ül-küttāb*. As their authority diminished more and more in course of time, so did their influence, and finally they were limited to preparing the *ṭug̲h̲ra*. According to Mouradjea d'Ohsson (*Tableau de l'Empire Ottoman*, iii, 373), the *nis̲h̲āndjīs* received from the state a salary of 6,620 piastres. On their official dress, see von Hammer, *GOR*, viii, 431, according to whom they wore red, in contrast to the other *k̲h̲odjagān* who wore violet.

Bibliography: See the article ṬUG̲H̲RA and the references there given; also J. von Hammer, *GOR*, i, 173, ii, 217, 229, iv, 3, viii, 431; idem, *Des Osmanischen Reiches Staatsverfassung und Staatsverwaltung*, Vienna 1815, i, 64, ii, 127, 135; M.Z. Pakalın, *Tarih deyimleri ve terimleri sözlüğü*, Istanbul 1946-53, ii, 694-7 s.v. *Nişan*, 697-700 s.v. *Nişancı*; *İA*, art. *Nişancı* (M. Tayyib Gökbilgin).

(F. Babinger)

NĪS̲H̲ĀPŪR, the most important of the four great cities of K̲h̲urāsān (Nīs̲h̲āpūr, Marw, Harāt and Balk̲h̲), one of the great towns of Persia in the Middle Ages.

The name goes back to the Persian Nēw-S̲h̲āhpūr ("Fair S̲h̲āpūr"); in Armenian it is called Niu-S̲h̲apuh, Arab. Naysābūr or Nīsābūr, New Pers. Nēs̲h̲āpūr, pronounced in the time of Yāḳūt Nīs̲h̲āwūr, now Nīs̲h̲āpūr (Nöldeke, *Ṭabarī*, 59, n. 3; G. Hoffmann, *Auszüge...*, 61, n. 530). The town occasionally bore the official title of honour, Īrāns̲h̲ahr.

Nīs̲h̲āpūr was founded by S̲h̲āhpūhr I, son of Ardas̲h̲īr I (Ḥamza al-Iṣfahānī, ed. Gottwaldt, 48), who had slain in this region the Turanian Pahlčak (Pālēžak) (*Städteliste von Ērān*, § 13); some authors say it was not founded till the time of S̲h̲āhpūhr II (al-Ṭabarī, i, 840; al-T̲h̲aʿālibī, ed. Zotenberg, 529).

In the wider sense, the region of Nīs̲h̲āpūr comprised the districts of al-Ṭabasayn, Kūhistān, Nisāʾ, Bāward, Abars̲h̲ahr, Djām, Bāk̲h̲arz, Ṭūs, Zūzan and Isparāʾin (al-Yaʿḳūbī, *Buldān*, ed. de Goeje, 278; cf. al-Ṭabarī, i, 2884); in the narrower sense, Nīs̲h̲āpūr was the capital of the province of Abars̲h̲ahr (Armen. *Apar as̲h̲kharh*, the "district of the Ἀπάρνοι"; Marquart, *Ērānšahr*, 74; idem, *Catalogue of the provincial capitals of Ērānshahr*, 52), which was in turn divided into 13 *rustāḳs* and 4 *ṭassūdj* (names in al-Iṣṭak̲h̲rī, 258; Ibn Ḥawkal, 313; Ibn K̲h̲urradād̲h̲bih, 24; al-Yaʿḳūbī, 278; Ibn Rusta, 171). The latter were: in the west Rēwand (now Rīwend), in the south al-S̲h̲āmāt, Pers. Tak-Āb, in the east Pus̲h̲tfrōs̲h̲an (now Pus̲h̲t Farūs̲h̲) and in the north Māzūl (now Māsūl); cf. al-Muḳaddasī, 314-21.

In the Rēwand hills to the northwest of the town was one of the three most sacred fire-temples of the Sāsānids, that of the fire Burzīn-Mihr (G. Hoffmann, *op. cit.*, 290). Yazdadjird II (438-57) made Nīs̲h̲āpūr his usual residence.

In the year 30/651 or 31/652 the governor of Baṣra, ʿAbd Allāh b. ʿĀmir [*q.v.*], took Nīs̲h̲āpūr (al-Ṭabarī, i, 3305; al-Balād̲h̲urī, 404), whose governor Kanārang (χαναράγγης: Marquart, *Ērānšahr*, 75) capitulated. The town was then insignificant and had no garrison. During the fighting between ʿAlī and Muʿāwiya (36-7/656-7), the Arabs were again driven out of Nīs̲h̲āpūr by a rising in K̲h̲urāsān and Ṭuk̲h̲āristān (al-Ṭabarī, i, 3249, 3350; al-Balād̲h̲urī, 408; al-Dīnawarī, 163). Pērōz III, the son of Yazdadjird III and of the daughter of the Kanārang of Nīs̲h̲āpūr, is said to have lived for a period in Nīs̲h̲āpūr. K̲h̲ulayd b. Kaʾs was sent in 37/657-8 by ʿAlī against the rebellious town (al-Dīnawarī, *op. cit.*). Muʿāwiya reappointed ʿAbd Allāh b. ʿĀmir governor of Baṣra in 41/661-2 and commissioned him to conquer K̲h̲urāsān and Sidjistān. The latter in 42/662-3 installed Ḳays b. al-Hayt̲h̲am al-Sulamī in Nīs̲h̲āpūr as governor of K̲h̲urāsān. Ziyād b. Abī Sufyān in 45/665-6 made K̲h̲ulayd b. ʿAbd Allāh al-Ḥanafī governor of Abars̲h̲ahr (Nīs̲h̲āpūr). ʿAbd Allāh b. K̲h̲āzim rebelled in 63/683 against the Umayyads. He fell in 73/692 at Marw fighting against ʿAbd al-Malik, whereupon Umayyad rule was restored in K̲h̲urāsān.

Until the time when the Ṭāhirid governor of K̲h̲urāsān ʿAbd Allāh b. Ṭāhir (213-30/828-45 [*q.v.*]) made it his capital, Nīs̲h̲āpūr was of less consequence than the Arabs' first capital, Marw [*q.v.*]. But soon, helped by its more salubrious climate, it overtook

Marw in political importance, and also became a centre of economic activity (above all for its famed textiles, including luxury *ᶜattābī* and *saḳlāṭūnī* cloths, cf. al-Thaᶜālibī, *Laṭāʾif al-maᶜārif*, tr. Bosworth, *The book of curious and entertaining information*, 133) and of cultural life. It ceased to be a provincial capital after the Ṣaffārid *amīr* Yaᶜḳūb b. al-Layth in 259/863 took over Khurāsān from the Ṭāhirids and entered the city, and for some 30 years control of it oscillated between the Ṣaffārids and various warlords and military adventurers like Rāfiᶜ b. Harthama [*q.v.*] until ᶜAmr b. al-Layth was defeated and captured by the Sāmānid Ismāᶜīl b. Aḥmad in 287/900 (see Barthold, *Turkestan down to the Mongol invasion*, 217-25; Bosworth, in *Camb. hist. of Iran*, iv, 114-21). But then under the Sāmānids (4th/10th century), it attained especial prosperity as the provincial capital of Khurāsān again and the base and residence of the commander-in-chief of that province. Arts and crafts, such as ceramic production, were notable, and the general prosperity of Nīshāpūr was reflected in the formation of an influential bourgeoisie, composed of merchants, craftsmen, officials and scholars and religious figures from the two main *madhhabs* of Khurāsān, the Ḥanafīs and the Shāfiᶜīs, and from their rivals for popular support there, the members of the ascetic and pietistic sect of the Karrāmiyya [*q.v.*]. From this social group, which R.W. Bulliet has called a patriciate, stemmed notable scholars like Abū Muḥammad al-Djuwaynī and his son the Imām al-Ḥaramayn Abu 'l-Maᶜālī [*q.vv.*] and the traditionist al-Ḥākim al-Naysābūrī, Ibn al-Bayyiᶜ [*q.v.*], and also ambitious statesmen like Maḥmūd of Ghazna's minister Ḥasanak [*q.v.*] from the Mīkālī [*q.v.*] family (see Bosworth, *The Ghaznavids, their empire in Afghanistan and eastern Iran 994:1040*, Edinburgh 1963, 145-202; Bulliet, *The patricians of Nishapur*, Cambridge, Mass. 1972). The large number of traditionists and lawyers which the city produced was undoubtedly a stimulus to the production of several biographical dictionaries of Nīshāpūr scholars, beginning with that of Ibn al-Bayyiᶜ (d. 405/1014) in eight or twelve volumes, the starting-point for various continuations and epitomes (see R.N. Frye, *City chronicles of Central Asia and Khurasan. The Taʾrīx-i Nīsāpūr*, in *Zeki Velidi Togan'a armağan*, Istanbul 1950-5, 405-20; facs. texts in idem, *The histories of Nishapur*, The Hague 1965; the *Muntakhab min al-siyāḳ li-taʾrīkh Naysābūr* of al-Ṣarīfīnī, ed. Muḥ. Aḥmad al-ᶜAzīz, Beirut 1409/1989).

The Arabic geographers describe Nīshāpūr at this time as a thickly populated town divided into 42 wards, 1 *farsakh* in length and breadth (al-Iṣṭakhrī, 254) and consisting of the citadel, the city proper and an outer suburb in which was the chief mosque built by the Ṣaffārid ᶜAmr. Beside it was the public market called al-Muᶜaskar, the governor's palace, a second open place called Maydān al-Ḥusayniyyīn and the prison. The citadel had two gates and the city four: the Gate of the Bridge, the Gate on the road from Maᶜḳil, the Gate of the Fortress (*Bāb al-Ḳuhandiz*) and the Gate of the Takīn Bridge. The suburbs also had walls with many gates. The best known market places were *al-Murabbaᶜa al-Kabīra* (near the Friday Mosque) and *al-Murabbaᶜa al-Ṣaghīra*. The most important business streets were about fifty in number and ran across the city in straight lines intersecting at right angles; all kinds of wares were on sale in them (on the products and exports of Nīshāpūr, see G. Le Strange, *The lands of the Eastern Caliphate*, 429-30). Numerous canals were led from the Wādī Saghāwar, which flowed down from the village of Bushtankār or Būshtaḳān and drove 70 mills, whence it passed near the city and provided the houses with an ample water supply. Gardens below the city were also watered in this way. The district of Nīshāpūr was regarded as the most fertile in Khurāsān.

The town suffered many vicissitudes after this period. A great famine broke out there in 401/1011. At the beginning of the 5th/11th century Nīshāpūr was the centre of the pietist Karrāmīs led by the anchorite Abū Bakr Muḥammad b. Isḥāḳ. The Saldjūḳ Ṭoghril Beg first occupied the town in 428/1037 and subsequently made it his capital. Alp Arslān also seems to have lived there (cf. Barhebraeus, *Chron. Syr.*, ed. Bedjan, 243). In Shawwāl 536/May 1142 the Khʷārazmshāh Atsïz took the town for a time from the Saldjūḳ sultan Sandjar. When it was sacked by the Ghuzz in 548/1153 the inhabitants fled, mainly to the suburb of Shādyākh which was enlarged and fortified by the governor al-Muʾayyid. Ṭughān Shāh Abū Bakr ruled the city during 569-81/1174-85 and his son Sandjar Shāh during 581-3/1185-7.

In Rabīᶜ I or II 583/May or June 1187 the Khʷārazmshāh Tekish took Nīshāpūr and gave it to his eldest son Malik Shāh. At the end of 589/1193 the latter received Marw and his brother Ḳuṭb al-Dīn Muḥammad became governor of Nīshāpūr. Malik Shāh died in 593/1197 in the neighbourhood of Nīshāpūr. ᶜAlāʾ al-Dīn Muḥammad (as Ḳuṭb al-Dīn called himself after his father's death) took Marw and Nīshāpūr in 598/1202 from the Ghūrids Ghiyāth al-Dīn and his brother Shihāb al-Dīn.

In addition to the wars and rebellions (e.g. 604-5/1207-8) which afflicted the town, it suffered from repeated earthquakes (540/1145, 605/1208, 679/1280). Yāḳūt who visited it in 613/1216 but stayed in Shādyākh, could still see the damage done by the first earthquake and by the Ghuzz, but nevertheless thought the town the finest in Khurāsān. The second earthquake was particularly severe; the inhabitants on this occasion fled for several days into the plain below the city.

In 618/1221 the Mongols under Čingiz Khān sacked the city completely (see Djuwaynī-Boyle, i, 169-78). Although Nīshāpūr's palmiest days were ended by the Mongol devastations, it soon revived from the effects of these. The city's centre had been displaced to Shādyākh after the earthquakes of the early 7th/13th century, and the same cause lay behind its reconstitution on a third site towards the end of that same century. Ḥamd Allāh Mustawfī describes it in the 8th/14th century as highly flourishing, with extensive protective walls (*Nuzha*, 148-9, tr. 147-8), whilst Ibn Baṭṭūṭa calls it "Little Damascus" for its fertility and productiveness, and praises the *madrasas* and throngs of students which he saw there (*Riḥla*, iii, 80-2, tr. Gibb, iii, 583-5).

Thereafter, Nīshāpūr slowly declined in importance until its modest revival in the later 19th century. In 1890 G.N. Curzon found the Nīshāpūr region still fertile, and the famous turquoise mines in the district called Bār-i Maᶜdin some 50 km/35 miles northwest of the town were still being profitably worked; but the walls of the town itself were ruinous (*Persia and the Persian question*, London 1892, i, 260-7). The modern town of Nīshāpūr is situated in lat. 36° 13' and long. 58° 49' E., and lies in an altitude of 1193 m./3,913 ft. and on the east side of a plain surrounded by hills. To the north and east of the town lies the ridge of Binālūd-Kūh, which separates it from the valley of Mashhad and Ṭūs. At its foot spring a number of streams, among them the Shūra Rūd and the river of Dizbād (Mustawfī) which irrigate the lands of

Nī**sh**āpūr and disappear in the salt desert to the west. North of the town in the mountains was the little lake of Ča**sh**ma Sabz out of which, according to Mustawfī, run two streams, one to the east and the other to the west. The tombs of her famous sons ᶜUmar **Kh**ayyām and Farīd al-Dīn ᶜAṭṭār [*q.vv.*] are still shown in the town. According to the 1365*sh*/1986 census, Nī**sh**āpūr had a population of 109,258.

Bibliography (in addition to references given in the article): 1. Sources. For these, see *EI*[1] art. s.v. (E. Honigmann), to which should be added *Ḥudūd al-ᶜālam*, tr. Minorsky, 102-3, comm. 325-6.
2. Studies. W. Tomaschek, *Zur historische Topographie von Persien*, in *SB Ak. Wien* (1883, 1885), i, 7708; Marquart, *Ērānšahr*, Berlin 1901, 47, 49, 68-9, 74-5, 293, 301; C.E. Yate, *Khurasan and Seistan*, Edinburgh 1900; Le Strange, *Lands*, 382-8; P.M. Sykes, *A sixth journey in Persia*, in *GJ*, xxxvii (1911), 1-19, 149-65; A. Gabriel, *Die Erforschung Persiens*, Vienna 1952, index; Sylvia A. Matheson, *Persia, an archaeological guide*², London 1976, 199-200; C. Wilkinson, *Nishapur. Some early Islamic buildings and their decoration*, New York 1986.

(E. Honigmann-[C.E. Bosworth])

NĪSHĀPŪRĪ, Ẓahīr al-Dīn, Persian author who wrote a valuable history of the Sal**dj**ūḳs during the reign of the last Great Sal**dj**ūḳ of Persia, Ṭo**gh**ril (III) b. Arslan [*q.v.*]; he must have died *ca.* 580/1184-5. Nothing is known of his life except that Rāwandī [*q.v.*] states (*Rāḥat al-ṣudūr*, ed. M. Iqbál, 54) that he had been tutor to the previous sultans Masᶜūd b. Muḥammad [*q.v.*] and Arslan b. Ṭo**gh**ril (II). His *Sal**dj**ūḳ-nāma* was long believed lost, but was known as the main source for Rāwandī's information on the Sal**dj**ūḳs up to the latter's own time (see *Rāḥat al-ṣudūr*, Preface, pp. XXVI, XXIX); hence it is essentially Nīshāpūrī's material which was utilised for the Sal**dj**ūḳs by later authors like Ra**sh**īd al-Dīn, Ḥamd Allāh Mustawfī and Ḥāfiẓ-i Abrū [*q.vv.*]. The *Sal**dj**ūḳ-nāma* is a concise, soberly-written history in Persian, of especial value for the history of the later sultans up to the accession of Ṭo**gh**ril (III) in 571/1176; see for an estimate of its worth, Cl. Cahen, *The historiography of the Seljuqid period*, in B. Lewis and P.M. Holt (eds.), *Historians of the Middle East*, London 1962, 73-6. After its rediscovery, it was indifferently published at Tehran in 1322/1953.

Bibliography (in addition to references in the text): Barthold, *Turkestan*, 30; Storey-Bregel, ii, 342-5 no. 639; K.A. Luther, *The Saljūqnāmah and the Jāmiᶜ al-tawārīkh*, in *Procs. of the colloquium on Rashīd al-Dīn Faḍlallāh, Tabrīz-Tehran 1348/1969*, Tehran 1971, 26-35. (C.E. Bosworth)

NITHĀR (a.), verbal noun of *nathara* "to scatter, spread abroad", in the pre-modern Middle East, the showering of money, jewels and other valuables on occasions of rejoicing, such as a wedding, a circumcision, the accession of a ruler, the victorious return from a military campaign, the reception of a diplomatic envoy, recovery from illness, etc. It was thus in part one aspect of the general practice of largesse and presentgiving by superiors to inferiors [see hiba, inᶜām, **kh**ilᶜa] but also an aspect of charity to the poor. On occasion, the whole of the state treasury might be disbursed in this way (see Spuler, *Iran*, 347). *Ni**th**ārs* are often mentioned in descriptions of court festivities under the early **Gh**aznawid [*q.v.*] sultans; see Gītī Falāḥ Rastgār, *ᶜĀdāb u rusūm u ta**sh**rīfāt dar bār-i **Gh**azna az **kh**ilāl-i Taʾrī**kh**-i Bayhaḳi*, in *Yād-nāma-yi Abu 'l-Faḍl-i Bayhaḳī*, Ma**sh**had 1349 *sh*/1970, 412 ff.

Bibliography: Given in the article. (Ed.)

In India. The occasions for the distribution of largesse to the court and to the multitudes attending processions have been detailed in marāsim. 5, and mawākib. 5, above; and references to the smaller coins used in the *ni**th**ār* are made in mu**gh**als. 11. Numismatics.

There are few specific references to *ni**th**ār* in Indian dynasties before the Mu**gh**al period, although it was an ancient Indian custom and so likely to have been perpetuated (cf. N.N. Law, *Ancient Hindu coronations and allied ceremonials*, in *Ind.Ant.* [June 1919], 84 ff.) in the Dihlī sultanate and elsewhere; for example, the shower of gold and silver coins, and jewels, over the head of a recent conqueror is referred to in the account of the conquest of Mālwā by Muẓaffar II of Gu**dj**arāt and by Sikandar b. Muḥammad Man**dj**hū in the *Mirʾāt-i Sikandarī*, and ᶜAlāʾ al-Dīn **Kh**al**dj**ī is said to have used *man**dj**anīḳs* [*q.v.*] to scatter coins and "golden stars" among the Dihlī populace.

There are many references in the early Mu**gh**al period to the practice under Bābur and Humāyūn (*Tūzuk-i Bāburī*, tr. Beveridge, 43; Gulbadan Begam, *Humāyūn-nāma*, 112 *et passim*), when not only small gold and silver coins but also small gold and silver fruits (almonds, walnuts and filberts) and flowers were so scattered. This would appear to have been a Ča**gh**ataʾī custom inherited by the Mu**gh**als, and it persisted until at least the time of Farru**kh**siyar. Fanny Parks (*Wanderings of a pilgrim in search of the picturesque*, London 1850) speaks of the custom of showering coins and jewels over the head of the new ruler in the Lakhnaʾū court. For the scattering of coins among the populace, besides the half- and quarter-rupees, smaller coins, usually thinner than those of the standard currency and not standing in any regular fractional relation to it, of gold as well as silver, and many of dainty and excellent workmanship, were known especially from the reign of **Dj**ahāngīr; *ni**th**ārī* was for a short time the name of his quarter-rupee, though *ni**th**ār*, *nūr af**sh**ān* and ***kh**ayr ḳabūl* are all used for largesse-coins in his reign. Occasions for the scattering of *ni**th**ār* were especially the Imperial festivals and processions on anniversaries of accession-date, the emperor's solar and lunar birthdays, the births and marriages of royal princes and princesses, the formal weighing of the emperor against gold, silver and jewels, the *āb-pā**sh**ī* ceremony, ceremonial visits to Akbar's tomb and to the tombs of certain *pīrs* (especially at Fatḥpur Sīkrī and A**dj**mēr), and so on. It seems certain that much largesse-money was struck at provincial mints, possibly in connection with imperial visits, as many of the dated *ni**th**ārs* correspond with dates in the chronicles.

Bibliography: In addition to references in the article, see especially S.H. Hodivala, *Niṣārs*, no. XIV in *Historical studies in Mu**gh**al numismatics*, Calcutta 1923; references *passim* in the coin catalogues mentioned in the *Bibl.* to mu**gh**als. 11.

(J. Burton-Page)

NIYĀḤA (a.) "lamentation", the noun of action from *nāḥa* "to weep with great cries, lamentations, sighings and affliction". The term is used to designate the activity of professional mourners who play a great role in funeral ceremonies all around the Mediterranean. If it is mentioned here, it is because this practice, considered to be a legacy of paganism, was condemned by the Prophet. Indeed, he is made to say "Three pre-Islamic customs (*a**kh**lāḳ*; *Usd al-**gh**āba, fiᶜl*) are not to be retained by the Muslims. They are: invoking the planets in order to receive rain (*istisḳāʾ bi 'l-kawākib*), attacking genealogies (*al-ṭaᶜn fi 'l-nisba*) and lamenting the dead (*al-niyāḥa ᶜalā 'l-mayyit*)" (al-

Ṭabarī, Appendix, extract from the *Dhayl al-Mudhayyal*, iii[4], 2387; Ibn al-Athīr, *Usd al-ghāba*, i, 299).

Weeping for the dead was something which could be done not only by women but also by men, some of whom become wellknown for this; the *Aghānī* cites, e.g. Ibn Suraydj (i, 99-100).

The pagan character of this practice is displayed in a text of Ibn Saᶜd, *Ṭabaḳāt*, i/1, 88, where it is written: "At the death of his son Ibrāhīm, the Prophet wept (*bakā*). Someone said to him, O Messenger of God, did you not forbid weeping?—He replied, I forbade raising one's voice (*nawḥ*) in two instances, both equally stupid and impious: a voice raised in a state of happiness (which shows itself) in celebrations, disporting and diabolical chantings (*mazāmīr shayṭān*) and a voice in times of misfortune (which shows itself) in mutilating one's face, tearing of clothes and a diabolical mourning cry (*rannat shayṭān* = the *nēnia* of the Romans = a funeral lament). My personal tears express my compassion (*raḥma*). Whoever has no compassion (for others), (these last) will have no compassion for him."

Another account, given by the same author (91), confirms the previous one. There was an eclipse of the sun on the day of Ibrāhīm's death; people saw in it a relationship of cause and effect. The Prophet rebutted this relationship and then let his tears flow. People said to him, "You are weeping, you, the Messenger of God!"—He replied, "I am a man; the eyes shed tears, the heart breaks and we say nothing which will irritate the Lord."

Finally, one should add that, amongst the ancient Arabs, the position of the woman weeping for her husband served as an indication of her future intentions. If she did this standing (*ḳāʾima*), it was assumed that she would not marry again (*Aghānī*, ii, 138).

Bibliography: In addition to references given in the article, see M. Abdesselem, *Le thème de la mort*, Tunis 1977, index s.vv. lamentations, mourners, etc.

(T. Fahd)

NIYĀZĪ, an Ottoman poet and mystic. Shams al-Dīn Meḥmed known as Miṣrī Efendi, Shaykh Miṣrī, whose *makhlaṣ* was Niyāzī, came from Aspūzī, the former summer capital of Malaṭya (cf. Ewliyā Čelebi, iv, 15; von Moltke, *Reisebriefe*, 349), where his father was a Naḳshbandī dervish. Niyāzī was born in 1027/1617-18. The statement occasionally found that Soghanlï was his birthplace is not correct.

His father instructed him in the teaching of the order, then he went in 1048/1638 to Diyārbakr, later to Mārdīn where he studied for three years and finally to Cairo. There he joined the Ḳādirī order, travelled for seven years and finally settled down in the Anatolian village of Elmalï, once notorious as a centre of heresy, to devote himself to study under the famous Khalwetī Shaykh Umm-i Sinān (d. 1069/1658). He stayed with him for twelve years until he was sent by the Shaykh as his deputy to ᶜUshshāḳ near Izmīr. After the death of his master, he moved to Bursa, where a pious citizen, Abdāl Čelebi, built a hermitage for him. The fame of his sanctity and his gifts of prophecy spread more and more and finally reached the ears of the grand vizier Köprülü-zāde Aḥmed Pasha [see köprülü], who invited him to Edirne, entertained him with great honour for 40 days and finally sent him back to Bursa. When in 1083/1672 the army set out for Kameniec in Podolia [see ḳamāničа], he was summoned to Edirne; where he had great audiences as a preacher. As he had allowed himself to drop Kabbalistic allusions (*kelimāt-i djifriyye*), he gave offence and was banished to Lemnos. There he spent some years in exile until he received permission to return to Bursa. The fact that during his stay on the island it was spared Venetian attacks was interpreted as a miracle wrought by this holy man. But when he stirred up the people by "kabbalistic" preaching he was again banished to Lemnos in Ṣafar 1088/May 1677. All kinds of prophecies which were fulfilled, as well as the story that his coming had been foretold by Ibn al-ᶜArabī [*q.v.*], strengthened his reputation as a holy man and miracle-worker. He spent ten years on Lemnos until in 1101/1689 the vizier Köprülü-zāde Muṣṭafā Pasha allowed him to return to Bursa. In the next year he was summoned to Edirne; he again excited the people by political utterances and mystical allusions so that the Ḳāʾimmaḳām ᶜOthmān Pasha had him taken, with all respect, by a guard of Janissaries and Čawushs out of the mosque and sent directly via Gallipoli to Bursa. From there he was again banished to Lemnos, but died on 20 Radjab 1105/17 March 1694. The date 1111/1699 given by von Hammer, *GOD*, iii, 588, must therefore be wrong.

Unfortunately, the contemporary notices give no information about the nature of the sermons by Niyāzī which gave offence from the political as well as religious point of view. The historian Demetrius Kantemir said Niyāzī was secretly a Christian. His *Dīwān*, in Arabic and Turkish, does not justify this suggestion, although the poem declared by von Hammer (*GOD*, iii, 589) to be apocryphal, given in translation by Kantemir, is really taken from his *Dīwān*, as Gibb, *HOP*, iii, 315, has proved. No study has yet been made of the *Dīwān* or of Niyāzī's position in the religious life of a Turkey generally.

The order founded by Niyāzī once possessed several monasteries on Greek soil, in Modoni, Negroponte (Eghriboz), Saloniki, Mytilene, also in Edirne, Bursa and Izmir. Cf. thereon the study by V.A. Gordlevski, *Tarikat Mïsri Niyazi*, in *Dokladï Akademii Nauk SSSR* (1929), 153-60.

The main source for the history of Niyāzī's life and work is the rare Turkish treatise of Moralïzāde Luṭfī (= Muṣṭafā Luṭfullāh), *Tuḥfat al-ᶜaṣrī fī manāḳib al-Miṣrī*, published at Bursa in 1308/1890-1.

Niyāzī's poems were repeatedly published 1254 and 1259 at Būlāḳ, also 1260 and 1291 in Istanbul; cf. thereon von Hammer, in *Wiener Jahrbücher*, lxxxv, 36, and *JA*, ser. 4, vol. viii, 261. On his numerous other works, only available in mss., cf. Bursalï Meḥmed Ṭāhir, *ᶜOthmānlï müʾellifleri*, i, 173-4, with references to where they are preserved, and Abdülbâkî Gölpınarlı, *İA* art. s.v.

Bibliography: In addition to the works mentioned by J. von Hammer, *GOD*, iii, 587 ff., and Gibb, *HOP*, iii, 312 ff., and Bursalï Meḥmed Ṭāhir, *ᶜOthmānlï müʾellifleri*, i, 172 ff., cf. also the biographies of Ottoman poets by Shaykhī, Sālim, ᶜUshshāḳī-zāde, etc.; Rāshid, *Taʾrīkh*, i, 89, 193; J.B. Brown, *The Darvishes*[2], London 1927, 203-5. On Niyāzī's religious attitude, cf. D. Kantemir, *Geschichte des osmanischen Reiches*, Hamburg 1745, 636-7, 642, also Mouradgea d'Ohsson, *Tableau de l'Empire Ottoman*, iv, 626, also von Hammer, *GOR*, vi, 337, 364, 578, vii, 161 (his tomb on Lemnos); L. Massignon, *al-Hallâj, martyr mystique de l'Islam*, i, Paris 1922, 428 ff., 440. The Vienna ms. no. 1928 (cf. Flügel, *Katal.*, iii, 474 ff.) contains besides the *Diwān* many other works of Niyāzī; cf. thereon Rieu, *Catal. of Turk. mss. in the Brit. Mus.*, 261.

(F. Babinger)

NIYĀZĪ BEY, Aḥmed (1873-1912), Young Turk officer and one of the protagonists of the Ottoman constitutional revolution of 1908. Niyāzī hailed from Resen (he was called Resnelī, i.e. "from Resen"), and was an Albanian by birth.

He went to military *rushdī* and *iʿdādī* schools in Monastir (Bitola) before entering the military academy (*Ḥarbiyye*) in Istanbul, where he graduated as a second lieutenant in 1896. After his graduation he saw service in the European provinces of the Empire and he made a name for himself during the battle of Beshpînar in the 1897 Greek-Ottoman war. He was promoted to first lieutenant, captain and eventually adjutant-major, while serving with the Third (Macedonian) Army between 1898 and 1908. Between 1903 and 1908 he was in command of the Third Light Rifle Batallion in Ohrid and constantly engaged in combating the guerrilla warfare of Bulgarian bands in the area.

When the *ʿOthmānlï Ḥürriyet Djemʿiyyeti* (Ottoman Freedom Committee), which later merged with the Paris-based *Ittiḥād we Teraḳḳī Djemʿiyyeti* [*q.v.*] (Committee of Union and Progress), began to spread among the officers of the Third Army, Niyāzī was an early member. In July 1908, the Society suspected that a decision to break up and divide the Ottoman Empire had been reached by King Edward VII of England and Tsar Nicholas during their discussions at Reval, and it decided to act to force the restoration of constitutional rule in order to ward off foreign intervention. Niyāzī was the first of a number of Young Turk officers, who, on the orders of the Committee, started an insurrection in Macedonia. On Friday, 3 July 1908 he took to the hills with about two hundred men and began to demand the restoration of the constitution in cables sent to the authorities. He was soon followed by other officers, such as Enwer [*q.v.*].

After the restoration of the constitution on 24 July, Niyāzī, together with Enwer, was launched by the C.U.P. as one of the *Ḥürriyyet Ḳahramānlarï* ("Freedom Heroes") and he toured the Empire, receiving a rapturous welcome from the crowds. Later in the year the C.U.P. decided to have Niyāzī's memoirs (which were partly ghosted) published as *the* account of the revolution to the exclusion of all others.

One reason for this was probably that, unlike most of his Young Turk colleagues, Niyāzī did not have political ambitions and devoted himself to military matters. When, on 13 April 1909, a counter-revolution broke out in Istanbul and the constitutionalists were driven from the city, Niyāzī was instrumental in raising the Albanian volunteers who made up an important part of the *Ḥareket Ordusu* ("Operational Army") that reconquered the capital for the C.U.P. and the constitution two weeks later.

Niyāzī fought in Tripolitania during the Ottoman-Italian war of 1911 and then retired to his native Resen. On 17 April 1913 he was killed by an Albanian nationalist in Valona, while on his way to Istanbul.

Bibliography: Ḳol Aghasï Resneli Aḥmed Niyāzī, *Khāṭirāt-ï Niyāzī yākhūd Tārīkhče-yi Inḳilāb-i Kabīr-i ʿOthmānīden bir ṣaḥīfa*, Istanbul 1326 [Rūmī] /1910, also published as İhsan İlgar (ed.), *Balkanlarda bir gerillacı. Hürriyet Kahramanı Resneli Niyāzī Bey'in anıları*, Istanbul 1975; İbrahim Alaettin Gövsa, *Türk meşhurları ansiklopedisi*, Istanbul n.d., 286; Feroz Ahmad, *The Young Turks. The Committee of Union and Progress in politics 1908-1914*, Oxford 1969, 176. (E.J. Zürcher)

NIYYA (A.), intention. The acts prescribed by the Islamic *sharīʿa*, obligatory or not, require to be preceded by a declaration by the performer, that he intends to perform such an act. This declaration, pronounced audibly or mentally, is called *niyya*. Without it, the act would be *bāṭil* [*q.v.*].

The *niyya* is required before the performance of the *ʿibādāt*, such as washing, bathing, prayer, alms, fasting, retreat, pilgrimage, sacrifice. "Ceremonial acts without *niyya* are not valid", says al-Ghazālī (*Iḥyāʾ*, Cairo 1282, iv, 316). Yet a survey of the opinions of the lawyers regarding the *niyya* in connection with each of the *ʿibādāt* would show that there is only unanimity about the *niyya* as required before the *ṣalāt*.

Further, the *niyya* must immediately precede the act, lest it should lose its character and become simple decision (*ʿazm*). It must accompany the act until the end (Abū Isḥāḳ al-Shīrāzī, *Tanbīh*, ed. Juynboll, 3). Its seat is the heart, the central organ of intellect and attention. Lunatics, therefore, cannot pronounce a valid *niyya*.

So the *niyya* has become a legal act of its own. It is usually called obligatory, but in some cases, e.g. the washing of the dead, commendable. It can even be asked what the intention of the *niyya* is. According to al-Bādjūrī (i, 57), four conditions must be fulfilled in a *niyya*: he who pronounces it must be Muslim, *compos mentis*, well acquainted with the act he wants to perform, and having the purpose to perform this act. In some instances *adjmaʿa* is used, where the later language has *nawā* (e.g. al-Nasāʾī, *Ṣiyām*, *bāb* 68; al-Tirmidhī, *Ṣawm*, *bāb* 33).

The term does not occur in the Ḳurʾān. It is found in canonical *ḥadīth*, but the passages show that is has not yet acquired in this literature the technical meaning and limitation described above. The development of this technical use appears to have taken place gradually, probably aided by Jewish influence. In Jewish law, the *kawwānā* has a function wholly analogous to the *niyya*. Al-Shāfiʿī (d. 204/820) appears to be acquainted with the *niyya* in its technical sense (*Kitāb al-Umm*). In canonical *ḥadīth*, i.e. the literature which, generally speaking, reflects the state of things up to the middle of the 2nd/8th century, neither the verb *nawā* nor the noun *niyya* appear to have any special technical connection with the *ʿibādāt*. On the contrary, *niyya* has here the common meaning of intention.

In this sense, it is of great importance. Al-Bukhārī opens his collection with a tradition, which in this place is apparently meant as a motto. It runs: "Works are only rendered efficacious by their intention" (*innamā 'l-aʿmāl bi 'l-niyya* or *bi 'l-niyyāt*). This tradition occurs frequently in the canonical collections. It constitutes a religious and moral criterion superior to that of the law. The value of an *ʿibāda*, even if performed in complete accordance with the precepts of the law, depends upon the intention of the performer, and if this intention should be sinful, the work would be valueless. "For", adds the tradition just mentioned, "every man receives only what he has intended"; or "his wages shall be in accordance with his intention" (Mālik, *Djanāʾiz*, trad. 36). In answer to the question how long the *hidjra* is open, tradition says: "There is no *hidjra* after the capture of Mecca, only holy war and intention" (al-Bukhārī, *Manāḳib al-Anṣār*, *bāb* 45; *Djihād*, *bāb* 1, 27; Muslim, *Imāra*, trad. 85, 86, etc.). This higher criterion, once admitted, may suspend the law in several cases (cf. Snouck Hurgronje, *Islam und Phonograph*, in *TBGKW*, xlii, 393 ff. = *Verspr. Geschriften*, ii, 419 ff.). So the intention, in this sense, becomes a work of its own, just as the intention in its juridical application. Good intention is taken into account by God, even if not carried out; it heightens the value of the work. On the other hand, refraining from an evil intention is reckoned as a good work (al-

Bu<u>kh</u>ārī, *Riḳāḳ*, *bāb* 31). In this connection, the (post-canonical) tradition can be understood, according to which the intention of the faithful is better than his work (*Lisān al-ʿArab*, xx, 223; cf. al-<u>Gh</u>azālī, *Iḥyāʾ*, iv, 330 ff., where this tradition is discussed). In similar instances, *niyya* comes near to the meaning of *i<u>kh</u>lāṣ* [*q.v.*].

Bibliography: Bā<u>dj</u>ūrī, *Ḥā<u>sh</u>iya*, Cairo 1303, i, 57; <u>Sh</u>aʿrānī, *al-Mīzān al-kubrā*, Cairo 1279, i, 135, 136, 161, ii, 2, 20, 30, 42; <u>Gh</u>azālī, *Kitāb al-Wa<u>dj</u>īz*, Cairo 1317, i, 11, 12, 40, 87, 100-1, 106, 115; idem, *Iḥyāʾ*, iv, book 7, also tr. into German by H. Bauer, Halle a.d. Saale 1916; C. Snouck Hurgronje, *Verspreide Geschriften*, i, 50, ii, 90; Th.W. Juynboll, *Handleiding*, index, s.v.; A.J. Wensinck, *Handbook of early Muh. tradition*, s.v. Intention; idem, *De intentie in recht, ethiek en mystiek der semietische volken*, in *Versl. Med. Ak. Amst.*, ser. 5, iv, 109 ff.

(A.J. Wensinck)

NĪZAK, ṬAR<u>KH</u>ĀN, ruler of the northern branch of the Hephtalite confederation which had in pre-Islamic times ruled both north and south of the Hindu Kush, from what is now Soviet Central Asia to northern India, that people known to the Arab historians as Hayṭal (<* Habṭal), pl. Hayāṭila [*q.v.*] (see on them, R. Ghirshman, *Les Chionites-Hephtalites*, Cairo 1958, 69 ff.). It is unclear whether the Ṭarkhān element of his name is in fact a personal name or the well-known Central Asian title (on which see Bosworth and Sir Gerard Clauson, in *JRAS* [1965], 11-12).

The power of the northern Hephthalites, whose dominions were centred on Bā<u>dh</u>ghīs [*q.v.*] in what is now northern Af<u>gh</u>ānistān, was threatened by the advance of Arab armies under the command of Ḳutayba b. Muslim [*q.v.*]. Uncertain of Nīzak's strength, Ḳutayba at first made peace with him, on condition that Nīzak provide military aid for his campaigns into Transoxania (87-90/706-9). But in 90/709 Nīzak led a rising against Ḳutayba of the Hephthalites and Turkish rulers of the upper Oxus lands, seeking help also from the Kābul-<u>Sh</u>āh, apparently fearing that the Arabs were going to secure an irreversible grip on these eastern fringes of <u>Kh</u>urāsān unless stopped. However, Ḳutayba and his brother ʿAbd al-Raḥmān defeated and captured Nīzak (91/710), and executed him, contrary to an earlier promise of *amān*, on the direct orders of the governor of the East al-Ḥa<u>djdj</u>ā<u>dj</u>. The collapse of the revolt marked the end of Hephthalite power north of the Hindu Kush, though the southern Hephthalite kingdom, centred on Zābulistān [*q.v.*], survived for some two centuries as a barrier to Muslim expansion through southern Afghanistan (see Bosworth, *Sīstān under the Arabs*, Rome 1968, index s.v. Zunbīl).

Bibliography: Balā<u>dh</u>urī, *Futūḥ*, 420; Yaʿḳūbī, *Taʾrī<u>kh</u>*, ii, 342; Ṭabarī, ii, 1184 ff., 1204-7, 1217-22, 1226; F.N. Skrine and E.D. Ross, *The heart of Asia*, London 1899, 56-9; J. Wellhausen, *Das arabische Reich und sein Sturz*, Berlin 1902, 271, Eng. tr. 435; H.A.R. Gibb, *The Arab conquests in Central Asia*, London 1923, 32, 37-8, 80; Ghirshman, *Les Chionites-Hephtalites*, 98-104; M.A. Shaban, *The ʿAbbāsid Revolution*, Cambridge 1970, 65-7. For Nīzak's coins, see Ghirshman, *op. cit.*, 25 ff.

(C.E. Bosworth)

NIẒĀM (A.), the honorific title which became characteristic of the rulers of the Indo-Muslim state of Ḥaydarābād [*q.v.*], derived in the first place from the fuller title Niẓām al-Mulk borne by the Mu<u>gh</u>al noble Ḳamar al-Dīn Čīn Ḳilič <u>Kh</u>ān [see NIẒĀM AL-MULK], who became governor of the Deccan in 1132/1720 and who also bore the title of Āṣaf <u>Dj</u>āh. The process of the identification of the title Niẓām with the rulership of Ḥaydarābād was strengthened by the long reign there (1175-1217/1762-1802) of Āṣaf <u>Dj</u>āh's fourth son Niẓām ʿAlī <u>Kh</u>ān, and henceforth the ruler was known in British Government of India parlance as "His Highness the Niẓām".

Bibliography: See H. Yule and A.C. Burnell, *Hobson-Jobson, a glossary of Anglo-Indian colloquial words and phrases*², London 1903, 628. (Ed.)

NIẒĀM BADA<u>KH</u><u>SH</u>Ī, Indo-Muslim scholar of the 10th/16th century. He studied law and *ḥadī<u>th</u>* under Mawlānā ʿIṣām al-Dīn Ibrāhīm and Mullā Saʿīd in his native province of Bada<u>kh</u><u>sh</u>ān in eastern Af<u>gh</u>ānistān and was looked upon as one of the most learned men of his age. He was also the *murīd* (disciple) of <u>Sh</u>ay<u>kh</u> Ḥusayn of <u>Kh</u>ʷārazm. His attainments procured him access to the court of Sulaymān, prince of Bada<u>kh</u><u>sh</u>ān, who conferred upon him the title of Ḳāḍī <u>Kh</u>ān. Subsequently, he left his master and went to India. At Kānpūr, he was introduced to the Mu<u>gh</u>al Emperor Akbar (963-1014/1556-1605). He received several presents, and was appointed *Parwānčī* writer. Akbar soon discovered in him a man of great insight, and made him a "Commander of One Thousand" (*yak hazārī*). He also bestowed upon him the title of <u>Gh</u>āzī <u>Kh</u>ān after he had distinguished himself in several expeditions. He died in Oudh at the age of seventy in 992/1584. He is the author of the following works: 1. *Ḥā<u>sh</u>iyat <u>Sh</u>arḥ al-ʿAḳāʾid*, a commentary on al-Taftāzānī's commentary on the *ʿAḳāʾid* of al-Nasafī; 2. several treatises on Ṣūfism.

Bibliography: ʿAbd al-Ḳādir al-Badāʾūnī, *Munta<u>kh</u>ab al-tawārī<u>kh</u>*, iii, 153; <u>Sh</u>āh Nawāz <u>Kh</u>ān, *Maʾā<u>th</u>ir al-umarāʾ*, ii, 857; Āzā<u>d</u>, *Darbār-i Akbarī*, 815; Abu 'l-Faḍl ʿAllāmī, *Āʾīn-i Akbarī*, tr. Blochmann, 440. (M. Hidayet Hosain)

NIẒĀM AL-DĪN AḤMAD B. MUḤAMMAD MUḲĪM AL-**HARAWĪ** (d. 1003/1594), a Persian historian, author of the celebrated *Ṭabaḳāt-i Akbar<u>sh</u>āhī*. He was a descendant of the famous *<u>sh</u>ay<u>kh</u>* of Harāt, ʿAbd Allāh Anṣārī. His father <u>Kh</u>ō<u>dj</u>a Muḳīm Harawī was major-domo to Bābur (932-7/1526-30 [*q.v.*]) and later vizier to the governor of Gu<u>dj</u>arāt Mīrzā ʿAskarī. Niẓām al-Dīn himself held several high military offices under the Great Mu<u>gh</u>al Akbar and became in 993/1585 *Ba<u>kh</u><u>sh</u>ī* of Gu<u>dj</u>arāt and in 1001/1593 even *Ba<u>kh</u><u>sh</u>ī* of the whole empire. According to Badāʾūnī (ii, 397), he died on 23 Ṣafar 1003/18 October 1594, aged 45. At his father's instigation he took up historical studies while quite a boy. His fondness for this subject increased as time went on and induced him to try writing himself. The lack of a complete history of India made him decide to fill the gap, and thus arose his celebrated work, called the *Ṭabaḳāt-i Akbar<u>sh</u>āhī* or *Ṭabaḳāt-i Akbarī* or *Taʾrī<u>kh</u>-i Niẓāmī* which was finished in 1001/1593. Niẓām al-Dīn used 27 different sources for this work, all of which he mentions by name, and in this way produced a very thorough piece of work on which all his successors have relied. He deals with the history of India from the campaigns of Sebüktigīn (366-87/977-97) to the 37th year of Akbar's reign (1001/1593). The work is divided into a *muḳaddima* which deals with the <u>Gh</u>aznawids, and nine *ṭabaḳāt* : 1. the Sultans of Dihlī from Muʿizz al-Dīn <u>Gh</u>ūrī to Akbar (574-1002/1178-1594); at the end of this part are biographies of famous men at Akbar's court, *amīrs*, *ʿulamāʾ*, poets, writers and *<u>sh</u>ay<u>kh</u>s*; 2. the rulers of the Deccan (748-1002/1347-1594): the Bahmanī, Niẓām<u>sh</u>āhī, ʿĀdil<u>sh</u>āhī and Ḳuṭb<u>sh</u>āhī ones; 3. the rulers of

Gudjarāt (793-980/1390-1572); 4. the rulers of Mālwa (809-977/1406-1569); 5. the rulers of Bengal (741-984/1340-1576); 6. the Sharḳī dynasty of Djawnpūr (784-881/1381-1476); 7. the rulers of Kashmīr (747-995/1346-1567); 8. the history of Sind from the Arab conquest (86/705) to 1001/1593; 9. the history of Multān (847-932/1444-1525). The whole work was to have as a *khātima* a topographical description of India, but it was apparently never finished by the author.

Bibliography: Rieu, *B.M. catalogue*, 220a-222a. Biography of the author: Elliot and Dowson, *History of India*, v, 178-80. Synopsis of contents, *ibid.*, v, 177-476; N. Lees, in *JRAS*, New Ser., iii, 451. Editions: lith. Lucknow 1870; B. De, *The Tabakat-i Akbari* (*or A History of India from the early Musalman invasions to the thirty-sixth year of the reign of Akbar*) (with Eng.tr.), Calcutta 1913 (*Bibl. Indica*, New Ser. 199). For mss., see Storey, i, 433-5.

(E. Berthels)

NIẒĀM AL-DĪN AWLIYĀʾ, Shaykh, a widely venerated saint of the Čishti order [see čishtiyya] who raised his *silsila* to a pan-Indian position, was born at Badāʾūn [*q.v.*] (in U.P.) *ca.* 640-1/1243-4. He was given the name Muḥammad but became known by his title Niẓām al-Dīn. His grandfather had migrated to India from Bukhārā under the stress of Mongol invasions. His father died when he was a boy of tender age. His mother, Bībī Zulaykhā, a lady of fervent piety, brought him up and moulded his thought and character. In Badāʾūn, Shādī Muḳrī taught him the Ḳurʾān, and Mawlāna ʿAlāʾ al-Dīn Uṣūlī gave instruction on the works of al-Ḳudurī and the *Hidāya*. At the age of sixteen he reached Dihlī in order to complete his education. Mawlānā Kamāl al-Dīn Zāhid, a pious and dedicated scholar, taught the *Mashāriḳ al-anwār* to him and he committed it to memory. During this early period Niẓām al-Dīn lived in Dihlī with his mother and sister under conditions of appalling poverty. At the age of twenty he left for Adjodhan (later known as Pak Pātan [*q.v.*], and joined the discipline of Shaykh Farīd al-Dīn Gandj-i Shakar [*q.v.*]. Three years later, the Shaykh appointed him as his chief successor and directed him to settle in Dihlī and work for the expansion of the order. For about half a century he lived and worked in Dihlī in order to propagate the Čishtī mystical way and transformed the Čishtī order into a movement for mass spiritual culture (Baranī's *Ḥasrat-nāma* as cited in *Siyar al-awliyāʾ*, 346-7). As a result, Čishtī *khānaḳāhs* came to be established all over the country. According to Ghawthī Shaṭṭārī, he sent 700 deputies to different parts of the country. Shaykh Niẓām al-Dīn Awliyāʾ died in Dihlī in 18 Rabiʿ II 725/3 April 1325. Muḥammad b. Tughluḳ [*q.v.*] built a dome over his grave. His mausoleum is visited by hundreds of thousands of people every year. The area where the tomb stands is known as *Basti Niẓām al-Dīn*.

The Shaykh maintained an attitude of dignified aloofness from the court and never meddled in political affairs. His *khalīfas* were not permitted to accept government service or to consort with kings.

An erudite scholar of *ḥadīth*, with deep insight in Islamic jurisprudence, he was respected for his learning and large numbers of the *ʿulamāʾ* of Dihlī owed spiritual allegiance to him. He gave a revolutionary direction to religious activity by emphasising that service of mankind brought greater spiritual reward then mere formal prayers (*Fawāʾid al-fuʾād*, 13-14). His *khānaḳāh* was a welfare centre where free food was served to all visitors, and money was distributed to the needy and the poor on a very large scale. Enormous *futūḥ* (unasked-for gifts) came to him, but he distributed everything and kept nothing for himself. Baranī (*Taʾrīkh-i Firūz-Shāhī*, 343-7) has given a graphic account of his popularity in Dihlī.

The Shaykh's way of thinking endeared him to the people. He believed in returning evil with good, forgiving the insolent and adopting non-violent and pacifist ways towards those inviting retaliation. He looked upon bringing happiness to the hearts of men as the *summum bonum* of his mystic activity. He believed in hating the sin, not the sinner. His heart went out in sympathy to the weak and the downtrodden, and the thought of people who had slept on the shops and the mosques without food made morsels stick in his throat (*Siyar al-awliyāʾ*, 128).

The principal *khalīfas* of the Shaykh who worked to propagate his teachings were: Shaykh Naṣīr al-Dīn Čirāgh in Dihlī, Shaykh Ḳuṭb al-Dīn Munawwar in the Pandjāb, Mawlānā Burhān al-Dīn Gharīb in the Deccan, Mawlāna Ḥusām al-Dīn in Gudjarāt, Mawlānā Wadjīh al-Dīn Yūsuf in Čanderi and Mawlānā Sirādj al-Dīn ʿUthmān in Bengal. Amīr Khusraw, the famous Persian poet, and Ḍiyāʾ al-Dīn Baranī, the famous historian of medieval India, and Mawlānā Shams al-Dīn Yaḥyā and Mawlānā Fakhr al-Dīn Zarrādī, eminent scholars of the period, were among his disciples. Fīrūz Shāh Tughluḳ referred to him as *Sulṭān al-mashāyikh* ("King of the saints"), and throughout the centuries people of all walks of life have paid respectful homage to his memory.

The site where Humāyūn's tomb now stands was then a village known as Ghiyāthpūr, and the Shaykh had his hospice there. Part of his *khānaḳāh*, the *Čilla-khāna*, still stands (Bāyazīd Bayāt, *Taʾrīkh-i Humāyūn wa Akbar*, Calcutta 1941, 234).

Bibliography: Two collections of his utterances —the *Fawāʾid al-fuʾād*, compiled by Ḥasan Sidjzī (Nawal Kishore, Lucknow 1884), and *Durar-i-Niẓāmī*, compiled by ʿAlī Djāndār (ms. Sālār Djang Museum, Ḥaydarābād 61/5-99), and two biographical accounts—*Ḳiwām al-ʿaḳāʾid* by Djamāl Ḳiwām al-Dīn (ms. Osmania University Library, Ḥaydarābād) and *Siyar al-awliyāʾ* of Mīr Khwurd (Muḥibb-i Hind Press, Dihlī 1885) supply all the basic details about his life, thought and activities. For other sources, Baranī, *Taʾrīkh-i Fīrūz Shāhī*, Calcutta 1860; Ḥamīd Ḳalandar. *Khayr al-madjālis*, ed. K.A. Nizami, ʿAlīgaṙh 1959; Ḥammād Kashānī, *Aḥsan al-aḳwāl*, conversations of Shaykh Burhān al-Dīn Gharīb, mss. Osmania University Library 478 and 1474; Akbar Ḥusaynī, *Djawāmiʿ al-kalim*, Kānpūr 1936; Rukn al-Dīn Kashānī, *Nafāʾis al-anfās*, ms. Nadwat al-ʿUlamāʾ Lucknow, no. 1366; Ghawthī Shaṭṭārī, *Gulzār-i abrār*, ms. As. Soc. Bengal D 262 ff. 26-8; Djamālī, *Siyar al-ʿārifīn*, Riḍwī Press, Dihlī 1315 A.H.; ʿAbd al-Ḥaḳḳ Muḥaddith, *Akhbār al-akhyār*, Mudjtabāʾī Press, Dihli 1309 A.H.; for detailed bibliography see Nizami, *The life and times of Shaykh Nizam al-Din Awliya*, Delhi 1991.

(K.A. Nizami)

NIẒĀM AL-DĪN, MULLĀ MUḤAMMAD, leading scholar and mystic of early 18th-century Awadh and the consolidator of the Niẓāmī *madrasa* curriculum which came to be used through much of South Asia down to the 20th century. Niẓām al-Dīn was the third son of Mullā Ḳuṭb al-Dīn Sihālwī whose murder in 1103/1692 led to the emperor Awrangzīb recompensing him and his three brothers by assigning them the property of a European indigo merchant in Lucknow and by granting them pensions to support their scholarship; they and their descendants came to be known as the Farangī Maḥall family [*q.v.* in Suppl.].

Niẓām al-Dīn, who was fourteen at the time of his father's death, studied under Mullās ʿAlī Ḳulī of Dja'is, Amān Allāh of Benares and Naḳshband of Lucknow. On finishing his education he established the teaching tradition in Farangī Maḥall, including amongst his many pupils not only members of his own family and the forerunners of the Khayrābād school of *maʿḳūlāt* studies but also students from Bengal and much of Awadh. At the same time through his powerful relationship with the illiterate Ḳādirī mystic, Sayyid ʿAbd al-Razzāḳ of Bānsa (d. 5 Shawwāl 1136/27 June 1724) he established his family's connections with the most dynamic saint of the region, who has been to the present day the prime source of the family's spiritual inspiration. He died on 1 Djumādā 1161/29 April 1748. His son ʿAbd al-ʿAlī Baḥr al-ʿUlūm (d. 12 Radjab 1225-13 August 1810) [*q.v.*] ranks with Shāh ʿAbd al-ʿAzīz of Dihlī [*q.v.*] as the leading Indian scholar of his day.

Niẓām al-Dīn's greatest achievement was the consolidation of the Dars-i Niẓāmiyya. Through this curriculum the tradition of *maʿḳūlāt* scholarship, which had been boosted by the migration of many Persian scholars to northern India from the time of Faḍl Shīrāzī's arrival at Akbar's court in 1583, and which had been brought to new heights by the scholars of Awadh in the late-17th and early-18th centuries, was spread through much of India. Tradition has it that in developing this curriculum Niẓām al-Dīn was merely giving form to the customs of his father. These meant directing the student only to the most difficult and most comprehensive books on each subject so that he was both forced to think and had a chance of finishing his education while still a youth. They also meant in practice a strong bias towards the rational as opposed to the transmitted sciences. Champions of the curriculum assert that this need not necessarily be the case; the *Dars* was not a specific course of books but a special way of teaching.

Niẓām al-Dīn's writings reveal him to be at the heart of the development of Persian traditions of *maʿḳūlāt* scholarship in northern India. Among his more prominent works were: his notes on Mullā Ṣadrā's commentary on al-Abharī's [*q.v.*] *Hidāyat al-ḥikma*, his notes on Djalāl al-Dīn Dawānī's [*q.v.*] commentary on the *ʿAḳā'id* of ʿAḍud al-Dīn Īdjī [*q.v.*] and his notes on the *Shams al-bāzīgāh* of Maḥmūd Djawnpūrī and his commentaries on the *Manār al-anwār* of Ḥāfiẓ al-Dīn al-Nasafī and on the *Musallam al-thubūt* of Muḥibb Allāh al-Bihārī [*q.v.*], his father's pupil. His writings also show him to be a supporter of the reformed understanding of Ibn al-ʿArabī promulgated by the 17th-century scholar and mystic, Shāh Muḥibb Allāh Ilāhābādī. This understanding is instinct in his record of the sayings and doings of his *pīr*, Sayyid ʿAbd al-Razzāḳ of Bānsa, *Manāḳib al-Razzāḳiyya*, in which, while supporting Ibn al-ʿArabī's concept of the "unity of being" (*waḥdat al-wudjūd*), he nevertheless insisted on a full observance of the *sharīʿa*. Niẓām al-Dīn's combination of *maʿḳūlāt* scholarship and moderate *wudjūdī* Ṣūfism remained the style of the Farangī Maḥall family and their followers through much of India down to the 20th century. Niẓām al-Dīn's shrine in Lucknow remains celebrated for the solace it can bring the mentally disturbed and scholars in difficulty.

Bibliography: The basic modern source for Niẓām al-Dīn is Muḥammad Raḍā Anṣārī, *Bānī-i Dars-i Niẓāmī*, Lucknow 1973; among other sources comprising the family tradition are: Niẓām al-Dīn Farangī Maḥallī, *Manāḳib al-Razzāḳiyya*, Lucknow 1313; Walī Allāh Farangī Maḥallī, *al-Aghṣān al-arbaʿa*, Nadwa ms., Lucknow; Alṭāf al-Raḥmān Ḳidwā'ī, *Aḥwāl-i ʿulamā'-i Farangī Maḥall*, 1907; ʿAbd al-Bārī, *Āthār al-uwal*, n.d., and *Malfūẓ-i Razzāḳī*, Kanpur 1926; Mawlawī ʿInāyat Allāh, *Tadhkira-yi ʿulamā'-i Farangī Maḥall*, Lucknow 1928; other major sources are: Ghulām ʿAlī Āzād Bilgrāmī, *Ma'āthir al-kirām*, Ḥaydarābād 1913, and *Subḥat al-mardjān*, Bombay 1303/1886; Faḳīr Muḥammad Lahawrī, *Ḥadā'iḳ al-ḥanafiyya*, Lucknow 1324/1906; Nawwāb Ṣiddīḳ Ḥasan Khān, *Abdjad al-ʿulūm*, Bhopal 1296/1878; Faḍl Imām Khayrābādī, *Tarādjim al-fuḍalā'*, Eng. trans. Bazmee Anṣārī, Karachi 1956; for broad context and interpretation see: F. Robinson, *Perso-Islamic culture in India from the seventeenth to the early twentieth century*, in R.L. Canfield, ed., *Turko-Persia in historical perspective*, Cambridge 1991; idem, *Scholarship and Mysticism in early eighteenth-century Awadh*, in A. Dallapiccola and S. Zingel-Ave Lallemant eds., *Islam and the Indian regions 1000-1750 AD*, forthcoming, and idem, *Problems in the history of the Farangi Mahall family of learned and holy men*, in N.J. Allen *et al.*, eds., *Oxford University Papers on India*, i/2, Delhi 1987. (F. Robinson)

NIẒĀM AL-MULK, Abū ʿAlī al-Ḥasan b. ʿAlī b. Isḥāḳ al-Ṭūsī, the celebrated minister of the Saldjūḳid sultans Alp Arslān [*q.v.*] and Malikshāh [*q.v.*]. According to most authorities, he was born on Friday 21 Dhu 'l-Ḳaʿda 408/10 April 1018, though the 6th/12th century *Ta'rīkh-i Bayhaḳ* of Ibn Funduḳ al-Bayhaḳī [*q.v.*], which alone supplies us with detailed information about his family, places his birth in 410/1019-20. His birth-place was Rādkān, a village in the neighbourhood of Ṭūs, of which his father was revenue agent on behalf of the Ghaznawīd government. Little is recorded of his early life. The *Waṣāyā-yi Khʷādja-yi Niẓām al-Mulk*, however (for a discussion of the credibility of which see *JRAS* [1931], *The Sar-gudhasht-i Saiyidnā*, etc.), contains several anecdotes of his childhood, and is also responsible for the statement that he became a pupil in Nīshāpūr of a well-known Shāfiʿī doctor Hibat Allāh al-Muwaffaḳ. On the defeat of Masʿūd of Ghazna at Dandānḳān [*q.v.* in Suppl.] in 431/1040, when most of Khurāsān fell into the hands of the Saldjūḳs, Niẓām al-Mulk's father ʿAlī fled from Ṭūs to Khusrawdjird in his native Bayhaḳ, and thence made his way to Ghazna. Niẓām al-Mulk accompanied him, and whilst in Ghazna appears to have obtained a post in a government office. Within three or four years, however, he left the Ghaznawid for the Saldjūḳ service, first attaching himself to Čaghrī-Beg's [*q.v.*] commandant in Balkh (which had fallen to a Saldjūḳid force in 432/1040-1), and later, probably about 445/1053-4, moving to Čaghrī's own headquarters at Marw. It seems to have been now, or soon after, that he first entered the service of Alp Arslān (then acting as his father's lieutenant in eastern Khurāsān) under his *wazīr*, Abū ʿAlī Aḥmad b. Shādhān. And he so far won Alp Arslān's regard as on Ibn Shādhān's death to be appointed *wazīr* in his stead (then, probably, receiving his best-known *laḳab*). During the period between the death of Čaghrī-Beg in 451/1059 and that of Ṭughrīl-Beg in 455/1063, therefore, Niẓām al-Mulk had the administration of all Khurāsān in his hands.

The fame which he thereby acquired, and the fact that by now Alp Arslān was firmly attached to him, played a considerable part in prompting Ṭughrīl-Beg's *wazīr* al-Kundurī [*q.v.*], first, before his master's death, to scheme for the throne to pass to Čaghrī's youngest son Sulaymān, and then, after it, to do his utmost to prevent Alp Arslān's accession. For he calculated that Alp Arslān, on becoming sultan, would retain Niẓām al-Mulk rather than himself in office. In the event, al-Kundurī, who soon found himself too weak to oppose Alp Arslān, and thereupon sought to retrieve his position by acknowledging his claim, was retained in his post on the new sultan's first entry into Rayy. But a month later Alp Arslān suddenly dismissed him and handed over affairs to Niẓām al-Mulk. Al-Kundurī was shortly afterwards banished to Marw al-Rūdh, where ten months later he was beheaded. His execution was undoubtedly due to Niẓām al-Mulk, whose fears he had aroused by appealing for help to Alp Arslān's wife.

During Alp Arslān's reign, Niẓām al-Mulk accompanied him on all his campaigns and journeys, which were almost uninterrupted. He was not present, however, at the famous battle of Malāzgird [*q.v.*], having been sent ahead with the heavy baggage to Persia. On the other hand, he sometimes undertook military operations on his own, as in the case of the reduction of Iṣṭakhr citadel in 459/1067. Whose, his or Alp Arslān's, was the directing mind in matters of policy, it is hard to determine. Its main points, however, appear to have been the following: first, the employment of the large numbers of Türkmens that had immigrated into Persia as a result of the Saldjūḳ successes, in raids outside the *Dār al-Islām* and into Fāṭimid territory: hence the apparently strange circumstance that Alp Arslān's first enterprise after his accession, despite the precarious condition of the empire he had inherited, was a campaign in Georgia and Armenia [see AL-KURDJ]; secondly, a demonstration that the sultan's force was both irresistible and mobile, coupled with clemency and generally with reinstatement for all rebels who submitted; thirdly, the maintenance of local rulers, Shīʿī as well as Sunnī, in their positions as vassals of the sultan, together with the employment of members of the Saldjūḳ family as provincial governors; fourthly, the obviation of a dispute over the succession by the appointment and public acknowledgement of Malikshāh [*q.v.*], though he was not the sultan's eldest son, as his heir; and lastly the establishment of good relations with the ʿAbbāsid caliph al-Ḳāʾim [*q.v.*], as the sultan's nominal overlord.

Niẓām al-Mulk did not really come into his own until after the assassination of Alp Arslān in 465/1072. But thenceforward, for the next twenty years, he was the real ruler of the Saldjūḳ empire. He succeeded from the outset in completely dominating the then eighteen-year-old Malikshāh, being assisted in this purpose by the defeat of Ḳāwurd's [*q.v.*] attempt to secure the throne for himself (for which service Niẓām al-Mulk received the title *atābeg* [*q.v.*], thus bestowed for the first time). Indeed, in one aspect the history of the reign resolves itself into repeated attempts by the young sultan to assert himself, always in vain.

Malikshāh undertook fewer campaigns and tours than his father, the prestige of the Saldjūḳ arms now being such that few would risk rebellion, and warlike operations being left largely to the sultan's lieutenants, as they had not been under Alp Arslān. Nevertheless, from Iṣfahān, which had by now become the sultan's normal place of residence, Malikshāh visited the greater part of his empire accompanied by Niẓām al-Mulk.

Policy continued on the same lines under Malikshāh as under his father. Niẓām al-Mulk, however, was notably less tender than Alp Arslān had been to insubordinate members of the Saldjūḳ family, insisting at the outset on the execution of Ḳāwurd, and, later, on the blinding and imprisonment of Malikshāh's brother Tekesh.

He also reversed during the earlier part of Malikshāh's reign the conciliatory policy originally pursued under Alp Arslān towards the caliph. He had been rewarded for the friendly attitude he first evinced—which formed a welcome contrast to that of al-Kundurī—by the receipt from al-Ḳāʾim of two new *laḳab*s, viz. *Ḳiwām al-Dīn* and *Raḍī Amīr al-Muʾminīn* (the latter believed to be the earliest of this type in the case of a *wazīr*); and up to 460/1068, his relations with the caliph's *wazīr* Fakhr al-Dawla Ibn Djahīr [see DJAHĪR, BANŪ] became more and more cordial; so much so, indeed, that al-Ḳāʾim in that year dismissed Ibn Djahīr, chiefly on account of his too-subservient attitude to the Saldjūḳ court. To secure this attitude in the caliph's *wazīr* was, however, the very aim of Niẓām al-Mulk; and on Fakhr al-Dawla's dismissal he sought to impose a nominee of his own in a certain al-Rūdhrāwarī, and subsequently in the latter's son Abū Shudjāʿ. Al-Ḳāʾim, to avoid this, reappointed Fakhr al-Dawla, though on condition that his relations with the Saldjūḳids should in future be more correct. In fact, they soon grew strained, till Niẓām al-Mulk came to attribute any unwelcome event in Baghdād to Fakhr al-Dawla's influence. For many years, matters were prevented from coming to a head by the tact of Fakhr al-Dawla's son, ʿAmīd al-Dawla [see DJAHĪR, BANŪ], who won Niẓām al-Mulk's favour so far as to marry in turn two of his daughters, Nafsā and Zubayda; but in 471/1078 Niẓām al-Mulk demanded Fakhr al-Dawla's dismissal, which the caliph al-Muḳtadī [*q.v.*] (who had succeeded in 467/1075), was obliged to grant. Niẓām al-Mulk now hoped to obtain the office for his own son Muʾayyid al-Mulk; but to this al-Muḳtadī would not agree. Henceforward, accordingly, his dislike was deflected to al-Muḳtadī himself, and to Abū Shudjāʿ, his former protégé, whom the caliph now created deputy *wazīr* in an effort to conciliate him, leaving the vizierate itself unoccupied till the next year, when he appointed ʿAmīd al-Dawla. But in 474/1082 Niẓām al-Mulk in turn demanded the dismissal and banishment of Abū Shudjāʿ, and at the same time composed his quarrel with Fakhr al-Dawla, when the latter was sent on a mission to Iṣfahān, concerting with him a plan by which Fakhr al-Dawla should watch his interests at Baghdād. As a result, al-Muḳtadī, who gave in with a bad grace, lost all confidence in the Banū Djahīr, and two years later replaced ʿAmīd al-Dawla with the offensive Abū Shudjāʿ; whereupon Fakhr al-Dawla and ʿAmīd al-Dawla fled to the Saldjūḳid headquarters. Niẓām al-Mulk, on this, vowed vengeance on al-Muḳtadī, and at first seems even to have contemplated the abolition of the caliphate (see Sibṭ Ibn al-Djawzī, *Mirʾāt al-zamān*), as a prelude to which he commissioned Fakhr al-Dawla to conquer Diyār Bakr from the Marwānids [*q.v.*], the sole remaining Sunnī tributaries of any consequence. The Marwānids were duly ousted by 478/1085, whilst al-Muḳtadī, on his side, showed himself consistently hostile to Niẓām al-Mulk. But the latter's feelings towards the caliph were in the following year completely transformed as a consequence of his first visit to Baghdād (for the wedding of al-Muḳtadī to Malikshāh's daughter). The caliph received him very graciously; and thenceforward he became a champion of the caliphate in face of the enmity which developed between al-Muḳtadī and Malikshāh as a result of the marriage.

The celebrity of Niẓām al-Mulk is really due to the fact that he was in all but name a monarch, and ruled his empire with striking success. It was not his aim to innovate. On the contrary, it was to model the new state as closely as possible on that of the G͟haznawids, in which he had been born and brought up. His position was similar to that of his forerunners, the Barmakids [see BARĀMIKA], and the notable Būyid *wazīr*, the Ṣāḥib Ismāʿīl b. ʿAbbād [*q.v.*]. All three may be said to have represented the old Persian civilisation (progressively Islamicised, of course) in the face of a rise to empire of barbarian conquerors, Arab, Daylamī and now Türkmen. The monarchs were in each case equalled, if not surpassed, by their *wazīrs*, and most of all in the case of Niẓām al-Mulk. For with him the invaders aspired to an emperor's position whilst still quite unacclimatised to their new habitat, so that his superiority in culture was the more marked (cf. Barthold, *Turkestan*, 308). But in revenge, the Sald͟jūḳs' lack of acclimatisation stood in the way of a complete realisation by Niẓām al-Mulk of the now traditional Perso-Muslim state. Hence the lamentations that recur in the *Siyāsat-nāma*.

The *Siyāsat-nāma* or *Siyar al-mulūk*, written by Niẓām al-Mulk in 484/1091 with the addition of eleven chapters in the following year, is in a sense a survey of what he had failed to accomplish. It scarcely touches upon the organisation of the *dīwān*, for instance, partly, it is true, because the book was intended as a monarch's primer, but also because Niẓām al-Mulk, having absolute control of the *dīwān*, as opposed to the *dargāh* (cf. again Barthold, 227), had succeeded with the assistance of his two principal coadjutors, the *mustawfī* S͟haraf al-Mulk and the *muns͟hī* Kamāl al-Dawla, in exactly modelling this, his special department, on traditional lines. Of the *dargāh*, on the other hand, Niẓām al-Mulk complains that the sultans failed to maintain a sufficient majesty. They were neither magnificent (though he approves their daily free provision of food), formal, nor awe-inspiring enough. At their court, accordingly, the formerly important offices of *ḥād͟jib*, *wakīl* and *amīr-i ḥaras* had declined in prestige. Nor, as had his model potentates, would they maintain a sound intelligence or *barīd* [*q.v.*] service, whereby corruption might be revealed and rebellion forestalled. The *Siyāsat-nāma* consists in all of fifty chapters of advice illustrated by historical anecdotes. The last eleven chapters, added shortly before the *wazīr*'s assassination, deal with dangers that threatened the empire at the time of writing, in particular from the Ismāʿīlīs (on the work, see *Bibl.*, 3).

Niẓām al-Mulk's situation resembled that of the Būyid administrators in another respect. He was faced, as they had been, with the problem of supporting a largely tribal army, and solved it likewise by a partial abandonment of the traditional tax-farming system of revenue collection for that of the *iḳṭāʿ* or fief [*q.v.*], whereby military commanders supported themselves and their troops on the yield of lands allotted to them. Since in the decay of the ʿAbbāsid power provincial *amīrs* had tended to assume the originally distinct and profitable office of *ʿāmil*, the way for this development had been paved. The Būyids had later attempted to restore the older system; but the establishment of numerous local minor dynasties had favoured the new. Niẓām al-Mulk now systematised it in the larger field open to him. In the *Siyāsat-nāma* he insists, however, on the necessity of limiting the rights of fief-holders to the collection of fixed dues, and of setting a short time-limit to their tenures (see on this subject, Becker, *Steuerpacht und Lehnswesen*, in *Isl.*, v [1914], 81-92, and IḲṬĀʿ).

In the absence of the intelligence service he desired, Niẓām al-Mulk contrived to intimidate potential rebels and suppress local tyranny by a judicious display of the might and mobility of the Sald͟jūḳid arms. He also insisted on the periodical appearance at court of local dynasts such as the Mazyadids [*q.v.*] and ʿUḳaylids [*q.v.*], and proclaimed the sultan's accessibility to appeals for the redress of wrongs by means of notices circulated throughout the empire and exposed in public places (see al-Māfarruk͟hī, *Maḥāsin-i Iṣfahān*). He also gained the powerful support of the *ʿulamāʾ*, especially those of the S͟hāfiʿī school, of which he was an ardent champion, by the institution of innumerable pious foundations, in particular of *madrasas*, the most celebrated being the Niẓāmiyya of Bag͟hdād (opened 459/1067), the earliest west of K͟hurāsān (see below), by the general abolition of *mukūs* (taxes unsanctioned by the *s͟harīʿa*) in 479/1086-7; and by undertaking extensive public works, particularly in connection with the *ḥad͟jd͟j*. After the Ḥid͟jāz had returned from Fāṭimid to ʿAbbāsid allegiance in 468/1076, he exerted himself to make the ʿIrāḳ road safe from brigandage for pilgrims, as well as to diminish their expenses; and from the next year until that of his death, the journey was accomplished without mishap. It was not until the second half of Maliks͟hāh's reign that the full effects of Niẓām al-Mulk's achievement made themselves felt. By 476/1083-4, however, such were the unwonted security of the roads and the low cost of living that reference is made to them in the annals.

Niẓām al-Mulk was naturally much sought after as a patron. The poet Muʿizzī [*q.v.*] accuses him of having "no great opinion of poetry because he had no skill in it", and of paying "no attention to anyone but religious leaders and mystics" (see Niẓāmī ʿArūḍī Samarḳandī, *Čahār maḳāla*, tr. Browne, 46). But though his charity, which was profuse (see for example, al-Subkī, *Ṭabaḳāt al-S͟hāfiʿiyya*, iii, 41), went in large measure to men of religion—among them the most notable objects of his patronage being Abū Isḥāḳ al-S͟hīrāzī [*q.v.*] and Abū Ḥāmid al-G͟hazālī [*q.v.*]—, he was clearly a lavish patron also of poets, as is attested by the *Dumyat al-ḳaṣr* of al-Bāk͟harzī [*q.v.*], the greater part of which is devoted to his panegyrists. In another sphere, the inauguration of the D͟jalālī calendar [*q.v.*] in 466/1074 was probably due to his encouragement, since at this time his ascendancy over Maliks͟hāh was at its most complete.

Niẓām al-Mulk's name is especially associated with the founding of a series of colleges whose ethos and teachings were closely connected with the As͟hʿarī *kalām* and the S͟hāfiʿī legal school, of which the vizier himself was an adherent. His reasons for the setting-up of a chain of *madrasas* in the main cities of ʿIrāḳ, al-D͟jazīra and Persia (and especially in his home province of K͟hurāsān) [see MADRASA. I. 4] are not entirely clear. But in the context of the age, with its reaction against Muʿtazilism in philosophy and dialectics and against political S͟hīʿism as manifested in the preceding Būyid and north Syrian amīrates and the still-powerful Fāṭimid caliphate in Egypt and southern Syria, it seems possible that he aimed at training a body of reliable, Sunnī-oriented secretaries and officials who would run the Great Sald͟jūḳ empire when Niẓām al-Mulk had moulded it along the right lines and thus further the progress of the Sunnī political and intellectual revival. In his patronage of such institutions as these colleges, he was by no means an innovator, for the Sunnī *madrasa*-building movement had been under way since the later part of the 4th/10th century, and other leading figures in the Sald͟jūḳ state were equally active in founding and endowing *madrasas* and associated institutions like hostels for students, such as the Ḥanafī official of Alp Arslān's, the *mustawfī* Abū Saᶜd, who built a *madrasa* attached to the shrine of Abū Ḥanīfa in Ba̲g̲h̲dād, and Niẓām al-Mulk's enemy at the court of Maliks̲h̲āh, the *mustawfī* Tād̲j̲ al-Mulk Abu 'l-G̲h̲anāʾim (d. 485/1093), founder of the Tād̲j̲iyya college there (see G. Makdisi, *Muslim institutions of learning in eleventh-century Baghdad*, in *BSOAS*, xxiv [1961], 1-56; C.E. Bosworth, in *Camb. hist. of Iran*, v, 70-4). Niẓām al-Mulk may have intended to give an impetus to the spread of his own As̲h̲ᶜarī and S̲h̲āfiᶜī views (although, in fact, the Bag̲h̲dād Niẓāmiyya, where the great Abū Ḥāmid al-G̲h̲azālī had taught, declined in the 6th/12th century, when the Ḥanbalī institutions of learning there showed greater vitality), but it seems reasonable to impute to him a wider vision of a Sunnī political, cultural and intellectual revival in the central and eastern lands of Islam, in which his own colleges would play a contributory role.

For the first seven years of Maliks̲h̲āh's reign, Niẓām al-Mulk's authority went altogether unchallenged. In 472/1079-80, however, two Turkish officers of the court instigated Maliks̲h̲āh into killing a protégé of the *wazīr*; and in 473/1080-1, again, the sultan insisted on disbanding a contingent of Armenian mercenaries against Niẓām al-Mulk's advice. Maliks̲h̲āh now began to hope, indeed, for the overthrow of his mentor, showing extraordinary favour to officials such as Ibn Bahmanyār and, later, Sayyid al-Ruʾasāʾ Ibn Kamāl al-Mulk, who were bold enough to criticise him. Ibn Bahmanyār went so far as to attempt the *wazīr*'s assassination (also in 473), whereas Sayyid al-Ruʾasāʾ contented himself with words. But in each case, Niẓām al-Mulk was warned; and the culprits were blinded. In the case of Ibn Bahmanyār, in whose guilt a court jester named D̲j̲aᶜfarak was also implicated, Maliks̲h̲āh retaliated by contriving the murder of Niẓām al-Mulk's eldest son D̲j̲amāl al-Mulk, who had taken D̲j̲aᶜfarak's execution into his own hands (475/1082). After the fall of Sayyid al-Ruʾasāʾ in 476/1083-4, however, the sultan left plotting till, some years later, a new favourite, Tād̲j̲ al-Mulk, caught his fancy.

All went well with Niẓām al-Mulk till 483/1090-1. In that year, however, occurred the first serious challenge to the Sald̲j̲ūḳid power, when Baṣra was sacked by a force of Ḳarmaṭians [see KARMAṬĪ]; and almost simultaneously their co-sectary the Assassin leader al-Ḥasan b. al-Ṣabbāḥ [*q.v.*] obtained possession of the fortress of Alamūt [*q.v.*], from which repeated attacks failed to dislodge him. Meanwhile, moreover, an awkward problem had arisen over the succession to the sultanate, on account of the death in turn of Maliks̲h̲āh's two eldest sons, Dāwūd (474/1082) and Aḥmad (481/1088). These sons had both been children of the Ḳarāk̲h̲ānid princess Terken K̲h̲ātūn (see Ras̲h̲īd al-Dīn, *D̲j̲āmiᶜ al-tawārīk̲h̲*), who had borne the sultan a third son, Maḥmūd, in 480/1087. She was eager for Maḥmūd to be formally declared heir. Niẓām al-Mulk, however, was in favour of Barkiyārūḳ [*q.v.*], Maliks̲h̲āh's eldest surviving son by a Sald̲j̲ūḳ princess. Hence Terken K̲h̲ātūn became his bitter enemy, and joined with Tād̲j̲ al-Mulk, who was in her service, in instigating Maliks̲h̲āh against the *wazīr*.

Tād̲j̲ al-Mulk accused Niẓām al-Mulk to the sultan, who by this time was in any case incensed with the *wazīr*'s championship of al-Muḳtadī, of extravagant expenditure on the army and of nepotism; and Maliks̲h̲āh's wrath was finally inflamed beyond bearing by an unguarded reply made by Niẓām al-Mulk to a formal accusation of these practices. But even so, he did not dare to dismiss him. (The earliest historian to assert that he was dismissed is Ras̲h̲īd al-Dīn Faḍl Allāh, who appears to have misunderstood the purport of some verses by al-Naḥḥās quoted in the *Rāḥat al-ṣudūr* of Rāwandī, and really composed after the *wazīr*'s death.)

Niẓām al-Mulk was assassinated on 10 Ramaḍān 485/14 October 1092 near Siḥna, between Kanguwar and Bisutūn, as the court was on its way from Iṣfahān to Bag̲h̲dād. His murderer, who was disguised as a Ṣūfī, was immediately killed, but is generally thought to have been an emissary of al-Ḥasan b. al-Ṣabbāḥ. Contemporaries, however, seem to have put the murder down to Maliks̲h̲āh, who died suddenly less than a month later, and to Tād̲j̲ al-Mulk, whom Niẓām al-Mulk's retainers duly tracked down and killed within a year. Ras̲h̲īd al-Dīn combines the two theories, stating that the *wazīr*'s enemies at court concerted it with the Assassins. The truth is therefore uncertain; but as Ras̲h̲īd al-Dīn is one of the earliest historians to whom the Assassin records were available, his account would seem to deserve attention.

The extraordinary influence of Niẓām al-Mulk is attested by the part played in affairs after his death by his relatives, despite the fact that only two appeared to have displayed much ability. For the next sixty years, except for a gap between 517/1123 and 528/1134, members of his family held office under princes of the Sald̲j̲ūḳid house.

Of Niẓām al-Mulk's family, Ḍiyāʾ al-Mulk is remarkable as being his son by a Georgian princess, either the daughter or the niece of Bagrat I, formerly married, or at least betrothed, to Alp Arslān, after the campaign of 456/1064.

See further, on the sons and descendants of Niẓām al-Mulk in the 6th/12th century, NIẒĀMIYYA.

Bibliography: 1. For the Arabic and Persian primary sources, see the *Bibl.* of the *EI*¹ article of H. Bowen.

2. Studies: E.G. Browne, *LHP*, ii, 167, 174-91, 212-17; M.T. Houtsma, *The death of Nizam al-Mulk and its consequences*, in *Jnal. of Indian History*, iii (1924), 147-60; Barthold, *Turkestan down to the Mongol invasion*, London 1928, 25-6, 306-10; H. Bowen, *The* sar-gudhasht-i sayyidnā, *the "Tale of the Three Schoolfellows" and the* wasaya *of the Niẓām al-Mulk*, in *JRAS* (1931), 771-82; Asad Talas, *La Madrasa Niẓāmiyya et son histoire*, Paris 1939; K.E. Schabinger-Schowingen, *Zur Geschichte des Saldschuqen-Reichskanzlers Nisāmu 'l-mulk*, in *Historische Jahrbücher*, lxii-lxix (1942-9), 250-83; idem, *Nisâmulmulk und das Abbasidische Chalifat*, in *ibid.*, lxxi (1952), 91-136; K. Rippe, *Über den Sturz Niẓām-ul-Mulks*, in *Fuad Köprülü armağanı*, Istanbul 1953, 423-35; İ. Kafesoğlu, *Sultan Melikşah devrinde Büyük Selçuklu imparatorluğu*, Istanbul 1953; ᶜAbbās Iḳbāl, *Wizārat dar ᶜahd-i salāṭīn-i buzurg-i Sald̲j̲ūḳī*, Tehran 1338/1959, 46-63; C.E. Bosworth, in *Camb. hist. of Iran*, v, Cambridge 1968, 66 ff., 99-102; A.K.S. Lambton, in *ibid.*, 211-17; Carla L. Klausner, *The Seljuk vezirate, a study of civil administration 1055-1194*, Cambridge, Mass. 1973, index; G. Makdisi, *Les rapports entre Calife et Sultân à l'époque Saljûqide*, in *IJMES*, vi (1975), 228-36; idem, *The rise of colleges. Institutions of learning in Islam and the West*, Edinburgh 1981, 23-4, 41, 54, 301-4, 306-7, 311; S.A.A. Rizvi, *Nizam al-Mulk Tusi, his contribution to statecraft, political theory and the art of government*, Lahore 1978; Lambton, *The dilemma of government in Islamic Persia*: *the* Siyāsat-nāma *of Niẓām al-Mulk*, in

Iran, *JBIPS*, xxii (1984), 55-66; eadem, *Concepts of authority in Persia: eleventh to nineteenth centuries A.D.*, in *ibid.*, xxvi (1988), 98; eadem, *Continuity and change in medieval Persia*, London 1988, 40-4 and index; Kafesoğlu, *İA*, art. *Nizâm-ül-Mülk*.

3. On the *Siyāsat-nāma*: see the studies given in 2. above, especially the works of Lambton. Numerous translations exist: (French) C. Schefer, Paris 1893, accompanying critical edition of text, Paris 1891; (Russian) B.N. Zakhoder, Moscow-Leningrad 1949; (Turkish) M. Şerif Çavdaroğlu, Istanbul 1954 (see on this, Kafesoğlu, *Büyük Selçuklu vezîri Nizâmü 'l-Mülk'ün eseri Siyâsetname ve türkçe tercümesi*, in *Türkiyat Mecmuası*, xii, 231-56); (German) Schabinger-Schowingen, Freiburg-Munich 1960; (English) H. Darke, London 1960, second, revised version London 1978, accompanying critical edition of text, Tehran 1340/1962.

(H. Bowen-[C.E. Bosworth])

NIẒĀM AL-MULK ČĪN ḲILIČ ḴHĀN, ḲAMAR AL-DĪN, founder of the Indian Muslim state of Ḥaydarābād in the early 12th/18th century and a dominant figure in the military affairs of the decaying Muḡhal empire from his appointment as governor of the Deccan by the Emperor Farruḵh-siyar [*q.v.*] till his death in 1161/1748. In the early years of his governorship he was the deadly foe of his rivals for influence in the empire, the Bārha Sayyids [*q.v.* in Suppl.], and after his victory over them at Shakarkheldā in 1137/1724, virtually independent ruler in Ḥaydarābād with the additional title of Āṣaf Djāh. For further details, see ḤAYDARĀBĀD, b. ḤAYDARĀBĀD STATE, and MUḤAMMAD SHĀH B. DJAHĀN SHĀH.

Bibliography: T.W. Haig (ed.), *The Cambridge hist. of India*, iv, *The Mughul period*, 331, 336, 341-3, 346-50, 377 ff., and see the bibls. to the articles mentioned above. (ED.)

NIẒĀM-SHĀHĪ (i.e. *Ilčī-yi Niẓām-shāhī* "ambassador of the Niẓām-Shāh" of the Dakhan), a Persian historian whose real name was Ḵhʷūrshāh b. Ḳubād al-Ḥusaynī. Born in Persian ʿIrāḳ, he entered the service of Sultan Burhān [see NIẒĀM-SHĀHĪS]. The latter being converted to the Shīʿa, sent Ḵhʷūrshāh as ambassador to Ṭahmāsp Shāh Ṣafawī. Reaching Rayy in Radjab 952/September 1545, he accompanied the Shāh to Georgia and Shīrwān during the campaign of 953/1546 against Alḳāṣ Mīrzā. He stayed in Persia till 971/1563, perhaps with occasional breaks. He died at Golkonda on 25 Dhu 'l-Ḳaʿda 972/24 June 1565.

Ḵhʷūrshāh's chief work is the *Taʾrīkh-i Ilčī-yi Niẓām-shāh*, a general history from the time of Adam based on such sources as al-Ṭabarī, al-Bayḍāwī, *Taʾrīkh-i guzīda*, *Ẓafar-nāma*, *Ḥabīb al-siyar*, the "Memoirs of Shāh-Ṭahmāsp", etc. The book is divided into a preface and seven *maḳāla*, each of which is again divided into several *guftār*. The most important part of this work is that which refers to the reign of Ṭahmāsp Shāh (in the Brit. Mus. ms. Or. 153, written in 972/1565, the events come down to 969/1561-2) and to the local dynasties of the Caspian provinces: Māzandarān, Gīlān, Shīrwān. The two manuscripts in the British Museum show differences in their contents: Add. 23,513 (written in 1095/1684) has passages added by some continuator and taken from the *Djihān-ārā* of Aḥmad b. Muḥammad Ghaffārī. The later additions of Or. 153 come down as late as 1200/1786.

According to Firishta, "Shāh Ḵhʷūrshāh", during the reign of Ibrāhīm Ḳuṭb-Shāh of the Deccan (957-988/1550-80) also wrote a history of the Ḳuṭb-Shāhīs [*q.v.*]. It is difficult to reconcile this with a continuous stay in Persia from 952 to 971.

Bibliography: Rieu, *Catalogue*, 107-11; Schefer, in his *Chrestomathie persane*, Paris 1885, ii, 56-103 (notes 65-133), printed the sections relating to the Caspian provinces. See also Storey, i, 113-14, 1239; Storey-Bregel, i, 406-8. (V. MINORSKY)

NIẒĀM SHĀHĪS, one of five Deccani dynasties, with its capital at Aḥmadnagar [*q.v.*] which emerged in South India as the Bahmanī [*q.v.*] kingdom disintegrated. The chroniclers of the Niẓām Shāhīs emphasise territorial and power disputes and religious (and possibly racial) tensions. The history of the dynasty splits into four periods. Under the first four rulers, 895-994/1490-1586, there was the vigorous establishment of the kingdom. Under the five rulers from 994-1008/1586-1600, there was intensive internal dissension. The period from 1008-35/1600-26, although with Niẓām Shāhī rulers on the throne, was dominated by a Ḥabashī (of black African origins) prime minister who restored much of the kingdom's economic and political viability. By 1041/1632 the state was destroyed, with formal dispersal of the territories of the Aḥmadnagar kingdom occurring in 1046/1636.

The founder of the dynasty, later known as Aḥmad Niẓām Shāh Baḥrī, was the son of a high official in the Bahmanī court. He held various posts under the Bahmanīs and in 895/1490 he declared independence from them and consolidated the areas in northern and western Mahārashtra under his rule as Aḥmad Niẓām Shāh. Under the first four rulers (Aḥmad, 895-915/1490-1510; Burhān I, 915-60/1510-53; Ḥusayn I, 961-72/1554-65; and Murtaḍā I, 972-97/1565-88) the kingdom prospered despite military skirmishing with neighbouring Islamic successor states, with the Hindu state of Vidjayanagar, and with the first Muḡhal incursions in the 990s/1580s. Burhān I converted to Shīʿism, the choice reflecting to some extent the underlying tension between those considered natives (*deshis*) and those considered outsiders (*pardeshis*). Potentially, there were racial implications as well. Many of the foreigners were generally fairer than the Deccanis, but there were many Ḥabashī officers in the court and the exact causes for the continuous realignment of loyalties are rarely clear.

Militarily, the high point of this period came in Djumādā II 972/January 1565. The six major Deccani states aligned and realigned themselves attempting to extend their boundaries. In the early 1560s, the armies of Vidjayanagar became particularly rapacious and the Islamic kingdoms reached an accommodation. The major armies gathered in Talikota to organise an assault on the Vidjayanagar forces and also, apparently, for a certain amount of pre-battle carousing. In Djumādā II 972/January 1565 the forces marched out of Talikota and moved against the enemy, decisively defeating them and putting an end to that kingdom.

The rapid turnover in Niẓām Shāhī rulers from 996/1588 to 1008/1600 reflects the dissension and turmoil in the higher ranks of the Aḥmadnagar court. Ḥusayn II, a parricide, ruled during 997-8/1588-9. He was succeeded by a paternal cousin, Ismāʿīl, who ruled in 998-9/1589-91. Ismāʿīl was succeeded by his own father, Burhān II, 999-1003/1591-5, who had been a member of the Muḡhal court for some years but, having manoeuvred his way on to the Niẓām Shāhī throne, had to deal with serious Muḡhal forays into the Deccan. Burhān II was succeeded by his son and Ismāʿīl's brother, Ibrāhīm, for four months in 1003/1595. Rival leaders put forth different candidates for the throne, and Bahādur, son of Ibrāhīm and strongly backed by Čand Bībī, was finally declared ruler only to be captured and imprisoned by the Mughals after the fall of Aḥmadnagar in Ṣafar 1009/August 1600.

Čand Bībī was a daughter of Ḥusayn I and, as part of unending Deccani negotiations and realignments, had been married to ʿAlī ʿĀdil Shāh of Bīdjāpūr [*q.v.*]. After his assassination in 1580, she was regent to their young son, Ibrāhīm ʿĀdil Shāh II. Later in the 1580s and in the early 1590s, Čand Bībī went back and forth between Bīdjāpūr and Aḥmadnagar as a sort of "emissary for safe keeping", as various leaders struck different bargains. After Burhān II was shot in 1003/1595, she was among those leaders who supported his grandson Bahādur to succeed him. By December of that year, the Mughals (led by Akbar's son Mūrād [*q.v.*], who died in Shawwāl 1007/May 1599 in the Deccan), who had been skirmishing, raiding, and attempting to seize territory in the Deccan, began the siege of Aḥmadnagar. In Djumādā II 1004/February 1596 they successfully mined one of the walls of the fort, and Čand Bībī valiantly led the rebuilding of that wall. She emerged with enough stature to unite some of the feuding Aḥmadnagar leaders and became a local heroine. In March, the occupants of the fort sued for peace and the Mughals withdrew.

In 1007/1599 the Mughals took Burhānpūr in Berār [*q.vv.*] which then served as their base of operations for attacking the Deccani states. The following year, accompanied by Akbar, the Mughals again set siege to Aḥmadnagar, this time led by his son Dāniyāl (died in Dhu 'l-Ḳaʿda 1012/April 1604 in the Deccan). In the town and fort of Aḥmadnagar, the internal feuding had reached such a pitch that one faction accused Čand Bībī of planning to betray the Niẓām Shāhī forces and incited a mob which killed her. In Ṣafar 1009/August 1600 the Mughals took Aḥmadnagar.

The third period of Niẓām Shāhī history was dominated by Malik ʿAnbar [*q.v.*], an Abyssinian slave who was a soldier in the Niẓām Shāhī armies, then went to Bīdjāpūr as a soldier, and finally returned to Aḥmadnagar in the 1590s. He fought for the Niẓām Shāhīs against the Mughals and oversaw the installation of the first two of the last three rulers, Murtaḍā II (1008-19/1600-10) and Burhān III (1019-41/1610-32), followed by Ḥusayn III (1041-2/1632-3).

The bickering and skirmishing continued in the Deccan, and Malik ʿAnbar, an able general and politician, carved out larger territories for the Niẓām Shāhīs. He formed new alliances, embracing Hindu leaders who were later to become leaders of the Marāthā [*q.v.*] forces. With these leaders, more effective ways of waging war were developed, and swift moving, mounted soldiers of the Niẓām Shāhī armies would quickly attack the Mughal forces and then retreat into the hills and prepare for the next swift attack and retreat. Dissension among the sons of Djahāngīr pervaded the Mughal court, which was also embroiled in power and territorial disputes, and helped to frustrate repeated Mughal attempts to occupy the Deccan. In the meantime, Malik ʿAnbar embarked on a major land reform, similar to that done by Rādjā Ṭodar Mall [*q.v.*] for Akbar. In 1025/1616 the Mughals put Aḥmadnagar under siege yet again. In the end, Djahāngīr's son Khurram was victorious and received the title Shāh-Djahān. Malik ʿAnbar's administration and generalship continued, as did Mughal inability to secure the Deccan.

In Shaʿbān 1035/May 1626 Malik ʿAnbar died at the age of 80. In Muḥarram 1036/October 1626 in Burhānpūr, Parwīs, heir apparent to the Mughal throne and in charge of the Mughal forces trying to invade the Deccan, died. A year later, Djahāngīr died, and was succeeded by his only living son, Shāh-Djahān. In 1039/1630 Shāh-Djahān returned to Burhānpūr in a re-attempt at conquering the Deccan. Malik ʿAnbar had been followed in office by his son Fatḥ Khān, who was a schemer rather than a leader and administrator, although he was finally imprisoned by the inept Burhān III. The cohesiveness of the state began to disintegrate, hastened by a terrible famine in the Deccan and Gudjarāt during 1039-41/1630-2. Shāh-Djahān worked on bribing and suborning the leaders of the Niẓām Shāhī factions. In 1038/1629, partially as a result of Mughal tactics, Burhān III attempted to murder a group of Marāthā leaders, driving several factions from his court to that of the Mughals.

At Burhānpūr in Dhu 'l-Ḳaʿda 1040/June 1631, however, Shāh-Djahān's wife died in childbirth (having already borne eight sons and six daughters for him). Shāh-Djahān ultimately returned to the north to plan and oversee the building of the Tāj Maḥall [*q.v.*] among other matters. Burhān III brought Fatḥ Khān back into power but, in 1041/1632, the latter poisoned the sultan and tried to put Ḥusayn Niẓām Shāh III on the throne. It was, in effect, the end of the dynasty. The following year, Fatḥ Khān had schemed himself into such a hopeless position that he took Ḥusayn III to Agra to petition Shāh-Djahān for help. In Rabīʿ I 1043/September 1633 Fatḥ Khān's lands were restored to him and Ḥusayn III was imprisoned.

In the Deccan, warring factions continued to fight. Shāhdjī Bhōnslē attempted to install a puppet, Murtaḍā Niẓām Shāh III, but was not successful. In 1045/1636 Shāh-Djahān reached an agreement with Ibrāhīm ʿĀdil Shāh which divided the Niẓām Shāhī territories between the two of them and specified that Shāhdjī Bhōnslē was not to enter the court of either of them until he surrendered the territories which he still held. Shāhdjī's son, Shivādjī, was the creator of the Marāthā confederacy, the armies of which, in 1761, attacked Shāh-Djahān's descendants on the plain of Pānīpat [*q.v.*], north of Dihlī.

During the years that Aḥmadnagar (founded in 899/1494) was the Niẓām Shāhī capital, it was (like Golkonda [*q.v.*] under the Ḳuṭb Shāhīs and Bīdjāpūr under the ʿĀdil Shāhīs) a centre not only for soldiers but also for travellers, traders, artisans, craftsmen, painters, writers, scholars, holy men, architects, builders and those dissatisfied with their lot in other places in South Asia, Persia and the Middle East and beyond. European travellers and traders visited the Niẓām Shāhī court. On the west coast, there was fierce competition among the Niẓām Shāhīs, the ʿĀdil Shāhīs, the rulers of Vidjayanagar, and other groups (including pirates) for the trade increasingly dominated by the Portuguese. For the Deccani rulers, the most important item in this trade was horses and the rulers of Vidjayanagar (until 972/1565) reputedly paid the full price assessed at embarkation for every horse delivered to them whether alive or dead.

The Niẓām Shāhīs and many of their high officials commissioned palaces, mosques, gardens, tanks, canals, bath houses, hospices, hospitals, tombs, etc., the remains of many of which are still extant. The early rulers and nobility commissioned many canals as well as palaces/pleasure houses/gardens. Indeed, a tomb near the impressive tomb of Aḥmad I is reputed to mark the burial site of the elephant which captured the ruler of Vidjayanagar in 1565. The most famous Niẓām Shāhī architect and builder was Ṣalābat Khān II, an official under Murtaḍā I and Ḥusayn II. He not only extended the system of canals and tanks, but rebuilt the Farāh Ba<u>kh</u>s<u>h</u> Gardens. His own tomb is outside the city on a hill; unlike other tombs of the period, it is an extremely tall building with stairs to the top. It is said he wished to make it even higher so that he could see as far as Dawlatābād [*q.v.*].

There was an interest in literature and painting as well; an illustrated *Taʿrif-i Ḥusayn Shāhī* (*ca.* 972-6/*ca.* 1565-9) survives at the Bharata Itihasa Samshodhaka Mandala in Poona and a portrait of Burhān II is in the Bibliothèque Nationale in Paris. Some other miniatures have been attributed to the Niẓām <u>Sh</u>āhī court and a few artists in the Mug<u>h</u>al court came from the Niẓām <u>Sh</u>āhī one. Unfortunately, the wars with the Mug<u>h</u>als and subsequently with the Marāthās led to the despoiling and destruction of the libraries that contained the volumes of literature and science, many no doubt illustrated, that must have been in Niẓām <u>Sh</u>āhī mosques, schools, and homes.

Bibliography: Firi<u>sh</u>ta; Sayyid ʿAlī Ṭabāṭabāʾī, *Burhān-i maʾā<u>th</u>ir* (tr. and abridged T. Wolseley Haig, in *The Indian Antiquary* [1920-3]);. Radhey Shyam, *The kingdom of Ahmadnagar*, Varanasi 1966, with bibl. (Marie H. Martin)

NIẒĀM-Ï <u>DJ</u>EDĪD (T.), literally, "new system, re-organisation", the new military units created by the Ottoman sultan Selīm III (1203-22/1789-1807 [*q.v.*]).

The Treaty of Sistova between the Ottoman Empire and Austria (August 1791) and that of Jassy between the Empire and Russia (January 1792) meant that Turkey had to recognise the loss of the Crimea and the fact of Russian control over much of the Black Sea, although Austria withdrew from its conquests in Serbia, Bosnia and the Danube Principalities. Moreover, the European powers were shortly to become increasingly pre-occupied with the threats posed to them by the extension of the French Revolutionary spirit and its ideas within Europe. Turkey thus had a breathing-space within which Selīm III could reorganise affairs in his remaining dominions and prepare against further threats to Turkey's territorial integrity. Above all, the sultan and his reform-minded advisers realised now that military and naval reforms were vital, although it was still hoped to reform and improve the existing military forces of the feudal cavalry, the Sipahīs, and the Janissaries, and the root-and-branch reform measures necessary to save the empire could not yet be contemplated and were probably not yet envisaged in the minds of contemporaries.

Selīm's efforts to improve the fighting efficiency and to reduce the bloated numbers of the traditional types of forces were not very successful, but reform was more successful in the newer, more technical arms: the artillery, the mortar-throwers, the mine-layers and sappers, the gun transport corps, etc., where younger officers trained by Baron de Tott two or three decades before and, after 1794, by further French advisers, made these corps the most efficient part of the Ottoman army.

However, the sultan decided that the only way forward in regard to the fighting forces themselves, sc. the cavalry and infantry, was to inaugurate a new infantry force parallel to, but entirely separate from, the older forces, so as not to alarm the latter unduly. Hence in 1793 Selīm created his "New Order", the *Niẓām-ï <u>Dj</u>edīd*, to be a corps of troops properly trained in the European manner, with European-type discipline and with modern weapons. To finance these and other reforms, he initiated a special fund, the "New Revenue", *Īrād-ï <u>Dj</u>edīd*, from taxes on brandy, tobaccoo, coffee, silk, wool, sheep and the yields from the fiefs of *tīmār*-holders in Anatolia who had neglected their duties in war and were therefore deprived of their fiefs.

The *Niẓām-ï <u>Dj</u>edīd* was originally a volunteer body, and was originally formed from various nationalities, including Austrian and Russian deserters who had fled to Turkish territory during the 1787-92 war with Austria and Russia, hence at first it enjoyed little prestige amongst the Turks themselves. But by 1800 it comprised three regiments, with barracks well-removed from proximity to the older troops, at Lewend Čiftlik to the north of Istanbul and at Üsküdār, and by July 1801 its strength had reached 27 officers and 9,263 men. After 1802, a system of conscription was introduced into Anatolia, although the greater power of local magnates in Rumelia prevented its extension to the Balkans. Hence by the end of 1806 the *Niẓām-ï <u>Dj</u>edīd* comprised 1,590 officers and 22,685 men, roughly half of them stationed in Anatolia and half in Istanbul. A large contingent of the new troops helped in the successful defence of Acre in Palestine led by Aḥmed <u>Dj</u>ezzār Pa<u>sh</u>a [see al-<u>dj</u>azzār pa<u>sh</u>a, aḥmad, in Suppl.] against the attacks of Bonaparte during March-May 1799. The sultan employed foreign officers and advisers, mainly from England, Sweden and Spain, to train the soldiers and to oversee the management of arsenals, ship-building yards and fortifications. Extensive barracks and ammunition depots were built. The "New Revenue" earmarked for military purposes and supplying the necessary funds, amounted by 1797-8 to 60,000 purses, i.e. 48 million francs (see <u>Dj</u>ewdet, *Taʾrī<u>kh</u>*, viii, 139-40).

Internal difficulties, and, especially, the increasing number of opponents of reform, prevented the sultan from completely realising his plans. In 1805-6 Selīm established a new *Niẓām-ï <u>Dj</u>edīd* corps at Edirne, with men to be recruited for it from the Balkans by conscription. But the power of local magnates there and the influence of the conservatives in the capital, including the Janissaries and the *ʿulamāʾ*, forced him to retreat from his design. A revolt against the sultan of Janissary auxiliaries (*yamaḳs*) broke out in May 1807; Selīm yielded to pressure from his enemies and disbanded the *Niẓām-ï <u>Dj</u>edīd* before his enforced abdication, and *Niẓām-ï <u>Dj</u>edīd* officers and men were hunted down and slaughtered in the general reign of terror. Under the new sultan, Muṣṭafā IV [*q.v.*], an attempt was made in 1808 by the *ser ʿasker* Muṣṭafā Pasha Bayraḳdār [*q.v.*] secretly to reconstitute the *Niẓām-ï <u>Dj</u>edīd* under the new designation of *Niẓāmlï ʿAsker*, with the Austrian renegade Süleymān Ag<u>h</u>a, who had previously commanded the corps stationed at Lewend Čiftlik, charged with this task, but without success (see Zinkeisen, *GOR*, vii, 552-3).

It was only after the murder of the imprisoned former sultan Selīm and the overthrow of the feeble puppet Muṣṭafā in favour of Maḥmūd II [*q.v.*], son of Selīm's predecessor ʿAbd al-Ḥamīd I [*q.v.*], that more successful and more lasting measures in the direction of modernising the Ottoman Empire, its administration and armed forces, could eventually be embarked upon. For by then it had become clear that the previous *Niẓām-ï <u>Dj</u>edīd* had represented merely a tinkering with an old system which was incapable of being transformed into a modern one; a totally new start was necessary.

Bibliography: <u>Dj</u>ewdet, *Taʾrī<u>kh</u>*, is the main primary source. See also: Zinkeisen, *GOR*, vii, 323, 342, 458 ff., 464, 471, 552; Jorga, *GOR*, v, 117 ff.; C. von Sax, *Geschichte des Machtverfalls Türkei*, Vienna 1908, 133-4; Enver Ziya Karal, *Nizâm-ı* *cedîde dâir lâyiklar*, in *Tarih Vesîkaları*, nos. 6, 8, 11-12 (1942-3); idem, *Selim III'in hatt-ı hümâyûnları, nizâm-ı cedîd*, Ankara 1946; S.J. Shaw, *The origins of Ottoman military reform*, in *Jnal. of Modern History*, xxxvii (1965), 219-306; idem, *The established Ottoman army corps under Sultan Selim III*, in *Isl.*, xl (1965), 142-84; idem, *Between old and new: the Ottoman empire under Sultan Selim III, 1789-1807*, Cambridge, Mass. 1971; idem, *History of the Ottoman Empire and modern Turkey*, i, Cambridge 1976, 262-6, 268, 270, 272, 274; *İA*, art. *Nizâm-ı Cedîd* (M. Tayyib Gökbilgin).

(F. Babinger-[C.E. Bosworth])

NIẒĀMĪ ʿARŪḌĪ SAMARḲANDĪ, Aḥmad b. ʿUmar b. ʿAlī, took the *ta<u>kh</u>alluṣ* of Niẓāmī and the honorific Na<u>dj</u>m al-Dīn (or Niẓām al-Dīn); he was usually called ʿArūḍī (the "prosodist") to distinguish him from other Niẓāmīs (particularly the great Niẓāmī of Gan<u>dj</u>a [*q.v.*], cf. the anecdote quoted by E.G. Browne, *Lit. hist. of Pers.*, ii, 339). According to Browne, Niẓāmī is one of the most interesting and remarkable Persian writers of prose: "one of those who throw most light on the intimate life of Persian and Central Asian Courts in the twelfth century of our era". He was a court poet who served faithfully the <u>Gh</u>ūrid [*q.v.*] princes for 45 years (he would thus be born at the end of the 5th/11th century), according to what he tells us at the beginning of the *Čahār maḳāla*, the only work by him that has come down to us. His verse has been lost, at least except for fragments; Dawlat<u>sh</u>āh (ed. Browne, 60-1) only gives one couplet which does not seem to be by him. ʿAwfī (*Lubāb*, ed. Browne, 207-8) quotes five poetical fragments (mostly occasional pieces) and adds that Niẓāmī composed several *ma<u>th</u>nawī*, the titles of which have not survived. The only biographical information we possess about Niẓāmī comes from himself. In 504/1110-11 he was in Samarḳand collecting traditions relating to the poet Rūdakī (*Čahār maḳāla*, text, 33); in 506/1112-13 he met ʿUmar <u>Kh</u>ayyām in Bal<u>kh</u> (*ibid.*, 63) and three years later he was living in Harāt (*ibid.*, 44); in the following year (510/1116-17), finding himself in poverty in Nī<u>sh</u>āpūr (*ibid.*, 9), he went to Ṭūs in the hope of gaining the favour of the Sal<u>dj</u>ūḳ Sultan San<u>dj</u>ar [*q.v.*] who was encamped outside the town (40-1); in Ṭūs he visited the tomb of Firdawsī (51) and collected information about him which he put in his book (47-8). Encouraged by Muʿizzī [*q.v.*], San<u>dj</u>ar's poet-laureate, he succeeded in attracting the prince's attention; his fame and fortune probably date from this time; in 512/1118-19 we find him again at Nī<u>sh</u>āpūr (69); and again in 514/1120-1 when he heard from the lips of Muʿizzī an anecdote about Maḥmūd and Firdawsī (50-51); in 530/1136 he returned to this town and visited the tomb of <u>Kh</u>ayyām (63); and in 547/1152 he fled into hiding after the defeat of the <u>Gh</u>urīd army by San<u>dj</u>ar near Harāt (87). His "Four Discourses" (*Čahār maḳāla*) were probably written in 551/1156. For the remainder of his life we have no data. There is reason to believe he practised medicine and astrology (cf. text, 65, 87). As to his poetry, in spite of the satisfaction he expresses with it, it is not of the first rank, to judge by the fragments that survive; in any case, it was very inferior to his prose, which Browne says is almost unequalled in Persian.

The *Čahār maḳāla* consists of four discourses, each of which deals with one of the classes of men whom the author regards as indispensable in the service of kings: secretaries, poets, astrologers and physicians. Each discourse begins with general considerations, which are followed by anecdotes, often from the writer's personal experience. The number of these anecdotes, which form the most interesting and valuable part of the book, is about forty; some give valuable information on the literary and scientific state of Persia. We may say that the "Four Discourses" (especially the second) and ʿAwfī's *Lubāb* are the two old works which deal systematically with Persian poetry. Dawlat<u>sh</u>āh made a great deal of use of it (cf. Browne, *Sources of Dawlat<u>sh</u>āh*, in *JRAS* [1899], 37-69). We may specially point out that it is to Niẓāmī that we owe the earliest notice of Firdawsī and the only contemporary reference to <u>Kh</u>ayyām. On the other hand, we must point out the historical inaccuracy of certain passages, even in the case of events in which Niẓāmī claims to have taken part. His book is mentioned or quoted by ʿAwfī (*Lubāb*), Ibn Isfandiyār (*Hist. of Ṭabaristān*), Mustawfī Ḳazwīnī (*Tārī<u>kh</u>-i guzīda*), <u>Dj</u>āmī (*Silsilat al-<u>dh</u>ahab*), <u>Gh</u>affārī (*Nigāristān*). Ḥā<u>djdj</u>ī <u>Kh</u>alīfa speaks of a *Ma<u>dj</u>mūʿ al-nawādir* which he thinks is different from the *Čahār maḳāla*; but Mīrzā Muḥammad Ḳazwīnī has shown that this is another title of the same book.

Bibliography: Niẓāmī ʿArūḍī's work has been edited in full by Mīrzā Muḥammad Ḳazwīnī and tr. by E.G. Browne, Pers. text, 1910, English tr., 1921, French tr. Isabelle de Gastines, *Les quatre discours*, Paris 1968; lith. ed. Tehran 1305/1887, and an edn. by Muḥammad Muʿīn, Tehran 1333 *<u>sh</u>.*/1954. Cf. *GIPh*, ii, index; Browne, *LHP*, ii, index; J. Rypka *et alii*, *History of Iranian literature*, Dordrecht 1968, 221-2; Ḥā<u>djdj</u>ī <u>Kh</u>alīfa, ed. Flügel, no. 4348; Riḍā Ḳulī-<u>Kh</u>ān, *Ma<u>dj</u>maʿ al-fuṣaḥāʾ*, i, 635; Muḥammad Nizám al-Dín, *Introd. to the Jawámiʿ ul-ḥikáyát*, London 1929, index.

(H. Massé)

NIẒĀMĪ GAN<u>DJ</u>AWĪ, <u>Dj</u>amāl al-Dīn Abū Muḥammad Ilyās b. Yūsuf b. Zakī Muʾayyad, one of the greatest Persian poets and thinkers. He was born and spent most, if not all, of his life in Gan<u>dj</u>a (called Elisavetpol and Kirovabad during the Imperial Russian and Soviet periods), Niẓāmī being his pen-name. In recognition of his vast knowledge and brilliant mind, the honorific title of *ḥakīm*, "learned doctor," was bestowed upon him by scholars. From his poetry, it is evident that he was learned not only in mathematics, astronomy, medicine, jurisprudence, history, and philosophy but also in music and the arts. His work is a synthesis of Persian literary achievements up to his time.

The traditional biographers, and some modern researchers, differ by six years about the exact date of his birth (535-40/1141-6), and as much as thirty-seven years about the date of his death (575-613/1180-1217). Now there is no doubt, however, that he died in the 7th/13th century, and the earlier dates must be discarded as erroneous. UNESCO recognised the 1141 date as his birth date and declared 1991 the year of Niẓāmī. To honour the 850th anniversary of his birth, there were international Niẓāmī congresses held in 1991 in Washington, Los Angeles, London and Tabrīz.

Usually, there is more precise biographical information about the Persian court poets, but Niẓāmī was not a court poet; he feared loss of integrity in this role and craved primarily for the freedom of artistic creation. His five masterpieces are known collectively as the *<u>Kh</u>amsa*, Quintet, or the *Pan<u>dj</u> gan<u>dj</u>*, the Five Treasures. The five epic poems represent a total of close to 30,000 couplets and they constitute a breakthrough in Persian literature. Niẓāmī was a master in the genre of the romantic epic. In erotic sensuous verse, he explains what makes human beings behave as they do, revealing their follies and their glories, all their struggles, unbridled passions and tragedies.

Though he did not write for the stage, he could be

called a master dramatist. The plot in his romantic stories is carefully constructed to enhance the stories' psychological complexities. The characters work and grow under the stress of action to discover things about themselves and others and to make swift decisions. He delineated simple people with as much insight and compassion as the princely heroes in his *mat͟hnawīs*. Artisans were particularly dear to him. Painters, sculptors, architects and musicians are carefully portrayed and often play crucial roles. The romance of K͟husraw and S͟hīrīn is a very important source of information about the role of artists in pre-Mongol Persia as well as the education and training methods of the artists. The *K͟hamsa* serves as a principal source of our knowledge of 6th/12th century Persian musical composition and instruments. There have been few poets other than Niẓāmī in the long and rich history of Persian literature who have had such an influence and impact on poets, calligraphers, miniature painters, musicians and, in recent times, on people of the theatre, film and ballet, and his influence has extended beyond Persia proper to such adjacent regions as Central Asia, the Caucasus, Asia Minor and Muslim India.

Considered as one of the greatest poems of the Near and Middle East, the number of imitations of, and sequels to, Niẓāmī's *K͟hamsa* or the separate poems of it is without precedent. The most popular have always been the three romantic epics: *K͟husraw wa S͟hīrīn, Laylā wa Mad͟jnūn*, and *Haft paykar*. Besides the *K͟hamsa*, an incomplete *Dīwān* of Niẓāmī's poetry exists.

Mak͟hzan al-asrār, The Treasury of Mysteries, is the first *mat͟hnawī* poem in Niẓāmī's *K͟hamsa*. It is a didactico-philosophical poem with mystical overtones. It is the shortest *mat͟hnawī* of the quintet and is comprised of some 2,260 couplets written in the *sarīʿ maṭwī mawḳūf* metre. Most probably it was completed in the year 582/1184-5, though the majority of scholars have tended to consider the year 570 or 572 as the date of its completion, and was dedicated to a patron of art and culture, Fak͟hr al-Dīn Bahrāms͟hāh of the Turcoman Mengüd͟jek [*q.v.*] dynasty of Erzind͟jan; according to some historians and biographers, Niẓāmī was richly rewarded by Bahrāms͟hāh for the poem.

To Niẓāmī, truth was the very essence of poetry. On this principle, he attacks the court poets who sell their integrity and talents for earthly returns. The Islamic law served as the loom on which the philosophy of his *Mak͟hzan al-asrār* was woven in intricate patterns. He was looking for universal justice, and is trying to protect the poor and humble people and to put under scrutiny the excesses of the powerful of the world. The guidelines for people in the poem are accompanied by warnings of the transitory nature of life. *Mak͟hzan al-asrār* is an emulation of Sanāʾī's *Ḥadīḳat al-ḥaḳīḳa*, and Niẓāmī acknowledges this but stresses his own superiority. The similarities between Sanāʾī's poem and Niẓāmī's are in the ethico-philosophical genre, but Niẓāmī used a different metre and organised the whole poem in a different way.

The language of Niẓāmī is unconventional. He introduces new and lucid metaphors and images as well as coining new words. Almost each couplet in *The Treasury of Mysteries* is enigmatic, making the poem one of the most difficult to understand in all of Persian literature. The difficult language, with its extremely austere ethical demands, made this poem not very popular among the general public. Nevertheless, it became a model for countless numbers of imitators throughout the East; in Persia alone, there were about forty first-class imitations of *Mak͟hzan al-asrār*.

Although some scholars consider *Mak͟hzan al-asrār* a mystical poem, the mysticism with its symbolism is apparent only in the introduction, which is infused with the essence of Ṣūfī thought. In the main body of the book one can detect scattered mystical overtones, but it is up to the reader to arrive at the final interpretation.

Structurally, the poem begins with a large body of introductory matter which contains about 825 couplets or a little more than one-third of the whole book. Here, Niẓāmī established a pattern for the introductory chapters not only of his later epics but also for almost all epics written thereafter. They include verses in worship of God, followed by a chapter of praise and veneration of the Prophet and a description of Muḥammad's ascension to the heavens. The twenty *maḳalāt* or discourses that follow cover some 1,400 couplets.

K͟husraw wa S͟hīrīn is the second poem of Niẓāmī's *K͟hamsa* and the first of his romantic epics. Its protagonists are K͟husraw II (590-628), the last great Sāsānid monarch, known as Parwīz [*q.v.*], the Victorious, and his mistress S͟hīrīn. Their love was recorded by many subsequent Islamic writers, and Firdawsī devoted more than 4,000 couplets to K͟husraw II's reign in his *S͟hāh-nāma*. It was Niẓāmī, however, who gave the story a real structural unity. Infusing it with his own profound experience of love and expanding it with his thoughts on religion, philosophy, and government, he created a romance of great dramatic intensity. The story has a constant forward drive with exposition, challenge, mystery, crisis, climax, resolution, and finally, catastrophe. The action increases in complexity as the protagonists face mounting complications. K͟husraw and S͟hīrīn are not able to meet for a long time, despite their untiring efforts and the help of their confidant. Then, after they do meet, they are forced apart by the political marriage of K͟husraw and Maryam. When K͟husraw promises S͟hīrīn to Farhād as a prize for completing a feat of daring and endurance, the story nearly comes to a premature conclusion.

After the death of Maryam and the murder-suicide of Farhād, it seems that all obstacles are removed and the lovers will be united. But Niẓāmī introduces an affair between K͟husraw and a girl from Iṣfahān that further complicates and delays his union with S͟hīrīn. Finally, on the lovers' wedding night, Niẓāmī creates a bizarre episode, a humorous entr'acte that gives the reader or listener a chance to take a deep breath before the epic's tragic climax. K͟husraw gets drunk and S͟hīrīn replaces her presence in the nuptial chamber with that of a knotty, wizened old crone. Through these dramatic devices, Niẓāmī makes a powerful commentary on human behaviour.

Niẓāmī's deep understanding of women is strongly expressed in *K͟husraw wa S͟hīrīn*. S͟hīrīn is the central character and there is no question that she is a poetic tribute to Niẓāmī's wife Āfāḳ. She is well educated, independent, fearless, resourceful, imaginative, erotic and humorous. Her loyalty knows no bounds. That she is a queen rather than a commoner, as is the case in Firdawsī's *S͟hāh-nāma*, gives the story a stately quality. Her association with Armenia is, perhaps, a reflection of its geographical proximity to Gand͟ja, and she is, like the Byzantine Maryam, a Christian; Niẓāmī was a pious Muslim, but he tolerated and respected other religions.

S͟hīrīn's sense of justice is so great that she forswears K͟husraw's love until he should regain his throne, thus fulfilling his responsibility to his people. Even after they are married, she continues to exert a strong influence on K̲h̲usraw, educating him as always through example and love; as a result, the country flourished, justice was observed and strengthened, and science, religion and philosophy thrived.

The tension between the strength of S̲h̲īrīn and the weakness of K̲h̲usraw is enhanced dramatically by Niẓāmī's tight control of plot and setting, and in his development of the towering figure of Farhād. Episodes of meeting and of missing, of searching and of waiting, are richly entwined with scenes of the barren desert and of luxurious court life; asceticism vies with sensuality.

Niẓāmī's use of allegories, parables and words with double meaning raised the Persian language to a new height. The poem is written in the light, flowing, graceful *hazad̲j̲ musaddas maksūr* metre, deliberately imitating that used by Gurgānī in *Vīs u Rāmīn*. There are about 6,500 couplets.

Its exact date of completion is uncertain. The year 576/1180 is given in some manuscripts, but many scholars believe, on internal evidence, that it was finished after 581/1184. Nor are the three dedicatory invocations—to the Sald̲j̲ū̲k̲ Sultan T̲og̲h̲ri̇̄l III and to his regents, the Atabegs Muḥammad Dj̲ahān Pahlawān and Ḳi̇̄zi̇̄l Arslan—useful in establishing a secure date. Although the first Atabeg was the ruler of Gand̲j̲a, where Niẓāmī lived, and the second one gave Niẓāmī title to a village, these dedications may well have been added by Niẓāmī for political reasons or may be later interpolations. The earliest extant text, dating from 763/1362, was written some 150 years after Niẓāmī's death and is suspected to contain many apocryphal verses.

The great Persian authority on Niẓāmī, Waḥīd Dastgirdī, calls *K̲h̲usraw wa S̲h̲īrīn* "the best historical fable of love and chastity, the treasure of eloquence, counsel and wisdom," whilst Bertels believed that *K̲h̲usraw wa S̲h̲īrīn* is "one of the great masterpieces of world literature. For the first time in the poetry of the Near East, the personality of a human being has been shown with all its richness, with all its contradictions and ups and downs."

Laylā wa Mad̲j̲nūn is perhaps the most popular romance in the Islamic world. Versions appear in prose, song, and poetry in almost every language within the vast area stretching from the Chinese border to the Atlantic ocean. But because of the psychological depth and universality invested in the story, Niẓāmī's epic still serves as the model for all others. It was commissioned by Abu 'l-Muẓaffar Ak̲h̲sitān S̲h̲irwān-S̲h̲āh, a Caucasian ruler proud of his Persian origin and a benefactor of Persian culture.

For centuries, the legend of Laylā and Mad̲j̲nūn had been a popular theme of the short love poems and songs of the Bedouins, and during the early days of the Muslim era, it had been absorbed and embellished by the Persians. Mad̲j̲nūn is traditionally identified with a poet known as Ḳays b. al-Mulawwaḥ, who probably lived in the second half of the 1st/7th century in the Nad̲j̲d desert of Arabia. Although it is probable that there was more than one love-crazed poet called Mad̲j̲nūn, possessed by a djinn or a genie, the Russian scholar Kračkovski in 1946 erased most doubts as to his historical identity.

Neither the arid desert setting nor the spare plot of Mad̲j̲nūn and Laylā's romance inspired Niẓāmī's poetic vision, but he could not refuse the royal commission. And so he expanded and deepened the plot and the personalities, creating from the fragmentary versions a full-scale dramatic poem.

For his romance, Niẓāmī chose an easy metre, the short *hazad̲j̲ musaddas*. *Laylā wa Mad̲j̲nūn* is comprised of at least 4,000 distichs. Niẓāmī wrote that it took him "less than four months" to compose it, which implies a trance-like state of writing. The exact number of distichs has long been a source of controversy, especially since those that are considered apocryphal alter the plot significantly. Waḥīd Dastgirdī's critical edition, based on thirty manuscripts copied between the 8th/14th and 11th/17th centuries, totals 4,650 distichs, of which Dastgirdī considers 600 to be spurious, added by later writers and scribes, who also transposed an additional 400 distichs to cover their handiwork. Gelpke consider Dastgirdī's the only authoritative text and based his prose adaptation of the poem upon it. Browne, Massé and Arberry, however, translated many passages as authentic which Dastgirdī and Gelpke consider interpolations. E.É. Bertels, the Russian editor of the Persian text published in 1965, found 4,659 distichs valid, using the ten most famous manuscripts. It is, of course, possible that Niẓāmī himself rewrote the poem, making his own changes and additions. Many of the great poets who imitated Niẓāmī included so-called spurious passages and plots, and their poetic sensibility should be respected.

Some manuscripts of *Laylā wa Mad̲j̲nūn* bear the date 584/1188 as the year of completion, others, 588/1192; still others, as was common in copied manuscripts, give both dates. The earlier year is supported in the text by an *abd̲j̲ad* dating. Whatever its length and its exact date of completion, there is no doubt that Niẓāmī used all the material, written and oral, available to him, adding, altering and transforming as his poetic genius prompted, in order to create this tragic masterpiece.

Niẓāmī's originality lies in his psychological portrayal of the richness and complexity of the human soul when confronted with intense and abiding love. Mad̲j̲nūn's compulsions, anxieties, frustrations, and passions are not slighted as he moves inexorably toward an ideal love that involves renunciation and, ultimately, transcendence. Many critics have interpreted this as mystical love; but if there is a mystic strain in Niẓāmī, it is subtle and covert; it never destroys or blurs the sharp psychological and the physical identity of its protagonist. It is virtually impossible to draw a clear line in Niẓāmī's poetry between the mystical and the erotic, the sacred and the profane. The psychological profile of Laylā is less deeply drawn, but her enduring love is no less extraordinary an achievement.

Laylā and Mad̲j̲nūn are scourged by separation, social ostracism, self-denial, and spiritual and physical suffering from the very beginning until their tragic ends. It is quite possible that, to soften the tragedy, Niẓāmī wrote a second version, weaving into it the love story of Zayd for his cousin Zaynab, which parallels that of Mad̲j̲nūn and Laylā; the couples become messengers for one another and to some degree are able to mitigate the relentless curse of separation.

The expanded version of *Laylā wa Mad̲j̲nūn* closes with a vivid dream sequence of Paradise. Mad̲j̲nūn and Laylā, sitting on magnificent carpets, are radiantly embracing, wine cups in hand. Many scholars believe this to be an interpolation, but if its date can be drawn from the moving dedication to the S̲h̲irwān-S̲h̲āh's crown prince, in which Niẓāmī counsels his own son Muḥammad, addressing him as a boy of fourteen, the entire Zayd-Zaynab addition may well be Niẓāmī's own work.

Imitators of Niẓāmī's *Laylā wa Mad̲j̲nūn* can be

listed by the hundreds, and the romance is popular even today. According to Bertels and A.A. Ḥikmat, counting only the most famous versions, there are twenty in Persian, forty in Turkish, three in Azeri Turkish, one in Uzbek, one in Kurdish and two in Tajik [see further, MADJNŪN-LAYLĀ].

Haft paykar is the fourth and the most intricate poem of Niẓāmī's *Khamsa*. It is a bedazzling exploration of the pleasures of love. At the same time, it can be interpreted as mystical. The seven stories told by the seven princesses can be interpreted as the seven stations of human life, or the seven aspects of human destiny, or the seven stages of the mystic way. In fact, the title of the story can be translated as the "Seven Portraits", the "Seven Effigies", as well as the "Seven Princesses". The poem is also known as the *Haft gunbad* or "Seven Domes".

In Islamic cosmology, the earth was placed in the centre of the seven planets: the moon, Mercury, Venus, the sun, Mars, Jupiter and Saturn. These were considered agents of God, and in their motion influenced beings and events on earth. Niẓāmī firmly believed as well that the unity of the world could be perceived through arithmetical, geometrical, and musical relations. Numbers were the key to the one interconnected universe; for through numbers multiplicity becomes unity and discordance, harmony. Hence Niẓāmī used seven, the number that has always been pre-eminent among the people of the East, as the major motif of *Haft paykar*; for in Islam, seven is considered as the first perfect number.

In *Haft paykar*, the phantasmagoric movement of its hero, Bahrām Gūr, as he visits each princess, covers a symbolic path between black, or the hidden majesty of the Divine, and white, or purity and unity. The princesses and their pavilions are manifestations of specific planets, specific climes, colours, and days. The pavilions are domed, representing the structure of the heavens. Niẓāmī illustrates the harmony of the universe, the affinity of the sacred and the profane, and the concordance of ancient and Islamic Iran.

The number seven casts its magic spell throughout the *Haft paykar*. Completed in the year 593/1197, the *Haft paykar* was commissioned by and dedicated to the prince of Maragha, ʿAlāʾ al-Dīn Kurp Arslan, who allowed the already famous Niẓāmī a free hand in choosing his theme. The poet chose an historical figure for his hero, the Sāsānid emperor and hero Bahrām Gūr, the "wild ass" or "the hunter of wild asses" [see BAHRĀM].

The main body of *Haft paykar* brings Niẓāmī's full creative power into play. It is made up of the stories told by the seven princesses to enchant Bahrām Gūr. Each has been installed in her own paradisial pavilion in a specially built seven-domed palace near to his own. Bahrām passes from one to another on succeeding days of the week, loving each and enthralled by each. There are stories within stories within stories, playing sensually on all the perceptions. The colours and ornamentation of the pavilions, the associated colours of the garments, the sparkling jewels of Bahrām and the princesses appeal to the visual instincts. The continuous background music pleases the ear. The musky perfumes and the pungent incense excite the olfactory nerves. Taste is aroused by mellow wines and exotic foods, and touch by the finest silks and brocades. All these serve as aphrodisiacs, stimulating sensual desire. But Niẓāmī, always true to moderation, tempers the erotic with restraint and hedonistic pleasure with responsibility to affairs of state. In spite of his delight in fabricating a myriad of tantalising scenes and metaphors, the essence of this *mathnawī* is that the physical passions are most preciously enjoyed when set in a context of virtue, simplicity, and kindness.

Haft paykar is written in graceful *khafīf* hexameters, and is estimated to contain from 4,637 to 5,136 couplets.

The Persian legend of Alexander the Great seems to overshadow all of the other fantastic Alexander stories, not only in the tales of the successful accomplishment of many a "mission impossible" but especially concerning the nature of his career. In Persia he rose from the stature of an evil foreign conqueror of the country to that of a national hero king, and even more, to that of a great prophet of God, preparing the nations for Islam [see AL-ISKANDAR].

Out of the many stories of Alexander in Persian literature, that of Niẓāmī is unsurpassed. It is a highly imaginative, dramatic and refined epic. In it, heroic behaviour is muted by psychological characterisation, piety and mysticism are balanced by common sense and situational humour, philosophy is counteracted by romanticism, and nationalism is softened by cosmopolitan ideals of Islam. The virtuosity of Niẓāmī's storytelling and his unbridled fantasy are matched by the brilliance of his language which is full of dazzling imagery and extended metaphor.

Niẓāmī's account of the adventures of Alexander the Great is probably the first work in Persian literature that is divided into two parts. The first half is called *Sharaf-nāma* (The Book of Honour) and the second part *Iḳbāl-nāma* (The Book of Wisdom). The two parts are also known, especially in India, as the *Iskandar-nāma-yi barri* (The Adventures of Alexander by Land), and the *Iskandar-nāma-yi baḥrī* (The Adventures of Alexander by Sea). The two parts, although constituting a full span of Alexander's life from birth to death under the general title of *Iskandar-nāma*, are treated by the poet as two separate entities, each covering a cycle in Alexander's life. In the first cycle, Alexander appears as the conqueror of the world, in the second, as the philosopher and prophet.

The introduction to the first part of the *Iskandar-nāma* is a little more than twice as long as the introduction to the second part. The introductions reflect the length of both parts; the *Sharaf-nāma* contains about 6,800 couplets and the *Iḳbāl-nāma* about 3,680 couplets, making *Iskandar-nāma*, with about 10,500 couplets, the longest poem of Niẓāmī's *Khamsa*.

Confusion has been created among scholars by various dates given for the completion of the poem, as well as by the various people to whom it or its parts are dedicated in the available manuscripts. Some of them have considered the *Iskandar-nāma* to be the fourth of Niẓāmī's epic quintet, written in 587/1191 and dedicated to ʿIzz al-Dīn Masʿūd I, the Zangid ruler of Mawṣil (572-89/1176-93). But because this date is contrary to many references and events in the text which would indicate a later date, some scholars believe that the work was dedicated to ʿIzz al-Dīn Masʿūd II, of the same dynasty (607-15/1211-18). If this is the case, then the span of Niẓāmī's life would have to be stretched and the date of his death moved from the traditional one of 599/1203 or 605/1209 to some time after ʿIzz al-Dīn Masʿūd II came to the throne in 607/1211.

In the preface to the *Sharaf-nāma*, Niẓāmī declares that he has already completed four *mathnawī*s. This would indicate that the *Iskandar-nāma* was the fifth and last of his epic poems and was, therefore, composed after 593/1197, the date of completion of *Haft paykar*.

Those whose names have come down to us in association with the manuscripts are: Nuṣrat al-Dīn

Djahān Pahlawān from the rulers of Ādharbāydjān, ʿIzz al-Dīn Masʿūd from the rulers of Mawṣil, and Nuṣrat al-Dīn Abū Bakr Pīshkīn (Bīshkīn) from the rulers in the Caucasus.

No doubt Pseudo-Callisthenes' account of the life of Alexander was known to Niẓāmī [see ISKANDAR NĀMA], but it was, however, Firdawsī who was his source of inspiration in composing the *Iskandar-nāma*. He, therefore, chose for it the heroic epic *mutaḳārib* metre which Firdawsī had employed in his *Shāh-nāma*. The *Sharaf-nāma*, the first portion of the *Iskandar-nāma*, is devoted to Alexander's conquest of the world. His conquest, however, was already shaped by the idea of his future prophetic mission. It was, therefore, not for an empire that Alexander set out to conquer but for the purpose of liberating oppressed peoples; assisting the Egyptians in their struggle against the Zangīs; rescuing Queen Nushāba from the hands of the Russians; freeing the Persian people from the enslavement of Darius and the Zoroastrian priests; securing safe passage through bandit territories; guiding travellers on land and sea; and assisting in building towns.

The second part of the *Iskandar-nāma*, the *Iḳbāl-nāma*, portrays Alexander as a great sage and prophet. With the advent of Islam, Alexander found his place as Dhu 'l-Ḳarnayn in Ḳurʾān, XVIII, 83/82-98, which encouraged Muslims to glorify him. After the conquest of the world, Alexander devoted his time to the spiritual gains of his conquests. He transported scholarly tomes from all parts of the known world to be translated for his library and surrounded himself with the greatest minds in the ancient world. Niẓāmī is not specific in describing Alexander's religion, but it is a kind of monotheism which prepares the way for Islam. Like Caesar who conquered the future lands of Christendom, Alexander conquered the future domain of Islam, so that he is the archetype of the ideal ruler and a wise prophet.

By comparison with his other *mathnawīs*, the *Iskandar-nāma* is very uneven. In the others, the stories not directly related to the main current are held together structurally, giving an impression of wholeness, whereas in the *Iskandar-nāma* they are loosely woven into the massive structure.

Bibliography: A. Texts. 1. Critical editions of *Khamsa*, *Dīwān* and miscellaneous verses. Waḥīd Dastgirdī, *Gandjīna-yi Gandjawī*, Tehran 1318; idem, *Hizār andarz-i Ḥakīm Niẓāmī*, Tehran 1319; *Kulliyyāt-i Khamsa*, ed. idem, Tehran 1318, 1335; *Kulliyyāt-i Khamsa*, Amīr Kabīr, Tehran 1341; M.Th. Houtsma, *Choix de vers tirés de la Khamsa de Nizami*, Leiden 1921; Saʿīd Nafīsī, *Dīwān-i ḳaṣāyid wa ghazaliyyāt-i Niẓāmī*, Tehran 1338; Maḥmūd Sipāsī, *Madjmūʿa-yi abyāt-i barguzīda az sukhanān-i Ḥakīm Niẓāmī*, Tehran 1348. 2. Critical editions of *Makhzan al-asrār*. Dastgirdī, Tehran 1313, 1334; ʿAbd al-Karīm ʿAlī Awghulī ʿAlī-zāda, Baku 1960; Ḥusayn Pizhmān Bakhtiyārī, Tehran 1344; N. Bland, London 1844. 3. Critical editions of *Khusraw wa Shīrīn*. Bakhtiyārī, Tehran 1343; Dastgirdī, Tehran 1313, repr. 1343; H.W. Duda, *Farhad und Schirin*, Monografie Archivu Orientalniho, 2, Prague 1933; L.A. Khetagurov and F. Babayev, Baku 1960. 4. Critical editions of *Laylā wa Madjnūn*. A.A. Alesker-zāde and F. Babayev, Moscow 1965; Bakhtiyārī, Tehran 1347; Dastgirdī, Tehran 1313, repr. 1335; Djalal Matīnī, *Khulāṣa-yi Laylī wa Madjnūn*, Mashhad, 1341. 5. Critical editions of *Haft Paykar*. Bakhtiyārī, Tehran 1344; Dastgirdī, Tehran 1315, repr. 1334; Muḥammad Muʿīn, *Taḥlīl-i Haft paykar-i Niẓāmī*, Tehran 1338; H. Ritter and J. Rypka, *Heft Peiker*, Monografie Archivu Orientalniho, 3, Prague 1934. 6. Critical editions of the *Sharaf-nāma*. Dastgirdī, Tehran 1316; Bakhtiyārī, Tehran 1345; ʿAlī-zāda, Baku 1947. 7. Critical editions of the *Iḳbāl-nāma*. Dastgirdī, Tehran 1317; Bakhtiyārī, Tehran 1335; Babayev, Baku 1947.

B. Translations. 1. *Makhzan al-asrār*. Gholam Hosein Darab, *Makzanol Asrar. The treasury of mysteries* (in English), London 1945; M. Gençosman Nuri, *Mahzen-i esrar* (in Turkish), Ankara 1964. 2. *Khusraw wa Shīrīn*. J.C. Bürgel, *Chosrou und Schirin* (in German), Zürich 1980; K.A. Lipskerov, *Khosrov i Shirin* (in Russian), Baku 1955; H. Massé, *Le Roman de Chosroès et Chîrîn* (in French), Paris 1970; Sabri Seuvesevil, *Hüsrev ve Şirin* (in Turkish), Istanbul 1955. 3. *Laylā wa Madjnūn*. P. Antokol'skiy, *Layli i Majnun* (in Russian), Moscow 1957; J. Atkinson, *Laili and Majnun* (in English), London 1836, and 1894, 1905, repr. 1968; R. Gelpke, *Lejla und Medshnun* (in German), Zürich 1963, ills.; idem, *The story of Layla and Majnun* (in English), London 1966, ills.; Ali Nihat Tarlan, *Leylâ ile Mecnun* (in Turkish), Istanbul 1943. 4. *Haft paykar*. A. Bausani, *Le sette principesse* (in Italian), Bari 1967; V. Derzhavin, *Sem' Krasavits* (in Russian), Moscow 1959; Gelpke, *Die sieben Geschichten der sieben Prinzessinnen* (in German), Zürich 1959; idem, *The story of the Seven Princesses* (in English), London 1976; C.E. Wilson, *The Haft Paikar* (in English, 2 vols.), London 1924. 5. *Iskandar-nāma*. H. Wilberforce Clarke, *The Sikander Nāmae Bará*, London 1881; E.É. Bertels, *Eskandarname, Part I, Sharafname*, Baku 1940; Lipskerov, *Eskandarname*, Moscow 1953.

C. General. Accademia Nazionale dei Lincei, *Il poeta Persiano Niẓāmī e la leggenda iranica di Alessandro Magno,* conference proceedings, Rome 1977; Akademia Nauk Azerbaidzankoi SSR, *Nizami Giandzevi*, Nizami conference proceedings, Baku 1947; G. Aliyev, *Legenda o Khosrovie i Shirin v literatura narodov vostoka*, Moscow 1960; R. Azada, *Nizami Ganjavi*, Baku 1981 (in English); W. Bacher, *Niẓâmî's Leben und Werke*, Göttingen 1871; E.É. Bertels, *Nizami: tvorcheskiĭ put' poéta*, Moscow 1956; idem, *Nizami i Fuzuli: izbrannye trudï*, Moscow 1962; idem, *Niẓāmī*, in *EI*[1]; L. Binyon, *The poems of Nizami, described by Laurence Binyon*, London 1928; K.R.F. Burrill, *The Farhād and Shīrīn story and its further development from Persian into Turkish literature*, in *Studies in art and literature of the Near East in honor of Richard Ettinghausen*, ed. P. Chelkowski, Salt Lake City and New York 1974; Chelkowski, *Mirror of the invisible world*, New York 1975; idem, *Nizami: master dramatist*, in Ehsan Yarshater (ed.), *Persian literature*, New York 1988; Fr. Erdmann, *Bahram Gur und die russische Fürstentochter*, Kazan 1844; Fuzuli, *Leyla and Mejnun*, tr. Sofi Huri, introd. and notes by A. Bombaci, London 1970; F. Gabrieli, *Le versione da Nizami*, in *AIUON*, x (1937-8), 31-72; Gelpke, *Liebe und Wahnsinn als Thema eines persichen Dichters: zur Mädschnun-Gestalt bei Nezami*, in *Symbolon*, no. 4 (Basel-Stuttgart 1964), 105-18; ʿAbd al-Naʿīm Ḥasanayn, *Niẓāmī al-Gandjawī*, Cairo 1954; ʿAlī Aṣghar Ḥikmat, *Romeo wa Juliet, muḳāyasa bā Laylī wa Madjnūn*, Tehran 1941; Houtsma, *Some remarks on the Dīwān of Niẓāmī*, in *E.G. Browne Festschrift*, Cambridge, 1922, 224-7; *Iranshenasi*, *Special issue celebrating the 850th year of the birth of Niẓāmī*, iii/3-4 (Bethesda, Md. 1991-2); A. Karbowska, *Einige Bermerkungen über Bahram Gur Epos und Geschichte*, in *Folia Orientalia*, xxii (1981-4); A. Kaziev, *Miniatiurï rukopisi Khamsa Nizami 1539-1543*, Baku 1964;

I. Yu. Kračkovski, *Die Frühgeschichte der Erzählung von Macnun und Laila in der Arabischen Literatur*, tr. H. Ritter, in *Oriens*, viii (1955), 1-50; H. Krenn, *Bermerkungen zu Versen von Niẓāmīs Epos Ḫosrou und Šīrīn*, in *WZKM*, liii (1956), 92-6; F.R. Martin and Sir Thomas Arnold, *The Nizami manuscript, illuminated by Bihzad, Mirak and Qasim Ali, written in 1495 for Sultan Ali Mirza Barlās, ruler of Samarqand, in the British Museum*, 24, 1, Vienna 1926; Martin, *The Khamsa of Niẓāmī, The Niẓāmī manuscript from the Library of the Shah of Persia now in the Metropolitan Museum at New York*, Vienna 1927; H. Massé and A. Zajączkowski, *Farhād wa-Shīrīn*, in *EI*²; M.V. McDonald, *The religious and social views of Niẓāmī of Ganjeh*, in *Iran*, i (1963), 97-101; Džamal Mustafaev, *Filosofiskie i etičeskie vozzreniya Nizami*, Baku 1962; Mehmet Emin Resulzade, *Azerbaycan şairi Nizamî*, Ankara 1951; Ritter, *Über die Bildersprache Niẓāmīs*, Berlin and Leipzig 1927; Rypka, *Das Sprichwort in Niẓāmīs Lajlí va Maǧnun*, in *Ar.Or.* (1969), 318-25; idem, *Der vierte Gesang von Niẓāmīs Haft Paikar neu übersetzt*, in *Oriens*, xv (1962), 234-41; idem, *Les Sept Princesses de Nizhami*, in *L'ame de l'Iran*, Paris 1951, 99-126; Saʿīdī Sīrdjānī, *Sīmā-yi dūzan, Shīrīn wa Laylā dar Khamsa-yi Niẓāmī*, Tehran 1368; G. Scarcia, *Glossa a un gioco di parole di Niẓāmī*, in *AIUON*, N.S. (1968), 207-13; Maeiétta Shaginian, *Etiudi o Nizami*, Erevan 1955; ʿAlī Akbar Shihābī, *Niẓāmī shāʿir-i dāstānsarā*, Tehran n.d.; Priscilla P. Soucek, *Niẓāmī on painters and painting*, in *Islamic art in the Metropolitan Museum of Art*, ed. R. Ettinghausen, New York 1972; Soucek, *Farhād and Ṭāq-i Būstān*, in *Studies in art and literature of the Near East in honor of Richard Ettinghausen*; Ali Nihad Tarlan, *Ganceli Nizamî divani*, Istanbul 1944; A. Wesselski, *Quellen und Nachwirkungen der Haft paikar*, in *Isl.*, xxii (1935), 106-19; Morteza Yamini, *Marlowe's Hero and Leander and Nizami's Khusraw and Shirin*, in *Bulletin of the Asian Institute*, iii-iv (Shiraz 1975); A. Zajączkowski, *À propos d'un épisode du* Khosrau u Shirin *de Nizami*, in *Mélanges H. Massé*, Tehran 1963, 405-16. (P. Chelkowski)

NIẒĀMĪ, Ḥasan, a Persian historian whose full name was Ṣadr al-Dīn Muḥammad b. Ḥasan. Born in Nīshāpūr, he went on the advice of his *shaykh Muḥammad Kūfī to* Ghaznī to give an opportunity to his remarkable talents as a stylist. A severe illness forced him to leave Ghaznī, and he went to Dihlī were he obtained an appointment as court historian to the Ghūrid Sultans and began, in 602/1206, his great historical work *Tādj al-maʾāthir fi 'l-taʾrīkh*, which brought him great fame. It deals with the history of the first three sultans of Dihlī—the Ghūrid Muḥammad b. Sām (588-602/1192-1206), and his slaves Ḳuṭb al-Dīn Aybak (602-7/1206-10) and Shams al-Dīn Iltutmish (607-33/1210-35). The book begins with the capture of Adjmēr by Muʿizz al-Dīn in 587/1191 and ends with the appointment of Nāṣir al-Dīn Muḥammad as governor of Lahore (614/1217). An Appendix contains a panegyric of Iltutmish and his campaigns of conquest. The work was very highly esteemed in the Muslim East as a model of elegant style. It is written in high-flown and difficult language and has a large number of poetical passages inserted in it. It is only with difficulty that the historical facts can be extricated from the medley of rhetoric, but nevertheless the book is of undeniable value for the history of India and Afghānistān.

Bibliography: Rieu, *Catalogue*, i, 239; Elliot and Dowson, *History of India*, ii, 204-43; N. Lees, in *JRAS* (1868), 433; Flügel, *Cat. Vienna*, ii, 173 (no. 951); W. Pertsch, *Die persischen Handschriften der ... Bibl. zu Gotha*, 53; E. Blochet, *Catalogue des mss. persans de la Bibl. Nationale*, Paris 1905, i, 333; C. Salemann and von Rosen, *Indices alphabet. codicum mss. persicorum ... in Bibl. Imper. Literarum Universitatis Petropolitanae*, St. Petersburg 1888, 12, no. 578; Storey, i, 493-5, 1310. On the biography of the author, see also Mīrkhwānd, lith. Bombay, i, 7.

(E. Berthels)

NIẒĀMIYYA, a term often used in the sources for Saldjūḳ history to designate the partisans and protégés of the great vizier Niẓām al-Mulk [*q.v.*], after his death attached to and operating with the sons and descendants of Niẓām al-Mulk. The influence of these partisans was especially notable in the years just after Sultan Malik Shāh's death in 485/1092, when they actively promoted the cause of and secured the sultanate for Berk-yaruḳ b. Malik Shāh [*q.v.*] against his infant half-brother Maḥmūd, the candidate of Malik Shāh's widow Terken Khātūn and her ally the vizier Tādj al-Mulk Abu 'l-Ghanāʾim. In this present article, it is the descendants of Niẓām al-Mulk, who filled many offices in the administrations of the Great Saldjūḳ sultans and also, at times, of the ʿAbbāsid caliphs, who will be considered.

At least nine of Niẓām al-Mulk's sons achieved some office, civil and/or military, in the decades after his assassination in 485/1092. There was a distinct feeling among contemporaries that, in accordance with the belief that the arcana and the expertise of certain professions or skills were handed down within the families of their original exponents, the supreme capability of Niẓām al-Mulk would manifest itself in his progeny. On the whole, this faith was unjustified.

Shams al-Mulk ʿUthmān was *ʿāriḍ al-djaysh* for Sultan Muḥammad b. Malik Shāh [*q.v.*], and then *mustawfī* and an inefficient vizier to Sultan Maḥmūd b. Muḥammad [*q.v.*] in the years 516-17/1122-3. No fewer than three of Niẓām al-Mulk's sons served Berk-yaruḳ as vizier: Muʾayyid al-Mulk ʿUbayd Allāh, Fakhr al-Mulk al-Muẓaffar and the drunken and incompetent ʿIzz al-Mulk Ḥasan. Fakhr al-Mulk also served Sandjar b. Malik Shāh [*q.v.*] as vizier until his assassination in Khurāsān in 500/1106 by a Bāṭinī. Muʾayyid al-Mulk was probably the most talented and competent of the sons of Niẓām al-Mulk, but was dismissed by the sultan in 488/1095 through the intrigues of Berk-yaruḳ's mother Zubayda Khātūn and Muʾayyid al-Mulk's rival Madjd al-Mulk al-Balasānī; after then, he served Muḥammad b. Malik Shāh as vizier until Berk-yaruḳ defeated his brother in battle at Hamadān in 494/1101 and executed his former vizier as a renegade. Fakhr al-Mulk had served Tutush b. Alp Arslan [*q.v.*], Saldjūḳ ruler in Syria, before entering the service of Berk-yaruḳ, and subsequently went to serve Sandjar until 500/1107 (his son Naṣīr al-Dīn Ṭāhir was also later to serve as Sandjar's vizier from 527/1133 till his own death in 548/1153). Djamāl al-Mulk Muḥammad b. Niẓām al-Mulk (d. 473/1080-1) was governor of Balkh during his father's lifetime; and ʿImād al-Mulk Abu 'l-Ḳāsim was vizier to Malik Shāh's brother Böri Bars (d. 488/1095), the governor of Herat.

Of the next generations, in addition to Fakhr al-Mulk's son Naṣīr al-Dīn Ṭāhir (see above), his brother Ḳiwām al-Mulk Ṣadr al-Dīn Muḥammad served Sandjar 500-11/1107-17, whilst Naṣīr al-Dīn Ṭāhir's son Niẓām al-Mulk Ḳiwām al-Dīn Ḥasan served Sulaymān Shāh b. Muḥammad, briefly sultan in Baghdād 555-6/1160-1. Another of Niẓām al-Mulk's great-grandsons, Shams al-Dīn Yaʿḳūb b. Isḥāḳ b. Fakhr al-Mulk, is mentioned as a patron of the local historian of Bayhaḳ, ʿAlī b. Zayd Ibn Funduḳ [*q.v.*] (Yāḳūt, *Irshād*, v, 216); with this generation, the descendants of Niẓām al-Mulk fade from public life and from mention in the sources.

Finally, of the great vizier's collaterals, his brother Abu 'l-Ḳāsim ʿAbd Allāh's son Abu 'l-Maḥāsin Shihāb al-Dīn functioned as Sandjar's vizier 511-15/1117-21; and Ibn Funduḳ mentions several other collateral relatives as living in the Bayhaḳ district in the later half of the 6th/12th century.

Bibliography: See M.F. Sanaullah, *The decline of the Saljūqid empire*, Calcutta 1938, 40 ff.; ʿAbbās Iḳbāl, *Wizārat dar ʿahd-i salāṭīn-i buzurg saldjūḳī*, Tehran 1338/1959; Carla L. Klausner, *The Seljuk vezirate, a study of civil administration 1055-1194*, Cambridge, Mass. 1973. There are genealogical tables of the family of Niẓām al-Mulk and his collaterals in Iḳbāl, *op. cit.*, after p. 318; the table in Zambaur, *Manuel*, 223, is incomplete and not wholly accurate.

(C.E. Bosworth)

al-**NIẒĀMIYYA**, al-**MADRASA**, the designation given to the colleges of Sunnī instruction founded in ʿIrāḳ, al-Djazīra and Persia by the great Saldjūḳ vizier Niẓām al-Mulk [*q.v.*]. See for these, madrasa, I. 4, and niẓām al-mulk. (Ed.)

NIZĀR b. **MAʿADD**, common ancestor of the greater part of the Arab tribes of the north, according to the accepted genealogical system. Genealogy: Nizār b. Maʿadd b. ʿAdnān (Wüstenfeld, *Geneal. Tabellen*, A. 3). His mother, Muʿāna bint Djahla, was descended from the pre-Arab race of the Djurhum [*q.v.*]. Genealogical legend, which has preserved mythological features and folklore relating to several eponyms of Arab tribes, is almost silent on the subject of Nizār (an etymological fable about his name: *Tādj al-ʿarūs*, iii, 563, 15-17 from the *Rawḍ al-unuf* of al-Suhaylī (i, 8, 8-10) is without doubt of very late origin, as is shown by the connection which is established with the prophetic mission of Muḥammad; the same etymology from *nazr* "insignificant" is further found in Ibn Durayd, *Kitāb al-Ishtiḳāḳ*, 20, 6; *Mufaḍḍaliyyāt*, ed. Lyall, 763, 16, without the story in question). Tradition has more to say about his four sons Rabīʿa, Muḍar, Anmār, Iyād and about the partition of the paternal heritage among them, in connection with which they visited the Djurhumī *ḥakam* al-Afʿā. Their adventures on the journey (they are able to describe minutely the appearance of a camel they have never seen from the traces it has left) form the subject of a popular story which has parallels among other peoples; its object is to make the origins of the *ḳiyāfa* [*q.v.*] go back to the most remote period (al-Mufaḍḍal b. Salama, *al-Fākhir*, 155-6, and the sources there quoted; al-Ṭabarī, i, 1108-10, etc.); it perhaps is of interest to note that the story was known to Voltaire who introduced it into his *Zadig*.

As Robertson Smith showed a century ago (*Kinship and marriage in early Arabia*², 5 ff., 283-9), and as Goldziher has confirmed by numerous quotations (*Muhammedanische Studien*, i, 78-92), the name Nizār only appears late in Arab poetry, while that of Maʿadd (which is found as early as the Byzantine historians Procopius and Nonnosus) appears quite early in it, although its ethnic character is rather vague (as to that of ʿAdnān, still more comprehensive, one of the oldest historians of Arab poetry, Muḥammad b. Sallām, d. 230/844-5, had already pointed out that his name was almost unknown in ancient poetry, *Ṭabaḳāt al-shuʿarāʾ*, ed. Hell, 5, 1; cf. Ibn ʿAbd al-Barr, *al-Inbāh ʿalā ḳabāʾil al-ruʾāh*, Cairo 1350, 48). Before the Umayyad period, the only trace we find of the use of Nizār as an ethnic is in a verse of the pre-Islamic poet Bishr b. Abī Khāzim (in the *Mufaḍḍaliyyāt*, 667, 15) and in another of Kaʿb b. Zuhayr (in al-Ṭabarī, i, 1106, 10); in the verse of Ḥassān b. Thābit, ed. Hirschfeld, lx, 2, the reference is to another Nizār, son of Maʿīṣ b. ʿĀmir b. Luʾayy (Wüstenfeld, *Tabellen*, P. 15) belonging to the Ḳuraysh. The line in Umayya b. Abi 'l-Ṣalt, ed. Schulthess, i, 10, in which the descent of the Thaḳīf from Nizār is celebrated, is apocryphal and is connected with the well-known dispute regarding the origin of the Thaḳīf. The story of the verdict of al-Aḳraʿ b. Ḥābis al-Tamīmī in favour of Djarīr b. ʿAbd Allāh al-Badjalī against Khālid b. Arṭāt al-Kalbī (*Naḳāʾiḍ*, ed. Bevan, 141-2; cf. Ibn Hishām, *Sīra*, ed. Wüstenfeld, 50), in which there is a reference to Nizār and which is placed before Islam, is not less suspect; its object is to defend the northern origin of the Badjīla (descendants of Anmār), often disputed, as well as that of their brethren the Khathʿam [*q.v.*], and to refuse the same origin to the Kalb, descendants of the Ḳuḍāʿa, to which it was attributed just at the time of the strife that raged around the succession to Yazīd I. The *radjaz* verses quoted by Ibn Hishām, *Sīra*, 49 (and often elsewhere; they are sometimes attributed to ʿAmr b. Murra al-Djuhanī, a contemporary of the Prophet, and sometimes to a certain al-Aflaḥ b. al-Yaʿbūb, otherwise unknown), in which we find used, with reference to Ḳuḍāʿa, the verb *tanazzara* "to announce oneself to be descended from Nizār" may be regarded as apocryphal. No stress need be laid on the isolated reference in al-Balādhurī (*Futūḥ*, ed. de Goeje, 276, 16) to the quarters (*khiṭaṭ*) of the Banū Nizār in Kūfa contrasted with those of the Yamanīs; his language simply reflects the position in the author's time or that of his sources, later than the great upheavals of the first century a.h.

It is only from this period, and, to be more exact, after the battle of Mardj Rāhiṭ (65/684 [*q.v.*]) won by the Kalb over the Ḳays, that we begin to find the name Nizār recurring with increasing frequency. It occurs mainly in political poetry: Djarīr, al-Farazdaḳ, al-Akhṭal, al-Ḳuṭāmī and Zufar b. al-Ḥārith use it to designate the common source of the tribes of the north, contrasting it with the terms "Yaman" or "Ḳaḥṭān". The expression *Ibnā Nizārⁱⁿ* "the two sons of Nizār" becomes regular; it indicates the Muḍar (Ḳays ʿAylān) and the Rabīʿa as belonging to one ethnic group; they were previously regarded as unrelated to one another. The tribes descended from Anmār (cf. above) and Iyād (the fourth son of Nizār; but other sources make him a son of Maʿadd) appear only rarely as members of the group. This is what the genealogical systematisation seeks to explain by alleged migrations of Anmār and Iyād into the groups of Yamanī tribes.

But the application of the term Nizār continued to remain vague, more so than those of Ḳays, Muḍar and Rabīʿa, which represent very large groups, but more precise than that of Maʿadd, of which it tends to take the place. This is due to the fact that the term Nizār corresponds to a political ideal rather than to a historical reality; in the latter, the reigning dynasty, claiming descent from Ḳuraysh (themselves, consequently, Nizārīs) had as their henchmen the Kalb, one of the most powerful Yamanī tribes, while the Azd, another tribe of the south, bound to the policy of their most illustrious representatives, the Muhallabids [*q.v.*], were sometimes on the side of the Umayyads and sometimes against them. It was this complicated position that gave rise to the attempt to separate the Ḳuḍāʿa (i.e. the Kalb) from the southern stock in order to make them descendants of Nizār. The story told in *Aghānī*, xi, 160-1, al-Bakrī, *Muʿdjam*, ed. Wüstenfeld, 14-15, is intended to explain the separation of the Ḳuḍāᶜa from the rest of the Nizār as a result of the murder of the Nizārī Yad̲h̲kur b. ᶜAnaza by the Ḳuḍāᶜī Ḥazīma b. Nahd. The lines in D̲j̲arīr (*Naḳāʾiḍ*, 994) sum up very completely the way in which the Ḳuḍāᶜa-Kalb were connected with the Nizār, while elsewhere (e.g. *ibid.*, 261: al-Farazdaḳ) Ḳuḍāᶜa and Nizār are opposed. Later, at the end of the Umayyad period and especially in the period of the struggle in K̲h̲urāsān which was the prelude to the fall of the dynasty, Nizār (also in the form *Nizāriyya*) became the regular designation which was contrasted with *Yamaniyya*: henceforth the Banū Nizār were to be the representatives of northern Arabism; as early as the period of decline of the Umayyads, the poet al-Kumayt b. Zayd al-Asadī [*q.v.*] had composed a long poem, the *Mud̲h̲ahhaba*, exalting the Nizār at the expense of the Ḳaḥṭān; nearly a century later, the Yamanī Diᶜbil [*q.v.*] replied to him; these poetical jousts on which the *ᶜaṣabiyya*, tribal rivalry, of the two great ethnic groups of the Arabs was nourished, continued down to quite a late date, especially among the Zaydīs of the Yaman.

From what has been said, it is evident that we cannot speak of Nizār as a tribe which had a real historical existence nor, as is the case with the Maᶜadd, as a comprehensive term indicating an effective grouping together of a number of tribes of different origin. Nizār is simply a fictitious invention, a label intended to serve political interests. One must, however, ask whence the name came and what were the precedents which suggested its use in the sense above outlined. It is possible that the history of the four sons of Nizār (cf. above), a popular story, the nature and diffusion of which seem to take it back to a very early period and which originally had nothing to do with genealogical tradition, supplied the names on which the *nassābūn* later gave their imagination free play. But this is a pure supposition, which would have to be confirmed by definite proofs.

Bibliography (in addition to references in the article): Wüstenfeld, *Register zu den geneal. Tabellen*, 337; Ibn al-Kalbī, *D̲j̲amharat al-ansāb* (ms. British Museum), fol. 3b; Ibn al-Kalbī-Caskel, i, *Tafeln*, 1, ii, *Register*, 1-2, 448; Ibn Ḳutayba, *Kitāb al-Maᶜārif*, ed. Wüstenfeld, 31; Ibn His̲h̲ām, *Sīra*, ed. Wüstenfeld, 7, 49-50; Ibn Saᶜd, i/1, 30; Nuwayrī, *Nihāyat al-arab*, ii, 327-8; *Kitāb al-Ag̲h̲ānī*; *Naḳāʾiḍ*; Ṭabarī, index. (G. Levi Della Vida)

NIZĀR b. al-**MUSTANṢIR**, Fāṭimid claimant, born on 10 Rabīᶜ I 437/26 September 1045. On the death of his father, having been displaced by his youngest brother al-Mustaᶜlī [*q.v.*], Nizār fled to Alexandria, took the title of al-Muṣṭafā li-Dīn Allāh, and rose in revolt early in 488/1095 with the assistance of the governor, Naṣr al-Dawla Aftakīn, who was jealous of al-Afḍal, and the population of the city. He was at first successful in driving back al-Afḍal and advanced as far as the outskirts of Cairo, supported by Arab auxiliaries. Al-Afḍal again took the field against him, and after a short siege in Alexandria he surrendered towards the end of the same year, was taken to Cairo, and there immured by order of al-Mustaᶜlī.

By the Ismāᶜīlī organisation in Persia [see al-ḥasan b. al-ṣabbāḥ and ismāᶜīliyya], Nizār was recognised as the rightful successor of al-Mustanṣir, and this, with its offshoots in Syria, formed a new group (*al-daᶜwa al-d̲j̲adīda*), opposed to the Mustaᶜlian group (*al-daᶜwa al-ḳadīma*), now known as K̲h̲ōd̲j̲as [*q.v.*] and Bohorās [*q.v.*] respectively. A party of the Nizāriyya at first held to the belief that Nizār was not dead and would return as the Mahdī or in company with him, but the majority held that the line of Nizār was continued by the Grand Masters of Alamūt [*q.v.*].

Bibliography: See that under al-mustaᶜlī; also Ibn K̲h̲allikān, tr. de Slane, i, 160-1 (from al-Nuwayrī); *Sid̲j̲illāt ... al-Mustanṣir biʾllāh*, ms., SOAS, London, nos. 35 and 43 (cf. *BSOS*, vii, 307 ff.); M.G.S. Hodgson, *The order of Assasins*, The Hague 1955, 46-7, 62-78; B. Lewis, *The Assassins, a radical sect in Islam*, London 1967, 34-5, 49, 74-5; Farhad Daftary, *The Ismāᶜīlīs, their history and doctrine*, Cambridge 1990, 261 ff., 324 ff. (H.A.R. Gibb)

NIZĀRĪ ĶUHISTĀNĪ, Ḥakīm Saᶜd al-Dīn b. S̲h̲ams al-Dīn b. Muḥammad, Persian poet, born 645/1247-8 in Bīrd̲j̲and [*q.v.*], where he died in 720/1320-1. The name Nizārī was not only his nom-de-guerre as a poet, but also seems to indicate the loyalty of his family to Nizār [*q.v.*], the pretender to the Fāṭimid imāmate in the late 5th/11th century whose claim was supported by most Persian Ismāᶜīlīs. Reliable facts concerning his life can only be deduced from his own works. According to Borodin, followed by Rypka, he would have been attached to the court of the Kart [*q.v.*] Maliks of Herat, but Bayburdi identified the patrons mentioned by Nizārī as local rulers and Mongol officials in the near vicinity of his native Ḳuhistān. The most important were S̲h̲ams al-Dīn ᶜAlī S̲h̲āh (reigned 688-708/1289-1308), who belonged to a dynasty ruling over Sīstān, and the *wazīr* ᶜAlāʾ al-Dīn Hindū, the representative of the Īl-K̲h̲āns in Khurasan. He worked for them both as an official and as a court poet. In 678-9/1280-1 he made a journey to the Transcaucasian lands, in his days the centre of Mongol power. In the *Mad̲j̲ālis al-ᶜus̲h̲s̲h̲āḳ* of Kamāl al-Dīn Gāzurgāhī mention is made of two encounters with Saᶜdī [*q.v.*] which however belong to the realm of biographical fiction. The same applies probably to the statement in the same source that he ended his life as a humble farmer.

The literary output of Nizārī was considerable, but it has only been preserved in few copies. The most important are the manuscripts of his collected works extant in libraries of St. Petersburg (Public State Library, dated 837/1434) and Dushambe (Academy of Sciences, dated 972/1564-5). They are both divided into fifteen parts, comprising volumes of *ḳaṣīdas*, *g̲h̲azals*, quatrains and other lyrical forms, as well as several *mat̲h̲nawīs*. His earliest work, the *Safar-nāma*, contains a lively and valuable description of his journey to Transcaucasia. *Adab-nāma* (695/1295-6), in the metre *mutaḳārib*, is a didactical poem after the fashion of Saᶜdī's *Būstān*. The romance *Azhar u Mazhar* (written about 700/1300-1), a poem in *hazad̲j̲* of about 10.000 lines, is situated in the Arabian desert. The plot was inspired by the *K̲h̲usraw-nāma* of Farīd al-Dīn ᶜAṭṭār [*q.v.*]. A *tenzone* between Night and Day, in the metre *k̲h̲afīf*, was written by Nizārī to vindicate himself when he was accused of heretical convictions. *Dastūr-nāma* (710/1310) is a short didactical work in *mutaḳārib* (edited and translated by Y̲e̲.E. Bertel's in *Vostočniy Sbornik*, Leningrad 1926, i, 37-104).

Nizārī's name remained relatively obscure in the history of Persian literature. His Ismāᶜīlī background is noticeable in his works although this is often hidden behind Imāmī S̲h̲īᶜī formulations more acceptable to his environment. There is also a strong Ṣūfī element, especially in the *g̲h̲azals*, which constitute the most important part of his lyrical poetry. Some of these poems were cited by the mediaeval anthologists D̲j̲ād̲j̲armī [*q.v.*] and Dawlats̲h̲āh. A competent critic like D̲j̲āmī [*q.v.*] compared his poetic "taste" (*salīḳa*) to that of Ḥāfiẓ [*q.v.*]. Modern Russian and Tadjik scholars have stressed his freedom of thought and the irreverent tone to be heard in his poetry.

Bibliography: Apart from the *Dastūr-nāma*, the works of Nizārī remained unpublished to date. A detailed analysis of his life and works can be found in Č.G. Bayburdi, *Žizn' i tvorčestvo Nizari*, Moscow 1966. See further: Dj̲ādj̲armī, *Muʾnis al-aḥrār*, ed. M.Ṣ. Ṭabībī, ii, Tehran 1350 *s̲h̲*/1971, 974-5, 1010-3, 1117-8; Dawlats̲h̲āh, 231-4; Dj̲āmī, *Bahāristān*, ed. Vienna 1846, 100; Amīn-i Rāzī, *Haft iḳlīm*, ed. Dj̲. Fāḍil, Tehran 1340 *s̲h̲*/1961, ii, 322-3; J. von Hammer-Purgstall, *Geschichte der schönen Redekünste Persiens*, Vienna 1818, 223-4; A. Sprenger, *Catalogue of the Library of the King of Oude*, Calcutta 1854, i, 524; B. Dorn, *Catalogue des manuscrits et xylographes orientaux de la Bibl. Impériale Publique de St. Pétersbourg*, St. Petersburg 1852, 365; H. Ethé, *Catalogue of the Persian ... manuscripts in the Bodleian Library*, Oxford 1889, 553; idem, in *Gr.I.Ph.*, ii, Strassburg 1904, 297; Browne, *LHP*, iii, 154-5; S.G. Borodin, *Ḥakīm Nizārī-yi Ḳuhistānī*, in *Farhang-i Īrānzamīn*, vi/2-3, 1337 *s̲h̲*/1958, 178-203; J. Dorri, *Stalinabadskiy ekzemplyar kulliyata Nizari*, in *Izvestiya otdeleniya obs̲h̲čestvennik̲h̲ nauk*, *AN Nauk Tadžikskiy SSR*, i, Dushambe 1958, 112-20 (description of the Dushambe *kulliyyāt*); Murt. Mud̲j̲tahidzāda, *Nasīm-i bahārī dar aḥwāl-i Nizārī*, Tehran 1344 *s̲h̲*/1965; J. Rypka, *History of Iranian literature*, Dordrecht 1968, 255-6; idem, in *Cambridge History of Iran*, v, Cambridge 1968, 604-5; A. Munzawī, *Fihrist-i nusk̲h̲ahā-yi k̲h̲aṭṭī-yi fārsī*, Tehran 1349 *s̲h̲*/1970, iii, 1895, and iv, 2811-2 (on *Dastūr-nāma*), 2911 (on *Safar-nāma*).

(J.T.P. de Bruijn)

NIZĀRIYYA, a major branch of the Ismāʿīliyya [*q.v.*], whose beginnings can be traced to the succession dispute following the death of the Fāṭimid [*q.v.*] Imām and caliph al-Mustanṣir bi'llāh (d. 487/1094). Those who gave their allegiance to Nizār, al-Mustanṣir's eldest son, as the designated successor and *imām*, and subsequently to those claiming descent from him, were called Nizāriyya. One of the most important figures in consolidating Nizārī identity in its early phase, particularly in Persia, was the well-known figure and *dāʿī* Ḥasan-i Ṣabbāḥ [*q.v.*], under whose leadership the Nizārīs were able to establish a confederation of principalities in Persia and Syria, linked to the mountain stronghold of Alamūt [*q.v.*]. The period also marks a re-interpretation of Fāṭimid Ismāʿīlī doctrine, with a greater emphasis on the role of the Imām as the authoritative interpreter of Muslim doctrine and practice.

The Nizārī polity in Persia lasted over 150 years, before its brutal destruction by the Mongols, ending in 654/1256. The various communities in Syria and Persia subsequently struggled to survive under sometimes adverse conditions, and much of their history and development during this period is little known. However, the *daʿwa* successfully initiated missionary activity leading to the emergence of a community in the Indian Subcontinent, principally in Pand̲j̲āb, Sind and Gud̲j̲arāt, referred to as the K̲h̲ōd̲j̲as [*q.v.*]. Over the next centuries, sporadic contact was maintained between the Imāms, living in different parts of Persia, and the Nizārī communities of Syria, the Subcontinent and Central Asia, each with their own distinctive literary heritage and tradition.

In its modern phase, Nizārī history has been distinguished by the transference of the *imāma* from Persia to British India in the 19th century and then to Europe, where the present headquarters of the current Imām, S̲h̲āh Karīm, Aga K̲h̲ān (*Ag̲h̲ā K̲h̲ān* [*q.v.*]) is located. Nizārī communities are found today in over 25 countries in Asia and Africa, as well as in Great Britain, Europe and the United States and Canada, where, based on a common constitution, they have organised strong community institutions. These are complemented by a development network headed by their Imām, concerned primarily with the development of the countries and peoples in which they live.

Bibliography (in addition to works and bibl. cited in ismāʿīliyya): F. Daftary, *The Ismāʿīlīs: their history and doctrines*, Cambridge 1990; Azim Nanji, *The Nizari Ismaili tradition in the Indo-Pakistan Subcontinent*, New York 1978; and for their literature, I. Poonawala, *Biobibliography of Ismāʿīlī literature*, Malibu 1977.

(Azim Nanji)

NIZĪB, Nīzīb, the Ottoman Turkish forms for modern Turkish Nizip, a town and district of southeastern Turkey, lying in the plain to the south-east of the Kurt Dağları mountain chain on the Nizip river, a right-bank tributary of the Euphrates, 17 km/10 miles to the west of Birecik [see bīred̲j̲ik], in lat. 37° 02′ N. and long. 37° 47′ E. at an altitude of 534 m/1750 feet. Nizīb and its surrounding district, extending to Kilis and the Syrian frontier, have long been famed for their extensive olive groves and sesame fields.

Ewliyā Čelebi visited Nizīb in the 11th/17th century and describes it as "an inhabited town in the middle of an unfertile district on the edge of a high hill, with inns, mosques, baths and a small market but without vineyards or gardens". Nizīb at this period was the residence of a judge on the salary scale of 150 *aḳčes*.

During the war (1831-40) between the Turks and Egypt under Muḥammad ʿAlī, Nizīb became the scene of a celebrated battle. Ibrāhīm Pas̲h̲a, adopted stepson and general of Muḥammad ʿAlī, had crossed the Syrian frontier by the end of 1831 and after several victories advanced as far as Ḳonya, where he inflicted such a defeat on the Turks at the end of 1832 that they had to cede by the peace of Kütāhiya (1833) the whole of Syria to Muḥammad ʿAlī and the government of Adana to Ibrāhīm himself, both recognising the sovereignty of the sultan. But neither the sultan nor Muḥammad ʿAlī were satisfied with this, and both made preparations for another war. For this purpose, Maḥmūd II combined the four *wilāyets* of Diyārbakr, K̲h̲arpūt, Raḳḳa and Sīwās under one governor with the title of vizier, Čerkes Ḥāfiẓ Meḥmed Pas̲h̲a (on his career, see *Sid̲j̲illi-i ʿot̲h̲mānī*, ii, 99-100), and commanded him to cross the Euphrates at the beginning of 1839. It was not till some time later, however, that fighting actually began. Moltke and the military experts in Čerkes Ḥāfiẓ Meḥmed's army then advised him not to cross the river but only to display his strength and frighten the Egyptian army into retreating; but Meḥmed Pas̲h̲a would not take this advice, crossed the Euphrates and fought a battle at Nizīb, where he was completely defeated by Ibrāhīm Pas̲h̲a on 24 June 1839.

Besides this great defeat on land, the Turks a few days later suffered an equally severe loss at sea. The traitorous *Ḳapudān-i Deryā* Aḥmed Fewzī Pas̲h̲a, known as Firārī (i.e. "fugitive", "deserter"; details in *Sid̲j̲ill-i ʿot̲h̲mānī*, i, 294-5), led the Turkish fleet, which was sent to Syrian waters at the time of the battle of Nizīb, to Alexandria and handed it over to Muḥammad ʿAlī. The Egyptians, however, were unable to take advantage of the victory at Nizīb because the Great Powers intervened and Muḥammad ʿAlī's aspirations were in 1841 limited to the hereditary governorship of Egypt. The defeat at Nizīb led in the domestic politics of Turkey to the speedy proclamation of the *tanzīmāt* reforms [*q.v.*].

The modern town of Nizip is in the *il* or province of Gaziantep and is the chef-lieu of an *ilçe* or district of the same name comprising 115 villages. In 1960, the estimated population of the town was 19,300 and of the district 68,200.

Bibliography: ʿAbd al-Raḥmān S̲h̲eref, *Taʾrīk̲h̲-i Dewlet-i ʿot̲h̲māniyye*, ii, Istanbul 1312, 338-9, 341-2; Ewliyā Čelebi, *Seyāḥat-nāme*, iii, Istanbul 1314, 145; ʿAlī Dje̲wād, *Taʾrīk̲h̲ we-Dj̲og̲h̲rāfiya lug̲h̲ātī*, iii, Istanbul 1314, 811 (wrongly identifies Nizīb and Niṣībīn); S. Lane-Poole, *Turkey*[5], London 1908, 345-50; Ḥ. Saʿdī, *Iḳtiṣādī dj̲og̲h̲rāfiya I. Türkiye*, Istanbul 1926, 277-80; K̲h̲alīl Edhem, *Düwel-i islāmiyye*, Istanbul 1927, 116; *Türkiye cümhuriyeti devlet yıllığı 1929-1930*, Istanbul 1930, 396-400; Hâmit ve-Muhsin, *Türkiye tarihi*, Istanbul 1930, 465-6, 630 ff.   (F. Bajraktarevic*)

NIZWA, a town of inner ʿUmān. It lies in an oasis on the eastern side of the Dj̲abal Ak̲h̲ḍār in central ʿUmān. It is divided between a walled lower town (*Nizwat al-Sufāla*) and an upper walled town (*Nizwat al-ʿAlāya* or *Samad al-Kindī*), which are situated on either side of the Wādī Kalbu. The water supply of ʿAlāya is provided by the *Faladj̲ Dāris* and that of Sufāla is provided by the *Faladj̲ G̲h̲unduḳ*. Sprenger suggested that Ptolemy's *Ravana/Rabana/Rouana basileion* should be identified with either Nizwa or Rustāḳ, but this remains unproven. At the onset of Islam, Nizwa appears to have been the seat of the local Azdī Āl Dj̲ulandā princes, and it was subsequently to become the capital of the country. Even during occupation by an ʿAbbāsid army under Muḥammad b. Nūḥ in 277/890 during the caliphate of al-Muʿtamid, Nizwa remained the capital of the country and the election place of the Ibāḍī *Imām*s of ʿUmān under the Āl Dj̲ulandā and under their successors. It was only in later times that it was supplanted by Rustāḳ and Maskaṭ, although it never lost its importance as a centre of Ibāḍī teaching and scholarship. From the death of the second Ibāḍī *Imām*, al-Wārit̲h̲, who drowned at Nizwa in a flood in the Wādī Kalbu, Nizwa was to become the usual burial place of the *Imām*s.

Al-Muḳaddasī in the 4th/10th century mentions Nizwa, listing it among the principal *ḳaṣaba*s of ʿUmān along with Maskaṭ, Ṣawḥar and Dj̲ulfār. Its name is merely mentioned by al-Idrīsī, but Yāḳūt in the 6th/13th century knew of it as a mountainous region with a number of large villages, where the local people were adherents of Ibāḍī doctrines [see IBĀḌIYYA]. In subsequent centuries, Nizwa seems to have retained its importance under its Nabhānī rulers, although it was eventually to give way to Rustāḳ and in the civil wars of the early 17th century, power shifted from the interior to the coast at Maskaṭ, with Nizwa losing its political importance.

The main mosque, the traditional place of election to the Imāmate, and *sūḳ* are in Sufāla, as is the *ḥiṣn*, a rectangular enclosure containing a massive circular tower, known as the *ḳalʿa*, ca. 43 m across at the level of the gun-platform. The *ḳalʿa* is the most prominent monument in Nizwa and the largest artillery tower in ʿUmān. It is attributed to the Yaʿrubī *Imām* Sayf b. Sulṭān (d. 1059/1649) and took 12 years and much gold and silver to build. It was designed to command the approaches to Nizwa from all directions, forming part of defences controlling the Wādī Samāʿil, the main access leading from the interior of ʿUmān to the Bāṭina coast. It was among the earliest towers in ʿUmān built as an artillery platform, and it was also able to withstand artillery bombardment because of its solid construction, with the lower 14 m of the main tower filled entirely with packed earth and stone. The water supply was secured by wells and a *faladj̲* which runs below the tower. According to Lt. Wellsted, dry well shafts in the tower were used as magazines for the artillery.

The first detailed description of the town was provided by Wellsted in 1835, who found Nizwa a stone-built town with houses of two storeys, an appearance which was little changed in 1975. In the early 1900s the largest tribe residing at Nizwa was the Banū Riyām, with a large number of houses of Banū Hina and Āl Bū Saʿīd, and a small number of households from other tribes.

The long association of Nizwa with the Imāmate revived in modern times when discontent with the Āl Bū Saʿīd sultan at Maskaṭ led to a coalition against his authority, culminating in 1913 in the election to the Imāmate of Salīm b. Ras̲h̲īd al-K̲h̲arūsī, supported by an alliance of al-G̲h̲āfirī and Hināwī tribal confederation, which seized Nizwa and installed the *Imām* at the ancient capital. Although a *modus vivendi* was eventually reached, Nizwa and its surroundings remained beyond the authority of Maskaṭ until 1955, when Sultan Saʿīd b. Taymūr entered Nizwa in a progress through the interior as far as Buraymī. However, between 1957 and 1959, the Imāmate based at Nizwa broke into open rebellion, backed by Saudi Arabia and by Arab nationalists in Cairo. The rebellion ended with the seizure of Nizwa by British troops and the Sultan's forces in 1959.

The surrounding oasis is said to have 25,000 palm trees, and accounts refer to the presence of sugar cane, cotton, and indigo among the crops of Nizwa. Traditional local manufactures include metal working, including gold and silver, and weaving. The latter is ancient, for Yāḳūt mentions a distinctive ornamental textile decorated with silk. According to Wellsted, the women would prepare cotton yarn, and men would work the looms. This division of labour was still apparent in the 1970s. In the 1970s, the oil wealth of ʿUmān brought growing prosperity to Nizwa and a transformation of its traditional economy, while the construction of tarmac roads improved its links with the rest of the country.

Bibliography: Muḳaddasī, 71; Idrīsī, tr. Jaubert, 153; Yāḳūt, *Buldān*, ed. Beirut, v, 281; J. Wellsted, *Travels in Oman*, London 1835, 120-7; Salīl b. Razīk, *History of the Imams and Seyyids of ʿOman from A.D. 661-1859*, tr. G.P. Badger, London 1871; Sirḥān b. Saʿīd, *Annals of ʿOman, from early to year 1728 A.D. From an Arabic ms. by Sheykh Sirhan bin Saʿid bin Sirhan b. Muhammad, of the Benu ʿAli tribe of ʿOman, translated and annotated by E.C. Ross, Political Agent of Muscat*, in *JASB*, xliii (1874), 111-96; A. Sprenger, *Die alte Geographie Arabiens*, Berne 1875, 281; S.B. Miles, *The countries and tribes of the Persian Gulf*, with a new introd. by J.B. Kelly, London 1966; E. d'Errico, *Introduction to Omani military architecture of the sixteenth, seventeenth and eighteenth centuries*, in *Journal of Oman Studies* (1983), 302-3; P.M. Costa, *Notes on settlement patterns in traditional Oman*, in *ibid.*, 253; J.G. Lorimer, *Gazetteer of the Persian Gulf, Oman, and Central Arabia*, Calcutta 1908, IIB, 1365-6.   (G.R.D. King)

NOGHAY, a Turkic-speaking people whose language belongs, together with Ḳazaḳ and Ḳaraḳalpaḳ, to the Caspian branch of the Ḳîpčaḳ-Turkic group. They number approximately 60,000, living mainly on a territory stretching to the west of the Caspian Sea between the Kuma and Terek rivers, a region sometimes referred to as the Nog̲h̲ay

Steppes. In the administrative aspect, the majority lived within the boundaries of the Dagestan Autonomous S.S.R., whilst others fell under the jurisdiction of Čečeno-Ingushetia and the Stavropol'skiy kray. All these regions belonged to the Russian Federation of the Soviet Union, but their administrative future within Russia, after the dissolution of the Soviet Union in December 1991, is unknown.

1. Ethnogenesis and early habitats. The stabilisation of the Noghay ethnos went hand in hand with the formation of the Noghay state. The latter was formed by Edigü (in Russian sources, Edigey), the famous military commander of the Tatar state of the Golden Horde. The Noghay *ulus* (appanage) seceded from the Golden Horde in the 1390s, their original homeland being the vast pasture lands between the Emba and Yayïḳ (now Ural) rivers. During the reign of Nūr al-Dīn, son of Edigü (1426-40), the Noghay tribes began to extend towards the Volga, and up to the 1550s they occupied the large territory between the Yayïḳ and the Lower Volga rivers. In the 15th-16th centuries the Noghay Horde was a significant Tatar state, one of the successor states of the Golden Horde, comprising various Turco-Mongolian tribes which later on took an active part in the formation of numerous modern Turkic peoples, including the Ḳazaḳs, the Ḳaraḳalpaḳs, the Bashkirs and the Ḳazan Tatars. The leading political force of the Noghay Horde was undoubtedly the Mangït tribe, from which Edigü himself, the founder of the state originated. That is why even their self-appellation during the first century of their stately independence was *Mangït* [*q.v.*].

The Noghay ethnos was formed of various Turkic and Turkicised Mongol tribes coming together under the sovereignty of Edigü's successors. Even the Mangït tribe was of Mongol origin, although the family genealogy of the Edigü clan, obviously due to pious Muslim influence, traced back their alleged descent to the Prophet Muḥammad's time. The widest extension of the Noghay Horde was in the first half of the 16th century, when its historical rôle was at its zenith, and they actively participated in the wars of Muscovy, the Ḳazan and the Crimean Khānates.

The application of the name Noghay to the Mangït-led confederation has not yet been satisfactorily explained. The term Noghay was first used for the Noghays in the Russian sources at the end of the 15th century, and it spread in Russia and Europe during the 16th century. According to the most accepted interpretation, the ethnonym Noghay is connected to the name of Noghay, famous warlord and *amīr* of the Golden Horde in whose army the Mangït tribe must have been a leading force. On the other hand, two facts severely hamper this theory: (a) it needs further elucidation why the ethnonym Noghay came into use only 150 years after Noghay's death in 1300; and (b) while Edigü's figure has been immemorialised in an extensive folk-epos, Noghay's personality has fallen out of folk-memory.

2. Economy and society. Up till the 1860s, the Noghays were *par excellence* nomadic stock-breeders (horse, sheep, cattle, camel). They had practically no agriculture (only millet was known) or handicrafts; all these products were acquired through trade and/or as booty. All adult males were warriors (200,000 in the 1550s), the total amount of inhabitants being approximately 350,000. Their society was organised according to clan and tribal principles, with an increasing number of feudal features from the 16th century onwards. The head of the political structure was the *biy*, whose sons and other male relatives, the *murzas*, stood at the head of the *ulus* or appanage. It was an amalgam of the clan and feudal system. The central power was very limited, and the *murzas* pursued sovereign foreign policies. Second in rank was the *nūraddīn* (called so after Edigü's son), whose duty was defending the western borderland, while the *kekovat* (third in rank) was in charge of the eastern frontier. The capital of the Noghays was Sarayčïḳ on the eastern bank of Lower Volga. In addition to the tribal-feudal aristocracy, the Muslim religious dignitaries, especially the *sayyids*, also played an important role in the Noghay social structure.

3. Noghay-Russian contacts. From 1489 onwards, exchange of envoys had become regular between Russia and the Noghay Horde. After Ismāʿīl's death (1563), the heyday of the Noghay Horde was over and it soon dissolved. Part of them accepted Russian suzerainty, other tribes fell under Crimean Tatar and Ottoman rule, while the eastern part was assimilated by the Ḳazaḳs. In the 17th-18th centuries, a few independent Noghay hordes survived (e.g. the Yedisan, the Djemboyluḳ, etc.), lingering between the Russian and Ottoman great powers. In the 1780s, subsequent to the annexation of the Crimean Khanate by the Russians, most Noghay groups fell under Russian jurisdiction. In 1858-66 a mass emigration of the Noghays to Turkey took place, but most of them were disappointed in their new homeland and returned to Russia. From the 1870s onwards, the Noghays have gradually been settled and forced to abandon their nomadism for agriculture. The vicissitudes of the Noghays continued in the Soviet era, their administrative borders being changed several times. During the past few years they have been struggling for more cultural and regional autonomy within the Russian Federation.

Bibliography: *Prodolženie drevney Rossiyskoy vivliofiki*, vii-xi, St. Petersburg 1793-5; *Pamyatniki diplomatičeskikh snosheniy drevney Rossii s deržavami inostrannïmi*, St. Petersburg 1895 (*Sbornik Russkogo Istoričeskogo Obshčestva*, 41); P. Melioranskiy, *Skazanie ob Edigee*, St. Petersburg 1905; V.V. Bartol'd, *Otets Edigeya*, in *Sočineniya*, ii/1, 797-804; A.A. Geraklitov, *Istoriya Saratovskogo kraya v XVI-XVIII vv.*, Saratov-Moscow 1923, 104-36; M.G. Safargaliev, *Nogayskaya Orda vo vtoroy polovine XVI veka*, in *Sbornik naučnïkh rabot mordovskogo gos. pedinstituta im. A. I. Poležaeva*, Saransk 1949, 32-56 (useful); B.-A.B. Kočekaev, *Klassovaya struktura nogayskogo obshčestva v XIX—načala XX vv.*, Alma-Ata 1969; V.M. Žirmunskiy, *Tyurkskiy geroičeskiy épos*, Leningrad 1974; E.A. Ponoženko, *Obshčestvennïy stroy Nogayskoy Ordy v XV-seredinï XVII vv.*, in *Vestnik Moskovskogo Universiteta*, seriya "Pravo" 1977/4; F.G. Garipova, *Dannïe toponimii o nogayskom komponente v étnogeneze kazanskikh tatar*, in *Issledovaniya po dialektologii i istorii tatarskogo yazïka*, Kazan' 1982, 123-8; *Posol'skaya kniga po svyazyam Rossii s Nogayskoy Ordoy 1489-1508 gg.*, Moscow 1984; B.-A.B. Kočekaev, *Nogaysko-russkie otnosheniya v XV-XVIII vv.*, Alma-Ata 1988 (important); *Obzor posol'skikh knig iz fondov-kollektsiy khranyashčikhsya v TSGADA (konets XV-načalo XVIII v.)*, Sostavitel' N.M. Rogožin, Moscow 1990, 166-71 (important).

(I. Vásáry)

NOUAKCHOTT, the capital of Mauritania [see MŪRĪTĀNIYĀ]. It was created *ex nihilo* near a site occupied by a small village and a ksar [see ḲAṢR]. The choice of its situation was made the object of serious studies, since it was necessary that it should be accessible, easily supplied with drinking water and distant enough from the Senegal River to escape inundations like that of 1950. Several plans of urban design were put forward even before independence was conceded to Mauritania (1960), and construction work, begun in 1958, has not ceased since that date in order to respond to a rapidly-increasing demographic growth because of the tendency of the nomads to become sedentarised and fixed and because of the massive migration of the peoples of the interior, driven forth by the desiccation which became severe during the years 1968-73 and searching for work. With an estimated population in 1974 of 100,000, the number of inhabitants rose to 600,000 by 1992.

Situated in the midst of sand dunes, 7 km from the ocean, Nouakchott is the only real town of the country, and comprises three parts: a westernised official and business centre (ministries, embassies, banks, trading establishments), better-quality residential quarters and, further out, the area of more or less precarious habitations of the less favoured population elements (in 1971, there were still 200 tents of nomads within the urban area). It has a relatively temperate climate (annual average of max. temp. 32°, and minima 11°); rainfall is very variable from year to year, but the average is considered to be 135 mm. Water supply, from the wells in the Trarza, is a serious problem, and the town has a water-purifying plant. Retail trade is in the hands of Lebanese immigrants, who are always very active. External trade, in particular represented by the import of manufactured products and foodstuffs, and by the export of copper, hides and gum, has developed since 1966, thanks to the construction of docks 7 km to the south-south-west of the capital. Electricity is provided by a central generator, and telephone installations exist in the government offices and in private homes. Communications within the town are not always easy since metalled roads are still sparse, and vehicles often get stuck in the sands once they leave the main roads. Connections with outside countries, and even with the interior of the country, are now more and more by air travel, thanks to the modern airport of Nouakchott and the improvised landing-strips which many places of middling importance possess. It is in fact extremely difficult to maintain roads and even tracks amidst moving sands.

There remains an interesting question: the origin of the name Nouakchott, which even the Mauritanian government, which uses the French language, customarily spells thus. Its etymology has given rise to apparently endless controversies. For Mokhtar Ould Hamidoun and Cyr Descamps, *Que veut dire Nouakchott?*, in *Notes Africaines*, no. 118 (1969), 62-4, the town's name means "place where, when one digs a well, the water appears at a level where shells are found profusely". In reality, the Arabic form *Anwāk<u>sh</u>ūṭ* is sufficiently clear, since it can be broken up as follows: *a-n-wak<u>sh</u>ut*, i.e. in Berber, "that of shells and shellfish", where *a* is a demonstrative pronoun, and *n* the copula introducing the state of annexation of the word *ake<u>sh</u><u>sh</u>uḍ* (whose final emphatic is normally unvoiced to pass into Arabic as *ṭ*). It should be noted that in the Berber speech of Morocco, in which this word exists, it means "woods".

Bibliography: This is quite abundant, and has been felicitously utilised by J.-R. Pitte, *Nouakchott, capitale de la Mauretanie*, Paris 1977, to which one can refer. (J.-F. STASZAK and ED.)

NOYAN (pl. *noyad*), a Mongolian title, rendered in the Muslim chronicles of the Mongol and Tīmūrid periods in the Arabic script as *nūyān*, *nūyīn*, *nuyīn*, etc. In the pre-Činggisid period the *noyad* were the hereditary clan chieftains. Under Činggis <u>Kh</u>ān and his successors, the title was granted initially as a military rank. According to the *Secret History of the Mongols*, § 191 [tr. Cleaves, 119], in 1203 Činggis <u>Kh</u>ān organised his army according to the decimal system so often used before in steppe armies, with groups of ten, a hundred and a thousand, each under the command of a *noyan*. Hence the term came to mean "commander" (Boyle) or "captain" (Cleaves). The *noyad* have been called the "new aristocracy" of the Mongol Empire, and were a means by which the Mongol rulers, in constructing their imperial machinery, were able to transcend the old clan system. The *noyad* were granted substantial rights of autonomy within their domains, and people and pasture in perpetuity. Under the Yüan régime in China, the term was used to refer to all officials serving in public posts (26,690 in the early 14th century, according to one reckoning).

Bibliography: F.W. Cleaves (tr.), *The Secret History of the Mongols*, Cambridge, Mass. 1982; G. Doerfer, *Türkische und mongolische Elemente im Neupersischen*, i, Wiesbaden 1963, 526-9; C. Hsiao, *The military establishment of the Yuan dynasty*, Cambridge, Mass. 1978; D.M. Farquhar, *The government of China under Mongolian rule*, Stuttgart 1990 (D.O. MORGAN)

NU^cAYM B. ḤAMMĀD al-<u>Kh</u>uzā^cī al-Marwazī, Abū ^cAbd Allāh, a traditionist originally from Marw al-Rū<u>dh</u> [*q.v.*] who lived for a while in Egypt but above all in Ba<u>gh</u>dād where, having been invited to recognise the created nature of the Ḳur^ɔān in the course of the *miḥna* [*q.v.*], he refused to give his opinion and was thrown into one of the prisons at Sāmarrā; he died there on 13 <u>Dj</u>umādā I 228/18 February 843 (but other dates around this are also given). He received from Sufyān b. Mu^cāwiya, ^cAlī b. al-Mubārak and other *muḥaddi<u>th</u>s* [see ḤADĪ<u>TH</u>] traditions which he in turn transmitted, notably to Yaḥyā b. Ma^cīn or al-Bu<u>kh</u>ārī. He is nevertheless judged to have been suspect and is even freely accused by some scholars, such as al-Nasā^ɔī and al-Dāraḳuṭnī, of fabricating *ḥadī<u>th</u>s* in support of the most rigorous form of Sunnī doctrine, of which he was a fervent defender. He is said, moreover, to have been a member of the <u>Dj</u>ahmiyya [*q.v.*] at one period, before changing his views and accusing Abū Ḥanīfa and ^cAmr b. ^cUbayd of having favoured the dissemination of this group's ideas. Whilst being thus discredited as a traditionist, he nevertheless acquired a reputation as a scholar regarding succession law (*farā^ɔiḍ* [*q.v.*]), to the point that he is sometimes dubbed Fāriḍ or Faraḍī.

His biographers attribute to him "some" books, but it is only known that he left behind a *Kitāb al-Fitan wa 'l-malāḥim*, of which there is a ms. in the B.L., London (9449) and which was abridged by Naṣr Allāh b. ^cAbd al-Mun^cim al-Tanū<u>kh</u>ī (604-73/1207-74; see F. al-Bustānī, *Dā^ɔirat al-ma^cārif*, s.v. Ibn <u>Sh</u>uḳayr, iii, 263c, who does not however cite this abridgement).

Bibliography: Abu 'l-^cArab-<u>Kh</u>u<u>sh</u>ānī, *Ṭabaḳāt ^culamā^ɔ Ifrīḳiya*, Algiers 1915-Paris 1920, i, 32; al-<u>Kh</u>aṭīb al-Ba<u>gh</u>dādī, *Ta^ɔrī<u>kh</u> Ba<u>gh</u>dād*, xiii, 306-14; Abū Nu^caym, *<u>Sh</u>a<u>dh</u>arat al-<u>dh</u>ahab*, ii, 66-7 (d. 228), 67 (second notice, d. 229); Ibn ^cAsākir, *Tabyīn ka<u>dh</u>ib al-muftarī*, Damascus 1928, 383-4; <u>Dh</u>ahabī, *Ta<u>dh</u>kirat al-ḥuffāẓ*, Ḥaydarābād 1376/1956, 418-20; idem, *Mīzān al-i^ctidāl*, iii, 238-9; Brockelmann, S I, 257 (cf. II, 929, no. 26); A. Amīn, *Ḍuḥā al-Islām*, ii, 126; G. Vajda, in *Arabica*, viii/1 (1961), 99; W. Madelung, *The Sufyānī between tradition and history*, in *SI*, lxiii (1986), 5-48 (based on Nu^caym's *K. al-Fitan*); J. Agnadé, *Eine Schrift des Nu^caim b. Ḥammād* *und ihre Überlieferung in Spanien*, in *Navicula Tubingensis. Studia in honorem Antonii Tovar*, Tübingen 1984; Ziriklī, ix, 14; Kaḥḥāla, xiii, 97; Sezgin, *GAS*, i, 104-5. (CH. PELLAT)

NUᶜAYMA, MĪKHĀʾĪL (spelled Naimy in English language publications), modern Arabic author (b. 1889, Biskinta, Lebanon, d. 1989 in Lebanon). He received his schooling at the "Russian" school founded by the "Russian Imperial Orthodox Palestine Society" in Biskinta, the training college instituted by the same society in Nazareth and the Diocesan Seminary in Poltava, Ukraine. In 1911 he joined his emigrant brothers in the USA, who financed his studies at the University of Washington in Seattle. There he became a member of the "Free Syria" movement which stood for an independent Syria and Lebanon under French protection. Later, he would become secretary of this movement in which most of Nuᶜayma's literary friends took part. It may be regarded as a forerunner of *al-Rābiṭa al-ḳalamiyya*.

Mīkhāʾīl Nuᶜayma obtained bachelor degrees in Law and in English Literature in 1916 and went to New York where his old-time friend Nasīb ᶜArīḍa was publishing the Arabic literary magazine *al-Funūn* ("The Arts"). In New York he established contacts with Djubrān Khalīl Djubrān [see DJABRĀN KHALĪL DJABRĀN], Rashīd Ayyūb and Īliyā Abū Māḍī. For his living he worked for the Russian delegation at the Bethlehem Steel Factories to purchase arms until Russia withdrew from the war in November 1917. He was then conscripted into the USA army and sent to France where he witnessed the last battles of the war. Early in 1919 he returned to New York and in 1920 he founded with his literary friends *al-Rābiṭa al-ḳalamiyya* (English, Arrabita = "The Pen League"). He earned his living as a travelling salesman. In 1932 he returned to Lebanon to devote himself to his pen.

Nuᶜayma's literary career started in Poltava, where he became acquainted with the works of the great Russian authors of that time. He especially admired Tolstoy and his Yasnaya Polyana. He composed poetry during this period and he kept a diary. During his stay in Seattle he began to contribute critical essays to *al-Funūn*, calling for drastic changes in Arabic poetry and in criticism. He also contributed a serialised play *al-Ābāʾ wa 'l-banūn* ("Parents and Children"), which appeared in book form in 1917 in New York. His critical essays were published in *al-Ghirbāl* ("The Sieve") in 1923 at Cairo with a foreword by Maḥmūd ᶜAbbās al-ᶜAḳḳād [*q.v.* in Suppl.]. In Seattle he became acquainted with the teachings of theosophy which were to have a permanent influence on his writings, culminating in the English-language publication *The book of Mirdad*, Beirut 1948, translated by the author as *Kitāb Mirdād*, Beirut 1952, and in books like *al-Yawm al-akhīr* ("The last day"), Beirut 1963, *Ayyūb* ("Job"), Beirut 1967 and *Yā ibn Ādam* ("O son of Adam"), Beirut 1969.

Nuᶜayma published one collection of poetry *Hams al-djufūn* ("Eyelids' whispering") Beirut [1943], which inspired Muhammad Mandūr [*q.v.*] to call this new type of poetry *shiᶜr mahmūs* ("whispered poetry"). Nuᶜayma further wrote some 80 stories which he collected in the volumes *Kān mā kān* ("Once upon a time"), Beirut 1937, *Akābir* ("Notables"), Beirut 1956 and *Abū Baṭṭa* ("The fat-calved man"), Beirut 1959.

Nuᶜayma's biography of Djubrān (Arabic edition, Beirut 1934, English edition, New York 1950), showing the weaker sides of Djubrān, produced a fierce shock to those who had already lifted Djubrān beyond good and evil. Nuᶜayma's most impressive work is his autobiography *Sabᶜūn* ("Seventy"), Beirut 1959-60, in which he describes his early years in Biskinta, Nazareth and Poltava (vol. i), his life in the USA and the formation of Arrabita (vol. ii), and his life in Lebanon from 1932 until 1959 (vol. iii).

Other works by Nuᶜayma include: *al-Marāḥil* ("Stages"), Beirut 1933; *Zād al-maᶜād* ("Food for the road"), Cairo 1936; *al-Awthān* ("The idols"), Beirut 1946; *Karam ᶜalā darb* ("A vineyard by the road"), Cairo 1946; *Liḳāʾ*, Beirut 1946, translated as *Till we meet ...*, Beirut 1957; *Ṣawt al-ᶜālam* ("The voice of the world"), Cairo 1948; *Mudhakkarāt al-arḳash*, Beirut 1949, translated as *Memoirs of a vagrant soul*, Beirut 1952; *al-Nūr wa 'l-daydjūr* ("Light and darkness"), Beirut 1950; *Fī mahabb ar-rīḥ* ("Windward"), Beirut 1953; *Durūb* ("Roads"), Beirut 1954; *Abᶜad min Mūskū wa-min Washintun* ("Very far from Moscow and from Washington"), Beirut 1957; *Hawāmish* ("Marginals"), Beirut 1965; *Fi 'l-ghirbāl al-djadīd* ("In the new sieve"), Beirut 1972; *Nadjwā al-ghurūb* ("Confidential whispers at sunset"), Beirut 1973; *al-Madjmūᶜa al-kāmila* ("The complete works") 8 vols., including *Maḳālāt mutafarriḳa* (= vol. vii, Uncollected essays) and *Rasāʾil* (= vol. viii, Letters), Beirut 1970-4.

Bibliography: Thurayyā Malḥas, *Mīkhāʾīl Nuᶜayma, al-adīb al-ṣūfī* ("M.N. the Ṣūfī author"), Beirut 1964; F. Gabrieli, *L'autobiografia di Mikhail Nuᶜaima*, in *OM*, xlix (1969), 381-7; N. Naimy, *Mikhail Naimy. An introduction*, Beirut 1967; Ṭunsī Zakkā, *Bayna Nuᶜayma wa-Djubrān* ("Between Nuᶜayma and Djubrān"), Beirut 1971; Shafī al-Sayyid, *Mīkhāʾīl Nuᶜayma*, [Cairo] 1972; Nadra Djamīl al-Sarrādj, *Thalāthat ruwwād min al-mahdjar* ("Three leading men of the Arab diaspora in the New World"), Cairo 1973; C. Nijland, *Mikhaʾil Nuᶜaymah, promoter of the Arabic literary revival*, Istanbul 1975; Nadīm Nuᶜayma, *Mīkhāʾīl Nuᶜayma, ṭarīḳ al-dhāt ilā al-dhāt* ("M.N. The way from the self to the self"), Beirut 1978; Nabil I. Matar, *Adam and the serpent: notes on the theology of Mikhail Naimy*, in *JAL*, xi (1980), 56-61; Nijland, *Mikhaʾil Nuᶜayma: the biography of Gibran and the autobiography*, in *al-ᶜArabiyya*, xv (1982), 7-15; A. Ghaith, *La pensée religieuse chez Ǧubran Ḫalīl Ǧubrān et Mīḫāʾīl Nuᶜayma*, Louvain 1990. (C. NIJLAND)

NŪBA, the mediaeval Islamic form for the land of Nubia, lying to the south of Egypt, and its peoples.

1. Definition

The names Nubia, Nubian, Nūba are commonly used without scientific precision and it is only in the linguistic sense that they have an unambiguous meaning. The frontier separating Nubia from Egypt proper is well defined as the first cataract of the Nile in the neighbourhood of Aswān, and the area where Nubian is spoken nowadays ends in the vicinity of the 18th parallel, but the southern limit of Nubia is sometimes placed as far south as the junction of the Atbara and the Nile or even the confluence of the two Niles. Nubia is often sub-divided into Lower Nubia from Aswān to Wādī Ḥalfa and Upper Nubia from Wādī Ḥalfa southwards, but neither term has any political or administrative significance.

The mediaeval Arabic writers are equally vague about the southern extent of Nubia: the region immediately bordering on Egypt, which bore the name of Marīs [*q.v.*], seems to have been regarded as Nubia *par excellence*; to the south of it lay Muḳurra with its capital at Dongola (Dunḳula, Dumḳula), and beyond this the kingdom of ᶜAlwa, the capital of which was Sōba, near the site of the modern Kharṭūm. According to the 4th/10th century author ᶜAbd

Allāh b. Aḥmad b. Salīm (Sulaym?, quoted by al-Maḳrīzī) Marīs and Muḳarra had distinct languages, and the frontier between them was situated three post-stations (*barīd*) to the south of the Third Cataract; politically, however, Marīs formed part of Muḳurra and this probably accounts for the fact that Ibn Salīm immediately afterwards places the commencement of Muḳurra at a day's journey from Aswān. The frontier between Muḳurra and ᶜAlwa was the district of al-Abwāb, a name still in use for the country round Kabūs̲h̲iyya in Berber province. ᶜAlwa is generally placed outside Nubia, and the preamble to the treaty which governed the political relations between Nubians and Arabs makes its provisions incumbent on "the chief of the Nubians and all people of his dominions .... from the frontier of Aswān to the frontier of ᶜAlwa"; yet al-Masᶜūdī speaks of ᶜAlwā as part of Nubia and states that it is under the political suzerainty of Muḳurra. According to Yaḳūt, *Buldān*, ed. Beirut, v, 308-9, Nubia extends along the Nile a distance of eighty days journey, Dongola being situated halfway at forty days' distance from Aswān; of ᶜAlwa he speaks, with obvious exaggeration of the distance, as a people beyond Nubia three months' journey from the king of the Nūba, whose official title is "King of Muḳurra and Nūba".

Bibliography: E. Quatremère, *Mémoire sur la Nubie* (= *Mémoires géogr. et hist. sur l'Égypte*, ii), Paris 1811, contains trs. of all the important passages from Arabic authors; J. Marquart, *Die Benin-Sammlung des Reichsmuseums für Völkerkunde*, Leiden 1913, pp. ccxlviii ff. See also ᶜALWA, DONGOLA, AL-MUḲURRA. (S. HILLELSON)

2. History

(a) Up to the Fāṭimid period

Nubia was called in Pharaonic times the Land of Kus̲h̲ [*q.v.*], and is vaguely mentioned in Herodotus and other Greek authors as part of the land of the Aethiopes; the name Nubia has been used since mediaeval times (see W.Y. Adams, *Nubia, corridor to Africa*, Princeton 1977, 13). In the Arabic sources it is often imprecisely described as part of the *Bilād al-Sūdān* "land of the blacks", although the term Sudan with concrete references to a political entity appears only after the Turco-Egyptian conquest of 1821 (Y.F. Hasan (ed.), *Sudan in Africa*, K̲h̲arṭūm 1985, 1 ff.).

Nubians were renowned as archers and were recruited by the Pharaohs and the Ptolemies as mercenaries. In Roman times, there were military camps in Dodekaschoinos, i.e. the northernmost part of Nubia, but the Roman military presence ended in 298 A.D. when Diocletian withdrew the last Roman guards from the region and established the Roman frontier at Syene (modern Aswān). Meanwhile, the rest of Nubia formed a separate kingdom, already in existence since 750 B.C., inhabited by an African people and with its capital first at Napata and then at Meroe. But the latter state collapsed in the mid-4th century with the invasion of king ᶜEzānā of Axum, after which various unknown peoples came in and merged with the existing population of Nubia, and amongst all these ethnic groups the names of the Blemmyes and Noubades are notable (see V. Christides, *Ethnic movements in southern Egypt and northern Sudan*: *Blemmyes-Beja in Late Antique and early Arab Egypt until 707 A.D.*, in *Listy Filologicke*, ciii [1980], 129-43; L. Török, *Late Antique Nubia*, Budapest 1986, 27 ff.). In spite of their rivalry, these two groups seem to have tried to unite against the Byzantines in the mid-5th century, but the Byzantine emperors used Nubia in a grandiose plan to dominate the Red Sea region and extend their influence as far as Yemen (see Christides, in *Annales d'Ethiopie*, ix [1972], 115-46). Within Nubia south of Dodekaschoinos, three independent kingdoms emerged, sc. Nobatia, Makuria or Muḳurra [*q.v.*] and Alodia or ᶜAlwa [*q.v.*].

The Arab conquest of Egypt inevitably affected Nubia, and according to the *Futūḥ al-Bahnasā*, Bed̲j̲a-Blemmyes [see BED̲J̲A] and Noubades participated in the Byzantine defence of Upper Egypt against the Arabs (see J. Jarry, in *Annales Islamologiques*, ix [1970], 9-20). The first Arab raids against Nubia took place before the final conquest of Egypt in 645 A.D., but these were probably defensive actions against the harryings of the Nubians rather than evidence of a definite plan to invade the distinctly inhospitable region of Nubia, just as the Arabs' use of the shipyard at Clysma or Ḳulzum [*q.v.*] was aimed at safeguarding the flow of grain across the Red Sea against Bed̲j̲a-Blemmyes pirates there. An Arab raid under Nāfiᶜ b. ᶜAbd al-Ḳays al-Fihrī took place in 21/641-2 and another by ᶜAbd Allāh b. Abī Sarḥ in 31/651-2, when the Muslims penetrated as far as Dongola [*q.v.*], destroying its basilica. After this, a truce was made between the Arabs and the Nubians, sealed by the celebrated *baḳṭ* (*q.v.*, and also P. Forand, *Early Muslim relations with Nubia*, in *Isl.*, xlviii [1971], and M. Hinds and H. Sakkout, in Wadād al-Ḳāḍī (ed.), *Studia Arabica et Islamica, Festschrift for Iḥsān ᶜAbbās*, Beirut 1981, 210 ff.). This comprised a trade agreement but was also a bilateral treaty of non-aggression and non-intervention between the two powers, and in future times was to play a significant role in Arab-Nubian relations.

During the Umayyad period, trade relations were important: Egyptian exports to Nubia included cereals and wine, whilst Nubia exported mainly slaves but also iron and camels, furnished by the Bed̲j̲a-Blemmyes. An Arabic papyrus of 141/758, just after the fall of the Umayyads, sent from the governor of Egypt to the king of Nubia, refers to the mistreatment of Arab merchants (see Hinds and Sakkout, *op. cit.*; J.M. Plumley, *An eighth-century Arabic letter to the King of Nubia*, in *Jnal. of Egyptian Archaeology*, lxi [1975], 241-5; and in general, Christides, *Nubia and Egypt from the Arab invasion of Egypt until the end of the Umayyads*, in *Procs. of the Seventh Internat. Conference for Nubian Studies, Geneva 1990*). Towards the end of the Umayyad period, the king Kyriakos invaded Egypt in order to release the Patriarch Anba Mīk̲h̲āʾīl, who had been imprisoned by the Muslims; and it was to Nubia that two children of the last Umayyad caliph, Marwān II [*q.v.*], fled after the ᶜAbbāsid Revolution (see Y.F. Hasan, *The Arabs in the Sudan*, Edinburgh 1967, 28 ff.; G. Vantini, *Christianity in the Sudan*, Verona 1981, 75 ff.).

During the ᶜAbbāsid period, Nobadia gradually became incorporated in Muḳurra, whilst ᶜAlwa followed a similar cultural pattern to the other states, so that a degree of homogeneity was achieved throughout Nubia; it was not however until the 9th century that the Bed̲j̲a-Blemmyes seem to have formed an organised kingdom, when we hear of a punitive raid into their land of 218/831 under the Arab general ᶜAbd Allāh b. D̲j̲ahm, ended by a peace agreement in which an annual tribute to the Arabs of camels was promised (see al-Yaᶜḳūbī, *Taʾrīk̲h̲*, i, 218; al-Maḳrīzī, *K̲h̲iṭaṭ*, ed. Wiet, Cairo 1927, iii, 272-5; Hasan, *The Arabs and the Sudan*, 38-41). Later in this century, the presence of gold mines in their land seems to have become generally known to the Muslims, for al-Mutawakkil in 241/855-6 sent his general Muḥammad b. ᶜAbd Allāh al-Ḳummī on a successful expedition against the Bedja in order to secure access to the gold mines in their country on the western shores of the Red Sea (al-Ṭabarī, iii, 1428-33, tr. J.L. Kraemer, Albany 1989, 141-5).

Over the next centuries, relations between Nubia and the Muslims revolved round the twin facts of the *baḳt*, with disputes over the number of black slaves to be delivered to the caliphs and with the penetration of Muslim traders into Nubia and the land of the Bedja-Blemmyes (seen in the number of Arabic inscriptions on tomb stones there from the mid-3rd/9th century onwards), and with the constant interference of the rulers of Nubia in the Christian church affairs of Egypt, since the Nubian kingdom was deeply theocratic, with the ruler as priest-king.

Under the Fāṭimids of Egypt, the *baḳt* continued to be sent, with the conqueror Djawhar sending an immediate embassy to King George II of Nubia (969-1002) regarding it, although the emphasis now seems to have been on the sending of beasts and exotica (see B.I. Beshir, *New light on Nubian-Fāṭimid relations*, in *Arabica*, xxii [1975], 15-24). The Fāṭimids managed to penetrate deeply into Nubia and to protect the maritime trade in the Red Sea, with a special fleet constructed against piracy there (al-Ḳalḳashandī, *Ṣubḥ*, iii, 468-9, 524). The Christian Church in Nubia continued to be dependent on the Patriarchate of Alexandria, with Monophysitism in the ascendant in Nubia after the Arab conquest of Egypt but with the emergence of a stronger Melkite element in the more tolerant Fāṭimid times, reflected in Nubia also; see U. Monneret de Villard, *Storia della Nubia cristiana*, Rome 1938, 128 ff.

Bibliography: Given in the article. But see also for the study of Islamic archaeological evidence, still in its infancy, W.Y. Adams, *Islamic archaeology in Nubia, an introductory survey*, in T. Hagg (ed.), *Nubian culture, past and present*, Stockholm 1987, 327-61, and Ali Osman Mohamed Salih, *Nationalist archaeology: the case of the Sudan*, in *Procs. of the Seventh Internat. Conference for Nubian Studies, Geneva 1990*, and for relations between mediaeval Nubia and Africa, P.L. Shinnie, *The culture of medieval Nubia and its impact on Africa*, in Hasan (ed.), *Sudan in Africa*, 42-50. See also D. Ayalon, *The Nubian Dam*, in *JSAI*, xii (1989), 372-90.

(V. Christides)

(b) From the Ayyūbid period to the 16th century

With the advent to power in Egypt of the Ayyūbids [*q.v.*] in 567/1171, Nubian affairs came into some prominence when in 568/1172-3 a coalition of the dispossessed Fāṭimids' black troops (*al-sūdān*) and the Nubians attacked an island just south of Aswān, provoking intervention by the troops of Ṣalāḥ al-Dīn under the sultan's brother Shams al-Dawla Tūrān Shāh, who devastated Ibrīm (which had apparently reverted to Nubian control since the Ikhshīdid capture of it in 345/957) and carried off a large number of captives. Soon after this, in *ca.* 1208, Abū Ṣāliḥ al-Armanī (see on him, Graf, *GCAL*, ii, 338-40) composed his account of the churches and monasteries of Egypt (ed. and tr. B.T.A. Evetts and A.J. Butler, Oxford 1894-5), which contains some interesting details about Marīs, al-Muḳurra, and ʿAlwa, but must be used with caution owing to the confusion in the writer's mind between Nubia and Abyssinia and his uncritical use of older authorities.

The factors which brought about the disintegration of the Nubian kingdom and the islamisation of the country were the immigration of Arab tribes, the rise of the Banu 'l-Kanz [*q.v.*], and the intervention in Nubian affairs of the Mamlūk rulers of Egypt, especially during the reigns of al-Ẓāhir Baybars [*q.v.*] and al-Manṣūr Ḳalāwūn [*q.v.*].

The Banu 'l-Kanz are first heard of in 397/1007 when the Fāṭimid caliph al-Ḥākim, as a reward for services rendered, conferred the hereditary title of *Kanz al-Dawla* on Abū Makārim Hibat Allāh, a chief of the Rabīʿa Arabs who had settled on the borderland between Egypt and the Sūdān. Already in the 4th/10th century the Rabīʿa had gained control of the mines of al-ʿAllāḳī and imposed their rule on the Bedja [*q.v.*] with whom they allied themselves by intermarriage. Another section, settled near Aswān, fraternised with the local Nubians, and the tribe, formed by this amalgamation and ruled by the Kanz al-Dawla dynasty, came to be known as the Banu 'l-Kanz; they are represented by the Kenūz of the present day. During the period of the Mamlūks, they were virtually in independent control of Upper Egypt, alternately in alliance with or in revolt against the Mamlūk government, and though repressed at times with a heavy hand, they remained a powerful tribe until the Ottoman conquest of Egypt. Before this event, however, they had played their part, together with nomad Arabs and Mamlūk troops, in the destruction of Nubian independence.

The Baḥrī Mamlūks, for reasons not apparent in our sources, departed from the traditional policy of Muslim Egypt, and actively intervened in Nubian affairs. The pretext for the expeditions undertaken by the generals of Baybars and Ḳalāwūn were non-payment of the tribute and, more frequently, the championship of Nubian pretenders who had solicited Egyptian support in order to gain the throne. On several occasions, such protégés of the Mamlūk government were installed in Dongola [*q.v.*] only to lose the throne again as soon as the Egyptian troops withdrew.

A formal treaty concluded with one of these kings virtually established an Egyptian protectorate. Meanwhile, the disintegration of the kingdom went on under the pressure of Arab immigration, and Arab chiefs who married into the royal house took advantage of the matrilinear line of succession to grasp at the throne. The age-long Christianity of Nubia was gradually undermined and in the 8th/14th century Muslim kings begin to appear. The first king to bear a Muslim name was Sayf al-Dīn ʿAbd Allāh Barshambū, a nephew of the Christian king David, who was installed by a Mamlūk force sent out by Sultan al-Nāṣir Muḥammad b. Ḳalāwūn under ʿIzz al-Dīn Aybak in 716/1316; the new king ʿAbd Allāh was, however, speedily overthrown by Kanz al-Dawla. From the manual for secretaries, *al-Taʿrīf bi 'l-muṣṭalaḥ al-sharīf* of Ibn Faḍl Allāh al-ʿUmarī [*q.v.*] (written in 741/1340), we learn that at this date Christian kings still alternated with Muslims, and Ibn Baṭṭūṭa in 753/1352 (iv, 396) speaks of the Nubians as Christians, but mentions a Muslim king (Ibn Kanz al-Dīn). Of the conversion of the common people we have no details: no doubt it was brought about by the absorption of the native inhabitants, or those who survived, in the Arab tribes.

The immigration itself has left little trace in the pages of the historians, though the outlines of the process can be reconstructed from occasional references and from oral tradition. The nomads who had entered Egypt in the wake of the first conquest can never have found that country congenial to their mode of life, and the rise of non-Arab dynasties tended to make conditions still less attractive, while the Sūdān seemed to offer all the advantages, from the nomads' point of view, that Egypt denied. For a long time, the kingdom of Dongola formed an effective barrier to southward expansion, but a gradual infiltration of Arabs must have begun at a comparatively early date, even though the end of the process was not accomplished for several centuries.

The early stages of the movement are seen in the conditions depicted in the story of Abū ʿAbd al-Raḥmān al-ʿUmarī, the events of which are laid in the reign of Aḥmad b. Ṭūlūn (i.e. the later 3rd/9th century) (al-Maḳrīzī's *Kitāb al-Muḳaffā*, quoted by Quatremère, *Mémoire sur la Nubie*, ii, 59-80). Arabs of Rabīʿa and Djuhayna, led into the Sūdān by that adventurous prince, have fraternised with the Bedja and exploit the mines of the Eastern Desert, but the Nile is forbidden them and Nubia is too strong to be attempted by force of arms. A fratricidal struggle in the Nubian royal house provides an opportunity for an alliance between the Arabs and a princely pretender to the throne. Acts of unblushing treachery are committed on both sides and in the end the Arabs have the worst of the encounter. The end of the process is seen in the 8th/14th century, when the kingdom of Nubia ceased to exist except as a puppet state controlled by the Muslim Arab tribes who gradually overran the country, a process noted by Ibn Khaldūn (*ʿIbar*, Beirut 1956-71, v, 922-3) as having led to something like anarchy in Nubia. The ascendancy of the nomads clearly affected Nubian Christianity adversely. The Churches of Alexandria and Nubia gradually became disassociated with each other, and churches and monasteries in Nubia must have been looted and dispersed at this time, although Nubian pilgrims were noted in Jerusalem (where in the 14th century the Nubians possessed a chapel in the Church of the Holy Sepulchre which soon, however, passed to the Armenians and then the Georgians) as late as *ca.* 1480.

Of ʿAlwa [*q.v.*] further to the south, little is heard at this time. It was a reservoir of slave manpower, frequented by Muslim slave traders and by merchants from al-Muḳurra to the north who came to collect slaves to pay the *baḳṭ*. Mamlūk pressure on al-Muḳurra (see above) was felt in ʿAlwa, and already in the time of Ibn Khaldūn (later 8th/14th century) we hear of branches of Djuhayna "close to the Abyssinians", that is to say no doubt on the upper reaches of the Blue Nile in the southern Djazīra. The kingdom of ʿAlwa nevertheless lingered on precariously and Nubian Christianity was still a living memory in the time of the Portuguese Alvarez (1520-7), but in *ca.* 1500 the capital Sōba fell to an alliance of Ḳawāsma Arabs (a branch of Rufāʿa-Djuhayna) and the negroid Fundj [*q.v.*], who here for the first time appear in history.

The 9th/15th century is almost completely barren of records relating to Nubia, and the historical memory of the present inhabitants remembers little of pre-Fundj days. With the coming of the Fundj, who soon extended their influence to Dongola, the history of Nubia is merged in that of the Sūdān, and the Nubians, now Muslims and deeply affected by racial mixture with their conquerors, survive only as a linguistic minority on the northern fringe of their ancient kingdom.

Lower Nubia, however, was politically separated from the Fundj kingdom by the Ottoman sultan Selīm I, who annexed the country south of Aswān as far as the neighbourhood of the Third Cataract, and garrisoned it with Turkish and Bosnian mercenaries (called Ghuzz by the people of the Sūdān).

For the subsequent history of the region, see FUNDJ; AL-MAHDIYYA; AL-SŪDĀN.

Bibliography: E. Quatremère, *Mémoire sur la Nubie*, in *Mémoires géographiques et historiques sur l'Égypte*, ii, Paris 1811; J. Marquart, *Die Benin-Sammlung des Reichsmuseums für Völkerkunde*, Leiden 1913, pp. CCXLVIII ff.; H.A. MacMichael, *A history of the Arabs in the Sudan*, Cambridge 1922; J.S. Trimingham, *Islam in the Sudan*, London 1965, 67-80; Yūsuf Faḍl Ḥasan, *The Arabs and the Sudan*, Edinburgh 1967, 96-132; W.Y. Adams, *Nubia, corridor to Africa*, Princeton 1984, 522 ff. On the Ottoman period, see M. Hinds and H. Sakkout, *Arabic documents from the Ottoman period from Qaṣr Ibrīm*, London 1986; Hinds and V. Ménage, *Qaṣr Ibrīm in the Ottoman period: Turkish and further Arabic documents*, London 1991.

(S. HILLELSON-[C.E. BOSWORTH])

3. Languages

The name Nub(i)a is first attested in Eratosthenes (*ca.* 200 B.C.). Its etymology is probably an autochthonous word for "slave". The term *Nūba* was originally applied by the Arabs to the Nile Nubians and later extended to cover other enslaved groups. It has since come to represent an ambiguous linguistic designation based on geography. About 50 tribes living in the Nūba Mountains (*Dār Nūba*) of Southern Kordofan province, Sudan (an area of about 30,000 square miles), can be denoted as *Nūba*. Many are from diverse racial and linguistic backgrounds, having fled to the region as a result of the Arab slave trade of the 17th-19th centuries. Almost all are Muslims, except for some Hill groups. Many *Nūba* tribes are named after the hills in which they reside.

The Nūba (Mountains) languages belong to two families: (1) (Niger-)Kordofanian, and (2) the East Sudanic branch of Nilo-Saharan, which contains Songhai, Fur, Maban, etc.

(Niger-)Kordofanian is subdivided into Niger-Congo, the Kadugli-Krongo group (thought by some to be Nilo-Saharan), and Kordofanian proper. The latter, whose linguistic development occurred in the Nuba Mountains, has the longest history. Among the better known Kordofanian languages are the Heiban group, Moro and Otoro. Some Kordofanian languages go by different designations; thus Koalib (30,000 speakers) is also called Ka/owalib, N(g)irere, Rere, Nuba, Lgalige and Abri.

East Sudanic is subdivided into eastern and western branches, plus Kuliak and Nilotic (e.g., Shilluk, Dinka, Bari). An example of a Proto-East Sudanic reconstruction is PES **te/o(ng)* "cow" > Birked *tei*, Kadaru *ti*, Majang *tang*, Murle *tang*, Gaam *tɔɔ* and Mongo *teenge* (Ross 1991).

The eastern group, which includes such languages as Daju (spoken in Chad), Nyimang and Temein, has three subdivisions: Eastern Jebel, Nubian and Surma. The Nubian group (disparagingly called *Barābra* by Arabs) is well documented, and has five constituents: (1) Central, including Birked (extinct) and Dongolāwī (Kenzī or Matoki); (2) Hill Nubian (Kadaru, Ghulfan, Debrī); (3) Unclassified Hill Nubian (Dair, Dilling, Karko, Wali); (4) Northern Nubian (Nobiin or Maḥas-Fadidja [Fadicca]); and (5) Western Nubian or M(e)īdōb. Thelwall and Schadeberg (1983) note that Birked and Hill Nubian once formed a single unit. Dongolāwī, with over a million speakers, is sometimes called Ratana, originally an Arabic pejorative label (< A. *raṭāna* "gibberish"), and has a 67% lexical similarity with Nobiin; cf. Nubi or Ki-Nubi (*rutáán núbi*), an East African Arabic creole emanating from the Sudan in the 19th century.

More is known about the Nubian past than that of

any other East Sudanic people. Although the Nubians established their Empire of Cush in *ca.* 850 B.C. with its capital at Meroe, Meroitic (written in a script derived from Egyptian Demotic) is unrelated to any form of Nubian. Lexicostatistics has shown that in the first millennium B.C., Nubians migrated from Dārfūr to the Nile. Old Nubian developed in the 6th century A.D. with the rise of the Christian Nubian kingdoms. It is a direct ancestor of Nile Nubian and is closest to Nobiin. All Old Nubian texts (the last in 1484 A.D.) appear to come from the Nobiin north. The geographical distribution of the two major Nubian dialects continues to remain puzzling. The Kenūz, who inhabit Upper Egypt north of Wadi Halfa and came from Dongola, speak a Nubian dialect hardly distinguishable from the Dongolāwī. However, these two groups are separated by the Nobiin, who are located along the Nile between them.

Bibliography: For older bibl., see Hillelson's *EI*[1] art. Of modern studies, see R. Thelwall and T.C. Schadeberg, *The linguistic settlement of the Nuba Mountains*, in *Sprache und Geschichte in Afrika*, v (1983), 219-31 (fundamental); Marianne Bechaus-Gerst, *Sprachliche und historische Rekonstruktionen im Bereich des Nubischen unter besonderer Berücksichtigung des Nilnubischen*, in *ibid.*, vi-vii (1984), 7-134 (useful); Schadeberg, *Kordofanian*, in *The Niger-Congo languages*, ed. J. Bendor-Samuel, Lanham, Maryland 1989, 67-80; J. Ross, *A preliminary attempt at the reconstruction of Proto-Eastern Sudanic phonology and lexicon*, Southern Illinois University, Carbondale, M.A. thesis, 1991, unpubl.; Aleya Rouchdy, *Nubians and the Nubian language in contemporary Egypt*, Leiden 1991 (useful). (A.S. Kaye)

4. The modern peoples of Nubia

The Barābra, as a separate group from the Danāgla, are collectively referred to by other Sudanese as Ḥalfāwiyyin (literally: those who come from the town of Ḥalfa). The term Nūbiyyin (Nubians), on the other hand, refers to both the Barābra and the Danāgla. The Barābra live in Aswān Province in upper Egypt and the Northern State of Sūdān. The Danāgla live only in the Northern State. Both groups are small-scale cultivators, skilful boatmen and are renowned for their domestic service. Date-palms are grown as a cash crop and cultivators have taken advantage of mechanical irrigation, introduced early this century, to cultivate more land with a variety of crops. The narrow strips of arable land on the banks of the Nile are insufficient to meet the demands of a rising population, hence the Barābra and Danāgla are forced to emigrate. They are adaptable and enterprising, the men seeking work opportunities in other parts of Egypt, Sūdān and, more recently, in the oil-rich countries of the Arab world where they are engaged in various professions. Wherever they go they maintain a strong cultural identity and keep links with their homeland. Though the Barābra and Danāgla have been influenced by Arab culture and Islam, their cultural identity is manifest in their dialects, traditions and attitudes. Even in urban centres in Sūdān and Egypt this identity is maintained in the social clubs which they have established.

As a result of the agreement between Sūdān and in Egypt in 1959 to resettle the Nubians affected by the creation of the High Dam reservoir lake (the Nūbā Lake in Sūdān and Lake Nāṣir in Egypt), it is estimated that about 50,000 Sudanese and 70,000 to 120,000 Egyptian Nubians lost their homes, land and their date-palms. The resettlement scheme, located in eastern Sūdān along the upper Aṭbara River near the Sūdān-Ethiopia border, known as K͟hashm al-Girba, absorbed 40,000 Sudanese Nubians in 1964-5. Here the relocated Nubians were granted landholdings and new homes; a new town was named Ḥalfa al-D̲j̲adīda (New Ḥalfa) as a replacement to old Ḥalfa which was inundated by the reservoir lake. The new villages established by the scheme were named after those which had been inundated in their homeland. Many amenities were introduced and planners were anxious to recreate the traditional architecture and physical layout of the submerged villages. Despite their displacement, the Nubians have accepted the inevitable and established good relations with the neighbouring nomadic tribes. The Nubians in Egypt, who were affected by the inundation, were resettled in the region of Kom Ombo, about 60 km/35 miles north of Aswān, and the resettlement area was named New Nubia.

Before and since Sūdān's independence in 1956, the Barābra and Danāgla have played a part in the country's cultural development and politics. They are generally devout Muslims and most of them belong to the Mīrg͟haniyya (K͟hatmiyya [*q.v.*]) *ṭarīḳa*. They are keen to take advantage of education facilities and show an aptitude for the educational professions and business. Many have achieved prominent positions in government, politics, the arts and in the civil service. Three Nubian singers are popular and famous: the late K͟halīl Faraḥ, Muḥammad Wardī and Ḥamza ʿAlāʾ al-Dīn. The most remarkable figure was Muḥammad Aḥmad [*q.v.*], the Mahdī of the Sūdān (d. 1885), who was a Dongolāwī, though his family claim to be *s͟harīf*s. Another Dongolāwī who has gained political prominence is D̲j̲aʿfar Muḥammad Numayrī, a military officer, who came to power through a military coup and ruled Sūdān from 1969 until 1985.

Bibliography (for older bibliography, see Hillelson, in *EI*[1]): S.F. Nadel, *The Nuba: An anthropological study of the hill tribes of Kordofan*, London 1947; D. Tothill (ed.), *Agriculture in the Sudan*, London 1948; R. Herzog, *Die Nubier. Untersuchungen und Beobachtungen zur Gruppenliederung, Gesellschaftsform und Wirtschaftsweise*, Berlin 1957; K.M. Barbour, *The republic of the Sudan. A regional geography*, London 1961; J. Vercoutter, *Sudanese Nubia and African history*, in *United Nations Review*, viii (1961); L. Greener, *High dam over Nubia*, London 1962; R. Herzog, *Dringliche Erforschung unter den Nubiern*, in *Bulletin of the International Committee on urgent anthropological and ethnological research*, v (1962); A. Kronenberg and W. Kronenberg, *Parallel cousin marriage in medieval and modern Nubia*, in *Kush*, xiii (1965); T. Little, *High dam at Aswan*, London 1965; J.S. Trimingham, *Islam in the Sudan*[2], London 1965; R. Fernea (ed.), *Contemporary Egyptian Nubia*, 2 vols., New Haven 1966; W.Y. Adams, *Continuity and change in Nubian cultural history*, in *Sudan Notes and Records*, xlviii (1967); Yūsuf Faḍl Ḥasan, *The Arabs and the Sudan*, Edinburgh 1967; J. Kennedy, *Nubian zar ceremonies as psychotherapy*, in *Human organisation*, xxvi (1967); idem, *Mushuhara: a Nubian concept of supernatural danger and the theory of taboo*, in *American Anthropologist*, lxix (1967); D. Lee, *The Nubian house: persistence of a cultural tradition*, in *Landscape*, xviii/1 (1969); Sondra Hale, *Nubians: a study in ethnic identity*, Khartoum 1971; G. Sorbo, *Economic adaptations in Kashm el-Girba: a study of settlement problems in the Sudan*, Khartoum 1971; C. Callender and Fadwa El Guindi, *Life-crises rituals among the Kenuz*, Cleveland and London 1971; Hussein M. Fahim, *Nubian resettlement in the Sudan*, Miami 1972; Marian Wenzel,

House decoration in Nubia, London 1972; Sondra Hale, *Nubians in the urban milieu: Great Khartoum*, in *Sudan Notes and Records*, liv (1973); Hassan Dafalla, *The Nubian exodus*, London 1975; R. Keating, *Nubian rescue*, London 1975; P.M. Holt and M.W. Daly, *The history of the Sudan. From the coming of Islam to the present day*, London 1980; J. Spaulding, *Kora. A theme in Nubian cultural history*, in *Africa Today*, xxviii/2 (1981); R.A. Lobban, *A genealogical and historical study of the Mahas of the "Three Towns". Sudan*, in *The International Journal of African Historical Studies*, xvi/2 (1983); W.Y. Adams, *Nubia. Corridor to Africa*², Princeton 1984; El Haj Bilal Omer, *The Danagla traders of Northern Sudan*, London 1985.

(Ahmed al-Shahi)

NŪBĀR PASHA (1825-99), a high-ranking official, statesman, and reformer of Armenian origin who held positions under six viceroys of Egypt at a time when the country was falling under European influence and control. Born in Smyrna and educated in France and Switzerland, Nūbār was translator for Ibrāhīm Pasha [*q.v.*], Chief Translator for ʿAbbās Ḥilmī I [*q.v.*], Secretary and Director of Communications and Railways for Saʿīd Pasha, and, under the Khedive Ismāʿīl Pasha [*q.v.*], Chief Translator, Director of Public Works, Head of Foreign Affairs, and Director of Commerce. He also served as President of the Council of Ministers under Ismāʿīl and two subsequent viceroys, and was foreign minister in fact for over two decades. Nūbār was personally involved in many of the major developments of the time, particularly the Alexandria-Cairo railway project (1851), the Suez Canal arbitration award (1864), the procuring of the 1873 *firmān*, the establishment of the Mixed Courts (1875), and the political crisis of 1875-9. He also served as an agent in negotiating some of the private and public loans taken out by Saʿīd and Ismāʿīl, and helped reorganise Egypt's transportation system.

Crucial to Nūbār's rise and success were the well-placed connections of his family, which included in-laws in Istanbul and a powerful uncle in the Egyptian court, who secured him his first position; the support of European diplomatic representatives (something which occasionally brought him into the ruler's disfavour); and his own extraordinary ability to make himself useful to viceroys in need of men who knew and understood Europe (Nūbār was entirely Western in culture and spoke all the major languages of Europe).

In his memoirs, Nūbār presents himself as a grand reformer and defender of Egypt. Declaring his aim to be that of limiting the power of both the European consuls and the viceroy, Nūbār discusses his strategy for the independence and development of Egypt, which included an increase in its transit trade, the build-up of the ports of Alexandria and Suez, the introduction of European technicians and expertise, and the establishment of the rule of law by means of Mixed Courts, which, he claims, could have protected the country against exploitation.

Yet Nūbār did more to advance the cause of Europe than any other official in the viceroy's service. The Alexandria-Cairo railway project (which Nūbār had suggested to ʿAbbās Ḥilmī I) increased British influence; the huge indemnity imposed upon Egypt by the Suez Canal arbitration enriched European money lenders and despoiled the Egyptian treasury; the loans Nūbār helped negotiate led to Egypt's bankruptcy and the establishment of European fiscal control (in his memoirs, Nūbār denies all responsibility for Egypt's debt); and the Mixed Courts became instruments of European political intervention. Between 1875 and 1879, Nūbār allied himself with Europe in a successful effort to bring down the ruler, Ismāʿīl Pasha, weakening the political structure and opening the way to a rebellion and the British occupation. Blinded by his own ambition to be maker of politics, Nūbār misjudged the amount of power that was left to local politicians and ended his days as an official in a British-controlled administration.

Bibliography: C.M. Bell, *Khedives and Pashas*, London 1884; E. Bertrand, *Nubar Pacha, 1825-1899*, Cairo 1904; M.B. Ghali, ed., *Mémoires de Nubar Pacha*, Beirut 1983; A. Holynski, *Nubar-Pacha devant l'histoire*, Paris 1886; F.R. Hunter, *Egypt under the Khedives, 1805-1879*, Pittsburgh 1984; M. Sabry, *L'Empire Égyptien sous Ismail et l'ingérence anglo-française*, Paris 1933; A. Schölch, *Egypt for the Egyptians*, London 1981; J. Tagher, *Portrait psychologique de Nubar Pacha*, in *Cahiers d'histoire Egyptienne*, i (1948), 353-72.

(F.R. Hunter)

NUBĀTA b. **ʿABD ALLĀH** al-Ḥimmānī al-Tamīmī, Abu 'l-Asad, minor poet of the early ʿAbbāsid period whose verses are known only from citations in other works and whose dates of birth and death are unknown. A native of Dīnawar in western Persia, he was in the circle of the caliph al-Mahdī's vizier al-Fayḍ b. Abī Ṣāliḥ Shīrawayh, and was a companion of the famous singer ʿAllawayh [*q.v.* in Suppl.].

Bibliography: Djahshiyārī, *Wuzarāʾ*, ed. al-Saḳḳā *et alii*, Cairo 1401/1980, 164; *Aghānī*¹, xvi, 62; Ziriklī, *Aʿlām*, viii, 320.

(Ed.)

NUBUWWA (a.), "prophecy", Hebrew *nǝbūʾa*, substantive derived from *nabī* "prophet", Hebrew *nābī(ʾ)*, term denoting in the first instance the precognition given by the divinity (Yahweh, the Baʿl, Allāh) to the prophet and the prediction made by the latter of future contingencies. In the second instance, *nubuwwa* is identified with *waḥy*, "revelation", which simultaneously comprises dogmas, cultic regulations, moral education, precepts of social and political order. In fact, for the early Muslims, prophecy was regarded as being the source of all knowledge having any degree of superiority. "The Prophet is the way and the prophets are the guides," wrote al-Kisāʾī (quoted by Yāḳūt, iv, 741).

In early times, the later Muslim *nabī* is almost identical to the Aramaic *ḥāzē* and to the Hebrew *rōʾeh* (cf. T. Fahd, *Divination*, 112 ff.). I Samuel ix, 9, reads: "In former times, in Israel, when a man went to enquire of God, he said 'Come, let us go to the seer (*rōʾeh*); for he that is now called prophet (*nabī*) was in former times called seer." It is for this reason that Muḥammad had considerable difficulty convincing his fellow-citizens that his inspiration was fundamentally different from that of seers of various specialities (*kāhin*, *ḥāzī*, *ʿarrāf*, etc.). He himself, at the outset of his vocation, dreaded being a *kāhin* (Ibn Saʿd, *Ṭabaḳāt*, i/1, 129-30). ʿUmar b. al-Khaṭṭāb, before his conversion, considered him as such (*Usd*, iv, 74). The intervention of revelation was required to convince him otherwise. "It is the word of an illustrious prophet," the Ḳurʾān states, "and it is not that of a poet, O men of little faith; nor is it that of a diviner, O men of little memory. It is a revelation (*tanzīl*) from the Master of the Universe" (LXIX, 40-3; cf. LII, 39-34; LXXXI, 19-25). The characteristic features of the Ḳurʾānic text sowed doubt in the minds of his fellow-tribesmen; the latter observed, especially in the first revelations, the distinguishing marks of the oracles of soothsayers, these being rhythm, the arrangement of components of a phrase, the concern for verbal equilibrium, the choice of a vocabulary full of images, the use of uncommon words, as well as the manner of "veiling the head" at the moment of inspiration and of "enwrapping himself" (cf. LXXIII, 1; LXXIV, 1; Ibn Hi<u>sh</u>ām, *Sīra*, 184; al-Ṭabarī, i, 1890, l. 10).

The triumph of Islam at Medina, followed by the conquest of Mecca, put an end to such reservations; the apostasy (*ridda*) of the Yemeni tribes of Ma<u>dh</u>ḥi<u>dj</u> in 11/632, under the leadership of al-Aswad, soothsayer and conjuror, who "entranced the hearts of those who heard him speak" (al-Ṭabarī, i, 1796), was the last manifestation of an entire Arab pagan tradition to which Islam put an end by the principle *lā kihāna baʿd al-nubuwwa* "no more divination after prophecy" (or rather, after "prophethood"). Henceforward, the gift of penetrating the mysteries of God is reserved for the Prophet alone, and the djinns who used to listen at the gates of Heaven, and inspire the *kuhhān*, are prevented from doing so by angels entrusted with the task of pelting them with shooting stars (XV, 15-18; XXXV, 6-9; XLV, 12; LXVII, 5; Ibn Hi<u>sh</u>ām, 129-30; Ibn Saʿd, i, 1, 110).

However, *kihāna* [*q.v.*] is not formally forbidden either in the Ḳurʾān or in the Sunna; what is forbidden is, first, to visit a *kāhin* and believe what he says: this is to deny the revelation made to Muḥammad (Wensinck, *Concordance*, iv, 196); and second, to charge a fee in the capacity of *kāhin* (*op. cit.*, 505). Nowhere in the Ḳurʾān is there a prohibition analogous to that of Leviticus, xix, 31, where it is written "Do not turn to those that evoke spirits nor to soothsayers; do not consult them lest you be defiled by them." "This reluctance of the Prophet to deny any intrinsic worth to the content of divination is due to the conception, current in his time, of prophecy and of its intermediaries" (T. Fahd, *Divination*, 68).

Prophecy was, in fact, regarded as an extension of divination. For Ibn <u>Kh</u>aldūn, for example, "a veil separates men from the unknown which nobody knows, except he to whom God reveals it in dreams or through the path of saintliness" (ii, 177/205). According to him, the difference between the prophet and the soothsayer resides, in the first place, in the absence of the ecstatic state in the case of the soothsayer, an absence which renders him incapable of a universal vision of the created being and of contingencies, and in the second place, in the imperfection of his source of information, subject to limitations which do not affect that of the prophet (i, 181-85/206-11; summarised in Fahd, *op. cit.*, 45 ff.).

As to this source of information, for the true prophets it emanates from angels, their inspirers and their guides; for soothsayers and false prophets it emanates from demons, their inspirers and seducers, while djinn, conceived after the fashion of man, can be either good or bad informants.

God has made the angels his envoys (*rusul*) (Ḳurʾān, XXXV, 1). The function of the "envoy" is to bear the message of the one who sends him. The demon is likewise an envoy and even the source of his message is the same as that of the angel; only the content is different. In fact, the angel who saved the life of Isaac, on the point of being sacrificed to Yahweh (Genesis, xxii, 11 ff.) was sent by the same Yahweh who permitted Satan, present before Him "with the sons of God", to test Job (Job, i, 6; cf. I Kings, xxii, 21 ff.)

Muslim authors, faced with the ambivalence of the divine message and its bearers, have established a distinction between "the angels of mercy", created from light, and "the angels of punishment", created from fire (al-Muṭahhar al-Maḳdisī, *Badʾ*, i, 160, quoting Ibn Isḥāḳ), a distinction inspired by Ḳurʾān, LXVI, 6, which gives the impression that angels exist which are spiritual (*rūḥānī*), corporeal (*<u>dj</u>ismānī*), capable of growth (*nāmī*) and inanimate (*<u>dj</u>āmid*) (*op. cit.*, 170), a notion comparable with the Neo-Platonic distinction between igneous and aerial demons and demons formed from earth (cf. Porphyrus, *De Abst.*, ii, 46; Proclus, *In Tim.*, ii, 11, 10; St. Augustin, *De civitate Dei*, x, 9, 2).

Demoniacal inspiration is opposed by the Ḳurʾān on account of the fascination which it exerts upon the minds of men. The typical example is that of poetic inspiration. Ḳurʾān, XXVI, 220-6, reads: "Shall I tell you to whom the demons (*<u>sh</u>ayāṭīn*) reveal? They reveal to every great liar and great sinner; they tell what they are supposed to have heard (at the gates of Heaven); but they are mostly liars. As for poets, they are followed only by the misled." It is not to be forgotten that the poets, described as *kilāb al-<u>dj</u>inn* "the dogs of the djinns", were originally givers of oracles for their tribes (al-<u>Dj</u>āḥiẓ, *Ḥayawān*, vi, 71; Goldziher, *Abhandlungen*, i, 17; Fahd, *Divination*, 74 f.).

The concept of inspiration and revelation in the formative years of Islam was influenced by that of angelology and of demonology, which was rudimentary and anthropomorphic (cf. in this context, T. Fahd, *Anges, démons et djinns en Islam*, in *Sources Orientales*, viii, Paris 1971, 155-213). The demeanour of the Prophet, at the moment of the onset of revelation, illustrates this point. Questioned about the processes of the revelation which he received, Muḥammad replied, "Revelation came to me in two manners: either <u>Dj</u>ibrīl brought it to me and communicated it to me as a man communicates with another man, but this eluded me; or it came to me like the ringing of a bell, such that it penetrated into my heart; this no longer eluded me" (Ibn Saʿd, i/1, 131 f.; cf. al-Bu<u>kh</u>ārī, ii, 309 = 59 *<u>kh</u>alḳ*, 6). "His physical condition was affected: he grew mournful, and his face darkened; he had the appearance of someone intoxicated and felt a great weight, to such an extent that his camel cried out and its legs buckled beneath him" (Ibn Saʿd, *loc. cit.*; Fahd, *Divination*, 76). A *ḥadī<u>th</u>* has him say, "The divine revelation comes to prophets in waking as well as in sleep," and he adds, "My eye sleeps, but my heart is awake" (Ibn Hi<u>sh</u>ām, 266; Ibn Saʿd, i/1, 113; other references in Fahd, *Divination*, 77, n. 1).

Finally, it should be noted that the initial identity of the source of information of the prophet and of the demon is further attested by the use of the verb *waḥā* "to reveal", and its derivatives, for one as for the other, as emerges from Ḳurʾān, VI, 111, where it is stated, "Thus we have appointed against every prophet an adversary (who is none other than) demons of human kind and of djinn who *reveal* to one another pleasing discourse (intended) to lead astray."

Still more suggestive regarding the manner of conceiving the phenomenon of prophecy in Islam are its "distinctive signs" (*ʿalāmāt, dalāʾil, imārāt al-nubuwwa*). An entire literature exists on this subject (cf. references in Fahd, *Divination*, 79, nn. 2 and 3). Ibn <u>Kh</u>aldūn supplies a summary of these signs. "The mark (*ʿalāma*) of this type of men," he writes, "is, first, that they are in a state, during the onset of revelation (*waḥy*), of absence (*<u>gh</u>ayba*) accompanied by choking (*<u>gh</u>aṭīṭ*), appearing to the eye like a loss of consciousness (*<u>gh</u>a<u>sh</u>y*) an unconsciousness (*i<u>gh</u>māʾ*), whereas in reality it is nothing other than a deep absorption (*isti<u>gh</u>rāḳ*) induced by the encounter with the spiritual kingdom and by the new faculty of comprehension which transcends the human faculty in an absolute manner. Then, from this ecstasy the man returns gradually towards a state of human awareness, either by hearing a sound of human speech which he attempts to understand, or by seeing represented before him the image of a person who speaks to him of that which the person has brought from the presence of God. Then this state is dissipated, once the man has absorbed that which has been communicated to him" (i, 165-6/185).

The second mark of the prophet is the moral infallibility (*ʿiṣma*), by virtue of which the man is naturally drawn towards goodness and purity (*ibid.*). The third mark is expressed in his activity on behalf of religion, of worship, prayer, alms and chastity, virtues which he practises and which he induces others to practise (i, 167/187). The fourth assumes that the prophet is of noble descent, well-regarded among his kinsfolk (i, 168/188). The fifth consists in miracles and marvels (in words and in actions, adds Ḥādjdjī Khalīfa, i, 427) which prove the veracity of his statements. The greatest miracle in Islam is the Ḳurʾān (i, 171/194).

But the most important of these marks, according to Ibn Khaldūn, is that faculty, granted by God to the prophet, of abstracting himself from human nature, in the state of inspiration and of ecstasy (i, 178/202). He who does not exhibit these signs has no right to claim the ability to penetrate the unknown; he is nothing other than a liar seeking to sell his wares (i, 209/240).

For more thorough information concerning these marks, see, in particular, al-Māwardī (d. 450/1058), *K. Aʿlām al-nubuwwa*, Cairo 1319/1901 ff.; Abū Ḥātim al-Rāzī, same title, extracts published by P. Kraus in *Orientalia*, n.s. v (1936), 35-56, 358-78; al-Djāḥiẓ (d. 255/869), *K. al-Ḥudjdja fī tathbīt al-nubuwwa*, ed. Sandūbī in *Rasāʾil al-Djāḥiẓ*, Cairo 1933; Abu 'l-Ḥusayn al-Rāwandī (d. 250/864), *K. al-Zumurrud*, in which the author opposes the traditional doctrine of prophecy and introduces some foreign elements (cf. P. Kraus, in *RSO*, xiv [1933-4], 93-129, 335-79); Fakhr al-Dīn al-Rāzī (d. 606/1209), *ʿIṣmat al-anbiyāʾ*, Cairo 1355/1936.

Other signs announce the coming or the presence of the Prophet. Ibn Saʿd classifies these in two categories: signs prior to the vocation of Muḥammad (i/1, 96-111) and signs following the start of the revelation (112-26). This is a collection of miraculous sayings and deeds relating to the birth and infancy of the Prophet, often belonging to a typology the elements of which were diffused in the popular domain, owing to apocryphal biographies of Jesus and of other prophets (cf. on this subject Fahd, *Problèmes de typology dans la Sira d'Ibn Isḥāq*, in *La vie du prophète Mahomet*, Paris 1983, 67-75).

This group of signs is augmented by a chorus of predictions announcing the coming of the Prophet, made by idols, soothsayers, leading personalities of the period, Jews, Christians, demons and djinns, etc., predictions emanating from the whole of nature, a kind of *praeparatio coranica*, testifying by their spirit, their form and their expression, to the concept held by early Islam of prophecy and of its intermediaries: a spirit removed from any metaphysical and psychological pre-occupation, a form showing small regard for realities and fundamentally marked by excess of imagination; finally, an expression which has no qualms about being simplistic, often full of picturesque imagery (for details, cf. Fahd, *Divination*, 81-8).

This conception evolved considerably with the elaboration of philosophy and of theology in Islam. For Ibn Sīnā, prophecy is "one of the conditions necessary to the order which is demanded by the unfolding of *fayḍ*, so that it may expand to the point required" (M.-A. Goichon, *La distinction de l'essence et de l'existence d'après Ibn Sīnā*, Paris 1937, 334, see also further, 314-34; *Shifāʾ*, lith. Tehran 1313/1886, ii, 646 ff.; *Nadjāt*, ed. Cairo 1331/1913, 498 ff.; *Ithbāt al-nubuwwa*, in *Tisʿ rasāʾil*, 6th *risāla*. On Ibn Sīnā's concept of prophecy, as it became known to scholars by means of Latin translations, cf. B. Decker, *Die Entwicklung der Lehre von der prophetischen Offenbarung von Wilhelm von Auxerre bis zu Thomas von Aquin*, diss. Breslau 1940, 15-24).

"For him, it is the Intelligences and the Souls of celestial bodies which transmit to the human soul certain hidden things, it being understood that the recipients possess particular perceptions and particular wills, emanating from a particular opinion" (Goichon, *Directives et remarques*, Paris-Beirut 1951, 507-8). And if the soul is of strong substance, it attains to ecstasy under a spiritual influence which sometimes "takes genuine control and then illumines the imagination in an evident manner". It is then that the soul is raised to the level of prophecy (*op. cit.*, 514). Finally, for him, the necessary conditions whereby a man may be a prophet are clarity and lucidity of intelligence, the perfection of the imaginative faculty and the ability to make himself obeyed by exterior matter (cf. *Psychologie d'Ibn Sīnā*, ed. Ján Bakoš, Prague 1956, i, 189-97 = *Shifā*, Physics, *fann* vi, *maḳāla* 4, ch. 4). See also L. Gardet, *Quelques aspects de la pensée avicennienne*, in *Revue Thomiste*, xlv (1939), 714; Decker, *op. cit.*, 16 ff. A brief analysis of Ibn Sīnā's doctrine concerning prophecy and the perception of the unknown is to be found in al-Shahrastānī, *Milal*, ed. Cureton, 309 ff. (Metaphysics) and 425 (Physics), German translation by Haarbrücker, ii, Halle 1851, 317-18, 327-32.

Al-Ghazālī accepted the doctrine of Ibn Sīnā and developed it further. In fact, in the last six chapters of the Latin version of *Maḳāṣid al-falāsifa* (tr. Dom. Gundisalvi, Venice 1506, of which the portion entitled *Metaphysics* has been edited by J.T. Muckle, *Algazel's Metaphysics, a medieval translation*, Toronto 1933; Arabic text ed. Cairo 1331/1912), which deal with vision, prophecy and marvels, al-Ghazālī revives Avicennan ideas (which he is to refute the same year, in 488/1095, in the *Tahāfut*, ed. M. Bouyges, Beirut 1927, 255-67; L. Gauthier, *La theorie d'Ibn Rochd sur les rapports de la religion et de la philosophie*, Paris 1909, 138-41) and reveals them in a clear and expressive style. For him, the vision of the unknown, in the state of waking, is subject to two conditions. On the one hand the soul must free itself from corporeal links and remove itself from the veil of the senses by a force which is peculiar to it; it is then elevated to the higher world where things appear to it in an instant brief as a lightning-flash. This is the first mode of prophecy. The other mode, decidedly imperfect in comparison to the first, comes about in the normal exercise of the senses. In fact, the temperament predisposed to melancholy and amazement and easily alienated from the senses enables the soul to withdraw from the body and to see and hear with eyes open that which normally it sees and hears only through the opaque veil of the senses (cf. *Metaphysics*, ii, 5,7, quoted by Decker, *op. cit.*, 25 f.). This agreement of the theologian with the philosopher on the subject of prophecy remains an isolated phenomenon; in fact, as M. Horten writes (*Texte zu dem Streite zwischen Glauben und Wissen in Islam. Die Lehre vom Propheten und der Offenbarung bei den islamischen Philosophen Farabi, Avicenna und Averroes*, Bonn 1913, 12), "in der Theorie über die

Prophetie stimmt er mit den Philosophen überein, die er sonst bekämpft." Whereas, in the *Tahāfut*, theories which present precognition and prophecy as the results of perfect nature, are countered by al-Ghazālī with the notion of revelation of things unknown, made by God to the prophet as to the dreamer, either directly or through the intermediary of an angel (see 260-1; cf. 252, 289, etc.).

Ibn Rushd does not share this view. For him, prophecy, dream and divination are three names denoting a single and identical reality. Our ignorance of the possible derives from our ignorance of the nature of being. Knowledge of this nature is either anterior to its object: it is the knowledge from which it follows, called *al-ʿilm al-ḳadīm*, prior or anterior knowledge; or it is posterior, *al-ʿilm al-ghayr ḳadīm*, or subsequent knowledge. "Knowledge of the unknown is nothing other than the knowledge of this nature" (*Tahāfut al-Tahāfut*, ed. Bouyges, Beirut 1930, 533, ll. 2-3). It is the result of this knowledge which is called, in popular usage, *ruʾyā*, dream, nocturnal vision, and, by the prophets, *waḥy*, revelation (*op. cit.*, 532-3; on Ibn Rushd's doctrine of prophecy, see L. Gauthier, *op. cit.*, 124-58). This represents a fairly deep fissure in the rationalist system which bears his name, on account of his role as an arbiter in the conflict, then current, between theology and philosophy.

With Maimonides (d. 601/1204, see IBN MAYMŪN), the brilliant disciple of Ibn Rushd, the Avicennan trend is revived. In fact, in chapters 32 to 48 of the second part of his monumental study of Jewish religious philosophy, intitled *Dalālat al-ḥāʾirīn* (= *Moreh Nebūkīm*), edited and translated into French by S. Munk under the title *Le guide des égarés. Traité de théologie et de philosophie*, i-iii, Paris 1856-66, Maimonides reveals at some length his opinion of prophecy and the various modes of perceiving the unknowable. According to him, prophecy is an emanation from God which, through the intermediary of an active intellect, influences first the rational faculty and subsequently the imaginative faculty; it is the highest degree of man and the ultimate perfection which the species may attain, and this state is the highest perfection of the imaginative faculty (ch. 35, tr. ii, 281). It assumes the existence in the man of a natural disposition which makes of him "a superior man, perfect in his rational and moral qualities" (ch. 32, tr. ii, 261 f.). Three perfections are required of the prophet: perfection of the rational faculty, perfection of the imaginative faculty and perfection of morals (ch. 36, tr. ii. 287). Dream and prophecy both belong to "the highest and most noble" activity of the imaginative faculty, which takes place only when the senses are in repose and cease to function; it is then that there occurs a certain emanation (*fayḍ*) which is the origin of true dreams and of prophecy and which "differs only in quantity and not in quality" (*Gen. Rabba*, c. 17, 44). In visions and in dreams, all the degrees of prophecy are contained (ch. 36, tr. ii, 282 ff. On Maimonides' conception of prophecy, see Z. Diesendruck, *Maimonides' Lehre von der Prophetie*, in *Jewish studies in memory of Israel Abrahams*, New York 1927, 82 ff.; Decker, *Entwicklung*, 37-8).

This close connection established by Maimonides between dream and prophecy corresponds precisely to the conception current in the early days of Islam. In fact, Tradition relates that before acceding to the full light of revelation as such, Muḥammad initially had dreams described as "veracious" (*ruʾyā ṣādiḳa*), supplying to him, in the words of L. Massignon (*Annuaire du College de France*, 41st year, 85), "in the form of isolated touches, light and sound, which he was unable to coordinate, that alphabet of ecstasy which he attempted later to represent, in the form of isolated consonants, at the heading of certain sūras (such is, at least, he adds, the reconciliation that we suggest)." This statement is based on the testimony of ʿĀʾisha, "The beginning of the prophecy of the Messenger of God, when God wished to make him His agent and the instrument of His mercy towards creatures, (was manifested) by veracious dreams; every dream which he saw in his sleep was as clear as the dawn. This made him love solitude; nothing was more pleasant to him than to be alone" (Ibn Hishām, 151; Ibn Saʿd, i/1, 129). A *ḥadīth* confirms this remark of ʿĀʾisha. The Prophet is quoted as saying, "There exist no signs announcing prophecy other than the good dream; the Muslim sees it or it is seen for him" (Ibn Saʿd, ii/2, 18; cf. Ibn Khaldūn, iii, 81/115). The term *bushrā* in Ḳurʾān, X, 64, is interpreted as *ruʾyā ḥasana* (al-Ṭabarī, *Tafsīr*, xi, 84 ff.). These "signs" or "preambles" form an integral part of prophecy, since the dream is said to be "a part of prophecy", an assertion repeated in all the prefaces of oneirocritical treatises. *Ḥadīth* goes further, specifying, following the Babylonian Talmud (*Berakhōt*, 57b, quoted by Maimonides, *op. cit.*, ii, 36), the proportions whereby dream is related to prophecy. The Prophet is quoted as saying: "The dream of the Believer is one of the forty (sixty, in the Talmud) parts of prophecy," a statement which al-Dīnawarī (*al-Ḳādirī fi 'l-taʿbīr*, ms. Paris, fol. 34b) explains as follows. "The Prophet means that the majority of prophets—peace be upon them!—did not see the angel, with the exception of a minority among them. It is during their sleep that they received the revelation." This amounts to saying that the Prophet first came to prophecy at the lowest level, i.e. the dream. It was at Ḥirāʾ that he graduated, for the first time, from dream to prophecy. In the year of his vocation—his fortieth year—he withdrew for a month of annual retreat (*taḥannuth*), accompanied by his wife. As he slept, the angel Gabriel appeared to him with a piece of some kind of silken fabric on which there was writing (*namaṭ min dībādj fīhi kitāb*). He said to him "Read!" "I cannot read" he replied. The angel stuffed the fabric into his mouth, almost suffocating him. "I believed," he says, "that this was death!" Then he released him, repeated the same question and inflicted the same treatment on him a second time, then a third. The fourth time, to escape this torture, Muḥammad asked him: "What must I read?", and the angel made him recite the beginning of the sūra *al-ʿAlaḳ* (XCVI, 1-5). Muḥammad adds, "I recited that which he had said, it was then that he finally left me. I woke up (*hababtu min nawmī*). (This phrase) was then as if inscribed in my heart. I went forth (wandering) and when I reached the middle of the mountain I heard a voice from Heaven saying 'O Muḥammad, you are the Messenger of God and I am Gabriel'. I stopped, watching him, neither advancing nor retreating, then I looked away from him towards the horizons and the sky; whichever way I turned, I saw him just as he was. I remained in this position, neither advancing nor retreating, until Khadīdja sent men to look for me. Her envoys arrived at the high places of Mecca and returned from there, and I was still in the same position. Then he parted from me and I parted from him, returning to my wife" (Ibn Hishām, 152-3; cf. the vision of Ezekiel, i, 4 ff.).

This account, combining the triple appeal of the vocation of Samuel with the initiation, through absorption of the prophetic message, of Ezekiel (ii, 8 ff.; cf. Jeremiah, v, 10) comprises two parts: the first took place in sleep, the second in a state of waking. Here there is a typical example of transference from dream to ecstasy (on dream and prophecy, cf. Fahd, *Divination*, 266-9, and on the dreams of Muḥammad, 255 ff.).

Bibliography: The essentials of the information contained in this article have been taken from T. Fahd, *La divination arabe. Études religieuses, sociologiques et folkloriques sur le milieu natif de l'Islam*, Leiden 1966, repr. Paris 1987. In addition to the numerous references cited in the text, see Tor Andrae, *Die Legenden von der Berufung Muhammeds* in *Le Monde Oriental*, vi (1912), 5-18; idem, *Die Person Muhammeds in Lehre und Glauben seiner Gemeinde*, Stockholm 1917 (reconciliation with the gnostic conception of prophecy); Asterios Argyriou, *Coran et histoire* (extract from the journal Θεολογία, liv (1983) and lv (1984), ch. iii (1) revelation, 62-7, (2) the prophets, 67-87 and Table no. iii: Ḳur'ānic prophetology); M. Jastrow Jr., *Ro'ēh and Ḥozēh in the Old Testament*, in *JBL*, xix (1900), 82-105; A. Jepsen, *Nabi. Soziologische Studien zur alt-testamentlichen Literatur und Religionsgeschichte*, Munich 1934; A. Haldar, *Associations of cult prophets among the ancient Semites*, Uppsala 1945; L. Gardet, *Quelques aspects de la pensée avicennienne*, in *Revue Thomiste*, xlv (1939), 708-20; A.R. Johnson, *The cultic Prophet in Ancient Israel*, Cardiff 1944; Kisā'ī, *Ḳiṣaṣ al-anbiyā'*, ed. J. Eisenberg, i-ii, Leiden 1922-3, Eng. tr. W.M. Thackston, *The tales of the prophets of al-Kisa'i*, Boston 1978; A. von Kremer, *Geschichte der herrschenden Ideen des Islams. Der Gottesbegriff, die Prophetie* (135-308) *und Statsidee*, Leipzig 1868, repr. Hildesheim 1961, 135-308; O. Pautz, *Mohammed's Lehre von der Offenbarung quellenmässig dargestellt*, Leipzig 1898; F. Rahman, *Prophecy in Islam*, London 1958; T. Robinson, *Studies in Old Testament prophecy presented to Prof. T.H. Robinson*, Edinburgh 1950; H.H. Schaeder, *Die islamische Lehre von vollkommenen Menschen, ihre Herkunft und ihre dichterische Gestaltung*, in *ZDMG* (1925), 213 ff. (reconciliation of the Islamic conception of prophecy with that of the Clementine Epistles, through the intermediary of Manichaeism); R.B. Serjeant, *Hūd and other pre-Islamic prophets of Ḥaḍramawt*, in *Le Muséon*, vi (1954), 121-79; A. Vinnikov, *The legend of the vocation of Muḥammad in the light of ethnography* [in Russian], in *Recueil ... Oldenburg*, Leningrad 1934, 125-46 (reviewed by B. Nikitine in *JA*, ccxxvi [1935], 337); A.J. Wensinck, *Mohammed und die propheten*, in *AO*, ii, Oslo 1923, 158-99; G. Widengren, *Muḥammed the Apostle of God and his Ascension (King and Saviour)*, in *Uppsala Universitets Årsskrift*, i, 1955.

(T. FAHD)

AL-**NUDJAYR**, a fortress in Ḥaḍramawt [*q.v.*] where in 12/633 during the caliphate of Abū Bakr [*q.v.*] rebels under al-Ash'ath b. Ḳays [*q.v.*] took refuge against Ziyād b. Labīb al-Anṣārī, the Prophet's governor.

Late in the year 11/633, Abū Bakr had decided that Islamic authority could only be effectively imposed on the Yemen by military force. In particular, he was worried by the situation in Ḥaḍramawt where al-Ash'ath b. Ḳays, the leader of Kinda, had refused to give him the oath of allegiance as caliph. Abū Bakr entrusted the task to al-Muhādjir b. Abī Umayya, the governor of Ṣan'ā', who marched eastwards from the capital to Ḥaḍramawt via Mārib. There al-Muhādjir received a letter from Ziyād, the Muslim governor in Ḥaḍramawt, urging him to proceed thither with speed. Leaving some of his army behind in Mārib, al-Muhādjir marched on Ḥaḍramawt. The rebels, in particular of Banū Mu'āwiya, a branch of Kinda (Mad'adj, 56, table 3), finally sought refuge in the fortress of al-Nudjayr. They could not, however, break out from the siege of the stronghold which was under the combined command of al-Muhādjir and Ziyād. The Banū Mu'āwiya finally surrended. Al-Ash'ath signed an agreement with the Muslim leaders, securing safe conduct for himself and his family. In return he opened the gates of al-Nudjayr. The Banū Mu'āwiya blamed al-Ash'ath for his betrayal, as many of their number were killed. However, the agreement put an end to serious anti-Muslim rebellion in Ḥaḍramawt and ensured a much stronger hold over the area by the Muslim authorities.

Al-Nudjayr is not mentioned further in the historical works and al-Hamdānī (87), writing in the 4th/10th century, describes the place as a ruin.

Bibliography: Ṭabarī, i, 2006-10; Yāḳūt, *Mu'djam al-buldān*, Beirut 1979, v, 272-3; 'Abd al-Muḥsin Mad'adj M. al-Mad'adj, *The Yemen in early Islam (9-233/630-847), a political history*, London 1988, 54-7.

(G.R. SMITH)

AL-**NUDJŪM** (A.), the stars. There are two words in Arabic carrying the notion of "star", *nadjm*, pl. *nudjūm* (from the root *n-dj-m*, "to rise"), and *kawkab*, pl. *kawākib* (see *WKAS*, i, 440 b 28; cf. already Babyl. *kakkabu*; a reduplication of a basic root *KB* "to burn, to shine"). For the etymologies of the two words, see Eilers [1], 96 ff.; [2], 115; [3], 6 f. Both words occur frequently in the Ḳur'ān. In LV, 6, it remains in dispute whether *al-nadjm*ᵘ is to be understood as "the plants, or grasses" (as maintained by I.Y. Kračkovskiy and A. Fischer) or as "the stars" (see the recent German translation by R. Paret, and his commentary, 465, also the English translation of R. Bell and his *A commentary on the Qur'ān*, Manchester 1991, ii, 330). *Al-nadjm* is also used, in Arabic, as an alternative name for the Pleiades (otherwise called *al-thurayyā*; see Kunitzsch [2], nos. 186, 306). The two words are used indiscriminately in the general sense of "star(s)", but *kawkab* can mean "planet(s)" specifically, according to context.

The following article is subdivided into three sections, for the fixed stars, the planets and other celestial objects.

I. THE FIXED STARS

The Arabs—inhabitants of the Arabian Peninsula, mostly Bedouins—had a good knowledge of the stars since ancient times. They used the fixed stars for orientation in their nightly desert travels (*ihtidā'*), to determine seasons and to predict weather, especially rain. They had proper names for a good dozen prominent stars or other celestial objects, names of old standing, the meanings of most of which had been obscured or lost in the course of time so that they became the object of speculation of the Arabic philologists and lexicographers of later times. For these, no modern "translations" can be given, cf. *al-'ayyūḳ* (α Aurigae, Capella), *al-shi'rā* (α Canis Maioris, Sirius—also mentioned in the Ḳur'ān, LIII, 49), *al-simāk* (*al-s. al-rāmiḥ*, "the lance-bearing Simāk", α Bootis, Arcturus; and *al-s. al-a'zal*, "the unarmed Simāk", α Virginis, Spica), etc.; cf. Kunitzsch [2], 20 f. For some of these old names there exist parallels in Babylonian astronomy; cf. Kunitzsch [8].

In addition, several hundred names for smaller, less conspicuous stars and asterisms were invented, most probably by poets, at various times and in various tribes and regions; see the name lists in Kunitzsch [2] and [7]. All these names were later assembled by the Arabic philologists and lexicographers in the so-called *anwā'* books (for these, see the bibliographies in AL-

ANWĀʾ and AL-MANĀZIL). In contrast to ancient Greek (and modern) astronomy, where large constellations are made up of numerous stars, in the indigenous Arabic stellar lore one star mostly represents one individual (mostly of a species of animals), a name in the dual represents two such individuals and a name in the plural represents a group of individuals. There are only a few Arabic constellations formed from a number of stars, such as e.g. the several *aṯẖāfī*, "fireplace(s) formed by a triangle of three stones on the ground" (cf. Kunitzsch [2], nos. 17-19). A classified survey of the asterisms of the old Arabs was given by Ideler, 407-28.

Of Iranian star names, only a few are known, and their astronomical identification remains uncertain; cf. Scherer 113 f., 118 f.; Eilers [1], [3]. Genuine Turkish star names are discussed by Bazin and Roux. In Islamic times the astronomers and poets of the Islamic world generally used the Arabic star names (but see the planets). Much of the Arabic stellar lore has lived on into modern times although the astronomical identifications and the calendrical usage may now differ; see the modern studies cited in AL-MANĀZIL and, for the Tuaregs, Bernus-Sidiyene.

Tradition has it that certain prominent fixed stars were worshipped by Arabic tribes in pre-Islamic times (cf. the allusion to *al-shiʿrā*, Sirius, in Ḳurʾān, LIII, 49), but, as it seems, these contentions still lack positive evidence; see Henninger.

Apart from perhaps some star names (see above), the old Arabs had also inherited from Babylonia—at unknown times, through unknown ways—some of the zodiacal constellations. But with them, several of these constellations were transferred to celestial areas different from their places in Babylonian and Greek (and modern) astronomy. Suffice it here to mention as a famous example *al-djawzāʾ* (a female name of uncertain signification) which, in the series of the zodiacal constellations, corresponds to Gemini, but which is located in the stellar figure known in Greek (and modern) astronomy as Orion; for more details, see MINṬAḲAT AL-BURŪDJ.

The old Arabs themselves developed a popular stellar system of so-called *anwāʾ* (sing. *nawʾ*), stars and asterisms mostly situated near the path of Sun and Moon which were used for calendrical purposes and weather predictions [see AL-ANWĀʾ]. Later, the *anwāʾ* were merged into the system of the 28 lunar mansions which the Arabs received from outside, perhaps from India, and which divided the ecliptic according to the Moon's monthly revolution into 28 portions, each mansion being marked by a star or asterism carrying the name of the corresponding *nawʾ* located in that place [see AL-MANĀZIL; also Varisco].

The old Arabic stellar lore was much used in poetry. The poets liked to cite star names and to use them for comparisons or for poetic allusions to calendrical and meteorological events connected with them, and the like; cf. Kunitzsch [10], items xxvi and xxvii; Kunitzsch-Ullmann.

The period of indigenous, old Arabic folk astronomy ended with the expansion of Islam, when the Arabs came into contact with ancient Greek and Hellenistic science. Through, and after, the translations from Greek (and sometimes Persian and Indian) into Arabic, the period of Greek-based "scientific" astronomy in the Islamic civilisation begins which, in some areas, continued down to the 19th century.

The knowledge of the fixed stars (*al-kawākib al-ṯẖābita*, or simply *al-ṯẖawābit*) in the "scientific" astronomy of the Islamic period was completely based on and influenced by ancient Greek theory and mate-

rial. The physical qualities and behaviour of the stars were understood according to the cosmological theories of Aristotle and Ptolemy: the stars were invariably fixed to the eighth sphere (beyond the planets), thus being unable to change places relative to each other, and were invariable in substance, size and colour. The eighth sphere (hence the stars fixed to it) performed a constant movement from West to East about the poles of the ecliptic, the so-called "precession" (*ḥarakat* or *sayr al-kawākib al-ṯẖābita*), which Ptolemy—following Hipparchus—assumed at a rate of 1° in 100 years. The astronomers of the caliph al-Maʾmūn arrived at an improved rate of 1° in 66½ years (*al-Zīdj al-mumtaḥan* [*Tabulae probatae*], 214/829-30), which afterwards—simplified as 1° in 66 years—was adopted by most of the succeeding authors of star catalogues (al-Battānī, al-Ṣūfī) and smaller star tables; another prominent value was 1° in 70 years (cf. the survey in Nallino, *al-Battānī, Opus astronomicum*, i, 292 f.; see also Mercier [1]).

The iconographical and topographical division of the stellar sky into constellations was also completely taken over from the Greeks. Here the main source was the star catalogue in Ptolemy's *Almagest* (epoch: A.D. 138) comprising 1,025 stars arranged in 48 constellations and registered with ecliptical coordinates, longitude and latitude, and (apparent) magnitudes. Of the *Almagest* several translations into Arabic were made from the late 8th to the late 9th centuries (cf. Kunitzsch [5], 15-82). The versions of al-Ḥadjdjādj and of Isḥāḳ b. Ḥunayn (the latter emended by Ṯẖābit b. Ḳurra) have survived into our time (the star catalogue from these two versions was edited by Kunitzsch [11], vol. i); the "old" version made before al-Ḥadjdjādj's was used in the star catalogue of al-Battānī, and many coordinate values from it are also cited by Ibn al-Ṣalāḥ. These sources supplied the Arabic-Islamic astronomers with the terminology and nomenclature of the 48 constellations and the 1,025 individual stars and provided them with the basic coordinate values for these stars (for a complete survey of the names of the 48 constellations, followed by Greek, Arabic and Latin indexes, see Kunitzsch [5], 169-212; the complete terminology for the individual stars, again followed by Greek, Arabic and Latin indexes, is given in *ibid.*, 212-370). The Arabs also knew Aratus (3rd cent. B.C.) as the inventor of the constellations and cited from his *Phaenomena* and the *Scholia in Aratum* (cf. Sezgin, vi, 75-7; further, al-Bīrūnī, *Tafhīm*, 72; Ibn al-Ṣalāḥ, 54 f., 71).

The Arabic term for "constellation" was *kawkaba*, pl. *kawkabāt* (adapted from Ptolemy's ἀστερισμός), or *ṣūra*, pl. *ṣuwar*.

Apart from the textual tradition, iconographic documents from (Late) Antiquity seem also to have reached the Islamic period conveying to the Muslim astronomers the outlines of the pictorial representation of the 48 classical constellations. An early example for the continuation of classical iconographic material into Islamic times is the fresco in the cupola of the bath in the desert castle of Ḳuṣayr ʿAmra (*ca.* 711-15 [see ARCHITECTURE]) showing a celestial hemisphere with constellation figures (cf. Saxl; Beer [1], [2]; Almagro). Also, instruments such as celestial globes and astrolabes of Greek provenience or tradition must have reached the Muslims; Ibn al-Ṣalāḥ (18, 72 f.) mentions the description of a Greek globe datable *ca.* A.D. 738, and Ibn al-Ḳifṭī (*Taʾrīkh al-Ḥukamāʾ*, 440) reports the existence of a globe made of copper (*nuḥās*), attributed to Ptolemy himself, in Cairo in 435/1043-4.

Several Islamic astronomers established star

atalogues in the manner of Ptolemy's catalogue: al-Battānī (only 533 out of Ptolemy's 1,025 stars; epoch A.D. 880; precession value = Ptolemy + 11°10′; dited in Nallino, *al-Battānī, Opus astronomicum*; cf. Kunitzsch [10], item v; Ibn al-Ṣalāḥ, Appendix ii, 7 ff.); Abu 'l-Ḥusayn al-Ṣūfī (complete, accompanied by drawings of the constellations; epoch 964; precession value = Ptolemy + 12°42′; *Kitāb Ṣuwar al-awākib*, ed. Ḥaydarābād 1373/1954, French tr. H.C.F.C. Schjellerup, St. Petersburg 1874, repr. Frankfurt-am-Main 1986; cf. Kunitzsch [10], item i); al-Bīrūnī (complete; epoch 1031; precession value = Ptolemy + 13°0; in *al-Ḳānūn al-masʿūdī*, ed. Haydarābād, iii, 1375/1956, Russian tr. S.A. Krasnovaya and M.M. Rozhanskaya, in *Istoriko-astronomičeskiye issledovaniya*, viii, Moscow 1962, 2-150, with comm. by B.A. Rosenfeld, in *ibid.*, 177-86); and Ulugh Beg (complete; epoch 1437; textually depending on Naṣīr al-Dīn al-Ṭūsī's Persian translation of al-Ṣūfī's Book on the Constellations; astronomically claiming his own observation for the majority of the stars and dependence on al-Ṣūfī for the rest; edited by Th. Hyde, Oxford 1665; a modern recension of the coordinate values was made by Knobel; cf. further, Evans, 162-5; Shevchenko).

Besides these great, complete catalogues, innumerable smaller star tables were drawn up by Muslim astronomers of all times, mostly listing fundamental stars for use on astronomical instruments such as the astrolabe (see Kunitzsch [10], item i; for some edited specimens, see *ibid.*, items ii-iv, and Kunitzsch [3], I A and XII A).

The pictorial representation of the 48 classical constellations in Islamic astronomy, in books, on celestial globes and elsewhere, mainly follows the patterns set up by the drawings in al-Ṣūfī's Book on the Constellations; al-Ṣūfī, in turn, must have followed traditions from Late Antiquity (for the textual description of the stars he generally follows the *Almagest* version by Isḥāḳ-Thābit; in the star coordinates he chooses between the various translations of the *Almagest* and faithfully repeats the *Almagest* values in his star tables, notwithstanding his criticism of many of them). For each constellation al-Ṣūfī gives two drawings, one as seen in the sky, the other as seen on the celestial globe where the figures are viewed from outside, on the convex surface of the globe, i.e. human figures seen in the sky looking towards the observer with their faces and front sides are seen on the globe with their back sides towards the observer; al-Ṣūfī, however, gives a "falsified" globe view, just the mirror image of the sky view representation; the reason for this is not obvious; most probably he just follows older models of Late Antique tradition; perhaps the intention was to keep the figures showing their faces to the observer under all conditions).

Outside the books, the fixed stars were used on various astronomical instruments. The astrolabe especially, but also quadrants, were instructed with the most important fundamental stars (see ASṬURLĀB; Kunitzsch [12]). While in the great star catalogues after Ptolemy, the stars were registered with ecliptical longitude and latitude, for use on the astrolabe another set of coordinates was more practical: *mediatio coeli* (*tawassuṭ*, or *mamarr*—passage at the meridian) and declination (*al-buʿd ʿan muʿaddil al-nahār*). These were usually obtained (from the ecliptical values) by calculation. Many astronomical handbooks (*zīdj*) and treatises on the astrolabe contain tables of astrolabe stars with one or both sets of these coordinates. Furthermore, the stars and their constellations used to be represented on celestial globes (up to now, a number of more than 130 celestial globes in the Islamic area has been found and registered, see Savage-Smith); here the stars were entered according to ecliptical coordinates; the styling of the constellation figures normally followed the models introduced by al-Ṣūfī. Celestial globes are the only form of mapping the entire sky known from Islamic astronomy; no plane star maps from the Islamic Middle Ages have been found, although some astronomers (e.g., al-Bīrūnī, *Kitāb Tasṭīḥ al-ṣuwar wa-tabṭīḥ al-kuwar*, ed. A. Saidan, in *Dirāsāt/al-ʿUlūm al-ṭabīʿiyya* [Univ. of Amman], iv [1977], 7-22; cf. Berggren; Richter-Bernburg) discuss the construction of plane star charts. Instead of complete star maps we only have al-Ṣūfī's isolated drawings of the individual constellations. The late Persian astrolabist Muḥammad Mahdī al-Yazdī produced two astrolabes, to each of which he added a plate carrying, on both sides, maps of the northern and the southern celestial hemispheres with all constellations. One of these instruments is dated 1065/1654-5 (in Riyāḍ; it was on display in the exhibition *Saudi-Arabia, yesterday and today* in Washington D.C., July 1989; see the accompanying catalogue *Islamic science and learning*, 14); the other one, dated 1070/1659-60, was described by W.H. Morley, *Description of a planispheric astrolabe...*, London 1856, 48 f. (repr. in *Arabische Instrumente in orientalistischen Studien*, ed. F. Sezgin, i, Frankfurt-am-Main 1990, 302 f.). These veritable sky maps are, however, inspired by contemporary European star charts; they include, in the southern hemisphere, near the South Pole, some of the non-classical southern constellations which were introduced in the 16th and 17th centuries. Hence these plates reflect a new development in Islamic astronomy, with the influx of modern Western knowledge.

The question, to what extent the star tables and catalogues of Muslim astronomers represent the result of their own independent observation, is not always easy to answer. It appears convincing that a star table or catalogue with ecliptical coordinates, whose latitudes are identical to Ptolemy's and whose longitudes show a constant increase over Ptolemy's, was obtained by calculation rather than by observation. When the latitudes differ and the longitudes show varying differences against Ptolemy's, one would rather be inclined to assume independent observation. A few well-known outstanding examples of independent observation are: the table of 24 stars measured by al-Maʾmūn's astronomers and transmitted in *al-Zīdj al-mumtaḥan* ("*Tabulae probatae*"; epoch 214/829-30; cf. Kunitzsch [10], item iii), or the star catalogue of Ulugh Beg (see above), although for this latter one the question seems not yet definitely answered. Personal observations of Ptolemy's stars were made by Ibn al-Ṣalāḥ (d. 1154), as can be understood in many places in his treatise *Fī sabab* .... Also, the most famous and most detailed Islamic author on the fixed stars, al-Ṣūfī (903-86), re-observed all of Ptolemy's stars and added, in his *Book on the Constellations*, to the description of each of the 48 constellations a special section reporting his criticism. Nevertheless, in the tables of his catalogue he merely repeated Ptolemy's coordinate values and did not enter any new or "better" values found by himself, except for the magnitudes. Since most of the *zīdj*s (astronomical handbooks with tables; cf. below) of the Islamic period are still unedited, it would be premature now to present final statements. It may be that in them one or another star table will be found that is built upon an author's own observations.

Surveys of the 48 Ptolemaic constellations are also

found—apart from the great star catalogues mentioned above—in some other works: Muḥammad b. Aḥmad al-Khwārazmī (*ca.* A.D. 980), *Mafātīḥ al-ʿulūm*, ed. G. van Vloten, Leiden 1895, 210-13; al-Bīrūnī, *Tafhīm* 69-72 (on 77-81 follows a survey of indigenous old-Arabic star names, and on 81-5 the lunar mansions are listed); Zakariyyāʾ al-Ḳazwīnī, *ʿAdjāʾib al-makhlūḳāt*, ed. Wüstenfeld, i, 29-41 (this section is extracted from al-Ṣūfī's *Book on the Constellations*; the section was separately edited and translated by L. Ideler and served as the nucleus for his voluminous study on the history of star names; on 41-51 follows a description of the 28 lunar mansions which is extracted from Ibn Ḳutayba's *Kitāb al-Anwāʾ*, cf. ed. Ḥaydarābād 1375/1956, 17 ff.). Of some interest for the continuity of the tradition is *Le traité sur les constellations* by Severus Sebokht, in Syriac, written in A.D. 660, i.e. in early Islamic times, but much before the famous Greek-Arabic translations; ed. F. Nau, in *Revue de l'Orient Chrétien*, xxvii (1929-30), 327-410, xxviii (1931-2), 85-100. About 600 years later another Syriac description of the 48 constellations was given by Bar Hebraeus (Abu 'l-Faradj b. al-ʿIbrī) in his *Livre de l'ascension de l'esprit*, ed. Nau, Paris 1899-1900, text i, 110 ff., tr. ii, 94 ff., which now, however, is a mixed text including both Syriac and Arabic elements (cf. Kunitzsch [1], 32 f.).

A rare use of the 48 constellations was made by the Persian poet Fakhr al-Dīn Gurgānī in his epic *Vīs u Rāmīn* (written *ca.* A.D. 1050), where he presents a horoscope which is greatly expanded by including all the constellations of the fixed stars in the astrological configuration (cf. Kunitzsch [10], item xxviii; in a subsequent article in *Isl.*, lx [1983], 297-301, O. Neugebauer has dated this horoscope to A.D. 968).

The Arab seafarers in the Indian Ocean in the 15th and 16th centuries, Aḥmad b. Mādjid and Sulaymān al-Mahrī, still knew and used some of the classical constellations and star names, though often in distorted form and in modified astronomical application. Especially Ibn Mādjid [*q.v.*] takes pride in naming the classical books he had studied, among them al-Ṣūfī's *Book on the Constellations* (here called *Kitāb al-Taṣāwīr*). On the other hand, the star nomenclature of these *muʿallims* contains several names of unknown and sometimes certainly non-Arabic origin. For discussions of these names, see the Index given in Kunitzsch [10], item xxix.

In astrology it was mostly the planets whose influence was considered. But since oldest times, the fixed stars could also be included in the astrological procedures. Already Ptolemy in his astrological handbook, the *Tetrabiblos* (*Kitāb al-Arbaʿa*), assigned to all the constellations and the major stars individually the "temperament" (κρᾶσις, A. *mizādj*, Lat. *complexio*, *temperamentum*) of one or two planets, cf. *Tetrab.* i, 9. Subsequently, lists of stars with their temperaments were drawn up, or in purely astronomical star tables the temperaments were added in a separate column. Further, to certain fixed stars was ascribed a bad influence on health, especially of the eyes, and also these stars were assembled in special lists. All this material reached the Arabic-Islamic civilisation, in the same way as the astronomical knowledge, and we find it reproduced directly, or in various adaptations, in Arabic texts.

Of the *Tetrabiblos* several Arabic translations were made (not all edited until now; cf. Sezgin, vii, 41 ff.). The famous astrologer Abū Maʿshar included in his comprehensive *al-Mudkhal al-kabīr*, ii, 1, a survey of the 48 classical constellations (without adding the astrological temperaments; see the facsimile ed.—made from ms. Istanbul, Carullah 1508, dated 327/938—by F. Sezgin, Frankfurt-am-Main 1985, 111 f.). For lists of stars doing harm to the eyes (cf. *Tetrab.*, iii, 12) see again Abū Maʿshar, *Mudkhal*, vi, 20 = facs. Frankfurt 351 f. (cf. Kunitzsch, *apud* Hübner 358 f.), and al-Bīrūnī, *Tafhīm*, 272-4 (§ 460). Another list of unlucky stars of Abū Maʿshar is in Kunitzsch [10], item xvii, 113-19. A very recent specimen for a horoscope introducing the fixed stars is the horoscope of Asad Allāh Mīrzā, 1830; cf. Elwell-Sutton (esp. 16-27, 94 f.). One ancient tradition on the "Thirty Bright Stars" appeared in Arabic under the name of Hermes; it must have come through (Middle) Persian mediation, because its badly distorted star names show signs of Persian influence (cf. Kunitzsch [10], item xiii), and the term for the fixed stars here used, *al-kawākib al-biyābāniyya* (in mediaeval Latin translation *stelle beibenie*), is Persian (from Pahlavi *a-wiyābān-īg*, which literally renders Greek ἀπλανής, the common term for the fixed stars; cf. W.B. Henning, *apud* Kunitzsch [10], item xiv, esp. 265; al-Bīrūnī's explanation of the term *al-kawākib al-biyābāniyya* as "desert stars", from New Persian *biyābān* "desert", in *Tafhīm*, 46 (§ 125), was mere guesswork and popular etymology). The Hellenistic astrological compilation in five parts ascribed to Zoroaster also reached the Arabs through a Persian intermediate stage; the star names in the chapter on the fixed stars of its fifth part, *Kitāb al-Mawālīd*, were transformed into Persian and were retained in this form in the Arabic version; cf. the ed. of the chapter in Kunitzsch [13]. Another tradition, on stars causing weather disturbances, tempest, etc., containing star names of unknown origin and meaning, has been found until now only in Byzantine and mediaeval Latin versions and it is uncertain whether an Arabic stage was also involved in its transmission; cf. Kunitzsch [10], items xv-xvi.

Yet another use of star names occurred in lot books (*kutub al-faʾl*) where they took the role of "judges" answering questions or guiding the interrogator to further questions. An example is the *Liber Alfadhol*, a lot book attributed to Hārūn al-Rashīd's astrologer al-Faḍl b. Sahl, of which also Latin and old German versions exist and which contains 144 "judges" carrying star names (including a few astronomical terms); cf. Kunitzsch, *apud* Lutz, 321-36, and idem, in *ZDMG*, cxviii (1968), 297-314, and cxxxiv (1984), 280-5. For other texts of this kind cf. Kunitzsch, *apud* Lutz, 321 n. 1; Kunitzsch [6], esp. 281 f.; Wetzstein.

In addition, it may be mentioned that Arabic texts of all the kinds described were translated into Western languages, into Byzantine Greek from the 11th century onwards and into Latin, in Spain, from the late 10th century onwards. In this way, Arabic star and constellation names became widely known in mediaeval and Renaissance Western science, and more than 200 "Arabic star names" can still be found in modern star atlases and astronomical textbooks today.

Since it is impossible to give here lists of the many Arabic star and constellation names, once more the literature is cited where all these names are completely listed and explained: for indigenous old Arabic star names, see Kunitzsch [2] and [7]; for the lunar mansions, see AL-MANĀZIL; for the zodiac, see MINṬAḲAT AL-BURŪDJ; for the nomenclature of stars and constellations derived from Greek sources, mostly the *Almagest*, see Kunitzsch [5]; for specimens of Arabic star names in Byzantine texts, see Kunitzsch [10], item ii (types I and II); for Arabic star names in mediaeval Western and modern astronomical use, see

Kunitzsch [1] and [3] and Kunitzsch-Smart; and for the special usage of names with the navigators of the Indian Ocean, see the Index in Kunitzsch [10], item xxix.

Arabic star names and their use in Western science have been the object of philological and historical studies over centuries, starting with G. Postellus' treatise *Signorum coelestium vera configuratio aut asterismus*, Paris 1553; cf. a short survey in Kunitzsch [1], 23 f. The Arabic matter in the popular book of R.H. Allen, *Star-names and their meanings*, New York 1899 (repr. New York 1963), is often incorrect and misleading, cf. the warnings in Kunitzsch [10], item xxiv. Also, modern Arabic authors have paid their tribute to the subject, cf. M.H. Jurdak [Djurdāḳ], A. Malouf [Maʿlūf] and A.H.M. Samaha [Samāḥa], cited in the bibliography of Kunitzsch [1]; the most recent author is A.R. Badr, *Asmāʾ al-nudjūm fi 'l-falak al-ḥadīth, uṣūluhā wa-taṭawwuruhā*, in *RAAD*, lix (1404/1984), 81-96, 290-333, 761-89, lx (1405/1985), 86-103.

II. THE PLANETS

As in all civilisations, the five planets visible to the naked eye were also known to the old Arabs, because they had names for them which were obviously originally Arabic and were not obtained, through translation, from outside. There seems, however, not to have existed a special term for the planets (as distinct from the fixed stars) with the Arabs in their "pre-scientific" period. Some commentators assume that the terms *al-khunnas* and *al-kunnas* in Ḳurʾān, LXXXI, 15-16, may refer to the planets; cf. *WKAS*, i, 387 a 2 ff., 442 b 41 ff. (not to be confused with the term *al-khussān* which, according to Ibn Durayd, *Djamhara*, i, 67 a 1-3, s.r. *kh-s-s*, designates the stars around the (North) Pole that never set, i.e. the circumpolar stars). In the "scientific" period of Arabic-Islamic astronomy which was based on translations from Greek, the most common terms for the planets (οἱ πλανώμενοι, sc. ἀστέρες) were (*al-kawākib*) *al-mutaḥayyira* (referring to the five planets alone) and (*al-kawākib*) *al-sayyāra* (for the five planets plus Sun and Moon), cf. al-Khʷārazmī, *Mafātīḥ*, 210, 228; al-Bīrūnī, *Ḳānūn*, iii 987; *WKAS*, i, 442 b 28 ff., 35 ff. Other terms, in certain translated texts, were *al-kawākib al-mutaḥarrika* (*WKAS*, i, 442 b 39), *al-k. al-sayyāḥa*, *al-k. al-djāriya* and *al-k. al-ḍālla* (*ibid.*, i, 580 b 27 ff.).

The following table shows the names of the planets in Arabic, adding some alternative names used in the Western Arabic and Spanish Arabic area, and in Persian:

	Arabic	Western Arabic	Persian
Moon	*al-ḳamar*		*māh*
Mercury	*ʿuṭārid*	*al-kātib*	*tīr*
Venus	*al-zuhara*		*[a]nāhīd*
Sun	*al-shams*		*mihr, khurshīd*
Mars	*al-mirrīkh*	*al-aḥmar*	*bahrām*
Jupiter	*al-mushtarī*		*hurmuz[d]*
Saturn	*zuḥal*	*al-muḳātil*	*kaywān*

For the etymologies of the names in Arabic and Persian, see Eilers [2] and [3]. The "Persian" name *kaywān* is of Babylonian origin (cf. *WKAS*, i, 518 b 9 ff.). For Jupiter another Arabic name of unknown background was *al-birdjīs*; cf. Ibn Ḳutayba, *Anwāʾ*, 126 f.; Eilers [3], 81 ff. A survey of the planets' names in seven languages (Arabic, Greek, Persian, Syriac, Hebrew, Sanskrit and Khʷārazmian) was given by al-Bīrūnī, *Āthār*, 192 (= tr. Sachau, 172). In Arabic poetry in ʿAbbāsid and later times, the Persian names were often used. In astronomy and astrology the names could be abbreviated by using only the last letter of the Arabic name, cf. Elwell-Sutton, 66. Further, the symbols for the planets introduced in Greek texts were also adopted by Arabic-Islamic astronomers and astrologers, see al-Bīrūnī, *Tafhīm*, 199 (§ 329); Ullmann, 345 f. The Arabic names shown above (including the Western Arabic alternative names) were also retained in many mediaeval Latin translations from the Arabic, in astronomical and astrological contexts. The complete set of the seven names even appears in Wolfram of Eschenbach's epic *Parzival* (*ca.* A.D. 1210), 782, 6 ff.; see Kunitzsch [4].

Planetary theory in Arabic-Islamic astronomy was mainly based on the teachings of Ptolemy in his *Almagest*. The planets rotate on seven successive spheres (*falak* [*q.v.*]) about the earth, the Moon being the nearest to the earth, in the first sphere, and Saturn being the farthest, in the seventh sphere; the eighth sphere was held by the fixed stars. The lower planets (below the Sun), Moon, Mercury and Venus, were called *al-kawākib al-sufliyya*, and the upper planets (beyond the Sun), Mars, Jupiter and Saturn, were *al-kawākib al-ʿulwiyya*. The lowest point in a planet's orbit was called *ḥaḍīḍ*, the farthest point was *awdj* (from Sanskr. *učča*, cf. D. Pingree, in *Viator*, vii [1976], 161; afterwards Latinised as *aux*, genitive *augis*). The two points of intersection of a planet's orbit with the ecliptic were each called by the Persian term *al-djawzahar* [*q.v.*] or—translated from Greek συνδεσμός—*ʿuḳda*, node. The ascending node (ἀναβιβάζων) especially was called *raʾs* (*al-tinnīn*) "(the Dragon's) head, *caput* (*draconis*)", and the descending node (καταβιβάζων) *dhanab* (*al-tinnīn*), "(the Dragon's) tail, *cauda* (*draconis*)". The planets performed a forward movement (*istiḳāma*) along the ecliptic (*ilā tawālī al-burūdj*); at certain times they became stationary (*wuḳūf, iḳāma*) and then performed a retrograde movement (*rudjūʿ*); this ended in a second stationary position after which they resumed the normal forward movement.

The knowledge about the planets' physical behaviour—motion, size, distances, etc.—was mainly laid down in the so-called *zīdj*s, i.e. comprehensive handbooks containing both theoretical chapters and the relevant tables. The word *zīdj* (pl. *zīdjāt, azyādj, ziyadja*) is of Persian origin (already in Pahlavi, *zīk*) and originally meant the thread(s) in weaving; from the arrangement of the threads in a piece of woven cloth it was extended to the network of lines drawn for astronomical tables and finally transferred upon complete works of tables with their introductory theoretical text. Very few such works have been edited so far, e.g. *al-Zīdj al-ṣābiʾ* of al-Battānī (ed. and tr. C.A. Nallino, i-iii, Milan 1899-1907); the Latin translation (by Adelard of Bath) of Maslama al-Madjrīṭī's redaction of the *Zīdj* of Muḥammad b. Mūsā al-Khʷārazmī (ed. A. Bjørnbo, R. Besthorn and H. Suter, Copenhagen 1914; Eng. tr. and comm. O. Neugebauer, Copenhagen 1962); al-Bīrūnī's *al-Ḳānūn al-masʿūdī* (ed. Ḥaydarābād, i-iii, 1954-6; Russian tr. P.G. Bulgakov *et alii*, i-ii, Tashkent 1973-76; survey of the contents in English by E.S. Kennedy, in *Al-Abḥāth*, xxiv [1971], 59-81). About 130 *zīdj*s were listed, and twelve of the most important abstracted, in Kennedy [1]. More abstracts are in Toomer [1]; Mercier [2]. Of great historical interest are also works such as *The Book of the reasons behind astronomical tables* (*Kitāb fī ʿilal al-zīdjāt*) of ʿAlī b. Sulaymān al-Hāshimī (ed.

and tr. F.I. Haddad, E.S. Kennedy and D. Pingree, New York 1981) which has preserved material lost, or not yet found, in the original; of the same character is *El libro de los fundamentos de las Tablas astronómicas* by the Spanish-Jewish scholar Abraham b. ᶜEzra (written in Latin in A.D. 1154; ed. J.M. Millás Vallicrosa, Madrid-Barcelona 1947).

Popular estimated values for the (sidereal) revolution of the planets are mentioned by Ibn Ḳutayba, *Anwāʾ*, 127. According to him, Saturn travels in each of the twelve zodiacal signs 32 months (i.e. a total revolution of 32 years); Jupiter 1 year (i.e. a total revolution of 12 years); Mars 45 days (i.e. a total of roughly 1½ years); the Sun 1 month (i.e. a total of 1 year); Venus 27 days (i.e. a total of 324 days); Mercury 7 days (i.e. a total of 84 days); and the Moon 2⅓ nights (i.e. a total of 28 nights). He also mentions that Venus and Jupiter are of bright white colour, Saturn is yellowish, Mars is red, and Mercury also red, but it is seen only rarely because of its vicinity to the Sun.

Scientific astronomy has received and continued to use the precise Greek data in the *Almagest* and has, in the course of time, improved upon many of them, based on new independent observation. For details, one has to consult the *zīdjs* and their abstracts mentioned above.

While, on the whole, Ptolemaic astronomy remained valid in the Arabic-Islamic civilisation until in recent times contacts began with modern Western astronomy, on the other hand serious criticism of Ptolemy's planetary theory was brought forward by several Muslim astronomers. Among the names here to be mentioned are Ibn al-Haytham (in Egypt, d. shortly after 432/1041; cf. Sezgin, v, 251 ff.); Djābir b. Aflaḥ (*Geber*, Spain, 1st half 12th cent.; cf. R.P. Lorch, *The Astronomy of Jābir ibn Aflaḥ*, in *Centaurus*, xix [1975], 85-107); al-Biṭrūdjī (*Alpetragius*, Spain, 2nd half 12th cent. [*q.v.*]; idem, *On the principles of astronomy*, ed. and tr. B.R. Goldstein, i-ii, New Haven 1971). In the East, an important name was further—besides Naṣīr al-Dīn al-Ṭūsī—Ibn al-Shāṭir (Damascus, 14th cent.), cf. the collection of papers *The life and work of Ibn al-Shāṭir*, ed. Kennedy and I. Ghanem, Aleppo 1976; Kennedy [2], section "Planetary theory"; idem, *Planetary theory*: *late Islamic and Renaissance*, in *Awrāḳ*, v-vi (1982-3), 19-24; Goldstein, *The status of models in ancient and medieval astronomy*, in *Centaurus*, xxiv (1980), 132-47; G. Saliba, *Theory and observation in Islamic astronomy*: *the work of Ibn al-Shāṭir of Damascus*, in *Journal for the History of Astronomy*, xviii (1987), 35-43. There have been observed similarities between certain new methods and solutions of problems in planetary theory by some 13th and 14th century Islamic astronomers and those of Copernicus. But it would be difficult to interpret these coincidences in terms of Arabic influence on Copernicus, since no direct lines of transmission from the Orient to Renaissance Western astronomers has been ascertained so far.

Islamic astronomers also devised—like Western scientists of late mediaeval and Renaissance times—instruments for the demonstration of the planets' movements, the so-called equatoria, see Kennedy [2], section "Equatoria"; Comes.

For the use of the planets in astrology and some of their astrological properties, see MINṬAḲAT AL-BURŪDJ.

III. OTHER CELESTIAL OBJECTS

a. *Nebulae*. Ptolemy in the star catalogue of the *Almagest* had described five of his 1,025 stars as "nebulous". However, all of these were star clusters or double stars appearing to the naked eye as "nebulous", but not nebulae according to modern astronomical understanding. It was Abu 'l-Ḥusayn al-Ṣūfī who, in his *Book on the Constellations*, independently and for the first time mentioned the Andromeda Nebula (M 31 = NGC 224), calling it *laṭkha saḥābiyya*, a "nebulous spot". In one of the drawings of the constellation of Andromeda he marked the position of the nebula by a number of small dots; see Kunitzsch [9]. As for the Magellanic Clouds, in the southern celestial hemisphere, near the South Pole, invisible from the Arabian Peninsula, a first reference to them seems to be in Yāḳūt, *Muᶜdjam al-buldān*, ed. Wüstenfeld, i, 501 f., where Yāḳūt cites several unnamed travellers (*ghayr wāḥid mimman shāhada tilka 'l-bilād*) who described that they saw in the sky a spot (*ṭāḳa*) about the size of the Moon looking like a white cloud (*ḳiṭᶜat ghaym bayḍāʾ*); this description may refer to the Larger Magellanic Cloud (Nubecula Maior) which is better visible than the Smaller one. Later, the Arabic navigators of the Indian Ocean, Aḥmad b. Mādjid (d. *ca.* 1500) and Sulaymān al-Mahrī (1st half 16th cent.), knew and described the Magellanic Clouds (*al-saḥābatān*) in their writings. Ibn Mādjid even specified (in his poem *al-Sufāliyya*) that one of them is clearly visible (*bayyina li 'l-ᶜayn*, i.e. the Larger Magellanic Cloud) and the other appears weak (*ṭamsāʾ*, i.e. the Smaller Magellanic Cloud); cf. I. Khoury, ed., *Sulayman al-Mahri's works*, iii, Damascus 1393/1972, 302. The assumption of L. Massignon that the asterism *al-baḳar* "the Cows", mentioned by al-Ṣūfī (cf. Kunitzsch [2], nos. 59 and 23), was identical with the Magellanic Clouds was rightly refuted by W. Petri, in *Die Sterne*, xxxviii (1962), 74-7.

b. *Comets*. The common Arabic term for a comet is (*kawkab*) *dhū dhanab* or *kawkab al-dhanab* "star with a tail". Also, the Greek term κομῆται was translated as *al-kawākib dhawāt al-dhawāʾib* (Aristotle). According to Greek cosmology, comets were regarded as atmospherical phenomena in the sublunar sphere, see Aristotle, *Fi 'l-samāʾ wa 'l-āthār al-ᶜulwiyya* (Meteorology), ed. A.R. Badawi, Cairo 1961, 15 ff.; *Aristoteles' Meteorologie*, ed. P.L. Schoonheim, Leiden 1978, 70 ff.; Ḥunayn b. Isḥāḳ, *Kompendium der aristotelischen Meteorologie*, ed. H. Daiber, Amsterdam-Oxford 1975, 58 ff.; *Aetius Arabus*, ed. Daiber, Wiesbaden 1980, 168 ff. Little attention was consequently paid to comets by the Islamic astronomers, because for them they were no regular celestial phenomena such as the planets, Sun and Moon and the fixed stars. On the other hand, since they were regarded as bad omens, they were often registered by historians, biographers, etc., and in astrology (cf. already Ptolemy, *Tetrabiblos*, ii, 9 and 13). In the latter category of literature, special subgroups of comets were distinguished according to their apparent forms in the sky and were given various extra names. Some such names were already mentioned by Ptolemy, *Tetrab.*, ii, 9; for more names in Antiquity, cf. *inter alios* Lydus, *De ostentis*, ed. C. Wachsmuth, Leipzig 1897, 28 ff., 35 ff., 165 f. (from Pliny, *Nat. hist.*), 166 f. A pseudepigraphic tradition ascribed a list of ten such names to Aristotle or Apuleius; see further A. Bouché-Leclercq, *L'astrologie grecque*, Paris 1899 (repr. Brussels 1963), 357 ff., esp. 359 n. 1.

For the Islamic area, see Kennedy [2], 311-18 (first published 1957); idem, *Astronomical events from a Persian astrological manuscript*, in *Centaurus* xxiv (1980), 162-77 (with an appendix by O. Gingerich, 178-80). Several of the texts published by L. Thorndike, *Latin treatises on comets between 1238 and 1368 A.D.*, Chicago 1950, reflect Arabic material of this sort.

c. *Shooting Stars*, *Meteors*. Together with comets,

shooting stars were included, in ancient cosmology, among the atmospherical phenomena of the sublunar sphere; see Aristotle, *Fi 'l-samā'*, ed. Badawi, 18 ff.; *Meteorologie*, ed. Schoonheim, 74 ff.; Ḥunayn b. Isḥāḳ, *Kompendium*, *loc. cit.* above; *Aetius Arabus*, *loc. cit.* above. The common Arabic terms for them were *shihāb*, pl. *shuhub*, and *nayzak*, pl. *nayāzik* (of Persian origin); cf. C.A. Nallino, *Raccolta di scritti*, v, Rome 1944, 377-93 (first published in *RSO*, viii [1919-21]). Their quick movement in the sky when falling towards the earth was well known and was described as *inkiḍāḍ*, *inṣibāb*, etc. Shooting stars (*shuhub*) are several times mentioned in the Ḳur'ān (XV, 18; XXXVII, 10; LXVII, 8-9); the implication here is that *djinns* or *shayṭāns* who try to spy on the angels are driven away by throwing *shuhub* at them. This myth (the "Sternschnuppenmythus") afterwards often served as a motif in poetry, cf. Kunitzsch [10], item xxvi, 248 f. with n. 23. The quick motion of the shooting stars was also often used in poetical comparison, especially in the description of animals, cf. Kunitzsch [10], items xxvi, 247 f., and xxvii, 104 with n. 18. In astrology, shooting stars mostly ranged in the same rank with comets as bad omens, cf. Ptolemy, *Tetrab.*, ii, 13; Bouché-Leclercq, *op. cit.*, 362; Pseudo-Ptolemaeus, *Centiloquium*, *apud* Nallino, *loc. cit.*

d. *Novae* or *Supernovae*. The Arabic language, and the Islamic astronomers, had no specific terms for novae. This was quite natural since, according to classical and the subsequent Islamic cosmology, the heavenly bodies—Sun, Moon, the planets and the fixed stars—were not capable of any changes in substance, magnitude or (for the fixed stars) location. Therefore the idea of "new" stars was basically alien to their imagination. If a phenomenon of this kind was really observed, it had to be subsumed under the well-known categories, mainly among the sublunar phenomena such as comets. Authors describing such objects had to use the terms current for other known phenomena. There are two famous supernovae that were reported by Islamic authors: one in A.D. 1006, see Goldstein, *Evidence for a supernova in A.D. 1006*, in *The Astronomical Journal*, lxx (1965), 105-14. The best source here is ʿAlī b. Riḍwān's commentary on Ptolemy's *Tetrabiblos*; in describing the object ʿAlī uses the terms *athar* (lit. "trace") and *nayzak* (properly, "shooting star"; cf. above). Ibn al-Athīr and Ibn al-Djawzī, in reporting the same event, spoke of *kawkab kabīr yushbihu 'l-zuhara*, "a large star similar to Venus" (Goldstein, *loc. cit.*, 107, 113 f.); the anonymous *Annales regum Mauritaniae* describe the object as *nadjm ʿaẓīm* [var. *gharīb*] *min dhawāt al-dhawā'ib*, "a great [var. wondrous] star from among the comets", and further on call it a *nayzak* ("shooting star"; Goldstein, *loc. cit.*, 108, 114). The second supernova was that of A.D. 1054; in mentioning it, Ibn Abī Uṣaybiʿa, *ʿUyūn*, ed. A. Müller, i, 242, 14-15, calls it *al-kawkab al-āthārī*, "the star leaving traces". On the subject, see also T. Velusamy, *Guest stars: historical supernovae and remnants*, in *History of Oriental Astronomy* (*IAU Colloquium 91*), Cambridge 1987, 265-70.

e. *Sunspots*. Ibn al-Ḳifṭī, *Ta'rīkh al-Ḥukamā'*, ed. Lippert, 156, cites from a book by Muḥammad b. Hilāl b. al-Muḥ[as]sin al-Ṣābi' a report copied by the latter from a notice on comets written by Djaʿfar b. al-Muktafī bi'llāh; here it is also reported that on Tuesday, 19 Radjab, in the year 225 (25 May 840), during the caliphate of al-Muʿtaṣim, there appeared in the Sun, near its centre, a black spot (*nukta sawdā'*); the report continues that al-Kindī said that this spot lasted for 91 days. It was taken as a bad omen, and indeed, some time afterwards al-Muʿtaṣim died. The report further says that al-Kindī had also maintained that the spot may have been caused by a passage of Venus in front of the Sun (*kusūf al-zuhara li 'l-shams wa-luṣūḳuhā bihā hādhihi 'l-mudda*).

f. *Paranatellonta*. The paranatellonta are constellations, or portions of constellations, co-ascending or reaching other fundamental points of the sphere together with the decans (i.e. sections of 10 degrees) of the zodiac. The observation of the paranatellonta has belonged to astrological practice since Antiquity. The constellations here used include, besides the classical Greek constellations, a number of exotic, Egyptian and other figures, the so-called *sphaera barbarica*. Texts describing the paranatellonta are known, *inter alia*, from Teukros the Babylonian (perhaps 1st cent. A.D.), in Arabic Tīnkalūs, or Tankalūshā al-Bābilī. An Arabic version of the paranatellonta for the 36 decans of the zodiac was inserted by Abū Maʿshar in his astrological *Kitāb al-Mudkhal al-kabīr*, Book vi, ch. 1. The text was edited by K. Dyroff as Appendix vi, *apud* F. Boll, *Sphaera*, Leipzig 1903, 482-539. Abū Maʿshar gives as the epoch for the positions of the constellations in his text the year 1160 Seleucid era = Oct. 848-Sept. 849. For each decan (here called *wadjh*) Abū Maʿshar registers in a first section the paranatellonta (*ṣuwar*) according to the "Persians, Chaldaeans and Egyptians". The ascription to the Persians is correct insofar as Abū Maʿshar used a Persian translation from a Greek redaction of Teukros' text probably dating from A.D. 542 and afterwards converted into new Persian (cf. Boll, *op. cit.*, 416; see also Sezgin, *GAS*, vii, 71 ff.). In a second section there follows the description of the paranatellonta according to the Indians. As Boll has shown, what there is described in this section are, however, not the paranatellonta, but rather the figures symbolising the decans themselves in Indian tradition (cf. Boll, 414 f.). The third section describes the paranatellonta formed from the 48 classical Ptolemaic constellations. Through Latin translations of Abū Maʿshar's work and through other channels, the paranatellonta and their nomenclature became of considerable influence in mediaeval and Renaissance Western astrological speculation (see the survey in Boll, 419 ff.). The astrologer Ibn Hibintā also included a description of the paranatellonta in his compilation *al-Mughnī* which, according to Sezgin, *GAS*, vii, 71 f., offers—at least in parts—a better text than Abū Maʿshar.

g. *Modern nomenclature of objects on the Moon, the planets and their satellites*. A last echo of the grandeur of the mediaeval Islamic astronomers is found in the modern nomenclature of features on the surfaces of the Moon, the planets and their satellites. In his map of the Moon (1651), Giovanni Baptista Riccioli introduced as names for the craters on her visible side the names of famous astronomers and scientists from various nations and times, a nomenclature which became standard until now in international astronomy. Among them there are the names of thirteen personalities of outstanding fame in astronomy and the science from the Islamic Middle Ages (two of them were added in 1837 by J.H. Mädler). All these names are spelled in their Latinised form as introduced and vulgarised in the West through the translations of the 12th century in Spain; examples are *Albategnius* [al-Battānī], *Alfraganus* [al-Farghānī], *Alhazen* [al-Ḥasan, Ibn al-Haytham], *Almanon* [the ʿAbbāsid caliph al-Ma'mūn, famous as a patron of the translations from Greek into Arabic and of the sciences generally], *Azophi* [al-Ṣūfī], etc.; for details, see Mohd. A.R. Khan, *Names of thirteen Muslim astronomers given to some natural features of the Moon*, in *IC*, xxvii (1953), 78-85. In recent times, after the exploration of the far side of the Moon, this kind of historical nomenclature has been continued. Among the names set up here—and which are approved of by the International Astronomical Union—there are five more of Islamic scientists: *Abul Wáfa* [Abu 'l-Wafā'], *al-Biruni* [al-Bīrūnī], *Avicenna* [Ibn Sīnā], *Ibn Yunus* [Ibn Yūnus] and *Omar Khayyam* [ʿUmar K̲h̲ayyām]. With the exploration of the planets and their satellites by spacecraft, the naming of objects on their surfaces continues and will honour many more of the astronomers and scientists of Islamic civilisation.

At the end of this article, it should be mentioned that the textual tradition of the astronomical and astrological literature in the Islamic area was accompanied by a rich tradition of illustrations. In purely astronomical texts we find—beside the tables—the geometrical and other diagrams illustrating the various technical demonstrations and—in al-Ṣūfī's *Book on the Constellations* and in his imitators such as al-Ḳazwīnī in the *ʿAd̲j̲āʾib al-mak̲h̲lūḳāt* or S̲h̲ahmardān in the *Rawḍat al-munad̲j̲d̲j̲imīn*—drawings of the constellations. In astrology, moreover, there are illustrations of the planets, the decans, the zodiacal signs, the paranatellonta and other items. This rich tradition was continued, together with the translations of texts, in the West where illustrations inspired by the Arabic manuscripts are found in innumerable manuscripts and many early printed editions of the 15th to the 17th centuries.

Final hints: for details on the seasonal asterisms of the old Arabs, see AL-ANWĀʾ; for the Poles, see AL-ḲUṬB; for the Milky Way, see AL-MAD̲J̲ARRA; for the lunar mansions, see AL-MANĀZIL; and for the zodiac, see MINṬAḲAT AL-BURŪD̲J̲.

Bibliography (in addition to the works cited directly in the article): 1. Arabic sources: Bīrūnī, *Tafhīm*, facs. ed. and tr. R.R. Wright, London 1934; Ibn al-Ṣalāḥ, *Zur Kritik der Koordinatenüberlieferung im Sternkatalog des Almagest* (*Fī sabab al-k̲h̲aṭaʾ wa 'l-taṣḥīf al-ʿāriḍayn fī d̲j̲adāwil al-maḳālatayn al-sābiʿa wa 'l-t̲h̲āmina min Kitāb al-mad̲j̲asṭī wa-taṣḥīḥ mā amkana taṣḥīḥuhu min d̲h̲ālika*), ed. and tr. P. Kunitzsch, Göttingen 1975; Ptolemy, *Almagest*, Star Catalogue: see below, Kunitzsch [11]. 2. Modern studies: M. Almagro *et alii*, *Qusayr ʿAmra. Residencia y baños omeyas en el desierto de Jordania*, Madrid 1975; L. Bazin, *Über die Sternkunde in alttürkischer Zeit*, in *Akademie d. Wiss. Mainz, Abh., Geistes- u. Sozialwiss. Kl.*, Jahrg. 1963, Nr. 5; Beer [1]: A. Beer, *The astronomical significance of the Zodiac of Quṣayr ʿAmra*, in K.A.C. Creswell, *Early Muslim architecture*, i, Oxford 1932, 296-303; Beer [2]: idem, *Astronomical datings of works of art*, in *Vistas in Astronomy*, ix (1967), 177-87 (with an addition by W. Hartner, at 225); J.L. Berggren, *Al-Bīrūnī on plane maps of the Sphere*, in *Journal for the History of Arabic Science*, vi (1982), 47-112; E. Bernus-E. ag-Sidiyene, *Étoiles et constellations chez les nomades*, in *Awal*, v (1989), 141-153; M. Comes, *Ecuatorios andalusíes, Ibn al-Samḥ, al-Zarqālluh y Abū-l-Ṣalt*, Barcelona 1991; Eilers [1]: W. Eilers, *Stern-Planet-Regenbogen. Zur Nomenklatur der orientalischen Himmelskunde*, in *Der Orient in der Forschung. Festschrift Otto Spies*, Wiesbaden 1967, 92-146; Eilers [2]: idem, *Zur Semasiologie der Himmelskunde*, in *Akten des VII. Kongresses für Arabistik und Islamwissenschaft*, Göttingen 1976, 115-19; Eilers [3]: idem, *Sinn und Herkunft der Planetennamen*, in *Bayerische Akademie d. Wiss., Phil.-hist. Kl., Sitzungsberichte*, Jahrg. 1975, Heft 5; L.P. Elwell-Sutton, *The Horoscope of*

Asadullāh Mīrzā, Leiden 1977; J. Evans, *On the origin of the Ptolemaic star catalogue: Part 1*, in *Journal for the History of Astronomy*, xviii (1987), 155-72; J. Henninger, *Über Sternkunde und Sternkult in Nord- und Zentralarabien*, in idem, *Arabica sacra*, Freiburg (Switzerland)—Göttingen 1981, 448-517 (first published in 1954); W. Hübner, *Die Eigenschaften der Tierkreiszeichen in der Antike*, Wiesbaden 1982; L. Ideler, *Untersuchungen über den Ursprung und die Bedeutung der Sternnamen*, Berlin 1809; Kennedy [1]: E.S. Kennedy, *A survey of Islamic astronomical tables*, in *Trans. Amer. Philos. Society*, N.S. xlvi (1956), 123-77 (repr. 1984); Kennedy [2]: idem, *Studies in the Islamic exact sciences*, Beirut 1983; E.B. Knobel, *Ulugh Beg's catalogue of stars*, Washington 1917; Kunitzsch [1]: P. Kunitzsch, *Arabische Sternnamen in Europa*, Wiesbaden 1959; Kunitzsch [2]: idem, *Untersuchungen zur Sternnomenklatur der Araber*, Wiesbaden 1961; Kunitzsch [3]: idem, *Typen von Sternverzeichnissen in astronomischen Handschriften des zehnten bis vierzehnten Jahrhunderts*, Wiesbaden 1966; Kunitzsch [4]: idem, *Die Planetennamen im "Parzival"*, in *Zeitschrift für deutsche Sprache*, xxv (1969), 169-74; Kunitzsch [5]: idem, *Der Almagest. Die Syntaxis Mathematica des Claudius Ptolemäus in arabisch-lateinischer Überlieferung*, Wiesbaden 1974; Kunitzsch [6]: idem, *Eine bilingue arabisch-lateinische Lostafel*, in *Revue d'histoire des textes*, vi (1976), 267-304; Kunitzsch [7]: idem, *Über ein anwāʾ-Tradition mit bisher unbekannten Sternnamen*, in *Bayerische Akademie d. Wiss., Phil.-hist. Kl., Sitzungsberichte*, Jahrg. 1983, Heft 5; Kunitzsch [8]: idem, *Remarks on possible relations between ancient Arabia and the neighbouring civilizations, as found in some old star names*, in *Studies in the history of Arabia*, ii, *Pre-Islamic Arabia*, Riyāḍ 1984, 201-5; Kunitzsch [9]: idem, *A medieval reference to the Andromeda Nebula*, in *The ESO Messenger*, no. 49 (Sept. 1987), 42 f.; Kunitzsch [10]: idem, *The Arabs and the stars*, Northampton 1989; Kunitzsch [11]: *Claudius Ptolemäus, Der Sternkatalog des Almagest. Die arabisch-mittelalterliche Tradition*, i, *Die arabischen Übersetzungen*, ed. and tr. Kunitzsch, Wiesbaden 1986; Kunitzsch [12]: idem, *Al-Ṣūfī and the astrolabe stars*, in *Zeitschrift für Geschichte der Arabisch-Islamischen Wissenschaften*, vi (1990), 151-66; Kunitzsch [13]: idem, *The chapter on the fixed stars in Zarādusht's Kitāb al-mawālīd*, in *ibid.*, viii (1992); P. Kunitzsch and T. Smart, *Short guide to modern star names and their derivations*, Wiesbaden 1986; P. Kunitzsch and M. Ullmann, *Die Plejaden in den Vergleichen der arabischen Dichtung*, in *Bayerische Akademie d. Wiss., Phil.-hist. Kl., Sitzungsberichte*, Jahrg. 1992; B.F. Lutz, *Das Buch 'Alfadol', Untersuchung und Ausgabe nach der Wiener Handschrift 2804*, Ph. diss. Heidelberg 1967, unpubl.; Mercier [1]: R. Mercier, *Studies in the medieval conception of precession*, in *Archives internationales d'histoire des sciences*, xxvi (1976), 197-220, xxvii (1977), 33-71; Mercier [2]: idem, *Astronomical tables in the twelfth century*, in *Adelard of Bath, an English scientist and Arabist of the early twelfth century*, London 1987, 87-118; L. Richter-Bernburg, *Al-Bīrūnī's Maqāla fī tasṭīḥ al-ṣuwar...*, in *JHAS*, vi (1982), 113-22; J.-P. Roux, *Les astres chez les Turcs et les Mongols*, in *RHR*, cxcv (1979), 153-92; E. Savage-Smith, *Islamicate celestial globes. Their history, construction, and use*, Washington D.C. 1985; F. Saxl, *The zodiac of Quṣayr ʿAmra*, in Creswell, *Early Muslim architecture*, i, 289-95; A. Scherer, *Gestirnnamen bei den indogermanischen Völkern*, Heidelberg 1953; Sezgin, *GAS*; M. Shevchenko, *An analysis of errors in the star catalogues of Ptolemy and Ulugh Beg*, in *JHA*, xxi (1990), 187-201; Toomer [1]: G.J. Toomer, *A survey of the Toledan Tables*, in *Osiris*, xv (1968), 5-174; Toomer [2]: idem, *Ptolemy's Almagest* (tr.), London and New York, etc. 1984; M. Ullmann, *Die Natur- und Geheimwissenschaften im Islam*, Leiden 1972; D.M. Varisco, *The origin of the* anwāʾ *in Arab tradition*, in *SI*, xxiv (1991), 5-28 (first draft printed, without corrections, in *JHAS*, ix [1991], 79-100); Wetzstein: *Die Königslose. J.G. Wetzsteins freie Nachdichtung eines arabischen Losbuches*, ed. G. Weil, Berlin-Leipzig 1929; *WKAS* = *Wörterbuch der Klassischen Arabischen Sprache*, i-, Wiesbaden 1973-(1983-). (P. KUNITZSCH)

In East Africa.

The Swahili people living along the East Coast of Africa between Mogadishu and Mozambique have a long tradition of sailing the Indian Ocean, to fish and to trade. Thus, from the Middle Ages, they have been familiar with the major stars and constellations of the tropical region as well as with the planets and their movements. Some of this vast knowledge of the Swahili navigators has been written down in manuscripts in Swahili in Arabic script. Some of these have survived and are now in the University Library, Dar es Salaam. In Swahili this science is called *elimu ya nujumu* or *elimu ya nyota* "knowledge of the stars", to be distinguished from *tanjimu* "astrology". So far, 105 Swahili names for planets, stars and constellations have been identified; the majority are adapted from Arabic. Native Swahili (i.e. Bantu) words are the sun *jua*, the moon *mwezi* and the Milky Way, *Njia Nyeupe* "the white path", also called *Mkokoto wa kondoo wa Sumaili* "the path along which Ismail's sheep was dragged", referring to the tale of the ram which God sent to replace Ismāʿīl as a sacrifice (Ḳurʾān, XXXVII, 107), an event still celebrated by Swahili Muslims. *Kilimio* "the Pleiades", lit. "What one cultivates by", is the Bantu-Swahili name; this constellation was well-known in pre-Islamic times because its appearance marks the moment when the rains should begin and so, the moment for the planting of millet.

A few of the star names are of Persian origin, e.g. *shahini* "royal white falcon" (Alshain, Beta Aquilae); *zanu* "knee" (Rukbat, Alpha Sagittarii); *bahu* "shoulder" (Gamma Orionis).

Most curious is the fact that the Swahili people have a solar calendar based on the Persian model; it is not known how, or when, this calendar came to be adopted by the Swahili. The New Year is called *nauruzi*, *noruzi*, or *nairuzi* (the latter form of this Persian word being the Indian alternant, though the Hindi dictionary gives *nauroj* for the Parsi New Year). This date falls when the sun enters the sign of Aries, the Ram (Swahili *Hamali*) on the 21st or 22nd of March [see further, NAWRŪZ. 2. In East Africa]. However, this calendar is now replaced by the Islamic lunar calendar, which in turn is regarded with less favour than the European (*Kizungu*) calendar since the latter permits a fairly accurate prediction of the start of the two rainy seasons.

Several other astronomical terms are also adapted from Arabic, e.g. the word for a comet, *shihabu* or *shuhubu*, also *nyota msafiri* "travelling star"; *ghurubu* "descent" and *shuruki* "ascent", though for the former *mshuko* is also used. The word for conjunction is *uungano* (Ar. *iḳtirān*); opposition is *uelekeano* (Ar. *muḳābala*, *muwādjaha*).

The most-watched heavenly body is the new moon, *hilali*, *mwezi mpya*, whose appearance is eagerly awaited on the last evening of Ramadhani. Loud cheers greet its appearance.

Swahili astrologers concentrate first and foremost on the signs of the Zodiac, *Buruji za Falaki*, whose names are all from Arabic:

Hamali,	Aries	*Mizani*,	Libra
Thauri,	Taurus	*Akarabu*,	Scorpio
Jauza,	Gemini	*Kausi*,	Sagittarius
Saratani,	Cancer	*Jadi*,	Capricornis
Asadi,	Leo	*Dalu*,	Aquarius
Sumbula,	Virgo	*Hutu*,	Pisces

Each sign creates a particular character in the person who was born under it, according to the Swahili *munajimu* or astrologer.

The Swahili names of the Planets are: Mercury, *Utaridi*; Venus, *Zuhura*; Mars, *Mirihi*; Jupiter, *Mushitari*; and Saturn, *Zohali*.

Bibliography: C. Velten, *Sitten und Gebräuche der Suaheli*, Göttingen 1903; G. Ferrand, *Introduction à l'astronomie nautique arabe*, Paris 1928; J. Knappert, *List of names for stars and constellations*, in *Swahili*, xxxv/1 (Dar es Salaam, March 1965); J.W.T. Allen, *The customs of the Swahili people, the Desturi za waswahili of Mtoro Bin Mwinyi Bakari*, Berkeley and Los Angeles 1981; R.B. Serjeant, *Hadramaut to Zanzibar: the Pilot Poem of the Nākhudā Saʿīd Bā Ṭāyiʾ of A.S. Al-Ḥāmī*, in *Paideuma*, xxviii (1982), 109-27, with bibl.; Knappert, *The Swahili names of stars, planets and constellations*, unpubl. (J. KNAPPERT)

NUDJŪM (AḤKĀM AL-), "decrees of the stars", expression denoting astrology [see also MUNADJDJIM].

Astrology comprises two branches: natural astrology, consisting in the observation of the influences of the stars on the natural elements, and judicial astrology, consisting in the observation of the influences of the stars on human destiny. The scientific term which describes them is Ptolemaism (derived from the astrological work of Ptolemy, entitled Κλαυδίου Πτολεμαίου τῶν πρὸς Σύρον ἀποτελεσματικῶν, ed. F. Boll and Ae. Boer, in *Bibliotheca Teubneriana*, Leipzig 1940, translated into Arabic under the title of *K. al-Arbaʿa* (= *Tetrabiblos*). With the *Centiloquium*, translated into Arabic as *K. al-Thamara* (= καρπός), which, being erroneously attributed to Ptolemy (cf. T. Fahd, *La divination arabe*, 233), is regarded by the Arabs as constituting the fifth book of the aforementioned, this work forms the basis of Arab astrology (cf. *Ptolemy's Tetrabiblos or Quadripartite being five books on the influence of the stars, newly translated into English from the Greek paraphrase of Proclus with notes..., followed by the Centiloquy*, translation by J.M. Ashmand, London 1822, 272 pp.; on the two works, see F. Sezgin, *GAS*, vii, 41 ff.).

According to Ibn Khaldūn, *Muḳaddima*, ii, 185-202/217-37, and Ḥadjdjī Khalīfa, *Kashf*, vi, 306 ff., the science of astrology has the object of drawing from the cyclical and permanent movements of the celestial bodies indications which have a bearing on this world of change and corruption. It comprises three parts: *mathematica* (*ḥisābiyyāt*), *physica* (*ṭabīʿiyyāt*) and *fantasmagorica* (*wahmiyyāt*). The first two are the ancestors of astrometry and astrophysics and constitute astronomy (*ʿilm al-hayʾa* [*q.v.*]), a science which has a merely descriptive role, while that of astrology is considerably more diverse. Astrology assumes a knowledge of astronomy, although it is probably anterior to it.

Under the heading of natural astrology, numerous procedures exist. Two of these are well known: *ʿilm al-anwāʾ* denotes the knowledge of the periods defined by the heliacal rising and the acronychal setting of certain stars (see ANWĀʾ, also Sezgin, *GAS*, vii, 336 ff., and Fahd, *Divination*², 412-17). The art of inspecting the sky to detect any signs of rain was known in Oriental and Greco-Roman Antiquity (cf. *ibid.*, 407-8). The pre-Islamic Arabs practised it; on account of its association with the astral cult, it was denounced by the Prophet (al-Bukhārī, i, 136).

More important is the art of drawing indications (*dalāʾil*) from the totality of atmospherical phenomena; these indications are gathered together in books bearing the title *malḥama*. The best known is that attributed to the Prophet Daniel (see MALĀḤIM, and *Divination*, 408-12).

This literary genre comprises a large number of astrological collections and agricultural almanacs, bringing together all the knowledge accumulated over the centuries in the region of the Near and Middle East, knowledge drawn from Arabic translation and adaptation of Sanskrit, Pahlavi, Greek and Syriac writings. One of these collections (Aya Sofya 2684, 139 fols., *naskhī* of 906/1499, 27.5 × 18 cm) has been described in *Divination*, 488-95. It is divided into three parts: (1) book of conjunctions, concerning relationships between the stars (fols. 1b-105a); (2) meteorological divination according to Daniel (fols. 106b-117a); and (3) the heliacal rising of Sirius according to Hermes (fols. 117-132). In an appendix, there is a compilation of indications drawn from the occasion of Nawrūz [*q.v.*], of the Coptic month of Ṭawba and the festival of Easter (fols. 137a-139b). For agricultural almanacs, see Fahd, *Le calendrier des travaux agricoles d'après* al-Filāḥa al-nabaṭiyya, in *Orientalia Hispanica* (*Mélanges Pareja*), i, Leiden 1974, 245-72; Sezgin, *GAS*, vii, 306 ff. on astrometeorology.

Since the articles ANWĀʾ and MALĀḤIM cover the subject of natural astrology in sufficient depth, the topic of judicial astrology may now be addressed; this too has been dealt with in a number of articles, in particular DJAFR, ḤURŪF and KHAṬṬ, which are processes of divination in which astrology plays an important role.

Judicial astrology is applied in two important areas of human life: genethlialogy (*mawālīd*) and hemerology (*ikhtiyārāt*), areas in which great interest was taken in the mediaeval Arab and Islamic world. A rich corpus of literature on these subjects is available.

I. *Genethlialogy*. This is the art of deducing portents from the position of the stars at the time of birth, an art already practised in Assyro-Babylonian times (cf. Ch. Fossey, *Présages tirés des naissances*, in *Babyloniaca*, v, Paris 1914; L. Dennefeld, *Babylonisch-assyrische Geburtsomina*, in *Assyriologische Bibliothek*, xxii, Leipzig 1914; B. Meissner, *Über Genethialogie bei den Babyloniern*, in *Klio*, xix [1925], 432-4).

The ancient Arabs deduced portents from signs and events observed at the time of birth, but without explicit reference to the stars; these tended rather to be omens relating to *faʾl* or to *djafr* [*q.vv.*]. Examples are to be found in *Divination*, 480-1. Genethlialogy was born in the ʿAbbāsid period under Persian influence; in this period, the practice of drawing the horoscope of the new-born became an established custom.

But the literature which has survived attributes the origin of this art to Hermes and Ptolemy. An anonymous manuscript of Aya Sofya (2704, fols. 27a-43a and 44a-60b, *naskhī*, undated, 20 × 14 cm) contains two opuscules entitled *K. Mawālīd al-ridjāl* and *K. Mawālīd al-nisāʾ ʿalā raʾy Hirmis wa-Baṭlamyūs* (on the numerous writings attributed to them in Arabic astrological literature, see Sezgin, *GAS*, vii, 41 ff., 50 ff.; cf. *Hermetis philosophi de revelationibus nativitatum*, ed. H. Wolf, Basel 1559; F. Boll, *Eine arabisch-byzantinische Quelle des Dialogs Hermippos*, in *SB Heidelberger Akad.* [1912], no. 18, ch. viii; *Taḥwīl sinī 'l-mawālīd li-Abī Maʿshar*, ed. C. Bezold, 23-5, text, and 8-12, German tr.).

A third source was known and used by the Arab astrologers, this being the Ἀνθολογίαι of Vettius Valens, an eminent astrologer of the period of Hadrian and Antoninus Pius; this work was translated into Pahlavi under the title of *Vizīdhak* (anthology), annotated by Buzurdjmihr, a courtier of Kisrā Anūshirwān (531-78), to whom it is attributed, and translated into Arabic as the *K. al-Mawālīd* (see Nallino, *Raccolta*, v, 238 ff.; Sezgin, *GAS*, vii, 38 ff.). The same title is also attributed to a Babylonian astrologer, Teukros, known to the Arabs as Tankalūsha, who lived at the beginning of the 1st century A.D. and who is the author of an astrological work, called Περὶ τῶν παρατελλόντων, translated into Pahlavi and thence into Arabic in the 2nd or 3rd/ 8th or 9th century as *K. al-Mawālīd ʿalā 'l-wudjūh wa 'l-ḥudūd*, used by Abū Maʿshar in his *K. al-Mudkhal al-kabīr*, according to an extract made by Rhetorios (6th century A.D.). The Arabic text was published and translated into German by K. Dyroff and F. Boll, *Sphaera*, Leipzig 1903 (repr. Hildesheim 1967), 482-539 (cf. Sezgin, *GAS*, vii, 11 ff., 71-3, 80-1; Nallino, *Raccolta*, v, 246 ff.; idem, *Tracce di opere greche giunte agli arabi per trafila pehlevica*, in *ʿAjab-náma, E.G. Browne Festschrift*, Cambridge 1922, 345-63; AL-NUDJŪM. III. f.).

A fourth source in Pahlavi was used by the Arab astrologers: this is the *K. Zarādusht fi 'l-nudjūm wa-taʾthīrātihā wa 'l-ḥukm ʿalā 'l-mawālīd*. On the Arabic writings attributed to Zarathustra, D. Pingree (quoted by Sezgin, *GAS*, vii, 84) writes: "Thus, as the original Zaradusht text, having a Hellenic origin, was revised in Sassanian Iran in about 550 and then expanded with material from the Pahlavi Dorotheos in about 650, so the latter was revised in about 400, when it was expanded with material both from the Pahlavi Valens and from a Pahlavi translation of a Sanscrit text" (*Māshāʾallāh: some Sassanian and Syriac sources*, in *Essays on Islamic philosophy and science*, New York 1975, 5-14, cf. 8; V. Stegemann, *Astrologische Zarathoustra—Fragmente bei den arabischen Astrologen Abū 'l-Ḥasan ʿAlī b. Abī 'r-Ridjāl* (*11. Jh.*), in *Orientalia*, N.S., vi [1937], 317-36).

From the Sanskrit, al-Bīrūnī (*Taḥkīk mā li 'l-Hind*, 122 ff.) translated the *K. al-Mawālīd al-ṣaghīr* (*ibid.*, 122) of Varāhamihira, identified by D. Pingree (*Astronomy and astrology in India and Iran*, in *Isis*, liv [1963], 234) with the *Laghujātaka*, and cited the *K. al-Mawālīd al-kabīr* by the same author, as well as a *K. al-Mawālīd* by Kalan Buram al-Malik (= Kaljana-Varnan). A *K. al-Mawālīd* is also attributed to Kanaka, astrologer at the court of Hārūn al-Rashīd (ms. Çorum 3001/5, fols. 156-159a, 11th/17th century; for the Pahlavi and Sanskrit writings, see Sezgin, vii, 68-97).

The first Arab astrologer to take an interest in genethlialogy is the eminent Jewish scholar Māshāʾallāh (d. *ca.* 200/815 [*q.v.*]). Two works bear his name: *K. al-Mawālīd*, where the topics addressed are as follows: (1) knowledge of the beginning of the formation of the foetus and the observation of its stages before birth, (2) knowledge of the position of the heliacal star at the moment of birth, (3) education, (4) knowledge of the age by means of *al-hīlādj* (the *alhyleg* of the Europeans), its positions and those of the stars which are responsible for it, and (5) the form of the body, its external appearance and temperament. This work is often quoted by Arab astrologers dealing with this question. It has been the subject of two Latin versions (cf. L. Thorndike, *The Latin translations of astrological works by Messahala*, in *Osiris*, xii [1956], 49-72; E.S. Kennedy and D. Pingree, *The Astrological History of Māshā'allāh*, Cambridge, Mass. 1971).

Ibn al-Nadīm mentions a *K. al-Mawālīd al-kabīr* by the same author, comprising 14 chapters, which is known only from its Latin translation, made by Hugo de Santalla, with the title *Libellus de navitatibus 14 distinctus capitulis* (Oxford, Bodl. Savile 15, 72 fols.). A *K. Taḥwīl sinī 'l-mawālīd*, quoted by Ibn al-Nadīm, is known only from a Latin manuscript (B.N. Paris, Latin 7324, fols. 1-24) bearing the title *De revolutionibus nativitatum*, a title also attributed to Abū Maʿshar, translated from the Greek according to F.J. Carmody (*Arabic astronomical and astrological sciences in Latin translation. A critical bibliography*, 95) and edited at Basel in 1559, under the name of Hermes (cf. L. Thorndike and Pearl Kibre, *A catalogue of incipits of medieval scientific writings in Latin*, revised and expanded ed., 1516).

A summary composed by ʿUmar b. al-Farrukhān using writings of Hermes, Dorotheos, Ptolemy and others, bearing the title *K. al-Mawālīd*, exists in mss. (cf. Sezgin, *loc. cit.*, 112). It was translated into Latin, under the title *De nativitatibus*, by Johannes Hispalensis (Carmody, 38-9) and edited by N. Pruckner as an appendix to *Firmicus maternus*, Basel 1551, 118-41.

Other writings bearing the same title, where the same sources are extensively quoted, are attributed to various eminent astrologers, including the following:

Abū ʿAlī al-Khayyāṭ, a disciple of Māshā'allāh, known to Europeans as Albohali. His work was translated into Latin as *De iudiciis nativitatum*, by Plato of Tivoli and Abraham b. Ḥiyya, known as Savasorda (cf. Carmody, 49-50; Sezgin, vii, 120-1, where the titles of the 38 chapters are given). This opuscule was edited by Joachim Heller in 1546 and 1549, and dedicated to Melanchthon (cf. M. Steinschneider, *Europ. Übersetz.*, 46).

Sahl b. Bishr, Zahel to Europeans, famous for his horoscopes; his work comprises two parts, of 8 and 10 chapters (Sezgin, vii, 126).

Abū Bakr al-Ḥasan b. al-Khaṣīb (or al-Khaṣībī), Abubather to Europeans; his work was translated into Latin, as *Liber de nativitatibus*, by Salio (or Solkeen), a canon of Padua, in 1218 (or 1248 or 1244), with the aid of a certain David Albubather, edited in Venice in 1492 and translated into German in the 15th century (cf. Steinschneider, *op. cit.*, 75, no. 107).

The author who brilliantly concludes this series of genethlialogical writings is Abū Maʿshar al-Falakī (d. 272/886 [*q.v.*]), the greatest astrologer of the Arab and Latin Middle Ages. Numerous examples of the genre bear his name: (1) *K. Aḥkām taḥwīl sinī 'l-mawālīd*, a horological work in 9 chapters, preserved in numerous manuscripts (cf. Sezgin, vii, 142). The Arabic text has been edited and partially translated into German by C. Bezold (see above), translated into Greek in the 10th century and edited by D. Pingree, Albumasaris, *De revolutionibus nativitatum*, Leipzig 1968. The editor describes its contents in the *Dictionary of scientific biography*, i, 1970, 37, no. 19. (2) *K. al-mawālīd* (*al-kabīr* and *al-ṣaghīr* according to Ibn al-Nadīm), of which numerous manuscripts exist (Sezgin, 144-5). (3) *K. Aḥkām al-mawālīd* (*ibid.*, 145; D. Pingree, *op. cit.*, 39). (4) *K. Mawālīd al-ridjāl wa 'l-nisā'*, on the subject of the birth of men and of women (several mss. indicated in Sezgin, vii, 145; for the contents, see J.M. Faddegon, *Notice sur un petit traité d'astrologie attribué a Albumasar* (*Abū Maʿshar*) in *JA*, ccxiii [1928], 150-58; D. Pingree, *op. cit.*, 38, no. 29).

With Abū Maʿshar, genethlialogical literature reached its apogee. The following generation confined itself to reproducing and annotating his writings (cf. *Divination*, 482-3).

II. *Hemerology and menology*. It has been observed that genethlialogy is concerned with the fate of individuals and permits the compilation of their horoscope, starting from the date of birth. The *ikhtiyārāt* (καταρχαί, choices) consist rather in establishing the calendar of the auspicious (*saʿd*) and of the inauspicious (*naḥs*). Choice depends upon years, months, days of the week and even hours. "Deciding the moment for action or for abstention, compiling, in terms of this moment, the list of things which may be undertaken with success and those which should be renounced, constituted one of the principal prerogatives of the astrologer who, in the ʿAbbāsid period, became a permanent functionary in the court of the caliph and at conferences of military leaders" (*Divination*, 483; cf. F. Boll, *Sternglaube und Sterndeutung. Die Geschichte und das Wesen der Astrologie*, 3rd ed. by W. Gunkel, Leipzig-Berlin 1926; C.A. Nallino, *Raccolta*, v, 38 ff.). Aḥmad Amīn, quoting al-Aṣmaʿī, states that the choice of *ḳāḍī* and of *imām* in the Umayyad period was made by means of astrological procedures (*Ḍuḥā 'l-Islām*, 27, 28 ff.).

The discernment of auspicious and inauspicious days has existed among many peoples (for the ancient Orient, see R. Labat, *Hémérologies et ménologies d'Assur*, Paris 1939; idem, *Le Calendrier babylonien des travaux, des signes et des mois*, Paris 1965; F. Chabas, *Le calendrier des jours fastes et néfastes de l'année égyptienne* (Papyrus Sallier iv), Paris undated; A. Lods, *Le rôle des oracles dans la nomination du roi, des prêtres et des magistrats chez les Israélites, les Égyptiens et les Grecs*, in *MIFAO*, lvi [1942], 91-100 = *Mélanges Maspero*, i).

The Arabs were aware of this procedure and practised it. Various accounts testify to it (cf. *Divination*, 483 ff. and IKHTIYĀRĀT, of which the current article is the completion). It emerges that it was under Persian influence that astrology acquired respectability in the court of the caliph and among the ruling class. "In order to imitate the Sāsānid kings, the ʿAbbāsid caliphs, who in most cases had Persian tutors (in particular al-Rashīd and al-Ma'mūn), adopted customs which were at odds with the Arab spirit and Islam. This process of adaptation gave rise to the translations from the Pahlavi made by Ibn al-Muḳaffaʿ, essentially comprising manuals for the education of princes (*Fürstenspiegel*), such as *Kalīla wa-Dimna*, the *K. al-Tādj* and the *K. al-Ā'īn*" (*Divination*, 485. On these writings, see F. Gabrieli, *Opera di Ibn al-Muqaffaʿ* in *RSO*, xiii [1932], 197-247; idem, *Etichetta di corte e costumi sasanidi nel* Kitāb aḫlāq al-mulūk *di al-Ǧāḥiẓ*, *ibid.*, xi [1928], 292-305).

According to the *Bāb al-ʿIrāfa*, attributed to al-Djāḥiẓ, "the astrologers had examined the days of the week, judging them and appraising them in the interests of the king. They said, 'Each day has its star (*ṭāliʿ*) which dominates it and its character which this star necessarily confers upon it.' Accordingly, they determined for each day of the week the tasks appropriate to it" (for details, see *Divination*, 485-6).

The auspicious and inauspicious character of days of the week depended on the planets to which they were dedicated. Similarly, the hours of the day were dedicated to the seven planets and characters conferred on them (cf. ms. Konya, Müze Kütüph. 5333, fols. 179a-181b, *naskhī* of 833/1429-30, 28 × 18 cm, *al-Ḳawl ʿalā 'khtiyārāt al-ayyām wa 'l-aʿmāl fīhā min al-khayr wa 'l-sharr*). Various procedures were employed for the arrangement of the material: enumeration of the days of the month with the comment "good" or "bad" for such-and-such a thing (ms. Esat Ef. 3554, *naskhī* of 1088/1677, 19.5 × 14 cm, attributed to Dja^cfar al-Ṣādiḳ), enumeration of actions advisable or inadvisable during the lunar months and the choice of days in any month, with justification (ms. Saray, Revan 1741, fols. 98a-107a, *naskhī*, 20 × 15 cm). More complex is the procedure described in the Köprülü ms. Fazıl Paşa 164, fols. 1-54b ((*naskhī* of 871/1466-7, 18 × 14 cm) arranged in the following manner: (1) Explanation of the method of application (fols. 1b ff.); (2) double column of actions; (3) circle of months; (4) thirty columns relating to the month and to the rubrics; (5) thirty rubrics: names of prophets, questions, positions of the moon, judgment according to the lunar houses; and (6) the lunar houses (for details, see *Divination*, 487).

The majority of Arab astrologers have left behind treatises or chapters relating to hemerology and menology. The following are the best known:

ᶜUmar b. al-Farrukhān al-Ṭabarī, one of the earliest Arab astrologers, *K. al-Ikhtiyārāt* (ms. Alexandria, Balad 2033-d/2, fols. 42a-52b, 6th/12th century).

Sahl b. Bishr, Zahel to the Europeans, *K. al-Ikhtiyārāt ᶜalā 'l-buyūt al-ithnay ᶜashar*, in 12 chapters corresponding to the number and names of the signs of the Zodiac (ms. Nuruosmaniye 2785/1, fols. 1-11b, 6th/12th century; Escurial, 919/2, fols. 36-44, 8th/14th century), translated into Latin as *De electionibus*, ed. Venice in 1493 and Basel in 1551, by Nicolas Pruckner, as an appendix to *Firmicus maternus*, 102-14 (Thorndike, *Cat.*, 985, 988; Carmody, 41), a dubious attribution according to Sezgin (*GAS*, vii, 127). Also attributed to him is *Fatidica* or *Fastitica pronostica*, translated by Hermann of Carinthia (Thorndike, 1424; Carmody, 44-5). In his *K. al-Awḳāt* (Escurial 919/4, fols. 47-53, 7th/13th century), translated into Latin as *Liber temporum* (Carmody, *op. cit.*), he gives the significations of times in judicial astrology; attributed to him also is *De significatione temporis ad iudicia*, ed. Venice 1493 (Thorndike, *Cat.*, 1411).

Abū Yūsuf Yaᶜḳūb al-Kindī, *Ikhtiyārāt al-ayyām* (ms. Leiden, Or. 199/2, fols. 19-20; cf. E. Wiedemann, *Über einen astrologischen Traktat von Al-Kindî*, in *Archiv für Gesch. d. Naturwiss. und Technik*, iii [1912], 224-6, where the contents are described).

Abū Maᶜshar, to whom three hemerological writings are attributed: *K. al-Ikhtiyārāt*, translated into Latin as *Electiones planetarum* (Carmody, 96); *Ikhtiyārāt al-sāᶜāt*, translated probably as *Flores de electionibus* by John of Seville (Thorndike, 180, 738, 945; Carmody, 97); *al-Ikhtiyārāt fī 'l-aᶜmāl wa 'l-hawāʾidj min umūr al-salāṭīn* (ms. Rabat D 769, fols. 1-73, 567/1171; cat. no. 2571).

ᶜAlī b. Aḥmad al-ᶜImrānī (d. 344/955), Haly Imrani to Europeans, *K. al-Ikhtiyārāt*, translated into Latin by Plato of Tivoli in collaboration with Abraham b. Ḥiyya, known as Savasorda (Thorndike, *Cat.*, 1363, 1007; Carmody, 138) and by John of Seville as *Regule de electionibus* (Thorndike, 1707; Carmody, 139).

Al-Isrāʾīlī, astrologer of al-Ḥākim bi-Amr Allāh (386-411/996-1021), wrote for his master a treatise on *ikhtiyārāt* in the form of 133 aphorisms, translated into Latin as *Liber capitulorum Almansoris*, by Plato of Tivoli (cf. J.-Cl. Vadet, *Les aphorismes latins d'Almansor. Essai d'interprétation*, in *Annales Islamologiques*, v [1963], 31-130).

Abū Saᶜīd al-Sidjzī, *K. al-Ikhtiyārāt*, in three lengthy sections (for the titles see Sezgin, *GAS*, vii, 179).

Abū 'l-Ḥasan Ibn ᶜAlī b. Abi 'l-Ridjāl, known to Europeans as Haly Aben Ragel or Abenragel or even Albohazan, author of popular astrological writings widely circulated in the East and the West. Attributed to him is a *De electionibus* in 103 chapters (ms. Vatican 4082, fols. 161-84; Thorndike, *Cat.*, 734; on his work, see V. Stegemann, *Beiträge zur Geschichte der Astrologie I*, Heidelberg 1935).

Fakhr al-Dīn al-Rāzī, *al-Ikhtiyārāt al-ᶜalāʾiyya*, in 9 chapters, translated by the author from Persian into Arabic (cf. ref. in M. Ullmann, *Die Natur- und Geheimwissenschaften*, 340).

As has been seen, the two main areas of judicial astrology considered in this article were widely known and practised in the mediaeval East and West. The principles which govern them derive from the observation and interpretation of the connections and interactions of stars. Knowledge of these connections constitutes the essence of astrological divination, of theurgy and of the talismanic art (cf. on this topic, Fahd's contribution to vol. vii of *Sources Orientales*, entitled *Le monde du sorcier en Islam*, Paris 1966, 157-204; summarised in *Encyclopedia of Religion*, art. *Magic*; reprinted in L.E. Sullivan (ed.), *Hidden truths. Magic, alchemy and the occult*, New York-London 1989, 122-30).

Bibliography: Numerous references to Arab astrological literature are to be found in vol. vii of Sezgin's *GAS*, Leiden 1979, 3-199 and in M. Ullmann's *Die Natur- und Geheimwissenschaften in Islam*, Leiden 1972, 271-358 (Handbuch d. Orientalistik, i, Abt., Erg. vi, 2. Absch.); see also C. Nallino, *Astrologia e astronomia presso i Musulmani*, summarised in J. Hastings (ed.), *ERE*, xii, 88-101, and published in full in *Raccolta di scritti editi e inediti*, v, Rome 1944, 1-41; in addition to historical and scientific information, this work contains an account of the polemics surrounding astrology (19 ff.); T. Fahd, *La divination arabe*², Paris 1987; Mūsā b. Nawbakht, *al-Kitāb al-Kāmil* (*fī asrār al-nudjūm*). *Horoscopos historicos*, ed. and tr. by Ana Labarta, preface by J. Vernet, Madrid-Barcelona 1982; L. Thorndike, *The true place of astrology in the history of sciences*, in *Isis*, xlvi (1955), 273-78; I. Goldziher, *Stellung der alten islamischen Orthodoxie zu den antiken Wissenschaften*, in *Abh. Akad. Pr.* (1915), no. 8; G. Thibaut, *Astronomie, Astrologie und Mathematik*, Strassburg 1899 (*Grundriss der indo-arischen Philologie und Altertumkunde*, 3, 9); V. Stegemann, *Astrologie und Universalgeschichte. Studien und Interpretationen zu den Dionysiaca des Nonnos von Panopolis*, *Stoicheia*, Heft 9; J. Bidez and Fr. Cumont, *Les mages hellénisés. Zoroastre, Ostanès and Hystaspe*, Paris 1938; Bīrūnī, *K. al-Tafhīm li-awāʾil ṣināᶜat al-tandjīm*, ed. from the B.L. London ms. with English tr. by R.R. Wright, London 1934; F.J. Carmody, *Arabic astronomical and astrological sciences in Latin translation. A critical bibliography*, Berkeley and Los Angeles 1956; L. Thorndike and Pearl Kibre, *A Catalogue of incipits of medieval scientific writings in Latin*, 2nd revised and expanded edn., London 1963; D. Pingree, *The Thousands of Abu Maᶜshar*, London 1968 (Studies of the Warburg Institute, 30); F. Rosenthal, *Das Fortleben der Antike im Islam*, Zürich and Stuttgart 1965 (Bibliothek des Morgenlandes). (T. FAHD)

NŪḤ, the Noah of the Bible, is a particularly popular figure in the Ḳurʾān and in Muslim legend. Al-Thaᶜlabī gives 15 virtues by which Nūḥ is distinguished among the prophets. The Bible does not regard Noah as a prophet. In the Ḳurʾān, Nūḥ is the first prophet of punishment, who is followed by Hūd,

Ṣāliḥ, Lūṭ, Shuʿayb and Mūsā. Ibrāhīm is one of his following (*shīʿa*) (XXXVII, 81). He is the perspicuous admonisher (*nadhir mubīn*, XI, 27; LXXI, 2), the *rasūl amīn* "the true messenger of God" (XXVI, 107), the *ʿabd shakūr*, "the grateful servant of God" (XVII, 3). God enters into a covenant with Nūḥ just as with Muḥammad, Ibrāhīm, Mūsā and ʿĪsā (XXXIII, 7). Peace and blessings are promised him (XI, 50). Muḥammad is fond of seeing himself reflected in the earlier prophets. In the case of Nūḥ, the Muslim Ḳurʾān exegetes have already noticed this (see Grünbaum, *Neue Beiträge*, 90). Muḥammad puts into the mouth of Nūḥ things that he would himself like to say and into the mouths of his opponents what he himself has heard from Nūḥ's opponents. Nūḥ is reproached with being only one of the people (X, 72-4). God should rather have sent an angel (XXIII, 24). Nūḥ is wrong (VII, 58), is lying, deceiving (VII, 62), is possessed by *djinn* (LIV, 9), only the lowest join him (XI, 29; XXVI, 111). When Nūḥ replies: "It is grievous to you that I live among you, I seek no reward, my reward is with God (X, 72-4; XI, 31); I do not claim to possess God's treasures, to know his secrets, to be an angel and I cannot say to those whom ye despise, God shall not give you any good" (XI, 31-3), we have here an echo of Muḥammad's defence and embarrassment about many of his followers. The Ḳurʾān pictures events as follows: God sends Nūḥ to the sinful people. Sūra LXXI, which bears his name, gives one of these sermons threatening punishment for which other analogies can be found. The people scorn him. Allah commands him to build an ark by divine inspiration. Then the "chaldron boils" (XI, 42; XXIII, 27). The waters drown everything; only two of every kind of living creature are saved and the believers whom Nūḥ takes into the ark with him. But there were very few who believed. Nūḥ appeals even to his son in vain; the latter takes refuge on a mountain but is drowned. When Nūḥ bids the waters be still, the ark lands on mount Djūdī ([*q.v.*] XI, 27-51). Not only Noah's son but also his wife (with Lūṭ's wife) are sinners (LXVI, 10). From the *Haggada* is developed, as Geiger shows, the following elements of this Ḳurʾānic legend of Nūḥ: 1. Nūḥ appears as a prophet and admonisher; 2. his people laugh at the Ark; 3. his family is punished with hot water (main passages: *Talm. Sanhedrin*, 108a-b; *Gen. Rabba*, xxix-xxxvi).

The post-Ḳurʾānic legend of Nūḥ, as in other cases, fills up the gaps, gives the names of those not mentioned in the Ḳurʾān, makes many links, e.g. connects Nūḥ with Farīdūn of the Persian epic, although it is pointed out that the Magi (Persians) do not know the story of the flood. Nūḥ's wife is called Wāliya and her sin is that she described Nūḥ to his people as *madjnūn*. The names of Nūḥ's sons, Sām, Ḥām and Yāfith are known to Ḳurʾān exegesis from the Bible, but this exegesis also gives the name of Nūḥ's sinful son who perished in the flood, Kanʿān, "whom the Arabs call Yām". The Ḳurʾānic statement that Nūḥ was 950 years of age at the time of the flood (*ṭūfān*) (XXIX, 13, 14) is probably based on Gen. ix. 39, which says Nūḥ lived 950 years in all. Also, it serves as a basis for calculations which make Nūḥ the first *muʿammar*; according to the *Kitāb al-Muʿammarīn* of Abū Ḥātim al-Sidjistānī (ed. Goldziher, in *Abh. zur arab Philologie*, ii), who begins his book with Nūḥ, he lived 1,450 years. Yet in his dying hour he describes his life as a house with two doors through one of which one enters, while he leaves through the other. Muslim legend knows the Biblical story of Nūḥ, his times and his sons, but embellishes it greatly, and in al-Kisāʾī it becomes a romance. From the union of Ḳābil's and Shīth's descendants arises a sinful people which rejects Nūḥ's warnings. He therefore at God's command builds the Ark from trees which he has himself planted. As he is hammering and building the people mock him: "Once a prophet, now a carpenter?", "A ship for the mainland?" The Ark had a head and tail like a cock, a body like a bird (al-Thaʿlabī). How was the Ark built? At the wish of the apostles, Jesus arouses Sām (or Ḥām) b. Nūḥ from the dead and he describes the Ark and its arrangements: in the lower storey were the quadrupeds, in the next the human beings and in the top the birds. Nūḥ brought the ant into the Ark first and the ass last; it was slow because Iblīs was clinging to its tail. Nūḥ called out impatiently: "Come in even if Satan is with thee"; so Iblīs also had to be taken in. The pig arose out of the tail of the elephant and the cat from the lion. How could the ox exist beside the lion, the goat alongside the wolf, or the dove beside the birds of prey? God tamed their instincts. The number of human beings in the Ark varies in legend between seven and eighty. ʿŪdj b. ʿAnaḳ was also saved along with the believers. Ḳābil's race was drowned. Nūḥ also took Adam's body with him, which was used to separate the women from the men, for in the Ark continence was ordered, for man and beast. Only Ḥām transgressed, and for this was punished with a black skin. The whole world was covered with water and only the Ḥaram (in al-Kisāʾī, also the site of the sanctuary in Jerusalem) was spared; the Kaʿba was taken up into heaven and Djibrīl concealed the Black Stone (according to al-Kisāʾī, the stone was snow-white until the Flood). Nūḥ sent out the raven, but finding some carrion it forgot Nūḥ; then he sent the dove, which brought back an olive leaf in its bill and mud on its feet; as a reward it was given its collar and became a domestic bird. On the day of ʿĀshūrāʾ every one came out of the Ark, men and beasts fasted and gave thanks to God.

There are many contacts with the *Haggada*: the (different, it is true) partitioning of the Ark, Nūḥ's anxiety about the animals, Ḥām's sin and punishment (*Sanhedrin*, 108a-b). The story that the giant ʿŌg escaped the Flood is also taken from the *Haggada* [see ʿŪDJ B. ʿANAḲ]. But Muslim legend goes farther than the Bible and Haggada in depicting Muḥammad, who sees himself in Nūḥ.

Bibliography: Principal passages are Ḳurʾān, VII, 57-62; XI, 27-51; XXIII, 23-31; XXVI, 105-22; XXXVII, 73-81; LXXI (whole); Ṭabarī, i, 174-201; Ibn al-Athīr, i, 27-9; Thaʿlabī, *Ḳiṣaṣ al-anbiyāʾ*, Cairo 1325, 34-8; Kisāʾī, *Ḳiṣaṣ al-anbiyāʾ*, ed. J. Eisenberg, i, 85-102, Eng. tr. W.M. Thackston, *The tales of the prophets of al-Kisaʾi*, Boston 1978, 91-109; A. Geiger, *Was hat Mohammed...*, Leipzig 1902^2, 106-11; M. Grünbaum, *Neue Beiträge*, 79-90; J. Horovitz, in *Hebrew Union College Annual*, ii (1925) 151; idem, *Koranische Untersuchungen*, Berlin 1926, 13-18, 22-9, 32-5, 49-51, esp. 46; J. Walker, *Biblical characters in the Koran*, Paisley 1931, 113-21; D. Sidersky, *Les origines des légendes musulmanes*, Paris 1933, 26-7; H. Speyer, *Die biblische Erzählungen im Qoran*, Grafenhainichen *ca.* 1938, 84-115.—On the name Nūḥ: Goldziher, in *ZDMG*, xxiv (1870), 207-11; on Nūḥ as *muʿammar*: Goldziher, *Abhandlungen zur arabischen Philologie*, ii, Leiden 1899, pp. lxxxix and 2. (B. HELLER)

NŪḤ (I) B. NAṢR B. AḤMAD, Sāmānid *amīr* of Transoxania and Khurāsān (331-43/943-54), given after his death the honorific of *al-Amīr al-Shahīd* ("the Praiseworthy").

Continuing the anti-Shīʿī reaction which marked the end of the reign of Nūḥ's father Naṣr [*q.v.*], the early years of the new reign were dominated by the vizierate of the pious Sunnī *faḳīh* Abu 'l-Faḍl Muḥammad Sulamī, but very soon, ominous signs of decline began to appear in the state. There were revolts in the tributary kingdom of Khwārazm [*q.v.*] and in Khurāsān under its governor Abū ʿAlī Čaghānī, whom Nūḥ attempted to replace by the Turkish commander Ibrāhīm b. Sīmdjūr. In 335/947 Abū ʿAlī succeeded in temporarily placing on the throne at Bukhārā Nūḥ's uncle Ibrāhīm b. Aḥmad. Although this putsch collapsed and the *Amīr* now appointed Manṣūr b. Ḳaratigin as governor of Khurāsān, Abū ʿAlī was able to withdraw to his family territories on the upper Oxus [see ČAGHĀNIYĀN] and to preserve a dominant role in the state and in external warfare against the Būyid *amīr* Rukn al-Dawla [*q.v.*] until *Amīr* Nūḥ died in Rabīʿ II 343/August 954.

The costs of quelling internal rebelliousness and of the wars in northern Persia caused a financial crisis during Nūḥ's reign, with the army often going unpaid and the subjects complaining of increased taxation burdens. Hence Nūḥ left to his son and successor ʿAbd al-Malik a divided and disaffected kingdom, whose fortunes no subsequent *amīr*s were able to restore.

Bibliography: The main primary sources are Gardīzī and Ibn al-Athīr, both utilising material from the lost *Taʾrīkh Wulāt Khurāsān* of Sallāmī; and Narshakhī, *Taʾrīkh-i Bukhārā*, tr. Frye, 97-8. Of studies, see Barthold, *Turkestan*, 246-9; R.N. Frye, in *Camb. hist. of Iran*, iv, 151; Erdoğan Mercil, *Sîmcûrîler. II. Ibrâhîm b. Sîmcûr*, in *Tarih Enstitüsü Dergisi*, no. x-xi (1979-80), 91-6. See also SĀMĀNIDS.

(C.E. BOSWORTH)

NŪḤ (II) B. MANṢŪR B. NŪḤ, Sāmānid *amīr* initially in Transoxania and Khurāsān, latterly in the first province only (366-87/977-97), given after his death the honorific *al-Amīr al-Raḍī* ("the Well-pleasing").

The last of his line to enjoy a reign of any significant length, Nūḥ succeeded his father Manṣūr (I) [*q.v.*] at the age of 13, real power being in the hands of his mother and the vizier Abu 'l-Ḥusayn ʿUtbī, the last vizier to the Sāmānids worthy of the title. However, authority in the state fell more and more into the hands of the great military commanders, such as Abu 'l-Ḥasan Sīmdjūrī and his son Abū ʿAlī, Fāʾiḳ Khāṣṣa and Tāsh. Warfare against the Būyids went badly, and only the death in 372/983 of ʿAḍud al-Dawla [*q.v.*] prevented a Būyid invasion of Khurāsān. In the confusion, Abū ʿAlī secretly connived with Bughra Khān Hārūn, chief of the Turkish Ḳarakhānids in the steppes to the north of Transoxania [see ILEK-KHĀNS], to partition the Sāmānid kingdom, with Abū ʿAlī to have the lands south of the Oxus. Bughra Khān entered Bukhārā in 382/992, but soon withdrew. With Khurāsān also out of his control, Nūḥ remained ruler of the Zarafshān valley only, and in 383/993 he called in Sebüktigin [*q.v.*] from Ghazna [see GHAZNAWIDS] against Abū ʿAlī and Fāʾiḳ. Sebüktigin and his son Maḥmūd [*q.v.*] established themselves in the former Sāmānid dominions, now threatened by a further Ḳarakhānid invasion from the north, but in 386/996 Sebüktigin and the Ḳarakhānid Ilig Naṣr made an agreement whereby the latter took over the whole basin of the Syr Darya, whilst Sebüktigin became complete master over Khurāsān. Nūḥ himself died in Radjab 387/July 997, with the final end of Sāmānid rule in Transoxania only two years away.

Bibliography: The main primary sources are ʿUtbī, Gardīzī, Narshakhī, tr. Frye, 99-100, and Ibn al-Athīr. Of studies, see Barthold, *Turkestan*, 252-64; M. Nāẓim, *The life and times of Sulṭān Maḥmūd of Ghazna*, Cambridge 1931, 30-2; R.N. Frye, in *Camb. hist. of Iran*, iv, 154-8; Erdoğan Mercil, *Sîmcûrîler. III*, in *Tarih Dergisi*, no. xxxiii (1980-1), 126-32, *Sîmcûrîler. IV*, in *Belleten*, no. 195 (1986), 547-67, *Sîmcûrîler. V*, in *Tarih Dergisi* (1987-8), 123-38. See also SĀMĀNIDS.

(C.E. BOSWORTH)

NŪḤ B. **MUṢṬAFĀ**, Ottoman theologian and translator, was born in Anatolia but migrated while still quite young to Cairo where he studied all branches of theology and attained a high reputation. He died there in 1070/1659. He wrote a series of theological treatises, some of which are detailed by Brockelmann, II², 407-8, S II, 432. His most important work, however, is his free translation and edition of Shahrastānī's celebrated work on the sects, his *Terdjeme-i Milal we-niḥal* which he prepared at the suggestion of a prominent Cairo citizen named Yūsuf Efendi (cf. Brockelmann, I², 551, S I, 763). It exists in manuscript in Berlin (cf. Pertsch, *Kat.*, 157-8), Gotha (Pertsch, *Kat.*, 76), London (cf. Rieu, *Cat.*, 35-6), Upsala (cf. Tornberg, *Codices*, 213), Vienna (cf. Flügel, *Kat.*, ii, 199) etc., and was printed in Cairo in 1263. On the considerable differences between this Turkish translation and the original Arabic, cf. Rieu in the British Museum Catalogue, 35b. In his *Mémoire sur deux coffrets gnostiques du moyen âge, du Cabinet de M. le Duc de Blacas*, Paris 1832, 28 ff., J. von Hammer gave some extracts from the latter part of the work. He also wrote on it in the *Wiener Jahrbücher*, lxxi, 50, and ci, 4.

In 1150/1741 a certain Yūsuf Efendi wrote a life of Nūḥ b. Muṣṭafā which exists in ms. in Cairo (*Cat.*, vii, 364).

Bibliography: In addition to references in the text, see Muḥibbī, *Khulāṣat al-athar*, Cairo 1868, iv, 458.

(F. BABINGER)

NUḤĀM (A.), substantive of collective type (*nomen unitatis, -a*), denoting in ancient Arabic texts the Greater Flamingo ("flaming one") or phoenicopter (the Φοινικόπτερος "purple-winged" of the Greeks and the *iṣṣūr nūri* "bird of light" of the Akkadians), this being *Phoenicopterus ruber roseus* or *antiquorum* of the order of the Phoenicopteridae (*nuḥāmiyyāt*) which resemble waders with their long legs and palmipeds with their webbed feet. The term *nuḥām*, drawn from the root *n-ḥ-m*, which evokes the notion of growling, was given to this large and graceful bird on account of its discordant cries composed of howls and bellows. The same applies to *mirzam*, another mediaeval name for the flamingo, as the root *r-z-m* also contains the notion of growling.

Among the six Phoenicoperidae classified according to ornithological systems, the Greater Flamingo, the only species known in Arab lands, is present throughout the periphery of the Mediterranean, on the western shores of the Red Sea, in the Persian Gulf and in Kuwait; its chosen habitat is in marshy regions such as the estuaries of the Nile, the Shaṭṭ al-ʿArab, the Shaṭṭ al-Djarīd in Tunisia and the Rhône (Camargue), from which it draws its subsistence, living in large flocks. The southern coasts of Arabia are occasionally visited by the Lesser Flamingo (*Phoenicopterus minor*) which normally inhabits Somalia and Eritrea; it has no specific name in Arabic, being confused with its larger cousin.

Each region of the Arabic language has given the flamingo names belonging to local dialects; thus in Egypt, it is the *basharūsh* (old French "becharu", "bacerux"), which in Tunisia has become *shabrūsh* by metathesis. Also found are the terms *nuḥāf*, *niḥāf*, *surkhāb*, and it is sometimes nicknamed *rahū 'l-mā'* "aquatic crane". For the Muslim bands of crossbow-archers (*rumāt ḳaws al-bunduḳ*) of the Middle Ages, the flamingo counted among the fourteen "obligatory birds" (*ṭuyūr al-wādjib*) required for scoring points in competitions. Hunters also called it *mirzam* and *turundjān*, this last term being the only one which refers to the striking colour of the plumage.

According to Islamic law, consumption of the flesh of the flamingo is permitted; it is said to be, apparently, quite agreeable, not tasting excessively of fish, and according to a *ḥadīth* (related by al-Damīrī but regarded as dubious), the Prophet is said to have eaten it. On the other hand, it is known that the Romans used the tongue of this bird in a number of sophisticated dishes. Gastronomic interest apart, the flamingo was credited with several specific qualities (*khawāṣṣ*) in the therapeutic field; its fat, used as an ointment, was a remedy against hemiplegia (*fālidj*) and maladies of the joints. The same afflictions could also be treated by means of a plaster consisting of a mixture of oil and the paste obtained after the whole body of the bird, including plumage, had been boiled for a long period. Finally, the tongue of the flamingo, dried and soaked in oil, then pounded, produced a medication for the treatment of otitis.

Of the ancient Arab naturalist writers, only al-Damīrī mentions the *nuḥām*, to which he attributes bizarre behaviour, resulting from total ignorance of the ethology of this elusive bird. Thus he says that the female flamingo is fertilised by an oral regurgitation on the part of the male and not by copulation. Once the eggs have been laid on the pyramid of dried mud which serves as a nest, the male comes and covers them with his droppings, and only the warmth of the sun guarantees their incubation. The chicks hatch in an inanimate state, and it is the female who brings them to life, breathing air into their beaks; all of this is pure fable.

In poetry, the only mention of the flamingo is found in the work of the poet Ṣafī al-Dīn al-Ḥillī of the 8th/14th century, who calls it *mirzam*, in a list of the fourteen "obligatory birds" contained in a long *urdjūza* of twenty-nine stanzas each with five hemistiches dedicated to the memory of the caliph al-Nāṣir li-Dīn Allāh (575-622/1180-1225 [*q.v.*]), who reorganised the *futuwwa* of crossbow archery.

Bibliography (in alphabetical order): anon. ms. Istanbul, Ayasofya 3636 (Egypt, 13th-14th centuries A.D.), fol. 118b; B. Al-Lūs (Allouse), *al-Ṭuyūr al-ʿirāḳiyya. Birds of Iraq*, Baghdād 1960, i, 136; A.E. Brehm, *L'homme et les animaux* (*les Oiseaux*), French ed. Z. Gerbe, Paris 1878, ii, 715-20; F.O. Cave and J.D. Macdonald, *Birds of the Sudan*, London 1955, 66; Damīrī, *Ḥayāt al-ḥayawān al-kubrā*, Cairo 1356/1937, ii, 323, 340; R.D. Etchecopar and F. Hue, *Les oiseaux du nord de l'Afrique* (Arabic names by F. Viré), Paris 1964, 76-8; P. Géroudet, *La vie des oiseaux* (*Les échassiers*), Paris-Neuchâtel ²1948, 63-8; E. Ghaleb, *al-Mawsūʿa fī ʿulūm al-ṭabīʿa, Dictionnaire des sciences de la nature*, Beirut 1966, ii (sub *nuḥām*); A. Hartmann, *al-Nāṣir li-Dīn Allāh (1180-1225), Politik, Religion, Kultur in der späten ʿAbbāsidenzeit*, Berlin-New York 1975, 92-108; H. Heinzel, R. Fitter, J. Parslow, *Oiseaux d'Europe, d'Afrique du Nord et du Moyen Orient*, Neuchâtel 1972, 42; F. Hue and R.D. Etchecopar, *Les oiseaux du Proche et du Moyen Orient*, Paris 1970, 86-9; Islamic Republic of Iran (Department of the Environment) *Parandagān-i Īrān, The Birds of Iran*, Tehran ²1983, 45-6, 356; R. Meinertzhagen, *Birds of Arabia*, London 1954, 411-12; R. Peterson, G. Mountfort, P. Hollom, *Guide to the birds of Europe*, French tr. P. Géroudet, Neuchâtel-Paris 1954, 59; Ṣafī al-Dīn al-Ḥillī, *Dīwān*, Beirut 1962, 231; F. Viré, *Le tir à l'arbalète-à-jalet et sa* futuwwa *dans l'Islam médiéval* (to appear in *REI*); D. Yeatman-Berthelot, *Atlas des oiseaux de France en hiver* (publ. Société Ornithol. de France), Paris 1991, 84-5.

(F. Viré)

NUḤĀS, the word most often used in Arabic for copper (Cu).

Next to gold and silver, this is one of the oldest known metals. The word is evidently common to all Semitic languages: Hebrew *nᵊḥōšeṯ*, Aramaic *nᵊḥāšā*, Ethiopic *nāḥes*; the Greek word χαλκός appears in transliteration as *khalḳūs*. Because the alchemists wanted the materials they used to be kept secret, there exist many pseudonyms for copper, which moreover were often changed and are for the greater part incomprehensible. The alchemists attach it to the planet al-Zuhara, i.e. Venus (see the survey in E. Wiedemann, *Aufsätze zur arabischen Wissenschaftsgeschichte*, ii, 603-4). Most of these pseudonyms cannot be defined unambiguously; they certainly do not only indicate pure copper but also copper minerals such as primary ore, secondary products of erosion or sedimentary formations. According to al-Bīrūnī, copper is called in Greek *khalḳūs*, in Syriac *nuḥāsā*, in Arabic *al-nuḥās*, *al-miss* (in ʿIrāḳ and Khurāsān) and *al-ḳiṭr* (i.e. brass) (*K. al-Djamāhir fī maʿrifat al-djawāhir*, Ḥaydarābād 1355/1936, 244-5). Shams al-Dīn al-Dimashḳī distinguishes three kinds of copper: the red-white Greek one (*rūmī*), the red and dry Cypriot one (*ḳubrusī*) and the blood-red one from Sūs (in Khūzistān). He describes the extraction as follows: the quicksilver in the quarry having attracted and absorbed the sulphur, the heat in the quarry causes the sulphur to dominate the quicksilver; after that, the mass is transformed into a red rock which has a pungent taste. Fire or a long stay in the earth occasionally makes it slate-like, occasionally it oxidises into verdigris (*zindjār*, the ἰός ξύστος of Dioscorides), or it acquires a surplus of sulphur in the quarry and then becomes antimony (*rūsakhtadj*), which is pulverised to obtain the collyrium called *rāsukht*. Dipped several times in bee honey, it takes on a golden colour. A needle, sickle, knife or sword made from copper thus treated and dipped in the blood of a billy-goat (*dam al-tays*) causes incurable wounds, and the sickle prevents the herb from growing (al-Dimashḳī, *Nukhbat al-dahr*, ed. A.F. Mehren, Leiden 1874, repr. Amsterdam 1964, Ar. text 54, tr. 59-60).

Of primary importance for Arabic mineralogy became the so-called "Book of Stones of Aristotle". Its influence can be perceived not only from the great number of manuscripts but also through the rich secondary tradition. In J. Ruska's edition, *Das Steinbuch des Aristoteles*, the "stone" copper is described under no. 59, where the best among the numerous kinds of copper is said to be the red one, mixed with black. Verdigris (*zindjār*) is explained as a green substance hidden inside this kind of copper, which can be extracted by the use of vinegar. When brass (*ṣufr*) is cast and vitriol (*zādj*) and borax (*bawraḳ* [*q.v.*]) are added, something emerges which resembles gold and is solid as if it were gold. Food and drink taken from a brass vessel are harmful, occasionally lethal. If a victim of facial paralysis (*laḳwa*) enters a darkened house and looks at himself in a mirror made of *ṭāliḳūn* (a copper alloy = μεταλλικόν, hardly καθολικόν as in Dozy, *Supplement*, ii, 19), the paralysis disappears. Hot *ṭāliḳūn* dipped in water drives flies off and prevents eyelashes from growing again after they have been depilated with a pair of tweezers. For these qualities of *ṭāliḳūn*, which probably is identical with "Chinese iron" (*k͟hār čīnī, ḥadīd ṣīnī*), see also J. Ruska (tr.), *Das Steinbuch aus der Kosmographie des... al-Ḳazwīnī*, Kirchhain, N.L. 1896, 28, and M. Ullmann, *Die Natur- und Geheimwissenschaften im Islam*, Leiden-Cologne 1972, 409 f.

Special healing properties were of old attributed to "burnt copper" (*aes ustum*), see Dioscorides, *De materia medica*, ed. M. Wellmann, v, 76, κεκαυμένος χαλκός/Arab. tr. ed. Dubler and Terés, v, 59, *al-nuḥās al-muḥraḳ*: this copper preparation possesses astringent, dehydrating, diluting and purifying power and scars sores. Taken with honey, it is an emetic. This copper is made from nails coming from destroyed or sunken ships. The nails, sprinkled with sulphur and salt, are made white-hot in a kiln inside a closed melting-pot made of clay. According to the description, the σῶρυ of Dioscorides (Greek text v, 102, Arab. tr. *ṣūrī*, v, 84) is also a product of the copper quarry and resembles burnt copper.

Al-Tamīmī describes how copper ore, set aglow in a kiln, disintegrates into its components, among which is copper; in the Nīs͟hāpūr region a copper quarry is said to exist, from which turquoise (*fayrūzad͟j*) was extracted at the same time and therefore said to be a "copper-like" substance; next, al-Tamīmī develops a theory on the nature of verdigris (see Jutta Schönfeld, *Über die Steine. Das 14. Kapitel aus dem "Kitāb al-Muršid" des Tamīmī*, Freiburg 1976, 57, 81, 119).

According to the *Ḥudūd al-ʿālam*, tr. Minorsky, there were layers of copper in the mountains of Bārd͟jān in the province of Kirmān (65), in Farg͟hāna (115-16), Georgia (68), Kirmān (124), Sardan (Fārs, 129), Spain (154) and Ṭūs (103). Elsewhere, too, Persia is mentioned as the most important land of copper export: from Sardan it was exported to Baṣra and other regions, lucrative layers of copper ore were found near Damindān (in Kirmān), in the region of Iṣfāhān and in D͟jibāl (Media) (see P. Schwarz, *Iran im Mittelalter*, 158, 268, 868). In the 3rd/9th century the copper quarries near Iṣfāhān paid taxes of 10,000 *dirhams*, and Buk͟hārā supplied copper for the shining domed roofs of the minarets (Mez, *Renaissance*, 416). According to Ibn K͟haldūn, the river bed of the Tiber (*sic*) was said to be covered with copper (Ibn K͟haldūn, tr. Rosenthal, i, 151).

Bibliography (in addition to references given in the text): M. Berthelot, *La chimie au Moyen Age*, i-iii, Paris 1893, repr. 1967, *passim* (very often), see indexes, i, 428, ii, 382-3, iii, 245-6; I. Löw, *Fauna und Mineralien der Juden*, ed. A. Scheiber, repr. Hildesheim 1969, 229-50, esp. 232-7; P. Kraus, *Jābir ibn Ḥayyān. Contribution à l'histoire des idées scientifiques dans l'Islam*, repr. 1986, 19, 21, 261; Dietlinde Goltz, *Studien zur Geschichte der Mineralnamen in Pharmazie, Chemie und Medizin von den Anfängen bis Paracelsus*, Wiesbaden 1972, 256 f., 262 f. On the healing qualities of copper (selected sources): Rāzī, *Ḥāwī*, xxi, 612-7 (no. 882); Harawī, *al-Abniya ʿan ḥaḳāʾiḳ al-adwiya*, Tehran 1346/1928, 335; Ibn al-D͟jazzār, *K. al-Iʿtimād*, facs. ed. Frankfurt 1985, 163; Ibn Sīnā, *Ḳānūn*, Būlāḳ 1294, i, 377; Ibn Hubal, *K.al-Muk͟htārāt*, Ḥaydarābād 1362/1943, ii, 135-6; Ibn Bayṭār, *al-D͟jāmiʿ*, iv, 178; Maimonides, *S͟harḥ asmāʾ al-ʿuḳḳār*, ed. Meyerhof, Cairo 1940, nos. 142, 357, 373; Ibn Rasūl al-G͟hassānī, *al-Muʿtamad*, Beirut 1395/1975, 520; Suwaydī, *K. al-Simāt fī asmāʾ al-nabāt*, ms. Paris ar. 3004, 185a-b; Anṭākī, *Tad͟hkirat ulī 'l-albāb*, Cairo 1371/1952, i, 329. (A. DIETRICH)

AL-**NUK͟HAYLA**, a town in ʿIrāḳ, near al-Kūfa. It is known mainly from the accounts of the battle of Ḳādisiyya [*q.v.*]. From the statements collected by Yāḳūt regarding its position, it appears that two different places of this name had later to be distinguished, namely one near al-Kūfa on the road to Syria, which is several times mentioned in the time of the caliphs ʿAlī and Muʿāwiya, and another, a watering station between al-Mug͟hīt͟ha and al-ʿAḳaba, 3 *mīls* from al-Ḥufayr, to the right of the road to Mecca. Several encounters took place there during the second battle of Ḳādisiyya. According to al-K͟halīl in al-Bakrī, this al-Nuk͟hayla was in the Syrian steppe (*al-bādiya*); Ibn al-Faḳīh also seems to be thinking of this region. Caetani assumes that the reference in both cases is to the same place on the edge of the desert. According to Musil, it perhaps corresponds to the modern K͟hān Ibn Nuk͟hayle about 22 km/14 miles S. S. E. of Karbalāʾ and 64 km/40 miles N. N. W. of al-Kūfa.

Bibliography: Yāḳūt, *Muʿd͟jam*, iv, 771-2; Ibn al-Faḳīh, 163; Bakrī, *Muʿd͟jam*, ed. Wüstenfeld, 577; Yaʿḳūbī, *Taʾrīk͟h*, ii, 162; Ṭabarī, i, 2201-2, 3259, 3345; ii, 545; Balād͟hurī, *Futūḥ al-buldān*, 245, 253-4, 256; Ibn Miskawayh, *Tad͟jārib*, ed. Caetani, 571; Masʿūdī, *Murūd͟j*, iv, 417, v, 213, 253 = §§ 1536, 1722, 1976, 2016; L. Caetani, *Annali dell' Islām*, iii/1, Milan 1910, 156, 254, 258, 261, A.H. 13, § 168, n. 2b, A.H. 14, § 11, 14a (with n. 3), 20; L. Massignon, in *MIFAO*, xxvii, 34b, 51, 53; A. Musil, *The Middle Euphrates*, New York 1928, 39, n. 31; 41, n. 32, 247, 329. (E. HONIGMANN)

AL-**NUKKĀR** (AL-NAKKĀRA, AL-NAKKĀRIYYA) "deniers": one of the main branches of the K͟hārid͟jī sect of the Ibāḍiyya [*q.v.*]. The existence of this sect has already been proved by E. Masqueray, A. de C. Motylinski and R. Strothmann; cf., however, the opinion of G. Levi della Vida, according to whom al-Nukkār is simply "an insulting epithet applied to K͟hārid͟jīs in general" [see ṢUFRIYYA]. The name al-Nukkār comes from the fact that the members of this sect refused to recognise the second Ibāḍī *imām* of Tāhert, ʿAbd al-Wahhāb b. ʿAbd al-Raḥmān b. Rustam [see RUSTAMIDS]. The other names given to this sect are: 1. *al-Yazīdiyya*, from the name of the chief theologian of the sect ʿAbd Allāh b. Yazīd al-Fazārī al-Ibāḍī (cf. below: to be distinguished from another Ibāḍī sect which bears the same name and was founded by a certain Yazīd b. Anīsa. 2. *al-S͟haʿbiyya*; we believe this name should be derived from that of S͟huʿayb b. al-Muʿarrif (see below). 3. *al-Mulḥida* (to be distinguished from another Muslim sect of this name = *al-Bāṭiniyya*). 4. *al-Nukkāt͟h* (*al-Nakkāt͟ha*); the *nisba* from this name is *al-Nākit͟hī*. 5. *al-Nad͟jwīya* (and not النجدية as Strothmann writes it, *Berber und Ibāḍiten*, 274, n. 4). 6. *Mistāwa*; this last name, which seems to be Berber (perhaps to be connected with the Berber tribe of *Meztaoua*, mentioned by Ibn K͟haldūn, *Histoire des Berbères*, i, 182) was with the Nukkār the most used.

The Ibāḍī historical tradition of North Africa, fixed towards the end of the 5th/11th century by Abū Zakariyyāʾ Yaḥyā b. Abī Bakr al-Ward͟jlānī [*q.v.*], places the first appearance of the Nukkār sect at the time of the election of ʿAbd al-Wahhāb (in 168/784-5, according to Ibn ʿId͟hārī, *al-Bayān al-mug͟hrib*, tr. Fagnan, Algiers 1901, 283), and names as the founder of the sect Abū Ḳudāma Yazīd b. Fendīn al-Ifranī, who was later joined by a learned dissenting Ibāḍī from Cairo, S͟huʿayb b. al-Muʿarrif. According to this tradition, the origins of the Nakkārī sect are closely connected with the Mag͟hrīb. On the other hand, from information supplied by the Ibāḍī theological works, one may judge that there were other founders of the Nakkārī sect in addition to Ibn Fendīn and Shuʿayb. They are mentioned in a *risāla* of Abū ʿAmr ʿUt̲h̲mān b. K̲h̲alīfa al-Mārig̲h̲nī (an Ibāḍī author of North Africa of this name was living in the 6th/12th century, cf. T. Lewicki, *Quelques textes inédits en vieux berbère*, in *REI* [1934], 278), dealing with the different Muslim sects (of which there is a manuscript in the library of the University of Lwów, no. 1088 II in the collection of mss.): ʿAbd Allāh b. Yazīd al-Fazārī, ʿAbd Allāh b. ʿAbd al-ʿAzīz, Abu ʾl-Muʾarrid̲j̲ ʿAmr b. Muḥammad al-Sadūsī, and Ḥātim b. Manṣūr (fol. 1 b). According to passages in the *Kitāb al-Siyar* of Abu ʾl-ʿAbbās al-S̲h̲ammāk̲h̲ī and Abū Zakariyyāʾ's book, one can distinguish among these individuals the representatives of three diverse tendencies in the Ibāḍiyya, or rather, of three separate schisms. The synthesis of these different ideas seems to have been the work of Shuʿayb after the death of Ibn Fendīn (E. Masqueray, *Chronique d'Abou Zakaria*, Algiers 1878, 74-5). The earliest was the schism of ʿAbd Allāh b. ʿAbd al-ʿAzīz, Abu ʾl-Muʾarrid̲j̲, Ḥātim b. Manṣūr and Shuʿayb, to which the Nakkārī sects owes its legal principles. The date of the secession of this group is perhaps rather earlier than the revolt of Ibn Fendīn: according to the Ibāḍī books, they detached themselves from the Ibāḍiyya in the time of Abū ʿUbayda Muslim b. Abī Karīma al-Tamīmī, the Ibāḍī *imām* of Baṣra who lived in the first half of the 2nd/8th century (cf. T. Lewicki, *Une chronique ibāḍite*, in *REI* [1934] 72). It should be noted that two doctors of this group, Shuʿayb and ʿAbd Allāh b. ʿAbd al-ʿAzīz, also fought against the Ḳadarī tendencies in the Ibāḍiyya represented by Ḥamza al-Kūfī and ʿAṭiyya; it is even said in connection with Shuʿayb that he had sympathies with the D̲j̲abriyya [*q.v.*]. Almost contemporary with the schism of Shuʿayb and his companions seems to have been that of ʿAbd Allāh b. Yazīd al-Fazārī, author of a theological system, later adopted by the Nakkārīs, and a traditionist highly esteemed by the Ibāḍīs (cf. T. Lewicki, *Une chronique*, 70). These two Ibāḍī schools were absorbed after 168/784-5 by that of Ibn Fendīn.

As to the latter, we know that he was one of the members of *al-s̲h̲ūrā*, the council constituted by ʿAbd al-Raḥmān b. Rustam following the example of ʿUmar b. al-K̲h̲aṭṭāb and composed of six men who, after the death of ʿAbd al-Raḥmān, were to choose the future *imām*. Ibn Fendīn had facilitated the election of ʿAbd al-Wahhāb, by conducting active propaganda in his favour among the Berbers, but afterwards he demanded of the new *imām* the adoption of two conditions (*s̲h̲arṭ*), quite in keeping no doubt with the Berber spirit of the Ibāḍīs of the Mag̲h̲rib but quite foreign to the principles of Ibāḍī teaching: firstly, that he should only act in concert with a regular *d̲j̲amāʿa*, and secondly, that he should resign if he found any one more worthy (*afḍal*) than himself. ʿAbd al-Wahhāb, supported by the Ibāḍī doctors of the east whom he consulted, opposed the views of Ibn Fendīn, who in his turn was supported by Shuʿayb, who came with his followers to Tāhert to join the malcontents. The "Deniers" attacked the partisans of ʿAbd al-Wahhāb, known as al-Wahbiyya (on this name, see Strothmann, *Berber und Ibāḍiten*, 274, n. 4). The sources mention two great battles, in which Ibn Fendīn was killed and ʿAbd al-Wahhāb won the day. The Nakkārīs withdrew, probably to the east of Barbary. Among the fugitives was Shuʿayb, who settled in Tripolitania. It was at this period that the complete rupture occurred between the Nakkār and the Wahbī section of the Ibāḍiyya, followed immediately by a

barāʾa or excommunication of Shuʿayb and his followers by the Wahbī doctors.

Soon the Nakkārī propaganda became very active, but it was not till the end of the 3rd/9th century, after the fall of the imāmate of Tāhert (in 296/908-9) and the establishment of the dynasty of the Fāṭimids in the Mag̲h̲rib, that the Nukkār acquired a preponderance among the Ibāḍīs of North Africa. The whole of the south of Tunisia and Algeria, from the D̲j̲abal Nefūsa [*q.v.*] to Tāhert, became Nakkārī. The historians speak of a vigorous propaganda by the Nukkār, the centres of which were, in addition to Tripolitania, the D̲j̲abal Awrās and the island of D̲j̲arba. As a result of this propaganda several Wahbī Ibāḍī districts were converted to the new sect. The Nakkārīs organised an imāmate separate from that of Tāhert. We know the name of a Nakkārī *imām* who lived towards the end of the 3rd/9th century: Abū ʿAmmār ʿAbd al-Ḥamīd al-Aʿmā. It was his disciple Abū Yazīd Mak̲h̲lad b. Kaydād [*q.v.*] who in the first half of the 4th/10th century was the leader of a formidable Nakkārī rising in the Mag̲h̲rib, which almost succeeded in its endeavour to destroy the Fāṭimid state. Abū Yazīd was elected by the Nukkār assembled in the D̲j̲abal Awrās as "the *s̲h̲ayk̲h̲*", of the true believers", Abū ʿAmmār giving place to him (in keeping with the teaching on *al-afḍal*). He tried to put into practice the teachings of Ibn Fendīn; he formed a council of twelve members called *ʿazzāba* who were to rule, in conjunction with him, the Nakkārī imāmate. But later he associated himself with the K̲h̲ārid̲j̲ī extremists by authorising *istiʿrāḍ* [*q.v.*] or religious murder on the model of the Azraḳīs [see AZĀRIḲA].

After the defeat and death of Abū Yazīd, the influence of the Nukkār diminished and several tribes went back to Wahbism. Nevertheless, the Nakkārīs again took part in the general rising of the Wahbīs against the Fāṭimids in 358/968-9 and later in 431/1039-40 we find them mentioned in connection with a great rising of this sect on the island of D̲j̲arba. In the 6th-8th/12th-14th centuries they are again mentioned in the district of Yefren to the east of D̲j̲abal Nafūsa, on the island of D̲j̲arba, among the Banū Warg̲h̲amma in southern Tunisia, and in the oases of Bilād al-D̲j̲arīd, Rīg̲h̲ and Wārd̲j̲lān. Remnants of the Nakkārī sect have survived to the present century and, according to A. de C. Motylinski, Nukkār could be found *ca.* 1900 on D̲j̲arba and in Zawāg̲h̲a.

Thanks to the exposition given by Abū ʿAmr, we are acquainted with the main principles which separated the Nukkār from the Wahbī Ibāḍīs. They number seven. Besides the doctrine regarding *s̲h̲arṭ*, mentioned above, a fundamental tenet of the Nukkār was their thesis that the names of God are created. Another Nakkārī tenet concerns the relations of man and woman. For other details of their teaching, see al-Barrādī, *Kitāb al-D̲j̲awāhir al-muntaḳāt*, Cairo 1302, ii, 171-2.

Several Wahbī Ibāḍī theologians refuted the Nakkārī teachings in their works, some of them quite early. For example, al-Barrādī mentions the refutations of the thesis of ʿAbd Allāh b. ʿAbd al-ʿAzīz and Shuʿayb by a Wahbī doctor of the 2nd/8th century named Abū ʿAmr al-Rabīʿ b. Ḥabīb (*Kitāb al-D̲j̲awāhir*, 172) and al-Wisyānī mentions a scholar of Sāhil in Tunisia named Muḥammad b. Abī K̲h̲ālid who lived earlier than the 5th/11th century and refuted the Nakkārī doctrines in his various works.

Bibliography: Abū Zakariyyāʾ Yaḥyā b. Abī Bakr al-Wārd̲j̲lānī, *Kitāb al-Sīra wa-ak̲h̲bār al-aʾimma*, ms. no. 23 in the Smogorzewski collection in the university of Lwów, fols. 17b-23a, 46a-50a, 51b-

53b, 56b; E. Masqueray, *Chronique d'Abou Zakaria*, Algiers 1878, 53-80, 226-51, 268, 270-8, 289, 290; Abu 'l-Rabīᶜ Sulaymān b. ᶜAbd al-Sallām al-Wisyānī, *Taʾlīf*, ms. no. 277 in the library of the Islamic Institute of the university of Lwów, fols. 27, 28, 30, 31, 33-8, 46, 73, 102, 125, 128, 129, 145, 189; an anonymous Ibāḍī chronicle contained in the same ms., fols. 218, 221, 249, 257, 265, 275, 276; Abu 'l-ᶜAbbās Aḥmad b. Saᶜīd al-Dardjīnī, *Kitāb Ṭabakāt al-mashāʾikh*, ms. no. 275 of the Islamic Institute of Lwów, fols. 16a-20a, 35a-37b, 77b, 144a-b; Abu 'l-Faḍl al-Barrādī, *Kitāb al-Djawāhir al-muntakāt*, Cairo 1302, 171-2, 174; Abu 'l-ᶜAbbās Aḥmad al-Shammākhī, *Kitāb al-Siyar*, Cairo 1301, 104-5, 109-10, 119-20, 145-54, 280-2, 338, 345, 358, 359, 368, 370, 376, 381, 395, 416, 432, 458, 480, 502-4, 530, 557, 590; A. de C. Motylinski, *Chronique d'Ibn Ṣaghîr*, in *Actes du XIVème congrès international des orientalistes*, Algiers 1905, 16-20, 72-7; Ibn al-Athīr, *Annales du Maghrib*, tr. E. Fagnan, Algiers 1901, 325, 338, 345, 367; Ibn ᶜIdhārī, *al-Bayān al-mughrib*, tr. Fagnan, Algiers 1901, i, 277, 311, 314-16; Tidjānī, *Riḥla*, tr. A. Rousseau, in *JA*, ser. 4, vol. xx (1852), 112, 167, 171, ser. 5, vol. i (1853) 123; Ibn Khaldūn, *Histoire des Berbères*, tr. de Slane, Algiers 1852-6, i, 232, 277, 285, ii, 530, 531, 537, iii, 201-12, 278, 286, 291, 301; Fournel, *Les Berbers*, ii, 225; Motylinski, in the *Bulletin de Correspondance Africaine*, iii, 16, no. 2; idem, *Le Djebel Nefousa*, Paris 1898-9, 69, 114; Dozy, *Supplément aux dictionnaires arabes*², Leiden-Paris 1927, ii, 722; M. Vonderheyden, *La Berbérie orientale*, Paris 1927, 48; R. Strothmann, *Berber und Ibāḍiten*, in *Isl.*, xvii (1928), 274, n. 4, 275. (T. Lewicki)

AL-**NUKRA**, a plain west of the Djabal Ḥawrān on the border of Trachonitis in Transjordan. The name *al-Nukra* ("the cavity") is quite modern. It is applied to an area which includes the two districts of al-Bathaniyya (with its chief town Adhriᶜāt) and Ḥawrān (west of the hills of the same name), i.e. the whole northern half of modern Jordan. In the wider sense, al-Nukra includes all the country from al-Ladjāʾ, Djaydūr and al-Balkāʾ to the foot of the Djabal Ḥawrān, in the narrower sense only the southern part of this; in any case it stretches from al-Ṣanamayn to the Djabal al-Durūz (Ḥawrān). To al-Nukra belong Mūᶜatbīn or Mūᶜtabīn, Tubnā (now Tibne), al-Mahadjdja, Obtaᶜ, ᶜOlmā, al-Musayfira and al-Faddayn already mentioned in Syriac texts of the pre-Muslim period.

Bibliography: Nöldeke, in *ZDMG*, xxix, 431, n. 1; F. Buhl, *Geographie des alten Palästina*, Freiburg i. B. and Leipzig 1896, 15, 43-4, 84; R. Dussaud, *Topographie de la Syrie*, Paris 1927, 323. (E. Honigmann)

NUKṬAT AL-**KĀF**, an early work on the Bābī [*q.v.*] movement.

In 1910, E.G. Browne published a work entitled *Kitáb-i Nuqṭatu 'l-Káf*, a Persian history of the early Bābī movement, based on a "unique" manuscript (Suppl. persan 1071) in the Bibliothèque Nationale. This manuscript had been bought by the library in 1884, in a sale of books belonging to the late Comte de Gobineau. Authorship of the history was ascribed by the Bābī leader Ṣubḥ-i Azal [*q.v.*] to Ḥādjdjī Mīrzā Djānī, a Kāshānī merchant killed in 1852.

Browne's text soon became the centre of a controversy that still continues. The Bahāʾī leader, ᶜAbbās Effendi ᶜAbd al-Bahāʾ, maintained that the work was a forgery produced by the Azalī Bābīs. This thesis was developed by the Bahāʾī scholar Mīrzā Abu 'l-Faḍl Gulpāygānī and his nephew Sayyid Mahdī in their *Kashf al-ghiṭāʾ* and, more recently, by H.M. Balyuzi. While this conspiracy theory is clearly unfounded, internal evidence suggests that the history was not written by Mīrzā Djānī. Recent conjectures favour authorship by his son or nephew, possibly in collaboration with a brother, using notes prepared by him. Some version of the *Nukṭat al-kāf* served as the basis for the later Bahāʾī *Tārīkh-i Djadīd* and its recensions. In spite of the controversy, there can be no doubt that the *Nukṭat al-kāf* remains one of the most important sources for the early history of Babism.

A full discussion of the problems of authorship, provenance, and dating may be found in MacEoin, together with a list of the twelve or so manuscripts now known to be in existence (Appendix 8).

Bibliography: H.M. Balyuzi, *Edward Granville Browne and the Bahá'í faith*, London 1970, ch. VII; E.G. Browne (ed.), *Kitáb-i Nuqṭatu 'l-Káf, being the earliest history of the Bábís, compiled by Ḥájjí Mírzá Jání of Káshán between the years A.D. 1850 and 1852*, Leyden and London 1910, Gibb Memorial Series, vol. XV; idem (ed. and tr.), *The New History (Táríkh-i-Jadíd) of Mírzá ᶜAlí Muḥammed, the Báb*, Cambridge 1903, repr. Amsterdam 1975; Mīrzā Abu 'l-Faḍl Gulpāygānī and Sayyid Mahdī Gulpāygānī, *Kashf al-ghiṭāʾ ᶜan ḥiyal al-aᶜdāʾ*. Tashkent n.d. [1919?]; D. MacEoin, *The sources for early Bābī doctrine and history: a survey*, Leiden 1992, chs. 6 and 7, Appendix 8; Muḥīṭ Ṭabāṭabāʾī, *Kitābī bī nām bā nāmī tāza*, in *Gawhar*, Year 2, parts 11-12 (1353/1974), 952-61; idem, *Tārīkh-i kadīm wa djadīd*, 2 parts, in *Gawhar*, Year 3, parts 5-6 (1354/1975), 343-8, 426-31. (D. MacEoin)

NUKṬAWIYYA, an offshoot of the Ḥurūfiyya sect [*q.v.*] that after an incubation lasting a century emerged as a significant movement of politico-religious opposition in Ṣafawid Persia and, in India, played some role in the origination of Akbar's *Dīn-i Ilāhī* [*q.v.*]. Given its similarities not only with Ḥurūfism but also with Nizārī Ismāᶜīlism, it may be regarded as one more link in the long chain of Persian heresies.

The designation Nukṭawiyya is said to be taken from the doctrine that earth is the starting point (*nukṭa*) of all things, the remaining three elements being derived from it; the term may also refer, however, to the use of two, three, or four dots, variously arranged, as cryptic abbreviations in the writings of the sect. The designation Maḥmūdiyya is also encountered, this being derived from the name of the founder, Maḥmūd Pasīkhānī. Born at the village of Pasīkhān near Fūman in Gīlān, Maḥmūd followed Faḍl Allāh Astarābādī (d. 796/1384), the founder of Ḥurūfism, until he was expelled from the movement for alleged arrogance (hence the epithets *Maḥmūd-i mardūd* "Maḥmūd the rejected" and *Maḥmūd-i maṭrūd* "Mahmud the banished"). He is said to have proclaimed himself the Mahdī and the bringer of a new dispensation in 800/1397, i.e. at the beginning of the 9th Islamic century. Virtually nothing is known of his life other than that he was still residing in Astarābād in 818/1415 when he finished the writing of one of his books, *Djawāz al-sāʾirīn*. He died in 831/1427-28, supposedly a suicide, having cast himself into the waters of the Aras, but this is dismissed as a calumny by the Nukṭawīs themselves.

Maḥmūd Pasīkhānī is said to have written sixteen books and 1,001 treatises (*nuskha*) in exposition of his doctrines; none of these has ever been published in full (for extracts from his principal work, *Mīzān*, see, however, Raḥīm Riḍā-zāda Malik's notes to his edition of Kaykhusraw Isfandiyār, *Dabistān-i madhāhib*, ii,

33-6, and Ṣādiḳ Kiyā, *Nuḳṭawiyān yā Pasīkhāniyān*, Tehran 1320 Sh./1941, 73-132).

Nuḳṭawī works were composed in an extremely opaque style and are marked by frequent recourse to abbreviations and special signs similar to those found in Ḥurūfī literature, but the main themes of Maḥmūd Pasīkhānī's teaching can easily be comprehended. They consist in the first place of a peculiarly materialist type of metempsychosis according to which the particles of the body do not disintegrate on death but are absorbed as a single mass into the soil. They then re-emerge in vegetable or solid form, possibly to be consumed by animals or men, the level of existence on which they are finally reintegrated being dependent on the degree of virtue and knowledge attained by their previous owner. When a being rises or descends from one level of existence to another, the traces of his former existence are still visible and can be discerned by the insightful, a process known as *iḥṣāʾ* "enumeration" (whence yet another designation for the sect, Iḥṣāʾiyya). Thus dogs can be recognised as having been Ḳizilbāsh Turks, their tails being a trace of the swords they once carried and the word used in Persian to shoo away a dog, *čikh*, being identical with Turkish *čiḳ*; and waterfowl should be identified as transmogrified clerics, still obsessed in their new existence with making ablutions. Maḥmūd Pasīkhānī himself claimed to be the reincarnation on a higher plane both of the Prophet Muḥammad (something allegedly indicated in Ḳurʾān, XVII, 79 "your Lord will raise you to a praiseworthy station", *maḳām maḥmūd*) and of ʿAlī, citing a *ḥadīth* in which the Prophet is reported to have said that he and ʿAlī were of one flesh. Other personal reincarnations are those of Moses in Ḥusayn b. ʿAlī and the Pharaoh in Yazīd; it was because Yazīd remembered being drowned in the Red Sea at the hands of Moses when he was the Pharaoh that he took care to keep Ḥusayn away from the water of the Euphrates.

Pasīkhānī is reputed never to have married, and his doctrine recommends celibacy. The celibate are said to have reached the rank of *wāḥid* (a word which has the crucial numerical value of 19) and to be capable of advancing to the rank of *Allāh*, this being none other than man in his ultimate essence, termed "the manifest compound" (*al-murakkab al-mubīn*); the Nuḳṭawīs therefore summarised their creed as *lā ilāha illā 'l-murakkab al-mubīn*. Nuḳṭawīs disinclined to celibacy (who for some reason are designated as *amīn*, "trustworthy") are advised to copulate not more than once a week. This disdain of marriage earned the Nuḳṭawīs accusations of incest, promiscuity and pederasty from their opponents.

Also central to Nuḳṭawī doctrine was a cyclical concept of time, one clearly influenced by Ismāʿīlī antecedents. The total life of the world is said to consist of 64,000 years, divided into four periods of 16,000 years that are known respectively as *ẓuhūr* "outwardness", *buṭūn* "inwardness", *sirr* ("concealment") and *ʿalāniyya* ("manifestation"). Each of these periods is divided in turn into an 8,000-year "Arab epoch" (*dawra-yi istiʿrāb*), during which the guidance of humanity is entrusted to a "perfected Arab messenger" (*mursal-i mukammal-i ʿArab*), and an 8,000-year "Persian epoch" (*dawra-yi istiʿdjām*), presided over by a "perfected Persian expositor" (*mubayyin-i mukammal-i ʿadjam*). The emergence of Maḥmūd Pasīkhānī signified the beginning of one such "Persian epoch". This exaltation of Persian-ness is apparent also in the assertion that Gīlān and Māzandarān have now superseded Mecca and Medina.

It was during the reign of Shāh Ismāʿīl I that the Nuḳṭawī movement first surfaced, significantly enough in the village of Andjudān near Kāshān, a principal centre of post-Alamūt Nizārī Ismāʿīlism. Shāh Ṭāhir, thirty-first Imām of the Muḥammad-Shāhī Nizārī line, is reported to have so angered Shāh Ismāʿīl by gathering around him in Andjudān Nuḳṭawīs and other religious deviants that he had to flee precipitately to India (Maʿṣūm ʿAlī Shāh Shīrāzī, *Ṭarāʾiḳ al-ḥaḳāʾiḳ*, ed. Muḥammad Djaʿfar Maḥdjūb, Tehran 1339 Sh./1960, iii, 136). Another instance of Nuḳṭawī-Ismāʿīlī symbiosis is provided by Murād Mīrzā, thirty-sixth Imām of the Ḳāsim-Shāhī Nizārī line, whose combined Nuḳṭawī and Ismāʿīlī following in Andjudān was broken up by Shāh Ṭahmāsp in 981-2/1573-4 and who was himself put to death (Aḥmad Thattawī, *Taʾrīkh-i Alfī*, cited in Kiyā, 36). Mention may also be made of two poets: Wuḳūʿī of Nīshāpūr whose beliefs are said to have been intermediate between Nuḳṭawism and Ismāʿīlism (Kiyā, 35), and Abu 'l-Ḳāsim Muḥammad Kūhpāyaʾī Amrī Shīrāzī, who praised two of the Ḳāsim-Shāhī Nizārī Imāms in his *Dīwān* and may have been a crypto-Ismāʿīlī (W. Ivanow, *A guide to Ismaʿili literature*, London 1933, 108).

Amrī Shīrāzī first came to the fore in the time of Shāh Ṭahmāsp, who entrusted him with the administration of *awḳāf*, belonging to the Ḥaramayn but located in Persia, and who also employed his brother, Mawlānā Abū Turāb, famed as a master of the occult sciences, as court calligrapher. Denounced for heresy in 972/1565, the brothers were blinded and went into seclusion. In 984/1576, the last year of Ṭahmāsp's reign, still more Nuḳṭawīs were apprehended in Kāshān; they included the poet Ḥayātī, who was jailed for two years in Shīrāz before making his way to India.

Other centres of Nuḳṭawī activity were developing meanwhile in Sāwa, Nāʾīn, Iṣfahān and—most importantly—Ḳazwīn. Nuḳṭawism was propagated in Ḳazwīn by Darwīsh Khusraw, the son of a well-digger, who had gone to Kāshān to learn the Nuḳṭawī doctrines and established his headquarters in a mosque on his return. Denounced by the *ʿulamāʾ*, he was interrogated by Shāh Ṭahmāsp but giving suitably evasive answers was released with instructions no longer to hold forth in the mosque. On the death of Ṭahmāsp, he resumed his public preaching with such success that he was able to build a *takya* which came to house two hundred of his followers. Despite a further round of executions of Nuḳṭawīs in Kāshān in 994/1586 which numbered among its victims two musicians, Afḍal Dū-tārī and Mīr Bīghamī, Darwīsh Khusraw remained unmolested throughout the reigns of Ismāʿīl II and Khudābanda into the early years of rule by Shāh ʿAbbās.

Shāh ʿAbbās began by establishing a friendly and even intimate relationship with Darwīsh Khusraw, and was even initiated into the Nuḳṭawiyya, with the grade of *amīn*, by Darwīsh Turāb and Darwīsh Kamāl Iḳlīdī. The Ṣafawid chroniclers (e.g. Iskandar Beg Munshī, *ʿĀlam-ārā-yi ʿAbbāsī*, Tehran 1350 Sh./1971, i, 444), followed by most later historians, maintained that Shāh ʿAbbās cultivated the Nuḳṭawīs only as a means of surveillance. It is, however, possible that he had a genuine interest in their teachings. They had already attempted to proclaim Shāh Ṭahmāsp as the Mahdī, and when they made a similar connection between their chiliastic theories and the person of Shāh ʿAbbās, he may well have contemplated the possibility of using Nuḳṭawism as a new ideological basis for the Ṣafawid state. It seems probable at the very least that his lifelong disregard for religious proprieties should have been in part the result of his exposure to Nukṭawī teachings (ʿAlī Riḍā Dhakāwatī Ḳarāgūzlū, *Nagāhī dīgar ba Nukṭawiyya*, 59-60).

The Nukṭawī movement was, however, not without its dangers for Shāh ʿAbbās. In 999/1591, a Nukṭawī insurrection centred on Iṣṭihbānāt broke out in Fārs; he had it mercilessly repressed, and the blinded poet Amrī was arrested in Shīrāz and torn to pieces at the bidding of the *ʿulamāʾ*. Shāh ʿAbbās's relations with Darwish Khusraw began to sour two years later when he was presumptuously warned by the Nukṭawī leader, on the eve of a campaign against rebels in Luristān, that unless he returned to Ḳazwīn by 1 Muḥarram 1302/27 September 1593, a Nukṭawī adherent, other than the Shāh himself, might be compelled for astrological reasons to seize the throne. When Shāh ʿAbbās was encamped at Kharraḳān, he was brought a similarly patronising message by Darwīsh Kūčik Bahla-dūz ("gauntlet-maker"), a principal lieutenant of Darwīsh Khusraw, warning him again to return as quickly as possible and offering to send 50,000 armed Nukṭawīs to aid in the suppression of the rebellion. By now thoroughly alarmed, Shāh ʿAbbās ordered Malik ʿAlī the *djārčībāshī* back to Ḳazwīn to attack the Nukṭawī *takya* and arrest its inmates in advance of his own return to the capital. The stealth employed in executing this command suggests that there was indeed the potential for a full-scale Nukṭawī insurrection in Ḳazwīn. The *djārčībāshī* surrounded the *takya* before dawn and sought an audience with Darwīsh Khusraw on the pretext of presenting him with a robe of honour. As he was draping the cloak around his shoulders, he suddenly felled him with a powerful blow to the head, and the soldiers rushed in, killing many Nukṭawīs and arresting the others. Among those captured was Darwīsh Kūčik; he committed suicide by ingesting a large amount of opium, promising to return swiftly in a new incarnation. Darwīsh Khusraw himself was interrogated by the *ʿulamāʾ* and publicly tortured to death over a period of three days, after which his body was exhibited on the gibbet for a week.

It happened that soon after these events a comet appeared in the heavens. This was interpreted by Djalāl al-Dīn Yazdī, the court astrologer, to mean that the king would be in mortal danger during 7-10 Dhu 'l-Ḳaʿda 1002/25-8 July 1594. He therefore proposed that a substitute ruler worthy of death be placed on the throne for the duration of the critical period. Shāh ʿAbbās then asked one of the Nukṭawī captives, Darwīsh Yūsufī Tarkish-dūz ("quiver-maker") for his interpretation of the comet, and he replied that it was a sign that one of the Nukṭawīs would soon assume rule. The monarch countered that Darwīsh Yūsufī was the most suitable Nukṭawī for the throne, and immediately divested himself of the paraphernalia of monarchy and seated Darwīsh Yūsufī on the throne. At the end of the three days, during which Darwīsh Yūsufī made use of his glory only to have himself surrounded by handsome youths, he went straight from the throne to the scaffold, and Shāh ʿAbbās took back his regalia. This curious episode, illustrative both of Shāh ʿAbbās's imaginative sadism and of his superstitiousness, has inspired at least two literary treatments: a short story by the Ādharbāydjānī writer Fatḥ ʿAlī Ākhūndzāda (= Akhundov, d. 1878: *Aldanmïsh kävakib*: *hekayati Yusufshah*, in *Äsärläri*, Bākū 1987, i, 209-34, Russian tr. Aziz Sharifov, *Obmanutyye zvezdy, rasskaz o Yusuf-shakhe*, in Akhundov, *Izbrannoye*, Moscow 1956, 29-57) and a novel by Djalāl Āl-i Aḥmad (d. 1969: *Nūn wa 'l-ḳalam*, Tehran 1340 *Sh.*/1961).

Mass arrests and executions of Nukṭawīs then ensued in other cities, including once again Kāshān, where the discovery of a list of leading Nukṭawīs among the papers of the poet Mīr Sayyid Aḥmad Kāshī permitted the sect to be uprooted from the area once and for all. Shāh ʿAbbās personally beheaded Kāshī when he was in the midst of reminiscing concerning a previous existence, and then deftly bisected his headless trunk before it fell to the ground. He had a further confrontation with Nukṭawīs during his pilgrimage to Mashhad in 1010/1600-1; he discovered that his caravan had been infiltrated by his erstwhile initiators into the sect, and they were accordingly put to death in the caravanserai at Kūsha. The last Nukṭawī to be executed during the reign of Shāh ʿAbbās was the astrologer Mullā Ayāz, put to death in 1020/1611.

Although curiously enough the Nukṭawīs continued to regard Shāh ʿAbbās as one of their own, discounting his hostility to them as a sign of immaturity, many of them found it prudent to take refuge in India. These refugees included an impressive number of poets: Wuḳūʿī Nīshāpūrī, Ḥayātī Kāshānī, ʿAlī Akbar Tashbīhī Kāshānī, Mullā Ṣūfī Māzandarānī (Āmulī), Ḥakīm ʿIbād Allāh Kāshānī and ʿAbd al-Ghanī Yazdī. Adjusting their calculations to make Akbar yet another candidate for millennarian rule, the Nukṭawīs found favour with the Mughal emperor and assisted him in the formulation of his imperial cult, the *Dīn-i Ilāhī*. One of their number, Mīr Sharīf Āmulī, even sat on the nineteen-member committee that elaborated the cult. It is possible, too, that Akbar's chief confidant, Abu 'l-Faḍl ʿAllāmī, had Nukṭawī sympathies; a letter from him was found among the papers of Mīr Sayyid Aḥmad Kāshī, and it was he who moved Akbar to write a letter to Shāh ʿAbbās, fruitlessly urging on him the merits of religious tolerance. The emperor Djahāngīr did not entirely turn his back on the Nukṭawīs, but their visible presence in India did not last long.

A brief resurgence of the Nukṭawī movement took place in Persia during the reign of Shāh Ṣafī I. In Ḳazwīn, a certain Darwīsh Riḍā who claimed alternately to be the Mahdī and his deputy gathered a vast following that allowed him to seize control of the city. The movement was bloodily suppressed and Darwīsh Riḍā was beheaded in 1041/1631-2. His followers expected him to return from the dead, and when the following year they discovered an obscure farrier who resembled him, they renewed their uprising, with the same result as before.

This marked the end of the Nukṭawiyya as a movement with insurrectionary capabilities. Some thirty years later, Raphael du Mans remarked on the presence in Iṣfahān of a ragged group of dervishes known as Maḥmūdīs (*Estat de la Perse en 1660*, ed. Ch. Schefer, Paris 1890, 87-8), but they were evidently too insignificant to warrant suppression. Despite its impressive longevity in the face of repression, the Nukṭawī movement never had a chance of long-term success, being composed almost entirely of artisans and literati in an age when the application of tribal power was decisive (the Ustādjlū chieftain Būdāḳ Dīn-oghlī was the sole member of the Ṣafawid military aristocracy whom the Nukṭawīs were able to recruit).

A few vestiges of the Nukṭawiyya can nonetheless be traced in post-Ṣafawid Persia. According to Muḥammad ʿAlī Nāẓim al-Sharīʿa, Sayyid Muḥammad ʿAlī the Bāb was taught the doctrines of Nukṭawism during his confinement in Mākū and incorporated them directly in his *Bayān* (*Ḥadīd-i muhammā*, quoted in Ḳarāgūzlū, *Nagāh-i tāzaʾī ba manābiʿ-i Nukṭawiyya*, 38). This is unproven, but there are undeniable similarities between Nuḳṭawism and Bābism: a belief in metempsychosis, extravagant interpretations of Ḳurʾān and *ḥadīth*, a claim to have abrogated the Islamic *sharīʿa*, and a fixation on the number nineteen. Also in the early nineteenth century, the Niʿmatullāhī Ṣūfī Zayn al-ʿĀbidīn Shīrwānī (d. 1253/1837-38) reports having met Nuḳṭawīs who concealed themselves in the guise of Ṣūfīs (*Bustān al-siyāḥa*, reprint, Tehran n.d., 182). A contemporary researcher, Nūr al-Dīn Mudarrisī Čahārdihī, mentions having met in Bihbahān a certain Bābā Muḥammad who regarded himself as a Nuḳṭawī, but he seems to have been nothing more than an isolated eccentric (*Sayrī dar taṣawwuf, dar sharḥ-i ḥāl-i mashāyikh wa aḳṭāb*, 320-1).

Bibliography (in addition to references in the text): Aziz Ahmad, *Safawid poets and India*, in *Iran*, xiv (1976), 131; B.S. Amoretti, *Religion in the Timurid and Safavid periods*, in *Cambridge history of Iran. vi. The Timurid and Safavid periods*, Cambridge 1986, 644-6; S.A. Arjomand, *The Shadow of God and the Hidden Imam*, Chicago 1984, 198-9; ʿAbd al-Ḳādir Badāʾūnī, *Muntakhab al-tawārīkh*, Calcutta 1864-9, ii, 286-8, iii, 204-6, 378-9; M. Ibrāhīm Bāstānī-Pārīzī, *Siyāsat wa iḳtiṣād dar ʿaṣr-i Ṣafawī*[4], Tehran 1367 *Sh*./1988, 31, 46, 54-6; Nūr al-Dīn Mudarrisī Čahārdihī, *Sayrī dar taṣawwuf, dar sharḥ-i ḥāl-i mashāyikh wa aḳṭāb*, Tehran 1361 *Sh*./1982, 312-29; Farhad Daftary, *The Ismāʿīlīs: their history and doctrines*, Cambridge 1990, 455-6; Naṣr Allāh Falsafī, *Zindagānī-yi Shāh ʿAbbās-i Awwal*[2], Tehran 1334 *Sh*./1965, ii, 338-44, iii, 40-51; Riḍā-Ḳulī Khān Hidāyat, *Rawḍāt al-ṣafā-yi Nāṣirī*, Tehran 1339 *Sh*./1960, viii, 273-8; Kaykhusraw Isfandiyār, *Dabistān-i madhāhib*, ed. Raḥīm Riḍā-zāda Malik, Tehran 1362 *Sh*./1983, i, 273-8, ii, 231-6 (attributed to Mīrzā Muḥsin Fānī, Calcutta 1809, 374-80); ʿAlī Riḍā Dhakāwatī Ḳarāgūzlū, *Nagāh-i tāzaʾī ba manābiʿ-i Nuḳṭawiyya*, in *Taḥḳīḳāt-i Islāmī*, ii/2 (1366 *Sh*./1987), 31-9; idem, *Nagāhī dīgar ba Nuḳṭawiyya*, in *ibid.*, iv/1-2, 55-62; Z. Kuli-zade, *Khurufizm i ego predstaviteli v Azerbaydzhane*, Bākū 1970, 249-55; K.K. Kutsiya, *Iz istorii sotsial'nykh dvizhenii v gorodakh sefevidskogo gosudarstva: dvizhenie nuktaviev*, in *Narody Azii i Afriki* (1966), no. 2, 69-75; Minūčihr Mīnuwī, *Salṭanat-i Yūsufī-yi Tarkish-dūz*, in *Yaghmā*, ii (1328 *Sh*./1949), 310-14; Maryam Mīr-Aḥmadī, *Dīn wa madhhab dar dawra-yi Ṣafawī*, Tehran 1363 *Sh*./1984, 93-9; Iskandar Beg Munshī, *ʿĀlam-ārā-yi Ṣafawī*, Tehran 1350 *Sh*./1971, 473-7 Eng. tr., R.M. Savory, *History of Shah ʿAbbas*, Boulder 1978, ii, 646-50; idem and Muḥammad Yūsuf, *Dhayl-i ʿĀlam-ārā-yi ʿAbbāsī*, ed. Suhaylī Khʷānsārī, Tehran 1317 *Sh*./1938, 83-85, 240; Maḥmūd b. Hidāyat Allāh Afūshtaʾī Naṭanzī, *Nuḳāwat al-āthār fī dhikr al-akhyār*, ed. Iḥsān Ishrāḳī, Tehran 1350 *Sh*./1971, 507-28; S.A.A. Rizvi, *Religious and intellectual history of the Muslims in Akbar's reign*, Delhi 1975, 431; Maʿṣūm ʿAlī Shāh Shīrāzī, *Ṭarāʾiḳ al-ḥaḳāʾiḳ*, ed. Muḥammad Djaʿfar Maḥdjūb, Tehran n.d., iii, 136; Zayn al-ʿĀbidīn Shīrwānī, *Bustān al-siyāḥa*, repr. Tehran n.d., 181-2; Hilmi Ziya Ülken, *İslam felsefesi tarihi*, Istanbul 1957, 57; ʿAbd al-Ḥusayn Zarrīnkūb, *Dunbāla-yi djustudjū dar taṣawwuf-i Īrān*, Tehran 1362 *Sh*./1983, 237-9.

(H. ALGAR)

AL-**NUʿMĀN** B. ABĪ ʿABD ALLĀH MUḤAMMAD b. Manṣūr b. Ḥayyūn, famous *ḳāḍī* of the Fāṭimid caliph al-Muʿizz li-dīn Allāh [*q.v.*], of whose origins and early life little is known. This small amount of information is insufficient to explain the exceptional rise and fortune of this obscure jurist of Ifrīḳiya after he had entered the service of the new masters of this province, the Fāṭimids. As a connection of the Banū Tamīm, to which the line of Aghlabid *amīrs* were attached, al-Nuʿmān rose rapidly in the hierarchy of the Shīʿī state to the high position of judge-in-chief (*ḳāḍī 'l-ḳuḍāt*) of the community.

Hence the date of his birth is unknown, as is likewise his social position and the calibre of his intellectual training at Ḳayrawān at the moment when, towards the end of the 3rd/9th century, the Shīʿī Berber rebellion broke out, first of all in Little Kabylia, which was to sweep away the orthodox dynasty of the Aghlabids [*q.v.*] and end in the foundation, in Ifrīḳiya, of the Fāṭimid anti-caliphate. However, our sources agree on placing in 313/925 his nomination to the service (*khidma*) of the first Fāṭimid caliph, al-Mahdī bi 'llāh [*q.v.*] in an office whose exact nature is unknown. The speed of his adhesion to the doctrine of the *Ahl al-Bayt* and also his *kunya* of Abū Ḥanīfa make one think that he belonged to the Ḥanafī law school, solidly represented at Ḳayrawān and less hostile to Shīʿīsm than that of Mālik. It is more plausible that he joined the Ismāʿīlī *daʿwa* before the foundation of the Fāṭimid caliphate, as I.K. Poonawala has shown; referring, in particular, to an old Sunnī source, the *Ṭabaḳāt ʿulamāʾ Ifrīḳiya* of al-Khushanī, one of Nuʿmān's contemporaries, he has had the pertinent idea of identifying a certain Muḥammad b. Ḥayyān, mentioned as being among the jurists of Ḳayrawān professing the doctrine of *tashrīḳ*, sc. that of the *mashāriḳa*, the eastern Ismāʿīlīs, as being undoubtedly the father of al-Nuʿmān and of consequently correcting Muḥammad b. Ḥayyān into Muḥammad b. Ḥayyūn.

Thus al-Muʿizz's famous judge seems to have been raised and educated in the doctrine of the *Ahl al-Bayt* by a father who had already long been won over to Shīʿism, before the proclamation of the Fāṭimid caliphate in 297/310. This would, moreover, explain his rapid rise from being the modest *ḳāḍī* of a province, Tripoli, to the highest office of supreme *ḳāḍī* in 336/948. It was in fact from that town that the Fāṭimid caliph Ismāʿīl al-Manṣūr [*q.v.*] summoned him to his new capital, al-Manṣūriyya, just after his triumph over the Khāridjite rebel Abū Yazīd [*q.v.*], the famous "man on the donkey", in order to appoint him to this high office, in conditions which al-Nuʿmān himself describes in his *Kitāb al-Madjālis wa 'l-musāyarāt*: "Al-Nuʿmān, as soon as he had arrived in al-Manṣūriyya, was solemnly invested one Friday by the caliph, who awarded him robes of honour woven in the royal workshops and ordered him to proceed immediately to Ḳayrawān, since al-Manṣūriyya had not yet got a mosque which could allow him to lead the Friday worship in a *masdjid djāmiʿ* and to give the *khuṭba* there. Al-Manṣūr had him escorted by the officers of the guard, who accompanied him, with drawn swords, all the way along both the outward and the return journey. Some days later, the caliph sent a written mandate (*tawḳīʿ*) to the chancery where a nomination patent (*ʿahd*) was made out appointing him *ḳāḍī* of al-Manṣūriyya, al-Ḳayrawān, al-Mahdiyya and other towns and provinces of Ifrīḳiya."

Al-Nuʿmān's elevation to the most coveted position amongst the body of *faḳīhs* thus coincided with the consolidation of the state and of Fāṭimid power, after the crushing of Khāridjism, as also with the enfeeblement of the Sunnī party and the deterioration of relations between the central organisation of the Ismaʿīlī *daʿwa* at al-Manṣūriyya with the Ḳarmaṭīs of Baḥrayn. The reform of Fāṭimid doctrine undertaken by al-Mahdī immediately on proclamation of the caliphate, with the obvious aim of adapting Ismāʿīlism to the realities of Ḳayrawānī orthodoxy in order the better to create a state maḏhhab, became more pronounced during the last years of al-Manṣūr's reign and became stronger all through the twenty years' reign in Ifrīḳiya of al-Muʿizz. Al-Nuʿmān's designation thus came at a specific moment when the supreme ḳāḍī was to have a prime role in the elaboration of the state doctrine. Whilst holding his office and giving to the position of ḳāḍī an exemplary image both by his own competence and by his high moral qualities, al-Nuʿmān was also to distinguish himself by his role as a fertile author who was to have the merit of constructing a juridical and doctrinal system accessible to the masses of Ifrīḳiya. From now onwards, he was to owe his fame to the elaboration and the teaching of a simplified and moderate doctrine (samāʿ al-ḥikma), at the same time giving to the office of ḳāḍī ʾl-ḳuḍāt amongst the Shīʿīs the weightiness and effulgence which a Saḥnūn [q.v.] had given to the Mālikī ḳaḍāʾ a century earlier.

The exercise of his judicial function was to entail, for al-Nuʿmān, a didactic task. Since his high office meant that he was to fulfil, at the side of the Imām, the role of theoretician of Ismāʿīlism, he now began to devote himself to compose treatises of fiḳh according to the doctrine of the Imāms and to render their contents more widely known by public courses of instruction (durūs al-ḥikma). These courses were held after the ʿaṣr worship, and then sessions devoted to discussion and controversy were held in a special chamber. This maḏjlis al-ḥikma soon became a genuine institution in the shape of a centre of studies and propaganda which the Sunnīs called dār al-Ismāʿīliyya.

Since the Imām was the depository of all learning, according to the doctrine of the Ahl al-Bayt, it was in close collaboration with him that the supreme ḳāḍī, in his function of official faḳīh of the dynasty, wrote treatises on fiḳh and doctrine meant for teaching and for the use of regional judges, for governors and for students. Thus al-Nuʿmān consulted al-Muʿizz regularly whilst composing his main theological works, comprising the K. Daʿāʾim al-Islām, the K. al-Himma and the K. Asrār al-taʾwīl, and also, having entitled an abridgement of the doctrine of the Ahl al-Bayt the K. al-Dīnār, he modified this title, on the advice of the Imām, to K. al-Iḵhtiṣār li-ṣaḥīḥ al-āṯhār ʿan al-aʾimma al-aṭhār. Al-Nuʿmān's merit thus consists in the construction of a juridical and legal system for the use of the state, one oriented in the direction of a reconciliation of the concepts of Ismāʿīlism with those of the orthodoxy of Ḳayrawān. Thus the points of doctrinal opposition between Sunnism and Shīʿism are not so flagrant, in al-Nuʿmān's works, as the geographical collections of biographies of orthodox scholars of Ḳayrawān would lead one to believe. If there remains a total divergence on the questions of the definition of faith or that of walāya (adhesion to the Imāms), the contradiction in fact concerns only minor questions concerning ritual and practice of the cult. Reading the K. Daʿāʾim al-Islām allows one to estimate the importance of al-Nuʿmān's endeavour to bring about a rapprochment between Ismāʿīlī doctrine and the theses of Sunnism. Endeavouring as much as he could to codify Fāṭimid fiḳh in a simple and clear manner and to popularise it in order to encourage obedience to a politics of moderation and realism, the supreme judge completed his task as official faḳīh with the intention, above all, of making out of a juridical and doctrinal system an instrument of politics adapted to the imperialist intentions of the Fāṭimid state. This explains al-Muʿizz's interest in the works which al-

Nuʿmān wrote under his ultimate direction. For the caliph, observes Madelung, doctrine was in effect an instrument of politics. Hence he impelled his supreme ḳāḍī to elaborate a juridical system accessible and conformable to the universalist concept of the imāmate. Thus if the Ismāʿīlī supreme ḳāḍī offered the same image of simplicity and modesty, with the additional technical and moral qualities inherent in his office, as did the Sunnī ḳāḍī ʾl-ḳuḍāt, he nevertheless lived and worked within a total dependence of power. He ceased to be the mouthpiece of the ʿāmma, the censor of the palace, listened to by the sovereign and feared by the aristocracy. In this way, various special traits contribute to the image of the figure of the supreme judge, who became in the Fāṭimid state an official personage, a man of law caught up in the service of a cause, that of the Ahl al-Bayt. Yet as a consummate theologian, a highly literate author and an official with recognised moral and technical qualities, al-Nuʿmān has the merit of being known as one of the most famous representatives of the Mālikīs and of preserving for the high office of ḳāḍī its dignity and lustre.

Bibliography: See above all Brockelmann, S I, 324-5; Sezgin, GAS, i, 575-8; R.J. Gottheil, A distinguished family of Fatimid cadis (an-Nuʿmān) in the tenth century, in JAOS, xxvii (1907), 217-96; A.A.A. Fyzee, Qadi al-Nuʿmān, the Fatimid jurist and author, in JRAS (1934), 1-32; idem, ed. of the K. Daʿāʾim al-Islām, Cairo 1951, introd.; Kāmil Ḥusayn, ed. of K. al-Himma, Cairo 1948, introd.; Ḥabīb Fiḳī, Ibrāhīm Shabbūḥ and M. Yaʿlawī, ed. of the K. al-Madjālis wa ʾl-musāyarāt, Tunis 1978, introd.; Wadād al-Ḳāḍī, ed. of K. Iftitāḥ al-daʿwa, Beirut 1970, introd.; F. Dachraoui, ed. of K. Iftitāḥ al-daʿwa, Tunis 1975, introd.; idem, Le califat fatimide au Maghreb (histoire politique et institutions), Tunis 1981; I.K. Poonawala, A reconsideration of al-Qāḍī al-Nuʿmān's madhhab, in BSOAS, xxxviii (1974), 572-9; W. Madelung, Fatimiden und Baḥrainqarmaten, in Isl., xxxiv (1959), 34-88; idem, Das Imamat in der frühen ismailitischen Lehre, in ibid., xxxvii-xxxviii (1961), 43-155.   (F. Dachraoui)

AL-NUʿMĀN B. BASHĪR AL-Anṣārī, Companion of the Prophet and governor of al-Kūfa and Ḥimṣ.

According to some Muslim authorities, al-Nuʿmān was the first Anṣārī to be born after the Hidjra. His father Bashīr b. Saʿd [q.v.] was one of the most distinguished of the Companions, and his mother, ʿAmra bint Rawāḥa, was the sister of the much-respected ʿAbd Allāh b. Rawāḥa [q.v.]. After the assassination of ʿUthmān, al-Nuʿmān, who was devoted to him, refused to pay homage to ʿAlī. According to some stories which seem rather apocryphal, he brought the bloodstained shirt of the caliph, according to others, the fingers cut from the hand of his wife Nāʾila, to Damascus and these relics were exhibited by Muʿāwiya in the mosque. In the battle of Ṣiffīn [q.v.] he faithfully stood by Muʿāwiya and he was always a favourite with him while the other Anṣār were kept at a suitable distance from the Umayyad court. In the year 39/659-60 al-Nuʿmān, by order of Muʿāwiya, undertook an expedition against Mālik b. Kaʿb al-Arḥabī, who had occupied in ʿAlī's name ʿAyn al-Tamr on the frontier between Syria and Mesopotamia and began to besiege it, but had to retire without accomplishing anything. Twenty years later he was given the governorship of al-Kūfa. He was not really fitted for this post, because his pronounced antipathy to ʿAlī and his followers did not suit the Shīʿī population of the town. In addition, he did not conceal his sympathy with the Anṣār, who were attacked by

Yazīd b. Muʿāwiya's favourite al-Akhṭal [*q.v.*], but freely expressed his opinion on the insult offered to his fellow-tribesmen.

After Yazīd had come to the throne in 60 Radjab/April 680, he nevertheless left al-Nuʿmān in office; but the latter did not long remain there. Al-Nuʿmān is described as an ascetic, and he knew the teachings of the Ḳurʾān thoroughly. But his asceticism was not of the strictest type, and his interest in musical entertainments was regarded as evidence of lack of dignity. In policy he proved very tolerant so long as it did not come to an open rising. When Muslim b. ʿAḳīl [*q.v.*], al-Ḥusayn's partisan, appeared in al-Kūfa to ascertain the feelings of the people and he found a number who were ready to pay homage to al-Ḥusayn, al-Nuʿmān adopted a neutral attitude and took no steps to check the vigorous propaganda. As a result, the followers of the Umayyads in al-Kūfa wrote to the caliph and called his attention to the fact that the threatening situation demanded a man of vigour who would be able to carry out the government's orders, while al-Nuʿmān, out of real or feigned weakness, was letting things take their course and only urging people to keep calm. When Yazīd was discussing this with his councillors, notably the influential Ibn Sardjūn, the latter showed him a document signed by Muʿāwiya shortly before his death, containing the appointment of the then governor of al-Baṣra ʿUbayd Allāh b. Ziyād [*q.v.*] to the same office in al-Kūfa. In spite of his antipathy to the proposal, Yazīd carried out his father's wish and made ʿUbayd Allāh governor of al-Kūfa without removing him from his post in al-Baṣra, whereupon al-Nuʿmān hastened back to Syria. When the people of Medina rebelled at the beginning of the year 63/682 and drove all the Umayyads out of the town, Yazīd wished to see what tact would do before resorting to arms and sent a mission to Medina under al-Nuʿmān to show the people the futility of armed resistance and to bring them to their senses. The mission was also instructed to go on to Mecca to induce the stubborn ʿAbd Allāh b. al-Zubayr to pay homage. Al-Nuʿmān's warnings and threats had no effect on his countrymen, however, and there was nothing left for the caliph but to subdue the rebels in the two holy cities by force of arms [see YAZĪD B. MUʿĀWIYA]. After the death of Yazīd in Rabīʿ I 64/Nov. 683, al-Nuʿmān, who had in the meanwhile become governor of Ḥimṣ, declared openly for ʿAbd Allāh b. al-Zubayr. In Dhu 'l-Ḥidjdja of the same year/July-Aug. 684 and Muḥarram 65/Aug.-Sept. 684, however, the latter's leading follower al-Ḍaḥḥāk b. Ḳays al-Fihrī [*q.v.*] was defeated at Mardj Rāhiṭ [*q.v.*], and thus the fate of al-Nuʿmān was also decided. He attempted to save himself by flight but was overtaken and killed. According to the Arab historians, the town of Maʿarrat al-Nuʿmān [*q.v.*] takes its name from al-Nuʿmān b. Bashīr.

Bibliography: Ibn Saʿd, vi, 35; Ṭabarī, see index; Ibn al-Athīr, i, 514, ii, 85, 303, 382, iii, 154, 228, 315, 430, iv, 9, 15, 17, 19, 75, 88, 120, 123-5; Yaʿḳūbī, *Taʾrīkh*, ii, 219, 228, 278, 301, 304-5; Dīnawarī, *al-Akhbār al-ṭiwāl*, ed. Guirgass, 239-40, 245, 247, 273; Masʿūdī, *Murūdj*, iv, 296-7, v, 128, 134, 204, 227-9 = §§ 1621, 1885, 1891, 1968, 1991; Abu 'l-Fidāʾ, ed. Reiske, i, 77, 385, 393, 405, 407; *Kitāb al-Aghānī*, see Guidi, *Tables alphabétiques*; Caetani, *Annali dell' Islām*, viii, 325, ix, 233, 355, x, 275 ff., see also index; Wellhausen, *Das arabische Reich und sein Sturz*, 47, 82, 94, 96, 110; Lammens, *Études sur le regne du calife omaiyade Moʿâwia Ier*, 43, 45, 58, 110, 116, 407; idem, *Le califat de Yazîd Ier*, 119 ff., 137, 140, 142, 207, 215, 221, 228; G. Rotter, *Die Umayyaden und der zweite Bürgerkrieg (680-692)*, Wiesbaden 1982, index.

(K.V. ZETTERSTÉEN)

AL-**NUʿMĀN** (III) B. AL-**MUNDHIR**, the last Lakhmid king of Ḥīra [*q.v.*] and vassal of Sāsānid Persia. He was the son of al-Mundhir IV [*q.v.*] and Salmā, the daughter of a Jewish goldsmith from Fadak. In the annals of the Lakhmids [*q.v.*], his reign (*ca.* A.D. 580-602) was the most memorable after that of his grandfather, al-Mundhir III (d. 554). His accession to the throne of Ḥīra he owed to ʿAdī b. Zayd [*q.v.*], the famous Christian poet and statesman of Ḥīra, and the Sāsānid Hormuzd celebrated that accession with an especially splendid crown.

Al-Nuʿmān was an assertive and strong ruler, and his reign witnessed tensions within Ḥīra and wars with the Arab tribes. The Ḥīra clan of the Banū Marīna had opposed his accession, and finally, the very friendly clan of the Banū Ayyūb was ranged against him. In addition to friction with the Taghlib tribe, he tried to withdraw the privilege of *ridāfa* (divisional leadership in battle) accorded to Yarbūʿ, a subdivision of the tribe of Tamīm, from them and transfer it to another subdivision, namely Dārim. Yarbūʿ contested this, and in a bloody encounter at Ṭikhfa, the Yarbūʿ were victorious. Al-Nuʿmān's brother Ḥassān and his son Ḳābūs led the Lakhmid troops but both were defeated and captured, and al-Nuʿmān had to ransom them for 1,000 camels.

The fall of the Ghassānids [*q.v.*] from grace *ca.* 580 brought about disarray in Ghassānid-Byzantine relations and with it a diminution of the Ghassānid military role in Byzantium's war with Persia in the 580s. Hence Lakhmid-Ghassānid encounters receive no mention in the sources, and these record only an echo of an expedition by al-Nuʿmān against Byzantine Circesium (Ḳarḳīsiyā [*q.v.*]). The conclusion of the Persian-Byzantine peace which lasted till the death of the emperor Maurice in 602 ruled out any serious Lakhmid military designs against Ghassānid or Byzantine territory. But before that peace was concluded, al-Nuʿmān had fought with Parwīz [*q.v.*], Hormuzd's son and successor, at the battle of al-Nahrawān against the rebel Bahrām Čūbīn.

During the reign of al-Nuʿmān, Ḥīra continued to develop as the greatest centre of Arab culture before the rise of Islam. In addition to the poetry of its most famous poet, the Christian ʿAdī b. Zayd, the splendid panegyrics of al-Nābigha al-Dhubyānī [*q.v.*], one of the poets of the *Muʿallaḳāt* [*q.v.*], were composed on this al-Nuʿmān. The earliest collection of Arabic poems are associated with his name, sc. panegyrics of various poets on members of the Lakhmid dynasty. The king converted to Christianity after most of his ancestors had resisted the temptation. But the Nestorianism to which he was converted was acceptable to Sāsānid Persia, and Parwīz himself had become well disposed towards Christianity after his marriage to the Christian Shīrīn and the peace with Byzantium in 591, which thus becomes the *terminus post quem* for al-Nuʿmān's conversion. Ḥīra became, even more than before, the centre of Arab Christianity in Sāsānid Persia, whence the Nestorian Church propagated Christianity among the Arabs of the Persian Gulf and Eastern Arabia.

The reign that started so auspiciously with the crown from Hormuzd ended disastrously for al-Nuʿmān, who, after harbouring suspicions towards ʿAdī b. Zayd to whom he owed his accession, had him incarcerated and put to death. ʿAdī's son, influential at the court of Parwīz, plotted against al-Nuʿmān in revenge for the murder of his father; al-Nuʿmān fled from Ḥīra after sensing that Parwīz was in pursuit of him and took refuge with the tribe of Bakr. He nevertheless finally surrendered to Parwīz, who had him trampled to death by elephants.

Al-Nuᶜmān's death represented the virtual end of the Lakhmid dynasty which had lasted for some three hundred years, the shield of Persia against the Arabs of the Peninsula. A few years later, the tribe of Bakr won the historic encounter of Dhū Ḳār [*q.v.*] against the Persians and their Arab condederates. It was the precursor of al-Ḳādisiyya [*q.v.*] fought in 637, the battle that was to remove Sāsānid Persia from the stage of Near Eastern history.

Bibliography: Ṭabarī, in Nöldeke, *Geschichte der Perser und Araber zur Zeit der Sasaniden*, Leiden 1879, repr. Graz 1973, 310-32, 346-7; Abu 'l-Baḳāʾ al-Ḥillī, *al-Manāḳib al-Mazyadiyya*, ed. S. Darādka and M. Khuraysāt, ᶜAmmān 1984, i, 265-9, ii, 386-403, 447-51; G. Rothstein, *Die Dynastie der Laḫmiden in al-Ḥīra*, Berlin 1899. (IRFAN SHAHÎD)

NUMAYR B. ᶜĀMIR B. ṢAᶜṢAᶜA, an Arab tribe (Wüstenfeld, *Geneal. Tabellen*, F 15) inhabiting the western heights of al-Yamāma and those between this region and the Ḥimā Ḍariyya: a bare and difficult country, the nature of which explains the rude and savage character of the Numayr. Their name like that of Namir and Anmār borne by other ethnic groups (there are also in the list of Arab tribes a number of other clans with the name Numayr: among the Asad, the Tamīm, the Djuᶜfī, the Hamdān, etc.) is no doubt connected with *nimr*, *namir* [*q.v.*], the Arabian panther; we know the deductions made by Robertson Smith from this fact and from other similar cases, to prove the existence of a system of totemism among the early Arabs (*Kinship and marriage in early Arabia*², 234). His theory is now abandoned.

The geographical dictionaries of al-Bakrī and Yāḳūt mention a large number of places in the land of the Numayr, especially their wells, and often even record a change of ownership from one tribe to another (e.g. Yāḳūt, *Muᶜdjam*, iii, 802: the well of Ghisl, which formerly belonged to the Tamīmī clans of the Kulayb b. Yarbūᶜ, later passed to Numayr); this wealth of references does not, however, mean that the Numayr played an important part in the history of Arabia. It is only due to the fact that the country of the Numayr is typically Bedouin in its scenery and lends itself to description by poets. The Numayr, besides, were much intermixed with the neighbouring tribes (especially the Tamīm, Bāhila and Ḳushayr) and the boundaries of their territory were rather vague.

The Numayr, a poor tribe without natural wealth, have always been brigands. The part they took in the pre-Islamic wars was a very modest one and they appear very rarely alongside of the other groups of the great tribe of ᶜĀmir b. Ṣaᶜṣaᶜa (they hardly played any part in the battle of Fayf-Rīḥ against the Banu 'l-Ḥārith b. Kaᶜb and their allies, *Naḳāʾiḍ*, ed. Bevan, 469-72). It is to this isolation that they owe the privilege of being known as one of the *Djamarāt al-ᶜArab*, i.e. a tribe which never allied itself with others (al-Mubarrad, *Kāmil*, ed. Wright, 372; *Naḳāʾiḍ*, 946; *Mufaḍḍaliyyāt*, ed. Lyall, 841; on the different tribes to which this title is given, cf. *Tādj al-arūs*, iii, 107); the other designation of the Numayr "the *Aḥmās* of the Banū ᶜĀmir", also gives them a special place within the great tribe from which they sprang; it indicates that they were thought not to have the same mother as the other clans of the Banū ᶜĀmir (*Mufaḍḍaliyyāt*, 259, 12-15 = 771, 2-4; the source is the *Djamhara* of Ibn al-Kalbī, Brit. Mus. mss., fols. 120b-121a, now edited). Neither during the life of the Prophet, nor at the beginning of the caliphate, did the Numayr make any stir; they appear neither as partisans nor as enemies of Islam. It is only from the Umayyad period that the name begins to appear in histories, but only to record their insubordination to the central power or their exploits as brigands; in the caliphate of ᶜAbd al-Malik, their refusal to pay tribute brought a punitive expedition against them (al-Balādhurī, *Futūḥ*, 139; cf. *Aghānī*, xvii, 112-13, xix, 120-1). Another expedition of the same kind but on a larger scale was that sent against them under the famous general of the caliph al-Mutawakkil, Bughā al-Kabīr [*q.v.*], in 232/846, to put an end to their systematic plundering; it ended in the complete dispersal of the tribe (al-Ṭabarī, iii, 1357-63, a most interesting account of Bedouin customs including on p. 1361 a detailed list of the Numayr clans, only one of which, the Banū ᶜĀmir b. Numayr, devoted itself to agriculture and grazing, while the others lived only by brigandage). It appears, however, that the Numayr soon resumed their old habits and another expedition was sent against them with the same object as the earlier ones in the 4th/10th century by the Ḥamdānid Sayf al-Dawla (Yāḳūt, iv, 378).

An event of little importance in itself has given the Numayr considerable fame in literary history, although little flattering to them: this is the satire directed against them by the poet Djarīr [*q.v.*] which is one of the most famous examples of the invective of the *hidjāʾ* (especially the hemistich: "Cast down thine eyes: thou belongest to the Numayr"). The occasion of it was the unfortunate intervention of the Numayrī poet al-Rāᶜī in favour of al-Farazdaḳ in the celebrated feud between him and Djarīr (*Naḳāʾiḍ*, 427-51, no. 53; *Aghānī*, vii, 49-50, xx, 169-71, etc.). The memory of this quarrel survived for a very long time. It was probably no accident that the man who urged the *amīr* Bughā to the expedition against the Numayr was the great-grandson of Djarīr, the poet ᶜUmāra b. ᶜAḳīl b. Bilāl b. Djarīr; the Numayr moreover had slain four of his uncles (Ibn Ḳutayba, *Shiᶜr*, ed. de Goeje, 284, where we must read Banū Ḍinna [b. ᶜAbd Allāh b. Numayr] in place of Banū Ḍabba). The enmity between the family of Djarīr and the Numayr was probably revived by the proximity of the latter to the tribe of the poet, the Banū Kulayb b. Yarbūᶜ.

To the Numayr belonged notable poets—in addition to al-Rāᶜī and his son Djandal—like Abū Ḥayya (in the early ᶜAbbāsid period) and Djirān al-ᶜAwd whose *Dīwān* has been published (Cairo 1350/1931, publications of the Egyptian Library), cf. Sezgin, *GAS*, ii, 217.

Bibliography: Wüstenfeld, *Register zu den geneal. Tabellen*, 340; Ibn Durayd, *Kitāb al-Ishtiḳāḳ*, ed. Wüstenfeld, 178-9; Ibn Ḳutayba, *Kitāb al-Maᶜārif*, ed. Wüstenfeld, 42; Ibn al-Kalbī, *Djamharat al-ansāb*, British Museum ms., fols. 147b-150a; Ibn al-Kalbī-Caskel, i, *Tafeln*, III, ii *Register*, 15-16, 450. (G. LEVI DELLA VIDA)

AL-**NUMAYRĪ, ABŪ ḤAYYA** [see ABŪ ḤAYYA AL-NUMAYRĪ in Suppl., and add to the *Bibl.* there: Y. al-Djubūrī, *Shiᶜr Abī Ḥayya al-Numayrī*, Damascus 1975; R.Ṣ. al-Tuwayfī, *Shiᶜr Abī Ḥayya al-Numayrī*, in *al-Mawrid*, iv/1 (1975), 131-52 (55 fragments), with the additions of S. al-Ghānimī, in *ibid.*, vi/2 (1977), 311-12. See also Sezgin, *GAS*, ii, 464-5, ix, 288].

NŪN, the 25th letter of the Arabic alphabet, transcribed /n/, with the numerical value 50, according to the oriental order [see ABDJAD]. Nūn is also a name of the 68th *sūra* [see ḲURʾĀN, SŪRA].

1. In Arabic

Definition: an occlusive, dental, voiced nasal (Cantineau, *Études*, 38-40; Fleisch, *Traité*, i, 58, 84-5).

Sībawayh distinguishes two kinds of *nūn*: (a) the one whose point of articulation is the tip of the tongue and the region a little above the incisors; this is a clear (*madjhūr*) and hard (*shadīd*) "letter", but it is accompanied by a resonance (*ghunna*) of the nose (*anf*). (b) the light (*khafīfa*) *nūn*, whose point of articulation is situated in the nasal cavities (*khayāshīm*) (*Kitāb*, ii, 452-4; Roman, *Étude*, i, 52, 56, 60).

For al-Khalīl, *nūn* is an apical (*dhalḳī*) letter, articulated with the tip of the tongue (*dhalḳ*) (*K. al-ʿAyn*, 65; Roman, *Étude*, i, 216-17).

As for Ibn Sīnā, he considers that *nūn* is realised by the tip of the tongue which touches the alveolar arch and holds in the air, then emits it through the nasal cavities (*khayāshīm*); the air becomes a resonance (*ghunna*) of the nose (*minkhar*) and a humming sound (*dawī*) (Roman, *Étude*, i, 263-4).

Phonologically, the phoneme /n/ is defined by the oppositions /n/-/m/, /n/-/r/ and /n/-/l/ (Cantineau, *Études*, 172).

Alterations: the realisation (*iẓhār*) of *nūn* can only take place before the four laryngeals /ʾ/, /h/, /ḥ/ and /ʿ/ and the two velars /kh/ and /gh/; before the bilabial /b/, there is conversion (*ḳalb*) to /m/; before the three pre-palatals /l/, /r/ and /y/ and the two bilabials /m/ and /w/, there is assimilation (*idghām*); before the other consonants, there is concealment (*ikhfāʾ*), i.e. reduction to the nasal resonance (Sībawayh, *Kitāb*, ii, 464-5; Roman, *Étude*, i, 306-7). See also TANWĪN.

Bibliography: J. Cantineau, *Études de linguistique arabe,* Paris 1960; H. Fleisch, *Traité de philologie arabe,* i, Beirut 1961; A. Roman, *Étude de la phonologie et de la morphologie de la koinè arabe*, Aix-Marseilles 1983; al-Khalīl, *K. al-ʿAyn*, ed. Darwīsh, Baghdād 1967; Sībawayh, *Kitāb*, ed. Dérenbourg, Paris 1889. (G. TROUPEAU)

2. In Turkish

The earliest form of Turkish known to us, that of the Orkhon inscriptions (8th century A.D.), distinguished in the so-called "Runic" script two separate forms for use in back- and front-vowelled syllables, for the dental nasal /n/, plus further forms for the velar nasal /ŋ/ and the palatal nasal /ń/ (Talat Tekin, *A grammar of Orkhon Turkic*, Bloomington-The Hague 1968, 23-4, 82-3, 92-3). A century or so later, the Uyghur script distinguished /n/, and /ŋ/, and the Brahmi script a further sign /ṃ/ for the nasalisation of vowels arising out of /n/ (A. von Gabain, *Alttürkische Grammatik*[2], Leipzig 1950, §§ 9, 25, 30-1).

In the Arabic script used for Ottoman Turkish, the dental nasal /n/ was conveyed by the letter *nūn*, whilst the gutterally pronounced /ñ/, largely disappeared in standard Ottoman pronunciation, was written with the so-called *ṣāghīr nūn*, the Persian *gāf* (ڭ, ݣ ; in Central Asian Turkish, نك). It should be noted that /n/ is very rare in word-initial position in true Ottoman Turkish words and /ñ/ never occurs thus (J. Deny, *Grammaire de la langue turque* (*dialecte osmanli*), Paris 1921, 19, 71-2, 76).

Bibliography: Given in the article. (ED.)

3. Indian sub-continent

Arabic, Persian and Turkish words with *nūn* occur frequently in Indian languages, and occasion no difficulties or differences in their orthography; the signs for nunation (*tanwīn*) remain unchanged, and the *tashdīd* is used for the geminated *-nn-* whenever Arabic orthography requires it (although it may be neglected in early inscriptions). The sound-systems of the Indo-Aryan languages, however, have resulted in certain modifications to the Perso-Arabic script, as follows.

In most Indian phonologies there are nasalised vowels; these are normally indicated by the usual *nūn* following the nasalised vowel, although when a nasalised long vowel stands finally in a word, or even morpheme, the final form of *nūn* is written without its *nuḳta*, and is then called *nūn ghunna*. This is derived from the purely calligraphic forms of the Persian *nastaʿlīḳ* script, but the Indian significance is different. Also, geminated consonants can arise morphophonemically; e.g. in the Urdū verb *bannā* "to be made", root *ban* + infinitive suffix *-nā*, the *-nn-* must be written with two *nūn*s and not with the *tashdīd*.

Most Indian sound-systems have a retroflex nasal (derived generally from a single intervocalic nasal in Middle Indo-Aryan) as well as the dental, but these have fallen together in standard Hindī and Urdū, and even where they are still differentiated in various rustic forms of speech they are never distinguished in the Urdū script. (They occur in Gudjarātī and Marāthī, but here there is no question of the Perso-Arabic script being used.) A retroflex nasal is required, however, in Sindhī and in Pashto, where new writing devices have been invented. In Pashto the *nūn*, medial or final, is written with its usual single *nuḳta* with the addition of a small subscript circle (or "bean") to either form. The Sindhī retroflex nasal substitutes a small *ṭāʾ* for the usual *nuḳta*. (Sindhī also distinguishes the velar and palatal nasals in speech, but the velar ṅ is represented by a *gāf* with two additional superscript *nuḳta*s, the palatal ñ by a *ḥāʾ* with two horizontal subscript *nuḳta*s.) The retroflex nasal also occurs in Pandjābī, but no standard writing system has yet been introduced.

Bibliography: Specimens of written (and printed) Pandjābī, Pashto and Sindhī are given in the appropriate volumes of G.A. Grierson, *Linguistic survey of India*. (J. BURTON-PAGE)

NŪR (A.), light, synonym *ḍawʾ*, also *ḍūʾ* and *ḍiyāʾ* (the latter sometimes used in the plural).

1. Scientific aspects

According to some authors, *ḍawʾ* (*ḍiyāʾ*) has a more intensive meaning than *nūr* (cf. Lane, *Arabic-English dictionary*, s.v. *ḍawʾ*); this idea has its foundation in Ḳurʾān, X, 5, where the sun is called *ḍiyāʾ* and the moon *nūr*. The further deduction from this passsage that *ḍiyāʾ* is used for the light of light-producing bodies (sun) and *nūr* on the other hand for the reflected light in bodies which do not emit light (moon), is not correct, if we remember the primitive knowledge of natural science possessed by the Arabs in the time of Muḥammad, nor is there any proof of it in later literature. The works on natural science and cosmology of the Arabs in the best period of the Middle Ages (Ibn al-Haytham, al-Ḳazwīnī [*q.vv.*] and later writers) in the great majority of cases use the term *ḍawʾ* and it therefore seems justified to claim this word as a technical term in mathematics and physics.

Besides dealing with the subject in his *Optics* (*Kitāb al-Manāẓir*), Ibn al-Haytham devoted a special treatise to it entitled *Ḳawl al-Ḥasan b. al-Ḥusayn b. al-Haytham fi 'l-ḍawʾ* which has been published with a German translation by J. Baarmann in *ZDMG*, xxxvi (1882), 195-237, from which we take the following details:

As regards light, two kinds of bodies are distinguished, luminous (including the stars and fire) and non-luminous (dark); the non-luminous are again divided into opaque and transparent, the latter again into such as are transparent in all parts, like air, water, glass, crystal etc., and such as only admit the light partly but the material of which is really opaque, such as thin cloth.

The light of luminous bodies is an essential quality

of the body, the reflected light of a body in itself dark being, on the other hand, an accidental quality of the body.

In the opinion of the mathematicians, all the phenomena of light are of one and the same character; they consist of a heat from fire which is in the luminous bodies themselves. This is evident from the fact that one can concentrate rays of light from the brightest luminous body, the sun, by means of a burning-glass on one point and thus set all inflammable bodies alight and by the fact that the air and other bodies affected by the light of the sun become warm. Light and heat are thus identified with each other or regarded as equivalent. The intensity of light, like that of heat, diminishes as the distance from the source increases.

Every luminous body, whether its light is one of its essential qualities (direct) or accidental (reflected), illuminates any body placed opposite it, i.e. it sends its light out in all directions. All bodies, whether transparent or opaque, possess the power of absorbing light, the former having further the power of transmitting it again; that a transparent body (air, water, etc.) also has the power of absorbing light is evident from the fact that the light becomes visible in it if it is cut with an opaque body: the light must therefore have already been in it.

The penetration of light into a transparent body takes place along straight lines (proof: the sun's rays in the dust-filled air of a dark room). This transmission of light in straight lines is an essential feature of light itself, not of the transparent body, for otherwise there must be in the latter specially marked lines along which the light travels; such a hypothesis is however disproved by admitting two or more rays of light at the same time into a dark room and watching them.

The ray is defined as light travelling along a straight line. The early mathematicians were of the opinion that the process of seeing consisted in the transmission of a ray from the eye of the observer to the object seen and the reflection from it back to the eye. Opposed to this is Ibn al-Hay<u>th</u>am's view that the body seen—luminous or opaque—sends out rays in all directions from all points of which those going towards the eye of the observer collect in it and are perceived as the image of the body (cf. *Optics*, book i, 23: "Visio non fit radiis a visu emissis" and also book ii, 23).

There is no absolutely transparent body; on the contrary, every body, even the transparent one, reflects a part of the light which strikes it (explanation of the phenomena of twilight). According to Aristotle, the heavens possess the highest and most perfect degree of transparency. Ibn al-Hay<u>th</u>am challenges this statement and shows from a use of the theory of the mathematician Abū Saʿd al-ʿAlāʾ b. Sahl (2nd half of the 4th/10th century, see Sezgin, *GAS*, vi, 232-3), which is based on the well-known rules of the refraction of light in passing through media of different densities, that the transparency has no limits and that for every transparent body an even more transparent one can be found.

An explanation of the origin of the halo around the moon, of the rainbow, its shape and its colours, and of the rainbow to be seen at night in the steam-laden atmosphere of the bath, is given by al-Ḳazwīnī in his *Cosmography*, i (*ʿA<u>dj</u>āʾib al-ma<u>kh</u>lūḳāt*, ed. Wüstenfeld, Göttingen 1849, 100-1; tr. Ethé, Leipzig 1868, 205 ff.). Al-Ḳazwīnī in his discussion replaces the raindrops by small looking-glasses; Ibn al-Hay<u>th</u>am, on the other hand, deals with the problem in a much more conclusive fashion by assuming a single or double reflection of light in spheres (cf. E. Wiedemann, in *Wied. Ann.*, xxxix [1890], 575).

Bibliography: Given in the article. New, corrected ed. of Ibn al-Hay<u>th</u>am's *al-Ḳawl fi 'l-ḍawʾ*, by ʿA.Ḳ. Mursī, Cairo 1938; critical Fr. tr. R. Rashed, *Le "Discours de la lumière" d'Ibn al-Haytham*, in *Revue d'histoire des sciences*, xxi (1968), 198-224. Cf. also the relevant chs. in Ibn al-Hay<u>th</u>am, *K. al-Manāẓir, maḳālāt* 1-3, ed. ʿA.Ḥ. Sabra, Kuwait 1983, tr. and comm. idem, *Ibn al-Haytham's Optics*, 2 vols., London 1989. (W. HARTNER)

2. Philosophical aspects

The doctrine that God is light and reveals Himself as such in the world and to man is very old and widely disseminated in Oriental religions as well as in Hellenistic gnosis and philosophy. We cannot here go into the early history; it will be sufficient to refer to some parallels in the Old and New Testaments, e.g. Gen., i. 3; Isaiah, lx. 1, 19; Zech., iv.; John, i. 4-9; iii. 19; v. 35; viii. 12; xii. 35; and Rev., xxi. 23-4.

How Muḥammad became acquainted with this teaching we do not know, but the Ḳurʾān has its "light" verses, notably XXIV, 35, the "light verse" proper; cf. XXXIII, 45 (Muḥammad as lamp); LXI, 8-9 (God's light); LXIV, 8 (the light sent down = revelation). The light verse runs (as rendered by Goldziher, in *Die Richtungen der Koranauslegung*, 183-5): "God is the light of the heavens and of the earth; His light is like a niche in which there is a lamp; the lamp is in a glass and the glass is like a shining star; it is lit from a blessed tree, an olive-tree, neither an eastern nor a western one; its oil almost shines alone even if no fire touches it; light upon light. God leads to his light whom He will, and God creates allegories for man, and God knows all things."

From the context it is clear that we have to think of the light of religious knowledge, of the truth which God communicates through his Prophet to his creatures especially the believers (cf. also XXIII, 40). It is pure light, light upon light, which has nothing to do with fire (*nār*), which is lit from an olive tree, perhaps not of this world (cf. however A.J. Wensinck, *Tree and bird as cosmological symbols in Western Asia*, in *Verh. Ak. Amst.* [1921], 27-8). Lastly, it is God as the All-Knowing who instructs men and leads them to the light of His revelation (cf. LXIV, 8). It is clear that we have here traces of gnostic imagery but those rationalist theologians, who—whether to avoid any comparison of the creature with God or to oppose the fantastic mystics—interpreted the light of God as a symbol of His good guidance, probably diverged less from the sense of the Ḳurʾān than most of the metaphysicians of light. Passages in which God appears as the Knowing (*ʿalīm*) and the Guiding (*hādī*) are very frequent in the Ḳurʾān. One did not need to look far for an exegesis on these lines. As al-A<u>sh</u>ʿarī observes (*Maḳālāt*, ed. Ritter, ii, 534), the Muʿtazilī al-Ḥusayn al-Na<u>djdj</u>ār interpreted the light verse to mean that God guides the inhabitants of heaven and earth. The Zaydīs also interpreted the light as God's good guidance [see <u>SH</u>Īʿa and ZAYDIYYA].

From *ca.* 100 A.H., we find references to a prophetic doctrine of *nūr*, and gradually to a more general metaphysics of light, i.e. the doctrine that God is essentially light, the prime light and as such the source of all being, all life and all knowledge. Especially among the mystics in whose emotional thinking being, name and image coalesced, this speculation developed. Meditation on the Ḳurʾān, Persian stimuli, gnostic-Hermetic writings, and lastly and most tenaciously, Hellenistic philosophy provided the material for new ideas. Al-Kumayt (d. 126/743 [*q.v.*])

had already sung of the light emanating through Adam via Muḥammad into the family of ʿAlī [see SHĪʿA]. The doctrine of light was dialectically expounded by Sahl al-Tustarī (d. 283/896) (see also Massignon, *Textes inédites*, 39, and SAHL AL-TUSTARĪ).

The first representatives of a metaphysics of light in Islam readily fell under the suspicion of Manichaeism, i.e. of the dualism of *nūr* and *ẓulma* (darkness) as the eternal principles. The tradition of al-Tirmidhī that God created in darkness [see KHALḲ] must have aroused misgivings. The physician al-Rāzī (d. 311/923), although a Hellenistic philosopher, adopted ideas from Persia and was for this refuted or cursed by various theologians and philosophers. Many mystics also (e.g. al-Ḥallādj; according to Massignon, *Passion*, 150-1, wrongly) were accused of this dualism.

But the speculations about *nūr* found powerful support from the 3rd/9th century in the monistic doctrine of light of the Neo-Platonists (we do not know of any Persian monism of light) which was compatible with the monism of Islam. The father of this doctrine is Plato, who in his *Politeia*, 506 D ff., compares the idea of the good in the supersensual world with Helios as the light of the physical world. The contrast is not therefore between light and darkness but between the world of ideas or mind and its copy, the physical world of bodies, in the upper world pure light, in the lower world light more or less mixed with darkness. Among the Neo-Platonists, the idea of the good = the highest God = pure light. This identification was also facilitated by the fact that, according to Aristotle's conception, light is nothing corporeal (*De anima*, ii, 7, 418b: [φῶς]... οὔτε πῦρ οὔθ' ὅλως σῶμα οὐδ' ἀπορροὴ σώματος). From the context, which is however not all clear, it appears that Aristotle regarded light as an effective force (ἐνέργεια). This is however of no importance here. Many Aristotelian forces and Platonic ideas are described by Neo-Pythagoreans and Neo-Platonists sometimes as forces and sometimes as substances (spiritual). With Aristotle, σκότος (darkness) was conceived not as something positive but as στέρησις (*privatio*, the absence of light).

From this developed the doctrine which we find in the Arabic *Theology of Aristotle*. Not far from the beginning (ed. Dieterici, 3) it is said: the power of light (*ḳuwwa nūriyya*) is communicated by the prime cause, the creator, to the *ʿaḳl* and by the *ʿaḳl* to the world soul, then from the *ʿaḳl* through the world soul to nature and from the world soul through nature to the things which originate and decay. The whole process of this creative development proceeds without movement and timelessly. But God who causes the force of light to pour forth is also light (*nūr*; occasional synonyms: *ḥusn*, *bahāʾ*), the "prime light" (51) or (44) the "light of lights". Light (51) is essentially in God, not a quality (*ṣifa*), for God has no qualities but works through His being (*huwiyya*) alone. The light flows through the whole world, particularly the world of men. From the supersensual original (150), the first man (*insān ʿaḳlī*), it flows over the second man (*insān nafsānī*) and from him to the third (*insān djismānī*). These are the originals of the so-called real men. Light is, of course, found in its purest form in the souls of the wise and the good (51). It should be noted also that *nūr* as a spiritual force (*rūḥānī*, *ʿaḳlī*) is distinguished from fire (*nār*) which is said to be only a force in matter with definite quality (85). Fire, of course, like everything else, has its supersensual original. But this is more connected with life than with light.

The elevation of the soul to the divine world of light corresponds to the creative descent of light (8). When the soul has passed on its return beyond the world of the *ʿaḳl*, it sees there the pure light and the beauty of God, the goal of all mystics.

Although the author of the *Liber de causis* is of the opinion that nothing can be predicated regarding God, yet he has to call Him the prime cause and more exactly pure light (§ 5, ed. Bardenhewer, 69) and as such the origin of all being and all knowledge (in God is *wudjūd* = *maʿrifa*; see § 23, p. 103).

The light emanated by God may, if it is regarded as an independent entity, be placed at various parts of the system. Most philosophers and theologians connect it with the *rūḥ* or *ʿaḳl* or identify it with them, sometimes also with life (*ḥayāt*), but this must be more closely investigated.

The great philosophers in Islam, al-Fārābī and Ibn Sīnā, connected the doctrine of light with the *ʿaḳl* in metaphysics as well as in psychology. Al-Fārābī is fond of using many synonyms for the light of God and the *ʿaḳl* (*bahāʾ*, etc.; see e.g. *Der Musterstaat*, ed. Dieterici, 13 ff.). In the biography of al-Fārābī in Ibn Abī Uṣaybiʿa (*ʿUyūn*, ed. Müller, ii, 134-40), a prayer is attributed to him in which God is invoked as the "prime cause of things and light of the earth and of heaven". Like al-Fārābī, Ibn Sīnā takes up the doctrine of light in theology and further develops it. In his psychological writings he regards the light as a link of the soul and body (cf. Sahl al-Tustarī, who places *nūr* between *rūḥ* and *ṭīn* in the four elements of man). In the *Kitāb al-Ishārāt* (ed. Forget, Leiden 1892, 126-7) he even reads the whole metaphysical doctrine of the *ʿaḳl* of the Aristotelians into the light verse of the Ḳurʾān. Light is the *ʿaḳl bi 'l-fiʿl*, fire the *ʿaḳl faʿʿāl* and so on. God's *nūr* is therefore like the *nous* of Aristotle! This discovery of Ibn Sīnā's was incorporated in the pious reflections of al-Ghazālī (in *Maʿāridj al-Ḳuds fī madāridj maʿrifat al-nafs*, Cairo 1927, 58-9).

On the idea of light amongst the Ṣūfīs, see TAṢAWWUF.

Bibliography: Ch. Clermont-Ganneau, *La lampe et l'olivier dans le Coran*, in *RHR*, lxxxi (1920), 213-59; W.H.T. Gairdner, *al-Ghazālī's Mishkāt al-Anwār and the Ghazālī problem*, in *Isl.*, v (1914), 121-53; idem, *al-Ghazālī's Mishkāt al-Anwār*, tr. with introduction, London 1924. See also ʿAḲL, AL-INSĀN AL-KĀMIL, ISMĀʿĪLIYYA, ISHRĀḲIYYŪN, AL-SUHRAWARDĪ (AL-MAḲTŪL). (TJ. DE BOER)

NŪR ALLĀH AL-SAYYID B. AL-SAYYID SHARĪF AL-MARʿASHĪ AL-ḤUSAYNĪ AL-SHUSHTARĪ, commonly called Ḳāḍī Nūr Allāh, was born in 956/1549. He was descended from an illustrious family of the Marʿashī Sayyids [*q.v.*] and settled in Shushtar. He left his native place for India and settled in Lahore where he attracted the notice of Ḥakīm Abu 'l-Fatḥ (d. 997/1588) and through his presentation to Emperor Akbar (963-1014/1556-1605), he was appointed *ḳāḍī* of Lahore in lieu of al-Shaykh Muʿīn (d. 995/1586). ʿAbd al-Ḳādir Badāʾūnī, iii, 137, says that he was, "although a Shīʿī, a just, pious and learned man." He was flogged to death in 1019/1610, on account of his religious opinions, by the order of the Emperor Djahāngīr (1014-37/1605-28). He is regarded as *al-Shahīd al-Thālith*, "the third martyr", by the Shīʿīs and his tomb in Akbarābād is visited by numerous Shīʿīs from all parts of India.

He is the author of innumerable works, of which the following may be quoted: 1. *Ḥāshiya ʿalā 'l-Bayḍāwī*, a supercommentary to al-Bayḍāwī's commentary on the Ḳurʾān entitled *Anwār al-tanzīl*: see Asiatic Society of Bengal mss., List of the Government Collection, 16; 2. *Ḥāshiya Sharḥ djadīd ʿalā 'l-Tadjrīd*, glosses to Ḳūshdjī's commentary on Naṣīr al-Dīn al-Ṭūsī's compendium of metaphysics and theology, entitled *Tadjrīd al-kalām*: see Loth, Ind. Off., no. 471, xv; 3. *Iḥkāḳ al-ḥaḳḳ wa-izhāḳ al-bāṭil*, a polemical work against Sunnism written in reply to Faḍl b. Rūzbahān's work entitled *Ibṭāl al-bāṭil*, a treatise in refutation of the *Kashf al-ḥaḳḳ wa-nahdj al-ṣidḳ* by Ḥasan b. Yūsuf b. ʿAlī al-Ḥillī; see Bankipore Library, Khudā Bakhsh cat., xiv, 172; Farangī Maḥall Library, Lucknow, fol. 108; Rāmpūr Library, 281; Asiatic Society of Bengal (List of Arabic mss., 23); 4. *Madjālis al-muʾminīn*, biographies of famous Shīʿīs from the beginning of Islām to the rise of the Ṣafawī dynasty in Persian: see Bankipore Library cat., 766; Asiatic Society of Bengal cat., 59; Ethé, Ind. Off., no. 704, and Rieu, *Cat. of Persian mss. in the Brit. Mus.*, 337a. Printed at Tehran 1268.

Bibliography: Muḥammad b. Ḥasan al-Ḥurr al-ʿĀmilī, *Amal al-āmil fī ʿulamāʾ Djabal ʿĀmil*, ed. al-Sayyid Aḥmad al-Husaynī, Baghdād 1385/1965-6, ii, 336-7 no. 1037; Muḥammad Bāḳir b. Zayn al-ʿĀbidīn al-Mūsawī, *Rawḍāt al-djannāt fī aḥwāl al-ʿulamāʾ wa 'l-sādāt*, iv, 220; ʿAbd al-Ḳādir al-Badāʾūnī, *Muntakhab al-tawārīkh*, iii, 137 and Rieu, *Cat. of Persian mss. in the Brit. Mus.*, 337b.

(M. Hidayet Hosain)

NŪR BĀNŪ Wālide Sulṭān (*ca.* 932-91/*ca.* 1525-83), Khaṣṣekī (principal consort) of the Ottoman sultan Selīm II [*q.v.*] and mother of the sultan Murād III [*q.v.*]. She was born on Paros [see para] as Cecilia, illegitimate daughter of Nicolo Venier (d. 1520), the penultimate sovereign ruler of the island and of Violante Baffo. The identity of this "Venetian Sultana" is often confused with that of her successor, the *Wālide Sulṭān* Ṣāfiye [*q.v.*]. Some Turkish historians persist in ascribing a Jewish origin to her. At the time of the conquest of the island in 1537, she was selected for deportation to the harem of the Sultan's palace and presented to Prince Selīm (II). Henceforward she is known as Nūr Bānū. In 953/1546 she gave birth to her eldest son, Murād. While at Maghnisa [*q.v.*] her daughters Shāh Sulṭān (951-88/1544-80), Djewher(-i Mülūk) Khān (? 951-86/1544-78), Ismikhān (Esmākhān) Sulṭān (952-93/1545-85) and Fāṭima Sulṭān (d. 988/1580) were born. Whether she was the mother of Selīm II's other six sons is not evident.

At the death of Selīm II (28 Shaʿbān 982/13 December 1574), it was she who ordered the corpse of the monarch to be put on ice to postpone burial till the time when her son arrived to succeed to the throne ten days later.

During the reign of Selīm II, her influence mainly affected official appointments by introducing the sale of offices. The imperial harem gradually extended its influence in this way to affairs outside the palace. During the reign of her son, Nūr Bānū was able to establish what is called the "Women's Sultanate" (*ḳadînlar salṭanatî*). Apart from her daughters, the leading members of her clique were the princess Mihr-i Māh (d. 985/1578 [*q.v.*]), the *kedbānū* ("Mistress of the Female Household") from 991 till 1003/1595, Djānfedā *Khātūn* and Rāḍiye *Khātūn* (*Ḳalfa*) (d. 1005/26 June 1597), a lady companion since Maghnisa days. (cf. Selānikī, *Taʾrīkh*, ed. İpşirli, 695). The Jewish *Kira* Esther Ḥandali (d. *ca.* 1590) also played a role in external contacts, e.g. with the financier Joseph Nasi, duke of Naxos (1514-69) [see nakshe]. The *bābüsseʿādet aghasî* Ghazanfer Agha (d. 1603) and the leading *müṣāḥib* Shemsī Aḥmed Pasha (d. 988/1580-1) belonged to Nūr Bānū's faction.

During her son's reign, one of her main preoccupations was the rivalry with Ṣāfiye, first *khaṣṣekī* of Murād III whom Nūr Bānū was able to relegate to the Old Saray at the time of his accession.

In her day already, Nūr Bānū was compared to the queen (mother) of France, Catherine de Médicis (1519-89). The two exchanged letters in 1581 and 1582. The presents from the French "*Wālide Sulṭān*" to her Ottoman opposite number arrived too late in April 1584 and were redirected to Ṣāfiye Sulṭān by Esther *Kira* instead! Some letters of Nūr Bānū and her *Kira* to the Doge and Senate as well as to the *bailo*, Giovanni Correr (in Istanbul 1578-80), apart from the many presents and tokens of respect received, are evidence of the sultana's lasting favourable interest in the affairs of Venice.

Her regular income came from the so called *bashmaklîḳ* ('slipper money') and *waḳf* endowments [see wālide sulṭān].

Nūr Bānū possessed her own palace near Edirne Ḳapî, where in 1580 her son retired during a serious attack of epilepsy (Charrière, iii, 922 and n. 1). The *ʿAtīḳ Wālide* (*Eski Valide*) mosque complex at Üsküdar-Toptashî was built on her orders. Construction lasted from 978/1570 to 991/1583 (designed by Sinān [*q.v.*]). Two small mosques were built in her name elsewhere in Istanbul.

After an illness, she died in her garden palace near Edirne Ḳapî (according to Selānikī, *Taʾrīkh*, ed. İpşirli, 141: Yeñi Ḳapî) on Wednesday, 22 Dhu 'l-Ḳaʿda 991/7 December 1583. Her son put on mourning dress (the first time ever reported of an Ottoman sultan on such an occasion). He carried her out of the palace gate and accompanied the coffin as far as the mosque of Fātiḥ, where the funeral *ṣalāt* was performed. Nūr Bānū is buried in the mausoleum of Selīm II at the Aya Sofya.

Bibliography: E. Rossi, *La Sultana Nûr Bânû (Cecilia Venier Baffo)*..., in *OM*, xxxiii (1953) 433-41; Selānikī, *Taʾrīkh*, ed. M. İpşirli in Latin script, *Tarih-i Selâniki*, 2 vols., Istanbul 1989, 98, 140 f., 155, 237, 502, 562, 587, 695; Muṣṭafā ʿĀlī, *Künh ul-akhbār*, quoted in J. Schmidt, *Pure water for thirsty Muslims. A study of Muṣṭafā ʿĀlī of Gallipoli's Künh ül-Aḫbār*, Leiden 1992, 105, 157, 243, 269, 271, 331 f.; Aḥmed Refiḳ [Altınay] *Ḳadînlar salṭanatî*, 4 vols., Istanbul 1332/1914, i, 94-112; *İA*, art. *Selim II* (Ş. Turan); İ.H. Uzunçarşılı, *Osmanlı devletinin saray teşkilâtı*, Ankara 1984², 154-71, 234; (M.)Ç. Uluçay, *Padişahların kadınları ve kızları*, Ankara 1985², 38, 40 ff., 43-4; İ.H. Konyalı, *Üsküdar tarihi*, 2 vols., Istanbul 1976, i, 141-9; von Hammer, *HEO*, vii, 11, 17, 49, 124-31, 160, 164, 165, 191, 194; E. Charrière, *Négociations de la France dans le Levant*, 4 vols., iii, Paris 1853, 831, 840, 922, iv, 1860, 36, 58, 123, 186 f., 236-41, 250, 273; P. Grunebaum-Ballin, *Joseph Naci, duc de Naxos*, Paris-The Hague 1968, 72-3, 82; J.H. Mordtmann, *Die Jüdische Kira im Serai der Sultane*, in *MSOS*, xxxii/2 (1929), 1-38; S.A. Skilliter, *The letters of the Venetian "Sultana" Nur Banu and her Kira to Venice*, in *Studia .... Alessio Bombaci ...*, Naples 1982, 515-36; eadem, *The Sultan's messenger Gabriel Defrens ...*, in *WZKM*, lxviii (1976), 47-59.

(A.H. de Groot)

NŪR DJAHĀN, name given to Mihr al-Nisāʾ, the famous queen of Djahāngīr, the Mughal Emperor. She was born at Ḳandahār in 985/1577 when her father, Ghiyāth Beg, was migrating from Persia to Hindustān (*Maʾāthir al-umarāʾ*, i, 129). In the reign of Akbar she was married to ʿAlī Ḳulī Beg, a Persian who had rendered distinguished military service to the Emperor and who, because of his bravery, was known as Shīr Afgan. The assassination of her first husband will always remain a matter of controversy, some regarding it as a repetition of the story of David and Uriah, others holding the view that he had been suspected of disloyalty. It was not, however, until four years later, in 1020/1611, that she became, at the age of thirty-four, the wife of Djahāngīr [*q.v.*]. In the eleventh year of that monarch's reign her name was changed from Nūr Maḥall to Nūr Djahān (*Tūzuk-i Djahāngīrī*, ed. Rogers and Beveridge, i, 319).

An extraordinarily beautiful woman, well-versed in Persian literature in an age when few women were cultured, ambitious and masterful, she entirely dominated her husband, until eventually Djahāngīr was king in name only. The chroniclers record that she sometimes sat in the *jharokā*, that coins were struck in her name, and that she even dared to issue *farmāns* (*Iḳbāl-nāma*, 54-7). She became the leader of fashion and is said to have invented the *ʿaṭr-i Djahāngīrī*, a special kind of rose-water. Her style in gowns, veils, brocade, lace, and her *farsh-i čandanī* (carpets of sandalwood colour) were known throughout the length and breadth of Hindūstān.

Ably assisted in political affairs by her father, now known as Iʿtimād al-Dawla, and her brother, Āṣaf Khān, she dispensed all patronage, thus falling foul of the older nobility led by Mahābat Khān [*q.v.*]. The history of the last years of Djahāngīr's reign is the history of Nūr Djahān's efforts at paving the way for the succession of her son-in-law, Prince Shahriyār. But the death of her father, combined with the fact that Āṣaf Khān was supporting the claim of his own son-in-law, Prince Khurram, considerably weakened her power. On the death of Djahāngīr, in 1037/1627, she was completely outwitted by Āṣaf Khān, her candidate was defeated, and Prince Khurram ascended the throne as Shāh Djahān. The historians of Mughal India record little of the last eighteen years of this remarkable woman's life during the reign of Shāh Djahān.

Bibliography: Muʿtamid Khān, *Iḳbāl-nāma-yi Djahāngīrī*, Calcutta 1865; Shāhnawāz Khān, *Maʾāthir al-umarāʾ*, in *Bibliotheca Indica*, i, 127-134; Beni Prasad, *History of Jahangir*, Allahabad 1940.

(C.C. Davies)

NŪR ḲUṬB al-ʿĀLAM, Sayyid, Ṣūfī saint of Pānduʾā [*q.v.*] in Bengal and pioneer writer in the Bengali vernacular, d. 819/1416. An adherent of the Čishtī order, he and his descendants did much to popularise it in Bengal and Bihār and to create an atmosphere favourable to the rise of the Bhakti movement there. In the literary field, he introduced the use of *rīkhta*, half-Persian, half-Bengali poetry. On the political plane, he secured the patronage of the Sharḳīs of Djawnpūr [*q.vv.*], and seems to have urged Sultan Ibrāhīm Sharḳī [*q.v.*] to attack the Islamised Hindu line of Rādjā Gaṇeśa [see rādjā ganesh] who were ruling in Bengal.

Bibliography: See bengali. ii, and čishtiyya. A.

(Ed.)

NŪR MUḤAMMADĪ (a.), the Muḥammadan light. It is one of the most prominent names given to Muḥammad's pre-existent entity which preceded the creation of Ādam [*q.v.*]. The concept has its parallels in Jewish, Gnostic and neo-Platonic ideas (see I. Goldziher, *Neuplatonische und Gnostische Elemente im Ḥadīt*, in *ZA*, xxii [1909], 317 ff.; T. Andrae, *Die Person Muhammeds*, Upsala 1917, *passim*. See also, L. Massignon, *Al-Ḥallāj*, Paris 1922, *passim*; idem, *Recueil...*, 1929, *passim*).

Not all Muslim scholars and theologians agreed on the nature of Muḥammad's pre-existence. Al-Ghazālī (d. 505/1111 [*q.v.*]) and Ibn Taymiyya (d. 728/1328 [*q.v.*]) claimed that the primordial creation (*khalḳ*) of Muḥammad did not signify pre-existence at all, only predestination (*taḳdīr*). They were opposed by Taḳī al-Dīn al-Subkī (d. 756/1355 [*q.v.*]), who supported the dogma of Muḥammad's pre-existence. There was also disagreement on whether Muḥammad was pre-existent in body or in soul. The controversy brought about the adoption of a somewhat neutral name for the primordial entity of Muḥammad: *al-ḥaḳīḳa al-Muḥammadiyya* (see a survey of the various opinions in Muḥammad b. Yūsuf al-Shāmī, *Subul al-hudā wa 'l-rashād fī sīrat khayr al-ʿibād*, Cairo 1990, i, 91, 99-100). The latter term, meaning "the Muḥammadan reality", emerges also in the discussions about *al-Insān al-Kāmil* [*q.v.*], i.e., the Perfect Man, the archetype of the universe and humanity, which is identified with Muḥammad. In these discussions allusion is most often made to the Ḳurʾānic verse of light (XXIV, 35). Specific elaborations on the concept are current in the Ismāʿīliyya [*q.v.*] and among other Shīʿī extremist sects (U. Rubin, *Pre-existence and light; aspects of the concept of Nūr Muḥammad*, in *IOS*, v [1975], 107-9).

The idea of Muḥammad's pre-existence is implied in early *ḥadīth* material, where it is stated that Muḥammad was the first of all prophets to be created (e.g. Ibn Saʿd, *Ṭabaḳāt*, Beirut 1960, i, 148-9). The idea is also implied in the commentaries on Kurʾān XXXIII, 7 (al-Ṭabarī, etc.) which mentions the covenant (*mīthāḳ* [*q.v.*]) of the prophets (Rubin, *art. cit.*, 69). Relevant are also the interpretations of Ḳurʾān VII, 172, which deals with the *dhurriyya* (offspring) of the children of Ādam (Rubin, *art. cit.*, 67-8).

In the early *ḥadīth* material, the Muḥammadan light is referred to as *nūr Muḥammad*, and is given a special function. It is identified with the spermatic substance of Muḥammad's ancestors. The light is said to have reached the corporeal Muḥammad from his progenitors through the process of procreation (see especially Abū Saʿd al-Khargūshī, *Sharaf al-Muṣṭafā*, ms. B.L., Or. 3014, fols. 7 ff.). This concept (traducianism) corresponds to the Arabian, pre-Islamic, belief that virtues, as well as vices, were passed on from the ancestors (Goldziher, *Muh. St.*, i, 41-2). Bearing (in their loins) the divine Muḥammadan substance, Muḥammad's Arab ancestors are presented as true Muslims, and sometimes even as "prophets" (Rubin, *art. cit.*, 71-83. See also the commentaries of al-Ḳummī, al-Ṭūsī, al-Ṭabarsī, al-Rāzī, al-Ḳurṭubī, etc. on Ḳurʾān, XXVI, 219: *wa-taḳallubaka fi 'l-sādjidīn*). The early *Sīra* of Ibn Isḥāḳ (d. 150/767 [*q.v.*]) already contains a detailed description of the emergence of a prophetic blaze (*ghurra*) on the forehead of ʿAbd Allāh, Muḥammad's father. It rested in his body till it was passed on to Āmina, when she became pregnant with Muḥammad (Ibn Hishām, 100 ff.). Shīʿī traditions hold that not only Muḥammad, but also ʿAlī [*q.v.*] and his family, including the Imāms, shared the same light. It is claimed that while being passed on through the ancestors, the light was split in two, so that both Muḥammad and ʿAlī received equal shares of it (Rubin, *art. cit.*, 83-98). There are also Sunnī counter-versions in which the first four caliphs are given a share in the Muḥammadan light (Rubin, *art. cit.*, 112 ff.).

There is also another kind of divine pre-existent light which is referred to as *Nūr Allāh*. It is said to have reached Muḥammad and the Shīʿī Imāms through the previous prophets (not the ancestors). It is being passed on at the end of each person's life, as part of his hereditary authority (*waṣiyya*) (see Rubin, *Prophets and progenitors in the early Shīʿa tradition*, in *JSAI*, i [1979], 41 ff.).

Bibliography: Given in the article.

(U. Rubin)

NŪR SATGUR (meaning "true teacher"), a person whose name is generally associated with the beginnings of the Nizārī [see NIZĀRIYYA] or Satpanth (i.e. the true path) Ismāʿīlism in India but who remains more as an enigmatic and a symbolic figure around whom the Nizārī tradition has woven a colourful tapestry of legends representing the emergence of its *daʿwa* in the Indian subcontinent. As far as the historical sources are concerned, we are on very tenuous ground because of scanty material. Most of our information is therefore derived from the Nizārī sources which tend to be hagiographic. The major source of his biography is the community's indigenous religious literature known as *ginān*s (derived from Sanskrit *jñāna*, meaning "contemplative or meditative knowledge"). The *ginān*s are poetical compositions in Indian vernaculars, such as Sindhī, Pandjābī, Multānī, Gudjarātī and Hindī, are polyglot in nature, and are ascribed to various *pīr*s [*q.v.*] who were active in preaching and propagating the *daʿwa*. They resemble didactic and mystical poetry and are often anachronistic and legendary in nature. Moreover, as this literature was preserved orally in the beginning before it was committed to writing in Khōdjkī (or Khʷādja Sindhī) script, and printed during the second half of the 19th century in Gudjarātī without any critical apparatus, it poses a different set of problems concerning its antiquity, authenticity, transmission, and interpolation. Based on some *ginān*s ascribed to Nūr Satgur, he probably came from Persia to Pātaṇ (in Gudjarāt), where he allegedly succeeded in converting the then reigning Rādjput king Siddharādja Djayasiṁha (1094-1143), the same king who is also reported to have been converted by the Mustaʿlī-Ṭayyibī [*q.v.*] *daʿwa*. The second narrative in those *ginān*s traces Nūr Satgur's activities in another region, Dharanāgarī, after his exploits in Pātaṇ, where he allegedly succeeded not only in converting the king but also in marrying the latter's daughter. (For details, see Azim Nanji, *The Nizārī Ismāʿīlī tradition in the Indo-Pakistan subcontinent*, Delmar, N.Y. 1978, 50-3, where the Nizārī tradition about the commencement of the Nizārī *daʿwa* is analysed.) The existence of a shrine located in Navsārī, near Sūrat, ascribed to him, and the chronogram on his tombstone giving the date of his death as 487/1094, are of very little help in locating him historically, as the shrine was actually constructed towards the end of the 18th century (Nanji, *op. cit.*, 60).

Bibliography: For a full description of older sources and works ascribed to him, see I. Poonawala, *Biobibliography of Ismāʿīlī literature*, Malibu, Cal. 1977, 298; F. Daftary, *The Ismāʿīlīs: their history and doctrines*, Cambridge 1990, 415, 478.

(I. POONAWALA)

NŪR AL-DĪN, ʿABD AL-ḲĀDIR, Algerian scholar and teacher, born at Biskra *ca.* 1892 and died in Algiers on 12 April 1987.

Of modest origins, he attended the primary school in his home town and at 15 entered the Algiers medersa. Under the guidance of eminent teachers, in particular, ʿAbd al-Ḳādir al-Madjdjāwī, ʿAbd al-Ḥalīm Ben Smāya, Muḥammad al-Saʿīd Ibn Zakrī and Muḥammad Ben Cheneb, he followed classical studies in Arabic and French and obtained the Diploma of Higher Studies. He completed his education by helping with the courses of well-known *ʿulamāʾ* such as ʿAlī Aḥmad b. al-Ḥadjdj Mūsā, Muḥammad b. Muṣṭafā b. al-Khūdja and Abu 'l-Ḳāsim al-Ḥafnāwī which they gave in the mosques of the capital. For several years, he functioned as adel (*ʿadl*, professional witness in the law courts) at Cherchell, but soon left this in order to devote himself in the future to teaching. He was appointed *mudarris* at Blida, then at Tlemcen and then, in 1945, at Algiers, in the al-Thaʿālibiyya *madrasa*, which became a Franco-Muslim lycée in 1951. Meanwhile, Nūr al-Dīn acted as *répétiteur* in Arabic at the Faculty of Letters in the University and *chargé de cours* at the Institute of Higher Islamic Studies. He had connections with the French Arabists, amongst others H. Pérès, M. Canard, J. Cantineau and H. Jahier of the Faculty of Medicine, and in collaboration with this last published five works concerned with medicine and the physicians of the Muslim West (see below).

In the course of his long teaching career, Nūr al-Dīn endeavoured above all to inculcate in his pupils the constitutive elements of the Arabic language and to bring to life the Arab-Islamic cultural heritage. This double task inspired his preferences and guided the choices which he made. On one hand, he put together a dozen manuals for lycée and medersa classes: précis of Arabic grammar, collections of classical and modern texts, with a lexicographical and grammatical commentary, followed by exercises, in which he strove to set forth the subject-matter in an easily comprehensible form. Having realised that certain ideas did not come easily to young minds, he tried to express them by concrete examples. Moreover, he thought that his pupils would more quickly grasp the syntactic relationships of words and would understand their functions better if he presented to them schematically certain examples, so that the arrangement of the different elements of the phrase might become clearer and more eloquent. All his educational works show great pedagogic care.

On the other hand, Nūr al-Dīn edited, translated into French and commented upon, in collaboration with Jahier, famous works of Ibn Rushd and Ibn Abī Uṣaybiʿa, wishing thereby to throw into relief that place which scientific texts, at the side of philosophical, religious and hagiographic ones, occupied in the Arabic literature of the Muslim West.

Of his historical works, one should mention his critical edition of *Ghazawāt ʿUrūdj wa-Khayr al-Dīn*, of a history of the town of Constantine by Ḥādjdj Aḥmad Ibn al-Mubārak and, above all, his *Ṣafaḥāt fī taʾrīkh madīnat al-Djazāʾir*, which is characterised by the solidity of its documentation, the clarity of its exposition and its easy style.

The essential quality of his publications shows that Nūr al-Dīn was a significant example of an Algerian *ʿālim*, with an Arabic and French education, who took up modern pedagogical methods and research techniques based on bibliography, the study of sources and manuscripts. With an absence of dogmatism and in a spirit of liberal-minded curiosity, he led a studious life devoted to learning. However, his published work is less important than the real value of the effects produced by his teaching, and it was in effect by his practical example that his influence was deepest. As a good teacher, well-informed, devoted and with a rare modesty, he brought much and inspired much not merely to his numerous pupils but also to his colleagues.

The chronological list of his writings is as follows:

A. Full-size works (all publ. Algiers unless otherwise stated)

1. *Muntakhab al-ḥikāyāt al-mithliyya*, 1346/1927. 2. *K. Ghazawāt ʿUrūdj wa-Khayr al-Dīn, chronique arabe du XVIe s.*, 1934. 3. *al-Ḳirāʾāt al-ifrīḳiyya al-mashrūḥa*, 1366/1937; 4. *Lāmiyyat al-afʿāl*, 1358/1940; 5. *al-Ḳawl al-maʾthūr min kalām al-Shaykh ʿAbd al-Raḥmān al-Madjdhūb*, n.d. 6. *al-Ādjurrūmiyya ʿalā ṭarīḳ al-suʾāl wa*

'l-djawāb, grammatical analysis with exercises. 1365/1946. 7. *al-Muṭālaʿa al-ʿarabiyya al-ʿaṣriyya*, 1366/1947. 8. *al-Risāla al-ṣarfiyya bi 'l-shakl al-tāmm*, n.d. 9. *Taʾrīkh madīnat Ḳusanṭīna li 'l-Ḥādjdj Aḥmad Ibn al-Mubārak*, 1952. 10. *ʿArīb b. Saʿīd al-Kātib al-Ḳurṭubī, Le livre de la génération du foetus et le traitément des femmes enceintes et des nouveaux-nés, tr. et annoté par H. Jahier et A. Noureddine*, 1956. 11. *Avicenne, Poème de la Médecine, texte arabe publié, traduit et annoté, accompagné d'une traduction latine du XIIIe siècle, par H.J. et A.N.*, Paris 1956. 12. Ibn Abī Uṣaybiʿa, *K. ʿUyūn al-anbāʾ bi-ṭabaḳāt al-aṭibbāʾ (chap. XIII: médecins de l'Occident musulman), publié, traduit et annoté par H.J. et A.N.*, 1377/1958. 13. *Ibid., chap. IV, V, et VI: Hippocrate et les hippocratiques, Galien et ses successeurs, les médecins alexandrins, publié, traduit et annoté par H.J. et A.N.*, 1958. 14. *K. Iʿrāb al-djumal*, 1377/1958. 15. Ibn ʿAbd al-Djabbār al-Fadjīdjī, *Rawḍat al-sulwān (Le Jardin de Consolation), publié, traduit et annoté par H.J. et A.N.*, 1378/1959. 16. *Anthologie de textes poétiques attribués à Avicenne, publié avec traduction française et notes par H.J. et A.N.*, 1960. 17. *al-Inshāʾ al-ʿarabī*, 1960. 18. *Asās al-ʿarabiyya li-taʿlīm al-ḥurūf al-hidjāʾiyya*, 1960. 19. *al-Muntakhab min ashʿār al-ʿArab*, 1961. 20. *K. al-Wasīla li-ʿilm al-ʿarabiyya*, n.d. 21. *Pages de la médecine arabe, avec préface et commentaire; gérontologie arabe au Moyen Âge*, n.d. 22. *Ṣafaḥāt fī taʾrīkh madīnat al-Djazāʾir*, Constantine 1385/1965. 23. *Mukhtaṣar fī 'l-ʿibādāt, trad. française*, n.d. 24. *Dictionnaire français-arabe de Ben Sedira, revu et augmenté par N.A.*, n.d.

B. Articles

1. *Un épisode de l'histoire de l'ancient Alger*, in *Mélanges E.F. Gautier*, 1937. 2. *Un philanthrope maure du XIXe siècle, El Hadj Abderrahmane El-Kinai. Essai d'une biographie critique et commentaire*, in *Feuillets d'El-Djezair*, no. 2 (Algiers, Sept. 1942), 57-63. 3. *Rapprochement littéraire*, in *BEA*, no. 21 (Algiers, Jan.-Feb. 1945), 7-8. 4. *Ibn Khallikān, notice biographique sur Avicenne extraite des Wafayāt al-aʿyān, texte arabe présenté et traduit par N.A. et H. Pérès*, in *ibid.*, no. 52 (March-April 1951), 36-43. 5. *Nubdha min ṣafaḥāt fī taʾrīkh madīnat al-Djazāʾir...*, in *Madjalla Kulliyyat al-Ādāb*, no. 1 (Algiers 1964), 3-32.

Bibliography: H. Pérès, *Critique de manuels d'arabe classique. I. Manuel de Noureddine*, in *BEA*, no. 39 (Sept.-Oct. 1948), 171-7; A. Merad, Compte-rendu de la publication du poème *Rawḍat al-sulwān*, in *RAfr.*, ciii/3-4 (1959), 409-10.

(R. Bencheneb)

NŪR AL-DĪN ARSLĀN SHĀH Abu 'l-Ḥārith b. Masʿūd b. Mawdūd b. Zangī, called al-Malik al-ʿĀdil, sixth ruler in Mawṣil of the Zangid line of Atabegs, reigned 589-607/1193-1211.

On the death of his father ʿIzz al-Dīn Masʿūd [*q.v.*], Nūr al-Dīn succeeded him, but for many years was under the tutelage of the commander of the citadel of Mawṣil, the eunuch Mudjāhid al-Dīn Ḳaymaz al-Zaynī, till the latter's death in 595/1198-9. Nūr al-Dīn's early external policy aimed at securing control of Niṣībīn [*q.v.*] from his kinsman, the Zangī lord of Sindjār ʿImād al-Dīn Zangī and the latter's son Ḳuṭb al-Dīn Muḥammad (594/1109), but was frustrated by the intervention in Diyār Bakr, leading to a siege of Mārdīn [*q.v.*], by the Ayyūbids al-Malik al-ʿĀdil and al-Malik al-Kāmil [*q.vv.*]. Nūr al-Dīn was victorious there in 595/1199 and drove al-Malik al-Kāmil back to Damascus, but had himself to return to Mawṣil through illness. Ḳuṭb al-Dīn Muḥammad retained his formal allegiance to al-Malik al-ʿĀdil (600/1203-4), and Nūr al-Dīn's capture of and attempt to hold Tell Aʿfar failed in the next year.

The pattern of alliances then changed, with a marriage union between Nūr al-Dīn's daughter and al-Malik al-ʿĀdil's son, when the Zangids of Mawṣil and the Ayyūbids for a while united Ḳuṭb al-Dīn, but this alignment changed with the intervention of the lord of Irbil, Muẓaffar al-Dīn Gökbüri, and the formation of an alliance against al-Malik al-ʿĀdil which now included the Saldjūḳ sultan of Rūm Kay Khusraw I [*q.v.*]. Nevertheless, in the end Ḳuṭb al-Dīn retained possession of Sindjār until 616/1219, but Nūr al-Dīn himself died in Radjab 607/January 1211, to be succeeded in Mawṣil by his son ʿIzz al-Dīn Masʿūd al-Malik al-Ḳāhir.

Nūr al-Dīn left behind a reputation in Mawṣil as a benefactor to the town, building *inter alia* a *madrasa* there for the Shāfiʿīs when he himself passed from the Ḥanafī *madhhab* to that of the Shāfiʿīs.

Bibliography: 1. Sources. Ibn al-Athīr, *Kāmil*, xii; idem, *Atabegs*, in *RHC, Historiens orientaux*, i, 71, 74, 82, 86, ii/2, 5, 346-62; Ibn Khallikān, ed. ʿAbbās, i, 193-4, tr. de Slane, i, 174-5. 2. Studies. H.M. Gottschalk, *al-Malik al-Kāmil von Ägypten und seine Zeit*, Wiesbaden 1958, 41-3; R.S. Humphreys, *From Saladin to the Mongols, the Ayyūbids of Damascus 1193-1260*, Albany 1977, 91, 114, 120, 128-21. See also Zambauer, *Manuel*, 226; *EI*[1] art. s.v. (K.V. Zetterstéen), of which the above article is a résumé.

(C.E. Bosworth)

NŪR AL-DĪN MAḤMŪD B. ZANKĪ, Zankid or Zangid sultan and successor to Zankī (d. 565/1174), who was murdered during the siege of Ḳalʿat Djaʿbar [*q.v.*] in Rabīʿ I 541/September 1146. The succession posed a series of problems since there were four heirs: Sayf al-Dīn Ghāzī, the eldest, represented his father at Mawṣil [*q.v.*], the second son, Nūr al-Dīn Maḥmūd, had accompanied his father in the majority of his military operations, the third, Nuṣrat al-Dīn Amīr-Amīrān, was to be governor of Ḥarrān [*q.v.*], the fourth son, Ḳuṭb al-Dīn Mawdūd [*q.v.*] was to succeed his eldest brother at Mawṣil. There was also a daughter who was to marry the *amīr* Nāṣir al-Dīn al-Ṣūrī.

After the death of his father, Nūr al-Dīn made his way to Aleppo [see ḤALAB], following the advice of Shīrkūh, a Kurdish *amīr* and friend of the former sultan. Sawār, the governor of the town, recognised Zankid sovereignty. Ḥamāt [*q.v.*], of which the titular *amīr* was Ṣalāḥ al-Dīn al-Yāghīsiyānī, also rallied to his cause. At Mawṣil, the situation was more complicated, but the pro-Zankid *amīrs* succeeded in bringing Sayf al-Dīn Ghāzī from Kurdistān and obtained from the sultan his appointment as ruler of Mawṣil.

Raymond of Poitiers, prince of Antioch, did not hear the news of the assassination of Zankī until seven days after the establishment of Nūr al-Dīn at Aleppo. He dispatched two forces, one against Aleppo and the other against Ḥamāt, whereupon the Muslims compelled their opponents to withdraw to Antioch [see ANṬĀKIYA]. Edessa, eastern bastion of Frankish expansion for the previous half-century (1098-1144 [see AL-RUHĀ]), came again under Muslim control, but Armenian elements who constituted the majority of the population there succeeded in neutralising the effectiveness of the local Muslim garrison and called upon the aid of Joscelin, who was the son of an Armenian mother. After six days of forced marches from Aleppo, Nūr al-Dīn was the first to arrive with siege machinery. The vigour of his operations induced the Armenians to evacuate the town. Joscelin found refuge at Sumaysāṭ on the right bank of the Euphrates. Edessa was then incorporated into the domain of Nūr al-Dīn. Relations between the latter and Sayf al-Dīn Ghāzī became strained until, on the occasion of his brother's investiture, Nūr al-Dīn addressed to him, from Aleppo, an official act of homage, recognising the primacy of his elder brother. He obtained guarantees for his eastern frontier where Ḥarrān took the place of Edessa and was charged with the responsibility of conducting the *djihād* [*q.v.*] against the enemy from the West.

Reviving the policy of his father, Nūr al-Dīn decided to take possession of Damascus [see DIMASHḲ] and to incorporate it into a Syrian federation, for political reasons in view of the presence of the Frankish kingdom of Jerusalem to the south, and for economic reasons since, being deprived of the Djazīra [*q.v.*], Syria needed the Biḳāʿ and also the Ḥawrān [*q.vv.*] to gain adequate supplies of cereals. In spring of 541/May 1147, Nūr al-Dīn and Muʿīn al-Dīn Unur together confronted the Franks in the Ḥawrān, where Altīntāsh, governor of Ṣalkhad and of Boṣrā [*q.vv.*] was seeking to make himself independent of Damascus with the aid of the Franks of Jerusalem, but the latter were forced to withdraw.

For the Latin states, the objective was to remove Nūr al-Dīn, but the absence of political direction among the Crusaders spared the latter a campaign which could have caused him serious problems. On 24 July 1148, following a series of debates in the Assizes of Jerusalem, the decision was taken to attack Damascus. In July, the Franks mustered at Tiberias and arrived before Damascus on the 24th. Muʿīn al-Dīn sent urgent appeals for help to Mawṣil and Aleppo and exploited the Zankid threat to repel the Franks, who raised the siege on 28 July.

The year 1149 was a time of considerable activity. Nūr al-Dīn was determined to counter the attacks of Raymond of Antioch. He decided, after receiving reinforcements from Damascus, to attack the region of Afāmiya [*q.v.*], then occupied by the Franks. He also laid siege to Inab which commanded the valley of the Ghāb [*q.v.*]. On 20 Ṣafar 544/29 June 1149, having defeated the Latins at a place known as ʿArḍ al-Ḥātim, Nūr al-Dīn occupied the land between the Rudj and the Orontes [see AL-ʿĀṢĪ]. He took Afāmiya and Ḳalʿat al-Muḍīḳ, and then Ḥārim [*q.v.*], where he installed a Muslim garrison and then resumed the siege of Antioch, where the antagonists concluded a truce.

On 23 Rabīʿ II 544/28 August 1149, on the death of Muʿīn al-Dīn Unur, there was tension in Damascus, where Mudjīr al-Dīn Aybak took control of the government. Seeking to intervene, Nūr al-Dīn found a pretext in the campaign currently being conducted by the Franks in the Ḥawrān. He appealed for the participation of a Damascene contingent in his support but, on the basis of previous agreements the Damascenes called upon the Franks of Jerusalem for help in resisting Nūr al-Dīn. Advancing with undiminished speed, the latter crossed the Biḳāʿ, traversed the Anti-Lebanon and deployed his army some ten km to the south-west of Damascus at a place known as Manāzil al-ʿAsākir, on 26 Dhu 'l-Ḥidjdja 544/25 April 1150. From his encampment, Nūr al-Dīn sent a declaration to the Damascenes, informing them that he had come to protect them from their supposed allies, the Franks. Since his supporters were still too few in number to control the city, Nūr al-Dīn decided to return to Aleppo, where his presence was necessary following the capture of Joscelin of Edessa by Turcomans in Dhu 'l-Ḥidjdja 544/April 1150 and his incarceration in the citadel of Aleppo. This event gave rise to various repercussions: in the month of Muḥarram 545, the Saldjūḳ ruler of Rūm, Masʿūd b. Muḥammad, set out to blockade Tell Bāshir and invited Nūr al-Dīn to join him. The latter accepted, not wishing to allow his rival to be the sole beneficiary of the situation. While Masʿūd succceeded in taking all the places situated in the valleys to the west of the Euphrates, Nūr al-Dīn attacked the region of upper ʿAfrīn [*q.v.*] in order to take control of the communications routes linking Antioch with the north. In autumn 545/1150 he occupied the region downstream of al-Bīra [*q.v.*] on the right bank of the Euphrates. The frontier of the *Dār al-Islām* was thus transferred from the Euphrates to the Orontes.

At the end of 545/spring 1151 the problem arose of the renewal of the treaty concluded between Damascus and Jerusalem. It was then that Nūr al-Dīn established his base to the south of Damascus and issued an appeal to the population but, failing to prevent contacts between the Damascenes and the troops of Baldwin III, he withdrew to the valley of the Baradā [*q.v.*]. The Franks entered the city and, before returning to Jerusalem, claimed a portion of the indemnity promised in July 1151. After their departure, Nūr al-Dīn renewed the siege of Damascus and engaged in negotiations: Damascus agreed to recognise his sovereignty, to mention him in the *khuṭba* [*q.v.*] and to strike coinage in his name, but in fact the city retained its independence.

In April-May 1152 the Zankid prince sent troops to the coast, taking Ṭarṭūs, a port situated between al-Lādhiḳiyya [*q.v.*] and Ṭarābulus al-Shām, thus severing communications between the County of Tripoli and the principality of Antioch.

Mudjīr al-Dīn preferred the Frankish protectorate to the Zankid ascendancy. To win over the population of Damascus to the cause of Nūr al-Dīn, his agents engaged in subtle propaganda, while he himself resorted to more persuasive tactics: he intercepted the food supplies arriving from the south. Prices rose and famine threatened. While the city starved, Nūr al-Dīn had dealings with the heads of the *aḥdāth* [*q.v.*] and with the *zuʿʿār* who were recruited among the porters and lower echelons of the souks. Mudjīr al-Dīn appealed to the Franks, but before they had time to intervene, Nūr al-Dīn launched his operation. When his troops entered the town, the middle classes barricaded their homes against them and the mob went on the rampage, but within a few hours Nūr al-Dīn restored order, distributed provisions and undertook to respect private property. The population was reassured. Mudjīr al-Dīn, isolated in the citadel, accepted Ḥimṣ [*q.v.*] in return for his capitulation. On the day of his departure, Nūr al-Dīn called a meeting, the participants including the *raʾīs* Raḍī al-Dīn al-Tamīmī and Nadjm al-Dīn Ayyūb, the *ḳāḍīs* and the *fuḳahāʾ*, as well as leading citizens and merchants. He repeated his conciliatory assurances and announced the abolition of taxes levied on the markets. The arrival of Nūr al-Dīn in Damascus marked the beginning of a new era for all the victims of previous régimes; thus the *amīr* Usāma b. Munḳidh, who had left the city ten years earlier, returned at the start of Rabīʿ II 549/June 1154.

In eight years, Nūr al-Dīn was to achieve, by gradual stages, his objective of a united Syria. He began by consolidating his position at Aleppo; as a means of suppressing the Shīʿīs, he revived with increased vigour the measures which Zankī had inaugurated: the imposition of Sunnī Islam was to be one of the major objectives of his policy. Having relocated his eastern frontier on the Balīkh, he was assured of the neutrality of his elder brother. He also participated in the dismemberment of the County of Edessa, as a result of which he had, in the north, a common frontier with his father-in-law Masʿūd,

Saldjūḳ sultan of Rūm. Whereas the power of Zankī had extended, from east to west, from Mawṣil to Aleppo, that of Nūr al-Dīn extended, in 549/1154, on a north-south axis from ᶜAzāz [*q.v.*] and al-Ruhā to Boṣrā and Ṣalkhad, guaranteeing the food-supplies of the Muslim towns.

The following year, Nūr al-Dīn demanded the submission of the *amīr* Ḍaḥḥāk al-Biḳāᶜī, since the region of Baᶜlabakk [*q.v.*] was dependent on the province of Damascus. When his demand was refused, he did not hesitate to send a detachment to rid himself of the rebel, who capitulated on 7 Rabīᶜ II/9 June 1155. This problem being settled, the treaty with Jerusalem renewed and another concluded with Antioch, Nūr al-Dīn was free to intervene in the struggle which had broken out between Saldjūḳs and Dānishmendids [*q.v.*] regarding the inheritance of his father-in-law who had recently died. He responded to the appeal of his brother-in-law Yaghī-basan, *amīr* of Sīwās, and took possession of the Saldjūḳ localities on the right bank of the Euphrates, including al-Bīra.

In the spring of 551/1156, weary of the skirmishes provoked by Renaud de Châtillon, the *amīr* Madjd al-Dīn, representative of Nūr al-Dīn in northern Syria, launched an attack in the direction of Ḥārim. Informed of the depredations committed by the Franks, Nūr al-Dīn left Damascus with a strong contingent to support the army of the north. Learning of his arrival, Renaud de Châtillon offered peace negotiations. An agreement was reached by which the treaty with Antioch was restored: Ḥārim remained in the hands of the Franks but produce and revenues were shared between the two states. Nūr al-Dīn returned to Damascus in Ramaḍān 551/November 1156 and renewed the treaty with Jerusalem, but at the end of Dhu 'l-Ḥidjdja 551/early February 1157 the Franks violated it. Baldwin III, pre-occupied by heavy debts and anticipating easy booty, launched an attack against the fertile region of the Djawlān [*q.v.*] where, under the terms of the treaty, Turcomans pastured a considerable number of horses and cattle; the Frankish cavalry seized these herds and took the herdsmen prisoner. This raid gave Nūr al-Dīn, who was eager to take possession of Baniyās [*q.v.*], an excellent pretext for intervention. In Ṣafar 552/early April 1157 he succeeded in persuading the Damascenes and the peasants of the Ghūṭa [*q.v.*] to contribute towards the cost of equipping his army with siege engines. Having reinforced the garrison of Baᶜlabakk to guard against possible intervention from the north, Nūr al-Dīn sent an army commanded by his brother Nuṣrat al-Dīn in the direction of Baniyās, where Frankish reinforcements were reported to have arrived. On 13 Rabīᶜ I/26 April 1157 the troops of Damascus inflicted a heavy defeat on the Franks and, although he succeeded in breaching the walls of Baniyās, Nūr al-Dīn learned of the advance of Baldwin, marching to the rescue of the besieged town, and taken by surprise, he gave the order to withdraw. Baldwin, believing that the troops of Damascus would not return, entrusted the task of restoring the town's defences to his infantry, and set out with his cavalry towards Galilee. Nūr al-Dīn set up an ambush near Djisr Banāt Yaᶜḳūb [*q.v.*] on the Jordan, and when the Franks halted on the shore of Lake Tiberias he surrounded them and took them prisoner. This success had the effect of uniting all the Frankish factions against him.

Learning that the Crusaders had established their head-quarters in the Buḳayᶜa [*q.v.*], not far from Ḥiṣn al-Akrād [*q.v.*], with the intention of attacking in the direction of the Middle Orontes, Nūr al-Dīn left Damascus in Radjab 552/August 1157 in order to repair the defences of fortresses damaged by the earthquakes of the previous month. Arriving at Sarmīn, he spent some time there. Shortly after the beginning of Ramaḍān 552/October 1157, he fell ill there and summoned Nuṣrat al-Dīn, Shīrkūh and his senior officers. Aware of the gravity of his condition, he gave instructions to be followed in the event of his death: he nominated Nuṣrat al-Dīn as his successor, to be resident at Aleppo; Nadjm al-Dīn Ayyūb was to remain military governor of Damascus and Shīrkūh was to be his representative there. In spite of intensive treatment, his condition worsened. The prince was transferred to Aleppo where he was lodged in the citadel. His health improving, he resumed the control of affairs and sent troops to occupy Shayzar. Henceforward the entire course of the Orontes was under the control of the Zankid power. Finally restored to health, Nūr al-Dīn returned to Damascus on 6 Rabīᶜ I 533/7 April 1158 and immediately set about mustering an army with the object of taking revenge for recent French raids against the Ḥawrān and Dārayyā in the Ghūṭa. The army left Damascus on 9 Rabīᶜ II 533/11 May 1158 with heavy equipment for laying siege to Ḥabīs Djaldaḳ, a cave fortified by the Crusaders which controlled Djawlān to the east and Lake Tiberias to the north-east. Learning that reinforcements were advancing, Nūr al-Dīn raised the siege and the two armies met near the Jordan on 14 Djumādā II/13 July. When some of the Muslim contingents were forced to give ground, Nūr al-Dīn ordered a strategic withdrawal; the Franks, fearing a trick on the part of the Damascenes, declined to pursue them.

In Dhu 'l-Ḥidjdja 553/December 1158-January 1159, Nūr al-Dīn once again fell ill in Damascus. Learning that Manuel was approaching from Cilicia, he urged the governors of the Syrian border regions to be vigilant. As his condition deteriorated, the prince summoned his senior *amīrs* to Damascus and warned his entourage against any sinister intentions towards him on the part of his brother Nuṣrat al-Dīn. To avoid any misunderstanding, he appointed as his successor his brother Ḳuṭb al-Dīn Mawdūd, ruler of Mawṣil.

At the beginning of 554/1159 Nūr al-Dīn was threatened by a proposed Franco-Byzantine coalition. He issued to his *amīrs* a summons to the Holy War, had an advanced bastion constructed at Aleppo and ordered the abandonment of certain sites which would be difficult to defend such as Kūrus. Learning that the Franks and the Basileus were intending to march against Aleppo, the prince set out to meet them. The latter had reached the ford of Balaneus on the ᶜAfrīn, whilst other elements were advancing from ᶜImm to the west of Aleppo. There then began a long series of negotiations which concluded, in Ṣafar 554/end of May 1159, with an agreement between Manuel and Nūr al-Dīn. An important element of this agreement was the latter's promise of support against Ḳilīdj Arslān II, the enemy of Byzantium. Manuel sought to conduct in northern Syria a policy of checks and balances, and it was fear of a Byzantine intervention which for many years prevented Nūr al-Dīn exploiting to the full his successes against the Franks. He entrusted Ḥarrān [*q.v.*] to the *isfahsālār amīr* Zayn al-Dīn ᶜAlī Küčük, ruler of Irbil [*q.v.*]. From Ḥarrān he descended towards the Euphrates and set about wresting control of al-Raḳḳa from the sons of the *amīr djāndār*, who had recently died. Worried by the ambitions of Ḳilīdj Arslān II, Nūr al-Dīn launched a campaign to coincide with a Byzantine expedition conducted against Eskishehir [*q.v.*]. Taking advantage of the troubles of Ḳilidj Arslān II, he occupied the former dependencies of the County of Edessa of which the Saldjūḳs had taken possession, and set out from Aleppo towards the north by way of Tell Bās̲h̲ir [*q.v.*]. He reached ʿAyntāb [*q.v.*] then took successively Raʿbān and Kaysūn, occupied Bahasnā then Marʿas̲h̲ [*q.v.*].

In 1160, Ḳilidj Arslān II succeeded in obtaining from his brother-in-law Nūr al-Dīn a cessation of hostilities since, as the Byzantine menace grew more serious, he needed all his troops. Ultimately, the Saldjūḳ sultan signed a peace agreement with Manuel.

After two years of respite, Baldwin III, knowing Nūr al-Dīn to be occupied in campaigning in the north, attacked territory dependent on Damascus, sending his troops towards the Ḥawrān. Nadjm al-Dīn Ayyūb negotiated the withdrawal of the Franks and obtained a truce of three months. As Nūr al-Dīn had not returned by the expiry of this respite, the Franks once again invaded the province of Damascus. Nūr al-Dīn returned to Damascus and, in the autumn of 555/1161, opened negotiations which concluded with a two-year treaty with Jerusalem. He was able to return to Aleppo, and from there he followed the course of events unfolding around the succession to the Saldjūḳ sultan in Hamad̲h̲ān [*q.v.*], a crisis which was keeping the troops of Ḳuṭb al-Dīn Mawdūd far from Syria.

The situation of Antioch having been settled in the interests of Manuel, the treaty with Baldwin being still valid and the army of Mawṣil at his disposal, Nūr al-Dīn had no fear of imminent interference with his domains, and he seized the opportunity to perform the *ḥadjdj* [*q.v.*] in 556/1161. He set out from Aleppo with S̲h̲īrkūh, passed through Damascus and took the *darb al-ḥadjdj* in order to reach the Holy Cities of the Ḥidjāz where he showed considerable generosity to the local inhabitants, particularly in the improvement of wells. At Medina he restored the defences of the town and arranged for the construction of a second perimeter wall complete with towers, to guarantee the protection of the population against raids by Bedouin marauders. On his return from the Pilgrimage in Ṣafar 557/February 1162, informed of Frankish plans to intervene in Egypt, Nūr al-Dīn decided to engage in diversionary operations in the north in the hope of restraining the campaign of the king of Jerusalem against Fāṭimid Egypt. At the end of 557/1162, Baldwin III fell seriously ill in Tripoli, and Nūr al-Dīn took advantage of the situation to muster an army at Aleppo and once again lay siege to Ḥārim. When the Franks arrived to within a short distance of this site, Nūr al-Dīn challenged them to a pitched battle, but the heavy rains of November cut the engagement short. Nūr al-Dīn decided to raise the siege, and Ḥarīm remained in the hands of the Crusaders.

In Rabīʿ I 558/February 1163, a new phase in the reign of Nūr al-Dīn began with the accession of Amaury. Henceforward, the Franks turned their attention towards Egypt, and Nūr al-Dīn could not afford to be absent from this new theatre of operations, as each of the local powers sought to establish sovereignty in Cairo. Aware of the progressive disintegration of Fāṭimid authority, the king of Jerusalem began to take an interest in Egypt, where the *amīrs* were in revolt against Ṭalāʾiʿ, a vizier of Armenian origin, converted to Twelver S̲h̲īʿī Islam. He had tried, on numerous occasions, to establish relations with Nūr al-Dīn, but he was the victim of two assassination attempts in 556/1161, the second, 18 Ramaḍān/10 September, proving successful. Egypt then collapsed into chaos, at a time when the Latin states of the Orient seemed to have regained their equilibrium in opposition to Nūr al-Dīn.

In the spring of 558/1163, intending to attack the County of Tripoli, Nūr al-Dīn set out with his army and encamped on the plain of al-Buḳayʿa at the foot of Ḥiṣn al-Akrād. Failing to take account of the fact that the Franks had recently gained reinforcements by sea, he was taken by surprise one day in May during the time of siesta. The Muslims were routed by the Frankish cavalry and Nūr al-Dīn, obliged to take flight for the sake of his own safety, did not halt until he reached the Lake of Qadesh (*Buḥayrat Ḳadis̲h̲*). A Romanesque fresco, dating from 1170, commemorates this battle in the Templars' chapel at Cressac in Charente. This defeat had a profound effect on the personality and the policies of Nūr al-Dīn since, after two successive defeats, he needed to restore confidence to the army and to the population. Henceforward, he was to embrace a life-style imbued with piety and religious observance, a development which earned him the respect of the religious classes and of the public but which was accepted only with some reservations by the *amīrs*. It was then that he decided to allocate *iḳṭāʿ*s to the orphans of combatants. Members of the religious classes, *ʿulamāʾ*, Ṣūfīs and Ḳurʾān readers received subsidies levied on the public treasury (*bayt al-māl* [*q.v.*]) but not on the spoils of war (*fayʾ* [*q.v.*]). Numerous inscriptions subsequent to 560/1165 feature two new composite titles in their protocol: *Nāṣir al-ḥaḳḳ bi 'l-barāhīn*, "Defender of the Truth by means of proofs" and *Munṣif al-maẓlūmīn min al-ẓālimīn*, "the Protector of the Oppressed against the Oppressors", titles expressing a part of the political programme of Nūr al-Dīn, that by which he sought to rally public support, presenting himself as the champion of the disadvantaged.

The course of events in Egypt was to pose an awkward problem for Nūr al-Dīn. In Rabīʿ I 559/January-February 1164, the vizier S̲h̲āwar, driven from Cairo by the revolt unleashed by the *amīr* Ḍirg̲h̲ām [*q.v.*] in Ramaḍān 558/August 1163, arrived at his court, imploring his aid. He reminded him that the deployment of Syrian units in Egypt would allow the creation of two fronts and the encirclement of the Latin kingdom of Jerusalem. S̲h̲āwar offered Nūr al-Dīn a third of the revenues of Egypt in exchange for his aid and the financing of the costs of the expedition. Furthermore, he promised to cede him part of the north-eastern province of the Delta and undertook to recognise his sovereignty. In D̲j̲umādā I 559/April 1164, impelled by public opinion, Nūr al-Dīn dispatched an army commanded by S̲h̲īrkūh with the objective of restoring S̲h̲āwar to power in Cairo. To protect the advance of this army, he conducted a diversionary manoeuvre in the direction of Baniyās, which enabled the troops accompanying S̲h̲āwar to reach the Delta of the Nile. Ḍirg̲h̲ām then issued a very urgent appeal to the Franks, offering Amaury a treaty of allegiance which, in the event of success on the part of the Franks, would have made Egypt a vassal of the Frankish kingdom of Jerusalem rather than a Syrian colony. Amaury accepted the offer but, harassed by the attacks of Nūr al-Dīn and not having sufficient troops to fight on two fronts, he was unable to send an army to Egypt in time to prevent S̲h̲īrkūh's arrival in the Delta. Having regained his authority in Cairo, S̲h̲āwar reneged on the promises made in Damascus, ultimately agreeing to accept the costs of the campaign but refusing to pay the promised tribute.

Nūr al-Dīn set out to invest Ḥārim, and the Franks

based in the northern Latin states reacted. The confrontation took place in the first ten days of Ramaḍān 559/end of July 1154. Nūr al-Dīn had deployed a significant quantity of heavy equipment but as the Franks advanced accompanied by Byzantine reinforcements, he raised the siege and, to avoid being encircled, he withdrew towards Artāḥ, not far from the ford of Balaneus to the east-south-east of the Lake of Antioch. Exploiting the tactic of withdrawal and counter-attack, *al-karr wa 'l-farr*, on 20 Ramaḍān 559/11 August 1164 he lured the Franks into a ferocious battle, in the course of which he inflicted heavy losses on them, a success which he immediately exploited, returning to Ḥārim, which capitulated the following day. This problem being settled, Nūr al-Dīn turned against the kingdom of Jerusalem, a large proportion of whose troops were then deployed in Egypt. He invaded Galilee and set about besieging Baniyās, which capitulated in Dhu 'l-Ḥidjdja 559/October 1164. Nūr al-Dīn installed a garrison there, agreed to a treaty with the Franks and insisted on sharing the revenues of the district of Tiberias. His policy had secured its objective, sc. to prevent the defeat of Shīrkūh.

In the spring of 561/1165, fearing an intervention by Manuel and not wanting to see Amaury prolong his stay in Antioch, Nūr al-Dīn agreed to free Bohemond III for a ransom of 100,000 gold pieces. In order to maintain the balance of forces in northern Syria to the advantage of Islam, he sought to avoid any action liable to provoke the anger of the Basileus. The same year, taking advantage of the capture of Raymond III of Tripoli, he crossed the Biḳāᶜ and regained from the Franks the fortress of Munayṭira.

While the second Egyptian campaign unfolded, Nūr al-Dīn, who had received reinforcements from Mawṣil, occupied the fortress of Ḥūnīn, not far from Bāniyās, in the Djabal ᶜĀmila.

Although disappointed by his campaign in Egypt, Shīrkūh brought back a considerable sum of money from Cairo when he returned to Damascus on 18 Dhu 'l-Ḳaᶜda 562/5 September 1167. To alleviate his disappointment, Nūr al-Dīn awarded him the fiefdom of Ḥimṣ, the wall and defences of which he had recently restored, then set out towards the coastal plain, where he laid siege to ᶜArḳā. Having taken possession of Ḥalbā, the army of Nūr al-Dīn took the fortress of al-ᶜUrayma, thus securing the lines of communication between Ṭarṭūs and Ṣāfīthā, but being unable to defend it he demolished it and returned to Ḥimṣ for the month of Ramaḍān 562/June-July 1167. After this success he fixed on the objective of Bayrūt [*q.v.*], in order to have a "window" on the Mediterranean and avoid the necessity of paying export dues to the Franks, but dissensions within the army prevented the realisation of this project.

In Radjab 563/April-May 1168 Bedouins of the tribe of the Banū Kalb [*q.v.*] captured Shihāb al-Dīn Mālik b. ᶜAli b. Mālik, ruler of Ḳalᶜat Djaᶜbar, while he was hunting to the north of the Euphrates. They took their prisoner to Nūr al-Dīn, who purchased him and held him in Aleppo. In exchange for Ḳalᶜat Djaᶜbar, he offered him money and a fief, but the offer was refused. Finally, it was Madjd al-Dīn Abū Bakr Ibn al-Dāya who succeeded, on 20 Muḥarram 564/26 October 1168, in persuading Shihāb al-Dīn to exchange the place for the important commercial centre of Sarūdj to the south-west of Edessa as well as the salt-flats of al-Djabbūl and Buzāᶜā [*q.vv.*] in the district of Aleppo. Henceforward, he controlled this section of the Euphrates and was assured of freedom of communication with Mawṣil.

In the middle of the month of Muḥarram 564/20 October 1168, the Franks launched an attack in the direction of Cairo. While the population resolved to resist, Shāwar warned the caliph al-ᶜĀḍid [*q.v.*] that the only chance of salvation was to appeal to Nūr al-Dīn, since the presence of Sunnīs was preferable to a Christian protectorate. The Fāṭimid caliph and Shāwar promised him a third of the revenues of Egypt as well as fiefs for the maintenance of the troops. Nūr al-Dīn decided to send a third expedition against the Delta, ordered Shīrkūh to Cairo and entrusted him with full powers. When the latter died on 22 Djumādā II/23 March 1169, his nephew, Ṣalāḥ al-Dīn, was appointed vizier by al-ᶜĀḍid and commander of the Syrian forces in Egypt by Nūr al-Dīn. Amaury, concerned at the latter's seizure of Egypt, issued appeals for help to the whole of Christendom. The Franks responded and decided on Damietta (Dimyāṭ [*q.v.*]) as an objective, but the lack of co-ordination between Byzantines and Franks led to the abandonment of the siege of this locality. After this retreat, al-ᶜĀḍid wrote to Nūr al-Dīn inviting him to recall to Syria the units sent as reinforcements to Egypt, keeping in Egypt only the original force commanded by Ṣalāḥ al-Dīn. The Syrian prince seems to have been worried by the attitude and the ambitions of the latter. He instructed Nadjm al-Dīn Ayyūb to remind his son that the struggle against the infidels was the first duty of the believers and that the ᶜAbbāsid *khuṭba* must be adopted in Cairo. Nadjm al-Dīn left Damascus on 27 Radjab 565/16 April 1170. To create a diversion, Nūr al-Dīn laid siege to al-Karak.

Following the great earthquake of 565/1170, Nūr al-Dīn left his headquarters at Tell ᶜAshtārā to attend to the repairs needed for the defences of Ḥimṣ, Ḥamāt, Bārīn and Aleppo.

On 1 Muharram 566/14 September 1170, the head of the Zankid family crossed the Euphrates opposite Ḳalᶜat Djaᶜbar and took possession of al-Raḳḳa [*q.v.*], its governor ceding the place to him in exchange for substantial compensation. Having taken control of the region of the Khābūr [*q.v.*], hitherto a dependency of Mawṣil, Nūr al-Dīn laid siege to Sindjār. At the approach of the Syrian troops, Fakhr al-Dīn placed himself under the protection of Shams al-Dīn Ildeñiz [*q.v.*]. The latter sent a deputation to Nūr al-Dīn forbidding to take any action against Mawṣil, but the Zankid, confident of the support of the caliph of Baghdād and that of the people of Mawṣil, made his entrance into the town on 13 Djumādā I 566/22 January 1171 and took up residence in the citadel. He suppressed all the *mukūs* and other abuses, and applied to the Djazīra the régime in force in Syria and in Egypt. He confirmed the authority of his nephew Sayf al-Dīn Ghāzī over Mawṣil and gave him the district of Djazīrat Ibn ᶜUmar [*q.v.*], while his nephew ᶜImād al-Dīn, son of Mawdūd, received Sindjār. Before leaving Mawṣil to return to Aleppo, he laid the foundations of the Great Mosque. Then, after returning to Damascus to observe the fast of Ramaḍān (May-June 1171), Nūr al-Dīn regained possession of Tell al-ᶜAshtārā, from which point he was able to observe the movements of the Franks of Jerusalem and eventually to support the operations of Ṣalāḥ al-Dīn.

Until the year 567/September 1171-August 1172, the relations between Nūr al-Dīn and Ṣalāḥ al-Dīn remained those between a chief and his subordinate. Thereafter, they soon found themselves in conflict over the manner in which the war against the Franks was to be waged; this was a conflict between two generations and two temperaments, one Turkish, the other Kurdish. Nūr al-Dīn, as Sir Hamilton Gibb (in

Setton and Baldwin, *A History of the Crusades*, i, 565) has underlined, operated within a political framework defined by the system of his times. For him, Syria was the principal field of battle against the Crusaders and Egypt represented nothing more than a source of additional revenue to cover the costs of the *dj̲ihād*. In that year, before attacking the County of Tripoli, he had ordered Ṣalāḥ al-Dīn to gather all available forces in Egypt and lead them towards Frankish Palestine, thus trapping the Franks in a pincer-movement. The first objective was the castle of al-Karak; after ten days of siege the garrison offered to surrender to Ṣalāḥ al-Dīn. For him, the elimination of all obstacles between Egypt and Syria was not desirable, since henceforward he would be at the mercy of Nūr al-Dīn. He decided to return to Cairo and sent a letter to his sovereign, claiming the pretext of unrest in Cairo fomented by the S̲h̲īʿīs. Nūr al-Dīn did not accept this excuse, and announced his intention of going to Egypt in person in order to depose Ṣalāḥ al-Dīn. The latter, on the advice of his father, re-affirmed his loyalty to Nūr al-Dīn, who relented, and tension abated.

In Rabīʿ I 568/October-November 1172, when Nūr al-Dīn had been resident in Damascus for more than three months, the Franks launched an attack against the Ḥawrān and advanced as far as S̲h̲ayk̲h̲ Miskīn. The prince of Damascus set out with his troops and encamped at Kiswa in the Mard̲j̲ al-Ṣuffar [*q.v.*]; the Franks withdrew towards S̲h̲allāla, where the Damascene army confronted them. Nūr al-Dīn established his camp at Tell al-ʿAs̲h̲tārā and dispatched cavalry units to raid the district of Tiberias.

Having repelled the Franks, Nūr al-Dīn turned his attention to northern Syria, where he was able to assist the Armenian Mleh to expel the garrisons of Maṣṣīṣa, Adana and Ṭarsūs [*q.vv.*]. He would have been glad to obtain the support of the Sald̲j̲ūḳ prince of Konya for operations against Antioch but, following a stern warning from Manuel, Ḳilid̲j̲ Arslān II rejected the overtures of Nūr al-Dīn and turned against his neighbour, the Dānis̲h̲mendid D̲h̲u 'l-Nūn. The latter sought refuge with Nūr al-Dīn, who was also joined by the ruler of Malaṭya [*q.v.*] and the *amīr* of al-Mad̲j̲dal. Nūr al-Dīn promised him his support and insisted that Ḳilid̲j̲ Arslān restore the property taken from the *amīr* of al-Mad̲j̲dal. When this ultimatum was refused, he felt justified in declaring war with a Muslim state; it was necessary for the interests of Islam since this prince was serving the cause of the infidels. While Mleh attacked Cilicia [*q.v.*] Nūr al-Dīn took Raʿbān, Marzubān, Ḳaysūn and Bahasnā, places held by the Sald̲j̲ūḳs on the right bank of the Euphrates. On 20 D̲h̲u 'l-Ḳaʿda 568/3 July 1173 he occupied Marʿas̲h̲. Shortly after this, Ḳilid̲j̲ Arslān II appealed to him for a truce. Nūr al-Dīn required him to free the prisoners taken in the region of Malaṭya and to participate in the Holy War, either sending a contingent to join the struggle with the Franks, or operating independently against Byzantium.

To mark his independence vis-à-vis the major atabegs, Nūr al-Dīn sent as an envoy to Bag̲h̲dād his trusted adviser Kamāl al-Dīn Abu 'l-Faḍl Muḥammad al-S̲h̲ahrazūrī to ask the caliph for a document conferring upon him all the territories and towns in which his authority was recognised. In granting this solemn deed of investiture to Nūr al-Dīn, the caliph deprived the successors of the Great Sald̲j̲ūḳs of any authority over the lands situated to the west of the Tigris.

Taking advantage of the absence of Amaury, who had returned to Antioch, Nūr al-Dīn put into operation a plan of attack against the land of Trans-Jordania. His objective remained the same: to take possession of al-Karak and S̲h̲awbak, where the Frankish garrisons cut the route between Egypt and Syria, interrupting caravan traffic and hindering the Pilgrimage. He also needed to gain the support of the nomads, many of whom did not hesitate to serve the Franks as auxiliaries or guides. Once again putting the good will of Ṣalāḥ al-Dīn to the test, he instructed him to attack al-Karak. The latter obeyed in mid-S̲h̲awwal 568/May 1173. The siege had been in effect for some time when Nūr al-Dīn crossed the southern border of Syria in D̲h̲u 'l-Ḥid̲j̲d̲j̲a 568/end of July 1173. When Ṣalāḥ al-Dīn learned that the Zankid army had reached al-Raḳīm, two days' march from al-Karak, he ordered his troops to return to Egypt, claiming, in a message to Nūr al-Dīn, that his father, Nad̲j̲m al-Dīn Ayyūb, was gravely ill in Cairo and that he feared lest, in the event of his father's death during his own absence, Egypt would slip away from the authority of Nūr al-Dīn and would be removed from the authority of the Sunna. Nūr al-Dīn, not deceived, pretended to understand the reasons for the departure of the Ayyūbid prince. Through this gesture on the part of Ṣalāḥ al-Dīn, the kingdom of Jerusalem gained a reprieve of forty years and Nūr al-Dīn was not to see in the al-Aḳṣā Mosque [*q.v.*] the wooden *minbar* [*q.v.*] which he had had made in advance in Aleppo as an *ex-voto* offering for the return of al-Ḳuds [*q.v.*] to Islam.

Returning from Aleppo in Muḥarram 569/September 1173 Nūr al-Dīn heard at Salāmiyya, to the south-east of Ḥamāt, the news of a Frankish attack against the Ḥawrān; while preparing to counter this, he was informed of the adversary's withdrawal. Returning to Damascus, he engaged in preparations for an expedition towards Egypt, the aim of which was to induce Ṣalāḥ al-Dīn to intervene against the Franks. According to his plan, he left in Syria, confronting the Franks, troops from Mawṣil, under the command of Sayf al-Dīn G̲h̲āzī, and he himself was to set out for Egypt with his squadrons after Ramaḍān 569/early May 1174. A few days after the *ʿĪd al-Fiṭr* [*q.v.*], Nūr al-Dīn fell ill with an inflammation of the throat. Confined to his bed in the palace which he had had constructed in the citadel of Damascus, he summoned, according to Ibn al-At̲h̲īr (*Kāmil*, ix, 124), two doctors including D̲j̲amāl al-Dīn Yūsuf b. Ḥaydar al-Raḥbī al-Dimas̲h̲ḳī, his personal physician. Despite their efforts, al-Malik al-ʿĀdil Nūr al-Dīn Maḥmūd b. Zankī died on Wednesday 11 S̲h̲awwāl 569/15 May 1174. At first interred in the citadel, his remains were transferred, when it was ready, to the funeral *madrasa* which he was having constructed to the south-west of the Great Mosque of the Umayyads. At the present time, his tomb is still the object of popular veneration.

Bibliography: For pre-1965 bibliography, see the very detailed one given by N. Elisséeff in *Nūr al-Dīn, un grand prince musulman de Syrie au temps des Croisades 511-569 H./1118-1174,* 3 vols., Damascus 1967, i, Bibliography, pp. XXI-LXXVII, and also Survey of sources, 1-85. The remainder of this bibliography deals with works published subsequently.

A. Arabic sources. ʿAlī b. Ṭāhir al-Sulamī, *K. al-D̲j̲ihād*, text and tr. E. Sivan, *La Genèse de la Contre Croisade: un traité damasquin du début du XIIe S.*, in *JA*, ccliv (1966), 197-224; Ibn ʿAsākir, *T. Dimas̲h̲ḳ*, facs. text ʿAmmān 1988, complete ed. in course of publication at Damascus; Ibn al-ʿAdīm, *Bug̲h̲yat al-ṭalab*, facs. ed. Frankfurt 1986-8, ed. Suhayl Zakkār, Damascus 1408-9/1988-9; Usāma b. Munḳid̲h̲, *K. al-Iʿtibār*, tr. A. Miquel, *Les enseignements de la vie. Souvenirs d'un gentilhomme syrien du temps des Croisades*, Paris 1983.

B. Studies. (a) Political history. K.M. Setton and M.W. Baldwin, *A history of the Crusades*, I², Philadephia 1969; J. Prawer, *Histoire du Royaume Latin de Jérusalem*, CNRS, Paris 1969, i, ch. III, 395-425, ch. IV, 427-59; H. Salame-Sarkis, *Contribution à l'histoire de Tripoli et de sa région à l'époque des Croisades*, Paris 1980; P.M. Holt, *The age of the Crusades*, London 1986, 466-52; Carol Hillenbrand, *A Muslim principality in Crusader times. The early Artuqid state*, Istanbul 1990. (b) *Djihād* and law. H. Laoust, *Les schismes dans l'Islam*, Paris 1965, 189-22; Sivan, *Le caractère sacré de Jérusalem dans l'Islam aux XIIe et XIIIe S.*, in *SI*, xxvii (1967), 149-82; idem, *L'Islam et la Croisade. Idéologie et propagande dans les réactions musulmanes aux Croisades*, Paris 1968, 3, 59-91; F.H. Russell, *The Just War in the Middle Ages, studies in medieval life and thought*, Cambridge 1975, 195-212; R. Peters (tr. and annotator), *Jihad in mediaeval and modern Islam. The chapter on jihad from Averroes' legal handbook* Bidayat al-mujtahid *and the treatise* Koran and fighting *by the late Shaykh al-Azhar, Mahmūd Shaltūt*, Leiden 1977; P. Rousset, *Histoire d'une idéologie: la Croisade*, Lausanne 1983. (c) Economy and society. H. Mason, *Two statesmen of mediaeval islam, Vizir Ibn Hubayra ... and Caliph an-Nâṣir li Dîn Allâh*, The Hague-Paris 1972; N.A. Faris, ch. *Arab culture in the twelfth century*, in N.P. Zacour, H.W. Hazard and K.M. Setton, *A history of the Crusades. v. The impact of the Crusades on the Near East*, Madison-Milwaukee 1985, 3-32.

(N. ELISSÉEFF)

NŪR AL-DĪN MUḤAMMAD, the fifth ruler of the Turkmen Artuḳid dynasty [*q.v.*] in Ḥiṣn Kayfā and most of Diyār Bakr, d. in Rabīʿ I 581/June 1185.

He succeeded on his father Ḳara Arslan's death, in 562/1166-7 according to the chronicles (although numismatic evidence suggests that the latter may have lived till 570/1174-5), having promised his father to continue support for the Zangid ruler Nūr al-Dīn Maḥmūd's [*q.v.*] *djihād* against the Franks, a commitment which he in fact honoured by bringing troops to Niṣibīn in 566/1170-1. But after the Zangid's death in 569/1174, Nūr al-Dīn Muḥammad transferred his allegiance to Ṣalāḥ al-Dīn [*q.v.*], and henceforth, he achieves prominence in the sources almost exclusively in the context of the Ayyūbid's career. Ṣalāḥ al-Dīn valued an alliance with the Artuḳids in Diyār Bakr as a check on the Saldjūḳ sultan of Rūm, Ḳilîdj Arslan II [*q.v.*]. Hence Muḥammad frequently sent troops to Ṣalāḥ al-Dīn on the latter's request. He was awarded possession of Āmid, long coveted by the Artuḳids of Ḥiṣn Kayfā, in 579/1183, as a reward for aid at the siege of Mawṣil in the previous year; henceforth, Āmid became the seat of power for Nūr al-Dīn Muḥammad's descendants. The Ayyūbid sultan bound his ally even more closely by an oath requiring the despatch of troops against the Franks whenever needed, and the Artuḳid was accordingly present at the siege of Karak in Djumādā I 580/August-September 1184. However, when Ṣalāḥ al-Dīn called for troops for his second attempt against Mawṣil, Nūr al-Dīn Muḥammad was too ill to go personally but sent a force to Dunaysir under his brother ʿImād al-Dīn. Muḥammad died within days, and his young son Ḳuṭb al-Dīn Sukmān II immediately established himself in Ḥiṣn Kayfā as his father's successor, with continued allegiance to Ṣalāḥ al-Dīn, whilst ʿImād al-Dīn had to be content with taking Khartpert, where he established a minor Artuḳid line.

Little is known of internal affairs in Ḥiṣn Kayfā and Āmid under Nūr al-Dīn Muḥammad, but it may be assumed that he continued the courtly traditions of his father which had been sophisticated enough to attract Usāma b. Munḳidh [see MUNḲIDH, BANŪ] to spend some of his declining years at Ḥiṣn Kayfā. The extant copper coins minted there in Muḥammad's name follow the numismatic traditions of the Turkmen dynasties of Mesopotamia for this century. As well as conventional Arabic inscriptions on one side, they bear figures copied from classical models; one coin depicts Nūr al-Dīn Muḥammad in the guise of Seleucus II (Lane Poole, *The coins of the Urtukí Turkumáns*, 125-7). The Aleppo Gate at Āmid has a celebratory inscription dated 579 AH announcing Muḥammad's occupation of the city. Van Berchem suggested that he may have taken the title of *sulṭān*, used by his successors, after his acquisition of Āmid; and he also quotes at length an anonymous, contemporary account describing in fulsome terms Muḥammad's just administration of the city (*Amida*, 71-2, 75-81).

Bibliography: 1. Sources. Abū Shāma, *Rawḍatayn*; Bar Hebraeus, *Chronography*; Ibn al-Athīr, xi-xii; Ibn Azraḳ al-Fāriḳī, *T. Mayyāfāriḳīn wa-Āmid*, B.L. ms. or. 5803, fols. 198b, 200b; Ibn al-Furāt, *Taʾrīkh*; Ibn Shaddād, *Nawādir*; Ibn Wāṣil, *Mufarridj*, ii; Michael the Syrian, *Chronicle*, tr. Chabot, iii; Sibṭ Ibn al-Djawzī, *Mirʾāt*, viii/2; Usāma b. Munḳidh, *Memoirs*.

2. Studies. S. Lane Poole, *The coins of the Urtukí Turkumáns*, in *The International Numismata Orientalia*, Pt. 2, London 1875, 16; idem, *The coins of the Turkumán houses of Seljook, Urtuk, Zengee, etc., in the British Museum*, London 1877, 125-7; M. van Berchem and J. Strzygowski, *Amida*, Heidelberg 1910, 71-81, 96; H.A.R. Gibb, *Al-Barq al-Shāmī ...*, in *WZKM*, lii (1953), 93-115; Helen Mitchell Brown, *Some reflections on the figured coinage of the Artuqids and Zangids*, in D. Kouymjian (ed.), *Near Eastern Numismatics, iconography, epigraphy and history. Studies in honor of George C. Miles*, Beirut 1974, 353-8.

(CAROLE HILLENBRAND)

NŪR AL-DĪN MUḤAMMAD II, Nizārī Ismāʿīlī *Imām* and the fifth lord of Alamūt (561-607/1166-1210). Born in Shawwāl 542/March 1148, he succeeded to the leadership of the Nizārī community and state on the death of his father, Ḥasan II, on 6 Rabīʿ I 561/9 January 1166. He devoted his long and peaceful reign of some forty-four years to managing the affairs of the Nizārī *daʿwa* and community, especially in Persia, from the central headquarters of the sect at Alamūt. A thinker and a prolific writer, he also contributed actively to the Nizārī teachings of his time.

Nūr al-Dīn Muḥammad II affirmed the Nizārid Fāṭimid genealogy of his father and, therefore, of himself; and, henceforth, the lords of Alamūt were acknowledged as *imāms*, descendants of Nizār b. al-Mustanṣir, by the Nizārī Ismāʿīlī community. In the doctrinal field, he systematically expounded and elaborated the important doctrine of the *ḳiyāma*, announced by his father in 559/1164, and placed the current Nizārī *imām* and his autonomous teaching authority at the very centre of that doctrine (see *Haft bāb-i Bābā Sayyidnā*, ed. W. Ivanow, in *Two early Ismaili treatises*, Bombay 1933, 4-42).

Aside from petty warfare, the history of the Nizārī state in Persia was politically uneventful under Nūr al-Dīn Muḥammad. However, the Syrian Nizārīs were more involved at this time in their own local alliances and conflicts. There are also indications that a widening rift had developed between this Nizārī *imām* and Rāshid al-Dīn Sinān [*q.v.*], the contemporary leader of the Syrian Nizārīs, although a complete break was avoided. Rashīd al-Dīn and other Persian historians also report a detailed story about how the Nizārīs of his time persuaded, initially through the intimidating dagger of one of their *fidāʾīs*, the famous Sunnī theologian Fakhr al-Dīn al-Rāzī (d. 606/1209 [*q.v.*]) to refrain from denouncing them in public. Having ruled longer than any other lord of Alamūt, Nūr al-Dīn Muḥammad II died, possibly of poison, on 10 Rabīʿ I 607/1 September 1210.

Bibliography: Djuwaynī, iii, 240-2; Djuwaynī-Boyle, ii, 697-9; Rashīd al-Dīn Faḍl Allāh, *Djāmiʿ al-tawārīkh, ḳismat-i Ismāʿīliyān*, ed. M.T. Dānishpazhūh and M. Mudarrisī Zandjānī, Tehran 1338 *Sh.*/1959, 170-3; Abu 'l-Ḳāsim ʿAbd Allāh b. ʿAlī Kāshānī, *Zubdat al-tawārīkh, bakhsh-i Fāṭimiyān wa Nizāriyān*, ed. M.T. Dānishpazhūh, ²Tehran 1366 *Sh.*/1987, 208-14; M.G.S. Hodgson, *The order of Assassins*, The Hague 1955, 160 ff., 180-4, 210-17, 225, 279-324 (containing the English tr. of the anonymous *Haft bāb*, the only Persian Nizārī work extant from this period); I.K. Poonawala, *Biobibliography of Ismāʿīlī literature*, Malibu 1977, 258-9; F. Daftary, *The Ismāʿīlīs. Their history and doctrines*, Cambridge 1990, 391-6, 400, 403-5, 687.

(F. Daftary)

NŪR AL-ḤAḲḲ AL-DIHLAWĪ, or Nūr al-Dīn Muḥammad al-Shāhdjahānābādī, a traditionist and historiographer of Mughal India who flourished in the 11th/17th century. The nickname "al-Turk al-Bukhārī" points to his origin from Central Asia. As a poet he adopted the pen name "Mashriḳī". He was the son of the scholar ʿAbd al-Ḥaḳḳ [*q.v.*] al-Dihlawī, a well-known *shaykh* of the Ḳādiriyya order. Nūr al-Ḥaḳḳ succeeded his father as a religious teacher and was appointed a judge at Agra under Shāh Djahān. His death at Dihlī occurred in 1073/1662.

In *Zubdat al-tawārīkh*, Nūr al-Ḥaḳḳ enlarged the *Tārīkh-i Ḥaḳḳī*, a chronicle of Indian history written by his father, bringing it up to 1014/1605, the beginning of the reign of Djahāngīr. He wrote two Persian commentaries on canonical collections of *ḥadīth*: *Taysīr al-ḳārī fī sharḥ Ṣaḥīḥ al-Bukhārī* and *Manbaʿ al-ʿilm fī sharḥ Ṣaḥīḥ Muslim*; the latter work was later revised and enlarged by his son Fakhr al-Dīn Muḥibb Allāh. *Nūr al-ʿayn*, an early work dedicated to his father, is a commentary on Amīr Khusraw Dihlawī's [*q.v.*] historical *mathnawī Ḳirān al-saʿdayn*; it is dated 1014 A.H. by a chronographical riddle (cf. Rieu, ii, 617b).

Bibliography: H.M. Elliot, *Bibliographical index to the historians of Muhammadan India*, i, Calcutta 1849, 281-97; idem and J. Dowson, *History of India*, London 1867-77, vi, 182-4; Ch. Rieu, *Catalogue of the Persian manuscripts in the British Museum*, London 1879, i, 224b-225a, 617; Brockelmann, S I, 263, no. 31, 266, no. 13; Storey i/1, 441, 501, 1309; A. Munzawī, *Fihrist-i nuskhahā-yi khaṭṭī-yi fārsī*, v, Tehran 1351 *sh*/1972, 3515, and vi, Tehran 1353 *sh*/1974, 4661. (J.T.P. de Bruijn)

NŪRBAKHSHIYYA, a Shīʿī offshoot of the Kubrawī Ṣūfī order [*q.v.*], which functioned for part of its existence as a distinct sect because of the intermittent claims to the status of *mahdī* [*q.v.*] of its eponym, Sayyid Muḥammad b. Muḥammad b. ʿAbd Allāh Nūrbakhsh. Its importance lies primarily in exemplifying the messianic-tinged Ṣūfī-Shīʿī ferment that preceded and, in some measure, prepared the way for the establishment of the Ṣafawid state.

Nūrbakhsh was born at Ḳāʾin in Ḳuhistān in 795/1392. His father, supposedly a descendant of the Imām Mūsā al-Kāẓim, had come from Ḳaṭīf, a Shīʿī region of eastern Arabia, on pilgrimage to Mashhad before settling in Ḳāʾin; he may therefore be presumed to have been a Shīʿī. Nūrbakhsh's grandfather was from al-Aḥsā [*q.v.*], likewise an area of Shīʿī settlement; this accounts for Nūrbakhsh's occasional use of the *takhalluṣ* Laḥṣawī. While studying in Harāt in his early youth, Nūrbakhsh was recruited into one branch of the Kubrawī order by a follower of Isḥāḳ Khuttalānī, the principal successor to Sayyid ʿAlī Hamadānī (d. 786/1384). Moving to the *khānaḳāh* at Khuttalān, he soon became the most prominent disciple of Khuttalānī, who bestowed on him the title Nūrbakhsh ("Bestower of Light") in accordance with an indication contained in a dream. The account given by Nūr Allāh Shushtarī (d. 1019/1610) in his *Madjālis al-muʾminīn* (ed. Tehran, 1375-6/1955-6, ii, 143-7)—followed almost unanimously by later writers—relates that on the basis of the same dream Khuttalānī also declared Nūrbakhsh to be the Mahdī and incited him to style himself Imām and caliph and to lay claim to rule. He swore allegiance to him himself and ordered his disciples to do the same; all obeyed, with the exception of Sayyid ʿAbd Allāh Barzishābādī (d. *ca.* 856/1452). Nūrbakhsh asked for a delay in starting his insurrection, but Khuttalānī refused, saying that the divinely-appointed time for rebellion (*khurūdj*) had arrived.

The beginnings of the episode are recounted somewhat differently by Ḥāfiẓ Ḥusayn Karbalāʾī, a spiritual descendant of the dissident Barzishābādī. He attributes a far more active role to Nūrbakhsh, claiming that he originated the claim to the status of *mahdī* himself and then had it endorsed by Khuttalānī, who was too senile and decrepit to stand in his way. Barzishābādī allegedly succeeded in having the endorsement temporarily withdrawn, but his influence over Khuttalānī was no match for that of Nūrbakhsh, and preparations for the uprising proceeded (Karbalāʾī, *Rawḍat al-djinān wa-djannāt al-djanān*, ed. Djaʿfar Sulṭān al-Ḳurrāʾī, Tehran 1349 *Sh.*/1970, ii, 249-50). This version of the affair seems at least as credible as that offered by Shushtarī. Nūrbakhsh certainly had a high estimate of his own worth; he claimed to possess superiority to Plato and Avicenna and absolute mastery of all the sciences. Moreover, he continued to advance claims to the status of *mahdī*, however sporadically, after the death of Khuttalānī and wrote a treatise, *Risālat al-Hudā*, attempting to vindicate these claims.

In 826/1423, Khuttalānī and Nūrbakhsh left the *khānaḳāh* in Khuttalān and ensconced themselves with their followers in the nearby castle of Kūh-tīrī. Before they could complete their military preparations, they were attacked and taken prisoner by Bāyazīd, the Tīmūrid governor of the area. Khuttalānī, together with his brother, was put to death almost immediately, despite his advanced age. Nūrbakhsh himself was spared and sent in chains to the presence of Shāhrukh in Harāt. The contrasting fates of the two men might be taken to confirm Shushtarī's depiction of Khuttalānī as the instigator of the whole affair; it is also possible, however, that Khuttalānī was singled out for death because of his long-standing ties to local rulers in Badakhshān who had sought to block the expansion of Tīmūrid power in the region (Devin DeWeese, *The eclipse of the Kubraviyah in Central Asia*, 60).

After interrogation, Nūrbakhsh was sent on from Harāt to Shīrāz; Ibrāhīm Sulṭān, Shāhrukh's governor of Fārs, subjected him to a further spell of imprisonment in Bihbahān before releasing him.

Nūrba<u>kh</u>s<u>h</u> then made his way in turn to <u>Sh</u>us<u>h</u>tar, Baṣra, Ḥilla (where he is said to have met the celebrated <u>Sh</u>īʿī scholar Ibn Fahd al-Ḥillī) and Baghdad. Next he proceeded to Kurdistān and the Ba<u>kh</u>tiyārī country where he revived with some success his claim to worldly sovereignty; loyalty was sworn to him and coins were struck, and the *<u>kh</u>uṭba* was read in his name. It happened that <u>Sh</u>āhru<u>kh</u> was campaigning in Ā<u>dh</u>arbāy<u>dj</u>ān at the time, and he had Nūrba<u>kh</u>s<u>h</u> seized and brought to his camp. Nūrba<u>kh</u>s<u>h</u> escaped and attempted to flee via <u>Kh</u>al<u>kh</u>āl back to Kurdistān, but he was soon recaptured and after fifty-three days spent at the bottom of a pit he was sent to Harāt with instructions to mount the *minbar* at the Mas<u>dj</u>id-i <u>D</u>jāmiʿ and publicly disavow his claims. This he did, with obvious reluctance, in the following ambiguous words: "They relate certain things from this wretch. Whether I said them or not, 'O Lord, we have wronged ourselves; if You do not forgive us and have mercy upon us, we will certainly be among the losers' (Ḳurʾān, VII, 23)." He was then released anew, on condition that he restrict himself to teaching the conventional religious sciences (*ʿulūm-i rasmī*), a condition he appears to have broken, for in 848/1444 he was re-arrested with orders for him to be ejected from the Tīmūrid realm into Anatolia. Instead he was confined in turn in Tabrīz, <u>Sh</u>īrwān and Gīlān, being definitively released on the death of <u>Sh</u>āhru<u>kh</u> in 850/1447. Thereupon he made his way to the village of Sulfān near Rayy, remaining there until his death in Rabīʿ I 869/November 1464. These last years of Nūrba<u>kh</u>s<u>h</u>'s life appear to have been relatively tranquil. It is probable that he reduced his public claims to spiritual eminence to those customary for a Ṣūfī *<u>sh</u>ay<u>kh</u>*, although he continued to designate himself by such suggestive terms as *maẓhar-i mawʿūd* ("the promised manifestation") and *maẓhar-i <u>dj</u>āmiʿ* ("the comprehensive manifestation").

Nūrba<u>kh</u>s<u>h</u> wrote a number of treatises, only one of which has ever been published (M. Molé, *Professions de foi de deux Kubrawis*: *ʿAlī-i Hamadanī et Muḥammad Nūrbaḫš*, in *BEO*, xvii [1961-2], 182-204: Arabic text and French translation of *al-Risālat al-Iʿtiḳādiyya*), as well as a considerable quantity of verse (for samples see Mawlawī Muḥammad <u>Sh</u>afīʿ, *Firḳa-yi Nūrba<u>kh</u>s<u>h</u>ī*, in *Maḳālāt*, ed. Aḥmad Rabbānī, Lahore 1972, ii, 45-74). The most interesting of his writings is perhaps the *Risālat al-Hudā* in which he clarifies his concept of the status of *mahdī*, one that deviates considerably from that of his ancestral Twelver <u>Sh</u>īʿism. Nūrba<u>kh</u>s<u>h</u> utterly rejects the occultation (*<u>gh</u>ayba*) of the Twelfth Imām, asserting that his body has decomposed and that his functions and attributes are now manifest (*bāriz*) in him, Nūrba<u>kh</u>s<u>h</u>. He defines "absolute imāmate" as reposing on four pillars: perfection of prophetic descent, perfection of knowledge, perfection of sanctity and the possession of temporal power. All the preceding Imāms, with the exception of ʿAlī b. Abī Ṭālib, lack the fourth pillar; Nūrba<u>kh</u>s<u>h</u>, destined as Mahdī to gain supreme political power, is therefore superior to them. The proofs cited by Nūrba<u>kh</u>s<u>h</u> for the status of *mahdī* consist largely of celestial signs and dreams and predictions by figures as varied as the Kubrawī saint Saʿd al-Dīn Ḥamūya (d. 650/1252) and the scholar Naṣīr al-Dīn Ṭūsī (d. 672/1274). Some of the dreams related here foretell setbacks as well as ultimate triumph in the form of a universal rule lasting seven or eight years; this suggests that the treatise may have been written after Nūrba<u>kh</u>s<u>h</u>'s coerced renunciation of the status of *mahdī* in Harāt (see Molé's synopsis of *Risālat al-Hudā* in *Les Kubrawiya entre sunnisme et shiʿisme*, in *REI*, xxix [1961], 131-6).

The most accomplished disciple of Nūrba<u>kh</u>s<u>h</u> was <u>Sh</u>ay<u>kh</u> Muḥammad Lāhī<u>dj</u>ī (d. 921/1515), author of the *Mafātīḥ al-iʿ<u>dj</u>āz fī <u>sh</u>arḥ-i Gul<u>sh</u>ān-i rāz*, one of the most widely-read later Ṣūfī texts in Persian. He established a Nūrba<u>kh</u>s<u>h</u>ī *<u>kh</u>ānaḳāh* in <u>Sh</u>īrāz, known as the Nūriyya, which was visited by <u>Sh</u>āh Ismāʿīl. The direction of this *<u>kh</u>ānaḳāh* was inherited by an apparently unworthy and dissolute son, <u>Sh</u>ay<u>kh</u>-zāda Aḥmad Lāhī<u>dj</u>ī, after whom there is no trace of this line of Nūrba<u>kh</u>s<u>h</u>ī transmission.

Nūrba<u>kh</u>s<u>h</u> had two sons: Sayyīd <u>D</u>jaʿfar, who went to the court of Ḥusayn Mīrzā Bāyḳarā in Harāt but, dissatisfied with the stipend offered him there, left for <u>Kh</u>ūzistān, where he spent the rest of his life; and <u>Sh</u>āh Ḳāsim Fayḍba<u>kh</u>s<u>h</u>, his principal heir. Fayḍba<u>kh</u>s<u>h</u> also spent a period in Harāt, where he is said to have acquired Bāyḳarā as a disciple and to have worsted Sunnī *ʿulamāʾ*, such as ʿAbd al-Raḥmān <u>D</u>jāmī, in public debate (<u>Sh</u>us<u>h</u>tarī, *Ma<u>dj</u>ālis al-muʾminīn*, ii, 149). One of Fayḍba<u>kh</u>s<u>h</u>'s sons, <u>Sh</u>āh Bahāʾ al-Dīn, was likewise close to Bāyḳarā, and under his protection established a Nūrba<u>kh</u>s<u>h</u>ī *<u>kh</u>ānaḳāh* in Harāt. In general, however, the Nūrba<u>kh</u>s<u>h</u>iyya appears to have been unable to strike root in <u>Kh</u>urāsān, and first Fayḍba<u>kh</u>s<u>h</u> and then Bahāʾ al-Dīn left Harāṭ for more westerly regions. Fayḍba<u>kh</u>s<u>h</u> took up residence on his father's holdings near Rayy, which were considerably enlarged by a grant of land from <u>Sh</u>āh Ismāʿīl. He died in 917/1511. Bahāʾ al-Dīn also initially enjoyed the favour of the Ṣafawid ruler, but after a few years he fell under suspicion and, as <u>Kh</u>ʷāndamīr delicately phrases it, "in accordance with the requirements of fate he was interrogated and passed away" (*Ḥabīb al-siyar*, ed. <u>D</u>j. Humāʾī, Tehran 1333 *<u>Sh</u>*./1954, iv, 611-12).

Relations between the descendants of Nūrba<u>kh</u>s<u>h</u> and the Ṣafawids were definitively ruptured in the time of Fayḍba<u>kh</u>s<u>h</u>'s grandson, <u>Sh</u>āh Ḳawām al-Dīn b. <u>Sh</u>āh <u>Sh</u>ams al-Dīn. Already in his grandfather's lifetime, Ḳawām al-Dīn attempted to establish himself as the dominant force in Rayy and its environs, silencing opponents and rivals by force. He also attempted to enlarge the family lands still farther, and when the poet Umīdī refused to surrender to him a large and desirable orchard, he had him assassinated, in either 925/1519 or 930/1524 (Sām Mīrzā Ṣafawī, *Tuḥfa-yi Sāmī, ṣaḥīfa-yi pan<u>dj</u>um*, ed. Iḳbāl Ḥusayn, Aligarh 1973, 32-3). Several years later, in the reign of <u>Sh</u>āh Ṭahmāsp, Ḳawām al-Dīn was imprudent enough to begin building castles and fortifications on the family lands, and using the unavenged blood of Umīdī as pretext, the monarch had him arrested and brought to Ḳazwīn, where he was tortured to death.

It appears that towards the end of the life of Nūrba<u>kh</u>s<u>h</u>, and still more after his death, attempts were made to normalise Nūrba<u>kh</u>s<u>h</u>ī beliefs by aligning them with those of conventional Twelver <u>Sh</u>īʿism. This is suggested by <u>Sh</u>us<u>h</u>tarī's assertion that <u>Kh</u>uttalānī had never really believed in the status of *mahdī* of Nūrba<u>kh</u>s<u>h</u>, viewing it simply as a device to incite an uprising against <u>Sh</u>āhru<u>kh</u> and to provide a transition to true <u>Sh</u>īʿism (*Ma<u>dj</u>ālis al-muʾminīn*, ii, 147). The messianic claim could, however, always be revived, and it was no doubt to eliminate the possibility of such a danger that the Ṣafawids—mindful of the circumstances under which they had risen to power—did away with the Nūrba<u>kh</u>s<u>h</u>īs of Rayy.

After the death of Ḳawām al-Dīn, there are traces of Nūrba<u>kh</u>s<u>h</u>ī presence in Kā<u>sh</u>ān, Naṭanz, Nāʾīn and Ḳum, but it is plain that the organised activity of the order was at an end. It is true that a Nūrba<u>kh</u>s<u>h</u>ī lineage has been reported for such luminaries of the

Ṣafawid period as Bahāʾ al-Dīn ʿĀmilī (d. 1030/1621 [*q.v.*]) and Mullā Muḥsin Fayḍ Kāshānī (d. 1091/1680 [see FAYḌ-I KĀSHĀNĪ, in Suppl.]), not to mention Ṣūfīs of the 12th/18th and even 13th/19th centuries. If such *silsila*s have any validity at all, they should be taken as indicating an intellectual filiation, not membership in an organised and functioning Ṣūfī order. It is curious that the anti-Ṣūfī polemicist Mullā Muḥammad Ṭāhir Ḳummī (d. 1098/1686) should nonetheless assert that "most Persians follow the Nūrbakhshī *silsila*" (*Tuḥfat al-akhyār*, Tehran 1336 *Sh.*/1957, 202; see too Section Nine of the same author's *Hidāyat al-ʿawāmm wa-fāḍiḥat al-liʾām*, ms. 1775, Āyatallāh Marʿashī Nadjafī Library, Ḳum). It may be that he wished to fix on all contemporary Persian Ṣūfīs the opprobrium of following Nūrbakhsh, who had falsely claimed the status of *mahdī* for himself. One indication that that claim had not been forgotten, despite subsequent adjustments in Nūrbakhshī doctrine, is provided by Mullā Muḥammad Bāḳir Madjlisī (d. 1110/1699) in his *ʿAyn al-ḥayāt* (Tehran 1341 *Sh.*/1963, 238), where he denounces Nurbakhsh for his gross and heretical error.

A prolongation of the original Nūrbakhshī movement took place in Kashmīr and Baltistān ("Little Tibet"), where it was introduced by Mīr Shams al-Dīn ʿIrāḳī, a disciple of Shāh Ḳāsim Fayḍbakhsh; for this, see ʿIRĀḲĪ, SHAMS AL-DĪN, in Suppl.

The supremacy of Sunnī Islam in Kashmīr after the period of Nūrbakhshī influence there was restored by Mīrzā Muḥammad Dughlāt when he invaded Kashümīr from Kāshghar in 940/1533. He sent the *Fiḳh-i aḥwaṭ*, a summation of Nūrbakhshī doctrine written by Shams al-Dīn (although sometimes erroneously attributed to Nūrbakhsh) to the *ʿulamāʾ* of India for their estimate, and invoking their condemnatory *fatwā* attempted to extirpate the Nūrbakhshiyya throughout Kashmīr (Dughlāt, *Tārīkh-i Rashīdī*, tr. N. Elias and E. Denison Ross, London 1898, 434-5). He also summoned Dāniyāl, one of the sons of Shams al-Dīn, from Iskardo, and had him beheaded in 957/1550. A recrudescence of Čāk [*q.v.* in Suppl.] dominance and Nūrbakhshī influence took place after Dughlāt's death the following year, and it was not until the full establishment of Mughal power in Kashmīr in the second decade of the 11th/17th century that the Nūrbakhshīs of Kashmīr were fully uprooted, despite occasional intervention on their behalf by the Baltistānī branch of the sect (Pardu, *A history of Muslim rule in Kashmir*, 303-4). The remaining Nūrbakhshīs merged into the Twelver Shīʿī population, to such a degree that the tomb of Shams al-Dīn ʿIrāḳī was favoured by the Sunnīs as a target of desecration during the communal riots that were frequent in Srinagar. It was ultimately relocated to a safer site at Chadur (G.M.D. Sufi, *Kashir*, i, 111-12).

The Nūrbakhshiyya survived much longer in Baltistān, which was after all an extremely remote region. Adherents of the sect (called "Keluncheh" by Vigne, *Travels in Kashmir, Ladak, and Iskardo*, ii, 254) captured power in the 12th/18th century. As late as the second half of the following century, travellers reported that fully one-third of the population of Baltistān was Nūrbakhshī; that the *Fiḳh-i aḥwaṭ* was still in circulation; and that the tombs of Mīr Mukhtār and Mīr Yaḥyā, two other sons of Shams al-Dīn ʿIrāḳī, in Kiris and Shigar, were still places of pilgrimage (J. Biddulph, *Tribes of the Hindoo Koosh*, Calcutta 1880, 118-25). A curious detail related by Biddulph is that the Nūrbakhshīs would pray with their hands folded like the Sunnīs in the winter and with their hands hanging loose like the Shīʿīs in the summer.

It remains finally to be noticed that Amīr Sulṭān (d. 833/1429), the Bukhāran saint who migrated to Bursa and married a daughter of Bāyezīd I, has also been described as a Nūrbakhshī. Although he is said, as a *sayyid*, to have had certain Shīʿī inclinations, it is chronologically impossible that he should have been a Nūrbakhshī. The origin of the error lies, no doubt, in the fact that Amīr Sulṭān's father, ʿAlī al-Ḥusaynī al-Bukhārī, was a disciple of Isḥāḳ Khuttalānī, together with Sayyid Muḥammad Nūrbakhsh (Medjdī Efendi, *Terdjüme-yi Shaḳāʾiḳ-i Nuʿmāniyye*, Istanbul 1269/1852, 77). That the Nūrbakhshiyya was unknown in Turkey is indicated by its frequent misidentification as a branch of the Khalwatiyya (see, for example, Şinasi Çoruh, *Emir Sultan*, Istanbul n.d., 29).

Bibliography (in addition to references in the text): Abu 'l-Faḍl, *Āʾīn-i Akbarī*, tr. H.S. Jarrett, Calcutta 1868, ii, 389; S.A. Arjomand, *Religious extremism* (Ghuluww), *Sufism and Sunnism in Safavid Iran 1501-1722*, in *Journal of Asian History*, xv/1 (1981), 14-17; P.N.K. Bamzai, *A history of Kashmir*, Delhi 1973, 532-4; M. Cavid Baysun, *Emir Sultan*, in *İA*, iv, 261-3; D. DeWeese, *The eclipse of the Kubraviyah in Central Asia*, in *Iranian Studies*, xxi/1-2, 59-63; Djahāngīr, *Tūzuk-i Djahāngīrī*, tr. A. Rogers and H. Beveridge, London 1909-14, ii, 149; Rasūl Djaʿfariyān, *Rūyārūʾ ī-yi faḳīhān wa ṣūfīyān dar ʿaṣr-i Ṣafawiyān*, in *Kayhān-i Andīsha*, xxxiii (Ādhar-Day 1369/November-December 1990), 112-13; F. Drew, *The Jummoo and Kashmir territories. A geographical account*, London 1875, 359; Muḥammad Ḳāsim Firishta, *Taʾrīkh-i Firishta*, tr. J. Briggs, Calcutta 1808-10, ii, 350; J.N. Hollister, *The Shiʿa of India*, London 1953, 145-8; Kaykhusraw Isfandiyār, *Dabistān-i madhāhib*, ed. Raḥīm Riḍā-zāda Malik, Tehran 1362 *Sh.*/1983, i, 44, 349, 353, 357; M.L. Kapur, *The Kingdom of Kashmir*, Jammu 1983, 328-31; W.L. Lawrence, *The Valley of Kashmir*, London 1895, 284; Muḥammad Mufīd, *Djāmiʿ-i Mufīdī*, ed. Īradj Afshār, Tehran 1340 *Sh.*/1961, iii, 104-7; Iskandar Beg Munshī, *Taʾrīkh-i ʿĀlam-ārā-yi ʿAbbāsī*, Tehran 1350 *Sh.*/1971, i, 145; R.K. Parmu, *A history of Muslim rule in Kashmir*, Delhi 1969, 192-203, 303-4; Abdul Qaiyum Rafiqi, *Sufism in Kashmir from the fourteenth to the sixteenth century*, Varanasi and Delhi n.d., 96, 215-20; S.A.A. Rizvi, *A history of Sufism in India*, Delhi 1978, i, 298-9; idem, *A socio-intellectual history of the Isna ʿAshari Shi'is in India*, Canberra 1986, i, 163-6, 168-75, 334; Ḥasan Rūmlū, *Aḥsan al-tawārīkh*, ed. C.N. Seddon, Baroda 1931, 123; Dj. Ṣadaḳiyānlū, *Taḥḳīḳ dar aḥwāl wa āthār-i Sayyid Muḥammad Nūrbakhsh Uwaysī Ḳuhistānī*, Tehran 1351 *Sh.*/1972; Meḥmed Shemseddīn, *Yādigār-i Shemsī*, Bursa 1332/1914, 4; Maʿṣūm ʿAlī Shāh Shīrāzī, *Ṭarāʾiḳ al-ḥaḳāʾiḳ*, ed. Muḥammad Djaʿfar Maḥdjūb, Tehran 1339 *Sh.*/1960, ii, 319-22, iii, 163, 215, 285; Ḳāḍī Nūr Allāh Shushtarī, *Madjālis al-muʾminīn*, Tehran 1354 *Sh.*/1975, ii, 143-56; G.M.D. Sufi, *Kashir*, Lahore 1948, i, 109-12; G.L. Tikku, *Persian poetry in Kashmir*, Berkeley and Los Angeles, 1971, 19-20; Ḥüseyin Waṣṣāf, *Sefīne-yi ewliyā*, ed. Mehmed Akkuş and Ali Yılmaz, Istanbul and Ankara 1990, i, 287; G.T. Vigne, *Travels in Kashmir, Ladak, and Iskardo*, London 1842, ii, 250-1, 254; ʿAbd al-Ḥusayn Zarrīnkūb, *Dunbāla-yi djustudjū dar taṣawwuf-i Īrān*, Tehran 1362 *Sh.*/1984, 183-7, 234-7, 263-4.

(H. ALGAR)

NURCULUK (T.), the name given by the modern Turkish press and authorities to the entire body of the teachings of Saʿīd Nursī [*q.v.*], while Nurcular ("Nurists") refers to his followers. The names seem to indicate that *nurculuk* is a sort of Muslim brotherhood (*ṭarīḳat*) not different from a variety of other Ṣūfī orders; but this is a misnomer. Nursī consistently rejected the view that he was a *sheykh* or *pīr*, bent on establishing his own *ṭarīḳat* and that his followers formed an organised body. He referred to his followers as *Risāle-yi Nūr ṭalebesi* (or *Ṭalebe-yi Risāle-yi Nūr*), that is, "students of the Book or Epistle of Light", but the word "disciples" is probably the best translation of *ṭalebe*. The negative image of the Nurists held in the West and by the secularists of Turkey was a direct consequence of politics; Nursī was repeatedly jailed for allegedly violating the secularist principles (article 163, now abolished) of the Penal Code. In the era of multi-party democracy, the Nurists have supported the Democratic Party and its successors, leading İsmet İnönü and his successors of the People's Republican Party leadership to accuse them of reactionary collusion.

The central concept of Nursī's philosophy is *nūr* conceived of as spiritual light (for the ordinary ray of light, he used the term *ṣua*). For Nursī's followers *nūr* is synonymous with *īmān* "faith", and their study is directed toward the achieving of divine illumination—the true faith through the study of the Ḳurʾān. The view that the Nurists are hierarchically organised into groups denominated as "student", "brother", *dost* "friend", and "beloved" according to their mastery of the teachings, veneration for the teacher, and devotion to the cause, is not supported by any definitive proof. The term *kardeş* "brother", commonly used by the *Risāle* students, is a general public form of address in Turkey and has no sectarian significance. Nonetheless, there is something of a natural selection among the Nurists; those who knew Saʿīd Nursī personally and who worked and lived with him for a long time, are held in higher esteem and respect than the latecomers to his philosophy. There are, of course, discussion groups and even periodic meetings usually held every three years for the consideration of his teachings. Originally, these meetings were regarded as religious seminars rather than devotional gatherings.

Nursī began to write the *Risāle*, which consists of his commentaries on the Ḳurʾān, in 1926, after he was forced to settle in Barla, in the province of Isparta, and after 1934 he wrote the last third part of his commentary in Kastamonu, but added supplementary sections right up until 1950. The *Risāle* was written originally in Arabic script and copied by hand. It was distributed first in Central Anatolia from a cluster of villages (Bedre, Islamköy, etc.) in Isparta province and then from Kastamonu. His first writings were called *Sözler* ("words"), but the name subsequently was changed to its present one due to what the author called a sort of divine inspiration. Sections of the *Risāle* have appeared in Latin script and been openly sold—despite occasional restrictions—mainly since 1958, under a variety of titles, e.g. *Şualar* (1960) and *Lem'alar* (Istanbul 1976). Increasingly, such titles are preceded by the general title *Risale-i Nur külliyatından*.

Various portions of the *Risāle* have been translated into English and published by the Risalat-i Nur Institute of America in California. After Nursī's death, a number of periodicals and newspapers, such as *Yeni Nesil* ("New Generation") and printing houses have become dedicated to publishing them and also commentaries on them. Some formal efforts at Nurist indoctrination were made, e.g. the brochure *Istikamet* ("Direction"), published in Istanbul in 1983. The periodical *Nur* is at present published in Turkish, Arabic, English and German and is widely distributed.

Contemporary *Risāle* students and discussion groups are concerned primarily with the meaning of Nursī's writings. His writings are at times quite ambiguous, sometimes rather cumbersome in style but interspersed with precise, clear and beautifully-written passages. The basic purpose of the Nurcular has been not to launch a religious movement or challenge the existing socio-political order. The Nurist publishing houses have been instrumental in popularising many scientific books, some being regarded as superior to the official textbooks; but Nursī opposed materialism and any other doctrine likely to undermine the spiritual essence of the human being. The Nurists, if they are a sufficiently well-defined group so as to be named, thus espouse an uncompromising religious orthodoxy, attaching the utmost importance to the faith reached through the study and understanding of the Ḳurʾān. However, on social, economic, and educational questions they adopt a middle-of-the-road ideology advocating humanitarianism, pluralism, fellowship, and national unity. (Nursī repeatedly stated that although he was a Kurd, he considered himself a member of the Turkish nation because of the Turks' lack of a sense of race, and for their faithful service to Islam.) The Nurists condemn both communism and capitalism for their excessive materialism and seem to favour a mild form of state intervention in the economy, provided it does not inhibit private initiative. This is a view that largely coincides with the economic policy of the recent Turkish governments. In social and political matters, the Nurists favour a pluralist approach, despite the danger that the advocacy of state-imposed social justice could provide justification for authoritarianism.

If the *Risāle* is considered in its entirety with regard to its theological message and preoccupation with human society, and taking into account the aspiration of those who follow its teachings and who come from every walk of life, then the Nurculuk must be regarded as one of the most democratic and advanced Islamic *iḥyāʾ* (rejuvenation) movements, and Nursī as among the foremost ranks of those Muslims who have attempted to reconcile the faith with their human and social environment. He was probably the first to advocate, in a doctrine openly based on the Ḳurʾān and Sunna, a total dedication to the faith along with acceptance of the philosophical, intellectual, and technological aspects of the modern age, whence Nurist groups have sprung up in a number of Muslim (Pakistan, Malaysia) and European (Germany) countries, making it in effect one of the strongest international Islamic revivalist movements. However, there is a latent danger of obscurantism as the movement spreads to the countryside and among the lower urban classes that tend to stress exclusively the devotional aspects of Nursī's teachings and ignore their modernist, change-oriented dimension. There has been lately a not unnatural tendency on the part of the dedicated Nurists to organise and regard themselves as forming a special group of illuminated, righteous ones and to develop an *esprit de corps* that gives the movement the appearances of a *ṭarīḳat*.

Nursī died without leaving a known disciple to continue his work and elaborate on his ideas. After his death, several newspapers and journals were published by the Nurists, one of them, *Yeni Asya*, taking a more activist stand. Differences and disagreements arose over the question of participation in the political process. The majority of Nurists seem to have supported Necmeddin Erbakan's Islamist parties, but felt betrayed when Erbakan in the late 1970s entered into a political coalition with the Republican People's Party, former persecutors of Saʿīd Nursī. After the restoration of political freedom in 1982-3, one group of Nurists continued to support Süleyman Demirel's Straight Path Party, while others backed the Motherland Party of Turgut Özal, who had proclaimed himself an adherent of the Naḳshbandiyya. Thus in general, the Nurists have supported right and centre parties, but the shifting course of Turkish political life has caused a certain reticence regarding politics amongst many Nurists. At the present time (1992), there are five major Nurist groups in Turkey, as well as that of Mehmet Kaplan in Germany.

Bibliography: On the organisational aspects of Nurculuk, see Ali Mermer, *Aspects of religious identity: the Nurcu movement in Turkey today*, diss., Univ. of Durham 1985, unpublished (this includes the most complete list of Nursī's published writings until 1985); Ursula Spuler, *Nurculuk. Die Bewegung des Bediuzzaman Said Nursi in der Modernen Turkei*, in *Bonner Orientalistische Studien*, xxvii (1973), 100-83. For contemporary Nurcu groups, see Mehmet Metiner, *Yeni bir dünyaya uymak*, Istanbul 1987; Ruşen Çakir, *Ayet ve slogan. Türkiye'de Islami oluşumlar*, Istanbul 1990. (KEMAL KARPAT)

NŪRĪ, a common name in the Near East for a member of certain Gipsy tribes. A more correct vocalisation would perhaps be *Nawarī* (so Hava, Steingass, etc.), with plural *Nawar*. Minorsky [see LŪLĪ, at V, 817a] gives *Nawara*. By displacement of accent we also find the plural form as *Nawār* (e.g. in Jaussen, *Coutumes des Arabes*, 90, and British Admiralty, *Handbook*, *Syria*, London 1919, 196, *Arabia*, London 1916, 92, 94). In Persia, the current name for Gipsy is *Lōrī*, *Lūrī* or *Lūlī* [*q.v.*]. It is not unlikely that by a natural phonetic transformation the form *nūrī* derives from *lūrī*, which, it has been suggested, originally denoted an inhabitant of the town of al-Rūr (or Arūr) in Sind. Quatremère advanced the theory (*Hist. des Sultans Mamlouks*, i/2, n. 5) that the name *nūrī* arose from the Arabic *nūr* (fire); he gives the form *n.ww.r.* because these vagrants were usually seen carrying a brazier or a lantern. Even today many of the *Nawar* earn their living as itinerant smiths. But it is more probable that the correct etymology is to be found in some Sanskritic dialect of northwestern India, the original home of the Gipsy tribes.

In the various countries of the Orient in which Gipsy families are located, we find several designations for them used. The older name, now much restricted in use, was Zuṭṭ [see ZUṬṬ] or Jatts. The Turkish name Čingana passed into European languages under such forms as Σιχάνος, Tzigane, Zingaro, Czigany, Zigeuner, etc. Dozy (*Supplément aux dictionnaires arabes*, i, 605), quoting Caussin de Perceval, records the occasional use of the name *Zandjiyya*, but this is inexact [see ZANDJ]. The commonest names, apart from those already mentioned, seem to be *Nawar* and *Kurbat* or *Ghurbat* (particularly in northern Syria and Persia), *Ghagar* and *Ḥalab* (especially in Egypt and North Africa) and *Dūman* (in ʿIrāḳ). For other sub-divisions, reference may be made to the bibliography, and particularly to E. Littmann's *Zigeuner-Arabisch*, which is an excellent summary of the whole subject, particularly on the linguistic side.

The collecting of data regarding the Gipsy tribes of the Orient is by no means easy. Even experienced orientalists and travellers have reached different conclusions regarding them. For example, Lane (in his *Modern Egyptians*, London 1836, ii, 108) in spite of his profound knowledge of Egypt, asserted that there were few Gipsies in the land, while numbers of well-educated local peoples today are still unaware of the presence of these tribes in their midst. The statistics of Massignon's *Annuaire musulman* (Paris ⁴1954, 271), however, gave the number of Gipsies in Egypt as 2% of the population, consisting, namely, of two tribes of Ghagar and Nawar respectively, and four tribes of Ḥalab.

The Gipsies as a rule seem, chameleon-like, to take their creed, such as it is, from their surroundings. In Muslim countries these tribes usually profess Islam, in so far as they may be said to profess any religious views, many of them, indeed, being very superstitious and reported to be scoundrels and vagabonds. The same applies to the Muslim Gipsies of what was formerly European Turkey (Admiralty, *Handbook of Turkey in Europe*, London 1917, 62). In the Balkans, many of them are Greek Orthodox.

Persian and Arabic writers preserve for us the tradition that tribes of Jats (or *Zuṭṭ*) from the Pandjāb were conveyed westwards by command of the Sāsānid monarch Bahrām Gūr (420-38 A.D.) and their descendants proved a troublesome problem some centuries later for the caliphs of Baghdād. Once more, numbers of them were dispersed to the borders of Syria, where many of them were captured by the Byzantines, and thus found their way into the Eastern Roman Empire, thence to continue their migrations to other ends of the East and West. Many of them are even said to have risen to high rank, e.g. al-Sarī b. al-Ḥakam b. Yūsuf al-Zuṭṭī, governor of Egypt (200-5/816-21). The name *Barāmika* is actually the designation in Egypt of a class of public dancers (*Ghawāzī*) of low moral character and conduct who have been regarded as of Gipsy blood, but it is more likely that the name arose from a parallel with the sad state of the fallen line of viziers. See L. Bouvat, *Les Barmécides d'après les historiens arabes et persans*, Paris 1912, 110, 125.

The German traveller Ulrich Seetzen and the American missionary Eli Smith gathered valuable material in the Near East regarding those nomadic peoples which proved useful to later scholars. They were followed by Capt. Newbold (1856) on the Gypsies of Egypt, Syria and Persia; von Kremer, Austrian Consul at Cairo, on the Egyptian Gypsies (1863); Sykes (1902) dealt with the Persian Gypsies, while an excellent treatise appeared in 1914 from R.A.S. Macalister on the language of the Nawar or Zuṭṭ, the nomad smiths of Palestine. Macalister in this work had the rather difficult task of reducing to writing a language almost completely unknown, and interpreting and analysing the Nūrī stories and folk-elements recounted to him by members of the Nūrī settlement north of the Damascus Gate in Jerusalem. He employed several of these Nawar in the course of his excavations there. A small Syrian Gypsy vocabulary received by Miss G.G. Everest of Beirut from a friend at Damascus was also published in the *Journal of the Gipsy Lore Soc.* (Jan. 1890), in an article by F.H. Groome. The philological aspect of the question has received, in recent years, the attention of scholars such as E. Galtier and E. Littmann (see *Bibl.*).

In Egypt, the Ḥalab (sing. Ḥalabī) are to be found mostly in Lower Egypt carrying on their special occupations at the various markets and *mawālīd* [see MAWLID], and as traders in camels, horses and cattle. Their womenfolk are noted seeresses and medicine-women, practicing all the arts of sorcery (*siḥr*): sand-divination (*ḍarb al-raml*), shell-divination (*ḍarb al-sadʿa*), bibliomancy (*fatḥ al-Kitāb*), etc. Their tribal subdivisions are variously given by Galtier (7) and

Newbold (291). Their name suggests some connection with Aleppo (Ḥalab), but they themselves proudly claim a South Arabian ancestry, their tribal chronicle being the popular broadsheet production, *Taʾrīkh Zīr Sālim*.

The Ghagar Gipsy tribe, however, have a rather unsavoury reputation, a fact that is reflected in the modern Egyptian colloquial Arabic verb *ghaggar* "to be abusive" (see M. Hinds and El-Said Badawi, *A dictionary of Egyptian Arabic*, Beirut 1986, 617). Their speech has fewer foreign ingredients, and Galtier is of the opinion that they are more recent arrivals in the Nile Valley, probably wanderers from Constantinople. The argot of the Egyptian Gipsies is called *al-Sīm*, and in modern colloquial Arabic in Egypt "to speak in enigmas" is *yatakallim bi 'l-Sīm* (see Hinds and Badawi, *op. cit.*, 446).

The word Nūrī in Egypt is almost synonymous with thief, and their thieving propensities are libellously associated in a popular proverb with the inhabitants of Damanhūr [*q.v.*] (*alf Nūrī wa-lā Damanhūrī*). According to the age-old policy of setting a thief to catch a thief, the Nawar are often recruited as estate watchmen (*ghuffār*).

Their pursuits and proclivities are varied in the extreme. Besides the myriad occupations of enchanters, amulet-sellers, quack-doctors, snake-eaters and astrologers, many of them travel about as hawkers, metal-workers, animal-trainers, professional tumblers, rope-dancers, acrobats, monkey-leaders, musicians and ballad-singers, while some are employed to circumcise Muslim girls, to tattoo lips and chins, and to bore ears and nostrils.

Bibliography: See LŪLĪ, ZUṬṬ, and further, de Goeje, *Bijdrage tot de geschiedenis der Zigeuners*, Amsterdam 1875, English tr. J. Snijders, publ. in D. MacRitchie, *Account of the Gypsies of India*, London 1886; idem, *Mémoire sur les migrations des Tsiganes à travers l'Asie*, Leiden 1903; *Journal of the Gypsy Lore Soc.* and *Index*; R.A.S. Macalister, *The language of the Nawar or Zutt = Gypsy Lore Soc.*, *Monographs*, no. 3, London 1914; E. Littmann, *Zigeuner-Arabisch, Wortschatz und Grammatik*, Bonn 1920; Pott, *Die Zigeuner in Europa und Asien*, Halle 1844-5; idem, *Über die Sprache der Zigeuner in Syrien*, in *Zeitschr. f. die Wissenschaft der Sprache*, Berlin 1846, 175-86; idem, in *ZDMG* (1849), 321-35, (1853), 389-90; U.J. Seetzen, *Reisen durch Syrien*, etc., Berlin 1854, 184-9; Newbold, *The Gypsies of Egypt*, in *JRAS* (1856), 285-312; A. von Kremer, *Aegypten*, Leipzig 1863, i, 138-48, and notes 70-2, 155, previously published in 1862 in Petermann's *Mittheilungen*, Gotha, ii, 41-4; R. Liebich, *Die Zigeuner, ihr Wesen und ihre Sprache*, Leipzig 1863, 10-11, reproduces the glossary of Gypsy words from von Kremer; R. Burton, *The Jew, the Gipsy and El Islam*, London 1898, is based on von Kremer; A.G. Paspates, *Études sur les Tchinghianés ou Bohémiens de l'Empire ottoman*, Constantinople 1870; F. Miklosich, *Über die Mundarten und Wanderungen der Zigeuner*, Vienna 1872-80; *Indian Antiquary*, index vol.; F.N. Finck, *Die Sprache der armenischen Zigeuner*, St. Petersburg 1907; E. Galtier, *Les Tsiganes d'Égypte et de Syrie*, in *MIFAO*, Cairo 1912, xxvii, 1-9; J. Walker, *The Gypsies of modern Egypt*, in *MW* (July 1933), 285-9; ʿAbd al-Raḥmān Ismāʿīl, *Ṭibb al-rukka*, Cairo 1310-12, 67, 68, 95, gives examples of Gipsy quack-doctoring; *ZDMG* (1870), 681-2, (1912), 339, 527, (1919), 233-42; Eutychius, *Annales*, ed. Cheikho, *Scriptores Arabici*, iii, vii, 60; Lammens, in *MFOB* (1906), 22; Dawkins, *A Gipsy stone*, in *JRAS* (1934), 787-90; C.E. Bosworth, *The mediaeval Islamic underworld*, Leiden 1976, i, 169-71, 176-9. (J. WALKER)

AL-**NŪRĪ**, ABU 'L-ḤUSAYN (or ABU 'L-ḤASAN) AḤMAD b. Muḥammad al-Baghawī, Ṣūfī mystic, of Khurāsānī background, was born (probably *ca.* 226/840, as he had met Dhu 'l-Nūn) in Baghdād, where he spent most of his life. He died in 295/907. The most extensive information about him is given by al-Sarrādj and al-Kalābādhī; the brief biographies of al-Sulamī and Abū Nuʿaym agree almost verbatim, as do the Persian notes in Anṣārī and Jāmī. ʿAṭṭār's biography elaborates on otherwise little-known details; Baḳlī devotes five chapters (§§ 95-9) of his *Sharḥ-i shaṭhiyyāt* to al-Nūrī.

It is said that he acquired his surname because "he radiated light when talking"; he claimed "I looked into the light until I became that light myself." A disciple of al-Sarī as-Saḳaṭī, he underwent extreme self-mortification: "Ṣūfism is leaving all pleasures of the *nafs*", and emphasised the true *faḳīr*'s reliance upon God alone. His best-known quality is *īthār*, i.e. that "it is a religious duty to prefer one's companions to oneself"; for "Ṣūfism consists not of forms and sciences but of *akhlāḳ*, good qualities." That is illustrated by his attitude during the trial of the Ṣūfīs by Ghulām Khalīl in 264/877, where he offered up his life for his friends, whereupon the caliph acquitted the Ṣūfīs. Al-Nūrī was quite emotional, and considered intellect to be "incapable"; contrary to the sober and prudent Djunayd he enjoyed participating in the *samāʿ*: "The Ṣūfī is one who hears the *samāʿ*", and Baḳlī asks in his threnody (*Sharḥ*, § 377) "Where is the singing, *tarannum*, of Nūrī?" That his death was caused by his running, in full ecstasy, into a freshly-cut reedbed and dying from wounds, fits into this picture, as does Anṣārī's remark that "he was more worshipping, *aʿbad*, than Djunayd." Al-Nūrī, who, according to ʿAṭṭār, was seen weeping along with the sad Iblīs, claimed to be a lover, *ʿāshiḳ*, which led the Ḥanbalīs to declare him a heretic; but for him, *maḥabba* (mentioned in Ḳurʾān, V, 59) was a higher stage than *ʿishḳ*, and "Love is to tear the veils and unveil the secrets." More dangerous seemed his remark "Deadly poison!", when hearing the *muʾadhdhin*'s call, but answering a dog's barking with *labbayka*; he intended to blame the one who performed religious duties for money, but understood every creature's praise of God, even from the dog's mouth.

Al-Kalābādhī mentions that al-Nūrī wrote about mystical sciences with *ishārāt*, symbolic expressions, but only recently did P. Nwyia discover his *Maḳāmāt al-ḳulūb*, which contains descriptions of the heart, that house of God, which is inhabited by the King Certitude, who is aided by two viziers, Fear and Hope. Such an allegorical interpretation of Ḳurʾānic data appears also in the comparison of the heart to a castle with seven ramparts (reminiscent of St. Theresa's imagery). The language of al-Nūrī, called by ʿAṭṭār *laṭīf ẓarīf*, "fine and elegant", is highly poetical, and a number of brief poems is attributed to him; the imagery of the heart as a garden which is fertilised, or else destroyed, by rain and in which laud and gratitude are the odoriferous herbs, prefigures Persian garden imagery. Al-Nūrī is called "the faithful one, *ṣāḥib al-wafāʾ*, and "prince of hearts", *amīr al-ḳulūb*, and, as a true love mystic, was one of the most remarkable companions of Djunayd, who said at his death, "half of Ṣūfism is gone".

Bibliography: Abū Naṣr al-Sarrādj, *Kitāb al-Lumaʿ fi 'l-taṣawwuf*, ed. R.A. Nicholson, London-Leiden 1914; Kalābādhī, *Kitāb al-Taʿarruf fī madhhab ahl al-taṣawwuf*, ed. A.J. Arberry, Cairo 1934; Abū Nuʿaym al-Iṣfahānī, *Ḥilyat al-awliyāʾ*, Cairo 1934 ff.; Sulamī, *Ṭabaḳāt al-Ṣūfiyya*, ed. N. Sharība, Cairo 1953; Ḳushayrī, *Risāla*, Cairo 1330/1912;

Anṣārī, *Ṭabaḳāt al-ṣūfiyya*, ed. ᶜA.Ḥ. Ḥabībī, Kabul n.d.; Hudjwīrī, *Kashf al-mahdjūb*, ed. V.A. Žukovski, Leningrad 1925, tr. Nicholson, London 1911; Rūzbihān Baḳlī, *Kitāb Sharḥ al-shaṭḥiyyāt*, ed. H. Corbin, Paris-Tehran 1966; Farīd al-Dīn ᶜAṭṭār, *Tadhkirat al-awliyāʾ*, ed. Nicholson, London-Leiden 1905-7; Suhrawardī, *ᶜAwārif al-maᶜārif*, Beirut 1966; Djāmī, *Nafaḥāt al-uns*, ed. M. Tawḥīdīpūr, Tehran 1957; L. Massignon, *Recueil de textes inédits*, Paris 1929; M. Dermenghem, *Vie des saints musulmans*, Algiers 1942; P. Nwyia, *Exégèse coranique et langage mystique*, Beirut 1970; L. Lopez Baralt, *Huellas del Islam en la literatura española* (ch. 4), Madrid 1985.

(ANNEMARIE SCHIMMEL)

NŪRĪ, SHAYKH FAḌL ALLĀH, the most notable of the anti-constitutionalist *ᶜulamāʾ* in the Persian Revolution of 1906.

Ḥādjdjī Shaykh Faḍl Allāh Nūrī was born in Tehran in 1259/1843-4 and went at an early age to study in the ᶜAtabāt [*q.v.* in Suppl.] under his uncle Mīrzā Muḥammad Ḥusayn Nūrī, and under Mīrzā Ḥasan Shīrāzī (M. Turkamān, *Shaykh-i shahīd Faḍl Allāh Nūrī*, Tehran 1362 *Sh*/1983, i, 9). In about 1300/1883 he returned to Tehran, where he gradually emerged as the leading scholar and jurist. He was active in the movement against the Tobacco Concession in 1308-9/1890-1, but otherwise not particularly prominent politically until 1321/1903, when ᶜAyn al-Dawla was appointed Ṣadr-i Aᶜẓam and passed on to Shaykh Faḍl Allāh the responsibility for government business in the *sharīᶜa* courts, which had previously come under the *mudjtahid* Sayyid ᶜAbd Allāh Bihbihānī (Mīrzā Muḥammad Nāẓim al-Islām Kirmānī, *Tārīkh-i bīdārī-yi Īrāniyān*, Tehran 1361 *Sh*/1982, i, 210). Shaykh Faḍl Allāh supported ᶜAyn al-Dawla's reforms of the finances in an attempt to preserve the traditional system of government and authority, but when the Ṣadr-i Aᶜẓam's régime collapsed in Djumādā II 1324/July 1906, Shaykh Faḍl Allāh was forced to join what became the constitutional movement, although he had previously expressed doubts about constitutionalism (Nāẓim al-Islām, *Bīdārī*, i, 321-4).

He found himself in eclipse, however, until the accession of Muḥammad ᶜAlī Shāh [*q.v.*] in Dhu 'l-Ḳaᶜda 1324/January 1907 gave him a powerful new ally. Having failed in discussion to modify the radical measures of the proposed Supplementary Fundamental Law he took *bast* [*q.v.*] or sanctuary in the Shrine of Shāh ᶜAbd al-ᶜAẓīm from 9 Djumādā II to 8 Shaᶜbān 1325/20 June to 16 September 1907, almost certainly financed by the Shah (Spring Rice to Grey, no. 143, 10 July 1907, FO 416/34 no. 136; Y. Dawlatābādī, *Tārīkh-i muᶜāṣir yā ḥayāt-i Yaḥyā*, ii, Tehran 1337 *Sh*/1958, 129). From there he published a series of propaganda leaflets in which he argued for *mashrūṭa-yi mashrūᶜa*, or more specifically *niẓām-nāma-yi islāmī*, an Islamic constitution (for the leaflets, see Turkamān, *Shahīd*, i, 231-368; H. Riḍwānī, *Lawāyiḥ-i Āḳā Shaykh Faḍl Allāh Nūrī*, Tehran 1362sh/1983). He also maintained that constitutionalism was contrary to the *sharīᶜa*, most notably on the point of equality before the law (Turkamān, *Shahīd*, 287-8, 291-2). Following the fear and disarray induced in the court at the assassination of the then prime minister Amīn al-Sulṭān, the Shah appears to have withdrawn his support and Shaykh Faḍl Allāh emerged from *bast*. He participated in the royalist demonstrations of Dhu 'l-Ḳaᶜda 1325/December 1907 but did not return to prominence until after the coup of Djumādā I 1326/June 1908. Then in a *fatwā* (M. Malikzāda, *Tārīkh-i inḳilāb-i mashrūṭiyyat-i Īrān*, Tehran 1351 *Sh*/1972, iv, 211-21) and in a work entitled *Tadhkirat al-ghāfil wa-irshād al-djāhil* (Turkamān, *Shahīd*, i, 56-75), he provided the Shah with a legitimising ideology for his refusal to restore the *madjlis*, arguing most notably that the Shah was one of the two pillars of Islam together with the *ᶜulamāʾ*, his role being to maintain order and stability (Malikzāda, *Mashrūṭiyyat*, iv, 217). He further contended that constitutionalism was pernicious, since it contradicted the five Muslim precepts (*al-aḥkām al-khamsa*), implying that it interfered with the soteriological purpose of Islam (V.A. Martin, *Islam and modernism: the Iranian Revolution of 1906*, London 1989, 178-9). In addition, he attacked the constitutionalists' source of legitimacy in representation of the will of the people, arguing that it had no basis for any claim to authority in Imāmī Shīᶜī law (Malikzāda, *Mashrūṭiyyat*, IV, 211; Turkamān, *Shahīd*, i, 67, 89-90; Martin, *op. cit.*, 181-3).

After the abdication of Muḥammad ᶜAlī Shāh in Radjab 1327/July 1909, Shaykh Faḍl Allāh declined the chance of refuge in the Russian Legation along with the Shah and his other prominent supporters (Malikzāda, *Mashrūṭiyyat*, v, 265, vi, 117). He was arrested, tried on 13 Radjab 1327/31 July 1909 and publicly executed immediately afterwards. On the scaffold he is said to have recited the verse, "If we were a heavy burden, we are gone; if we were unkind, we are gone" (E.G. Browne, *The Persian revolution 1905-9*, Cambridge 1910, 444; see also Nāẓim al-Islām, *Bīdārī*, ii, 535).

Bibliography (in addition to references in the article): A. Arjomand, *The ᶜulama's traditionalist opposition to Parliamentarianism: 1907-9*, in *MES*, xvii/2 (1981), 174-90; Browne, *The press and poetry of modern Persia*, Cambridge 1914; H.A. Burhān, *Shaykh Faḍl Allāh wa dār kishīdan-i ū*, in *Waḥīd*, no. 203 (1335 *Sh*/1956), 876-80; Faḍl Allāh Nūrī, *Suʾāl wa-djawāb*, Bombay 1893; A.H. Hairi, *Shīᶜism and constitutionalism in Iran*, Leiden 1977; A. Kasrawī, *Tārīkh-i mashrūṭa-yi Īrān*, Tehran 2537 *shāhān-shāhī*/1978; Y. Richard, *Le radicalisme islamique du Sheykh Fazlollah Nuri et son impact dans l'histoire de l'Iran contemporain*, in *Les intégrismes: la pensée et les hommes*, xxix/2, Brussels 1986, 60-86.

(VANESSA MARTIN)

NURI KILLIĞIL [see ENWER PASHA].

NŪRĪ AL-SAᶜĪD, fourteen times Prime Minister of ᶜIrāḳ under the monarchy (1921-58) and one of the most robust Arab politicians of his generation, was born in Baghdād in 1888, the son of a minor administrative official, and was killed at the hands of a hostile crowd in Baghdād on the day after the ᶜIrāḳī Revolution of 14 July 1958. Nūrī attended military schools in Baghdād and Istanbul, receiving his commission in 1906; after four years soldiering in ᶜIrāḳ, he returned to the Staff College in Istanbul, participating in campaigns in Macedonia (1911) and in the Balkan Wars (1912-13). In common with many of his fellow Arab officers, he was attracted to the liberal aims of the Committee of Union and Progress [see ITTIḤĀD WE TERAḲḲĪ DJEMᶜIYYETI], only to be disappointed by the increasingly centralising and pro-Turkish policies which it pursued when in power. Along with several other ᶜIrāḳīs, Nūrī joined *al-ᶜAhd*, a secret society of Arab officers in the Ottoman Army, founded by ᶜAzīz ᶜAlī al-Miṣrī.

At the outbreak of the First World War, Nūrī was in Baṣra where he surrendered to the British occupying forces. He was sent briefly to India and eventually made contact with ᶜAzīz ᶜAlī al-Miṣrī, whom he joined in Cairo at the end of 1915. Shortly afterwards he was asked to take part in the British-sponsored Arab

Revolt, which the Sharīf Ḥusayn of Mecca [*q.v.*] proclaimed against the Ottomans (or more specifically against the government of the Committee of Union and Progress), on 5 June 1916. Al-Miṣrī was the first commander of the Sharīfian forces, but he soon fell out with the Sharīf and returned to Egypt. His place was taken by Djaʿfar al-ʿAskarī, captured by the British in the Western Desert a few months earlier, who was doubly Nūrī's brother-in-law—the two men were married to each other's sisters. Nūrī himself became "coordinator and adviser-in-chief to the Sharīfian forces" and then "Chief of Staff" (Lord Birdwood, *Nuri as-Said: a study in Arab leadership*, London 1959, 45, 59). During his time in the Ḥidjāz and Syria, Nūrī developed close personal relationships with a number of British officers, and also with Ḥusayn's second son, Fayṣal (1885-1933 [*q.v.*]), remaining at the latter's side from August 1917 until, and well beyond, the capture of Damascus in October 1918. In the course of the War Nūrī received two British decorations for gallantry, the C.M.G. and the D.S.O.

In common with those with whom he was most intimately concerned, Nūrī would have had no clear idea of Britain's plans for the Arab provinces of the Ottoman Empire in event of the defeat of the Central Powers in the First World War. However, since Britain had given its backing to Sharīf Ḥusayn and his sons, it was reasonable to assume that they would be involved in whatever future settlement of the area might be reached. Early in November 1918, Fayṣal invited Nūrī to accompany him on his journey from Syria to London (via France) and then to the peace conference in Paris, where he was to represent the Ḥidjāz. The French made it clear to Fayṣal that they had no intention of recognising the "Arab kingdom" which he had established in Syria in October 1918.

Encouraged, perhaps, by the fact that almost a year passed before sufficient French troops arrived in Syria to enforce French policy, Fayṣal's supporters there were determined not to give up their state. The First Arab Congress, held in Damascus on 7-8 March 1920, proclaimed Fayṣal King of Syria and his brother ʿAbd Allāh King of ʿIrāḳ. A few weeks later, under the terms of the Treaty of San Remo, France was given the mandate for Syria and Lebanon, and Britain the mandate for ʿIrāḳ and Palestine-Transjordan. By this time there was a substantial French military presence in Syria; on 14 July 1920 the French delivered an ultimatum to Fayṣal to accept the terms of the mandate, and when this was not accepted, defeated his army at Khān Maysalūn [see MAYSALŪN] a few miles outside Damascus, ten days later. Fayṣal, with Nūrī at his side, left for Egypt, and eventually for discussions in London in the late autumn of 1920.

In the immediate aftermath of the First World War, British plans for the territory which was to become ʿIrāḳ were by no means clear. Most of the British administrators there had served in India, where they were used to a system of direct rule by British officials, and had little understanding of any expression of "national" or "Arab nationalist" aspirations. In the late summer of 1920 there was an uprising in ʿIrāḳ against the British occupation, which elicited a fundamental change in British policy. A provisional Arab government was formed at the end of October, and at the Cairo Conference in March 1921 it was decided to offer Fayṣal the throne of ʿIrāḳ, thus giving substance to the negotiations which had taken place in the course of his own and Nūrī's visit to London the previous October. Fayṣal arrived in Baṣra at the end of June, and was duly enthroned in Baghdād on 23 August.

Meanwhile, Nūrī had returned to Baghdād in January 1921, where he was made Chief of Staff of the ʿIrāḳī Army under his brother-in-law Djaʿfar, Minister of Defence in the provisional government. For most of the 1920s Nūrī concentrated on building up the ʿIrāḳī Army, in his capacity either as Chief of Staff (1921-2) or as Minister of Defence, an office he held in seven of the nine cabinets formed between November 1922 and March 1930. Between March 1930 and October 1932 he served as Prime Minister, and was intimately involved in the negotiations for the Anglo-ʿIrāḳī Treaty of 1930 which provided for the official withdrawal of British control over ʿIrāḳ and for ʿIrāḳ's entry into the League of Nations in 1932.

King Fayṣal's premature death in August 1933 left a power vacuum at the centre of ʿIrāḳī politics. His son Ghāzī, then aged 21, was both inexperienced and lacking in political acumen, with the result that control of the country passed increasingly to former or serving military officers. In October 1936, General Bakr Ṣidḳī led a coup against the government of (former Major-General) Yāsīn al-Hāshimī, in which Nūrī was serving as Minister of Foreign Affairs and Djaʿfar as Minister of Defence. Djaʿfar was shot at Ṣidḳī's instigation while trying to negotiate with the coup leaders; Yāsīn died in exile a few months later, and Nūrī was smuggled out of the country via the British Embassy. He returned to ʿIrāḳ in the autumn of 1937, a few months after the overthrow of Bakr Ṣidḳī, and proceeded to wage a relentless vendetta against the perpetrators of the coup of October 1936 in general, and in particular against those involved in his brother-in-law Djaʿfar's murder. Eventually, Nūrī formed his third cabinet, and, apart from a crucial few months out of office between January and October 1941, served as Prime Minister for much of the period between December 1938 and June 1944, often holding the Defence and/or Foreign Affairs portfolios at the same time.

Two incidents during these years were to have lasting effects upon Nūrī's subsequent career, and generally to alienate him from public esteem. The first of these was the persistent allegation that he was in some way involved in Ghāzī's death in a motor accident in April 1939. Nūrī was openly contemptuous of Ghāzī (whose evident character defects were redeemed in the eyes of many ʿIrāḳī "nationalists" by his anti-British posturings), and his death and replacement by his more malleable cousin ʿAbd al-Ilāh as Regent for Ghāzī's son Fayṣal II (who was four years old in 1939), certainly simplified matters for Nūrī and his British patrons. In any case, whether or not this allegation had any foundation was less important than the fact that it was widely believed (see Hanna Batatu, *The old social classes and the revolutionary movements of Iraq; a study of Iraq's old landed classes and its Communists, Ba'thists and Free Officers*, Princeton 1978, 342).

The second incident was the complex of events surrounding ʿIrāḳ's participation in the Second World War. There is little doubt that the anti-British movement initiated in 1940-1 by the so-called Golden Square (four Arab nationalist Army colonels, all some ten years younger than Nūrī) and their political mouthpiece Rashīd ʿAlī al-Gaylānī [*q.v.*], had immense popular appeal. Especially after the fall of France in 1940, the notion that ʿIrāḳ should either remain neutral—in defiance of the provisions of the Treaty of 1930—or even, in the minds of some, call upon Germany to force Britain out of ʿIrāḳ, began to gain ground. In April 1941 the Golden Square staged a coup which brought Rashīd ʿAlī to power. Nūrī and ʿAbd al-Ilāh fled to Jordan with British assistance, while the ʿIrāḳī Army fought a somewhat quixotic one-month campaign against a British force. The defeat of the ʿIrāḳī Army was followed by a "second British occupation"; as for the Regent and Nūrī, "their return from abroad only after the country had been subdued by British power made them so odious among the people that, regardless of what they did afterwards, they were never able to command public confidence" (Batatu, *op. cit.*, 345).

By this time certain guiding principles of Nūrī's conduct may be discerned. As the First World War ended, he seems to have realised that some form of foreign control over the Arab provinces of the former Ottoman Empire was inevitable, and that his own career would be best served by a pragmatic acceptance of this situation. Nūrī saw the future of the Arab world in terms of a loose confederation of regions (and eventually of individual states) under the general aegis of Britain, and, if more reluctantly, of France. His patron Fayṣal's translation to ʿIrāḳ in 1921 gave Nūrī the opportunity to assist in building up a state which was independent at least to the extent that it was no longer part of the Ottoman Empire, and which might eventually emerge as a leading regional force, largely through the agency of the Army, whose construction and organisation was one of his principal concerns throughout the 1920s and 1930s.

The major flaw in this design was that because Fayṣal and the Hāshimite house on the one hand, and Nūrī and his circle on the other, were regarded by members of the "Old Social Classes" first as foreigners and outsiders and secondly (because of their lower class origins) as upstarts, both were forced to rely on Britain in ways which became more and more intolerable to the politically conscious sections of the ʿIrāḳī population. Fayṣal died before these tensions had developed beyond the point of no return, although he earned considerable opprobrium towards the end of his life because of his acceptance of the restrictions on ʿIrāḳ's independence in the Anglo-ʿIrāḳī Treaty of 1930.

Realising the extent of his own isolation within ʿIrāḳ, Nūrī tried to secure his base by placing trusted friends and colleagues in key positions in the army, so that in 1936, all of the Army's 3 major-generals, 3 of its 4 brigadiers and 6 of its 11 colonels were former Sharīfian officers. In addition, as he gradually gained greater control of the state machinery, he was able to win over the tribal *shaykh*s and urban notables by co-opting them both politically and economically (see Batatu, *op. cit.*, *passim*), a process greatly facilitated during and after the Second World War by this group's hostility to and fear of a burgeoning spectrum of "opposition" parties and groups.

On his return to power after the Anglo-ʿIrāḳī "War" of 1941, Nūrī began to root out the Pan-Arab supporters of the Golden Square from within the Army, while putting forward his own modest version of Arab nationalism, the "Fertile Crescent" scheme, in 1943. This involved the creation of a "Greater Syria" out of Syria, Jordan, Lebanon and Palestine, with which ʿIrāḳ would be associated, possibly leading to a wider federation which might embrace Egypt and Saudi Arabia. Needless to say, this arrangement (whose details were extremely vague) was to come into being under the benevolent auspices of Britain. The Egyptians, Syrians and Saudis were intensely suspicious of anything that might smack of Hāshimite domination, and in its place the Arab League, a loose arrangement which maintained the structures of the existing states and was designed to foster cooperation rather than Arab unity, came into being in May 1945.

British relations with ʿIrāḳ, or more accurately with Nūrī and the Regent, remained close until the Revolution of July 1958, although British officials were often bothered by the extent to which "our eggs are concentrated in Nūrī's somewhat unstable basket" (quoted in Batatu, *op. cit.*, 347). Throughout the 1940s, and especially after the ill-fated attempt to extend the Anglo-ʿIrāḳī Treaty of 1930 at Portsmouth in January 1948, the political situation in ʿIrāḳ was characterised by mounting repression and increasingly dictatorial régimes, presided over either by Nūrī himself or by his acolytes and supporters. Britain tolerated this state of affairs for a number of reasons, not least among which were its concern to maintain the free flow of oil from ʿIrāḳ, and to preserve the British air bases there, but also because no amount of prodding seemed sufficient to persuade Nūrī to change his ways, or to train up a less compromised successor. At the same time, Nūrī's relative lack of concern over Palestine, and his imperturbable championing of unpopular causes (notably ʿIrāḳī membership of the Baghdād Pact in 1955) made it easier for Britain to overlook his shortcomings.

In time, popular resentment against Nūrī and his circle reached a crescendo, although, given the nature of the political system, it was impossible for the régime to be ousted other than by force. In the course of the 1950s, a conspiratorial movement of Free Officers emerged in the Army, which eventually took advantage of military manoeuvres in July 1958 to direct units commanded by its sympathisers to take control of key locations in Baghdād. On the morning of 14 July the Royal Palace was surrounded, and the King (Fayṣal II had attained his majority in 1953) and his uncle (the former Regent, now Crown Prince), were killed. Nūrī went into hiding, but was discovered on the afternoon of the next day; his body, and that of the Crown Prince, both of whom were the objects of particular hatred, were dragged through the streets and eventually torn to pieces by the mob.

Possibly as a result of their reluctance to face harsh realities, few British diplomats concerned with ʿIrāḳ in the 1950s thought that a major change in the status quo was imminent (see here W.R. Louis, *The British and the origins of the Iraqi Revolution*, in R.A. Fernea and W.R. Louis, *The Iraqi Revolution of 1958: the Old Social Classes revisited,* London and New York 1991, 31-61). It is clear now that the perpetuation of the immense social inequalities over which Nūrī presided (which increased with the rapid rise in oil revenues and the inauguration of the Development Board in the early 1950s), together with his dictatorial style and his constant manipulation of the electoral and parliamentary systems, were major causes of the chaos and violence which erupted when the dam finally broke in July 1958. It is not clear either that this was "inevitable", or that Nūrī had "no choice" in acting as he did. While Nūrī was clearly Britain's most faithful servant in ʿIrāḳ, the nature of his contribution to the history of his own country remains rather more difficult to assess.

Bibliography: In addition to works cited in the text, see Marion Farouk-Sluglett and P. Sluglett, *Iraq since 1958: from revolution to dictatorship*, 2nd revised ed. London 1990; W. Gallman, *Iraq under General Nuri: my recollections of Nuri al-said [sic], 1954-1958*, Baltimore 1964; Majid Khadduri, *Independent Iraq 1932-1958: a study in Iraqi politics,* 2nd ed., London 1960; idem, *General Nuri's flirtation with the Axis Powers*, in *MEJ*, xvi (1962), 328-36; W.R. Louis, *The British Empire in the Middle East 1945-1951: Arab nationalism, the United States and postwar imperialism,*

Oxford 1984; Reeva S. Simon, *Iraq between the two world wars: the creation and implementation of a nationalist ideology*, New York 1986; P. Sluglett, *Britain in Iraq 1914-1932*, London 1976; Mohammad Tarbush, *The role of the military in politics: a case study of Iraq to 1941*, London 1982. (P. SLUGLETT)

NURSĪ, SHEYKH BADĪᶜ AL-ZAMĀN SAᶜĪD (Modern Tkish. Bediuzzaman Said Riza-Nursi) (*ca.* 1876-1960), religious leader, of Kurdish origin, in late Ottoman and Republican Turkey.

Saᶜīd Nursī, the author of the *Risāle-yi Nūr* "Epistle of Light" (or "Wisdom") from which the intellectual-religious movement known as Nurculuk [*q.v.*] sprang, was born in the village of Nurs in the province of Bitlis [see BIDLĪS] in eastern Turkey. His father apparently belonged to a local family of notables, as indicated by his surname Mīrzā. Nursī started his education in the *medrese* of Seyyid Nūr (the names of many places and people with whom he was associated, including that of his mother, Nūriyye, derived from *nūr* "light"), but he soon changed to an intensive, three-month-long study under Sheykh Meḥmed Djelālī in Beyazit; he received the title of Mollā [*q.v.*], and from then on he continued his education on his own. During his travels around the province he developed an interest in the life of the common people and a deep feeling for nature that stayed with him all his life. His growing erudition, communal involvement and occasional confrontation with Ottoman officials earned him first the title of *Meshhūr* ("famous") and later, around 1894, that of *Badīᶜ al-zamān* or "beauty of the age". In 1909 he started to call himself *gharīb* ("stranger" or "dissident") in order to show that his way of thinking and behaving differed from that of his contemporaries, a strangeness displayed outwardly by his native garb and the gun and knife in his belt, resembling more his fellow-Kurdish tribesmen than a refined city *ᶜālim*.

After spending two years in Bitlis as the guest of ᶜÖmer Pasha, Nursī moved to Van in 1894, where he lived in the house of the provincial *wālī* or governor Ishḳodralî Ṭāhir Pasha. There he acquainted himself with the physical and natural sciences and began to apply their methodology both to the teaching of Islam and to demonstrate the truth of the faith. At about this same time he began to move closer to the Ottoman establishment, away from the Naḳshbandiyya Khālidiyya Ṣūfīs with whom he first studied and closer to the Ḳādiriyya. After making the acquaintance of modern science, Nursī adopted the view that progress and salvation lay not in the faith alone but also in the sciences and in government action. (The preoccupation with "philosophy", as he called it, engaged him until about 1920, when he rediscovered the superiority of faith.) During his stay in Van, according to his biographer, Nursī read a declaration attributed to Gladstone, the British Liberal statesman known for his anti-Turkish views, that "we [the British] cannot dominate the Muslims as long as we do not take the Koran away from them" (Şahiner, 1988, 73); he now swore to prove to the world that "the Ḳurʾān was a spiritual sun and indestructible" (*ibid.*). His religious dedication, coupled with his association with Ottoman officials, eventually secured for Nursī in 1907 an introduction to Sultan ᶜAbd ül-Ḥamīd II. However, his coarse appearance, his petition for the establishment of modern schools in Bitlis province and his assertion that "Islam does not sanction tyranny" landed him first in the Yîldîz military court and then in a mental hospital (in order to avoid the possible imposition of severe punishment). This incident shows clearly the difference between the two forms of Islamism or Pan-Islamism [*q.v.*] that dominated Ottoman society in the period 1870-1908. On the one hand, there was the caliph's Pan-Islamism that relied on the government, its bureaucracy and the traditional religious establishment for its survival; on the other hand, there was the populist, grass-roots form of religion that relied on community support. Nursī's advocacy of this latter, populist Islamism before the foremost proponents of the traditional view did not sit well with the bureaucrats.

He was, in fact, the product of socio-political changes occurring in Anatolia, which had passed from the rule of local feudal lords, thanks to the centralising policy of the government, but now came under the spiritual domination and the social guidance of the *ṭarīḳat sheykhs*, since, although theoretically under the rule of the new bureaucracy, the hinterlands were not in fact brought completely under the influence of the centre, allowing the *sheykhs* more power as leaders of local society. However, Nursī's communal, Naḳshbandī Islam was also increasingly confronted not only by ᶜAbd ül-Ḥamīd's state-sponsored Pan-Islamism but also by the positivist and the liberal ideology of the growing modernist intelligentsia. Nursī accepted in varying degrees some of the tenets of all these ideologies, in the end opting fully for religious orthodoxy while evolving an Islamic-modernist-national philosophy of his own. His aims were not only to rejuvenate the faith but also to revitalise the society in which the faith found its expression. This preoccupation with the living society had the effect of elevating the local culture and the vernacular (Nursī only learned Turkish around the age of 14) to respectability and gave love of country (*waṭan*) and the natural aspects of human existence the sanction of religion. Yet the same forces that conditioned modernist and nationalist views also created disunity in society and a penchant for materialism, and these ills became Nursī's ultimate target.

From roughly 1895 to 1921, Nursī lived the life of an up-and-coming Ottoman rural intellectual. He came to share the patriotic and nationalist-religious views of this group of people as well as their search for social status and position which socio-economic and political change offered the opportunity to achieve. Thus he at first joined the Young Turk Revolutionaries, delivering in Salonica in 1908 a fiery speech glorifying the virtues of political liberalism; but later, in reaction to the positivist secularism of the Young Turks, he helped found the *Ittiḥād-î Muḥammedī* (Muslim Union), which staged the abortive counter-revolution of 1909. Arrested and tried, but acquitted, he went back to his native region where he taught for a while. Then he participated in the Turkish war effort and helped prepare the call to *djihād* against the Allies. In 1915, he went by submarine to Libya, in order to work with the Sanūsiyya [*q.v.*] against the Italians. Returning home, he took part in the defence of Bitlis, was captured by the Russians, but escaped in 1917 and returned home via Warsaw and Vienna. He held a teaching job in Istanbul for about three years, after which the ascetic, spiritual "new" Saᶜīd replaced the activist, worldly "old" Saᶜīd.

The change was caused as much by Nursī's increasing age as by the establishment of the Republic, the abolition of the caliphate (which he apparently accepted), and the passing of the old Ottoman order. Probably the "old" Saᶜīd would have long been forgotten if the "new" one had not emerged. Nursī described his life until the early 1920s as a time of preparation and training necessary for the creation of the man who subsequently made himself into the voice of the community and the faith. He criticised not the new régime, or even its reforms, but the spiritual and ethical void which it had created in society in the name of science and progress, which it saw as synonymous with "secularism". From 1925 almost until his death in 1960, Nursī was viewed as the enemy of the new régime, although the truth of this view was never proved. In 1925 he was arrested for alleged involvement in the Kurdish revolt of Sheykh Saᶜīd, and although he was once more acquitted, he was forced to settle in the town of Barla in the Isparta province, where he wrote two-thirds of his *Risāle-yi Nūr* (originally called *Sözler*). He began to attract an increasingly large group of followers who copied by hand his writings in the Arabic script and distributed them all over Anatolia; eventually he permitted the printing of the *Risāle* in Latin script. Nursī repeatedly stated that all the persecutions and hardships inflicted on him were God's blessings, serving to define more clearly his path and his mission to save the faith. He held that the secularist régime in Ankara, having destroyed the formal religious establishment, had unwittingly left popular Islam as the only authentic faith of the Turks, allowing Saᶜīd Nursī to become its spokesman, symbol and martyr.

Alarmed by the growing popularity of Nursī's teachings, which had spread even among the intellectuals and the military officers, the government arrested him again in 1934 and sent him, first, to Eskişehir and, later, to seven years' enforced exile in Kastamonu. He was subsequently arrested again in 1943, 1948 and 1952 for allegedly violating laws mandating secularism, but was finally acquitted in 1956. This was the result, among other things, of the official opinion issued by the *Diyanet* (Religious) Affairs Directorate which finally stated that Nursī's teachings were spiritual and Islamic. He had returned meanwhile to Isparta, which he considered his home, and there openly cast his vote for the Democratic Party, which had restored some religious freedom. He died in Urfa on 23 March 1960 and was buried there, but the military government that came to power on 27 May 1960 exhumed the remains (supposedly in response to his brother's request) and buried him in secret in an unknown place in the mountains of Isparta.

The broad range of Saᶜīd Nursī's teachings rested on the fact that he considered himself not a *sheykh* but an *imām*, similar to al-Ghazālī and Aḥmad Sirhindī [*q.vv.*], and followed the orthodoxy of ᶜAbd al-Ḳādir al-Djīlānī [*q.v.*]. Absolute faith (*īmān*) in God was the foundation of his belief. In this respect he departed from the Ṣūfī personalised love and search for unity with God as well as from the Naḳshbandī concept of the *ṭarīḳat* or brotherhood as the vehicle of the faith. He adopted the notion of *millet* (the nation) as the collectivity of the Muslims, with *Islāmiyyet* (the faith), the whole of this superseding ethnic, linguistic and local differences. The *millet* was, in fact, a new type of political-social entity, in which nature and humanity existed in harmony and balance, both being viewed as God's creations and the proof of His existence.

Religion, according to Nursī, operated in a social and human environment and had to take into consideration the changing nature of society and the needs of the human being. He regarded modern society—notably that of the West—and that espoused under the positivist-materialist policy of the Turkish government in the name of "secularism" as the source of materialism and spiritual impoverishment. He considered that the level of development of the faith was conditioned by the intellectual, moral, and economic level of development in society, and upheld the virtue of labour (*say-etmek, çalışkanlık* "exertion" or "activity"), mutual help, self-awareness and property rights, moderate acquisitiveness being a natural, God-given instinct. He criticised the *ulema* for turning their back on the physical sciences; in fact, he advised them to study these sciences. For him, ignorance (*cehalet*), poverty (*fakirlik*), and dissension were the worst enemies of society. Nursī's teachings lacked the dogmatism and rigidity that infected many other fundamentalist movements and appeared at times to say many things at once. This vagueness appealed to a variety of groups, ranging from modernists to moderate conservatives and dedicated Islamists. Above all, however, it was the example of the man and his life that has won him a wide following: a simple Kurdish villager with limited formal education, who eventually opted for membership in the newly-formed Turkish nation (he dropped the name Saᶜīd-i Kurdī) as having the potential best to represent the brotherhood of Muslims.

Bibliography: The best and most comprehensive biography is that of Necmeddin Şahiner, *Bilinmeyen taraflariyle Bediuzzaman*, 7th ed. Istanbul 1988. Others include Cemal Kutay, *Tarih sohbetleri*, vols. i-vi, Istanbul 1966-7; *Nurculuk*, Ankara 1968; Şerif Mardin, *Religion and social change in modern Turkey*, Albany, N.Y. 1989; Sefa Mürsel, *Bediüzzaman Said Nursi ve devlet felsefesi*, Istanbul 1976; Hamid Algar, *Said Nursi and the Risale-i Nur*, in *Islamic perspectives. Studies in honour of Sayyid Abul Ala Mawdudi*, Leicester 1979, 313-33. (KEMAL KARPAT)

NUṢAYB al-Aṣghar, Abu 'l-Ḥadjnāᵓ (not to be confused with Nuṣayb b. Rabāḥ [*q.v.*], who is sometimes given the *kunya* of Abu 'l-Hadjnāᵓ), a negro poet of the Arabic language originally from Yamāma.

He is described as *mawlā 'l-Mahdī* to distinguish him from his homonym, because the future ᶜAbbāsid caliph had bought him and freed him during the reign of al-Manṣūr (136-58/754-75). It was he who gave him his *kunya* and married him to a female slave named Djaᶜfara. Once established on the throne (158/775), al-Mahdī, whose companion he had become, offered him property in the Sawād and entrusted him with various missions, one of which is given considerable prominence by the biographers: having been sent to the Yemen to buy *mahriyya* camels [see MAHRA, at VI, 83 a-b) for a sum of 20,000 dīnārs which the governor was ordered to deliver to him, he spent this money on his personal needs and pleasures; imprisoned in the Yemen, then taken to Baghdād in chains, he gained the caliph's pardon as a result of the intervention of a certain Thumāma b. al-Walīd al-ᶜAbsī to whom he expressed his gratitude; he was furthermore a friend of the latter's brother, Shayba, over whose death he wept. He also expressed his appreciation of al-Mahdī in a long *ḳaṣīda* (-*ᶜu* rhyme, metre *ṭawīl*) and some other pieces (notably a poem in -*ᵓuhā*, metre *ṭawīl*). His daughter Ḥadjnāᵓ, also a talented versifier, addressed adulatory poems to the caliph and to his daughter ᶜAbbāsa [*q.v.*]. After the death of al-Mahdī (169/785), Nuṣayb is encountered in the entourage of al-Rashīd (170-93/786-809), who even appointed him head of a province of Syria, where he exploited his authority for his own enrichment. Naturally enough, he composed, in a long *ḳaṣīda* (-*lū* rhyme, metre *ṭawīl*), the eulogy of this caliph, whose wife Zubayda [*q.v.*] was also the object of his praises, on the occasion of her pilgrimage to Mecca (-*mī* rhyme, metre *ṭawīl*).

During this period, he also maintained amicable

relations with the Barmakids, in particular with al-Faḍl b. Yaḥyā (d. 193/808 [*q.v.*]), who offered him both a house and property. There is a general impression that at least some of his work is inspired by the exchanges of gifts with other, lesser-known individuals, by gratitude for the presents solicited or by anger when his expectations were disappointed. Although he is described by the *Aghānī* as *hadjdjāʾ malʿūn*, there are barely any traces of *hidjāʾ* in what has survived of his work, other than a satirical poem addressed to the governor of Ṣanʿāʾ, who had accepted his adulation but had not rewarded him (*-rī* rhyme, metre *ṭawīl*).

The *Fihrist* (163, Cairo edition, 231-2) estimates his corpus as comprising 70 compositions, but of this only a few verses have survived. The critics have been unstinting in their praises for his talent. They place him at the same level as his homonym, declare that al-Rashīd preferred him to other poets and speak highly of his qualities in the domains of amorous poetry, panegyric, satire and description, but it is difficult to corroborate their judgment.

Bibliography: The principal biography is that of the *Aghānī*, xx, 25-34 = ed. Beirut, xxiii, 400-37. See also Abū Tammām, *Ḥamāsa*, i, 273; Djāḥiẓ, *Burṣān*, 107, 108, 314; Ibn al-Muʿtazz, *Ṭabaḳāt*, ed. Eghbal, 68-9; Yāḳūt, *Irshād*, vii, 216-18 = *Udabāʾ*, xix, 234-7; Ziriklī, *Aʿlām*, viii, 356; Sezgin, *GAS*, ii, 539. (Ch. Pellat)

NUṢAYB al-Akbar b. **RABĀḤ**, Abū Miḥdjan, a negro poet of the Arabic language who is said to have belonged, originally, to a Kinānī of Waddān, a small village close to Medina (see al-Masʿūdī, *Murūdj*, Arabic index, s.v.); it could, however, be supposed that the locality in question is rather the main settlement of the oasis of Djufra [*q.v.*] which bears the same name, since the available information regarding the biography of Nuṣayb indicates that he was a native of Africa. In any case, attempting to establish his origin would be futile, since this has been the object of so many speculations that it is impossible to draw any firm conclusions (Abu 'l-Faradj reproduces these speculations conscientiously, without deluding himself as to their reliability). To explain the colour of his skin, he is supposed to have had Nubian parents, but according to the most trustworthy version, he was the son of a slave who was made pregnant by her master, who died before the birth of the child; his paternal uncle having offered him for sale, he was bought by a Kinānī of Waddān, but it is quite certain that accounts relating to this period of his life have no historical validity. The circumstances of his attainment of freedom are also variously explained. According to the most often repeated story, when he began to compose poetry the dignitaries of the tribe intervened on his behalf with his master, who sent him to Egypt where, after a long period of waiting, he succeeded in delivering a eulogy, at Ḥulwān, to ʿAbd al-ʿAzīz b. Marwān [*q.v.*], governor of Egypt. The Umayyad prince having bought and then freed him, he became for posterity the *mawlā ʿAbd al-ʿAzīz*, as Nuṣayb al-Aṣghar [*q.v.*] was to become the *mawlā 'l-Mahdī*. He took on the role of accredited panegyrist of his benefactor, whom he mourned when he fell victim to an epidemic of plague in 85/704. He had already sung the praises of Bishr b. Marwān (d. 74/693-4 [*q.v.*]), and he went on to address eulogies to the caliphs ʿAbd al-Malik b. Marwān (d. 86/705), Sulaymān b. ʿAbd al-Malik (d. 99/717) and ʿUmar b. ʿAbd al-ʿAzīz (d. 101/720), and to other aristocrats of Medina; he lived in fact in the Holy City, but also resided in Damascus. He died between 108 and 113/726-31.

In the course of his career as a panegyrist, he had occasion to exchange verses with al-Farazdaḳ, Djarīr and ʿUmar b. Abī Rabīʿa, and he was also sometimes at odds with al-Kumayt or Dhu 'l-Rumma, but he always refrained from the practice of *hidjāʾ* [*q.v.*]. Ibn Sallām places him in the sixth rank of poets of the Islamic period, and critics are particularly appreciative of his *nasīb*, always pure, and his *madīḥ*, which was in some respects his speciality and for which he possessed an acknowledged talent, although his panegyrics lack originality. In part, he owes his renown to the fact that some of his verses were set to music by Isḥāḳ al-Mawṣilī, who also devoted a monograph to him, *Akhbār Nuṣayb*, preceding al-Zubayr b. Bakkār, writer of another work with the same title.

Nuṣayb had married a white woman, whom he celebrated in the lyrical section of his work in such terms that he has been reckoned among the poetic lovers according to the ʿUdhrī tradition. (It is remarkable that the passage of the *Aghānī* relating to his wife was suppressed in the Cairo edition.) However, an original theme of his poetry was inspired by the colour of his skin on account of which he suffered considerable and intolerable racist abuse. He consoled himself, however, by insisting on his integrity and his greatness of soul. In this context, B. Lewis (*Race and color in Islam*, New York 1971, 12 ff. and *passim*; French tr., *Race et couleur en pays d'Islam*, Paris 1982, 29 ff. and *passim*) has raised the question of the extent to which awareness of his birth and his race affected this talented poet, of whom he recalls that he was one of the *aghribat al-ʿArab*, the "ravens of the Arabs". It is furthermore astonishing that the great champion of the Negroes, al-Djāḥiẓ (d. 255/869 [*q.v.*]) only quotes a few of his verses (*Bukhalāʾ*, ed. Ḥādjirī, 188; *Bayān*, i, 219; *Ḥayawān*, i, 30 (anonymous verse), iii, 206) and, in particular, does not include him among the number of his racial brothers whom he celebrates in his *Fakhr al-Sūdān ʿalā 'l-bīḍān*, where his name is not even mentioned.

Bibliography: To the references quoted above, the first source to be added is the *Aghānī*, which contains the most thorough biography (i, 129-50 = Beirut edition, i, 302-51). Another useful source is Yāḳūt, *Irshād*, vii, 212-16 = *Udabāʾ*, xix, 228-34. Fragments of his work (which amounted to 50 pieces, *Fihrist*, 163) have been assembled by U. Rizzitano, *Alcuni frammenti poetici di ... Nuṣayb*, in *RSO*, xxii (1945), 23-35, and by D. Sallūm, *Shiʿr Nuṣayb b. Rabāḥ*, Baghdād 1967. The most complete modern articles are those of Rizzitano, *Abū Miḥğan Nuṣayb b. Rabāḥ*, in *RSO*, xx (1943), 421-71; of R. Blachère, *HLA*, 603-6 (with valuable bibliography), and of Sezgin, *GAS*, ii, 410-11 and index. For the rest, see Ibn Sallām, *Ṭabaḳāt*, 348, 529, 544-50; Abū Tammām, *Ḥamāsa*, index; Ibn Ḳutayba, *Shiʿr*, 242-4 = Cairo ed., 371-4; Washshāʾ, *Muwashshā*, 84; Zadjdjādjī, *Amālī*, 31-5; Marzubānī, *Muwashshah*, *passim*; Yāḳūt, *Muʿdjam*, index; Ibn Taghrībirdī, *Nudjūm*, i, 262-3; Anṭākī, *Tazyīn al-aswāḳ*, Cairo 1291, i, 98-100; Brockelmann S I, 99; Nallino, *La letterature arabica*, French tr., 238, 248-9; Rescher, *Abriss*, i, 194-6; Gabrieli, *Storia*, 120-1; Ziriklī, *Aʿlām*, viii, 355. (Ch. Pellat)

NUṢAYRIYYA, a Shīʿī sect widely dispersed in western Syria and in the south-east of present day Turkey; the only branch of extreme (*ghuluww*) Kūfan Shīʿism which has survived into the contemporary period.

1. Etymology

Pliny (*Hist. nat.*, v, 81) mentions a *Nazerinorum tetrarchia* in Coelesyria, situated opposite Apameia, beyond the river Marsyas (not identified; probably the right-hand tributary of the Orontes passing to the east of the town), but this name is evidently not related to that of the sect. The Nuṣayriyya themselves derive the name from that of their eponym Ibn Nuṣayr, which would appear to be correct. In Arab-Islamic texts, the name is not attested in Syria before the establishment of the sect at al-Lā<u>dh</u>iḳiyya in the 5th/11th century.

2. Current distribution

In Syria, the heartland of the Nuṣayriyya is the <u>D</u>jebel Anṣāriyye (known today as *<u>D</u>jabal al-ʿAlawiyyīn*) between al-Ḥaffa to the north and Tall Kala<u>kh</u> to the south. From this nucleus, the Nuṣayriyya have spread out to occupy parts of the surrounding plains: the coastal plain to the west, the <u>Gh</u>āb to the east and the plain of ʿAkkār to the south-west. Nevertheless, the towns which surround the <u>D</u>jebel have always maintained a non-Nuṣayrī majority (al-Lā<u>dh</u>iḳiyya, <u>D</u>jabala, Bāniyās, Ṭarṭūs, Ṣāfītā, Tall Kala<u>kh</u>, Ḥimṣ, Maṣyāf, Ḥamāt). Nuṣayrī minorities are distributed to the south of Ḥimṣ, on the plateau between Maṣyāf and the Orontes, to the north-east of Ḥamāt and in the regions of Maʿarrat al-Nuʿmān, Idlib and Aleppo, as well as in Damascus. In 1964, the number of Nuṣayriyya in Syria was estimated at 600,000, or 11% of the population (more recent assessments do not exist). In Lebanon there is a Nuṣayrī minority immediately to the south of the Syrian frontier. Within the current boundaries of Turkey, sizeable minorities are to be found on the plateau of al-Ḳuṣayr, at Antakya (Antioch), on the plain of the Lower Orontes between Antakya and the estuary of the river, and on the coastal plain to the south-west of Iskenderun. Since the 19th century, Nuṣayrī colonies have become established in Cilicia, especially at Tarsus and Adana as well as in the surroundings of these two towns (approximately 80,000 in 1921; the current figures are not known. Cf. the maps in Weulersse, i, 58 f.).

3. Origins

The sect was formed in Irak in the mid-3rd/9th century. According to al-Nawba<u>kh</u>tī, 78 (cf. al-Ḳummī, 100-1; al-Ka<u>sh</u><u>sh</u>ī, 520-1; Halm, *Gnosis*, 282-3), Muḥammad b. Nuṣayr al-Namīrī was a supporter of the tenth <u>Sh</u>īʿī *imām* ʿAlī al-Hādī (d. 254/868). He proclaimed the divine nature of the *imām* (who cursed him for this reason; al-Ka<u>sh</u><u>sh</u>ī, 520, 999) and claimed for himself the status of a prophet; he professed metempsychosis (*tanāsu<u>kh</u>*) and antinomianism (*ibāḥa*). At the court of Ba<u>gh</u>dād, he was supported by the *kātib* Muḥammad b. Mūsā b. al-Ḥasan b. al-Furāt al-<u>D</u>juʿfī (al-Ka<u>sh</u><u>sh</u>ī, 302, 554). According to Nuṣayrī tradition, Ibn Nuṣayr was the favourite disciple of the eleventh *imām* al-Ḥasan al-ʿAskarī (d. 260/874), who entrusted to him a new revelation which was to constitute the nucleus of the Nuṣayrī doctrine. In the most ancient sources (al-Nawba<u>kh</u>tī, al-Ḳummī; even al-Ba<u>gh</u>dādī, 255-6), the sect is called *al-Namīriyya* (from the *nisba* of Ibn Nuṣayr); from the 5th/11th century onwards, the name *al-Nuṣayriyya* becomes current (Ibn al-<u>Gh</u>adāʾirī, d. 411/1020-1, quoted by al-Astarābādī, *Manha<u>dj</u> al-maḳāl*, 314; Ibn Ḥazm, *Milal*, quoted by Friedlander in *JAOS*, xxix [1908], 126 ff.; al-Samʿānī, fol. 562 b [ed. Hyderabad xiii, 121 ff.]; al-<u>Sh</u>ahrastānī, 143-5).

The literature of the Nuṣayrīs has revealed to us the lineage of the disciples of the founder, who wield authority in the tradition of the secret doctrine. Of Ibn Nuṣayr's successor, Muḥammad b. <u>D</u>jundab, nothing is known other than his name. His disciple Abū Muḥammad ʿAbd Allāh al-<u>D</u>junbulānī al-<u>D</u>jannān ("the gardener"), d. 287/900, seems to have been a Persian immigrant from the region of Fārs in ʿIrāḳ (<u>D</u>junbulāʾ is situated between Kūfa and Wāsiṭ). It is probably he who was responsible for certain quasi-Iranian features of the Nuṣayrian doctrine, for example the adoption of the Iranian festivals of the equinoxes, *nawrūz* and *mihrgān* [*q.vv.*], which are celebrated by the Nuṣayrīs as the days when the divinity of ʿAlī is manifested in the sun. Al-<u>D</u>junbulānī is the hero of a book intitled *Kitāb al-Akwār wa 'l-adwār al-nūrāniyya* ("The aeons and the cycles of the light"), from which numerous quotations have been preserved in the Calendar of festivals of the Nuṣayrīs and of which the author was possibly the disciple and successor of Ibn <u>D</u>jundab, al-<u>Kh</u>aṣībī.

Abū ʿAbd Allāh al-Ḥusayn b. Ḥamdān al-<u>Kh</u>aṣībī (d. 346/957) was the head of the Nuṣayrī community of the suburb of al-Kar<u>kh</u> to the south of Ba<u>gh</u>dād, but he seems to have led a peripatetic existence. He was a poet of considerable talent (his *Dīwān* has been preserved) and seems to have earned his living as such at the courts of the Būyids in ʿIrāḳ and in western Persia, later at the courts of the Ḥamdānids of Mawṣil and Aleppo. It was evidently he who conveyed the doctrines of the sect to northern Syria; he dedicated his *Kitāb al-Hidāya al-kubrā* to Sayf al-Dawla, the Ḥamdānid *amīr* of Aleppo (*Taʾrī<u>kh</u> al-ʿAlawiyyīn* [= *TA*], 260, 318). Al-<u>Kh</u>aṣībī died at Aleppo in 346/957 (*TA*, 257-9) or 358/969 (al-Astarābādī, *Manha<u>dj</u> al-maḳāl*, 112-23), and left behind numerous works. His tomb to the north of Aleppo, known by the name of <u>Sh</u>ay<u>kh</u> Yābrāḳ, is still venerated by Nuṣayrīs today (*TA*, 259).

The successor of al-<u>Kh</u>aṣībī at Aleppo was Muḥammad b. ʿAlī al-<u>D</u>jillī (from al-<u>D</u>jilliyya on the estuary of the Orontes). He survived the reconquest of Cilicia and of Antioch by the Byzantine emperor Nicephorus Phocas (358/969) and of the Syrian coast by John Tzimisces (363/975) and was for a period of time a prisoner of the Christians. He died, probably in Aleppo, after 384/994 (*TA*, 260).

Surūr b. al-Ḳāsim al-Ṭabarānī, successor of al-<u>D</u>jillī at Aleppo, left the town in 423/1032 on account of the incessant warfare in the region and settled at al-Lā<u>dh</u>iḳiyya (Laodicea), which at this time was still under Byzantine domination. Here, he was the true founder of the Syrian Nuṣayrī community; according to *TA*, 327, the local dynasty of al-Lā<u>dh</u>iḳiyya, the Tanū<u>kh</u>, adopted Nuṣayrī doctrines. Unhindered by any Muslim authority, al-Ṭabarānī seems to have converted the peasants (possibly still pagan) of the mountainous hinterland of the town. Al-Ṭabarānī, whose works form the major part of the written tradition of the Nuṣayrīs, died at al-Lā<u>dh</u>iḳiyya in 426/1034-5; his tomb, still venerated, is located inside the mosque of al-<u>Sh</u>aʿrānī not far from the port (*TA*, 262-5).

4. History

The history of the Nuṣayri community in mediaeval times is obscure; the accounts contained in the *TA*, compiled at the beginning of the 20th century, are of dubious value; a study of this period has yet to be undertaken. In the early years of the 12th century, the western part of the territory of the Nuṣayrīs was conquered by the Crusaders; in 496/1103 al-Lā<u>dh</u>iḳiyya was captured by the Norman Tancred after a long siege. From this time onward, the northern area of what is now the <u>D</u>jabal Anṣāriyya formed a part of the Norman principality of Antioch, but Christian penetration of the mountain region seems to have been ineffectual; in the <u>D</u>jabal itself, fortresses and other relics of the Crusaders are quite rare (cf. *TAVO*, maps B viii 8, 10 and 12). In Latin sources, the Nuṣayrīs (*Nossorite*) are seldom mentioned (cf. Dussaud, 21-7, 30).

In 527/1132-3 the fortress of al-Ḳadmūs was sold by the *amīr* of al-Kahf to the Nizārī Ismāʿīlīs of Alamūt, who subsequently took possession of numerous fortresses in the southern Djabal: al-Kahf, al-Kharība (531/1136-7) and Maṣyāf (535/1140-1), then al-Khawābī, al-Ruṣāfa, al-ʿUllayka and Manīḳa. The establishment of Ismāʿīlīs (the *assassini* of the Latin sources) in the region provoked conflicts with the Nuṣayrīs; this is probably the context in which belongs the Nuṣayrī tradition of a "council" at ʿĀna (on the middle Euphrates) where representatives of the Nuṣayrī communities—two each from Baghdād, from ʿĀna, from Aleppo, from al-Lādhiḳiyya and from the Djabal—tried in vain to find a formula of conciliation (*tawḥīd*) with the Ismāʿīlīs (*TA*, 258, 365). The council (*al-madjlis al-dīnī*) of ʿĀna is undated; a second is recorded as having taken place in 690/1291 at Ṣāfītā, with equal lack of success (*TA*, 365).

Following the capture of Djabala, al-Lādhiḳiyya and the Frankish fortresses of Ṣahyūn and Balāṭunus by Ṣalāḥ al-Dīn in 584/1188, the Djabal became part of the Ayyūbid sultanate. It is at the end of the Ayyūbid period that Nuṣayrī tradition places an event of extraordinary importance: the settlement in the Djabal of Bedouin tribes from the Djabal Sindjār, led by the *amīr* Ḥasan al-Makzūn al-Sindjārī. Answering an appeal from the Nuṣayrīs for help in repelling the attacks of the Ismāʿīlīs, the *amīr* invaded the Djabal for the first time in 617/1220. After being defeated, he withdrew to the Djabal Sindjār, returning in 622/1223 and establishing himself definitively in the region of Abū Ḳubays and of Siyānū; from his troops were to emerge the Nuṣayrī tribes of the Ḥaddādiyya, Matāwira, Mahāliba, Darāwisa, Numaylātiyya and Banū ʿAlī (*TA*, 358-64; for the expansion of the various tribes, cf. Weulersse, i, 330-1, and figs. 136 and 137).

In the Mamlūk period, Baybars, having taken the fortresses of the Ismāʿīlīs to the south of the Djabal, made numerous attempts to convert the Nuṣayrīs to Sunnism; he forbade initiations into the sect and ordered the construction of mosques throughout the country. After an uprising by the Nuṣayrīs, sultan Ḳalāwūn re-imposed the ban on all proselytism and repeated the order to construct in every township a mosque, for the maintenance of which the local population was to be responsible. But Ibn Baṭṭūṭa, touring the region in the mid-8th/14th century, relates that these mosques had been abandoned or even transformed into cattle-sheds or stables (Ibn Baṭṭūṭa, i, 177). The well-known *fatwā* of Ibn Taymiyya (d. 728/1328 [*q.v.*]) condemned the Nuṣayrīs as more heretical even than idolators and authorised *djihād* against them (S. Guyard, *Fetwa*; Dussaud, 28-31). Ibn Ḳāḍī Shuhba, *Taʾrīkh*, tells of an expedition in 745/1344 in the course of which "books containing the dogmas of the Nuṣayrīs" were confiscated.

But the sect survived these persecutions and remained active until the Ottoman period, during which oppression seems to have eased. According to C. Niebuhr, who crossed the Djabal in 1766, the Nuṣayrīs were governed by four *muḳaddams* (at Bahlūliyya near al-Lādhiḳiyya, at Sumrīn, at the Bilād al-Shawābī and at Ṣāfītā), who were subsidiary to the Pasha of Tripoli (*Reisebeschreibung*, ii, 439). Such was still the situation in 1832 when the Egyptian general Ibrāhīm Pasha b. Muḥammad ʿAlī [*q.v.*] crushed the resistance of the *muḳaddam* of Ṣāfītā. After 1854, the Turkish government was content to control the Djabal indirectly through the appointment of a local chieftain, the *mushīr al-djabal* Ismāʿīl Beg, governor of the district of Ṣāfītā; installing himself at Dreykīsh (close to Ṣāfītā), he put an end to the constant wrangling of the different rival families and subjected them to his authority. In exchange for a fixed tribute, the government allowed him unlimited power in the Djabal. But in 1858 this potentate was reckoned to have become too powerful, and he was deposed by Ṭāhir Pasha. On numerous occasions, in particular in 1870 and 1877, Ottoman troops ravaged the territory of the Nuṣayrīs and succeeded finally in breaking the power of the tribes and establishing a direct administration there (levying of taxes; recruitment of soldiers); mosques were constructed but they remained empty (Dussaud, 32-8).

During the last years of the Ottoman empire, a Nuṣayrī of Adana, Muḥammad Amīn Ghālib al-Ṭawīl, the chief of police in several *wilāyets*, composed his "History of the Alawites" (*Taʾrīkh al-ʿAlawiyyīn*), which was published in 1924 in Arabic. In this book, the term *Nuṣayrī*, in usage since the Middle Ages, was replaced for the first time by *ʿAlawī*, which was henceforward to be the norm. The *Taʾrīkh* had the object of ridding the Nuṣayrīs of their reputation for being heretics or even pagans and showing that in fact they were true Twelver Shīʿīs. It is for this reason that, from 1920 onward, "Djaʿfarī" (i.e. Twelver) judges were appointed in the towns of the south of the country (*EI*[1], s.v. *Nuṣairī*).

Following the disintegration of the Ottoman empire and the establishment of the French mandate in Syria, the territory of the Nuṣayriyya was divided into three parts: Cilicia was ceded to the Republic of Turkey, while the *sandjāḳ* of Alexandretta (Iskenderun) was separated from the remainder of Syria and placed under special administration. On 31 August 1920 the French established the "Autonomous Territory of the Alawites", which consisted of the former *sandjāḳ* of al-Lādhiḳiyya, the northern sector of the *sandjāḳ* of Tripoli and part of the *ḳaḍāʾ* of Maṣyāf (*sandjāḳ* of Ḥamāt). On 12 July 1922, the Territory was proclaimed a State which, with the States of Damascus and Aleppo, formed the "Federation of States of Syria". At the beginning of 1924, the Federation was dissolved and the State of the Alawites became the "Independent State of the Alawites" headed by a French governor (Cayla; after 1925 Schoeffler) and a Council composed of nine representatives of the various minorities (9 ʿAlawīs, 3 Sunnīs, 3 Orthodox Christians, 1 Ismāʿīlī and 1 representative of the other Christian minorities). In 1930, the State of the Alawites was renamed "Government of Lattakia", and on 10 January 1937 it was transformed into a province (*muḥāfaẓa*) of the new Syrian State; the flag of the Alawites (a sun on a white background) was replaced by the Syrian tricolour. In 1939 the French ceded the *sandjāḳ* of Alexandretta to Turkey.

5. Doctrines

As *ghulāt*, the Nuṣayriyya venerate ʿAlī b. Abī Ṭālib as supreme and eternal God (*al-ilāh al-aʿẓam, al-ḳadīm al-azal*). The basis of Nuṣayrī doctrine is a cosmogony of gnostic nature (Sulaymān, *Bākūra*, 59-61; Halm, *Gnosis*, 298 ff.). In the beginning of time, the souls of the Nuṣayrīs were lights, surrounding and praising God; then they rebelled against Him, disputing His divinity. From then onwards, they have been hurled down from the celestial heights and exiled on the earth, where they are enclosed in material bodies and condemned to metempsychosis (temporal *nāsūkhiyya* for the elect, eternal *nāsūkhiyya* for the damned). During their fall, the supreme God appears to them seven times, calling for their obedience, but they refuse. In each manifestation, God, who is called "the Essence" (*maʿnā*), is accompanied by two subordinate hypostases, "the Name" (*ism*) which is also called "the Veil" (*ḥidjāb*) and the "Gate" (*bāb*). In earthly life, this trio is revealed in numerous instances: the *maʿnā* is incarnated successively in Abel, Seth, Joseph, Joshua, ʿAṣaf, St. Peter and ʿAlī b. Abī Ṭālib, then in the *imāms* as far as the eleventh one, al-Ḥasan al-ʿAskarī; all of these are therefore manifestations of divinity. However, their true character is veiled by the presence of the *ḥidjāb* or *ism* (Adam, Noah, Jacob, Moses, Solomon, Jesus and Muḥammad), each of them is accompanied by a *bāb*. The central trio of the Islamic period is ʿAlī (*maʿnā*), Muḥammad (*ism, ḥidjāb*) and Salmān al-Fārisī (*bāb*). The *abwāb* of the eleven *imāms* are the intermediaries between the concealed divinity and initiated believers; for example, the eponym of the Nuṣayriyya, Muḥammad b. Nuṣayr, was the *bāb* of the eleventh *imām* al-Haṣan al-ʿAskarī, whose secret revelations he confided exclusively to the Nuṣayriyya. He who recognises the identity of the *maʿnā* is saved and may escape from metempsychosis; his soul, released from the body and transformed into a star, resumes its journey back across the seven heavens to arrive at the ultimate objective (*ghāya*), sc. contemplation (*muʿāyana*) of the divine light. Women are excluded from this because they are born of the sins of devils; for this reason, they are not entitled to participate in the rites of men (Sulaymān, *Bākūra*, 61). The popular religion of the Nuṣayriyya, especially that of women, retains traces of paganism (veneration of high places, of springs, of green trees). For the cult of saints (*ziyārāt*), cf. Weulersse, i, 255-62; for rites of initiation and festivals, cf. Dussaud, 104 ff., 136 ff., Weulersse, i, 259-61; Halm, *Gnosis*, 303 ff.

Bibliography: Sulaymān Efendī, *al-Bākūra al-sulaymāniyya fī kashf asrār al-diyāna al-nuṣayriyya*, Beirut 1864; S. Guyard, *Le Fetwa d'Ibn Taimiyyah sur les Nosairis*, in *JA*, 6ᵉ sér., xviii (1871), 158-98; Cl. Huart, *La poésie religieuse des Noṣairīs*, in *JA*, 7ᵉ sér., xiv (1879), 190-261; H. Lammens, *Au pays des Nosairis*, in *ROC*, iv (1899), 572-90, v (1900), 99-117, 303-18, 423-44; R. Dussaud, *Histoire et religion des Noṣairīs*, Paris 1900; Muḥ. A. Gh. al-Ṭawīl, *Taʾrīkh al-ʿAlawiyyīn*, al-Lādhiḳiyya 1924, ³Beirut 1979; L. Massignon, *Esquisse d'une bibliographie nusayrie*, in *Mél. R. Dussaud*, ii (1939), 913-22 (= *Opera minora*, i, 640-9); idem, *Les Nusayris*, in *L'Elaboration de l'Islam, Colloque de Strasbourg*, Paris 1961, 109-14 (= *Opera minora*, i, 619-24); E. de Vaumas, *Le Djebel Ansarieh. Etudes de géographie humaine*, in *Revue de Géographie Alpine*, xlviii (1960), 289 ff.; J. Weulersse, *Le Pays des Alaouites*, 2 vols., Tours 1940; R. Strothmann, *Festkalender der Nuṣairier*, in *Isl.*, xxvii (1944-6); idem, *Seelenwanderung bei den Nuṣairī*, in *Oriens*, xii (1959), 89-114; Cl. Cahen, *Note sur les origines de la communauté syrienne des Nusayris*, in *REI*, xxxviii (1970), 243-9; H. Halm, "*Das Buch der Schatten*". *Die Mufaḍḍal-Tradition der Ġulāt und die Ursprünge des Nuṣairiertums*, in *Isl.*, lv (1978), 219-66, lviii (1981), 15-86; idem, *Die islamische Gnosis. Die extreme Schia und die Alawiten*, Zürich 1982 (with complete bibl.). (H. HALM)

AL-**NŪSHĀDIR**, also *nushādir*, *nawshādir*, Sanskrit *navasadara*, Chin. *nao-sha*, sal-ammoniac. The etymology of the word is uncertain; perhaps it comes from the Pahlavi *anōsh-ādar* "immortal fire" as we find the form *anūshādhur* in Syriac.

The oldest references to the occurrence of sal-ammoniac in a natural state are in the reports of Chinese embassies of the 6th-7th centuries, which were the subject of very full investigation in connection with a geological problem, the question of volcanoes in Central Asia, by H.J. von Klaproth, A. von Humboldt and C. Ritter. The reference was to mountains of fire, Pe-Shan, on the northern slopes of the Tien-Shan south of Ḳuldja [*q.v.*], Ho-Chou on the south side of the Tien-Shan near Turfan and the sulphur pits of Ürümči/Ürümqi. The mountain Pe-Shan was said to pour forth fire and smoke continually; on one side of it all the stones burn, and are melted and then after flowing some miles solidify again. *Nao-sha* and sulphur were obtained there for medicinal purposes but the stones could only be collected in winter when the cold had cooled the ground. Humboldt and Ritter do not accept a reference to the burning of coal by which sal-ammoniac and sulphur are obtained. The statement that the volcanoes of Central Asia produce sal-ammoniac in immense quantities is found in G. Bischof, and even G. von Richthofen still held the volcano theory. The botanist and geographer Regel, who travelled in these regions about 1879, was the first to dispute the existence of volcanoes. After Nansen, Le Coq and others had been unable to confirm the existence of volcanoes but established the fact that there were large deposits of coal on the surface, the old sources in Central Asia are now generally attributed to the burning of coal.

Almost all the Arab geographers who refer to Central Asia, from al-Masʿūdī, al-Iṣṭakhrī, Ibn Ḥawḳal, to Yāḳūt and al-Ḳazwīnī, give fantastic stories about the method by which sal-ammoniac is procured in the Buttam hills east of Samarḳand. Here again the details suggest the burning of the earth rather than volcanic exhalations. The Persian traveller Nāṣir-i Khusraw [*q.v.*], however, mentions deposits of sal-ammoniac and sulphur at Demāwend, and Ibn Ḥawḳal is acquainted with the volcanic sal-ammoniac of Etna; the latter was still exported to Spain in the 12th century. At an earlier date, they had begun to procure sal-ammoniac from the soot of camel dung. This product remained into modern times an important import by the Venetian traders and was only driven from the market by the modern cheap methods of production from gas liquor, etc.

The use of sal-ammoniac as a remedy in cases of inflammation of the throat, etc., is already mentioned by ʿAlī b. Rabbān al-Ṭabarī. Ibn al-Bayṭār also quotes from other authors all kinds of remarkable uses of it, on which no stress need be laid. Djābir b. Ḥayyān reckons sal-ammoniac among the poisons, which is true of large doses.

The part played by sal-ammoniac in alchemy is much more important. Djābir adds it as a fourth to the three πνεύματα of the Greeks, quicksilver, sulphur and sulphide of arsenic (AsS or As_2S_3), and it is used by all Persian-Arab alchemists in countless recipes. The preparation of carbonate of ammonia through distillation of hair, blood and other materials is already fully described in the "Seventy Books" and other works of Djābir. These methods seem to have given the stimulus to the discovery of the Egyptian method of obtaining sal-ammoniac. All these things came with alchemy to Spain and thence into western alchemy.

In the earliest Latin translations, sal-ammoniac is still called *nesciador*, *mizadir*, etc., i.e. transliterations of the Arabic name. The general term *al-ʿuḳāb* is also found in the forms *aliocab*, *alocaph* or translated by *aquila*. The identification of this salt with the salt of the oasis of Ammon already mentioned by Herodotus is first found in Syriac authors and lexicographers.

Bibliography: H.E. Stapleton, *Sal-ammoniac: a study in primitive chemistry*, in *Mem. As. Soc. Bengal* (1905), i, no. 2; M. Berthelot, *Archéologie et histoire des sciences*, in *Mém. Ac. Sc.* (1906), xlix; J. Ruska, *Sal ammoniacus, Nušādir und Salmiak*, in *SB Heid. Ak. d. Wiss.*, phil.-hist. Klasse (1923), treatise 5.; idem, *Die Siebzig Bücher des Ǧābir ibn Ḥajjān*, in *Festschr. f. E.O. v. Lippmann*, 1927, 38 ff.; idem, *Der Salmiak in der Geschichte der Alchemie*, in *Zt. f. angew. Chemie* (1928), xli, 1321 ff.; Sezgin, *GAS*, iv, 18 (on the importance of the early knowledge of *nūshadir* for the history of Arabic chemistry); cf. also Bīrūnī, *K. al-Ṣaydana fi 'l-ṭibb*, ed. al-Ḥakīm Muḥ. Saʿīd, Karachi 1973, 364-65. (J. Ruska)

AL-NŪSHARĪ or AL-NAWSHARI, Abū Mūsā ʿĪsā b. Muḥammad, general (said to be Turkish, but perhaps an Iranian from Khurāsān, since al-Samʿānī, *Ansāb*, ed. Ḥaydarābād, xiii, 201-2, derives the *nisba* al-Nūsharī (*sic*) from Nūshār, a village in the district of Balkh) from the guard of the ʿAbbāsid caliphs at Sāmarrā and governor of Damascus on various occasions during the caliphates of al-Muntaṣir, al-Mustaʿīn and al-Muʿtazz [*q.vv.*] from 247/861 onwards. At the accession of al-Muʿtazz in 252/866, he expanded southwards into Palestine, displacing the Arab governor of Ramla [*q.v.*], ʿĪsā b. al-Shaykh [*q.v.*], and subsequently defended his territories against rivals; but thereafter he fades from historical mention.

Bibliography: Scattered references in Yaʿḳūbī, Ṭabarī, Ibn al-Athīr and Ṣafadī, cited by M. Forstner, *Al-Muʿtazz billāh (252/866-255/869). Die Krise des abbasidischen Kalifats im 3./9. Jahrhundert*, Germersheim 1976, 86, 98-9, 106. (C.E. Bosworth)

NŪSHIRWĀN [see ANŪSHIRWĀN].

NUSKHA (A.). 1. In the central Islamic lands. *Nuskha* is the common Arabic word for "transcript", "copy", and in the manuscript era used in the meaning of "manuscript". Semantically directly related derived forms of the stem *n.s.kh* are *nassākh* are *nāsikh*, "copyist", and forms I, VIII and X of the verb *nasakha*, all meaning "to transcribe, to copy". In the following, *nuskha* will be more specifically used in order to denote the medium of the transmission of Islamic texts with exclusive reference to manuscripts. Other words for "manuscripts" which are commonly used are the Arabic *makhṭūṭāt*, the Persian *nuskha-hā-yi khaṭṭī*, and the Turkish *yazmalar*. Where in the following the examples are mostly taken from Arabic literature, one must realise that, especially for the earlier period, no significantly different circumstances are applicable to the transmission of Persian texts, or Turkish or other Islamic texts for that matter. It must in this connection be borne in mind that the process of transmitting handwritten texts in an Islamic cultural environment persisted till well into the 20th century, in contradistinction to the transmission of European texts, which were almost exclusively distributed in printed form ever since the art of printing became practiced, from the second half of the 15th century A.D. onward. The following aspects of *nuskha* in this sense will be distinguished here.

(a) *The rôle of the book in Islam.* The importance of the written word in Islam can hardly be underestimated. Muslims have always insisted that the Ḳurʾān, the divine revelation to the Prophet Muḥammad and God's own word, was Islam's own miracle, the *muʿdjiza* [*q.v.*], that was on equal footing with the miracles by which the earlier prophets had proved the truth of their mission. Also, the non-Muslims are divided in the *Ahl al-Kitāb*, the People of the Book who did have a divine revelation, corrupted as it had become in the course of time, and those unbelievers who had no book at all. The concept of the Celestial Book was not alien to other, pre-Islamic, cultures in the Middle East, of course, and this culture of the written word did, of course, not originate in 7th-century Arabia. The Nabataean, Syriac, Hebrew, Aramaic, Coptic, Greek, Latin, Persian, Indian and Ethiopic literatures were there already, before Islam, with a considerable production of texts. According to a report by Ibn al-Kalbī [*q.v.*], Arabic books seem even to have existed in pre-Islamic al-Ḥīra [*q.v.*]. Islam's innovation seems to have been that the Book was given divine status, or rather that this divine status was so rigorously enforced. It is probably this new accent on the importance of the Holy Book that gave the book in Islam its central rôle. In the course of time, this pivotal importance of the book in Islamic culture has only increased and the result is, today, that there are many millions of Islamic manuscripts ranging in age from the earliest period till the beginning of the 20th century. When expressed in mere numbers of texts, the Islamic literature of the manuscript era can claim to be the largest literature on earth.

The Islamic book had become in less than two centuries after the death of the founder of Islam the repository of all knowledge of an increasingly internationally orientated culture, just as the Arabic language had developed into a main vehicle of that culture. Whereas in the earlier period the language of the manuscripts was Arabic, with the emergence of the local languages and the spread of Islam, manuscripts in the other Islamic languages, most notably Persian and Turkish, were made with the use of Arabic script. The number of languages for which Arabic script is used is only surpassed by those for which the Latin script is employed. In later time, Islamic manuscripts were also written in other alphabets than the Arabic. This mostly happened on the periphery of the Middle East, in countries such as China, Thailand, Sri Lanka and Indonesia. Within the Near Middle East, Albanian Islamic manuscripts may be mentioned in this respect.

(b) *Material aspects of the manuscript.* The study of the material, physical, aspects of the handwritten book is called codicology. This technical term for the study of the codex [see DAFTAR] is, by extension, also employed for the study of the non-codex forms of manuscripts. The earliest writing materials in the Islamic era were papyrus, *bardī* in Arabic, and parchment [see DJILD, RAḲḲ]. There are reports on a great variety of materials on which the earliest fragments of the Ḳurʾān were recorded (see the survey in Nöldeke and Schwally, *Geschichte des Qurāns*, ii, Leipzig 1919, 13-14), but, with the possible exception of leather or parchment and palm leaves, none of those can have been in regular use for the recording of texts in the Ḥidjāz during and shortly after the Prophet Muḥammad's lifetime. It is probably because of Islam's main orientation to the Hellenistic and Mediterranean civilisations that it chose papyrus and parchment as its prime writing materials, rather than palm leaf and tree bark, which were the common writing materials of South Asia at the time. When the Chinese techniques of manufacturing of paper [see KĀGHAD] were introduced from Central Asia into the Middle East in the course of the 8th century A.D., the production of manuscripts must have received an extra impulse. The advantages of paper over papyrus and parchment are obvious. Paper is a stronger material than papyrus and cheaper, though less durable, than parchment.

The bulk of Islamic manuscripts have been written on paper, although parchment has remained in use for special purposes, such as copies of the Ḳurʾān or special letters or documents, for a long time, and more in the Islamic West than elsewhere. Manuscripts made of a mixture of materials, paper and parchment, are known as well. The Leiden Latin-Arabic glossary (Or. 231), which recently was dated (by P.S. van Koningsveld, *The Latin-Arabic glossary of the Leiden University Library*, Leiden 1976, 38-9) to Toledo 1193 A.D., consists of quires of which the outer and inner leaves are of parchment and the remainder of paper. Even if this particular manuscript was a codicological anachronism or exception, its mixed composition conveys an impression of the gradual westbound introduction of paper as *the* material of which manuscripts are made. Locally used writing materials, dating from early, possibly even pre-Islamic times, have remained in use in many areas. An example of this is apparently the use of wooden chips for notarial documents in North Africa. Another example is the use in Indonesia (see 2. below) of a great variety of natural products for the production of manuscripts, both Islamic and non-Islamic ones. For comparative codicology, the results of Beit-Arié's research in the field of Hebrew manuscripts are significant, since Hebrew copyists in the Middle East, and elsewhere, tended to use local materials and to adopt local bookmaking techniques.

The common shape of the book was, from the earliest period of Islam onwards, that of the codex as it had developed in Europe in the post-classical period (quires consisting of folded sheets, sewn through their hearts and then sewn together as to constitute a book). This shape had, well before the advent of Islam, superseded the scroll, which was the common shape of the book in classical antiquity. It would appear that Gregory's law (see Beit-Arié) concerning the positioning of parchment leaves was not observed in Islamic manuscripts. The most common composition of quires in the entire Middle East is that of five sheets, folded into ten leaves containing twenty pages.

In the entire manuscript period, however, scrolls have remained in use in the Islamic realm as vehicles for special texts, e.g. genealogies, amulets and prayers, and for special features such as micrography. The common proportions of the Islamic manuscript are vertically orientated, meaning that its height is larger than its width. Only during a relatively short period of time, Kūfic Ḳurʾānic manuscripts are known to have been made exclusively in an oblong format. A tendency in Western Islam seems to have been to produce manuscripts in an almost square format, or at least with less difference between height and width than was commonly done in the East. Yet another shape, which was in use for notebooks, is the *safīna*. Its architecture is that of an oblong-shaped book, but it is used in a vertical position, the sewing of the leaves being in the top edge, very much as present-day noteblocks.

Whereas there developed an extensive indigenous paper production in the Islamic East and West, this only seems to have lasted till the end of the 9th/15th century. Islamic papers had no watermarks, but different types of chain lines in the paper can be distinguished. Sometimes the paper mould of Middle Eastern paper makers must have had such a fine sieve that no marks at all are visible in the structure of the indigenous paper. Natural, vegetal, components are often visible in this type of paper. Especially the older "medieval" papers have a certain thickness, sometimes verging on cardboard quality (which is particularly the case with one of the very oldest dated Arabic manuscripts on paper, the Leiden manuscript Or. 298, *G͟harīb al-ḥadīt͟h* by Abū ʿUbayd al-Qāsim b. Sallām, which dates from 252/866). Papers are often coloured, usually shades of brown or cream, whereas paper of different colours (bluish, pink) was often used to liven up a quire. By the end of the 9th/15th century, paper production had developed a firm footing in the countries across the Mediterranean, most notably in Italy. It was from there that increasingly paper was exported to the Middle East, and to such an extent that the indigenous industry became almost extinct. Only paper of very coarse quality continued to be made locally, and this was seldom used for the manufacture of the handwritten book. The Italian papers were often provided with downright Islamic watermarks, such as the *trelune*, the three crescents, or with watermarks that were not offensive to Muslims. Crosses, crowns or coats of arms of unbelieving kings in watermarks were apparently avoided in papers destined for export to Islamic countries. These imported papers were often given an extra touch, such as an extra coating, a slight colouring and a thorough polishing, so that they would have the same appearance as the earlier indigenously produced papers, which would make them more attractive to Muslims.

As a necessary by-product of the codex, the Islamic art of bookbinding (A., *tasfīr*) developed. The typical Islamic binding of the "classical" period consists of a full leather binding with a flap covering the fore-edge. The boards and flap often have a blind or gold stamped ornament in geometric shape. It might be rewarding if ornaments on Islamic bookbindings could be studied in comparison with those on Oriental carpets. Sometimes the title of the book is stamped on the outer side of the flap, but usually it is written with ink on the lower edge of the paper. Books were stored in a flat position on book shelves, and that is how their titles could be read. In a later period and more to the East (Persia and beyond, from around the 18th century onwards) also lacquer bindings were used. For Ḳurʾān manuscripts, especially those divided into a number of *ad͟jzāʾ*, special types of furniture, cases, boxes and the like developed. About the production of ink we are reasonably well informed [see MIDĀD], but there is hardly any information on the practical use of different types of ink in Islamic manuscripts. There exists in Islam an extensive technical literature on the making of handwritten books, the manufacture of bookbindings and the production of inks.

(c) *Palaeographical aspects of the manuscript.* In the course of time, important and significant developments in the styles of writing of the Arabic script can be distinguished [see K͟HAṬṬ. ii, iii]. These can roughly be divided into a number of periods, and, in the later period, into geographically defined styles. The script employed in a handwritten book can, therefore, be used as a tool for the determination of the age and origin of a manuscript. From the methodological point of view, however, it must be added that the style of script is but one of a number of determining factors, and that it can, at best, be used as a corroborating argument, only in combination with other codicological and philological evidence. A holistic approach in this respect is the only safe way of looking at the handwritten book.

The discussion on the Arabic script must begin with the mention of the pre-Islamic development of the Nabataean script in and around the Arabian peninsula, which is only known from epigraphic evidence. There are no Islamic manuscripts written in this script. It is the direct forebear of the Arabic script which was used in Mecca and Medina in the first half of the 7th century A.D. to note down the divine revelation. Its basic set of graphemes had probably come into use in the Ḥidjāz around the middle of the 6th century A.D. There are reports by early Islamic historians pointing to another, ʿIrāḳī, origin of the Arabic script, but concrete evidence for this is entirely lacking. In the early Islamic period, the geometrically stylised and highly monumentalised calligraphic script of the Ḳurʾān manuscripts developed into several sub-styles. The original manuscript of the ʿUthmanic recension of the Ḳurʾān—the first book in Islam—and its direct copies do not appear to have been preserved, nor any other of the manuscripts of early texts, notebooks and registers, for that matter. Only Arabic papyri give contemporary evidence for this stage in the development of the Arabic script.

The best distinguished types of these so-called Kufic styles of writing are *māʾil* (used in the Ḥidjāz in the 2nd/8th century, with its characteristically right-leaning shafts), *mashḳ* (used in the Ḥidjāz and Syria, with its typically horizontal extensions, mainly for Ḳurʾān manuscripts and always in oblong format), western Kūfī (with round shapes) and eastern Kūfī (also called *ḳarmāṭī*, with its typically edgy forms). Later direct developments of these Kūfī script styles are *maghribī* (used in al-Andalus and till the present day in the Maghrib [*q.v.*]) and *sūdānī* (used in sub-Saharan West Africa). The Kūfī and Ḥidjāzī styles, in turn, developed in the central lands of Islam into several types of bookhands. These can be seen in the (not too numerous) dated manuscripts which have survived from the 3rd/9th and 4th/10th centuries. Comparative evidence for these, now obsolete and somewhat archaic-looking bookhands is adduced in the older Christian Arabic manuscripts of that period, although the dated ones in this group appear to be even more scarce than the Islamic ones. There is no survey of this corpus of manuscripts. Only quite recently, François Déroche has succeeded in producing a more detailed typology of the script in early Ḳurʾān manuscripts on the basis of the collection in the Bibliothèque Nationale in Paris. Application of this typology to other collections, most notably the *Şam Evrakı* in Istanbul and the fragments found in the Great Mosque of Ṣanʿāʾ, seems promising.

At the same time there developed from the earliest period of Islam onwards, for daily life purposes, mainly in Arabic papyri of administrative and occasionally also literary contents, cursive styles of scripts, in which the protoforms of the later classical styles of script can already be distinguished. The canonisation of these cursives into well-regulated and respectable calligraphic forms is in the Arabic tradition usually connected with the names of famous calligraphers such as the ʿAbbāsid *wazīr* Ibn Muḳla (died 328/939 [*q.v.*]) and Ibn al-Bawwāb (died 423/1032 [*q.v.*]), who are said to have invented these styles of writing and to have laid down their rules of orientation and proportion. There is a problem of authenticity of evidence, however. The description of the different calligraphic styles is, in most cases, not based on authentic models originating from the great calligraphers themselves or even from their lifetime, but rather on reports by historians such as Ibn al-Nadīm or al-Ḳalḳashandī [*q.vv.*]. The models that are available are often reconstructions and interpretations by later calligraphers.

The classical six styles of calligraphy, called *al-aḳlām al-sitta*, which developed near the end of the 4th/10th century, are *naskh* (the most often used style of writing, the common indication for "bookhand", in which many styles can be distinguished, and—after a long development—the forebear of present-day printing type fonts of Arabic), *thuluth* (a monumental and decorative script which is used for titles, inscriptions, calligraphic panels and the like, but hardly ever to copy entire texts), *muḥaḳḳaḳ* (till the 8th/15th century in use for calligraphic Ḳurʾān copies), *rayḥānī* (a smaller and more slender version of *muḥaḳḳaḳ*), *tawḳīʿ* (used in the ʿAbbāsid chanceries, a script with round and flowing shapes with many interconnections) and *riḳāʿ* (a smaller version of *tawḳīʿ*, mostly used in titles, *sūra* headings, colophons and diplomas (*idjāza* [*q.v.*]). About the first of these six classical styles, *naskh*, the bookhand, it must be added that this is, in fact, an unworkable category. In the 4th-5th/10th-11th centuries *naskh* was a clearly distinguished style of writing, but in the course of time numerous styles of writing, which are very much different from one another, have been designated as *naskh*, thereby making the term itself useless.

The most important later, regionally distinguished styles are *taʿlīḳ* (a development of *tawḳīʿ* and used in important documents and diplomas; there are two variants, Persian *taʿlīḳ* and Ottoman *taʿlīḳ*), *nastaʿlīḳ* (originated in the 8th-9th/14th-15th centuries as a mixture of *naskh* and *taʿlīḳ* and is now very much in use in Iran and the Indian subcontinent), *shikasta* (a highly cursive style developed from *taʿlīḳ* and *nastaʿlīḳ*, and now mostly in use in Iran, where it has become a means of expression of the new Islamic Iranian identity), *dīwānī* (developed in the Ottoman chanceries, of uncertain origin and in the Arab world still in use for decorative epigraphy), *dīwānī djalī* (a decorative variant of Ottoman *taʿlīḳ*), *ruḳʿa* (an edgy cursive style with remarkable contrast between thick and thin which developed in the end of the 12th/18th century in the Ottoman Empire and which has reached calligraphic peaks. A more common variant of this script has now become the cursive for daily use throughout the Middle East) and *siyāḳa* (a curious stenographic-like Arabic script in which diacritics are not used; it is of uncertain origin and was in use in the lower administrative echelons of the Ottoman Empire for cash registers [see DAFTAR] and the like). See for a more extensive description of the characteristics of these styles of writing, KHAṬṬ. ii, iii.

(d) *The manuscript as the medium of transmission of texts.* It should be borne in mind that, throughout the history of Islamic literatures, manuscripts have been abundantly available. They were never a rare commodity, though not all texts were available at all places at all times. The numbers given for the contents of royal libraries, exaggerated as they may seem and often are, are nevertheless a sign that numerous manuscripts were found there. Private collections of manuscripts, often with large and important holdings, were, and still are, a common feature in the Islamic world. Their existence was often guaranteed by converting them into a *waḳf* [*q.v.*]. The fact that a literary or theological education has always been an honorable pursuit and rewarding occupation for a Muslim has added to this. One can maintain that the combination of scholarly activities with texts and the respect for the book has resulted in this stupendous accumulation in Islam of handwritten books. They are in fact so numerous that their number in millions cannot precisely be estimated. The first effort ever to make a complete bibliographical survey of all Islamic manuscripts in the world is being undertaken by the London-based Al-Furqan Islamic Heritage Foundation, which was founded by Sheikh Ahmad Zaki Yamani. The publication by this Foundation of a

World survey of Islamic manuscripts has been in progress since 1992. It is an inventorisation of all known and as yet unknown collections containing Islamic manuscript materials, not only in Arabic, Persian and Turkish, but in a great number of other languages as well, including numerous materials in scripts other than Arabic.

The progress of bibliography can be illustrated by an example taken from Arabic literature. The Ottoman Turkish bibliographer Ḥādjdjī Khalīfa (died 1067/1657 [see KĀTIB ČELEBI]) mentioned around 15,000 titles in his great bibliography, *Kashf al-ẓunūn*. Almost three centuries later, Carl Brockelmann mentions around 25,000 different titles in the index of his *Geschichte der arabischen Litteratur*. Brockelmann's figures concern titled works that have been preserved. Now, almost fifty years after Brockelmann, these figures must probably be multiplied by several times, due to the enormous growth of cataloguing activities in the past years.

The view by Pedersen, *The Arabic book*, 20, that scholarly activities were mainly centred on the mosque [see also MASDJID] is too narrow, even if it is exclusively applied to the pursuit of the theological sciences. Writing, reading, discussing, commenting upon books (and buying and selling them as well!) were mostly private activities which were widespread in all periods of time and in many strata of Islamic civilisation, but not primarily in a purely religious connection. With a Book as its distinguishing miracle, Islam was—one may say—bound to devote special attention and a central position to the book as a source of learning, and, thereby, give learning itself a special emphasis. It may be surmised that literacy was relatively high among Muslims and producing texts must have been a common occupation in an Islamic environment. The ensuing interrelatedness of different texts on the same subject is a problem with which philologists must try to cope.

These scholarly activities involved the copying of manuscripts and the transmission of texts. This could happen in many ways. Many manuscripts carry on their title-pages, in their margins or near their colophons information on their readership (*samāʿāt, ḳirāʾāt*), on the authorisation to use a certain text (*idjāza*), or on its chain of transmission (*riwāya*). Manuscripts often reveal traces of their collation (*muḳābala*) with the exemplar (*aṣl*), and sometimes with other copies as well. All these marks provide an insight in the use and manufacture of a handwritten book. They are hardly less important for our knowledge of the status of a text than the text of the manuscript itself.

The production of the handwritten book was, in most cases, a private affair between author or teacher and reader or student. Anyone who wished to own a manuscript either had to buy it, or to borrow and copy it if it was not for sale. If he wished to read it with the author or a respected authority in the field, he often had to travel around (*ṭalab al-ʿilm*). In Islamic higher education it was not uncommon that students noted down (*istimlāʾ* [see MUSTAMLĪ]) what their teacher dictated (*imlāʾ*) from his own work to them, with the casual remarks of the author often written in the margin (sometimes provided with the note *min fam al-muṣannif*, "from the mouth of the author"). From this it is clear that scriptoria of the mediaeval European type were not a common source of book production in the Islamic realm. It is known, however, that for a quick and multiple publication of a text in the manuscript era mass dictation was used. The exact circumstances of this type of mass production of manuscripts are unknown.

Royal or noble patronage made it possible that lavishly illustrated or illuminated manuscripts were produced, often in magnificent bindings, and from the Ottoman and Mughal sultans it is known that they instituted palace workshops for the production of royal copies of important texts.

(e) *The end of the manuscript era*. The art of printing became widespread in the Middle East only in the course of the 19th century, although it had been practiced by Muslims in Istanbul since 1729 [see MAṬBAʿA. B.2]. In the end, printing superseded copying by hand. The age of transition is in this respect the 19th century. It can be observed that the manufacture and distribution of texts took place, for a while, in the shape of printed and handwritten books simultaneously. This could even mean that manuscripts were copied from printed exemplars. Those authors who had, for whatever reason, no access to the new medium of printing were more or less obliged to revert to the traditional, time-proven way of copying by hand, for the distribution of their texts. In course of time this decreased. The outward appearance of the manuscript had its direct influence on the typographical design of the early printed book. This is particularly evident from the lithograph editions, of which many have been made in the Islamic world. Lithography involves a minimum of technical requirements and therefore became immensely popular, notably in India, Persia and Morocco, to name but the best-known areas. But also the Egyptian editions from Būlāḳ, made with movable type, betray in their lay-out their handwritten models.

Bibliography: M. Beit-Arié, *Hebrew codicology. Tentative typology of technical practices employed in Hebrew dated manuscripts*[2], Jerusalem 1981; G. Bosch, J. Carswell and G. Petherbridge, *Islamic bindings and bookmaking*, Chicago 1981; F. Déroche, *Les manuscrits du Coran. Aux origines de la calligraphie coranique*, Paris 1983; idem (ed.), *Les manuscrits du Moyen-Orient*. Actes du Colloque d'Istanbul, Istanbul-Paris 1989; idem, *The Abbasid tradition. Qurʾans of the 8th to the 10th centuries AD*, in J. Raby (ed.), *The Nasser D. Khalili collection of Islamic art*, London 1992; G. Endress, *Handschriftenkunde*, in W. Fischer (ed.), *Grundriss der arabischen Philologie*, Band I. *Sprachwissenschaft*, Wiesbaden 1982, 271-96; idem, *Die arabische Schrift*, in *ibid.*, 165-97; A. Gacek, *A select bibliography of Arabic language publications concerning Arabic manuscripts*, in *MME*, i (1986), 106-8; B. Gray (ed.), *The arts of the book in Central Asia. 14th-16th centuries*, Paris-London 1979; A. Grohman, *Arabische Paläographie*, Teil I-II, Vienna 1967-71; D. Haldane, *Islamic bookbindings in the Victoria and Albert Museum*, London 1983; Mohamed A. Hussein, *Vom Papyrus zum Codex*, Leipzig 1970; D. James, *The master scribes. Qurʾans of the 10th to 14th centuries AD,* and idem, *After Timur. Qurʾans of the 15th and 16th centuries*, in *The Nasser D. Khalili collection of Islamic art*, ii-iii, London 1992; M. Levey, *Mediaeval Arabic bookmaking and its relation to early chemistry and pharmacology*, Philadelphia 1962; J. Pedersen, *The Arabic book*, Princeton 1984; Y. Porter, *Peinture et art du livre*, Paris-Tehran 1992; G. Roper (ed.), *World Survey of Islamic manuscripts* (in progress), London 1992- ; F. Rosenthal, *The technique and approach of Muslim scholarship*, Rome 1947; Y.H. Safadi, *Islamic calligraphy*, London 1978; Annemarie Schimmel, *Die Schriftarten und ihr kalligraphischer Gebrauch*, in *Gr. ar. Ph.*, i, 198-209; eadem, *Calligraphy and Islamic culture*, New York-London 1984; R. Sellheim, *The cataloguing of Arabic manuscripts as a literary problem*, in *Oriens*, xxiii-xxiv (1974), 306-11; J.J. Witkam, *Arabic Manuscripts in the Library of the University of Leiden ... A General Introduction to the Catalogue*, Leiden 1982; and idem, *Establishing the stemma. Fact or fiction?*, in *MME*, iii (1988), 88-100. The scholarly journals *Islamic Art, Manuscripts of the Middle East* and *Muqarnas* contain articles on many aspects of the Islamic handwritten book. Electronic databases on codicological aspects of Middle Eastern manuscripts are maintained by M. Beit-Arié (Hebrew manuscripts) and François Déroche (early Islamic manuscripts).

(J.J. Witkam)

2. In Indonesia

Naskah designates here old manuscripts, Islamic or otherwise, alongside indigenous-language terms which designate the literary form and the basic text (*ḥikayat, carita, kidung, babad, serat tarikh sejarah, wawacan, pus(t)aka, pustaha)* and also the original text before being printed. Islam brought the Arabic script of the Ḳurʾān and the Arabic words necessary for its teaching. On the model of the extra characters added to the Arabic alphabet for Persian, Turkish and Urdu, Arabic characters were adapted for the vernaculars, and were called *pegon*, *jawi* or *melayu*, for these, see INDONESIA. iii. Languages, and for the *pegon* script of West Java, see H. Sukanda, *Agama Islam ngabudayakeun Basa jeung Sastra Sunda*, in *Kongres Bahasa Sunda,* Bogor 1988. The ways of writing have not been codified, but one can distinguish two sorts of scribes: the graduates of a *pesantren* [*q.v.*] and those of a *paguron* (Sukanda-Tessier, *Centres d'enseignements traditionnels de l'Islam...* , in *Séminaire Kiyai Haji Wasyid*, Banten 1988). (The term "Nusantarian", from Nusantara, is now used for all cultural matters relating to pre-Independen (17 August 1945) Indonesia, the term "Indonesian" being used only for post-1945 matters.)

The manuscripts in indigenous scripts correspond to three socio-cultural strata, distinguished as follows: (1) The pre-Islamic mss. have as their bases olla, *lontar*, palm leaves, *nipah*, tree bark prepared for writing, *daluwang*, thin sheets of bamboo, gold leaf or sheets of red copper. The characters used, of Indian origin, are called *aksara* (Balinese, Bugi/Makasar/Bima, Javanese/Kawi, Sumatranese (Batak, Karo, Lampung, Mandailing, Rejang, Toba), Sasak, Old Javanese, Old Malay and Old Sundanese, corresponding to the respective languages. The oldest texts, in Old Javanese, come from the 12th-14th centuries, and in Old Sundanese from the middle of the 15th century (see J. Noorduyn, *Bujangga Manik*, in *BKI* [1982]). There are numerous catalogues and critical editions of Malay and Javanese mss., but the Old Sundanese ones present difficulties of decipherment not yet completely resolved, neither for those in the Manuscript Collection of the National Library at Jakarta and in foreign collections nor for those in numerous special collections in Indonesia and the *kabuyutan* (Sukanda-Tessier, *Le triomphe de Sri en pays soundanais*, in *PEFEO*, ci [Paris 1977]).

(2) The Islamic mss. have the same materials, with the following chronology: olla, 15th-18th centuries; tree bark, 16th-19th centuries; filigrained European papers, 17th-20th centuries; Dutch registers, local folio papers and note books, 19th-20th centuries. The Ḳurʾān, *ḥadīt͟h*, the combined precepts of the *rukun (al)-Islam* and *rukun (al)-Iman (share'at), fiḳh (safīnat ul-nad͟jā, farāʾiḍ* and *duʿā)* are written in Arabic characters. Works on Ṣūfism, *tarekat Satariyah* and *Kodiriyah, duʿā, sulūk, ʿilmu (l)-ladunī, adab*, Arabic hagiography and epics of the Islamisation of Java/Malay, Javanese and Sundanese chronicles, not to mention an important corpus of works on the *ʿilmu falak*, cosmogony, medicinal plants, customs, rites and ancestral prayers linked to the agricultural round, calendars and propitiatory formulae of Hindo-Buddhist origin, are all written in *pegon*. The Islamic mss. are numbered in thousands, whether Malay from the various sultanates of Sumatra, Malaysia, Kalimantan, Maluku, Sulawesi and Lombok/Sumba/Sumbawa, or Sundanese from the sultanal courts of Banten and Cirebon or the princely ones of Banten, Galuh/Banyumas and Sumedang regions, or Javanese from the sultanates of Pajang, Demak, Mataram, Surakarta and Yogyakarta, or Balinese. The oldest of them, mostly from S͟hāfiʿī milieux, come from the beginning of the 16th century, including those of Sumatra and Banten. A large number of them are concerned with *taṣawwuf* [*q.v.*] and *ʿilm al-uṣūl*, whilst the *fiḳh* texts are comparatively few, contrary to the tendency visible from the second quarter of the 20th century and assimilated to a "fourth" wave of Islamisation. The Old Javanese mss. only stem from West Java from the middle of the 17th century onwards, legitimated by the sultanate of Mataram. Some of them, recopied in the course of Islamisation—a process which lasted for several centuries—contain a few Arabic words, such as *mas͟hhūr, sarwāl, wafāt, Nabī Muḥammad*, and are written in *aksara*.

(3) The first epics about Islamisation stem from pre-Islamic epics, oral and manuscript, salvaged by Islam from the 15th century onwards. Written in *aksara* on *lontar*, such as *Carita Nabī Yūsuf*, they represent a type of *daʿwa* through the didactic aspect of their message, which is no longer delivered in the form of a harangue or sermon. The heroes are of Arab origin, such as Amir Hamdjah, Umarmaya, Lukmanul Hakim, Sama'un, Ahmad Muhammad, ('ab) Durrahman-('ab)Durrahim, Abu(n) Nawas, or Malay, such as Hang Tuah, Ken Tambuhan, Indraputra and Muhammad Hanafiah, or Sundanese like Silihwangi, Kean Santang, Ogin Amarsakti, Munding Sari Wiramantri, Hasanuddin and Walangsungsang, or Javanese like Damarwulan, Candrakirana, Rara Mendut, Sekartaji, Sunan Rahmat, Raden Patah and Senapati. The historical texts recount either the first contacts with Islam (?12th-15th centuries), which met with strong resistance in West Java, or else the second Islamisation (16th century), which only affected the northern coastlands of Java and the merchant sultanates outside Java, or else the third wave of Islamisation (17th to the beginning of the 20th century).

These epics belong to a living tradition of the preservation of writings. For the scribes who copy them, the readers, reciters and listeners, they are a *amal* and a *ganjaran (baraka)* which will earn merit in the Next Life, just like good acts which are non-obligatory, *sunna*, which can entail the pardoning of sins, or the equivalent of *ʿibāda*. These much-revered epic texts are read and chanted in West Java from sunset to sunrise according to *belŭk*, a vocal art which is in course of disappearing, marking religious, family and agrarian rites, and they are hedged by a narrow surveillance when, if they are very ancient ones, they were considered as sacred and preserved in the *kabuyutan* where they could only be seen at every twelfth *Mulud* (12 Rabīʿ I), together with ancient Arabic mss.

The indigenous Indonesian mss., which are of an unusual richness and number, have contributed extensively to unifying an entire nation in respect of the vast spread of differing religions and cultures. They have, moreover, given to Indonesian Islam its exceptional image of tolerance and examplariness.

Bibliography: This is voluminous, and only the main catalogues will be mentioned. T. Behrend, *Katalog Induk Naskah Museum Radio Pustoko*, Jakarta 1990; J.L.A. Brandes, *Beschrijving der Javaansche, Balineesche en Sasaksche hds ... Batavia*, 4 vols., 1901-26; *Catalogue des mss. soundanais*, Afd. Oosterse Handschriften, U.B. Leiden (ms.); *Collection of Sundanese mss. in the National Library of Australia*, Canberra 1973 (ms.); E.S. Ekadjati *et alii*, *Naskah Sunda: inventaire et liste*, Bandung 1988; N. Girardet *et alii*, *Descriptive catalogue of the Javanese manuscripts...*, Wiesbaden 1983; Y. Jusuf and Tuti Munawar, *Katalog Koleksi Naskah Melayu*, Jakarta 1982; idem, *Katalogus Koleksi Naskah Kitab Babad Museum Pusat*, Jakarta 1973; Y. Yusuf, *Katalogus Naskah-Naskah Sunda di Museum Pusat*, Jakarta n.d.; H.H. Juynboll, *Catalogus van de Maleische en Sundaneesche Handschriften der Leidsche Univ.-Bibliotheek*, Leiden 1899; idem, *Suppl. op den Catal. van de Sundaneesche Hand...*, Leiden 1912; F.H. van Naerssen, Th.G.Th. Pigeaud and P. Voorhoeve, *Catalogue of Indonesian mss.*, Copenhagen 1977; Partini Sardjono *et alii*, *Naskah Sunda Kuno*, Bandung 1987; Pigeaud, *Literature of Java*, The Hague, 4 vols., 1967-80; R.M.Ng. Poerbatjaraka, *Beschrijving der Hand. Menak*, Bandoeng 1940; idem, Voorhoeve and C. Hooykaas, *Indonesische Handschriften*, Bandung 1950; M.C. Ricklefs, *An inventory of the Javanese mss. coll. in the British Museum*, in *BKI*, cxxv (1969); idem and Voorhoeve, *Indonesian mss. in Great Britain...*, Oxford 1977; Ph.S. Ronkel, *Catalog. der Mal. Hand. in het Museum van het B.G....*, in *VBG*, lvii (1909); idem, *Suppl. to the catal. of the Arabic mss. ...*, Batavia 1913; Rosad Amidjaja *et alii*, *Naskah kuno yang bersifat keagamaan di Kec. Banjaran*, Bandung 1982; G.P. Rouffaer and W.C. Muller, *Catalogus der Koloniale Bibl. van het KITLV*, The Hague 1908; Rd. Memed. Sastrahadiprawira, *Korte inhoud en Lijst van de in de Bibl. van het B.G. en in de Catal. voorkomende Soendase mss.*, Batavia 1928 (ms.); Sukanda-Tessier and Hasan Muarif Ambary, *Katalog raisonné Naskah Islam di Jawa Barat*, Jakarta 1992 (in press); Voorhoeve, *Handlist of Arabic mss. in the Library of the Univ. of Leiden...*, Leiden 1957; idem, *Les mss. malais de la Bibliothèque Nationale de Paris*, in *Archipel*, vi, Bandung 1973; A.C. Vreede, *Catalogus van de Javaansche en Madoereesche hds...*, Leiden 1892; Y. Yogaswara, *Naskah dan Kitab Lama Cisondari*, Bandung 1976. (VIVIANE SUKANDA-TESSIER)

NUṢRATĀBĀD, the more recent name for the town of eastern Persia known in mediaeval Islamic times as Isfīdh, Sipih, Safīdj (written in al-Iṣṭakhrī and Ibn Ḥawḳal as Sanīdj, for *Sabīdj/Safīdj). It lay on what was the highway from Kirmān to Sīstān [*q.vv.*], and some of the classical Islamic geographers attributed it administratively to Sīstān and others to Kirmān, reflecting its position on the frontier between these two provinces. Muḳaddasī and others describe it as a flourishing and populous town with its water from *ḳanāt*s, the only town in the Great Desert. The ruins of the old town were still called by the local Balūč nomads, according to Sykes (1895), Ispi. Its modern successor Nuṣratābād (lat. 29°54′ N., long. 59°59′ E.), on the Kirmān-Bam-Zāhidān road, is the chef-lieu of a *bakhsh* or subdistrict of the same name in the *shahrastān* of Zāhidān; in *ca.* 1960 it had a population of 700 Balūč.

This Nuṣratābād is to be distinguished from the town of the same name in Sīstān proper, in the 19th century the administrative centre of the region and the modern Shahr-i Zābul; for this, see SĪSTĀN.

Bibliography: Iṣṭakhrī, 162; Ibn Ḥawḳal, ed. Kramers, 402-3, 413, 423, tr. 393, 402, 410; Muḳaddasī, 495; *Ḥudūd al-ʿālam*, tr. 125, s.v. Sibih, com. 375; Yāḳūt, *Buldān*, ed. Beirut, i, 180, s.v. Asfīdh, iii, 269, s.v. Sanīḥ (*sic*); Sir Percy Sykes, *Ten thousand miles in Persia*, London 1902, 36, 416; Le Strange, *Lands*, 325-6; Schwarz, *Iran im Mittelalter*, 250-1; A. Gabriel, *Die Erforschung Persiens*, Vienna 1952, index s.v. Nasratabad (Sipih); Razmārā, *Farhang-i djughrāfiyā-yi Īrān*, viii, 410-11. (C.E. BOSWORTH)

NUṢRATĪ, MUḤAMMAD NUṢRAT, Deccani Urdu poet of the 11th/17th century, whose work marks a stage in the history of Urdu language and literature. Born in the Carnatic as a relative of the ruling family there, he at first lived as a dervish but then moved to Bīdjāpūr [*q.v.*], where he became an official and the poet-laureate of the ʿĀdil-Shāhī ʿAlī II b. Muḥammad (1066-83/1656-72 [see ʿĀDIL-SHĀHS]. He wrote many poems, including *ḳaṣīda*s and *ghazal*s, but more especially a number of *mathnawī*s of substantial length. The most important of these was his *ʿAlī-nāma*, a eulogy of his patron and the history of his wars with the Mughals and Marāthās [*q.vv.*], and this he claimed to be a new form, an amalgam of Hindu and Persian epics; Sadiq, 48, states that this was no idle claim. His romantic *mathnawī*s include the *Gulshan-i ʿishk*, *Guldasta-yi ʿishk* and *Taʾrīkh-i Iskandarī*.

The language of this poetry is archaic and difficult compared with modern Urdu, and characterised by hyperbole and conceits, but according to Saksena, 40, sweet, flowing and melodious.

Bibliography: Ram Babu Saksena, *A history of Urdu literature*, Allah-abad 1927, 12, 39-40; Muhammad Sadiq, *A history of Urdu literature*, Oxford 1964, 46-9. (J.A. HAYWOOD)

NUṢUB (A.), pl. *anṣāb*, Hebrew *maṣṣebōt*. The plural, more often used, denotes the blocks of stone on which the blood of the victims sacrificed for idols (*awthān*, *aṣnām*) was poured, as well as sepulchral stones and those marking out the sacred enclosure (*ḥimā*) of the sanctuary (cf. J. Wellhausen, *Reste*², 101-2; W. Robertson Smith, *Religion of the Semites*, 201 ff.). In nomadic circles, the *nuṣub* has been regarded in a few rare instances as the symbol of the divinity (cf. Ibn Saʿd, *Ṭabaḳāt*, iv/1, 159-60; R. Dozy, *Essai sur l'histoire de l'Islamisme*, translated from the Dutch by V. Chauvin, Paris-Leiden 1879, 9, quoting, after Ibn Ḳutayba, a contemporary of the Prophet, Abū Radjāʾ al-ʿUṭāridī. For the two examples, see T. Fahd, *Panthéon*, 26). Among sedentary populations, the *nuṣub*, a rough stone, has become the *ṣanam*, "a stone carved with the image of the idols of the Kaʿba" (Yāḳūt, *Buldān*, iv, 622: *fa-nahata-hu ʿalā ṣūrat aṣnām al-Bayt*). "In every house", writes Ibn Hishām, "the occupants took an idol (*ṣanam*) which they worshipped. Whenever one of them set out on a journey, the last thing which he did before leaving, and the first on his return, was to touch it" (*Sīra*, 54 = al-Azraḳī, *Akhbār*, 78: *tamassaḥa bihi*; cf. Gen. xxxi, 14), as a token of benediction for a successful enterprise and as an act of thanksgiving (on the *masḥ* and its magical and therapeutic power, see Ibn Saʿd, ii/2, 14, 47; Goldziher, in *Or. Stud. Th. Nöldeke gewidmet*, i, 327, where numerous references to *ḥadīth* are to be found). To explain the proliferation of *anṣāb*, Ibn Hishām (51-2) makes them symbols of the Kaʿba, brought with them by the sons of Ishmael when they finally left Mecca, while Yāḳūt (iv, 622) asserts that "the cult of stones among the Arabs in their encampments has its origin in their deep attachment to the idols (*aṣnām*) of the *ḥaram*." These texts reflect a state of affairs prior to the reform of Ḳuṣayy [*q.v.*]. Comparing them with certain Biblical texts, one should in fact, regard them as an echo of very ancient Semitic traditions (in particular, Gen. xxxi, 13, 19, 34-46). The *teraphīm* of the Canaanites, the *elōhīm* of the Hebrews and the *ilānī* of the Assyrians long outlasted monotheism in the shrines fashioned in stone, in sand mixed with milk (*Panthéon*, 91) and in wood (Ibn Hishām, 335) of pagan Arabia (on the equivalence between *elōhīm*, *teraphīm* and *ilānī*, cf. C. Gordon, *Parallèles Nouzéens aux lois et coutumes de l'Ancient Testament*, in *RB*, xliv [1935], 35-6; idem, in *JBL*, liv [1935], 139-44; cf. *Divination*, 132-50). Among the commonest finds in archaeological excavations are figurines representing "new divinities" worshipped in Egypt, Palestine, Syria and Babylonia (cf. among others, Petrie, *Memphis*, i, pls. 8-13 and p. 7; E. Pilz, in *ZDPV*, xlvii, 165 ff.; J.B. Pritchard, *Palestine figurines in relation to certain goddesses*, 5-31; Parrot, *Sumer*, 238 and *passim*; idem, *Assur*, 250 and *passim*; J.B. Connelly, *Votive offerings from hellenistic Failaka: evidence for Herakles cult*, in *L'Arabie préislamique et son environnement historique et culturel*, Leiden 1989, 145-58).

The cult of stones, deeply rooted among the Arabs of the Ḥidjāz, was not transformed as quickly as elsewhere into a cult of statues. It was in the mid-3rd century A.D. that Nabataean and Syro-Palestinian influences had the effect of promoting, in urban centres, the representational phase of the Arab pantheon; it was only then that the sacred stone became an idol. Wellhausen rightly asserts that "Die Bilder sind nicht echt arabischen; *wathan* und *çanam* sind importierte Worte und importierte Dinge" (*Reste*^{2}, 102). Henceforward, the *ṣanam*, made of wood (Ibn Hishām, 303) gradually took the place of the *nuṣub* made of stone. ʿIkrima, the son of Abū Djahl, Muḥammad's greatest enemy, was a maker of idols; merchants offered these to the Bedouin who purchased them and set them up in their tents. In Mecca, there was not a single house which did not have its own idol (al-Azraḳī, *Akhbār Makka*, 77-8).

After the triumph of Christianity in the Orient, the Ḥidjāz remained the sole bastion of paganism; carvers of idols could still make a living there. It comes as no surprise to find that at the time of Muḥammad's arrival in Mecca there were three hundred and sixty idols in the Kaʿba (al-Azraḳī, 77; Ibn al-Athīr, ii, 192), a number which probably has a symbolic significance but which confirms an abundance well corroborated by other sources.

The process of expansion of the cult of idols is described by Ibn al-Kalbī in the following terms: "The Arabs devoted themselves to the cult of idols: some constructed a sanctuary (*bayt*; regarding this term see *Divination*, 132 ff.), others acquired an idol (*ṣanam*); anyone who could neither possess an idol nor have a sanctuary constructed would set up a stone of his choice, facing the *ḥaram* or some other place, and then he would perform processions around it, as in the sanctuary (of Mecca). These stones were called *anṣāb* (as opposed to) *aṣnām* and *awthān*, which were statues (*tamāthīl*), and the procession made around them was called *dawār*" (*K. al-Aṣnām*, ed. Aḥmad Zakī Pasha, Cairo 1914, 21, quoted in *Panthéon*, 59). On this evolution and the various names given to the idols, see the summary of a *Kitāb al-Aṣnām* by al-Djāḥiẓ, no longer available, in his *K. al-Ḥayawān*, i, 5; this information is also presented in *Divination*, 249-50.

Thus the *anṣāb* are represented as replicas of the Black Stone of the Kaʿba. They take on the form of sacred stones in nomadic and semi-nomadic societies. The contribution of sedentary civilisations reinforces and enriches the cults and the rites of the nomads, but at the same time introduces confusion and adds to the difficulties facing the historian of religions, who is inclined to seek out connections and influences and to establish comparisons and similarities (*Panthéon*, 182).

Nevertheless, whatever were the forms given to the divinities of the Arab pantheon, the Arab religions retained their quite primitive internal structure. The development of the "artistic" representation of gods had no effect on the conceptual evolution of the cult. The present writer's study, in *Le panthéon de l'Arabie Centrale à la veille de l'hégire*, illustrates the static nature of the Arab religions, rooted in a desert environment.

Bibliography: The material contained in this article is borrowed for the most part from T. Fahd, *Panthéon*, Paris 1968, and from the same author's *La divination arabe. Études religieuses, sociologiques et folkloriques sur le milieu natif de l'Islam*, Leiden 1966, ^{2}Paris 1987. Abundant references and quotations relating to the subject are to be found in these two works. Other sources include W.W. Baudissin, *Über die Entwicklung des Gottesbegriffs in den Religionen der semitischen Völker, mit Nachträgen*, Giessen 1929; C. Brockelmann, *Allah und die Götzen. Der Ursprung des islamischen Monotheismus*, in *ARW*, xi (1923), 92-121; E. Dhorme, *Religion primitive des Sémites*, in *RHR*, cxxviii (1944), 1-27; idem, *Les religions arabes préislamiques*, review of G. Ryckmanns, in *ibid.*, cxxxiii (1947), 34-48 (*Recueil Ed. Dhorme*, Paris 1951, 736 ff.); A. Jamme, *Le panthéon sud-arabe préislamique d'après les sources épigraphiques*, in *Le Muséon*, lx (1947), 57-147; L. Krehl, *Über die Religion der vorislamischen Araber*, Leipzig 1863 (study of a page of al-Shahrastānī, *Milal*, ed. Cureton, 432); H. Lammens, *Le culte des Bétyles et les processions religieuses chez les Arabes préislamites*, in *BIFAO*, xvii (1919-20), 39-101; idem, *Les sanctuaires préislamites dans l'Arabie Occidentale*, in *MUSJ*, xi (1926), 39-173; G. Ryckmans, *Les religions arabes préislamiques*, ^{2}1953 (*Bibl. du Muséon* 26/1951) = Quillet, *Hist. gen. des religions*, ^{2}Paris 1960, ii, 199-228; J. Starcky, *Palmyréniens, Nabatéens et Arabes du Nord avant l'Islam*, in *Hist. des religions*, Paris 1956, iv, 201-37; Djurdjī Zaydān, *Anṣāb al-ʿArab al-ḳudamāʾ*, Cairo 1906.

(T. FAHD)

AL-**NUWAYRĪ**, MUḤAMMAD B. AL-ḲĀSIM al-Iskandarānī, local historian of his home Alexandria, who lived in the 8th/14th century but whose precise dates are unknown.

Between 767/1365-6 and 775/1373-4 he wrote a three-volume history of the city, the *K. al-Ilmām fīmā djarat bihi 'l-aḥkām al-maḳḍiyya fī wāḳiʿat al-Iskandariyya* purporting to describe the calamity of Muḥarram 767/October 1365 when the Frankish Crusaders, led by Pierre de Lusignan, king of Cyprus, descended on Alexandria, occupied it for a week and sacked it (see S. Runciman, *A history of the Crusades*, London 1952-4, iii, 444-9; A.S. Atiya, in H.W. Hazard (ed.), *A history of the Crusades*, iii, Madison, Wisc. 1975, 16-18). Ibn Ḥadjar al-ʿAsḳalānī [*q.v.*], however, cited by al-Sakhāwī [*q.v.*], states that al-Nuwayrī spent so much time on the earlier history of the city that he barely had space to deal with the events of 767/1365. The work has now been edited by Atiya, 6 vols. Ḥaydarābād 1388-93/ 1968-73.

Bibliography: A.S. Atiya, *A Fourteenth-Century Encyclopedist from Alexandria. A Critical and Analytical Study of al-Nuwairy al-Iskandarānī's "Kitāb al-Ilmām"*, Salt Lake City 1977; F. Rosenthal, *A history of Muslim historiography*^{2}, Leiden 1968, 155, 458-9 (= tr. of Sakhāwī's *Iʿlān*); Brockelmann, II^{2}, 44-5, S II, 34.

(C.E. BOSWORTH)

AL-**NUWAYRĪ**, S̲H̲IHĀB AL-DĪN AḤMAD B. ʿABD AL-WAHHĀB al-Bakrī al-Tamīmī al-Ḳuras̲h̲ī al-S̲h̲āfiʿī, Egyptian encyclopaedist and historian.

Born at Ak̲h̲mīm [q.v.] on 21 D̲h̲u 'l-Ḳaʿda 677/5 April 1279, died in Cairo on 21 Ramaḍān 733/5 June 1333, he is the author of one of the four best-known encyclopaedias of the Mamlūk period. His family may have originated from a small township of the Egyptian Ṣaʿīd, al-Nuwayra, but he had no direct links with this locality. He claims only, and on numerous occasions in the course of his work, to be descended from the caliph Abū Bakr.

His father, Tād̲j̲ al-Dīn Abū Muḥammad ʿAbd al-Wahhāb (618-99/1221-99), who was possibly an official in the sultan's administration (Kratschowsky, Taʾrīk̲h̲ al-adab al-d̲j̲ug̲h̲rāfī al-ʿarabī, 408, and EIⁱ, s.v.), lived for most of his life in Cairo. According to an obituary notice written by his son, it is also known that he was born in the capital, at Miṣr, in an Ayyūbid madrasa known by the name of Manāzil al-ʿIzz. Speaking of him, his son stresses in particular his remarkable piety, his life and his death both demonstrating his close affinity with matters of faith. He died on 21 D̲h̲u 'l-Ḥid̲j̲d̲j̲a 699/7 September 1299 in al-madrasa al-Ṣāliḥiyya al-Nad̲j̲miyya, in a room reserved for Mālikī teaching. Birth in a madrasa could be proof that his father belonged to the world of the ʿulamāʾ. He probably had another son, older than the author, named Muḥammad. A final point worth mentioning in connection with his father is that he was buried in the turba [q.v.] of the Mālikī supreme ḳāḍī Ibn Mak̲h̲lūf al-Nuwayrī al-D̲j̲azūlī (d. 718/1318), an important figure in the world of the ʿulamāʾ who was supreme ḳāḍī for thirty-four years, during crucial periods in the history of Egypt and of Syria in the Mamlūk period, and who was probably the patron of the al-Nuwayrī who is the subject of this article. He had the same nisba as the latter, and according to al-Ṣafadī, he was a native of Nuwayra, but there is no indication that they were related.

Snippets of information gleaned from his vast encyclopaedia give the impression that before 698/1298, al-Nuwayrī must have lived for at least some of the time in Upper Egypt and in general in Egypt. Thus in the sections devoted to agriculture (M. Chapoutot-Remadi, L'agriculture de l'Empire mamluk au Moyen Âge d'après al-Nuwayrī, in CT, xxii [1974], 23-45) it seems that he is speaking from personal experience of regions visited and observation of practices. Similarly, in dealing with animals, he mentions the teeth of elephants which he saw at Ḳūṣ in 697/1298. Although not definitely established, it is probable that he stayed in Upper Egypt at least until this date.

It is difficult to compile an accurate list of his masters. It is known, however, that he attended courses given by some of the leading masters of his time such as ʿAbd al-Muʾmin al-Dimyaṭī (d. 705/1305 [q.v.]), from one of whose books, entitled Kitāb Faḍl al-k̲h̲ayl (Aleppo 1930), he frequently quotes. His second master, Ibn Daḳīḳ al-ʿĪd (d. 702/1302 [q.v.]), was a specialist in ḥadīth. The third is the grand ḳāḍī Ibn D̲j̲amāʿa (d. 733/1332 [q.v.]), who was s̲h̲ayk̲h̲ of the k̲h̲ānḳāh [q.v.] al-Nāṣiriyya. His biographers also mention among his s̲h̲uyūk̲h̲ the s̲h̲ayk̲h̲a Zaynab bint Yaḥyā b. ʿAbd al-Salām (d. 735/1334). He continued throughout his life to take an interest in the teaching of ḥadīth, and in particular he attended seminars of transmission of the Ṣaḥīḥ of al-Buk̲h̲ārī held by the s̲h̲ayk̲h̲a Wazīra bint Munad̲j̲d̲j̲ā (d. 716/1316) in 715/1315, as well as those held by the s̲h̲ayk̲h̲ al-Ṣāliḥī al-Ḥad̲j̲d̲j̲ār (d. 730/1329) at al-madrasa al-Manṣūriyya.

He heard the s̲h̲ayk̲h̲ Ibn al-Ṣābūnī (d. 720/1320) transmit the Sunan of Abū Dāwūd, Zayn al-Dīn ʿAbd al-Ḥaḳḳ b. Fityān b. ʿAbd al-Mad̲j̲īd al-Ḳuras̲h̲ī, the Kitāb al-S̲h̲ifāʾ bi-taʿrīf ḥuḳūḳ al-Muṣṭafā in 708/1308 at al-madrasa al-Nāṣiriyya, and the S̲h̲arīf ʿIzz al-Dīn al-Dimas̲h̲ḳī (d. 715/1315), the Muwaṭṭaʾ of Mālik and the Ṣaḥīḥ of Muslim. He also received an id̲j̲āza [q.v.] from the s̲h̲ayk̲h̲ ʿIzz al-Dīn al-Fārūt̲h̲ī al-Wāsiṭī al-Rifāʿī.

For the first time, following his recording of his birth (xxx, 386-7), al-Nuwayrī mentions, in his account of the events of the year 698/1298, his recruitment to the dīwān al-k̲h̲āṣṣ in Cairo and his residence at al-madrasa al-Nāṣiriyya, inaugurated by al-Malik al-ʿĀdil Kitbug̲h̲ā (694-96/1295-7) and acquired by Muḥammad b. Ḳalāwūn on his return to power in 698/1298. He speaks at length of this institution and reproduces the text of its waḳf. He openly criticises the administration of Ṭawās̲h̲ī S̲h̲ud̲j̲āʿ al-Dīn ʿAnbar al-Lālā (d. 724/1324), the tutor of the sultan who was entrusted with administration of the waḳf, accusing him of embezzlement and even demanding that he return some of the money owed to the staff of the madrasa.

Al-Nuwayrī travelled to Syria in the month of D̲j̲umādā II 701/January 1301, at the request of the sultan, to manage the property of the state, the dīwān al-k̲h̲āṣṣ. Syria had then been in a state of turmoil since 699/1299 following the large-scale invasion of G̲h̲āzān K̲h̲ān [q.v.]. He participated in a battle against the Mongols on 29 S̲h̲aʿbān 702/18 April 1303 alongside Mug̲h̲ulṭāy [q.v.], and could thus describe the war against the Mongols and the victory of S̲h̲aḳḥab as an eye-witness. In 702/1303, the sultan appointed the amīr Sayf al-Dīn Balabān al-D̲j̲ukāndār al-Manṣūrī to be s̲h̲ādd of crown property, and the two men became friends. Al-Nuwayrī seems to have travelled round the country; he mentions for example a journey in the G̲h̲awr, and he describes the G̲h̲ūṭa of Damascus with the same attention to detail which he demonstrated in his description of Upper Egypt. He seems to have amassed a small fortune; in 703/1303, he possessed no fewer than ten horses, but an equine epidemic destroyed this resource, leaving him without even a horse for his own use. He stayed in Damascus for two years and four months.

Recalled to Cairo in Ramaḍān 703/April 1303, he resumed his administrative activities and, in his capacity as mubās̲h̲ir amlāk al-k̲h̲āṣṣ al-s̲h̲arīf, he administered the dīwān al-k̲h̲āṣṣ, the bīmāristān [q.v.] al-manṣūrī and the whole range of manṣūrī waḳfs. Control was exercised, apparently, by the supreme ḳāḍī Ibn Mak̲h̲lūf. He took up residence again in the madrasa, and was thus a witness to the early stages of the dispute between Ibn Taymiyya [q.v.] and the ʿulamāʾ of Egypt and Ibn Mak̲h̲lūf in particular. It was in the madrasa al-Nāṣiriyya that this affair began, lasting from 705/1305 to 709/1309. Al-Nuwayrī was induced to play a minor mediating role between his patron, implacable enemy of Ibn Taymiyya, and the governor of Damascus, D̲j̲amāl al-Dīn Aḳḳūs̲h̲ al-Afram, ardent defender of the eminent s̲h̲ayk̲h̲. Numerous details indicate that al-Nuwayrī remained in Cairo during this period. In 705/1305, Ibn Ṣaṣrā [q.v.] was appointed supreme ḳāḍī of Cairo, and al-Nuwayrī was instrumental witness in some of the matters submitted to his judgment. At the time of the death of the amīr al-Turkumānī, al-Nuwayrī, who was then in the service of the sultan, was entrusted with the task of sequestering and liquidising his assets. The sultan subsequently instructed him to erect a turba for the amīr and to establish a maintenance waḳf with what remained of his property. Muḥammad b. Ḳalāwūn made his way in person to al-Ḳarāfa to draw the plan of this *turba* on the ground.

The sultan Muḥammad b. Ḳalāwūn, wearying of the tutelage exercised by the senior *amīrs*, abdicated and went to establish himself in the governorate of al-Karak [*q.v.*] in 708/1308. Baybars II took power in Cairo. Five months later, in Rabīʿ II 709/September 1309, al-Nuwayrī, a loyalist, joined Muḥammad b. Ḳalāwūn at al-Karak and only returned to Cairo with the sultan, who regained his throne at the end of Ramaḍān/early March of the same year. After this triumphant return, one of al-Nuwayrī's patrons, the steward of the sovereign, *wakīl al-khāṣṣ*, Ibn ʿAbbāda (d. 710/1310), allowed him to work quite closely with the sovereign. This Ibn ʿAbbāda was himself the appointee of the supreme *ḳāḍī* Ibn Makhlūf, who had given him the task of administering the property left behind by Ḳalāwūn. This individual rose very quickly in the favour of the sultan. In his turn, he seems to have noticed the talents of al-Nuwayrī, entrusting to him the administration of the great complex constructed by Ḳalāwūn and of *al-madrasa al-Nāṣiriyya*. Through his good offices, al-Nuwayrī had regular access to Muḥammad b. Ḳalāwūn, and in numerous instances had occasion to work directly on his behalf. This excessively rapid promotion seems to have turned his head (*al-Ṭāliʿ*, 46; *Sulūk*, ii, 91; *Durar*) and he spoke disparagingly of his patron, for whom he had little regard. This conduct displeased the sultan, who denounced him to Ibn ʿAbbāda and gave the latter permission to punish him as he saw fit. Ibn ʿAbbāda did not hesitate to have him flogged and to confiscate his property; shortly afterwards he was sent away to Syria, but he does not even hint at this misfortune in his work and mentions only his transfer to Tripoli. In the course of the same year, Ibn Abbāda died; al-Nuwayrī devoted to him a dry and brief obituary in which he has considerably more to say about his successor than about the deceased.

He arrived at Tripoli in Ṣafar 710/July 1310 as *ṣāḥib dīwān al-inshāʾ*, head of the office of correspondence. He replaced a senior functionary who had made a name for himself in this occupation, Tādj al-Dīn al-Ṭawīl (d. 711/1311), *mustawfī 'l-dawla*. A few months later, in the same year, he was appointed *nāẓir al-djaysh*, replacing another functionary of Tripoli who had recently died, a certain Nadjm al-Dīn al-Ḳaṣīr, and he travelled extensively during his time in Tripoli, as he had done previously in Upper Egypt and in Damascus. He stayed in Tripoli until 712/1312 and witnessed the defection to the Mongols of the *nāʾib* of Damascus Djamāl al-Dīn Aḳḳūsh al-Afram. This *amīr-nāʾib*, before 708/1308, had been among the opponents of the restoration of Muḥammad b. Ḳalāwūn; following his return to the throne the sultan, stung by his experience of two depositions, attempted to eliminate all the senior *amīrs* who could eventually pose a threat to his rule. Thus the governor of Aleppo, Shams al-Dīn Ḳarāsunḳur, realising that his only hope of survival lay in flight, sought to win over to his side certain *amīrs* including the *nāʾib* of Tripoli, possibly with the intention of provoking an insurrection in Syria. Al-Nuwayrī, claiming amicable relations with the governor, sought to dissuade him from following Ḳarāsunḳur. He recounts his conversation with him and the arguments which he posed to convince him. In spite of everything, the *amīr* took flight and attempted to induce him to join him as well as the *amīrs* of Tripoli. He relates how he succeeded in persuading the latter not to follow him, with only one exception, and how he induced them to renew their oath of allegiance to the sultan. Al-Nuwayrī, who, with the exception of his father, never speaks of his immediate family—it is not known whether he was married or had children—mentions the *ḳāḍī* ʿImād al-Dīn al-Nuwayrī (d. 717/1317), his father's cousin in the maternal line, who died in Tripoli where he was *ṣāḥib al-dīwān*; he had previously been *nāẓir* in numerous places in Syria. Al-Nuwayrī left Tripoli in Djumādā I 712/September 1312 and arrived in Cairo on 20 Radjab/20 November of the same year, after a brief stay in Damascus during the return journey. The circumstances of his departure from Tripoli are obscure; the formula that he uses is ambiguous. His sojourn in Tripoli perhaps explains the place which it occupies in his chronicle. He describes the conquest of Tripoli by Ḳalāwūn, then retraces its history from the Arab conquest to 688/1289 and finishes by providing a list of its *nuwwāb*, governors, up to the year 725/1325. This passage is furthermore a synthesis of data compiled by his predecessors and contemporaries, and of information which he gathered himself. His interest in Tripoli persists throughout his work, and thus he does not omit to note, every year, the changes taking place, the appointments of *amīrs* and of functionaries, the cadastral revision, information concerning the Nuṣayriyya and climatic phenomena.

According to his biographers, on returning to Cairo he was appointed *nāẓir al-dīwān* of two provinces of the Nile Delta, al-Daḳhaliyya and al-Murtāḥiyya (*Ṭāliʿ*, 46). He speaks of them indirectly in a biographical article concerning a major figure in the administration, a *ṣāḥib dīwān al-djaysh*, the *ḳāḍī* Ibn Ḥashīsh (d. 729/1328; *Aʿyān al-ʿaṣr*, iii, 312; *Sulūk*, ii, 315). It may be assumed that at least until 716/1316, al-Nuwayrī was engaged in administering the revenues of these provinces, while residing in Cairo, probably until the end of his life. It seems that he continued to reside in *al-madrasa al-Nāṣiriyya*, since he mentions a dream which he had at that time which took place in one of the *īwāns* of the *madrasa*, called *al-Īwān al-Baḥrī*, on the eve of Friday 13 Dhu 'l-Ḳaʿda 729/8 September 1329. It is not known at exactly what date al-Nuwayrī abandoned administration to devote himself exclusively to the composition of his monumental work, but before turning to the latter, it would be useful to summarise the main points of his life and career.

The reconstructed biography of al-Nuwayrī shows a man often involved in the important events of his time such as the war against Ghāzān Khān and the victory of Shaḳhab, in which he was a participant. Even in *al-madrasa al-Nāṣiriyya*, which played such an important role in his life, he dared to challenge the administrator of the foundation, Ṭawāshī Shudjāʿ al-Dīn ʿAnbar al-Lālā, the sultan's tutor, insisting that he pay to the staff the salary owed to them; from the same vantage-point, he witnessed the controversies surrounding Ibn Taymiyya. During the reign of Baybars II, al-Nuwayrī sided with Muḥammad b. Ḳalāwūn, whom he regarded as the only legitimate sultan, joining him in exile at al-Karak. While resident in Tripoli, decidedly at the centre of important events, al-Nuwayrī tried to dissuade the governor Djamāl al-Dīn Aḳḳūsh al-Afram from defecting to the Mongols with Ḳarāsunḳur; failing in this, he nevertheless succeeded in limiting the damage. Through his contacts, he was well informed concerning affairs of state, and he took advantage of his duties to travel widely in Egypt and Syria. His career was in itself quite distinguished; he played a major role in the administration of the three most important *dīwāns*, those of *al-khāṣṣ*, *al-inshāʾ* and *al-djaysh*.

During the course of his career, he forged numerous amicable relationships with highly-placed members of the Mamlūk régime. In Damascus, his friends included three *amīr*s, Sayf al-Dīn Balabān al-Djukāndār al-Manṣūrī (d. 706/1306), Ẓāhir al-Dīn Mukhtār al-Manṣūrī (d. 716/1316) and ʿAlāʾ al-Dīn Mughulṭāy (d. 707/1307) whom he had previously known in Cairo, and among the *ʿulamāʾ*, members of the most distinguished Damascus families, Ibn Ṣaṣrā (d. 717/1317), Ibn al-Ḳalānisī (d. 715/1315) and his son Muḥibb al-Dīn Maḥmūd (d. 730/1330). In Tripoli, he showed the same propensity for making friends, among members of the Mamlūk élite as well as among his colleagues in the *dīwān al-inshāʾ* and the *dīwān al-djaysh*. He was also acquainted with some of the senior *kuttāb* of the Mamlūk administration, letters from whom he reproduces in numerous instances in his encyclopaedia. Each time, the terms which underline his privileged relations with one or the other are *rāfaḳtuhu* or *ṣāḥabtuhu*. As a man of his time, al-Nuwayrī was also acquainted with Ṣūfī *shaykhs*.

After a career of at least eighteen years, approximately from 698/1299 to 716/1316, he retired from public life and devoted himself to *adab* and to the writing of his encyclopaedia. From his administrative life, he would have learned *kitāba*, the establishment of roles, exercised *ḥisba*, land-surveying (*al-muḳāyasāt*), the management of accounts and revenues, *al-muḥāsaba wa 'l-taḥṣīlāt*, *naẓar*, inspection of crops and of presses (*al-ghallāt wa 'l-iʿtiṣār*), forage, sales (*al-mubāyaʿāt*). He read and contemplated a great deal over the years and conceived the idea of writing a book, or rather a work large enough to provide a compendium of the fruits of his reading and of his administrative experience. He expresses it in his introduction in these terms: "I mounted the war-horse of reading and investigation and spurred him on. I then galloped in the region of consultation. When I succeeded in taming the horse and the source of knowledge became clear to me, I then undertook to compose a work which would keep me company and in which I would find my bearings, having recourse to my own administrative experience. I called upon God the Great and Merciful and I have produced five great Books (*funūn*) harmoniously composed and divided into sections and sub-sections."

Al-Nuwayrī died on 21 Ramaḍān 733/5 June 1333, at the age of fifty-six years, having composed a monumental work of 9,000 pages in thirty-one volumes which he intitled *Nihāyat al-arab fī funūn al-adab*. He thus bequeathed to posterity his experience and his culture in the form of a *summa*. His capacity for work was extraordinary since, while working on his encyclopaedia, he made copies of it which he sold before composition of the whole was complete. The first volume (p. 16) bears the date 714/1314. A single autograph manuscript survives from the first version of his encyclopaedia, volume 19 (corresponding to xxi in the printed edition, p. 540); it is dated 9 Djumādā II 718/8 August 1318. Volumes 29 and 30 are dated 725/1325, but it is certain that he made additions to volume 30, after 728/1328. It seems that he began making a second copy, the first volume of which was completed on 20 Dhu 'l-Ḳaʿda 721/11 December 1321, the fifth on 22 Djumādā I 722/8 June 1322, the seventeenth on 7 Ramaḍān 722/19 September 1322 and the eighteenth on 26 Ramaḍān/8 October, just 19 days later. He must thus have copied eighteen volumes in less than ten months. His biographers have noted his ability to fill three manuscript notebooks in a day, and this performance seems unequivocally confirmed, with the addition to what he copied and sold of eight copies of the *Ṣaḥīḥ* of al-Bukhārī. He was deemed an excellent calligrapher and bookbinder. He must then have written the totality of his work between 714/1314 and 731/1330, over a period of seventeen years, since his chronicle finishes in 731/1331, two years before his death.

The work is divided into five *funūn*; each *fann* comprises five parts which, in turn, consist of a certain number of chapters or *abwāb* (from two to fourteen). The first is a description of the Universe. Al-Nuwayrī begins with a cosmographic vision and then proceeds to the Earth and the elements of which it is composed. Earth and Heaven were conceived by God for Man's benefit. The *fann* concludes with a description of Egypt, its inhabitants and archaeological remains. The three succeeding volumes are devoted to living beings: Man is the principal theme of the second, while the third and fourth are concerned with fauna and flora. History is the subject of the fifth and last, and this is by far the most important; it represents more than two-thirds of the work. This section is conceived as a universal history, covering the period from Creation to 731/1331. Crucial episodes in this history are the story of the Prophet and of Arab expansion, then the ʿAbbāsid period and finally, the history of Egypt since the Fāṭimids. The major preoccupation of al-Nuwayrī seems to lie in providing the reader with succinct summaries of the principal historical events. The work is conceived primarily as a work of reference, and the manner of compilation displays a concern to inform the reader in a qualitative manner; only works bearing authority are summarised here. The final volume of this important historiographer differs somewhat from the remainder. These are annals, or rather notes taken from day to day; the text is condensed and even displays a certain dryness. It contrasts strongly with the rest of the work, in which the style is in general mannered, sometimes even lapsing into rhymed prose. This abridged account of events personally experienced may have been written with a view to later revision, but he died without making any amendments.

In all, with a work gigantic in terms of the variety of subjects studied, the breadth of the information contained, al-Nuwayrī not only achieved his avowed object but even went further, since not only did he succeed in providing the sum of practical knowledge necessary for a good secretary and for the administrative world in general but he also reached a much broader public. The literary form of the work and the spectrum of subjects exposed, summarised and classified in the most accessible manner possible, clearly show that al-Nuwayrī wanted, beyond his readership of administrators, to contribute to the formation of a kind of "well-informed man". He states this himself occasionally.

Al-Nuwayrī was greatly inspired by the geographical encyclopaedia of his predecessor, al-Waṭwāṭ (d. 718/1318 [*q.v.*]) entitled *Mabāhidj al-fikar wa-manāhidj al-ʿibar* (partial edition, Kuwait 1981), for the subdivision into *fanns* and even for the content. The four *fanns* of al-Waṭwāṭ recur in the work of al-Nuwayrī, who added history to form a fifth section. Furthermore, he mentions him by name, as he does with the majority of his sources. In the books devoted to natural history, fauna and flora, he makes a synthesis between three types of pre-occupation, naturalist, medical and literary. He thus describes the animal or the plant, mentions its medical and other attributes, the legends concerning his subject and the poems of which it has been the object. Science and *adab* are thus united. Amīna Muḥammad Djamāl al-

Dīn (see Bibl.) has listed seventy-five poets quoted in the book on fauna (148). The work reflects the author's education with his constant references to *ḥadīth*; the impact of traditions is also evident in his very approach of *khabar*, since he always adds to a work compiled by an authoritative person details gleaned either from his direct observation or from the testimony of a trustworthy person. He sometimes exhibits scepticism when he relates a story which he regards as fantasy, "this saying derives, in my belief, from the fables of the Arabs (*khurāfāt al-ʿArab*)" (ix, 276, or x, 209), but he has no qualms about relating marvels for the entertainment of the reader. Throughout his work he is guided by three principles: to adhere to the stated plan, not to go to excess over details and to avoid repetition. In the introduction to Book III, which concerns animals, he writes, "Were it not for the risk of saying too much, we could have composed an epistle for each animal, but we prefer to confine ourselves to the writing of others rather than to our own accounts" (ix, 225). He engages in a constant dialogue with the reader and explains his approach. To avoid repetitions, he often has recourse to postponements; he even has a system of double postponement which demonstrates simultaneously his attention to minute detail in his conception of the work as a whole and his unwillingness to weary the reader with repetitions (ix, 333, xii, 2). There remains a final important remark which is valid for the work as a whole; al-Nuwayrī's professional travels across parts of Syria and Egypt led him to take a constant interest in the countries and regions visited, and it is from this source that he draws all the concrete examples which are scattered throughout his work. Such personal notes occur on numerous occasions and in all parts of his encyclopaedia, on Tripoli, on Damascus, Upper Egypt, the Delta and Cairo, and in the historical section he borrows constantly from Syrian authors such as al-Djazarī or al-Birzālī, in a manner which enables him to sketch in, for each year, information concerning at least the places in which he has lived and worked at one time or another. Similarly, in the sections devoted to administration, his personal experience enables him to convey important information regarding the machinery of the financial administration of Mamlūk Egypt, with precise and meticulous descriptions. Furthermore, under the heading of administrative and financial information, al-Nuwayrī reveals indirectly, and without departing from his primary intention, certain aspects of the rural economy in the 8th/14th century. Thus his surveys of fiscal policy convey information on types of soil, crops, certain problems inherent in climatic or hydrographic conditions. In the same Book II, taking advantage of his access to important state documents and under the pretext of supplying models for the benefit of the *kātib*, he reproduces a series of letters emanating from, in particular, great sovereigns such as Baybars, Ḳalāwūn and his son Muḥammad. Other documents reproduced include certificates of investiture and records of *wakf*s.

The first four *funūn* cover only ten volumes, while the section reserved for history accounts in itself for twenty-one. The importance of Book V accounts for the fact that his biographers consider al-Nuwayrī a historian before all else. He reveals his methodology in the introduction to his historical section: "When I saw that all those who wrote the history of the Muslims had adopted the annalistic form rather than that of dynastic history, I realised that by this method the reader was being deprived of the pleasure of an event which held his preference and of an affair which he might discover. The chronicles of the year draw to a close in a way which denies awareness of all the phases of an event. The historian changes the year and passes from east to west, from peace to war, by the very fact of passing from one year to another... The account of events is displaced and becomes remote. The reader can only follow an episode which interests him with great difficulty... I have chosen to present history by dynasties and I shall not leave one of them until I have recounted its history from beginning to end, giving the sum of its battles and its achievements, the history of its kings, of its kingdom and of its highways" (xiii, 2). Little (*Introduction to Muslim historiography*, 31; idem, *The historical and historiographical significance of the detention of Ibn Taymiyya*, in *IJMES*, iv [1973], 315) has already drawn attention to the originality of the method adopted by al-Nuwayrī in his willingness to break with chronology in order to give more coherence to his narrative. When he does this he alerts the reader and explains himself, then, when he has finished with his exposure of a topic, he writes as a general rule *wa-l-nardjiʿ li-siyāḳat al-akhbār* (or *al-taʾrīkh*) (Or 2n, fol. 15b) or *wa-l-nardjiʿ ilā baḳiyyat ḥawādīth al-sana* (Or 2n, fol. 29a). Following the stated pattern, proposing for example to deal with the history of the Mongols, he writes: "We shall give a brief account of (Čingiz Khān's) story and the circumstances of his appearance, his development and his reign. We shall explain this by means of what we have gained from our reading and by means of oral testimony which we have gathered... This kingdom was remote and vast, historians have not learned a great deal about it, we have not been able to verify... We have taken as our basis al-Nasawī and his Djalālī history (*Sīrat Djalāl al-Dīn Mangubirtī*) and Ibn al-Athīr and his *Kāmil*... If there are other historians who have studied this question, their work is not available to us" (xxvii, 300). These pre-occupations are very modern and they illustrate the author's constant concern to instruct his reader in the best way possible, providing him with the most reliable written and oral sources. But even in its historical section, al-Nuwayrī stresses the literary nature of his work, "Our book is not based on history only; it is a book of *adab*" (xiii, 5).

In the last part of his work which is devoted to the Mamlūk empire, Egypt, Syria and the Ḥidjāz, al-Nuwayrī departs from the stated plan and, for each sultan, after a biographical presentation, he gives an account of his battles, then of the events which took place under his reign, according to chronological order, giving obituary notices of distinguished persons at the end of each year. In spite of his wish to avoid repetitions, this pattern induces him to make them in numerous instances. Born some thirty years after the beginning of this dynasty, he begins by borrowing from his elders, Ibn ʿAbd al-Ẓāhir, Abū Shāma and Ibn Shaddād, then his contemporaries, al-Djazarī, al-Yūnīnī, al-Birzālī and Baybars al-Manṣūrī. As in other parts of his work, he usually mentions them by name but sometimes he is content to indicate his borrowings with *ḳāla* (or *ḥakā*) *al-muʾarrikh*; he sometimes adds the title of the work. He quotes the majority of his contemporaries, without saying whether he has known them personally. He adds to their material that which he has obtained from his friends and his professional contacts. He explains the choice of the plan which he has adopted at every opportunity (Or 2n, fols. 3a, 5b, 15b, 16a ...) even though, he says, he has not always conformed to the rules of history (*al-khurūdj ʿan al-ḳāʿida al-taʾrīkhiyya*).

Several authors have borrowed from the *Nihāya*;

reference should be made to the comparison of sources made by Little (*Introduction*...), with the aid of numerous passages, in order to attempt a clarification of the circulation of borrowings between the different authors of the Mamlūk period, while the severity of Ashtor's judgment of this work (*Studies*, 15) needs some attenuation, since its dimensions and its characteristics render impossible such an unequivocal judgment of the merits of this encyclopaedia.

The edition of the *Nihāya*, begun in Egypt by Aḥmad Zakī Pasha in 1923, came to a halt with volume xviii in 1955, was then resumed in the 1970s and, after further interruptions, volume xxx appeared in 1991; however the two preceding ones, xxviii and xxix, are not yet available. The edition will comprise more volumes than the manuscript work, since the thirtieth which has just appeared deals with the beginnings of the Mamlūk period, while the years 678-731 have yet to be edited. Manuscripts of the *Nihāya* are to be found almost everywhere in Europe, in particular in Paris, Rome and Leiden, but also in Egypt. The work has been known and exploited for a long time [see *EI*[1], s.v.], but much remains to be drawn from it.

Bibliography: Brockelmann, II, 175, S II, 173-4; Adfuwī, *al-Ṭāliʿ al-saʿīd*, Cairo 1966, 96, no. 51; Ibn al-Dawādārī, *Kanz al-durar wa-djāmiʿ al-ghurar*, Cairo 1971, viii, 391; al-Mufaḍḍal Ibn Abi 'l-Faḍāʾil, *al-Nahdj al-sadīd wa 'l-durr al-farīd*, Freiburg 1973, 55; Ṣafadī, *Wāfī*, vii, 165, no. 3097; idem, *Aʿyān al-ʿaṣr*, Frankfurt 1990, i, 82; Ibn Ḥadjar, *Durar*, i, 209, no. 507; Ibn Ḥabīb, *Durrat al-aslāk*, Amsterdam 1846, ii, 358; idem, *Tadhkirat al-nabīh fī ayyām al-Manṣūr wa-banīh*, Cairo 1982, ii, 246; Maḳrīzī, *Sulūk*, ii, 363; idem, al-*Muḳaffaʿ*, Beirut 1991, 521, no. 508; Ibn Taghrībirdī, *Nudjūm*, ix, 299; idem, *al-Manhal al-ṣāfī*, i, 381, no. 203; idem, *al-Dalīl al-shāfī*, i, 58, no. 199; Suyūṭī, *Ḥusn al-muḥāḍara*, i, 255; ʿAli Mubārak, *al-Khiṭaṭ al-tawfīḳiyya*, xvii, 15-16; Ziriklī, *al-Aʿlām*, i, 158; Ḥādjdjī Khalīfa, *Kashf al-ẓunūn*, ed. Flügel, iv, 397-8 no. 14069; Y. Sarkīs, *Muʿdjam*, 1884; Ismāʿīl Pasha, *Hadiyyat al-ʿārifīn*, i, 108; E. Ashtor, *Some unpublished sources for the Baḥrī period*, in U. Heyd (ed.), *Studies in Islamic history and civilisation* (*Scripta Hierosolymitana*, ix), Jerusalem 1961, 11-30; R. Blachère, *Quelques réflexions sur les formes de l'encyclopédisme en Egypte et en Syrie du VIIIe/XIVe siecle à la fin du IXe/XVe siecle*, in *BEO*, xxiii (1970), 7-20; Cl. Cahen, *Mea culpa sur Djazarī/Nuwayrī*, in *IOS*, iii (1973), 293; M. Chapoutot-Remadi, *Al-Nuwayrī encyclopédiste et chroniqueur égyptien de l'époque mamlūke*, in *Les Africains*, Paris 1978, x, 311-45; eadem, *Les encyclopédies arabes de la fin du Moyen âge*, in *L'encyclopédisme, Proceedings of the Symposium of Caen 12-16 Jan. 1987*, Paris 1990, 267-79; Amīna Muḥammad Djamāl al-Dīn, *al-Nuwayrī wa-kitābuhu Nihāyat al-arab fī funūn al-adab, maṣādiruhu al-adabiyya wa-ārāʾuhu 'l-naḳdiyya*, Cairo 1984; Shah Morad Elham, *Kitbuġā und Lāǧīn, Studien zur Mamluken-Geschichte nach Baybars al-Manṣūrī und Nuwairī*, Freiburg 1977, 27-37, 38-43, 54-61, 68-73; U. Haarmann, *Quellenstudien zur frühen Mamlukenzeit*, Freiburg 1969; idem, *L'édition de la chronique Mamlūke syrienne de Šams al-dīn Muḥammad al-Ǧazarī*, in *BEO*, xxvii (1974), 195-203; Muḥammad ʿAbd Allāh ʿInān, *Muʾarrikhū Miṣr al-Islāmiyya*, Cairo 1969, 62-75; S. Kortantamer, *Ägypten und Syrien zwischen 1317 und 1341 in der Chronik des Mufaḍḍal b. Abi 'l-Faḍāʾil*, Freiburg 1973, 24-7; ʿUmarī, *Masālik al-abṣār fī mamālik al-amṣār*, ed. A. Miquel and Ayman Fuʾād Sayyid, Cairo 1985, 7-12.

(M. Chapoutot-Remadi)

NUZHA [see miʿzaf].

O

OB, one of the major rivers of Siberia, which flows from sources in the Altai Mountains to the Gulf of Ob and the Kara Sea of the Arctic Ocean. Its course is 3,680 km/2,287 miles long and 5,410 km/3,362 miles long if its main left-bank affluent, the Irtysh [see irtish in Suppl.] is included. Its whole basin covers a huge area of western Siberia.

In early historic times, the lands along the lower and middle Ob were thinly peopled with such groups as the Samoyeds and the Ugrian Voguls and Ostiaks (in fact, the indigenous population of these regions today, only the upper reaches of the river in the Altai region being ethnically Turkish territory; see M.G. Levin and L.P. Potapov (eds.), *Narodi Sibiri*, Eng. tr. *The peoples of Siberia*, Chicago and London 1964, 305-41, 511-70). These Ugrian peoples are the ones whom the early Muslim geographers and travellers in Inner Asia knew as the Yūra (mediaeval Russ. *Yugra*) who lived beyond the Bulghārs [*q.v.*] towards the *Baḥr al-Ẓulumāt* "Sea of Darkness", i.e. the Arctic, and supplied furs to the more southerly peoples by dumb barter (see J. Marquart, *Ein arabischer Bericht über die arktischen (uralischen) Länder aus dem 10. Jahrhundert*, in *Ungarische Jahrbücher*, iv [1924], 289 ff., 303 ff., 321 ff.; V. Minorsky, *Sharaf al-Zamān Ṭāhir Marvazī on China, the Turks and India*, London 1942, tr. 34, comm. 112-15; K. Donner, *La Sibérie*, Paris 1946, 124 ff.; P.B. Golden, in *The Cambridge history of early Inner Asia*, Cambridge 1990, 253-4).

It is probable that the Ob is to be identified with the river beyond the Ili, the Irtysh and a nameless one, and which Maḥmūd Kāshgharī calls the Yamār, locating along its shores the tribe of the Yabaḳu, who had their own language (? or dialect) but also spoke Turkish (*Dīwān lughāt al-turk*, tr. Atalay, i, 29, 30, 79, iii, 28, etc. = tr. R. Dankoff and J. Kelly, *Compendium of the Turkic dialects*, Cambridge, Mass. 1982-4, i, 83, 117, ii, 161, etc.; Brockelmann, *Mitteltürkischer Wortschatz*, 244, identifies the Yamār "probably" with the Ishim, a left-bank tributary of the Irtysh, hence further west than the Ob, but this seems too far west, in the light of the relative positions of the Turkish tribes in its vicinity, see below). The map accompanying Kāshgharī's text (reproduced by Dankoff and Kelly at i, 82; according to A. Herrmann, *Die älteste türkische Weltkarte*, in *Imago Mundi*, i [1935], 27, this is possibly by the author himself or was drawn according to his specifications) places the Yamār river beyond the lands of the Ḳay and Čömül tribes on the nameless river, again described as being beyond the Yabaḳu, but the Ḳay and Čömül territories may well have extended from the Irtysh to the

Ob, as apparently did those of the Basmil also (see Minorsky, *Ḥudūd al-ʿālam*, comm. 285, 305; idem, *Marvazī*, comm. 96). There is also the precious information in Kās͟hg͟harī about an expedition northwards led by one Arslan-tigin (presumably a Ḳarak͟hānid [see ILEK K͟HĀNS]) against infidels who were led by a certain Budrač and who were routed, and the Turkish verses which Kās͟hg͟harī quotes mention the crossing of the Ili and the Yamār; also hostile to the Muslims were the Basmil (*Dīwān*, tr. Atalay, i, 144, 452, iii, 356 = tr. Dankoff and Kelly, i, 163, 340, ii, 330-1). Kās͟hg͟harī derived information directly from one of the participants in this *g͟hazw*, hence it must have taken place in the early or mid-5th/11th century, although the episode very soon became enshrouded in legendary accretions (Barthold, *Zwölf Vorlesungen über die Geschichte der Türken Mittelasiens*, Berlin 1935, 95-6, Fr. tr. *Histoire des Turcs d'Asie Centrale*, Paris 1945, 76-7).

Islam never penetrated to the Ugrian peoples of the lower and middle Ob, and the Turkic peoples of the upper reaches remained shamanists also. In the later 16th century, Kučum K͟hān, ruler of the Turco-Mongol k͟hānate of Sibir [*q.v.*] centred on Isker on the middle Irtysh, was finally defeated by Russian forces in August 1598 on the Ob; the Russians had already penetrated to the Ob basin in their thrust eastwards through Siberia. A Russian army had reached the shores of the Ob in 1584; a fort was founded at Tomsk in 1604, and this place was later to be the seat of the first university in Siberia, inaugurated in 1888; Surgut was founded in 1595 and Barnaul erected into a town in 1771 (see Donner, *La Sibérie*, 144-6; J. Forsyth, *A history of the peoples of Siberia, Russia's north Asian colony 1581-1990*, Cambridge 1992, 28 ff.). The river itself, navigable on its upper course for some 190 days a year, became an important means of communication. Novosibirsk, where the Trans-Siberian railway crosses the Ob, was founded in 1893 and soon eclipsed Tomsk, later becoming the largest city of Soviet Asia. At present, the Ob basin falls within the Russian Republic, with only the river's headwaters in the Gorno-Altai Autonomous Oblast'.

Bibliography: Given in the text. See also *BSE*², xviii, 267-8, and SIBIR. (C.E. BOSWORTH)

OCHIALY [see ʿULŪDJ ʿALĪ].

OCHRIDA [see OK͟HRI].

OCSONOBA [see UKS͟HUNŪBA].

ODJAḲ (T.), "fireplace, hearth, chimney", a word which survives with a rather wide range of meanings in all Turkish languages and dialects. Originally *otčoḳ* < *otčaḳ* with the elements *ōt* "fire" and *-čaḳ* (perhaps to be connected with a rare suffix denoting a place, cf. S. Tezcan, *Eski Uygurca Hsüan Tsang biyografyası X. bölüm*, Ankara 1975, n. 1074; idem, *Das uigurische Insadi-Sutra*, Berlin 1974, n. 275). The connotation "iron ring (for a prisoner or criminal)" appears only in *Sanglāk͟h* and in S͟heyk͟h Süleymān Buk͟hārī (G. Doerfer, *Türkische und Mongolische Elemente im Neupersischen*, Wiesbaden 1965 ii, 10-2, no. 421; G. Clauson, *An etymological dictionary of pre-thirteenth century Turkish*, Oxford 1972, 22). The term passed into Arabic (*wudjāḳ*), Persian and most Balkan languages (A. Škaljić, *Turcizmi u srpskohrvatskom-hrvatskosrpskom jeziku*, Sarajevo ³1973, s.v. *odžak*, etc.). There are place names derived from it, like Odžaci (district of Sombor, Bačka) and Odžak (a town in Bosnia, district Doboj and a locality near Livno).

Synonymously used with *yurt* [*q.v.*] in the sense of "family, inherited possession", *odjak* or *odjaklïḳ* means a special sort of *timar* (K. Röhrborn, *Untersuchungen zur osmanischen Verwaltungsgeschichte*, Wiesbaden 1973, 46 ff.) or a semi-independent *sandjaḳ* (N. Göyünç, *Yurtluk-ocaklık deyimleri hakkında*, in *Prof. Dr. Bekir Kütükoğlu'na armağan*, Istanbul 1991, 269-77).

The *odjaḳ* was equally a unit of recruitment in the Ottoman military administration [see ʿADJAMĪ OG͟HLĀN, BOSTĀNDJÎ, DJEBEDJI]. The Janissaries in their totality were *the odjaḳ* par excellence [see YEÑI ČERI]. Their cognomen *Odjagh-i̊ Bektās͟hiyān* was coined for their close relation to the fraternity [see BEKTĀS͟HIYYA]. The Turkish soldiery in the Mag͟hrib and Egypt was also referred to as the *odjaḳ* (M. Colombe, *Contribution à l'étude du recrutement de l'Odjaq d'Alger*, in *RAfr.*, lxxxvii [1943], 166-83; A. Raymond, *Artisans et commerçants au Caire au XVIII*ᵉ *siècle*, Damascus 1973-4, *passim*).

In the civil sphere we find groups of workmen formed into *odjaḳ*s (e.g. L. Fekete, *Die Siyāqat-Schrift in der türkischen Finanzverwaltung*, i, Budapest 1955, 761; C. Orhonlu, *Osmanlı imparatorluğunda şehircilik ve ulaşım*, Istanbul 1984, 33: *ocağ-ı ahenger*).

The technical vocabulary of fraternities like the Bektās͟hiyya and the Mawlawiyya [*q.v.*] assigns to the *odjaḳ* a special place in their *tekkes*. Bektās͟hī *tekkes* used to have an *odjaḳ* in front of the *ḳibla* between the *post* of Seyyid ʿAlī and the *K͟horāsān postu*. In Mewlewī-k͟hānes, *odjaḳ* was another word for the *maḳām* of the cook (*as͟hdji̊ dede*). Amongst the Alevis of Anatolia, *ocak-zâdes* are spiritual guides who belonged to one of the lineages stemming from the twelve imams (K. Kehl-Bodrogi, *Die Kızılbaş-Aleviten*, Berlin 1988, 167-79).

At the beginning of the 20th century, *odjaḳ* became an emotive word with nationalist overtones for the Turkist movement (seen in the *Türk Odjaghi̊* founded in 1911-12). The youth organisations of the more recent Milliyetçi Hareket Partisi were called *Ülkü Ocakları Dernekleri* (1968-78).

The traditional name for the month of January was replaced in 1945 by a literal translation (*calque sémantique*) from *Ḳānūn-i t͟hānī* to *Ocak* (law no. 4696).

Bibliography (in addition to references in the article): Gibb and Bowen, index; Pakalın, s.v. (K. KREISER)

ODJAḲLÎ [see ODJAḲ].

OFEN, first the German name of Pest [see PES͟HTE] (this meaning "cave or lime-kiln"), later and until recent times that of Buda [see BUDĪN], both today parts of the capital of Hungary.

OGĀDĒN, a vast arid expanse in the south-eastern part of Ethiopia approximately delimited by the Wadi Shebille to the south-west, the frontier of the former Somaliland to the north-east, the line Ferfer-Werder (the administrative capital) - Doomo to the south-east and the line Degeh Bur - Degeh Medo to the north-west. It is ranged over by Somali nomads belonging to the Dārōd group, the Ogādēn (from whom the region gets its name), and formed part of the province of Harargé (Harar) until 1991, when a new administrative set of arrangements on ethnic and cultural bases placed it within the "Somali province". It is claimed by the Republic of Somalia, and the fact that it actually belongs at present to Ethiopia explains the chevron-like shape of the Somalia territory. Certain fringe regions of Ogādēn (those of Jigjiga and the valley of the Shebelle) are cultivated by Somalis or by peasants who have come from other parts of Ethiopia. Explorations have revealed the presence there of natural gas.

It was after the conquest of the Muslim amirate of Harar [*q.v.*] in 1887 that the King of Shoa Menelik, the future Emperor of Ethiopia (b. 1844, regn. 1889-1913), ordered the conquest of Ogādēn, which was completed in 1890. Carried out in the context of colonial expansion within the Horn of Africa (Britons, Italians and French installed themselves there in the years 1880-1890), this annexation was confirmed internationally by agreements concluded with Britian, which renounced part of the Haud pastures in favour of Ethiopia (1897), and with the Italians (1908), without however the frontiers being clearly delimited. Despite a certain amount of tension with the two European powers (the frontier incident of Wal-Wal in December 1934 was the pretext for the Italian agression against Ethiopia of 1935-6), the situation remained thus until 1960.

During the rebellion of 1900-20 of the *sayyid* Muḥammad ʿAbdille Ḥassān, the so-called "Mad Mullah" (who was of Ogādēn ancestry [see MUḤAMMAD B. ʿABD ALLAH B. ḤASSĀN]) against the British, some of the military operations took place in the territory of the Ogādēn, and these last made appeals to the Ethiopians for help on various occasions.

In 1960 the two former Italian and British colonies, Somalia and Somaliland, became independent and united to form the Republic of Somalia [*q.v.*]. Impelled by a militant pan-Somalia feeling, the new state proclaimed its rights over Ogādēn, claiming the provinces of Harargé (Harar), Bale, Sidamo and Arssi, hence much more than those territories actually inhabited by Somalis. It also claimed the French Coastal Region of the Somalis (which later became the French Territory of the Afars and Issas and then, after its achievement of independence in 1977, the Republic of Djibouti) and part of northern Kenya. From this time onwards, Ogādēn became one of the five territorial entities populated by Somalis and symbolised by the five points of the star in the national flag, to whose unity Somalian nationalism aspires.

The first war between Somalia and Ethiopia was begun by the former in 1964, and only international pressure prevented the Ethiopian military advance. The Khartoum Agreements in the spring of that year confirmed the status quo. After the fall of Emperor Haile Selassie in 1974, the Somalis took advantage of the disorder within Ethiopia to make another attempted invasion (1977). The Ethiopians only retrieved their position thanks to the Soviet Russian volte-face when the Soviets abandoned Somalia, their ally until 1970, for the Marxist Ethiopian régime and replaced American aid by their own. Thus the quite local problem of Ogādēn took on an international dimension.

The grave difficulties into which Somalia has fallen since 1991 have removed the imminent acuteness of the Ogādēn problem.

Bibliography: Material may be found in the general works dealing with Ethiopia, Somalia and the geopolitics of the Horn of Africa and the Red Sea regions. The following first two titles reflect the Ethiopian case in the Ogādēn dispute: Wolde-Mariam Mesfin, *The background of the Ethio-Somalia boundary dispute*, Addis Ababa 1964; S.P. Petrides, *The boundary question between Ethiopia and Somalia*, New Delhi 1983; I.M. Lewis, *A modern history of Somalia*³, London and Boulder, Colo. 1988. It may also be recalled that A. Rimbaud put together a *Rapport sur l'Ogadine* from the notes of the Greek merchant Sottiro (*Comptes-Rendus des Séances de la Société de Géographie, Paris* [1884]). (A. ROUAUD)

ÖGEDEY or ÖGÖDEY, the second Great K͟hān of the Mongol Empire. Born probably in 1186, he was the third son of Čingis K͟han (Čingiz K͟hān [*q.v.*]) by his principal wife Börte. He was the first of the Mongol rulers to adopt the title Ḳaʾan: D͟juwaynī always refers to him thus, almost as though it was regarded as a personal name. Čingis had during his lifetime indicated that Ögedey should succeed him, in preference to his other surviving sons Čag͟hatay and Toluy. It is often suggested that Ögedey was a generally acceptable conciliatory figure, and the empire seems to have been administered by Ögedey on the basis of family consultation rather than imperial autocracy. Ögedey does appear to have been, by Mongol standards, an unusually benevolent ruler, if the numerous anecdotes illustrating his tolerance and generosity which are preserved by D͟juwaynī and Ras͟hīd al-Dīn are to be believed.

Čingis's death in 1227 was, however, followed by a two-year interregnum before Ögedey was confirmed as Great K͟hān at a *ḳuriltay* in 1229 convened by his younger brother Toluy. Thereafter, the Mongol Empire continued to expand in both east and west. The conquest of the Chin Empire in north China was completed in 1234, and Mongol armies under the generals Čormag͟hun and Bayd͟ju campaigned in northern Persia from 1229. The most spectacular campaign undertaken during Ögedey's reign was that in Russia and eastern Europe. In 1235 a *ḳuriltay* decided to launch this expedition, which was to be headed by Batu [*q.v.*], son of Čingis's (deceased) eldest son D͟joči, to whom the lands to the west had been allotted as his *ulus*. The campaigns, conducted triumphantly between 1237 and 1241, culminated in an invasion of eastern and central Europe, from Poland to Hungary and Austria, which was abruptly terminated in early 1242, probably at least in part because the news had reached Batu of the death of Ögedey on 7 December 1241 (possibly as a result of over-indulgence in drink: a not uncommon end among the Mongol notables). The enduring result of the expedition was the establishment of Batu's and his descendants' rule over what Westerners called the Golden Horde (known in the Islamic world as the K͟hanate of Ḳïpčaḳ).

The achievements of Ögedey's reign were not solely warlike. It was at this time that the Mongol Empire acquired a capital: Ḳaraḳorum, in the Ork͟hon [*q.v.*] valley of central Mongolia. Čingis seems previously to have used the site, but it was Ögedey who in 1235 had the city walled and who built the substantial though (according to the Franciscan traveller William of Rubruck, who was there in the 1250s) not enormously impressive buildings. Another significant achievement was the establishment in 1234 of the imperial communications system, the *Yām* [see MONGOLS, section 5]. This network of post stations was initially set up by Ögedey in the territories subject to his own direct rule, and it was then extended to include the lands subject to Čag͟hatay, Toluy and Batu. The reign saw the height of the (by no means unchallenged) influence of the Sino-Khitan minister Yeh-lü Ch'u-ts'ai, who managed to exercise some restraint on the Mongol leaders' more rapacious instincts; it is he who is credited with foiling the suggestion that the population of north China should be exterminated, and the land turned over to pasture for the Mongols' flocks and herds.

Bibliography: 1. Primary sources. Mongolian: *The Secret History of the Mongols*, English trs. F.W. Cleaves, Cambridge, Mass. 1982; I. de Rachewiltz, in *Papers in Far Eastern history*, 1971-85, and U. Onon, Leiden 1990; French tr. P. Pelliot, Paris 1949. Chinese: *Yüan-shih*, tr. W. Abramowski, *Die chinesischen Annalen von Ögödei und Güyük— Übersetzung des 2. Kapitels des Yüan-shih*, in *Zentralasiatische Studien*, x [1976], 117-67. Persian: D͟juwaynī, and tr. D͟juwaynī-Boyle;

Ras̲h̲īd al-Dīn, relevant section of the *Djāmiʿ al-tawārīkh*, ed. E. Blochet, GMS, Leiden and London 1911, or (better) ed. A. Alizade, Moscow 1980, tr. J.A. Boyle, *The Successors of Genghis Khan*, New York and London 1971.

2. Secondary sources: All general studies of the Mongol Empire contain some account of Ögedey and his reign. More detail is to be found in Barthold, *Turkestan*[4], London 1977, ch. 5, and L. de Hartog, *Genghis Khan: Conqueror of the World*, London 1989, chs. 13-15. On Yeh-lü Ch'u-ts'ai (conspicuous by his absence from the Islamic sources), see de Rachewiltz, *Yeh-lü Ch'u-ts'ai (1189-1243): Buddhist idealist and Confucian statesman*, in A.F. Wright and D. Twitchett (eds.), *Confucian personalities*, Stanford 1962, 189-216.

(D.O. Morgan)

OG̲H̲UL (T.), a word common to all Turkic languages (cf. W. Radloff, *Versuch eines Wörterbuches der Türk-Dialecte*, St. Petersburg 1888-1911, i/2, cols. 1015-16), found as early as Ork̲h̲on Turkic and meaning "offspring, child", with a strong implication of "male child", as opposed to *ḳiz* "girl" [*q.v.*] (Sir Gerard Clauson, *An etymological dictionary of pre-thirteenth century Turkish*, Oxford 1972, 83-4), original plural *og̲h̲lan*, still thus in Kās̲h̲g̲h̲arī (*Dīwān lug̲h̲āt al-turk*, facs. ed. Atalay, iv, *Dizini*, 425-6; C. Brockelmann, *Mitteltürkischer Wortschatz*, Budapest 1928, 126).

In connection with the sense of "offspring, descendant", attention may be called to certain formations, such as *odjaḳ og̲h̲lu*, "son of a good house", *ḳul og̲h̲lu*, which used to be applied to the sons of the Janissaries. *Og̲h̲ul* is very frequently found in family names where it takes the place of the Persian *zāde* or the Arabic *ibn*, e.g. Ḥekīm-og̲h̲lu or Ḥekīm-zāde for Ibn al-Ḥekīm, or Ramaḍān-og̲h̲lu for Ramaḍān-zāde or Ibn Ramaḍān (where it should be remembered that the Arabic *ibn* does not mean exclusively "son" but "descendant"). An incomplete survey of such formations in an early period is to be found in *Sidjill-i ʿot̲h̲mānī*, iv, 778-812. Atatürk's law on family names has led in Republican Turkey to many names incorporating the element *oğlu* after the name of famous persons, families or tribes (e.g. Osmanoğlu, Şahsevenoğlu) or after the names of practitioners of trades and crafts (e.g. Saraçoğlu, Ekmekçioğlu, Tarakçıoğlu, Fırıncıoğlu, Dülgeroğlu).

From being an original plural, *og̲h̲lan* evolved into an independent singular, meaning "youth, servant, page, bodyguard", also found in certain compounds, e.g. *ič og̲h̲lan*, "sultan's page", *dil og̲h̲lan*, "language-boy", "interpreter". From *og̲h̲lan* we also get German Uhlan, the name for light cavalry.

Bibliography: Given in the article; see also *İA* art. *Oğul* (F. Rahmeti Arat).

(F. Babinger-[C.E. Bosworth])

OG̲H̲UZ [see g̲h̲uzz].

OG̲H̲UZ-NĀMA, a term which designates the epic tradition of the Og̲h̲uz [see g̲h̲uzz], Turkish tribes mentioned for the first time in the Ork̲h̲on [*q.v.*] inscriptions.

After the fall of the empire of the Kök or Celestial Turks (7th-8th centuries), the Og̲h̲uz tribes migrated westwards. From the 8th and 9th centuries onwards, they are found installed in the basin of the middle and upper Syr Darya, between Lakes Aral and Balkas̲h̲ in the modern Kazak̲h̲stan Republic, where they formed tribal confederations. The Saldjūḳs, who invaded the Persian world and Asia Minor from the 11th century onwards, were part of these. The epic tradition of the Og̲h̲uz rests on earlier legends and epic tales dating from before their adoption of Islam. The geographical setting reflects the regions of the Syr Darya. Like popular poetry and ethnic origin legends, this epic tradition was at first transmitted orally.

The title *Og̲h̲uz-nāma* denotes the legend going back to the eponymous hero Og̲h̲uz. The tales were transmitted by the *ozans* [*q.v.*] who recited and sang them to the accompaniment of the *kopuz*. Written *Og̲h̲uz-nāmas* are signalled from the 13th century onwards, during the Saldjūḳ period, but none has come down to us. The oldest text is that given by the Persian historian Ras̲h̲īd al-Dīn (646-718/1248-1318 [*q.v.*]) in his *Djāmiʿ al-tawārīkh* begun in the time of the Il-K̲h̲ānid G̲h̲azan (694-703/1294-1304 [*q.v.*]) and presented to his successor Öldjeytü (703-16/1304-16 [*q.v.*]). The author based himself on oral information in which legend and reality are mixed together, which is why his history of the Og̲h̲uz belongs more to the realm of folklore than history. Ras̲h̲īd al-Dīn's *Og̲h̲uz-nāma* relates happenings from before the Og̲h̲uz's conversion to Islam, but it also contains historical facts concerning the Saldjūḳ conquests. The author must have used in the first place a text written in Turkish and then translated into Persian, since his narrative contains vocabulary elements from Mongolian and Eastern Turkish. He has added to this Ḳurʾānic verses and poetic quotations from the *S̲h̲āh-nāma*, as well as certain phrases aimed at making the subject more vivid, such as "in the towns of Talas and Sayram, Muslim Turks are living today".

In the Bibliothèque Nationale of Paris there is preserved an *Og̲h̲uz-nāma* in Uyg̲h̲ur script (Suppl. turc 1001, fonds Schefer). According to P. Pelliot, it must have been written *ca.* 700/1300 in the region of Turfān, but the manuscript itself must have been copied in K̲h̲ʷārazm at the beginning of the 9th/15th century. The story contains no Islamic traces, but Iranian influences and some Mongolian words have been detected in it. The story rests on the epic tradition of the ancient Turks. Cosmogonic myths and the confused memory of great exploits are linked with the eponymous hero Og̲h̲uz. There is a totemistic substratum, such as the appearance of the "grey wolf". The heroes in it are the legendary Og̲h̲uz K̲h̲ān, of heavenly origin, and his Begs, who represent symbolically the Og̲h̲uz tribes and confederations of tribes. The epic tradition was written between the 7th/13th and 9th/15th centuries. The copyists made no change at all to the basic text, apart from a certain Islamic gloss. They added details stemming from various periods and from various places inhabited by the Turks. An *Og̲h̲uz-nāma* of 65 lines was inserted into the *Taʾrīk̲h̲-i Āl-i Saldjūḳ* of Yazïdjï-og̲h̲lu ʿAlī, who lived in the time of sultan Murād II (824-48, 850-5/1421-44, 1446-51 [*q.v.*]). Except for the latest part dealing with events contemporary with the author, the work is a translation of Ras̲h̲īd al-Dīn's *Djāmiʿ al-tawārīkh* for the Og̲h̲uz and of Ibn Bībī for the Saldjūḳids.

The *Og̲h̲uz-nāma* gave birth to two works of fundamental importance. The first is the *Book of Dede Ḳorḳut*, preserved in two manuscripts dating from the end of the 10th/16th century, one in the Vatican Library and the other at Dresden. Its subject is the epic-chevaleresque cycle of the Og̲h̲uz and their fights with the evil Christian believers. Added to Central Asian motifs is material stemming from the 8th-9th/14th-15th centuries, when the Aḳ Ḳoyunlu occupied the lands of Persian Ād̲h̲arbaydjān and eastern Anatolia. The hero of the story, Bayïndïr, bears the name of an ancestor of the Aḳ Ḳoyunlu. Dede Ḳorḳut, to whom the story is attributed, represents the *ozan*, preserver of the oral epic tradition, who recites and sings the noble deeds of the old heroes. The second work drawn from the origins of the ancient *Oghuz-nāmas* is that of Abu 'l-Ghāzī Bahādur (1012-74/1603-63 [*q.v.*]), a khān of Khwārazm who led an adventurous life, who belonged to the family of the Uzbek or Özbeg [*q.v.*] Shībānī and who was a descendant of Čingiz Khān. He wrote two works, one on the ethnic origins of the Turkmens, the *Shadjara-yi Tarākima*, and another, the *Shadjara-yi Turk*, written at Khīwa in the year of his death and forming a genealogical history of the Turks. The author used Rashīd al-Dīn's history, but he states that he used seventeen historical chronicles. The tradition of the legendary Oghuz lived on in Central Asia, where numerous *Oghuz-nāmas* written between the 9th/15th and 13th/19th centuries are to be found. On some occasions, Oghuz appears in them as a Muslim hero summoning his people to adopt the Islamic faith.

Bibliography: W. Bang and G.R. Rahmati, *Die Legende von Oghuz Kaghan*, in *SBAW Berlin* (1932), 683-724; W. Barthold, *Histoire des Turcs d'Asie Centrale*, Paris 1945, Tkish. version, *Orta Asya Türk tarihi hakkında dersler*, Ankara 1975; L. Bazin, *Notes sur les mots "Oghuz" et "Türk"*, in *Oriens*, vi (1954), 315-22; A. Bombaci, *Histoire de la littérature turque*, Paris 1968, 102-3, 162-71, 183-99; J. Eckmann, *Die Tschagataische Literatur*, in *PTF*, ii, Wiesbaden 1964, 382-5; A.-M. von Gabain, *Die alttürkische Literatur*, in *ibid.*, 218-20; R. Giraud, *L'empire des Turcs Célestes*, Paris 1960; K. Jahn, *Die Geschichte der Oghuzen des Rašīd-ad-Dīn*, Vienna 1969; A.N. Kononov, *Rodoslovnaya Turkmen*, Moscow-Leningrad 1958; H. Korogly, *Oguzskiy geroičeskiy epos*, Moscow 1976; B. Ögel, *Türk mitolojisi*, i, Ankara 1971; P. Pelliot, *Sur la légende d'Oghuz Khan en écriture ouïgoure*, in *T'oung Pao*, xxvii (1930), 247-538; A.M. Sherbak, *Oguz-nāme-Muhabbatnāme*, Moscow 1959; F. Sümer, *Oğuzlar*, in *İA*; idem, *Oğuzlar'a ait destanı mahiyetde eserler*, in *AÜDTCF Dergisi*, xvii (1960), 359-455; Z.V. Togan, *Umumî Türk tarihine giriş*, i, Istanbul 1946; idem, *Oğuz destanı, Reşideddin Oğuznâmesi*, Istanbul 1972.

(Irène Mélikoff)

OHRID [see OKHRI].

OKČU-ZĀDE, Meḥmed Shāh Beg (970-1039/1562-1630), Ottoman *nishāndji* and prose stylist.

Okču-zāde Meḥmed Shāh (or Shāhī) Beg was born in 970/1562, the son of a long-serving Ottoman chancery official, later *beglerbegi* [*q.v.*] Okču-zāde Meḥmed Pasha (d. *ca.* 995/1587). His own chancery career spanned 44 years. Appointed *kātib* of the *dīwān-i hümāyūn* [*q.v.*] (988/1580), he held office as *re'īs ül-küttāb* (1005/1596), *defter emīni* (1006/1597), and *nishāndji* [*q.vv.*] (1007-10/1599-1601). He then served as *defterdār* [*q.v.*] of Egypt with the rank of *sālyāne begi* (1013-16/1605-8). After several years without official employment, he was reappointed *defter emīni* (*ca.* 1029/1620), then *nishāndji* briefly at the start of ʿOthmān II's Polish campaign (1030/1621), and again for a short final period (*ca.* 1031-3/1622-3) coinciding approximately with the second sultanate of Muṣṭafā I and the tenure of the office of *shaykh ül-Islām* by his friend and patron Yaḥyā Efendi. Okču-zāde died in 1039/1630 (Newʿī-zāde ʿAṭā'ī, *Dheyl-i Sheḳā'iḳ-i nuʿmāniyye*, Istanbul 1268/1852, ii, 730-1).

Considered by ʿAṭā'ī as second only to Tādjī-zāde Djaʿfer Čelebi for his skill as *nishāndji*, Okču-zāde's *inshā'* style is comparable with that of ʿAzmī-zāde, Nergisī and Weysī [*q.vv.*]. His principal works are: (i) *Münshe'āt al-inshā'*, a collection of about 80 letters, first compiled *ca.* 1038/1629, with a valuable autobiographical introduction; various manuscript versions exist. (ii) *Aḥsen al-ḥadīth* (published Istanbul 1313/1895-6), an elegant versification, with prose commentary, of *ḳirḳ ḥadīth* (cf. A. Karahan, *İslam-Türk edebiyatında Kırk Hadis toplama, tercüme ve şerhleri*, Istanbul 1954, 218-22). (iii) A prose translation of Kāshifī's [*q.v.*] *Tuḥfet al-ṣalāt* (completed 1021/1612). Samples of his verse are also found in *tedhkires* under the *makhlaṣ* Shāhī.

Bibliography: ʿAṭā'ī, ii, 730-1, and Okču-zāde's *Münshe'āt*, Istanbul University Library TY 3105, fols. 1b-8b; derived from ʿAṭā'ī are Kātib Čelebi, *Fedhleke*, Istanbul 1267/1851, 127-8; Aḥmed Resmī, *Khalīfet er-rü'esā* [*Sefīnet er-rü'esā*], Istanbul 1269/1853, 23-5; *Sidjill-i ʿOthmānī*, iv, 153; *ʿOthmānlï mü'ellifleri*, ii, 78-9. For other references, see C. Woodhead, *Ottoman inşa and the art of letter-writing: influences upon the career of the nişancı and prose stylist Okçuzade (d. 1630)*, in *Osmanlı araştırmaları*, vii-viii (1988), 143-59.

(Christine Woodhead)

OKHRĪ, Ohrid, a former Ottoman *sandjaḳ* capital and centre of an extensive *ḳaḍā'*, today a town of *ca.* 20,000 inhabitants situated in the south-westernmost part of the former Yugoslav republic of Macedonia. The Ottoman name of Okhrī derives from the Slav Ohrid, which in turn goes back to the antique name Likhnidos. Throughout recorded history it was a major centre of Slav Christianity, the seat of an autocephalous patriarchate (976-1767 A.D.) and from 971 to 1018 capital of the West Bulgarian or Slav-Macedonian empire of Tsar Samuel. During the greater part of the Ottoman period (1385 or 1395-1912), it was the centre of a *sandjaḳ* which comprised the south-western corner of modern Slav Macedonia and large stretches of central Albania. During the reorganisations of the *Tanẓīmāt* [*q.v.*], it was degraded to a *ḳaḍā'* in the *sandjaḳ* of Manastïr [*q.v.*], which was also the centre of the *wilāyet* of Manastïr. Okhrī was further an Islamic centre of regional importance, possessing a number of mosques, *medreses* and dervish lodges, of which that of the Ḥayātiyye was the central *tekke* of this Khalwetiyye branch of supra-regional importance, having a large number of *tekkes*, especially in southern Albania.

Okhrī is situated at an altitude of 806 m/2,643 feet above sea level on the shores of Lake Ohrid, and is picturesquely built on the slopes of a promontory, which is on three sides surrounded by the lake and still carries the well-preserved castle and city walls of Tsar Samuel's time, repaired in the Middle Ages and maintained by the Ottomans till the 19th century. Its easily defensible position, on a lake full of fish and at the head of a fertile plain, ensured that the town was inhabited throughout recorded history as well as in pre-historic times. Moreover, Okhrī commands the Via Egnatia on the eastern approaches of Albania.

The old Ottoman chroniclers (ʿĀshïḳ-pasha-zāde, Orudj, Neshrī, Anonymus Giese) do not mention the conquest of Ohrid and present an inaccurate picture of the conquest of the adjacent districts (Manastïr, Pirlepe/Prilep to the east and Ḳarlï-Ili = Central Albania to the west), which are supposed to have been conquered in 787/1385. This date in fact represents a raid into Albania, ending with the Battle of the Vijoshe, after which a number of Albanian lords accepted Ottoman overlordship. It is possible that at that time the Albanian ruler of Ohrid, the Grand Župan Andrew Gropa, who in 1378 is mentioned as such on the foundation inscription of the church of Old St. Clement, was removed and direct Ottoman rule installed. It is nevertheless difficult to imagine

Okhrī, ruin of Imaret Mosque, late 15th century. (Photo: M. Kiel, 1990)

Okhrī, Hayati Tekke, early 19th century. (Photo: M. Kiel, 1990)

direct rule over the Ohrid area as long as Constantin Dejanović and Marko Kraljevič were still ruling over almost all of Slav Macedonia (till their deaths in 1395) as Ottoman vassals. The town of Ohrid seems to have surrendered to the Ottomans without a fight and the annexation of the district went through without great disturbance. On one side, this is reflected in the fact that the Ohrid Christians continued to live inside the old walled town and kept almost all their old churches. Moreover, the flourishing Slav Christian arts of the 14th century, architecture, icon painting and wall painting, continued to flourish after the Ottoman administration was installed. This is shown by a long list of newly-built or painted churches in the villages around Ohrid and in the town itself (Radožda, 1400; Višni, 1400-5, Elšani, 1407-8; Njivica (Psarades), 1409-10; Velestovo, 1444, Godivlje, *ca.* 1450; Lešani Monastery 1451-2, Stefan Pancir-Gorica, 1450-60; Sts. Constantin and Helena in Ohrid, 1460; Leskoec, 1461-2; St. Nicolas Bolnica in Ohrid, 1467 and 1480-1; Kosel, 1490, mostly built by local Ohrid noblemen). Interesting is the gap between the 1410s and 1430s, an indication of the unsettled conditions during the civil war between the sons of Sultan Bāyezīd I and its aftermath under Murād II. The artists of this 15th-century "School of Ohrid" also left their works in present-day Greek territory (Banitsa, now Vevi, near Vodena-Edessa, 1460): in Bulgaria, Monastery of Dragalevtsi near Sofia, 1475-6; the Monastery of St. Demetrius of Boboševo near Dupnica, 1487-8, and the Monastery of Matka near Skopje, painted in 1496-7 at the expense of Lady Milica, also a member of the old nobility. Some churches have a list of their property in land and orchards, others mention the bishop in whose time the building was erected or painted, or they mention the ruling Ottoman Sultan, styled as "Tsar". As a whole, these preserved monuments of Christian art mirror the situation in the Ohrid *ḳaḍā*ʾ in a manner not recorded in any chronicle.

After the conquest, the Ottomans confiscated two of the major churches of Ohrid and turned them into mosques for the Muslim settlers who came to form the nucleus of the Muslim Turkish population of the town. The first church was the cathedral of St. Sofia, built in 1056 by the Byzantine archbishop Leo on the site of an older church, perhaps going back to K͟hān or Tsar Boris or Michael after the Bulgarians/Macedonians had converted to Christianity (865 A.D.) and enlarged by a monumental exo-narthex by Archbishop Gregory in 1317. An Ottoman account of sizeable repairs of this building, dated 955/1548 (Maliyeden Müdevver no. 55, p. 522), gives us the name of the ruler responsible for the transformation of the church into a mosque: "the father of Sultan Murād K͟hān, Sulṭān Meḥemmed K͟hān", which is Meḥemmed I (1413-21). This sultanic mosque did not get a *waḳf* of its own. The expenditure for its maintenance and for the large staff of its servants (according to an account of 1047/1636-7, sixteen persons) was paid by the income of the Ok͟hrī *muḳāṭaʿa* (BBA, Maliyeden Müdevver no. 5625, p. 26). The second church, the then episcopal church of St. Clement, a tri-conchos, built in the late 9th century by St. Clement himself, must have been seized by Sultan Meḥemmed II when visiting the town during his Albanian campaign of 1466. In that year, there had been disturbances, of a further unspecified nature, in Ohrid, in which the Archbishop Dorothej and a part of the Ohrid clergy and nobility had been involved. This group was deported to Istanbul and to the town of Elbasan, newly-founded by Meḥemmed in that same year. The confiscation of the church is seen as an act of punishment.

This action would explain why the mosque is locally known as the "Mosque of Sultan Meḥemmed". In the last decade of the 15th century, the by then 600 year-old church was demolished, and on its foundations the large, single-domed mosque which we see today was erected in the pure Ottoman style of the time of Bāyezīd II. Before the confiscation, the Ohrid Christians were allowed to dig up the relics of St. Clement and to take all the icons and church books to the large monastery church of Panayia Perivleptos, built in 1295 by the Albanian lord Progon Sguros, son-in-law of the Byzantine emperor Andronicus II. In this way, the Perivleptos church, thereafter called "St. Clement"', became the richest repository of mediaeval icons and manuscripts. It became the seat of the Patriarchate of Ohrid, and it remained there till the end of this institution, able to function legally within the framework of Ottoman law.

The walled town of Ohrid encloses a space of nearly 32 ha. Using the well-known formula of 130 to 150 inhabitants per hectare for a mediaeval walled settlement, this would indicate a population of about 4,000 inhabitants, which is a lot for its time and place. As, however, the western half of the enclosure was almost certainly empty (steep slopes, and no traces of mediaeval buildings whatsoever), we might suggest a pre-Ottoman population of 2,500-3,000. In the 15th century the number of the original inhabitants of Ohrid must have diminished. Almost immediately after the conquest of Constantinople, the Jews of Ohrid were deported to the new Ottoman capital. In 947/1540 the Jews from Ohrid living in Istanbul numbered only 16 families (Tapu Defter no. 210, pp. 45-72). In 1466 Sultan Meḥemmed II deported an unknown number of Ohrid Christians to his newly-founded town of Elbasan, an event only recorded in an marginal note in a Slavic church book. The Ottoman census register T.D. 367 from 1528-9, p. 432, describing Elbasan, gives an impression of the extent of this deportation. Out of the 174 households of Christians, 73 households are mentioned as deportees (*d͟jemʿat-i sürgünān-i gebrān-i nefs-i Ilbaṣan*), paying until then considerably lower taxes. The first preserved detailed survey of the urban population of Ohrid is apparently the census of 1583, contained in the *mufaṣṣal defter* of the Ohrid *sand͟jaḳ* preserved in the Cadaster Office in Ankara (Kuyudu Kadime, no. 25). It gives the names of 25 Christian *maḥalla*s in Ohrid, mostly called after their churches, having altogether 263 households. The Muslims are mentioned as one group with a total of 270 households. The names of the heads of households show us that a considerable part of them were converts to Islam in the first generation (ibn-i ʿAbd Allāh), 21% of the total. As a whole, the town might have numbered 2,600-2,800 inhabitants, including the military and the administration, or just about as many as in the 14th century. The 1583 register explicitly states that the Christians as well as the Muslim citizens were freed from paying the *ʿawāriḍ* and *tekālif* taxes [see ʿAWĀRIḌ] because they had long been entrusted with the maintenance of the town walls.

For the villages of the *ḳaḍā*ʾ of Ohrid, we have population numbers from 1519 and 1583 for the Muslims and the Christians, and for 1634 for the Christians only. The best available numbers for the late Ottoman population, from Vasil Kănčev, shortly before 1900, show us the end of the development. Especially in the 16th and 17th centuries, this shows a totally atypical demographic trend. For the two towns of the *ḳaḍā*ʾ (Ohrid and Ustruga/Struga) and 55 of its villages, constituting almost two-thirds of the whole, we have comparable numbers. In 1519 these settlements contained 2,745 households, of which 7% were Muslim, all living in the two towns. Instead of showing a massive population growth, as known from most of the Balkans and Anatolia (and all over Europe), the Ohrid area stagnated. In 1583 the Christians numbered 2,490 households, only 35 more than in 1519. The Muslims, on the other hand, had increased from 200 to 523, or to 17% of the total surveyable population. The numbers of 1634 (Nat. Libr. Sofia, Oh. 6-7) show that the Islamisation of a part of the population of the villages and the towns must have continued, but as a whole the total population suffered only a slight decline, and not the drastic losses known to have taken place elsewhere, in the Balkans, especially in the Greek lands and in Central Anatolia. The poll tax register of 1634 shows that the Christian population of the town of Ohrid had decreased to 210 households. A codex entry of the year 1664 mentions that the town had 142 Christian houses but no less than 37 churches. In 1670 Ewliyā Čelebi visited the town, which he describes as counting 160 well-built Christian houses, all situated within the castle walls, and over 300 Muslim houses, also well constructed and palace-like. These numbers look quite reliable. The mid-17th century seems to reflect the lowest point for the Ohrid Christians. In the subsequent period, they recovered, when the town again was witnessing expansion. The same is true for the village population. Some villages, which in the late 16th century seemed to be on the road toward total Islamisation (Delogožda, Livada, Mislešovo, Moroišta, Novo Selo, Orovnik, Trebeništa, Vapila and Volino), had by 1900 no Muslims at all. Some later prominent Muslim villages, as Radolišta, Vešta or Zagračani, on the other hand, were in 1583 already one-third Muslim, showing that this process is much earlier than the 17th century, with its grave economic difficulties, than is usually assumed.

After the Ottoman conquest, the town of Ohrid began to spread outside the city walls. A *ḥammām* on the Struga road, to the north-east of the castle, with pronounced 15th-century features, still stands as an illustration of this process. The most important genuine Ottoman building in the town is the so-called "ʿImāret Dj̲āmiʿi", or "Emperor's Mosque" (Careva Džamija). Local legend connects it with Meḥemmed the Conqueror. In fact, it was built immediately before 897/1490-1, when its *waḳf-nāme* was written. In this important source, the founder was Sinān al-Dīn Yūsuf Čelebi, son of Ḳāḍī Maḥmūd. This Sinān Čelebi is mentioned in 1479 as inspector of the sultanic *k̲h̲āṣṣeler* in Bosnia. He died in Radj̲ab 898/April 1493 and was buried in the graveyard next to his mosque, where his *türbe* and tombstone are still preserved. According to local legend, Sinān was a Pas̲h̲a and a descendant of a local Ohrid noble family. The *waḳf-nāme* provides for a *zāwiye*, a school and an *ʿimāret* where the poor of all creeds were fed daily. Very probably, Sinān Čelebi dedicated the mosque to Sultan Bāyezīd II, when the latter on his Albanian campaign of 1492 visited Ohrid. To the *waḳf* property belonged the large villages of Vraništa and Ležani near Ohrid, which he had received from Sultan Bāyezīd as a present, as well as a *k̲h̲ān* in Karaferya/Verria and some shops and water mills in and around Ohrid. The *ʿimāret* mosque fell into ruins in the late 19th century, but its four walls remain standing, the whole showing pronounced features of the architectural fashion of Bāyezīd II's time. All other Islamic buildings of any importance are situated outside the old town, to the east and the south of it, along the flat lake-side and on the plain along the roads to Manastīr/Bitola and Struga. Besides the above-mentioned buildings, the *waḳf* section of the 1583 census (BBA, TD 717, a *suret* from 1613, pp. 741-53) gives the names of a number of mostly small Islamic institutions and their buildings: the school (*muʿallim-k̲h̲āne*) of Süleymān Bey, the *mesdj̲id* of Iskender Bey, the *mesdj̲id* and school of Maḥmūd Čelebi, son of Ḥādj̲dj̲ī Ṭurg̲h̲ut, the mosque of S̲h̲eyk̲h̲ S̲h̲udjāʿ b. Barak, the school of ʿAlī Čelebi b. Ḥamza, the school and *mesdj̲id* of Yūnus Voyvode and the *mesdj̲id* of Ḥamza the Bazargān. Ok̲h̲rī-zāde Muṣṭafā Čelebi, who founded a school in Struga, was the builder of a *ḥammām* in Ohrid, most probably the one on the Struga road. The fact that Islam was slowly spreading in the Ohrid villages is illustrated by the fact that a Meḥmed Bey b. Isḥāḳ had constructed a *mesdj̲id* and a school in the village of Delogožda, where in 1583 14 Muslim households were living, besides 73 Christian households (in 1900 Delogožda was entirely Muslim). The register also mentions the mosque of Ḥādj̲dj̲ī Ḳāsīm in Ohrid but gives no details on its *waḳf*. The Aya Sofya mosque/church is not mentioned because it had no *waḳf* of its own, but was maintained from other sources.

In 1081/1670-1, Ewliyā Čelebi visited Ohrid, and he mentions that the town had 17 mosques and *mesdj̲ids*, of which the mosque of Ḥādj̲dj̲ī Ḳāsīm, the Ḳulog̲h̲lu mosque, the mosque of Ḥaydar Pas̲h̲a and that of Ḥādj̲dj̲ī Ḥamza were the most important, besides of course the Aya Sofya mosque/church and that of Sinān Čelebi, who in the 1583 lists and by Ewliyā is styled Ok̲h̲rī-zāde or Ok̲h̲rī-zāde Sinān Čelebi. Of *medreses*, Ewliyā mentions the "*tekke-medrese*" of Sultan Süleymān and the *medrese* of Siyāwus̲h̲ Pas̲h̲a, both unknown from the extant sources, including the comprehensive work of Cahid Baltacı. The official Ottoman list of *medreses* of Rūmeli from *ca.* 1660 (Özergin 1974), however, mentions the only *medrese* then active in Ohrid as being that of Ḥamza Bey, a person certainly identical with the founder of the mosque of "Ḥādj̲dj̲ī Ḥamza" as mentioned by Ewliyā and the "Ḥamza Bazargān" of the 1583 *defter*. Besides these buildings, there were three *k̲h̲āns* in Ohrid and two *ḥammāms*. Illustrative is Ewliyā's remark that the Aya Sofya mosque was only used on Fridays, when its guards and servants came to pray there, but that on other days, against a small payment, Christians were admitted to perform their own ceremonies. Taken in all, the Ohrid of the 17th century was still a small town, in spite of its being the centre of an important *sandj̲aḳ*.

In 1767 the Ottomans, advised by the Greek Patriarchate of Constantinople, dissolved the autocephalous archbishopric of Ohrid, which until that time still had the metropolitans of Kastoria, Prilep/Bitola, Strumica, Korça/Elbasan, Berat, Drač/Durazzo, Vodena/Edessa, Grevena and Sisanion under its jurisdiction, as well as the bishoprics of Debar/Kičevo, Veles, Prespa, Moglena, Gora-Mokra and Drimkol. In 1557 Ohrid had already lost its northern districts (Kalkandelen/Tetevo, Üsküp/Skopje, Istip/Štip, Gorna Džumaya-Nevrokop and Razlog), which came under jurisdiction of Serbian Patriarchate of Ipek/Pač, then restored by the Ottoman administration.

In the second half of the 18th century, the K̲h̲alwetiyye S̲h̲eyk̲h̲ Meḥmed Ḥayātī lived and worked in Ohrid and founded the Āsitāne-yi Ḥayātiyye, the mother *tekke* of a large number of others in

Macedonia and especially in Albania, as well as in the Greek Macedonian town of Kesriye/Kastoria. Meḥmed Ḥayātī is said to have studied in Edirne under the famous Ḥasan Sezāʾī (died in 1151/1738) and took the *khilāfet* from Shaykh Hüseyin of Siroz/Serres, after which he settled in Ohrid and transformed an old *medrese* into the first *tekke* of his new Khalwetī suborder, which he and his followers propagated successfully.

From the end of the 18th century till 1830, Ohrid and its district was ruled by the Albanian *derebey* Djemāl al-Dīn Bey, son of the Wezīr Aḥmed Pasha, who is remembered locally for the restoration of the Ohrid town walls, done with harsh forced labour from the local Christian population. He also brought good drinking water to the town, a feat commemorated in a long Ottoman inscription on the Iḥtisāb Česhme in the old town square "Čınar", a work of the poet Süleymān Fehim (1203-62/1789-1846), dated 1237/1821-2. In 1830, the reformed Ottoman army, on its way to suppress the Būshātlî Wezīrs of Iskenderiyye/Shkodër, drove him away and reinstalled a regular Ottoman administration. In 1262/1846 the Ottoman *Ḳāʾim-maḳām* Sherīf Bey constructed a large new *medrese* in Ohrid, of which a long inscription still remains. In the course of the 19th century, a number of mosques were repaired or rebuilt in the style of the period. The most important is the domed ʿAlī Pasha mosque in the market-place.

In the course of the 18th century, the population of the town of Ohrid and its *ḳaḍāʾ* began to grow. This growth gained momentum in the 19th century and is in accordance with the general trend in Europe and in the Ottoman dominions. One of the characteristics was that the Christians grew considerably faster than the Muslims, having bigger families. The result was that by 1900, when Kănčev did his research, which is generally held to be the most reliable, the town's population, in 1583 fifty-fifty Muslim-Christian and in the mid-17th century two-thirds Muslim, became two-thirds Christian. Kănčev gives for Ohrid 8,000 Bulgarian-Macedonian Christians, 300 Albanian and 460 Vlach Christians, 5,000 Turks and 500 Albanian Muslims. In the three *nāḥiye*s of the *ḳaḍāʾ* of Ohrid, great changes had occurred. The mountainous *nāḥiye* of Debrica in the north-east had entirely kept its Christian character but in the *nāḥiyes* of Ohrid, and especially that of Ustruga/Struga, Islam had gained considerably, partly through conversion of the local Slav-Macedonian population, partly through the settlement of Muslim Albanians coming from the west. The large villages of Boroec, Labunište, Oktisi and Podgorci had become half-Muslim but had remained Slav-speaking; the villages of Bogovica, Delogožda, Frangovo, Kalište, Mislodežda, Novo Selo, Poum, Radolišta, Velešta and Zagračani had become entirely Albanian Muslim. Turkish-speaking Muslims were only living in the towns of Ohrid and Struga. As a whole, the population of the *ḳaḍāʾ* had risen to 60,305 inhabitants, of whom 16,837, or 28%, were Muslim. The Ottoman *Nüfūs Defter* of 1889 gives 36,621 Christians and 16,230 Muslims (= 31%), the difference being caused by the fast-growing Christian community. The *Sālnāme* of the Manastîr *wilāyet* of 1305/1887-8, intended for public use, gives falsified numbers (17,345 Christians and 29,360, 63%, Muslims!)

Nineteenth-century Ohrid was a prosperous place. The Christian population particularly flourished and lived in large and well-built houses, the fur industry being their principal occupation. J.G. von Hahn, travelling in the early 1860s, especially noted that there were very few poor people in Ohrid. In his time, the *ʿimāret* of "Sinān Pasha" was still functioning, but it had lost most of its income. Like Ewliyā Čelebi 200 years before him, Hahn praises this institution, distributing food to the needy regardless of their religion.

During the Balkan Wars, on 29 November 1912, the Serbian-Montenegrin army took Ohrid, which was then incorporated in the Serbian state. Late Ottoman Ohrid counted, according to the *Sālnāme* of the Manastîr *wilāyet* of 1308/1890-1, 13 *khāns*, two *ḥammāms*, nine mosques, two *tekkes* and one *medrese*. In 1934 Fehim Bajraktarević noted 12 mosques in Ohrid. Most of his names are the same as those encounted by Ewliyā Čelebi. After 1912 the St. Sofia church/mosque was reconverted to a church. The Ottoman additions, except for the fine marble *minbar*, were removed. In the years after World War II, the many surviving mediaeval churches and their paintings were restored and studied. To a lesser extent the same was done with the Ottoman monuments. In 1955-6 an important part of the Turkish-speaking Muslims of Ohrid and Struga emigrated to Turkey. Their place was taken by Albanian Muslims, who in the 20th century witnessed an expansive growth, turning Ohrid from a Turkish-Muslim into an Albanian-Muslim town, especially as the Christians hardly grew any more. The Asitāne of the Ḥayātī order under the leadership of Sheykh Ḳadrī (born 1932), a direct descendant of Meḥmed Ḥayātī, is functioning unbrokenly, its buildings in perfect shape (December 1992). This *tekke*, which is one of the most important of Macedonian Islam, shared in the general renaissance of Islam after the downfall of old Yugoslavia.

The various censuses of the 20th century, only available for the western half of the old *ḳaḍāʾ* of Ohrid, show that the Albanian Muslims and the Pomaks [*q.v.*] survived the turbulences of the Balkan Wars and the two World Wars. In 1900 the 39 settlements later constituting the Yugoslav district of Struga, basically the plain of Ohrid and the mountains facing Albania, contained 24,640 inhabitants, of which 38% was Muslim. In 1914 it stood at 25,970 inhabitants, 39% Muslim; in 1944; 31,341 inhabitants, of which 42% Muslim; in 1953; 33,319, 46% Muslim; and 1969; 40,172, 52% Muslim. Thus the 19th century pattern has been completely reversed, the Muslims having the larger families, and the Slav Christian population, especially since the 1970s, being almost static. In the early 1990s, the Muslim population, Albanian, Slav Macedonian and Turkish-speaking, must have reached two-thirds of the total population of the same area.

Since World War II, the entire old town of Ohrid has been declared a Monument of National Culture, to be preserved for the coming generations. The town, with its many monuments and oriental flavour, and the lake side, has developed into a centre of international tourism, the most important one of Slav Macedonia.

Bibliography: For the 1519 and 1583 *ṭahrīrs* see Sokoloski, 1971. Ewliyā Čelebi, *Seyāḥat-nāme*, viii, Istanbul 1928, 735-43; J.G. von Hahn, *Reise durch die Gebiete des Drin und Wardar*, in *Denkschriften der Akad. der Wiss.*, Phil. Hist. Cl., Vienna 1865, no. 14, pp. 120-2; H. Gelzer, *Der Patriarchat von Achrida, Geschichte und Urkunden*, in *Abh. der Phil. Hist. Cl. der Sächsischen Gesellschaft der Wiss.*, Leipzig 1902; V. Kănčev, *Makedonija etnografija i statistika*, Sofia 1900 (repr. in *Izbrani proezvedenija*, Sofia 1970, 552-5); Meḥmed Tewfīḳ, *Manastîr wilāyetiniñ tārīkhčesi*, Manastîr 1327/1911; Iv. Snegarov, *Istorija na Ohridskata arhiepiskopija/patriaršija*, Sofia 1932; F.

Mesesnel, *Ohrid, varoš i jezero, starine, okoline*, Skopje 1934; D. Kočo, *Klimentoviot manastir Sv. Pantalejmon i razkopkata pri Imaret vo Ohrid*, in *Godišen Sbornik na Filosofski Fakultet*, Skopje 1948; I. Dujčev, *La conquête turque et la prise de Constantinople dans la littérature slave contemporaine*, in *Byzantinoslavica*, xiv (Prague 1953), 14-54 (text of the deportation of 1466); F. Bajraktarević, *Turski spomenici u Ohrid* (with lengthy French summary) in *Prilozi za Orientalnu Filologiju*, v (Sarajevo 1954-5), 111-34; B. Čipan, *Stara gradska arhitektura vo Ohrid*, Skopje 1955; D. Bošković-K. Tomovski, *L'architecture médievale d'Ohrid* (Serbian and French), in *Sbornik/Receuil de travaux du Musée National d'Ohrid*, 1961, 71-100; A. Nikolovski, D. Ćornakov, K. Balabanov, *The cultural monuments of the People's Republic of Macedonia*, Skopje 1961, 209-59; *Enciklopedija Jugoslavije*, vi, Zagreb 1965, 372-5; Semavi Eyice, *Ohri'nin Türk devrine ait eserler*, in *Vakıflar Dergisi*, vi (Ankara 1965), 137-45; G. Palikruševa-Krum Tomovski, *Les Tekkes en Macedoine, aux 18e-19e siècle*, in *Atti del Secondo Congresso Intern. di Arte Turca, Napoli*, 1965, 203-11; K. Popovski, *Demografski dviženija*, in V. Malevski (ed.), *Struga i Struško*, Struga 1970, 23-37 (rare 20th century censuses); M. Sokoloski, *Ohrid i Ohridsko vo XVI vek*, in *Makedonska Akademija na Naukite i Umetnostite, Prilozi*, ii/2 (Skopje 1971), 5-37 (fundamental); Hasan Kaleši, *Najstariji vakufski dokumenti u Jugoslaviji na Arapskom Jeziku*, Priština 1972, 111-43 (Okhrī-zāde Sinān Čelebi's *wakfiyye*); Kemal Özergin, *Eski bir rûzname göre Istanbul ve Rumeli medreseleri*, in *Tarih Enstitüsü Dergisi* (Istanbul 1973) 4-5 [1973-4], 262-90; A. Matkovski, *Crkovni davački (kilise resimleri) vo Ohridskata arhiepiskopija (1371-1767)*, in *MANU Prilozi*, ii/2 (Skopje 1971); *Ohrid i Ohridsko niz istorija, kniga vtora*, Skopje 1978; G. Subotić, *Ohridska slikarska škola XV veka*, Belgrade 1980 (with long French summary; fundamental); A. Stojanovski, *Gradovite na Makedonija od Krajot na XIV do XVII vek*, Skopje 1981 (esp. ch. I); Džemal Ćehajić, *Derviški redovi u Jugoslovenskim zemljama*, Sarajevo 1986, 112-15. (M. Kiel)

OKTAY [see ögedey].

OKTAY RİFAT (Horozcu), Turkish author and poet, born in Trabzon in 1914. He was the son of Samih Rifat, author and poet and Governor of Trabzon. He finished at the Faculty of Law in 1936 and was sent to Paris on a government grant to further his studies. After three years he had to come back to Turkey without completing his doctorate because of the start of World War II (1940). He worked at the Directorate of Press and Information and later practiced law. He died in Istanbul on 18 April 1988.

His friendship with Orhan Veli, whom he met at secondary school, continued until his death. He wrote only poetry until 1960, drama after 1960 and novels after 1970. In all his works, his literary style and themes show great variation because he liked trying his hand at different forms of expression, always renewing himself. Expression of his feelings and his thoughts, and the symbols which he created, all stemmed from his keen observation of real life.

Bibliography: 1. His works. (a) Poetry. *Garip*, 1941 (with Orhan Veli Kanık and Melih Cevdet Anday); *Güzelleme*, *Yaşayıp ölmek*, *Aşk ve avarelik üstüne şiirler*, 1945; *Aşağı yukarı*, 1952; *Karga ile tilki*, 1954; *Perçemli sokak*, 1956; *Aşık merdiveni*, 1958; *Elleri var özgürlüğün*, 1966; *Şiirler*, 1969; *Yeni şiirler*, 1973; *Çobanıl şiirler*, 1976; *Bir cıgara içimi*, 1979; *Elifli*, 1980; *Denize doğru konuşma*, 1982; *Dilsiz ve çıplak*, 1984; *Koca bir yaz*, 1987. (b) Plays. *Bir takım insanlar*, 1961; *Kadınlar arasında*, 1966; *Atlar ve filler* (staged in 1962); *Yağmur sıkıntısı* (staged in 1970); *Dirlik düzenlik* (staged in 1975); *Çil horoz* (staged in 1988). (c) Novels. *Bir kadının penceresinden*, 1976; *Danaburnu*, 1980; *Bay Lear*, 1982.

2. Studies. M. Kaplan, *Cumhuriyet devri Türk şiiri*, Ankara 1990; M. Ünlü and Ö. Özcan, *20.yüzyıl Türk edebiyatı*, Istanbul 1990; *Yazko edebiyat dergisi*, Şubat/Temmuz 1981; T. Uyar, *Milliyet sanat dergisi*, 15 Ekim 1984; S.K. Aksal, *Cumhuriyet gazetesi*, 3 Mayıs 1988. (Çiğdem Balım)

OKYAR, ʿAlī Fetḥī (1880-1943), Turkish statesman and diplomat, was born and brought up in Macedonia, then under Ottoman rule. He entered the War College and Staff College in Istanbul, graduating as a Staff Captain in 1904. At the War College, he formed a lifelong friendship with Muṣṭafā Kemāl [Atatürk]. During service with the 3rd Army, he joined the Committee of Union and Progress [see ittiḥād we teraḳḳī djemʿiyyeti], which brought about the revolution of 1908. He was then posted as Military Attaché in Paris (1908-11) before returning to serve in what is now Libya (1911) and in the first Balkan war (1912). He was briefly elected to the Ottoman Chamber of Deputies in 1912, and in 1913 he resigned from the army to become Ambassador in Sofia (1913-17). After re-election to parliament in December 1917, he joined the cabinet formed by ʿIzzet Pasha at the very end of the Great War. In March 1919 he was imprisoned by the succeeding government of Dāmād Ferīd Pasha [*q.v.*], and then transferred by the British to internment in Malta until 1921. After his release, Fetḥī joined the nationalist government led by Muṣṭafā Kemāl, becoming Minister of the Interior in October 1921, and twice Prime Minister (August to November 1923, and November 1924 to March 1925). He then left parliament, to become Turkish Ambassador in Paris. In August 1930 he returned to Turkey to establish the Free Republican Party (*Serbest Cumhuriyet Fırkası*). This was set up with Atatürk's encouragement as a Liberal opposition to the ruling Republican People's Party. Unfortunately the experiment proved premature since, against Fethi's intentions, the party attracted the support of those opposed to the secular institutions of the republic. Accordingly, it was wound up in October 1930. Fethi was appointed Ambassador to London in 1934, staying there until 1939, when he re-entered the Turkish parliament. He served a term as Minister of Justice, but retired in 1942, and died after an illness in 1943.

Bibliography: W.F. Weiker, *Political tutelage and democracy in Turkey: the Free Party and its aftermath*, Leiden 1973; *Türk Ansiklopedisi*, xxv, Ankara 1977, s.v. (W. Hale)

ÖLDJEYTÜ, Ghiyāth al-Dīn Muḥammad Khar-(later Khudā-)Banda Öldjeytü Sulṭān, eighth Mongol Īlkhān of Persia and the penultimate direct descendant of Hülegü to rule (704-16/1304-16). Born in 680/1282, he was like his predecessor Ghazan a son of Arghun, the fourth Īlkhān. He succeeded his brother without serious difficulty, and began a reign which was unusually peaceful by Mongol standards. Öldjeytü does not appear to have been a notable soldier, and his reign saw only three major military expeditions. In 706/1307 he attempted, at considerable cost, forcibly to incorporate the Caspian province of Gīlān, which had remained independent, into the Īlkhānate. In 712/1312-13 he mounted the last Īlkhānid invasion of Mamlūk territory, unsuccessfully besieging Raḥbat al-Shām [see raḥba] on the Euphrates; and in 713/1314 he was obliged to march east to ward off an invasion of Khurāsān by forces from the Čag̲h̲atay K̲h̲ānate. The early years of the reign had in fact seen an attempt, successful for a time, to re-establish peace and harmony between the various K̲h̲ānates of the Mongol Empire. Öld̲j̲eytü refers to this in a Mongolian letter of 1305 to King Philip the Fair of France (A. Mostaert and F.W. Cleaves, *Les Lettres de 1289 et 1305 des ilkhan Arγun et Öljeitü à Philippe le Bel*, Cambridge, Mass. 1962).

Domestically there seems to have been considerable continuity with the previous reign; the reform programme associated with G̲h̲azan continued in force, though it may perhaps have been pursued with reduced enthusiasm. The great *wazīr* and historian Ras̲h̲īd al-Dīn continued to hold office throughout the reign, though his tenure was not untroubled. His colleague Saʿd al-Dīn Sāwad̲j̲ī fell from power and was executed in 711/1312, to be succeeded by Tād̲j̲ al-Dīn ʿAlī-S̲h̲āh. Relations between Ras̲h̲īd al-Dīn and Tād̲j̲ al-Dīn eventually became so bad that the empire had to be divided into two administrative spheres so that the *wazīrs*' responsibilities should as far as possible not overlap: Ras̲h̲īd al-Dīn took the centre and south of the empire while Tād̲j̲ al-Dīn was made responsible for the north-west, Mesopotamia and Anatolia. Early in the next reign, that of Öld̲j̲eytü's son Abū Saʿīd, Tād̲j̲ al-Dīn was able to engineer Ras̲h̲īd al-Dīn's fall and execution (718/1318) before himself achieving the unparalleled feat, for an Īlk̲h̲ānid *wazīr*, of dying of natural causes.

Ras̲h̲īd al-Dīn presented to Öld̲j̲eytü his history of the Mongols which G̲h̲azan had commissioned, and which was to form the first part of the *D̲j̲āmiʿ al-tawārīk̲h̲*. Öld̲j̲eytü asked him to continue the work as a memorial to G̲h̲azan. This continuation was to contain accounts of all the peoples with whom the Mongols had come into contact: the unique "world-history" sections of Ras̲h̲īd al-Dīn's great history.

Öld̲j̲eytü's personal religious pilgrimage was complex even by the standards of the day, encompassing at one time or another almost every currently available faith. No doubt a residual shamanist, he had in infancy been baptised a Christian, with the name of Nicholas in honour of Pope Nicholas IV, with whom his father had negotiated. Subsequently he became a Buddhist, but after G̲h̲azan's decisive conversion to Islam, he became a Sunnī Muslim, dallying in turn with the Ḥanafī and S̲h̲āfiʿī *mad̲h̲habs*. Thereafter he became a S̲h̲īʿī.

For much of the reign work continued on a new capital, Sulṭāniyya [*q.v.*], on the plain to the south-east of modern Zand̲j̲ān. The city had been founded by Arg̲h̲un; it was completed in 713/1313-14. Since Öld̲j̲eytü maintained the nomadic habits of his ancestors, migrating seasonally from summer to winter quarters, Sulṭāniyya should perhaps be called his "chief seasonal residence" rather than his capital (C.P. Melville, *The itineraries of Sultan Öljeitü, 1304-16*, in *Iran*, xxviii [1990], 55-70). It is said that Öld̲j̲eytü wished to transfer the mortal remains of the S̲h̲īʿī imāms ʿAlī and Ḥusayn to a new shrine in Sulṭāniyya. This remarkable mausoleum eventually became, instead, Öld̲j̲eytü's own. It still stands, the only important building of the new capital to survive and the most striking positive memorial of the Mongol period in Persian history.

Bibliography: Primary sources: The most important is Abu 'l-Ḳāsim Ḳās̲h̲ānī, *Taʾrīk̲h̲-i Ūljāytū*, ed. M. Hambly, Tehran 1969. The unique ms., Aya Sofya 3019, ff. 135a-240b, should if possible be consulted. See also Waṣṣāf, *Taʾrīk̲h̲-i Waṣṣāf*, lith., ed. M.M. Iṣfahānī, Bombay 1852-3. Sources from the Tīmūrid period are also of value, e.g. Ḥāfiẓ Abrū, *D̲h̲ayl-i D̲j̲āmiʿ al-tawārīk̲h̲*, ed. K. Bayānī, 2nd ed., Tehran 1972, as are Mamlūk sources, especially ʿUmarī, in K. Lech, *Das mongolische Weltreich*, Wiesbaden 1968.

Secondary sources: J.A. Boyle in *Cambridge History of Iran*, v, Cambridge 1968, 397-406; Spuler, *Mongolen*[4], Leiden 1985, 90-8.

(D.O. Morgan)

OLENDIREK, Ottoman form of the Greek Lidoriki, a small borough in the central Greek Eparchy of Doridos, Nomos Efthiotis, 46 km west of Amphissa/Salona (16 km as the crow flies) and only urban centre of a large and particularly mountainous rural area. In Ottoman times it was the centre of a *ḳāḍīlīk*, first of the *sand̲j̲aḳ* of Tirhala, after 1530 of Inebak̲h̲tī-Lepanto, which after that date was organised as a separate *sand̲j̲aḳ*. It would remain within Inebak̲h̲tī until the end of the Ottoman period (here 1827). In the 17th and 18th centuries it was an Islamic centre of local importance.

Olendirek is situated in a small plain, 630 m above sea level, at the foot of the Giona Mountains (2510 m), at the crossing of the pass roads from Athens and Thebes (Istife) to Inebak̲h̲tī and from the Morea, via the small port of Vitrinitsa-Vodrunce, over the mountains to the Spercheios valley at Badračïḳ-Ypate in the north, and further to Thessaly and Macedonia, a route in modern times rarely used.

The place is mentioned as a seat of an Greek Orthodox bishopric from the late 9th century onward. After 1204 it belonged to the Despotate of Epirus and in 1327 it was included in the Catalan Duchy of Athens, as property of the Fadrique family. Sultan Yïldïrïm Bāyezīd reportedly occupied it in 1394 but lost it to the Despot of the Morea, Theodore Paleologus, three years later. Mediaeval Lidoriki must have had a castle, but nothing remains of it and nothing is known about it among the local population. S. Bommeljé and P. Doorn suggested that the castle of Velouchovo (now Kallion), 3 km outside the town, where antique and mediaeval ruins are preserved, is identical with the *Lodorich castrum* of the sources.

The exact date of the definitive Ottoman conquest of Olendirek is not known. Most probably it was taken during the reign of Murād II (1421-51) because the adjacent area immediately to the west, the likewise very mountainous district of Kravari, which also belonged to the *sand̲j̲aḳ* of Tirhala, was firmly in Ottoman hands in 1454. This can be seen in the *Taḥrīr defter*, Mal. Müd. 10, which contains frequent references to an earlier Ottoman census of the same district. The section on Olendirek is not preserved in this incomplete register.

At the very beginning of Ottoman rule, a small Muslim Turkish colony was settled in the town, which became the nucleus of the much larger Muslim population of later times. According to the Ottoman census of 1466 (Mal. Müd. 66), the town was the centre of a district with 10 villages and 34 *katuns* (semi-permanent settlements of Albanian or Vlach cattle breeders) and had 24 Muslim households and 146 Christian ones. According to the 1569-70 census, (Ankara KuK 50) the Muslims had stagnated at 19 households, whereas the Christians had gone up to 243 households. The town had a privileged status as a *derbend* settlement, guarding the road from Morea, Ḳarlï-ili and Inebak̲h̲tī to the inland of Greece in exchange for exemption from the *ʿawāriḍ* [*q.v.*] and *tekālīf* taxes and giving sons to the Janissary corps.

The sources for the 11th/17th century show partly a general decline of the population, and partly the effects of Islamisation of a large part of the local population. In 1642 there were 85 Christian households liable to pay the *djizye* (BBA. Mal. Müd. 1000, 252), in 1646 69 households (Mal. Müd. 1000, p. 5), but in 1688-9 only 27 households (Sofia, Nat. Libr. F. 195/2), on top of which an unknown number of families must be counted who were too poor to pay, or otherwise exempted. An official Ottoman list of *ḳāḍīliḳ*s of the European provinces of the empire, dating from 1670, mentions Olendirek in the eleventh of the 12 ranks of *ḳāḍīliḳ*s, a pointer to the relative unimportance of the place (M. Kemal Özergin, *Rumeli kadılıklarından 1078 düzenlemesi*, in *Ord. Prof. Ismail Uzunçarşılı'ya armağan*, Ankara 1976, 276). Ewliyā Čelebi, who in 1081/1669-70, on his way from Salona to Karpenisi (Krenbesh), must have passed through Olendirek, does not mention it, as his travel notes of this section were apparently in disorder.

In 1805 the French traveller François Pouqueville describes Olendirek as a *bourg* of 180 families, Greeks and Turks all speaking the same language because the Muslims were "des apostats indigènes" (*Voyage de la Grèce*, iv, Paris 1826, 56-7). It was still the centre of a *ḳāḍīliḳ*, having 42 villages. The Greek bishop and the Christian notables were residing in the nearby village of Klima.

In 1825, during the Greek War of Independence, the town was the centre of an Ottoman military district under ʿAbbās Pasha Dibra. In 1827 the Ottomans, the military and the civilians were driven out of town and district forever. Information on the modest Islamic spiritual life, or on Muslim building activity, seems to be non-existent, but the *Cevdet Evkaf Tasnifi* in the BBA may yield some names of mosques, schools or *tekke*s.

Throughout its history Lidoriki-Olendirek has remained very small. Bommeljé and Doorn thought that 1500-1600 inhabitants were the maximum in all times. In 1928, a peak of 1537 inhabitants was reached. During the Second World War, the town and the villages around it were destroyed by the Wehrmacht. In 1961 the town again had 1338 inhabitants, or just as many as in the Süleymānic age.

Bibliography: J. Koder and F. Hild, *Tabula Imperii Byzantini*, Vienna 1976, 205; *Megali Elleniki Enkyklopedeia*, xvi, 101-2; S. Bommeljé and P.K. Doorn, *Aetolia and the Aetolians, towards the interdisciplinary study of a Greek region*, Utrecht 1987, with exhaustive bibliography. The Ottoman sources mentioned in the text are unpublished.

(M. Kiel)

OLGHUN, MEḤMED ṬĀHIR (Tahir Olgun, Tâhir-ül Mevlevî), Turkish writer and literary critic, born in Istanbul on 13 September 1877, died in 1951. He graduated from the Gülkhāne Rüshdiyye-i ʿAskeriyyesi (military high school) and Menshe'-i küttāb-i ʿaskeriyye. While working as a secretary at the War Ministry, he attended the Fātiḥ Mosque *medrese* and received his *idjāzet-nāme* from Methnewīkhʷān Selānikli Meḥmed Esʿad Dede Efendi, whence his name Tâhir-ül Mevlevî. After 1903 he taught Persian, the history of Islam, history and literature in many schools, including the Dār üsh-shafaḳa high school and the Kuleli military high school. During his later years he worked in the cataloguing committees of the Istanbul libraries. He is known for his work on the leading figures of Islamic religion and on the history of Turkish literature.

Bibliography: 1. Selected works. *Mir'āt-i Ḥaḍret-i Mewlānā*, 1898; *Naẓīm we eshkāl-i naẓīm*, 1913; *Manzum bir muhtıra* (Tanzimat öncesi edebiyatı özeti), 1931; *Edebiyat lûgatı*, 1936; *Fuzuli'ye dair*, 1936; *Şair Nev'ı ve Suriye kasidesi*, 1937; *Baki'ye dair*, 1937; *Müslümanlıkta ibadet tarihi*, 1946; *Germiyanlı Şeyhi ve Harnâme'si*, 1949.

2. Studies. İbnülemin M.K. İnal, *Son asır Türk şairleri*, Istanbul 1970; K.E. Kürkçüoğlu, *Tahir-ül Mevlevî: Edebiyat lügatı*, Istanbul 1973; S.K. Karalioğlu, *Türk edebiyatı tarihi*, Istanbul 1986.

(Çiğdem Balim)

ʿOMAR KHAYYĀM [see ʿumar-i khayyām].

OMDURMAN (Umm Durmān), a town on the west bank of the Nile at the confluence of the Blue and White Niles (lat. 15°38′ N., long. 32°30′ E.), now linked with Khartoum (al-khurṭūm [*q.v.*]) and Khartoum North as the principal conurbation of the Republic of the Sudan. The etymology of the name is unknown, although several fanciful explanations have been given.

Omdurman is first mentioned as the village of a holy man, Ḥamad b. Muḥammad al-Mashyakhī, known as Wad (i.e. Walad) Umm Maryūm (1055-1142/1645-6 to 1729-30) (see Ibn Ḍayf Allāh, *Kitāb al-Ṭabaḳāt*, ed. Yūsuf Faḍl Ḥasan, ²Khartoum 1974, 174-82; cf. H.A. MacMichael, *History of the Arabs in the Sudan*, Cambridge 1922, ii, 242, no. 124). A Nile-crossing from Omdurman to the Djazīra, i.e. the peninsula between the Blue and White Niles, was used by the invading Turco-Egyptian army under Ismāʿīl Pasha in 1821. A fort, constructed to guard the western approaches to the capital, Khartoum, was surrendered to the forces of the Mahdī Muḥammad Aḥmad b. ʿAbd Allāh [see al-mahdiyya] on 5 January 1885, and Khartoum itself fell three weeks later.

The Mahdī, now the victorious head of a Sudanese Muslim state, transferred the capital to Omdurman, where he died on 22 June 1885 and was buried. Under his successor, the Khalīfa ʿAbd Allāh b. Muḥammad al-Taʿā'ishī [*q.v.*], the early settlement grew into a town. Like the Mahdī's earlier seats during the revolutionary war, it was officially styled *Buḳʿat al-Mahdī*, and the Mahdī's tomb (*ḳubbat al-Mahdī*) was a place of pilgrimage in lieu of the *ḥadjdj* to Mecca. Beside the tomb (now restored) are the Khalīfa's house (now a museum) containing a labyrinth of rooms, and to the west the great walled space which formed the mosque. Other official buildings were the arsenal-storehouse (*bayt al-amāna*, now a football stadium), the treasury (*bayt al-māl*), and the prison (*al-sāyir*, from the name of the gaoler). A great wall protected the inner city. From this central area ran three main roads: one southwards to the former Fort Omdurman (*al-kāra*), garrisoned by the Khalīfa's black troops (*djihādiyya*); one westwards to the parade-ground at the desert-fringe; and the ominously-named *darb al-shuhadā'* (the martyrs' road) northwards to the assembly-point for expeditions to Egypt. Around these roads, the greater part of Omdurman consisted of an unplanned huddle of dwellings, ranging from brick houses to straw huts, sprawling along the Nile bank for about 9 km/6 miles. Its depth of about 1½ km/a mile was limited by the distance to which river-water could conveniently be carried. For a detailed plan of Mahdist Omdurman, see R.C. Slatin, *Fire and sword in the Sudan*, London 1896 and later edns. The population of the town was greatly increased in 1888-9, when the Khalīfa more or less forcibly brought his tribesmen, the Taʿā'isha, and other Baḳḳāra [*q.v.*] from Dār Fūr [*q.v.*] to Omdurman, where they formed a privileged élite, oppressive to, and highly unpopular with, the more sophisticated riverain sedentaries (*awlād al-balad*). Like other migrations to the presence of the living or dead Mahdī, this movement was designated *hidjra*. Accounts of life in

Omdurman by three former European prisoners, Slatin (as above), Father Joseph Ohrwalder (in F.R. Wingate, *Ten years' captivity in the Mahdi's camp*, London 1892), and Charles Neufeld, *A prisoner of the Khaleefa*, London 1899, have found a wide readership. It should be borne in mind that the first two were produced under the auspices of Wingate as Director of (Egyptian) Military Intelligence, while the third is an apologia by an adventurer, whose exploits aroused European disapproval. Sudanese accounts are provided by S.M. Nur (ed.), *A critical edition of the memoirs of Yūsuf Mīkhāʾīl*, unpubl. Ph.D. thesis, London 1962; Bābikr Badrī, *Taʾrīkh ḥayātī*, ?Khartoum 1959, tr. Y. Bedri and G. Scott, *The memoirs of Babikr Bedri*, i, London 1969.

During the Anglo-Egyptian Condominium (1899-1955), with the restoration of Khartoum as the capital, Omdurman lost its unique status, but acquired a new significance as the centre of Sudanese politics and culture. For example, in consequence of the settlement there of migrants from all parts of the country, the speech of Omdurman became the standard Sudanese colloquial Arabic (cf. J.S. Trimingham, *Sudan colloquial Arabic*, ²London 1946, Preface; V.A. Yagi, *Contes d'Omdurman*, Antibes 1981). An Islamic religious college, *al-Maʿhad al-ʿilmī*, was established with government assistance in 1912, and developed after independence into the Islamic University of Omdurman. The Graduates' General Congress, founded in 1938 but the successor to an older grouping, with its headquarters in Omdurman, became the leading nationalist organisation and the seedbed of future political developments.

Bibliography: In addition to works cited in the text, there are frequent references to Omdurman in standard works on the Mahdiyya and Condominium; e.g. P.M. Holt, *The Mahdist state in the Sudan 1881-1898*, ²Oxford 1970; M.W. Daly, *Empire on the Nile*, Cambridge 1986; idem, *Imperial Sudan*, Cambridge 1991. (P.M. Holt)

ʿÖMER ʿĀSHİḲ famous Ottoman Turkish *saz* poet of the 11th/17th century, d. 1119/1707.

Apart from one or two sources, information on him stems mainly from what he says in his own *dīwān*. Basing themselves on such statements, some scholars (Bursalī Meḥmed Ṭāhir, Fuad Köprülü and Cahit Öztelli) have regarded him as coming from Gözleve (Gezlevi) in Konya province, whilst others (S. Nüzhet Ergun and, especially, Şükrü Elçin) place his home at Gözleve in the Crimea. Information in the *Menāḳıb-nāme* of Ketkhudāzāde ʿĀrif (94), in a poem discovered by Üsküdārlī Ṭalʿat (Ergun, 6), in the *Medjmūʿa-yi tewārīkh* and in Şükrü Elçin's work, all strengthen the hypothesis that he came from the Crimea but settled in Aydîn. After what was believed to have been a long life, he died in 1119/1707, according to Üsküdārlī Ḥasīb's line *ola ʿāshiḳ ʿÖmeriñ djilwegehi ʿadnī djelīl* ("may ʿÖmer's promenade be the exalted heaven!").

From his poems, ʿÖmer is known to have had a certain level of education, including a knowledge of Persian and Arabic. He gives his personal name as ʿÖmer and his pen-name as ʿAdlī, although he most frequently used ʿÖmer, ʿĀshıḳ ʿÖmer, the pen-name Derwīsh Nihānī, and rarely, ʿAdlī. It is very probable that he was an adherent of the Mewlewī order [see MAWLAWIYYA]. In addition to the *saz*, he played other stringed instruments like the *ṭanbūr* and is known to have been a *ḥāfiẓ*, i.e. one who knew the Ḳurʾān by heart. In his *Shāʿir-nāme* he speaks of one Sherīfī, possibly his teacher, of whom he counted himself a follower. Whilst a Sherīfī, allegedly from the Crimea, appears in several of the *tedhkires* of Ottoman poets, such as those of Riḍā, Sālim and Ṣafāyī, this is not the same person as the Sherīfī named by ʿÖmer. He is also known from his poems to have been a Janissary and to have travelled widely in the course of participation in warfare (Varna, Sakız, Bursa, Sinop, Istanbul, Edirne, etc.).

The oldest manuscript copy of his *Dīwān* is the 517-page one, formerly in the Yaḥyā Efendi Dergāhī, now housed in the Süleymaniye Library (Haci Mahmud 5097), copied in 1141/1728-9. Another important copy is Mevlana Museum, Konya 99, compiled 50 years later by Ḥüseyin Aywansarāyī in 1191/1782. There is also a lithograph edition from 1306/1888. Since he was widely read, his poems figure in almost every *djönk* or manuscript collection of folk poetry. The verse forms of both *dīwān* and folk literatures, such as the *destān, ḳoshma, ghazel, murabbaʿ, takhmīs, müseddes* and *semāʿī*, are encountered in his *dīwān*; the examples of the folk literature ones are the more successful of the two. Among his well-known poems is the *Shāʿir-nāme*, consisting of 34 quatrains giving the names of the important poets, the *Istanbul destānī* describing various places in the capital, and the Bursa and Pire *destāns*. Influenced by such poets as Nesīmī, Fuḍūlī, Aḥmed Pasha and Khaṭāyī, ʿÖmer in turn had an impact on poets who were his contemporaries as well as on those following him. Although post-*Tanẓīmāt* poets like Ḍiyā Pasha and Muʿallim Nādjī disparaged him, they themselves could not deny having been influenced by him in their formative years. Many of his poems have been set to music; the miniaturist Lewnī made a miniature of him. Sünbülzāde Wehbī, Müstaḳīm-zāde and Üsküdārlī Mewlewī Ḥasīb mention him, and ʿIzzet Mollā wrote a poem in emulation of one of his hemistichs employing the same metre and rhyme scheme (*taḍmīn*).

Bibliography: Emīn Ef., *Menāḳib-i Ketkhudā-zāde el-Ḥādjdj Meḥmed ʿĀrif Ef. Ḥaḍretleri*, Istanbul 1305/1888, 94; Bursalī Meḥmed Ṭāhir, *ʿOM*, ii, 312; M. Fuʾād Köprülü, *ʿĀshıḳ ʿÖmere ʿāʾid baʿdi notlar*, in *Ḥayāt Medjmūʿasi*, no. 24 (12 May 1927), 2-3; idem, *Türk saz şairleri. II*, Ankara 1962, 253-69; Saʿdeddin Nüzhet Ergun, *Aşık Ömer hayatı ve şiirleri*, Istanbul n.d. [1936?]; Cahit Öztelli, in *Türk Ansıklopedisi*, xxvi, 1977, art. s.v., 257; Günay Kut-Turgut Kut, *Ayvansarayi Hafız Hüseyin b. İsmail ve eserleri*, in *Istanbul Üniv. Tarih Dergisi*, xxxiii (1980-1) [1982], 432-3; Şükrü Elçin, *Âşık Ömer*, Ankara 1987; Saim Sakaoğlu, *Türk saz şiiri*, in *Türk Dili Özel Sayısı III* (Halk Şiiri), no. 445-50 (Jan.-June 1989), 138-42; Abdülkadir Karahan, *Âşık Ömer*, in *Türkiye Diyanet Vakfı Islâm Ansiklopedisi*, iv, 1991, 1; Ḥüseyin Aywansarāyī, *Medjmūʿa-yi tewārīkh.*, ed. Fahri Ç. Derin-Vâhid Çabuk, Istanbul 1985, 369. (Günay Kut)

ʿÖMER EFENDI, an Ottoman historian, according to popular tradition originally called Elkazović or Čaušević, who belonged to Bosna-Novi (Bosanski-Novi). Of his career we only know that he was acting as *ḳāḍī* in his native town when fierce fighting broke out on Bosnian soil between the Imperial troops and those of Ḥekīm-Oghlu ʿAlī Pasha (1150/1737). ʿÖmer Efendi at this time wrote a vivid account of the happenings in Bosnia from the beginning of Muḥarram 1149/May 1736 to the end of Djumādā I 1152/end of March 1739; written in a smooth, easy style, this work is of considerable importance for social history. It seems to have been called *Ghazawāt-i Ḥekīm-Oghlu ʿAlī Pasha*, but is usually quoted as *Ghazawāt-i diyār-i Bosna*, and sometimes as *Ghazawāt-nāme-yi Bānālūḳā* (i.e. Banjaluka in Bosnia).

As a reward for this literary effort, ʿÖmer Efendi was promoted to be one of the six judges (*rütbe-i welāy-i sitte*). Of his further life and death, nothing more is known. It is certain that he ended his days in Bosna-Novi and was buried there. The site of his grave is still pointed out but the tombstone has disappeared.

ʿÖmer Efendi's little book is fairly common in mss. (usually copies of the first printed text); cf. F. Babinger, *GOW*, 277, to which should now be added: Zagreb, South Slav Acad. of Sciences, coll. Babinger, no. 390, 391, as well as no. 631, iv (here called *Ghazawāt-nāme-yi Bānālūḳā*). The printer Ibrāhīm Müteferriḳa [*q.v.*] revised and corrected ʿÖmer Efendi's narrative (cf. Ḥanīf-zāde, in Ḥādjdjī Khalīfa, no. 14533: *Ghazawāt-i diyār-i Bosna*) and published it under the title *Aḥwāl-i ghazawāt der Diyār-i Bosna* (8 + 62 pp., Istanbul 1154; cf. Babinger, *Stambuler Buchwesen im 18. Jahrh.*, Leipzig 1919, 17). On later editions cf. Babinger, *GOW*, 277. The book is also accessible in a rather bad German translation and a not very successful English one, cf. *GOW*, 277.

Bibliography: Safvetbeg Bašagić, *Bošnjaci i Hercegovci u islamskoj kniježevnosti*, Sarajevo 1912, 152; Babinger, *GOW*, 276-7; Meḥmed Handžić, *Kniježevni rad bosanski-hercegovačkikh muslimana*, Sarajevo 1934, 39-40; Muḥammad al-Bosnawī (i.e. Meḥmed Handžić), *al-Djawāhir al-asnā fī tarādjim ʿulamāʾ wa- shuʿarāʾ Bosna*, Cairo 1349, 112; *İA*, art. *Ömer Efendi* (A. Cevat Eren). (F. Babinger)

ʿÖMER SEYF ül-DĪN (Ömer Seyfeddin), late Ottoman and early modern Turkish writer (1884-1920).

A major figure of Turkish fiction, ʿÖmer Seyf ül-Dīn (modern rendering Seyfeddin or Seyfettin) was a pioneer of realism and the use of the common idiom. A 1903 graduate of the Istanbul War College, he served as an officer, saw action, fell captive, and retired upon his release in 1913. Having published poems, short stories and essays since 1900, he joined his nationalist colleagues ʿAlī Djānib and Ḍiyā (Ziyā) Gökalp in Salonica (1911) where they published the influential magazine *Genč Ḳalemler* ("Young Pens"). From 1914 until his death on 6 March 1920 he lived in Istanbul, where he served as a teacher of literature, editor-in-chief of the journal *Türk Sözü* ("Turkish Speech"), and a member of the Istanbul University Linguistic Research Board.

His 16-volume complete works comprise poetry, essays, children's stories, etc., in addition to fiction. He was not an accomplished poet. His articles and essays, which exerted considerable influence in launching the ideals of nationalism in literature for the benefit of a wider reading public, are concise, lucid and deft. Among his published translations are those of parts of the *Iliad* and *Kalevala*.

His fame rests essentially on his 138 short stories, mostly derived from childhood recollections, military life including combat, and everyday events. Many of them make use of traditional folk tales and legends, often recounting heroic deeds. In some, ʿÖmer Seyf ül-Dīn criticised entrenched institutions and superstitions. With a progressive spirit, he articulated the prospects offered by the awakening of Turkish nationalism for a better future. He took a stand against Ottomanism, cosmopolitan culture, and imitation of European models. He expressed faith in traditional Turkish culture blended with modernisation. He was one of the earliest among literary pioneers who brought the Anatolian countryside into urban literature. Reacting against the ornate élite poetry and prose of his predecessors, who were influenced by the Arabs and Persians, he wrote for and often about the common man in an attempt to make literature accessible "to the people."

His major novel, *Efrūz Bey* (1919), is an acerbic satire of the life and times of an opportunistic, quixotic pseudo-intellectual and is the author's most mature and most compelling work of realistic fiction. With several dozen of his well-made short stories, two or three novellas, and *Efruz Bey*, he brought new dimensions to, and earned an enduring place in, the history of Turkish fiction.

Bibliography: Ali Canip Yöntem, *Ömer Seyfettin, hayatı ve eserleri*, Istanbul 1935; O. Spies, *Die türkische Prosaliteratur der Gegenwart*, in *WI*, xxv (1943); Hikmet Dizdaroğlu, *Ömer Seyfettin*, 1964; Yaşar Nabi Nayır, *Ömer Seyfettin, hayatı, sanatı, eserleri*, 1965. (Talat Sait Halman)

ON IKI ADA, Turkish rendering of the Dodecanese (Dodekanesos, "Twelve Islands"), the greater part of the Southern Sporades archipelago; they are grouped in a north-west to south-east direction in the south-eastern segment of the Aegean along the Turkish coast. The concept and even the number is somewhat artificial and underwent different interpretations and political expressions in the course of history, hence the relativity of the definition as to how many and which islands constitute this archipelago. The earliest mention seems to occur under the Byzantine emperor Leo III the Isaurian (717-40), when the "Dodecanese or Aigion Pelagos" formed one of his three naval commands. In the later Middle Ages Italian maritime control asserted itself over much of the Aegean, and some of the Dodecanese became a Venetian possession, but others passed under the sway of the Knights of St. John of Jerusalem after their establishment in Rhodes (1310). It was from the latter two powers that Ottoman Turkey seized control of the Dodecanese: those pertaining to the Knights as a result of the conquest of Rhodes in 1522, and those belonging to Venice during the *ḳaptan pasha* Khayr al-Dīn Pasha [*q.v.*] Barbarossa's two campaigns in 1537 and 1538. It was then that twelve islands within this archipelago acquired a special status of "privileged islands" that gave the inhabitants a sense of cohesive identity and firmly established their group as a geopolitical unit; the islands were: Ikaria, Patmos, Leros, Kalimnos, Astipalea, Nisiros, Tilos, Simi, Chalki, Karpathos, Kasos and Meis; this was the result of their voluntary submission and consequent treaty sanctioned by Süleymān I, to be confirmed by a number of later *firmāns*; the mostly Greek and Orthodox islanders had self-rule, against payment of a fixed annual sum (*maḳṭūʿ*). An illustration of the administrative rather than geographical nature of this Ottoman Dodecanese is the fact that the group included Meis (also known as Kastellorizon, Italian Castelrosso), an islet by the southern Anatolian coast near Kas to the east of Rhodes, but not Rhodes itself; like Rhodes, Kos too was excluded, although geographically situated in the midst of the group. The islands of Simi, and later Patmos, appear to have constituted the centre of political gravity and representation of the islanders in their dealings with the Porte and eventually also with other powers.

The inhabitants extracted some livelihood from their deforested islands (fruit, olives, wheat, tobacco), but for the most part they depended on the sea: local shipping, fishing, and especially sponge-diving, were their traditional occupations. Their smooth relations with the Porte began to suffer with the appearance of Greek as well as Turkish nationalism in the 19th and early 20th century. Istanbul first tried to cancel the islands' privileged status and, following the constitutional movement of 1909 and against the islanders' expectations, attempted to impose measures that amounted to incipient Turkicisation. The upheavals caused by the Italo-Turkish War of 1911-12, the Balkan War of 1912-13, and World War I brought about the final separation of the Dodecanese from Turkey and its establishment, enlarged by Rhodes as the administrative centre, as an Italian possession (Possedimenti Italiani dell'Egeo). Only in 1948 did the entire archipelago pass to Greece.

The Muslim Turkish population of the islands, numbering some 10,000, did not face any great changes during the period of Italian rule, and the community's newspaper, *Selām*, continued to appear in Arabic characters. But during World War II, from 1941 to 1944, the islands were occupied by the Germans (and the Jewish minority largely deported for extermination at Auschwitz), and then the Treaty of Paris of 1947 awarded the Dodecanese to Greece. From then on, under the pressure of Hellenisation, emigration to the Turkish mainland, especially to Izmir, accelerated; most of those who remained became Greek subjects, though retaining their Turkish language, with only a few of them retaining the Turkish citizenship which they had been able to keep since the time of Italian rule. In 1974 there were *ca.* 4,000 Muslims in their two main centres, Rhodes and Kos, those of Rhodes mainly in the town of Rhodes but those of Kos in a village popularly known as Türk Köyü. The communities are at present ageing ones since, under Greek aegis, young people find career prospects on the islands very confined, and the communities seem destined for gradual disappearance.

Bibliography: Jeanne Z. Stephanopoli, *Les Îles de l'Egée, leurs privilèges, avec documents et notes historiques*, Athens 1912, 33-47; Pīrī Re'īs, *Bahrije*, ed. P. Kahle, Berlin 1926, ii, 61-88; idem, *Kitabi Bahriye*, Ankara 1935, 191-242; [J.N.L. Myres], Naval Intelligence Division, Geographical Handbook Series, *Dodecanese*, 2nd ed. London 1943; E. Armao, *In giro per il mare Egeo con Vincenzo Coronelli*, Florence 1951, 179-221; Michele Nicolas, *Une communauté musulmane de Grèce (Rhodes et Kos)*, in *Turcica*, viii (1976), 58-69; İ. Parmaksızoğlu, *On iki ada*, in *Türk Ansiklopedisi*, xxv, Ankara 1977, 443-4. See also RODOS. (S. SOUCEK)

ORĀMĀR, URMAR, modern Turkish Oramar, a district (*nahiye*) of the extreme south-east of Turkey, just to the north of the frontier with ʿIrāḳ, and in the modern *ilçe* or district of Gawar (Yüksekova) in the *il* or province of Hakkari, with its chef-lieu of the same name (lat. 37°23′ N., long. 44°04′ E., altitude 1,450 m/4,756 ft.). In 1955 the settlement of Oramar itself had a population of 943, whilst the nine villages comprising the *nahiye* had a total population of 3,632.

The boundaries of Orāmār are on the north Ishtāzin and Gawar; on the south Rēkān; on the west Djilū, Bāz and Tkhūma and Artush; in the east Sāt [see SHAMDĪNĀN]. Orāmār is a group of hamlets scattered on the two sides of a rocky mountain spur above the Rūdbār-i Sin. On the spur itself, which is called Gaparāni Zhēr, at the place named Gīre Būti, is the capital of the group and the residence of the *agha*s, the Nāw Gund or "the middle of the town". A large cemetery occupies the promontory at the end of the spur. The name Gīre Būti, explicable as the "hill of the idol", seems to indicate the antiquity of the settlement. The fact that the slopes separated by the Gaparān are very carefully cultivated and present a complicated system of little terraces, each of which is a field or tiny kitchen garden, leads one to believe that man chose this site for habitation a long time ago, perhaps simply on account of its extreme isolation in the centre of a wild country.

Orography. Orāmār is at the east end of the curve traced by the system of the Djilū Dāgh. According to Dickson, the chains and valleys of Turkish Kurdistān run roughly along the parallels of latitude and take a south-eastern direction as they approach the Persian frontier and at the point where they change their axis form a complicated system of heights and valleys. The most complicated part near the centre of the change of axis in question may be called Harki-Orāmār.

Road system. Although they are really nothing but tracks used for intertribal communications, these routes must have played a more prominent part in ancient times. Orāmār is connected with Gawar via Shamsiki, the pass of Bashtazin, ʿAlī Kānī, Bāžirgā and Dizza. It is a road which shows traces of works undertaken at the more dangerous places. To the south, the road going through a very narrow defile leads first to Nerwa (cf. below) where it forks to the west and to the east. A third road goes from Nerwa to Nehri, the centre of Shamdīnān, via Razga, the heights of Peramizi (frontier of the three tribes—Rekāni, Harki, Duskāni), Deri, defile of Harki (Shīwa Harki), Begor, Mazra, Nehri.

Ethnography. The following Kurdish tribes may be mentioned in Orāmār itself and in the vicinity, with ramifications inevitable as a result of the Kurd migrations. After the name of each tribe that of the district and the number of households in *ca.* 1930 is given: Duskānī Zhüri (Orāmār, 2,000); Nirwei (Nerwa, *ḳaḍā'* of Amādiya, 800); Dîri (Gawar and Gelia Dîri, 1,000): Peniānish (between Gawar and Djulāmerk, and the part of the Pirhulki, near Bashḳalʿa 4,000); Duskāni Zhēri (*ḳaḍā'* of Dehuk, 2,000); Mizūri Zhēri (*ibid.*, 5,000); Berwāri (*ibid.*, 4,000); Guwei, nomads (wintering at Dehuk; summering at Gawar and Orāmār, 1,400); Čeli (Djulāmerk, 6,000); Artūshi (summering at Firashin; wintering at Beriei Zhengār, 6,000); Artūshi (sedentary: Albāk, 1,000; Nurdîz, 1,000); parts of Artūshi: Gewdan, Mām Khōran, Zhirki (around Djulāmerk, 6,000).

History. Orāmār has a rich history full of associations with the Nestorian Christianity of south-eastern Turkey and adjoining areas. (V. Cuinet, *La Turquie d'Asie*, Paris 1892, ii, 757, says that "the 40 Nestorian rayas domiciled in Orāmār are entrusted with the care of the two Nestorian churches in the Kurdish town (*sic*)"; one of these churches, that of Mār Dāniyāl at Nāw Gund was turned into a mosque towards the end of the 19th century or in the early 20th century.

A local tradition even suggests that the ancestor of the modern *agha*s came long ago into this Christian district and by stratagems and intrigues succeeded in driving out its inhabitants. The toponymy of Orāmār seems to confirm this. The name Orāmār is probably ancient, and the district was probably inhabited at a very early date. There are similar place-names elsewhere in the region: Ora Bishu, one of the slopes of Kiria Tawka; Orishu, a village beyond Gelia Nu; Uri, a Nestorian clan; finally Urmiya itself.

Bibliography: Cuinet, *loc. cit.*; B. Nikitine and E.B. Soane, *The tale of Suto and Tato. Kurdish text with translation and notes*, in *BSOS*, iii (1923-5), 69-106, see p. 69; Nikitine, *Le systèm routier du Kurdistan (le pays entre les deux Zab)*, in *La Géographie*, lxiii (1935), 363-85 (includes general view of Oramar from a photograph); H. Bobek, *Forschungen im zentralkurdischen Hochgebirge zwischen Van und Urmia-See*, in *Petermanns Mitteilungen* (1938), 152-62, 215-28; P. A. Andrews, *Ethnic groups in the Republic of Turkey*,

Wiesbaden 1989, 218-19; İA, art. Oramar (Nikitine and Besim Darkot). On the Nestorians of the region, see M. Chevalier, Les montagnards chrétiens du Hakkâri et du Kurdistan septentrional, Paris 1985, index s.v. Oramar.   (B. NIKITINE *)

ORAN [see WAHRĀN].

ORBAY, ḤÜSEYIN RAʾŪF (1881-1964), Turkish naval commander, statesman and diplomat, was educated as a naval officer. He served in the Turco-Italian war of 1911, before winning national fame in the Balkan wars of 1912-13 as the commander of the cruiser Ḥamīdiyye which carried out daring raids on enemy ports and warships. During the Great War he served as Chief of Naval Staff, becoming Minister of Marine in October 1918. In the same month, he headed the Ottoman delegation which signed the armistice of Mudros [see MONDROS]. He resigned from the navy in May 1919, and joined Muṣṭafā Kemāl (later Atatürk) and Fetḥī Okyar [q.vv.] in organising the national resistance movement in Anatolia. As a leading nationalist and a member of the last Ottoman Chamber of Deputies, Raʾūf was arrested by the British in March 1920 and deported to Malta. He returned to Turkey in March 1921 and was appointed Prime Minister in August 1922, but had serious disagreements with ʿIṣmet [İnönü], the chief Turkish delegate at the Lausanne Peace Conference. In August 1923 he resigned from the premiership, and became part of the opposition to Muṣṭafā Kemāl. Like other opposition leaders, Raʾūf feared Atatürk's dictatorial tendencies, and wished to clip his wings, but not to overthrow him entirely. In November 1924 he played a leading role in establishing the Progressive Republican Party (Teraḳḳīperwer Djümhuriyyet Fīrḳasī). After the forcible closure of the party in June 1925, Raʾūf went abroad for medical treatment. In August 1926, following the unsuccessful attempt on Atatürk's life in Izmir, Raʾūf and other leading members of the nationalist movement were placed on trial. Although the court could not show that he had played any part in the murder plot, he was sentenced to ten years imprisonment in absentia. He benefited from an amnesty proclaimed in 1933 and returned to Turkey in 1935, but did not fully clear his name until 1939. Following his political rehabilitation, he served as Turkish Ambassador in London between 1942 and 1944.

Bibliography: Türk Ansiklopedisi, xxv, Ankara 1977, s.v.; E.J. Zürcher, The Unionist factor: the role of the Committee of Union and Progress in the Turkish National Movement, 1905-1926, Leiden 1984.

(W.M. HALE)

ORDU (T.), thence in Mongolian, orda, "the royal tent or residence, the royal encampment", a term which became widespread in the mediaeval Turco-Mongol and then in the Persian worlds, acquiring from the second meaning that of "army camp".

1. In early Turkish and then Islamic usage

The word ordu appears in some of the earliest known texts of Turkish, sc. in the Kül-tigin inscription (Talât Tekin, A grammar of Orkhon Turkish, Bloomington 1968, 237), and may have passed from such an Inner Asian people as the Hsiung-nu into Chinese as wo-lu-to (*oludu = ordu) (G. Doerfer, Türkische und mongolische Elemente im Neupersischen. ii. Türkische Elemente im Neupersischen, Wiesbaden 1965, 35). Already in the Sāmānid period (4th/10th century), the geographer al-Muḳaddasī, 263, 275, mentions *Urduwā as "the residence of the ruler of the Turkmen", and in the ensuing Ḳaraḵẖānid period Urdū is recorded as a mint in Transoxania, possibly to be equated with their capital at Balāsāḡẖūn (E. von Zambaur, Die Münzprägungen des Islam, i, Wiesbaden 1968, 42).

The cross-continental movements of the Turco-Mongol peoples in the 13th and 14th centuries ensured for the word a wide diffusion into Eastern Europe, including the East Slavonic, Magyar, Balkan and New Greek linguistic areas, finally entering such Western European languages as English and French horde, German Horde, etc. (Doerfer, op. cit., 38).

Under the Ottoman Turks, ordu-yu hümāyūn was a general term for the imperial army, and appears also as an element in the names of various functionaries connected with the army, e.g. the ordudju baṣẖī/aghasī, who was the chief of a staff of tradesmen and technicians (ehl-i ḥiref, arbāb-i ḥiref) who accompanied the Janissaries [see YEÑI ČERILER] on their campaigns away from the capital (see İ.H. Uzunçarṣılı, Osmanlı devleti teskilâtından kapıkulu ocakları, Ankara 1943-4, i, 368-73; M.Z. Pakalın, Tarih deyimleri ve terimleri sözlüğü, Istanbul 1946-54, ii, 728-9).

In South Asia, through usage amongst the Mughals [q.v.] of India, with the royal residence at Dihlī styled the urdu-yi muʿallā "exalted camp", the term zabān-i urdu was used for the mixed Hindustani-Persian-Turkish language of the court and the army, now the Urdu language of a large proportion of the Muslims in the subcontinent (see Yule and Burnell, Hobson-Jobson, a glossary of Anglo-Indian colloquial words and phrases,[2] 639-40; HIND. iii. Languages; and URDU). The term was still used in Ṣafawid Persia (cf. the Tadhkirat al-mulūk, tr. Minorsky, London 1943, tr. 51, 62), but must by the time when the latter work was written (early 18th century) have been archaic and obsolete.

Bibliography: Given in the article.

(C.E. BOSWORTH)

2. In Mongol historical usage

In sources dealing with the period of the Mongol Empire, ordu is normally used in the sense of the camp or household of a Mongol prince, which would be under the supervision of one of his wives. He might therefore have several ordus. During the Īlkhānate, "to go to the ordu" meant to travel to the ruler's presence, whether that was to be found at one of the fixed capitals such as Tabrīz, or wherever the royal encampment happened to be. This kind of usage was no doubt the origin of the Western term "Golden Horde" for what in the Islamic world was usually known as the khānate of Ḳıpčaḳ. Quatremère (Raschid-Eldin, Histoire des Mongols de la Perse, Paris 1836, 98, n. 25) suggested that the word ughruḳ was sometimes used to indicate, to some extent by contrast, the military camp in a more general sense. During his journey to Mongolia in the 1250s, William of Rubruck, whose Latin word for ordu is generally curia, picked up a confusion between ordu and orta ("middle"): "The court is called in their language orda, meaning 'the middle', since it is always situated in the midst of the men" (The mission of Friar William of Rubruck: his journey to the court of the Great Khan Möngke 1253-1255, tr. P. Jackson and ed. Jackson and D.O. Morgan, London 1990, 131 and n. 4). The transformation in English of the meaning of "horde" from the camp to the nomadic warrior people who (in large numbers) inhabited it was already established by the time of the OED's first cited reference (1555).

Bibliography: G. Doerfer, Türkische und mongolische Elemente im Neupersischen, ii, Wiesbaden 1965, 32-9.

(D.O. MORGAN)

ORDŪBĀD, a town in eastern Transcaucasia on the left bank of the middle course of the Araxes or Aras River, lying in lat. 38°54′ N. and long. 46° 01′ E. and at an altitude of 948 m/2,930 ft.

The Turco-Persian name "army town" implies a probable foundation during the period of the Mongol invasions or of the ensuing Il-Khānids, especially as the latter made Ādharbāydjān the centre of their power. Certainly, Ḥamd Allāh Mustawfī (mid-8th/14th century) describes it as a provincial town, one of the five making up the *tūmān* of Nakhčiwān [*q.v.*], watered by a stream coming down from Mount Ḳubān (= the modern Gora Kapydzik, 4,200 m/12,800 ft.) to the north (*Nuzha*, 89, tr. 90; cf. Le Strange, *Lands*, 167). In subsequent centuries, the khānates of both Eriwān [see REWĀN] and Nakhčiwān were dependencies of Persia, with Ordūbād forming the main town of the district of Āzā-Djirān in the eastern part of the khānate of Nakhčiwān; but after the Russo-Persian War of 1827 and the resultant Treaty of Turkmančay of 1828, these were ceded to Imperial Russia, so that henceforth, Ordūbād fell within Russian territory. Since the breakup of the Soviet Union, it is now within the Nakhčiwān region of the Azerbaijan Republic, forming an enclave of territory between the Armenian Republic and Iran.

Bibliography: In addition to references given in the article, see D. Krawulsky, *Iran—das Reich der Īl-ḫāne. Eine topographisch-historische Studie*, Wiesbaden 1978, 543.

(C.E. Bosworth)

ÖRIK, NAHĪD ṢIRRĪ (Nahit Sırrı Örik), Turkish author, journalist and literary researcher, born on 22 May 1894 in Istanbul, died in 1960. He was the grandson of Aḥmed Nāfidh Pasha of Olti, who was also a poet and the son of Örik Aghasî-zāde Ḥasan Ṣirrī, who was a government official and translator. Nahit Sırrı attended Galatasaray lycée, graduating in 1913. He lived in Europe until 1928, and after his return to Turkey, worked as a correspondent for the newspaper *Cumhuriyet* and as a translator for the Ministry of Education. He travelled in Anatolia and wrote articles, mostly concerning the archaeological and historical antiquities of the places he visited. He continued to work as a journalist until his death on 18 January 1960, never having married.

Nahit Sırrı admired and loved Istanbul deeply, and this is reflected in his works. The style he adopts for his historical novels is the objective, calm and good-humoured reporting of events with life in the Istanbul of the past a dominant subject for his works and his language remaining faithful to refined Ottoman style.

Bibliography: 1. First editions. (a) Stories: *Zeyneb, la Courtisane*, 1927; *Kırmızı ve siyah*, 1929; *Sanatkârlar*, 1932; *Eski resimler*, 1933. (b) Novels: *Eve düşen yıldırım*, 1934; *Kıskanmak*, 1946; *Hayat ve kadınlar*, 1946; *Sultan Hamîd düşerken*, 1957. (c) Plays: *Sönmeyen ateş*, 1933; *Muharrir*, 1934; *Oyuncular*, 1938; *Alın yazısı*, 1952. (d) Research and criticism: *Edebiyat ve sanat bahisleri*, 1933; *Tarihi çehreler etrafında*, 1933; *Yüzelli yılın Türk meşhurları ansiklopedisi*, 1933; *Roman ve hikâye*, 1933. (e) Travel notes: *Anadolu*, 1939; *Bir Edirne seyâhatnamesi*, 1941; *Kayseri-Kırşehir-Kastamonu*, 1955.

2. Studies. T. Alangu, *Cumhuriyetten sonra hikâye ve roman, I*, Istanbul 1959; H. Yavuz, *Roman kavramı ve Türk romanı*, Istanbul 1972; O. Önertoy, *Türk roman ve öyküsü*, Ankara 1984; M. Ünlü and Ö. Özcan, *20. yüzyıl Türk edebiyatı*, Istanbul 1988.

(Çiğdem Balim)

ORISSA [see URISA].

ORKHAN, the son of the founder of the Ottoman dynasty, ʿOthmān I [*q.v.*], and of the daughter of *sheykh* Edebali, who seems to have exercised considerable influence upon his son-in-law through his connections with the fraternity of the *Akhīs* [*q.v.*] and with the group of dervishes known as the *Abdālān-i Rūm*. According to the Ottoman tradition, Orkhan had a brother, ʿAlāʾ al-Dīn [*q.v.*], who resigned from their father's possessions and accepted the office of the vizierate. Little is known about Orkhan's early life as most of the Turkish sources reporting about him were written more than one century after his death and are of a legendary character. Yakhshī Faḳīh, the son of his *imām*, wrote a chronicle about the house of ʿOthmān, which unfortunately has not been preserved in its original form but incorporated within a later chronicle, that of ʿĀshīk-Pasha-zāde (see V.L. Ménage, *The* Menāqib *of Yakhshi Faqīh*, in *BSOAS*, xxvi [1963], 50-4). One can find precise information about him in a few Ottoman documents, some of them preserved in the original, the oldest of which is of the year 1324; also in the Byzantine sources, especially the works of Gregoras and Cantacuzenus.

According to the Turkish sources, Orkhan was married to Nilüfer, the daughter of the Byzantine lord of Yār-Ḥiṣār, who, together with her father, was taken prisoner when this fortress was captured by ʿOthmān's soldiers, presumably in 1299. From this union were born Süleymān Pasha, the conqueror of Rūm-ili, and Murād, who succeeded his father [see MURĀD I]. Names of several members of Orkhan's family are known through Ottoman documents and also through the history of Cantacuzenus, who, among other things, describes a banquet in which Orkhan participated, accompanied by his four sons.

Orkhan took part in many military operations organised by his father, who resided in the region of Sögüt and Yeñi-Shehir. When he ascended the throne, in 1326, his father's troops had with their frequent raids reached the littoral opposite Constantinople, while the Byzantine towns of Bithynia had been blockaded for many years. Bursa [*q.v.*] surrendered in the same year and became the Ottoman capital. Orkhan continued his father's military activity directed against the Byzantines by raiding their territories. He was surrounded by several military chieftains bearing the title of *ghāzī* or *alp* [*q.vv.*]. A campaign organised by the Byzantine emperor Andronicus III Palaeologus in 1329 in order to expel the Turks from Bithynia ended with the defeat of his army, first in Pelekanon, and immediately afterwards in Philokrene. Nicaea/Iznik surrendered in 1331 and soon became a centre of Muslim intellectual life through its *medreses*. The Byzantine emperor was forced to conclude a treaty with Orkhan in 1333, undertaking to pay 12,000 *hyperpera* a year, while Orkhan promised to leave in peace the fortresses situated on the coast of Mesothynia. Nevertheless, in 1337 the port of Nikomedeia/Iznikmīd (later Izmīd) surrendered also to Orkhan, who in this same year, perhaps encouraged by the Genoese of Pera, performed his first important raid on Thrace reaching the suburbs of Constantinople.

According to the Egyptian author al-ʿUmarī and to the Moroccan traveller Ibn Baṭṭūṭa, who visited the Ottoman lands, the amirate of Orkhan was one of the strongest in Asia Minor in the early 1330s and he himself had much prestige resulting from the holy war that he continuously carried out against the "infidel" Christians. However, his power increased impressively during the last years of the Byzantine civil war (1341-7) between the legitimate heir to the throne, John V Palaeologus, and the pretender John VI Cantacuzenus. When the war began the latter obtained military support from the *amīr* of Aydîn, Umur; but in 1344, he appealed to Orkhan, who promptly responded, sending troops to Thrace to fight on Cantacuzenus' side. The alliance was corroborated by the marriage of Orkhan with the daughter of Cantacuzenus, Theodora. Under these circumstances, the

Ottoman troops learned the topography of Thrace and Macedonia, while they became rich by pillaging the property of Cantacuzenus' opponents and by taking them into captivity together with the peasants, who had remained faithful to the legitimate heir, in order to sell them as slaves. Cantacuzenus himself confesses that he could not control his Turkish allies. During the same period, around 1346, the Ottomans annexed the adjacent amirate of Ḳarasi [q.v.] thus gaining access to the Aegean Sea. Orkhan, who had a fleet of at least 36 vessels as early as the 1330s, acquired thus the important fleet of the Ḳarasi Turks who, experienced in naval warfare, began to collaborate successfully with the Ottomans by organising raids on the Greek littoral. The alliance between Cantacuzenus and Orkhan continued after the end of the civil war in 1347, because the former, insecure and suspecting that some of the Thracian towns were ready to revolt against him, frequently appealed to his son-in-law for military support. Orkhan's son, Süleymān Pas̲h̲a, often resided in Thrace at the head of troops sent to assist Cantacuzenus.

The war between Genoa and Venice, which broke out in 1351 and in which the Byzantines were eventually involved, gave Orkhan the opportunity to emerge on the international scene. He supported the Genoese by supplying them first with victuals and later with soldiers, and he placed a little fleet consisting of 9 vessels at their disposal. In 1351-2 the first Genoese-Ottoman treaty was concluded. Around the same time, the powerful kral of Serbia Stefan Dušan, whose territories were harassed by the Ottoman raids, tried also to conclude an alliance with Orkhan and proposed to give his own daughter in matrimony to one of his sons. It is not certain that the marriage ever took place.

In 1352 Süleymān Pas̲h̲a accomplished the first Ottoman conquest in Europe by occupying the fortress of Tzymbe. In 1354 an earthquake destroyed the walls of several towns in Thrace, including the strategically important fortress of Kallipolis/Gelibolu [q.v.]. The Turks who were encamped in the countryside proceeded immediately to occupy them, while their inhabitants fled before them to escape captivity. Süleymān Pas̲h̲a immediately took care of Kallipolis by restoring its walls and by inviting some prominent Turks to settle in it. In this same year the Ottomans occupied two important towns in Asia Minor, Ankara and Krateia Gerede. The Ottoman expansion was temporarily halted in 1357, when Orkhan's son K̲h̲alīl was captured by Genoese pirates and taken to Phocaea, a town nominally under Byzantine rule. Orkhan was obliged to ask for the help of the Byzantine emperor, who put forward as a condition the end of the Ottoman raids. A treaty was concluded and the Byzantines had a period of peace. Nevertheless, the Ottomans resumed their raids on Thrace, perhaps as a result of the activity of the papal legate Pierre Thomas, who visited Constantinople with his fleet and then proceeded to an attack on Lampsakos in the autumn of 1359. It was probably in 1361 that the Ottomans conquered Didymoteichon/Dimetoḳa [q.v.].

Orkhan died in March 1362 (P. Schreiner, Die Byzantinischen Kleinchroniken, ii, Vienna 1977, 290-1). He left a state extending over Asia Minor and Europe. He had consolidated his rule by organising the administration of his territory, which was divided into domains governed by his sons and by some military chiefs. According to the Ottoman chronicles, in his years, besides the irregular force of the aḵindj̲is [q.v.], a cavalry was created consisting of müsellems

[q.v.] and an infantry of yayas. The information given by Idrīs Bidlīsī [q.v.] that the corps of the Janissaries was founded in Orkhan's days seems to be inaccurate (see V.L. Ménage, Some notes on the Devshirme, in BSOAS, xxix [1966], 64-78). Regulations regarding dress produced a clear distinction between the Ottoman army and that of the other amirates, and ʿAlāʾ al-Dīn induced his brother to adopt the white cap (börk) for his soldiers.

Orkhan founded several mosques, establishments for dervishes, charitable institutions and schools. Religious life was vigorous in his days and aḵẖī fraternities were active in the towns, as well as orders of dervishes, who remained popular religious leaders often inspired by heterodox doctrines. However, orthodox Islamic traditions became gradually predominant through the growing influence of theologians indicated in the sources as dānis̲h̲mend. On the other hand, there existed close relations with the local Christian population, and the early Ottoman chronicles mention many a Byzantine lord, or even groups of Christians, who collaborated with the Ottomans. In 1354 Gregory Palamas, Metropolitan of Thessalonica and distinguished theologian, was taken a prisoner to the Ottoman territories, where he had the opportunity to meet the Christian communities and also to participate in a public theological debate organised by Orkhan in Nicaea.

The economic situation of the state which Orkhan left behind, was apparently prosperous. The currency was the silver aḵče [q.v.] struck in his name. Apart from agriculture and cattle-raising, the revenues of his state derived from booty, which was important as it included war captives sold as slaves or liberated after paying ransom; from the annual tribute paid by the Byzantines and the other Christian states and from the money paid by Christian states in order to be allowed to recruit soldiers within his amirate; and finally, from customs duties since trade was carried out, as suggested by the commercial treaty concluded with the Genoese.

Bibliography: Irène Beldiceanu-Steinherr, Recherches sur les actes des règnes des sultans Osman, Orkhan et Murad I, in Acta Historica, iv, Munich 1967; C. Imber, The Ottoman Empire 1300-1481, Istanbul 1990; H. Inalcik, The Ottoman Empire. The classical age 1300-1600, London 1973; idem, The question of the emergence of the Ottoman state, in International Journal of Turkish Studies, ii (1980), 71-9; idem, in The Cambridge history of Islam, i. The central Islamic lands, Cambridge 1970, 295-353; Irène Mélikoff, L'Islam hétérodoxe en Anatolie, in Turcica, xiv (1982), 142-54; eadem, Les origines centre-asiatiques du soufisme anatolien, in Turcica, xx (1988), 7-18; A.Y. Ocak, La révolte de Baba Resul ou la formation de l'hétérodoxie musulmane en Anatolie au XIIIe siècle, Ankara 1989; Anna Philippidis-Braat, La captivité de Palamas chez les Turcs: dossier et commentaire, in Travaux et Mémoires, vii (1979), 109-221; M.M. Pixley, On the date of Orhan's accession, in The Turkish Studies Association Bulletin, v (1981), 32-3; İ.H. Uzunçarşılı, Osmanlılarda ilk vezirlere dair mutalea, in Belleten, iii (1939), 99-106; idem, Gazi Orhan bey vakfiyesi, in Belleten, v (1941), 277-88; idem, Orhan gazi'nin vefat eden oğlu Süleyman paşa için tertip ettirdiği vakfiyenin aslı, in Belleten, xxvii (1963), 437-51; E. Werner, Die Geburt einer Grossmacht—Die Osmanen, Forschungen zur Mittelalterlichen Geschichte 32, 4th ed., Weimar 1985; P. Wittek, The rise of the Ottoman empire, London 1938; idem, Zu einigen frühosmanischen Urkunden, in WZKM, liii (1957), 300-13; idem, Zur Geschichte Angoras in Mittelalter, in Festschrift G. Jacob, ed. Th. Menzel, Leipzig 1932, 329-54; E.A. Zachariadou, *'Ιστορία καὶ Θρύλοι τῶν Παλαιῶν Σουλτάνων 1300-1400*, Athens 1991; eadem, *S'enrichir en Asie Mineure au quatorzième siècle*, in *Hommes et richesses dans l'empire byzantin*, ed. V. Kravari et al., ii, Paris 1991, 215-24; eadem, *Trade and Crusade, Venetian Crete and the Emirates of Menteshe and Aydin (1300-1415)*, Library of the Hellenic Institute of Byzantine and Post-Byzantine Studies, xi, Venice 1983. (E.A. Zachariadou)

ORKHAN KEMĀL, Meḥmed Rāshid (Orhan Kemâl Öğütçü), Turkish short story writer and novelist, born in Adana, Ceyhan, on 15 September 1914, died in 1970. His father ʿAbd ül-Ḳādir Kemālī was a lawyer who became a first-term MP (1920-3) and Minister of Justice for a while and founded the Ehālī Djümhūriyyet party in Adana but was forced to flee to Syria upon the closure of his party. Orhan Kemâl left secondary school and went with his father, and for a year they lived in Syria and Lebanon, where he worked at a printing house (reflected in his later novel *Baba evi*). In 1932 his father died and Orhan came back to Adana, working as a labourer, weaver, secretary and stock-taker in the cotton mills (1932-8). During his spare time he read extensively and began to write adventure novels and plays. While doing his military service, he wrote poetry under the pseudonym Raşit Kemali (later he also used that of Orhan Raşit). He was arrested on the allegation that he had engaged in political propaganda and was imprisoned for 5 years (1938-43). He published his first story *Balık*, in 1940, and between 1941-3, his stories were published in *Yeni edebiyat, Yürüyüş, İkdam, Yurt ve dünya*, and *Adımlar*. In Bursa prison he met Nâzım Hikmet [*q.v.*] and wrote prose under his influence, and in 1945, the literary journal *Varlık* declared him to be the most popular story writer. In 1943 he had come back to Adana, and when he could no longer find employment, moved to Istanbul with his family and tried to make a living as a writer. In 1949 *Ekmek kavgası* and his first novel *Baba evi* were published, and he then became famous; in 1958 *Kardeş payı* and in 1969 *Önce ekmek* won literary prizes. He still had to write for his living, and produced novels, short stories, interviews, scripts for cinema and theatre. In 1970 he was invited to Bulgaria, where he died on 2 June.

In his works Orhan Kemâl told of the small people who struggled to earn their daily bread—labourers who worked in the fields and factories of the Çukurova, people who lived in the slums of the big city. His characters therefore are workers, small government officials, beggars, garbage collectors, inmates, villagers, drivers, whores and the like. He played a great role in introducing "life in the prison" as a theme to Turkish short story. He was keen to reflect the social state of women and children in his works. His women have the traditional positive attributes, and his child heroes begin to work before they can enjoy their childhood. Some of his works reflect the conditions after the war years: effects of industrialisation, capitalism, changing traditions of the lower classes, especially in the Adana region. He reflected on his childhood, and the stories he heard from his inmates during his imprisonment. His works after 1946 are about the class war, and the bitter indifference of the big cities to poor people became a dominant theme. He does not describe the psychological dispositions of his characters, but this is reflected instead in the dialogues of the characters themselves. His language and style are plain, without metaphors and similes. Most of his works have been made into films, with the scripts by the author himself.

Bibliography: 1. First editions. (a) Novels: *Baba evi*, 1949; *Avare yıllar*, 1950; *Murtaza*, 1952; *Cemile*, 1952; *Bereketli topraklar üzerinde*, 1954 (in French: *Sur les terres fertiles*, Paris, Gallimard, 1971); *Suçlu*, 1957; *Devlet kuşu*, 1958; *Vukuat var*, 1959; *Gâvurun kızı*, 1959; *Dünya evi*, 1960; *El kızı*, 1960; *Hanımın çiftliği*, 1961; *Gurbet kuşları*, 1962; *Eskici ve oğulları*, 1962; *Sokakların çocuğu*, 1963; *Kanlı topraklar*, 1963; *Bir Filiz vardı*, 1965; *Müfettişler müfettişi*, 1966; *Yalancı dünya*, 1966; *Evlerden biri*, 1966; *Arkadaş ıslıkları*, 1968; *Sokaklardan bir kız*, 1968; *Üç kağıtçı*, 1969; *Kötü yol*, 1969; *Kaçak*, 1970. (b) Stories: *Ekmek kavgası*, 1949; *Sarhoşlar*, 1951; *Çamaşırcının kızı*, 1952; *72. koğuş*, 1954; *Grev*, 1954; *Arka sokak*, 1956; *Kardeş payı*, 1957; *Babil kulesi*, 1957; *Serseri milyoner*, 1957; *Küçücük*, 1960; *Mahalle kavgası*, 1963; *Dünyada harp vardı*, 1963; *İşsiz*, 1966; *Önce ekmek*, 1968; *Küçükler ve büyükler*, 1971.

2. Studies. Y. Kenan Karacanlar, *Orhan Kemal*, Istanbul 1974; H. Altınkaynak, A. Bezirci, *Orhan Kemal*, Istanbul 1977; O. Önertoy, *Türk roman ve öykü̈sü*, Ankara 1984; C. Kudret, *Türk edebiyatında hikâye ve roman*, Istanbul 1990. (Çiğdem Balim)

ORKHAN SEYFĪ (Orhan Seyfi Orhon), Turkish poet and journalist, born in 1890 in Istanbul, died in 1972. He was the son of Colonel Emīn and Niʿmet. After finishing Mekteb-i Ḥuḳūḳ (Istanbul Darülfünūn Ḥuḳūk Fakültesi, i.e. Faculty of Law) in 1914, the same year he became a secretary at the Othmānlï Medjlis-i Mebʿūthānï until its suspension. In 1913 he published a small book of poems *Fïrṭïna ve ḳār* in *ʿarūḍ* metre. His second book, *Peri ḳïzï ile čoban ḥikāyesi*, a poetic tale with a Turkic theme written in syllabic metre, was published in 1919. He taught literature at several schools in Istanbul, and then in 1922 he began to publish *Aḳ baba*, the famous satirical magazine, with Yūsuf Ziyā. In 1924 he launched *Resimli dünyā*, a children's magazine, followed by *Güneşh*, *Papaghan* and *Yeñi ḳalem* magazines in 1927. In 1932 he published *Edebiyat gazetesi*, in 1935 *Ayda bir*, and in 1942 *Çınaraltı*. In 1946 he became an MP for the Halk partisi (Republican People's Party) from Zonguldak. In 1960 he returned to journalism. In 1965 he joined the Adalet partisi (Justice Party) as an MP from Istanbul. From 1969 until his death on 22 August 1972, he worked as a journalist.

Throughout his life, he wrote for many newspapers and magazines, including *Taṣwīr-i efkār, Cumhuriyet, Ulus, Zafer* and *Son Havadis*. As a poet, his first poems are in *ʿarūḍ/aruz*, but later he became one of the famous promoters of syllabic metre of the National literary movement between 1908-12. In fact, he is known as one of the group of young poets called the "Five poets of the syllabic metre" (Faruk Nafiz Çamlıbel, Enis Behiç Koryürek, Halit Fahri Ozansoy and Yusuf Ziya Ortaç being the others). His popular poems have been set to music.

Bibliography: 1. Selected works. (a) Poetry: *Fïrṭïna we ḳār*, 1919; *Peri ḳïzï ile čoban ḥikāyesi*, 1919; *Gönülden sesler*, 1922; *O beyaz bir kuştu*, 1941; *Kervan*, 1964; *İşte sevdiğim dünya*, 1965; *Şiirler*, 1970. (b) Novel: *Çocuk adam*, 1964. (c) Satire: *Asrî Kerem*, 1942. (d) Collected articles: *Dün, bugün, yarın*, 1943; *Kulaktan kulağa*, 1943; *Hicivler*, 1951. (e) Short story: *Düğün gecesi*, 1957.

2. Studies. Ş. Kurdakul, *Şairler ve yazarlar sözlüğü*, Istanbul 1971; N.S. Banarlı, *Türk edebiyatı tarihi*, Ankara 1984; S.K. Karaalioğlu, *Türk edebiyati tarihi*, Istanbul 1986. (Çiğdem Balim)

ORKHON, a river of the northern part of what is now the Mongolian People's Republic; it joins the Selenga to flow northwards eventually into Lake Baikal.

For Turcologists, the banks of this river are of supreme importance as the locus for the Old Turkish inscriptions, carved in the middle decades of the 8th century in a so-called "runic" script, in fact derived ultimately from the Aramaic one [see TURKS. Languages]. These inscriptions are the royal annals of the Köktürk empire, centred on this region till its fall in 744 and supersession by a Uyghur [q.v.] grouping based on Ḳara Balg̲h̲asun on the Ork̲h̲on; these Uyg̲h̲urs were in turn dispossessed by the Ḳīrg̲h̲īz [q.v.] in 840 and forced to migrate southwards to Kan-su and Turfan [q.vv.]. No Islamic geographers mention the Ork̲h̲on, but we know something of Ḳara Balg̲h̲asun (whose ruins are still visible) from the visit to it by a Muslim traveller Tamīm b. Baḥr al-Muṭṭawwiʿ, which probably took place, in Minorsky's view, in 821 A.D.; this is the only first-hand Muslim account of the Uyg̲h̲ur kingdom in Mongolia.

Bibliography: See V. Minorsky, *Tamīm ibn Baḥr's journey to the Uyghurs*, in *BSOAS*, xii (1948), 275-305.   (C.E. BOSWORTH)

OROMO, a people of eastern Africa, partly Islamised, present in Ethiopia but also, although in small numbers only, in Kenya, Somalia and even in the Sudan. Among its constituent groups are the Arssi (Arusi), Boran, Guji, Karayu, Leqa, Macha, Raya (Azebo), Tulama, Wello, etc. The Amharas, amongst whom they have become installed, have for a long time given them the name of "Galla", whose etymology is uncertain.

Numerically, the Oromo form one of the leading ethnic groups of Africa. In Ethiopia they represent 40% of the total population, i.e. between some ten and fourteen millions. Linguistically, they are the majority, ahead of the Amhara speakers. Their language is called by themselves *afaan oromo* and by the Amharas *oromeñña* or *galleñña*, and belongs to the Cushitic group [see KŪS̲H̲] at the side of Afar, Agaw, Bedja, Saho and Somali. The writing of Oromo in Latin characters seems now to be becoming generalised, even though the Ethiopian or Arabic alphabets have sometimes been used for it also.

Religious differences (they include Christians faithful to the national church, Catholics and Lutherans, also Muslims, and also followers of their traditional religions), as well as the cultural diversity of their groups and the denial of their existence as a people before 1975, have not prevented the gradual formation of a common identity among the Oromo. This is based on a substantial degree of linguistic intercommunication and on common values (such as the *gada* system). For some people it shows itself in a nationalism which the setting-up of a new, decentralised Ethiopian administrative system (1992), which endeavours to regroup the Oromo lands into an entity called "Oromia", would probably not satisfy completely.

The cradle of the Oromo, originally nomads, is believed to have been the region which stretches from Lake Abaya to the upper course of the Webi Shebele. The most important warrior raids and migrations which pushed them northwards began in the middle of the 16th century. They were favoured, if not provoked, by the disorder brought about by the wars which had set the Christian empire against the Muslims in the first half of that century, and especially against the sultanate of Harar [q.v.]. These migrations brought them to the Blue Nile, to Tigré and, in the northeast, to Harar, in the midst of peoples whose customs and beliefs, and even language, they often adopted. In this way, some of them early became Muslim.

From the 18th century onwards, Muslim political entities took shape, often engaged in trading. In the north, the Tajju and Wello were capable of having an influence on the political evolution of the Christian states until 1853. In the south, petty kingdoms (Ennarya, Jimma, Gera, Gomma and Guma), originating from the middle of the 18th century, became Muslim under the influence of merchants, mainly Harari ones. Divided by internal rivalries, they were integrated into the empire by Menelik between 1881 and 1897, together with the Arssi region which had become Muslim in the second half of the century and the sultanate of Harar itself.

Oromo Islam is far from "orthodox", and its devotees are sometimes Muslim only in name. The famous pilgrimage to the *ḳubba* of S̲h̲ayk̲h̲ Nūr Husen takes place in the Arssi territory, and the rites practised there strongly resemble those of the traditional pilgrimages at Abba Mudda. The influential *ṭarīḳa*s have come from the Sudan (Tīd̲j̲āniyya, Sammāniyya) or from Arabia (Aḥmadiyya, Ḳādiriyya).

Bibliography: Information on Oromo Islam is very scattered. In addition to the bibls. published on Ethiopia, Kenya and Somalia, one may consult J.S. Trimingham, *Islam in Ethiopia*, London 1952; A. Trudnos, *Oromo documentation. Bibliography and maps*, Warsaw 1984; P.T.W. Baxter, *The present state of Oromo studies: a resumé*, in *Bull. des Études Africaines de l'Inalco*, vi, no. 11 (1986), 53-82.
                                        (A. ROUAUD)

ORONTE(s) [see AL-ʿAṢĪ].

ORTA (T.), literally "centre", in Ottoman Turkish military terminology, the equivalent of a company of fighting men in the three divisions (the *Segmen*, the *Djemāʿat* and the *Bölük*) of which the Janissary corps was eventually composed [see OD̲J̲AḲ and YEÑI ČERILER].

The number of *orta*s within the corps varied through the ages, but eventually approached 200; d'Ohsson reckoned the total at 229. The strength of each *orta* likewise varied; in the time of Meḥemmed II Fātiḥ [q.v.], they are said to have been composed of 50 men, but in the low hundreds at subsequent periods. The commander of an *orta* was called the *Čorbad̲j̲ī* (literally, "soup purveyor" [q.v.]), and amongst the officers below him were, *inter alios*, the *Āshd̲j̲ī* ("cook") and the *Bas̲h̲ Ḳara Ḳullukd̲j̲u* ("head scullion"), reflecting the origin of much Janissary nomenclature in culinary terms. The several officers in an *orta* seem to have reflected a variety of military functions rather than a hierarchy of ranks, as in modern armies. Also, each *orta* had its own clerk, *oda yazīd̲j̲ī*, who kept the rolls of the soldiers on the company's strength.

Bibliography: İ.H. Uzunçarşılı, *Osmanlı devleti teşkılâtından kapukulu ocakları*, Ankara 1943-4, index; M.Z. Pakalın, *Tarih deyimleri ve terimleri sözlüğü*, Istanbul 1946-54, ii, 730-1; H.A.R. Gibb and H. Bowen, *Islamic society in the West*, i/1, London 1950, index and esp. 60-3, 314-20.   (ED.)

ORTA OYUNU (T.), "entertainment staged in the middle place", a form of popular Turkish entertainment so-called because it takes place in the open air, *palanka*, around which the spectators form a circle. One side is reserved for the men, the other for the women. Behind the spectators is found the place where the actors get ready to enter the stage by means of a passage which is left free. The décor consists solely of a chair—or a table—called *dükkān* "shop, booth" and a folding screen, *yeñi dünyā* "new world". An orchestra made up of a *zurna*, oboe, a *čifte naḳḳāre* "double drum" and a *dawul* "big drum" plays a tune for dancing, and the dancers (*köček*) enter the stage, followed by the *d̲j̲urd̲j̲unad̲j̲ī*s "comic dancers". After this preliminary demonstration, the actors proper appear. The two main characters, Ḳawuḳlu and Pīshekār, have, respectively, the same characteristics of those of Karagöz and Hacivad in the shadow theatre [see KARAGÖZ], likewise the character of Zenne "lady" (here a male actor in woman's dress) and the various other types representing the minority groups of the Ottoman empire: Jew, Armenian, Frank (here the Frenchman, or European, resident in Turkey) and the Anatolian peasant, here called Türk. The role of Bebe Ruhi of the shadow plays is here played by an actor genuinely a dwarf and hump-backed.

There are a large number of themes in common with the shadow theatre, and several of these are drawn from the repertoire of popular romances like those of Ferhād and Shīrīn, Leylā and Medjnūn, etc. As in the Karagöz plays, these are stripped of their serious nature, enriched by comic elements and provided with a happy ending. What distinguishes the Orta Oyunu from Karagöz is, so it would appear, its mode of presentation: the coming together of living persons who are entirely free to draw comic effects from the mimes. A burlesque dialogue between Ḳawuḳlu and Pīshekār is called *čene yarîshî* "chin competition", a term signifying in Turkish "contest in gossiping, talking at length"; the two actors, drawing upon the term's ambiguity, reinforce their repartee with a miming contest which consists of twisting and deforming the chin to produce the most comic effects of the face.

Certain types of *taḳlīd* "comic imitation" of the Turkish tradition attested from the 12th century onwards have some common features with the Orta Oyunu, but only the imitative element can be traced back to there. The same applies to the spectacle known as *ḳol oyunu* "entertainment with troupes" about which Ewliyā Čelebi speaks. One could also compare the Orta Oyunu with the improvised street displays of rural areas. Nevertheless, with the full array of its characteristics, the Orta Oyunu is only attested in written sources after the beginning of the 18th century.

Some Orta Oyunu texts, transcribed rather late, have been published in the works of Martinovitch (one text in translation) and of Cevdet Kudret (nine texts). In the work of Selim Nüzhet Gerçek appears a list of 46 titles.

Bibliography: I. Kunos, *Das türkische Volksschauspiel: Orta Ojunu*, Leipzig 1908; E. Saussey, *Littérature populaire turque*, Paris 1936; N.N. Martinovitch, *The Turkish theatre*, New York 1933; Ahmet Kutsi Tecer, *Köylü temsilleri*, Ankara 1940; Th. Menzel, *Meddāḥ, Schattentheater und Orta-Ojunu*, Prague 1941; Selim Nüzhet Gerçek, *Türk temaşası: Meddah, Karagöz, Orta oyunu*, Istanbul 1942; A. Bombaci, *Orta-oyunu*, in *WZKM*, lvi (1960), 285-97; Sükrü Elçin, *Anadolu köy orta oyunları*, Ankara 1964; Helga Uplegger, *Das Volksschauspiel*, in *PTF*, ii, Wiesbaden 1964, 147-58, 169-70; Metin And, *Geleneksel Türk tiyatrosu*, Ankara 1969, 172-242; Cevdet Kudret, *Orta oyunu*, Ankara 1973.

(P.N. BORATAV)

ORTAČ, YŪSUF ḌIYĀ (Yusuf Ziyâ Ortaç), Turkish poet and journalist, born on 23 April 1895 in Istanbul, the son of engineer Süleymān Sāmī and Ḥurriyye, died in 1968. He finished *Wefā Iʿdādīsī* in 1915. By then he had already showed an interest in writing poetry and had won a prize for one of his poems, which was published in *Türk yurdu*. He taught literature first in İzmit, then at Galatasaray lycée. His poetry followed the tradition of the nationalist poets of the time. His first book of poems, *Aḳîndan aḳîna* was published in 1916, followed by *Djenk ufuḳlarî* in 1917, a work which aimed to give moral support to the army and the nation during the war. In 1918 he began to write satirical poems. He launched a journal called *Shāʿir* and wrote in the journal *Diken* using the pseudonym of Čimdik. In 1919 he published his satirical poems in *Shen kitāb*, comprising twenty poems which criticise the social and administrative life of Istanbul. In 1922, he published *Aḳ baba*, a satirical magazine, with Orkhan Seyfī [*q.v.*], which became the forerunner of the journals of satire during the first years of the Republic. Yusuf Ziyâ wrote for the newspapers *İkdam* and *Cumhuriyet* between the years 1927 and 1933. In 1935, he published *Ayda bir* with Orhan Seyfi Orhon as well as *Her ay*, a journal devoted to arts, economy and politics, and also the journal *Çınaraltı*. He left journalism to work as a literature teacher and later became an MP between the years 1946-54. In 1962 he published his last book *Bir rüzgâr esti* and until 1967 he worked for the magazine *Akbaba*. He died on 11 March 1968.

Bibliography: 1. Selected works. (a) Collections of poetry: *Aḳîndan aḳîna*, 1916; *Djenk ufuḳlarî*, 1917; *ʿĀshîklar yolu*, 1919; *Shāʿiriñ duʿāsî*, 1919; *Shen kitāb*, 1919; *Yanardağ*, 1928; *Bir servi gölgesi*, 1938; *Bir rüzgâr esti*, 1962. (b) Plays: *Biñ nāz*, 1917; *Kördüğüm*, 1919; *Nikāḥta kerāmet*, 1923; *Nâme veya eski mektup*, 1938. (c) Novels: *Üç katlı ev*, 1953; *Göç*, 1961. (d) Travel books: *Göz ucuyla Avrupa*, 1958. (e) Collection of articles: *Ocak*, 1943; *Sarı çizmeli Mehmet Ağa*, 1956; *Gün doğmadan*, 1960. (f) Memoirs: *Bir varmış bir yokmuş: portreler*, 1960; *Bizim yokuş*, 1966.

2. Studies. Ahmet Kabaklı, *Türk edebiyatı 3*, Istanbul 1972; Fethi H. Gözler, *Hece vezni ve hecenin beş şairi*, Istanbul 1980; Mehmet Önal, *Yusuf Ziyâ Ortaç*, Ankara 1986. (ÇİĞDEM BALIM)

ORUDJ [see URUDJ].

OSMAN DAN FODIO [see ʿUTHMĀN IBN FŪDĪ].

OSMAN DIGNA [see ʿUTHMĀN ABŪ BAKR DIGNA].

OSMAN NŪRĪ [see ERGIN, OSMAN NŪRĪ].

OSRUSHANA [see USRUSHANA].

OSSETIANS, an Iranic-speaking people who live in the central part of the North Caucasus, primarily in the North Ossetian ASSR and neighbouring areas on the southern slopes of these mountains in Georgia. According to the 1989 census, of the approximately 598,000 Ossetians in the former Soviet Union, 335,000 live in North Ossetia and 164,000 in Georgia. Sixty-five thousand of the Ossetians living in Georgia live in what was the South Ossetian AO.

The Ossetians are divided into two major religious groups, the Orthodox Christian Ossetians (*Iron* and *Tuallag*) and those professing Sunnī Islam, the *Digor* Ossetians. The Iron, or Eastern Ossetians, live primarily in eastern North Ossetia, and the Tuallag in Georgia. The Digors live primarily in the mountains and valleys of the northwestern part of Northern Ossetia, in a small portion of eastern Kabarda, and in the major Ossetian urban centre of Vladikavkaz.

The Muslim Ossetians are a relatively small minority, constituting between 20 to 30% of the Ossetian population. The ancestors of the Digors accepted Islam under the influence of the neighbouring Kabardinians between the 16th to 19th centuries. Although both Christianity and Sunnī Islam are represented in Ossetia, both of these faiths form only a thin veneer over a strong residual influence of the ancient polytheist and animist beliefs of the north Caucasian tribes. Pagan rituals, deities and folkways of Caucasian culture have survived throughout Ossetia, mixing with traditional Christian and Islamic beliefs and practices. For example, polygamy was practiced well into the Soviet period among both Christian and Muslim Ossetians, and both groups appear to have been relatively casual in practicing their respective faiths. This syncretic blend has resulted in a curiously unique and distinct Ossetian culture. In addition to adopting many beliefs of the local Caucasic peoples among whom they lived, including the Balkars, Ingush, Kabardinians, and Georgians, the Digors and other Ossetians also maintain fragments of the ancient cultural practices of their nomadic ancestors, the Alans.

The Ossetians are considered to be descendants of the ancient Scythian and Sarmatian tribes who inhabited the steppe region north of the Black Sea. In the fourth century A.D., the Alans, descendants of these tribes, were forced southward from their steppe homelands by more powerful nomadic tribes, including the Huns and the Mongols. Although they generally maintained their nomadic way of life, the Alans formed a loosely structured state called Alania in the foothills and mountain valleys between the upper Kuban River and the Darial Gorge of the Caucasus. Strong ties were established between Alania and the Byzantine Empire, and, in the 10th century, Christianity became the offical religion of Alania [see further, ALĀN].

Following the Mongol invasions of the 13th century, the Alans scattered. One group migrated to what is now Hungary and parts of western Europe; another followed the Huns to China. The Alans who remained in the Caucasus region moved deeper into the mountain valleys and on to the southern slopes of the mountain range, abandoning their nomadic way of life for the more sedentary Caucasian life style of stock raising and agriculture. After intermarrying and culturally mixing with the local Caucasian peoples, the Alans re-emerged three centuries later as a distinct ethnic group now known as the Ossetians.

The Ossetic language is the only survivor of the northeastern branch of Iranian languages, also known as Scythian. Ossetic is divided into two main dialects: "eastern" or Iron and "western" or Digor. Among the Digor Ossetians, a form of Ossetic developed incorporating linguistic elements from Kabardinian (Circassian), a Caucasic language. Many archaic linguistic terms and structures that no longer exist in Iron or Tuallag Ossetic were preserved in Digor. Iron and Tuallag are more heavily influenced by the Russian and Georgian languages, respectively. In the late 19th century a distinct Digor literary language was created, which used Arabic characters. At the same time, the Iron dialect was written in the Cyrillic alphabet and Tuallag in the Georgian alphabet. In 1923, all dialects of Ossetic were changed to the Latin alphabet, and in 1939, the Digor literary language was abolished and replaced by standard literary Iron, which again used the Cyrillic alphabet.

In 1944 the Digor were deported to Central Asia along with other Muslim peoples of the North Caucasus. In the late 1950s, the survivors of the deportations were permitted to return to homelands in the North Caucasus, and the Digor were resettled more or less in their traditional territories in the Digor Valley and the foothills of western North Ossetia, along the border of Kabarda. Today, the Digors live primarily by animal husbandry, settled agriculture, and many work in the nickel mining industry of North Ossetia. There are no major cities in the Digor region of North Ossetia and the Digor remain less urbanised than their Christian Iron neighbours and kinsmen.

Bibliography: R. Wixman, *Language aspects of ethnic patterns and processes in the North Caucasus*, University of Chicago, Department of Geography Series, no. 191, 1980; idem, *The peoples of the USSR. An ethnographic handbook*. Armonk, N.Y. 1988; S. A. Shuiskii, *Ossetians*, in *Muslim peoples: a world ethnographic survey*, ii, ed. R.V. Weekes, second edition, Westport, Conn. 1984; *Osetini*, in *Narodi Kavkaza*, ii, Moscow 1956; T. Trilati, *Literature on Ossetia and the Ossetians*, in *Caucasian Review*, no. 6 (1958). See also *The modern encyclopedia of Russian and Soviet history*, ed. J.L. Wieczynski, xxvi, Gulf Breeze, Fla. 1982; *Atlas Cevero-Osetinskaya ASSR*, Moscow 1967. (NANCY E. LEEPER)

OSTĀDSĪS [see USTĀDHSĪS].

ʿOTHMĀN, ĀL-I ʿOTHMĀN [see ʿOTHMĀNLĪ].

ʿOTHMĀN I, eponymous founder of the Ottoman dynasty. It is impossible to establish the dates of his birth or of his accession to sovereignty. He was active during the first quarter of the 8th/14th century, and Ottoman tradition asserts that he died shortly after his son Orkhan's [*q.v.*] conquest of Bursa (on 6 April 1326. For this date, see P. Schreiner, *Die Byzantinischen Kleinchroniken*, ii, Vienna 1977, 231). However, this story which makes a son assume leadership already during his father's lifetime, may have originated in the early 9th/15th century simply as an ideal model of succession to contrast with the contemporary practice of succession by fratricide. A *wakfiyya* of ʿOthmān's son Orkhan, dated Rabīʿ I 724/March 1324 (İ.H. Uzunçarşılı, *Gazi Orhan Bey vakfiyesi*, in *Belleten*, v/19 [1941], 277-88) already bears Orkhan's *tughra* [*q.v.*], suggesting—but by no means proving—that he had succeeded to full sovereignty by this date. In which case, ʿOthmān's death should perhaps be placed before March 1324. (For an argument in favour of 724/1324 as the date of Orkhan's succession, see İ.H. Uzunçarşılı, *Gazi Orhan Beğin hükümdar olduğu tarih*, in *Belleten*, ix/33 [1945], 207-11.)

ʿOthmān's origins are unknown. However, Turkish sources beginning with the *Iskender-name* (*ca.* 1400) of Aḥmedī [*q.v.*] (ed. İsmail Ünver, Ankara 1983, 65b) are unanimous in naming his father as Ertoghrul [*q.v.*], and a silver coin stamped on the obverse and reverse "Struck (by) ʿOthmān son of Ertoghrul" supports this claim (İ. Artuk, *Osmanlı beyliğinin kurucusu Osman Gaziye ait sikke*, in *1st International Congress on the Social and Economic History of Turkey. Papers*, Ankara [1983], 27-33). The names of ʿOthmān's children, apart from Orkhan, are also known, as they appear as witnesses to Orkhan's *wakfiyya* of 724/1324. They are Čoban, Ḥamīd, Melik, Pazarlu and Faṭma Khātūn. The Malkhatun daughter of ʿÖmer Beg, whose name also appears as a witness to the same document, may have been ʿOthmān's wife. Ottoman tradition from ʿĀshiḳ-pasha-zāde [*q.v.*] onwards name his wife as Malkhun, daughter of the legendary dervish Edebali. Neshrī [*q.v.*], however, while taking over ʿĀshiḳ-pasha-zāde's tale of ʿOthmān's marriage, adds a separate anecdote about ʿOthmān's love-affair with a lady called Malkhatun (ed. F. Taeschner, *Ğihānnümā. Die altosmanische Chronik des Mevlānā Mehemmed Neschrī*, i. Text of Codex Menzel, Leipzig 1951, 24. The copyist of the Manisa ms. renders this name as Malkhun Khātūn. See Taeschner, *Ğihānnümā*, ii. Text of Codex Manisa 1373, Leipzig 1955, 29). These tales may conceivably represent folk-memories of a real Malkhatun, a wife of the historical ʿOthmān.

The *Anonymous chronicles* (ed. F. Giese, *Die Altosmanischen Anonymen Chroniken*, Breslau 1922, 7) and Oruč (Oruč b. ʿĀdil, ed. F. Babinger, *Tevārīkh-i Āl-i ʿOthmān*, Hanover 1925, 12, 15-16) attribute only two sons to ᶜO<u>th</u>mān: Or<u>kh</u>an and ᶜAlī Pa<u>sh</u>a. ᶜĀ<u>sh</u>ıḳ-pa<u>sh</u>a-zāde (ed. ᶜAlī, *Tevārī<u>kh</u>-i Āl-i ᶜO<u>th</u>mān*, Istanbul 1332/1913-14, 39-40) adopts this scheme, but re-names ᶜAlī Pa<u>sh</u>a as ᶜAlāʾ al-Dīn Pa<u>sh</u>a [*q.v.*, ᶜAlāʾ al-Dīn Bey]. Most later historians follow ᶜĀ<u>sh</u>ıḳ-pa<u>sh</u>a-zāde. However, the figure of ᶜAlī Pa<u>sh</u>a/ᶜAlāʾ al-Dīn Pa<u>sh</u>a is wholly fictitious, despite inclusion in the *Encyclopaedia of Islam*. (For the origin and development of this legend, see C. Imber, *Canon and apocrypha in early Ottoman history*, in C. Finkel and C.J. Heywood (eds.), *Festschrift for V.L. Ménage*, Istanbul.)

The survival of a coin stamped with ᶜO<u>th</u>mān's name confirms the Ottoman tradition that he declared himself an independent ruler, since the issue of coinage served as a declaration of sovereignty. There are no other Ottoman texts or artefacts from his reign. The only contemporary source to mention ᶜO<u>th</u>mān is the Byzantine chronicle of George Pachymeres (1242-*ca.* 1310) (ed. I. Bekker, *De Michaele et Andronico Palaeologo,* Bonn 1835, ii).

Pachymeres' references to ᶜO<u>th</u>mān are confused. His chronicle records a victory which ᶜO<u>th</u>mān won over the Byzantine *hetaireiarches* Mouzalon at Bapheus, identified as the district around Nikomedia/Izmit (Pachymeres, *op. cit.*, 333). The battle, Pachymeres claims, "was the beginning of great trouble for the whole region." In a second attempt to defeat ᶜO<u>th</u>mān, the Byzantine Emperor Andronicus II sent another force against him under the *stratopedarch* Siouros. ᶜO<u>th</u>mān defeated this army in a night attack near a fortress called Katoikia, which he had also occupied (Pachymeres, *op. cit.*, 414). Pachymeres follows his account of this victory with a statement that ᶜO<u>th</u>mān next occupied Belokome/Bile<u>dj</u>ik [*q.v.*], thereby "gaining great wealth and living in prosperity, and using the fortresses as places of safekeeping for treasures" (Pachymeres, *op. cit.*, 414-15). The exact sequence of events is, however, unclear. In a slightly earlier passage, Pachymeres already refers to the loss of Belokome, together with Angelokome (İnegöl?), Melangeia (İnönü?), Anagourdia and Platanea (unidentified), without, however, attributing these conquests to ᶜO<u>th</u>mān (Pachymeres, *op. cit.*, 413). It would perhaps be reasonable to assume that it was ᶜO<u>th</u>mān who captured all these places, at about the time of his victory at Katoikia. Pachymeres reports that he also laid siege to Prousa/Bursa [*q.v.*] and to Pegai on the coast, where the besieged population suffered famine and plague (Pachymeres, *op. cit.*, 414), and finally that he made a determined but unsuccessful assault on Nikaia/Iznik [*q.v.*] (Pachymeres, *op. cit.*, 637). His final reference to ᶜO<u>th</u>mān reads: "So in this way ᶜO<u>th</u>mān was greatly inspired to ambitious plans. There was nothing in the regions around Nikaia, Pythia and everywhere right down to the coast which he did not control" (Pachymeres, *op. cit.*, 642). The disjointed sequence of events that Pachymeres describes must have occurred before 707-8/1308, the closing date of his chronicle. One can infer from this source that by this date the occupation of Belokome/Bile<u>dj</u>ik and other fortresses had given ᶜO<u>th</u>mān a secure base in the Sakarya valley and that he controlled the countryside westwards as far as the Sea of Marmara.

The earliest Ottoman lists of ᶜO<u>th</u>mān's conquests also indicate that his secure base was the Sakarya valley. The *Iskender-nāme* of Aḥmedī (*loc. cit.*) credits him with the capture of Bile<u>dj</u>ik, Inegöl and Köprüḥiṣār, at least the first two of which correspond with Pachymeres' narrative. A *Chronological list* of 824/1421 lists Bile<u>dj</u>ik, Yarḥiṣār, Inegöl and Yeñi<u>sh</u>ehir (Ç.N. Atsız, *Osmanlı tarihine ait takvimler*, Istanbul 1961, 25), and the subsequent chronicles by <u>Sh</u>ükrullāh (*ca.* 1460) (ed. Th. Seif, *Der Abschnitt über die Osmanen in Šükrullah's persischer Universalgeschichte*, in *MOG*, ii [1923-6], 81) and Enwerī (*ca.* 1465) (ed. M.H. Yınanç, *Düstūr-nāme-yi Enwerī*, Istanbul 1928, 82-3) offer permutations of these earlier lists. The *Anonymous chronicles* (ed. Giese, 6), Oruč (ed. Babinger, 12) and ᶜĀ<u>sh</u>ıḳ-pa<u>sh</u>a-zāde (ed. ᶜAlī, 18), all deriving their information from a common source of *ca.* 825/1422, also refer to ᶜO<u>th</u>mān's conquest of a fortress called Ḳara[<u>dj</u>a]ḥiṣār ("Black Fortress"). This toponym may correspond to the Melangeia of Pachymeres, since alternative forms of this name are Melagina/Melaina, which resemble the Greek word *melaina* (f. sing. "black") and suggest that the Turkish name is a calque of the Greek. The correspondence of these places with the general locations of ᶜO<u>th</u>mān's conquests to be inferred from Pachymeres suggests that in these few particulars the Ottoman tradition is historically accurate.

In general, however, Turkish traditions about ᶜO<u>th</u>mān are clearly unhistorical and should be understood as belonging to the literary genres of folk-epic (*dāstān* [*q.v.*]) and *manāḳib* [*q.v.*]. These traditions appear in their most primitive and disjointed form in the *Anonymous chronicles* and Oruč, which derive the core of their material from the "common source" of *ca.* 825/1422. The *History* of ᶜĀ<u>sh</u>ıḳ-pa<u>sh</u>a-zāde presents a fuller and more coherent narrative, adding a great deal to the stories which it shares with these two chronicles. For this reason, it is ᶜĀ<u>sh</u>ıḳ-pa<u>sh</u>a-zāde whose narrative has come to form the basis of the modern historiography of ᶜO<u>th</u>mān's reign. However, ᶜĀ<u>sh</u>ıḳ-pa<u>sh</u>a-zāde's additional material is similar in type to what he took from the "common source". For example, he also derives the names of ᶜO<u>th</u>mān's followers and companions from toponyms, and creates battle stories both from folk-etymologies of place-names and from the sites of shrines. An example of this last type is ᶜO<u>th</u>mān's supposed victory over the Byzantines at Ḳoyunḥiṣār, which modern historians have over-optimistically identified with the Bapheus in Pachymeres. The original story comes from the "common source", and locates the battle at the site of a shrine, which popular tradition came to associate with the tomb of a fictitious relative of ᶜO<u>th</u>mān who supposedly fell in a battle at that spot (Oruč b. ᶜĀdil, *op. cit.*, 13). ᶜĀ<u>sh</u>ıḳ-pa<u>sh</u>a-zāde (ed. ᶜAlī, 21) adopts the same tale, but removes the battle-site to nearby Dinboz. This clearly reflects the influence of a tale preserved in the *Ottoman history* of Theodore Spandugino (for the recension of 1513, see *La cronaca italiana di Teodoro Spandugino*, in C. Villain-Gandossi, *La Méditerranée aux XII-XVIe siècles*, London 1983, 158-60; for the recension of 1538, see C. Sathas, *Documents inédits relatifs à l'histoire de la Grèce au moyen-âge*, ix, Paris 1890, 138-9) of an Ottoman victory over the infidels at Dinboz. The starting point of Spandugino's story is the name Dinboz itself, which he understands as deriving from Turkish *dīn boz-* ("to destroy religion") and as being so named in commemoration of an Ottoman victory over the Greeks. ᶜĀ<u>sh</u>ıḳ-pa<u>sh</u>a-zāde has simply conflated the two stories to create a new account of a battle, and this procedure is typical of his entire narrative.

In the 20th century, a number of historians have adapted Ottoman traditions relating to ᶜO<u>th</u>mān and his forbears in order to construct new theories of the origins of the Ottoman Empire. M. Fuad Köprülü (*Les origines de l'Empire Ottoman*, Istanbul 1935) accepted that the Ottoman tradition making ᶜO<u>th</u>mān a leader of the Ḳayı̊ [*q.v.*] tribe is, at least in essence, true. R.P. Lindner (*Nomads and Ottomans in mediaeval Anatolia*, Bloomington 1983) also postulated a tribal origin for ᶜOthmān and his followers, but greatly modified the traditional stories to accord with modern anthropological theory. P. Wittek (*The rise of the Ottoman Empire*, London 1938) rejected the traditions of ᶜOthmān as leader of a tribe, in favour of the view that he was leader of a *ghāzī* corporation and that these *ghāzī* origins pre-determined the future trajectory of the Ottoman Empire. (On the intellectual roots of Wittek's famous theory, see C.J. Heywood, *Wittek and the Austrian tradition*, in *JRAS* [1988], 7-25; idem, *"Boundless dreams of the Levant": Paul Wittek, the George-Kreis, and the writing of Ottoman history*, in *ibid.* [1989], 30-50. See also R.C. Jennings, *Some thoughts on the gazi-thesis*, in *WZKM*, lxxvi [1986], 151-61.) Another thesis harmonises the "nomad" and "*ghāzī*" theories (Halil İnalcık, *The question of the emergence of the Ottoman state*, in *International Journal of Turkish Studies*, ii/2 [1981-2], 71-80). Another view is that the Ottoman traditions concerning ᶜOthmān's origins and forbears are myths, most of which developed during the course of the 9th/15th century and had the function of legitimising Ottoman dynastic rule (C. Imber, *The Ottoman dynastic myth*, in *Turcica*, xix [1987], 7-27; on the legitimising functions of the Ottoman genealogy, see Wittek, *op. cit.*, 1-15; Barbara Flemming, *Political genealogies in the sixteenth century*, in *Osmanlı Araştırmaları*, vii-viii [1988], 123-37).

Bibliography: Given in the article.

(C. Imber)

ᶜOTHMĀN II, sixteenth sultan of the Ottoman empire (regn. 1027-31/1618-22), was born on 19 Djumādā II 1012/15 November 1603; cf. *Sidjill-i ᶜothmānī*, i, 56), the son of Sultan Aḥmed I. After the death of his father in November 1617, the brother of the latter had been proclaimed sultan as Muṣṭafā I [*q.v.*] but ᶜOthmān, taking advantage of the weak character of his uncle and supported by the *Muftī* Esᶜad Efendi and the *Ḳîzlar Aghasî* Muṣṭafā, seized the throne on 26 February 1618 by a coup d'état.

The youth of the new sultan at first assured the promoters of the coup d'état of considerable influence. To them was due the replacement of Khalīl Pasha [*q.v.*] as grand vizier by Öküz Meḥmed Pasha [*q.v.*] in January 1619. Khalīl had just concluded a treaty of peace with Shāh ᶜAbbās I of Persia, after a campaign which had been indecisive. The relations with the other powers, Austria and Venice, with which the capitulations were renewed, were also peaceful. But in January 1620, after Meḥmed Pasha had been replaced by the very influential favourite Güzeldje ᶜAlī Pasha [*q.v.*], who removed from the court all possible rivals, the chances of war increased. This time it was a war with Poland, which broke out through the intrigues of the voivode of Moldavia. In the battle of Jassy on 20 September 1620, the Polish army was annihilated by the *ser-ᶜasker* Iskender Pasha. The grand vizier, who held office mainly by satisfying the avarice of the young sultan, never lost an occasion to irritate and provoke the enmity of Austria and Venice. He died on 9 March 1621 and under his successor Ḥüseyn Pasha of Okhri, ᶜOthmān II took part in person in the campaign of 1621 against Poland. This campaign ended in a check for the Turks and the Tartars, who, with great losses, had in vain tried to storm the fortified Polish camp on the Dniester near Choczim. A preliminary peace was signed under the same conditions as before under Süleymān I, and the sultan appointed a new grand vizier, Dilāwer-zāde Ḥüseyn Pasha.

Since the time when ᶜOthmān, still considerably under the influence of the Ḳîzlar Aghasî Süleymān and his Khodja, Mollā ᶜÖmer, had begun to act independently, he had not been able to gain the sympathy of the army on account of his brutal treatment of the Janissaries, nor of the people chiefly as a result of his avarice, nor of the *ᶜulemā*ʾ. The latter were particularly horrified at the sultan's wish to take four legitimate wives from the free classes of his entourage; he actually married the daughter of the *Muftī* Esᶜad. His unpopularity increased still further when he wished to put himself at the head of an army to fight Fakhr al-Dīn Maᶜn [*q.v.*], the Druze *Amīr*, and to go on and make the pilgrimage to Mecca. Preparations had already been made for this expedition when on 18 May 1622, a mutiny broke out among the Janissaries and Sipāhīs, who plundered the house of Mollā ᶜÖmer. Next day, the rebels secured the cooperation of the chief *ᶜulemā*ʾ and demanded the heads of the Ḳîzlar Aghasî, the Khodja, the grand vizier and three other high officials. ᶜOthmān at first refused, but after the rebels had forced the third wall of the palace he had to sacrifice the grand vizier and the Ḳîzlar Aghasî. But in the meantime, his uncle Muṣṭafā had been brought out from his seclusion in the harem to be proclaimed sultan. ᶜOthmān tried during the night to secure his throne through the influence of the Agha of the Janissaries, but the latter was killed on the following morning and he became the prisoner of the Janissaries, who took him to their barracks. The rebels had no intentions against his life, but meanwhile the direction of affairs had passed to Dāwūd Pasha, the favourite and son-in-law of Māh-Peyker, the mother of Sultan Muṣṭafā. Dāwūd Pasha, being appointed grand vizier, had ᶜOthmān taken to the castle of Yedi Kule, where he was put to death in the evening of 20 May 1622. He was buried in the *türbe* of his father Aḥmed I. ᶜOthmān is praised for his skill as a horseman and for his intelligence. He was also a poet with the *makhlaṣ* of Fārisī. He was the first of three sultans to lose his life in a rising, the others being Ibrāhīm and Selīm III.

Bibliography: The Turkish sources are the works of Naᶜīmā, Pečewī, Ḥasan Bey-zāde, the *Rawḍat al-abrār* of Ḳara Čelebi-zāde, and the *Fedhleke* of Ḥādjdjī Khalīfa. The *Waḳᶜa-yi Sulṭān ᶜOthmān Khān* of Ṭūghī is specially devoted to the deposition of ᶜOthmān (tr. by A. Galland; cf. *GOW*, 157), while his whole reign is described in a *Shah-nāme* by Nādirī (*GOW*, 169). Among contemporary western accounts, see the *Relazione* quoted by von Hammer, in the note on p. 806 of *GOR*², ii, and that of Sir Thomas Roe. See also the general histories by von Hammer, Zinkeisen and Jorga; İ.H. Uzunçarşılı, *Osmanlı tarihi*, iv/1, 337-41, iv/2, 370 ff.; A.D. Alderson, *The structure of the Ottoman dynasty*, Oxford 1956, index; S.J. Shaw, *History of the Ottoman empire and modern Turkey*, i, Cambridge 1976, 246; R. Mantran (ed.), *Histoire de l'empire ottoman*, Paris 1989, index; *İA*, art. *Osman II* (Şinâsî Altındağ).

(J.H. Kramers)

ᶜOTHMĀN III, twenty-fifth sultan of the Ottoman empire (regn. 1168-71/1754-7) and son of Muṣṭafā II, succeeded his brother Maḥmūd I on 14 December 1754. He was born on 2 January 1699 (*Sidjill-i ᶜothmānī*, i, 56) and had therefore reached an advanced age when he was called to the throne. No events of political importance took place in his reign. The period of peace which had begun with the peace of Belgrade in 1739 continued; at home only a series of seditious outbreaks in the frontier provinces indicated the weakness of the empire. In the absence of any outstanding personality, the sultan was able to rule as he pleased, but his activities were practically confined to changing his grand vizier frequently (six times). His favourite, Silihdār ᶜAlī Pa<u>sh</u>a, grand vizier from 24 August to 22 October 1755, had his career terminated by execution. The appointment on 13 December 1756 of Rā<u>gh</u>ib Pa<u>sh</u>a [*q.v.*] was an important one, as for five years this great statesman showed himself an excellent administrator of the empire under the following sultan Muṣṭafā III. ᶜO<u>th</u>mān III's other activities were the suppression of cafés, of the liberty of women to show themselves in public and the regulation of the dress of his non-Muslim subjects. His name is associated with the great mosque of Nūr-i ᶜO<u>th</u>mānī (Nuruosmaniye), which had been begun by Maḥmūd I and was solemnly opened in December 1755. The reign of this sultan is remembered for the great fires in the capital in 1755 and 1756. He died on 30 October 1757 and was buried, like Maḥmūd I, in the tomb of the Yeñi <u>Dj</u>āmiᶜ.

Bibliography: The *Taʾrī<u>kh</u>* of Wāṣif is the principal source. The reign is described in the great histories of von Hammer, Zinkeisen and Jorga. See also A. Danon, *Contributions à l'histoire des sultans Osman II et Mouçtafâ I*, in *JA*, 11th ser., xiv (1919), 69-139, 243-310; İ.H. Uzunçarşılı, *Osmanlı tarihi*, iii/1, 132 ff., iii/2, 385 ff.; A.D. Alderson, *The structure of the Ottoman dynasty*, Oxford 1956, index; S.J. Shaw, *History of the Ottoman empire and modern Turkey*, i, Cambridge 1976, 191-3; R. Mantran (ed.), *Histoire de l'empire Ottoman*, Paris 1989, index; *İA*, art. *Osman II* (Şinâsî Altındağ).

(J.H. Kramers)

ᶜO<u>TH</u>MĀN ḤAMDĪ (b. Istanbul, 1842; d. Kuruçeşme, 1910; buried in Eskihisar), Ottoman painter and archaeologist.

He was the eldest son of Ibrāhīm Edhem Pa<u>sh</u>a [*q.v.*], grand vizier under ᶜAbd al-Ḥamīd II, and brother of Ismāᶜīl <u>Gh</u>ālib [*q.v.*] and <u>Kh</u>alīl Edhem (Eldem [*q.v.*]). Sent to Paris *ca.* 1857 in order to study law, ᶜO<u>th</u>mān Ḥamdī gravitated toward the École des Beaux-Arts, where he studied painting under the leading proponents of Academic painting, in particular G. Boulanger and J.-L. Gérôme; he also attended courses in archaeology. From his teachers he absorbed a knowledge of classical antiquity, a precise descriptive technique and a taste for "Oriental" themes. In 1867 he functioned as representative for the Ottoman section of the Exposition Universelle in Paris visited by Sultan ᶜAbd al-ᶜAzīz. On his return to the Ottoman Empire in 1869, ᶜO<u>th</u>mān Ḥamdī spent two years in Ba<u>gh</u>dād in the service of Midḥat Pa<u>sh</u>a, then governor of ᶜIrāḳ. For the 1873 International Exposition in Vienna he served as Head of the Turkish section and compiled a book, *Les costumes populaires de la Turquie*. During the 1870s, he served in various administrative posts, pursued his artistic interests and became associated with the newly established Müze-yi Hümāyūn (Imperial Museum; continues as Arkeoloji Müzeleri). In 1881 he was appointed director of this museum and shortly thereafter participated in founding the Ṣanāyiᶜ-i Nefīse Mektebi (School of Fine Arts, continues as Güzel Sanatlar Akademisi). During his years as museum director (1881-1910), ᶜO<u>th</u>mān Ḥamdī was also responsible for overseeing archaeological activities in Ottoman territory and was instrumental in drafting the 1884 *Ā<u>th</u>ār-i ᶜAtīḳa Niẓām-nāmesi*, a law which declared all antiquities to be the property of the State, forbidding to archaeologists a share of their finds and making clandestine excavation and antiquities smuggling criminal offences; the basic provisions of this law remain in force today. His father's position as Minister of the Interior (1883-5) facilitated the speedy enforcement of this law, which was soon to give the Müze-yi Hümāyūn an outstanding collection of antiquities as well as an archive of tablets excavated in ᶜIrāḳ and Anatolia. ᶜO<u>th</u>mān Ḥamdī's zeal for preserving the relics of the past led him to undertake excavations where finds of antiquities were reported. Most notable was his 1887 excavation of a necropolis in Sidon which yielded a sarcophagus portraying battles of Greeks and Persians initially thought to have been made for Alexander of Macedon. The finds from Sidon were published by ᶜO<u>th</u>mān Ḥamdī in collaboration with Théodore Reinach (*Une nécropole royale à Sidon. Fouilles de Hamdy Bey*, Paris 1892). Antiquities from Sidon and other sites soon made it necessary to build a proper museum near the Çinili Köşk of Topkapı Palace which had been used since 1876 to house objects collected from pre-Islamic and Islamic sites in the Ottoman Empire. ᶜO<u>th</u>mān Ḥamdī gained international recognition as archaeologist and museum director; among other awards for him were the title of Grand Officier of the Légion d'Honneur (1906) and the degree of Doctor Honoris Causa from Oxford University (1909).

Throughout his career as administrator and archaeologist ᶜO<u>th</u>mān Ḥamdī continued to paint, and his works were exhibited in both Turkey and Europe. Most of his compositions were close variants of types used by his teacher, J.-L. Gérôme, and are characterised by a painstaking attention to detail in the rendering of setting, figures and ancillary objects. Because of this, it is possible to discern that many paintings are self-portraits or contain likenesses of his immediate family. Most of the settings are also recognisable, and include buildings in Bursa, Karaman and Istanbul. Several have as a background the Çinili Köşk and some of the objects he portrayed are known to have been part of the museum's collection. As a painter, administrator and scholar, ᶜO<u>th</u>mān Ḥamdī devoted his life to the study and preservation of the artistic and cultural heritage of the Ottoman Empire, laying the foundations for institutions which continue to function in the Turkish Republic.

Bibliography: Mustafa Cezar, *Sanatta batı'ya açılış ve Osman Hamdi*, Istanbul 1971, and *Bibl.*, 629-36; Refik Epikman, *Osman Hamdi*, Ankara 1967; Arif Müfid Mansel, *Osman Hamdi Bey*, in *Belleten*, xciv (1960), 291-301; V. Belgin Demirsar, *Osman Hamdi tablolarında gerçekle ilişkiler*, Ankara 1989; H. Metzger (ed.), *La correspondance passive d'Osman Hamdi Bey*, Limoges-Paris 1990; *Türk Ansiklopedisi*, xviii (1970), 433-5, s.v. Hamdi Bey, Osman.

(P. and S. Soucek)

ᶜO<u>TH</u>MĀN PA<u>SH</u>A, Özdemir-O<u>gh</u>lī, Ottoman grand vizier and celebrated commander in the Ottoman-Ṣafawid war of 1578-90.

Born in Egypt in 933/1526-7, his father was Özdemir Pa<u>sh</u>a [*q.v.*], a *mamlūk* who became Ottoman governor (*beylerbeyi*) of Yemen and conqueror of Abyssinia (Ḥabe<u>sh</u> [*q.v.*]). The earliest documentary evidence of ᶜO<u>th</u>mān's holding office in Egypt dates from <u>Dh</u>u 'l-Ḥi<u>dj</u><u>dj</u>a 957/December 1550; yet it is claimed that by the age of twenty he was a *san<u>dj</u>aḳbeyi*, the rank he held in Rabīᶜ I 968/December 1560 when appointed Egyptian *amīr al-ḥa<u>djdj</u>*.

ᶜO<u>th</u>mān followed his deceased father as *beylerbeyi* of Ḥabe<u>sh</u>, probably in late 968/mid-1561. It has been suggested (Orhonlu, *Habeş eyaleti*, 49), though without supporting evidence, that he was chosen because he had earlier served there under his father and was familiar with the province's lands and peoples.

During his six years in this office, ᶜO͟thmān Pa͟sha apparently operated mainly in the coastal region south from Maṣawwaᶜ [*q.v.*], seeking to forestall Abyssinian contacts with the Portuguese. He may also have taken measures aimed at linking Ḥabe͟sh with Upper Egypt to counter the Fund͟j [*q.v.*] tribes, who in 971-2/1564 besieged Sawākin, the province's administrative centre.

Released from Ḥabe͟sh in Ṣafar 975/August 1567, ᶜO͟thmān returned to his native Cairo. There he shortly learned that, from 14 D͟jumādā II 975/16 December 1567, he had been appointed governor of Ṣanᶜāʾ, then one of two *beylerbeyiliks* in Yemen [see MAḤMŪD PA͟SHA] where a Zaydī rebellion was out of control. Although ordered to depart for Yemen immediately with a modest force in advance of a larger one under the *serdār* (commander-in-chief) Muṣṭafā Pa͟sha Lala [*q.v.*], ᶜO͟thmān lingered in Cairo and became drawn to Muṣṭafā Pa͟sha in his bitter rivalry with Ḳod͟ja Sinān Pa͟sha [*q.v.*], the governor of Egypt. When finally he left Suez early in 976/mid-1568 with 3,000 troops, ᶜO͟thmān's status had been elevated to *beylerbeyi* of the reunited single province of Yemen. His troops rescued the beleaguered Ottoman garrison at Zabīd in D͟jumādā II 976/November-December 1568 and quickly recovered Taᶜizz in the interior. But ᶜO͟thmān shortly came under close Zaydī siege until relieved in D͟hu 'l-Ḳaᶜda 976/April 1569 by Ḳod͟ja Sinān Pa͟sha, then *serdār* in place of Muṣṭafā Pa͟sha. Subsequent cooperation between the *beylerbeyi* and *serdār* proved elusive, owing to their dislike of each other. Thus the *serdār* exercised his discretionary authority to dismiss and expel ᶜO͟thmān from Yemen.

The next several years of ᶜO͟thmān Pa͟sha's career remain somewhat obscure. Proceeding to Istanbul during 977-8/1570, he was initially refused domicile in the city by the grand vizier Ṣoḳollu Meḥmed Pa͟sha [*q.v.*], to whom Ḳod͟ja Sinān Pa͟sha had reported on him adversely. Nevertheless, his friend Muṣṭafā Pa͟sha Lala [*q.v.*], now the popular conqueror of Cyprus, commended him to Sultan Selīm II and secured for him the governorship of al-Ḥasā in eastern Arabia. After a year there, he was transferred to al-Baṣra, where, as instructed, he organised for an assault on Hurmuz, before being named *beylerbeyi* of Diyār Bakr (980/1572-3). ᶜO͟thmān held this office for four years, and, when replaced by a relative of Ṣoḳollu Meḥmed, he sought to escape the latter's machinations by remaining in Diyār Bakr.

When it was decided in 985/1578 to make war on Ṣafawid Persia, Muṣṭafā Pa͟sha Lala, who was chosen *serdār*, invited ᶜO͟thmān Pa͟sha to participate. ᶜO͟thmān accepted and was commissioned for the campaign on 20 Muḥarram 986/29 March 1578. Advancing with the main army east from Erzurum in the summer of 1578, ᶜO͟thmān commanded forces which scored two decisive victories over the Ṣafawids, the first on 5 D͟jumādā II 986/9 August 1578 at Čildir, and the second a month later near the Alazan River. These successes both gained ᶜO͟thmān renown and made possible the Ottoman occupation of, respectively, Georgia and S͟hirwān, including the key centres of S͟hamāk͟hī and Derbend. Muṣṭafā Pa͟sha subsequently withdrew the army to winter near Erzurum, having persuaded ᶜO͟thmān to stay and defend the conquests with a modest army, the rank of vizier, and the status of governor-general of S͟hirwān and Dāg͟histān.

Predictably, the Ṣafawids reappeared once the main Ottoman army had departed. Despite the arrival of a support contingent of Crimean Tatars, ᶜO͟thmān was compelled, after two sieges during Ramaḍān 986/November 1578, to abandon S͟hamāk͟hī and retreat to Derbend on the Caspian. He maintained this Ottoman foothold in the Caucasus until S͟haᶜbān 987/October 1579, when, at Sultan Murād III's bidding, Meḥmed Girāy, the Crimean *k͟hān*, arrived with a substantial force. Although shortly afterwards ᶜO͟thmān Pa͟sha and the Tatars recovered S͟hamāk͟hī and swept the Ṣafawids from S͟hirwān, Meḥmed Girāy returned home, leaving only a token Tatar contingent under his brother, G͟hāzī Girāy (II [*q.v.*]).

Thereafter, ᶜO͟thmān withdrew to Derbend, his base until 991/1583. His communicating with the sultan directly to report his desperate circumstances resulted in the arrival at Derbend via the Crimea, towards the end of 990/1582, of an army of Rumelian reinforcements. With these, ᶜO͟thmān Pa͟sha the following spring won his greatest victory when he defeated a formidable Ṣafawid army between the Samur River and S͟hābirān. This engagement, known as the "Battle of the Torches (*Me͟shᶜale Sawa͟shī*)" because of the use of torches to fight by night, raged during 14-18 Rabīᶜ II 991/7-11 May 1583 and resulted in the expulsion of the Ṣafawids from S͟hirwān and Dāg͟histān for some time hence.

ᶜO͟thmān Pa͟sha left the Caucasus in S͟hawwāl 991/October 1583, with more than five years' continuous service there and a reputation as a brilliant commander. He returned through the Crimea, under orders to execute Meḥmed Girāy K͟hān for not supporting the war in the Caucasus after 987/1579, and to instal as *k͟hān* a brother being sent from Istanbul. Meḥmed Girāy was eventually assassinated, but only after the arrival of the Ottoman fleet in the spring of 1584 forced him to lift his 37-day siege of ᶜO͟thmān in Kaffa and flee. The celebrated warrior reached Istanbul in early summer and received a hero's welcome by all but the envious viziers of the dome [see ḲUBBE WEZĪRI] and suspicious palace factions. Following an audience with Murād III, to whom he related his experiences, ᶜO͟thmān was appointed grand vizier (*ṣadr-i aᶜẓam*) on 20 Rad͟jab 992/28 July 1584.

When in Ramaḍān 992/September 1584 it was learned that there was renewed conflict in the Crimea, the grand vizier himself volunteered to resolve it. But while in winter quarters in Anatolia, the ailing ᶜO͟thmān learned that matters in Bāg͟hče Sarāy had been settled satisfactorily. He shortly also learned that he was to succeed Ferhād Pa͟sha [*q.v.*] as *serdār* of the eastern front. With a vast army, ᶜO͟thmān departed from Erzurum for Tabrīz; and, although too ill to mount up, on 28 Ramaḍān 993/23 September 1585 he oversaw the Ottoman occupation of Tabrīz that would endure nearly twenty years.

Özdemir-og͟hlī ᶜO͟thmān Pa͟sha died in D͟hu 'l-Ḳaᶜda 993/October 1585 while returning from Tabrīz, and was buried in the city of Diyār Bakr, as he wished. Surviving him was his wife, a Dāg͟histān princess said to have been a woman of remarkable beauty. Although a tireless warrior like his father, he was not without his critics, including Koči Bey [*q.v.*], who accused him of being the first both to meddle with the system of awarding military fiefs and to admit non-*ḳuls* into *ḳapuḳulu* regiments.

Bibliography: Ms. sources include the versified *S͟hed͟jāᶜat-nāme* by Dāl Meḥmed Čelebi Āṣafī (who was ᶜO͟thmān Pa͟sha's secretary and assistant); Muṣṭafā ᶜĀlī's *Künh ül-ak͟hbār* and *Nuṣrat-nāme* (the latter an eye-witness account of the 1578-9 campaign); the three works by Raḥīmī-zāde Ibrāhīm Ḥarīmī Čawu͟sh entitled *Ẓafer-nāme-i ḥaḍret-i Sulṭān Murād K͟hān*, *Gend͟jīne-i fetḥ-i Gend͟je*, and *Ḳünd͟je-yi bāg͟h-i Murād*; the *Tebrīziyye* by Taᶜlīḳī-zāde Meḥmed Čelebi Ṣubḥī; and the *G͟hazawāt-nāme-i*

Özdemiroghlî ᶜOthmān Pasha by Ebūbekir b. ᶜAbdullāh (cf. A.S. Levend, *Gazavât-nâmeler*, 87).

Printed materials are Nahrawālī, *al-Barḳ al-Yamānī* = *Ghazawāt al-Djarākisa*, ed. al-Djāsir, Riyāḍ 1967, 205-45 *passim;* the anonymous relation in E. Albèri, *Relazioni*, Florence 1844, ser. 3, ii, 427-70; G.T. Minadoi, *Historia della Guerra fra Turchi et Persiani*, Rome 1587, 78-103, 257-78, 320-50; G. Le Strange (ed. and tr.), *Don Juan of Persia*, London 1926, 147-55, 176-86; Iskandar Beg Munshī, *Taʾrīkh-i ᶜālam-ārā-yi ᶜAbbāsī*, Tehran 1955, i, *passim* (tr. R.M. Savory, *History of Shah ᶜAbbas the great*, Boulder, Col., 1978); R. Knolles, *The Turkish history*, 6th ed., London 1687, i, 658-66, 686-8, 696-701; Selānīkī, *Taʾrīkh*, Istanbul 1281/1864-5, 97-8, 146-202 *passim;* Pečewī, *Taʾrīkh*, Istanbul 1283/1866-7, ii, 17-18, 39-102 *passim;* Münedjdjim Bashî, iii, 539-58 *passim;* Hammer-Purgstall, *GOR*, iii, 551-6, iv, 71-7, 88-97, 170-4; ᶜOthmān-zāde Ṭāʾib, *Ḥadīḳat ül-wuzarāʾ*, Istanbul 1271/1854, 38-41; *Sidjill-i ᶜOthmānī*, iii, 416 (faulty); Sāmī, *Ḳāmūs ül-aᶜlām*, Istanbul 1306-12, 3126-7; N. Jorga, *Geschichte des osmanischen Reiches*, Gotha 1910, iii, 236-45; Sheref, *Özdemir-oghlî ᶜOthmān Pasha*, in *TOEM*, iv (1329/1911), 1289-1303, 1353-69, 1417-43, 1482-1516, v (1330/1912), 1-12; İ.H. Danişmend, *Osmanlı tarihi kronolojisi*, Istanbul 1963, ii, 374, 376-80, iii, 17-99 *passim;* İ.H. Uzunçarşılı, *Osmanlı tarihi*, 2nd ed., Ankara 1977, iii/2, 2 ff., 342 ff.; B. Kütükoğlu, *Osmanlı-Iran siyasi münasebetleri 1578-90*, Istanbul 1962; M. Sālim, *al-Fatḥ al-ᶜUthmānī al-awwal li 'l-Yaman*, Cairo 1969, 243-54; C.M. Kortepeter, *Ottoman imperialism during the reformation*, New York 1972, 53-75, 85-91; C. Orhonlu, *Habeş eyaleti*, Istanbul 1974, 48-52; C. Fleischer, *Bureaucrat and intellectual in the Ottoman empire*, Princeton 1986. (J.R. Blackburn)

ᶜOTHMĀN PASHA, YEGEN, leader of *lewends* [*q.v.*], bandit, vizier, and *serᶜasker* of the Ottoman army in Hungary. In 1096/1685 he was *bölük-bashî* [*q.v.*] of the *lewends* of *serdār* Sheyṭān/Melek Ibrāhīm Pasha in Hungary. After fleeing from the theatre of war, he sacked villages and towns between Sivas and Bolu (in Anatolia). Afterwards, he became the chief *bölük-bashî* of Khalīl Pasha, who was responsible for the pursuit of the bandits (*teftīshdji*). When the latter was dismissed (Djumādā II 1089/April 1689), ᶜOthmān Pasha obtained the *sandjak* of Ḳaraḥiṣār-i Ṣāḥib [see afyūn ḳara ḥiṣār] with two horsetails (*tugh*) and was ordered to go on campaign with five hundred *segbāns* [*q.v.*] (Silāḥdār, *Taʾrīkh*, ii, Istanbul 1928, 266; M. Cezar, *Osmanlı tarihinde levendler*, Istanbul 1965, Fotokopi no. 6). In the capital he also enforced his nomination as *serčeshme*, i.e. leader of all *lewends*, and, being considered powerful, he was honoured several times by the sultan. After the Ottoman army had been defeated near Mohács [*q.v.*] on 3 Shawwāl 1098/12 August 1687 and the Grand Vizier Ṣarî Süleymān Pasha had fled, ᶜOthmān Pasha took part in the meeting of the army commanders in which Siyāwush Pasha was made *serdār* and an account drawn up for the sultan. He did not, however, join the rebellious army in its advance against the capital, but stayed back at Edirne. He then proceeded to Istanbul, but pitched his tents before the city and carefully remained distant. After Meḥemmed IV had been deposed and Süleymān II had ascended the throne (2 Muḥarram 1099/8 November 1687), Siyāwush Pasha appointed him *beglerbegi* of Rumelia, but before ᶜOthmān Pasha could march off, the Grand Vizier was killed by the rebels. His successor Ismāᶜīl Pasha did not want to take command of the campaign personally, and had ᶜOthmān Pasha appointed vizier, *beglerbegi* of Aleppo and *serdār*. The new vizier reinforced his *lewend* troops, extorted money on their behalf and had relatives and followers appointed as *sandjaḳbeg*s and *beglerbegi*s. When it became known that he had his eyes on the grand vizierate, he was removed from the supreme command, officially because he was going to be appointed *beglerbegi* of Bosnia. In fact, however, a legal prosecution was introduced against him (*firmān* at the end of April 1688, in A. Mumcu, *Osmanlı devletinde siyaseten katl*, Ankara 1963, 215 ff.), and the units of the *ṣarîdja*s and *segbāns*, the bases of his power, were disbanded. But the new Grand Vizier Bekrī Muṣṭafā Pasha confirmed him in his function because the Imperial troops were about to attack Belgrade and a new army command could not be organised in due time. At the advance of the enemy, ᶜOthmān Pasha abandoned the camp before Belgrade and retreated to Niš, his *lewends* having looted the *bezistān* [see ḳayṣariyya] and the *khāns* [*q.v.*] (Silāḥdār, *Taʾrīkh*, ii, 373). Although now entrusted with the defence of the frontier, ᶜOthmān Pasha, while looting villages, retreated further to Sofia, allegedly to spend the winter there. At consultative meetings held in the capital during the winter of 1688-9, it was again decided to disband the *ṣarîdjas* and the *segbāns*, and to put an end to the function of *serčeshme*. It was also decided to raise a general troop levy (*nefīr-i ᶜamm*) against ᶜOthmān Pasha (Silāḥdār, *Taʾrīkh*, ii, 409-11; the *firmāns* of *ewāʾil Rebīᶜ ül-ewwel* 1100/end of December 1688 are in the Başbakanlık Arşivi, *Mühimme defterleri* 98, 132-5). With a dwindling number of followers, ᶜOthmān Pasha fled westwards, but at İpek (Peć [*q.v.*]) they were outmanoeuvred and killed by Maḥmūd Beg-zāde Maḥmūd (Djumādā II 1100/March-April 1689, Silāḥdār, *Taʾrīkh*, ii, 423-4; Defterdār, *Zübde-yi weḳāyiᶜāt*, ii, 170-1). Such a rise of Anatolian-Turkish *lewends* to leading positions in the Ottoman empire was symptomatic of the times, but remained only an episode.

Bibliography: Rāshid, *Taʾrīkh*, i-ii, Istanbul 1282/1865; Silāḥdār, *Taʾrīkh*, ii, Istanbul 1928; Defterdār Ṣarî Meḥmed Pasha, *Zübde-yi weḳāyiᶜāt*, ed. Abdülkadir Özcan, Defterdar Sarı Mehmed Paşa, *Zübde-i vekayiat*, ii, Istanbul 1977. *Sidjill-i ᶜOthmānī*, ii, 421; Cengiz Orhonlu, *Osmanlı imparatorluğunda aşiretleri iskân teşebbüsü (1691-1696)*, Istanbul 1963, 8-9; Mustafa Cezar, *Osmanlı tarihinde levendler*, Istanbul 1965, 221-6, 229, 232, 292-3, 300, 481; Mustafa Akdağ, *Genel cizgileriyle XVII. yüzyıl Türkiye tarihi*, in *Tarih Araştırmaları Dergisi*, iv/6-7 (1966) 236, 238-40; H.G. Majer, *Ein Brief des Serdar Yeğen Osman Pascha an den Kurfürsten Max Emanuel von Bayern vom Jahre 1688 und seine Übersetzungen*, in *Islamkundliche Anhandlungen aus dem Institut für Geschichte und Kultur des Nahen Orients an der Universität München, Hans Joachim Kißling gewidmet von seinen Schülern*, Munich 1974, 130-45; Halil İnalcık, *Military and fiscal transformation in the Ottoman Empire 1600-1700*, in *Archivum Ottomanicum*, vi (1980), 299-302. (H.G. Majer)

ᶜOTHMĀN PAZAR (in modern Turkish orthography, Osman Pazar; in Bulgaria since 1934, Omurtag), the name of a minor town (population in 1981, 10,339) in central Bulgaria, situated at an altitude of 540 m/1,771 feet above sea level on an infertile wooded plateau to the north of the Balkan Mountains. In late Ottoman times (till 1878) the town was the centre of a *ḳaḍāʾ* of the same name, which besides ᶜOthmān Pazar contained three small towns: Ḳazghan/Kotel, Virbiče/Vărbitsa and Čitaḳ (after 1934: Tiča), and 82 villages with a total population of

44,220 Muslims and 9,660 Christians, the latter concentrated in the above four townlets and in two mixed villages (Konak and Kabdağ-i Zir/ Dolnja Kabda). The 19th century *ḳaḍāʾ* of O<u>th</u>mān Pazar, an area of some 50 km in length and 25 km wide, was composed of two historical landscapes with different geographic features, a different settlement history and a different administrative history. The south-eastern half of the *ḳaḍāʾ* is a hilly basin 300 m above sea level, which is surrounded on all sides by mountains. At least since the early 14th century, it was known by the Old Bulgarian name of Gerlovo, which became the Ottoman "Gerīlova" or "Gerīlābād" (first mentioned so in the *Tahrīr* fragment OAK 45/29 (Sofia), from 1479). The north-western half of the *ḳaḍāʾ*, in popular parlance known as Tozluk/Tuzluk (officially, Slannik), constituted since at least the late 15th century the *nāḥiye* of Ala Kilise/Kenisa. This name is apparently first mentioned in the *Tahrīr* no. 77 of 925, 1519 (BBA), which notes that a group of Yürüks of the Rhodopes (Tanrı Dağ) in southern Bulgaria had "forty years ago migrated to a place called Ala<u>dj</u>a Kilise in Gerilova, in the direction of Dobru<u>dj</u>a." Ala, or Ala<u>dj</u>a, Kilise refers to the ruins of a conspicuous church, built of alternating courses of white stone (from the nearby Preslav Balkan) and red bricks in the style of the Bulgaro-Byzantine Middle Ages. Tozluk, or the district of Ala Kilise is an infertile plateau of about 600 m above sea level, largely covered with woods or shrubs. The population of this district, living in more than 50 small villages and hamlets (*maḥalles*), was in the past exclusively Turkish-speaking Muslim, disregarding the two mixed villages of Konak and Kabdağ on the northern edge of the area.

Very little is known about the pre-Ottoman Gerlovo. Its centre appears to have been Gerilgrad, the forerunner of Văbitsa, which is situated on the banks of the Gerila brook, a tributary of the Golema Kamčija. The ruins of a Byzantine castle are still to be seen on the hill of Grădište, where hundreds of Byzantine coins from the 12th century have been found. In the 15th and 16th centuries, Vărbitsa was by far the largest settlement of Gerlovo and almost wholly Christian. In Gerlovo are at least twenty deserted sites called Kiliselik, pointing to disappeared pre-Ottoman settlements. Bulgarian historiography has suggested that these sites were destroyed during the Ottoman conquest. Yet the only site which has been excavated in a proper manner, that near the village of Kara Demir (after 1934, Vinica), showed that this settlement, around a church, existed from the 9th till the 12th centuries. It seems that the great European economic and demographic crisis of the 14th century caused Gerlovo to become deserted, the inhabitants moving to the much more fertile lowlands, where after the depopulations there was enough room to settle. Vărbitsa, Čitaḳ (pointing to a pre-Ottoman Christian Turkic population) and Kotel remaining the corner stones of the Christian settlements in the area. Yürük settlers from Asia Minor arrived in Gerlovo as early as the second half of the 15th century. The oldest preserved *Tahrir* of the area, the incompletely preserved *Icmal* of 1479 (*Turski Izvori*, ii, 1966) mentions six *mezraʿas* in "Gerilova" which were worked by Yürüks (*Yürükler ekerler*): Ak Dere Yakası, Bolu'lu Süleyman, Dobroka (later known as Sağırcık), Gagrašentsi, Hisar Bey and Veysel. Together they paid 2900 *aḳčes*, which might indicate a population of 40-50 Yürük families. Ak Dere, Dobroka/Sağırcık and Veysel later developed into villages which still exist today (as Bjala Reka, Rătlina and Orlovo). According to the *Tahrir* of 1516, contained in the *Tapu Defter* 370 (BBA), pp. 549-55, which was compiled around 1530, the Christian population of Gerlovo still dominated. The Muslims lived in more than 20 very small villages, mostly bearing the name of their founders or the occupations of the first settlers. In the 16th century they witnessed a rapid expansion, partly through high birthrates but largely through the arrival of new settlers. The place names suggest a largely heterodox adherence (Aşıklar, Abdallar, Şah Veli, etc.). In 1936 Vasil Marinov found that the villages of Alvanlar, Küçükler, Topuzlar and Veledler were almost exclusively inhabited by Ḳīzīlba<u>sh</u>. Most likely the bulk of the Gerlovo Turks arrived after the suppression of the Ḳīzīlba<u>sh</u> in the reign of Selīm I and after the Ḳalendero<u>gh</u>lu rebellion, causing great unrest in Anatolia. The settlement of these Turkish nomads must have caused unrest in the area. To keep the Christian population in its place, the Ottoman government gave the three above-mentioned Christian settlements *derbend* status, so that they could defend themselves, and in the course of the 16th century formed Kabdağ and Konak as other gathering points for Christians, who moved from some small settlements, which became deserted afterwards (Dočina, Gerlova, Polane and Selište, in 1516 together 30 households), whereas "Dobrofča" became "Dobru<u>dj</u>a" and Islamised completely after the end of the 16th century. So the ethno-religious composition remained thus till the 19th century, the only fluctuation being the number of households, which for both groups went up in the 16th century, down in the 17th and early 18th and steeply up again since the second half of the 18th century. Throughout that time, Ḳaz<u>gh</u>an/Kotel was the largest settlement of the area, with an almost entirely Christian Bulgarian population. Čitaḳ was partly Islamised; Vărbitsa came to house an important group of Crimean Tatars, who around 1780 followed the deposed Ḳal<u>gh</u>ay Mesʿūd Giray. Their descendants still live in Vărbitsa, Meedalı Giray serving a number of decades as deputy in the Bulgarian Parliament (beginning of the 20th century). Their monumental late 18th century *saray* was destroyed by Bulgarian nationalists during the aftermath of the assimilation campaign of 1985. Vărbitsa is apparently the only place of the *ḳaḍāʾ* of ʿOthmān Pazar which is mentioned in the early Ottoman chroniclers, where Ne<u>sh</u>rī in the Codex Manisa has it as "Virpič" (in other manuscripts and in the printed edition, very much mutilated and misidentified).

Of the district of Ala Kilise in pre-Ottoman times even less is known. It is much less fertile than Gerlovo and considerably cooler, little suited to agriculture. Disregarding the later Turkified village of Dobrofča/Dobru<u>dj</u>a (1516, 25 Christian households; 1580, 43 of them), it must have been almost uninhabited when the first Turkish settlers arrived. Only extensive archaeological research might modify this picture. The village of Ala Kilise, 10 km to the west of ʿO<u>th</u>mān Pazar, was also known as Ḥasan Faḳīh. It is first mentioned in the 1752 *Mufassal Avariz Tahrīr*, but might have existed before. The Ottoman registers (1516, 1525, 1550, 1580, 1642 and 1752) give a picture of a unstable settlement pattern, with many very small tribal villages, continuously splitting into new *maḥalles*, often changing names and with many settlements being given up after a certain time. According to the ethnographic and linguistic research of Gadžanov at the beginning of the 20th century, the original settlers must have come from the region of Kastamonu in northern Anatolia. The Anatolian origin of the Muslim population of the district of ᶜOth̲mān Pazar is also not denied by modern Bulgarian historiography (cf. art. "Omurtag", in *Encikl. na Bălg.*, 1984), but usually the colonisation is thought to have taken place in the 17th and 18th centuries, whereas in reality the bulk of the settlers arrived shortly after 1500. Especially for the case of Gerlovo, the majority of the Muslims are held to be Turkified, former Bulgarian Christians (especially held by V. Marinov), whereby the case of a few isolated villages (Huyvan/Ivanovo, Trnovitsa, Jamna and Čerkovna, all situated inside Gerlovo but outside the *ḳaḍāʾ* borders of the past) are taken to have been the general pattern.

In the 15th and 16th centuries, both the districts of Gerlovo and Ala Kilise were *nāḥiye*s of the *ḳaḍāʾ* of Sh̲umnu/Šumen. In the 1530s the northern part of this large *ḳaḍāʾ* was cut off and added to the newly-formed *ḳaḍāʾ*s of D̲jumᶜa-yi ᶜAtīḳ/Eski D̲jumᶜa (now Tărgovište) and Hezārgrad/Razgrad. In the 1630s the *nāḥiye* of Ala Kilise was upgraded to the status of *ḳaḍāʾ*, and ᶜOth̲mān Pazar, then just founded, was made its seat.

The town of ᶜOth̲mān Pazar itself came into being in the first half of the 17th century as a centrally-located market place for the entire village network. At the locality of Irincik near the town are the ruins of a Late Antique castle, which in the early 9th century was restored by the Turco-Bulgarian Khan Omurtag; the modern name of the town refers to that fact. According to local legends, written down by Felix Kanitz *ca.* 1870, the town was founded by the Turkish cartwright ᶜOth̲mān, who "about 300 years ago" built an inn on the lonely plateau, which became the nucleus of the new settlement. The *Avariz Defter* MM 7086 from 1052/1642 (BBA) is apparently the first source which explicitly states that Ala Kilise was an independent *ḳaḍāʾ* and that ᶜOth̲mān Pazar, then counting 22 Muslim households, was its centre. This place was to develop relatively rapidly. The *Mufassal Cizye Defter* of the *ḳaḍāʾ* of Ala Kilise from 1102/1690-1 (MM 3801, BBA) mentions that no less than seventy adult male Christians were found in the *ḳaṣaba* of ᶜOth̲mān Pazar doing their jobs but were not permanent residents from there. The *Mufassal Avariz Defter* of 1165/1752 (BBA) calls the district: "*Ḳaḍāʾ* of Ala Kilise, also known as [*ḳaḍāʾ* of] ᶜOth̲mān Pazar." The village to which the district owes its name "Ala Kilise, also known as Ḥasan Faḳīh", than contained 25 Muslim households, all mentioned person by person. According to the same source, a complete new *Tahrir* of a number of *ḳaḍāʾ*s in north-eastern Bulgaria, the town had 103 households, of which two were of convert origin. There were only two permanently settled Christian households. It is remarked that, "according to the old register", the town had but one *maḥalle.* Now there were two, the Maḥalle of the Mosque of Meḥmed Pas̲h̲a and Orta Maḥalle. After this date, the town saw a rapid development into the leading centre of crafts, especially textiles (abas, goat-hair blankets) and metalwork.

In the mid-19th century, the old *ḳaḍāʾ* of ᶜOth̲mān Pazar was considerably enlarged. It came to include the entire basin of Gerlovo (formerly only the western parts), which until that time had been a part of the *ḳaḍāʾ* of Sh̲umnu/Šumen, and the important Christian villages of Konak and Kapdağ-i Zir, which were detatched from Hezārgrad. On the other hand, the whole chain of old Bulgarian villages to the south of the Pre-Slav Balkan, which for long had belonged to Gerlovo (Smolvçe/Čāʾūs̲h̲köy, Jamla, Tirnovitsa, Čerkovna and Vardun) were now attached to the *ḳaḍāʾ* of Eski D̲jumᶜa. According to the *Sālnāme* of the Tuna *wilāyet* of 1290/1873-4, which contains the results of a census of six years earlier, the district had 86 settlements, of which only two had non-Turkish place names. The town of ᶜOth̲mān Pazar then contained *ca.* 5,000 inhabitants, of which one-fifth was Christian (Aubaret, Kanitz). According to the *Sālnāme* of 1291/1874-5, the town had 958 houses, eight mosques, 310 shops, one *ḥammām* and one church.

During the Russo-Turkish War of 1877-8, which led to the independence of Bulgaria, the town was burned down and suffered an eclipse because of the flight of an important section of its Turkish population. According to the Bulgarian census of 1887, ᶜOth̲mān Pazar counted 3,755 inhabitants, of which 1,371 were Bulgarians and 2,382 Muslims, besides a few Gypsies, all Turkish-speaking. The town stagnated till after World War II, in 1934 its population being almost the same as in 1887, the religious-ethnic composition also remaining as it was. The same can be said for the villages of the former *ḳaḍāʾ* of ᶜOth̲mān Pazar. In Gerlovo, groups of old Turkish inhabitants emigrated to Turkey, and their place was taken by Bulgarians from elsewhere (details by V. Marinov). The north-western part of the old *ḳaḍāʾ*, Tozluk/Tuzluk, remained overwhelmingly Turkish.

Throughout the late Ottoman period the three other urban centres of the *ḳaḍāʾ*, Čitaḳ, Kotel and Vărbitsa, enjoyed a lively trade and developed crafts, especially the fabrication of abas and carpet (*kilim*) weaving, tailoring and wood turning. Kotel and Čitak, in particular, were the native towns of a disproportionally large number of writers, politicians and university professors, who played an important role in the intellectual development of Bulgaria after 1878. All three suffered a collapse after the country became independent, the merchants and craftsmen moving to the lowland cities, from which the Turkish inhabitants had largely fled or emigrated after 1878. Between 1878 and 1926 the three mountain towns lost more than one-third of their population. Kotel and Vărbitsa recovered more or less in the decades after World War II, Čitak/Tiča sank back to a village, being in 1972 still much smaller than in 1873.

In 1934 the entire historical toponomy of the old *ḳaḍāʾ* of ᶜOth̲mān Pazar was Bulgarised by decree of the new nationalist government. Only Kotel, Konak, Kabdağ and Vărbitsa kept their names. During the forced Bulgarisation campaign of 1985, the Gerlovo villages offered stubborn resistance, focussing on the Ḳîzîlbas̲h̲ village of Alvanlar (since 1934, Jablanovo; population in 1972, 2,989).

In 1972 there were still three mosques in ᶜOth̲mān Pazar: the Muftī, or Yuḳarî D̲jāmiᶜ, with an inscription on the minaret referring to a repair in 1219/1804-5, the Fîndîḳ D̲jāmiᶜi (serving as workshop), with a number of 18th and 19th century gravestones in its cemetery, and the Tekke D̲jāmiᶜ on the southern edge of the town, once part of the Tekke of Meḥmed Baba.

Its cemetery contained some 19th century tombstones, the oldest from 1250/1834-5. The church of St. Dimitri, rebuilt in 1860 in a grandiose style and testifying to the wealth of the small Christian community of ᶜOth̲mān Pazar, is now a recognised historical monument. The Müftī D̲jāmiᶜi survived the upheavals of 1985 and still serves the Muslim community, which, since 1990 is reconstituting itself.

In 19th century ᶜOth̲mān Pazar, there lived and worked the Ottoman scholar Niyāzī S̲h̲eykh Ismāᶜīl Efendi, who was born in the Gerlovo village of Kara Ehadlar (since 1934, Vrani Kon) and died in ᶜOth̲mān Pazar in 1312/1894-5.

Bibliography: G. Aubaret, *Province du Danube*, in

Bulletin de la Société de Géographie, VIᵉ Série, T. xii (Paris 1876), 167; F. Kanitz, *Donau-Bulgarien und der Balkan*, Leipzig 1875-9, ²1882, iii, 44-6; D.G. Gadžanov, *Vorläufiger Bericht, Reise im Auftrage der Balkan-Kommission zur türkischen Dialekt-Studien in Nord-Ost Bulgarien*, in *Anzeiger der Kais. Akad. der Wissensch.*, Phil. Hist. Klasse, xlvi (Vienna 1909, Jahrg. 1911), 28-42; idem, *Zweiter Vorläufiger Bericht*, in 1912, no. 3, 13-20; D.G. Gadžanov, *Gerlovo, kratki etnografični beležki*, in *Sbornik v čest na L. Miletič*, Sofia 1912, 104-14; L. Stefanov, *Grad Omurtag, prinos kăm istorijata na grada*, Omurtag 1935; V. Marinov, *Gerlovo, oblastno geografsko izučavane*, Sofia 1936; Ž. Čankov, *Geografski rečnik na Bălgarija*, Sofia 1939; M. Tayyib Gökbilgin, *Rumeli'de Yürükler, Tatarlar ve Evlâd-i Fâtihân*, Istanbul 1957; P. Mijatev, *Epigrafski proučavanija ina pametnitsi s arapsko pismo v Bălgarija*, in *Arheologija*, iv (1962), no. 1; N. Todorov–B. Nedkov, *Turski izvori za Bălgarskata istorija*, ii, Sofia 1966, 222-5, 234-5; Vera Antonova, *Srednovekovno selište v čašata na jazovir Vinitsa, Šumensko*, in *Izvestija na Narodenija Muzej Šumen*, iv (Varna 1967), 3 ff., 35 ff.; A. Kuzev, *Zwei Notizen über einige mittelalterliche Festungen in Nordostbulgarien*, in *Studia Balcanica. Recherches de géographie historique*, Sofia 1970, 129-39; V.A. Marinov, *Gerlovo, kraevedski očerk i maršruti*, Sofia 1970; H.J. Kornrumpf, *Zwei weniger bekannte islamische Denkmäler in Bulgarien*, in *Südost-Forschungen*, xxx (1971), 291-6; I. Nikolov, *Grad Omurtag*, Sofia 1973; M. Penkov, *Sledi ot izčesnali selišta v Gerlovo*, in *Vekove*, v (1973), 69-73; Kornrumpf, *Die Territorialverwaltung im östlichen Teil der europäischen Türkei, 1864-1878*, Freiburg 1976; Iv. Jakimov, *Nazvanie i samonazvanie na Kazălbašite v Gerlovo*, in *Godišnik Muzeite v Sev. Bălgarija*, no. 9 (1983), 155-61; M. Kiel, *Anatolia transplanted? Patterns of demographic, religious and ethnic changes in the district of Tozluk (N.E. Bulgaria) 1479-1873*, in *Anatolica*, xviii (Leiden 1991), 1-29; Ivanička Georgieva (ed.), *Bălgarskite aliani, sbornik etnografski materiali*, Sofia 1991; K. Popkonstantinov and A. Konakliev, *Za dva epigrafski pametnika ot Gerlovo*, in G. Dančev and V. Tăpkova-Zaimova, *Turskite zavoevanija i sădbata na Balkanskite narodi XIV-XVIII vek*, Veliko Tărnovo 1992, 134-41; Kiel, *Mevlana Neşrī and the towns of medieval Bulgaria*, in the forthcoming *Festschrift V.L. Ménage*, Istanbul 1993. For the correct date of the important register O.A.K. 45/29 in Sofia (1479 instead of "vers le milieu du XVe s."), see S. Dimitrov, *Za datirovkata na njakoj osmanski registri ot XV v.*, in *Izvestija na Bălgarskoto Istoričesko Družestvo*, Kn xxvi (1968), 244. The Ottoman sources used here, preserved in the Turkish archives, are not published. (M. Kiel)

ᶜOTHMĀN-ZĀDE Aḥmed Tāʾib, a notable Ottoman poet, scholar and historian of the end of the 17th and first third of the 18th century. The son of the *rūz-nāmedji* (*māliyye tezkeredji*) of the pious foundations, ᶜOthmān Efendi, he took up a theological career. The year of his birth is not recorded. From 1099/1687 he held the post of *müderris* in various *medreses* in Istanbul. At intervals he also worked in other places. For example, in 1107/1695 he went to Damascus with Kemānkesh Meḥmed Pasha when the latter was appointed governor there. In 1124/1712 he was appointed *müderris* at the Süleymāniyye, a post he had aimed at from the very beginning. He then went as chief judge (*Ḥaleb mollāsī*) to Aleppo in 1126/1716, and lastly as *Miṣr mollāsī* (chief justice of Cairo) to Cairo, where he died at the end of his year of office on 2 Ramaḍān 1136/25 May 1724. According to Bursalī Meḥmed Ṭāhir, there is in existence a biography of ᶜOthmān-zāde composed by Ibn al-Emīn Maḥmūd Kemāl Bey.

ᶜOthmān-zāde was regarded by his contemporaries as the most important poet of his period. He was particularly celebrated for his chronograms (*taʾrīkh*) and *ḳiṭᶜa*. A chronogram on the birth of prince Ibrāhīm (1133/1720-1) made such an impression on Sultan Aḥmed III (1115-43/1703-30) that he gave ᶜOthmān-zāde first, the title "chief poet" (*reʾīs-i shāᶜirān*, and then that of "king of poets" (*malik [sulṭān] al-shuᶜarāʾ*) and granted him a special *khaṭṭ*. ᶜOthmān-zāde left behind him a *dīwān* of the usual type (*müretteb dīwān*) which consists of 12 *ḳaṣīdas*, 32 chronograms and 77 *ghazels*. Along with these are isolated poems, e.g. a satire (*hadjw*) on Thāḳib Efendi composed in 1124/1712. He also wrote in verse a commentary on the 40 *ḥadīths* entitled *Sharḥ-i Ḥadīth-i arbaᶜīn*, which is also known as *Ṣiḥḥat-ābād*; it was written in 1128/1715.

It is, however, to his prose works that he owes his fame with posterity, especially his historical works, some of which are still popular and valuable at the present day. The most important is his biographical collection *Ḥadīḳat al-wüzerāʾ*, a most estimable and still important collection of lives of the first 92 grand viziers of the Ottoman empire, from ᶜAlāʾ al-Dīn ᶜAlī Pasha to Rāmī Meḥmed Pasha, who was dismissed in 1115/1703. The work was composed six years before his death. It was printed at Istanbul in 1271/1854. ᶜOthmān-zāde's idea was later taken up by others. His biographical collection was continued by: Dilāwer Agha-zāde ᶜÖmer Efendi (ᶜÖmer Waḥīd), a friend of Rāghib Pasha's who wrote a *Dheyl-i Ḥadīḳat al-wüzerāʾ*, also called *Idjmāl-i menāḳib-i wüzerāʾ-i ᶜiẓām* or *Gül-i zībā*, which covers the period from the grand vizier Ḳowanos Aḥmed Pasha to Saᶜīd Meḥmed Pasha; also by Aḥmed Djāwīd Bey, who compiled a continuation entitled *Wird al-muṭarrā* which covers the period 1172-1217/1758-1802, from Rāghib Pasha to Yūsuf Ḍiyā Pasha, the conqueror of Egypt; finally, by ᶜAbd al-Fettāḥ Shefḳat-i Baghdādī, entitled *Berk-i sebz*, covering the period 1217-71/1802-54 from Ḍiyā al-Dīn Yūsuf Pasha to ᶜĀlemdār Muṣṭafā Pasha.

All three continuations are printed as an appendix to the *Ḥadīḳat* of ᶜOthmān-zāde, while the later continuation by Rifᶜat Efendi, *Wird al-ḥaḳāʾiḳ*, appeared in a lithograph separately and the continuation by Meḥmed Saᶜīd Shehrī-zāde entitled *Dheyl-i Ḥadīḳat al-wüzerāʾ* or *Gül-i zībā* or *Gülshen-i mulūk*, which deals with 31 grand viziers from Nishāndjī Aḥmed or Siliḥdār Meḥmed Pasha to Saᶜīd Meḥmed Pasha, is still only available in mss.

The two sketches of Turkish history by ᶜOthmān-zāde also attained great popularity. The longer one, *Idjmāl-i menāḳib* (or *tewārīkh*)*-i Salāṭīn-i Āl-i ᶜOthmān*, deals with the first 24 Ottoman sulṭāns, from the founder of the dynasty to Aḥmed III. The shorter version, *Fihrist-i Shāhān* or *Fihrist-i Shāhān-i Āl-i ᶜOthmān* or *Mukhtaṣar-i Taʾrīkh-i Selāṭīn* or *Tuḥfet al-mülūk* or *Ḥadīḳat al-mülūk* covers the period from ᶜOthmān to Muṣṭafā II. The number of varying titles shows the popularity of the work. The book, sometimes quoted as *Faḍāʾil-i Āl-i ᶜOthmān*, dedicated to Dāmād Ibrāhīm Pasha [see al-dāmād], seems to be only a variant title of one of these books.

In the year of his death (1136/1724), ᶜOthmān-zāde wrote a history of Fāḍil Aḥmed Pasha entitled *Taʾrīkh-i Fāḍīl Aḥmed Pasha*, which like most of his works is only accessible in mss. The *Munāẓare-yi dewletayn* ("struggle between the two kingdoms") in the form of questions and answers is also dedicated to Ibrāhīm Pasha (ms. in Vienna) and is an interesting contribuion to the very highly developed *munāẓara* literature. As further independent works may be mentioned *Idjāz naṣāʾiḥ al-ḥukemāʾ* and *Tuḥfet al-nuʿmān*. Here we may mention his anthology *Djāmiʿ al-leṭāʾif* (a collection of anecdotes, jests etc.). His stylistic collection *Münsheʾāt-i Tāʾib Efendi* was intended for practical purposes; it is a collection of letters in three *faṣls* and a concluding chapter.

His extracts from and editions and translations of other works are very numerous. The greater part of his work is collected in his *Külliyyāt* with an introduction by Aḥmed Ḥanīf-zāde. Some titles, cited by von Hammer and Bursalï Meḥmed Ṭāhir, which apparently go back to Ḥanīf-zāde, the continuator of the *Kashf al-ẓunūn* of Ḥādjdjī Khalīfa, are probably not correct and refer to double or subsidiary titles.—Translations by him are: *Meshāriḳ al-anwār* and *Meshāriḳ sherīf*, the latter entitled: *Ṭawāliʿ al-maṭāliʿ* on *ḥadīth*.—Extracts from or versions of other works are: *Akhlāḳ-i Muḥsinī* (or *Mukhtaṣar-i Akhlāḳ-i Muḥsinī* or *Khulāṣat al-Akhlāḳ*) from the *Ethics* of Ḥusayn b. ʿAlī Kāshifī, who is known as Wāʿiẓ al-Harawī (d. 910/1504 [*q.v.*]). The original work, which was written in Persian for Mīrzā Muḥsin b. Ḥusayn Bayḳara, was translated by Pīr Meḥmed known as Gharamī, with the title *Anīs al-ʿārifīn* in 974/1566; *Akhlāḳ-i ʿAlāʾī*, an extract from the work of ʿAlī b. Amr Allāh, known as Ibn Ḥinnāʾī (Ḳïnalï-zāde [*q.v.*]) which was written for the Amīr al-Umarāʾ of Syria, ʿAlī Pasha, and therefore called after him; the *Menāḳib-i Imām-i aʿẓam*, i.e. of Abū Ḥanīfa. We also have from his pen a synopsis of the *Hümāyūn-nāme*. The *Anwār-i Suhaylī*, the Persian version of Ibn al-Muḳaffaʿ's Arabic version from the original Indian (Pahlawī) of Bidpāī, was the work of Ḥusayn Wāʿiẓ Kāshifī, court-preacher to Ḥusayn Bayḳara of Harāt. This *Anwār-i Suhaylī* was translated into Ottoman Turkish by ʿAbd al-Wāsiʿ ʿAlīsī Mollā ʿAlī Čelebi b. Ṣāliḥ, known as ʿAlī Wāsiʿ or Ṣāliḥ-zāde al-Rūmī, with the title *Humāyūn-nāme* and dedicated to Sultan Süleymān. ʿOthmān-zāde abbreviated the *Hümāyūn-nāme* to about a third of its length. This version was printed in Istanbul in 1256/1840 under the title *Thimār al-asmār*. In the *Külliyyāt* this extract is entitled *Zübdet al-naṣāʾiḥ*.

The version of the *Naṣāʾiḥ* (*Naṣīḥat*) *al-mulūk* of Reʾīs Efendi Sarï ʿAbd Allāh entitled *Talkhīṣ al-ḥikam* is also described as a synopsis of the *Humāyūn-nāme*. A synopsis of the *Medjālis al-akhbār* of ʿĀlī is also attributed to ʿOthmān-zāde.

Bibliography: Sālim, *Tedhkere*, Istanbul 1314, 178-81; Faṭīn, *Tedhkere*, Istanbul 1271, 32; Ḥādjdjī Khalīfa, *Kashf al-ẓunūn*, ed. Flügel, esp., however, Aḥmed Ḥanīf-zāde, *Nova opera* (*Athār-i new*), *ibid.* in vol. vi; idem, *Kashf al-ẓunūn*, Istanbul 1321, i, 428; Thüreyyā, *Sidjill-i ʿothmānī*, i, 242; Muʿallim Nādjī, *Esāmī*, Istanbul 1308, 92; Sāmī, *Ḳāmūs al-aʿlām*, iii, 1261; Bursalï Meḥmed Ṭāhir, *ʿOthmānlï müʾellifleri*, ii, 116-17; Hammer, *GOR*, ix, 238; idem, *GOD*, iv, 120-31; Babinger, *GOW*, 254 ff. et *passim*; the ms. catalogues by Flügel (Vienna), Pertsch (Berlin), Aumer (Munich), Rieu (Brit. Museum) and Uppsala, no. 292; *İA*, art. *Osman-zâde Tâib* (A. Karahan); W. Björkman, in *PTF*, ii, 448.

(Th. Menzel)

ʿOTHMĀNDJÏḲ, modern Turkish Osmancık, the administrative centre of an *ilçe* or district of the same name in the *il* or province of Çorum [see čorum] in northern Anatolia, in the southern part of classical Paphlagonia. It lies on the Halys or Ḳïzïl Irmaḳ [*q.v.*] at an important crossing-point of that river by the Tosya-Merzifun road (lat. 40°58′ N., long. 34°50′ E., altitude 430 m/1,310 ft.).

The town is situated in a picturesque position at the foot of a volcanic hill which rises straight out of the plain and is crowned by a castle which formerly commanded the celebrated bridge said to have been built by Bāyezīd I. The settlement is probably very old, as is evident from the numerous rock chambers cut out of the cliffs; it is probably on the site of classical Pimolisa (see *PW*, xx/2, cols. 1386-7 [W. Ruge]). The importance for us of the place, however, lies entirely in the part it has played in Islamic history. The name ʿOthmāndjïḳ is connected with that of ʿOthmān I [*q.v.*], the founder of the Ottoman dynasty, and it is said that ʿOthmān I took his name from this place which had been granted him as a fief. This suggestion, which is found as early as the 15th century (probably for the first time in the *Geschicht von der Turckey* of Meister Jörg v. Nürnberg, Memmingen n.d. but about 1496, and again in Spandugino, van Busbeek, etc.), has little claim to credibility although it has been revived in modern times, e.g. by Cl. Huart, in *JA*, ser. 11, vol. ix (1917), 345 ff., and by J.H. Kramers, in *AO*, vi (1927), 242 ff.; cf. thereon, W.L. Langer and R.P. Blake, in *American Historical Review*, xxxvii (1932), 496, note with other references. It is probable that ʿOthmān is the arabicised form of a Turkish name which may have sounded something like Atman, Azman, and we must not forget Ibn Baṭṭūṭa's assertion that the founder of the dynasty called himself ʿOthmāndjïḳ, i.e. "Little ʿOthmān" to distinguish himself from the third caliph. The Turkish sources are contradictory: Ḥādjdjī Khalīfa says that the town of ʿOthmāndjïḳ took its name from the fact that in the 10th(!) century a leader named ʿOthmān conquered it. Ewliyā Čelebi (1647-8) says (ii, 180 ff.) that many see in ʿOthmāndjïḳ the birth-place of the *amīr* ʿOthmān. This opinion had become the current one about the middle of the 17th century, as may be seen from a passage in *Les voyages et observations* of François le Gouz (Paris 1653, 65). The place does not appear in the clearer light of history till 794/1392 when it was taken by Bāyezīd I from the lord of Kastamuni, Bāyezīd Kötürüm, and definitely incorporated in the Ottoman empire. The fact is worth mentioning that there was evidently a considerable Bektashī settlement here at an early date, and the tomb of the famous Bektashī saint Ḳoyun Baba [*q.v.*] in ʿOthmāndjïḳ has always been much visited. The inhabitants, according to Ḥādjdjī Khalīfa, belonged almost entirely to the order of the Bektashīs. See on this point, in reference to events in 1546, *Le voyage de Monsieur d'Aramon*, ed. Ch. Schefer, Paris 1887, 66 (where Cochiny-Baba should be read Ḳoyun Baba). Makarius of Antioch mentions a place called ʿOthmāndjïḳ near Marʿash. He visited the site where there was said to have been formerly a large town of this name also called Osman Dada (= ʿOthmān Dede?) (*Travels*, ii, 453 ff.).

The plain around modern Osmancık is a fertile agricultural region for cereals, fruit and vegetables. In 1953 the town had a population of 5,559.

Bibliography: Ewliyā Čelebi, *Seyāḥat-nāme*, ii, 180 ff.; Ḥādjdjī Khalīfa, *Djihān-numā*, 625, middle; Maercker, in *ZGE*, xxxiv (Berlin 1899), 376; F. Taeschner, *Das anatolische Wegenetz*, i, 199-200, 205, 216; J.G.C. Anderson, *Studia Pontica*, i, Brussels 1903, 103 (with a picture of the bridge built by Bāyezīd II, not I); Von Flottwell, *Aus dem Stromgebiet des Qyzyl-Yrmaq*, in *Pet. Mitt.* (1895), Ergänzungsheft, no. 114, p. 11 (according to whom ʿOthmāndjïḳ is inhabited by the Ḳïzïlbash); F.W. Hasluck, *Christianity and Islam under the Sultans*, i, Oxford 1929, 95 ff. (on the saint Pambuk Baba); on the name, see also F. Giese, in *ZS*, ii (1923), 246 ff.

and A.D. Mordtmann, in *ZDMG*, xxx (1876), 467; Sāmī Bey, *Ḳāmūs al-aᶜlām*, Istanbul 1894, iv, 3127 ff.; Admiralty Handbooks, *Turkey*, London 1942-3, ii, 577-8; *İA* art. s.v. (Besim Darkot).

(F. Babinger*)

ᶜOTHMĀNIYYE [see ergani].

ᶜOTHMĀNLİ, the name of a Turkish dynasty, ultimately of Oghuz origin [see ghuzz], whose name appears in European sources as Ottomans (Eng.), Ottomanes (Fr.), Osmanen (Ger.), etc.

I. Political and dynastic history
II. Social and economic history
III. Literature
IV. Religious life
V. Architecture
VI. Carpets and textiles
VII. Ceramics, metalwork and minor arts
VIII. Painting
IX. Numismatics

I. Political and Dynastic History

1. General survey and chronology of the dynasty

The Ottoman empire was the territorially most extensive and most enduring Islamic state since the break-up of the ᶜAbbāsid caliphate and the greatest one to be founded by Turkish-speaking peoples. It arose in the Islamic world after the devastations over much of the eastern and central lands of the *Dār al-Islām* by the Mongols and survived the further onslaught at the opening of the 15th century of Tīmūr. Also, it originated on the periphery of the Islamic world, in Anatolia, into which Muslim Turks had been infiltrating by the time of the establishment of the Saldjūḳ sultanate of Rūm [see saldjūḳs] and was to play a dominant role in the processes of Turkicisation and Islamisation—even though this was not to be completed till the very end of the Ottoman dynasty, in 1922—of the formerly Greek and Armenian land of Anatolia [see anadolu]. A further consequence of the rise of the Ottomans was the overrunning of most of mainland Greece and many of the Aegean islands, Albania, the Slav lands of the Balkans and much of Hungary, by the 10th/16th century, and although this tide of conquest subsequently receded, Turkish occupation has left permanent traces in the Balkans in the forms of pockets of Muslim Turks and of the indigenous peoples who adopted Islam [see muslimūn. 1. The old-established Muslim communities of Eastern Europe] (and even of Turks who adopted Christianity [see dobrudja]).

Operating in Bithynia in northwestern Anatolia, the Ottomans gradually encircled the Byzantine empire, weakened as it latterly was from the Latin occupation of Constantinople in the 13th century, and eventually, in 1453, conquered Constaninople, the age-old goal of Muslim arms [see al-ḳusṭanṭīniyya. 1], at a time when ancient Balkan kingdoms such as Bulgaria and Serbia had already been overrun. Other states such as Wallachia and Bosnia were made tributary, and after 1526 [see mohácz], two-thirds of Hungary fell under Ottoman domination. In the east, the sultans took over the Arab provinces of Syria (1516) and Egypt (1517) from the Mamlūks [*q.v.*], and constituted themselves as the defenders of the orthodox Sunnī world against the Shīᶜī Ṣafawids [*q.v.*], even carrying the war for a short time into the Persian province of Ādharbāydjān. The sultans had at this time a far-reaching political and diplomatic policy, which included links with the Crimean Tatars to the north of the Black Sea [see ḳïrïm] and with the South Indian and Malaysian sultanates threatened by Portuguese and other colonial powers' expansion along the Indian Ocean shores; in the Muslim West, the sultans supported the corsair states of North Africa [see ḳurṣān. 1].

The achievements of Ottoman culture, an amalgam of native Turkish traditions with Persian and Arabic literary and artistic currents, were quantitatively great and often of the highest aesthetic standard (see sections V-VIII below). The alliance of the sultans with the Sunnī *ᶜulamā*ᵓ and with such Ṣūfī orders as the Mewlewīs [see mawlawiyya], later strengthened by the fact that they tacitly assumed for themselves the caliphate after the demise of the ᶜAbbāsid puppet caliphs of Cairo in 1517 [see khalīfa. (i)], led to the dominance of the Ḥanafī *madhhab* of Islamic law over the central Turkish lands and over much of the Arab lands also, an influence not quite extinguished today [see maḥkama, 1, 2, 4, and medjelle].

But after the high point in the 17th century of the occupation of Crete (1645-69) and the siege of Vienna (1683), a period of slow decline set in for the empire. In the early centuries, the Ottomans had been vigorous and expansionist and the scourge of Christian Europe. Now, however, the stimuli to intellectual enquiry from the Renaissance and Reformation and the dying-down of religious passions in Europe after 1648, enabled the West to forge ahead scientifically and technologically, with the application of new ideas to the art of war and to economic and commercial activities, so that the Ottoman empire fell more and more on to the defensive, its frontiers vulnerable to superior military and naval techniques and its craft industries and commerce vulnerable to industrial mass production and new financial mechanisms evolved in the West. In the 19th century, the new forces of ethnic and linguistic nationalism released by the French Revolution meant that the subject peoples of the Balkans, for centuries peoples without history, were no longer content to accept a clearly-defined but subordinate place in the Ottoman empire, especially as, by reaction, it began in the later 19th century to grow more specifically Turkish [see pan-turkism]. Hence the frontiers of the empire receded in the Balkans, until by 1913 only Eastern Thrace remained of the European territories. Nor were the Arab lands of the empire unaffected by the new ethnic and cultural nationalisms, and already by 1914 the increasingly shadowy Ottoman authority in the North African countries and Egypt had been thrown off. Turkey's decision in November 1914 to enter the First World War on the side of the Central Powers proved the crowning disaster for the empire, and in the wake of the new Turkish nationalism aroused by the post-War dismemberment of the Ottoman empire, there was no place by 1924 for the Ottoman ruling family and the old Islamic religion-based culture which it epitomised.

Chronology of the Ottoman sultans

	Ertoghrul, d. *ca.* 679/1280
680/1281	ᶜOthmān I Ghāzī
724/1324	Orkhan
761/1360	Murād I
791/1389	Bāyezīd I Yïldïrïm
(804/1402	Tīmūrid invasion)
805/1403	Meḥemmed I Čelebi (at first in Anatolia only, after 816/1413 in Rumeli also)
806/1403	Süleymān I (in Rumeli only until 814/1411)
814/1411	Mūsā Čelebi (counter-sultan in Rumeli until 816/1411)
824/1421	Murād II, first reign

824/1421 Muṣṭafā Čelebi, Düzme (counter-sultan in Rumeli until 825/1422)
848/1444 Meḥemmed II Fātiḥ ("the Conqueror"), first reign
850/1446 Murād II, second reign
855/1451 Meḥemmed II, second reign
886/1481 Bāyezīd II
918/1512 Selīm I Yavuz
926/1520 Süleymān II Ḳānūnī ("the Magnificent")
974/1566 Selīm II
982/1574 Murād III
1003/1595 Meḥemmed III
1012/1603 Aḥmed I
1026/1617 Muṣṭafā I, first reign
1027/1618 ᶜOthmān II
1031/1622 Muṣṭafā I, second reign
1032/1623 Murād II
1049/1640 Ibrāhīm
1058/1648 Meḥemmed IV
1099/1687 Süleymān III
1102/1691 Aḥmed II
1106/1695 Muṣṭafā II
1115/1703 Aḥmed III
1143/1730 Maḥmūd I
1168/1754 ᶜOthmān III
1171/1757 Muṣṭafā III
1187/1774 ᶜAbd ül-Ḥamīd I
1203/1789 Selīm III
1222/1807 Muṣṭafā IV
1223/1808 Maḥmūd II
1255/1839 ᶜAbd ül-Medjīd I
1277/1861 ᶜAbd ül-ᶜAzīz
1293/1876 Murād V
1293/1876 ᶜAbd ül-Ḥamīd II
1327/1909 Meḥemmed V Reshād
1336/1918 Meḥemmed VI Waḥīd ül-Dīn (last sultan)
1341-2/1922-4 ᶜAbd ül-Medjīd II (as caliph only)
(Republican régime of Muṣṭafā Kemāl)

See further, Zambaur, *Manuel de chronologie et de généalogie*, 160-74, with genealogical table O; A.D. Alderson, *The structure of the Ottoman dynasty*, Oxford 1956; Bosworth, *The Islamic dynasties*, 136-40.

(C.E. BOSWORTH)

2. The foundation and expansion of the Ottoman Empire

Recent research on the subject of the founding of the Ottoman state, especially epigraphic, numismatic and archival discoveries, have made clear many things that formerly had been seen mainly through the medium of Ottoman historical tradition as reflected in the sources belonging to the second half of the 9th/15th century and later, namely, the different versions of the chronicles of *Āl-i ᶜOthmān* and half-legendary sources of mystic orders known as *menāḳib-nāmes* and *wilāyet-names*.

The nucleus of the state of the Ottomans was a far advanced outpost (*udj*) in the region of the Sakarya [*q.v.*] river, which for many centuries constituted the frontier zone between the old Saldjūḳ state of Rūm and that of the Byzantines. The former had gradually relapsed into anarchy after its defeat by the Mongol army at the battle of Kösedağ [see KÖSE DAGH] in 1243. Asia Minor at that time had already been turcicised to a large degree; the greater part of the Anatolian Turks belonged to the Oghuz tribes [see GHUZZ] who invaded the country during the second half of the 5th/11th century, especially after the battle of Malāzgird [*q.v.*] (1071). Moreover, in the first half of the 13th century, the Mongol advance in Asia caused a new migration of Turkish tribes and of fugitives into the country; many of these fugitives came from the former Khwārazmian state and were Persians. Part of the Anatolian Christian population, not abandoning its old religion, continued to live in the Saldjūḳ state in which there was no sharp social division between Muslims and Christians. On the contrary, there was a conflict between the townspeople and the nomads or Turkomans, who were roving all through Asia Minor, as they did also in the adjacent territories of Syria, Mesopotamia and Persia. These Turkomans had still preserved many pre-Islamic religious traditions within the particular form of Islam to which they adhered. This form of Islam was the result of the preaching of wandering dervishes, known under the name of Ḳalenderiyye and Ḥayderiyye, who spread from the 5th/11th century all over northern Persia and Transoxania; their preaching was imbued with mystical doctrines containing a large amount of heterodox elements. After their immigration into Asia Minor, the Turkomans had remained under the same influences and those who exercised religious authority amongst them, called *babas*, had still much resemblance to the pre-Islamic *shamans*. Under these religious leaders in 1239, the fearful revolt of the Bābāʾīs [*q.v.*] had taken place (cf. A.Y. Ocak, *La révolte de Baba Resul ou la formation de l'hétérodoxie musulmane en Anatolie au XIIIe siècle*, Ankara 1989). The government at that time had been able at last to suppress the revolt, but the heterodox opposition among the lower classes in Asia Minor still deeply influenced the history of the first centuries of the Ottoman Empire. These Turkomans were indeed far more numerous that the governing classes and the townspeople, as is shown by the present geographical nomenclature of Asia Minor; numerous villages, rivers and mountains have pure Turkish names of tribes such as Ḳayî, Salur, Bayat and Čepni (cf. Köprülü-zāde Fuat, *Oguz etnolodjisine tārīkhī notlar*, in *Türkiyyāt Medjmūᶜasî*, i, 185 ff.). Insofar as the Turkoman tribes were still militant, the best use that could be made of them was as frontier guards and as conquerors of new territory. After settling down, they may have mixed with a good deal of the original rural population and this mixture explains the curious half-Christian views and customs that are reported in later times as existing among the lower classes in Anatolia.

The Saldjūḳ government and the higher classes of society had followed the orthodox Sunnī Islamic tradition, which is to be traced back to the times of the Sāmānid empire in Khurāsān and Transoxania. These were also the regions with which the Anatolian Turks had always been in constant contact. The higher culture was mainly Persian in character. These contacts explain also how the Ḥanafī *madhhab* became officially predominant in Anatolia and afterwards in the Ottoman empire. The upper classes of society were not free themselves from a strong mystical influence of a higher order. It had likewise its source in Khurāsān, whence had come the theologian and mystic Djalāl al-Dīn Rūmī [*q.v.*], who lived in the Saldjūḳ capital Konya and who influenced for centuries Ottoman Turkish culture through the Mewlewī order [see MAWLAWIYYA]. So the townspeople were likewise familiar with the formation of fraternities on mystical lines, entering within the category of the *futuwwa* [*q.v.*]. One of the fraternities which played an important rôle was that of the *Akhīs* (*q.v.*, and cf. F. Taeschner, in *Islamica*, iv/1 [1929]); a similar fraternity was formed by the *Ghāziyān*. On this basis of religious and social controversy is to be understood the development of events since the end of the 7th/13th century. In the many small principalities that appeared during the break-up of the Saldjūḳ state we see sometimes the influence of the orthodox element and at other times that of the heterodox Turkoman element as predominant.

When the Ottoman state was founded in Bithynia, presumably around 1299, it was one among several other small Turkish states, such as that of the Ḳarasî-oghlu [*q.v.*], the Ṣarukhān-oghlu [*q.v.*], the Aydîn-oghlu [*q.v.*], the Menteshe-oghlu [*q.v.*], the Djandar-oghlu or Isfendiyār-oghlu [*q.v.*], the Ḳaramān-oghlu [*q.v.*], the Germiyān-oghlu [*q.v.*], the Ḥamīd-oghlu, etc. All these states had this in common with the Ottoman one, that they were established between the former Saldjūḳ state and the Byzantine empire, on the frontier zone, that is, in the most remote regions from the Islamic cultural centre of Anatolia; their lords, bearing the Turkish title *beg* [*q.v.*] or the equivalent Arabic title *amīr* [*q.v.*], were descendants of the Turkoman chieftains who were frontier guards (*udj begleri*). Furthermore, they had the possibility to expand by attacking the coastal regions ruled by the Byzantines and the islands ruled by the Italian colonists. It was this opportunity of westward expansion, which proved most favourable for the ᶜOthmān-oghlu and secured them in the end the superiority over the other principalities.

The historical tradition of the Ottomans has preserved reminiscences of the Turkoman nomadic origin of the founders of the state. The father of ᶜOthmān, Ertoghrul [*q.v.*], is said to have established himself with his little tribe in the neighbourhood of Söğüt [*q.v.*] and the pedigree given for Ertoghrul and his father Süleymān Shāh shows them as belonging to the Ḳayî [*q.v.*] division of the Oghuz Turks. As the various reports about Ertoghrul have a good deal of a legendary character, his very existence was put under doubt until a coin of ᶜOthmān also bearing his father's name, was found (İ. Artuk, *Osmanlı beyliğin kurucusu Osman gazi'ye ait sikke*, in *Papers presented to the First International Congress on the Social and Economic History of Turkey, Hacettepe University 1977*, Ankara 1980, 27-33). When Ertoghrul died, ᶜOthmān took over the leadership. It is not certain that his name was ᶜOthmān, that is, a prestigious Arabic name; his contemporary the Byzantine historian George Pachymeres wrote the name down as Atman, which is a simple Turkic name (cf. L. Bazin, *Antiquité méconnue du titre d'Ataman?*, in *Harvard Ukrainian Studies, Essays presented to O. Pritsak*, iii-iv [1979-80], 61-70). He was, at any rate, one of the *ghāziyān-i Rūm* and surrounded by other *ghāzīs* (Turkish *alp*) as well as by people belonging to the fraternity of the *Akhīs*. His father-in-law, the *sheykh* Edebali, was deeply involved with the group of dervishes known as the *Abdālān-i Rūm*, which was connected with the mystic order of the Bektāshīs (*q.v.*, and cf. Irène Mélikoff, *Un ordre de derviches colonisateurs: les Bektachis*, in *Memorial Ömer Lûtfi Barkan*, Paris 1980, 149-57). As a result of collaboration of these various elements, a small amirate was established. Its centre was the fortress of Ḳaradja Ḥiṣār, the exact location of which remains unknown; its identification with the Byzantine Melagina proposed by von Hammer is not valid anymore (V. Laurent, *La Vita retractata et les miracles posthumes de Saint Pierre d'Atroa*, Brussels 1958, 10, 66, 74). During ᶜOthmān's reign, the history of the amirate was not different from that of the contemporary Anatolian principalities. By organising raids against the Byzantine territories, but also by stratagems and personal relations, he succeeded in extending his rule. In 1302 he inflicted a serious defeat on the Byzantines at Bapheus and his troops reached the littoral opposite Constantinople. At his death, in 1326, the Sakarya was practically the eastern boundary of the state, while the Byzantine towns of Bithynia had been blockaded for several years. During the early years of his son and successor Orkhan [*q.v.*], important towns, unable to resist any more, surrendered: Bursa, which became the capital, in 1326, Iznik (Nicaea) in 1331 and Iznikmid/Izmid (Nicomedeia) in 1337. In this year Orkhan also performed his first important raid on Thrace. On the other hand, he added the adjacent amirate of Ḳarasî to his dominions, around 1346, and by this acquisition his state became one of the prominent maritime amirates since the Ḳarasî Turks possessed fleets of light vessels and were experienced in naval warfare.

In Orkhan's years, the more orthodox Islamic traditions gradually became predominant, though the dervishes remained in high esteem as popular religious leaders. It is a noteworthy fact, however, in the history of ᶜOthmān and Orkhan that there apparently existed close relations with local Christian chiefs and commanders; the most representative of them was Köse Mīkhāl, lord of the fortress of Kharmankaya, who collaborated with ᶜOthmān, eventually embraced Islam and was the ancestor of a notable military family in the Ottoman Empire [see MĪKHĀL-OGHLU]. This early collaboration with Christian Greek elements makes it probable that, in this way, Byzantine traditions and customs early entered the Ottoman state, in the same way as was the case in some other contemporary maritime amirates. Both the Christian and the Muslim heterodox element were gradually assimilated by the growing influence of the orthodox *mollās*, often indicated in the older sources as *dānishmend*; some of these belonged to the *Akhī* circles, as is said of the Ḳāḍī Djandarlî Ḳara Khalīl, later vizier to Murād I under the name of Khayr al-Dīn Pasha; many of them had also come from the more eastern parts of Asia Minor. During Orkhan's reign these fairly different elements contributed to the foundation of a typical form of administration and civilisation, from which the later development of the Ottoman state must be explained. The administration, similar to that of the other contemporary amirates, was basically a military one, following Saldjūḳ tradition. The state belonged to the family and it was ruled by the father considered as the senior lord, or in Turkish, *ulu beg*. It was he who concluded treaties, struck coins and was apparently commemorated in the Friday public prayer. The territory of the amirate was divided into domains governed by his sons. Military chiefs were also granted territory by the *ulu beg* and this institution may have reposed on earlier Byzantine or Saldjūḳ ones [see IḲṬĀᶜ]. Apparently under Orkhan there was created a cavalry force of *müsellems* [*q.v.*] and an infantry of *yayas*, as the irregular force of the *aḳindjis* [*q.v.*], originally composed of Turkoman tribesmen, was no longer adequate. In this time also the title *pasha* [*q.v.*], originally peculiar to military dervishes, began to be given to statesmen (e.g. Sinān Pasha under Orkhan) and military commanders.

The natural extension of the young state was towards the west, in keeping with the naval raids of the Ṣarukhān-oghlu and mainly of the Aydîn-oghlu on the isles and on the Greek coast. Orkhan's military expeditions on the Thracian littoral became more frequent since the annexation of the Ḳarasî amirate, but the rise of his power is notably connected with his alliance with the emperor John VI Cantacuzenus during the Byzantine civil war which erupted in 1341. In 1352, however, began the conquest of towns on the European side when Orkhan's son Süleymān occupied the fortress of Tzymbe. In 1354 the Ottomans, profiting from an earthquake, occupied the strategically-important town of Kallipolis or Gallipoli [see GELIBOLU]. In the meantime they established diplomatic relations with the Republic of Genoa and a commercial treaty was concluded in 1352. After Orkhan's death, in 1362, military operations were launched by Murad I, who conquered all the Byzantine territory to the west of Constantinople; Adrianople (Edirne [*q.v.*]), captured in 1369, became soon afterwards the European Ottoman capital. Then followed the wars against the Bulgarians and the Serbians, and the latter were crushed in the battle of Maritsa in 1371 [see MERIČ]. This victory assured to the Ottomans the greater part of the present state of Bulgaria while the Serbians and Byzantines were reduced to the status of tribute-paying vassals of the Ottoman sultan (cf. G. Ostrogorsky, *Byzance état tributaire turc*, in *Zbornik Radova*, v [1958], 49-58). The Serbians were crushed for a second time in the battle of Ḳoṣowa [*q.v.*] in 1389, where Murād was killed.

Bāyezīd I's military expeditions extended over a still wider range, including Hungary, Bosnia and southern Greece, but in these regions the Ottoman conquests were not yet permanent, notwithstanding the victory won at Nicopolis in 1396 over the allied Hungarian, French and German armies [see NĪKBŪLĪ]. Bāyezīd began a siege of Constantinople and the end of the Byzantine state seemed to have come. On the other hand, the Ottomans began to extend their rule in Asia Minor. Murād I acquired a large part of the Germiyān-oghlu territory, which included important mines of alum, as a wedding present to his son, and also the amirate of Ḥamīd-oghlu by sale. Bāyezīd I continued the conquest of the Anatolian amirates but in a brutal manner and with the assistance of his Christian vassals. Ṣarukhān, Aydîn and Menteshe were annexed in 1390 and the amirate of the Isfendiyār-oghlu in 1391. His policy provoked the intervention of the Turco-Mongol *khān* Tīmūr [*q.v.*] who invaded Anatolia with his army, crushed Bāyezīd's army in the battle of Ankara (1402) and captured him. Bāyezīd committed suicide in captivity in 1403.

While the sultans conducted the military operations, the organisation was in the hands of their statesmen, among whom Djandarlî Ḳara Khalīl is the most notable (see DJANDARLÎ and cf. F. Taeschner-P. Wittek, *Die Vezierfamilie der Čandarlyzade und ihre Denkmäler*, in *Isl.*, xviii [1929], 61-115). To him is attributed the institution of the Janissaries [see YEÑI-ČERI] in connection with the reservation of a fifth part of the war booty for the sultan. The Janissaries were usually taken from the captured Christians, but a Greek source indicates that the *devshirme* [*q.v.*] was already applied in Bāyezīd's days. Their organisation on the lines of a fraternity after the model of the *Akhīs* and the *ghāzīs*, and their connection in this respect with the dervish order of the Bektāshīs [see BEKTĀSHIYYA], shows again the influence of the peculiar religious tradition of the state.

The first *begs* of the Ottoman dynasty, in the older sources generally bearing the titles of *khān* and of *khūnkār*, had originally taken over some of the Saldjūḳ customs and traditions, such as the bearing of *laḳabs* [*q.v.*] composed with *dīn* and *dunyā*, but from the time of Murād I this custom was abandoned. Murād I is also the first to take the title *sulṭān* [*q.v.*] in inscriptions, although the Moroccan traveller Ibn Baṭṭūṭa [*q.v.*], who visited the Ottoman lands, mentions Orkhan with the title of sultan. These rulers followed also the traditions of other Anatolian rulers by marrying high-born Christian ladies: Orkhan was the first to take a Byzantine princess for his wife. To the same early time is to be traced back the investiture of the sultan by the girding on of a sword, which perhaps symbolised originally his admission to the order of the *ghāzīs* (*ḳîlîdj alay* [see TAḲLĪD AL-SAYF]). An important fact of the first century of Ottoman history was the enforced migration of populations (*sürgün*), which ancient oriental custom was particularly applied by Bāyezīd I, mostly from the east to the west.

When Tīmūr left Asia Minor again, the country was as divided as it had been a hundred years before; from the river Euphrates up to the Aegean coast the amirates had been restored to their former lords. The Ottoman state passed through a period of political instability combined with dynastic war and social strife, and it remained divided until 1413. This period is known as the interregnum (*fetret dewri*), during which four sons of Bāyezīd staked a claim to leadership over the Ottomans, while the Christian states tried to take the maximum advantage from the division of the Ottomans by supporting one prince against the others. Although the European possessions, where a son of Bāyezīd, Süleymān, resided, had been left untouched by the Mongols, the restoration of the Ottoman state had again its centre in Anatolia, where another son, Meḥemmed, established himself as a master of a considerable territory having Amasya [*q.v.*] as its capital. Süleymān first concluded a treaty with the Christian powers of Romania (1403), making territorial concessions to them, abolishing taxes paid by them and confirming old commercial privileges. Then he crossed to Anatolia to fight against his rival brothers, ʿĪsā and Meḥemmed; another brother, Mūsā Čelebi [*q.v.*], appeared in the European territories and obliged him to return there.

It was Meḥemmed I who finally emerged victorious from the fratricide strife and restored the unity of the Ottoman state in 1413. Three years later, in 1416, this state was shaken by a revolt with deep social roots, apparently under the spiritual leadership of *sheykh* Bedr al-Dīn [*q.v.*], the ex-*ḳāḍīʿasker* of Mūsā. Meḥemmed suppressed the revolt by a huge massacre.

After a short period of peace, the chief military activity of the Ottomans was given to the expansion of their power in Europe. The sultans themselves resided most of the time there and led many campaigns in person. The campaigns became more frequent after Meḥemmed I's death (1421) under his son and successor Murād II. Since the second half of the 14th century, the chief opponent of the Ottomans in the Balkans had been Hungary. The conflict was exacerbated in the late 1430s and in the 1440s, and desire to control the silver-producing mines of Novobrdo in Serbia was one of the reasons. After some military operations, Murād II defeated the Hungarians and their allies first at Varna in 1444 and then at Ḳoṣowa in 1448. Despite warfare, most of the European territory was left under the administration of the old lords, who now were the sultan's vassals responsible for paying an annual tribute and offering military aid to him. Also, Constantinople and the rest of the Byzantine possessions kept for a long time their semi-independence in this way and succeeded even several times in defying a siege.

During the reigns of Meḥemmed I and of Murād II there began a second incorporation of the various Anatolian amirates into the Ottoman state, but this time this was effected gradually and without much bloodshed, with the exception of the Ḳaramān-oghlu state, the old rivals of the ʿOthmān-oghlu. But even there the Ottomans began by following a remarkably conciliatory policy. The descendants of these dynasties were generally granted high military posts in Europe. During Murād's reign trade began to thrive. Venetian, Genoese, Ragusan and other merchants developed important activity in several Ottoman cities, which expanded considerably, such as Bursa with its silk market.

Murād II died in 1451 and was succeeded by his son Meḥemmed II [*q.v.*], who immediately began preparations to put an end to the Byzantine empire, which was then limited to the city of Constantinople, a few islands and some towns on the western Black Sea coast. Constantinople fell on 29 May 1453, and the Ottoman empire succeeded the Byzantine one. The capture of Constantinople, which made such a profound impression among the Turks as well as in the Occident, was only the realisation of a part of a political scheme of Meḥemmed II, that of bringing the whole Balkan peninsula under the direct government of the Ottoman state. After continuous military campaigns this scheme had nearly become a reality. There were still Venetian enclaves in the Morea and Albania, and in the north Belgrade was still held by the Hungarians; but even Bosnia had now passed under Ottoman rule. The large Aegean islands, except Rhodes, were incorporated in the same manner. Only the Danube principalities, Wallachia and Moldavia, and, since 1475, the Crimean K͟hānate, had remained vassals. Meḥemmed II also finished the conquest of Anatolia proper by the conquest of the empire of Trebizond in 1461 and when at last the Ḳaramānid dynasty was extinguished, in 1475, the Ottoman empire stood face to face with the Aḳ Ḳoyunlu [*q.v.*] dynasty in the east and the Mamlūk state in the south-east. The dangerous policy of the Aḳ Ḳoyunlu lord Uzun Ḥasan [*q.v.*] came to an end in 1473 when Meḥemmed II defeated him at Otluk Beli. Under Bāyezīd II, this neighbour was succeeded by the young Ṣafawid dynasty of Persia; still, until the reign of this sultan, the Ottoman territory was not enlarged on the Asiatic front, though there were several inglorious frontier wars with the Mamlūk forces in Syria.

During all this time, the Christian powers were scheming and planning crusades to expel the Turks from Europe, while trying also to contract alliances with their Asiatic opponents. But no really great enterprise was ever undertaken; only temporary damage was done by the Hungarian Hunyádi, the Wallachian Wlad Dracul, the Albanian Skander Beg [see ISKENDER BEG] and by some Venetian naval expeditions. All these Ottoman military successes in Europe would not have been possible without the strong base in Turkish Anatolia. Still more astonishing is, perhaps, the permanence of the Ottoman occupation. The reason may be sought mainly in the lack of any sufficiently great political Christian power in the much-divided Balkan peninsula, and also in the deep hatred between the Greek Orthodox and the Roman Catholic Church.

During Meḥemmed II's reign the Ottoman political system developed, but the beginnings of this inner evolution are to be sought in the reign of Murād II, parallel with the consolidation of the Ottoman type of religious orthodoxy. The overwhelming importance of the person of the sultan for the existence of the state is still more accentuated during this period. This is shown by the menace of military revolts after the death of nearly every sultan and the artifices by which his death was kept secret until the arrival of his successor, also by the grave disturbances caused by pretenders and the tradition of fratricide, probably inaugurated by Bāyezīd I but officially decreed by Meḥemmed II. The supporting of Ottoman pretenders was justly considered as one of the most effective means available to Christian enemies of the empire.

The new leading men in the state and in the army were now for the greater part of Christian origin, Albanians, Slavs, Greeks or, even more, westerners. They derived from war prisoners, the *dews͟hirme* levies, or they were simple renegades. The older families that had come from Asia Minor, such as the Mīk͟hāl-og͟hlu or the Ewrenos-og͟hlu [*q.v.*], receded into second place as owners of large land properties on the Danube and in Macedonia; the high position of the D͟jandarlĭ family as viziers ended with the execution of K͟halīl Pas͟ha shortly after the fall of Constantinople. The newly-converted Christians served the state to their best, but the all-dominating authority of the sultan and perhaps also the democratic tradition of Islam prevented the formation of a hereditary nobility; statesmen and military commanders (as *beglerbegi*s and *sand͟jaḳbegi*s) were the slaves (*ḳullar*) of the sovereign and much less independent than they had been in the 8th/14th century. Less dependent was the class of the scholars and jurists who provided the religious hierarchy with the *S͟heyk͟h al-Islām* at the head; among them there are signs of an upper class of theologians. So there was formed an Ottoman ruling class composed for the greater part of non-Turkish elements recruited from the ranks of the Christians. Under these circumstances, it was inevitable that the administrative institutions should show the influence of Byzantine ideas, as was also the case with the court organisation. By *Ḳānūn-nāmes* [*q.v.*], of which those of Meḥemmed II and later of Süleymān the Magnificent are the best known, the hierarchy of officials was minutely regulated.

Besides the older troops of irregular *aḳĭnd͟jĭ*s and *ʿazabs* [*q.v.*] the army consisted chiefly (a) of the cavalry of the *sipāhī*s, whose organisation was intimately connected with the military administration of the territory [see TĪMĀR], and (b) of the Janissaries, apparently levied in the time of Murād II by the *dews͟hirme*. Agriculture, constituting the financial support of the cavalry, was closely connected to the *tīmār* system. Firearms may also have been used for the first time during Murād II's reign [see BĀRŪD. iv]. The fleet [see GELIBOLU and DARYĀ-BEGI] was mainly manned with Christian renegades, *ʿazab*s and Christian prisoners as galley slaves. It began to be well-organised under Meḥemmed II.

The revenues of the state or rather of the sultan consisted for the most part of the constantly-increasing *d͟jizye* [*q.v.*] and *k͟harād͟j* [*q.v.*], both of them levied on non-Muslim subjects, and of the annual tributes paid by the vassal states. The different kinds of custom-duties were also considerable. Trade remained largely in the hands of the *d͟himmī*s, the merchant class having increased in number by the massive arrival of Jews from Spain and Central Europe. Exports and imports were also largely in the hands of foreigners, especially Italians, who had their communities in Constantinople [see G͟HALAṬA in Suppl.] and some other towns. These communities were treated in the same way as the indigenous non-Turkish communities; they were allowed considerable autonomy under their consuls, including consular jurisdiction. These privileges were granted by the sultans in the well-known form of "capitulations", in which were prescribed also the commercial duties to be paid by the foreigners, who, in accordance with the principles of Muslim law, were considered as *müsteʾminūn* [see IMTIYĀZĀT].

The civilisation of the Ottoman Empire of the later Middle Ages was not yet separated from central and western Europe by the wide gap that became characteristic for later centuries. It has been pointed out that the friendly relations between Meḥemmed II and Italian princes and artists and his liking for pictorial art entitles him, in a way, to a place among the Renaissance rulers of the time. In the days of his successor Bāyezīd II, however, the Muslim attitude to life began to be again more predominant.

Bibliography: F. Babinger, *Mehmed the Conqueror and his time*, tr. R. Manheim, ed. W.C. Hickman, Princeton 1978; N. Beldiceanu, *Le timar dans l'Empire Ottoman (début du XIVe-début XVIe siècle)*, Wiesbaden 1980; Irène Beldiceanu-Steinherr, *En marge d'un acte concernant le pengyek et les aqingi*, in *REI*, xxxvii (1969), 21-47; B. Braude, *Foundation myths in the Millet system*, in *Christians and Jews in the Ottoman Empire. The functioning of a plural society*, ed. B. Braude and B. Lewis, i, *The Central Lands*, London-New York 1982, 69-88; S. Christensen, *European-Ottoman military acculturation in the Late Middle Ages*, in *War and peace in the Middle Ages*, ed. B.P. McGuire, Copenhagen 1987, 227-51; G. Dennis, *The Byzantine-Turkish treaty of 1403*, in *Orientalia Christiana Periodica*, xxxiii (1967) 72-88; C. Imber, *The Ottoman Empire 1300-1481*, Istanbul 1990; H. Inalcik, *Bursa and the commerce of the Levant*, in *JESHO*, iii (1960), 131-47; idem, in *The Cambridge history of Islam*. i. *The central Islamic lands*, Cambridge 1970, 295-353; idem, *The Ottoman economic mind and aspects of the Ottoman economy*, in *Studies on the economic history of the Middle East*, ed. M. Cook, London 1970; idem, *The Ottoman Empire. The classical age 1300-1600*, London 1973; idem, *The policy of Mehmed II toward the Greek population of Istanbul and the Byzantine buildings of the city*, in *Dumbarton Oaks Papers*, xxiii-xxiv (1969-70) 231-49; idem, *The question of the closing of the Black Sea under the Ottomans*, in *Archeion Pontou* ("Black Sea", Birmingham, 18-20 March 1978), xxxv (1979), 74-110; H.J. Kissling, *Das Menakybname Scheich Bedr ed-Dīn's des Sohnes des Richters von Simavna*, in *ZDMG*, c (1950), 112-76; M. Fuad Köprülü, *Les origines de l'empire ottoman*, Paris 1935, Tkish. version, *Osmanlı devleti'nin kuruluşu*, Ankara 1959, Eng. tr. and commentary G. Leiser, *The origins of the Ottoman empire*, Albany 1992; K.P. Matschke, *Die Schlacht bei Ankara und das Schicksal von Byzanz*, Forschungen zur Mittelalterlichen Geschichte 29, Weimar 1981; Irène Mélikoff, *L'Islam hétérodoxe en Anatolie*, in *Turcica*, xiv (1982) 142-54; eadem, *Les origines centre-asiatiques du soufisme anatolien*, in *Turcica*, xx (1988) 7-18; V.L. Ménage, *Some notes on the Devshirme*, in *BSOAS*, xxix (1966), 64-78; S. Vryonis, *The decline of medieval Hellenism in Asia Minor and the process of Islamization from the eleventh through the fifteenth century*, Berkeley and Los Angeles 1971; E. Werner, *Die Geburt einer Grossmacht-Die Osmanen*, Forschungen zur Mittelalterlichen Geschichte 32, 4th ed., Weimar 1985; P. Wittek, *De la défaite d'Ankara à la prise de Constantinople*, in *REI*, xii (1938), 1-34; idem, *The rise of the Ottoman Empire*, London 1938; E.A. Zachariadou, *Süleyman Çelebi in Rumili and the Ottoman chronicles*, in *Isl.*, lx (1983), 268-96; eadem, *Ἱστορία καὶ Θρύλοι τῶν Παλαιῶν Σουλτάνων 1300-1400*, Athens 1991.

(J.H. Kramers-[E.A. Zachariadou])

3. The empire at its zenith

After the relatively peaceful reign of Bāyezīd II, there is no more question about Asia Minor or the Balkan Peninsula. The struggle continued in Albania and Morea, but had on the whole a local character. The empire was now strong enough to face its new Asiatic neighbours. The war waged against Persia by Selīm I was in a way a continuation on an international scale of the former internal struggle against the Shīʿī opposition in Asia Minor itself. This war secured Turkey the temporary possession of Ādharbāydjān and the lasting domination over Kurdistān and northern Mesopotamia. Very soon afterwards the Egyptian state of the Mamlūks, with whom the Ottoman empire had clashed under Bāyezīd II in a rather inglorious way, was incorporated by Selīm in one single campaign. The consequence was the extension of Turkish overlordship to the holy cities of Islam and soon to Yaman. Finally, under Süleymān I the Magnificent, the empire obtained its greatest extension by the conquest of the greater part of Hungary, one of the two great mediaeval opponents in Europe; in the same campaign the Turks went even so far as to besiege Vienna. Only the other old rival, Venice, was not broken by the victorious empire. After Meḥemmed II's death, official wars with Venice had become rather an exception. The Ottoman empire never had acquired an absolute maritime superiority, and this weakness appeared almost immediately after the great period of conquest was over, in the battle of Lepanto. Rhodes was conquered, but Malta has never been Turkish and the maritime exploits of Kemāl Reʾīs [*q.v.*] under Bāyezīd and those of Barbarossa Khayr al-Dīn [*q.v.*] and others, which assured Turkey's political authority in the age of Süleymān on the north coast of Africa and in the Indian Ocean, never wholly lost the character of piracy. On the Asiatic front, the continuation of the conflict with Persia led for the time to the conquest of Baghdād and ʿIrāḳ, so that the sultan was now in reality *sulṭān al-barrayn wa 'l-baḥrayn*.

At the end of the reign of Süleymān I, the Ottoman empire found itself between two powerful continental neighbours: the Austrian monarchy in Europe and the Ṣafawid empire in Asia. In Europe, the Turkish provinces of Bosnia and Hungary were the bulwarks against Austria, while farther to the east the half-independent principalities of Transylvania, Wallachia and Moldavia, and the Tatar Crimea were allowed to exist; from the Turkish point of view also, Poland with its Cossacks, and even Muscovy, held similar intermediate positions between the two empires; during this period Turkey raised more than once claims to the suzerainty of the last-mentioned countries. In Asia, the geographical situation did not allow for the existence of this intermediary kind of state, with the exception of Georgia [see al-Kurdj] which was invaded and brought under Turkish authority in 1578. In Asia, however, the Turkish feudal system left places for a number of petty local rulers who were given the title of Pasha. They were found on the Persian frontier in Kurdistān (the princes of Bitlis), but also in Syria (the Druse amīrs). The *sharīf* of Mecca occupied likewise a vassal position, while Yaman, after its reconquest in 1568-70, was again partly a more direct Ottoman possession. After 1550 the Turks had even obtained a footing in Maṣawwaʿ [*q.v.*] on the African coast and had begun to interfere with Abyssinian affairs; the opportunities here came to an end after the unlucky war of 1578. Egypt was at this time still somewhat under the control of the Turkish Pasha [see Miṣr. D. 6]; the Barbary states were nearly independent; the *sharīf* of Morocco recognised in 1580 the authority of the Turkish sultan.

This general political system of the empire was maintained throughout the third period, a kind of equilibrium being established between the Ottoman empire and the great continental powers.

Under Selīm II, or rather under the administration

of Meḥmed Soḳollu Pas̲h̲a, Cyprus was conquered (1570-1), but this conquest occasioned immediately the naval defeat in the battle of Lepanto [*q.v.*] in 1571, considered to be the first great military blow inflicted on the Turks. The impossibility of further military expansion brought about an inner weakening of the Empire that was marked on the whole by unsuccessful campaigns against Austria (defeat of Mezőkeresztes [*q.v.*] in 1596) and against Persia (loss of Tabrīz and Eriwān in 1603 and 1604) and found its expression in the unfavourable peace treaty of Zsitvatorok with Austria in 1606 and the peace of 1612 with Persia, then under the strong rule of S̲h̲āh ʿAbbās the Great. In the last decade of the 16th century, Transylvania [see ERDEL] and the Rumanian principalities even made themselves for some time independent; from 1572 Poland also played often an active role in the complicated political and military course of events on these northern frontiers of the Turkish empire. The raids of the Cossacks in the Crimea had not yet the dangerous aspect of a century later, when the Muscovite power began to appear on the horizon. A favourable circumstance for Turkey was the weakening of Central Europe by the Thirty Years' War; among the west European countries the already existing friendly relations with France, followed in 1580 by England and in 1603 by Holland, were on the whole profitable for the empire, while Spain had ceased since the end of the century to be a serious maritime danger. In view of the never very strong maritime position of Turkey, the relations with Venice remained subject to surprises on both sides, such as the annexation of Cyprus; during the 17th century this was followed by the conquest of Crete (1645-69) and about 1655 by the important Venetian conquests in Morea and in the archipelago, so that for a moment even Istanbul was threatened. Still, the relations with Venice were on the whole friendly, Turkey being the stronger power on account of its continental position. On the Asiatic frontier, Turkey's weakness led temporarily to the loss of Bag̲h̲dād in 1623 and a renewed Persian danger. But here the old position of the empire was restored by the revival of its military strength under Murād IV; under his reign and after S̲h̲āh ʿAbbās's death, Persia was invaded by Ottoman troops, and Eriwān and Tabrīz, and finally Bag̲h̲dād reconquered (1638); in 1639 there began a long period of peace with Persia. After 1640 the stronger position of the empire was used, as well as for the conquest of Crete, for strengthening the authority of the Porte in Transylvania and the Danube principalities, and for a fortification of the frontier to the north of the Black Sea, where Azov was taken from the Cossacks, now under Muscovite authority, and fortified in 1660. In this same year the hostilities with the now-recovered Austria began again and took on at first a crusading character; even France was this time an ally of Austria (Turkish defeat of St. Gotthard 1664). But this was only a prelude to the final struggle with Austria that began in 1683 with the unsuccessful siege of Vienna, and finished in 1688 with the loss of the Ottoman province of Hungary and the invasion of the Balkan peninsula by Austrian armies, followed at last by the peace of Carlowitz (1699 [see ḲARLOFČA]) in which Turkey, considerably weakened again, had to give up nearly the whole of Hungary and its claim on Transylvania, while it had to recognise the authority of Venice in Morea.

The weakening of the Ottoman empire at the beginning of this period was mainly due to domestic reasons. During the 16th century it had already been observed that the empire in this form could only subsist by continuous warfare; it had to be adapted now to peaceful conditions, and this went beyond the possibilities of the personal rule of the sultan, which was based essentially on military conquest. The successors of Süleymān the Great were not equal to the task of meeting these new conditions; it is true that Meḥemmed III, ʿOt̲h̲mān II and Meḥemmed IV occasionally accompanied their armies, but Murād IV was the last sultan to revive the military traditions of his dynasty, the last real *g̲h̲āzī*. So the sultans, whatever their personal qualities were, became less directly concerned in the administration of the state, though their personality remained surrounded with the traditional veneration. This did not prevent, however, the deposition and murder of ʿOt̲h̲mān II in 1628, nor the deposition of Ibrāhīm in 1648 and of Meḥemmed IV in 1688. Instead of the sultans, the statesmen and generals became now more prominent, first in time and in importance Meḥmed Soḳollu Pas̲h̲a [see SOḲOLLU] under Selīm II, Sinān Pas̲h̲a [*q.v.*], the great enemy of the Austrians, under Meḥemmed III, Murād Pas̲h̲a [*q.v.*] and K̲h̲alīl Pas̲h̲a [*q.v.*] under Aḥmed I and ʿOt̲h̲mān II; and in the second half of the century the great members of the Köprülü family [*q.v.*]: Meḥmed Pas̲h̲a, his son Aḥmed Pas̲h̲a and their cousin Muṣṭafā Pas̲h̲a; to the same period belonged also Ḳara Muṣṭafā Pas̲h̲a [*q.v.*], the besieger of Vienna in 1683. These military statesmen belonged to the numerically feeble renegade class and were supporters of the typical Ottoman government system as it had been perfected under Süleymān I, but they did not represent any considerable group of the strongly diverging population of the empire. There was not yet an Ottoman Turkish nation. Several other groups were competing with them in the direction of the state affairs; the most formidable being the military corps of the Janissaries and the Sipāhīs, who several times, especially after serious military defeats as at the time of the enthronement of Murād IV in 1632 and of Meḥemmed IV's deposition in 1688, were masters of the political situation. The Janissaries were now even less recruited in the ancient way from the Christian populations, while many abuses had ruined the former discipline of their corps. Several Grand Viziers fell victims to their fury. Another powerful group, that made occasional use of these military elements, was the court circle, led several times by a powerful *Wālide Sulṭān* or by a *Ḳi̊zlar Ag̲h̲asi̊*. Finally, the *ʿulemā*ʾ with the *S̲h̲eyk̲h̲ al-Islām* succeeded repeatedly in playing a decisive part in the direction of the state affairs (e.g. the *muftī* Saʿd al-Dīn under Meḥemmed III); the deposition of sultan Ibrāhīm was sanctioned by *fetwā* of the *S̲h̲eyk̲h̲ al-Islām*. These symptoms of decay were truly analysed in Ḳoči̊ Bey's [*q.v.*] famous *Risāla*. Only Murād IV was able to suppress, often by violent means, the influence of these different groups; he succeeded even in raising a new military force (the Segbāns) alongside of the Janissaries. In the capital there were several times outbursts of religious fanaticism directed against the Christians, as happened under Ibrāhīm I, but it cannot be said that political events were influenced by them; the great statesmen showed on the contrary a remarkable tolerance.

The non-Muslim element, though excluded from all direct influence on the government, had adapted itself to the circumstances. A new Greek aristocracy had arisen in Istanbul, which by wealth and intrigue had powerful relations in Turkish circles, as well as in the leading circles of the Christian principalities on the Danube; they likewise were able to control the nomination of the Greek patriarchs. To this time belongs also the definite turn of the Ottoman Greeks towards Greek Orthodoxy under the influence of the patriarch Cyrillus Lucaris (executed in 1638); the consequence was a decisive rupture with the Roman Christian world and indirectly a strengthening of the Ottoman empire. The Ottoman Turks had still many religious traditions in common with the Greeks, and Christian saints were also venerated in Turkish circles. Next to the Greeks, the Jewish element, considerably strengthened since the arrival of the Spanish and Portuguese Jews under Bāyezīd I, played a great social role, chiefly as bankers; the best known representative of this group was Joseph Nasī [see NAḲSHE and NASĪʾ], the favourite of Selīm II.

The lower classes in Asia Minor participated as little in the direction of the state as those of European Turkey. Some dangerous revolts proved, however, that the old religious traditions of the 13th and 14th centuries had not wholly disappeared. In 1599 began the movement of Ḳara Yazîdjî [*q.v.*] in Urfa; much more dangerous for the unity of the empire was the revolt of Ḳalender-oghlu in Ṣarukhān (1606), who ruled for some years independently over a great part of western Anatolia, until he was crushed by Murād Pasha. Soon afterwards, in 1623-8 took place the insurrection of Abāẓa Meḥmed Pasha [*q.v.*], the relentless persecutor of the Janissaries. Farther to the east, the movement for independence under the Kurd Djānbulāṭ [*q.v.*] in northern Syria like that of the Druse Fakhr al-Dīn Maᶜn [*q.v.*] in the Lebanon had to be tolerated to some extent. The inclination to mysticism and veneration for mystic *sheykh*s (such as Maḥmūd of Scutari, where several grand viziers found asylum under ᶜOthmān II) continued its hold on all classes of the population; several new mystical orders were founded during this period. The foreign trade remained as before in the hands of foreigners, Venetians and other Italians; of Italian origin were also many of the leading personalities of the Turkish navy that was rebuilt after the battle of Lepanto, such as Čighale-zāde Sinān Pasha [*q.v.*].

4. The period of decline

During the 18th century the inevitable action of the elements of decay began to be felt more and more in the empire and brought about a situation that has been, too superficially, described as decadence. The causes of the decline were to be sought mainly within the body politic; they were still the consequences of the transition from a conquering state to a peaceful administration, but they were now ever more exploited by foreign powers. Among these Austria was in the beginning still a formidable opponent; after the war of 1716-18 the peace of Passarowitz [see PASAROFČA] meant the loss of what had been left to Turkey of Hungary and Transylvania, and even of Belgrade, but the peace of Belgrade in 1739, in which this town itself was restored, proved that from the Austrian side the real danger had ceased. Moreover, in 1715, Morea had been reconquered from the Venetians by the grand vizier Djinn ᶜAlī Pasha [see MORA], which success had shown that Venice also was no more to be feared. A new and formidable enemy had risen, however, in the form of the now much enlarged Russia, which, to the Orthodox Christians of Rumania and Serbia, seemed a more welcome liberator than even Austria had ever been. The war of 1711 with Peter I, intimately connected with the coming of Charles XII of Sweden to Turkey, ended with a Turkish victory at Poltava and brought back Azov to the empire in 1712, and the war of 1732, equally successfully closed by the already-mentioned Treaty of Belgrade in 1739, was not yet disastrous for Turkey; Russian navigation in the Black Sea was even formally prohibited. After 1739 there followed a period of peace for the empire in Europe. The military and peaceful relations with Persia during this time were mainly influenced by the political events in that empire, by which the Turks sought to profit. The successes of Nādir Shāh [*q.v.*] of Persia in 1730 were for a moment threatening; they even occasioned the deposition of Aḥmed III, but at last the peace of 1736 restored the frontiers of the time of Murād IV. The real military weakness of the Ottoman empire was finally revealed in the conflict with Russia that had begun in 1768 with a Turkish declaration of war; this war brought the Russian armies deep into Bulgaria and was ended by the memorable treaty of Küčük Ḳaynardja [*q.v.*] in 1774, by which the Crimea became wholly independent (to be annexed in 1783 by Russia), while Turkey had to recognise the Russian protectorate in the Danube principalities. The right of religious protection accorded to the sultan with regard to the Muslims in the Crimea, was the beginning of the religious claims of Turkey that were to acquire such importance in its international relations in the 19th century. After an equally unhappy war with Karīm Khān Zand [*q.v.*] in Persia (1776), in which Baṣra was temporarily lost, the Ottoman empire again suffered serious losses to the Russians by the war of 1784-92, closed by the peace of Jassy; this time the Dniepr became the frontier between the two empires. Austria also had tried to profit by this war and had occupied Bucharest, but in the separate peace of Zistowa (1791) Austria did not gain the expected profits.

During all this time, the friendly relations with the western countries, France, Britain and Holland, to which Sweden was added in 1737, Denmark in 1756 and Prussia in 1763, had often been of great value to Turkey by the services rendered by them as intermediaries in the peace negotiations; especially France, which obtained in 1740 its well-known final capitulations, had considerable influence by its right to protect the Roman Catholics. At the end of the century, however, the Ottoman empire began to be a factor in the new expansionist schemes of the western powers, in connection with their colonial acquisitions and political influence in South and East Asia. These interests did not show at that time any wish to possess Ottoman territory, but the rising colonial powers needed between themselves and their possessions a state over which they could exert control, since they saw the necessity of communicating with the Persian Gulf and India by a more direct way than the southern sea-route. The more immediate cause of the occupation of Egypt by the French in 1798 was the rivalry between France and Britain; this made for the moment Britain and even Russia allies of Turkey. But in 1802 peace with France was restored, to be followed some years later by a new war with Russia and hostilities with Britain (the British fleet before the capital in 1807). By the peace of Bucharest (1812), the Ottoman Empire again lost territory (Bessarabia [see BUDJĀḲ]) to Russia, while Britain, after the elimination of France's colonial power in India and the weakening of the Ottoman authority in Egypt, was for the moment satisfied. The empire was again severely affected by the ups and downs of the Greek insurrection that began in 1820 and ended in 1830 with the recognition of the independence of Greece, not, however, before a disastrous war with Russia—that had played from the beginning an important part in the Greek troubles—had obliged Turkey to conclude the peace of Adrianople (1829). Still, the action of the other European powers had prevented Russia from realising its territorial aims; it had to be contented with a strong political ascendancy over Turkey, as was proved in 1833 by the Treaty of Kh̲ünkār Iskelesi, which, in a secret article, forced Turkey to become Russia's ally in the matter of the navigation in the Black Sea. This unnatural alliance with Russia was occasioned by the action of Muḥammad ʿAlī [*q.v.*] of Egypt (begun in 1831), who threatened for a moment to deprive the empire of Egypt, Syria and Cilicia, but led at the end only to the recognition of Egypt as a privileged part of the Empire under a hereditary dynasty (1840). This time again the intervention of the European powers had been decisive for the territorial status of the empire. The existence of the Ottoman empire was justly considered as a political necessity; already in 1789 there had been a treaty between Prussia and Austria to guarantee the northern frontiers of the Empire. About the year 1830, moreover, Turkey concluded several new treaties, on the lines of the capitulations, with the United States of America, Belgium, Portugal and Spain. The conquest of Algiers by France (1827-57) [see AL-D̲JAZĀʾIR] could hardly be called a loss to the empire.

The administrative system of the empire remained much the same during this period; in every direction the central authority was, however, losing its influence. At the beginning of the 18th century this was not yet very perceptible. Istanbul was still the brilliant capital of a powerful empire, where the court of Aḥmed III set the example of a luxurious life; to this time falls the curious passion for the cultivation of tulips, that makes the epoch known as *lāle dewri* [*q.v.*]. To this period also belongs the expansion of higher literary, specifically Ottoman, culture beyond the class of the *ʿulemāʾ*; a new class of literati came into existence, who were the precursors of the intellectual Turkish middle class that originated in the beginning of the 19th century. The abortive beginning of Muslim Turkish printing in 1727 [see IBRĀHĪM MÜTEFERRIḲA and MAṬBAʿA. 2] is likewise intimately connected with the new cultural orientation of the higher classes. Most of them served the government in higher or lower functions, and from this class came forth Grand Viziers, such as Dāmād Ibrāhīm and Rāg̲h̲ib Pas̲h̲a [*q.vv.*]. This changed considerably the ancient military character of the government system; the home and foreign affairs of the empire were now treated in a more statesmanlike way by the Sublime Porte (Bāb-i ʿĀlī), and the modest office of the Reʾīs al-Küttāb [*q.v.*] now became more and more important, since the holders began to act as competent Ministers of Foreign Affairs; one of them, Aḥmed Rasmī [*q.v.*], is well known as one of the first Ottoman ambassadors. Still, this new class of functionaries was, according to tradition, the sultan's slaves; only under Maḥmūd II was their position regulated in a more liberal way. The new upper classes had manifold relations with the cultivated Greek Phanariots of their time [see FENER], many of whom occupied high offices in the government service, especially as dragomans (as e.g. Nikusios and Mavrocordato); there were no ties with the lower Muslim classes. Under these governing functionaries, the Janissaries and Sipāhīs, now that their discipline was loosened, more than once interfered in a dangerous way. The Janissary rebellion under Patrona Kh̲alīl [*q.v.*] in 1730, which cost Aḥmed III his throne, seems to have been directed mainly against this new aristocracy. After Aḥmed III, court life became much more sober. The ruling classes and most of the sultans with them had begun to realise the weakness of the empire and sought now a remedy in the introduction of military reforms, in which they were aided by several foreigners, of whom the Frenchman Bonneval (d. 1747 [see AḤMAD PAS̲H̲A BONNEVAL]) is the best known. Another French officer, De Tott, worked in the same direction under Muṣṭafā III, but the Russian war that broke out under this sultan showed how little effective the measures had been.

Selīm III undertook army reforms with much more energy, but even in his time very few leading people had real understanding for these things; the institution of the new troops (*niẓām-i d̲jedīd* [*q.v.*]) provoked another formidable rebellion of the Janissaries, seconded by a large proportion of the *ʿulemāʾ*. Maḥmūd II, finally, took up the question of reforms with more deliberateness; this sultan finally concluded there was no other way of imposing the reforms than by the famous massacre of the Janissaries in Istanbul on 16 June 1826; at the same time, the Bektās̲h̲ī dervish order [see BEKTĀS̲H̲IYYA] was persecuted. The events showed, however, that so far, more destructive than constructive work had been done; still, this sultan succeeded at least in subjecting a number of powerful semi-independent local dynasts [see DEREBEY]. The weakening of the central authority had indeed been characteristic of the Ottoman empire of the 18th century. Algiers, Tunis and Tripoli were ruled by hereditary Beys; only Tripoli was brought by Maḥmūd again under the direct authority of the Porte. Egypt had seen in 1767 the usurpation of ʿAlī Bey. In Rūm-ili some powerful vassals had come forth from the ranks of the great *tīmār* [*q.v.*] holders or timariots; they were called *aʿyān* [*q.v.*]. Under Selīm III and Maḥmūd II the most noteworthy were ʿAlī Pas̲h̲a Tepedelenli [*q.v.*] of Yanina and Paswān-og̲h̲lu [*q.v.*] at Vidin. In Anatolia there had been in 1739 the dangerous insurrection of Ṣarī Beg-og̲h̲lu, after which the so-called *derebeys* were as good as independent, as was also the case in Kurdistān. In Mesopotamia and ʿIrāḳ the same conditions were prevalent; in 1706 was formed in ʿIrāḳ the powerful Bedouin confederation of the Muntafiḳ [*q.v.*], and under Selīm III Bag̲h̲dād was ruled autocratically by Süleymān Pas̲h̲a (d. 1810). In Syria, the Druses of the Lebanon had their own *amīrs* [see DURŪZ. ii], and on the coast ruled, in Selīm III's time, D̲jazzār Pas̲h̲a [*q.v.*] of ʿAkkā. In Arabia, the Wahhābīs [see WAHHĀBIYYA] had taken Mecca in 1803, and Yaman and ʿAsīr could hardly be called parts of the Turkish empire. On the islands of the Aegean archipelago, hardly any Turks were to be found; here, as in Syria, there was strong European influence. Still, although the Ottoman real power had sunk everywhere, the Ottoman type of administration had put its seal on the cultural life of all these different regions; the great Ottoman tradition held them together and enabled Maḥmūd II and the statesmen who, after him, continued the centralisation of the Empire, to keep together their political unity for a century more to come.

5. The beginnings of reform and westernisation, and the end of the dynasty

In this period, the transition of the Ottoman empire to a national Turkish state was completed, but in a way not intended by the Christian powers, nor expected by the Turkish ruling classes themselves. The new course followed in the administration by the gradual application of the *Tanẓīmāt* measures [*q.v.*] had meant to establish, mainly after the French model, a modern state where all citizens, whatever their religion, had equal political and civil rights, under the direct authority of the Ottoman government; only Egypt, the Danube principalities and Serbia (since 1815) and in Asia the Ḥid̲jāz were allowed a privileged position. The ideal of the new Ottoman state was, however, far from the democratic ideals that worked in Europe and which by now began to show their effect, especially among the Christian populations. The democratic revolutionary movement of 1849 in Moldavia and Wallachia [see BOGHDĀN and EFLĀḲ] was equally opposed by Turkey and by Russia, but had as result the convention of Balta Liman, by which the Turkish authority in these principalities was reduced to a negligible point. When Russia, as a result of a conflict over the Holy Places in Jerusalem, invaded again the principalities, in 1853, the Ottoman empire found Britain and France at its side; this was the beginning of the Crimean War. By the peace treaty of Paris (1856) the integrity of the empire seemed secured. In reality, the intervention of Britain and France and soon again of Russia was now more firmly established than ever. This was not only the case in political questions, as for instance the armed intervention in the Lebanese and Syrian troubles of 1845 and 1860, after the troubles of Djidda in 1858, and in the international regulation of the position of Crete in 1866. For the influence of the foreign powers was likewise extended to many points of internal administration, which kind of intervention was made possible by the capitulations. These originally unilateral privileges were looked upon now as bilateral treaties, but their contents had become incompatible with the new state conception that the *Tanẓīmāt* tried to realise. From 1856, indeed, the Porte had tried in vain to get rid of this international servitude, which, at the end of the 19th century, had taken on the character of a collective tutelage of all countries possessing capitulations. Not till 1914 did the conflict between the European powers enable the Turkish government to put the capitulations aside [see IMTIYĀZĀT].

In 1862 the Ottoman government was able to restore its authority in Montenegro [see ḲARA DAGH] and Herzegovina, while, on the other hand, Serbia, and the two Danube principalities, since 1861 united in one state, recovered a nearly complete independence in 1865. Twelve years later the Bulgarian troubles again brought about an armed conflict with Russia, which country, in 1870, had already broken the conventions of 1856 about the Black Sea. The preliminaries of San Stefano (1878), mitigated by the Treaty of Berlin (1879), brought the definite loss of Serbia, Montenegro and Rumania, while Bulgaria was constituted a semi-dependent principality; on the Caucasian frontier, Turkey lost Ḳars and Batum [*q.vv.*], and Britain obtained the administration of the isle of Cyprus [see ḲUBRUS]. This abandonment of Britain's policy hitherto followed of respecting the integrity of Ottoman territory was followed in 1882 by the occupation of Egypt [see KHEDĪW and MIṢR. D. 7]. The remaining dates in the dismemberment of Turkey in Europe are the Greco-Turkish war (1897), by which the Greek territory was enlarged towards the north, the autonomy of Crete (1898) and, after the deposition of ʿAbd ül-Ḥamīd II, in 1909, the declaration of independence of Bulgaria and the annexation of Bosnia and Herzegovina by Austria. Then, after Tripoli had been lost in the war with Italy (1912, Peace of Lausanne), the Balkan War of 1912-13 reduced the territory of Turkey in Europe to Eastern Thrace, including Edirne, which town had even been occupied for some time by the Bulgarians.

During the 19th century, the relations with Persia had been on the whole peaceful; conflicts were only occasioned by frontier questions, such as the dispute about authority over the Kurdish territory of Sulaymāniyya [*q.v.*], which was settled in 1847 in favour of Turkey. The territory round the Persian Gulf had come more and more under the control of the British, but the territorial status in Asia remained for a long time unchanged. In the meantime, Turkey had been drawn gradually into the economic expansion schemes of the German empire as manifested by the project of the Baghdād railway; this diminished Britain's interest in the territorial integrity of the Ottoman state. So, when in the first year of the First World War, Turkey joined the Central Powers, Russia and Britian co-operated for the first time to take away Turkish territory. The attempts of the Allies to enter the Dardanelles by sea and by land failed, however, during the war; but the combined action of the French and British troops in Palestine and Syria, and the different British campaigns in ʿIrāḳ and Mesopotamia, succeeded at last in conquering these provinces from the Ottoman armies. In Syria, they were aided by forces of the Sharīf of Mecca, who had made himself independent in 1917 as king of the Ḥidjāz. The Russians, in the meantime, had made considerable progress in north-eastern Anatolia, but from this side the danger came abruptly to an end with the Russian Revolution, and the peace of Brest-Litowsk (3 March 1918) gave back to Turkey the lost territory, besides Ḳars, Ardahān and Batum. Soon afterwards, the war with the other powers came to an end by the armistice of Mudros [see MONDROS] (30 October 1918). Subsequently, Istanbul was occupied by Allied troops; France occupied the whole of northern Syria and Cilicia, Britian occupied the so far unconquered parts of northern Mesopotamia, including Mawṣil, and Italian troops landed in Antalya. Greece was allowed to occupy eastern Thrace and Izmīr in May 1919. All this the Istanbul government had to witness passively. The Turkish parliament, convoked in January 1920, took for a moment a firmer attitude by adopting the so-called National Pact (*mīthāḳ-i millī* [*q.v.*]); but when in March the Allied occupation of Istanbul was rendered more severe, the parliament was dissolved. Finally, in August, the Ottoman government was compelled to sign the Treaty of Sèvres, by which large parts of the remaining Ottoman territory, including Istanbul and Izmīr, were brought under the control of one or more foreign powers. In the meantime, another, interior, enemy had risen against the Ottoman government as a result of the organised national opposition against the foreign occupations, especially the Greeks' landing in Izmīr. In the course of 1920, the Istanbul government lost gradually all control over Anatolia, and the measures undertaken with Allied help to restore its authority failed. Under the growing successes of the nationalists, the authority of the sultan's government increasingly dwindled, and the Great National Assembly of Ankara, under the leadership of Muṣṭafā Kemāl Atatürk [*q.v.*], was able at last to pronounce on 1 November 1922 the abolition of the Istanbul government and the deposition of sultan Meḥemmed VI Waḥīd al-Dīn. This meant nothing less than the extinction of the Ottoman empire and its dynasty. Istanbul and eastern Thrace were occupied by nationalist troops and the last sultan left his capital, which now ceased to be the capital of Turkey. The only remnant of the dynastic tradition was that ʿAbd ül-Medjīd II, son of sultan ʿAbd ül-ʿAzīz, continued to reside in Istanbul as *Khalīfa*. This dignity was abolished by decree of the Great National Assembly of 2 March 1924; ʿAbd ül-Medjīd, as well as all other members of the dynasty of ʿOthmān, were at the same time banished from Turkey; it was to be some fifty years before they were allowed back into Turkey.

Such was the outcome of a long series of events, in which the inner development of the empire played no less a part than the outward political circumstances. The *Tanẓīmāt* period, in fact, was a no less powerful factor in the dissolution than the political interest of foreign powers. The *Tanẓīmāt* [*q.v.*] were a more deliberate continuation of the reforming measures under Selīm III and Maḥmūd II, and they were by no means the execution of a programme supported by a large group of the population. Re**sh**īd Pa**sh**a, ʿĀlī Pa**sh**a and their helpers wanted to turn Turkey into a modern state ruled by a council of ministers, whose president kept the title of *ṣadr-i aʿẓam*, but their methods were those of an absolute government in the name of the sultans, who did not in the beginning interfere. When, however, the first real constitution was elaborated by Midḥat Pa**sh**a [*q.v.*], it happened that the new sultan ʿAbd ül-Ḥamīd II preferred to govern himself, and with the same absolutist methods as his predecessors; only his aim became ever less the copying of a western European state, but rather the strengthening and the securing of the position of the sovereign, to which end there was finally developed the notorious system of censorship and espionage which has made known this period in Turkish history as *dewr-i istibdād* "the period of despotism". This period cannot be called reactionary in that it abolished the institutions of the *Tanẓīmāt*; it opposed only some consequences of the reforms. The reforms had brought into existence a middle class of intellectuals of Turkish speech and Islamic religious tradition, mostly divided between the army and the state functionaries and, in a less degree, the *ʿulemāʾ*. These intellectuals, of very different extraction, had developed a new ideal of patriotism, as reflected most eloquently in Nāmıḳ Kemāl's [*q.v.*] *Waṭan*, and they had begun to form a public opinion that claimed a certain influence in the government of the state. About this time was also born the Turkish daily press [see DJARĪDA. iii]. Gradually, as this social group took more definite forms, it became ever more separated from the different groups of the Christian and Jewish population, and also from the non-Turkish speaking Muslims in the Asiatic provinces. At the same time, however, relations between Christianity and Islam had worsened since the beginning of the 19th century as a result of the subjection of many Islamic countries to the rule of Christian powers.

By this process was generated Pan-Islamic feeling [see PAN-ISLAMISM] and Istanbul, as the capital of the relatively most powerful independent Islamic state, became the political capital of Islam. With a great many of the Turkish intellectuals, and among them chiefly the *ʿulemāʾ*, Pan-Islamic feeling surpassed the still somewhat vague patriotism. Moreover, Islamic sentiment found sympathy with the lower classes of the Turkish population, still strongly imbued with mystical traditions, and with the non-Turkish Muslims of the empire. ʿAbd ül-Ḥamīd, while emphasising his dignity as *Khalīfa*, relied mainly on Islamic sentiment, though, in course of time, the persons who surrounded the ever more suspicious monarch came to be of the worst kind. Utterances of patriotism were opposed in the most drastic way and many intellectuals had to take refuge abroad. The growing opposition against the *istibdād* found at last a means of organising itself in the province of Macedonia, since 1906 governed by a Turkish governor under European control. Salonica became the centre of the new patriotic, more conscious, Young Turkish movement, led by the Committee of Unity and Progress [see ITTIḤĀD WE TERAḲḲĪ DJEMʿIYYETI] and supported to a great extent by the army. Its influence obliged the sultan to promulgate again the constitution of Midḥat Pa**sh**a on 24 June 1908 and to abolish at once the onerous system of censorship and espionage. In November, the first Ottoman parliament came together [see MADJLIS. 4. A. ii], but in the troubled years that followed this parliament never had the opportunity to exert a real influence on the government. On 13 April 1909 followed an attempt to re-establish the sultan's former authority; this time the Young Turkish cause could only be saved by the occupation of the capital by the Macedonian army and the deposition of the sultan (27 April).

Then, for a time, Ottomanism became the political ideal, meaning the equality of all Islamic and non-Islamic elements in the state. But it soon appeared that these elements were already too much estranged from each other, so that the foundation of a strong state on these principles became impossible. The Young Turks, under the influence of the ideas of Pan-Turkism [*q.v.*], began now a policy with the final object of making the Ottoman empire a state where the Turkish element should be predominant; they turned to the lower Turkish-speaking classes, especially in Anatolia, to form a real Turkish nation. Pan-Islamism, too, was propagated again by several persons as a way of attaining this aim, but this course was gradually abandoned, although used occasionally for outward political manifestations. The very unfavourable international development after the revolution, however, brought the Young Turkish rulers to measures that certainly were not originally on the programme, such as the Armenian massacres during the war and the severe government in Syria. And as a consequence of the final loss of nearly all non-Turkish territory in the war, Turkish nationalism was born at last, the simplest and at the same time the most effective form of Turkish patriotism, not hampered by any ideas of religion or original racial connections.

The statesmen who had carried out the *Tanẓīmāt* programme had been careful not to offend the religious scruples of the leaders of orthodox Islam. In spite of the remonstrances of foreign representatives, no measures were taken that were in direct conflict with the *sharīʿa*, though the application in practice might have been changed. The *sharīʿa* was also the basis of the new Civil Code or *Medjelle* [*q.v.*]. In Midḥat's constitution, Islam was declared the state religion and the *Sheykh al-Islām* was given a rank as high as the grand vizier. This wise religious policy could not prevent, however, occasional religious outbursts of which Christians were the victims, as in 1858 at Djidda and in 1860 at Damascus, both places situated outside the purely Turkish provinces. Under ʿAbd ül-Ḥamīd, religious activity was mainly under the influence of Pan-Islamism, shown in the various attempts to enter into relations with Muslims in all parts of the world. Even the Young Turkish government did not refrain from proclaiming the Holy War on its entering the First World War. In their internal administration, the Young Turks clearly opposed the influence of the religious authorities, as was proved by their attempt in 1917 to bring the *medreses* under the administration of the Ministry of Public Instruction. Another break with the Islamic tradition was the reform of the calendar. In 1789 the Greek Julian calendar had already been introduced officially for the financial administration, but by a curious compromise the era of the Hidjra was preserved (*sene-yi māliyye*); and in 1917 the Gregorian calendar was adopted. The Christian era came gradually into use after the war.

It was also through the *Tanẓīmāt* measures that

domestic administration was separated from the military by the laws concerning the *wilāyets*. The chief occupation of the Department of the Interior was still for a long time tax-gathering. The Europeanisation and centralisation of the financial system proved to be one of the chief difficulties, as a reliable corps of functionaries had to be created at the same time. After the Crimean War, Turkey was able to conclude a number of foreign loans, but the money was not well administered nor well-used. In 1876, a state bankruptcy had to be declared, with foreign intervention as a consequence and the establishment of the service of the Public Debt, which was very much resented in all Turkish circles. A serious hindrance for the recovery of the finances was also the antiquated custom rules of the capitulations, although the original dues of 3% were several times raised. After the Young Turk Revolution, however, the greatest difficulties seemed to have been overcome.

The new Turkish army created gradually by conscription, after the suppression of the Janissaries, had during this period many occasions to show its valour. It contributed considerably to the strengthening of the patriotic Turkish spirit and played an important role in the Revolution. After 1856 it was theoretically admitted that Christians and Jews also could be enrolled, but in practice they always liberated themselves by paying an exemption tax, the *bedel-i ʿaskerī* [see BADAL]. It was only after the Young Turk Revolution that these non-Turkish elements also became Turkish soldiers.

Bibliography: Among the sources of Ottoman political history the historiographical literature of the Ottoman Turks themselves takes the first place. For this literature it is sufficient to refer to F. Babinger, *Die Geschichtsschreiber der Osmanen und ihre Werke*, Leipzig 1927. The study of documentary sources is still in its beginnings; historical documents have been published in various places, as in the *TOEM* (*TTEM*) and in the works of the Turkish historian Aḥmed Refīḳ. Some of the *Ḳānūn-nāmes* have been published in *TOEM* and other Turkish publications. For the treaties of the Ottoman empire, a most valuable collection is to be found in Gabriel Effendi Noradounghian, *Recueil d'actes internationaux de l'Empire Ottoman*, 4 vols., Paris 1897-1903. On the epigraphical sources there are important monographs, such as those of K͟halīl Edhem and the less ancient publications of Mubārek G͟hālib. The chief work on Ottoman numismatics is still Ismāʿīl G͟hālib, *Taḳwīm-i meskūkāt-i ʿOt͟hmāniyye*, Istanbul 1307, besides other publications (such as Aḥmed Refīḳ, *ʿOthmānlī imperator lug͟hunda meskūkāt*, in *TTEM*, nos. 6, 7, 8, 10; *British Museum catal. oriental coins*, viii); but see further on this, below, IX. Numismatics.

Of non-Turkish literary sources, the Oriental ones have been partly treated by Babinger in his bibliographical work. Among the Western sources, the Byzantine historians are of extraordinary importance for the first centuries of the Ottoman empire (Phrantzes, Ducas, Chalcocondyles, Critobulos). Since the 15th century a very important place is also taken by the *Relazioni* of the Venetian bailos, to be consulted in the great publications of Albèri (Florence 1839-63) and Barozzi and Berchet (Venice 1856-77). To them were added in course of time the reports of the representatives of other governments that entered into relations with the Porte. To the same category may be reckoned the numerous descriptions of travels in the Ottoman empire by European travellers, beginning in the 16th century. Not sharply separated from the travel literature are the many descriptions of the Turks and of the Ottoman empire, of which the best known is d'Ohsson, *Tableau général de l'Empire Ottoman*, 3 vols., Paris 1787-1820. This kind of literature continued all through the 19th century (the important works of Ubicini) and the beginning of the 20th century.

The first great "general" work on Ottoman Turkish history was Josef von Hammer's *Geschichte des osmanischen Reiches*, 10 vols., Pest 1827-35; zweite verbesserte Ausgabe, 4 vols., Pest 1834-6 (French translation by J.J. Hellert, *Histoire de l'Empire Ottoman*, 9 vols., Paris 1835-43). This work is for the greater part based on Turkish literary sources and ends with the peace of Küčük Ḳaynard͟ja in 1774; vol. x contains an extensive list of works concerning Ottoman history which had appeared in Europe until 1774. A work of the same scope is J.W. Zinkeisen, *Geschichte des Osmanischen Reiches in Europa*, 7 vols. (until 1812), Hamburg 1840 and Gotha 1854-63; Zinkeisen used Western sources much more than von Hammer, but did not draw directly from original Turkish sources. The same is the case with N. Jorga, *Geschichte des Osmanischen Reiches*, 5 vols. (until 1912), Gotha 1908-13. The *Histoire de l'Empire Ottoman* of de la Jonquière, 2 vols., Paris 1914, is important for its historical treatment of the end of the 19th and the beginning of the 20th century. Among the several works that treat only a certain period of Ottoman history may be mentioned G. Rosen, *Geschichte der Türkei* (*1826-56*), Leipzig 1866.

As a result of the greater interest in Turkish history after the First World War, there began to be published in 1922 the *Mitteilungen zur Osmanischen Geschichte*, by F. von Kraelitz and P. Wittek, the first journal published in the West, before the advent of *Archivum Ottomanicum*, specifically devoted to Ottoman studies; it unfortunately ran for only two years, but more recently, various specialised journals and series have appeared in Turkey itself, such as *Belleten, Tarih Dergisi*, etc. carrying on the tradition of the Ottoman period and after *TOEM* (see above).

Of more recent works on Ottoman history, there is first of all a good bibliography by H.-J. Kornrumpf, *Osmanische Bibliographie mit besonderer Berücksichtigung der Türkei in Europa*, Leiden-Köln 1973. Of general works covering the post-1500 period, see R.H. Davison, *Turkey, a short history*, Englewood Cliffs, N.J. 1968, repr. Beverley, Yorks. 1981; İ.H. Danişmend, *İzahlı Osmanlı tarihi kronolojisi*, 2nd ed. 5 vols., Istanbul 1971-2; S.J. and Ezel Kural Shaw, *History of the Ottoman empire and modern Turkey*, 2 vols., Cambridge 1976-7 (extensive bibls.); R. Mantran (ed.), *Histoire de l'empire ottoman*, Paris 1989 (authoritative chapters by various specialists).

For the earlier part of this post-1500 period, see İ.H. Uzunçarşılı, *Osmanlı tarihi*, ii-iv, Ankara 1949-59; Halil Inalcik, *The Ottoman empire, the classical age 1300-1600*, London 1973; M.A. Cook (ed.), *A history of the Ottoman empire*, Cambridge 1976 (= chs. from the *Camb. hist. of Islam* and the *New Camb. modern history*).

For the later part of this same period, there is the unsatisfactory work of H.A.R. Gibb and H. Bowen, *Islamic society and the West*, 2 vols., London 1950-7, and the classic by B. Lewis, *The emergence of modern Turkey*, London 1961, revised ed. London 1968; see also the chs. by H.J. Kissling, H. Scheel and G. Jäschke in *The Muslim world, a historical survey* (= Hdb. der Orientalistik), iii. *The last great Muslim empires*, Leiden 1969, iv. *Modern times*, Leiden 1981.

For the Dhimmī communities, see the papers collected in B. Braude and B. Lewis (eds.), *Christians and Jews in the Ottoman empire, the functioning of a plural society*, 2 vols., New York 1982.

(J.H. Kramers*)

II. Social and Economic History

The periodisation current in Ottoman political history (see I. above) is only to a limited extent usable by social and economic historians. An alternative periodisation uses the manner of taxing the population as a starting point: a formative period down to the middle of the 9th/15th century, a "classical" age dominated by the *tīmār*, lasting to the end of the 10th/16th century, a "tax farming" period down to the middle of the 13th/19th century, followed by an age in which direct taxation gained ground, and which lasted to the end of the empire.

An alternative periodisation is based upon the development of commerce: again, a formative period lasts till the middle of the 9th/15th century, characterised by limited regional and local trade and concentration of international commerce in a few centres, principally Bursa. The second period continues to the end of the 10th/16th century, and its salient feature is the development of Istanbul into a giant city, by far the largest in both Europe and the Mediterranean region, providing a proportional stimulus to internal trade. A third period begins with the political and economic crisis of the 990s/1580s, when northern European merchants enter the Mediterranean in force. Their demands change patterns in the spice and silk trades and have an impact on production in certain regions, such as Syria or the Aegean seaboard. After the crisis of the late 10th/16th and early 11th/17th centuries, there is some recovery, which, however, is soon interrupted by the Habsburg-Ottoman war of 1095/1683 to 1110-11/1699. In the early 12th/18th century, most regions enter upon a prolonged expansion in commerce and manufacturing, whose end in the 1170s and 1180s/1760s-1770s coincides with a period of prolonged warfare. This decade should be regarded as the end of the third period. Economic dislocation and penetration by European powers characterise the fourth period, which can be subdivided by a date marking the time at which the transition of the most developed European countries to the factory system began to affect the empire's economy. Traditionally, the Anglo-Ottoman trade convention of 1254/1838 has been favoured; but since recent research has cast doubt on the significance of this date, the end of the Napoleonic Wars in 1815 constitutes an alternative "turning point". This second division of the fourth period continued until the end of the Ottoman empire. Scholars working within dependency and world systems paradigms stress the late 10/16th century as the period when the Ottoman economy was first affected by European penetration, and the years around 1215/1800 when final incorporation ensued.

Thus periodisations according to different socio-economic criteria have resulted in "turning points" at about the same dates, and there is some similarity to the periodisation used in political history. This may be due to the strong impact of the Ottoman state upon the economic life of its subjects, but also to the habituation of present-day historians to these particular "turning points".

The governing class and its subjects

Ottoman society before the *Tanẓīmāt* [*q.v.*] was divided into *ʿaskerī*s who served the Sultan as soldiers or officials, owing allegiance to him alone (many of them slaves, *ḳul*), and the tax-paying subjects or *reʿāyā* [see raʿiyya. 2]. *ʿAskerī*s were exempt from most taxes, and society's wealth was concentrated in their hands. Ottoman authors of the 10th/16th and 11th/17th centuries, particularly the historian Muṣṭafā ʿĀlī, emphasised the rigidity of the *reʿāyā-ʿaskerī* boundary. In their view, *ʿaskerī*s were to be recruited from among the sons of *ʿaskerī*s, except in the case of officials with religious-juridical training (*ʿulemā*), the study of the *sheriʿat* being open to all. In reality, other *ʿaskerī*s were also recruited from among the *reʿāyā*. Soldiers distinguishing themselves on the frontier were awarded a *timār* and thus joined the ranks of the *sipāhī*s. Christian peasant boys recruited through the *dewshirme* [*q.v.*] might rise to the rank of vizier, and the financial bureaucracy, which as a separate career evolved in the 10th/16th century, was entered by men from diverse social backgrounds. However, the status of many officials from non-*ʿaskerī* families and who were not recruited through the *dewshirme* was often precarious, with some of them experiencing denunciation and demotion.

As a *ḳul*, an Ottoman official was beholden for his entire career to the sultan, who could promote, demote and even execute him at will. His children did not inherit the right to any specific official post, even though by the 10th/16th century, the sons of *sipāhī*s by virtue of their birth could apply for a *timār* when they had reached the appropriate age. Other officials introduced their sons to potential patrons who might further their career in the military, scribal or financial services. Special rules of promotion applied to *ʿulemā*, who after completing their studies taught in a sequence of progressively higher-ranking *medrese*s before they became eligible for the office of *ḳāḍī* [see ʿilmiyye]. Alone among the *ʿaskerī*s, *ʿulemā*ʾ officials' estates reverted to their heirs, while the estates of *ḳul*s were in principle confiscated. The extreme dependence of *ḳul* officials upon the ruler reminded contemporaries of slavery: an Egyptian *shaykh* of the 10th/16th century challenged Ottoman officials as unworthy of ruling over free Muslims, unless they could present formal proof of manumission.

The ascendancy of the *ḳul*s within the Ottoman ruling group dates to the reign of Meḥemmed II the Conqueror (848-50/1444-6 and 855-86/1451-81 [*q.v.*]). He severely curtailed the role of the Anatolian Turkish aristocracy, from which his first Grand Vizier Čandarlīzāde Khalīl Pasha (killed 857/1453 [see djandarlī]) had come. Khalīl Pasha was executed, and many magnates were forcibly separated from their adherents by resettlement in Rūmeli. Numerous large landholdings and pious foundations were confiscated and converted into *timār*s. This measure increased the number of warriors at the disposal of the central state. But after Meḥemmed II's death, his son Bāyezīd II (886-918/1481-1512 [*q.v.*]) returned many properties and pious foundations to their previous holders.

The 10th/16th century saw the *dewshirme*-recruited *ḳul*s at the height of their power. Their number included Grand Viziers such as Ḳānūnī Süleymān's one-time favourite Ibrāhīm Pasha (killed 942/1536) and his successors Rüstem Pasha (died 968/1561) and Sinān Pasha (died 1004/1596). While recruitment through the *dewshirme* remained a privilege of the sultan, high-ranking officials sometimes trained young *ḳul*s in their own households; these might be taken over into the sultan's service. Prominent administrators often had their relatives and countrymen recruited through the *dewshirme*; this gave rise to the formation of patronage networks and regional groupings. A particularly successful example was the Ṣoḳollu [*q.v.*] clan, founded by Ṣoḳollu Meḥmed Pas͟ha (killed 987/1579), who acted as Grand Vizier to Ḳānūnī Süleymān (926-74/1520-66 [*q.v.*]), Selīm II (974-82/1566-74 [*q.v.*]) and Murād III (982-1003/1574-94 [*q.v.*]). In the later 10th/16th century, the "easterners", who came from the Caucasus and often had seen service in the Persian administration, opposed the "westerners", a group which included Serbs, Croats and Albanians.

In the 11th/17th century, the *dews͟hirme* became less important as a mode of recruitment into the Ottoman ruling group. High-level officials now took promising young men into their households and launched them on to their careers, thereby securing their own positions. Loyalty to one's patron constituted one of the principal virtues of an Ottoman gentleman. Rivalries between members of different households were commonplace. The household of the *S͟heyk͟h ül-Islām* Fayḍ Allāh Efendi (killed 1115/1703), well-documented through the *S͟heyk͟h ül-Islām*'s autobiography, demonstrates the manner in which the system operated; yet Fayḍ Allāh in part fell from power because of excessive nepotism. Patronage relations continued to be important well through the *Tanẓīmāt* period, even though the differences in legal status between *ʿaskerī*s and *reʿāyā*, as well as the sultan's right to execute his servitors at will, were abolished by the guarantees of life, liberty and property promulgated by the *Tanẓīmāt fermānı̊*.

The coherence of the political structure was ensured by the sultan, in whose name the *ʿaskerī*s ruled and collected taxes. As the victor over heretics and infidels, the sultan legitimised the entire state. Spectacular failure in war was a reason for deposing a ruler, thus Meḥemmed IV (1058-99/1648-87 [*q.v.*]) and Muṣṭafā II (1106-15/1695-1703 [*q.v.*]) lost their thrones due to the outcome of the Ottoman-Habsburg war of 1095-1111/1683-99. Down to the late 10th/16th century, the ruler was expected to take the field in person, and the historian Muṣṭafā ʿĀlī censured Murād III for failing to do so. Well into the reign of Ḳānūnī Süleymān, the ruler dined regularly in front of his soldiers even in peacetime, thereby documenting his good health and preparedness for war. However, in his later years, Ḳānūnī Süleymān developed a different style of palace life; now the remoteness of the ruler and the fact that he rarely spoke in public were regarded as proof of his dignity. From the later 10th/16th century onwards, the sultan was no longer required to take an active role in government, and administration lay in the hands of Palace dignitaries and the Grand Vizier; the Grand Vizier's power was particularly great during the Köprülü vizierates (1066-1122/1656-1710 [see KÖPRÜLÜ]).

Tension between *ʿaskerī*s and *reʿāyā* focused on the status of men serving as soldiers without possessing the rights of *ʿaskerī*s. In the 11th/17th and 12th/18th centuries, provincial governors recruited and paid their own forces; the latter possessed no official status and lost their jobs when the employing *pas͟ha* lost his, a frequent occurrence. In the 11th/17th century, these men often rose in rebellion to safeguard their positions, or else forced the employing *pas͟ha* to do so. Unemployed mercenaries turned to highway robbery, against which Anatolian villagers at the end of the 10th/16th and 11th/17th centuries defended themselves by organising their own militias. Conflicts between mercenaries in the service of a *pas͟ha*, unemployed soldiers and village militias constituted the civil wars known as the D͟jelālī rebellions [*q.v.* in Suppl.]. In Rumeli mercenaries of *reʿāyā* background fighting on the frontier were thrown out of employment when the Ottoman empire lost territory in the peace of Ḳarlofča (1110-/1699 [*q.v.*]) and later peace treaties; this was the background of the *hayduk* rebellions.

Peasant status and power in the countryside

Down to the end of the 10th/16th century, the Ottoman élite's principal means of controlling the *reʿāyā* was the *tīmār*. *Tīmār* holders (*sipāhī*s) at this time constituted the backbone of the army, but also were in charge of local administration. Peasants were not permitted to leave their farmsteads without the permission of the *sipāhī*. If they did, the *tīmār* holder could have them returned by applying to the *ḳāḍī*'s court within a delay varying between ten and twenty years according to the locality. However, the responsibility of proof was on the *sipāhī*, and many migrants were able to provide witnesses testifying to their residence for the requisite period. Ottoman regulations accepted the existence of *reʿāyā* not included in the official tax registers (*taḥrīr*) (*k͟hārid͟j ez defter*). The latter migrated, and only if they continued to reside in the same place for a prolonged period of time, were they entered in the *taḥrīr* register.

Farmland and pasture normally belonged to the state, and the peasant owned only his house, gardens and vineyards. Peasant tenures passed from father to son, other relatives inherited against payment of an entry fine (*resm-i ṭapu*). Daughters were originally excluded; with the increasing impact of *s͟herīʿat* inheritance rules from the end of the 10th/16th century onwards, they were admitted in the absence of sons. Peasants in the 10th/16th century were forbidden to sell their tenures without the consent of the relevant *tīmār* holder, foundation administrator or grantee of crown lands. However, such permission was often granted, and by the end of the century in some regions we encounter a lively land market. In the Kayseri area, fields formally owned as private property became widespread in the course of the 12th/17th century. The Ottoman land law of 1274-75/1858 [see MARʿĀ. 3. In Turkey] sanctioned the transition to private property, which in the Ottoman core lands had been going on for several centuries. But in those areas where land had been tribally owned this law furthered the formation of large-scale private property, as tribal leaders registered communal lands as their own.

Taxation rates varied from region to region; the determining factor was often historical circumstance, rather than the productivity of a given area. The tithe (*ʿös͟hür*) was higher than one-tenth, as a share for the tax collector (*salāriyye*) was usually included. In parts of eastern and central Anatolia, where taxes were shared between the state and private landowners, the peasants paid a double tithe (*mālikāne-dīwānī*). In Syria and Palestine, tithes might amount to a quarter or a third of the crop. Tithes were demanded in kind; in addition, the peasants paid money taxes both to the *tīmār* holder and to the central administration. The proportion of total dues payable in money varied according to time and place.

In the early Ottoman period, peasants provided labour services for their *sipāhī* (*yedi ḳulluḳ*, "seven services"). When the regulations preceding Ottoman tax registers, the so-called *ḳānūn-nāme*, codified peasant-*sipāhī* relations in the 9th/15th and 10th/16th centuries, most labour dues had been commuted to payments in money and in kind. However, even at this time, peasants were obliged to build a tithe barn for their owner, and cart the *sipāhī*'s grain to the nearest market. The judges' protocols (*ḳāḍī sidjilleri*) of certain provinces record the tensions ensuing from these relationships, such as disputes as to what constituted the nearest market. Conversion of dues in kind into money payments caused difficulties in areas remote from the main thoroughfares, where opportunities for commercialisation were few. In the late 10th/16th and early 11th/17th centuries, *reʿāyā* attempts to shake off *sipāhī* control can also be traced through the justice rescripts (*ʿadālet fermānlarī*). The *ʿadālet-nāme* of 1058/1648 explains that it was not sufficient if peasants paid their taxes to the *sipāhī* or other legal claimant to the village revenue; they also owed him submission and obedience. But the *sipāhī*'s frequent absence on campaign, the limited material means at his disposal and peasant access to the *ḳāḍī*'s court made it impossible for the former to exercise full control over the peasants.

Down to the mid-9th/15th century, the Ottoman state probably was a "light" state, demanding but limited prestations from the *reʿāyā*. But the campaigns of Meḥemmed the Conqueror led to an increase in peasant taxes, and the contemporary chronicle of ʿĀs̲h̲iḳ-pas̲h̲a-zāde reflects the dissatisfaction of a member of the Anatolian aristocracy with the newly-emerging, much more costly state. In the 9th/15th and 10th/16th centuries, taxes were normally collected by the holders of *timār, zeʿāmet* and *k̲h̲āṣṣ*, who owed military or administrative service and therefore did not remit much cash to the central administration. From the later 10th/16th century onward, the increasing costs of war induced the central administration to progressively substitute tax farming [see MÜLTEZIM]. Tax farmers acquired the right to collect taxes at auction. The contract in principle was awarded for three years, but could be terminated earlier if a higher bid was received. A tax farmer also acted as local administrator, but could be from the *reʿāyā*. A wealthy villager might bid for the taxes of a single settlement, while the major tax farmers were rich men and occasionally women, often close to the court.

In 1106-7/1695, a new kind of tax farm was instituted, the *mālikāne* [*q.v.*], which combined features of the *timār* and the old style tax farm. The *mālikāne* holder paid a large sum of money to the treasury upon entering possession. For the remainder of his or her life, annual payments were fixed at a moderate level. *Mālikāne* holders had to be part of the Ottoman ruling group. The *mālikāne* was instituted to ease the pressure upon the *reʿāyā*, as it was claimed that long-term holders would be concerned about the future of their tax base, while ordinary *iltizām* holders were concerned only with short-term gain. However, frequent subletting for short periods tended to nullify this advantage.

Tax farmers of different types were an important component of the *aʿyān* [*q.v.*], local power holders who from the late 11th/17th century onward dominated growing sectors of the Ottoman countryside without necessarily being landowners. A major source of *aʿyān* power was the right to apportion taxes, levied *en bloc* by the central administration, among individual settlements. This allowed *aʿyāns* holding land to spare "their" peasants at the expense of their neighbours, and thus to gather a clientèle. Prominent power holders became tax gatherers for absent provincial governors, and in coastal regions with opportunities for export, marketed the produce gathered as taxes in kind, along with the saleable surpluses belonging to villagers. The Ḳara ʿOt̲h̲mān-og̲h̲ullarī of Izmir and Manisa, for instance, rose to power in this fashion. Even though the sultans of the 11th/17th and 12th/18th centuries often had the heads of *aʿyān* families executed, the treasury needed the family's services, and thus the following generation was allowed to follow in their fathers' footsteps.

Only in the reign of Maḥmūd II (1233-55/1808-38 [*q.v.*]) was this policy reversed; this sultan relied on European, particularly British, support to eliminate internal opposition. Many *aʿyāns* were executed and their possessions confiscated; those who remained were often still wealthy but no longer a political threat to Ottoman central government. Even though the major *aʿyāns* of the 12th/18th and 13th/19th centuries had considerable military forces at their disposal, only a few of them seem to have aimed at political independence. Culturally speaking, they looked toward Istanbul, and in their residences imitated the mural paintings then current in the Palace and the wealthy dwellings of the capital. Some of them fostered an interesting adaptation of rococo and empire decorative styles.

Landholdings in the hands of wealthy power holders are known as *čiftliks* [*q.v.*]. Recent research downplays the importance of market-oriented large-scale production before the 13th/19th century. Such production occurred, by the end of the 11th/17th century, in the western Black Sea region with a view toward the Istanbul market. In the 12th/18th century, *čiftliks* spread to Macedonia, and part of their production was now destined for export. Many *čiftliks* used sharecroppers in addition to wage labourers and a small number of slaves. Most of them were not large, and those that were, often appropriated some of the product which, under the earlier régime, had been left in the hands of the peasants. Saleable surpluses were normally produced by peasants, and the power holders reserved for themselves the profits of commercialisation.

Peasant production

In its vast majority, the Ottoman population consisted of settled peasants producing mainly for their subsistence and controlling their family farms. Peasants grew wheat and barley, leaving a one-year fallow period between crops. Rye and millet were of secondary importance. Oil was gained from plants, such as sesame, linseed or poppy; melted butter was also widely consumed. Olives were important in northern Syria, Crete and northwestern Anatolia. But olive oil was largely used for lighting; its use as a food seems to have been secondary. Grapes were consumed as raisins and grape syrup, most towns being surrounded by a belt of gardens and vineyards. Non-Muslims also produced wine, which Ḳānūnī Süleymān forbade them to sell in public. But at least in Ottoman Hungary, the prohibition was hard to enforce, as the *timār* holders of this area had taken over the monopoly of wine sales during part of the year (*monopolya*). Honey was also produced.

Certain regional specialities were highly esteemed; thus English merchants of the 11th/17th century were granted the privilege of exporting a small quantity of Aegean raisins for the table of their king. During the same period, Malatya was already renowned for high-quality fruit, while hazel nuts were found on the Black Sea coast. Cotton cultivation, according to 10th/16th century tax registers, was significant in certain parts of Syria [see KUṬN. 2. In the Ottoman empire], in the Adana region and on the Aegean coast, while flax was grown in northwestern Anatolia. Tobacco appeared in the central Anatolian countryside by the beginning of the 12th/17th century, introduced by soldiers who had become accustomed to its use on the Hungarian frontier. Tobacco cultivation spread in spite of repeated prohibitions. Many specialty crops have persisted in the same locations for several centuries.

In the 10th/16th century, rice [see RUZZ] was still a luxury. It was cultivated mainly in the areas of Filibe (Plovdiv) and Boyabat in northern Anatolia. Rice was rarely grown by ordinary peasants, but by specialised labourers, working under supervision and without any farms of their own. They were exempt from the taxes payable by other peasants. Possibly they had originally been war captives, although there is room for debate whether rice growers were better or worse off than ordinary peasants. Maize entered western Rumeli and northern Anatolia during the 11th/17th and 12th/18th centuries. Villagers dependent on landlords (so-called *čiftlik* villagers) sometimes cultivated wheat for their masters and maize for their own consumption.

Small-scale irrigation [see MĀʾ. 8. Irrigation in the Ottoman empire] was widespread throughout the Empire, even though 10th/16th century plans to make a "second Egypt" out of the lake districts of central Anatolia did not come to fruition. Water power was used for industrial purposes, particularly the milling of flour; 10th/16th century tax registers record the number of mills in each village, and often the number of months during which available water supplies permitted operation. In villages near 10th/16th and 11th/17th century Salonica, water power was used for the fulling of woollen cloth, while in the Bursa-Izmit area, sawing mills were also water-driven. These activities were market-oriented and therefore located in the vicinity of larger towns.

Urban merchants in certain regions intervened in village production. In the second half of the 10th/16th century, Ankara merchants had angora wool spun in steppe villages, while in the more immediate vicinity of the city, cloth was woven. Similar arrangements existed in the Bursa and Aydın cotton manufactures. This putting-out system coexisted with the direct marketing of rural products by peasants.

Most peasant marketing was probably undertaken to earn the cash needed for taxes. In many parts of 10th/16th century Anatolia, markets expanded as population increased. Only occasionally did rural dwellers demand urban goods and services, such as jewelry or repairs to a heavy plough. Itinerant artisans catered for some of this demand, repairing copper kettles or putting up mudbrick walls. These migrant artisans, sometimes enrolled in the Janissary corps, competed with urban craftsmen. Peasant-nomad exchanges were less unequal; these took place at seasonal fairs, often sited on summer pastures used by both villagers and nomads.

Nomads and other herdsmen

Nomads in Rūmeli and Anatolia often grew some wheat, barley or cotton in their winter quarters. As many villagers on the Aegean and Mediterranean coasts migrated into the mountains in summer to escape the danger of malarial infection, social differences between peasants and nomads were less pronounced here than in sub-desert areas. Yet this did not preclude disputes about fields and gardens damaged by nomad flocks, or outright robbery on the part of armed and mounted tribesmen. Nomads and semi-nomads were important to the urban transport economy, as they raised the horses, camels and mules needed by merchants and officials.

But nomads were more difficult to tax than settled peasants, and due to their possession of horses and firearms, the administration regarded them as potential robbers and rebels. The settlement of Anatolian nomads was therefore officially encouraged. Animal taxes were sometimes levied in such a manner as to endanger the reproduction of flocks. If a degree of settlement had been reached, nomad groups were reclassified as low-level districts (*nāḥiye* [*q.v.*]) settled by peasants. In the 10th/16th century, Anatolia was a land of peasants, with a nomad minority varying in size according to the region. Migration from eastern to western Anatolia probably resulted in a higher percentage of nomads in the 12th/17th century, which the earliest official attempts at forcible settlement did not change. Settlement projects continued in the 12th/18th and particularly 13th/19th centuries, after the immigration of Muslim inhabitants from the Crimea and Balkan territories lost by the Empire necessitated the creation of new opportunities for peasant settlement. Particularly in southeastern Anatolia, commercial agriculture became possible after large numbers of nomads had been forcibly settled.

In Rūmeli nomads were an important component of the population, mainly in Thrace. These *yürük*s [*q.v.*] were detribalised at an early stage, and given a military organization. The *yürük*s were organized in units called *od̲j̲ak*s [*q.v.*], some members participating in campaigns while the others financed the campaigners' equipment. From the 10th/16th century onward, nomads were no longer employed as fully-fledged soldiers but mainly as auxiliaries. Yet their services were still needed, and therefore the central administration penalised *yürük*s who settled by increasing their taxes. Ottoman Rumeli also was inhabited by Christian migrant herdsmen, the Vlachs, who enjoyed tax exemptions. With trade between central Europe and the Balkans increasing in the 12th/18th century, many Balkan herdsmen prospered as transportation entrepreneurs.

Trade

The bulk of Ottoman trade was internal. Istanbul was supplied through interregional trade, involving the shores of the Black Sea, the Aegean and even Egypt. Down into the 13th/19th century, wheat and barley came mainly from the western coasts of the Black Sea. Fruit, both fresh and dried, was supplied mainly by western Anatolia and Thessaly, while meat on the hoof came to Istanbul from the Balkan peninsula and to a lesser extent Anatolia. The capital's needs for timber and firewood were supplied largely from northwestern Anatolia, where certain forests had been set aside for the Imperial Arsenal. Around the turn of the 12th/17th century, Istanbul Janissaries were active in both the legal and the illegal trade in wood, the latter responding to the high demand for this commodity in Cairo. Melted butter arrived at the capital from the steppes to the north of the Black Sea. Agriculture and forestry in the region surrounding Istanbul thus conformed quite well to the ring pattern analysed by Von Thünen, modified by the fact that the Bosphorus permitted easy access to both the Black Sea and the Mediterranean. Aleppo's hinterland was less vast, but still encompassed southeastern Anatolia and northern Syria. The city received grain, cotton thread and cloth, silk, soap and olive oil from the surrounding region. Cairo was supplied by the Nile valley; at its ports there arrived grain, linen, linseed and vegetables.

But as the capital of the Empire, Istanbul possessed an economic advantage: as the taxes of the entire state accumulated there, purchasing power was concentrated in the city. Provincials, with limited access to the gold and silver imported through foreign trade, delivered agricultural produce and manufactured goods to Istanbul in order to earn back the cash previously paid out as taxes. According to the price lists (*narkh defterleri* [see NARKH]) of Istanbul, fabrics, leather, copperware and other specialties arrived from remote provinces. But due to the city's political advantage, its inhabitants did not pay for the goods and services they received by offering others in return.

In the 9th/15th century, Anatolian manufactured goods were exported, principally to the countries north of the Black Sea. In exchange, oil, honey, skins and hides reached Ottoman territory. The merchants conducting this trade were mainly Muslims; the conquest of Genoese Black Sea bases gave the Ottomans an advantage over the Italians, and in the course of the 10th/16th century, the Black Sea was closed to non-Ottoman traders. After the conquest of the Arab provinces Ottoman merchants and administrators controlled the trade routes passing through Egypt and Syria. Traders based in Cairo dealt with India, importing Indian fabrics and spices by way of the Red Sea. The importation of coffee from Yemen became economically significant in the second half of the 10th/16th century [see ḲAHWA]. This trade was profitable enough to counterbalance the loss of transit trade in spices to Venice, after the Dutch had monopolised the importation of spices to Europe at the beginning of the 11th/17th century. Aleppo was a major entrepot of the silk trade, where raw silk from Persia was sold to Ottoman, Venetian, English and French merchants [see ḤARĪR. ii. The Ottoman empire]. Damascene traders supplied the pilgrimage caravans, and also delivered manufactured goods to the Ḥidjāz. This expansion of the area in which Ottoman traders operated stimulated the economy in general.

While the Venetians had specialised in the transit trade in silks and spices, the English merchants, who entered the Mediterranean during the closing years of the 10th/16th century, paid for the silk they purchased with moderately-priced English cloth; their competition caused the woollens of Salonica to disappear from the market. French merchants from Marseilles bought and sold a wide range of goods, which in the 12th/18th century included woollen cloth from Languedoc. They also purchased olive oil and grain in Tunisia, and acted as shippers. The depredations of pirates and corsairs gave European ships a competitive advantage over Ottomans [see ḲURṢĀN. 2. In Turkish waters], as they were able to offer better security, and by the 12th/18th century, even trade between ports of the Ottoman Empire was largely effected in European ships.

During the 11th/17th century, Ottoman non-Muslims gained ground *vis-à-vis* their Muslim competitors, benefiting from the expansion of European trade. As the capitulatory rights granted European merchants also became more important during this period [see IMTIYĀZĀT], many members of the minorities were able to gain tax privileges by registering as servitors of foreign consulates. However, this did not preclude lively competition between Ottoman and foreign merchants. In the 12th/18th century Greek traders benefited from French involvement in wars to expand their merchant marine and establish a successful diaspora not only within the Ottoman, but also the Habsburg and Russian empires. Syrian Catholics traded in Egypt, Serbs were active in Vienna, while the woollen cloth weavers of Filibe (Plovdiv) marketed their goods throughout Anatolia. In many areas, the transformation of local economies away from manufactured goods and toward the provision of grain and raw materials to European buyers did not take place until the 13th/19th century. Capital resources accumulated by non-Muslim merchants were often used to bolster the resistance of local economies against foreign control.

Integration into the European-dominated world market during the 13th/19th century did, however, politicise pre-existing communal tensions. In the 1260s-1270s/1840s-1850s Damascus merchants involved in the supply trades encountered serious difficulty due to the increasing export of grain to Europe in which non-Muslims were active. This was the economic background to an attack on the Christian quarters of Damascus in 1276/1860.

The Ottoman government of the *Tanẓīmāt* period (1255-93/1839-76 [*q.v.*]) responded to the threat of economic and political disintegration by the construction of railways and telegraph lines, and permitted the modernisation of the major ports. However, these investments were expensive, particularly the kilometric guarantees demanded by foreign investors in the railways, so that the latters' benefit to the Ottoman economy is open to question. Most lines linked a port to the hinterland or, in cases where the government imposed its will, strategic rather than economic considerations determined the course of the railways. Ottoman spending on war and infrastructure having led to bankruptcy in 1296-97/1879, major sources of revenue were pledged to the settlement of debts and committed to administration by a consortium of creditors known as the *Dette Ottomane*. For the remainder of the empire's existence, Ottoman public spending was limited by the constraints imposed by this consortium.

Monetary developments

While the use of cash continually expanded throughout Ottoman history, even the *timār* system in its early shape could not operate without a money economy. Down to 882/1477-78, when the first Ottoman gold coin was minted, roughly corresponding in weight and fineness to the Venetian ducat, the Ottoman mints turned out silver coins only. The *aḳče* [*q.v.*] before the devaluation effected by Meḥemmed the Conqueror weighed 1.01 gr. and 0.83 gr after this event. Throughout most of the 10th/16th century, the *aḳče* stood at 0.73 gr; a new wave of devaluation occurred at the end of the 10th/16th century, at a time when imports of silver from the New World had also resulted in a price rise. The latter was viewed by contemporaries as a major calamity, affecting not only the conduct of trade but the legitimacy of the state. In spite of several currency reforms, in the course of the 11th/17th and 12th/18th centuries the *aḳče* was devalued to such an extent that it disappeared from the market and only survived as a money of account. Its place was taken by the *pāra* [*q.v.*], originally an Egyptian coin valued at twice or three times the rate of the *aḳče*, and by a number of European silver coins collectively known as *ghurūsh*. These were also debased, as the importation of low-quality European coins constituted a major business at the end of the 11th/17th century. Local mints virtually ceased operation. There was a brief experiment with a trimetallic system in the late 11th/17th century. Copper, which hitherto had been used only in small transactions, was now declared legal tender. Uncontrolled inflation led to a return to the bimetallic standard after three years.

Debasement as a means of raising revenue was abandoned in 1260/1844, when a new bimetallic system was established, based on the silver *ḳurush* and gold *lira* (100 *ḳurūsh* = 1 *līra*). This standard was adhered to till the very end of the Ottoman Empire, as monetary stability was now regarded as essential to the needs of trade. To cope with budget deficits, the authorities occasionally issued paper money and then allowed it to depreciate, or contracted the loans which finally caused the bankruptcy of 1296-97/1879 (see further, below, IX. Numismatics).

Urban artisans

Many urban producers were organised in guilds, which had adopted rituals of the *Akhīs* [*q.v.*], organisations of young men which Ibn Baṭṭūṭa encountered in many early 8th/14th century Anatolian towns; however, the *Akhīs* were not organised by craft, and the exact link between guilds and *Akhīs* is little understood. Guilds were headed by a *sheykh*, whose role was in decline by the 12th/18th century. Daily business was conducted by the *ketkhüdā* and *yigitbashi*, who were elected by the guildsmen and confirmed by the administration; guild officials purchasing their offices are also on record. Guilds were composed of masters; apprentices and hired labourers (*ishčis*) were not members, and masters tried to discipline their employees through their guilds. In some places, such as 10th/16th century Jerusalem or 12th/18th century Bursa, the guilds could be entered easily. At times, it was probably sufficient to pay the requisite taxes to be considered a guild member. But in other instances, masters refused the entry of newcomers under the pretext of insufficient skills; in Bursa, where such cases are also on record, rejected masters sometimes formed new "business centres" on the outskirts of the city.

Guildsmen often procured raw materials collectively, by agreement with the farmer of a mine or else another guild. *Yigitbashis* and *ketkhüdās* were in charge of distribution among individual artisans, and often the small masters complained that their more successful colleagues obtained more than their due; or else suppliers found it advantageous to sell to merchants at higher prices, particularly if the goods in question were also in demand in the export market. If the artisans whose interests were hurt by this intrusion of the free market made their complaints heard in Istanbul, export prohibitions were promulgated. In other cases, guildsmen preferred to abandon collective purchases altogether.

In the 11th/17th to early 13th/19th centuries, guildsmen developed a form of property known as the *gedik* [see ṢINF], which encompassed the locale and tools necessary for the exercise of a given trade. This was a response to increased demands for rent from property owners, particularly *waḳifs*, which resulted from the demand for revenue placed upon the latter by the Ottoman administration. Once a given property had been recognised as forming part of a *gedik*, it could only be turned over to another guildsman, and guild officials had to approve the transaction. This arrangement protected the interests of craftsmen in contracting trades, but made overall adjustments to changing demand more difficult. The Ottoman administration, torn between the need for increased revenue from *waḳifs* and the wish to protect its urban tax base, did not prevent *ḳāḍīs* from recognising the *gedik*.

From the government's point of view, the guilds were important as a means of securing control over the urban population. In wartime, the guilds were obliged to provide artisans accompanying the army and undertaking the maintenance and repair work needed by the soldiers. Other guilds were obliged to find rowers for the navy. Assessment was not equal, and gave rise to frequent disputes.

Prices demanded by artisans were decreed by the market inspector (*muḥtesib* [see ḤISBA]) or *ḳāḍī*, after consultation with the heads of the relevant guilds. In Istanbul and other large cities, official prices were recorded in special registers or entered into the *ḳāḍī sidjilleri*; in smaller towns only the prices for basic foodstuffs were officially promulgated. The Palace often demanded goods at less than the official price. Profit margins for artisans ranged between 10 and 20 per cent, while long-distance traders were much less closely controlled. Capital formation by artisans was difficult, although there were instances of craftsmen branching out into trade without severing their links to manufacture.

Craft guilds retained their vitality throughout the 13th/19th century, particularly in Istanbul. With European investment growing, especially in the transportation sector, guilds defended the interests of dockyard workers and others whose livelihoods were threatened by technical and organisational reshaping of enterprises. The Ottoman government, both before and after the revolution of 1326/1908, saw the revendications of these guilds as a means of augmenting its own bargaining power *vis-à-vis* foreign interests, and adopted a neutral or even favourable stance. In the long run, however, the restructuring of enterprises within the framework of dependent capitalism weakened the power of the guilds.

Not all urban handicraft workers were guild members. In 10th/16th and 11th/17th century Bursa, slaves were employed by silk weavers and merchants; after manumission, some of them set up independent businesses and then joined the guilds. Women working for artisans also were not usually members. New migrants to the city, unable to enter a guild, often made a living as street sellers; this was resented by the guildsmen, as these unorganised competitors paid no taxes. During the migrations which accompanied the Djelālī rebellions (late 10th/16th-early 11th/17th centuries) many such migrants were active in towns along the principal routes to Istanbul. Some of the migrants were destitute; at the end of the 10th/16th century, a prison was built in Üsküdar to facilitate catching these people and sending them back to their places of origin.

Urban society and spatial structure

In Ottoman cities, most artisan activities took place in the *čarshi*, a district filled by *khāns*, the covered market (*bedestān*) and *waḳif*-owned shops. Only transients renting accommodation in a *khān* resided in the *čarshi*. Down to the middle of the 13th/19th century, construction in residential quarters was not planned by any central authority, which only from time to time decreed that encumbrances in public thoroughfares needed to be removed, or that non-Muslims must not reside in Muslim quarters so that existing mosques would be ensured of a congregation. Most day-to-day affairs were in the hands of the *ketkhüdās* of town quarters or communities, disputes being adjudicated by the *ḳāḍīs*. From the *Tanẓīmāt* period onwards, newly-founded town quarters were sometimes designed according to a master plan; the Ottoman administration was concerned about securing streets wide enough for wheeled traffic and the passage of fire trucks. In Istanbul and Bursa, neighbourhoods in fashionable areas were reorganised according to criteria derived from contemporary French urban planning; by the late 13th/19th century, the results of such planning were seen in Anatolian provincial towns as well. To administer these projects, special administrations were instituted; these involved the creation of representative bodies through which urban élites influenced planning.

Building styles in vernacular architecture varied according to the region but also the time period involved. The impact of Istanbul models can be discerned in 13th/19th century houses in present-day Greece, Bulgaria and Albania and also in western and central Anatolia. In the area where Istanbul influences were strong, such as in Ankara from the late 11th/17th century onwards, multi-story buildings were common; in certain places, upper floors were often reserved for summer use. Houses of this type contained numerous windows overlooking the street, with special arrangements to prevent passers-by from looking in. In Syria, houses were built around a courtyard, turning only a blind wall to the street. Normally a house was inhabited by a single family, but exceptions to this rule were numerous, such as poor families sharing a single courtyard. "Apartments" were in use in Cairo and possibly also in parts of 12th/18th century Istanbul.

Social dynamics

In the 9th/15th and 10th/16th centuries, high and medium-level officials as well as merchants possessed opportunities for capital formation, but *ᶜaskerīs* were the dominant group. *ᶜAskerīs* enjoyed greater revenues than *reᶜāyā*, although apart from the *ᶜulemāʾ* they were not usually able to transfer their fortunes to their heirs. *ᶜAskerīs* also controlled the economic power of the state apparatus, which was the largest single entrepreneur in the land. Mines were mostly owned by the state, and large enterprises such as the Arsenal and major building sites were financed and run by the central administration. Ottoman authors emphasised the submission of all officials to the will of the sultan, but many *ᶜaskerīs* were able to use political opportunities for private gain. Merchant-*ᶜaskerī* conflicts are only documented indirectly; late 10th/16th and 11th/17th century texts wax eloquent concerning the corrupting power of money, but nowhere do we find the assumption that the handling of money is exclusively the province of the merchant. Some Ottoman officials subscribed to the view, derived from the teachings of Ibn Khaldūn, that gainful activity should be reserved for the *reᶜāyā*, but this view was challenged by others. In most instances, *ᶜaskerīs* viewed their economic interests as coinciding with those of the state in general. The Ottoman state should not be viewed as an abstract entity totally separate from the *ᶜaskerī* class.

Down to the second half of the 12th/18th century, Ottoman power rested on the agricultural revenues of a vast territory and on the control of internal trade routes. Revenues from international commerce were of secondary importance. Commercialisation of agricultural revenues was important from at least the 9th/15th century, and increased particularly in the 10th/16th and 12th/18th centuries. In the 9th/15th and 10th/16th centuries, Muslims dominated a large share of Ottoman trade, including certain branches of international commerce. Non-Muslims rose to prominence with the expansion of trade with Europe; but down to the late 12th/18th century, Muslims continued to be very active as merchants, although they had lost control of shipping, and certain, though not all, local industries succumbed to European competition. The role of many non-Muslim merchants involved not only co-operation with Europeans but also strenuous competition. The Ottoman realm was integrated into the world economy dominated by Europe only after a protracted struggle.

Bibliography: Ömer Lütfi Barkan, *Türk-Islam toprak hukuku tatbikatının Osmanlı imparatorluğunda aldığı şekiller: malikâne-divani sistemi*, in *Türk Hukuk ve Iktisat Tarihi Mecmuası*, ii (1939), 119-84; idem, *Türk toprak hukuku tarihinde Tanzimat ve 1274 (1858) tarihli arazi kanunnamesi*, in *Tanzimatın 100. yıldönümü münasebetiyle*, Istanbul 1940, 1-101; idem, *XV ve XVI ıncı asırlarda Osmanlı imparatorluğunda zirai ekonominin hukuki ve mali esasları. I, Kanunlar*, Istanbul 1943; R. Anhegger, *Beiträge zur Geschichte des osmanischen Bergbaues. I. Europäische Türkei*, 3 vols., Istanbul-Zürich-New York 1943-5; Çagatay Ulucay, *Karaosmanoğullarına ait düşünceler*, in *III. Türk Tarih Kongresi, Kongreye sunulan tebliğler*, Ankara 1948, 241-59; Ismail Hakkı Uzunçarşılı, *Osmanlı devletinin merkez ve bahriye teşkilatı*, Ankara 1948; F. Babinger, *Mehmed der Eroberer und seine Zeit, Weltenstürmer einer Zeitenwende*, Munich 1953; M. Tayyib Gökbilgin, *Rumelide yürükler, tatarlar ve evlad-ı fatihan*, Istanbul 1957; X. de Planhol, *De la plaine pamphylienne aux lacs pisidiens, nomadisme et vie paysanne*, Istanbul-Paris 1958; Halil Inalcık, *Osmanlı'larda raiyyet rusumu*, in *Belleten*, xxiii (1959), 69-94; idem, *Bursa and the commerce of the Levant*, in *JESHO*, iii/2 (1960), 131-47; idem, *Bursa I. XV. asır sanayi ve ticaret tarihine dair vesikalar*, in *Belleten*, xxiv/93 (1960), 45-110; Fahri Dalsar, *Türk sanayi ve ticaret tarihinde Bursa'da ipekçilik*, Istanbul 1960; T. Stoianovich, *The conquering Balkan Orthodox merchant*, in *Jnal. of Economic History*, xx (1960), 234-313; R. Mantran, *Istanbul dans la seconde moitié du XVIIe siècle. Essai d'histoire institutionelle, économique et sociale*, Istanbul-Paris 1963; Cengiz Orhonlu, *Osmanlı imparatorluğunda aşiretleri iskân teşebbüsü (1691-1696)*, Istanbul 1963; B. Papoulia, *Ursprung und Wesen der "Knabenlese" im Osmanischen Reich*, Munich 1963; Bistra Cvetkova, *Recherches sur le système d'affermage (iltizam) dans l'Empire Ottoman au cours du XVᵉ-XVIIIᵉ s. par rapport aux contrées bulgares*, in *RO*, xxvii/2 (1964), 111-32; Lütfi Güçer, *XV.-XVI. asırlarda Osmanlı imparatorluğunda hububat meselesi ve hububattan alınan vergiler*, Istanbul 1964; Mustafa Cezar, *Osmanlı tarihinde leventler*, Istanbul 1965; H. İnalcık, *Adaletnameler*, in *Belgeler*, ii/3-4 (1965), 49-145; Uzunçarşılı, *Osmanlı devletinin ilmiye teşkilatı*, Ankara 1965; T. Stoianovich, *Le maïs dans les Balkans*, in *Annales ESC*, xxi (1966), 1026-40; R. Davis, *Aleppo and Devonshire Square. English traders in the Levant in the eighteenth century*, London 1967; N. Beldiceanu and Irène Beldiceanu-Steinherr, *Recherche sur la province de Qaraman au XVIᵉ siècle. Étude et actes*, in *JESHO*, xi (1968), 1-129; H. Inalcık, *Capital formation in the Ottoman empire*, in *JEH*, xix (1969), 97-140; idem, *The policy of Mehmed II toward the Greek population of Istanbul and the Byzantine buildings of the city*, in *Dumbarton Oaks Papers*, xxiii-xxiv (1969-70), 231-49; Ahmet Türek and Çetin Derin, *Feyzullah Efendi'nin kendi kaleminden hal tercümesi*, in *Tarih Dergisi*, xxiii (1969), 205-18, xxiv (1970), 69-93; G. Baer, *The administrative, economic and social functions of Turkish guilds*, in *IJMES*, i (1970), 28-50; Inalcık, *The Ottoman Empire, the classical age, 1300-1600*, London 1973; R. Jennings, *Loan and credit in early 17th century judicial records: the sharia court of Anatolian Kayseri*, in *JESHO*, xvi (1973), 168-216; K. Röhrborn, *Untersuchungen zur osmanischen Verwaltungsgeschichte*, Berlin 1973; N. Steensgard, *The Asian trade revolution of the seventeenth century: the East India Companies and the decline of the caravan trade*, Chicago-London 1973; A. Raymond, *Artisans et commerçants au Caire au XVIIIe siecle*, 2 vols., Damascus 1973-4; Rifa'at Abou-El-Haj, *Ottoman attitudes toward peacemaking: the Karlowitz case*, in *Isl.*, li (1974), 131-7; Metin Kunt, *Ethnic-regional (cins) solidarity in the seventeenth century Ottoman establishment*, in *IJMES*, v (1974), 233-9; Mustafa Akdağ, *Türk halkının dirlik ve düzenlik kavgası, "Celali İsyanları"*, Ankara 1975; Mehmet Genç, *Osmanlı maliyesinde malikane sistemi*, in Osman Okyar and Ünal Nalbantoğlu (eds.), *Türkiye iktisat tarihi semineri, metinler, tartışmalar, 8-10 Haziran 1973*, Ankara 1975, 231-96; M. Kunt, *Kulların kulları*, in *Boğaziçi Üniversitesi-Hümaniter Bilimler Dergisi*, iii (1975), 27-42; Cvetkova, *Les registres des celepkeşan en tant que sources pour l'histoire de la Bulgarie et des pays balkaniques*, in *Hungaro-Turcica. Studies in honour of Julius Nemeth*, Budapest 1976, 325-35; G. Veinstein, *"Ayan" de la region d'Izmir et commerce du Levant (deuxième moitié du XVIIIe siècle)*, in *Études balkaniques*, iii (1976), 71-83; Huri Islamoğlu and Çağlar Keyder, *Agenda for Ottoman history*, in *Review*, i (1977), 31-55; W.-D. Hütteroth and Kamal Abdulfattah, *Historical geography of Palestine, Transjordan and Southern Syria in the late 16th century*, Erlangen 1977; Kunt, *Derviş Mehmed Paşa, vezir and entrepreneur: a study in political-economic theory and practice*, in *Turcica*, ix (1977), 197-214; D. Quataert, *Limited revolution: the impact of the Anatolian railway on Turkish transportation and the provisioning of Istanbul, 1890-1908*, in *Business History Review*, li (1977), 139-60; R. Jennings, *Kadi, court and legal procedure in 17th c. Ottoman Kayseri*, in *SI*, xlviii (1978), 133-72; B. Braude, *International competition and domestic cloth in the Ottoman Empire, 1500-1650, a study in undevelopment*, in *Review*, ii (1979), 437-54; Huri Islamoğlu and Suraiya Faroqhi, *Crop patterns and agricultural production trends in sixteenth-century Anatolia*, in *Review*, ii (1979), 401-36; F. Taeschner, *Zünfte und Bruderschaften im Islam. Texte zur Geschichte der Futuwwa*, Zürich-Munich 1979; A. Raymond, *The Ottoman conquest and the development of the great Arab towns*, in *Internat. Jnal. of Turkish Studies*, i (1979-80), 84-101; N. Beldiceanu, *Le timar dans l'état Ottoman (début XIVe-début XVIe siècle)*, Paris 1980; Murat Çızakça, *Price history and the Bursa silk industry: a study in Ottoman industrial decline, 1550-1650*, in *JEH*, xl (1980), 533-50; C.V. Findley, *Bureaucratic reform in the Ottoman Empire, the Sublime Porte, 1789-1922*, Princeton 1980; H. Gerber, *Social and economic position of women in an Ottoman city: Bursa 1600-1700*, in *IJMES*, xii (1980), 231-44; Inalcık, *Military and fiscal transformation in the Ottoman Empire, 1600-1700*, in *Archivum Ottomanicum*, vi (1980), 283-337; C. Issawi, *The economic history of Turkey 1800-1914*, Chicago-London 1980; N. Todorov, *La ville balkanique aux XVe-XIXe siècles*, Bucharest 1980; B. McGowan, *Economic life in Ottoman Europe*, Paris-Cambridge 1981; R. Owen, *The Middle East in the world economy 1800-1914*, London-New York 1981; A. Abdelnour, *Introduction a l'histoire urbaine de la Syrie ottomane (XVIe-XVIIIe siècle)*, Beirut 1982; Fikret Adanır, *Heiduckentum und osmanische Herrschaft. Sozialgeschichtliche Aspekte der Diskussion um das frühneuzeitliche Räuberunwesen in Südosteuropa*, in *Südost-Forschungen*, xli (1982), 43-116; Inalcık, *Rice cultivation and the çeltükçi-re'aya system in the Ottoman empire*, in *Turcica*, xiv (1982), 69-141; Ayda Arel, *Osmanlı konut geleneğinde tarihsel sorunlar*, Izmir 1982; Kunt, *The Sultan's servants. The transformation of Ottoman provincial government, 1550-1650*, New York 1983; Mübahat Kütükoğlu, *Osmanlılarda narh müessesesi ve 1640 tarihli narh defteri*, Istanbul 1983; R.P. Lindner, *Nomads and Ottomans in medieval Anatolia*, Bloomington, Ind. 1983; A. Marcus, *Men, women and property: dealers in real estate in 18th century Aleppo*, in *JESHO*, xxvi (1983), 137-63; Quataert, *Social disintegration and popular resistance in the Ottoman Empire, 1881-1908. Reactions to European economic penetration*, New York 1983; Elizabeth Zachariadou, *Trade and crusade, Venetian Crete and the emirates of Menteshe and Aydın (1300-1415)*, Venice 1983; Abou-El-Haj, *The 1703 rebellion and the structure of Ottoman politics*, Istanbul-Leiden 1984; Faroqhi, *Towns and townsmen of Ottoman Anatolia, Trade, crafts and food production in an urban setting, 1520-1650*, Cambridge 1984; Genç, *Osmanlı ekonomisi ve savaş*, in *Yapıt*, xlix/4 50, 5 (1984), 52-61, i/5 (1984), 86-93; P. Sluglett and Marion Farouk-Sluglett, *The application of the 1858 Land Code in Greater Syria: some preliminary observations*, in Tarif Khalidi (ed.), *Land tenure and social transformation in the Middle East*, Beirut 1984, 409-24; Nihal Atsız, *Aşıkpaşaoğlu tarihi*, Ankara 1985; Çızakça, *Incorporation of the Middle East into the European world-economy*, in *Review*, vii (1985), 353-77; Ilber Ortaylı, *Tanzimattan Cumhuriyete yerel yönetim geleneği*, Istanbul 1985; D. Panzac, *La peste dans l'Empire Ottoman, 1700-1850*, Louvain 1985; Linda Schatkowski Schilcher, *Families in politics, Damascene factions and estates of the 18th and 19th centuries*, Wiesbaden-Stuttgart 1985; J.P. Thieck, *Décentralisation ottomane et affirmation urbaine à Alep à la fin du XVIIème siècle*, in *Mouvements communautaires et espaces urbains au Machreq*, Beirut 1985, 117-168; E. Werner, *Die Geburt einer Grossmacht—die Osmanen (1300-1481). Ein Beitrag zur Geschichte des türkischen Feudalismus*, Weimar 1985; Engin Akarlı, *Gedik: Implements, mastership, shop usufruct and monopoly among Istanbul artisans, 1750-1850*, in *Wissenschaftskolleg Berlin, Jahrbuch* (1986), 223-31; A. Bryer and H. Lowry (eds.), *Continuity and change in late Byzantine and early Ottoman society*, Birmingham-Washington D.C. 1986; Yavuz Cezar, *Osmanlı maliyesinde bunalım ve değişim dönemi (XVII. yy.'dan Tanzimat'a mali tarih)*, Istanbul 1986; Zeynep Celik, *The remaking of Istanbul. Portrait of an Ottoman city in the nineteenth century*, Seattle-Washington 1986; C. Fleischer, *Bureaucrat and intellectual in the Ottoman Empire. The historian Muṣṭafā ʿĀlī (1541-1600)*, Princeton 1986; Gülru Necipoğlu, *Architecture, ceremonial and power*, Cambridge, Mass. 1991; Elena Frangakis-Syrett, *Greek mercantile activities in the Eastern Mediterranean, 1780-1820*, in *Balkan Studies*, xxviii (1987), 73-86; Huri Islamoğlu-Inan, *State and peasants in the Ottoman Empire: a study of peasant economy in north-central Anatolia during the sixteenth century*, in eadem, (ed.), *The Ottoman Empire and the world economy*, Paris-Cambridge 1987, 101-59; I. Wallerstein, Hale Decdeli and Reşat Kasaba, *The incorporation of the Ottoman Empire into the world economy*, in Islamoğlu-Inan (ed.), *op. cit.*, 88-100; E. Akarlı, *Provincial power magnates in Ottoman Bilad Al-Sham and Egypt, 1740-1840*, in Abdeljelil Temimi (ed.), *La vie sociale dans les provinces arabes à l'époque ottomane*, iii, Zaghan 1988, 41-57; Caroline Finkel, *The administration of warfare: the Ottoman military campaigns in Hungary, 1593-1606*, Vienna 1988; Gerber, *Economy and society in an Ottoman city: Bursa, 1600-1700*, Jerusalem 1988; Yusuf Halaçoğlu, *XVIII. yüzyılda Osmanlı imparatorluğunun iskân siyaseti ve aşiretlerin yerleştirilmesi*, Ankara 1988; Reşat Kasaba, *The Ottoman Empire and the world economy. The nineteenth century*, Albany 1988; B. Masters, *The origins of western economic dominance in the Middle East. Mercantilism and the Islamic economy in Aleppo 1600-1750*, New York 1988; Şevket Pamuk, *100 soruda Osmanlı-Türkiye iktisadi tarihi, 1500-1914*, Istanbul 1988; Leslie Peirce, *Shifting boundaries. Images of Ottoman royal women in the 16th and 17th centuries*, in *Critical Matrix*, iv (1988), 43-82; Veinstein, *Du marché urbain au marché du camp: l'institution ottomane des orducu*, in Temimi (ed.), *Mélanges Professeur Robert Mantran*, Zaghouan 1988, 299-328; C.A. Bayly, *Imperial meridian, the British Empire and the world 1780-1830*, London 1989; Faroqhi, *Merchant networks and Ottoman craft production (16th-17th centuries)*, in Takeshi Yukawa (ed.), *Urbanism in Islam. The proceedings of the international conference on urbanism in Islam...*, Tokyo 1989, i, 85-132; Findley, *Ottoman civil officialdom, a social history*, Princeton 1989; A. Marcus, *The Middle East on the eve of modernity, Aleppo in the eighteenth century*, New York 1989; Ahmet Akgündüz, *Osmanlı kanunnameleri ve hukuki tahlilleri*, 3 vols. to date, Istanbul 1990- ; Sina Akşin (ed.), *Türkiye tarihi*, 4 vols., new ed., Istanbul 1990; D. Goffman, *Izmir and the Levantine world, 1550-1650*, Seattle-London 1990; Cemal Kafadar, *Les troubles monétaires de la fin du XVIe siècle et la prise de conscience ottomane du déclin*, in *Annales ESC*, xlii (1991), 381-400; Çağlar Keyder and Faruk Tabak (eds.), *Landholding and commercial agriculture in the Middle East*, Albany 1991; Doris Behrens-Abouseif, *Institutions and foundations in Ottoman Cairo* (in press); S. Pamuk, *From akçe to lira: a monetary history of the Ottoman empire* (in preparation). (Suraiya Faroqhi)

III. Literature

The literature to which the name of Ottoman is now generally given arises out of the literature of the Og̲h̲uz Turks, who settled in Asia Minor in the Sald̲j̲ūḳ period and later in the time of the Ottomans in Rūm-ili, where they founded a powerful empire. This literature, which had an uninterrupted development from the time of the Sald̲j̲ūḳs up to the beginning of the 20th century, was based on the literatures of still older dialects and remained in touch with these in all periods of its evolution. Especially since the 16th century, it became the most important and richest branch of all the Turkish literatures and exercised an influence on the literature of the other dialects. Here the general evolution of this literature will be sketched, noting its main genres and principal personalities. We shall deal not only with the classical literature which was confined to the upper classes, but also—in their general features—with the literature of the masses, that of the poet musicians (*sāz s̲h̲āʿirleri*) and the literature of the various mystic groups.

Ottoman literature may be divided into three great periods, corresponding to the general development of the history of Turkey:

a. Muslim literature from the 13th century to the end of the 16th century.

b. After 1600 AD.

c. European-type and national literature, arising out of the development of the nationalist movement, to the end of the Ottoman dynasty.

These will be examined in chronological order, in order to avoid arbitrary distinctions.

(a) Until 1600 A.D.

1. *The beginnings*

We find the first written examples of Ottoman Turkish literature already flourishing in the 13th century, and the works of that literature can be divided into three types:

1. Classical mystical (Ṣūfī) literature;
2. Religious mystical folk literature; and
3. Classical (later called *Dīwān*) literature.

Given that the Mongol invasion of Anatolia gave an impetus to the spreading of mystical views there and to the literary activities based on them, we shall have to consider this period as the starting point. During the Mongol invasions, the migration from Persia and Turkestan to Anatolia was intensified: scholars, Ṣūfīs and dervishes of various sects (e.g. Nad̲j̲m al-Dīn Kubrā (d. 1226 [*q.v.*]), Ḳuṭb al-Dīn Ḥaydar), and rich merchants settled down in Anatolia. Amongst them were major poets as well, such as Fak̲h̲r al-Dīn ʿIrāḳī (d. 1289 [*q.v.*]), author of the theosophical poem *Lamaʿāt*, Awḥad al-Dīn Kirmānī and S̲h̲eyk̲h̲ Nad̲j̲m al-Dīn Dāya (d. 1256). These Ṣūfīs settled in the cultural centres of Anatolia, such as Tokat, Kayseri and Sivas, and enjoyed the patronage and respect of the Rūm Sald̲j̲ūḳ sultans, and attracted extensive popular followings. In this way, Ṣūfī concepts and ideas spread effectively amongst the folk masses over wide areas. In addition, when we consider that Ibn ʿArabī (d. 1240), and his step-son and interpreter Ṣadr al-Dīn Ḳonawī, both settled in Konya after having found peace and tolerance at the Sald̲j̲ūḳ court, we can assume that already in the 13th century a cultural milieu for the future development of classical Ṣūfī literature had been prepared. Moreover, Rūmī both elaborated and popularised Ibn ʿArabī's mystical ideas within the spiritual and formal framework of classical Islamic literature. Thus he introduced the aesthetic conceptions and formal constructions of classical Islamic literature to Anatolia; he also played a most important role in the furthering of both classical (*Dīwān*) literature and the classical Ṣūfī literature of the Mewlewī order which arose after him [see mawlawiyya].

The foundations of Ṣūfī literature were laid by Ḥad̲j̲d̲j̲ī Bektas̲h̲ Walī, one of the dervishes of Ḳuṭb al-Dīn Ḥaydar who also came from K̲h̲urāsān and settled in Sulud̲j̲a .Ḳara Höyük, in the vicinity of Ḳirs̲h̲ehir, spreading his Bābāʾī-Bāṭinī views. As with Mawlānā, he also laid the foundations of the so-called Bektas̲h̲ī literature, the literature of the Ṣūfī order named after him, that which was greatly developed later on in Janissary circles [see bektās̲h̲iyya].

Alongside this Ṣūfī folk literature there developed a religious folk literature based on the tradition of singing of poetry with musical accompaniment (*sāz*) [see also nefes]. This became widespread among the army and the city folk, the Turcoman tribes and the frontier *g̲h̲āzī*s, and the folk minstrels, under the influence of the religious atmosphere, and it included heroic epic cycles and also short pious tales (e.g. the *Baṭṭāl-nāme, Dānis̲h̲mend-nāme*, the Tale of the Gazelle, Tale of the Dove, etc.) This religious folk literature should accordingly be added to the Turkish literature of the 13th century.

The works belonging to the classical Ṣūfī literature of this period were composed with the metres and forms of classical Islamic literature. This meant that the first poets had to face the difficult task of applying the rules of the *ʿarūḍ* metre to the phonetic system of Turkish. As a result, we witness in these early poems a lot of unnatural and forced expressions. Amongst these works we should mention the following: two religious *mat̲h̲nawī*s, the *Čark̲h̲-nāme* and the *Ewṣāf-i mesād̲j̲id-i s̲h̲erīfe* of Ḥad̲j̲d̲j̲ī Aḥmed Faḳīh [*q.v.* in Suppl.] from Ḳonya, the Turkish *g̲h̲azel*s of Mawlānā Rūmī (d. 1273 [*q.v.*]), the Turkish poems found in Sulṭān Weled's (d. 1312 [*q.v.*]) *Rebāb-nāme* and *Ibtidāʾ-nāme*, Ṣeyyād Ḥamza's *g̲h̲azel*s and his *mat̲h̲nawī* called *Dāstān-i Yūsuf*, and Ṣūlī Faḳīh's *Yūsuf u Zuleyk̲h̲ā* which deals with the same story.

One may also include yet another version of this very popular biblical story, the *mat̲h̲nawī Yūsuf we Zuleyk̲h̲a*, translated by K̲h̲alīl-og̲h̲lu ʿAlī from a Ḳipčaḳ original composed by a certain Maḥmūd from the Crimea into Anatolian Turkish, using the syllable metre and quatrain form typical of traditional folk poetry.

The first example of classical Turkish literature in this century came from the pen of K̲h̲od̲j̲a Dehhānī, poet at the court of ʿAlāʾ al-Dīn III at Ḳonya; he wrote *ḳaṣīde*s and especially *g̲h̲azel*s with non-religious themes, and was the first Turkish classical poet to sing of the beauty of nature, and of carnal love, wine and the other pleasures of life.

2. *The 14th and 15th centuries*

With the collapse of the Saldjūḳ central government in Ḳonya around 1300, Turkish culture and art came to flourish in the capital cities of the beyliks, such as Kütahya, Aydïn, Antalya, Kastamonu, Kayseri, Sivas and Ḳonya. The material wealth of these cities and their lords, who did not know any language other than Turkish, attracted poets and writers who started to produce their literary works in their mother tongue. When the Ottomans started getting the upper hand over the Anatolian beyliks, cultural and artistic activities were channelled into the emerging Ottoman centres situated on important trade routes such as Bursa, Edirne, Amasya and Manisa (1410-53), and finally to Istanbul, so that the scholars, poets and writers who used to be active at the courts of the Anatolian beyliks now began to produce their works under the direct patronage of the Ottoman sultans and princes and of Ottoman dignitaries.

Among those poets who formerly served Germiyān-oghlu Yaʿḳūb II (1387-1428) and who transferred themselves to the court of the Ottomans, were Aḥmedī (1334-1413), Sheykh-oghlu (1350-?), Aḥmed-i Dāʿī (d. after 1421), and Sheykhī (d. 1429); they were finally active at the courts of Bāyezīd I, his son Amīr Süleyman (d. 1412), Meḥemmed Čelebī (d. 1421) and Murād II (d. 1451). These rulers were frequently poets themselves, e.g. Murād II had the pen-name Murādī, Meḥemmed II the Conqueror used that of ʿAwnī, Prince Ḳorḳud (d. 1512) that of Harīmī and Bāyezīd II (d. 1512) that of ʿAdlī. From amongst these sultan-poets, Meḥemmed II, his son Djem (d. 1495) and Bāyezīd II wrote enough poetry to form independent *dīwāns*.

The Ottomans took special care to promote culture and the arts in order to preserve their cultural identity and not to be absorbed by the neighbouring Byzantine Christian culture. To achieve this goal, they also had to prove themselves victorious in the cultural rivalries that had been going on for some time among the Anatolian principalities. The following example will illustrate just how strong this rivalry was. When Mollā Fenārī was seriously offended by the Ottoman sultan, he transferred to Ḳonya, where the Ḳaramān-oghlu ruler offered him a salary of 1000 *aḳčes* per day, as well as 100 *aḳčes* for each of his students, unheard of until that time. The flourishing economy of the Ottoman state (see section II, above) greatly contributed to the success of these literary and cultural activities, so that the living standards in provincial cities located on the trade routes across Anatolia to southeastern Europe such as Amasya, Trabzon, Bursa, Manisa, Antalya and Edirne increased significantly. That Meḥemmed Čelebi became governor of Amasya, Prince Ḳorḳud in Manisa, Prince Selīm (II) in Trabzon, Djem Sulṭān in Ḳastamonu and Ḳaramān, was not at all accidental! They brought with them their own scholars and poets, but they also encouraged and protected local literary figures. For instance, Nedjātī Bey [*q.v.*] (d. 1509), one of the greatest poets of the 15th century, was first at the court of the crown prince ʿAbd Allāh in Ḳaramān, and after the prince died, he also served as the head of the *dīwān* of the crown prince Maḥmūd in Manisa.

The most striking characteristic of the cultural and literary activities of the Ottomans during the 15th century was the admiration which the Ottomans felt towards the art and literature of the Tīmūrids at their courts in Samarḳand and Harāt, and especially towards Čaghatay literature; it would not be unfair to say that classical Ottoman literature was under the spell of Mīr ʿAlī Shīr Nawāʾī [*q.v.*] whose influence reached its apogee at the end of the 15th and beginning of the 16th century, including also in the Persian literature of the time. Indeed, Persian literature, music, miniature painting and architecture were greatly refined under the patronage of the Tīmūrid sultans Shāhrukh (d. 1447), Ulugh Beg (d. 1449) and Ḥusayn Bayḳara (d. 1506) [*q.vv.*], and the attraction of this renaissance of Persian culture under Turkish political hegemony strongly influenced the Ottoman court, with echoes of that influence felt up to the 19th century.

The Tīmūrid court was taken as a model first in the political field. As is well known, at the cultural centres of Samarḳand and Harāt, the Uyghur alphabet was used side-by-side with the Arabic alphabet in literary texts as well as in the chancery. Wishing to compete with this Central Asian Turkish court, the Ottoman sultan Murād II (d. 1451) kept at his court in Edirne secretaries capable of composing *firmāns* in the Uyghur alphabet. The crown princes themselves were taught the Uyghur alphabet. Even at later dates, some Ottoman *firmāns* were composed in Čaghatay and written down in both the Arabic and Uyghur alphabets. Thus Meḥemmed II announced his victory over the Aḳ Ḳoyunlu Uzun Ḥasan in the form of a *fetḥ-nāme*, in which he addressed the local rulers of Eastern Anatolia in Čaghatay written down in Uyghur letters with an interlinear text in Arabic letters. However, all the Ottoman *firmāns* addressed to the European powers in Ottoman Turkish were in the Arabic script.

The Tīmūrid court was also taken as a model in the literary and artistic fields, since Ottoman poets and intellectuals took a great interest in Čaghatay and Persian literature. Aḥmed Pasha, who was Meḥemmed II's vizier and later on Bāyezīd II's *sandjaḳ-bey* of Bursa, used to await with enthusiasm and excitement ʿAlī Shīr Nawāʾī's latest *ghazels* carried with the caravans to Bursa. At one point, Nawāʾī sent 33 *ghazels* to Bāyezīd II, and Aḥmed Pasha wrote *naẓīras* to them at the order of the sultan. To write *naẓīras* to Nawāʾī's poems remained fashionable among Ottoman poets up until the 19th century, and even the greatest and proudest Ottoman poets such as Nedīm [*q.v.*] and Sheykh Ghālib followed that fashion. In the field of science many young men went to Central Asia to get a good education, and scholars and scientists from these lands were esteemed on Ottoman soil. One of these was the famous Uzbek *sheykh* Süleymān Efendi who dedicated his Čaghatay-Ottoman dictionary to ʿAbd ül-Ḥamīd II. The influence of the courts in Samarḳand and Harāt found its echoes in the music festivals of the Manisa court of the crown prince Ḳorḳud, so that during the 17th century Ewliyā Čelebi talks about music festivals called *Ḥusayn Bayḳara faṣïllarï*.

An important characteristic of the 14th and 15th centuries was the intensive translation movement from Arabic and Persian texts. Even though the Anatolian beyliks and the early Ottomans considered themselves as Islamic political entities, they still had not completely broken away from their ancestral Central Asian traditions, nor had they fully assimilated the new civilisation of which they were now part. So in order to bring Islamic culture to a wider audience, a concerted effort was undertaken to translate works in every field of Islamic learning and practice into a simple and clear Turkish. These translations may be classified as follows:

1. Works of *ʿilm-i ḥāl*, a kind of catechism of the

basic principles of worship and of behaviour within the family and the community. Alongside these, or perhaps later, there were made interlinear translations of the Ḳurʾān and translations of *tafsīr*, of the stories of prophets (*ḳiṣaṣ al-anbiyāʾ*), legends of saints (*menāḳib al-awliyāʾ*), etc.

2. Encyclopaedic manuals on medicine and drugs, on geography, astronomy and the interpretation of dreams, music treatises and dictionaries.

3. Translations in *mat͟hnawī* form of love stories of typical Near Eastern content, as well as mystical Ṣūfī *mat͟hnawī*s. The first texts to be translated in this category were Niẓāmī's (d. 1140) *K͟husraw wa S͟hīrīn*, ʿAṭṭār's (d. 1193) *Manṭiḳ al-ṭayr* and Firdawsī's (d. 1020) *S͟hāh-nāma*.

It must be emphasised that these so-called translations were not direct word-for-word ones, but rather adaptions made by the Turkish writers, who, besides putting in their own phrases, frequently added chapters and their own corrections or improvements, so that sometimes the translation would be three times as long as the original.

The strongest supporter of the translation effort was Murād II, who was a passionate lover of poetry and the fine arts and who attracted large numbers of artists and writers to his court.

Naturally, original creations exist side-by-side with these translations. Amongst them are to be noted the *G͟harīb-nāme* of ʿĀs͟hiḳ Pas͟ha (d. 1332 [*q.v.*]) which resembles Rūmī's *Mat͟hnawī*, the allegorical *mat͟hnawī Čang-nāme* of Aḥmed-i Dāʿī (d. after 1421) which expresses man's longing for immortality, the *K͟har-nāme* by S͟heyk͟hī [*q.v.*] which is one of the best satirical works in the entire Turkish literature, the *K͟hawāṣṣ-nāme* by Tād͟jī-zāde D͟jaʿfar Čelebi (d. 1516) which describes Istanbul, the *Mewlid* of Süleymān Čelebi [*q.v.*] which narrates the Prophet's birth, his *miʿrād͟j* and death, and finally, the *Muḥammediyye* of Yazīd͟jī-og͟hlu Meḥmed (d. 1449 [*q.v.*]) which also deals with the Prophet's life and his miracles. Besides all this, we have to mention the greatest mystical folk poet, Yunūs Emre [*q.v.*] who has a place of his own within Turkish literature; soon after he died, many poets imitated his style, without however attaining the universalism of his appeal.

All these literary activities raise the issue of the history of the written language: was the Old Anatolian Turkish in existence before the migrations from Central Asia? Or did it arise in Anatolia after the migration? Some scholars have argued that the Og͟huz tribes had established their own written language already in central Asia before their migration into Anatolia. However, this assumption does not seem to meet the basic precondition for the creation of a written language, namely that there should be a distinct political entity under whose auspices the written language can develop. Such a political structure existed in Ḳonya after the 11th century, but was absent for the Turkomans in Transoxiana. Thus we have to assume that the Turkomans established their written language for the first time under the political patronage of the Rūm Sald͟jūḳs and the beys of the Anatolian principalities. There is strong material evidence for this, namely, the fact that in the very first Old Anatolian Turkish texts we witness a typically Ḳurʾānic orthography: defective writing of the vowels and excessive usage of *tanwīn*s for Turkish endings and any final syllables of words. This would indicate that they did not bring with them an orthography already established in Central Asia, where the Ḳarak͟hānid system was based on the full (*plene*) writing of the vowels.

3. *Classical Ottoman literature during the 16th century*

At the beginning of the 16th century, the Ottomans were established as a world-empire, and the literature of this century reflects well the new political situation. Starting from the most famous poets like Bāḳī (d. 1600) and Fuḍūlī (d. 1556) [*q.vv.*] down to lesser poets, one finds a strong feeling of confidence and self-assurance. Of course, this feeling finds diverse expressions. In Fuḍūlī it becomes a sense of pride that defies the world, especially in his famous complaint, *S͟hikāyet-nāme*, whereas in Bāḳī and in other poets it is evident in their majestic style and their placing themselves on a equal footing with the famous Persian poets. In Uṣūlī (d. 1538), Ḥayretī (d. 1534) and K͟hayālī (d. 1557 [*q.v.*]) it appears as an expression of disdain for the worthless material world, but in most works one can detect a celebration of victory and denial of humility. Considering that this atmosphere, one taken for granted in the historical writings, permeates love tales and even lyric poetry, one has to acknowledge that the psychology of triumph brought about by the successes of the Ottoman expansion deeply affected the literary works of this period. For instance, the love tale *D͟jem-S͟hāh ü ʿĀlem-S͟hāh* of Ramaḍān Bihis͟htī, a less than first-rate poet, which was dedicated to Süleymān the Magnificent (d. 1566), clearly expresses this ideal image of world domination in between the lines, for all that the poet presented his poem to his audience as a symbolic work expressing his own mystical ideas.

The literature of this age is mostly preoccupied with the material and living world, despite the great number of religiously-inspired works. The simple religious atmosphere of the previous centuries had vanished, and with it the simple language, which now gives way to a flowery idiom of word-plays and refined rhetorical devices. In prose, however, Turkish entered a mature period of clarity and accuracy of expression, despite the heavy borrowings from the Arabic and Persian vocabulary. The scribes of the secretarial class, increasing in size along with the empire's expansion, especially those attached to the *reʾis ül-küttāb* and the *nis͟hānd͟jī* [*q.vv.*], well-versed in poetry and chancery skills (*fünūn-i kitābet*), played a significant role in the emerging literary trends. A good number of the poets of this period came from this class of government officers, e.g. Muṣṭafā ʿĀlī Efendi (d. 1599 [*q.v.*]) the famous historian, who wrote the *Künh ül-ak͟hbār* and first introduced critical method into Ottoman historiography. It is not surprising that these secretary-poets had to extoll the pleasures of the material world, as this was part of their duties to please and entertain their superiors, up to the sultan himself. This would explain why suddenly the *ḳaṣīde* or ode became fashionable, and every poet of significance had to compose *ḳaṣīde*s for the sultan and the high dignitaries. Thus, in this period when the *ḳaṣīde* was so widespread, the poet was in essence forced to arrange both his inner and outer worlds according to the palace hierarchy: the sun, moon and stars of the nature became the sultan in the centre, with the Grand Vizier and other dignitaries around him; the sultan is the rose and his officials the other flowers; the beloved is the sultan, those around the beloved are the dignitaries of the palace and the lover, i.e. the poet, is the sultan's slave. The sultan was the centre of the universe and of the poet's personal world. This imagery was already present in its incipient form in the earlier centuries, but now acquired precision, continuing until this literature exhausted itself.

The most important representative of the classical literature flourishing in the palace circles was Bāḳī, the court poet of Süleymān the Magnificent who was himself also a poet writing under the pen-name Muḥibbī. Bāḳī wrote *ḳaṣīde*s for Süleymān and his successors, Murād II (d. 1595) and Meḥemmed III (d. 1603). His superb skill in composing meticulously designed, geometrical and artistic poems remained unsurpassed by contemporary or even later poets, a skill seen in the elegy which he composed while still in his forties for the dead sultan.

Bāḳī's *dīwān* is quite voluminous, revealing not only refined feelings but a brilliant intelligence and eloquence. Eschewing ugliness, he made nature and realistic love his themes, showing his skill by hiding the intended image under perfectly chosen words.

The second most important poet of this period is Fuḍūlī, who excelled because of the liveliness of his artistic skill and the sincerity of his emotions in his *ḳaṣīde*s dedicated to the prophet Muḥammad and the sultan Süleymān. What distinguished him sharply from all other Ottoman poets is that he was not a poet from the capital but from Baghdād, which he greatly praises in his Turkish poems, all written in Ādharī or Azerī Turkish. He was influenced by the Ṣūfī poet Nesīmī (d. 1418 [*q.v.*]) and especially by ʿAlī Shīr Nawāʾī; the latter's poems provided inspiration for a lot of his compositions. He may be considered the poet of suffering. All his poems express a suffering and love that directly emanate from his nature. For all that his skills are as superb as Bāḳī's, this is not immediately apparent, since it takes a careful reading to unveil the complex images (*maḍmūn*) and word relationships hidden behind a seemingly effortless pleasing verse (*sehl-i mümteniʿ*).

In the 16th century, the *mathnawī* was still a very popular genre. In fact, we see an increasing number of poets who wrote love tales as well as mystical and religious subjects in the *mathnawī* form. Among the poets who wrote *mathnawī*s in the fashion of the famous Persian poet Niẓāmī [*q.v.*], with his *Khamsa*, two well-known poets can be mentioned here. One of these was Ṭashlîdjalî Yaḥyā (d. 1582 [*q.v.*]). His *Khamsa* consists of the following five *mathnawī*s: *Gendjīne-i rāz, Uṣūl-nāme, Shāh u gedā, Yūsuf u Züleykhā* and *Gülshen-i enwār*.

The second poet, who not only wrote one but two *Khamsa*s, was Lāmiʿī Čelebi (d. 1532 [*q.v.*]), very well versed in Persian culture and literature, as well as Čaghatay literature, and very much influenced by the works of Djāmī (d. 998/1492 [*q.v.*]), Mīr ʿAlī Shīr Nawāʾī and other famous Persian poets. As a result of this, he translated their works into Anatolian, namely, Ottoman Turkish. Because of his great interest in Djāmī and because of his translations of the latter's works, he was given the title of Djāmī-i Rūm ("the Djāmī of Anatolia"). Lāmiʿī was an outstanding figure in both Ottoman verse and prose. Being very productive, he introduced works of diverse forms into Turkish literature. Among them, his *mathnawī*s included: *Absāl u Salāmān, Wāmiḳ u ʿAdhrā, Wīs u Rāmīn, Ferhād u Shīrīn, Tuḥfe-yi Lāmiʿī, Shehrengīz-i Bursā, Guy u Čewgān, Maḳtel-i Ḥusayn, Shemʿ u perwāne*, and *Heft peyker* (unfinished at his sudden death).

Along with the poets writing in the elaborate classical style we should mention Tatawlalî Maḥremī (d. 1535) and Edirneli Naẓmī (d. 1548 [*q.v.*]) who represent a group of poets who tried, with reasonable success, to apply the *ʿarūḍ* metres to a Turkish relatively purified of foreign borrowings. Whether writing love or mystical poetry, there was a conscious effort to address the larger audience of the folk masses; it may be that these poets took their inspiration from the popular story-tellers and their stories recited at various meeting places.

The absence of a religious and mystical atmosphere from classical poetry is the characteristic peculiarity of this period. (This is the only period during which the above peculiarity is valid for all poetry.) This is not to say that there is no mystical thought in these poems, only that this is pushed into the background. These poets used Ṣūfī terminology, but expressed their own personal emotions, so that there emerges, for the first time, a distinction between the mystical (Ṣūfī) and the mystical-style (*mutaṣawwif*) poet. Even in the love *mathnawī Leylā we Medjnūn* of Fuḍūlī, which is permeated with a mystical atmosphere, a story of worldly but Platonic love is narrated with same intensity as the love adventures and sufferings of two living people in love. The same can be said of the *mathnawī Shāh u gedā* by the period's greatest *mathnawī* writer, Ṭashlîdjalî Yaḥyā.

This interest in the material world made the poets of this period less and less interested in the classical themes of Persian literature, and they started to turn to stories taken directly from real life, to their immediate vicinity and to contemporary human types, along with the traditional classical topics; this so-called *maḥallīleshme* movement continued well into the 17th and 18th centuries, but, with the exception of Nedīm, eventually lost its impetus without ever achieving the creativity and universality which the poets were hoping for.

The main reason for this tendency to be interested in the real and material world is perhaps connected with entertainment literature. Translation activity here had started in the 15th century, but was now intensified. In particular, Djelāl-zāde Ṭāhir Čelebi translated the tales of Firūz-Shāh and the extensive story collection in Persian *Djāmiʿ al-ḥikāyāt wa-lawāmiʿ al-riwāyāt* of Muḥammad ʿAwfī [*q.v.*] for the benefit of the sultans and grand viziers. However, these stories were not read only in palace circles; the people would listen to them in coffee houses and public gatherings. Story-tellers had been active narrating religious-heroic cycles, love stories and excerpts from the *Shāhnāma* from the 13th century onwards. During the 16th century, their repertory came to include unusual events and characters taken from everyday life. The custom of employing such story-tellers in the palace had been going on since the reign of Bāyezīd I, but acquired new significance in the 16th century, when the court story-tellers started being educated persons, to the point that some of them became the sultan's personal courtiers. New themes emerged. For instance, Muṣṭafā Djinānī (d. 1585) wrote his collection of stories for Murād II, who loved the new stories. Most likely the same motivation was behind the collection *ʿIbrat-nümā* of Lāmiʿī, the very knowledgeable translator of the Persian poet Djāmī. (It is in the *ʿIbrat-nümā* that we find the first serious mention of Naṣr al-Dīn Khodja [*q.v.*] and his extremely popular anecdotes.)

Finally, we have to mention one event of lasting consequence. In the 16th century the Ottomans became in closer touch with the Western world. This was the result both of accident and necessity, and the relations with the West were not deliberate and conscious but passive. The following example will illustrate how these contacts were reflected in literature: a writer using the pen-name Esīrī ("prisoner") narrates in his *Sergüdhesht* the story of his captivity during one of the Ottoman campaigns, his escape and adventures before reaching home again.

Another significant event in this regard was the introduction of the printing press into the empire since the reign of Bāyezīd II by the non-Muslim subjects, including Christians and the Jews who had been welcomed into the Ottoman domains after their expulsion from Spain in 1492. Books on Judaism, on Christianity and on the works of European Renaissance-period authors were published, and their influence on Ottoman Muslim society, though not direct, cannot be dismissed altogether. Moreover, the old Turkish theatrical representations, *Orta oyunu* [*q.v.*], greatly expanded in the 17th century and were certainly influenced by the Sephardic Jewish theatrical traditions and the Italian folk-comedy, given that the Ottomans had close political and commercial relations with Genoa, Venice and other Italian principalities.

Throughout the 16th century, then, Ottoman literature and culture was still considerably influenced by the Turco-Persian literature flourishing in the courts of Khurāsān and Samarḳand, while themes from everyday life inevitably crept into them as well; furthermore, Ottoman society, was beginning to be influenced by the West, without being fully aware of it.

Bibliography: See the articles on the various literary figures mentioned in the article and the general surveys of earlier Turkish literature given in the more detailed *Bibl.* at the end of this section on Literature. (GÖNÜL ALPAY TEKIN)

4. *Historical and geographical prose literature and popular poetry during the 16th century*

Prose in this century assumes a heavier and more artificial form; exaggerating Persian models, the simplest ideas are expressed by the most complicated images to the detriment of the subject. This lack of taste is found in the greatest stylists of the period: Lāmiᶜī, Kemāl Pasha-zāde [*q.v.*], Djelāl-zāde Muṣṭafā Čelebi [*q.v.*], Feridūn Beg [*q.v.*], ᶜAẓmī, the translator of the *Humāyūn-nāme*, ᶜAlī Čelebi, Ḳinalī-zāde ᶜAlī Čelebi [*q.v.*], Khʷādja Saᶜd al-Dīn [see KHODJA EFENDI] and others. This artificial tendency had a much more marked influence on prose than on poetry. Works written in simple language were despised by the educated classes. We find, however, that in very long works, it was only the preface that was written in this turgid and clumsy style. Many literary, historical, religious or moralising works of the period were in fact written in more simple language. The same applies to official correspondence and other state documents. In religious works intended for the people, every endeavour was made to write as simply as possible. The prose which we possess by Bāḳī and Fuḍūlī shows an elegant and comparatively simple language.

We shall begin with the historical works, a field in which great progress was made in this century, mainly on account of the interest taken by the educated classes in the military successes of the empire. Beside the rhymed chronicle, in continuation of the Saldjūḳ tradition, we find from the time of Bāyezīd II and Selīm I historical works in prose. The official Ottoman history written in Persian by Idrīs Bidlisī was translated into Turkish by his son. Other general histories were those of Ibn Kemāl, Djelāl-zāde Muṣṭafā Čelebi, entitled *Ṭabaḳāt al-mamālik*, of Muḥyī al-Dīn Djemālī, of Luṭfī Pasha [*q.v.*], of Khʷādja Saᶜd al-Dīn and of ᶜAlī [*q.v.*]. There are also a number of special histories, dealing with particular periods or certain events (the *Feth-nāmes*) and biographical works (like the *Djawāhir al-manāḳib* relating to Ṣoḳollu Meḥmed Pasha). At the same time, the office of *Sheh-nāmedji* was maintained at the court. In the time of Süleymān, it was filled by Feth Allāh ᶜĀrif Čelebi, whose successors included Eflāṭūn Shirwānī, Seyyid Luḳmān and Taᶜlīḳī-zāde (d. 1013/1604). These were also Turkish poets, but tradition demanded that the official *Sheh-nāme* should be written in Persian in the *mütekārib* metre, until Meḥemmed III ordered it to be written in Turkish. From the time of Taᶜlīḳī-zāde, prose began to appear scattered through the text. From the historical point of view, these *Sheh-nāmes* are naturally of less importance than the non-official chronicles. While works like the *Tādj al-tawārīkh* of Saᶜd al-Dīn were regarded as models of style, the *Taʾrīkh* of Luṭfī Pasha, whose style more resembles that of the old chronicles, and especially his *Āṣaf-nāme*, are very important for our knowledge of the social history of this period. The *Taʾrīkh* of Selānikli Muṣṭafā Efendi shows how corrupt the administration was at the end of the century. We must regard ᶜĀlī as the greatest historian of the time, and his other works reveal him as a man of almost encyclopaedic learning. Not only his *Künh al-akhbār*, but also his *Naṣīḥat al-salāṭīn, Ḳawāᶜid al-madjālis* and *Menāḳib-i hünerwerān* show that the author was a severe critic, well informed about the conditions of life of his time. The style of his historical works is relatively simple (on his life and works, see the introduction by Ibn ül-Emīn Maḥmūd Kemāl to the edition of the *Menāḳib-i hünerwerān*, Istanbul 1926). To this century also belongs the *Shaḳāʾiḳ-i Nuᶜmāniyye* written in Arabic by Ṭashköprü-zāde [*q.v.*] and translated into Turkish with additions by Medjdī [*q.v.*] of Edirne and Khākī of Belgrade; also, an extensive biographical literature among which the biographies of the Turkish Ṣūfī *sheykhs* are of considerable historical interest. A similar interest is contained in a few light works of badinage (*mizāḥ*) like the *Nafs al-amr-nāme* of Lāmiᶜī and of Nīksārī-zāde (see *Millī Tetebbuᶜlar Medjmūᶜasi*, no. 3).

Among historical works, those which deal with literary history occupy an important place. The first Ottoman *tedhkere* is the *Hesht bihisht* written in 945/1538 by Sehī [*q.v.*], in imitation of the *Madjālis al-nafāʾis* of Nawāʾī. He was followed by Laṭīfī [*q.v.*], ᶜĀshiḳ Čelebi [*q.v.*], ᶜAhdī of Baghdād and Ḥasan Čelebi [*q.v.*]. ᶜAlī also gives important notices of poets in his *Künh al-akhbār*. The compilation of collections of *naẓāʾir* on poems of other poets, like the *Djāmiᶜ al-naẓāʾir* written in 918/1512 by Ḥādjdjī Kemāl, containing poems by 266 poets, and others, is a custom which is also found in the 16th century and has contributed greatly to our knowledge of Turkish poets.

It is in this century that we find geographical works and travels beginning to appear. In the 15th century we have only translations and excerpts from al-Ḳazwīnī and Ibn al-Wardī as well as a translation from the Greek of Ptolemy. In the 16th century, these two works are again translated, as well as those of Abu 'l-Fidāʾ (by Sipāhī-zāde) and al-Iṣṭakhrī (by Sherīf Efendī) and ᶜAlī Ḳūshdjī's work on mathematical geography, and geographical descriptions of Egypt. A *Čīn seyāḥat-nāmesi* written in Persian by the merchant ᶜAlī Ekber Khiṭāyī was translated into Turkish for Murād III. The celebrated *Baḥriyye* of Pīrī Reʾīs [*q.v.*] written in 935/1529, was a result of the maritime policy of the Turkish empire. It is based in part on older cartographers like Ṣafāʾī and on Italian maps. As a result of Süleymān's campaigns by land, we have Matrāḳdjī Naṣūḥ's [*q.v.*] work, full of admirable little sketches. Seyyidī ᶜAlī Reʾīs wrote his *Muḥīṭ* as a result of his unfortunate exploit in the Indian Ocean, although the book is based entirely on earlier Arab works. The *Mirʾāt al-mamālik* by the same author is much more original. After it we have the *Seyāḥat-nāme* in verse of the merchant Aḥmed b. Ibrāhīm, describing his voyage to India. The *Menāẓir al-ᶜawālim* of

Meḥmed ᶜĀs͟hı̊ḳ of Trebizond is very important; based on the old Arab geographies, it gives valuable new information about the Ottoman lands. Finally, we may mention a *Taʾrīk͟h-i Hind-i g͟harbī* on the discovery of the New World, translated in 990/1582 from a European language by Meḥmed Yūsuf al-Herewī (on this literature see F. Taeschner, in *ZDMG*, lxxvii [1923]).

Alongside classical Turkish literature, we find the literature of the people increasing, the knowledge of which was spread by the *ḳiṣṣa-k͟hʷān*, the *meddāḥ* and the *ḳaragözd͟ji* in the popular cafés and in the barracks of the Janissaries. Many classical poets also wrote *türküs* [*q.v.*] intended for the masses. These *türküs* are in the *ᶜarūḍ* metre and in the form of *mürebbaᶜ*; later they were called *s͟harḳī* [*q.v.*]. This form of poem goes back to the earliest forms of verse among the Turks. But the works of unlettered poets, like Enwerī, T͟hiyābī, Rāyī, Raḥīḳī and others, written in imitation of the classical poets, were more to the taste of the people. In popular gatherings such themes as *Abū Muslim*, the *Ḥamza-nāme, Baṭṭāl G͟hāzī*, etc. were enthusiastically received. This encouraged Ḥās͟himī of Istanbul to write the *met͟hnewī* entitled *Barḳī we-pūlād* taken from the *Ḥamza-nāme*, and inspired several authors and poets to write similar works. Sultān Süleymān had the story of *Fīrūz-s͟hāh* translated into Turkish in 8 vols. by Ṣāliḥ Efendi, translator of the *D͟jāmiᶜ al-ḥikāyāt* of ᶜAwfī. There were *ḳiṣṣa-k͟hʷān*s even in the palaces of the sultans. Alongside of old Islamic and Persian subjects, we find also collections of stories of everyday life like the *Bursalı̊ K͟hʷād͟ja ᶜAbd al-Reʾūf Efendi ḥikāyesi* by the poet Waḥdī, also called *Ana Bad͟jı̊ ḥikāyesi*. The stories of everyday life by Muṣṭafā D͟jinānī of Bursa in an unaffected style give us a valuable insight into different aspects of the life of the people in these days. Another poet of this kind is Medḥī [*q.v.*], whose real name was Derwīs͟h Ḥasan, who was the *meddāḥ* of Murād III (see Rieu, *Cat. of Turk. mss.*, 42).

In the 16th century we are a little better informed regarding the activities of the *ozan* [*q.v.*], although they are now generally known as *ᶜās͟hiḳ* or *čögürd͟jü*. These wandering musicians were to be found wherever the people congregated and used to recite their poems in syllabic metres, love-songs, heroic tales, *mert͟hiye*s and *türküs*. At the beginning of this century we have a portion of Bak͟hs͟hī's epic on the Egyptian campaign of Selīm I, and at the end of the century we have the names of Ḳul Meḥmed (d. 1014/1605), Öksüz Dede, K͟hayālī and Körog͟hlu, and, in the garrisons of the Mag͟hrib, Čirpanlı̊, Armudlu, Ḳul Čulk͟ha, Gadāmuṣlu (see also Köprülüzāde M. Fuʾād, *Türk sāz s͟hāᶜirleri*, Istanbul 1930). The influence of the various classes of society on one another even had the result that syllabic metre was sometimes used among the cultured classes (but especially in the *hezl*) and the *ᶜarūḍ* metre in popular poems, just as had been the case formerly for poems of a religious character. The mystic poets however, following the tradition of Yūnus Emre, wrote their *ilāhīs* in syllabic metre. We may note the names of Ummī Sinān (d. 958/1551), Aḥmed Sārbān (d. 952/1545), Idrīs Muk͟htefī (d. 1024/1615) and Seyyid Seyf Allāh K͟halwetī (d. 1010/1601). But the greatest successors of Yūnus and Ḳayg͟husuz were found among the Bektās͟hīs and Ḳı̊zı̊lbas͟hs, such as Ḳul Himmet and his pupil Pīr Sulṭān Abdal, a native of Sīwās who was executed in 1008/1600 by order of K͟hiḍr Pas͟ha (cf. Saᶜd al-Dīn Nüzhet, *Pīr Sulṭān Abdāl*, Istanbul 1929). Other products of the popular literature of the period were *Ḥasan-og͟hlu türküleri, Ḳara-og͟hlan türküsü* and *Geyik destānı̊*.

(b) After 1600 A.D.

1. *The 17th century*

In spite of the political decline of the empire, we still find intellectual and literary life pursuing its normal course. The knowledge of the Ottoman literary language spread among the Muslim lower classes generally and also through districts with a non-Turkish population or speaking a non-Ottoman Turkish dialect like eastern Anatolia (Ād͟harī dialect) and the Crimea. The Crimea [see ḲIRIM] began to produce a number of Ottoman poets, among them actually some of the K͟hāns. The influence of Turkish literature and culture is found as early as the 16th century in the use of Arabic characters by the Muslim Hungarians and Croats (cf. *Ungarische Bibliothek*, Budapest 1927, no. 14). There is also a Turkish-Serbian dictionary in verse, called *Potur s͟hāhidiyye*, composed by Hawāyī (*Bull. of the Soc. of Sciences Skoplije*, iii, 189-202), a similar Turkish-Bosniak vocabulary by Uskūfī and several rhymed Turco-Greek glossaries.

Istanbul was always the centre to which men of letters and learning flocked from all parts of the empire and from beyond its frontiers. With the exception of Murād IV, no sultan took an interest in literature, and among statesmen there were relatively few patrons of literature like Ilyās Pas͟ha, Muṣāḥib Muṣṭafā Pas͟ha, Rāmī Pas͟ha and the *S͟heyk͟h al-Islām*s Yaḥyā and Behāyī. In spite of this and of the decline in the *medrese*s, this century saw scholars of ability like Ṣarı̊ ᶜAbd Allāh [*q.v.*], Ismāᶜīl Anḳarewī, Isḥāḳ K͟hʷād͟jası̊, Aḥmed Efendi, and others. The various branches of religious learning and Arabic philology have, however, no great representatives in this century, and the conflict between the *medrese*s and the *tekke*s known as the "question of the Ḳāḍī-zādes" shows what a narrow point of view still prevailed in the *medrese*s. The persecutions of the Ṣūfī orders, which sometimes had a political object also, did not however prevent these orders from continuing to prosper throughout the empire.

The "classical" Turkish poetry of the 17th century was in no respect below the level of the Persian models. But in place of devoting themselves to imitations and translations, the Turkish poets were now working on original subjects. It is true, on the other hand, that the influence of contemporary Persian and Indo-Persian poets is still felt. Nefᶜī shows the inspiration of ᶜUrfī, Nābī of Ṣāʾib and Nāʾilī-yi Ḳadīm that of S͟hawḳat.

Nefᶜī [*q.v.*] may be regarded as the greatest Turkish master of the *ḳaṣīde*, on account of the power of his imagination, the richness of his language and the harmony of his style. His *g͟hazel*s and his *hid͟jw* on the other hand are less successful. The influence of Nefᶜī was always great on his successors, although his period saw several eminent *ḳaṣīded͟ji*s, like Newᶜī-zāde ᶜAṭāyī, Ḳāf-zāde Fāʾiḍī, Riyāḍī, Ṣabrī and Riḍāyī. The greatest representative of the *g͟hazel* is the *S͟heyk͟h al-Islām* Yaḥyā [*q.v.*] who may be regarded as the successor of Bāḳī, especially on account of his great power to express feelings and emotions. His fame likewise survived into the following centuries. Other representatives of the school of Bāḳī and Yaḥyā are the *S͟heyk͟h al-Islām* Behāyī and Wed͟jdī. In contrast to the latter, the poets Fehīm [*q.v.*], Nāʾilī-i Ḳadīm [*q.v.*], S͟hehrī and even the poet Nābī [*q.v.*] were under the influence of contemporary Persian poetry. Nābī, on whom can be noticed the influence of Ṣāʾib, became renowned for his *met͟hnewī k͟hyriyye*s and his *g͟hazel*s. His poems are characterised by the preponderance of intellectual conceptions, but this has not affected his popularity. In many of his poems he describes and criticises the social life of his time. His young contemporary T͟hābit [q.v.] endeavours to show his originality by mingling proverbial expressions with his poetry. Among the masters of the g͟hazel in the 17th century we may also mention Nis͟hāṭī Mewlewī, D͟jewrī and Rāmī Meḥmed Pas͟ha.

ᶜAẓmī-zāde Ḥāletī [q.v.] excelled in all poetical genres and is best known for his rubāᶜīs. The lug͟hz [q.v.] and the muᶜammā became very popular, as did the taʾrīk͟h (chronogram). The hidjw and mizāḥ, composed in different forms, caused poets of the first rank to write very coarse things. Some products of this genre, however, can be appreciated, like the tedhkere in the form of a met͟hnewī by Güftī in which the author depicts contemporary poets; the hidjw of Fehīm and of D͟jewrī, written in the form of mulammaᶜ, are curious because the text is scattered with passages in non-Turkish languages.

Some met͟hnewīs of the first half of the century show a remarkable perfection. The subjects of the old k͟hamsas are gradually replaced by more topical subjects. The greatest representative of the style is Newᶜī-zāde ᶜAṭāyī [q.v.] who acquired his great reputation with his K͟hamsa, the subjects of which are taken from the life of his time. This poet reveals the influence of his Turkish predecessors like Yaḥyā of Tas͟hlīdja and D͟jinānī (see above). After him we may note the following authors of met͟hnewīs: Ḳāf-zāde Fāʾiḍī, G͟hanī-zāde Nādirī and Riyāḍī. It was mainly in this century that it became fashionable to write Sāḳī-nāmes in imitation of the Persian poet Ẓuhūrī, although this genre is already found earlier, as is shown by the ᶜIs͟hret-nāme of Rewānī (16th century). Among the Sāḳī-nāmes we may specially note those of ᶜAṭāyī, Riyāḍī and Ḥāletī; all are tinged with mysticism. The met͟hnewī thus served for all sorts of subjects taken from daily life, stories, descriptions, speculative works, tales of actual events, etc.

The number of religious and mystical works, lives of Ṣūfī saints and didactic works connected with the different ṭarīḳas, is very great in this century. Poetical forms were often used for them. Very well-known is the Miᶜrādjiyye of Nādirī. Then there were panegyrics of the Prophet (naᶜt), translations in verse of the Ḥadīth-i arbaᶜīn, of mawlids etc. Among the Ṣūfī poets there were some who used the syllabic metre; we may note Niyāzī-i Miṣrī, founder of the Miṣriyye branch of the K͟halwetiyye order, whose poems were long popular; the Bektās͟hīs also numbered several poets in their ranks. There are also a large number of historical works in verse, S͟hāh-nāmes, G͟hazā-nāmes, etc., like the S͟hāh-nāme of Nādirī of the time of ᶜOt͟hmān II and others. The S͟hehins͟hāh-nāme written by Mülhemī by order of Murād IV has only the preface in Turkish; the rest is Persian in keeping with the old tradition. It is in this century also that the custom begins of writing brief Ottoman histories in verse; we have that of Ṭālibī, written in 1017/1608, of Nit͟hārī (d. 1075/1664) written for Meḥemmed IV, and the Fihrist-i S͟hāhān, dedicated to Meḥemmed IV by Ṣolaḳ-zāde Hemdemī, and continued by a series of poets down to Ḍiyā (Ziyā) Pas͟ha in the 19th century. This kind of work has neither much historical nor literary value.

Literary prose follows the same lines as in the preceding century. The great stylists (müns͟hī), like Weysī, Nergisī [q.v.], Oḳdju-zāde [q.v.] and others, carried affection of language to a still more advanced degree. A fine specimen is given by the official documents addressed to the Persian court and written by müns͟hīs like Ḥükmī; this same style was sometimes used even in private correspondence. The works

which were considered to have no literary value in their day are those which are now most appreciated, like those of Ḳočī Beg, Kātib Čelebi, Ewliyā Čelebi and Naᶜīmā. Histories, in this century also, take first place among prose works. There are several which have the character of semi-official chronicles like the S͟hāh-nāme written in prose by Ṭas͟hköprüzāde [q.v.] for ᶜOt͟hmān II. Murād IV appointed Ḳābilī as waḳᶜa-nüwīs for the Eriwan campaign. In 1074/1664 the nis͟hāndjī ᶜAbd al-Raḥmān Pas͟ha was appointed by Meḥemmed IV to chronicle events, as was Meḥmed K͟halīfa [q.v.] of Fīndīḳlī by Muṣṭafā II. It is only later that Naᶜīmā was appointed waḳᶜa-nüwīs. The historical works of this century are translations of the general histories of Islam, original works on the same subject, general and special works and monographs on Ottoman history. From the historical point of view, the most important are the Djāmiᶜ al-duwal, written in Arabic by Müned͟jdjim Bas͟hī [q.v.], the Fed͟hleke of Kātib Čelebi, the Taʾrīk͟h of Pečewī and the best that of Naᶜīmā. The great encyclopaedist Kātib Čelebi [q.v.] also reveals himself in his Mīzān al-ḥaḳḳ and Dastūr al-ᶜamal as a historian of penetrating insight. Pečewī [q.v.], who made use of Christian sources, is also very valuable for his sound judgment and impartiality. Naᶜīmā [q.v.] who possessed descriptive powers of the first order, gives vivid psychological analyses of historical characters. Ḳočī Beg [q.v.] examines in his celebrated Risāle the causes of the decline of the empire. Ḳara Čelebi-zāde is a müns͟hi rather than a historian. We must also mention chroniclers like Wed͟jīhī, Ḥasan Bey-zāde and Ṣolaḳ-zāde, as well as the dheyl to the S͟haḳāʾiḳ-i nuᶜmāniyye by Newᶜī-zāde ᶜAṭāyī and the continuation by ᶜUs͟hs͟hāḳī-zāde.

The tedhkere is much below the level of the 16th century; the most notable is that of Riyāḍī written in 1018/1609. The Riyāḍ al-s͟huᶜarā of Ḳāf-zāde Fāʾiḍī composed in 1030/1621 also contains specimens of the work of the poets dealt with in it. There is also the dheyl to this work by Meḥmed ᶜĀṣim (d. 1086/1675), the concise tedhkere of Riḍā and that of Güftī already mentioned. The Maṭāliᶜ al-naẓāʾir by K͟hiṣālī (1062/1652) is a collection of maṭlaᶜs.

In the field of geography, the most important works are those of Kātib Čelebi and Abū Bakr Dimas͟hḳī. They use European as well as Muslim sources. The Seyāḥat-nāme of Ewliyā Čelebi [q.v.] is important for the history of all aspects of social life. In spite of its defects it is a work without an equal in Turkish literature. In this century also the first sefāret-nāmes appear.

The great popularity of the s͟hehnāmedji, meddāḥ, karagözdji, etc. continued in this century in all classes of society. At Bursa we have Derwīs͟h Kāmilī, Ḳurbānī ᶜAlīsi and others, at Erzerūm Ḳaṣṣāb Kurd, Ḳandilli-og͟hlu, etc. In Istanbul there were eighty meddāḥs, who were organised in a gild (eṣnāf); the best known is Ṭiflī [q.v.] who was nedīm to Murād IV. Towards the end of this century, the meddāḥ Ḳīrīmī (d. 1120/1708) flourished.

The musician-poets (sāz s͟hāᶜirleri) became very numerous in the 17th century. We find them among the Janissaries, the sipāhīs [q.v.], the lewends [q.v.], the Djelālīs [see DJALĀLĪ in Suppl.], and in the religious bodies like the Ḳīzilbas͟h and the Bektās͟hīs. They were always to be found in military retinues. The writer of this article succeeded in collecting and identifying the works and names of about thirty musician-poets of this century. The most notable are Gewherī and ᶜÖmer ᶜĀs͟hiḳ [q.v.]; the latter has almost become the patron saint of the sāz s͟hāᶜirleri (cf. Köprülü-zāde

M. Fuʾād, *Türk sazşairlerine ait metinler we-tetkikler*, i-v, Istanbul 1929-30). The influence of this popular literature is felt even among the upper classes, as in the poems of the Khān of the Crimea, Meḥmed Girāy, who wrote under the *makhlaṣ* of Kāmil, and a *merthiye* of ᶜAfīfe Sulṭān, one of the favourites of Meḥemmed IV. Several "classical" poets also wrote *sharḳī*s for the masses. The poem on the hero *Gendj ᶜOthmān* by Ḳayîḳdjî Muṣṭafā has actually given rise to a folk-tale which still survives in Anatolia (Köprülü-zāde, *Kayıkcı kul Mustafa we-genc osman hikayesi*, Istanbul 1930). It is probable that several other folk-tales originated in this century, like those called *ᶜĀshîḳ Kerem*, *ᶜĀshîḳ Ghārib*, and *Shāh Ismāᶜīl*. Lastly, we see from the statements of Ewliyā Čelebi that it was in this century that the *orta oyunu* [*q.v.*] began to be popular with the people.

2. *The 18th century*

Literature and culture in this century continued to follow the same lines as in the preceding centuries. There was a vast output in prose and poetry, while the intellectual links with Persia and Transoxania continued to exist. Persian poets, especially Shawḳat and Ṣāʾib, exercised a great influence on Turkish poetry. But in spite of all this, the tendency to a more individual development gained in strength and was shown in the endeavours to simplify the language. It is mainly due to the great poets of the beginning of this century that classical Turkish poetry entered on a path entirely independent of contemporary Persian poetry.

The period of Dāmād Ibrāhīm Pasha [see IBRĀHĪM PASHA, DĀMĀD] is a very important one. Many works were written and translated by his orders or those of Sultan Aḥmed III. Committees were appointed to translate important works rapidly. Among the poets of this period we may mention ᶜOthmān-zāde Aḥmed Tāʾib [*q.v.*], who was called the king of poets, Seyyid Wehbī, Sāmī, Rāshid, Neylī, Ṣelīm, Kāmī of Edirne, Durrī, Thāḳib, ᶜĀrif, Sālim, Čelebi-zāde ᶜĀṣim, and ᶜIzzet ᶜAlī Pasha. Nedīm [*q.v.*] in particular acquired a great reputation in the second half of the century and later. His *ghazel*s and his *sharḳī*s recall the period of Saᶜdābād [see LĀLE DEWRI] and by his original subjects, rich imagination and harmonious language, he surpasses his predecessors and his contemporaries. In the *sharḳī* he reached a level which neither Nāẓim before him nor Fāḍil Enderūnī after him attained. It was also through the patronage of Dāmād Ibrāhīm Pasha that Ibrāhīm Müteferriḳa [*q.v.*] was able to inaugurate Muslim Turkish printing [see MAṬBAᶜA. 2]; but for several reasons printing remained confined to a very restricted sphere throughout this century and did not exercise any particular influence on intellectual or artistic life.

Among the great poets of this century we must also make special mention of Ḳodja Rāghib Pasha [*q.v.*], the greatest representative of the school of Nābī, and Sheykh Ghālib [*q.v.*], the last great poet of the classical period. In the *ḳaṣīde* it was the influence of Nefᶜī that dominated, while in the *ghazel* there was a rivalry between the disciples of Nedīm and Sāmī on the one hand and admirers of Nābī on the other. But towards the end of the century, a decline in both schools became apparent; poets like Fāḍil Enderūnī [*q.v.*] and Sünbül-zāde Wehbī [*q.v.*] are only mere imitators. The poets of this century practised all forms of poetry and special attention was devoted to genres characteristic of an epoch of decadence, like the *hidjw*, the *hezl*, the *muᶜammā* (enigma) and the *taʾrīkh* (chronogram), while immorality and a general decline in good taste increased. On the other hand, true religious inspiration still continued, as may be seen from the *munādjāt* and the *naᶜt* of Naẓīm [*q.v.*], the *Miᶜrādjiyyes* of poets like Nāyī ᶜOthmān Dede, Naḥīfī [*q.v.*] and ᶜĀrif Süleymān Bey and the verse translation of the *Methnewī* of Mewlānā by Naḥīfī. The *methnewī*s of this period are numerous but of little literary value, the old subjects of the *khamsa* are entirely dropped, with the exception of the *Ḥusn-u ᶜishḳ* of Sheykh Ghālib, the last masterpiece of this class. Finally, the rhymed historical works of this period and the Ṣūfī poems by initiates of the various orders are of little importance.

Literary prose tends to become gradually simpler, although we still find imitations of the style of Nergisī and Okčî-zāde. A well-known stylist like ᶜOthmān-zāde Tāʾib openly declared against exaggerated artificiality in prose. Historical works occupy the first place. Among authors serving as *waḳᶜa-nüwīs* [*q.v.*] we may mention Rāshid, Čelebi-zāde ᶜĀṣim and Wāṣif, but none of them can be compared to their predecessors like Naᶜīmā, although hundreds of people were writing biographical and historical works. The political and military decline of the empire caused a large number of *lāyîḥa* ("memoirs") to be written investigating the causes. The most remarkable of these memoirs is that of Ḳodja Segbān Bashî. From the point of view of geography, we may note a number of important *sefāret-nāme*s, of which the *Fransa sefāret-nāmesi* of Yirmi-Sekiz Čelebi Meḥmed Efendi [see MEḤMED YIRMISEKIZ] is a typical example; these works were occasionally, although rarely, written in verse. The *sūr-nāme*s written to celebrate the splendid festivals held by the sulṭāns are important sources for sociological research. Those best known are the *Sūr-nāme*s of Seyyid Wehbī and of Ḥashmet. The collections of biographies of poets are even more numerous than in the preceding century. We may mention the *tedhkere*s of Ṣafāyī and Sālim and that of Belīgh [*q.v.*]; the *tedhkere* of Esrār Dede [*q.v.* in Suppl.] is specially devoted to Mewlewī poets; to this century belong also the *Waḳāʾiᶜ al-fuḍalāʾ* of Sheykhī, which is the final continuation (*dheyl*) of the *Shaḳāʾiḳ*. Lastly, the *Tuḥfe-yi khaṭṭāṭīn* of Mustaḳīm-zāde [*q.v.*]—whom we may regard as the greatest encyclopaedist of this century—is the most important source for the Muslim and Turkish calligraphers (*khaṭṭāṭ*). In the field of geography we have only translations and excerpts from European works.

The *meddāḥ*, *ḳaragözdji* and *orta oyundju* continued to enjoy the same popularity among all classes of society. The works of the musician-poets were also known everywhere; we may mention Ḳīmetī, Nūrī, Lewnī, Ḳaba Saḳal Meḥmed and Faṣīḥī, but the popularity of Gewherī and ᶜĀshîḳ ᶜÖmer continued; some of these poets were of Armenian origin, like Medjnūn and Warṭan who lived at the beginning of the century. This influence of Turkish musician-poets on the poems of the Armenian *ashūgh* perhaps begins as early as the 16th century (see KÖPRÜLÜ-ZĀDE, in *Edebiyyāt Fakültesi Medjmūᶜasi* [1922], i, 1-32). The best example of the way in which the literary taste of the people had penetrated among the upper classes is the fact that the great poet Nedīm also wrote a *türkü* in the popular metre. This tendency became more marked as the century advanced.

3. *The 19th century*

At the beginning of this century, Ottoman literature had sunk to a very low level which continued till the period of the *Tanẓīmāt*. Wāṣif Enderūnī [*q.v.*] and ᶜIzzet Molla [*q.v.*] alone show some originality. Wāṣif appeals to the popular taste and shows the influence of Nedīm as well as that of Fāḍil

Enderūnī. ʿIzzet Molla, while strongly influenced by Nedīm and Sheykh Ghālib, is, however, a much greater poet than Wāṣif, especially as regards the purity of his language and his poetical technique; in addition to *ḳaṣīdes* and *ghazels*, he wrote quite good *methnewīs*; he is the last "master" of classical poetry before the *Tanẓīmāt*. It is true that even after the *Tanẓīmāt*, many poets wrote *ḳaṣīdes* and *ghazels* in the ancient style, and among them the great advocates of literary innovations like Nāmiḳ Kemāl and Ḍiyā Pasha; to this period also belong Ghālib Bey of Leskofča, ʿAwnī Bey and ʿĀrif Ḥikmet Bey [*q.v.*], all imitators of Nāʾilī and Fehīm-i Ḳadīm. They had, however, no influence on the course of literary development. It was only natural that the old literary tradition could not disappear at one stroke; Shināsī and his school had to maintain a long and hard struggle against the old school.

The prose of the period before the *Tanẓīmāt* is not of much value, although the production was not less than in preceding centuries. In history, the *Taʾrīkh* of Müterdjim ʿĀṣim [*q.v.*] is remarkable for its style and critical ability; the author uses even simpler language in his translation of the *Burhān-i ḳāṭiʿ* and of the *Ḳāmūs*. The *waḳʿa-nüwīs* Esʿad Efendi [*q.v.*], translator of the *Mustaṭraf* of al-Ibshīhī and author of the well-known *Üss-i ẓafer* on the extermination of the Janissaries, is far below ʿĀṣim, with his insipid language and confused style. The same writer edited the *Taḳwīm-i weḳāʾiʿ*, and Sultan Maḥmūd II reproached him with the obscurity of his language in an account of a journey of the sultan which he had drawn up in this capacity. On the other hand, in his translation of the *Mustaṭraf*, he recommends the use of Turkish instead of Arabic and Persian words and the simplification of literary style, which shows to what an extent the movement to simplify the language had made progress. Lastly, we must not forget the celebrated poet and stylist Meḥmed ʿĀkif Pasha [*q.v.*] who, in spite of several poems written in the popular metre and some works in simple prose, ought not to be regarded as the first to spread literary innovations. ʿĀkif Pasha, indeed, remained entirely unaffected by European culture and was one of the last representatives of the old literature.

Among the representatives of the popular literature we have information about the *meddāḥs* Pič Emīn, Ḳi̊z Aḥmed, Ḥādjdjī Müʾedhdhin, Kör Ḥāfiẓ and others, as well as of some writers of shadow-plays (*khayāldji̊*) like Sherbetdji Emīn, Ḥāfiẓ of Ḳāsi̊m Pasha, Muṣāḥib Saʿīd Efendi; it is only towards the end of the century that Kātib Ṣāliḥ in breaking with the ancient tradition began to imitate the modern theatre.

The best known musician-poets of this century are Derdli, Dhihnī of Bayburt and Emrāḥ of Erzerum, who acquired a great and well-merited popularity in Anatolia as well as in Istanbul among all classes (see KÖPRÜLÜ-ZĀDE, *Erzurumlu Emrah*, Istanbul 1929). Down to the end of the reign of ʿAbd al-ʿAzīz, these *ʿāshi̊ḳs* used to assemble in a café in Ṭawuḳ Pazari̊. They had an organisation of their own with a chief (*reʾīs*) at their head, recognised by the government. This organisation was broken up later on, but in the early 20th century there were still found musician-poets in Anatolia.

This classical Turkish literature and especially the poetry had lost almost all its vigour and originality by the time the *Tanẓīmāt* began. Classical poetry had lost the ability to create anything new within its narrow limitations, and the poets could only produce imitations (*naẓīre*) of the great masters of the past, or in their efforts to show a little originality, fall into artificiality and platitude. As a result of continually repeating the same conceptions by the same limited means of expression, all the vitality of Turkish poetry was destroyed. Even great artists like Nedīm and Sheykh Ghālib had not been able to escape the rigid rules of the old models. On the other hand, the attempts to draw upon the language and literature of the people and to appeal more to popular taste and language, efforts such as we observe in Fāḍil Enderūnī and Wāṣif, only resulted in vulgarity and banality. In spite of the political and economic connection with Europe which had existed for centuries, the social structure of the Ottoman people had never emerged from the frame of traditional Islamic civilisation, which had kept it imprisoned in a mediaeval system of ideas. It is true that the continual military defeats and the gradual economic decline had impressed upon thinking people the material and technical superiority of Europe and that, as early as the 18th century, they had begun to take advantage of European skills to reorganise the army and the fleet. But it was much more difficult to admit the superiority of Europe in the field of culture. The *medreses*, which were in a very backward state compared with earlier centuries, still clung tenaciously to the mentality and tastes of the Middle Ages. Modern science was beginning to be introduced only in institutions founded for the army, like the Engineering School (*mühendis-khāne*) and the Medical School (*ṭibb-khāne*). These innovations owed a great deal to a few individuals, who had studied western languages and modern sciences, like Khodja Isḥāḳ Efendi, Gelenberī and Shānī-zāde. It was the need felt by Selīm III, and especially by Maḥmūd II, to reorganise the army and navy and to establish a central administration to prevent the empire being parcelled out between feudal chiefs, that led them to consent, in spite of the opposition of the *medreses*, to the reform of the teaching of mathematics and natural sciences.

From the end of the 18th century, there were in Turkey men who knew French and recognised the cultural superiority of Europe. In bringing teachers from France and sending students to Europe, the movement of Europeanisation was encouraged in Turkey. It was natural then that, as a result of all these needs, European influence began to show itself little by little in every branch of life, including the fields of thought and art.

(c) "European-type" Turkish literature. The period of the *Tanẓīmāt* and the new literature

The great industrial and capitalist development in Europe as well as the political expansion and rivalry of the imperialist Great Powers could not long ignore so vast and rich a field of exploitation as Turkey. At the same time, the mediaeval institutions of the empire had lost their power of resistance, and the revolutionary movements in France had propagated the principle of nationality among the non-Muslim elements. All these circumstances made the urgent need felt of introducing reforms in the social and administrative institutions of the empire. These reforms were to meet with considerable resistance, not only among the lower classes but also among those members of the educated classes who had been educated in the *medreses*. It was due to Muṣṭafā Reshīd Pasha [*q.v.*] and his little group of followers that the reforms were gradually introduced into the country. In Turkish history these reforms are known as *Tanẓīmāt* [*q.v.*].

The *Tanẓīmāt* were not confined to the fields of administration, justice and finance; with the object of securing the progress of education among the Muslim Turks, primary and secondary schools were opened and plans made to found a university. An *Endjümen-i dānish* was formed to prepare schoolbooks (1269/1853) and students were sent to Europe. The *Endjümen-i dānish* was soon replaced by the *Djemʿiyyet-i ʿilmiyye-yi othmāniyye* (1277/1860), which began to publish its own organ, *Medjmūʿa-yi fünūn*. In the following year, the Girls' School was opened and in 1279/1862 University courses were begun. In 1282/1865 was formed a *Terdjeme djemʿiyyeti*, in 1284/1867 the Civil School of Medicine (*Ṭibbiyye-i mülkiyye mektebi*) began its lectures, and in the following year, the Lycée of Galata Saray was opened, the curriculum of which was adapted from western secondary schools and French was used for teaching alongside of Turkish. The University (*Dār ül-Fünūn*) was opened in 1286/1869, but the intrigues of the conservative elements forced it to be closed two years later. In 1287/1870 the School of Law (*Ḥuḳūḳ mektebi*) was opened and in 1294/1877 a School of Political Sciences (*Mekteb-i mülkiyye*). At the same time, museums and libraries were founded as well as technical schools such as the engineering, agricultural and commercial schools. Thus there was gradually created an educated class outside the *medreses*. All this activity was accompanied by a gradual development of the daily press. In 1247/1831 the official publication *Taḳwīm-i weḳāʾiʿ* began to appear, which was followed by the *Djerīde-yi ḥawādith* in 1256/1840, the *Terdjümān-i aḥwāl* in 1276/1859 and the *Taṣwīr-i efkār* in 1278/1861 [see DJARĪDA. iii. Turkey]. These two last mark an important stage in the history of modern developments for it was through them that Shināsī, founder of the new literary school, and his disciple Nāmïḳ Kemāl addressed the public. Down to the period when the absolutism of ʿAbd ül-Ḥamīd II prevented any kind of publication, the Turkish press developed very rapidly. Many scientific and literary works were translated from European languages, especially from French, and the Turkish language began to be simplified, at the same time enriching itself with a large number of scientific expressions.

The three great figures of the new literature are Shināsī [*q.v.*] who had been educated in France, his great disciple Nāmïḳ Kemāl [see KEMĀL, MEḤMED NĀMÏḲ] and Ziyā (Ḍiyā) Pasha [*q.v.*], both of whom had lived in France as exiles. Through these circumstances the new school was imbued with the French literature of the 18th and 19th centuries, and the principles proclaimed during the political revolutions in France. The innovators wished to sweep away the old feudal literature and proclaim the ideas of "fatherland" (*waṭan*), "liberty" (*ḥurriyyet*), "democracy" (*khalḳdjïlïḳ*) and "constitutionalism (*meshrūṭiyyet*); and they aimed at creating a "bourgeois" literature. It was in this way that journalism, political and literary criticism, the theatre, the translation of western literary works, the novel and the philosophical and sociological study began. Shināsī was neither a brilliant stylist nor a great poet, but his programme was well defined; he wished to free himself from the trammels of the old unintelligible language, and although he was not able to realise all this programme, his theories exercised a great influence on those around him. Ziyā Pasha, by his translations of Rousseau and Molière and by his literary and political criticism, gave great support to this movement. He was well versed in the classical literature, yet he went so far as to allege that this literature had no relation to the Turkish character; he upheld the thesis that one ought to follow nature, i.e. borrow from the popular language and literature. In reality, Ziyā Pasha had neither the strength nor the courage to put these theories into force.

It was undoubtedly Nāmïḳ Kemāl who assured the definite success of the new school. He was a great artist, a keen fighter, a prolific author and a great patriot. For him, art was a means of provoking a revival in the land and he contributed vigorously to the cultural and political revolution in Turkey by his political articles, his dramas, his novels, his patriotic poetry, his historical works, his critical essays and even by his private letters. He exercised a profound influence. The presentation of *Waṭan* was a great political event in the country. He attacked the old literature even more bitterly than Ziyā Pasha and thought that it was impossible to write Turkish poetry in the *ʿarūḍ* metre. However, not even Kemāl could cast off the old traditions entirely, nor could his friends. It is for this reason that Saʿd Allāh Pasha was able to write in 1297/1880 in an anonymous article in the journal *Waḳt*, that pupils should only be given literal translations of western works because the "new" writers had not been able to produce in reality anything really new.

ʿAbd al-Ḥaḳḳ Ḥāmid [*q.v.*], a pupil of Nāmïḳ Kemāl, brought about a great revolution in the field of poetry, which hitherto had not been able to free itself from ancient forms. This extremely prolific poet introduced into Turkish the lyric and the drama in which his models were Dante, Racine, Corneille and Shakespeare. Even Nāmïḳ Kemāl acknowledged that the new Turkish poetry begins with Ḥāmid. Other important figures were Redjāʾī-zāde Ekrem [see EKREM] and Sāmī Pasha-zāde Sezāʾī [*q.v.*], but in proportion as the pressure of despotism increased, the second generation of the period of the *Tanẓīmāt* began to pursue purely artistic ends.

Many other thinkers or writers contributed to the cultural evolution of the country. We may mention the famous historian Aḥmed Djewdet Pasha [*q.v.*], Aḥmed Wefīḳ Pasha [*q.v.*], Süleymān Pasha, and the great writer and encyclopaedist Aḥmed Midḥat Efendi [*q.v.*], as well as the lexicographer Shams al-Dīn Sāmī Bey [*q.v.*]. Djewdet Pasha, well versed in Islamic learning and author of a Turkish grammar in collaboration with Fuʾād Pasha, wrote beautiful prose in Turkish. Aḥmed Wefīḳ, animated by western ideas, wished to revive national culture, and proclaimed the fact that the Turks of Anatolia were a branch of the great Turkish nation. He compiled the first dictionary of Anatolian Turkish, collected proverbs and translated the *Shadjara-yi Turk* of Abu 'l-Ghāzī. By his adaptations of the comedies of Molière, he played a great part in the development of the Turkish theatre. Süleymān Pasha, who reorganised the military schools, was a great patriot. He claimed that the language and literature should be called "Turkish" and not *ʿOthmānli*; and in his *Taʾrīkh-i ʿĀlem* he devoted a special chapter to the early Turks, taking his material from J. de Guignes and other sources.

Lastly, Aḥmed Midḥat wrote and translated hundreds of volumes of a popular nature, beginning with books of the alphabet; he thus trained the people to read and contributed to raising the level of education, which was his only aim, for his books have no scientific or literary value. Sāmī Bey showed himself a worthy successor of Wefīḳ Pasha in his *Ḳāmūs al-aʿlām* and *Ḳāmūs-i türkī*.

At the end of the 19th century appeared Muʿallim Nādjī [*q.v.*], who obtained great fame under the protection of Aḥmed Midḥat. Nādjī was well versed in

Islamic culture and wrote *g͟hazel*s in the classical style alongside good poems in the new style. The followers of the old school expected from him almost a resurrection of classicism, although Nād͟jī was not at all a champion of such a reaction, as is shown by his beautiful simple prose (as in *ᶜÖmeriñ čod͟juḳlug͟hu*). His quarrels with Ekrem Bey originated rather in personal reasons. At the same time Nābī-zāde Nāẓim, who died very young, came to the front; his novel *Zehrā* makes him a figure of first importance in literary history.

The most important event at the end of the 19th century is the literary movement begun by a group of youthful men of letters who had associated themselves, at the instigation of Red͟jāʾī-zāde Ekrem, with the periodical *T͟herwet-i Fünūn* [*q.v.*]; this movement marks the second and last stage of the Europeanisation of Turkish literature. It is dominated by the figures of Tewfīḳ Fikret and K͟hālid Ḍiyā (Ziyā) [*q.vv.*] and is very much under the influence of the literary movements in France at the end of the 19th century. Started in a period of absolute despotism and having only a short life of five or six years, this movement produced works of a neurotic and pessimistic sentimentality. Its motto was "art for art's sake". If we except D͟jenāb S͟hihāb al-Dīn, who acquired after the revolution the reputation of a great prose writer, Süleymān Naẓīf, who may be considered a pupil of Nāmīḳ Kemāl with an originality of his own, Fāʾiḳ ᶜĀlī, an imitator of ᶜAbd al-Ḥaḳḳ Ḥāmid, and Ismāᶜīl Ṣafā, an independent figure, who found his subjects in everyday life, all the poets who wrote in the *T͟herwet-i Fünūn* were imitators of Tewfīḳ Fikret. K͟hālid Ziyā, who had a very choice style, was the true founder of the literary novel in Turkish. He takes his subjects generally from the upper middle classes, but some of his short stories describe the life of the people. The latter genre was more successfully treated by the novelists Aḥmed Ḥikmet and Ḥüseyn D͟jāhid, in more simple language. Meḥmed Raʾūf [*q.v.*] was a novelist who made excellent psychological analyses, but his language was imperfect. In the field of science, philosophy and criticism, the collaborators on the *T͟herwet-i Fünūn* did no more than translate. But the severe censorship and the short life of the group did not enable them to show greater vitality.

While the school of Tewfīḳ Fikret and K͟hālid Ziyā reflected only the life of the upper classes, Ḥüseyn Raḥmī [*q.v.*] depicted in his novels various aspects of the life of the people; and at the same time the notable publicist Aḥmed Rāsim [*q.v.*] was dealing in several of his works with the same subject. Among the poets of this period, we may further mention Riḍā (Rizā) Tewfīḳ [*q.v.*] who wrote the finest lyrics in the style of the *ᶜās͟hiḳ* poets and Bektās͟hīs, but in syllabic metre, the poetess Nigār K͟hānîm and lastly Meḥmed Emīn Bey [*q.v.*], who suddenly became celebrated during the Turco-Greek war by his *Türkče s͟hiᶜrler*. Meḥmed Emīn employed a very simple language in the syllabic metre and wished to reach the people directly (*k͟halḳa dog͟hru*), although the existing popular literature with its mentality, tastes and traditional forms were entirely unknown to him. As a man of letters he was entirely of the school of Fikret; he was not, however, an individualist like his contemporaries but imbued with the populist spirit (*k͟halḳd͟jîlîḳ*). This was the first occasion on which a Turkish poet had descended to the level of the people. Perhaps it is right to charge him with a lack of lyrical feeling, but this does not prevent us from regarding him as an interesting figure in literary history. At the same time, the movement to simplify the language continued and even gave rise to an exaggerated purism. By the translation of the works of European scholars, the early history and culture of the Turks became known, while the journalistic activities of the young Turks abroad began to envisage Turkish nationalism from the political point of view. These were the main elements in the cultural and literary life of Turkey before the Young Turk Revolution of 1908.

This event, having brought about the abolition of the censorship, caused an extended literary activity. The patriotic pieces of Kemāl and Ḥāmid re-appeared on the stage and a large number of works of a sociological, philosophical and historical nature were translated into Turkish. At the same time, great improvements were made in education and the relations with Europe raised the general cultural level to a height never before reached.

The most important literary movement after the Revolution was that of the *Fed͟jr-i ātī* [*q.v.*], although it was a literary circle which lasted only a short time; its members began by following the school of Fikret and K͟hālid Ziyā, but the majority of them ended up as members of the national literary movement. Aḥmed Hās͟him alone continued to develop in the way he had first chosen. He never abandoned the *ᶜarūḍ* metre nor the conception of "art for art's sake" in its strictest form. Besides, he had ideas of his own on the relation between music and poetry (see H. Duda, *Aḥmed Häschim*, in *WI*, ii [1928], 200-44). The poet Yaḥyā Kemāl (Beyatlı) [*q.v.*], who had a great influence after 1912, had literary views entirely different from those of Aḥmed Hās͟him, for he sought music rather in the exterior elements of his poems, while he retained the motto "art for art's sake". Another poet who remained outside the national literature, was Meḥmed ᶜĀkif (Ersoy), the advocate of Pan-Islamism [*q.v.*] and unrivalled master of the *ᶜarūḍ* metre; in simple language he described the life of the people in its most realistic aspects. ᶜĀkif, whose lyrics sometimes rose to great heights, remained quite uninfluenced by western poetry; he was a democratic poet, born of the people. In the work of these three poets, very different from one another, we see Turkish poetry striving to free itself from the too limited sphere of Tewfīḳ Fikret and his school; but under the stimulus of the great development of the nationalist movement, which manifested itself in the whole domain of art, poetry also ended by entering on new paths.

(d) The national literature

After the Revolution of 1908, it was the ideal of Ottomanism (*ᶜot͟hmānlîlîḳ*) that animated the governing classes. But the political events which rapidly followed, soon proved that this ideal was a chimera, by the attitude of the Muslim elements no less than by that of the Christians. The Turkish element, which was dominant in the empire, thus needed a new ideal; this was the national ideal, which had already revealed itself in the period of the *Tanẓīmāt* and which had existed through the Ḥamīdian period in a cultural form. After the revolution also, this movement began by assuming a cultural aspect. On 28 December 1908, the society *Türk Derneği* was founded, the object of which was to study the past and present of the Turkish peoples, to simplify the Turkish language and to make it a language of science. This society had not much power, but in November 1911 the periodical *Türk Yurdu* began to appear and on 12 March 1912, the *Türk Od͟jag͟hî* was founded. This movement was not confined to a few Turkish patriots; associated with it were a number of Turkish intellectuals from other countries who had fled from Russian expansionism, like Ag͟haog͟hlu Aḥmed, Ḥuseyn-zāde ᶜAlī and Aḳ Čora-og͟hlu ūsuf. The movement was violently opposed by the llowers of a badly-understood occidentalism (*gharb-ilik*) on the one side, and by the partisans of Pan-lamism (*ittiḥād-i Islām*) on the other. At the same me, the periodical *Gendj Ḳalemler*, published at alonika, again started, under a pretentious name, a mpaign to purify the Turkish language, and Ziyā)iyā) Gök Alp [see GÖKALP, ZIYĀ] a member of the ommittee of Union and Progress [see ITTIḤĀD WE ERAḲḲĪ DJEMᶜIYYETI] began his activities. With the ansfer of the central office to Istanbul, Ziyā Gök Alp ined the *Türk Yurdu*. Later, after the disastrous con-usion of the Balkan War, the younger generation lso rallied to the national movement. The time was ery opportune for the success of the national ideal; it nly required a man capable of directing the national lea and laying down a programme and giving it a hilosophical basis. It was Ziyā Gök Alp who did this. Ie exercised a great influence on the youth by his niversity courses, by his lectures and by his articles nd poems; all his life, from the time of the Balkan Var to the Armistice, when he was exiled to Malta, nd later during his sojourn in Diyār Bakr and nḳara, he displayed an uninterrupted activity: the ésumé of his teaching is contained in his book *'ürkdjülüğüñ esāslarî* (Ankara 1339/1923, Istanbul 940, Eng. tr., *Principles of Turkism*, 1968). His death, oon after, was a cause of general mourning through-ut the land.

As in all branches of life, the national movement iade its influence felt in literature: the syllabic metre ttained the dominant position in poetry; the inguage was simplified; the motto "art for art's ake" was replaced by "art for life"; writers began to orrow from popular literature and its traditional orms; literature began to reflect the life and charac-eristics of all branches of society. Philological and istorical studies were made on the works of the nusician-poets, on the popular literature, the music f the people. In brief, the science of Turkology was ounded, in large measure through the efforts of Aeḥmed Fuᵓād Köprülü (1890-1966 [*q.v.*]). All this ontributed greatly to give a definite direction to the ew literary movement.

Among the poets of this movement we may give rst place to Fārūḳ Nāfidh, who in his last poems lepicts the scenery of Anatolia, then Orkhān Seyfī *q.v.*], Enīs Behīdj, Yūsuf Ziyā, Khālid Fakhrī and Nedjīb Fāḍil. All these show the influence of Ziyā Gök Alp and Yaḥyā Kemāl rather than of Meḥmed Emīn. n prose, progress was still more marked and the vriters in it have still greater force. The greatest igure of the period is Khālide Edib Khanîm (Adıvar *q.v.*]). After the stories of love and passion which are haracteristic of her first period she wrote books in the tyle of *Ateshden gömlek* in which she describes the truggle of Anatolia for independence. ᶜÖmer Seyfed-līn [*q.v.*], who died young, has left a number of very good little stories, some of which, like *Bombā*, are nasterpieces of national literature. Refīḳ Khālid Karay [*q.v.*]), who is perhaps the best writer of simple Turkish, describes in his *Memleket ḥikāyeleri* realistic cenes of Anatolian life, hitherto unknown to iterature; his realism is however expressed in a mer-ciless sarcasm, quite devoid of sympathy and feeling. Yaᶜḳūb Ḳadrī (Karaosmanoğlu [*q.v.* in Suppl.]) even n his novels, is more a stylist and a mystic poet than a story-teller. Other well-known figures in the new prose are Fāliḥ Rîḳī (Atay [*q.v.* in Suppl.]), who lescribes in *Atesh we-günesh* episodes of the war in Palestine, and Rūshen Eshref. Among the novelists Reshād Nūrī (Güntekin [*q.v.*]) achieved fame by his novel *Čalî ḳushu*.

The Western-type theatre enjoyed a great spurt in popularity as a result of the Young Turk Revolution and increased political liberalisation after the restoration of the constitution. Many of the plays of this period were patriotic ephemera only; but significant for the future evolution of the drama in Turkey was the first appearance in 1919 of a Turkish Muslim woman actress on the stage [see further, MASRAḤ. 3. In Turkey].

Bibliography: For general works on Ottoman literature and its various genres, see J. von Hammer-Purgstall, *Geschichte der osmanischen Dichtkunst bis auf unsere Zeit*, 4 vols., Pesth 1836-8; E.J.W. Gibb, *A history of Ottoman poetry*, 6 vols., London 1900-9; P. Horn, *Die türkische Literatur*, in *Die Kultur der Gegenwart*, i/7 (1906), 269-81; A.F. Krîmski, *Istoriya Turtsii i e'e literaturî*, 2 vols., Moscow 1916; Th. Menzel, *Die türkische Literatur*, in *Die Kultur der Gegenwart*, i/7, 2nd printing, 1926, 283-331; M.F. Köprülü, *Türk edebiyyātî taᵓrīkhi*, Istanbul 1926-8; F. Babinger, *Die Geschichtschreiber der Osmanen und ihre Werke*, Leipzig 1927; Hasan Ali Yücel, *Türk edebiyatına toplu bir bakış*, Istanbul 1932, German tr. O. Reşer, *Ein Gesamtüberblick über die türkische Literatur*, Istanbul 1941; A. Bombaci, *Storia della letteratura turca*, Milan n.d. [1956], French tr. Paris 1968 (good bibl.); Fahir İz, *Eski türk edebiyatında nesir*, Istanbul 1966; idem, *Eski türk edebiyatında nazım*, Istanbul 1966-7. See also *PTF*, ii, chs. *Die klassisch-osmanische Literatur* (W. Björkman), 427-65, *La littérature moderne de Turquie* (Kenan Akyüz), 465-634 (copious bibls.); W.G. Andrews, *Poetry's voice, society's song. Ottoman lyric poetry*, Seattle, etc. 1985; V.R. Holbrook, *Originality and Ottoman poetics: in the wilderness of the new*, in *JAOS*, cxii (1992), 440-54. See also ḤIKĀYA. 3; GHAZAL. iii; ḲAṢĪDA. 3; MASRAḤ. 3, and *İA* art. *Türkler. Türk edebiyatı*.

(M.F. KÖPRÜLÜ*)

IV. RELIGIOUS LIFE

Religious life all through the life of the Ottoman empire, and indeed until Atatürk's secularist reforms of the mid- and late 1920s, had a two-fold aspect. First, there was the official religious institution of the *ᶜulamāᵓ* and *fuḳahāᵓ*, in varying extents connected with the ruling dynasty and headed by the *Sheykh ül-Islām* in Istanbul, whose functions included amongst others that of *muftī* or issuer of legal opinions or *fatwās*. The training of these *ᶜulamāᵓ* rested on an extensive structure of orthodox Sunnī *madrasas* scattered throughout the empire (whose curricula still warrant further investigation), and the finished products filled various official posts, often by a kind of *cursus honorum*, as *müderris*, *ḳāḍīs*, *nāẓirs* of pious endowments or *ewḳāf*, *khaṭībs*, etc. They were expected to use their intellectual training and polemical powers, in the earlier centuries of the empire's existence, against the threats from syncretism, within the Ottoman lands of Anatolia and Rumelia, with the previously-dominant Greek, Armenian and Balkan Christianity, and in the 9th/15th to 11th/17th centuries against Shīᶜism amongst Türkmen elements of eastern Anatolia and the Ottomans' Ṣafawid enemies in Persia. In subsequent times, the religious classes, including the numerous class of theological students, *softas*, were often a politically and socially reactionary element, at critical periods involved in riots and revolts in the capital Istanbul, as in 1808, 1876 and 1909.

Hence for this official religious institution, see FATWĀ. ii; ḲĀḌĪ. Ottoman empire; ḲĀḌĪ ᶜASKER; KÜLLIYYE; MADRASA; MÜLĀZAMET; MULĀZIM; SOFTA; ᶜULAMĀᵓ.

Second, there has always been a strong current of Ṣūfī mysticism in Turkish religious life and in popular devotion, a current which in Anatolia went back to the time of the Saldjūḳs of Rūm, the Dānishmends [q.vv.] and the succeeding beyliks. Before they reached Anatolia, the Turks' Central Asian background had been strongly influenced by the Ṣūfism of such holy men of Turkistān as Aḥmad Yasawī [q.v.], and this was subsequently reinforced in Anatolia by the establishment in Ḳonya [q.v.] during the time of the Mongol invasions of the father of Djalāl al-Dīn Rūmī, Mawlānā himself and his son Sulṭān Walad [q.vv.], making this capital of the Saldjūḳs and then city of the Ḳaramānids [q.v.] a centre of spirituality whose luminaries included also a figure like Ṣadr al-Dīn Ḳōnawī [q.v.], the stepson of Ibn ʿArabī; the influence of Ibn ʿArabī [q.v.] was to be important in later Turkish mystical thought and poetry. As well as these religious elements of pre- and early Ottoman religious life stemming from Khurāsān, there seems also to have been considerable interaction at the popular level with the Christian and even pre-Christian substrata in Anatolia.

This is probably the case with a Ṣūfī order like that of the Bektāshiyya [q.v.], in which a distinct Shīʿī tinge is also discernible. The Bektāshīs became especially strong amongst the Turkish communities of the Balkans, and remained so up to the 20th century, latterly in a somewhat clandestine manner after the official suppression of the order's patrons, the Janissaries, in 1826. The Mewlewī [see MAWLAWIYYA] contribution to the Turkish mystical tradition—in some ways a more aristocratic one, the order being linked with the dynasty and the higher reaches of the administration—included an especial emphasis on their own particular forms of *dhikr* and *samāʿ* [q.vv.]. But numerous other orders such as the Khalwatiyya, Shādhiliyya and Naḳshbandiyya [q.vv.] were to play important roles until the official suppression of the orders and their *tekke*s by Atatürk in 1926, and the Ṣūfī element in Turkish popular religious life is by no means unimportant today [see e.g. NURCULUK].

A product of this very perceptible Ṣūfī imprint is further seen in Ṣūfism's contribution to Ottoman literature, in both its Turkish and Persian embodiments, in the tradition of the simple mystical poems and hymns of Yūnus Emre (d. 721/1321 [q.v.]), exemplified in the Bektāshī hymns of the 9th/15th century poet Ḳayghusuz Abdāl [q.v.]. Also, prose hagiographical works in both Persian and Turkish became a distinct element of Ottoman literature [see MANĀḲIB].

See, in addition to the references given above to articles, ʿĀSHİḲ; BABA; NEFES; PĪR. 1; ṬARĪḲA; TAṢAWWUF; WALĪ. (ED.)

V. ARCHITECTURE

In the 14th century, Ottoman architecture developed from the simple cubes of such small mosques as that of Ḥādjdj Özbek at Iznik (734/1333). Tiled domes were later replaced by lead. A portico was important as a meeting-place. Early Ottoman rule required dervish centres, and so the mosque-*zāwiye* plan emerged in Anatolia and Thrace, such as that of Bāyezīd Pasha at Amasya (822/1419). A portico admitted to an inner court with a pool under the largest dome lit by an oculus. From this court, steps led to the prayer hall with a fine wooden *minbar* and tiled *miḥrāb* [q.vv.]. The bays on each side of the court formed open rooms, while the winter rooms off them had hearths and ornamental shelving. The plan consisted therefore of two large domes flanked by pairs of smaller domes, and the interior functions of a monument could be read from outside. The apotheosis of the plan in all its permutations was the Green Mosque (Yeşil Cami) at Bursa (822/1420), with sumptuou royal apartments on an upper floor. Tiles and orna ment of all kinds were rivalled by those of th mausoleum (*türbe*) of Meḥemmed I (823/1421 [q.v.]) Viziers' foundations developed the mosque-*medres* [see MADRASA] plan, as at that of Isḥāḳ Pasha at Inegö (887/1482), where the college faces the mosque por tico. With arcades added and the ground paved, thi form became a hallmark of the Ottoman style.

The conservative tradition flowered into the 2 domes of the Ulu Cami (Great Mosque) at Burs (802/1400). The plain square or multi-facetted Ot toman tomb whittled away the elaboration of it Saldjūḳ roots. By the 15th century, major monument were built of ashlar limestone, although the Byzantin system of brick mixed with stone courses survived.

In the mid-15th century, Murād II built Üç Şerefel Cami, the mosque of the Three Balconies, with a revolutionary central dome 24 m in diameter. Thi was carried on six massive piers, of which two wer free-standing. The lateral areas were not walled of but were still roofed with twin domes. The larg courtyard was also an innovation as were the (even tually) four minarets at each corner. The name of th architect is unknown, but by this date the names o builders emerge as ideas developed beyond those o masons working within a tradition. After the conques of Constantinople, the influence of the twin half-domes of the church of Hagia Sophia was absorbed. Yet the urge to combine domed units continued. Fatih Cami (875/1470), the mosque of Meḥemmed II [q.v.] in Istanbul, built by ʿĀtīḳ Sinān, failed to accommodate this influence, but the mosque of Bāyezīd II (911/1505) achieved a rigid version. Both mosques had grand courtyards and re-used Byzantine columns. At the Bāyezīdiyye, the bulky minarets [see MANĀRA] set abnormally far apart were the last before the evolution of the slender, stone style which were emblems of Ottoman supremacy.

In 1537, Sinān ʿAbd ül-Mennān [q.v.] was appointed chief architect. As a soldier, he was trained in organising large work forces and supplies. His strictly-disciplined subordinates could carry out his plans independently from the immaculate mosque of Selīm II, at Karapınar (971/1564) to the elaborate foundation of Murād III, at Manisa (944/1586). At Sinān's memorial complex to Meḥemmed Shehzāde in Istanbul (955/1548), four semi-domes brought the centralised plan to a logical conclusion, but the subordinate buildings of the complex lacked significant unity. This was achieved with the much larger educational and charitable complex (see KÜLLIYYE) built for Süleymān I in Istanbul (964/1557). The mosque is set on a vast esplanade raised on massive vaults. The fine quality of the decoration, including Iznik [q.v.] tiles, contrasts with the puritanical structure where no stone is purely ornamental. The subordinate courtyards are remarkable, and in that of the hostel, where the corner columns are the same size as the rest, a sense of flowing movement is achieved in the Italian Renaissance manner.

Sinān was skilled in the use of awkward sites. At the mosque-*medrese* of Ṣoḳollu Meḥmed Pasha [q.v.] in Kadırga, Istanbul (980/1572), a broad stairway admits to the courtyard under the central hall of the college. The tiled *miḥrāb* wall is unrivalled. At Edirne [q.v.], Sinān built his masterpiece for Selīm II. The use of eight piers inside create a sense of circular movement, and the decoration is sparingly but splendidly used. The four minarets abutting the dome are the tallest in Islam (70.89 m) and the dome is as broad as that of Hagia Sophia (31.28 m). Only the work of

Sinān's most gifted student, Dāwūd Agha, absorbed the influence of the Selīmiyye at the mosque of Nishāndjī Meḥmed Pasha in Istanbul (997/1588). The mosque of Meḥmed Agha in Istanbul (1026/1617) and the belated Yeni Valide Camii at Eminönü (1074/1663) ended the Sinān era.

The palaces of Topkapı and at Edirne expanded pavilion-by-pavilion, and the Baghdād Köshk (1048/1638), built for Murād IV at the former of these, is the noblest Ottoman room. Grander domestic architecture centred on a first floor chamber with rooms at each corner. The 18th and 19th centuries built standard wooden-frame mansions capable of infinite variation, often to create rectangular spaces where a site was misshapen.

Newshehirli Ibrāhīm Pasha and Aḥmed III [*q.vv.*] imported a modified French rococo which blossomed into elegant water kiosks [see SABĪL]. The flowering of ornament did not disguise the square form of prayer halls: thus the decoration of the Nuru Osmaniye Camii in Istanbul, is superficial except for the horseshoe shape of the court. The Ayasma Cami at Üsküdar (1174/1760) and the Laleli one in Istanbul (1177/1763), however, achieved some freedom of interior planning. Ottoman bridges and aqueducts derived from Roman or Saldjūḳ precedents, in particular, Sinān's monumental bridge at Büyükçekmece (975/1587). Bridging techniques were applied to the foundations of major monuments. Fortresses such as Rūmeli Ḥiṣār [*q.v.*] on the Bosphorus were massively built, but their architecture owed much to that of their enemies. *Köshks* (kiosks, belvederes) were, in a sense, permanent tents.

The 19th century was dominated by the buildings of the Balian family, whose palaces included those at Dolmabahçe (1270/1853) and Beylerbey (1282/1865) on the shores of the Bosphorus. They built extensively in the Beaux Arts style. Foreign architects dominated commercial building, but Kemāl ül-Dīn led a revivalist movement. His fourth Waḳf Khan in Istanbul (1335/1916) achieved monumentality, but generally, pastiche replaced that discipline which was at the heart of Ottoman architecture.

Bibliography: Edhem Pasha, *L'architecture ottomane*, Istanbul 1873; C. Gurlitt, *Die Baukunst Konstantinopels*, 4 vols., Berlin 1912; A. Gabriel, *Monuments turcs d'Anatolie*, 2, Paris 1931-4; idem, *Voyages archéologiques dans la Turquie orientale*, Paris 1940; idem, *Une capitale turque, Brousse (Bursa)*, Paris 1958; E. Egli, *Sinan der Baumeister osmanischer Glanzzeit*, Zurich 1954; U. Vögt-Göknil, *Les mosquées turques*, Zurich 1953; İbrahim Hakkı Konyalı, *Mimar Koca Sinan*, Istanbul 1948; Behçet Ünsal, *Istanbul Turkish-Islamic architecture 1071-1923*, London 1959; Tahsin Öz, *Istanbul camileri*, 2 vols., Ankara 1962-5; Suut Kemal Yetkin, *L'architecture turque en Turquie*, Paris 1962; Aptullah Kuran, *The mosque in early Ottoman architecture*, Chicago 1962; Oktay Arslanapa, *Turkish art and architecture*, London 1971; G. Goodwin, *A history of Ottoman architecture*, London 1971; Ömer L. Barkan, *Süleymaniye cami'i ve imareti inşaati, 1550-57*, 2 vols., Ankara 1972-9; Jale N. Erzen, *Mimar Sinan dönemi cami cepheleri*, Ankara 1981; Mustafa Cezar, *Typical commercial buildings of the Ottoman Classical period and the Ottoman construction system*, Istanbul 1983; Kuran, *Sinan, the Grand Old Master of Ottoman architecture*, Washington 1987.

(G. GOODWIN)

VI. CARPETS AND TEXTILES

The Ottoman court was an important patron of textiles and carpets since the 15th century, and commerce in carpets and textiles formed an important part of the Ottoman economy. Silk-weavers and carpet-weavers were listed among the *ehl-i ḥiref* of the court from the reign of Meḥemmed II (1451-80) onward, although no carpets from this period have heretofore been identified with certainty. The popularity of Turkish rugs in the West led to their export in large quantities from early times; in the year 1503, for example, the customs registers of Braşov in Transylvania list over 500 Turkish carpets passing through this single frontier post in a eight-month period. The history and commercial diffusion of Turkish carpets are further documented by their extensive representation in European paintings, especially those of Italy, Holland, and Flanders, as well as of Germany, England, Spain, and France.

Although knotted-pile carpet-weaving as an art form may have existed in Asia Minor prior to the Saldjūḳ invasions of the late 11th century and onward, the on-going artistic traditions of rug-weaving in Anatolia, both commercial and traditional, that have survived into our own time appear to have most of their artistic roots in a Turkic and nomadic tradition that came west from Central Asia. In Ottoman times, Anatolian commercial rug-weaving consisted of two types: carpets with geometric and emblematic designs that probably originate in the nomadic past—including, among others, the so-called Lottos, Holbeins, Memlings, and Crivellis—and carpets whose designs were derived from other media, at first from architectural decoration and then later from the arts of the book—including, among others, the Uşak and other commercial carpets with medallion, star, "chintamani" and "bird" designs [see BISĀṬ in Suppl.].

The carpets termed by scholars "Ottoman" are in fact an atypical sub-group of Turkish carpets, utilising a technique technically related to that of the Mamlūk carpets of Egypt, and patterns stemming from 16th-century designs created in the *naḳḳāsh-khāne* [*q.v.*] in Istanbul. Once assumed to be a fairly homogeneous group of weavings produced in Cairo, these carpets are in fact a diverse group in both technical and artistic quality; they were probably woven in a variety of locales, including Egypt and various places in Anatolia or Thrace, from at least as early as the mid-16th century until well into the 17th. The quality of the "Ottoman" carpets varies widely; the best examples may well have been woven to the specific order of the court in Istanbul, but many large examples woven in Ottoman court designs in Cairo appear to have been made expressly for sale in Europe. The Ottoman carpets had an enormous influence on later commercial and traditional weaving in Anatolia, and by the 19th century even certain nomadic carpets in traditional formats exhibited the influence of the lotus palmettes, sinuous *saz* leaves, and vine arabesques of the earlier court designs. The court-design carpets themselves were woven until the end of the 17th century, with later examples tending to be of a much lower technical and artistic quality.

The Ottoman court practice of collecting and preserving ceremonial robes of the sultans and their families has resulted in the survival of a remarkable sequence of Ottoman silks in Istanbul, while the extensive export of Ottoman silks to western, central and eastern Europe has resulted in the preservation of early pieces in many European collections. Documents dealing with Ottoman silks and other textiles, such as woollen, cotton, and mohair fabrics, are quite numerous both in Turkey and in the lands to which these luxury textiles were exported; the remarkable commerce in high-quality silks between Istanbul and Moscow in the 16th and 17th centuries, for example, is extensively documented in Russian archives, and the Orthodox sacerdotal garments made from Ottoman silk frequently bear embroidered Russian dates and inscriptions.

The artistic as well as the commercial history of silk in the Ottoman empire is enormously complex [see ḤARĪR]. While it has long been known that the Bursa silk market was a major source of cocoons for the Italian silk-weaving industry, it now appears that there was close collaboration between Turkey and Italy in weaving finished silks as well; many fine silk fabrics which technically appear to be within the Italian orbit exhibit impeccably Ottoman designs. Both artistic traditions emerged in the 15th century, owing much to the Mamlūk silks woven in Syria or Egypt, including the popular ogival or diapered design format. Typically Turkish floral motifs, such as the ubiquitous tulip blossom, actually appear in Italian 15th-century silks depicted by *quattrocento* painters such as Uccello, while the earliest surviving Turkish examples with the motif probably date from the early sixteenth century. Fifteenth-century Turkish sources abound with references to Ottoman silks, such as the famous *čatma* velvets of Bursa, but few examples seem to have survived.

By the mid-16th century Ottoman silks are more easily documentable, in part through their appearance in dateable European paintings, in part from their use in dateable European sacerdotal garments, but primarily through their depiction in Turkish historical manuscript illustrations and through the growing use of designs originating in the *naḳḳāsh-khāne* in the arts of textile-weaving, ceramics, carpets, bookbinding, and architectural decoration, each of which may help serve as collateral dating for the others. Large numbers of 16th- and 17th-century Ottoman silks are preserved in museums and collections worldwide.

In the 16th century and later, Bursa continued to be a major source of velvets (*čatma, kadīfe*), whose designs tended to be more traditional; the brocaded silks (*seraser, kemkha, serenk* and *zerbāft*), on the other hand, appear to have been woven in or near Istanbul, and their designs show an astounding variety based on the full repertoire of motifs and styles in use in the *naḳḳāsh-khāne*. In addition, an important subgroup of 16th- and 17th-century Ottoman silks with figural designs and Christian—specifically Orthodox—iconography was woven for use in Orthodox churches both within the Empire and in Russia.

Some of these textiles appear to have been woven directly under court control or on court commission by members of the *ehl-i ḥiref*; new research indicates that there is a wide variety of technical quality exhibited in pieces of similar design, possibly an indication of differences between finer pieces woven for the court on commission, and somewhat coarser silks woven for export or for sale in the bazaar. Ottoman documents from the early 16th century onward indicate that maintaining standards of quality in textiles was a concern both for the *müḥtesib* [see ḤISBA] and for the law courts.

In addition to the artistically important carpets and silks, Ottoman weaving centres from Damascus to Kavalla produced simple and cheap carpets and textiles for commercial sale; many such manufactories also produced goods destined for the army. It is quite difficult to identify specific surviving examples of this kind of weaving, as they are without dateable design or ornamentation. Because of their low value very few examples have been preserved, except occasionally as military booty and trophies in European collections.

Later Ottoman woven textiles in general show a marked decline in artistic and technical quality from those of the 15th until the 17th centuries; the exception is the tradition of Ottoman domestic embroidery, which continued to produce works of very high artistic quality through the 19th century.

Bibliography: T. Öz, *Türk kumaş ve kadifeleri*, i, Ankara 1950, and ii, Istanbul 1951; L. Mackie, *The splendor of Turkish weaving*, Washington 1974; W. Denny, *Ottoman Turkish textiles*, in *Textile Museum Journal*, iii/3 (1972), 55; idem, *Origins and development of Ottoman court carpets*, in *Oriental carpet and textile studies*, ii (1986), 243; idem, *Textiles*, in Y. Petsopoulos (ed.), *Tulips, arabesques and turbans*, London 1982. (W.B. DENNY)

VII. CERAMICS, METALWORK AND MINOR ARTS

(a) *Ceramics*

The Saldjūḳ tradition of glazed pottery and tiles of a hard, white composite ware found at Konya and at Ḳubādābād [*q.vv.*] in the 12th-13th centuries AD was superseded in Anatolia by a crude red earthenware, covered with a white slip and decorated in blue, green, purple or black under a lead glaze. This simple, utilitarian ware, misnamed "Miletus" ware after large quantities were exacavated in that town [see MĪLĀS], was in fact produced at Iznik. At Bursa in the early 15th century, the Yeşil Cami and Yeşil Türbe were elaborated and decorated with *cuerda seca* tiles, in Tīmūrid style; the names of the tilemakers, "the masters of Tabrīz" and "Muḥammad al-Madjnūn", are recorded on the tilework, as well as the fact that the decoration in the Yeşil Cami was completed in 1424 AD by ʿAlī b. Ilyās ʿAlī (Naḳḳāsh ʿAlī). The Yeşil Türbe contains the elaborated tiled cenotaph of Meḥemmed I (1413-21) and a fine *miḥrāb* in similar style. In the second Ottoman capital, hexagonal tiles of off-white ware decorated in underglaze blue with a wide variety of designs are found in the mosque of Murād II, built in 1435. The *miḥrāb* is a mixture of *cuerda seca* and underglaze elements, and these, like the hexagonal tiles, betray a strong influence of imported Yüan and early Ming Chinese porcelain, arguing that such imported blue-and-white was already a current feature of Ottoman life before the conquest of Constantinople in 1453.

With the establishment of the capital in Istanbul, a new industry flourished at Iznik, to supply both vessels and tiles. Both were made of a hard, white composite ware similar in composition to the fritware produced in Ḳāshān described in Abu 'l-Ḳāsim's treatise on ceramic manufacture of 1301 AD, suggesting an influx of new technology rather than the development of the existing Edirne-Iznik tradition. Initially decorated in cobalt blue, a supplementary turquoise was added by the first quarter of the 16th century, and later a full range of softer colours by the mid-16th century, culminating in the brilliant colours of the mature Iznik style from *ca.* 1565 onwards, with cobalt and turquoise blue, viridian, and a relief red aptly compared to sealing-wax in appearance. While the early monochrome blue designs were in a taut, manuscript style with strong Chinese influence, by the middle of the 16th century Iznik ware develops a distinctive iconography of elaborate floral and arabesque forms. Tiles in similar style were produced in great quantity for the new mosques, palaces and other buildings in the city; acknowledged as the finest is the mosque of Rüstem Pasha [*q.v.*] (1561). Iznik ware was also appreciated outside Ottoman Turkey, and has been found as far afield as the Crimea, in Hungary, England, Germany and Nubia.

The history of the Iznik industry is further complicated by the existence of a parallel industry at

Mosques of Shehzāde and Süleymān, Istanbul.

Arz Odasi, Topkapı Sarayı, Istanbul.

Meḥemmed II Mosque, Istanbul.

Rūmeli Ḥiṣār, Istanbul.

Mosque of Selīm II, Edirne.

Central fountain, Mosque of Selīm II, Edirne.

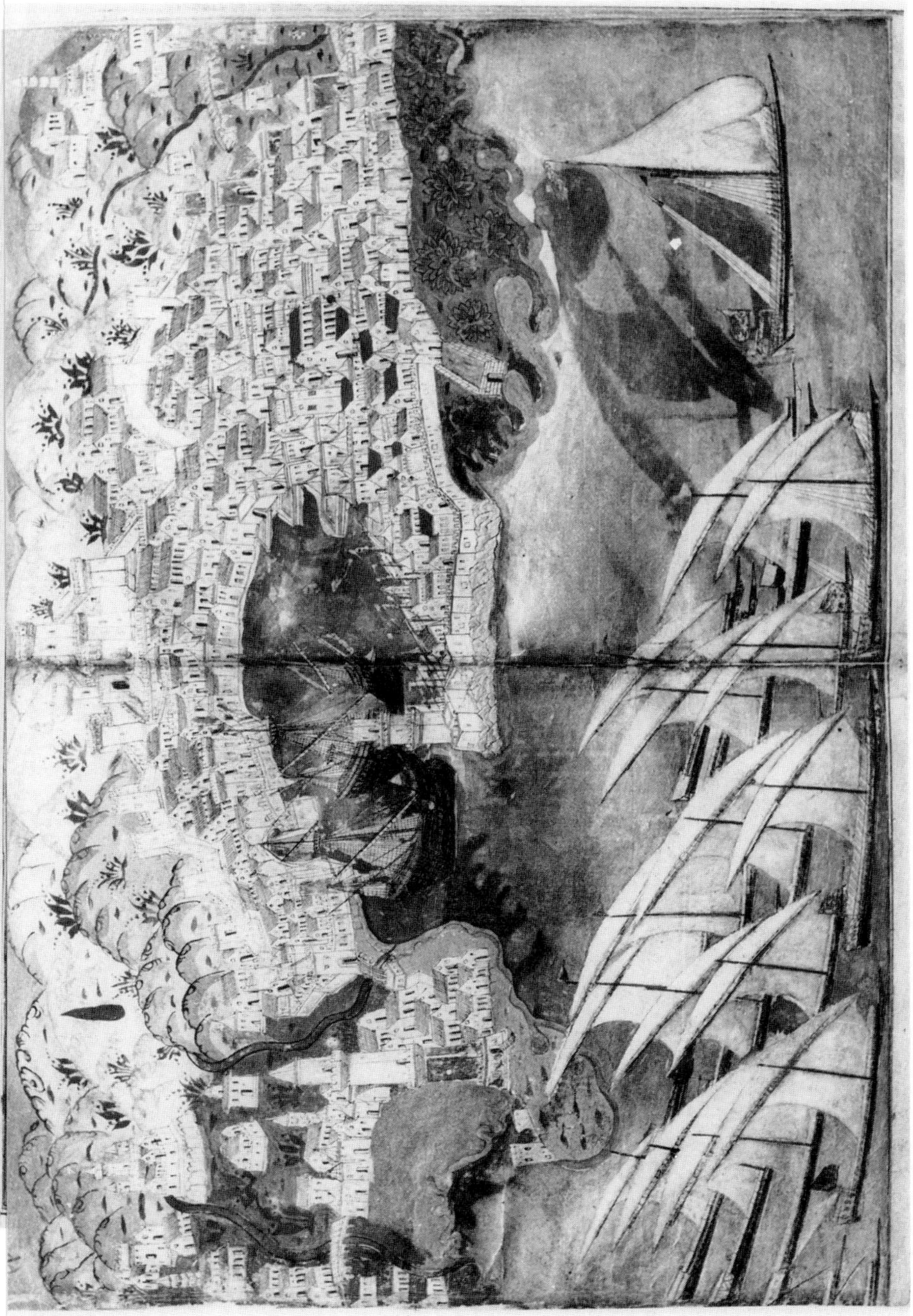

The city of Genoa, *Süleymān-nāme*, written and illustrated by Nāṣūḥ al-Maṭrāḳī al-Silāḥī, TSM (Topkapı Sarayı Müzesi), H. 1608, fol. 32v-33r, ca. 1537.

Süleymān leading his troops, *Hüner-nāme*, Vol. II, written by Seyyid Loḳmān, TSM, H. 1524, fol. 278r, attributed to painter Osman, dated 1588.

Christ ascended to Heaven while a man named Feltiyanus is caught mistakenly to be crucified, *Zübdat al-Tevārīkh*, written by Seyyid Lokmān, TSM, H. 1321, fol. 46r, dated 1583-86.

Kütahya [*q.v.*] in western Anatolia; two inscribed and dated pieces of 1510 and 1529 AD have Armenian texts and refer to Kütahya as the place of manufacture; they are in the general Iznik style. Further, texts refer to the continuing production of Kütahya ware in the 16th and 17th centuries, and the precise identification of these wares is the subject of current research.

By the mid-17th century, the Iznik industry had more or less collapsed, with the withdrawal of Ottoman court patronage, and a minor factory was established at Tekfūr Saray in Istanbul, as well as provincial manufacturies in Diyarbakir and in Syria, working in a sub-Iznik style. A major work was the restoration of the Ḥaram al-Sharīf in Jerusalem, undertaken by Sultan Süleymān from 952/1564-5 onwards. The Jerusalem tiles were made *in situ* by Persian craftsmen who had previously been employed for the decoration of a number of royal structures in Istanbul in the *cuerda seca* technique. In Jerusalem, the decoration is in tile mosaic and *cuerda seca*, and underglaze tiles developed independently of the Iznik tradition. An inscription above the north porch is signed "ʿAbd Allāh of Tabrīz" and dated 959/1551-2.

In the 18th century, the Kütahya industry came into its own, with Armenian potters producing both tiles and pottery in a new style. A major enterprise was the manufacture of a series of tiles with Biblical subjects, originally intended for the refurbishment of the Holy Sepulchre in Jerusalem in 1719 AD; the majority of these were subsequently installed in the Armenian Cathedral of St James in Jerusalem *ca.* 1727. A variety of cups, dishes, bowls and other forms were delicately decorated with underglazed floral designs, and enjoyed a wide popularity outside Turkey. In the 19th century, grotesquely decorated lead-glaze earthenware was produced at Çanakkale, on the Dardanelles; and Tokat has recently been identified as another centre for lead-glazed pottery in the 18th-19th centuries, many examples with incised and dated Turkish inscriptions and some with stamped Armenian monograms.

Armenian potters from Kütahya were brought to Jerusalem under the British mandate after World War I for the repair of the Ḥaram al-Sharīf, and subsequently settled in that city. The modern Kütahya industry has been largely concerned with the production of debased Iznik designs for the tourist industry, but in recent years there have been signs of a new aesthetic vitality.

(b) *Metalwork*

Ottoman metalwork can be divided into two categories, the utilitarian and the decorative. Predominant in the former is the huge quantity of arms and armour used by the Ottoman army [see DJAYSH. iv and ḤARB. iv], of which much was stored in the Byzantine church of Hagia Irene in the grounds of the Top Kapu Palace, and marked accordingly with a crook-like emblem in an incised ring; a large quantity is now in the Military Museum in Istanbul, whose collection also includes important examples of European arms. Turkish arms include shields, helmets, swords and daggers, and horse trappings with characteristically Ottoman *chanfrons*. Much of the finer armour is gilt-plated (*ṭombaḳ*). For everyday use, there was a large production of metal vessels in a wide variety of forms, and from the mid-17th century onwards, an increasing amount of tinned-copper vessels, many of the domestic examples being engraved with maker's and owner's names and dates.

Decorative metalwork was in great demand at the Ottoman court, and was executed both in gold and silver and often encrusted with gems. In the late 15th century there was a considerable production of silver vessels, particularly of bowls with *repoussé* and engraved decoration, of Balkan origin; a number of these are stamped with the *ṭughra* of Bāyezīd II (1481-1512), and it has been noted that their patterns of interlacing arabesques had a direct influence on the design of early Iznik monochrome blue ceramic ware of the same period. Like the other arts, decorative metalwork reached its peak during the mid-16th century, and many examples remain in the Ottoman treasury of Top Kapu Saray, amongst the most distinguished of which is undoubtedly the sword made for Süleymān the Magnificent with its *chinoiserie* panels of dragons and phoenixes in relief, its ivory hilt inlaid with gold arabesques and cloud-scrolls, and its elegant gold relief Arabic *thulth* inscription on both sides of the steel blade dedicating it to Süleymān and dated 933/1526-7; see Rogers and Ward (1988), no. 83. The spine bears Persian *nastaʿlīḳ* verses and the name of the craftsman, Aḥmed Tekkelu.

Mention should also be made of the use of gold inlay and gem settings on vessels of other materials, such as jade, zinc and even imported Chinese porcelain (Krahl, 1986).

(c) *Bookbinding*

The art of bookbinding in the Ottoman empire continued the general tradition of Islamic bookbinding, the salient features of which were the use of a triangular envelope flap to protect the fore-edge of the textblock, the linkstitch sewing of the gatherings or fascicules, the use of traditional Islamic chevron endbands, often of contrasting coloured threads, and the joining of the textblock to the covers with hinged doublures. See Bosch, Carswell and Petherbridge (1981) for a detailed description of these characteristic features, based on an analysis of mediaeval bindings, early bookbinders' manuals (cf. Bosch, 1961) and modern practice in the Islamic world.

The design of Turkish bindings follows the Tīmūrid tradition of the 14th-15th centuries as exemplified at Harāt and Tabrīz (cf. Aslanapa, 1979), often with a pointed central medallion either stamped or built up from individual *petit fer* motifs, with quarter-medallions at the corners. Titles were often incorporated on the spine (Islamic books being designed to be stored horizontally, rather than vertically as in the European tradition). A particularly Turkish feature was the use of marbled papers (*ebrū*) for the lining of the covers. For more lavish courtly bindings, instead of pasteboard, covers were made of expensive materials such as jade, tortoise-shell, and gold and silver cloth, further embellished with precious stones, jewels and pearls set in gold mounts.

The binders themselves would have been an integral part of the *naḳḳāsh-khāne* [*q.v.*] or court scriptorium, generally credited with being the inspiration and source of designs for all the Ottoman crafts, though the importance of the role of the *naḳḳāsh-khāne* in standardising Ottoman taste may be somewhat exaggerated. While the tradition of arabesque ornament continues, along with foreign elements such as the Chinese cloud-scroll, specifically Ottoman elements include spiral designs of tiny rosettes, bold assymetrical compositions in the feathery *sāz* style, and even the use of naturalistic floral motifs—all of which parallel Turkish design in other crafts, notably in ceramics and textile design.

(d) *Glass-making*

Although the Ottoman empire came to include a region of great importance for the history and evolution of glass-making, sc. the Syro-Egyptian littoral, the indigenous tradition in Syria was ended by

Tīmūr's deportation in 1400 of the Syrian craftsmen to Samarḳand. In a curious reversal of roles, the Near East then began, from the time of Bāyezīd II onwards, to be supplied by glass from Venice. In particular, there is a record from 1569 of the Venetian ambassador to the Ottomans, Marcantonio Barbaro, ordering from Venice for Istanbul 900 mosque lamps of two different types, for which he supplied two drawings.

But at least as early as the late 16th century, there was glass-making in Istanbul itself, for in 1582 a Turkish guilds procession included glassblowers on their float and with furnaces. Throughout the 17th century, imported European glass was very popular, often featuring in diplomatic exchanges of presents, and by the early 18th century Bohemian glass became a significant export of the Habsburg empire. There were Bohemian glass warehouses in Istanbul, Izmir, Beirut and Cairo. Even English and Spanish glass was imported into Turkey at this time.

From the late 18th century onwards, the local glass-making tradition was well established in Turkey, with a factory founded at Beykoz on the Anatolian shore of the Bosphorus, and workshops sprang up in nearby villages throughout the 19th century. The earliest Beykoz ware appears to have been of clear glass, often with sprigged gold decoration; the more typical opaque glass with enamel decoration dates from the mid-19th century. The most popular form was the rose-water sprinkler, with a threaded, pierced glass stopper and floral decoration in gold and enamel colours. Other shapes included ewers, cups and tulip-shaped vases, dishes and covered bowls, and also fantastic pieces in the shapes of doves and pistols. The highly-successful modern glass industry at Paşabahçe is located close to Beykoz on the Asiatic shore.

Bibliography: (a) Ceramics. O. Aslanapa, *Osmanlı devrinde Kütahya çinileri*, Istanbul 1949; A. Lane, *The Ottoman pottery of Isnik*, in *Ars Orientalis*, ii (1957); idem, *Later Islamic pottery*², London 1971; J. Carswell and C.J.F. Dowsett, *The Kütahya tiles and pottery from the Armenian Cathedral of St. James, Jerusalem*, 2 vols., Oxford 1972; Carswell, *Six tiles*, in *Islamic art in the Metropolitan Museum of Art*, New York 1972; idem, *Some fifteenth-century hexagonal tiles from the Near East*, in *Victoria and Albert Museum Yearbook*, cxi (London 1972); idem, *Syrian tiles from Sinai and Damascus*, in *Archaeology in the Levant*, Warminster 1978; idem, *Ceramics*, in *Tulips, arabesques and turbans*, ed. Y. Petsopoulos, London 1982; idem, *The tiles in the Yeni Kaplıca baths at Bursa*, in *Apollo*, cxx (1984); Aslanapa, S. Yetkin and A. Altun, *The Iznik tile kilns excavation, 1981-1988*, Istanbul 1989; N. Atasoy and J. Raby, *Iznik, the pottery of Ottoman Turkey*, Istanbul-London 1989; M.S. Tite, *Iznik pottery: an investigation of the methods of production*, in *Archaeometry*, xxxi/2 (1989); Altun, Carswell and G. Oney, *Turkish tiles and ceramics: the Sadberk Hanim Museum*, Istanbul 1991.

(b) Metalwork. Ü. Yücel, *Türk kılıç ustaları*, in *Türk Etnografya Dergisi*, vii-viii (1964-5), 59-99; idem, *Thirteen centuries of Islamic arms*, in *Apollo*, xcii (1970), 46-9; J. Raby and J.W. Allan, *Metalwork*, in *Tulips, arabesques and turbans*, 17-73; R. Krahl, *Porcelain with Ottoman jewelled decoration*, in *Chinese porcelain in the Topkapi Saray Museum*, i, London 1986, 833-77; C. Köseoğlu, *Topkapı, the Treasury*, ed. J.M. Rogers, London 1987.

(c) Bookbinding. G.K. Bosch, *"The staff of the scribes and the implements of the discerning"* (ᶜUmdat al-kuttāb wa ᶜuddat dhawī al-albāb, *by Tamīm ibn al-Muᶜizz ibn Bādīs*), in *Ars Orientalis*, iv (1961), 1-13; Kemal Çiğ, *Türk kitap kaplari*, Istanbul 1971; O. Aslanapa, *The art of bookbinding*, in *The arts of the book in Central Asia*, ed. B. Gray, UNESCO, Paris 1979, 59-71; Bosch, J. Carswell and G. Petherbridge, *Islamic bindings and bookmaking*, The Oriental Institute, Univ. of Chicago 1981; F. Çağman and Z. Tanındı, in *Topkapı, the albums and illustrated manuscripts*, ed. J.M. Rogers, London 1986; Rogers and R.M. Ward, *Bindings*, in *Süleyman the Magnificent*, London 1988, 75-6.

(d) Glass-making. R.J. Charleston, *The import of Western glass into Turkey: sixteenth-eighteenth centuries*, in *The Connoisseur* (May 1966); idem, *The import of European glass into the Near East, 15th-16th centuries*, in *Annales du 3ᵉ Congrès des Journées Internationales du Verre*, Liège 1966; K. Hettes, *Influences orientales sur the verre de Bohème du XVIIIᵉ au XIXᵉ siècles*, in *ibid.*; Fuat Bayramoğlu, *Turkish glass and Beykoz-ware*, Istanbul 1976; J.M. Rogers, *Osmanisches Glas*, in *Türkisches Kunst und Kultur aus osmanischer Zeit*, ii, Recklinghausen 1985, 332-8; Önder Küçükerman, *The art of glass and traditional glassware*, Istanbul 1985; *Proceedings, First International Anatolian Glass Symposium, April 26th-27th, Istanbul 1988*, Istanbul 1990; J. Carswell, *The rosewater sprinkler—Beykoz or Bohemia?*, in *Art at auction 1989-90*, Sotheby's, London 1990, 246-7. (J. Carswell)

VIII. Painting

Manuscript illustration was the dominant form of pictorial art among the Ottomans, who developed a painting school with distinctive characteristics that showed continuity from the 15th to the 19th centuries. Ottoman imperial records indicate that the production of illustrated manuscripts was an institutional activity in the court where there was the *naḳḳāsh-khāne* [*q.v.*], the imperial workshop, composed of artists who illustrated manuscripts commissioned by the sultan and his officials. Its permanent staff consisted of artists of diverse provenances within the empire and were supplemented when needed by the local guilds in Istanbul. Artists collaborated on a manuscript under the supervision of the chief artist, and sometimes a single illustration was executed by more than one *naḳḳāsh*.

The earliest illustrated manuscripts date from the 15th century and are attributed to the palace workshop in Edirne, the earlier capital of the Ottoman Empire. An illustrated copy of Aḥmedī's *Iskender-nāme* (Biblioteca Marciana, cod. or XC) and Kātibī's *Külliyyāt* (Topkapı Saray Müzesi, R. 989), dating from the mid-15th century, are rather provincial works revealing traces of Shīrāz painting. When Meḥemmed II (1451-81) moved the capital to Istanbul after 1453 and built the Ṭopḳapï Palace, he established a studio which through the years absorbed the one in Edirne, producing most of the illustrated manuscripts until the 19th century. Meḥemmed II invited European painters and medallists, such as Gentile Bellini and Costanzo da Ferrara, to execute his portrait and his reign is an important era in Ottoman painting for establishing a tradition of imperial portraiture. These Italian artists inspired local painters such as Sinān Bey, who, portraying the sultan, adopted European norms of portraiture to Islamic canons of manuscript illustration (TSM, H. 2153). Although his successor Bāyezīd II (1481-1512) was less interested in European painting, manuscripts illustrated in his reign reflect certain western influences in the treatment of landscape and architecture (e.g. Amīr Khusraw Dihlawī's *Khamsa* dated 903/1498 in TSM. H. 799, and Hātifī's *Khusraw wa Shīrīn* dated 904/1498-9 in the Metropolitan Museum, New York 69.27).

With the expansion of the empire's eastern and

western frontiers during the reigns of Selīm I (1512-20) and Süleymān I (1520-66), an increasing number of artists joined the *naḳḳash-khāne* from Persia, Syria and Egypt in the east and the Balkan provinces in the west, bringing an eclectic style into Ottoman painting. The literary taste of the time called for Persian classics and for works in Čaghatay Turkish by ʿAlī Shīr Newāʾī. Illustrated copies of Newāʾī's works (*Khamsa* dated 937/1530-1 in TSM, H. 802, and *Dīwāns ca.* 1530 in TSM, R. 804, 806) combine features from the Harāt, Shīrāz and Tabrīz schools of painting as well as some western elements retained from the style of Bāyezīd II's period. It was with the illustrated historical manuscripts produced in Süleymān I's reign that a distinctive school of painting was established, to reach its classical age in the reign of Murād III (1574-95).

The outstanding feature of Ottoman painting is the genre of illustrated histories unmatched by any other Islamic painting school. Predominating in the 16th century, these histories written by the official paid annalists, the *shāh-nāmedjis*, and illustrated at the court studios, visually recreated the achievements of the sultans, their appearance and activities with documentary realism. When illustrating scenes of accession ceremonies, military campaigns, receptions or royal hunts, the Ottoman artist had to introduce a new iconography for which no prototypes existed in other schools of Islamic painting. The monumental illustrated history of the Ottoman Empire written in five volumes by ʿĀrifī, annalist at Süleymān I's court, documented historical events and served as a prototype for future artists in iconography and compositional schemes (e.g. *Süleymān-nāme*, TSM, H. 1517 dated 965/1558). A series of histories were written in the second half of the 16th century by Loḳmān, ʿĀrifī's successor, and illustrated by a group of artists headed by ʿOthmān, in which a classical Ottoman style was achieved by eliminating foreign elements and formalising rigidly observed compositions, strong colours and powerful figures. The *Tārīkh-i Sulṭān Süleymān* on the life of Süleymān I (Chester Beatty Library, T. 413, dated 987/1579), *Shāh-nāme-yi Selīm Khān* on Selīm II (TSM, A. 3595, dated 989/1581), the two-volume *Hüner-nāme* covering the history of the Ottomans (TSM, H. 1523 and 1524, dated 1584 and 1588) and the *Sur-nāme* narrating the royal circumcision festival of 1582 (TSM, H. 1344, dated *ca.* 1582) replete with illustrations, all realistically documenting the events, personages and their settings, mirror the political and social history of the empire in the 16th century.

This realistic approach was maintained in religious manuscripts as well. The Ottomans' interest in their ancestry resulted in the production of world histories where the sultans are linked genealogically with the prophets. The illustrations in Loḳmān's *Zübdet al-tewārīkh* (Türk Islam Eserleri Müzesi, 1973, TSM, H. 1321 (BL, T. 414, dated 1583-86) and the six-volume work on the life of Prophet Muḥammad, the *Siyer-i Nebī* dated 1595 (TSM, H. 1221, 22, 23, CBL, T. 419 and New York Public Library), follow the compositional schemes in the historical manuscripts.

One other distinctive genre in Ottoman painting is royal portraiture. Set by Meḥemmed II, the tradition of portraiture continued into the 16th century with works by Nigārī, who painted Süleymān I, Selīm II and Khayr al-Dīn Barbarossa [*q.v.*] (TSM, H. 2134). Later in the century, portrait albums were produced. A *Shemāʾil-nāme* describing the appearance of the first twelve sultans, written by Loḳmān in 1579 and illustrated by ʿOthmān, set a model for all later images of the sultans (TSM, H. 1563, Istanbul Üniversitesi Kitapliği T. 6088).

Interest in imperial histories resulted in one other feature of Ottoman painting, namely topographical illustration, which was foreshadowed early in the 16th century in the works of Pīrī Reʾīs [*q.v.*], captain and cartographer known for his sea charts and map of the Atlantic Ocean. The works of Nāsūḥ al-Maṭraḳī al-Silāḥī [*q.v.*], an officer and historian who wrote and illustrated Süleymān I's campaigns, are the basic examples of this genre (e.g. *Beyān-i menāzil-i sefer-i ʿIrāḳayn*, IUK, T. 5964, dated 944/1537-8, *Süleymān-nāme*, TSM, H. 1608, dated *ca.* 1543). Topographical illustrations continued throughout the 16th and 17th centuries in historical manuscripts.

With the empire entering a period of stagnation in the 17th century, there was a decline in the production of illustrated histories. The artist, no longer having to record imperial achievements, turned to single-figure studies and scenes from daily life. Along with the westernising efforts of the sultans in the 18th century, painting took a new course. During Aḥmed III's reign (1703-30) the last manuscript of a historical nature was produced by the poet Wehbī and painter Lewnī. The illustrations of the *Sur-nāme* (TSM, A. 3593) relating the circumcision festival of 1721 are full of innovative elements such as shading and perspective. Lewnī and his contemporary Bukhārī also painted single figures dressed in glorious costumes. Costume studies were produced throughout the century, the best examples being displayed in the *Khubān-nāme* and the *Zanān-nāme* of 1206/1793 (IUK, T. 5502), where figures seem to have acquired European postures and more volume. The same is true for the sultans' portraits painted in the 18th and 19th centuries. Manuscript illustration ended in the 19th century, and other forms of painting, such as painting on walls and small furniture, emerged with easel painting in the western sense taking over at the end of the century.

Bibliography: R.M. Meriç, *Türk nakış tarihi araştırmaları*, Ankara 1953; V. Minorsky, *The Chester Beatty Library: a catalogue of the Turkish manuscripts and miniatures*, Dublin 1958; F.E. Karatay, *Topkapı Sarayı Müzesi kütüphanesi Türkçe yazmalar kataloğu*, Istanbul 1961; *Farsça yazmalar kataloğu*, Istanbul 1961; R. Ettinghausen, *Turkish miniatures from the 13th to the 18th century*, Milan 1965; I. Stchoukine, *La peinture turques d'après les manuscrits illustrés. Ire partie: de Suleyman à Osman II*, Paris 1966; S.K. Yetkin, *L'ancienne peinture turque du XIIe au XVIIIe siècle*, Paris 1970; Stchoukine, *La peinture turque d'après les manuscrits illustrés. IIème partie: de Murad IV à Mustafa II*, Paris 1971; N. Atasoy, *Türk minyatür sanatı bibliografyası*, Istanbul 1974; idem and F. Çağman, *Turkish miniature painting*, Istanbul 1974; G. Renda, *Batılılaşma döneminde Türk resim sanatı*, Ankara 1977; M. And, *Turkish miniature painting*, Istanbul 1978; E. Binney, *Turkish treasures from the collection of Edwin Binney*, Portland, Oregon 1979; Çağman, *Turkish miniature painting*, in *Art and architecture of Turkey*, Fribourg 1980; E. Atil, *Art of the book*, in *Turkish art*, Washington D.C. 1980; N. Titley, *Miniatures from Turkish manuscripts*, London 1981; Atil, *The age of Suleyman the Magnificent*, Washington D.C. 1987; *Suleymanname*, Washington D.C. 1987; Çagman and Z. Tanındı, *Topkapı Saray Museum. Albums and illustrated manuscripts*, ed. J.M. Rogers, London 1986; G. Renda, *Traditional Turkish painting and the beginnings of Western trends*, in *A history of Turkish painting*, Seattle-London 1988; Rogers and R.M. Ward, *Suleyman the Magnificent*, London 1988.

(Günsel Renda)

IX. Numismatics

When ʿO<u>th</u>mān b. Ertog<u>h</u>rul (*ca.* 699-724/1300-24) established his base in Sögüd in Bithynia there was probably very little coinage of any kind in circulation. The principal Islamic coin he would have encountered was the Rūm Sal<u>dj</u>ūḳ *dirham*. The Byzantine *basilikon*, the Venetian *grosso* and smaller *denier*-sized silver from various European mints may also have been found in trade or as booty of war. The Rūm Sal<u>dj</u>ūḳ coinage continued to be based on the classic Islamic *dirham*, weighing 2.8-2.9 gr, until the coinage reform of the Il-<u>kh</u>ān Maḥmūd <u>Gh</u>azan (694-703/1295-1304) in 696/1297. However, with the continued devaluation of the new coinage under <u>Gh</u>azan's successors, Öl<u>dj</u>eytü (703-16/1304-16) and Abū Saʿīd (716-36/1316-35 [*q.vv.*]), the eastern Islamic world gave up the long-established currency system of *dīnār*s and *dirhams*, whose metrology was enshrined in the *<u>Sh</u>arīʿa*, for one where the weight standard was regularly manipulated (and usually devalued) by the governing power.

Öl<u>dj</u>eytü's early 8th/14th century coinage in Western Anatolia consisted of light silver *dirhams* weighing about one gramme, but the earliest known Ottoman coin, struck in the name of ʿO<u>th</u>mān b. Ertog<u>h</u>rul, weighs 0.62 gr. Following his capture of the city of Bursa, *ca.* 726, Or<u>kh</u>an b. ʿO<u>th</u>mān (724-61/1324-60) issued his first coin, an *aḳče* weighing about 1.10 gr based on a conventional Il<u>kh</u>ānid prototype, with the *kalima* and the names of the four Orthodox Caliphs on the obverse, and that of the ruler and mint (*Brusa*) on the reverse with the date 726 written out in Arabic in the margin. Or<u>kh</u>an issued several subsequent series of *aḳče*s, all without mint names or dates, the last of which, introduced after the Ottomans obtained their first foothold on the European shore of the Dardanelles at Gallipoli *ca.* 752, was notable because it omitted his father's name. A special five-*aḳče* weight, 5.80 gr, issue of this type was also struck, probably as a donative for Or<u>kh</u>an's victorious troops.

Or<u>kh</u>an's son and successor, Murād I (761-91/1360-89) issued three types of *aḳče*, one, *ca.* 762, with a line dividing the reverse field, a second, *ca.* 772, with two lines dividing the obverse and reverse fields, and a third, *ca.* 782, which was the first to omit the *kalima* from the coinage, with three lines dividing the reverse field. Murād also struck copper *man<u>gh</u>ir*s in his own name, one with the unusual date of Ramaḍān 790.

Bāyezīd I (791-804/1389-1402) continued his father's practice of numbering his issues. The first has a numeral 4 and the date 792 on the reverse, and the second, *ca.* 802, has a pellet on the dividing lines. These early issues simply give the names of the rulers without any titles. When Tīmūr invaded Western Anatolia and overthrew Bāyezīd at the Battle of Ankara in 804/1402, Bāyezīd's four sons competed for the former Ottoman territories. Amīr Süleymān held Rumelia and struck coins in Edirne dated 806 and 813. Meḥemmed Čelebi held Bursa and Amasya, where he issued coins first acknowledging Tīmūr as overlord, then, after Tīmūr's death, in his own right. Mūsā Čelebi struck coinage in Edirne in 813 and Muṣṭafā in Edirne and Serez in 822 and 824.

After his consolidation of power Meḥemmed I (816-24/1413-21) struck coins dated 816 on which he called himself *al-Sulṭān*, but he removed this title, probably at the urging of the Tīmūrids, on his 822 issue. Murād II (824-48 and 850-5/1421-44 and 1446-51) struck a one-year issue dated 824 and a second in 825 from various mints in Rumelia and Anatolia. On these he inscribed his name in a *ṭug<u>h</u>ra*, a practice introduced by Amīr Süleymān in 806. On Murād's third issue of 834 the obverse and reverse are divided by two interlaced lines without a *ṭug<u>h</u>ra*. After his first abdication his son Meḥemmed II (first reign 848-50/1444-6) issued *aḳče*s bearing the date 848, and when Murād II resumed power he copied his son's coinage, unobtrusively changing the order from Meḥemmed b. Murād to Murād b. Meḥemmed by moving the position of the word *ibn* from the left to the right of the names.

Until the 848 issue the weight of the *aḳče* had remained roughly constant at 1.1 gr, but during Meḥemmed II's second reign (855-86/1451-81) it was regularly reduced each time a new issue was introduced, first in 855, and then in 865, which was the first coinage to bear the mint name *Ḳusṭanṭīniyya*, conquered in 857. With his fourth issue in 875, Meḥemmed experimented by striking a ten-*aḳče* coin, the *aḳče-i buzurg*. His fifth issue was dated 880, and two years later he brought out the first Ottoman gold coin, the *sulṭānī*, which adopted the weight standard of the Venetian ducat, *ca.* 3.52 gr. A second gold issue was dated 883 and a third 885. In the last year of Meḥemmed's life his sixth and last series of *aḳče*s was struck with the date 886. After the death of the Tīmūrid <u>Sh</u>ah Ru<u>kh</u> (807-50/1404-46), Meḥemmed cast aside his inhibitions over the use of titles, and introduced two royal styles that were to remain in use for centuries. The first was *Sulṭān al-barrayn wa-<u>kh</u>āḳān al-baḥrayn al-Sulṭān ibn al-Sulṭān* and the second *Ḍārib al-naḍr wa-ṣāḥib al-ʿizz wa 'l-naṣr fi 'l-barr wa 'l-baḥr*. Like his forebears he also struck *man<u>gh</u>ir*s in his own name in several mints.

On the accession of Bāyezīd II (886-918/1481-1512) it was decided to date the coinage by the sultan's accession year rather than by issue as had been the previous practice. This was probably to avoid public anger caused by the repeated debasements of the *aḳče* under Meḥemmed II. The short-lived rebellion of <u>D</u>jem b. Meḥemmed was marked by an issue of *aḳče*s from Bursa following the design of his father's last coinage dated 886. Bāyezīd II also struck coins in Gelibolu (Gallipoli) and Trabzon (Trebizond). The dies for the latter may actually have been cut by his son and successor Selīm <u>Sh</u>āh whose private craft was die-cutting. Until the end of his reign, Bāyezīd II's coinage from both Rumelia and Anatolia was uniform in style, and was, in effect, the "national" coinage of the Ottomans.

With the conquests of Selīm I (918-26/1512-20) and his son Süleymān I (926-74/1520-66) the character of the Ottoman coinage developed from a national to an imperial one. After Selīm conquered Syria and Egypt he continued the coinage of the Bur<u>dj</u>ī Mamlūks who struck gold *a<u>sh</u>rafī*s substantially lighter than the contemporary Ottoman *sulṭānī*s, and silver *medin*s based on the half-*dirham*, which by then was considerably heavier than the Ottoman *aḳče*. Selīm also introduced the custom of striking conquest coins to signal the submission of the important towns he had captured, including Āmid (Diyarbakır), Bitlīs, Dima<u>sh</u>ḳ (Damascus), Ḥalab (Aleppo), al-<u>D</u>jazīra, Ḥiṣn Kayf and al-Ruhā (Urfa/Edessa) [*q.vv.*].

Süleymān I retained a uniform *aḳče* coinage for Rumelia and Anatolia. After the Ottomans conquered the Mag<u>h</u>rib the broad flan heavy weight gold coinage of the Ziyānids of Tilimsān (Tlemcen) remained in use, as did the square silver *naṣrī* of formerly Ḥafṣid Tunisia. After the conquest of ʿIrāḳ and Ā<u>dh</u>arbāy<u>dj</u>ān from the Ṣafawids, a heavier *mit<u>h</u>ḳāl*-weight silver coinage was introduced for use in these lands, but shortly thereafter its weight was reduced by a quarter. Under Süleymān's son Selīm II (974-82/1566-74) minting activity declined, but Murād III (982-1003/1574-95) and Meḥemmed III (1003-12/1595-1603) expanded the number of mints to no fewer than fifty, the greatest in Ottoman history.

During Murād III's reign the Empire was engulfed by a tidal wave of silver from the New World. European traders imported silver in coin and bullion in order to purchase gold which they then exported and sold in Westen Europe at considerable profit. As a result the *aḳče* suffered a rapid devaluation, producing both inflation and great hardship for the peoples of the empire. This decline in prosperity was reflected by a decrease in the number of active mints and a great scarcity of gold coinage struck in the names of Aḥmed I (1012-26/1603-17), Muṣṭafā I (1026-7 and 1031-2/1617-8 and 1622-3), ʿO̲th̲mān II (1027-31/1618-22), and Murād IV (1032-49/1623-40). The quick succession of sultans demanded frequent distributions of *d̲j̲ulūs bak̲h̲s̲h̲īs̲h̲i*, accession donations, which regularly emptied the treasury just when money was most needed to defend the state against its enemies.

ʿO̲th̲mān II was the first to issue ten-*aḳče* coins in large numbers, because by then the one *aḳče*'s weight had fallen to 0.30 gr and a larger coin was needed for everyday use. The ten-*aḳče* was rapidly debased under Muṣṭafā I and in the economic crises of Murād IV's reign. Midway through the latter Kemankes̲h̲ Ḳara Muṣṭafā Pas̲h̲a attempted to revive and protect the coinage by closing down most of the provincial mints in Rumelia and Anatolia, and introduced the *para*, valued at five *aḳče*s, to the Constantinople currency. This reform was continued in Ibrāhīm's reign (1049-58/1640-8), when the Constantinople coinage consisted of the 10, 5, 2 and 1-*aḳče*, and Egypt's of the gold *sulṭānī*, the *medin* valued at 3 *aḳče*s and the 1-*aḳče*. Since the reign of Bāyezīd II, the striking of copper *mang̲h̲ir*s had been the prerogative of local tax farmers who forced the public to buy new issues in return for payment in silver or gold. By now, however, the purchasing power of copper had fallen so low that it had virtually disappeared from circulation.

The spiral of economic decline continued under Meḥemmed IV (1058-99/1648-87), when the striking of silver and gold virtually ceased in Constantinople, and the value of the Ottoman gold *sulṭānī* decreased markedly against the Venetian ducat, or sequin. It continued to appear sporadically in Algeria, Tunisia and Tripoli, and there are also unique examples of gold coins from Belgrade and Bag̲h̲dād. During the 11th/17th century European coinage virtually supplanted that of the Ottomans in their own territories, because the population had lost trust in the products of their local mints. In the last year of Meḥemmed's reign a European renegade called Frenk Muṣṭafā was called upon to reform the Constantinople mint. His first act was to prepare dies of very high artistic quality to return a sense of pride to the imperial mint, and a few specimens of this work have survived.

The accession of Süleymān II (1099-1102/1687-91) saw three major reforms. The first was to strike broad flan gold coins for conversion into jewellery, the second introduced a large-sized silver coinage on the European pattern made up of the *zolota*, 18.5-19.7 gr, and half-*zolota*, 8.65-9.85 gr, and, most important, a new copper coinage to compensate for the great shortage of silver *aḳče*s. The new *mang̲h̲ir* bore the sultan's *ṭug̲h̲ra* on the obverse and was originally valued at one *aḳče*. Its great popularity led to the opening of a second mint for copper in Saray Bosna (Sarajevo) in 1099, and for a time its value rose to two *aḳče*s. By the time Aḥmed II (1102-6/1691-5) acceded, however, its value had plunged to virtually nothing, and it was withdrawn soon after. Aḥmed II's coinage followed the pattern established by Süleymān II.

Fresh attempts at reform were made under Muṣṭafā II (1106-15/1695-1703). He added mints in Edirne, Izmir and Erzurum to that of Constantinople so that European and Ṣafawid coins could be restruck as they reached the frontiers of the state. A new gold coinage called the *as̲h̲rafī*, bearing the sultan's *ṭug̲h̲ra*, was introduced to replace the discredited *sulṭānī*, as was a *ḳurūs̲h̲* valued at 120 *aḳče*s compared to the 90-*aḳče zolota*, but both these reforms failed because of the economic chaos caused by the wars with Austria.

During the reign of Aḥmed III (1115-43/1703-30) the coinage was repeatedly taken in hand, and a degree of stability was established. In the early years the *as̲h̲rafī* and *zolota* with the mint name *Ḳusṭanṭīniyya* were the dominant coins. These were succeeded by a gold *funduḳ*, or *zind̲j̲irli altun*, bearing only the sultan's *ṭug̲h̲ra* on the obverse and *ḍuriba fī Islāmbol* on the reverse, accompanied by the new *ḳurūs̲h̲*, valued at 40 *para*s or 120 *aḳče*s, whose theoretical weight was approximately 24 gr, with its fractions half, quarter and eighth. In the last years of Aḥmed's reign, a three-quarters weight gold coin, 2.64 gr, was introduced, called the *zar-i maḥbūb*. Both this and the *funduḳ* had fractional and multiple denominations in the broad-flan *zīnet*, ornamented jewellery coins. This coinage pattern continued under Maḥmūd I (1143-68/1730-54) and ʿO̲th̲mān III (1168-71/1754-7). The Barbary regencies continued to strike gold coins whose weight was comparable to the Venetian sequin and the Constantinople *funduḳ*, while the silver coinage maintained various standards based on local usage, but was struck in the name of the sultan as nominal overlord. These coins were dated by the actual year of their striking rather than by accession year only, as they were in Constantinople and Cairo.

Under Muṣṭafā III (1171-87/1757-74), the coinage of Constantinople became even more complex, consisting of the gold *funduḳ* and half-*funduḳ*, the *zar-i maḥbūb* and its half, the *zīnet* 5, 3 and 1½ *funduḳ*, the silver *ḳurūs̲h̲* series, full, 40 *para*, half, 20 *para*, quarter, 10 *para* and eighth, 5 *para*, and the double *zolota*, 60 *para*, the *zolota*, 30 *para* and the half-*zolota*, 15 *para*. There was also the *para* valued at three *aḳče*s and the *aḳče* itself. At this time the Constantinople mint modified the traditional dating system by placing the actual year of striking on the coin, abbreviated to (1171) 1-9 and (11) 80-87 as well as the accession year. With the accession of ʿAbd ül-Ḥamīd I (1187-1203/1774-89) came the final change when coins were dated both by accession year and *d̲j̲ulūs* (regnal) year. (The actual date of striking is found by substracting one from the number of regnal years and adding the remainder to the accession year.) In 1203, the last year of ʿAbd al-Ḥamīd's reign, the double *ḳurūs̲h̲*, 80 *para*, was introduced to meet the cost of the war with Russia. Selīm III (1203-22/1789-1807), added the silver 100 *para* (2½ *ḳurūs̲h̲*) to the series. Towards the end of his rule an imbalance in the gold and silver ratio caused an increase in the amount of gold and a decrease in that of silver placed in circulation.

The coinage of Egypt, always the Ottomans' primary source of gold, whose tribute was of the greatest importance to the imperial finances, became more prominent during this period. Its minor coinage was still based on the *medin*, now a debased and ugly little coin which people stored in their cheeks to keep it from being lost in the seams of their robes or blown away by the *K̲h̲amsīn* winds. Following ʿAlī Pas̲h̲a's revolt in 1183 Egypt struck its first large-size silver coins, the *kurūsh*, half and quarter. When the French seized Egypt during Selīm III's reign the Cairo mint issued *kurūsh*, halves and quarters bearing the regnal year 13, and then, when Ottoman authority was restored, another issue with the "sun" of Shemsī Pasha to the left of the *tughra* was struck in the year 16.

Selīm's overthrow in 1222/1807 led to the enthronement of the feeble Muṣṭafā IV (1222-3/1807-8). By this time the coinage of Algiers, Tunis and Tripoli (Ṭarābulus al-Gharb) had undergone a major revival thanks to the proceeds of piracy in the Mediterranean. The Algerian Deys issued *sulṭānī*s, halves and quarters in gold, but allied their silver coinage to the Spanish eight reales, striking double, single, half and quarter *real dirhams* with the approximate weight and fineness of the Spanish silver coinage. The Beys of Tunis were too poor to sustain a gold coinage, and issued a billon *riyāl/kurūsh*, half and quarter. In Ṭarābulus al-Gharb, now held by the Ḳaramānlī dynasty [*q.v.*], the *sulṭānī* remained in use, with frequent silver issues of varying quality forced into circulation largely as a means of raising taxes from their unhappy subjects.

The coinage of Maḥmūd II (1223-55/1808-39) is the most complex in Ottoman history, and the word chaos might most aptly describe it. Many points concerning it are still obscure. At the beginning of the reign it was still traditional in form, but the tremendous political and economic upheavals of the time transformed it into something new and different. A bewildering variety of gold and silver coins were in circulation whose exchange rates fluctuated constantly, whose weights and alloys were inconsistent with one another, and whose designs and legends departed from past conventions. Added to this was the usual host of foreign coins circulating in the Empire, as well as counterfeit coins which created further confusion in the public mind.

The financial situation was never easy, and often desperate, with the state living from hand to mouth, and the manipulation of coinage was seen as an unavoidable expedient to help close the wide gap between income and expenditure. By this time the government fully appreciated that debasing the coinage was self-defeating, and that a stable medium of exchange had to be created if the state was to achieve its broader goals of renewal and reform.

The Constantinople currency was altered no fewer than eight times in Maḥmūd's reign, and that of Cairo under Muḥammad ʿAlī Pasha [*q.v.*] four times. The virtually independent state of Algiers was the first whose mint installed a European coinage press in 1236/1821. The French invasion of 1245/1830 ended the Algerian Deys' coinage, but the Bey of Constantine continued to strike coins in Maḥmūd's name until 1253/1837. Tunis maintained a silver billon coinage throughout the reign, and the Ḳaramānlī Beys of Ṭarābulus al-Gharb struck a multitude of issues, sometimes several in a year, as a means of taxation. Their mint was closed after the Ottomans retook the province in 1250/1834. In the east a limited copper coinage was struck in Wan, and a more extensive one in Baghdād during the final years of the local Mamlūk dynasty.

After Egypt had reformed its coinage under Muḥammad ʿAlī in 1251/1835 the impetus for reform in Constantinople gathered speed, and by the end of Maḥmūd's reign the establishment of an Ottoman coinage on the European pattern was being considered for inclusion within the reforms of the forthcoming Imperial Rescript [see TANẒĪMĀT], issued in 1255/1839. While the Egyptian coinage reform had introduced a 100-*kurūsh* coin with the weight of an English guinea as its principal gold coin, and the 20-*kurūsh taler* weighing 28 grams patterned on the Maria Theresa thaler, as its main silver coin, the Constantinople government preferred to rectify the coinage by striking the silver 20-*kurūsh medjīdiyye* which weighed 24 gr of 833 parts fine silver, and the gold *lira* valued at 100 *kurūsh* weighing 7.20 gr of 916 parts fine gold. This coinage was to last unchanged until the end of the Empire in 1341/1923. The gold denominations were 500, 250, 100, 50 and 25 *kurūsh*, the silver 20, 10, 5, 2 and one *kurūsh*, and 20 *para*, and the copper 40, 20, 10, 5 and one *para*. The copper coinage was discontinued at the end of ʿAbd ül-Medjīd's reign because people refused to accept coins that could not be freely converted into silver and gold. Perhaps the most important part of the currency reform reduced seigniorage to the point where it merely covered the costs of running the mint. In the absence of any other means of raising revenue the government was forced to close the shortfall between tax receipts and expenditures through the expedient of contracting foreign loans. This brought about the bankruptcy of the Empire and the fall of ʿAbd ül-ʿAzīz (1277-93/1861-76). He was succeeded by Murād V, who ruled for three months in 1293/1876, ʿAbd ül-Ḥamīd II (1293-1327/1876-1909), Meḥemmed V Reshād (1327-36/1909-18) and finally Meḥemmed VI Wāḥid al-Dīn (1336-41/1918-22). The new coinage carried the reigning sultan's *tughra* on the obverse, with the regnal year beneath, and on the reverse the legend *ʿAzza naṣruhu ḍuriba fī Ḳusṭanṭīniyya* with the accession year. A gold *zīnet* coinage was introduced during ʿAbd ül-Ḥamīd's reign, the proceeds from which were used to help fund the state pensions scheme.

The most popular denominations in the currency series were the *lira* and the five-*kurūsh* (quarter-*medjīdiyye*). The small gold coins were used as presents on the occasion of circumcision celebrations or gifts for brides, while the large ones were converted into jewellery to be kept as family savings. The Imperial mint also struck special series of coins to commemorate the sultans' visits to Edirne in 1247/1831, Edirne in 1262/1846, Bursa in 1277/1861, Bursa in 1327/1909, Edirne in 1328/1910 and Selānik (Salonica), Monastīr (Bitola) and Ḳoṣowa (Prishtina) in 1329/1911. The striking of the *medjīdiyye* (20 *kurūsh*) was suspended in 1295 after the rapid fall in the price of silver following the development of the Comstock Lode in the United States. It was reintroduced in the last year of the First World War to pay the Turkish troops fighting in Syria and Palestine.

Egypt's coinage was hampered because the minting machinery could not keep up with the needs of the province, and foreign coins circulated more freely than did local pieces. However, the Cairo mint did strike a full range of denominations: gold 500, 100, 50, 25, 10 and 5 *kurūsh*; silver 20, 10, 5, 2½, 1 *kurūsh*, 20 and 10 *para*, and copper 40, 20, 10, 5, 4 and 1 *para*. After the British Protectorate was established the coinage was taken in hand and struck in European mints from 1302/1884 onwards. This coinage continued to bear the name, and accession and regnal year of the Ottoman Sultan until the Ottomans joined the German side in the First World War, whereupon the British deposed the Khedive ʿAbbās Ḥilmī II [*q.v.*] and made his brother Ḥusayn Kāmil [*q.v.*] sultan of Egypt. In Tunis the Ḥusaynid Beys started to place their own names on the coinage during the reign of ʿAbd ül-Medjīd. They introduced European coinage machinery in 1263, and based their unit of value on the *riyāl* [*q.v.*] weighing 3.20 gr. The gold coinage consisted of the 100, 50, 25, 10 and 5 *riyāl*; silver of the 5, 4, 2, 1 and ½ *riyāl* (8 *kharrūb*), and copper of the 8, 4, 2, 1, ½ and ¼ *kharrūb*. These coins were struck in the names of both the Ottoman Sultan and the Bey of Tunis until the establishment of the French Protectorate in 1298/1881.

Bibliography: There is an extensive literature on Ottoman numismatics, much of it in short articles, but only the principal works are mentioned in this bibliography.

S. Lane Poole, *Catalogue of oriental coins in the British Museum*, viii, London 1875-90; Edhem Ismāʿīl Ghālib, *Taḳwīm-i meskūkāt-i ʿOthmāniyye*, Constantinople 1307; Khalīl Edhem, *Meskūkāt-i ʿOthmāniyye I. Meskūkāt-i ḳadīmī-yi Islāmiyye, ḳism* vi, Constantinople 1334/1916; F. Sultan, *La monnaie égyptienne*, Paris 1914; E. Kolerkılıç, *Osmanlı imparatorluğunda para*, Ankara 1958; C. Ölçer, *Son altı Osmanlı padişahı zamanında İstanbul'da basılan gümüş paralar*, Istanbul 1966; idem, *Yıldırım Bayezid'in oğullarına ait akće ve mangırlar*, Istanbul 1968; N. Pere, *Osmanlılarda madeni paralar*, Istanbul 1968; C. Ölçer, *Sultan Mahmud II zamanında darp edilen Osmanlı madeni paraları*, Istanbul 1970 (addendum published Istanbul 1990); İ. and C. Artuk, *İstanbul Arkeoloji Müzeleri teshirdeki İslâmî sikkeler kataloğu*, ii, Istanbul 1971; İ. Artuk, *Kanuni Sultan Süleyman adına basılan sikkeler*, Ankara 1972; C. Ölçer, *Sovyet Rusya müzelerindeki (Moskova ve Leningrad) nadır Osmanlı madeni paraları*, Istanbul 1972; A. von Schaendlinger, *Osmanische Numismatik*, Brunswick 1973; C. Ölçer, *Nakışlı Osmanlı mangırları*, Istanbul 1975; idem, *Sultan Abdülmecid Han devri Osmanlı madeni paraları*, Istanbul 1978; idem, *Sultan Abdülaziz Han devri Osmanlı madeni paraları*, Istanbul 1969; idem, *Avrupa müzelerinde nadır Osmanlı madeni paraları*, Istanbul 1984; idem, *Sultan Murad V ve Sultan Abdülhamid II dönemi Osmanlı madeni paraları*, Istanbul 1986; idem, *Sultan Mehmed Reşad ve Sultan Mehmed Vahdeddin dönemi Osmanlı madeni paraları*, Istanbul 1987; idem, *Sultan Yavuz Selim Şah bin Bayazid Han dönemi Osmanlı sikkeleri 917-926 AH/1512-1520 AD*, Istanbul 1989; idem, *Darphane Müzesi: Osmanlı madeni paraları kataloğu*, Istanbul 1985. See also AḲČE and PARA.

(R.E. DARLEY-DORAN)

OTRANTO [see ITALIYA].

OTRĀR [see UTRARI].

ÖTÜKEN, a forested, mountain area of Inner Asia which had a special religious and moral significance for the early Turkish peoples.

It seems to have been located in the eastern part of the Khangai Mts. around the headwaters of the Orkhon and Tamir rivers (the latter river corresponding, according to R. Giraud, *L'Empire des Turcs célestes. Les règnes d'Elterich, Qapghan et Bilga (680-734)*, Paris 1960, 207, to the *ïduḳ yer sub* "sacred places and watercourses" of the old Turkish inscriptions), generally along the co-ordinates of long. 101° E. and lat. 47° N., in the western part of what is now the Mongolian People's Republic (see *ibid.*, 172-3). It was the heartland of the Ḳaghans of the Eastern Türk or T'ukiieh when they constituted their empire in the later 7th century A.D. (see W. Thomsen, *Alttürkische Inschriften aus der Mongolei*, in *ZDMG*, lxxviii [1924], 123-6; R. Grousset, *L'Empire des steppes*[4], Paris 1951, 131-2, 154, Eng. tr. 106, 561 n. 2). It was a region of cosmic significance for these Turks, the navel of the world, a holy site, *ïduḳ Ötüken yïsh* "sacred, forested Ötüken", mentioned many times in the Kül Tigin and Tonyuḳuḳ inscriptions of the Eastern Türk empire and also in the Tariyat and Sine Usu ones from the 750s of the Uyghurs who succeeded in Mongolia to the Eastern Türk Ḳaghans, although it was probably not the only sacred site for the Turks. In the annals of T'ang China, it appears as Yu-tou-kin (see P. Pelliot, *Le mont Yu-tou-kin (Ütükän) des anciens Turcs*, in *T'oung-Pao*, xxvi [1929], 212-19).

The religious significance of Ötüken later passed to the Mongols who came to this region of Inner Asia, appearing in the 13th century as the Mongol earth and fertility goddess Ätügän or Itügän (John of Plano Carpini's Itoga, see W. Heissig, *The religions of Mongolia*, Berkeley and Los Angeles 1980, 101-4; the Mongols' sacred mountain region of Burkhan Galdun played for them the rôle which Ötüken had earlier played for the Turks).

Only the name, without consciousness of Ötüken's part in the life of the early Turks, persisted into the Islamic period: Maḥmūd Kāshgharī (late 5th/11th century [*q.v.*]) defines *Utūkān* as "the name of a place in the Tatār deserts near the Uyghur" (*Dīwān lughāt al-turk*, Tkish. tr. Atalay, i, 138, Eng. tr. R. Dankoff and J. Kelly, *Compendium of the Turkic dialects*, Cambridge, Mass. 1982-4, i, 159), but on the map accompanying the manuscript of his dictionary he apparently places it somewhere near the source of the Irtish river [*q.v.* in Suppl.] and the steppe of the Yimäk [see KIMÄK] (schematic reproduction of the map in Dankoff and Kelly, *op. cit.*, i, at p. 82, and see also V. Minorsky, *Sharaf al-Zamān Ṭāhir Marvazī on China, the Turks and India*, London 1942, comm. 73-4); obviously, Kāshgharī had only the haziest idea of Ötüken's real location.

Bibliography (in addition to references given in the article): J.P. Roux, *Les inscriptions de Bugut et de Tariyat sur la religion des Turcs*, in *Studia turcologica memoriae Alexii Bombaci dicata*, Naples 1982, 459-60.

(C.E. BOSWORTH)

OUDH [see AWADH].

OUJDA [see WADJDA].

OXUS [see DJAYḤŪN].

ỌYỌ, a West African Yoruba empire in what is now Nigeria [*q.v.*] and rivalling Ife, where kingship existed from at least the 12th century. Ọyọ grew in importance from the 16th century with the rise of the Atlantic slave trade. The empire linked northern trade routes along the Niger with the Atlantic. Muslims from Borno, Hausa, Nupe and the former Mali and Songhay were resident in its capital and along the route to the sea, but the Alafin, the local chief, and the vast majority of the people followed their traditional religion.

Struggle between central and provincial government produced a series of serious internal crises. At the death of the Alafin Awolẹ in 1796, the governor of Ilorin, Afọnja, broke from Ọyọ. To secure his independence against a resuscitating Ọyọ, he allied himself in 1817 with Fulani Muslims [see FULBE] connected with Sokoto [*q.v.*]. Their leader, Ṣāliḥ, conducted a successful *djihād* against Ọyọ with the help of pastoral Fulani and Muslim town residents and slaves. His son ʿAbd-al-Salām turned on Afonja and was recognised by Sokoto as "Amīr of Yoruba". After a sustained campaign, by 1836 the capital, Ọyọ Ile, was destroyed and the heartland of the empire incorporated into the Ilorin amirate.

Ilorin's *djihād* to the sea met resistance from new Ọyọ, Ibadan, and later the British in Lagos, but was ultimately blunted by the disappearance of its economic target, the Atlantic slave market.

Bibliography: S. Johnson, *The history of the Yorubas*, London 1921; R. Smith, *Kingdoms of the Yoruba*, London 1969; J.F.A. Ajayi and R. Smith,

Yoruba warfare in the nineteenth century, Cambridge 1971; J.A. Atanda, *The new Ọyọ empire*, London 1973; S.O. Biobaku, *Sources of Yoruba history*, Oxford 1973. See R. Law, *The Ọyọ empire c. 1600-c. 1836*, Oxford 1977, for more references. (J. Kenny)

OZAN (T.), in Turkish society "troubadour poet/singer/story-teller". The term comes from the verb *oz-* "to outstrip, go ahead in the race" (see Clauson, *Etymological dictionary of pre-thirteenth century Turkish*, 279), already attested in Kā<u>sh</u><u>gh</u>arī's [*q.v.*] *Dīwān lu<u>gh</u>āt al-turk* (5th/11th century), as also in the living tongues of Kirgiz, Sagay and Koybol of Central Asia and in the Turkish of Anatolia. The term *ozan* was used for the singers who accompanied the army in Sal<u>dj</u>ūḳ times. An Anatolian Turkish poet of the 9th/15th century called himself Ozan. In Turkmen, the term is archaic and is replaced by *bagsı* "popular poet". In the Turkish of Turkey, from the 10th/16th century onwards it was replaced by *ʿā<u>sh</u>iḳ (âşık)*. Nevertheless, in certain contemporary dialects of Anatolia, it has survived with the meaning "poet/singer", as also as an element of the terms *ozanlama* "assonantal sayings, proverbs", *ozancı* "garrulous person", *ozanlık* "pleasantry" and *ozannama* "improvised story, song". At the present day, in modern Turkish, it has replaced the Arabic term *<u>sh</u>āʿir (şair)*.

Bibliography: Attilâ Özkırımlı, *Türk edebiyatı ansiklopedisi*, Istanbul 1982; *Türkiye'de halk ağzından söz derleme dergisi*, iii, 1947; P.N. Boratav, *Halk hikâyeleri ve halk hikâyeciliği*, Istanbul 1988; Köprülüzāde Meḥmed Fuʾād, *Türk edebiyyātında ilk müteṣawwiflar*, Istanbul 1918, 273-4; idem, *Meddāḥlar*, in *Türkiyyāt Me<u>dj</u>mūʿasī*, i (1925), 2-3; idem, *Türk dili ve edebiyatı hakkında araştırmalar*, Istanbul 1934, 273-93; Hamit Zübeyr-Ishak Refet, *Anadilden derlemeler*, 2 vols., Ankara 1932-52; K.-K. Yudahin, tr. Abdullah Taymas, *Kırgız sözlüğü*, Ankara 1945; Maḥmūd Kā<u>sh</u><u>gh</u>arī, *Dīwān lu<u>gh</u>āt al-turk*, ed. Kilisli Rifʿat Bey, Istanbul 1914-17; W. Radloff, *Proben der Volksliteratur der türkischen Stämme*, i-x, St. Petersburg 1866-1904. (P.N. Boratav)

ÖZBEG (Ūzbak, Ūzbīk) (T.), a term with a variety of uses in pre-modern times.

1. Historical aspects

(a) As a generic term, it was applied to the Turko-Mongol nomadic tribal groups in Central Asia, especially Trans- and Cis-Oxiana and <u>Kh</u>ʷārazm, which from the mid-15th century onwards comprised the military support for <u>Dj</u>ūčid-Čingīzid lineages such as the <u>Sh</u>ībānids [*q.v.*] (ʿArab<u>sh</u>āhids) of <u>Kh</u>ʷārazm (16th and 17th centuries), the <u>Sh</u>ībānids (Abu 'l-<u>Kh</u>ayrids) of Trans- and Cis-Oxiana (16th century) and the Tuḳāy Tīmūrids (<u>Dj</u>ānids [*q.v.*]) in Trans- and Cis-Oxiana (17th century).

By the 16th century, there were two well-established traditions listing 32 or 92 distinct "Özbeg" tribes (*īl, ḳawm, ūlūs, ṭāʾifa*) (T.I. Sultanov, *Kočevye plemena pri-Aral'ya v XV-XVII vv.*, Moscow 1982, 7-51). Of these, the ones which figure most prominently in the history of <u>Kh</u>ʷārazm (<u>Kh</u>īwa [*q.v.*]) and Trans- and Cis-Oxiana from the beginning of the 16th to the end of the 19th centuries, are the Mangīt, Ḳungrāt, Ar<u>gh</u>ūn, Ḳipčāḳ, Ḳirgīz, Ḳārlūḳ, Kalmuk [*q.v.*], Alčīn, Ḳiyāt, Uyrāt (Oyrat), Nāymān, Ḳaṭa<u>gh</u>an, Ḳānglī (Ḳānḳulī), Utārči, Dūrman, Arlāt, Kerāyit, Mīng, Yūz, <u>Dj</u>alāʾir, Sarāy, Onggut, Tānggut, Merkit (Makrīt), Ḳārī, Ö<u>gh</u>lān, Ū<u>sh</u>ūn, Kenīkas, Tātār, Ḳirḳ, Ḳū<u>sh</u>čī, Uy<u>gh</u>ūr and Bahrīn. Many of these tribal entities, or at least their names, disappeared over the centuries from written records; others, like the Mangīt, Kenīkas, Ḳaṭa<u>gh</u>an, Ḳungrāt, Mīng and Yūz survived the eventual breakdown of Čingīzid authority in the region and formed successor amīrates (or begates) which survived to modern times.

The meaning of the term Özbeg is closely linked to the emergence of two new <u>Dj</u>ūčid lineages at the beginning of the 16th century in Central Asia, the Abu 'l-<u>Kh</u>ayrid and the ʿArab<u>sh</u>āhid or Yādgārid. Both traced their origins to <u>Sh</u>ībān b. <u>Dj</u>ūčī b. Čingīz Khan. Their supporters, apparently because of their earlier affiliations with the <u>Dj</u>ūčid Golden Horde and Uzbek Khan, are known (in Persian) as the *Ūzbakān* or *Ūzbakiyya*. When allied with the Ča<u>gh</u>atāy Čingīzids, however, these same Turko-Mongol tribal groups are called *Mu<u>gh</u>uls* (see e.g. Ẓahīr al-Dīn Muḥammad Bābur, *Bābur-nāma*, tr. A.S. Beveridge, London 1922, 2; also Section IV of the introduction, E.D. Ross (ed.) and N. Elias (tr.), *A history of the Moghuls of Central Asia, being the Tarikh-i-Rashidi of Mirza Muhammad Haidar Dughlát*, London 1898). To contemporary observers like Bābur and later Iskandar Beg Mun<u>sh</u>ī [*q.v.*], the term meant both the Turko-Mongol supporters of the Central Asian Čingīzids and, by extension, and, in the Persian case, derogatorily, the Čingīzids themselves.

The <u>Dj</u>ūčid agnates held exclusive right to the titles *<u>kh</u>ān* (sovereign) and *sulṭān* (prince), while their Özbeg military backers were generally distinguished by the title of *amīr*. Although a court ceremonial with apparently ancient antecedents established a traditional hierarchy of the Özbeg tribal groups, it had little to do with their actual political power. The early 17th century writer Maḥmūd b. Amīr Walī wrote a detailed description of court protocol at Bal<u>kh</u> which, when compared with the biographies he also compiled of contemporary *amīrs*, shows no clear correspondence between court status and political prominence (see R.D. McChesney, *The Amirs of seventeenth century Muslim Central Asia*, in *JESHO*, xxvi, 41-2).

The leading *amīrs* were granted rights in revenue known variously as *iḳṭāʿ*, *suyur<u>gh</u>āl*, *tiyūl* [*q.vv.*] (see e.g. M.A. Abduraimov, *Očerki agrarnī<u>kh</u> otno<u>sh</u>enii v Bu<u>kh</u>arskom <u>kh</u>anstve*, Tashkent 1966-70, ii, 100-24), which gave them and their kinsmen and allies an interest in the regions from which they derived this income. Through the 16th and early 17th centuries the Čingīzid sovereigns followed a policy of periodically transferring their amīrid backers, perhaps to limit the degree of attachment they might feel to any particular locale. By the middle of the 17th century, this policy was becoming more and more difficult to enforce. Attempts by Na<u>dh</u>r Muḥammad [*q.v.*] (*r.* at Bal<u>kh</u> 1015-51/1606-42 and 1055-61/1645-51), for example, to move *amīrs* like Yalangtū<u>sh</u> Bī Alčīn from what was a long-time *iḳṭāʿ* in the region south of Bal<u>kh</u> contributed to his downfall after a brief reign at Bu<u>kh</u>ārā (1642-5). His Čingīzid successors did not make the same mistake.

Through the 18th century, the Özbeg groups consolidated their local ties and by the beginning of the 19th century some of them had established independent dynasties—at Bu<u>kh</u>ārā and Samarḳand (Mangit), Maymana (Mīng), <u>Kh</u>oḳand (Mīng), Ḳunduz (Ḳaṭa<u>gh</u>an), <u>Kh</u>īwa (Ḳungrāt) and <u>Sh</u>ahr-i Sabz (Kenīkas). The new petty dynasts tended to prefer the title *amīr* or *mīr*, perhaps in deference to the power which the idea of Čingīzid legitimacy still retained long after the last of the Čingīzids had disappeared from the scene.

(b) More specifically, the term was also used as part of a proper name, perhaps designating urbanised Turkish-speakers who did not identify themselves with any of the above tribal organisations. In the archives of the <u>Dj</u>ūybārī *<u>sh</u>ay<u>kh</u>s* of Bu<u>kh</u>ārā (see

P.P. Ivanov (tr.), *Khozyaĭstvo dzhuibarskikh sheikhov*, Moscow-Leningrad 1954) appear names of property-owners like "Āķ Bīga, daughter of ʿĀdil Bī Özbeg" (134), "Tūlūm Beg, daughter of Bilāl Bī Özbeg" (240) and "Khʷādjā Muḥammad Mīr Özbeg" (177). However, of the several thousand names in this archive less than a dozen are so distinguished.

(c) Contemporary indigenous sources often applied the term Özbeg to uncultured and unlettered individuals, usually nomads or rural peasants (see e.g. for the mid-17th century, Maḥmūd b. Amīr Walī, *Baḥr al-asrār fī manāķib al-akhyār*, i, ed. and Russian tr. as *More tain otnositel'no doblestei blagorodnikh*, Tashkent 1977, 1 of the Persian text, for a contrast between the intellectuals who inhabited Andīdjān before the "Özbegs" settled in the region; Muḥammad Ṭālib Djūybārī, *Maṭlab al-ṭālibīn*, Tashkent IVAN ms. no. 3757, fol. 147b, where Imām Ķulī Khān (*r.* 1020-51/1612-42) is described as angered at "the Özbegs, the desert-dwellers (*ṣaḥrā-nishīnān*) of that region", and fol. 214b, where a *shaykh* has an encounter with a drunken "Özbeg" in a Bukhāran street).

(d) Finally, in the late 19th and early 20th centuries the term Özbeg was used by the politically-dominant Durrānī Afghāns for long-term residents in northern Afghānistān, whether Turkish-speaking or not (see R.D. McChesney, *Waqf in Central Asia*, Princeton 1991, 303-4; N. Tapper, *Bartered brides: politics, gender and marriage in Afghan tribal society*, Cambridge 1991, 39).

Bibliography (in addition to works cited in text): General works: Ya. G. Gulyamov (ed.), *Istoriya Uzbekskoi SSR*, i, Tashkent 1967; I.M. Muminov (ed.), *Istoriya Samarkanda*, i, Tashkent 1969; B.A. Akhmedov, *Istoriko-geografičeskaya literatura Srednei Azii XVI-XVII veka*, Tashkent 1985 (survey of the Persian and Turkish sources); idem, *Gosudarstvo kočevikh Uzbekov*, Moscow 1965.

16th century: (Trans- and Cis-Oxiana, Khʷārazm, Khurāsān) anon. (possibly Muḥammad Ṣāliḥ), *Tawārīkh-i guzīda-yi nuṣrat-nāma*, facs. text ed. A.M. Akramov, Tashkent 1967; Khʷāndamīr, Tehran 1333/1954, iv; (Trans- and Cis-Oxiana) Ḥāfiẓ-i Tanīsh Bukhārī, *Sharaf-nāma-yi shāhī*, text, Russian tr. and comm. M.A. Salakhetdinova, i, Moscow 1983-.

17th century: (Khʷārazm) Abu 'l-Ghāzī Bahādur Khān, *Shadjara-yi Turk*, text and Fr. tr. P.I. Desmaisons, *Histoire des Mongols et des Tatares*, Amsterdam 1970 (repr. of St. Petersburg 1871-4 ed.); (Trans- and Cis-Oxiana) Maḥmūd b. Amīr Walī, *Baḥr al-asrār fī manāķib al-akhyār*, vi/4, India Office Library, ms. no. 575, esp. fols. 124a-126b, 277b-286a, 290b-304b, 387b-389a; Muḥammad Yūsuf Munshī, *Mukim-khanskaya istoriya*, ed. and tr. A.A. Semenov, Tashkent 1966; (Kāshghar) Shāh Maḥmūd Čurās, *Tārīkh*, text, Russian tr. and comm. O.F. Akimushkin, Moscow 1976.

18th and 19th centuries: (General) E. Schuyler, *Turkistan*, repr. New York 1966; A. Vambery, *Travels in Central Asia*, New York 1970 (repr. of 1865 edition); (Bukhārā) Mīrzā ʿAbd al-ʿAẓīm Sāmī, *Tārīkh-i Salāṭīn-i Manghītiyya*, text, Russian tr. and comm. L.M. Epifanova, Moscow 1962; (Khoķand) Muḥammad Ḥakīm Khān, *Muntakhab al-tawārīkh*, facs. ed. A. Mukhtarov, 2 vols., Dushanbe 1983-5; T.K. Beisembiev, "*Tarikh-i Shakhrukhi*" *kak istoričeskii istočnik*, Alma-Ata 1987.

(R.D. McChesney)

2. Ethnography

The Özbegs are one of the predominant ethnic groups of Turkistān [*q.v.*] or Central Asia, with their territory extending from the Caspian Sea to Sinkiang. They are found in the former Soviet republics of Türkmenistān, Özbegistān, Tādjikistān, Ķirghizia, Ķazākhstān, across northern Afghānistān and in Kābul, the capital of Afghānistān, and in the People's Republic of China. In the former Soviet Union, there are approximately 20 million Özbegs, indicating a rapidly increasing population. The number of Özbegs in Afghānistān [*q.v.* (ii)] has probably been underestimated as one million since the 1960s. In Sinkiang there are about 14,000 Özbegs, about whom little is known in the outside world.

Pakistan, Saudi Arabia, Turkey and now Europe and the United States have provided a home for Özbegs who have left their traditional territory because of political, economic and social disruption related either to Soviet or Chinese expansionism or the on-going Afghānistān conflict. During Russian and later Soviet control in Central Asia, the Özbegs periodically rebelled and through spontaneous uprisings expressed nationalistic feelings [see BASMAČIS]. In Afghānistān, competition and hostility has been directed most toward the Pashtūns [see AFGHĀNS], a group economically and politically dominant there. Özbegs from northern Afghānistān are currently (1992) involved in the Afghān resistance movement against the Marxist government.

The groups of Özbegs divided by national boundaries have been somewhat isolated from each other during much of the 20th century. For example, Özbeg was traditionally written in Arabic script, but since 1940 Cyrillic script has been used in the Soviet Union, hampering communication with those in other countries who retain Arabic script as in Afghānistān or those who utilise Latin script such as Turkistānī exiles in Turkey. However, recent contacts between Özbegs have been facilitated by construction of the Ķaraķorum highway through Pakistan and the disintegration of the Soviet Union.

The Özbeg khānates of the late 19th century [see BUKHĀRĀ, KHĪWA and KHOĶAND] had a complex socio-political organisation with dynastic rulers, standing armies, governmental and religious bureaucracy, social stratification and specialisation. Villages were traditionally led by an *aķsaķal*, a respected older headman who mediated disputes. The ethnographic literature and travellers' accounts indicate that Özbegs had become sedentary by the 20th century. Vestiges of a semi-nomadic past remain for some who still construct *yurts*, portable felt-covered round tents with wood frames, in the household courtyards for use during the summer. Agricultural Özbegs live in permanent villages which are either compact with surrounding agricultural lands or dispersed with homesteads in linear arrangements following irrigation canals. Some rural and urban household compounds are still built of adobe brick, most with flat roofs, but some structures exhibit a "beehive" style.

Agriculturist Özbegs grow rice, cotton, wheat, barley, sorghum, alfalfa, various vegetables and fruits, especially melons, and raise sheep, goats, cows and horses. Mulberry, which has leaves used in the raising of silkworms, is cultivated. Traditional commercial activities include black-, tin-, lock- and coppersmithing; silk, textile, saddle, sheepskin coat, leather, felt and pottery manufacture, soap making, barbering, oil pressing, butchering, baking, rice hulling and milling. Carved plaster made of gypsum and decorative wood work are important decorative crafts. Özbeg women are known for their flat-weave rugs and embroidery. A brightly dyed silk cloth made into cloaks and dresses is another specialty.

Men's and women's activities are spatially regulated. Women traditionally perform their duties of cooking, cleaning, sewing, bread making and animal care in the private space of the household courtyard while men work in the public area of the marketplace or fields. This division is adhered to most strictly in urban areas in northern Afg̲h̲ānistān, where traditional Özbeg women begin wearing the veil around the age of puberty. In the former Soviet republics, Özbeg women work outside the home in factories, offices and agriculture. However, they remain the primary homemakers.

Historically, tax-farming was the primary land tenure system, especially north of the Amū Daryā [*q.v.*]. In the k̲h̲ānate of Buk̲h̲ārā [*q.v.*], provinces were divided into tax districts administered by appointees of the *amīr* of Buk̲h̲ārā. Each *beg* retained the amount of revenue which he considered necessary to maintain his court and forwarded the rest to the *amīr*. The situation of the common people was not substantially altered after the Russian annexation of Central Asia except in Farg̲h̲ānā [*q.v.*], where the Russians instituted cotton mono-cropping and eliminated the traditional bureacracy.

In the late 1920s to 1930s, agriculture was collectivised in Turkistān. Despite Sovietisation, many Özbegs continued to market some of their own crops. Increasing cotton production in the late 19th to 20th centuries has led to integration into the world market. Depending on location, one-third to one-half of urban Özbegs in the former Soviet republics currently own their own households. In northern Afg̲h̲ānistān the most important land tenure system is currently freehold or private ownership which entails full rights and disposal through sale and inheritance. Most of the holdings are small, typically 5-10 acres.

The basic kin group is known as the *ḳawm* (other terms are also used), which in its basic sense consists of related households comprising a community. The *ḳawm* contains several groups of patrilineally-related families who regard themselves as descended from a common ancestor. However, *ḳawm* is a structural category which is adjusted by the people to suit their own social situation. The word is used to include not only agnates, but also persons who assist each other, share goods and live nearby, including affinal kinsmen and even unrelated people who marry in and become viewed as part of the group. Ideally, the nearest households in the village or urban neighbourhood who have close co-operative relationships and who may have their own mosque or other common interests form a *ḳawm*. A village may be composed of one or more *ḳawms*. An urban *ḳawm* is often associated with a craft or occupation. An important feature of kinship terminologies is the emphasis on special terms for older brother, *aḳa*, and older sister, *āpa*.

In the traditional marriage system, marriage preference is for one to whom a kin connection can be traced. There are norms against marriage with members of other ethnic groups. Although polygamy has become rare, parental arrangement and consent to marriage have been retained. A cash payment from the groom's side to the bride's is part of marriage negotiations, part of which may be used to buy household items for the bride. Divorce is governed by Islamic law or by the laws of the country, although community pressure limits its use.

The ideal is the patrilocal extended family with the senior married couple, their sons, the sons' wives and children and the unmarried daughters of the senior couple all residing in the same household compound. Nuclear families are also common, since extended families may break up as the sons mature and the senior pair ages.

Özbegs generally favour large families. In northern Afg̲h̲ānistān, the baby is strapped into a special wooden cradle on rockers beginning forty days after birth. Outside of the cradle, the baby is swaddled. Circumcision of boys, practiced by all Özbegs, is generally done at some time between the second and fourth year. A Ḳurʾānic education was traditional, but now public high school and university education are increasingly common, especially for boys.

The ruling dynasties in the Central Asian k̲h̲ānates from the end of the 18th to the 20th centuries were the tribal groups of Mangit [*q.v.*] in Buk̲h̲ārā [*q.v.*] and Ḳungrāt [*q.v.*] in K̲h̲ʷārazm [*q.v.*], which came to be called K̲h̲īwa [*q.v.*]. The leaders of the K̲h̲oḳand k̲h̲ānate were from the Mīng tribe. Some Özbegs still remember a tribal designation and may use this as part of their personal identity. Important tribes are Ḳungrāt, Mangit, Ḳipčaḳ, Ḳangli, Naʾimān, K̲h̲itay, Dürmen, Čag̲h̲atay, Mīng, Kenīkas and Lakai. Other "non-tribal" Özbegs use either a district or town as an identity marker. Gender, age, dialect and Islamic observance are important components of personal identity and status.

The Özbegs are Sunnī Muslims who follow the Ḥanafiyya [*q.v.*] legal tradition. Naḳs̲h̲bandiyya [*q.v.*] Ṣūfism has been a social and political force. For some, folk beliefs like the evil eye and harmful possessing spirits, *d̲j̲inn* [*q.v.*] or *parī* [*q.v.*], are part of daily life and necessitate the use of amulets or written verses of the Ḳurʾān. Diseases may be classified as "hot" or "cold," with oppositely-classified foods used in their curing. The *ʿulamāʾ*, religious scholars and teachers, traditionally were very influential, since Buk̲h̲ārā was for long a centre of Islamic learning. Shamanistic healing, especially the removal of spirits, was done by a practitioner called a *bāk̲h̲s̲h̲ī*, *parīk̲h̲ʷān* or *duʿāk̲h̲ʷān*, often a *mullā* learned in the Ḳurʾān. In the folk tradition, there is also belief in *albastī*, a witch-like *d̲j̲innī*.

In addition to the celebration of Islamic festivals and holy periods such as Ramaḍān, a non-Islamic holiday, the New Year, held at the beginning of spring, is celebrated by the distribution of a pudding-like food made of sprouted wheat, *sūmūlak*, to family and friends. Özbegs are known for their cuisine, which includes many noodle dishes such as *mantū*, a steamed dumpling. The musical tradition includes indigenous instruments such as the two-stringed *dūtār* and the *dāʾira*, a tambourine, for use in public and private entertainment. To celebrate weddings and circumcisions, men play *ūlaḳ*, a sport in which men on horseback battle to carry the carcass of a cow to a goal.

Bibliography: E. Schuyler, *Turkistan: notes of a journey in Russian Turkistan, Khokand, Bukhara, and Kuldja*, 2 vols., London 1876; B. Chagatay and A.N. Sjoberg, *Notes on the Uzbek culture of Central Asia*, in *Texas Journal of Science*, vii/1 (1955), 72-112; E. Bacon, *Central Asians under Russian rule*, Ithaca 1966; E. Allworth, *Central Asia, a century of Russian rule*, New York 1967; I.M. Djabbarov, *Crafts of the Uzbeks of Southern Khorezm in the late nineteenth and early twentieth centuries*, in *Soviet Anthropology and Archeology* (1973-5); G.P. Snesarev, *Remnants of Pre-Islamic beliefs and rituals among the Khorezm Uzbeks*, in *Soviet Anthropology and Archeology* (1970-4); E. Naby, *The Uzbeks in Afghanistan*, in *Central Asian Survey*, iii/1 (1984), 1-21. (AUDREY C. SHALINSKY)

ÖZBEG B. **MUḤAMMAD PAHLAWĀN**, Muẓaffar al-Dīn (reigned 607-22/1210-25), the fifth and last Atabeg of the Ildegizid or Eldigüzid family [see ILDEÑIZIDS] who ruled in Ādharbāydjān during the later Saldjūḳ and Khwārazmshāhī periods. He married Malika Khātūn, widow of the last Great Saldjūḳ sultan Ṭoghrïl III (killed in 590/1194 [*q.v.*]).

During the early part of his career, he ruled in Hamadhān as a subordinate of his brother Nuṣrat al-Dīn Abū Bakr, during the time when much of Ādharbāydjān and ʿIrāḳ ʿAdjamī was falling into anarchy in the post-Saldjūḳ period. His freedom of action was often circumscribed by powerful Turkish *amīrs*, nominally his agents and protectors, such as Ay-Aba, Gökče and Ay-Ṭoghmïsh, until in 607/1210 he succeeded Abū Bakr as Atabeg in Tabrīz and head of the family.

Under military pressure from the resurgent Georgians [see AL-KURDJ], he had to come to an arrangement with the Khwārazm-Shāh ʿAlāʾ al-Dīn Muḥammad whereby he was confirmed in Ādharbāydjān and Arrān but as the Shāh's vassal, acknowledging him in the *khuṭba* and *sikka* (614/1217). In 617/1220 the Mongols first came to Tabrīz, and on their third reappearance Özbeg abandoned the city for Nakhčiwān [*q.v.*], but was back again by the autumn of 619/1222. In 621/1224 a fresh wave of Mongol troops entered Persia, defeated the Khwārazmians at Rayy and pushed on to Tabrīz, compelling Özbeg to extradite to them the Khwārazmian refugees who had fled thither. In Radjab 622/June 1225, however, the Shāh Djalāl al-Dīn [*q.v.*] occupied the Ildegizid capital, whilst Özbeg withdrew to Gandja [*q.v.*], and the Shāh forced Özbeg to divorce his wife Malika Khātūn, whom he married himself, till intervention by the Ayyūbid al-Malik al-Ashraf rescued her and brought her to Khilāṭ. Özbeg now lost Gandja also, and died in humiliation at the fortress of Alindja (622/1225), so that his line came to an end.

Özbeg is very severely judged by the chroniclers for his indolence and love of luxurious living; but it must be said in extenuation that he faced redoubtable foes in the Georgians, the Khwārazmians and the Mongols. His court was famed as a centre for art and letters, with his vizier Rabīb al-Dawla being a noted patron of poets.

Bibliography: 1. Sources. Rāwandī, *Rāḥat al-ṣudūr*; Ḥusaynī, *Akhbār al-dawla al-saldjūḳiyya*; Ibn al-Athīr; Nasawī, *Sīrat al-Sulṭān Djalāl al-Dīn*; Mustawfī, *Taʾrīkh-i Guzīda*.

2. Studies. C. Defrémery, *Recherches sur quatre princes d'Hamadan*, in *JA*, ix (1847), 148-86; Bosworth, in *Camb. hist. of Iran*, v, 183-4; Boyle, in *ibid.*, 325-7; Minorsky, *EI*[1] art. *Uzbek b. Muhammad Pahlawān*, of which detailed article the present one is a résumé. (C.E. BOSWORTH)

ÖZBEGISTAN [see UZBEKISTAN].

ÖZDEMIR PASHA, Ottoman *beylerbeyi* (governor) of Yemen and, subsequently, of coastal Abyssinia (Ḥabesh [*q.v.*]), and the individual most instrumental in establishing the sultan's authority in both provinces during the mid-10th/16th century.

An Egyptian *mamlūk* of Circassian origin whose master is said to have been one Kaykāwūs Shewkat Bey, Özdemir took service with the Ottomans after Selīm I conquered Egypt in 922-3/1517. He held a number of minor offices in the provincial administration until, by 945/1538, he had gained the position of *kāshif* (district prefect). In this year he enrolled for service in the sizeable naval expedition launched from Suez against the Portuguese in India under the command of Süleymān Pasha [*q.v.*].

Upon the armada's return from India to coastal Yemen, where Süleymān Pasha secured Ottoman rule at Zabīd under a *sandjaḳ beyi*, Özdemir remained there as an *amīr*. Ewliyā Čelebi's claim (*Seyāḥat-nāme*, x, 220, 939) that he next served in southern Egypt against the expansionist Fundj [*q.v.*] is without corroboration. Yet Özdemir is next noticed only in Dhu 'l-Ḥidjdja 953/February 1547 as a participant in the Ottoman capture of Taʿizz [*q.v.*]. When shortly Uways Pasha, the Ottoman governor (*beylerbeyi*), was assassinated, Özdemir, by then a *sandjaḳ beyi*, was elected locally as interim commander (*serdār*). He resolved to capture Ṣanʿāʾ, the Zaydī capital, which ambition was realised on 7 Radjab 954/23 August 1547. Although it was nearly another two years before he was confirmed as *beylerbeyi* of Yemen, he maintained pressure on the weak and divided Zaydīs. The high point of Ottoman domination was reached in 959/1552 when, after five years of unavailing warfare, the Zaydī leader al-Muṭahhar [*q.v.*] and Özdemir Pasha concluded a peace treaty whereby the former acknowledged Ottoman suzerainty in return for limited autonomy.

Özdemir was dismissed from Yemen during 961/1554, probably in Djumādā I/April. Attracted by the prosperity of the eastern Red Sea port of Sawākin, where he landed while returning from Yemen, and filled with enthusiasm to conquer the Abyssinian littoral to further Islam and check Portuguese ambitions, Özdemir subsequently persuaded Sultan Süleymān in person to appoint him commander (*serdār*) of an Egyptian force of 3,000 to achieve that goal. When an initial attempt to reach his objective via the Nile River failed, Özdemir established his base at Sawākin, the centre of the new Ottoman province of Ḥabesh, which was officially created on 15 Shaʿbān 962/5 July 1555 with Özdemir Pasha as *beylerbeyi*. From Sawākin, the Ottoman forces first seized and secured the Abyssinian coastlands, including the key port of Maṣawwaʿ [*q.v.*], before in 965/1558 commencing successful forays into the province of Tigre. An inland Ottoman base was secured in 966/1559 at Debārwā, where a fortress and mosques were constructed.

It was at Debārwā that Özdemir Pasha died during 967/1560, after which the vastly outnumbered Ottoman troops began retreating towards the coast. His body was interred at Debārwā, but later it was transferred for burial in a mausoleum erected at Maṣawwaʿ by his son ʿOthmān Pasha [*q.v.*], who succeeded him as *beylerbeyi* of Ḥabesh and who eventually became Grand Vizier (*ṣadr-ï aʿẓam*). Özdemir is usually portrayed as an indefatigable warrior with frugal personal habits and an incorruptible loyalty to the Ottoman sultan.

Bibliography: Ms. sources include, in Arabic: ʿĪsā b. Luṭf Allāh, *Rawḥ al-rūḥ*, and Ibn Dāʿir, *al-Futūḥāt*; and, in Turkish: Rüstem Pasha, *Tārīkh* (paraphrased by L. Forrer, *Die osmanischen Chronik des Rustem Pascha*, Leipzig 1923, 159-74, 187-9), Luḳmān b. Sayyid Ḥusayn, *Mudjmal al-ṭūmār*, Muṣṭafā ʿĀlī, *Künh al-akhbār*, and the Turkish rendering of *al-Barḳ* (see below) by ʿĀlī ʿAlī, *Akhbār al-Yamānī* (for differences from the Arabic original).

Published materials: Nahrawālī, *al-Barḳ al-Yamānī* = *Ghazawāt al-Djarākisa*, ed. Ḥ. al-Djāsir, Riyāḍ 1967, 98-128 *passim*; Yaḥyā b. al-Ḥusayn, *Ghāyat al-amānī*, ed. S. ʿĀshūr, Cairo 1968, ii, 698-715; Pečewī, *Tārīkh*, Istanbul 1283/1866-7, i, 32-3; Ḥādjdjī Khalīfa, *Djihān-numā*, 550; Münedjdjim Bashï, iii, 239-42; *Sidjill-i ʿOthmānī*, i, 444; Rāshid, *Tārīkh-i Yemen*, Istanbul 1291/1874-5, i, 84-104 *passim*; Sheref, *Özdemiroghlu ʿOthmān Pasha*, in *TOEM*, iv (1289); Wüstenfeld, *Jemen*, Göttingen

1884, 8-9; C. Orhonlu, *Osmanlıların Habeşistan siyaseti 1554-1560*, in *Tarih Dergisi*, xv (1965), 39-54; idem, *Habeş eyaleti*, Istanbul 1974, 33-48 (rich in Ottoman documents); and Blackburn, *The Ottoman penetration of Yemen*, in *Archivum Ottomanicum*, vi (1980), 55-100 (for an annotated translation of Özdemir's *fatḥ-nāme* for the conquest of Ṣanʿāʾ).

(J.R. BLACKBURN)

ÖZI, Özü, the Turkish name of three related features: the river Dnepr, the coastal fortress of Očakov (both in the Ukraine), and the Ottoman *eyālet* alternately called Özi or Silistre (roughly a coastal area bracketed by the lower Özi/Dnepr on the east and the lower Danube with the nearby river port city of Silistre on the south-west; its *beylerbeyi* resided at Aḳḳirmān or Silistre but not at Özi/Očakov, more often the seat of a *sand̲j̲aḳ beyi*).

Both the river and the fortress played an important but complex role in the history of the two Turkish Muslim powers in the Black Sea area, the Crimean Tatars and the Ottomans. The river's lower course first represented a dividing line between the Lithuanians and Poles on the west and the Tatars on the east, and later, in a similar manner, between the *eyālet* of Silistre (Özi) and the k̲h̲ānate, although within the framework of the Ottoman empire of which the k̲h̲ānate became a vassal. The Dnepr approaches the Black Sea from the east through a long and wide estuary which also receives the river Bug from the north; this estuary, known by its Russian term (but possibly a loanword from Ottoman Turkish) as *liman*, at the same time separates the mainland from the Crimean peninsula which ends up in a spur named Kinburnskaya kosa ("Kinburn spur", lit. "scythe", a distortion of the Ottoman name Ḳïlburun "Hair-[thin] cape") two km/1.3 miles south of Očakov. It was on the western bank of the Bug's estuary that King Vytautas of Lithuania built a fort named Das̲h̲iv in *ca.* 1400, which was renamed D̲j̲ānkirmān after the Crimean K̲h̲ān Mengli Giray [*q.v.*] acquired it in 1492. D̲j̲ānkirmān became a direct Ottoman possession in 1538. Until its final fall to the Russian army and navy two-and-a-half centuries later, Özi—as D̲j̲ānkirmān came to be called by the Ottomans—played an important strategic role in the long struggle between the Turks and Tatars on the one hand, and the Lithuanians, Poles, Cossacks and finally Russians, on the other, involving a contest for the control—especially naval control—of the Black Sea, the Crimea, and the Danubian provinces. Although Özi failed to deter the Cossacks (who founded their famous base of Sič further upstream on the Dnepr) from raiding it and sailing past it on their forays all over the Black Sea, it did help the Ottomans maintain their own presence on this frontier and delay the success of the eventual Russian onslaught. Nevertheless, by the 18th century the latter showed its force in two Russo-Turkish wars: that of 1736-9 and that of 1787-92. Özi was taken on both occasions (July 1736, but the Peace Treaty of Belgrade, 1739, restored it to Turkey; and, definitively, in December 1788, with the Peace Treaty of Jassy, 1792). This final stage was memorable, among other things, for the series of naval engagements between the Ottoman fleet under the able but inadequately-supported *ḳaptanpas̲h̲a* G̲h̲āzī Ḥasan Pas̲h̲a and the Russian one, marked by the rivalry between its two commanders, John Paul Jones (a hero of the American Revolution) and the German prince Charles of Nassau-Siegen.

A matter of some interest is Özi's earlier name, D̲j̲ānkirmān (and another such form given by Ewliyā Čelebi, Dehkirmān), as well as that of Očakov. The specific origin of the name D̲j̲ānkirmān is obscure, but it clearly consists of two elements, *d̲j̲ān* (possibly the Persian term "soul, something dear") and *kirmān* (Persian "fortress"); the latter word appears in a number of place names in the Ukraine (for example Aḳḳirmān, the Slavic Belgorod), but not elsewhere (except for the Persian cities of Kirmān and Kirmāns̲h̲āh); a Scythian (thus Iranian) origin is probable, a remarkable case of the permanence and resilience of toponyms. Although the place became known in Ottoman Turkish by the name of the river as Özi ḳalesi (but was on occasion also called Uzun ḳale), the citadel part was called Ačï-ḳale, which was then extended in Russian and Ukrainian (as Očakov and Očakiv) to the whole fortress.

Bibliography: Ewliyā Čelebi, *Seyāḥat-nāme*, 173-213 (esp. 179-85, where a thorough description of Ottoman Özi/Očakov is given); İ.H. Uzunçarşılı, *Osmanlı tarihi*, iii, iv, *passim*, see index; S.J. Shaw, *History of the Ottoman Empire and modern Turkey*, Cambridge 1976, i, 191, 198, 260, 287; idem, *Between old and new, the Ottoman empire under Sultan Selīm III, 1789-1807*, Cambridge, Mass. 1971, 29-67; *Istoriya mist i sil Ukrains'koy RSR* ("History of the cities and towns of the Ukrainian SSR"), xv, Kiev 1971, 614-31 (entry *Očakiv*); Süleymān Nuṭḳī, *Muṣawwer muḥārebat-ï bahriyye-i ʿot̲h̲māniyye*, Istanbul 1307/1889, 85-88; R.C. Anderson, *Naval wars in the Levant*, Liverpool 1952, 318-47; S.E. Morison, *John Paul Jones*, Boston 1985, 361-84; G. Veinstein, *L'occupation ottomane d'Očakov et le problème de la frontière lituano-tatare, 1538-1544*, in *Passé turco-tatar, present soviétique. Études offertes à Alexandre Bennigsen*, Paris 1986, 123-55.

(S. SOUCEK)

ÖZKEND, ŪZKEND, sometimes written in the sources Yūzkand or Ūzd̲j̲and, a town of mediaeval Islamic Farg̲h̲āna [*q.v.*] in Central Asia, lying at the eastern end of the Farg̲h̲āna valley and regarded as being near the frontier with the pagan Turks.

Already in the mid-3rd/9th century, Özkend had a local ruler called by the Turkish name K̲h̲ūrtigin (?Čūr-tigin) (Ibn K̲h̲urradād̲h̲bih, 30). The geographers of the next century (i.e. that of the Sāmānids) describe it as having the tripartite pattern typical of eastern Islamic towns, with a citadel in the *madīna* or inner city and a suburb; from it led the way towards Semirečye and the Turkish lands (Ibn Ḥawḳal, ed. Kramers, 513-14, tr. Wiet, 491-2; al-Muḳaddasī, 272; *Ḥudūd al-ʿālam*, tr. 116, comm. 255; Yāḳūt, ed. Beirut, i, 280; Le Strange, *Lands*, 476).

Under the Ḳarakhānids [see ILEK-K̲H̲ANS], it became the capital at the opening of the 5th/11th century of the Ilig Naṣr b. ʿAlī, and then the capital of the eastern wing of the confederation, with Yūsuf Ḳadïr K̲h̲ān b. Hārūn Bug̲h̲ra K̲h̲ān minting coins there from 416/1025. Maḥmūd Kās̲h̲g̲h̲arī mentions Ūzkand and defines it as the chief town of Farghāna and as meaning in Turkish *balad anfusinā* "city of our souls" = "our own, special city" (*Dīwān lughāt al-turk*, tr. Atalay, i, 343 = R. Dankoff and J. Kelly, *Compendium of the Turkic dialects*, Cambridge, Mass. 1982-4, i, 270). It remained a centre of the Ḳarak̲h̲ānids until the invasions of Čingiz K̲h̲ān, and Ḳarak̲h̲ānid coins were minted there up to 610/1213 (E. von Zambaur, *Die Münzprägungen des Islam*, i, Wiesbaden 1968, 58). But after Mongol times it declined, since the Mongol *maliks* of Farghāna made Andid̲j̲ān [*q.v.*] their centre there. In modern times, it is a mere village in the district of Andid̲j̲ān (Barthold, *A short history of Turkestan*, in *Four studies on the history of Central Asia*, Leiden 1962, i, 23, 48).

Bibliography: See also Barthold, *Turkestan*, 156-7, 260, 285-6, 353, 363.

(C.E. BOSWORTH)

P

PĀʾ or *bāʾ-i fārsī* or *bāʾ-i ʿadjamī*, i.e. the *bāʾ* with three points subscript, invented for Persian as supplement to the Arabic *bāʾ* and to represent the unvoiced, as opposed to the voiced, bilabial plosive (for the voiced *b*, see BĀʾ). It is sometimes interchangeable with *bāʾ* (e.g. *asp* and *asb*, *dabīr* and *dapīr*) and, more frequently, with *fāʾ* (e.g. *sapīd* and *safīd, Pārs* and *Fārs*). The regular use of the letter in manuscripts is comparatively modern, but it is found in good ones of the 7th/13th century while at the same time it is often omitted in manuscripts of much later date (*GIPh*, 1/iv, 74; G. Lazard, *La langue des plus anciens monuments de la prose persane*, Paris 1963, 142).

The usage of the letter *pāʾ* passed into Ottoman Turkish, for both original Turkish words (early Turkish had distinguished both voiced and unvoiced versions of the sound, and the first writing system for Turkish, that of the Yenisei and Orkhon inscriptions (7th-8th centuries A.D.), had had separate signs for *p* and *b*, see Talât Tekin, *A grammar of Orkhon Turkic*, Bloomington, Ind. 1968, 24, 27 n. 10, 75) and for Persian loanwords (see J. Deny, *Grammaire de la langue turque (dialecte osmanli)*, Paris 1921, 51-2, 77-8). *Pāʾ* is likewise used in Urdu both for Persian and Turkish loanwords and for words stemming from the Indo-Aryan basis of the language.

In loanwords into Arabic, *pāʾ* may be rendered as *bāʾ*, e.g. in *bāshā* for Turkish *pasha*; *būsta*/*būsṭa* for Italian *posta*; *batrūl* for Fr./Eng. *pétrole*/*petrol*. But it was often rendered, especially in Classical Arabic at a time when Persian cultural influences were strong, as *fāʾ* also, e.g. *furāniḳ* < MP *parvānak*, NP *parwāna* "messenger, courier with despatches"; *fānīdh* < Skr. *phāṇita*, NP *pānīd* "sugar-cane syrup"; *firind* < NP *parand* "damascening on a sword" (see A. Siddiqi, *Studien über die persischen Fremdwörter im klassischen Arabisch*, Göttingen 1919, 71).

(R. LEVY-[C.E. BOSWORTH])

PĀDHŪSPĀN [see RŪYĀN].

PĀDISHĀH (P.), the name for Muslim rulers, especially emperors. The Persian term *pād-i shāh*, i.e. (according to M. Bittner, in E. Oberhummer, *Die Türken und das Osmanische Reich*, Leipzig 1917, 105) "lord who is a royalty" in which the root *pad* is connected with Sanskrit *patis*, lord, husband, fem. *patni*, Greek πότνια and δεσ-πότης, Lat. *potens* (G. Curtius, *Griech. Etymol.*, 377), was originally a title reserved exclusively for the sovereign, which in course of time and as a result of the long intercourse of the Ottomans with the states of the West also came to be approved for certain Western rulers. In the correspondence of the Porte with the Western powers, the grand vizier Ḳuyudju Murād Pasha (d. 7 Djumādā II 1021/5 Aug. 1612) probably for the first time applied the title *pādishāh* to the Austrian emperor Rudolf II. At the conference of Nemirow (1737), Russia demanded the title for its Tsars (cf. J. von Hammer, *GOR*, vii, 488) and claimed it again at the negotiations at Bucharest (1773; cf. *ibid.*, viii, 412). When *pādishāh* came to be applied to the sultan, the *pādishāh-i āl-i ʿOthmān*, does not seem to be exactly known. In any case it is found in conjunction with all kinds of rhyming words as early as the beginning of the 10th/16th century in Ottoman documents. *Pādishāh* therefore may have come to be used towards the end of the 9th/15th century, presumably instead of *khunkʲār* (from *khudāwendkʲār*; cf. *JA*, ser. ii, vol. xv, 276/572), an obsolete word, as well as *sulṭān* (cf. *Isl.*, xi [1921], 70) already found in dervish Ṣūfism, and was regularly used till the end of the sultanate (cf. the cry of *pādishāhīmīz čoḳ* or *biñ yasha* with which the sultan was greeted by his troops and subjects).

In Persian usage, followed by that of the Indo-Muslim rulers such as the Mughal emperors, *pādishāh* became a normal designation for the ruler, though regarded as lower than that of *shāhanshāh* [see SHĀH], and in more recent times it was used by Persian monarchs in diplomatic documents addressed to European kings. Already the *Ḥudūd al-ʿālam* (end of the 4th/10th century) uses *pādshā(h)* "ruler" and *pādshāʾī*/*pādshāy* even for petty princes of the upper Oxus region and northern Afghānistān (tr. Minorsky, 108, 109, § 23.65, 75; idem, *Addenda to the Ḥudūd al-ʿālam*, in *BSOAS*, xvii [1955], glossary, 257). When ʿAlī, son of the head of the Ṣafawī order Ḥaydar b. Djunayd, adopted the title of *pādishāh* in his struggle with the Aḳ Ḳoyunlu [*q.v.*] towards the end of the 9th/15th century, it was a clear indication of the ambitions of the Ṣafawī family (see R.M. Savory, *Iran under the Safavids*, Cambridge 1980, 20). In the later half of the 19th century, A. de Biberstein Kazimirski noted that some of the officials of Nāṣir al-Dīn Shāh [*q.v.*] had taken to describing their master, not only as *shāhanshāh*, but also as *pādishāh-i kull-i mamālik-i Īrān*, apparently in imitation of the Tsar's designation "Emperor of all the Russias" (*Menoutchehri, poète persan du 11ème siècle de notre ère (du 5ième de l'hégire)*, Paris 1887, 359-60).

Bibliography (in addition to references given in the article): St. Kekulé, *Ueber Titel, Aemter, Rangstufen und Anreden in der offiziellen osmanischen Sprache*, Halle a. d. S. 1892, 3, and P. Horn, *Grundriss der neupersischen Etymologie*, Strassburg 1893, 61, no. 266 (where, however, another derivation is given, from Old Persian *pad*, protector, and *shāh*, ruler; cf. thereon Horn, in *GIPh*, i/1, 274, 309, and i/2, 41, 88, 97, 159, where the Old Persian, Pahlavi, etc., forms are given); M.Z. Pakalın, *Osmanlı tarihi deyimleri ve terimleri sözlüğü*, Istanbul 1946-54, ii, 749-51; *İA*, art. *Padişah* (Halil Inalcik); B. Lewis, *The political language of Islam*, Chicago and London 1988, 98.

(F. BABINGER-[C.E. BOSWORTH])

PADRI, the name of a major Islamic revivalist movement in Minangkabau [*q.v.*], Sumatra, 1803-38. The appellation Padri is derived from *orang Pidari* "men of Pedir (Pidië)", in reference to those who made the pilgrimage to Mecca by way of the Atjèhnese port of Pidië. The Padri built on earlier Minangkabau reform movements initiated by the two major Ṣūfī *tarekat* which had been the instrument for converting the central highlands of Sumatra, the Naksyabandiyah (Naḳshbandiyya [*q.v.*]) and the Syattariyah (Shaṭṭāriyya [*q.v.*]). Operating by the late 18th century in a society which was only very partially Islamicised, these *tarekat* flourished around *surau* or centres for religious studies which attracted hundreds of students from throughout Minangkabau.

In the 1780s the hilly regions surrounding some of the major *surau* in the valley districts of Agam, Tanah

Datar and Limapuluh Kota in the Minangkabau highlands were experiencing a major economic revival caused by European and American demand for coffee and cassia. Overcome by booming demand, the society exhibited an inability to organise a secure trading network to the coastal ports or a suitable method of settling disputes in the marketplace. It was the *surau* which was able to offer an alternative to the existing mode of regulation, especially in commercial affairs. Both the Syattariyah and Naksyabandiyah *tarekat* had instigated "back to the *syariat* (*sharīʿa* [*q.v.*])" movements in other parts of the Islamic world, and now for the first time in central Sumatra conditions became ripe for a similar movement: for Minangkabau Muslim *surau*, such as those of the Syattariyah *syekh* (*shaykh*) Tuanku Nan Tua in Agam, to challenge further accommodation with society, and to couch this challenge in terms of elevating Islamic law, including the commercial provisions of the *syariat*, to a position of pre-eminence.

It was against this background that in 1803 there returned to Minangkabau three pilgrims who had observed the Wahhābī conquest of Mecca [see WAHHĀBIYYA]. They were well aware of the difference between "back to the *syariat*" and a return to the fundamental tenets of the Prophet and his Companions. The most distinguished of these three Padri was Haji Miskin, who had worked with Tuanku Nan Tua prior to his departure for Mecca. He now settled in the coffee village of Pandai Sikat in Agam and worked to improve the state of the marketplace and to rationalise commerce. He gained the support of certain lineage heads and in fact during the Padri movement a number of religious teachers and *adat* [see ʿĀDA] leaders worked together to introduce a new commercially favourable régime where cockfighting would disappear from the market and bandit villages would be eliminated. It is certainly misleading to see the Padri movement as an uncomprising attack on the *adat* leadership.

Ultimately driven out of Pandai Sikat, Haji Miskin joined the religious teacher Tuanku Nan Rinceh in the coffee- and cassia-rich hill area in the north of Agam. Also a pupil of Tuanku Nan Tua, Tuanku Nan Rinceh had been trying to put his master's ideas into practice, but piecemeal action no longer seemed adequate when Haji Miskin was able to indicate another way. Tuanku Nan Rinceh now concluded that each village must be turned into an Islamic community as rapidly as possible, using the simplicity of the Wahhābī system as a model along the lines of which such new communities were to be organised. He proclaimed a *djihād* and announced to his own village the régime of extreme puritanism which must henceforth be followed. The outward signs of a revivalist village were to be the abandonment of cockfighting, gambling and the use of tobacco, opium, *sirih* and strong drink; white clothes symbolising purity were to be worn, with women covering their faces and men allowing their beards to grow; no part of the body was to be decorated with gold jewellery, and silk clothing was to be eschewed. Needless to say, prayer five times a day was obligatory. A system of fines was instituted for infringement of these rules.

How successful the Padri were at imposing a Wahhābī-style administration on the villages they conquered is difficult to say. It seems that the village traditional leaders in their council continued to play an important role, although each conquered or converted village was obliged to appoint a *kadi* (*ḳāḍī* [*q.v.*]) who functioned side by side with the village council. The village was also required to appoint an *imam*, to be occupied with expounding the Ḳurʾān and carrying out religious ceremonies in the newly-built mosque. Apart from this, the most characteristic mark of the Padri village was its participation in organised violence against villages which would not submit to the Padri notion of an Islamic community.

Violence was particularly marked among the Padri of Tanah Datar, the home of Tuanku Lintau, who became notorious for his slaughter, in 1815, of many members of the Minangkabau royal family at a meeting arranged for negotiations. He went on to pursue a career of raiding and burning of opposition villages. In fact, throughout the Padri period all villages were heavily fortified and their male population kept almost constantly on a war-footing.

Just as a Padri victory over the whole of Minangkabau seemed certain, the Dutch returned to the chief Minangkabau coastal port of Padang in 1819. Invited into the highlands by anti-Padri *adat* leaders and remnants of the royal family, in February 1821 they signed a treaty in which these suppliants surrendered Minangkabau to Dutch sovereignty. So began the Padri War of 1821-38, in which, despite strong Padri resistance, the colonial forces were ultimately victorious. Prominent among the Padri war leaders was Tuanku Imam Bonjol. Having established his village at Bonjol, north of Agam, in 1807, like other Padri leaders he tried to build up a trading network to the west coast, away from outside control. The Dutch after their return in 1819 were a threat to this, and Bonjol launched its first attack on Dutch forces in the interior in 1822. From this period until 1837, Dutch and Bonjol forces were periodically engaged despite Bonjol's attempt to expand away to the north into the Batak country. Bonjol finally fell to the Dutch in 1837, Tuanku Imam Bonjol was exiled and Dutch victory over the last Padri remnants took place at Daludalu in 1838.

During this period, the Padri movement itself altered in character. Mecca had been lost to the Wahhābīs since 1813, and by the 1820s Minangkabau began to pay attention to the reports of returning pilgrims and the rigours of the original Padri system began to soften. The returning *haji*s were aided by the fact that no Padri leader had ever been able to acquire unchallenged dominance over a wide area and there was no monolithic Padri political system to break down. Nevertheless, the Padri left a lasting mark on Minangkabau and their legacy was powerful enough to be revivified as occasion demanded.

Bibliography: H.M. Lange, *Het Nederlandsch Oost-Indisch Leger ter Westkust van Sumatra (1819-1845)*, 2 vols., 's Hertogenbosch 1852; H.A. Steijn Parvé, *De Secte der Padaries (Padries) in de Bovenlanden van Sumatra*, in *Tijdschrift voor Indische Taal-, Land- en Volkenkunde*, iii (1855); Ph.S. van Ronkel, *Inlandsche getuigenissen aangaande den Padri-oorlog*, in *Indische Gids*, xxxvii/2 (1915); D.D. Madjolelo and A. Marzoeki, *Tuanku Imam Bondjol. Perintis Djalan ke Kemerdekaan*, Jakarta and Amsterdam 1951; M. Radjab, *Perang Paderi di Sumatera Barat (1803-1838)*, Jakarta 1954; M.D.Mansoer *et alii*, *Sedjarah Minangkabau*, Jakarta 1970; C. Dobbin, *Islamic revivalism in a changing peasant economy: Central Sumatra, 1784-1847*, Scandinavian Institute of Asian Studies Monograph Series no. 47, London and Malmö 1983, repr. 1987; eadem *Kebangkitan Islam dalam ekonomi petani yang sedang berubah, Sumatra Tengah, 1784-1847*, Jakarta 1992.

(CHRISTINE DOBBIN)

PAHANG [see MALAY PENINSULA].

PAHLAWĀN (P.), from *Pahlaw*, properly "Parthian'', acquired in pre-modern Persian and thence in Turkish, the sense of "wrestler, one who engages in hand-to-hand physical combat", becoming subsequently a general term for "hero, warrior, champion in battle". From this later, broader sense it is used as a personal name in the Persian world, e.g. for the Eldigüzid Atabeg [see ILDEÑIZIDS] Nuṣrat al-Dīn Djahān-Pahlawān (reigned in ʿĀdharbāydjān, d. 581 or 582/1186 [see PAHLAWĀN, MUḤAMMAD B. ILDEÑIZ; and see Justi, *Iranisches Namenbuch*, 237, for other bearers of this name]. The word's appearance in Arabic as *bahlawān* is clearly a secondary development, and has in more recent times acquired the meaning of "acrobat, tightrope walker in a circus, etc.", as was noted by Lane in early 19th century Cairo, where it was gypsies who by then practised these skills (*The manners and customs of the modern Egyptians*, ch. xx "Serpent-charmers, and performers of legerdemain tricks, etc."; see also Spiro, *Arabic-English dict. of the colloquial Arabic of Egypt*, repr. Beirut 1973, 61, and Barthélemy, *Dict. arabe-français des dialectes de la Syrie*, Paris 1935-54, 66). In the most recent colloquial of Cairo, it has become a pejorative term for "tricky person" (Hinds and Badawi, *A dict. of Egyptian Arabic, Arabic-English*, Beirut 1986, 110), cf. also *fahlawī* "clever" and *fahlawa* "cleverness".

The topic of wrestling, as a sport and as an expression of manliness and chivalry, thus linking up with the *futuwwa* [*q.v.*], was the subject of a classic study, primarily of its Arabic aspects, by M. Canard (*La lutte chez les Arabes*, in *Cinquentaire de la Faculté de Lettres d'Alger (1881-1931)*, Algiers 1932, 1-64, repr. in *L'expansion arabo-islamique et ses répercussions*, Variorum Reprints, London 1974, no. XI), largely utilised here. Wrestling and fighting, with the aim of bringing the opponent to the ground, was an expression of classical Greek and Roman athleticism; but the sports most probably developed in parallel ways, rather being a continued influence upon the Arabic and Persian worlds. In ancient Arabia, wrestling seems to have been one of the spectacles at the pre-Islamic fair of ʿUkāẓ [*q.v.*]; in the *Sīrat ʿAntar* as it later developed [see ʿANTAR, SĪRAT], the hero ʿAntara b. Shaddād [*q.v.*] practised this sport as did, according to some traditions, the caliph ʿUmar I. The terms most commonly used for this in Arabic were *ṣurʿa* and *ṣirāʿ*, with the basic idea of hurling one's opponent to the ground. It may have continued in mediaeval Arabic times as a popular sport; in 251/865, during the disturbances at the caliphal capital of Sāmarrā during al-Mustaʿīn's time, citizens there hired *muṣāriʿūn* to defend their houses against the violence of the Turkish soldiery (al-Ṭabarī, iii, 1540, tr. G. Saliba, *The crisis of the ʿAbbāsid caliphate*, Albany 1985, 31).

However, it was in Persia that wrestling was developed to a fine art, being associated with the heroes of legendary times. Firdawsī's *Shāh-nāma* contains several episodes of wrestling and combat, often illustrated in manuscripts of the national epic; three centuries or so later, Saʿdī often cites the *pahlawān* or wrestler in situations where a moral of some sort can be pointed. Above all, this national pastime from ancient Iran has survived in the often-described special gymnasia for wrestling, the *zūr-khānas* [*q.v.*], with ritualistic methods of fighting and a special garb of tight-fitting trousers [see SIRWĀL in *EI*[1]] and belt.

From the Persians it passed to the Turks and was a significant element of the military prowess for which the race was famed in the mediaeval Islamic world. It was practised amongst the Mamlūks of Egypt and Syria as part of their military training, *ṣirāʿ* being a skill ascribed to some of the great masters of *furūsiyya* [*q.v.*] (see D. Ayalon, *Notes on the Furūsiyya exercises and games in the Mamluk sultanate*, in *Scripta Hierosolymitana*, ix, Jerusalem 1961, 57, 61-2, repr. in *The Mamlūk military society*, Variorum Reprints, London 1979, no. II). Turkish troops took these skills as far as the Maghrib, and *bahlawānāt turkiyya* were found in the entourage of the Beys and Pashas of Tunis up to the 19th century. In the Ottoman empire, wrestlers were included in each Janissary company (*orta* [*q.v.*]), and in 11th/17th century Istanbul, wrestlers were organised into a corporation of *pelhiwāns* (*sic*, in this metathesised form), on the evidence of Ewliyā Čelebi.

Bibliography: Given in the article.

(C.E. BOSWORTH)

PAHLAWĀN, MUḤAMMAD B. ILDEÑIZ, NUṢRAT AL-DĪN, Atābeg of Ādharbāydjān in the later 6th/12th century. His father Ildeñiz [*q.v.*] had in course of time risen to be the real ruler in the Saldjūḳ empire; the widow of Sultan Ṭoghrïl [*q.v.*] was Pahlawān's mother and Arslān b. Ṭoghrïl [*q.v.*] his step-brother. In the fighting between Ildeñiz and the lord of Marāgha, Ibn Aḳsunḳur al-Aḥmadīlī, Pahlawān played a prominent part [see MARĀGHA]. From his father he inherited in 568/1172-3 Arrān, Ādharbāydjān, al-Djibāl, Hamadhān, Iṣfahān and al-Rayy with their dependent territories and a few years later he also took Tabrīz, which he gave to his brother Ḳïzïl Arslān. Like Ildeñiz, Pahlawān also became the real ruler. Sultan Arslān b. Ṭoghïl was completely under his control, as was also his young son Ṭoghrïl [*q.v.*], whom Pahlawān put on the Saldjūḳ throne, after Arslān had been disposed of by poison. Pahlawān died in Dhu 'l-Ḥidjdja 581/February-March 1186 or the beginning of 582/1186 and his brother Ḳïzïl Arslan succeeded him.

Ibn al-Athīr (xi, 346) pays a high tribute to Pahlawān's statesmanlike qualities, and during his tenure of office peace and prosperity prevailed in his governorship. After his death, however, bloodshed and unrest broke out. In Iṣfahān the Shāfiʿīs and Ḥanafīs fought one another, and at al-Rayy the Sunnīs and Shīʿīs, until order was gradually restored.

Bibliography: Ibn al-Athīr, xi, xii, s. index; Ḥamd Allāh Mustawfī Ḳazwīnī, *Taʾrīkh-i Guzīda*, ed. Browne, i, 466, 470, 472-5; C. Defrémery, *Histoire des Seldjoukides*, in *JA*, ser. 4, xiii, 15 ff.; Mīrkhʷānd, *Historia Seldschukidarum*, ed. Vullers ch. 34; Bundārī, *Zubdat al-nuṣra*, in *Recueil de textes relatifs à l'histoire des Seldjoucides*, ed. Houtsma; Houtsma, *Some remarks on the history of the Saldjuks*, in *AO*, iii, 136 ff.; K.A. Luther, *Rāvandī's report on the administrative changes of Muḥammad Jahān Pahlavān*, in *Iran and Islam, a volume in memory of Vladimir Minorsky*, ed. C.E. Bosworth, Edinburgh 1971, 393-406; Bosworth, in *Camb. hist. of Iran*, v, 168-9, 179-80; F. Sümer, *İA* art. *Pehlivan*. See also the *Bibl.* to ILDEÑIZIDS.

(K.V. ZETTERSTÉEN)

PAHLAWĪ, PAHLAVĪ, the name of the short-lived dynasty which ruled in Persia from 1925 to 1979. Its two members were Riḍā Shāh (*r.* 1925-41) and his son Muḥammad Riḍā Shāh (*r.* 1941-79) [*q.vv.*].

PĀʾĪ (Hindi "quarter"), English form "pie", the smallest copper coin of British India = $^{1}/_{12}$ of an anna. Originally, in the East India Company's early experiments for a copper coinage, the pie, as its name implies, was the quarter of an anna or pice [see PAYSĀ]; after the Acts of 1835, 1844 and 1870, however, the pie was $^{1}/_{3}$ of a pice.

Bibliography: Yule and Burnell, *Hobson-Jobson, a glossary of Anglo-Indian colloquial words and phrases*[2], 705.

(J. ALLAN)

PAI YEN-HU (Muḥammad Ayyūb), a noted leader of northwestern Chinese Muslim rebellions against the Ch'ing-Manchu rule during the 1860s and 1870s.

A native of Ching-Yang in Shensi province, he was born in 1841 into a traditional *ahung* family. In 1862 he joined the Muslim rebels in Shensi province, his military skills and family background making him one of eigthteen rebel leaders. After most of these had defected to or been killed by the Imperial troops, Pai assumed overall leadership of the anti-Manchu campaigns. When some of his own "Old Teaching" followers defected in 1869, he was driven out of Shensi and joined forces with Ma Hua-Lung [*q.v.*] at Chin-chi-pao, Kansu, but deserted him again when he realised that Ma also intended to surrender. Pai and his troops next took the area around Hsi-Ning, but were evicted by the veteran pacification general, Tso Tsung-T'ang, in 1873. From here they fled to Chinese Turkestan, where they joined forces with Yaᶜḳūb Beg [*q.v.*], whom they assisted in defending Dzungaria. They were again defeated by Tso. Yaᶜḳūb Beg died (the cause is unknown) at Kurla in May 1877, precipitating the dissolution of his Kā<u>sh</u>g<u>h</u>aria amīrate. By this stage severely weakened, Pai and his followers were forced to flee to Kuča, further westwards to Aḳsu, U<u>sh</u> Turfan and eventually into the Naryn River valley in Russia, where they found asylum. In 1879 they moved to Pi<u>sh</u>pek (present-day Frunze) [*q.v.*], where Pai is said to have died of illness on 22 July 1882.

The descendants of Pai and his followers form the main stock of the Dungan minority now living in the Kirghiz, Kazakh and Uzbek Republics of the former Soviet Union. Recent research suggests that they have preserved their ethnic identity and some elements of Chinese Islam. Their first mosques were built in the Chinese manner, and they still speak Shensi and Kansu dialects, using Chinese in Cyrillic characters.

Bibliography: An Wei-Chun *et alii* (eds.), *Kansu Hsin T'ung-Chih* ("New Kansu province gazetteer"), n.p. 1909; I-Hsin *et alii* (eds.), *P'ing-Ting Shen-Kan Sinkiang Fang-Lueh* ("Documents relating to the suppression of the Muslim rebellions in Shensi, Kansu and Sinkiang"), repr. of 1896 edition, Taipei, Cheng-Wen 1968; Mu Shou-Chi (ed.), *Kan-Ning-Ch'ing Shih-Lueh* ("Historic records of Kansu, Ninghsia and Ch'inghai provinces"), repr. of 1936 ed., Taipei, Kuang-Wen 1973; Pai Shou-I (ed.), *Hui-Min Chi-I* ("Collections of documents on Muslim rebellions during the late Ch'ing period"), iii-iv, Shanghai, Shen-Chou Kou-K'uan-She 1952; Svetlana Rimsky-Korsakoff Dyer, *Soviet Dungan kolkhozes in the Kirghiz S.S.R. and the Khazakh S.S.R.*, Oriental Monograph Series, no. 25, A.N.U. Canberra 1979; Sung Po-Lu *et alii* (eds.), *Shensi Hsu T'ung-Chi Kao* ("New gazetteer of Shensi province"), repr. of 1934 ed., Taipei, Hua-Wen 1969; Tso Tsung-T'ang, *Tso Wen-Hsing-Kung Ch'uan-Chi* ("Collected works of Tso Tsung T'ang"), repr. of 1907 ed., Taipei, Wen-Hai 1979; Wan Shu-Tan (ed.), *Sinkiang T'u-Chih* ("A gazetteer of Sinkiang province"), revised ed., T'ien-Chin, Po-Ai 1911.

(CHANG-KUAN LIN)

PAISĀ [see PAYSĀ].

PĀK PĀTAN, a *taḥṣīl* in the Montgomery district of the Pan<u>dj</u>āb in Pākistān, famous for its association with <u>Sh</u>ay<u>kh</u> Farīd-al-Dīn Masᶜūd Gan<u>dj</u>-i <u>Sh</u>akar [*q.v.*]. It was founded by a prince of the Yaudhaya tribe and was named A<u>dj</u>odhan. It appears from Greek accounts that the place existed at the time of Alexander's invasion. When <u>Sh</u>ay<u>kh</u> Farīd settled there, it was a deserted town, having forests full of ferocious beasts and reptiles. Gradually, it became a great centre of spiritual culture and people from far and near were attracted to the *<u>dj</u>amāᶜat-<u>kh</u>āna* of <u>Sh</u>ay<u>kh</u> Farīd. Ajodhan stood at a strategic place on the Multān-Dihlī road. Caravans and armies passed through it and carried the <u>Sh</u>ay<u>kh</u>'s fame to different regions (*Fawāʾid al-fuʾād*, Lucknow 1885, 99; Ibn Baṭṭūṭa, *Riḥla*, Cairo 1928, i, 13). The name Pāk Pātan was given by the Mu<u>gh</u>al emperor Akbar in homage to the memory of the saint. Situated on a high mound, it has a complex of buildings: a Friday mosque, tomb of the <u>Sh</u>ay<u>kh</u> and his descendants <u>Sh</u>ay<u>kh</u> <u>Sh</u>ihāb al-Dīn and <u>Sh</u>ay<u>kh</u> ᶜAlāʾ al-Dīn, a *samaᶜ-<u>kh</u>ana* (hall for musical sessions), residential quarters and various graves.

Bibliography: *Imperial gazetteer of India*², xix, 332-3; Abdullah Chaghtai, *Pakpattan and Baba Farid Ganj-i Shakar*, Lahore 1968; Ahmad Nabi Khan, *The mausoleum of Šaiḫ ᶜAlāʾ al-Dīn at Pākpattan (Punjāb). A significant example of the Tughluq style of architecture*, in *EW*, N.S., xxix/3-4 (September-December 1974), 311-26; M. Irving, *The shrine of Baba Farid Shakarganj at Pakpattan*, in *Jnal. of the Punjab Historical Society*, i/1 (1911), 70-7; D. Ibbetson, *A glossary of the tribes and castes in the Punjab and North-West Frontier Provinces*, Lahore 1914, iii, 342-3; K.A. Nizami, *The life and times of Shaikh Farid-uʾd-din Masᶜud Ganj-i Shakar*, ᶜAlīgaṙh 1955.

(K.A. NIZAMI)

PĀKISTĀN, the Islamic Republic of Pākistān or *Islām-i <u>Dj</u>umhūriyya-yi Pākistān* is bounded by Iran, Af<u>gh</u>ānistān, the former Soviet Union, China, India and the Arabian Sea. It covers an area of 706,495 km² and has a population of 114,071,000 (1990 estimate which includes the population of the disputed state of <u>Dj</u>ammū and Ka<u>sh</u>mīr as well as Af<u>gh</u>ān refugees). The country is divided into four distinct physical regions. In the north, sections of the Himalayan and Karakoram ranges reach an average of more than 6,100 m/20,000 ft. and include some of the world's highest peaks. The Balūčistān plateau to the west and south-west is a broken highland region crossed by many ridges. The western portion of the Indo-Gangetic plains—the Indus valley—extends southwards from the Potwar plateau to the Arabian Sea. It is watered by five major rivers—the Indus, Chenab, Jhelum, Ravi and Satlaj—and their tributaries, and is Pākistān's most prosperous agricultural region. The Thal, Cholistan and Thar desert areas are found in the south-east of the country, bordering on India. The climate is characterised by extremes of temperature and aridity. A weak form of tropical monsoon climate occurs over much of the country with arid conditions in the north and west where the wet season is from December to March. Elsewhere, rain is mainly between July and December. Summer temperatures are high, in places exceeding 45°C., but the mountains in the north experience cold winters.

Pākistān is made up of the four provinces of the Pan<u>dj</u>āb, Sind, Balūčistān [*q.vv.*] and North-West Frontier Province (NWFP), together with the Tribal Areas, Gilgit Agency [*q.v.* in Suppl.], Islāmābād Capital Territory and Āzād Ka<u>sh</u>mīr, whose possession is disputed with India. The bulk of the population is concentrated in the Indus Valley plain and remains rural in occupation. Rural to urban migration, however, has resulted in rapidly growing cities such as Karachi, Lahore, Rawalpindi, Multān, Fayṣalābād and Ḥaydarābād, together with the accompanying problems of inadequate housing and transport facilities. Pākistān has a developing mixed economy, largely based on agriculture, light industries and services. Agriculture, which is almost dependent on an extensive irrigation system, employs more than 50% of the labour force and in 1986 provided 26% of GNP and 45% of foreign exchange earnings. The main crops are wheat, cotton, maize, sugar cane and rice. The country is agriculturally self-sufficient although there are often shortages of staple products. Industry employs only about 10% of the labour force and produces nearly 20% of GDP. Textiles, especially cotton, are the main manufacture and leading export commodity. Under-employment is widespread and there has been significant emigration by professional and skilled workers, in particular to the Middle East and Gulf States. Social welfare and health facilities are limited. *Zakāt* [*q.v.*] has been used by governments to provide funds for welfare provision. Although primary education is free, less than half the number of school-aged children attend and literacy remains limited to only about one-quarter of the population and only one-sixth of women.

The national language is Urdu, but English is used in central government and business. The main regional languages are Pandjābī, Sindhī, Balūčī, Pashto, Brahui and Siraiki. No single language is common to the population as a whole. According to the 1981 census, 96.68% of the population are Muslims, with Christians (1.55%), Hindus (1.51%), Parsees and Buddhists making up very small religious minorities. Most Muslims are Sunnīs and belong to the Ḥanafī school. There is a significant Shīʿī minority which is divided into sub-sects, primarily the Ithnā ʿAsharīs and Ismāʿīlīs, both Aghā-Khānīs and Bohrās. Members of the small but influential sect of the Aḥmadiyya [*q.v.*] are also found.

Pākistān, which achieved independence on 14 August 1947, was the first modern state to be set up on the grounds of religion. Its name, meaning "land of the pure", is said to have been constructed in 1933 by Chaudhri Raḥmat ʿAlī, an Indian Muslim student at Cambridge, from letters taken from the names of its component provinces (Pandjāb, North-West Frontier or Afghāniyya, Kashmīr, Sind and Balūčistān). Its creation was seen as the logical outcome of the so-called two-nation theory which argued that Indian Muslims (only about one-fifth of the total population of India) formed a distinct nation and had the right to a separate state at independence. The origins of Pākistān, however, are generally seen as linked to the effect which British rule in India had on the relationship between the different communities making up the population of the subcontinent. The interaction of its impact with processes of religious revival and reform meant that groups belonging to these communities gradually came to see themselves as being distinct or separate in political terms. In this context, the emergence of the Indian National Congress as the leading all-Indian political organisation by the beginning of the 20th century helped to bring about a reaction among some Muslims who considered the Congress to be dominated by Hindus and therefore sought their own political representative. This occurred in 1906 with the formation of the All-India Muslim League. Suspicion of Congress was especially common in parts of northern India where Muslims, although a small minority, still enjoyed the legacy of their former status as rulers of the region during the period of Mughal rule. They feared that Congress agitation, Hindu revivalism and constitutional reform would undermine their position, and hence supported policies of protecting Muslim "rights" and culture. Aligarh College, founded by Sir Sayyid Aḥmad Khān [*q.v.*] in 1877, played an important part in generating the kind of Muslims who were attracted to this political path. The diversity of India's Muslims, however, prevented them from coming together in a single political organisation until the 1940s. Indeed, the intervening years saw periods of collaboration with Congress, such as 1919-22 when Muslims from all over India joined with Hindus in the Khilāfat-Non-Cooperation movement [*q.v.*] to agitate against British rule. In Muslim majority provinces such as the Pandjāb and Bengal, there was also significant support for provincial parties which represented class rather than communal interests. League activity remained slack for much of the 1930s, as highlighted by its poor showing in the provincial elections of 1937. But constitutional reforms which retained communal electorates meant that Muslims were increasingly encouraged to think of themselves as a separate political category, while the growth in communal feeling on the part of both Hindus and Muslims reinforced this trend.

The turning point for the League came with the outbreak of the Second World War. Efforts made at the centre by its leader, Muḥammad ʿAlī Djināḥ [*q.v.*] (Jinnah) meant that the British recognised the League as the representative of Muslim aspirations and, in the face of Congress opposition to the way in which India had been taken into the conflict, an alternative organisation through which to legitimise the war effort. Under these circumstances, in which more people were listening to what it had to say, the League in March 1940 issued its Lahore demand for a separate Muslim state or states, the precise meaning deliberately vague in order to keep the League's options open. The party's main task was to persuade its co-religionists in the Muslim majority provinces that provincial autonomy would not protect their position if Congress held power at the centre. Gradually, it won over local landowning and religious élites and with them their considerable political influence. This success was reflected in the striking gains made in the 1946 elections in which the League won an overwhelming majority of Muslim seats. Deadlock in negotiations with Congress, together with growing communal tension, resulted in a British plan to partition India, including the Pandjāb and Bengal which the League had expected to receive in full. Jinnah, therefore, was not happy with the "truncated" and "moth-eaten" state which it was offered, but, with the alternative of conceding power completely to the Congress, the League finally accepted this option in the summer of 1947.

Pākistān faced independence with both strengths and weaknesses. On the one hand, it could be argued that, composed of an overwhelming majority of Muslims, it had the basis of a strong national identity with which to contemplate the future. On the other hand, it still had to contend with the fact that, although predominantly Muslim, its people were divided ethnically, linguistically, theologically and by caste and class. In addition, it had the added problem that its two wings—East and West Pākistān—were separated by over 1,600 km of Indian territory. In the event, these obstacles to a united Pākistān proved too great and the country, in the form that it was created, survived only 24 years before East Pākistān broke away to form Bangladesh. Pākistān's new leaders by and large had supported Jinnah's campaign, not so much because they desired an Islamic state, but because Congress rule had become synonymous with Hindu domination. Islam represented different things to them, ranging from an ethic on which to base personal behaviour within a modern democratic state to a total way of life requiring a theocracy. With the removal of the direct threat of a Hindu majority, these, together with other non-religious differences, became more apparent. As a result, Pākistān's history has been characterised by the failure of the new state to build workable political institutions which could reflect the diversity present within the country. Provincial rivalry, the intervention of the military in politics and recourse to Islam as a potential source of unity have been important features of Pākistān's political development since 1947. In particular, the country's "Islamic" identity has generated tensions within the political system, caused to a great extent by the need to reconcile Pākistān's creation as a homeland for Indian Muslims with pressure to translate it into some kind of more self-consciously Islamic state.

Pākistān's position in the years immediately following independence was fraught with difficulties. There was the immense task of resettling about eight million refugees known as *muhādjirs* [*q.v.*] who had begun to stream across the border at partition, as well as the need to establish its economy in the aftermath of a war fought with India over the disputed state of Djammū and Kashmīr. The task of framing a constitution was entrusted to a Constituent Assembly which also functioned as an interim legislature. The structure of the state was a federal one, with the Governor-General and the Constituent Assembly at the centre and governors and provincial assemblies in the provinces. Jinnah's death in September 1948 meant that power passed into the hands of Liyāḳat ʿAlī Khān [*q.v.*] (Liaqat Ali Khan), someone who shared his commitment to a democratic and essentially secular state but whose power base was considerably weaker. Pākistān had been created as a state for Indian Muslims, but there was a significant distinction between this and an Islamic state. Indeed, Jinnah himself had stressed that religion was to be an essentially private affair from the point of view of the state. Liaqat's position, however, meant that he needed to gain support where he could, and so in 1949 he wooed the country's religious spokesmen by issuing a resolution on the aims and objectives of the constitution which emphasised Islamic values. The debate on the relationship between religion and the state continued in the Constituent Assembly where religious groups played an active role. It was affected by the appointment of Khwaja Nizamuddin, an individual of great personal piety, as Governor-General following Liaquat's assassination in October 1951, as well as by religio-political campaigns such as that led by the Aḥrārs demanding both the purification of political life in general and, in 1953, the outlawing of the Aḥmadiyya sect in particular. This action led to rioting in some of the country's larger cities, and martial law was imposed to restore order in Lahore. When Pākistān finally achieved its first constitution in 1956, it tried to resolve the debate by accommodating as many different opinions as possible. The constitution embodied the Islamic provisions of the 1949 Objectives Resolution and declared Pākistān to be an Islamic republic. Its preamble accepted Allāh's sovereignty over man; Clause 204 envisaged the formation of an Institute of Islamic Research "to assist in the reconstruction of Muslim society on a truly Islamic basis"; and Clause 205 reiterated that "all new laws were to conform to the Ḳurʾān and Sunna" and no existing law would be repugnant to them. In reality, however, these provisions were little more than a statement of intent as no mechanisms were actually established to determine whether or not a law was un-Islamic. The constitution also confirmed the merger of the West Pākistānī provinces into One Unit carried out in 1955 to create parity between the two wings of the country. This was an attempt to reconcile East Pākistānī differences with the centre, which Bengalis saw as dominated by West Pākistānī interests and which had been reflected in the crushing defeat of the Muslim League in provincial elections in East Pākistān in 1954. Finally, the power of the military-bureaucratic élite was reflected in the far-reaching powers granted to the President in relation to the federal and provincial parliaments.

Growing factionalism and economic problems reinforced disillusionment with politicians, and meant that there was little opposition when the military under General Ayyūb Khān (Ayub Khan) intervened by instituting martial law in October 1958. In March 1962 Pākistān received its second constitution. This constructed a more centralised system of government, with the executive branch under the full control of an indirectly-elected President chosen by an electoral college of Basic Democrats. The powers of the central and provincial legislatures were severely restricted but parity between East and West Pākistān was preserved. Initially, the constitution did not envisage political parties but subsequently a restricted role was engineered for them. Modernisation was the watchword for Ayub's régime. Accordingly, his government displayed a modernising zeal in relation to the role of Islam. Unlike its predecessor, the constitution did not at least initially call Pākistān an "Islamic republic" (the adjective had been dropped in 1958 and it was not until the Amendment of 1963 that the title was restored), nor did it recognise the Ḳurʾān and the Sunna as the sole inspiration for the country's law. It did, however, reiterate that no law should be repugnant to Islam and established various councils to advise on these matters. All the same, the government was not popular with religious leaders who objected to the treatment of Islam in the 1962 constitution. It confirmed their alienation, much enhanced by the Family Laws Ordinance of 1961 which had included notable reforms such as the restricting of polygamy. Religio-political parties, such as the Djamāʿat-i Islāmī led by Mawlānā Sayyid Abu 'l-ʿAlāʾ Mawdūdī [*q.v.*], increased their support. Modernisation under Ayub, however, took place above all in the economic field, which experienced increased growth during the 1960s. But this growth was unevenly distributed, and the imbalance between East and West Pākistān increased, leading to greater disquiet among Bengalis. Despite victory over Miss Fatima Jinnah in the presidential election of January 1965, Ayub's problems mounted in the aftermath of an unsuccessful war against India also in 1965. In March 1969 the strength of opposition to his government finally forced him to hand over responsibility to General Yaḥyā Khān, who once again placed the country under martial law.

Yahya immediately set about dismantling Ayub's political system. In March 1970 he published the Legal Framework Order which defined Pākistān as a federal democratic republic with a Muslim head of state; representation was once again to be on the basis of population rather than parity between east and west; and West Pākistān was redivided into its former provinces. Elections were held in December 1970 but produced the unexpected result of a decisive victory for the East Pākistānī Awami League with 167 out of 300 seats. Faced with the loss of power at the centre and the Awami League's call for virtual autonomy for

East Pākistān, West Pākistānī politicians, notably Zulfikar Ali (D͟hu 'l-Fiḳār ʿAlī) Bhutto, leader of the Pakistan People's Party (PPP), decided to boycott the National Assembly. The country's military leadership, equally dismayed by the shift in power which was taking place, cooperated by suspending the Assembly. This in turn led the Awami League's leader, Shaikh Mujibur Rahman, to call for complete secession. The Pākistānī authorities launched Operation Searchlight and arrested Mujib, but a stalemate ensued which was only broken with the entry of India into the war in December 1971 on the side of the Bengalis. With its help, the East Pākistānī *Mukti Bahini* (Bengali freedom fighters) took Dhaka (Dacca) and established the independent state of Bangladesh in January 1972.

The main victor in what remained of Pākistān was Bhutto, who established a patriotic image for himself at negotiations at the United Nations in New York and was sworn in as President following Yahya's resignation at the end of December 1971. Pākistān's third constitution adopted in April 1973 sought to reach consensus on the sharing of power between the federal government and the provinces, the divisions of responsibility between President and Prime Minister, and the role of Islam in politics. Bhutto's advocacy of Islamic socialism led to little tangible change but did provide, in the short term, a way of keeping Islamic fundamentalism at arm's length. The populism of his economic and social programme was also successful at first, but its failure to live up to popular expectations led to growing disillusionment with his government. This was reinforced by increasingly autocratic tendencies on the part of Bhutto and other PPP members. The drift to the opposition, in particular to religio-political alternatives, gathered pace and demonstrated its threat during elections in March 1977. Although the PPP won a large victory, the opposition coalition, known as the Pakistan National Alliance (PNA), claimed that massive vote rigging had taken place. Mounting protest brought chaos to Pākistān's cities and Bhutto was himself forced to proclaim martial law. Eventually, the military under the Chief of Staff of the Army, General Muḥammad Ḍiyāʾ al-Ḥaḳḳ (Zia-ul Haq), took over power in July 1977.

The new military régime, in line with its Operation Fairplay, announced that it intended to restore democracy and that fresh elections would be held within 90 days. Following Bhutto's arrest in early September on charges of attempted murder, however, these elections were postponed, supposedly to allow for Bhutto's trial to take place. In reality, it was clear that Bhutto remained the only politician with mass national appeal. Bhutto was eventually hanged in April 1979 following a Supreme Court review of the case, but elections promised for November 1979 were again postponed, political parties banned and strict censorship imposed on the press. Meanwhile, Zia had proclaimed himself President. In February 1979, he embarked on his programme of Islamisation by introducing Islamic criminal punishments. Zia's own strongly held religious views, however, did not disguise the political motives which were at the root of his policies on Islam. Zia firmly believed that Pākistān's political system had to be Islamised in order ostensibly to forge national unity, and he used Islamisation as a populist weapon to disarm the moral opposition to his régime. His determination was helped by changes in the international climate caused by the Soviet Union's intervention in Afg͟hānistān in December 1979. Substantial support provided by the United States and Muslim countries such as Saudi military while the influx of millions of Afg͟hān refugees produced enormous amounts of foreign economic aid. In March 1981, despite the failure of a specially-appointed committee of scholars, jurists and *ʿulamāʾ* to reach a consensus on recommendations for the structure of an Islamic system of government, Zia promulgated a Provisional Constitutional Order which allowed martial law to continue indefinitely and gave the President powers to amend the constitution. Its main provisions included the setting up of a *Madjlis-i S͟hūrā* or Federal Consultative Council on the grounds that parliamentary democracy was not compatible with Islam. Partisan political activity, however, was allowed to resume gradually albeit subject to official censure. An amendment to the Political Parties Act of 1962 meant that parties could be denied registration if their manifestos did not include Islamic provisions. A referendum held in December 1984 Arabia allowed him to strengthen the position of the confirmed Zia's Islamisation policy, which included economic reforms to the banking system as well as the controversial Zinā Ordinance, which limited the role and rights of women. Opposition groups strongly contested the result. The official majority of 98% was also taken as a mandate for Zia to remain in office for a further five years.

National and provincial elections, boycotted by the opposition, were held on a non-party basis the following February and Muhammad Khan Junejo was appointed Prime Minister. By then, however, Zia had moved to concentrate political power even more firmly in presidential hands by promulgating an order which introduced sweeping changes in the 1973 constitution. Martial law was eventually lifted in December 1985 and the constitution, in its amended form, restored in full. Zia remained President as well as Chief of Staff for the Army which effectively redefined the relationship between civilians and the army. In January 1986 Junejo revived the Pākistān Muslim League and later in the year Bēnaẓīr Bhutto, daughter of Zulfikar Ali Bhutto, returned from exile to lead the PPP. Anti-government agitation increased, as did levels of ethnic violence in the province of Sind and in Karachi in particular. Zia stepped in to dissolve the national and provincial assemblies in May 1988, accusing them of corruption, and once again announced elections within 90 days. As before they were postponed until November 1988, but in August Zia himself was killed in an unexplained aircrash along with other senior military officers and the United States ambassador to Pākistān. The Chairman of the Senate, Ghulam Ishaq Khan, became acting President and proclaimed a state of emergency promising that the elections would take place as scheduled later in the year.

Benazir Bhutto's PPP failed to win an overall majority but, with the help of coalition partners, came to power as the largest party in the new National Assembly, and Bhutto herself became the first woman in modern history to be elected premier of a Muslim state. Ghulam Ishaq Khan was subsequently chosen by an electoral college to serve a five-year term as President. In the context of severe economic difficulties and mounting ethnic violence in Sind, Bhutto's hold on power became increasingly tenuous. The government's failure to introduce a populist socio-economic programme increased widespread dissatisfaction, and party members were also dismayed at their leaders' attempts to win over the opposition by apparently compromising the party's position.

In August 1990, the President dismissed Bhutto

and an interim premier, Ghulam Mustafa Jatoi, was appointed. Elections were held in October in which the opposition Islāmī Djumhūrī Ittiḥād (IJI) and its allies won convincing victories on both the national and provincial level. All four provinces returned anti-PPP majorities. While the voting was generally considered to be free of rigging, the low turn-out of no more than 50% reflected continuing popular disillusionment with the political process. The IJI leader, Nawaz Sharif, a Pandjābī industrialist and former protege of Zia, was sworn in as Prime Minister. Pākistān was badly affected by the Gulf crisis 1990-91. Remittances from workers employed in the Middle East, already declining, dropped further, and the government was caught in a dilemma between honouring long-standing alliances with the West and strong pro-ʿIrāḳ sentiment at home. In the event, Pākistānī troops were sent to Saudi Arabia with the provision that they did not come under United States command. In 1991, the government succeeded in passing the Shariat Bill which confirmed Pākistān as an Islamic state but which, like previous attempts at legislating Islamic principles into the constitution, appeared to lack the necessary mechanisms to give much weight to the changes which it introduced.

Bibliography: For the growth of Muslim separatism, the Muslim League and the demand for Pakistan, see P. Hardy, *The Muslims of British India*, Cambridge 1972; F. Robinson, *Separatism among Indian Muslims: the politics of the United Provinces' Muslims, 1860-1923*, Cambridge 1974; G. Minault, *The Khilafat Movement: religious symbolism and political modernization in India*, Columbia 1982; A. Jalal, *The sole spokesman: Jinnah, the Muslim League and the demand for Pakistan*, Cambridge 1985; D. Gilmartin, *Empire and Islam*, Berkeley 1989; and as a bridge between pre-independence and post-independence trends, Aziz Ahmad, *Islamic modernism in India and Pakistan, 1857-1964*, Oxford 1967. For Pakistan's own subsequent history, focusing in particular on the interaction between religion, the state and the military, see: L. Binder, *Religion and politics in Pakistan*, Berkeley 1961; L. Ziring, *The Ayub era, politics in Pakistan, 1958-69*, Syracuse 1971; K.K. Aziz, *Party politics in Pakistan, 1947-1958*, Islamabad 1976; S.J. Burki, *Pakistan under Bhutto, 1971-1977*, London 1980; Khalid B. Sayeed, *Politics in Pakistan: the nature and direction of change*, New York 1980; S.P. Cohen, *The Pakistan Army*, Berkeley 1984; Hasan Askari Risvi, *The military and politics in Pakistan: 1947-86*, Lahore 1986; O. Noman, *Pakistan: political and economic history since 1947*, London 1990; and A. Jalal, *The state of martial rule: the origins of Pakistan's political economy of defence*, Cambridge 1990. The break-up of Pakistan and the secession of Bangladesh are examined in: R. Jahan, *Pakistan: failure in national integration*, New York 1972; and T. Maniruzzaman, *The Bangladesh revolution and its aftermath*, Dhaka 1980; while M. Ayub Khan, *Friends not masters: a political autobiography*, London 1967; and Zulfikar Ali Bhutto, *If I am assassinated* ..., New Delhi 1979, provide valuable insights on their régimes. (Sarah Ansari)

PĀLĀHANG (p.), Ottoman Turkish form *pālāheng*, literally "string, rope, halter, cord", is applied to the belt worn around the waist by dervishes, especially the Bektāshīs [see bektāshiyya], and on which is fixed a disc of stone (of jasper, found near the tomb of Ḥādjdjī Bektāsh at Ḥādjdjī Bektāsh Köy in Anatolia, of crystal or of translucent stone from Nadjaf in ʿIrāḳ) with twelve flutings at the edge; these are said by the Bektāshīs to symbolise the Twelve *Imāms*, the Twelve Disciples of Jesus or even the Twelve Tribes of Israel (see J.K. Birge, *The Bektashi order of dervishes*, London-Hartford 1937, 255-6, 268 and illustr. no. 10, object 8). Its introduction is ascribed to the *pūsh-neshīn* or master of the *tekke* at Ḥādjdjī Bektāsh Köy in the time of sultan Bāyezīd II (*ibid.*, 57).

Very similar in shape and substance is the smaller, twelve-fluted disc worn on a cord, sometimes with smaller stones strung along the cord (the *dürr-i Nedjef* "pearls of Nadjaf"), around the neck and called the *teslīm tashi* "stone of submission", given to the young dervish at the end of his novitiate (see *ibid.*, 217, 233-4, 247, 270, and illustr. no. 10, object 4).

Bibliography (in addition to references given in the article): Th. Ippen, *Skutari und die nordalbanische Küstenebene*, Sarajevo 1907, 78 (with reference to the Bektāshīs of Kruja in Albania); J.P. Brown, *The dervishes or oriental spiritualism*², ed. H.A. Rose, London 1927, 214. (F. Babinger-[Ed.])

PALAMAW ("place of refuge"), the name of what is now a District in the Bihār State of the Indian Union. It straddles the plateau region of Čhoṭa Nāgpur. It was also the name of two fortresses which were built by the Rādjput Čero Rādjās of Palamāw, which were attacked in the middle decades of the 11th/17th century by the Mughal commander Dāwūd Khān Ḳurayshī, who made the Rādjās tributary and erected several fine Islamic buildings at Palamāw. In the early years of the 20th century, Muslims constituted 8% of the population of the District.

Bibliography: *Imperial gazetteer of India*², xix, 334-44; and see bihār. (Ed.)

PĀLĀNPUR, a former, Muslim-ruled princely state of India, now in Gujarat State of the Indian Union but in British Indian times included in the Western India States Agency. The territory incorporated in this agency included the area formerly known as Kāthiāwār together with the Cutch and Pālanpūr agencies. Its creation in October 1924 marked the end of the political control of the Government of Bombay and the beginning of direct relations with the Government of India. The old Pālanpūr Agency with its headquarters at the town of Pālanpūr was a group of states in Gudjarāt [*q.v.*] lying between 23° 25′ and 24° 41′ N. and 71° 16′ and 71° 46′ E. It was bounded on the north by the Rādjput states of Udaypūr and Sirohi; on the east by the Mahī Kāntha Agency; on the south by the state of Barōda and Kāthiāwār; and on the west by the Rann of Cutch.

The state of Pālanpūr was conquered towards the end of the 10th/16th century by Lohāni Paṭhāns, subsequently known as Djāloris. A short account of its history under the Mughal emperors will be found in the *Gazetteer of Bombay*, v, 318-24, and in the *Mirʾāt-i Aḥmadī* (Ethé, no. 3599, fol. 741). British relations with this state date back to the year 1809, when, through British influence, arrangements were made for the payment of tribute to the Gaekwar of Barōda (Aitchison, vi, no. lxxxix). This engagement was further strengthened by an agreement signed on November 28, 1817 (*op. cit.*, no. xci). In 1848, the appointment of an agent from the Gaekwar was abolished and the finances of the state remained under British supervision until 1874, when the ruler of Pālanpūr was entrusted with the management of his own finances.

Pālanpūr was still ruled by its princes up to 1947 and the merging of the princely states within the Indian Union by Lohānī Paṭhāns. It had in 1933 a population of 264,179, of whom 245,000 spoke

Gudjarātī, when the distribution of population according to religion was as follows: Hindus, 222,714; Muslims, 28,690 and Jains, 12,542. Since Partition, many of the Muslims have emigrated to Pākistān.

Bibliography: C.U. Aitchison, *Treaties, engagements and sanads*, vi, 1909; *Census of India*, x, *The Western States Agency*, Bombay 1933; *Gazetteer of the Bombay Presidency*, v, Bombay 1880; *Imperial gazetteer of India*[2], xix, 345-55; ʿAlī Muḥammad Khān, *Mirʾāt-i Aḥmadī* (India Office, Ethé, nos. 3597-3599); *Selections from the records of the Bombay Government*, no. xxv, 1856. (C.C. Davies)

PALEMBANG, the capital city of the province of *Sumatera Selatan* (South Sumatra) in Indonesia, situated on the shores of the Musi river. It lies in long. 104° 45′ E. and lat. 2°59′ S., and has a population of *ca.* 790,000 (1990), of whom some 85% are Muslims.

The area of Palembang, united with neighbouring Malayu (Jambi), was the centre of the (Mahayana-) Buddhist empire of Sri Vidjaya (4th-14th centuries A.D.), renowned especially in the 8th-10th centuries for its famous study centres for Buddhism and Sanskrit. After the 11th century, tantric Kāla-Čakra-Buddhism with a strong magical component became dominant. In 1377 Palembang was conquered and partly destroyed by the ruler of Madjapahit, the great Hindu-Javanese empire (14th-15th centuries). A royal prince, after his escape, founded Malacca [*q.v.*] in 1403 and became its first sultan after adopting Islam in 1413. The Javanese-Chinese *adipati* of Palembang, Arya Damar (after his conversion to Islam: Arya Dilah = ʿAbd Allāh, 859-91/1455-86), became the ancestor of the later sultans of "Palembang Darussalam". Sultan Susuhunan Arya Kusuma ʿAbd ar-Raḥīm (1069-1118/1659-1706) was the first ruler to adopt this title. After a power struggle between Sultan Mahmud Badaruddin and Sultan Ahmad Najamuddin in 1811-21, a struggle used by the British and Dutch for their conflicting interests, the Dutch finally exiled the last sultan, Najamuddin's son, in 1825, following a last abortive attempt to regain his independence. Thus the history of the sultanate came to an end.

In the second half of the 18th century especially, some Muslim scholars from Palembang achieved international fame, such as ʿAbd al-Ṣamad al-Palimbānī [*q.v.*]. At present, Palembang is the site of an influential *Institut Agama Islam Negeri* (State Islamic Institute, *IAIN*), to promote Islamic education.

Bibliography: M.O. Woelders, *Het sultanaat Palembang*, 's-Gravenhage 1975 (= VKI 72); G.W.J. Drewes, *Directions for travellers on the mystic path*, The Hague 1977; Taufik Abdullah, *Beberapa aspek perkembangan Islam di Sumatera Selatan*, in K.H.O. Gadjahnata (ed.), *Masuk dan berkembangnya Islam di Sumatera Selatan*, Jakarta 1986, 53-66. (O. Schumann)

PAMIRS, the name (of unknown etymology) of a mountain massif of Inner Asia. Its core is in the modern Gorno-Badakhshan Autonomous oblast of the former USSR, but it spills over into Kirghizia and Tadjikistan to the north and west, and into the Sinkiang Uighur Autonomous Region of China to the east, and Afghānistān (including the Wakhān corridor) and Pākistānī Kashmīr (Āzād Kashmīr) to the south. Comprised mainly of east-west-running ranges, its many river valleys being right-bank affluents of the upper Oxus (here called the Pandj "Five [rivers]", its mountains reach a height of 7,495 m/24,584 ft. on Communism Peak. It is extremely thinly populated: the population of the western Pamirs is in the main ethnically Tadjik and Ismāʿīlī Shīʿī in faith, whilst that of the eastern Pamirs is mainly Turkish Kirghiz and Sunnī Muslim (some of these last, from the Wakhān corridor, fled via Gilgit and eventually settled in Turkey after the 1978 Communist takeover in Afghānistān; see MUHĀDJIR. 2. In Turkey and the Ottoman lands, at vol. VII, 353b). As a typical refuge area, it is in the Pamirs region that there survive certain archaic eastern Iranian languages, such as Shughnī, Ishkāshmī, Wakhī, Yāzghulāmī, Sanglīčī, Mundjī, etc. [see ĪRĀN, iii. Languages, in Suppl.].

Being so topographically and climatically unattractive to all but a few agriculturists in the valleys and nomads on the plateaux, the only part of the region of historical significance has been the upper Oxus valley, along which an important commercial route led to passes across the Hindū Kush [*q.v.*] mountains to the Pandjhīr [*q.v.*] valley of Afghānistān and southwards into Čitrāl [*q.v.*] and Gilgit [*q.v.* in Suppl.]. It was doubtless for this reason that the region was known to the Chinese, with Shughnān [*q.v.*] appearing in Chinese sources, such as the travel account of the early 7th century Buddhist pilgrim Hsüen-Tsang, as *She-kʾi-nior* "the kingdom of the five *She-ni* (gorges)", apparently referring to the Oxus's name here of Pandj. In Islamic times, al-Yaʿḳūbī, *Buldān*, 292, tr. Wiet, 109, mentions the principality in "upper Ṭukhāristān" [*q.v.*] of (?) Khumār-Beg or Khumār-Tigīn, ruler of Shiḳinān (Shughnān) and Badakhshān [*q.v.*]; the people there were still pagan, though apparently tributary to adjoining Muslim princes (see Ibn Ḥawḳal, ed. Kramers, 467, tr. Kramers and Wiet, 449-50; Barthold, *Turkestan*[3], 65). The *Ḥudūd al-ʿālam* (4th/10th century) situates in the Pamirs region the "Gate to Tibet", *dar-i Tubbat*, and the seat of the *malik* of Wakhān at Ishkāmish, its chef-lieu (tr. Minorsky, 120-1, § 26.12-18, comm. 363-9; cf. Marquart, *Ērānšahr*, 224-6).

Towards the end of the 13th century, Marco Polo passed through the Pamirs region, from Badakhshān to the Wakhān valley and thence northwards to Kāshghar [*q.v.*]; he describes the sparse inhabitants there as warlike Muslims, with a chief called (?) *None* (Yule-Cordier, *The book of Ser Marco Polo*[3], London 1903, i, 170-9 and Itinerary map no. III).

Subsequently, the upper Oxus region of the Pamirs was mainly under the political authority of Nizārī Ismāʿīlī hereditary *mīrs* based on Shughnān, who managed to survive pressure and attacks from the local Tīmūrid governors; this isolated Ismāʿīlī community has been significant for its rôle in preserving many theological and legal texts of the sect (see F. Daftary, *The Ismāʿīlīs: their history and doctrines*, Cambridge 1990, 436, 441, 486-7, 544). Toward the end of the 19th century, the upper Oxus/Pandj river was established, after disputes between the Amīr of Afghānistān ʿAbd al-Raḥmān Khān [*q.v.*], the Amīr of Bukhārā and the Russians, as the political boundary between Russian Central Asia and Afghānistān (the Russo-Afghan Agreement of 1895) (see L. Dupree, *Afghanistan*, Princeton 1973, 424).

Bibliography: Given in the article, but see also *BSE*[2], xix, 127-9, and the bibls. to BADAKHSHĀN, SHUGHNĀN and WAKHĀN. (C.E. Bosworth)

PAN-ARABISM, an ideology advocating an overall union of Arabs (*waḥdat al-ʿArab, al-waḥda al-ʿArabiyya*). Ideologues of Pan-Arabism have consistently recommended such union on the basis of several elements of commonality: (a) Language and culture, considered the ultimate expression of the entire Arab nation and one of its major links with the past (including the Islamic past; many Arabs have expressed their nationalism in Islamic terms). (b) History, preoccupation with which afforded immersion in a common past glory differing from the 20th-century situation. (c) Ethnic-origins, increasingly called "race" in the first half of the 20th century. (d) Territorial contiguity from the coasts of Morocco to those of ᶜIrāḳ and Saᶜūdī Arabia, which maintained a common culture and history and could naturally promote political and economic relations. The methods advocated and variously attempted generally focused on the establishment of federations and confederations as a step towards a general union, to be achieved either by persuasion or force.

The history of Pan-Arabism is largely a record of these attempts. In the early 20th century, several writers and journalists, such as Negib Azoury, discussed the Arab nation in terms of long-extant primordial sentiments. Their works were mostly read by relatively small élitist circles, however, and rarely served as guidelines for achieving an all-Arab union. Only after the end of the First World War, with the consequent breakdown of the Ottoman Empire and the establishment of mandated Arab entities [see MANDATES], were political moves made by several Arab leaders towards federating Arab-inhabited territories. The Hā<u>sh</u>imite rulers in ᶜIrāḳ and Transjordan were prominently active in this sphere.

The long-range aim of Fayṣal I [*q.v.*] of ᶜIrāḳ was to establish a confederation, embracing ᶜIrāḳ, Syria, Transjordan, Palestine and the Ḥi<u>dj</u>āz. He sought to bolster his own position and that of his country in a highly competitive environment, while gaining access to Mediterranean shores. French-mandated Syria was the key to Fayṣal's success or failure; he strove to persuade the Syrians, French and British of his plans' feasibility. Certain nationalist groups supported Fayṣal and his Pan-Arab plans during the 1920s and 1930s, not only in ᶜIrāḳ, but in Syria as well. In the Pan-Islamic Congress that convened in Jerusalem in 1931 [see PAN-ISLAMISM], a group of activists from Damascus and Jerusalem met and drew up a Pan-Arab charter, whose first paragraph declared the indivisibility of the Arab nation and Arab lands. Pan-Arabists from ᶜIrāḳ, Lebanon and Egypt proclaimed their solidarity with this charter. Plans to convene an all-Arab congress in 1932 floundered, however, because of the strife between ᶜIrāḳ and Saᶜūdī Arabia, as well as British opposition.

Following Fayṣal I's death in 1933, his brother ᶜAbd Allāh [*q.v.*], then *Amīr* of Transjordan, intensified his own efforts at achieving a partial Arab union. Having been involved in Syria's affairs in the 1920s, in the succeeding decade ᶜAbd Allāh renewed his plans to create a confederation of Transjordan with Syria (and ᶜIrāḳ and Palestine, eventually), with himself as its ruler. Once the British had ousted the Vichy French forces from Syria, he again tried to promote his Greater Syria project, persisting in these efforts after the Second World War as well. His failure was due not only to Saᶜūdī opposition and Egyptian reservations, but also to the activities of the ᶜIrāḳī Prime Minister Nūrī al-Saᶜīd [*q.v.*], who was working along the same lines on behalf of his own state, attempting to persuade the British to help in shaping up a union among ᶜIrāḳ, Syria and Palestine (including Transjordan). ᶜAbd Allāh, however, opposed this scheme, which would have diminished his own chances of heading such a union. Another complicating factor was a proposal in 1936-7 by ᶜAbd al-ᶜAzīz Āl Saᶜūd [*q.v.*], King of Saᶜūdī Arabia, to set up an Arab federation headed by himself.

The more factors involved in such moves, the less practicable they became. Even Egypt joined these efforts. Since the early 20th century, a significant part of the political spectrum had identified with supranational objectives and defined itself in Pan-Arab or Pan-Islamic terms, based on the commonality of the Arabic culture and language for an all-Arab nation. Egyptian Pan-Islamists, too, considered Pan-Arabism as a vital step in the struggle for their own ideals. In the 1930s, political groups advocated Pan-Arabism, emphasising Egypt's solidarity with Arabs elsewhere. At the same time, élitist groups in ᶜIrāḳ and Syria expressed themselves in similar political language. Cultural cooperation among Arab governments and other organisations also increased in the 1930s and early 1940s, much of it expressed in political action; cultural and professional associations were formed and politico-literary conventions held. Pan-Arab terminology was increasingly employed by these groups and others.

Towards the end of the Second World War, chiefly after 1943, Arab wishes and British interests combined to bring about consultations for the establishment of the Arab League (*<u>Dj</u>āmiᶜat al-duwal al-ᶜArabiyya*, literally, the League of Arab States [see AL-<u>DJ</u>ĀMIᶜA AL-ᶜARABIYYA in Suppl.]). A preparatory committee met in 1944 and the League itself was set up in Cairo in the following year by Egypt, Saᶜūdī Arabia, ᶜIrāḳ, Syria, Lebanon, Transjordan and Yemen (along with a representative of Palestine's Arabs). It has meanwhile grown to comprise twenty-two states, including Mauritania, Somalia and Djibuti. The League, the most important organisational instrument of Pan-Arabism, could not have been founded without the increase in the number of factors propounding Arab unity; its rather limited political success, on the other hand, reflects strong elements of divisiveness. The League's main objective has been to promote all-Arab unity through cooperation and policy coordination amongst its member states in economics, culture, health, law, communications and social affairs. Its committees have achieved results in all these areas, but much less so in politics and military matters, due to clashes of interests amongst its members and power struggles between rival groups of members states. Paragraph 7 of the League's charter, which allows for vetoing any decision, reflected this situation. Consequently, cardinal decisions in inter-state relations have been reached by direct negotiations between the states, not via the Arab League, where members agree to disagree. The League's most important service to Pan-Arabism remains its very existence as a regional organisation of sovereign Arab states, a framework for debate and consultation amongst its members and an instrument for crisis management, as in its mediation in the civil war in Lebanon during the 1980s (it failed, however, in its attempt to mediate between ᶜIrāḳ and Kuwayt in 1990).

Twelve summit meetings of Arab heads-of-state or their delegates took place between 1964 and 1982 in various capitals. These were useful occasions to coordinate policies regarding the Palestine problem and to attempt to resolve conflicts of interest among Arab states. They accomplished but little, however, insofar as *rapprochement* was concerned. More meaningful were various moves for unification, starting with Egypt and Syria (in February 1958), soon joined by Yemen, and the ᶜIrāḳi-Jordanian unification shortly thereafter. These, however, proved ephemeral, as did several similar moves, e.g. in North Africa. While widely proclaimed as steps towards an all-Arab union, they were regarded by many as merely intended to serve regional self-interests. Djamāl ʿAbd al-Nāṣir [*q.v.* in Suppl.] did succeed in arousing Pan-Arab sentiment in Egypt and elsewhere, especially during the 1950s; he was seen by many as a natural leader of a future Arab union. Similarly, various groups and political parties, chiefly in Syria and Lebanon, strove to promote Pan-Arabism. Of these, the most important was the Baʿth movement. Its particular importance lies in its widespread impact (it has numerous branches in various Arab countries), due to its Pan-Arab appeal mingled with a version of neo-Marxism. Furthermore, the continuous rule of rival Baʿth factions in Syria (since 1963) and ʿIrāḳ (since 1970) implies that the movement is indeed capable of enforcing its ideology: Syria did so by becoming a near-dominant force in Lebanon since 1990 (Arab critics, however, accuse it of "Pan-Syrianism" rather than Pan-Arabism); and ʿIrāḳ by raising irredentist claims against Iran in both the Shaṭṭ al-ʿArab and Khūzistān since the early 1980s, then in Kuwayt in 1990.

Still, the failure of Pan-Arabism to achieve any meaningful results during the entire 20th century has led several Arab intellectuals to mourn "The end of Arabism" as in the title of a much-discussed essay by Fouad Ajami (*Foreign Affairs* [Winter 1978-9]). Ajami argued that the myth of Pan-Arabism had been declining, possibly since the 1967 war, supplanted by the particularist interests and national ideologies of individual Arab states. He also mentioned the minorities, such as the Christians in Lebanon, who oppose Pan-Arabism that would submerge them. Not even Libya's Muʿammar Ḳadhdhāfī could revive Pan-Arabism, according to Ajami. Other Arabs replied, asserting that Pan-Arabism was alive and well. Centres for Studies on Arab Unity (*Markaz dirāsāt al-waḥda al-ʿArabiyya*) in Cairo and Beirut strive to prove this. Whatever the issues, Pan-Arabism, while declaratively still popular, appears underrated in practice by certain new élites which are more oriented towards other universalist ideologies (such as Pan-Islamism), state nationalism, or socio-economic problems of development. Nevertheless, the outpouring of emotional support among Arab masses in several countries for Ṣaddām Ḥusayn and his ʿIrāḳī policies in 1990-2 is an indication that the latent ideal of Pan-Arab unity is maintained and chiefly observable among Sunnīs.

Bibliography: A bibliography on Arab nationalism (with little on Pan-Arabism, however) is F. Clements, *The emergence of Arab nationalism from the nineteenth century to 1921*, Wilmington, Delaware 1976. This is updated by P.J. Vatikiotis's *Between Arabism and Islam*, in *MES*, xxii/4 (Oct. 1986), 576-86. For the Arab League: Asher Gōren, *Ha-Līga ha-ʿAravīt 1945-1954* (Hebrew: *The Arab League, 1945-1954*), Tel Aviv 1954; Michel Laissy, *Du Panarabisme à la Ligue Arabe*, Paris 1948; B.Y. Boutros-Ghali, *The Arab League 1945-1955*, New York 1955; Muhammad Khalil, *The Arab States and the Arab League: A documentary record*, 1-11, Beirut 1962; R.W. MacDonald, *The League of Arab States: a study in the dynamics of regional organization*, Princeton, N.J. 1965; Hussein A. Hassouna, *The League of Arab States and regional disputes: A study of Middle East conflicts*, Dobbs Ferry, N.Y. 1975; Markaz dirāsāt al-waḥda al-ʿArabiyya, *Djāmiʿat al-duwal al-ʿArabiyya: al-wāḳiʿ wa 'l-ṭumūḥ*, Beirut 1983; Abū Khaldūn Sāṭiʿ al-Ḥuṣrī, *Thaḳāfatunā fī Djāmiʿat al-Duwal al-ʿArabiyya*, Beirut 1985; I. Pogany, *The Arab League and peacekeeping in Lebanon*, Aldershot, (U.K.) 1987. See also Negib Azoury, *Le Reveil de la nation arabe*, Paris 1905; Jean Lugol, *Le Panarabisme: passé-présent-future*, Cairo 1946; M.J. Steiner, *Inside Pan-Arabia*, Chicago 1947, 197-208; Fayez A. Sayegh, *Arab unity: hope and fulfillment*, New York 1958; W.A. Beling, *Pan-Arabism and labor*, Cambridge, Mass. 1961; M.M.H. Shehab Eddin, *Pan-Arabism and the Islamic tradition*, Ph.D. diss. American Univ., Washington D.C. 1966; J.W. Ryan, *An inquiry into the problem of building political community beyond the nation-state: a comparative analysis of the Pan-Arab and Pan-African movements*, Ph.D. diss. Univ. of Massachusetts, Amherst 1967; Aref S. Hajjaj, *Der Panarabismus Gamal Abdel-Nassers*², Ph.D. diss. Heidelberg Univ. 1971, 54-96; ʿAbd al-ʿAzīz al-Ahwānī, *Azmat al-waḥda al-ʿArabiyya*, Beirut 1972; Munīf al-Razzāz, *al-Waḥda al-ʿArabiyya: hal lahā min sabīl*, Beirut 1973; ʿAbd al-ʿAzīz al-Rifāʿī, *al-Waḥy al-ʿArabī wa-waḥdat Miṣr wa-Lībiyā*, Cairo 1974; Khaldun S. Husry, *King Fayṣal I and Arab unity*, in *Journal of Contemporary History*, x/4 (Apr. 1975), 323-40; Maḥmud Kāmil, *al-Islām wa 'l-ʿUrūba: taḥlīl li-ʿawāmil al-waḥda bayn ʿishrīn dawla ʿArabiyya*, n.p. [Cairo] 1976; Shaukat Ali, *Pan-movements in the Third World: Pan-Arabism, Pan-Africanism, Pan-Islamism*, Lahore n.d. [1976]; M. Shafīḳ, *al-Waḥda al-ʿArabiyya fi 'l-taʾrīkh al-ʿArabī, in Dirāsāt ʿArabiyya*, xiii (June 1977), 55-72; Saʿd al-Dīn Ibrāhīm, *Ittidjāhāt al-raʾy al-ʿāmm al-ʿArabī naḥw masʾalat al-waḥda*, Beirut 1980; Yūsuf Aḥmad Maḥmūd al-Ḳawsī, *al-Waḥda fī taʾrīkh al-ʿArab al-ḥadīth wa 'l-muʿāṣir*², Cairo 1981; Israel Gershoni, *The emergence of Pan-Arabism in Egypt*, Tel Aviv 1981; William Sulaymān Ḳilāda, *al-Shaʿb al-waḥīd wa 'l-waṭan al-waḥīd: dirāsa fī uṣūl al-waḥda al-ʿArabiyya*, n.p. [Cairo] 1982; Avraham Selaʿ, *Aḥdūt bĕ-tōkh perūd ba-maʿarekhet habeyn-ʿAravīt* (Hebrew: *Unity in disunity in the inter-Arab system*), Jerusalem 1983; S. Reiser, *Pan-Arabism revisited*, in *MEJ*, xxxvii/2 (Spring 1983), 218-33; idem, *Islam, Pan-Arabism and Palestine: an attitudinal survey*, in *Journal of Arab Affairs*, iii/2 (Fall 1984), 189-204; L.L. Snyder, *Macro-nationalisms: a history of the Pan-movements*, Westport, Conn. 1984, ch. 8; Y. Porath, *Abdallah's Greater Syria programme*, in *MES*, xx/2 (April 1984), 172-89; idem, *Nūrī al-Saʿīd's Arab unity programme*, in *ibid.*, xx/4 (Oct. 1984), 76-98; T. Mayer, *The end of Pan-Arabism?*, in *Middle East Review*, xvi/4 (Summer 1984), 31-6; Djūrdj Djabbūr, *Khawāṭir mudjaddada ḥawl mustaḳbal al-waḥda al-ʿArabiyya*, Damascus 1984; Fawzi Mellah, *De l'unité arabe: essai d'interprétation critique*, Paris 1985; Fārūḳ Yūsuf Aḥmad, *Miṣr wa 'l-ʿālam al-ʿArabī*², Cairo 1985; Porath, *In search of Arab unity, 1930-1945*, London 1986; Shukrī ʿAyyāḍ, *al-Adab al-ʿArabī: taʿbīruh ʿan al-waḥda al-ʿArabiyya*, Beirut 1987; Madjdī Ḥammād, *al-ʿAskariyyūn al-ʿArab wa-ḳaḍiyyat al-waḥda*, Beirut 1987, chs. 10-12; T.E. Farah (ed.), *Pan-Arabism and Arab nationalism: the continuing debate*, Boulder, Col. 1987; C.E. Dawn, *The formation of Pan-Arab ideology in the interwar years*, in *IJMES*, xx/1 (Feb. 1988), 67-91; Yūsuf Khūrī (ed.), *Mashārīʿ al-waḥda al-ʿArabiyya, 1913-1987*, Beirut 1988; Ilyās Faraḥ, *al-Ḳawmiyya al-ʿArabiyya wa 'l-waḥda al-ʿArabiyya amām taḥaddī al-maṣīr*, Baghdad 1988; ʿAbd al-ʿAzīz al-Dūrī *et alii*, *al-Waḥda al-ʿArabiyya, tadjāribuhā wa-tawaḳḳuʿātuhā: buḥūth wa-munāḳashāt*, Beirut 1989; E. Tauber, *Rashīd Riḍā's Pan-Arabism before World War I*, in *MW*, lxxix/2 (Apr. 1989), 102-12; Bassam Tibi, *Arab nationalism: a critical enquiry*², London 1990, 123-207; D. Pipes, *Greater Syria: the history of an ambition*, New York 1990; E. Kienle, *Baʿth versus Baʿth: the conflict between Syria & Irak*, London 1990;

Menahem Klein, *Arab unity: a nonexistent entity*, in *Jerusalem Journal of International Relations*, xii/1 (Jan. 1990), 28-44; J.M. Landau, *Irredentism and minorities in the Middle East*, in *Immigrants and Minorities* (London), ix/3 (Nov. 1990), 242-8; M. Strohmeier, *al-Kullīya as-Ṣalāḥīya in Jerusalem: Arabismus, Osmanismus und Panislamismus im ersten Weltkrieg*, Stuttgart 1991; Hilal Khashan, *The revival of Pan-Arabism*, in *Orbis*, xxxv/1 (Winter 1991), 107-16; N. Masalha, *Faisal's Pan-Arabism, 1921-33*, in *MES*, xxvii/4 (Oct. 1991), 679-93. (J.M. LANDAU)

PAN-ISLAMISM (in Arabic *al-Waḥda al-Islāmiyya*; in Ottoman Turkish *Ittiḥād-i Islām*, in modern Turkish *İslam ittihadı*), the ideology aiming at a comprehensive union of all Muslims into one entity, thus restoring the situation prevalent in early Islam. The religious element of the unity of all Muslims had been advocated since the days of Muḥammad, but acquired an added political significance in the 19th century. The Turkish term was used politically by Turkish writers and journalists since the 1860s, while "Pan-Islam" seems to have been coined by Arminius Vambéry in early 1878 (probably on the model of "Pan-Slavism") and then was popularised by the French journalist Gabriel Charmes in his articles in the *Revue des Deux Mondes* of 1881-2, reprinted in bookform as *L'Avenir de la Turquie: le Panislamisme* (Paris 1883). Charmes's main argument was that the Sultan ʿAbd ül-Ḥamīd II [*q.v.*] was urging Muslims to unite against France's invasion of Tunisia. Charmes was not far off the mark, which is probably why his writings stirred serious concern in French and other European chancelleries. In reaction to the loss of Cyprus (1878), Tunisia (1881) and Egypt (1882), both orthodox and secular intellectuals energetically strove to formulate political ideologies and recommend pragmatic steps directed against European penetration—political, military, economic and missionary.

Hence, political Pan-Islam originated essentially as a defensive policy, mainly aimed at saving all Muslims from foreign, non-Muslim domination by uniting them. Not surprisingly, then, this movement came into being during the last third of the 19th century, when European colonialism reached its peak, and the Great Powers of the day were already ruling many foreign territories and carving out others for themselves. Not a few of these were densely inhabited by Muslim populations. The few independent Muslim states of the day—Afg̲h̲ānistān, Persia, the Ottoman Empire and Morocco—troubled by internal economic, social and political dissension, also felt threatened externally by European expansionism. Of these, Afg̲h̲ānistān and Morocco were rather peripheral, geographically, while Persia, overwhelmingly S̲h̲īʿī, was less suited than others to promote a Pan-Islamic policy among preponderantly Sunni populations. The Ottoman Empire, both centrally located and territorially the largest, was decidedly more appropriate.

ʿAbd ül-Ḥamīd II subsidised several Pan-Islamic ideologues (such as D̲j̲amāl al-Dīn al-Afg̲h̲ānī [*q.v.*]), to write and publish in Turkish, Arabic or Persian, as well as agents to spread Pan-Islamic propaganda—both openly and covertly—within and without the Ottoman Empire. This sultan claimed to be the caliph [see K̲H̲ALĪFA], therefore leader and commander of all Muslims everywhere, in the old tradition of Islam where spiritual and temporal rule were one. The propaganda which he fostered, intended to offset as far as possible the Empire's military and economic weakness, seems to have had two major policy objectives: (a) Favouring the central government over the periphery, and the Ottoman Empire's Muslims at the expense of others, in education, official and economic opportunities; special attention was given in this context to Turks and Arabs, and less to Albanians and Bosnians. (b) Launching a major effort to recruit the Empire's Muslims and many others outside it, in response to the activities of some of the Powers who were encouraging nationalist and secessionist trends among the Empire's Muslims; the sultan-caliph could threaten these Powers with incitement of the Muslims in their empires (French, British and Russian, in particular). The results of ʿAbd ül-Ḥamīd II's Pan-Islamic policies were modest in practice: expressions of support and fund-raising, particularly during times of war, as with Greece over Crete in 1897. However, his efforts were taken seriously enough by several European Powers, which refrained from attacking the Ottoman Empire while ʿAbd ül-Ḥamīd was engaged in Pan-Islamic and other activities.

Following ʿAbd ül-Ḥamīd's deposition in 1909, Italy invaded Tripolitania, and the Balkan peoples annexed some additional Ottoman territories to bolster their independence. The Young Turks, less dedicated to Pan-Islam (some of them were even lukewarm in their religious commitment), did not hesitate to exploit it in the First World War. The Ottoman declaration of war on 11 November 1914 was accompanied by a proclamation of *d̲j̲ihād* [*q.v.*], and the pronouncement of five *fatwā*s, or legal opinions, by the S̲h̲eyk̲h̲ ül-Islām. These ordered all Muslims everywhere to unite and join the Ottoman Empire, with life and property, in the *d̲j̲ihād* against Russia, Great Britain and France. Separate circulars, sent out by the Young Turks, defined the aim of the war as "liberating the Islamic world from the domination of the infidels." Indeed, these three states (and the Netherlands) were then ruling most of the non-independent Muslim populations. Ottoman Pan-Islamic propaganda, with full German co-operation, was intensive throughout the First World War, most particularly during the first two years, until its inefficacy became evident through its inability to induce Muslims—both civilians and soldiers in the Allied Forces—to revolt. The failure of Pan-Islam in the First World War and the defeat and dismemberment of the Ottoman Empire brought about an almost total lethargy in the generation following the end of the war, both in ideological writing and organisational attempts, chiefly in convoking five Pan-Islamic congresses during the inter-war period: in Mecca, 1924; Cairo, 1926; Mecca (again), 1926; Jerusalem, 1931; and Geneva, 1935.

In Tsarist Russia, during the second half of the 19th century, the rise of political Islam and Pan-Islam was chiefly due to two main factors of the official policy, Russification and Christianisation. The Government of Tsarist Russia, aware of potential problems with the numerous groups in the huge empire, undertook a campaign of forced Russification in the schools and cultural life of the minorities. In a co-ordinated, parallel manner, missionaries worked to proselytise local Muslims. These efforts were only partly successful, as they caused considerable resistance led by the *mullā*s or Muslim religious functionaries. However, another element joined the resistance to Russification and Christianisation. Since the middle of the 19th century, a commercial bourgeoisie had been growing, chiefly among the Tatars and the Azeris. These merchants were better educated than others in the Muslim population and more aware of general conditions both in the Tsarist Empire and abroad. Some members of this new class, intellectual-y oriented, developed nationalist aspirations from the hird quarter of the 19th century onwards. While nostly centred on the specific problems of the Tatars, Azeris and some other groups, their nationalist sentiments borrowed heavily from both Pan-Islam and Pan-Turkism [*q.v.*]. The reason was self-evident; solated from one another by huge empty spaces or by nasses of other populations (non-Turkic and non-Islamic), the Tatars, Azeris and others sought the support of their brethren-in-faith, and particularly that of the largest independent Islamic state of the time, the Ottoman Empire. Three congresses of Russian Muslims, in 1905-6, served to sharpen nationalist and Pan-Turk sentiments and even create several organisational elements. In 1917, these Pan-Islamic and Pan-Turkic organisations intensified their political activities, but were soon broken down by the new Soviet régime and its Red Army. During Soviet rule, at least until recently, a persistent atheist propaganda was carried out, intensified by anti-Pan-Islamic activities. Many Soviet publications of the time reveal a basic fear of the competition of Pan-Islam with the régime's own universalist ideology, Communism.

In another part of the globe, India was one of the largest concentrations of Muslims masses. While signs of an Islamic revival were noticeable even before the First World War, it was mainly subsequent to that war that political Pan-Islam came into being there, soon becoming a significant force. Hemmed in by what they perceived as a threat by the huge Hindu majority, political leaders of India's Muslims naturally sought allies among Muslim populations abroad, with increasing emphasis being placed on the Pan-Islamic element of commonality. Moreover, India's Muslims, like the Hindus there, already had a tradition of organising politically on European lines, a feature rarely observable elsewhere. The spark which ignited Pan-Islamic political activity in India was the threat to Turkey and, most particularly, to the caliphate, immediately after the end of the First World War. The defeated Ottoman Empire was being dismembered, Constantinople had been occupied by the Allied Powers and the office of the sultan—who claimed to be the caliph—was being threatened. Two brothers, Muḥammad ʿAlī [*q.v.*] and S̲h̲awkat ʿAlī, and other Muslim political leaders in India, organised a Khilafat movement [see KH̲ILĀFA] to save the caliph and the caliphate. This comprised hundreds of thousands of adherents, collected large sums, which were sent to Turkey, organised mass demonstrations, published manifestoes and newspapers, and despatched missions abroad to intercede with the Allied Powers. The movement grew during the early 1920s, but petered out after 1924, when the Republic of Turkey abolished the caliphate and exiled the last sultan-caliph. This act deprived the Pan-Islamic movement of its titular head and dealt it a blow from which it has not yet recovered, remaining without a common leader to look up to.

Thus in the inter-war period, particularly since the mid-1920s, political Pan-Islam receded in such important Muslim centres as Russia, India and Turkey. The Pan-Islamic congresses in that period, mentioned above, only served to emphasise this retreat. Most of its activities and publications focused in the Arab-populated countries of the Middle East and North Africa. However, in these, too, Pan-Islam had to compete with rival ideologies, such as modernisation, secularisation, nationalism, and Pan-Arabism [*q.v.*]. But the first expressions of the revival of Islam comprised an obvious element of Pan-Islam as well, for example in Egypt, where the organisation of the Muslim Brethren, set up in 1928, adopted some of the slogans of Pan-Islam, as in the speeches and writings of its founder, Ḥasan al-Bannāʾ [*q.v.*]. This could be noticed even better, at the time and subsequently, in Saudi Arabia which, after all, had been established on the foundations of classical Islam which served as the most prominent element cementing the inter-tribal union on which rested the new Kingdom of Saudi Arabia.

The situation changed radically after the Second World War. The number of independent states with Muslim populations grew visibly. Although only some of these emphasised their Islamic character, it soon became clear that Islam was again a factor to be reckoned with in local, regional and international politics. True, Islam and Pan-Islam had to compete increasingly not only with the impact of Europe, as before (to which that of the United States was added later), as well as with that of nationalism, particularism and secular modernism, but also with the influence of rival universal ideologies in Muslim lands, like Pan-Arabism, Pan-Turkism and Pan-Iranism. An answer was found by the Pan-Islamists in due course, on both the ideological and pragmatic-organisational levels.

On the ideological level, the more extreme Pan-Islamists, rooted in faith, still advocated a religio-political union of all Muslims; their model was the early history of Islam, as warmly preached by Muslim fundamentalists everywhere; for these, a religious and political Pan-Islam was a *sine qua non*. For numerous others, more moderate, some accommodation with reality was deemed necessary. Well aware of the immense power of nationalism in many of the new Muslim states, they argued for solidarity among all these, as a transitional stage to the universal state canvassed by fundamentalists and their partisans. They maintained, moreover, that complete solidarity—political, military, economic and cultural—would create a huge force, capable of achieving its own ends in any conflict or clash of interests with European and other Powers. On the pragmatic level, no less significantly, it appeared for the first time that achieving Pan-Islam, at least on the level of solidarity, was feasible. Not only were there independent Muslim states who had the political means to promote the fulfillment of Pan-Islam, such as Saudi Arabia and Pakistan, and later Egypt, Persia and Libya; but at least some of these also had the economic capacity to do so. Indeed, some—chiefly Saudi Arabia, Persia and Libya—had become gigantic oil producers since the 1973 boycott. Several, notably Pakistan and Saudi Arabia, had set up efficient structures for furthering the political and economic aims of Pan-Islam, largely in the context of promoting solidarity and co-operation. Three of the most important organisations should be mentioned specifically.

(a) The Muslim World Congress was set up in Karachi in 1949, very probably with official Pakistani encouragement; it now comprises some thirty-six member states, although branches exist in sixty countries. Among its tenets are propagating Islam, co-operating with all Muslim lands in order to promote Islamic unity, persuading Muslim governments and peoples to renounce their differences, instilling Arabic as a *lingua franca* of all Muslims, co-operating in trade policies, framing constitutions and laws based on the *s̲h̲arīʿa* (or Islamic jurisprudence). (b) The Muslim World League was founded in Mecca in 1962 as an unofficial agency of the Saudis. It serves, however, as an umbrella organisation of many other Islamic associations and groups. Richly funded by the Saudis, the League's activities in all five continents have been varied. As a non-governmental body, it is concerned not only with Islamisation and propaganda for religious education, but also with promoting Islamic solidarity (and paying for it): it promotes many publications and international seminars, preaches unified Islamisation and Islamic law and assists Muslim minorities with the aim of drawing them into a common Islamic activity, both political and economic. (c) The Organisation of the Islamic Conference, also Saudi-inspired, was established in 1969 as an association of Muslim states complementary to the Muslim World League. The Organisation of the Islamic Conference, made up of some forty-five states, combines the principles of Islam with the mechanisms of a contemporary international body. Both its charter and its activities emphasise the consolidation of Islamic solidarity, co-ordination and co-operation, with a view to strengthening the integration of all Muslim states in the future. For this purpose, the Organisation has set up the instruments for active policies—political, economic and cultural. Meetings of the Organisation's Heads-of-State and Foreign Ministers have initiated and furthered some common institutions, as an Islamic Development Bank (modelled on the World Bank), an Islamic Educational, Scientific and Cultural Organisation (patterned on UNESCO), and an Islamic Academy for Jurisprudence (to achieve the unity of the Islamic world in the legal sphere). See further, MUʾTAMAR.

Bibliography: For a recent detailed bibliography, J.M. Landau, *The politics of Pan-Islam: ideology and organization*, Oxford 1990, 382-425. See also Landau, *Some Soviet works on Muslim solidarity*, in *MES*, xxv (1989), 95-8; Yaacov Ro'i, *The Islamic influence on nationalism in Soviet Central Asia*, in *Problems of Communism* (Washington, D.C.), xxxix/4 (July-Aug. 1990), 49-64; Masayuki Yamauchi, *The Green Crescent under the Red Star: Enver Pasha in Soviet Russia 1919-1922*, Tokyo 1991 (= *Studia Culturae Islamicae*, 42); M. Strohmeier, *al-Kullīya as-Ṣalāḥīya in Jerusalem: Arabismus, Osmanismus und Panislamismus im Ersten Weltkrieg*, Stuttgart 1991 (= *Abhandlungen für die Kunde des Morgenlandes*, 49/4); G.R. Fuller, *Islamic fundamentalism in the Northern Tier countries*, Santa Monica 1991, 5 ff.; H.L. Müller, *Islam, ğihād und Deutsches Reich: ein Nachspiel zur wilhelminischen Weltpolitik im Maghreb 1914-18,* Frankfurt a/M 1991, 173 ff.; Cezmi Eraslan, *II. Abdülhamid ve İslâm birliği*, Istanbul 1991; Azmi Özcan, *Pan-Islamizm: Osmanlı devleti, Hindistan Müslümanları ve İngiltere (1877-1914)*, Istanbul 1992.

(J.M. LANDAU)

PAN-TURKISM, one of the Pan-ideologies originating in the late 19th century. It expresses strong nationalist interest in the welfare of all Turks and members of Turkic groups, recognisable by kindred languages and a common origin, history and tradition. It addresses itself chiefly to those in Turkey, Cyprus, the Balkans, the former Soviet Union, Syria, ʿIrāḳ, Persia, Afg͟hānistān and East Turkistan (or Sinkiang). Pan-Turkism should be distinguished from Turanism (sometimes called Pan-Turanism), a broader concept, whose ideologues hail as fellow-Turks all those originating from Tūrān, a mythical plateau in Central Asia; this would include all the above groups as well as the Finns, Estonians, Hungarians, Yakuts, Mongols, Manchurians (even the Chinese and Japanese). Generally termed *Türkçülük* in modern Turkish, Pan-Turkism is confounded at times with *Türklük*, or Turkism, which more usually refers to the commonality of Turkish civilisation. It is not always easy to distinguish, historically, between the more moderate cultural Pan-Turkism, aiming at solidarity, and the relatively extreme political trend, seeking an irredentist union for all Turkic groups and the lands they inhabit. As in some other Pan-ideologies (such as Pan-Slavism), the cultural trend frequently precedes the political movement, with the latter generally predominating afterwards.

While Arminius Vambéry, the Hungarian-Jewish Turcologist, seems to have been the first to use the term Pan-Turkism, in the late 1860s, and to consider its political potential, it was left to intellectuals from the Tatars, Azeris, and other Turkic groups in Tsarist Russia to work out an ideology and attempt to set up organisational structures. Practically all of them were Muslims, resentful of policies of Russification and Christianisation being carried out by the ruling classes of Tsarist Russia. In defence, Muslim sentiment grew stronger and nationalist feeling began to spread. The latter, which proudly asserted the characteristics of each Turkic group, instinctively sought allies amongst its ethnic and linguistic kinsfolk, all of which led to the concept of Pan-Turkism. These nationalist intellectuals tended to be secular-minded, without being anti-religious. Their rallying slogans were Turkism and Pan-Turkism, to which Islam and Pan-Islam [*q.v.*] were occasionally added. Indeed, their call for the latter seems to have been in direct ratio to their isolation and their need for allies.

Not surprisingly, among Pan-Turkism's most prominent initiators in Tsarist Russia were the Tatars, who had endured Russian rule longest and were the chief sufferers from the effects of Pan-Slavic-minded Russification. Further, although they were surrounded by non-Tatars, they were located relatively close to the Ottoman Empire with its preponderant Turkish-minded élites. A Tatar bourgeois class had been developing, and in the late 19th century it had found itself capable of raising the twin banners of nationalism and Pan-Turkism. The Tatars were well aware that linguistic commonality was the key factor in a rapprochement and ensuing joint activity among the Turkic groups. Realising that literacy levels were low and that linguistic and dialectal variations prevented effective co-operation, they strove for improved education and language reform, and the publication of journalistic propoganda. The life's work of Ismāʿīl Gaspîralî [*q.v.*] examplifies this trend. A schoolmaster and mayor, he revised the curriculum in his town to include Turkish, along with Arabic; then he devised a *lingua franca* for schools and newspapers (he himself published a newspaper, called *Terd̲j̲ümān* "Interpreter", from 1883), emphasising the common vocabulary of the Turkic languages and attempting to minimise phonological differences. Preaching "unity in language, thought and action," Gaspîralî's brand of Pan-Turkism was chiefly cultural.

Other Tatars, like Yūsuf Akčura, ʿAlī Ḥüseyinzāde and ʿAbd ül-Res̲h̲īd İbrāhīm, and Azeris like Aḥmed Ag̲h̲aog̲h̲lu, preached political Pan-Turkism. Akčura, in particular, in his lengthy article *Üč ṭerz-i siyāset* ("Three systems of government"), anonymously published in Cairo in 1903, rejected Ottomanism and Pan-Islam, arguing that Pan-Turkism was the only feasible ideology for unity, which ought to be a union of all Turks, with Turkey at its centre. These and others were encouraged in their action by the revolutionary trends current in Russia of that period. In addition to publishing newspapers, they organised three congresses of all Russia's Muslims (1905-6), presided over, again, by Tatars, in which a Pan-Turk union was discussed; Azeris and Turkestanis joined in. Such meetings were repeated in 1917 and revolts occurred in Ādharbaydjān, Turkistān, Bukhārā, Khīwa and Khōḳand. Most of these uprisings were suppressed by the Red Army in the following years. The Soviet authorities banned Pan-Turkism, along with other universal ideologies competing with Communism. A harsh campaign of propaganda for Communism, strict censorship, and personal and economic pressures drove Pan-Turkism underground until the breakdown of the Soviet Union, when it is showing signs of a revival.

In most other areas where Turks and Turkic groups have held a minority status, Pan-Turkism has been low-keyed in expression, making itself heard mainly in times of discrimination or persecution. It was only in the Ottoman Empire, chiefly in its last decade, that it flourished. Writers and journalists, émigrés from Tsarist Russia and other countries, promoted it, joined by such distinguished Turkish intellectuals as ʿÖmer Seyfeddīn and Meḥmed Emīn [Yurdakul] [*q.vv.*], or even Żiyā Gök Alp, a Kurd, and Tekīn Alp, a Jew. Their literary and political organisations inspired further activities, and their books and newspapers have remained the treasured heritage of Pan-Turkism to this day. No less important politically is the fact that from *ca.* 1910, a part of the ruling Committee for Union and Progress adopted Pan-Turkism as the official state ideology. Chiefly supported by Enwer Pasha, the Committee used the state bureaucracy (including secret agents) and finances for Pan-Turk propaganda and activity both within the Empire and abroad, among Turkish-Turkic concentrations. The very entry of Turkey into the First World War was at least partly motivated by Pan-Turk, anti-Russian ambitions. Enwer Pasha, by then Minister for War, pursued these aims unremittingly and, towards the end of the war, sent his forces into southern Russia with the aim of carving out a new Pan-Turk empire to take place of the rapidly disintegrating Ottoman one. His own death in Bukhārā, fighting the Russians, in 1922, has rendered him a hero to Pan-Turkists to this day.

Discredited in war, Pan-Turkism had little place in the Republic of Turkey. Moreover, the Republic's founding father and first President, Atatürk [*q.v.*], was very critical of such universalist ideologies as Pan-Turkism and Pan-Islam, replacing them with his own popular brand of local nationalism, focused on Turkey and its Turks. A further consideration must have been that Pan-ideologies were certain to embroil Turkey with its neighbours at a time when it badly needed peace to reconstruct itself politically, economically and culturally. So Pan-Turkism entered a latent stage in Turkey, with its few adherents keeping a low profile and initiating rare publications (only since the 1930s), which seemed to have had few readers and were severally banned. After Atatürk's death in 1938, the number of Pan-Turk periodicals increased, although there was no change in the government's anti-Pan-Turk policy. Their main ideological quarrel was with Atatürk's brand of Turkish nationalism—which the Pan-Turks termed, derogatorily, Anatolianism—as well as with Communist-inspired Soviet (and, later, Chinese) rule which they interpreted as oppressive and perilous to Pan-Turkism. The main contributors to these periodicals were from among the émigrés, referred to above. There were also some others; among the Turks, two brothers were particularly active, Hüseyin Nihal Atsız (1905-75) and Necdet Sancar (1910-75), whose writings, particularly during the Second World War, were frankly racist; their main standard for being Turk was one of race, which conformed with Nazi principles.

The Second World War seemed, indeed, to offer Pan-Turkism a unique opportunity for reasserting itself, as it might well have been able to change the international *status quo*. Apparently encouraged by Nazi propaganda and funding, Pan-Turkists attempted, unsuccessfully, to persuade the Turkish government to enter the war against the Soviet Union, first in their newspapers, then by street demonstrations, led by Atsız and Sancar. These failed, but after the end of the war, Pan-Turkism began to be somewhat more popular than before, and tried to stage a comeback into the mainstream of politics, as one of many competing ideologies since the 1950s to-date. Increasingly, hostility to Communism and its sponsors, and sympathy for the complaints of Turkish-Turkic minorities in the Soviet Union, China, ʿIrāḳ, Greece, Cyprus and, in the late 1980s, Bulgaria, brought some potential support. Nonetheless, organisationally Pan-Turkism in Turkey itself remained weak and limited to élitist circles.

This situation was partly changed by Alparslan Türkeş. Born in Nicosia in 1917, he emigrated with his family to Turkey and chose a military career, reaching the rank of colonel. His connections with the Pan-Turkists began at least as early as the mid-1940s, when he participated in their street demonstrations. A controversial figure, he entered politics in 1965, when he took over the leadership of a medium-size political party whose name he changed to the Nationalist Action party (*Milliyetçi Hareket Partisi*). This ultranationalist grouping, active in politics until the military intervention of 1980, which banned all parties, and subsequently re-established as the Industriousness Party (*Çalışma Partisi*), still with Türkeş as chairman, obtained—at least for a while—the support of Pan-Turkists. In recent years, though, they have abandoned it, since Türkeş did not achieve results that satisfied them, and, also, because Türkeş increasingly took a pro-Islamic stand (in order to gain more votes), which Pan-Turkists did not consider consistent with their basic ideology.

In the late 1980s and early 1990s, there seems to have occurred, again, an upsurge in Pan-Turk sentiment, in Turkey, where public feelings identified with the "Outside Turks" (*Dış Türkler*) first in Bulgaria, then in the Union of Independent States, heir to the Soviet Union, as both sides of the border increasingly wished for greater co-operation and solidarity. Nonetheless, the ideal of a Pan-Turk union has not been achieved, for several reasons. Among external factors, the general reluctance of the Powers to alter the *status quo* has co-operated with opposition by the former Soviet Union and by China, as well as their protégés, to political (and even cultural) Pan-Turkism. Among internal ones, no less crucial, have been opposition by most of Turkey's political establishment, strong competition by rival ideologies, paucity of numbers (and no grassroots support) and lack of efficient organisation.

Bibliography: Several periodicals in Turkey still carry the message of Pan-Turkism. Some of these advocate the cause of a specific area and are edited and published largely by émigrés. Such are *Azerbaycan, Türkistan* and *Emel* (the last caters to Tatars). Two scholarly periodicals advocate Pan-Turkism more generally, the monthly *Türk Kültürü* (Ankara) and the bi-monthly *Türk Dünyası Araştırmaları* (Istanbul). A detailed bibliography on Pan-Turkism, updated to 1980, is given by J.M. Landau, *Pan-Turkism in Turkey*, London 1981, Greek tr. Athens 1985, Chinese tr. Urumchi 1992. See also: Shirin Akiner, *Islamic peoples of the Soviet Union*, London 1983; J.M. Landau, *Tekinalp, Turkish patriot 1883-1961*, Istanbul and Leiden 1984; L.L. Snyder, *Macro-nationalism: a history of the Pan-movements*, Westport, Conn. 1984, ch. 6; A. Benningsen and S.E. Wimbush, *Muslims of the Soviet empire: a guide*, London 1985, index; Benningsen, *Panturkism and Panislamism in history and today*, in *Central Asian Survey*, iii/3 (1985), 39-49; Landau, *The fortunes and misfortunes of Pan-Turkism*, in *ibid.*, vii/1 (1988), 1-5; idem, *The ups and downs of irredentism: the case of Turkey*, in Naomi Chazan (ed.), *Irredentism and international politics*, Boulder, Colo. 1991, 81-96; Margaret Bainbridge (ed.), *The Turkic peoples of the world*, London 1992. (J.M. Landau)

PANDJ PĪR, Pačpiriyā, followers of the Five Saints, Urdu *pānč pīr*, especially in northern and eastern India, whose myths and legends (there is no real historicity or hagiology about them) are attached to a primitive form of shrine worship with as many Hindū as Muslim adherents (Kipling in *Kim*, ch. 4, speaks of the "wayside shrines—sometimes Hindu, sometimes Mussulman—which the low caste of both creeds share with beautiful impartiality". For "caste" among the lower grades of Muslim society see hind. ii, Ethnography). They have no formal organisation, and belong to the general north Indian cultus of *pīr* and *shahīd*. The number *five* of course holds, affectionate associations, at least for a more formal Islam, in the *pandjtan-i pāk*: Muḥammad, ʿAlī, Fāṭima, Ḥasan and Ḥusayn; although in the sub-continent today a list of five great saints might be Bahāʾ al-Ḥaḳḳ of Multān, Rukn-i ʿĀlam of Lakhnaʾū, Shams-i Tabrīz of Multān, Makhdūm Djahāniyā Djahāngasht of Uččh, and Farīd al-Dīn "Shakargandj" of Pākpattan, although the list is variable. There are also, for example, the five hours of prayer, and the five duties of Islam, and the five "fingers" of the *pandja* used as one of the *ʿalams* in the Muḥarram ceremonies, or of the "hand of Fāṭima" commonly used as a talisman.

With the Pačpiriyā, however, the list is more variable: Crooke, for example, cites five different enumerations of the Pānč Pīr in Banāras alone, and refers to groupings in Bihār which include Langṛā Tār, a piece of crooked wire, and Subarnā Tīr, the bank of the Subarnā river, clearly crude fetishism; the only constant figure in the various enumerations is Ghāzī Miyān [*q.v.*], i.e. Sayyid Sālār Masʿūd, nephew of Maḥmūd of Ghaznī, killed in battle against the Hindūs of Bahrayč [*q.v.*] in 425/1034 and claimed as one of the first martyrs of Islam in India, and his tomb and shrine at Bahrayč—and cenotaphs elsewhere in north-eastern India—are visited as much by Hindūs as by Muslims. The "doubtfully Islamic fair" referred to in the art. manēr, above, is part of this cultus. For Hinduism the Panč Pāṇḍava, the five heroes of the *Mahābhārata*, or a set of five valiant Rādjpūt warriors, may even be referred to as the Pānč Pīr.

One possible connecting link among the various enumerations of the Pānč Pīr is the idea of martyrdom, since the tomb of a *shahīd*—which may come to have its own attached *pīr*—commonly attracts a particular devotion. For example, away from north India there is a modern mosque known as Pānč Pīr at Tālikoṭā [*q.v.*], the site of the battle wherein the Vidjayanagara army was defeated in 972/1565 by the confederated armies of the five sultanates of the Deccan; the mosque contains five tombs said to be of Deccan soldiers killed in the battle, which are now visited and venerated by Muslims and Hindūs alike.

The worshippers were described by E.A.H. Blunt, *The caste system of northern India*, Oxford 1931, as belonging to some 53 castes, 44 of which were "wholly or partly Hindu", and he puts the number of Hindū worshippers of the Five at some thirteen and a half million. R. Greeven, *op. cit.* below, gives two theories of the origin of the worship: (i) that low-caste Hindū converts to Islam degraded its purer doctrines into a species of more intelligible idolatry; (ii) that the Hindū low castes, under the influence of terror, deified certain of the earlier Muslim conquerors, into whose worship the humbler converts, never wholly emancipated from idolatry, relapsed by an easy passage. Two facts are apparently not disputed: (i) that the worshippers belong to low castes—indeed one authority declares that they are almost entirely sweepers; (ii) that even among Hindū devotees the Muslim origin of the cult is not forgotten, villagers speaking of the Five as the "Muslim deities" (*musulmānī dewtār*), and have certain ceremonies performed by Muslim drummers (*dafālī*, strictly "tambourinist"). Crooke's lists, which enumerate the offerings (not excluding spirituous liquor) presented to the Five at different places and by different *ḳawm*, show an amazing diversity of practice between one community and another, as though the Five were Hindū household or village gods, and as though any conformity were only a matter of *ḳawm* organisation. The household worship of the Five may simply be directed to an iron bar or three-pointed spear, representing Ghāzī Miyān, or five wooden pegs in the floor of the courtyard. There may be some cohesion through the songs of the itinerant *dafālīs*, but otherwise the Pačpiriyā have no formal organisation; the cult is discouraged by orthodox Muslims, and their "priests" are nothing but opportunists operating upon an illiterate and gullible public.

Specimens of the ballad poetry of the *dafālīs* and others, given by Greeven, are largely adaptations to Muslim ideas of tales found in the Indian epics, and the glorification of Ghāzī Miyān and his family.

Bibliography: W. Crooke, *Popular religion and folklore of northern India*, Allahabad 1894, esp. ch. 4, "The worship of the sainted dead"; R. Greeven, *The Heroes Five, an attempt to collect some of the songs of the Pachpiriya ballad-mongers in the Benares division*, Allahabad 1898; *ERE*, ix, 600 ff.

(D. S. Margoliouth-[J. Burton-Page])

PANDJĀB (p., "land of the five rivers"), a province of the northwestern part of the Indo-Pakistan subcontinent. In pre-Partition British India it comprised all that part of the Indian Empire, with the exceptions of the North West Frontier Province and Kashmīr, north of Sindh and Rādjpūtāna and west of the river Djamna. Geographically therefore it includes more than its name implies, for, in addition to the country watered by the Djhelum, Čināb, Rāwī, Beās, and Satledj, it embraces the table-land of Sirhind between the Satledj and Djamna, the Sind-Sāgar Dōāb between the Satledj and the Indus, and the district of Dēra Ghāzī Khān. Since 1947, the province has been divided between Pākistān and India, the eastern, Indian portion being now divided into the states of Pandjāb, Haryana and Himachal Pradesh (see 2. below).

Under British rule, the province of Pandjāb was administratively divided into two parts, British territory and the Pandjāb States. British territory, which had an area of 99,265 square miles and a population in 1931 of 23,580,852, was divided into 29 districts, each administered by a deputy-commissioner. These districts were grouped into the five divisions of Ambāla, Djullundur, Lahore, Rāwalpindi, and Multān, each under a commissioner. The Pandjāb States had an area of 37,699 square miles and a population in 1931 of 4,910,005. The conduct of political relations with Dudjānā, Patawdī, Kalsia, and the 27 Simla Hill States was in the hands of the Pandjāb Government. The remaining states of Lohāru, Sirmūr, Bilaspūr, Mandi, Suket, Kapurthālā, Malēr-Kōtla, Farīdkōt [*q.v.*], Čambā, Bahāwalpūr [*q.v.*], and the Phūlkian states of Pattiālā, Djind, and Nabhā, were directly under the Government of India.

1. History until 1911

The history of this area has been profoundly influenced by the fact that the mountain passes of the north-west frontier afford access to the Pandjāb plains. For this reason, it is ethnologically more nearly allied to Central Asia than to India. The excavations conducted since 1920 at Harappa in the Montgomery district are evidence of a culture which probably flourished in the Indus valley about 3000 B.C., and which bears a general resemblance to that of Elam and Mesopotamia (Sir John Marshall, *Mohenjo-Daro and the Indus Civilization*, 3 vols., London 1931). But the first migration of which we have any evidence is that of the Aryan-speaking peoples who established themselves on the Pandjāb plains in pre-historic times. Centuries later, successive waves of invaders swept like devastating torrents through the mountain passes of the north-west. Persian, Greek, and Afghān, the forces of Alexander and the armies of Maḥmūd of Ghazna, the hosts of Tīmūr, Bābur, and Nādir Shāh, and the troops of Aḥmad Shāh Durrānī [*q.vv.*], all advanced by these routes to lay waste the fertile plains of the Pandjāb. All these migrations and invasions added to the heterogeneity of the existing population in the land of the five rivers. The history of invasions from Central Asia proves that the Pandjāb and the frontier zone from the banks of the Indus to the Afghān slopes of the Sulaymān range have never presented any real barrier to an enterprising general. The Sulaymān range itself has seldom formed a political boundary, for the Persians, Mauryas, Graeco-Bactrians, Sakas, Pahlawas, the Kushān branch of the Yüeh-či, and the Hūṇas all bestrode this mountain barrier.

The capture of Multān [*q.v.*] by Muḥammad b. Ḳāsim [*q.v.*], in 94/713, extended Arab power to upper Sind and the lower Pandjāb, but the real threat to Hindustān came from the direction of modern Afghānistān. The Ghaznawid invaders found the powerful Hindūshāhiyya dynasty of Wayhand [see HINDŪSHĀHĪS] ruling between Lamghān and the Čināb. The power of this Hindu state was completely shattered by Maḥmūd of Ghazna [*q.v.*], who annexed the Pandjāb, which became a frontier province of his extensive empire with its capital at Lahore (Lāhawr [*q.v.*]) and the sole refuge of his descendants when driven out of Ghazna by the Shansabānī sultans of Ghūr [see GHŪRIDS]. Multān and the surrounding country had remained in Muslim hands since the days of the Arab conquest, but the fact that its rulers were heretical Ḳarmaṭians (i.e. Ismāʿīlīs) was one reason for Maḥmūd's attack in 396/1006. Muḥammad Ghūrī annexed the Pandjāb in 582/1186 and on his death in 602/1206 it definitely became a province of the Sultanate of Dihlī under the rule of Ḳuṭb al-Dīn Aybak [*q.v.*]. With the exception of occasional rebellions and raids from Central Asia, it remained under the Sulṭāns of Dihlī until the defeat of Ibrāhīm Lōdī [*q.v.*] by Bābur at Pānīpat [*q.v.*] in 932/1526 paved the way for the foundation of the Mughal empire. Under Akbar [*q.v.*] the modern province of the Pandjāb was included in the *ṣūba*s of Lahore, Multān, and Dihlī, a detailed description of which will be found in the *Āʾīn-i Akbarī* (tr. Jarrett, ii, 278-341).

The more intransigent policy of Akbar's immediate successors, above all, of Awrangzīb [*q.v.*], led to the growth of Sikh political power in the Pandjāb and transformed a band of religious devotees, founded by Guru Nānak [*q.v.*] in the second half of the 15th century, into a military commonwealth or Khālṣa animated with undying hatred toward Muslims [see SIKHS]. The weakness of the central government and the unprotected condition of the frontier provinces under the later Mughals exposed Hindūstān to the invasions of Nādir Shāh [*q.v.*] and Aḥmad Shāh Durrānī [*q.v.*]. On the bloodstained field of Pānipat, in 1761, the Marāthās [*q.v.*], who were aspiring to universal sovereignty, sustained a crushing defeat at the hands of the Afghān invader. In the following year, at Barnāla near Ludhiāna, Aḥmad Shāh disastrously defeated the Sikhs who had taken advantage of his absence in Kābul to possess themselves of the country around Lahore. The Sikhs, however, soon extended their sway to the south of the Satledj and ravaged the country to the very gates of Dihlī, but their further advance was checked by the Marāthās who had rapidly recovered from their defeat at Pānipat. It was the defeat of the Marāthās by Lord Lake, in 1803, which facilitated the rise of Randjīt Singh and enabled him to found a powerful Sikh kingdom in the Pandjāb. His attempts to extend his authority over his co-religionists, the cis-Satledj Sikhs, brought him into contact with the British, and, by the treaty of 1809, he pledged himself to regard the Satledj as the north-west frontier of the British dominions in India (Aitchison, viii, no. liii). After the death of Randjīt Singh in 1839, his kingdom rapidly fell to pieces under his successors. Revolution succeeded revolution, and during the minority of Dalīp Singh the Khālṣa soldiery became virtually rulers of the country. Unprovoked aggression on British territory produced two Sikh wars which ended with the annexation of the Pandjāb in 1849.

At first the newly-conquered territories were placed under a Board of Administration. This was abolished in 1853, its powers and functions being vested in a Chief Commissioner. In 1859, after the transfer of the Dihlī territory from the North-Western (subsequently the United) Provinces, the Pandjāb and its dependencies were formed into a Lieutenant-Governorship.

The annexation of the Pandjāb by advancing the British administrative boundary across the Indus brought the Government of India into closer contact with the Pathān tribes of the north-west frontier and the Amīr of Afghānistān [*q.v.*]. Because this frontier was too long and too mountainous to admit of its being defended by the military alone, much depended upon the political management of the tribes. At first there was no special agency for dealing with the tribal tracts, and relations with the tribesmen were conducted by the deputy-commissioners of the six districts of Hazāra, Peshāwar, Kōhāt, Bannū [*q.vv.*], Dēra Ismāʿīl Khān, and Dēra Ghāzī Khān [see DĒRADJĀT]. In 1876, the three northern districts formed the commissionership of Peshāwar, the three southern ones that of the Dēradjāt. The system of political agencies was not adopted until 1878, when a special officer was appointed for the Khyber [see KHAYBAR] during the Second Afghān War. Kurram [*q.v.*] became an agency in 1892, while the three remaining agencies of the Malakand, Tochi, and Wāna were created between 1895 and 1896. The Malakand was placed under the direct control of the Government of India from the outset, all the other agencies remaining under the Pandjāb Government. This was the arrangement until the creation of the North-West Frontier Province in 1901.

The Pandjāb attained its latest dimensions within British India in 1911 when Dihlī became a separate province. It was not, however, until 1921 that it was raised to the status of a governor's province.

Bibliography: In addition to the standard works on the history of India, see C.U. Aitchison, *Treaties, engagements, and sanads,* viii, 1909; Muftī ʿAlī al-Dīn, *ʿIbrat-nāma* (India Office, no. 3241); J.D. Cunningham, *History of the Sikhs*, Oxford 1918; M.L. Darling, *The Punjab peasant in prosperity and debt*, London 1925; C.C. Davies, *The problem of the North-West Frontier 1890-1908*[2], London 1975; C. Gough and A.D. Innes, *The Sikhs and the Sikh War*, London 1897; L.H. Griffin, *The Rajas of the Punjab*, Lahore 1870; idem, *The Punjab chiefs*, Lahore 1890; idem, *Ranjit Singh*, Oxford 1892; *Indian Statutory Commission*, x, 1930; S.M. Latif, *History of the Panjāb*, Calcutta 1891; idem, *Lahore, its history, architectural remains and antiquities*, 1892; M. Macauliffe, *The Sikh Religion*, 6 vols., Oxford 1909; Ghulām Muḥyī 'l-Dīn, *Tārīkh-i Pandjāb* (India Office, no. 3244); Muḥammad Naḳī, *Shīr Singh-nāma* (India Office, no. 3231); T.C. Plowden, *Kalīd-i-Afghāni*, 1875; H. Priestley, *Hayat-i-Afghāni,* 1874; *Punjab administration reports* (published annually); H.A. Rose, *A glossary of the tribes and castes of the Punjab and North-West Frontier Province*, 3 vols., Lahore 1911-19; A.B.M. Habibullah, *The foundation of Muslim rule in India*[2], Allahabad 1961; K.K. Aziz, *Britain and Muslim India, 1857-1947*, London 1963. See also the *Bibls.* to LAHAWR and MULTĀN and to section 2. below. (C.C. DAVIES*)

2. History after 1911

The course of British policy profoundly influenced political developments in the region after 1911. The British created a system of control based on their alliance with rural powerholders. They also encouraged the growth of an "agriculturalist" political identity which cut across communal lines. This policy was largely dictated by the need to secure rural stability in a region which was the major centre for recruitment to the Indian Army. The Government of India's introduction of improved communications, the spread of western education and missionary activity, however, stimulated religious revivalism. The communities of the Pandjāb's towns thus developed a communal political ideal which challenged the British definition of society. Two systems of politics emerged, the rural politics of mediation, and the urban politics of faith.

The Government of India's political institutions largely excluded the urban communities from power. Only members of the statutory "agriculturalist" tribes could stand for election in the rural constituencies which accounted for the majority of the seats in the Provincial Assembly, newly created in 1937. Because the rural voting requirements were low and large numbers of soldiers were enfranchised, agriculturalists comprised nearly three-quarters of the restricted electorate. This greatly handicapped both the Indian National Congress and the All-India Muslim League, as their supporters were concentrated in the Pandjāb's towns.

The Unionist Party was the dominant political force. The Party was founded in 1923. It won the support both of the Muslim landholders from the West Pandjāb and the Hindu Jat peasants of the eastern Ambāla division. Its main policies concerned the elimination of rural indebtedness. Its cornerstone was the 1900 Alienation of Land Act which limited land transfers and divided Pandjābi society into the categories of "agriculturalist" and "non-agriculturalist".

Urban politicians, however, stressed communal identities. The Aḥrārs championed the rights of Kashmiri Muslims and also attacked the heterodox Aḥmadī community [see AḤMADIYYA]. The Khāksārs preached a revolutionary Islamic nationalism. The Sikh Akālīs were the first to successfully infuse communal values into rural politics. They wrested power from the landholders of the Khālsa National Party through their militant struggle in the early 1920s to secure control of the Sikh shrines and temples. Muslim politics continued to move along the same track as before. The Unionist Party triumphed in the 1937 Provincial elections, reducing the Muslim League to a single seat. Jinnah received some consolation when the new Unionist Premier, Sikandar Ḥayāt Khān, agreed to support him in All-India politics in their Pact of October 1937. But the cost was the Unionist domination of the reorganised Pandjāb branch of the Muslim League.

The Second World War dealt a series of blows to the Unionist Party. It had to agree to the unpopular measure of the forced requisition of grain. The War also undermined it by raising Jinnah's status and signalling an imminent British departure from India. Simultaneously, the Party was internally weakened by the sudden deaths of Sikandar and Chhotu Ram, its leading Jat figure. Khiḍr (Khizr) Ḥayāt Khān Tiwana succeeded Sikandar as Premier early in 1943. He remained wedded to the Party's intercommunal stance, but he lacked his predecessor's ability to unite all its Muslim factions. Jinnah seized the opportunity to reassert his authority over the Pandjāb Muslim League. After protracted negotiations, he expelled Khiḍr from the party in May 1944. Thereafter there was a steady drift of Muslim Unionists into the Muslim League, while their Hindu counterparts joined the Congress.

The Unionist Party was reduced to a rump of 21 members following the 1946 Provincial elections. Khiḍr remained as Premier of a Coalition Ministry until March 1947. His resignation sparked an outbreak of communal violence which had become endemic by the summer of 1947. The disintegration of the police and other services helps explain the chaos which afflicted the region following the British departure.

The Partition of the Pandjāb resulted from the acceptance of the 3 June Plan. The boundary commission drew a line passing between Lahore and Amritsar. The decision to award an area of about 5,000 square miles of contiguous Muslim majority areas to India to retain the "solidarity" of canal and road systems evoked great controversy. In the chaotic two-way flight of August to November 1947, 13 million people crossed the new boundaries. In 1956 the Patiālā and East Pandjāb States Union was merged with the Indian Pandjāb State. This was, however, further reorganised along linguistic lines in 1966 with the Hindi-speaking areas being carved out into the new State of Haryana. The Himalayan Hill Tracts were also taken away to form part of what became the State of Himachal Pradesh. The Sikhs were left as a majority in their homeland for the first time. By 1981 they omprised 56% of the State's population of 6,800,000. The West Pandjāb has undergone much ess territorial reorganisation. It has incorporated the ormer State of Bahāwalpūr [*q.v.*]. From 1955-70 it was merged into the single province of West Pākistān. When it was reconstituted, it comprised 28 districts in ive divisions and a population of 37,400,000.

Both the Indian and Pākistānī Pandjāb were istorically well placed to benefit from the Green Revolution of the 1960s. They possessed good existing oads and canals and agriculturally skilled populaions. With the introduction of the improved seeds and technology of the Green Revolution, agricultural production was further increased, with the result that they became the wealthiest regions in their respective ountries. The Pākistānī Pandjāb possessed the addiional favourable inheritance of a stranglehold over military recruitment.

The colonial legacy has also shaped political developments in the Pandjāb region. The Akālī Dal's dominant position in Sikh politics dates from its capure of the resources of the Sikh shrines and temples. The genesis of the Khālistān demand is complex and s rooted mainly in the social changes brought by the Green Revolution and the Centre-State conflicts engendered by Mrs Gandhi's rule. Nevertheless, the sharpened Sikh communal identity during the colonial era, and Sikh distrust of the Congress following he failure of the Sikhistān demand in 1947, are important historical influences.

An important colonial legacy for the politics of the Pākistānī Pandjāb, and indeed for Pākistān as a whole, has been the region's establishment as a major army recruitment centre. For the virtual exclusion of non-Pandjābīs from the continued military association with power has reinforced regional imbalances and increased alienation from the centre. Military service, landholding and political power have become increasingly intermeshed. Equally important, however, has been the inheritance of an unresolved tension between a political authority based on the mediation of local leaders and Islamic ideals. This boiled over in the anti-Aḥmadī riots in Lahore of 1953 which were reminiscent of the Ahrārs' agitations of the 1930s. The riots resulted in the introduction of martial law in Lahore and the downfall of the Premier of Pākistān. This paved the way for the military to assume a larger role in the nation's politics [see further, PĀKISTĀN].

Bibliography: Punjab Unionist Party, *Rules and regulations*, Lahore 1936; S. Zaheer, *Muslim Līg awr Yūnyūnist Partī: Pandjāb meṅ ḥakk o bāṭil ki kashmakash*, Bombay 1944; Punjab Provincial Muslim League, *Manifesto of the Punjab Provincial Muslim League*, Lahore 1944; Punjab Government, *Report of the Government Inquiry constituted under Punjab Act II of 1954 to enquire into the Punjab disturbances of 1953*, Lahore 1954; A.H. Batalvi, *Iḳbāl ke ākhiri do sāl*, Karachi 1969; S. Lavan, *The Ahmadiyah movement*, Delhi 1974; W. Ahmad, *Letters of Mian Fazl-i-Husain*, Lahore 1976; P. Chowdhry, *Punjab politics: the role of Sir Chhotu Ram*, New Delhi 1984; R.G. Fox, *Lions of the Punjab: culture in the making*, Berkeley 1985; I.H. Malik, *Sikander Hayat Khan (1892-1942): a political biography*, Islamabad 1985; R. Kapur, *Sikh separatism: the politics of faith*, London 1986; I. Talbot, *Punjab and the Raj, 1849-1947*, New Delhi 1988; I. Ali, *The Punjab under imperialism, 1885-1947*, Princeton 1988; D. Gilmartin, *Empire and Islam: Punjab and the making of Pakistan*, Berkeley 1989; J.S. Grewal, *The Sikhs of the Punjab*, Cambridge 1990. (I. TALBOT)

PANDJĀBĪ is only loosely to be defined as the Indo-Aryan language of the Pandjāb [*q.v.*]. Most linguists follow the narrower definition proposed by Grierson in the *Linguistic survey of India*, according to which "Pandjābī proper" is restricted to the speech of the central and eastern districts only, in distinction from the western dialects separately classified under Lahndā [*q.v.*].

1. *Historic status and dialects*. Pandjābī is thus placed between Lahndā to the west and the Khaṛī bōlī of the Dihlī region, which forms the base of Urdū and of modern standard Hindī, to the south-east. As is so often the case in the uncertain internal taxonomies of Indo-Aryan, its relations with these two immediate neighbours are complex, being marked by a range of features shared with one or the other, and being further confused by numerous borrowings.

The intermediate status of Pandjābī was explained by Grierson in terms of his insecurely based theory of "Outer" and "Central" groups of Indo-Aryan languages, according to which Pandjābī was the product of the innovating "Central" type, exemplified by Western Hindī, having come partially to overlay the conservative "Outer" Lahndā.

A more satisfactory explanation requires to be more closely linked to the historical evidence. This is admittedly very scanty for the beginning of the new Indo-Aryan period, which is here roughly contemporary with the Ghaznawid conquests of the 11th century. Widespread acceptance has, however, been secured for the argument first advanced by Ḥ.M. Shērānī that Pandjābī was one of the principal Indo-Aryan components of the early Muslim *lingua franca* of India, as might be deduced from the known patterns of conquest and settlement. The language of both the often garbled vernacular utterances occasionally included in some early Dihlī *malfūẓāt* [*q.v.* in Suppl.] and the amply preserved corpus of early Dakanī Urdū literature (*ca.* 1500-1650) clearly exemplifies this former Pandjābī predominance, largely eliminated in later varieties of Urdū where Khaṛī bōlī norms have become the rule. Such Pandjābisms notably include the preference for the retention of Middle Indo-Aryan geminates, e.g. *akkh* "eye" versus modern Urdū *āṉkh*, the use of vocabulary now distinctively Pandjābī, e.g. *ākh-* "say" besides *kah-* (now alone used in modern Urdū), and numerous morphological features, e.g. future *ākhsī* "he will say" (versus modern *kahēgā*), or ablative singular *prēmōṉ* "from love" (versus modern *prēm sē*).

Within the Pandjāb itself a similar pattern of influence from west to east may discerned in the premodern period. The local Muslim literary language, as often as not described by its authors in the usual Indo-Muslim fashion as "Hindī" or "Hinduī" rather than "Pandjābī" freely incorporates many Lahndā forms alongside those more strictly characteristic of the central Mādjhī dialect of Lahore, the provincial capital. This may be accounted for by the continuing importance of Multān as a spiritual and political centre in the south-west, and by the fact that many of the most important writers came from the districts west of Lahore, where Pandjābī shades into Lahndā. The broad dialectal base of the literary language is to be seen in the simultaneous use of numerous western (Lahndā), mid-western (Lahndā-Pandjābī) and central (Mādjhī) forms, e.g. feminine plural *akkhīṉ*, *akkhiyāṉ*, *akkhāṉ* "eyes", or future *akhēsi*, *ākhsī*, *ākhēgā* "he will say". Only from *ca.* 1750 is it possible clearly to distinguish the Sirāikī of south-western Pandjāb, more exclusively based on Lahndā [*q.v.*] from this composite Muslim Pandjābī literary idiom.

2. *Muslim Pandjābī literature*. The prolonged cultural

supremacy of Persian in the Pandjāb, only ended by the imposition of Urdū following the British conquests in the mid-19th century, accounts for the quite restricted nature of the typical genres of pre-modern Muslim Pandjābī literature, whose linguistic base has been indicated above. Written in Persian script and drawing extensively upon Perso-Arabic vocabulary, this Muslim literature may largely be considered in isolation from the contemporary Sikh scriptural and post-scriptural literature, whose dialectal base incorporates many more Hindī forms alongside their Pandjābī equivalents, which is recorded in the sacred Gurmukhī script, and whose abstract vocabulary is largely Sanskritic in origin. The two literatures coincide only in the isolated small corpus of pre-16th century *shalōk* and hymns attributed to Farīd al-Dīn Gandj-i Shakar (571-664/1175-1265 [*q.v.*]) which is preserved in the Sikh *Ādi Granth* (1604). While valuable as uniquely early examples of Muslim vernacular poetry in the Pandjāb, and as linguistic records (especially since the Gurmukhī script records such archaic features as morphemically significant distinctions of short vowels, never systematically indicated in the Persian script), these verses must in many ways be regarded separately from the later Muslim literature.

This abounds in the difficulties of attribution and dating, not to speak of the uncertainties of textual transmission, to be expected from its semi-popular character in relation to Persian. Also consistent with its popular nature is the fact that it is all composed in verse, whose patterns are based not upon the learned *ʿarūḍ* certainly familiar to many of its authors but on local metres characterised by regular accentual beats. The literature may be classified under three broad headings. The first consists of versified Islamic treatises on fundamentals of the faith or prescriptions of the *sharīʿa*. Although quite copious in quantity, this genre is of the least literary interest, even in the well preserved works of its first and best known exponent, Mawlawī ʿAbd Allāh "ʿAbdī" of Lahore (d. 1075/1664).

A far greater literary significance attaches to the Ṣūfī lyric associated with *ḳawwālī* performance. Here the premier genre is the *kāfī*, a lyric consisting of rhymed couplets or short stanzas having a refrain repeated after each verse, and normally following the usual Indian poetic convention whereby the poet assumes a female persona, typically that of a young girl yearning to be united with her husband/lover, allegorically to be understood as an expression of the soul's yearning for God. The 16th-century *malāmatī* of Lahore, Shāh "Mādhō Lāl" Ḥusayn, is considered to be the first exponent of the Pandjābī *kāfī*, although it must observed that the transmission of the verse attributed to him has been largely through the oral *ḳawwāl* tradition. The master of the genre is the Ḳādirī, ʿAbd Allāh "Bullhe Shāh" (1680-1758), whose tomb is at Ḳaṣūr, and in whose *kāfī*s the combination of a lyrical poignancy underpinned by imagery from local legends and local life with wide-ranging Islamic references creates a local expresion of Ṣūfī teaching and ideals still rightly regarded as classic. His reputation is matched only by that of another Ḳādirī, Sulṭān Bāhū of Jhang (d. 1102/1691), whose more sober poetry is cast in the quatrain form called *dōhṛā*.

The third genre consists of longer narrative poems, composed in one or other of the two local metres called *baint*, and arranged by rhyme either in *mathnawī*-style couplets, or more usually in stanzas (*pauṛī*) of four or more lines, whose contents are often headed by Persian prose rubrics. Although more obviously designed for reading than the Ṣūfī lyric, at least the most famous of these narratives are equally performed as ballads to more or less set tunes. One category of such narratives indeed consists of historical ballads (*vār*) on martial themes, the best known examples being the 18th-century *Nādir Shāh dī vār* by Nadjābat, and the mid-19th century *vār* on the Anglo-Sikh wars by Shāh Muḥammad.

The largest and most popular class of narrative poems belongs, however, to the romance or *ḳiṣṣa*. Well attested from the 17th century, the Pandjābī *ḳiṣṣa* reaches its apogee in the *Hīr Rāndjhā* by Wārith Shāh (1180/1766). Comprising some 4,000 lines, this version of one of the most famous local legends is rightly regarded as the masterpiece of Muslim Pandjābī literature, not merely for its narrative skill but for its encyclopaedic vision of Pandjābī society, its exploitation of the total stylistic range of language from the most rarefied Perso-Arabic to the most earthily obscene, and its challenging mixture of the sardonic with the romantic. Classic treatments of other local legends, besides adaptations from the Persian of such widely diffused romances as Laylā-Madjnūn or Shīrīn-Farhād, followed in the early 19th century, and many further imitations were inspired by the development of Lahore as a major publishing centre from the 1860s. The only later *ḳiṣṣa* to achieve a popularity rivalling that of the Wārith Shāh *Hīr* was, however, the lengthy and elaborate re-working of the Arabian Nights' romance of *Sayf al-Mulūk* (1272/1855) by the Ḳādirī Miyān Muḥammad Bakhsh of Mīrpūr (Kashmīr) in some 10,000 lines as a Ṣūfī allegory incorporating a vast range of references to Islamic learning and local culture, characteristically concluding with the first history of Muslim Pandjābī literature.

3. *Modern Pandjābī*. While Pandjābī literature of a traditional type, if no longer of very high quality, continues even now to be produced in Pākistān, pre-modern patterns have been increasingly affected by the major linguistic and political changes which have overtaken the Pandjāb in the 20th century.

The intimate association in modern South Asia between Urdū and Islām facilitated the ready acceptance during the British period by educated Pandjābī Muslims of Urdū in place of Persian as their main cultural language. The creation and development of a modern standard Pandjābī was therefore left to the Sikh reformists and writers who from 1900 onwards used it as the medium of a modern prose literature. Being written in the Gurmukhī script, this literature was, however, unintelligible to nearly all Muslim readers, from whose ranks only a very small number of writers began to experiment with newer poetic forms, including adaptations of Urdū and English models into Pandjābī. This profound cultural barrier was naturally reinforced by the partition of the Pandjāb in 1947, and the wholesale exchange of populations between its Indian and Pākistānī parts [see PANDJĀB. 2. after 1911].

The place of Pākistān Pandjāb as one of the stoutest continuing bastions of Urdū in South Asia was challenged in the succeeding decades only by very small groups of intellectuals and writers who began to lay the foundations of a modern standard Pākistānī Pandjābī, inevitably profoundly influenced by Urdū, but consciously differentiated from it by the adoption of some elements from modern Sikh Pandjābī, and of a more carefully distinguished orthography (e.g. through the adoption of super-dotted *nūn* to mark the retroflex *ṅ*). The efforts of these pioneers have borne some fruit in recent decades, when political evelopments have encouraged an increasing role for nguistic and other manifestations of local ethnicity in ākistān. Their reversal of direction in the historic atterns of influence from west to east has served to ase the written language more closely on the Mādjhī f Lahore, but at the cost of emphasising its distinctiveness from other regional standards, notably the iräikī of Multān-Bahāwalpūr. For the present, therepre, Urdū continues to represent an attractive alterative to the greater adoption of Pandjābī as literary anguage, even in the specialised world of Pākistānī Pandjābī scholarship.

Bibliography: 1. Language. G.A. Grierson, ed., *Linguistic survey of India*, ix, part I, *Western Hindī and Pañjābī, 607-825*, Calcutta 1916, contains a full bibliography of the earlier sources. The significance of Pandjābī in the early formation of Urdū was first argued in Ḥ.M. Shērānī, *Pandjāb meṉ Urdū*, Lahore 1930. More recent studies are best consulted through O.N. Kaul and M. Bala, *Punjabi language and linguistics, an annotated bibliography*, Patiala 1992. There is no systematic account of Muslim Pandjābī comparable to the description of modern standard Sikh Pandjābī in H.S. Gill and H.A. Gleason, *A reference grammar of Punjabi*, Patiala 1969.

2. Literature. There is a lengthy composite account (in Urdū) in *Pandjābī adab*, in *Tārīkh-i adabiyyāt-i musulmānān-i Pākistān ō Hind*, ed. Fayyāḍ Maḥmūd, xiii, part I, Lahore 1971, 185-433. The earlier period is surveyed in C. Shackle, *Early vernacular poetry in the Indus valley*, in *Islam and Indian regions*, ed. A.L. Dallapiccola and S. Zingel-Avé Lallemant, Stuttgart 1993, i, 259-89. For the Ṣūfī poetry, L. Rama Krishna, *Pañjābi Ṣūfī poets, A.D. 1460-1900*, Calcutta 1938, still awaiting its long overdue English replacement, may be supplemented by *Bulleh Shah* [*sic*], *a selection*, tr. Taufiq Rafat, Lahore 1982. A comprehensive bibliography of English and other sources for the Wārith Shāh *Hīr* (and to the *ḳiṣṣa* poetry generally) is provided in C. Shackle, *Transitions and transformations in Vāris Shāh's* Hīr, to appear in *The Indian narrative: perspectives and patterns*, ed. idem and R. Snell, Wiesbaden 1993.

3. Modern Pandjābī. The changing status of the language is examined in C. Shackle, *Punjabi in Lahore*, in *Modern Asian Studies*, iv (1970), 239-67; idem, *Language, dialect, and local identity in northern Pakistan*, in *Pakistan in its fourth decade*, ed. W.-P. Zingel, Hamburg 1983, 175-87; idem, *Some observations on the evolution of modern standard Punjabi*, in *Sikh history and religion in the twentieth century*, ed. J.T. O'Connell, Toronto 1988, 101-9. (C. Shackle)

PANDJDIH (Pendjdeh), a village now in the Turkmenistan Republic, situated to the east of the Kushk river near its junction with the Murghāb at Pul-i Kishti. The fact that the inhabitants of this area, the Sarik Turkomans, were divided into five sections, the Soktīs, Harzagīs, Khurāsānlis, Bayrač, and the ʿAlī Shāh, has been put forward as a possible explanation of the origin of the name Pendjdeh, but it carries no weight as the Sariks were only 19th-century immigrants, whereas the name was in use in the 15th century.

This obscure oasis owes a somewhat melancholy importance to the "Pandjdih Incident" of 1885, when an Afghān force suffered heavy losses in an engagement with Russian troops, and which threatened to become a major Anglo-Russian military confrontation in Central Asia. History proves that an ill-defined boundary is a potential cause of war. It was a knowledge of this and the Russian occupation of Marw in 1884, with an intention in Imperial Russian minds of extending power over all the Turkmen peoples of the region, that gave the necessary impetus to negotiations which ended in the appointment of an Anglo-Russian Boundary Commission for the delimitation and demarcation of the northern boundary of Afghānistān. Trouble immediately arose in this quarter, for while the Russians contended that the inhabitants of Pandjdih were independent, the British held the view that they were subjects of the *Amīr* of Afghānistān. According to the British, the district of Pandjdih, which comprised the country between the Kushk and Murghāb rivers from the Band-i Nādir to Ak Tepe, together with the rest of Bādghīs, formed part of the Harāt province of Afghānistān. During the first quarter of the 19th century, Pandjdih had been occupied by Djamshīdīs and Hazāras. Towards the end of this period, some Turkomans of the Ersari tribe, whose settlements were scattered along the banks of the Oxus between the Čardjuy and Balkh, moved to Pandjdih and obtained permission to settle there. Salor Turkomans had also settled in this area. About 1857, the Ersaris migrated from the oasis of Pandjdih, and soon afterwards the Sarik Turkomans, forced southwards by their more powerful neighbours, the Tekkes, occupied Yulatan and Pandjdih and compelled the Salor families to migrate elsewhere. Although, therefore, Pandjdih had from time to time been occupied by various tribes, they had all, whether Djamshīdīs, Hazāras, Ersaris, Salors or Sariks, acknowledged they were on Afghān soil and paid tribute to the *nāʾib* or deputy of the Afghān governor of Harāt. The Sarik Turkomans had even supplied the *Amīr* with troops. The British therefore contended that the district of Bādghīs, of which Pandjdih formed a part, had long been under Afghān rule (Foreign Office mss. 65, 1205).

The Russians, on the other hand, contended that the people of this oasis had always enjoyed independence. Lessar, a Russian engineer, who visited Pandjdih in March 1884, discovered no trace of Afghān authority, but a Russian doctor, named Regel, who visited it in June of the same year reported the presence of an Afghān detachment. In their opinion, therefore, Pandjdih had only recently been occupied by Afghān troops.

The fact that the Afghāns had not permanently garrisoned this area was no proof of its independence. On the contrary, it was only natural that, after the Russian occupation of Marw and Pul-i Khātūn, ʿAbd al-Raḥmān Khān should have taken steps to indicate his sovereign rights over this area. When, therefore, an Afghān garrison occupied Pandjdih, the Russian Government immediately protested and disputed the *Amīr*'s claim to the territory. While negotiations were taking place between London and St. Petersburg, events moved swiftly on the frontiers of Afghānistān. On 29 March 1885, General Komarov sent an ultimatum demanding the withdrawal of the Afghān garrison. The Afghāns resolutely refused to withdraw, whereupon the Russians attacked them, driving them across the Pul-i Kishti with the loss of some 900 men. It must be admitted that the posting of Afghān troops in Pandjdih, and the Russian advance to Yulatan on the Murghāb and to Pul-i Khātūn on the Harī Rūd, were both provocative actions almost certain to precipitate war. The whole incident should have been avoided, but the confusing reports of Sir Peter Lumsden, the British Commissioner, to the Foreign Office, and the delay of Zelenoi, the Russian Commissioner, in arriving at Sarakhs complicated matters still more.

At the time, this incident seemed likely to embroil Russia and Britain in war, but, fortunately, the good sense of the *Amīr*, who was at this critical moment on a State visit to Rawalpindi, and the diplomatic skills of the Viceroy, Lord Dufferin, prevented this, for even the pacific Liberal government of Gladstone had proposed to Parliament that £11,000,000 should be expended on preparations for war.

It was finally agreed that Pandjdih should be handed over to Russia in exchange for Dhu 'l-Fiķār, and by the year 1886 the northern boundary of Afghānistān had been demarcated from Dhu 'l-Fiķār to the meridian of Dukči within forty miles of the Oxus. After a dispute as to the exact point at which the boundary line should meet the Oxus, the process of demarcation was completed in 1888. This recognition of a definite frontier between Russia and Afghānistān led to a decided improvement in the Central Asian question.

In the history of mediaeval Islamic literature, Pandjdih appears as the home, or the place of ultimate origin, of at least two poets: Abū Ḥanīfa Pandjdihī, whose Arabic verses are quoted in al-Bākharzī, *Dumyat al-ķaṣr*, ed. al-Ḥilū, Cairo 1388-91/1968-71, ii, 257 no. 303 = ed. al-ʿĀnī, Baghdād 1390-1/1960-1, ii, 154; and Muẓaffarī Pandjdihī Marwī (Marwarrūdhī ?), a Persian poet included by Niẓāmī ʿArūḍī, *Čahār maķāla*, ed. Ķazwīnī, 28, and ʿAwfī, *Lubāb al-albāb*, ed. Browne and Ķazwīnī, ii, 63-5, amongst the eulogists of the Ghaznawids.

Bibliography: *Délimitation Afghane. Négociations entre la Russie et la Grande-Bretagne*, 1872-85, 1886; *Parliamentary Papers, Central Asia*, 1884-5, lxxxvii, c. 4387-9, 4418; *Public Record Office*, London, Foreign Office mss. 65, 1205; 1238-45; C.E. Yate, *Northern Afghanistan*, or *Letters from the Afghan Boundary Commission*, London 1888; Sir Alfred Lyall, *The life of the Marquis of Dufferin and Ava*, London 1905, ii, 90-3; V. Gregorian, *The emergence of modern Afghanistan. Politics of reform and modernization 1880-1946*, Stanford 1969, 117, 156-7; L. Dupree, *Afghanistan*, Princeton 1973, 421-3; M. Bence-Jones, *The Viceroys of India*, London 1982, 138-9.

(C.C. Davies)

PANDJHĪR, the name of a river and its valley in the northeastern part of Afghānistān. The river flows southwards from the Hindū Kush [*q.v.*] and joins the Kābul River at Sarobi, and near this point a barrage was constructed in the 1950s to supply water for Kābul. The Pandjhīr valley has always been important as a corridor for nomads who winter in the Lāmghānāt-Djalālābād [*q.vv.*] regions and then travel to summer pastures in Badakhshān [*q.v.*].

In mediaeval Islamic times, Pandjhīr was a famed centre for silver mining [see maʿdin at V, 964, 967, 968 for details], and coins were minted there by the Ṣaffārids [*q.v.*], Abū Dāwūdids or Bānīdjūrids [*q.v.* in Suppl.] and Sāmānids [*q.v.*] (see E. von Zambaur, *Die Münzprägungen des Islam*, i, Wiesbaden 1968, 79). Pandjhīr seems to have produced a poet in Persian of some renown (the "well-known" al-Bandjhīrī of Yāķūt, *Buldān*, ed. Beirut, i, 499?), Abu 'l-Muẓaffar Makkī al-Pandjhīrī, eulogist of the Ghaznawids; see ʿAwfī, *Lubāb al-albāb*, ed. Browne and Ķazwīnī, London-Leiden 1903-6, ii, 46.

In the 1980s, the Pandjhīr valley was a particular centre of *Mudjāhid* [*q.v.*] resistance to the Communist régime in Kābul and its Soviet Russian supporters.

Bibliography: See Le Strange, *Lands*, 417-19; J. Humlum *et alii*, *La géographie d'Afghanistan, étude d'un pays aride*, Copenhagen etc. 1959, 32, 41, 44, 311.

(Ed.)

PANDJWĀY [see ķandahār].

PĀNDUʾĀ, a mediaeval Islamic town of the Bengal Sultanate [see bangāla], now in the Mālda District of the West Bengal State of the Indian Union and situated about 16 km/10 miles to the south of modern Mālda town, in lat. 25° 8′ N. and long 88° 10′ E. It was the residence of Shams al-Dīn Ilyās Shāh of Bengal (746-59/1345-58) and his five successors, and it was at Pānduʾā that he mounted the throne. Pānduʾā continued as the capital of the Bengal Sultanate till the reign of Djalāl al-Dīn Muḥammad Shāh (817-35/1414-31), who transferred the capital to Gawr or Lakhnawtī [*q.v.*]. On coins, Pānduʾā is referred to as Fīrūzābād. It was deserted due to its unwholesome climate and the rise of swamps and marshes. It is now a deserted town—a square mound, five miles in diameter with archaeological evidence of fortification.

Pānduʾā developed as a brisk centre of spiritual activity in Bengal. Djalāl al-Dīn Tabrīzī established his *khānaķāh* at Deotala, near Pānduʾā. In 742/1342 ʿAlāʾ al-Dīn ʿAlī Shāh built his tomb at Pānduʾā. Shaykh Sirādj al-Dīn ʿUthmān, known as Akhī Sirādj, a distinguished disciple of Shaykh Niẓām al-Dīn Awliyāʾ [*q.v.*], planted the Čishtī order at Pānduʾā. His successors—Shaykh ʿAlāʾ al-Ḥaķķ, Nūr Ķuṭb-i ʿĀlam and others—played an important role in the cultural life of the place. Shaykh ʿAlāʾ al-Ḥaķķ (d. 800/1398) pushed further the work of his distinguished predecessors and made Pānduʾā the centre of a powerful religious and intellectual movement. His son Nūr Ķuṭb-i ʿĀlam built there a big *madrasa* and a hospital. The land granted by ʿAlāʾ al-Dīn Ḥusayn Shāh to his *khānaķāh* continued up to recent times. According to the *Riyāḍ al-salāṭīn*, Ḥusayn Shāh used to come from Ekdala every year on foot to visit the tomb of Nūr Ķuṭb-i ʿĀlam. We find eminent saints, like Shaykh Aḥmad ʿAbd al-Ḥaķķ of Rudawlī, visiting his shrine (*Anwār al-ʿUyūn*, ʿAlīgaŕh 1905, 12-14).

The site of Pānduʾā contains some splendid Muslim buildings, mostly in a ruinous condition, including the remarkable Ādīna or Friday Mosque, the largest in the subcontinent, built by the second Ilyās Shāhid, Sikandar Shāh I (759-92/1358-90), completed in Radjab 776/December 1374-January 1375 according to an inscription in the mosque; the 10th/16th century Ķuṭb Shāhī mosque; and several significant tombs (see A.H. Dani, *Muslim architecture in Bengal*, Dacca 1961, 55-73, 76-83, 168-70; G. Michell (ed.), *The Islamic heritage of Bengal*, UNESCO, Paris 1984, 109-14, 155-64).

Bibliography: *Imperial gazetteer of India*², xix, 392-4; M. Abid Ali Khan, *Memoirs of Gaur and Pandua*, revised by H.E. Stapleton, Calcutta 1931; M.A. Rahim, *Social and cultural history of Bengal*, i, Karachi 1963, 183-4; M.R. Tarafdar, *Husain Shahi Bengal, a socio-political study*, Dacca 1965, 128-9; A. Karim, *Corpus of the Muslim coins of Bengal*, Dacca 1960; Ghulam Rasool, *Chishti Nizami Sufi order of Bengal*, Dihlī 1990.

(K.A. Nizami)

PANGULU [see penghulu].

PĀNĪPAT, a town of northern India (lat. 29° 24′ N., long. 76° 58′ E.) situated 86 km/57 miles north of Dihlī; it is also the name of the southernmost *taḥṣīl* in the Karnāl District of what was in British Indian times the province of the Pandjāb [*q.v.*] but has since 1947 been in the eastern or Indian part of the divided province of the former Pandjāb, at present in Haryana province of the Indian Union.

On three occasions has the fate of Hindustān been decided on the plain of Pānīpat: in 1526, when Bābur q.v.], the Barlās Turk, defeated Ibrāhīm Lōdī [q.v.]; n 1556, when Akbar [q.v.] crushed the forces of Hēmū; and lastly, in 1761, when the Marāthās [q.v.] were defeated by Aḥmad Shāh Durrānī [q.v.]. The geographical factor combined with internal decay and a weak system of frontier defence has been chiefly responsible for this. From the strategic background of Afghānistān the path for invaders lay along the lines of least resistance, the Khyber, Kurram, Tochi, and Gomal passes, on to the Pandjāb plains, for the Indus has never proved an obstacle to an enterprising general. Checked on the south by the deserts of Rādjputāna, invading armies were forced to enter the Ganges and Djamnā valleys through the narrow bottleneck between the north-eastern extremity of the desert and the foot of the Himālāyas.

Hence because of this strategic position, Pānīpat has always been important, and is mentioned in the *Mahābhārata* and in the historical sources on the Dihlī Sultanate [q.v.]. In the first battle of Pānīpat, Bābur defeated and killed Ibrāhīm b. Sikandar Lōdī on 8 Radjab 932/20 April 1526. His success was attributed by earlier scholars to an extensive use of cannon, 700 *ʿarabas* [q.v.] being mentioned in the *Bābur-nāma*, tr. Beveridge, 463 ff., see esp. 468-9 n. 3; but these must have been for the conveyance of baggage, not gun carriages. Bābur certainly had an unspecified number of cannon, and his Master Gunner Ustād ʿAlī-Ḳulī had *farangī*, *ḍarbzan* and *dēgh* cannon which were lashed together for action [see further BĀRŪD. vi. India]. The battle sealed the fate of the Lōdī dynasty [q.v.], but much tougher resistance to Bābur was offered to him in the following year at the battle of Khānuʾā, when he routed the Rādjpūt Rānā Sāṅgā of Mēwāṛ [q.v.] and brought about the extinction of Mēwāṛ as a separate kingdom (see *Bābur-nāma*, tr. 558-75).

The second battle of Pānīpat took place on 2 Muḥarram 964/5 November 1556, when Akbar, soon after his accession, defeated the usurping Hindu minister Hēmū, who had assumed the title of Rādjā Vikramaditya, this victory being the first major step in Akbar's constituting the Mughal empire.

The third battle of Pānīpat took place on 7 Djumādā II 1174/14 January 1761, when the Marāthās, having managed to occupy Dihlī, were nevertheless put to flight by the Afghān *amīr* of Ḳandahār, Aḥmad Shāh Durrānī. Although Aḥmad Shāh returned to Afghānistān shortly afterwards and Marāthā power revived, the battle had long-term effects in preserving the Muslim state of the Niẓām in Ḥaydarābād [q.v.] and in allowing the British to consolidate their position in Bengal.

The modern town of Pānīpat still retains its fort and a wall with 15 gates, and amongst its monuments are the ruins of a mosque in the Kābulī Bāgh built to commemorate the first battle of Pānīpat. In 1971 Pānīpat had a population of 87,981.

Bibliography: *Imperial gazetteer of India*², xix, 397-8; A.S. Beveridge (tr.), *Bābur-nāma*, ii, London 1921; Abu 'l-Faḍl ʿAllāmī, *Akbar-nāma*, tr. H. Beveridge, Calcutta 1897-1921, ii, 58 ff.; ʿAlī Muḥammad Khān, *Mirʾāt-i Aḥmadī* (Ethé, no. 3598, fols. 583-4); *Nigār-nāma-yi Hind*, Orme 1896 (see also *Asiatic Researches*, iii, and Elliot and Dowson, *History of India*, viii, 396-402); *Selections from the Peshwa's Daftar, Letters and Dispatches relating to the Battle of Panipat, 1747-1761*, 1930; Hari Ram Gupta, *The Marathas and Panipat*, Delhi 1961; *Haryana District gazetteers. Karnal*, Chandigarh 1976, 513-16.

(C.C. DAVIES-[C.E. BOSWORTH])

PANTELLERIA [see ḲAWSARA].

PANTHAY, a term applied to the Chinese Muslims of Yunnan and their rebellion in the 19th century.

In the second half of the 19th century, Chinese Muslims in Yunnan province (in south-west China, bordered by Burma, Thailand and Vietnam) were known to the Europeans as *Panthay*, a term which had never been used anywhere in China. The Yunnanese Muslims were known as *Huei-Huei* up to 1949, when the incoming communist government referred to them as *Huei-Min* or *Huei-Tsu*.

Views differ as to the etymology of the term *Panthay*. If it derives from Chinese, it may have meant indigenous (*Pen-ti*) or rebellious brigand (*Pan-Tsei*), although there is no reliable evidence. If, alternatively, it derives from Persian or Burmese, it might have been a corruption of *Pan-see*, a Burmese term, referring to Indo-Burmese of northern Arakan, who had converted to Islam in the early 13th century, and originating from Persian *Parsi* of which the *r* sound was dropped by Burmese, who called Muslims *Pathi* or *Passi*. The most likely etymology is that the term was a British coinage, corrupted by colonial officers in British India from the Burmese term *Pan-see* to designate the Yunnanese Muslims during their 1855-73 rebellion against the Manchu authorities. For today's Yunnanese Muslims in Burma, *Panthay* carries a pejorative meaning.

Sources concerning the first entry of Muslims and Islam to Yunnan vary in accuracy and credibility. Tang (618-906 A.D) and Sung (960-1279 A.D) records have left no adequate summary of the religious status and activities of Central Asian migrants in Yunnan, although archaeological evidence from the Tang period suggests that they were enslaved in the Buddhist Tali Kingdom of the native Yunnanese at that time. This accords with the fact that, when Tibet invaded the Tali Kingdom in 801, many of those taken prisoner were found to be conscripts from Samarḳand. An unofficial history of the Tali Kingdom dating from the Sung period maintains that the first Muslims were Persian merchants and Southeast Asians on a tribute mission. According to Chinese Muslim legend, however, the first settlers were Arab merchants in the middle years of the Tang dynasty, and there is no evidence of Islam taking root in Yunnan prior to the Mongol conquest of the whole of China (1279), after which mass Muslim immigration into Yunnan was carried out by the central government through their own Muslim generals.

After the conquest, Muslims migrated to Yunnan in three waves, in 1253, 1256 and 1267. Various Muslim ethnic groups (Tanguts, Tatars, Uyghurs, Persians, etc.) were introduced, following their overlords there as the province was settled. The Muslim immigrants were allocated lands and scattered all over the province, so that camps or villages, known as *Huei-Huei Yin* or *Huei-Huei Chun*, gradually developed. Furthermore, Central Asian Muslim soldiers were continually sent thither from other parts of China as part of a political and military strategy aimed at pacifying Burmese or local insurgents. This also served to promote social integration in that the Muslims began to intermarry with native or Han women or to adopt non-Muslim orphans and bring them up as Muslims to become natural suitors for their daughters.

In order to maintain control of the Muslim population, the Mongol-Yüen court appointed Muslim generals as provincial governors, amongst whom the most eminent was the Bukhārī general, Sayyid Adjall Shams al-Dīn ʿUmar, who was entrusted by Ḳubilay

Khān [*q.v.*] with the task of sinicising not only the local tribes but probably also the Muslims. Under his governorship, many mosques were built, although he did not intentionally promote Islam. By the end of the Yüen period, the Muslims had gradually abandoned their Central Asian traditions in order to adopt Chinese customs and had developed their religion into a syncretised one.

During the Ming period (1368-1644), Muslim migration continued. However, unlike the Mongols, who had allowed their non-Han subjects to retain their traditions, the Ming rulers imposed Confucianism in an attempt to eliminate all non-Han culture. Under these conditions, Muslims were forced further to integrate, but managed to preserve their religious freedom and their numbers grew. As military activity decreased, soldiers engaged in other occupations, the most important of which, in mineral-rich Yunnan, was mining. The early Ming period also saw the start of the caravan trade, and eventually six trade routes linked Yunnan, Burma, Tibet and other parts of China. Porcelain manufacture also flourished. *Huei-Ch'ing* (Islamic blue) was made chiefly in Yunnan for Muslim patrons abroad. By the onset of the Manchu-Ch'ing period (1644-1911), leather and carpet manufacture also significantly contributed to the Yunnanese economy. By the mid-19th century, the province of Yunnan was home to the second largest Muslim population centre next to that of Northwest China [see KANSU].

Under the Mongols, Muslims had enjoyed more political privileges and higher social status than the Han Chinese. Even under the Ming, they were still able to live without political and social discrimination. However, under the Manchus, Muslims found it increasingly difficult to uphold their religious freedom in the face of oppressive Confucianisation and Han chauvinism, which discriminated against all non-Han cultural elements. The resulting resentment led to serious uprisings in Muslim population centres in northwestern China. In Yunnan, where imperial law was only weakly enforced, social order broke down still further as the Yunnanese Muslims began to take up arms against the Han.

Chief among the factors contributing to the Yunnanese Muslim rebellion of 1855-73 were religio-cultural and economic conflicts and institutionalised oppression by Han officials. Muslim traditions, preserved from their ancestors, particularly dietary customs, set them apart from Han society. Muslims abhorred pork, while the Han reared cattle only as draught animals. Other cultural and religious disparities, which caused conflict, included methods of worship (Muslims considered the Han idolatrous), dress, language, wedding and funeral customs.

The national economic crisis prevailing in the 19th century was chiefly reflected in Yunnan in the mining industry, in which there was much Han-Muslim rivalry. Both groups had constantly to look for new veins of ores, and ownership disputes frequently occurred. The Han resented the Muslims' superior techniques and trade acumen and would wrest wealth from their opponents by force.

The maintenance of social order had previously been the responsibility of the local gentry, but during the 19th century the whole social system increasingly became corrupt and local government all but collapsed. Instead of restraining wayward elements, many of the gentry were themselves a source of disturbance, particularly in firing Han Chinese hatred against Muslims. They colluded with local officials, secret societies and local militia in order to oppress the Muslims for their own interests. With all these factors ranged against them, the Muslims vainly tried to seek justice from the central government, but eventually they were driven to rebel against the Manchu authority itself.

The rebellions took place in the early 1850s in most parts of Yunnan, but were concentrated around Yunnan Fu (present-day Kunming), the provincial capital in the east, and the Tali region in the west. From the middle of 1856 onwards, local, uncoordinated insurrections gradually gravitated towards a few centres of leadership in eastern Yunnan. Here, the grand *imām*, Yūsuf Ma (Chinese name *Ma Te-Hsing* or *Ma Fu-Chu*) was elected as spiritual leader, but military responsibility was in the hands at first of his *ahund* disciples, mainly Hsu Yüen-Chi, later a military degree holder, Ma Ju-Lung.

Imām Ma, a prolific writer and Islamic educationalist, under whom Yunnan became one of the three Islamic learning centres in China, was a moderate theologian who advocated a negotiated solution to the Muslims' problems. On the other hand, Ma Ju-Lung, who had also been one of the *imām*'s disciples, was an opportunist who sought privileges with the ruling Manchu.

Muslim forces were able to lay siege to Yunnan Fu three times between 1855 and 1862, causing severe strains on the imperial army and local Han militia, but failed to take the city. The response of the Manchu provincial government was to adopt a policy of "Pardon and Pacification" and to reward the eastern rebel leaders with governmental posts and honorary titles. Imām Ma was appointed the Beg of Yunnan, which was the equivalent of *Shaykh al-Islām* of Yunnan. This bought off the loyalty of the eastern rebels, who later became the main force led by Ma Ju-Lung to subdue the rebellion in the west.

This had been led by Tu Wen-Hsiu, also known as Sultan Sulaymān to the Europeans, who was more committed to the political and religious cause of Islam. His experience of the brutality of Manchu rule towards the Muslims in northwest China during the Djahriyya (a Naḳshbandiyya [*q.v.*] Ṣūfī sub-order) movement, inclined him not to yield to the Manchu's inducements and to hold out instead for a independent Muslim state within China.

Thus in western Yunnan, the situation was different. Here, the rebels seized Tali as capital of their sultanate (*Ping-Nan-Kuo*, in Chinese, "Southern Pacified Kingdom") in 1855. An Islamic court was set up and Islamic law implemented, but this only applied to Muslims, while the old Ming laws were re-adopted and applied to non-Muslim subjects. Islamic learning was encouraged, Islamic schools were established to educate Muslims and many conversions took place, although these were not forced.

During the course of the rebellions, the two rebel groups were at odds and the only opportunity for them to unite to drive the Manchu out of Yunnan was wasted for two reasons. First, Tu Wen-Hsiu offered Ma Ju-Lung a high-ranking post in his court. Ma, who was politically and militarily more ambitious, rejected this, saying that he could serve under no-one other than the grand *imām*, Ma Te-Hsing. Secondly, there was considerable sectarian conflict. The eastern rebels belonged to the traditional conservative Kê-Ti-Mu (Ar. *al-Ḳadīm*) who opposed new teaching or reform. The Tali court, on the other hand, was dominated by the Djahriyya reformists who had been exiled to Yunnan after the suppression of their movement in northwestern China by the Manchu government. The grand *imām*, who himself belonged to the

Kê-Ti-Mu, was once courteously invited by the Tali Sultan to lead religious affairs, but the invitation was turned down. Under these circumstances, the Kê-Ti-Mu rendered assistance to the Manchu government to suppress the Tali rebellion for the sake of preserving their own religious interests.

After only 18 years, the Tali sultanate collapsed. Its fate was sealed following the defection to the Manchu of most of its Han leaders and its lack of modern weaponry in order to continue to fight. The defection of the Han leaders resulted from unbalanced power-sharing in the Tali court. The sultan was accused of favouring his Muslim followers in administrative and military affairs. Towards the end of its rule, the Tali court sought military assistance from Western powers. At the beginning of 1872 a Pant͟hay mission, mediated by the British Government of India, and headed by the sultan's adopted son, Prince Ḥasan, was sent to London to secure arms and recognition from Queen Victoria as a tributary of Britain. However, at that time the British government's relations with Peking, from whom they hoped to gain further trade advantages, outweighed other considerations and the mission was not well received. Nor did it obtain the support of the Ottoman government in Istanbul, where it stopped on its way back to Yunnan.

The Yunnanese Muslim rebellion was not simply a political uprising against Manchu corruption, as it has been sometimes viewed. It was in reality a search for ethno-religious identity and social status. Prior to the Manchu period, Muslims were included in the Middle Kingdom, China, as Muslim Chinese and were treated equally with their Han counterparts. Under Manchu rule, they were classified as a minority, and their previous equal rights were gradually eroded. In these circumstances, a rejection of Manchu rule developed and was fanned by the religious undercurrents of reform brought by the Ṣūfī D̲j̲ahriyya movement, these currents thus crystalising in the ideology of a secession movement, fighting for its own separate future.

The suppression of the rebellion was highly significant in Chinese history. It was another triumph of the Han supremacy and Confucianism which had never been challenged or set aside by non-Han elements. The status of Yunnanese Muslims was now reduced to its lowest level. They were forced to abandon their ethno-religious identity and to assimilate further into Confucian society. Many of those who did not want to live under these conditions fled to Burma [*q.v.*] and formed solid communities there in order to maintain their traditions, these being the forebears of the present-day Chinese Muslims in Burma.

Bibliography: 1. Primary sources. India Office, London: *India Office Records, India Political and Foreign Proceedings*, vols. 1-65, 1861-73; Public Record Office, London, *Foreign Office Records, China 17/284-918*; G. Cordier, *Les musulmans du Yunnan*, Hanoi: Imprimerie Tonkinois, 1927; E. Rocher, *La province chinoise du Yun-nan*, 2 vols., Paris 1879-80; G.W. Clarke, *Kweichou and Yunnan provinces*, Shanghai: China Inland Mission, 1884; idem, *The province of Yunnan, past, present and future*, Shanghai: China Inland Mission, 1885; Documents on Yunnan Muslim rebellions collected in the first and seconds vols. of *Huei-Min Chi-'i* ("Documents on Muslim revolt"), 4 vols., ed. Pai Shou-I, Shanghai: Shen-Chou Kuo-Kwang-Shih, 1953; Documents collected in Yunnan *Huei-Min Chi-'i Shih-Liao* ("Historical sources on Yunnan Muslim rebellions"), ed. Chin Te-Hsing, Kunming: Min-Tsu Publisher, 1986.

2. Secondary sources. T.L. Bullock, *The Great Mohammedan Rebellion in Yunnan*, in *China Review*, xvi/2 (1887-8), 83-95; G. Cordier, *Nouveaux documents sur la révolte musulmane au Yunnan*, in *Revue Indo-Chinoise* (1909), 656-75; idem, *Les Musulmans du Yunnan, leur attitude,* in *RMM*, xxiv (1913), 318-26; A.C. Hanna, *The Panthays of Yunnan*, in *MW*, xi (1931), 69-74; Ho Huei-Ch'ing, *Yunnan Tu Wen-Hsiu Chien-Kuo Shih-Pa-Nian Shih-Mo* ("Eighteen years of Tu Wen-Hsiu's régime"), in *I-Ching*, xii (1936), 9-16; xiii, 34-6; xiv, 36-9, xv, 32-8; xvi, 29-33; Li Shou-K'ung, *Hsien-Fêng Liu-Nien Yun-nan Shung-Chung Mieh-Huei K'ao* ("Research on the Kunming massacre of Muslims in the 6th Year of the Hsien-Fêng period"), in *Ta-Lu Tsa-Chih*, xx/6 (1960), 10-3; idem, *Wan-Ch'ing Yun-nan Huei-Pien Shih-Mo* ("Accounts of the Yunnan Muslim Rebellion in the late Ch'ing period"), in *Chung-Kuo Chin-Tai-Shih Lun-Wen-Chi*, ii, Taipei: Commercial Press, 1985, 427-533; T'ien Ju-K'ang, *Yu-Kuan Tu Wen-Hsiu Tei-Wai Kuan-Hsi ti Wen-Ti* ("Inquiry into Tu Wen-Hsiu's foreign relations"), in *Li-Shih Yen-Chiu*, iv (1963), 141-50; M. Yegar, *The Panthay (Chinese Muslims) of Burma and Yunnan*, in *J. of Southeast Asian History*, vii (1966), 73-85; W.K. Chan, *Ma Ju-Lung: from rebel to turncoat in the Yunnan Rebellion*, in *Papers on China*, xx (1966), 86-118; idem, *The Panthay embassy to Britain, 1872*, in *St Antony's Papers*, xx (1967), 101-17; Li Ching, *T'an-T'an Kuan-Yü Tu Wen-Hsiu ti Chi-Chien Shih-Liao* ("On some historical sources about Tu Wen-Hsiu"), in *Huei-Tsu-Shih Lun-Chi*, Yinchwan: Jen-min Publisher, 1983, 373-85; B. Evans, *The Panthay mission of 1872 and its legacies*, in *J. of Southeast Asian Studies*, xvi/1 (1985), 117-28; Ma Hsing-Tung, *Yunnan Huei-Tsu Yuen-Liu T'an-Suo* ("Inquiry into the origins of Yunnanese Muslims"), in *Yunnan Min-Tsu Hsueh-Pao*, no. 4 (1988), 25-34; no. 1 (1989), 50-6; Chang-Kuan Lin, *Chinese Muslims of Yunnan, with special reference to their revolt (1855-73)*, Aberdeen Univ. Ph.D. thesis 1991, unpubl.

(Chang-Kuan Lin)

PAPYRUS, a term of Greek origin, πάπυρος, is one of the world's oldest writing materials; it seems to have been used in Egypt, the land of its provenance, since the 6th dynasty, *ca.* 2470-2270 A.D. As an equivalent for this word the Arabs, after their conquest of this country, used *bardī, abardī*, or better still *warak al-bardī*. However, these expressions were not of widespread usage, and in Egypt the term employed was *fāfīr*, corresponding more closely to the original Greek. Elsewhere, the word *ḳirṭās* was also used, derived from the Greek χάρτης, through the intermediary of the Aramaic *ḳarṭīs*. And since this last term denoted not only papyrus but also parchment and later even paper, it became necessary in this context to add the adjective *miṣrī* "Egyptian", as was done by Ibn al-Nadīm in his *Fihrist*, 21, ll. 10 f.

The use of this material extends over some seven centuries, lasting until the 8th/14th century. Its utilisation increased following the arrival of the Arabs in Egypt and remained dominant even in the 3rd/9th century, despite the introduction of paper [see kāg̲h̲ad].

Arabic papyrology is the scientific study of texts written on papyrus, although it is conventional, as A. Grohmann (*Einführung*, 3, l. 1) has pointed out in his definition of this branch of scholarship, to include automatically within its scope non-literary documents written on other materials, such as leather, parchment, cloth, paper, ostraca, bone or wood. However, the mass of documents on papyrus is by far the most important.

Despite the antiquity of papyrus as a writing material in Arabic culture, Arabic papyrology has developed quite recently. In fact it was only in 1824 that the subject first emerged as a science in its own right, this being the year in which two papyri were discovered in a small sealed pottery, located in a tomb or in a well near the Pyramids of Saḳḳāra (see Grohmann, *Aperçu*, table IX; N. Abbott, *The rise*, table IV). A. Silvestre de Sacy published them and thus became the founder of this discipline, which was nevertheless not to attain real prominence until 1877, the year in which sensational discoveries of papyri were made in the ruins of the old Arsinoe-Krokodilopolis (Kōm Fāris and Kōm al-K͟haryāna) to the north of the town of al-Fayyūm. In subsequent years excavations continued, bringing to light a mass of material. The pieces found were sold to the museums of Berlin, to the Bodleian in Oxford, and to the National Library of Vienna, where the Archduke Rainer of Austria purchased 1,000 pieces; thus began the gradual development of the famous PER collection (Papyri Erzherzog Rainer), which currently holds the world's greatest accumulation of Arabic pieces and which celebrated its centenary in 1983 (see *Festschrift zum 100-jährigen Bestehen...*). Sales continued and other collections came into being around the world: in Hamburg, Heidelberg, Strasbourg and elsewhere. Excavations also continued in the hills of Old Cairo (Fusṭāṭ), in other ruins including those of the Memphis Necropolis, Abūṣīr al-Malaḳ, and those of Ahnās (Herakleopolis), and, with fewer pieces found, at al-Us͟hmūnayn (Hermopolis Magna) and Kōm Es͟hḳawh (Aphrodito) where in 1901, during the digging of a cistern, two metres of papyri were found. Other discoveries were made in Upper Egypt, at Ak͟hmīm (Panopolis), at Gabalayn (Pathyris), the source of part of the Heidelberg collection (see the works of C.H. Becker and R.G. Khoury) and also at Edfu (Apollinopolis Magna) where the Institut Français d'Archéologie Orientale of Cairo found some important pieces, including the well-known codex on papyrus of *al-Ḏj̲āmiʿ* by ʿAbd Allāh Ibn Wahb (d. 197/812) (see the edition by J. David-Weill), the only relatively complete book written on papyrus which has been preserved.

Outside Egypt, there have been few discoveries of papyri. In Palestine some 600 pieces were found (including about a dozen in Arabic) in the course of British excavations conducted at ʿAwd̲j̲āʾ al-Ḥafīr in 1936-7, and a few other texts, which Grohmann has published, were discovered by Bedouins in the cave of K͟hirbet el-Mird.

Collections, of varying degrees of importance, have thus been gradually assembled in both the eastern and the western world. In the East, it is the Cairo collection which is the most important; in the former Khedival Library (currently the Dār al-Kutub), some 2,000 pieces are to be found: papyri, parchments, papers, a few ostraca and a rare fragment of a wooden tablet. The founder of this collection was B. Moritz, director of the afore-mentioned Library from 1896 to 1914 (with reference to this collection, see B. Moritz, *Arabische Schrift/Arabic script*; Grohmann, *Einführung*, 36 ff.; R.G. Khoury, *Papyruskunde*, 253-54). But it is Grohmann who deserves the greatest credit for his study of these papyrological materials, devoting to them a series of ten volumes, the first six of which were published in his lifetime, while the four final volumes remain in manuscript form (see Grohmann, *APEL*).

In America, most worthy of mention is the University of Chicago, where the Oriental Institute has assembled, since 1929, a collection comprising numerous documents, in particular historical, literar and Ḳurʾānic texts. Chiefly responsible for th publication of these was Nabia Abbott (see *Bibl.*). A the Library of the University of Michigan (Ann Ar bor) there are also a few pieces, and the same applie to the Museum of the University of Philadelphia Other small collections exist, which have not bee catalogued or which are not sufficiently well known t have attracted academic interest.

In Europe, as in the world at large, by far the mos important collection is that of the National Library o Vienna, which owes its success to "a very thoroug collaboration" between the merchant Theodor Gra (on his visits to Cairo), the director of the Library Joseph von Karabacek, a papyrologist in his own righ (see *Bibl.*) and the already-mentioned Archduk Rainer. Currently, it contains more than 50,00 pieces and fragments, including more than 10,00 papyri, 340 parchments, some thirty thousan papers, 33 pieces of cloth, a text on bone and te ostraca. Not included in this list are all those item which have yet to be classified and made available t scholars, as well as countless fragments. Karabace and Grohmann have studied several hundreds o these, in various forms, as have, more recently Khoury, W. Diem and Y. Rāg͟hib (Ragheb) (se *Bibl.*).

In Germany, numerous collections exist: in Giessen, and especially in Hamburg where A. Dietrich has conscientiously published various letter or documents (see *Bibl.*), and also in Berlin (formerl East Berlin), where there is an important collection consisting primarily of business letters and a variety o documents, some of which have been studied by Grohmann, Khoury and Rāg͟hib. Particular importance is attached to the Heidelberg collection, which contains some rare and particularly precious items: (1) the most important collection of administrative correspondence, dating from the year 91/710, of Ḳurra b. S͟harīk [*q.v.*], Umayyad governor of Egypt, which has been published by C.H. Becker (see Becker, *PSR* I, and *Arabische Papyri*); (2) the oldest existing version of the life of the Prophet Muḥammad (*Mag͟hāzī*) and the story of King David (*Ḥadīt͟h Dāwūd*); and (3) the only papyrus scroll preserved from the entirety of Arab-Islamic culture. (Khoury has published all these texts; see *Wahb b. Munabbih* with reference to the first two, and *ʿAbd Allāh b. Lahīʿa*, for the third.) This collection, known as *PSR* (Papyri Schott-Reinhardt), in memory of the collector and patron Schott, who purchased a large proportion of the material and then presented it to the University of Heidelberg, also contains a variety of other texts, letters of all kinds, etc. (with regard to publications relating to these categories, see E. Seidel; Grohmann, *CPR*; K. Jahn; Dietrich, *Zum Drogenhandel*, also, most relevant to this article, in particular, Diem, *Arabische Briefe*).

In France, in the Louvre and in Strasbourg, there are hundreds of contracts and letters of all kinds, including texts or fragments of texts belonging to the celebrated correspondence of the governor Ḳurra b. S͟harīk. J. David-Weill began the systematic study of these collections, in particular that of the Louvre (see *Bibl.*) and this work has been continued by Cl. Cahen and most notably Rāg͟hib, who has edited two unpublished letters of Ḳurra b. S͟harīk and has undertaken, with considerable success, to classify series of papyri according to common central themes (see *Bibl.*).

In England, there is a small but valuable collection in the British Museum, and another, of equal impor-

.nce, in the John Rylands Library at Manchester; ıe Bodleian Library of Oxford holds about a hundred ·xts, to which more have recently been added.

In Italy, there are a few items in Milan and in lorence. In addition, Arabic pieces have come to ght from time to time almost everywhere: in Oslo, stanbul, Geneva and, in particular, St. Petersburg nd Moscow. Prague also has about a thousand agments. There exist, besides these, many other braries which hold Arabic papyri, as well as private ɔllections, often unknown to the academic communi- /; not only here, but especially in the important col- :ctions mentioned above, in the East and in the Vest, there is an enormous quantity of material to be lassified, examined and studied, which cannot be tilised until it has been treated and placed at the isposal of specialists. All these items need to be close- / examined, as has been done, for example, in Vien- ıa, Heidelberg and elsewhere, with the object, first of ll, of saving the pieces from destruction; they can hen be subjected to the appropriate scientific crutiny.

It is unnecessary to stress the importance of papyri or the study of Arabic paleography and orthography, n spite of the fact that it is possible only to trace in art the history of these two auxiliary disciplines and o give examples of the possible methods of writing. Iowever, since papyri constitute the preferred mate- ial for writing used in the period before the prolifera- ion of paper, documents on papyrus have acquired a re-eminent importance, not only in the two areas ust mentioned, but also, and especially, in that of the Arabic language: scrutiny of such documents does not elate exclusively to the study of certain particular philological phenomena, such as, for example, the history of Ḳurʾānic vocabulary, an area in which fragments on papyrus are very numerous (see especially the analysis of Abbott, *The rise,* 60-91), but also to the study of classical Arabic of the first three centuries of the Islamic calendar, as has been shown by S. Hopkins (*Studies in the grammar*...). Furthermore, it is clear that papyri afford considerable interest to scholars of the later centuries of the Arabic language, in particular the language of the Middle Ages (for more detail on this point, see Grohmann, *Einführung*, 88 ff.; Khoury, *Papyruskunde*, 263-68; G. Endress, *Herkunft und Entwicklung der arabischen Schrift*, in *GAP*, i, 165-97; and *Handschriftenkunde*, in *ibid.*, 271-96). This is to say nothing of the sometimes unique value of much of the testimony, authentic and usually dated, supplied by the papyri, of which more will be said in due course.

Particularly interesting are those documents which may be classified as texts of protocols, official or private documents:

(1) *Protocols*. As early as the Byzantine period, for example, the start of each scroll was usually introduced by an official formula or protocol (πρωτόκολλον). The Arabs borrowed this method at a quite early stage, no doubt from the Byzantines: this is attested for the first time (among the texts currently available) in a bilingual text found at ʿAwdjāʾ al-Ḥafīr and bearing the date Dhu 'l-Ḳaʿda 54/674. Around 105/724 the unilingual genre began to replace the bilingual.

(2) *Official and private documents*. Unfortunately the number of official documents available is too small to permit close study of the functioning of Islamic institutions in the early years. In the majority of cases one is at the mercy of later historians and scholars, who have not always left a reliable picture of preceding periods; this fact has been definitively established by the celebrated correspondence of the above-mentioned governor of Egypt, Ḳurra b. Sharīk (90-5/709-14). All of the important elements of this correspondence published so far (Becker, *PSR*, i; Abbott, *The Ḳurrah papyri*; Rāghib, *Lettres nouvelles*), show him in a quite different light to his received image: equitable, zealous for the public good, resolute, etc. These administrative letters are all the more important in that they constitute a source of a unique kind, and that nothing comparable regarding the other Islamic provinces has survived in original and authentic form. We thus remain dependent on these letters, which are of considerable elegance, concerning the functioning of the administration of the earliest Islamic periods.

It is appropriate to draw attention to the opening of these letters, which usually begin with the *basmala*, followed by the name of the governor, who is himself the sender, and that of the addressee of his letter. The final formula *al-salām ʿalā man ittabaʿa 'l-hudā* ("peace be upon him who follows the Guidance") accompanies every letter written by a Muslim to a non-Muslim; in general, and notably in the correspondence under consideration here, the letter concludes with the name of the scribe and the date of composition (concerning such usages, see for example, al-Ṣūlī, *Adab al-kuttāb*, 225; al-Ḳalḳashandī, *Ṣubḥ*, vi, 344, 366). Other official letters, of equal rarity and of no less worth, do not contain, for the reasons stated above, the above formula but conclude with the classical phrase *wa 'l-salām ʿalayka wa-raḥmat Allāh* ("may peace be upon you, and the mercy of God"), before introducing the name of the scribe and the date of the letter.

As for private documents, these concern official or strictly private relations between individuals: marriage, divorce, purchase, sale, complaints and legal proceedings of all kinds, etc. Grohmann undertook in his *CPR* (see *Allgemeine Einführung*, 17-88), and subsequently in his *Einführung*, 107-30, a study of the theory of diplomatic study (*Urkundenlehre*) of the papyri. The form of these documents varies to some degree according to the content: ratification of a marriage contract, simple business contract, receipt concerning a sum of money received or outstanding, business letter, etc. In spite of the efforts made in this area, by Grohmann, Jahn and others, a comprehensive account of the theory of diplomatic has yet to be written. For such a project it would be necessary to examine the maximum possible number of papyri and to compare all the documents which bear a resemblance, close or distant, to others, first within the Arab-Islamic culture, subsequently in the neighbouring civilisations (Byzantine, Coptic), from which Islam profited in this respect.

The value of the various documents of papyrus cannot be over-stressed, value for the study not only of purely philological problems, but in particular of those relating to the administration and the social and private life of the early Islamic centuries in general, all the more so since this type of source is authentic, and often unique in its original authenticity. This opens the way to more reliable methods of scientific investigation and constitutes a firm basis for further, more thorough studies.

Bibliography: N. Abbott, *An Arabic papyrus in the Oriental Institute, Stories of the Prophets*, in *JNES*, v (1946), 169-80; eadem, *Arabic marriage contracts among Copts*, in *ZDMG*, xcv (1941), 59-81; eadem, *Arabic palaeography, The development of early Islamic scripts*, in *Ars Islamica*, viii (1941), 65-104; eadem, *Arabic papyri of the reign of Ǧaʿfar al-Mutawakkil ʿalā llāh*, in *ZDMG*, xcii (1938), 88-135; eadem, *Studies in Arabic literary papyri I, Historical texts*, Chicago 1957; II, *Qurʾānic commentary and tradition*, 1967; III, *Language and literature*, 1972 (The University of Chicago Or. Inst. Publications, 75-7); eadem, *The Ḳurrah papyri from Aphrodito in the Oriental Institute*, Chicago 1938 (The University of Chicago Or. Inst. Studies in Anc. Or. Civil., 15); eadem, *The monasteries of the Fayyum*, Chicago 1957 (*ibid.*, 16); eadem, *The rise of the North Arabic script and its Ḳurʾānic developement with a full description of the Ḳurʾān manuscripts in the Oriental Institute*, Chicago 1939 (1st series, 50); M. Adda, *Les collections de papyri arabes du Louvre*, in *La Revue du Louvre et des Musées de France*, 1978, 69-72; C.H. Becker, *Arabische Papyri des Aphroditofundes*, in *ZA*, xx (1907), 68-104; idem, *Beiträge zur Geschichte Ägyptens unter dem Islam*, 1-2, Strasbourg 1902-3; idem, *Neue arabische Papyri des Aphroditofundes*, in *Isl.*, ii (1911), 245-68; idem, *Papyri Schott-Reinhardt* I (= *PSR* I), Heidelberg 1906; idem, *Papyrusstudien*, in *ZA*, xxii (1909), 137-54; Cl. Cahen, *Information sur des travaux de papyrologie arabe entrepris par M. Cl. Cahen*, in *Académie des Inscriptions et Belles-Lettres, Comptes rendus* (Nov.-Dec. 1977), 680-5; idem (with Y. Ragheb and M.A. Taher), *L'achat et le waqf d'un grand domaine égyptien*, in *Annales Islamologiques*, xiv (1978), 59-126; idem, *Makhzūmiyyāt, Études sur l'histoire économique et financière de l'Égypte médiévale*, Leiden 1977; H. Cadell, *Recherches de papyrologie*, i-iv, Paris 1961-7; J. David-Weill, *Contrat de travail au pair, papyrus Louvre 7348*, in *Etudes d'orientalisme dédiées à la mémoire de Lévi-Provençal*, Leiden 1962, 509-15; idem, *Le Djâmiʿ d'Ibn Wahb*, 2 vols., Cairo 1939-48 (*PIFAOC*); idem, *Papyrus arabes du Louvre*, i-ii, in *JESHO*, viii (1965), 277-311, xiv (1971) 1-24; iii (idem, with Cl. Cahen *et alii*), *ibid.*, xxi (1978), 146-64; W. Diem, *Arabische Briefe auf Papyrus und Papier der Heidelberger Papyrussammlung*, Wiesbaden 1991; idem, *Der Gouverneur an den Pagarchen; ein verkannter Papyrus vom Jahre 65 der Hiǧra*, in *Isl.*, lx (1983), 104-11; idem, *Einige frühe amtliche Urkunden aus der Sammlung Papyrus Erzh. Rainer*, in *Le Muséon*, xcvii (1984), 109-58; idem, *Philologisches zu den arabischen Aphrodito-Papyri*, in *Isl.*, lxi (1984), 251-75; idem, *Vier Dienstschreiben an ʿAmmār. Ein Beitrag zur arabischen Papyrologie*, in *ZDMG*, cxxxiii (1983), 239-62; A. Dietrich, *Arabische Briefe aus der Papyrussammlung der Hamburger Staats- und Universitäts-Bibliothek*, Hamburg 1955; idem, *Arabische Papyri aus der Hamburger Staats- und Universitäts-Bibliothek*, Leipzig 1937; idem, *Die arabischen Papyri des Topkapı Sarayı-Museums in Istanbul*, in *Isl.*, xxxiii (1958), 37-50; idem, *Die arabischen Urkunden*, in *Zeitschrift für Vergleichende Rechtswissenschaft*, lx (1957), 211-37; idem, *Eine Eheurkunde aus der Aiyūbidenzeit*; in *Documenta islamica inedita*, Berlin 1952, 121-54; idem, *Zum Drogenhandel im islamischen Ägypten. Eine Studie über die arabische Handschrift Nr. 912 der Heidelberger Papyrus-Sammlung*, Heidelberg 1954; *Festschrift zum 100-Jährigen Bestehen der Papyrussammlung der Österreichischen Nationalbibliothek. Papyrus Erzherzog Rainer*, 2 vols., Vienna 1983; G. Frantz-Murphy, *Saving and investment in medieval Egypt*, diss. Univ. of Michigan 1978; unpubl.; eadem, *A comparison of the Arabic and earlier Egyptian contract formularies*, Part I, *The Arabic contracts from Egypt (3d/9th-5th/11th centuries)*, in *Arabic and Islamic studies in honor of N. Abbott*, *JNES*, xl (1981), 203-25; eadem, *A new interpretation of the economic history of medieval Egypt. The role of the textile industry 254-567/868-1171*, in *JESHO*, xxiv (1981), 274-97; eadem, *The agrarian administration of Egypt from the Arabs to the Ottomans*, Cairo 1986 (Suppl to *AI*, ix); A. Grohmann, *Allgemeine Einführung in die arabischen Papyri, nebst Grundzügen der arabischen Diplomatik*, Vienna 1924 (*CPR*, iii, 1); idem, *Aperçu de papyrologie arabe*, in *Etudes de papyrologie 1*, Cairo 1932, 23-95; idem, *Arabic papyri from Ḫirbet el-Mird*, Louvain 1963; idem, *APEL = Arabic papyri in the Egyptian Library*, i-vi, Cairo 1934-61; idem, *Arabische Chronologie*, in *Handb. d. Or.*, Leiden-Cologne 1966; idem, *Arabische Paläographie*, i, ii, Vienna 1967, 1971; idem, *Arabische Papyri aus den Staatl. Museen zu Berlin*, in *Isl.*, xxii (1934), 1-68; idem, *Arabische Papyri aus der Sammlung Carl Wessly im Or. Institute zu Prag*, in *Arch. Or.*, x (1938), 149-62, xi (1940), 242-89, xii (1941), 1-85, 99-112, xiv (1943), 161-260; idem, *Arabische Papyruskunde*, in *Handb. d. Or.*, Leiden-Cologne 1966; idem, *CPR = Corpus Papyrorum Raineri Archiducis Austriae*, iii, Ser. Arab. i/1, *Allgemeine Einführung* (see above), i/2, Protokolle, Vienna 1924; idem, *Die arabischen Papyri aus der Gießener Universitätsbibliothek. Mit Beiträgen von F. Heichelheim*, Gießen 1960; idem, *Edizione di testi arabi*, in A. Vogliano, *Publicazioni della Università di Milano. Papiri della R. Università di Milano*, i, Florence 1937, ²1966, 241-69; idem, *Ein Qorra-Brief vom Jahre 90 a.H.*, in *Aus fünf Jahrtausenden morgenländischer Kultur. Festschrift Max Freiherr von Oppenheim*, Berlin 1933, 37-40; idem, *Einführung und Chrestomathie zur arabischen Papyruskunde, I Einführung*, Prague 1954; idem, *Einige bemerkenswerte Urkunden aus der Sammlung der Papyrus Erzherzog Rainer an der Nationalbibliothek zu Wien*, in *Arch. Or.*, xviii/3 (1950), 80-119; idem, *From the world of Arabic papyri, with a foreword by Prof. Shafik Ghorbal-Bey*, Cairo 1952; idem, *Probleme der arabischen Papyrusforschung*, in *Arch. Or.*, iii (1931), 381-94; v (1933), 273-83; vi (1934), 125-49, 377-98; idem, *Zum Papyrusprotokoll in frühislamischer Zeit*, in *Jahrbücher der Österreichischen Byzantinischen Gesellschaft*, ix, Graz-Cologne 1960, 1-19 (see also under R.G. Khoury); *GAP = Grundriß der arabischen Philologie*, i, ed. W. Fischer, Wiesbaden 1982; S. Hopkins, *Studies in the grammar of early Arabic. Based upon papyri datable to before 300 A.H./912 A.D.*, Oxford 1984; K. Jahn, *Vom frühislamischen Briefwesen. Studien zur islamischen Epistolographie der ersten drei Jahrhunderte der Hiǧra aufgrund der arabischen Papyri*, in *Arch. Or.*, ix (1937), 153-200; J. Karabacek, *Ägyptische Urkunden aus den Königl. Museen zu Berlin*, in *WZKM*, xi (1897), 1-21; idem, *Das arabische Papier*, in *Mitteilungen aus der Sammlung der Papyrus Erzherzog Rainer II-III*, Vienna 1887, 87-178; idem, *Der Papyrusfund von el-Faijûm*, in *Denkschriften der Kaiserl. Akademie der Wissenschaften, Phil.-hist. Classe*, xxxiii, Vienna 1883, 207-42; idem, *Papyrus Erzherzog Rainer. Führer durch die Ausstellung*, Vienna 1894; R.G. Khoury, *ʿAbd Allāh Ibn Lahīʿa (97-174/715-790), juge et grand maître de l'École Égyptienne. Avec édition critique de l'unique rouleau de papyrus arabe conservé à Heidelberg*, Wiesbaden 1986 (*CAA = Cod. Arab. Antiqui*, IV); idem, *(arab.) Papyruskunde*, in *GAP*, i, 251-70; idem, *Bemerkungen zu einigen arabischen Papyri aus der Wiener Sammlung und der Chester Beatty Library*, in *Festschrift zum 100-Jährigen Bestehen der Papyrussammlung der Österr. Nationalbibliothek* (see above), Vienna 1983, 113-120; idem, *Chrestomathie de papyrologie arabe. Documents relatifs à la vie privée, sociale et administrative dans les premiers siècles islamiques*, préparée par A. Grohmann, retravaillée et élargie par R.G. Khoury, Leiden 1993 (*Handb. d. Or.*); idem, *Papyrologische Studien zum privaten und gesellschaftlichen*

Leben in den ersten islamischen Jahrhunderten, vorbereitet von A. Grohmann, neu bearbeitet und erweitert von R.G. Khoury, Wiesbaden 1994 (*CAA*, V); idem, *Die Bedeutung der arabischen literarischen Papyri von Heidelberg für die Erforschung der klassischen Sprache und Kulturgeschichte im Frühislam*, in *Heidelberger Jahrbücher*, xix (1975), 24-39; idem, *Die ältesten erhaltenen historischen und administrativen Zeugnisse des Islam: Arabische Raritäten der Heidelberger Papyrussammlung*, in *Jahrbuch der Heidelberger Akademie der Wissenschaften für 1985*, Heidelberg 1986, 127-32; idem, *Al-Layth ibn Saʿd (94/713-175/791), grand maître et mécène de l'Égypte, vu à travers quelques documents islamiques anciens*, in *Arabic and Islamic studies in honor of Nabia Abbott*, in *JNES*, xl/3 (1981), 189-202; idem, *Les légendes prophétiques dans l'Islam depuis le Ier jusqu'au IIIe siècle de l'Hégire d'après le manuscrit d'Abū Rifāʿa ʿUmāra b. Waṯīma al-Fārisī: Kitāb Badʾ al-ḫalq wa-qiṣaṣ al-anbiyāʾ*, avec éd. critique du texte, Wiesbaden 1978 (*CAA*, III); idem, *Quelques remarques supplémentaires concernant le papyrus de Wahb b. Munabbih*, in *BSOAS*, xl (1977), 15-24; idem, *Wahb b. Munabihh. 1. Der Heidelberger Papyrus PSR Heid. Arab. 23. Leben und Werk des Dichters*, (= ed. of the *Maghāzī* and of the Story of David, with German tr. and monograph on Wahb). 2. *Faksimiletafeln*, Wiesbaden 1972 (*CAA*, I); M.J. Kister, *Notes on the papyrus text about Muḥammad's campaign against the Banū al-Naḍīr*, in *Arch. Or.*, xxxii (1964), 233-6; idem, *On the papyrus of Wahb b. Munabbih*, in *BSOAS*, xxxvii (1974), 547-71; H. Lammens, *Un gouverneur omaiyade d'Égypte Qorra ibn Šarîk d'après les papyrus arabes*, in *BIE*, 5th Series, ii (1908), 99-115; H. Loebenstein (ed.), *Koranfragmente auf Pergament aus der Papyrussammlung der Österreichischen Nationalbibliothek*, Vienna 1982; O. Loth, *Zwei arabische Papyrus*, in *ZDMG*, xxxiv (1880), 685-91; D.S. Margoliouth and E.J. Holmyard, *Arabic documents from the Monneret Collection*, in *Islamica*, iv (1930), 249-71; idem, *Arabic papyri in the Bodleian Library reproduced by the collotype process with transcription and translation*, London 1893; idem, *Catalogue of Arabic papyri in the John Rylands Library Manchester*, Manchester 1933; Y. Ragheb/Rāġib, *Contrat d'affermage d'un pressoir à huile en 205/821*, in *S Ir, Mélanges offerts à R. Curiel*, xi (1982), 293-99; idem, *Lettres arabes*, i, in *AI*, xiv (1978), 15-35; ii, in *ibid.*, xvi (1980), 1-29; idem, *Lettres nouvelles de Qurra b. Šarīk*, in *Arabic and Islamic studies in honor of N. Abbott, JNES*, xl/3 (1981), 173-87; idem, *Marchands d'étoffes du Fayyoum au IIIe/IXe siècle d'après leurs archives (actes et lettres)*, i, *Les actes des Banū ʿAbd al-Muʾmin*, in *Suppl. aux Annales Islamol.*, Cahier 2, Cairo 1982; II, *La correspondance administrative et privée des Banū ʿAbd al-Muʾmin*, in *ibid.*, Cahier 5, 1985; III, *Lettres des Banū Ṭawr aux Banū ʿAbd al-Muʾmin*, in *ibid.*, Cahier 14, 1992 (vols. on other themes are envisaged); idem, *Pour un renouveau de la papyrologie arabe. Comment rassembler les archives dispersés de l'Islam médiéval*, in *Académie des Inscriptions et Belles-Lettres, comptes rendus*, Paris 1984, 68-77; idem, *Quatre papyrus arabes d'Edfou*, *AI*, xiv (1978), 1-14; idem, *Trois documents datés du Louvre*, *ibid.*, xv (1979), 1-9; idem, *Un contrat de mariage sur soie d'Égypte fatimide*, *ibid.*, xvi (1980), 31-7 (see also Cahen); E. Seidel, *Medizinisches aus den Heidelberger Papyri Schott-Reinhardt*, in *Isl.*, i (1910), 145-52, 238-68; ii (1911), 220-30; iii (1912), 273-91; A.I. Silvestre de Sacy, *Mémoire sur quelques papyrus écrits en arabe et récemment découverts en Égypte*, in *Journal des Savants* (1825), 462-73, and *Mémoires de l'Institut Royal de France, Acad. des Inscriptions et Belles-Lettres*, ix (1831), 66-85. (R.G. Khoury)

PARA (Gk. Paros), Turkish name of an important Aegean Cycladic island, west of Naḳshe and north-east of the once-attached Antiparos (1981 pop.: 8,516), celebrated since Antiquity for its marble, still popular in the 15th century according to the Italian travellers Buondelmonti (ed. Legrand, 53 ff.) and Cyriacus of Ancona (cf. Miller-Lampros [= M-L], ii, 380, 397), and rich in Byzantine, post-Byzantine and Catholic (Capuchin) monuments. The Byzantine period (to 1207) saw the island's incorporation in the Aegean maritime theme after *ca.* 843 (see Malamut, *Les îles...*, 47 ff., s.v. Paros, Paronaxia), as well as several Arab raids, due to its strategic position in Aegean sea routes (see naḳshe), mostly from the amīrate of Iḳrīṭish [*q.v.*] in the 9th-10th centuries, chief among them being those of 837, directed by Nis(i)r and associated with legendary St. Theoctiste of Lesbos, who died on the island (872), and of 904, directed by the renegade conqueror of Thessalonica [see selānik], Leo of Tripoli; the devastations of such raids are vividly recorded in the *Vita S. Theoctistae* (see Christides, *Conquest of Crete*, 6, 166-7, 211 ff.; Malamut, 109, 112, 136, 142-3, 269, 401 and s.v.; more refs. in A. Savvides, *Notes on Naxos and Paros-Antiparos* [in Gk.], in *Pariana*, xlii [1991], 227-37).

Turkish raids began within the intricate period of the Archipelago Duchy (1207-1566), when successive Latin families strove for power; Naḳshe, Para and Antiparos were ravaged by Turcoman and Christian corsairs from the early 15th century, to the effect that the Loredani fortified the Antiparian capital "Kastron" and the Sommaripae transferred the Parian capital from Paroikiā, on the north-west, to the eastern fortress of Kēphalos, following an Ottoman raid of 1490 (M-L, ii, 372, 381; Pitcher, 67; Krantonelle, 50, 379, n. 114, 400, 437, 443). The first Ottoman raid against Para was led by admiral Čalī Bey at the head of the Gelibolu fleet and was caused by the Archipelago Duke's failure to greet sultan Meḥemmed I at Izmīr as master of the western Anatolian coast; extensive looting was followed by the abduction of many Parians (Ducas, ed. Bonn, 109; Critobulus, ed. Reinsch, 92; cf. M-L, ii, 371; Krantonelle, 25, 192, 257, 400; Uzunçarşılı, *Osmanlı tarihi*, ii[5], 1988, 30; Melas, 10), yet subsequent treaties (1419, 1426, 1446, 1454) acknowledged Venetian overlordship over the Duchy. Bāyezīd II's 1490 raid aimed at the Duke Sommaripa's overthrow, but the Venetian Admiral Capello hindered the Ottoman expedition (M-L, ii, 394), while the information that extensive ravages took place in that raid is to be taken with reservations (Th. and N. Aliprantes, *Paros-Antiparos*[2], 48-9, 168). Being a base for western espionage against the Sultanate in the early 16th century made Para one of the targets of Khayr al-Dīn Pasha [*q.v.*] in the latter's Cycladic raids; its last ruler, Sagredo, surrendered Kēphalos fortress (Dec. 1537) and 6,000 Parians and Antiparians suffered massacre, the young men ending up as oarsmen in the Pasha's vessels and young girls entering his harem, apart from many spoils (see naḳshe; cf. M-L, ii, 404, 406, 407 ff.; Pitcher, 138 and map XIV; Vakalopoulos, iii, 151 and map; Krantonelle, 142, 160, 206, 405; Slot, *The Turkish conquest of the Cyclades*, 1537-8 [in Gk.], in *Kimoliaka*, vii [1978], 62 ff.; idem, *Archipelagus*, 73 ff.; Frazee, 83, 90, 253; M. Roussos-Melidones, in *Pariana*, xxxvi, [1990], 20 ff. [acc. to W. sources]). Ottoman control was ratified by the 1540 treaty, which allowed for semi-autonomy under a *ḳapudan pasha*, while a semblance of Latin power continued until the eventual annexation of 1566 (see Th. and N. Aliprantes, 49-50, 66 ff., 156, 168-9); the local influential families were also directly involved in the island's affairs, predominantly the Kondylai and the Mavrogenai (see Th. Blancard, *Les Mavrogeni*, Paris 1909; cf. *Pariana*, xviii [1985], 71 ff. [Mavroi]; xxvi [1987], 113 ff. [Sphaelloi]; xxxvi [1909], 95 ff. [Desyllai]; also refs. in N. Aliprantes, in *DEGEE*, v [1985], 42-119 [on families and coats of arms]).

After the Jewish Duke Nasi's death in 1579 [see NAḲSHE], extensive privileges were granted by Murād III (*ʿahd-nāme* of 1580, renewed by Ibrāhīm in 1646, shortly after the ravages against Para in 1645-6) (cf. Zinkeisen, iv, 766; Vakalopoulos, iii, 491, 502, n. 2; Polemis, *Hist. of Andros*, 74-5, 80-1); Naḳshe became the seat of the Cycladic *sandjak*, enjoying privileges until the early 19th century, while Para was to suffer from incessant piratical raids in the course of the Turco-Venetian wars of the 16th-17th centuries (Vakalopoulos, ii², 139, n. 39, 144 ff.; iii, 503; iv, 134 and map, 192, 198; N. Kephalleniades, in *Pariana*, xiv-xv [1984]; Krantonelle, 35, 49, 60, 121, 176, 241-5, 290, 357, 405 and s.v. Paros). Meanwhile, the first waves of Capuchins and Jesuits established themselves on Para, particularly on its northern fortified harbour of Naoussa (cf. Vakalopoulos, ii², 148; iii, 404 ff.; iv, 120 ff., 132 ff.; Th. and N. Aliprantes, 53 ff., 170). Ottoman fleets used to collect *kharādj* annually from Naoussa and Dryo ports, and it was off Dryo that the Venetian Admiral Mocenigo scored a spectacular victory over the Ottomans bringing succour to the besiegers of Crete in mid-1651 or 1652, capturing 5,000 Turks (Muṣṭafā Naʿīmā, v, 98 ff.; Sathas, *Turkish-dominated Greece*, 263-4; Vakalopoulos, ii², 141; iii, 499-500; iv, 38; cf. *Pariana*, vii [1981], 100 ff.), while in 1666 or 1668 the *ḳapudan pasha* Muṣṭafā Ḳaplan, while chasing Latin corsairs, sacked Paroikiā with 63 vessels, executing publicly the local notable Kondyles and abducting 400 Parians, and moreover pillaging the celebrated 6th-century Ekatontapylianē (= Our Lady of one hundred gates) church (cf. E. Kriaras, *The sack of Paroikiā: Cretan verses of the 17th c.* [in Gk.], *Athenā*, xlviii [1938], 120-62; Vakalopoulos, ii², 142; Th. and N. Aliprantes, 51-2, 53 ff.); meanwhile, the Turco-Venetian war in Crete brought waves of Cretan refugees on Para, which was terrorised by the "Saldar" of Aḳ Deñiz (= Aegean) in 1674; in 1676-7 another Ottoman fleet, in chase of western pirates, landed at Naoussa and looted it (cf. Vakalopoulos, ii², 145-6).

From the late 17th century local administration was carried out by a *voivode*, 2 annual *ḳodja-bashī*s and a *ḳāḍī*. In *ca.* 1700, however, the French traveller Tournefort records that the local magnate Constantine Kondyles secured the Porte's favour and became acting *voivode*, to be accused of harbouring pirates and overthrown by the *ḳapudan pasha* Djānīm Khodja, who had him executed (1716); these developments caused new waves of refugees to Smyrna (Vakalopoulos, iv, 148-9, 446, 448, 482; V. Sphyroeras, in *Mikrasiatika Chronika*, x, 1963, 172 ff.; Mathiopoulos, 27 ff.; *Pariana*, xvl [1991], 73 ff.). In the course of the first Turco-Russian war (1668-74), the Russian fleet under admirals Orlov and Svyridov seized Naḳshe, Para and Antiparos, using Naoussa as their base until 1774, when ousted by the Ottomans according to the Küčük Ḳaynardja treaty [*q.v.*], before materialising their plan to sell Para-Antiparos to the British or French (cf. testimony of the Dutch Pasch van Krienen, in Sathas, 516-17, 520; Vakalopoulos, iv, 412 ff.). There ensued hard decades for the Parians, whose penury is vividly depicted in their 1820 petition to the *ḳapudan pasha*; yet both Parians and Antiparians were among the first islanders to join the 1821 Greek War for Independence, with distinguished personalities, like Demetrakopoulos, Delagramates and the legendary heroine Manto Mavrogenous (E. Konstantinou, *Parian fighters for independence*, and *Cycladian fighters for independence*, Athens 1985; cf. Vakalopoulos, v, 406 ff.; vi, 515-16, 718-19 and s.v.; vii, 384, 726, 811 ff.; cf. *Pariana*, xvi-xvii [1984-5]; xxx [1988], 145 ff.; xxxvii [1990], 71 ff. [all in Gk.]). In the course of the uprising, both islands suffered from domestic pirates [see NAḲSHE], until incorporated into the newly-founded Greek Kingdom between 1830-2 (cf. Roussos-Melidones, in *Paria-na*, xxx [1988], 152 ff.). A most interesting case of Christianisation of an ex-Muslim Turkish woman is recorded in 1823 (see *Pariana*, x [1982], 106 ff.), the same year of the Maltese Knights' abortive attempt to purchase Naḳshe, Para and Antiparos from the temporary Greek government (Vakalopoulos, vi, 486).

Bibliography: See references in NAḲSHE; older references in D. Moustakas-D. Paschales, *Paros*, in *MEE*, xix, 742-4 and G. Georgalas-D. Moustakas-C. Karamanos, *Antiparos*, in *MEE*, iv, 914-5 (fundamental); general accounts [in Gk.]: P. Mathiopoulos, *Paros, an historical island in the heart of the Aegean*, Athens 1963; D. Sophianou, C. Georgousses *et alii*, *Hist. of Paros and Antiparos*, Municipality of Paros 1989; comprehensive Parian bibliographies in the following in Gk.: Th. and N. Aliprantes, *Paros-Antiparos*, Athens 1968² (with detailed chronology); N. Aliprantes, *ibid.*, rev. ed., 1978³ (with Engl. appx. on Ekatontapylianē [Katapolianē] church by Th. Aliprantes); *The toponymics of Paros*, 1990 (fundamental); J. Kampanelles, *The holy metropolis of Paronaxia through the ages*, 1991. On Parian-Antiparian fortifications [in Gk.]: M. Philippa-Apostolou, *The castle of Antiparos. A contribution to the study of medieval fortified settlements in the Aegean*, 1978, unpubl. diss.; J. Gikas, *Castles-voyages in Greece*, ii, 1981, 181-93, 194-9; on Buondelmonti's 15th-century description, cf. J. Melas, *The Cyclades in the early 15th c.*, in *Kykladika*, i/1 (1959), 9-21, esp. 17-18 (Paros-Antiparos-Naxos). Various important articles [in Gk.] in *EEKM*, i-xi, 1960-84 (mostly by D. Paschales), and *Pariana*, i-xli (1980-91); other contributions (esp. on the Turkish period) include N. Aliprantes, *Unedited Parian documents of the Turkish domination*, in *Athenā*, lxxv (1974-5), 95-119; *Clerics of Paros during Turkish domination*, in *Ekklesiastike Rizareios Paideia*, ii, 1980, 503-23; B. Sphyroeras, *The dragomans of the fleet*, 1965; *Greek crews of the Turkish fleet*, 1965; H. Koukkou, *Communal institutions in Cyclades during Turkish domination*, i-ii, 1980-9; T. Gritsopoulos, *Paronaxian episcopal affairs of the 17th c.*, in *EEKM*, xiii (1985-90), 203-44 [all in Gk.]. (A. SAVVIDES)

PĀRA (P. "piece, fragment"), a Turkish coin of the Ottoman and early Republican periods. It was originally a silver piece of 4 *aḳče*s, first issued early in the 18th century; it soon replaced the *aḳče* as the monetary unit. The weight, originally 16 grains (1.10 grammes), sank to one-quarter of this weight by the beginning of the 19th century and the silver content also depreciated considerably. The multiples of the silver *pāra* were 5 (*beshlik*) *pāra*s; 10 (*onliḳ*); 15 (*onbeshlik*); 20 (*yigirmiparalīḳ*); 30 (*zolota*) and 40 (*ghurūsh* or piastre). Higher denominations: 60 (*altmīshlīḳ*); 80 (*ikilik*, i.e. two piastres); and 100 (*yüzlik*) *pāra*s were occasionally issued.

In the new Medjidiyye currency of 1260/1844, the *pāra* became a small copper coin with multiples 5 (*beshpāralīḳ*), 10 (*onpāralīḳ*), 20 (*yigirmipāralīḳ*) and 40 (*ghurūsh*). In the later years of the Ottoman empire, the larger copper pieces were replaced by nickel. The āra under the republic was a money of account, the 00 *pāra* or 2½ piastre piece of aluminium bronze eing the smallest denomination issued. With the ost-World War II inflation, the *pāra* eventually lisappeared from use in Turkey; in present-day Turkey, *para* has acquired, by a process of semantic volution akin to that of Arabic *fulūs* [see FALS], the eneral meaning of "money".

When Serbia became independent, it retained the ame *pāra* for its smallest coin, as did Montenegro lso. The name survived in the former Yugoslavia luring the interwar period, where the nickel 50 *pāra* iece was the smallest coin issued. During the Russian ccupation of Moldavia and Wallachia in 1771-4, opper coins were issued with the value in *pāras* and kopecks.

Bibliography: Lane-Poole, *Catalogue of oriental coins in the British Museum*, viii, London 1881; Belin, in *JA*, ser. 6, iii, 447-51. (J. ALLAN)

PARČĪN-KĀRĪ (P.), a technique of inlaywork used in the architecture of the Indo-Pakistan subcontinent, in Urdū *paččī-kārī*.

It is usually set in marble in a technique which reached its fullest development in Hindūstān under Djahāngīr and Shāh-Djahān in the 11th/17th century, by then as an essential element in imperial symbolism. The craft of using semi-precious stones in floral or foliate compositions in the equivalent of the Florentine *commesso di pietre dure* appears to have arisen from a long regional tradition of stone intarsia work with a stimulus from imported Florentine pieces, and possibly European craftsmen. The Tīmūrid use of faience mosaic, *kāshī-tarāshī* [*q.v.*], following a somewhat comparable development in Persia and greater Khurāsān, provided the model for compositions in specific architectural situations: it was already used extensively at Bīdar [*q.v.*] in the *madrasa* of Maḥmūd Gāwān [*q.v.*] (877/1472), under direct Persian influence, probably *via* Māhān (the plan is derived from Khargird). Although the technique of wood inlay was well known to the Tīmūrids, they had not transferred it to stone, except in marble dados inlaid with geometric networks, as at Gāzurgāh (832/1429) and Ṭaybād (848/1444) or with tesserae of stone or bisque tile and faience. Stone inlay may therefore be regarded as a medium developed in Hindūstān, whose use can be distinguished in three stages: first the use of strips or bands of contrasting stone, then the use of a more varied range of colours in geometrical compositions based on the Persian tradition of cut-brick or tile profiles (see Wulff, *op. cit.* in *Bibl.*, fig. 187), and finally the freely-drawn work in coloured stones inlaid and polished *in situ*. The origins of this third stage have been investigated since 1839, and their foreign origin disputed, but the arguments have been admirably collated, and an Italian connection clearly demonstrated, by Koch (in *Bibl.*).

The effect of contrasting marble with stone masonry was already recognised in the Afhā'ī-din-kā Djhōnpṛā mosque at Adjmēr (595/1199), where a single white *miḥrāb* with swirling scrolled carving is set against the *ḳibla* wall. A similar contrast is used for the *miḥrāb* in the mosque at Sulṭān Ghārī (629/1231) and for the *miḥrāb* and cenotaph in Iltutmish's tomb at Dihlī (*ca.* 1235). Inset marble first appears there under the Khaldjī sultanate in the ʿAlāʾī Darwāza (711/1311), where white architrave fillets, inscribed bands, lotus-bud arches, colonnettes and arched niches are deftly alternated with elements in red stone, articulated by changes in plane, and united by the imposition of a mesh of similar deeply incised carving on both. The inserts of black marble and blue schist suggest a connection with Gudjarātī work.

The vocabulary is extended in the tomb of Ghiyāth al-Dīn Tughluḳ (*ca.* 725/1325), where marble spandrels and a fretted tympanum contrast with grey panels in the red stone, and the treatment is echoed in the interior. At Dhār the *miḥrāb* of the Kamāl Mawlā Masdjid (795/1392-3) is surrounded with black and white fillets in the architrave, and in the Djāmiʿ Masdjid (Lāt Masdjid) (807/1404-5) this treatment is extended to white lines trimming the black spandrels. In the Djāmiʿ Masdjid at Aḥmadābād (827/1424), all five *miḥrāb*s are carved in carefully assorted marbles, with an open flower in coloured stones that may be the first application of true *pietre dure*. By 858/1454 contrasting marble trims to the *miḥrāb* of the Djāmiʿ Masdjid at Māndū are combined with the use of blue tile infill between the merlons of a frieze above; the trim and contrasting spandrels are repeated in the main entrance. Combinations of this kind reached a sophisticated level in the Purānā Ḳilʿa complex at Dihlī a century later, where intersecting white arches surround panels of ultramarine tile mosaic, alternately geometric and floral, with traces of turquoise green: these suggest a technique imported from Persia by Humāyūn [*q.v.*] on his return in 1555. In his Shēr Mandal (*pre*-1556) the dados at both levels outside are filled with geometric inlay, white marble stars and kite-shaped lozenges in the Iranian range of cut brick shapes set in linear rosettes of structural stone. The spandrels are trimmed with a single white line, and inlaid with a six-pointed star on either side. The internal dados, however, are of faience. At the roughly contemporary Masdjid-i Kuhna nearby, the tympanum of the central bay is filled with square and rectangular panels of this geometric inlay, framed with white strips, while the inner architrave is of successive rectangular panels inlaid with frets of white lines to form a geometric spider's web. Black outlines to the inscribed panels define *miḥrābī* cartouches which were to be used regularly thereafter. The white semidome of the *miḥrāb* is divided into sectors by a fine black trim. Use of tilework combined with stone, both in contrasting colours, continued until the mosque and tomb of ʿĪsā Khān were built in 954/1547-8.

Geometric marble set in a red stone matrix, however, gained ascendancy in the metropolitan style fostered by the harem faction under Persian influence during Akbar's [*q.v.*] minority. The elegant little tomb of Ätägä Khān (974/1566-7) at Niẓām al-Dīn has a fully Persian *pīshṭāḳ* [*q.v.*] with inlaid white geometric tesserae on both dados and spandrels, the latter alternating with smaller areas of dark blue tile and green centres. Those in the lateral panels are reticulated in black lines rather than the red background stone; yet tile mosaic is fitted to the blind arches of the western enclosure wall. Larger-scale marble inlay appears in the merlon frieze and in a display of six-pointed stars among hexagons on the drum. This appears again on the drum of Humāyūn's tomb (969/1561-2 to 1570), probably reflecting his preoccupation with astrology, and notably in stars set in the floor of the main chamber, though the exterior is trimmed only in the earlier linear style. It has been suggested by Lowry (*op. cit.* in *Bibl.*, 140-5) that the choice of red and white here refers deliberately to India's tradition under the Sultanate, in contrast to Transoxania where such stone is absent, and that the star was used to symbolise both Humāyūn and his successors. Tessellated inlay is consummated in the great mosque at Fatḥpur Sīkrī (979/1571-2), where geometric networks are used extensively on the intrados of arches and in bands framing blind arches, niches, and rectangular panels, mostly inside: again, some are set off with black lines and some with accents of faience. The main *miḥrāb* is inlaid with black and white marbles, but the lateral ones, though on the same model, vary in detail, two being set with tilework in four colours.

The transition to floral forms is marked by the southern gateway to Akbar's tomb at Sikandra (1022/1613). Though the wings are decorated with superimposed panels of geometric work, the background alternates in buff and red. The framing bands are in *bannāʾī* technique, and the spandrels carry diagonal palmettes with arabesque scrolling—both translating Tīmūrid practice into stone. The tall extrados within the *pīshṭāḳ* transforms the usual interlocking rosettes into boldly stylised petals and leaves in a sequence of giant flowers reminiscent of block-printing: black, white, and green marble are used. The scheme is repeated in the *pīshṭāḳ* of the tomb itself. In the gateways to the tomb of Iʿtimād al-Dawla (1031-7/1621-7) at Āgra the character of these features is already changed: the inlay on the extrados is intrincately laced, and the spandrel arabesques are spread more loosely but more evenly, while the side elevations are articulated with arched outlines framing vases and flasks. The tomb, wholly in white marble, astonishes by its wealth of meticulous surface ornament of polished *pietra dura* work, establishing a fully Persianate vocabulary under the aegis of Nūr Djahān [*q.v.*], and epitomising the new technique and its overall use; the inlay is in black, grey, brown, buff and white, blue accents being introduced only in the pavilion roof near the skyline. The material includes *khattū*, agate, jasper and yellow porphyry. The dados both outside and in are in continuous geometrical work, some of interlocking angular pieces. Similar panels on the upper wall outside are subdivided by plain marble fillets, with borders of countered arabesque meanders throughout, and vivaciously coiled arabesques in the spandrels. The arch reveals are decorated with grouped trees, flasks, flower-vases and cups set within outlines of niches, cartouches, and lobed roundels, the round corner towers with ovate pole-medallions. As the interior is largely painted, it is clear that this work was intended for more exposed positions. The floor of the upper chamber, however, is inlaid with swirling arabesques. It may be noted that there is little difference between the types of designs chosen and those of the faience mosaic still used to face the Čīnī-ka Rawḍā (*ca.* 1048/1638) not far away, though there floral motifs predominate: the prototypes may well have been worked out in the Pandjāb [*q.v.*], where tiles were the usual ornament, in such buildings as the Sarāy Doraha (*ca.* 1610) west of Sirhind (see Begley, *op. cit.* in *Bibl.*, pl. 6). Under the same patronage, Djahāngīr's [*q.v.*] tomb (*ca.* 1627) at Shāhdara in Lāhawr [*q.v.*] is clad outside in red and white work with the same pervasion, while the access corridor, the floor, walls and cenotaph of the tomb chamber are inlaid with *pietre dure*, including floral designs in which the petals are shaded in differing colours. The inscriptions, too, are inlaid in black marble. The work, now referred to as *parčīn-kārī* or *parčīn* in both the *ʿAmal-i Ṣāliḥ* and the *Pādshāh-nāma*, established the standards and the vocabulary used throughout Shāh Djahān's reign.

At Āgra Fort [see MAḤALL], geometrical work is no longer in evidence. The Muthamman Burdj apartments (1628-30) combine floral and arabesque inlay with floral relief carving in the marble dados, and for the first time the faceted columns are inlaid from base to scrolled brackets; even the sculpted leaves of the pool spread among inlay. The *djarōkhā* of the public audience hall (1037-46/1628-37), with three trefoil arches and a *čīnī-khāna* wall at the rear, is of a more curvilinear design, in which the convex arched soffits, the concave ceiling coving, and the swelling capitals are inlaid. The spandrel arabesques are without central palmettes, and the ceiling is articulated with foliate strapwork with sharp angles and clasps at intervals like wrought iron work. As Koch has pointed out (*op. cit.*, 20), the increasingly florid fullness in marble forms is in contrast to an increasing stylisation, slenderness, and symmetry of the floral inlay accompanying them. The deliberate choice of white marble as an image of purity was combined with a floral evocation of paradise referring to both legendary and Ḳurʾānic sources, as both inscriptions and contemporary historians consistently make clear. The developed medium thus played an essential rôle in the Mughal idea of divinely-endowed kingship. By 1045/1635 the Dawlat-khāna-yi Khāṣṣ was built with marble columns in which the inlay is differentiated between powerfully serrated leaves framing the pedestal carving, and delicately framed floral repeats in the collars; all the dados are bordered with floral strapwork of the angular type.

This répertoire is that of the Tādj Maḥall (1041-57/1632-47 [*q.v.*]). The relatively bold spandrel scrolling still centres on palmettes, or a lyre-shape, and vestigial use is made of the coarser technique of alternating chevrons for framing dados, but the work tends to incorporate tiers of paired flowers, and tendrils converted to strapwork: it is subordinate to the sculptured forms. The mosque and its counterpart continue the older red stone style, with geometric inlay on the dome drum.

The great mosques at Āgra (1058/1648) and at Dihlī (1066/1656) make no use of the finer technique, though their red stone is set off by white accents and outlined panelling, with chevron work at Āgra and reeding at Dihlī, both extending to the bulbous domes themselves. At Dihlī a new element is introduced in an outlined network of panels in the curved zone of transition under the domes. It appears that the imagery of floral inlay was appropriate only to the palace. It is significantly absent in the marble court mosques at Āgra, the Mīnā Masdjid, the Nagīna Masdjid, and the Mōtī Masdjid, though the quintessence of the material can be seen in the serene black outlines of the *djā-yi namāz* on the floor. At those in Lāhawr and Dihlī it is allowed a discrete appearance on the skyline.

A final stage in the development can be recognised in the Red Fort at Dihlī (1048-58/1638-48), where the tendrils in borders are wiry meanders linking predictably-placed foliage and flowers. The main floral motifs, though finely executed, are reduced to a display of buds and blooms scarcely connected by their stems. The Bangālī vault of the baldachin in the public audience hall is plainly elaborated from that at Āgra, with its convex arch soffit and coving. It is the wall behind this which is clad with work from Florence, with a figure of Orpheus at the apex and surrounding panels of birds amongst foliage and fruit, with lions at the foot, unique in Mughal architecture. The black matrix of these 318 panels, typical of the Grand Ducal workshops, is itself an innovation, accommodated by dint of composing it in an arboreal setting with Indian birds on the usual white ground, probably done *in situ* by local craftsmen. Koch has shown (*op. cit.*, 23-33) that the whole is to be interpreted as a Solomonic setting for the ruler, as bringer of harmony to nature, hence of natural justice, with reference to David's pacification of the natural world through music.

In this instance, a convergence between the in-erests and crafts of the Mug͟hal and European courts ould lead to a cross fertilisation which, however, eems to have led no further. That the main impetus or the development of *parčīn-kārī* came from faience nosaic is clear in such details as the inclusion of cen-res of a different colour in peripheral leaves. A timulus may well have been received from Bīdar, as he Rangīn Maḥall there (*ca.* 1542-80) was decorated ot only with faience mosaic but exceptionally fine nother-of-pearl inlay on dark basalt; S͟hāh D͟jahān ad passed through Bīdar during his rebellion of 623-4, and the complex seems to have been emulated t the Mut͟hamman Burd͟j at Āgra on his accession. 'atterns on textiles, and the floral painting as found n some tombs at Burhānpur, are likely to have con-ributed to its evolution.

With the exception of the Mōtī Masd͟jid at Dihlī 1073/1662-3), little use was made of *parčīn-kārī* after hāh D͟jahān's death, and the craft had so declined by he mid-19th century that it could only be revived by British initiative (Koch, *op. cit.*, n. 24). At the Pād-hāhī Masd͟jid in Lāhawr (1084/1673-4), the exterior nakes further use of red and white work, but though ome strips are inlaid flush, the central *pīs͟htāḳ* is or-amented with marble inlay standing out in relief: the pandrel scrolling is centred on a sunflower, with etals, leaves, and tendrils all embossed, and the soffit f the arch carries continuous floral scrolling ar-iculated by a sequence of vases, both highly stylised, nd possibly under Italian influence (Chaghatai, *op. it.* in *Bibl.*, 1972, 26-7). The contrast between culpted marble and inlay is thus finally resolved by culpting the white inlay itself.

Technique. The Muslim craftsmen still practising t Āgra, who claim descent from those who worked or S͟hāh D͟jahān, state that the work is properly called *baččī-kārī*, from a Hindi root meaning "joined, stick-ng", as in Platts' dictionary. The design, *k͟hākā*, is first drawn in pencil, and then chiselled out with a urin, *narza* (?), tapering conically to 1.5 mm with a 30° point held between the fourth and fifth fingers like a pen; another chisel, *tāṅkī* (*tanḳīh*?), with a point 2.5 mm square is used to clean out the edges with a dig-ging action, *narzāna*. The white marble *sang-i marmar*, for the background is from Makrāna, some 100 km/60 miles west of D͟jaypur. The inlaid stones include malachite, *dāna-farang*, lapis lazuli, *lād͟jward*, cor-nelian, *ʿaḳīḳ*, mother of pearl, *sīp*, black onyx, *sang-i mūṣā*, coral, *mard͟jān*, turquoise, *fīrūza*, besides garnet, moonstone, smoky topaz, golden or yellow topaz, and all types of agate. Of these the malachite is now from the Congo, the lapis lazuli from Afg͟hānistān, the cor-nelian from India, the mother-of-pearl is abalone from Australia, and the coral is from Sicily—a black variety is more expensive. The inlay in general is called *pačče*; the petals and leaves are *pattī*, and the stems *dand*. The flowers, seen as roses, *gulāb*, or jasmine, *čamēlī*, are inlaid first, and then the stems.

The marble, once blasted, is cut with a bamboo bow, *kamāna*, with a wire blade: seven pieces can be cut at once with seven blades. It is then reduced with a hammer, *hatōṛā*, and chisel, *čhēnī*, to the required shape, *s͟hakl*; its edges are ground, *ghisnā*, with a broken piece of grinding wheel, *sān*. The inlay is cut roughly to shape with shears, *kāṅtī*, and ground on a wheel, *ca.* 30 cm diameter by 2.5 cm thick, set on a steel axle and operated by a bow 90 cm long. The composition of this wheel, regarded as the essential secret of the craft, is of river sand, sugar-cane juice, and brown resin: it should last 30 years, and if pitted can be restored by heating it with charcoal and rubbing it with marble. The flat surface of the wheel is used to grind the inlay surface, and its bevelled edge for the profile; it takes half an hour to shape a flower of 3 or 5 petals by eye, *raḳam banānā*, to fit one another. The marble is usually hollowed, *katyānā*, to twice the depth of the inlay, the profile being exact. After the fit of each piece has been tested, a glue mixed from white cement, plaster of Paris, and beeswax, is put in the hollow and softened by holding a red hot coal over it with tongs, *čimta*, for 5-10 seconds, and the stone pressed in place: it sets in 25 seconds. In some cases the parts of a flower are pre-assembled with heated resin, *sarēs*, on a mica table. Once set, the work is ground smooth, *ṣāf karnā*, with a piece of grindstone, water, and river sand, and finally polished with white zinc powder, water, and a soft cloth. A piece of work some 40 cm across takes two craftsmen seven hours to complete (informant: Ustād Muḥammad Āṣaf K͟hān b. Muḥammad ʿAbd al-K͟hān b. ʿAbd al-Salām b. ʿAbd al-Asad, 1981).

Bibliography: For a summary of the present state of research, see the extensive notes in E. Koch, *Shah Jahan and Orpheus. The pietre dure decoration and the programme of the throne in the Hall of Public Audiences at the Red Fort of Delhi*, Graz 1988. For earlier discussion of the origins, see J.H. Marshall in *ASI, AR* (1902-3), 26-8, and in *ASI, AR* (1904-5), 1-3; Sir Sayyid Aḥmad K͟hān, *Āt͟hār al-ṣanādīd*, Dihlī 1263/1847, as ed. K͟halīd Naṣīr Has͟hmī, Cawnpore (Kānpur) 1904, repr. Delhi 1965, 102-6, tr. R. Nath in *Monuments of New Delhi*, New Delhi 1979, 12 ff.; N. Chatterji, *Italians and Mughal pietra dura*, in *Journal of the U.P. Historical Society*, x (1937), 80-7; M.A. Chaghtai, *Pietra dura decoration of the Taj*, in *IC*, xv (1941), 465-72; Sir Jadunath Sarkar, preface, in S.K. Saraswati, *Glimpses of Mughal architecture*, Calcutta 1953; R. Nath, *Colour decoration in Mughal architecture*, Bombay 1970, 33-7. For the Italian viewpoint, see L. Bartoli and L. Zangheri, *I raporti tra la Firenze dei Medici e l'India nella prima metà del 17° secolo*, in *Europa und die Kunst des Islam: 15. bis 18. Jhdt., Akten des XXV. Internationalen Kongresses für Kunstgeschichte*, v, Vienna 1985, 55-73, pls. 22-8.

For Tīmūrid use of stone in dados, see B. O'Kane, *Tāybād, Turbat-i Jām and Timurid vaulting*, in *Iran*, xvii (1979), 87, pls. Ib, IIb, and fig. 5; idem, *Timurid architecture in Khurasan*, Costa Mesa 1987, 60-1, fig. 25.5 and pl. 25.4; L. Golombek and D. Wilber, *The Timurid architecture of Iran and Turan*, Princeton 1988, 134, 309, col. pls. VIIa-b, IXb, and pls. 125, 175. For the Persian cut brick and tile forms, see H.E. Wulff, *The traditional crafts of Persia*, Cambridge, Mass. and London 1966, 122-5.

Adequate illustrations of the buildings referred to above are not always readily available, but may be found in the following general works, some in colour, marked (c). P.A. Andrews, *The architecture and gardens of Islamic India*, in B. Gray (ed.), *The arts of India*, Oxford 1981, 94-124; P. Brown, *Monuments of the Mughul period*, in *The Cambridge history of India*, iv, Cambridge 1937, 523-76 and plates; idem, *Indian architecture (the Islamic period)*, Bombay 1942; J. Burton-Page, *Lahore Fort, The Red Fort, Fatehpur Sikri*, and *Taj Mahal*, in Sir M. Wheeler (ed.), *Splendours of the East*, London etc. 1965, 83-93, 131-41, 142-53, 154-65; B. Gascoigne, *Die Großmoguln*, Gütersloh 1987; G. Hambly, *Cities of Mughal India*, New York 1968; E. la Roche, *Indische Baukunst*, v, Munich 1922; Sir J. Marshall, *The monuments of Muslim India*, in *Cambridge history of India*, iii (*Sultanate*), Cambridge 1928, 568-640 and plates; R.

Nath, *Colour decoration in Mughal architecture*, Bombay 1970; idem, *Agra and its monumental glory*, Bombay 1977; idem, *Calligraphic art in Mughal architecture*, Calcutta 1979; O. Reuther, *Indische Paläste und Wohnhäuser*, Berlin 1925; Sir E.W. Smith, *Moghul colour decoration of Agra*, Allahabad 1901; Sir M. Wheeler, *Five thousand years of Pakistan*, London 1950.

For specific buildings in the sequence mentioned, see as follows: Dihlī, Tomb of Iltutmish, ʿAlāʾī Darwāza, Tomb of Ghiyāth al-Dīn Tughluḳ: Andrews, *op. cit.* 1981, figs. 113-15; Hambly, *op. cit.* 1968, pl. 4, 6 (c), 10. Māndū, Djāmiʿ Masdjid: G. Yazdani, *Mandū, city of joy*, Oxford 1929, pl. x; Gascoigne, *op. cit.*, 42 (c). Dihlī, Masdjid-i Kuhna: Andrews, *op. cit.* 1981, fig. 118; Brown, *op. cit.* 1937, ills. 8, 9, and idem, *op. cit.* 1942, pl. lxiii; Nath, *op. cit.* 1979, pl. xvii. Dihlī, Tomb of Ātägä Khan, Brown, *op. cit.* 1937, ill. 13. Dihlī, Humāyūn's Tomb: Andrews, *op. cit.* 1981, fig. 123 (c); G.D. Lowry, *Humāyūn's tomb: form, function and meaning in early Mughal architecture*, in *Muqarnas*, iv (1987), 133-48; Fatḥpur Sīkrī, Djāmiʿ Masdjid: Brown, *op. cit.* 1937, ills. 38-40; idem, *op. cit.* 1942, pl. lxxii; Burton-Page, *op. cit.* 1965, 150 (c); Nath, *op. cit.* 1979, pls. xxvi-ix; Saiyid A.A. Rizvi and V.J.A. Flynn, *Fatḥpūr Sīkrī*, Bombay 1975, pls. 53-5; E.W. Smith, *The Moghul architecture of Fatḥpur Sīkrī*, in *ASI, NS*, Allahabad 1894-7. Sikandra, Akbar's Tomb: Brown, *op. cit.* 1937, ills. 49-51 and idem, *op. cit.* 1942, pl. lxxvii; Gascoigne, *op. cit.* 1987, 120, detail 142 (c); Hambly, *op. cit.* 1968, pls. 39-41; Nath, *op. cit.* 1977, pls. 33-54, details; idem, *op. cit.* 1979, pls. xxxviii-xlii. Āgra, Tomb of Iʿtimād al-Dawla, gateway: Nath, *op. cit.* 1977, pl. 56. Tomb: Andrews, *op. cit.* 1981, fig. 130 (c); Brown, *op. cit.* 1937, ills. 53-6; Gascoigne, *op. cit.* 1987, detail 159 (c), 155; Hambly, *op. cit.* 1968, pls. 42-5 (c), 53-4; Nath, *op. cit.* 1977, pls. 58-61; idem, *op. cit.* 1979, pls. xlv-vi. Sarāy Doraha: W.E. Begley, *Four Mughal caravanserais built during the reigns of Jahāngīr and Shāh Jahān*, in *Muqarnas*, i (1983), 167-79. Lāhawr, Djahāngīr's Tomb: Burton-Page, *op. cit.* 1965, 82-3 (c); Sir R.E.M. Wheeler, *Five thousand years of Pakistan*, London 1950, pls. xi-xii; K.K. Mumtaz, *Architecture in Pakistan*, Singapore 1985, figs. 4. 19-20; and S. Mahmood, *Islamic inscriptions in Pakistani architecture to 1707*, unpubl. Ph.D. thesis, Edinburgh 1981, 471-7. Āgra Fort: Brown, *op. cit.* 1937, ills. 59, 63, and idem, *op. cit.* 1942, pl. lxxxix; Gascoigne, *op. cit.* 1987, 192 (c); Koch, *op. cit.* 1988, pls. 3, 7; la Roche, *op. cit.* v. 1922, Abb. 302-3, and Taf. 111-18 (large b & w, 115 (c); Nath, *op. cit.* 1977, pls. 7-9, 19-24, and idem, *op. cit.* 1979, pls. lix-lxvi; Reuther, *op. cit.* 1925, Taf. 51-6 (large b & w). Āgra, Tādj Maḥall: Brown, *op. cit.* 1937, ills. 84-5; Burton-Page, *op. cit.* 1965, 155, 158-9, 163-4; Hambly, *op. cit.* 1968, pl. 74 (c), 57, 68-71; Nath, *op. cit.* 1970, idem, *op. cit.* 1977, pls. 69-81, and idem, *op. cit.* 1979, pls. lix-lxvi; especially H. Rau, *Taj Mahal*, in *Lynkeus* (house magazine of Dr. K. Thomae GmbH) Biberach an der Riss n.d. [1904], *passim.* (30 outstandingly good colour plates, with details); Agra, Djāmiʿ Masdjid; Brown, *op. cit.* 1937, ills. 77-8, and idem, *op. cit.* 1942, pl. lxxxvi; Hambly, *op. cit.* 1968, pl. 84 (c); Nath, *op. cit.* 1979, pls. xlix-li, Dihlī, Djāmiʿ Masdjid: Brown, *op. cit.* 1937, ills. 79-80; Hambly, *op. cit.* 1968, pl. 86 (c); Nath, *op. cit.* 1979, pls. lii-iv. Āgra, marble court mosques: Brown, *op. cit.* 1937, ill. 62; Nath, *op. cit.* 1977, pls. 25, 28-9, and idem, *op. cit.* 1979, pls. lv-vi. Lāhawr, Mōtī Masdjid: Burton-Page, *op. cit.* 1965, 86. Dihlī, Red Fort: Andrews, *op. cit.* 1981, fig. 128; Brown, *op. cit.* 1937, ills. 68, 71-4, and idem, *op. cit.* 1942, pls. lxxvii-viii, lxxx-iii; Gascoigne, *op. cit.* 1987, detail 193 (c); Koch, *op. cit.* 1988, (*passim* for *djharōkhā*, c); la Roche, *op. cit.* v, 1922, Abb. 316, 319-20, 323, and Taf. 120-4 (large b & w); Reuther, *op. cit.* 1925, Taf. 63-71 (large b & w). For the inlay at Bīdar, see G. Yazdani, *Bidar, its history and monuments*, Oxford 1948, 44-5, 96, pls. xii-xiv, and E. Merklinger, *The madrasa of Maḥmūd Gāwān in Bīdar*, in *Kunst des Orients*, xi, 1-2, fig. 3. Dihlī, Mōtī Masdjid; Brown, *op. cit.* 1937, ills. 73, 75. Lāhawr, Pādshāhī Masdjid: Brown, *op. cit.* 1937, ill. 87; A. Chaghatai, *The Badshahi Masjid, history and architecture*, Lahore 1972, pls. 3b, 12-4; Gascoigne, *op. cit.* 1987, 227. (P. A. Andrews)

PARDA-DĀR (P.), literally "the person who draws the curtain", a term used among the dynasties of the eastern Islamic world from the Saldjūḳ period onwards as the equivalent of Arabic *ḥādjib*, i.e. for the court official, the chamberlain, who controlled access to the ruler, the latter being normally veiled from public gaze. For this function, see ḤĀDJIB. (Ed.)

PARENDĀ, a small town and fortress, formerly in the native state of Ḥaydarābād, now in the Sholapur District of Mahārashtra State of the Indian Union (lat. 18° 16′ N., long 75° 27′ E.) The fortress is attributed, like many of those in the Deccan, to the Bahmanī minister Maḥmūd Gāwān [*q.v.*], i.e. to the third quarter of the 9th/15th century, but may well be earlier [see BURDJ. III. at vol. I, 1323b]. Parendā was for a short time the capital of the Niẓām Shāhīs [*q.v.*] after the capture of Aḥmadnagar [*q.v.*] by Akbar's forces in 1014/1605, but was conquered by Awrangzīb when he was governor of the Deccan in Shāh Djahān's reign. The fortress and old town subsequently fell early into ruins.

Bibliography: *Imperial gazetteer of India*², xx, 1-2. (Ed.)

PARGANA, a Hindi word, ultimately from a Sanskrit root "to compute, reckon up", a term in Indo-Muslim administrative usage denoting an aggregate of villages, a subdivision of a district or *sarkār* [see MUGHALS. 3. Administrative and social organisation]. In later Anglo-Indian usage, the term was often rendered as *pergunnah*, see Yule and Burnell, *Hobson-Jobson, a glossary of Anglo-Indian colloquial words and phrases*, 698-9. The first reference to this term in the chronicles of the Sultanate of Dihlī appears to be in the *Taʾrīkh-i Fīrūz Shāhī* of Shams-i Sirādj ʿAfīf (*Bibliotheca Indica,* Calcutta 1891, 99), for it is not used by Ḥasan al-Niẓāmī in his *Tādj al-maʾāthir* or by Minhādj al-Dīn Djūzdjānī in his *Ṭabaḳāt-i Nāṣirī*. Although it first came into prominence in the 8th/14th century, partially superseding the term *ḳaṣba*, it is, in all probability, based on still more ancient divisions in existence before the Muslim conquest. The exact date of its creation is therefore uncertain.

An account of the internal working of a *pargana* occurs in the chronicles of the reign of Shīr Shāh Sūrī (947-52/1540-5), who learned the details of revenue administration in the management of his father's two *parganas* at Sasarām in Bihār. When he became ruler of Hindustān he organised his kingdom into administrative units known as *sarkārs* which were divided into collections of villages termed *parganas*. Each *pargana* was in charge of a *shiḳdār* or military police officer who supported the *amīn* or civil officer. The *amīn* had for his civil subordinates a *fotadār* or treasurer and

[t]wo *kārkuns* or clerks, one for Hindi and the other for [P]ersian correspondence. It does not seem correct to [h]old the view that in this respect he was an ad[m]inistrative innovator, for the provincial officials and [in]stitutions which he has been credited with creating [w]ere already in existence before he ascended the [th]rone. This remained the administrative system until [A]kbar organised the Mug͟hal empire into *ṣūbas* (prov[in]ces), which were divided into *sarkārs*. The smallest [fi]scal unit under Akbar was the *pargana* or *maḥall*. [T]hus, for example, the *ṣūba* of Oudh was divided into [fi]ve *sarkārs* and thirty-eight *parganas* (*Āʾīn-i Akbarī*, tr. [J]arrett, *Bibl. Indica*, Calcutta 1891, ii, 170-7).

Under the Mug͟hal emperors, the chief *pargana* of[fi]cials were the *ḳānungo*, the *amīn* and the *s͟hiḳdār*, who [w]ere responsible for the *pargana* accounts, the rates of [a]ssessment, the survey of lands, and the protection of [t]he rights of the cultivators. Similarly, in each village [a] *patwāri* or village accountant was appointed whose [f]unctions in the village resembled those of the *ḳānungo* [i]n the *pargana*. It must not be imagined that the [p]*argana* was a stable and uniform unit. Not only did it [v]ary in area in different parts of the country, but often [a] new land settlement was followed by a fresh division [a]nd re-distribution of these fiscal units. The co[e]xtensiveness of a *pargana* with the possessions of a [c]lan or family has given rise to the suggestion that it [w]as not only a revenue-paying area but that it was [f]ounded on the distribution of property at the time of [i]ts creation.

The Twenty-four *Parganas*: these were a [d]istrict of Bengal lying between 21° 31′ and 22° [5]7′ N. and 88° 21′ and 89° 6′ E. It derives its name [f]rom the number of *parganas* comprised in the *zamīn[d]ārī* ceded to the English East India Company in 1757 [b]y Mīr D͟jaʿfar [*q.v.*], the Nawāb Nāẓim of Bengal. [T]his was confirmed by the Mug͟hal emperor ʿĀlamgīr [I]I in 1759 when he granted the Company a perpetual [h]eritable jurisdisdiction over this area. In the same [y]ear, Lord Clive, as a reward for services rendered by [h]im to Mīr D͟jaʿfar, was presented with the revenues [o]f this district. This grant, which amounted to [£]30,000 per annum, made Clive both the servant and [t]he landlord of the Company. The sum continued to [b]e paid to him until his death in 1774, when, by a [d]eed sanctioned by the emperor, the whole pro[p]rietary right in the land and revenues reverted to the [C]ompany.

Bibliography: Given in the article.

(C.C. Davies)

PARĪ (p., t. *peri*, borrowed into English as *peri*, French *péri*), a supernatural being of stories and legends, and likewise forming a whole category of popular beliefs. The word stems from Pers. *par* "wing"; and the being is sometimes pictured as being winged. Turkish tradition considers it as a beneficent spirit. However, amongst the Kazaks it is sometimes represented as an evil genie. In the Anatolian tradition, it is conceived as a being belonging to both sexes, and the compound form *peri kızı* "girl peri" is used for peris of the female sex. It was believed that marriage with human beings was possible. Peris form the main characters of the action in a whole category of tales of marvels; they bring aid to good persons but punishment for the evil ones.

Bibliography: W. Radloff, *Proben der Volksliteratur der türkischen Stämme*, i-x, St. Petersburg 1866-1904; J.-J.P. Desmaisons, *Dictionnaire persan-français*, Rome 1908; W. Eberhard-P.N. Boratav, *Typen türkischer Volksmärchen*, Wiesbaden 1953; Boratav, *100 soruda Türk folkloru*, Istanbul 1984, 75, 77; idem, *Halk hikâyeleri ve halk hikâyeciliği*, Istanbul 1988, 67, 69; idem, *100 soruda Türk halk edebiyatı*, Istanbul 1988, 104; N.R. Baltacıoğlu, *Anadolu'da cinlere, perilere ve devlere dair inanışlar*, in *Türk Folklor Araştırmaları*, no. 35 (Istanbul 1952), Saim Sakaoğlu, *Gümüşhane masalları*, Ankara 1973, 250-1.

(P.N. Boratav)

In Persian.

The Avestan *pairikās*, defined as "a class of female supernatural beings of malicious character, who seek to beguile and harm mankind" (Boyce, 85), gave their name to the New Persian *parī*, but little else of the characteristics ascribed to them by the Zoroastrians. The *parīs* of Islamic times are not unlike the fairies of European folklore (cf. *Enzyklopädie des Märchens*, iv, Berlin-New York 1984, s.vv. *Fairy, Fee*). They are introduced in oral tales and written literature as benevolent spirits appearing in splendid and alluring beauty to human beings. Sexual love and marriage between *parīs* and humans are recurrent motifs. Such unions can only be reached, however, after many obstacles of a magical nature are overcome. The *parīs* have two sexes, though females are much more frequent than males, and they beget children. They live long but are not immortal. In the sphere of mythical beings they form a nation, ruled by a king whose daughter is a leading character in many fairy tales. The land of the fairies lies far away but can be reached by ordinary travel. It is sometimes situated near the mountain Ḳāf [*q.v.*]. In spite of their association with beauty and elegance, they can be fierce fighters. They are able to fly and can change into animals, monsters and demons. Their main enemies are the demons (*dīw* [*q.v.*]), the sorcerers and the witches. One may enchant them in a magic circle, and they are unable to free themselves when they are chained. In spite of their elusive nature, they are generally of good will and keep their promises. Some of them are even believers.

Many of these features are mentioned in the anonymous *Iskandar-nāma*, a mediaeval prose version of the Alexander saga recounting a journey to a country ruled by the fairy queen Arāḳīt, which Iskandar subdues in a long war ending in the dispersal of the *parīs* and the return of the land to its original human inhabitants. The story is strongly influenced by legends about Sulaymān and Bilḳīs [*q.v.*], the queen of Sheba. Both Bilḳīs and Arāḳīt were said to be of mixed human and fairy blood (cf. Southgate, 210-11; B. Carra de Vaux, *EI*[1] s.v. *Bilḳīs*). Features of the *parīs* as they appear in Persian fairy tales have been summarised by Christensen and Marzolph.

To the classical poets, comparisons with the beauty of the *parī* were commonplace. In a single hemistich ʿUnṣurī (d. 431/1039-40) described his beloved as a *parīzāda parīrūʾī parīčihrī parīpaykar* ("a fairy-child with a fairy-face, with the traits of a fairy and shaped like a fairy"; *Dīwān*, ed. Y. Ḳarīb, Tehran 1341 *s͟h*./1962, 100). Ḥāfiẓ put the fairies on a par with the *ḥūr* of the Islamic Paradise (*Dīwān*, ed. P.N. K͟hānlarī, Tehran 1362 *s͟h*./1983, 121, 210, 391, 404, 425). In the epic they were included in the armies of the primeval kings of Iran, together with *dīws*, animals and birds. A trace of the malice of the ancient *pairikās* is still apparent in the figure of the sorceress (*zan-i d͟jādū*) who tried to seduce the heroes Isfandiyār and Rustam in the shape of a beautiful woman (cf. Christensen, *Démonologie*, 64-5). Folkloristic elements are also reflected in romantic and didactic *mat͟hnawīs*. In the *Ilāhī-nāma* of Farīd al-Dīn ʿAṭṭār [*q.v.*] the desire of a young prince for the daughter of the king of the fairies is denounced by his father as the "cult of lust" (*s͟hahwatparastī*). The first story of Niẓāmī's *Haft paykar*, told by the Indian princess in the Black Pavilion, is a typical instance of the delusions experienced in a fairy-land. Another example of the use of folklore in polite literature is *Dāstān-i Djamāl wa Djalāl* by the Tīmūrid poet Muḥammad Āṣafī (d. 923/1517), an allegorical *mathnawī* about the search of prince "Glory" for "Beauty", the latter being personified as the daughter of the king of the *parīs*.

The unique copy of the last-mentioned work, preserved in the Uppsala University Library (Nova 2, dated 1502-5), is also an important source for the iconography of the *parī* in Persian miniature painting. The fairies were depicted like angels, as the latter were commonly represented in Tīmūrid art (see Stchoukine, 116). Other subjects giving occasion for picturing *parīs* were Niẓāmī's story of the Black Pavilion (see e.g. Robinson, *Rylands*, no. 418) and throne scenes of Sulaymān and Bilḳīs (cf. e.g. Titley, 98, Pl. 14).

Bibliography: M. Boyce, *A history of Zoroastrianism*, i, Leiden 1989², 85-7; A. Christensen, *Essai sur la démonologie iranienne*, Copenhagen 1941, 14-5, 60-68, 78; idem, *Persische Märchen*, Düsseldorf-Köln 1958, 290-1; U. Marzolph, *Typologie des persischen Volksmärchen*, Beirut 1984, 29-30, 273-4 (Motivindex s.v. *Fee*); *Iskandar-nāma*, ed. by Ī. Afshār, Tehran 1964, tr. M.S. Southgate, New York 1978; Farīd al-Dīn ʿAṭṭār, *Ilāhī-nāma*, ed. F. Rūḥānī, Tehran 1339 *sh*./1960, 26-38, tr. J.A. Boyle, Manchester 1976, 30-45; Niẓāmī, *Haft paykar*, ed. H. Ritter and J. Rypka, Prague 1934, 121-50; K.V. Zetterstéen and C.J. Lamm, *The story of Jamāl and Jalāl. An illuminated manuscript in the Library of Uppsala University*, Uppsala 1947; I. Stchoukine, *Les peintures des manuscrits Tîmûrides*, Paris 1954; B.W. Robinson, *Persian paintings in the John Rylands Library*, London 1980; Norah M. Titley, *Persian miniature painting*, London 1983.

(J.T.P. de Bruijn)

PARIAS (the word arose from such Latin accountancy terms as *paria facere* "to settle an account" already current in Imperial Latin; Du Cange considered Mediaeval Latin *pariae* as from the Spanish) in the mediaeval Iberian peninsula "tribute paid by one ruler to another in recognition of his superior status".

The term is rarely used except of tribute paid by Muslims to Christians. There was no universally recognised tariff for such payments, nor any set form of contract setting out what was received in exchange for the *parias*, although there clearly was a presumption that payment secured protection from extortion at the hands of other Christians. Du Cange regarded *parias* as a type of feudal due ("*feudalis redditus, honores, homagia*"). Whether that is an accurate characterisation is doubtful; *parias* were paid when Christian rulers were powerful, refused when the Andalusī Muslims themselves or their Muslim protectors from North Africa felt safe to do so. The system appeared at the end of the Umayyad period and in the first Ṭāʾifa period (5th/11th century), apparently *ca.* 1010 with Ramon Berenguer I of Barcelona, and at times led to the transfer of considerable sums to the Christians. The taxes raised to pay the *parias*, quite illegal from the Islamic point of view (Muslim sources could only regard them as an inversion of the relationship of *dhimma* [*q.v.*], and, indeed, they are not infrequently termed *djizya* [*q.v.*]), were a factor in the collapse of the Ṭāʾifa régimes. The *Poema de Mio Cid* and Castilian chronicle narratives have al-Muʿtamid of Seville [*q.v.*] complain to Alfonso VI because the *parias* paid had not brought him safety from Christian freebooters; the Cid was despatched southwards to chastise the trouble-makers and to collect instalments overdue. (That we have to do with historical reality here is unlikely; what is important is that this was how the system was thought to function.) During the period following the Almoravid collapse, and again as Almohad power waned, payments resumed. From the initial agreement between the Castilian crown and Muḥammad I Ibn al-Aḥmar [see naṣrids] in 1246 onwards, *parias* formed an important part of the relationship between Granada and Castile. As seen by Castile, such tribute was a sign of the vassal status of the Naṣrid kingdom; as seen by the Granadans *parias* were a way of buying respite from damaging *talas* ("forays"). Carriazo has shown that the story that the penultimate Naṣrid ruler, Abu 'l-Ḥasan ʿAlī, refused to pay *parias* to Isabel, saying "the kings of Granada who used to give *parias* were dead, and the places in Granada where they used to strike the coins to pay the tribute were being used to forge lance-heads" is apocryphal.

Bibliography: Du Cange, *Glossarium mediae et infimae latinitatis*, Niort 1886 s.v. *pariae*; I. de las Cagigas, *Los mudéjares*, 2 vols., Madrid 1948-9; J. de Mata Carriazo, *Las treguas con Granada de 1475 a 1478*, in *Al-And.*, xix (1954), 317-64; R. Menéndez Pidal, *La España del Cid*⁵, Madrid 1956, esp. 257-60; H. Grassotti, *Para la historia del botín y las parias en Leon y Castilla*, in *Cuad. Hist. Esp.* (1964).

(L.P. Harvey)

PĀRSĀʾIYYA, a sub-order of the Central Asian Naḳshbandiyya [*q.v.*] Ṣūfī *ṭarīḳa* and the most prominent *shaykhly* family of Balkh from the middle of the 9th/15th century. The eponymous founder of the line was Khwādja Muḥammad b. Maḥmūd (or Muḥammad) al-Ḥāfiẓī al-Bukhārī (d. 822/1419), who adopted the nickname *Pārsā* ("the devout"). His tomb in Medina became a shrine for Central Asian pilgrims and the burial place of at least one Central Asian grand khān, the Tuḳāy-Tīmūrid, Imām Ḳulī (r. 1020-51/1611-41).

Khwādja Muḥammad Pārsā's son, Abū Naṣr, seems to have been the first of the line associated with Balkh. When he died there in 864 or 865 (1459-60 or 1460-1), his patron, the Tīmūrid general Mīr Mazīd Arghūn, erected a "high domed building" (*gunbadh-i ʿālī*) (*ca.* 867/1462-3), which became the centre of the order and survives in much-renovated form to the present. A no-longer extant *madrasa* was also built at the site sometime in the middle of the 10th/16th century.

The Pārsāʾīs remained prominent in Bukhārā well into the first half of the 10th/16th century, but the headquarters of the family and its order shifted to Balkh. The appointment of a great-grandson, ʿAbd al-Hādī b. Abū Naṣr (II) (d. *ca.* 967/1559) as *shaykh al-islām* at Balkh during the reign of the Abu 'l-Khayrid/Shībānid ʿUbayd Allāh (r. 940-6/1533-40) established the family in an official position which it would hold at least until the beginning of the 12th/end of the 17th century. Pārsāʾīs appearing in the literary record after the mid-10th/16th century are almost always from Balkh. Among the most prominent members of the family were ʿAbd al-Walī Pārsā (alias Khwādja Djān Khwādja, d. *ca.* 995/1587), who is portrayed as populist leader, political advisor and mediator; Ḳāsim Khwādja, architect of the royal *madrasa* constructed by Nadhr Muḥammad Khān [*q.v.*] before 1045/1635 as well as *shaykh al-islām*; and Ṣāliḥ Muḥammad (*fl.* 1100s/1690s), who was briefly installed as vice-khān (*ḳaʾlkhān*) at Balkh in 1107/1696. From the early 18th century onward, the

[fa]mily's fortunes appear to have ebbed along with [th]ose of the city, although the survival of the shrine [su]ggest that the family and the order it administered [re]tained at least a local importance for some time.

Bibliography: Khʷāndamīr, Tehran 1333/1954, iv, 4-5; Zayn al-Dīn Wāṣifī, *Badāʾiʿ al-waḳāʾiʿ*, Moscow 1961, 230-1; Khʷādja Bahāʾ al-Dīn Ḥasan Nithārī Bukhārī, *Mudhakkir al-aḥbāb*, New Delhi 1969, 319-21; Sulṭān Muḥammad b. Darwīsh Muḥammad, *Madjmaʿ al-gharāʾib*, Institut Vostokovedeniya Akademii Nauk (IVAN), Uzbekistan, ms. no. 1494, fols. 16a-b; Ḥāfiẓ-i Tanīsh Bukhārī, *Sharaf-nāma-yi shāhī*, Moscow 1983, i, fols. 81b-82a, 111a-b (Russian translation 183-4, 240-1); Maḥmūd b. Amīr Walī, *Baḥr al-asrār fī manāḳib al-akhyār*, India Office Library ms. no. 575, fols. 332a-b, 364b-365a, 366a, 374a; Muḥammad Ṭāhir b. Abi 'l-Ḳāsim, *ʿAdjāʾib al-ṭabaḳāt*, Royal Asiatic Society ms. no. 179, p. 87; B.A. Akhmedov, *Istoriya Balkha*, Tashkent 1982, 26-7; A. Mukhtarov, *Pozdnesrednevekovi Balkh*, Dushanbe 1980, 56-8. (R.D. McChesney)

PĀRSĪS (Pahlavi, *pārsīk*, NP *pārsī*, lit. "inhabitants [o]f Fārs", "Persian"), the name given to those [d]escendants of the Zoroastrians who migrated to In[d]ia, mostly to Gudjarāt [*q.v.*], from the 4th/10th cen[t]ury onwards [see MADJŪS].

This movement is described in the *Ḳiṣṣa-yi Sandjan*, [w]ritten in 1600 but using older oral tradition. In detail [i]t is unlikely to be historically reliable but it probably [h]as a valid overall perspective. It reflects the Pārsī [c]onviction that their move to India was divinely-[i]nspired and that they have been treated tolerantly by [t]he Hindu majority.

From the 17th century onwards, when European traders were arriving in western India, Pārsīs emerg[e]d from their previous relative obscurity to rise to positions of considerable wealth, significant educa[t]ional status (both in terms of building schools and colleges and in attending them), from which base they introduced the industrial revolution into India (first in the textile industry, then in steel), developed Indian commerce (notably banking and insurance), were foremost in many of the professions in western India (notably law and medicine) and became leaders in Indian politics, especially before the rise of the militants in the Indian National Congress in 1906. The major figures were Dadabhai Naoroji (1825-1917), popularly known as the "Grand Old Man of India", who was a founder of the Indian National Congress and the only person to be its president three times (1886, 1893, 1906). He was also the first Asian to be elected a Member of the British Parliament (1892-5). (The only other two Asian M.P.s elected prior to the 1980s were also Pārsīs: Bhownagree (elected in 1895) and Saklatvala (elected in 1923).) Two other major Pārsī politicians in India were Sir Pherozeshah Mehta (1845-1915) and Sir Dinshah Wacha (1844-1915). The former was especially important, not only in the Indian National Congress, but also in the government of India's commercial capital, Bombay. A brilliant lawyer and orator, he was mentor to many Indian politicians, especially Muhammad Ali Jinnah, founder of Pākistān [see DJINĀḤ] (Jinnah had several Pārsī connections, notably his wife and his doctor, who nursed him throughout his final illness).

The popular image of 20th century Pārsīs is of a community in decline. Numerically that may be true. In the 1981 census they totalled 71,630 throughout India, a decline of 20% in a decade, and subsequent demographic studies suggest that the rate of decline is likely to increase. The cause is partly emigration, but also a low fertility rate due to late marriages (Pārsī living standard expectations being high, young people commonly delay marriage until the age of 30), and with high levels of female education and career success many do not marry at all. Converts are not accepted, at least in the traditional areas of Gudjarāt and Bombay, though in Delhi the children of mixed marriages may be accepted as Zoroastrians.

However, Pārsīs are typically a high-status social group, mostly professionals (the civil service, law and medicine), leading figures in commerce, with some important political figures. (Mrs Indhira Gandhi was married to an active Pārsī politician, Feroze, so Pārsīs sometimes claim that her sons were Pārsīs; this is especially claimed for Rajiv who is said to have resembled his father.) Since independence, Pārsīs have held the post of head of each branch of India's armed forces. They own India's largest industry, Tatas, and South Asia's largest private company, Godrej Brothers. Recent studies have further established that the general standard of living of the average Pārsī in Bombay is higher than that of the general population of the city and this is almost certainly true for other parts of India, with the possible exception of parts of rural Gudjarāt. Throughout their history in India, Pārsīs have been noted for their charitable activities, not only among their own people but also among the wider community in the subcontinent, back in Iran [see MADJŪS, at V, p. 1115] and indeed on a wider international scale.

From India, Pārsīs have migrated to most continents in pursuit of trade and education. The first Pārsī to visit China was Hirjee Jivanjee Readeymoney in 1756. Their main bases were in Hong Kong (some Pārsī traders were there before the British take-over in 1841), Canton (the Zoroastrian Association was started in 1845) and Shanghai (the Association was founded in 1854). The main Pārsī business was opium, but they diversified into many branches of the import-export trade and into property and banking.

The first Pārsī to visit Britain arrived in 1723, but it was the mid-19th century before Pārsīs came in any numbers. Mostly they came for education, both formal university studies and informal studies of British industry, especially the textile trade and engineering. Others came for business. The first Indian firm in Britain was that of the Pārsī Cama brothers (with Naoroji) which opened in London and Liverpool in 1855. The Zoroastrian Association was formed in 1861, the first Asian religious body in Britain. A burial ground was purchased in 1861 and the first building obtained in 1909. Prior to World War II, there were about 200 Pārsīs in Britain at any one time. More Zoroastrians migrated, along with other South Asians, in the 1960s and after. They came mostly from urban centres, above all Bombay, but also from Pākistān and East Africa. Typically, they are well educated (over 70% have a university education), concentrated in London and are professionals. There are a few Iranian Zoroastrians who settled in the 1970s and 80s.

Also from the 1960s Pārsīs began to migrate to Canada and to America. There are now some 21 Zoroastrian Associations on the continent with buildings in New York (opened in 1977), Toronto (1980), Los Angeles (1982), Chicago (1983), and Vancouver (1987). Following the fall of the Shāh a number of Zoroastrians migrated from Iran and they settled mostly in New York, Vancouver and California. It was an Iranian Zoroastrian, Arbab Rustom Guiv and the charitable foundation he endowed, which provided most, in some cases practically all, of the funds to open the Zoroastrian buildings. It is typically the very well-educated Pārsīs and Iranian Zoroastrians who have migrated (in America most are scientists). Precise numbers are unknown and estimates vary greatly. They are steadily increasing, mostly through migration, but it is also a young population so that the birth-rate exceeds the death-rate. Current plausible estimates suggest around 10,000.

The latest centre for migration is Australia. The Sydney-based "Australian Zoroastrian Association" was formed in 1971 and its building was opened in 1986. The other main group in Melbourne was founded in 1987. Numbers in Australia are probably little over 1,000, but they are increasing for the same reasons as in America.

The problems facing the younger Pārsīs in the "New World" and Australasia are those experienced by most South Asian migrants: the changing perceptions of successive generations; debates on intermarriage and problems posed by perceived racial prejudice. Typically, these diaspora communities give greater emphasis to religious education than do the communities in the "old country" because the elders are conscious of the dangers of acculturation. The result, over a number of years, could be that the Zoroastrian youth in the diaspora know more about their history and teachings then do those in the "old country". However, what they are taught tends to be those facets of the religion more readily intelligible in the "West" than in South Asia (for example, certain philosophies or ritual interpretations are stressed rather than the purity laws). Consequently, the result of the geographical dispersal could result in a greater religious diversity.

There are also Pārsī communities in Muslim lands (other than Iran). The most important of these is in Pākistān, mostly in Karachi, but with about 100 in Lahore (and until recently Quetta). Pārsīs played a significant role in the development of Karachi. The first Pārsī firm to move to Sind was Jessawalla and Co in (approximately) 1825 and several others soon followed. The burial ground was opened in 1839; the first temple was built in 1849 and the first Pārsī school in 1859. Numbers grew so that a second temple was built in 1869 and another *dakhma* ("Tower of Silence") was opened in 1875. The main trade pursued by the growing number of settlers was as suppliers to the British, especially during the Afghan Wars. Numbers peaked around 1940 with approximately 4,000 Pārsīs. That was also the era of one of the community's great leaders, Jamshed Mehta (1862-1952). He was President of the Municipality for 13 years and the first Lord Mayor of Karachi. He was universally respected as a man of total integrity and deep commitment to his city. When he died Karachi came to a standstill as people of all communities mourned. When Pākistān was declared an independent Muslim state, some Pārsīs feared for their future because of their memories of their fate in Iran. That, as well as the educational and career attractions of the "West", was why many migrated and numbers declined to below 3,000. In fact, however, the community has been secure, especially in Karachi where numbers and wealth are concentrated. Several have achieved significant status, a judge in the Supreme Court, brigadiers and majors in the army, two M.P.s and one Pārsī, Jamsheed Marker, has successively held the post of Pākistān's ambassador to France, America and the United Nations. Various Pārsī firms have been important in the shipping business, hotels, pharmaceuticals and property. Their reputation for charitable work is outstanding, especially in the medical and educational fields. As Islam has become ever more prominent in Pākistān's life, so Pārsīs have been required to provide their own children with a religious education. Numbers attending temple are commonly reported to be increasing. Whereas Pārsīs in the West are seen as prone to secularism, in Pākistān typically they are traditional, distanced but not alienated from the wider society.

There are also long-standing Pārsī communities in East Africa. The pioneer in this development was the family firm of the Cowasji Dinshaws (1824-1900). The father was largely responsible for the development of technology in Aden, above all the dockyard. He also owned a fleet of ships and was agent for several British firms. He, too, was known for his charitable work. Contemporary with the Pārsī move to Aden was their settlement in Zanzibar. The first to arrive was M.A. Mistry in 1845. Others did not follow until the 1870s-1890s. The Zoroastrian Association was formally started in 1875. In 1884 the Cowasji Dinshaws were persuaded to move here from Aden. They became leaders in the community, building a temple and running the Association. After World War II there were 184 Zoroastrians in Zanzibar, but subsequent to the 1964 revolution, numbers declined and now in the 1990s there are only two families left.

Zoroastrian traders probably arrived on the east coast of Africa centuries ago, but the first known to have been on the mainland, Jehangir Bhedwar, came in 1870 and built the dockyard at Mombasa. The architect, Sorabji Mistry, was an important early arrival for he built many of the major municipal buildings. From around 1896 many lawyers, engineers and accountants came in connection with the building of the East African railway. The Zoroastrian Association was started in 1897 and began to acquire land in Nairobi from 1902. The main period of growth was post-World War II when numbers reached about 400 in each city, but with the process of Africanisation in the 1960s most emigrated, some to India and Canada but most to Britain. At present (early 1990s) there are only approximately 40-50 Zoroastrians in the two cities, mostly business men and professionals.

In East Africa, as in Pākistān, Pārsīs have remained within their own tightly-knit communities (though there have been strong internal divisions) and as a result have, on the whole, remained traditional in their religious beliefs and practices. They have not been subject to the same processes of acculturation that those in the West have. Whereas Pārsīs in Bombay have been subject to marked Hindu influences, not only in dress and language but also in customs and concepts (e.g. wedding rites, symbolic decorations around the home, ideas on caste and rebirth, veneration for modern Hindu holy men), the deep reservations which have arisen from Islamic persecution in Iran have in practice meant that most, though not all, Pārsīs in Muslim lands have sought to preserve their distinctiveness. Although many feared for their fate in the 20th century, they have not experienced overt oppression from Muslims. Their situation in Iran is documented elsewhere [see MADJŪS]. The homeland remains the country in which there is the most widespread concern for their future. Many feel vulnerable and oppressed, generally their career prospects are limited (especially in government and the forces) but some stress that there has been no actual persecution and a few Zoroastrian businesses continue to flourish. Government estimates put the number of Zoroastrians in Iran in the 1990s at over 90,000—

hich if accurate would mean that there has been a ourfold increase in 30 years. Unfortunately, it is mpossible to give an account of the reported 500 Pārsīs working as traders and professionals in the Arab Gulf States because no formal Associations have been stablished and no records preserved.

Bibliography (in addition to works cited under MADJŪS): there is an overview of the literature in J.R. Hinnells, *The Parsis: a bibliographical survey*, in *Journal of Mithraic Studies* (*JMS*), iii (1980), 100-49, and a compendium of textual materials in M. Boyce, *Sources for the study of Zoroastrianism*, Manchester 1984. On the *Ḳiṣṣa-yi Sandjan* as a historical source, see P. Axelrod, *Myth and identity in the Indian Zoroastrian community*, in *JMS* (1980), 150-65. On the early sources, see R.B. Paymaster, *Early history of the Parsees in India*, Bombay 1954, and for the travellers' accounts see N.K. Firby, *European travellers and their perceptions of Zoroastrians in the 17th and 18th centuries*, Berlin 1988. The history of the Pārsīs in Bombay is outlined in *EIr.*, IV, 339-46; see also Hinnells, *Parsis and the British*, in *Journal of the Cama Oriental Institute* (*JCOI*), Bombay, xlvi (1978), 1-64. Two books which give a helpful account of the Pārsīs in their main 19th century base, Bombay, are C. Dobbin, *Urban leadership in Western India*, Oxford 1972, and G. Tyndall, *City of Gold, the biography of Bombay*, London 1982. The main biography of Naoroji is R.P. Masani, *Dadabhai Naoroji: the Grand Old Man of India*, London 1939; on Mehta, see H. Mody, *Sir Pherozeshah Mehta*, Bombay 1963. Important studies of the Pārsī role in Indian politics include: A. Seal, *The emergence of Indian nationalism*, Cambridge 1968; J. Masselos, *Towards nationalism*, Bombay 1974; and G. Johnson, *Provincial politics and Indian nationalism*, Cambridge 1973. See also D. Mellor, *The parliamentary life of Dadabhai Naoroji*, in *JCOI*, lii (1985), 1-113, and C. Monk, *The Parsis and the emergence of the Indian National Congress*, in *ibid.*, 115-245. The main study of the great Pārsī philanthropist is J.R.P. Mody, *Jamsetjee Jejeebhoy*, Bombay 1959. On the work of Saklatvala, see M. Squires, *Saklatvala: a political biography*, London 1990, and S. Saklatvala, *The fifth commandment*, Salford 1991. The main biography of the leading Pārsī industrialist is F. Harris, *Jamsetji Nusserwanji Tata*, Bombay 1958. There are numerous demographic studies of the community; most are listed in Hinnells' bibliography listed above. Later studies include: M. Karkal, *Survey of Parsi population of Greater Bombay-1982*, Bombay 1984; S. Bose and A. Khullar, *Socio-economic survey of the Parsis of Delhi*, Delhi 1978; S. Taraporewala, *Religiosity in an urban setting: a study of Parsi college students in the city of Bombay*, Ph.D. thesis, Kalina University Bombay 1985 (unpubl.); K. Gould, *Singling out a demographic problem: the never married Parsis*, in *JMS*, iiii (1980), 166-84. At the time of writing there is little published on the Pārsīs outside India. Two works are in preparation: J.R. Hinnells and R. Writer, *The living flame: a study of the Zoroastrians in Britain*, Manchester (this will also include a study of the otherwise neglected Pārsī M.P., M.M. Bhownagree); and Hinnells, *An ancient religion in contemporary exile: the Zoroastrian diaspora*. On Karachi, there is J.F. Punthakey, *The Karachi Zoroastrian Calendar* (Eng. tr. F.H. Punthakey), Karachi 1989 (a historical overview of Pārsīs in the city). On Pārsīs in Hong Kong, there is K.N. Vaid, *The overseas Indian community in Hong Kong*, Hong Kong 1972, ch. 3, and for Kenya, C. Salvadori, *Through open doors: a view of Asian cultures in Kenya*, Nairobi 1983, ch. 1. (J.R. HINNELLS)

PARTAI ISLAM SE MALAYSIA (PAS), an Islamic-oriented political party of Malaysia.

The Partai Islam Se Malaysia (formerly Malaya), or Pan Malaysian (Malayan) Islamic Party (PMIP), was formed in the 1950s. Its ideological origins lie in the Islamic reformist movement in Malaya at the beginning of the 20th century. A party began to take shape in the 1940s as the religious wing (*Hizbul Muslimin*) of the radical but essentially secular Malay Nationalist Party (MNP). In 1948 the Majlis Tertingi Agama (supreme religious council; its acronym, MATA, is the Malay word for "eye") was set up at the religious college at Gunong Semanggol (in the west-coast state of Perak), which remained the centre for Islamic politics for several years. The radical Malay movement collapsed under the Emergency Regulations issued to counter the communist insurrection in 1948, and in 1951, pulling clear of the MNP, religious activists formed the All-Malaya Islamic Association (or Pan-Malayan Islamic Association, Persatuan Islam Sa-Tanah Melayu). At first, the Association co-operated with the United Malays National Organisation (UMNO), which was the strongest Malay political party and appealed more to ethnicity than to Islam, but when UMNO formed the Alliance with the Malayan Chinese Association (later joined by the Malayan Indian Congress), the All-Malaya Islamic Association became alienated from the mainstream of the Malay nationalist movement. Registering as a political party (the Pan-Malayan Islamic Party or Partai Islam Se Malaya), it opposed the Alliance in Malaya's first federal elections of 1955, two years before independence from British rule. Of the 52 electable seats, the Alliance (dominated by UMNO) won 51 seats while PAS was victorious only in the constituency of Krian (Perak).

The party was put on a stronger footing when Dr Burhanuddin Al-Helmy (formerly president of the MNP, 1946-7, and leader of the *Hizbul Muslimin*) became its president in December 1956. Blending a strong appeal to communal chauvinism with an avowed commitment to Islam as the basis for a Malay-dominated Malaya, Burhanuddin attracted support from rural Malays, and PAS came to rely upon Malay teachers in religious schools or *pondok*s [see PESANTREN] in the Malay-majority states of the north-west (Kedah and Perlis) and east coast (Trengganu and Kelantan). At the 1959 elections, PAS secured the government of Trengganu and won a landslide in Kelantan. Although it relinquished the former in the 1964 elections, it maintained control over the latter until late 1977.

During the bitterly contested election campaign of 1969, which polarised politics on communal lines, PAS claimed that UMNO had failed the Malays during the years since independence because it had compromised with infidels and neglected the needs of the rural community. Though the UMNO-dominated Alliance secured a majority in the Dewan Rakyat (federal parliament), it lost the vital two-thirds majority allowing it to amend the constitution. Non-Malay parties, notably the Democratic Action Party and Gerakan, won 25 seats, while PAS gained 12 (and 23.7% of the total vote). These elections and the bloody aftermath of communal violence (the "13 May 1969 incident") represent a watershed in modern Malaysian politics and a spur to economic and social restructuring; the Alliance was refashioned as the Barisan National (BN, national front), of which UMNO was the major component, and the government launched a series of five-year plans in support of the New Economic Policy, whose objectives were to sustain economic growth, project Malays into the modern sector and, ultimately, break down communal compartments. PAS joined the ruling coalition in 1974 and, campaigning as part of the BN, it won 14 of the 154 federal seats in the elections of 1974. Led by Mohamed Asri Haji Muda (acting president 1964-71, president 1971-82), PAS reached the high-point in its electoral fortunes in 1969-74, but in the late 1970s it went into decline. Torn by internal disputes, PAS lost control of Kelantan and was forced out of the Barisan National; at the end of 1977 the federal government established "emergency rule" in Kelantan, and elections the following year (which PAS fought in opposition to the Barisan) not only confirmed the end of PAS rule in Kelantan but also reduced the party's seats in the federal parliament from 14 to 5.

Nonetheless, PAS kept up its attacks upon UMNO and, from the late 1970s onwards, these coincided with the upsurge of fundamentalism elsewhere in the Islamic world, notably the Iranian revolution. After Asri resigned as president following another poor performance in the elections of 1982 (when PAS won five seats), the more militant Yusuf Rawa (president 1982-89) assumed the leadership of PAS. Under the influence of the *ulama* and professing its goal to be the creation of an Islamic state, PAS issued a *fatwa* declaring all supporters of UMNO to be infidels. The phenomenon of one Malay Muslim branding another as infidel—known as the "*kafir-mengkafir* dispute"—became particularly intense in Trengganu, Kelantan and Kedah, where UMNO and PAS vied with each other for support and where Malay kampongs divided in their allegiance to one or other of the parties.

Competition between UMNO and PAS for power and authority has been a major feature of Malay politics while Dr Mahathir has been president of UMNO and Prime Minister of Malaysia (1981 to date). PAS ideas were spread by speakers at *ceramah* (private political meetings) and through the distribution of thousands of audio-visual cassettes. In its attacks both upon UMNO as guardian of Malay nationalism and mainstay of the Malaysian government and upon the Barisan's New Economic Policy, PAS received backing from Islamic universities, many Malays in local higher education institutions and Malay students overseas. It also established links with ABIM (Angkatan Belia Islam Malaysia, the Malaysian Islamic Youth Movement) led by Anwar Ibrahim. Committed though it was to Malay interests, UMNO could not countenance an ideology that rejected secular nationalism and worldly materialism; UMNO leaders rejected the PAS strategy as a recipe for disaster in a country where Malays (i.e. Muslims) amounted to only a little over half of the total population. UMNO took the *dakwah* (Islamic revivalist) challenge seriously, however, with the result that government adopted a more obviously Islamic stand on certain issues (such as banking, higher education and the construction of mosques). Moreover, in 1982 Mahathir co-opted Anwar Ibrahim into the government, thereby diminishing the influence of ABIM. In 1984 a TV debate between UMNO and PAS leaders vying for legitimacy in the eyes of Malaysia's Muslims was cancelled at the last minute on the intervention of the Agong (Malaysia's king). Tension did not fade; on the contrary, confrontation between government and PAS came to a head at Memali (Kedah) in November 1985, when Malay policemen opened fire on Malay farmers, and PAS acquired 14 martyrs for Islam.

UMNO's hold over Malays appeared to be endorsed by the 1986 elections when only one PAS candidate was returned to the federal parliament, whose total membership had been increased to 177. UMNO's success can be put down to its efficiency and control of the media, the five-fold increase in the election deposit required of candidates, and, perhaps most significantly, PAS's overtures to Chinese voters. Its attempt to line up an opposition front in co-operation with non-Malays, though vain, compromised its "Malay-ness"; Malay voters opted for ethnic interests rather than Islamic principles.

Although circumscribed by government restrictions, not least the Internal Security Act, PAS was provided with an opportunity to advance its position by a power struggle that racked UMNO in 1987-90. In 1987 UMNO was split by a vicious leadership battle when Tengku Razaleigh challenged Dr Mahathir for the presidency of UMNO. A new political configuration seemed to be taking shape; the multi-racial coalition of the Barisan, which Mahathir's UMNO continued to dominate, was for the first time challenged by an alternative coalition of racially and ideologically disparate parties. PAS and Semangat '46 ("spirit of '46", a party composed of UMNO dissidents led by Tengku Razaleigh) formed the Angatan Perpaduan Ummah (Muslim solidarity movement), and together they joined the Chinese-dominated Democratic Action Party in the Gagasan Rakyat or People's Front. During the 1990 electoral campaign, PAS tempered its fundamentalism and adopted the slogan "Developing with Islam", but the three disparate parties failed to resolve their differences. The Barisan as a whole and UMNO in particular were returned with formidable majorities; Malays rejected PAS and Semangat '46, except in Kelantan, where APU formed the state government, while in the federal parliament PAS increased its representation from one to seven.

To some extent, the myth of Malay solidarity has been cracked in recent years by the emergence of PAS's challenge to UMNO and by the latter's internal rifts. Both UMNO and PAS have inherited and continue to appeal to the traditions of Malay culture, but, whereas PAS has presented itself as a fundamentalist Islamic movement, UMNO's reputation as guardian of Malay nationalism, its command of government since independence, its capacity to respond to and generate social and economic change, and the breadth and depth of its organisation have all assisted its continuing political dominance.

Bibliography: G.P. Means, *Malaysian politics*², London 1976; C.S. Kesseler, *Islam and politics in a Malay state: Kelantan 1838-1969*, Ithaca 1978; N.J. Funston, *Malay politics in Malaysia. A study of the United Malays National Organisation and Party Islam*, Kuala Lumpur 1980; Judith Nagata, *Religion and social change: the Islamic revival in Malaysia*, in *Pacific Affairs*, liii (Fall 1980), 405-39; Mohamad Abu Bakar, *Islam and nationalism in contemporary Malay society*, in Taufik Abdullah and Sharon Siddique (eds.), *Islam and society in Southeast Asia*, Institute of Southeast Asian Studies, Singapore 1986, 155-74; Hussin Mutalib, *Islam and ethnicity in Malay politics*, Singapore 1990; Means, *Malaysian politics: the second generation*, Singapore 1991. (A.J. STOCKWELL)

PARWĀN [see FARWĀN].

PARWĀNA [see MUʿĪN AL-DĪN SULAYMĀN PARWĀNA].

PARWĀNAČĪ, "relater", term used in Persian administration for the official who noted down the instructions for the promulgation of deeds, and who forwarded them to the chancery.

The function is recorded for the first time under īmūr, and is then found among the Tīmūrids, the ara Ḳoyunlu, the Aḳ Ḳoyunlu [*q.vv.*] and in the ear- Ṣafawid period. According to Khʷāndamīr, there ere usually two relaters, one in charge of the Council r Army Inspection (*dīwān-i towāčī*), the other of the ouncil for Finances (*dīwān-i māl*) and of the ad- ninistration of the *Ṣadr (sarkār-i ṣidārat)* [see ṢADR]. Only occasionally did each of these three departments ave its own relater, or did there exist one single elater for the three together. In addition to Persians, ere were also Turkish *amīrs* under the relaters. In ank they were above the secretaries of the chancery *nunshīs* [*q.v.*]), but subordinate to the viziers. As a ule, they apparently transmitted the orders for the eeds to the chancery in writing. The related ocuments were called *parwāna, parwānača* or *risāla*, nd they were sealed with the *muhr-i-parwāna* [see UHR], which usually was in the hands of a keeper f the seal (*muhrdār*) and only exceptionally (see Khʷāndamīr, *Dastūr al-wuzarāʾ*, Tehran 2535 *hāhānshāhī*, 401) in those of the relater.

Bibliography: H. Busse, *Untersuchungen zum islamischen Kanzleiwesen*, Cairo 1959, 69 ff.; G. Herrmann, *Der historische Gehalt des "Nāmä-ye nāmī" von Ḫāndamīr*, Ph.D. thesis Göttingen 1968, unpubl., 31, 92 ff., 207 ff.; Sh. Ando, *Timuridische Emire nach dem Muʿizz al-ansāb*, Berlin 1992, 106, 172-3, 194-5, 198, 211-12, 249.

(G. Herrmann)

PARWĪN IʿTIṢĀMĪ, celebrated female poet of ran, was born on 16 March 1907 in Tabrīz. Her ather, Yūsuf Iʿtiṣāmī (d. 2 January 1938), was a espected author known chiefly for his translations of rench and Arabic works into Persian. He was also he founder and principal writer of the literary nagazine *Bahār*, which appeared from April 1910 till November 1911 and again from April 1921 till December 1922. Parwīn received her early instruction n Persian and Arabic literature from her father. When she was still small, her father moved the family o Tehran. There she attended the American High School for Women. Following her graduation, she was employed for some time to teach at the same in- titution. It is reported that Riḍā Shāh wanted her to ct as private tutor to the queen, but she declined. In 1934 she married a cousin of her father, and went to ive in Kirmānshāh where her husband was a police officer. The union, however, did not last, and ended n divorce after a few months. In 1936 the Iranian Ministry of Culture gave her a medal ranking third in order of importance. The poetess is said to have turn- ed down the award which, in its poor choice, was clearly an offence to her self-respect. In 1939 Parwīn worked for some months as librarian in Dānish-sarā- yi ʿĀlī, University of Tehran. On 5 April 1941 she died after a brief illness caused by typhoid fever, and was buried at Ḳum in the family tomb next to her father.

According to Malik al-Shuʿarā Bahār, Parwīn started composing poetry when she was eight years old. In her poetical training during the initial period, the main guiding figure was most probably her father. He would give her his prose translations of French, Arabic and Turkish poems and encouraged her to put them into verse. Already at an early age, Parwīn demonstrated a remarkable artistic maturity. Consequently, some individuals were disposed to take the sceptical view that the poems in her name were actually composed by her father. In the beginning, her poems appeared in her father's journal during its second period. Before her death she is said to have destroyed a portion of her poetical output which did not come up to her expectations. A book containing her collected poems appeared for the first time in 1935, and an enlarged edition was published soon after her death in 1942.

Parwīn Iʿtiṣāmī may be regarded as a poet in the classical mould. Among the literary influences detected in her poems are chiefly those associated with such former poets as Nāṣir-i Khusraw, Anwarī, ʿAṭṭār, Saʿdī, and Rūmī [*q.vv.*]. Barring a few exceptions, her poems adhere to conventional verse forms, and include *ḳaṣīdas*, *mathnawīs*, *ḳiṭʿas*, and *ghazals*. As regards the subject matter of her poetry, it is dominated by moralistic and ethical themes. The poetess is largely indifferent to the real social concerns of her time, and shows only a passing appreciation of the problems pertaining to her own sex. Still, Parwīn's poetry has a charm of its own resulting from a deep feeling of tenderness and compassion. As her favourite device, she uses the form of *munāẓara* (strife poem) [*q.v.*] and dialogue, a technique borrowed from earlier sources but featuring more extensively and devoted to better use in her works.

Bibliography: Parwīn Iʿtiṣāmī, *Dīwān*, 3rd edition (with introd. by Malik al-Shuʿarā Bahār), Tehran 1944; idem, *Matn-i kāmil-i dīwān-i Parwīn Iʿtiṣāmī*, ed. Aḥmad Karīmī (with introd. by Sīmīn Bihbihānī), Tehran 1369/1990; *Madjmūʿa-yi maḳālāt wa ḳiṭaʿāt-i ashʿār ki bi-munāsabat-i dargudhasht wa awwalīn sāl-i wafāt-i Khānum Parwīn Iʿtiṣāmī niwishta wa surūda shuda ast* (published by Abu 'l-Fatḥ Iʿtiṣāmī), Tehran 1944; M. Ishaque, *Sukhanwarān-i Īrān dar ʿaṣr-i ḥāḍir*, i, Calcutta 1933; idem, *Four eminent poetesses of Iran*, Calcutta 1950; Saʿīd Nafīsī, *Parwīn Iʿtiṣāmī*, in *Payām-i naw*, i/2, Tehran 1323/1944; Muḥammad Bāḳir Burḳaʿī, *Sukhanwarān-i nāmī-yi muʿāṣir*, i, Tehran 1229/1950; ʿAbd al-Ḥamīd Khalkhālī, *Tadhkira-yi shuʿarā-yi muʿāṣir*, Tehran 1333/1954; Munibur Rahman, *Post-revolution Persian verse*, Aligarh 1955; idem, *Djadīd Fārsī shāʿirī*, Aligarh 1959; ʿAlī Akbar Mushīr Salīmī, *Zanān-i sukhanwar*, i, Tehran 1335/1956-7; J. Rypka *et alii*, *History of Iranian literature*, Dordrecht 1968; ʿAbd al-ʿAlī Dastghayb, *Hadiyya-yi fikr wa shiʿr yā dīwān-i Parwīn Iʿtiṣāmī*, in *Payām-i nuwīn*, ii/6, Tehran 1960; Buzurg ʿAlawī, *Geschichte und Entwicklung der modernen persischen Literatur*, Berlin 1964; Aḥmad Aḥmadī and Ḥusayn Razmdjū, *Sayr-i sukhan*, ii, Mashhad 1345/1966; F. Machalski, *La littérature de l'Iran contemporain*, ii, Wrocław-Warszawa-Kraków 1967; Kashāwarz Ṣadr, *Az Rābiʿa tā Parwīn*, Tehran (?) n.d.; Muḥammad Ḥusayn Shahriyār, *Parwīn Iʿtiṣāmī* (poem dealing with the author's personal impressions about Parwīn Iʿtiṣāmī), in *Rahnamā-yi kitāb*, January-March 1971; Heshmat Moayyad, *Parvin's poems: a cry in the wilderness*, in *Islamwissenschaftliche Abhandlungen*, ed. R. Gramlich, Wiesbaden 1974; Ḥusayn Namīnī (ed.), *Djāwidāna Parwīn Iʿtiṣāmī* (essays on life and poetry of Parwīn Iʿtiṣāmī by various authors and a selection of her poetry), Tehran 1362/1983; Naẓmī Tabrīzī, *Duwīst sukhanwar*, Tehran 1363/1984; Heshmat Moayyad and A. Margaret Arent Madelung (tr.), *A nightingale's lament* (selections from the poems of Parwīn Iʿtiṣāmī), Lexington, Ky. 1985; ʿAbd al-Rafīʿ Ḥaḳīḳat, *Farhang-i shāʿirān-i zabān-i Pārsī*, Tehran 1368/1990.

(Munibur Rahman)

PARWĪZ, KHUSRAW (II), Sāsānid emperor 591-628, and the last great ruler of this dynasty before the invading Arabs overthrew the Persian empire. The MP name *Parwīz* "victorious" is explained in al-Ṭabarī, i, 995, 1065, as *al-muẓaffar* and *al-manṣūr*; the name was Arabised as Abarwīz (see Justi, *Iranisches Namenbuch*, 19).

For the main events of his long reign (dominated by the struggles with the Byzantines over the buffer-state Armenia and over control of the Fertile Crescent in general, culminating in the Persian invasion of Egypt in 619, but then the riposte by the Byzantine emperor Heraclius, which brought the Greek armies as far as Mesopotamia in 627-8), see Christensen, *L'Iran sous les Sassanides*², Copenhagen 1944, 445-96, and R.N. Frye, *The political history of Iran under the Sasanians*, in *Camb. hist. of Iran*, iii/1, 165-72. Most relevant for us here are Khusraw Parwīz's relations with the Arabs on the fringes of Mesopotamia and, in particular, with the Lakhmid dynasty of al-Ḥīra [*q.v.*], outlined in LAKHMIDS and chiefly significant for the fact of Khusraw Parwīz's overthrow of the last Lakhmid king al-Nuʿmān III b. al-Mundhir IV in 602 and the establishment of direct Persian rule soon afterwards, ending the power of this Arab dynasty which had acted as a protective force against pressure from the Bedouins of the Arabian interior. The Sāsānids' flank in western Mesopotamia was laid open to attack, and a foretaste of the Muslim Arab invasions of the 630s given in the battle or, more probably, skirmish of Dhū Ḳār [*q.v.*] in central ʿIrāḳ, when the tribe of Bakr b. Wāʾil defeated a coalition of other Arab tribes plus Persian regular troops, demonstrating that the Persian army was not invincible (see further, C.E. Bosworth, *Iran and the Arabs before Islam*, in *Camb. hist. of Iran*, iii/1, 607-9).

In later Islamic literature, such as *adab* works and the Mirrors for Princes [see NAṢĪḤAT AL-MULŪK], Khusraw Parwīz became renowned for the splendour and luxury of his court. He was a devotee of music and poetry, and the famous musician Bārbadh, allegedly the inventor of the rhythmic musical modes known as *dastānāt* (see H.G. Farmer, *A history of Arabian music*, London 1929, 198-9), was one of his courtiers. His famous horse Shabdīz is mentioned, but above all he is linked with his favourite wife, the Christian Shīrīn, as part of the very popular theme in Persian literature of Shīrīn and her humble lover Farhād, dealt with by *inter alios* Niẓāmī and Amīr Khusraw Dihlawī [*q.vv.*; see FARHĀD WA-SHĪRĪN]. See further on Parwīz's image in later literature, Niẓām al-Mulk, *Siyāsat-nāma*, index, and al-Ghazālī, *Naṣīḥat al-mulūk*, Eng. tr. F.R.C. Bagley, *Ghazālī's Book of counsel for kings*, London 1964, 192, 194 and the references there.

Bibliography: Given in the article.

(C.E. BOSWORTH)

PASANTREN [see PESANTREN].

PASAROFČA, the Ottoman Turkish form of the Yugoslavian town of Požarevac, better known in European history under its Germanic form Passarowitz. Požarevac is now a prosperous commercial town, situated in lat. 44°37′ N. and long. 21°12′ E. some 60 km/40 miles to the southeast of Belgrade in the fertile plain of Serbia between Morava and Mlava, and only a short distance from the Danube port of Dubravica.

The town, whose name is popularly connected with the Serbo-Croat word *požar* ("fire") (M.D. Milićević, *Kneževina Srbija*, Belgrade 1876, 172, 1058), is first mentioned towards the end of the 9th/15th century. It must, however, have been previously in existence and have become Turkish like the surrounding country in 1459. According to the Turkish treasury registers of Hungary of 1565 (A. Velics, *Magyarországi török kincstári defterek*, ii, Budapest 1890, 734), Pasarofča belonged to the Turkish *sandjak* of Semendre (Semendria, Smederevo), and in the middle of the 11th/17th century, Ḥādjdjī Khalīfa describes it as the seat of a judge (*ḳāḍīlīḳ*) (cf. *Spomenik*, xviii, Belgrade 1892, col. 26). Towards the end of the century, many Serbs migrated from Pasarofča and at the beginning of the 18th century it is sometimes mentioned as a village.

Pasarofča was, however, destined soon to become famous through the peace which ended the Austro-Turkish war of 1716-18. At the end of 1714, the Ottoman sultan Aḥmed III [*q.v.*] had already declared war on Venice on the pretext that the peace of Carlowitz [see ḲARLOFČA] was not being observed and in 1715 occupied the Morea and some of the Ionian Islands. Austria, which at first intervened to negotiate as an ally of Venice, in 1716 entered the war herself and her armies, led by Prince Eugene of Savoy, won three great victories, at Peterwardein, Temesvár and Belgrade, so that England intervened to secure peace. After long preparations (see von Hammer, *GOR*², iv, 159-64), the congress of Passarowitz was convoked. The negotiations at which plenipotentiaries of Turkey, Austria, Venice with England and Holland as mediators took part began on 5 June 1718 and the Treaty of Passarowitz was signed on 21 July.

Peace was concluded on a basis of the territory actually held by the opponents at the time (*uti possidetis*). Austria retained the eastern part of Sirmia, the banate with Temesvár, the whole of northeastern Serbia with Belgrade, Požarevac, etc., and Little Wallachia. Venice also retained a few places she had taken on the Dalmatian and Albanian coasts, received certain commercial preferences and the island of Cerigo (Kythera), but had to restore to Turkey the whole of the peninsula of the Morea and the southeastern districts of Hercegovina. By a commercial agreement which was also concluded at Passarowitz on 27 July, Austria secured certain trading, consular and other privileges such as preferential tariffs, in the Ottoman Empire. The Imperial Ostend Company was formed to exploit these concessions, and in 1719 commercial activity began from the new "free port" of Trieste. The actual Treaty of Passarowitz in effect proclaimed that the Ottomans were no longer a serious military danger to their European neighbours.

Following the traditional formalities observed after the conclusion of a treaty of peace, the first Turkish plenipotentiary Ibrāhīm Pasha Newshehirli went to Vienna with his retinue and Count Wirmont, the Austrian representative in the negotiations, to Constantinople. A member of the Turkish embassy wrote in 1726 an interesting account which has been published by Fr. van Kraelitz in text and translation (*Bericht über den Zug des Gross-Botschafters Ibrahim Pascha nach Wien im Jahre 1719*, in *SB Ak. Wien*, clviii [1908]; in *TOEM*, vii [1332/1916], 211-27, the Turkish text of this edition was reprinted by A. Refīḳ).

During the Austrian occupation (1718-39), Pasarofča was the most important place in this territory. In the Serbian war of independence against Turkey, it was besieged for a long period, but had finally to surrender to the Serbs (1804). In 1813, the town again fell into Turkish hands but became Serbian again in 1815.

In the years of peace that followed (1815-1915), Požarevac developed. Prince Miloš in 1825 made it his second residence and had two *ḳonaḳs* (palaces) built there. Shortly afterwards, a Prussian officer visited the town and left interesting notes on the conditions there (Otto von Pirch, *Reise in Serbien im Spätherbst 1829*, Berlin 1830, part i, 119-71). In the second half of the 19th century, the population increased steadily, ut otherwise the town offered "little of interest" (F. Kanitz, *Serbien*, Leipzig 1868, 13).

At the beginning of the 20th century Požarevac was ne of the most important towns in Serbia. In the irst World War, it was occupied by the Germans in 915 and by the Bulgarians (from October 1916), but n the autumn of 1918 it was again occupied by the erbs. Since then it has belonged to Yugoslavia now 1993) coming within the Serbia-Montenegro rump of he Yugoslavian Republic.

Bibliography (in addition to the references in the text): V. Bianchi (the Venetian plenipotentiary at the peace negotiations), *Istorica relazione della pace di Posaroviz*, Padua 1719; ʿAbd al-Raḥmān Ṣheref, *Taʾrīk̲h̲-i Dewlet-i ʿothmāniyye*, ii, 1312/1894, 140-7; G. Noradounghian, *Recueil d'actes internationaux de l'empire ottoman*, i, Paris 1897, 61-2 (nos. 308-9), 108-16 (Latin text of the treaty of peace with Austria) and 216-20 (French résumé of it); Drag. M. Pavlović, *Požarevački mir (1718. g.)*, in *Letopis matice srpske*, Novi Sad 1901, part 207, pp. 26-47, and part 208, pp. 45-80 (good historical study on the peace of Požarevac); V. Popović, in *Narodna enciklopedija*, iii, Zagreb 1928, 428; *Almanah kraljevine Jugoslavije*, Zagreb 1930, i, 561; M.A. Purković, *Požarevac*, Požarevac 1934 (first attempt at a monograph on the town and its history); Lavender Cassels, *The struggle for the Ottoman empire, 1717-1740*, London 1966, 14, 47; S.J. Shaw, *History of the Ottoman empire and modern Turkey*, i, Cambridge 1976; A.N. Kurat, *The retreat of the Turks, 1683-1730*, in *The New Cambridge Modern History*, vi, 640-2; *İA* art. *Pasarofça* (Cemal Tukin).

(F. Bajraktarević*)

PASÈ, the name of a district on the north coast of Atjeh [*q.v.*] in Sumatra, which according to the prevalent local view stretches from the Djambō-Ajé river in the east to the other side of the Pasè river in the west. The whole area is divided up into a number of little states each with an *ulèibalang* or chief.

Pasè at one time was a kingdom known throughout eastern Asia. The north coast of Atjeh was in the middle ages on the trade route by sea from Hindustān to China. Islam followed this route and firmly established itself from India on this coast, the first point in the East Indian archipelago which it reached. In the 7th/13th century we know there were already Muslim rulers here. One of these was Malik al-Ṣāliḥ (d. 1297), according to native tradition founder of the state and the man to make the country Muslim; his tomb made of stone imported from Cambay in India has been discovered along with several other gravestones on the left bank of the Pasè river, not far from the sea. The capital of the kingdom is said to have been here. A second capital, rather more to the west, was Samudra; it was the royal residence when Ibn Baṭṭūṭa in the middle of the 8th/14th century twice visited the land, on his way to China and on the return journey. The present name of the island of Sumatra, by which it is known in the west, comes from Samudra (in Ibn Baṭ-ṭūṭa: Sumaṭra). Pasè was then a flourishing country on the coast; the ruler was king of the port, who himself sent out trading-ships; a ship belonging to him was seen by Ibn Baṭṭūṭa in the harbour of Ch'ünchou (Fukien) in South China. Life at the court was modelled on that of the Muslim courts of India. The ruler at this time was an ardent Muslim, who took a great interest in learning. He waged a victorious *d̲j̲ihād* on the natives in the hinterland. Leaden coins struck in the country and Chinese crude gold were the means of exchange. The chief food was rice.

Shortly after Ibn Baṭṭūṭa left the country, the king

had to recognise the suzerainty of the Javanese Hindu empire of Madjapahit (before 1365). A tomb of a queen or princess found near Lhō' Sukon has an Arabic inscription, dated 791/1389 at the top of the stone, and at the bottom an inscription in much weathered old Javanese script. The Chinese envoy Cheng Ho remarked in 1416 that the land was involved in continual war with Nago (Pidië). He mentions rice, silkworms and pepper as its products. The last-named attracted the Portuguese there. From 1521 they had a fortified settlement in Pasè, but in 1524 they were driven out by the sultan of the rising kingdom of Atjeh (i.e. Great Atjeh). Henceforth, Pasè was a dependency of Atjeh. The tombs of the rulers of the former kingdom were still an object of pilgrimage to the most famous sultan of Atjeh, Iskandar T̲h̲ānī, as late as 1048/1638-9; but at the present day, even the memory of the old kingdom is extinct. The mouth of the Pasè river is silted up and the place where the capital stood is no longer recognisable.

Pasè exercised through the years a considerable influence in the Malay Archipelago through its Muslim scholars and missionaries. Javanese and Malay tradition have preserved its memory.

Bibliography: C. Snouck Hurgronje, *Verspreide geschriften*, iv/1, 402 ff., iv/2, 101 ff.; Ibn Baṭṭūṭa, iv, 228 ff.; W.P. Groeneveldt, *Notes on the Malay Archipelago and Malacca*, in *Miscellaneous Papers relating to Indo-China and the Indian Archipelago*, ser. 2, vol. i, London 1887, 171, 208 ff.; J.P. Moquette, *De eerste vorsten van Samoedra-Pasè (Noord-Sumatra)*, in *Rapporten Oudheidk. Dienst Nederlandsch-Indië* (1913), 1 ff.; *Oudheidk. Verslag*, in *ibid.* (1915), 127 ff.

(R.A. Kern)

PASHA (т., from the Pers. *pādis̲h̲āh*, probably influenced by Turkish *bas̲k̲ak*), the highest official title of honour (ʿunwān or *laḳab*) in use in Turkey until the advent of the Republic and surviving for sometime after that in certain Muslim countries originally part of the Turkish empire (Egypt, ʿIrāḳ, Syria). It was always accompanied by the proper name, like the titles of nobility in Europe, but with this difference from the latter, that it was placed after the name (like the less important titles of *bey* and *efendi*). In addition, being neither hereditary nor giving any rank to wives, nor attached to territorial possessions, it was military rather than feudal in character. It was however not reserved solely for soldiers but was also given to certain high civil (not religious) officials.

The title of *pas̲h̲a* first appears in the 7th/13th century. It is difficult to define its original use exactly. The word had in any case early assumed the vague meaning of "seigneur" (*dominus*) (cf. *Dīwān-i türkī-i Sulṭān Weled*, 14; text of the year 712/1313, where Allāh himself is invoked in the phrase *Ey Pas̲h̲a!*). At this same period, the title of *pas̲h̲a* like that of *sulṭān* was sometimes given to women (cf. Ismāʿīl Ḥaḳḳī, *Kitābeler*, Istanbul 1927, index, s.v. Ḳadem pas̲h̲a, Selčuk pas̲h̲a), a practice which recurs only once again, and then exceptionally, in the 19th century in the case of the mother of the K̲h̲edive [see WĀLIDE SULṬĀN].

Under the Saldjūḳs of Anatolia, the title of *pas̲h̲a* (in as much as it was an abbreviation of *pādis̲h̲āh* and always by analogy with that of *sulṭān*) was given occasionally to certain men of religion, who must also have at the same time been soldiers and whose history is not yet well known. To judge from the genealogy which ʿĀs̲h̲ïḳ-pas̲h̲a-zāde claims for himself, the title of *pas̲h̲a* was already in use in the first half of the 7th/13th century. Muk̲h̲liṣ al-Dīn Mūsā Baba, alias S̲h̲ayk̲h̲ Muk̲h̲liṣ or Muk̲h̲liṣ Pas̲h̲a had, according to ʿAlī

Efendi, seized power before the Ḳaramānog͟hlu [*q.v.*] and in the same region, after the defeat of the Saldjūḳ Sultan G͟hiyāt͟h al-Dīn Kayk͟husraw II [*q.v.*] at Köse Dag͟h which took place in 641/1243 (cf. Gibb, *A history of Ottoman poetry*, i, 177).

At the end of the same century, the title of *pas͟ha* seems to have been added to the names of certain members (restricted in number) of the petty Turkish and Turkoman dynasties which shared Asia Minor; these are sometimes rulers, sometimes members of their families. It was the same in the principalities of Tekke, Aydi̊n, Deñizli and Ḳi̊zi̊l-Aḥmadli̊ and probably also in other little kingdoms of Anatolia (cf. for Saruk͟han, ʿAlī Pas͟ha, according to S͟hihāb al-Dīn Ibn Faḍl Allāh al-ʿUmarī, *al-Taʿrīf bi 'l-muṣṭalaḥ al-s͟harīf*, quoted by al-Ḳalḳas͟handī, *Ṣubḥ al-aʿs͟hā*, viii, 16, l. 14).

In the family of ʿOt͟hmān, two individuals are credited with the title of *pas͟ha*: ʿAlāʾ al-Dīn, son of ʿOt͟hmān, and Süleymān, son of Ork͟han.

The case of ʿAlāʾ al-Dīn is very obscure. Two different individuals of this name have even been distinguished: the one being ʿAlāʾ al-Dīn Bey, son of ʿOt͟hmān, the other ʿAlāʾ al-Dīn Pas͟ha, *wazīr* [*q.v.*] of ʿOt͟hmān, and the two may have been confounded (cf. Ḥüseyin Ḥüsāmeddīn, *ʿAlāeddīn Bey*, in *TTEM*, years xiv and xv, 4 articles). It may be added that the same individual or one of the two individuals in question may also have been a *beylerbeyi* (cf. Orudj's chronicle, ed. Babinger, 15, l. 15). Whatever be the case with this insoluble problem, it seems certain that the title of *pas͟ha* was given early to statesmen (cf. a Sinān Pas͟ha under Ork͟han).

The title of *pas͟ha* in any event very soon became the prerogative of two classes of dignitaries: 1. the *beylerbeyi*s of the provinces, and 2. the *wazīr*s of the capital. It was later extended to officials with similar functions.

In the second half of the 8th/14th century (in 760/1359 or 763/1362?), Lala S͟hāhīn who, according to the Ottoman historians, was the first (?) *beylerbeyi* of the ʿOt͟hmānli̊s, was given the title of *pas͟ha* at the same time as he received this office. The same title was then given to the *beylerbeyi* of Anatolia (thus keeping up the idea of the two *beylerbeyi*s, one of the right and one of the left wing) and later as new posts were created in the growing empire, extended to the other *beylerbeyi*s or *wālī*s "governors-general".

It was the same with the *wazīr*s, of whom the first (?) according to the Ottoman historians, was Djandarli̊ K͟halīl surnamed K͟hayr al-Dīn Pas͟ha (in 770/1368-9) [see DJANDARLI̊]. The number of the *wazīr*s who were called *ḳubbe wezīrleri* down to the time of Aḥmed III was raised to three and then to nine and the title of *wazīr*, also given to high officials like the *ḳapudan pas͟ha*, the *nis͟hāndji̊* and the *defterdar* [*q.vv.*], became more and more one of honour, carrying with it the title of *pas͟ha*; but since at the beginning and for a considerable time in the capital itself there was only one *wazīr*, the title of *pas͟ha*, par excellence and without any addition, came to be applied to the prime minister (later *ulu wezīr* or *ṣadr aʿẓam* [*q.v.*]), whence the expression *pas͟ha ḳapi̊si̊* which was later replaced by that of *bāb-i ʿālī* "Sublime Porte, the door of the first minister".

The increase in the number of *pas͟ha*s was not at first very rapid. M. d'Aramon mentions only 4 or 5 *pas͟ha*s or *wezīr-pas͟ha*s and at the time he wrote (in 1547), there were only three (Ayaz, Güzeldje Ḳāsim and Ibrāhīm, all three of Christian origin). It is true that here he is referring only to the capital.

In the provinces they were, and became, more numerous, and two classes of *pas͟ha*s were distinguished: 1. the *pas͟ha*s of 3 horse-tails (*tug͟h*) or *wazīr* (a rank which became more and more one of honour and extending to the provinces gradually absorbed that of *beylerbeyi*); 2. the *pas͟ha*s of 2 horse-tails or *mīr-mīrān* [see MĪR-I MĪRĀN] (rank at first the Persian synonym for the Turkish *beylerbeyi* and the Arabic *amīr al-umarāʾ* but gradually became a lower rank). Besides, the old *sandjaḳ-beyi*s having in principle a right to only one horse-tail were promoted *mīr-mīrān* and thus became *pas͟ha*s in their turn.

After the *Tanẓīmāt* [*q.v.*], the title of *pas͟ha* was given to the four first (out of 9) grades of the civil (1. *wezīr*, 2. *bālā*, 3. *ūlā*, 4. *sāniye ṣi̊nfi̊ ewweli*) or military (1. *müs͟hīr*, 2. *birindji ferīḳ*, 3. *ferīḳ*, 4. *liwā*) hierarchy and to the notables (3. *rūmeli beylerbeyi*, 4. *mīr-mīrān*, with in practice unjustified extension to the fallen *emīr-ül-ümerāʾ*, in this case to the purely honorary rank of the sixth grade).

The table of ranks having been abolished after the fall of the Ottoman Empire, the Turkish Republic retained the title of *pas͟ha* for soldiers only. It was finally abolished by the Grand National Assembly of Ankara (26 November 1934). Instead of *pas͟ha*, one now uses *general* and in place of *müs͟hür*, *mares͟hal*.

In western usage, the word was at first pronounced *bas͟ha* (the pronunciation *pas͟ha* does not appear till the 17th century): Ital. *bascia*, Low Latin *bassa*, Fr. *bacha* or *bassa*, Engl. *bashaw*, to say nothing of variant spellings. In Greek on the contrary, the form *pas͟ha* is the oldest (14th century) but probably under western influence we also find *bas͟ha* (16th century); cf. Ducange, *Glossarium mediae et infimae Graecitatis*, s.v. μπασίας.

The pronunciation as *bas͟ha* by Europeans is due either to the influence of Arabic in Egypt or to a confusion with the old Turkish title of *bas͟ha* (see the end of the article).

Etymology of the word *pas͟ha*: we shall examine the various etymologies that have been proposed.

1. Pers. *pāy-i s͟hāh* "foot of the sovereign". This explanation, which was based on the fact that in ancient Persia there were officials called "eyes of the king", is found already in Trévoux's Dictionnaire (s.v. *bacha*) and was revived by J. von Hammer. It is to be rejected.

2. Turk. *bas͟h* "head, chief" already suggested by Antoine Geuffroy (*Briesve description de la Court du Grand Turc*, 1542) and by Leunclavius (Löwenklau), *Pandectes historiae turcicae*, suppl. to his *Annales* (1588). Cf. also Trevoux's *Dict.* and Barbier de Meynard, *Suppl.* It is to be rejected; see the following word.

3. Turk. *bas͟h-ag͟ha* taken (for the purposes of proof) in the meaning of "elder brother". This is the etymology accepted in Turkey until the end of the 19th century (Meḥmed T͟hüreyyā, *Sidjill-i ʿOt͟hmānī*, iv, 738; S͟hams al-Dīn Sāmī, *Ḳāmūs-i türki*, s.v. *pas͟ha*) and based on the fact that Süleymān Pas͟ha and ʿAlāʾ al-Dīn Pas͟ha were the elder brothers of Ork͟han and ʿOt͟hmān respectively. ʿĀlī Efendi in his *Künh ül-ak͟hbār* written in 1001-7/1593-9 (v. 49, l. 23) and ʿOt͟hmān-zāde Aḥmed Ṭāʾib (d. 1136/1724) called attention to this use of the word *pas͟ha* among the Turkomans (*Ḥadīḳat al-wüzerāʾ*, Istanbul 1271, 4, l. 16). Heidborn (*Manuel de droit public et administratif ottoman*, Vienna 1908, 186, n. *a*) also says that *pas͟ha* means "elder brother" among the Greeks of Karamania, but there seems to be nothing to confirm these isolated statements. Some Turkish lexicographers like Aḥmad Wefīḳ (under باشه) and Ṣalāḥī admitted this etymology, but by two stages: *pas͟ha* comes from the Turkish title *bas͟ha* which is for *bas͟h-ag͟ha*. The title of *bas͟ha*, to be discussed below,

does really seem to come from *bash-agha* but, contrary to what the present writer at first thought, has nothing to do with *pasha*.

4. Pers. *pādishāh* "sovereign". This etymologically, the only admissible one (with however the possibility of the influence mentioned under 5), was proposed by the Turkish-Russian dictionary of Boudagov (1869) and later revived by the Russian encyclopaedia of Brockhaus and Efron. It had previously been proposed by d'Herbelot (under *pascha*, à propos of the spelling with final *h*). This explanation is based on the use of the words *sulṭān* and *pādishāh*, as the titles most often placed after the names when applied to individuals of high rank in the religious world (dervishes). Cf. F. Giese, in *Türkīyāt Medjmūʿasi*, i (1925), 164. It seems that one can even explain by *pādishāh* the obscure phrase spoken by Orkhan to ʿAlāʾ al-Dīn Pasha in ʿĀshiḳ-pasha-zāde (ed. Giese, 34-5) before the latter asks leave to retire (cf. above). Orkhan says "You will be *pasha* for me." Now a few lines earlier he had asked him to be a *čoban pādishāh*, i.e. a shepherd for his people.

On the other hand, it will be noted that the title of *pasha* is often used not only as an alternative for *pādishāh* but also for *shāh*. Here are a few examples: Shudjāʿ al-Dīn Sulaymān, of the dynasty of Ḳizil Aḥmedli, is called Sulaymān Pādishāh in Ibn Baṭṭūṭa (ii, 343) and Sulaymān Pasha in al-ʿUmarī, *al-Taʿrīf bi 'l-muṣṭalaḥ al-sharīf*, Cairo 1312, 4 (written *basha*, following the Arabic script) and in Munadjdjim Bashi (iii, 30). The son and successor of this ruler, Ibrāhīm, is called *shāh* in al-ʿUmarī and *Pasha* in Münedjdjim Bashi. In the *Düstūr-nāme-i Enwerī* (ed. Mükrimīn Khalīl, 83-4), Süleymān Pasha, son of Orkhan, is called Shāh Sulaymān (with poetical inversion). ʿAlī b. Čiček (Čeček), the Īlkhānid governor of Baghdād (d. 736/1336), is called ʿAlī Pasha by al-ʿUmarī. According to Naẓmī-zāde (*Gülshen-i khulafāʾ*, Istanbul 1143), he is also found in some mss. as ʿAlī Shāh. He is also called ʿAlī Pādishāh (Cl. Huart, *Histoire de Bagdad*, 10). In the eastern Turkish dialects the title of *pādishāh* is given to petty local rulers; there it has taken the form not of *pasha* but of *patsha* (Kirghiz) and *pōtshō* (Özbeg).

5. Turk. *basḳaḳ* (variants *bashkak*?, *bashkan*?) "governor, chief of police" (Pavet de Courteille, *Dictionnaire*, and under *basmaḳ* in that of Boudagov). This word of the "Kh^{w}ārazmian language", according to Vullers, came into use in Persia (Īlkhānid period). Among the Mongols, it meant the commissioners and high commissioners sent by them to the conquered provinces (or the West only?), notably in Russia. The accepted etymology is from the verb *basmaḳ* "to press, impress (e.g. of a seal)" (not, however, with the extended meaning of "to oppress, tyrannise over", giving the meaning of "oppressor" for the *basḳaḳ*, an official whose main duty was to collect taxes and tribute, cf. G. Doerfer, *Türkische und mongolische Elemente im Neupersischen*, ii, Wiesbaden 1965, 241-3). However extraordinary such an explanation of an official title may appear, it seems to be confirmed by the parallelism with the Mongol equivalent of *basḳaḳ*, which is *darugha* or *darogha* [*q.v.*] and which may be compared with *darukhu*, a Mongol verb synonymous with *basmaḳ* in the sense of "to impress". These may, however, be popular etymologies.

Schefer, in his edition of the *Voyage de M. d'Aramon* (238, n. 3), says "The etymology of the word pacha given by Geuffroy (from the Turkish *bach*) is wrong. Pacha is a softened form of the word *bachqaq* or *pachqaq* which means a military governor."

Carpini calls the Mongol *basḳaḳs baschati* (variants in the ms.: *bascati*, *bastaci*; cf. *The texts and versions of John de Pl. Carpini...*, Hakluyt Soc., London 1903, 67 and 261, notes). In the edition of 1598 (Hakluyt) there is a marginal note "Basha, vox Tartarica qua utuntur Turci". This also implies a confusion between the words *basḳaḳ* and *pasha*.

It is not impossible that there was actually some confusion among the Turks themselves between *pādishāh* (*pasha*) and the title *basḳaḳ*, the synonym of the Mongol *darugha*. It may be noted that the title of *pasha* (which is not found in Persian sources, according to Muḥammad Ḳazwīnī) was applied either to Anatolians, subject in fact or in theory to the Mongols, or to officials of the Mongol Īlkhāns (like the governor of Baghdād mentioned above; cf. also *piser-i ʿAlī Pasha* alluded to in the *Bezm-ü rezm* of ʿAzīz b. Ardashīr Astarābādī (ed. Köprülü, 249, l. 8). The confusion could be explained the more easily as one finds (rarely) the form *bashkaḳ* (Djuwaynī, *Taʾrīkh-i Djahān-gushā* of 658/1260, ed. Muḥammad Ḳazwīnī, ii, 83, n. 9, tr. Boyle, i, 351; in this passage there is a reference to a Kh^{w}ārazmian official of 609/1212-13, i.e. before the Mongol conquest).

It may be suggested that, but for the influence of this confusion with the title *bashkaḳ*, that of *pasha* would never have attained such importance.

The Turkish title of *basha*. This title, which is not to be confused with the preceding, nor with the Arabic or old eastern pronunciation of it, was also put after the proper name but was applied only to soldiers and the lower grades of officers (especially Janissaries) and, it seems, also to notables in the provinces (Meninski, *Thesaurus*, i, col. 662 and 294, l. 18; *Onomasticon*, col. 427; d'Herbelot, s.v. *pascha*; Viguier, *Éléments de la langue turque*, 1790, 218, 309, 327; Zenker, 164, col. 2 (probably following Meninski); De La Mottraye, *Voyages*, 1727, i, 180 n. *a*; cf. Ewliyā Čelebi, v, 107^{6}, 216^{18}; Naʿīmā, v, 71^{11}; Ismāʿīl Ḥaḳḳī, *Kitābeler*, سفر بشه, 41 and 8). De La Boullaye-Le-Gouz (*Voyages*, 1657, 59, and 552) also distinguishes the title from *bacha* and translates it by "monsieur". Meninski, *loc. cit.*, also notes the pronunciation *bashi* (بشى), which is not to be taken as the word *bash* followed by the possessive suffix of the 3rd pers. *-i*; Meninski knew Turkish too well to make such a mistake. As to the pronunciation *beshe* (given by Chloros, s.v. *pasha*), it comes from the spelling بشه (cf. e.g. Aḥmad Wefīḳ Pasha, *Zoraki Ṭabīb*, act i, sc. 2, ironically applied to a woman) but Meninski pronounces *basha*, even with this spelling.

As the lexicographers have sometimes confused *basha* and *pasha*, some have thought that *basha* also meant "elder brother" (Meḥmed Ṣalāḥī, *Ḳāmūs-i ʿothmānī*, ii, 291 ff., followed by Chloros). It seems that there are two separate problems and that *basha* is really for *bash-agha*, but with the meaning of "*agha* (military title) in chief". The *kawas* (also called Janissaries or *yasaḳčī*) were called *bash-agha* (according to Roehrig). On the other meanings of *bash-agha*, and in general for more details on some of the points dealt with here, see Deny, *Sommaire des Archives turques du Caire*, Cairo 1930.

A note on the accentuation: In the word *pasha*, the tonic accent is on the last syllable (*pashà*). In the word *basha*, it is on the first (*bàsha*), as is shown by the weakening of the final vowel in the pronunciation *bàshi*, already mentioned.

Bibliography: In addition to references in the article, see M.Z. Pakalın, *Osmanlı tarih deyimleri ve terimleri sözlüğü*, Istanbul 1946-54, s.v. *Paşa*.

(J. Deny*)

PASHA ḲAPUSU, WEZĪR ḲAPUSU, a term of

Ottoman administration denoting the building presented by Sultan Meḥemmed IV in 1064/1654 to the Grand Vizier Derwīsh Meḥmed Pasha and intended to serve both as an official residence and as an office; after the *Tanẓīmāt* [*q.v.*] period it became known as the Bāb-i ʿĀlī [*q.v.*] or Sublime Porte, and soon came to house most of the administrative departments of the *Dīwān-i Hümāyūn* [*q.v.*].

Bibliography: M.Z. Pakalın, *Osmanlı tarih deyimleri ve terimleri sözlüğü*, Istanbul 1946-54, ii, 757.

(Ed.)

PASHALÎḲ (t.), means 1. the office or title of a *pasha* [*q.v.*]; 2. the territory under the authority of a *pasha* (in the provinces).

After some of the governors called *sandjak-beyi* (or *mīr-liwā*) had been raised to the dignity of *pasha*, their territories (*sandjak* or *liwā* [*q.vv.*]) also received the name of *pashalîḳ*.

Early in the 19th century, out of 158 *sandjak*s 70 were *pashalîḳ*s. Of these, 25 were *pasha sandjaghî*, i.e. *sandjak*s in which were the capitals of an *eyālet*, the residence of the governor-general or *wālī* of a province. For further details, cf. Mouradgea d'Ohsson, *Tableau général de l'Empire Othoman*, vii, 307.

Bibliography: See M.Z. Pakalın, *Osmanlı tarih deyimleri ve terimleri sözlüğü*, Istanbul 1946-54, ii, 758.

(J. Deny)

PASHTO [see afghān].

PASHTŪNISTĀN, a name given to a projected political unit based on the North West Frontier province (NWFP) of Pākistān. The project had a dual origin, in the NWFP and in Afghānistān.

Although Pashtūns possessed a strong sense of cultural identity deriving from language, genealogy, law and custom, there is no evidence before the 1920s of any desire for political expression of that identity. A precondition of the formulation of political demands was the creation of a political arena in the form of the NWFP. The origins of the province may be traced to the conquest of the trans-Indus lands of the former Durrānī empire by the Lahore state between 1819 and 1837. In 1849 this region of the Sikhashāhī passed into British hands and in 1901 four trans-Indus districts (Peshāwar, Kōhāt, Bannū and Dēra Ismāʿīl Khān), together with the cis-Indus district of Hazāra, were formed into the NWFP. The tribal regions (to which Afghānistān had been persuaded to relinquish her claims by the 1893 Durand Agreement) on the mountainous western borderland of NWFP did not form part of the province but were grouped into five political agencies. The peculiar problems of the NWFP led to its exclusion from the British Indian constitutional reforms of 1909 and 1919. Resentful Pakhtūns (the alternative forms Pashtūn(istān) and Pakhtūn(istān) reflect the regional differences between the Pashto of the southwestern group of dialects (the so-called "soft" ones) and that of the northeastern ("hard") group, see afghān. (ii) The Pashto language) of the Peshāwar valley formed the *Andjuman-i Islām al-Afāghina* which in 1929 became the *Afghān Djirga* [see djirga in Suppl.] which merged with the Hindu-Sikh dominated provincial branch of the Indian National Congress Party in 1931 to form a party commonly known as the *Khudā-yi Khidmatgār* (KK) after the name of its paramilitary organisation, also called Red Shirts. The aims of the Pakhtūns (notably the brothers ʿAbd al-Ghaffār Khān and Dr Khān Ṣāḥib), who controlled the KK, are uncertain although the evidence of speeches, memoirs and the periodical *Pakhtūn* (founded 1928) suggest a vaguely articulated concept of an ill-defined region referred to as Pakhtūnkhawā which might become a highly autonomous component of an all-India confederation. The KK dominated political life in NWFP under British rule until 1947, when the party began to lose support to the Muslim League, which demanded that the NWFP became part of the projected Pākistān. When it became clear that there was little support for NWFP joining what was perceived as Hindu-dominated India, the KK switched to advocacy of an independent Pakhtūnistān (Pathānistān). This option, however, was not included in the referendum of July 1947, which was boycotted by the KK and yielded an overwhelming majority for Pākistān. Thereafter, the KK accepted the decision and agitated for the greatest degree of provincial autonomy within Pākistān, and this became the main plank of the programme of its successor party, the National ʿAwāmī Party led by ʿAbd al-Wālī Khān, the son of ʿAbd al-Ghaffār. A permanent problem for the Pakhtūn nationalists was the circumstance that Pakhtūns were not a majority within the NWFP, despite their dominant position in the adjacent tribal areas.

Afghānistān's interest in the fate of the frontier Pakhtūns derived from an historic claim (Afghānistān contended that the Durand Agreement, although frequently confirmed by Afghān governments, notably in the 1921 Anglo-Afghān treaty, had been accepted by Afghānistān under duress and had lapsed in 1947), ethnic links, geographical propinquity and political concern about Pakhtūn interference in Afghān politics (as in 1930). On several occasions after 1919, particularly during the Second World War, Afghān governments raised claims to the trans-Indus lands, including the territory of Balūčistān [*q.v.*] and its dependencies, possession of which would have given Afghānistān an outlet to the sea. In 1947 Afghānistān modified its position (following contacts with the KK) and demanded that the Pakhtūns of NWFP should be offered a choice between joining Afghānistān and an independent Pashtūnistān. Afghānistān maintained this demand after 1947 and in 1949 encouraged the emergence of a phantom national assembly of Pashtūnistān with the Faḳīr of Ipi [*q.v.* in Suppl.] as president. During the prime ministership of Muḥammad Dāwūd (1953-63 [*q.v.*]) the dispute between Afghānistān and Pākistān over Pashtūnistān reached its height, especially after the merger of NWFP in West Pākistān's one-unit scheme in 1955. Diplomatic relations were suspended in 1955 and 1961, and during 1960-1 there were armed clashes in Bādjawr. In 1963 the dispute was patched up, but Pashtūn nationalists in Afghānistān maintained the claims. During the period 1973-5 relations deteriorated again (although mainly because of the insurgency in Balūčistān rather than NWFP) and during the 1980s the Afghān government gave encouragement to dissident Pakhtūns in Pākistān. The extent of the territory embraced in the Afghān claim for Pashtūnistān was uncertain. It included not only the NWFP but also the tribal territories, areas outside the NWFP inhabited by Pakhtūns, and, in some versions, Balūčistān as well. The Pashtūns of the Afghān Pashtūn tribal belt were never included, however. Although India and the USSR occasionally issued vaguely sympathetic statements, neither they nor any other state supported Afghān claims.

Bibliography: Sir Olaf Caroe, *The Pathans, 550 BC-AD 1957*, London 1958; Sir William Barton, *India's North-West Frontier*, London 1939; Khalid B. Sayeed, *Pakistan: the formative years, 1857-1948*², London 1968; A.T. Embree (ed.), *Pakistan's western borderlands: the transformation of a political order*, New Delhi 1977; S.M. Burke and L. Ziring, *Pakistan's* *foreign policy: an honest analysis*², Karachi 1990; L. Dupree, *Afghanistan*, Princeton 1973; J.C. Griffiths, *Afghanistan: key to a continent*, London 1981; Mehrunisa Ali, *Pak-Afghan discord: a historical perspective (Documents 1855-1979)*, Karachi Pakistan Study Centre, University of Karachi 1990; D.G. Tendulkar, *Abdul Ghaffar Khan*, Bombay 1967; Abd al-Qaiyum Khan, *Gold and guns on the Pathan frontier*, Bombay 1945; *Pathans—the people of Pakistan*, Ministry of Information, Government of Pakistan 1964; Abd al-Rahman Pazhwak, *The Pakhtunistan question*, Afghanistan Information Bureau, London 1957. (M.E. Yapp)

PASIR, a former sultanate in southeastern Borneo, now in the province of Kalimantan Timur of the republic of Indonesia. It comprises the valley of the Pasir or Kendilo river, which, rising in the north on the borders of Kutei runs in a southeasterly direction along the eastern borders of the Beratos range and, turning east, finally reaches the straits of Makassar through a marshy district. The country, about 1,125 km² in area, still contains primitive forest, in so far as the scanty population, which is found mainly in Pasir, the residence of the sultan, and in Tanah Grogot, that of the official administration, has not cleared the trees to make ricefields. Although some gold, petroleum and coal are found in Pasir, Europeans have not exploited them, still less do they practice agriculture. A European administrative official was first stationed in 1901 at Tanah Grogot at the mouth of the Kendilo river. Pasir was therefore a good example of the Borneo coast state which, as regards Islam, developed independently of European influence. The population of the sultanate was in the 1930s estimated roughly at 17,000. It consists of Dayaks who live by growing rice, of immigrant Bandjarese and Buginese from Celebes, who control the trade; they are found chiefly in the flat country at the river mouth. On the coast, the Badjos, a people of fishermen, live in their villages built on piles in the sea. Of the 9,000 Dayaks, about 4,000 had by the 1930s adopted Islam, while 5,000 in the highlands were pagans. The Buginese have a predominating influence in view of their large numbers and their prosperity; the Bandjarese are of less importance. There are very few Europeans and a small number of Chinese and Arabs in Pasir.

Half of the population are therefore foreigners, but like the Dayaks they belong to the Malay race and mix with one another.

Whilst Borneo formed part of the Netherlands East Indies, i.e. until 1949, Pasir was despotically ruled by the sultan and the members of his family; the people had no voice in the government. Alongside of the sultan and his presumed successor was a council of five notables, which the sultan consulted on important occasions; this was also the highest court of the country. These notables and a number of other members of the sultan's family had estates as fiefs. Since 1844 each sultan on his accession concluded a treaty with the Netherlands East Indian authority. In 1908 they declared themselves vassals of that government. In 1900 the right to collect duties on imports and exports and taxes, as well as the monopoly of opium and salt, was ceded to the government in return for compensation. This amounted in the 1930s to 16,800 gulden yearly, of which 11,200 went to the sultan and 5,600 to the notables.

The sultan still collected the following taxes: a poll-tax from adult males; 1/10 of the yields of the rice-fields and forest products; 2 coconuts from each fruit-bearing tree; and military service. He also had an income from the administration of justice in the capital.

From the very legendary history of the country, it may be gathered that this despotic government, which is foreign to the Dayaks, was introduced from eastern Java. Under the ruling caste were the chiefs of lower rank, priests and landowners and freemen as a middle class. At the beginning of the 20th century, there were still slaves and debtor-slaves as the lowest class in Pasir, although slavery had long been abolished in other states of the Indies under Dutch influence. As was usual among other Dayak tribes, slaves went about like free men, took part in all festivities and games, might own property and were not even distinguished by dress. If their debt was paid to their master by someone, they went over to the latter. Slaves were not sold.

The following remarks are confined to the pagan Dayaks and their Muslim relatives, the Pasirese.

According to tradition, an Arab (Tuan Said) brought Islam to Pasir. His marriage with the daughter of the reigning chief did much to further the progress of Islam in the country.

As to the Pasirese, their social life was only superficially affected by Islam. In their daily life, a pagan conception of the worship of the deity and of the world of spirits still prevails. The old belief in the important influence of spirits on the fate of man and reliance upon their signs are evidence of this. The fact also is significant that, throughout Pasir, there was in the 1930s only one *missigit* and a few smaller places of worship. The number of Muslim religious leaders and *ḥādjdjī*s was also small, nor was the enthusiasm to make the pilgrimage to Mecca great. On important occasions, appeal is made for assistance to the spirits; this is particularly the case with illness among the Pasirese, who hold the pagan *blian* feasts, which are also celebrated in South Borneo. Amid a great din of gongs and drums which can be heard a long way off, the pagan priest (*balian*) becomes possessed by the spirit which then communicates to him the remedy for the illness. Even in the capital Pasir, exclusively inhabited by Muslims, the advice of the *bàlian* is sought; only during the month of Ramaḍān did the sulṭan forbid this.

How attached the upper classes of Pasir were to animistic views is evident from the legend still current according to which sultan Adam in the middle of the 19th century used to isolate himself for several days in the year on the mountain of the spirits, Gunung Melikat; he had concluded, it was said, a marriage there with a female *djinn* from which a son named Tendang was born. This son, who has the gift of making himself invisible, is said to live on the island of Madura where he married a princess of the *djinn*. He appears from time to time in Pasir, when he is invited by a great sacrificial feast (formerly also human sacrifice). These feasts are still celebrated occasionally, especially in order to free the land from misfortune and sickness. In the village of Busui, a house was built for Tendang with a roof in three parts, which was built on a large pole and thus resembled a dove-cote.

The revenues of the priests consist of what they collect at the end of the month of fasting in *zakāt* and *piṭra*, everyone giving what he can and the chiefs exercise no pressure. A priest also receives a small fee at a marriage or divorce.

The calendar now in general use in the sultanate is the Islamic one. As elsewhere among the Dayaks, the tilling of the fields begins when a particular constellation becomes visible in the heavens.

The family life of the Pasirese has developed to some extent according to Muslim ritual. Among the followers of Islam, marriage is performed through the intermediary of a religious leader, with the father or another man as *wālī*, but only after an agreement has been come to about the very considerable dowry. This is paid to the parents of the bride; she herself only receives a small part of it. According to Dayak custom, young people are allowed to meet very freely before marriage. A marriage feast is marked by a very considerable consumption of palm-wine. The man remains at least a year in the home of his parents-in-law before he can take a home of his own. Divorce is very frequent because attention is seldom paid to the wishes of the woman in the negotiations between the parents. Man and woman retain their property after marriage; after a divorce, this goes back to the family. Property acquired during marriage is divided into two equal portions between husband and wife. After the death of one or the other, the survivor inherits all. Only a few families follow the Muslim law. The followers of Islam are buried with Muslim rites.

Bibliography: A.H.F.J. Nusselein, *Beschrijving van het landschap Pasir*, in *BTLV* (1905); see also INDONESIA.

(A.W. NIEUWENHUIS)

PASISIR (Old Javanese, *pasisi* or *pasir*; Indonesian, *pesisir* "shore, coast") originally an administrative unit of the Central Javanese kingdom of Mataram emcompassing Java's northern littoral from Cirebon in the west to Surabaya in the east. Historically, its importance comes from the establishment during the 15th-16th centuries of small Muslim enclaves within the prevailing religious mix of Hindu, Buddhist, and animistic beliefs. While traditions of the conversion to Islam at the hands of the *wali sanga*, or Nine Saints, differs from place to place, common to them are direct experience of Islam in the Middle East, or transmission by one who had such experience, and an element of Islamic egalitarianism. Under the guidance of the *wali sanga* these enclaves rapidly developed into independent Islamic principalities.

Explanations for Java's conversion to Islam at this time range from those emphasising the "mood of the times," through influences of the Ṣūfī *ṭarīḳas* [*q.v.*] to a race with Christianity. More significant here is the region's response to the changing economic environment. With an increased volume of East-West trade, which tended to be dominated by Muslim merchants, the states of the *pasisir* provided an congenial urban environment for international commerce and Islamic religious centres. The formation of political confederations among *pasisir* states—Demak in the 15th century and Cirebon-Banten in the 16th—led to armed conflict with the inland states, providing a complementary process ultimately furthering Islamic interests in the island.

Culturally, the *pasisir* played a key role in the introduction of important Arabic texts, especially those dealing with the *sharīʿa* [*q.v.*]. Of those cited in the early 19th century *Serat Centini*, only a half-dozen are attributable to the *pasisir* era. These include the *Mukharar* (*al-Muḥarrar* of Abu 'l-Ḳāsim ʿAbd-al-Karīm b. Muḥammad al-Rāfiʿī) [see AL-NAWAWĪ], the *Kitab Nawawī* (*Minhādj al-ṭālibīn* of al-Nawawī), the *Kitab Ibnu Kadjar* or *Kitab Tuhpah* (*Tuḥfat al-muḥtādj li-sharḥ al-Minhādj* of Ibn Ḥadjar al-Haytamī [*q.v.*]), the *Ilah* (*Īḍāḥ fi 'l-fiḳh*), and the *Sujak* (*al-Mukhtaṣar fi 'l fiḳh ʿalā madhhab al-Imām al-Shāfiʿī* of Aḥmad b. al-Ḥasan b. Aḥmad al-Iṣfahānī). To these can be added an important work on Ṣūfism, the *Hulumodin*, a corrupted title of the *Iḥyāʾ ʿulūm al-dīn* of al-Ghazālī [*q.v.*].

Bibliography: H.J. de Graaf and Th.G.Th. Pigeaud, *De eerste moslimse vorstendommen op Java; studien over de staatkundige geschiedenis van de 15de en 16de eeuw*, and their companion volume *Islamic states in Java 1500-1700; a summary, bibliography and index*, in *Verhandelingen van het Koninklijk Instituut voor Taal-Land- en Volkenkunde*, lxix, lxx (1974, 1976); Th.G.Th. Pigeaud, *Literature of Java, catalogue raisonné of Javanese manuscripts in the Library of the University of Leiden and other public collections in the Netherlands*, 3 vols., The Hague 1966-70; Soebardi, *Santri-religious elements as reflected in the book of Tjentini* in *BTLV*, cxxvii/3 (1971), 331-49.

(M.C. HOADLEY)

PASSAROWITZ [see PASAROFČA].

PASWAN-OGHLU (written *Pāsbān-oghlī*, as if from Pers. *pāsbān* "guard, shepherd", cf. *Ḳāmūs al Aʿlām*, ii, 1467) or *Pāzwānd-oghlī* (as in ʿAbd al Raḥmān Sheref, *Taʾrīkh*, ii, 280) or, according to modern Turkish orthography, Pazvantoğlu (Hami and Muhsin, *Türkiye tarihi*, 423), but on his own sea "Pāzwānd-zāde ʿOthmān" (in Orěškov, see *Bibl.*), the rebel Pasha of Vidin (1758-1807). His family originated in Tuzla in Bosnia, but his grandfather Paswan Agha, for his services in the Austrian wars was granted two villages near Vidin [*q.v.*] in Bulgaria in *ca.* 1739. ʿOthmān's father ʿÖmer Agha Paswan-oghlu not only inherited these villages but as *bayraḳdār*, etc., was also a rich and prominent man (*aʿyān*); on account of his defiant attitude, however, he was put to death by the local governor.

ʿOthmān himself only escaped death by escaping into Albania, but after taking part in the war of 1787-9 as a volunteer, he returned to his native town. Very soon he was in the field again and fought with distinction, returning to Vidin in 1791. From there he organised with his men raiding expeditions into Wallachia and Serbia. When the sultan wanted to punish him for this, he cast off his allegiance in 1793, took to the mountains and at the end of 1794 captured Vidin with his robber band and became the real ruler in the *pashalïḳ* there. Vidin, which he fortified again, thus became a meeting-place for robbers and discontented Janissaries who were driven out of Serbia in 1792, and he himself became the popular leader of all those who opposed the reforms of Selīm III.

In 1795 Paswan-oghlu even attacked the governor of Belgrade, Ḥādjdjī Muṣṭafā Pasha, a supporter of the reformers, who had been given the task of disposing of him; strong bodies of troops were sent by the Porte but without success. In consequence, negotiations were begun at the end of 1795 but Paswan-oghlu remained practically independent in the whole of Upper Bulgaria.

But since the Porte did not also formally recognise him, Paswan-oghlu drove the official governor out of Vidin and in 1797 attacked the adjoining *pashalïḳs*; in the east his forces occupied or threatened a number of places in Bulgaria (but they were defeated at Varna), and in the south they attacked Nish [*q.v.*] without success; in the west they advanced up to Belgrade, occupied the town, but were driven back from its fortress by the resistance of the Turks and Serbs whom Ḥādjdjī Muṣṭafā had armed. As a result of this and because of Paswan-oghlu's negotiations with France and Russia, the Porte in 1798 sent an army of 100,000 men against him under Admiral Küčük Ḥuseyn Pasha. He besieged Vidin in vain until October, and had to withdraw with heavy losses. This defeat and Bonaparte's invasion of Egypt induced Turkey to come to terms, nominally at least, with Paswan-oghlu and to give him the rank of Pasha of three tails (1799).

Nevertheless, he declared himself against the reforms, against the central government and even against Selīm III; he also sent several expeditions to plunder Wallachia (1800 and 1801) and incited the Janissaries, who had in the meanwhile returned to Belgrade, to occupy the fortress (in the summer of 1801) and to murder Ḥādjdjī Muṣṭafā Pas̲h̲a (at the end of the year).

At this time, he repeatedly asked the Tsar to number him among his faithful subjects and also offered his services to France. The Porte, which shortly before had forgiven Paswan-og̲h̲lu everything, from 1803 declared war on him again, but the Serbian rising of 1804 diverted their attention. Paswan-og̲h̲lu himself had to fight in the western part of his territory against Pintzo's rising (1805). The appearance of the Russians on the left bank of the Danube (1806) induced him to offer his services to the Porte, but the latter instead gave the supreme command to the commander of Rusčuk [q.v.]. This embittered him so much that he resolved to defend only his own territory against the allied Russians and Serbians, but he died soon afterwards on 27 January 1807.

That Paswan-og̲h̲lu was able to hold out so long was due to the state of the Ottoman empire at the time, to his personal ability and foresight (he never abandoned Vidin), but for the most part to luck. Within his area he collected customs and taxes, ruled strictly and despotically, although not entirely without mildness and justice. In Vidin, he was active in public works, building a mosque, madrasa and library (see F. Kanitz, Donau-Bulgarien und der Balkan, Leipzig 1882, 4, 8). Although his health was rather poor as a result of too great mental strain, ambition led him to aim at independence, as evidence of which we have the coins struck by him and known as Pazvančeta.

Bibliography: Various notes on Paswan-og̲h̲lu are already found in the contemporary travels of G.A. Olivier (1801) and L. Pouqueville (1805), but it is not till the Notes sur Passvan-Oglou 1758-1807 par l'adjudant-commandant Mériage, of the French agent in Vidin (1807-8), that we have a complete picture of him which is still the best account of his career; these Notes were edited by Grgur Jakšić in La Revue Slave (i [Paris 1906], 261-79, 418-29; ii [1906], 139-44, 436-48; iii [1907], 138-44, 278-88) and tr. in the Glasnik zemaljskog muzeja (xvii [Sarajevo 1906], 173-216) into Serbo-croat. See also J.W. Zinkeisen, GOR in Europa, vii, Gotha 1863, 230-41; C. Jireček, Geschichte der Bulgaren, Prague 1876, 486-503; Iv. Pavlović, Ispisi iz francuskih arhiva, Belgrade 1890, esp. 103-28 (diplomatic reports regarding Paswan-og̲h̲lu, 1795-1807); M. Gavrilović, in La Grande Encyclopédie, xxvi, Paris n.d., 68; St. Novaković, Tursko carstvo pred srpski ustanak 1780-1804, Belgrade 1906, 332-89; M. Vukićević, Karadorde, i, Belgrade 1907, 166-76, 185-208; P. Oreškov, Několko dokumenta za Pazvantoglu i Sofroni Vračanski (1800-1812) [from the Russian Foreign Ministry], in Sbornik of the Bulgarian Academy of Science, iii [Sofia 1914], article 3, pp. 1-55; V. Ćorović, in Narodna enciklopedija, iii, Zagreb 1928, 272; S̲h̲. Sāmī, Ḳāmūs al-aʿlām, ii, 1467; G. Lebel, La France et les principantés danubiennes du XVIème siècle à la chute de Napoléon Ier, Paris 1955; İA, art. Pazvand-oğlu (A. Cevat Eren). (F. BAJRAKTAREVIĆ*)

PĀṬAN, one of the oldest and most renowned towns of Gudjarāt [q.v.] in the Aḥmadābād district of Bombay. It was founded in 746 by the Čavadas of Gudjarāt. Originally known as Anhilwāra, the Arab geographers refer to it as Nahrwāla [see NAHRAWĀL]. Later, it became known as Pāṭan. According to the Mirʾāt-i Aḥmadī, the Hindus used the word Pāṭan for a big or capital town. The poet Farruk̲h̲ī [q.v.] says that

on its possession "Bhīm prided himself over the princes of India" (Nāẓim, The life and times of Sulṭān Maḥmūd of G̲h̲azna, Cambridge 1931, 217). Sultan Maḥmūd of G̲h̲azna attacked and conquered it but did not annex it. In 573/1178 the G̲h̲ūrid S̲h̲ihāb al-Dīn attacked it but did not succeed in defeating the rādjā. However, in 591/1195 Ḳuṭb al-Dīn Aybak defeated its ruler and collected enormous booty. After many ups and downs, Muslim power was established there under ʿAlāʾ al-Dīn K̲h̲aldjī, who retained Pāṭan as the capital. Pāṭan continued as the capital of Muslim power in Gudjarāt till the time of Aḥmad S̲h̲āh I, who shifted it to Aḥmadābād after his accession in 813/1410.

Pāṭan was a great centre of Muslim culture, with imposing mosques, splendid madrasas, k̲h̲ānaḳahs zāwiyas and dāʾiras. S̲h̲ayk̲h̲ Niẓām al-Dīn Awliyāʾ [q.v.] sent his disciple S̲h̲ayk̲h̲ Ḥusām al-Dīn to implant the Čis̲h̲tī order there. Due to the very large number of graves of saints, it came to be called Pīrān Pāṭan. Muẓaffar I and Muḥammad S̲h̲āh Tatār K̲h̲ān were also buried there. It was perhaps in view of this background that Muḥammad b. Tug̲h̲luḳ deputed there a grandson of S̲h̲ayk̲h̲ Farīd al-Dīn Gandj-i S̲h̲akar [q.v.] to deal with the recalcitrant elements. A highway—with hundreds of thousands of trees on both sides—connected Pāṭan with Baroda [q.v.]. The entire region was prosperous and fertile. Its trade potential attracted the Ismāʿīlī Bohrā [q.v.] community to it. During the time of Akbar, the region was in the grip of Mahdawī [see MAHDAWĪS] and anti-Mahdawī activities.

The earliest mosque was constructed in Pāṭan in 655/1257. Its madrasas enjoyed a wide academic reputation and had big libraries attached to them. A madrasa known as Fayḍ-i Ṣafāʾ, founded during the reign of Awrangzīb, had hostels, a mosque and baths attached to it. S̲h̲ayk̲h̲ Matā's madrasa produced eminent scholars like S̲h̲ayk̲h̲ Djamāl al-Dīn Muḥammad b. Ṭāhir, author of the Madjmaʿ biḥār al-anwār.

Bibliography: Imperial Gazetteer of India², xx, 24; M.S. Commissariat, A history of Gujarat, i, London 1938, ii, Bombay 1957; Sayyid ʿAbd al-Ḥayy, Yād-i ayyām, Lucknow 1926; Sayyid Abū Ẓafar Nadwī, Gudjarāt ki tamadduni tārīk̲h̲, Aʿẓamgaŕh 1962; idem, Tārīk̲h̲-i Gudjarāt, Dihlī 1958; J. Tod, Travels in Western India, repr. Dihlī 1971. (K.A. NIZAMI)

PATANI (Thai: Pattani), a region of Southeast Asia, formerly a Malay Sultanate but now included in Thailand (as a result of the Treaty of Bangkok, 1909, between Great Britain and Siam), and at present comprised of the four southern provinces of Pattani, Narathiwat, Yala (Jala) and Satun. The population of these four provinces is approximately 1,500,000, 80% of whom are Malay Muslims.

From the 14th to 18th centuries, Patani was a leading entrepôt for trade between China and Southeast Asia. The conversion of the royal court to Islam, reportedly in the mid-15th century, enabled it to profit from the economic and political advantages which affiliation with the Muslim community offered. Because of the relatively early date (in the local context) of official identification with Islam, Patani is regarded as one of the cradles of Islam in Southeast Asia.

For the history of Islam, Patani is chiefly famous for two reasons. The first is a lengthy and continuing tradition of kitab literature, that is, works on fiḳh, kalām, and taṣawwuf written in Jawi (Malay using the Arabic script). The founder of this tradition and its most prolific author was Dāwūd b. ʿAbd Allāh b. Idrīs al-Faṭānī [q.v.]. He has been followed by a line of influential and versatile scholars, the most prominent of whom was Aḥmad b. Muḥammad Zayn (1856-1906), who supervised the Malay printing press in Mecca and attracted many pupils from the Malay-speaking world, among them Tok Kenali (1868-1933), a famous teacher and influential figure for the practice of Islam in Northeast Malaya. Aḥmad b. Muḥammad Zayn is remembered chiefly for *al-Fatāwā al-Faṭaniyya*, which is a substantial collection of his rulings. They are technically excellent, show a secure command of Arabic sources and illustrate the adaptation of Islam to the realities of Malay life in the late 19th century. The tradition of *kitab* writing is maintained to this day and is influential in the northern Malaysian states of Kelantan, Kedah and Perak, as well as Patani itself.

Second, and related to the first reason, Patani was, and to some extent remains, famous as the home of a distinct tradition of Islamic education and learning as conducted in the *pondok* (literally "hut") schools [see PESANTREN]. These are privately-run traditional Islamic institutions, headed by a *Tok Guru* (religious teacher), often with Middle Eastern education, where young Muslim men and women are instructed in a wide range of Islamic subjects. Traditionally, many *pondok* graduates went on to study in Mecca, Medina and Cairo (al-Azhar), and, more recently, also in the Philippines, Malaysia and Indonesia. The *pondok* is regarded by Patani Muslims as a guardian of their religion, language and culture and for that reason has been an object of considerable concern to the Thai government throughout this century.

This brings us to the final point. Patani, and the present northern Malaysian states, came under Siamese (now Thai) domination during the 19th century. The relationship between Thais and Muslims was, and remains, strained, Thais still referring to Malays as *khaek* (aliens, visitors). In the modern state of Thailand the Muslims of the south are a tiny minority (3% of Thailand's 50 million largely Buddhist population). The history of Patani Muslims has been one of prolonged struggle to remain independent in religion, language and culture. The traditional past is kept alive by a vigorous tradition of oral and written histories which emphasise the pre-19th century period, when Patani was outside the sphere of Siamese control. The policy of the Bangkok government towards the southern Muslims has oscillated between a grudging tolerance on the one hand, and an aggressive policy of Thaiicisation on the other. The latter was especially prominent in the 1940s and 1950s, giving rise to strong local reaction and bloody clashes between the government and the Malay Muslims. Imprisonment of religious leaders resulted in an even greater determination by their followers to sustain their traditional Islamic way of life.

From the 1960s to the present, Bangkok's attitude tends to be one of assimilation, as expressed in policies such as grants to religious schools providing that they teach secular subjects as well as Islam; attempts to set up councils of religious leaders to advise (but as yet there are no *s̲h̲arīʿa* courts); the publication of Thai language translations of the Ḳurʾān, and some concessions to the wearing of Muslim dress. These policies are viewed by Muslims, rightly, as attempts to diminish the practice of their religion. In fact, throughout this century, the Muslim response to efforts at assimilation has been to strengthen their devotion to Islam.

The economic condition of Muslims in the four southern provinces has been deteriorating since the 1950s and 1960s. In the 1970s, Bangkok recognised that the subsistence-level living standard of the Malays was a factor in the increasing political unrest, banditry and separatist activities which were occurring in the area. Efforts to improve the economic conditions of the region have so far met with little long-lasting success, the reasons being complex, but including a reluctance to invest capital in an area whose history has been so troubled.

There are a number of separatist movements among the Malays, which since the late 1940s have struggled for either independence or irredentism with Malaysia. Since the displacement of their traditional rulers by the Thais, the people have turned to religious teachers for leadership, and the four existing national fronts have leaders from this group. These movements have been dealt with severely by the Thais and are currently in a period of quiescence. The occasional separatist violence is followed by rapid suppression, but the determination of the separatists, and their continued support by Muslims outside Thailand, indicates that the "problem" will be an ever-present one for the Bangkok government.

Bibliography: There is as yet no standard reference work on Patani. The following Bibliography has been divided into subject headings for ease of reference.

1. *Traditional histories*. A. Teeuw and D.K. Wyatt, *Hikayat Patani: The Story of Patani*, 2 vols. The Hague 1970.

2. *Recent local histories with a nationalist purpose*. *Patani Dahulu dan Sekarang*; Ibrahim Shukri, *Sejarah Kerajaan Melayu Patani*, Kelantan n.d., English tr. C. Bailey and J.N. Miksic, as *History of the Malay Kingdom of Patani*, Columbus, Ohio 1985.

3. *Modern studies*. Uthai Dulyakasem, *Muslim-Malay separatism in Southern Thailand: factors underlying the political revolt*, in Lim Joo-Jock and S. Vani (eds.), *Armed separatism in Southeast Asia*, Singapore 1984; T.M. Fraser, *Fishermen of Southern Thailand: the Malay villagers*, New York 1966; Nantawan Haemindra, *The problem of the Thai Muslims in four southern provinces of Thailand*, in *Journal of Southeast Asian Studies*, vii/2 (1976), viii/1 (1977); Margaret L. Koch, *Patani and the development of a Thai state*, in *Journal of the Malaysian Branch of the Royal Asiatic Society*, l/2 (1977); W.K. Che Man, *Muslim separatism: the Moros of southern Philippines and the Malays of southern Thailand*, Singapore 1990; Surin Pitsuwan, *Islam and Malay nationalism; a case study of the Malay-Muslims in southern Thailand*, Harvard Ph.D. thesis, 1982, unpubl.

4. *Islam*. W.A. Bougas, *Some early Islamic tombstones in Patani*, in *JMBRAS*, lix/1 (1986); Omar Farouk, *The origins and evolution of Malay-Muslim ethnic nationalism in southern Thailand*, in Taufik Abdullah and Sharon Siddique (eds.), *Islam and society in Southeast Asia*, Singapore 1986; Virginia Matheson and M.B. Hooker, *Jawi literature in Patani: the maintenance of an Islamic tradition*, in *JMBRAS*, lxi/1 (1988).

(VIRGINIA MATHESON HOOKER)

PATE, a small town on an island of that name in East Africa. It lies in lat. 2°05′ S., and long. 41°05′ E., off the Kenya coast in the Lamu [*q.v.*] archipelago. The use by Arab sailors of the *Mkanda*, the channel between it and Lamu, is mentioned in the *Periplus of the Erythraean Sea*, written *ca.* A.D. 50. Aḥmad b. Mād̲j̲id al-Nad̲j̲dī identifies it as *Batā*, and several epitaphs spell the adjective *Batāwī*. H.N. Chittick excavated the periphery of the site in the 1960s, and claimed that it was not occupied before the 14th century. An excavation by Athman Lali, Curator of the Lamu Museum, and T.R. Wilson, as yet un-ublished, disclosed Sāsānid-Islamic pottery in levels f *ca. ante* 750, below a 15th-century mosque with two *iḥrābs*, one incorrectly orientated. The former large wn is much depopulated, leaving a large ruin field, which numerous Arabic epitaphs, none of them ecorded, protrude from cemeteries which are vergrown by tobacco crops. The growing of tobacco r snuff is the principal industry.

At least twelve versions are extant of the *Habari za ate*, the traditional Swahili history. They record the abhānī dynasty, claiming that it was founded *ca.* .D. 1200. It is not claimed that the rulers were escended from the Nabhānī *maliks* of ʿUmān [see ABHĀN], but rather from collaterals of the same tribe. Videly-held Swahili traditions report that it and other wahili towns were founded under the Umayyad aliph ʿAbd al-Malik b. Marwān. In spite of their 9th-century date, recent archaeological evidence ere and in the vicinity at some twenty-six sites sugests that there is some nucleus of truth: they may be plausible reminiscence of the increase in demand for nangrove roofing timbers consequent upon the extenive building operations of that reign.

This dynastic history records thirty-five rulers, and s remarkable in repeating a complete *isnād* for each of he first twenty-five. It appears to be a composite vork, the account of the first twenty-five rulers having een composed *ca.* 1810, with additions in distinct tyles *ca.* 1888 and 1911. A highly glossed version was ublished in English by C.H. Stigand, with some islocations of the dynastic order. The best version, in Swahili in Arabic script, Document 157 in the University Library, Dar es Salaam, has never been published.

The Portuguese had a customs post on the island from *ca.* 1510 until 1698, and an Augustinian mission from 1596. The most important trade was in mangrove poles and ivory, and later in tobacco. The island came under ʿUmānī suzerainty in 1698, intermittently paying customs dues to Zanzibar. Following a revolt, the island was garrisoned from Zanzibar in 1861, when the Nabhānī *sulṭān*, with his family, slaves and followers, migrated to Witu on the mainland.

A surviving item of the regalia of Pate, an intricately carved ivory horn, with an Arabic inscription, is exhibited in the Lamu Museum.

Bibliography: L. Casson, *The Periplus Maris Erythraei*, Princeton 1989; H.N. Chittick, *A new look at the history of Pate*, in *Journ. of African Hist.*, x/3 (1969); G.S.P. Freeman-Grenville, *The Swahili Coast, 2nd to 19th centuries*, London 1988, with abundant references; M.D. Horton, *Shanga, 1980: an interim report*, National Museums of Kenya, Nairobi 1980; T.A. Shumovski, *Tri neizvestnie lotzii Aḥmada ibn Mād̲j̲ida*, Moscow 1957; C.H. Stigand, *The land of Zinj*, London 1912; G.R. Tibbetts (ed.), *Arab navigation*, with translation of Aḥmad b. Mād̲j̲id al-Nad̲j̲dī, *Kitāb al-Fawāʾid*, London 1971; M. Ylvisaker, *Lamu in the nineteenth century*, Boston 1979; information kindly communicated by Bwana Athman Lali, and personal observation on site.

(G.S.P. Freeman-Grenville)

PAṬHĀN [see AFG̲H̲ĀN].

PAṬNĀ, a city in Bihār Province of the Indian Union, situated on the right bank of the Ganges (lat. 25° 37′ N., long. 85° 8′ E.) and with a population (1971 census) of 474,000. In the years 1912-36, it was the capital of the province of Bihar and Orissa of British India, and subsequently, of Bihar alone.

From 1116/1704 onwards, it is known in Muslim chronicles as ʿAẓīmābād, after Awrangzīb's grandson ʿAẓīm al-S̲h̲aʾn who made his court here. Paṭnā, however, had already been selected as the Muslim provincial capital of Bihār [*q.v.*] by the Afg̲h̲ān ruler S̲h̲īr S̲h̲āh in 948/1541. At that time it was the seat of the local government, but as yet an insignificant town. S̲h̲īr S̲h̲āh built a great fort, and we subsequently see Paṭnā become one of the largest cities of the province of Bihār. It remained a governor's seat during the Mug̲h̲al period. D̲j̲ahāngīr's reign is especially noted for the mosques constructed in Paṭnā. On account of its commercial importance, Paṭnā also attracted European merchants as early as 1620. Peter Mundy, who came to Paṭnā in 1632, does not fail to mention the *madrasa* of Paṭnā, which was famous throughout the Muslim world. Bānkīpūr, the western suburb of the city, is well known for its collection of Arabic and Persian manuscripts in the K̲h̲udā Bak̲h̲s̲h̲ Library [see BĀNKĪPŪR].

Bibliography: Numerous chronicles, such as the *Taʾrīk̲h̲-i S̲h̲īr S̲h̲āhī*, the *Taʾrīk̲h̲-i Dāwūdī* and the *Ṭabaḳāt-i Akbarī*, mention Paṭnā *passim*; useful information can also be found in N. Kumar, *Bihar District Gazetteer: Patna*, Patna 1970, and *Imperial gazetteer of India*², xx, 54-70.

(A. Wink)

PATRAS [see BALIABADRA].

PAṬRĪK, patriarch, the form found in Ottoman Turkish (see Redhouse, *Turkish and English lexicon*, s.v.) for the Patriarchs of the Greek Orthodox and Eastern Christian Churches in the empire, of whom by the 19th century there were seven. It stems from the Arabic form *biṭrīḳ/baṭrīḳ* [*q.v.*] "patricius", confused with *baṭriyark/baṭrak* "patriarch", also not infrequently found in mediaeval Arabic usage as *faṭrak*. See G. Graf, *Verzeichnis arabischer kirchliche Termini*², Louvain 1954, 84; C.E. Bosworth, *Christian and Jewish religious dignitaries in Mamlûk Egypt and Syria...*, in *IJMES*, iii (1972), 68-70.

(Ed.)

PATRONA K̲H̲ALĪL, Ottoman rebel (d. 14 D̲j̲umādā I 1143/25 November 1730). Of Albanian origin, he belonged to the protégés of the *Ḳapudān-Pas̲h̲a* Muṣṭafā and ʿAbdī Pas̲h̲a (*ca.* 1680-5 and later). He was born at K̲h̲urpis̲h̲te (Khroupista, now Argos Orestikon, to the south of Kastoria, Greece). He served as a Lewend [*q.v.*] on board the flagship of the Ottoman vice-admiral, the Patrona (for this term, see RIYALA) whence probably his name. Transferred from naval service, he was able to join the Seventeenth *Orta* of the Janissary Corps in which he served till the peace settlement of 1718. While on garrison duty in Vidin [*q.v.*] he became involved in a rebellion, managed to escape to Istanbul where he lived thereafter as an unskilled labourer, travelling salesman and *ḥammām* attendant. During the successive stages of his career he seems always to have enjoyed protection in high places, since he always escaped the punishments which he incurred because of his repeated misbehaviour and criminal acts.

Together with Muslu Bes̲h̲e, a greengrocer and former Janissary, Emīr ʿAlī, a coffeemaker, and others, Patrona K̲h̲alīl started the rebellion on Thursday, 15 Rabīʿ I 1143/28 September 1730 which led to the abdication of Sultan Aḥmed III [*q.v.*]. The cause of this revolt may have been a conservative reaction against the westernising tendencies of the so-called "*Lāle Dewri*" [*q.v.*]. The rebels claimed that their aim was the restoration of the rule of Islamic law. The movement was instigated by a group of disaffected, high-ranking *ʿulemāʾ*, hostile to the powerful faction of the grand vizier Dāmād News̲h̲ehirli Ibrāhīm Pas̲h̲a [see IBRĀHĪM PAS̲H̲A, NEVS̲H̲EHIRLI]. There are data pointing to an element of ethnic solidarity: all the leading rebels were of Albanian origin. The moment was well chosen: the losses in the war with Ṣafawid

Persia worsened the effects of the socio-economic problems of the day. The *Dīwān* was not in session that day; the sultan and grand vizier were absent from Istanbul and the *ḳāʾim-maḳām* [*q.v.*] was at his private residence in Čengel Köy on the Bosphorus. The government was not able to organise any effective resistance. The rebellious *ʿulemāʾ*, led by Arnawud Zulālī Ḥasan Efendi, a former *ḳāḍī* of Istanbul dismissed in 1140/1728, successfully pressed the sultan to appoint a new government. Before this the Grand Vizier Newshehirli Ibrāhīm Pasha and other prominent members of the government were murdered (18 Rabīʿ I 1143/1 October 1730). The new sultan Maḥmūd I [*q.v.*], who acceded to the throne on 6 October, was urged to grant a general amnesty to the rebels following a *hüddjet* issued by the new *Sheykh ül-Islām* (14 Djumādā I 1143/11 November 1730). Patrona Khalīl, instead of seeking high office, aimed at securing a lasting influence on affairs. His domination endured for two weeks only, until the Imperial *Dīwān* decided in secret to make an end to it. The factions of the seraglio, led by the *Ḳîzlar Aghasî* Beshīr Agha and the new Grand Vizier, Silāḥdār Meḥmed Pasha, united forces and created their own power base to effect a counter coup. Ḳabaḳulaḳ Ibrāhīm Agha (notorious for his bloody suppression of the revolt in Egypt), the admiral Djanîm Khodja Meḥmed Pasha, and a former khān of the Crimea, Ḳaplan Girāy, organised it. On 14 Djumādā I 1143/25 November 1730, Patrona Khalīl, accompanied by his fellow-rebel leaders, was invited to attend the meeting of the *Dīwān*, at which the sultan was to appoint him *beglerbegi* of Rumeli. During the meeting in the seraglio, the three leading rebels were set upon and killed. *ʿUlemāʾ* such as Zulālī Efendi were arrested and secretly executed later. In Ramaḍān 1143/March 1731 a riot ensued, purportedly instigated by a group of Albanians in revenge for their fellow-countryman Patrona Khalīl; this was quickly suppressed by the newly appointed grand vizier Ḳabaḳulaḳ Ibrāhīm Pasha.

Paintings of these bloody events were made by the French painter Jean-Baptiste Vanmour (Rijksmuseum Amsterdam, Inv. A 2012 and A 4082 i.a.).

Bibliography: Munir Aktepe, *Patrona isyanı (1730)*, Istanbul 1958 (basic, with bibl.); idem (ed.), *Şemdānī-zāde Fındıklılı Süleymān Efendi tarihi Mür'i't-tevarih*, 3 vols. in 4, Istanbul 1976-81, vol. i, 6-19; Ahmed Refik Altınay, *Lâle devri*, ed. H.A. Diriöz, Ankara 1973, 110-53 (original ed. Istanbul 1912); A. Vandal, *Une ambassade française en Orient. La mission du Marquis de Villeneuve 1728-1741*, Paris 1887, 147-67; *Destari Salih tarihi*, ed. B.S. Baykal, Ankara 1962; A. Boppe, *Les peintres du Bosphore au dix-huitième siècle*, new illustr. ed. C. Boppe-Vigne and T. Florenne, Courbevoie, Paris 1989, 35-7 (original ed. Paris 1911); G.R. Bosscha Erdbrink, *At the Threshold of Felicity*, Ankara 1975, 93-8; [M. Cezar *et alii*], *Mufassal Osmanlı tarihi*, 6 vols., Istanbul 1957-63, v, 2460-6, 2468-76; Hammer-Purgstall, *Histoire*, xiv, 219-46; R.E. Kocu, *Patrona Halil*, Istanbul 1967 (romanticised biography, with detailed information); Ch. Perry, *A view of the Levant particularly of Constantinople, Syria, Egypt and Greece*, London 1743.

(A.H. de Groot)

PAWLĀ, the name given in the Mughal emperor Akbar's monetary system to the ¼ *dām* (¼ *paysā*).

(J. Allan)

PAYĀS, the Ottoman Turkish form of modern Turkish Payas, a small town at the head of the Gulf of Alexandretta 18 km/12 miles north of Iskandarūn [*q.v.*] (lat. 36° 46′ N., long. 36° 10′ E.). Lying as it does in the very narrow coastal corridor between t sea and the Amanus Mts. or Djabal al-Lukkām [*q.v.* the modern Turkish Gavur Dağları, Payās has alwa been a strategically important point on the route fro Cilicia to Antioch; the name itself goes back to that the classical Greek town of Baiae (see *PW*, ii/2, cc 2775 (Ruge)).

In the early Islamic period, Payās was on the ro connecting Iskandarūn with the frontier fortre against the Byzantines of al-Maṣṣīṣa [*q.v.*] (Mo suestis), and the classical Arabic geographers name as Bayyās, a flourishing small town. Under the O tomans, with their acquisition of Syria, it became i the 10th/16th century quite a significant port; th vizier Ṣoḳollu Meḥmed Pasha [*q.v.*] built there a larg caravanserai, a mosque, *madrasa*, *ʿimāret* and baths. I the next century, Ewliyā Čelebi describes the port a strongly fortified and with batteries of cannon. In th 19th century it came within the *wilāyet* of Adana, an Cuinet numbered its population at 6,325, slightl more than half of whom were Muslims. With the 192 agreement between France and the Nationalis Turkish government in Ankara, Payās came jus within the boundaries of Turkey. After the 1939 in corporation of the Hatay *vilâyet* in Turkey, Payās wa included within this last, and is at present the chef-lie of a *nahiye* in the *ilçe* of Dört-Yol in the Hatay/Antaky *il*. The population in 1950 was 2,653.

Bibliography: Ewliyā Čelebi, *Seyāhat-nāme* Istanbul 1314/1896-7, iii, 42-3; Sāmī Bey, *Ḳāmū al-aʿlām*, Istanbul 1894, ii, 1571; V. Cuinet, *La Tu quie d'Asie*, Paris 1891, ii, 105-8; Le Strange *Palestine under the Moslems*, 422; R. Dussaud *Topographie historique de la Syrie antique et médiévale* Paris 1927, 435, 503; *İA*, art. *Payas* (Besim Darkot) on which the above article is based.

(C.E. Bosworth)

PAYGHŪ (t.), a Turkish name found e.g among the early Saldjūḳs, usually written *P.y.ghū* o *B.y.ghū*. In many sources on the early history of th Saldjūḳs these orthographies seem to reflect the ol Turkish title *Yabghu*, which goes back at least to th time of the Orkhon inscriptions (see C.E. Boswort and Sir Gerard Clauson, in *JRAS* [1965], 9-10), an it was the Yabghu of the western, Oghuz Turks whor the eponymous ancestor of the Saldjūḳs, Duḳā Temir-Yalïgh "Iron-bow" served (see Cl. Cahen, i *Oriens*, ii [1949], 42; Bosworth, *The Ghaznavids, thei empire in Afghanistan and eastern Iran 994-1040*, Edin burgh 1964, 219 and n. 46). But the orthography *P.y.ghū*, *B.y.ghu*, is so frequent in the sources that i has been suggested (e.g. by P. Pelliot and O. Pritsak) that we have here a totemistic personal name used by the early Saldjūḳs, stemming from *bïghu*/*pïghu* "a typ of falcon" (see M.Th. Houtsma, *Ein türkish-arabisches Glossar*, Leiden 1894, 28). See the lengthy discussion in J. Marquart, *Über das Volkstum der Komanen*, in W. Bang and Marquart, *Osttürkische Dialektstudien*, in *AGW Göttingen*, N.F. xiii, Berlin 1914, 42-3 n. 5, 44. In support of this, it is true that the name/title Payghū / Bīghū Khān re-appears amongst the Ḳarakhānids [see ilek-khans] in the 6th/12th century (see Pritsak, *Die Karachaniden*, in *Isl.* xxvi [1953-4], 54).

Bibliography: Given in the article.

(C.E. Bosworth)

PAYSĀ, Paisā (Hindi), English form pice, a copper coin of British India = 3 pies or ¼ anna. Under the Mughals, the name *paisā* became applied to the older *dām*, introduced by Shīr Shāh, 40 of which went to the rupee, as the unit of copper currency; the name found on the coins however is usually simply *fulūs* or *rewānī*. *Paisā* is the general name for the extenve copper coinage coined in the 18th and 19th centuries by the numerous native states which arose out f the Mughal empire (see J. Prinsep, *Useful tables*, ed. . Thomas, London 1858, 62-3). In the currencies of modern India and Pakistan, 100 *paisās* = one rupee, nd in that of Bangladesh, one taka.

Bibliography: Yule and Burnell, *Hobson-Jobson, a glossary of Anglo-Indian colloquial words and phrases*², 703-4. (J. ALLAN)

PEČENEGS, a Turkic tribal confederation of mediaeval central and western Eurasia. Their ethnonym appears in our sources as Tibet. *Be-ča-nag*, Arabo-Persian *Bdjnāk, Bdjānāk, Bdjynh*, Georg. *Pačanik-i*, Arm. *Pacinnak*, Greek Πατζιναχῖται, Πατζινάκοι, Rus'. *Pečeneg'*, Lat. *Pizenaci, Bisseni, Bysseni, Bessi, Beseneu*, Pol. *Pieczyngowie* and Hung. *Besenyő* (< *Beshenägh*) = *Bečenäk/Pečenäk*. It has been etymologised, with some uncertainty (cf. Pritsak, *Pečenegs*, 211; Bazin, *À propos du nom des Petchénèques*), as a variant of *badjanak/badjïnak* "in-law" (>Old Church Slav. *Pashenog*), i.e. "the in-law clan/tribe."

Their earliest history and origins are unclear. They have been identified with the *Pei-ju* (= Middle Chin. Pək-ńźi̯ʷok = Pečeneg (?), according to Pelliot, *Quelques noms*, 226, n.1), noted in a 7th century A.D. Chinese source, the *Sui-shu*, a T'ieh-lê tribe, located near the En-ch'ü (Onoghur?) and A-lan (Alans). But, this is far from certain. More reliable is a notice in a Tibetan translation of an 8th century Uyghur source on the "Northern peoples" which tells of *Be-ča-nag* hostilities with the *Hor* (Oghuz), probably in the Syr Darya region (Bacot, *Reconnaissance*, 147; Ligeti, *Rapport*, 170, 172, 175, 176). Oghuz traditions (cf. Jahn, *Geschichte der Oġuzen des Rašīd ad-Dīn*, 24-5; Abu 'l-Ghāzī Bahādur Khān, *Shadjara-yi Tarākima*, ed. Kononov, 41-2) appear to confirm this. The presence in their union of the Ḳangar/Kenger (Κάγγαρ) subconfederation (Const. Porph., *De admin. imperii*, 170-1) may also point to a tie to this region. Ḳangar has been connected with the Kengeres people mentioned in the Kül Tegin inscription and the *Kangarāyā* (< **Khangarāyē*) nomads who settled in Transcaucasia. These, in turn, may be related to the Türk toponym Kengü Tarban and the Chinese *K'ang-chü* (a term designating the middle Syr Darya and adjoining lands, see Klyashtornïy, *Drevnetyurkskie pamyatniki*, 156-78) and Old Iran. *Kangha*. Pritsak (*Pečenegs*, 212-14) derives this ethno-toponym from Tokharian **kāñk* "stone" (cf. Turk. Tashkent "Stone City," *Kengeres* < *kāñk* + Ἄορσοι > **āvrs* > *ārs* > *ās* = **Kenger As*) and suggests that they were Tokharian-speaking, mercantile city-oasis (Tashkent) dwellers. The difficulty here is that although *Kang*, etc., may be connected with **kāñk*, *As* cannot be derived from Ἄορσ (= Iran. *Aoruša* which produces *Urs/Ors*). Pritsak further conjectures that the Ḳangars, driven into the steppe by an Oghuz-Ḳarluḳ-Kimek coalition, became nomads, forming a confederation consisting of Tokharian, Eastern Iranian and Bulgharic Turkic elements. Their connection with Eastern Iranian elements is hinted at in the remark of al-Bīrūnī (*Taḥdīd*, tr. ʿAlī, 19) regarding a people that "are of the race of al-Lān and that of al-Ās and their language is a mixture of the languages of the Khwārazmians and the Badj(a)nāk." This is echoed in the Old Rus' translation of Josephus Flavius (ed. Meshčerskiy, 454) which adds "the Yas, as is known, descended from the Pečeneg clan/tribe." Németh, followed by Ligeti, however, on the basis of their fragmentary linguistic remains, view them as Common Turkic-speakers (most probably, Ḳïpčaḳ, see Németh, *Die Inschriften*, 16, 50-1; Ligeti, *A magyar nyelv*, 362, 506, and Györffy, *A Besenyők nyelve*, 170-91). Anna Comnena (ed. B. Leib, ii, 142) remarks that the Pečenegs (whom she calls "Seythians") speak the same language as the Komans (= Ḳuman-Ḳïpčaḳ). Maḥmūd al-Kāshgharī (tr. Dankoff, i, 84), however, seems to lump them together with the Bulghār and Suwār speaking a "Turkic of a single type with clipped ends." The available linguistic material points rather in the direction of Ḳïpčaḳ. The possibility that they adopted Turkic is not to be excluded.

Islamic geographers (cf. al-Iṣṭakhrī, 10; al-Masʿūdī, *Tanbīh*, 180-1) were aware that the Pečenegs had entered the Western Eurasian steppes in a series of migrations, the source of some confusion regarding the Pečeneg habitat in other Islamic authors. This confusion is furthered by the use of the ethnonym *Basdjirt/Bashdjirt*, etc., to denote both the Bashkirs (Bashḳort) and the Hungarians in both their Bashkirian (Magna Hungaria) and Pannonian homelands. Warfare with the Oghuz (who absorbed some of them, cf. the Oghuz *Pečene*), Ḳarluḳs and Kimäks drove the Pečenegs from Central Asia into the Volga-Ural/Yayïḳ mesopotamia and later, with added Khazar pressure in the late 9th century (Const. Porph., *DAI*, 166-7), into the Pontic steppes. Here, they nomadised from the Don to the Danube. They were, as Kāshgharī notes (tr. Dankoff, i, 92), the closest, of all the Turkic peoples, to Rūm. The Islamic authors, without indicating which of their abodes is meant, note that they were the objects of annual raiding (for slaves and booty) by the Khazars, Burdās/Burṭās and others of their neighbours (Ibn Rusta, 140; Gardīzī/Barthold, 35, 36; *Ḥudūd al-ʿālam*, 101, 142, 160 (commenting that the slaves brought from Khazaria to the Islamic lands "are mostly from here" i.e. the "Khazarian Pečenegs"); al-Bakrī, ed. tr. Kunik and Rozen, 42). Gardīzī/Barthold, 35, however, perhaps using information pertaining to their earlier homeland, describes them as rich in cattle, horses and sheep and possessing "many vessels of gold and silver. They have many weapons. They have silver belts..."

The Byzantines, in Constantine Porphyrogenitus' day (d. 959) were eager to use them to control the steppe approaches to the Empire. According to the *De adm. imp.*, the Pečeneg union was composed of 8 tribal groupings (lit. θέματα "provinces"), headed by "great princes," four on each side of the Dnieper (reflecting Turkic bipartite, left-right organisational principles). These further subdivided into 40 "districts" (μέρη), clan groupings (?). This internal organisation, like other steppe polities, was dynamic. Thus Cedrenos (ii, 581-2) reports 13 tribes in the 11th century. The names of the 8 tribal groupings, consist of two parts, the name proper, usually a horse colour, and with some possible exceptions, the titles of their rulers, e.g. Χαβουξιν-γυλά *Ḳabuḳsïn-Yula* "the tribe of the Yula with bark-coloured horses," Συρου-κουλπέη *Suru Kül Bey* "the tribe of the Kül Bey with greyish horses." The *De adm. imp.* also notes the names of the "great princes" (hereditary positions, passed from cousin to cousin) at the time they were expelled from their Volga-Ural/Yayïḳ habitat, *ca.* 889 (*DAI*, 166-9; Németh, *Die Inschriften*, 50-1; Ligeti, *A magyar nyelv*, 507-11). None of the contemporary sources (Byzantine, Rus' or Islamic) notes the presence of a supreme executive authority in this tribal confederation. The *Ḥudūd*, 101, merely comments that they were ruled by an "elder" (*mihtar*) and had no towns. The notice in Abū Saʿīd (d. 1286, preserved in Abu 'l-Fidā, d. 1331), reporting that they had a town, Badjanākiyya, and were ruled by a Khāḳān (Abu 'l-Fidā, *Taḳwīm*,

205), should be viewed as a *topos*. The Pečenegs, like most of the nomadic polities in the Western Eurasian steppes, were stateless.

The Bulgarian Tsar Symeon (893-927), used them to defeat the Hungarians, allies of Byzantium during his war with the Empire (894-6). Formal relations with Rus' were established in 915 so that the Pečenegs, now Byzantine allies, could attack Bulgaria. After 920, Pečenegs-Rus' relations were largely hostile. On occasion, Pečenegs served as mercenaries in Rus' campaigns (e.g. Igor's 944 raid on Byzantium, *PSRL*, i, cc. 42, 43, 45). Sometimes, they were brought in as "allies" in Rus' throne struggles. They never undertook the permanent conquest of Rus'. The Byzantines used them during Svyatoslav's Balkan wars, eventually leading to their fatal ambush of the Rus' ruler in 972 (*PSRL*, i, cc. 72, 73). Relations with Rus' worsened under Vladimir I (978-1015), producing several decades of war (988-*ca.* 1006-7). They were decisively defeated by Yaroslav of Kiev in 1036 and thereafter pushed (by Rus', Oghuz and Ḳuman-Ḳîpčaḳ pressure) toward the Byzantine Danubian frontier (*PSRL*, i, cc. 150-1; Diaconu, *Les Petchénègues*, 39-49) which now became their primary area of focus. Military defeat and the loss of pasturages led to internal conflicts which resulted ultimately in their movement into Byzantine lands from which a weakened Empire could not dislodge them. The Rus' defeat of the Western Oghuz (1060) and the entrance of the Ḳuman-Ḳîpčaḳs into the Pontic steppe increased the pressure on the Pečenegs, who retaliated with their own depredations. The Byzantine Emperor Alexius I (1081-1118), aided by the Ḳuman-Ḳîpčaḳs, delivered a mortal blow to Pečeneg military might at Levunion in 1091. Some Pečenegs fell under Ḳuman-Ḳîpčaḳ overlordship, others took service as borderguards with Byzantium, the Hungarian kingdom (where they also settled) or Rus' (where they became part of the *Černii Kloboutsi* ("Black cowls" noted in Rashīd ad-Dīn, ed. Alizade, ii/1, 162-3, as the *ḳawm-i kulāh-i siyāhān*), a Turkic, nomadic force in service to the Kievan rulers.

In their heyday, the Pečenegs had extensive commercial ties with Rus' (where they sold horses, cattle and sheep) and the Islamic world. Al-Masʿūdī notes the presence among them of merchants from Khazaria, the North Caucasus (Bāb al-Abwāb, Alania) and elsewhere (Const. Porph., *DAI*, 48-51; al-Masʿūdī, *Murūdj*, ed. Pellat, i, 237). On occasion, the Pečenegs threatened the "route from the Varangians to the Greeks" (Const. Porph., *DAI*, 56-63), but never seriously affected trade.

We know little of Pečeneg culture and customs. Al-Idrīsī, ed. Bombaci *et al.*, viii, 918, reports that like the Rus' they burnt their dead. "Some of them shave their beards. Some plait it. Their clothing consists of short tunics." A late Rus' source (the *Nikon chronicle*, in *PSRL*, ix, 57, 64) places their introduction to Christianity in the late 10th century (the conversions of Metigay and Küčük by Vladimir, himself newly converted, in 988 and 991). Latin Christianity was propagated by Bruno of Querfort (early 11th century), the consequences of which are unclear. Al-Bakrī (ed. Kunik and Rozen, 43), however, reports that the Pečenegs were *madjūsī*, but in 400/1009-10, under the influence of a captive *faḳīh*, converted to Islam, precipitating internecine strife from which the Muslims emerged victorious. Manichaeanism, along with Orthodox Christianity also came to them from the Balkans (see Vasil'evskiy, *Vizantiya i Pečenegi*, 38-43).

Bibliography: 1. Sources.

(a) *Chinese*. E. Chavannes, *Documents sur les Tou-ki (Turcs) Occidentaux, recueillis et commentés suivi de Not Additionelles*, St. Petersburg 1903, 1904, repr. Pari 1941, Taipei, 1969; Mau-tsai Liu, *Die chinesische Nachrichten zur Geschichte der Ost-Türken (T'u-küe*, Wiesbaden 1958.

(b) *Tibetan*. J. Bacot, *Reconnaissance en Haute As septentrionale par cinq envoyés ouïgours au VIIIe siècle*, i *JA*, ccxliv (1956), 137-53.

(c) *Turkic*. Abu 'l-Ghāzī Bahādur Khān, *Shadjara-y Tarākima/Rodoslovnaya Turkmen*, ed. tr. A.N Kononov, Moscow-Leningrad 1958.

(d) *Arabic*. Abu 'l-Fidā, *Taḳwīm al-buldān/Géograph d'Aboulfeda*, ed. Reinaud and de Slane, Paris 1840 Bakrī, in A. Kunik and V. Rozen (ed. tr.), *Izvestiy al-Bekri i drugikh avtorov o Rusi i slavyanakh*, 102 (pt 1 supplement to the *Zapiski Imperatorskoy Akadem Nauk*, xxxii [1876]); Bīrūnī, *Kitāb Taḥdīd nihāyāt a amākin*, tr. Djamīl ʿAlī, Beirut 1962; Ibn Faḍlān *First Risāla*, ed. S. Dahhān, Damascus 1960; Ib Rusta; Ibn Saʿīd, *Kitāb al-Djughrāfiya*, Beirut 1970 Idrīsī, *Kitāb Nuzhat al-mushtāḳ, Opus geographicum* ed. A. Bombaci *et al.*, Naples-Leiden-Rome 1970 84; Iṣṭakhrī; Masʿūdī, *Murūdj*, ed. Ch. Pellat Beirut 1966 ff.; idem, *Tanbīh*.

(e) *Persian*. Anon., *Ḥudūd al-ʿālam*, tr. Minorsky Gardīzī, *Zayn al-akhbār*, in V.V. Bartol'd (Bar thold), *Otčet o poezdke v Srednyuyu Aziyu s naučno tsel'yu 1893-1894 gg.*, in *Zapiski Imperatorsko Akademii Nauk*, ser. VII, t. i, 74-175. Pers. text an Russ. tr. repr. in *Sočineniya*, Moscow 1963-73, viii 23-62; Rashīd al-Dīn, *Djâmi' al-Tawârîkh*, ed. A.A Alizade *et al.*, Baku-Moscow 1980[3]; idem, in K Jahn (ed. tr.), *Die Geschichte der Oġuzen des Rašīd ad Dīn*, facs. ed., Vienna 1969.

(f) *Byzantine*. George Cedrenos, *Georgii Cedreni com pendium historiarum*, ed. I. Bekker, Bonn 1893; Ann Comnena, *Alexiade*, ed. tr. B. Leib, i-iii, Paris 1937 45; Constantine Porphyrogenitus, *De administrand imperio*, ed. Gy. Moravcsik, tr. R. Jenkins Washington, D.C. 1967.

(g) *Russian*. Josephus Flavius, in N.A. Meshčer skiy, *Istoriya yudeyskoy voynî iosifa flaviya drevnerusskom perevode*, Moscow-Leningrad 1958; *Polnoe sobranie russkikh letopisey*, St. Petersburg Petrograd/Leningrad-Moscow 1841-.

2. Studies.

L. Bazin, *À propos du nom des Petchénègues*, in *Pass turco-tatar, présent soviétique. Études offertes à Alexandre Bennigsen*, Louvain-Paris 1986, 66-77; K. Czeglédy, *A kangarok (Besenyők) a vi. századi szír forrásokban*, in *A magyar tudományos akadémia nyelv és irodalom-tudományi ostályának közlemenyei*, v/1 4 (1954), 243-76; P. Diaconu, *Les Petchénègues au Bas-Danube*, Bucharest 1970; H. Göckenjan, *Hilfsvölker und Grenzwächter im mittelalterlichen Ungarn* (Quellen und Studien zur Geschichte des östlichen Europas, 5), Wiesbaden 1972; P.B. Golden, *The migrations of the Oğuz*, in *Archivum Ottomanicum*, iv (1972), 45-84; idem, *The people nwkrda*, in *Archivum Eurasiae Medii Aevi*, i (1975), 21-35; idem, *The peoples of the South-Russian steppes*, in D. Sinor (ed.), *The Cambridge history of early Inner Asia*, Cambridge 1990, 256-84; idem, *Aspects of the nomadic factor in the economic development of Kievan Rus'*, in I.S. Koropeckyj (ed.), *Ukrainian economic history*, Cambridge, Mass. 1991, 58-102; idem, *An introduction to the history of the Turkic peoples*, Wiesbaden 1992, 264-70; Gy. Györffy, *A Besenyők nyelve*, in *Besenyők és Magyarok*, in *A Magyarság keleti elemei*, Budapest 1990; A.N. Kurat, *Peçenek tarihi*, Istanbul 1937; S.G. Klyashtornîy, *Drevnetyurkskie runičeskie pamyatniki kak istočnik po istorii Sredney Azii*, Moscow 1964; L. Ligeti, *À propos du rapport sur les rois demeurant dans le Nord*, in *Études tibetaines dédiées à la mémoire de Marcelle Lalou*, Paris 1971; idem, *A magyar nyelv török kapcsolatai a hongfoglalás előtt és az Árpád-korban*, Budapest 1986; A. Pálóczi Horvath, *Pechenegs, Cumans, Iasians. Steppe peoples in medieval Hungary*, Budapest 1989; P. Pelliot, *Notes sur l'histoire de la Horde d'Or suivies de Quelques noms turcs d'hommes et de peuples finissant en -ar (-är)...* (*Oeuvres posthumes*, II), Paris 1949; O. Pritsak, *The Pečenegs: a case of social and economic transformation*, in *Archivum Eurasiae Medii Aevi*, i (1975), 211-35; Gy. Németh, *Die Inschriften des Schatzes von Nagy-Szent-Miklós* (Bibliotheca Orientalis Hungarica, II), Budapest 1932; L. Rásonyi, *Hidak a Dunán*, Budapest 1981, Tkish. tr. *Tuna köprüleri*, Ankara 1984; A.N. Shčerbak, *Znaki na keramike i kirpičakh iz Sarkela-Beloy Veži*, in *Materialī i issledovaniya po arkheologii SSSR*, no. 75 (1959); E. Tryjarski *et al.*, *Hunowie europejscy, Protobułgarzy, Chazarowie, Pieczyngowie*, Wrocław-Warszawa-Gdańsk 1975; V.G. Vasil'evskiy, *Vizantiya i Pečenegi*, in idem, *Trudī*, i, St. Petersburg 1908.

(P.B. Golden)

PEČEWĪ, Ibrāhīm (982-*ca.* 1060/1574-*ca.* 1649-50), Ottoman historian.

Pečewī was born in 982/1574 in Pécs in south-western Hungary, whence his epithet Pečewī (or, alternatively, Pečuylu, from the Croatian پچوی). His family had a long tradition of Ottoman military service. Both his great-grandfather Ḳara Dāwūd and his grandfather Djaʿfer Beg served as *alay begi* in Bosnia; his father (name unknown) took part in campaigns in Bosnia, and in ʿIrāḳ during the 1530s (Pečewī, *Taʾrīkh*, i, 87, 102-6, 436-7, ii, 433). Pečewī's mother was a member of the Ṣoḳollu [*q.v.*] family. At the age of 14, after the death of his elderly father, he joined the household of his maternal uncle Ferhād Pasha, *beglerbegi* [*q.v.*] of Buda, and then that of another Ṣoḳollu relative, Lala Meḥmed Pasha [*q.v.*], in whose service he remained for 15 years until the Pasha's death while Grand Vizier in 1015/1607 (*Taʾrīkh*, ii, 323). He participated in many of the campaigns of the Ottoman-Habsburg war of 1593-1606. Thereafter, Pečewī was appointed *taḥrīr* (land census) recorder in the Rumelian *sandjaḳ*s of Egriboz, Inebakhtī and Ḳarlī-ili (1015/1606), then *muḳābeledji* (clerk) to the Grand Vizier Ḳuyudju Murād Pasha (*ca.* 1607-11). Following a fire at his home in Pécs, he returned to Hungary for several years, but by 1031/1622 was again in Istanbul, where he witnessed the deposition of ʿOthmān II (*Taʾrīkh*, ii, 380-8). He subsequently resumed an official career, serving as *defterdār* [see daftardār] of Diyār Bakr (*ca.* 1033/1623-4), from where he was sent as *beglerbegi* of Raḳḳa [*q.v.*] with 200 *sekbān* troops to the defence of Mārdīn (1033/1624), and then as *defterdār* of Toḳat (1034/1625) (*Taʾrīkh*, ii, 391-2, 394-5, 403). His next recorded post was *defterdār* of the Tuna (Danube) province, from which he was dismissed in 1041/1631-2 to be appointed *defterdār* of Anadolu (*Taʾrīkh*, ii, 421). His next post may have been as governor of Istolni Belgrad (1042-5/1632-5), after which he became *defterdār* of Bosnia (1045/1635-6) and then of Temesvár (1047/1638) (*Taʾrīkh*, ii, 445, 442). Retiring from official employment in 1051/1641, Pečewī spent his last years in Buda and Pécs writing his history.

Pečewī's *History* as published (2 vols., Istanbul 1261-3/1864-6; repr., 1 vol., with intro. and index, ed. F.Ç. Derin and V. Çabuk, Istanbul 1980) covers the period from the accession of Süleymān in 1520 to the death of Murād IV in 1640, and is one of the principal sources for Ottoman history, particularly for the period *ca.* 1590-1632 when the historian was a close observer of many events. It is a compilation (described repeatedly by Pečewī as a *medjmūʿa*) drawing upon the histories of Djelāl-zāde Muṣṭafā [see djalālzāde], Ramaḍān-zāde, ʿĀlī, Ḥasan Beg-zāde [*q.v.*], Kātib Meḥmed [see kātib čelebi] *inter alios* (*Taʾrīkh*, i, 3; on his use of the Hungarian histories of Heltai and Istvánffy, see Karacson Imre, *Pečevi İbrahim'in tercüme-i hali*, in *Türk derneği* [1327], 1/3, 89-96), but also including much unique material gained orally from leading viziers and other Ottoman officials and military men. It is particularly rich for events on the Hungarian and Bosnian frontiers, incorporating details which Pečewī learnt from his family and local acquaintances, and for the critical period of the early 1620s. Though written in relatively simple Ottoman Turkish, the text contains much anecdotal material and some less usual terms (occasionally of Hungarian origin) which render it lively but not without difficulty. There is a strong authorial presence, which contributes to its value as an original source.

Pečewī's *History* was a major source for Kātib Čelebi's *Fedhleke*, Naʿīmā [*q.vv.*] and Djewrī, and was used extensively by von Hammer. No other historical work by him is known.

Bibliography: In addition to references in the article, see F. von Kraelitz, *Der osmanische Historiker İbrâhîm Pečewî*, in *Isl.*, viii (1918), 252-60; Aḥmed Refīḳ, *ʿĀlimler we ṣanʿatkārlar*, Istanbul 1924, 129-50; *GOW*, 192-5; *İstanbul kütüphaneleri tarih-coğrafya yazmaları kataloğu. I. Türkçe tarih yazmaları*, 2 fascs., Istanbul 1944, 225-30; Ş. Turan, art. *Peçevî*, in *İA*, ix, 543-5 (with further references).

(F. Babinger-[Christine Woodhead])

PECHINA [see badjdjāna].

PÉCS (Ottoman *Pečūy*, German Fünfkirchen, Latin Quinque Ecclesiae), town and centre of a *sandjaḳ* in Transdanubian Hungary.

Founded on the site of Roman Sopianae and preserving remnants of buildings from the first centuries of Christianity, Pécs became an episcopal see in 1009, housed the first university of the country (established in 1367) and was the most important economic centre south of Lake Balaton throughout the Middle Ages.

The town surrendered without fight to the forces of Ḳāsim, *sandjaḳ-begi* of Mohács [*q.v.*], and Murād, *sandjaḳ-begi* of Pozsega (Pōzhegha), during Süleymān the Magnificent's sixth Hungarian campaign, on 17 Rabīʿ II 950/20 July 1543. Until 1570, it belonged to the *sandjaḳ* of Mohács, although the name of this administrative unit alternated between Szekcső (Sekčōy) and—rarely—Pécs. Around the middle of September 1595, the *liwā* of Pécs was attached to the newly-created *wilāyet* of Szigetvár (Sigetwār) (cf. Istanbul, Başbakanlık Osmanlı Arşivi, Kâmil Kepeci Tasnifi 344, p. 362) and remained so until 1597. Then it was transferred to the province of Kanizsa [*q.v.*], established in 1600. There was one serious but unsuccessful attempt by Count Nicholas Zrínyi to retake Pécs in 1664, which caused great damage. Ottoman domination ended on 3 Dhu 'l-Ḥidjdja 1097/21 October 1686 when Louis of Baden captured the town.

The 16th century Ottoman surveys present the original population of Pécs as purely Hungarian. Their number shows a markedly decreasing tendency, as in most administrative centres of Hungary. This meant that out of 531 married and 58 unmarried Christian heads of households with their 10 priests in 1546 (Başbakanlık Osmanlı Arşivi, Tapu defteri 441, fols. 5b-9a) there were only 195 heads of families and 2 widows left by 1579 (*ibid.*, Tapu defteri 585, fols.

5b-7a). On the other hand, the number of Ottoman mercenaries getting regular pay diminished from 828 in 1545 to 220 in 1568. Some of them, however, had received *tīmārs*, 237 persons being so listed in 1570. In the same year, there served 22 *zaʿīms* and 98 timariots plus their *djebelüs* in the *sandjak* (Tapu defteri 480). Muslim civilians are not listed in the *defters* at all. The total number of inhabitants can be estimated at 4,500-5,000 in 1546 and at 2,500-3,000 around 1580. Population data from the 17th century are very scarce. The first Habsburg survey in 1687 found 363 houses, mostly within the city walls, which permits us to draw the conclusion that there had been no radical changes in the meantime. The Muslim majority may have become dominant with a not-negligible Slav infiltration.

The Reformation (Unitarian, Calvinist and also Lutheran) strongly affected the town, which was the scene of open disputes among Protestant theologians. In the 17th century, however, the Jesuits restored Catholicism.

Local grain and grape cultivation was modest. In spite of that, the town was a significant centre of viticulture, producing wine from the crops of the neighbouring settlements. In 1687, as many as 3,334 units of vineyards, cultivable in one day, were registered, naming 387 actual and/or former owners, the latter being mostly Muslims. The number of mills was traditionally high, amounting to 40 wheels both in 1546 and 1687, some of which being ruinous at the latter date.

Pécs remained an important emporium in Ottoman times as well. Transit cattle and horses passed through the town both in the directions of Vienna and Venice. Local shops were numerous (46 in 1570), mostly in Muslim, rarely in Christian possession.

The town had remarkable Muslim religious and cultural institutions. Among the *sheykhs* of its *mevlewī-khāne* there were outstanding personalities such as Aḥmed Dede, later head of the *Yeñi-ḳapī mevlewī-khānesi* in Istanbul (cf. Gábor Ágoston, *16-17. asırlarda Macaristan'da tasavvuf ve mevlevîlik*, in *1. Milletlerarası Mevlâna Kongresi. Tebliğler*. Konya 1987, 228-9). Today, two *djāmiʿs* (those of Ghāzī Ḳāsim Pasha and Yaḳowalī Ḥasan Pasha) and a *türbe* (that of Idrīs Baba) still survive in their original form.

Bibliography: Antal Velics–Ernő Kammerer, *Magyarországi török kincstári defterek* ("Turkish fiscal defters from Hungary"), ii, Budapest 1890, 45, 387, 411-12, etc.; Pál Zoltán Szabó, *A török Pécs, 1543-1686* ("The Turkish Pécs, 1543-1686"), Pécs 1941; Ede Petrovich, *Pécs utcái és házai 1687-ben* ("The streets and houses of Pécs in 1687"), in *Baranyai helytörténetírás 1969*, Pécs [1969], 193-217; Lajos Nagy, *A Császári Udvari Kamara pécsi prefektúrájához tartozó* terület 1687-ben ("The territory belonging to the Pécs prefecture of the Imperial Court Chamber in 1687"), in *Baranyai helytörténetírás 1978*, Pécs 1979, 15-55 (esp. 19-27); Győző Gerő, *Pécs török műemlékei* ("The Turkish monuments of Pécs"), Budapest 1960. (G. DÁVID)

PEDROCHE [see BIṬRAWSH].

PEHLEWĀN [see PAHLAWĀN].

PELOPONNESUS [see MORA].

PEMBA, an island of East Africa. It appears in Yāḳūt and other authors as al-Djazīra al-Khaḍrāʾ, and lies to the north of Zanzibar [*q.v.*] off the Tanzanian coast. There has been much debate whether the Menouthias mentioned in the *Periplus of the Erythraean Sea* is Pemba or Zanzibar, with the balance in favour of the former. At *ca.* A.D. 50, it attests Egyptian and Arab trade in the area.

Nothing is heard of it until al-Djāḥiẓ (d. 255/868-9), who mentions *Landjūya*, a corruption of al-Ungudja, the Swahili name for Zanzibar, pairing it with an island of forests and valleys which he calls Ḳanbalū. Geographically this is satisfactory, for Pemba is hilly and wooded, as opposed to the flatness of Zanzibar. Al-Masʿūdī travelled thither with ʿUmānī shipowners in 304/916, and gives an account of its trade. Buzurg b. Shahriyār (d. *ca.* 956) speaks of it as a trading station on the way to Sofāla, but in spite of these dates the thirty ancient sites so far identified have yielded no archaeological evidence earlier than the 10th century. At these the principal remains are of mosques, some in actual use, and occasional houses.

Yāḳūt mentions two cities on the island, called *Mtanby* and *Mkanbalū*, recognisable in modern Swahili as Mtambwe and Mkumbuu [see MTAMBWE MKUU]. Each had a *sulṭān*. The first-named had as ruler an Arab who is stated to have emigrated from al-Kūfa. At this place in 1985-6 a hoard of more than 2,000 silver pieces was recovered, naming ten local rulers accompanied by seven Fāṭimid *dīnārs*. The ten rulers covered three to four generations in a hoard formed *ca.* 1070, which would place the earliest of them in the 10th century. Al-Masʿūdī speaks of kings (*mulūk*) of the Zandj people (*Murūdj*, iii, 6, 29-30 = §§ 848, 871), and it may be suggested that (like the Ayyūbids) these would have reigned in different places at the same time. There is no historical record of their vicissitudes.

Pemba was a vassal of the Portuguese Crown from 1506 until 1695, with a king. After 1698 it fell to the ʿUmānīs. It served Mombasa as a rice-growing area, for which its very rainy climate (76″ av. p.a.) made it suitable. Under Sayyid Saʿīd of ʿUmān and Zanzibar (1806-56), clove cultivation was introduced *ca. post-*1822, making it eventually, with Zanzibar, the greatest clove exporter in the world. The clove plantations were almost all in Arab hands, and exploited until 1873 by slave labour. A disastrous hurricane had destroyed many plantations in the preceding year, and the abolition of slavery came as a further disaster.

Bibliography: L. Casson (ed. and tr.), *The Periplus Maris Erythraei*, Princeton 1989; H.N. Chittick and R.I. Rotberg, *East Africa and the Orient*, New York 1975; C. Clark and M. Horton, *Zanzibar Archaeological Survey*, Ministry of Information, Culture and Sport, Zanzibar 1985; Djāḥiẓ, *Fakhr al-Sūdān ʿalā 'l-bīḍān*, in *Rasāʾil*, ed. Hārūn, Cairo-Baghdād 1385/1965; idem, *Kitāb al-Ḥayawān*, ed. Hārūn, Cairo 1359/1940; idem, *Bayān*, ed. Hārūn, Cairo 1368/1949; J.M. Gray, *History of Zanzibar from the Middle Ages to 1856*, Cambridge 1962, with full bibl.; G.S.P. Freeman-Grenville, *A find of silver coins at Mtambwe Mkuu, Pemba Island, Zanzibar, Tanzania*, in *Antiquaries Jnal.*, lxvi/2 (1986); idem (ed.), Buzurg b. Shahriyār, *The wonders of India*, London 1981; F. Hirth and W.W. Rockhill, *Chao Ju-Kua*, St. Petersburg 1911; M.C. Horton, H.M. Brown and W.A. Oddy, *The Mtambwe hoard*, in *Azania*, xxi (1986); Ibn Baṭṭūṭa, *Riḥla* ii, 192-3, tr. Gibb, ii, 379-80; W.H. Ingrams, *Zanzibar, its history and its people*, London 1931.

(G.S.P. FREEMAN-GRENVILLE)

PENANG (Malay name Pulau Pinang), a state of the Federation of Malaysia consisting of the island of Penang (113 sq. miles) in the Straits of Malacca and a strip of land on the mainland opposite known as Province Wellesley or Seberang Prai (285 sq. miles) linked by a road bridge since 1985. The capital, Georgetown, ranks with Johor Bahru as Malaysia's second most populous urban centre (both a little over

)0,000 in 1980) behind the Federal capital Kuala umpur.

The sparsely inhabited island was acquired from ıe Sultan of Kedah in 1786 for the East India Comany as an entrepôt for country trade. After initial ıccess, it was overtaken by Singapore, remaining a ıbsidiary centre until the establishment of plantaons in eastern Sumatra stimulated it again early this ·ntury. From 1805 it briefly had the status of a residency under the English East India Company, om 1829 joined with Malacca and Singapore as the traits Settlements, governed from Singapore after 836, and in 1867 became a British colony. After the ıpanese interregnum from 1942 to 1945, Penang was ıined to the rest of Malaya in 1948 as a state of the ederation of Malaya (since 1963, Malaysia [*q.v.*]). It etained the free-port status it had enjoyed under ritish rule for some time. In 1970 it opened Ialaysia's first free trade manufacturing zone, and oon became a significant centre for electronics comonent manufacturing.

Reflecting the commercial history of the settlement, ıe population is ethnically mixed. There is a Chinese ıajority, Penang having the lowest proportion of Ialays found in any peninsular Malaysian state Malays being dominant numerically and politically ı the Federation as a whole: see MALAYSIA). ieorgetown is a predominantly Chinese city (68% in 980), with Malays (19%) and Indians (13%) in the ıinority. Muslims in Penang comprise the whole Ialay community and a small proportion of the Inian population, including the so-called Jawi 'eranakan or Jawi Pekan, Muslims of South Indian xtraction who have to some degree adopted Malay ınguage and customs. The latter, being urbanised, ave provided political and intellectual leadership to 'enang Muslims. Unlike Singapore, Penang has not ad an important Arab community. As elsewhere in outheast Asia, the Shāfiʿī law school is followed.

In the Malay states, the hereditary Ruler (Sultan) s head of religion, administering and regulating slamic affairs through the agency of an advisory ouncil of religious notables (Majlis Ugama Islam) nd secretariat (see MALAY PENINSULA, 8). Such conrol was absent in the British colonies, beyond the apointment of a Muslim Advisory Board and a Muslim nd Hindu Endowments Board to regulate *waḳf*. In 957 under the independence constitution, Islam ecame the official religion of the Federation of Malaya, of which Penang was a component state. The ead of Islam in Penang was thenceforth the Federal Ruler or Yang Dipertuan Agung (chosen in rotation rom the hereditary Rulers of the Malay states) and a eligious administration parallel to that of the Malay tates was set up under the Administration of Muslim Law Enactment of 1959. This provided for a Majlis Jgama Islam headed by a state Muftī, including ımong its activities the support of Islamic schools, ropagation of Islam, supervision of the *khuṭba*, and ıdministration of *zakāt* and *fiṭra*. A system of *ḳāḍī* ourts (Mahkamah Kadi) to administer *sharīʿa* law was also instituted, though as elsewhere in Malaysia his jurisdiction extends only to Muslims in the areas of family and testamentary law, immorality, false preaching, and failure to fulfil religious obligations.

Given their cosmopolitan urban society, historically higher educational levels, and lack of governmental concern with religious matters, the British Straits Settlements became, in Roff's words, "sniping posts" for critics and reformers. In education, reformist ideals found expression in the foundation of the Madrasa al-Mashhūr in 1916, which used Arabic and English as the media of instruction, while the Jawi Peranakan in general embraced the government English education stream. In the 1920s, thanks in large measure to the scholar-publisher Sayyid Shaykh al-Hādī, a Malacca-born Malay of Ḥaḍramī descent, Penang emerged as the centre of reformist thought and Muslim publishing in Malaysia, promoting the values of the young Turks or *kaum muda*, who stood for informed *idjtihād* rather than blind *taḳlīd*. Reformist journals like the Malay-language *Al-Ikhwān* (1927-31) circulated from Penang throughout Malaya, southern Thailand and Sumatra. Through the correspondence pages of the related and similarly-titled newspaper *Saudara* ("Brothers", 1928-41), arose Malaya's first national organisation, PASPAM or Persaudaraan Sahabat Pena Malaya ("Malayan Brotherhood of Pen-friends"), which espoused the economic and social progress of the Malay community. During this period, two Muslim presses in Penang were active among publishers of *kitāb* literature (Ḳurʾānic commentaries, manuals of *fiḳh*, etc.: see INDONESIA, vi. 5), and tracts, including some by Aḥmadiyya [*q.v.*] activists, as well as modern novels adapted from English and contemporary Egyptian works.

Within Malaysia, Penang has retained its nonconformist milieu, as an urban centre removed from the centre of power. From Penang in the 1970s and 80s, Chandra Muzaffar, born in Kedah of Indian background, has been prominent in advocating the need for a liberal Islamic sociology unfettered by ethnicity in a modern plural society.

Bibliography: W. Roff, *The origins of Malay nationalism*, New Haven 1967 (standard work); J. Nagata, *Malaysian mosaic*, Vancouver 1979, ch. 4; M. Yegar, *Islam and Islamic institutions in British Malaya*, Jerusalem 1979; M.B. Hooker, *Islamic law in South-East Asia*, Singapore 1984; H. Fujimoto, *The South Indian Muslim Community and the evolution of the Jawi Peranakan in Penang up to 1948*, Tokyo 1988.

(I. PROUDFOOT)

PENČE (T., from Persian *pandja* "palm of the hand"), a term of Ottoman Turkish diplomatic. It was a mark, somewhat resembling an open hand and extended fingers, affixed (on either of the left- or right-hand margins or at the foot of the scroll) to documents, such as *fermāns* [see FARMĀN] and *buyuruldus* [*q.v.*], issued from the Ottoman chancery by higher officials such as viziers, *beglerbeg*s and *sandjaḳ beg*s.

Bibliography: F. Kraelitz-Greifenhorst, *Studien zur osmanische Urkundenlehre. 1. Die Handfeste (Penče) der osmanischen Wesire*, in *MOG*, ii (1923-6), 257 ff.; İ.H. Uzunçarşılı, *Tuğra ve pençeler ile ferman ve buyuruldulara dair*, in *Belleten*, v, nos. 17-18 (1941), 111-18, 131-57 and pls. XXXIV-LIV; idem, *Osmanlı devletinin merkez ve bahriye teşkilâtı*, Ankara 1948, 135-6; M.Z. Pakalın, *Tarih deyimleri ve terimleri sözlüğü*, Istanbul 1946-54, ii, 769-71. See also DIPLOMATIC. iv. Ottoman empire.

(ED.)

PENDJIK (T., from Persian *pandj yak* "fifth"), a term of Ottoman Turkish financial and administrative usage. It denoted the fifth which the sultan drew as the ruler's right (equivalent to the Arabic *khums* [*q.v.* in Suppl.]) from booty captured in the *Dār al-Ḥarb*. This involved, in particular, the collection of young boys from the Christian Balkans and Greece by the process of the *dewshirme* [see DEVSHIRME], and these were then trained for either palace or military service as the *ḳapi ḳullari*; the official in charge of the process of thus extracting the sultan's fifth was termed the *pendjikči bashi*.

Bibliography: İ.H. Uzunçarşılı, *Osmanlı devleti*

teşkilâtından kapukulu ocakları, Ankara 1943-4; M.Z. Pakalın, *Tarih deyimleri ve terimleri sözlüğü*, Istanbul 1946-54, ii, 766-9. (Ed.)

PENGHULU (Indonesian and Malay), literally, "headman, chief, director", used in Southeast Asia as a title for secular and religious leaders. In areas where Malay was the common language the word has often been used for chiefs of tribes and clans. In older Malay writings it is also used as an honorific title for the prophet Muḥammad, indicating him as "leader of all the prophets" (*penghulu para nabi*). In more Javanised areas the word indicated the highest religious officials, both at the central courts of the various sultanates and at places where the authority was exercised by a provincial governor (*regent, bupati*). In these places the *penghulu* exercised authority in all religious affairs, with the implementation of Islamic jurisprudence as his first and the administration of the mosque as his second task. The common Javanese and Sundanese term for this functionary was also *pangulu*. Here will be discussed several developments in the role and position of the Islamic judges in Indonesia through history and also the role of judges in areas outside Java even if they had other names such as, *inter alia*, *hakim, hukum, serambi* (after the place of the religious court: in the *serambi* or front veranda of a mosque), *qadhi, mufti, syarat* or even "priest" and "chief priest" (*hoofd-priester*) by the Dutch colonial government.

In Malay historical writings since the 16th century, religious functionaries under a rich variety of colourful titles took a position at the court of the sultanates. Very often these religious dignitaries also received important tasks in the general administration of the country. S͟hams al-Dīn al-Samatranī (*ca.* 1605-30) as well as a later successor Nūr al-Dīn al-Ranīrī (1637-43) served the Achehnese court not only in religious affairs, but also as a Minister of Foreign Affairs. Collections of Malay law show a clear awareness of the differences between customary law and Islamic law, with priority given in most cases to customary law and only verbal respect to the latter. Only in matters of family law and inheritance was the judgment of the Islamic officials to be taken as the final decision. (Cf. Liaw Yock Fang, *Undang-undang Melaka: the laws of Malakka*, The Hague 1976.)

Classical Islamic Javanese literature since the 17th century depicts the *penghulu* as the court official assigned to execute Islamic regulations, as being often in conflict with mystical wanderers and teachers. In masterpieces of this literature such as the *Serat Jatiswara* and the *Serat Centhini*, the *penghulu* (sometimes together with his following called *kaum*) is depicted as a stubborn official and as being not reliable as a guide for religious matters. Also, in the poetical genre of *suluk* (shorter mystical poems) we find many descriptions of the *penghulu* as a stupid and ridiculous figure, clearly of a lower standard than the mystical teacher, *kyahi* or *guru*, living in his *pondok* or *pertapaan* (hermitage, outside the towns), centres of real spiritual life. At the end of the 19th century Snouck Hurgronje found a cleavage between the *penghulus*, closely related to the realm of politics, and the *kyahis*, religious teachers at *pesantren* [*q.v.*], independent of, neglected or sometimes even opposed by the "administrative" religious leaders. Snouck Hurgronje felt that there was a clear preference for the independent leaders on the part of the Indonesian population. He related a number of cases where the *penghulus* urgently needed the scholarly advice of good leaders of the *pesantren* [*q.v.*] (*Verspr. geschr.*, iv/1, 281; idem, *Adviezen*, 's-Gravenhage 1957, 762-97). Still, at several Javanese courts the *penghulu* held a high position. In many cases he was a member of the family of the ruler. Several *penghulus* are also well known for their literary skills and are also known as authors of *babad*, traditional Javanese history-writing.

The rich variety of Islamic administration in the dozens of Muslim kingdoms in the vast Malay archipelago became more centralised after the tightening of colonial rule in the 19th and early 20th centuries. The Dutch administration in the 19th century recognised the Islamic courts in the traditional fields of family law and inheritance, while a *penghulu* also was nominated as adviser to the higher law-courts. The various editions of the basic colonial legislation (*Regeringsreglement*, 1815, 1830, 1836, 1854) recognised the indigenous rulers (sultans and *regents*) as "head of religion", with the task to supervise and control the "Islamic priests" (i.e. *penghulus*, *hajis* and religious teachers). The *penghulu* then was only nominated by the Governor-General in his function as adviser to general law-courts. In 1882 the first law on religious courts was promulgated. This law made the "priest" (i.e. *penghulu*) the chairman of a judiciary council. After many debates (started between L.W.C. van den Berg, the main author of the 1882 law, and Snouck Hurgronje, who denied the "priesthood" of Muslim judges and the collegial character of Islamic courts), the 1931 regulation on *penghulu* courts corrected this law. An effect of the 1882 law was the diminishing influence of the local native rulers on Islamic courts because the *penghulu* as religious judge became nominated by the Governor-General. This tendency became stronger after C. Snouck Hurgronje was nominated as "Adviser for Native Affairs" (1889-1906). Snouck and his successors were deeply involved in the functioning of the *penghulu*, especially as religious judges. They gave advice for nominations, reprimanded corrupt and ignorant *penghulus* and finally even organised formal examinations of candidates (a number of examples in G. Pijper, *Studiën over de geschiedenis van de Islam in Indonesia, 1900-1950*, Leiden 1977, 63-96). The various activities of this colonial office created a climate of centralised administration in the field of religion, taken over by the Indonesian government and its Ministry of Religion since January 1946.

In 1895 the colonial government issued a Regulation of Marriages (*Huwelijksordonnantie*), which enhanced the position of the Islamic officials, because on the islands of Java and Madura, for which this Regulation was promulgated, the *penghulu* and his local staff now also received an (often indirect) jurisdiction at village level.

In January 1931 a new regulation introduced the term *penghulu* court for the religious courts as a substitute for the former term of *priesterraad* (lit. "council of priests", used in the 1882 regulation). The acknowledgment of the *penghulu* as a sole judge was considered a recognition of Islamic law. For the islands of Java and Madura, however, cases of inheritance were taken out of the religious courts, which meant a loss of importance for the religious administration versus *adat* or customary law. Still, decisions of the *penghulu* courts were bound before and after to an approval of general courts of justice in order to become effective, a regulation that was considered as a subordination of the religious courts to the secular courts. The 1931 Regulation also prescribed the foundation of an Islamic Court of Appeal, which took effect only in 1938 because of the economic crisis of the 1930s. A fixed salary to be paid by the central government, in place of presents from clients r the fixed allowance of 10% of the amount of money nvolved in a case of inheritance, was decided upon in 931, but never took effect during the colonial period. 'he *penghulu* and his staff gained their income only om a small allowance as advisers to general courts of stice and from free gifts presented to them as heads f mosques and judges in religious courts.

Since the independence of the Indonesian Republic nd the creation of a Ministry of Religious Affairs 1946), the title of *penghulu* has been officially abolish-d. His tasks in the field of religious courts have been aken over by the *Kepala Pengadilan Agama*, head of the eligious courts in a district (*kabupaten*), while his tasks s administrator of marriages, divorces and recon-iliations are committed to the *Kepala Kantor Urusan gama*, head of the local branch of the Ministry of Religion on the sub-district level (*kecamatan*) and his taff. The administration of mosques has commonly ecome a private undertaking, not directly related to he government. Many Muslims, however, are still sing the officially abolished term for the *Kepala Kantor Jrusan Agama* in his function as administrator of mar-iages.

In 1974 the parliament of the Republic of Indonesia assed a bill on marriage which strengthened the posi-ion of the personnel of the Ministry of Religion, ecause all cases of divorce now had also to be con-ented to by this part of the bureaucracy. During the 1980s, the Ministry of Religion carried out an exten-sive survey concerning the procedures at religious courts, and in 1989 the parliament passed a bill on religious courts, where the subordination of these courts to the general courts was abolished; the former no longer need the approbation of the latter. Also, the differences between Java-Madura and the (outer) islands were abolished by the laws of 1974 and 1989, which meant the ultimate centralisation of the Islamic administration.

Bibliography: A.H. van Ophuijsen, *De Huwelijksordonnantie en hare uitvoering*, Leiden 1907; *Adatrechtbundels* nos. 28 and 29, 's-Gravenhage 1927-8; J.J. van de Velde, *De godsdienstige rechtspraak in Nederlandsch-Indië*, Leiden 1928; J. Prins, *Adat en islamitische plichtenleer in Indonesië*, 's-Gravenhage 1954; D. Lev, *Islamic courts in Indonesia*, Berkeley and Los Angeles, 1972; J. Prins, *De Indonesische huwelijkswet van 1974*, Nijmegen 1977; Deliar Noer, *The administration of Islam in Indonesia*, Ithaca, N.Y. 1978; H. Zaini Ahmad Noeh and H. Abdul Basit Adnan, *Sejarah Singkat Pengadilan Agama Islam di Indonesia*, ²Surabaya 1983 (first ed. 1980); M.B. Hooker, *Islamic law in South-East Asia*, Oxford 1984; S. Pompe, *A short note on some recent developments with regard to mixed marriages in Indonesia*, in *BTLV*, cxlvii (1991), 261-72.

(K.A. Steenbrink)

PERA [see istanbul].

PERAK, a sultanate on the west coast of the Malay peninsula. It became politically independent in the early 16th century following the fall of its overlord Malacca [*q.v.*] to the Portuguese in 1511. Sometime after 1528, the elder son of the refugee Malacca sultan fled to Perak where the people accepted him as ruler. Perak was already known for its extensive tin deposits, and under this new régime it began to expand economically. But although it inherited many of Malacca's cultural traditions, including adherence to Sunnī Islam and Shāfiʿī law, Perak never developed into a similar Muslim centre because it remained a distribution point for tin and jungle products rather than being fully integrated into the international Islamic trade network.

The 18th century court text, the *Misa Melayu*, nonetheless suggests that by this time a loose Islamic hierarchy was already developing. Like other Malay courts, Perak attracted a number of Ḥaḍramī Sayyid migrants who were accorded great respect and who have been seen as a powerful impetus to the growth of religious orthodoxy. However, the ability of the Perak court to act as a patron of Islam diminished sharply from about 1800 because of a series of succession disputes, invasion by neighbouring states, and a growing Chinese mining population. In 1874, one of the contenders for the throne signed the Pangkor Treaty with the British, which obliged him to accept a Resident whose advice he was to follow in all matters "except custom and religion". But this secular-religious distinction proved impossible to maintain because Islam was so much a part of Malay life. In order to facilitate their own administration, British advisors, through the sultan and the State Council, actively fostered the clarification of Malay Islamic law and the establishment of a statewide religious hierarchy and court system. In the development of Malay Islam during the colonial period, Perak is important because many measures were initially introduced here and later adopted in the other Malay states.

When the Federation of Malaya (later Malaysia [*q.v.*]) gained independence in 1957, each state was given responsibility for administering Islamic law. In Perak, as in the other Malay states, Islam was confirmed as the state religion, headed by the sultan who acts in consultation with the Majlis Agama Islam dan Adat Melayu (Council of Religion and Malay Custom). The Majlis is empowered to issue *fatwas* and through its executive arm, the Religious Affairs Department, supervises matters such as the collection of *zakat* and *fitrah*, and the teaching of Islamic doctrine. A system of *syariah* (*sharīʿa* [*q.v.*]) law courts is maintained to deal with religious offences committed by Muslims. Like the rest of Malaysia, however, Perak stops short of being a fully Islamic state because of the necessity of accommodating its considerable non-Muslim population.

Bibliography: Barbara Watson Andaya, *Perak, the Abode of Grace: a study of an eighteenth century Malay state*, Kuala Lumpur 1979; T.F. Willer, *Religious administrative development in colonial Malay states, 1874-1941*, Ph.D. thesis, University of Michigan 1975, unpubl.; Moshe Yegar, *Islam and Islamic institutions in British Malaya; policies and implementation*, Jerusalem 1979; M.B. Hooker, *Islamic law in South-East Asia*, Singapore 1984.

(Barbara Watson Andaya)

PERIM [see mayyūn].

PERTEW PASHA, the name of two Ottoman statesmen.

I. Pertew Meḥmed Pasha, Ottoman admiral and *wezīr*, started his career on the staff of the imperial harem, became *ḳapudji bashi* [see ḳapīdjī], later Agha of the Janissaries, and in 962/1555 he was advanced to the rank of *wezīr;* in 968/1561 he was appointed third *wezīr*, in 982/1574 second *wezīr* and finally commander (*serdār*) of the imperial fleet under the *ḳapudan pasha* Muʾedhdhin-zāde ʿAlī Pasha. He had fought at the Battle of Lepanto [see aynabakhtī]. He later fell into disgrace and died in Istanbul, where he was buried in his own *türbe* in the cemetery of Eyyūb.

Bibliography: J. von Hammer, *GOR*, iii, 382, 438; Meḥmed Thüreyyā, *Sidjill-i ʿothmānī*, ii, 37-8.

II. Pertew Meḥmed Saʿīd Pasha, Ottoman dignitary and poet (1785-1837). He was of Tatar descent and was born in the village of Darīdja near Urmiya. In his early youth he came to the capital

Istanbul and entered upon an official career. In Muḥarram 1240/September 1824 he became *beylikdji efendi*, i.e. State referendary, and in Shaʿbān 1242/March 1827 head of the imperial chancery (*reʾīs al-küttāb*). Two years later he lost the post of chancellor and went on a special mission to Egypt. On his return he became in 1246/1830 assistant (*kāhya*) to the Grand Vizier. On 23 Dhu 'l-Ḳaʿda 1251/ 12 March 1836 he was appointed minister for civil affairs (*mülkiyye nāẓiri*) and given the title of marshal (*müs̲h̲īr*). In the spring of 1836 he was given the title of Pas̲h̲a but was dismissed by the autumn. In the beginning of September 1836 he was banished by Maḥmūd II to Scutari in Albania. Pertew Pas̲h̲a set out a few weeks after his banishment to his place of exile but did not reach it. He died in Edirne on 5 Ramaḍān 1253/3 December 1837, three hours after a banquet which the governor there, Muṣṭafā Pas̲h̲a, gave in his honour (according to Gibb, *HOP*, iv, 333: Emīn Pas̲h̲a), and was buried there. No-one doubted that his sudden death was due to poison, and public opinion ascribed the crime to Maḥmūd himself. On his family, see *Sidjill-i ʿot̲h̲mānī*, ii, 38. His son-in-law, who shared his views, was the intrigue-prone private secretary to Maḥmūd II, Waṣṣāf Bey, a highly educated man but lacking in character and accessible to bribery, who lost his office about the same time as Pertew Pas̲h̲a and was banished to Toḳat in Anatolia; cf. G. Rosen, *Geschichte der Türkei*, i, Leipzig 1866, 255-6. Pertew Pas̲h̲a's successor was his political opponent ʿAḳif Pas̲h̲a, cf. Babinger, *GOW*, 357-8. As a statesman Pertew Pas̲h̲a took up a pronounced anti-Russian attitude and was no less hostile to the Christians, whom he oppressed with long obsolete and forgotten laws. His feeling against the Christians increased with advancing years.

As a poet, Pertew Pas̲h̲a composed a *Dīwān*, which was esteemed as a model of the poetical art of the period of Maḥmūd II. There are two editions of it: Būlāḳ 1253 (8°, 91 pp.) and Istanbul 1256 (8°, 130 pp.). On other works by Pertew Pas̲h̲a, see Bursalī Meḥmed Ṭāhir, *ʿOt̲h̲mānli müʾellifleri*, ii, 114-15. His valuable library, rich in manuscripts, was in what was formerly the Selīmiyye monastery in Üsküdar, and is now in the Süleymaniye Kütübhanesi.

This Pertew Pas̲h̲a is not to be confused with the statesman and poet Pertew Edhem Pas̲h̲a, who died on 7 Dhu 'l-Ḳaʿda 1289/6 January 1873 as governor of Ḳastamuni [*q.v.*], a number of whose poems have been published e.g. a *S̲h̲āhnāme* and *Lāḥiḳa*, n.p. [Istanbul] n.d., and *Iṭlāḳ al-afkār fī ʿaḳd al-abkār*, Istanbul 1304. On him, see Meḥmed Ṭāhir, *op. cit.*, ii, 114-15; *IA*, art. Pertev Paşa (Şerâfeddin Turan).

Bibliography: G. Rosen, *Geschichte der Türkei*, i, Leipzig 1866, *passim*, esp. 255-6; Gibb, *HOP*, iv, 332-5, with references to Jouannin and J. van Gaver, *Turquie*, Paris 1843, for an account of the death of Pertew Pas̲h̲a in Edirne; Meḥmed Thüreyyā, *Sidjill-i ʿot̲h̲mānī*, ii, 38; Sāmī Bey Frās̲h̲erī, *Ḳāmūs al-aʿlām*, 1494-5; Bursalī Meḥmed Ṭāhir, *ʿOt̲h̲mānli müʾellifleri*, ii, 114.

(F. Babinger)

PERZERIN [see PRIZREN].

PESANTREN, Javanese "*santri*-place", the educational institution of Indonesia where students (*santri*) study classical Islamic subjects and pursue an orthoprax communal life. *Pondok* ("hut, cottage"; cf. Ar. *funduḳ*) is an alternative term, meaning "lodgings" and, by extension, "Islamic religious boarding school". *Pesantren* is used most often in Indonesia (especially Java), whereas *pondok* is the preferred term in Malaysia and the Patani region of southern Thailand. Sometimes the two terms are combined in Indonesia, when the speaker means to make clear that a traditional Islamic boarding school a "*pondok pesantren*", and not merely a religious day school (such as the more modern *madrasa*), is meant. The Minangkabau [*q.v.*] region of Sumatra has a parallel type of Islamic school, called *surau*. This article treats mostly the Indonesian institution, although some references to peninsular Malaysia are included.

The indigenous origins of the Javanese *pesantren* are thought by some scholars to be in the rural Javanese Hindu-Buddhist *mandala* schools of East and Central Java, where ascetical *gurus* imparted religious doctrine and mystical wisdom to students residing together in a communal setting (Koentjaraningrat, 1985, 55, 321-3; Soebardi and Woodcroft-Lee, 1982, 183-4). With the gradual Islamisation of Java—driven in no small measure by both *ṭarīḳa* and popular Ṣūfism—and the conversion of such *gurus*, the *mandala* evolved into the *pesantren*, in which the traditional charismatic teacher—versed in magical and healing arts—became the *kiai* ("venerable religious teacher, respected old man", cf. *s̲h̲ayk̲h̲*) of Islamic times. The traditional Islamic Ḳurʾān school—the *kuttāb*—easily blended with the Javanese prototype, which helped to domesticate and, through a dominant S̲h̲āfiʿī *fiḳh*, in form and integrate, if not unify, Islam in Java. There was also considerable Ṣūfī content in the programmes of many *pesantren*s; and although not dominant, Ṣūfism continues to be an important factor in a sector of *pesantren* life in Indonesia (see Madjid, 1983; Nasution *et alii*, 1990). The historical evolution of the *pesantren* is a complex matter, requiring analysis of its premodern existence in a dynamic, triadic relationship with the rulers (*kraton*) and the market (see Abdullah, 1986), before it became more of an independent, somewhat separatist venture in Islamic communal life in late colonial times and even more in the present.

The origins of the Malay *pondok* were probably in Patani [*q.v.*] (southern Thailand) in the 15th-16th century. Patani Muslims are proud of their tradition in Islamic education, their close ties to the Islamic Middle East, their success in resisting assimilation to Thai language and customs (in large part because of the *pondok* system of sustaining an Islamic microcosm), and the many Malay religious books written in Arabic script (*kitab jawi*). To this day, Patani and neighbouring Kelantan in Malaysia have a strong *pondok* tradition, which resembles that of Indonesia in most respects (see Matheson and Hooker, 1988, 43-6; Winzeler, 1975).

The *pesantren* was well established in rural Java by the 17th century and has contributed much to the spiritual, cultural, social and economic character of Islamic village life down to the present (see Geertz, 1956, 144 ff.; Oepen and Karcher, 1988, *passim*). The Javanese *pesantren* was the dominant Islamic educational institution in Indonesia during the colonial period, when it was a bulwark against Dutch penetration into Islamic faith and order in the countryside (see Rahardjo, 1985, 245, on the gradual postindependence shift of *pesantren*s from closed, guarded institutions to more open and cooperative ventures).

Usually, *pesantren*s have been built in undeveloped space near a village or in a separate part of a settled location. Most students have traditionally travelled to attend *pesantren*s outside their native districts. Travelling for study was a hallmark of early Islamic education in Java, and it had both pre-Islamic Javanese as well as classical Islamic precedent. Thus there is often a somewhat alien character attaching to *santris*, because they are not connected with the local kinship ıd *adat*. In recent years, *pesantren* students at selected ıstitutions have begun to provide some social and :onomic services in their rural locations, as part of ıodern rural development. One "specialised" ıkhassus) *pesantren*, Darul Fallah, in Bogor, West ıva, is sponsored by teachers from the Bogor Agri- ıltural Institute, for the purpose of training students ı farming and crafts within a strong Islamic ethos evoted to useful careers in rural development (for an verview, see S. Widodo, in Oepen and Karcher, 987, 140-5). But East Java's "Pondok Modern" tudents, for example, are forbidden to have social ontact with the townspeople of Gontor and the idea f service to the immediate community is lacking. Iowever, "Pondok Modern" does have a strong ense of being a *wakf* that belongs to the world-wide Auslim community (*Short description*, 26).

In Java (as in Nazareth) it is thought inappropriate or a spiritual leader to have been educated in his own ommunity; the one who has returned, however, after aining wisdom and power through foreign ex- erience and travel, may find a receptive attitude in is home territory. In addition, the *pesantren* holds up n ideal of affinity based on a common, transcending slamic faith and discipline, whereas so much of ar- hipelago life centres on local custom and traditional ocial patterns. On the other hand, *pesantren* life pro- ides for youth a laboratory for self-government and ocialisation into that larger community of ogetherness and consensus that residents of the Malaysian-Indonesian archipelago also value highly.

Pesantren-educated Muslims have tended to criticise heir compatriots for what they perceive to be their ess than pure Islamic belief and lax ritual observance. This Islamist attitude has given Indonesia (mostly in he 20th century) its (much analysed) *santri* type of or- hoprax Muslim, as contrasted with the vast popula- tion of *abangan* people, with their blending of local custom and Islamic belief (Geertz, 1960b, 5-7; see Ricklefs, 1979, 118-125 for a detailed review of the nuances of Javanese socio-religious distinctions).

Although traditionally the vast majority of students in *pesantrens* have been male, there have also been female students for a long time and today they com- prise a sizeable proportion of *pesantren* populations. The sexes are always educated and lodged separately in *pesantrens*, and there is never social mixing, but facilities are often on adjoining campuses while shar- ing the same *kiai* and faculty, which may include teachers of both sexes. Female students are not numerous in Malaysian *pondoks*, where they usually reside in the *guru*'s house under a watchful eye. In Patani, however, females and males attend *pondok* (after puberty) in large numbers.

Although the *pesantren* usually maintains a separate kind of social presence in a rural locale, its central figure—the *kiai* (*guru* in Malaysia and Thailand)—is often a well-known, strong-willed, local personage with charismatic gifts combining Islamic learning with the occult powers of the shaman-like *dukun* (cf. Geertz, 1960a; Rahardjo, 1985). The *pesantren* would not exist without the *kiai*, who is its founder, sus- tainer, and absolute master. Former students, whether in the Javanese *pesantren* or the Malay *pondok*, have vivid memories of occasional corporal punish- ment at the hands of their masters, and being required to serve him in the fields and other tasks. Sometimes the *kiai* has been a local person who returned from Islamic study abroad or from the *ḥadjdj*, whereupon he started providing more-or-less orthodox Islamic teaching or was sought out by the locals for healing and spiritual guidance. *Kiai*s, in the colonial period more than in recent reformist times, often provided Ṣūfī indoctrination, both to the *santri*s and to people in the community.

Of no small consequence is the *kiai*'s personal property—land and buildings—which may be in- herited, donated as *wakf*, or acquired by means of his industry. Whatever goes on in the way of teaching an Islamic curriculum—and this has varied greatly in the past, although today standardisation of the cur- riculum has widely set in—the *kiai* nevertheless bestows on the operation a special blessing and legitimacy. There have been extremely learned *kiai*s (and *gurus*), with advanced training in Mecca or Cairo, and there have been virtually untutored ones, with strong personal charisma and little in the way of formal Islamic education in the Arabic classical cur- riculum. Although often a *pesantren* perishes when the *kiai* dies, sometimes institutions endure and even flourish in the hands of the *kiai*'s heirs, who may in- clude former students who marry the *kiai*'s daughters and carry on the teaching tradition.

The physical plant of a typical *pesantren* consists of the *kiai*'s house and lodging for assistants, a building for regular prayers and instruction, an open space for community activities and sports, latrines/bath with ablution facilities, student dwellings (the *pondok* prop- er), and utility buildings such as granaries, and sur- rounding fields that are worked by the students. There is a great range of physical accommodation found among *pesantrens*, from minimal necessities (the majority) to elaborate campuses, such as the Pondok Modern, in Gontor, East Java, with its Friday mosque, tall minaret, staffed library, bookstore, stu- dent laundry, guest quarters, playing fields, ball courts and other facilities.

Earlier accounts remark on the extreme filth of the students' quarters, clothing and persons (e.g. Snouck Hurgronje, 1906, ii/30-1), resulting among other things in chronic skin disease. In the writer's visits to *pesantren*, the range of personal cleanliness and housekeeping among males has appeared to be about what one would find in men's college dormitories in the west, that is, from acceptable to unsanitary. Female lodgings have appeared to be clean and order- ly and the women students very well groomed.

The *pesantren* served as the main form of Islamic educational institution in Indonesia until the early 20th century, when modern schools—such as the *madrasa*—began to be established. A distinctive aspect of the *pesantren* is its character as a nearly total institu- tion. Although students freely come and go, and although the curriculum is often largely accessed by means of private study and individual interaction with the *kiai*, or his assistants, the régime of the typical *pesantren* is a 24-hour-a-day way of life, with morning classes and/or tutorials, Ḳurʾān recitation, afternoon study and work in the fields, with the rest of the time spent preparing meals and taking care of personal maintenance tasks, perhaps doing errands for the *kiai* and his staff, and honourable begging (in earlier periods especially). The all-important regular prayers punctuate each day's progress.

The *pesantren* is often a place of little comfort, ex- treme crowding, and scanty means. Student body sizes range from scores to thousands, with some Javanese establishments drawing students from throughout Indonesia and abroad (see *Direktori Pesan- tren*: I, *passim*, for specific enrollment figures and cur- ricula of 255 selected institutions from the more than 5,000 in Indonesia). As no or minimal fees are charg- ed, depending on the institution, poor students can benefit from the régime of strict moral and religious training, socialisation into community self-government, and time for meditation on life from an Islamic perspective. Students generally range in age from around ten to twenty-one, although in some cases children as young as seven attend a *pesantren* (as at the Pesantren Ihyaul Ulum, near Gresik, East Java). In larger *pesantren*s, the older students act as preceptors for the younger ones and self-government is the rule, with the *kiai* standing aloof, his house and his face turned away from the *pondok* part of the campus where the students reside. He is approached for help and intervention only for special and urgent reasons.

The *pesantren* curriculum has always been centred on the Ḳurʾān, both its recitation and interpretation, and Arabic language (or Malay or Javanese in Arabic script) texts on jurisprudence, doctrine, classical Arabic grammar and rhetoric, ethics, mysticism, *ḥadīth* and devotional practices (e.g. collections of prayers, praise, invocations, blessings). (See Matheson and Hooker, 1988; and van Bruinessen, 1990, for genres and titles of Arabic script books used in *pesantren*s and *pondok*s over the past century.) *Pesantren* textbooks are often referred to as *kitab kuning* "yellow books" because of the orange-tinged paper they have often been printed on. Modernist *pesantren*s, such as have been supported by the Muhammadiyah, use textbooks in Romanised Indonesian (as well as Arabic language and script), which are called, by contrast, *buku putih* "white books." The distinction between the two types of Islamic education—traditionalist and progressive—symbolised by the colours, is much less pronounced than a generation ago.

Today, most Indonesian *pesantren*s have augmented their traditional course of studies to provide instruction in modern subjects in a curriculum divided into three levels: *ibtidaiyah* ("primary" with *ca.* 60% general content); *tsanawiyah* ("middle" with *ca.* 40-50%); and *aliyah* ("higher" with only 20%) (Rahardjo, 1985, 241). Some *pesantren*s also have an advanced level, *takhassus*, "specialised", where students study only Islamic subjects, such as Ḳurʾānic studies, *fiḳh*, *taṣawwuf* and others. Many *pesantren*s are still rural and provincial, with a curriculum dominated by Islamic subjects taught by rote. Arabic proficiency varies considerably, but there are *kiai*s who are able to raise students' competence to a level sufficient for studying advanced classical texts rather than simpler summaries. Moreover, students are often obliged to study at more than one *pesantren* (whether in Indonesia or the Malay world) if they would cover a sufficient range of the classical Islamic studies curriculum. However, the contents and methods of *pesantren* instruction have undergone considerable modernisation in the more progressive institutions, such as the aforementioned ones at Gontor and Bogor, where modern secular subjects—such as social studies, natural science, mathematics, history and English—are also taught.

Traditional *pesantren*s, based on individualised instruction under the authority of a *kiai*, although still serving a mostly (but not exclusively) poor, rural clientèle, have steadily diminished in numbers and importance since independence, when the more modern *madrasa*s, in Islamic education, and the *sekolah* or "secular" school, with a minimum of religious instruction, have come to dominate. The bureaucratically regulated (whether by government or voluntary religious associations) *madrasa* offers modern subjects alongside Islamic studies, but, unlike the *pesantren*, has neither *kiai* nor an all-encompassing social environment of Islamic discipline. The *madrasa* continues to be a major part of Indonesian education although the *sekolah* is continually gaining ground as universal public education gradually becomes a reality in Indonesia (see Steenbrink, 1986).

The modern type of *pesantren* is far different from the old-style institution. At Gontor, for example, the more than 1,900 students are required to converse socially only in Arabic and English (Indonesian is the instructional medium in general courses, with Arabic the medium in Arabic and Islamic studies and English for teaching that language). Lapses into Indonesian or Javanese in daily life are punished by a short haircut which is a major humiliation for youth acquainted with rock culture and Jakarta or Surabaya street life (to be "sent to a *pondok pesantren*" is a proverbial parental threat when children become unruly at home). The strict Arabic- and English-only rule testifies to the institution's commitment to training its students to be capable participants in both the global Islamic and economic communities. A number of outstanding Indonesian religious, civic, governmental and educational leaders have graduated from Gontor which since the later 1960s has also granted the B.A. degree (in *uṣūl al-dīn*). And unlike most old-time *pesantren*s, the "Pondok Modern" has been placed on a secure foundation for continuing development and growth as a rational organisation with a large and capable professional staff and foreign as well as internal funding (e.g. the Saudi government provided the resources for a major academic building on the campus).

The modern *pesantren*, whether in Bogor, Gontor or a number of other places, does not exist in name only, for it continues, like its predecessor, to sustain a closely regulated, full-time Islamic communal ethos set apart from the differing but equally worrisome seductions of syncretistic Javanese culture and modern secular materialism. Java, particularly, is experiencing increasing urban encroachment on its rural areas, so that once isolated *pesantren*s are being surrounded by inexorable development. It is likely that some of the special qualities of *pesantren* education will be preserved, but in new ways. One widespread development in Indonesia is *pesantren kilat* ("express pesantren"), intensive Islamic education for youth during the summer vacation, held on university campuses and in other facilities. As the Indonesian social scientist, Taufik Abdullah, has summarised the situation, "the future of the *pesantren* will be determined by its ability to maintain its identity as an *ulama*-dominated educational system, while at the same time clarifying its role as a complementary feature of national education" (102).

Bibliography (in alphabetical order of authors): T. Abdullah, *Pesantren in historical perspective*, in T. Abdullah and S. Siddique (eds.), *Islam and society in Southeast Asia*, Singapore 1986, 80-107; M. van Bruinessen, *Kitab kuning: books in Arabic script used in the pesantren milieu*, in *BTLV*, xlvi/2-3 (1990), 226-69 (detailed survey of the "top 100" titles in *pesantren* curricula); Z. Dhofier, *Tradisi pesantren* ("The *pesantren* tradition"), Jakarta 1982 (translation of author's important Ph.D. dissertation, "The *pesantren* tradition: a study of the role of the *kyai* in the maintenance of the traditional ideology of Islam in Java," ANU, Canberra 1980); *Direktori pesantren: I*, Jakarta 1986; C. Geertz, *Religious belief and economic behavior in a Central Javanese town: some preliminary considerations*, in *Economic development and cultural change*, iv/2 (Jan. 1956), 134-58; C. Geertz, *a: The Javanese kijaji: the changing role of a cultural broker*, in *Comparative studies in society and history*, ii/2 (Jan. 1960);

C. Geertz, *b: The religion of Java*, Glencoe, Ill. 1960; Koentjaraningrat, *Javanese culture*, Singapore 1985; N. Madjid, *Pesantren dan tasauf* ("Pesantren and Sufism"), in M.D. Rahardjo (ed.), *Pesantren dan Pembaharuan* ("Pesantren and reform"), Jakarta 1974, 95-120 (the volume has several useful articles on contemporary *pesantren*); V. Matheson and M.B. Hooker, *Jawi literature in Patani: the maintenance of an Islamic tradition*, in *JMBRAS*, lxi/I/254 (1988), 1-86; J. Nagata, *The reflowering of Malaysian Islam: modern religious radicals and their roots*, Vancouver 1984, 38-42 (describes *pondok* in context of Islamic education in Malaysia); H. Nasution (ed.), *Thoriqot Qodiriyyah Naqsabandiyyah: sejarah, asal-usul, dan perkembangannya* ("The Ḳādiriyya-Naḳshbandiyya order: its history, origin-nature, and development"), Tasikmalaya, Indonesia 1991 (scholarly essays commemorating the 85th anniversary of the Ṣūfī-oriented Pondok Pesantren Suryalaya in W. Java, and its celebrated *kiai*); M. Oepen and W. Karcher (eds.), *The impact of pesantren in education and community development in Indonesia*, Jakarta 1988 (essays from 1987 Berlin seminar); S. Prasodjo *et alii*, *Profil pesantren*, Jakarta 1974 (quantitative studies of several *pesantrens* in the Bogor region of W. Java); S. Prasodjo, *The kyai, the pesantren, and the village: a preliminary sketch*, in A. Ibrahim, S. Siddique, and Y. Hussain, compilers, *Readings on Islam in Southeast Asia*, Singapore 1985, 240-6; M.C. Ricklefs, *Six centuries of islamization in Java*, in N. Levtzion (ed.), *Conversion to Islam*, New York 1979, 100-28 (important review of sources and theories); *A short description of Islamic educational institution Pondok-Modern and its Daarussalaam University*, Gontor-Ponorogo, Indonesia n.d.; C. Snouck Hurgronje, *The Achehnese*, 2 vols., Leiden 1906; S. Soebardi and C.P. Woodcroft-Lee, *Islam in Indonesia*, in R. Israeli (ed.), *The crescent in the east: Islam in Asia Major*, London 1982, 180-210; S. Soebardi, *Santri-religious elements as reflected in the Book of Tjentini*, in *BTLV*, cxxvii/3 (1971), 331-49 (struggle between Javanese mysticism and legalistic Islam *ca.* 17th-18th c.); K.A. Steenbrink, *Pesantren, madrasah, sekolah: recente ontwikkelingen in indonesisch islamonderricht*, Nijmegen 1974 (also published in Indonesian under same main title, Jakarta 1986); S. Widodo, *Rural vocational training in pesantren*, in Oepen and Karcher, *op. cit.*, 140-5; R.L. Winzeler, *Traditional Islamic schools in Kelantan*, in *JMBRAS*, xlviii/1 (May 1975), 91-103 (illustrated).

(F.M. Denny)

PESHĀWAR, a city of Muslim India, in the northwestern part of the subcontinent, now in Pakistan (lat. 34° 01′ N., long. 71° 40′ E., altitude 320 m/1,048 ft.). In modern Pākistān, it is also the name of various administrative units centred on the city (see below). The district is bounded on the east by the river Indus, which separates it from the Pandjāb and Hazāra, and on the south-east by the Nīlāb Ghasha range which shuts it off from the district of Kōhāt. Elsewhere it is bounded by tribal territory. To the south lie the territories of the Ḥasan Khēl and Kōhāt Pass Afrīdīs; westwards, the Khaybar Afrīdīs and Mullāgorīs. Farther north, across the Kābul river, the various Mohmand clans stretch to the Swāt river. The northern boundary of the district marches with the territories of the Utmān Khēl, the Yūsufzays of Swāt and Buner, the Khudu Khēl, Gaduns and Utmānzays. Mountain passes famous in frontier history connect it with the surrounding tribal tracts. In the northeast, the Mora, Shākot, and Malakand passes lead into Swāt. The historic gateway of the Khyber (Khaybar [*q.v.*]) connects it with Afghānistān, while, to the south, the Kōhāt Pass runs through a strip of tribal territory, known as the Djowaki peninsula, into the neighbouring district of Kōhāt [*q.v.*].

References to the district occur in early Sanskrit literature and in the writings of Strabo, Arrian, and Ptolemy. It once formed part of the ancient Buddhist kingdom of Gandhāra, for, from the Khyber Pass to the Swāt valley, the country is still studded with crumbling Buddhist stupas. Here, too, have been unearthed some of the best specimens of Graeco-Buddhist sculpture in existence, while one of Aśoka's rock edicts is to be found near the village of Shāhbāzgarha in the Yūsufzay country. Both Fa-hien, in the opening years of the 5th century A.D., and Hiuen Tsang, in the 7th century A.D., found the inhabitants still professing Buddhism. It is also on record that Purushapura was the capital of Kanishka's dominions. Through centuries of almost unbroken silence we arrive at the era of Muslim conquest, when, between the 7th/13th and 10th/16th centuries, numerous Paṭhān tribes from Afghānistān spread over and conquered the country roughly corresponding to the modern North-West Frontier Province (T.C. Plowden, *Kalīd-i Afghānī*, chs. i-v; Selections from the *Tārīkh-i Muraṣṣaʿ*).

The town of Peshāwar is an ancient one, and as Parashawara or Purushapura was once the capital of Gandhāra; it was also called Begram, appearing as such in early Pashto poetry. The present name of the town is popularly ascribed to the Mughal Emperor Akbar [*q.v.*] and is said to derive from Persian *pēsh-āwar* "frontier [town]". Islam first appeared there in the time of the Ghaznawids [*q.v.*]. Sebüktigin fought over the surrounding region against its then possessor, the Hindūshāhī [see HINDŪ-SHĀHĪS] ruler Djaypāl in *ca.* 376/986-7, and his son Maḥmūd likewise combatted and defeated there Djaypāl's son Anandpāl in 396/1006. Thereafter, it came firmly within the Ghaznawid dominions, forming an important link in the route down from the Afghān plateau to the Ghaznawid capital in northern India, Lahore (Lāhawr [*q.v.*]). In 575/1179-80 Peshāwar was captured by the Ghūrid Muʿizz al-Dīn Muḥammad b. Sām [*q.v.*], but destroyed by Čingiz Khān some forty odd years later. Although Peshāwar obviously retained its strategic importance, it is somewhat surprising that Peshāwar is so little mentioned in the Indo-Muslim sources.

Towards the end of the 9th/15th century, according to local tradition, two large branches of Pathān tribes, the Khakhay and the Ghōriyya Khēl, migrated from their homes in the hilly country around Kābul to the Djalālābād valley and the slopes of the Safīd Kōh. The most important divisions of the Khakhay were the Yūsufzay, Gugiyanī and Tarklānrī; the Ghōriyya Khēl were divided into five tribes, the Mohmands, Khalīls, Dāwūdzays, Čamkannīs and Zerānīs. The Yūsufzays, advancing into the modern Peshāwar district, expelled the inhabitants, known as Dilazāks, and finally conquered the country north of the Kābul river and west of Hoti Mardān. By the opening years of the 10th/16th centuries, the Ghōriyya Khēl had also reached the Khaybar area. Eventually these powerful tribes dispossessed the original inhabitants, driving some to the Swāt Kōhistān and forcing the Dilazāks across the Indus. Later, the Ghōriyya Khēl attempted to oust the Khakhay branch but were signally defeated by the Yūsufzays.

Since the modern Peshāwar district lay athwart the route of invading armies from the direction of Central Asia, much of its history resembles that of the Pandjāb. The Paṭhāns of this part of the frontier proved a thorn in the side of the Muslim rulers of India, and, although nominally incorporated in the Mughal empire, they were never completely subjugated, even Akbar and Awrangzīb contenting themselves with keeping open the road to Kābul. Bābur [*q.v.*] had used Peshāwar as a base for campaigns into Kōhāt, Bannū [*q.v.*] and Bangash, and Awrangzīb's governor of Kābul, Mahābat Khān b. ʿAlī Mardān Khān (not to be confused with Mahābat Khān Zamāna Beg [*q.v.*]), used Peshāwar as his winter capital, building there his great mosque (see below). With the decline of Mughal power, Peshāwar was in the 12th/18th century ceded to the Persian invader Nādir Shāh Afshār [*q.v.*] and then subsequently taken over by the Afghān chief Aḥmad Shāh Durrānī [*q.v.*] of Ḳandahār; under his son and successor Tīmūr Shāh, the Mughal practice was revived of using Kābul as the summer capital and Peshāwar as the winter one.

With the militant expansionism in the Pandjāb of the Sikhs in the early 19th century, Peshāwar in 1834 was captured by the Italian commander in Sikh service, General Paolo di Bartolomeo Avitabile, but with the defeat of the Sikhs by British forces in 1849 and the annexation of the Pandjāb, the Peshāwar valley came under British control for nearly a century; administratively, it remained part of the Pandjāb until the formation of the North-West Frontier Province in 1901. (For British administration and policy with the various Paṭhān tribes of the region, see C. Collin Davies, *The problem of the North-West Frontier 1890-1908*, 2nd ed. London 1975.) In the 1930s, the Peshāwar region was violently disturbed by the agitation of the *Khudāʾī Khidmatgārs* or "Red Shirts" of ʿAbd al-Ghaffār Khān [see KHĀN, ʿABD AL-GHAFFĀR, in Suppl.], allied with the Indian National Congress; this rather unnatural alliance, against all the trends in other Muslim parts of India, gave a peculiar flavour to NWFP local politics in the run-up to Partition in 1947, although after that date the Muslim League took over from the previous Congress-inclined provincial government (see J.W. Spain, *The Pathan borderland*, The Hague 1963, 165-73, 211 ff.).

Peshāwar city was the capital of the NWFP of Pākistān for eight years, until in 1955 the NWFP was amalgamated, together with the provinces of the Pandjāb, Sind and Balūčistān, into the "one-unit" province of what then became West Pakistan. The city (population in 1981, 555,000, since Partition, almost entirely Muslim, the great majority ethnically Paṭhāns) is situated near the left bank of the Bāra river about 21 km/13 miles east of the Khyber Pass. Its importance as a trading centre on the main route between India and Afghānistān increased after the construction of the Khyber railway to Landī Kōtal in 1925. It has 16 gates which are closed every night and opened before sunrise. The richest part is the Andarshahr where before Partition the wealthier Hindus had taken up their abode. In this quarter, conspicuous on account of its high minarets of white marble, stands the mosque of Mahābat Khān. On the north-west the city is dominated by a fort known as the Bālā Ḥiṣār. The Shāhī Bāgh with its spacious and shady grounds is a favourite resort of the inhabitants in the spring. The fame of the Ḳiṣṣa Khʷānī or Storytellers' Bazaar is known throughout the length and breadth of the frontier and beyond.

Two miles to the west of the city are the cantonments, the principal military station in the province. Some three miles to the west of the cantonments is the former Islāmiyya College, since 1950 erected into Peshawar University and now with five constituent and eighteen affiliated colleges.

Peshāwar is also the chef-lieu of a district and of a division (area 38,322 km²/14,798 sq. miles) which comprises the districts of Mardān, Hazāra, Kōhāt and Peshāwar plus tribal agencies.

Bibliography (in addition to works given in the article): H.R. James, *Report on the settlement of the Peshawar district*, Calcutta 1865; M. Foucher, *Notes sur la géographie ancienne du Gandhara*, Paris 1902; *Imperial gazetteer of India*², xx, 11-26; *Peshawar District gazetteer*, vol. A, 1933; Sir Olaf Caroe, *The Pathans 550 BC-AD 1957*, London 1958, index; D. Dichter, *The North-West Frontier of West Pakistan, a study in regional geography*, Oxford 1967, 104-15.

(C.C. DAVIES-[C.E. BOSWORTH])

PĒSHWĀ, a Persian word for "leader" with various connotations (Pahl. *pēshōpay*). As a title, it was used for one of the ministers of the Bahmanī sultans of the Dakhan and, more specifically, the hereditary ministers of the Marāṭhā kings of Satara [see MARĀṬHĀS].

At first, the Pēshwā was only the *mukhya pradhān* or "prime minister" of Śivādjī's Council of Eight, and this post was not hereditary up to 1125/1713, the year of the accession of Bālādjī Visvanāth, when the Pēshwā began to outstrip the other *pradhāns* and the Pratīnīdhī in importance. When the Pēshwā transferred his capital to Pūna [*q.v.*] (Poona), the Council of Eight fell into disuse. With the promotion of Bālādjī Visvanāth to the Pēshwāship by Shāhū, a great number of Brahmans from his subcaste of the Citpāvans or Konkanasthas began to migrate from the Konkan to the Dakhan. Brahmans of all subcastes had figured prominently in the early part of Shāhū's reign, but by the 1730s the Citpāvans had already gained ascendancy in the Marāṭhā state. Before the rise of Marāṭhā power, these Brahmans had occupied a rather low position in the Brahman hierarchy. Now, however, they began to derive a sense of caste superiority from their association with the Pēshwā.

Bālādjī Visvanāth in 1131/1719 obtained the *farmāns* for *svarādjya, čawth and sardeśmukhī* from the Mughal emperor, after which he began to re-organise the revenue administration through the promulgation of an elaborate scheme of quota repartition, both in the Western Dakhan and the newly conquered areas where the Marāṭhās had not yet obtained full control but only levied *čawth* and *sardeśmukhī*. Marāṭhā expansion to the north began to gain momentum under Bālādjī Visvanāth's son Bādjī Rāo, who succeeded him in the Pēshwāship in 1132/1720. This proved to be of great importance for the consolidation of the Pēshwā's power in opposition to the older Marāṭhā *sardārs*, who were adherents of the Rādjā of Satara but jealous of the Pēshwā's supremacy. The Pēshwās later gave out to have received sanction from the Mughal emperor for levying tribute from the *ṣūbas* of Gudjarāt and Mālwā. According to the *Shāhū caritra*, the Pēshwā's attempts to extend Marāthā power in Gudjarāt, Mālwā and Hindustān were for some time opposed with success by the Pratīnīdhī, who proposed an expansionist policy into the Konkan and the Karnataka, to complete the conquests begun by Śivādjī. But it was the Pēshwā who received the Rādjā's sanction to pursue the expansion to the north as the latter's delegate, and from then on the Pēshwā steadily acquired more and more power and wealth. The Rādjā of Satara became almost entirely a figurehead already under Bādjī Rāo, who promoted his own *sardārs*, Pawār, Holkar and Śindhīyā, to strategic commands in the north. Bādjī Rāo himself was also, up to his death in 1153/1740, incessantly campaigning: in Mālwā, the Dakhan, Gudjarāt and in the Konkan.

Bādjī Rāo was succeeded by his eldest son, Bālādjī ādjī Rāo, in 1153/1740. Now the conquests of ſālwā and Gudjarāt were completed. And it is to ālādjī's reign that many of the Brahman families ho were prominent at the turn of the 18th century ate their rise. There now arose two distinct groups of ırdārs: on the one hand, the relations and adherents f the Rādjā of Satara, the Bhōnslē of Nāgpur [q.v.] ıe remainder of the Council of Eight and the Pratīnīhī; on the other, the new men put forward by the ēshwā, most important of which were Śīndhīyā and Iolkar. In 1153/1740 Bālādjī's claim to Mālwā was ecognised by an imperial *farmān* of the *nā᾿ib-ṣūbadārī* ır "deputy governorship" of that province. Between 153/1740 and 1161/1748 the same Pēshwā organised our other expeditions to the north: twice to ʀādjāstān, to Bihār, Bengal and Bundelkhand, and gainst the Afghān Aḥmad Shāh Abdālī [q.v.] in Hinustān. After the death of the Marāthā king Shāhū in 162/1749, Bālādjī assumed power in all but name. The new king of Satara, Rāmrādjā, was left in almost omplete isolation; the Rādjā's attempts to regain ontrol were unsuccessful, and in 1164/1751 he, in efect, renounced all sovereign power, agreeing to sancion the Pēshwā's policies unconditionally. Shāhū's vidow Tarabai subsequently made a final attempt to ubvert "the Brahman government" of the Pēshwā, ut again without success. The Rādjā, however, coninued to invest each new Pēshwā with the *khilʿāt* or obes of honour [see KHILʿA] and similar ceremonial of tate. The Pēshwā continued to travel, as the Rādjā's 'prime minister", to Satara every year in order to ubmit the revenue accounts.

Bālādjī did not survive the catastrophic Battle of Pānīpat [q.v.] in 1174/1761, in which the Marāthās were defeated by the Afghāns. His son Mādhav Rāo hen received the investiture from the Rādjā, who remained in confinement. Mādhav Rāo reigned for eleven years, a period in which he succeeded in restoring the prestige of the Brahman rādj. Citpāvan power reached its peak under Nānā Phadnis, the regent in the name of the child of Mādhav Rāo's murdered brother Narāyan Rāo. Still, the Rādjā of Satara continued as the *de jure* sovereign. From 1188/1775 to 1209/1795, Nānā Phadnis's power was supreme, although he was constantly fearing the Marāthā leaders rallying around the Rādjā. The new threats, however, did not come from the Marāthā royal clique but from the Pēshwā's own *sardārs*, Śīndhīyā and Holkar. The Pēshwā had to take from Śīndhīyā and assume for himself the title of *wakīl-imuṭlaḳ* of the Mughal empire. Śīndhīyā grew more powerful in Hindustān. In 1210/1796 Bādjī Rāo II was elevated to the Pēshwāship by the military power of Śīndhīyā. The fear of Śīndhīyā and Holkar ultimately, in 1217/1802, induced the Pēshwā to conclude the Treaty of Bassein with the British, resulting in the establishment of a subsidiary force in Pūna, for the protection by which the Pēshwā sacrificed his independence. This was the first result of the "subsidiary system" devised by Lord Wellesley. The latter appears to have been unaware of the existence of the Rādjā of Satara and spoke of the Pēshwā as a "sovereign". Under Nānā Phadnis, in fact, the relationship of the Pēshwā and the Rādjā had, even in its ceremonial aspect, approached one of equality. However, by 1810, the same forms of external respect towards the Rādjā were re-introduced as were observed when the Rādjā was the effective sovereign and the Pēshwā merely his prime minister. Nevertheless, all treaties with the British were concluded by the Pēshwā alone. In 1818 an outbreak of hostility led to the Third Anglo-Marāthā War, the expulsion of the Pēshwā, and British annexation of the Dakhan.

Bibliography: *Pēshwā Daftar* (Pūna Archives); P.M. Joshi (ed.), *Selections from the Peshwa Daftar (New Series)*, 3 vols., Bombay 1957-62; A. Pawar (ed.), *Tārābāīkālīn kāgadpatre*, 3 vols., Kolhapur 1969-72; V.K. Rajvade (ed.), *Marāthyāṉcyā itihāsācīṉ Sādhaneṉ*, 22 vols., Pūna, Bombay, etc. 1898-1919; G.S. Sardesai (ed.), *Selections from the Peshwa Daftar*, 45 vols., Bombay 1930-34; G.S. Sardesai, Y.M. Kale and V.S. Vakaskar (eds.), *Aitihāsik patreṉ yādī vagaire*, Pūna 1930; R.B.G.C. Vad, P.V. Mawji and D.B. Parasnis (eds.), *Sanadāpatreṉ*, Bombay 1913; R.B.G.C. Vad, D.B. Parasnis, *et alii* (eds.), *Selections from the Satara Rajas' and Peishwas' diaries*, 9 vols., Pūna and Bombay 1905-11; V.K. Bhave, *Pēshwekālīn Mahārāshtra*, Pūna 1935; J. Grant Duff, *History of the Marathas*, 2 vols., Delhi 1971; S.N. Sen, *Administrative system of the Marathas*, Calcutta 1976; A. Wink, *Land and sovereignty in India: agrarian society and politics under the eighteenth-century Maratha Svarājya*, Cambridge 1986. (A. WINK)

PEST (Ottoman *Peshte*), formerly a separate town, in Ottoman times centre of a *nāḥiye* in the *sandjaḳ* of Budīn [q.v.], today part of the capital of Hungary.

It was an earlier settlement than Buda, with mostly German inhabitants. After the Mongol invasion in A.D. 1241-2, with the creation of the fortification on the Castle Hill of present-day Buda (called new Pest for a period), Pest slowly lost some of its importance and was overshadowed by the capital, to which also the Germans moved. Nevertheless, the population of Pest reached some 7-8,000 souls at the end of the 15th century.

Although surrounded by walls and a channel with morasses, the town was quite vulnerable and fell into Ottoman hands without fight in 1541. One year later, a large Habsburg imperial army, headed by Joachim, Elector of Brandenburg, attempted to reconquer Pest, but failed due mainly to bad organisation and the lack of resoluteness. Another siege on 6 October 1602 brought success, and Pest was in Habsburg hands for almost two years. On 30 June 1684, the forces of Charles of Lorraine marched into the castle abandoned by the Turks. Four months later, however, after the abortive attack against Buda, the Ottomans were able to return. The final retaking by the same Duke's army took place on 17 June 1686.

The 16th century Ottoman surveys show that the indigenous population of Pest was Hungarian. Their number diminished rapidly, as in most administrative centres of Hungary: 122 Christian heads of families were found here in 1546, of which there remained 63 by 1590 (intermediate values: 1559-110, 1562-98, 1580-66 heads of families; cf. Gyula Káldy-Nagy, *A Budai szandzsák 1546-1590. évi összeírásai. Demográfiai és gazdaságtörténeti adatok* ("Registers of the *sandjaḳ* of Buda in 1546-1590. Data on demography and economy"), Budapest 1985, 490.) As regards Muslims, our knowledge is limited to mercenaries, who were almost 1,000 in 1541, close to 1,500 in 1543, and 734 in 1628. The total number of the population could not have exceded 2,500-3,000 people, although it is difficult to guess at the proportion of possible Muslim civilians.

The role of Pest as a commercial centre was significant both for local and transit trade. Its importance was enhanced by the immense floating bridge erected in 1566 when Ṣoḳollu Muṣṭafā was governor of Buda.

The *nāḥiye* of Pest was the largest within the *liwā* of Buda, with more than 200 settlements and *mezraʿ*as.

Bibliography: Ferenc Salamon, *Budapest története* ("The history of Budapest") i-iii, Budapest 1878-85; Lajos Fekete, *Budapest a törökkorban* ("Budapest in Turkish times"), Budapest 1944; L. Fekete, *Buda and Pest under Turkish rule*, in *Studia Turco-Hungarica*, ed. Gy. Káldy-Nagy, iii, Budapest 1976.
(G. Dávid)

PETRO VARADIN [see WARADĪN].

PETRUS ALFONSI, Andalusian polemicist and translator (*fl.* A.D. 1106-*ca.* 1130), convert to Christianity in 1106, composed his *Dialogi contra Iudaeos* in 1108 or 1110. Staged as a debate between his former Jewish self (Moses), and his present Christian self (Peter), the *Dialogi* ridicule Talmudic Aggadah, showing that they contradict principles of Graeco-Arabic philosophy and science (in particular astronomy); the *Dialogi* became the most widely-read anti-Jewish text of the Latin Middle Ages.

In the fifth chapter of the *Dialogi* Alfonsi attacks Islam, following—to a large extent—the Arabic text attributed to ʿAbd al-Masīḥ b. Isḥāḳ al-Kindī [*q.v.*]. Alfonsi portrays Muḥammad as a charlatan driven by lust and political ambition, ill-tutored in religious matters by a heretical Christian, Sergius [see BAḤĪRĀ] and two heretical Jews, Abdias (ʿAbd Allāh b. Salām [*q.v.*]) and Chabalahabar (Kaʿb al-Aḥbār [*q.v.*]). He gives a curious description of pre-Islamic cult rituals at Mecca (based, it seems, on Spanish Jewish sources), asserting that current Islamic practice is tainted by these pagan origins. Later Latin writers on Islam used Alfonsi's tract extensively.

Alfonsi taught astronomy in England and France. In 1116, he produced an inept Latin adaptation of the *Zīdj al-Sindhind* of al-Khwārazmī [*q.v.*]; subsequently, Adelard of Bath (probably with Alfonsi's help) produced a somewhat better version. He later wrote an *Epistola ad Peripateticos*, urging French scholars to study astronomy and arguing for the superiority of Arab texts to those of Latin authors such as Macrobius.

Alfonsi's *Disciplina clericalis* is a collection of proverbs accompanied by short, illustrative fables; it is one of the earliest Latin texts to contain stories of Arabic provenance. The *Disciplina* was extremely popular for centuries (both in Latin and in its many vernacular translations); its fables were used by preachers as *exempla*, incorporated by Boccaccio into the *Decameron*, and resurfaced in the 15th and 16th centuries in printed editions of Aesop.

Bibliography: The best edition of the *Dialogi contra Iudaeos* is that of K.-P. Mieth, diss. Berlin 1982, although the older edition by J.P. Migne, in *Patrologia latina cursus completus*, clvii, 527-672, is more widely available. *Disciplina Clericalis*, A. Hilka and W. Söderhjelm (eds.), in *Acta Societatis Scientiarum Fennicae*, xxxviii/4, Helsinki 1911; E. Hermes (tr.), *Die Kunst, vernünftig zu Leben (Disciplina clericalis)*, Zürich and Stuttgart 1970. The *Epistola ad Peripateticos* is edited by J. Tolan (see below). The translation of the *Zīdj al-Sindhind* is edited by O. Neugebauer, in *The astronomical tables of al-Khwārizmī*, Copenhagen 1962. On Alfonsi, see B. Septimus, *Petrus Alfonsi on the cult at Mecca*, in *Speculum*, lvi (1981), 517-33; G. Monnot, *Les citations coraniques dans le "Dialogus" de Pierre Alphonse*, in *Cahiers de Fanjeaux*, xviii (1983), 261-77; J. Tolan, *Petrus Alfonsi and his medieval readers*, Gainesville, Fla. 1993.
(J. Tolan)

PHILBY, Harry St. John Bridger (1885-1960), Arabian explorer and traveller, adviser to King ʿAbd al-ʿAzīz b. Suʿūd (Ibn Suʿūd) [see SUʿŪD, ĀL] and British convert to Islam.

Born of parents connected with planting and with official service in the Indian subcontinent, he had a conventional public school and Cambridge University education, and himself entered the Indian Civil Service in 1908. Already he showed a flare for learning Indian languages and for immersing himself in the cultures of India, until the First World War found him in ʿIrāḳ (1915-17), where he first acquired what became a lasting love for the Arab world and made his first trip into the interior of Arabia as part of a government mission in 1917-18 to persuade Ibn Suʿūd (Ibn Saud) to attack Ḥāʾil and its pro-Turkish rulers the Āl Rashīd [*q.vv.*]. After the War, he remained in the Middle East, with Sir Percy Cox in ʿIrāḳ and then in the newly-created kingdom of Transjordan.

But in 1924 he decided to resign from government service, disillusioned with British policy in the Middle East and its failure to recognise the new forces of Arab nationalism. In the ensuing lean years, he became involved, with little success, in business ventures in the Middle East and in pro-Arab, anti-British press polemics. He had often mentioned the potential advantages for his business activities in becoming a Muslim, and in 1930 became one at the hands of Ibn Suʿūd, though most Arabs were subsequently to consider him insincere and most Europeans to regard his Islam as a convenience rather than an act of genuine faith. It did, however, give him the entrée to Ibn Suʿūd's court and the King's companionship. He was now able to make his great cross-Arabian Desert journeys, including of the Rubʿ al-Khālī [*q.v.*] in 1932 (although he had been beaten to this by Bertram Thomas two years previously), and in 1936-7 around the southern fringes of Nadjd [*q.v.*] and the northern fringes of the region to the east of the Aden Protectorate, where his appearance with a Suʿūdī armed party prompted British fears that his mission involved Suʿūdī designs on the South Arabian shaykhdoms; a deliberate intention in various of his journeys of enlarging Suʿūdī borders was in fact almost certainly a motive as well as the pure love of exploration (see J.B. Kelly, Jeux sans frontières: *Philby's travels in southern Arabia*, in C.E. Bosworth *et alii* (eds.), *The Islamic world, from classical to modern times. Essays in honor of Bernard Lewis*, Princeton 1989, 701-32). Philby's journeys were nevertheless heroic ones, during which he took meticulous records of all aspects of natural phenomena (much of this material is deposited with the Royal Geographical Society, London). Further business projects involved him with American oil companies and with the import of Ford cars. He was back in Britain during the Second World War, but returned to Arabia in 1945, and between 1950 and 1953 undertook further journeys of exploration—to Ḳaryat al-Fāw [see AL-FĀʾW], to Midian [see MADYAN SHUʿAYB] and into the south, where he gathered petroglyphs and Thamudic and South Arabian inscriptions. But the new king, ʿAbd al-ʿAzīz's son Suʿūd, was displeased at Philby's denunciations in his writings of the laxity of morals and habits of luxury amongst the ruling élite which newly-found oil wealth had brought; in 1955 he had to leave Saudi Arabia for Beirut; and after returning twice to al-Riyāḍ [*q.v.*], died in Beirut in 1960.

Philby's various public careers were vitiated by his at times immoderate language and hectoring behaviour, for he lacked the qualities of the diplomat and conciliator. His fame rests upon his many books about the peninsula and his acute observation of its geographical and scientific features. He never claimed to be a professional historian, and was careless about checking dates and consulting parallel sources in his books on Suʿūdī history (see G. Rentz, *Philby as a historian of Saudi Arabia*, in *Studies on the history of Arabia*, i/2, al-Riyāḍ 1399/1979, 25-35). Despite this, his many talents and remarkable experience of Arabia give his writings a permanent value.

Bibliography (in addition to references in the article): G. Ryckmans, *H. Saint John B. Philby, le "Sheikh ʿAbdallah", 3 avril 1885-30 septembre 1960*, Istanbul 1961 (outline bibl. of Philby's works, 23); Elizabeth Monroe, *Philby of Arabia*, London 1973 (official biography; bibl. of Philby's works, incomplete, at 307-12). (C.E. Bosworth)

PHILIPPINES, a group of islands between 4° and 21° N. lat, and 117° and 127° E. long. (Greenwich) on the western rim of the Pacific Ocean. Although the Philippines comprise 7,107 islands, about 10% are uninhabited and most of the population is on the eleven largest islands, with the two largest, Luzon and Mindanao, accounting for 65% of the country's land area and 60% of its population. Some seventy Austronesian languages are spoken, as well as English, with Tagalog (Pilipino), the language of the people around the capital, Manila, being the national language. Before colonisation by Spain in the 16th century A.D., the population of the Philippines lived mostly in small, self-contained communities (*barangays*), except in the south where Muslim sultanates had been established. In the lowland areas, these small communities quickly came under Spanish influence, with most of the population being converted to Christianity. Today, somewhat less than 10% of the national population of almost 50 million is Muslim. Apart from a growing urban population in Metro Manila, the Muslim communities are concentrated in the south: in the Sulu Archipelago, in western and southern Mindanao and coastal areas of southern Palawan. Thirteen ethno-linguistic groups have been distinguished among them, the three largest—Maranao, Maguindanao and Tausug—accounting for three-quarters of the total Muslim population. Archaeological evidence, however, suggests that the Tausug migrated to Sulu from the northern Philippines no earlier than the 11th century, largely displacing the indigenous Samal (the fourth largest Muslim ethno-linguistic group). As in most of Southeast Asia, Philippine Muslims are predominantly Sunnīs of the S͟hāfiʿī school, though as commentators have often observed, in some Muslim communities Islam has blended into earlier folk religions.

1. *Islamisation in the Philippines*

From around the 9th century A.D., Arab and Indian merchants, and subsequently Muslim missionaries, travelled, and probably established settlements, along the trade routes which linked Arabia and China through Southeast Asia. Initially on the periphery of this trade, by the 14th century Jolo, the largest island in the Sulu archipelago, had become a significant entrepôt centre. In a sacred grove outside Jolo there is a Muslim grave dated 710 A.H. (1310 A.D.) which Cesar Majul takes as evidence of a settlement of foreign Muslims on Jolo by the late 13th or early 14th century. Local genealogies (*tarsilas*) record that a Tuan Masha'ika arrived in Sulu around this time, marrying the daughter of a local chief and raising their children as Muslims. They also speak of a Karīm ul-Mak͟hdūm (Tuan S͟harīf Awliyā)—possibly a Ṣūfī missionary—who settled on Jolo, at Buansa, in the second half of the 14th century, preaching Islam and building a place of worship. Soon after this a nobleman from the Minangkabao region of Sumatra, Rajah Baguinda, arrived in Sulu with a small army and established himself in authority in Buansa. That he was able to do so, it has been argued, suggests that by the late 14th or early 15th century there was, around Buansa at least, a significant population of sympathetic Muslims. Baguinda married the daughter of a local chief and consolidated the process of Islamisation in the area. Around 1450 another Arab visitor, Sayyid Abu Bakr, joined Baguinda, marrying his daughter, Paramisuli, and on Baguinda's death assuming political control in Buansa. Abu Bakr, known in Sulu as S͟harīf ul-Hās͟him, founded the Sultanate of Sulu. He promoted the spread of Islam, converting the hill people in the interior of Jolo, introduced organised religious study, and established social and political institutions along Islamic lines. At its height, the influence of the Sulu Sultanate spread from Basilan and the coast of southern Zamboanga in the east, to Palawan in the north and Borneo in the west. (Later Philippine claims to the Malaysian state of Sabah refer back to this period.)

The introduction of Islam to the island of Mindanao, however, is believed to have come not from Sulu but from Johore, with the arrival at the mouth of the Pulangi River (the present site of Cotabato) around 1515 of S͟harīf Muḥammad Kabungsuwan and a group of Samal people. (Maguindanao legends also tell of earlier visits by the foreign Muslims S͟harīf Awliyā and S͟harīf Maraja, who married Awliyā's daughter.) Kabungsuwan, the son of an Arab father from Mecca and allegedly descended from the Prophet, and a Malaccan princess, is a powerful figure in Philippine Muslim history. He is generally credited with the spread of Islam in Mindanao, by a combination of proselytising, military conquest and diplomacy, and he provided the foundation for the Maguindanao Sultanate, though it appears to have been his great-great-grandson, the celebrated Kudarat, who first adopted the title of sultan. From the Cotabato area, Islam spread inland to Lanao and other parts of western and central Mindanao, from the north coast to the Gulf of Davao in the south.

In the late 15th to early 16th centuries Islam also spread from Borneo to Mindoro and southern Luzon in the northern islands of the Philippines. Muslim leaders Rajah Sulaymān and Rajah Lakandula, both kin of the Sultan of Brunei, controlled areas around Manila and Muslim influence extended south of Manila into what is now Batangas.

Thus by the 16th century Islam was well established in Sulu and western Mindanao and was spreading eastwards on Mindanao and to the northern islands. In the southern Philippines there were powerful sultanates and, encouraged by visits from foreign missionaries, religious institutions were growing in number and influence. Jolo was an important centre for trade, and intermarriages linked Philippine Muslims with Malay states to the west and south.

2. *Islam in the colonial Philippines*

When the Spanish arrived in the Philippines in 1521 they recognised among the local Muslims their old adversaries the "Moro", and in effect resumed the crusades in Southeast Asia. Following their permanent settlement in the islands in 1565, the Spaniards reversed the spread of Islam in the north and embarked upon a series of Moro Wars against the Muslims in Sulu and Mindanao as well as in Borneo. Spanish policy in the Philippines was to Hispanise and Christianise the native population, and the commander of the first military expedition to Mindanao and Sulu was specifically instructed to prevent the teaching of the "doctrine of Mahoma" and to destroy places in which "that accursed doctrine has been preached". The Spaniards partially succeeded in halting the easterly spread of Islam on Mindanao and established footholds in western Mindanao, notably at Zamboanga. In addition to religious and political objectives, Spain sought to displace Moros in local and regional trade, to stop Moro piracy against Spanish shipping, and to put an end to Moro raids against Spanish and Christianised *indio* settlements in Luzon and the Visayas. These objectives were pursued strongly in the 17th and 18th centuries as Dutch commercial activity in the area increased, as Jolo became a major entrepôt in the European trade with China, and as attacks on Visayan settlements increased along with the growing importance of slavery to the regional economy.

In 1637 Lamitan, the capital of Sultan Kudarat of Maguindanao, fell to Spanish forces; Jolo was captured the following year. Eight years after the fall of Lamitan, however, the Spaniards withdrew, signing a treaty with Kudarat which recognised his sphere of influence from Zamboanga to the Gulf of Davao and eastwards to Maranao territory. Fighting broke out again in 1656 with a *djihād* led by Kudarat and the sultans of Sulu, Ternate and Makassar. In 1663 the Spaniards again withdrew, not returning until 1718, when another round of the Moro Wars began. Finally, with increasing European rivalry in the area, the balance of advantage shifted in favour of Spain with the introduction of steam gunboats in the mid-19th century. In 1860 Spanish authorities set up a "Government of Mindanao", and eighteen years later the Sultan of Sulu acknowledged Spanish sovereignty. When in 1898 the Philippines were ceded by Spain to the USA under the Treaty of Paris, the Muslim areas of Sulu and Mindanao were still not fully under Spanish control, but this did not prevent their being included in the settlement, notwithstanding Muslim protests.

Under an agreement signed with the Sultan of Sulu in 1899 the occupying US army at first adopted a position of "non-interference" in the Muslim areas. This was soon abrogated, however, and replaced by policies designed to "develop, civilise and educate" the Muslims. The American administration made some attempt to accommodate aspects of Muslim social life, particularly in relation to Islamic law and *adat* on domestic matters, but Muslims justifiably feared an undermining of traditional authority and attempts to assimilate them into the larger, Christian, society. Resistance to American rule resulted in a series of military confrontations, culminating in the battle of Bud Bagsak on Jolo in 1913. Two years later the Sultan of Sulu surrendered his temporal authority to the US government. Under a "policy of attraction" health and education services were improved and public works programmes undertaken.

Initially administered by US army officers as the Moro Province, Mindanao and Sulu subsequently came under a separate department headed by a civilian governor and later (until 1935) under the Bureau of Non-Christian Tribes. With increasing Filipinisation of government, however, the special provisions granted to the Muslim areas of Mindanao and Sulu were progressively withdrawn, including, in 1936, recognition of civil titles such as sultan and datu. In response, there were several local uprisings and in a series of petitions in the 1920s and 1930s Moro leaders asked the colonial government either to incorporate Mindanao and Sulu, with special provisions, within the USA or to recognise the separate independence of a Moro Nation.

3. *Islam in the independent Republic*

What came to be referred to as "the Moro Problem" (though Peter Gowing suggested as a more appropriate term, "the Moros' 'Christian Problem' ") was inherited by the independent Philippine Republic in 1946. Moreover, heavy immigration from the northern islands, encouraged by the colonial government earlier in the century but increasing in scale after the Second World War, exacerbated the situation insofar as it created tensions between Muslim communities and immigrant settlers, especially over land ownership, and undermined the political authority of Muslim leaders. In 1954 a special committee of the Philippines Congress was created to investigate "the Moro Problem". As a result of its report a Commission on National Integration was set up to promote "the economic, social, moral, and political advancement of the non-Christian Filipinos", but it achieved little before being abolished in 1975. A subsequent report of a Senate Committee on National Minorities identified immigration and land grabbing as the major sources of Muslim grievances, but provided no solutions to the growing unrest.

As in earlier periods of Moro history, a feeling of grievance among Muslim communities promoted a heightened sense of Islamic identity. In the 1950s and 1960s this growing Islamic consciousness was reinforced by tendencies towards "Islamic reassertion" internationally. Within the Philippines it was reflected in a proliferation of mosques and *madāris*, a burgeoning of Islamic organisations, increasing contacts with overseas Muslims including missionaries, and a growing sense of resentment against the Christian-dominated government in Manila. A significant reflection of this was the formation in 1968 of the Muslim Independence Movement (MIM) under Datu Udtog Matalam. The MIM's stated objective was to create an independent Islamic Republic of Mindanao, Sulu and Palawan. The following year a group of young Muslims, recruited through the MIM, began guerilla training in neighbouring Malaysia. This group became the nucleus of a more radical Muslim separatist group, the Moro National Liberation Front (MNLF). Elections in 1971 proved to be something of a watershed in Muslim-Christian relations in the southern Philippines. With the positions of a number of traditional Muslim politicians under threat from Christian immigrants, and with increasing Christian-Muslim tension, the election campaign in Mindanao was marked by a number of violent incidents. When the following year Philippine President Marcos declared martial law, the conflict in the southern Philippines was listed as a reason for such action.

In 1972 leadership of the Moro movement was assumed by Nur Misuari as chairman of the MNLF. The MNLF received assistance initially from Sabah and subsequently from Libya. Leadership of the MNLF came mostly from the young men of traditional élite families, though Misuari himself was a commoner and had been associated with the Left while at the University of the Philippines. As well as demanding restitution of Muslim lands and recognition of a separate Bangsa Moro Republic, the MNLF also called for social reform within Moro society to reduce the power of the traditional aristocracy. A second prominent Moro organisation, the élite-dominated Bangsa Moro Liberation Organization (BMLO), began with similar ethno-nationalist objectives but decided to co-operate with the Marcos government; in 1974 its leader, Rashid Lucman, was recognised by President Marcos as the "Paramount Sultan of Mindanao and Sulu".

Over the next few years the MNLF maintained a

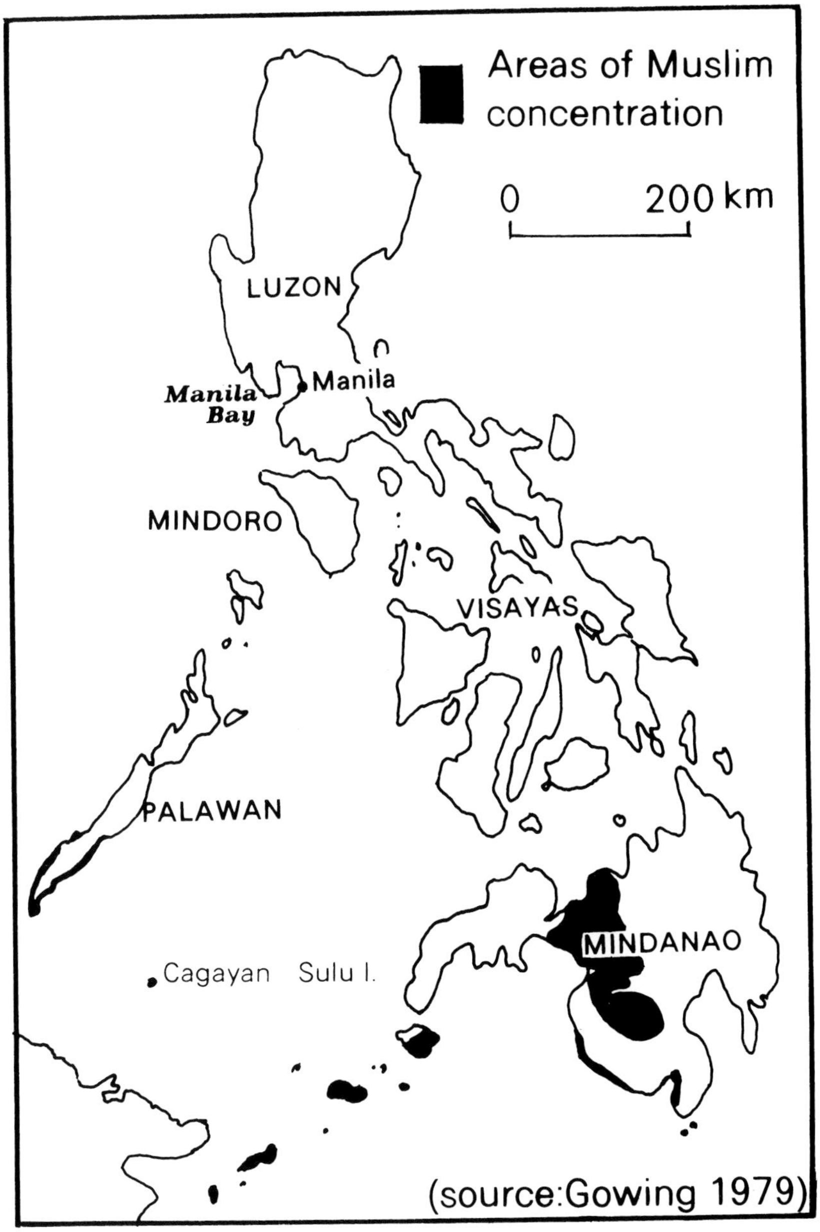

Map of the Philippines

state of insurgency against the Philippine government, with heavy casualties on both sides and considerable disruption of Muslim communities. Over 100,000 Philippine Muslims took refuge in Sabah. The MNLF's demands were supported by the Organization of Islamic Conference and the Islamic Conference of Foreign Ministers. Following negotiations in 1976, the "Tripoli Agreement" was signed by representatives of the MNLF and the Philippines government. The agreement contained general provision for the granting of autonomy in the Muslim areas of Mindanao and Sulu; by this time, however, as a result of decades of immigration, only five of the twenty-three provinces of Mindanao and Sulu contained Muslim majorities and disputes arose between the MNLF and the Philippines government over the terms of a proposed plebiscite on autonomy. In the event, the MNLF rejected the plebiscite, which was heavily boycotted, and further talks broke down. The government nevertheless went ahead to set up autonomous governments in the two administrative regions with substantial Muslim populations, though these were generally judged to be ineffective. As well, the Marcos government adopted a number of measures to promote Muslim interests. These included commitment to the codification of Muslim laws and the introduction of Sharia courts, establishment of a Muslim Amanah Bank, removal of restrictions on the historic barter trade between the Muslim Philippines and Borneo; creation of an Institute of Muslim Studies within the University of the Philippines, proclamation of Muslim holidays; and several economic development programmes in Mindanao-Sulu. Grants of land, jobs, and scholarships were offered to MNLF surrenderees.

Between 1977 and 1982 there were two major splits in the MNLF, the first with the formation of the Moro Islamic Liberation Front (MILF), a second with the breakaway of a MNLF-Reformist Group. These splits reflected personal, ideological, and ethnic divisions within the movement. There was also during the 1980s some scaling down of the armed conflict.

Following the overthrow of President Marcos in the "People Power Revolution" of 1986, the incoming government of President Aquino secured a cease-fire with the MNLF and reopened negotiations with Misuari, and the new constitution of 1987 made specific provision for autonomy in "Muslim Mindanao". Negotiations again broke down, however, and implementation of the autonomy provisions was marked by acrimonious debate in which Muslim-Christian rivalry was strongly evident. In a subsequent plebiscite, only four of the thirteen provinces and none of the nine cities polled opted for autonomy.

Given the demographic situation of Philippine Muslims, outnumbered in all but a few parts of their traditional homeland, attempts to resolve age-old tensions through the granting of Muslim autonomy on a geographical basis are bound to run into problems. However, while inequalities persist and separatist sentiments remain strong, Philippine governments appear to be showing greater sensitivity to the demands of Philippine Muslims and many Muslims are playing important roles in national social and political affairs.

Bibliography: E.H. Blair and J.A. Robertson, *The Philippine Islands 1493-1898* (55 volumes), Cleveland 1903-9; N.M. Saleeby, *The history of Sulu*, Manila 1908 (repr. 1963); M. Mednick, *Encampment on the lake: the social origin of a Moslem-Philippine (Moro) people*, Chicago 1965; T.M. Kiefer, *The Tausug: violence and law in a Philippine Muslim society*, New York 1972; C.A. Majul, *Muslims in the Philippines*, Quezon City 1973; P.G. Gowing and R.D. McAmis (eds.), *The Muslim Filipinos. Their history, society and contemporary problems*, Manila 1974; M. Saber and A. Madale (eds.), *The Maranao*, Manila 1975; Gowing, *Mandate in Moroland. The American government of Muslim Filipinos 1899-1920*, Quezon City 1977; idem, *Muslim Filipinos—heritage and horizon*, Quezon City 1979; N.T. Madale, *The Muslim Filipinos. A book of readings*, Quezon City 1981; J.F. Warren, *The Sulu Zone 1768-1898*, Singapore 1981; T.J.S. George, *Revolt in Mindanao: the rise of Islam in Philippine politics*, Kuala Lumpur 1980; R.J. May, *The Philippines*, in M. Ayoob (ed.), *The politics of Islamic reassertion*, London 1981, 211-32; F.L. Jocano (ed.), *Filipino Muslims. Their social institutions and cultural achievements*, Quezon City 1983; Datu M.O. Mastura, *Muslim Filipino experience. A collection of essays*, Manila 1984; C.A. Majul, *The contemporary Muslim movement in the Philippines*, Berkeley 1985; M. Boransing, F.V. Magdalena and L.Q. Lacar, *The Madrasah institution in the Philippines*, Iligan City 1987; Gowing (ed.), *Understanding Islam and Muslims in the Philippines*, Quezon City 1988; May, *The Moro movement in Southern Philippines*, in C. Jennett and R. Stewart (eds.), *Politics of the future. The role of social movements*, Melbourne 1989, 321-39; R. Laarhoven, *Triumph of Moro diplomacy. The Maguindanao Sultanate in the 17th century*, Quezon City 1989; W.K. Che Man, *Muslim separatism. The Moros of Southern Philippines and the Malays of Southern Thailand*, Singapore 1990.

(R.J. May)

PICKTHALL, Mohammed Marmaduke William (1875-1936), English traveller, novelist, polemicist and educationist, who became a convert to Islam at a time when British converts to Islam were much rarer than later in the 20th century, and is now best remembered for his Ḳurʾān translation, *The meaning of the Glorious Koran*.

Born in London, the son of an Anglican clergyman and with two step-sisters who were Anglican nuns, his boyhood and formative years were spent in rural Suffolk, from which he acquired a nostalgic view of a countryside way of life which was then passing. He was at school at Harrow as a contemporary of Winston Churchill, and after failing to enter the Army and the Levant Consular Service, lived as a country gentleman in Suffolk, a life interspersed with extensive travels in the Near East, where he became fluent in Arabic (and later, also in Turkish and Urdu). His extended stay in Palestine, Lebanon and Syria of 1894-6, with a return through Ottoman Turkey and the Balkans, inspired him with a romantic view of the Islamic East which was to determine the future course of his life. He subsequently became a fervid partisan of the Ottomans and of the Young Turk reformers [see yeñi ʿoth̲mānlîlar], thereby ranging himself with such contemporaries as the Conservative MPs and Middle Eastern publicists Aubrey Herbert and Sir Mark Sykes in his dislike for Philhellenes and Gladstonian liberals.

All this time he had been writing novels, and after 1903 was publishing one a year, either with British (mainly Suffolk) settings or Near Eastern ones. The best-known of the latter was *Said the Fisherman* (1903) (reprinted, with an introduction on Pickthall by P. Clark, London 1986), set in Syria and Egypt during the latter half of the 19th century and which went through fourteen editions; another of these novels, *Knights of Araby* (1917), was set in the 11th century Yemen of the Ṣulayḥids and Nad̲j̲āḥids [*q.vv.*].

The First World War, with his beloved Turkey

ranged on the side of the Central Powers, gave him a profound emotional shock. He campaigned for a separate peace with Turkey, and in 1917 announced his conversion to Islam, at once becoming a leader among the small band of the indigenous British Muslims and functioning as Acting Imām of the London mosque, then in Notting Hill. His acceptance of Islam came from an empathy which had existed for some two decades between his own naturally conservative temperament and the faith, with its attitudes of dignity and fortitude in the face of suffering and adversity and, as he saw it, its essential justice and tolerance. In 1920 he was invited by Indian Muslim colleagues to the subcontinent, and spent fifteen years there as a Muslim journalist and in Ḥaydarābād, Deccan [*q.v.*], as Principal of a Muslim high school and as an adviser and publicist for the Niẓām [*q.v.*]; he felt that in Ḥaydarābād he was living in a society were the traditions of the old Mug̲h̲al empire still lived on and where a benevolent, paternalistic ruler over a mass of Hindus exemplified the Islamic ideals of wisdom and tolerance. Retiring to England in 1935, he died there on 19 May 1936.

It was whilst living in Ḥaydarābād that he became editor of the journal *Islamic Culture*, founded under the patronage of the Niẓām, but above all put together his *The meaning of the Glorious Koran*, an explanatory translation (New York 1930, London 1939; cf. J.D. Pearson, *Bibliography of translations of the Qurʾān into European languages*, in A.F.L. Beeston *et alii* (eds.), *Camb. hist. of Arabic lit. Arabic literature to the end of the Umayyad period*, Cambridge 1983, 510). For this work of translation, he spent a period in Egypt with traditional scholars there, but was also familiar with European Ḳurʾān criticism, which he accepted and applied selectively. His book has had a great vogue, and has been itself the basis for further translations, e.g. into Portuguese (in Mozambique) and into Tagalog (for the Moros of the Philippines); it is still (1991) in print.

Bibliography: Ann Fremantle, *Loyal enemy*, London 1938; P. Clark, *Marmaduke Pickthall: British Muslim*, London 1986. (C.E. Bosworth)

PĪLKH̲ĀNE [see fīl].

PĪR (p.), literally, "old person, elder" (= Ar. *s̲h̲ayk̲h̲*). In Islamic law, these terms were used for people in their fifties or even in their forties (see al-Tahānawī, *Kas̲h̲s̲h̲āf iṣṭilāḥāt al-funūn*, Calcutta 1862, 731), whilst those even older are often qualified as *harim, fānī* "decrepit, worn out".

1. In the Persian and Turkish worlds

In general Persian usage, *pīr* is often, as with Arabic *s̲h̲ayk̲h̲*, used in compound expressions by metonymy, e.g. *pīr-i dihḳān* "well-matured wine" (see Vullers, *Lexicon persico-latinum*, i, 392a), or in a title, e.g. *pīr-i Sarandīb* = Adam, *pīr-i Kanʿān* = Jacob, *pīr-i Harī* = ʿAbd Allāh al-Anṣārī al-Harawī [*q.v.*].

Its more generalised usage in religious parlance is as a Ṣūfī term, again corresponding to Arabic *s̲h̲ayk̲h̲* and Turkish *baba*. Hence the *pīr* is the *murs̲h̲id* or spiritual director, and may be the founder of a Ṣūfī order or *ṭarīḳa* [*q.v.*]. As a person who has already followed the path (*sulūk*) to God and has acquired spiritual powers (*wilāya*), he is qualified to encourage and direct the aspiring novice (*murīd* [*q.v.*]) on the Ṣūfī path and finally to lay hands on the novice and bestow on him the Ṣūfī cloak or *k̲h̲irḳa* [*q.v.*], thereby admitting him to the spiritual fellowship of the order. A Turkish Ṣūfī author, Rusūk̲h̲ al-Dīn Ismāʿīl b. Aḥmad al-Anḳarawī (d. 1042/1632-3, see Brockelmann, II², 590-1, S II, 662), divides *pīrs* into four types: (1) *sālik-i ṣirf*, the *pīr* known for his scholarship but not to be followed, since he is not free from the trammels of self; (2) *mad̲j̲d̲h̲ūb-i ṣirf*, who is not to be followed either, since the divine attraction (*d̲j̲ad̲h̲be*) has brought him to the state of annihilation of self (*fanāʾ* [*q.v.*]); (3) *sālik-i mad̲j̲d̲h̲ūb*, also not to be followed since he has reached a state of ecstasy almost beyond consciousness; and (4) *mad̲j̲d̲h̲ūb-i sālik*, who is to be followed, since this person has passed beyond the stages of ecstasy and *fanāʾ* and is fit to instruct seekers and to perfect their discipleship (*Minhād̲j̲ al-fuḳarāʾ*, Istanbul 1286/1869-70, 28 ff.).

Amongst the Ṣūfīs also, the *čahār pīr* "four *pīrs*" denote al-Ḥasan, al-Ḥusayn, Kumayl b. Ziyād and al-Ḥasan al-Baṣrī, to whom the *k̲h̲irḳa* was allegedly given by ʿAlī b. Ṭālib (al-Tahānawī, *Kas̲h̲s̲h̲āf*, Calcutta 1862, 737).

Bibliography (in addition to references given in the article): R.A. Nicholson, *Studies in Islamic mysticism*, Cambridge 1921; J.P. Brown, *The dervishes, or oriental spiritualism*, Oxford 1927; *IA*, art. *Pir* (Tahsin Yazıcı), from which material for this article has been derived. (C.E. Bosworth)

2. In Indo-Muslim usage

In mystic parlance, this is generally used for a spiritual mentor; in popular usage, it is applied as prefix or suffix with different terms in a variety of senses. (i) To distinguish between different types of spiritual affiliation: *pīr-i-ṣuḥbat*, a saint from whose company one derives spiritual benefit; *pīr-i-ṭarīḳat*, a saint to whom one owes spiritual allegiance. (ii) To describe mystical customs: *pīr kā nayza*, standard carried in procession to the grave of some saint. (iii) To denote religious heads: *pīr-i-ḥaram* and *pīr-i-kalīsa*. The famous Urdu poet Muḥammad Iḳbāl [*q.v.*] has used these terms frequently in his verses to denote leaders of Muslim and non-Muslim religions. Note also *pīr-Mug̲h̲ān*, literally chief priest of the Magi, but generally used for a tavern keeper. (iv) As part of proper names to emphasise spiritual qualities; e.g. *Pīrān Pīr* (for S̲h̲ayk̲h̲ ʿAbd al-Ḳādir Gīlānī [*q.v.*]). (v) To denote spiritual links with some *k̲h̲ānaḳāh*, community etc.: as Pīr Manki S̲h̲arīf, Pīr Taunsa S̲h̲arīf, Pīr Pagaro, etc. (vi) To specify certain religious donations or endowments: e.g. *pīr awtār*, daily allowance paid to *faḳīrs* from collective village sources; *pīr pāl*, land endowed for assistance of the *pīr* or for maintenance of some mausoleum; *pīrān*, charity lands bestowed on the poor in honour of a saint. (vii) To indicate spiritual kinship: e.g. *pīr bhāi*, disciple of the same spiritual mentor and therefore brother; *pīr bahn*, woman owing spiritual allegiance to the same spiritual mentor and therefore sister; *pīr zāda*, son of the *pīr*. (viii) In sayings: *pīr d̲j̲ī kī sagāʾī mīr d̲j̲ī kay yahan*, *pīr* has his relations with *mīr*, with people of the same status; *pīr ko na faḳīr ko, pahlay kanay čur ko*, a low status man receiving precedence over *pīr* and *faḳīr*; *pīr-i man k̲h̲as ast, iʿtiḳād-i man bus ast*, my *pīr* may be (worthless) like straw, but my faith in him is firm; *pīr to ap dar manda hayn, s̲h̲afāʿat kis ki karain gay*, the *pīr* is himself helpless, how will he help others; *pīr miyan bakrī, murīd miyan banga, a gaʾi bakrī čap gai banga*, the *pīr* is the goat and his disciples the fodder; *barh d̲j̲āyen to amīr, g̲h̲aten to faḳīr, maren to pīr*, if they thrive they are nobles; if they decline they are holy ascetics; when they die they are saints; *pānī pid̲j̲yay čāhan kay aur pīr kid̲j̲yah d̲j̲ān kay*, drink water after straining, select *pīr* after scrutiny. (ix) In mythology: *Pīr Bhučrī*, *pīr* of the eunuchs; *Pīr Bhučrī ki karhaī*, food distributed while admitting a eunuch to the fold; *Pīr Hatailay*, a mythical figure, like S̲h̲aykh Saddo, in whom woman have great faith; *Pīr-i Dīdār*, a legendary saint who arranges intermixture of breeds; *Pīr Dīdār kā kunda*, offering made by women longing for the return of some relative. (x) To indicate

ings old and aging: *pīr-i āsmān* or *pīr-i falak*, or *pīr-i* *hkān falak*, for the sky; *pīr-i khazaf*, old man without nses; *pīr duta*, man with a bent back; *pīr-i zal*, an old an with gray hair; *pīr-i Sarandīp*, Adam; *pīr-i Kanᶜān*, cob; *pīr-i hasht khuld*, Riḍwān; *pīr-i fānī*, an old man out to die; *pīr-i fartūt*, very old; *pīr mard*, old man; r-i nā bāligh, old man with child-like habits; *pīr-i zan* *pīr-i zal*, old woman. (xi) In a derogatory sense: a ever and crooked old man; *pīr-i kharābāt*, a *pīr* free om the bonds of *sharīᶜat* law; owner of a tavern. (xii) proverbs: *pīr-i tasma pa*, one difficult to get rid of; r *khaylna*, to behave as if under the influence of some vil spirit; *pīr ana*, under the spell of some evil spirit; r-i *payghambar manānā*, to pray, to beseech for the lfilment of some desire; *pīr-i shahīd manānā*, to bless e soul of some saint through offerings. (xiii) To ow cultural status: *bay pīr*, without a *pīr* and there- re, uncultured and uncouth (Sir Syed Ahmad, *Sīrat-farīdiyya*, Agra 1896, 37). Thus in Indo-Muslim sage, the term *pīr* either becomes symbolic of ex- essive attachment with a spiritual mentor, or else it ecomes surrounded by superstitious and ythological concepts or assumes a derogatory con- otation and passes into proverbs and sayings.

Bibliography: J.T. Platts, *A dictionary of Urdu, classical Hindi and English*, Lucknow, repr. 1984; S.W. Fallon, *Urdu-English dictionary*, Lahore, repr. 1986; Athar Lakhnawī, *Farhang-i Athar*, Lucknow 1961; Nūr al-Ḥasan Nayyār, *Nūr al-lughāt*, Lucknow 1345 A.H.; *A dictionary of Urdu*, iv, Urdu Development Board, Karachi 1982; J. Shakespear, *Dictionary, Urdu-English and English-Urdu*, repr. Lahore 1980; Sayyid Ahmad Dihlawi, *Farhang-i Āṣafiyya*, i, *Tarakkī-yi Urdū* Board Edition, Dihlī 1974; Nadjm al-Dīn, *Nadjm al-amthāl*, v, Dihlī 1876.

(K.A. Nizami)

PĪR ṢADR al-DĪN, Indian Muslim holy man, considered to be the founder of the Khodja [*q.v.*] Nizārī Ismāᶜīlī community in India. Most of our biographical information is derived from the *ginān*s (poetical compositions in Indian vernaculars), the largest number of which is ascribed to him, hence we are not on firm ground. He lived probably between the second half of the 8th/14th and the beginning of the 9th/15th centuries. The centre of his activity was around Koṭri and Uččh in Sind, where he converted large numbers of Hindus from the Lohaṇa caste and gave them the title of Khodjas (derived from Persian *khʷādja*, honorary title like "sir") because the Lohaṇas were addressed by the honorary title *thākur* in Hindi. He seems to have played a key role in the communal organisation and is credited with the establishment of the first *djamāᶜat-khāna* (a congregation hall for the community) in Koṭri. He is also said to have visited the Imām Islām Shāh in Persia to hand over the *dasondh* (tithes) collected from the Indian community. His shrine is located in Djetpur, near Uččh, but the overseers of his shrine consider themselves as Twelver Shīᶜīs and call the Pīr Ḥādjdjī Ṣadr Shāh.

Bibliography: For a full description of his works and sources, see I. Poonawala, *Biobibliography of Ismāᶜīlī literature*, Malibu, Cal. 1977, 301-2; Azim Nanji, *The Nizārī Ismāᶜīlī tradition in the Indo-Pakistan subcontinent*, New York 1978, 72-7; F. Daftary, *The Ismāᶜīlīs: their history and doctrines*, Cambridge 1990, 479.

(I. Poonawala)

PĪR SHAMS or **SHAMS al-DĪN**, Indian Muslim holy man, regarded as the second important figure after Nūr Satgur [*q.v.*], whose name is traditionally associated with the commencement of Nizārī [*q.v.*] or Satpanth (i.e. the true path) Ismāᶜīlism in Sind. Historically he is an obscure figure surrounded by legends. Most of our information is derived from *ginān*s ascribed to him. The latter, being poetical compositions in Indian vernaculars resembling didactic and mystical poetry, are often anachronistic and legendary in nature. The dates mentioned for his activities, centred in Sind and working within a Hindu-Muslim milieu, cover a long period from the first half of the 6th/12th to the 8th/14th centuries. The overseers of his alleged mausoleum at Multān, however, identify him with Shams-i Tabrīz [*q.v.*], the spiritual guide of Mawlānā Djalāl al-Dīn al-Rūmī [*q.v.*], and a descendant of the Twelver Imām Mūsā al-Kāẓim [*q.v.*]. The Nizārī community of the Shamsīs living in Pandjāb and chiefly in Multān, on the other hand, claim to have been converted by Pīr Shams and have preserved the *ginān*s of the Pīr in Pandjābī dialect.

Bibliography: For a full description of his works and sources, see I. Poonawala, *Biobibliography of Ismāᶜīlī literature*, Malibu, Cal. 1977, 299-300; Azim Nanji, *The Nizārī Ismāᶜīlī tradition in the Indo-Pakistan subcontinent*, New York 1978, 53-5, 62-8, 103-5, 121-2; F. Daftary, *The Ismāᶜīlīs: their history and doctrines*, Cambridge 1990, 415, 478-9.

(I. Poonawala)

PĪRĪ MEḤMED PASHA (?-939/?1532-3), an Ottoman Grand Vizier, belonged to Amasya and was a descendant of the famous Djalāl al-Dīn of Aḳsarāy and therefore traced his descent from Abū Bakr. He took up a legal career and became successively *ḳāḍī* of Sofia, Siliwri and Galata, administrator of Meḥemmed II's kitchen for the poor (*ᶜimāret*) in Istanbul, and at the beginning of the reign of Bāyezīd II attained the rank of a first *defterdār* (*bash defterdār*). In the reign of Selīm I, he distinguished himself by his wise counsel in the Persian campaign (see J. von Hammer, *GOR*, ii, 412, 417 ff.), was sent in advance to Tabrīz to take possession of this town in the name of the sultan, and at the beginning of Shaᶜbān 920/end of September 1514 was appointed third *wezīr* in place of Muṣṭafā Pasha, who had been dismissed (see *GOR*, ii, 420). He temporarily held the office of a *ḳāʾim-maḳām* of Istanbul, and after the end of the Egyptian campaign was appointed Grand Vizier in place of Yūnus Pasha, who had been executed on the retreat from Egypt in 923/1517. In this capacity he took part in the conquest of Baghdād in 927/1521. Soon after the occupation of Rhodes, Pīrī Pasha fell from the sultan's favour as a result of the slanders of the envious Aḥmed Pasha, who coveted his office, and was dismissed with a pension of 200,000 aspers on 13 Shaᶜbān 929/27 June 1523. His successor was Ibrāhīm Pasha [*q.v.*], a Greek from Parga. Pīrī Meḥmed lived another ten years and died in 939/1532-3 at Siliwri, where he was buried in the mosque founded by him. One of his sons, Meḥmed Beg, had predeceased him in 932/1526 as governor of Ič-il. Pīrī Meḥmed Pasha created a number of charitable endowments, among them a mosque in Istanbul called after him (cf. Ḥāfiẓ Ḥuseyin, *Ḥadīḳat al-djawāmiᶜ*, i, 308), a *medrese* and a public kitchen as well as what was known as a *tāb-khāne*. While his *laḳab* was Pīrī, he used Remzī as a *makhlaṣ* for his poems, which are of moderate merit (cf. von Hammer, *Geschichte der osmanischen Dichtkunst*, ii, 327 ff., with the wrong year of death and also i, 187, under *Pīrī* without the identity of the two being recognised, also Laṭīfī, *Tedhkire*, 168 under *Remzī*).

Bibliography: Meḥmed Thüreyyā, *Sidjill-i ᶜothmānī*, ii, 43, more fully in ᶜOthmānzāde Meḥmed Tāʾib, *Ḥadīḳat al-wuzarāʾ*, Istanbul 1271, 22 ff., and the Ottoman chroniclers of the 10th/16th century; *İA*, art. *Pîrî Mehmed Paşa* (Şerâfeddin

Turan).—Bursalï Meḥmed Ṭāhir, *ʿOthmānlï müʾellifleri*, ii, 111 ff., deals with Pīrī Meḥmed Pasha as a literary man. According to him, he wrote a small collection of poems (*dīwānče*) and an exposition of a part of the *methnewī* and of the *shāhidī* entitled *Tuḥfe-yi mīr*, but both works are described by Meḥmed Ṭāhir as still in mss. (F. BABINGER)

PĪRĪ REʾĪS b. Ḥādjdjī Meḥmed, a Turkish mariner, cartographer and author (b. probably Gallipoli, date of birth unknown; d. Cairo, 961/1553-4). His uncle, Kemāl Reʾīs [*q.v.*], served as a captain in the Ottoman fleet but was especially notorious among Mediterranean Christians for his exploits as a corsair; it was in this earlier profession by his uncle's side that Pīrī Reʾīs first learned the trade of seaman. Generally welcomed by their Arab fellow-Muslims to use the coasts of Tunisia and Algeria as a base, refuge and place for selling their booty, they preyed upon Christian shipping and the coasts of Spain, France, western and southern Italy and the islands of the Western Mediterranean. During these campaigns, which spanned much of the first half of Bāyezīd II's reign (sc. 886-900/1481-95), Pīrī Reʾīs acquired an intimate knowledge of both the Mediterranean and of the "haven-finding art"—various tools aiding navigation and the expertise in using them—as it existed among his fellow-sailors of that sea. Both personal experience and assiduous gathering of sources (primarily Italian and Catalan), combined with an original creative mind, later enabled Pīrī Reʾīs to produce a remarkable body of cartographic and hydrographic work.

The second stage in Pīrī Reʾīs's life began in 900/1495 when the sultan summoned his uncle to serve in the Ottoman fleet. From then on until Kemāl Reʾīs's death (either in 916/1510 or 917/1511; for this date see S. Soucek, *Piri Reis and Turkish map-making after Columbus*, 164), he participated, always by his uncle's side, in various naval assignments such as conveying supplies to Mamlūk Egypt or patrolling the sea-lanes between Istanbul and various points of the Aegean and Eastern Mediterranean, molested by the Hospitallers of Rhodes [see RODOS]; Kemāl Reʾīs especially distinguished himself during the 1499-1502 war with Venice, an event again witnessed by Pīrī Reʾīs, who had by then commanded a ship in his own right; this independence may also have saved his life when his uncle went down with his ship during a storm in the eastern Aegean.

Kemāl Reʾīs's death signalled a third and most productive stage in Pīrī Reʾīs's life, for from then on he spent more time at Gallipoli [see GELIBOLU; until 1518 it was the chief naval base of the Ottoman empire] and devoted himself to the theoretical side of the seaman's profession—marine cartography and science of navigation. His first and most dazzling achievement occurred in 1513, when he made a world map of which only a part—probably one-third—has survived. This map is anchored in a double tradition: that of the Mediterranean portolan chart, and that of the world map of the age of Great Discoveries (see T. Campbell, *Portolan charts from the late thirteenth century to 1500*, in *The history of cartography*, ed. J.B. Harley and D. Woodward, i, 371-458; S. Soucek, *Islamic charting in the Mediterranean*, in *The history of cartography*, ii/1, 269-72; idem, *Piri Reis*, 49-79); a third type of tradition could be added here, that of the "presentation specimen chart": for its lavishly coloured and aesthetically appealing form, as well as several topical legends relating such events as the discovery of America or describing the new continent's memorabilia, revealed a purpose that went beyond serving as a tool for sailors but aimed to impress an important recipient. The extant part (Istanbul, Topkapı Palace library, Revan 1633 mükerrer; dimensions: 90 × 63 cm, parchment), is the western third or half of the original, and includes a colophon which reads: "Composed by the poor Pīr son of Ḥādjdjī Meḥmed, known as paternal nephew of Kemāl Reʾīs, may God pardon them both, in the city of Gallipoli, in the month of Muḥarram the sacred year nine hundred and nineteen [March-April 1513]." It shows the Atlantic with the adjacent coasts of Europe and Africa, and the New World as far as Pīrī Reʾīs could piece it together from up to five cartographic sources: a map made by Columbus, as well as between one and four Portuguese charts, according to the author's own statements and to internal evidence. The map is torn longitudinally in such a way that what must have been its major part, including the bulk of Europe and Africa and all of Asia, is missing; how and when the mutilation occurred is unknown, but it may have happened in Cairo where Pīrī Reʾīs had sailed with several ships of the Ottoman navy at the conclusion of Selīm I's 1517 conquest of Egypt, for he states in another work, the *Kitāb-i Baḥriyye* (p. 5 in the 1935 facs. ed.; see below), that the sultan had at that point graciously accepted the map. It then lapsed into oblivion until its 1929 discovery in the Topkapı Palace library; the map's identification as a work partly based on an early but no longer extant map made by Columbus had an effect that transcended the bounds of scholarly interest, and it became an international sensation as well as a matter of pride for the young Turkish republic, especially for its founder Kemal Atatürk. Upon instructions from the president, the Turkish Historical Society published in 1935 a facsimile together with, in a separate brochure, a full transcription as well as translation of its legends into modern Turkish, German, French, English and Italian (*Piri Reis haritası*; repr. in 1966; many smaller scale reproductions exist, the best in M. Mollat du Jourdin and Monique de La Roncière, *Sea charts of the early explorers: 13th to 17th century*, New York 1984, pl. 28). The documentary value of the chart, which has sometimes received such inaccurate labels as "the earliest map of America" or "the lost map by Columbus in a Turkish translation" is indeed considerable, and could be even greater if it had survived in its entirety, for Pīrī Reʾīs tells us that he had used both European and Oriental sources in the construction of the map. Put in modern terms, the result must have been a work of unique kind and value. Even in its truncated state, the map is viewed as one of the prime treasures of the Topkapı Palace; the world-wide interest it has stirred has also provoked some eccentric interpretations.

The recent and ongoing interest in Pīrī Reʾīs's world map stands in sharp contrast to the apparent indifference with which it met in the author's lifetime. Another work of his, the *Kitāb-i baḥriyye* ("Book on seafaring"; completed in 1521, and reworked in a second version in 1526; a facsimile of one of its best manuscripts, Aya Sofya 2612, now in the Süleymaniye library, was in 1935 published by the Turkish Historical Society concurrently with the facsimile reproduction of the 1513 world map; our references are to the page numbers of this edition (Piri Reis, *Kitabi Bahriye*)) fared better, however, judging from the many copies produced during the 16th and 17th centuries. It too is anchored in the tradition of portolan texts and portolan charts (but also in that of the closely related genre of *isolarii*). Although both pertain to the universal category of sailing directions nd marine charts, their "portolan" label further pecifies a genre created and perfected in the Mediter- anean between the 13th and 17th centuries; more- ver, it was a primarily Christian (Italian and atalan) speciality, with only marginal Muslim (Arab nd Turkish) participation. The *Kitāb-i baḥriyye* is an p to a point original and remarkable exception, not nlike the author's 1513 world map, for Pīrī Reʾīs gain gave free rein to his genius and produced a olume of texts and charts such as none of his Christ- an models had ever done: a description of the entire lediterranean subdivided into chapters, each chapter ccompanied by a chart of the area described. More- ver, a long versified introduction written for the econd version discusses subjects related to naviga- ion, oceanic geography and the ongoing voyages of iscovery. The first version consists of 130 chapters nd charts, the second of 210. Both have a brief pre- ace in which Pīrī Reʾīs tells why he composed the vork: to provide a manual for his Turkish fellow- ailors, and to offer a present to Sultan Süleymān on he occasion of his accession. This preface in prose is hen followed by the versified introduction in the econd recension (pp. 7-85), and by the main body of he text in prose with charts (86-848); the second ver- ion ends in a versified epilogue (849-55), in which the uthor tells how in 1524 the Grand Vizier Ibrāhīm ʾas͟ha [*q.v.*] had encouraged him to produce a more olished version of the work and thus worthier of the ugust recipient. Neither recension's autographs are nown to have survived, but copies of both (23 and 0, respectively, plus several adaptations and nodifications; a list of the known manuscripts compil- d by T. Goodrich can be found in *The history of car- ography*, ii/1, 290-1) have survived and mostly carry n either original's structure, form and function. Those of the first version are less polished but meant as manuals for sailors; those of the second are often calligraphied, and their lavishly coloured charts per- tain to the art of miniature illustration and were clear- y produced not for use at sea but as bibliophile ar- ifacts for wealthy or important customers. Especially striking are elaborate sketches of many port cities, in- cluding topographic views of Istanbul, Venice and Cairo (Walters Art Gallery, Baltimore, ms. 658, and its twin ms. Yıldız Türkçe 6605, Istanbul University library, are the best examples). Despite all these addi- tional documentary and artifactual features, however, the second version does not quite supersede the first; in fact, one of the special assets of Pīrī Reʾīs's portolan—personal and topical reminiscences from the Turkish corsairs' main base, eastern Algeria and Tunisia—exists in the second version only in an abridged form. Moreover, this truncation may have been performed not by Pīrī Reʾīs himself but by one Seyyid Murād or Murādī, the editor of K͟hayr al-Dīn Barbarossa's [*q.v.*] *G͟hazawāt*, who claims to have ghost-written also the second version of the *Kitāb-i baḥriyye* (see H. Yurdaydın, *Kitab-i bahriryye'nin telifi meselesi*, in *AÜDTCFD* x [1952], 143-6).

In 935/1528-9 Pīrī Reʾīs produced his last known work, another map of the world of which again only a fragment—probably one-sixth—has survived (Topkapı Palace library, Hazine 1824; parchment, 69 × 70 cm; see colour reproduction in *The history of cartography*, ii/1, pl. 21). It covers the north-western part of the Atlantic and the New World from Venezuela to Newfoundland and the southern tip of Greenland. This map, too, is signed by the author, and combines the artifactual qualites of a "presentation copy" with those of a valuable document. The quality of this fragment suggests that in its original state, the map may have been another brilliant example of the subsequently stifled attempt by Muslim cartography to join Renaissance Europe's exploration of the world.

Aside from writing and cartographical work between 1513 and 1529, all we know of Pīrī Reʾīs during this period is that he may have on occasion accompanied K͟hayr al-Dīn Barbarossa to North Africa, and that he must have remained active as a pilot in the Empire's home waters, as his assignment to steer Ibrāhīm Pas͟ha's ship to Egypt (1524) suggests. After 1529, however, all trace of him disappears until he re-emerges in 1547 as commander of the Ottoman fleet based at Suez. In this capacity, Pīrī Reʾīs carried out the reconquest of Aden (1549); but his luck turned in 1552-3 when reports of the approach of an enemy relief fleet made him raise the siege of Portuguese-held Hurmuz [*q.v.*] and withdraw to Baṣra; worse still, his subsequent decision to leave the bulk of his ships there and return with three vessels (one of which was lost en route) to Suez led to a death sentence by the government which was carried out at Cairo (Cengiz Orhonlu, *Hint kaptanlığı ve Piri Reis*, in *Belleten*, xxxiv [1970], 234-54). This bizarre end of the great cartographer does not seem to have been questioned by Ottoman observers, but it has puzzled modern historians; some have wondered if two namesakes are not being confused (the age factor for example: by 1553 the cartographer would probably have been an octogenarian). A more likely explanation is the fact that the Ottoman élite, with the exception of Ibrāhīm Pas͟ha, failed to grasp the value of his cartographic and hydrographic work, and that, personally, Pīrī Reʾīs never managed to penetrate the otherwise broad spectrum of that élite and thus receive the totally different treatment reserved for its members (as exemplified by the case of K͟hādim Süleymān Pas͟ha [*q.v.*], who in 1538 failed before Diu much as Pīrī Reʾīs did before Hurmuz but instead of being executed became Grand Vizier). [See also SELMĀN REʾĪS, SEYYIDĪ ʿALĪ REʾĪS, TAʾRĪK͟H-I HIND-I G͟HARBĪ.]

Bibliography: Given in the article, and S. Soucek, *Islamic charting in the Mediterranean*, in *The history of cartography*, Chicago 1992, ii/1, 263-92 (see also this volume's bibliographical index, 521-45); idem, *Piri Reis and Turkish mapmaking after Columbus*, London 1992, 162-75; idem, review article discussing the literature on Pīrī Reʾīs, in *JAOS* (forthcoming). (S. SOUCEK)

PĪRĪ-ZĀDE MEḤMED ṢĀḤIB EFENDI (1085-1162/1674-1749), Ottoman *S͟heyk͟h al-Islām* [*q.v.*] in Istanbul and the pioneer translator into Turkish of Ibn K͟haldūn.

Ibn K͟haldūn's *Muḳaddima* was quite early known in Ottoman Turkey, being cited by e.g. Maḥmūd b. Aḥmed Ḥāfiẓ al-Dīn (d. 937/1550) and by Ḥād͟jd͟jī K͟halīfa in his *Kas͟hf al-ẓunūn*. But during the years 1138-43/1725-30 Pīrī-zāde translated the *Muḳaddima* from the beginning to the end of the fifth chapter, i.e. about two-thirds of the whole, and this was lithographed at Cairo in 1275/1859, with Aḥmed D͟jewdet Pas͟ha [*q.v.*] shortly afterwards translating the final, sixth chapter. Pīrī-zāde's translation circulated in manuscript, and thus helped considerably in making Ibn K͟haldūn a familiar figure in 18th and 19th century Turkey.

Bibliography: Babinger, *GOW*, 282-3, with the Ottoman biographical sources; Fındıkoğlu Z. Fahri, *Türkiyede Ibn Haldunizm*, in *Köprülü armağanı*, Istanbul 1953, 159-60; F. Rosenthal, *The Muqaddima, an introduction to history*, New York 1958, i, pp. cvii-cviii; *İA* art. *Ibn Haldun* (Abdülhak Adnan Adıvar), at cols. 740b-741b. (C.E. BOSWORTH)

PIRLEPE, PRILEP, a town of more than 40,000 inhabitants situated on the northern edge of the fertile Pelagonian Plain at the foot of the Babuna Mountains in the southern part of the former Yugoslav Macedonia. In the Middle Ages, Prilep was the capital of a Slav principality. In Ottoman times (1395-1912) it was the centre of an extensive ḳāḍīlik̲ stretching from the modern Greek border in the south (Nidže and Kajmakčalan Mountains, 2521 m/8,268 ft) and the Solunska Glava (the highest mountain of Macedonia, 2540 m/8,331 ft) in the north, an area which in 1900 contained 141 villages. Especially in late Ottoman times, Prilep was the commercial metropolis of northern Macedonia. It was also an Islamic centre of regional importance.

Prilep is first mentioned in the edicts of the Byzantine emperor Basil the Bulgar-Slayer (1014), but must be much older. From the early 11th century till 1201, Prilep was in Byzantine hands; from 1201 till 1246 it was included in the Second Bulgarian Empire; then Byzantine again till 1334, when the troops of the Serbian king (later Tsar) Dušan conquered it and included it in the short-lived Serbian empire. After Dušan's death, it was included in the principality of Vukašin, who in 1366 declared himself king in Prilep. During the wars of the 14th century, both sides made use of Turkish mercenaries. After the death of King Vukašin in the Battle of the Maritsa (1371) against the Ottomans, his son Marko Kraljević came to rule over Prilep as an Ottoman vassal, serving in the major campaigns of the Sultans until his death in 1395 in the Battle of Rovine. Portraits of Vukašin and Marko are preserved in the fresco decorations of the church of St.

Michael in the Archangel's Monastery above the old town of Prilep, which was refurbished by the two rulers. The old Ottoman chroniclers place the conquest of Prilep in the 1380s, which is an evident mistake. The town and its district were annexed without a struggle or great disturbance after Marko's death. A part of his troops went over to direct Ottoman service, to become the Christian sipahīs known from the 15th century census registers.

Mediaeval Prilep was situated below a mountain-top castle (first mentioned in 1240) from which the town took its name (Prilep = "stuck on a mountain"). The greater part of this mediaeval settlement, with many Byzantino-Slavic churches with wall paintings of high quality, as well as a large monastery, is still preserved, the site being called "Kale Varoš" or "Prilep-Varoš." The town we see today is an Ottoman creation, situated 2 km/1 mile down in the plain. The Arabic inscription on the oldest preserved mosque of the town, the Çarşı Camii, from 881/1476-7, gives an indication of the time at which the new settlement came into being. Throughout history, Prilep-Varoš remained an exclusively Christian settlement, whereas the new town was first entirely Turkish but, especially since the 18th century, became predominantly Christian. For Prilep and its district, a relatively large number of Ottoman taḥrīr defters have been preserved and are partly published (Sokoloski, 1971), or have been the basis of demographic research (Stojanovski, 1981). Together with some Poll Tax registers preserved in Sofia, and with the numbers collected by Vasil Kănčev during his solid research shortly before 1900, they give the following picture:

Year of registration	Christian households	Muslim households	Total households	Approximate total population	Percentage of Muslims
1445	350	10	360	1,500 to 1,600	3%
1455	300	21	321	1,380 to 1,420	6%
1478	386	141	530	2,200 to 2,300	27%
1528	463	210	673	3,000 to 3,200	31%
1544	492	189	681	3,000 to 3,200	28%
1570	326	279	605	2,700 to 2,900	46%
1614	135	(ca. 400)	(ca. 550)	2,200 to 2,400	72%
1900	3,000	1,400	4,400	24,540	29%

It is clear that during the rule of Meḥemmed the Conqueror, the town of Prilep received an important group of Muslim Turkish settlers, mostly craftsmen, as the registers show (tanners, coppersmiths, tailors, weavers, etc.). The link between the arrival of this group and the construction of a large mosque in 1476-7 is evident. At first, the settlers developed along natural patterns, but after the mid-16th century the Muslim community grew, especially through the conversion and linguistic assimilation of a part of the local Christians. The early defters also show that the villages on the plain, which in the late Ottoman period were inhabited by Albanian Muslims (Aldanci, Belušino, Borino, Crnilište, Desovo, Drenovo, Gorno Žitoše, Norovo, Sačevo and Vrboec) were still almost entirely Slavic and completely Christian, only a few incidental Albanian households being registered. The later, entirely Slav Muslim villages (Pomak/Torbeš) of Debrešte, Lažani and Peštalevo, were also entirely Christian. The nine Muslim Turkish villages which the ḳaḍāʾ was to have later did not exist in 1445 and 1455. Ali Obası (Alinci), Dedebalcı and Şeleverci are mentioned as places where a few Yürük families lived, serving in the army in time of war. Dedebal(ci) and the no-longer-existing hamlet of Timur existed

already in the time of Murād II. The same defter also mentions groups of Christian eshkündjis, serving in the Ottoman army in time of war and enjoying important tax facilities. The important monasteries of the Archangels of Prilep and that of Treskavac, 10 km/6 miles from the town, a Byzantine imperial foundation, were the property (mülk) of the Metropolitan of Prilep, David.

In the second half of the 16th century, almost the entire nāḥiye of Moriovo, constituting the mountainous south of the ḳaḍā of Pirlepe, was transformed from k̲h̲āṣṣ to waḳf property of the Süleymāniye complex in Istanbul. The waḳfiyye of this largest of all Ottoman socio-religious foundations, written between 1558 and 1566, does not yet mention these villages among the waḳf property of the foundation. They must have been added later, most probably towards the end of the 16th century, when the wave of inflation caused financial difficulties. The Djizye Defter F 16 A, a.e. 60 A, in the Sofia National Library, a newly-made taḥrīr from the year 1023/1614, mentions 28 villages and the number of their households, from which djizye was part of the waḳf, together with all other taxes. Four of these villages were situated outside the nāḥiye of Moriovo, four others no longer ‹ist, and 20 of them survive to the present day. The ‹ct that the Moriovo *nāḥiye* was part of this important *akf* helped them to survive the difficulties and ar-‹trariness of the 17th and 18th centuries. When ‹any other villages wholly or partly converted to ‹slam to escape fiscal and other pressures, the entire ‹loriovo remained Christian and some of its villages ‹rew from a few dozen households into the largest of ‹e entire *ḳaḍā*ʾ. This little-known phenomenon finds ‹arallels in the clusters of *wakf* villages in Central ‹reece (*wakf* of the Wālide Sulṭān Kösem ‹lāhpeyker) and in Bulgaria (Plevna, *wakf* of ‹līkhāloghlu ʿAlī Bey) and elsewhere.

In the first quarter of the 16th century, six more ‹luslim Turkish villages came into being in the plain ‹outh of the town: Budaklar (now called Budjakovo), ‹üyük Oba (Golemo Kojnari), Elekler (Erekovci), ‹anatlarcı, Küçük Oba (Malo Kojnari) and Musa ‹Obası (Musinci). Their names and notes in the *defters* ‹ell us that they were Yürük villages. Their migration ‹o Macedonia must be seen in connection with the ‹ersecution of the Ḳîzîlbash ʿAlewī groups in Anatolia ‹nder Selīm I. In the important village of Kanatlarcı ‹here was since a long while back a large Bektāshī ‹ekke*, which still exists today, being together with the ‹ne in Kırçova/Kičevo, the only *tekkes* of this order ‹urviving in Slav Macedonia.

Ewliyā Čelebi, who visited Prilep in 1071/1660-1, ‹lescribes it as a town of 1,000 houses, divided into ‹ver ten *maḥalles*. He mentions the Mosque of the ‹Alay Bey, which was particularly lofty, and that of ‹Arslan Pasha, besides a number of *mesdjids*, 200 ‹hops, a pleasant *ḥammām*, a *khān* and some *medreses*, ‹*mektebs* and *tekkes*. These numbers look reasonable. That of the houses must be too high. Most of the public buildings of Ottoman Prilep were the work of Ḳodja Arslan Pasha, who seems to have been still alive when Ewliyā visited the town. In the course of the 17th century, the administrative subdivisions of Macedonia changed. Previously, Prilep was part of the Pasha Liwāsî. Ḥādjdjī Khalīfa mentions the *ḳaḍā*ʾ as part of the *sandjaḳ* of Üsküb. In the 19th century it was attached to the *wilāyet* of Manastîr.

Throughout the 15th, 16th and 17th centuries, numerous churches were either newly-built and painted or else thoroughly reconstructed, beginning with the new church of Bogorodica Prečiste in Prilep-Varoš itself, from 1420, and with the paintings of the Treskavac Monastery from 1430 and the choir of the monastery church of Zrze, shortly after 1400. Some of the newly-built and painted churches, such as in Dolgaec, from 1454-5, explicitly mention "Tsar Mehmet Tsalapi" as ruling Sultan. The paintings in the nave of the monastery church of Treskavac, from 1480-90, belong to the best of the entire Balkans. Highlights of 16th century painting are those in the Monastery of Zrze, the work of the Albanian artist Onufre of Elbasan. Zrze has also good examples of paintings from 1625 and 1636. Other important and well-preserved works of the 17th century are the village churches of Rilevo and Slepče, built and painted in 1617 and 1627. The difficult economic and social conditions of the late 17th and 18th century did not allow Christian art under the Ottomans to flourish.

In 1807 François Pouqueville visited Prilep and describes it as a town of 1,000 to 1,100 houses, illustrating the stagnation of the 18th century. Prilep's great time was to come in the 19th century, when the population almost quintupled, the Macedonian Christians growing at a much faster rate than the Muslims. In this time, Prilep became the commercial metropolis of inland Macedonia. A disastrous fire of 1273/1856-7 could not stop this expansion. In 1861 von Hahn noted a "richly-stored, newly-built bazaar". In these years the entire town centre was rebuilt on a regular chess board plan. A monumental Clock Tower was added and the old mosque from 1476-7 was restored and doubled in size by a huge annex.

At the end of the 19th century, the town had more than 24,000 inhabitants, 16,700 being Macedonian Christians, 6,200 Muslim Turks and the remainder Gypsies. Sāmī Bey in his *Ḳāmūs al-aʿlām*, ii, Istanbul 1316/1898-9, describes Prilep as having ten mosques, three *tekkes*, five *medreses*, two *ḥammāms*, a Rüshdiyye school, an Ibtīdāʾıyye school, seven Muslim primary schools, six Christian primary schools and two churches. He also mentions the famous Prilep Fair in August-September. The greater part of the population was, according to Sāmī Bey (but this is an incorrect source), Muslim. The Muslims spoke Ottoman Turkish and Albanian, the Christians spoke Bulgarian and Rumanian.

For the composition of the population of the district of Prilep in the late Ottoman period, we have the data from the *Nüfūs Defters* of 1884 and 1890, the numbers of the *Sālnāme* of 1305/1888, and Kănčev's detailed and reliable numbers. They are as follows:

The population of the ḳaḍāʾ *of Pirlepe according to various late 19th century sources*

	Nüfūs Defter 1884	*Sālnāme* 1888	*Nüfūs Defter* 1890	*Kănčev* c. 1900
Bulgarians/Macedonian Christians	44,759	29,041	50,916	57,213
Muslims	13,753	30,271	13,342	13,415
Vlachs	753	498	528	745
Gypsies	709	in the above	1,634	1,775
Totals	59,974	59,312	66,420	73,146
Percentage of Muslims	24%	50,2%	22%	20%

It is evident that the numbers of the *Sālnāme*, intended for public use, are gross distortions, of a kind known also from elsewhere [see OKHRĪ]. The real state of affairs is reflected in the numbers of mosques and churches in the 141 villages of the *ḳaḍā*ʾ of Pirlepe as given by Sāmī Bey on the basis of the *Sālnāme*: 34 mosques, in the 18 villages with Muslim inhabitants and the town together, and 101 churches in the 122 Christian villages. The proportion of Muslims to Christians was 20% to 80%, that of mosques and churches 25% to 75%, or almost the same.

During the First Balkan War, Prilep was taken by the Serbian Army in 1912. Town and district remained part of Serbia, later Yugoslavia, till 1992, although interrupted by harsh Bulgarian occupations during both World Wars. The population of the town changed considerably through the emigration of a large part of the Muslim citizens to Turkey in the 1950s. In the post-war years, the town, which had stagnated in the interwar period because of changes in the trade routes and economic system, was "modernised", in which process most of the Ottoman buildings disappeared. In 1990 the old mosque of 1476 was still standing, together with the Clock Tower from 1280/1863-4 and one wall of the monumental Kurşunlı *khān* of Ḳodjā Arslan Pasha from the 17th century.

In the villages of the former *ḳaḍāʾ*, the changes were less drastic. The greater part of the Pomak [*q.v.*] and Albanian Muslim populations remained where it was, although both communities grew, but slowly, due to emigration. The Turkish population of the former Yürük villages is also still present and saw a slow growth from *ca.* 2,000 to a little below 3,000 souls, living in Budaklar, Elekler, Kanatlarcı and Musa Obası/Musinci. The other originally Turkish villages had by 1970 completely lost their Muslim population, their place being taken by Macedonians.

Bibliography: Ewliyā Čelebi, *Seyāḥat-nāme*, v, Istanbul 1315/1897-8, 570-2; J.G. von Hahn, *Reise von Belgrad nach Saloniki*, Vienna 1861, 110; V. Kančev, *Makedonija, etnografija i statistika*, Sofia 1900 (repr. in *Izbrani proizvedenija*, Sofia 1970,) 544-8 (generally accepted to be the most reliable population numbers on late Ottoman Macedonia); L. Schulze-Jena, *Makedonien, Landschafts- und Kulturbilder*, Jena 1927 (information collected in 1916-18 and 1923-4), 159-60; A. Nikolovski, D. Ćornakov, K. Balabanov, *The cultural monuments of Macedonia*, Skopje 1961, 157-79; *Enciklopedija Jugoslavije*, vi, Zagreb 1965, 616-17; Sv. Radojčić, *Jedna slikarska škola iz druge polovina XV veka*, in *Zbornik za Likovne Umetnosti*, i (Novi Sad 1965), 68-104; J. Trifunoski, *Bitolsko - Prilepsko kotlina, antropogeografski proučvanja*, Skopje 1970; M. Sokoloski, A. Stojanovski, *Turski dokumenti za istorijata na Makedonskiot narod, Opširen Popiski Defter no. 4*, Skopje 1971, 37-130 (full publication of the Ottoman *Taḥrīr* of 1454-5 (Ursinus), wrongly dated 1467-8); *Prilep i Prilepsko niz istorijata, kniga prva*, Prilep 1971; Boško Babić, *Srednovekovna naselba, crkva i nekropola Sv. Dimitrija, Prilop-Varoš*, in *Arheološki Pregled*, xiv (Belgrade 1972); idem, *Some of the essential characteristics of the origin and development of medieval Prilep*, in *Balcanoslavica*, vi (Prilep 1977), 29-35; M. Kiel, *Some little-known monuments of Ottoman Turkish architecture in the Macedonian province: Štip, Kumanovo, Prilep, Strumitsa*, in *Güney-Doğu Avrupa Araştırmaları Dergisi*, 6-7 (Istanbul 1978), 153-78 (updated repr. in Kiel, *Studies on the Ottoman architecture of the Balkans*, Variorum, London 1990); A. Stojanovski, *Gradovite na Makedonija od krajot na XIV do XVII vek*, Skopje 1980; Elica Maneva, *Srednovekoven nakit od Makedonija*, Skopje 1992, 186-7 (plan of the mediaeval town). (M. Kiel)

PĪSHDĀDIDS, a mythical dynasty of ancient Persia, given a considerable role in the national historical tradition of Persia. This tradition was essentially put together in the *khʷadāy-nāmags* of late Sāsānid times and, like most of our information on Sāsānid history, has to be reconstructed from post-Sāsānid, mainly early Islamic sources. Hence we find information on the Pīshdādids in such sources as al-Ṭabarī, al-Masʿūdī, Ḥamza al-Iṣfahānī and al-Thaʿālibī.

Ḥamza, ed. Beirut n.d. [*ca.* 1961], 13, 16-17 makes the Fīshdādiyya the first *ṭabaḳa* of the kings of Persia (the second being the [also legendary] Kayāniyya, the third the Ashghāniyya or Arsacids and the fourth the Sāsāniyya), with nine monarchs whose rule totalled 2,470 years. The Persian national history begins in fact with Kayūmarth or Gayōmard the first world-king, and it is his grandson or great-grandson Hūshang (OP Haošyanha), called *paradhāta* (NP *pīshdād*) "the one who first establishes the law" (see Justi, *Iranisches Namenbuch*, 126), who, as bearer of the "royal glory" (*hvarna, farrah*), is regarded as the founder of the Pīshdādids. Subsequent members of the dynasty include such heroic figures as Ṭahmūrath, Djamshīd, Farīdūn, Manūčihr and Garshāsp, and the national history records their struggles with the tyrant Dahāk and with the leader of Tūrān [*q.v.*] Afrāsiyāb [*q.v.*]. Then after the reigns of Garshāsp and Zāb, often described as co-rulers, came an interregnum and the advent of the new dynasty of Kayānids.

Bibliography: In addition to references given in the text, see Ṭabarī, i, 170-2, 174-6, 179-83 (tr. F. Rosenthal, *The history of al-Ṭabarī*. i. *General introduction and from the Creation to the Flood*, Albany 1989, 341-2, 344-5, 348-52), 201-10, 225-30 (tr. W. Brinner, *ibid.* ii. *Prophets and Patriarchs*, Albany 1987, 1-10, 23-7), 430-40; Masʿūdī, *Murūdj*, ii, 110-19 = §§ 535-41; idem, *Tanbīh*, 85-8, tr. 122-7; *Thaʿālibī, Taʾrīkh Ghurar al-siyar*, ed. and tr. H. Zotenberg, Paris 1900, 5 ff.; E. Yarshater, *Iranian national history*, in *Camb. hist. Iran*, iii/1, 370-4.

(C.E. Bosworth)

PĪSHKASH (P.) as a general term designates a present, usually from an inferior to a superior. As a technical term it denotes a "regular" tax (*pīshkash-i mustamarrī*) and an *ad hoc* tax levied by rulers on provincial governors and others, and an *ad hoc* impost laid by governors and officials in positions of power on the population under their control. The offering of presents to rulers and others was known from early times (cf. Abu 'l-Faḍl Bayhaḳī, *Tārīkh-i Bayhaḳī*, ed. A.A. Fayyāḍ, Mashhad 1350 *sh*/1971, 655, 679, 705, 734-5, 789, 815). With the proliferation of dues which took place under the Īlkhānate, the giving of gifts to the ruler and his officers was transformed into an *ad hoc* impost known by such terms as *saʾuri* and *tuzghü* rather than *pīshkash* (see G. Doerfer, *Türkische und mongolische Elemente im Neupersischen*, Wiesbaden 1963-75, i, 335). Under the Tīmūrids and the Turkoman dynasties the term *pīshkash* for such imposts is common. It was levied on the population of a district collectively (*pīshkash-i djamʿī*) and on individuals (*pīshkash-i ghayr-i djamʿī*) (see Sayyid Hossein Modarressi Tabataba'i, *Farmānhā-yi Turkamānān-i Ḳarā Ḳoyunlū wa Āḳ Ḳoyunlū*, Ḳum 1352 *sh*/1973-4, 103, 115, 126). Under the Ṣafawids, *pīshkash* is attested both as a due or tax paid on a regular basis and as an *ad hoc* levy; it constituted an important source of revenue. An official of the royal secretariat (*daftar-khāna*), known as the *pīshkash-niwīs* (the registrar of presents), recorded the number and value of *pīshkash*. This official is found until the second half of the 19th century (cf. W. Ouseley, *Travels in various countries of the East, more particularly Persia, etc.*, London 1819, ii, 172-3). Provincial governors paid *pīshkash* on appointment and thereafter annually at the Naw Rūz [see nawrūz] (cf. K. Röhrborn, *Provinzen und Zentralgewalt Persiens im 16. und 17. Jahrhundert*, Berlin 1966, 92).

Iṣfahān, Masdjid-i Shāh, entry īwān (N) from inside, 1020-5/1611-6.

Konya, İnce Minareli Medrese, main portal, *ca.* 656-78/1258-79.

Konya, Büyük Karatay Medresesi, main entrance, 649/1251.

Sivas, Cüveyni Dar ül-hadisi (Çifte Minareli Medrese), 670/1271.

Sivas, Buruciye Medresesi, 670/1271.

Holders of *tuyuls* and *soyurghals*, unless given immunity, were subject to the payment of *pīshkash*, as also were the leaders of *dhimmī* communities (cf. documents in A.D. Papazyan, *Persidskie dokumentï Matenadarana. 1. Ukazï, vïpusk pervï (XV-XVI vv.)*, Erivan 1956 and idem, *Persidskie dokumentï Matenadarana. 2. Ukazï, vïpusk vtoroy (1601-1650)*, and H. Busse, *Untersuchungen zum islamischen Kanzleiwesen*, Cairo 1959, 212-13). As in the case of other taxes and funds, drafts were sometimes drawn on *pīshkash* and collected locally. The *Dastūr al-mulūk* of Mīrzā Rafīʿā (Muḥammad Taḳī Dānish-pazhūh, *Dastūr al-mulūk-i Mīrzā Rafīʿā wa Tadhkirat al-mulūk-i Mīrzā Shafīʿā*, in *Tehran University, Rev. de la faculté des lettres et sciences humaines*, xv/5-6 [1968], xvi/1-6 [1968-9]) and the *Tadhkirat al-mulūk* (Persian text in facsimile, tr. and explained by V. Minorsky, London 1943) record late Ṣafawid practice and also the levy of commissions and fees on *pīshkash* made for various officials. Occasions for the exaction of *ad hoc pīshkash* were numerous. They included conquest of a town or district, the circumcision of princes, royal marriages, royal "progresses" and the progress of governors through their provinces. If the Shāh visited one of his subjects, his host was expected to give him a present in return (R. du Mans, *Estat de la Perse en 1660*, ed. C. Schefer, Paris 1890, 33). The grant of immunity from *pīshkash* is attested in a number of documents (cf. Sayyid Hossein Modarressi Tabataba'i, *op. cit.*, and Papazyan, *op. cit.*) and *farmāns* (cf. a *farmān* of Shāh Ṭahmāsp, dated 932/1526, engraved at the entrance of the Amīr ʿImād al-Dīn mosque in Kāshān (ʿAbd al-Ḥusayn Nawāʾī, *Shāh Ṭahmāsp-i Ṣafawī madjmūʿa-yi asnād wa mukātabāt-i tārīkhī*, Tehran 1350 *sh*/1971-2, 509).

The levy of "regular" *pīshkash* and *ad hoc pīshkash* continued under the Ḳādjārs (cf. United Kingdom, Parliament. Accounts and Papers. Report on Persia, A&P 1867-68, quoted by C. Issawi, *The economic history of Iran 1800-1914*, Chicago 1971, 366, and also the agreement made between the Imām of Muscat and the Persian Government dated 1272/1886 in Djahāngīr Ḳāʾim-Maḳāmī, *Yak ṣad wa pandjāh sanad-i tārīkhī*, Tehran 1348 *sh*/1969-70, 215-16. See also Muḥammad Djaʿfar b. Muḥammad Ḥusayn Nāʾīnī, *Djāmiʿ-i Djaʿfarī*, ed. Īradj Afshār, Tehran 1353 *sh*/1974-5, 592, 593-4; Afḍal al-Mulk, *Afḍal al-tawārīkh*, ed. Manṣūra Ittiḥādiyya (Niẓām Māfī); and Sīrūs Saʿdwandiyān, Tehran 1361 *sh*/1982-3, 391, 435). Its levy pressed heavily on the population (cf. Lady Sheil, *Glimpses of life and manners in Persia*, London 1856, 393). Open criticism of the practice of the levy of *pīshkash* was not to be expected, but voices against it were sometimes heard. One such was that of Muḥammad Shafīʿ Ḳazwīnī, a hatter (*kulāh-furūshī*) of Ḳazwīn, who commented on the evils of *pīshkash* in an essay written between 1264/1848 and 1266/1850, which he sent to the Amīr Kabīr, Nāṣir al-Dīn's first minister (*Ḳānūn-i Ḳazwīnī*, ed. Īradj Afshār, Tehran 1370 *sh*/1991).

Bibliography: Haphazard references to *pīshkash* are to be found in historical texts and documents. See also A.K.S. Lambton, *Pīshkash: present or tribute?*, in *BSOAS*, lvi (1993).

(ANN K.S. LAMBTON)

PISHPEK, a settlement of early and mediaeval Islamic times in the Ču [*q.v.*] valley of the Semirečye in Turkestan, during the Soviet period forming the city of Frunze (lat. 42° 54′ N., long. 74° 36′ E.). The region of Pishpek and nearby Toḳmaḳ is known to have been in mediaeval Islamic times a centre of Nestorian Christianity, and inscribed grave stones, the oldest of which date back to the time of the Ḳara Khiṭay [*q.v.*] (6th/12th century), have been found there (see W. Barthold, *Zur Geschichte des Christentums in Mittel-Asien bis zur mongolische Eroberung*, Tübingen and Leipzig 1901, 1-2, 37-8 *et passim*).

In the early 19th century, the Khāns of Khoḳand [*q.v.*] founded a fort at Pishpek, captured in 1862 by the advancing Russians, who then founded in 1878 a town there. When the Kirghiz SSR was created as part of the Soviet Union in 1926, Pishpek became its capital and was re-named Frunze after the Bolshevik commander M.V. Frunze, sent by Lenin in 1919-20 to Central Asia in order to combat the Basmači fighters there for local independence. In 1970 Frunze had a population of 431,000. With the break-up of the former Soviet Union, the city has now been re-named Bishkek, within the Kyrgyzstan Republic.

Bibliography: See also *BSE*², xxviii, cols. 316-19.

(C.E. BOSWORTH)

PĪSHṬĀḲ (P.), literally, "the arch in front", hence the portal of an important building, the term being appropriate to the advancing of the structure, at least in its developed form, forward from the plane of the façade: it is formally typified by this projection, and the articulation of receding planes to the entrance within. Though initially used throughout the Middle East and Hindūstān, the portal came to be most typical of Perso-Indian architecture. The Persian concept appears to be connected with the Arabic *dihlīz* as the palace vestibule where the ruler appeared for public audience, as at ʿAmman [*q.v.*]. It draws on the images of pre-Islamic wonders, particularly on the great Sāsānid Ṭāḳ-i Kisrā [*q.v.*] at Ctesiphon (3rd century A.D.), as extolled by, for example, al-Buḥturī [*q.v.*] in the 3rd/9th century (*loc. cit.* in *Bibl.*), and ultimately on Solomon's buildings, with which the Bāb Djayrūn became identified (see Soucek, *op. cit.* in *Bibl.*). As Golombek and Wilber have pointed out, the scale of the portal appears to reflect the status of the founder (*op. cit.* in *Bibl.*, 206-7), height, *irtifāʿ*, being a standard metaphor for exaltation; it often displayed his name conspicuously. It is also suggested (Bloom, *op. cit.* in *Bibl.*, 26) that portals may have symbolised a source from which *baraka* might emanate (cf. *Bāb* in *Encycl. Iranica*), especially in a Shīʿī context; this may have extended to some tombs. In mosques their inscriptions often identify them as entrances to the world of prayer, and ultimately paradise. Hillenbrand has also inferred that in some later tomb towers, as at Basṭām (700/1301), it may have had a cultic significance (*op. cit.* 1982, in *Bibl.*, 249). Mosque entrances remained flush until the Fāṭimids introduced the projection in the early 4th/10th century.

The features characteristic of the developed portal include a rectangular front taller than its width, surrounded by successive architrave friezes of running ornament and inscriptions, some in different planes, or comprising superimposed arched niches, enclosing an archway whose spandrels are set off with bosses, panels, or later with arabesque designs; its recessed rear wall in turn houses a smaller arch, later joined to it by a semivault, either through *muḳarnas* [*q.v.*] or squinch netting, leaving a tympanum over the doorway. Both arches may have round angle shafts. As such the organisation is close to that of the *miḥrāb* [*q.v.*], and appears to have developed in parallel with it. The format also applies, especially in the Perso-Indian context, to the handling of *īwān* fronts [*q.v.*], here used in the arthistorian's sense.

In the pre-Islamic phase, the *īwān* arch at Ctesiphon is flush with the screen wall on either side, to which it relates much as that at the Parthian palace at Assur, itself derived from Roman prototypes, as was that at Hatra; it formerly had an arcuated archivolt. In niches at the palace at Bis̲h̲āpūr (A.D. 260) the arch is framed by key-pattern friezes within the flanking pilasters. The gateway of the 6th century Sāsānid palace at Dāmg̲h̲ān, now in the Philadelphia Museum of Art, incorporates two concentric arches recessed one well within the other. The roughly contemporary rock-hewn *īwāns* of the Ṭāḳ-i Bustān near Kirmāns̲h̲āh incorporate stucco angels in the spandrels and a garlanded archivolt. A façade shown on the post-Sāsānid Fortress Plate in the Hermitage, which as Pope showed has features in common with the Parthian shrine at Tak̲h̲t-i Sulaymān, already shows the arched door set in a clearly defined rectangular frame, of which the upper panel ends in a cresting different from that on the flanking walls. The pre-Islamic prototypes thus occur in both sacred and palace buildings. This dual use was to continue in Muslim buildings.

Creswell (*op. cit.* in *Bibl.*, 1958, 197) identified the *līwān* arch on the south side of the Court of Honour at al-Uk̲h̲ayḍir (*ca.* 140-60/760-80 [*q.v.*]) as the first example of the *pīs̲h̲ṭāḳ*, but it has fallen, and the reconstruction of a rectangular frame is conjectural; it does, however, show the taller arch as the inevitable expression of a wide central bay in a wall of smaller arcading. The *īwān* of the Tārik K̲h̲āna Mosque at Dāmg̲h̲ān (4th/10th century) was probably comparable, with a frame rising from above the crowns of the lateral arcades, much as in the Masd̲j̲id-i D̲j̲āmiʿ at Nāʾīn (*ca.* 340/950). In the Great Mosque at Sāmarrā (234-7/848-52), the complete format can already be recognised in the *miḥrāb*, with its tall, recessed rectangular frame, two concentric pointed arches supported on paired angle shafts of rose marble on each side, and mosaic spandrels. At Córdoba, the Bāb al-Wuzarāʾ (Puerta de San Estéban) of 241/855-6 has a horseshoe arch recessed close within a rectangular frame (*alfiz*) set above the level of the door lintel, a treatment which persists in the Mag̲h̲rib: there are traces of flanking elements on either side in the flush wall. The full expression of this raised framing, with a cresting of five intersecting arches above, survives in a side door built by al-Ḥakam II in *ca.* 364/965. In the tomb of the Sāmānids at Buk̲h̲ārā (pre-331/943) the portal is still flush, but two concentric arches rest on angle shafts, with a decorated tympanum over the door, geometric panels in the spandrels, and a framing frieze of roundels. The entire front of the mausoleum of ʿArab Atā (367/977-8) at Tīm in Uzbekistan is a *pīs̲h̲ṭāḳ* rising between polygonal shafts at the corners to screen the lower part of the dome, and a deep cavetto moulding within the frame enhances the recession, with a striking row of three blind arches above the entry. In the Būyid D̲j̲urd̲j̲ir portal (4th/10th century) at Iṣfahān, the arch is joined to the entrance wall by two quadrants of a semidome, with a window between. The implications of the dominant façade at Tīm are realised in the three Ḳarak̲h̲ānid [see ILEK K̲H̲ĀNS] tombs at Uzgend in Kyrgyzstan (Ḳïrgïzstan) (*ca.* A.D. 1012-1187), where the diapered terracotta, while derived from the Sāmānid tomb, is now clearly articulated within successive frames reaching the ground, but without the intervention of an arcade; it includes early geometric frets. The Ḳarak̲h̲ānid mausoleum of ʿAlambardār at Āstāna-Bābā (*ca.* 395/1005?) in Türkmenistan has an advanced *pīs̲h̲ṭāḳ* housing one arch recessed within another, and what appears to have been a full architrave frame (its top is missing) as the centre bay of a tripartite arched front (Pugachenkova, *op. cit.* in *Bibl.*, 268-74). A century later, the Sald̲j̲ūḳ mausoleum at Tākistān in western Persia still has, by contrast, a single, full-front façade, with the outer frame uniting repeatedly recessed frames for the three sections, and rows of flat trilobed *muḳarnas* in the top of each (Hillenbrand, *op. cit.* 1972 in *Bibl.*).

The use of superimposed blind niches to flank the main arch derived from Roman practice, as can be seen in the projecting portal of the great mosque at Mahdiyya (308/920-1) [see BĀB, pl. xxv *a*], whence it appears to have been brought to Fāṭimid Egypt, in the Mosque of al-Ḥākim (393/1003) and the Mosque of al-Aḳmar (519/1125) at Cairo: the latter has a semidomed arch with radial ribbing, flanked by similar superimposed niches with angle shafts and, for the first time, square-framed *muḳarnas* hoods over the lower pair. The absence of minarets in these mosques is due to the connection between the portal itself and the call to prayer in Fāṭimid Egypt. The Aḳmar front is angled so as to adjust the line of a pre-existing street to the *ḳibla*-orientated interior. The derivation may have proceded separately in Persia.

The 18 m outer arch of the Ribāṭ-i Malik on the Buk̲h̲ārā-Samarḳand road (pre-1078), standing 6 m higher than the walls, is framed by a broad architrave of contiguous stars in relief, housing a smaller entry arch within a plain outlined frame for contrast. That of Sand̲j̲ar's Ribāṭ-i S̲h̲araf (508/1114-15 [*q.v.*]) on the Marw-Nīs̲h̲āpūr road is framed by a Kūfic inscription in deep relief contrasted with smooth mouldings, around a similar four-centred archivolt and diapered spandrels; in the comparable inner portal the inscription rises from piers indented with tall arched niches on either side. By the early 6th/12th century the sanctuary *īwān* of the Masd̲j̲id-i D̲j̲āmiʿ at Iṣfahān probably had a *pīs̲h̲ṭāḳ* rising more than twice the height of the two-storied wings on either side, whose original form appears to have incorporated lateral frames of arched panels set one over the other, and a pronounced archivolt; the north entrance was built in 515/1121, and, according to Māfarrūk̲h̲ī, was flanked by paired minarets. The Sald̲j̲ūḳ format of a four-centred arch flanked by superimposed niches is established clearly but simply in the *īwāns* of the Masd̲j̲id-i D̲j̲āmiʿ at Zawāra (530/1135-6) and that at Ardistān (555/1160), concurrently with the appearance of the four-*īwān* plan in D̲j̲ibāl province. The mosque of Imām Ḥasan at Ardistān (late 6th/12th century) has a portal once crowned by two minarets, possibly the earliest of the type to have survived. Records of the portal at the mausoleum of Muʾmina K̲h̲ātūn at Nak̲h̲čiwān (582/1186) (Useynov *et alii, op. cit.* in *Bibl.*, 89, 92) show it to have had a tall arch framed between two cylindrical minarets rising from the ground. In G̲h̲ūrid work, as at the S̲h̲āh-i Mas̲h̲had *madrasa* (571/1175-6) in G̲h̲ard̲j̲istān, and the Masd̲j̲id-i D̲j̲āmiʿ (*ca.* 1200) at Harāt [*q.v.*], the emphasis remains on broad, highly ornamented Kūfic frames. The east *īwān* at Zawzan (616/1219) incorporates both epigraphic frieze and elaborate *muḳarnas* vaulting. Subsequent structural and decorative developments were to be variations on this scheme. The classic form is achieved in the Masd̲j̲id-i D̲j̲āmiʿ at Warāmīn (726/1326), with a generous arch, splayed flanks to the projection, and fully integrated faience and terracotta decoration. This splay led later to the Tīmūrid incorporation of *pīs̲h̲ṭaḳ* in the *has̲h̲t bihis̲h̲t* plan type.

A type distinguished by a *muḳarnas* hood spanning from front wall to entry wall emerged in Syria, first in shallow stucco at the Muristān Nūrī at Damascus (549/1154) and then in full depth in stone in the *madrasa* of S̲h̲ādbak̲h̲t (589/1193) or the Ribāṭ Nāṣirī

(635/1237-8) at Aleppo [see BĀB, pl. xxvi]; it results in a triangular profile of successive arcs on the façade. This was subsequently used on mosques. It reached Egypt in the *madrasa* of Baybars (662/1264). Though keel-vaulted entrances were still used for some caravanserais in Anatolia, it was already used there by ca. 1200 in the Halifet Gazi mausoleum at Amasya (traditionally dated 540/1145-6) with wriggling torus frames around an arch set on elongated corbels, in the Sitte Melik Kümbeti at Divriği (592-1195-6) with its more sober cranked frame, and in the Mama Hatun Kümbeti (1200-20) at Tercan, where it is flanked by tall angular niches. By 656/1258 it appeared in the mosque of Sahib Ata at Konya flanked by a pair of pleated brick minarets above two diminutive superimposed niches framed by knotted strapwork and mouldings. This type with minarets achieved full expression in the Çifte Minareli Medrese at Erzurum (639/1242?), and the Gök Medrese and Çifte Minareli Medrese, both of 670/1271, in Sivas. A variant with a flat-topped hood appeared in parti-coloured marble in the Büyük Karatay Medrese, Konya, of 649/1251, with cabled angle shafts. Other, highly sculptural Anatolian forms in this wonderfully inventive period are in the İnce Minareli Medresesi, Konya (*ca.* 1258-79), with an inner arch tied by a knotted inscription band through a semidomed outer arch to an arcuated cresting, and the Ulu Cami at Divriği (626/1228-9), where the swarming, heraldic ornament all but obscures the form. The full Egyptian form is to be seen 37 m high in the mosque of Sulṭān Ḥasan in Cairo (760/1359), apparently deriving from the Gök Medrese, with its two minarets: the hood climbs to a cusped semidome at the apex, a Syrian detail already used in the Great Mosque of Baybars (667/1269) in its lateral niches [see BĀB, pl. xxv*b*]. Ottoman portals were to incorporate flattened variants of the triangular Säldjük hood [*ibid.* pl. xxix*a*], but their significance was usually reduced by the use of an arcade in front.

The format with double minarets, apparently adopted from Ādharbāydjān, was to be characteristic of 8th/14th century Persia under the Mongols. In the Masdjid-i Djāmiʿ at Ashtardjān (715/1315) they are set back behind the plane of the *pīshṭāḳ* frame to rise on top of the structure. The height of the arch is three times its width, housing a *muḳarnas* semi-dome divided from the entry arch by a horizontal inscription frieze, all flanked by three tall superimposed arched niches; subtle use is made of blue glazed brick. Other examples are the portals of the *khānaḳāh* at Naṭanz (707/1307-8) and the Masdjid-i Niẓāmiyya at Abarḳūh (*ca.* 725/1325), culminating in the *pīshṭāḳ* of the great mosque at Yazd (*ca.* 730/1330, reconstructed in 765/1364), twice its width in height, with four tiers of niches, where extra buttressing is required behind the façade. In that at Kirmān, built under the Muẓaffarids in 750/1349, the format is transformed by an overall reventment of mosaic tile, with arabesques in the spandrels. The use of a cable moulding to frame the main arch may be a reference to Solomon's supposed ability to mould stone, as told of cabled shafts in Jerusalem (see MIḤRĀB, pl. 1, for the *miḥrāb* of Sulaymān in the Ḳubbat al-Ṣakhra). The squinch nets first devised under the Muẓaffarids, though already implicit in the star vaults at Iṣfahān, appear in Tīmūrid work by the end of the century: they are used structurally in the *īwān*s of the Mosque of Fīrūzshāh at Turbat-i Djām (846/1442-3), but were later to be false. By the second half of the 9th/15th century they were widely to replace *muḳarnas* as the means of transition, though they survived longer in portals than elsewhere, sometimes in combination with nets, as in the much-restored *īwān* of ʿAlī Shīr Nawāʾī at Mashhad.

The Great Mosque of ʿAlī Shāh at Tabrīz (*ca.* 710-20/1310-20) incorporates a vast *īwān* (30.15 m span) in deliberate emulation of Ctesiphon (22.86 m). Not only its size, but the marble columns of the courtyard, and the great marble slabs in the entrances, were to be copied by Tīmūr in his Masdjid-i Djāmiʿ at Samarḳand (806/1403-4) (17 m, and 19 m high), after his even larger portal for the Āḳsarāy at Shahr-i Sabz (781-98/1379-96) (22.30 m, *ca.* 50 m high). These may have been influenced by a late 8th/14th century mosque at Sulṭāniyya, no longer extant, since in all three the flanking minarets sprang from the ground (Golombek and Wilber, *op. cit.*, cat. 211). In all, too, the cabled moulding is prominent. This was to be a model for subsequent Tīmūrid, Ṣafawid, and Mughal *pīshṭāḳ*s.

Hindūstān. The introduction of arched stone frontal screens [see MASDJID. II. In Muslim India] gave the central bay a new potential. The form and articulation of the Ribāṭ al-Sharaf front was to be emulated in the deeply-carved screen of the Masdjid Ḳuwwat al-Islām (595/1199) at Dihlī [*q.v.*], and more closely in that of the Aṛhāʾī-din-kā Djhōṅpṛā mosque at Adjmēr (607-33/1211-36), with its cusped lateral arches, but this time with two non-functional reeded minarets set on top of the 17 m central bay: the Harātī (?) architect cited the Ḳuṭb Minār in their profile [see MANĀRA. 2. In India], probably as a symbol of dominion, thus giving them a new semantic purpose to be resumed elsewhere. In form, he seems to have anticipated the Anatolian double type. The implication, rather than the form of such treatment was continued in the massive domed entrances and *īwān*s of Tughluḳid mosques. That at Djahānpanāh (Begampur, Dihlī *ca.* 744/1343) incorporates a projecting *čahārṭāḳ* porch with battered walls, enhanced by a wedge of access steps, and a towering *pīshṭāḳ* to the prayer hall between tapering round angle turrets, in which the arch is almost as tall as the parapet, dwarfing the triple entrance within. This tendency was taken still further at Djawnpur, as at the Atāla Masdjid (811/1408), where the sides of the *pīshṭāḳ* frame are expressed as battered rectangular piers, still housing niches, with an architrave bridging the arch at the top; in front of the prayer hall, the structure forms a pylon five stories high, outtopping the dome, 17 m wide at the base and 23 m high; the arch itself houses five tiers of grouped openings. The *guldasta*, a shaft-like pinnacle, is introduced in Tughluḳid work as a prolongation of the angle turret, and is subsequently transformed. Exceptionally, in the Lōdī mosque at Khayrpur, Dihlī (900/1494), a façade directly based on the Mustanṣiriyya at Baghdād (1233) is modified by advancing the central bay. A Tīmūrid form first appears in the Masdjid-i Kuhna at Dihlī (*ca.* 1540), with reeded angle shafts recalling the Ḳuṭb, rising into *guldasta* among merlons at the skyline, black fillets trimming an epigraphic frieze, and the first use of geometric white marble inlay in the flat tympanum. Red sandstone is henceforward the normal matrix, with inlaid work [see PĀRČĪN-KĀRĪ]. By 969/1561-2, the Khayr al-Manāzil, *ca.* 1568-70, incorporates a semidome for the first time. The portal of Akbar's mosque in the Čishtī Dargāh at Adjmēr (977/1570) projects between splayed reveals, with one tall arch recessed within another [see MUGHALS. 7. Architecture, pl. xx, 1]. His Buland Darwāza at Fatḥpur Sīkrī returns in 983/1575-6 to the monumental scale, 39.62 m wide and 40.84 m high, at the top of a vast flight of steps. The projection is hemioctagonal, with shafts at the angles, the great arch of the main face housing a hemioctagonal recess with a squinch-netted semidome above. Each splayed face and the three internal sides are articulated in three storeys, with a cresting of small open domed kiosks in series on the skyline. The inscriptions carved in cartouches on the architrave celebrate prayer as a gateway to paradise. The *pīshṭāḳ* acquires a new independence in the Nīl Kanth belvedere at Māndū (982/1574-5), where three are grouped to surround a courtyard with a cascade.

In Akbar's tomb at Sikandra, the gateway (1022/1613) has the arched format of Adjmēr, but is flanked by wings each housing two superimposed arches of the same depth. The inlay is the first to include floral motifs. Above each bevelled corner stands a tall marble minaret, still reeded at the base. The rise of the *pīshṭāḳ* inherently tended to obscure the dome of a *maḳṣūra* behind it, as evident at Fatḥpur Sīkrī [see MUGHALS. 7, pl. xx, 2]. A solution to the problem was found in the little Nagīna Masdjid (*ca.* 1630) in the Āgra Fort, where the newly popular Bangālī curve was used to raise the *čhadjdja* line over the centre bay. Other devices were tried in smaller mosques [see MASDJID, vol. VI, at 697-8]. In the major metropolitan mosques at Āgra (1058/1648), Dihlī (1060-6/1650-6), and Lāhawr (1084/1673-4), however, the *pīshṭāḳ* was retained, with a relatively wide arch surrounded by an unpunctuated architrave, framed by angle shafts enlarged to slender, lanterned minarets, and a single entry arch within [see MUGHALS. 7, pls. xxxi-xxxii]. Palace pavilions [see MAḤALL] generally had straight, uninterrupted eaves, and the function of the *pīshṭāḳ* at court was restricted to entrance gates, often with a raised gallery for the musicians [see MUGHALS. 7, pls. xxiv, 2 and xxviii, 2].

Bibliography: For parallel material, see BĀB (some parts of sequence now outdated). For the image of Ctesiphon, see Buḥturī, tr. G.E. von Grunebaum, in *Kritik und Dichtkunst*, Wiesbaden 1955, 59. The general theme of prototypical images is discussed by B. Finster, in *Architekturbeschreibungen arabischer Autoren des 9.-14. Jahrhunderts*, in *Forschungsforum* ii (Orientalistik), Bamberg 1990, 56-63, and P. Soucek, *The temple of Salomon in Islamic legend and art*, in J. Gutman (ed.), *The temple of Solomon*, 1976. The legend of the cabled moulding is cited by R. Jairazbhoy from J.E. Hanauer, *Folklore of the Holy Land*, London 1935, 41.

Other works cited are, alphabetically: J.M. Bloom, *The mosque of al-Ḥākim in Cairo*, in *Muqarnas*, i (1983), 15-36; K.A.C. Cresswell, *A short account of early Muslim architecture,* Harmondsworth 1958; L. Golombek and D. Wilber, *The Timurid architecture of Iran and Turan*, Princeton 1988; R. Hillenbrand, *Saljuq monuments in Iran. II. The "Pīr" mausoleum at Takistān*, in *Iran, JBIPS*, x (1972), 45-55; idem, *The flanged tomb tower at Basṭām*, in *Art et Société dans le monde iranien*, Paris 1982, 237-61; idem, art. *Pishtaq*, in *Dict. of the Middle Ages*, ix, New York 1987; G.A. Pugačenkova, *Putui razvitiya arkhitekturui yuzhnogo Turkmenistana*, Moscow 1958; M. Useynov (Hüseynov), L. Bretanitskiy, A. Salamzade, *Istoriya arkhitekturui Azerbaydzhana*, Moscow 1963.

Illustrations of Nāʾīn, Ribāṭ-i Sharaf, Ardistān, Zawāra, Zawzan, Bisṭām, Ashtardjān and Warāmīn can conveniently be found in A. Hutt, *Islamic architecture Iran*, 1, London 1977, and Kirmān, in *ibid.*, 2, London 1978. See also D. Hill and O. Grabar, *Islamic architecture and its decoration*, London 1967 (including Üzgend), and J.D. Hoag, *Islamic architecture*, New York 1977. For the Saldjūḳ examples in Persia, see A. Godard, *Ardistan et Zaware*, in *Athar-è Iran* ii/1 (Paris 1937), and *Isfahan*, in *ibid.* For the Īl-Khānid ones, Godard, *Abarquh*, in *Athar-è Iran* i/1, Paris 1936, and D. Wilber, *The architecture of Islamic Iran: the Il Khānid period*, Princeton 1955. For Anatolian examples, see A. Gabriel, *Monuments turcs d'Anatolie*, ii, Paris 1934 (Amasya, Divriği), and A. Kuran, *Anadolu medreseleri*, i, Ankara 1969. For India, see the bibliographies under DIHLĪ, HIND, MASDJID, and MUGHALS, and E. Koch, *Mughal architecture, an outline of its history and development*, Munich 1991. (P.A. ANDREWS)

PIST (P.), a kind of food compounded of the liver of gazelles or almonds, etc. A daily portion of the size of a pistachio (*pista*) is taken by those derwīshes and others who undertake long fasts, e.g. the *čilla* or forty-day fast, and is sufficient to maintain life.

Bibliography: Vullers, *Lexicon Persico-Latinum*, s.v. *pist, čilla.* (R. LEVY)

PIYĀLE PASHA, Ottoman Grand Admiral, came according to St. Gerlach, *Tage-Buch* (Frankfurt a/M. 1674, 448), from Tolna in Hungary and is said to have been the son of a shoemaker, probably of Croat origin. Almost all contemporary records mention his Croat blood (cf. the third series of the *Relazioni degli ambasciatori Veneti al Senato*, ed. E. Albèri, Florence 1844-5, and esp. iii/2, 243: *di nazione croato, vicino ai confini d'Ungheria*; 357: *di nazione croato*; iii/3, 294: *di nazione unghero*; 418). Following the custom of the time, his father was later given the name of ʿAbd al-Raḥmān and described as a Muslim (cf. F. Babinger, in *Litteraturdenkmäler aus Ungarns Türkenzeit*, Berlin and Leipzig 1927, 35, n. 1). Piyāle came in early youth as a page into the Serai in Istanbul and left it as *ḳapudjī bashī* [see ḲAPÎDJÎ]. The year 961/1554 saw him appointed Grand Admiral (*ḳapudan pasha* [*q.v.*]) with the rank of a *sandjaḳbey*, and four years later he was given the status of a *beylerbey* (J. von Hammer, *GOR*, iii, 406). He succeeded Sinān Pasha, brother of the Grand Vizier Rüstem Pasha [*q.v.*], in the office which he had held from 955-61/1548-54. When after his capture of Djerba and other heroic achievements at sea he thought he might claim the rank of *wezīr* with three horse-tails, Sultan Süleymān, thinking it too soon for this promotion and regarding it as endangering the prestige of the vizierate (see Ḥādjdjī Khalīfa, *Tuḥfat al-kibār*, first edition, fol. 36, and *GOR*, iii, 406), married him to his grand-daughter Djewher Sulṭān, a daughter of Selīm II (see *GOR*, iii, 392: summer of 1562). It was not till five years later that he received the three horse-tails as a *wezīr* related by marriage (*dāmād*) like Meḥmed Ṣoḳollu Pasha.

Meanwhile, he had carried out several of his great exploits at sea and attained the reputation of one of the greatest of Ottoman admirals. Along with Torghud Reʾīs, at the instigation of the French ambassador d'Aramon, he had harassed the coast around Naples, besieged and taken Reggio and carried off its inhabitants into slavery. In 982/1555 he endeavoured in vain to besiege Elba and Piombino (see *GOR*, iii, 418), and finally took the fortified harbour of Oran in Algeria with 45 galleys. In the following year, with 60 warships he occupied the port of Bizerta (Bent-Zert) and a year later ravaged Majorca with 150 galleys and burned Sorrento near Naples. In 965/1558 he lay inactive with his fleet, 90 in number, before Valona in Albania in order to watch the enemy fleets there which were preparing an enterprise against Djerba and Tripoli. The 31 July 1560 saw his greatest exploit at sea, namely, the capture of Djerba, which had shortly before been taken by the Spaniards; this he did with 120 ships setting out from Modon. On 27 September 1560, he held his triumphal entry into Istanbul, to which he had sent in advance the news of his victory by a galley (see *GOR*, iii, 421 ff.). The Grand Admiral did not take to sea again till four years later when, in August 1564, he took the little rocky island of Peñón de Vélez de la Gomera from the Spaniards in order to prepare for the conquest of Malta, which the sultan's favourite daughter Mihrimāh [see RÜSTEM PASHA] was conducting with all her resources. This time, however, fortune no longer favoured him, for the siege of Malta in June-July 1565 failed against the heroic courage of the Christian defenders, who performed miracles of bravery and inflicted heavy losses on the Ottomans. During the Hungarian campaign of Süleymān in the spring of 973/1566, Piyāle Pasha was placed in charge of the harbour and arsenal of Istanbul (see *GOR*, iii, 438), after previously undertaking a successful raid on Chios and the Apulian coast (*ibid.*, iii, 506 ff.), in which the island of Chios and its harbour passed into his hands (Easter Sunday 1566).

Under Selīm II, his father-in-law, he was disgraced and deprived of office of Grand Admiral because, it was alleged, he had kept the greater part of the booty of Chios for himself (according to the report of the embassy of Albrecht de Wijs of May 1568, in von Hammer, *GOR*, iii, 782), and replaced by Muʾedhdhinzāde ʿAlī Pasha. He at once endeavoured to regain the imperial favour by new exploits at sea. In Dhu 'l-Kaʿda 977/April 1570, he set sail with 75 galleys and 30 galleots, landed first of all on the island of Tine which he captured and next took part in the conquest of Cyprus. On 20 January 1578—according to Ottoman sources on 12 Dhu 'l-Kaʿda 985/21 January 1578—he died in Istanbul, according to Stephan Gerlach (cf. his *Tage-Buch*, 448). His vast estates passed in part to the imperial treasury and in part to his widow and children. His widow later married the third *wezīr* Meḥmed Pasha and his second son became *sandjak bey* of Klis (Clissa) above Split (Spalato in Dalmatia) in 992/1584 (cf. the Italian record quoted by von Hammer, *GOR*, iv, 104, n. 1: *La Sultana fo moglie di Piale ora di Mohammedbassa terzo vezir, ha ottenuto dal Sign. il Sangiaco di Clissa per il secondo suo figlio con Piale*). Piyāle Pasha was buried in Istanbul in the Kāsim Pasha quarter in the mosque founded by him (cf. Ḥāfiẓ Ḥuseyin Aywansarāyī, *Ḥadīkat al-djawāmiʿ*, ii, 25 ff.).

Bibliography: In addition to works quoted in the text, see the histories of Zinkeisen and Iorga, and Rāmiz Pasha-zāde Meḥmed Efendi, *Kharīṭa-yi Ḳapudānān-i Deryā*, Istanbul 1285; also Meḥmed Thüreyyā, *Sidjill-i ʿothmānī*, ii, 41-2; Jurien de la Gravière, *Les corsaires barbaresques et la marine de Soliman le Grand*, Paris 1887; *İA*, art. *Piyâle Paşa* (Şerâfeddin Turan). (F. BABINGER)

PLEVEN [see PLEWNA].

PLEWNA (Ottoman Turkish orthography, پلونه), the modern city of Pleven in northern Bulgaria. It is situated at an altitude of 105 m/336 ft in a depression of the Pleven plateau which is formed by the small river Tučenica, a tributary of the river Vit, which passes the city 6 km/3½ miles to its west. The important road and railway from Sofia to Bucarest and the Black Sea port of Varna passes through this town. In Ottoman times (1393-1878) it was a centre of Islamic life, with many mosques and some important *medreses*, and was the centre of a *ḳaḍāʾ* containing 46 villages. Throughout most of the Ottoman period it belonged to the *sandjak* of Nīkbūlī [*q.v.*] (Nigbolu, Nikopol). After the reorganisation of the provincial administration in 1864, it became part of the *sandjak* of Rusčuk [*q.v.*] (Russe) in the *wilāyet* of Ṭūna. The present city is an Ottoman foundation from the last decade of the 9th/15th century, founded around a *külliyye* consisting of a mosque, a large *medrese* (with 30 student cells), an *ʿimāret*, a *zāwiye*, a primary school and a *ḥammām*, founded by the well-known *akîndjî* leader Mīkhāl-oghlū [*q.v.*] ʿAlī Bey. The town gained international fame during the siege of 1877, which held up the Russian invasion of the Ottoman Balkans for over five months and seriously influenced the outcome of the war (see below).

Plewna is the indirect successor of the Roman town of Storgosia, which was destroyed by the Huns (A.D. 441-8) but which was apparently reconstructed later, as is indicated by archaeological finds from the 6th century. Around 600 A.D., during the invasions of the Slavs and the Avars, this settlement, which was situated at the site of Ḳayalîk above the present town, ceased to exist. In the Bulgaro-Byzantine Middle Ages, a castle and a *suburbium* of some size must have existed, but information on it is very meagre: some coins from the First Bulgarian Empire (10th century), a few dozen Byzantine coins from the Comneni emperors (12th century), a Jewish tombstone with an inscription from A.D. 1266, a few silver coins of Tsar Michael Šišman (1323-30) and Tsar Ivan Alexander (1330-71) and, curiously enough, a bronze Buddha statue of the Pala-Sena period (11th-12th centuries). In the mediaeval written sources, Plewna is mentioned only once, in 1266, during the Bulgarian campaign of the Hungarian King Stephen the Great, when his troops took the "castrum Pleun." From this information, Bulgarian historiography has constructed a thriving military and commercial centre.

The capture of the castle of Plewna by the Ottomans is not recorded in local or early Ottoman sources. Its capture has to be connected with the 790-1/1388-9 campaign of the Grand Vizier Djandarlîzāde ʿAlī Pasha, when after the capture of the nearby Nigbolu/Nikopol [see NĪKBŪLĪ], the Ottoman army could have taken it on its way back to Edirne, via Plewna and Lofča (Loveč). Neshrī [*q.v.*], who is the only source describing this campaign with any detail, giving lists of important towns and castles of Bulgaria, is silent about Plewna and Lofča. It is possible that, on this occasion, the mediaeval Plewna was destroyed. It is also possible that this happened in 1444 during the Crusade of Varna, when most north Bulgarian towns were put to the torch, but the principal account of that campaign, by Michael Behaim, is silent about it. Yet this source is incomplete. It does not mention the conquest of Lofča by the Crusaders, a fact which we know from an Ottoman source, *Ghazawāt-nāme-yi Sulṭān Murād Khān*. What Ewliyā Čelebi reports about the conquest is purely legendary and based on misidentifications of the various members of the Mikhāl-oghlu clan, which he associates with it. The castle of Plewna survived into the 10th/16th century, probably serving as a basis for Mikhāl-oghlu ʿAlī Bey, the first of this family about whom we can be certain that he resided in or near Plewna since *ca.* 866/1462. The castle is mentioned in the *taḥrīr* of 922/1516, where, at "High Plewna" (Plewne-yi Bālā), "a castle survives from the time of the unbelievers." The settlement of Plewne-yi Bālā itself is first mentioned in a large fragment of the oldest preserved Ottoman *taḥrīr* of the Nigbolu *sandjak*, an *idjmāl* from 884/1479-80, as having ten Christian and nine civilian Muslim households (ed. N. Todorov and B. Nedkov, *Turski izvori za Bălg. istorija*, ii, Sofia 1966, 244-5). In spite of this small size, it was the administrative centre of a *nāḥiye*. Below it, a settlement called Plewne-yi Zīr existed. This place is mentioned in another fragmentarily preserved *taḥrīr*, from *ca.* 890/1485, as having three households, two widows and two *müdjerreds*, all Christians (Sofia, National Library Kiril i Metodii, Or. Dep. N.K. a.e. 12/9, fol. 10).

In the 1480s, these two places, and 20 uninhabited sites (*mezraʿa*), were acquired as *mülk* property by Mikhāl-oghlu Ghāzī ʿAlī Bey, who subsequently brought together several hundred Bulgarian Christian and Muslim Turkish settlers, with whom he founded 20 villages and the town of Plewna, built in the depression below the ruined castle, at the site of Plewne-yi Zīr. The new town developed around the socio-religious buildings provided by ʿAlī Bey, among which were many shops. In the *ewāsiṭ* of Radjab 901/end of March 1496, all this was made into a *wakf*. The *wakfiyye* is preserved in several copies, in Arabic and in a Turkish translation of the poet-*müderris* Ḍaʿīfī from 962/1554-5, and is partly published by A.S. Levend (*Gazavāt-nāmeleri*, 359-60). The settlers of the town were attracted by freedom from the *ʿawāriḍ* and *tekālif* taxes. The Christians of the town and the villages paid only half the *djizye*. ʿAlī Bey had also invited Spanish Jews to his new town, who came by way of Selānik and Sofia (1516: 69 families). In 910/1505 an important addition, *dheyl*, was made to the *wakf*, of which a Bulgarian extract remains (Trifonov, *Grad Pleven*, 40-1). ʿAlī Bey died in 913/1507-8 and was buried in a *türbe* behind his mosque. His life as a warrior of Islam was sung by the poet Sūzī Čelebi of Prizren. His sons and grandsons continued his policy of promoting the town, adding numerous fountains and paving for the streets (*kaldïrïm*). In 981/1573-4, Süleyman Bey completed the Ḳurshunlu Djāmiʿ, a monumental, domed mosque in the best classical Ottoman style (good photograph by Trifonov, at 45). Khiḍïr Bey added a second *medrese*, where the poet Ḍaʿīfī worked as *müderris*. Together with the great *medrese* of ʿAlī Bey, this made Plewna an important provincial centre of Islamic learning. Besides these buildings, the 957/1550 *taḥrīr* mentions five smaller mosques. The 987/1579 *taḥrīr* mentions a mosque of Khadīdje Sulṭān, the daughter of ʿAlī Bey's successor Meḥmed, and the new Friday mosque of Süleymān Bey, son of Ḥasan Bey b. ʿAlī, and a number of *mesdjids*. When in 932/1526 the Ottomans took Buda(pest), a part of the Jews of that city was invited to settle in Plewna (according to the 957/1550 *taḥrīr*, T.D. 382, pp. 685-6, 41 families). The same source also mentions 62 households of Jews from Germany, of which seven were headed by widows, and 84 households (15 headed by widows) of Jews from the Latin lands (*Yahūdiyān-i Frenk*). In the 1570s, these Jewish groups rose to over 200 households, making Plewna one of the largest Jewish centres of the Balkans. Throughout the centuries, Plewna remained a predominantly Muslim town, which in the course of time absorbed and turkified a part of the local Bulgarian population (in 1550, 20% of the Plewna Muslims were of convert origin). A survey of its demographic development, based on the Ottoman *taḥrīrs*, a *mufaṣṣal ʿawāriḍ defter, djizye defters*, the census results in 1290/1873-4, the *Sālnāme-yi Wilāyet-i Ṭūna* and the first Bulgarian censuses, is given in the following Table:

IN HOUSEHOLDS

	Muslims	*Christians*	*Jews*	*Gypsies*	*Total*	*Percentage of Muslims*
1479	9	10	/	/	19	47%
1516	200	99	69	11	379	54%
1550	472	185	104	36	797	59%
1579	558	180	209	44	991	56%
1751	441	125	n.d.	n.d.		
1845	n.d.	660	20	n.d.		
1873	1,241	1,477	75	65	2,858	43%
1887	450	2,580	81	40	3,151	14%
1926	525	5,915	115	105	6,660	8%
1934	560	6,690	60	115	7,425	7%

In the 11th-12th/17th-18th centuries, the town apparently declined, a process which, in addition to internal reasons, was triggered off by the sack and the destruction of the town by the Rumanians under Michael the Brave in 1064/1596, who also carried off thousands of the inhabitants of the *wakf* villages and forcibly settled them in Wallachia. After the invasion, the ruins of the mediaeval castle were taken down and the stones used for the construction of a large new *khān* with 70 fireplaces, flanking the *bedesten*.

In 1659 the town was visited by the Bulgarian Catholic archbishop Philipp Stanislavov (ed. Fermandžiev, 1887), who mentions as its inhabitants 500 Orthodox Bulgarians, having two churches, and no less than 5,000 Turks with seven mosques. Three years later, Ewliyā Čelebi visited the town (*Seyāḥat-nāme*, vi, 1898-9 164-5; more detailed in the autograph, Topkapı Sarayı Müzesi, Revan Köşk, no. 1457, fol. 59a), who recalls the Wallachian raid of 1064/1596; but most of his "history" is purely legendary or, at best, full of misidentifications of historical persons. In his time, Plewna consisted of "2,000 houses", which is a gross exaggeration. The *ʿimāret* of Ghāzī ʿAlī Bey, which according to its *wakfiyye* served everyone twice daily with cooked food, regardless of his religion or origin, was still in full operation. Ewliyā noted that there were seven *mektebs* in the town, six *tekkes* and six *khāns*.

Especially in the prosperous 10th/16th century, the Christian *wakf* villages around Plewna, and the monasteries of St George near the town and Sadovec outside it, developed an important scribal activity, writing Bibles and church books for the Bulgarian Orthodox churches of northern Bulgaria (survey of preserved copies by Trifonov, 53-6). Of great importance was the literary production of the Plewna Jews, of whom Joseph ben Ephraim Karo, who came from Spain and worked as *Ḥāḥām* in the Plewna synagogue, should be mentioned.

At the end of the 11th/17th century, the land around Plewna suffered badly from the passage through northern Bulgaria on their way to the Hungarian front of the army of the Crimean Tatars under their Khān Selīm Giray, "no cattle, woman and girls being left behind", according to a marginal note in a church book dated October 1689. This event is also recorded in some grafitti in grottos near Plewna, where the people had taken shelter. In 1131/1719, the town suffered much damage when a flood swept away the houses and shops of the lower iarters of the town. According to the *mufaṣṣal ʿawārid̲ fter* of 1164/1751 (BBA, Kepeci, Mevkufat, 2913), ie town was considerably smaller than in the late 0th/16th century, having *ca.* 2,500 inhabitants, of hom almost three-quarters were Muslims. The ames of the *maḥalle*s were largely the same as in 87/1579. After the end of the 12th/18th century, but articularly throughout the entire 13th/19th century, ie town again witnessed a rapid expansion, especially f the Christians, who outnumbered the Muslims at ie end of the Ottoman period. During the reforms of 1aḥmūd II, the Mīk̲h̲āl-og̲h̲lu family, living as *iütewellī*s of the *wak̲f*s of their ancestors, succeeded in eeping most of their property. A *fermān* of Maḥmūd I from 1238/1823 (published by Ihčiev) confirmed hem in their possessions. Ḥād̲j̲d̲j̲ī ʿÖmer Bey Aütewellī was reported to be the richest man of the ntire north-western Bulgaria. The tax revenue of the 8 *wak̲f* villages was estimated at one million piastres. The *Sālnāme* of the Ṭūna *wilāyet* of 1286/1869-70 noted hat Plewna contained 18 mosques, two churches, one ynagogue, 925 shops, a *ḥammām* and 30 *k̲h̲ān*s. The *Sālnāme* of 1285/1868-9 adds three *medrese*s and five *tek̲-es*. In the very last years of the Ottoman period, the ;eographer Felix Kanitz noted 1,627 Muslim houses and 1,474 Christian ones, giving a total population of about 17,000 inhabitants; with the Christians having arger families than the Muslims, the former would iave had a slight majority. During the Russo-Turkish War of 1877-8, Plewna became world-famous for its ;allant defence of more than five months under the in-spired command of (G̲h̲āzī) ʿOt̲h̲mān Pas̲h̲a. After crossing the Danube on July 1877, the Russians ap-peared before Plewna, where they met unexpected resistance. Their attacks from 20 to 30 July were repulsed. The town was not fortified. ʿOt̲h̲mān Pas̲h̲a used the excellently defensible position of the sur-rounding hills, where he had extensive earthworks thrown up. On 11 and 12 September the Russians and the Rumanians, who had been summoned to their assistance, made a third attempt to take Plewna by storm, and again were repulsed with heavy losses. After further failures on 18 September and 19 Oc-tober, the allies decided upon a regular siege of the town, which was conducted by the Russian general Totleben, the hero of Sebastopol. On 10 November the Russians succeeded in cutting off Plewna from the outside world in an effort to starve the fortress into submission. A month later, on 10 December, ʿOt̲h̲mān Pas̲h̲a undertook a last desperate sortie in an attempt to break through the western lines of the besieging army of 120,000 men (including the Tsar in person), which, after an initial success, failed. ʿOt̲h̲mān Pas̲h̲a, "the Lion of Plewna", was himself wounded and finally forced to surrender with some 40,000 men. The five months' siege had cost the Rus-sians and their allies over 40,000 men. The fall of Plewna opened the way for the Russians to Edirne and on to San Stefano, where they dictated the peace which was concluded there on 3 March, on the basis of a truce made at Edirne a month before [see also BULGARIA].

The capture of Plewna by the Russians led to a drastic transformation of the town, half-destroyed during the siege. The entire Turkish population fled from fear of the bands of Bulgarian irregulars, and only a third of them returned when, under the new Bulgarian state, ordered life returned. A member of the Mīk̲h̲āl-og̲h̲lu family even occupied a seat in the Bulgarian Parliament in Sofia. The place left vacant by the departed Turks was immediately filled by Bulgarian newcomers from the villages. With their much bigger families, the number of Bulgarians in the town also grew in a natural way, eroding the percen-tage of Muslims ever faster. In the decades before World War I, most of the Ottoman buildings of the town were demolished. A huge Russian neo-Byzantine mausoleum came to occupy the site of the mosque, *medrese* and *ʿimāret* of G̲h̲āzī ʿAlī Bey. The mosque of Süleymān Beg was still standing in 1931, but was then replaced by the Military Club. On the site of the great Kerwānserāy, the new building of the provincial administration was erected. Great tree-lined boulevards and squares came to replace the old Turkish quarters. A name like "Tekiiskija Bair" still keeps the memory of the great *zāwiye* of ʿAlī Bey. The bones of the Russian and Rumanian soldiers of "77" were partly placed in the huge mausoleum, partly in large war cemeteries, the Rumanians having their own one, New Grivitsa, where they had fallen in the furious fights around the Grivitsa Redoubt. The village of Grivitsa had been until the end of the Ot-toman period one of the major possessions of the *wak̲f* of G̲h̲āzi ʿAlī Bey. The skeletons of the tens of thousands of Ottoman soldiers, however, were dug up and sold to a British firm to be turned into fertiliser used for English agriculture. A part of the earthworks and trenches of ʿOt̲h̲mān Pas̲h̲a was maintained as a memorial and can still be seen. In the 1970s, an enor-mous memorial building, with a magnificent panorama of the battlefield, was constructed, one more beautiful even than that commemorating the Battle of Borodino (1812) near Moscow.

G̲h̲āzī ʿOt̲h̲mān Pas̲h̲a's defences around Plewna left a deep imprint on subsequent Western fortifica-tion, the Plewna profile and concept of defence being used in the newer works around Verdun, the principal fortress of France, as well as in the "Position Amster-dam" and in the forts of Chatham (Twydale Redoubt).

After World War II, the city of Pleven, which already before the war had a considerable amount of industry (textiles, canned food, chocolate and metalwork) shot up to become one of the largest in-dustrial centres of northern Bulgaria, with a present population of over 100,000. Until the early 1970s, on-ly one miserable wooden mosque was still standing in Pleven, no longer used by the minuscule Muslim community. Disregarding the earthworks of 1877, not a single Ottoman building remains to testify to the long Islamic past of the town, a situation exemplary for the fate of Islamic culture in south-eastern Europe after the end of Islamic rule.

Bibliography: F. Kanitz, *Donau-Bulgarien und der Balkan*[2], Leipzig 1882, ii, esp. 76 ff. (remarks on early history are worthless); Mouzaffer Pascha-Talaat Bey, *Défence de Plevna d'après les documents of-ficiels et privés réunis sour la direction de muchir Ghazi Osman Pascha*, Paris 1889; C. Jireček, *Das Fürsten-thum Bulgarien*, Prague-Vienna-Leipzig 1891, 189, 286, 545; E.W. von Herbert, *The Defence of Plevna*, London 1895, repr. Ankara 1990 (Turkish tr. Nureddin Artan, *Plevne müdafaası*, Istanbul 1945); J. Trifonov, *Istorija na grada Pleven do osvoboditelnata voina*, Sofia 1933 (rich material); Ž. Čankov, *Geografski rečnik na Bălgarija*, Sofia 1939, 340-2; Agâh Sırrı Levend, *Ġazavāt-nāmeler ve Mihaloğlu Ali Bey'in Ġazavāt-nāmesi*, Ankara 1956; R. Furneaux, *The siege of Plevna*, London 1958 (rich and balanced ac-count); I. Penkov, *Pleven*, Sofia 1962; Şerafettin Turan, *İA*, art. *Plevne*; M. Tayyib Gökbilgin, *İA*, art, *Mihaloğlu*; Tsv. and G. Todorova, *Pleven, putevoditel*, Sofia 1977; Mihaila Stajnova, *Osmanskite biblioteki v bălgarskite zemi*, Sofia 1982, 150-4; *Ent-

siklopedija Bălgarija, v, Sofia 1986, art. *Pleven*. The Ottoman sources used here are unpublished, and have not been used previously by those writing about Pleven; hence the picture of the early history of the town as given here differs greatly from that in the works cited above.

The date of construction of the important Ḳurs͟hunlu D̲j̲āmiʿ is given as a chronogram, *mesd̲j̲id-i aḳṣā-yī t̲h̲ānī oldī* (Trifonov, 44-5), which Trifonov and those following him took for 927/1521, instead of the correct 981/1573-4. (M. Kiel)

PLOVDIV [see FILIBE].

POLEY [see BULĀY].

POMAKS, the name given to a Bulgarian-speaking group of Muslims in Bulgaria and Thrace, now divided amongst Bulgaria, Greece and the Macedonian Republic of Yugoslavia. This name, which is usually given them by their Christian fellow-countrymen, used also to be given occasionally by Bulgarians to Muslims speaking Serbian in western Macedonia. There, however, the Serbian Muslims are usually called *torbeši* (sing. *torbeš*) by their Christian fellow-citizens, sometimes also *poturi*, more rarely *kurki*, etc. How far these Serbian Muslims were still called Pomaks by some people in the early 20th century depended mainly on the influence of the Bulgarian school and literature, and would only be correctly applied when used of Muslims who had actually migrated from Bulgaria, e.g. in 1877-8 (cf. J.H. Vasiljević, *Južna Stara Srbija*, i, 187-8, 207, 236). In the Rhodopes, the Bulgarian Muslims are also called *achrjani* (*ch* = *k̲h̲*) or *agarjani* (Ischirkoff, ii, 15). In some parts of Southern Serbia and Bulgaria, the name *čitak* (pl. *čitaci*) is occasionally heard, and it used sometimes to be said (e.g. by A. Urošević, in *Glasnik Skopskog naučnog društva*, v [1929], 319-20) that this name was only given to Serbs converted to Islam; the truth seems to be, however, that this name is limited to Turks in the two countries (cf. H. Vasiljević, *Muslimani...*, 34, and Elezović, in *Srpski književni glasnik*, xxviii [1929], 610-14, and in *Rečnik kosovskometohiskog dijalekta*, ii, 449). No more correct is the statement that *apovci* is the name given to Serbian Muslims in Southern Serbia, for this seems to be a name applied to one another only by Albanians who are closely related to one another (brothers and cousins, according to H. Vasiljević, *Muslimani...*, 34).

The origin and the etymology of these names are in part more or less obscure and arbitrary. The usual explanation that the name Pomak comes from the verb *pomoći* "to help" and means helper (*pomagači*), i.e. auxiliary troops of the Turks, was first given by F. Kanitz (*Donau-Bulgarien und der Balkan*, ii, Leipzig 1882, 182), but was soon afterwards (1891) declared by Jireček (see *Bibl.*) to be inadequate. Another equally improbable popular etymology is that which explains Pomak by the Bulgarian word *măk* = "torment, force", and justifies this explanation by saying that the conversion of the Bulgars to Islam on a considerable scale was carried out by force and constraint (Ischirkoff, ii, 15). In 1933, Iv. Lekov (see *Bibl.*) explained the name Pomak from *poturnjak* (lit. "one made a Turk"). Whether the word *čomaḳ*, which in Turkish means "club, cudgel", in Uyg̲h̲ur "Muslim" and in South Russia "pedlar" (cf. Barthold, *Histoire des Turcs d'Asie Centrale*, Paris 1945, 73-4), is in any way connected with Pomak, or has been influenced by the Bulgarian *poturnjak* or confused with it, has still to be investigated.

1. History of the Pomaks from their origin to the Second World War.

The history of the conversion of the "Pomaks" and "Torbeši" is very little known in detail. In any case the adoption of Islam did not take place everywhere at once but was gradual and at different periods. A beginning was made immediately after the battle of Marica (1371) and after the fall of Trnovo (1393); many Serbs and Bulgars at this time, and especially, as Jireček thought, the nobles and the Bogomils among these, adopted Islam. After these first conversions under Bāyazīd II, considerable numbers of converts were made according to native tradition in the reign of Selīm I (1512-20); for this purpose he is said to have sent his "favourite Sinān Pas̲h̲a" into the territory of the Šar mountains. The highlands of Čepino (in the Rhodopes) were converted, according to local histories, in the beginning of the 17th century; according to Jireček (*Fürstenthum*, 104), however, not till the middle, in the reign of Meḥemmed IV (1648-87); the Grand Vizier Meḥmed Köprülü is said to have taken a leading part in the work. The conversion to Islam of the Danube territory (Loveč, etc.) is put in this period. Towards the end of this century (sc. the 17th) further conversions took place among the Serbs in the Debar region. In some districts Islam only gained a footing on a large scale in the course of the 18th century and sometimes not till the beginning of the 19th (e.g. in Gora, south of Prizren).

Until the early 20th century, one was very often inclined to believe that these conversions to Islam were made under compulsion, even by force of arms, but subsequently the view began to prevail that the authorities never took any direct steps to proselytise their Christian subjects; conversion was on the contrary voluntary and for quite different reasons except in a few exceptional cases (cf. e.g. H. Vasiljević, *Muslimani...*, esp. 53-61).

Towards the end of the 19th century, when the process of conversion had ceased for decades everywhere, the great majority of the Slav Muslims (Bulgar and Serb) were to be found in the Rhodopes and the mountains of eastern Macedonia and in groups of considerable size up and down Macedonia as far as the Albanian frontier, a wide area which stretched in the north from Plovdiv (Philippopolis) to Salonika in the south and in the east from the central course of the Arda over the Vardar and even beyond the Crni Drim, i.e. across the districts of Ohrid, Debar, Gostivar and Prizren to the west. At that time only a small part of this territory, which was interspersed with Christian areas, belonged to the principality of Bulgaria; the greater part was still Turkish, and only after the Balkan War passed to Serbia or after the First World War to the former Yugoslavia. In addition to the main body of Muslim Bulgars in the Rhodopes mountains, there were at the same time also sporadic groups north of the Balkan range in the Danube territory, in the circles of Loveč, Pleven (Plevna) and Orehovo (Rahovo).

Since then, however, the frontiers of the "Pomaks" have receded considerably. During the siege of Plevna almost all the Bulgarian Muslims fled from the Danube districts to Macedonia; although they returned in 1880, they soon afterwards migrated into Turkey. After the union of eastern Rumelia and Bulgaria in 1885, the Rhodopes "Pomaks" also began to emigrate. The frontiers of the "Torbeši" likewise were not unaffected. The Balkan War and the First World War brought about certain changes which resulted in the migration of some bodies of Serbian Muslims out of Southern Serbia.

As regards the distribution of these Muslim Slavs according to countries, the following statistics may be quoted. In what used to be the principality of ulgaria Jireček estimated (1891) their number at ıost 28,000 souls, and before the Balkan War there ere within the old frontiers of Bulgaria (according to fficial statistics of 1910) 21,143 (0.49% of the opulation). In the lands acquired in the Balkan War Southern Bulgaria there were, however, many ıore Pomaks, mainly in the regions of the rivers Ara, Mesta and Struma, so that the official census of 920 makes their number 88,399 (1.82% of the whole opulation). A somewhat higher figure was given by ıe *Annuaire du Monde Musulman* for 1929 (305), namely 16,000 Pomaks in Bulgaria proper and 75,337 in 'hrace, i.e. 91,337 in all. The 1926 census gave 02,351 Bulgarian-speaking Muslims in Bulgaria, i.e. .87% of the population, while the number of Auslims in Bulgaria without distinguishing their anguages was then 789,296 or 14.41% of the population. Of these 102,351 Bulgarian-speaking Muslims nly 5,799 lived in the towns and the remaining 6,552 in the villages. Literate Pomaks in the whole f Bulgaria in 1926 numbered only 6,659 in 1926 (of vhom 5,534 were men).

The number of Pomaks (in reality of Muslim lavs) in Macedonia was, according to S. Verkovič 1889; see *Bibl.*) 144,051 men.

As regards the number of Serbian-speaking Auslims in Southern Serbia, they were estimated y H. Vasiljević (*Muslimani*..., 11 ff.), whose calculaions were, however, to some extent based on the ituation before the Balkan War, at 100,000 souls; in 935 the figure was put at 60,000 and the number of erbo-Croat-speaking Muslims in the whole of the ormer Yugoslavia at about 900,000 (exact figures ould not be given because the statistics according to eligions had not been published).

For Thrace, the figure of 75,337 Muslim Bulgars ıas already been given from the *Annuaire*; in Western Thrace there were, according to the inter-Allied cenus (of March 1920), 11,739 (cf. *La question de la Thrace*, ed. by the Comité suprême des réfugiés de Thrace, Sofia 1927).

On these statistics, the following observations may oe made. The Bulgars (e.g. Kănčov) usually included as "Pomaks" all the Macedonian Slavs of Muslim aith, i.e. including Serbs from Southern Serbia. On he other hand, on account of their religion these Muslim Slavs were sometimes carelessly counted with he Turks. Moreover, some statistics were not completely free from chauvinistic and political bias. The European estimates, finally, were based on approximations or were quite arbitrary.

In spite of the fact that the Pomaks and Torbeši are occasionally included among the Turks and in spite of the fact that they sometimes call themselves Turks, they are nevertheless the purest stratum of the old Bulgarian or Serbian population, as the case may be, who have preserved their Slav type and Slav language (especially archaic words) very well, sometimes even better—as a result of their being cut off from the Christians and their isolation in outlying districts—than their Christian kinsmen, who have been constantly exposed to admixture from other ethnic elements. They have a certain feeling of aversion for the Turks, whose language they do not understand. It is only in the towns that we find that in course of time some of these Slavs have adopted the Turkish language. What bound them to the Ottomans was not language, but principally a common religion, with its prescriptions and customs (e.g. the veiling of women), which along with Turkish rule naturally imposed upon them many Arabic and Turkish words. In spite of this, there have survived among them many pre-Islamic customs and reminiscences of Christianity (observation of certain Christian festivals, etc.).

That the Bulgar Muslims in particular occasionally (esp. in 1876-8) fought alongside the Turks against the Christian Bulgars may be ascribed to the fact that, as a result of their low cultural level, they made no clear distinction between nation and religion and that their Christian fellow-countrymen treated them as Turks and not as kinsmen. These mistakes were repeated in the Balkan War, when the victorious Bulgar troops and the Orthodox priests were led so far as to convert the Pomaks in the Rhodopes and other districts to Christianity, mainly by pressure and force of arms. But on the conclusion of peace, they returned to Islam again. This was frankly admitted by the Bulgarian geographer Iširkov (Ischirkoff) and the Bulgarian writer Iv. Karaivanov (in his Bulgar periodical *National Education*, Küstendil 1931, according to Ćamalović [see *Bibl.*]).

A century or so ago, the songs and ballads of the "Pomaks" were the subject of much dispute. A Bosnian ex-cleric, Stefan Verković (1827-93), an antique dealer in Seres, published under the title of *Veda Slavena* (i.e. the "Veda of the Slavs", Belgrade 1874, vol. i) a collection of songs which were alleged to have been collected mainly among Pomaks and which celebrated "pre-Christian and pre-historic" subjects (the immigration into the country, discovery of corn, of wine, of writing and legends of gods with Indian names, of Orpheus, etc.). A. Chodzko, A. Dozon (*Chansons populaires bulgares inédites*, Paris 1875; cf. also *Revue de littérature comparée*, xiv [1934], 155 ff.) and L. Geitler (*Poetické tradice Thrákŭ i Bulharů*, Prague 1878) also strongly supported belief in this "Veda"; it was even assumed that the Pomaks were descended from the ancient Thracians, who had been influenced first by Slav culture and then by Islam.

But of ballads on such subjects neither the Muslim nor the Christian Bulgars knew anything, and Jireček, who investigated the question on the spot, repeatedly described this "Slav Veda" as the fabrication of some Bulgarian teachers (*Fürstenthum*, 107[1]). We now know that Verković's chief collaborator was the Macedonian teacher Iv. Gologanov (cf. Pentscho Slawejkoff, *Bulgarische Volkslieder*, Leipzig 1919, 15).

In view of the fact that the Muslims in question consist mainly of conservative dwellers in the mountains and villages, they were for the most part illiterate and there could be no possibility of any literary activity among them. The only people among them who could write are the khōdjas, who frequently used the Turkish language and Arabic alphabet when writing. They also frequently used the latter alphabet when writing their mother tongue. (It is interesting to note that, even today (1993), the Pomaks in Greek Western Thrace have new Ottoman Turkish schoolbooks in the Arabic script.) Of earlier generations of Bulgar Muslims, many distinguished themselves in the Turkish army or otherwise in the Turkish service.

Bibliography (in addition to works mentioned in the text): C. Jireček, *Geschichte der Bulgaren*, Prague 1876, 356, 457, 520, 568 and 578; idem, *Das Fürstenthum Bulgarien*, Prague-Vienna-Leipzig 1891, 102-8 (the principal passage), 310, 346, 353, 453-6; S.I. Verkovič, *Topografičesko-ethnografičeskij očerk Makedonij*, St. Petersburg 1889 (gives full tables of the numbers of Pomaks in some districts and even villages); V. Kănčov, *Makedonija etnografija i statistika*, Sofia 1900, 40-53 (where a portion of the older literature is given, esp. p. 42) with an ethnographical map of Bulgaria on which these

"Muslim Bulgar" settlements are specially marked; J. Cvijić, *Osnove za geografiju i geologiju Makedonije i Stare Srbije*, i, Belgrade 1906, 182; Vl. R. Đorđević, *U Srednjim Rodopima, putopisne beleške od Plovdiva do Čepelara*, in *Nova iskra*, Year 8 (Belgrade 1906), 172-6, 198-205 (interesting description of a Serbian journey in the year 1905 on the life and customs of the Pomaks); M. Gavrilović, in *Grande Encyclopédie*, s.v.; A. Ischirkoff, *Bulgarien, Land und Leute*, ii, Leipzig 1917, 14-17; J. Hadži Vasiljević, *Muslimani naše krvi u Južnoj Srbiji*[2], Belgrade 1924; idem, *Skoplje i njegova okolina*, Belgrade 1930, 314; J.M. Pavlović, *Maleševo i Maleševci*, Belgrade 1929, 35, 244-5, 251; S. Ćemalović, *Muslimani u Bugarskoj*, in *Gajret*, Year 8 (Sarajevo 1932), 345-5, 364-5, 375-6 (also in *La Nation Arabe* for 1932, nos. 10-12); A. Bonamy, *Les musulmans de Pologne, Roumanie et Bulgarie*, in *REI* (1932) (deals with the Pomaks (p. 88) very superficially); Iv. Lekov, *Kăm văpros za imeto pomak* (On the question of the name "Pomak"), in *Sbornik poluvekovna Bălgarija*, Sofia 1933, 38-100 (cf. *Bibliographie Géographique Internationale*, Paris 1933, 317, which also quotes a short article by G. Ivanov on the history of the Loveč-Pomaks (*Za minaloto na lovčenskite pomaci*), appeared in *Loveč i Lovčensko*, v, Sofia 1933); *Annuaire statistique du royaume de Bulgarie*, Sofia 1934, 23, 25, 28.

(F. Bajraktarević)

The preceding article skilfully brings together what was known of the Pomaks on the eve of the Second World War. One can, however, add to the bibliography for that period certain items not noted there or which have appeared since 1935, such as: L. Miletič, *Lovčanskite Pomaci*, in *Bălgarski Pregled*, v/5 (Sofia 1899), 67-78; St. Šiškov, *Pomacite v trite bălgarski oblasti: Trakija, Makedonija i Mizija*, Plovdiv 1914 (cf. a notice on this work, *Les Bulgares mahometans des Rhodopes et les traces du christianisme dans leur vie*, in *En terre d'Islam*, vi/51 [Nov.-Dec. 1931], 387-8); idem, *Bălgaro-mohamedanite (Pomaci). Istoriko-zemepisen i narodoučen pregled s obrazi*, Plovdiv 1936 (cf. an especially useful review by M.S. Filipović, in *Pregled*, xi/166 [Sarajevo, Oct. 1937], 673-9; Ahmet Cevat Eren, *Pomaklar*, in *İA*, ix, 572-6; idem, *Pomaklara dair*, in *Turk Kültürü*, i/4 (Ankara 1963), 37-41; Ch. Vakarelski, *Altertümliche Elemente in Lebensweise und Kultur der bulgarischen Mohammedaner*, in *Zeitschr. für Balkanologie*, iv (Berlin 1966), 149-72; N. Kaufman, *Pesni na Bălgarite mohamedani ot Rodopite*, in *Rodopski Zbornik*, ii (Sofia 1969), 41-130; B. Lory, *Une communauté musulmane oubliée: les Pomaks de Loveč*, in *Turcica*, xix (1987), 95-116.

In regard to the thorny problem of the Islamisation of the Pomaks, see the viewpoint of St. Dimitrov, *Demografski otnošenija i pronikvaneto na islama v zapadnite Rodopi i dolinata na Mesta prez XV-XVI v.*, in *Rodopski Zbornik*, i (1965), 165-84.

2. The Pomaks during the Second World War.

Being one of the Axis Powers, Fascist-controlled Bulgaria was awarded by Hitler, on the one hand, the southern territories of contemporary Serbia (or Old Serbia, *Stara Srbija* or *Južna Srbija*) and on the other, western Thrace (belonging to Greece), which meant that, from 1941 to 1944, the Pomaks of the Balkans found themselves united within one state. Our knowledge of their situation at that time varies from region to region, but everywhere it was extremely bad: social and economic deprivation, a deplorable health position and continual discrimination on the part of the authorities, religious and cultural oppression, driving the Pomaks towards a "religious fanaticism", according to the expression used b[y] Bulgarian authors themselves.

On the Bulgarian occupation of south Serbi[a] (which in 1944 became part of Yugoslavia[n] Macedonia), see the collective work (from a pro[-] Macedonian, extremely anti-Bulgarian viewpoint[)] called *Denacionalizatorska dejnost na bugarskite kulturno[-] prosvetni institucii vo Makedonija (Skopska i Bitolska okupa[-] ciona oblast 1941-1944)*, Skopje 1974.

On the Pomaks of Bulgaria proper, see V. Božinov[,] *Bălgarite mohamedani prez Vtorata svetovna vojna (1939[-] 9.IX.1944)*, in *Iz minaloto na Bălgarite mohamedani [v] Rodopite*, Sofia 1958, 137-44; idem, *Bălgarit[e] mohamedani i văorăženata borba sreštu fašizma*, in *ibid.* 144-51, where some further references can be found[.] (It should be mentioned in passing that a law is sai[d] to have been passed on 8 July 1942 concerning th[e] compulsory Bulgarisation of names borne by th[e] Pomaks, and that 60,000 of them had to change thei[r] names at this time.) On the participation of som[e] Pomaks in the anti-Fascist struggle at the side of th[e] "partisans" (i.e. Bulgarian Communists) towards th[e] end of 1944, see *Iz minaloto*..., 148-51; Ju. Memišev[,] *Učastieto na bălgarskite Turci protiv kapitalizma i fašizm[a] 1919-1944*, Sofia 1977.

As for the Pomaks of Greek Western Thrace (th[e] southern part of the Rhodope Mountains) at thi[s] time, we possess a piece of evidence (rapid and in complete, it is true, but completely first-hand) fron the Orthodox Bulgarian Patriarch Kiril, who visite[d] these regions in 1943-4: Kiril, patriarh bălgarski *Bălgaromohamedanski selišta v Južni Rodopi (Ksantijsko Gjumjurdžinsko) toponimno, etnografsko i istoričesko izsled vane*, Sofia 1960. This contains much information or the daily life of this people (especially on the ethnographic level), but also on the general atmosphere in these isolated mountain villages. The local Pomaks were often hostile to their visitor; they spoke Bulgarian and knew no Turkish whatsoever, their womenfolk were only very rarely veiled; polygamy was unknown; divorce was very rare; but the villages adjacent to the plain were, more and more, becoming slowly Turkicised. On the religious and cultural level should be noted the survival of certain Christian customs, the fact that the dead were buried in the direction of Mecca and the existence of mosques in the villages (but only one *tekke* is mentioned, in the district of Šahin, whilst the *medreses* were all in ruins).

3. The Pomaks from the end of the Second World War to the present time.

Since 1945, the history of the Pomaks in the Balkans can be followed in two countries only, Bulgaria and Greece, in the light of the fact that, the Communist Yugoslavian authorities having set up a "Socialist Federal Republic of Macedonia", all the Slavonic-speaking Muslims of the region became *ipso facto* the Muslim Macedonians. There are, moreover, relatively few works on this group of Muslims of former Yugoslavia. See e.g. J.F. Trifunoski, *Za torbešite vo porečieto na Markova Reka*, in *Godišen Zbornik (Fil. Fak.)*, iv/1 (Skopje 1951), 3-11; D.Hr. Konstantinov, *Makedonci muslimani*, in *Prilozi, Društvo za nauka i umetnost*, xv (Bitola 1970), 139-46; and above all, N. Limanoski, *Etno-socijalne karakteristike islamizevanih Makedonaca*, Belgrade 1991 (unpubl. thesis); and then, in a much wider perspective, A. Popovic, *L'Islam balkanique. Les musulmans du sud-est européen dans la période post-ottomane*, Berlin-Wiesbaden 1986; idem, *Les musulmans yougoslaves (1945-1989). Médiateurs et métaphores*, Lausanne 1990. One can nevertheless wonder whether the present dissolution of the Comunist countries into ethnic and regional groups may ot bring about the re-appearance some day of the rmer entities of this land, such as the omaks/Pomaci, the Čitaks/Čitaci, the Torbeš/ 'orbeši, the Gorans/Corani, etc. We shall know at me future time, but at the present moment, mongst these diverse groups, the Gorani (Slavonic-peaking Muslims of Skopska Crna Gora) alone speak f themselves and seem to display a certain ohesiveness, through the medium of a handful of pokesmen, notably vis-à-vis the Turkish and Alba-ian Muslims of Macedonia.

The Pomaks of Bulgaria (peasants and shepherds of he Rhodopes and the region of Razlog and a few ther places, numbering from 150,000 to 200,000 per-ons) continued to endure an extremely difficult situa-ion, within a climate of permanent hostility from the ulgarian Communist authorities. They speak ulgarian and have no knowledge of Turkish, which xcludes them from the very strong Turkish com-nunity of the land, three or four times more umerous and much more structured. Being for the nost part illiterate until recent times and never aving had, in practice, a local "intelligentsia", it vould have been logical to conclude until very recent-y that their assimilation was only a question of time. Meanwhile, they are considered in Bulgaria (and they re still taken into consideration) rather as "lost hildren" of the nation. Their religiosity (which is, in act, more like an attachment to a sort of "popular slam") has had to suffer since 1945 the ravages of ime (notably under the continual attacks of Soviet-style "scientific atheism"). Official Bulgarian ublications on the local Pomaks (since 1945) are omewhat condescending. They set forth unanimous-y their very backward cultural state in relationship to he rest of the Orthodox Bulgarian populaltion, but trongly insist that they are indigenous Bulgarians vhich various forces and "malevolent" tendencies nave tried, on many occasions, either to assimilate to he Turks or to separate from their ethnic brothers nd homeland. See e.g. P. Marinov, *Iz mirogleda na sredno rodopskite Bălgari-mohamedani*, in *Bălgarski narod*, i/1, Sofia 1947; N. Vrančev, *Bălgari mohamedani (Pomaci)*, Sofia 1948; V. Božinov, *Bălgarite mohamedani pri narodnata vlast*, in *Iz minaloto...*, 151-6; K. Vasilev, *Rodopskite Bălagari-mohamedani*, Plovdiv 1961; *Narodnostna i bitova obštnost na rodopskite Bălgari*, Sofia 1969; *Bălgarite mohamedani-nerazdelna čast ot bălgarskija narod (preporačitelna bibliografija)*, Blagoevgrad 1971 (with a lengthy bibl.); C. Monov, *Prosvetnoto delo sred Bălgarite s mohamedanska vjara v rodopskija kraj prez godinite na narodnata vlast (1944-1968)*, in *Rodopski Zbornik*, iii (1972), 9-51; A. Promovski, *Bit i kultura na rodopskite Bălgari*, Sofia 1974; P. Petrov, *Razprostranenie na islama v Rodopite*, in *Rodopite v bălgarska istorija*, Veliko Tărnovo 1974, 62-86; K. Kanev, *Srednorodopski (svadbeni) nravi i običai*, in *Rodopi*, 1974/10, 22-6; idem, *Srednorodopski običai*, in *Rodopi*, 1974/11, 22-4; etc. For a diametrically opposed view, amongst numerous publications of this type, see *Rodoplardaki son Türk katliâmının iç yüzü*, Istanbul 1972.

The attempts at forcible (and all other means) assimilation of the Pomaks by the Bulgarian Communist authorities increased to a brutal pitch after 1979 (see e.g. K. Yanatchkov, *Entre le croissant et le marteau: les musulmanes bulgares*, in *L'Alternative* [Paris, Jan.-Feb. 1980] 22-3), culminating dramatically in the events of February-March 1985. From this date onwards, the Western press began to speak on numerous occasions of several dozen (even, of several hundred) deaths: murders committed in the course of the Bulgarisation of names campaign (first amongst the Pomaks, then amongst the Turks of Bulgaria), an action which involved not only the change of names of living persons but also (by means of the civil government registers and the gravestones in cemeteries) those of parents and ancestors. The fall from power of Communism stopped this barbarous policy, and the governments formed after this time have made numerous acts of appeasement and goodwill towards the local Pomaks, especially since the necessity of a coalition (probably tactical and ephemeral) with the political Party of the Bulgarian Turks.

We are relatively well informed about the life of the Pomaks of Greece (around 25,000 to 30,000 persons, and living in the Rhodopes, along the Bulgarian frontier) during this period. These form an exclusively village society, apart from those settled in the towns and settlements of Western Thrace, where they are undergoing a slow Turkification process because of the presence there of a Turkish community, much better organised and three or four times as numerous. It is very much an introspective community, living in a mountain region to which access (since it is a military zone) was forbidden until very recent times to Greeks and foreigners alike and only to be entered with a special permit, difficult to get. The cultural level of this population seems to have remained fairly modest, and in any case we do not have (as is the case for the Pomaks of Bulgaria) any written eye-witness information. What we know at present of it rests on several works which are mainly of an ethnographical and sociological nature. See e.g. B. Vernier, *Rapports de parenté et rapports de domination ... Représentation mythique du monde et domination masculine chez les Pomaques*, diss. Paris, EHESS 1972 unpubl. (a brief analysis of it in Popovic, *L'Islam balkanique*, 169-70); E. Arvanitou, *Turcs et Pomaks en Grèce du Nord (Thrace Occidentale). Une minorité religieuse ou deux minorités nationales, sous une administration hellénique chrétienne*, diss. Univ. de Paris VII, unpubl.; F. de Jong, *Names, religious denomination and ethnicity of settlements in Western Thrace*, Leiden 1980; E. Sarides, *An ethnic-religious minority between Scylla and Charybdis. The Pomaks in Greece*, in *La transmission du savoir dans le monde musulman périphérique. Lettre d'information*, 5 (April 1986), 17-25; idem, *Ethnische Minderheit und zwischenstaatliches Streitobjekt. Die Pomaken in Nordgriechenland*, Berlin 1987. As for the official attitude of the Greek authorities (and of some local authors), this is disconcerting. It is currently maintained that this is a Greek population (or else the descendants of ancient Thracian tribes) completely separate from the Bulgarian Pomaks, a population which was allegedly first of all Bulgarised, and then Islamised, some time later. See e.g. N. Xirotiris, *Personal remarks on the distribution of the frequencies of blood groups amongst the Pomaks* [in Greek], Salonica 1971; Ph. Triarkhis, *The Rhodope administrative district yesterday and today* [in Greek], Salonica 1974; Pan. Photeas *The Pomaks of Western Thrace (a small contribution to a great subject)* [in Greek], Komotini 1976; and finally, three works, also in Greek, recently have appeared: P. Hidiroglou, *The Greek Pomaks and their relations with Turkey*, Athens 1989; Y. Magriotis, *The Pomaks or Rodopeoi*, Athens 1990; and P. Mylonas, *The Pomaks of Thrace*, Athens 1990, on which one can find a lucid analysis by M. Anastasiadou, *Trois livres sur les Pomaks de Grèce*, in *La transmission du savoir ... Lettre d'information*, xi (March 1991), 64-6, who writes specifically, "The feeling which one gets from reading these three works is that the Greek state is not only resolved to begin a new process of assimilating the Pomaks—until now condemned to isolation—but above all wishes to prevent at any price the Pomaks from drawing closer to the Turks of Western Thrace". There is, moreover, no doubt that the fall of the Communist régime in Bulgaria will have as a result the opening-up of this region of Greece and, as a result, the end of the isolation of the local Pomaks.

Bibliography: Given in the article.

(A. Popovic)

PONDOK [see PESANTREN].

PONTIANAK, the name of a part of the former Dutch residency "Wester-Afdeeling" of Borneo, also of the sultanate in the delta of the river Kapuas and of its capital; these are now in the Kalimaintan [*q.v.* in Suppl.] region of the republic of Indonesia [*q.v.*].

As a Dutch province Pontianak included the districts of Pontianak, Kubu, Landak, Sanggau, Sĕkadau, Tajan and Mĕliau. The administration was in the hands of an assistant-resident whose headquarters were in Pontianak where the Resident of the "Wester-Afdeeling" also lived. The Dutch settlement is on the left bank of the Kapuas, where also is the Chinese commercial quarter. The Malay town lies opposite on the right bank.

The sultanate of Pontianak with its capital of the same name was independent under the suzerainty of the Netherlands and was 4,545 km² in area. In 1930 the population consisted of 100,000 Malays and Dayaks, 562 Europeans, 26,425 Chinese and 2,378 other Orientals. The term Malays includes all native Muslims, among them many descendants of Arabs, Javanese, Buginese, and Dayaks converted to Islām. The Dayaks in the interior are still heathen. Roman Catholic missions are at work among the latter and the Chinese. The very mixed population is explained by the origin and development of Pontianak.

The town was founded in 1772 by the Sharīf ʿAbd al-Raḥmān, a son of the Sharīf Ḥusayn b. Aḥmad al-Ḳadrī, an Arab who settled in Matan in 1735 and who in 1771 died in Mampawa as vizier, revered for his piety. In 1742 ʿAbd al-Raḥmān was born, the son of a Dayak concubine, and very early distinguished himself by his spirit of enterprise. He attempted to gain the ruling power, successively in Mampawa, Palembang and Bandjarmasin, from which he had to retire with his band of pirates, although the sultan had been his patron, after he had taken several European and native ships. By this time, he had married a princess of Mampawa and Bandjarmasin and possessed great wealth. On his return to Mampawa, his father had just died. As he met with no success here, he decided to found a town of his own with a number of other fortune-seekers. An uninhabited area at the mouth of the junction of the Landak with the Kapuas, notorious as a dangerous haunt of evil spirits, seemed to him suitable. After the spirits had been driven away by hours of cannon fire, he was the first to spring ashore, had the forest cut down and built rude dwellings there for himself and his followers.

The favourable position of the site and the protection which trade enjoyed there soon attracted Buginese, Malay and Chinese merchants to it so that Pontianak developed rapidly and Sharīf ʿAbd al-Raḥmān was able by his foresight and energy to hold his own against the neighbouring kingdoms of Matan, Sukadana, Mampawa and Sanggau.

He appointed chiefs over each of the different groups of people and regulated trade by reasonable tariffs. He was able to impress representatives of the Dutch East Indian Co. in Batavia to such an extent that they gave him the kingdoms of Pontianak and Sanggau as fiefs after the company had bought off the claims of Banten to Western Borneo. As early as 1772 the Buginese prince Radja Ḥādjdjī had given him the title of sultan. After his death in 1808, his son Sharīf Ḳāsim succeeded him. He was the first to change the Arab ceremonial at the court for more modern ways.

According to the treaty concluded with the Dutch Indies government in 1855, the sultan received a fixed income from them while they administered justice and policed the country. The relationship to the Dutch Indies government was defined in a long agreement of 1912, which also settled the administration of justice and the taxes. From the local treasury, then constituted, the sultan received 6,800 guilders a month; he also received 50% of the excise on agriculture and mines.

In keeping with the nature of its origin, Pontianak is predominantly Muslim in character and a relatively large number take part in the pilgrimage to Mecca. For these pilgrims, who are known as Djāwa Funtiana, the sultan, when he performed the pilgrimage in the 1880s, founded several *wakf* houses in the holy city.

The main support of the whole population is agriculture and along with it trade in the products of the jungle. The exports are copra, pepper, gambir, sago, rubber and rotan, especially to Singapore and Java. Rice, clothing and other articles required by Europeans and the more prosperous Chinese and Arabs are imported. The import and export trade is mainly in the hands of the Chinese. They live together in the Chinese quarter in the European half of Pontianak on the left bank where also the other foreign Orientals have settled. This is therefore the centre of trade and commerce in the valley of the Kapuas.

In the swampy lands of Pontianak, intercourse with the outer world is amost exclusively by water. Only in the 1920s and 1930s were motor-roads laid over the higher ground from Pontianak to Mampawa and Sambas, to Sungei Kakap and from Mandor to Landak.

Bibliography: P.J. Veth, *Borneo's Wester-Afdeeling*; J.J.K. Enthoven, *Bijdragen tot de geographie van Borneo's Wester-Afdeeling*, in *Tijdschrift Kon. Aardrijkskundig Genootschap* (1912, 203-10).

(A.W. Nieuwenhuis)

POONA [see PŪNA].

PORPHYRY [see FURFŪRIYŪS].

PORT SAʿĪD (A. Būr Saʿīd), a seaport on the Mediterranean coast of Egypt at the northern extremity of the Suez Canal and on its western bank (lat. 31° 16′ N., long. 32° 19′ E.). It is connected with Cairo, 233 km/145 miles away, by a standard-gauge railway constructed in 1904 via Zagāzīg and Ismāʿīliyya, and also with Damietta and Alexandria. After the construction of the Suez Canal, it became the second seaport of Egypt after Alexandria, and is now the chef-lieu of a governorate (*muḥāfaẓa*) of the same name. The population of the governorate (1986 estimate) was 382,000 and of the town itself 374,000.

Port Saʿīd was founded in 1859, as soon as the Suez Canal was decided, during the reign of Saʿīd Pasha [*q.v.*], Viceroy of Egypt, and was named after him. Except for the strip of sand which, varying in width between 200 and 300 yards, separates Lake Manzala from the Mediterranean, the site of the present town was under the water. This site was selected by a party of engineers under Laroche and de Lesseps, not on account of being the nearest point across the isthmus to Suez, but because the depth of the water there corresponded most favourably to the requirements of the projected canal. As soon as work was started on the

Canal, five wooden houses were constructed above the water, supported on massive piles and equipped with a bakery and a water-distillery for the use of the pioneers. A year later, dredgers began to deepen the waters of the newly established harbour, and the mud thus raised was immediately utilised for more buildings, besides the workshops, covering 30,000 square metres in all. This, however, did not suffice for the rapid growth of the population as the work on the Canal progressed towards Ismāᶜīliya. To meet this emergency, and in the absence of stone quarries within reasonable reach of Port Saᶜīd, the manufacture of artificial stones capable of resisting the action of sea-water was begun by Messrs. Dussaud in 1865. Details of this process are given in ᶜAlī Pas̲h̲a Mubārak's *K̲h̲iṭaṭ* (x, 38-40). These stones weighed about 22 tons each and were used both for the construction of the two huge breakwaters of the outer harbour and for the creation of further building ground. In the same year, mail boats sailed up the Canal to Ismāᶜīliya while others brought imports to Port Saᶜīd. In 1868 the breakwaters were finished, and in 1869 the Canal was completed. As a result, the town was thronged by consuls and representatives of many nations, and the population reached 10,000.

By the end of the 19th century, Port Saᶜīd was the world's largest coal bunkering station, primarily for the Canal transit trade, and in the early 20th century the point of export for cotton, rice and other agricultural products of the eastern Nile Delta region and also a centre for fish processing. Its many public buildings included the headquarters of the Suez Canal Company, and by 1907 the population numbered 49,884. Its outer harbour, covering an area of 570 acres, its two moles or breakwaters built in such a way as to protect the Canal from the continuous onrush of sea-water and sand-drifts, and its docks numbering originally three on the western bank, all had to be extended. A large floating dock (259 ft. long, 85 ft. wide and 18 ft. deep, with a lifting capacity of 3,500 tons) was constructed; and, further, in the years 1903-9, new docks were established on the eastern bank. To accommodate the workmen on these docks, the new town of Port Fuʾād, named after the then King of Egypt, Fuʾād I [*q.v.*], sprang up on the east side.

To safeguard the ships approaching the Canal by night, the K̲h̲edive Ismāᶜīl ordered four lighthouses to be erected at the expense of the Egyptian Government at Rosetta, Burullus, Burd̲j̲ al-ᶜIzba near Damietta, and Port Saᶜīd. The latter one was 174 ft. high and its beam distinct from those of the other three and visible at a distance of 20 miles. It lay at the base of the western mole which, at its seaward extremity, carried a colossal statue of Ferdinand de Lesseps by E. Fermiet, unveiled in 1899.

In 1956 the Egyptian President Gamāl ᶜAbd al-Nāṣir (Nasser) [see ᶜABD AL-NĀṢIR, D̲J̲AMĀL in Suppl.] nationalised the Suez Canal. In the ensuing war of Britain, France and Israel against Egypt during late October-early November 1956, Port Saᶜīd was severely damaged by air attacks and during the British and French landings, with the statue of de Lesseps, amongst other things, being destroyed. After the war, the damages were repaired and the Canal re-opened, but during the Six Days' War of June 1967 Israeli forces advanced to the eastern bank of the Canal and occupied the territory of western Sinai up to that bank. The Canal remained closed for several years. But after the Camp David Accords of 1978 and the Israel-Egypt Peace Treaty of 1979, the use of the Canal revived and the revenue from transit dues has become a significant part of Egypt's income, with Port Saᶜīd returning to something of its former prosperity.

Bibliography: The chief contemporary source is ᶜAlī Pas̲h̲a Mubārak, *al-K̲h̲iṭaṭ al-Tawfīḳiyya*, 20 vols., Cairo (Būlāḳ) 1305-6. See also 1. publications on the Suez Canal and its history; 2. the annual *Taḳwīm*s, Annuaires statistiques and the Trade Returns issued by the Egyptian Government and the Suez Canal Company; 3. guides to Egypt such as Baedeker's, Murray's (ed. Mary Brodrick) and Cook's (ed. Sir E.A. Wallis Budge).

(A.S. ATIYA*)

POSTA (Ital. *posta*), borrowed into Ottoman Turkish and Arabic in the 19th century in the forms *p/bōsta, p/bōsṭa* to designate the new conception of European-style postal services in the Near East. In more recent times, it has been replaced at the formal level by *barīd* [*q.v.*], a revival of the mediaeval Arabic term for the state courier and intelligence services, but *būsta/būsṭa* and *būstad̲j̲ī* "postman" continue in use in the Arab Levant at the informal level, and *posta* remains the standard term in Modern Turkish. In modern Persian also *post*, from the French *poste*, is used. (ED.)

POSTA, postage stamps. Postage stamps (Ar. *ṭābiᶜ* [*barīdī*]; Pers. *tambr*; Tk. *pul*) are a Western innovation. The world's first postage stamp—the "penny black" bearing the portrait of young Queen Victoria—was issued by Great Britain in 1840. There exists an evident connection between the spread of the "postage stamp revolution" and European overseas expansion. Besides Great Britian, other European countries, above all France, but also Austria, Germany, Italy and Spain were responsible for the founding of postal services and the diffusion of stamps in North Africa and the Middle East. Foreign post offices of these countries were opened e.g. in Lebanon, Syria, Palestine, Morocco, Libya, and Egypt. They issued the stamps of their countries, and as a result the dispatching point of these stamps is only to be identified by the postal cancellations. Later, overprints were added. Here, as in other cases, the foreign post offices cut into revenues that would otherwise have gone to the national post office. The first Middle Eastern countries which joined the parade of stamp-issuing states were: India (1854 with a portrait of Queen Victoria on the first issued stamp, after using issues of the East India Company for two years); the Ottoman Empire (1863); Egypt (1866); Persia (1868); and Afg̲h̲ānistān (1871). The first three of them opened post offices in their "satellite states" using the same practice as the European countries.

Despite the more than one hundred year-old history of stamps in North Africa and the Middle East, "Islamic philately" has not received much attention until recently. This intensified interest is mainly to be explained by the fact that, since the 1960s and the 1970s, the themes on stamps have been diversified and several Islamic countries have begun to use postage stamps as instruments of propaganda. Philately is considered as an ancillary historical and social science discipline, although its skilled use as such is rarely revealed. Unlike its honoured sister numismatics, philately cannot of course provide information on dark periods where written evidence is scarce or unavailable. But it can be of additional value for the analysis of official viewpoints and of cultural and political history; stamps are excellent primary sources for the symbolic messages which governments seek to convey to their citizens and to the world. The same is true of banknotes, because "both are a monopoly—i.e. a sovereign attribute of the state as well as an efficient iconographic propaganda vehicle thereof. They can tell us something about the official discourse of the state, the one for which it attempts to ensure ideological hegemony'' (Sivan 1987, 21). For modern times, the symbolism of stamps is more useful for the historian than that of coins because stamps are more varied and less conservative.

Which types of historical evidence are to be found on stamps in detail? Stamps can be studied from the "inside" and the "outside". Under the latter we understand the stamp as a "physical and economic object" (cf. Hazard 1959/1980, 200 ff.), made up of paper, ink, glue, etc., marked by inscriptions, overprints and denominations. An enquiry into the quantity and quality of these components (kind of paper, method of printing, perforation, watermark, overprint types and settings, etc.) is not merely of limited interest for the collector or the historian of printing technology and paper manufacturing; an investigation of these aspects can give indications concerning the political and economic situation of the issuing country. A large quantity of new issues has normally two causes: either the state is fully appreciating the propaganda value of stamps (as was the case, for instance, in Iran under the last Shāh, in Libya since the mid-1970s and also in ʿIrāḳ at present under the leadership of Ṣaddām Ḥusayn), or else it is seeking additional revenue. Numerous countries, mostly small and poor, have abandoned their prerogative to represent themselves in favour of financial advantages. They have entrusted Western agencies with the production of stamps on any possible occasion and with their promotion to dealers and collectors. Many of these stamps never touch the shores of the countries that issue them. The stamps display themes which have mostly nothing to do with the heritage of the issuing countries: astronauts, European paintings, famous people of the world (such as J.F. Kennedy, the Prince of Wales and Princess Diana), or international sports events. For the Islamic countries, this practice was used e.g. by Afghānistān under the reign of Ẓāhir Shāh, by North Yemen (since 1962), by Mauritania, Ḳaṭar (since 1961), and the poor Persian Gulf shaykhdoms (ʿAdjmān, with even special issues for its exclave Manāma, Dubayy, Fudjayra, Raʾs al-Khayma, al-Shāriḳa, Umm al-Ḳaywayn) in the 1960s, with the noticeable exception of Abū Ẓaby that possesses 90% of the present-day's United Arab Emirates' oil wealth. The other extreme is found in Lebanon, where no stamps were printed in 1976-7, in 1979, and between 1985 and 1987. Due to the civil war, Lebanon issued not more than 100 stamps over the last 14 years. More direct money-raising methods include the issuance of souvenir sheets (also used as a propaganda instrument), postal tax (also called revenue) stamps (several Arab countries, e.g. Syria, printed such stamps for the wars against Israel and subsequent military needs; the Ottoman Empire issued tax stamps during the Balkan War of 1911-12, and the young Turkish Republic printed a large quantity in 1920, reflecting the disastrous situation of the country during these years), and "semi-postal" stamps with premiums for charitable or public purposes (including relief for refugees from the Druze war—Lebanon and Syria, 1926—and for victims of earthquakes, of volcanic eruptions, etc.). A decline in the quality of printing, paper, and perforation points to economic difficulties. For the printing of the Ḥaydarābād stamp of 1946, commemorating the Second World War Victory, many types of paper were used; this is attributable to the scarcity of paper during and immediately after the War (Nayeem 1980, 198-9). Similar problems are suggested in the case of Iran after the Revolution in 1979. A possible reason why the watermark of the Pahlavī stamps was not altered until 1981 is because of a paper shortage. Libya used Egyptian watermarks until 1960; the stamps were printed in Rome, Naples, Cairo or by Bradbury. This dependence on foreign technology can be explained by the extreme poverty of this North African state until the large-scale production and export of oil in the mid-1960s.

Overprints and surcharges are of great historical interest, since they always arise as a result of an emergency. One of the earliest surcharges became necessary when a Persian Postmaster-General resigned and thereafter considered a huge quantity of stamps as his own property, refusing to return them to the post office (nos. 94 ff./1897-9). After the Ottoman entry into the First World War, the Ottoman Post Office ran out of the stocks of the 1914 pictorial set, the plates of which were inaccessible in London. It had to resort to overprinting old stocks of superseded issues. More often, overprints have been used by occupying (see e.g. ʿIrāḳ, occupied in 1918 by units of the Indian army, where Turkish stamps overprinted "BAGHDAD IN BRITISH OCCUPATION" were used; or Lebanon as occupied territory, where Turkish stamps overprinted "E.E.F.", for "Egyptian Expeditionary Force", were issued; or Syria, where in 1919 French stamps were overprinted "T.E.O.", for "*Territoires ennemis occupés*", later changed to "O.M.F.", for "*Occupation militaire française*"), protecting, mandatary, and colonial powers. The date and type of overprints indicate the severity of foreign rule, the degree of dependence and control. Whereas Egypt had the right to issue special stamps of its own, other Ottoman provinces were less autonomous, as was true for ʿIrāḳ; it had to use Turkish postage stamps until the Ottoman Empire was replaced by the British mandatary power. Algeria, being constitutionally part of metropolitan France, had stamps of its own only after 1924. In that year, French stamps were overprinted "ALGÉRIE". Even the post-war issues have continued to omit Arabic, to stress French culture and interests to the exclusion of Arab ones, and to emphasise French dominance. Similar was the practice of the Italian colonial power in Libya, whereas the French protectorate in Tunisia replaced the monolingual inscription "RÉGENCE DE TUNIS" in 1906 by another one in French and Arabic; Palestine as a British mandate after 1920 even used a trilingual inscription in Arabic, English and Hebrew. The autonomy of the ʿAlawī areas, guaranteed by the French after 1924, can be deduced from French stamps overprinted "ALAOUITES-AL-ʿALAWIYYĪN". In the case of nominally independent shaykhdoms, like al-Kuwayt or al-Baḥrayn, the stamps indicate that they were actually under firm British control. After using Indian stamps with no indication of the issuing state's name, the stamps were overprinted (in 1923-4 and 1933 respectively) "KUWAIT/BAHRAIN". After the Partition of India (1947), the same was done with British stamps. The complex postal history of Morocco under foreign control, and of war-time Libya, becomes clear by observing the diversity of overprints and used stamps.

Pākistān's first stamps illustrate the hasty creation of the nation. The first issue consisted of Indian stamps (portrait of King George VI) overprinted "PAKISTAN" by the Indian Security Press at Nasik. Owing to the events after Partition, grave shortages of stamps occurred in many places. It was therefore necessary to supplement the Nasik prints by local overprints in Pākistān. Machine-printed, hand-stamped, typewritten and manuscript overprints thus appeared in many places and under varying conditions; they were sanctioned by the central or provincial governments, and sometimes even by minor authorities down to the village postmaster. All these issues were governed by the same conditions, namely, an acute shortage of Pākistān stamps, a surplus stock of unwanted Indian stamps, and the determination to do something in order that the posts could carry on (Martin 1959/1974, VII, 2). A similar situation in independent Algeria caused at the outset the overprinting of former French issues with the initials "E.A." for "*État Algérien*".

Overprints indicating the new state's name, and similar techniques like the obliterating with black bars of the former ruler's portrait, have been employed in other countries following a drastic change in régime in order to use up old stocks of stamps while demonstrating a complete departure from the past (see e.g. Egypt, 1953, or Iran, 1979). Sometimes former sets are overprinted in order to commemorate an important event in the history of a particular country; in Transjordan, for instance, stamps of 1927 were overprinted one year later, in Arabic script, with the word *dustūr* in order to mark the promulgation of the constitution. Frequent changes in denomination may well reveal economic problems and inflation.

We have yet to mention some further conclusions which can be drawn from the mono- or bilingual inscriptions. The exclusive use of the national language in Islamic countries either underlines the continuity with the Islamic past (by confirming the sanctity of the Arabic script and language; see also the using of Islamic/Christian dates) or growing nationalistic feelings. To quote some examples: Ottoman stamps up to 1876 used exclusively the Turkish language and "Turkish"-style numerals. The inscriptions translate "The Ottoman Empire" and "Postage" (the latter being the western-derived *pōsṭa*, however, rather than the Arabic *barīd*). In 1876 a French inscription and a "Western"-style numeral were added to a set of stamps in order to conform to membership of the new-established Universal Postal Union. With the alphabet reform of 1928, the Arabic script gave way to Latin, after a brief transitional use of both scripts for writing Turkish (1926-8). Ḥidjāzī stamps (1916-25) used only Arabic (compare Yemenī stamps from 1926 till 1930); not until four years after the unification with Nadjd, in 1929, did the Latin script appear for the recording of the state and value. National feelings in Egypt came through, when, during Ismāʿīl's rule, Arabic replaced Turkish as the usual language of administration. The first Egyptian stamps of 1866 (nos. 1-7) bear Turkish-language inscriptions; one year later, Arabic replaced Turkish on stamps (nos. 8 ff./1867). The change in the language came at the time of Ismāʿīl's hard-won acquisition of the title of Khedive, and a few years later (nos. 14 ff./1872) the stamps proudly displayed the Khedivial title. After the recession of British influence on Egypt in 1922, an overprint exclusively in Arabic announced the formal independence of "The Egyptian Kingdom" in that year (nos. 69-81/1922; notice also nos. 82-93/1923-4). This nationalistically-induced omitting of any Western script except for a numeral of value was obviously soon found impractical, because French reappears from 1925 onwards (nos. 94 ff.).

Multilingual inscriptions on postage stamps can also indicate the use of several national languages or be interpreted as a concession to linguistic minorities. Postage stamp series of Ḥaydarābād from 1871 show a value label in four languages (English, Marāthī, Persian-Urdu and Telugu). The secession of East Pākistān (later Bangladesh) can be observed on Pākistānī stamps by the reduction of the former trilingual inscription (English, Urdu, Bengali) to a bilingual one.

Stamps may be considered as a *prima facie* evidence of the existence of postal services, but not as an evidence of postal sovereignty, as the cases of Manāma and Bahāwalpūr [*q.vv.*] show. Until 1947 Bahāwalpūr was a princely state in British India, afterwards forming part of Pakistan; it issued its own stamps between 1947 and 1949, although the post offices in Bahāwalpūr used stamps of Pakistan. The introduction of airmail and special delivery stamps ordinarily indicates the initiation of such a service in a particular country.

The studying of the stamp's "inside", i.e. of its iconography, can be quite illuminating and will be of central concern here. Several factors predestine stamps to propaganda purposes. First, since the discovery of offset printing, stamps are easy and cheap to produce; second, a worldwide spread is potentially possible; third, visual messages are not difficult to understand, i.e. it is possible to make them accessible to persons who are not reached by other communication means; this is especially true of Third World countries, where the percentage of illiterates is high; in regard to Arabic countries, one has to bear in mind also the problem of diglossia. But, whereas the message which is intended to be transmitted to the observer of the stamps is comparatively easy to discern, it is almost impossible to assess its impact upon its target population.

Subjects often dealt with on stamps can be grouped in the following way: national symbols; local deceased heroes; cultural heritage; significant historical and political events and commemoratives; reforms, national progress, and social, economic or cultural achievements; foreign policy (regional, Arabic or Islamic solidarity, international ties); diverse (expositions and fairs, international congresses, etc.).

Primary visual symbols of the modern state include, beside the national flag, emblems, coats of arms, official seals, the personified state, i.e. the presiding head of state (a hereditary monarch or an elected president). With regard to the head of state's portraits it is interesting to find out when the first portraits appeared, on which occasions they are issued, how often the head of state is portrayed, in which manner he is represented, and how he is dressed. Further, the question arises whether there is any difference between monarchies and republics.

Several Islamic countries followed in the beginning the Islamic proscription of portraits. Instead, they employed—as the Ottoman stamps did until 1913—three specialised motifs: the crescent [see HILĀL], sometimes accompanied by a star; a coat of arms; and the *ṭughrā* [*q.v.*], along with more general calligraphical and arabesque designs. The turning-point in Ottoman stamp design came in 1913, when a set of stamps showing the Istanbul post office swept aside the tradition of avoiding pictorial designs (nos. 212-21/1913). In 1914, a further step was made by portraying Sultan Meḥemmed V Reshād (no. 245/1914). On the other hand, in Persia, where a vigorous tradition of pictorial painting had long flourished, the Shāh appeared on stamps as early as 1876 (nos. 19-22). In Egypt, religious inhibitions about portraying living things have been ignored since 1924 (nos. 82-93), and Islamic symbols were replaced by monarchical watermarks after 1926. King Fayṣal of ʿIrāḳ followed this example in 1927/31. Afghānistān was beginning to portray its monarchs in 1937; afterwards, the rulers of Afghānistān were often depicted, but President Taraki looks like being, until now (1992) the last one in this series. States with a special Islamic legitimation like Saudi Arabia (and its forerunners Ḥidjāz and Nadjd), Yemen (first as a kingdom, later as a republic), and Pākistān, avoided portraits of the rulers until the 1960s. Saudi Arabia and Yemen began with a small portrait of a human figure (1952 and 1948 respectively); the king of Saudi Arabia (Fayṣal) was portrayed for the first time in 1964, in the following period several times, in contrast to North Yemen where the only president ever portrayed until now has been President Ḥamdī in 1978. Ayyūb Khān was the first president to be shown on Pākistānī stamps (nos. 229-30/1966); thereupon also the portraits of the deceased national heroes Muḥammad ʿAlī Djinnāḥ and Muḥammad Iḳbāl could appear on stamps (1966-7); previously, the days of their death were commemorated and their contributions to the establishment of Pākistān were honoured by showing a memorial inscription or their monograms (e.g. nos. 44-6/1949 or nos. 96-8/1958). Republics such as Turkey, Syria, Lebanon, Tunisia and ʿIrāḳ depicted the portraits of their presidents from the beginning. Another practice was followed in Egypt and Libya after the revolutions there. Despite his popularity and the personality cult of him allowed in other media, President ʿAbd al-Nāṣir (Nasser) kept his portrait off Egyptian stamps except on three occasions (1964, 1965, 1967). After his death, however, he was commemorated on Egyptian stamps in 1970-2, and on stamps of several other Arabic countries. Al-Ḳadhdhāfī (Gaddafi) appeared for the first time on a souvenir sheet in 1975; in subsequent years he has become the central figure on the stamps. Remarkable exceptions are Algeria and Iran after 1979. No Algerian president has appeared until now on stamps during his lifetime (H. Boumedienne/Hawārī Būmadyan was for the first time portrayed after his death in 1979); on the occasion of the (re-)election of Boumedienne or Shādhlī b. Djadīd, instead of a portrait, inscriptions in Arabic were used which translate "Election of Brother ... as President ...". Whereas in the Shāh's days a profile of the monarch was almost always displayed, the Islamic Republic of Iran has only honoured "martyrs" on stamps (see also banknotes). For this reason, Āyatullāh Khumaynī was depicted for the first time after his death (1989 ff.), although already in his lifetime huge posters of him were plastered on walls of most Iranian towns and were carried in processions. As Chelkowski has pointed out, "This is a clever symbolic manipulation to suggest that Khomeini has not imposed his rule but is the 'chosen' representative of the people who carry his portrait out of love and devotion" (1990, 92-3).

Several monarchs of Islamic countries (Egypt since Fuʾād I, Afghānistān under Ẓāhir Shāh, Iran since the Pahlavīs, Jordan under the reign of Ḥusayn II, and Morocco under the reign of Ḥasan II) have flooded their countries with regular issues bearing their portraits on the occasion of commemorating special royal events: births and birthdays (especially of the male heir), royal birthdays; weddings; deaths and coronations (esp. Iran, nos. 1365-7/1967), etc. Another practice was followed, for instance, in Libya, where King Idrīs I was only once portrayed, directly after independence. Ruling predecessors are honoured, sometimes together with the reigning monarch, to show the continuity of the particular dynasty. The Pahlavīs even tried to base their reign on a fictitious continuity of the Persian monarchy since the time of the Achaemenids. This intention was revealed also in 1935 when Persia was renamed Iran (nos. 149 ff.: "*Postes iraniennes*", instead of "*Postes persanes*"). Regularly, the hereditary heads of state have attempted to enhance their legitimacy, either by combining their rule (in a portrait) directly with symbols of progress (see below), or by stressing the dynasty's role in the fight for independence (e.g., in Morocco under Muḥammad V and his son, and in Jordan). In this respect, differences between monarchies and republics seem to be blurred: republican heads of state are portrayed on similar occasions, as Independence or National Day, Revolution Day, etc.; the personality cult of Ḥabīb Bourguiba (Abū Raḳība) is intertwined with his role of Supreme Mudjāhid, his life history marking the major milestones of the Tunisian fight against the French. Other heroes of that same era appear on stamps only if they are long dead. Bourguiba was often shown together with female figures; this is an allusion to the improvement of the women's status as a result of the revised Personal Status Code in 1956. Sometimes even the birthdays of the presidents (e.g. of Ṣaddām Ḥusayn since 1984) are celebrated on stamps; frequently, they invoke their contributions to the modernisation process. Turkish presidents present themselves as the sons of the "Father of the Turks". A souvenir sheet (no. 25) in 1987 shows the hitherto-existing presidents from Atatürk to Evren in the shape of a family tree; the picture seems to suggest that Turkey is still firmly adhering to the political principles and aims of Atatürk. On another stamp issued in 1939 (no. 1052), the role of Atatürk is compared to that of George Washington for the United States.

Monarchs often appear on stamps in traditional (Bedouin) headgear and robes (see Fayṣal I of ʿIrāḳ in the 1920s, and his brother ʿAbd Allāh in Transjordan, and moreover, the rulers of the U.A.E. and Saudi Arabia), later, they also underlined their links to the army (see Riḍā Shāh Pahlavī) by wearing military uniform, or their support for reforms and westernisation by appearing bare-headed and clothed in Western style. The first presidents (e.g. of Turkey, Syria) were shown as modern townsmen in Western-style coats and ties, thereby expressing their intent to modernise and secularise the country. The fez, once a modern symbol, disappeared gradually and by the 1950s it was finally becoming old-fashioned. Soldier-politicians, as Atatürk or Sādāt, alternated between military uniform and civilian garb; Asad was always depicted in civilian clothes despite his military vocation, thereby underscoring his legitimacy, while Sādāt preferred the military uniform. Al-Ḳadhdhāfī is shown in different garbs; the most favourite one, beside the military uniform, seems to be Bedouin garb; sometimes the "revolutionary leader" is sitting on a horse, surrounded either by fighting people, or jubilating masses, or "Green Books", propagated as his "Third Universal Theory", with a liberating message for the whole world. The described style of illustration is itself a hint at the contents of the "Green Book" (here part 3), where the author is praising the Bedouins for their practising of "national sports" (e.g. mounted games), instead of merely watching sporting events. Like Ṣaddām Ḥusayn (1988), al-Ḳadhdhāfī is represented on stamps as an ideal Muslim on the *ḥadjdj* or during the Muslim worship (1985). This confirmation seemed necessary after al-Ḳadhdhāfī's open shift to "de facto-secularisation" in 1975 and his unorthodox interpretation of Islam since

en (rejection of the Sunna as a source of Islamic law,
c.).

Other important and specific national symbols and
mblems which are often seen on stamps should be
mentioned. In the case of Persia, the national emblem
ext to the portrait of the S̲h̲āh was the Lion and the
un, under the Pahlavī crown; for Lebanon it is still
ne cedar, for Morocco the pentagram. After the Ira-
ian Revolution, the red tulip, symbolising love and
acrifice in Persian poetry, has been made an official
mblem. The word *Allāh* in the shape of a red tulip apears on stamps, as on the 100-rial bill and on coins.
'urkey used sometimes (1926, 1929, 1931, 1961) the
nythical grey wolf (*bozkurt*), an embodiment of the
nification of its people. An allegorical figure, the em-
odiment of the nation, usually represented in the
orm of a woman, so popular on French stamps,
epresents Syria in one case (1956), but this particular
ymbolism seems to have been too foreign to the
slamic tradition to have taken root in Syria.

Another category of symbols of power is that of
nistorical notables or local heroes. Every régime has
ts own pantheon, and this becomes clear on stamps
oo. The emphases shift with the change of régimes,
lthough local heroes are generally more often
nonoured than famous persons who have had an im-
nact on the whole Arab-Islamic world. Whereas
nonarchies have emphasised the role of their
ncestors, especially the founder of a particular dynas-
y (e.g. monarchical Egypt frequently depicted
Muḥammad ʿAlī; Libya the founder of the Sanūsiyya,
S̲īdī Muḥammad b. ʿAlī al-Sanūsī; Saudi Arabia
hose Ibn Saʿūd), republican régimes have issued
stamps to commemorate a variety of nationalists (e.g.
Turkey memorialised Namiḳ Kemāl and Ḍiyāʾ (Ziya)
G̲ökalp; Egypt ʿUmar Makram, ʿUrābī Pas̲h̲a and
Muṣṭafā Kāmil; ʿIrāḳ honoured Sāṭiʿ al-Ḥuṣrī, progenitor of the various pan-Arab ideological trends;
Syria, instead, preferred to honour a native-born
theoretician of Pan-Arabism, al-Kawākibī), reformers
ʿal-Ṭaḥṭāwī, al-Afg̲h̲ānī, ʿAbduh, Ṭāhir Ḥaddād,
etc.), freedom fighters (e.g. Pākistān 1979, 1989-90),
and cultural leaders (in literature, arts or creative
fields). A myth of the peoples' continuous struggle for
independence is created in some cases (e.g. on Libyan
stamps since 1971-2, esp. since 1980, and on Iranian
stamps after 1979). The Islamic Republic of Iran
marked the abrupt departure of the past and the
changing orientation from Western ideology and ap-
parel of the S̲h̲āh's era to the traditional Islamic attitudes by a series of stamps (since 1979) devoted to
the "forerunners of the Islamic movement". The role
of the clerical opposition is overemphasised; but,
besides firm supporters of K̲h̲umaynī (like Āyatullāh
Bihis̲h̲tī, died in 1981), or forerunners of an Islamic
republic (as Faḍl Allāh Nūrī, died in 1909), other
famous persons are represented in this set who would
not have supported the "reign of the Āyatullāhs", if
they were still living (e.g., Mīrzā Kučik K̲h̲ān,
Muṣaddiḳ, Āl-i Aḥmad, S̲h̲arīʿatī, Ṭāliḳānī). Most of
the forerunners are considered as "martyrs" for the
"right cause", pointing to the glorified idea of martyrdom which is also one characteristic of S̲h̲īʿism.
Another S̲h̲īʿī feature commemorated on postage
stamps is that of the S̲h̲īʿī Imāms or works connected
with them, such as the *Nahd̲j̲ al-balāg̲h̲a* [*q.v.*] (e.g. in
1981). The search for historical heroes to honour on
Lebanese stamps is a difficult task. The choice of
Druze and Maronite princes is an indication of Christian dominance there till the outbreak of the Civil
War and of the neglect of the Islamic heritage.

Harmless illustrations of traditional costumes, na-

tional handicraft, festivals and musical instruments,
animals and flora, fauna, scenery, as well as antiquities, archaeological excavations, historical
monuments (mosques, forts, and palaces etc.) and
modern buildings (hotels, banks, museums, etc.) are
found on the stamps of nearly every country with the
aim of underlining the national heritage and, probably, of convincing the public of a clear-cut national
identity. So, even the representation of antiquities
and other common motifs can throw light upon the
political aims or the ideological orientation of a régime
and its self-identification. Despite the post-colonial
Pan-Arabic and Pan-Islamic rhetorics of some
régimes, they often lay particular stress on the pre-
Islamic and pre-Arabic history, a sign of the specific
national pride and patriotism. In Egypt, Pharaonic
monuments are as prevalent today as they were in
1866 when the first issues bore a pyramid watermark.
All stamps issued between 1867 and 1913 featured
pyramid-and-sphinx designs, and the Giza pyramids
have been a favourite subject ever since, although
after 1952, as the interest in other themes increased,
the pre-Islamic heritage was less often depicted. ʿIrāḳ
places great emphasis on its Babylonian forerunners
(cf. already a set from 1963, here together with
Islamic monuments; and from 1988, on the occasion
of the Babylon Festival), especially since Ṣaddām Ḥusayn shifted from extremist Pan-Arabic policies
towards a specifically ʿIrāḳī *waṭaniyya*; a Mesopo-
tamian-inspired culture is seen as a convenient vehicle
to introduce and support the change in fundamental
ideology (compare the results of A. Baram's study,
Mesopotamian identity in Baʿthi Iraq, in *MES,* xix [1983],
425-55). Jordanian stamps frequently show the
Nabataean city of Petra or the Temple of D̲j̲aras̲h̲
(since 1933). This pattern is repeated also in other
Arab (Algeria, Tunisia) and Islamic (Pākistān,
Afg̲h̲ānistān, etc.) countries.

Depicting antiquities or other signs of national
heritage can be seen as a means of advertisement and
as evidence for the tourist industry (e.g. Lebanon in
the 1960s until 1975; Egypt since the 1950s, with a
short interruption as a result of the 1967 events). But,
as Sivan has pointed out, the impressive continuity in
the patterns of postage stamps produced over the last
thirty years shows that touristic considerations have
not reigned supreme in this domain. A comparison
with the monetary iconography of the same era
(issued in Egypt, Syria, and Jordan) shows that the
recurrence of certain images on postage stamps has
not been a purely aesthetic tendency but the result of
conscious political decision. These visual symbols
should be mainly interpreted as official attempts to
create a common national identity and loyalty to the
territory. "Thus, the ancient past is part and parcel
of the legitimating genealogy of the modern state"
(Sivan 1987, 23). Noteworthy exceptions are the Gulf
emirates with no past to speak of, and Saudi Arabia,
where the pre-Islamic past of its territory is associated
with the paganism of the D̲j̲āhiliyya. An extraordinary
shift has occurred in Iran. Whereas the emphasis in
the S̲h̲āh's days was almost exclusively on pre-Islamic
architecture and art, the revolutionary Islamic régime
started to neglect the pre-Islamic era; in this context
one has to recall the strong protests of the Islamic
religious classes against the S̲h̲āh's bombastic celebration of the twenty-five centuries old history of Iran.
Lebanon, again, is a special case in the opposite direction, because of the Maronite élite's support of the
"Phoenician ideology".

Stamps illustrate most of the period of colonial expansion, as well as its end. After using their own

stamps, with or without overprints, the colonial powers in the Islamic lands under their control passed on to the "colonial-picturesque style", i.e. one foreign from the paper to the design; the favourite subjects on pictorial sets were scenes of monuments and landscapes; local allusions were rare, natives appeared only occasionally on horse or on camel, whereas representatives of European colonialism (as Marshal Lyautey on Moroccan stamps (1935/1948, 1951), General Gordon on Sudanese ones (1931/37, 1935)) were commemorated. While the colonial powers were shown as civilised and modernised, the dependent territories were depicted as backward countries and societies, needing the import of progress through colonialism. After independence, postage stamps rapidly became a means of asserting sovereignty, of seeking for self-definition, and of furthering economic and social development. The pictorials now often employ a semi-abstract style and international iconography: the national flag represents independence; broken chains and rising suns, flames etc. stand for liberation and a very promising future; doves for peace; globes for universal themes; balance scales for justice; the Asclepian serpent and staff for medicine; books and torches for education.

In tracing the evolution of some national holidays and memorial days, we find instances of discontinuity (particularly in revolutionary states) and continuity (mostly in conservative ones). But all these memorial days have a common feature, that they celebrate national events, as e.g. Independence (National) Day; Evacuation Day, to commemorate the departure of foreign forces (e.g. the British evacuation of the Suez Canal Zone, the evacuation of US bases in Libya, the evacuation of French occupation forces in Syria); Revolution Day (8 March 1963 in Syria; 1 September 1969 in Libya), which signalled the change in legitimation; or Army Day (when the army was the vehicle of the revolution, as in ʿIrāḳ). Other major political events and changes in legitimation which may be memorialised philatelically include constitutional, legal or programmatic reforms (e.g. Pākistān 1973, on the occasion of the promulgation of the new constitution; Algeria, 1976 (new constitution, *Charte Nationale*), 1986 (*Charte Nationale*)); overthrows of authoritarian régimes (Sudan, 1986; Tunisia, 1988); the first regular elections after a long period of military/authoritarian rule (Turkey, 1950; Pākistān, 1970); decisive plebiscites (Iran, referendum of 1979, commemorated in 1984, 1991; Pākistān, 1985, "overwhelming mandate by the people" for Ḍiyāʾ al-Ḥaḳḳ and his Islamisation policy in the 1984 referendum); nationalisations (of the Suez Canal in Egypt, 1956, 1961/66, or of the oil industry (Iran, 1953, ʿIrāḳ, 1973)); and the "corrective revolution" or accession day of the present ruler (Asad's Syria or Sādāt's Egypt). Several authoritarian régimes commemorate the single mass party (as in Tunisia, the Destour, later PSD; in South Yemen, the National Liberation Front, later Yemen Socialist Party; in Syria and ʿIrāḳ, the Baʿth; in Egypt, the Arab Socialist Union, and in Algeria, the FLN).

Postage stamps reinforce a myth of popular struggle for independence. Turkish stamps memorialised famous battles during the Liberation War (e.g. that at İnönü). Libya somehow managed to find two dozens of major and minor battles against the Italian occupiers during the period of 1911-43 (stamps issued since 1980). Iranian stamps after the Revolution in 1979 have frequently recalled the heavy toll of lives, also mentioned in the constitution, so that their characterisation as "stamps of blood" is justified. The Iranian stamps reflect the central theme of the revolution, the "Karbalāʾ-martyrdom-paradigm". The uprising of 5 June 1963 is seen as the beginning of the revolutionary movement (1979, 1982, etc.)—an obvious, but typical, misrepresentation of the facts.

After military coups toppled monarchies, "the people" begin to be shown on the stamps (e.g. post-1952 Egypt). For the first time, social groups such as peasants and industrial workers appeared, joining soldiers, whose role as the people's vanguard was stressed (e.g. Libya 1969/nos. 284-9 and 1970/nos. 290-95 with the inscription *dj̲ays̲h̲unā dirʿunā al-wāḳī* "our army is our protective shield"). The scarcity of pictures of other classes and occupational groups was not accidental at that time. Most of the women are shown in modern dress; whereas in conservative countries, either no females are featured, or they are shown in their traditional role, or in typical female professions, South Yemen and Libya even depicted women as factory workers (South Yemen 1975, 1979-80; in the case of the People's Republic of South Yemen this is to be seen in connection with the labour shortage and the encouragement of working women) and in military uniform (South Yemen 1971/77; Libya 1984). Turkey honoured Halide Edip (1966), Egypt the national pioneer feminists Ḳāsim Amīn (1958) and Hudā S̲h̲aʿrāwī (1973). A set of Turkish stamps on the occasion of the Twelfth International Women's Congress was issued in 1935, i.e. one year after the introduction of universal suffrage for women.

Concerning the Islamic Republic of Iran, the changed orientation of the new régime becomes evident in this aspect also; women are rarely depicted, but if they are, they are veiled, marching in a crowd under a banner, portrayed in a militant way (with a rifle over the shoulder), or as the mothers of future martyrs, following the "model women" of S̲h̲īʿī Islam, i.e. Fāṭima, the daughter of the prophet and mother of the third Imām Ḥusayn, or Zaynab, the sister of Ḥusayn.

Despite the protests from the side of conservative religious circles, some states propagate their promotion of family planning on stamps, symbolised by a three-, mostly four-headed-family (Pākistān, 1969; Iran, 1972; Egypt and Tunisia, 1973; Algeria, 1986).

Whereas a revolutionary ideology is shown in ʿAbd al-Nāṣir's Egypt in a less explicit way, Libya after 1977 has turned to propagating the contents of the "Green Book", e.g. by quoting central statements in Arabic and English on postage stamps.

Since the 1950s and 1960s, particularly, symbols of national development and progress are standard. A difference between monarchies and republics is not noticeable any more, with the exception of the Islamic Republic of Iran which stresses much less than Muḥammad Riḍā S̲h̲āh achievements in the economic and social spheres (compare regular issues commemorating the reforms since the "White Revolution" in 1962). The symbols follow the Western ideals of progress: cogwheels and smokestacks, etc. stand for a modernised industry; tractors or modern irrigation works for the mechanisation of agriculture. Favourite themes on stamps include the improvement of the communication and transportation networks (building of streets, railroads, seaports, airports, bridges, installation of telegraphs), urbanisation (modern buildings and cities), industrialisation (industrial plants, esp. steel and cement works, oil refineries), electrification and irrigation (high dams, irrigation pumps). The importance of the water problem in the Middle East is nown by the underlining of great irrigation projects, s the Libyan one (*al-nahr al-ṣināʿī* "the artificial iver", illustrated as the lifework of the "revolu- onary leader"), which has beome one of the main ubjects on stamps since 1983; Saudi Arabia and the Gulf states depict plants for the desalination of sea vater (e.g. Saudi Arabia 1974, 1989). Scenes from the il industry are illustrated on stamps from several rab countries ("petro-philately"), and trace the Middle East's growth as an oil-producing region. A ortfolio of Arab countries' stamps portrays almost he entire process of bringing oil from the ground to s various users; some of the most detailed oil in- lustry stamps have been printed for Dubayy and Kuwait. Other main export articles also appear on tamps (cotton on Egyptian and Syrian stamps, jute n Pākistānī ones (before the secession of the Eastern art), coffee on Yemeni stamps). Economic plans pro- nise a prosperous future.

Stamps indicate the interest in providing free ducational and medical services; new university and chool buildings are illustrated proudly, alphabetisa- ion campaigns are propagated. Occasionally, new hemes and technologies (pollution control or solar nergy) are advertised philatelically (ʿIrāḳ, 1985; Tunisia, 1988).

Stamps alluding to foreign relations are related to regional as well as international ties. Demonstrations of regional solidarity (e.g. with the R.C.D./Regional Cooperation for Development between Turkey, Iran, and Pākistān, existent till 1979, or the Gulf Coopera- tion Council) are of minor interest, if compared to the philatelically-delineated regional tensions and border disputes which are pieces of evidence for territorial claims. Since the annexation of a part of the former Spanish Sahara in 1975, Morocco has printed annual- ly a stamp on the occasion of the so-called "Green March", firstly, to underline its legitimate claims on this territory, and secondly, to use this cause as a uni- fying national factor (compare Mauritania, the oc- cupier of the other part of Spanish Sahara—according to an agreement with Morocco—which has only once (1976) printed a stamp showing the map of North-Africa with the inscription *Mauritanie réunifiée*). On the other hand, Algeria (1976) demonstrates its solidarity with the POLISARIO guerilla movement there. Afghānistān issued several stamps supporting the cause of an independent Pashtūnistān [*q.v.*]; the first one in this series (no. 367-8/1951) caused—in contrast to the later stamps (1952 ff.)—political friction with Pākistān and had to be withdrawn. Since the achieve- ment of full sovereignty in 1919, and since the establishment of Pākistān, Afghānistān has demanded the rescinding of the Durand Treaty (1893) which delimited the border between British India and Afghānistān. The conflict over Pashtūnistān reached its climax in the early 1960s when Pākistān occupied the "Tribal Areas" and closed the whole frontier to Afghānistān. Asad's dream of a "Greater Syria" is revealed on one stamp (no. 1510/1981). Pākistān's conflicts with India over Kashmīr have been depicted three times (1960, 1967, 1973). The stamps of Iran and ʿIrāḳ since 1981 and 1982 respectively concen- trate on the Gulf War. The stamps issued until 1992 are an excellent example of the functioning of war propaganda. Both countries have revived episodes from Islamic history (Ḳādisiyya or Karbalāʾ [*q.vv.*]) for the mobilisation of the population. Thus one Ira- nian stamp bears a red flag, symbolising blood and sacrifice, on a cupola of the tomb of Imām Ḥusayn at Karbalāʾ; inscribed in calligraphic Arabic on that stamp are the words "Every day is ʿĀshūrāʾ, the whole earth is Karbalāʾ, all months are Muḥarram". ʿIrāḳ has issued several stamps propagating "Ṣad- dām's Ḳādisiyya" (1981, 1985-6). Special com- memorative issues on the occasion of innovated Memorial Days ("The Preparation Day", "Mobilisation of the Oppressed", "Day of the Ar- my", etc.) are printed. War victims are glorified as martyrs on both sides. ʿIrāḳ accuses Iran of commit- ting war crimes and *vice-versa* (1988). ʿIrāḳ even refers to the Geneva Convention on one stamp (nos. 1275- 8/1985). The aggressor celebrates the armistice as ʿIrāḳ's Victory Day (nos. 1413-15/1988), whereas Iran shows the resolution no. 598 of the UN with an interrogation mark (1989), indicating thereby its doubts concerning the durability of the agreement. The reconquest of occupied territory (ʿIrāḳ, 1988; Iran, 1985) and later, the reconstruction of destroyed areas (1989 for both countries) is celebrated.

Pan-Arabic themes became popular since the 1940s. In general, events associated with the Arab League, Arab conferences on different subjects, Arab Boy Scout Jamborees, Pan-Arab games, the Arab Postal Union, etc., are commemorated. An exception is found on stamps commemorating the unification at- tempts of several Arab states, e.g. the formation of the U.A.R. in 1958 was proudly marked by stamps show- ing an arch uniting the maps of Egypt and Syria. The eagle, a revolutionary symbol which had appeared earlier, and the new U.A.R. flag were frequent sub- jects on stamps from then onwards. Regular annual issues celebrating the anniversaries of the short-lived union followed. After the break-up (1961), only the continuing use of the name "United Arab Republic" by Egypt remained.

Nearly all Arabic countries, and some Islamic ones, frequently print stamps demonstrating their solidarity with the Palestinian cause. Standard are issues show- ing the Dome of the Rock or al-Aḳṣā in Jerusalem with an inscription indicating solidarity; the memorialising of massacres (e.g. the Dayr Yāsīn one in 1948; Ṣabrā and Shātīlā in 1982); and issues poin- ting to the refugee problem (see esp. Jordan, 1969) or the outbreak of the *Intifāḍa* and the proclamation of the Palestinian state. More militant standpoints are expressed on stamps of South Yemen, Syria, ʿIrāḳ, Iran, Libya and Kuwait. Whereas the majority of these states seem to see the only chance for the libera- tion of Palestine in armed struggle, Libya is addi- tionally advising the adoption of the "Third Univer- sal Theory" and Iran the establishment of an Islamic republic. Iran, characteristically, is calling the begin- ning of the *Intifāḍa* "the Uprising of the Muslim People of Palestine" (1980). Both countries com- memorate annually (since the early 1980s) the "Universal Day of al-Ḳuds". South Yemen has been, until 1992, the only country that issued a stamp with the portrait of Yāsir ʿArafāt, the PLO's chairman (1983).

Religious loyalties are commonly expressed by printing stamps on the occasion of the beginning of the 15th century A.H., of Islamic conferences or of the pilgrimage to Mecca. Mediaeval Islamic history is referred to on stamps through monuments, per- sonalities and events dating from that period. Still, it is noteworthy that many of the Islamic symbols are usually local mosques (apart from the Kaʿba in pilgrimage stamps and the famous mosques of Jerusalem). Mediaeval Islamic personalities are quite often native sons. Mediaeval persons who do not per- tain to the country on whose stamps they appear are usually those representing the Muslim contribution to world civilisation (esp. science and technology, such as Avicenna/Ibn Sīnā, Averroes/Ibn Rushd, al-Fārābī, al-Kindī, Rhazes/al-Rāzī). Conservative countries such as Saudi Arabia, significantly enough, do not carry such persons on their stamps, preferring to depict in their stead such people as the founders of the four Islamic schools of law (in the shape of an inscription; nos. 625-28/1977). The anti-Crusader myth has been expoused by almost all Arab countries (in most cases by commemorating the battle at Ḥiṭṭīn [*q.v.*] and the victorious Ṣalāḥ al-Dīn/Saladin). The only exception was Maronite Lebanon, which celebrated the Crusaders as allies of Maronites. The total neglect of a country's Islamic past, as for instance in Lebanon, can also reflect the ruler's secular attitude, as was the case in pre-revolutionary Egypt. Most of the countries hesitate to exploit Islamic sentiments because of the growing fundamentalist opposition. A remarkable exception is again given by the Islamic Republic of Iran; here, stamps commemorate the calling of Muḥammad to the prophethood (*ʿĪd al-mabʿath*, commemorated since 1982) and the birthday of the Mahdī (celebrated since 1980), which is called "The Universal Day of the Oppressed". Islamic unity is the subject of stamps issued annually on the birthday of the Prophet Muḥammad. Most of these feature the Holy Kaʿba surrounded by the faithful of all races. Such stamps attempt to depict Iran as a unifying force for all Muslims; they bear the message that the Islamic Republic of Iran is a leader of world-wide resurgent Islam. By its frequent use of Ḳurʾānic quotations, the régime is trying to depict itself as a vanguard of the Islamic world.

Solidarity with other fundamentalist movements and the intention of exporting the revolution are reflected on Iranian stamps which honour the martyrdom of Muḥammad Bāḳir Ṣadr (an old friend of Khumaynī and a noted theologian, executed by the ʿIrāḳi régime; no. 2023/1982), President Sādāt's assassin (Khālid al-Islāmbūlī; no. 2029/1982), an Egyptian soldier who shot Israeli civilians (Sulaymān Khāṭir; no. 2146/1986), or a leading ideologist of the Egyptian Muslim Brothers (Sayyid Ḳuṭb; no. 2078/1984); solidarity is expressed with the Afghān resistance (1985-8) and the militant Ḥizb Allāh in Lebanon (no. 2208/1987). The intention to export the state's ideology is also revealed on Libyan stamps since 1977. Yet before this, the Egyptian régime under ʿAbd al-Nāṣir had cheered the arrival of new converts to the leftist camp; stamps marking the ʿIrāḳi and Yemenī Revolutions and Algeria's independence from France (1958, 1963, 1962) reflect a feeling of triumph and revolutionary brotherhood. Algeria showed its solidarity for Vietnam (1973), Zimbabwe and Namibia (1977). Some countries are underscoring their ties with Africa (Egypt, 1964, 1965; Mauritania, 1966, 1973, etc.) and to the non-alignment movement (e.g. Algeria, 1973).

Anti-Americanism is shown on Iranian and Libyan stamps. A series of Iranian stamps were issued to represent the hostage crisis that occurred during the Carter administration (1983, 1985, 1987); Libyan stamps condemn the USA for its aggression against Libya in 1986, representing Ḳadhdhāfī in the same moment as the peacemaker (nos. 1719-24/1986). In contrast to these examples, Turkey depicted its engagement in the Korean War on the side of the Western powers (nos. 1337-40/1952) and the ensuing alignment with NATO (1954, 1959, 1964, 1989). Afghānistān since 1980 printed several stamps portraying Lenin—a sign of the occupation by Russian forces at that time; stamps marking the centenary of Lenin's birth were, however, frequently printed in other Islamic states (e.g. Egypt and Syria, 1970). Standardised international subjects have been frequently featured on stamps since the 1960s, honouring UNICEF, WHO, FAO, UNRWA, and UNESCO, as well as the parent UN itself. Other world themes have included an International Day for the Elimination of Racial Discrimination, Mothers' Day, Childrens' Day, etc. A major exception is again to be found on an Iranian stamp, issued in 1983 for United Nations Day, which indicates a criticism of the five superpowers' veto power in the Security Council and the struggle of the Islamic Republic against this unjust distribution of power. Anti-racism is interpreted as an Islamic achievement by depicting a black *muʾadhdhin*, an allusion to the first *muʾadhdhin* in the history of Islam [see BILĀL B. RABĀḤ]. These internationalist subjects are also stressed for economic reasons, for they are popular with stamp collectors around the world.

National pride and heritage is sometimes revealed on stamps which treat the subjects of sport and traditional activities. As an instance of this intention, one may mention Iranian or Libyan stamps which depict "old Iranian" or "national" sports; Afghānistān has issued several stamps with the motif of traditional mounted games; Turkey and Pākistān have displayed wrestling and hockey respectively, and the Arabic states of the Gulf, falconry.

Bibliography: The information and comments on stamps in this article are based either on the *Michel-Katalog* (*Asien 1991/92, Übersee*, v/1-2, Munich 1991; *Afrika 1989, Übersee*, iii/1-2, Munich 1989; *Europa-Katalog West 1992/93*, part 2, Munich 1992), or on observation of the stamps themselves. The number (or series of numbers) or years of issues in the parentheses refer to the number under the relevant country in *Michel*. Other standard reference works are the following catalogues: *Catalogue de timbres-postes*, Yvert et Tellier Publications, Paris, not revised and enlarged annually; *Minkus new world wide postage stamp catalog*, 2 vols., New York, issued annually; *Scott's standard postage stamps catalogue*, 2 vols., New York, issued annually; *Stanley Gibbons' priced postage stamp catalogue*, London, issued annually.—Specialised catalogues: M.H. Bale, *The stamps of the Palestine Mandate*, rev. and enlarged ed., Ilfracombe, England 1978; ʿAbd al-Ḥ. al-Kīlānī, *al-Dalīl al-ʿarabī li'l-ṭawābiʿ al-ʿarabiyya al-miṣriyya*, Cairo 1967; *Scott's Zeheri catalogue for postage stamps of Egypt, U.A.R., and the Sudan*, ed. by Mehanny Eid (8th ed., Cairo 1987).

Basic information on special philatelic terms and on the postage stamps of Islamic countries can be found in philatelic dictionaries or handbooks, e.g. C. Brühl, *Geschichte der Philatelie*, 2 vols., Hildesheim etc. 1985-6; W. Grallert and W. Gruschke, *Lexikon der Philatelie*, Berlin 1976; U. Häger, *Großes Lexikon der Philatelie*, Gütersloh 1973; G. Schenk, *Sie war dabei. Die Geschichte der Briefmarke*, Gütersloh 1959; J.A. Mackay, *The dictionary of stamps in color*, New York 1973.

Special articles and monographs on stamps issued in Islamic countries: T. Azzabi, *De la poste arabe au timbre poste tunisien*, Tunis 1986; R. Badry and J. Niehoff, *Die ideologische Botschaft von Briefmarken – dargestellt am Beispiel Libyens und des Iran*, Tübingen 1988; B. Bryan, *The private posts of Morocco*, in *Philatelic Literature Review*, x/2 (1961), 12 ff.; P. Chelkowski, *Stamps of blood*, in *The American Philatelist* (June 1987), 556-66; idem, *Khomeini's Iran as seen through banknotes*, in D. Menashri (ed.), *The Iranian revolution and the Muslim world*, Boulder, Col.

1990, 85-101; R.K. Clough, *British post offices and agencies in Morocco 1857-1907 and local posts 1891-1914*, Lancashire 1984; J.H. Coles and H.E. Walker (eds.), *Postal cancellations of the Ottoman Empire*, i-iii, London-Bournemouth 1984-90; N. Donaldson, *The postal agencies in Eastern Arabia and the Gulf*, Batley, West Yorks. 1975; P.R. Feltus, *Catalogue of Egyptian revenue stamps with Sudanese revenues and Egyptian cinderellas*, Southfield, Mich. 1982; J. Firebrace, *British Empire campaigns and occupations in the Near East, 1915-1924: a postal history*, London-Bournemouth 1991; H.W. Hazard, *Islamic philately as an ancillary discipline*, in *The world of Islam. Studies in honour of Philip K. Hitti*, ed. J. Kritzeck and R.B. Winder, New York 1980 (repr. of 1959), 199-232; W. Hoexter and S. Lachmann, *The stamps of Palestine*, Haifa 1959; D. Keep, *History through stamps. A survey of modern world history*, London-Vancouver 1974 (see, above all, 72 ff.); D.R. Martin, *Pakistan overprints on Indian stamps, 1948-49*, London 1959 (rev. ed. 1974, repr. Lahore); M.A. Nayeem, *Hyderabad philatelic history*, New Delhi 1980; R.S. Newman, *Orientalism for kids: postage stamps and "creating" South Asia*, in *Journal of Developing Societies* (Leiden), v (1989), 70-82; R. Obojski, *Mosques, minarets and stamps*, in *Aramco World Magazine*, xxxii/2 (1981), 8-11; *Palestine: stamps (1865-1981)*, Beirut-Cairo 1981; A. Passer, *The stamps of Turkey*, London 1938; F.W. Pollack, *The stamps of Palestine Mandate*, Tel Aviv 1961; D.M. Reid, *The symbolism of postage stamps: a source for the historian*, in *Journal of Contemporary History*, xix (1984), 223-49 (fundamental); idem, *Egyptian history through stamps*, in *MW*, lxii (1972), 209-29; idem, *The postage stamp: a window on Saddam Hussein's Iraq*, in *MEJ*, xlvii (1993), 77-89; R. Schuessler, *Petrophilately*, in *Aramco World Magazine*, xxxix/1 (1988) 38-41; E. Sivan, *The Arabs nation-state in search of a usable past*, in *Middle East Review*, ix/3 (1987), 21-30 (fundamental). (Roswitha Badry)

POTIPHAR [see ḲIṬFĪR].

PRANG SABIL, the name in Malay of the *d̲j̲ihād* [*q.v.*] in the East Indian archipelago; *prang* = war.

The course of recent history has made it difficult for Muslims to fulfil their duties with respect to the *d̲j̲ihād*. The representatives of the law, however, still teach and the masses readily believe that arms should only be allowed to rest against the *kāfir* so long as any success must be despaired of. In a Muslim country under non-Muslim rule, as were the Netherlands East Indies under Dutch colonial rule, the teachers, however, preferred to be silent. At most they said that under the prevailing conditions there was no legal inducement to conduct the *d̲j̲ihād*, in view of the superior forces and the comparative freedom enjoyed by believers. Or, on the other hand, they expounded particularly those texts which removed the more serious feuds between Muslim and *kāfir* to the next world. When political events, catastrophes, misfortunes of any kind resulted in disturbances, it was not at all uncommon for the Muslim population of what is now Indonesia to look at these things from a religious point of view. It may happen on such an occasion that the feeling of being bound to fight the unbeliever is aroused again. If the leaders utter the war-cry *prang sabil*, it finds a ready answer. It is true that according to the law, the signal for the *d̲j̲ihād* should be given by the *imām*. There is now no *imām*; but even in the time when the Ottoman sultan was still recognised as *imām*, any misgivings were easily overcome if the *imām* remained inactive. Outside the boundaries of the territory in which the holy war is proclaimed, the silent sympathy of the believers was with the fighters. Any forcible conversion which took place anywhere in the East Indies, was generally praised by Muslim chiefs and represented as a fulfilment of the more solid obligations of the *d̲j̲ihād*.

This practical teaching of the *prang sabil* was of particular importance in Atjeh [*q.v.*] in the last quarter of the 19th century. Circumstances were very much in its favour. The Atjehnese were a self-satisfied people, convinced of their own superiority, and also of a warlike disposition. Non-Muslims were everywhere hated or at least despised. At the same time, those individuals who were in any way connected with the Muslim cult were held in great honour. These qualities were, however, not in themselves sufficient to conduct a *prang sabil* with success against a disciplined attacking power. A military leader was necessary. There was indeed a sultan in Atjeh, but he was a negligible factor as regards the situation in the country. The chiefs, the real rulers of the land, preferred to confine themselves to their own territory; they were not fitted for co-operation. Bands of armed men ravaged the country, doing the *kāfir* as much damage as possible, but they could raise no claim for general co-operation and assistance as they were not waging war in the way Allah had willed. The law lays down the sources from which the costs of the *d̲j̲ihād* can be met; pillage and plundering, as was the practice of these bands, could never be blessed by Allah. In addition the organisation of these bands was such that they never held together long. In these circumstances it was the *ʿulamāʾ* (also used as a singular) who took in hand the organisation of the war; among these the most prominent were the *ʿulamāʾ* of Tirò, from olden times a centre of study of sacred learning. They reproached the chiefs with their slothfulness and the people with preferring worldly advantages to heavenly rewards. Going up and down the country, they preached the doctrine of the *d̲j̲ihād* and there was no one who could openly oppose them; indeed, they represented the divine law. In order to be able to wage war, a war-chest was needed. The *ʿulamāʾ* claimed the share of the *zakāt* set aside for Allah's purposes; the *ʿulamāʾ* of Tirò in particular used it to train a strong force of duly converted recruits. The *ʿulamāʾ* were for a long time the soul of the war. It is, however, clear that the authority which they had gained over the secular rulers could only last so long as they were able to inspire the people to continue fighting. When the war was over, they returned to their old, still very influential position as representatives of the holy law. Various writings which, together, formed a regular war literature, proved an effective means of inspiring their warriors with enthusiasm. They were an accompanying feature of the *prang sabil*. *ʿUlamāʾ* wrote pamphlets and epistles in which attention was called to the duty of waging the holy war; emphasis was laid on the heavenly reward that awaited the martyr or *s̲h̲ahīd*, and the *kāfirs* to be overcome were painted in the blackest colours. An elaborate poem, the *Hikajat Prang sabi(l)*, of which there were many versions, was specially intended to be declaimed in order to increase the courage and contempt for death of those who heard it.

Bibliography: C. Snouck Hurgronje, *De Atjèhers*, Batavia 1893-4, i, 183 ff.; ii, 123; idem, *Verspreide Geschriften*, iv/2, 233 ff.; H.T. Damsté, *Atjehsche oorlogspapieren*, in *Indische Gids*, i (1912), 617 ff., 776 ff.; idem, *Hikajat Prang Sabil* (text and tr.), in *BTLV*, lxxxiii, 545 ff. (R.A. Kern)

PRĒM ČAND (1880-1936), Indian writer of fiction in Urdu/Hindi, best known for his short stories, which gained him wide recognition as a pioneer of the genre.

During his lifetime, and a hundred years previously, apart from English the official language of the British Government of India was often called Hindūstānī. It was usually written in Persian-style script by and for Muslims, and in Dēvanāgarī script by and for Hindus. The former type, when used as a literary language, was also referred to as Urdū ("the language of the army camp, *urdū* [see ORDO]) and the latter type as Hindī (formerly Hindawī). When written in the Persian script, Hindūstānī was characterised by considerable Arabic-Persian vocabulary. In the Dēvanāgarī script, the literary language had much vocabulary taken from Sanskrit and the Prākrit vernaculars. Even before Independence in 1947, Urdu and Hindi began to be considered distinct languages, and they were recognised as official languages in Pākistān and India (Bhārat) respectively. It must, however, be noted that when we read of Prēm Čand writing novels or short stories in Urdu or Hindi, and then translating them from one language to the other in subsequent editions, we should not assume that major alterations were made in translation. Changes were largely in the script used than in the actual text. Thus Prēm Čand's fiction should be regarded as a single corpus, rather than as two separate corpora from a bilingual author. He depicted social life and preached social reform in the India of his time, with its rich variety of races, classes and religions, but he dealt more with rural than urban life and more with Hindus than with Muslims.

Prēm Čand was born in a village near Benares (Banāras) and named Dhanpat Rāʾē. At the start of his literary career he adopted the nom-de-plume first of Nawāb Rāʾē and then of Prēm Čand. His father was a poor postal clerk, and Prēm Čand's education was somewhat haphazard, and depended increasingly on private studies and tuition. At one time he had to walk ten miles to Benares for lessons, yet in 1919 he graduated B.A. as an external student. His home and family life was not easy; he was orphaned, and had to look after the rest of the family. Before this, his father had arranged Prēm Čand's marriage at the age of 15. Some years later, Prēm Čand married a second and younger wife, by whom he had a son and two daughters. He was never robust in health, and always had to work very hard for his living. He acquainted himself with earlier and contemporary Urdu fiction, ranging from the *dāstān* to the works of Surūr, Sarshār, ʿAbd al-Ḥalīm Sharar and Mīrzā Muḥammad Hādī Ruswā [see ḲIṢṢA. 5. In Urdu]. He obviously had ambitions as a writer, especially of fiction, though he began as a dramatist at the age of 14, writing two plays, both now unfortunately lost. Earning a living presented problems, and he changed his occupation several times. He started as a teacher, then as an inspector of education. He later worked for publishers, including the well-known Nawal Kashōr in Lucknow. For a time he kept a shop. Finally, he went to Bombay as a film script writer. But he could not get on with directors and producers, and was ill at ease in the film studio environment. He returned to Benares, where he died in 1936.

He was a prolific writer. As we have seen, his juvenilia included two plays. Later in life he wrote a major historical drama, *Rambhūmī* ("Earthly terror") in Hindi, the title of whose Urdu version, *Karbalā*, indicates its theme from Arab-Islamic history. Prēm Čand had studied Persian for eight years, and at first showed preference for the Urdu script. But despite his brilliant command of the language, he did not find favour with Urdu readers, and increasingly wrote in the Dēvanāgarī script. After his death, however, he became recognised as a master of Urdu, particularly for his short stories. He also wrote numerous magazine articles, many published in *Zamāna* from 1901 onwards. He championed Hindu-Muslim co-operation and social reform. Strange to say, he first won fame as a writer of novels: some short, others full length, some published in parts, some in instalments, others as a whole, some originally in Urdu, others in Hindi. Saksena, writing presumably in about 1926, mentions several Hindi novels which he says are to be published in "Urdu translation" (*op. cit.* in *Bibl.*, 344). His short novel, *Asrār-i-maḥabbat*, appeared in 1898, and his Hindi novel *Prēmā* in 1904. *Bāzār-i-ḥusn* ("Brothels") described by Sadiq (*op. cit.* in *Bibl.*, 346-7) as "perhaps the most satisfactory of his novels", appeared in 1918 in two parts. It is the story of a reformed "fallen woman" who finds that the world will not forgive her. She is led astray by a wealthy prostitute, and ends up "saved" and working as head of an orphanage. An account of this and other novels will be found in Muhammad Sadiq, *op. cit.*, 344 ff. These novels are now somewhat dated and appear to have lost some of their popularity.

It is for his short stories that he had gained lasting fame. These, numbering over 200, were published in eleven collections between 1907 and 1936, among the best known being *Prēm Paččīsī*, *Prēm Battīsī* and *Prēm Čālīsī*. Many of them deal with the misfortunes of poor village-dwellers who are "more sinned-against than sinning". They perhaps justify Sadiq's description of him as "an idealist ... a reformer ... and a dreamer". Many of them are masterpieces, though Saksena's paean of praise is as excessive in its way as is Sadiq's lukewarmness. Allowance must surely be made for the taste of readers and writers for melodrama in those days. The rich harvest of Urdu and Hindi short stories in the Subcontinent during the last hundred years owes a great debt to Prēm Čand. Moreover, as Sayyid Waḳḳār ʿAẓīm says, *op. cit.* in *Bibl.*, 592, Prēm Čand's fiction "paints a true picture of social and political life in the early 20th century".

Bibliography: A detailed bibl. would contain few works in English but a good deal not only in Urdu but also in Hindi. Reference should be made to the bibl. in Sayyid Waḳḳār ʿAẓīm's art. *Prēm Čand*, in *Urdu Encyclopaedia of Islam*, v, Lahore 1390/1970, 590-4. For general accounts, see Muhammad Sadiq, *A history of Urdu literature*, London 1964, 344-55, a very perceptive and informative account, which some may find rather severe. Ram Babu Saksena, *A history of Urdu literature*, Allahabad 1927, 343-4, contains a little additional information and is full of enthusiasm, but was written a little too early, while Prēm Čand was still alive, and is very brief. There are many editions of Prēm Čand's short stories in both Urdu and Hindi, and most anthologies of prose in both languages include examples. Among general works on Urdu fiction containing useful sections on Prēm Čand, see Shāʾista Akhtar Bānū Suhrawardī, *A critical survey of the Urdu novel and short-story*, London 1945; and, in Urdu, ʿIbādat Brēlwi, *Tanḳīdī zāwiyē*, 304-82, Karachi 1957, a detailed history of the Urdu short story.

(J.A. HAYWOOD)

PREVEZE, PREVESE, Greek Prevesa, a coastal town in the southernmost part of Epeiros, in western Greece, situated on the upper entrance of the Ambracian Gulf opposite the ancient Cape Actium and associated with the Italian *prevesione* (= "provisioning"), the Slavonic *perevoz* (= "passage") and the

Albanian *prevëza* or *prevëzë* (= "transportation") (cf. Phourikes, *Zur Etymologie von Prevesa*, in *Philolog. Wochenschr.*, xvii [1927], 509; idem, in *EEBS*, i, 283-93, and in *Epeir. Chr.*, iv, 265-6; Soustal-Koder, 242). The old mediaeval settlement's foundation (Palaeoprevesa) is associated with the destruction of the nearby Nicopolis, 6 km/4 miles north of modern Prevesa, by the invasion of the Turcophone Uzes (Ouzoi) in central and southwestern Hellas (1064-5) (*Chronicle of Galaxeidi*, ed. E. Anagnostakes, Athens 1985, 20-2, 78; cf. A. Savvides, art. *Turks* [in Greek], in *World History*, ii, Athens 1990, 360 D). In the scantily-documented mediaeval period, the first definitive reference appears in the Greek version of the *Chronicle of the Morea* (ed. P. Kalonaros, Athens repr. 1989, vv. 9108, 9119; see also Italian version, ed. K. Hopf, *Chroniques gréco-romanes*, Athens repr. 1961, 468 and French versions, ed. J. Longnon, Paris 1911, §§ 636, 649, with references to the *vieille cité de la Prevasse* and to the latter's harbour as *port de Saint Nicolas de Tort*), which is, however, connected with the new mediaeval Prevesa and its despoliation in 1292 by the Genoese allies of the Byzantine emperor Andronicus II Palaeologus, during the latter's operations against the Epeirot despot Nicephorus I (cf. Phourikes, in *EEBS*, i, 281 ff. and in *Epeir. Chr.*, iv, 266 ff.; Schreiner, *Kleinchroniken*, ii, 528; Soustal-Koder, 242; D. Nicol, *The Despotate of Epiros 1267-1479*, Cambridge 1984, 38 ff., 229 f.). The only direct reference between 1292 and the Ottoman conquest of the 15th century, associates new mediaeval Prevesa with *Nicopolim vetustissimam civitatem*, according to the antiquarian humanist Cyriacus Anconensis, who visited the Ambracian area in 1436-7 (cf. E. Ziebarth, *Cyriacus of Ancona in Epeiros* [in Greek], in *Epeir. Chr.*, i [1925], 111, 114; Phourikes, in *Epeir.;Chr.*, iii [1928], 141 and iv, 271-2; Soustal-Koder, 214).

The gradual Ottoman annexation was recorded by four Byzantine anonymous short chronicles (cf. Schreiner, i, 422, 548, 552, and ii, 528; Soustal-Koder, 242): no. 71/7 dates the conquest to A.M. 6986 (= A.D. 1477-8), i.e. to Meḥemmed II's reign, while nos. 58/23a and 70/39 date the first Ottoman "foundation" (Greek *ktisis*, here signifying "fortification") to A.M. 6995 (= A.D. 1486-7), i.e. to Bāyezīd II's reign. Finally, no. 58/23b dates the second Ottoman fortification to A.D. 1495. In the course of the 1499-1502 Turkish-Venetian war, a Venetian attack on the town's Ottoman garrison, recorded by Saʿd al-Dīn (*Tac-üt-tevarih*, ii, 97) and short chronicle no. 36/30 (Schreiner, i, 295, dating it to A.M. 7008 = A.D. 1500), failed despite extensive damages and, therefore, a supposed Venetian occupation of the town from 1499-1500 to 1529-30 is to be discarded (cf. Phourikes, in *Epeir. Chr.*, iv, 274-6; Hammer-Purgstall, *GOR*, ii, 325 ff.; İ.H. Uzunçarşılı, *Osmanlı tarihi*, ii, Ankara 1988⁵, 217 f., 222). The first Ottoman occupation (1477-8 to 1684) witnessed the most important events in the area's history, i.e. the victory of Khayr al-Dīn Pasha [*q.v.*] over an allied western fleet under Andrea Doria in September 1538 (cf. Phourikes, *op. cit.*, 276-8; Uzunçarşılı, *op. cit.*, 375 ff.; D.E. Pitcher, *An historical geography of the Ottoman Empire*, Leiden 1972, 115, 117 and map XIII-A2; K. Setton, *The Papacy and the Levant 1204-1571*, iii, Philadelphia 1984, 445 ff.). Following a brief western recapture of the town (1605), the Venetians under Francesco Morosini succeeded in capturing Prevesa (1684) during the 1684-1718 Turkish-Venetian War (*Short Chronicle*, no. 58/23, in Schreiner, i, 422; cf. Phourikes, *op. cit.*, 279-83). The first Venetian rule (1684-1701) was followed by the second Turkish rule (1699 and 1701 to 1717-18), while the ensuing second Venetian rule (1717-18 to 1797) was terminated by a brief French rule (1797-8), which ended abruptly by the decimation of the French guard and the destruction of the town by ʿAlī Pasha Tepedelenli [*q.v.*] in October 1798 (Phourikes, *op. cit.*, 280-9). The first ʿAlī Pasha period (1798-9) was followed by the third Turkish rule (1800-7), following the Turkish-Russian treaty of 1800, and the second ʿAlī Pasha rule (1807-20), connected with widespread property confiscations and terrorist involvements of Bekir's Albanian guard, but also with an extensive plan of fortifications and building constructions, was eventually followed by the fourth and final Turkish rule (1820-1912) (Phourikes, *op. cit.*, 289-94). The Ottoman period in Prevesa ended during the First Balkan War with the entry of a revolutionary corps of Prevesians in the town on 21 October 1912, following the defeat of the Turkish forces near ancient Nicopolis.

Bibliography: For older references, see P. Phourikes, *Prevesa. Location-foundation-name* [in Greek], in *Epeteris Etaireias Byzantinon Spoudon* (= *EEBS*), i (1924), 274-94; idem, *A small contribution to Epeirot history*, pt. II: *Prevesa* [in Greek], in *Epeirotika Chronika* (= *Epeir. Chr.*), iv (1929), 263-94. See also P. Schreiner, *Die byzantinischen Kleinchroniken*, i-ii, Vienna 1975-7; P. Soustal-J. Koder, *Nikopolis und Kephallenia*, Tabula Imperii Byzantini, no. 3, Vienna 1981, 93 ff., 213-14, 242. Full references in A. Savvides, *The Turkish capture of Prevesa according to the Short Chronicles* [in Greek], in *Tetramena*, fasc. xlvi-xlvii, 1991, 3053-68; idem, *On the problems concerning the foundation of medieval Prevesa* [in Greek], in *Acts XIIth Panhellenic Hist. Congr.*, Thessaloniki 1992, 73-85; M. Delibaşi, *History of Preveze in the 16th century according to the Ottoman taxation registers*, in *Osmanli Araştırma ve Uygulama Merkezi Dergisi*, ii (Ankara 1991), 53-62. (A. Savvides)

PRISHTINA (Serbo-Croat, Priština), a town in Serbia, the administrative centre of the region of Kosovo. It is situated in the valley of a small river called the Prištevka (a western affluent of the Sitnica) and on the eastern fringe of the Kosovo Plain (Kosovo Polje), at the foot of the western part of the Butovac mountain, at an altitude varying (according to the different quarters of the town) between 585 m/1,918 ft. and 670 m/2,197 ft. The origin of its name is unknown.

Archaeological investigations have shown that the district of the town has been inhabited since the Neolithic period (300-2500 B.C.) and then in the Bronze and Iron Ages. The first Illyrian colonies come from the 4th century B.C. In Roman times, the place was known as an important crossroads, notably between the towns of Naissus (Niš [see NISH]), Lissum (Lješ) and Skupi (Skoplje), but also as a centre for roads leading towards Bosnia and Dalmatia. In the 2nd century A.D., at about 12 km/8 miles from the modern Prishtina, the Roman town called Ulpiana (Lipljan) grew up, the centre of the province of Dardania. It was rebuilt in the 6th century by Justinian I, and the town became "Justiniana Secunda", but then disappeared completely after the Slavic invasions and the Slav peoples' installation in these districts.

In the mediaeval Serbian state, Prishtina was early known as the main town of the Kosovo region. Its rise was linked with mineral exploitation in the nearby region of Novo Brdo and Kopaonik; with the fertility of the Kosovo plain, which was always a real agricultural granary; and with its position, moreover, as the crossroads of the main communication routes in the Balkans. Soon afterwards, at the time of the first exploitation of mineral resources in the reign of king Milutin (1282-1321), Prishtina became the capital (first the royal one, then the imperial one) of the Serbian state (at that time under the Nemanid dynasty, founded by Stevan Nemanja, 1170-96). The king Stevan Dečanski (Stephen Uroš III, 1321-31) often lived there, but much more frequently, his son (king, then emperor) Stephen Uroš IV, known as "Dušan the Strong" (Dušan Silni, 1331-55). It was in his palace at Prishtina that Dušan in 1342 received the Byzantine emperor John Cantacuzenus when the latter had fled from Constantinople, and it was there that Dušan issued a certain number of imperial charters (e.g. that of 1351). According to the description left by Cantacuzenus, Dušan's palace was situated in the area which is today between the Clock Tower and the Pazar mosque (Čarshî Djāmiᶜ), very likely on the site of the present-day headquarters of the military garrison. Prishtina continued to be the capital under the next king, Stephen Uroš V (1355-71); and then (at a time when the capital of Serbia, in face of the Ottoman menace, was moved further north, first to Kruševac and then to Belgrade) it became the capital of the son-in-law of the "Tsar" (in reality of the Prince) Lazar, Vuk Branković (d. 1398), and this even after the decisive defeat of the Serbian armies by the Ottomans on the "Field of Blackbirds" (Kosovo Polje) not far from Prishtina (June 1389). One might finally add that it was always at Prishtina that the descendants of the Serbian royal family continued to reside until the end of the 15th century.

In the first half of the 15th century, corresponding to the period of the Serbian "despotate", Prishtina remained one of the main commercial and trading centres of mediaeval Serbia. In particular, there was an important colony of merchants from Ragusa [*q.v.*], who also operated a sophisticated banking system, linked on one hand to the customs duties and on the other to the possibilities of cash loans granted to merchants and local business men and to various passing Ragusan emissaries. Thus it is known that the "despot" Djuradj (George) Branković granted to the Ragusans of Prishtina the customs rights in 1411 and 1415. It was also within the framework of this grant that the workshops for refining the silver ore extracted from the nearby silver mines of Novo Brdo and Trepča functioned, and at Prishtina that the famous knightly tournaments took place, in which not only local people from the town and its neighbourhood took part but also people coming from a distance, such as the citizens and nobility of Ragusa.

The Ottoman advance was felt more and more, through the numerous raids which made the roads less safe and to a large extent injured trade. On the fall of the Serbian "despotate" in 1439, the Ottomans installed as their representative in Prishtina ᶜĪsā Bey of Skoplje, son of Isḥāḳ Bey [see BOSNA. 2. (a), at vol. I, 1263a], and a Turkish *ḳāḍī* is mentioned in the town from 1448. Prishtina became definitively Ottoman in 1455. The palace of the Serbian kings was destroyed at a time when the first Ottoman buildings appeared, some of which, however, had been already built at the time of the last Serbian "despots". This was notably the case of the "Pazar mosque" (situated in the eastern part of the main market of the town), founded by Murād II (824-55/1421-51) and completed by Meḥemmed Fātiḥ (855-86/1451-81). The latter also had a further mosque built in Prishtina bearing his own name. Finally, it may be mentioned that not far from the town was constructed the *türbe* of Murād I, killed during the battle of Kosovo Polje in 791/1389 [see ḲOSOWA].

Under the Ottomans, Prishtina (now only the centre of a *nāḥiye*) lost its political and administrative importance to the town of Vučitrn, the centre of the *sandjaḳ* before 1462. Prishtina remained nevertheless an important economic centre, thanks mainly to the Ragusan colony and to the permanent consulate there of Ragusa; to the proximity of rich mining centre (lead and zinc); and to the numerous trading establishments filled with goods of all kinds handled by the Ragusan and Italian merchants (e.g. those from Verona, Genoa, Mantua and Florence). The 16th century travellers (one could mention the celebrated Felix Petancius (Ragusinus Dalmata), diplomat at the court of the king of Hungary Vladislas II) underline its importance and richness. In the 17th century, it is mentioned by several authors: in a report addressed to the Vatican in 1685, the Catholic archbishop of Sofia and Skoplje, Pjetër Bogdani (of Albanian origin), classes Prishtina among the category of Serbian towns with as many as 3,000 houses, and he underlines the fact that this was an unfortified town. For Kātib Čelebi, it was a "medium-sized" town, whilst Ewliyā Čelebi (who visited it in 1660-1) records that it was a *ḳāḍīlîḳ* of 150 *aḳčes*, and that it had 2,060 houses ("spacious and in good repair"), among which were distinguished the palace of Alay Bey and the building of the legal tribunal (*meḥkeme*), and also 300 shops, 11 *khāns* and two public baths (*ḥammāms*). It is known that the Ragusan colony there still existed at this time, possessing some twenty houses, and that silver mining still continued (but apparently at a reduced level).

The town suffered a great deal in the Austro-Turkish War, that of the "Holy League" (1683-99), especially in 1689 at the time of the famous raid of the Austrian general Piccolomini, which managed to seize Prishtina and Skoplje (aided in this by local Serbian insurgents led by the Patriarch Arsenije III Čarnojević and by Catholic Albanians led by the archbishop Pjetër Bogdani). Piccolomini's staff headquarters at this time were actually in Prishtina. A plague epidemic which broke out carried off a large number of people, including the Albanian archbishop and the Austrian general. At the time of the precipitate retreat by Austrian forces in 1690, a large part of the Serbian population of the region, fearing future Ottoman reprisals, emigrated northwards en masse. It was this emigration (and also that taking place in similar conditions in 1737, under the patriarch Arsenije IV Jovanović Šakabenta, at the time of a fresh Austro-Turkish War) which was the origin of the installation of Serbian groups in Hungary (at Budapest, Szentendre, Eger, Szekesfehervár and elsewhere) and the beginning of the mass invasion of the Kosovo region by Muslim Albanians from Albania, a process which the Ottoman authorities naturally helped as far as possible (see S. Skendi, *The Albanian national awakening 1878/1912*, Princeton 1967, 7).

Prishtina declined greatly in the course of the 18th century, firstly because of a fresh epidemic of plague in 1707, and then because of a new Austro-Turkish War (that of 1737) and its consequences. From that time, profiting from the growing anarchy in the European lands of the Ottoman empire (an anarchy which made the Ragusan colony and foreign merchants leave), Prishtina and its district fell under the control of an Albanian Muslim family, the Gjinolli (in Albanian, Gjinollëve, in Serbo-Croat Džinići), a domination which lasted, in the shape of an hereditary *pashalîḳ*, for about a century. Towards the end of this century, the town was fortified by means of solid pallisades and had around 7,000 inhabitants; at this time it was the seat of a *pasha*.

There is naturally a lot to say about Prishtina in the

ʼth century. In 1812, France opened a consulate ere, followed soon afterwards by other powers, in-uding (in 1889) the kingdom of Serbia. In *ca.* 1836, e town had a population of about 9,000 (the figures ed in the course of this century vary between 9,000 12,000), and it was often described as "a small wn fortified by a double wall, and rather dirty in ap-arance". But it was also mentioned as an important ading centre "between Sarajevo and Istanbul", here two fairs were held annually (in April and in eptember), frequented by merchants "coming from iš, Bosnia, Albania, Edirne and Salonica". After e two great fires of 1859 and 1863, which seriously amaged the town, there was only one fair annually eld in the second half of May and lasting for two eeks, frequented by traders "from Sarajevo, kadar, Peć and Prizren" (hence within a much more estricted radius). Despite a famed body of local ar-sans, the town's economy continued to decline, specially as the "local Turks" (in reality, more Muslim Albanians than Turks proper) in 1873 revented the line of the railway coming through the wn, thus cutting Pri<u>sh</u>tina off from its commercial elations with Skadar and Sarajevo. At that time, fterwards "hardly anything except sheep and goat kins" were exported from it. However, in 1877 ri<u>sh</u>tina became the seat of the newly-created *wilāyet* f Kosovo (in place of that of Prizren), but not for ng, since a dozen years later, in 1888, the seat of the rovince was transferred to Üsküb/Skoplje, and ri<u>sh</u>tina became once more a mere *palanka*. During his short period (1877-88) there appeared at Pri<u>sh</u>tina ve *Sālnāme-yi wilāyet-i Ḳoṣowa* (in 1878-9, 1882-3, 884-5, 1886-7 and 1887-8), forming an interesting istorical source which has not yet been sufficiently tilised. During the period between Serbian-Turkish Vars of 1876-8 and the Balkan Wars of 1912-13, the nore or less continuous terror perpetrated by the local Albanian governors (often in open or latent conflict with the Ottoman central government) on the local Orthodox Serbian population of the town reached eights of savagery. In *ca.* 1910 Pri<u>sh</u>tina had (accord-ng to J. Cvijić) "about 4,000 houses, Albanian, erb, Jewish, Gypsy and Čerkes, including 3,200 of Muslims, 531 of Orthodox Christians and 65 of ews".

The town was liberated by the Serbian army of 1912. From this time onwards there began an exodus of the local Muslim population which continued all hrough the First World War and even after it. In 1913 the town had 18,174 inhabitants. In 1915, Pri<u>sh</u>tina was occupied by the Bulgarian army, then again liberated by the Serbian one in 1918. From then ill 1941, it formed part of the "Kingdom of the Serbs, Croats and Slovenes" and then of the "Kingdom of Yugoslavia". During 1941-4 it was incorporated with the entire region of Kosovo and of Metohija) in-o a Fascist "Greater Albania", at that time under Italian and then German domination.

After the end of the Second World War, it formed part of the "People's Federal Republic of Yugoslavia" as the main town of the "Autonomous Region of Kosovo and Metohija" (and then simply, "of Kosovo"). As the cultural and political centre of the Albanian minority in Communist Yugoslavia, during this latter period it played a preponderant role in the more or less clandestine (but in fact upheld in a perfectly obvious fashion by the Titoist authorities) action aimed at making the non-Albanian population of the region (Serb, Montenegrin and Turkish) flee by terror and intimidation or simply by demographic pressure, an action marked by various abrupt changes of policy, but one in the end successful. As a result, the Albanian population (which is 95% Muslim and 5% Catholic) now forms 90% of the total population of Kosovo and Metohija. Pri<u>sh</u>tina is now the seat of the official "Muslim community of Serbia" and of a *madrasa* (of lower rank in relation to that of Sarajevo), the "Alaudin medresa", where instruction is given in the Albanian language. The Albanian Muslim religious journal called *Edukata Islame* (which is generally considered as a version, meant for the Albanian population of the region, of the official Yugoslavian Muslim journal, *Glasnik Vrhovnog Islamskog Starješinstva* of Sarajevo) appears there and also a Muslim annual in Albanian called *Takvim*.

Bibliography: V. Radovanović, art. *Priština*, in *Narodna Enciklopedija*, Zagreb 1928; O. Savić, art. *Priština*, in *Enciklopedija Jugoslavije*, Zagreb 1965, vi, 619-20; *Kosovo nekad i danas/Kosova dikur e sot* (a collective work published in Serbo-Croat and Albanian), Belgrade 1973, 853 ff.; *Istorija srpskog naroda* (collective work, still in course of appearance), i-vi, Belgrade 1981-6, see index. (A. Popovic)

PRIZREN (in Ottoman Turkish orthography, Perzerīn), the second largest city of the former Yugoslav autonomous district of Kosovo-Metohija with about 40,000 inhabitants, the greater part of which are Albanian-speaking Muslims, the remainder Orthodox Serbians, Muslim Turks, Orthodox Vlachs, Roman Catholic Albanians and some Gypsies. Prizren is the only trilingual city of the Balkans. Until the dismemberment of Yugoslavia, Albanian, Serbian and Turkish were fully recognised, with newspapers and periodical published in all three languages and trilingual street name plaques. Till today, Prizren preserved its Ottoman physionomy of the 19th century better than any other city of the Balkans, entire districts being placed under protection of the law on monuments of culture.

In Ottoman times (1455-1912), Prizren was one of the largest cities of the Balkans interior and was an Islamic centre of considerable importance, possessing dozens of mosques and baths, a number of *medreses* and dervish convents of no less than seven different orders (among which is the *Āsitāne* of the Ḳarabā<u>sh</u>iyye branch of the <u>Kh</u>alwetiyye) and a library with many old Islamic manuscripts. It was the centre of a *san<u>dj</u>aḳ* throughout the Ottoman period, and a number of important poets and writers of Ottoman literature lived and worked in this city.

Prizren is situated at the southern edge of the fertile plain of Metohija, at the place where the small river Bistritsa (a tributary of the Beli Drim) comes out of the picturesque Duvska Klisura (gorge). The town is partly built on the northern slopes of the Shar Mountains, beneath the ruins of a huge mediaeval and Ottoman citadel, and partly in the plain. Prizren is situated 55 km/34 miles north-west of Üsküb/Skopje and 125 km/77 miles east of the important north Albanian city of Iskenderiye/<u>Sh</u>koder, with which it is linked by a good road over a pass through the Albanian mountains, one since 1912 largely disused, however.

According to C. Jireček and those following him, the present town is the successor of the Roman city of Theranda; but extensive archaeological research in the present town has found nothing older than the Middle Byzantine period. The town is first mentioned in 1019 as the seat of an Orthodox bishop. It seems that between 1169-90, as a result of the Serbo-Byzantine wars, the town was in Serbian hands. In this last-mentioned year it became again Byzantine, and in 1204 it was included in the Second Bulgarian Empire. In the mid-13th century, when the Bulgarian state collapsed, Prizren was again taken by the Serbians and remained part of their kingdom (later empire) until the Ottoman conquest in 1455. In these two centuries, the Serbians erected a number of important buildings in and around the town. In 1307 King Milutin reconstructed and enlarged the episcopal church of the Byzantines and had it adorned with high-quality fresco paintings. This is the church of Bogorodica Ljeviška, one of the most important monuments of Orthodox Christian art of the Balkans and still in perfect shape. Just outside the town, in the gorge of the Bistritsa, Tsar Dušan (1331-55) constructed the huge marble monastery of the Archangels, which became his imperial sepulcre after his death. Dušan had made Prizren the capital of the Serbian state. Milutin's and Dušan's noblemen constructed a number of other churches in Prizren, of which some are still preserved, largely in original shape (Sv.Spas below the castle).

In 1455, during the war against Vilk-oğlu (George Branković) the Ottomans took Prizren. The fact is apparently not mentioned in the early Ottoman chroniclers, who only mention the capture of the nearby silver mine towns of Novo Brdo and Trepča. Prizren was immediately made the seat of a *sandjak bey*. There are some vague indications of an earlier conquest of the town, under Murād I, but this had no lasting consequences, if it took place at all. The sultan had a garrison stationed in the Prizren castle, and converted the cathedral of King Milutin into a Friday Mosque, which became known as Djāmiᶜ-i ᶜAtīḳ, or Djumᶜa Djāmiᶜ, by which name it is known in the *wakf-nāme* of Kukli Bey from 944/1537-8, and as: "Djāmiᶜ-i Sulṭān Meḥemmed Khān" in the census register Tapu Defter 368 (p. 43), which dates from the time of the first Grand Vizierate of Rüstem Pasha (1544-53). In the Serbian literature, the conversion is supposed to have taken place in the course of the 18th century, the Ottoman sources and the reports of the Catholic bishop-visitator Pietro Masarechi from 1623-4 being wholly ignored. It seems that the monastery of the Archangels was plundered by the Ottomans during the conquest, but survived and functioned throughout most of the 16th century. The *mufaṣṣal* registers of *ca.* 1550 (T.D. 368, p. 51) and from 1569-70 (T.D. 495, p. 46) still mention the "Manastīr-i Arhangel" paying 50 *aḳčes* per year as tax for its pr perty. In the town itself, the Christians kept a numb of churches for their own use.

There are no records about the size and appearan of mediaeval Serbian Prizren. The walled town, bu on a hill which is surrounded by a loop of the Bistrits covers two ha and could have contained 300-400 i habitants. The greater part of the open town w clustered on the steep slopes below this citadel, but t preserved cathedral of B. Ljeviška in the plain, sever hundred metres to the north of the castle, sugges that the town also spread out there, following the riv and the main road to the north. In the words of t best scholar of the old Serbian culture of bygone day Jireček, it should not be imagined as being more th a *Bretterbudenstadt*. Perhaps the town had 2,000-2,5(inhabitants, which for the time and the place was co siderable.

At the time of the conquest, a sizeable group Muslim Turkish colonists must have settled in t town, setting up their own *maḥalles*, especially in t plain beneath the castle. The first reliable numbers o the population of Prizren are contained in the Ta Defter no. 167 from 1530-1, which is based on the i formation taken during the census of the first years the reign of Süleymān the Magnificent. At that tim the Muslims, 273 households in all, of which 40 we *aḳïndjïs*, lived in four *maḥalles*. The Christians, 39 households, lived in nine *maḥalles*. The town mig have had 3,300-3,400 inhabitants. Islamic life was st little developed. Besides the Mosque of Sulta Meḥemmed, there were only a few *mesdjids*, finance from their own *wakfs*. The Defter mentions: *Mesdjid* Yaᶜḳūb Bey, *Rikābdār* of Sultan Meḥemmed Khā *Mesdjid* of Kātib Sinān and the *Mesdjid* of Ayās Be The Mosque of Sultan Meḥemmed had no *wakf* of i own but was financed from the poll-tax of the distri of Prizren, a rather common procedure for sultan mosques in the Balkans (cf. Mal. müd. 5625, p. 17

In the course of the 16th and early 17th centurie the town did not grow very much, but gained slowl a predominantly Islamic character, due to the slo conversion of the local population (1570: 13% co verts) and through the erection of a large number c Muslim buildings. This process of change can be fo lowed with help of the three *taḥrīr defters* available some poll-tax registers and a *mufaṣṣal ᶜawāriḍ defter*:

Year of registration	*Muslim households*	*Christian households*	*Muslim maḥalles*	*Christian maḥalles*	*Approximate total population*	*Percentage of Muslims*
1530	270	396	4	9	3,300	40%
1550	278	252	4	11	2,700	52%
1570	428	254	8	11	3,500	63%
1591	n.d.	97	n.d.	7		
1643	466	113	14	3	2,900	80%

1530 = T.D. 167, p. 372; 1550 = T.D. 368, pp. 440-45; 1570 = T.D. 495, pp. 37-46; 1591 = Mal. müd. 14930, pp. 2-4; 1643 = Kepeci 2607 Mevkufat 62, pp. 4-8.

The stability of the internal situation in the 16th century can be seen from the size of the garrison of the castle of Prizren; in 1530 and 1550 it contained only twenty soldiers, serving under a *Dizdār*, a *Ketkhüdā* and an *Imām*. The Ottoman registers allow us to follow the expansion of Islamic life in the town. In 1513 the poet Sūzī Čelebi, writer of the important *Ghazawātnāme-i Mīkhāl-oghlu ᶜAlī Bey*, had the *wakfiyye* for his mosque and school in Prizren drawn up. Sūzī Čelebi (real name: Meḥmed b. Maḥmūd b. ᶜAbd Allāh) died in 1522 and was buried in a *türbe* behind his mosque. Both buildings are still extant. Two year later another poet of Prizren, Nehāri (Ramaḍān Efendi), allegedly Sūzī's brother, died and was buried ir the same *türbe*. The tombstones of both men are likewise preserved. In Shawwāl 944/March 1538, the *sandjak bey* Kukli Meḥmed Bey founded a mosque in the town, which still exists today, and had the road from the Albanian ports of Lesh and Shkoder secured by the construction of 17 caravanserais. In the town, he built 117 shops providing revenue for his foundations. Another indicator to the growing commercial imporance of the town is the presence of 80 shops belonging to the *wakf* of Ewrenos-oghlu Aḥmed Bey (died 1506) and a *ḥammām*, providing revenue for his foundations in Yeñidje-yi Vardar in (Greek) Macedonia. In 1570 the number of shops had grown to 99. In 1573 the *sandjak bey* of Iskenderiye/Shkoder, Meḥmed Pasha, had a large domed mosque erected in Prizren, which later became known as the Bayraḳlî Djāmiᶜ. This foundation included a *medrese*, a *mekteb*, a large double bath, a library and a *türbe* for the founder. All these buildings still exist today, the mosque and the *ḥammām* largely in original shape. The library contains a large number of manuscripts, on religion, medicine, mathematics and history. The Grand Vizier Yemen Fātiḥi Sinān Pasha was to add books to this library in 1589. The *medrese* of Meḥmed Pasha functioned till 1947. In 1022/1613, the vizier Ṣofu Sinān Pasha, a native Albanian from the Prizren area, erected the largest mosque in the town, whose huge dome became one of the architectural dominant features of the town. A *medrese* once belonged to it. For the construction of the mosque, the stones of the by now deserted Monastery of the H. Archangels were used, and these are clearly visible at the structure. In the literature, Sinān Pasha is often confused with Yemen Fātiḥi Sinān Pasha, who originated from the same district (Lume belonging to Prizren), as did Ṣofu Sinān, who was governor of Buda, Bosnia and finally of Damascus. He died around 1615. His Prizren mosque belongs to the largest and most monumental ones of the entire Balkans. The expansion of Islamic life in the town can best be shown in a table, based on the surveys of the *wakfs* as indicated in the *taḥrīrs*:

1520	*1550*	*1573*
1 mosque	1 mosque	4 mosques
4 *mesdjids*	7 *mesdjids*	13 *mesdjids*
1 *ḥammām*	1 *ḥammām*	2 *ḥammāms*
1 *mekteb*	2 *mekteb*	3 *mektebs*
	2 caravanserais	2 caravanserais
		1 *medrese*
		1 library

In 1606 and 1614 Prizren is described enthousiastically in the reports of the visiting Catholic bishops Mario Bizzi and Pietro Masarechi, who praised the beauty of the houses, all having courtyards and fountains and a multitude of green and trees. Bizzi maintains that Prizren contained 8,600 houses, of which only 30 were Roman Catholic, having their own church. There were many schismatics (Orthodox), with two churches of their own. It is interesting to remark that the bishop maintains that "in this part of Serbia the inhabitants speak Albanian", a remark also made by Masarechi as pertaining to the town itself. For the villages, the presence of Albanians is confirmed by the Ottoman *taḥrīrs*. In Serbian historiography, the Albanisation and Islamisation of Kosovo has to be seen as a result of the mass emigration of the Serbs after the Christian revolts and Habsburg invasion at the end of the 17th century and the subsequent settlement of Albanians on the vacated lands. The conversion of the great church of Bogorodica Ljeviška is therefore also placed in the early 18th century. According to Masarachi, Prizren had 12,000 Turkish (= Muslim) inhabitants, 600 Serbian inhabitants and 200 Catholics. Only the numbers of the two Christian communities look more or less realistic when compared with the Ottoman data.

Prizren and its district suffered terribly from the invasion of the Habsburg army under Piccolomini in the winter of 1689-90, during which the city was burnt down and a large part of the Muslim population slaughtered. According to the late 19th century historian Ṭāhir Efendi, who used local memory and now unavailable sources, only 60 Muslim families survived. With the help of Albanian Muslims from the unoccupied mountains, the Ottomans succeeded in driving back the Habsburgs and their Serbian and Albanian-Christian auxiliaries, after which terrible vengeance was taken on the remaining Christians. This led to the "Great Exodus" of the Serbs of Kosovo under their Patriarch Arsenije III Crnojević. The Austrian invasion of 1737 led to a repetition of these events. After these disturbances a certain Ṣāliḥ Agha from the village of Nenkovac near Prizren, who had exerted himself in the expulsion of the Austrians, repaired many mosques and schools in Prizren and reorganised normal life in the district, for which he received the title of Pasha. Ṣāliḥ Pasha is the founder of the hereditary dynasty of the (Albanian) Pashas of the Rotulla family, which was to rule Prizren till well into the 19th century. Ṣāliḥ was succeeded by his son Emr Allāh Pasha. The son of the latter, Ṭāhir Pasha, fought against Ḳara Maḥmūd Bushaṭlî, the powerful Albanian *derebey* [*q.v.*] of Shkoder, who occupied Prizren in 1795 and drove Ṭāhir Pasha away. In 1805 Saᶜīd Pasha, son of Ṭāhir, became *sandjak bey* of Prizren. In 1806 he fought against the rebellious Serbs, a fact memoralised in numerous folksongs. From 1809 till 1836 Prizren was governed by Maḥmūd Pasha, the most important of the Rotulla dynasty. In 1809 he helped to destroy the Serbian insurgents near Niš [see NISH] and subsequently conquered Semendere/Smederevo and Belgrade. As symbols of his victory, he took the bells of the clock towers of Smederevo with him and placed them in three new clock towers which he constructed in the citadel of Prizren and in the large villages of Orahovica and Mamusha. In 1821 Maḥmūd Pasha participated in the suppression of the Greek Revolt. He is especially known for the large mosque, the *medrese* and the *mekteb* he had erected in Prizren. Maḥmūd Pasha also rebuilt the mosque in the Prizren castle and repaired the great *ḥammām* of Meḥmed Pasha and the Mosque of Ḥādjdjī Ḳāsîm, which is already mentioned in the *wakfiyye* of Kukli Meḥmed Bey from 1537-8. In 1831 Maḥmūd Pasha sided with the rebellious Albanian vizier Muṣṭafā Bushaṭlî but was beaten by the forces of Reshīd Pasha. He was finally removed in 1836, banished to Anatolia and executed there. His brother Emīn Pasha Rotulla succeeded him and remained in charge till his death in 1259/1843. In 1247/1831, Emīn Pasha constructed the last great mosque of Prizren and the fourth and last *medrese* of the city. The mosque still stands, a large domed structure which is visibly inspired by the 200 years' earlier mosque of Ṣofu Sinān Pasha. Emīn Pasha had only one child, his daughter Umm Kulthūm, which is the reason that the rule of the Rotulla pashas over Prizren ended. In 1327/1909, Umm Kulthūm, then living in the Istanbul suburb of Üsküdār, drew up her *wakfiyye* for the *mekteb* she had founded in Prizren.

In 1843, within the framework of the reorganisation of the *eyālets*, Prizren became the capital, instead of Üsküp/Skopje, of a large administrative unit. This had a positive effect on the population of the town, which grew rapidly. In 1865 the experienced traveler Johann Georg von Hahn called "Prisrend" the "largest city of Albania", bigger than Yenişehir/Larissa, Yannina or Shkoder, and probably even bigger than Monastîr. According to the statement of the Austrian consular agent Dr. von Petelenz, who lived many years in the city, there were 11,540 houses, of which 8,400 were Muslim, 3,000 Orthodox and 150 Catholic. In them lived 46,000 inhabitants, 36,000 of whom were Muslims. According to the same source, Prizren had 26 mosques, two Orthodox churches and one Catholic church, as well as 17 *mektebs* for boys and nine for girls, one Rüshdiyye school, and a school for the Orthodox and Catholic communities each. At this time, Prizren was the arms factory of the Balkans, producing swords, all sorts of rifles and pistols as well as excellent saffian leather and a large textile production; silversmiths were especially famous. The population was Turkish, Albanian, Bulgarian/Serbian and Vlach, and most people spoke all these languages because they lived mixed together and not in segregated *maḥalles*, a situation which can be seen as early as 1643 in the *ʿawāriḍ defter* of that year. From 1868 till 1874, Prizren was the capital of the *wilāyet* of Perzerīn. In 1288/1871, a bilingual Turkish-Serbian weekly *Perzerin* started its existence. In 1874, however, the large *wilāyet* was split up into several different units, apparently to counteract the too strong Albanian influence. After this date, the expansion of the city began to stagnate, especially when the new railway from Selānik/Thessaloniki to Kosovo caused a change in the trade network and left Prizren largely outside it. From 1878 till 1881, the Albanian nationalist movement called the "League of Prizren" met in the *derskhāne* of the *medrese* of Meḥmed Pasha in Prizren, trying to keep the "Four Albanian *wilāyets*" (Shkoder, Kosovo, Manastir and Yanya) together and to prevent Serbian and Greek annexation, attempts which ultimately failed.

In October 1912, during the First Balkan War, the Serbian army under General Janković took Prizren, which was accompanied by a massacre of the Muslim population, according to contemporary press reports amounting to 12,000 victims. After the conquest, the citadel and all its buildings were blown up, the mosque of Sultan Meḥemmed the Conqueror was made into a church and the buildings of Rotulla Maḥmūd Pasha, the victor of Belgrade and Smederevo, were totally destroyed. Later, a beginning was made at demolishing the great mosque of Ṣofu Sinān Pasha, but violent popular protests saved the greater part of the building, its three-domed porch being lost. From the events of 1912 and from the subsequent neglect in the interwar period, Prizren never recovered. In 1961 it still numbered as few as 28,056 inhabitants. Even after the settlement of some industry and the connection with the railroad network after World War II, the city remained smaller than it had been at its height in the 19th century. Neglect and poverty, however, saved it from ugly modernisations. After the War, extensive works of restoration and conservation were carried out on the Christian as well as on the Muslim historical monuments.

In the 16th century Prizren was, in the words of the biographer and prolific writer ʿĀshıḳ Čelebi [*q.v.*], himself a native of Prizren (born 1518 or 1520, died in Üsküb/ Skopje 979/1571), a "fountain of poets". Besides Sūzī Čelebi, Nehārī and ʿĀshıḳ himself, there lived the poet Muʾmin and the mystical poet Semʿī Behārī. Saʿyī from Prizren wrote a *Fetḥ ḳalʿa-yi Belgrad*. Sudjūtī, who is often represented as a native of Kalkandelen/Totovo, was in fact from Prizren; he wrote a *Selīm-nāme* during that sultan's reign and built a bridge at Prizren. Tedjelli (d. Dhu 'l-Ḳaʿda 1100/August-September 1689) is another poet worth mentioning because of his *dīwān*. An important 18th century literary ʿĀdjizī figure was the poet and dervish leader Süleymān Efendi, the founder of the ʿĀdjiziyye branch of the Saʿdiyye dervish order, who lived and died in Prizren (1151/1738). His *türbe*, with a magnificent wooden dome, is still extant and held in veneration. The most important 19th century figure is Khōdja Ṭāhir Efendi, teacher in the *medrese* of Emīn Pasha, whose great work is a *Tārīkh-i Perzerin*, written in Arabic rhyming prose, the publication of which is an urgent desiratum for the history of Ottoman culture in the Balkans.

Prizren was and still is a centre of dervish life. The presence of the Sināniyye order dates from 998/1589-90, when Sheykh Mūsā Efendi founded a *tekke* of this order in the Ṭabaḳ-khāne Maḥalle. The Ḳādiriyye order apparently came in 1066/1655-6, when Sheykh Ḥasan, son of Sheykh Maḳṣūd, founded the still-existing *tekke* of this order in the Ḳuril Maḥalle. The Ḳarabāshiyye branch of the Khalwetiyye came into being in 1111/1699-1700; Sheykh ʿOthmān Efendi from Serres founded the still existing *tekke* of this order. A second *tekke* of the Sināniyye was founded in 1118/1706-7. The ʿĀdjiziyye branch of the Saʿdiyye has already been mentioned. The Bektashī order is also said to have been active in Prizren, and some Melāmī groups still exist. Of more recent date is the now very active Rifāʿiyye, whose *tekke* was wholly rebuilt in 1972 by the present (1993) Sheykh Džemali Zukić, replacing a late 19th century foundation. The *Newrūz* ceremony in this *tekke* is one of the greatest events in dervish life of all of the former Yugoslav territories.

Bibliography: J.G. von Hahn, *Reise durch die Gebiete des Drin und Wardar*, in *Denkschr. Akad. Wiss. Wien*, Phil.-Hist. Classe, xiv (1865); F. Rački *Isveštaj Barskog Nadbiskup Marina Bizzia*, in *Starine Jugoslovenska Akademija znanosti i umjetnosti, Zagreb* (1887), 119-20; Sami Fraşeri, art. *Perzerīn*, in *Ḳāmūs ul-aʿlām*, ii, 1490-6; C. Pauli, *Kriegsgreuel, Erlebnisse im türkisch-bulgarischen Kriege 1912*, Minden in Westfalen 1913, 50; A. Olesnički, *Suzi Čelebi iz Prizrena Turski pesnik-istorik XV-XVI veka*, in *Glasnik Skopskog Naučnog Društva*, xiii (Skopjle 1934), 67-82; K. Draganović, *Izvješće Petra Masarechija, apostolskog visitatora Bugarske, Srbije, Slavonije i Bosne, o stanju katolicisma 1623 i 1624*, in *Starine Jugoslovenska Akademija Znanosti i Umjetnosti*, xxxix (Zagreb 1938), 28-9; Hasan Kaleši, *Jedna Prizrenska i dve Vučitrnske Kanunname*, in *Glasnik Muzeja Kosova i Metohije*, ii, (Priština 1957), 289-300; Kadri Halimi, *Derviški redovi i njihova kultna mjesta na Kosovu i Metohiji*, in *ibid.*, 193-206; H. Kaleši and Ismail Redžep, *Prizrenac Kukli Beg i njegove zadužbine*, in *Prilozi za Orientalnu Filologiju*, viii-ix (Sarajevo 1958-9), 145-68 (with ed. of *waḳfiyye*); D. Panić, *Bogorodica Ljeviška*, Belgrade 1960; H. Redžić, *Pet osmalijskih potkupolni spomenika na Kosovu in Metohiji*, in *Starine Kosova i Metohije, Antikitete të Kosovë Metohis*, i (Priština 1961), 95-112; Ḥ. Kaleši, *Kada je crkva Svete Bogorodice Ljeviške u Prizrenu pretvorena u camiju*, in *Prilozi za Književnost, Jezik, Istoriju i Folklor*, xxvii/3-4 (Belgrade 1962), 253-61; idem, *Prizren kao kulturni centar za vreme Turskog perioda*, in *Gjurmime Albanolojike*, i (Priština 1962), 91-118; M. Radovanović, *Stanovništvo Prizrenskog Podgora*, in *Glasnik Muzeja Kosova i Metohije* (1964), 253-415; art. *Prizren* in *Enciklopedia Jugoslavije*, vi, Zagreb 1965, 621-2; Mehmed Mujezinović, *Nadpisi na nadgrobim spomenicima Suzi-Čelebija i Neharija u Prizrenu*, in *Prilozi za Orientalnu Fililogiju*, xii-xiii (1965), 265-8 (with large facs. of both texts); Hasan Kaleshi-H.J. Kornrumpf, *Das Wilajet Prizren, Beitrag zur Geschichte der türkischen Staatsreform im 19. Jahrh.*, in *Südost-Forschungen*, xxvi (1967), 176-283 (with list of *sandjaḳ beys* from 1553 till 1908 and genealogical tree of the Rotulla Pas͟has); S. Nenadović, *Dušanova zadužbina Manastir Svetih Arhandjela kod Prizrena*, Belgrade 1967 (= *Spomenik Srpska Akademija Nauka i Umetnosti*, cxvi, N.S. 18); K. Özergin, H. Kaleşi, I. Eren, *Prizren kitabeleri*, in *Vakıflar Dergisi*, vii (1968), 75-96; P. Bartl, *Die albanische Muslime zur Zeit der nationalen Unabhängigkeitsbewegung 1878-1912*, Wiesbaden 1968 (on the League of Prizren); Nimetullah Hafiz, *Prizrenli Şeyh Hacı Ömer Lutfi ve onun edebi yapıtları*, in *Sesler*, no. 60 (Skopje 1971), 57-65; H. Kaleši, *Najstariji vakufski dokumenti u Jugoslaviji na Arapskom jeziku*, Priština 1972, 257-74 (on the identity of the two Sinān Pas͟has); Madžida Bećirbegović, *Prosveteni objekti islamske arhitekture na Kosovu*, in *Starine Kosova*, vi-vii (Priština 1972-3), 81-96; Roksanda Timotijević, *Crkva Sv. Spasa u Prizren, same Starine*, in *ibid.*, 65-79; H. Kaleši-I. Eren, *Prizrenac Mahmud-Paša Rotul, njegove zadužbine i vakufnama*, in *ibid.*, 23-64; Selami Pulaha, *Nahija e Altun-Ilisë dhe popullsia e saj në fund të shekullit XV*, in *Gjurmime Albanolojike*, i (Priština 1972), 194-272 (French résumé; shows early presence of Albanians in Prizren area); Nimetullah Hafiz, *Hacı Ömer Lutfunun tarihi eserleri*, in *VIII. Türk Tarih Kongrese*, ii, Ankara 1981, 1216-22; Džemal Ćehajić, *Derviški Redovi u Jugoslovenskim Zemljama*, Sarajevo 1986; Jusuf Sureja, *Prizrenski turski govor*, Priština 1987; A. Popović, *Les dervisches balkaniques. I. La Rifaiyya*, in *Zeitschrift für Balkanologie*, xxv/2 (Berlin 1989), 167-98; *II*, in xxvi/2, 142-83; art. *Aşık Çelebi*, in *Türkiye Diyanet Vakfı İslâm Ansiklopedisi*, iii, Istanbul 1991, 549-50.

The Ottoman *taḥrīrs* from 1530, 1550 and 1570, and the *d͟jizye* and *ʿawāriḍ defters* from 1591 and 1643, preserved in the Başbakanlık Arşivi in Istanbul, have not yet been published. (M. Kiel)

PROCLUS [see buruḳlus].

PTOLEMY [see baṭlamiyūs].

P'U SHOU-KENG, Chinese Muslim merchant and official. Although somewhat neglected by classical Chinese and Muslim writers, P'u Shou-keng, whose surname was probably derived from Arabic "Abū", was born in the mid-13th century. As to his place of origin, one theory suggests he was born into a sinicised Central Asian family that had settled in Sze-chuan during the early Sung and later moved to Ch'üan-chou (known as Zaytūn to Muslim and Western travellers in mediaeval times [see al-ṣīn]). Another has it that his family migrated there from Champa in Southeast Asia in the second half of the Sung period. The third, and most likely, maintains that he was from a South Arabian family who had settled in Kuang-chou.

P'u was one of the wealthiest sea traders in the provinces of Fu-kien and Canton. In about 1250 A.D. he was appointed as Superintendent of Shipping Trade in Ch'üan-chou, a post he held for thirty years. Through this post he monopolised trade profits and amassed great wealth. However, towards the end of the Sung, his defection to the Mongols (attributable to his anger at the misappropriation by the Sung court of his personal fortune to finance the war against the Mongols) led directly to the Mongol conquest of all China. Following the establishment of the Mongol-Yüan Dynasty, P'u was appointed Commissioner for Infantry and Cavalry for Defence and Attack. Later he became Assistant Civil Councillor of Kiang-si Province and in 1281 one of the two Executive Assistants of the Fu-kien Provincial Secretariat. Thereafter he is little mentioned in sources and doubtless at some point died. His family flourished in government posts throughout the Yüen period.

P'u and his family were devout Muslims, sponsoring Muslim communities in Fu-kien, donating money to repair Ch'üan-chou city wall and *waḳf* land for Muslim cemeteries. P'u's son donated money for the reconstruction of the city's Ch'ing-chin-ssu mosque. Ch'üan-chou became the biggest trade port and important centre for Muslim missionaries and travellers to China. During the Ming period (1368-1644), however, its significance declined and P'u's descendants were banned from civil posts by the Ming rulers on acount of his previous disloyalty to the Sung. One, however, distinguished himself as a writer during the Manchu-Ch'ing period (1644-1911). P'u Sung-ling's *Liao-Chai Chih-i* ("Strange tales from a Make-up Studio") contains Central Asian characters and reflects many Islamic traditions.

Bibliography: Chang, Hsiu-min, *Chan-ts'êng Jên Chams Yi-ju Chung-kuo Kao* ("On the Cham people's migration into China"), in *Hsüeh Yüen*, ii/7 (1948), 41-59; Ch'en, Mao-jên, *Ch'üan-nan Tsa-chih* ("Miscellanea on South Ch'üan-chou"), in *Pao-yen-chai Mi-ji*, vol. x, reprint of *Shêng-shih Shang-chai* edition, Taipei: Yi-wen [n.d.]; Fujita, Toyohachi, *Yule Shi Chū Malco Polo Kikō Hosei Nisoku* ("Two corrections to H. Yule's *Ser Marco Polo*"), in *Tōyō Gaku Ho*, iii (1913), 443-8; Huai, Yin-pu (eds.), *Ts'ung-hsiu Ch'üan-chou Fu-chih* ("Revised gazetteer of Ch'üan-chou") 4 vols., repr. of 1870 edition, Tainan: City Archive Office, 1953; Kuwabara, Jitsuzô, *On P'u Shou-keng*, in *Memoirs of the Research Department of Tōyō Bunko*, ii (1928), 1-79, vii (1935), 1-104; Lo, Hsiang-lin, *P'u Shou-keng Chuan* ("Biography of P'u Shou-keng"), Taipei: Chung-hua Wen-hua Publisher, 1955; Sugimoto, Naojirō, *Bojuku no Kokuseki Mondai* ("On P'u Shou-keng's nationality"), in *Tōyōshi Kenkyu*, xi/5-6 (1956), 66-76). (Chang-Kuan Lin)

PŪNA, now officially *Pūne*, conventional European rendering Poona, a city of South India located in a District with the same name, on the Dakhan plateau, at 18° 31′ N. latitude and 73° 51′ E. longitude. The Pūna district is first mentioned in Ras͟htrakuta inscriptions of the 2nd/8th century as *Punya Vis͟haya* and *Punaka*, which had "a thousand villages." The town can be identified for the first time in the *Punaka-vādi* of another Ras͟htrakuta inscription of the 4th/10th century. According to local tradition, Pūna was a hamlet of about fifteen huts in 613 A.D.

There are no historical records concerning Pūna from the 5th/11th to the 8th/14th centuries. During the reign of ʿAlāʾ al-Dīn K͟hald͟jī [see k͟hald͟jīs], the Sultan of Dihlī from 696/1296 to 716/1316, Pūna came under Muslim control. Hindu temples were now converted into *dargāhs*, the town became a Muslim *ḳaṣaba* and a military base surrounded by a mud-wall. Within the wall there were the Muslim army and a few villagers, outside were the Hindu cultivators, traders, village officials, and brahmans. Pūna commanded the communications to its immediate hinterland, the Maval Hills, but was not situated along any of the major trade routes of the Dakhan. The *ḳaṣaba* was subsequently included in the Bahmanī Sultanate [*q.v.*], from the 8th/14th century onwards, and in the Niẓām S͟hāhī Sultanate [*q.v.*] in the late 9th/15th and early 10th/16th centuries, both Dakhan-based Muslim powers, which did not, however, make Pūna their capital. The Russian traveller Nikitin mentions D͟junnar, not Pūna, as the main town, while travelling through the area in the late days of the Bahmanī Sultanate.

In 1004/1595 the *ḳaṣaba* of Pūna, with its surrounding district, was part of a *d͟jāgīr* [*q.v.*] conferred by the

Niẓām Shāhī government on the ancestors of the future Marāthā king Śivādjī. The town was destroyed several times, worst in 1040/1630, when it was captured and burnt by the ʿĀdil Shāhī army. About 1047/1637 Śivādjī's father first made his residence in the town of Pūna, which started to increase substantially in size. Śivādjī, however, spent most of his time at Satara, in his hill-forts, or campaigning. Pūna changed hands between the Mughals and the Marāthās [*q.vv.*] before it came into the possession of the Pēshwās [*q.v.*] early in the 12th/18th century. Due to the Mughal presence, the number of mosques increased, as did the Muslim population of the town. Khāfī Khān speaks of Pūna in the time of Awrangzīb as "situated in a treeless plain." By 1133/1720, the old *ḳaṣaba* may have had a total population of 20,000 to 30,000. By 1164/1750, Pūna had officially been acknowledged as the Marāthā capital, and, as the residence of the Pēshwās, expanded dramatically, while "a million mango trees" were planted in and around the town. The Pēshwās built the Shanwar Palace, the most magnificent building of Pūna, which was, however, destroyed by fire in 1243/1827. Numerous temples were erected, especially on Parvati hill, to the south-west of the city. From about 1143/1730 to 1234/1818, Pūna was the city of the Pēshwās, a bureaucratic-military capital with a largely Citpāvan-brahman constituency. It did not have the economic base of such Muslim cities as Āgra, Dihlī, Lahore, or Murshidābād, nor did it have the commercial promise of the new British cities of Madras, Bombay or Calcutta. Pūna had a peculiarly brahman character, and, for the most part, was a creation of the Pēshwās, who transformed it into a city of 150,000. Muslims were only a small community in 12th/18th-century Pūna, and many of them were converts from the Hindu population of the period before the rise of Śivādjī. But both Shīʿī and Sunnī groups were represented. Later in the same century, Muʾmins and Bohorās [*q.v.*] came to the city to trade, and there were also a small number of Sīdīs, descendants of African Muslims, and mercenary Arabs. In 1225/1810 there were in Pūna 412 Hindu temples and 10 Muslim shrines or mosques. The Pēshwās' generosity towards Muslim shrines in Pūna (as elsewhere) is nevertheless on record. In general, life in Pūna was much influenced by Indo-Muslim culture. The Pēshwās, for instance, affected a semi-Mughal style of dress for formal occasions.

In 1233/1817 Pūna was occupied by the British, and British troops remained in Pūna until 1368/1948, in a separate cantonment. The population increased again, to 276,000 in 1360/1941. In the post-Independence period, Pūna became an industrialised city of over 800,000 in 1391/1971, and over 1,500,000 in the 1400s/1980s. The percentage of Muslims in the city has, from the mid-12th/18th century onwards, never been more than ten, and is less now. But the Muslim population in Pūna is still sizeable, and there is considerable communalist tension.

Bibliography: V.D. Divekar, *Survey of material in Marathi on the economic and social history of India. 3*, in *The Indian Economic and Social History Review*, xv/3 (July-Sept. 1978), 404-5; B.G. Gokhale, *Poona in the eighteenth century: an urban history*, Delhi 1988; J.-Y. Le Guillou, *Le voyage au-delà des trois mers d'Afanasij Nikitin (1466-1472)*, Quebec City 1978; K.V. Purandare (ed.), *Purandare daftar*, Puna 1929; S.B. Sawant, *The city of Poona: a study in urban geography*, Puna 1978.

(A. Wink)

PŪR-I BAHĀʾ-i Djāmī, Tādj al-Dīn b. Bahāʾ al-Dīn, a Persian poet who was active in the second part of the 7th/13th century when Persia was ruled by the Mongols. Most of the biographical information is based on statements to be found in his verses. His *takhalluṣ* was Pūr-i Bahāʾ. He was a native of Djām in Khurāsān and was born into a family of *ḳāḍīs* and scholars; his ancestors had held the post of *ḳāḍī* in the *wilāyat* of Djām since the days of the Sāmānids, but by Pūr-i Bahāʾ's time had lost this function. In his youth he lived in Harāt, where Mawlānā Rukn al-Dīn Ḳubāʾī and Saʿīd-i Harawī were his masters in poetry.

Pūr-i Bahāʾ was the *maddāḥ* of several high officials, who all belong to the reign of the Īlkhān Abaḳa (1265-82 [*q.v.*]). While living in Khurāsān he praised ʿIzz al-Dīn Ṭāhir al-Faryūmadī (d. *ca.* 668/1270) and his son Wadjīh al-Dīn Zangī (executed in 685/1287) who both were appointed *wazīr*/*nāʾib* of that province, the former in 1265, the latter in 1270 and again in 1282. Another prominent *mamdūḥ* was Naṣīr al-Dīn Ṭūsī (d. 672/1274 [*q.v.*]). When Pūr-i Bahāʾ left his native province he lived in Tabrīz, Iṣfahān and Baghdād where he became the panegyrist of several members of the Djuwaynī family: Shams al-Dīn the *ṣāḥib dīwān* (executed 1284), ʿAlāʾ al-Dīn ʿAṭā Malik, the famous historian and governor of Baghdād (d. 1283 [*q.v.*]) and Bahāʾ al-Dīn b. Shams al-Dīn, the governor of Iṣfahān (d. 1279). Nothing is known of his fate after the death of these patrons, a fact which must also have affected his life considerably.

Ḥamd Allāh Mustawfī Ḳazwīnī (d. after 740/1339-40) confirms in his *Taʾrīkh-i guzīda* that Pūr-i Bahāʾ's *dīwān* was well-known. Verses of Pūr-i Bahāʾ are quoted in anthologies, biographical or historical works. By far the most comprehensive collection of his poems is to be found in a comparatively late manuscript dated 1029/1619-20, written for the Ḳuṭb-Shāhīs [*q.v.*] of Ḥaydarābād in South India, and entitled *Kitāb-i Pūr-i Bahāʾ*; but as it does not contain all the verses cited in other sources it can hardly represent his complete *dīwān*.

This manuscript comprises 41 *ḳaṣāʾid*, 13 *muḳaṭṭaʿāt*, 1 *tarkīb-band*, 1 *mathnawī* called *Kār-nāma-yi awḳāf*, 2 *ghazals* and 73 *rubāʿiyyāt*, altogether totalling 25,216 verses. With the exception of the *rubāʿiyyāt*, his poetry is devoted to panegyrics (*madḥ*), satire (*hadjw*) or quite often a mixture of both. Sanāʾī and Sūzanī were his favourite poets and admired models.

Pūr-i Bahāʾ shows a predilection for complicated metres and rare words. He makes frequent use of financial and administrative technical terms, and is famous for his macaronic pieces that mix Persian with Mongolian and Eastern Turkic vocabulary, so that most of his verses are not easily understood. There are many comments on the political and social grievances of the time, such as excessive taxation or the improper behaviour of state officials, and allusions to otherwise unknown or little-known individuals. The satirical *mathnawī Kār-nāma-yi awḳāf* criticises the bad state of affairs prevailing within the pious endowments. For his criticism and satire, Pūr-i Bahāʾ indulges in pornographic images and obscene words; this may have been the true motive for the copying of his poems for the Ḳuṭb-Shāhī ruler's library.

Bibliography: 1. Mss. (a) BL Or. 9213: *Kitāb -i Pūr-i Bahāʾ*, *Dīwān* of Tādj al-Dīn b. Bahāʾ al-Dīn (= Pūr-i Bahāʾ-i Djāmī), copied for the library of Muḥammad Ḳuṭb-Shāh at Ḥaydarābād in 1029/1619-20. Cf. G.M. Meredith-Owens, *Handlist of Persian manuscripts*, 56. (b) Cambridge University Library, E.G. Browne Collection V.5 (7), *Madjmūʿa of ancient dīwāns*, ff. 225b-226b. Cf. *Descriptive catalogue*, Cambridge 1932, 2250.

2. Editions and translations: Browne, *LHP*, iii, 111-15; Dihḵhudā, *Lughat-nāma*, s.v. *Pūr-i Bahāʾ*; V. Minorsky, *Pūr-i Bahāʾs "Mongol Ode"*, in *BSOAS*, xviii (1956), 261-78 (also in *Iranica, twenty articles by V. Minorsky*, Tehran 1964, 274-91); idem, *Pūr-i Baha and his poems*, in *Charisteria orientalia (Festschrift for Jan Rypka)*, Prague 1956, 186-201 (also in *Iranica, twenty articles*, 292-305); Iradj Afshār, *Kār-nāma-yi awḵāf. Aṯhar-i Tādj al-Dīn Nasāʾī*, in *Farhang-i Īrān-zamīn*, viii (1339/1960), 5-22, based on a 7th/13th century manuscript, wrongly ascribed to a certain Tādj al-Dīn Nasāʾī, who is only a protagonist of that satire. This edition of the *Kār-nāma-yi awḵāf* was compared to its more comprehensive version in the *Kitāb-i Pūr-i Bahāʾ*, re-ed. with German tr. Birgitt Hoffmann, *Von falschen Asketen und «unfrommen» Stiftungen*, in *Proceedings of the first European Conference of Iranian Studies*, in Turin, 7-11 September 1987, Part 2, 409-85.

3. Biographical notes on Pūr-i Bahāʾ and/or specimens of his poetry in historical or biographical works. Mustawfī, *Taʾrīkh-i guzīda*, ed. ʿAbd al-Ḥusayn Nawāʾī, Tehran 1339*Sh*/1960, 724; Sayfī Harawī, *Tārīkh-nāma-yi Harāt*, ed. Siddīqī, Calcutta 1944, 346-7; Dawlatshāh Samarḳandī, *Tadhkirat al-shuʿarāʾ*, ed. Ḥādjdjī Muḥammad Ramaḍānī, Tehran 1338 *sh*/1959, 136-8; Faṣīḥ Aḥmad b. Djalāl al-Dīn Muḥammad Khʷāfī, *Mudjmal-i Faṣīḥī*, ed. Maḥmūd Farrūḵh, ii, Tehran 1340 *sh*/1961, 337, 340. For further references, see Dhabīḥ Allāh Ṣafā, *Taʾrīkh-i adabiyyāt dar Īrān*, iii/1, Tehran 1363 *sh*/1984, 660-71. (B. Hoffmann)

PŪR-I DĀWŪD, Ibrāhīm, Persian scholar, poet and patriot, born in 1886/1264 at Rasht [*q.v.*], the son of a merchant-landowner of Sayyid descent. From boyhood he delighted in poetry, and himself became an acclaimed romantic and patriotic poet (Browne, p. XVIII; Rypka, 376). As a student in Tehran in 1906 he witnessed the struggle for constitutional reform, which affected him deeply. He studied law briefly in Paris, but abandoned it for ancient Iranian studies, which he pursued in France and Germany for a number of years. In 1924 the Pārsīs [*q.v.*] invited him to translate Zoroaster's *Gāthās* into modern Persian. He accordingly spent some time in India, where this translation was published in 1927, to be followed by renderings of the Avestan *Yašts* (1931), *Khorda Avesta* (1932) and *Yasna* (1934) (Tarapore, 14, 19-22, 34-6). His great aim was both to serve Iranian Zoroastrians and enlighten Iranian Muslims about their cultural heritage. In 1938 he became professor of Avestan, Pahlavi and ancient Iranian history at Tehran University, publishing thereafter other scholarly works on Iranian religion, history and folklore, as well as poems. He died in 1347 *sh*/1968.

Bibliography: E.G. Browne, *The press and poetry of modern Persia*, Cambridge 1914; J. Rypka, *et alii*, *History of Iranian literature*, Dordrecht 1968, 385; J.C. Tarapore, in *Professor Poure Davoud memorial volume*, ii, Bombay 1951, 1-48. Further sources in his obituary, in *Rāhnamā-yi Kitāb* xi/9 (1347/1968), 486. (Mary Boyce)

PUSHTŪNISTĀN [see pashtūnistān].

PŪST (p.), skin, Turkish *pōst* or *pōstakī*, a tanned sheepskin, used as the ceremonial seat or throne of a *pīr* or *shaykh* of a dervish order. The head, sides and foot had mystical significances ascribed to them. It corresponds to the Arabic *bisāṭ*. According to Ewliyā Čelebi (Istanbul 1314/1896-7, i, 495), the *murīd*, after passing the test by the *pīr*, is called *ṣāḥib pūst*. On ceremonial occasions amongst the Bektāshī order, the hall or convent was said to have been set out with twelve *pūst*s of white sheepskin in remembrance of the twelve *Imām*s or standing symbolically for twelve great figures in Bektāshī history, but in the last days of the order's open existence in Turkey (i.e. before 1925; see bektāshiyya), the number of special *pūst*s was restricted to not more than four, in the experience of Birge (see *Bibl.*).

Bibliography: J.P. Brown, *The darvishes*, Oxford 1927; G. Jacob, in *Türkische Bibliothek*, ix, Berlin 1908; H. Thorning, in *ibid.*, xvi, 1913; J.K. Birge, *The Bektashi order of dervishes*, London and Hartford, Conn. 1937, 176 (with illustr. no. 2), 178-9. (R. Levy*)

PŪST-NESHĪN (p.), lit. "the one sitting on the [sheep's] skin", the title given to the *baba* or head of a dervish *tekke* in Persian and Ottoman Turkish Ṣūfī practice, e.g. amongst the Bektāshīs [see bektāshiyya].

Bibliography: J.K. Birge, *The Bektashi order of dervishes*, London 1937, 57 n. 2, 269. (Ed.)

PUWASA [see Suppl.].

R

RĀʾ the tenth letter of the Arabic alphabet, transcribed as /r/, and with a numerical value of 200, according to the eastern letter order [see abdjad].

Definition. Vibrant, apical, alveolar and voiced. This trilled consonant is produced by a series of movements of the tongue produced a little behind the gums of the incisors. Sībawayh calls the consonant /r/ "hard" (*shadīd*) and "repeated" (*mukarrar*), because of the repetition (*takrīr*) of the tongue's movement during the sound's production. For al-Khalīl, the /r/ is a "pointed" (*dhawlaḳī*) consonant because it is produced with the tip (*dhawlaḳ*) of the tongue. In phonology, the phoneme /r/ is defined by the oppositions /r - l/, /r -n/ and /r - gh/; the phoneme /r/ is thus non-lateral, non-nasal and anterior.

Velarisation (*tafḵhīm*). As well as the simple realisation of /r/, the grammarians describe an emphatic realisation /ṛ/ brought about by the phonetic surroundings. The /r/ is velarised (*mufakhkham*) when it is followed by the vowel /a/ or the vowel /u/, or by one of the seven "high" (*mustaʿliya*) consonants: /ṭ/, /ḍ/, /ẓ/, /ṣ/, /ḳ/, /kh/ and /gh/, itself followed by /a/ or /u/; contrariwise, the /r/ is not velarised if it is followed by the vowel /i/ or the semi-vowel /y/. This emphatic realisation is a combinatory variant of the same phoneme, and has only a phonetic, extra-phonological value. One of the properties of the emphatic /ṛ/ is to prevent, through its proximity, the inclination (*imāla*) of the vowel /a/ towards /i/. The opposition of non-emphatic /r/ and emphatic /ṛ/ exists also in Arabic dialects. In most eastern dialects, the opposition remains purely phonetic, with no distinctive character, and the causes producing emphasisation are the same as those in literary Arabic; but in certain eastern dialects and in the western ones, the opposition of the two forms of /r/ has a distinctive value, and one can speak of two phonemes, non-emphatic /r/ and emphatic /ṛ/.

Assimilation (*idghām*). Because of its specific character, the trilling or repetition (*takrīr*) which accompanies its emission, Sībawayh considers that /r/ cannot be assimilated (*mudgham*) to another consonant, since it would lose its character; however, the assimilations of /-rl-/ into /- ll -/ are found amongst certain "readers" (*ḳurrāʾ*) of the Ḳurʾān.

In modern Arabic dialects, /r/ undergoes very few conditioned alterations and is subject to only one non-conditioned alteration; in certain sedentary dialects, both eastern and western, the /r/ may be realised as a voiced velar spirant /gh/.

Bibliography: Sībawayh, *al-Kitāb*, ed. Derenbourg, Paris 1889, ii, 283-93, 454, al-Khalīl, *K. al-ʿAyn*, ed. Darwīsh, Baghdād 1967, 57, 65; Ibn Yaʿīsh, *Sharḥ al-Mufaṣṣal*, ed. Cairo, ix, 61-2, x, 143; Astarābādhī, *Sharḥ al-Shāfiya*, ed. Cairo, iii, 20-3, 264; J. Cantineau, *Etudes de linguistique arabe*, Paris 1960, 48-50, 172, 200; H. Fleisch, *Traité de philologie arabe*, Beirut 1961, i, 57-61, 87-8; A. Roman, *Etude de la phonologie et de la morphologie de la koinè arabe*, Aix-Marseilles 1983, i, 52, 70-2, 217, 259-60.

(G. Troupeau)

RABʿ (a., pl. *ribāʿ*) originally means home, domicile, home town or home country; the verb *rabaʿa* means "to dwell". In the context of Cairene architecture, it designates a type of urban dwelling which is a rental multi-unit building founded for investment. It can also refer to the living quarters belonging to a religious institution.

In his description of Cairo in the 5th/11th century, Nāṣir-i Khusraw [*q.v.*] mentions tenant buildings that sheltered as many as 350 dwellers, and ʿAbd al-Laṭīf al-Baghdādī (d. 629/1231-2) writes about *rabʿ*s in Cairo which included 50 living units (*bayt*) (*al-Ifāda wa 'l-iʿtibār*, 55, 58; de Sacy, *Relation*, 374-411). Many travellers have described multi-storied houses in Fusṭāṭ which are also mentioned in Geniza documents (Goitein, *A Mediterranean society*, iv, 58-9). It is not clear, however, whether the multi-storied houses should necessarily be identified with rental buildings. Apart from the multi-storied houses, there were buildings consisting of shops or stores on the street level with living units on the upper level having an independent entrance (*ibid.*, 17). Both the multi-storied house and the rental apartment complex are documented in papyri concerning large Egyptian cities of the Ptolemaic period (Nowicka, *Maison privée*, 108, 125). In the Fāṭimid sources, large dwelling complexes are designated by the term *dār*; it cannot be definitely stated whether or not these were the equivalent of the Roman *insulae*. The *rabʿ* in the specific sense of a Cairene dwelling type consisting of a row of living units built above a row of shops or a commercial structure is not documented before the Mamlūk period.

The most common type of living-unit in a *rabʿ* is called *ṭabaḳa* (pl. *ṭibāḳ*); larger apartments are referred to as *riwāḳ* or *ḳāʿa*. The *ṭabaḳa* was a kind of duplex with a vestibule (*dihlīz*), a recess for water jars, a latrine and a main room consisting of a slightly raised *īwān* and a *dūrḳāʿa*. An inner staircase led up to a mezzanine (*mustaraḳa*) used for sleeping. Each unit had its own enclosed private roof. A *ṭabaḳa* may also be a triplex with an additional room above the mezzanine.

The *rabʿ* was often built on the second floor above a row of shops or store-rooms or above any type of caravanserail like a *wakāla*, a *khān*, a *funduḳ* or *ḳaysariyya*. In the first case it was built along the street. If it was associated with a commercial structure, it was adapted to its layout, i.e. it was built around a courtyard. As the basic study of L. Ali Ibrahim demonstrates (see *Bibl.*), the windows of the living units, as a rule, overlooked the street whenever they could be located on the street side, which contradicts the wide-spread conception that residential architecture in Egypt is introverted. Each *rabʿ* was served by an independent staircase which was reached through a separate entrance from the street. The staircase led to a gallery leading to the living units. There were also *rabʿ*s built independently without commercial structures, with living units also on the ground floor. Since the 9th/15th century the *rabʿ* type of housing was adopted to serve as living quarters for the community of the *khānḳāh*s and *madrasa*s instead of the traditional cells. Such *rabʿ*s were built by Sultan Barsbāy and Amīr Ḳurḳumās at their respective religious-funerary complexes in the cemetery. A different kind of *rabʿ* was the *rabʿ al-zaytī* mentioned by Maḳrīzī (*Khiṭaṭ*, ii, 78). Located in the green outskirts of Cairo, along the Nāṣirī Canal, its apartments on four sides overlooked gardens and orchards. It was frequented by a licentious clientèle (*yanziluhā ahl al-khalāʿa li 'l-ḳaṣf*).

The rental *rabʿ*s were built by members of the ruling class and other wealthy investors who made them into *waḳf*, i.e. they alienated their revenues either to endow philanthropic and religious foundations or for their private family trusts. The dwellers of the *rabʿ* were not poor, but middle-class citizens who were able to pay the rent that made this form of dwelling a lucrative investment. The *waḳf* archives of Cairo provide a wealth of *rabʿ* descriptions from the Mamlūk as well as the Ottoman periods (see H. Sayed). From the Mamlūk period only *rabʿ*s built by the ruling establishment have survived, those of the sultans Barsbāy, Īnāl, Ḳāyitbāy, al-Ghūrī and Amīr Ḳurḳumās. From the Ottoman period there are still a good number of *rabʿ*s built by *amīr*s and other notables.

Bibliography: 1. Sources. Nāṣir-i Khusraw, *Safar-nāma*, Fr. tr. Ch. Schefer, Paris 1881, Eng. tr. W.M. Thackston, Albany 1986; ʿAbd al-Laṭīf al-Baghdādī, *K. al-Ifāda wa 'l-iʿtibār*, Cairo 1931, Fr. tr. S. de Sacy, *Relation de l'Egypte par Abd Allatif, médecin arabe de Baghdad*, Paris 1810; Maḳrīzī, *Khiṭaṭ*, Būlāḳ 1270.

2. Studies. M. Nowicka, *La maison privée dans l'Egypte ptolemaique*, Warsaw-Cracow 1969; L. Ali Ibrahim, *Middle-class living units in Mamluk Cairo: architecture and terminology*, in *Art and Archaeology Research Papers*, xiv (1978), 24-30; A. Raymond, *The Rabʿ: a type of collective housing during the Ottoman period*, in *Architecture as symbol of self-identity. Proceedings of Seminar Four (1980) held in Fez, Morocco ... 1979*, The Aga Khan award for architecture, Cambridge, Mass. 1980; M. Zakariya, *Le Rabʿ de Tabbāna*, in *AI*, xvi (1980), 275-96; S.D. Goitein, *A Mediterranean society*, iv, Berkeley, etc. 1983; J.Ch. Depaule *et alii*, *Actualité de l'habitat ancien au Caire. Le Rabʿ Qizlar*, CEDEJ Dossier 4, Cairo 1985; H. Sayed, *The Rabʿ in Cairo. A window on Mamluk architecture and urbanism*, unpubl. diss M.I.T., Cambridge, Mass. 1987; M.M. Amin–L. Ali Ibrahim, *al-Muṣṭalaḥāt al-miʿmāriyya fi 'l-wathāʾiḳ al-mamlūkiyya*, Cairo 1990.

(Doris Behrens-Abouseif)

The *rab^c* of Sultan al-Ghawrī at his *wakāla* near al-Azhar.

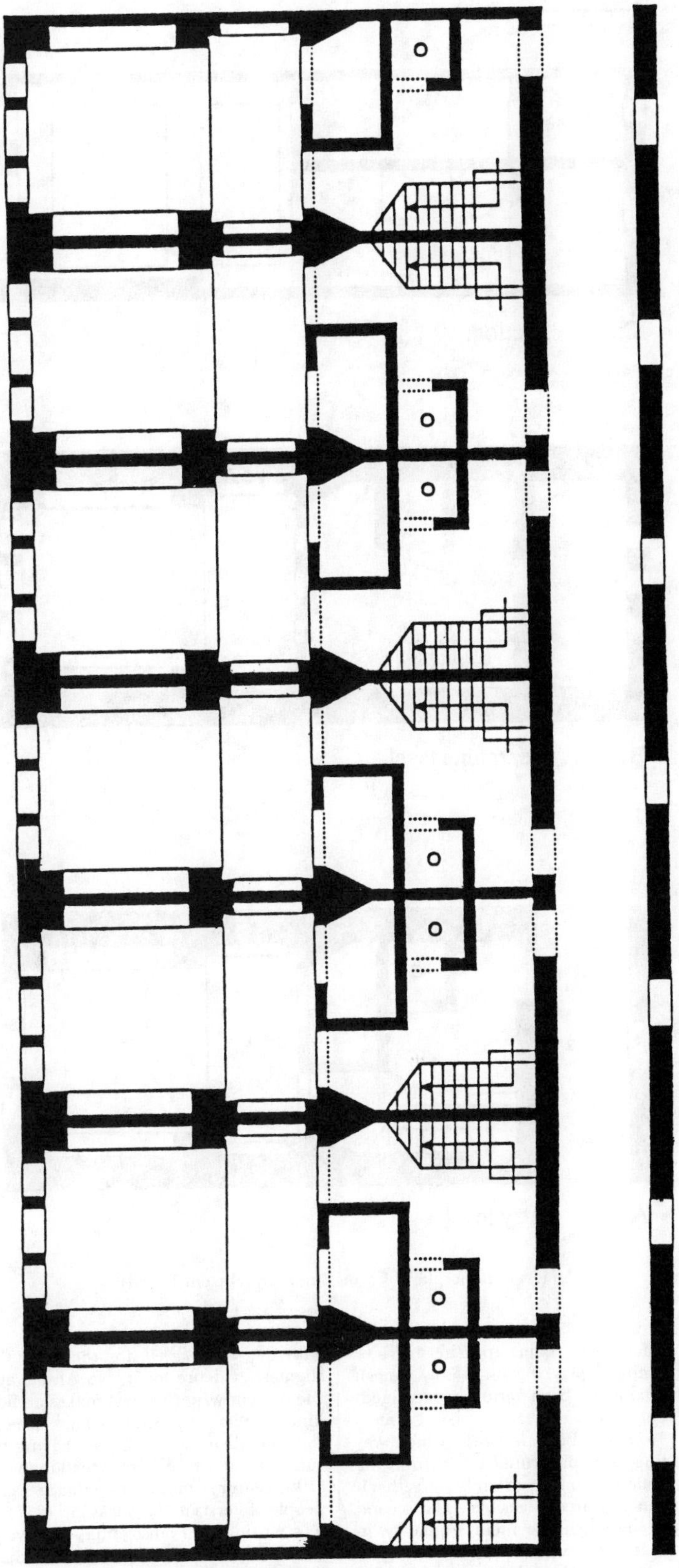

Diagrammatic plan of a *rab*^c block (by Hazem Sayed).

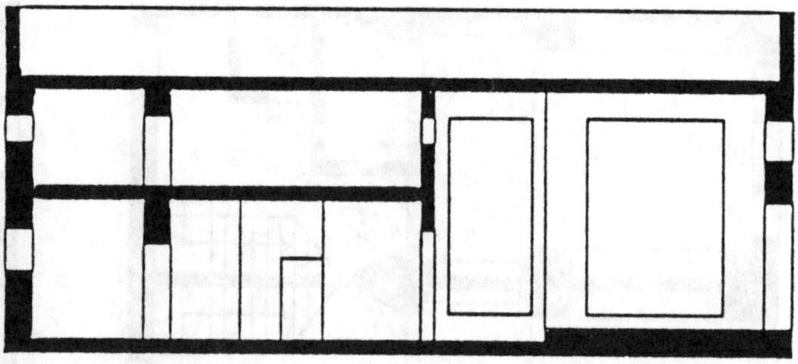

C: Section.

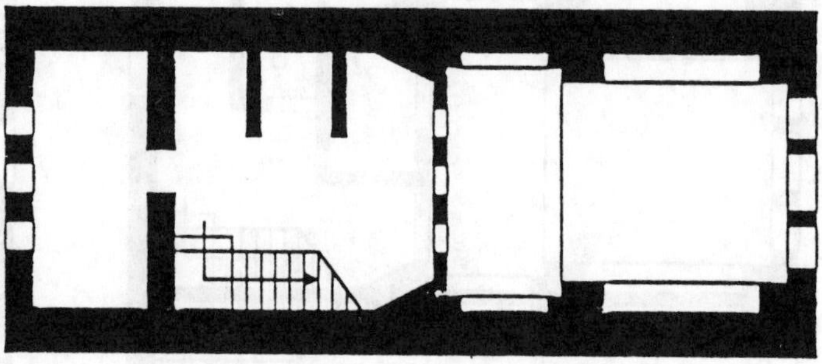

B: Mezzanine level.

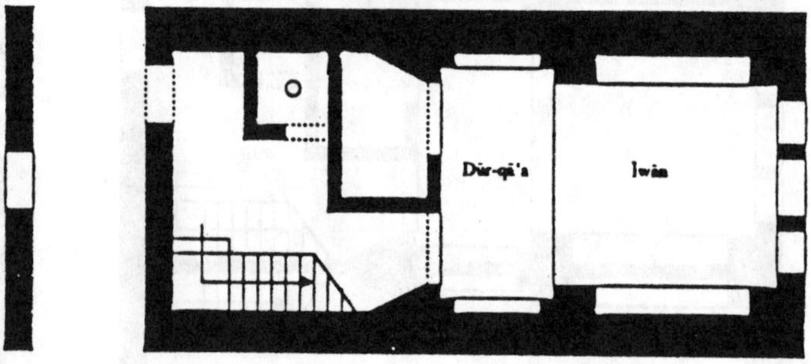

A: Entry level.

Diagrammatic plan of a *rab*ᶜ unit (by Hazem Sayed).

RABĀB (A.), the generic name for the viol, or any stringed instrument played with a bow (*ḳaws*). The origin of the name has been variously explained: *a.* from the Hebrew *lābab* (*l* and *r* being interchangeable); *b.* from the Persian *rubāb*, which was played with the fingers or plectrum; and *c.* from the Arabic *rabba* (to collect, arrange, assemble together). The first derivation is scarcely feasible. The second has a *raison d'être*, although the mere similarity in name must not be accepted without question. In spite of the oft-repeated statement that the Arabs admit that they borrowed the *rabāb* from the Persians, together with the word *kamān* for the bow, there is not the slightest evidence for it. No Arabic author (so far as the present writer knows) makes an admission of this kind, nor have the Arabs adopted the word *kamān* for the bow, their own term *ḳaws* having been considered sufficient. It is true that we read in the *Mafātīḥ al-ᶜulūm* (10th century) that "The *rabāb* is well known to the people of Persia and Khurāsān" (237), but this author was writing in Transoxania, and we know from al-Fārābī that the *rabāb* was also well known in Arabian lands. One argument against the alleged borrowing from Persia is that the *rubāb* with the Persians was always a plucked and not a bowed instrument. Still, the Arabs may have borrowed the plucked instrument and adapted it to the bow. On the other hand, the Arabic root *rabba* as the parent of the word *rabāb* has much in its favour. As the Arabic musical accousticians point out, plucked instruments such as the *ʿūd* (lute), *ṭunbūr* (pandore), etc., gave short (*munfaṣil*) sounds, but bowed instruments such as the *rabāb* gave long or sustained (*muttaṣil*) sounds. It was application of the bow which "collected, arranged, or assembled" the short notes into one sustained note, hence the term *rabāb* being applied to the viol (see Farmer, *Studies*, i, 99).

The *rabāb* is mentioned as early as the Arabic polygraph al-Djāḥiẓ (d. 255/869) in his *Madjmūʿat al-rasāʾil*. Yet we cannot be sure whether this was the bowed *rabāb* or the plucked *rubāb*. At any rate, it already had a legendary history when he wrote. According to the *Kashf al-humūm* (15th-16th century), it is first found in the hands of a woman of the Banū Ṭayyiʾ (fol. 263). Turkish tradition ascribed its "invention" to a certain ʿAbd Allāh Fāryābī (Ewliyā Čelebī, *Seyāḥat-nāme*, i/2, 226, 234). An Andalusian legend places its invention within the Iberian peninsula (Delphin and Guin, *Notes sur la poésie et la musique arabes*, 59). One thing is certain: even if we have iconographic evidence of the viol in the 8th or 9th century (see below), the earliest literary evidence of the use of the bow comes from Arabic sources, i.e. from al-Fārābī (d. 950), the Ikhwān al-Ṣafāʾ (10th century), Ibn Sīnā (d. 1037), and Ibn Zaylā (d. 1048), as I have fully demonstrated elsewhere (*Studies*, i, 101-5).

Seven different forms of viol are known to Islamic peoples, viz. 1. the Rectangular Viol, 2. the Circular Viol, 3. the Boat-Shaped Viol, 4. the Pear-Shaped Viol, 5. the Hemispherical Viol, 6. the Pandore Viol, and 7. the Open Chest Viol.

1. The Rectangular Viol. This consists of a wooden frame, more or less rectangular, over the face (*wadjh*) and back (*ẓahr*) of which is stretched a membrane (*djilda*). The neck (*ʿunuḳ*) is cylindrical and is of wood, whilst the foot (*ridjl*) is of iron. It has either one or two strings (*awtār*), generally of horsehair. Al-Khalīl (d. 791) says that "the ancient Arabs sang their poems to its [the *rabāb*'s] voice [or sound]" (Farmer, *Studies*, i, 100). In the *Kashf al-humūm* (fol. 267) we read that it was used to accompany the pre-Islamic *ḳaṣīda* and the elegiac poem. Probably the pre-Islamic *rabāb* was of this rectangular form. Lane (*Lexicon*, 1005) held this latter view. Ibn Ghaybī (d. 1435) describes this viol of the Bedouin as rectangular (*murabbaʿ*) and with a membrane face and back and one string of horsehair (fol. 78b). Niebuhr (i, 144) says that it was still called the *murabbaʿ* in the 18th century. We certainly have a rectangular instrument shown in the frescoes of Ḳuṣayr ʿAmra (Musil, pl. xxxiv), but it is played with the fingers and not with a bow. Yet even in modern times the *rabāb* of the desert was to be found played in this way as well as with a bow (Crichton, ii, 380; Burckhardt, *Bedouins*, 43; idem, *Travels*, i, 389; Burton, *Personal narrative*, iii, 76). Niebuhr (Tab. xxvi, F) delineates a rectangular viol of two strings, although he says that he saw a viol of one string in Cairo. Villoteau (722-4, 913-18) distinguishes between the two instruments. In Egypt, he says, the *rabāb al-shāʿir* (poet's viol) had one string, whilst the *rabāb al-mughannī* (singer's viol) had two strings. Lane (*Mod. Egypt.*, chs. xviii, xxi) also describes them. These instruments never form part of a concert orchestra, being relegated to the folk. For other delineations of the instrument, see Fétis (*Hist.*, ii, 145), Engel (*Catalogue*, 211; *Researches*, 88), Chouquet (204), Sachs (*Reallex.*, 317). Actual specimens abound in museums, e.g. Brussels, no. 382 and New York, nos. 242, 391.

2. The Circular Viol. The modern instrument of this form consists of a circular wooden frame or pan, the face, and sometimes the back, being covered with a membrane. There is no foot. There is no special reference to this form in Arabic literature nor is there any definite inconographic evidence of it earlier than the 18th century, when it is described and delineated by Niebuhr (i, 144; Tab. xxvi, G), who found it at Baṣra. It had but one string. It is still found among the folk of Palestine (Sachsse, 30, 40, Tab. 3, 17) and the Maghrib (Chottin, 50), where it is still known as the *rabāb* or *ribāb*. For other delineations, see Lavignac (2790) and Chottin (pl. vi).

3. The Boat-Shaped Viol. This form is confined to the Maghrib. It consists of a piece of wood hollowed out into the shape of a boat. The chest (*ṣadr*) is covered with thin metal or wood pierced with ornamental rosettes (*nuwwārāt*), whilst the lower part is covered with a membrane. The head (*raʾs*) is at right angles to the body, and it is generally furnished with two strings. It seems to have been used by the Arabs and Moors of Spain since their invasion of the peninsula. It is praised by their 10th and 11th century writers Abū Bakr Yaḥyā Ibn Hudhayl (see al-Shalāḥī, fol. 15), and Ibn Ḥazm (see Muḥammad b. Ismāʿīl, 473), and doubtless they refer to either this instrument or the Pear-Shaped Viol (see below, 4) since the *Glossarium Latino-Arabicum* (11th century) equates *rabāb* with *lira dicta a varietate*. If we have no iconographic evidence of this viol from Arabian or Moorish sources, it certainly existed among the Spaniards, since the instruments in the *Cantigas de Santa Maria* (13th century) show definite oriental features; see Riaño (129) and Ribera (pl. xi). Ibn Khaldūn (d. 1406) is the first to describe this viol, although not very clearly (*Prolegomena*, in *Notices et extraits*, xvii, 354). It is not until the time of ʿAbd al-Raḥmān al-Fāsī (*ca.* 1650) that we get any musical details of the instrument (*JRAS* [1931], 366). European travellers (Addison, Windhus, Höst, Shaw) mention the instrument as popular in the Maghrib, and today it is one of the principal instruments in concert music. Höst gives us one of the earliest delineations of the instrument from Eastern sources (Tab. xxxi, 2). For a 19th century description, see F. Salvador-Daniel (80), and for a design, see Christianowich (pl. 1). Several delineations of both instruments and players may be seen in al-Ḥafnī (pls. 34, 39-52), Mahillon (i, 416-17), Fétis (*Hist.*, ii, 146), Engel (*Cat.*, 143), Chouquet (205), Sachs (*Reallex.*, 317), etc. For the instrument of Northern India called the *sārangi*, see Lavignac (350) and Fétis (ii, 298).

4. The Pear-Shaped Viol. Probably, the earliest Arabic reference to this instrument is that made by Ibn Khurradādhbih (d. *ca.* 912) who, in an oration before the caliph al-Muʿtamid (d. 893), says that the Byzantines had a wooden instrument of five strings called the *lūra* which was identical with the *rabāb* of the Arabs (al-Masʿūdī, *Murūdj*, viii, 91). We can probably identify the instrument in the famous Carrand Casket at Florence which dates from the 9th century (*L'Arte*, 1896, 24). From the Siculo-Moorish woodwork of the Palatine Chapel at Palermo (12th century) we see to better advantage what the Arabian instrument was like (*BZ* [1893], ii, 383). It was this form of the *rabāb*, probably, with which al-Fārābī (d. 950) deals (see Land, *Researches*, 130, 166). He gives full details of both the *accordatura* and scales. We know little about this instrument in Arabic-speaking lands

after the 13th-14th centuries, until it is described by Niebuhr (i, 143; Tab. xxvi, D) in the 18th century, and even then it appears to have been favoured only by the Greek population. It had three strings. It may have been used in the Mag͟hrib (Jackson, 159-60), but neither Villoteau nor Lane know of it in Egypt. In Turkey, it appears to have been adopted from the Greeks, possibly in the 17th century, and with the *ʿūd* and *lawta* plays a prominent part in concert music today (Lavignac, 3015). Recently, an attempt has been made to introduce this *rabāb turkī* or *arnaba*, as it is now called, into Egypt (al-Ḥafnī, 661, pl. 35). Designs of the instrument may be found in Engel (*Cat.*, 210) and Crosby Brown (iii/1, 22), where they represent specimens in collections at South Kensington (London) and New York.

5. The Hemispherical Viol. This is, perhaps, the best known form of the viol in the Islamic east. The body consists of a hemisphere of wood, coconut, or a gourd, over the aperture of which a membrane is stretched. The neck is of wood, generally cylindrical, and there is a foot of iron, although sometimes there is no foot. It is often known in Arabic as the *kamānd͟ja* or more rarely as the *s͟hīs͟hak*. The former is derived from the Persian *kamānča* (dim. of *kamān*, "bow") whilst the latter is derived from the Persian and Turkish *s͟hīs͟hak*, *s͟hūs͟hak*, *g͟his͟hak*, *g͟hižak*, *g͟hičak*, etc., which may have had their origin in the Sanskrit *g͟hos͟haka*, an instrument mentioned in the pre-Christian *Nāṭya-s͟hāstra* (ch. xxxiii). The present writer believes that the words *s͟hīs͟hal and s͟hīzān* mentioned in the Ik͟hwān al-Ṣafāʾ (Bombay ed., i, 97) and al-S͟halāḥī (fol. 12) respectively, are copyist's errors for *s͟hīs͟hak* and *s͟hīzāk*. The word *kamānd͟ja* is first mentioned in Arabic by Ibn al-Faḳīh (*ca.* 903) who says that it was used by both the Copts and the people of Sind. Of course, this need not mean that the instrument mentioned was a hemispherical viol, because, being a Persian by origin, the author may have used the word *kamānd͟ja* in its Persian generic sense meaning a viol. That Egypt had an early liking for the *kamānd͟ja* is borne out from various sources. Although in Egypt the hemispherical viol is nowadays called the *rabāb miṣrī* (Egyptian viol), in earlier days it was acknowledged that Egypt borrowed the instrument from Persia (*Kas͟hf al-humūm*, fol. 106). The *kamānd͟ja* was certainly popular at the courts of the Ayyūbid al-Kāmil (d. 1238) and the Mamlūk Baybars (d. 1277); see al-Maḳrīzī, i/1, 136; Lane-Poole, *Hist. of Egypt*, 249. In the Persian *Kanz al-tuḥaf* (14th century) the hemispherical viol is described and figured as the *g͟hičak*, but in Ibn G͟haybī, where both the *g͟hižak* and the *kamānd͟ja* are described, the former is a larger type of the latter, having, in addition to its two ordinary strings, eight sympathetic strings (*Kanz al-tuḥaf*, fol. 261b; Ibn G͟haybī, fol. 78). In the 18th century the *kamānd͟ja* is delineated by Russell (i, 152-3, pl. iv), and Niebuhr (i, 144, Tab. xxvi, E). Both Villoteau (900, pl. BB) and Lane (*Mod. Egyptians*, ch. xviii) give minute details of the construction and *accordatura*. Mus͟hāḳa [*q.v.*] also describes the Syrian *kamānd͟ja* (*kamand͟ja*) of his day (*MFOB*, vi, 25, 81). For the modern Persian instrument, see Advielle (14 and pl.) and Lavignac (3074). Turkoman instruments are given by Fitrat (45) and Belaiev (54). For Malaysia, see Kaudern (178); for India, Lavignac (349) and Fétis (ii, 295). For other designs, see Farmer (*Studies*, i, 76), Fétis (*Hist.*, ii, 136-7), Chouquet (203), Sachs (*Reallex.*, 207).

6. The Pandore Viol. This form is practically a *ṭunbūr, sitār*, or the like, which is bowed instead of being plucked by the fingers or a plectrum. The two best-known examples from India are the *esrār* and *ṭāwūs*. The former has a membrane on its face and has five strings played with the bow together with a number of sympathetic strings. The latter is practically identical with the former, but is adorned with the figure of a peacock (hence its name) at the bottom of the body of the instrument. See Lavignac (351) and Mahillon (i, 131) for designs and details. With the Persians and Turkomans we see various kinds of pandores used with the bow. See Advielle (14), Lavignac (3074), Mironov (27) and Kinsky (26).

7. The Open Chest Viol. This is unknown to the peoples of North Africa and the Near East, although it is popular in the Middle East and the Subcontinent. Unlike the preceding forms of the viol, the upper part of the face of the body or sound-chest is left open. The best-known example of this is the *sārindā* of India which has three strings. See Fétis (ii, 296), Lavignac (351), Mahillon (i, 137) and Kinsky (27), for both designs and details. In Turkestan a similar instrument known as the *ḳūpūz* is very popular. It has two strings. See Belaiev (52), Mironov (25) and Fitrat (43).

Bibliography: 1. Printed books: Farmer, *Studies in oriental musical instruments*, London 1931; Sachs, *Reallexikon der Musikinstrumente*, Berlin 1913; Land, *Recherches sur l'histoire de la gamme arabe*, in *Actes du VIème Congr. Inter. Orient.*, Leiden 1883; Niebuhr, *Voyage en Arabie*, Amsterdam 1776; Villoteau, in *Description de l'Égypte, État moderne*, i, Paris 1809-26; Fétis, *Hist. gén. de la musique*, Paris 1869; Engel, *Descr. catalogue of the musical instruments in the S. Kensington Museum*, London 1874; idem, *Researches... violin family*, 1883; Chouquet, *Le Musée du Conservatoire National de Musique*, Paris 1884; Sachsse, *Palästinensische Musikinstrumente*, in *ZDPV*, (1927); Lavignac, *Encyclopédie de la musique*, 1913 etc.; Muḥammad b. Ismāʿīl, *Safīnat al-mulk*, Cairo 1309; Ibn K͟haldūn, *Muḳaddima*, in *NE*, xvii, 354; Höst, *Nachrichten von Marokos und Fes*, Copenhagen 1781; Salvador-Daniel, *La musique arabe*, Algiers 1879; Ḥafnī, *Recueil des travaux du Congrès de Musique Arabe ...*, Cairo 1934; Mahillon, *Catalogue... du Musée... du Conservatoire royal de Musique de Bruxelles*; Crosby Brown, *Catalogue of the Crosby Brown coll. of musical instruments...*, New York 1904; Russell, *Nat. hist. of Aleppo*, London 1794; Advielle, *La musique chez les Persans en 1885*, Paris 1885; Fitrat, *Uzbik ḳilāssiḳ mūsīḳāsī*, Tas͟hkent 1927; Belaiev, *Muzïkalnïe instrumentï uzbekistana*, Moscow 1933; Mironov, *Obzor musïkalnïk͟h kultur uzbekov i drugik͟h narodov vostoka*, Samarḳand 1931; Kaudern, *Musical instruments in Celebes*, Goteborg 1927; Kinsky, *Geschichte der Musik in Bildern*, Leipzig 1929; Chottin, *Corpus de musique marocaine*, ii, Paris 1933.

Manuscripts: Ibn G͟haybī, *D͟jāmiʿ al-alḥān*, Bodleian Library, Marsh 282; Ibn Sīnā, *Kitāb al-S͟hifāʾ*, India Office, no. 1811; Ibn Zaylā, *Kitāb al-Kāfī*, British Library, no. 2361, now printed, ed. Z. Yūsuf, Cairo 1964; *Kas͟hf al-humūm*, Top Kapu, Istanbul; ʿAbd al-Raḥmān al-Fāsī, *Kitāb al-D͟jumūʿ fī ʿilm al-mūsīḳī*, Berlin Staatsbibl., Lgb., no. 516; *Kanz al-tuḥaf*, British Library, Or. 2361; *The new Grove dictionary of music and musicians*, London 1980, xv, 521-2.

(H.G. Farmer)

RABAḌ (A., pl. *arbāḍ*), district or quarter of a town situated outside the central part or *madīna* [*q.v.*]. This term, which is very frequently found in mediaeval Islamic historical texts of both the Occident and Orient, lies at the origin of the Spanish word *arrabal*, which has the same meaning. In the strongholds (*ḥiṣn* or *ṣak͟hra*) of Muslim Spain, the name *rabaḍ* was given to the civil quarter situated below the strictly

Mosque of Meḥmed Pa<u>sh</u>a (Bayraḳlî <u>D</u>jāmi[c]), 980-1/1573. (Photo: M. Kiel)

Mosque of Ṣofu Sinān Pa<u>sh</u>a, 1023/1614-5. The date is given as chronogramme, written on the *miḥrab*: mi<u>th</u>āl-i <u>d</u>jennet (= 1023).

Ḳādiriyye Tekke, founded 1066/1655-6. *Türbe* with the tombs of the eleven Shaykhs since the foundation, all direct descendants of the *tekke*'s founder Shaykh Ḥasan (*silsile* by Ćehajić, Derviški Redovi). Photo: M. Kiel)

Mosque of Emīn Pasha Rotulla, interior view, 1247/1831-2. (Photo: M. Kiel)

military quarter; it was also applied to the quarters of the lepers and of prostitutes, whilst amongst the Spanish Christians, it designated a parish.

These quarters of a town generally bore a special name. Thus we know the names of 21 of the 4th/10th century suburban quarters of the caliphal capital Cordova [see ḲURṬUBA]. Rabaḍ Shaḳunda or simply al-Rabaḍ was the southern quarter of Cordova, where the celebrated revolt called "that of the suburb" broke out. Situated on the left bank of the Guadalquivir, it was inhabited by the Cordovan plebs, but also by artisans and merchants, as well as by Mālikī fuḳahā᾿ who had made it a centre of opposition to the Umayyad authorities. A conspiracy hatched by the notables of the quarter in Djumādā II 189/May 805 had failed and 72 of those involved had been executed; in the following year, an outbreak of discontent had likewise been followed by several condemnations to death. For about a dozen years, the trouble-makers amongst the *fuḳahā᾿* seem to have maintained an attitude of mind which provoked a popular rising on 18 Ramaḍān 202/25 March 818 (and not in 198/204, the date generally accepted before Lévi-Provençal's revision of this in *Hist. Esp. Mus.*, i, 165 n. 1). The immediate cause of the uprising was the *amīr* al-Ḥakam I's decision to impose new, extraordinary taxes and to entrust the task of raising them to the chief of his police force, a Christian called Rabīᶜ, but the actual pretext was the murder of a tradesman by one of the police. Since al-Ḥakam was, on his return from a hunting session in the Campiña [see ḲANBĀNIYYA], jeered at by the population of the quarter, he had some ten of those involved executed, which enraged the mob. It surged en masse towards the bridge over the Guadalquivir with the intention of going to seize the *amīr*'s palace situated on the right bank. The bridge guards were on the point of being overwhelmed when two officers, the *ṣāḥib al-ṣawā᾿if* ᶜUbayd Allāh b. ᶜAbd Allāh al-Balawī and Isḥāḳ b. al-Mundhir, crossed the river at a ford with a rapidly-assembled force of cavalrymen and, taking the mob in its rear, speedily suppressed the insurrection. The *amīr* then allowed the soldiery to give free rein to pillaging and massacring with an unheard-of ferocity. At the end of three days, the killing was halted, and al-Ḥakam allegedly put to death 300 of the notables. The remainder of the inhabitants of the quarter were compelled to flee Cordova, the Rabaḍ was razed to the ground and, right until the end of the 4th/10th century, the prohibition of erecting any sort of building there was respected by his successors.

The bloody repression of the revolt gave to this last the name of Rabaḍī, which was also given to those victims compelled to swarm all over al-Andalus. A number of these exiles fled to Morocco where, in the newly-founded town of Fās, they gave their name to the ᶜUdwat al-Andalus(iyyīn), the bank of the Andalus (see R. Le Tourneau, *Fès avant le Protectorat*, Casablanca 1950, 136-47 and index).

Bibliography: See E. Lévi-Provençal, *L'Espagne musulmane du Xème siècle*, Paris 1932, 151, 203, 207; idem, *Hist. Esp. mus.*, i, 161-2 and index; R. Dozy, *Supplément*, s.v. (E. LÉVI-PROVENÇAL)

AL-**RABADHA**, an early Islamic settlement in western Arabia, now essentially an archaeological site marked by the *birka* or cistern of Abū Salīm. It lies in the eastern foothills of the Ḥidjāz mountain chain some 200 km/124 miles east of Medina. In early Islamic times it lay on the main pilgrimage route from Kūfa in ᶜIrāḳ to Mecca, later known as the Darb Zubayda [*q.v.* in Suppl.], with such facilities as food and drinking water for the pilgrims. Today, the area is green for much of the year and is used by Bedouins for grazing their flocks.

Originally an extensive *ḥimā* [*q.v.*] which Abū Bakr confiscated from the Banū Thaᶜlaba, al-Rabadha was a thriving place, and not the contemporary equivalent of Siberia, when the Companion and puritan activist Abū Dharr [*q.v.*] was either exiled to al-Rabadha by the caliph ᶜUthmān or withdrew there of his own free will, according to some sources, dying there in 31 or 32/651-3 (see ABŪ DHARR and also A.J. Cameron, *Abû Dharr al-Ghifârî, an examination of his image in the hagiography of Islam*, revised ed. London 1982, 67-8, 73, 78, 80, 89-90, 107-9). The early Arab historians often mention it and the geographers described it as flourishing until 319/931, when warfare of its people with those of Ḍariyya to its east in Nadjd brought about the intervention and destruction of the town by the Ḳarāmiṭa or Carmathians [see ḲARMAṬĪ]; al-Muḳaddasī, 108, characterises it as having only brackish water and being ruinous.

The modern archaeological site covers an area of approx. 1,740 hectares, and several seasons of excavations have revealed various types of buildings, including palaces, houses, two mosques, large reservoirs and underground water-storage tanks. There is evidence of small-scale artisanal activity such as tanning, dyeing, smelting and metal-working. Many Umayyad and ᶜAbbāsid period dirhams and dīnārs have been found, together with a variety of ceramics, including polychrome and lustre ware, steatite and glass objects.

Bibliography: In addition to the references given in the article, see Yāḳūt, *Buldān*, ed. Beirut, iii, 24-5; Ḥamad al-Djāsir, *al-Rabadha fī kutub al-mutaḳaddimīn*, in *al-ᶜArab*, i/5-8 (1386/1967); and above all, S.ᶜA.ᶜA. al-Rashid, *Al-Rabadhah, a portrait of early Islamic civilisation in Saudi Arabia,* Riyāḍ 1986, giving the earlier sources and the results of recent excavations. (S.ᶜA.ᶜA. AL-RASHID)

AL-**RABAḤĪ**, YŪSUF B. SULAYMĀN b. Marwān al-Anṣārī, Abū ᶜUmar, b. 367/978, d. at Murcia 448/1056, grammarian of Muslim Spain. Best known as such, he is equally credited with competence in *fiḳh*, poetry, metrics and genealogies. It appears that he played a certain role in the reconciliation of the various grammatical schools in al-Andalus. A *Radd ᶜalā 'l-Kabrī* and a *Radd ᶜalā Abī Muḥammad al-Aṣīlī* are attributed to him, but do not seem to have survived.

Bibliography: Ibn Bashkuwāl, *Ṣila*, Cairo 1374/1955, ii, 640 no. 1499; Kaḥḥāla, *Mu᾿allifīn*, Damascus 1376-80/1957-61, xiii, 303. (ED.)

AL-**RABAᶜĪ**, Abu 'l-Ḥasan ᶜAlī b. ᶜĪsā, grammarian of Baghdād of the 4th/10th century and contemporary of Ibn Djinnī.

He was born at Baghdād in 328/940, and studied grammar there under the direction of al-Sīrāfī [*q.v.*] before moving to Shīrāz in order to follow the teaching of al-Fārisī [*q.v.*] over a period of almost 20 years. He then returned to Baghdād where he died, at an advanced age, in 420/1029. His eccentricities, seen in a fear of dogs, prevented him from having any pupils. Amongst his works, none of which have survived, are mentioned commentaries (*sharḥ*), such as one on the *K. al-Īḍāḥ* of al-Fārisī and one on the *K. al-Mukhtaṣar* of al-Djarmī, and two treatises on grammar, the *K. al-Muḳaddima* and the *K. al-Badīᶜ*.

Bibliography: Ibn al-Anbārī, *Nuzha*, 201-3; Ḳifṭī, *Inbāh*, ii, 297; Suyūṭī, *Bughya*, 344-5; Yāḳūt, *Irshād*, v, 283-7; Kaḥḥāla, *Mu᾿allifīn*, vii, 163-4; Brockelmann, S I, 491; Sezgin, *GAS*, ix, 185. (G. TROUPEAU)

RABAT [see AL-RIBĀṬ].

RABB (A.), lord, God, master of a slave. Pre-Islamic Arabia probably applied this term to its gods or to some of them. In this sense the word corresponds to the terms like Baʿal, Adonis, etc. in the North-western Semitic languages, where *rabb* means "much, great" (see A. Jeffery, *The foreign vocabulary of the Qurʾān*, Baroda 1938, 136-7). In one of the oldest sūras (CVI, 3) Allāh is called the "lord of the temple". Similarly, al-Lāt bore the epithet *al-Rabba*, especially at Ṭāʾif where she was worshipped in the image of a stone or of a rock. In the Ḳurʾān, *rabb* (especially with the possessive suffix) is one of the usual names of God. This explains why in *Ḥadīth*, the slave is forbidden to address his master as *rabbī*, which he must replace by *sayyidī* (Muslim, *al-Alfāẓ min al-adab*, trads. 14, 15, etc.). The abstract *rubūbiyya* is not found in either Ḳurʾān or *Ḥadīth*, but is in common use in mystic theology.

In pre-Islamic times, *rabb* was one of the titles given to certain of the *kāhins* [*q.v.*]; Lammens gives numerous references for this topic (see his *Le culte des bétyles et les processions religieuses*, in *BIFAO*, xvii [1919], 39-101). The name *r b y*, associated with *ś h r* (the Moon), designated in the kingdom of Ḳatabān a class of priest-officials who had the duty of administering the divinity's domains (G. Ryckmans, *Les religions arabes preislamiques*², Louvain 1953, 30). For the usage of *rabb* in the Ḳurʾān, see J. Chelhod, in *Arabica*, v (1958), 159-67. For further details, see T. Fahd, *La divination arabe*, Paris 1987, 107-8.

Bibliography: In addition to references in the text, see the Arabic lexica and the Ḳurʾān commentaries, s.v. (A.J. WENSINCK-[T. FAHD])

RABGHŪZĪ, NĀṢIR AL-DĪN B. BURHĀN AL-DĪN, early writer in Central Asian Turkish, was born somewhere in the second half of the 13th century, possibly in the still unidentified encampment of Ribāṭ Oghuz in Transoxiana (Western Turkestan), then under the hegemony of the Čaghatay Khānate [*q.v.*]. Being himself a Turk and a judge by profession, he also had some rather good relations with the Mongol ruling élite. The date *post quem* for his death is 710/1310. These scarce facts all stem from his own work and no other source so far has come to light revealing anything more about his identity.

Rabghūzī gained his fame as author of the first Middle Turkic version (in prose) of the *Ḳiṣaṣ al-anbiyāʾ* [*q.v.*] genre, commonly referred to as the *Ḳiṣaṣ-i Rabghūzī*, and written in 710/1310 at the instigation of Nāṣir al-Dīn Tuḳ Bugha, a young (not yet identified) prince of Mongol lineage, but of Muslim faith. The text is enriched with some seventy poems in Arabic and Türki (cf. H. Boeschoten and M. Vandamme, 1990); also, it contains some 1200 Arabic quotations from the Ḳurʾān and the *ḥadīth*.

First extracting material from a large range of sources, Rabghūzī then recomposed this chosen material in a number of cyclic stories. However, since the identification of these sources is still problematical, this will not be elaborated here; see, however, Dorleijn (1986) and Boeschoten (1992, 55-6).

Albeit much is still indistinct, Rabghūzī's kind of Turkic, which he himself calls "Türki", is commonly referred to as Khʷārazm Turkish, the literary Turkic language of Central Asia of the 13th and 14th centuries. It is commonly characterised as the transition stage from the Ḳarakhānid literary language to (early) Čaghatay. As a whole, Rabghūzī's Khʷārazm Turkish offers the picture of a hybrid language which has been infiltrated by forms from various dialects, notably those spoken by Oghuz and Ḳïpčaḳ tribes (Boeschoten and Van Damme, 1987, and Boeschoten, 1991, 23 ff.). As to language and contents, the *Ḳiṣaṣ-i Rabghūzī* stands very close to Maḥmūd b. ʿAlī's *Nahdjatü l-farādīs*, written before 1358 (facsimile publ. by J. Eckmann, Ankara, 1956, and S. Tezcan and H. Zülfikar, TDK, 518).

Although the archetype has been lost, the *Ḳiṣaṣ-i Rabghūzī* has become the focus of a Central Asiatic tradition which lived on well into this century. This may be summarised briefly as:

(a) The old mss. (13th-16th centuries), of which five are still extant (Boeschoten, 1991, 3-4). Up to now, only one facsimile has been produced (Grønbech, 1948).

(b) A period of loss of interest, the cause of which is still unknown, somewhere in the 17th-18th centuries.

(c) A host of new mss. (18th-20th centuries), which have the particularity of showing rather conservative versions as to the contents, but which were modernised versions seen from the language aspect.

For a listing of the most important mss. and older printed editions, see Hofman (1969), iii/1, 88-9, Jarring (1980), 17-18 and J. Eckmann in *PTF*, i, 104; ii, 218-19.

Bibliography: H.E. Boeschoten, *The Leningrad mss. of Rabghuzi's Qisas*, i, in *Türk Dilleri Araştırmaları*, iii (1991), 47-9; idem, *Iskandar-Dhulqarnain in den Qiṣaṣ-i Rabghuzi*, i: *De Turciis aliisque rebus*, in *Commentarii Henry Hofman dedicati*, Utrecht Turcological Series, iii, 1992, 39-57; H.E. Boeschoten and M. Van Damme, *The different copyists in the London ms. of the Qiṣaṣ-Rabghuzi*, Utrecht Turcological Series, ii, 1987, 177-183; idem, *The poetry in Rabghuzi's Qiṣaṣ l-Anbiyā'*, in *L'Asie Centrale et ses voisins, influences réciproques*, Paris 1990, 9-36; M. Dorleijn, *De verhalen van Ilyas en Hizir door Rabghuzi*, 1986, unpubl. M.A. diss., Utrecht University, unpubl.; K. Grønbech, *Rabghuzi. Narrationes de Prophetis. Cod. Mus. Brit. Add. 7851, reproduced in facsimile*, Copenhagen 1948; H.F. Hofman, *Turkish literature. A biobibliographical survey*, iii/1, Leiden 1969; G. Jarring, *Literary texts from Kashgar*, Lund 1980 (which includes a substantial bibl.); M. Van Damme, *Rabghuzi's Qiṣaṣ al-Anbiyā reconsidered in the light of Western Medieval studies: Narrationes vel Exempla*, i, in *Commentarii Henry Hofman dedicati*.

(M. VAN DAMME)

RABĪʿ (A.), the name of the third and fourth months of the Muslim calendar. The Syriac equivalent *rbīʿā* is used in the Peshitta as a translation of the Hebrew *malḳōsh* (late rain). This and the fact that the two months following Rabīʿ II are called Djumādā (month of frost) suggested to Wellhausen that these four months originally fell in winter and that the old Arab year began with the winter half-year [see AL-MUḤARRAM]. Rabīʿ means originally the season in which, as a result of the rains, the earth is covered with green; this later led to the name Rabīʿ being given to spring. Al-Bīrūnī expressly describes autumn (*kharīf*) as the season indicated by Rabīʿ. As a result of the Ḳurʾānic prohibition of intercalation [see NASĪʾ], since the beginning of the Muslim era the two months no longer fall at a regular season.

Bibliography: Wellhausen, *Reste*², 97; Brockelmann, *Lexicon Syriacum*², s.v.; Bīrūnī, *Āthār*, ed. Sachau, 60, 325. (M. PLESSNER)

AL-**RABĪʿ** B. **YŪNUS** B. ʿABD ALLĀH B. ABĪ FARWA (so-called from his entering Medina with a fleece on his back), emancipated slave of al-Ḥārith al-Ḥaffār, himself the emancipated slave of ʿUthmān b. ʿAffān [*q.v.*]. He was really a man of obscure origin, born in slavery at Medina about 112/730. He was ought by Ziyād b. ʿAbd Allāh al-Ḥārithī, who resented him to his master Abu ʾl-ʿAbbās al-Saffāḥ, ne first ʿAbbāsid caliph. All his life, he served, with arying fortune, three more ʿAbbāsid caliphs: al-Manṣūr, al-Mahdī and al-Hādī.

He reached the zenith of his power under al-Manṣūr (136-58/754-75 [*q.v.*]), who, finding him a apable and useful courtier, appointed him *ḥādjib* and afterwards made him his *wazīr* in succession to Abū Ayyūb al-Mūriyānī [*q.v.*]. His son al-Faḍl b. al-Rabīʿ [*q.v.*], who was destined to play a prominent part in he forthcoming intrigues against the house of Barmak, succeeded to his father's duties as *ḥādjib*. After he foundation of Baghdād, the new town was divided nto four quarters, one of which was given as a land-grant by al-Manṣūr to al-Rabīʿ and was thus named after him (*ḳaṭīʿat al-Rabīʿ*).

During the reign of al-Mahdī (158-69/775-85 [*q.v.*]), his influence seems to have dwindled for some time. Abū ʿUbayd Allāh became *wazīr*. From that time onwards, al-Rabīʿ participated in an intrigue which led to the downfall of his rival by exposing his son as a heretic (*zindīḳ* [*q.v.*]) in 163/779-80 and bringing about his execution (see Sourdel, *Vizirat*, 103-11 and index). Even then, al-Rabīʿ only retained his old office as *ḥādjib* and never became al-Mahdī's *wazīr*. It was ʿAbd Allāh Abū Yaʿḳūb b. Dāwūd who succeeded the disgraced minister, but, at the end of 168/middle of 785, the absentee caliph made him his delegated representative in Baghdād. He took part in the intrigues which arose around the succession to al-Mahdī, but on his accession, al-Hādī [*q.v.*] pardoned him and appointed him to the vizierate, the *ḥidjāba* and the chancery. However, the vizierate was taken back from his control shortly afterwards, and the only office which he retained was the *dīwān al-azimma*. The exact date of his death is uncertain. Whilst al-Djahshiyārī and al-Ṭabarī place it in 169/785-6, al-Khaṭīb al-Baghdādī and Ibn Khallikān assert that he died at the beginning of 170/786.

Details about his administration are scanty, but it is certain that he was an able, industrious, temperate and tactful man of affairs. Even al-Mahdī, who was never lavish in showering favours on al-Rabīʿ, once described him as the model of a good administrator (al-Yaʿḳūbī, ii, 486). The literary sources, however, do not single him out as a patron of letters.

Bibliography: 1. Texts. See the indices of the following works: al-Khaṭīb al-Baghdādī, *Taʾrīkh Baghdād*, Cairo 1931, viii, no. 4521; Djahshiyārī, *Kitāb al-Wuzarāʾ*, ed. H. v. Mžik, Leipzig 1926; Ṭabarī, ii and iii; Ibn Khallikān, *Wafayāt*, ed. I. ʿAbbās, ii, 294-9, tr. de Slane, i, 521-6; Yaʿḳūbī, *Taʾrīkh*; idem, *Buldān*; Bar Hebraeus, *Taʾrīkh Mukhtaṣar al-duwal*, Beirut 1890; Ibn Ḳutayba, *ʿUyūn al-akhbār*, 4 vols., Cairo 1925-30; Iṣbahānī, *Aghānī*, i and iii, 112 ff.; Djāḥiẓ, *Bayān*; Masʿūdī, *Murūdj*; idem, *Tanbīh*; Ibn al-Athīr, v, 383-4; Suyūṭī, *Taʾrīkh al-Khulafāʾ*.

2. Studies. G. Weil, *Geschichte der Chalifen*, Mannheim 1846-51; Sir W. Muir, *Caliphate*, ed. T.H. Weir, Edinburgh 1924; Cl. Huart, *Histoire des Arabes*, Paris 1912-13; G. Le Strange, *Baghdad during the Abbasid Caliphate*, Oxford 1924; E. de Zambaur, *Manuel de généalogie*, etc., Hanover 1927; S. Lane-Poole, *Mohammadan dynasties*, Paris 1925; D. Sourdel, *Le vizirat ʿabbāside*, 118-21 and index.

(A.S. Atiya*)

RABĪʿ B. ZAYD, Arabic name of a Mozarab Christian [see MOZARABS] whose true name was Recemundo (Recemundus in Latin = Raymond) and who owes his place in the *EI* to the role which he played in the service of the Umayyad caliphs of Spain ʿAbd al-Raḥmān III al-Nāṣir (who reigned from 300 to 350/912-61 [*q.v.*]) and al-Ḥakam II al-Mustanṣir (350-68/961-76 [*q.v.*]), and to his involvement in the presentation of the well-known *Calendar of Cordova*.

Recemundo was a Cordovan who, with his command of Latin and of Arabic, was able to render considerable services to the caliphal chancellery which employed him, but history remembers him on account of a mission which he undertook in Frankfurt at the court of Otto I the Great, king of Germany (from 936 onward) and Roman emperor (962-73), who had held ʿAbd al-Raḥmān III responsible for depredations and extortions committed by the Moors in Provence [see FRAXINETUM and add to the Bibl., Ph. Senac, *Musulmans et Sarrasins dans le sud de la Gaule (VIIIe-XIe siècles)*, Paris 1980, and idem, *Provence et piraterie sarrasine*, Paris 1982]. In 953 Otto I, who had considered insolent an initial message sent from Cordova in 950, dispatched a monk named John of Gorze to deliver a letter of protest to the caliph. (The biography of this monk was related by an abbot of St. Arnulph, also known as John, in his *Vita Johannis Gorziensis* (*Monumenta Germaniae Historica, Scriptores*, Hanover 1841, iv, 338-77); the passage (369 ff.) concerning these exchanges was utilised by R. Poupardin in *Le royaume de Bourgogne*, Paris 1907, 94-5; cf. E. Lévi-Provençal, *HEM*, ii, 160-1.) It is stated here that Otto's messenger was detained in Cordova and could thus have been aware of the departure, in the spring of 955, of Recemundo, who returned in June 956, having completed his mission but apparently without much success. It may also be noted that the *Antapodosis* of Liutprand (*Mon. Germaniae Hist.*, 265 ff.) is dedicated to Recemundus. He is mentioned again, but under the name of Rabīʿ b. Zayd, in connection with another mission, this time to Constantinople and Syria, with the object of acquiring works of art for Madīnat al-Zahrāʾ [*q.v.*], under construction since 325/956. He returned with "a basin of sculpted and gilded marble and a fountain of green onyx decorated with bas-reliefs representing human figures" (Lévi-Provençal, *HEM*, ii, 148, quoting al-Maḳḳarī, *Analectes*, i, 372-3; see also H. Terrasse, *L'art hispano-mauresque*, 102). As a reward for his services, ʿAbd al-Raḥmān III had him appointed bishop of Elvira (but, if no errors and omissions have occurred, he is not mentioned in the section of vol. xii of *España sagrada* which is devoted to Iliberis).

It is not only for his missions that he is of interest to historians of Muslim Spain, since he participated—perhaps without knowing it—in the development of the *Calendar of Cordova* (although Sezgin, who is unaware of him, devotes only one line of his *GAS*, i, 327, to the co-author of the work, the continuator of al-Ṭabarī, ʿArīb b. Saʿd; see below).

Recemundo was popular at the court of al-Ḥakam II, who appreciated his expertise in philosophy and astronomy. Since this caliph, to whom the *Calendar* is dedicated, acceded to the throne in 961, the editor of this work, R. Dozy, dated it in this year, but it could have been composed at another date, and in stages. Whatever the case may be, this composite almanac has a history all of its own. Libri had discovered and inserted in his *Histoire des sciences mathématiques en Italie* (Paris 1838, i, 461 ff.) a *Liber Anoe* attributed to *Harib filii Zeid episcopi* (*sic*), and it was not until 1866 that a ms., in the Arabic language but in Hebrew characters, corresponding to the Latin text published by Libri, was found to exist in the B.N. of Paris (see further G. Vajda, *Index général*, Paris 1953, 653). Dozy copied this ms. and sent it to Simonet, who translated into Spanish the liturgical part of the text, precisely that which may with some confidence be attributed to Recemundo, and published it under the title of *Santoral hispano-mozárabe escrito en 961 por Rabi ben Zaid, obispo de Iliberis* (in *Ciudad de Dios*, v [1871], 105-16, 192-212). Two years later, at Leiden, Dozy decided to publish the original, this time in Arabic characters, and the Latin version, entitling the whole *Le calendrier de Cordoue de 961*. Finally, the author of the present article has revived the Arabic text and the Latin version, combining the two and offering in addition an annotated French translation. The whole, entitled *Le Calendrier de Cordoue* (omitting *de l'année 961*), was published at Leiden in 1961, thus exactly a thousand years after the date assumed by Dozy for the composition of the work. The Arabic text (improved by reference to the *Kitāb al-Anwāʾ* of Ibn Ḳutayba [*q.v.*], which had recently been edited), lacks a title (but it is easy to observe that the Latin expression *Liber Anoe* corresponds exactly to *Kitāb al-Anwāʾ*) and gives as the name of the author ᶜArīb b. Saᶜd al-Kātib (d. *ca.* 370/980 [*q.v.*]), whereas the Latin version is headed *Harib filii Zeid episcopi quem composuit Mustansir imperatori*, with an unexpected genitive and a relative pronoun which refers to no expressed term. The phrase needs therefore to be completed, to read, for example, *Harib filii* (*Sad liber cum libro* or (according to Saavedra) *additamentis Rabi filii*) *Zeid episcopi*. As for the full name of Rabīᶜ b. Zayd, it is supplied by Ibn Saᶜīd (*apud* al-Maḳḳarī, *Analectes*, ii, 125), who specifies his role as *usḳuf* (bishop) and attributes to him, and to him alone, a *Kitāb Tafṣīl al-zamān wa-maṣāliḥ al-abdān*, while the colophon of the Arabic text reads *tamma kitāb ᶜArīb fī tafṣīl*, etc., which does nothing to simplify the issue.

In view of the fact that the almanac comprises a book of traditional *anwāʾ* [*q.v.*] and a liturgical calendar, it seems logical to assert that the latter is the work of Rabīᶜ b. Zayd and that the former is to be attributed to ᶜArīb b. Saᶜd. However the solution is not so simple, since the statement of Ibn Saᶜīd and the colophon of the ms. are utterly contradictory. It has to be assumed therefore that an understandable confusion has arisen between the names of the two authors (which are, it may be observed, anagrams one of the other) and that the blending is so perfect that, towards the end of the introduction, a paragraph relating to Christian festivals gives the impression that the work is attributable to a single author. As for information concerning agricultural activities, hygiene, daily life, etc., so precious in the view of historians, it is not unreasonable to give the credit to ᶜArīb rather than to Rabīᶜ, since the former was apparently more apt to respect the tradition of *kutub al-anwāʾ*, which themselves contain facts of this type as well as material concerning astronomy and meteorology. In view of the fact that a *Kitāb Tafṣīl al-zamān*, etc., evidently as a result of confusion, is attributed to each of the two authors, the problem remains unsolved.

Bibliography: In addition to the references indicated in the text of the article, see Dozy's introduction to his edition of the *Calendrier*; idem, *Die Cordowaner ᶜArīb ibn Saᶜd der Secretär, und Rabīᶜ ibn Zayd der Bischof*, in *ZDMG*, xx (1866), 595-609; Simonet, *Historia de los mozárabes de España*, Madrid 1897-1903, index; Dom Ferotin, in appendix to *Liber ordinum*, in F. Cabrol and H. Leclercq, *Monumenta Ecclesiae liturgica*, v, Paris 1904, 451 ff.; F. Viré, *La volerie dans l'Espagne du Xᵉ siècle*, in *Arabica*, xii/3 (1965), 306-14; J.D. Latham, review of the ed. of the *Calendrier* by Ch. Pellat, in *JSS*, viii (1963), 300 ff.; idem, *Loanwords from the Arabic in the Latin translation of the Calendar of Cordova*, in B.C Bloomfield (ed.), *Middle East studies and libraries: felicitation volume for Professor J.D. Pearson*, Londo 1980, 103-13.

(Ch. Pellat)

RABĪᶜA and **MUḌAR**, the two largest an most powerful combinations of tribes in ar cient Northern Arabia.

The name Rabīᶜa is a very frequent one in th nomenclature of the Arab tribes. More importar tribes of this name within the Muḍar group are th Rabīᶜa b. ᶜĀmir b. Ṣaᶜṣaᶜa, from which came th Kaᶜb, Kilāb and Kulayb, then the Rabīᶜa b. ᶜAb Allāh b. Kaᶜb, Rabīᶜa b. Kilāb, Rabīᶜa b. al-Aḍba and Rabīᶜa b. Mālik b. Djaᶜfar; also the Rabīᶜa b ᶜUḳayl and Rabīᶜa b. Djaᶜda; three branches of th ᶜAbd Shams also bear this name. Of larger Yeme tribes may be mentioned: the Rabīᶜa b. al-Khiyār Rabīᶜa b. Djarwal and Rabīᶜa b. al-Ḥārith b. Kaᶜ (Wüstenfeld, *Register*, 377-8). (Banū) Rabīᶜa simply o Banū Abī Rabīᶜa is a clan of the Shaybān (*ᶜIḳd*, iii $60_{,27\text{-}8}$, $65_{,25\text{-}6}$). The name Rabīᶜa al-kubrā or al wusṭā and al-ṣughrā is given to three clans of the Tamīm: the Rabīᶜa b. Mālik b. Zayd Manāt, also called *Rabīᶜat al-Djūᶜ* "Hunger Rabīᶜa", the Rabīᶜa b. Ḥanẓala b. Mālik b. Zayd Manāt and Rabīᶜa b. Mālik b. Ḥanẓala; the plural al-Rabāʾiᶜ includes al these (*LA*, ix, $469_{,9}$ ff.; *ᶜIḳd*, ii, $47_{,26}$, $43_{,1}$). In contrast to Rabīᶜa, the name Muḍar hardly occurs elsewhere (perhaps only as a variant of Maṭar b. Sharīk: *ᶜIḳd*, iii, $74_{,2}$; cf. Wüstenfeld, *op. cit.*, 290).

Genealogies. According to the genealogists, the common ancestor of the greatest part of the North Arabian tribes Nizār b. Maᶜadd b. ᶜAdnān [*q.v.*] by his wife Sawda bint ᶜAkk b. ᶜAdnān had two sons Muḍar and Iyād [*q.v.*] and by Djadāla bint Waᶜlān of the pre-Arab family of the Djurhum the sons Rabīᶜa and Anmār (al-Ṭabarī, i, 1108; al-Batanūnī (see *Bibl.*), 25, has also Ḳuḍāᶜa; but cf. Wüstenfeld, *op. cit.*, 137-8). In addition to the well-known story of the division of their father's inheritance at which Muḍar received the epithet *al-ḥamrāʾ* (on account of the red tent: Goldziher, *Muh. Stud.* i, 268; cf. however, *LA*, vii, $26_{,17}$) and Rabīᶜa the name *Rabīᶜat al-Faras* ("Rabīᶜa with the horse"), it is also related that Rabīᶜa was buried alongside of Nizār; Muḍar, who settled, however, in Mecca, was buried in al-Rawḥāʾ, two days' journey from Medina, where his grave is said to have been a place of pilgrimage (al-Diyārbakrī, *Taʾrīkh al-Khamīs*, Cairo 1283, i, $148_{,6}$; al-Ḥalabī, *Sīra*, Cairo 1292, i, $21_{,17}$).

According to the genealogical plan, Muḍar had two sons: al-Yās (or Ilyās, Alyās) and ᶜAylān al-Nās, the ancestor of large and famous tribes [see ḳays ᶜaylān; there also the question of the descent of the Muḍar is discussed]. Al-Yās had three sons by his wife Laylā bint Ḥulwān known as Khindif (see Wüstenfeld, *op. cit.*, 133), from whom her descendants are called Banū Khindif: Mudrika, Ṭābikha and Ḳamaᶜa (Ibn ᶜAbd al-Barr, *al-Inbāh*, 72 ff.). The two first in turn became the ancestors of large and important tribes: Mudrika's sons were Hudhayl [*q.v.*] and Khuzayma; the latter again is the ancestor of the Asad [*q.v.*] and Kināna [*q.v.*], from whom the Ḳuraysh [*q.v.*] are descended amongst others. Udd b. Ṭābikha had as sons Ḍabba [*q.v.*], ᶜAbd Manāt, ᶜAmr, whose descendants are known as Muzaina from the name of his wife, Murr and Ḥumays. Tamīm [*q.v.*] b. Murr is again the ancestor of one of the largest Arab tribes.

The sons of Rabīᶜat al-Faras were Aklub, Ḍubayᶜa and Asad; the latter's sons were ᶜAmīra, ᶜAnaza [*q.v.*] and Djadīla, to whom the ᶜAbd al-Ḳays [*q.v.*], al-Namir and Wāʾil b. Ḳāsiṭ trace their descent. Wāʾil was the ancestor of two of the most powerful Arab tribes: Bakr [q.v.] and Taghlib [q.v.]. From Bakr are descended the tribes of Ḥanīfa [q.v.], Shaybān, Ḏhuhl, Ḳays b. Thaʿlaba and others (see Ibn Durayd, Ishtiḳāḳ, 189-216).

From the introduction to Bakrī's Muʿḏjam we get the following idea of the dwelling-places of the two tribes. At the partition of Arabia among the descendants of Maʿadd, the Muḍar received the frontiers of the sacred territory as far as al-Sarawāt and the land on this side of al-Ghawr with the adjoining territory; the Rabīʿa received the slopes of the hills of Ghamr Ḏhī Kinda and the central part of Ḏhāt ʿIrḳ with the adjoining parts of al-Nadjd as far as al-Ghawr in al-Tihāma. Both tribes increased their lands by driving the other sons of Maʿadd from Mecca and the district. After the withdrawal of the ʿAbd al-Ḳays to Baḥrayn, a number of Rabīʿa tribes occupied the highlands of Nadjd and Ḥidjāz and the frontiers of Tihāma where al-Dhanāʾib, Wāridāt, al-Aḥaṣṣ, Shubayth, Baṭn al-Ḏjarīb und al-Taghlamān were their settlements. As a result of a war, the various clans separated and, pushing forward, for the most part reached Mesopotamia, where they occupied the lands which later bore their names: Diyār Rabīʿa and Diyār Bakr [q.vv.] (Wüstenfeld, Wohnsitze, 107, 136-7, 161 ff., 168; Blau, in ZDMG, xxiii [1869], 579-80).

After the withdrawal of the Rabīʿa from the Tihāma, the Muḍar remained in their settlements until the Ḳays, defeated by the Khindif, advanced into the lands of Nadjd. Dissensions among the Khindif caused the Ṭābikha to migrate to Nadjd, Ḥidjāz and adjoining territories. Clans of the Ṭābikha went as far as Yamāma, Hadjar, Yabrīn and ʿUmān; some groups settled between Baḥrayn and Baṣra. Several Mudrika tribes, however, remained in the Tihāma, like the descendants of Naḍr b. Kināna in the vicinity of Mecca (Wüstenfeld, Wohnsitze, 169 ff.). The Muḍar who migrated to Mesopotamia gave their name to Diyār Muḍar, which Blau, op. cit., 577, recognises in the Arab tribe of the Μαυζανῖται mentioned there in the 4th century A.D.

History. Down to the overthrow of the Ḥimyar kingdom by the Abyssinians, the Rabīʿa and Muḍar were under the suzerainty of Yaman, which they were able several times to cast off when they all obeyed one ruler. Of battles in these wars there are recorded al-Baydāʾ, al-Sullān and Khazāz(ā) in which the Maʿaddī tribes were victorious (Reiske, Primae lineae hist. regn. arab...., ed. Wüstenfeld, 180 ff.; al-Yaʿḳūbī, ed. Houtsma, i, 257; Yāḳūt, ii, 432 ff., iii, 114-15). They belonged for a time to the kingdom of the Kinda [q.v.], the rulers of which bore the title king of the Maʿadd (or Muḍar) and Rabīʿa (A. Sprenger, Geogr., 216). Like the Bakr and Taghlib, the rest of the Rabīʿa and Muḍar recognised the Kindī al-Ḥārith b. ʿAmr al-Maḳṣūr, who led them successfully against the Ghassānid and Lakhmid kings but lost his conquests again (Ḥamza al-Iṣfahānī, ed. Gottwaldt, i, 140). When after his death the kingdom of Ḏhū Nuwās collapsed under the Abyssinians and the Kindīs no longer recognised the suzerainty of Yemen, the Basūs war [q.v.] broke out between the Bakr and the Taghlib. The "first day of al-Kulāb" or "day of Kulāb of the Rabīʿa", so-called because both tribes were descended from Rabīʿa b. Nizār, ended in favour of the Taghlib, and the Bakr turned to the king of Ḥīra al-Mundhir III, who now extended his rule over the Rabīʿa and Muḍar and other Central Arabian tribes (al-Yaʿḳūbī, op. cit.; Yāḳūt, iv, 294-5). To this period belongs the irruption into Mesopotamia of the Taghlib, who were probably the

first of the Rabīʿa to settle there; they were followed by the Banū Namir b. Ḳāsiṭ and other Rabīʿa tribes. The hostilities between the Taghlib and Bakr did not cease, and in the battle of Dhū Ḳār [q.v.] they were on opposite sides. The victory of the Bakr, celebrated as a great success of the Rabīʿa over the Persians (cf. Nöldeke, Sasaniden, 310 ff.; an earlier encounter, Yāḳūt, ii, 735 ff.), liberated the Central Arabian tribes from foreign rule and paved the way for Islam.

Legend records very old connections of the Muḍar with the Meccan sanctuary; the Ḏjurhum [q.v.], the lords of Tihāma and guardians of the Kaʿba, were driven out of Mecca by the Iyād and Muḍar. In the fight for the possession of the sanctuary the Muḍar were victorious but had to hand over the administration of the Kaʿba and of Mecca to the Khuzāʿa [q.v.], so that only three purely religious offices were left to them connected with the pilgrimage (the idjāza of ʿArafāt, the ifāḍa of Muzdalifa and the idjāza of Minā) and these remained with Muḍar families also after the redistribution by Ḳuṣayy [q.v.] (Ibn Khaldūn, ʿIbar, ii, 333, 335; al-Yaʿḳūbī, i, 274). The influential office of time-reckoner also fell to a Muḍarī under the Kinda (Sprenger, Geogr., 225). While Christianity was widespread among the Rabīʿa in Muḥammad's time, the Muḍar remained more faithful to the old pagan ways and were less susceptible to Aramaic influence than the tribes on the frontier ("this perhaps partly explains their estrangement from the Rabīʿa": Wellhausen, Reste², 231). Radjab was the sacred month of the Muḍar (hence Radjab Muḍar; cf. Wellhausen, op. cit., 97; a strange explanation of this from Ibn al-Mudjāwir in A. Sprenger, Moḥammad, iii, 301), Ramaḍān of the Rabīʿa (cf. al-Dimishḳī, Nukhbat al-dahr, tr. Mehren, 403). From their practices during iḥrām, all the Rabīʿa and many groups of the Muḍar, including the Ribāb league, belonged to the Ḥilla (al-Yaʿḳūbī, i, 298). In al-Dimashḳī, 385, we find the peculiar view that the Copts are descended from Rabīʿa "or" Taghlib who had migrated into Egypt in search of food.

The Muzayna [q.v.] boasted of being the first Muḍar tribe to pay homage to the Prophet (as early as 5 A.H. it is said; Sprenger, op. cit., iii, 201). In 8/630 Khālid b. al-Walīd destroyed the idol al-ʿUzzā in Nakhla, which was revered by the Ḳuraysh, Kināna and "all the Muḍar" (al-Tabarī, i, 1648). In the "year of the Deputations" (9/631), several large clans of the Muḍar and Rabīʿa like the Tamīm, Thaḳīf, ʿAbd al-Ḳays and Bakr b. Wāʾil adopted Islam, but this does not imply the submission of the whole of Central Arabia. The lament of the deputation of the ʿAbd al-Ḳays to Muḥammad is significant: "between thee and us dwell Muḍar tribes and we can only come to thee in the sacred months" (Sprenger, op. cit., iii, 374; cf. 301, n. 1). In the year 11 a saying of the followers of the false prophet Musaylima [q.v.], who belonged to the Rabīʿa, is recorded: "a deceiver of the Rabīʿa is dearer to us than a true prophet of the Muḍar" (perhaps the variant "than a deceiver of the Muḍar" is better: al-Tabarī, i, 1936-7; perhaps the earliest clearly expressed contrast between the Rabīʿa and Muḍar?). When in the same year the "Rabīʿa" in Baḥrayn proclaimed a king of their own, this can only refer to the tribes of Ḳays b. Thaʿlaba and ʿAbd al-Ḳays (al-Tabarī, i, 1960; al-Balādhurī, Futūḥ, 83-4). The tribes of Rabīʿa and Muḍar are from now onwards mentioned as important contingents in the Muslim armies, but sometimes the large numbers given for them are doubtful (cf. Caetani, Annali, 12 A.H., § 188, n. 5). When al-Muthannā invaded al-Sawād in 13/635, he surprised the Rabīʿa and Ḳuḍāʿa assembled at the Sūḳ al-Khanāfis, who still recognised the suzerainty of the Sāsānids (al-Ṭabarī, i, 2202-3); five years later a considerable force was sent against al-Raḳḳa, Naṣībīn and the nomadic Rabīʿa and Tanūkh (Ibn Khaldūn, *ʿIbar*, ii/2, 107-8).

It is unnecessary to follow the history of the Rabīʿa and Muḍar farther, as it is clear from the above that the two names stand only for a few clans and not for the whole confederation of tribes, as the genealogists say (Rabīʿa usually means the Bakr and Taghlib or only one of them). Sometimes we even find the whole Rabīʿa group included in the Muḍar (*ʿIḳd*, ii, 39,$_{30}$) which further increases the confusion. The beginnings of the two tribes are further put at so early a date that it is difficult to decide whether they really existed as such, or like Maʿadd and Nizār are only artificial conceptions. Goldziher (*Muh. Stud.*, i, 94-5) surmised that the antagonism between North and South Arabia had its roots in the rivalry between Ḳuraysh and Anṣār, and he regarded the early wars between Maʿadd and Yemen as a later invention. "Maʿadd and Muḍar," he lays down, "is primarily contrasted with the name Anṣār." When tribal antagonism became intensified by political developments, and after the battle of Mardj Rāhiṭ [*q.v.*] in 65/684, the tendency to form confederacies spread ever more widely, and finally the Tamīm with the Ḳays joined the large party of the Muḍar. On the other hand, the Azd [*q.v.*] joined the rest of the Yemenīs, among whom in Khurāsān [*q.v.*] were also included the Rabīʿa (Bakr); finally, the Syrian Ḳuḍāʿa (Kalb) also joined them (Wellhausen, *Das arabische Reich*, 44-5). The effects of this dualism between Muḍar (Tamīm and Ḳays) and Yemen (Azd and Rabīʿa) which wiped out the other antagonisms and polarised the whole Arab world are presented in their main outlines in the article ḲAYS ʿAYLĀN.

Bibliography: 1. The Arabic dictionaries and genealogical handbooks. Ibn al-Kalbī-Caskel, *Tabellen*, 1, *Register*, 476-83; F. Wüstenfeld, *Register* and *Tabellen*, A-Z; Ibn Durayd, *Kitāb al-Ishtiḳāḳ*, ed. Wüstenfeld, Göttingen 1854, esp. 189-216; Ibn Ḥazm, *Djamharat ansāb al-ʿarab*, ed. Hārūn, Cairo 1382/1962, 10-11, 466-70, 479-84; Ḳalḳashandī, *Nihāyat al-arab fī maʿrifat ansāb al-ʿarab*, Baghdād 1332, 215-18, 340, 345-6; Suwaydī, *Sabāʾik al-dhahab fī maʿrifat ḳabāʾil al-ʿArab*, Bombay 1296, lith. 20 ff.; Ibn ʿAbd al-Barr, *al-Inbāh ʿalā ḳabāʾil al-ruwāh*, Cairo 1350, 64, 96-100; Wüstenfeld, *Die Wohnsitze und Wanderungen der arabischen Stämme*, in *Abh. Ges. Wiss. Gött.*, xiv (1868-9), 107, 136-7, 161 ff., 167-8, 169 ff.

2. Other primary sources. Ṭabarī; Balādhurī; Masʿūdī, *Murūdj*; *Kitāb al-Aghānī*; *Naḳāʾiḍ*, ed. Bevan, indices; Wensinck, *Handbook*, s.v. Embassy; Ibn Khaldūn, *ʿIbar*, Būlāḳ 1284, ii, 298-338; Ibn ʿAbd Rabbihi, *al-ʿIḳd al-farīd*, Cairo 1316, esp. ii, 37-47, 263-7, iii, 256-7; Batanūnī, *al-Riḥla al-Ḥidjāziyya*, Cairo 1329, 25-6.

3. Studies. A. Sprenger, *Die alte Geographie Arabiens*, Bern 1875, 216, 225; idem, *Das Leben und die Lehre des Moḥammad*, Berlin 1865, iii, pp. CXXXVIII ff., 201, 301, 374; J. Wellhausen, *Reste arabischen Heidentums*[2], Berlin 1897, 97, 231, 245; Th. Nöldeke, *Geschichte der Perser und Araber zur Zeit der Sasaniden*, Leiden 1879, 46, 203, 310 ff., 330; idem, in *ZDMG*, xl (1886), 178; Caussin de Perceval, *Essai sur l'histoire des Arabes...*, Paris 1847-8, i, 110, 116, 185-94, 218-21, 240, 348, ii, 259-394 *passim*. For the later period, see I. Goldziher, *Muhammedanische Studien*, Halle 1888-90, i, 80, 83 ff., 92-8, 180, 206, 268; A. Müller, *Der Islam im Morgen- und Abendland*, Berlin 1885-7, esp. i, 316, 346, 377, 445, 451 ff.; Wellhausen, *Die religiö politischen Oppositionsparteien...*, in *Abh. Ges. Wis Gött.*, N.S., v (1901), 6, 23, 58, 83; idem, *D arabische Reich und sein Sturz*, Berlin 1902, esp. 43 ff 122, 130-1, 156, 163, 196, 205, 242 and chs. 8 an 9 *passim*.

(H. KINDERMANN)

RĀBIʿA AL-ʿADAWIYYA AL-ḲAYSIYYA (a double *nisba* because she was attached to a family, the Ā ʿĀtik, of ʿAdī b. Ḳays (of Ḳuraysh; see Ibn al-Kalb Caskel, tab. 35)), famous mystic and saint c Baṣra.

One cannot go so far as to throw into doubt he historical existence, but the traditions about her lif and teachings include a very large proportion c legend which today can hardly be distinguished fron authentic information. With this qualification born in mind, one may nevertheless be permitted to presen a portrait of the saint as it was conceived by her co religionists over the course of the centuries.

She is said to have been born in 95/714 or 99/717 18 and to have breathed her last at Baṣra in 185/801 where her tomb was shown outside the city (see al Harawī, *Ziyārāt*, ed. and tr. J. Sourdel-Thomine 81/88). In the evolution of Ṣūfī mysticism, she becam one of the three most famous female mystics of Baṣra the two others being Muʿādha al-ʿAdawiyya, wife o the "ascetic" ʿĀmir b. ʿAbd al-Ḳays al-ʿAnbar [*q.v.*], and a certain Umm al-Dardāʾ (see Pellat, *L milieu baṣrien*, 104).

Born into a poor home, she was stolen as a child and sold into slavery (she is even sometimes made into a *ḳayna* [*q.v.*]), but her sanctity secured her freedom, and she retired to a life of seclusion and celibacy, at first in the desert and then in Baṣra, where she gathered round her many disciples and associates, who came to seek her counsel or prayers or to listen to her teaching. These included ʿAbd al-Wāḥid b. Zayd (d. 177/793; see Pellat, *Milieu*, 102-3 and index), Mālik b. Dīnār [*q.v.*], the ascetic Rabāḥ al-Ḳaysī, the traditionist Sufyān al-Thawrī [*q.v.*] and the Ṣūfī Shaḳīḳ al-Balkhī. Her life was one of extreme asceticism and otherworldliness. Asked why she did not ask help from her friends, she said, "I should be ashamed to ask for this world's goods from Him to Whom they belong, and how should I seek them from those to whom they do not belong?" (it should be noted that al-Djāḥiẓ, more conscious of the neatness of this reply than of its deeper sense, cites it at least twice (in *Ḥayawān*, v, 589, and *Bayān*, iii, 127) and does not mention any other details concerning Rābiʿa, which seems to show that, in the 3rd/9th century, the legend around her had not yet totally crystallised. On the other hand, this tradition, perhaps authentic, is contradicted by a piece of evidence according to which she possessed a *khādim/khādima* and by the mention, in al-Ḥusaynī, of another saint called Maryam al-Baṣriyya, her servant and disciple, to whom she had communicated her doctrine of pure love, *ʿilm al-maḥabba*).

To another friend she said, "Will God forget the poor because of their poverty or remember the rich because of their riches? Since He knows my state, what have I to remind Him of? What He wills, we should also will." Miracles were attributed to her as to other Muslim saints. Food was supplied by miraculous means for her guests, and to save her from starvation. A camel, which died when she was on pilgrimage, was restored to life for her use; the lack of a lamp was made good by the light which shone round about the saint. It was related that when she was dying, she bade her friends depart and leave the way free for the messengers of God Most High. As they went ut, they heard her making her confession of faith, nd a voice which responded, "O soul at rest, return thy Lord, satisfied with Him, giving satisfaction to Iim. So enter among My servants into My Paradise" sūra LXXXIX, 27-30). After her death, Rābiʿa was en in a dream and asked how she had escaped from Iunkar and Nakīr [*q.v.*], the angels of the tomb, vhen they asked her, "Who is your Lord?", and she eplied, "I said, return and tell your Lord, 'Notwithtanding the thousands and thousands of Thy reatures, Thou hast not forgotten a weak old woman. , who had only Thee in all the world, have never orgotten Thee, that Thou shouldst ask, Who is thy ord?'"

Among the prayers recorded of Rābiʿa is one she vas accustomed to pray at night upon her roof: "O ord, the stars are shining and the eyes of men are losed and kings have shut their doors and every lover s alone with his beloved, and here am I alone with Thee." Again she prayed, "O my Lord, if I worship Thee from fear of Hell, burn me therein, and if I worship Thee in hope of Paradise, exclude me thence, but f I worship Thee for Thine own sake, then withhold not from me Thine Eternal Beauty." Of Repentance, he beginning of the Ṣūfī Path, she said, "How can anyone repent unless his Lord gives him repentance and accepts him? If He turns towards you, you will urn towards Him." She held that Gratitude was the vision of the Giver, not the gift, and one spring day, when urged to come out to behold the works of God, she rejoined, "Come rather inside to behold their Maker. Contemplation of the Maker has turned me aside from contemplating what He has made." Asked what she thought of Paradise, Rābiʿa replied, "First the neighbour, then the house" (*al-dj̲ār t̲h̲umma 'l-dār*) and al-G̲h̲azālī, commenting on this, says she implied that no one who does not know God in this world will see Him in the next, and he who does not find the joy of gnosis here will not find the joy of the Vision there, nor can anyone appeal to God in that world if he has not sought His friendship in this. None may reap who has not sown (*Iḥyā*ʾ, iv, 269). The otherworldliness of her teaching is shown in her declaration that she had come from that world and to that world she was going, and she ate the bread of this world in sorrow, while doing the work of that world. One who heard her said derisively, "One so persuasive in speech is worthy to keep a rest-house" and Rābiʿa responded, "I myself am keeping a rest-house; whatever is within, I do not allow it to go out and whatever is without, I do not allow to come in. I do not concern myself with those who pass in and out, for I am contemplating my own heart, not mere clay." Asked how she had attained to the rank of the saints, Rābiʿa replied, "By abandoning what did not concern me and seeking fellowship with Him Who is eternal."

She was famed for her teaching on mystic love (*maḥabba*) and the fellowship with God (*uns*) which is the pre-occupation of His lover. Every true lover, she said, seeks intimacy with the beloved, and she recited the lines:

I have made Thee the Companion of my heart,
But my body is present for those who seek its company,
And my body is friendly towards its guests.
But the Beloved of my heart is the guest of my soul.
(*Iḥyā*ʾ, iv, 358, margin)

Questioned about her love for the Prophet she said, "I love him, but love of the Creator has turned me aside from love of His creatures"; and again, "My love for God has so possessed me that no place remains for loving any save Him." Of her own service to God and its motive-force, she said, "I have not served God from fear of Hell, for I should be but a wretched hireling if I did it from fear; nor from love of Paradise, for I should be a bad servant if I served for the sake of what was given me, but I have served Him only for the love of Him and desire of Him." The verses often ascribed to her (but now shown by G.J.H. van Gelder to be originally a secular love poem, see his *Rābiʿa's poem on the two kinds of love: a mystification?*, in *Verse and the fair sex, a collection of papers presented at the 15th Congress of the UEAI ... 1990*, ed. F. de Jong, Utrecht 1993, 66-76) on the two types of love, that which seeks its own ends and that which seeks only God and His glory, are famous and much quoted, translated and commented upon:

I love Thee with two loves: a selfish (or concerned, impassioned, instinctive) love
and a love of which Thou [alone] art worthy.
The selfish love makes me turn away from all that is not Thou, making me think only of Thee
But as for that love of which Thou [alone] art worthy.
Thou raisest the veils so that I may see Thee.
In neither the one case nor the other have I any merit, but the praise for the first and the second is wholly Thine.

Al-G̲h̲azālī again comments, "She meant, by the selfish love, the love of God for His favour and grace bestowed and for temporary happiness, and by the love worthy of Him, the love of His Beauty which was revealed to her, and this is the higher of the two loves and the finer of them" (*Iḥyā*ʾ, iv, 267). Like all mystics, Rābīʿa looked for union with the Divine (*waṣl*). In certain of her verses she says, "My hope is for union with Thee, for that is the goal of my desire", and again she said, "I have ceased to exist and have passed out of self. I have become one with God and am altogether His."

Rābiʿa, therefore, according to the traditions about her, differs from those of the early Ṣūfīs who were simply ascetics and quietists, in that she was a true mystic, inspired by an ardent love, and conscious of having entered into the unitive life with God. She was one of the first of the Ṣūfīs to teach the doctrine of Pure Love, the disinterested love of God for His own sake alone, and one of the first also to combine with her teaching on love the doctrine of *kas̲h̲f*, the unveiling, to the lover, of the Beatific Vision.

The semi-legendary personality of Rābiʿa has inspired romantic biographies and even two Egyptian films, but one should remember a curious phenomenon, which has its origin in an account which shows the saint holding in one hand fire and in the other water, and replying to some youths who had asked her where she was going: "...towards the heavens, in order to throw some fire into Paradise and some water on Hellfire, so that both of them may disappear and that human beings may contemplate God without hope or fear, for if neither hope for Paradise nor fear of Hellfire existed, would they worship al-Ḥaḳḳ and submit to it?" This text, which appears in Persian in the *Manāḳib al-ʿārifīn* (ms. India Office Library, no. 1670, fol. 114a) of Aflākī (8th/14th century [*q.v.*]), is found again almost word-for-word in the *Mémoires du sieur de Joinville*, ed. Paris 1854, 195, with this difference that a Preaching Friar called Yves the Breton, sent to the "soudan" of Damascus by the King of France Louis IX (the future Saint Louis), meets en route an old woman carrying fire and water, etc. It is not certain that the heroine of this story is our Rābiʿa al-ʿAdawiyya, since the locale is Damascus, where there is said to have lived, equally in the 2nd/8th century, another holy woman called Rābiᶜa bint Ismāᶜīl al-ᶜAdawiyya. It is astonishing that the oldest attestation in the Islamic world goes back no further than the 8th/14th century when a French chronicler introduces the story a century earlier. In any case, the bishop J.-P. Camus (1582-1653) illustrates pure love by developing the story in question in a work called *La Caritée ou le pourtraict de la vraye charité, histoire dévote tirée de la Vie de Saint-Louis*, Paris 1641.

Bibliography: 1. Sources. Makkī, *Ḳūt al-ḳulūb*, Cairo 1310, i, 103, 156 ff., iii, 84; Kalābādhī, *Taᶜarruf*, ed. Arberry, Cairo 1934, 73, 121; Ḳushayrī, *Risāla*, Būlāḳ 1867, 86, 173, 192, also ed. Maḥmūd and Ibn al-Sharīf, Cairo 1385/1966; Ibn al-Djawzī, *Ṣifat al-ṣafwa*, Ḥaydarābād 1355-6/1936-7, iv, 17; Sharīshī, *Sharḥ*, ii, 251 ff.; ᶜAṭṭār, *Tadhkirat al-awliyā*ʾ, ed. Nicholson, i, 59 ff.; Shaᶜrānī, *al-Ṭabaḳāt al-kubrā*, Cairo 1299, 56; Djāmī, *Nafaḥāt al-uns*, ed. Nassau Lees, 716 ff.; Ḥusaynī, *K. Siyar al-ṣāliḥāt al-muʾmināt al-khayyirāt*, ms. B.N. Paris 2042, fols. 26a ff.; M. Zihni, *Mashāhīr al-nisā*ʾ, Lahore 1902, 225; Ibn Khallikān, *Wafayāt*, ed. I. ᶜAbbās, ii, 285-8, tr. de Slane, i, 515-17; Munāwī, *al-Kawākib al-durriyya*, ms. B.L. Add. 23,369, fols. 50 ff. The sayings attributed to Rābiᶜa have been collected together by ᶜAbd al-Raḥmān Badawī, in *Shahīdat al-ᶜishḳ al-ilāhī, Rābiᶜa al-ᶜAdawiyya*, Cairo n.d. [? 1952].

2. Studies. L. Massignon, *Essai sur les origines du lexique de la mystique musulmane*, Paris 1922, 193-5; idem, *Recueil de textes inédits*, Paris 1929, 6-9; Margaret Smith, *Rābiᶜa, the woman saint*, in *MW*, xx, 337-43; eadem, *Rābiᶜa the mystic and her fellow-saints in Islam*, Cambridge 1928; L. Gardet, *La connaissance et l'amour de Dieu...*, in *Revue Thomiste* (Jan.-March 1946), 143; idem, *Expériences mystiques en terres non-chrétiennes*, Paris 1953, 108-14; idem, *Dieu et la destinee de l'homme*, Paris 1967, 338-44; idem and G. Anawati, *La mystique musulmane*, Paris 1961, 166-70; Ch. Pellat, *Le milieu baṣrien*, 104-6, where one should suppress "bint Ismāᶜīl"; R. Casper, *Rābiᶜa et le pur amour de Dieu*, in *IBLA*, cxxi/1 (1968), 71-95; J. Baldick, *The legend of Rābiᶜa of Baṣra. Christian antecedents, Muslim counterparts*, in *Religion*, xx (1990), 233-47. On an interesting usage, see V. Loewenstein, *Saint Magdalene, or Bibi Rabi'a Basri in Mogul painting*, in *IC*, xiii (1939), 466-9.

(MARGARET SMITH-[CH. PELLAT])

RABĪB AL-DAWLA ABŪ MANṢŪR B. ABĪ SHUDJĀᶜ MUḤAMMAD B. AL-ḤUSAYN, vizier of the ᶜAbbāsids and Saldjūḳs. When the vizier Abū Shudjāᶜ Muḥammad al-Rūdhrāwarī [*q.v.*] made the pilgrimage to Mecca in 481/1089, he appointed his son Rabīb al-Dawla and the *naḳīb al-nuḳabā*ʾ Ṭirād b. Muḥammad al-Zaynabī his deputies, and in 507/1113-14, on the death of Abu 'l-Ḳāsim ᶜAlī b. Fakhr al-Dawla Muḥammad b. Djahīr [see DJAHĪR, BANŪ], Rabīb al-Dawla was appointed vizier of the caliph al-Mustaẓhir [*q.v.*]. In Dhu 'l-Ḥidjdja 511/April 1118 the fourteen-year old Maḥmūd b. Muḥammad [*q.v.*] succeeded his father as Saldjūḳ sultan and, when he was looking around for an able vizier, he was recommended to choose someone who had had the necessary training in the service of the caliph (*min tarbiyat dār al-khilāfa*), allegedly because there was no suitable man in the train of the young sultan. The choice therefore fell upon Rabīb al-Dawla who was at once summoned from Baghdād to Iṣfahān but, as the nominee of the *amīrs* and great men of state, proved himself a somewhat ineffectual vizier until his death after a brief tenure of office in Rabīᶜ I 513/June-July 1119; according to another statement he died as early a[s] 512/1118-19.

Bibliography: Ibn al-Athīr, x, 111, 349, 37[3], 387, 394; Bundārī, in Houtsma, *Recueil*, ii, 115-2[6]; ᶜAbbās Iḳbāl, *Wizārat dar ᶜahd-i salāṭīn-i buzurg-i saldjūḳī*, Tehran 1338/1959, index; C.L. Klausner *The Seljuk vezirate*, Cambridge, Mass. 1973, 61, 87, 107.

(K.V. ZETTERSTÉEN)

RĀBIGH (Bandar Rābigh, Rābugh), a port i[n] the Ḥidjāz province of Saudi Arabia, in lat. 22° 48′ N., and long. 39° 1′ E., half-way between Djud[d]a [*q.v.*] and Yanbuᶜ. It may perhaps be identifie[d] with Ptolemy's Ἄργα χώμη (Sprenger, *Die alt[e] Geographie*, no. 38). North of Rābigh lies al-Abwā [*q.v.*], now called al-Khurayba, the reputed buria[l] place of the Prophet's mother Āmina [*q.v.*]. In th[e] past, the port had no proper harbour. Ships anchore[d] at Sharm Rābigh, an inlet about 3 km long, which of[-]fered excellent anchorage (Hogarth, *Hejaz*, 29). From there cargoes were transferred on local sailing craft t[o] Rābigh proper, a group of four hamlets and extensive date-groves, about 6 km from Sharm Rābigh. It used to be the place [see MĪḲĀT] where pilgrims to Mecca, coming overland from Syria, Egypt and the Maghrib, put on the *iḥrām* [*q.v.*] (see Ibn Baṭṭūṭa, *Rihla*, i, 297, tr. Gibb, i, 186). As such, Rābigh had succeeded the village of al-Djuḥfa which lies in a valley reaching the sea just south of the port. Pilgrims coming down the Red Sea entered into *iḥrām* as their ships passed Rābigh. It was the centre of the Banū Zubayd, a sub-section of the Banū Masrūḥ who, together with the Banū Sālim, were the main sections of the Banū Ḥarb [*q.v.*], the dominant tribe in the area between Mecca and Medina (Hogarth, *Hejaz*, 38). Before an asphalt highway joined Mecca and Medina via Djudda, Rābigh and Badr, secondary routes (see Hogarth, *Hejaz*, 114-21) ran from Rābigh northward through the mountains to Medina, providing a more direct but more difficult approach than the *al-Ṭarīḳ* (or *al-Darb* "narrow mountain pass") *al-Sulṭānī*, which follows the coast. In 1924 ᶜAbd al-ᶜAzīz Āl Saᶜūd, the future king of Saudi Arabia, sent the *Ikhwān* [*q.v.*] to capture Rābigh, cutting the communications between Djudda and Medina. In 1925 he declared Rābigh an official pilgrim port.

Bibliography: See AL-ḤIDJĀZ; MAKKA; D.G. Hogarth, *Hejaz before World War I, a handbook*, repr. Cambridge 1978; R. Baker, *King Husain and the Kingdom of Hejaz*, Cambridge 1979; *Western Arabia and the Red Sea*. Naval Intelligence Division, London 1939-45, 541-2; Ibn Baṭṭūṭa, *Travels A.D. 1325-1354*, tr. H.A.R. Gibb, Cambridge 1958-71.

(ED.)

RĀBIḤ B. **FAḌL ALLĀH**, an adventurer attached to the ivory and slave trader of the eastern Sudan, Zubayr Pasha [*q.v.*]. After the fall of Zubayr in 1291/1874 and the subsequent death of his son Sulaymān, Rābiḥ assumed leadership of Sulaymān's followers. By 1305/1887 he had become associated with the Mahdiyya [*q.v.*] movement in the eastern Sudan. Between 1309-10/1892 and 1310-11/1893 he attacked and defeated the sultanates of Baghirmi and Wadai.

There then followed a period during which Rābiḥ entered into an association with Hayatu dàn Saʾidu, a disaffected grandson of Muhammadu Bello [*q.v.*], first caliph of Sokoto, to conquer Borno [see BORNŪ] and then Sokoto [*q.v.*]. The conquest of Borno was accomplished at the battle of Ngala in 1311/1893, but at that point Hayatu and Rābiḥ quarrelled and the projected attack on Sokoto failed to develop.

Rābiḥ now moved south and occupied Dikwa,

which became his headquarters. After several clashes with the French, he was defeated and killed at the battle of Kusseri in 1900.

Bibliography: J.F. Ajayi and M. Crowder (eds.), *History of West Africa*, ii, London 1974, 114-15; M. Hiskett, *The development of Islam in West Africa*, London and New York 1984, 198-200. His relations with Hayatu are dealt with in H. Jungraithmayr and W. Günther (eds. and trs.), *Sultan Saʾidu bi Hayatu tells the story of his and his father's life*, in *Abhandlungen der Marburger Gelehrten Gesellschaft*, Jahrgang 1977, Nr. 2.

(M. HISKETT)

RABĪʿIYYĀT. In Ottoman literature.

There is no special literary genre called *rabīʿiyyāt* (*bahāriyyāt*) in Ottoman literature (from now on referred to as *dīwān* literature). Spring, however, has an important place within *dīwān* literature, as is the case for every other national literature. Spring, with its different functions fitting the structure of almost every kind of literary style and genre, was given its own special place in diverse literary genres coeval with the beginnings of written Ottoman literature in the second half of the 13th century. Since this literature favoured the *methnewī* genre, in which all sorts of religious stories, religio-mythological works, histories, semi-religious books of advice pertaining to literary edification and romances were written, spring acquired a place in romances written in the style of the 13th and 14th centuries, especially those dealing with love adventures. It did so whilst serving two functions: as a sort of setting-décor, but also, beyond that obvious function, as a means to convey certain symbolic-mythological meanings.

Spring in Ottoman literature was naturally connected with the descriptions of orchards and gardens in springtime, thus bringing together the categories of time and space and carrying out the task of creating in the reader/listener the impression of verisimilitude. In this literature most lovers meet or are introduced to one another in the setting of a green, blossoming orchard full of flowers and plants coming back to life. Spring is connected here with the image of an orchard and with the idea of eternal life as the plants that have wilted and died in winter come back to life, and through these two motifs it is further related to the notion of Paradise (that includes an idealised version of all the elements of nature in springtime, such as meadows, gardens, flowers, trees, birds, running waters, light, cool breezes and the like) and its eternal happiness. Thus, in the descriptions of spring it is the notion of Paradise and its central role in the religion and beliefs of Islam that is at the back of the poet's intention and imagery. For instance, Meḥmed, in his *methnewī ʿIshk-nāme* (15th century) has the two lovers meet in an orchard at springtime, and the description of spring is presented in the above-mentioned terms (cf. 102, ll. 1716-1728; 116, ll. 2300-16). Likewise, the first love scenes take place in the same setting, as do the wedding ceremonies (cf. 81-2, ll. 872-91; 248-9 ll. 8081-8100; 225 l. 8409). Descriptions of spring in the same terms are also found in the 14th century *methnewīs Djemshīd ü Khurshīd* of Aḥmedī of Germiyān, and in the *Khurshīd-nāme* of Sheykh-oghlu Muṣṭafā (ed. Hüseyin Ayan, Erzurum 1979, 176-7, ll. 1263-1319; 192, ll. 1706-29. For the meeting of the lovers in an orchard, cf. 239-40, ll. 2959-87).

In the *methnewīs*, spring is presented in close association with the sun. For instance, in the *Khurshīd-nāme* of Sheykh-oghlu Muṣṭafā, the garden specially ordered by Sultan Siyāwush for his son Khurshīd is described as a garden in eternal springtime. All the flowers, trees and vegetation in this garden preserve their blossoming in an eternal spring. This garden is in fact an image of paradise. It has been arranged as an eternally unwilting garden, and moreover, it is the garden of a god (cf. 176-7). The owner of this garden is Khurshīd, and if we consider the etymology of the word *khurshīd* we realise that the owner of the garden is the sun. Furthermore, Khurshīd in this work is dressed in green from head to toe, with a green crown and a green veil; in other words, he has been described as a Khiḍir [*q.v.*] figure (cf. 240, ll. 12979, 1981). At the same time, the garden is a symbol of Khurshīd (cf. further *Khurshīd-nāme*, 19-92), since it is a *gülistān* (cf. l. 1653). In this manner, both the image and the concept of the orchard's association with the sun, spring and the rebirth of life at springtime, as well as the thought that the orchard belongs to the beloved or the sun or the ruler, are reminiscent of the Hanging Gardens of Babylon, of the blessed divine gardens (whose gardener is a Sumerian or Akkadian king), of the even more ancient Sumerian temples, of the Sumerian concept of Akat's paradise named Dilmun, and, finally, of the Paradise of the Torah and the gardens of Solomon in eternal springtime as described in the Song of Solomon in the Old Testament. Likewise, the traditional and typified theme in the *methnewīs* of the meeting of the two lovers in gardens of eternal springtime, and their holding festivities and wedding ceremonies there, may be traced back to the older tradition of the New Year festivals, mostly a tradition orally transmitted for thousands of years and only a small part of which is reflected in written traditions. For instance, the scene of the washing and decoration of Ferāhshād before the meeting of the lovers in the eternal spring garden in the *Khurshīd-nāme* is clearly a distant echo of the ritual washing and decoration of the gods and goddesses before their wedding in the New Year festival (cf. 248-9; cf. also G. Alpay-Tekin (ed.), *Aḥmed-i Dāʿī, Čeng-nāme*, in *Sources of Oriental Languages and Literature*, 16, Harvard University 1992; the ninth and tenth part of the text are a spring and garden description and the celebration of New Year in the spring at the ruler's garden).

These mythological elements preserved their identity during the 14th and 15th centuries but not thereafter, when they were reduced to mere decorative elements after losing their lively character and deeper meaning with the onset of a changing world view that paralleled the changing living conditions, social classes and economic conditions of the Ottoman empire. In the hands of the poets of *dīwān* literature, spring and everything associated with it became means for creating all sorts of literary figures and word plays on the level of style and rhetoric. Nonetheless, the words expressing these mythological viewpoints relating to spring, used in a stereotyped manner both in the *methnewīs* and in other literary genres to be examined, were used only for the purpose of background description and word plays in the following centuries, while viewpoints whose meaning had been more or less changed were combined with concepts and used, always, in the same stereotyped associations. In the following are outlined the main characteristics of these associations with reference to these particularities:

1. As mentioned above, spring was presented in terms of the association garden-spring-eternal-life-Paradise.

2. Spring was always expressed together with the emotion of eternal happiness, either in connection with Paradise or with youth. In the following centuries, however, the quality of the eternal withered

away and happiness was associated with the transitory quality of spring and depicted as a happiness with an end drawing near. Uzun Firdewsī started depicting spring along with the transitoriness of happiness and youth in his *Ḳuṭb-nāme* (ed. 21.)

3. Spring is the symbol of youth and therefore represents the beloved and beautiful lady. For instance, in the *Yūsuf u Zulaykhā* of the 16th century poet Kemāl Pasha-zāde, spring represents youth, and autumn and winter old age (ed. Mustafa Demirel, Ankara 1983, 183-4, ll. 1850-6; for a classic depiction of spring, see 70-1, ll. 553-70). Spring, garden, beautiful lady, beloved, are all also found in the work *Leylā ile Medjnūn* of the most famous poet of the 16th century, Fuḍūlī (d. 1556 [*q.v.*]). In this case, Leylā, who enters a garden in springtime for a walk with her friends, does not meet her lover there, yet one of her companions gives her tidings of Medjnūn by reading to her a poem of his. Thus the picture which has been painted of spring, the garden and the meeting of the two lovers in it has here been modified. Nevertheless, Leylā is depicted as the symbol of the flower that blossoms in spring and represents youth and beauty, hence the garden is presented in terms of the traditional associations (ed. Necmettin Halil Onan, Istanbul 1956, 133-42, ll. 1321-1418).

4. The relationship between spring and sun is presented mostly in the following fashion. Because at the spring equinox night and day are equal, the sun is considered a symbol of justice and spring is the season when this justice is applied. Moreover, it is because of the sun's beneficial effects that vegetation comes back to life in the spring. Thus generosity is a quality that comes about by the joining of spring and the sun. As a result, in *dīwān* literature, the sun, because of its associations with justice and generosity, has always been conceived in terms of spring and the ruler, on account of his close relation to the sun, has been presented as an indivisible part of spring.

5. Spring has always been considered together with the rains of April and the concepts of blessing and mercy. Moreover, through the coming into being of the pearl out of the raindrop of April that falls into an oyster, the image of the pearl, its preciousness, perfection and beauty are added to these concepts.

6. Spring in *dīwān* literature is frequently presented together with the celebrations, drinking and music at evening gatherings held in gardens in connection with the spring festivals.

Different social and military conditions entered the above general picture after the second half of the 15th century and especially during the 16th century. For instance, the elements used in describing spring started to stand for the different ranks of Ottoman hierarchy, in accordance with the social relations of the time. Thus the rose (*gül*) was the sultan, the tulip (*lāle*) the *sandjaḳ-beyi*, the iris (*süsen*) the *silāḥdār*, the narcissus the *emīr-i tādjdār* and the spring clouds the ruler's tents. As for the cypress and the plane-tree (*čīnar*), they were the servants of the ruler standing around him (*Khayālī Bey Divanı*, ed. Ali Nihad Tarlan, Istanbul 1945, 93-4, ll. 3-5). Likewise, spring was connected to the military and war system: the manifestations of spring on the meadows were the soldiers, and the cypress their banner (*liwā*). Spring itself was the young hero (*pehlewān*). The violet was the mace and the rose the shield, and the iris had its sword girded. (*Yahyā Bey Divanı*, ed. Mehmet Çavuşoğlu, Istanbul 1977, 58-9, ll. 1-3, etc.)

During the 17th and 18th centuries, spring was represented in a more realistic way in poetry. These descriptions were in close association with festivities, drinking and music sessions, and spring was greete[d] as a season of mirth and joy (e.g. Nābī, *Khayriyye*, ed. İ. Pala, Istanbul 1989, 147-50: *der beyān-ï ferāḥ-ï faṣl bahār*). In this way, in every century, new meaning[s] and allegorical allusions peculiar to the century wer[e] added to the descriptions of spring. Thus during th[e] 14th century and the first half of the 15th century spring was full of symbolic, legendary (romance) allusions, whereas during the second half of the 15th an[d] the whole of the next century spring was associate[d] with the wars, social hierarchy and majestic pomp o[f] the expanding empire. Finally, in the 17th and 18t[h] centuries it was described in a realistic language tha[t] had more to do with nature and human life, the environment in which people live. However, for all tha[t] spring was presented from all these different point o[f] views, it was always described in terms of th[e] stereotyped expressions presented earlier on. Moreover, in the cases where there was no special sectio[n] devoted to spring itself, these expressions about spring were sprinkled, without much sense of unity an[d] order, in all genres of *dīwān* literature (*methnewī*, *ghazel*, *ḳaṣīde*, *ḳiṭʿa*, *turkī* and *terdjīʿ*). For instance, we find the standard images of classical poetry where th[e] cheek of the beloved was compared to a rose, the locks of hair to hyacinth, the elegant stature to a cypress, etc.

Spring was sometimes the topic of the *nesīb* (*teshbīb*) [see NASĪB] section of the literary genre of the *ḳaṣīde*. In fact *ḳaṣīdes* frequently start with a description of nature, which may have to do with one of the four seasons, and the poem is termed, accordingly, a *bahāriyye*, or a *shitāʾiyye* or a *temmūziyye*. Just like the descriptions of autumn and winter, those of spring are a means for the poet to effect the transition to the short *girizgāh* part, serving as an introduction to the praise (*medḥiyye*) section of a *ḳaṣīde* which he has composed in order to praise his patron-ruler or another high member of the Ottoman hierarchy, such as a Grand Vizier or a pasha or a vizier, or even just a person near and dear to him.

The *ḳaṣīdes*, for all that they conform to the descriptions of spring presented above and are faithful to the whole network of stereotypical relations between themes and concepts, are the poems that best reflect not only the political and social developments of the Ottoman empire but the changing conceptions of spring paralleling those. There are plenty of poets in *dīwān* literature who are famous for their *ḳaṣīdes*, including Aḥmed Pasha and Nedjātī for the 15th century, Fuḍūlī, Bāḳī, Newʿī, Yaḥyā Bey for the 16th, Khayālī and especially Nefʿī for the 17th, and Nedīm for the 18th. Almost all of these poets treated spring as the subject of the *nesīb* section of their *ḳaṣīdes*. There is little doubt that, among these *bahāriyyes*, the most famous is the one dedicated by Nefʿī (d. 1634 [*q.v.*]) to Sultan Murād IV, whose *maṭlaʿ* begins:

Esdi nesīm-i newbahār ačïldï güller ṣubḥ-dem
Ačsun bizim de gönlümüz sāḳī mede ṣun djām-ï Djem
(*Dīwān*, Istanbul 1249, 47).

Another very famous *ḳaṣīde* beginning with a spring depiction was written in the 18th century by Nedīm (d. 1730). This poem that puts to words the excitement and joy of spring is one of the most beautiful examples of *dīwān* literature and was composed in praise of Sultan Aḥmed III. Here is its opening distich:

Gel ey faṣl-ï bahārān māye-i ārām u ḫābïmsïn
Enīs-i khāṭïrïm kām-ï dil-i pür ïḍṭïrābïmsïn

The following distich is still popularly remembered:

Gülüm shöyle gülüm böyle demekdir yāre muʿtādïm
Seni ey gül sever djānïm ki djānāna khiṭābïmsïn

(Nedīm, *Dīwān*, ed. A. Gölpınarlı, İnkilāp Kitabevi, Istanbul 75.)

The influence of the depictions of spring in *dīwān* literature is so strong that even when writing *shitāʾiyyes* or *temmūziyyes*, poets compare that season to spring. It is also worth mentioning that sometimes a word having to do with the spring répertoire is the rhyming word of the *ḳaṣīde*, even if there is no proper *nesīb* section dealing with spring, and the *ḳaṣīde* is then named according to that rhyme word, e.g. the *gül ḳaṣīdesi* or the *nergīs ḳaṣīdesi*, etc.

A third literary genre (besides the romance *methnewīs* and the *ḳaṣīdes* describing spring in their *nesīb* sections and sometimes therefore named *bahāriyye*) that may deal with spring is the *Sāḳī-nāme*. This genre, which is in fact written in *methnewī* style, was developed especially after the 16th century. Spring in this genre is more closely associated with music and drinking gatherings.

It should be noted that there is a fourth genre dealing with spring, the *münāẓare* [see MUNĀẒARA], even though there appears to be only one extant example, Lāmiʿī Čelebi's prose work *Münāẓare-yi Sulṭān-ī Bahār bā Shehriyār-ī Shitā*. As may be understood from its title, this work deals with a competition between the two seasons.

Apart from all these, the only work of *dīwān* literature entirely devoted to the springtime New Year festivals is the *Čeng-nāme* of Aḥmed-i Dāʿī, who lived in the first half of the 15th century. Except for the last, synonymous work of 70-80 lines by the Persian poet Saʿdī, this work appears to be the only one connecting not just Ottoman but Islamic literature with the New Year festivals of ancient times. In *methnewī* style, it was written to express the desire of man, alone and a stranger in this world, to return to man's real homeland and to find eternal life. The lyre (*čeng*), which represents exactly such a man, is played at a musical gathering on a spring day, entertaining everyone. In the first part of the work there is a description of a spring festival in which the son of Bāyezīd I, Prince Süleymān, is participating. In the second part, the lyre played at this festival tells the poet the adventures of its coming to this strange world through the stories of the cypress, the gazelle, the horse and the silk worm, the origins of the four constituent parts of the lyre. The heroes of the four stories are victims to the chain of eternal change, birth and death, of the material world and at the same time are eaten with the desire to return to their homelands, the source of eternal life. In the *Čeng-nāme*, the lyre celebrating spring and the man wishing for eternal life (symbolised by spring) are joined into one figure.

Bibliography: Given in the article.

(G. ALPAY TEKIN)

RABĪʿIYYAT: In Arabic [see ZAHRIYYĀT].

RĀBIṬA (A.), term employed in al-Andalus to denote a fortified enclosure, a bastion constructed on the coast to deter enemy attacks from the sea. This term sometimes served as a substitute for *ribāṭ* [*q.v.*], a term which no longer extended to the concentration point occupied by combatants in a holy war, but was almost reduced to the sense of *djihād* [*q.v.*] or even replaced *ghāra* "sudden attack, raid".

In a *rābiṭa*, "volunteers, who were periodically relieved, maintained a vigilant watch, while practising spiritual exercises and striving to lead an ascetic life. "The best known of these fortified monasteries, on the Mediterranean, was that of the Cape of Gata, at the eastern point of the bay of Alméria... Another known *rābiṭa*, on the other side of the Straits of Gibraltar, was that of al-Tawba or "Penitence"; it stood, opposite Huelva, not far from the estuary of the Río Tinto, on the same site where today stands the famous monastery of the Rabita, whose presence, since the end of the Middle Ages, has continued to uphold the Muslim monastic tradition" (E. Lévi-Provençal, *Hist. Esp. mus.*, iii, 111-12).

Current Spanish toponymy preserves, in the forms Rápita, Rávita, Rábida, the memory of the existence, in other parts of al-Andalus, of hermitages which were places of retreat for persons considered to be saints, accompanied by their disciples. This term thus became synonymous with *zāwiya* [*q.v.*], and it is this which has been adopted by the Spanish language, which uses *rábida* to denote a monastery or a hermitage.

Long before the arrival in the Maghrib of the wave of mysticism and the development in these regions of the "maraboutism" characteristic of religious activity, *rābiṭa* was also used there in concurrence with *zāwiya* (see al-Bādisī, *Maḳṣad*, tr. G.S. Colin, in *AM*, xxvi [1926], 240).

Bibliography: L. Torres Balbás, *Rábitas hispanomusulmanas*, in *al-And.*, xiii/2 (1948), 475-91; C. Villanueva, *Rábitas granadinas*, in *Miscelánea de estudios árabes y hebraicos*, iii (1954), 79-86. (ED.)

AL-RĀBIṬA AL-ISLĀMIYYA (A.), literally "the Islamic league."

Pan-movements in the Muslim world have been usually rendered by Arabic terms like *waḥda*, *ittiḥād*, *rābiṭa* or *djāmiʿa*. *Rābiṭa* ("bond") in eastern Muslim mystic tradition originally meant the relationship of a *murīd* to his master (R. Gramlich (tr.), *ʿAwārif al-maʿārif. Die Gaben der Erkenntnisse des ʿUmar as-Suhrawardī*, Wiesbaden 1978, 107-8) and hence a close friendship (*rābiṭa-yi ukhuwwat*, Saʿd al-Dīn Khodja Efendī, *Tādj al-tawārīkh*, as cited in Fr.A. Mesgien Meninski, *Lexicon arabico-persico-turcicum*, Vienna 1780, iii, 2-3). It underwent a significant semantic change in the 19th century, when *rābiṭa* became a political notion in Ottoman usage (in the sense of "league", X.T. Bianchi, *Dictionnaire français-turc*, Paris 1846, ii, 300), reflecting the emergence of an Islamic political language. *Djāmiʿa* [*q.v.*] as a noun signifies a gathering, a universality which embraces everything (hence from about 1850 onwards, also meaning a university). In modern usage, *djāmiʿa* has also been used to characterise a political, united movement. It is this sense which made these two terms popular among Muslim intellectuals and politicians in the second half of the 19th century. With the term *islāmiyya* attributed to it, *rābiṭa* and *djāmiʿa* soon became notions to render the European word Pan-Islam [see PAN-ISLAMISM]. Another earlier equivalent is the Ottoman-Turkish term *ittiḥād-i Islām* ("Union of Islam", arabicised as *al-waḥda al-islāmiyya*) which came into use in 1871 at the latest (e.g. Nāmiḳ Kemāl [*q.v.*] in 1872, see Landau, *The politics of Pan-Islam, ideology and organization*, Oxford 1990, 23-4). European travellers identified this political tendency as an Islamic form of the then common pan-movements and accordingly rendered this term with Pan-Islam (Vambéry, see Lee, *Origins*, 278-87), or in German with Panislamismus (Murad Effendi [Franz von Werner], *Türkische Skizzen*, Leipzig 1877, i, 95) from 1877 onwards. The concept of Pan-Islam again was re-arabicised to *al-djāmiʿa al-islāmiyya* or *al-rābiṭa al-islāmiyya* when after 1894 Pan-Islamism became a major concept of contemporary Islamic politics in the Ottoman Empire (see e.g. *al-Manār*, ii [1317/1899], 337-45, where Rashīd Riḍā stated that "today", Djamāl al-Dīn al-Afghānī's call to Islam should be rendered as *al-djāmiʿa al-islāmiyya*).

These dates suggest that after 1880, Islamic politics were primarily conceived as a movement to reunify the Muslim countries and, as al-Afg͟hānī put it in 1884, "to preserve [our] nation's honour, to grieve for what hurts it, and to co-operate to defend a total union against whomsoever attacks it." (al-Afg͟hānī-ʿAbduh, *al-ʿUrwa al-wut͟hḳā*, 71, tr. Landau, in *op. cit.*, 319). Consequently, Islamic politics construed the mass of the whole Islamic *umma* as superseding any national boundaries of Muslim politics (see *al-ʿUrwa al-wut͟hḳā*, 48).

Pan-Islamic rhetorics were of great importance during the reign of the two Ottoman sultans ʿAbd al-ʿAzīz and ʿAbd al-Ḥamīd II [*q.vv.*]. They used the concept of Islamic unity to develop a new form of foreign policy which aimed at mobilising the peoples of the Muslim world in favour of the Ottoman Empire. Though ʿAbd al-Ḥamīd II, who now stressed his identity as caliph, tried to establish a network of Islamic propagandists, the success of his appeal to Islamic unity and of Pan-Islam as an "imperial ideology" (Landau, *op. cit.*, 9-72) was very small. Obviously, national policy was much more able to mobilise Muslim intellectuals, since the nation state offered real positions of power, whereas Pan-Islamism referred to an Islamic *umma* which had only a nebulous existence. Only in India were the activities of the Ottoman emissaries rather more successful.

Since *ca.* 1900, *rābiṭa* has also become a technical term to denote political organisations (e.g. the All-India Muslim League, established in the context of local politics by partisans of Sayyid Aḥmad K͟hān's (1817-98 [*q.v.*]) reform movement in 1906 (W.C. Smith, *Modern Islām in India*, London 1946, 246-92, Lahore 1969, 297-358; Landau, *op. cit.*, 185), in Arabic called *al-rābiṭa al-muslima* (Masʿūd al-Nadwī, *Taʾrīk͟h al-Daʿwa al-islāmiyya fi 'l-Hind*, Beirut 1370/1950, i, 249)). In 1909-10, the famous Egyptian nationalists Ibrāhīm Nāṣīf al-Wardānī (1886-1910) and S͟hafīḳ Manṣūr (1886-1925) called their small, militant organisation either *d̲jamʿiyyat al-rābiṭa al-islāmiyya, d̲jamʿiyyat al-ittiḥād al-islāmī* or simply *d̲jamʿiyyat al-rābiṭa al-ak͟hawiyya*.

During the First World War, the Central Powers, especially Germany, induced the Ottoman empire to strengthen its Pan-Islamic activities, hoping that they would serve to mobilise the Muslim world to join the war against the Allies. Again, however, this propaganda failed, since national identities of local élites predominated over trans-national forms of self-identification [see further on this, PAN-ISLAMISM].

Islamic policy formulated as Pan-Islamism was often, but not invariably, connected to the *Salafiyya* [*q.v.*] movement. It continued to be an important field of propaganda, especially in Muslim minority communities and among dissident Muslim political groups. ʿAbd al-Raḥmān al-Kawākibī (1848-1902 [*q.v.*]) elaborated the idea of Pan-Islamism in construing a fictive Muslim congress that should have taken place in Mecca in 1898-9. He stressed the importance of the civil identity of Pan-Islamism as being for him the only policy that could guarantee Muslim social, cultural and political welfare (*Umm al-ḳurā*, Beirut 1982, 38-9; Kramer, *Islam assembled*, 30-5). The congress idea aroused a brief enthusiastic response in 1907-8 and again after the abolition of the caliphate in Turkey on 4 March 1924. From 1926 to 1931, three international Islamic congresses were held (Mecca 1926, Cairo 1926 and Jerusalem 1931), each of which aimed at helping establish an Islamic public opinion on special issues (the question of the Holy Places, the question of the caliphate, and the question of the Sanctuaries in Jerusalem).

The more such independent Islamic groups as the Egyptian Muslim Brotherhood (*d̲jamʿiyyat al-ik͟hwān al-muslimīn* [see AL-IK͟HWĀN AL-MUSLIMŪN]) or the Muslim Youth Organisation (*d̲jamʿiyyat al-s͟hubbān al-muslimīn*) were able to spread their propaganda and to articulate an Islamic policy which was directed more to a local public than to an imagined Islamic *umma* (the influence of Ras͟hīd Riḍā [*q.v.*] is notable), the more the traditional concept of Pan-Islam lost its influence. Following Ras͟hīd Riḍā, most Islamic activists now favoured a unity of Islamic avant-garde organisations (*rābiṭa islāmiyya*) which would represent "the polity of Islam" (*dawlat al-Islām*) in contrast to the undifferentiated unity of the Islamic *umma* (*d̲jāmiʿa islāmiyya*) (cf. Ras͟hīd Riḍā, *Taʾrīk͟h al-Imām al-Ustād͟h Muḥammad ʿAbduh*, i, Cairo 1350/1931, 318-20, 328). It is in this sense that the term *rābiṭa* ("league") has been widely used since the 1930s. In Syria, Morocco, ʿIrāḳ, Algeria and Sudan, for instance, Muslim scholars have founded so-called "leagues" (*rābiṭat al-ʿulamāʾ*), which show that the term *rābiṭa* has now become a word signifying an independent Muslim élite organisation, mostly of *Salafī* orientation.

After the Second World War, Pan-Islamism as a label for independent, trans-national Islamic policy faded out. Instead, national politics of the newly-established or re-established states began to incorporate Pan-Islamic ideals into their own propaganda (Egypt, Jordan, Pakistan, Saudi Arabia) and set up different trans-national Islamic bodies which would attest the Islamic identity of the national régimes, e.g. the Islamic World Congress (1949-52), the General Islamic Congress of Jerusalem (1953), the Higher Council of Muslim Affairs (1960) or the Muslim World League (1962) (Schulze, *Internationalismus*, 104-22). During the so-called Arab Cold War (M.H. Kerr, *The Arab Cold War*, New York-London 1970), Pan-Islamism served as a cornerstone of either faction: Egyptian Nasserists and Saudi Royalists both used Pan-Islamic rhetoric in order to internationalise their policy. In the 1970s, the strengthening of independent Islamic politics led to a competition in the field of trans-national Islamic politics. On the one hand, patronising Muslim states reacted positively to the Saudi call to found an inter-state Islamic organisation (*Munaẓẓamat al-Muʾtamar al-Islāmī*, 1969, 1972) which would serve to establish Islamic solidarity through government policy. On the other hand, however, Islamic politicians favoured the trans-national co-operation of homogenous Islamic tendencies which would serve to establish a network of congenial Islamic organisations. The most famous trans-national league is *Rābiṭat al-ʿĀlam al-Islāmī* (Muslim World League), founded in 1962 at Mecca. Its members claimed to "represent [the Muslim world] in the fields of dogmatics and belief" and to work for the establishing of a "union of the Muslim world" (*d̲jāmiʿat al-ʿālam al-islāmī*) (*Mad̲jallat Rābiṭat al-ʿĀlam al-Islāmī*, i/1 [1383/1963], 8; Schulze, *op. cit.*, 215). Hence *rābiṭa* now means a political and cultural avant-garde of Muslim scholars and intellectuals whose task is, according to Ḳurʾān, III, 103, to propagate the message of "the true Islam" in order to create a true union of Muslim peoples, whereas *d̲jāmiʿa* continues to signify the political unification of Muslim states.

Bibliography: In addition to the *Bibls.* of PAN-ARABISM, PAN-ISLAMISM and PAN-TURKISM, see D̲jamāl al-Dīn al-Afg͟hānī-Muḥammad ʿAbduh, *al-ʿUrwa al-wut͟hḳā*², Cairo 1958; ʿAbd al-Raḥmān al-Kawākibī, *Sid̲jill mud͟hakkirāt d̲jamʿiyyat umm al-ḳurā ay ḍabṭ mufāwaḍāt wa-muḳarrarāt muʾtamar al-nahḍa al-*

islāmiyya al-munᶜaḳid fī Makka al-mukarrama sanat 1316, Port Said [1899], ²Beirut 1402/1982; A. Vambéry, Pan-Islamism, in The Nineteenth Century and After, lx (1906), 547-58, lxi (1907), 860-72; V. Bartol'd, Khalif i Sultan, in Mir' Islama (St. Petersburg), i (1912), 203-26, 345-400; Ismāᶜīl Ṣidḳī, Ḥayy ᶜalā 'l-intibāh, Istanbul 1329/1913; Djelāl Nūrī [Ileri], Ittiḥād-i Islām. Islāmiñ māḍīsi ḥālī istiḳbāli, Istanbul 1331/1913; Shakīb Arslān, Ḥāḍir al-ᶜālam al-islāmī (= annotated tr. of L. Stoddard, The new world of Islam, London 1921), i-iv, Cairo 1352/1933-4; D.E. Lee, The origins of Pan-Islam, in American Hist. Review, xlvii (1942), 278-87; A.-M. Goichon, Le panislamisme d'hier et d'aujourd'hui, in L'Afrique et l'Asie (Paris), ix (1950), 18-44; Sylvia Haim, Intorno alle origini della teoria del panislamismo, in OM, xxxvi (1956), 409-21; A. Reid, Nineteenth-century Pan-Islam in Indonesia and Malaysia, in Jnal. of Asian Studies, xxvi (1966-7), 267-83; S.A. Zenkovsky, Pan-Turkism and Islam in Russia, Cambridge, Mass. 1967; Nikki R. Keddie, Pan-Islam as proto-nationalism, in Jnal. of Modern History, xli (1969), 17-28; M. Kramer, Islam assembled. The advent of the Muslim congresses, New York 1986; R. Schulze, Islamischer Internationalismus im 20. Jahrhundert, Leiden 1990. (R. SCHULZE)

RAḌĀᶜ or **RIḌĀᶜ**, also RAḌĀᶜA (A.), suckling; as technical term, the suckling which produces the legal impediment to marriage of foster-kinship.

1. Legal aspects.

From the manner in which the Ḳurʾān presents its ruling, it may be supposed that the question was already familiar to those addressed. Sūra IV, 23, falls into two sections comprising lists of those with whom the Muslim may not contract marriage. The first, dealing with blood relatives, begins with the natural mother. The second, opening with the foster-mother and the foster-sister, that is, any female to whom the foster-mother has also given suck, suggested for foster-relations duplication of the list already given for blood-relations. To foster-mother and foster-sister came to be added the foster-niece, the foster-aunt (maternal and paternal), and foster-daughter. Nor may a man simultaneously wed or own two women who are foster-sisters, nor a woman and either of her foster-aunts.

An early and long-lived point of contention, expressed in traditions involving the Prophet's own immediate household, concerned the foster-uncle, that is, the brother of the husband of the wet-nurse. These reports frequently state that discussion of the status of the foster-uncle arose subsequent to the imposition of the segregation of the sexes. What was in view was the need to identify all males with whom females, in terms of interpretation of sūra IV, 23, read in conjunction with XXIV, 31, might lawfully dispense with the inconvenience of the *ḥidjāb*. The latter verse failed to mention the uncle, although sūra IV prohibits marriage with nieces. Informality was taken to be restricted to persons between whom marriage was not permitted. Al-Shāfiᶜī argued that the extension of the range of foster-relationship had been based on both the lay-out of sūra IV and the elucidation of the passage supplied by the Prophet in the traditions just mentioned. Some of these illustrate the maxim: "Foster-relationship prohibits precisely what blood-relationship prohibits."

The addition of the foster-uncle to the relations of forbidden degree, as well as the idea, promoted in a series of traditions, that marriage was also prohibited between the foster-children of two wives or slaves of the same man, by including relationship by marriage in foster-relationship, adds to the impediment to marriage by reason of fostership a further impediment on grounds of a relationship in law. Resistance to the idea that the relation established between nurse and infant extended to the nurse's husband and, through him, to his brother, was expressed in variants of the above traditions, one of which exposes the principle underlying the proposed extension. This is the concept of "the sire's milk". It was thought that there inhered in breast-milk some quality similar to that residing in blood. The semen of the husband caused the flow of milk. That was what underlay the ban created by the act of nursing and it was, therefore, of necessity, implicated in its legal consequences. Incorporation of relationship in law within the structure of foster-relationships was upheld but, at least in this aspect, was abandoned by al-Shāfiᶜī under the influence of contrary traditions.

Foster-relationship is to a degree specific. The *fuḳahāʾ* are agreed that, whereas it exists between a man and all his descendants and his nurse and all her foster- and blood relatives, and for the majority, all her husband's ones as well, no foster-relationship is assumed between a man and the ascendants or lateral relatives of his foster-brothers and sisters, or between the nurse and the ascendants or lateral relatives of her foster-child.

Since the Ḳurʾān envisages the employment for hire of wet-nurses, the duration of the breast-feeding had to be ascertained, under the rules governing hire. As to the age of the infant, that and the question of the period of his feeding had been addressed in II, 233, which suggested that the complete course would be of two years. For the majority, therefore, only suckling that occurs in infancy and is indispensable for the physical development of the child creates the legally significant bond. The point was illustrated using hypothetical illustrations. A husband, coming to the aid of his wife whose milk is slow to flow, is not barred from future marital relations with her if he should inadvertently swallow any of her milk. Nor can a jealous wife prevent legitimate sexual relations between her husband and any younger co-wife whom he chooses to marry by the expedient of nursing her. The response to such situations was conveyed in traditions traced to prominent Companions, or to the Prophet himself: *innamā 'l-raḍāᶜa min al-madjāᶜa* "valid suckling is that which alone staves off hunger." Traditions of the kind were directed against the artificial foster-relationship to which we shall shortly return.

The majority of the *fuḳahāʾ* accepted that the suckling provided during the first two years of life was alone legally relevant and (despite the wide circulation of traditions from the Prophet to the contrary), that the swallowing of only a single drop of breast-milk at that age established the legally-recognised affiliation.

The discussion of both these questions had as its background a debate on the legal efficacy of the suckling of non-infants, referred to in the literature as *raḍāᶜ al-kabīr*. Various wives of the Prophet are reported to have arranged that certain infants be suckled by their sisters or by the daughters of their brothers, to ensure that, in their later years, such males would be able to visit them. The traditions in question make the point that a minimum number, usually five or ten, of suckling sessions had to be completed if the plan were to succeed. Where the number of sessions fell below the stated minimum, the underlying intent was frustrated. That, it is explained, is why Sālim b. ᶜAbd Allāh could never call upon ᶜĀʾisha. The discussion on numbers merged with the separate tradition on the plight of a particular family unit. When the wife of a prominent Companion told the Prophet that, following the revelation of sūra XXXIII's negation of the reality of legal adoption, her husband resented the continued presence in their home of their adopted son, now grown to full manhood, the Prophet counselled her to suckle the man on five separate occasions. A variant says ten separate occasions. Alone among the Prophet's widows, ʿĀʾis͟ha is said, on the basis of this episode, to have adopted the principle that the suckling of an adult is legally efficacious. Rebuked by the Prophet's other widows, ʿĀʾis͟ha is reported to have replied that she merely followed a precedent established by the Prophet and alluded to XXXIII, 21. This argument from the Sunna proving inadequate in the face of an equal weight of contrary traditions traced to the remaining widows, showing that they regarded that as having been a specific concession granted by the Prophet and never intended for general application, resort had to be made to higher authority. ʿĀʾis͟ha is said to have claimed that a Ḳurʾān verse had been revealed to the Prophet setting the minimum number of suckling sessions required to establish the marriage ban at ten. The verse had subsequently been withdrawn and replaced by a second verse setting the limit at five. ʿĀʾis͟ha is further held to have stated that this second verse was still being recited as part of the Ḳurʾān when the Prophet died. Mālik reproduced this report in his *Muwaṭṭaʾ* merely to dismiss it, but it became a crucial element in al-S͟hāfiʿī's bitter polemic against the Mālikīs of his day. Ḥanafīs and Mālikīs are agreed that one single session suffices to establish the ban; three opinions are transmitted from Aḥmad which show him somewhat equivocal on the matter. Al-Layt͟h b. Saʿd and the Ẓāhirīs Dāwūd and Ibn Ḥazm argued for this limit of five sessions, and defended the legal efficacy of suckling an adult, although al-S͟hāfiʿī had already abandoned this element of the tradition as curtly as Mālik had dismissed any minimum number greater than one.

The discussion incidentally furnished the theorists on *nask͟h* [*q.v.*] with what were claimed to be two attested instances of the phenomenon. The ten sucklings verse exemplified *nask͟h al-tilāwa wa 'l-ḥukm*, suppression of both wording and ruling of a Ḳurʾān verse, while the five sucklings-verse represented suppression of the wording, but not the ruling of a revealed verse, *nask͟h al-tilāwa dūna 'l-ḥukm*. That the Mālikīs treated both verses as suppressed in respect of wording and ruling shows that they traced their view directly to IV, 23. The verse used the preterite of the verb which can be realised in a single act, an interpretation illustrated in a tradition attributed to ʿAbd Allāh b. ʿUmar: "God's word is superior to ʿĀʾis͟ha's word. God merely says 'Your foster-sisters are prohibited'; He does not say 'One suckling' nor 'two sucklings'."

To prove foster-kinship, many authorities were content with the testimony of the foster-mother. But, as the foster-mother may be either free or a slave, Muslim or *d͟himmī*, Mālik is said to have expected the evidence of at least two women, although his followers are divided on this. The Ḥanafīs demanded two men, or, failing that, one man and two women (II, 282).

Bibliography: Wensinck, *Concordance*, s.v. *raḍāʿ*; Juynboll, *Handbuch des islāmischen Gesetzes*, 219; idem, *Handleiding*[3], 185; D. Santillana, *Istituzioni di diritto musulmano malichita*, i, 161; for the Imāmīs, Querry, *Droit musulman*, i, 657 ff.; J. Schacht, *The origins of Muhammadan jurisprudence*, Oxford 1950; J. Burton, *The collection of the Qurʾān*, Cambridge 1977; idem, in St. Andrews University, School of Abbasid Studies, *Occasional Papers*, 1 (1986); idem, *The sources of Islamic law*, Edinburgh 1990; S͟hāfiʿī, *Umm*, Cair 1321/1903, v, 20 ff., vi, 240, vii, 208, 246-; S͟hawkānī, *Nayl al-awṭār*, Cairo 1345/1926, vi 113 ff., Beirut 1393/1973, vii, 113 ff.

(J. Schacht-[J. Burton])

2. In Arabian society.

Before Islam, the Meccans habitually gave their ir fants to wet-nurses, choosing these for preferenc amongst the Bedouins; hence Muḥammad was en trusted to Ḥalīma, of the tribe of Saʿd b. Bakr (al Balād͟hurī, *Ansāb al-as͟hrāf*, ed. Ḥamīdallāh, Cair 1959, i, 93). It was normal for such services to b recompensed, and Ḳurʾān, II, 233, stipulates that th wet-nurse should be rewarded according to th custom. Curiously, it is also envisaged that a husban should make a payment to the mother whom he ha repudiated as a wife so that she can suckle her chil born of him. If there is any dispute over the amoun of this recompense, the mother can refuse to provid milk without the father being able to exert an pressure or compulsion on her. In such a case, th parents can only entrust their child to a wet-nurs (LXV, 6).

Suckling creates fraternal bonds which have widespread social and moral effect. As a vital elemen which embodies a sacred principle, milk produces ar effect comparable to that of blood, of which it is sometimes a synonym. This is why children suckled from the same breasts were considered as brothers, so tha S͟hīmā, daughter of the wet-nurse Ḥalīma, was the foster-sister of Muḥammad. When she was capturec on the Day of Ḥunayn [*q.v.*], she identified herself tc the Prophet, who accorded her a welcome worthy o a sister (al-Balād͟hurī, *Ansāb*, i, 93).

The mystical bond of relationship created by suckling gave rise to a number of marriage prohibitions (see 1. above). The prohibition of marrying a foster-sister was pre-Islamic. In order to prevent ʿAntar from consummating his marriage, a rival tried to make him believe that he was the milk-sister of his wife ʿAbla, on the grounds that the latter had allegedly sucked the breasts of Zabība, ʿAntar's mother. In addition to the Ḳurʾānic prohibition (see 1. above), a *ḥadīt͟h* adds "suckling prohibits what birth prohibits" (*al-raḍāʿa tuḥarrimu mā tuḥarrimu al-wilāda*) (Muslim, *Ṣaḥīḥ*, *k. al-raḍāʿa*, Cairo 1334, iv, 162), and another tradition states "what is prohibited through fostering is the same as what is prohibited by blood relationship" (*yaḥrumu min al-raḍāʿa mā yaḥrumu min al-nasab*) (al-Buk͟hārī, *Ṣaḥīḥ*, *k. al-nikāḥ*, Cairo 1376, vii, 9). When a husband learnt that he had been suckled at the same breast as had his spouse, he consulted the Prophet, who ordered him to divorce her (*ibid.*, vii, 10). Since the wet-nurse's husband was considered as a father, the latter's brother became the uncle of the man who had been suckled, i.e. a foster-uncle (see 1. above).

One question to be considered concerns the provenance or source of the milk. Only a woman's milk creates bonds of kinship; if a man suckles a child with milk secreted by his breasts, no prohibitions result (al-S͟haʿrānī, *Mīzān*, Cairo 1322, ii, 143).

Bibliography: Given in the article.

(J. Chelhod)

RADD (a.), the normal term used in classical Islamic literature to denote a response to an adversary, intended to refute his statements or opinions. A number of works, especially those belonging to the earlier period (2nd-4th centuries A.H.), bore the title *Kitāb al-Radd ʿalā...* "response, reply to...": cf. *Fihrist*, ed. Tad͟jaddud, Tehran 1971, index, 109-11; Sezgin, *GAS*, i, 903-4; viii, 369; ix, 378-9. Also often sed, with the same meaning, was the expression *[K]itāb ʿalā...*, cf. *Fihrist*, index, 132. There are also instances where the word *radd* is interposed in the second element of the title; thus, in the field of theological polemic, the *K. Ikhtilāf al-lafẓ wa 'l-radd ʿalā 'l-Djahmiyya wa 'l-mushabbiha* of Ibn Ḳutayba, the *K. al-intiṣār wa 'l-radd ʿalā Ibn al-Rāwandī* of al-Khayyāṭ [*q.v.*], the *K. al-Lumaʿ fī 'l-radd ʿalā ahl al-zaygh wa 'l-bidaʿ* of al-Ashʿarī, the *K. al-Tamhīd fī 'l-radd ʿalā 'l-mulḥida wa 'l-muʿaṭṭila...* of al-Bāḳillānī. Another term in frequent usage is *naḳḍ* "refutation", although *naḳḍ* is principally employed in reference to a book (*K. Naḳḍ Risālat al-Shāfiʿī*, *K. Naḳḍ K. Ibn al-Rāwandī fi 'l-imāma*, etc.; if the refutation applies to an individual, the expression used is *K. al-Naḳḍ ʿalā...*); cf. *Fihrist*, index, 159-60. The refutation of a work may in its turn be refuted; thus the *Naḳḍ al-Lumaʿ* of ʿAbd al-Djabbār (a refutation of the *K. al-Lumaʿ* of al-Ashʿarī) was followed by a *K. Naḳḍ al-Naḳḍ* of al-Bāḳillānī (cf. *Arabica* [1985], 187, n. 12).

All topics liable to give rise to divergent points of view, between individuals or between schools, could provide material for refutation. Thus in the writings of grammarian-lexicographers, refutations are to be observed, in opposition to Sībawayh, al-Khalīl, al-Farrāʾ, al-Mubarrad, al-Mufaḍḍal b. Salama, Thaʿlab, Ibn Khālawayh, etc. (cf. *GAS*, viii and ix, index of titles). In the field of *fiḳh*, attention may be drawn, among others, to refutations of Mālik by Abū Yūsuf (*Fihrist*, 257, ll. 2-3), of Muḥammad b. al-Ḥasan by al-Shāfiʿī (*ibid.*, 264, l. 22), of al-Shāfiʿ ī by the Mālikī Ibrāhīm b. Ḥammād (*ibid.*, 252, ll. 29-30) and the Imāmī Abū Sahl al-Nawbakhtī (*ibid.*, 225, l. 17). But it is in the field of dogmatic theology that refutations are most abundant; it is accepted, furthermore, that if, in Islam, theology has come to be known as the "science of speech" (*ʿilm al-kalām* [*q.v.*]), it owes this title to the fact that it was, at the outset, of an essentially polemical and apologetic nature (cf., most recently, J. van Ess, *Theologie und Gesellschaft im 2. und 3. Jahrhundert Hidschra*, i, Berlin-New York 1991, 48-55). The adversaries in question are, on the one hand, all adherents of doctrines other than Islam: Jews, Christians, Mazdaeans, Dualists, "Zindīḳs" [*q.v.*], *dahriyya* [*q.v.*], disciples of Aristotle, practitioners of astrology, partisans of "natures" (*ṭabāʾiʿ*), believers in metempsychosis, "sophists", etc. On the other hand, within the context of Islam, there are all the schools or "sects" reckoned to uphold—from the point of view of the author in question—doctrines which are erroneous and which deserve, for this reason, to be opposed: Murdjiʾa, Djahmiyya, Ḳadariyya, Muʿtazila, "assimilationists" (*mushabbiha*), "corporealists" (*mudjassima*), *hashwiyya* [*q.v.*], "coercionists" (*djabriyya* or *mudjbira*), Khāridjites, "Rāfiḍīs" [*q.v.*], extreme Shīʿīs (*ghulāt*), etc. As among grammarians and jurists, the polemic is also often of an individual nature: in the bibliography of the Muʿtazilī Bishr b. al-Muʿtamir [*q.v.*], for example, there figures a whole series of refutations of this kind, in opposition to, among others, Abu 'l-Hudhayl, al-Naẓẓām, Ḍirār, Ḥafṣ al-Fard, Hishām b. al-Ḥakam, Abū Bakr al-Aṣamm (*Fihrist*, 185, ll. 2-6).

A uniform model of refutation does not exist. It is possible, however, to identify two principal types. Either the refutation is purely unilateral; the author presents successively each of the assertions of the adversary ("he says", *ḳāla*), and in each case gives his reply ("he is answered", *yuḳālu lahu*), and this is the model followed for example—although in very different registers—by Ibn Ḥanbal in the first section of his *K. al-Radd ʿalā 'l-zanādiḳa* and by al-Khayyāṭ in his *Intiṣār*; or else the refutation is presented in the form of an imaginary controversy (*munāẓara* [*q.v.*]), with a series of questions and answers [see AL-MASĀʾIL WA 'L-ADJWIBA], where, naturally, the author gives himself the best lines and effortlessly reduces his interlocutor to a state of confusion ("he will be asked", *yuḳālu lahu...*, "and if he says", *fa-in ḳāla...*, "he will be answered", *ḳīla lahu...*, "and if he says", etc.). A good example—among a hundred others—of this second method is the *Tamhīd* of al-Bāḳillānī (see especially the chapters opposing the Mazdaeans and the Christians).

Bibliography: Given in the article.

(D. GIMARET)

AL-**RĀDHĀNIYYA**, a name by which is known a group of Jewish merchants whose origin, identity and activities have been the subject of an endless series of questions, opinions, commentaries and contradictory judgments, none of which have proved finally convincing.

These speculations have been inspired by a passage of the *Kitāb al-Masālik wa 'l-mamālik* of Ibn Khurradādhbih [*q.v.*] composed between 232 and 272/846-85. This text, which has been copied and summarised, but never genuinely corroborated by contemporary or later authors, Muslim or non-Muslim, has been avidly studied by a series of scholars who will be mentioned below. It appears in its entirety in the edition-translation of the *K. al-Masālik* produced by Barbier de Meynard (in *JA* [1865]), in the standard edition of M.J. De Goeje (*BGA*, vi, 1885, 153-5), in the edition-translation of M. Hadj-Sadok (*Description du Maghreb et de l'Europe au IIIᵉ/IXᵉ siècle*, Algiers 1949, 20-2) and, partially, in the *Extraits des principaux géographes arabes du Moyen Âge* by R. Blachère (Paris 1957, 28-9). It has furthermore been the object of a quite considerable number of translations into English (for specific references see *Bibl.*) by Sprenger, Jacobs, Adler, Lopez-Raymond, Katz, Rabinowitz (1948 = Jacobs' translation with commentary by I. Friedlander), Goitein (1954), Roth, Baron, Serjeant; into German, by Aronius, Caro, Jacobi; into Hebrew, by Dinur; into Yiddish, by Schipper (this version was also translated into Hebrew).

The best method of introducing the subject is to offer a literal translation of this text:

"Itinerary/itineraries of the Jewish merchants (known as) Rādhāniyya, who speak Arabic, Persian, *Rūmī* (= Greek?), Frankish (= French?), Andalusian (= Romance) and Slavonic, and travel from the East to the West and vice-versa, by land and by sea. From the West they import eunuchs (*khadam*), young slaves of both sexes (*djawārī* and *ghilmān*), silk brocade (*dībādj*), beaver fur (*djulūd al-khazz*), [pelts of] the sable (*sammūr*) and [other] furs, as well as swords."

[*First itinerary*] "They embark in the land of the Franks (Firandja [see IFRANDJ]) on the Western Sea (= the Mediterranean) and disembark at al-Faramā (= ancient Pelusium), then they transport their merchandise by land (*ʿalā 'l-ẓahr*) as far as al-Ḳulzum [*q.v.*] (ancient Clysma), a distance of 25 parasangs; they then traverse the Eastern Sea (= the Red Sea) from al-Ḳulzum to al-Djār (the port of Medina; see Yāḳūt, *Buldān*, s.v.) and to Djudda [*q.v.*]. From here, they continue their journey to Sind [*q.v.*], to India [see AL-HIND] and to China [see AL-ṢĪN]. From China, they bring back musk (*misk* [*q.v.*]), wood of aloes (*ʿūd*), camphor (*kāfūr* [*q.v.*]), cinnamon (*dār ṣīnī* [*q.v.* in Suppl.]) and other (products) which are imported from these countries. Thus they return to al-Ḳulzum, then transport their [consignment] to al-Faramā and embark on the Mediterranean. Sometimes, they made a detour through Constantinople with their merchandise, which they sold to the Byzantines. Sometimes furthermore, they went to sell them [in the land of the] king of Firandja."

[*Second itinerary*] "When they chose to do so, on leaving Firandja, they transported their merchandise by sea, on the Mediterranean, disembarking at Antioch (Anṭākiya [*q.v.*]), whence they made their way, in three overland stages, to al-Djābiya (see below); they then sailed on the Euphrates (al-Furāt [*q.v.*]) to Baghdād, then on the Tigris (Didjla [*q.v.*]) to al-Ubulla (see *EI*[1], s.v. AL-OBOLLA), and from here they gained access to Oman (ʿUmān [*q.v.*]), Sind, India and China, all these countries being contiguous with one another."

After the succinct description of these two itineraries, the text moves on to the "Russian traders", who are not to be confused with the Rādhāniyya; not only, in fact, do "they call themselves Christians", but moreover their journeys, confined to the Orient, have Baghdād as their western limit. The paragraph devoted to them is possibly an interpolation owed to a copyist, but it is equally possible that the author himself has inserted a few lines regarding these merchants; this would then be one of those intercalations through association of ideas which are such a feature of mediaeval Arab writings, especially in the process of revision, and it is known that Ibn Khurradādhbih adapted his own text. On the subject of the Russians, al-Masʿūdī, who does not know of the Rādhāniyya, speaks (*Murūdj*, ii, 18 = § 458) of the Lūdhʿāna (?) "who come in pursuit of trade to Spain, to Rome, to Constantinople and Khazaria". J. Marquart (*Streifzüge*, 33), D.M. Dunlop (*Khazars*, 209) and A. Seippel (p. xxviii) have proposed various readings and identifications, but it would be tempting to see this name as an adaptation of Rādhāniyya; the author of the present article was rash enough to suggest such a connection (Arabic index of the *Murūdj*, s.v. Lūdhʿāna): Jacobi (252-3) also speculates cautiously on the possibility of the al-Lūdhʿāna = al-Rādhāniyya equation and shows equal circumspection in considering a passage of the *Kitāb al-Tanbīh* of the same author (140; ed. Cairo, 121-2) where it is said that the Byzantine city (*sic*) of Musannāt impounds ships of the Kūdhkūna (= Rādhāniyya ?) and of other Russians.

It is particularly important not to overlook, as R. Blachère has, the continuation of the account of Ibn Khurradādhbih, who returns to the Rādhāniyya without introducing them other than by a personal pronoun (*hum*), which could equally well refer to the Russian merchants. So, having described in the first part of the text two itineraries of the Jewish merchants who, on the outward journey at least, traverse the Mediterranean from end to end, the author moves on to a *Third itinerary*, to

"Their overland route: those among them who set out from al-Andalus or from Firandja, cross over (the strait) to Lower Sūs (al-Sūs al-Akṣā [*q.v.*]) and arrive at Tangier, whence they make their way to Ifrīḳiya [*q.v.*] (approximately equivalent to present-day Tunisia, but more specifically Ḳayrawān), to Miṣr [*q.v.*] (Egypt, but more specifically al-Fusṭāṭ); they subsequently pass through al-Ramla [*q.v.*] (in Palestine), Damascus (Dimashḳ [*q.v.*]), Kūfa [*q.v.*], Baghdād, Baṣra [*q.vv.*] (these last three in ʿIrāḳ), al-Ahwāz [*q.v.*] (in Khūzistān), Fārs and Kirmān [*q.vv.*], arriving in Sind, India and China."

[*Fourth itinerary*] "Sometimes they take a route to the rear of Rome (Rūmiya), through the land of the Slavs (al-Ṣaḳāliba [*q.v.*]), reaching Khamlīdj (or Khamlīkh see *Ḥudūd al-ʿālam*, comm. Minorsky, 454 and index) capital of the Khazars [*q.v.*], then [they sail] on the sea of Djurdjān (= the Caspian), [arriving] at Balkh [*q.v.*] (in northern Afghanistan) and in Transoxiana (Mā warā' al-Nahr [*q.v.*]) before attaining the camp (*wurt*; see below) of the Toghuzghuz [*q.v.*] and moving into China."

The first orientalist to have drawn attention to this passage was A. Sprenger who, in 1844, undertook an English translation of it. Shortly after this, J.-T. Reinaud had occasion to quote it, and C. Barbier de Meynard annotated it in his edition-translation of the *K. al-Masālik*, all of this before historians of the Jewish people or of international trade began to utilise and to analyse it. Among the latter, the most authoritative is undoubtedly W. Heyd who, although having no direct access to the Arabic text, posed some pertinent questions, regarding in particular the land of origin of these Jews, whom he perceived nevertheless as westerners, since they set out from the West. Since then, studies and commentaries have followed in rapid succession: I. Schipper concurred with Heyd and stressed the fact (in his *Anfänge* and *Anteil*) that, among Jewish merchants, only those from the West travelled worldwide, the orientals among them remaining within the limits of the Islamic world. In fact, the issue of the origin or the home-base of the Rādhāniyya has been discussed by numerous scholars who, in general, have considered them to be natives of Spain or of France. M. Lombard has even declared that they set sail from Narbonne, without providing evidence in support of this claim. In this company, only Barbier de Meynard displayed sound judgment, logically linking their name to that of the district of the Sawād of Baghdād known as Rādhān (see Yāḳūt, *Buldān*, s.v.). J. Jacobs, for his part, has sought to locate them at Rayy [*q.v.*], and S. Katz, while appearing to support this hypothesis, has made the remark that between Spain and China there were enough Jewish communities to explain the details of the itineraries described by Ibn Khurradādhbih. In 1957, S.W. Baron (328, n. 39) wrote that the latter undoubtedly included Jewish merchants of Khazaria among the Rādhāniyya, who are not necessarily all of the same origin; this scholar considered that these polyglot travellers could not be linked to any specific place and, rejecting the suggestion of Barbier de Maynard and of Simonsen (see below), he supported the explanation proposed by De Goeje of *rāh-dān* ("itinerant merchants").

Setting aside the question of their name, which will be examined here at a later stage, the problems posed by the Rādhāniyya are not always dealt with, by the authors who mention them, in relation to a wider context. Thus for example, G. Wiet, writing in 1937, described this text as "crucial" and translated it in part, but did not dwell on it and did not even mention the name of the group. In 1954, R. Brunschvig (in *EI*[2], s.v. ʿABD, at i, 32a), on the basis of this "famous" passage, gave prominence to the role of the Jews in the traffic of "Slavs" (i.e. slaves) across eastern and western Europe and even made a connection with the "eunuch factory" situated at Verdun [see KHAṢĪ, at iv, 1083b]. Occasional references such as this exist in abundance, none of them throwing the least light on the problems posed by the Rādhāniyya. The first thorough study of the text in question was due to J. Rabinowitz who, following his survey of *The routes of the Radanites* (1944), devoted a monograph to these merchants, entitled *Jewish merchant adventurers. A study of the Radanites*. This senior South African rabbi reckoned it necessary to consider in the first place the general situation of the world in the 9th century in order to identify and locate the "Radanites", in reference to whom he asserted (11), quoting Jacobs (194), that "His (Ibn Khurradādhbih's) account gives the key to the whole economic history of the Jews in the Middle Ages" and observed that the members of this group present three unusual features: they begin their journey in Europe; they follow overland routes between Khurāsān and China; they cover half of the fourth itinerary before reaching Islamic territories. In any event, he added, circumstances were favourable to the Radanites, since the trade routes between Christian Europe and the Islamic world were closed, except for the Jews. S.D. Goitein (1955), who was well aware of the work of Rabinowitz, considered the history of the Radanites in the light of documents from the Geniza and saw in their activity the first example of Jewish commerce in the early years of Islam. Writing in 1967, this same scholar attributed in part the major role played by Jews in the silk industry to the Rahdāniyya (*sic*), who could have had the opportunity, during their visits to China, to become acquainted with the professional intricacies of silk production. Goitein was unaware of a seminal article *Y a-t-il eu des Rahdānites*? by Cl. Cahen, who was the first historian (in 1964) to subject the text of Ibn Khurradādhbih to close analysis. The scepticism suggested by the title is explained by the fact that the passage in question—which is not corroborated, it will be remembered, by any independent source—raises a number of queries which, taken together, amount to the question: is it necessary to take Ibn Khurradādhbih's account as valid testimony, such that study of it is confined to critical examination of certain striking details or, on the contrary, if the whole is not to be rejected, should its authenticity at least be seriously questioned, bearing in mind that it is possibly a case of interpolation, the product of the intervention of some copyist? No historian has gone so far as this, not even Cl. Cahen, nor B. Blumenkranz who, writing in 1960, has shown considerable scepticism and has criticised the modern scholars who "by means of ingenious but barely reliable exegesis" locate the Rādhāniyya in the valley of the Rhône (an allusion to Simonsen; see below). He adds "An organisation into commercial companies has been invented for them" and "All the merchants who are known to have traded between the West and the East are automatically assumed to be Jews", but this author criticises above all "the invention" of Jewish merchants, without contributing anything new with regard to the Rādhāniyya. For his part, Cl. Cahen bases his doubts on certain points of the four itineraries described briefly by the geographer. He finds it astonishing that, in the first, al-Faramā is portrayed as a very busy commercial port and he is surprised that, in the second, Antioch should be the port of disembarkation of the Rādhāniyya, for this ancient city, which had lost much of its importance since the Arab conquest, was not a known market. Furthermore, the name of al-Djābiya is suspect (and it hard to understand how Blachère, *op. cit.*, 28, n. 12, discovered that it refers to "a small locality on the Euphrates", whereas the name in question [*q.v.*] is only that of a small town situated to the south of Damascus, and it seems unlikely that itinerant merchants would have made such a detour. In fact, this toponym features in only one of the two mss. of Ibn Khurradādhbih and was omitted by Ibn al-Faḳīh (see below). On the other hand, if it is accepted that the name of al-Djābiya is not an addition owed to a copyist but simply replaces that of the locality which is thought to be meant, sc. Bālis [*q.v.*], it is not necessarily a fluvial port which is involved, since the text says simply: *thumma yarkabūn fi 'l-Furāt*. The third itinerary caused even greater astonishment to Cl. Cahen, who justifiably described as "incomprehensible" a "maritime detour leading from France or from Spain to the Atlantic coast of Morocco". (This is also the opinion of Hadj-Sadok who, considering the reading *al-Sūs al-Aḳṣā* an error, with reason corrected it to *al-Sūs al-Adnā*, which is closer to reality. It is possible that confusion arose in the mind of the author, who was unfamiliar with the Islamic West, between Sūs and the Maghrib, but such an error does not compromise the veracity of the account.) Then, Cahen found it doubtful that the journey between Kirmān and Sind could have been made by overland route "on the terrible Persian coast". Finally, the fourth itinerary crosses central Europe and, via Khazaria, leads to China by way of the Caspian, Balkh, Transoxiana and the Camp of the Toghuzghuz, in other words through the "traditional passes of the Silk Road". (The word *wurt* in the text should no doubt be read *yūrt* or *yurt*, "tent" or "encampement" [see KHAYMA. iv. Central Asia].)

Without rejecting the whole of the paragraph, Cahen questioned the general image of the "Rahdānites". He doubted that Spain could, in this period, have exported beaver furs, that Jewish merchants would have adopted four quasi-specific itineraries, and that there would have been a "Rahdānite" organisation. He admitted, however, the plausible existence of a kind of association between people speaking various languages among those mentioned above and travelling between the West and the Far East.

This explosive article was bound to provoke reactions among historians. Writing in 1965, B. Lewis (in *EI*², s.v. IFRANDJ, at iii, 1044b) supported the sceptical attitude of Cahen. In 1970, E. Ashtor expressed equal surprise at certain sections of the itineraries and considered that Ibn Khurradādhbih without doubt "included in his survey material which does not conform to the conditions of his period, such as the journey to the Indies by way of the Red Sea". In his opinion, the geographer's intention was to indicate the principal routes of worldwide commerce, at a time when Jews played a dominant role in exchanges between the Christian and Muslim worlds.

The most detailed response to Cahen has been that of Jacobi who, in his article *Die Rādāniyya*, has offered a veritable monograph comprising: (1) a German translation of the text, in which the four itineraries are clearly separated (with recourse to the passages mentioned above, by Ibn al-Faḳīh and al-Masʿūdī which Marquart was the first to link together in his *Streifzüge*); (2) acceptance of its authenticity; (3) its credibility: discussion of points of detail regarding the languages spoken by the Rādhāniyya, the itineraries (with references, 257 n. 1, to the role of al-Faramā as a commercial port, the role on which Cahen cast doubt). Jacobi contradicts the latter, who had asserted that al-Ubulla was "enclosed within the Muslim city of Baṣra". In regard to the overland itinerary, he sees in the expression al-Sūs al-Aḳṣā a synonym of al-Maghrib al-Aḳṣā, which is evidently inaccurate. In view of the fact that Ibn Khurradādhbih indicates (84-9, ed.-tr. Hadj-Sadok, 2-10/3-11) a more detailed overland route, there is a temptation to use it to supplement the itinerary across North Africa which is more succinctly described in the passage studied here; but it does not seem appropriate to accept extrapolations of this kind. Jacobi examines the different types of merchandise mentioned and supplies, for each of them, references which in general do not contradict Ibn Khurradādhbih's version. The religion of the group poses no problem, the role of the Jews in worldwide commerce being well known; its organisation, however, is a mystery. (4) Etymology and origin: it is specifically in regard to the meaning and etymology of the term that Jacobi presents an interesting hypothesis worthy of serious consideration. Recalling that the author of the *K. al-Masālik* was a member of the managerial staff of the postal organisation (*barīd*) and thereby, of an information service, he proposes to see in the word *rādhāniyya*, not a name as such, but a technical term denoting a group of intelligence agents who, being Jews, were able to move from one community to another without attracting too much attention, using their commercial activity as a cover. This interpretation deserves to be taken seriously, but judgment must be suspended so long as there is no new source available to throw a decisive light on this problem.

The dialogue has not stopped here, and Cl. Cahen returned to the attack with an article intitled *Quelques questions sur les Radanites*. He thanks Jacobi for having corrected a few minor errors and judges "plausible, though unproven" his "interpretation of the word *Ra(h)daniya*", but returns to the major questions posed by the problem of the "Radanites". He adds that the text of Ibn Khurradādhbih gives the impression of "an organisation of people travelling from one end to the other along specific itineraries", which appears to conflict with the information supplied a little later by "the documents of the Geniza, according to which there never was a single commercial route directly followed from the West to the Indian Ocean." Above all, how is it to be explained that Ibn Khurradādhbih should be the only one to speak of the Rādhāniyya, that there was no western testimony regarding their journeys and that Europe knew nothing of the Far East?

The latest, chronologically, to take an interest in the Rādhāniyya has been M. Gil (1974), who presents a historical survey of works devoted to this subject and of answers to some of the questions posed by Cahen. Refusing to follow Kmietowicz (see below) and Jacobi, he sets out to study the relative value of the sources (a comparison with Ibn al-Faḳīh), the point of departure and the itineraries (on which he comments at length), the meaning of Firandja (which he prefers to interpret as meaning Italy), the types of merchandise transported (which are subjected to thorough analysis) and finally the land of the Rādhānites: Gil revives the notion that they take their name from Rādhān, a toponym which is the object of a very detailed study. The conclusion (323) is that "they were no organisation, nor association, nor group; they only had in common their country of origin."

An issue which has so far been left to one side is the widely debated question of the etymology of the name of the Rādhāniyya. Reinaud was the first to associate it with a "Persian" word, *rāh-dān*, translating it as "knowers of the way", and it is in fact a Persian origin which has been proposed by the scholars who have tackled the subject, with the exception of those who, like Barbier de Meynard or Gil, see Rādhān as an ethnic term. In his *Glossarium* to the *BGA*, De Goeje followed Reinaud, justifying his acceptance of *rāh-dān* with the reading Rāhdāniyya of Ibn al-Faḳīh al-Hamadhānī [*q.v.*] who, in his *Mukhtaṣar Kitāb al-Buldān* (270, tr. H. Massé, *Abrégé du Livre des Pays*, Damascus 1973, 324), summarised the passage of Ibn Khurradādhbih. However, in the course of editing this translation, the author of the present article has established that the Mashhad ms. of the *Mukhtaṣar* also featured *Rādhāniyya*, thus a reading identical to that which De Goeje retained in his edition of the *K. al-Masālik*. In 1907, D. Simonsen returned to the etymological problem and, rejecting the solution of Barbier de Meynard, since the Rādhāniyya came from Europe, he revived Sprenger's hypothesis and suggested that they should be seen as "sea voyagers from the Rhône" (*nautae*) *Rhodanici*. Furthermore in 1931, in a book in Hebrew on the subject of Israel in the diaspora, B. Dinur accepted this etymology, and he was not the only one to do so (see F. Kmietowicz, 166), but it had been rejected as early as 1908 by De Goeje (in his *Opuscula*), for a phonetic reason, a transformation from *o* to *ā* being impossible. Jacobs and Katz, who saw the Rādhāniyya as coming from Rayy [*q.v.*] in Djibāl, where Ibn Khurradādhbih was employed as head of the *barīd*, sought to link their name to this town, although the corresponding ethnic term is Rāzī. In 1957, S.W. Baron considered De Goeje's explanation (= itinerant merchants) more plausible than that of Simonsen. Cl. Cahen (1951, 1964, 499, n. 4) seemed willing to accept *rāhdān*, rejecting *rāhdār* ("custodian of the road"), which could equally well be proposed; he made the point, however, that the orthography of the name of the group is far from being established. He no longer accepted a possible harmonisation with the reading of al-Muḳaddasī (*Aḥsan al-taḳāsīm*, 30), who mentions a plural *rahādina* and explains it as meaning "sellers of linen and cotton goods". Dozy, who took this reference into account (*Suppl.*, s.v. *r-h-d-n*), added that he had encountered in the ms. of the *Riyāḍ al-nufūs* of al-Mālikī (mid-6th/11th century), the same plural designating (fol. 29b) a quarter of Ḳayrawān and (fol. 91b) traders who used their children to sell their merchandise (cf. R. Brunschvig, *Ḥafṣides*, i, 354, ii, 204); there was also at Ḳayrawān a Bāb al-Rahādina (al-Muḳaddasī, *op. cit.*, 225; partial ed.-tr. Pellat, *Description de l'Occident musulman au IVe/Xe siècle*, Algiers 1950, 14/15). In 1970, Kmietowicz took a direction radically different from that of all his predecessors, deriving *rādhāniyya* from *veredarii* "couriers" and positing a phonetic evolution *veredarii-rēdārii-rēdhānī*, a somewhat far-fetched notion and one made all the more difficult to justify by the fact that the Latin *veredus* has given to Arabic *barīd* "post and information" and to Berber *abrīd* "road". It emerges that it is precisely espionage which Jacobi had in mind (261-2), accepting the etymology proposed by Reinaud. Finally, the last chronologically, M. Gil (306), is noteworthy for his assertion that the name of these merchants is based *in all probability* on the Syriac *rhadhan*. This rapid survey has shown that, in spite of the erudition or the imagination of scholars, the problem posed by the origin of the term *rādhāniyya* remains unsolved. Other unanswered questions include, whether this name was known throughout the itineraries described, or whether it was current only in the East of the Islamic world or even known only in the services of the *barīd*; was it a kind of password used by spies, assuming that Jacobi's suggestion is to be taken seriously?

What is to be concluded now from examination of the principal works devoted to the Rādhāniyya? If it is accepted that they did really exist—and nobody seriously doubts this—it is beyond doubt that they were merchants who followed numerous itineraries between western Europe and China. On the outward and return journeys they conveyed a number of types of costly merchandise which are carefully listed by Ibn hurradādhbih. The latter also informs us that they poke numerous languages, and it may be supposed hat each individual was familiar with two or three mong the languages mentioned and that they would have employed a common traders' argot, probably containing many Hebrew elements. This is all that can be said with confidence.

The scholars whose opinions have been summarised above have posed questions which they have attempted to answer with varying degrees of success. They have seized the opportunity to demonstrate their knowledge of international commerce in the Middle Ages and of the economic role of the Jews, but as regards the Rādhāniyya specifically, all their speculations have not brought any discernible progress. For so long as new sources remain undiscovered it is appropriate to avoid both hypercriticism and imprudence and to admit that Ibn Khurradādhbih, occasional geographer, musicologist and above all *ṣāḥib al-barīd wa 'l-khabar*, constituted himself the echo of information which circulated—perhaps confidentially—in the governmental circles of his time.

Bibliography (in alphabetical order): E.W. Adler, *Jewish travellers*, London 1930, 2-3; J. Aronius, *Regesten zur Geschichte der Juden im fränkischen und deutschen Reiche*, Berlin 1902, no. 113; E. Ashtor, *Quelques observations d'un orientaliste sur la thèse de Pirenne*, in *JESHO*, xiii (1970), 166-94, esp. 181-8; C. Barbier de Meynard, *Le livre des routes et des provinces par Ibn Khordadhboh*, in *JA*, vi/5 (1865), 115 ff., 262; S.W. Baron, *A social and religious history of the Jews*, iv, New York 1957, 180-1, 328 n. 39; R. Blachère, *Extraits des principaux géographes arabes du Moyen Âge*, Paris 1932, ²1957, 27-9; B. Blumenkranz, *Juifs et Chrétiens dans le monde occidental, 430-1096*, Paris 1960, 13 ff.; R. Brunschvig, *Naṣrides*, i, 364, ii, 204; Cl. Cahen, review of Rabinowitz, *Adventurers*, in *RH*, ccv (1951), 119-20; idem, *Y a-t-il eu des Rahdānites?*, in *REJ*, 4 sér., iii/3-4 (1964), 499-505; idem, *Quelques questions sur les Radanites*, in *Isl.*, xlviii/2 (1972), 333-4; G. Caro, *Social- und Wirtschaftsgeschichte der Juden*, Frankfurt 1924, i, 126-7; M.J. De Goeje, *Internationaal Handelsverkeer in de Middeleeuwen*, in *Opuscula*, Amsterdam 1908, iv, 6 ff.; B. Dinur, *Israël in the diaspora* [in Hebrew], Tel-Aviv 1961, i/1, 366-7; R. Dozy, *Supplément*; D.M. Dunlop, *The history of the Jewish Khazars*, Princeton 1954; *Encyclopaedia Judaica*, Jerusalem, xiii (1971), col. 1495; W. Fischel, *Jews in the economic and political life of mediaeval Islam*, London 1937; idem, *The Jews of Central Asia and Khorasan*, in *Historia Judaica*, vii (1945), 29; M. Gil, *The Rādhānite merchants and the land of Rādhān*, in *JESHO*, xvii (1974), 299-327 (with copious bibl.); S.D. Goitein, *Jews and Arabs*, New York 1955, ²1964, 105-7; idem, *A Mediterranean society*, i, Berkeley-Los Angeles 1967, 104; J. Guttmann, *Die wirtschaftliche und soziale Bedeutung der Juden in Mittelalter*, in *MGWJ*, li (1907), 257 ff.; W. Heyd, *Histoire du commerce du Levant au Moyen Âge*, Leipzig 1885-6, ²1925, i, 126-8; Ibn al-Faḳīh, *Mukhtaṣar Kitāb al-Buldān*, 270, Fr. tr. H. Massé, 324; J. Jacobi, *Die Rādāniyya*, in *Isl.*, xlvii (1971), 252-64; J. Jacobs, *Jewish contributions to civilization*, Philadelphia 1919, 184-214; S. Katz, *The Jews in the Visigothic and Frankish kingdoms of Spain and Gaul*, Cambridge, Mass. 1937, 134; Fr. Kmietowicz, *The term Ar-Rādanīya in the work of Ibn Ḫurdādhbeh*, in *Fol. Or.*, xi (1970), 163 ff.; M. Lombard, *La route de la Meuse et les relations lointaines des pays mosans entre le VIIIᵉ et le XIᵉ siècle*, in P. Francastel (ed.), *L'Art mosan*, Paris 1953, 9-10; R.S. Lopez and I.W. Raymond, *Medieval trade in the Mediterranean world*, New York 1955, 29 ff.; J. Marquart, *Osteuropäische und ostasiatische Streifzüge*, Leipzig 1903, 342-53; Masʿūdī, *Murūdj al-dhahab*, ed. and tr. Pellat, Arabic index s.v. al-Lūdhʿāna; idem, *al-Tanbīh wa 'l-ishrāf*, ed. De Goeje, in *BGA*, viii, Leiden 1894; Muḳaddasī, *Ahsan al-taḳāsīm*, ed. De Goeje, in *BGA*, ii, Leiden 1877, 30, 225, partial tr. Ch. Pellat, *Description de l'Occident musulman au IVᵉ/Xᵉ siècle*, Algiers 1950, 14/15); H. Pirenne, *Mahomet et Charlemagne*, ⁶1937, 235; L. Rabinowitz, *The routes of the Radanites*, in *JQR*, N.S., xxxv (1944-5), 251 ff.; idem, *Jewish merchant adventurers. A study of the Radanites*, London 1948 (to be used with care); J.-T. Reinaud, *Introduction générale à la géographie des Orientaux*, Paris 1848, i, pp. LVIII ff.; C. Roth, *The world history of the Jewish people*. ii. *The Dark Ages. Jews in Christian Europe, 711-1096*, Tel Aviv 1966, 23-9, 386, nn. 12-20; I. Schipper, *Anfänge des Kapitalismus bei den abendländischen Juden im früheren Mittelalter*, Vienna 1907, 18; idem, *Der Anteil der Juden am europaïschen Grosshandel mit dem Orient*, in L. Kellner (ed.), *Heineker*, Berlin 1912, 141; idem, *Economic history of the Jews* [in Yiddish], Warsaw 1930, 29-33, Hebrew tr. Tel-Aviv 1935, 24-32; A. Seippel, *Rerum normannicarum fontes arabici*, Christiana 1896, p. XXVIII; R.B. Serjeant, *Material for a history of Islamic textiles*, in *Ars Islamica*, xv-xvi (1968), 85; D. Simonsen, *Les marchands juifs appelés "Radanites"*, in *REJ*, liv (1907), 141-2; A. Sprenger, *Some original passages on the early commerce of the Arabs*, in *JASB*, xiv/2 (1844), 519-26; G. Wiet, *L'Egypte arabe*, in G. Hanotaux (ed.), *Histoire de la nation égyptienne*, iv, Paris 1937, 167; Yāḳūt, *Muʿdjam al-buldān*.

(CH. PELLAT)

RĀDHANPŪR, a former princely state, headed by a Nawwāb [*q.v.*], of British India, at that time in the Pālānpūr [*q.v.*] Agency of Bombay Province, now in the Gujarat State of the Indian Union. It is also the name of its capital (lat. 23° 49′ N., long. 7° 39′ E.), lying 90 km/56 miles to the southwest of Pālānpūr and to the east of the Rann of Cutch.

The rulers of Rādhanpūr traced their descent from a Muslim adventurer who came to India from Iṣfahān about the middle of the 11th/17th century. His descendants became *fawdjdārs* and farmers of revenue in the Mughal province of Gudjarāt [*q.v.*]. Early in the 12th/18th century Djawān Mard Khān Bābī, the head of the family at that time, received a grant of Rādhanpūr and other districts (*Mirʾāt-i Aḥmadī*, ms. in Ethé, no. 3599, fol. 742). With the decline of the Mughal empire these districts passed into the hands of the Marāthās [*q.v.*], but the Bābī family were confirmed in the possession of Rādhanpūr by Damādjī Rāō Gaekwār.

British relations with Rādhanpūr date back to the year 1813 (Aitchison, vi, c). Some years later, the British were called upon to rid Rādhanpūr of plundering tribes from Sind who were committing serious depredations in the Nawwāb's territories. In return for this the Nawwāb agreed to become a tributary of the British government, but a few years later this tribute was remitted because it was felt that the state was unable to bear the expense. After the Sepoy Mutiny of 1857-8, in 1862, the ruler of Rādhanpūr received an adoption *sanad* from the governor-general (*op. cit.*, cii). It was not until 1900 that the Djorawarsai currency previously in use was discontinued and replaced by British currency.

In the last years of British rule, Rādhanpūr covered an area of 1,150 square miles and supported a population of 70,530, of whom only 8,435 were Muslims.

The town of Rādhanpūr, the capital of the state, had a total population of 11,225, of whom 3,694 were Muslims (1931 Census Report).

Bibliography: See that to PĀLANPŪR, and also *Imperial gazetteer of India*², xxi, 22-5.

(C. COLLIN DAVIES)

AL-**RĀḌĪ BI 'LLĀH**, ABU 'L-ʿABBĀS AḤMAD (MUḤAMMAD) B. AL-MUḲTADIR, the twentieth ʿAbbāsid caliph.

He was born in Rabīʿ II 297/December 909; his mother was a slave named Ẓalūm. He was proposed for the caliphate immediately after the assassination of his father al-Muḳtadir [*q.v.*], but the choice fell upon al-Ḳāhir [*q.v.*]. The latter had him thrown into prison; after the fall of al-Ḳāhir, he was released and put upon the throne (Djumādā I 322/April 934). As his adviser in this difficult period, al-Rāḍī chose al-Muḳtadir's vizier ʿAlī b. ʿĪsā [*q.v.*] who asked, however, to be excused on account of his great age, whereupon Ibn Muḳla [*q.v.*] was given the office. The most influential official, however, continued to be Muḥammad b. Yāḳūt [*q.v.*] and only after his fall in Djumādā I 323/April 935 did Ibn Muḳla gain control of the administration, while the caliph himself fell completely into the background. But Ibn Muḳla's rule did not last long; in Djumādā I 324/April 936 he was seized by al-Muẓaffar b. Yāḳūt, brother of the above-mentioned Muḥammad, and the impotent caliph had to dismiss him and in the same year summon the governor of Wāsiṭ and Baṣra, Muḥammad b. Rāʾiḳ [*q.v.*], to Baghdād and entrust him with complete authority as *amīr al-umarāʾ*. This meant a complete breach with the past; the caliph was only allowed to retain the capital and its immediate vicinity and to abandon all influence on the business of government, while Ibn Rāʾiḳ in combination with his secretary decided all the more important questions. Ibn Rāʾiḳ held power for nearly two years; his name was actually mentioned in the *khuṭba* for the reigning dynasty along with that of the caliph; in Dhu 'l-Ḳaʿda 326/September 938, however, he was replaced by Badjkam [*q.v.*].

To the financial difficulties and the constant quarrels of the viziers and *amīrs* there was now added war with foreign foes. In 323/935 al-Rāḍī endeavoured to remove from office the governor of al-Mawṣil Nāṣir al-Dawla [*q.v.*], but failed, and a few years later Badjkam, accompanied by the caliph, attacked the Ḥamdānids in order to force them to pay tribute levied upon them, but had to make peace because the fugitive Ibn Rāʾiḳ suddenly appeared in Baghdād. The war with the Byzantines was also continued; the Ḥamdānids, however, in this war came forward as defenders of Islam. In Egypt Muḥammad b. Ṭughdj [*q.v.*] founded the dynasty of the Ikhshīdids and at the same time Badjkam had to fight with the Būyids, who were advancing on several sides and a few years later victoriously entered Baghdād.

In the capital itself al-Rāḍī had to take measures against the fanatical Ḥanbalīs (323/935), who had many followers among the common people and committed all kinds of excesses. They entered private houses, destroyed musical instruments, ill-treated women singers, poured away wine that they found, interfered in business, annoyed passers-by in the streets, beat Shāfiʿīs and generally behaved as arbitrarily as if they represented a kind of tribunal of the Inquisition.

Al-Rāḍī died in the middle of Rabīʿ I 329/December 940 of dropsy. The Arab historians praise his piety, justice, clemency and generosity as well as his interest in literature and it is said of him, for example (Ibn al-Ṭiḳṭaḳā, *al-Fakhrī*, 380): "He w the last caliph, by whom a collection of poems exist the last who retained his independence as a ruler, th last to preach a sermon from the pulpit on Fridays, th last to mix freely with his friends and to welcome me of learning, and the last who followed the principles the earlier caliphs as regards rank, tokens of favou servants and chamberlains." This characterisatio may well be correct in its main lines, but al-Rāḍī wa not independent; he was on the contrary a ready to in the hands of his viziers and *amīrs*.

Bibliography: ʿArīb, 33, 43-5, 57, 79, 92, 11 139, 155, 168, 180, 183, 185; Masʿūdī, *Murūdj*, 166, viii, 308-44, ix, 31, 48, 52; idem, *Tanbīh*, 10 122, 154, 174, 193, 388-97; Ibn al-Athīr, viii, se index; Abu 'l-Fidāʾ, *Annales*, ed. Reiske, ii, 383 ff. Ibn Khaldūn, *al-ʿIbar*, iii, 396 ff.; Abu 'l-Maḥāsi b. Taghrībirdī, *al-Nudjūm al-zāhira*, ed. Juynbo and Matthes, ii, see index; Ibn al-Ṭiḳṭaḳā, *al Fakhrī*, ed. Derenbourg, 370-1, 374, 379-85 Amedroz and Margoliouth, *The eclipse of the ʿAbbasi caliphate*, see index; Ḥamd Allāh Mustawfī Ḳaz wīnī, *Taʾrīkh-i guzīda*, ed. Browne, i, 339, 344-6 778, 788; Ṣūlī, *Akhbār ar-Rāḍī wa 'l-Muttaḳī*, ed J.H. Dunne, Cairo 1354/1935; Weil, *Gesch. de Chalifen*, ii, 650, 655-78; Muir, *The Caliphate, its rise decline and fall*, new ed. by Weir, 569-72; L Strange, *Baghdad during the Abbasid Caliphate*, 155 194-5; H. Busse, *Chalif und Grosskönig, die Buyiden im Iraq (945-1055)*, Beirut-Wiesbaden 1969, index.

(K.V. ZETTERSTÉEN)

RAḌĪ AL-**DĪN ḤASAN** AL-**ṢAGHĀNĪ** [see AL-ṢAGHĀNĪ].

RADĪF (A.), lit. "one who rides behind", "pillion rider", is used metaphorically in several technical senses (for a poetical figurative use in Turkish, cf. *ordū-yi ẓafer-redīf* "the victorious army [one which has victory on its croup]" in *Tārīkh-i Djewdet*, Istanbul 1270/1853-4, i, 22):

1. In astronomy it has two meanings, which seem, however, not very amply attested: (a) *al-Radīf*, and also, better attested, *al-Ridf*, is the ancient Arabic name for *Dhanab al-Dadjādja*, i.e. the star *Deneb* (α Cygni), called thus because it "rides pillion" to the "Horsemen" (*al-Fawāris*)—δγεζ Cygni. (b) *Radīf* refers to a star or constellation that is rising (*yanūʾu*, cf. also ANWĀʾ) at sunrise, while its opposite (*raḳīb*) is setting. For both meanings see *LʿA* and Lane, s.v., for *al-Ridf* also al-Khʷārazmī, *Mafātīḥ* 212, 6, and P. Kunitzsch, *Arabische Sternnamen in Europa*, Wiesbaden 1959, 82, 143.

2. In Persian and Persianate prosody the term denotes a word or a whole phrase that follows the rhyme letter (*rawiyy*) and recurs in every line of the poem. In Western languages various renditions of the term have been used, such as "over-rhyme" (Schimmel, 21), "echo rhyme" (Bombaci, in *PTF*, ii, pp. xxii, xxv), "refrain" (Thiesen, 76, n. 5), and "hypermeter" (J. Deny, in *EI*¹, s.v. REDĪF). However, "refrain" normally refers to entire lines or even stanzas repeated throughout a poem, while the *radīf* is always shorter than a hemistich, and "hypermeter" denotes a metrically superfluous element, which the *radīf* is decidedly not. The *radīf* is a metrically and semantically necessary element of the line, as Shams-i Ḳays (*Muʿdjam*, 258) and other authorities stress. The following line by Ḥāfiẓ (*q.v.*; *Dīwān*, edd. Ḳazwīnī and Ghanī, no. 233) may serve as an example:

Dast az ṭalab nadāram tā kām-i man bar āyad
yā tan rasad bi-djānān yā djān zi tan bar āyad.

"I do not cease striving, until my desire comes about:

either the body reaches the friend or the soul
comes up from the body."

The rhyme (*ḳāfiya*) in this ghazal is *-an* (the *rawiyy* being *-n*) and the *radīf* is *bar āyad*. Clinton (*Manūčihrī*, 51) calls the overall rhyme scheme in such cases very aptly "multiple rhyme", but goes on, as do others as well, to call this ensemble a *radīf*, which is not correct usage: *ḳāfiya* and *radīf* are considered two separate elements.

The length of the *radīf* may vary between one word and several words almost filling the hemistich. Extreme examples are (*radīfs* underlined):

zihī fuzūda djamāl-ē tu zīb u ʾārā rā
shikasta sunbul-i zulf-ē tu mushk-i sārā rā
(Rūdakī [*q.v.*], *apud* Elwell-Sutton, 225)

and

sarw-rā gul-bār nabwad w-ar buwad nabwad čunīn
sarw-e gul-rukhsār nabwad w-ar buwad nabwad čunīn
dīdam-ash way bar sar-ē gulbār u guftam rāstī
sarw dar gulbār nabwad w-ar buwad nabwad čunīn
(Khʷādjū [*q.v.*], *apud* Elwell-Sutton, 225)

or, from Čaghatay Turkish:

Meni shaydā ḳila durghan bu köngül dür, bu köngül,
Khōr u ruswā ḳila durghan bu köngül dür, bu köngül.
Oḳ tegin ḳāmatimizni ḳara ḳashlighlar üčün
Muttaṣıl ya ḳila durghan bu köngül dür, bu köngül...
Luṭfī [*q.v.*], *apud* J. Eckmann, in *PTF*, ii, 310)

Mere suffixes following the *rawīyy are not considered a radīf* (cf. e.g. Djāmī, *Ḳāfiya*, 1), and statements to the contrary in the secondary literature should be amended. It is true that Naṣīr al-Dīn-i Ṭūsī (*Miʿyār al-ashʿār*, 200-1) prefers to consider everything that follows the *rawiyy-cum waṣl* (see below) a *radīf* but, as al-Tahānawī (*Kashshāf*, i, 576, 23-4) notes, this is against the *communis opinio* (*wa īn khilāf-i mutaʿāraf ast*). The strength of this general opinion is shown by the fact that the early modern Turkish critic Muʿallim Nādjī (*Istılahat*, 51) who would likewise subsume the suffixes under the general heading *radīf*, defends his position with a personal statement to this effect (*Aciz kanaatimizce, revíden sonra her ne gelirse redif sayılmak daha doğrudur*). The suffixes, or rather the letters that make up the suffixes, have special names in "orthodox" *ʿilm-i ḳāfiya*, the first letter after the *rawiyy* being called *waṣl*, the second *khurūdj*, the third *mazīd*, and the fourth, fifth and sixth—which is said to be the maximum—*nāʾira*.

The *radīf* is supposed to have the same meaning throughout the poem. If it does not, a special artifice results (*radīf mutadjānis*, see al-Tahānawī, *Kashshāf*, i, 576) with complete paronomasia between *radīfs*.

Another specific type is the internal *radīf*, called *ḥādjib*, which precedes the rhyme rather than following it. In the following example the *ḥādjib* is *sulṭān* and the rhyme, *-ūr*:

Sulṭān Malik ast u bar dil-ē sulṭān nūr
har rūz bi-rūy-i ū kunad sulṭān sūr etc.
(Masʿūd-i Saʿd-i Salmān, *apud* Elwell-Sutton, 226)

Even more sophisticated is a combination of *ḥādjib* and double rhyme (*dhu 'l-ḳāfiyatayn*), as in the following lines from Muʿizzī [*q.v.*] (*ibid.*), where the first rhyme is *-ān*, followed by the *ḥādjib dārī*, in turn followed by words containing the second rhyme *-akht*:

Ay shāh-i zamīn bar āsmān dārī takht
sust ast ʿadū tā tu kamān dārī sakht etc.

A poem with *radīf* is called *muraddaf*. This should not be confused with the term *murdaf*, which means "provided with a *ridf*". The *ridf* is a letter of prolongation (*alif, wāw, yāʾ*) immediately preceding the *rawiyy*, as in the Arabic rhymes *nāru, nīru, nūru* (spelled *naHru, niyru, nuwru* [*H* = *alif*]); in Persian rhyme theory there is the additional *ridf-i zāʾid* which denotes a consonant intervening between the *ridf* and the *rawiyy*, as in *dūst* (spelled *duwst*), where *w* is the *ridf*, *s* the *ridf-i zāʾid* and *t* the *rawiyy*. Since both *muraddaf* and *murdaf* are terms used in rhyme theory, confusion is not easily avoided.

As for history and the poetics of the phenomenon, much remains to be studied. The first thing to be said is that the *radīf* is unknown to the Arabs, as a critic like Rashīd al-Dīn-i Waṭwāṭ (*Ḥadāʾiḳ*, 79-80) was well aware, except, he says, for innovations of the Moderns. As an example he adduces a *ḳiṭʿa* by al-Zamakhsharī [*q.v.*] in praise of ʿAlāʾ ad-Dawla Khʷārazmshāh in which the *laḳab* of the *mamdūḥ* is used as *radīf*. First line:

al-faḍlu ḥaṣṣalahū ʿAlāʾu l-Dawlah
wa l-madjdu aththalahū ʿAlāʾu l-Dawlah

In the Arabic poetry of Persian poets this is actually not uncommon (e.g. Khāḳānī, *Dīwān*, ed. Sadjdjādī, 950-3, a panegyric on the city of Baghdād with its name as *radīf*).

Elwell-Sutton, 176, 178, 225, makes the point that the *radīf* occurs in Persian poetry at a very early date, already in those satirical jingles from the late 7th and early 8th centuries A.D. preserved in Arabic sources. Here the *radīf* is not even preceded by a regular rhyme, but by assonances at best, which may represent an earlier stage in the development. Köprülü, in discussing the origins of the *radīf* (*redīf*) in Turkish poetry, denies that it was taken over from Persian, "car les origines de ce procédé de *redīf* qui, d'ailleurs, est tout à fait conforme à la structure de la langue turque, se trouvent dans l'assonance de la poésie turque ancienne" (*PTF*, ii, 259). It is probably closer to the truth to say that existing rhyme phenomena in pre-Islamic Turkish poetry facilitated the adoption of the Persian *radīf* technique.

Waṭwāṭ alleges that "most" Persian poems have a *radīf* (*Ḥadāʾiḳ, loc. cit.*). In the case of Manūčihrī [*q.v.*] poems with and without *radīf* are about evenly divided (Clinton, *Manūchihrī*, 51). But simple percentages do not tell much without due consideration of the various kinds of *radīfs* that are attested. The most common, and probably most ancient, type is the verbal *radīf* consisting of a simple and mostly rather nondescript verb (cf. the line from Ḥāfiẓ quoted above). This may be expanded into longer phrases and even complete sentences, such as *bar na-tābad bēš az īn* "more than this is not feasible" serving as a *radīf* in a *ḳaṣīda* of seventy-nine lines by Khāḳānī (*q.v.*; Reinert, *Ḫāqānī*, 40; cf. *Dīwān*, 337-40). As for nominal *radīfs*, Khāḳānī does not follow the fad of his time which was to choose just any noun in order to display one's artistic virtuosity; the nouns he selects always have a bearing on the theme of the poem, such as using *khāk* "dust", as a *radīf* in a dirge of forty-two lines (*ibid.*; cf. *Dīwān*, 237-9), or the noun construct *sag-i kūy-at*, "the dog of your street", in a *ghazal* of fifteen lines in which the poet describes himself as the most despicable dog in the beloved's lane (Schimmel, 403, n. 26, cf. *Dīwān*, 575). These nominal *radīfs* can acquire an iconic character, as in a *tardjīʿ-band* by Djannatī Biyā, quoted by ʿAwfī (*Lubāb*, ed. Browne, ii, 394), where they denote various precious stones (*gawhar, laʿl, zumurrud*), thus forming a necklace of sorts for the poem itself (Schimmel, 156). This possibility is also alluded to in a poem by the Mughal poet Ashraf who says about a celadon bowl with craquelé glaze:

You cannot describe it in a quatrain or a *ghazal* -
I think of a *ḳaṣīda* with the *radīf* "Hair"
(Schimmel, 149).

Similarly, almost every poet in Persia, Turkey, and

Muslim India attempted at least one poem with the *radīf gul*, "rose" (Schimmel, 389, n. 65), and in Ottoman poetry such poems with *gül* (and also *nergis*) as *radīf* almost form subgenres of the *ḳaṣīda* [see RABĪᶜIYYĀT, toward the end].

Bibliography: 1. Mediaeval works on prosody. Rashīd al-Dīn-i Waṭwāṭ, *Ḥadāʾiḳ al-siḥr fī daḳāʾiḳ al-shiᶜr,* ed. ᶜAbbās Iḳbāl, Tehran 1308/[1929]); Shams-i Ḳays, *al-Muᶜdjam fī maᶜāyīr ashᶜār al-ᶜadjam*, ed. Muḥammad Ibn-i ᶜAbd al-Wahhāb-i Ḳazwīnī and Mudarris-i Raḍawī, Tehran n.d. [before 1961]; Naṣīr al-Dīn-i Ṭūsī, *Miᶜyār al-ashᶜār dar ᶜilm-i ᶜarūḍ wa ḳawāfī-i shiᶜr-i ᶜarabī wa fārsī,* lith. Tehran 1325 *sh.*; Waḥīd-i Tabrīzī, *Risāla-yi Djamᶜ-i Mukhtaṣar*, ed. A.E. Bertel's, Moscow 1959, 119 (Persian text); Djāmī, *Risāla-i Ḳāfiya*, in H. Blochmann, *The prosody of the Persians*, Calcutta 1872; al-Tahānawī, *Kashshāf iṣṭilāḥāt al-funūn*, ed. A. Sprenger *et alii*, Calcutta 1862.

2. Modern works on prosody. Muallim Naci (Muᶜallim Nādjī), *Istılahat-ı edebiyye. Edebiyat terimleri,* edd. A. Yalçın and A. Hayber. Ankara n.d. [1984]; *Philologiae Turcicae Fundamenta* [*PTF*], ii, Wiesbaden 1964 (see, in particular, M.F. Köprülü, *La métrique ᶜarūz dans la poésie turque*, 252-66); L.P. Elwell-Sutton, *The Persian metres,* Cambridge 1976; N.S. Pekin and N.N. Karaman, *Temel edebiyat bilgileri*, Istanbul 1982, 68; F. Thiesen, *A manual of Classical Persian prosody*, Wiesbaden 1982.

3. Modern studies of poetry. A. Schimmel, *A two-colored brocade. The imagery of Persian poetry*, Chapel Hill and London 1992; B. Reinert, *Ḫāqānī als Dichter. Poetische Logik und Phantasie*, Berlin and New York 1972; J.W. Clinton, *The Divan of Manūchihrī Dāmghānī. A critical study*, Minneapolis 1972. (W.P. HEINRICHS)

3. In Turkish military usage. Maḥmūd II [*q.v.*] gave the name of *redīf* (*ᶜasākir redīfe-yi manṣūre*) to the reserve army created in 1834 (Jouanin and van Gaver, *Turquie*, 425). The historian Luṭfī (iv, 144), speaking of the project for this army, under the year 1249/1833-4, explains the meaning of the term by saying that it was a force that "came after" the regular army (*muwazzafe-ye redīf olarak*). They were, therefore, not soldiers who had, at need, to mount behind the cavalry on the croup, like the Roman *velites*. *Redīf* was contrasted with *niẓām* or *ᶜasākir-i niẓāmiyye* or *ᶜasākir-i muwaẓẓafe*, taken in the strict sense of active or regular army (standing army), and with *iḥtiyāṭ* "reserve of the regular army". For the lack of an exact equivalent, we may say "militia" in English and "armée de reserve" or "garde nationale" in French. The German term "Landwehr" is perhaps nearest to it, but in the former Prussian rather than the Austrian sense. Sometimes the *redīf* are included in the *niẓāmiyye*, taking the latter term in a wider sense of regular or disciplined troops (synonym *müretteb*). Luṭfī (*loc. cit.*) calls the *redīf bir newᶜ-i ᶜasākir-i niẓāmiyye* "a kind of regular troops".

The characteristic feature of the *redīf* army was the existence of permanent cadres, whence its mixed character. It was linked with the regular army by its officers and with the reserve by its men (*efrād-ī redīfe*). It was the object of its creators that this army should provide a large number of men, if necessary, without imposing too long a period of service on the rural population (Luṭfī, *op. cit.*).

It was decided from the first that the *redīf* should consist of battalions (*tabur*), and, indeed, this organisation by battalion depots (*tabur dāʾireleri*) remained in force as long as the *redīf* existed. The commanders of these battalions (*biñbashī*) were at first chosen from the chief local families (*maḥalleri khānedānīndan*). The first battalions formed in 1250/1834-5 were those of the *sandjaḳs* [*q.v.*] of Ḳaraḥiṣār Ṣāḥib, Anḳara Kangïrï (Čankïrï), Siro and Menteshe. Ismāᶜīl Bey, hereditary Kurdish governor of Palu, was appointed colonel of the three battalions in the *ḳaḍāʾ*s known as those of the "Imperial Mines" (*meᶜādin-i hümāyūn*) in the *eyālet* of Sīwās (Luṭfī, iv, 171). There were three to four battalions to the *sandjaḳ*, thus 10 to 12 to the *eyālet*. The officers received a quarter of the usual pay, but were only expected to serve and wear uniform two days a week (Muṣṭafā Nūrī Pasha, *Netāʾidj ül-wuḳūᶜāt*, iv, 109).

In 1252/1836-7, the *redīf* was organised in wide groups with a high command: *müshīrlik* (*müshürlük*) or "marshal-ship" [see MÜSHĪR] of *redīf*, conferred upon the *wālī*s. The first were those of the *eyālets* of Ḳaramān (Ḳonya), Khudāwendigār (Bursa: guard or *khāṣṣe*), Anḳara, Aydïn, Erzurum and Edirne. At the same time, plans were made to raise the money required for this purpose. The *wālī*-marshals were given the *ḥarwānī* (*kharmānī*) or cloaks of their new rank. Just as the troops of the line (*menṣūre*) were distinguished from those of the guard (*khāṣṣe*), so there were *redīf-menṣūre* and *redīf-i khāṣṣe*. The appointment of commanders of divisions was to follow (for details, see the *Taḳrīr-i ᶜālī* or report of the grand vizier Meḥmed Emīn Raʾūf Pasha, in Luṭfī, v, 165-70). If we may believe the *khaṭṭ-ï hümāyūn* [*q.v.*] promulgated on this occasion by Maḥmūd II, these first steps gave every satisfaction (*ibid.*, 74).

When the Military School (*mekteb-i ḥarbiyye*) instituted in 1251/1835-6 began to supply officers, the *redīf* under arms was converted into active forces and the officers were sent back to their *odjāḳ*s (*Netāʾidj ül-wuḳūᶜāt*, iv, 109-10). The service as *redīf* (*khidmet-i redīfe*) was now definitely to assume the character of a kind of period of service in the reserve or intermittent service, the duration of which (*müddet-i redīfe*) was to be fixed under conditions which we shall explain below.

In the *khaṭṭ-ï hümāyūn* of Gülkhāne (30 November 1839), there is an allusion to an approaching improvement in the system of regional recruiting. In 1838, five years had been fixed as the period of service in the regular army, previously practically unlimited (one saw young married soldiers leaving their families for life), but this measure did not immediately make its effect felt (cf. von Moltke, *Lettres sur l'Orient*, n.d., 211, letter no. xlvii).

On 6 September 1843, the military law of the *serᶜasker* Riḍā Pasha (Engelhardt, i, 71) was promulgated, a law of fundamental importance, half-French and half-German in character, the principles of which survived even into the early Republican period; it confirmed the period of regular service at five years (later reduced to four), to be followed by a period of seven years during which a *redīf* could be recalled to the colours for a month each year (later every two years). Each *ordu* (army corps) was to have its *redīf* contingent (*ṣïnf-ï redīf*) placed in time of peace under the orders of a brigadier-general (*liwā*, brigade) who lived at the headquarters of the *ordu*. In 1853 (Ubicini, i, 456) the *redīf* was organised into 4 (out of 6) *ordus*, namely, those of *khāṣṣe* (Üsküdār [Asia] and Izmīr), Deriseᶜādet (Istanbul and Anḳara), Rumeli (Manastïr) and Anatolia (Harput). The *ordus* of ᶜArabistān and ᶜIrāḳ were still to be organised. Ubicini adds this observation: "By means of this organisation the government has secured.... a force at its disposal equal to the regular army and capable of eing moved in a few weeks either to the line of the Balkans or to any other point in the empire." According to Bianchi (*Guide de la conversation*, 1852, 230), the organised reserve (*müretteb redīf*) was then 150,000 men compared with 300,000 of the regular army.

Ḥüseyn ʿAwnī Pasha's law of 1869, more clearly French in character (Aristarchi, iii, 514; Engelhardt, i, 37 ff.), provided for 4 years' active service and one of *iḥtiyāṭ* or in the active reserve, a period of 6 years in the *redīf* in two bands (*ṣinf-i mukaddem and ṣinf-i tālī*) of 3 years each (according to Engelhardt, of 4 and 2 years respectively). In practice, in 1877 there were 3 bands, the third (*ṣinf-i thālith*) being represented by the territorial army (*mustaḥfiẓ*) then mobilised (Zboiński, 98). A conscript who obtained a lucky number in the draw was drafted directly into the *redīf* army (art. 17).

The law of 27 Ṣafar 1304/13 Teshrīn-i thānī 1302 25 November 1886; résumé by Lamouche, 77, and Young, ii, 394) prepared by a commission of reorganisation which included Muẓaffar Wālī Riḍā Pasha and von der Goltz Pasha, fixed the period of *redīf* service at 9 years, but was soon afterwards followed by a special law (*redīf kanunu*) of 10 Muḥarram 1305/28 September 1887. According to this, which was, however, not put into force till 1892, the period of *redīf* service was 8 years. The ranks in the *redīf* were the same as in the regular army from general of division down to sergeant-major. These officers formed at the same time the personnel of the recruiting offices for the whole army.

According to the law regulating the uniforms of the army on land (*elbise-yi ʿaskeriyye niẓām-nāmesi*) of 29 Djumādā I 1327/5 Ḥazīrān 1325 (18 June 1909), the *redīf* soldiers wore as distinctive badge a dark green (*neftī*) piping (*zīh*, Pers. *zih*, Ar. *zīk*) at the bottom of the collar (*yaka*) of the tunic (*djaket* or *djeket*, modern spelling *caket, ceket*). The officers wore a piece of cloth of the same colour 7 cm in length fastened on the collar of the undress tunic (*ceket*) or the full dress tunic (*setre*, older *setri*; cf. Pers. *sudre*) (*Düstūr, Tertīb-i thānī*, i, 276; A. Biliotti and Aḥmad Sedād, *Législation ottomane*, Paris 1912, 171 ff.).

The *redīf* system was abandoned by the Young Turks. The law of 18 Ramaḍān 1330/18 Aghustos 1328 (31 August 1912), without proclaiming the dissolution of the corps, ordered the formation of units of *mustaḥfiẓ* with elements furnished by the battalion depots in the second inspection (*müfettishlik*) or *redīf* (*Düstūr, Tertīb-i thānī*, iv, 615). The Young Turks were reproached for this measure, and some even saw in it the cause of the Turkish defeat in the Second Balkan War.

Bibliography: L. Lamouche, *L'organisation militaire de l'Empire Ottoman*, Paris 1895; H. Zboiński, *Armée ottomane* (*loi de 1869*), Paris 1877; L. von Schlözer, *Das türkische Heer*, Leipzig n.d.; Ubicini, *Lettres sur la Turquie*, Paris 1853; E. Engelhardt, *La Turquie et le Tanzimat*, Paris 1882; Aristarchi Bey, *Législation ottomane*, publ. by Démétrius Nicolaïdes, part 3, Constantinople 1874; G. Young, *Corps de droit ottoman*, ii, Oxford 1905; M.Z. Pakalın, *Osmanli tarih deyimleri ve terimleri sözlüğü*, Istanbul 1946-54, iii, 21. (The collections of Turkish laws or *düstūr* generally refrain from including the principal laws relating to the army and the two works of Aristarchi and Young contain only a very few.)

(J. DENY)

RAḌIYYA, in full, Raḍiyyat al-Dunyā wa 'l-Dīn, female sultan of Dihlī during the period of the Slave Kings (634-8/1236-40) and daughter of the Sultan Iltutmush [*q.v.*] by a daughter of Ḳuṭb al-Dīn Aybak. She was the only female ruler in mediaeval Islamic India, and her rule was a source of wonder to later Indo-Muslim historians.

In 629/1231 she was appointed by her father Iltutmush to govern Dihlī whilst he was away campaigning against Gwalior [see GWĀLIYĀR], and shortly afterwards he nominated Raḍiyya as his heir. However, when in 634/1236 he died, the army commanders and courtiers disregarded his wishes and raised to the throne one of his sons, Rukn al-Dīn Fīrūz. Fīrūz wasted his time in riotous living, all power being in the hands of his mother Shāh Turkān. The latter's excesses led to a popular revolt. Raḍiyya appeared in red garments before the Dihlī populace, and they and a section of the army raised her to the throne, despite traditionalist objections to a woman ruler. She was astute enough to steer a course between the factions of the Turkish commanders, favouring instead the *Ḥabashī* Malik Djamāl al-Dīn Yāḳūt, the *amīr-i ākhur* [*q.v.*]. Only towards the end of her reign did she appear in men's clothing and unveiled.

Eventually, the Turkish *amīrs* rebelled against her rule, and deposed and imprisoned her, replacing her by her half-brother Bahrām Shāh (Ramaḍān 638/March-April 1240). However, the governor of Bhattinda [*q.v.*], Ikhtiyār al-Dīn Altuniya, to whom she had been entrusted, decided to espouse her cause and married her. The two of them advanced towards Dihlī with their forces, but were defeated by the new sultan, Bahrām Shāh, near Kaithal, captured, and both put to death (Rabīʿ II 638/December 1240), Raḍiyya having reigned three-and-a-half years.

Bibliography: The only contemporary, in part eye-witness, source for her reign is Djūzdjānī's *Ṭabaḳāt-i Nāṣirī*, ed. Ḥabībī, Kābul 1342-3/1963-4, i, 457-62, tr. Raverty, i, 637-48; see also ʿIṣāmī, *Futūḥ al-salāṭīn*, ed. A.S. Usha, Madras 1948, and Yaḥyā b. Aḥmad Sirhindī, *Taʾrīkh-i Mubārak-Shāhī*, ed. Hidāyat Ḥusayn, Calcutta 1931. Of secondary sources, see M.A. Ahmad, *Political history and institutions of the early Turkish empire of Delhi (1206-1290 A.D.)*, Lahore 1949; A.B.M. Habibullah, *The foundation of Muslim rule in India*, Allahabad 1961.

(M. ATHAR ALI)

RADJʿA (A.) (or *karra*), lit. "return", a term that has several distinct meanings in the doctrines of Shīʿī groups:

(1) The passing of the soul into another body either human or animal (i.e. metempsychosis), or

(2) the transmigration of the spirit of holiness from one Imām to the next. Both are more usually referred to as *tanāsukh*. It was mainly members of various *ghulāt* sects [*q.v.*] that believed in them.

(3) Return of power to the Shīʿa (see further under no. 5).

(4) Return from concealment, usually of a particular Imām at the end of his occultation (*ghayba* [*q.v.*]). Already ʿUmar is said to have initially denied Muḥammad's death, arguing that he had gone into temporary concealment, like Moses before him. Belief in the return of an Imām is first attested among various chiliastic movements in the Umayyad and early ʿAbbāsid periods. A group of Sabaʾīs, the followers of ʿAbd Allāh b. Sabaʾ [*q.v.*], for example, reportedly held that ʿAlī was not dead and would return to install a reign of jusice; similarly, Abū Karib, founder of the Kuraybiyya subsect of the Kaysāniyya [*q.vv.*], denied that Ibn al-Ḥanafiyya had died and predicted that he would return to wreak vengeance on the Umayyads. These beliefs are reflected in the poetry of Kuthayyir [*q.v.*] and later of al-Sayyid al-Ḥimyarī [*q.v.*]. Belief in the disappearance and future return of the Imām as Mahdī is characteristic of many Wāḳifī sects. It some-

times incorporates docetic elements: the corpse taken to be that of the Imām is said actually to have belonged to someone else. In Twelver Shīʿism the term *radjʿa* ordinarily has the sense given in the next paragraph, and the most commonly used term for the appearance of the last Imām is *ẓuhūr*.

(5) The return to life of some of the dead before the Resurrection. The earliest adherents of this doctrine are also to be found among subsects of the Sabaʾiyya and Kaysāniyya. Thus some Sabaʾīs claimed that ʿAlī was dead but would be brought back to life (*yubʿathu*) together with others before the Resurrection; and the followers of the Kaysānī Ḥayyān al-Sarrādj believed that Ibn al-Ḥanafiyya had died in the Raḍwā mountains and would return to life with his supporters before the *yawm al-ḳiyāma*. In Imāmī reports, however, Ḥayyān is said to have denied the death of Ibn al-Ḥanafiyya and to have predicted that, like Jesus, he would return (see e.g. Ibn Bābawayh, *Ikmāl al-dīn*, Nadjaf 1389/1390, 34-5). Early proponents of the idea of *radjʿa* are said to have included Djābir b. Yazīd al-Djuʿfī and Bashshār b. Burd [*q.vv.*].

By the early ʿAbbāsid period, belief in *radjʿa* had spread among a number of Zaydī groups, though it was rejected by mainstream Zaydism; more significantly, it became a constituent element of Imāmī, and subsequently of Twelver, Shīʿism. The doctrine is described by al-Ashʿarī (ed. Ritter, 46) as common to most of the Rāfiḍa [*q.v.*]; and al-Khayyāṭ (*K. al-Intiṣār*, 97), who ascribes it to the Rāfiḍa as a whole, asserts that they concealed it from outsiders—a claim which appears to find support in Imāmī texts.

According to Imāmī exegetes, there are a number of Ḳurʾānic verses which prove that the *radjʿa* will take place. Already Djābir b. ʿAbd Allāh al-Anṣārī [*q.v.* in Suppl.] is said to have interpreted the *maʿād* of XXVIII, 85, as referring to the *radjʿa*. Other verses repeatedly cited are II, 243, 259, XVII, 6, XXIV, 55, XXVIII, 5-6, and particularly XXVII, 83 ("On the day when We shall muster out of every nation a troop"). There is also a Shīʿī *ḳirāʾa* [*q.v.*] of III, 185 ("Every soul shall taste of death"), in which the word *wa-manshūra* ("and shall be brought back to life") is added to the canonical text and interpreted as referring to the *radjʿa* (al-Ḥasan b. Sulaymān al-Ḥillī, *Mukhtaṣar baṣāʾir al-daradjāt*, 17).

Some Imāmī traditions say that the *radjʿa* will occur before the coming of the Mahdī, some place it during his coming, and some after his coming. The identity of the Imāms who will be brought back to life was likewise a moot point. A number of traditions refer only to al-Ḥusayn, emphasising that he will reign until he reaches a great age. According to other traditions, al-Ḥusayn will be followed by ʿAlī (often referred to as *ṣāḥib al-karrāt*), who will avenge himself on all those who fought against him. Elsewhere it is claimed that all Imāms (with the exception of the Mahdī) and all prophets will be brought back to life to fight at ʿAlī's side. In addition, some of their followers and opponents will also be returned; in a prelude to the events of the final Day of Judgment, the followers will triumph and the opponents will be punished for their deeds. Then both parties will die to await the Resurrection and their respective eternal reward or punishment. The opponents are typically identified as Ḳurashīs or Umayyads; they will be decapitated, or else the Mahdī will cut off the hands and legs of some and will crucify or gouge out the eyes of others. There is agreement that the *radjʿa* (which is sometimes referred to as *ḥashr khāṣṣ*, "specific resurrection", in contradistinction to the Resurrection which is the *ḥashr ʿāmm*) will involve believers and unbelievers only from Muḥammad's community, and not from earlier communities.

The growing influence of Muʿtazilism on Imāmī thought during the Buwayhid period did not lead to the rejection of the doctrine of *radjʿa*, which remained a subject of dispute between the two sides. It was perhaps in order to accommodate Muʿtazilī objections that a minority among the Imāmiyya interpreted *radjʿa* as referring to the return of power (*dawla* [*q.v.*]) to the Shīʿa during the time of the Mahdī; but this view was rejected by the leading Imāmī scholars of the Buwayhid period. Their main concern was to prove that there was no contradiction between the doctrine of *radjʿa* and Muʿtazilī views about reason and divine justice. A case in point is al-Shaykh al-Mufīd (d. 413/1022 [*q.v.*]), who was told by a Muʿtazilī critic that if *radjʿa* were to take place, this would give the enemies of Shīʿism a chance to repent and thus escape punishment. Al-Mufīd's answer is that the Imāms have made it clear that these enemies will never repent; and even if they were to do so, God would not accept their repentance, just as He did not accept the repentance of Pharaoh. The Muʿtazilī argues that if this were so, then the *radjʿa* would constitute an enticement to disobedience (*al-ighrāʾ bi 'l-ʿiṣyān*) during the period of renewed life that followed it, since God's enemies would know that even if they were to change their ways, their repentance would not be accepted. Al-Mufīd responds that their past experience of punishment after death will deter them from adding to it by further evil deeds when brought back to life (al-Murtaḍā, ʿAlī b. al-Ḥusayn, *al-Fuṣūl al-mukhtāra*, Beirut 1405/1985, 115-9, cited in McDermott, *The theology of al-Shaikh al-Mufīd*, 268-9). The subject of *al-ighrāʾ bi 'l-ʿiṣyān* is also tackled by the Muʿtazilī Abu 'l-Ḳāsim al-Balkhī al-Kaʿbī (d. 319/931). He asserts that if people were to know that they would have a chance to repent following the *radjʿa*, this would incite them to acts of disobedience in this life. Abū Djaʿfar al-Ṭūsī (d. 460/1067) replies that since only some will be brought back to life, and it is not known who they are, no-one can safely act on the assumption that he will be among them (*Tibyān*, i, 255).

This doctrine of *radjʿa* continued to be a favourite subject of attack by opponents of Shīʿism, who claimed that it was a borrowing from Judaism that had no basis in Islam. Such criticism led some Imāmī apologists to minimise its importance. For example, the contemporary Lebanese scholar Muḥammad Djawād Maghniyya maintains that not all Imāmī doctors adhere to this doctrine; he asserts that it is only transmitted in reports (*aḥādīth, akhbār*) of a type which may be accepted or rejected, and that it is not among the principles of the religion (*uṣūl al-dīn*) (*al-Shīʿa fi 'l-mīzān*, Beirut n.d., 54-5).

(6) The return to life of all of the dead before the Resurrection (sometimes referred to as *al-radjʿa al-ʿāmma*). Belief in this idea is ascribed to a number of extremist Shīʿī sects.

The term *radjʿiyya* or *aṣḥāb al-radjʿa* may refer to adherents of any of the doctrines described here.

Bibliography (in addition to the sources cited in the article): ps.-Nāshiʾ, *Masāʾil al-imāma*, ed. J. van Ess, Beirut 1971, 27-9; al-Faḍl b. Shādhān al-Naysābūrī, *al-Īḍāḥ*, ed. Djalāl al-Dīn al-Ḥusaynī al-Urmawī, Tehran 1392/1972, 381-432; Djāḥiẓ, *al-Bayān wa 'l-tabyīn*, ed. ʿAbd al-Salām M. Hārūn, 3rd ed., Cairo 1388/1968, i, 24; Nawbakhtī, *K. Firaḳ al-shīʿa*, ed. H. Ritter, Istanbul 1931, 25-6, 33, 37, 68, 80-1, 89-90; Saʿd b. ʿAbd Allāh al-Ḳummī, *K. al-Maḳālāt wa 'l-firaḳ*, ed. Muḥammad

Djawād Mashkūr, Tehran 1963, 27, 37, 45, 50, 71, 90, 107, 115-6; Khayyāṭ, *K. al-Intiṣār*, ed. A.N. Nader, Beirut 1957, 14, 80, 95-7; ᶜAlī b. Ibrāhīm al-Ḳummī, *Tafsīr*, ed. Ṭayyib al-Mūsawī al-Djazāʾirī, Nadjaf 1386-7, i, 106, 312-3, ii, 36, 65, 75-6, 130-3, 147, 170, 256, 261, 283, 290-1, 327, 391; ᶜAyyāshī, *Tafsīr*, ed. Hāshim al-Rasūlī al-Maḥallātī, Ḳumm 1380-1, i, 210, ii, 112-4, 259-60, 281-2, 306; Abū Ḥātim al-Rāzī, *K. al-Zīna*, iii, in ᶜAbd Allāh S. al-Sāmarrāʾī, *al-Ghuluww wa 'l-firaḳ al-ghāliya fī 'l-ḥaḍāra al-islāmiyya*, Baghdād 1392/1972, 311-2; Malaṭī, *K. al-Tanbīh wa 'l-radd*, ed. S. Dedering, Istanbul 1936, 14-5, 120; Ibn Bābawayh, *Risālat al-Iᶜtiḳādāt*, Tehran 1917, 88-90, tr. A.A.A. Fyzee, *A Shiᶜite creed*, London 1942, 62-5; idem, *ᶜUyūn akhbār al-Riḍā*, Nadjaf 1390/1970, ii, 201-2; Maḳdisī, *al-Badʾ wa 'l-taʾrīkh*, ed. Cl. Huart, Paris 1899-1919, v, 129-30; al-Mufīd, *Awāʾil al-maḳālāt*, ed. ᶜAbbās-ḳulī Ṣ. Wadjdī, Tabriz 1371, 13, 50-1; idem, *Taṣḥīḥ al-iᶜtiḳād*, printed in the same volume as the *Awāʾil al-maḳālāt*, 40; ᶜAbd al-Djabbār, *al-Mughnī*, xx/2, Cairo n.d., 177-8, 181, 185; *Aghānī*, ed. Beirut, ix, 4, 15-9; ᶜAbd al-Ḳāhir al-Baghdādī, *Farḳ*, Beirut n.d., 56, 59; al-Murtaḍā, ᶜAlī b. al-Ḥusayn, *Djawābāt al-masāʾil al-rāziyya*, in *Rasāʾil al-Sharīf al-Murtaḍā*, Ḳumm 1405, i, 125-6; Ibn Ḥazm, *al-Fiṣal*, ed. Muḥammad Ibrāhīm Nuṣayr and ᶜAbd al-Raḥmān ᶜUmayra, Beirut 1405/1985, v, 35-7; Abū Djaᶜfar al-Ṭūsī, *al-Tibyān fī tafsīr al-Ḳurʾān*, ed. Aḥmad Shawḳī al-Amīn and Aḥmad Ḥabīb Ḳuṣayr al-ᶜĀmilī, Nadjaf 1376-83, i, 254-5, ii, 283, viii, 120; Abu 'l-Muẓaffar al-Isfarāyīnī, *al-Tabṣīr fī 'l-dīn*, Cairo 1374/1955, 38; al-Faḍl b. al-Ḥasan al-Ṭabrisī (al-Ṭabarsī), *Madjmaᶜ al-bayān fī tafsīr al-Ḳurʾān*, Beirut 1380/1961, i, 257, ii, 270, xx, 251-3; Shahrastānī, *al-Milal wa 'l-niḥal*, ed. ᶜAbd al-ᶜAzīz Muḥammad al-Wakīl, Cairo 1387/1968, i, 27-8, 147, 165-6, 168, 173-4, ii, 17; Nashwān al-Ḥimyarī, *al-Ḥūr al-ᶜīn*, Cairo 1367/1948, 43, 159, 260; Ibn Abi 'l-Ḥadīd, *Sharḥ Nahdj al-balāgha*, ed. Muḥammad Abu 'l-Faḍl Ibrāhīm, Cairo 1959-64, vii, 59; Ibn Ṭāwūs, *Saᶜd al-suᶜūd*, Nadjaf 1369/1950, 64-6, 116-7; idem, *Kashf al-mahadjdja*, Nadjaf 1370/1950, 54-5; Ibn al-Murtaḍā, *Ṭabaḳāt al-muᶜtazila*, ed. S. Diwald-Wilzer (*Die Klassen der Muᶜtaziliten*), Beirut-Wiesbaden 1380/1961, 30; al-Ḥasan b. Sulaymān al-Ḥillī, *Mukhtaṣar baṣāʾir al-daradjāt*, Nadjaf 1370/1950, 17-51, 176-212; Radjab al-Bursī, *Mashāriḳ anwār al-yaḳīn fī asrār amīr al-muʾminīn*, Beirut n.d., 210, 212; Abū Ḥāmid al-Maḳdisī, *Risāla fī 'l-radd ᶜala 'l-rāfiḍa*, Bombay 1403/1983, 194; al-Madjlisī, *Biḥār al-anwār*, Tehran 1956-74, liii, 39-144; al-Ḥurr al-ᶜĀmilī, *al-Īḳāẓ min al-hadjᶜa fī 'l-burhān ᶜala 'l-radjᶜa* ed. Hāshim al-Rasūlī al-Maḥallātī, Ḳumm 1381, passim; ᶜAlī al-Ḥāʾirī, *Ilzām al-nāṣib*, Beirut 1404/1984, ii, 308-79; J. Wellhausen, *The religio-political factions in early Islam*, ed. R.C. Ostle, tr. R.C. Ostle and S.M. Walzer, Amsterdam and New York 1975, 153-4, 158; I. Friedlaender, *The heterodoxies of the Shiites according to Ibn Ḥazm*, New Haven 1909, 23-30 and index; idem, *ᶜAbdallāh b. Sabaʾ, der Begründer der Šīᶜa, und sein jüdischer Ursprung*, in *ZA*, xxiii (1909), 296-327, xxiv (1910), 1-46, at 10-15, 18; idem, *Jewish-Arabic studies*, in *JQR*, N.S. ii (1911-2), 481-516; Āghā Buzurg al-Ṭihrānī, *al-Dharīᶜa ilā taṣānīf al-shīᶜa*, Nadjaf 1936-8, Tehran 1941-78, i, 90-5, x, 161-3; M.G.S. Hodgson, *How did the early Shīᶜa become sectarian?*, in *JAOS*, lxxv (1955), 1-13, at 6-7; H. Corbin, *En Islam iranien*, Paris 1971-2, i, 275; W.F. Tucker, *Bayān b. Samᶜān and the Bayāniyya*, in *MW*, lxv (1975), 241-53, at 251; Wadād al-Ḳāḍī, *al-Kaysāniyya fī 'l-taʾrīkh wa 'l-adab*, Beirut 1974, index; eadem, *The development of the term ghulāt in Muslim literature with special reference to the Kaysāniyya*, in *Akten des VII. Kongresses für Arabistik und Islamwissenschaft*, ed. A. Dietrich, Göttingen 1976, 295-319; M.J. McDermott, *The theology of al-Shaikh al-Mufīd (d. 413/1022)*, Beirut 1978, index; A.A. Sachedina, *Islamic messianism*, Albany 1981, 166-73, 178; H. Halm, *Die islamische Gnosis*, Zurich-Munich 1982, index; idem, *Die Schia*, Darmstadt 1988, 25, 99; M. Momen, *An introduction to Shiᶜi Islam*, New Haven and London 1985, index, s.v. *Return*; R. Freitag, *Seelenwanderung in der islamischen Häresie*, Berlin 1985, 29-34 and index; D.K. Crow, *The death of al-Ḥusayn b. ᶜAlī and early Shīᶜī views of the Imamate*, in *Alserāt* [= *al-Ṣirāṭ*], xii (1986), 71-116; D. Gimaret and G. Monnot, *Livre des religions et des sectes*, i, Louvain-Paris 1986, index; J. van Ess, *Theologie und Gesellschaft im 2. und 3. Jahrhundert Hidschra*, i, Berlin and New York 1991, 285-308. (E. Kohlberg)

RĀDJĀ GANESH (the latter part of the name being the Hindu name Gaṇésa, appearing in Arabic script as G.n.s or G.n.sī), a local Hindu landowner of northern Bengal, who successfully usurped authority in Bengal during the latter years of the first period of power of the Ilyās Shāhī line, probably in the first decade or so of the 9th/15th century.

The sources are unclear, but it seems that Rādjā Ganesh wielded the real power in the state under the nominal rule of the Ilyāsids, and then in 817/1414 placed on the throne his young son Djadu, who became a Muslim and assumed the name of Djalāl al-Dīn Muḥammad Shāh. The latter ruled until 835/1432, when he was succeeded by his son Shams al-Dīn Muḥammad Shāh, who held power in Bengal till the restoration of the Ilyās Shāhīs in 841/1437. This family of Islamised Hindus had clearly enjoyed considerable support from both the class of Muslim landholders and notables and the Hindus, and it had ruled over a powerful sultanate which extended as far as the Kusi River in the north-west of Bengal to Chittagong [*q.v.*] in the south-east.

Bibliography: R.C. Majumdar (ed.), *The history and culture of the Indian people, vi. The Delhi Sultanate*, Bombay 1960, 205-11; C.E. Bosworth, *The Islamic dynasties*, 193, 195. (C.E. Bosworth)

RADJAB, the seventh month of the Islamic calendar, was observed as a holy month in the period of the Djāhiliyya in spring. It was the month of the sacrifices of the *ᶜatāʾir* offered to the pagan deities as a token of gratitude for the augmentation of their flocks and herds. It was also the time of invocations of their deities to increase the number of their flocks. It was as well the month of the sacrifices of the *furuᶜ*, the firstlings of the flocks and herds. The owner of the flock had to sacrifice one ewe out of fifty (or hundred) of his herd.

The holy month of Radjab was also the month of peace in the Arab peninsula; the tribes refrained from raids and warfare. The month was called *al-aṣamm* "the deaf" because no sound of weapons was heard during that month and *al-aṣabb* "the pouring" because the unbelievers of Mecca used to say that the mercy is pouring forth in this month. Another by-name of Radjab was *al-radjm* "the stoning" because the Satans were stoned in that month and were expelled from the dwellings of the tribes. Other by-names attached to Radjab were: *al-muḳīm* "the constant," because its sanctity was a firm one, since Radjab is one of the four *ḥurum* months; *al-harim* "the aged" because the sanctity of the month was an ancient one, dating from the time of Muḍar b. Nizār; as the tribes of Muḍar venerated this month, it was also named *radjab Muḍar*. Because of the comprehensive peace among the tribes and their abstaining from hostilities, the month was called *munṣil al-all* and *munṣil al-asinna*, pointing to the fact that the spearheads were removed, weapons laid down and no fighting among tribes was launched. The name *al-muʿallā* "the elevated" was attached to Radjab because it was a month highly respected among the Arab tribes. The name *al-mubriʾ* "the clearing [from fault]" was given to the month because warlike activity was given up, no iniquity was committed and no act of hypocrisy was perpetrated during the month. A peculiar name granted to Radjab was *al-muḳashḳish* "the exonerating," denoting that Radjab distinguished between the people who stuck to the tenets enjoining abstention from fighting during the month and those who violated the sanctity of the month by fighting. Finally, the month was called *al-ʿatīra* because the sacrifices of the *ʿatīra* were carried out during this month.

According to tradition, the month of Radjab was a time of devotional practices, exertions and fasting. Invocations against the iniquitous and the wrong-doers in this month were especially efficacious.

The opinions of the scholars of Islam as to the permission to continue these practices in Islam were divergent, controversial and even contradictory. The differences in their opinions are clearly exposed in the utterances attributed to the Prophet in the collections of *ḥadīth*.

An utterance attributed to the Prophet and recorded in the early collection of ʿAbd al-Razzāḳ (d. 211/826) says that the Prophet approved of the sacrifice of the *ʿatīra* which the people used to practice in Radjab. The Prophet said, "Do it, and name it *al-radjība*."

The utterance of the Prophet enjoining sacrifice of the *ʿatīra* and naming it the *radjība* is opposed by an utterance attributed to the Prophet enjoining annulment of the sacrifice of the firstlings and the sacrifice of the Radjabī *ʿatīra* . It is recorded in the same collection and is formulated plainly: *lā faraʿa wa-lā ʿatīra* "there is no [sacrifice] of the firstlings nor of the *ʿatīra*."

This prohibitive tradition was, however, changed by the interpretation given to it by al-Shāfiʿī: there is no sacrifice of the *ʿatīra* nor of the *faraʿa* "as an obligatory practice", adds al-Shāfiʿī. This comment of his changes, of course, the meaning of the tradition and its significance.

In the same way was interpreted the utterance of the Prophet *ʿalā ahl^{i} kull^{i} bayt^{in} an yadhbaḥū shāt^{an} fī kull^{i} radjab^{in} wa-fī kull^{i} aḍḥā shāt^{an}*. The expression *ʿalā kull^{i} ahl^{i} bayt^{in}* is, however, interpreted not as an enjoinment but only as a recommendation. The utterance has to be understood as recommendation for every family group to sacrifice a ewe during every month of Radjab and to sacrifice a ewe on every *aḍḥā* celebration.

An utterance of the Prophet about the *ʿatīra* permits the sacrifice of the *ʿatīra* in any month of the year and enjoins the practice of charity, dividing among the poor the meat of the slaughtered beasts. It is obvious that the sanctity of Radjab was, according to this tradition, fairly limited, or even abolished, while the advice of charity was especially stressed.

A tradition reported on the authority of ʿĀʾisha says that the Prophet enjoined the slaughter of the firstling of the herd numbering fifty, which tallies with the prevalent Djāhilī practice. But another tradition attributed to the Prophet says, "Practice the sacrifice of the *faraʿa* if you want". Thus the sacrifice was left to the discretion of the believer.

A peculiar utterance of the Prophet turns th sacrifice of the *faraʿa* into a voluntary practice, with special reservation of the Prophet changing the aim c the practice. The Prophet permitted the practice bu remarked that it would be preferable to feed the came until it grows up and to ride it on expeditions an raids for the cause of God; similarly, it is preferabl to feed the ewe until it grows up, to sacrifice it and t divide the meat among the poor.

Similarly, the utterance of the Prophet in which h is said to have approved of the *faraʿa*, saying *al-faraʿ ḥaḳḳ*, was considerably changed by the added reserva tion that it would be better to feed the destine sacrificial animal until it grows up and can be used t ride on it in a raid for the cause of God (in the cas of a camel) or to slaughter it (in the case of a ewe) an give the meat as charity to a needy widow.

Scholars of Islam stress that the slaughter o animals in Radjab was continued in the first period o Islam and was only later abrogated. Al-Khaṭṭābī (d. 388/998) considered the *ʿatīra* compatible with th principles of Islam: it was in the period of Islam sacrificed to God in contradistinction to the Djāhili *ʿatīra*, which was sacrificed to the idols. There is indeed a report saying that Ibn Sīrīn (d. 110/729) used to slaughter the *ʿatīra* in Radjab.

Strictly orthodox scholars stressed that there is no valid tradition concerning the virtues of Radjab. There were, however, scholars, especially from among the pious and devoted, who favoured the widely-circulated popular traditions allegedly uttered by the Prophet, emphasising the virtues of Radjab and encouraging the carrying-out of the various practices considered laudable and right. The Prophet is said to have named Radjab "the month of God", *shahr Allāh*, because it was the month of the people of the *ḥaram* (i.e. the people of Mecca) who were called *āl Allāh*. The problem of the sacrifices during the month of Radjab was only one aspect of the disputes among the Muslim scholars as to the ritual practices performed in the Muslim community in that month.

A significant tradition ascribed to the Prophet singled out the peculiar sanctity of three months of the year: "Radjab is the month of God, Shaʿbān is my month and Ramaḍān is the month of my people." As the month of Radjab was put on par with the two other months there was an obvious tendency to competition between these holy months regarding the rewards of the ritual practices performed during these months, the exceptional position of certain nights of the months and the prayers during these months. The competition between Radjab and Shaʿbān is clearly presented in a tradition reported on the authority of Zayd b. Aslam. The Prophet was informed about people fasting during Radjab. He remarked, "How far are they from the virtues of the people fasting during Shaʿbān!" Zayd observed, "Most of the fasting of the Prophet, except in Ramaḍān, was in Shaʿbān." The partisans of Radjab quoted a report of Ibn al-ʿAbbās saying that the Prophet used to fast so many days in Radjab that his Companions did not think that he would break his fast; and he used to break his fast so that they doubted whether he would resume it.

As against the people venerating Shaʿbān, the partisans of Radjab had recourse to utterances attributed to the Prophet in which the fasting of Radjab was recommended and very high rewards were promised to people who were fasting in it. The Prophet is said to have stated that the month of Radjab is of a high position and that the good deeds of the believer gain multiple rewards. He who fasts one day in Radjab is in the position of a believer who would fast a year. He who fasts nine days, for him the gates of Hell are closed; he who fasts eight days, for him the eight doors of Paradise are opened; he who fasts ten days, God will fulfill for him every wish; he who fasts fifteen days, a herald will announce from Heaven that God forgave him every sin which he had committed in the past. In the month of Radjab God carried Nūḥ (Noah) in the ark; he fasted during Radjab, and bade his people to fast during it, thus expressing their gratitude to God for their salvation.

Aḥmad b. Ḥanbal said that he had in his possession a tradition recording the rewards for fasting of every day of Radjab; he considered, however, the *ḥadīth* a forged one. The fasting of the whole month of Radjab was nevertheless frowned upon and sometimes forbidden in order not to create a similarity with Ramaḍān. The practices of fasting during Radjab were censured by Abū Bakr, ʿUmar and people of the *ṣaḥāba*, says Ibn Taymiyya.

Some nights of Radjab are considered to be replete with God's graces. In the first night of Radjab, God will grant every supplication of the believer. It is one of the five chosen nights in the year. Another prayer strongly censured by Ibn Taymiyya was the prayer practised in the midst of Radjab called *ṣalāt Umm Dāwūd*.

A night highly praised by those who observed Radjab was the night of the *ṣalāt al-raghāʾib* "the night of the prayer for extensive and desirable gifts"; it starts on the eve of the first Friday of Radjab; the prayers and supplications contained hundreds of invocations, prostrations, *rakʿas* and recitations of some sūras of the Kurʾān. The believer is requested to fast on Thursday preceding this night. A night of Radjab distinguished by the rich rewards is the night of the twenty-seventh of Radjab. The believer spending this night in vigils: praying; thanking God; repeating a hundred times the various phrases of gratitude, the oneness of God, invocations and supplications; performing prostrations and *rakʿas*; and reading a sūra of the Kurʾān and fasting the next day, will be highly rewarded by God; he will attain God's grace as if he fasted a hundred years and practiced vigils for a hundred years. On that night, Muḥammad was sent as a prophet.

The significant events connected with the life of the Prophet which allegedly happened in Radjab turn the month into one of the most distinctive periods of the year. According to a tradition, the mother of the Prophet conceived him on the first evening of Radjab; another tradition claims that he was born in Radjab. Some traditions assert that the event of the *laylat al-miʿrādj* occured in Radjab. Other traditions claim that the date of the *isrāʾ* was the twenty-seventh day of Radjab.

The struggle of the orthodox scholars against those practices of Radjab widely approved by pious ascetics and Ṣūfīs was not entirely successful. These practices have survived and form until the present time an essential part of Muslim popular belief and ritual.

Bibliography: ʿAbd al-Razzāḳ, *al-Muṣannaf*, ed. Ḥabīb al-Raḥmān al-Aʿẓamī, Beirut 1391/1972, iv, 342, no. 8000, iv, 341, no. 7998, iv, 341, no. 7999, iv, 340, no. 7997, iv, 337, no. 7989, iv, 337, nos. 7990-1, iv, 340, no. 7996, and see *ibid.*, iv, 338, nos. 7992-3, iv, 292, no. 7858, iv, 317, no. 7927; Ibn Abī Shayba, *al-Muṣannaf fi 'l-aḥādīth wa 'l-āthār*, ed. ʿAbd al-Khāliḳ al-Afghānī, repr., n.p. n.d., viii, 64-7; Abū Yaʿlā al-Mawṣilī, *al-Musnad*, ed. Ḥusayn Salīm Asad, Damascus-Beirut 1407/1987, x, 282, no. 5879 (and see the abundant references of the editor); Subkī, *Ṭabaḳāt al-shāfiʿiyya al-kubrā*, ed. ʿAbd al-Fattāḥ Muḥammad Ḥulw and Maḥmūd Muḥammad al-Ṭannāḥī, Cairo 1383/1964, ii, 111; Munāwī, *Fayḍ al-ḳadīr, sharḥ al-djāmiʿ al-ṣaghīr*, Beirut 1391/1972, vi, 435, no. 9914, iv, 321, no. 5457, iv, 375, no. 5674, iii, 454, no. 3953; ʿAbd al-Raḥmān al-Ṣaffūrī, *Nuzhat al-madjālis wa-muntakhab al-nafāʾis*, Beirut, n.d., 189-95; Ibn Taymiyya, *Iḳtiḍāʾ al-ṣirāṭ al-mustaḳīm mukhālafat aṣḥāb al-djaḥīm*, ed. Muḥammad Ḥāmid al-Fiḳī, Cairo, ʿĀbidīn 1369/1950, 293, 302; Abū ʿUbayd al-Ḳāsim b. Sallām al-Harawī, *Gharīb al-ḥadīth*, ed. Muḥammad ʿAẓīm al-Dīn, Ḥaydarābād 1385/1966, ii, 4-6; ʿAbd Allāh b. Muḥammad b. Djaʿfar b. Ḥayyān, Abu 'l-Shaykh al-Anṣārī, *Ṭabaḳāt al-muḥaddithīn bi-Iṣbahān wa 'l-wāridīn ʿalayhā*, ed. ʿAbd al-Ghafūr ʿAbd al-Ḥaḳḳ Ḥusayn al-Balūshī, Beirut 1407/1987, i, 279-82, nos. 27-9 (and see the references of the editor); ʿUmar b. Badr al-Mawṣilī, *al-Mughnī ʿan al-ḥifẓ wa 'l-kitāb*, Cairo 1342, 33, 36; Ḳurṭubī, *al-Djamiʿ li-aḥkām al-Ḳurʾān = Tafsīr 'l-Ḳurṭubī*, Cairo 1387/1967, vi, 326; Ibn ʿAsākir, *Taʾrīkh Dimashk*, ed. ʿAbd al-Ḳādir Badrān, Beirut 1399/1979, vi, 246, vii, 347 inf.-348 sup.; Bayhaḳī, *Faḍāʾil al-awḳāt*, ed. ʿAdnān ʿAbd al-Raḥmān Madjīd al-Ḳaysī, Mecca 1410/1990, 89-90, no. 7, 106-7, 311-12, no. 149, 95-8, nos. 11, 12; Wadjīh al-Dīn ʿAbd al-Raḥmān b. Khalīl al-Adhruʿī, *Bishārat al-maḥbūb bi-takfīr al-dhunūb*, ed. Madjdī al-Sayyid Ibrāhīm, Cairo n.d., 41, no. 98; Bayhaḳī, *al-Djāmiʿ li-shuʿab al-īmān = Shuʿab al-īmān*, ed. ʿAbd al-ʿAlī ʿAbd al-Ḥamīd Ḥāmid, Bombay 1409/1988, vii, 382-3, no. 3520, 390-3, no. 3529, 393-5, nos. 3530-1; Khaṭīb al-Baghdādī, *Taʾrīkh Baghdād*, Cairo-Baghdād 1349-1931, viii, 331, no. 4421; ʿAbd al-Raḥmān al-Suhaylī, *al-Rawḍ al-unuf*, ed. ʿAbd al-Raḥmān al-Wakīl, Cairo 1387/1967, i, 70; Nūr al-Dīn al-Haythamī, *Madjmaʿ al-zawāʾid wa-manbaʿ al-fawāʾid*, Beirut 1967, iii, 188, 191; Murtaḍā al-Zabīdī, *Itḥāf al-sāda al-muttaḳīn bi-sharḥ asrār iḥyāʾ ʿulūm al-dīn*, Beirut n.d., iii, 422-5; Ibn Ḥadjar al-ʿAskalānī, *Tabyīn al-ʿadjab bi-mā warada fī faḍl radjab*, ed. Abū Asmāʾ Ibrāhīm b. Ismāʿīl Āl ʿAṣr, Beirut 1408/1988; Ibn Himmāt al-Dimashḳī, *al-Tankīt wa 'l-ifāda fī takhrīj aḥādīth khātimat sifr al-saʿāda*, ed. Aḥmad al-Bazra, Beirut 1407/1988, 96-7, 112-13; Maḳrīzī, *al-Khabar ʿan al-bashar*, ms. Dār al-Kutub 947, Taʾrīkh, p. 444; ʿIzz al-Dīn b. ʿAbd al-Salām al-Sulamī, *Kitāb al-Fatāwā*, ed. ʿAbd al-Raḥmān b. ʿAbd al-Fattāḥ, Beirut 1406/1986, 117; ʿAbd al-Wāsiʿ b. Yaḥyā al-Wāsiʿī, *al-Mukhtaṣar fī targhīb wa-tarhīb ḥadīth sayyid al-bashar*, Cairo 1345, 26 ult.-27; al-Ḥasan b. Muḥammad al-Khallāl, *Faḍāʾil shahr radjab*, ed. ʿAmr ʿAbd al-Munʿim, Ṭanṭā 1412/1972; ʿAlī b. Sulṭān al-Ḳārī, *al-Adab fī radjab*, ed. ʿAmr ʿAbd al-Munʿim, Ṭanṭā 1412/1992, also ed. ʿAbd Allāh ʿAwda in *JSAI*, forthcoming; Badr al-Dīn al-Shiblī, *Maḥāsin al-wasāʾil fī maʿrifat al-awāʾil*, ms. B.L., Or. 1530, fol. 56b; ʿAlī Maḥfūẓ, *al-Ibdāʿ fī maḍārr al-ibtidāʿ*, Cairo 1388/1968, 296-7; Muḥammad b. Aḥmad b. Djubayr al-Kinānī, *Riḥla*, Beirut 1388/1968, 98-104; Muḥammad b. ʿAlī b. Ṭūlūn al-Dimashḳī, *Faṣṣ al-Khawātim fī-mā ḳīla fi 'l-walāʾim*, ed. Nizār Abāẓa, Damascus 1402/1982, 92-4. For additional bibl., see M.J. Kister, *Radjab is the month of God*, in *IOS*, i (1971), repr. Variorum, London 1980, *Studies in Jāhiliyya and early Islam*, no. XII.

(M.J. Kister)

RĀDJĀSTHĀN [see Suppl.].

RADJAZ (A.) indicates an Arab metre. The proper meaning of the word is "tremor, spasm, convulsion (as may occur in the behind of a camel when it wants to rise)''. It is not clear how this word became a technical term in prosody. The other etymological meaning of *radjaz* ''thunder, rumble, making a noise'', may perhaps be taken into consideration. In that case, there might be an allusion to the iambic, monotonous and pounding rhythm of these poems (cf. *ka-mā samiʿta radjaza l-ṣawāʿiḳī*, Abū Nuwās, ed. E. Wagner, ii, 299; for the etymology, see also T. Fahd, *La divination arabe*, Leiden 1966, 153-8). A poem composed in this metre is called *urdjūza*.

1. Prosody

In the system of Arabic metres, the *radjaz* occupies a special place. Whereas in other metres the lines of verse consist of two symmetrical half-lines, separated by a caesura, the line of verse of the *radjaz* is in one part only and has no caesura. In general, the *radjaz* lines are only half as long as the lines of other metres. The basic element is the dipody which consists of four syllables. The first and second syllables can be long or short, but the third one must be short and the fourth one long ⏓ ⏓ ⏑ –. Three such dipodies form a trimeter, which is by far the most widely used form of the *radjaz* poem. In its acatalectic form it has the following scheme: ⏓ ⏓ ⏑ – | ⏓ ⏓ ⏑ – | ⏓ ⏓ ⏑ – (e.g. *innaka lā tadrī ghadan mā fī ghadī*, Ruʾba, no. 20, v. 23). In the catalectic form, the second syllable in the third dipody must be long, while the third (short) syllable is missing: ⏓ ⏓ ⏑ – | ⏓ ⏓ ⏑ – | ⏓ – – (e.g. *nasḳī 'l-ʿidā ghayẓan ṭawīla l-djaʾzī*, Ruʾba, no. 23, v. 10). A brachycatalectic variant seldom occurs.

Next to the trimeter there is a less frequent dimeter (*manhūk al-radjaz*), which again can be acatalectic, catalectic or (rarely) brachycatalectic. An example is Abū Nuwās's panegyric poem for al-Faḍl b. al-Rabīʿ, which begins as follows: *wa-baldatin fīhā zawar | ṣaʿrāʾa tukhṭā fī ṣaʿar | martin idhā 'l-dhiʾbu ḳtafar* (*Dīwān*, ed. E. Wagner, i, 161 ff.; Abu 'l-Fatḥ ʿUthmān b. Djinnī, *Tafsīr urdjūzat Abī Nuwās*, ed. Muḥammad Bahdjat al-Atharī, Damascus 1966; see also E. Wagner, *Abū Nuwās*, Wiesbaden 1965, 216). A monometrical *radjaz* poem consisting of 17 verses was once composed by Salm al-Khāsir (*urdjūza ʿalā djuzʾ wāḥid* or *mukaṭṭaʿ al-radjaz*, cf. G.E. von Grunebaum, in *Orientalia*, N.S. xix [1950], 66, no. 15).

By analogy with the other metres, the *radjaz* is sometimes constructed as a distich. In this case, two verses are linked to one another, the first verse becoming the first half-line, the second verse the second half-line. The end of the first verse, lying between the two halves, becomes the caesura, and the rhyme occurs only in the second (half-)verses. Examples are the poems by Ḳaʿnab b. Ḍamra al-Ghaṭafānī, al-Naẓẓār b. Hāshim al-Faḳʿasī (cf. al-Akhfash al-Aṣghar, *K. al-Ikhtiyārayn*, Damascus 1974, no. 54; Aḥmad b. Abī Ṭāhir Ṭayfūr, *K. al-Manthūr wa 'l-manẓūm*, xii/1, Beirut 1977, 103-8), Ibn al-Rūmī (ed. Naṣṣār, i, no. 165), Ibn al-Muʿtazz, Ibn Durayd (the famous *Maḳṣūra*, ed. Maḥmūd Djāsim Muḥammad, Beirut 1986, with commentary by Ibn Khālawayh), al-Maʿarrī, Ṣafī al-Dīn al-Ḥillī, and others. Such a distichal poem was composed by Aḥmad b. ʿAbd al-Raḥmān b. Nafāda (d. 601/1204), who in a playful way introduced four different rhymes in the 2nd, 3rd, 4th and 6th dipodies (cf. al-Ṣafadī, *Wāfī*, vii, 44).

A further variety of the old *urdjūza* is the *muzdawidj* [*q.v.*] poem, in which the principle according to which one and the same rhyme is obligatory for the entire poem is abandoned. Instead, only two verses rhyme. This type of poem came into being in the ʿAbbāsid period. By restricting the constraint imposed by the rhyme, it became possible to compose narrative, historical or didactic poems of some length. In this way, Abān b. ʿAbd al-Ḥamīd al-Lāḥiḳī (d. *ca.* 200/815; Sezgin, ii, 515-16) retold the book of fables *Kalīla wa-Dimna* [*q.v.*] (cf. al-Ṣūlī, *K. al-Awrāḳ*, i, 46 ff.). This poem is said to have comprised 14,000 verses. Later, Muḥammad b. al-Habbāriyya [*q.v.*] (d. 509/1115-16) and ʿAbd al-Muʾmin b. al-Ḥasan al-Ṣāghānī (Brockelmann, SI, 235) also presented the same material in *muzdawidj* verses. Proverbs and aphorisms were treated in this type of verse by Abu 'l-ʿAtāhiya (*Dīwān*, ed. L. Cheikho, 346-8; ed. Sh. Fayṣal, Damascus 1965, 444-66), while historical subjects were treated in this way by ʿAlī b. al-Djahm, Ibn al-Muʿtazz, Ibn ʿAbd Rabbih (cf. J.T. Monroe, *The historical Arjūza of Ibn ʿAbd Rabbihi*, in *JAOS*, xci [1971], 67-95), ʿAbd al-Djabbār al-Mutanabbī and Lisān al-Dīn b. al-Khaṭīb. In general, any subject-matter, when versified for the sake of instruction, was preferably presented in the form of an *urdjūza muzdawidja*. Such poems exist on astronomy (ʿAbd al-Raḥmān al-Ṣūfī), medicine (Ibn Sīnā), agriculture (Ibn Luyūn), navigation (Ibn Mādjid), grammar (*Mulḥat al-iʿrāb* by al-Ḥarīrī, the *Alfiyya* by Ibn Mālik), metrics, law of inheritance, chess, hippology, archery and many other subjects. The simple, rhythmical verses were an easy vehicle for memorising.

Next to the *muzdawidj*, in which every two verses have the same rhyme, other groups were developed. In the *urdjūza muthallatha* every three verses are rhymed, in the *murabbaʿa* every four, in the *mukhammasa* every five, in the *muʿashshara* every ten. In these forms the strophic poem thus becomes visible. These poems, too, serve to present scientific doctrines, lexical problems, various descriptions and travel accounts.

2. Historical development

In pre-Islamic times, the *radjaz* was only used for short poems. They originated from a concrete situation, were mostly improvised [see IRTIDJĀL] and as a rule comprised only three to five verses. It is true that these compositions in *radjaz* were correct prosodic units, but they were no poems in the sense of works of art. Initially, the *radjaz* was not a ''literary'' metre. During the *Djāhiliyya* [*q.v.*], no-one composed a *ḳaṣīda* in the *radjaz*.

A typical situation was the man-to-man fight, in which two adversaries came forward from their battle array. Both heroes called their names and boasted about their strength. Abū Ḥayya al-Fazārī, for instance, said *anā Abū Ḥayyata wa-smī Wadʿān / lā ḍaraʿun ṭiflun wa-lā ʿawdun fān / kayfa tarā ḍarbī ruʾūsa l-aḳrān* (cf. al-Āmidī, *Muʾtalif*, ed. ʿAbd al-Sattār Aḥmad Farrādj, Cairo 1961, 146). The purpose of such utterances was to intimidate the adversary and to make him insecure. Self-praise (*fakhr*) was here linked to cursing (*hidjāʾ*) the enemy. The factual power of words should hit the adversary and weaken him. Here it becomes clear that magic was one of the ancient elements of the *radjaz*.

Hidjāʾ also indicates another group of *radjaz* poems, namely, trivial mocking verses of an erotic and obscene content. Occasionally, a dialogue is then staged between man and wife during intercourse, the dialogue being divided by conventional expressions such as *ḳultu...ḳālat*. A typical example is the poem by al-Aghlab al-ʿIdjlī, in which he ridicules the pseudo-prophets Musaylima [*q.v.*] and Sadjāḥi (cf. Djumaḥī, *Ṭabaḳāt*, ed. Maḥmūd Muḥammad Shākir, Cairo 1974, 740-2).

Radjaz is also the metre for tunes, sung at rhythmical activities such as urging camels or drawing water [see GHINĀʾ]. Rhythmical games are also accompanied by *radjaz* verses: mothers used to sing such erses when making their children dance in a circle cf. W. Walther, *Altarabische Kindertanzreime*, in *Studia Orientalia in memoriam Caroli Brockelmann*, Halle 1968, 17-33). Finally, incantations were also composed in *radjaz*. Hind bint al-Khuss [*q.v.*] was able to cast, with such verses, a spell on birds that were flying by *Aghānī*[1] ix, 175; [3]xi, 36).

In the old days, the *radjaz* therefore was only artless folk poetry. Great poets such as al-Nābigha al-Dhubyānī, Zuhayr, Ṭarafa, ʿAntara, Imruʾ al-Ḳays, etc., hardly used this metre and the few verses in it ascribed to them cannot be vouched for as being authentic. In the early Islamic period a change gradually becomes apparent. According to the Arab literary historians, al-Aghlab b. Djusham al-ʿIdjlī, who allegedly fell in the battle of Nihāwand in 21/641, is said to have been the first to compose longer poems in *radjaz* (Sezgin ii, 163-4; collection of fragments by Nūrī Ḥammūdī al-Ḳaysī, in *Madjallat al-Madjmaʿ al-ʿIlmī al-ʿIrāḳī*, xxxi/3 [1980], 104-44). But Labīd b. Rabīʿa al-ʿĀmirī and al-Shammākh b. Ḍirār al-Ghaṭafānī, together with his companions Djabbār b. Djazʾ, Djundab and al-Dhulayḥ, also composed several *urdjūzas* which comprise as many as 40 verses. They contain parts of the real *ḳaṣīda*, like the *nasīb* [*q.v.*], the ride through the desert or the description of the bull antelope. The Hudhalī Mulayḥ b. al-Ḥakam composed an *urdjūza* of 94 verses (*Ashʿār al-Hudhaliyyīn*, ed. J. Wellhausen, no. 278; German tr. H.H. Bräu, in *ZS*, v [1926], 277-82).

This development of the *radjaz* into a metre for real literary poems continued in the second half of the 1st/7th century. It culminated in two eminent poets, namely, ʿAbd Allāh b. Ruʾba b. Labīd, called al-ʿAdjdjādj [*q.v.*] (d. *ca.* 91/710, Sezgin ii, 366-7) and his son Ruʾba (d. *ca.* 145/763, Sezgin ii, 367-9). Both composed verses exclusively in *radjaz* and did not use any other metre. But as far as the contents are concerned, their poems are full *ḳaṣīdas*, which start with the complaint addressed to the remains of the abandoned camp (*aṭlāl*), pass into the desert ride (*raḥīl* [*q.v.*]) and end in a request to the patron. They contain the usual images which are developed into independent episodes, and all the other elements of the traditional *ḳaṣīda*. Both poets are inclined to exaggeration and immoderation. Their phrasing is marked by rudeness and coarseness, and their arsenal of words of abuse is inexhaustible. But it looks as if even the greatest self-glorification and the devastating scoffing of the adversary are not meant that seriously. Again and again, ironic and humoristic turns of phrase are woven into their diatribes, and irony does not exempt their own persons. Sarcastic, grotesque, comical and humoristic elements may be said to turn al-ʿAdjdjādj's and Ruʾba's *urdjūzas* into a persiflage of the regular two-hemistich *ḳaṣīda*.

Next to these two poets mention should be made of their contemporary al-Faḍl b. Ḳudāma al-ʿIdjlī, called Abu 'l-Nadjm [*q.v.*], of whose poems, apart from a *lāmiyya* (ed. ʿAbd al-ʿAzīz al-Maymanī, *al-Ṭarāʾif al-adabiyya*, Cairo 1937, 55-71), only fragments have been preserved (collected by ʿAlāʾ al-Dīn Aghā, al-Riyāḍ 1981). Other *radjaz* poets of this period are Muḥammad b. Dhuʾayb al-Fuḳaymī, called al-ʿUmānī (collection of fragments by Ḥannā Djamīl Ḥaddād, in *RIMA*, xxvii/1 [1983], 73-119), Abū Nukhayla al-Ḥimmānī [*q.v.* in Suppl.], al-Zafayān, Ḥumayd al-Arḳaṭ [*q.v.*], Manẓūr b. Marthad al-Asadī and Himyān b. Ḳuḥāfa al-Saʿdī.

As for the great poets of the Umayyad period, they were not as unfavourably disposed towards the *radjaz* metre as had been their colleagues of the *Djāhiliyya*. There exist at least 20 *urdjūzas* by Djarīr (d. 111/729 [*q.v.*]), some of which contain more than 40 verses. They deal mainly with satire, but some are undoubtedly fragments of original *ḳaṣīdas*. Typical Bedouin *ḳaṣīdas* are also the 10 *urdjūzas* which have been transmitted in the *dīwān* of Ghaylān b. ʿUḳba, called Dhu 'l-Rumma (d. 117/735-6 [*q.v.*]). Among them are long pieces of 60 to 80 verses. This metre is also used by the poets of the ʿAbbāsid period. Bashshār b. Burd [*q.v.*] (d. 167/783), for instance, composed lengthy *ḳaṣīdas* in *radjaz* after the old fashion. They contain mainly panegyrics on the governors Dāwūd b. Yazīd, ʿUḳba b. Salm and Yazīd b. Ḥātim. Two of these poems contain more than 160 verses (*Dīwān*, ed. Muḥammad al-Ṭāhir b. ʿĀshūr, Cairo 1950-7, i, 134 ff., 140 ff.; ii, 219 ff.; iii, 92-3, 178 ff.). Important and lengthy *urdjūzas* were also composed by Ibn al-Rūmī [*q.v.*] (*Dīwān*, ed. Ḥusayn Naṣṣār, Cairo 1973 ff., nos. 60, 76, 91, 141, 217, 293, 310, 340, 355, 357, 368, 415, 438, 440, etc.). They are for the greater part defamatory poems (*hidjāʾ* [*q.v.*]), whose contents are grossly obscene. Abū Tammām, al-Buḥturī, al-Sharīf al-Murtaḍā and his brother al-Raḍī, al-Aʿmā al-Tuṭīlī and many other poets occasionally also used this metre, moulding all the usual themes of the earlier poets. Worth mentioning is that Maḥmūd b. al-Ḥusayn al-Sindī, called Kushādjim (d. *ca.* 350/961 [*q.v.*]), often uses the *radjaz* in description poems (*ekphrasis, waṣf*). He depicts a fried fish (*Dīwān*, ed. Khayriyya Muḥammad Maḥfūẓ, Baghdād 1970, no. 5), an abacus (no. 24), a wine filter (no. 30), a cake (nos. 48, 63), sugar-cane (no. 50), ink and reed pen (no. 53), fodder beans (nos. 55, 143), figs (no. 86), the polo game (no. 108), a hen (no. 136), a cloud (nos. 151, 153), asparagus (no. 160), a melon (no. 166), a mill (no. 206), a quince (no. 223), and many other objects. He thus asserted the rights of the *radjaz* in a field which otherwise is dominated by other metres (cf. A. Giese, *Waṣf bei Kušāğim*, Berlin 1981).

A special place is taken by the hunting poems (*ṭardiyyāt*). Unlike the hunting descriptions of ancient poetry, in which a poor man is hunting for antelopes and onagers in order to secure his sustenance, the *ṭardiyyāt* deal with descriptions of courtly hunting, organised by high-placed personalities as a pastime and for pleasure. These poems are composed almost exclusively in *radjaz* and are, from their beginning onwards, largely standardised in their motives and wording. They very often start with the striking of camp in early morning, the formula *ḳad aghtadī wa 'l-ṣubḥu...* occurring quite repeatedly; or it is simply said, *anʿatu kalban...* The hunting animals are dogs and cheetahs, and as trained birds of prey are named the hawk (*bāzī, zurraḳ*), the saker or lanner (*ṣaḳr*), the peregrine (*shāhīn*), the merlin (*yuʾyuʾ*), the eagle (*ʿuḳāb*) and the sparrowhawk (*bāshiḳ*). The quarry are antelopes, hares, foxes, cranes, bustards (*ḥubārā*), francolins, geese and other birds. The dog is said to fly away without wings or, when running, to resemble a falling star. Its muzzle looks like burning coal, the falcon's plumage like a piece of embroidery, its claws like spearheads or a butcher's knives. At the end, the preparation of the game for the meal is often described, and the poet praises his dog or falcon.

The beginnings of this poetry are apparently to be found with al-Shamardal b. Sharīk al-Yarbūʿī, a contemporary of al-Farazdaḳ. From his work, 17 *urdjūzas* are transmitted, but most of these are only small fragments (ed. T. Seidensticker, *Die Gedichte des Šamardal*, Wiesbaden 1983, nos. 19-29, 36-41). Al-Shamardal was the model for Abū Nuwās, in whose *Dīwān* the *ṭardiyyāt* take up a full chapter (ed. Āṣāf,

Cairo 1898, 206-34; ed. E. Wagner, ii, 176-327; cf. also Wagner, *Abū Nuwās*, Wiesbaden 1965, 265-89). Even if, according to the transmitters, many of them are not authentic, yet the full range and richness of this literary genre are shown in Abū Nuwās. More than others he strongly influenced later poets when they were writing about hunting. Among other poems, ʿAbd al-Ṣamad b. al-Muʿadhdhal (d. *ca.* 240/854; Sezgin ii, 508) composed one on hunting with the cheetah (*fahd*), 49 verses of which are transmitted by Kushādjim (*Maṣāyid*, Baghdād 1954, 190 ff.). Among the hunting poems of ʿAbd Allāh b. al-Muʿtazz (d. 296/908) are 48 *urdjūza*s, and only 5 in other metres (*Dīwān*, ed. B. Lewin, iv, 2-44; ed. Yūnus A. al-Sāmarrāʾī, ii, Baghdād 1978, 405 ff.). His contemporary ʿAbd Allāh b. Muḥammad al-Nāshiʾ al-Akbar (d. 293/906; Sezgin, ii, 564 ff.) also composed numerous *urdjūza*s on falcons, dogs and on fox-hunting (cf. the inventory of his poems in J. van Ess, *Frühe muʿtazilitische Häresiographie*, Beirut 1971, 155-61; see also ʿAlī b. Muḥammad al-Shimshāṭī, *K. al-Anwār wa-maḥāsin al-ashʿār*, Baghdād 1976, 284-5, 300, 305, 311, 322). Kushādjim, too (see above), composed a number of hunting *urdjūzas* (*Dīwān*, ed. Khayriyya Muḥammad Maḥfūẓ, Baghdād 1970, nos. 2, 12, 88, 172, 259, 260, 267, 321, 354, 371, etc.). He was very familiar with this métier. In his *K. al-Maṣāyid wa 'l-maṭārid* he also quotes numerous hunting poems by other poets. Finally, mention should be made of Ṣafī al-Dīn al-Ḥillī (d. 749/1349; Brockelmann, II, 159, S II, 199), who composed 7 *urdjūza*s on hunting with falcons, cheetahs and dogs (*Dīwān*, Beirut 1962, 257 ff.). One of his *muwashshaḥāt* [*q.v.*] (*Dīwān*, 245 ff.) is also composed in *radjaz*. He describes in it bird-hunting with the crossbow (*ḳaws al-bunduḳ*), a theme already treated by Abū Nuwās.

3. Special characteristics

As said above, the length of line of the *radjaz* is in general only half of that of the other metres. The *ḳarīḍ* verse contains an average of 8, 9 words, while the *radjaz* trimeter consists of only 4, 3 words. This means that every fourth or fifth word must be a rhyme word (in the dimeter the relations are even less favourable), and thus the poet is quite limited in the choice of his words. Nowhere does the *ḍarūrat al-shiʿr* impose itself so strongly as in the *radjaz*. If, for instance, the poet chooses the *-ayn* rhyme, almost every fourth word must be a dual. In Ruʾba's poem no. 32 the rhyme is *-āṭī*. Consequently, almost all the rhyme words of the 94 verses must be nouns in the genitive. In the *-ītū* rhyme (Ruʾba, no. 10) the forms of the first person perfect of the *verba tertiae infirmae* dominate, and in al-ʿAdjdjādj's poem no. 40, which has the *-iyyū* rhyme and which comprises 200 verses, innumerable *nomina relativa* (*nisba*) occur. The part of speech, the case and the grammatical person thus are largely determined by the requirements of the rhyme, and so the syntax of the verses is fixed to a high degree. It is also evident that a full sentence can only rarely be accomodated in the short lines of verse. Nowhere does enjambment (*taḍmīn*) occur so often as in the *radjaz* (cf. G.J.H. van Gelder, *Breaking rules for fun ..., On enjambment in classical Arabic poetry*, in *The challenge of the Middle East: Middle Eastern studies at the University of Amsterdam*, 1982, 25-31, 184-6; idem, *Beyond the line*, Leiden 1982, 123-4). The choice of words, too, depends on the requirements of the rhyme. Since the lexicon of literary speech is not sufficient for the rhymes of a long *urdjūza*, the poet searches for rare words, i.e. expressions which have become obsolete or which originate from certain dialects, or he reaches even for foreign words. In order to meet the requirements of the rhyme, the poet furthermore often has to change, to mutilate or to expand the words; he has to replace one sound by another, to form irregular plurals, and so on. Metre and rhyme had to be taken into account correctly in any case, while sounds, forms and syntax could eventually be changed. All this gives the *radjaz* poems their unmistakable, distinctive hall-mark. They belong to the most difficult texts of Arabic literature.

Bibliography: 1. Editions: Muḥammad Tawfīḳ al-Bakrī, *Arādjīz al-ʿArab*, Cairo 1313/1895 (2nd ed. Cairo 1346/1927); W. Ahlwardt, *Die Dīwāne der Reǵezdichter Elʿaǵǵāǵ* und *Ezzafajān*, Berlin 1903; idem, *Der Dīwān des Reǵezdichters Rūba ben Elʿaǵǵāǵ*, Berlin 1903; (German tr. Berlin 1904); R. Geyer, *Altarabische Diiamben*, Leipzig-New York 1908; idem, *Al-ʿAǧǧâǧ und az-Zafayân*, in *WZKM*, xxiii (1909), 74-101; idem, *Beiträge zum Dîwân des Ruʾbah*, in *SBAk. Wien*, clxiii (1909), III. Abh.; ʿIzzat Ḥasan, *Dīwān al-ʿAdjdjādj*, Aleppo-Beirut 1971; ʿAbd al-Ḥafīẓ al-Saṭlī, *Dīwān al-ʿAdjdjādj*, i-ii, Damascus 1971.

2. Secondary literature: A. Schaade, *EI*[1] s.v. *Radjaz*; C.A. Nallino, *La littérature arabe*, tr. Ch. Pellat, Paris 1950, 146-70; M. Ullmann, *Untersuchungen zur Raǧazpoesie*, Wiesbaden 1966; Djamāl Nadjm al-ʿUbaydī, *al-Radjaz, nashʾatuhū, ashhar shuʿarāʾihī*, Baghdād 1971; Khawla Taḳī al-Dīn al-Hilālī, *Dirāsa lughawiyya fī arādjīz Ruʾba wa 'l-ʿAdjdjādj*, i-ii, Baghdād 1982; E. Wagner, *Grundzüge der klassischen arabischen Dichtung*, i, Darmstadt 1987, 43-7, ii, 46-58; G.R. Smith, *Hunting poetry* (ṭardiyyāt), in Julia Ashtiany *et alii* (eds.), *ʿAbbasid belles-lettres* [= *Camb. hist. of Arabic lit.*, ii], Cambridge 1990, 167-84. (M. Ullmann)

4. As a term of non-metrical poetry

In some early Arabic traditions the term *radjaz* is used not in its metrical sense, but to denote poetry defined by "halved" (*mashṭūr*), i.e. three-foot, lines without caesura. Since poetry in the *radjaz* metre is, at least for the most part, also characterised by tripodies (see above under 1.), the two applications of the term are certainly related. The priority may lie with the *mashṭūr* meaning, which would then have been narrowed down to the one metre in which *mashṭūr* verses occurred most.

The first early attestation of this use is in al-Akhfash al-Awsaṭ (d. 215/830 or 221/836 [*q.v.*]), *Ḳawāfī*, 67-8, where poetry is divided into *ḳaṣīd, ramal,* and *radjaz*, which are defined as having lines that are *tāmm, madjzūʾ*, and *mashṭūr*, i.e. "complete", "shortened by one foot per hemistich", and "halved". In terms of metres, the *ḳaṣīd* comprises *ṭawīl, basīṭ, kāmil, madīd, wāfir*, and *radjaz* (sic, here meant as the *radjaz* hexameter with caesura), the *radjaz* includes everything with three feet and no caesura (thus presumably the *radjaz* and the *munsariḥ* trimeter), and the *ramal* [*q.v.*] covers everything else (thus the metres *ramal, hazadj*, the metres of the Fourth [unless they are trimeters] and the Fifth Circles, and all *ḳaṣīd* metres, if they are *madjzūʾ*).

A slightly different system is found in al-Djawharī (d. 393/1003 or later [*q.v.*]), *Ḳawāfī*, fols. 34b-35b. Here we have the following fourfold division:

1. *ḳaṣāʾid tāmm*	*ṭawīl, al-basīṭ al-tāmm, al-wāfir al-tāmm, al-kāmil al-tāmm, al-radjaz al-tāmm,* [some say *al-khafīf al-tāmm*]
2. *ramal madjzūʾ*	*madjzūʾ al-madīd, madjzūʾ al-basīṭ, madjzūʾ al-wāfir, madjzūʾ al-kāmil,* and the like (sic).

. radjaz	mashṭūr	mashṭūr al-radjaz, mashṭūr al-munsariḥ
.	manhūk	manhūk al-radjaz, manhūk al-munsariḥ

The difference is the addition, in al-Djawharī, of the *manhūk* metres, i.e. the "emaciated" dimeters, which however do not have their own name. The rest seems to be identical, although for lack of a complete enumeration of the metres covered by each term in both authors we cannot be certain. A system similar to al-Djawharī's is quoted by al-Tahānawī, *Kashshāf*, i, 745, where the last category is called *khafīf*.

Of particular interest are the various functions attributed to these formal types of poetry. Al-Akhfash says that *ḳaṣīd* is sung (*taghannā*) by the caravan riders, while *radjaz* is chanted (*tarannama*) to accompany work, to drive herds, and to urge on riding-camels (the function of *ramal* is not mentioned). Al-Djawharī offers a similar picture with slight changes: *ḳaṣāʾid* are for chanting and singing when mounted, *ramal* for social rank disputes, praises and lampoons, *radjaz* for chanting at the market places, during work and while driving the camels, and the *manhūk* metres for urging on the camels, for letting little children dance (*tarḳīṣ*), and for drawing water from wells.

These various divisions are explicitly attributed to the *ʿArab*, the Bedouins, and they soon fell into desuetude. Al-Djawharī says that all four genres were later also used in situations different from the original ones mentioned.

Bibliography: al-Akhfash al-Awsaṭ, *K. al-Ḳawāfī*, ed. ʿIzzat Ḥasan, Damascus 1390/1970; Djawharī, *K. al-Ḳawāfī*, ms. Istanbul, Atıf Efendi 1991, fols. 34a-60a (cf. W. Heinrichs, *Al-Ǧauharīs Metrik*, in *ZDMG, Supplement* viii, Stuttgart 1990, 140-9 [esp. 148-9]); Tahānawī, *Kashshāf iṣṭilāḥāt al-funūn*, ed. A. Sprenger *et alii*, Calcutta 1862; H. Gätje (ed.), *Grundriss der Arabischen Philologie*, ii, *Literaturwissenschaft*, Wiesbaden 1987, 191-2.

(W. Heinrichs)

RADJʿIYYA (A.), also irtidjāʿ, the term coined in modern Arabic for reaction in the political sense (from *r-dj-ʿ* "to return"). Towards the same end of the political spectrum appear also the terms *muḥāfiẓ* "conservative" and *muḥāfaẓa* "conservatism"; cf. A. Ayalon, *Language and change in the Arab Middle East*, New York-Oxford 1987, 125. (Ed.)

RADJM (A.), the casting of stones. *R-dj-m* is a Semitic root, derivatives from which are found in the Old Testament with the meaning of "to stone, to drive away or kill by throwing stones" an abominable creature; *radjma* is "a heap of stones, an assembly of men, cries, tumult".

In Arabic, the root means "to stone, to curse"; *radjam*, "heap of stones", also means simply the stones placed upon tombs either as flagstones or in a heap, a custom which *ḥadīth* condemns, recommending rather that a grave should be level with the surface of the ground. On the *ḥadīth* of ʿAbd Allāh b. Mughfal, it is discussed whether *lā turadjdjimū ḳabrī* means "do not build my grave in a mound" or "do not utter imprecations there".

The lapidation and heaps of stones at Minā [*q.v.*] are called *djamra*, and *djamarāt al-ʿArab* means the groups of Bedouin tribes; we find there the two old meanings of the root which can be taken back to *dj-m*, in Arabic *djamma* and *djamaʿa* "to reunite". The Arab grammarians derive *djamra* "lapidation" from *djamarāt al-ʿArab*.

In addition to the meaning of "ritual stoning as a punishment for fornication", *radjm* means the casting of stones at Minā, which is one of the pre-Islamic rites preserved by Muḥammad and inserted among the ceremonies of the pilgrimage. See here djamra, ḥadjdj and minā with their bibliographies.

The Ḳurʾān does not mention this rite, but it knows *radjama* in its Biblical sense of "stoning of prophets by unbelievers", and also *radjīm* (= *mardjūm*) as an epithet of Satan, "driven away and struck with projectiles of fire by the angels", and lastly (XVIII, 21) in an abstract sense which indicates a long semantic evolution.

The rite of casting stones at Minā was regulated by *ḥadīths* in the classical collections. There is a model *ḥadjdj*, that of the Prophet which we find in the manuals of *manāsik al-ḥadjdj*, e.g. in the *Risāla* of Ibn Taymiyya (cf. Rifʿāt, i, 89 ff.). Some *ḥadīths* of archaic form (e.g. al-Bukhārī, *Nikāḥ, bāb* 2; *Salam, bāb* 1 and 2; *ʿUmda*, viii, 489) show that Muḥammad had to lay down rules for the essential question of the *wuḳūf*, the culmination of the *ḥadjdj*. The *Ḥums*, i.e. the Ḳuraysh and their allies, observed it at Djamʿ (Muzdalifa [*q.v.*]), in the *ḥaram*; the others, the *ʿArab*, at ʿArafa, outside of the *ḥaram* of Mecca. Having to choose between his companions of two different origins, the *Muhādjirūn* and the *Anṣār* [*q.vv.*], Muḥammad decided with the latter for ʿArafa; but he retained a secondary *wuḳūf* at Muzdalifa, and the two *ifāḍas*, the new combination of rites culminating in the throwing of stones at ʿAḳaba.

Situated at the bottom of the valley of Minā, on the slope of the defile towards Mecca, al-ʿAḳaba is "not in Minā but it is its boundary on the side of Mecca" (*ʿUmda*, iv, 770). On the morning of 10 Dhu 'l-Ḥidjdja, the pilgrim goes down into the valley, passes without saluting them in front of the great *djamra*, 500 yards farther on the middle one, and 400 yards beyond he comes to *djamrat al-ʿAḳaba* (Rifʿat, i, 328). There he throws 7 stones, and this is one of the four ceremonies which on the tenth day are intended to remove his state of sanctity. He must also have his hair shaved (*ḥalḳ*), sacrifice a victim (*naḥr*) and return in procession to Mecca (*ifāḍa*). This last rite prepares the sexual deconsecration; the three others together abolish the prohibitions of the *ḥadjdj*, but the legists are not agreed on the order in which they have to be accomplished. The *ḥadīths* say that the Prophet replied to the pilgrims who were worried, not having followed the order in which he had himself followed them, *lā ḥaradja* "no harm (in that)" (al-Bukhārī, *Ḥadjdj*, *bābs* 125, 130 etc.). It is explained that the Prophet on this day of rejoicing did not wish to hurt the feelings of the ignorant Bedouins. We may imagine that these *ʿArab* did not follow the customs of the Ḳuraysh and that Muḥammad had neither the time nor the inclination to impose his own choice between the varying customs.

Muḥammad began with the lapidation at al-Aḳaba. After the *ḥalḳ*, the sacrifice and the *ifāḍa*, he returned to spend the night in Minā. Then on the 11th, 12th and 13th days, he cast 7 stones at the three *djamarāt*, ending with that of al-ʿAḳaba. The pilgrims imitating him ought therefore to throw $7 + (7 \times 3 \times 3) = 70$ stones. But in general, they take advantage of the liberty (*rukhṣa*) given them by the *ḥadīth* to leave Minā finally on the 12th day and therefore only to throw $7 + (7 \times 2 \times 3) = 49$ stones. It is probable that there was no ancient usage; the presence of the bodies of the sacrificial victims made Minā a horrible place. It is difficult to see how Wavell (*Pilgrim*, 202) threw 63 stones, i.e. $7 \times 3 \times 3$; this is, however, the number of victims which, according to tradition, Muḥammad sacrificed with his own hand, one for each year of his life.

The stoning of al-ʿAḳaba is done on the 10th day by

the pilgrims in *iḥrām*; those of the three days following by the deconsecrated pilgrims. The whole business is not a fundamental element of the pilgrimage (*rukn*).

Little stones are thrown, larger than a lentil, but less than a nut, what the old Arabs called *ḥaṣa 'l-khadhf* which were thrown either with the fingers or with a little lever of wood forming a kind of sling (*mikhdhafa*: al-Tirmidhī, iv, 123). A *ḥadīth* forbids this dangerous game, which might knock out an eye but is not strong enough to kill an enemy; it must therefore have had something magical or pagan in its character. The stones have to be collected of the proper size and not broken from a rock. Gold, silver, precious stones, etc., are condemned; but some texts allow, in addition to date-stones, a piece of camel-dung or a dead sparrow, which we find are also the means used by the women of the *Djāhiliyya* at the end of their period of isolation to remove the impurity of their widowhood and prepare a new personality. It is recommended that the seven stones for the lapidation of al-ʿAḳaba should be gathered at the *mash̲ʿar al-ḥaram* at Muzdalifa, outside of Minā. As a rule, the 63 others are gathered in the valley of Minā, but outside of the mosque and far from the *djamarāt* to avoid their having already been used (Ibn Taymiyya, 383). Besides, it is thought that stones accepted by Allāh are carried away by angels. Stones collected but not used should be buried; they have assumed a sacred character which makes them dangerous.

The model pilgrimage of the Prophet fixed the time of the *djamrat al-ʿAḳaba* for the day of the 10th D̲h̲u 'l-Ḥid̲jd̲ja. It shows him beginning the *ifāḍa* of Muzdalifa after the prayer at dawn (*fad̲jr*) and casting the stones after sunrise. But by survival of an ancient custom more than for reasons of convenience, other times are allowed by law. Al-S̲h̲āfiʿī, against the three other imāms, permits the ʿAḳaba ceremony before sunrise (Rifʿat, i, 113); in general, the time is extended to the whole morning (*ḍuḥā*), till afternoon (*zawāl*), till sunset, till night, till the morning of the day following; these infractions of the normal routine are atoned for by a sacrifice or alms, varying with the different schools. The *djamarāt* of the three days of the *tashrīḳ* take place in the *zawāl*: here again there are various opinions (al-Bukhārī, *Ḥad̲jd̲j*, *bāb* 134). In fixing the time of the lapidations, the law has always endeavoured to avoid any Muslim rite, e.g. prayer, coinciding with one of the three positions of the sun by day, rising, noon, setting. A.J. Wensinck asserted (in ḤAD̲JD̲J, at vol. III, 32b) the probability of the solar character of the pagan *ḥad̲jd̲j*.

Muḥammad made his lapidation at al-ʿAḳaba from the bottom of the valley, mounted on his camel, turned towards the *djamra*, with the Kaʿba on his left and Minā on his right, standing at a distance of five cubits (eight feet). But there are other possible positions. Rifʿat (i, 328) gives the *djamra* the following dimensions: 10 feet high and 6 feet broad on a rock 5 feet high (see the photographs, *ibid.*). It is said to have been removed at the beginning of Islam and replaced in 240/854-5 (al-Azraḳī, 212). Muḥammad made the lapidations of the other two *djamarāt* on foot, turning towards the *ḳibla*. In brief, the stones are cast in the attitude one happens to be in. The position facing the Great Devil is explained by the nature of the ground, but it would also be in keeping with the idea of a curse cast in the face of a fallen deity. The position which makes the pilgrim turn towards the Kaʿba is due to the Muslim legend of the tempter Satan and to the rule of the *takbīr*, which will be explained below.

According to the *sunna*, the stones are placed on the thumb and bent forefinger and thrown, one by one,

as in the game of marbles. However, the possibility of the stones having been thrown together in a handful has been foreseen, and it was decided that this should only count as one stone and that the omission could be made good. The stone should not be thrown violently nor should one call "look out! look out!" (al-Tirmidhī, iv, 136), a pagan custom which the modern Bedouins still retained until quite recently (Rifʿat, i, 89). It seems that Muḥammad put some strength into it, for he raised his hand "to the level of his right eyebrow" (al-Tirmidhī, iv, 135) and showed his armpit (al-Bukhārī, *Ḥad̲jd̲j*, *bāb* 141).

In Islam, the casting of each stone is accompanied by pious formulae. It is generally agreed that the *talbiya* is no longer pronounced at ʿArafa or at least before the lapidation of al-ʿAḳaba (al-Bukhārī, *Ḥad̲jd̲j* *bāb* 101); some writers however approve of it after al-ʿAḳaba. The *tahlīl* and *tasbīḥ* are permitted, but it is the *takbīr* which is recommended (Ibn Taymiyya, 382; al-Bukhārī, *Ḥad̲jd̲j*, *bāb*s 138, 143). The spiritual evolution of the rites even sees in this the essential feature of the rite, the throwing of the stone and the figure formed in throwing it by the thumb and forefinger forming an *ʿuḳd* which represents 70, being no more than symbolical and mnemonic gestures. "The throwing of the stones was only instituted to cause the name of God to be repeated" (al-Tirmidhī, iv, 139). To al-G̲h̲azālī (*Iḥyāʾ*, i, 192), it is an act of submission to God and of resistance to Satan, who seeks to turn man away from the fatigues of the *ḥad̲jd̲j*, but the rite is without rational explanation *min g̲h̲ayrⁱ ḥazzⁱⁿ li 'l-ʿaḳlⁱ wa 'l-nafsⁱ fīhi* (cf. Goldziher, *Richtungen*, 252). The devout man adds a prayer (*duʿāʾ*) which is as a rule quasi-ritual. The usual one is *Allāhumma 'd̲jʿalhu ḥad̲jd̲jⁱᵃⁿ mabrūrᵃⁿ wa-d̲h̲anbᵃⁿ mag̲h̲fūrᵃⁿ wa-saʿyᵃⁿ mashkūrᵃⁿ* "Lord, make this pilgrimage a pious one, pardon our sins and recompense our efforts!" There is, as a matter of fact, after the stoning, a halt, a *wuḳūf*, before the two higher *djamarāt*, that at the second being especially long: the duration is calculated by the recitation of the sūra of the Cow (II), or of Joseph (XII), or of the Family of ʿImrān (III) by altering the indication in the *ḥadīth* (al-Bukhārī, *Ḥad̲jd̲j*, *bāb*s 135-7). This would take the place of an ancient ceremony of imprecation.

Breaches of the rules for the performance of these diverse ceremonies, especially as regards the number of stones thrown and the time when they are thrown (*ʿUmda*, iv, 767 ff.; Rifʿat, i, 113), are punished by atonements, the exact nature of which the legists delight to vary, from the sacrifice of an animal to the giving of a *mudd* of food in alms.

The Muslim teachers have sought to explain the lapidations of Minā. Some exegetes (e.g. al-Ṭabarī, *Tafsīr*, xxv, 167) have seen quite clearly that they represent ancient rites and have compared the *ramy* of the tomb of Abū Rid̲jāl. Others are known, for example at the well of D̲h̲u 'l-Ḥulayfa (Lammens, *Bétyles*, 94). The works quoted [see ḤAD̲JD̲J] show the spread of this rite and the cases in which we are certain that it is a question of the driving away or the expulsion of evil. Stones used to be thrown behind an individual whom one wished never to return (al-Hamad̲h̲ānī, *Maḳāmāt*, ed. Beirut, 23). At Alexandria, tired people used to go and lie down on a fallen pillar, throw 7 stones behind them on a pile "like that of Minā", then go away quite recuperated (al-Ḳalḳas̲h̲andī, *Ṣubḥ al-aʿs̲h̲ā*, iii, 322). But comparisons would take us out of the region of Arabia (Lods, *Prophètes d'Israël*, 354).

Popular legend has connected the lapidation, like many other rites, with Abraham. It was Abraham or Hagar or Ishmael, or even Muḥammad, that Satan wished to deter from accomplishing the rites of the *ḥadjdj* and who chased him, whoever this was, away with stones. If we conclude that he is *radjīm*, we are some way to the explanation of sūra LXVII 5 (see above).

One would like to be able to locate the lapidations among the rites of the pre-Islamic pilgrimage. One would first have to have a clear idea of the meaning and details of the ceremonies and of the part played by lapidations and sacred piles of stones in Semitic and Mediterranean antiquity. Stoning seems to have been a rite of expulsion of evil which coincided with the deconsecration of the pilgrim and seems to protect his return to everyday life. It is possible that lapidations at one time followed the sacrifices which perhaps took place at ʿArafa and Muzdalifa.

To sum up, the lapidation at Minā has been by turns interpreted as a vestige of the cult of the dead (refs. in Lammens, *Le culte des bétyles*, 39 and esp. 96 ff.); a rite honouring protective deities, after the manner of the Ἑρμαῖον (refs. in Fahd, *La divination arabe*, 189 n. 1); a symbol of the expulsion of malevolent spirits (*averuncatio*), in the sense given by Tradition to the rite at Minā (refs. in *ibid.*, 189); a gesture of cursing against certain tombs of persons of sinister memory (*ibid.*, n. 3); and, finally, as an act of scopelism born out of the hatred of the nomads for the sedentaries (see V. Chauvin, *Le jet de pierres au pèlerinage à la Mekke*, in *Annales de l'Académie Royale d'Archéologie*, 74, 5th sér., iv [Antwerp 1902], 272-300, a thesis refuted by Van Vloten and Th. Houtsma; refs. in Fahd, 189 n. 4).

In regard to the basic sense of *djamra* [*q.v.*], pl. *djimār*, which designates, among other things, the tribe (*ḳabīla*), this rite seems merely to have been in origin a simple gesture of coming together, done by means of a ballot. In practice this term denotes essentially the internal uniting of all the fractions of a tribe or a tribal grouping (see *TA*, iii, 129: *al-djamra al-ḳabīla inḍammat fa-ṣārat yad^an wāḥidat^an lā tanḍammu ilā aḥad^in wa-lā tuḥālifu ghayra-hā*). Thus "the secondary sense, expressed in *djamra*, pl. *djimār*, 'pile of pebbles', allows the gesture of union, which renews the tribe periodically or occasionally, to be represented as being like the throwing of a pebble on a precise spot, near to a sacred site or in the midst of an encampment, done by all the members of the tribe or by the heads of the clans composing it, and thus symbolising the indissoluble unity of the tribe and its adhesion to a decision which has been taken. The standing at Minā which ends the sacred sequence of the Pilgrimage, before entry into the sacred city, lends itself well to the idea of a renewal of a pact of union between clans and tribes. In short, the basic aim of the Meccan Pilgrimage was to serve as a rallying point for all the Arab tribes, involving the exclusion of all outsiders, in order to put an end to the internal quarrels between tribes and in order to undertake common action aimed at permanently opposing all outside intervention in this inviolable centre of the Arabian peninsula" (Fahd, *op. cit.*, 190).

Bibliography (in addition to references given in the article): Ibrāhīm Rifʿat Pasha, *Mirʾāt al-Ḥaramayn*, Cairo 1344/1925-6, 2 vols.; Ibn Taymiyya, *Risālat Manāsik al-ḥadjdj*, in *Madjmūʿat al-rasāʾil al-kubrā*, Cairo 1323/1905, ii, 355; T. Fahd, *La divination arabe*, Paris 1987, 188-95.

(M. Gaudefroy-Demombynes-[T. Fahd])

RĀDJMAHĀL, a former city of Muslim Bengal during Mughal times, now a small town 6 km/4 miles to the east of the ruinous Mughal site, in the Santāl Parganas District of Bihār Province in the Indian Union (lat. 25° 3′N, long. 87° 50′E.). To its west run the basaltic Rādjmahāl Hills of central Bihār. Rādjmahāl city grew up in the strategically important gap between the Hills and the right bank of the Ganges, a corridor defended in Mughal times by the fortress of Teliāgarhi.

When the Rādjput governor of the Mughals, Mān Singh [*q.v.*], had in 1000/1592 conquered Orissa [see Úrisā], he made the existing settlement Agmahāl into Rādjmahāl and into the capital of Bengal, and it remained the capital until this was moved to Dacca/Dhaka [*q.v.*] in 1069/1659. European travellers testify to the importance of Rādjmahāl, which, with Dhaka, was one of Bengal's two minting centres. It still had probably some 25,000 to 30,000 inhabitants in the early 19th century, but its prosperity was adversely affected by changes in the channels of the Ganges. It is now notable for a remarkably large number of significant monuments of Mughal architecture, many now ruinous, including the Akbarī mosque, the Čhoṭa ("small") mosque, the Djumma mosque, the enormous Djāmiʿ mosque, etc.

Bibliography: *Imperial gazetteer of India*², xxi, 76-8; Catherine B. Asher, in G. Michel (ed.), *The Islamic heritage of Bengal*, UNESCO Paris 1984, 116-27, with further references. (C.E. Bosworth)

RĀDJPŪTĀNA [see Rādjāsthān in Suppl.].

RĀDJPŪTS, inhabitants of India, who claim to be the modern representatives of the Kshatriyas of ancient tradition. (From the Sanskrit *rādjaputra* "a king's son". For the connection between Rādjanya and Kshatriya see Macdonell and Keith, *Vedic index*, i, s.v. Kṣatriya) The term Rādjpūt has no racial significance. It simply denotes a tribe, clan, or warlike class, the members of which claim aristocratic rank, a claim generally reinforced by Brahman recognition.

The origin of the Rādjpūts is a problem which bristles with difficulties. The theory which was held earlier this century was that propounded by Bhandarkar, Smith and Crooke. According to this theory, the Rādjpūts can be divided into two main classes, the foreign and the indigenous. The foreign clans, such as the Čawhāns, Čālukyas, and Gurdjaras, are the descendants of invaders of the 5th and 6th centuries of the Christian era. The indigenous Rādjpūts include the Rāshtrākūtas of the Deccan, the Rāthors of Rādjpūtāna proper, and the Čandēls and Bundēlas of Bundēlkhand.

The theory that certain Rādjpūt clans are of foreign extraction is chiefly based on Rādjpūt legends and folklore, according to which there are three branches of Rādjpūts: the Sūradjbansi, or Solar race; the Čandrabansi, or Lunar race; and the Agni Kula, or Fire-group. The legend relates how the Agni Kula Rādjpūts, that is, the Čawhāns, Čalukyas, Parihārs (Pratihāras), and the Pramāra, originated in a fire-pit around Mount Abu in southern Rādjpūtāna. From this it has been concluded that the four clans in this group are related and that the fire-pit represents a rite of purgation by which the taint of foreign extraction was removed. Since these writers believed the Parihārs to be invaders of Gurdjar stock, it was concluded that the other three Agni Kula clans were also invaders.

According to Smith, the Gurdjaras were invaders who founded a kingdom around Mount Abu. In time the rulers of this kingdom, who were known as Gurdjara-Pratihāras, conquered Kanawdj [*q.v.*] and became the paramount power in northern India about 800 A.D. Smith contends that the Pratihāras were a clan of the Gurdjara tribe. This seems to be the chief evidence produced by these writers for the foreign extraction of certain Rād͟jpūt clans.

It seems wrong to base this theory of foreign descent principally upon the Agni Kula legend, for Waidya and other writers have proved this to be a myth first heard of in the *Prit͟hwīrād͟j-rāisā* of the poet Čand, who could not have composed this work before the 12th century A.D. Recent research has brought to light the fact that the inscriptions of the Pratihāras and Čawhāns before the 12th century represent them as Solar Rād͟jpūts, while the Čālukyas are represented as of the Lunar race. The Agni Kula legend does not therefore deserve the prominence given to it by Smith and other writers. Even the contention that the Pratihāras were a branch of the Gurd͟jara tribe has met with much hostile criticism.

According to the orthodox Hindu view, the Rād͟jpūts are the direct descendants of the Ks͟hatriyas of the Vedic polity, but this claim is based on fictitious genealogies. The Ks͟hatriyas of ancient India disappear from history, and this can probably be explained by invasions from Central Asia which shattered the ancient Hindu polity. It is accepted that these invading hordes, such as the Yüeh-či and Hūṅas, became rapidly Hinduised, and that their leaders assumed Ks͟hatriya rank and were recognised as such. Out of this chaos arose a new Hindu polity with new rulers, and the families of invaders which became supreme were recognised as Ks͟hatriyas or Rād͟jpūts. In later times, many chiefs of the so-called aboriginal tribes also assumed the title of Rād͟jpūt.

It is therefore safe to assert that the Rād͟jpūts are a very heterogeneous body and probably contain some survivors of the older Ks͟hatriyas. A mass of legend arose assigning to the various clans a descent from the sun and the moon, or from the heroes of the epic poems. These are the legendary pedigrees recorded in great detail by Tod. The main argument which can be brought forward in support of the foreign descent of certain Rād͟jpūt clans is the incorporation of foreigners into the fold of Hinduism to which the whole history of India bears testimony. Even though the Agni Kula legend be discredited, it is still possible to argue that the Rād͟jpūts are not a race. Anthropologically they are definitely of mixed origin. That some Rād͟jpūts were of foreign origin can be proved by the acceptance of the Hūṅas in the recognised list of Rād͟jpūt tribes.

Whatever may be the origin of the Rād͟jpūts, we know that disorder and political disintegration followed the death of Hars͟ha, and that until the Muslim invasions of northern India the chief characteristic of this period was the growth and development of the Rād͟jpūt clans. Except for about two hundred years, when the Gurd͟jara-Pratihāras were the paramount power in Hindustān, there was constant internecine warfare between the various Rād͟jpūt kingdoms. This weakness considerably facilitated the Muslim conquest. It was not, however, until the days of Muḥammad of G͟hūr that the Rād͟jpūt dynasties in the plains were finally overthrown [see MUḤAMMAD B. SĀM, MUʿIZZ AL-DĪN]. Driven from Dihlī and Kanawd͟j, they retreated into modern Rād͟jpūtāna [see RĀD͟JĀSTHĀN in Suppl.] where they eventually built up a strong position and were able to resist the Muslim invader, for it cannot be said that the Sultans of Dihlī ever really subdued the Rād͟jpūts of Rād͟jpūtāna. Nevertheless, throughout this period there was constant warfare, fortresses and strongholds frequently changing hands. The Rād͟jpūts nearest to Dihlī were naturally the weakest because the eastern frontier of Rād͟jputāna was exposed to attack. The Sultans of Dihlī appear to have realised the value of communications with the western coast, and we find that the route between Dihlī and Gud͟jarāt via Ad͟jmēr was usually open to imperial armies. The chief menace to the Rād͟jpūts was not from Dihlī but from the independent Muslim kingdoms of Gud͟jarāt [*q.v.*] and Mālwā [*q.v.*].

The outstanding feature of the period from the end of the so-called Sayyid rule to the final invasion of Bābur [*q.v.*] was the growth of Rād͟jpūt power in northern India under Rānā Sāṅgā [*q.v.*] of Mēwāṙ [*q.v.*]. Taking advantage of the weakness of the Lōdīs [*q.v.*] under Ibrāhīm and of the war between Gud͟jarāt and Mālwā, he had extended his sway over the greater part of modern Rād͟jpūtāna. The battle of K͟hānuʾā in 1527, when Bābur shattered his power, marks a turning-point in the history of Muslim rule in India, for the Rād͟jpūts never again attempted to regain their lost dominions on the plains and contented themselves with remaining on the defensive. After K͟hānuʾā, the place of the Sesodias in Rād͟jpūt politics was taken by the Rāthors, the growth of whose power under Maldēō of Mārwār was facilitated by the struggle between Humāyūn [*q.v.*] and S͟hēr S͟hāh. Akbar's Rād͟jpūt policy was based on conquest and conciliation. The fall of Čitawṙ and Ranthambhōr made him master of the greater part of Rād͟jputāna, with the exception of Mēwāṙ [*q.v.*], which was not completely subdued until the reign of D͟jahāngīr [*q.v.*]. The reversal of Akbar's conciliatory policy produced the great Hindu reaction of Awrangzīb's reign, when, faced at the same time with the Rād͟jpūts of the north and the Marāṭhās [*q.v.*] of the Deccan, Awrangzīb [*q.v.*] was unable to concentrate on either campaign. But internal dissensions once more prevented the Rād͟jpūts from taking advantage of the decline of Mug͟hal power, and, in the second half of the 18th century, they proved no match for the Marāṭhās, who easily overran their country. It was not until the beginning of the 19th century, when the British were at war with the Marāṭhās, that they entered into political relations with the Rād͟jpūt states. Before the end of the year 1818, the group of states which in British Indian times comprised Rād͟jpūtāna had been taken under British protection.

In British India of the 1930s, there were 10,743,091 Rād͟jpūts distributed throughout the country as follows: United Provinces, 3,756,936; Pand͟jāb, 2,351,650; Bihār and Orissa, 1,412,440; Rād͟jputāna, 669,516; Central Provinces and Berār, 506,087; Gwāliōr, 393,076; Central India, 388,942; Bombay, 352,016; D͟jammū and Kas͟hmīr, 256,020; Western India States, 227,153; Bengal, 156,978; Baroda, 94,893; and Ḥaydarābad 88,434 (1931 *Census report*). It will be noted that, in Rād͟jpūtāna, only 669,516 Rād͟jpūts were to be found out of a total population of 11,225,712. The native states of Rād͟jpūtāna were ruled by Rād͟jpūts, with the exception of Tonk, which was Muslim, and Bharatpur and Dholpur, which was D͟jāt. the chief Rād͟jpūt clans in Rād͟jpūtāna are the Rāthor, Kačhwāha, Čawhān, D͟jādon, Sesodia, Ponwar, Parihār, Tonwar and D͟jhāla. Rād͟jasthānī is the mother tongue of 77% of the inhabitants of this area. It is interesting to note that in some parts of India, Rād͟jpūts have embraced Islam, as for example the Manhās, Kātils and Salahria of the Pand͟jāb.

Bibliography: In addition to the standard works on the history of India, see C.U. Aitchison, *Treaties, engagements, and sanads*, iii, 1909; D.R. Bhandarkar, *Gurjaras*, in *JBBRAS*, xxi (1902-4); W. Crooke, *Rājputs and Mahrattas*, in *J.R. Anthropological Institute*, xi (1910); K.D. Erskine, *The Western Rajputana States*, 1909; R.C. Majumdar, *The Gurjara-*

Pratihāras, in *Journal of the Department of Letters*, Calcutta University, x (1923); M.S. Mehta, *Lord Hastings and the Indian States*, 1930; G.H. Ojha, *Rājpūtāne kā Itihās*, fasc. i, Adjmēr 1925, ii, 1927; B.N. Reu, *History of the Rāshtrakūtas* (*Rāthōdas*), Jodhpur 1933; A.H. Rose, *Glossary of the tribes and castes of the Punjab and North-West Frontier Province*, 1914, iii, s.v. Rajputs; R.V. Russell, *Tribes and castes of the Central Provinces*, iv, 1916; V.A. Smith, *The Gurjaras of Rājputana and Kanauj*, in *JRAS* (1909); J. Tod, *Annals and antiquities of Rajasthan*, 3 vols., 1920; C.V. Vaidya, *History of mediaeval Hindu India*, 3 vols., Poona 1921-6; R.C. Majumdar *et alii* (eds.), *The history and culture of the Indian people. v. The struggle for empire*², Bombay 1966, 61 ff., 161 ff.; *ibid.*, vi. *The Delhi Sultanate*, Bombay 1960, 326-61; A. Wink, *Al-Hind. The making of the Indo-Islamic world*, i, Leiden 1990, 277-303.

(C. Collin Davies)

RĀDKĀN, the site of a mediaeval Islamic monument in northern Persia. The tomb tower (Iranian National Monument 145) sits on the edge of an isolated, 1,300 metre long valley in the Alburz Mountains north of the Nikā River, 70 km/43 miles east of Nikā in the province of Māzandarān. It is often known as Rādkān West to distinguish it from another tomb tower, the Mīl-i Rādkān at Rādkān East near Ṭūs in Khurāsān. The cylindrical tower (height 35 m; exterior diameter 9.8 m; interior diameter 5.80 m) is built of baked brick and is topped with a conical roof. An inscription plaque in terra cotta once stood over the entrance doorway, and another inscription band in Pahlavi and Arabic (illustrated in kitābāt, Pl. XIX, no. 22) encircles the tower below the roof. Both record that the patron was the *amīr* and *ispahbad* Abū Djaʿfar Muḥammad b. Wandarīn Bāwand and that the building was constructed during his lifetime between Rabīʿ II 407/September-October 1016 and 411/1020-1. He was a member of the first branch of the Bāwand [*q.v.*] dynasty, the Kayūsiyya, which ruled the mountainous area south of the Caspian 45-397/665-1006. The family lost power when the *ispahbad* Shahriyār revolted against the Ziyārid Ḳābūs b. Wushmgīr [*q.v.*], was captured, and later executed, but several local princes such as Muḥammad b. Wandarīn continued to rule in isolated localities. The tomb tower at Rādkān exemplifies a type of funerary construction which became common in the area at the time (the most striking example is the stellate tower that Ḳābūs ordered in 397/1006-7 at nearby Gunbadh-i Ḳābūs) and is remarkable for its superb inscriptions in plaited Kūfic script.

Bibliography: E. Diez, *Churasanische Baudenkmäler*, Berlin 1918, 36-9, 87-100; *RCEA*, nos. 2312-13; E. Herzfeld, *Postsasanidische Inschriften*, in *Archaeologischen Mitteilungen aus Iran*, iv (1933), 140-7; S.S. Blair, *The monumental inscriptions from early Islamic Iran and Transoxiana*, Leiden, 1991, no. 31.

(Sheila S. Blair)

al-**RĀDŪYĀNĪ**, Muḥammad b. ʿUmar, author of the first Persian treatise on rhetoric, the *Kitāb Tardjumān al-balāgha*. The little that can be inferred about the author's life is known from the *Tardjumān* itself; no other source mentions him. According to the researches of A. Ateş, he seems to have lived in Transoxania, and his book was written between 481/1088, the beginning of the Karakhānid Aḥmad Khān's incarceration at the hand of Malik Shāh, as mentioned in one of the poems quoted, and 507/1114, the date of the unique ms. of the *Tardjumān*, the *madjmūʿa* Istanbul, Fatih 5413, fols. 233a-290a.

As al-Rādūyānī explicitly states (*Tardjumān*, 3), his book was modelled on the Arabic *Maḥāsin al-kalām* of Abu 'l-Ḥasan Naṣr b. al-Ḥasan al-Marghīnānī, recently published by G.J. van Gelder as *K. al-Maḥāsin fi 'l-naẓm wa 'l-nathr* (see *Bibl.*). However, in spite of his assertion, there are substantial differences between the two works in size and structure, e.g. the *Maḥāsin* has about 33 rhetorical figures as opposed to 73 in the *Tardjumān*, the figures being slightly misleading because of different taxonomies; also, the *Maḥāsin* uses examples from Ḳurʾān and Ḥadīth, which are totally lacking in the *Tardjumān* (see further, Ateş, Introd. to *Tardjumān*, 39-42).

The *Tardjumān* in turn was known to Rashīd al-Dīn-i Waṭwāṭ (d. 573/1177 [*q.v.*]), who found it lacking and wrote his own *Ḥadāʾiḳ al-siḥr fī daḳāʾiḳ al-shiʿr* to supersede it (*Ḥadāʾiḳ*, 1). He does not mention the author's name. Later sources do not seem to have had direct access to the *Tardjumān* and uniformly attribute it to the poet Farrukhī (d. 429/1037-8 (?) [*q.v.*]).

Whereas Waṭwāṭ adduces both Persian and Arabic examples, all poetic examples in the *Tardjumān* are in Persian. Due to its early date it is an important source for the beginnings of Persian poetry (see Ateş, *Etude*, and Lazard).

Bibliography: Ahmed Ateş (ed. and introd.), *Kitāb Tarcumān al-balāġa yazan Muhammed b. ʿOmar ar-Rādūyānī*, Istanbul 1949 (contains also a facs. of the ms.), an earlier version of the introd. in a German tr. by H. Ritter, in *Oriens*, i (1948), 45-52; idem, *Etude sur le Tarcumān al-balāġa et sur la manière dont la poésie persane s'est conservée jusqu'à nos jours*, in *Türk Dili ve Edebiyatı Dergisi*, iii (1949), 257-65; G.J. van Gelder (ed.), *Two Arabic treatises on stylistics: al-Marghīnānī's* al-Maḥāsin fi 'l-naẓm wa-'l-nathr *and Ibn Aflaḥ's* Muqaddima, *formerly ascribed to al-Marghīnānī*, Istanbul 1987; Rashīd al-Dīn-i Waṭwāṭ, *Ḥadāʾiḳ al-siḥr fī daḳāʾiḳ al-shiʿr*, ed. ʿAbbās Iḳbāl, Tehran 1339/[1960]; G. Lazard, *Les premiers poètes persans* (*IXe-Xe siècles*), 2 vols., Tehran 1964.

(W.P. Heinrichs)

RAḌWĀ, the name of the crags west of Medina, occasionally mentioned in connection with the mountain Thabīr (*Sīrat al-Ḥabasha*, 86). Lying behind Yanbuʿ, between the regions of Madyan [see madyan shuʿayb] and Mecca, they were known to Ptolemy (Sprenger, *Die alte Geographie*, nos. 28, 30) and are mentioned by Ibn Isḥāḳ (*The life of Muhammad*, tr. 413, 542). Al-Hamadhānī quotes a tradition, according to which the Prophet said: "May God be satisfied (*raḍiya*) with it (Raḍwā)!" Abū Karib, leader of the Kuraybiyya [*q.v.*], a sub-sect of the Kaysāniyya, is said to have believed that Muḥammad b. al-Ḥanafiyya, a son of ʿAlī b. Abī Ṭālib, was alive hidden in the mountains of Raḍwā.

Bibliography: Ḥasan b. Aḥmad al-Ḥaymī, *Sīrat al-Ḥabasha*, ed. and tr. E. van Donzel, Stuttgart 1986; A. Sprenger, *Die alte Geographie Arabiens als Grundlage der Entwicklungsgeschichte des Semitismus*, repr. Amsterdam 1966; Ibn Isḥāḳ, *The life of Muhammad*, tr. A. Guillaume, London-New York 1955; Ibn al-Faḳīh al-Hamadhānī, *Abrégé du Livre des Pays*, tr. H. Massé, ed. by Ch. Pellat, Damascus 1973, 25, 30, 257; D.H. Hogarth, *The penetration of Arabia*, New York 1904, 182, 289; A. Musil, *The northern Ḥeǧāz, a topographical itinerary*, New York 1926; A. Al-Wohaibi, *The northern Hijaz in the writings of the Arab geographers 800-1150*, Beirut 1973.

(Ed.)

RAFʿ (a.), literally, "elevation, the act of raising something".

1. *As a technical term of Arabic grammar*

Here it denotes the vowel /u/ which affects the final

consonant of words (nouns and verbs) which are inflected (*muᶜrab*). The term indicates not a function but the position of the tongue "raised" (*marfūᶜ*) towards the top of the palate in order to pronounce the vowel /u/. European grammarians see in this vowel the mark of the nominative case of nouns and the mark of the indicative mood in verbs.

Nouns "raised" (*marfūᶜāt*) by the vowel /u/ are of five kinds:

(1) The inchoative (*mubtadaʾ*), which is to be connected (*musnad*) with an item of information, and which is stripped (*mudjarrad, muᶜarrā*) of any regent (*ᶜāmil*) which is expressed (*lafz̲ī*); it is "raised" by the fact of beginning a piece of speech utterance (*ibtidāʾ*), which is an understood (*maᶜnawī*) regent.

(2) The noun which is a predicate (*k̲h̲abar*), to which the inchoative is connected (*musnad ilayhi*). For certain of the Baṣran grammarians (including Sībawayh and Ibn al-Sarrādj), it is "raised" at the same time by both the act of beginning and by the noun which forms this; for other Baṣran grammarians, it is "raised" by the act of beginning by means of (*bi-wāsiṭa*) the noun which forms this; for the Kūfans, it is "raised" solely by the act of beginning.

(3) The noun which is an agent (*fāᶜil*) built upon a verb formed (*buniya*) for it and to which it is connected; it is "raised" by this verb, which is what one is talking about (*mā yuḥaddat̲h̲ ᶜanhu*).

(4) The noun which is a direct object (*mafᶜūl bihi*) built upon a verb formed by it and to which it is connected, but whose agent is not named (*summiya*); it is "raised" by this verb, which is what one is talking about (*mā yuḥaddat̲h̲ ᶜanhu*).

(5) The noun which is assimilated (*mus̲h̲abbah*) to the agent in actual utterance (*lafz̲*). This noun comes after incomplete verbs, such as *kāna* and its sisters, which are not genuine (*ḥaḳīḳī*) verbs, since they express only time. It can also come after two negative particles assimilated to these verbs, such as *mā* and *lāta* in the dialect of the Ḥidjāz; it is "raised" by this verb or by this particle.

As for the "similar" (*muḍāriᶜ* [*q.v.*]) verb, it is "raised" by an understood (*maᶜnawī*) regent, which is the fact that it occupies (*wuḳūᶜ*) the place (*mawḳiᶜ*) of a noun, whatever its inflexion might be.

Bibliography: G. Troupeau, *Lexique-Index du Kitāb de Sībawayhi*, 101-2; Mubarrad, *K. al-Muḳtaḍab*, ed. ᶜUḍayma, i, 8-9, iv, 126-35; Ibn al-Sarrādj, *K. al-Uṣūl*, ed. Fatlī, i, 58-98, ii, 146-7; Ibn al-Anbārī, *K. Asrār al-ᶜarabiyya*, ed. Seybold, 28-41, 124-9; Ibn Yaᶜīs̲h̲, *S̲h̲arḥ al-Mufaṣṣal*, ed. Cairo, i, 74-101, vii, 12-14.   (G. Troupeau)

2. As a technical term in the science of Muslim tradition = *ḥadīt̲h̲* [*q.v.*].

Beside the verbal noun, the passive participle *marfūᶜ* (plural *marfūᶜāt*), "lifted up", is commonly used. An *isnād* [*q.v.*] of a tradition is *marfūᶜ*, when it is, as it were, "lifted up", sc. to the level of the Prophet Muḥammad, supporting a *matn* (= text) containing either his words and/or describing some activity of his as transmitted by one of his Companions. (In contrast, when the transmission of such a tradition is put in the mouth of a Successor, who could not possibly have been present, or someone who lived even later, one speaks of a *mursal* [*q.v.*] *isnād*; on the other hand, when the text of a tradition does not contain a mention of the Prophet, but describes the words and/or deeds of a Companion or somebody later, tradition science defines that as a *mawḳūf* tradition, a qualification also applied to its *isnād*, since it has literally "stopped" at the Companion.)

During the initial stages of *ḥadīt̲h̲* transmission, a time roughly coinciding with the first three quarters of the 1st/7th century, the necessity of naming one's source(s) was not yet generally felt. In the course of the last few decades of that century, however, the *isnād* as authentication device came into use. In order to validate a report of which one claimed that it described an event of the past, one was requested to call an older authority to witness. The earliest *isnād*s contained only one name, mostly that of an alleged expert in legal or ritual matters, a Companion or somebody of a later generation, resulting in a *mawḳūf isnād* strand, or the Prophet himself, resulting in a *mursal isnād*, thus without a Companion. But, as a result of inaccurate handling of *isnād*s and/or because of widespread *isnād* fabrication, they became subject to a more sophisticated evaluation, which resulted in the course of time in fully-fledged *isnād* criticism. Merely supplying *mawḳūf* or *mursal isnād*s in an attempt to guarantee the veracity of a report which one wished to circulate was no longer sufficient, and the call for *isnād*s ending in a Companion, who reported on the authority of the Prophet, became louder. Muslim tradition scholars generally credit the founder of the legal school that bears his name, Muḥammad b. Idrīs al-S̲h̲āfiᶜī (d. 204/820) [*q.v.*], with the foresight of having been the first to emphasise the authority of *marfūᶜ isnād*s, more so than the other types of *isnād* strands. This was also underlined in western studies, notably in those of J. Schacht (cf. his *The origins of Muhammadan jurisprudence*, Oxford 1950, ch. 3). As from al-S̲h̲āfiᶜī's days, the prestige of these latter types began to diminish and traditions supported by them gradually failed to attract the attention of tradition collectors, while supplying *marfūᶜ isnād* strands, which in the beginning were vastly outnumbered by the other types as is especially clear in the pre-canonical *ḥadīt̲h̲* collections, became the rule.

The qualification *marfūᶜ* for an *isnād* strand does not necessarily imply that it is at the same time beyond criticism. To be considered unassailable, the strand has to show up an uninterrupted string of names of known transmitters, from the Prophet to the collector in whose collection that strand turns up. At the same time, each pair of transmitters in that string of names must be believed to have transmitted from one another. For this quality of a strand the technical term *muttaṣil* is used. Because not each *muttaṣil* strand is *marfūᶜ*, but can "stop" at a Companion (= *muttaṣil mawḳūf*) and because not every *marfūᶜ* is at the same time *muttaṣil* (e.g. a *munḳaṭiᶜ marfūᶜ*), a strand deemed genuinely reliable has to be both *marfūᶜ* as well as *muttaṣil*; for both terms taken together the technical term *musnad* [*q.v.*] came into use. It is only a tradition with a *matn* supported by a *musnad isnād* strand which may have a claim to be considered *ṣaḥīḥ* [*q.v.*], "sound".

The Arabic root *r-f-ᶜ* has given rise to yet another derivative being widely used in a technical sense in the context of *ḥadīt̲h̲*. With the prestige of *marfūᶜ* strands gradually increasing, but especially after al-S̲h̲āfiᶜī's insistence on them, many transmitters became known as *raffāᶜūn*, i.e. people who developed the habit of frequently "raising" *isnād* strands "to the level" of *marfūᶜāt*, either by inserting the name of a Companion in *mursal* strands which they had, or replacing the actor in a *mawḳūf*-supported *matn* by the Prophet.

In later times certain form rules were less strictly observed. Thus the mention of the Prophet was often dropped in a saying ascribed to him by the mere addition of the adverbially used *marfūᶜan* after the name of the Companion of that saying's *isnād* strand. Alternative loose formulae for this were the verbal forms *yarfaᶜu ʾl-ḥadīt̲h̲, yanmīhi, yablug̲h̲u bihi* or *riwāyatan* im-

ADDENDA AND CORRIGENDA

VOLUME II
P. 862b, **FĀṬIMIDS,** *add to Bibl.*: H. Halm, *Das Reich des Mahdi. Der Aufsteig der Fatimiden (875-973)*, Munich 1991.

VOLUME III
P. 736b, **IBN BAṬṬŪṬA,** *add to Bibl.*: H.A.R. Gibb (tr.), *The travels*, iii, Cambridge 1971; R.E. Dunn, *The adventures of Ibn Battuta, a Muslim traveller of the 14th century*, Berkeley and Los Angeles 1986.

VOLUME V
P. 231b, **KITĀBĀT.** 9. Iran and Transoxania, *add to Bibl.*: Sheila S. Blair, *The monumental inscriptions from early Islamic Iran and Transoxania* (Studies in Islamic art and architecture, supplements to *Muqarnas*, v), Leiden 1992.

VOLUME VI
P. 750a, **MASRAḤ.** 1. In the Arab East, *add to Bibl.*: S. Moreh, *Live theatre and dramatic literature in the medieval Arabic world*, Edinburgh 1992.

VOLUME VII
P. 977a, **NASHWĀN B. SAʿĪD,** *add to Bibl.*: Ismāʿīl b. ʿAlī al-Akwaʿ, *Naschwān Ibn Saʿīd al-Ḥimyarī und die geistigen, religiösen und politischen Auseinandersetzungen seines Epoche*, in Werner Daum (ed.), *Jemen*, Innsbruck and Frankfurt/Main 1987, 205-16 (English ed. 1988).

ISBN 90 04 09811 9

PRINTED IN THE NETHERLANDS

E ENCYCLOPAEDIA OF ISLAM

NEW EDITION

PREPARED BY A NUMBER OF
LEADING ORIENTALISTS

EDITED BY

. E. BOSWORTH, E. VAN DONZEL, W. P. HEINRICHS AND G. LECOMTE

ASSISTED BY P.J. BEARMAN AND MME S. NURIT

UNDER THE PATRONAGE OF
THE INTERNATIONAL UNION OF ACADEMIES

VOLUME VIII

FASCICULES 137-138

RAFʿ — RIḌĀ SHĀH

TUTA SUB AEGIDE PALLAS · 1683 ·

LEIDEN
E.J. BRILL
1994

All correspondence on editorial matters should be addressed to the Editors, at the following address:

The Encyclopaedia of Islam, c/o E.J. Brill, P.O. Box 9000, 2300 PA Leiden, The Netherlands

AUTHORS OF ARTICLES IN THESE FASCICULES:

Feroz Ahmad, University of Massachusetts. 511
A. Arioli, University of Rome. 389
[F. Babinger, Munich]. 391, 393, 419, 422
M.A. Bakhit, University of Amman, Jordan. 385
Çiğdem Balim, University of Manchester. 484
[E. Berthels]. 478
Th. Bianquis, University of Lyon. 396
[W. Björkman, Uppsala]. 481
F.C. de Blois, Royal Asiatic Society, London. 445
C.E. Bosworth, University of Manchester. 385, 386, 393, 403, 404, 417, 450, 453, 460, 463, 469, 470, 473
Barbara Brend, London. 453
J.T.P. de Bruijn, University of Leiden. 423
Kathleen Burrill, Princeton, NJ. 490
Y. Callot, University of Tours. 481
Sheila R. Canby, British Museum, London. 510
J. Chabbi, University of Paris. 506
P. Chelkowski, New York University. 465
M. Chenoufi, University of Tunis. 402
F. Daftary, Institute of Ismaili Studies, London. 443
[C.C. Davies, Oxford]. 426
[J. Deny, Paris]. 483
W. Ende, University of Freiburg im Breisgau. 448
Suraiya Faroqhi, University of Munich. 406, 489
Maribel Fierro, University of Madrid. 480
J. Fontaine, Institut des Belles Lettres Arabes, Tunis. 471
Teresa Garulo, University of Madrid. 407
D. Gimaret, Ecole Pratique des Hautes Etudes, Paris. 399
L.E. Goodman, University of Hawaii at Manoa. 477
A.H. de Groot, University of Leiden. 480
M. Guettat, Institut Supérieur de Musique, Tunis. 449
H. Halm, University of Tübingen. 438, 468
A. Havemann, Free University, Berlin. 403
G.R. Hawting, University of London. 466
W.P. Heinrichs, Harvard University. 428
[B. Heller, Budapest]. 397
Carole Hillenbrand, University of Edinburgh. 440, 461
[E. Honigmann]. 424, 435
M.B. Hooker, Australian National University, Canberra. 483
Virginia Matheson Hooker, Australian National University, Canberra. 491
Halil İnalcik, Bilkent University, Ankara. 487
Renate Jacobi, University of the Saar, Saarbrücken. 398, 467
G.H.A. Juynboll, The Hague. 385, 421
O. Kahl, Frankfurt am Main. 417
[R.A. Kern, Leiden]. 433
R.G. Khoury, University of Heidelberg. 409, 478
G.R.D. King, University of London. 436, 437
A. Knysh, University of Northern Colorado, Greeley. 430
E. Kohlberg, The Hebrew University, Jerusalem. 389, 463
Remke Kruk, University of Leiden. 407
[E. Lévi-Provençal, Paris]. 441
D. MacEoin, University of Durham. 451
W. Madelung, University of Oxford. 454
[G. Marçais, Paris]. 415
[D.S. Margoliouth, Oxford]. 400
[H. Massé, Paris]. 431, 511
K. McPherson, University of Western Australia, Nedlands. 469
M. Meinecke, Museum für Islamische Kunst, Berlin-Dahlem. 414
[V. Minorsky]. 473
J.-P. Molénat, Centre National de la Recherche Scientifique, Paris. 474
D.O. Morgan, University of London. 444
D.W. Morray, University College Dublin. 460
E. Neubauer, University of Frankfurt. 422
B. O'Kane, American University of Cairo. 509
[H. Pérès, University of Algiers]. 420
[M. Plessner, Jerusalem]. 418
L. Pouzet, Saint-Joseph University, Beirut. 460
Nasser Rabbat, Massachusetts Institute of Technology, Cambridge. 433, 506
Munibur Rahman, University of Oakland, Rochester, Mich. 442, 448
F. Rosenthal, Yale University, New Haven. 451
A. Rouaud, Centre National de la Recherche Scientifique, Paris. 438
E.K. Rowson, University of Pennsylvania, Philadelphia. 390
[J. Schacht, New York]. 400, 493
Annemarie Schimmel, Bonn. 416
J. Schmidt, University of Manchester. 509
[Moḥammad Shafīʿ, Lahore]. 386, 459
Elizabeth M. Sirriyeh, University of Leeds. 439
P. Sluglett, University of Durham. 446
G.R. Smith, University of Manchester. 454, 457
S. Soucek, Princeton. 403
W. Stoetzer, University of Leiden. 421
M. Talbi, University of Tunis. 466
J.F. Troin, University of Tours. 508
Odile Verberkmoes, Wijk bij Duurstede. 407
D.J. Wasserstein, Tel-Aviv University. 479
O. Weintritt, University of Freiburg. 465
R. Weipert, University of Munich. 401
[A.J. Wensinck]. 397, 455, 459
J.J. Witkam, University of Leiden. 410
Christine Woodhead, University of Durham. 441
E.J. Zürcher, University of Nijmegen. 486
A. Zysow, University of Washington, Seattle. 425

Names in square brackets are those of authors of articles reprinted or revised from the first edition of this Encyclopaedia.

The preparation of these fascicules of the Encyclopaedia of Islam was made possible in part through grants from the Research Tools Program of the National Endowment for the Humanities, an independent Federal Agency of the United States Government; the British Academy; the Oriental Institute, Leiden; Académie des mediately following the name of the Companion in an *isnād* strand. Reports, furthermore, in which Companions are alleged to have said: "We used to do (or say) such and such a thing in the time of the Prophet", were considered *mawḳūf* as to the actual wording but *marfūᶜ* as to the underlying meaning, since they implied Muḥammad's tacit approval, in Arabic *taḳrīr* (plural *taḳrīrāt*). Moreover, although Muḥammad's name is not mentioned, additional statements in a *matn* such as: "... while the Ḳurʾān was still being revealed", or a Companion's assertion that a certain Ḳurʾān verse pertained to one particular situation to which he bore witness, were likewise considered to be *marfūᶜ*-supported, but only by implication.

Bibliography: For the usages of the derivatives of *r-f-ᶜ* and accompanying casuistry, including juridical authority, see Ibn al-Ṣalāḥ, *al-Muḳaddima* [*fī ᶜulum al-ḥadīth*], ed. ᶜĀʾisha ᶜAbd al-Raḥmān Bint al-Shāṭiʾ, Cairo 1974, 122-30; Nawawī, *Taḳrīb*, tr. W. Marçais in *JA*, 9ᵉ série, xvi (1900), 506-13; Suyūṭī, *Tadrīb al-rāwī*, ed. ᶜA. ᶜAbd al-Laṭīf, 183-93; al-Khaṭīb al-Baghdādī, *al-Kifāya fī ᶜilm al-riwāya*, Ḥaydarābād 1357, 415-24; Ṣubḥī al-Ṣāliḥ, *ᶜUlūm al-ḥadīth wa-muṣṭalaḥuhu*, Damascus 1959, 226 ff.; for the role of the *rafᶜ* phenomenon in the proliferation and fabrication of traditions, as well as a list of *raffāᶜūn*, see G.H.A. Juynboll, *Muslim tradition. Studies in chronology, provenance and authorship of early* ḥadīth, Cambridge 1983, index s.v. *rafᶜ* and *raffāᶜ*; idem, *Some notes on Islam's first* fuqahāʾ *distilled from early* ḥadīth *literature*, in *Arabica*, xxxix (1992), 287-314. (G.H.A. Juynboll)

RAFᶜ [see ṬALĀḲ].

RAFAḤ, conventional modern rendering Rafah, originally a town 5 km/3 miles inland from the eastern Mediterranean (lat. 31° 18′ N., long. 34° 15′ E.), on the borders of Egypt and Palestine and now administratively divided between Egypt and the Israeli-occupied Gaza Strip as two separate towns.

The name is ancient, and appears in Egyptian records of *ca.* 1300 BC as RPH. In Byzantine times it was part of Palestina Prima and a prosperous place, depicted on the famous Madaba map. At the time of the Arab invasions, it seems to have surrendered to ᶜAmr b. al-ᶜĀṣ on condition of paying the poll-tax and the *ᶜushr* [*q.v.*] in return for security of life and property: subsequently, it was included in the *djund* [*q.v.*] of Filasṭīn. The Arabic geographers often mention it as a stage on the route between Damascus and Egypt and as being in the zone of *djifār*, sand dunes difficult to traverse. However, water was easily available through digging, and in the 18th century Asad al-Luḳaymī (d. 1765), en route for Jerusalem, compared the water from Rafaḥ's well to that of the Nile in its sweetness. The geographer al-Muhallabī (d. 376/986), cited by al-Ḳalḳashandī, says that the population of this *madīna* was composed of Lakhm and Djudhām tribesmen; it had a market, a mosque with a *minbar, funduḳ*s, and was administered by a *wālī al-maᶜūna* who had a force of soldiers at his disposal. Modern archaeological surveys and investigations have disclosed a number of derelict settlements in the neighbourhood, including on the coast, Tall Rafaḥ, which served as the town's landing-place. Yāḳūt describes Rafaḥ as ruinous in his own time, and for several centuries it is hardly mentioned.

But in the 19th century it regained some of its old importance, being from 1865 a telegraph station on the Damascus-Cairo line. In 1870 the Khedive Ismāᶜīl visited the place, and two granite columns were erected to define the border there of Egypt and Ottoman Syria. Subsequently, however, Rafaḥ became a point of dispute. In 1898 ᶜAbbās Ḥilmī [*q.v.*] visited it after threats of an Ottoman annexation of the Sinai peninsula, discouraged at this time by British diplomatic intervention; but in April 1906 the Ottomans occupied Rafaḥ, removed the two columns and uprooted the telegraph poles. Negotiations followed, and the borders were defined in October 1906, with the telegraphic service restored and telephone and camel postal services introduced. During the First World War, British forces under Sir Archibald Murray occupied Rafaḥ in June 1917, establishing a military camp; a double-track, standard-gauge railway from al-Ḳanṭara to Rafaḥ, thence to Beersheba, was built. The town later grew by the settlement of Bedouins there and, after 1948, of Palestinian refugees; and in 1956 and 1967 it was occupied by Israeli forces. Following the Camp David Accords and the peace treaty between Israel and Egypt of 1978, Palestinian Rafaḥ was again separated from its Egyptian counterpart.

Bibliography: 1. For the classical Arabic sources, see Le Strange, *Palestine under the Moslems*, 517, and Marmardji, *Textes géographiques arabes sur la Palestine*, 80, also Ibn Faḍl Allāh al-ᶜUmarī, *Masālik al-abṣār*, ed. Ayman Fuʾād Sayyid, Cairo 1985, 95; Ḳalḳashandī, *Ṣubḥ*, iii, 232, iv, 75-7, 89; Mudjīr al-Dīn al-ᶜUlaymī, *al-Uns al-djalīl*, ᶜAmmān 1973, ii, 67.

2. Studies. Naᶜūm Shuḳayr Bey, *The history of Sinai*... (in Arabic), Cairo 1916, 19, 122, 175-9, 252-3, 588-616; H.C. Luke and E. Keith-Roach, *The handbook of Palestine and Trans-Jordan*², London 1930, 286-7; Naval Intelligence Division, Admiralty Handbooks, *Palestine and Jordan*, London 1943, index; U. Heyd, *Ottoman documents on Palestine 1552-1615*, Oxford 1960, 125-7; Muḥammad Ramzī, *al-Ḳāmūs al-djughrāfī li 'l-bilād al-miṣriyya*, Cairo 1963, ii/4; art. *Rafa*, in *Encyclopaedia Judaica*, xiii, 1510; arts. on history and education and on the town of Rafaḥ itself, in *al-Mawsūᶜa al-Filisṭīniyya*, Beirut 1990. (M.A. Bakhit)

RĀFIᶜ b. **HARTHAMA**, a soldier of fortune who disputed control of Khurāsān with other adventurers and with the Ṣaffārid Amīr ᶜAmr b. al-Layth [*q.v.*] in the later 3rd/9th century, d. 283/896.

Rāfiᶜ had been in the service of the Ṭāhirids [*q.v.*], and after the death in 268/882 at Nīshāpūr of the previous contender for power in Khurāsān, Aḥmad al-Khudjistānī, he set himself up as *de facto* ruler of Khurāsān, subsequently securing legitimisation from the ᶜAbbāsid caliphs when al-Muwaffaḳ [*q.v.*] broke with the Ṣaffārids. By 283/896, however, ᶜAmr managed to defeat Rāfiᶜ and to drive him out of Khurāsān to Khʷārazm, where he was killed.

Bibliography: R. Vasmer, *Über die Münzen der Ṣaffāriden und ihrer Gegner in Fārs und Ḫurāsān*, in *Num. Zeitschr.*, N.F., xxiii (1930), 138 ff.; C.E. Bosworth, in *Camb. hist. of Iran*, iv, 118-20; idem, *The Ṣaffārids of Sistan and the Maliks of Nīmrūz*, Costa Mesa, Calif. 1993. (C.E. Bosworth)

RĀFIᶜ b. al-**LAYTH** b. **NAṢR** b. **SAYYĀR**, apparently the grandson of the last Umayyad governor of Khurāsān Naṣr b. Sayyār [*q.v.*] and rebel against the ᶜAbbāsid caliphate in the opening years of the 9th century A.D.

In 190/806 Rāfiᶜ led a rising in Samarḳand which turned into a general rebellion throughout Transoxania against the harsh rule and financial exploitation of the caliphal governor of Khurāsān, ᶜAlī b. ᶜĪsā b. Māhān [see IBN MĀHĀN]. As well as receiving support from the local Iranian population, Rāfiᶜ secured help from the Turks of the Inner Asian steppes, the Toghuz-Oghuz [see GHUZZ] and Ḳarluḳ [*q.v.*]. Hārūn al-Rashīd sent against him the commander Harthama b. Aʿyan [*q.v.*], and was about to take charge of the campaign against Rāfiʿ personally when he died at Ṭūs in 193/809. Only after Hārūn's death did Rāfiʿ surrender to the successor as ʿAbbāsid governor in the East, al-Maʾmūn, and receive from him *amān* or pardon, after which Rāfiʿ fades from historical mention.

Bibliography: Barthold, *Turkestan down to the Mongol invasion*, 200-1; E.L. Daniel, *The political and social history of Khurasan under Abbasid rule 747-820*, Minneapolis and Chicago 1979, 172-7; C.E. Bosworth (tr.), *The History of al-Ṭabarī. xxx. The ʿAbbāsid caliphate in equilibrium*, Albany 1989, index, with the other primary sources (Yaʿḳūbī, Masʿūdī, Gardīzī, Narshakhī, etc.) indicated at 259 n. 891 and 261 n. 894. (C.E. BOSWORTH)

RAFĪʿ AL-**DĪN**, MAWLĀNĀ SHĀH MUḤAMMAD B. SHĀH WALĪ ALLĀH B. ʿABD AL-RAḤĪM AL-ʿUMARĪ (after the caliph ʿUmar b. al-Khaṭṭāb), was born in 1163/1750 in Dihlī, in a family which enjoyed the highest reputation in Muslim India for learning and piety, from the 18th century onwards, and produced a number of eminent *ʿulamāʾ* up to the Sepoy Rebellion of 1837-8 (see Ṣiddīḳ Ḥasan Khān, *Itḥāf al-nubalāʾ*, Kānpur 1288, 296-7; *JASB*, xiii, 310). He studied *ḥadīth* with his father, Shāh Walī Allāh [see AL-DIHLAWĪ, SHĀH WALĪ ALLĀH] who was the most celebrated traditionist in his time, in India.

After the death of his father in 1176/1762-3, he was brought up by his elder brother Shāh ʿAbd al-ʿAzīz (1159-1239/1746-1823), with whom he completed his studies in the usual sciences, being specially interested in *ḥadīth*, *kalām* and *uṣūl*. When about twenty, he entered upon his career as *muftī* and *mudarris*, and later succeeded in these capacities his brother and teacher, who, in his old age, had lost his eyesight, and had indifferent health. He died on 6 Shawwāl 1233/9 August 1818, at the age of 70 (lunar years), of cholera, and was buried in their family graveyard outside the city of Dihlī.

He wrote about 20 works, mostly in Arabic and Persian, and a few in Urdū. He is praised for the subtlety of his ideas and the conciseness of his style. Among his works are:

In Urdū: 1. a translation of the Ḳurʾān, interlinear to the Arabic text, which it follows closely and faithfully. He and his brother ʿAbd al-Ḳādir [*q.v.*] were the pioneers in this field, though their work was considerably facilitated by their father Shāh Walī Allāh's Persian translation of the Ḳurʾān (entitled *Fatḥ al-Raḥmān fī tardjamat al-Ḳurʾān*). The first edition of Shāh Rafīʿ al-Dīn's translation appeared in Calcutta in 1254/1838-9 and another, in 1266/1849-50. For some of its numerous editions (from 1866 onwards) see Blumhardt, *Cat. of the Hindustānī printed books of the Libr. of the British Museum*, London 1889, 290-1, and its *Supplement*, London 1909, 403.

In Arabic: 2. *Takmīl al-ṣināʿa* or *Takmīl li-ṣināʿat al-adhhān*, dealing with a. logic, b. *taḥṣīl*, i.e. principles of dialectics, teaching, learning, authorship and self-study, c. *mabāḥith min al-umūr al-ʿāmma* (some metaphysical discussions) and, d. *taṭbīḳ al-ārāʾ* (i.e. an enquiry into the causes and the criteria for judging conflicting opinions in religious matters). A considerable portion of the work has been quoted in the *Abdjad al-ʿulūm*, 127-35 and 235-70; 3. *Muḳaddimat al-ʿilm*; see *Abdjad al-ʿulūm*, 124; 4. *Risālat al-Maḥabba*, a discourse on the all-pervading nature of love; see *Abdjad al-ʿulūm*, 254; 5. *Tafsīr Āyat al-Nūr*, a commentary on sūra XXIV, 35; 6. *Risālat al-ʿArūḍ wa 'l-ḳāfiya*; see *Abdjad*, 915; 7. *Damgh al-bāṭil*, dealing with some abstruse problems of the *ʿilm al-ḥaḳāʾiḳ*; 8. a gloss on Mīr Zāhid al-Harawī's commentary on Ḳutb al-Dīn al-Rāzī's *Risālat al-Taṣawwurāt wa 'l-taṣdīḳāt* (see *GAL*, II², 271); 9. *Ibṭāl al-barāhīn al-ḥikmiyya ʿalā uṣūl al-ḥukamāʾ*.

In Persian: 10. *Ḳiyāmat-nāma* (Lahore 1339; Ḥaydarābād, undated ed.), on the last judgment also called *Maḥshar-nāma* (see Browne's *Supplementary handlist*, 189). For the two poetical versions, in Urdū, of this popular work, viz., *Āthār-i maḥshar* (chronogrammatic name, which gives 1250/1834-5 as the date of composition), and *Āthār-i ḳiyāmat*, see Sprenger, *Oudh catalogue*, 624, and Blumhardt, *Cat.*, 290, and for an Urdū prose version, *Ḳiyāmat-nāma* or *Daʾb al-ākhirāt*, see Blumhardt, *loc. cit.*; 11. *Fatāwā*, Dihlī 1322; 12. *Madjmūʿat tisʿ rasāʾil*, Dihlī 1314, small treatises on religious and mystical topics; 13. *Sharḥ al-Ṣudūr bi-sharḥ ḥāl al-mawtā wa 'l-ḳubūr*, an eschatological work, in a ms. copy in the Dār al-ʿUlūm, Deoband, which institution also possesses the ms. of his 14. *Laṭāʾif khamsa*, a mystical work (ff. 32).

Bibliography: Besides the references given above, *Malfūẓāt Shāh ʿAbd al-ʿAzīz Muḥaddith Dihlawī* (composed 1233/1818), Meerut 1314, 79, 83-4; Muḥammad b. Yaḥyā (commonly known as al-Muḥsin) al-Tirhutī, *al-Yāniʿ al-djanī fī asānīd al-Shaykh ʿAbd al-Ghanī* (lithogr. on the margin of the *Kashf al-astār ʿan ridjāl maʿāni 'l-āthār*, and composed in Medīna in 1280/1863), Deoband 1349, 75; Ṣiddīḳ Ḥasan Khān, *Abdjad al-ʿulūm*, Bhopāl 1295, 124, 914-15, and other places mentioned in the article; Karīm al-Dīn, *Farāʾid al-dahr*, Dihlī 1847, 410; Sayyid Aḥmad Khān, *Āthār al-ṣanādīd*, Dihlī 1270, 106; Faḳīr Muḥammad Djihlamī, *Ḥadāʾiḳ al-ḥanafiyya*, Lucknow 1891, 469; Raḥmān ʿAlī, *Tadhkira ʿulamāʾ-i Hind*, Lucknow 1914, 66 (and 4, 24, 51, 63, 223, 276 for notices, etc., of the Shāh's sons and pupils); Bashīr al-Dīn Aḥmad, *Wāḳiʿat Dihlī*, Agra 1918, ii, 588-9; Garcin de Tassy, *Histoire de la littérature hindoue et hindoustanie*, 2nd ed., Paris 1870, ii, 548-9; Saksena, *History of Urdu literature*, Allāhābād 1927, 253; *Maʿārif* (an Urdū monthly published from Aʿẓamgaṛh, India) for Nov. 1928, 344 ff.; *The Oriental College Magazine, Lahore* (an Urdū quarterly) for Nov. 1925, 42-9 (life, including a biogr. notice from the unpublished *Nuzhat al-khawāṭir* by Mawwī ʿAbd al-Ḥayy of Lucknow, and a list of works). (MUḤAMMAD SHAFĪʿ)

AL-**RĀFIḌA** OR AL-RAWĀFIḌ, a term that refers to (i) the proto-Imāmiyya (and, subsequently, the Twelver Shīʿa); (ii) any of a number of Shīʿī sects. In this article it is used in the former sense unless otherwise indicated.

The origin of the term is a matter of dispute. 1. Early Imāmī heresiographers maintain that the name was first applied to the adherents of Djaʿfar al-Ṣādiḳ by al-Mughīra b. Saʿīd (executed in 119/737), immediately after they had dissociated themselves from him [see MUGHĪRIYYA]. 2. Other reports, in contrast, relate it to the abortive uprising of Zayd b. ʿAlī against the Umayyads (in 122/740). According to these reports (including one from the Kūfan historian ʿAwāna b. al-Ḥakam and another from Abū Mikhnaf [*q.vv.*]), some Kūfans who had initially joined Zayd's camp made their continued support conditional on his rejection (*rafḍ*) of Abū Bakr and ʿUmar (or of the entire *ṣaḥāba*). When Zayd refused to accede to their demands they deserted him (*rafaḍūhu*), thus bringing about his defeat. The term *Rāfiḍa* is therefore variously said to recall the desertion of Zayd, the rejection of the first two caliphs, or both.

The name is used to refer to the proto-Imāmiyya in

statements of dubious authenticity ascribed to the traditionist al-Shaʿbī (d. 103/721 or 110/728), and was current by the mid-2nd/8th century, when it was reportedly used by (among others) the Zaydī Sulaymān b. Djarīr. Not surprisingly, Ḥasanid circles were particularly active in propagating anti-Rāfiḍī traditions. Zayd himself is said to have quoted the Prophet as telling ʿAlī that he should kill any Rāfiḍī whom he meets; the reason given is that they are polytheists (Nashwān al-Ḥimyarī, *al-Ḥūr al-ʿīn*, Cairo 1948, 185). Muḥammad is also said to have declared: "At the end of time there will appear a group ... called *Rawāfiḍ* who will reject (*yarfuḍūna*) Islam." According to an account attributed to al-Suddī (d. 127/744-5), Zayd compared the Rāfiḍī desertion with the Khāridjī revolt against ʿAlī (Ibn ʿAsākir, *Taʾrīkh Madīnat Dimashk*, facsimile ed., vi, 648). Detractors argue that *rafḍ* is based on Judaism; they allege that ʿAbd Allāh b. Sabaʾ [*q.v.*] was of Jewish origin, and claim that anthropomorphism (*tashbīh*), allegedly a hallmark of Judaism, was first introduced into Islam by the Rāfiḍa (cf. J. van Ess, *Theologie und Gesellschaft*, i, 399-403).

While *Rāfiḍa* was originally intended as a pejorative term, the Imāmīs soon turned it into an honorific. The traditionist al-Aʿmash [*q.v.*] quotes Djaʿfar al-Ṣādiḳ as explaining that it was bestowed on the Shīʿīs by God and is preserved in both the Torah and the Gospels. According to al-Ṣādiḳ, there were seventy men among the people of Pharaoh who rejected their master and chose to join Moses instead. God therefore called them *Rāfiḍa*, i.e. those who rejected evil, and ordered Moses to write this word, in the original Arabic, in the Torah. After Muḥammad's death, when most of the early adherents of Islam began to stray from the path of truth, only the Shīʿīs rejected evil. They thus became the successors of the original Rāfiḍa. According to another version, those who renounced Pharaoh were not Egyptians but Israelites who had adopted (or perhaps been born into) Pharaoh's religion; having later become aware of their error, they rejoined their erstwhile co-religionists (al-Kulīnī, *al-Kāfī*, ed. ʿAlī Akbar al-Ghaffārī, Tehran 1375-7, viii, 34). Yet another account states that the term was originally applied to Aaron and his followers by the worshippers of the golden calf, whence it was given to the followers of ʿAlī (al-ʿĀmilī al-Bayāḍī, *al-Ṣirāṭ al-mustaḳīm ilā mustaḥiḳḳī 'l-taḳdīm*, ed. Muḥammad Bāḳir al-Bihbūdī, Tehran 1384, i, 323); this reflects the well-known Imāmī tradition that equates ʿAlī's position with regard to the Prophet with that of Aaron with regard to Moses. A retrojection of the term into an even earlier period occurs in an Imāmī account about Idrīs [*q.v.*]. According to this account, Idrīs lived during the reign of the infidel tyrant Bīwarāsb (i.e. al-Ḍaḥḥāk, cf. al-Masʿūdī, *Murūdj*, ed. Pellat, §537), who belonged to the progeny of Cain; those who rejected the tyrant and counted themselves among the followers (*shīʿa*) of Idrīs were called *Rāfiḍa* (al-Masʿūdī, *Ithbāt al-waṣiyya*, Nadjaf 1955, 20-1). Another version, finally, states that the first Rāfiḍa were the seventy followers of Noah (ʿAbd al-Djalīl Ḳazwīnī, *Kitāb al-Naḳḍ*, 585-6).

Rāfiḍism, which first emerged in Kūfa, had spread to Ḳumm by the end of the 2nd/8th century. Ḳumm became a bastion of Rāfiḍī orthodoxy, in contrast to Kūfa, where the various Shīʿī sects were in continual conflict with each other. It was primarily in Ḳumm that Rāfiḍī traditions were sifted and collected. The Ḳummī traditionists were largely Arabs, whereas those of Kūfa were mostly *mawālī*. Rāfiḍī centres which arose in the 3rd/9th century included Ahwāz, Rayy and Naysābūr; by the 4th/10th century, Rāfiḍism had spread to Ṭūs, to Bayhaḳ and to various places in Ṭabaristān and Transoxania, and Baghdād (particularly the Karkh quarter) had become a stronghold of Rāfiḍī rationalist *kalām* (see W. Madelung, *Religious trends in early Islamic Iran*, Albany 1988, 78-86).

The early Rāfiḍīs combined extreme anti-Sunnī positions with political quietism. Their most prominent theologians included Zurāra b. Aʿyan (d. 150/767), Shayṭān al-Ṭāḳ, Hishām al-Djawālīḳī and Hishām b. al-Ḥakam (d. 179/795-6 [*q.v.*]). They were divided into a number of subsects, some of which are noted in the list which the prefect of police Ibn al-Mufaḍḍal drew up for the caliph al-Mahdī (al-Kishshī, *Ridjāl*, Nadjaf n.d., 227). While disagreeing on points of detail (as indicated for example by the title of one of Hishām b. al-Ḥakam's works, *Kitāb al-Radd ʿalā Hishām al-Djawālīḳī*), most Rāfiḍīs shared a number of basic doctrines. They affirmed that God has a form, that his attributes are essentially subject to change, and that he may reverse his rulings [see BADĀʾ]. On the question of the imāmate they maintained that ʿAlī had been appointed as Muḥammad's successor by an explicit designation (*naṣṣ*) and that the majority of the Companions were sinners or even unbelievers for failing to support him after the Prophet's death. The Rāfiḍīs asserted further that ʿAlī's enemies deleted or changed passages in the Ḳurʾān in which ʿAlī's rights were mentioned; as a result the Ḳurʾān as we have it is not identical with the original revelation. They maintained that both the Imāms and their community were created of a heavenly substance and are thus sharply distinguished from the outside world. Only members of this community are believers; they remain in a state of belief even when they sin, and are guaranteed entry into Paradise. The Imāms are immune from error and sin [see ʿIṢMA] and are the supreme authority since they possess virtually limitless knowledge; their teachings formed the basis for the Rāfiḍī legal system. The Rāfiḍīs held that self-protection through dissimulation (*taḳiyya* [*q.v.*]) is often permitted and sometimes obligatory, and believed that there will be a return to this world before the resurrection [see RADJʿA]. As noted by al-Ashʿarī, some Rāfiḍīs had by the 3rd/9th century adopted Muʿtazilī ideas about God's unity and about the Ḳurʾān.

In practice, the Imāms' authority manifested itself chiefly in religious guidance. Muḥammad al-Bāḳir and Djaʿfar al-Ṣādiḳ [*q. vv.*] laid down the principles of Rāfiḍī doctrine and law and taught them to a circle of students in Medina. With the advent of the ʿAbbāsids, the Imāms' activities were severely hampered by the restrictions placed on their movements; they were often incarcerated or placed under house arrest, and so had little direct contact with their followers. This, combined with the geographical expansion of the Rāfiḍa, led naturally to the growth of a local leadership, to which the Imāms delegated some of their authority. In the mid-3rd/9th century, for example, Aḥmad b. Muḥammad al-Ashʿarī served as leader of the Rāfiḍī community in Ḳumm and as the upholder of Rāfiḍī orthodoxy. In addition, the Imāms relied on a network of financial agents for the collection of the *khums*. The groundwork was thus laid for the assumption of responsibility by the *ʿulamāʾ* after the onset of the Occultation [see GHAYBA].

The Rāfiḍīs were attacked by representatives of most other religious groups; Ibn al-Nadīm, for example, records three works entitled *al-Radd ʿalā 'l-rāfiḍa*, one by the Ibāḍī ʿAbd Allāh b. Yazīd, a second by the

Muʿtazilī Bis̲h̲r b. al-Muʿtamir and the third by the Zaydī al-Ḳāsim b. Ibrāhīm (on which see W. Madelung, *Der Imam al-Qāsim ibn Ibrāhīm*, 98; ed. B. Abrahamov, in *The theological epistles of al-Ḳāsim ibn Ibrāhīm*, Ph.D. diss., Tel-Aviv University 1981, unpubl.). While some Sunnī scholars permitted traditions to be transmitted on the authority of Rāfiḍīs, others did not (al-K̲h̲aṭīb al-Bag̲h̲dādī, *al-Kifāya fī ʿilm al-riwāya*, Ḥaydarābād 1357, 120-5). Opposition to the Rāfiḍīs also came to the fore in the legal sphere: the *ḳāḍī* of Kūfa Ibn Abī Laylā (d. 148/765 [*q.v.*]) reportedly refused to accept their testimony (Wakīʿ, *Ak̲h̲bār al-ḳuḍāt*, Cairo 1366-9/1947-50, iii, 133; al-Mad̲j̲lisī, *Biḥār al-anwār*, lxviii, 156), while one of his successors as *ḳāḍī*, the Kūfan traditionist Ḥafṣ b. G̲h̲iyāt̲h̲ al-Nak̲h̲aʿī (d. 194/809-10), is said to have denied permission for women to marry them. His stated reason was that the Rāfiḍīs consider a triple repudiation (*ṭalāḳ*) pronounced in one session to be tantamount to a single repudiation, and hence revocable; Rāfiḍīs who pronounced this formula therefore regarded themselves as still married (Wakīʿ, *Ak̲h̲bār al-ḳuḍāt*, iii, 185, 188; *Taʾrīk̲h̲ Bag̲h̲dād*, viii, 193-4). The ascription of this view to Ḥafṣ has polemical overtones, since he was generally regarded as pro-ʿAlid. Sunnī authors often contrast *rafḍ* with *tas̲h̲ayyuʿ*, a favourable attitude to ʿAlī and members of the Prophet's family which in itself is not objectionable.

As already noted, the appellation *Rāfiḍa* had wider applications. For example, K̲h̲us̲h̲ays̲h̲ b. Aṣram (d. 253/867), as cited by al-Malaṭī, refers to fifteen Rāfiḍī groups, most of whom were extremist S̲h̲īʿīs, and al-S̲h̲ahrastānī also includes the *g̲h̲ulāt* in the term *Rāfiḍa*; and the Rāfiḍīs whose veneration for ʿAlī is likened in some traditions to the Christian deification of Jesus may likewise be the *g̲h̲ulāt*. Ibn Ḥanbal (as cited in Ibn Abī Yaʿlā, *Ṭabaḳāt al-ḥanābila*, i, 33), Ibn Ḳutayba, ʿAbd al-Ḳāhir al-Bag̲h̲dādī, Abu 'l-Muẓaffar al-Isfarāyīnī and others used the term Rāfiḍa to refer, *inter alia*, to the Zaydīs.

Yet in general the term continued to denote the Twelver S̲h̲īʿīs throughout the Middle Ages and into the modern era, particularly in a polemical context. Of late it has again been used in a positive sense, as when the Lebanese S̲h̲īʿī leader Mūsā al-Ṣadr described the S̲h̲īʿīs as men who reject evil (*rāfiḍūn*) and who revolt against tyranny (cited by Fouad Ajami, *The vanished Imam*, Ithaca and London 1986, 155).

Bibliography (in addition to the sources given in the article): (pseudo)-Nās̲h̲iʾ, in J. van Ess, *Frühe muʿtazilitische Häresiographie*, Beirut 1971, Ar. text, 46; Buk̲h̲ārī, *al-Taʾrīk̲h̲ al-kabīr*, Ḥaydarābād 1360-4, i, 279-80, no. 897; Ibn al-Iskāfī, *al-Miʿyār wa 'l-muwāzana*, ed. (as a work of al-Iskāfī) Muḥammad Bāḳir al-Maḥmūdī, Beirut 1402/1981, 32-3, 38, 41-2, 76; Aḥmad b. Ḥanbal, *Musnad*, ed. Aḥmad Muḥammad S̲h̲ākir, i, 136-7, no. 808; al-Faḍl b. S̲h̲ād̲h̲ān al-Naysābūrī, *al-Īḍāḥ*, ed. D̲j̲alāl al-Dīn al-Ḥusaynī, Tehran 1392/1972, 301-4, 473-6; D̲j̲āḥiẓ, *Ḥayawān*, ed. ʿAbd al-Salām Muḥammad Hārūn, Cairo 1356-64/1938-45, i, 7, vi, 289; Ibn Ḳutayba, *al-Maʿārif*, Beirut 1390/1970, 267; Barḳī, *K. al-Maḥāsin*, ed. D̲j̲alāl al-Dīn al-Ḥusaynī, Tehran 1370, i, 157; al-Ṣaffār al-Ḳummī, *Baṣāʾir al-darad̲j̲āt*, Ḳumm 1404, 149; Saʿd b. ʿAbd Allāh al-Ḳummī, *K. al-Maḳālāt wa 'l-firaḳ*, ed. Muḥammad D̲j̲awād Mas̲h̲kūr, Tehran 1963, index; Nawbak̲h̲tī, *K. Firaḳ al-s̲h̲īʿa*, ed. H. Ritter, Istanbul 1931, 20, 54-5; As̲h̲ʿarī, *Maḳālāt*, ed. H. Ritter, index; Ṭabarī, ii, 1700; K̲h̲ayyāṭ, *Kitāb al-Intiṣār*, ed. A.N. Nader, Beirut 1957, 11, 12, 14, 15, 21, 22, 28, 37, 48, 50, 55, 59, 68, 72, 75, 77-80, 85, 93, 96, 98-117, 123; Abū Ḥātim al-Rāzī, *K. al-Zīna*, iii, in ʿAbd Allāh S. al-Sāmarrāʾī, *al-G̲h̲uluww wa 'l-firaḳ al-g̲h̲āliya fi 'l-ḥaḍāra al-islāmiyya*, Bag̲h̲dād 1392/1972, 259, 270-1, 302, 305; Malaṭī, *K. al-Tanbīh wa 'l-radd*, ed. S. Dedering, Istanbul 1936, 14-28, 29, 72, 118-26; Abū Muṭīʿ al-Nasafī, *Kitāb al-Radd ʿalā ahl al-bidaʿ wa 'l-ahwāʾ*, ed. M. Bernand, in *AI*, xvi (1980), at p. 63; Ibn al-Nadīm, *al-Fihrist*, ed. Riḍā Tad̲j̲addud, Tehran 1391/1971, 223-6, 244-7; Maḳdisī, *al-Badʾ wa 'l-taʾrīk̲h̲*, ed. Cl. Huart, Paris 1899-1919, v, 124; ʿAbd al-Ḳāhir al-Bag̲h̲dādī, *Farḳ*, Beirut n.d., 21-4, 29-72, 225-8, 230, 232-53, 270, 272-3; idem, *al-Milal wa 'l-niḥal*, ed. A.N. Nader, Beirut 1970, 47-56; ʿAbd al-D̲j̲abbār, *al-Mug̲h̲nī*, xx/ii, Cairo n.d., 179 (citing Balk̲h̲ī); Muḥammad b. D̲j̲arīr b. Rustam al-Ṭabarī, *K. Dalāʾil al-imāma*, Beirut 1408/1988, 251; Ibn Abī Yaʿlā, *Ṭabaḳāt al-ḥanābila*, ed. Muḥammad Ḥāmid al-Fiḳī, Cairo 1371/1952, i, 30, 36; Ibn Ḥazm, *al-Fiṣal*, ed. Muḥammad Ibrāhīm Nuṣayr and ʿAbd al-Raḥmān ʿUmayra, Beirut 1405/1985, iv, 156-75, 179, v, 5, 19, 35-50; Abu 'l-Muẓaffar al-Isfarāyīnī, *al-Tabṣīr fi 'l-dīn*, Cairo 1374/1955, 30, 32-45, 120; S̲h̲ahrastānī, *al-Milal wa 'l-niḥal*, ed. ʿAbd al-ʿAzīz Muḥammad al-Wakīl, Cairo 1387/1968, i, 155, 160; ʿAbd al-D̲j̲alīl Ḳazwīnī, *K. al-Naḳḍ*, ed. D̲j̲alāl al-Dīn al-Ḥusaynī al-Muḥaddit̲h̲, Tehran 1980, index; Ibn al-D̲j̲awzī, *Talbīs Iblīs*, Beirut 1403/1983, 112-6; idem, *al-Muntaẓam*, ed. Muḥammad ʿAbd al-Ḳādir ʿAṭā and Muṣṭṭafā ʿAbd al-Ḳādir ʿAṭā, Beirut 1412/1992, vii, 210-1; Fak̲h̲r al-Dīn al-Rāzī, *Iʿtiḳādāt firaḳ al-muslimīn wa 'l-mus̲h̲rikīn*, Cairo 1356/1938, 52-66; Ibn Taymiyya, *Minhād̲j̲ al-sunna al-nabawiyya*, Cairo 1322, i, 2-16; Murtaḍā b. Dāʿī Rāzī, *Tabṣirat al-ʿawāmm*, ed. ʿAbbās Iḳbāl, Tehran 1313 S̲h̲./1934, index; D̲h̲ahabī, *Siyar aʿlām al-nubalāʾ*, ed. S̲h̲uʿayb al-Arnaʾūṭ, Beirut 1402-9/1982-8, viii, 506-7, ix, 27; Ibn al-Murtaḍā, *Ṭabaḳāt al-muʿtazila*, ed. S. Diwald-Wilzer (*Die Klassen der Muʿtaziliten*), Beirut-Wiesbaden 1380/1961, 52; Abū Ḥāmid al-Maḳdisī, *Risāla fi 'l-radd ʿala 'l-rāfiḍa*, Bombay 1403/1983, 190 ff., 434-6, 443, 448-57; Fak̲h̲r al-Dīn al-Ṭurayḥī, *Mad̲j̲maʿ al-baḥrayn*, ed. Aḥmad al-Ḥusaynī, Nad̲j̲af 1378/1959, iv, 206-7; al-Mad̲j̲lisī, *Biḥār al-anwār*, Tehran 1376-94, xxvi, 36, lxviii, 96-8; I. Friedlaender, *The heterodoxies of the Shiites*, New Haven 1909, ii, 137-59 (= Appendix A); G. Vajda, *Deux "histoires de Prophètes" selon la tradition des Shīʿites duodécimains*, in *REJ*, xvi (1941-5), 124-33; W. Montgomery Watt, *The Rāfiḍites: a preliminary study*, in *Oriens*, xvi (1963), 110-21; idem, *The formative period of Islamic thought*, Edinburgh 1973, index; J. Wellhausen, *The religio-political factions in early Islam*, tr. R.C. Ostle and S.M. Walzer, Amsterdam and New York 1975, 163-4; W. Madelung, *Der Imam al-Qāsim ibn Ibrāhīm und die Glaubenslehre der Zaiditen*, Berlin 1965, index; idem, *The Shiite and Khārijite contribution to pre-Ashʿarite kalām*, in *Islamic philosophical theology*, ed. P. Morewedge, Albany 1979, 120-39; J. Calmard, *Le chiisme imamite en Iran à l'époque seldjoukide, d'après le Kitāb al-Naqḍ*, in *Le monde iranien et l'Islam*, i, Geneva and Paris 1971, 43-67; Wadād al-Ḳāḍī, *al-Kaysāniyya fi 'l-taʾrīk̲h̲ wa 'l-adab*, Beirut 1974, 28-9, 354; T. Nagel, "*Die Urǧūza al-Muḫtāra*" *des Qāḍī an-Nuʿmān*, in *WI*, N.S., xv (1974), 96-128; idem, *Rechtleitung und Kalifat*, Bonn 1975, 155-224 and index; P. Crone and M. Hinds, *God's Caliph*, Cambridge 1986, 99-105; E. Kohlberg, *The term "Rāfiḍa" in Imāmī Shīʿī usage*, in *JAOS*, xcix (1979), 677-9; idem, *Belief and law in Imāmī Shīʿism*, Aldershot 1991, index; D. Gimaret and G. Monnot, *Livre des religions et des sectes*, i, Peeters-Unesco 1986, index; J. van Ess, *Theologie und Gesellschaft im 2. und 3. Jahrhundert Hidschra*, i, Berlin and New York 1991, 272-403. See also SHĪʿA. (E. KOHLBERG)

AL-**RĀFIʿĪ**, ʿABD AL-KARĪM B. ABĪ SAʿĪD MUḤAMMAD b. ʿAbd al-Karīm al-Shafiʿī, Abu 'l-Ḳāsim Imām al-Dīn, Shāfiʿī scholar, born at Ḳazwīn in 555/1160 and died there in 623/1226. He is best known by his *nisba* of al-Rāfiʿī and, because of this, occasionally confused in some oriental sources with the poet of Ṭabaristān Rāfiʿī Naysābūrī and with a poet of Ghūr called Abu 'l-Ḳāsim Rāfiʿī, whilst Browne, *LHP*, iii, 88, 381, takes him for al-Yāfiʿī.

Skilled in *fiḳh*, he was the author of several works, numbering ten if one examines the sources which contain notices of his scholarly works: (1) *K. al-Muḥarrar*; (2) *K. al-Tadwīn fī dhikr ahl al-ʿilm bi-Ḳazwīn*; (3) *al-Amālī al-shāriḥa li-mufradāt al-Fātiḥa*; (4) *Sawād al-ʿayn fī manāḳib Abu 'l-ʿālamayn Aḥmad al-Rifāʿī*; (5) *al-Tadhnīb*; (6) *Sharḥ al-Wadjīz* (sc. by al-Ghazālī); (7) *Sharḥ Musnad al-Shāfiʿī*; (8) *al-Sharḥ al-ṣaghīr*; (9) *al-Tartīb*; (10) *K. al-Īdjāz fī akhtār al-Ḥidjāz*. The first six are to be found in Brockelmann (I, 393, S I, 678), and the others in al-Subkī (*Ṭabaḳāt*, Cairo 1965, v, 120). To underline al-Rāfiʿī's high standing amongst Sunnī scholars, one may merely note that the famous *Minhādj al-ṭālibīn* of al-Nawawī [*q.v.*] (Fr. tr. L.W.C. Van Den Berg, Batavia 1882) is a compendium of his *K. al-Muḥarrar*.

However, one should also note the value for the history of Ḳazwīn and its region of his *K. al-Tadwīn*, a dictionary containing over a thousand biographies, listed more or less alphabetically, spread out over the first six centuries of Islam and devoted to the Sunnī *ʿulamāʾ*, above all the Shāfiʿī ones, of Ḳazwīn. The pre-eminence of this *madhhab* there is confirmed by it, even if, in the Ṣafawid period, another scholar of the town, Raḍī al-Dīn Ḳazwīnī, who was fiercely critical of the *Tadwīn* and its author, was to endeavour, in his *Ḍiyāfat al-ikhwān* (ed. al-Sayyid Aḥmad al-Ḥusaynī, Ḳumm 1977), by somewhat dubious methods, to exaggerate the importance of the Imāmīs in Ḳazwīn, by bringing to light a good number of them concealed amongst the persons listed in the *Tadwīn*; such is the remarkable case of Muntadjab al-Dīn [*q.v.*], one of the most famous Imāmī Shīʿī scholars of the period and who was, moreover—a testimony to the strength of *taḳiyya*—one of al-Rāfiʿī's masters.

But the book's value can especially be seen in the four chapters prefixed to the actual biographies (of which preliminary chapters, lengthy extracts translated into Persian may be found in Sayyid ʿAlī Gulrīz's *Mīnūdar yā bāb al-djanna Ḳazwīn*, Tehran 1337). They provide rich historical and geographical information which was extensively used, a century later, by Ḥamd Allāh Mustawfī Ḳazwīnī [*q.v.*] in the 6th chapter of his *T.-i Guzīda* and even, in a very synthetic fashion, in the passages on Ḳazwīn in his *Nuzhat al-ḳulūb*. Since the formal dependence of this section of the *T.-i Guzīda* on the *Tadwīn* is demonstrable, one will need to reconsider the importance of this history, which has generally been considered as one of the main sources on Ḳazwīn, since its information dates from a century before.

As well as the Persian extracts from the *Tadwīn* mentioned above, there exists an index of the persons listed in it compiled by Mīr Djalāl al-Dīn Ḥusayn (*Fihrist asmāʾ al-ridjāl* [Tehran] 1374), who has used only a single one of the mss. of this work.

Bibliography: A. Arioli, *Il Kitāb al-tadwīn I*, in *Annali di Ca' Foscari*, xvii/3 (1978) (Serie Orientale, 9), 39-50 (with full bio-bibliographical references to the oriental sources); idem, *Su una fonte di Mustawfī Qazwīnī*, in *La Bisaccia dello Sheikh. Omaggio ad Alessandro Bausani islamista nel sessantesimo compleanno*, Venice 1981, 29-41; idem, *Dei dotti contesi. Note alla Ḍiyāfat al-ikhwān di Raḍī d-dīn Qazwīnī (XVII sec.)*, in *Cahiers d'onomastique arabe*, C.N.R.S. Paris 1981, 67-79. (A. ARIOLI)

RAFSANDJĀN, a town of Kirmān province, central Persia (lat. 30° 25′ N., long. 56° 00′ E., altitude 1,572 m/5,156 ft.), situated on the Yazd road 120 km/74 miles to the west of Kirmān city. It is the chef-lieu of a *shahrastān* or district of the same name. Known also as Bahrāmābād, in 1991 it had an estimated population of 87,798 (*Preliminary results of September 1991 census*, Statistical Centre of Iran, Population Division). Its chief claim to fame is as the home of the present (1993) head of state of the Islamic Republic of Iran "President and Prime Minister" ʿAlī Akbar Hāshimī Rafsandjānī.

Bibliography: Razmārā (ed.), *Farhang-i djughrāfiyā-yi Īrān-zamīn*, viii, 207. (ED.)

AL-**RĀGHIB** AL-**IṢFAHĀNĪ**, ABU 'L-ḲĀSIM AL-ḤUSAYN b. Muḥammad b. al-Mufaḍḍal, religious and Arabic literary scholar. Despite the considerable popularity of his works, at least a dozen of which are extant, and his demonstrable influence on al-Ghazālī and other later figures, al-Rāghib's name is missing from almost all the standard biographical collections, and information about his life is extremely scanty. Although late sources place him in the 6th/12th century, more recent scholarship has confirmed al-Suyūṭī's statement (*Bughya*, ii, 297) that he died early in the 5th/11th. In his literary anthologies he alludes a number of times to contemporaries who can be identified as members of the circle of the Būyid vizier Ibn ʿAbbād (d. 385/995 [*q.v.*]); and the fact that he refers to Ibn ʿAbbād's successor, Abu 'l-ʿAbbās al-Ḍabbī (d. 399/1008), exceptionally, by his full title suggests that he may have been writing during the latter's vizierate. There is no sound evidence that al-Rāghib ever visited Baghdād or left his native Iṣfahān.

Further knowledge of al-Rāghib comes almost entirely from his own works, whose variety made it difficult for later biographers to pigeonhole him; al-Suyūṭī calls him simply an "author" (*ṣāḥib al-muṣannafāt*). His best-known work, the *Muḥāḍarāt al-udabāʾ wa-muḥāwarāt al-shuʿarāʾ wa 'l-bulaghāʾ* (2 vols., Beirut 1960, and earlier editions), is a comprehensive *adab* encyclopaedia, organised in twenty-five chapters covering such topics as intellect, rulership, crafts, food, courage, love, death, and animals, and including poetry and short prose anecdotes from all periods of Islamic history in approximately equal proportions; particularly prominent are verses by al-Mutanabbī and al-Sharīf al-Raḍī [*q.vv.*] and poetry and prose by Ibn ʿAbbād. Similar in scope, and overlapping in content, is the *Madjmaʿ al-balāgha* (ed. Muḥammad ʿAbd al-Raḥmān al-Sārīsī, ʿAmmān 1986), which differs from the *Muḥāḍarāt* in purpose, however, being essentially a thesaurus of elegant expressions for the use of the aspiring littérateur; this title is not recorded by the biobibliographical sources, but is probably to be identified with the *Kitāb al-Maʿānī al-akbar* referred to by Ḥādjdjī Khalīfa (ed. Flügel, v, 616), quoting from the extant but unpublished introduction to al-Rāghib's own *Durrat al-taʾwīl* (see below). A third literary work by al-Rāghib, preserved without proper title in a Yale manuscript (ms. Landberg 165) and dealing with the standard rhetorical figures of poetry, is perhaps to be identified with the *Afānīn al-balāgha* mentioned by al-Suyūṭī and later sources.

Al-Rāghib's predilection for subtle semantic analysis, apparent in the *Madjmaʿ al-balāgha*, is even more pronounced in his alphabetical lexicon of Ḳurʾānic vocabulary, the *Mufradāt alfāẓ al-Ḳurʾān* (ed. Nadīm Marʿashlī, Beirut 1972, and other editions). This work, whose influence can be traced in later *tafsīr* as well as lexicography, was one of a series of monographs by al-Rāghib on the Ḳurʾān; in its introduction the author refers to his previous *Risāla munabbiha ʿalā fawāʾid al-Ḳurʾān* and *Risāla fi 'l-ḳawānīn al-dālla ʿalā taḥḳīḳ munāsabāt al-alfāẓ*, both apparently lost, and promises a further work specifically on the "obscure distinctions" to be drawn between apparent synonyms in the Holy Book. The latter is probably to be identified with the *Durrat al-taʾwīl fī mutashābih al-tanzīl*, a study of phrases repeated in the Ḳurʾān in slightly varying forms, offering explanations for the significance of such minor variations. This work is extant in a number of manuscripts with varying titles, and has been shown by Muḥammad ʿAbd al-Raḥmān al-Sārīsī to be substantially identical, except for its introduction, with the *Durrat al-tanzīl wa-ghurrat al-taʾwīl* (Beirut 1973, and other editions) attributed to al-Khaṭīb al-Iskāfī (d. 421/1030), a contemporary and compatriot of al-Rāghib and a member of the circle of Ibn ʿAbbād in Rayy; whatever the source of the confusion, al-Rāghib's authorship seems to be supported on stylistic grounds, as well as by an internal reference to the author's *Djāmiʿ al-tafsīr*, which accords with other information on al-Rāghib but not on al-Iskāfī.

Al-Rāghib's *tafsīr*, of which only the initial sections are known to be extant in manuscript, is quoted in the *tafsīrs* of al-Bayḍāwī (anonymously) and Fakhr al-Dīn al-Rāzī (explicitly). It may never have been completed. Most celebrated was its methodological introduction, which was often copied separately and has been printed several times (most recently, as a *mulḥaḳ* to al-Nāhī, *al-Khawālid* [see *Bibl.*]). A model of clarity, this brief essay combines traditional philology with concepts derived directly from the philosophical tradition in an elegant and novel way.

The same combination of traditional religious scholarship and *falsafa* is even more apparent in al-Rāghib's best-known ethical work, *al-Dharīʿa ilā makārim al-sharīʿa* (ed. Abū Yazīd al-ʿAdjamī, Cairo 1985, and earlier editions). This work is structured in terms of a Platonic-Aristotelian psychology, with separate chapters on man's faculties in general, his intellect, the concupiscent and irascible faculties, justice, labour and money, and human acts. The pervasive philosophical influence is highly reminiscent of Miskawayh [*q.v.*] (who died and was buried in Iṣfahān in 421/1030), although no textual parallels between the two authors' works have been identified (except for a few brief quotations from Miskawayh in the *Muḥāḍarāt*). Al-Rāghib's *falsafa* is, however, considerably more Islamicised than Miskawayh's, with virtually every assertion being backed up by appropriate citations from Ḳurʾān and *ḥadīth*. The statement by al-Bayhaḳī (*Taʾrīkh ḥukamāʾ al-Islām*, ed. M. Kurd ʿAlī, Damascus 1946, 112-13) that al-Rāghib combined *sharīʿa* and *ḥikma* in his works is particularly apposite to the *Dharīʿa*. The work's ultimate influence was considerable, as it was al-Ghazālī's direct source for a good half of his *Mīzān al-ʿamal*, as well as for significant sections of his *Iḥyāʾ ʿulūm al-dīn* and *Maʿāridj al-ḳuds*. Al-Rāghib also wrote a companion piece to the *Dharīʿa*, the *Tafṣīl al-nashʾatayn wa-taḥṣīl al-saʿādatayn* (ed. ʿAbd al-Madjīd al-Nadjdjār, Beirut 1988), which presents many of the same ideas but stresses even more explicitly the complementarity of *ʿaḳl* and *sharʿ*.

Influence from the *falsafa* tradition is equally apparent in a theological treatise by al-Rāghib published (very imperfectly) under the title *al-Iʿtiḳādāt* (ed. Shamrān al-ʿAdjalī, Beirut 1988). Its proper title is unknown, although one of the three known manuscripts of the work calls it (rather implausibly) *Taḥḳīḳ al-bayān fī taʾwīl al-Ḳurʾān*, a title referred to by the author himself in his *Dharīʿa*. In this work, al-Rāghib deals with a series of standard *kalām* topics, such as the attributes of God and the problem of free will, but much of his argumentation is philosophical, including his conception of God as the Necessary Existent (*wādjib al-wudjūd bi-dhātihi*) and the Unmoved Mover. Repeated attacks on the Muʿtazilīs, and occasional ones on the Shīʿa, show traditional questions about al-Rāghib's adherence to either of these positions to be groundless, although the existence of such questions from an early period suggests that this work was never widely known. Al-Rāghib's actual theological stance seems in fact to have been close to that of the Ashʿarīs, although he attacks them once for denying the existence of a rational moral order in the universe; his pointed omission of Abū Ḥanīfa from a list of major formative figures in jurisprudence can be added to other evidence for his adherence to the Shāfiʿī school in law. He also explicitly supports Ṣūfism in some form.

Al-Sārīsī has noted the existence of four brief epistles by al-Rāghib in an Istanbul manuscript (Esad Efendi 3645), with the titles *R. fī anna faḍīlat al-insān bi 'l-ʿulūm*, *R. fī dhikr al-wāḥid wa 'l-aḥad*, *R. fī ādāb mukhālaṭat al-nās*, and *R. fī marātib al-ʿulūm*. The status of a few other titles in manuscript catalogues and bibliographical sources remains to be investigated. Apparently uninfluenced by his contemporary Ibn Sīnā, al-Rāghib is significant as a precursor of al-Ghazālī in accepting and utilising a more diffuse form of *falsafa* in maintaining a rationalised but relatively conservative Islamic stance.

Bibliography (in addition to references in the article): Māfarrūkhī, *Maḥāsin Iṣfahān*, ed. al-Ṭihrānī, Tehran 1312/1933, 32; Fakhr al-Dīn al-Rāzī, *Asās al-taḳdīs*, Cairo 1935, i, 5; Dhahabī, *Siyar aʿlām al-nubalāʾ*, Beirut 1981, xviii, 120-1; Ṣafadī, *Wāfī*, xiii, 45; Zarkashī, *al-Burhān fī ʿulūm al-Ḳurʾān*, Cairo 1957, index; Suyūṭī, *al-Muzhir fī ʿulūm al-lugha wa-anwāʿihā*, Cairo 1945, i, 201; Ḥādjdjī Khalīfa, index; Khwānsārī, *Rawḍāt al-djannāt*, Ḳumm 1970, iii, 197-227; Āghā Buzurg Ṭihrānī, *al-Dharīʿa ilā taṣānīf al-shīʿa*, Nadjaf 1936–, i, 374, iv, 351-2, v, 45-6, vii, 73, viii, 95, x, 25-6, x, 28, xx, 128, xxi, 364; Brockelmann, I, 289, S I, 505-6, S II, 83; W. Madelung, *Ar-Rāġib al-Iṣfahānī und die Ethik al-Ġazālīs*, in *Islamwissenschaftliche Abhandlungen Fritz Meier zum 60sten Geburtstag*, ed. R. Gramlich, Wiesbaden 1974, 152-63; Ṣalāḥ al-Dīn ʿAbd al-Laṭīf al-Nāhī, *al-Khawālid min ārāʾ al-Rāghib al-Iṣfahānī fī falsafat al-akhlāḳ wa 'l-tashrīʿ wa 'l-taṣawwuf*, ʿAmmān 1987; ʿUmar ʿAbd al-Raḥmān al-Sārīsī, *al-Rāghib al-Iṣfahānī wa-djuhūduhu fi 'l-lugha wa 'l-adab*, ʿAmmān 1987. (E.K. Rowson)

RĀGHIB PASHA, Khodja Meḥmed (1111-76/1699-1763), Ottoman Grand Vizier and littérateur. He was born in Istanbul, the son of the *kātib* Meḥmed Shewḳī, and was soon on account of his unusual ability employed in the *dīwān*. He then acted as secretary and deputy-chamberlain to the governors of Van, ʿArifī Aḥmed Pasha, and Köprülü-zāde ʿAbd al-Raḥmān Aḥmed Pasha [*q.v.*], and, lastly, to Ḥekīm-zāde ʿAlī Pasha. In 1141/1728 he returned to the capital and in the following year went back to Baghdād as deputy to the *re'īs efendi*. Soon after the conquest of Baghdād in 1146/1733 he was appointed *defterdār* there, but very soon received the post of chief of the petition department of the *māliyye* office in Istanbul. Two years later he accompanied the governor Aḥmed Pasha, who had been appointed as *ser'asker* of Baghdād, as deputy of the *re'īs efendi*, and returned to the capital as chief of the poll-tax office (*djizye müḥāsebedjisi*). In this capacity he went into the field in 1149/1736 and took a leading part in the peace negotiations of Nimirov. In Dhu 'l-Ḥidjdja 1153/ February 1741 he succeeded the *re'īs efendi* Muṣṭafā in his office, and three years later was promoted to be governor of Egypt. For five years he struggled there with the factions of the Mamlūks [*q.v.*], but had finally in Ramaḍān 1161/September 1748 to yield to the superior power of the begs. He returned to the capital, and as *nishāndjī-bashī* was given a seat in the *dīwān*. After brief periods as governor in Raḳḳa and Aleppo, he was appointed to the highest office in the state, the Grand Vizierate, in succession to Muṣṭafā, who had been dismissed on 20 Rabī' I 1170/13 December 1756. He filled this office gloriously for seven years till his death, and was the last outstanding Grand Vizier of the Ottoman empire. He died in Istanbul on 24 Ramaḍān 1176/8 April 1763 and was buried in the garden of the noble library founded by him (see J. von Hammer, *GOR*, viii, 249).

Meḥmed Rāghib Pasha was not only one of the greatest of Ottoman statesmen but is one of the classical authors of Turkish literature. His works, which are distinguished by beauty of style as well as by graceful presentation, cover all possible fields (see J. von Hammer, *GOR*, viii, 255-6). He was also a distinguished political historian. His state documents and letters of congratulation known as *telkhīṣāt* were famous as models of perfect writing (see *GOR*, ix, 626, nos. 3338-3653). His translations into Turkish of two Persian histories, Mīrkhwānd's [*q.v.*] *Rawḍat al-ṣafā'* and 'Abd al-Razzāḳ b. Isḥāḳ al-Samarḳandī's history of the Tīmūrids, *Maṭla' al-sa'dayn*, unfortunately only survive in fragments but even in this state are masterpieces of Ottoman prose. Rāghib Pasha is no less highly esteemed as a poet. His *Dīwān* (printed at Būlāḳ in 1252 and n.p. [= Būlāḳ] in 1253) contains his most important poems, some of which are in praise of great contemporaries.

On mss. of his works, see Babinger, *GOW*, 290 (to which may be added Istanbul, Ḥamīdiyye, no. 598; Zagreb Acad. of Sciences, orient. coll., no. 833, 1 and 2 (with *Dīwān*), both containing his *telkhīṣāt*; Uppsala, no. 706 (see Zettersteen, *Cat.*, ii, 106-7) obviously contains another work).

Bibliography: See F. Babinger, *GOW*, 288 ff., and the sources given on 290; *İA*, art. *Râgıp Paşa* (Bekir Sıtkı Baykal-Abdülkadir Karahan)

(F. Babinger)

RAGHŪSA, the mediaeval Arabic form of the name of the Dalmatian city of Ragusa, until the advent of Bonaparte a free state, the modern Dubrovnik in Croatia (see 2. below), situated in lat. 42° 40′ N., long. 18° 07′ E.

1. History up to the beginning of the 19th century.

Ragusa, the Roman Ragusium (see *PW*, 2. Reihe, 1.A. 1, col. 130), is situated on the south side of a peninsula which runs out into the Adriatic, picturesquely situated (50 feet) at the foot and on the slopes of Mount Sergius, and was founded in the 7th century by Romance fugitives from Epidaurus which had been destroyed by the Slavs; it later belonged to Byzantine Dalmatia which had been settled by a Romance population. At the end of the 10th century the town, which had became strong and rich through its prosperous maritime trade, was paying homage to the Venetians, under whose suzerainty it remained after various interludes continuously from 1204 to 1358. In this year, Ragusa passed to Hungary and soon attained such power through its flourishing trade that it formed a free state with an aristocratic form of government. Authority was in the hands of the nobles (Grand Council) who chose the Senate (45 members). The latter chose the Little Council (10, later 7 members) which chose every month a Rector (*rettore*) as head of the state. Al-Idrīsī [*q.v.*] mentions Ragusa in his *Opus geographium* (761, 769, 790, 791) as رغوسه (other readings: رغوص, رغوصة), and is evidently quoting Frankish sources (cf. thereon W. Tomaschek, *Zur Kunde der Hämus-Halbinsel: II. Die Handelswege im XII. Jahrh. nach den Erkundungen des Arabers Idrisi*, in *SB Ak. Wiss. Wien*, phil.-hist. Kl., vol. cxiii [1887], fasc. 1). In the Ottoman period, the Slav name Dubrovnik is found exclusively, in place of Ragusa.

Ragusa's relations with Islam, at first completely hostile, go back to a remote date. When the Arabs in the 9th century conquered Sicily and established themselves on the mainland in Bari (Apulia), they besieged Ragusa on one occasion, which defended itself bravely and was relieved by the navy of the emperor Basil I (867-86). Under the emperor Romanus III (1028-34) the Ragusans distinguished themselves in the sea-fights between Byzantines and Arabs. It was not till a later date that relations became more peaceful, when Ragusan commerce, which extended to Egypt and Syria, to Tunis and as far as the Black Sea, began to flourish. As early as the 14th century, corn was exported to Ragusa from the harbours of Anatolia and the relations to the beyliks (*ṭewā'if-i mülūk*) in Anatolia were well established. The first documented relations between Ragusa and the Ottoman empire belong to the period of Bāyezīd I Yîldîrîm (791-805/1389-1403 [*q.v.*]), as the relations of the free state with Orkhan [*q.v.*] and Murād I [*q.v.*] mentioned in later Ragusan histories will not bear serious investigation. It is, however, certain that at quite an early date it became necessary for the Ragusans to remain on good terms with the Ottomans, who were advancing westward, for the sake of their trade. They were able to deal with tact and skill with their new neighbours. Ragusan trade in Turkey developed considerably as the many frontiers and customs offices of the numerous petty rulers of the Balkans, who had been dispossessed by the Turks, disappeared and the Turkish duties were uniform and low. Articles manufactured in Ragusa itself, like cloth, metal, soap, glass, wax, etc., or goods imported from Italy for the Balkan peninsula, were taken into the interior on safe roads. There was a caravan trade which went from Ragusa via Trebinje, Tientište, Foča, Goražde, Plevlje, Prijepolje, Trgovište, Novibazar, Niš [see nish], Sofia and Plovdiv to Edirne and later to Istanbul (cf. C.J. Jireček, *Die Handelsstrassen und Bergwerke von Serbien und Bosnien während des Mittelalters*, Prague 1879, 74 ff.: *Von Ragusa nach Niš*). In the interior of the Peninsula, there were the factories of the Ragusans like Rudnik, Prizren, Novo Brdo, Priština [see prishtina], Zvornik, Novibazar, Skoplje and Sofia, with many other settlements extending as far as the mouths of the Danube. On 12 May 1392 the Little Council of Ragusa gave the nobleman Teodoro Gisla in Novo Brdo orders to travel to the Turkish sultan and to

Nudjūm, ed. Popper, ii, 34) in the caliphate of al-Maʾmūn (198-218/813-33) (a legendary embellishment of the story of its foundation by ʿUmar al-Bisṭāmī, in Yāḳūt, ii, 764). The new foundation was in the form of a long, rectangular head cloth (*ṭaylasān*). After the death of its founder (Ibn al-Athīr, vii, 188) in 260/873-4, he was succeeded as ruler of the town by his son Aḥmad, who was, however, driven out of it in 270/883 by Muḥammad b. Abi 'l-Sādj, lord of al-Anbār, Ṭarīḳ al-Furāt and Raḥbat Ṭawḳ (al-Ṭabarī, iii, 2039).

The Ḳarmaṭī Abū Ṭāhir al-Djannābī took the town on 8 Muḥarram 316/3 March 928 and killed many of its inhabitants (Miskawayh, *Tadjārib*, ed. Amedroz, i, 182-3; al-Masʿūdī, *Tanbīh*, 384-5; Ibn al-Athīr, viii, 132; ʿArīb, 134). In the following decades, the town suffered much from civil wars until ʿĀdil, who had been sent from Baghdād by Badjkam, in 330/941-2 took possession of the town and the whole province of Ṭarīḳ al-Furāt and a part of al-Khābūr (Ibn al-Athīr, xiii, 266-7, 295). In the reign of the Ḥamdānid Nāṣir al-Dawla, the Taghlibī Djamān rebelled in al-Raḥba, and the town suffered very much; he was finally driven out and was drowned in the Euphrates (*op. cit.*, 357-8). After the death of Nāṣir al-Dawla (358/969), his sons Ḥamdān, Abu 'l-Barakāt and Abū Taghlib disputed for the possession of the town, which finally fell to the last-named, who had its walls rebuilt (Ibn al-Athīr, viii, 437-8). He lost it again in 368/978-9; it then passed to the Būyid ʿAḍud al-Dawla (Ibn al-Athīr, viii, 511-12). Bahāʾ al-Dawla in 381/991-2, at the wish of the inhabitants, appointed a governor to al-Raḥba (Ibn al-Athīr, ix, 64). Soon afterwards the town passed to Abū ʿAlī b. Thimāl al-Khafādjī, who was killed by the ʿUḳaylid ʿĪsā b. Khalāṭ in 399/1008-9. The latter in turn was defeated by an army sent by al-Ḥākim from Egypt and slain. The ʿUḳaylid Badrān b. Muḳallid was, it is true, able to drive back the Egyptian army but Luʾluʾ of Damascus soon afterwards brought al-Raḳḳa and al-Raḥba into Egyptian power.

A citizen of the town, Ibn Muḥkān, next made himself its independent master and also took ʿĀna, an enterprise in which the Kilābī Ṣāliḥ b. Mirdās of al-Ḥilla at first supported him but later killed him in order to make himself master of al-Raḥba (Ibn al-Athīr, ix, 148; Ibn Khaldūn, *ʿIbar*, ed. Būlāḳ, iv, 271). Between 447/1055 and 450/1058, Arslān al-Basāsīrī [*q.v.*] fled to al-Raḥba in order to join up with the Egyptian caliph al-Mustanṣir from there (Yāḳūt, i, 608). Ṣāliḥ's son, Thimāl, later lord of Aleppo, followed him in possession of the town (Ibn al-Athīr, ix, 163). In the spring of 452/1060 his brother ʿAṭiyya (Ibn al-Athīr, x, 8) captured it. He was driven from Aleppo in 457/1065 by his nephew Maḥmūd, but remained lord of al-Raḥba, Aʿzāz, Manbidj and Bālis (Kamāl al-Dīn, *Historia Merdasidarum*, tr. J.J. Müller, 59). To the district of al-Raḥba at this time (455/1063) there also belonged al-Khānūḳa, Ḳarḳīsiya and Duwayra (Ibn al-Ḳalānisī, ed. Amedroz, 116). Malikshāh in 479/1086-7 granted al-Raḥba with the country round it, Ḥarrān, Sarūdj, al-Raḳḳa and al-Khābūr to Muḥammad b. Sharaf al-Dawla (Ibn al-Athīr, x, 105). In 489/1096 Karbūḳa of al-Ḥilla seized and plundered the town (Ibn al-Athīr, x, 177). After his death it passed in 495/1102-3 to Ḳāymāz, a former general of Alp Arslan, then to the Turk Ḥasan. It was taken from him by the ruler of Damascus, who sent the Shaybānid Muḥammad b. al-Sabbāḳ to govern it (Ibn al-Athīr, x, 249). On 24 Ramaḍān 500/19 May 1107, Djāwalī, the general of ʿImād al-Dīn Zangī, took the town through treachery (Ibn al-Athīr, x, 297; Ibn al-Ḳalānisī, ed. Amedroz, 156-7; Michael Syrus, tr. Chabot, iii, 193, iv, 592; Barhebraeus, *Chron. syr.*, ed. Bedjan, 273). ʿIzz al-Dīn Masʿūd b. al-Bursuḳī took it in 521/1127 shortly before his death (Ibn al-Athīr, x, 360-1; Mich. Syr., iii, 228, v, 610; Barhebr., *Chron. syr.*, 287). His successors killed one another fighting for the succession and al-Raḥba then passed to ʿIzz al-Dīn's young brother, for whom Djāwulī governed it as vassal of Zangī (Ibn al-Athīr, x, 453-4). Ḳuṭb al-Dīn, son of Zangī, in 544/1149-50 occupied the town (Ibn al-Athīr, xi, 93). On 4 Radjab 552/12 August 1157, al-Raḥba with Ḥamāt, Shayzar, Salamiyya and other towns were destroyed by an earthquake (Ibn al-Ḳalānisī, ed. Amedroz, 344; Mich. Syr., iii, 316; Barhebr., *Chron. syr.*, 325-6). The Khafādja tribe who in 556/1161 had plundered the district of al-Ḥilla and al-Kūfa returned to Raḥbat al-Shaʾm, followed by the government troops, where they were reinforced by other nomads and scattered the enemy (Ibn al-Athīr, xi, 182-3). Nūr al-Dīn granted the Kurd Asad al-Dīn Shīrkūh b. Aḥmad b. Shādī of Dwīn, Ṣalāḥ al-Dīn's uncle, in 559/1164, al-Raḥba and Ḥimṣ (Mich. Syr., iii, 325; Barhebr. *Chron. syr.*, 330). The latter entrusted the government of al-Raḥba to an officer named Yūsuf b. Mallāḥ. Shīrkūh built al-Raḥbat al-Djadīda with a citadel about a *farsakh* (3 miles) from the Euphrates, because the town of Raḥbat Mālik b. Ṭawḳ was now in ruins (Abu 'l-Fidāʾ, *Taḳwīm al-buldān*, ed. Reinaud, 281; Ḥādjdjī Khalīfa, *Djihān-nümā*, Istanbul 444). The new town of al-Raḥba became an important caravan station between Syria and the ʿIrāḳ, as we learn from Ibn Baṭṭūṭa amongst others (iv, 315) who travelled from there via al-Sukhna to Tadmur.

The town remained for a century in Shīrkūh's family until in 662/1264 Baybars installed an Egyptian governor there (Ibn al-Athīr, xi, 341, xii, 189; Abu 'l-Fidāʾ, *Annales muslem.*, ed. Reiske-Adler, iv, 142, v, 16). Sunḳur al-Ashḳar of Damascus, who rebelled against Ḳalāʾūn in 678/1279, fled after a defeat to al-Raḥba to the *amīr* ʿĪsā and from there appealed to the Mongol Abaḳa for protection (Barhebr., *Chron. syr.*, 543).

The Mongols under Kharbanda besieged al-Raḥba in 712/1312-13 on their way to Syria. On his return, Kharbanda left his siege artillery behind, whereupon it was taken by the defenders of the town into the citadel (Abu 'l-Fidāʾ, v, 268-9; al-Ḥasan b. Ḥabīb b. ʿUmar, *Durrat al-aslāk fī dawlat al-atrāk*, in H.E. Weijers, in *Orientalia*, ed. Juynboll, ii, Amsterdam 1846, 319). Its governor at the time, Ibn al-Arkashī, died in 715/1315-16 in Damascus (Abu 'l-Fidāʾ, v, 300). Al-Muhannā and his family, the ʿĪsā, were driven from the district of Salamiyya in the spring of 720/1320 and pursued by the Syrian troops as far as Raḥba and ʿĀna (Abu 'l-Fidāʾ, v, 340-1); the town was perhaps destroyed on this occasion.

In 731/1331 the Euphrates inundated the country round al-Raḥba (Ibn al-Athīr, Vienna ms. in Musil, *The Middle Euphrates*, 3, n. 3).

According to the Muslim geographers, al-Raḥba lay on the Euphrates (Ḳudāma, 233; al-Muḳaddasī, 138; al-Idrīsī, tr. Jaubert, ii, 137-8; al-Dimashḳī, ed. Mehren, 93; Abu 'l-Fidāʾ, ed. Reinaud, 51) and also on the canal Saʿīd led off from it at Fam Saʿīd on the right bank, which rejoined the Euphrates below the town, the gardens of which it watered, and above al-Dāliya also called Dāliyat Mālik b. Ṭawḳ (Suhrāb, ed. von Mžik, in *Bibl. arab. Histor. u. Geogr.*, v, Leipzig 1930, 123; Yāḳūt, iv, 840; Abu 'l-Fidāʾ, *Taḳwīm*, 281). The town lay 3 *farsakh*s from Ḳarḳīsiya (al-ʿAzīzī, in Abu 'l-Fidāʾ, ed. Reinaud, 281) and, according to al-Muḳaddasī, 149, a day's journey each from this town, al-Dāliya and Bīrā (the latter statement is quite inaccurate; cf. Musil, *op. cit.*, 253-4). Musil (*ibid.*, 250) wrongly takes al-Dāliya to be al-Ṣāliḥiyya, which is impossible, as 8-10 miles above it the Euphrates flows close to the foot of Djabal Abu 'l-Ḳāsim, so that the Saʿīd canal must have flowed north of it back into the Euphrates (cf. the *Karte von Mesopotamien* of the Prussian Survey, Feb. 1918, 1: 400,000, sheet 3c: ʿĀna; Cumont, *Fouilles de Doura-Europos*, Paris 1926, Atlas, pl. i.: *Cours de l'Euphrate entre Circesium et Doura-Europos d'après l'Aéronautique de "l'Armée du Levant"* on the same scale and the maps in Sarre-Herzfeld, *Arch. Reise*). The town of al-Raḥba was a Jacobite bishopric (a list of the bishops in Mich. Syr., iii, 502); that it—for a time at least—was also a Nestorian bishopric is shown from a life of the Catholicos Eliyā I (on him, see Baumstark, *Geschichte der syr. Literatur*, 286-7) who, shortly before his death on 6 May 1049, appointed a bishop to this town (Assemani, in *BO*, iii, 263).

In the statements of the Arab geographers, it is clear that the old Raḥbat Mālik b. Ṭawḳ lay on the bank of the Euphrates (al-Iṣṭak̲h̲rī, 13, 72; Ibn Ḥawḳāl, ed. de Goeje, 17, 138; al-Muḳaddasī, 138; Yāḳūt, iii, 860; Ibn K̲h̲urradādhbih, 233), i.e. it presumably corresponded to the modern al-Miyādīn (pl. of *maydān*) (G. Hoffmann, *Auszüge aus syr. Akten pers. Märtyrer*, 165; Herzfeld, *Arch. Reise*, ii, 382, n. 1; A. Musil, *The Middle Euphrates*, 3, 253, 340), while the new al-Raḥba, as we saw, was built a *farsak̲h̲* from it, where in the south-west of al-Miyādīn there still are the ruins of the citadel al-Raḥaba or al-Raḥba. According to Abu 'l-Fidāʾ (ed. Reinaud, 281), towers were still standing among the ruins of the old town. Opposite al-Raḥba on the left bank of the Euphrates stood a fortress taken by Marwān II (127-32/744-50) in the fighting with His̲h̲ām (Maḥbūb of Manbidj, *Kitāb al-ʿUnwān*, ed. Vasiliev, in *Patr. Orient.*, viii, 517-18). In this fortress Musil (*op. cit.*, 338-9) has recognised al-Zaytūna (al-Balādhurī, Futūḥ, 180; al-Ṭabarī, ii, 1467-8; Ibn K̲h̲urradādhbih, 74) and the ancient Ζαυδά which is still called al-Marwāniyya after this caliph, but is not really opposite al-Miyādīn but fourteen miles farther down.

Ibn Ḥawḳal, 155, praises the fertility of the well-watered region of Raḥba, where the orchards on the east bank of Euphrates also produced date-palms; their quinces were also famous (al-Muḳaddasī, 145). The *Karte von Mesopotamien* (1 : 400,000) marks at "Mejādin" "the first (most northerly) palm". Dates really only ripen in specially favourable weather in the region of Albū Kamāl (Musil, *op. cit.*, 342). According to al-Iṣṭak̲h̲rī, 77, Raḥbat Mālik b. Ṭawḳ was larger than Ḳarḳīsiya; al-Muḳaddasī, 142, calls it the centre of the Euphrates' (*ʿamal al-Furāt* or *nāḥiyat al-Furāt*), as in the early Islamic period the fertile plain from Dayr al-Zawr to Albū Kamāl with the towns of al-Raḥba, Dāliya, ʿĀna and al-Ḥadītha was called (Herzfeld, *op. cit.*, ii, 382). According to him, the town was built in a semi-circle on the edge of the desert and defended by a strong fortress.

Yāḳūt visited the town, which according to him was eight days' journey from Damascus, five from Aleppo, 100 *farsak̲h̲s* from Bag̲h̲dād and a little over 20 *farsak̲h̲s* from al-Raḳḳa. In al-Dimas̲h̲ḳī, 202, it is called Raḥbat al-Furātiyya. In the time of K̲h̲alīl al-Ẓāhirī (*Zubda*, ed. Ravaisse, 50) it belonged to Aleppo. According to al-ʿUmarī, Syria, or, to be more exact, its eastern marches with the capital Ḥimṣ, reached as far as al-Raḥba; he mentions there "a citadel and a governorship and there are Baḥriyya, cavalry, scouts

and mercenaries stationed there" (al-ʿUmarī, tr. R. Hartmann, in *ZDMG*, lxx, 23, 30). Ibn Baṭṭūṭa calls the town "the end of al-ʿIrāḳ and the beginning of al-S̲h̲aʾm". Ḥādjdjī K̲h̲alīfa reckons from ʿĀna to al-Raḥba three days' journey and from there to al-Dayr one days' journey (*Djahān-nümā*, 483; cf. thereon, Musil, *op. cit.*, 257).

The Venetian jeweller Gasparo Balbi, who passed by the town on 6 February 1588 on the Euphrates, says (*Viaggi dell' Indie orientali*, Venice 1599, without pagination) *vedemmo castello Rahabi appresso il qual castello si vede una città rovinata, ma in alcuni lati di essa habitata da alcune poche persone di nome di Rahabilatica* (on the form Raḥabī, cf. M. Hartmann, in *ZDPV*, xxii, 44, at no. 390). Pietro Della Valle (*Viaggi*, Venice 1544, i, 571) saw the town of "Rachba" at some distance from the Euphrates and heard that there were some old buildings there. Tavenier (*Les six voyages*, i, Paris 1676, 285) mentions a place called "Mached-raba", i.e. Mas̲h̲had al-Raḥba (six miles to the southwest of al-Raḥba).

The mediaeval Arabic texts on al-Raḥba have now been published over the last half-century. For the period 640-1060, for which no further publication of importance is to be expected, a tentative sketch of its history has been made by Th. Bianquis, *Raḥba et les tribus arabes avant les Croisades*, in *BEO*, xli-xlii (1989-90), with a detailed bibliography.

As for the period 452-923/1060-1517, the work of extracting information from the texts is still in progress. Ibn al-Dawādārī's history, especially rich on the sieges of al-Raḥba (see, in particular, the year 711/1311-12), has not been exploited, and the appearance of chronicles from the 7th/13th and 8th/14th centuries is announced. Until an extended study on al-Raḥba and the middle Euphrates in general during the Arab period shall appear, a survey of some recently acquired pieces of information is given here.

Numerous projects have been carried out since 1970 on the material culture of the region in mediaeval and post-mediaeval times. Archaeological excavations have been made on the site from 1976 to 1981 by the General Directorate of the Syrian Museum of Antiquities, the Institut Français d'Études Arabes de Damas and the University of Lyons II. Subsequently, Syrian, European and American multi-disciplinary teams, working on the societies of the desert margins, have carried out surveys on both banks of the Euphrates and on those of the K̲h̲ābūr. Our knowledge of the past of al-Raḥba and its region has thus been considerably enlarged, but the sparse publications so far available are still only provisional.

Work has been carried out at three sites. To the south of the town of al-Miyādīn, a stretch of territory on the banks of the Euphrates, near an old Ottoman caravanserai, was excavated from 1976 to 1981, mainly revealing dwellings from the Ayyūbid period and with abundant material. The excavation had to be relinquished in the face of contemporary building operations just when an old level, probably ʿAbbāsid (4th/10th century) had been uncovered beneath a layer of material abandoned when irrigated gardens were laid out, corresponding to an urban decline in the 5th/11th century. The coins discovered at this site have been published by A. Nègre, *Les monnaies de Mayādīn*, in *BEO*, xxxii-xxxiii (1980-1), and the pottery will shortly be published also. Some urban life then continued along the Euphrates banks long after the earthquake of 551/1156.

The great citadel on a cliff some 2.5 miles/4 km from the Euphrates (for earlier illustrations of this, see

Musil, *The Middle Euphrates*, 7, fig. 2, and Sarre-Herzfeld, *Arch. Reise*, iii, pls. LXXIX ff.) is now deteriorating rapidly, with erosion eating away the supports of the walls. A study made 1976-81 allowed the drawing up of plans and elevations of the site, bringing out the complexity of the building, which was destroyed, rebuilt and enlarged on several occasions; see J.L. Paillet, *Le château de Raḥba, étude d'architecture militaire islamique médiévale*, diss. Univ. of Lyons II 1983, unpubl. Large numbers of featherings for arrows, cut out of the paper of registers, have been found, souvenirs of sieges by the Mongols. From the Ottoman period onwards, the building no longer had any military value and provided shelter for sheep-raising villagers.

From 1976 to 1978, work was undertaken at the foot of this fortress in the abandoned ruins of an urban settlement. A great enclosure, quadrangular in shape with sides of some 30 m, surrounded by a wall one metre thick, restored on various occasions and in some places more than 4 m in height, has been partially revealed. One can guess at an ensemble comprising a public building—a *khān*, a cavalry barracks or a great mosque, probably including a small oratory—with a complex network of canals for the bringing in of fresh water and for carrying away waste and dirty water. The pottery and coins which have been analysed are mainly Mamlūk, with some Ayyūbid sherds in the deeper layers. The houses around this great building have not yet been excavated but offer a clearly more rural aspect than the houses spread along the Euphrates banks.

Until the end of the 5th/11th century al-Raḥba was a riverine port to which came caravans arriving via Tadmur or Palmyra from Damascus, Ḥimṣ, Salamiyya and Ḥamāt. After then, this river traffic declined, for reasons not yet clear; lack of wood for the construction of river craft? Decrease in the amount of water through desiccation? Insecurity? Caravan traffic running parallel to the river, on the plateau above the right bank, now enjoyed a corresponding increase. The ability to survey the steppe lands, which stretch as far as eye can see, always justified the building of a progressively stronger citadel on the river banks. To the north-east, it dominated the valley and could easily block or hold up the advance of an army venturing into the 4 km-wide plain along the right bank of the Euphrates. The fortress being at a lower level, on the edge of the cliff, on the alluvial plain, and unable to command a view of the steppes at a higher level, lost some of its value.

Al-Raḥba formed part of various types of regional groupings: the Euphrates valley in the context of the administration of the *ṭarīḳ al-Furāt*, the Djazīran principality of Mawṣil under the Ḥamdānid Nāṣir al-Dawla, Fāṭimid Egypt and southern Syria at the beginning of the 6th/12th century, northern Syria under the Kilābī Mirdāsids after 416/1025, the Saldjūḳ principality of Damascus at the end of the 5th/11th century and the Syrian steppe principality extending from Salamiyya to the Euphrates in the Zangid and Ayyūbid periods. Under the Mamlūks, the citadel was rebuilt and held an important garrison, and it protected the new town which had grown up right at its feet. The *nāʾib* commanding it had a high place in the military hierarchy. It played a notable role at the time of the Turco-Mongol invasions between 1260 and 1400, forcing these invaders to detach from their fighting force powerful contingents to watch over and besiege the fortress. There are several mentions of al-Raḥba in the *Taʾrīkh* of Ibn Ḳāḍī Shuhba, ed. Adnan Darwich, Damascus 1977; on p. 479 the author states that, in 795/1392-3, when Tīmūr Lang had conquered Mesopotamia, he sent messages to the *nāʾib* of al-Raḥba, who after having read them, put the Turco-Mongol emissaries to death.

Bibliography (in addition to references given in the article): Ibn Djubayr, ed. Wright, 250; Ḳalḳashandī, *Ḍawʾ*, Cairo 1324, 291, cf. Gaudefroy-Demombynes, *La Syrie à l'époque des Mamelouks*, Paris 1923, 77-80, 183, 245-6, 254, 259; R. Hartmann, *Die geographischen Nachrichten über Palästina und Syrien in Khalīl al-Ẓāhirī's Zubdat Kashf al-Mamālik*, diss. Tübingen 1907, 62; K. Ritter, *Erdkunde*, xi, 268, 693-4, 706, 1433; G. Hoffmann, *Auszüge aus syr. Akten pers. Märtyrer*, 165; M. Hartmann, in *ZDPV*, xxiii, 42, 44-50, 49, 61, 68, 113, 124, 127; *OLZ*, ii (1899), col. 311; B. Moritz, *Zur antiken Topographie der Palmyrene*, in *Abh. Pr. Ak. W.* (1889), 36, 37 n. 4; E. Sachau, *Reise in Syrien und Mesopotamien*, Leipzig 1883, 279 ff.; G. Le Strange, *Lands of the Eastern Caliphate*, Cambridge 1905, 105, 124; idem, *Palestine under the Moslems*, London 1890, 517-18; R. Hartmann, in *ZDMG*, lxx (1916), 30, n. 9; E. Reitemeyer, *Die Städtegründungen der Araber* (diss. Heidelberg), Munich 1912, 85; R. Dussaud, *Topographie historique de la Syrie antique et médiévale*, Paris 1927, 252-3, 259, 454 n. 2, 514; A. Musil, *The Middle Euphrates*, New York 1927, 340-5 and *passim*, cf. index, 415-16, s.v. ar-Raḥba, Raḥba Ṭowḳ, etc.; A. Poidebard, *La trace de Rome dans le désert de Syrie*, text, Paris 1934, 93, 104; E. Herzfeld in Sarre-Herzfeld, *Archäologische Reise im Euphrat- und Tigris-Gebiet*, ii, Berlin 1920, 382-4, and B. Schulz, *ibid.*, 384-6, figs. 367-9; iii, Berlin 1911, pls. LXXIX ff.

(E. Honigmann-[Th. Bianquis]

RAHBĀNIYYA (A.), monasticism. The term is derived from *rāhib* [*q.v.*] "anchovite, monk"; it occurs in the Ḳurʾān once only, in a complicated passage (sūra LVII, 27) that has given rise to divergent interpretations: "And we put in the hearts of those who followed Jesus, compassion and mercy, and the monastic state (*rahbāniyya*); they instituted the same (we did not prescribe it to them) only out of a desire to please God. Yet they observed not the same as it ought truly to have been observed. And we gave unto such of them as believed, their reward; but many of them have been doers of evil."

According to some of the exegesis, the verb "we put" has two objects only, viz. compassion and mercy, whereas the words "and the monastic state" are the object of "they instituted". Accordingly, the monastic state or *rahbāniyya* appears here as a purely human institution, which, moreover, has been perverted by evil-doers.

According to others, however, the object of the words "and we put" is compassion, mercy and the monastic state. According to this exegesis, monasticism is called a divine institution, although not prescribed for mankind. But it has been perverted by evil-doers. This exegesis seems preferable to the other, although the juxtaposition of compassion, mercy and the monastic state seems rather unnatural. Of the two, the first interpretation displays a much less favourable attitude to the monastic state than the second. L. Massignon pointed out that this latter exegesis is the older one; the younger one expresses a feeling hostile to monasticism, which coined the tradition "No *rahbāniyya* in Islam."

This tradition does not occur in the canonical collections. Yet it is being prepared there. When the wife of ʿUthmān b. Maẓʿūn [*q.v.*] complained of being neglected by her husband, Muḥammad took her part, saying: "Monasticism (*rahbāniyya*) was not prescribed for us" (Aḥmad b. Ḥanbal, vi, 226; al-Dārimī, *Nikāḥ, bāb* 3). The following tradition is less exclusive: "Do not trouble yourselves and God will not trouble you. Some have troubled themselves and God has troubled them. Their successors are in the hermitages and monasteries, 'an institution we have not prescribed for them'" (Abū Dāwūd, *Adab, bāb* 44).

Islam, thus rejecting monasticism, has replaced it by the *d̲j̲ihād*: "Every prophet has some kind of *rahbāniyya*; the *rahbāniyya* of this community is the *d̲j̲ihād*" (a tradition ascribed to Muḥammad, in Aḥmad b. Ḥanbal, iii, 266; and to Abū Saʿīd al-K̲h̲udrī, *ibid.*, iii, 82). See also ṬARĪḲA, ZUHD.

Bibliography: L. Massignon, *Essai sur les origines du lexique technique de la mystique musulmane*, 123 ff.; the commentaries of the Ḳurʾān on sūra LVII, 27; Ibn Saʿd, *Ṭabaḳāt*, ed. Sachau, iii/1, 287; Ḥarīrī, *Maḳāmāt*, ed. de Sacy, 570-1; Zamak̲h̲s̲h̲arī, *al-Fāʾiḳ*, Ḥaydarābād 1324, i, 269; Ibn al-At̲h̲īr, *Nihāya*, s.v.; A. Sprenger, *Das Leben und die Lehre des Mohammad*, i, 389; I. Goldziher, *Muhammedanische Studien*, ii, 394; idem, in *RHR*, xviii, 193-4, xxxvii, 314; E. Beck, *Das christliche Mönchtum im Koran*, Helsinki 1946. (A.J. WENSINCK)

RĀHIB (A., pl. *ruhbān, rahābīn, rahābina*), a monk. The figure of the monk is known to pre-Islamic poetry and to the Ḳurʾān and Tradition. The pre-Islamic poets refer to the monk in his cell, the light of which the traveller by night sees in the distance and which gives him the idea of shelter.

In the Ḳurʾān, the monk and the *ḳissīs*, sometimes also the *aḥbār*, are the religious leaders of the Christians. In one place it is said that rabbis and monks live at the expense of other men (sūra IX, 34) and that the Christians have taken as their masters instead of God their *aḥbār* and their monks as well as al-Masīḥ b. Maryam (IX, 31). In another passage, the Christians are praised for their friendship to their fellow-believers, which is explained from the fact that there are priests and monks among them (V, 87). In *Ḥadīt̲h̲*, the *rāhib* is frequently encountered in stories of the nature of the *ḳiṣaṣ al-anbiyāʾ* (see al-Buk̲h̲ārī, *Anbiyāʾ*, *bāb* 54; Muslim, *Zuhd*, trad. 73; *Tawba*, trad. 46, 47; al-Tirmid̲h̲ī, *Tafsīr*, sūra LXXXV, trad. 2; *Manāḳib*, trad. 3; al-Nasāʾī, *Masād̲j̲id*, trad. 11; Ibn Mād̲j̲a, *Fitan*, trad. 20, 23; al-Dārimī, *Faḍāʾil al-Ḳurʾān*, trad. 16; Aḥmad b. Ḥanbal, i, 461; ii, 434; iii, 337, 347; v, 4; vi, 17 *bis*).

From the fact that in the Islamic literature of the early centuries A.H. the epithet *rāhib* was given to various pious individuals, it is evident that there was nothing odious about it then; see, however, the article RAHBĀNIYYA.

Bibliography: See that to RAHBĀNIYYA. (A.J. WENSINCK)

RĀḤĪL, in the Bible Rachel, wife of Jacob, mother of Joseph and Benjamin, is not mentioned in the Ḳurʾān. There is, however, a reference to her in sūra IV, 27: "Ye may not have two sisters to wife at the same time; if it has been done formerly, God now exercises pardon and mercy." This is said to allude to Jacob's marriage with Liyā and Rāḥīl; before Moses revealed the Tora, such a marriage was valid. Al-Ṭabarī gives this explanation in his *Annals*, i, 356, 359-60. Ibn al-At̲h̲īr, i, 90, adopts it. But already in *Tafsīr*, iv, 210, al-Ṭabarī explains the verse correctly: Muḥammad forbids for the future marriage with two sisters but he does not dissolve such marriages concluded before the prohibition.—Islamic tradition generally adopts the view that Yaʿḳūb only married Rāḥīl after Liyā's death. So already in al-Ṭabarī, i, 355, al-Zamak̲h̲s̲h̲arī, al-Bayḍāwī, Ibn al-At̲h̲īr, etc. Al-Kisāʾī even thinks that Yaʿḳūb only married Rāḥīl after the death of Liyā and of his two concubines. Here again Muslim legend differs from the Bible, in making him not marry Rāḥīl until after 14 years of service; in the Bible, Jacob serves seven years, marries Leah and, after the wedding week, Rachel and serves another seven years. Yaʿḳūb's wooing and Lāban's trick by which he substitutes Liyā for Rāḥīl as "neither lamp nor candle-light" illuminate the bridal chamber, is embellished in Muslim legend.

Rāḥīl is also of importance in the story of Yūsuf. Yūsuf inherits his beauty from Rāḥīl; they had half of all the beauty in the world, according to others two-thirds, or even according to the old Haggadic scheme (*Ḳiddus̲h̲in*, 49b), nine-tenths (al-T̲h̲aʿlabī, 69). When Yaʿḳūb left Lāban, he had no funds for the journey; at Rachel's suggestion, Yūsuf steals Lāban's idols. As Yūsuf, sold by his brothers, passes the tomb of Rāḥīl he throws himself from his camel on the grave and laments: "O mother, look on thy child, I have been deprived of my coat, thrown into a pit, stoned and sold as a slave." Then he hears a voice: "Trust in God." The old Haggada does not know this touching scene. But it has found its way into the late mediaeval book of stories *Sefer Hayas̲h̲ar* (ed. Goldschmidt, 150). The Judaeo-Persian poet S̲h̲āhīn (15th century) adapts this motif from Firdawsī's *Yūsuf u Zulayk̲h̲ā* in his book of Genesis.

Bibliography: Ṭabarī, i, 355-60, 371; idem, *Tafsīr*, iv, 210; T̲h̲aʿlabī, *Ḳiṣaṣ al-anbiyāʾ*, Cairo 1325, 69, 74; Ibn al-At̲h̲īr, i, 90; Kisāʾī, *Ḳiṣaṣ al-anbiyāʾ*, ed. Eisenberg, 155-6, 160, tr. W.M. Thackston, *The Tales of the Prophets of al-Kisaʾi*, Boston 1978, 165, 167, 181; Neumann Ede, *A muhammedán József monda*, Budapest 1881, 12, 39-40; Grünbaum, *Gesammelte Aufsätze zur Sprach- und Sagenkunde*, ed. F. Perles, Berlin 1901, 523, 534-8, 548; W. Bacher, *Zwei jüdisch-persische Dichter, Schahin und Imrāni*, Budapest 1907, 119. See also YAʿḲŪB and YŪSUF. (B. HELLER)

RAḤĪL (A.), "travelling by camel", a term applied in Arabic poetry to themes involving a desert journey. In its specific meaning it denotes a section of the polythematic *ḳaṣīda* [*q.v.*], following the *nasīb* [*q.v.*], where the poet describes his camel and his travels. The term is derived from the verb *raḥala* "to saddle a camel" or "to mount a camel". In Arabic poetics, the *raḥīl* is not classified among the "genres" (*ag̲h̲rāḍ*) of poetry, nor is the term used in a technical sense. Mediaeval critics usually paraphrase the theme (cf. Ibn Ḳutayba, *S̲h̲iʿr*, 14).

In the *D̲j̲āhiliyya* [*q.v.*], poets allude to the perilous desert journey at the beginning of their self-praise [see MUFĀK̲H̲ARA], introducing it, like other themes of *fak̲h̲r*, by *wāw rubba* ("and many a...") or by *ḳad* preceding a verb in the imperfect tense ("and often I..."). But already in early texts, there is a tendency to connect the *raḥīl* with the *nasīb*. The poet, after his disappointment in love, turns to his camel for consolation, or he asks whether it will be strong enough to carry him to his beloved. Then usually follows a detailed description of the camel (*waṣf al-d̲j̲amal*), embellished by scenes of animal life, introduced as comparisons, the camel being compared to a wild bull, an onager, an ostrich, and, very rarely, to an eagle. If the ode ends with a *madīḥ* [*q.v.*], the poet sometimes adds, by way of transition (*tak̲h̲alluṣ*), that he is travelling towards the *mamdūḥ*, the addressee of his panegyric. From the corpus of pre-Islamic verse it appears that the *raḥīl* originally formed a theme of *fak̲h̲r*, and that its interpretation as a journey to the *mamdūḥ* is a secondary development. For poets in the *Djāhiliyya* do not travel towards a destination; travelling is the mode of Bedouin life, and the camel is its most significant symbol. By turning to his excellent mount after the emotional crisis of the *nasīb*, the "Bedouin hero" regains his equanimity and his ability to perform the tasks demanded of him by tribal society.

During the first part of the 7th century, a transformation of the camel-section sets in, which is continued in the Umayyad period. As a result, the traditional description of the poet's camel is replaced by a *raḥīl* to the *mamdūḥ*, by which the poet emphasises the dangers and hardships which he took upon himself on his way. In the Umayyad *raḥīl*, the destination is always stated, and the length of the way dwelled upon. The poet mentions a group of travellers and their mounts, and describes their state of weariness and exhaustion. Some odes begin with a *raḥīl*, which is often blended with the *madīḥ* in an ingenious way. Thus the *raḥīl* is now entirely determined by the panegyrical function of the ode, as described by Ibn Ḳutayba (*loc. cit.*), who evidently had the Umayyad *ḳaṣīda* in mind, when explaining the genre (cf. R. Jacobi, *The camel-section of the panegyrical ode*, in *JAL*, xiii [1982], 1-22).

In the early ʿAbbāsid period, the *raḥīl* is gradually reduced in length or omitted altogether (Jacobi, *op. cit.*, 19-21). ʿAbbāsid odes are as a rule bipartite in structure, a development already beginning in the Umayyad period. However, later poets occasionally fall back upon traditional patterns, and there are some original variations of the travel theme. As part of the panegyrical ode, the *raḥīl* survives until modern times.

Bibliography: In general works, the *raḥīl* is treated in connection with the *ḳaṣīda*, cf. *GAP*, ii (index), *CHAL*, ii (index); E. Wagner, *Grundzüge der klassischen arabischen Dichtung*, i-ii, Darmstadt 1987-8 (Index). Studies limited to the *Djāhiliyya*: R. Jacobi, *Studien zur Poetik der altarabischen Qaṣide*, Wiesbaden 1971, cf. 49-65; A. Hamori, *The poet as hero*, in idem, *On the art of medieval Arabic literature*, Princeton 1974, 3-30; W. Rūmiyya, *al-Riḥla fi 'l-ḳaṣīda al-djāhiliyya*, 1975. (R. Jacobi)

RAḤĪM [see ALLĀH].

RAḤMA (A.), a Ḳurʾānic term (attested 114 times), denoting either kindness, benevolence (synonym of *raʾfa*) or—more frequently—an act of kindness, a favour (synonym of *niʿma* or *faḍl*). Almost invariably, the term is applied to God; in only three verses is there reference to the *raḥma* which humans have, or should have, in their relationships with others: sons towards their father and mother (XVII, 24), married couples between themselves (XXX, 21), Christians among themselves (LVII, 27).

The French translation by "miséricorde", although often used, is misleading, since in current usage, particularly in religious vocabulary, "miséricorde" essentially includes the notion of forgiveness, this being the kindness whereby God forgives men for their sins (the same observation applies moreover, although less precisely, to the English "mercy" and the German "Gnade"). It is true that the indulgence of God with regard to sinners is an eminent form of his kindness, and in fact in some instances the Ḳurʾān associates the two notions (cf. for example XVIII, 58; XXXIX, 53; XL, 7). It is also possible to understand in this sense (although not necessarily, cf. al-Ṭabarsī's commentary) the formula of VI, 12 and 54: *kataba ʿalā nafsih al-raḥma*. But in the majority of cases, the notion of the forgiveness of sins is totally absent from Ḳurʾānic usages of *raḥma*. As previously stated, this term is to be understood most often as a simple equivalent of *niʿma*. It represents a "kindness" which God grants (*ātā, wahaba*) to men (cf. III, 8; XI, 28; XVIII, 10, 65), a good which He "makes them taste" (*adhāḳa*), as opposed to the evils which he inflicts upon them, *raḥma* being, in such instances, opposed to *ḍurr, ḍarrāʾ*, or *sayyiʾa* (cf. X, 21; XI, 9; XXX, 33, 36; XLI, 50; XLII, 48); sometimes, in fact, it is an affliction (*sūʾ, ḍurr*) which He wills upon them, and sometimes a *raḥma* (cf. XXXIII, 17, and XXXIX, 38).

These *raḥmas* which God gives as benefits to men, or to one or another individual, are of various kinds. There is the "Book given to Moses", described as *hudā wa-raḥma* (VI, 154; VII, 154), *imān wa-raḥma* (XI, 17; XLVI, 12); the Ḳurʾān itself, also frequently described as *hudā wa-raḥma* (XXVII, 77; XXXI, 3; etc.) or as *shifāʾ wa-raḥma* (XVII, 82); Jesus (XIX, 21); Muḥammad (XXI, 107). Also a *raḥma* is the fact of having given to Moses, to assist him, his brother Aaron (XIX, 53), to Zachariah a son (XIX, 2); of having saved from annihilation Hūd and his supporters (VII, 72; XI, 58). *Raḥma* is furthermore the treasure destined to the two orphans of XVIII, 82; the wall erected by Dhu 'l-Ḳarnayn (XVIII, 98); the maintenance (*rizḳ*) which the Prophet awaits from God (XVII, 28); the rain (VII, 57; XXV, 48; XXVII, 63; XXX, 50); and the alternation of day and night (XXVIII, 73).

There is disagreement among the early exegetes regarding the original meaning of the term, a disagreement which essentially divides, it seems, lexicographers from theologians. For the former, *raḥma* denotes at the outset an aggregate of related emotional states, of which the most characteristic is that of *riḳḳat al-kalb*, which may be translated, for want of a better choice, by "sensibility", the "fact of having a sensitive heart". Al-Mubarrad would define *raḥma* by *taḥannun* ("tenderness") *wa-riḳḳa* (according to al-Zadjdjādjī, *Ishtiḳāḳ asmāʾ Allāh*, Beirut 1986, 41, 8), *riḳḳa wa-taʿaṭṭuf* ("benevolence") (according to Abū Ḥātim al-Rāzī, *al-Zīna*, ii, Cairo 1958, 23, 7-8; cf. also *LA*). In his "exoteric" commentary on the *basmala*, al-Shahrastānī gives the following definition: "In Arabic, *raḥma* denotes sensibility (*riḳḳat al-ḳalb*), compassion (*shafaḳa*), softness (*līn*) and gentleness (*rifḳ*); this term has for antonyms hardness (*faẓāẓa*) and severity (*ghilẓat al-ḳalb*)" (*Mafātīḥ al-asrār*, facs. ed. Tehran 1989, fol. 33b). Lending force to this interpretation is a saying of Ibn ʿAbbās, glossing *raḥmān* with *raḳīḳ* and *raḥīm* with *ʿāṭif* (cf. Gimaret, *Les noms divins en Islam*, Paris 1988, 379). The question which is posed is, for a theologian, whether, thus understood, *raḥma* can truly be used in connection with God. On account, no doubt, of what this term implies in the sense of vulnerability, fragility, it is generally reckoned in fact that *riḳḳa* could not be counted among the divine attributes (thus al-Khaṭṭābī and al-Ḥusayn b. al-Faḍl al-Badjalī, according to al-Bayhaḳī, *al-Asmāʾ wa 'l-ṣifāt*, Cairo 1939, 51, 13-18). A *riḳḳa*, explains al-Ghazālī, is a cause of suffering, and it is in order to alleviate this suffering that the "sensitive" man performs an act of beneficence; God, on the other hand, is not susceptible to suffering (*al-Maḳṣid al-asnā*, Beirut 1961, 66, 1-11). For this reason al-Zamakhsharī considers that, when *raḥma* is applied to God, it is to be taken in a figurative sense, signifying His beneficence (*inʿām*) towards His creatures (*al-Kashshāf*, Cairo 1385/1966, i, 44-5). For al-Mubarrad, the term is frankly ambiguous. Applied to men, it signifies "tenderness and sensibility"; applied to God, it means "beneficence and generosity" (*inʿām wa-ifḍāl*) (al-Zadjdjādjī, *Ishtiḳāḳ*, 41, 8-9). Al-

Djubbāʾī, for his part, goes further; for him, the true sense of *raḥma* is that which makes it an equivalent of *niʿma*; if a man of sensitive heart is described as *raḥīm*, it is in fact because such a man is beneficent (ʿAbd al-Djabbār, *al-Mughnī*, xx/b, 207, 6-8). The same point of view is expressed by Ibn Bābawayh (*al-Tawḥīd*, Nadjaf 1387/1968, 203-4).

The question of the origin and meaning of the divine name *al-Raḥmān*, as well as of the formula *al-Raḥmān al-Raḥīm*, has already been discussed [see BASMALA and AL-ḲURʾĀN. 4.c]. For almost all the ancient commentators—the single exception being Thaʿlab—there is no doubt that *raḥmān* and *raḥīm* are quite simply two parallel qualificatives, both derived from the root *r-ḥ-m*, one in the *faʿlān* form, the other in *faʿīl*, both attesting that the person thus described practises the virtue of *raḥma*. Some, including the grammarian Abū ʿUbayda, even saw the words as pure doublets, analogous, they declared, to the pair of *nadmān* and *nadīm*, the only difference being that *raḥmān* could be applied only to God (thus, in particular, al-Ashʿarī, according to Ibn Fūrak, *Mudjarrad*, Beirut 1987, 47, 21-3; al-Djuwaynī, *Irshād*, Cairo 1950, 145, 4-6). However, later authorities—these being the majority—attribute to *raḥmān* a stronger quality, precisely because the word is applied only to God, and because, according to a frequent exegesis, *raḥmān* is reckoned to have a broader "extension" than *raḥīm*. It is said that God is *raḥmān* for all men, believers or non-believers, while He is *raḥīm* only for believers (in conformity with Ḳurʾān, XXXIII, 43, *wa-kāna bi 'l-muʾminīna raḥīm*[an]). For al-Ḥalīmī, for example, God is *raḥmān* in that He gives to all men the means of finding their salvation, so that they have no excuse not to worship Him; He is *raḥīm* for the believers in that He rewards them without stinting (al-Bayhaḳī, *al-Asmāʾ*, 49, 20-1). Some writers (for example, Ibn Bābawayh, *al-Tawḥīd*, 203, 13-14) furthermore assert that, if God alone is described as *raḥmān*, while *raḥīm* can be applied to anyone who has compassion for the suffering of others, this is because God alone has, in addition, the power of removing this suffering (on this area of speculation, see Gimaret, *Noms divins*, 379-82).

Bibliography: Given in the article.

(D. GIMARET)

RAḤMA B. **DJĀBIR** [see ḲURṢĀN. iii].

RAḤMĀN [see BASMALA; ḲURʾĀN].

RAḤMĀNIYYA, Algerian Ṣūfī order (*ṭarīḳa*) called after Muḥammad b. ʿAbd al-Raḥmān al-Gashtulī al-Djurdjurī al-Azharī Abū Ḳabrayn, who died in 1208/1793-4. It is a branch of the Khalwatiyya [*q.v.*] and is said to have at one time been called Bakriyya after Muṣṭafā al-Bakrī al-Shāmī. At Nafṭa [*q.v.*], in Tunisia, and some other places it is called ʿAzzūziyya after Muṣṭafā b. Muḥammad b. ʿAzzūz.

Life of the founder. His family belonged to the tribe Ayt Smāʿīl, part of the Gashtula confederation in the Ḳābiliyya Djurdjura; having studied at his home, and then in Algiers, he made the pilgrimage in 1152/1740, and on his return spent some time as a student at al-Azhar in Cairo, where Muḥammad b. Sālim al-Ḥafnawī (d. 1181/1767-8: *Silk al-durar*, iv, 50) initiated him into the Khalwatī order, and ordered him to propagate it in India and the Sūdān; after an absence of thirty years he returned to Algeria, and commenced preaching in his native village, where he founded a *zāwiya*; he seems to have introduced some modifications into Khalwatī practice, and in his Seven Visions of the Prophet Muḥammad made some important claims for his person and his system; immunity from hell-fire was to be secured by affiliation to his order, love for himself or it, a visit to himself, stopping before his tomb or hearing his *dhikr* recited. His success in winning adherents provoked the envy of the local *murābiṭs*, in consequence of which he migrated to Ḥamma in the neighbourhood of Algiers. Here, too, his activities met with opposition from the religious leaders, who summoned him to appear before a *madjlis* under the presidency of the Mālikī *muftī* ʿAlī b. Amīn; through the influence of the Turkish authorities, who were impressed by the following which he had acquired, he was acquitted of the charge of unorthodoxy, but he thought it prudent to return to his native village, where shortly afterwards he died, leaving as his successor ʿAlī b. ʿĪsā al-Maghribī. His corpse is said to have been stolen by the Turks and buried with great pomp at Ḥamma with a *ḳubba* and a mosque over it. The Ayt Smāʿīl, however, maintained that it had not left its original grave, whence it was supposed to have been miraculously duplicated, and the title *Abū Ḳabrayn* "owner of two graves" was given to him.

History and propagation of the order. ʿAlī b. ʿĪsā al-Maghribī was undisputed head from 1208/1793-4 to 1251/1835; his successor died shortly after, and from the following year, though the order continued to win adherents, it divided into independent branches. This was owing to the objections raised by the Ayt Smāʿīl to the succession of al-Ḥādjdj Bashīr, another Maghribī; in spite of the support of the *amīr* ʿAbd al-Ḳādir [*q.v.*], he had to quit his post, which was held for a time by the widow of ʿAlī b. ʿĪsā, who, however, owing to the dwindling of the revenues of the *zāwiya*, had ultimately to summon Bashīr back. Meanwhile, the founders of other *zāwiya*s were assuming independence. After the death of Bashīr in 1259/1843, the widow's son-in-law al-Ḥādjdj ʿAmmār succeeded to the headship of the order. Finding his influence waning owing to his failure to participate in the attack on the French organised by Bū Baghla, in Dhu 'l-Ḥidjdja 1272/August 1856 he called his followers to arms and obtained some initial successes; he was, however, compelled to surrender in the following year, together with his wife (or mother-in-law) at the head of a hundred *khwān* shortly afterwards. ʿAmmār retired to Tunis, where he endeavoured to continue the exercise of his functions, but he was not generally recognised as head of the order, and his place among the Ayt Smāʿīl was taken by Muḥammad Ameẓẓyān b. al-Ḥaddād of Ṣaddūḳ, who at the age of 80 on 8 April 1871 proclaimed *djihād* against the French, who had recently been defeated in the Franco-Prussian War. The insurrection met with little success, though it spread far, and on 13 July Ibn al-Ḥaddād surrendered to General Saussier, who sent him to Bougie. The original *zāwiya* was closed as a precautionary measure.

His son ʿAzīz, who had been transported to New Caledonia, succeeded in escaping to Djudda, whence he endeavoured to govern the community; but various *muḳaddam*s who had been appointed by his father, as well as other founders of *zāwiya*s, asserted their independence. Lists have been given by Depont and Coppolani of these persons and their spheres of influence, which extended into Tunisia and the Sahara. In their work, the numbers of the adherents to the order were reckoned at 156,214 (1897). In 1954, L. Massignon revised this number to 156,000 adherents, with 177 *zāwiya*s, whilst in 1961 Fauque estimated them at 230,000. It should be said that the Raḥmāniyya constitute the most important Ṣūfī order in Algeria, with more than one-half of the *khwān* of the land. It predominates in the towns of the Constantinois such as Constantine, ʿAnnāba, Souk-Ahrag, Batna, Biskra, etc., and naturally in Kabylia, where it originated. Rinn noticed that the Raḥmāniyya of Tolga regularly maintained good relations with the French authorities.

Practices of the order. The training of the *murīd* consists in teaching him a series of seven "names", of which the first is the formula *lā ilāhᵃ illa 'llāhᵘ*, to be repeated from 12,000 to 70,000 times in a day and night, and followed by the others, if the *shaykh* is satisfied with the neophyte's progress; these are: 2. *Allāh* three times; 3. *huwa*; 4. *ḥakk* three times; 5. *ḥayy* three times; 6. *ḳayyūm* three times; 7. *ḳahhār* three times (Rinn's list differs slightly from this). Rinn stated that the *dhikr* of the order consists in repeating at least 80 times from the afternoon of Thursday to that of Friday the prayer ascribed to al-Shādhilī [*q.v.*], and on the other weekdays the formula *lā ilāhᵃ illa 'llāhᵘ*. Favourite lessons are the "Verse of the Throne" followed by sūras I, CXII-CXIV (prescribed in the Founder's diploma, translated by A. Delpech, in *RA* (1874), and the Seven Visions mentioned above (translated by Rinn, 467).

Literature of the order. Most of this would seem to be still in ms.; the founder is credited with several books. A. Cherbonneau, in *JA* (1852), 517, describes a catechism called *al-Raḥmāniyya* by Muḥammad b. Bakhtarzī with a commentary by his son Muṣṭafā, perhaps identical with a work called by French writers *Présents dominicaux*. Another work belonging to the order which they mention is called *al-Rawḍ al-bāsim fī manāḳib al-Shaykh Muḥammad b. al-Ḳāsim*.

Bibliography: E. de Neveu, *Les Khouan*, Paris 1846, repr. Algiers 1913; L. Rinn, *Marabouts et Khouan*, Alger 1884; O. Depont and X. Coppolani, *Les confréries religieuses musulmanes*, Algiers 1897; H. Garrot, *Histoire générale de l'Algérie*, Algiers 1910; M. Simian, *Les confréries islamiques en Algerie*, Algiers 1910; A. Berque, *Essai d'une bibliographie critique des confréries musulmanes algériennes*, in *Bull. de la Soc. de Geogr. et d'Arch. d'Oran*, xxxix (1919), 135-74, 193-283; L. Massignon, *Annuaire du monde musulman*, Paris [4]1954, 235; L.P. Fauque, *Où en est l'Islam traditionnel en Algérie?*, in *L'Afrique et l'Asie*, lv (1961), 17-22; A. Merad, *Le reformisme musulman en Algérie de 1925 à 1940*, Paris-The Hague 1967, 55, 59-60.

(D.S. MARGOLIOUTH*)

RAHN (A.), pledge, security; *rāhin*, the giver and *murtahin*, the taker of the pledge. The Ḳurʾān (II, 283), obviously in confirmation of pre-Islamic legal usage, provides for the giving of pledges (*rihānᵘⁿ maḳbūḍa*) in business in which a definite period is concerned, if the preparation of a written document is impossible. The part here played by the security as evidence of the existence of an obligation is in Islamic law much less important than that of securing the fulfilment of a demand. From the latter point of view, the traditions are mainly concerned with two questions: *a*. whether the security in case of non-fulfilment passes without more ado into the ownership of the creditor or not (the two answers are crystallised in the legal maxims *al-rahn bi-mā fīh* or *al-rahn lā yaghlaḳ*); and *b*. who is entitled to use it and is bound to maintain it (the answer often found in earlier authorities that the taker of the pledge may enjoy its use if he sees to its maintenance, later fell out into disuse). According to the doctrine of Islamic law, the giver of the pledge is bound to maintain it, but can enjoy the use of it only according to the Shāfiʿīs; its use by the taker of the pledge is also forbidden (except by the Ḥanbalīs); the yield (increase) belongs to the giver of the pledge but also becomes part of the security (except with the Shāfiʿīs); the taker of the pledge is responsible for it according to the Ḥanafīs and (with limitations) the Mālikīs. Among the Shāfiʿīs and the Ḥanbalīs, the agreement regarding the security is regarded as a bailment relationship (with much less responsibility). The basis for the condition of a pledge must be a claim (*dayn*); the accessory character of the security is in general allowed; but exceptional cases are recognised in which the debt is extinguished by the disappearance of the security, i.e. the risk passes to the taker of the pledge. While the ownership of the pledge remains with the debtor, he has no power of disposal over it and possession passes to the creditor; the latter has the right to sell it to satisfy his claim if the debt becomes overdue or is not paid. Mortgage is unknown, as well as a graded series of rights to the same object of pledge. To be distinguished from the pledge is the detention (*ḥabs*) of a thing to enforce fulfilment of a legal claim, which represents a concrete right afforded by the law in individual cases so that it has contacts with the legal right to pledge.

Bibliography: J. Schacht (ed.), *G. Bergsträsser's Grundzüge des islamischen Rechts*, Leipzig 1935, 55-6; Guidi-Santillana, *Sommario del diritto malechita*, Milan 1919, ii, 285 ff.; López Ortiz, *Derecho musulmán*, 192-3; Sachau, *Muhammedanisches Recht*, Stuttgart and Berlin 1897, 323 ff.; Querry, *Droit musulman*, Paris 1871-2, i, 443 ff.; Th.W. Juynboll, *De hoofdregelen der Sjafiʾitische leer van het pandrecht*, dissertation, Leiden 1893; Schacht, *An introduction to Islamic law*, Oxford 1964, 138-40.

(J. SCHACHT)

AL-**RĀʿĪ**, *laḳab* of a poet of the Banū Numayr [*q.v.*] who lived in the 1st/7th century. His real name was ʿUbayd b. Ḥuṣayn (see his genealogy in Ibn al-Kalbī, *Djamharat al-nasab*, ed. W. Caskel, Leiden 1966, Taf. 92 and 112; for other sources see R. Weipert, *Studien*, 27-8), but he was commonly known as al-Rāʿī al-Numayrī. His *kunya* Abū Djandal refers to his son Djandal, who inherited his father's poetical talent and produced some poems (for a collection of some fragments see N.Ḥ. al-Ḳaysī and H. Nādjī, *Shiʿr al-Rāʿī*, 8-13).

Al-Rāʿī was a *sayyid* of his tribe and commanded great respect. He spent a considerable part of his life in ʿIrāḳ, especially in Baṣra, where he was on good terms with Umayyad rulers and governors, e.g. Bishr and ʿAbd al-Malik b. Marwān, Yazīd and ʿAbd Allāh b. Muʿāwiya [*q.vv.*], Khālid b. ʿAbd Allāh b. Khālid b. Asīd and Saʿīd b. ʿAbd al-Raḥmān b. ʿAttāb, to whom he addressed his panegyrical odes. It is evident that he kept these close relations with wealthy men of political influence for his personal profit, because, as many of his invectives against other tribes and poets like ʿAdī b. al-Riḳāʿ, al-Akhṭal, and Djarīr [*q.vv.*] show, he did not get on easily with neighbours or fellow poets. When he interfered in the *naḳāʾiḍ* [*q.v.*] between Djarīr and al-Farazdaḳ [*q.v.*] and gave preference to the latter, Djarīr was deeply hurt and reacted by composing his famous *ḳaṣīda* "*al-dammāgha*" (see his *Dīwān*, ed. Nuʿmān Muḥammad Amīn Ṭāhā, Cairo 1969 f., ii, 813 ff. no. 3), in which he slighted al-Rāʿī and the Banū Numayr entirely. This poem silenced al-Rāʿī at once and, as many traditions say, led to his premature death less than a year after this event (see M.N. Ḥidjāb, *al-Rāʿī*, 76-7, who fixes the date of his death in 96/714 or 97/715).

Al-Rāʿī's verses are a typical example of Old Arabian Bedouin poetry; he excels in the description of the camel and its shepherd (hence his nick-name), the wild bull, the oryx, the wild ass, and other animals of the desert. The Arab literary critics highly esteemed al-Rāʿī's qualities and ranked him besides Ḥumayd b. Thawr and Ibn Muḳbil [*q.vv.*] at the head of the Muḍar poets (see al-Aṣmaʿī, *Fuḥūlat al-shuʿarāʾ*, ed. C.C. Torrey, in *ZDMG*, lxv [1911], 500). According to Ibn Sallām, who called him "*faḥl Muḍar*" (see his *Ṭabaḳāt*, i, 503), he belonged to the first class of Islamic poets and was equal in value to Djarīr, al-Farazdaḳ, and al-Akhṭal.

His *dīwān* was transmitted by his *rāwī* Dhu 'l-Rumma [*q.v.*], whose own poetry is strongly influenced by al-Rāʿī's style (see Ibn Sallām, *Ṭabaḳāt*, ii, 551). About a century later, al-Aṣmaʿī [*q.v.*] composed the first philological recension of his *dīwān*, which was largely used by Abū ʿUbayd al-Bakrī [*q.v.*] in his *Muʿdjam ma 'staʿdjam* (see the index). Other recensions are due to al-Sukkarī [*q.v.*], Ibn al-Anbārī [see AL-ANBĀRĪ, ABŪ BAKR], and Thaʿlab [*q.v.*] (see R. Weipert, *Studien*, 34-5). Thaʿlab's recension and commentary was still known to Yāḳūt [*q.v.*], who often quoted it in his *Muʿdjam al-buldān* (see the index).

Though al-Rāʿī's *dīwān* has been cited and valued by many lexicographers, philologists and *udabāʾ*, no manuscript of it has been discovered so far. Fortunately, Muḥammad b. al-Mubārak b. Maymūn (d. 591/1201) selected from the *dīwān* twenty complete *ḳaṣīdas* for his *Muntahā 'l-ṭalab min ashʿār al-ʿarab* (ms. Yale 389, fols. 135b-163a). These long poems, which are missing in the obsolete collections of G. Oman and N. al-Ḥānī, form the basis of the comprehensive editions of al-Rāʿī's poetical remains, published by R. Weipert and, less critically, by N.Ḥ. al-Ḳaysī and H. Nādjī in 1980, each of them containing about 1,300 verses, to which only a dozen may be added today.

Bibliography: The main biographies are in Abū ʿUbayda, *Naḳāʾiḍ Djarīr wa 'l-Farazdaḳ*, ed. A.A. Bevan, Leiden 1905 ff., i, 427-32; Ibn Sallām al-Djumaḥī, *Ṭabaḳāt fuḥūl al-shuʿarāʾ*, ed. Maḥmūd Muḥammad Shākir, Cairo 1974, i, 502-21; Ibn Ḳutayba, *Shiʿr*, 246-8; *Aghānī*³, xxiv, 205-16; Ibn ʿAsākir, *Taʾrīkh madīnat Dimashḳ*, ed. Shākir al-Faḥḥām, in *MMIA*, lxii (1987), 669-84.

Modern studies: Muḥammad Nabīh Ḥidjāb, *al-Rāʿī al-Numayrī ... ʿaṣruhu, ḥayātuhu, shiʿruhu*, Cairo 1383/1963; R. Weipert, *Studien zum Diwan des Rāʿī*, Freiburg 1977 (Islamkundliche Untersuchungen 44).

Editions: G. Oman, *Un poeta pastore: al-Rāʿī*, in *AIUON*, xiv (1964), 311-87, xvi (1966), 89-100; Nāṣir al-Ḥānī, *Shiʿr al-Rāʿī al-Numayrī wa-akhbāruhu*, Damascus 1383/1964, corrected and supplemented by Hilāl Nādjī, in *al-Mawrid*, i/3-4 (1972), 237-76; Nūrī Ḥammūdī al-Ḳaysī and Hilāl Nādjī, *Shiʿr al-Rāʿī al-Numayrī*, Baghdād 1400/1980; R. Weipert, *Dīwān al-Rāʿī*, Beirut 1401/1980 (BTS 24). For further bibliographical references see F. Sezgin, *GAS*, ii, 388 f. and ix, 283; R. Weipert, *Beiträge zur Geschichte des arabischen Schrifttums*, in *ZGAIW*, ii (1985), 261; idem, *Literaturkundliche Materialien zur älteren arabischen Poesie*, in *Oriens*, xxxii (1990), 355-6.

(R. WEIPERT)

AL-RĀʾID AL-TŪNUSĪ ("The Tunisian Scout"), the first official newspaper to be published in the Arabic language, appearing on 22 July 1860 and thereafter on a weekly basis. Considered the third-oldest newspaper of the Arab world [see DJARĪDA], after *al-Waḳāʾiʿ al-miṣriyya* (1828) and the Algerian *Moniteur*, *al-Mubashshir* (1847), this leading light of the Tunisian press was created by the twelfth Ḥusaynī Bey Ṣādiḳ (1859-82), at the instigation of the minister Khayr al-Dīn [*q.v.*], champion of the Tunisian reformist movement, with the object of promoting the reforms set in motion by the promulgation, in 1857, of the *Fundamental Pact* (*ʿAhd al-Amān* [see DUSTŪR]) and provoked by the combined effect of European economic penetration, the French occupation of Algiers in 1830 and the *Tanẓīmāt* (1839 and 1856).

The creation of *al-Rāʾid*, as well as that of the first Arabic printing-press [see MAṬBAʿA. 2.] followed on from attempts to introduce lithographical presses, private and governmental, in progress since 1847; these were at first, in the frantic race for concessions, granted to a British subject, Richard Holt, who published on an experimental basis, in April 1860, several issues of a weekly, in Italian, *La Gazetta di Tunisi*. But this private agreement was soon revoked by the Beylical government which, by a decree of 17 July 1860, inaugurated *al-Rāʾid al-Tūnusī* and *al-Maṭbaʿa al-rasmiyya*, placing them under the direct authority of the President of the Municipal Council, General Ḥusayn (d. 1887), and specifying that "no political issue is to be addressed without express authorisation from the above-named President".

Pascal-Vincent (alias Manṣūr) Carletti (1822-90), a French subject, born in Nicosia of Italian parentage, brought up in Syria, former pupil of Silvestre de Sacy and founder of the weekly *ʿUṭārid* ("Mercury"), which appeared first in Marseilles in 1858, then in Paris in 1859, was engaged both as editor (*munshī*) of *al-Rāʾid* and as supervisor of the printing-press. Pro-French, Carletti succeeded in retaining his post for seventeen years, until the downfall, in 1877, of his patron, General Khayr al-Dīn.

He contributed, however, to ensuring his own replacement by Tunisian personnel: Shaykh Maḥmūd Ḳābādū (d. 1871), author of the first editorials of the 1860s and inventor of the title of the journal; Bayram V (d. 1889); and Muḥammad al-Sanūsī (d. 1900).

With a circulation of about a thousand (in a population of a million, the vast majority being illiterate), and with an average annual frequency of 40 to 50 issues, drawing its revenue from subscriptions imposed on more than 400 officials and from a government subsidy, *al-Rāʾid* was sold for one *riyāl* (piastre), or 60 centimes, per copy. Consisting of four pages *in plano* 50/28, each of three columns, it appeared with a headline bearing the title, surmounted by the Tunisian flag—a revealing sign of the aspirations for independence of the Regency in relation to the Sublime Porte—surrounded by palms and Beylical heraldic symbols. From 1870, the headline bore, in addition, a supposed *ḥadīth*: *ḥubb al-waṭan min al-īmān* ("love of country is part of faith").

The contents of al-*Rāʾid* fell under two major headings: an official section (*ḳism rasmī*), devoted to the publication of laws and decrees, and a non-official section (*ghayr rasmī*), devoted to national news (*ḥawādith dākhiliyya*) and international news (*khāridjiyya*), commercial activity (*matdjar*) and literary and scientific items. Sources were Beylical governmental ordinances for the *ḳism rasmī*, and European, principally French journals, for international news.

Although providing strictly-regulated information, and in spite of three intermissions (1867-8, 1875 and 1880-2), *al-Rāʾid* is of undeniable documentary and historical interest for the pre-colonial period of Tunisia (1860-81); it was definitely the chronicler of the constitutional era, from 1860 to 1864 (promulgation in April 1861 of the first Tunisian constitution [see DUSTŪR] and the lavish festivities which marked the event), and of the reforms of Khayr al-Dīn between 1870 and 1877, in his capacity as controlling Minister (*mubāshir*) and as Prime Minister.

During the peasant insurrection of 1864, led by Ibn

Ghidhāhum [*q.v.* in Suppl.], *al-Rāʾid*, although experiencing a few very brief interruptions, displayed objectivity and calmness, all relative of course, but worthy of recognition.

It compensated for the interruption of the publication of the texts of laws and decrees relating to reforms with the publication of literary articles, consisting in most cases of excerpts from works published by the *maṭbaʿa* (some 70 titles, from 1860 to 1880).

Thus, as admitted by the eminent historian Ibn Abi 'l-Ḍiyāf (1802-74 [*q.v.*]), *al-Rāʾid* constituted both the best complement and the most faithful continuation to the *Itḥāf*, which came to an end in 1872. It remains, furthermore, a first-hand source for the study of the rise of modern Arabic culture.

Under the French Protectorate and since Independence, *al-Rāʾid* has continued to appear into the present day, as an official journal, *stricto sensu*, bilingual and bi-weekly.

Bibliography: Besides the references cited in DJARĪDA. B. North Africa, see Ibn Abi 'l-Ḍiyāf, *Itḥāf ahl al-zamān bi-akhbār mulūk Tūnis wa-ʿahd al-amān*, Tunis 1964, iv, 31-2, vi, 117-40; M. Chenoufi, *Le problème des origines de l'imprimerie et de la presse arabes en Tunisie dans sa relation avec la renaissance "Nahḍa" (1847-1887)*, i-ii, thesis reproduction service, University of Lille III, 1974, *passim*.

(M. CHENOUFI)

RĀʾIḲA, a slave singing-girl (*ḳayna* [*q.v.*]) in the earliest days of Islam. She is mentioned as being in the poetry and music-making circles of Medina in ʿUthmān's caliphate, i.e. the middle years of the 7th century A.D., and as being the teacher (*ustādha*) of the celebrated singer ʿAzza al-Maylāʾ [*q.v.*].

Bibliography: *Aghānī*¹, xvi, 13 = ³xvi, 162; H.G. Farmer, *A history of Arabian music*, London 1929, 46, 54, 147.

(ED.)

RAʾĪS (A.), pl. *ruʾasāʾ*, from *raʾs*, "head", denotes the "chief, leader" of a recognisable group (political, religious, juridical, tribal, or other). The term goes back to pre-Islamic times and was used in various senses at different periods of Islamic history, either to circumscribe specific functions of the holder of the office of "leadership" (*riʾāsa*) or as a honorific title (*laḳab* [*q.v.*]).

1. In the sense of "mayor" in the central Arab lands.

Here, the *raʾīs* most commonly referred to was the head of a village, a city or a city-region. He emerged as a kind of local "mayor" and was particularly active from the 4th/10th to the 6th/12th centuries. Although references to such *ruʾasāʾ* well before that time do exist, the exact date of origin, as well as its place, remains open to question. The areas of activity of the *ruʾasāʾ* were located in ʿIrāḳ and the Persian regions, in Syria and the Djazīra. Thus *ruʾasāʾ* (in the sense of mayors) established their position mainly in territories under Būyid, Fāṭimid and Saldjūḳ rule.

The degree of power exercised by the *raʾīs* was dependent on the weakness or strength of the political authorities. Just as, if not more, important were groups of the local population who lent support to the *raʾīs*. Most famous were native-born, non-professional militias of "young men", the *aḥdāth* [*q.v.*], as they were called in Syria and the Djazīra, and the *fityān* [see FATĀ] or *ʿayyārūn* [see ʿAYYĀR], in ʿIrāḳ and Persia. Together with such popular elements, the *raʾīs*, himself as a rule of local origin, constituted a dynamic force of urban self-representation vis-à-vis the central rulers, usually foreigners. This situation was most evident in Syrian cities, in Damascus more than in Aleppo, when the *raʾīs* succeeded in transforming "classical" government offices, such as that of the police (*shurṭa* [*q.v.*]), the supervision of the market and public order (*ḥisba* [*q.v.*]), and the vizierate (*wizāra* [*q.v.*]), into local self-representative institutions. Things evolved so far that the *ruʾasāʾ* complemented or even replaced the official rulers and their garrisons. In time, they became institutionalised collaborators within the régimes. By forcing the authorities to recognise the *raʾīs al-aḥdāth* as the *raʾīs al-balad* ("mayor of the city"), symbolised through the grant of robes of honour [see KHILʿA] and estates, the latter rose to a semi-official position. Competition or even cooperation between the *raʾīs* and the central government became more frequent than resistance by local leaders against foreign rule (which earlier had been the case when the *raʾīs* was only leader of the *aḥdāth*). An illustrative example of this new arrangement of power was the appointment of several *ruʾasāʾ* in Damascus to the office of vizier. Another was the political and military cooperation against common enemies from outside. With the increase of functions attributed to or gained by the *raʾīs*, some cities established hereditary dynasties of *ruʾasāʾ*, comparable with the dynasties of *ḳāḍīs* [*q.v.*] in Syrian coastal cities (Tyre, Tripoli) at that time, but lacking in their degree of "urban independence". Concerning the social origin of the *ruʾasāʾ*, it seems that some of them came from a low social milieu, even from rural background. This holds true for those *ruʾasāʾ* who did not acquire official recognition through the rulers. On the other hand, most *ruʾasāʾ* obviously were members of wealthy families—a fact which also may have eased their access to a semi-official position.

After the middle of the 6th/12th century, the urban office of the *raʾīs* started to experience a gradual, but irresistible decline. Due to a new policy of centralising rule by the Saldjūḳids and their successors, who installed military commanders (*shiḥna* [*q.v.*]) at the head of each city, the *raʾīs* was doomed to political insignificance. Military, political, and administrative functions were now exercised by the *shiḥna*, and the control of the urban economy was returned to the classical holder of this office, the *muḥtasib*. The *raʾīs* as mayor of the city became much more rarely mentioned by the sources, only to disappear from them altogether during the second half of the 7th/13th century.

With regard to ʿIrāḳ and also Persia, many cities also had a *raʾīs* who appears sometimes to have been the *raʾīs* of the *fityān* or *ʿayyārūn* in his place. Parallels to conditions in Syria are existent, but just as important are dissimilarities which also must be seriously taken into consideration, if one wants to understand the varieties of the institutional history of Islamic cities.

Bibliography: E. Ashtor-Strauss, *L'administration urbaine en Syrie médiévale*, in *RSO*, xxxi (1956), 73-128; Th. Bianquis, *Damas et la Syrie sous la domination fatimide (359-468/969-1076)*, 2 vols., Damascus 1986-9; Cl. Cahen, *Mouvements populaires et autonomisme urbain dans l'Asie musulmane du moyen âge*, in *Arabica*, v (1958), 225-50; idem, in *Arabica*, vi (1959), 25-56, 233-65; N. Elisséeff, *Nūr ad-Dīn, un grand prince musulman de Syrie au temps des Croisades (511-569 H./1118-1174)*, 3 vols., Damascus 1967, 830-2; A. Havemann, *Riʾāsa und qaḍāʾ. Institutionen als Ausdruck wechselnder Kräfteverhältnisse in syrischen Städten vom 10. bis zum 12. Jahrhundert*, Freiburg i.Br. 1975; idem, *The vizier and the raʾīs in Saljuq Syria: the struggle for urban self-representation*, in *IJMES*, xxi (1989), 233-42; idem, *Non-urban rebels in urban society—the case of Fatimid Damascus*, in M.A. al-

Bakhit and R. Schick (eds.), *Bilād al-Shām during the Abbasid period* (= *Proceedings of the Fifth International Conference on the History of Bilād al-Shām*...), Amman 1991, 81-90; G. Hoffmann, *Kommune oder Staatsbürokratie?*, Berlin (GDR) 1975; B. Lewis, *The political language of Islam*, Chicago-London 1988, 59; R.P. Mottahedeh, *Loyalty and leadership in an early Islamic society*, Princeton, N.J. 1980, 129-35, 150-7.

(A. Havemann)

2. In the sense of "mayor" in the Eastern Islamic lands.

Here, as in the lands further west also, the *riyāsa* was an office that was of concern to both the state and to the urban bourgeoisie and notables what Bulliet has styled, with regard to Nīshāpūr, the patriciate although the actual functions of a *raʾīs* are less easy to pinpoint than those of e.g. the *khaṭīb* and the *ḳāḍī*, who were in a similar, dual position as state nominees and as socially significant members of the local *aʿyān* or notables. In general, the *ruʾasāʾ* of the 4th-5th/10th-11th centuries seem to have been prominent in those towns which did not form normally the residences or courts of rulers; thus they are seldom mentioned for Shīrāz and Rayy in the Būyid and Saldjūḳ periods or for Bukhārā under the Sāmānids, although under the Būyids, the *ruʾasāʾ* of quite small towns in provinces like rural Fārs and Gurgān could play significant political roles (see R.P. Mottahedeh, *Loyalty and leadership in an early Islamic society*, Princeton 1980, 150-3).

In Khurāsān, the position of the *ruʾasāʾ* of Nīshāpūr is quite well known to us because of the plethora of biographical information on its scholars and notables. One of the greatest of Nīshāpūr families, the Mīkālīs [*q.v.*], who were the confidantes of and diplomatic representatives for princes, held the office there for most of the Sāmānid period and that of the Ghaznawids, i.e. till *ca.* 431/1040, interspersed with members of the Ḥanafī Ṣāʿidī family and one Ibn Rāmish, equally from top Nīshāpūr families. From the pages of the Ghaznawid historian Abu 'l-Faḍl Bayhaḳī, it emerges that, during Sultan Masʿūd's reign at least, when firm control over Khurāsān in the face of the Turkmen incursions was vital to the ruler, the state nominated or at least approved the *raʾīs* and marked him out by the award of official robes, a fine horse, etc., the *raʾīs* being then responsible to the central government for the town's internal security and taxation (see Bosworth, *The Ghaznavids*, 180 ff., 184-5; R.W. Bulliet, *The patricians of Nishapur. A study in medieval Islamic social history*, Camb., Mass. 1972, 66-8).

In Saldjūḳ times, the central government certainly appointed the *raʾīs* on some occasions, e.g. the vizier Niẓām al-Mulk [*q.v.*] appointed to Nīshāpūr an outsider from Marw al-Rūdh, Abū ʿAlī Ḥassān al-Manīʿī, as *shaykh al-Islām* and *raʾīs* of the town, intending to use him as the agent for favouring Ashʿarī theology and Shāfiʿī law there, with Abū ʿAlī holding office there *ca.* 465-82/1073-89; but after al-Manīʿī's death, the office of *shaykh al-Islām* reverted to a member of the Ṣāʿidī family, a former persecutor of the Ashʿarīs in Nīshāpūr (Bulliet, *op. cit.*, 45, 52 n. 13, 66, 68, 74, 170). During the 6th/12th century, the Saldjūḳ sultans continued to nominate *ruʾasāʾ* for the larger towns, although in the smaller ones, the *ruʾasāʾ* tended to emerge from the local urban notables without any outside interference. We possess the texts of various administrative documents nominating these heads of towns or regions, such as that for Tādj al-Dīn Abu 'l-Makārim Aḥmad as *raʾīs* over Māzandarān, Gurgān and Dihistān during Sandjar's reign, in which Tādj al-Dīn is granted by the sultan's *dīwān* full civil powers over the populations there and is invested with splendid insignia of office consonant with the exaltedness of his office. As before, the *raʾīs*, whether appointed by an outside ruling body or not, was not simply a salaried official of the state but the representative of his town and its interests *vis-à-vis* the provincial or central government, above all, over questions of the taxation due from the town, and he could report back to the sultan's *dīwān* if any of the state officials were grossly abusing their power locally. The *raʾīs* seems often to have had an office or *dīwān* of his own and to have been paid for his official duties by dues (*rusūm*) levied locally; but most *ruʾasāʾ* were men of substance anyway (see A.K.S. Lambton, in *Camb. hist. of Iran*, v, 251-2; eadem, *The administration of Sanjar's empire as illustrated in the* ʿAtabat al-kataba, in *BSOAS*, xx [1957], 383-7; H. Horst, *Die Staatsverwaltung der Großselǧūqen und Ḫōrazmšāhs (1038-1231)*, Wiesbaden 1964, 53-6 and index s.nn. *raʾīs, riyāsat*).

The *raʾīs* recedes from mention in the history of the Persian lands by the time of the Mongol invasions, but it should be noted that the Āl-i Burhān, the line of Ḥanafī *ruʾasāʾ* in the Transoxanian city of Bukhārā, held hereditary office there from the mid-6th/12th century well into the middle years of the 7th/13th one, with the additional title, expressive of their religious leadership also in the city, of *ṣadr al-ṣudūr* [*q.v.*] or *ṣadr-i djahān* (see Bosworth, *EIr* art. *Āl-e Borhān*).

Within Persia, during Aḳ Ḳoyunlu, Ṣafawid and subsequent times, up to the 19th century, many of the functions of the earlier *raʾīs* were assumed, as the link between the central government and the taxpayers, by the headman of a town or district, who was then known as the *kalāntar* [*q.v.*], although the parallels are not completely exact.

Bibliography: Given in the article.

(C.E. Bosworth)

3. In the sense of "sea captain".

Here *raʾīs*, in Turkish *reʾīs*, with its derivation from *raʾs* "head", followed the same semantic process as "captain" from *caput* "head", and came to mean "ship's captain" in Ottoman Turkish. The names of most major figures of the empire's naval history from the 15th and 16th centuries are followed by this epithet: Kemāl Reʾīs, Pīrī Reʾīs, Selmān Reʾīs, Seyyidī ʿAlī Reʾīs, Turghut Reʾīs [*q.vv.*]. Towards the end of the 16th century, further nuances appeared. In the imperial navy, *reʾīs* began to be restricted to captains of single units, while *ḳapudan* or *ḳaptan* was applied to those who commanded actual fleets (see ḲAPUDAN PASHA). Meanwhile, in the semi-independent *beylerbeyilik* of Algiers [see AL-DJAZĀʾIR], the term became associated with commanders of corsair ships (the *ṭāʾifa* of the *ruʾasāʾ*), an institution that vied with the Turkish *odjaḳs* of Janissaries or their offspring (the *ḳul-oghlus* [*q.v.*]) for political power. In modern Turkish, the word, spelt *reis*, means "captain of a small merchant vessel, skipper; able-bodied seaman" (*Redhouse Yeni türkçe-ingilizce sözlük*, Istanbul 1974, 953). For the completely different usage in Ottoman bureaucracy, see REʾĪS ÜL-KÜTTĀB.

Bibliography: İ.H. Uzunçarşılı, *Osmanlı devletinin merkez ve bahriye teşkilâtı*, Ankara 1948, 432 and *passim*; Kātib Čelebi, *Tuḥfat ul-kibār fī esfār il-biḥār*, Istanbul 1329, *passim*. (S. Soucek)

RAʿIYYA (A.), pl. *raʿāyā*, literally "pasturing herd of cattle, sheep, etc.", a term which in later Islam came to designate the mass of subjects, the tax-paying common people, as opposed to the ruling military and learned classes.

1. In the mediaeval Islamic world.

Ḳurʾānic use of the verb *raʿā* and its derivatives

covers the two semantic fields of "to pasture flocks" (e.g. XX, 56/54; XXVIII, 23) and "to tend, look after someone's interests" (e.g. XXIII, 8; LVII, 27; LXX, 32). Since other Near Eastern religions and cultures have evolved the image of the ruler, in both a theocratic and a secular sense, as the shepherd superintending his flock, sc. the subjects (the obvious example being that of Christianity with Jesus as the Good Shepherd), it is not surprising that Islam evolved similar ideas. In the later developments of the personality and role of Muḥammad—developments which were in many cases influenced by the figure of Christ, his characteristics and his miracles, in Eastern Christianity—the Prophet is said by the *Ḳāḍī* ʿIyāḍ al-Yaḥṣubī (d. 544/1149 [*q.v.*]) to have been awarded the epithets *al-raʾūf* "the kindly one" and *al-raḥīm* "the merciful one" by God from amongst His own Most Beautiful Names [see AL-ASMĀʾ AL-ḤUSNĀ] (*al-Shifāʾ bi-taʿrīf ḥuḳūḳ al-Muṣṭafā*, cited in T. Andrae, *Die Person Muhammeds in Lehre und Glauben seiner Gemeinde*, Upsala 1917, 254), and he is described by the mystic Muḥammad b. ʿAlī al-Ḥakīm al-Tirmidhī (*flor.* later 3rd/9th and early 4th/10th centuries, see Brockelmann, I², 216, S I, 355-7, and Sezgin, i, 653-9) as the shepherd of mankind, whose sheep the latter are: he guides them in the right way, gives them pure water, provides them with winter and summer pasture, keeps them from the dangerous places, cares for the newly-born lambs, etc. (*Nawādir al-uṣūl fī maʿrifat akhbār al-rasūl*, cited in Andrae, *op. cit.*, 254-5).

Both the image from Islamic ethics of the secular ruler (as opposed to the Prophet) as *rāʿī* "shepherd" and that of his subjects as *raʿiyya* "flock" appear in the manuals of constitutional law and the "mirrors for princes" literature [see NAṢĪḤAT AL-MULŪK]. But there further developed, in the eastern Islamic world in particular, the additional concept—foreign to the emphases of early Islam on piety and worthiness of God's grace as ideally determining the conduct of worldly affairs—that the *raʿiyya* were the lowest stratum of a hierarchical social structure, the taxable classes of traders and cultivators, whilst above them were the ruling military and civilian classes, the *ahl al-sayf wa 'l-ḳalam*. The roots of this conception probably lay in Sāsānid Persia, where society had been divided into the military aristocracy; the secretaries; the Zoroastrian clergy; and finally, the peasants, artisans and merchants, who paid taxes. Certainly, the duties of treating the *raʿiyya* with benevolence and equity are stressed in the mirrors and in other sententious and moralising literature. Thus ch. 5 of Niẓām al-Mulk's [*q.v.*] *Siyāsat-nāma* deals with the holders of land grants, *muḳtaʿān*, and the need for their enquiring into the condition of the *raʿāyā*; and solicitude for the interests of the taxpayers who financed the armies and administration of the Mongol Il-Khāns is expressed by Rashīd al-Dīn [*q.v.*] in the maxim "there are no *raʿiyyat* if there is no justice."

But the ethical aspect of the ruler-subject relationship, the ruler's duty to further agriculture and trade and the prosperity of the cultivators and artisans, tended to fall into the background in the face of relentless financial exigencies in which the duties of the docile taxpayers were emphasised but not the reciprocal duties of the rulers. The lot of the peasantry in particular deteriorated in the Saldjūḳ and Mongol periods, not least from the incessant warfare in the lands stretching from northern Syria to Transoxania and from the alienation of much land to feudatories, with a consequent loss of direct control by the ruler [see IḲṬĀʿ]. Although legally free in status, their freedom was in practice a fiction, and they were oppressed and ill-treated, liable e.g. for forced labour (*bīgārī, ḥashar*); for housing and feeding officials, messengers, soldiers, etc. and their staffs (*nuzūl*); and for providing mounts for the postal courier service (*olagh*). These requirements had, of course, existed before, but they became much more onerous in the central and eastern lands of Islam from the 5th/12th century onwards (see A.K.S. Lambton, *Landlord and peasant in Persia*, London 1953, chs. II-IV; I.P. Petrushevsky, in *Camb. hist. of Iran*, v, 492-4, 515, 527 ff.; 535-7; B. Fragner, in *ibid.*, vi, ch. 9).

Hence it was during these times that the word *raʿiyya* became narrowed down in the eastern lands to its present meaning in Persia, sc. that of "peasantry" pure and simple, and this meaning was carried into Indo-Muslim society, yielding the Anglo-Indian term *ryot* = "farmer, cultivator" (see *Hobson-Jobson, a glossary of Anglo-Indian words and phrases*, new ed. London 1903, 777). *Raʿiyya* also tended increasingly, in the central and eastern Islamic lands of the later mediaeval period, to have the connotation of "those classes in society who were not allowed to bear arms", and this usage passed into Ottoman official terminology, for which see section 2. below.

Bibliography: Given in the article.

(C.E. BOSWORTH)

2. In the Ottoman empire.

Here, the plural *reʿāyā* was commonly used. In the Ottoman context down to and including the 12th/18th century, the term denotes the tax-paying subject population as opposed to the servitors of the Ottoman state (*ʿaskerīs*). The *reʿāyā* paid taxes and possessed few opportunities for legitimate political activity. From the 12th/18th century onwards, the term is increasingly used for the Christian taxpayers only; 13th/19th century population counts distinguish between *reʿāyā* and Islām; all statements in the present context refer to members of the subject population regardless of religion. In the 9th/15th and 10th/16th centuries, *reʿāyā* status was proven by showing that the person in question or his father had been recorded in the Ottoman tax registers as one of the *reʿāyā*. In later periods, the evidence of witnesses was regarded as decisive.

Reʿāyā *and* ʿaskerīs: *boundaries and boundary crossing*.

Exemption from certain taxes, particularly the *ʿawāriḍ-i dīwāniyye* [*q.v.*], were quite readily granted to *reʿāyā* performing special services to the Ottoman state, such as the guarding of dangerous passes, the repairing of bridges or auxiliary services to the military. Down to the 10th/16th century, *reʿāyā* soldiers formed special corps in the Ottoman army, known as *yaya* and *müsellem* [*q.v.*]. Certain members of those corps performed military service, while others engaged in agriculture on special landholdings (*čiftliks* [*q.v.*]) to finance their fellows' campaign expenses. Detribalised nomads in the Balkans (*yürüks* [*q.v.*]) also were originally employed as soldiers. But from the late 10th/16th century onwards, the *yaya* and *müsellem* corps were abolished and their members demoted to the status of ordinary peasants, while the *yürüks* increasingly were confined to guard duties. In principle, tax exemptions for special services did not place a *reʿāyā* classified as *muʿāf* (or *muʿāf we müsellem*) in the *ʿaskerī* category. However, certain *reʿāyā* doubtlessly used tax-exempt status as an opportunity to claim the privileges of the ruling group.

From the point of view of established *ʿaskerīs*, people born as *reʿāyā* could only under very specific conditions legitimately abandon their station. The study of religious law and subsequent careers as *ḳāḍī*, *müftī* and *müderris* were open to all Muslims. While minor mosque personnel often were reconsidered ʿ*askerī* only for the duration of their appointments, the higher ranks of the ʿ*ilmiyye* [*q.v.*] permanently left their subject status behind. More problematic was the position of *zāwiyedārs* in charge of the numerous Ottoman dervish convents; in the 9th/15th and 10th/16th centuries, they could sometimes claim ʿ*askerī* status by default, if able to demonstrate that in the contemporary tax registers they had not been recorded as *raʿiyyet*. Dervishes suspected of heterodoxy were occasionally reclassified as *reʿāyā* by way of punishment. Down to the 11th/17th century, the levy of boys (*dew<u>sh</u>irme* [*q.v.*]) normally permitted the young men thus recruited unchallenged entry into the Ottoman ruling group, provided they survived the often arduous training period. In later centuries, it was possible to enter the ranks of the ʿ*askerīs* by service in the household of a high official. In particular, the sultan could move the young men he called into his service from their humble status as *reʿāyā* to a position of power. More problematic was the status of mercenaries of *reʿāyā* background who were awarded *tımārs* [*q.v.*] for service on the frontiers. Such promotions occured, for instance during the Hapsburg-Ottoman "Long War" (1001-15/1593-1606), but the beneficiaries might find their status challenged at a later time.

ʿ*Askerīs* could frequently count upon support from the Ottoman sultans in their attempts to limit upward mobility on the part of the *reʿāyā*. In the later 10th/16th and throughout the 11th/17th century, the *reʿāyā* best placed to wage a struggle for ʿ*askerī* privileges were the musket-armed mercenaries who now constituted the bulk of Ottoman armed forces on the Hapsburg and Persian frontiers. Time and again, the attempts of these former peasants turned mercenaries to obtain the regular pay and privileges of Janissaries and other regular military corps resulted in full-scale civil war. The authorities armed peasant militias (*il erleri*) against the rebellious mercenaries, and in extreme cases mobilised militias over entire provinces (*nefīr-i ʿāmm* [see NEFĪR]). Some mercenaries of *reʿāyā* background doubtlessly gained admission to the ʿ*askerī* class in the course of this unrest, but most were unable to shake off their subject status.

From the 11th/17th century onwards, merchants and craftsmen increasingly protected themselves from unforeseeable demands for supplementary taxes by joining the Janissary and other military corps of the major cities. By paying fixed dues to the corps to which they adhered, the Muslim merchants and artisans of *reʿāyā* origins became pro-forma soldiers and joined the lowest ranks of the ʿ*askerīs*. This process has been particularly well studied in the case of Cairo, where it was virtually completed by the middle of the 12th/18th century.

Competition for economic resources.

The *reʿāyā* constituted a political and not an economic category. In terms of economic activity, this group was extremely diverse; town dwellers, nomads and peasants all counted as *reʿāyā*. Disparities of wealth were equally great. While rich merchants of *reʿāyā* status were active in 9th/15th century Bursa or 10th-11th/16th-17th century Aleppo and Cairo, the majority of *reʿāyā* were peasants of modest income, who, from the evidence of their estate inventories, must have reproduced their families with great difficulty. Moreover, in the 9th/15th and 10th/16th centuries substantial merchants of *reʿāyā* status could not compare in wealth with even quite modest ʿ*askerīs*.

In principle, *reʿāyā* were able to transfer their wealth to their descendants, while the inheritances of ʿ*askerīs* were largely confiscated. However, debts to the fisc, incurred particularly by tax farmers, led to the confiscation (*müṣādere* [see MUṢĀDARA]) of *reʿāyā* estates as well. Heirless estates reverted to the state; the right to collect these properties was often farmed out and sometimes gave rise to major abuses. Toward the end of the 12th/18th century, previous rules concerning *müṣādere* were frequently disregarded, as the central administration confiscated the estates of wealthy *reʿāyā* in an effort to raise cash.

The competition between *reʿāyā* and ʿ*askerīs* for the control of economic resources constitutes an important aspect of Ottoman commercial history. While substantial merchants of *reʿāyā* status engaged both in internal and external trade, governors and other important officials had the grains, cottons and other products of their *<u>kh</u>āṣṣ* [*q.v.*] marketed, and gained economic advantage from their political position. Ottoman officials sometimes also used their political power to make loans to peasants, or to market peasant produce. After the institution of the *mālikāne* [*q.v.*] (life-time tax form) in 1106/1695, ʿ*askerīs* gained a further advantage over their *reʿāyā* competitors, as the latter were barred from direct access to this form of investment. The attempts of Christian *reʿāyā* merchants to gain tax-exempt status by association with European consulates thus may be seen as a move in their challenge to the economic supremacy of the ʿ*askerīs*.

The Ottoman system of taxation depended upon the marketing of peasant produce. Peasants were obliged to carry the *tımār* holders' grain to the nearest market, while tax farmers supplied provincial towns and thereby remitted to the central administration in money taxes which they had collected in kind. In the 9th/15th century, low-level administrative districts (*ḳaḍāʾ*) generally possessed a single market; but by the end of the 10th/16th century, markets in villages, and in some areas even in the open countryside, multiplied. In Thessaly and Thrace during the same period, minor local fairs developed into centres for inter-regional and at times even international exchange. Pious foundations profited by this upsurge of rural trade by providing shops and booths and by collecting rents in return. From the later 10th/16th century onwards, peasants also made money by selling, often illegally, grain, cotton or raw silk to European merchants.

However, the profits from this trade were not for the most part retained by the peasantry but collected by the central government or local administrators in the shape of taxes or interest on loans. In addition, a 10th/16th century peasant paid at least 15% and up to 50% of his gains from agriculture in the form of tithes and other taxes; this percentage does not include the money which he needed to set aside for dues such as ʿ*awāriḍ* and *sürsat*, whose level was not predetermined as it depended on the demands of current campaigns. When comparing the estates of peasants and townsmen from one and the same area, the substantially lower standard of living in the villages immediately strikes the eye. (On farming and peasant tenure, see ʿOTHMĀNLĪ. II. Social and economic history.)

Peasant reʿāyā *and local government.*

Most Ottoman peasants ran their smallholdings independently, with minimal involvement on the part of *tımār* holders and other tax grantees. But since the tax registers specified that taxes in kind were levied on specific crops, and the taxes were assessed on the village as a whole, the pressure to conform to locally established crop patterns was very strong. This situation did not, however, preclude changes in response to market conditions. The expansion of a town or city encouraged the conversion of fields into gardens and vineyards, and from the 11th/17th century onwards the villages surrounding Bursa switched over to mulberry orchards and silk cultivation.

Disputes between peasants and local administrators focussed on taxes and the manner of their collection. Frequent tours of inspection on the part of governors, accompanied by numerous armed men, resulted in spoliation of the *reᶜāyā*; concern about peasant flight and erosion of the tax base caused Sultan Murād III to totally prohibit these armed incursions in the 990s/1580s. This prohibition did not last long, but *reᶜāyā* complaints continued to refer to their existence for a much longer time. Monetisation of the economy formed another source of complaints, as tax collectors increasingly demanded payments in coin from peasants whose access to markets remained limited. *Reᶜāyā* at times sought redress of their grievances by complaining to the *Dīwān-i̊ hümāyūn* [*q.v.*] and demanding an official commission in charge of redressing grievances (*me<u>kh</u>āyif müfetti<u>sh</u>i*). At the height of the <u>D</u>jelālī rebellions [see <u>D</u>JALĀLĪ in Suppl.], some villages also built strongholds for use in emergencies. Others fled to neighbouring provinces, the cities or remote areas. The frequent flight of *reᶜāyā* to some degree checked the abuses committed by local administrators, as such events were considered "bad points" in the official's record on the part of the central government. However, financial considerations often induced the latter to allow governors and tax farmers notorious for their oppression of the *reᶜāyā* to go unpunished.

The abolition of reᶜāyā *status.*

With the *<u>Kh</u>aṭṭ-i̊ <u>sh</u>erīf* [*q.v.*] of Gül<u>kh</u>āne, promulgated in 1255/1839, all subjects of the Ottoman sultans were accorded equal rights, and the disappearance of *ᶜaskerī* privileges entailed the abolition of the *reᶜāyā* as a special legal category. However, increasing nationalist and communal rivalries among the inhabitants of the Ottoman Empire and the political, economic and cultural interventions of the various European powers nullified the attempt to create a unified Ottoman citizen body irrespective of social, religious and national differences.

Bibliography: M. Tayyib Gökbilgin, *Rumeli'de Yürükler, Tatarlar ve Evlad-ı Fâtıhan*, Istanbul 1957; Mustafa Akdağ, *Celâlî isyanları* (*1550-1630*), Ankara 1963; B.D. Papoulia, *Ursprung und Wesen der "Knabenlese" im Osmanischen Reich*, Munich 1963; Lütfi Güçer, *XVI-XVII asırlarda Osmanlı imparatorluğunda hububat meselesi ve hububattan alınan vergiler*, Istanbul 1964; Cengiz Orhonlu, *Osmanlı imparatorluğunda derbend teşkilâtı*, Istanbul 1967; Ömer Lütfi Barkan, *Osmanlı imparatorluğunda bir iskân ve kolonizasyon metodu olarak vakıflar ve temlikler*, in *Vakıflar Dergisi*, ii (1972), 279-386; A. Raymond, *Artisans et commerçants au Caire au XVIII siècle*, 2 vols., Damascus 1973-4; G. Veinstein, "*Aᶜyān*" *de la region d'Izmir et commerce du Levant*, in *Etudes balkaniques*, iii (1976), 71-83; Halil İnalcık, *Military and fiscal transformation in the Ottoman Empire, 1600-1700*, in *Archivum Ottomanicum*, vi (1980), 283-337; idem, *Rice cultivation and the* çeltükçi-reʾāyā *system in the Ottoman Empire*, in *Turcica*, xiv (1982), 69-141; Suraiya Faroqhi, *The peasants of Saideli in the later sixteenth century*, in *Archivum Ottomanicum*, viii (1983), 215-50; Huri Islamoğlu-Inan, *State and peasant in the Ottoman Empire—a study of peasant economy in north-central Anatolia during the sixteenth century*, in eadem (ed.), *The Ottoman Empire and the world economy*, Cambridge-Paris 1987, 101-59; Orhonlu, *Osmanlı imparatorluğunda şehircilik ve ulaşım üzerine araştırmalar* ed. Salih Özbaran, Izmir 1984; Caroline Finkel *The administration of warfare: the Ottoman military campaigns in Hungary, 1593-1606*, 2 vols., Vienna 1988 Halime Doğru, *Osmanlı imparatorluğunda yaya müsellem-taycı teşkilâtı*, Istanbul 1990; Mehmet Öz *Population, taxation and regional economy in the district of Canık ... 1455-1576*, unpubl. Ph.D. diss., Cambridge 1990; Huricihan Islamoğlu-Inan, *Osmanlı imparatorluğunda devlet ve köylü*, Istanbul 1991; Faroqhi, *Political activity among Ottoman taxpayers and the problem of sultanic legitimation (1570-1650)*, in *JESHO*, xxxv (1992), 1-39; Chr. Neumann and Fikret Yılmaz, *Kontrolle der Lokalbehörden durch die Zentralverwaltung im Osmanischen Reich*, in *Periplus* (forthcoming).

(SURAIYA FAROQHI)

RAKᶜA (A.), literally "the act of bowing, bending", a sequence of utterances and actions performed by the Muslim believer as part of the act of worship or *ṣalāt*, involving utterance of the *takbīr* and *Fātiḥa*, then the bending of the body from an upright position (*rukūᶜ*) and then two prostrations (*su<u>d</u>jūd*). See further ṢALĀT.

(ED.)

AL-**RAḲĀ<u>SH</u>Ī** [see ABĀN B. ᶜABD AL-ḤAMĪD].

RAḲĪB (A.), from a root signifying "to guard", "to wait", "to observe, watch over", is one of the names of God, with the sense of "guardian, vigilant one who knows everything that takes place", but it is especially familiar as a term in Arabic love poetry, *<u>gh</u>azal* [*q.v.*], where it denotes the person who, by watching or simply being present, prevents the lovers from communicating with each other. The character first appears in the amorous poetry of the Umayyad period (B. Blachère, *Les principaux thèmes de la poésie érotique au siècle des Umayyades de Damas*, in *AIEO*, v [1934-41], 82-128 = *Analecta*, Damascus 1975, 333-78), in particular, in the poetry which Blachère (*Histoire de la littérature arabe des origines à la fin du XVᵉ de J.-C.*, iii, 620 ff.) calls "of Ḥi<u>d</u>jāzian spirit", in company with other enemies of lovers, such as the *kā<u>sh</u>iḥ*, "secret, spiteful enemy", the *wā<u>sh</u>ī*, "slanderer" and the *ᶜā<u>dh</u>il*, "censorious person", who, in the poems of ᶜUmar b. Abī Rabīᶜa [*q.v.*], appear to make reference to real individuals (Ibn Abī ᶜAtīḳ [*q.v.*], for example), but who, very soon, become fictional characters inhabiting the world of the lovers.

In this early period, the figure of the *raḳīb* appears relatively infrequently (it does not appear in the *dīwān* of <u>D</u>jamīl al-ᶜU<u>dh</u>rī [*q.v.*]), in comparison with that of the *kā<u>sh</u>iḥ* and especially that of the *wā<u>sh</u>ī*. The same applies to the poetry of al-ᶜAbbās b. al-Aḥnaf (d. 193/808 [*q.v.*]) but, in the course of the 3rd/9th century, through the influence, perhaps, of amorous narratives and the romanticised biographies of love poets, the *raḳīb* becomes one of the principal obstacles to the union of the lovers. He appears as such in the treatises on love written by the Arabs, in particular in the work of those authors who are more interested in the psychology of love or in the situations in which lovers find themselves (Ibn Dāwūd, Ibn Ḥazm and Ibn Abī Ḥa<u>d</u>jala [*q.vv.*]), than in the ethical problems posed by unrestrained love. Ibn Ḥazm, who devotes three chapters of the *Ṭawḳ al-ḥamāma* to the *ᶜā<u>dh</u>il*, the *wā<u>sh</u>ī* and the *raḳīb*, classifies the last-mentioned according to three categories: the unwelcome, but not malevolent witness to the meeting of the lovers; the curious who seeks to discover, by observing the lovers, whether his suspicions are justified; the guardian charged with watching over the loved one—this last being, in his opinion, the one about whom the poets complain. The similarity between this type of *raḳīb* and the *gardador*, or between the *wās̲h̲ī* and the *lauzengier*, in the poetry of the troubadours, constitutes one of the arguments in favour of establishing links between Hispano-Arab and Provençal poetry (R. Menéndez Pidal, *Poesía árabe y poesía europea*, Madrid 1941; A.R. Nykl, *Hispano-Arabic poetry and its relations with the old Provençal Troubadours*, Baltimore 1946, 371 ff.; R. Boase, *The origin and meaning of courtly love. A critical study of European scholarship*, Manchester 1977).

The *raḳīb* appears quite frequently in the poetry of al-Andalus (H. Pérès, *La poésie andalouse en arabe classique au XIe siècle*, Paris 1953, 417-20). With the *wās̲h̲ī* and the *ʿād̲h̲il*, he is the subject of a brief monograph by the later poet Ibn K̲h̲ātima [*q.v.*] (S. Gibert, *Un tratadito de Ibn Jātima sobre los enemigos de los amantes (Notas sobre el ms. 5974 de la B.N. de Paris)*, in *Al-Andalus*, xviii [1953], 1-16). Predictably, this theme of amorous poetry plays a significant role in the *muwas̲h̲s̲h̲aḥāt* (A. Jones, *OCCAM. Computer-based study of the Muwaššaḥ and the K̲h̲arja*, in F. Corriente and A. Sáenz-Badillos (eds.), *Poesía estrófica. Actas del Primer Congreso Internacional sobre Poesía Estrófica Árabe y Hebrea y sus Paralelos Romances (Madrid, diciembre de 1989)*, Madrid, Facultad de Filologia, UCM-ICMA, 1991, 187-200, Appendix A), and is even introduced into the *k̲h̲ard̲j̲as* in Hispanic vernacular (E. García Gómez, *Las jarchas romances de la serie árabe en su marco*, Madrid 1965, nos. IV, XXVIII).

Bibliography: Given in the article.

(TERESA GARULO)

RĀḲID (A.) "the sleeping child". This term (in Mag̲h̲ribī dialects, *rāged* or *bū mergūd*) is used to indicate a foetus which is considered to have stopped its development, continuing to stay in the womb in an unchanged condition for an indefinite period of time, after which it may "wake up" again and resume its development until it is born. The "falling asleep" and "waking up" may either take place spontaneously or (at least in the Mag̲h̲rib) be induced by a religious scholar (*fḳīh*) or by a midwife (*ḳābla*) with the help of charms (a written charm to that effect is found in ms. Leiden Or. 14048, B2 fol. 12b) and herbs (see Gaudry, *Société féminine*, 370).

This belief is firmly rooted in Islamic culture as far back as the earliest Islamic times, and has been incorporated in the legal systems of the four leading *mad̲h̲āhib*. Some famous cases are mentioned by Ibn Ḳutayba (*K. al-Maʿārif*, Cairo 1960, 594-5), among them Mālik b. Anas, the founder of the Mālikī law school; by Mālik himself (*Muwaṭṭaʾ*, Cairo 1951, 740, = *K. al-Aḳḍiya*, no. 21), where a case is discussed that dates back to D̲j̲āhiliyya days; and by ʿArīb b. Saʿīd al-Ḳurṭubī, *K̲h̲alḳ al-d̲j̲anīn*, 32. The latter text, which is of a medical nature, also illustrates the fact that Islamic physicians were little inclined to include the idea of the *rāḳid* in their theoretical considerations; they took their ideas from the Greek rather than from the ancient Arabian tradition, which implied that the eleven-month pregnancies sometimes allowed for by Hippocrates were the maximum that they were prepared to consider.

From early Islamic times onwards, jurists have disagreed about the possible duration of the prolonged pregnancy; some saw two years as a maximum, but according to others it could last much longer. Even in the midst of the 20th century, Libyan Courts of Appeal were prepared to accept pregnancies of up to twelve years, as A. Layish's research into the practice of Libyan *S̲h̲arīʿa* courts (which have yielded a number of cases of children legally born after prolonged pregnancies) has shown (*Divorce in the Libyan family*, New York etc. 1991, 161). Recent law reforms in Muslim countries have generally abolished the practice and have put the maximum duration of pregnancy at one year, although sometimes allowing for extension, as for instance in the Moroccan Civil Code of 1958, the *Mudawwana* (arts. 76, 84).

Although the idea of the *rāḳid* is accepted by all four Sunnī law schools, it seems to have taken root mainly under Mālikī law, especially in North Africa, where until very recent times it was firmly incorporated into the social system, thus creating a device to protect women as well as children against the sanctions attached to pregnancies and births out of wedlock: a *rāḳid* might be born legally long after its parents' marriage had come to an end by death or divorce. At the same time, the system offered barren wives an escape from the odium of infertility and the practical and psychological consequences attached to it, such as depression, loss of social status and repudiation.

Bibliography (in addition to references given in the article): ʿArīb, *K. K̲h̲alḳ al-d̲j̲anīn wa-tadbīr al-ḥabālā wa 'l-mawlūdīn*, ed. and tr. H. Jahier and N. Abdelkader, Algiers 1956; Wans̲h̲arīsī, *al-Miʿyār al-muʿrib wa 'l-d̲j̲āmiʿ al-mug̲h̲rib ʿan fatāwā ʿulamāʾ Ifrīḳiya wa 'l-Andalus wa 'l-Mag̲h̲rib*, Fez 1897, iii, 224-5, iv, 335, 353, 542; G.H. Bousquet and H. Jahier, *L'enfant endormi. Notes juridiques, ethnographiques et obstétricales*, in *Revue algérienne, tunisienne et marocaine de législation et jurisprudence* (Feb. 1941), 17-36, 28-30, 153-4; L. Buskens, *Islamitisch recht en familiebetrekkingen in Marokko*, diss. Leiden 1993, unpubl., 392-3; M. Gaudry, *La société féminine au Djebel Amour et au Ksel*. Algiers 1961, 192-4, 370, 485-90; W. Jansen, *Mythe of macht. Langdurige zwangerschappen in Noord-Afrika*, in *Tijdschrift voor Vrouwenstudies*, 1982/2, 158-79; Y. Linant de Bellefonds, *Traité de droit musulman comparé III. Filiation, incapacités, liberalités entre vifs*. Paris etc. 1973, 36; J. Mathieu and R. Maneville, *Les accoucheuses musulmanes traditionelles de Casablanca*, Paris 1952, 45-8, 73-4, 81-7; O. Verberkmoes, *Raged. Hoe een foetus in de baarmoeder in slaap valt en pas jaren later geboren wordt*, MA diss., Utrecht 1988, unpubl.

(ODILE VERBERKMOES and REMKE KRUK)

AL-**RAḲĪḲ** AL-**ḲAYRAWĀNĪ** [see IBN AL-RAḲĪḲ].

AL-**RAḲĪM** [see AṢḤĀB AL-KAHF].

RAḲḲ, RIḲḲ (A.), parchment.

1. History of the use of parchment in the Islamic world.

Raḳḳ is the term employed by the Arabs to denote parchment, alongside certain other terms used in a less specific manner, such as *ḳirṭās* [*q.v.*] (from the Greek χάρτης, through the intermediary of Aramaic) denoting papyrus, a sheet of papyrus or even a scroll of papyrus; *waraḳ*, which was later to be reserved for paper; and *d̲j̲ild* [*q.v.*] (leather). Furthermore, all these words occur from time to time, in reference to the early years of Islam, to denote writing materials in general, whereas *bardī* or *waraḳ al-bardī* was the particular term for papyrus [see PAPYRUS] and *raḳḳ* the particular term for parchment. The latter is derived from the verb *raḳḳa* "to be thin, fine" (hence the explanatory terms observed at a later stage, such as *d̲j̲ild raḳīḳ*, or "fine leather"). Parchment (on the subject of which Grohmann wrote a very fine article, see *Bibl.*) was fashioned initially, in most cases, from the hide of certain animals such as sheep, goats or calves, but sometimes also from the hide of gazelles (see below).

Its usage in Arabia may conceivably be attested from the 5th century A.D., as may be observed in the *Ḳaṣīda* of Ḳudam b. Ḳādim (A.D. 400-80) (on this see Griffini, *Il poemetto*, 352, v. 56), if this is not—as seems very probable—later ʿAlid or ʿAbbāsid propaganda (Caskel); at a later stage, Ṭarafa speaks of *ḳirṭās al-Shām*, and Labīd mentions a *ṭirs nāṭiḳ* ("speaking parchment"). *Ṭirs* is a palimpsest, of which only a few exist dating from the Arabic period. Such a fragment is preserved in the papyrological collection of Florence: on the *recto* is a Latin fragment of the Bible, Exodus viii, 16, and on the *verso* an Arabic economic text of the 1st century A.H. (on this, see Vaccari, and on Labīd, see A. von Kremer, *Über die Gedichte des Labîd*, 583).

Before the time of the Arabs, parchment had been in use among the ancient Babylonians, and, in particular, among the Egyptians from the 2nd century B.C., and it was subsequently to become ever more important. The Prophet Muḥammad is said to have used, alongside leather, a very fine variety of parchment for his correspondence; evidence of this is a document allocating territory to the Tamīm tribe, written by ʿAlī and mentioned by Ibn Durayd, *K. al-Ishtiḳāḳ*, ed. Wüstenfeld, 226, n.*b*. The Ḳurʾān itself (LII, 2-3) declares that it is written on *raḳḳ manshūr* ("unfolded parchment"). It is known that certain fragments (*riḳāʿ*), containing what the Prophet left behind, must have contained verses of the Ḳurʾān, some of them written on parchment (cf. al-Suyūṭī, *Itḳān*, 137, ll. 11-13; idem, *Muḳaddimatān*, i, 36, l. 22; 49, l. 8; L. Marraccius, *Prodromus*, i, 257; A. Sprenger, *Das Leben*, iii, 39); the corpus of the Holy Book of Islam, the assembly of which was undertaken by Zayd b. Thābit, must have been written on parchment, *waraḳ* (on this, see Sprenger, *ibid.*, iii, 40; al-Suyūṭī, *Itḳān*, 138, l. 3); the ancient sections of the Ḳurʾān which have survived provide convincing evidence of this (see e.g. the Vienna collection, published by Loebenstein).

This tradition was continued under the Rightly-Guided Caliphs, as is noted by Ibn Khaldūn (see *Muḳaddima*, index; cf. Karabacek, *MPER*, ii/3, 1887, 119), since by this means their correspondence, their instructions and their edicts had a more artistic and attractive appearance, and were better assured of long-term survival; furthermore, use of this material added to the renown of the scribes.

In the Umayyad period, the situation was unchanged (see e.g. Abu 'l-Faradj al-Iṣfahānī, *Aghānī*, xvi, 111, ll. 3-5, where the subject is the biography of the poet Dhu 'l-Rumma). Furthermore, the caliph Muʿāwiya personally instructed the officials of his administration to use parchment, in order to underline the importance of the edicts emanating from it (see Quatremère, tr. of Rashīd al-Dīn, *Histoire des Mongols de la Perse*, Paris 1836, i, 134; Karabacek, *MPER*, ii/3, 1887, 152). It would, moreover, be surprising if sections of the *Akhbār* of ʿAbīd/ʿUbayd b. Sharya, lively tales related to this caliph in Damascus and put into writing by order of the same sovereign, were not written, at least in part, on parchment, in view of the high regard in which Muʿāwiya held them, particularly admiring their innumerable verses (see, on this subject, R.G. Khoury, *Kalif, Geschichte und Dichtung*, 214-15).

Even in the early years of the ʿAbbāsid caliphate, parchment continued to be used, albeit alongside papyrus, the use of which was dominant, and paper, the use of which was becoming ever more widespread but which did not command, at the outset, the same degree of acceptance. Ibn Ḥanbal himself, when asked which method of writing he preferred, replied, "A pen of reed, shining ink and fine hide" (al-Manūfī, *Laṭāʾif*, fol. 100a); this is definitely a reference to parchment, this being the meaning of *djild raḳīḳ*, which is the expression used in this phrase; the lexicographer al-Djawharī, *Ṣiḥāḥ*, ii, 85, 28 f., provides testimony in support of the use of these two words. And when the *dīwāns* were ransacked, under Muḥammad b. Zubayda, the caliph al-Amīn [*q.v.*], the parchments taken from them, from which the texts had been obliterated, were re-used as writing materials (*ṭirs*). At Kūfa and Edessa (al-Ruhā [*q.v.*]), parchment of the finest quality was produced. But as paper progressively gained acceptance in administrative circles, the use of parchment declined, before coming to a definitive end. In the 11th and 12th centuries A.D. it was still being used alongside paper (see *ʿUmdat al-kuttāb*, Codex gothanus 1357, fol. 11b).

In al-Andalus, as late as the time of al-Muḳaddasī, who composed his work after 373/985, parchment was still being used for all copies of the Ḳurʾān and books of accounts (*Aḥsan al-taḳāsīm*, 239). As for the Maghrib, the situation there was the same, as has been proved by the discovery of hundreds of literary codices on parchment in the mosque of Sīdī ʿUḳba at Ḳayrawān (see G. Marçais *et alii, Objets kairouanais*). Recent discoveries in the Great Mosque of Ṣanʿāʾ also confirm this well-established tradition.

Besides the other types of hide described above, the fine hide of gazelles was also used for the making of parchment, especially for copies of the Ḳurʾān, as is attested by codices preserved e.g. in Cairo (see *Fihrist al-kutub al-ʿarabiyya*, i, 2; Ahmed Moussa, *Zur Geschichte der islamischen Buchmalerei*, 45-6; Muḥammad Ṭāhir al-Makkī al-Khaṭṭāṭ, 81) or in Medina (Spies, 102-3). Furthermore, in the various collections of papyrus, which contain not only documents on papyrus but also texts written on hide and all other kinds of ancient material, striking examples of all types of parchment are to be found (see A. Grohmann, *Einführung*, 3; Khoury, art. *Papyrus* in *EI²*; *Chrestomathie*, 7).

Initially, it was usually the *recto*, this being the smoother surface, which was written on; when space was insufficient, the *verso* was used. Judicial documents were often bound up with a strip of leather or a thread of some kind. The dimensions of parchments vary between 85.2 × 82 cm (see P. Lond. B.M. Or. 4684/III) and 4.8 × 1.8 cm (see *PER Inv. Perg. Ar.*, 53). Some of the Vienna fragments are saffron coloured and there is no way of knowing whether the material has been dyed or if this is merely the effect of long-term storage. On the other hand, there is at least one undisputed example of the use of blue dye: this is a leaf which belonged to a Ḳurʾānic manuscript of Mashhad (Persia) datable to the 2nd/8th century. In addition, manuscripts on purple parchment are well known among mediaeval Latin documents.

The earliest known and datable Arabic parchment is a fragment which Ernst Kühnel saw in the possession of a German consul in Luxor, of which neither Grohmann, during his stay in Egypt, nor the writer of this article, have succeeded in finding any trace. The most recent is from the year 498/1105 (P. Berol. 9160). Naturally, these observations apply to known parchments; it is possible that there are others which will come to light in the future, either in private collections or in the unclassified stocks of certain libraries.

Bibliography (in addition to references in the article): 1. Sources. Djawharī, *Tādj al-lugha wa-ṣiḥāḥ al-ʿarabiyya*, Cairo 1282/1865; Manūfī, *Laṭāʾif akhbār al-uwal fī man taṣarraf fī Miṣr min arbāb al-duwal*, ms.; Suyūṭī, *al-Itḳān fī ʿulūm al-Ḳurʾān*, Calcutta 1857; idem, *Muḳaddimatān fī ʿulūm al-Ḳurʾān*, ed. A. Jeffery, Cairo 1954; Ṭarafa, *Muʿallaḳa*, in Zawzanī, *Sharḥ al-Muʿallaḳāt al-sabʿ*, Beirut 1963, v. 31 (cf.

F.A. Arnold, *Septem Moʿallaḳât*, Leipzig 1850, 46).

2. Studies. L. Marraccius, *Prodromus ad refutationem Alcorani*, Rome 1691; A. Sprenger, *Das Leben und die Lehre des Mohammed*, 3 vols., Berlin 1861-5; A. von Kremer, *Über die Gedichte des Labîd*, in *SBWAW*, phil.-hist. Cl., xcviii (1881); Khedival Library, Cairo, *Fihrist al-kutub al-ʿarabiyya al-maḥfūẓa bi ʾl-Kutubk̲h̲āna al-K̲h̲idīwiyya*, Cairo 1892-3; E. Griffini, *Il poemetto di Ḳudam ben Ḳādim*, in *RSO*, vii (1916), 293-363; Ahmed Moussa, *Zur Geschichte der islamischen Buchmalerei in Ägypten*, Cairo 1931; O. Spies, *Die Bibliotheken des Hidschas*, in *ZDMG*, xc (1936), 83-120; Nabia Abbott, *The rise of the North Arabic script and its Ḳurʾānic development, with a full description of the Ḳurʾān manuscripts in the Oriental Institute*, Chicago 1939; Muḥammad Ṭāhir al-K̲h̲aṭṭāṭ, *Taʾrīk̲h̲ al-k̲h̲aṭṭ al-ʿarabī wa-ādābihi*, Cairo 1939; G. Marçais, L. Poinssot, L. Gaillard, *Objets kairouanais, IXe au XIIIe siècle*, 2 vols., Tunis 1948-52; A. Vaccari, *Frammento biblico latino*, in *PSI*, xii/2 (1951), no. 1272, 97-110; A. Grohmann, *Einführung und Chrestomathie zur arabischen Papyruskunde, i, Einführung*, Prague 1954; idem, *Arabische Paläographie*, 2 vols., Vienna 1967-71, s.v. *Pergament*, at i, 108b-111b (utilised as a basis for this present article); R.G. Khoury, *Kalif, Geschichte und Dichtung. Der jemenitische Erzähler ʿAbīd/ʿUbayd ibn Sharya am Hofe Muʿāwiyas*, in *ZAL*, xxv (1993) [= *Festschrift für W. Fischer*], 204-18 (cf. Ibn al-Nadīm, *Fihrist*, ed. Flügel, 89-90); idem, *EI²* art. *Papyrus*; idem and Grohmann, *Chrestomathie de papyrologie arabe*, Hdb. der Or., Leiden 1993.

Sigla for collections of papyri: P. Berol. = papyri of the Berlin Museums; P. Cair. = papyri of the Egyptian Nat. Libr. (Dār al-Kutub); PER = Papyri Erzherzog Rainer, Vienna; PERF = *ibid.*, *Führer durch die Ausstellung Wien 1894* (of Karabacek); P. Lond. = Papyri in the Brit. Museum; PSR = Papyri Schott-Reinhardt, Heidelberg. For other sigla, see Khoury, in Khoury and Grohmann, *Chrestomathie*, bibl.

(R.G. Khoury)

2. The production of parchment and modern knowledge of Islamic parchment.

Parchment was used in the early Islamic period as one of the common durable writing materials for books, chancery documents, letters and registers, the less durable material being papyrus. In Europe, it remained in use till well in the 15th century. In Ethiopia, which may have given Islam the term *muṣḥaf* [*q.v.*], parchment remained in use as a writing material for religious and superstitious texts till well in the 20th century. Although its primary and main use in the Middle East was as a writing material, it was used for other purposes as well. Most notable in this respect is its use in musical instruments and in puppets for shadow plays [see K̲h̲AYĀL AL-ẒILL]. For these uses, parchment may have been made of the skin of other, larger, animals as well.

Parchment is manufactured by cleaning the skin from hair and impurities, by applying lime or certain other preserving materials to it and by then letting it dry under tension, the skin being stretched on a frame. This stretching and the absence of tanning make parchment different from leather. In many parchments it is still possible to discern the flesh side from the hair side, the latter being recognisable from its grained appearance caused by the roots of the hairs. Techniques were developed in mediaeval times visually to diminish this difference as much as possible. This was done either by finely thinning and scrubbing or chafing the skin or by splitting it. The use of the skin of unborn animals also vouches for a soft and minimally hairy appearance of the parchment.

Being of natural origin, parchment had its limit in size determined by the size of the animal it was made of. Many of the large Ḳurʾānic manuscripts of the early period consist of single or at best double leaves of parchment only. For smaller-sized books, the parchment may have been folded once or twice more, thereby making quarto or octavo arrangements. Depending on whether the first fold was in the length or in the width, the quarto quire resulting from this operation would be oblong shaped or not. The square shape of Mag̲h̲ribī books on parchment may be explained by supposing that the animal-shaped material was first folded two times in the width and then once in the length, whereby a quire of six almost square leaves of moderate size was produced. In the Middle East, Gregory's rule, by which parchment leaves in a quire are so arranged that flesh sides would only face flesh sides and hair sides only hair sides, was as often as not unobserved. This rule apparently did not matter as much in the Middle East as it did in Europe.

The basic tools for a comprehensive study of the Middle Eastern parchment book are lacking. A catalogue of a corpus of parchment codices does not exist. There are a few large collections of parchments books and fragments that together would constitute the main elements of such a corpus. The most important of these are the Ḳurʾānic fragments in the Bibliothèque Nationale of Paris (a varied collection which served as the source of the typology of the graphics of the early Ḳurʾān codex as developed by François Déroche); the Nasser D. Khalili collection in London, which contains coloured fragments as well (extensively described by Déroche); the fragments that were discovered in *ca.* 1970 in the Great Mosque of Ṣanʿāʾ and that are now kept in the Dār al-Mak̲h̲ṭūṭāt in Ṣanʿāʾ (studied by G.-H. Puin, H.C. Graf von Bothmer and Ursula Dreibholz; no major description published as yet); and, finally, the Ṣ̲am Evrakı, the Ḳurʾānic fragments that were transferred some one hundred years ago from the Umayyad Mosque in Damascus to Istanbul and that are now kept in the Türk ve Islam Eserleri Müzesi in Istanbul (studied by Déroche; no major description published as yet). The library of the Monastery of St. Catherine in Sinai contains an important number of Christian Arabic codices on parchment. It would seem that the use of parchment persisted longer with the Oriental Christians than among Muslims. Parchment of several types has continued to be used for religious reasons by Oriental Jewry till the present day. Their extensive technical literature on the subject is also of relevance to the study of Islamic parchment. Many parchment fragments of the Ḳurʾān, and to a limited extent also of other Islamic texts, have surfaced since *ca.* 1970 in the international art market, a fact witnessed by their frequent appearance in the auction catalogues of Christie's and Sotheby's of London. Parchment material is present in virtually all larger collections of Middle Eastern manuscripts.

Bibliography: F. Déroche, *Les manuscrits du Coran. Aux origines de la calligraphie coranique*. Paris 1983; idem, *The Abbasid tradition. Qurʾans of the 8th to 10th centuries*. (The Nasser D. Khalili Collection of Islamic Art, vol. i), London 1993; idem, *A propos d'une série de manuscrits coraniques anciens*, in *Les manuscrits du Moyen-Orient* [= *Varia turcica*, VIII], Istanbul-Paris 1989, 101-11; P. Rück (ed.), *Pergament. Geschichte, Struktur, Restaurierung, Herstellung*, Sigmaringen 1991. Particular use has been made for the present article of the contributions in this volume by Michael L. Ryder, Menahem Haran, Gerhard Endress, Robert Fuchs, Ursula Dreibholz, J. Visscher and of the bibliography by Stefan Janzen and Angelika Manetzki. For Arabic language publications, see A. Gacek, *A select bibliography of Arabic language publications concerning Arabic manuscripts*, in *MME*, i (1986), 106-8.

(J.J. Witkam)

al-**RAḲḲA**, a mediaeval Islamic town on the left bank of the Middle Euphrates, at the junction of its tributary the Nahr al-Balīkh. Today it is the administrative centre of the al-Raḳḳa governorate of the Arab Republic of Syria; in mediaeval Islamic historic topography it was considered to be the capital of Diyār Muḍar [*q.v.*] in al-Djazīra/Northern Mesopotamia.

The origin of settlement on opposite sides of the Nahr al-Balīkh is attested by the Tall Zaydān and the Tall al-Bīᶜa, the latter identified with the Babylonian city of Tuṭṭūl (excavated since 1980; reports published in *MDOG*, cxiii [1981] and later). To the south of the Tall al-Bīᶜa, on the border of the Euphrates, Seleucus I Nikator (301-281 B.C.) founded the Hellenistic city of Nikephorion, later probably enlarged by Seleucos II Kallinikos (246-226 B.C.) and named Kallinikos/Callinicum after him. Destroyed in A.D. 542 by the Sāsānid Khusraw I Anūshirwān [*q.v.*], the emperor Justinian (527-65) soon after rebuilt the town in the course of an extensive fortification programme at the Byzantine border alongside the Euphrates (on the pre-Islamic city, see the article by M. al-Khalaf and K. Kohlmeyer in *Damaszener Mitteilungen*, ii [1985], 133-62).

The classical city was conquered in 18/639 or 19/640 by the Muslim army under ᶜIyāḍ b. Ghanm, who became the first governor of the Djazīra (in this connection, see W.E. Kaegi, *Byzantium and the early Islamic conquests*, Cambridge 1992). Renamed al-Raḳḳa, the Muslim faith was heralded by a congregational mosque, founded by the succeeding governor Saᶜīd b. ᶜĀmir b. Ḥidhyam, which was subsequently enlarged to monumental dimensions of c. 73 × 108 m. Recorded by the German scholar Ernst Herzfeld in 1907, the mosque, together with the square brick minaret (Pl. XXVI, 1), supposedly a later addition from the mid-4th/10th century, has since vanished completely.

In 36/656 ᶜAlī crossed the Euphrates at al-Raḳḳa on his way to Ṣiffīn [*q.v.*], the place of the battle with Muᶜāwiya b. Abī Sufyān, the governor of Damascus and founder of the Umayyad dynasty. Located near the village of Abū Hurayra opposite the mediaeval citadel of Ḳalᶜat Djaᶜbar [*q.v.*] *ca.* 45 km/28 miles west of al-Raḳḳa, the burials of ᶜAlī's followers remained venerated places of Shīᶜī pilgrimage (listed extensively in al-Harawī's *Kitāb al-Ziyārāt*). The last of those tombs located in the Muslim cemetery on the western fringes of the early Islamic city of al-Raḳḳa, the mausoleum of Uways al-Ḳaranī, recently had to give way to a huge pilgrimage centre. Another witness from the early days of Islam, a stone column supposedly depicting an autograph of ᶜAlī from the Mashhad quarter of al-Raḳḳa, was already in the 6th/12th century transferred to Aleppo, where it was incorporated in the Masdjid Ghawth (E. Herzfeld, *CIA*, part ii, Northern Syria, *Inscriptions et monuments d'Alep*, i, Cairo 1955-6, 271-2 no. 142).

Throughout the Umayyad period al-Raḳḳa remained an important fortified stronghold protected by a garrison, occasionally involved in revolts and internal fighting over supremacy in the Djazīra, as described by al-Ṭabarī. Opposite al-Raḳḳa, near the south bank of the Euphrates, the Umayyad caliph Hishām b. ᶜAbd al-Malik (105-25/724-43), residing mainly at al-Ruṣāfa [*q.v.*] *ca.* 50 km/31 miles further to the southwest in the Syrian desert, created the agricultural estate of Wāsiṭ al-Raḳḳa, irrigated by two canals named *al-Hanī wa 'l-Marī*. Further north, at a distance of *ca.* 72 km/45 miles, near the river al-Balīkh, another member of the Umayyad family, the famous military commander Maslama b. ᶜAbd al-Malik (d. *ca.* 121/739 [*q.v.*]), a half-brother of the caliph Hishām, founded the residential estate of Ḥiṣn Maslama, which served as an advanced outpost towards the Byzantine frontier (on the ruins of Madīnat al-Fār, probably to be identified with Ḥiṣn Maslama, see the report by C.-P. Haase in *Bilād al-Shām during the Abbasid period. Proceedings of the fifth International conference on the History of Bilād al-Shām*, ed. Muḥammad ᶜAdnān al-Bakhīt and R. Schick, Amman 1991, 206-13).

Though the treaty between the inhabitants of al-Raḳḳa and the victorious Muslim general ᶜIyāḍ b. Ghanm, as quoted by al-Balādhurī, 173-4, stipulated that the Christians should retain their places of worship but were not allowed to build new churches, the non-Muslim community is recorded to have thrived well into the Middle Ages. Till the 6th/12th century a bishop is attested to have resided there, and at least four monasteries are frequently mentioned in the sources, the most famous of which, the Dayr Zakkā, can be identified with recently excavated ruins on the Tall al-Bīᶜa (on the Christian sources and the newly-detected remains, see M. Krebernik, in *MDOG*, cxxiii [1991], 41-57). To this monastery belonged the estate of al-Ṣāliḥiyya, a favourite halting place for hunting expeditions (described by al-Bakrī, iii, 582, and Yāḳūt, ii, 644-5), possibly to be associated with the ruins of al-Ṣuwayla near the river al-Balīkh, *ca.* 4 km/2.5 miles to the northeast of al-Raḳḳa (recently investigated archaeologically and recorded in *Damaszener Mitteilungen*, ii [1985], 98-9). There also existed a large Jewish community maintaining an ancient synagogue, still operating during the visit of Benjamin of Tudela in about 1167 (see his *Travels*, tr. M.N. Adler, London 1907, 32).

The early ᶜAbbāsid period. Early in the ᶜAbbāsid period the programme of border fortifications in all of the Muslim empire resulted in the construction of an entire new city about 200 m/660 feet west of al-Raḳḳa. Named al-Rāfiḳa, "the companion (of al-Raḳḳa)", the city, according to al-Yaᶜḳūbī (*Taʾrīkh*, i, 238) was already conceived in the time of the first ᶜAbbāsid caliph al-Saffāḥ (132-6/749-54); nevertheless, al-Ṭabarī attributes the foundation of al-Rāfiḳa to his brother and successor al-Manṣūr (136-58/754-75), who in 154/770-1 decided on the construction of the city, which was eventually implemented by his son and heir-apparent al-Mahdī from 155/771-2 onwards. Construction work was still continuing when, in 158/775, al-Mahdī was summoned to Baghdād to be invested as caliph upon the sudden death of his father. Purposely modelled after the only recently completed residential city of Baghdād, the partly surviving city fortifications testify to the military might of the ᶜAbbāsid empire. In the form of a parallelogram surmounted by a half circle with a width of *ca.* 1300 m/4,265 feet, the city was protected by a massive wall of almost 5000 m/16,400 feet in length (Pl. XXV, 1). Fortified by 132 round projecting towers, an advance wall and a moat further improved the defence system (see Murhaf al-Khalaf, in *Damaszener Mitteilungen*, ii [1985], 123-31). Originally accessible by three axial entrances, the recently excavated northern gate (Pl. XXV, 2) has revealed stately dimensions, with a portal opening of four metres/13 feet. Remains of iron door posts attest the existence of massive or metal-plated doors, which attracted special praise in the Arabic chronicles. One of the doors, according to the mediaeval tradition, is identified with spoils from the Byzantine city of Amorion or ʿAmmūriya [*q.v.*] in Asia Minor, transported by al-Muʿtaṣim (218-27/833-42) in 223/838 to his newly-founded residence at Sāmarrāʾ in central Mesopotamia, from where it supposedly reached al-Raḳḳa towards the end of the 3rd/9th century. Only about half-a-century later, the door was again dismantled in 353/964 on behalf of the Ḥamdānid Sayf al-Dawla ʿAlī (333-56/945-67), to be later incorporated in the Bāb al-Ḳinnasrīn at Aleppo (E. Herzfeld, *CIA*, part ii, Northern Syria, *Inscriptions et monuments d'Alep*, i, 60).

In the centre of al-Rāfiḳa another Great Mosque was constructed with monumental proportions of 108 x 93 m/354 x 305 feet in order to serve the garrison of soldiers from Khurāsān (Pl. XXVI, 3). Built with massive mud brick walls, strengthened by burnt brick facing and encircled by a chain of round towers, the plan layout is characterised by triple aisles on brick piers in the prayer hall and by double arcades on the three other sides of the interior courtyard (see Creswell, *Early Muslim architecture*, ii, Oxford 1940, 45-8, and recent project reports). This first pillar mosque in Islamic architecture obviously served as a model for later Friday mosques at Baghdād (enlarged from 192/808 till 193/809 by Hārūn al-Rashīd), Sāmarrāʾ (both mosques of al-Mutawakkil, inaugurated in 237/852 and 247/861 respectively) and at Cairo (Mosque of Aḥmad b. Ṭūlūn, completed in 265/879).

Al-Raḳḳa as capital of the ʿAbbāsid empire. The new city al-Rāfiḳa alone almost matches the traditional Syrian capital Damascus in size; but the two sister cities of al-Raḳḳa and al-Rāfiḳa together formed the largest urban entity in Syria and northern Mesopotamia, probably only surpassed by the ʿAbbāsid centre of power, Baghdād, in central Mesopotamia. Therefore, it was a logical choice that the caliph Hārūn al-Rashīd (170-93/786-809), when searching for an alternative residence in 180/796, settled on al-Raḳḳa/al-Rāfiḳa, which remained his base for a dozen years till 192/808. This resulted not only in additions to the city fortification (inscription on the eastern gate of al-Rāfiḳa, the Bāb al-Sibāl, quoted by Ibn Shaddād, iii/1, 71), but more importantly, in the construction of an extensive palatial quarter to the north of the twin cities. This caliphal residence of almost 10 km², as attested by aerial photographs, includes about twenty large-size complexes, of which the most monumental of *ca.* 350 x 300 m/1,148 x 984 feet in a central position obviously served as the main residence of Hārūn al-Rashīd (Pl. XXVII, 1), probably to be identified with the Ḳaṣr al-Salām mentioned by Yāḳūt. The other structures were evidently used for housing the family members and court officials residing with Hārūn al-Rashīd at al-Raḳḳa, or else were devoted to service functions.

The huge area of ruins outside the twin cities has since 1944 attracted archaeological investigations. First trial soundings were conducted by the Syrian Antiquities Service at the Main Palace, but were soon discontinued due to the poor state of preservation. Instead, another major complex of *ca.* 120 x 150 m/393 x 492 feet, only 400 m/1,312 feet north of the city wall of al-Rāfiḳa, named Palace A, was partly excavated. Excavations eventually continued at three other complexes to the east of the Main Palace: Palace B (1950-52), Palace C (1953), and Palace D (1954 and 1958), all of rather monumental dimensions measuring *ca.* 170 x 75 m/557 x 246 feet, 150 x 110 m/492 x 360 feet and 100 x 100 m/328 x 328 feet respectively; (see the series of reports by Nassib Saliby in *Les Annales Archéologiques de Syrie*, iv-v [1954-5], 205-12, Arabic part 69-76; vi [1956], Arabic part 25-40). Additionally, further soundings in the vicinity of and at Palace A were implemented between 1966 and 1970 (summarised by Kassem Toueir in the excavation review by P.H.E. Voûte [ed.], in *Anatolica*, iv [1971-2], 122-3). Since the modern town development caused the overbuilding of most of the palace city, the German Archaeological Institute in Damascus has conducted ten seasons of rescue excavations from 1982 till 1992. At the eastern fringes of the site, four larger buildings bordering on a public square were investigated: the so-called Western Palace of *ca.* 110 x 90 m/360 x 295 feet divided into representative, living and infrastructural units; the North Complex of *ca.* 150 x 150 m/492 x 492 feet, probably the barracks of the imperial guards; the East Complex of *ca.* 75 x 50 m/246 x 164 feet, mostly of recreational functions; and the Eastern Palace of *ca.* 70 x 40 m/230 x 131 feet, reserved entirely for representative purposes. On the northeastern limits of the palace area, another large-size complex with an extension of *ca.* 300 x 400 m/984 x 1,312 feet was also partly excavated, revealing an elongated double courtyard structure encircled by round towers, which was obviously left unfinished (see the reports by J.-Chr. Heusch and M. Meinecke).

All the investigated buildings depended on mud as the major construction material, either in the form of sun-dried bricks or of stamped mud, only occasionally strengthened by burnt bricks. The ground plans, on the other hand, are generally characterised by precisely calculated geometrical subdivisions, indicating the careful laying-out of the built fabric. The publicly visible parts, on the exterior as well as in the interior, received a coating of white plaster, masking and protecting the mud core of the walls. On the representative units the buildings were decorated by stucco friezes in deep relief (Pl. XXVII, 2-3), depicting mostly vine ornament in numerous variations (partly documented by Meinecke, in *Rezeption in der islamischen Kunst*, ed. B. Finster, forthcoming). Genetically, these patterns are only vaguely related to Umayyad predecessors; instead, the dependence on classical models indicates an intended revival of the ornamental corpus of the monuments from the 2nd and 3rd centuries A.D. at Palmyra (see Meinecke and A. Schmidt-Colinet, in the exhibition catalogue by E.M. Ruprechtsberger [ed.], *Syrien. Von den Aposteln zu den Kalifen*, Linz 1993, 352-9). Selections of excavation finds and decorative elements from the Raḳḳa palaces are exhibited at the Damascus National Museum and at the archaeological museum at al-Raḳḳa.

Though the investigated complexes lack building inscriptions pointing to their original function or to the patron, their history can be clearly defined by the numismatic evidence. Among the coins collected during the recent excavations on the eastern border structures of the palace belt, examples minted at al-Rāfiḳa in the year 189/804-5 in the name of Hārūn al-Rashīd are especially numerous, while only individual items minted at al-Rāfiḳa in the reigns of the succeeding sons al-Maʾmūn (208/823-4 and 210/825-6) and al-Muʿtaṣim (226/840-1) have been recorded (on the ʿAbbāsid mint at al-Rāfiḳa, see now L. Ilisch, in *Numismatics – witness to history. IAPN publication*, viii [1986], 101-21). Consequently, those structures investigated recently must have been in use towards the end of Hārūn al-Ras͟hīd's tenure of power at al-Raḳḳa. After the removal of the court back to Bag͟hdād on the death of Hārūn al-Ras͟hīd in 193/809, the palaces were obviously in use only briefly and occasionally.

This extensive residential city was evidently founded in 180/796 by Hārūn al-Ras͟hīd and continuously further enlarged for over a decade. These buildings formed the backstage of the political events of this period, described in great detail by al-Ṭabarī and others. From there, the yearly raids (*ṣawāʾif*, sing. *ṣāʾifa* [*q.v.*]) into the Byzantine empire and the frequent pilgrimages to the Holy Cities of Mecca and Medina were organised. In these palaces lived the family of the caliph, including his wife Zubayda and his heirs apparent, al-Amīn, al-Maʾmūn and al-Ḳāsim, and also al-Muʿtaṣim, for much of their youth (as described by N. Abbott, *Two queens of Baghdad*, Chicago 1946). Here was the military centre with the army command and the administrative centre of the vast ʿAbbāsid empire, where the treasuries and the material wealth of the caliph were safeguarded (al-Ṭabarī, iii, 654). Here the members of the Barmakid family managed the affairs of the state until they were executed or imprisoned in 187/803 [see AL-BARĀMIKA].

For his periodic centre of administration, Hārūn al-Ras͟hīd also improved the infrastructure decisively. For the irrigation of the palace city, two canals were laid out: one channelling the water of the Euphrates from about 15 km/9 miles further west, and another of over 100 km/62 miles collecting water from the Anatolian mountains to the north. According to Yāḳūt, one of these (probably the Euphrates canal) was named Nahr al-Nīl (described by Kassem Toueir, in *Techniques et pratiques hydro-agricoles traditionelles en domaine irrigué. Actes du Colloque de Damas*, ed. B. Geyer, Paris 1990, 217-20).

About 8 km/5 miles to the west of the city, the Euphrates canal passes by another monument to be associated with Hārūn al-Ras͟hīd. Surrounded by a circular enclosure wall of 500 m/1,640 feet in diameter, with round buttresses and four portals on the cardinal points, the centre is occupied by a massive square building of *ca.* 100 m/328 feet for each side. Accessible on the ground level only are four vaulted stately halls on the main axis, from where ramps lead to the upper storey, which was not, however, completed. This curious stone structure, recently also investigated archaeologically, with the traditional name of Hiraḳla obviously alluding to the conquest of the Byzantine city of Heraclea by Hārūn al-Ras͟hīd in 190/806, can be interpreted as a victory monument. The stone material used seems to have originated from churches of the frontier region whose dismantling was ordered in 191/806-7 by the caliph (Ibn S͟haddād, iii/1, 342). Obviously, due to the departure of the imperial patron to K͟hurāsān in 192/808 and his death shortly thereafter, the building was left unfinished (see Toueir, in *World Archaeology*, xiv/3 [1983], 296-303, and in *La Syrie de Byzance à l'Islam, VIIe-VIIIe siècles, Actes du Colloque International*, ed. P. Canivet and J.-P. Rey-Coquais, Damascus 1992, 179-86).

The extensive construction programme at al-Raḳḳa was accompanied by accelerated industrial activities; these are attested by a string of mounds with large piles of ashes outside the northern wall of the city of al-Raḳḳa/Nikephorion. Recently investigated archaeologically at two points, workshops for pottery and glass production have been detected, for which the numismatic evidence points to their use in the time of Hārūn al-Ras͟hīd. The expertly-potted ceramics with incised or moulded decoration, as well as the fragile glass vessels featuring incised, relief or lustre decoration, which are known from the inventories of the excavated palaces, were thus evidently for the most part fabricated locally.

The later ʿAbbāsid period. Shortly after the sudden death of Hārūn al-Ras͟hīd, his widow Zubayda in 193/809 organised the transfer of the vast state treasures to Bag͟hdād, where her son al-Amīn (193-8/809-13) was enthroned as ruler of the ʿAbbāsid empire (al-Ṭabarī, iii, 775). While this marks the reinstallation of Bag͟hdād as the administrative centre of the Muslim world, the city of al-Raḳḳa remained of regional importance as seat of the governor of the D̲jazīra province until the mid-4th/10th century.

In opposition to al-Maʾmūn (198-218/813-33), who succeeded in capturing Bag͟hdād from his brother al-Amīn, a revolt caused the destruction by fire of the market quarter between the sister cities of al-Raḳḳa and al-Rāfiḳa in 198/813 (Michael Syrus, ed. J.-B. Chabot, iii, 26). To police the situation, al-Maʾmūn sent the general Ṭāhir b. al-Ḥusayn [*q.v.*] as governor of the D̲jazīra to al-Raḳḳa, followed by his son ʿAbd Allāh b. Ṭāhir [*q.v.*] until 210/825-6, when he was nominated governor of Egypt. In the time of the Ṭāhirids, the palace belt outside the city walls was already evidently falling into disrepair. Nevertheless, a last reactivation is attested for the time of al-Muʿtaṣim on the basis of fresco inscriptions with his name found at the Palace B to the east of Hārūn al-Ras͟hīd's central residence (A. Grohmann, *Arabische Paläographie*, ii, Vienna 1971, pl. 18). This is to be connected with the last military campaign into the Byzantine empire conducted from al-Raḳḳa, which resulted in the conquest of the city of ʿAmmūriyya/Amorium in 223/838 (Ibn S͟haddād, ii/1, 341). From there, the caliph carried off the famous iron doors to his newly-founded capital of Sāmarrāʾ, to be set up at the main entrance, the Bāb al-ʿĀmma, of his residential palace, then under construction.

Instead of utilising the palace city of Hārūn al-Ras͟hīd, new structures were built up on top of the suburb between the sister cities; soundings conducted by the Syrian Service of Antiquities (1953 and 1969) have revealed stucco decorations in the bevelled style of Sāmarrāʾ from the mid-3rd/9th century. About the same time also, the prayer-niche of the Great Mosque at al-Rāfiḳa received a new stucco decoration with similar features. A series of stone capitals, now scattered to many museum collections, featuring the characteristic slant cut and related ornamental patterns, bear witness to continuous building activities (M.S. Dimand, in *Ars Islamica*, iv [1937], 308-24; Meinecke, in *Bilād al-Shām during the Abbasid period*, in *Proceedings of the fifth International Conference on the History of Bilād al-Shām*, 232-5).

Though the size of the inhabited area became drastically diminished, the city of al-Raḳḳa remained the only real antipode to Bag͟hdād. Therefore, it was the obvious alternative for caliphs in exile or seeking refuge, as it was the case with al-Mustaʿīn in 251/865, al-Muʿtamid in 269/882, al-Muʿtaḍid in 286/899 and 287/900, and finally with al-Muttaḳī in 332-3/944, as recorded by al-Ṭabarī and other historians. But the fame of the city at that period did not result from political might or artistic achievements but from the scholars living and teaching at al-Raḳḳa, for instance the famous astronomer Abū ʿAbd Allāh Muḥammad al-Battānī (d. 317/929 [*q.v.*]), or Muḥammad b. Saʿīd al-Ḳus͟hayrī (d. 334/945), the author of a *Taʾrīk͟h al-Raḳḳa*, ed. Ṭāhir al-Naʿsānī, Ḥamā 1959.

The first period of decline. The decline of the

1. City walls of al-Rāfiḳa (photo German Archaeological Institute Damascus: P. Grunwald 1985).

2. North Gate of al-Rāfiḳa (photo German Archaeological Institute Damascus: M. Meinecke 1984).

1. Great Mosque of al-Raḳḳa/Nikephorion, minaret (photo G.L. Bell 1909; courtesy Gertrude Bell Photographic Archive: Department of Archaeology, The University of Newcastle upon Tyne).

2. Great Mosque of al-Rāfiḳa, minaret (photo German Archaeological Institute Damascus: P. Grunwald 1984).

3. Great Mosque of al-Rāfiḳa, aerial view *ca.* 1930 (reproduced from M. Dunand, *De l'Amanus au Sinai*, 1953).

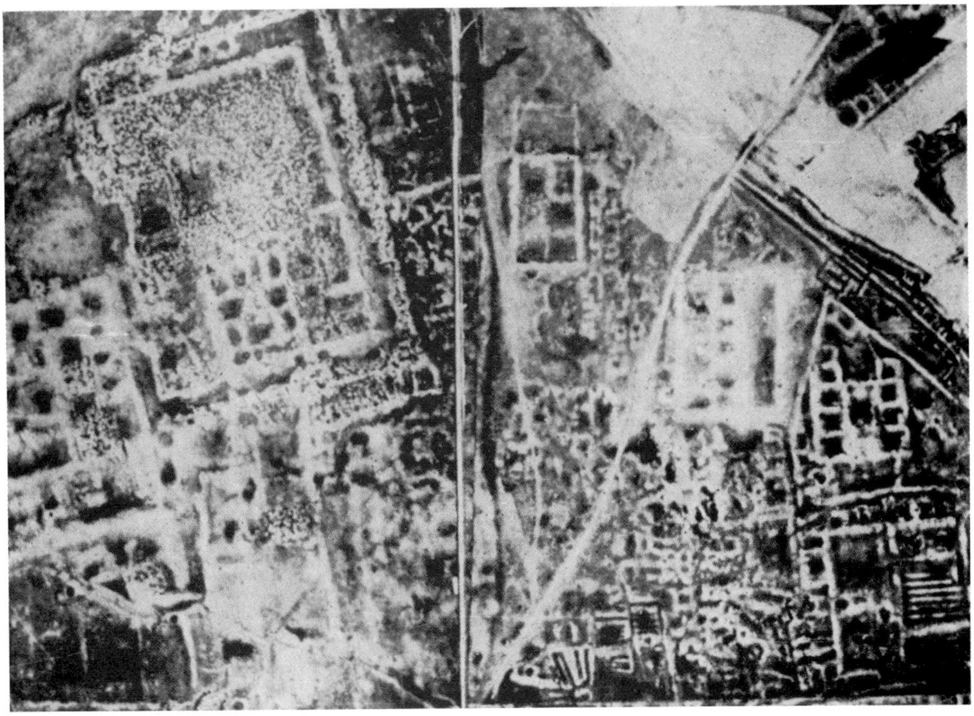

1. Palace City of Hārūn al-Rashīd, main palace and neighbouring structures on the southeast, aerial view *ca.* 1930 (reproduced from M. Dunand, *De l'Amanus au Sinai*, 1953); for identification see map.

2. Western Palace, stucco frieze (photo German Archaeological Institute Damascus: P. Grunwald 1985).

3. Western Palace, stucco frieze (photo German Archaeological Institute Damascus: P. Grunwald 1985).

1. Bāb Baghdād (photo German Archaeological Institute Damascus: K. Anger 1983).

2. Palace of Djamāl al-Dīn Muḥammad al-Iṣfahānī/Ḳaṣr al-Banāt, domed corner room (photo German Archaeological Institute Damascus: K. Anger 1983).

ANCIENT CIVILIZATIONS FROM SCYTHIA TO SIBERIA

An International Journal of Comparative Studies in History and Archaeology

E.J. BRILL

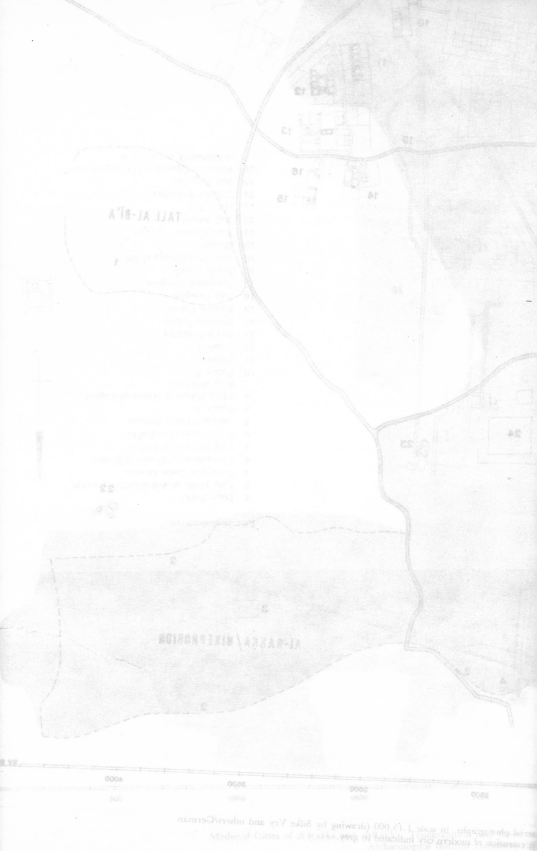

central administration of the ʿAbbāsid caliphate affected also the city of al-Raḳḳa. Since the conquest by the Ḥamdānids in 330/942, the urban centre on the Euphrates was contested between the rulers of Mawṣil and Aleppo, as being the gate for supremacy in Northern Mesopotamia. The founder of the Aleppo branch of the Ḥamdānid dynasty, Sayf al-Dawla ʿAlī, (333-356/945-967) is blamed by Ibn Ḥawḳal and Ibn Shaddād for the devastation of the Djazīra and the former capital al-Raḳḳa. Political instability caused, for instance, the destruction by fire of part of the city of al-Raḳḳa/Nikephorion in 332/944, resulting in a gradual depopulation of the initial urban settlement. The dismantling in 353/964 of the iron doors from an entrance gate to the city is another proof for a marked reduction of the population (on the history of this period in general, see M. Canard, *Histoire de la dynastie des H'amdânides de Jazîra et de Syrie*, i, Algiers-Paris 1951). This development is also mirrored by the Umayyad Great Mosque, which, according to the position of the minaret in the interior courtyard, only remained in use with part of the initial prayer hall.

After the Ḥamdānids there followed a century of turmoil, when the governorship of al-Raḳḳa was fought over by the Arab tribal dynasties of the Numayrīds, the Mirdāsids and the ʿUḳaylids (described in great detail by Ibn Shaddād, iii/1, 74-8). Nothing is attested as having been added to the urban fabric; on the contrary, the shrinking population retreated increasingly from the initial city al-Raḳḳa to the ʿAbbāsid foundation of al-Rāfiḳa, which according to Yāḳūt, followed by al-Dimashḳī, eventually also took over the name of the sister city.

The revival of al-Raḳḳa in the Zangid and Ayyūbid periods. The fate of the city only changed with the appearance of the Zangids in the region (on the history of that period, see C. Alptekin, *The reign of Zangi (521-541/1127-1146)*, Erzurum 1978). Conquered by ʿImād al-Dīn Zangī in 529/1135, al-Raḳḳa was soon to regain importance, as attested by building activities (listed partly by Ibn Shaddād, iii/1, 71). When Zangī was murdered in 541/1146 whilst besieging Ḳalʿat Djaʿbar further up the Euphrates, he was first buried at Ṣiffīn, but soon afterwards his corpse was transferred to a domed mausoleum constructed for this purpose in the Mashhad quarter of al-Raḳḳa (Ibn al-ʿAdīm, ii, 285). Following the death of Zangī, his *wazīr* Djamāl al-Dīn Muḥammad al-Iṣfahānī organised from al-Raḳḳa the succession of Zangī's son, Nūr al-Dīn Maḥmūd (N. Elisséeff, *Nūr ad-Dīn*, Damascus 1967, 390-2). In this connection a palace is mentioned, which may eventually be identified with the Ḳaṣr al-Banāt (Pl. XXVIII, 2), a ruined structure from that period (on the archaeological investigation since 1977, see Toueir, in *Damaszener Mitteilungen*, ii [1985], 297-319). Ibn Shaddād in addition also mentions a *khānḳāh* of the same patron, as well as another commissioned by Nūr al-Dīn Maḥmūd, together with a hospital (*bīmāristān*) and two *madrasas*, one for Shāfiʿīs and the other for Ḥanafīs, presumably all erected by or in the time of the same ruler. Most indicative for the reactivation of the city during this period is the ʿAbbāsid Great Mosque of al-Rāfiḳa, which already attracted minor construction and decoration activities in 541/1146-7 and 553/1158, as recorded on re-used inscription fragments (photographed by G.L. Bell in 1909) and on newly-discovered inscription panels (excavated in 1986, now on display at the Raḳḳa Museum). The surviving parts of the mosque, the façade or the *ḳibla riwāḳ* and the cylindrical minaret (Pl. XXVI, 1), are due to the reconstruction programme of Nūr al-Dīn Maḥmūd, completed in 561/1165-6.

The reduced size of the reactivated mosque, limited to the former prayer hall, mirrors the comparatively modest population of the town, which only occupied the eastern half of the ʿAbbāsid city, where evidently most of the lost other religious buildings mentioned were also located. As the main entrance to the mediaeval city, there functioned the Bāb Baghdād at the southeast corner of the ʿAbbāsid city walls, according to the brick decoration erected at this time (Pl. XXVIII, 1) (re-dated by J. Warren, in *Art and Archaeology Research Papers*, xiii [1978], 22-3; and R. Hillenbrand, in *The art of Syria and the Jazira 1100-1250*, ed. J. Raby, Oxford 1985, 27-36).

With the conquest by Ṣalāḥ al-Dīn in 578/1182, the city passed into the control of the Ayyūbids. As one of the chief towns of the principality of Diyār Muḍar, al-Raḳḳa was especially favoured by the Ayyūbid prince al-Malik al-ʿAdil Abū Bakr, who took up residence at the city between 597/1201 and 625/1128. He is attested to have constructed palaces and bath complexes, and laid out many gardens with extensive plantations (Ibn Shaddād, iii/1, 71-2). Of these Ayyūbid additions to the town, nothing has survived. But in this period, al-Raḳḳa emerged as a major production centre for glazed ceramics of high artistic perfection, which were exported widely. Most frequent among these are figural or vegetal designs in black under a transparent turquoise glaze, but other variations with lustre on turquoise and purple glazes, or coloured designs, including red, under a colourless glaze, are also recorded (see the detailed studies by E.J. Grube, in *Kunst des Orients*, iv [1963], 42-78; V. Porter, *Medieval Syrian pottery (Raqqa ware)*, Oxford 1981; and also the extensive bibliography by Cr. Tonghini and Grube, in *Islamic Art*, iii [1989], 59-93). The pottery workshops were located in the immediate vicinity of the urban settlement, even partly within the ʿAbbāsid city walls to the south of the Great Mosque (on a kiln excavated in 1924 immediately outside the east wall of the city, see J. Sauvaget in *Ars Islamica*, xiii-xiv [1948], 31-45).

The Ayyūbids successfully repulsed occasional attacks on the city by the Saldjūḳs of Asia Minor and the Khʷārazmians, but finally had to yield to the Mongol forces, who invaded northern Mesopotamia in 657/1259 (on the history of that period, see R.S. Humphreys, *From Saladin to the Mongols*, Albany 1977). Urban settlement at Diyār Muḍar ceased in the early years of the Mamlūk era, when in 663/1265 all the fortified cities on the middle Euphrates were destroyed for tactical reasons, including al-Raḳḳa (L. Ilisch, *Geschichte der Artuqidenherrschaft von Mardin zwischen Mamluken und Mongolen 1260-1410 AD*, Münster 1984, 51-2).

The Ottoman period. Throughout the Mamlūk period, al-Raḳḳa remained practically deserted, as certified by Abu 'l-Fidāʾ. Only after the Syrian campaign of the Ottoman sultan Selīm I (918-26/1512-20), which resulted in the downfall of the entire Mamlūk empire in 923/1517, was it reactivated as a military outpost. In the time of sultan Süleymān II Ḳānūnī (926-74/1520-66), al-Raḳḳa was the nominal capital of a province of the Ottoman empire, probably in memory of its past glory. A building inscription commemorating the restoration of a castle and a sacred building (*ḥaram*) by Sultan Süleymān b. Selīm Khān remains the only testimony to this limited reactivation as a military and administrative centre (originally located at the Mausoleum of Uways al-Ḳaranī, now on display in the archaeological museum of the modern city). Due to destruction by Türkmen and Kurdish tribes, the governorship was transferred to the city of al-Ruhā/Urfa *ca.* 135 km/84 miles further north (according to Ewliyā Čelebi, *Seyāḥat-nāme*, tr. J. von Hammer, i/1, London 1834, 95, 101, 104, 110; tr. Danişman, v, Istanbul 1970, 41, 52-3). On the visit of Ewliyā Čelebi in winter 1059/1649, the place was deserted following recent raids, though the ruins of the glorious past and formerly-irrigated gardens still remained visible.

The site was only repopulated in the late 19th century, when the Turkish government settled there a group of Circassians in order to police the region. Initially a village of only a few houses near the southwest corner of the ʿAbbāsid city, the population grew slowly but steadily, counting somewhat less than 5,000 inhabitants by the middle of the 20th century. Since then, due to the agricultural revival of the region, the settlement has reached a population of nearly 90,000 inhabitants in 1981 (Syrian ... Central Bureau of Statistics (ed.), *Statistical abstract*, xxxvii, Damascus 1984). Now the capital of a province administered by a governor, and an active commercial and industrial centre, the city has reached a size larger than ever in its history, consequently submerging most of the historic fabric. This in turn has motivated an extensive programme of archaeological research and architectural conservation for the monuments from the Islamic past.

Bibliography (in addition to the references in the text): Arabic texts. For Yaʿḳūbī, Ibn al-Faḳīh, Muḳaddasī, Ibn Ḥawḳal, Yāḳūt, and other geographical works, see the convenient index by C. Corun, *Atlas du monde arabo-islamique à l'époque classique, IXe-Xe siècles*, Leiden 1985, 21-2, s.v. Rāfiqa and Raqqa. In addition see Balādhurī, *Futūḥ*, 173-4, 178-80, 297; Ṭabarī (tr. in 39 vols. with annotation and index in progress); Bakrī, *Muʿdjam mā istaʿdjam*, ed. Muṣṭafā al-Saḳḳā, Cairo 1945-51; Harawī, *K. al-Ziyārāt*, ed. J. Sourdel-Thomine, Damascus 1953, 63 (tr. eadem, Damascus 1957, 141-2); Ibn al-ʿAdīm, *Zubdat al-Ḥalab*, ed. Sāmī al-Dahhān, 3 vols., Damascus 1951, 1954, 1968; Muḥammad Ibn Shaddād, *al-Aʿlāḳ al-khaṭīra*, ii/1, ed. A.-M. Eddé in *B. Ét. Or.*, xxxii-xxxiii (1980-1); ed. Yaḥyā ʿAbbāra, 2 vols., Damascus 1878, 69-82; Dimashḳī, *Nukhbat al-dahr*, ed. A.F. Mehren, St. Petersburg 1866; Abu 'l-Fidāʾ, *Taḳwīm*, 277.

General works and publications on the monuments of al-Raḳḳa. E. Sachau, *Reise in Syrien und Mesopotamien*, Leipzig 1883, 241-6; G. Le Strange, *Palestine under the Moslems*, London 1890, 518; idem, *Lands of the Eastern Caliphate*, London 1905, 101-2; H. Violet, *Description du Palais de al-Moutasim, fils d'Haroun-al-Raschid à Samara et de quelques monuments arabes peu connus de la Mésopotamie*, in *Mémoires présentés par divers savants à l'Académie des Inscriptions et Belles-Lettres*, xii/2 (1909), 568-71; G.L. Bell, *Amurath to Amurath*, London 1911, 54-60; F. Sarre and E. Herzfeld, *Archäologische Reise im Euphrat- und Tigris-Gebiet*, i, Berlin 1911, 3-6 (M. van Berchem), 156-61; ii, Berlin 1920, 349-64; iv, Berlin 1920, 20-5; A. Musil, *The Middle Euphrates*, New York 1927, 91, 325-31; K.A.C. Creswell, *Early Muslim Architecture*, ii, Oxford 1940, 39-48, 165-6; M. Dunand, *De l'Amanus au Sinai*, Beirut 1953, 94-7; Creswell, *A short account of early Muslim architecture*, Harmondsworth 1958, 183-90; M. Abû-l-Faraj al-ʿUsh (ed.), *Catalogue du Musée National de Damas*, Damascus 1969, 166-76; Abdul-Kader Rihaoui, *Aperçu sur la civilisation de al-Jazira et de la Vallée de l'Euphrate à l'époque arabe-musulmane*, in *Les Annales Archéologiques Arabes Syriennes*, xix (1969), 84-7, Arabic part 56-9; D. Sturm, *Zur Bedeutung der syrischen Stadt ar-Raqqa von der arabischen Eroberung bis zur Gegenwart*, in *Hallesche Beiträge zur Orientwissenschaft*, i (1979), 35-72; M. Meinecke, *Raqqa*, in *Land des Baal*, ed. K. Kohlmeyer and E. Strommenger, Mainz 1982, 261-3, 274-84; H.G. Franz, *Palast, Moschee und Wüstenschloß. Das Werden der Islamischen Kunst, 7.-9. Jahrhundert*, Graz 1984, 121-4, 126, 128; J.-C. Heusch und M. Meinecke, *Grabungen im ʿabbāsidischen Palastareal von ar-Raqqa/ar-Rāfiqa 1982-1983*, in *Damaszener Mitteilungen*, ii (1985), 85-105; idem, *Die Residenz des Harun al-Raschid in Raqqa*, Damascus 1989; Creswell, *A short account of early Muslim architecture*, revised and supplemented by J.W. Allen, Aldershot 1989, 243-8, 270-8; Meinecke, *Raqqa on the Euphrates: recent excavations at the residence of Harun er-Rashid*, in *The Near East in Antiquity: German contributions to the archaeology of Jordan, Palestine, Syria, Lebanon and Egypt*, ed. S. Kerner, ii, Amman 1991, 17-32.

(M. MEINECKE)

RAḲḲĀDA, a city of the Maghrib which was the centre of power of the Aghlabid *amīrs* of Ifrīḳiya about 6 miles south of Ḳayrawān, was founded in 263/876 by Ibrāhīm II, seventh prince of the dynasty. Until then the Aghlabids [*q.v.*] had resided in ʿAbbāsiyya [*q.v.*] nearer the capital. A chance trip into the country by Ibrāhīm, it is said, determined the site of the new residence. The *amīr* was suffering from insomnia and on the advice of his physician, Isḥāḳ b. Sulaymān, went out to take the air. Stopping in a certain place, he fell into a deep sleep and decided to build a palace there which was called Raḳḳāda, the "soporific". The story is probably based on a popular etymology of the name, which is found elsewhere in North Africa. Another explanation, equally suspect, is that which attributes the name to the memory of a massacre of the Warfadjūma by the Ibāḍī chief Abu 'l-Khaṭṭāb [*q.v.*] in 141/758 and the many dead left lying there.

In the same year that the work of building was begun, Ibrāhīm settled in Raḳḳāda in the Castle of Victory (*Ḳaṣr al-Fatḥ*). He was to live there the rest of his life, as were his successors, except for the stays the *amīrs* made in Tunis. Raḳḳāda became a regular town just as al-ʿAbbāsiyya had been before it. Besides Ḳaṣr al-Fatḥ (or Ḳaṣr Abi 'l-Fatḥ), there were several other castles in it: Ḳaṣr al-Baḥr (the castle on the lake), Ḳaṣr al-Ṣaḥn (castle of the court), Ḳaṣr al-Mukhtār (castle of the elect) and Ḳaṣr Baghdād, a large mosque, baths, caravanserais and *sūḳ*s. Al-Bakrī says that it had a circumference of 24,040 cubits (over 6 miles); al-Nuwayrī makes it smaller (14,000, nearly 4 miles). A wall of brick and clay surrounded this vast area, and this wall was renovated by the last Aghlabid with a view to a final effort at resistance. Al-Bakrī further tells us that the greater part of the enceinte was filled with gardens. The soil was fertile and the air temperate. The *amīrs* and their followers enjoyed in Raḳḳāda a liberty of conduct which would have caused a scandal in Ḳayrawān. The sale of *nabīdh* [*q.v.*], forbidden in the pious old city, was officially permitted in the royal residence.

It was from Raḳḳāda that Ziyādat Allāh III, the last of the Aghlabids, fled on the approach of the Shīʿī Fāṭimids. The victorious Abū ʿAbd Allāh [*q.v.*] installed himself in Ḳaṣr al-Ṣaḥn. His master, the Mahdī ʿUbayd Allāh, lived in Raḳḳāda until 308/920 when he moved to al-Mahdiyya [*q.v.*]. After being deserted by the ruler, Raḳḳāda fell into ruins. In 342/953 the Fāṭimid caliph al-Muʿizz ordered what was left of it to be razed to the ground and ploughed over. The gardens alone were spared.

A few traces of the Aghlabid foundation are still to be seen at the present day. A great rectangular reservoir with thick walls strengthened by buttresses may be identified with the lake (*baḥr*) which gave its name to one of the palaces. A pavilion (?) of four stories stood in the centre. Nothing is left of it, but on the west side of the reservoir may be seen the remains of a building which must have been reflected in the great mirror of water. Three rooms may still be distinguished with their mosaic pavements. The technique and style of decoration closely connect these Islamic buildings of the 3rd/9th century with the Christian art of the country.

Excavations under the auspices of the National Institute of Archaeology of Tunisia have been carried on at the site since 1962. The finds have only been very partially studied until now (1993), but are preserved in a rich National Museum of Islamic Art established not far from the ruins, whilst awaiting a fuller examination.

Bibliography: Nuwayrī, in Ibn Khaldūn, *Hist. des Berbères*, tr. de Slane, Algiers 1852-6, i, 424, 441; Bakrī, *al-Masālik wa 'l-mamālik*, ed. de Slane, Algiers 1911, tr. idem, *Description de l'Afrique septentrionale*, Algiers 1913, 62-3; Ibn ʿIdhārī, *Bayān*, ed. Dozy, i, 110, 144-5, 147, 157, tr. E. Fagnan, i, 152, 202, 205-6, 218-19, ed. G. Colin and E. Lévi-Provençal, Leiden 1948-51; Ibn al-Abbār, *al-Ḥulla al-siyarāʾ*, ed. Müller, Munich 1866, 261; Ibn al-Athīr, vii, 215-22, viii, 34, tr. Fagnan, *Annales du Maghreb et de l'Espagne*, Algiers 1892, 253-5, 297; *K. al-Istibṣār*, tr. Fagnan, 11-21; M. Vonderheyden, *La Berbérie orientale sous la dynastie des Benoû 'l-Arlab*, Paris 1927, 193 and passim; G. Marçais, *Manuel d'art musulman*, 2 vols., Paris 1926-7, i, 42-4, 52; Ḥ.Ḥ. ʿAbd al-Wahhāb, *Villes arabes disparues*, in *Mél. William Marçais*, Paris 1950; idem, *Waraḳāt ʿan al-ḥaḍāra al-ʿarabiyya bi-Ifrīḳiya al-tūnisiyya*, 3 vols., Tunis 1965-72, i, 360-75; J. Solignac, *Recherches sur les installations hydrauliques de Kairouan et des steppes tunisiennes, du VIIe au XIe siècles (J.-C.)*, in *AIEO Alger*, x (1952), 5-273; H.R. Idris, *La Berbérie orientale sous les Zirides*, Paris 1962; M. Talbi, *L'émirat aghlabide, 184-296/800-909*, Paris 1966, index; A. Lézine, *Architecture de l'Ifriqiya. Recherches sur les monuments aghlabides*, in *Arch. Med.*, ii (1966); Ennabli-Mahjouni-Salomson, *La necropole romaine de Raqqâda*, 2 vols., Tunis 1971-3; F. Dachraoui, *Le califat fatimide au Maghreb 296-362/909-973, histoire politique et institutions*, Tunis 1981, 111 ff.; H. Halm, *Das Reich des Mahdi. Der Aufsteig der Fatimiden (875-973)*, Munich 1991, 114 ff., 133 ff.

(G. Marçais*)

RAKKĀṢ (A.), in French *rekkas*, a term which has several meanings but which only merits an entry in the *EI* because, amongst several technical senses, it particularly denotes, in the Muslim West, a messenger who travels on foot long distances in order to carry official or private mail. The name is derived from the noun *raḳṣ* meaning "trotting" (of a horse or camel; see *LA*, s.v.), but is also applied to a man who "trots", as is the case with the *raḳḳāṣ*. The development of various means of communication has put an end to this calling, now unnecessary, and the word *raḳḳāṣ* can now only denote an occasional messenger, above all in time of war.

Dozy, *Supplément*, s.v., gathered together a certain number of references in the Arabic sources (notably al-Maḳḳarī, *Analectes*, i, 557, since the term was used in Spain, as P. de Alcala indicates in his *Vocabulista*) and in the accounts of Western travellers, and also indicated various other technical senses of *raḳḳāṣ*, notably "pendulum", "hand of a watch" (cf. Fr. "trotteuse"), "trigger of a fire-arm" and, after Mehren (in *Acts of the Royal Society of Sciences*, Copenhagen 1872, 28), "part of a mill which produces a noise through the movement of the millstone". It is nevertheless also useful to note that the Kabyle *arəḳḳas* (with de-emphasisation of the sibilant) is equally applied to the hand of a watch and the pendulum of a clock, as well as to a piece better described by J. Dallet (*Dictionnaire kabyle-français*, Paris 1982, 732) than by Mehren: "a simple contrivance of a water-mill made from a pin fixed on a small stick floating above the moving mill-stone; this pin, fixed to the trough containing grain, transmits a vibration to it which ensures the regular feeding of the grain into the mouth of the mill."

Bibliography: Given in the article. (Ed.)

RAKṢ (A.), dance. The following article deals with the dance in Ṣūfism.

During recent decades, one could sometimes read in American newspapers about "Courses in Sufi Dance", and "Sufi dance" became a fashionable way of cultivating one's soul. However, the topic of dancing is frowned upon in Islam, for dancing is connected, in the history of religions in general, with ecstasy. It takes the human being out of his/her normal movement and makes him/her gyrate, so to speak, around a different centre of gravity. To be sure, cheerful parties of well-to-do people in the Islamic Middle Ages often ended with music and dancing, but in the context of religion, the dance, basically an epi-phenomenon of music or melodious recitation, was felt to contradict the nomos-oriented character of Islam because it could make the individual stray from the divinely ordered way, the *sharīʿa*. Therefore, normative Islam has opposed dancing, and, based on sūra VIII, 35, it also opposed handclapping and related movements. Treatises and articles against dancing have been written throughout the centuries, for one saw here demonic influences; hence musicians and dancers should not serve as witnesses at court. Typical is a *risāla* attributed to Ibn Taymiyya [*q.v.*] about *raḳṣ* and *samāʿ* [*q.v.*] which are, as he claims, as dangerous for the believers as is their obedience to the Mongols (more than one later scholar has seen in the Ṣūfī dance an influence from or reminiscence of shamanistic dancing). Even the sober Ṣūfīs themselves blamed those for whom dancing constituted the main feature of Ṣūfism and who joined the Ṣūfī movement because they wanted to indulge in such ecstatic experiences.

They agreed with Hudjwīrī [*q.v.*], who wrote in the 5th/11th century "Dancing has no foundation in the religious law or the Path ... frivolous imitators have made it a religion..." (*Kashf al-maḥdjūb*, Eng. tr. Nicholson, 416).

The first known *samāʿ-khāna* or place for religious music-making and dancing was founded in Baghdād in the second half of the 3rd/9th century. There, Ṣūfīs could listen to the musical recitation of poetry, during which some were borne into a whirling movement. Sometimes, their ecstatic state led them to tear their robes; the pieces were carefully collected, since they were thought to be filled with *baraka* [*q.v.*], "blessing and charismatic power." The question was whether beginners on the Ṣūfī path should be allowed to participate, so that their sensual lusts might be dissipated (thus the Ṣūfī *shaykh* of Khurāsān Abū Saʿīd [*q.v.*]), or should be prohibited from listening and dancing. Another problem was, whose mystical "state" was loftier, that of a Ṣūfī who left himself to whirl at the sound of music, or the one who, like al-Djunayd [*q.v.*], refrained from showing movement?

Stamping and handclapping were part of such

dances, which might end in a frenzied group ecstasy (as the poet Djāmī [*q.v.*] describes it ironically in his *Silsilat al-dhahab*), and numerous miniatures, mainly from the Persian world, show Ṣūfīs in whirling dances, with their long sleeves resembling wings. The normative believer disliked the fact that the presence of a *shāhid*, a handsome young man, was regarded as necessary during the *samā*ᶜ; in fact, the very contemplation of such a person might induce the Ṣūfī involuntarily to dance (as would any overwhelming experience).

It is related that al-Ḥallādj [*q.v.*] (executed in 309/922) went dancing in his fetters to the execution, and a "dance in chains" occurs as a literary cliché, as does the Persian expression of the *raḳṣ-i bismil*, the "dance" of a ritually slaughtered bird, that is, the convulsions of the lover who resembles "a headless chicken".

Although dance as part of the *samā*ᶜ occured in various dervish groups, especially among the Čishtiyya [*q.v.*], it was institutionalised only in the Mewlewī order [see MAWLAWIYYA]. Mawlānā Djalāl al-Dīn Rūmī (604-72/1207-73 [*q.v.*]) had composed most of his lyrical poetry while listening to music, and many of his *ghazal*s [*q.v.*] can easily be accompanied by rhythmical handclapping. Terms like "clapping", "stamping" and the like abound in his lyrics, especially in his *rubāᶜiyyāt* [*q.v.*], for the *rubāᶜī* was the poetical form generally used in *samā*ᶜ sessions. For Rūmī, the whole universe is moving in a wonderful dance, from the moment that Not-Being heard God's primordial address "Am I not your Lord?" (sūra VII, 172) and came into existence by dancing (*Dīwān*, no. 1832), an idea alluded to as early as in Djunayd's sayings. Dance and *samā*ᶜ are the ladder to heaven, that is, the true *miᶜrādj*, and angels and demons participate in it. Stamping the ground makes the water of life gush forth; it is like treading the grapes out of which the spiritual wine is made. The trees, touched by the spring breeze, move their twigs in happy dance. Rūmī's son Sulṭān Walad [*q.v.*] institutionalised the music and dance from which his father had drawn much of his inspiration. Thus the dance of the Mewlewīs is by no means a wild ecstatic act but rather a well-organised "ballet" in which the individual dervish, however, may experience something like an ecstatic rapture. But it is "a dance for God", a way of praising God. The whirling is often compared to the movement of the stars around the central sun, or the dance of the moth around the candle in order to become annihilated; it is experiencing *fanā*ʾ "annihilation" in God in order to reach a higher level of consciousness. Later Mewlewī poets such as Ghālib Dede in Istanbul (d. 1213/1799 [*q.v.*]) took over this symbolism into their poetry as did Indo-Persian poets, most outspokenly Mīrzā Ghālib (d. 1869 [see GHĀLIB, MĪRZĀ ASAD ALLĀH KHĀN]) in his *ghazal* with the *radīf ba-raḳṣ*.

Among the dervishes, and in particular the Mewlewīs, funerals were often accompanied by ecstatic dance, and so was the *ᶜurs*, the celebrations to commemorate a dead saint. It is therefore not astonishing that some Ṣūfīs claimed that there was dance in Paradise (thus reminding the western reader of Fra Angelico's paintings), and Rūzbihān-i Baḳlī (d. 605/1209 [*q.v.*]) saw himself dancing with the archangels and with the Prophet, symbolising the end of his mystical journey as a "dance with God".

As for folk dances in Islamic countries, they are usually performed by either men or women, and in cases when both sexes participate—as is the case among some Berber tribes—dancing is frowned upon by both normative believers and serious Ṣūfīs. The fact that, nowadays, even women participate in dervish dances in "modernised" orders contradicts all classical tradition because the dervish dance does not aim at sensual goals, especially as conservative, traditionalist critics of Ṣūfism like the Ḥanbalī Ibn al-Djawzī [*q.v.*] in his *Talbīs Iblīs* branded dancing as a demon-inspired, "immoral" activity.

Bibliography: H. Corbin, *Quiétude et inquiétude de l'âme dans le soufisme de Rūzbihān Baqlī*, in *Eranos Jahrbuch*, xxvii (1958); S. Haq, *Samā*ᶜ *and Raqṣ of the derwishes*, in *IC*, xviii (1944); J. During, *Musique et extase*, Paris 1988; A. Gölpınarlı, *Mevlâna'dan sonra mevlevilik*, Istanbul 1953; Hudjwīrī, *Kashf al-maḥdjūb*, tr. R.A. Nicholson, London 1911; Ibn al-Djawzī, *Talbīs Iblīs*, Beirut n.d.; D.B. Macdonald, *Emotional religion in Islam as affected by music and singing. Being a translation of a book of the Iḥyā*ʾ *ᶜulūm ad-Dīn*, in *JRAS* (1901), 195-252, 705-48; (1902), 1-28; F. Meier, *Abū Saᶜīd-i Abū l-Ḫair*, Leiden-Tehran-Liège 1976; idem, *Der Derwischtanz*, in *Asiatische Studien*, viii (1954), 107-36; J.R. Michot, *Musique et dance selon Ibn Taymiyya*, Paris 1991; M. Molé, *La danse extatique en Islam*, in *Les danses sacrées*, Sources orientales, Paris 1963, 146-280; H. Ritter, *Das Meer der Seele*, Leiden 1955; J. Robson, *Tracts on listening to music*, Oriental Translation Fund, NS XXXIV, London 1938; Rūmī, *Dīwān-i kabīr*, ed. B. Furūzānfar, 10 vols., Tehran 1957-72; A. Schimmel, *The Triumphal Sun*, The Hague-London 1978, repr. Albany 1993; G. Vajda, *Un libelle contre la danse des Soufis*, in *SI*, li (1980), 163-77; G. van der Leeuw, *In den himel is een dans*, Amsterdam 1930.

(ANNEMARIE SCHIMMEL)

RĀM-HURMUZ (the contracted form *Rāmiz*, *Rāmuz* is found as early as the 4th/10th century), a town and district in Khūzistān [*q.v.*] in south-western Persia. Rām-Hurmuz lies about 55 miles southeast of Ahwāz, 65 miles south-south-east of Shūshtar, and 60 miles north-east of Bihbihān. Ibn Khurradādhbih, 43, reckons it 17 *farsakh*s from Ahwāz to Rām-Hurmuz and 22 *farsakh*s from Rām-Hurmuz to Arradjān. Ḳudāma, 194, who gives a more detailed list of stages, counts it 50 *farsakh*s from Wāsiṭ to Baṣra, thence 35 *farsakh*s to Ahwāz, thence 20 *farsakh*s to Rām-Hurmuz, and then 24 *farsakh*s to Arradjān. The importance of Rām-Hurmuz lay in the fact that it was situated at the intersection of the roads from Ahwāz, Shūshtar, Iṣfahān and Fārs (via Arradjān); that it is the natural market for the Bakhtiyārī and Kūh-gilū tribes [see LUR] and that there is oil in its vicinity. The town lies between the rivers Āb-i Kurdistān and Gūpāl. The first of these (also called Djibur) is made up of the following streams: Āb-i Gilāl (Āb-i Zard), Āb-i Aᶜlā (coming from Mungasht), Rūd-i Pūtang and Āb-i Darra-yi Kūl. A canal is led from the right bank of the Djibur to supply the town of Rām-Hurmuz. Farther down, the Djibur joins the Āb-i Mārūn which comes from the southeast in the region of Bihbihān and of the old town of Arradjān [*q.v.*]. Their combined waters are known as the Djarrāḥī. The other little river (Gūpāl) runs north of Rām-Hurmuz and is lost in marshes. Rām-Hurmuz (160 m/500 feet above sea-level, in lat. 31° 15 'N., long. 49° 38' E.) is situated above the plain to the northeast of which rise the hills of Tūl-Gorgūn 490 m/1,600 feet high.

The town is rarely mentioned by historians. The Pahlavi list of *the towns of Iran*, § 46 (ed. Markwart, *A catalogue of the provincial capitals of Ērānshahr*, 19, 98) attributes the building of Rām-Hurmuz to Hurmuzd b. Shāhpuhr (272-3) (cf. also al-Ṭabarī, i, 833). According to Ḥamza, ed. Gottwald, 46-7, the town was built by Ardas̲h̲īr I and its name was *Rām-(i) Hurmizd Ardas̲h̲īr*, which Marquart explains as "the delight of Ahura Mazda is Ardas̲h̲īr". According to a tradition recorded by al-Iṣṭak̲h̲rī, 93, Mānī was executed in Rām-Hurmuz, but al-Ṭabarī, i, 834, says that Mānī was exposed on the "gate of Mānī" at D̲j̲undī-Sābūr (cf. also al-Bīrūnī, *Chronology*, 208). The Nestorian bishops of Rām-Hurmuz are mentioned in the years 577 and 587 (Marquart, *Ērānšahr*, 27, 145). Al-Muḳaddasī, 414, says that ʿAḍud al-Dawla built a magnificent market near Rām-Hurmuz and that the town had a library founded by Ibn Sawwār (according to Schwarz, the son of Sawwār b. ʿAbd Allāh, governor of Baṣra, who died in 157/773), and was a centre of Muʿtazilī teaching. According to Ibn K̲h̲urradād̲h̲bih, 42, Rām-Hurmuz was one of the 11 *kūra*s of K̲h̲ūzistān (Ḳudāma, 242, and al-Muḳaddasī, 407: one of the 7 *kūras*). Its towns (al-Muḳaddasī) were Sanbil, Īd̲h̲ad̲j̲ [*q.v.*], Tyrm(?), Bāzank, Lād̲h̲, G̲h̲.rwa(?), Bābad̲j̲, and Kūzūk, all situated in the highlands. To these Yāḳūt, i, 185, adds Arbuk (with a bridge, 2 *farsak̲h̲*s from Ahwāz). On the other places in the *kūra* of Rām-Hurmuz (Asak, Būstān, Sasān, Ṭās̲h̲ān, Ūr) see Schwarz, *op. cit.*, 341-5. According to al-Muḳaddasī, 407, Rām-Hurmuz had palm-groves but no sugar-cane plantations (in the 8th/14th century, however, Ḥamd Allāh Mustawfī, *Nuzhat al-ḳulūb*, 111, says that Rām-Hurmuz used to produce more sugar than cotton); among the products of Rām-Hurmuz, al-Iṣṭak̲h̲rī (93) mentions silks (*t̲h̲iyāb ibrīsam*) and al-Dimas̲h̲ḳī, 119, tr. 153, the very volatile white napththa which comes out of the rocks.

Oil seepages in the region between S̲h̲ūs̲h̲tar and Rām-Hurmuz were noted as commercially exploitable from the beginning of the 20th century, and Rām-Hurmuz has in recent decades benefited from the expansion of the K̲h̲ūzistān oil industry, with the Haft Gel oilfield just to its north and the Ag̲h̲a D̲j̲ārī one just to its south. It also remains, with other towns of the northern rim of the province like Dizfūl and Masd̲j̲id-i Sulaymān, a market centre for the tribespeople of the adjacent Zagros massif. The population of Rām-Hurmuz was in 1991 34,059 (*September 1991 census, Statistical Centre of Iran, Population Division*). The ethnic composition of the Rām-Hurmuz region includes, as well as Persians, Arabs of the Āl K̲h̲amsīn from the D̲j̲arrāḥīs.

Bibliography: J. Macdonald Kinneir, *A geographical memoir*, London 1813, 457; Rawlinson, *Notes on a march from Zoháb*, in *JRGS* (1839), ix, 79 (region of Mungas̲h̲t, to the north-east of Rām-Hurmuz); Bode, *Travels*, London 1845, i, 281 (Bihbihān-Tās̲h̲ūn-Mand̲j̲ānik-Tūl-Mālamīr-S̲h̲ūs̲h̲tar), ii, 39, 76, 82 (distribution of tribes); Layard, *Description of Khūzistān*, in *JRGS* (1846), 13 (country round Rām-Hurmuz; in the town 250 families, taxes 3,000-5,000 *tumans*), 66 (valley of D̲j̲arrāḥī); Herzfeld, *Eine Reise durch Luristan*, in *Pet. Mitt.* (1907) (Ahwāz-S̲h̲āk̲h̲-i Gūpāl-Medibčiye (*Mīr-bača?) - Rāmūz (*sic*) - Palīn-D̲j̲ayzūn-Bihbihān); Ritter, *Erdkunde*, ix, 145-52; Schwarz, *Iran im Mittelalter*, i, 332-5, cf. also the index; Le Strange, *The Lands of the Eastern Caliphate*, 243, 247; Admiralty Handbooks. *Persia*, London 1945, index; Razmārā (ed.), *Farhang-i d̲j̲ug̲h̲rāfiyā-yi Īrān*, vi, 186; Barthold, *An historical geography of Iran*, Princeton 1984, 190, 194.

(V. Minorsky-[C.E. Bosworth])

RAMAD (a.), an eye disease, "ophthalmitis; ophthalmia, conjunctivitis". *Ramad*, nomen verbi of *ramida*, follows the morpheme *faʿal* which is commonly used to denote chronic and congenital diseases. Being a genuine Arabic word, *ramad* occurs in pre- and early Islamic poetry in the broad sense of inflammation of the eye (ophthalmitis). Accordingly, the Arab lexicographers often explain *ramad* by referring to one or another symptom of ophthalmitis, i.e. pain, oedematous swelling, increased lachrymation, redness, itching, hyperaemia *et alia*. In the course of the transmission of Greek medicine, especially the *Corpus Galenianum*, to the Arabs during the late 2nd/8th and 3rd/9th centuries, *ramad* became a proper medical term. It was used by the Arab physicians in the specifically narrowed sense of inflammation of the conjunctiva, based upon Galen's observation that an inflammation of the eye usually means an inflammation of its mucous membrane (*multaḥim*, ἐπιπεφυκώς): ὀφθαλμία ἡ τοῦ [ἐπι]πεφυκότος ὑμένος φλεγμονή (thence ophthalmia = conjunctivitis). Clinically, the disease was classified into "[acute] conjunctivitis" (*ramad*, ὀφθαλμία/φλεγμονή τοῦ ἐπιπεφυκότος), "chronic c." (*r. muzmin*, πολυχρόνιος ὀφθαλμία), "inveterate c." (*r. ʿamīḳ*, κεχρονισμένη ὀφθαλμία), and "severe c." (*r. ṣaʿb*/*s̲h̲adīd*, χήμωσις); the initial stage was called "irritation [of the conjunctiva]" (*takaddur*, τάραξις).

Bibliography (selected): B. Lewin, *A vocabulary of the Hud̲h̲ailian poems*, Göteborg 1978, 164; ʿAbda b. al-Ṭabīb (*fl.* 20/641), in *The Mufaḍḍalīyāt. An anthology of ancient Arabian odes*, ed. C.J. Lyall, Oxford 1921, i (Ar. text), 279 no. 32; Ibn Manẓūr, *Lisān al-ʿarab*, Beirut 1388/1968, iii, 185a; M. Meyerhof, *The book of the ten treatises on the eye ascribed to Hunain ibn Is-hâq (809-877 A.D.)*, Cairo 1928, 55-6 (tr.), 128-9 (Ar. text), 188-9 (gloss.); J. Hirschberg and J. Lippert, *Die Augenheilkunde des Ibn Sina*, Leipzig 1902, 27-9; idem, *Ali ibn Isa. Erinnerungsbuch für Augenärzte*, Leipzig 1904, 130-1; M. Ullmann, *Die Medizin im Islam*, Leiden-Köln 1970, 15, 235.

(O. Kahl)

RAMAḌĀN (a.), name of the ninth month of the Muslim calendar. The name from the root *r-m-ḍ* refers to the heat of summer and therefore shows in what season the month fell when the ancient Arabs still endeavoured to equate their year with the solar year by intercalary months [see nasīʾ].

Ramaḍān is the only month of the year to be mentioned in the Ḳurʾān (II, 181/165): "The month of Ramaḍān (is that) in which the Ḳurʾān was sent down", we are told in connection with the establishment of the fast of Ramaḍān. Concerning the origins of this, to what is said in *EI*[1] ṣawm should be added the researches of S.F. Goitein, *Zur Entstehung des Ramaḍān*, in *Isl.*, xviii (1929), 189 ff., who in connection with the above-mentioned verse of the Ḳurʾān calls attention to the parallelism between the mission of Muḥammad and the handing of the second tablets of the law to Moses, which according to Jewish tradition took place on the Day of Atonement (*ʿās̲h̲ūrāʾ*, the predecessor of Ramaḍān) and actually was the cause of its institution. Goitein suggests that the first arrangement to replace the ʿĀs̲h̲ūrāʾ [*q.v.*] was a period of ten days (*ayyām maʿdūdāt*, sūra II, 180/184), not a whole month, which ran parallel with the ten days of penance of the Jews preceding the Day of Atonement and survives to the present day in the 10 days of the *iʿtikāf* [*q.v.*]. If we consider further that the Muslim ideas of the *Laylat al-Ḳadr* which falls in Ramaḍān, in which according to Ḳurʾān, LXXXVII, 1, the Ḳurʾān was sent down, coincide in many points with the Jewish ones on the Day of Atonement, we must concede a certain degree of probability to Goitein's suggestions, in spite of the undeniable chronological difficulties (alteration of the length of the period of the

shield for their sciences and treasures'' (*fa-dja*ᶜ*alū hādhihi 'l-rumūz*ᵃ *sitr*ᵃⁿ ᶜ*alā* ᶜ*ulūmihim wa-kunūzihim*, Ibn Waḥshiyya, 91-2). The latter clearly refer to the hieroglyphs, and a number of them are easily recognisable, albeit fancifully explained, in Ibn Waḥshiyya's book. The double function of these symbols becomes clear: they are said to encode (a) occult (alchemical, magical, astrological) knowledge, and (b) information about hidden treasures. In his book on the pyramids, Abū Djaᶜfar al-Idrīsī (d. 649/1251) reports about people who claim to be able to decode—*ḥall al-rumūz*—the hieroglyphs (*al-ḳalam al-birbāwī*) and thus to find the hidden treasures (*Ahrām*, 36, 61, 141). As a result of this idea *Ḥall* (or *Fakk*) *al-rumūz fī kashf al-kunūz* becomes a very popular book-title, not only in the field of the occult sciences (cf. Brockelmann, I², 139-40, S I, 144, 430, 531, 712, 783, S II, 768, etc., and the indices of *GAS*).

In all this, it is important to be aware of the fact that the *ramz*, whether linguistic or graphic symbol, can be used for encoding as well as for decoding, and that the latter, interpretive, function may be applied to texts that were not encoded in the first place. Allegories of non-allegorical technical writings (cf. e.g. Kraus, *Jābir*, p. 12-13, n. 7) and symbolic interpretation of hieroglyphs are both instances of this phenomenon.

(b) *Ramz* as "symbolic action". This may refer to cryptic messages conveyed by sending certain objects that the recipient needs to interpret. In a chapter entitled "cryptic remarks (*rumūz*) current among literary men and their playing with allusions (*ma*ᶜ*ārīḍ*) which only the eloquent can understand", Abu 'l-ᶜAbbās al-Djurdjānī (d. 482/1089) enumerates many cases in which the *rumūz* are enigmatic references to poetical lines, but also some where the language of objects is used. These, he says, are very hard to solve, because they are restricted to the mere acts (*al-iḳtiṣār* ᶜ*alā mudjarrad al-fi*ᶜ*l*) without words (*Kināyāt*, 71-85, esp. 79). Al-Ḳalḳashandī (d. 821/1418 [*q.v.*]) gives a few examples of such wordless messages as used in diplomacy (*Ṣubḥ al-a*ᶜ*shā*, ix, 249-51 [= ch. on *al-rumūz wa 'l-ishārāt allatī lā ta*ᶜ*alluḳ lahā bi 'l-khaṭṭ wa 'l-kitāba*], tr. C.E. Bosworth, in *Arabica*, x [1963], 148-53). In a different way, the term *ramz* is used by Ibn Abī ('l-)Sarḥ (wrote 274/887) to denote the superstitious acts of the ancient Arabs, on which he was the first to write a comprehensive work (*Rumūz*, ed. Ḥusayn, 641-42; tr. Bellamy, 227). He actually uses the construct *ramz al-nafs*, not yet satisfactorily explained, and divides the *rumūz* into three categories: supernatural, natural, and mixed.

(c) *Rumūz* as "sigla". This modern meaning is already attested in mediaeval contexts. Muḥammad b. ᶜAbd al-Raḥmān al-ᶜUkbarī (*fl.* 665/1267), in his *Madjma*ᶜ *al-aḳwāl fī ma*ᶜ*ānī al-amthāl*, uses thirty different abbreviations to indicate his sources after each proverb and calls these signal *rumūz* (see A.J. Arberry, in *JAL*, i [1970], 109-10).

Bibliography: 1. Rhetorical meaning: Sakkākī, *Miftāḥ al-*ᶜ*ulūm*, ed. Nuᶜaym Zarzūr, Beirut 1403/1983; J. Garcin de Tassy, *Rhétorique et prosodie des langues de l'orient musulman*, repr. Amsterdam 1970; A.F.M. von Mehren, *Die Rhetorik der Araber*, repr. Hildesheim and New York 1970.—Ibn Rashīḳ, *al-*ᶜ*Umda fī maḥāsin al-shi*ᶜ*r wa-ādābih wa-naḳdih*, ed. Muḥammad Muḥyī al-Dīn ᶜAbd al-Ḥamīd, 2 vols., Cairo ³1383/1963-4, i, 305-6; Sidjilmāsī, *al-Manza*ᶜ *al-badī*ᶜ *fī tadjnīs asālīb al-badī*ᶜ, ed. ᶜAllāl al-Ghāzī, Rabat 1401/1980.—Related meanings: Isḥāḳ b. Ibrāhīm Ibn Wahb al-Kātib, *al-Burhān fī wudjūh al-bayān*, ed. Aḥmad Maṭlūb and Khadīdja al-Ḥadīthī, Baghdād 1387/1967; P. Kraus, *Jābir ibn Ḥayyān. Contribution à l'histoire des idées scientifiques dans l'Islam*, 2 vols., Cairo 1942-3, ii, index, s.v. *ramz*; Ibn Waḥshiyya, *Shawḳ al-mustahām fī ma*ᶜ*rifat rumūz al-aḳlām*, ed. and tr. J. Hammer, as *Ancient alphabets and hieroglyphic characters explained*, London 1806; Abū Djaᶜfar al-Idrīsī, *Anwār* ᶜ*ulwiyy al-adjrām fi 'l-kashf* ᶜ*an asrār al-ahrām*, ed. U. Haarmann, Beirut 1991; al-Ḳāḍī Abu 'l-ᶜAbbās Aḥmad b. Muḥammad al-Djurdjānī al-Thaḳafī, *al-Muntakhab min kināyāt al-udabā*ᵓ *wa-ishārāt al-udabā*ᵓ, ed. [together with Thaᶜālibī, *K. al-Kināya wa 'l-ta*ᶜ*rīḍ*] Muḥammad Badr al-Dīn al-Naᶜsānī al-Ḥalabī, Cairo 1326/1908; Ḳalḳashandī, *Ṣubḥ al-a*ᶜ*shā*, ix, Cairo 1334/1916, introd., tr. and annot. C.E. Bosworth, *Some historical gleaning from the section on symbolic actions in Qalqashandī's* Ṣubḥ al-Aᶜšā, in *Arabica*, x (1963), 148-53; Ibn Abī ('l-) Sarḥ, *K. al-Rumūz*, ed. S.M. Ḥusayn, in *RAAD*, ix, 1931, 641-55; tr. and ann. J. Bellamy, in *JAOS* (1961), 224-46.

(W.P. Heinrichs)

3. In mystical and other esoterical discourse. Like its counterpart, *ramz* originally meant "gesture" or "sign", usually a silent one, especially a speechless movement of the lips practiced by interlocutors in order to conceal the contents of their conversation from a third party. By extension, the term also denotes any silent gesture made by the hand, the head, the eyes, the eyebrows, etc. (see *LA*, s.v. *r-m-z*; al-Fīrūzābādi, *al-Ḳāmūs*, Beirut n.d., ii, 183-4). In this sense, *ramz* appears in the Ḳurᵓān, III, 41, where God bids Zakariyyāᵓ "not to speak to the people except by gesture" (*ramz*ᵃⁿ). While the majority of commentators agree that *ramz* here is synonymous with either *ishāra* or *īmā*ᵓ (yet another word for a silent sign), al-Ṭabarī adds that in pre-Islamic poetry it also meant an unintelligible murmur or whisper (see al-Ṭabari, *Djāmi*ᶜ *al-bayān*, Beirut 1984, iii, 259-60). For al-Thaᶜālibī, *ramz* is "movement indicative of what is [concealed] in the heart of the gesturer (*rāmiz*)", and also "a speech deflected from its apparent meaning (*muḥarraf* ᶜ*an ẓāhirihi*)", i.e. a symbolic and allegoric speech *par excellence* (see his *Djawāhir al-ḥisān*, Beirut n.d., i, 264-5). In both cases, *ramz* is viewed as the opposite of *taṣrīḥ*, an unequivocal declaration of one's feelings and intentions. These two terms, together with their synonyms, became closely associated with the major opposition between the explicit style of thinking and narration and that involving deliberate ambiguity, an opposition that pervades Muslim intellectual culture as a whole [see ẒĀHIR and BĀṬIN].

As a statement implying more than its words and thus evoking a host of various associations, *ramz* was employed by mediaeval literary critics (see above, section 1.). In its broader meaning, *ramz* was often used to describe literary works which utilised the allegoric language, vague symbols, allusions and obliquities, e.g. "an allegorised poem" (*ḳaṣīda marmūza*), mentioned by al-Maḳḳarī [*q.v.*] (*Analectes*, i, 608).

In early Ṣūfī literature, it was also overshadowed by *ishāra*. A striking example of the wide currency enjoyed by the latter word is Abū Ḥayyān al-Tawḥīdī's [*q.v.*] *al-Ishārāt al-ilāhiyya*, in which Ṣūfī knowledge is forthrightly equated with the capacity to comprehend mystical symbols and allusions. Throughout the work, the author constantly referred to them as *ishārāt* but never as *rumūz* (see al-Tawḥīdī, *op. cit.*, ed. Wadād al-Ḳāḍī, ²Beirut 1982). In other Ṣūfī writings, *ramz* almost invariably appears in conjunction with, or as an explanation of, *ishāra*. According to early Ṣūfī authors, symbolic language and allusions play a double role. On the one hand, they are the only way to convey the elusive spiritual experiences and ineffable visions bestowed upon the "friends of God" (*awliyā*ʾ [see WALĪ]). On the other, they effectively preserve the essence of these higher mysteries and insights from the uninitiated, who should satisfy themselves with the "externals" (*ẓāhir*) of religion. Hence the knowledge of *rumūz* pertains exclusively to the Ṣūfī masters, and is not to be divulged to the outsiders (see *Adab al-mulūk. Ein Handbuch zur islamischen Mystik aus dem 4./10. Jahrhundert*, ed. B. Radtke, Beirut 1991, 20, 34, 70-1). Attesting the importance of the word *ramz* for the mystical doctrines of the Ṣūfīs, Abū Naṣr al-Sarrādj (d. 378/988) included *ramz* in his list of the specifically Ṣūfī terms. According to this author, *ramz* designates "an inner meaning hidden under the guise of outer speech, which no one will grasp except for its people (*ahluhu*)." Such symbols should be looked for primarily in the correspondence between the Ṣūfī masters, rather than in works addressed to the uninitiated reader (al-Sarrādj, *al-Lumaʿ*, ed. ʿAbd al-Ḥalīm Maḥmūd and Ṭāhā Surūr, Baghdād 1960, 414, cf. 314). Rūzbihān Baḳlī Shīrāzī (d. 606/1209 [*q.v.*]), who cites a similar definition of *ramz*, adds that it allows one to grasp "the mysteries of the unseen by means of the subtleties of knowledge, which, in turn, find their expression in the language of mystery through the words opposite to their meanings" (*Commentaire sur les paradoxes des soufis*, ed. H. Corbin, Tehran-Paris 1966, 561). Thus, when dealing with the language of the Ṣūfīs, one should be careful in distinguishing between the verbal shell (*lafẓ*) and the kernel of an allusion (*ramzuhu*). A person unaware of such a symbolic method of expression can be easily misled by some Ṣūfī utterances and condemn them as an expression of the worst kind of unbelief. At the same time, a more perspicacious interpreter will find them in complete accord with the inner meaning (*bāṭin*) of the Ḳurʾān and the Sunna (see Ibn ʿAbd al-Salām al-Sulamī, *Ḥall al-rumūz wa-mafātīḥ al-kunūz*, Cairo 1961, 5-20, *et passim*). In a sense, the opposition between *lafẓ* and *ramz* reflects the irreducible contradiction between the normative, outward aspects of religion (*sharīʿa* [*q.v.*]), and its spiritualised interpretation and interiorisation practiced by the Ṣūfī gnostics (*ḥaḳīḳa* [*q.v.*]). To Ṣūfī authors, *rumūz* appeared to be the most convenient way to express the latter without disclosing it to those from whom it ought to be withheld (see al-Ghazālī, *Mishkāt al-anwār*, ed. Abu 'l-ʿAlāʾ ʿAfīfī, Cairo 1382/1964, 40).

Ibn al-ʿArabī (d. 638/1240 [*q.v.*]), who often treats *ramz* as a synonym of *lughz* [*q.v.*] (puzzle or enigma), defines it as "a speech which does not convey the meaning implied by the speaker". In his view, the use of *ramz* is not an end in itself, because what matters is the implicit meaning behind it. Due to his overall proclivity toward allegorisation of reality, Ibn al-ʿArabī tends to envision the whole cosmos as a giant arrangement of symbols that require an explanation. In keeping with their ability (or inability) to comprehend the true meaning of these cosmic symbols (which, in many respects, are similar to the verbal symbols and allusions permeating revelation), people are divided into several categories ranging from the greatest knowers, the "men of symbols" (*ridjāl al-rumūz*), who can grasp the allegorical meaning of all things and events through supersensory unveiling (*kashf* [*q.v.*]), to the ignorant populace, who accept everything at face value and are, therefore, doomed to wander in darkness. Ibn al-ʿArabī's *magnum opus, al-Futūḥāt al-makkiyya*, abounds in descriptions of various symbolic events and personalities, whose real meaning is sometimes disclosed but, more often, is tantalisingly left open to a wide variety of interpretations. On many occasions, Ibn al-ʿArabī draws close parallels between Ṣūfī modes of self-expression and poetic language, both of which, in his view, endeavour to clothe their meanings in intricate symbols and allegories. No wonder that in his major works, *al-Futūḥāt al-makkiyya* and *Fuṣūṣ al-ḥikam*, this author normally introduces his daring insights in the form of symbolic verses, then proceeds to elucidate them in prose (*al-Futūḥāt al-makkiyya*, ed. O. Yaḥyā and I. Madkūr, Cairo 1972–, i, 67, 218, 251, iii, 120, 196-7, 201, etc.; *Fuṣūṣ al-ḥikam*, ed. Abu 'l-ʿAlāʾ ʿAfīfī, Beirut 1946, *passim*; cf. idem, *Dīwān*, Bulāḳ 1271/1855, *passim*). Stressing Ibn al-ʿArabī's propensity for an abstruse and allegoric style meant to hide his real intentions, his compatriot Ibn Khātima [*q.v.*] wrote that this Ṣūfī thinker "spoke from behind the veil (*ḥidjāb*), fortifying himself with [the use of] *ramz* in an impenetrable mountain citadel, and seeking refuge in the *ishāra* of dubious import" (see al-Maḳḳarī, *Azhār al-riyāḍ fī akhbār ʿIyāḍ*, ed. Muṣṭafā al-Saḳḳā, Ibrāhīm al-Abyārī and ʿAbd al-Ḥafīẓ Shalabī, Cairo 1361/1942, iii, 54-5).

Ibn Sīnā's [*q.v.*] usage of *ramz* is a corollary to his theory of prophecy which, in his view, should of necessity be communicated to the masses in a symbolic or allegorical form lest they misinterpret the prophetic message, thus ruining the divinely-established order. Therefore, the prophet "should inform them (sc. the masses) about God's majesty and greatness through symbols (*rumūz*) and images (*amthila*) derived from things that for them are majestic and great." The same is true concerning other articles of faith, e.g. divine punishment and reward, destiny (*ḳadar*), etc. Basically, however, symbols communicate the same knowledge that can be stated in demonstrative or expository language employed by the rational philosophers (see D. Gutas, *Avicenna and the Aristotelian tradition*, Leiden 1988, 300-1). Because "the majority of humans are ruled not by pure intellect but rather by their lower passions", they are unqualified to grasp such an abstract language and the syllogistic argumentation it conveys. Conversely, symbols and images primarily appeal to imagination and not to intellect. Hence they are more likely to be comprehended by uncultured minds (see P. Heath, *Allegory and philosophy in Avicenna,* Philadelphia 1992, 150-2). Irrespective of whether or not Ibn Sīnā actually regarded the allegorical method of communication as inferior to the demonstrative and expository (Gutas, *op. cit.*, 302; cf. Heath, *op. cit.*, 153-65), he was convinced that "those individuals with philosophical propensities" were in a position to penetrate the authentic meaning of the symbols found in the revelation, and would eventually acquire a philosophical vision of the universe (Gutas, *op. cit.*, 307). A similar view of the function of *ramz* was adopted by the later philosophers of Muslim Spain, namely Ibn Ṭufayl and Ibn Rushd [*q.vv.*]. According to the former, "pure truth does not at all suit the vulgar, enslaved by senses." In order "to penetrate those materialistic intelligences, ... it is obliged to clothe itself with the wisdom that constitutes the revealed religions", in other words, with symbols and allegories (L. Gauthier, *Ibn Thofaïl*, Paris 1909, 63). Symbols can also be helpful as a means to present some abstract philosophical ideas. Thus Ibn Ṭufayl's *Ḥayy b. Yaḳẓān* [*q.v.*] may be taken as a symbolic representation of the evolution undergone by the human active intellect. Ibn Rushd seems to have envisaged *ramz* as an essential part of rhetoric argument (as opposed to demonstrative and dialectical), which the prophets address to their communities because most of the people are not intellectually mature enough to understand the more sophisticated types of discourse. This fact accounts for the necessity to explicate revelation allegorically [see TAʾWĪL] with a view to reconciling it with the conclusions reached through the syllogistic argument.

Proponents of messianic expectations, who sought to substantiate their claims regarding the imminent advent of the *mahdī* [*q.v.*] by exploiting the numerical values and occult properties of the Arabic characters, often viewed the latter as *rumūz*—esoteric signs pointing to the inevitable fulfillment of their predictions. To decipher such signs contained, for instance, in the mysterious letters preceding some Ḳurʾānic sūras and the divine names [see AL-ASMĀʾ AL-ḤUSNĀ, and cf. above, section 2(a), first para.], Muslim esotericists—primarily, the S͟hīʿa, including the Ismāʿīlīs, and some Ṣūfī leaders harbouring messianic hopes—practiced elaborate divinatory techniques known as *d̲j̲afr* [*q.v.*; see also ḤURŪF]. Ḳurʾānic stories and certain *ḥadīt̲h̲*, mostly of an esthatological nature, were also treated by the esoterically-minded Muslims as symbols and signs, whose true meaning could only be elucidated by means of an allegoric interpretation. A curious mixture of Ismāʿīlī and Ṣūfī views utilising both types of *ramz* can be observed in a divinatory poem by a purported Ismāʿīlī *dāʿī* [*q.v.*], ʿĀmir b. ʿĀmir al-Baṣrī, d. in the early 8th/14th century (see Y. Marquet, *Poésie ésotérique ismaïlienne*, Paris 1985, 73-4, 81, 101, etc.; cf., however, Ibn ʿArabī, *ʿAnḳāʾ mug̲h̲rib*, Cairo n.d., where in similar predictions the word *ramz* is never mentioned).

Aḥmad al-Būnī (d. 622/1225 [*q.v.* in Suppl.]), the celebrated fortune teller and master of "letter magic" (*sīmīyya*), considered the usage of *rumūz* to be part and parcel of the occult sciences permitting to predict the future. As in the case with the philosophers and Ṣūfīs, symbols, according to al-Būnī, perform the twofold function. They conceal the secrets of the divinatory procedures from the uninitiated, while at the same time helping to impart them to the deserving few (see *Manbaʿ uṣūl al-ḥikma*, Cairo 1370/1951, 5, 6, 325).

Interestingly, *ramz* (spelt *rams*) is one of the few Arabic words mentioned by the great Catalan philosopher, missionary, and mystic Ramon Llull (d. 1316), for whom it apparently meant a tropological-moral purport behind some scriptural parables (see Ch. Lohr, *Christianus arabicus*, in *Freiburger Zeitschrift für Philosophie und Theologie*, xxxi [1984], 59). Normally, however, when referring to the moral lessons contained in the Ḳurʾānic text, Muslim exegetes would rather use such terms as *mat̲h̲al* [*q.v.*] and *ḥadd* (see G. Böwering, *The mystical vision of existence in classical Islam*, Berlin 1980, 138-41).

4. In modern Arabic literature.

In this literature, which took shape under the strong influence of European literary trends, *ramz* became an exact equivalent of the Western term "symbol" defined as "a deliberate use of a word or a phrase to signify something else, not by analogy (for, unlike metaphor and simile, it lacks a paired subject), but by implication and reference" (S. Jayyusi, *Trends and movements in modern Arabic poetry*, Leiden 1977, ii, 709). As in the West, in the Middle East also, an acute interest in, and extensive use of, symbols gave rise to a literary movement known as "symbolism" (*al-ramziyya*) that flourished from the 1920s to the 1940s, but then gradually lost ground as a cohesive literary trend. Its representatives, primarily poets such as Adīb Maẓhar, Saʿīd ʿAḳl, Bis̲h̲r Fāris, and, to a lesser extent, Abu 'l-Ḳāsim al-S̲h̲ābbī have employed symbol as "a vehicle for feelings, for complex and valuable states of awareness" as well as a means to express an idea or a set of ideas. While most of the Arab symbolists drew their inspiration from the European literary notions of "universal relationships" and "latent affinities" which they sought to convey through symbolist imagery (K. Abu Deeb, *Al-Jurjānī's theory of poetic imagery*, Warminster, Wilts. 1979, 124-6; Jayyusi, *op. cit.*, 478-81), they seem to have neglected the fact that similar approaches to creative process had already been maintained, albeit spontaneously and unconsciously, by their Muslim predecessors, namely, Ibn al-Fāriḍ, D̲j̲alāl al-Dīn Rūmī and many other mediaeval Ṣūfī poets, who communicated their nonrational and intuitive perception of being by having recourse to elaborate symbols and allegories (see e.g. Ibn al-Fāriḍ's masterful use of wine symbolism to convey his mystical vision of reality, Ibn al-Fāriḍ, *Dīwān*, Beirut 1962, 140-3). Ṣūfī imagery and symbols were more readily adopted by the less Westernised poets and prose writers, who, being well versed in the Islamic *turāt̲h̲*, succeeded in creating original works in which Islamic and Western influences were inextricably intertwined (see, e.g. Nad̲j̲īb Maḥfūẓ, Adūnīs, Muẓaffar al-Nawwāb, D̲j̲amāl al-G̲h̲īṭānī, etc.). On the other hand, some symbols, which became particularly popular with the modern Arab poets (e.g. the sea, the rain, the wind etc.), have suffered from over-use and have gradually developed into mere conventions devoid of any poetic originality (Jayyusi, *op. cit.*, 710).

Bibliography: Given in the article.

(A. KNYSH)

RAN [see NĀẒIM ḤIKMET].

RĀṆĀ SĀṆGĀ (reigned 915-35/1509-28), Rād̲j̲pūt ruler of the kingdom of Mēwāŕ [*q.v.*] on the borders of Rād̲j̲āsthān and Mālwā, with his capital at Čitawŕ. He was a strenuous opponent of the Muslim rulers of northern and western India in the years before Bābur's establishment of the Mug̲h̲al empire, and under him, Mēwāŕ became a major power in India.

In the first 15 years of his reign, he made firm his power within Mēwāŕ and strengthened his position vis-à-vis his Muslim neighbours. The reaction of the ruler of Mālwā, Maḥmūd II K̲h̲ald̲j̲ī, against the ascendancy of his Rād̲j̲pūt *wazīr* Mēdinī Rāʾī [*q.v.*], led in 923/1517 to Maḥmūd's seeking military assistance from Muẓaffar II of Gud̲j̲arāt [*q.v.*], whereupon Mēdinī Rāʾī in Māndū sought in turn the aid of Rāṇā Sāṇgā. In 925/1519 the latter decisively defeated Maḥmud, capturing him and only releasing him the next year on payment of a war indemnity and the provision of hostages at the Mēwāŕ court, and in the next year Rāṇā Sāṇgā successfully repelled an attack by the forces of Gud̲j̲arāt under Muẓaffar's general Malik Ayāz [*q.v.*].

He was, however, disposed to make peace because of his ambitions on the Dihlī Sultanate [*q.v.*] itself (after 923/1517 under the rule of Ibrāhīm Lōdī [see LŌDĪS]). A Lōdī invasion of Mēwāŕ was repelled, in part because of the temporary treachery of Ibrāhīm's Afg̲h̲ān commander Ḥusayn K̲h̲ān Farmulī, and the power of Mēwāŕ was extended into Mālwā as far as Kalpī [*q.v.*] on the D̲j̲amnā river. Rāṇā Sāṇgā now proposed to the Mug̲h̲al Bābur [*q.v.*] a concerted attack on Ibrāhīm Lōdī. Bābur accordingly defeated Ibrāhīm at the first battle of Pānīpat [*q.v.*] in 932/1526, but was now obviously aiming at establishing a kingdom in northern India for himself. Rāṇā Sāṇgā secured in effect control over Gud̲j̲arāt, but at the battle of K̲h̲ānuʾā near Fatḥpūr Sīkrī in 933/1527 the numerically superior Rād̲j̲pūt army was completely routed by Bābur. Rāṇā Sāṇgā himself died a year later at the age of 46 and with him, Mēwāŕ lost its power as an independent kingdom.

Bibliography: R.C. Majumdar (ed.), *The history and culture of the Indian people. The Delhi Sultanate*, Bombay 1960, 167-9, 183, 328, 339-47; G.N. Sharma, in M. Habib and K.A. Nizami (eds.), *A comprehensive history of India. v. The Delhi Sultanate*, New Delhi 1970, 797-802; and see the *Bibls.* to MĒDINĪ RĀʾĪ and MĒWĀŔ. (ED.)

RANGĪN, the *takhalluṣ* of several Indian poets. The *Riyāḍ al-wifāḳ* of Dhu 'l-Fiḳār ʿAlī, biographies of Indian poets who wrote in Persian, and the *Tadhkira* of Yūsuf ʿAlī Khān (analysed by Sprenger, *A catalogue of the Arabic, Persian and Hindustan mss... of the King of Oudh*, i, 168, 280) mention five of them. The first, a native of Kashmīr, lived in Dihlī in the reign of Muḥammad Shāh (1719-48): his *ghazals* were sung by the dancing-girls.—The most celebrated, however, was Saʿādat Yār Khān of Dihlī. His father, Ṭahmāsp Beg Khān Tūrānī, came to India with Nādir Shāh and settled in Dihlī where he attained the rank of *haft-hazārī* and the title of Muḥkim. al-Dawla. In his turn, Saʿādat Yār Khān entered the service of Mīrzā Sulaymān Shikūh, son of the emperor Shāh ʿĀlam II, who lived in Lucknow. He was a good horseman and able soldier; for a time he commanded a part of the artillery of the Niẓām of Ḥaydarābād, but he gave up this post to go into business. He was in his youth a friend of the poet Inshāʾ [*q.v.*] in Lucknow; a pupil of the poet Muḥammad Ḥātim of Dihlī (cf. Ram Babu Saksena, *A history of Urdu literature*, 48; Sprenger, *op. cit.*, 235), he afterwards submitted all his verses to the criticism of Nithār (cf. Sprenger, 273), then of Muṣḥafī [*q.v.*] (Saksena, 90); he died in 1251/1835 aged eighty (or a year later; cf. Garcin de Tassy).—The following are his works in Urdu: *Mathnawī dilpazīr*, a poem of romantic adventures (1213/1798); *Īdjād-i Rangīn, a mathnawī* of fables and anecdotes (Lucknow 1847, 1870); another *mathnawī* of anecdotes: *Mazhar al-ʿadjāʾib* or *Gharāʾib al-mashʿūr* (lith. Agra and Lucknow); four *dīwāns* collectively known as *Naw ratan* ("the Nine Jewels"), the two first lyrical, the third humorous and partly in *rekhti* (language peculiar to women), the fourth in this same language with a preface by Rangīn explaining the principal words (on the development of *rekhti* and Rangīn's skill in this licentious genre (see URDŪ, and Saksena, *op. cit.*, 94); in prose a treatise on horsemanship (*Faras-nāmā*, 1210/1775, several times edited) and a collection of critical observations on a number of poets, entitled *Madjālis-i Rangīn*. In Persian (if the work is really his; cf. Sprenger, *op. cit.*, 54, no. 462), Rangīn under the title *Mihr u-māh*, sang of the adventure of a son of a *sayyid* and of a daughter of a jeweller, based on an incident that occurred in Dihlī in the reign of Djahāngīr (cf. *GrIPh*, ii, 254).

Bibliography: In addition to the references in the text, see Garcin de Tassy, *Litt. hindouie et hindoustanie*², i, 45, ii, 2; Pertsch, *Die Handschriften-Verzeichnisse der Königl. Bibl. zu Berlin*, iv, index, 1157; Blumhardt, *Cat. of the..... Hindustani mss. in the British Museum*, no. 74. (H. MASSÉ)

RANGOON, a city of the Pegu district of Burma and the country's capital, situated on the Rangoon (Hlaing) River (lat. 16° 47′ N., 96° 10′ E.). It was developed as a port in the mid-18th century by the founder of the last dynasty of Burmese kings, with a British trading factory soon established there and with flourishing groups of Parsee, Armenian and Muslim merchants. In 1852, during the Second Anglo-Burmese War, it passed definitively under British control, and Rangoon became a more modern city, and also, through immigration, largely Indian in composition. These last included Muslims, who in 1931 comprised 17% of the city's population. But the Indian and European population was reduced by the Japanese occupation of 1941-5, and after Burma's opting for independence in 1948, the Indian and Muslim element in Rangoon was reduced still further by the policies of governments hostile to non-Burmese in general and Muslims in particular (for these in Burma, see ARAKAN, BURMA, MERGUI). Today, 90% of Rangoon is Burmese, with Muslims only a small part of the remaining 10%.

Bibliography: *Imperial gazetteer of India*², xxi, 213-21; M. Yegen, *The Muslims of Burma, a study of a minority group*, Wiesbaden 1972; idem, *The Muslims of Burma*, in R. Israeli (ed.), *The crescent in the East, Islam in Asia Major*, London 1982, 102-39. (ED.)

AL-**RĀNĪRĪ** [see INDONESIA. vi].

RANK (P.), literally "colour, dye", a term used in mediaeval Arabic sources primarily to designate the emblems and insignia of *amīrs* and sultans in Egypt, Syria, and al-Djazīra. Mamlūk historians occasionally also use it as a generic term for emblem in general, such as the *ranks* of merchants' guilds (al-Ḳalḳashandī, *Ṣubḥ al-aʿshā*, Cairo 1913-18, v, 207), those of Bedouin chieftains in Tunisia (Ibn Shaddād, *Taʾrīkh al-Malik al-Ẓāhir*, Wiesbaden 1983, 196), and, oddly, the *rank* of Ḳassām, a Damascene rebel under the Fāṭimids who lived even before the word was in common use (Ibn al-Dawādārī, *al-Durra al-muḍiyya fī akhbār al-dawla al-Fāṭimiyya*, Cairo 1961, 195, 210). There is no indication otherwise that the term, or the practice of having *ranks*, was known beyond the historic or geographic limits of the Ayyūbid and Mamlūk states.

From the Ayyūbid period there are a number of references to *ranks* (Ibn Taghrībirdī, *al-Manhal al-ṣāfī*, Cairo 1988, v, 296; Ibn al-Dawādārī, *al-Durra al-dhakiyya fī akhbār al-dawla al-turkiyya*, Cairo 1971, 56-7) but no corresponding, conclusive material to show how they looked. The fleur-de-lis associated with Nūr al-Dīn Maḥmūd b. Zangī (541-70/1146-74 [*q.v.*]), and the truncated bicephalic eagle in the Cairo Citadel attributed to Ṣalāḥ al-Dīn (Saladin) are no longer accepted as *ranks* (L. Mayer, *Saracenic heraldry*, Oxford 1938, 152, 195; M. Meinecke, *Zur mamlukischen Heraldik*, in *Mitteilungen des Deutschen Archäologischen Instituts Abteilung Kairo*, xxviii [1972] 215-16). The earliest firmly established *rank* is the feline motif of al-Ẓāhir Baybars (658-76/1260-77 [*q.v.*]), many more or less identical examples of which are attested on buildings, coins, and other objects. From Baybars's time until the end of the Mamlūk period, *ranks* were adopted by sultans, *amīrs*, and perhaps other high officials. They were carved on buildings, painted on glass, wood, and pottery, engraved on metalwork, struck on coins, and embroidered or dyed on textiles. But the profusion of material evidence is not matched by contemporary textual testimony. Mayer counted less than fifty references in the sources he knew. Today, we have perhaps seventy. This paucity of historical information led early studies to consider *ranks* in terms of European heraldry, but most authors today caution against doing this and try to study *ranks* on their own terms.

Mamlūk *ranks* come in different shapes and forms. They may be monochromatic or multicolored, free-standing or enclosed in round, pointed, or polygonal shields. They first appeared as single-element emblems. Horizontal strips, called *shaṭfa* in the sources, were introduced to the shields in the early

14th century, and, in the 15th and early 16th centuries, *ranks* developed into composite shields with three fields, each containing one sign or more. Some rare *ranks* may be termed representative, such as the felines of Baybars, which may have implied power and courage or illustrated his own name *bay bars*, meaning "chief panther" in Ḳipčaḳ Turkish. Others are denotative, displaying the attribute of the office held by the *amīr*, such as Ḳawṣūn (d. 743/1342) who started his career as a cupbearer (*sāḳī*) and who carried a *rank* showing a cup. Still others combine more than one sign of office, or a sign and an image, such as the *rank* of Ṭuḳuztamur (d. 746/1345) which includes an eagle over a cup.

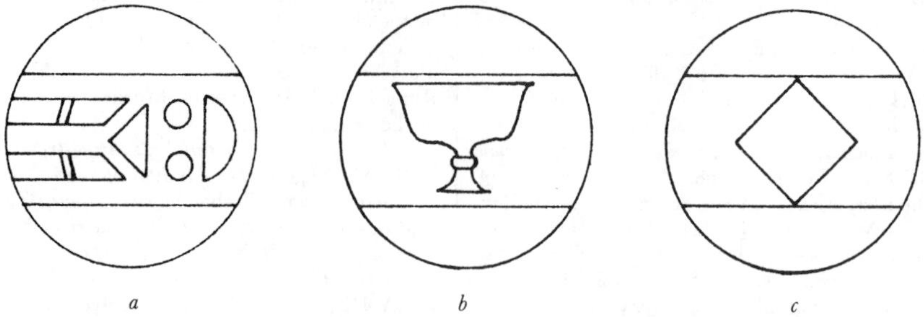

a *b* *c*

Fig. 1. Examples of single-element *ranks*: a) *rank* of *dawadar* (secretary); b) *rank* of *sāḳī* (cupbearer); c) *rank* of *d̲j̲amdar* (wardrobe master). (Drawing Nasser Rabbat 1993).

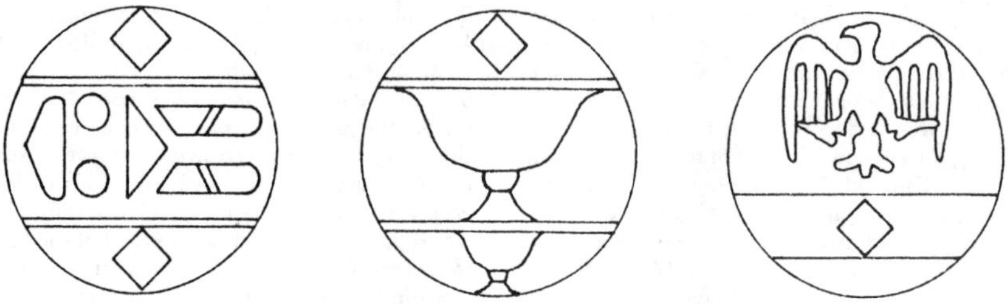

Fig. 2. Examples of composite *ranks*. (Drawing Nasser Rabbat 1993).

Initially, the sultan assigned *ranks* to his newly appointed *amīrs* as symbols of their positions at court (Ibn Tag̲h̲rībirdī, *op. cit.*, vii, 4). Thus, for instance, the *rank* of a *dawādār* (secretary) [*q.v.*] was a pen box or an inkwell, and that of a *d̲j̲amdār* (wardrobe master) [*q.v.*] was a lozenge. This practice may have been inherited from earlier Islamic rulers, notably the K̲h̲ʷārazm-S̲h̲āh Muḥammad b. Tekis̲h̲ (596-617/1200-20), who is said to have honoured his close pages with emblems (designated by the Arabic term *ʿalāma*) representing their offices (Abu 'l-Fidāʾ, *Kitāb al-Muk̲h̲taṣar fī ak̲h̲bār al-bas̲h̲ar*, Beirut 1979, vi, 49). *Amīrs* usually held their *ranks* for their entire careers, whether or not they subsequently held other offices. Midway in the Mamlūk period, *ranks* appear to have become the choice of the individual *amīr*, irrespective

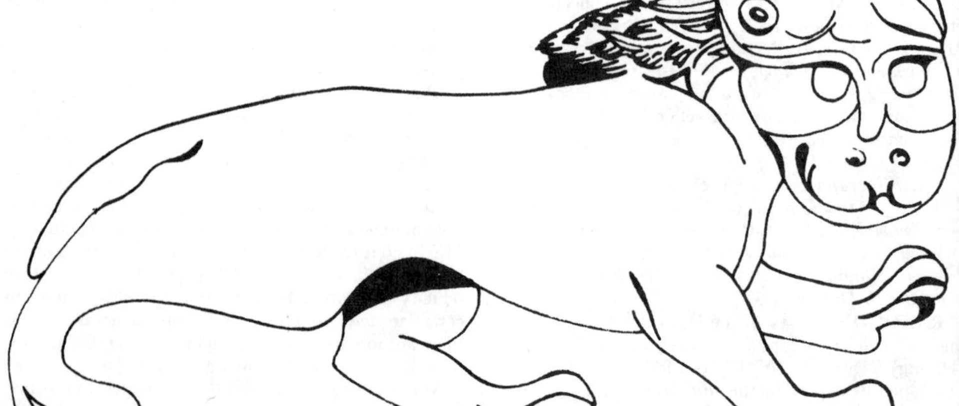

Fig. 3. Line drawing of the feline *rank* of Baybars (658-76/1260-77) as it appears on a recently-uncovered tower at the Citadel of Cairo. (Drawing Nasser Rabbat 1993).

Feline *rank* from the entrance of Khān al-Wazīr, Aleppo (1682).

Composite *rank* on the metal sheathing of the entrance to the Khān of Khāyir Bek, Aleppo (1516).

f the insignia associated with his original office (al-.alkashandī, *Ṣubḥ*, iv, 61-2). Later still, *ranks* became omposite, each containing a number of elements om a fixed repertoire disposed in three strips. Mayer oted that the composite *ranks* of a group of *amīrs* who ere *mamlūks* of a given sultan exhibited the same ar-angement (*Saracenic heraldry*, 29-33). They appear to ave differed chiefly in the attribute of the position eld by each individual which was inserted some-here in his own *rank*. This may mean that *ranks* had y then become an indication of an affiliation with a oyal household in addition to being a sign of office see Meinecke, 258-78). Furthermore, additions to anks appear to have been made as the *amīr* ascended p the Mamlūk hierarchy. Yashbak Min Mahdī *al-'awādār* added a lion (*sabuʿ*) to his *rank* in 885/1480 efore he led a campaign to Anatolia (Ibn Iyās, *adāʾiʿ al-zuhūr fī waḳāʾiʿ al-duhūr*, Cairo 1982-84, ii, 27).

Ranks of sultans were different from those of *amīrs*. ound, tripartite shields with the name, title, and a hort motto inscribed on one, two, or all three strips ecame the norm in sultans' *ranks* from the beginning f the 14th century. But they were not exclusively tilised, especially in the Burdji period (784-922/1382-517) when most sultans were former *amīrs* with enotative *ranks*, which they sometimes displayed longside their inscribed shields.

Very little is known about the significance of *ranks* n Mamlūk society. Like European nobility, sultans nd *amīrs* seem to have used their *ranks* both as ecipherable codes and as signatures displayed on heir buildings and objects or on those they wanted to laim as their own (Ibn Taghrībirdī, *op. cit.*, xiii, 99). But, unlike coats-of-arms in Europe, *ranks* do ot seem to have carried any heraldic potential. In are instances, sons of *amīrs* who became *amīrs* them-selves inherited their fathers' *ranks*. But even then, hese individuals did not acquire the offices or rivileges that had originally pertained to their athers' *ranks*, perhaps because of the peculiar struc-ure of the Mamlūk ruling class whose members pass-d their power to recruited *mamlūks* rather than to heir own sons [see MAMLŪK]. This apparent absence f a hereditary mechanism may have been the major eason why the institution of *rank* died out after the fall of the Mamlūks and the coming of the Ottomans in 922/1517.

Bibliography: In addition to the works cited in the text, see Meinecke, *Die Bedeutung der mamlukischen Heraldik für die Kunstgeschichte*, in *ZDMG* (1974), Suppl. II. XVIII Deutscher Orientalistentag, Vorträge, 213-40; W. Leaf and S. Purcell, *Heraldic symbols, Islamic insignia and Western heraldry*, London 1986; Estelle Whelan, *Representations of the Khassakiyah and the origins of Mamluk emblems*, in *Content and context of visual arts in the Islamic world*, Philadelphia 1988, 219-43.

(NASSER RABBAT)

RAPAK (Javanese; A. *rafʿ*) is a technical term used among the Javanese, in this one case only, for the charge made by the wife, at the court for matters of religion, that the husband has not fulfilled the obligations which he took upon himself at the *taʿlīḳ* of *ṭalāḳ* or divorce [see ṬALĀḲ]. These obligations are of a varied and changing nature. Among the conditions the following always occurs: "If the man has been absent a certain time on land or (longer) over seas" i.e. without having transmitted *nafaḳa*, i.e. payment for maintenance to his wife. A clause that is never omitted is the following: "If the wife is not content with this." She is therefore at liberty to be quite satisfied with the husband's non-fulfilment of his vows, without taking steps for a divorce. The work of the court is only to ascertain the fulfilment of the condition and the arising of *ṭalāḳ*. As always, the *ṭalāḳ* is still entered in a register. It is evident that this procedure guarantees the integrity of the law otherwise endangered.

Bibliography: C. Snouck Hurgronje, *De Atjèhers*, Batavia 1893, i, 382; Th.W. Juynboll, *Handleiding tot de kennis van de Moh. wet*, Leiden 1925, 210.

(R.A. KERN)

RAʾS (A. pl. *ruʾūs/arʾus*), "head", in geography the common word for "cape" (cf. Latin *caput* → cape), but it is also used with the meaning of "headland, promontory". The Musandam Peninsula in ʿUmān is sometimes called Raʾs Musandam, while the small territory occupying the northern tip of the Peninsula is called Ruʾūs al-Djibāl "the Mountain tops". Raʾs Tannūra [*q.v.*], the terminal of pipelines in eastern Saudi Arabia, derives its name from the tip of a small peninsula, at which the modern port is situated. In the name Raʾs al-Khayma [*q.v.*] "Tent Point", the word *raʾs* is not geographical, but refers to a large tent formerly used as a navigational device.

(ED.)

RAʾS AL-ʿĀM (A.) means New Year's Day, lit. "beginning of the year", i.e. 1 al-Muḥarram. For the difference with *Raʾs al-sana*, see Lane, *Lexicon*, s.v. *ʿām*. Sunnī Muslim law does not prescribe any particular celebration for the first month of the year, except that a voluntary fast-day is recommended on the tenth [see ʿĀSHŪRĀʾ]. However, the first ten days of the month are considered as particularly blessed (Lane, *Manners and customs*, chs. ix, xxiv). The Shīʿa know several celebrations during this month [see MUḤARRAM; TAʿZIYA]. In most Islamic countries, New Year's Day has long been indicated by the Persian word *Nawrūz* [*q.v.*], Arabic variant *Nayrūz*. (ED.)

RAʾS AL-ʿAYN or ʿAYN WARDA, Syriac Rēsh ʿAynā, a town of classical and mediaeval Islamic times of al-Djazīra, deriving its name ("spring-head") from the famed springs of the locality (see below). It is situated on the Greater Khābūr [*q.v.*] affluent of the Euphrates in lat. 36° 50 ′ N. and long. 40° 02′ E. It is now little more than a village straddling the modern border between Syria and Turkey, with the Syrian settlement still known as Raʾs al-ʿAyn and the Turkish one as Resülayn or Ceylânpınar.

In classical times it was known as Resaina-Theodosiopolis, receiving from the Emperor Theodosius I (379-95) urban rights and its latter name, one also borne by the Armenian town of Karin (Erzurūm [*q.v.*]), probably from the time of Theodosius II (408-50), so that it is sometimes difficult in the sources to distinguish which one is meant. The Persian general Ādharmahan twice (in 578 and 580) destroyed Rēsh ʿAynā, according to Michael Syrus, and in the reign of the Emperor Phocas the Persians captured the rebuilt town.

In 19/640 ʿIyāḍ b. Ghanm, after the subjection of Osrhoëne, marched against the province of Mesopotamia and by ʿUmar's orders sent ʿUmayr b. Saʿd against the town of ʿAyn Warda or Raʾs al-ʿAyn, which was besieged and stormed by him (al-Balādhurī, ed. de Goeje, 175-7). When a portion of the people of the town abandoned it, the Muslims confiscated their property. Among the rebels who rose against the caliph ʿAbd al-Malik in *ca.* 700 was ʿUmayr b. Ḥubāb of Raʾs al-ʿAyn (Abu 'l-Faradj, *Kitāb al-Aghānī*, Būlāḳ, xx, 127; Ibn al-Athīr, iv, 254-5; Mich. Syr., ii, 469; Barhebraeus, *Chron. syr.*, ed. Bedjan, 111). In the reign of al-Maʾmūn, Ḥubayb took the town in 1125 Sel. (A.D. 814) (Mich. Syr., iii, 27; Barhebraeus, *op. cit.*, 137). The Jacobite patriarch Yōḥannān III died on 3 December 873 in Rēsh ʿAynā (Mich. Syr., iii, 116; Barhebraeus, *Chron. eccles.*, ed. Abbeloos-Lamy, i, Lyons 1872, col. 387). After their campaign against Dārā and Naṣībīn (A.D. 942) the Byzantines in 943 took Raʾs al-ʿAyn, plundered it and carried off many prisoners (Ibn al-Athīr, viii, 312). A man from Raʾs al-ʿAyn, Aḥmad b. Ḥusayn Aṣfar Taghlib, called al-Aṣfar, disguised as a dervish, in 395/1005 with a body of Arabs made a raid into Byzantine territory as far as Shayzar and Maḥrūya near Anṭākiya but was driven back by the Patricius Bīghās. The governor Nicephorus Uranus in the following year undertook a punitive expedition to the region of Sarūdj, defeated the Banū Numayr and Kilāb and had al-Aṣfar thrown into prison by Luʾluʾ, lord of Aleppo in 397/1007 (Yaḥyā b. Saʿīd al-Anṭākī, in *Patrol. Orient.*, xxiii, 1932, 466-7; Georg. Kedren.-Skylitz., Bonn, ii, 454, 8; Barhebraeus, *Chron. syr.*, ed. Bedjan, 229). In *ca.* 523/1129 the Franks were lords of the whole of Syria and Diyār Muḍar and threatened Āmid, Naṣībīn and Raʾs al-ʿAyn. The latter was taken by Joscelin and a large part of the Arab population killed and the remainder taken prisoners (Mich. Syr., iii, 228; Barhebr., *Chron. syr.*, ed. Bedjan, 289). But the Franks cannot have held the town for very long.

Sayf al-Dīn of Mawṣil and ʿIzz al-Dīn Masʿūd of Aleppo in 570/1174-5 attacked Ṣalāḥ al-Dīn and besieged Raʾs al-ʿAyn, but were soon afterwards defeated by him at Ḳurūn Ḥamā. In 581/1185-6 Ṣalāḥ al-Dīn crossed the Euphrates and marched via al-Ruhāʾ, Raʾs al-ʿAyn and Dārā to Balad on the Tigris. His son al-Afḍal in 597/1200-1 received from al-ʿĀdil the towns of Sumaysāṭ, Sarūdj, Raʾs al-ʿAyn and Djumlīn; when he then marched on Damascus, Nūr al-Dīn of Mawṣil and Ḳuṭb al-Dīn Muḥammad of Sindjār again took Djazīra from him, but fell ill at Raʾs al-ʿAyn in the heat of summer and concluded peace again. In 599/1202-3 al-ʿĀdil took from al-Afḍal the towns of Sarūdj, Raʾs al-ʿAyn and Djumlīn (other fortresses also are mentioned). When the Kurdj [*q.v.*] (Georgians), who had advanced as far as Khilāṭ in 606/1209-10, learned that al-ʿĀdil had reached Raʾs al-ʿAyn on his way against them, they withdrew (Kamāl al-Dīn, tr. Blochet, in *ROL*, v, 46). Al-Malik al-Ashraf, who had defeated Ibn al-Mashṭūb in 616/1219-20 forgave him for rebelling and gave him Raʾs al-ʿAyn as a fief (Kamāl al-Dīn, *op. cit.*, 61; according to Barhebraeus, *Chron. syr.*, 439, however, Ibn al-Mashṭūb died in prison in Ḥarrān).

Ṣalāḥ al-Dīn's nephew al-Ashraf in 617/1220-1 was fighting against the lord of Mārdīn. The lord of Āmid made peace between them, when Raʾs al-ʿAyn was ceded to al-Ashraf, al-Muwazzar and the district of Shabakhtān [*q.v.*] (around Dunaysir) to the lord of Āmid. In exchange for Damascus, al-Ashraf, in 626/1229 gave his brother al-Kāmil the towns of al-Ruhāʾ, Ḥarrān, al-Raḳḳa, Sarūdj, Raʾs al-ʿAyn, Muwazzar and Djumlīn (Kamāl al-Dīn, in *ROL*, v, 77; Barhebraeus, *Chron. syr.*, 458) who occupied them in 634/1236-7 (Kamāl al-Dīn, *op. cit.*, 92). After the defeat of the Khʷārazmians at Djabal Djalahmān near al-Ruhāʾ, the army of Aleppo in 638/1240-1 took Ḥarrān, al-Ruhāʾ, Raʾs al-ʿAyn, Djumlīn, al-Muwazzar, al-Raḳḳa and the district belonging to it (Kamāl al-Dīn, in *ROL*, vi, 12). But in 639/1241-2 the Khʷārazmians, who had made an alliance with al-Malik al-Muẓaffar of Mayyāfāriḳīn, returned to Raʾs al-ʿAyn, where the inhabitants and the garrison, including a number of Frankish archers and crossbowmen, offered resistance. An arrangemer was made by which they were admitted to the town b the inhabitants, whose lives were promised them, an captured the garrison. When al-Malik al-Manṣūr ha returned to Ḥarrān and al-Muẓaffar had retired t Mayyāfāriḳīn with the Khʷārazmians, they sent thei prisoners back (Kamāl al-Dīn, in *ROL*, vi, 14). In th same year also, the Mongols came to Raʾs al-ʿAy (*ibid.*, 15). When the Khʷārazmians and Turkmen raided al-Djazīra, the army of Aleppo under the *am* Djamāl al-Dawla in Djumādā II 640/1242-3 went ou against them, and the two armies encamped opposit one another near Raʾs al-ʿAyn. The Khʷārazmian combined with the lord of Mārdin, and finally a peac was made by which Raʾs al-ʿAyn was given to the Ar tuḳid ruler of Mārdīn (Kamāl al-Dīn, in *ROL*, vi, 19)

In a Muslim cemetery in the north of Raʾs al-ʿAyn M. von Oppenheim found an inscription of the yea 717/1317-18. The Syrian chroniclers mention Rēsh ʿAynā as a Jacobite bishopric (11 bishops between 79 and 1199 are given in Mich. Syr., iii, 502) in whic a synod was held in 684 (Barhebraeus, *Chron. eccl.*, i 287). Towards the end of the 8th/14th century th town was sacked by Tīmūr.

Raʾs al-ʿAyn is built at a spot where a number o copious, in part sulphurous, springs burst forth which form the real "main source" of the Khābūr (al Dimashḳī, ed. Mehren, 191). The Wādī al-Djirdjib which has not much water in it and starts furthe north in the region of Wirānshehir, and which may b regarded as the upper course of the Khābūr, only afte receiving the waters from the springs of Raʾs al-ʿAy becomes a regular river, known from that point as th Khābūr. According to M. von Oppenheim (cf. hi map in *Petermanns Mitteil.* [1911], ii, pl. 18), th springs at Raʾs al-ʿAyn are ʿAyn al-Ḥuṣān, ʿAyn al Kebrīt and ʿAyn al-Zarḳāʾ; according to Taylo (*JRAS*, xxxviii, 349 n.), ʿAyn al-Bayḍāʾ and ʿAyn al Ḥasan are the most important; he also gives th names of 10 springs in the north-east and 5 in th south of the new town. The Arab geographers talk o 360, i.e. a very large number of springs, the abundance of water from which makes the vicinity of th town a blooming garden. One of these springs, ʿAyn al-Ẓāhiriyya, was said to be bottomless. According t Ibn Ḥawḳal, Raʾs al-ʿAyn was a fortified town with many gardens and mills; at the principal spring there was according to al-Muḳaddasī a lake as clear as crystal. Ibn Rusta (106) mentions Raʾs al-ʿAyn, Ḳarḳīsiyā, and al-Raḳḳa as districts of al-Djazīra. Ibn Djubayr in 580/1184-5 saw two Friday mosques, schools and baths in Raʾs al-ʿAyn on the bank of the Khābūr. According to Ḥamd Allāh Mustawfī (8th/14th century), the walls had a circumference of 5,000 paces; among the rich products of Raʾs al-ʿAyn he mentions cotton, corn and grapes. The historical romance *Futūḥ Diyār Rabīʿa wa-Diyār Bakr* (10th/16th century?) wrongly ascribed to al-Wāḳidī, which contains much valuable geographical information, mentions at Raʾs al-ʿAyn a plain of Muthaḳḳab and a Mardj al-Ṭīr (var. al-Dayr); it also mentions a Nestorian church in the town and several gates (in the translation by B.G. Niebuhr and A.D. Mordtmann, in *Schriften der Akad. von Hamburg*, i, part iii, Hamburg 1847, 76, 87. The "gate of Istacherum" in the east and the "Mukthaius or gate of Chabur" are not precisely located.

At Raʾs al-ʿAyn were the Jacobite monasteries of Bēth Tirai and Spequlos (*speculae*; Ps.-Zacharias Rhet., viii, 4, tr. Ahrens-Krüger, 157, 2; so also for Asphulos in Mich. Syr., iii, 50, 65, cf. ii, 513, n. 6; Saphylos in Mich. Syr., iii, 121, 449, 462;

Barhebraeus, *Chron. eccl.*, ed. Abbeloos-Lamy, i, 281-2; Sophiclis, *ibid.*, 397-8, probably so to be read throughout).

A little to the southwest of Raʾs al-ʿAyn on the right bank of the Khābūr is the great mound of ruins, Tell Ḥalāf, where M. von Oppenheim excavated the ancient palace of Kapara (see *Bibl.*).

Bibliography: The Arab geographers and historians and Syriac chroniclers already mentioned; also Khwārazmī, *Kitāb Ṣūrat al-arḍ*, ed. von Mžik, in *Bibl. arab. Hist. u. Geogr.*, iii, Leipzig 1926, 21 (no. 296); Suhrāb, *ʿAdjāʾib al-aḳālīm*, ed. von Mžik, in *ibid.*, v, 1930, 29 (no. 256) *Ḥudūd al-ʿālam*, tr. Minorsky, 141, § 34.7; on Resaina in Antiquity: Weissbach, in Pauly-Wissowa, s.v. *Resaina*, i, A, cols. 618-19; s.v. *Theodosiopolis*, no. 1, vol. v, A, cols. 1922-3; Assemani, *Dissert. de monophysit.*, in *BO*, ii, 9; Carsten Niebuhr, *Reisebeschreibung nach Arabien u.a. umliegenden Ländern*, ii, Copenhagen 1778, 390; K. Ritter, *Erdkunde*, xi, 375 ff.; Taylor, in *JRGS* (1868), xxxviii, 346-53; G. Le Strange, *The lands of the Eastern Caliphate*, Cambridge 1905, 87, 95-6, 125; V. Chapot, *La frontière de l'Euphrate de Pompée à la conquête arabe*, Paris 1907, 302-3; M. von Oppenheim, in *ZG Erdk. Berl.*, xxxvi (1901), 88; idem, *Der Tell Halaf und die verschleierte Göttin*, in *Der Alte Orient*, year X, fasc. 1, Leipzig 1908, 10-11; idem, *Der Tell Halaf, eine neue Kultur im ältesten Mesopotamien*, Leipzig 1931, 69-70 (cf. also index, 274, under Raʾs al-ʿAyn); A. Poidebard, *La trace de Rome dans le désert de Syrie*, Paris 1934, 130, 151-2, 158, 164; M. Canard, *Hist. de la dynastie des H'amdanides*, 97-8.

(E. Honigmann*)

RAʾS AL-KHAYMA (officially Ras-al-Khaimah), a constituent Amirate of the United Arab Emirates federation [see al-imārāt al-ʿarabiyya al-muttaḥida in Suppl.], to which it acceded in February 1972. It is also the name of the capital of the Amirate. The town seems to take its name from a configuration of hills on the coast which, seen from seaward, suggest the profile of the pole ridge of a nomad tent. The name is known to Portuguese geographers by the 16th century, but it is not until the 18th century that Raʾs al-Khayma supplants its predecessor, Djulfār, whose deserted tells lie immediately north of the suburbs of the town. The capital of the Amirate is divided into several major areas, of which the oldest is the old town, where the fort of the Āl Ḳāsimī rulers is situated. It has a good port as a result of dredging. There is also an airport.

The Amirate is ruled by the Āl Ḳāsimī, members of the Hawālā Arab tribe, who, according to their tradition, originate in ʿIrāḳ. The present Amirate constitutes the remains of very much larger Āl Ḳāsimī territories which once encompassed most of the ʿUmān peninsula, as well as places on the Persian coast opposite. The borders of the present Amirate are complex and, at certain points, they are subject to dispute. The main Raʾs al-Khayma territory lies in the far north of the U.A.E., principally bordered by the neighbouring Amirates of Umm al-Ḳuwayn and Fudjayra. In the north, it borders the Sultanate of ʿUmān's territory on the Musandam Peninsula. There is also a large enclave of Raʾs al-Khayma territory further south, centring on Ḥuwaylāt and Wādī al-Ḳawr, bordering the Amirate of Fudjayra, and the eastern enclaves of the Amirates of al-Shāriḳa (i.e. Sharjah) and ʿAdjmān, and the Sultanate of ʿUmān. Raʾs al-Khayma also formerly held two Gulf islands known as the Tunbs until they were seized by Iranian forces on 30 November 1971.

The indigenous population of the Amirate is Arab and Sunnī, with marked Wahhābī sentiments since the late 18th century. The inhabitants of the mountains are Shiḥūh, who continue into the ʿUmānī territory of Musandam. There is also a nomadic element to the population. Migrant workers including Indians, Pakistanis and Persian Balūč have settled in the Amirate in recent years.

The main coastal settlement in the past was the port of Djulfār, before it gave way to Raʾs al-Khayma town. Other coastal settlements which belong to the Amirate include Shaʿm, al-Rams and Djazīrat al-Ḥamrāʾ. Between the coastal strip and the Djabal Ḥadjar highlands there is a belt of agricultural land irrigated by rainfall, wells and *aflādj*. The Shiḥūh farm small plots of land on the top of the Djabal Ḥadjar chain.

The Amirate preserves a large number of archaeological sites testifying to settlement in ancient times, especially during the Bronze and Iron Age: there are numerous tombs associated with the 3rd-1st millennium in northern Raʾs al-Khayma, on the Daya plain and around Shimāl. There are also early sites further south at al-Khaṭṭ and along the course of Wādī al-Ḳawr in southern Raʾs al-Khayma. Ceramic finds suggest activity in the 3rd century A.D. on Djazīrat al-Hulayla on the coast, north of al-Rams.

The main town for much of the Islamic period was Djulfār. In its broadest application, the place-name Djulfār seems to have related to successive settlements between Raʾs al-Khayma town in the south and the Djazīrat al-Ḥulayla area in the north. Indeed, it now seems likely that before Islam and in the early Islamic period, Djulfār was centred on al-Ḥulayla. The name of Djulfār is mentioned in context of the early Islamic sea-borne expeditions against Persia when ʿUthmān b. al-ʿĀṣ in *ca.* 16/637 sailed with a force from Djulfār. Umayyad and ʿAbbāsid caliphs repeatedly used Djulfār to disembark armies engaged in campaigns against the Ibāḍī community of ʿUmān. This reflects the fact that Djulfār's harbour was the finest in the lower Gulf. In the 4th/10th century, al-Muḳaddasī, 70-1, numbered Djulfār among the *ḳaṣabas* of ʿUmān and on an equivalent level with Maskaṭ, Ṣuḥār and Nizwa [*q.vv.*].

Around the 7th/14th century the centre of Djulfār shifted to the area of tells known as al-Maṭāf and al-Nudūd on the northern edge of modern Raʾs al-Khayma town. The port was engaged in pearl fishing and commerce with China and south-east Asia, as well as India; imported Chinese porcelain and celadon found in quantity at the site bear witness to this trade. By the 7th/14th century, Djulfār was under the jurisdiction of the sultans of Hurmūz [*q.v.*], whose coinage it used, and when Hurmūz passed under Portuguese control, they established a garrison at Djulfār. The Portuguese remained in control of the coast until 1043/1633 when they were finally driven out by the ʿUmānī Imām, Nāṣir b. Murshid al-Yaʿāriba. Thereafter, Djulfār declined, possibly because of the silting channels into the port, and the town of Raʾs al-Khayma to the south increasingly supplanted Djulfār.

The Persian ruler Nādir Shāh [*q.v.*] sent a force through Djulfār in 1149/1737 to occupy much of ʿUmān, establishing garrisons at a number of places, including Djulfār and al-Khaṭṭ (in the Amirate of Raʾs al-Khayma today). The Persians were finally expelled in 1157/1744. During the latter part of the 12th/18th century, Raʾs al-Khayma passed under the Āl Ḳāsimī *shaykhs*, of the Ḥawāla Arab tribe, which has elements on both the Arab and the Persian coasts. The Āl Ḳāsimī have continued to rule Raʾs al-Khayma until the present time. In the framework of the traditional ʿUmānī factions, they espouse the Ghifārī cause as opposed to the Hināwī.

The Āl Ḳāsimī *shaykhs* adopted Wahhābism under the influence of the Āl Suʿūd, with whom they still maintain good relations. As a sea-borne power, they engaged in piracy in the Gulf in the latter years of the 18th and the early 19th century, challenging East India Company shipping and the British Navy. In 1224/1809 British and Indian forces from Bombay attacked Raʾs al-Khayma to suppress the "Joasmee" (Ḳawāsimī) forces. These operations were repeated in 1234/1819, which led to the reduction of the Āl Ḳāsimī and the demolition of their fortresses, the destruction of their fleet and a brief British occupation of Raʾs al-Khayma. A General Treaty between the British and the Āl Ḳāsimī was signed at al-Falāya near to Raʾs al-Khayma town in 1235/1820, aimed at suppressing piracy in the Gulf: it was to this treaty that other *shaykhs* along the coast acceded, creating the foundation of the Trucial ʿUmān states. The Treaty was finally reinforced by The Perpetual Maritime Truce of 1853 which set the framework of relations between the various shaykhdoms and the British until 1971. Raʾs al-Khayma underwent a period of decline with its power sharply reduced by the British attack. The main political concern of the Āl Ḳāsimī during the following years was to prevent incursions on their territory by ʿUmān and by the Banū Yās of Abū Ẓabī.

The Āl Ḳāsimī ruled their territories from either Sharjah or Raʾs al-Khayma, but after 1921 the family territories were conclusively divided and Raʾs al-Khayma was recognised by the British as an independent Amirate. The British recognition of the Amirate of Fudjayra in 1952 marked the formal ending of al-Ḳāsimī control of this part of the east coast of the ʿUmān Peninsula: today the border of Raʾs al-Khayma with Fudjayra lies at the western edge of the Djabal Ḥadjar.

With the ending of the British treaty relationship with the Trucial States in 1971, Raʾs al-Khayma acceded to the newly created United Arab Emirates on 10th February, 1972. The Ruler of Raʾs al-Khayma since 1948, *Shaykh* Ṣaḳr b. Muḥammad al-Ḳāsimī, is a member of the Supreme Council of the U.A.E. Today, Raʾs al-Khayma, lacking oil in any quantity, is one of the poorer members of the U.A.E. Its major exports are stone from the Djabal Ḥadjar and cement, and its manpower contributes to the federal administration and the armed forces.

Bibliography: Muḳaddasī, *loc. cit.*; Duarte Barbosa, *The Book of Duarte Barbosa*, ed. M.L. Dames, London 1918, i, 73-74; J.S. Buckingham, *Travels in Assyria, Media, and Persia*, London 1830, 208 ff.; R.M. Burrell, *Britain, Iran and the Persian Gulf: some aspects of the situation in the 1920s and 1930s*, in *The Arabian Peninsula. Society and politics*, London 1972, 171-9; B. de Cardi and D.B. Doe, *Archaeological survey in the northern Trucial States*, in *East and West*, xxi/3-4 (Sept.-Dec. 1971), 225-87; M. Deakin, *Ras al-Khaimah, flame in the desert*, London (1976); W. Dostal, *The traditional architecture of Rās al-Khaimah (North)*, Wiesbaden 1983; J. Hansman, *Julfār, an Arabian port*, London 1985; F. Heard-Bey, *From Trucial States to United Arab Emirates*, London and New York 1982; G.R.D. King, *Excavations of the British team at Julfār, Ras-al-Khaimah, U.A.E.: interim report on the first season (1989)*, in *Procs. Seminar for Arabian Studies*, xx (1990), 79-93; idem, *Excavations by the British team at Julfār, Ras-al-Khaimah, U.A.E.: interim report on the second season* (1990), in *ibid.*, xxi (1991), 123-34; idem, *Excavations of the British team at Julfār, Ras-al-Khaimah, U.A.E.: interim report on the third season*, in *ibid.*, xxii (1992), 47-54; J.G. Lorimer, *Gazetteer of the Persian Gulf, ʾOmān and Central Arabia*, Calcutta 1908-15, i-ii; T. and H. Sasaki, *Japanese excavations at Julfār: 1988, 1989, 1990 and 1991 seasons*, in *Procs. Seminar for Arabian Studies*, xxii (1992), 105-20; A.T. Wilson, *The Persian Gulf*, London 1928. (G.R.D. King)

RAʾS MUSANDAM, a rocky peninsula that lies at the northernmost point of the promontory that terminates the Djabal Ḥadjar mountain range, the spine of the Oman Peninsula. It is attached to the mainland by the narrow Maḳlab isthmus. The Peninsula is deeply indented by creeks, of which the most important are Khawr al-Shamm, Khawr Ḥabalayn and Khawr Ghubb ʿAlī. Khawr al-Shamm is known as Elphinstone Inlet after Mountstuart Elphinstone, Governor of Bombay when the Court of Directors of the East India Company initiated a coastal survey of the western side of the Oman Peninsula, starting in the neighbourhood of Musandam in 1820. Buckingham comments on the depth of the water in the inlets of Musandam, but also remarks on the area's dangers as an anchorage and the risks entailed to shipping entering the channels (J.S. Buckingham, *Travels in Assyria, Media and Persia*, London 1830, ii, 385-6).

In modern usage, the term "Musandam" encompasses the dramatic cliffs of the mountainous mainland, properly termed Ruʾūs al-Djibāl (J.G. Lorimer, "Ruūs al Jibāl", in *Gazetteer of the Persian Gulf, ʾOmān, and Central Arabia*, ii/B, 1604-14; S.B. Miles, *The countries and tribes of the Persian Gulf²*, 378, 449; A.T. Wilson, *The Persian Gulf*, London 1959, 3) and the term also indicates the northernmost territory of the Sultanate of Oman (ʿUmān).

The term "Musandam" is taken by D.G. Hogarth (*The penetration of Arabia*, repr. Beirut 1966, 230) to mean "Anvil Head". The name is not known to the Classical or Arabic geographers and it seems to enter the literature in the Portuguese period, and, thereafter, the northern tip of the Oman Peninsula regularly appears as Raʾs Musandam.

Raʾs Musandam and Ruʾūs al-Djibāl reflect marked geological activity in the late Quaternary. The highlands are formed of limestones and dolomites, while sandy gravels form slope deposits and alluvial fans, a characteristic of the entire Oman Peninsula.

The earliest reference to Raʾs Musandam dates to 326 B.C., when Alexander's admiral Nearchos saw it from the Persian side of the straits of Hurmuz and was told it was called Maketa. It is further mentioned by Eratosthenes and Strabo, and possibly by Pliny, whilst the *Periplus of the Erytraean Sea* refers to the mighty range of the *Asabon*; Miles (*op. cit.*, 10) suggested that *Asabon* is preserved in the place-name Khaṣab, a village on the northern end of the promontory.

Al-Muḳaddasī (70-1) refers to a sequence of places between Masḳaṭ and Djulfār, but makes no reference to the villages of Raʾs Musandam that we know today. Al-Idrīsi refers to al-Khayl, al-Djabal or Ḥabal lying between Masḳaṭ and Djulfār (*Opus geographicum*, ed. A. Bombaci *et alii*, Naples-Rome 1972, ii, 162, tr. Jaubert, i, 157). The reading al-Djabal, if correct, is an appropriate reference to Djabal Ḥadjar, Ruʾūs al-Djibāl and Raʾs Musandam.

Evidence of early settlement at Raʾs Musandam is slender, although the accumulation of gravels in the alluvial fans may mask early archaeological sites. The earliest evidence of settlement in the region is indicated by a site on Djazīrat al-Ghanam attributed to the Sāsānid period (B. de Cardi, *A Sasanian outpost in northern Oman*, in *Antiquity*, xlvi, no. 184 [1973], 305-

10; eadem, *Archaeological survey in Northern Oman, 1972*, in *EW*, xxv [1975], 24-6). It included foundations of rectangular buildings along the foreshore to which a date after S̲h̲apūr II had occupied parts of eastern Arabia has been suggested (early 4th century A.D.), based on ceramic evidence. Evidence of Sāsānid occupation is limited elsewhere in this area and most ceramics recovered from the Musandam settlements indicate a 14th to 15th century A.D. date range.

Information increases about Ra's Musandam with the coming of the Portuguese. A Portuguese fleet is shown off "Cabo de Mocamdam" in the *Livro de Lizuarte de Abreu* of *ca.* 1564. K̲h̲aṣab (Casapo) is marked in Fernao Vaz Dourado's map drawn at Goa in 1571: S̲ībī is indicated in Dourado's map of 1575. Ruy Freyre de Andrada visited Kumzār and K̲h̲aṣab in 1620 during the last period of Portuguese dominion. Finding a fort at K̲h̲aṣab, de Andrada reinforced and garrisoned it (C.R. Boxer (ed.), *Commentaries of Ruy Freyre de Andrada*, London 1930, 189; Miles, 446; De Cardi, *Archaeological survey in Northern Oman, 1972*, 28). An inscription in the fort also records restoration in 1649 by the Portuguese. There are other Portuguese forts at Lima, at D̲jazīrat al-G̲h̲anam and Sīfa Maḳlab, the latter appearing to be 17th century.

From the second half of the 18th century, the Sulṭan of Masḳaṭ [*q.v.*] would collect taxes at Ra's Musandam on commerce passing through the straits of Hurmuz (Miles, 291). The deep creeks of Ra's Musandam gave cover to Ḳawāsimī pirates [see AL-ḲAWĀSIM] in the early years of the 19th century, and Buckingham describes the use of the Musandam creeks by pirates with their oar-driven boats sailing out to prey on shipping. From 1809, East India Company vessels in alliance with the Sulṭan of Masḳaṭ took up station off Ra's Musandam, in order to control the piracy of the Ḳawāsim (Miles, 314). Colonel Lewis Pelly, the British Resident in the Gulf, proposed in 1862-3 the siting of a British station near K̲h̲aṣab from which to control local disputes and the slave trade.

In 1862-4 a cable was laid for the Indo-European Telegraph across Ra's Musandam, running through Elphinstone Inlet (K̲h̲awr al-S̲h̲amm) and Malcolm Inlet (K̲h̲awr Ḥabalayn). The cable system remained in use until 1955 (C.P. Harris, *The Persian Gulf submarine telegraph of 1864*, in *GJ*, cxxxv/2 [June 1969], 170-90).

According to Lorimer, the population of Ru'ūs al-D̲jibāl was 13,750 in 1908 ("Oman", in *op. cit.*, ii/B, 1411, and "Ruūs al-Jibāl", 1605). Estimates in 1970-1 suggested that the population remained much as in Lorimer's time, but with a greater concentration in the coastal settlements (A. Coles, in *EW*, xxx [1975], 16). The majority of the people are S̲h̲iḥūh, dominating the mountain summits and the coasts alike, with elements of the much smaller D̲h̲āhiriyya residing at Buk̲h̲a and K̲h̲aṣab among other places.

Ra's Musandam has little cultivable lowland, and the people of Kumzār take their flocks by boat to D̲jazīrat al-G̲h̲anam to graze. By contrast, K̲h̲aṣab and Buk̲h̲a on the coast of Ru'ūs al-D̲jibal have somewhat more extensive date groves. Fish, shell fish and pearling remain part of the economy as they have since ancient times, when people of this area were termed *Ichthyophagi* by the Classical sources.

Isolated and inaccessible farmsteads characterise the mountains, where the terraced fields depend on rainfall for irrigation. Various types of distinctive, stone-built structures have been developed in the highlands, including the *bayt al-kifl*, a storage grain building.

Politically, Ra's Musandam and Ru'ūs al-D̲jibāl are under the jurisdiction of the Sultanate of ʿUmān (Oman), although the southern areas of Ru'ūs al-D̲jibāl lie in the Amīrate of Ra's al-K̲h̲ayma, while Dibba is under the joint jurisdiction of ʿUmān, al-Fud̲jayra (Fujairah) and al-S̲h̲āriḳa (Sharjah).

Bibliography (in addition to references given in the article): B. de Cardi, with sections by C. Vita-Finzi and A. Coles, in *EW*, xxv (1972), 9-75; L. Casson, *The Periplus Maris Erithraei*, Princeton 1989; P.F.S. Cornelius, *The Musandam expedition 1971-72. Scientific results*, in *GJ*, cxxxix (1973), 400-25; P.M. Costa (ed.), *Musandam*, London 1991; N.L. Falcon, *The Musandam (Northern Oman) expedition (1971/1972)*, in *GJ*, cxxxix (1973), 1-19; C. Ptolemy, *Geography*, tr. E.L. Stevenson, with an introd. by J. Fischer, New York 1932; Strabo, *Geography*, tr. H.L. Jones, Loeb edn.; B. Thomas, *The Musandam Peninsula and its people the Shihuh*, in *Journal of the Royal Central Asian Society*, xvi (1929), 71-86; idem, *Alarms and excursions in Arabia*, Indianapolis 1931; P. Ward, *Travels in Oman on the track of the early explorers*, Oleander 1987, 453-77.

(G.R.D. KING)

RA'S (AL-) TANNŪRA, a cape in eastern Saudi Arabia on the Persian Gulf, in lat. 26° 40' N., 50° 13' E., north of al-Ḳaṭīf [*q.v.*]. The word *tannūr* occurs in Ḳur'ān, XI, 42, and XXIII, 27, in the story of Noah, meaning "oven". It also indicates any place from which water pours forth (Lane, *Lexicon, s.v.*). In July 1933 King ʿAbd al-ʿAzīz gave the concession for drilling oil in the eastern part of Saudi Arabia to the Standard Oil Company of California. The first consignment of Saudi oil was sent away from Ra's Tannūra in 1939. Its refinery is connected by a pipeline with the Dammām field, about 60 km/37 miles away.

Bibliography: G. de Gaury, *Faisal. King of Saudi Arabia*, London 1966; H.I. Anderson, *Aramco, the United States and Saudi Arabia. A study of the dynamics of foreign oil policy 1933-1950*, Princeton 1981; H. Blume, *Saudi-Arabien*, Tübingen-Basel 1976, index *s.v.*; see also the Bibl. to NAFṬ. 3. (ED.)

RASHĀ'IDA, *ḳabīlat al-Rashā'ida*, an Arab and Muslim nomadic people of the eastern Sudan and Eritrea, which emigrated from the coast of Arabia in the middle of the 19th century. Installed in the first instance on the *sāḥil* between Sawākin (Suakin) and ʿAḳīḳ, they were forced by the Mahdiyya [*q.v.*] to move southwards. Some of them then returned to the Anglo-Egyptian Sudan, so that today they can be found dispersed along the coast from Port Sudan to Massawa [see MAṢAWWAʿ] and on the left bank of the Atbara beyond Kassala. In the Sudan, their number was estimated in 1922 at one to two thousand and in 1986 at 40,000. They are less numerous in Eritrea.

They herd goats in the more confined areas and, more often, camels in the wider expanses. The most northerly group nomadises, for example, along the axis of the Atbara over 500 km/310 miles. In the wet season, from the end of June to October, the herds (from 50 to 70 head) are between Kassal and Goz Regeb. In the dry season, they go down towards Doka and the Dinder National Park in order to graze on the fields of sorghum which have just been watered.

The Rashā'ida have other resources. The camel rearers of the fringes are carriers and have benefitted from the Eritrean war up to 1991. Certain of them sometimes engage in agriculture. One group has even tried to live by fishing on two of the Dahlak [*q.v.*] islands.

They do not ally either with the Cushitic peoples of whom they are neighbours (Bichari, Hadendowa, etc.) nor with other Arabs, and have preserved their own dialect and traditions. They live in small family groups (*dār*) of two to eight tents, grouped together in the dry season in an encampment (*farīg*) of 100 to 200 persons who recognise the authority of an *ʿomda*. The cohesion of the community as a whole is not kept together by any central authority able to represent them vis-à-vis the political authorities.

The men wear a long shirt over trousers with wide legs, have on their heads a voluminous turban and never move anywhere without a long whip. The womenfolk wear long black robes and a veil of material and leather decorated with embroidery in which two square holes are made for the eyes. Among the young girls, the veil, decorated with cowrie shells, hides only the nose and mouth.

Bibliography: W. Young, *The effect of labour migration on relations of exchange amongst the Rashaayda Bedouin of Sudan*, in *Revue européenne des migrations internationales*, ii/1 (1986), 121-36; idem, *The Days of Joy: a structuralist analysis of weddings among the Rashaayda Arabs of Sudan*, diss. UCLA 1988; I. Köhler-Rollefson *et alii, The camel pastoral system of the southern Rashaida in eastern Sudan*, in *Nomadic Peoples*, xxix (1991), 68-76. (A. Rouaud)

RASHĪD, Rosetta, a town in Egypt, situated in lat. 31° 24′ N., long. 30° 24′ E., on the western bank of the western branch of the Nile. The town which is situated near the site of the ancient Bōlbouthiō (Greek Bolbitínē) seems not to have existed before the Arab conquest. Even at the beginning of the 8th century A.D., the papyri mention only the name of Bolbitínē as emporium for merchandise from Upper Egypt (Bell, *The Aphrodite papyri*, 1414, 1. [59], 102, etc.). Till the 9th century A.D., ships sailed direct to Fuwwa; but owing to the excessive depositing of the silt in this region, Rashīd began to take its place.

Rashīd is first mentioned in 132/750 when the Copts of the town revolted against the caliph Marwān II who had taken refuge in Egypt from the ʿAbbāsids (al-Kindī, *Wulāt*, 96). In 278/891-2, al-Yaʿkūbī (*Buldān*, 338) mentions its port. When the Fāṭimid heir-apparent (the future caliph al-Ḳāʾim) tried to conquer Egypt in 307/920, his fleet was prevented by an ʿAbbāsid squadron from sailing into the mouth of the Rashīd branch of the Nile, and was then annihilated (al-Kindī, *Wulāt*, 276).

Rashīd is numbered among the *kūras* [*q.v.*] of Egypt (al-Yaʿkūbī, *loc. cit.*; al-Ḳuḍāʿī, quoted by al-Maḳrīzī, *Khiṭaṭ*, ed. Wiet, i, 311, 1. 5). After the reorganisation of the provinces of Egypt, probably during the reign of the Fāṭimid caliph al-Mustanṣir (427-87/1035-94), it became a unit of its own, not belonging to any of the newly-created provinces of the Delta. Al-Idrīsī, *Opus geographicum* (ed. E. Cerulli *et alii*), 343, describes it as a commercial town and mentions the fishery activities on the Nile and the Sea and the export of pickled mussels (*dallīnas*). The Arab geographers usually qualify Rashīd as a frontier station (*thaghr*), where probably customs were levied. In the 8th/14th century, its revenues were given as an *iḳṭāʿ* to Mamlūk officers; but *ca.* 885/1480, under sultan Ḳāyit Bāy, it was part of the crown-lands (*al-khāṣṣ al-sulṭānī;* Ibn al-Djīʿān, *al-Tuḥfa*, ed. B. Moritz, Cairo 1898, 138). In the last years of the 8th/14th century, Ibn Duḳmāḳ (*al-Intiṣār*, ed. Vollers, Cairo 1893, v, 113-14) calls Rashīd a *ribāṭ* and says that the inhabitants of the town were exclusively volunteers (*murābiṭūn*).

After the Ottoman conquest of Egypt in 1517 and the decay of European trade through Alexandria, Rashīd became an important centre for maritime trade with Istanbul and the Aegean territory of the Turkish Empire. The viceroy ʿAlī Pasha, in 915/1509, restored its old *khāns* (warehouses) and *funduḳs* (hostelries), built new ones, and cleared the silt from its docks. Till modern times, its wall was maintained for defence against Arab raids. At the mouth of the River, near Kōm al-Afrāḥ, two castles guarded the waterway entrance to the town. Vansleb, who visited Rashīd in May 1672, gives a description of the castles and their garrison (*State of Egypt*, London 1678, 105). When Carsten Niebuhr passed through Rashīd in November 1761, the town was the residence of a French and a Venetian consul; it served as port of trans-shipment for the trade between Cairo and Alexandria (*Reisebeschreibung*, i, 56-7 and pl. VI). In 1799, in the neighbourhood of the town, Boussard, an officer of the French Expedition, discovered the famous Rosetta Stone with its trilingual inscription (now in the British Museum). In 1218/1803 Rashīd witnessed al-Bardīsī's victory over the combined sea and land forces of the Ottoman Porte; and in 1222/1807 it was seized by the British who came to help al-Alfī and his Mamlūk successors.

The town continued to flourish until Muḥammad ʿAlī [*q.v.*] reconstructed the Maḥmūdiyya Canal for navigation between Alexandria and the Nile, and thus diverted the course of trade from Rashīd, which declined rapidly to a mere fishing town with but a few minor local industries such as rough cotton weaving, rice production and oil manufacture. Its population in 1907 was only 16,660, but in 1970 the population of the town, which still benefits from coastal trade and fisheries, had risen to 36,711.

Bibliography: ʿAlī Pasha Mubārak, *al-Khiṭaṭ al-Tawfīḳiyya*, Būlāḳ 1884-9, xi, 75; Maspéro-Wiet, *Matériaux*, 99-100, 173-91; M. Ramzī, *al-Ḳāmūs al-djughrāfī li ʾl-bilād al-Miṣriyya*, Cairo 1953-68, ii/2, 300; H. Halm, *Ägypten nach den mamlukischen Lehensregistern, II. Das Delta*, Wiesbaden 1982, 769, map 49. (A.S. Atiya-[H. Halm])

RASHĪD, ĀL, an Arabian tribal dynasty belonging to the ʿAbda clan (*ʿashīra*) of the Shammar tribes and ruling over parts of northern and central Arabia from 1251/1835 until 1340/1921. Although the area under their control fluctuated with their political fortunes, their essential power base was in the Djabal Shammar region of northern Nadjd where they could rely on tribal allegiance and make the small town of Ḥāyil [*q.v.*] their centre of government.

The history of Āl Rashīd is closely linked with that of Āl Suʿūd [see suʿūd, āl], at first as their allies and supporters, later as their rivals for domination over central Arabia. The founder of the Rashīdī dynasty, ʿAbd Allāh b. Rashīd, is usually presented as a close friend and supporter of the Suʿūdī *amīr* Fayṣal b. Suʿūd and, on a religious and military level, enthusiastic to promote the Wahhābī cause. He managed to establish himself as ruler in Ḥāyil in 1251/1835 after a power struggle with cousins from the rival family of Ibn ʿAlī, but to what extent he owed his position to the Suʿūdīs or to his personal abilities and tribal backing is a subject of dispute. He was noted for his largely successful efforts to enforce security, despite resentment in some quarters of his pro-Suʿūdī and Wahhābī stance. He was succeeded on his death in 1264/1847 by his eldest son Ṭalāl.

Ṭalāl's rule from 1264-84/1847-67 saw the achievement of a high point in commercial prosperity and stability due to his encouragement of trade. More religiously tolerant than his father, he accepted the settlement of Shīʿī merchants from ʿIrāḳ, generally hated by the Wahhābīs. His apparently accidental death from a gunshot wound led to a brief period of internecine struggle, characteristic of the Rashīdīs and a major cause of their downfall, before Muḥammad, a younger brother of Ṭalāl, came to power following his massacre of all Ṭalāl's sons.

Despite its bloody beginnings, the long reign of Muḥammad b. Rashīd (1289-1315/1872-97) witnessed the expansion of Rashīdī power over al-Ḳaṣīm [q.v.] and the Wahhābī heartlands of southern Nadjd, including the Suʿūdī capital, al-Riyāḍ [q.v.]. After a long contest with Āl Suʿūd he defeated them decisively at the battle of al-Mulayda in 1309/1891, expelling them from Nadjd, after which they sought refuge in al-Kuwayt, among them the young ʿAbd al-ʿAzīz [q.v.], future founder of the modern kingdom of Suʿūdī (Saudi) Arabia. The *amīr* Muḥammad was noted for his military skills and the energy with which he sought to control recalcitrant tribes. European visitors to Ḥāyil during his reign included C.M. Doughty, the poet Wilfred Scawen Blunt and his wife, Lady Anne.

Following the death of their last great *amīr*, Āl Rashīd sank into their final decline, faced with the rising new power of ʿAbd al-ʿAzīz b. Suʿūd as well as political and economic pressures exerted by the Ottomans and British, especially during World War I and its aftermath. Muḥammad's immediate successor, his nephew ʿAbd al-ʿAzīz, was killed in battle with the Suʿūdīs, and the Rashīdīs then fell prey to savage internal quarrels reminiscent of the time before Muḥammad's accession. Four *amīrs* were murdered by their own relatives in the period from 1325/1907 to 1339/1920. The last two *amīrs*, who ruled only briefly, were forced to surrender to Ibn Suʿūd in 1339-40/1921.

Bibliography: The local Nadjdī historian ʿUthmān b. Bishr (d. 1288/1871), *ʿUnwān al-madjd fī taʾrīkh Nadjd*, Mecca 1930; Lady Anne Blunt, *A pilgrimage to Nejd*, London 1881; C.M. Doughty, *Travels in Arabia Deserta*, Cambridge 1888; J.C. Lorimer, *Gazetteer of the Persian Gulf, ʿOmān and Central Arabia*, Calcutta 1908-15, i/1B, 1161-78; Dharīʿ b. Rashīd, *Nubdha taʾrīkhiyya ʿan Nadjd*, al-Riyāḍ 1966; ʿAbd Allāh al-ʿUthaymīn, *Nashʾat imārat Āl Rashīd*, al-Riyāḍ 1981; M. Al Rasheed, *Politics in an Arabian oasis, the Rashidi tribal dynasty*, London 1991, combines historical and anthropological approaches.

(Elizabeth M. Sirriyeh)

AL-**RASHĪD** [see HĀRŪN AL-RASHĪD].

AL-**RĀSHID** BI'LLĀH, ABŪ DJAʿFAR AL-MANṢŪR, the thirtieth ʿAbbāsid caliph, the son of al-Mustarshid [q.v.] and a slave girl called Khushf, was probably born around 501/1107-8 since the sources record the date of his *walī al-ʿahd* ceremony as 2 Rabīʿ I 513/13 July 1119 when he was aged twelve (Ibn al-Athīr, x, 377). Al-Rāshid became caliph after al-Mustarshid's murder in Dhu 'l Ḳaʿda 529/August 1135 (Sibṭ Ibn al-Djawzī, 158; Ibn al-Athīr, xi, 16) and died in 532/1138.

His reign was tragically short. He was drawn immediately into a bitter and ultimately fatal battle of wills with the Saldjūḳ sultan Masʿūd b. Muḥammad [q.v.] who now, after his clashes with al-Mustarshid, wanted a malleable caliph ready to stay put in Baghdād and to confine himself to religious matters (Ibn al-Azraḳ, 73). Al-Rāshid, however, was of a different ilk, demanding vengeance for his father's murder and no doubt cherishing hopes of continuing al-Mustarshid's aim of expelling the Saldjuḳs from ʿIrāḳ. The sources record in some detail the deteriorating relationship between caliph and sultan.

Shortly after al-Rāshid's accession, Masʿūd demanded tribute from him, but this the caliph refused to disgorge. Indeed, he proceeded to prepare for conflict by raising troops and fortifying Baghdād (Ibn al-Djawzī, x, 54; Ibn al-Athīr, xi, 22; Bar Hebraeus, 262; Ibn al-ʿImrānī, 222), whilst factions hostile to Masʿūd, notably his nephew Dāwūd b. Maḥmūd, and Zangī, converged on the city in Ṣafar 530/November 1135 and persuaded al-Rāshid to make common causes with them. After the *khuṭba* had been pronounced in Dāwūd's name on 14 Ṣafar 530/23 November 1135 (Ibn al-Djawzī, x, 55; Ibn al-Athīr, xi, 23), Masʿūd hastened to besiege Baghdād and the intimidated rebels soon dispersed in disarray. After an initial display of bravado, al-Rāshid fled in panic with Zangī to Mawṣil (al-Bundārī, 180; Ibn al-Azraḳ, 76-7; Ibn al-Djawzī, x, 59; Ibn al-Athīr, *Atābegs*, 51).

It was a serious blunder for al-Rāshid to vacate the traditional seat of caliphal power. In Dhu 'l-Ḳaʿda 530/August 1136, Masʿūd entered Baghdād peacefully and engineered the deposition of the absent caliph. A group of *ʿulamāʾ* summoned by Masʿūd declared al-Rāshid unsuitable for office, accusing him of wine-drinking and immorality and of breaking a solemn oath to Masʿūd that he would never leave Baghdād or take up arms against him (Ibn al-Azraḳ, 72) and producing a document to this effect signed by al-Rāshid (Ibn al-Athīr, xi, 26; Ibn al-Djawzī, x, 60; Bar Hebraeus, 263). A *fatwā* deposing al-Rāshid was pronounced by the Shāfiʿī *ḳāḍī*, ʿImād al-Dīn Ibn al-Karkhī (Ibn al-Athīr, *Atābegs*, 53; Ibn al-Azraḳ, 78). Al-Rāshid's uncle al-Muḳtafī [q.v.] was proclaimed caliph in his stead.

Zangī's support for the exiled al-Rāshid proved short-lived. The ex-caliph soon felt too insecure to remain in Mawṣil and he moved to Ādharbaydjān to join Dāwūd and a coalition of Turkish *amīrs* who resolved to restore him to the caliphate (al-Ḥusaynī, 108-9; al-Bundārī, 180; Ibn al-Athīr, xi, 39-40). These and other offers of support soon evaporated (*ibid.*, xi, 41; Ibn al-Azraḳ, 81) and after wandering from place to place, the hapless al-Rāshid was finally killed outside Iṣfahān on 25 or 26 Ramaḍān 532/6 or 7 June 1138. Although some sources blame the Assassins for his murder (ʿImād al-Dīn al-Iṣfahānī, *apud* Sibṭ Ibn al-Djawzī, 168; Ibn al-Athīr, *Atābegs*, 55), Saldjūḳ complicity seems likely, since Masʿūd could clearly no longer tolerate the way that the peripatetic al-Rāshid was arousing rebellion within the western Saldjūḳ sultanate. What is indisputable, however, is that two successive ʿAbbāsid caliphs, father and son, who had ventured forth from Baghdād and defied the Saldjūḳ sultan, had now been eliminated.

Al-Rāshid was buried in the Friday mosque of Shahristān in a *turba* set aside exclusively for him (al-Bundārī, 181; Sibṭ Ibn al-Djawzī, 168). His caliphate had lasted about eleven months (Ibn al-Athīr, xi, 27).

Little is known of al-Rāshid's personality, although his recorded conduct suggests that he was ambitious, foolhardy and easily embroiled in intrigue. It was his misfortune to clash with Masʿūd, a ruthless warrior sultan who in difficult times contrived to stay in power for twenty years. Al-Rāshid's sexual precocity was legendary—by the age of nine he had fathered a son from one of al-Mustarshid's concubines and he had allegedly sired twenty more by the time of his accession (Sibṭ Ibn al-Djawzī, 158; Ibn al-Azraḳ, 73). Like his father, he had a ruddy complexion and dark blue eyes and was of medium stature (Ibn al-ʿImrānī, 224).

Bibliography: 1. Primary sources. Bar Hebraeus, *Chronology*, tr. E.A.W. Budge, London 1932, i, 260, 262-5; Bundārī, *Zubdat al-nuṣra*, ed. M.T. Houtsma, 178-81, 183; Ḥusaynī, *Akhbār al-*

dawla al-Saldjūkiyya, ed. M. Iḳbāl, Lahore 1933, 108-9; Ibn al-Athīr, *Taʾrīkh al-dawla al-atābakiyya*, ed. A. Ṭulaymāt, Cairo 1963, 50-5; idem, *Kāmil*, xi, 17, 22-4, 26-8, 39-41; Ibn al-Azraḳ, *Taʾrīkh Mayyāfariḳīn*, ed. and tr. C. Hillenbrand, in *A Muslim principality in Crusader times*, Leiden 1990, 69, 72-4, 76-8, 80-1, 138; Ibn al-Djawzī, *Muntaẓam*, x, 54-7, 59-62, 66-8, 70-1; Ibn al-ʿImrānī, *al-Inbāʾ fī taʾrīkh al-khulafāʾ*, ed. al-Samarrai, Leiden 1973, 222-4; Ibn al-Ḳalānisī, *Dhayl taʾrīkh Dimashḳ*, ed. H.F. Amedroz, Leiden 1908, 256-7, 259, 264, 267; Ibn al-Ṭiḳṭaḳā, *Fakhrī*, tr. C.E.J. Whitting, 297-8; Rāwandī, *Rāḥat al-ṣudūr*, ed. M. Iḳbāl, London 1921, 228-9; Sibṭ Ibn al-Djawzī, *Mirʾāt al-zamān*, Ḥaydarābād 1951, viii/1, 157-8, 164, 167-8.

2. Secondary sources. *Cambridge History of Iran*, v, 127-8; *EI*[1], art. *al-Rāshid* (K.V. Zettersteen). (CAROLE HILLENBRAND)

AL-**RASHĪD** (MAWLĀY) B. AL-SHARĪF B. ʿALĪ B. MUḤAMMAD B. ʿALĪ, ʿAlid sultan of Morocco and the real founder of the dynasty which still rules the Sharīfian empire. He was born in 1040/1630-1 in Tāfīlālt [*q.v.*] in the south of Morocco, where his ancestors, the Ḥasanī Shurafāʾ (Shorfāʾ [*q.v.*]) of Sidjilmāsa [*q.v.*], had founded a flourishing *zāwiya* [*q.v.*] and gradually acquired a fairly considerable political influence, which increased with the decline of the Saʿdian [*q.v.*] dynasty. Morocco being at this time plunged into anarchy, the Shorfāʾ of Tāfīlālt were able rapidly to become masters of the great tracts of steppe-like country to the north of the cordon of oases which formed their appanage. The eldest son of the chief of the *zāwiya*, Mawlāy Maḥammad, having successfully fought the marabout of the *zāwiya* of Īligh in Tāzarwālt (in the south-west of Morocco), ʿAlī Abū Ḥassūn, who had political ambitions of his own, assumed a royal title in 1050/1646. He did not, however, yet succeed in crushing the power of the marabouts of the *zāwiya* of al-Dilāʾ [*q.v.* in Suppl.] in central Morocco; he had to be content, after a very brief occupation of Tāzā and Fās in 1060/1650, with effective sovereignty over eastern Morocco only.

On the death of Mawlāy al-Sharīf in 1069/1659, his son, Mawlāy al-Rashīd, not trusting his brother, Mawlāy Maḥammad, left the ancestral *zāwiya* for the rival *zāwiya* of al-Dilāʾ, where in spite of a superficially warm welcome, he was soon given the hint to go; he proceeded to Āzrū, then to Fās, which, regarded as an undesirable by the lord of the city, the adventurer al-Duraydī, he was not allowed to enter. He next went to eastern Morocco, and very soon succeeded in gaining a large number of followers, particularly, in the important tribe of the Banū Īznāssen (Benī Snassen), the Shaykh al-Lawātī, a religious dignitary, then of great influence. At the same time he attacked a very rich Jew, who behaved like a great lord and lived in the mountains of the Banū Īznāssen, at the little town called Dār Ibn Mashʿal: al-Rashīd slew him and seized his wealth. This coup vividly impressed the imagination of the people of the district and was to give rise, as P. de Cenival brilliantly showed, to a legend, the memory of which still survives in the annual festival which follows the election of the "sultan of the *ṭulbāʾ*" at Fās. Mawlāy al-Rashīd by this murder not only acquired considerable material resources but also a real ascendancy over the people of the neighbourhood. In 1075/1664, the large tribe of the Angād rallied to his authority, and he set up in Oujda [see WADJDA] as a regular ruler. On the news of the proclamation of al-Rashīd, his brother Mawlāy Maḥammad, much disturbed, hurried from Tāfīlālt to eastern Morocco; his troops were met by those of al-Rashīd, and Mawlāy Maḥammad having been killed early in the battle, his men then went over to the surviving prince. Thenceforth, Mawlāy al-Rashīd went on from success to success.

He very soon seized Tāzā without difficulty, and directly threatened Fās, but he first of all took care to secure his power solidly at Tāfīlālt, the cradle of his line, and added to his lands the mountains of the Rīf [*q.v.*] on the shores of the Mediterranean, which were then ruled by an enterprising individual named Abū Muḥammad ʿAbd Allāh Aʿarrāṣ. This *shaykh* had made an agreement, first with the English and then with the French, for the establishment of factories on the Rīf bay of Alhucemas [see AL-ḤUSAYMA in Suppl.] (transcribed in the documents of the period as Albouzème). Mawlāy al-Rashīd deprived him of the Rīf in Ramaḍān 1076/March 1666, just when the Marseillais Roland Fréjus, having obtained from the King of France the privilege of trading in the Rīf, was landing on the Moroccan coast. Fréjus then went to see Mawlāy al-Rashīd at Tāzā, but the negotiations into which he endeavoured to enter with the *shaykh* soon collapsed.

Al-Rashīd without delay turned his attention to the capital of northern Morocco, Fās, which still withstood his authority. He laid siege to it and took it by storm on 3 Dhu 'l-Ḥidjdja 1076/6 June 1666; the adventurer in command there, al-Duraydī, took to flight. Al-Rashīd took vigorous steps to punish certain of the notables of the town, and the people proclaimed him sultan. He was at the same time able to rally to his side the important group of Idrīsid Shorfāʾ in the capital.

The years that followed were used by Mawlāy al-Rashīd to extend his possessions towards west and south. He first made an expedition against the Gharb, out of which he drove the chief al-Khaḍir Ghaylān, and seized al-Ḳaṣr al-Kabīr [*q.v.*] (Alcazarquivir); he also took Meknes [see MIKNĀS] and Tetuan [see TIṬṬĀWĪN] as well as Tāzā, the inhabitants of which had rebelled. In 1079/1668, he took and destroyed the *zāwiya* of al-Dilāʾ after having routed its chief Maḥammad al-Ḥādjdj at Baṭn al-Rummān. The same year, Mawlāy al-Rashīd seized Marrākush and put to death there the local chief ʿAbd al-Karīm al-Shabbānī, surnamed Karrūm al-Ḥādjdj. In 1081/1670, he undertook an expedition into the Sūs [*q.v.*], where agitators still disputed his authority. He took Tārūdānt [*q.v.*] and the fortress of Īligh and returned to Fās, now lord of all Morocco. At this time, says the chronicler al-Ifrānī, "all the Maghrib, from Tlemcen to the Wādī Nūl on the borders of the Ṣaḥārā, was under the authority of Mawlāy al-Rashīd".

The next year the sultan went from Fās to Marrākush, where one of his nephews was endeavouring to set up as a pretender to the throne. During his sojourn in the southern capital, Mawlāy al-Rashīd, not yet 42, died as the result of an accident on 11 Dhu 'l-Ḥidjdja 1082/9 April 1672; the horse he was riding having reared, he fractured his skull against a branch of an orange tree. He was buried at Marrākush, but later his body was brought to Fās, where he was interred in the chapel of the saint ʿAlī Ibn Ḥirzihim (vulg. Sīdī Ḥrāzem). His brother, Mawlāy Ismāʿīl [*q.v.*], who succeeded him, was proclaimed sultan on the 15 Dhu 'l-Ḥidjdja following.

The brief political career of Mawlāy al-Rashīd was, as has been seen, particularly active and fruitful. The Muslim historians of Morocco never tire of praising this ruler, whose memory is still particularly bright, especially in Fās. It was he who built in the town the

'*Madrasa* of the Ropemakers'' (*Madrasat al-Sharrāṭīn*), the bridge of al-Raṣīf, the *ḳaṣaba* of the Sharārda Casba of the Cherarda) and 2½ miles to the east of 'ās, a bridge of nine arches over the Wādī Sabū Sebou).

Bibliography: Ifrānī, *Nuzhat al-ḥādī*, ed. and tr. Houdas, in *PELOV*, 3rd series, iii, Paris 1889, 301-4 (text) and 501-3 (tr.); Zayyānī, *al-Turdjumān al-muʿrib*, ed. and tr. Houdas (*Le Maroc de 1631 à 1812*, in *PELOV*, 2nd series, xviii), Paris 1886; Akansūs, *al-Djaysh al-ʿaramram*, Fās 1336/1918, i, 58-63; Nāṣirī, *Kitāb al-Istiḳṣāʾ* Cairo, iv, 1312/1894-5, tr. Fumey, in *AM*, ix, Paris 1906 (*Chronique de la dynastie ʿalaouie au Maroc*), index; Ḳādirī, *Nashr al-mathānī*, Fās, ii, 3-6, tr. E. Michaux-Bellaire, in *AM*, xxiv, Paris 1917, 211-17; most of the other Moroccan biographers (cf. E. Lévi-Provençal, *Les historiens des Chorfa*, Paris 1922, index); Mouëtte, *Histoire des conquêtes de Mouley Archy* [= al-Rashīd], *connu sous le nom de roy du Tafilet, et de Mouley Ismaël*, Paris 1683; H. de Castries, *Les sources inédites de l'histoire du Maroc*, Paris, 2nd series, *passim*; P. de Cenival, *La légende du juif Ibn Mechʿal et la fête du sultan des tolba à Fès*, in *Hespéris*, v (1925), 137-218; A. Cour, *L'établissement des dynasties des Chérifs au Maroc et leur rivalité avec les Turcs de la Régence d'Alger (1509-1830)*, Paris 1904; Ch.A. Julien, *Histoire de l'Afrique du Nord*, Paris 1931, 487-90 (reproduction of a portrait [authentic?] of Mawlāy al-Rashīd, fig. 225, p. 481); H. Terrasse, *Histoire du Maroc*, Paris 1949-50; P. Shinar, *Essai de bibliographie sélective et annotée sur l'Islam maghrébin contemporain, ... 1830-1978*, Paris 1983. See also ʿALAWĪS; AL-MAGHRIB; SHORFĀ; SIDJILMĀSA; TĀFĪLĀLT.

(E. LÉVI-PROVENÇAL)

RĀSHID, MEḤMED (?-1148/1735), Ottoman historian and poet. He was born in Istanbul, the son of *ḳāḍī* Muṣṭafā Efendi from Malaṭya. From 1116/1704 he held a regular series of posts as a *müderris* culminating in appointment to the Süleymāniyye in 1130/1718, the latter held concurrently with the post of *Ḥaremeyn müfettishi*, inspector of the *awḳāf* of Mecca and Medina. He then served as *ḳāḍī* of Aleppo 1135-7/1723-4. His career thereafter was irregular by comparison, and much influenced by political considerations, in particular by his closeness to the Grand Vizier Newshehirli Ibrāhīm Pasha [*q.v.*] and his consequent identification with the palace culture of the *Lāle dewri* [*q.v.*] period (described in Aḥmed Refīḳ Altınay], *ʿĀlimler ve ṣanatkārlar*, Istanbul 1924, 311-22). In 1141/1728-9, Rāshid went as Ottoman ambassador to Iṣfahān, and shortly afterwards was appointed *ḳāḍī* of Istanbul (1141-3/1729-30). Following the Patrona Khalīl [*q.v.*] rebellion of 1730, Rāshid spent three years in exile, first in Bursa, then on the island of Limni. His final appointment, in 1147/1734, was as *ḳāḍī ʿasker* [*q.v.*] of Anatolia, in which post he died in 1148/1735.

Although enjoying a contemporary reputation also as a leading poet and prose stylist, Rāshid is remembered principally as an historian, successor to Naʿīmā [*q.v.*] as official Ottoman historiographer. In 1126/1714 he was commissioned by the Grand Vizier Dāmād ʿAlī Pasha [see DĀMĀD] to write the history of the reign of Aḥmed III, from his accession in 1115/1703. For this purpose he was given the title *wekāyiʿ-nüwīs* (or *waḳʿa-nüwīs* [*q.v.*]), allowed access to official documents, and required to attend in person on the Morea and Waradīn campaigns of 1714 and 1716 respectively. In 1130/1718 at the request of Newshehirli Ibrāhīm Pasha, newly-appointed Grand Vizier, Rāshid then revised his work to begin in 1071/1660, at the point where Naʿīmā's history ceased. The *Taʾrīkh-i Rāshid* terminates in 1134/1722. Rāshid was succeeded as *waḳʿa-nüwīs* by Küčük Čelebi-zāde Ismāʿīl ʿĀṣim Efendi [*q.v.*].

The *Taʾrīkh-i Rāshid* has been published twice: in 1153/1741, by the Müteferriḳa press, 3 vols., and 1282/1865, 5 vols. (both editions also include the continuation by Küčük Čelebi-zāde Ismāʿīl ʿĀṣim Efendi for the period 1134-41/1722-8; cf. Babinger, *GOW*, 268-70).

Bibliography: For the biography and a list of Rāshid's works, see M. Kemal Özergin, *İA*, *Râşid*, with detailed bibl.; see also *Taʾrīkh-i Rāshid*, i, 4-10, v, 449-54, and *passim*. (CHRISTINE WOODHEAD)

RĀSHID, N.M., modern Urdu poet (1910-75). His real name was Nadhar (Nadhr) Muḥammad, but he is universally known by his literary name, Nūn Mīm Rāshid.

He was born in the township of ʿAlīpūr Ćaťťha (formerly Akālgaŕh) in the Gūdjarānwāla district of the Pandjāb in present-day Pākistān. His father, Faḍl Ilāhī Ćishtī, was in the provincial educational service from which he retired as District Inspector of Schools. Rāshid pursued his early education in his native town passing his high school examination in 1926. Thereafter, he studied in Lāyalpūr and Lahore respectively, and received his M.A. in economics from Government College, Lahore, in 1932. After completing his education he was employed from 1932 to 1934 as editor of *Nakhlistān*, a semi-literary journal published by the Punjab government's Rural Welfare Department. During 1934 and 1935 he worked as assistant editor for the literary journal *Shāhkār*, which was published from Lahore. He was associated with All-India Radio from 1939 until 1943, after which he joined the Indian Army as Public Relations Officer in Inter-Services Directorate. His job in that capacity lasted until 1947, and involved his stay in outside countries such as Iran, ʿIrāḳ, Egypt and Ceylon (presently Sri Lanka). In 1947 he rejoined All-India Radio as Assistant Regional Director. Following the partition of the sub-continent in 1947, he transferred himself to Radio Pakistan, where he remained until 1951. In October 1952 he joined the United Nations as Information Officer, rising eventually to the position of Director, U.N. Information Centre. In that position he was posted in 1967 to Tehran, where he was stationed until his retirement in 1974. Thereupon, he took up permanent residence in England, and died in London on 9 October 1975 of a heart attack. In accordance with his own wish, his body was cremated instead of being buried as required under Muslim custom.

Rāshid's first volume of poetry appeared in 1941 under the title *Māwarā* (''Beyond''), which immediately established him as a non-traditional poet of considerable originality and boldness. His next collection was published in 1955, entitled *Īrān meṅ adjnabī* (''A stranger in Iran''), and contained, in part, a group of poems arranged collectively under the same name. This work was followed in 1969 by *Lā = Insān* (''X = Man''), the poems of which indicated a more complex symbolistic style. Rāshid's last poetical collection was *Gumān kā mumkin* (''The possibleness of doubt''), which was published in 1977 after the poet's death. Finally, a complete edition of his entire verse (*Kulliyyāt*) was published in 1988.

Apart from original works, Rāshid also made a number of translations from foreign languages such as Alexander Kuprin's *Yama the pit* (1939), William Saroyan's *Mama I love you* (1956), and an anthology published under the title *Djadīd Fārsī shāʿirī* (''Modern

Persian poetry") (1987), which contained Urdu translations from modern Persian poets as well as notices on the life and works of the authors.

The dominant note of Rā**sh**id's poems is personal, often interspersed with political subjects. Sexual themes are prominent in the poems which belong to his early and middle periods, but in his later works he shows an increasing disposition towards complex human and personal issues. An overly-Persianised idiom pervades his diction, and his expression is complicated and difficult. His poetic technique has given impetus to the widespread use of *naẓm-i āzād* (the Urdu form of "free verse"), and he is regarded as one of the pioneers whose influence has been of paramount importance in giving a new direction to modern Urdu poetry.

Bibliography: N.M. Rāshid, *Kulliyyāt-i Rāshid*, Lahore 1988; Mālik Rām, *Tadhkira-yi muʿāṣirīn*, iii, Delhi 1978; Mughnī Tabassum and Shahriyār, *Nūn Mīm Rāshid: shakhṣiyyat awr fan*, Delhi 1981; *Nayā dawr* (special issue on Rāshid), 71 and 72, Karachi n.d.; Muhammad Sadiq, *Twentieth century Urdu literature*, Karachi 1983; *Annual of Urdu studies*, v (Chicago 1985); M.A.R. Habib (tr.), *The dissident voice: poems of N.M. Rashid*, Madras 1991; *Pakistani literature*, i/1, Islamabad 1992; Kathleen Grant Jaeger and Baidar Bakht (tr.), *An anthology of modern Urdu poetry*, i, Delhi 1984; *Mahfil: a quarterly of South Asian literature*, vii/1-2 (Chicago 1972) (contains English translations of Rāshid's poems by Carlo Coppola and Munibur Rahman).

(MUNIBUR RAHMAN)

RĀSHID AL-DĪN SINĀN, the greatest of the mediaeval Nizārī Ismāʿīlī leaders in Syria, d. 588/1192 or 589/1193. Also referred to as Sinān Rāshid al-Dīn by the Nizārīs, his full name was Rāshid al-Dīn Sinān b. Salmān (or Sulaymān) b. Muḥammad Abu' 'l-Ḥasan al-Baṣrī. He was born into an Imāmī Shīʿī family during the 520s/1126-35, near Baṣra, where he converted to Nizārī Ismāʿīlism in his youth. Subsequently, Rāshid al-Dīn Sinān went to the central headquarters of the Nizārī *daʿwa* at Alamūt [*q.v.*], in northern Persia, to further his Ismāʿīlī education. There, Sinān became a close companion, and possibly a schoolfellow, of the then lord of Alamūt's heir apparent Ḥasan, the future Ḥasan II *ʿalā dhikrihi 'l-salām*. Soon after his accession in 557/1162 to the central leadership of the Nizārī *daʿwa* and state, Ḥasan II dispatched Sinān to the Nizārī community in Syria, which henceforth became the centre of his activities.

Initially, Sinān spent some time at Kahf, a major Nizārī stronghold in the Djabal Bahrāʾ region of central Syria, making himself extremely popular locally as a schoolmaster. The death of Shaykh Abū Muḥammad, who had led the Syrian Nizārīs for some years, resulted in unprecedented succession disputes within the community, but soon Sinān was appointed by Alamūt as the chief Nizārī *dāʿī* in Syria, a post he held for some thirty years until his death.

Immediately upon his appointment, Sinān, who normally resided at the fortresses of Kahf, Maṣyāf or Ḳadmūs, began the task of reorganising the Nizārī *daʿwa* and community in Syria and also of fortifying the existing sectarian strongholds and acquiring new ones in the Djabal Bahrāʾ. He also paid special attention to establishing a corps of *fidāʾīs* (or *fidāwīs*), the self-sacrificing devotees who would undertake missions to remove prominent enemies of their sect. The absolute obedience of the *fidāʾīs* and their seemingly irrational behaviour, as well as the much exaggerated reports about their assassination attempts, gave rise to a number of imaginative legends, especially in the Crusaders' circles, regarding the strange practices of the sectarians (known to the mediaeval Europeans as the Assassins) and their awe-inspiring chief, Sinān, who now became famous in the occidental sources as the "Old Man of the Mountain"; or, "*le Vieux de la Montagne*" (see William of Tyre, *Willelmi Tyrensis Archiepiscopi Chronicon*, ed. R.B.C. Huygens, Turnholt 1986, ii, 953-4; L. Hellmuth, *Die Assassinenlegende in der österreichischen Geschichtsdichtung des Mittelalters*, Vienna 1988, 78-116).

When Ḥasan II proclaimed the *ḳiyāma* within the Persian Nizārī community in 559/1164, it fell upon Sinān to inaugurate the new dispensation in Syria. A while later, Sinān did ceremonially announce the spiritual Resurrection of the Syrian Nizārīs; and he taught his own version of the *ḳiyāma* doctrine, which evidently never acquired any deep roots in the community (see S. Guyard, *Fragments relatifs à la doctrine des Ismaélîs*, Paris 1874, text 17-9, 66-9, tr. 99-101, 204-9; Ibn Faḍl Allāh al-ʿUmarī, *Masālik al-abṣār fī mamālik al-amṣār*, ed. A.F. Sayyid, Cairo 1985, 77-8).

Sinān played a prominent part in the regional politics of his time, successfully resorting to diplomacy and other suitable policies in the interest of safeguarding the independence of the Syrian Nizārī community. To this end, he entered into an intricate and shifting web of alliances with the major neighbouring powers and rulers, especially the Crusaders, the Zangids and Ṣalāḥ al-Dīn.

When Sinān assumed the leadership of the Syrian Nizārīs, the ardently Sunnī Nūr al-Dīn [*q.v.*], who ruled over the Zangid dominions in Syria, was at the height of his power, posing a greater threat to Sinān than the Crusaders, who had been sporadically fighting the Nizārīs for several decades over the possession of various strongholds. The Nizārīs were also under pressure by the Hospitallers and Templars [see DĀWIYYA and ISBITĀRIYYA in Suppl.], who acted rather independently and often successfully demanded tribute. Hence, from early on Sinān aimed to establish peaceful relations with the Crusaders; and, in fact in 569/1173, he sent an embassy to king Amalric I, seeking a formal rapprochement with the Latin state of Jerusalem. On Nūr al-Dīn's death in 569/1174, Sinān came to be confronted by Ṣalāḥ al-Dīn, leader of the Muslim holy war against the Crusaders, who was then extending his own authority over Syria. Sinān now allied himself temporarily with the Zangids of Aleppo, equally threatened by Ṣalāḥ al-Dīn's rise, and he dispatched *fidāʾīs* to kill the latter on two occasions without success during 570-1/1174-6 (see B. Lewis, *Saladin and the Assassins*, in *BSOAS*, xv [1953], 239-45). In vengeance, Ṣalāḥ al-Dīn then laid siege to Maṣyāf. However, hostilities soon ceased permanently between Sinān and Ṣalāḥ al-Dīn, who had reached some sort of truce. Towards the end of Sinān's life, relations seem to have deteriorated once again between the Crusaders and the Syrian Nizārīs. According to Ibn al-Athīr (*anno* 588 A.H.) and other sources hostile to Ṣalāḥ al-Dīn, the murder of Conrad of Montferrat, the Frankish king of Jerusalem, in 588/1192 at the hands of *fidāʾīs*, had been instigated by Ṣalāḥ al-Dīn.

Sinān enjoyed an unprecedented popularity within the Syrian Nizārī community, which enabled him, alone amongst the Syrian Nizārī leaders, to act somewhat independently of Alamūt in managing the affairs of his community. There are, indeed, reports indicating that serious disagreements had developed between Sinān and Ḥasan II's successor at Alamūt, Nūr al-Dīn Muḥammad II (561-607/1166-1210 [*q.v.*]).

But there is no evidence suggesting that Sinān was ever acknowledged as an *imām* by the Syrian Nizārīs, who were sometimes called by the outsiders as the Sinānīs after his name (Ibn Khallikān, tr. de Slane, iii, 340). An outstanding organiser, strategist, and statesman, Rāshid al-Dīn Sinān led the Syrian Nizārīs to the peak of their power and laid solid foundations for the continued existence of the Nizārī community and *daʿwa* in Syria. He died in 589/1193, or, less probably, a year earlier.

Bibliography (in addition to the works cited in the article): 1. Sources: References to Rāshid al-Dīn Sinān may be found in most of the general Muslim histories and the regional chronicles of Syria dealing with his period, and in the occidental chronicles of the Third Crusade. However, the chief primary sources on Sinān's life and career are: (i) *Faṣl min al-lafẓ al-sharīf*; or *Manāḳib al-mawlā Rāshid al-Dīn*, ed. and tr. S. Guyard in his *Un grand maître des Assassins au temps de Saladin*, in *JA*, 7 série, ix (1877), 387-489; a new ed. of its Arabic text in M. Ghālib, *Sinān Rāshid al-Dīn*, Beirut 1967, 163-214, which is a Syrian Ismāʿīlī hagiographical work attributed to the Nizārī *dāʿī* Abū Firās Shihāb al-Dīn al-Maynaḳī (*flor.*, 10th/16th century); and (ii) Kamāl al-Dīn Ibn al-ʿAdīm's biography of Sinān in a still undiscovered volume of his *Bughyat al-ṭalab*, as preserved in later recensions, ed. and tr. B. Lewis in his *Kamāl al-Dīn's biography of Rāšid al-Dīn Sinān*, in *Arabica*, xiii (1966), 225-67; repr. in his *Studies in Classical and Ottoman Islam*, London 1976, no. X.

2. Studies: E.M. Quatremère, *Notice historique sur les Ismaëliens*, in *Fundgruben des Orients*, iv (1814), 353 ff.; C. Defrémery, *Nouvelles recherches sur les Ismaéliens ou Bathiniens de Syrie*, in *JA*, 5 série, v (1855), 5-32; W. Ivanow, art. *Rāshid al-Dīn Sinān*, in *EI*[1]; M.G.S. Hodgson, *The Order of Assassins*, The Hague 1955, 185-209; B. Lewis, *The Ismāʿīlīs and the Assassins*, in *A history of the Crusades*, ed. K.M. Setton, i, *The first hundred years*, ed. M.W. Baldwin, [2]Madison 1969, 120-7; idem, *The Assassins*, London 1967, 110-8; N.A. Mirza, *Rashid al-Din Sinan*, in *The great Ismaili heroes*, Karachi 1973, 72-80; I.K. Poonawala, *Biobibliography of Ismāʿīlī literature*, Malibu, Calif. 1977, 289-90; F. Daftary, *The Ismāʿīlīs: their history and doctrines*, Cambridge 1990, 332, 396-403, 689-91; idem, *The Assassin legends*, London 1994. (F. Daftary)

RASHĪD AL-DĪN ṬABĪB, Persian statesman and the greatest historian of the Īlkhānid period (*ca.* 645-718/*ca.* 1247-1318).

Rashīd al-Dīn Faḍl Allāh b. ʿImād al-Dawla, Abu 'l-Khayr, was born in Hamadān into a Jewish family with a professional medical tradition: his father was an apothecary. He himself was originally trained as a physician (hence he remained known as Ṭabīb), and in that capacity he entered the service of the Mongol court during the reign of the Īlkhān Abaḳa (r. 663-80/1265-82). He had converted from Judaism to Islam at around the age of 30. His Jewish religious background remained throughout Rashīd al-Dīn's career a potential embarrassment, and the demonstration of his Islamic orthodoxy and respectability may well have been his principal motive for writing a number of somewhat derivative works on Islamic theology (see J. van Ess, *Der Wesir und seine Gelehrten*, Wiesbaden 1981, and the comments in A.Z.V. Togan, *The composition of the History of the Mongols by Rashīd al-Dīn*, in *CAJ*, vii [1962], 60-72). It may be that he should be identified with the Rashīd al-Dawla who, according to Bar Hebraeus, was prominent in the household of the Īlkhān Gaykhatu (r. 690-4/1291-5) during the troubles caused by the introduction of paper currency, *ch'ao*, on the Chinese model (J.A. Boyle, introduction to Rashīd al-Dīn, *The successors of Genghis Khan*, New York and London 1971, 3).

Rashīd al-Dīn did not achieve high political office until 697/1298, during the reign of Ghazan, when after the fall of Ṣadr al-Dīn Zandjānī (to whom Rashīd al-Dīn had briefly acted as deputy) he was appointed associate *wazīr* to Ṣadr al-Dīn's successor, Saʿd al-Dīn Sāwadjī. He remained at the summit of state affairs for the rest of his life, though always with a colleague; he was never sole chief minister. He is usually credited with having been the principal architect of Ghazan's great programme of administrative reforms. His position, though always, like that of all Īlkhānid ministers, precarious, was one of great power and influence, and he accumulated vast wealth, such that he was able to construct quarters in both the capitals, Tabrīz and Sulṭāniyya. The *waḳf-nāma* for his quarter in Tabrīz, the Rabʿ-i Rashīdī, survives, in part in his own hand (facsimile ed. Tehran 1972, printed ed., Tehran 1977-8, both ed. Ī. Afshār and M. Mīnovī). His interests extended beyond history and administration including, as well as theology, agriculture and related subjects, on which he left a treatise, the *Āthār wa aḥyāʾ* (ed. M. Sutūda and Ī. Afshār, Tehran 1990). (A volume of letters attributed to him and known as the *Mukātabāt-i Rashīdī*, ed. M. Shafīʿ, Lahore 1945, or as *Sawāniḥ al-afkār-i Rashīdī*, ed. M.T. Dānishpazhūh, Tehran 1980-1, is now generally regarded as a spurious compilation, perhaps of the Tīmūrīd period.)

Rashīd al-Dīn's last colleague, during the reign of Öldjeytü (r. 703-16/1304-16), Tādj al-Dīn ʿAlī Shāh, was also a bitter rival. Relations between them eventually became so bad that administrative responsibility had to be divided, with Rashīd al-Dīn taking the centre and south of the empire, and Tādj al-Dīn the north-west, Mesopotamia and Anatolia. During the reign of Öldjeytü's son and successor, Abū Saʿīd, Tādj al-Dīn's intrigues were ultimately successful in bringing about Rashīd al-Dīn's overthrow. He was charged with having poisoned Öldjeytü, and together with his son Ibrāhīm was executed in 718/1318. His property was confiscated and the Rabʿ-i Rashīdī looted; but later in the reign, his son Ghiyāth al-Dīn followed his father in the office of *wazīr*.

Rashīd al-Dīn's enduring fame rests more on his work as a historian than on his career as a prominent official. His *Djāmiʿ al-tawārīkh* is undoubtedly the most important single historical source for the Mongol Empire as a whole, not merely of the realm of the Īlkhāns. The work was commissioned by Ghazan, who seems to have feared that the Mongols, as they settled down as Muslims in Persia, might be in some danger, ultimately, of forgetting who they were and where they had come from. It initially contained an account of the history of the Mongols and their steppe predecessors. This part, which became known as the *Taʾrīkh-i Ghāzānī*, was presented to Öldjeytü after the death of his brother and predecessor. Öldjeytü asked Rashīd al-Dīn, as a memorial to Ghazan, to continue the work so as to provide a history of all the peoples with whom the Mongols had come into contact. It is this part of the history that justified Boyle's description of Rashīd al-Dīn as "the first world-historian". The history, when completed (there appears to have been an earlier, shorter version), consisted of the following parts: (1) The Mongol and Turkish tribes; the Mongols, from Činggis Khān to the death of Ghazan; (2) A history of Öldjeytü (of which no copy is known, though Togan claimed to have seen one in

Mashhad in 1923), followed by the "universal history": Adam and the Patriarchs, the pre-Islamic kings of Persia, Muḥammad and the caliphs, the dynasties of Persia in the Islamic period, the Oghuz and the Turks, China, the Jews, the Franks, and India; (3) The *Shuʿab-i pandjgāna* [the "Five genealogies" of the Arabs, Jews, Mongols, Franks and Chinese: unpublished but surviving as Topkapı Sarayı ms. 2932]; (4) The *Ṣuwar al-aḳālīm*, a geographical compendium of which no copy has yet come to light. These sections are very uneven in length: the first is by far the largest. In 1908 E.G. Browne produced a scheme for publication of the whole, organised more manageably (*Suggestions for a complete edition of the Jami 'ut-Tawarikh of Rashidu'd-Din Fadlu'llah*, in *JRAS* [1908], 17-37). Much, though not all, of this has since been accomplished (for details of the more important editions and translations of the various sections of part 1, see the *Bibl.* to MONGOLS).

Study of the *Djāmiʿ al-tawārīkh* is not without its problems. Even the authorship of the book has been questioned. Togan (*art. cit.*) contended, not very persuasively, that it was a translation from a Mongol original. The author of the most important surviving contemporary source for the reign of Öldjeytü, Abu 'l-Ḳāsim Ḳāshānī, maintained that he was himself the true author of the work, for which Rashīd al-Dīn had stolen not only the credit but also the very considerable financial rewards (Ḳāshānī, *Taʾrīkh-i Ūldjāytū*, ed. M. Hambly, Tehran 1969, 240). It is not easy to judge what justification there may have been for this claim. Rashīd al-Dīn was of course a busy government minister, whose available time for scholarship must have been limited; he tells us that he wrote his history between morning prayer and sunrise. It may well have been that he was obliged to use one or more research assistants to deal with the collection of material and perhaps the initial writing up, and that Ḳāshānī was among these; this was Barthold's hypothesis (*Turkestan*, 47).

The various parts of the *Djāmiʿ al-tawārīkh* differ greatly in their value to the historian. Not all of them can be regarded as primary. Much of Rashīd al-Dīn's material on the period after the death of Činggis Khān, for example, is lifted straight from his predecessor Djuwaynī [*q.v.*], and has limited independent significance. The "universal history" sections are of undeniable historiographical interest because they are evidence of so unprecedented an intellectual endeavour; but no one would go to them to find out what happened in China, India or Europe. On the other hand, Rashīd al-Dīn's account of the life and career of Činggis Khān is of the first importance, even though he was writing a century after the events. This is because his material is derived from a now lost Mongolian chronicle, the *Altan debter*, whose contents appear to have been conveyed to him by Bolad Chingsang, the representative in Persia of the Great Khān in China. So far as can be judged by comparison with Chinese use of the same chronicle, the Persian version accurately preserves what was in the original (see P. Pelliot and L. Hambis (ed. and tr.), *Histoire des campagnes de Gengis Khan*, i, Leiden 1951).

For the historian, by far the most important section is Rashīd al-Dīn's history of the Īlkhāns, the period of which he was a contemporary, and for much of which he held high office and was, presumably, well placed to gather full and accurate information. There can be no doubt that Rashīd al-Dīn's position at the centre of affairs makes his history of those affairs uniquely authoritative. Yet this creates its own problems: not, perhaps those of accuracy as such, but of perspective and partisanship (see D.O. Morgan, *The problems of writing Mongolian history*, in S. Akiner (ed.), *Mongolia today*, London 1991, 1-8). Rashīd al-Dīn, inevitably had a point of view and a set of assumptions: those of a Persian bureaucrat, which were by no means necessarily identical with those of his Mongol masters who are rarely represented directly in our sources. We almost always see the Mongols through the eyes of others.

Equally, as both chief minister and, in effect, "official" historian to Ghazan and Öldjeytü, Rashīd al-Dīn had an interest in painting the troubles of the pre-Ghazan era in colours as black as possible and in depicting Ghazan's reforms as a total success. This should be treated with a degree of scepticism. The *Taʾrīkh-i Ghāzānī* provides us with the full texts of the reforming edicts (*yarlīghs*), which are vivid, convincing and full of detail. There may be less reason, however, for supposing that the edicts were in fact universally implemented. Rashīd al-Dīn was a remarkable historian of great importance; but it should not be supposed that he was an impartial one.

Bibliography: Given in the article. See also Browne, *LHP*, iii; Spuler, *Mongolen*⁴, Leiden 1985; *CAJ*, xiv (1970), an issue which contains numerous valuable articles on aspects of Rashīd al-Dīn's life and work, e.g. Ī. Afshār, *The autograph copy of Rashīd al-Dīn's Vaqfnāmeh*, 5-13, J.A. Boyle, *Rashīd al-Dīn and the Franks*, 62-7, K. Jahn, *Rashīd al-Dīn and Chinese culture*, 134-47, I.P. Petrushevsky, *Rashīd al-Dīn's conception of the state*, 148-62.

(D.O. MORGAN)

RASHĪD AL-DĪN Muḥammad b. Muḥammad b. ʿAbd al-Djalīl al-ʿUmarī, known as **WAṬWĀṬ**, secretary and prolific author in Arabic and Persian. A reputed descendant of the caliph ʿUmar, he was born either in Balkh or Bukhārā, but spent most of his life in Gurgāndj, the capital of Khʷārazm. He died, according to Dawlatshāh, in 578/1182-3, in his 97th year, which would put his birth in 481/1088-9; Yāḳūt (at least in the published text) has him die 5 years earlier.

Rashīd al-Dīn was chief secretary (*ṣāḥib dīwān al-inshāʾ*) under the Khʷārazmshāh Atsïz (521-51/1127-56) and his successor Īl-Arslān (d. 568/1172). His loyalty to Atsïz earned him the enmity of the Saldjūḳ Sandjar who, according to Djuwaynī, resolved at one point to cut Rashīd al-Dīn into 30 pieces, but was dissuaded from doing so by his own chief secretary, Muntadjab al-Dīn al-Djuwaynī, the uncle of our informant's great-grandfather. We possess a considerable number of Rashīd al-Dīn's highly ornate letters, including those which he wrote on behalf of his two masters (in Arabic to the caliphs and their entourage, in Persian to Sandjar and others) and also his private letters in both languages. Two bilingual collections of epistles were compiled by Rashīd al-Dīn himself, *Abkār al-afkār fī 'l-rasāʾil wa 'l-ashʿār* and *ʿArāʾis al-khawāṭir wa nafāʾis al-nawādir*, and others are preserved elsewhere. The Persian letters found in the two collections were edited by Ḳ. Tūysirkānī (Tehran 1338 *Sh.*/1960), and a large number of Arabic letters were published (from an unidentified source) by Muḥammad Fahmī under the title *Madjmūʿat rasāʾil Rashīd al-Dīn al-Waṭwāṭ*, 2 parts, Cairo 1315/1897-8. Ten of the latter are translated in H. Horst, *Arabische Briefe der Ḫōrazmšāhs an den Kalifenhof aus der Feder des Rašīd ad-Dīn Waṭwāṭ*; in *ZDMG*, cxvi (1966) 24-43, and the same author has summarised many of the Persian letters in his *Die Staatsverwaltung der Großselǧūqen und Ḫōrazmšāhs*, Wiesbaden 1964.

Rashīd al-Dīn's Persian *dīwān* contains more than

,500 verses in S. Nafīsī's edition (Tehran 1339 *h*./1960) and consists largely of poems eulogising Atsïz. Modern Persian critics have in general not had high estimate of their merits. But the best known of his works is *Maṭlūb kull ṭālib min kalām amīr al-muʾminīn ʿAlī b. Abī Ṭālib*, or *Tardjama-yi ṣad kalima*, consisting of the 100 Arabic sayings of ʿAlī said to have been collected by al-Djāḥiẓ [*q.v.*]; each apothegm is followed by a verbose Arabic paraphrase, then a Persian commentary and finally a poetic paraphrase in the form of a mostly rather pedestrian Persian *dubaytī*. It has frequently been printed in the East—though in many of the editions (and mss.) one or both of the prose commentaries are omitted—also with a Latin translation by Stickel (Jena 1834), with a German version by Fleischer (Leipzig 1837) and with an English verse rendering (but without the prose versions) by Harley (Calcutta 1927). Rashīd al-Dīn subsequently gave the same treatment to 100 sayings of each of the three first caliphs, with his works entitled *Tuḥfat al-ṣadīḳ ilā 'l-ṣadīḳ min kalām amīr al-muʾminīn Abī Bakr al-Ṣiddīḳ*, *Faḍl al-khiṭāb min kalām amīr al-muʾminīn ʿUmar b. al-Khaṭṭāb* and *Uns al-lahfān min kalām imām al-muʾminīn ʿUthmān b. ʿAffān*; these remain unpublished, though mss. are available. Another work of comparable nature, *Laṭāʾif al-amthāl wa ṭarāʾif al-aḳwāl*, is a collection of several hundred Arabic proverbs, each with a Persian prose translation and often extensive commentary. It was published by S.M.B. Sabzwārī (n.p. 1358 *Sh*./1979) on the basis of an old ms. found in Medīna. Further paraenetic works survive in manuscript.

His much-admired handbook of rhetorical figures, *Ḥadāʾiḳ al-siḥr fī daḳāʾiḳ al-shiʿr*, is available in a richly annotated edition by ʿAbbās Iḳbāl (Tehran 1308 *Sh*./1929-30; reprinted, but without the editor's introduction and endnotes, in the appendix to Nafīsī's edition of the *dīwān*, and again, with a Russian translation by N.Yu. Čalisova, Moscow 1985). It is strongly dependent both on al-Marghīnānī's *al-Maḥāsin fī 'l-naẓm wa 'l-nathr*, from which many of the Arabic prose and verse quotations are derived, as well as on Rādūyānī's *Tardjumān al-balāgha*, whence Rashīd al-Dīn has virtually all of the illustrative quotations from early Persian poets (see the editions of the two books by Van Gelder and Ateş respectively), but he added a good number of citations from Persian poets of the 6th/12th century as well as from his own poems in both languages. He has also been credited with a Persian dictionary (*Ḥamd wa thanā*, or *Nuḳūd al-zawāhir wa ʿuḳūd al-djawāhir*, extant in both prose and verse versions) and a short treatise on metre (*Risāla-yi ʿarūḍ*), but the question of their authenticity requires closer scrutiny.

Bibliography: ʿAlī b. Zayd al-Bayhaḳī, *Tatimmat Ṣiwān al-ḥikma*, ed. M. Shafīʿ, Lahore 1935, 166-8 of the Arabic section; Muḥammad b. Muḥammad al-Kātib al-Iṣfahānī, *Kharīdat al-ḳaṣr* (the relevant entry was published by M. Shafīʿ in *Oriental College Magazine* [1934-5], at the end of fascicules xi/1, xi/2, xi/3, xii/4, separate pagination); Yāḳūt, *Udabāʾ*, vii, 91-5; ʿAwfī, *Lubāb* i, 80-6; Djuwaynī ii, 6-14, 18; Zakariyyāʾ b. Muḥammad al-Ḳazwīnī, *Āthār al-bilād*, ed. Wüstenfeld, Göttingen 1848, 223-5; Dawlatshāh, 87-92; Browne, *LHP*, ii, 330-3; Brockelmann, I 275-6, S I 486; A. Ateş, *Raşīd al-Dīn Vaṭvāṭ'ın eserlerinin bazı yazma nüshaları*, in *Tarih Dergisi*, x (1959) 1-24; Storey, iii/1, 85-7, 176-8. See also the editors' introductions to Rashīd al-Dīn's various works (listed in the article).

(F.C. de Blois)

RASHĪD ʿALĪ AL-GAYLĀNĪ (al-Djīlānī), Prime Minister of ʿIrāḳ on four occasions in the 1930s and 1940s and for long a symbol of ʿIrāḳī resistance to British interests. He was a descendant of the famous religious leader ʿAbd al-Ḳādir al-Djīlānī [*q.v.*] and a member of a cadet branch of the family which held the office of *naḳīb al-ashrāf* [*q.v.*] in Baghdād several times in the 19th and 20th centuries (b. Baghdād 1892, d. Beirut 1965).

Rashīd ʿAlī qualified as a lawyer and became an appeal court judge in 1921; in 1924 he became Minister of Justice in the cabinet of Yāsīn al-Hāshimī, perhaps his most intimate political colleague. Together with other opponents of Nūrī al-Saʿīd [*q.v.*], he and Yāsīn were co-founders of the Party of National Brotherhood (*Ḥizb al-Ikhāʾ al-Waṭanī*) formed to spearhead opposition to the Anglo-Iraqi Treaty of 1930. However, after the treaty had come into effect and ʿIrāḳ had become at least theoretically independent of Britian, both men came to adopt a more pragmatic approach. Rashīd ʿAlī accepted his first premiership on 20 March 1933 and held office until the end of October of the same year. After this he remained out of power until March 1935, but he and Yāsīn spent much of the intervening period attempting to incite the Middle Euphrates tribes to rise against the governments of their rivals ʿAlī Djawdat and Djamīl Midfaʿī. Their efforts succeeded to the extent that tribal demonstrations in Baghdād prevented Djawdat and Midfaʿī from forming cabinets, and in March 1935 Yāsīn became Premier, with Rashīd ʿAlī as Minister of Interior, in a government which lasted until Bakr Ṣidḳī's coup d'état in October 1936.

By the latter part of the 1930s, especially after the Palestine rebellion and the failure of the Franco-Syrian independence negotiations, Britain and France had become widely unpopular in the Arab Middle East. At the same time, the governments of Italy and Germany were held up by Arab nationalists as exemplars of states whose strength lay in their national unity. Pan-Arab nationalism had little following in ʿIrāḳ outside the officer corps, but the weakness of the central institutions of the state after the death of King Fayṣal, the existence of widely shared aspirations for genuine independence from Britain, the arrival of al-Ḥādjdj Amīn al-Ḥusaynī, Muftī of Jerusalem [*q.v.* in Suppl.] in Baghdād in October 1939, and the fact that a clique of four powerful nationalist officers, the so-called "colonels of the Golden Square" had come to exercise a pivotal influence on ʿIrāḳī politics, combined to heighten anti-British feeling, and also to create a climate of opinion in ʿIrāḳ which was either neutral or benevolent towards the Axis powers at the beginning of the Second World War.

Rashīd ʿAlī became the chief political ally of the nationalist colonels of the Golden Square, and became Prime Minister for the third time in March 1940, after the fall of Nūrī al-Saʿīd's fifth ministry. Nūrī, who stayed on under Rashīd ʿAlī as Minister of Foreign Affairs, was unpopular because of his staunchly pro-British past, but he thought that a government headed by Rashīd ʿAlī, who had been famous for his opposition to the Anglo-Iraqi Treaty, would be both less compromised because of the latter's anti-British record and better able to resist the more extreme demands of the Golden Square. However, after the fall of France in June 1940, and under the combined influence of the Golden Square, the Muftī and prominent Syrian politicians in exile in Baghdād, Rashīd ʿAlī gradually adopted a more openly anti-British and pro-Axis stance.

Under the terms of the Anglo-Iraqi Treaty of 1930, the ʿIrāḳī government was obliged to allow the transit of British troops across its territory in wartime. Britain requested this facility in June 1940, and permission was eventually if somewhat grudgingly given in mid-July. However, in spite of requests from Britain, the ᶜIrāḳī government refused to break off relations with Italy when Italy declared war on Britain in June 1940, and the Italian legation developed into a centre of anti-British intrigue. In addition, the ᶜIrāḳī government now began to approach the legations of Italy and Japan for arms supplies, and in August 1940 Rashīd ᶜAlī and the Muftī entered into direct if somewhat fruitless negotiations with Berlin (for details, see Majid Khadduri, *Independent Iraq 1932-1958: a study in Iraqi politics*², London 1960, 181-2, 378-80, and U.S. Department of State, *Documents on German foreign policy 1918-1945*, Series D, vol. x, 141-4, 154-5, 275, 415-16, 558-60).

Matters came to a head, when Rashīd ᶜAlī, who now had the support of most of the armed forces, refused to yield to British pressure to resign in November 1940 in the face of his unwillingness to allow British troops to land in or pass through ᶜIrāḳ. He was forced to step down temporarily as Prime Minister in January 1941 but returned to power on 12 April; by this time the Regent, Nūrī and other pro-British politicians had fled to Transjordan.

On 17 and 18 April 1941 British troops landed at Baṣra; there was no doubt that Rashīd ᶜAlī and his government enjoyed widespread support (cf. Khadduri, *op. cit.*, 214; Hanna Batatu, *The old social classes and the revolutionary movements of Iraq; a study of Iraq's old landed classes and its Communists, Ba'thists and Free Officers*, Princeton 1978, 453-62), but, given the balance of forces involved, the defeat of the ᶜIrāḳī army in May 1941 was a foregone conclusion. The German assistance which Rashīd ᶜAlī had requested never materialised, and he was obliged to flee first to Iran, and then to Germany, where he arrived in November 1941.

Rashīd ᶜAlī stayed in Germany until May 1945, and then found his way to Saᶜūdī Arabia, where he remained until 1954. He returned to ᶜIrāḳ a few weeks after the overthrow of the monarchy in July 1958, apparently hoping that his previous services would be duly acclaimed. When adequate recognition was not forthcoming he set about planning the sort of coup that he had engineered successfully in the mid-1930s, inciting rebellion among the tribes of the Middle Euphrates in a quixotic attempt to unseat the government of ᶜAbd al-Karīm Ḳāsim [*q.v.*]. He was arrested in December 1958, tried and condemned to death, but the sentence was commuted by Ḳāsim, and he was eventually released from prison in October 1961. He died in Beirut on 30 August 1965.

Bibliography: Given in the article.

(P. SLUGLETT)

RASHĪD RIḌĀ, whose full name was Muḥammad Rashīd b. ᶜAlī Riḍā b. Muḥammad Shams al-Dīn b. Muḥammad Bahāᵓ al-Dīn b. Munlā (i.e. Mullā) ᶜAlī Khalīfa (1865-1935), one of the most productive and influential authors of Islamic reform [see IṢLĀḤ], of Pan-Islamism [*q.v.*] and also, to a certain extent, of Arab nationalism [see ḲAWMIYYA]. His name is connected with the journal *al-Manār* [*q.v.*] in the first place, whose editor he was from its foundation in 1898 till his death.

Rashīd Riḍā was born on 27 Djumādā I 1282/23 September 1865 in Ḳalamūn, a village near Tripoli (Ṭarābulus al-Shām [*q.v.*]) on the Mediterranean coast in northern Lebanon (for his day of birth, see Sharabāṣī, 102). The inhabitants of Ḳalamūn were exclusively Sunnī Muslims and the great majority of them claimed descent from the Prophet (for the allegedly Ḥusaynid pedigree of Rashīd Riḍā's famil see Shakīb Arslān, 809-11, and Sharabāṣī, 103-7).

Rashīd Riḍā received his first education in the *ku tāb* [*q.v.*] of Ḳalamūn, and after that in an Ottoma state school in Tripoli and, above all, in the *madra waṭaniyya*, founded there in 1879. The director of th school was Shaykh Ḥusayn al-Djisr (1845-1909). was from this scholar that Rashīd Riḍā received th incentives that were essential for his intellectu development, such as, for instance, those regardin the modernistic interpretation of scientif achievements. Later, he also had heated differences opinion with al-Djisr (see Sharabāṣī, 231-46; Eber index, 188; for other teachers of Rashīd Riḍā i Lebanon, see Sharabāṣī, 246 ff.).

In the winter of 1897-8, Rashīd Riḍā travelled t Egypt. Already the day after his arrival in Cairo h went to see Muḥammad ᶜAbduh [*q.v.*] in order to ex pound to him his aim of publishing a journal dealin with Islamic reform. The first issue of this journal, *a Manār*, appeared on 22 Shawwāl 1315/mid-Marc 1898.

The house which Rashīd Riḍā acquired at Cairc after some time, served as private residence, printin establishment, bookshop and bookstore (Sharabāṣ 137). Notwithstanding the success of many of hi publications and the occasional gifts of friends an patrons, he apparently was seldom free from financia worries (Sharabāṣī, 166-9, based, among othe sources, on letters of Rashīd Riḍā to Shakīb Arslān)

Some information on his being married three time (the first two marriages broke down after a short time and on his children can be found in Sharabāṣ 216-27.

After the Ottoman constitution had been re instated in 1908, Rashīd Riḍā visited *Bilād al-Shām* On this journey, as well as on later journeys to Istan bul (1909-10), to India (1912; on his way back h visited Masḳaṭ and Kuwayt), to the Ḥidjāz (1916 an again in 1926), to Syria (1919-20), to Europe (1921-2 and to the Pan-Islamic Congress in Jerusalem (1931) he each time reported in *al-Manār* (partly reprinted i Yūsuf Ibish (ed.), *Riḥalāt*; see also Sharabāṣī, 145-61)

For Rashīd Riḍā, all these journeys were connecte with specific political aspirations, but he was no seldom disappointed in his immediate expectations For instance, during the journey to Syria in 1908, ar incident in the Umayyad mosque in Damascus and subsequent riot made it clear to him that he had t reckon there with considerable opposition, and that h could not rely unconditionally on support from th Young Turks (Ibish, 29-40; cf. Arslān, 147-8 anc Commins, nn. 129-31). His stay in Istanbul (Octobe 1909-October 1910) was aimed at removing misunderstandings in the relationship between Arabs and Turks. Rashīd Riḍā also wanted to establish ir Istanbul a modern Islamic institution of higher education, whose graduates —much better scholars than the ᶜ*ulamā*ᵓ educated in the traditional way—would be able to defend Islam according to modernis standards.

After some initial successes, Rashīd Riḍā came tc the conclusion that both aims could not be attained —in any case not according to his own conceptions— mainly because of the opposition of influentia members of the *Ittiḥād we Teraḳḳī Djemᶜiyyeti* [*q.v.*], the ruling Committee of Union and Progress (Tauber, 104-6; al-Shawābika, 193 ff.). Disappointed, he returned to Egypt and immediately started preparations for establishing an association that should serve as the basis for the planned institution of higher education. The latter was indeed founded in 1911, under the name of *Dār al-Daʿwa wa ʾl-Irshād*. Regular instruction began in March 1912, but had to be discontinued soon after the outbreak of the First World War for want of financial donations (Tauber, 106; for the curriculum, see *RMM*, xviii [1912], 224-7).

As a result of his disappointment with the Young Turks, Rashīd Riḍā began to develop political plans on the lines of Pan-Arabism [*q.v.*]. Already in 1902-3 *al-Manār* had printed in instalments the work of ʿAbd al-Raḥmān al-Kawākibī [*q.v.*], *Umm al-ḳurā* (see for this and for the further political context, Kramer, esp. 30-5). Now, from 1911-2 onwards, Rashīd Riḍā adhered to the public agitation against the Young Turks and at the same time founded a secret political association with Pan-Arabic aims, the *Djamʿiyyat al-Djāmiʿa al-ʿArabiyya*. Its purpose was, on the one hand, to reconcile the rulers of the Arabian Peninsula with one another, and on the other, to put the Arabic secret associations in touch with one another (Tauber, 106-11). These activities led Rashīd Riḍā to establish relations with most of the rulers of the Arabian Peninsula, such as Ibn Suʿūd and the Sharīf of Mecca, but they also burdened for years to come, especially during the First World War, his contacts with those of his friends who, like Shakīb Arslān, associated themselves, notwithstanding many reservations, with the Ottoman Empire (Arslān, 152-6).

During the First World War, Rashīd Riḍā supported the "Arab Revolt" in the Ḥidjāz and even after the War's end he belonged for some time to the propagandists of its aims. During his journey to Syria in 1919-20 he was elected president of the "Syrian Congress", but he returned to Egypt after the French mandatary troops had marched into Syria.

In the following years, his relations with the King of the Ḥidjāz, Ḥusayn b. ʿAlī, and with the Hashimite dynasty in general, deteriorated. After the Wahhābī Āl Suʿūd had taken over power in the Ḥidjāz, and the Hāshimites had been expelled (1924-6), Rashīd Riḍā came to belong to those authors who tried, on historico-political grounds, to justify this development (see Boberg, esp. 290-314).

The most important proof of this attitude is his work *al-Wahhābiyyūn wa ʾl-Ḥidjāz* (Cairo 1925-6), a collection of articles which had appeared in *al-Manār* and in the daily newspaper *al-Ahrām* (see also Kawtharānī, 191-238, 290-318). Until his death in 1935 he repeatedly explained how and why his judgement of the Wahhābiyya had changed: in his youth, under the influence of Ottoman propaganda, he had regarded the Wahhābīs as fanatical sectarians; after his arrival in Egypt, however, through reading the chronicle of al-Djabartī [*q.v.*] and works of other authors and through direct information, he had understood that it was the Wahhābīs, not their opponents, who defended true Islam, even if they were inclined to certain exaggerations. Parallel to this, Rashīd Riḍā aimed at the rehabilitation of authors like Ibn Taymiyya [*q.v.*] and of his school (see Laoust, *Essai*, 557-75, and idem, *Le réformisme*, esp. 181-2; cf. Rashīd Riḍā's preface to Muḥammad Bashīr al-Sahsuwānī, *Ṣiyānat al-insān ʿan waswasat al-Shaykh Daḥlān*, 3rd ed., Cairo 1958-9, 8-9).

This change of views, for which he also referred to remarks made in private by his mentor Muḥammad ʿAbduh, necessarily led to a deterioration of his relations with the Shīʿīs and of his judgement on the rôle of the Shīʿa in Islamic history. Already earlier, separate articles in *al-Manār* had provoked protests by Shīʿī scholars (see, for example, Sayyid Muḥsin al-Amīn al-ʿĀmilī, *al-Ḥuṣun al-maniʿa fī radd ma awradahu ṣāḥib al-Manār fī ḥaḳḳ al-Shīʿa*, Damascus 1910, new impr. Beirut 1985). In opposition to these protests, however, there existed numerous statements of Rashīd Riḍā and other authors of *al-Manār* in favour of Pan-Islamic unity and of interconfessional overtures. After his overt endorsement of the Wahhābiyya, Rashīd Riḍā became the chosen target of Shīʿī polemics, as for instance in the work of the above-mentioned Sayyid Muḥsin al-Amīn al-ʿĀmilī, *Kashf al-irtiyāb fī atbāʿ Muḥammad b. ʿAbd al-Wahhāb*, Damascus 1927-8, re-impr. Tehran *ca.* 1973. Rashīd Riḍā's objections against these polemics are resumed in his *al-Sunna wa ʾl-Shīʿa aw al-Wahhābiyya wa ʾl-Rāfiḍa*, i, Cairo 1929-30, ii, 2nd ed. 1947.

Already at an early stage, Rashīd Riḍā, who in his younger years had been for a while a *murīd* of the Naḳshbandī order, criticised ideas and practices which appeared to him as false and harmful Ṣūfism. His increasingly critical statements on the rôle of the Ṣūfī orders, especially of those of his own day, which later also brought him in conflict with leading scholars of al-Azhar, are not, however, to be understood as a radical refusal of all forms of Ṣūfism (Hourani, *Rashīd Riḍā and the Sufi orders*).

In the internal Islamic debates on the past and the future of the caliphate [see KHILĀFA, KHILĀFAT MOVEMENT], Rashīd Riḍā, after the First World War, opted more and more for a renewed, Arabic caliphate. His work *al-Khilāfa aw al-imāma al-ʿuẓmā* (Cairo 1923) is an answer to the fact that the Great Turkish National Assembly had abolished the sultanate on 1 November 1922, i.e. had stripped the caliphate of all secular authority (for the contents of this work, see H. Laoust's annotated translation, *Le califat*, and M. Kerr, 151-86). Rashīd Riḍā took a lively part in the further discussions on the caliphate, in the preparations of several Pan-Islamic congresses [see MUʾTAMAR] as well as in their sessions (see Kramer, index, 248; Shawābika, 337-54).

Many aspects of his political activities, such as his attitude towards the British occupation forces in Egypt, require further investigation (Shawābika, 264-75; Tauber, 105, 110).

The extraordinary influence exercised by Rashīd Riḍā in many parts of the Islamic world as the spokesman of the *Salafiyya* [*q.v.*], as well as the development of his views in a great number of individual questions concerning theology and the *Sharīʿa*, cannot be dealt with here. For this, see the articles IṢLĀḤ, AL-MANĀR, and the literature given in the *Bibliography*, in particular the works of Adams, Jomier, Kerr, Marrākushī and Sāmarrāʾī.

Bibliography: Numerous publications of Rashīd Riḍā consist of series of articles published first in *al-Manār* and later brought together in book form. A useful (even if not faultless) survey is given by Yūsuf Asʿad Dāghir, *Maṣādir al-dirāsa al-adabiyya*, ii/1, Beirut 1956, 396-401; see also Brockelmann, S III, 321-4; Khayr al-Dīn al-Ziriklī, *al-Aʿlām*, 3rd ed. Beirut 1969, vi, 361-2; ʿUmar Riḍā Kaḥḥāla, *Muʿdjam al-muʾallifīn*, Damascus 1960, ix, 310-2, and *Mustadrak*, Beirut 1985, 639.

Since 1970, certain texts from *al-Manār* have been selected thematically and reprinted in bookform. See especially: 1. Ṣalāḥ al-Dīn al-Munadjdjid and Yūsuf Ḳ. Khūrī (eds.), *Fatāwā ʾl-Imām Muḥammad Rashīd Riḍā*, 6 vols., Beirut 1970; 2. Yūsuf Ibish, *Riḥalāt al-Imām Rashīd Riḍā*, Beirut 1971; 3. Wadjīh al-Kawtharānī, *Mukhtārāt siyāsiyya min madjallat al-Manār*, Beirut 1980. A general survey of the contents of the individual volumes of *al-Manār* is found in Anwar al-Djundī, *Taʾrīkh al-ṣiḥāfa al-*

islāmiyya. i. al-Manār, Cairo 1983. A *mukhtaṣar* of his *Tafsīr*, already begun by Rashīd Riḍā, was completed and published by Muḥammad Aḥmad Kanʿān and Zuhayr al-Shāwīsh as *Mukhtaṣar tafsīr al-Manār*, 3 vols., Beirut-Damascus 1984.

From the extensive secondary literature in Arabic, there may be mentioned Shakīb Arslān, *al-Sayyid Rashīd Riḍā aw ikhāʾ arbaʿīn sana*, Damascus 1937; Ibrāhīm Aḥmad al-ʿAdawī, *Rashīd Riḍā, al-imām al-mudjāhid*, Cairo n.d. [*ca.* 1965]; Aḥmad al-Sharabāṣī, *Rashīd Riḍā, ṣāḥib al-Manār*, Cairo 1970; Ḥasīb al-Sāmarrāʾī, *Rashīd Riḍā al-mufassir*, Baghdād 1977; Muḥammad Ṣāliḥ al-Marrākushī, *Tafkīr Muḥammad Rashīd Riḍā min khilāl madjallat al-Manār*, Tunis-Algiers 1985; Muḥammad Aḥmad Durnayḳa, *al-Sayyid Rashīd Riḍā, iṣlāḥātuhu al-idjtimāʿ-iyya wa 'l-dīniyya,* Tripoli-Beirut, 1986; Aḥmad Fahd Barakāt al-Shawābika, *Muḥammad Rashīd Riḍā wa dawruhu fi 'l-ḥayāt al-fikriyya wa 'l-siyāsiyya*, ʿAmmān 1989.

In Western languages: C.C. Adams, *Islam and modernism in Egypt*, New York 1933; H. Laoust, *Le réformisme orthodoxe des "salafiyya"*, in *REI*, vi (1932), 175-224; idem, *Le califat dans la doctrine de Rashīd Riḍā*, Beirut 1938; idem, *Essai sur les doctrines sociales et politiques de Taḳī-d-Dīn Aḥmad b. Taimīya*, Cairo 1939, 557-75; J. Jomier, *Le commentaire coranique du Manâr*, Paris 1954; A. Hourani, *Arabic thought in the Liberal Age*, London 1962, 222-44; idem, *Rashīd Riḍā and the Sufi orders: a footnote to Laoust*, in *BEO*, xxix (1977), 231-41; M. Kerr, *Islamic reform. The political and legal theories of Muḥammad ʿAbduh and Rashīd Riḍā*, Berkeley, etc. 1962; R. Wielandt, *Offenbarung und Geschichte im Denken moderner Muslime*, Wiesbaden 1971, 73-94; A. Busool, *Shaykh Muḥammad Rashīd Riḍā's relations with Djamāl al-Dīn al-Afghānī and Muḥammad ʿAbduh,* in *MW*, lxvi (1976), 272-86; M. Kramer, *Islam assembled,* New York 1986; E. Tauber, *Rashīd Riḍā as Pan-Arabist before World War I*, in *MW*, lxxix (1989), 102-12; E.E. Shahīn, *Muḥammad Rashīd Riḍā's perspectives on the West as reflected in al-Manār*, in *ibid.*, 113-32; D.D. Commins, *Islamic reform. Politics and social change in late Ottoman Syria*, New York-Oxford 1990; D. Boberg, *Ägypten, Nadjd und der Ḥidjāz*, Berne 1991; J. Ebert, *Religion und Reform in der arabischen Provinz. Ḥusayn al-Djisr*, Frankfurt a.M. 1991.

(W. Ende)

RASHĪD YĀSIMĪ, modern Persian poet and scholar, born on 4 December 1896 at Kirmānshāh and died in 1951. His real name was Ghulām Riḍā, but he is popularly known as Rashīd Yāsimī in literary and intellectual circles. He came from a cultured and well-educated family, which counted as one of its respected members the author of the novel *Shams u ṭughrā*, namely Muḥammad Bāḳir Mīrzā Khusrawī (1849-1950), who was his maternal uncle. After completing his early education in his native town, Rashīd Yāsimī proceeded to Tehran in 1333/1914-15 and joined the Saint Louis High School, from where he graduated with proficiency in French language and literature. Simultaneously, he devoted his attention to the pursuit of Persian studies as well as to the study of Arabic, Pahlavi and English. Having finished his education, he served for some time as principal of a local high school in Kirmānshāh. But soon afterwards he returned to Tehran, where he joined Malik al-Shuʿarāʾ Bahār (d. 1951 [see BAHĀR]) in founding the journal *Dānishkada*, which began to appear in 1918 as the organ of the literary association bearing the same name. Among his contributions to this journal were a series of articles which he published under the title *Inḳilāb-i adabī* describing the history of changes in French literature from the 18th to the 20th century. Translated for the most part from French sources, these articles were of special value to Persian readers in so far as they contained useful information about French writers and their works. His early writings also appeared in such journals as *Dunyā-yi imrūz*, *Shark*, *Naw bahār* and *Armān*.

Rashīd Yāsimī held a number of government jobs before he was appointed in 1933 to the chair of Islamic history in the Faculty of Letters, Tehran University and the Advanced College for Teachers. Subsequently, he was also made a member of the Iranian Academy. In 1944 he travelled to India as part of a cultural delegation representing the Iranian government. He died in early May 1951 after a prolonged illness.

Rashīd Yāsimī was the author of numerous books covering a variety of subjects. These included biographical accounts of Ibn Yamīn (d. 769/1368) and Salmān Sāwadjī (d. 778/1376), editions of the poetical works of Masʿūd Saʿd Salmān (d. 515/1121) and Hātif Iṣfahānī (d. 1198/1783-4), publication of Djāmī's *mathnawī Salāmān u Absāl*, and translation of the fourth volume of E.G. Browne's *Literary history of Persia* as well as of books from other writers. His creative writing consisted mainly of a modest collection of poetry which was first published in 1337/1958. On the basis of the dates appended to most of his poems, it may be assumed that his poetic career began around 1295/1916-17. His verse is characterised by a lyrical outlook and love of nature. It contains a moral tone tending towards philosophising. His literary position may be best described as that of a transitional poet representing preliminary changes from traditionalism in the 20th century Persian poetry.

Bibliography: Rashīd Yāsimī, *Dīwān-i Rashīd Yāsimī*, 2nd ed., Tehran 1362/1983; Muḥammad Isḥāḳ (ed.), *Sukhanwarān-i Īrān dar ʿaṣr-i ḥāḍir*, i, Delhi 1933; Muḥammad Bāḳir Burḳaʿī (ed.) *Sukhanwarān-i nāmī-yi muʿāṣir*, i, Tehran 1329/1951; F. Machalski, *La littérature de l'Iran contemporain*, ii, Wrocław-Warszawa-Kraków 1967; Jiří Bečka (ed.), *Dictionary of oriental literatures*, iii, London and New York 1974, s.n.; Mahdī Ḥamīdī (ed.), *Daryā-yi gawhar*, iii, Tehran 1367/1988; Dhabīḥ Allāh Ṣafā (ed.), *Gandj-i sukhan*, iii, Tehran 1367/1988; Abū Ṭālib Raḍawī-nizhād (ed.), *Čahār-sad shāʿir-i Pārsī-gūy*, Tehran 1369/1990. (Munibur Rahman)

AL-**RASHĪDIYYA**, *al-Djamʿiyya al-Rashīdiyya li 'l-Mūsīḳā al-Tūnisiyya*, a Tunisian musical society founded in November 1934.

A general assembly of 71 participants (including a singer-actress, Shāfiya Rushdī), from all walks of life—artisans, members of the liberal professions, musicians, poets and men of letters—decided to create an "association to safeguard the heritage of Tunisian music and its spread amongst the coming generations". Muṣṭafa Ṣfar, mayor of the Medina of Tunis, was unanimously elected its first president. Various names were proposed before that of Rashīdiyya was chosen, thereby glorifying the work of the music-loving Bey Muḥammad al-Rashīd (d. 1172/1759). During its period of evolution, the Rashīdiyya was to assume the work of an Institute, whence its name *al-Maʿhad al-Rashīdī li 'l-mūsīḳā al-tūnisiyya, ca.* 1945).

The setting-up of this famous institution was not fortuitous. It formed part of the Tunisian nationalist movement founded at the beginning of the century, and for which the 1930s formed a period of transition on the cultural and artistic level. It marked the beginning of a period of intense activity, of recovery and

:eservation and of creativity on behalf of an identity ·hich felt itself threatened. In practice, music had uring this period become the profession of a despised ass, whose depraved morals and avidity for nothing ut financial gain had ended in dragging the whole rt, and as a result, the artist's status, down to a eplorable situation. Just as there were many factors ading to a series of attempts aiming at the rehabilita- on of Tunisian music, so these were favoured by everal important events concerning the poetic and usical spheres. Such a spirit had already taken shape hanks to the creative impetus of Shaykh Aḥmad al- Wāfī (1850-1921) and the genius of Khumayyis Tar- ān (1894-1964), both reared, like so many others, in he pure tradition of the *zāwiya*s of the Ṣūfī rotherhoods, and to the efforts of Baron Rudolphe 'Erlanger (d. 1932) and of the musicians and usicologists gathered round his palace of Sīdī Bū aʿīd. In 1931 the famous Syrian musician Shaykh Alī Darwīsh of Aleppo arrived in Tunisia and within he Khaldūniyya gave the first courses in tonic sol-fa, nd in the modes and rhythms of Arab music, as well s tuition in the *nāy*. There was also the first congress f Arab music at Cairo (14 March-3 April 1932), which was an event of great artistic importance. The Tunisian delegation included various famous figures, uch as Ḥasan Ḥusnī ʿAbd al-Wahhāb, Mannūbī nūsī, Ḥassūna Ben ʿAmmār, and a musical ensem- le composed of Muḥammad Ghānin (*rabāb*), Khumayyis Tarnān (*ʿūd ʿarabī*), ʿAlī bin ʿArfa (*ṭār*), Khumayyis al-ʿĀṭī (*nakkārāt*) Muḥammad al-Mukrānī nd Muḥammad Billaḥsan (singers). In this way, the Rashīdiyya, whose setting up had been for music the ulmination of a concatenation of circumstances, very oon became "a real bed of flowers", as Shāfiya Rushdī liked to stress, a nursery of high-quality ar- ists, poets and musicians who succeeded, "through work and faith", in rehabilitating Tunisian musical rt.

The Rashīdiyya was controlled by a legal charter which gave it civil and financial autonomy, and its irecting committee was composed of a dozen members from amongst its most faithful supporters nd patrons, chosen by the duly qualified electors and with a mandate which was renewable. It had three ommissions: literary, musical and the sphere of ublic relations; the first two sat in the form of a com- mittee of sifting and selection. In 1935, a first concert was given in its provisional headquarters, on the patio of the patron Belaḥsen Laṣram, before it acquired its own centre. An initial competition was held to stimulate creative activity amongst Tunisian artistes. Thereafter, a lively activity was embarked upon, en- visaging three vital objectives:

(1) Safeguarding the musical heritage (and more specially, the *maʾlūf* or popular one), against all cur- ents of deformation, preserving it intact against the effects of time and the blurring of the collective memory, giving it fresh impetus and spreading it widely. A long work of recovery and transcription was envisaged, a somewhat arduous and delicate mission, given that the music of an oral tradition, difficult to pin down in a fixed, standard notation, was involved, and that numerous versions, making up a field of great richness, had to be gathered together. Hence the effort was carried out on two fronts: collection and transcription (led by M. Trīkī), and restoration, the giving of fresh impetus and new compositions (a work given effect by Kh. Tarnān). The text and music of thirteen complete *nawba*s [*q.v.*], as well as those of numerous traditional pieces of music, instrumental and vocal, were gathered together, transcribed and published (cf. the nine fascicules of the Tunisian musical heritage). The greater part of this repertoire was likewise recorded.

(2) Laying the foundations for a centralised musical teaching, involving mainly national and Arab music. Through the seriousness and successfulness of this policy, the Rashīdiyya speedily became an Institute for educating cadres who were well qualified to keep up this role until 1972, when its courses were transfer- red to the National Centre for Folk Music and the Arts.

(3) Launching a vigorous movement of musical creativeness and high quality poetic activity, as much on the level of the texts as the music and interpreta- tion. Tunisian song had its genuine creative spirits, composers, song-writers, instrumentalists and singers of great talent, notably the famous group *Taht al-Sūr* ("below the city wall") or *ʿAskar al-līl* ("soldiers of the night"), artistes, intellectuals and bohemians who were known by the name of the famous café which gave them shelter.

One by one, the new wave of musicians and poets were to help in the building of a new edifice, all bring- ing their contribution to the Tunisian song, for which they provided an impulse which brought it to the forefront of Arab music. The Rashīdiyya did much to render respectable practical musical-making. A tradi- tion of weekly concerts was begun, and, according to Trīkī, one went there "as to the mosque".

The founding of a national radio network (Tunis R.T.T. in 1936), which began to transmit its own emissions towards the end of 1938, helped the rise of the Tunisian song and probably contributed to pro- mote the efforts of the Rashīdiyya, notably through the live transmission of its weekly concerts. However, this institution gradually lost its potentialities once an orchestra had been created (1948), and then a choir (1957), both belonging to the R.T.T. and which at- tracted the best artistes of the time. At the present time, the Rashīdiyya, with its headquarters in the rue du Dey, no. 5, comes under the Ministry of Culture and is supported financially by the municipality of Tunis. A new breath has been recently given to it so that it may recover its former status.

Bibliography: On Muḥammad al-Rashīd Bāy, see Kaḥḥāla, ix, 246, and Ziriklī, vi, 336. On the Rashīdiyya, see the works published under its aegis: *al-Maʿhad al-Rashīdī, histoire de l'institution*, Tunis n.d., and two monographs devoted to two of its leading figures, Aḥmad al-Wāfī and Khumayyis Tarnān. In general, see S. al-Mahdī, *Maḳāmat al-mūsīḳa al-ʿarabiyya*, Tunis n.d.; M. Guettat, *La musique classique du Maghreb*, Paris 1980, 214-27; idem, *La Tunisie dans les documents du Congrès du Caire*, in *Musique arabe. Le Congrès du Caire 1932*, Cairo 1992, 69-86; idem, *Visages de la musique tunisienne*, in *IBLA*, no. 160, 227-40; M. Marzūḳī and Ṣ. al-Mahdī, *al-Maʿhad al-Rashīdī li 'l-mūsīḳī al-Tūnisiyya*, Tunis 1981; Tunisian Ministry of Culture, *al-Turāth al-mūsīḳī al-tūnisī*, 9 fascs. so far appeared, Tunis 1967-79; S. Rizgī, *al-Aghānī al-tūnisiyya*, Tunis 1967; M. Skāndjī, *al-Rashīdiyya, madrasat al-mūsīḳī wa-ghināʾ al-ʿarabī fī Tūnis*, Tunis 1986. See also the *Bibl.* to NAWBA.

(M. GUETTAT)

RASHT, RESHT, a town of the Persian province of Gīlān [*q.v.*], in the Caspian Sea lowlands and lying on a branch of the Safīd Rūd [*q.v.*] in lat. 37° 18′ N. and 49° 38′ E. It has long been the commercial centre of Gīlān, with its fortunes fluctuating with the state of sericulture and silk manufacture. However, the town is not mentioned by the early Arabic geographers, who localise the silk industry in the province of Ṭabaristān to the east [see MĀZANDARĀN], and it is the *Ḥudūd al-ʿālam* which first gives the name, but as a district, not a town (tr. Minorsky, 137, § 32.25). It does appear as a town in Ḥamd Allāh Mustawfī, writing soon after the Mongol conquest of Gīlān in 706/1307, and by that time, the silk of Gīlān was famous and, according to Marco Polo, sought after by Genoese merchants whose ships had recently appeared on the Caspian waters. Subsequently, Rasht became the seat of a minor dynasty of Gīlān, the Isḥāḳids of Fūmin, until these rulers were replaced by the Kiyā princes of Lāhidjān [*q.v.*], and then, in 1000/1592, Shāh ʿAbbās the Great [*q.v.*] annexed Gīlān to the Persian state.

Among the events of this period was the establishment in Gīlān, of which Rasht became the administrative and economic centre, of the "Muscovite Company" founded in 1557 by Anthony Jenkinson, Richard and Robert Johnson, who, taking the Russian route, sent ten expeditions into Persia between 1561 and 1581. It is to noteworthy that the last independent ruler of Gīlān, Aḥmad Shāh, sent ambassadors to Moscow to seek help against Shāh ʿAbbās and obtained promises of protection which, however, came to nothing. The Cossacks at the same time were plundering in Gīlān and Rasht and trying to gain the support of the Persian court. The most notable invasion was that of Stenka Razin who sacked Rasht in 1045/1636. On 2 Ṣafar 1082, the day of Stenka's execution, the Persians in Moscow at the time were invited to be present at it (cf. the journal *Kāweh*, 12, N.S., 1 December 1921). From 1722 to 1734, Rasht and Gīlān were occupied by the Russians (Shipov, then Matushkin) invited by the governor who was threatened by the Afghāns. In 1734, Gīlān was restored to Persia after a treaty. Rabino quotes a Persian testimony in favour of the Russian occupation. For military reasons the Russians cleared the jungle round Rasht.

The history of Gīlān and that of Rasht, which has always played a preponderant part in it, merges into the general history of Persia after its annexation. During the Persian Revolution, a body of Social Democrats was sent by the Regional Committee of the Caucasus to Rasht, and there helped in February 1909 to overthrow the authority of the Shāh and to establish a revolutionary committee which elected as governor the Sipihdār ʿAẓam, who played a prominent part in the history of the period along with Sardār Asad Bakhtiyārī (cf. *Persia v borbé za nezavisimost*, by Pavlovič and Iranskii, Moscow 1925). Rasht then became the base of operations of the northern revolutionary army. A few years later, during the First World War, Rasht again attracted attention in connection with the movement of the *Djangalīs*, created by Mīrzā Kūčak Khān [*q.v.*]. Assisted by German (von Passchen), Turkish and Russian officers, an armed force was organised to oppose the passage of the British troops under General Dunsterville on their way to Bākū, without, however, much success (battle of Mandjīl, 12 June 1918). The British were able to force their way through with the help of Bičerākhov's detachment of Cossacks and established a garrison in Rasht. A second battle with the *Djangalīs* in the town itself on 20 July 1918 also ended in British victory. On 25 August peace was signed with Kūčak Khān at Enzelī. At one time, at the end of March 1918, the position of Kūčak Khān was so strong that the capture not only of Ḳazwīn, but even of Tehran, was feared (cf. *The adventures of Dunsterforce* by Maj. Gen. L.C. Dunsterville, London 1920).

Rasht again became the arena of the revolutionary *Djangalī* movement, aimed at the pro-British government in Tehran of Mushīr al-Dawla in 1920. After the capture of Bākū on 28 April 1920 by the Reds, the White Fleet sought refuge in the port of Enzelī, which was held by the British. Enzelī fell to the Soviet forces who then twice occupied Rasht. But after the Perso-Soviet agreement of May 1921, Russian and British troops left Persian territory, Kūčak Khān's movement was suppressed by Riḍā Khān's [see RIḌA SHĀH PAHLAWĪ] Cossack Brigade, and Persian authority re-established in Gīlān and Rasht.

Rasht was again occupied by Russian forces in the Second World War. At the present time, it is the administrative centre of the *ustān* of Gīlān. It has road connections with Tehran and Bandar Anzalī and an airport. In 1972 it had an estimated population of 160,000.

Bibliography: H.L. Rabino, *Les provinces caspiennes de la Perse. Le Guîlân*, in *RMM*, xxxii (1915-16), 1-499; Le Strange, *Lands*, 174-5; Admiralty Handbooks. *Persia*, London 1945, 532-3 and index; Razmārā, *Farhang-i djughrāfiyā-yi Īrān*, ii, 130-2; Barthold, *An historical geography of Iran*, Princeton 1984, 236-7. (B. NIKITINE-[C.E. BOSWORTH])

RASHTĪ, SAYYID KĀẒIM B. ḲĀSIM (d. 1259/1844), the head and systematiser of the Shaykhī school of Shīʿism after Aḥmad al-Aḥsāʾī [*q.v.*]. The son of a merchant, Sayyid Kāẓim was born in Rasht [*q.v.*], in northern Persia, between 1194/1784 and 1214/1799-1800. Details of his early life are sparse and contradictory. Educated in Rasht he underwent mystical experiences and, somewhere between his mid-teens and early twenties (between 1809 and 1814?), became a pupil of al-Aḥsāʾī, then living in Yazd. He also studied under and received *idjāzāt* from other *mudjtahids*.

The Sayyid soon came to hold an important position among al-Aḥsāʾī's entourage, acting as his *nāib* or deputy and spokesman, answering questions on his behalf, continuing and translating some of his writings, and defending him from the attacks of hostile *ʿulamāʾ*. On al-Aḥsāʾī's death, Rashtī succeeded him as head of the central group of his pupils in Karbalāʾ. This led to the emergence of a sort of order for the transmission of inspired knowledge within orthodox Shīʿism, with Rashtī as "the bearer of innate knowledge" (Kirmānī) and the interpreter of al-Aḥsāʾī's words. Although he denied trying to establish a new *madhhab*, he became embroiled in major public debates with leading *ʿulamāʾ*. These disputes, and Rashtī's own development of an esoteric teaching divulged to a privileged circle of students, made it inevitable that Shaykhism should be viewed as a school of heterodox opinion within Twelver Shīʿism.

In spite of this, Rashtī acquired considerable political influence in Karbalāʾ and Persia, where he numbered many members of the ruling Ḳādjār family among his admirers. His death on 11 Dhu 'l-Ḥidjdja 1259/1 January 1844 sparked off a leadership struggle within the school, resulting in the emergence of two sharply opposed branches: that of Karīm Khān Kirmānī, which attempted a rapprochement with orthodoxy, and that of ʿAlī Muḥammad Shīrāzī [*q.v.*], which grew into the Bābī sect.

Bibliography: D. MacEoin, *From Shaykhism to Babism. A study in charismatic renewal in Shīʿī Islam*, diss. Cambridge 1979 unpubl., ch. 3, at 95-124; H. Corbin, *Les successeurs de Shaykh Ahmad Ahsaʾi*, in *En Islam iranien. Aspects spirituels et philosophiques. IV*, Paris 1972, Livre VI *L'Ecole Shaykhie*, ch. II, at 232-6; A.L.M. Nicolas, *Essai sur le Cheikhisme. II. Séyyèd Kazem Rechti*, Paris 1911; Abu 'l-Ḳāsim b. Zayn al-

ʿĀbidīn [Khān Kirmānī], *Fihrist-i kutub-i Shaykh Aḥmad Aḥsāʾī wa sāʾir mashāyikh-i ʿiẓām*, ^{3}Kerman [1977], 112-28, 288-359 (a brief biography and a comprehensive listing of Rashtī writings).

(D. MacEoin)

RASHWA (A.) or, apparently preferred by purists, *rishwa/rushwa*, pl. *rushā*, Persian *rishwat*, *rishwe*, *rushwa*, Turkish *rüşvet*, the legal term for "bribe." Like English "bribe", its connotation is absolutely negative and whatever is called *rashwa* is strictly forbidden by law. The word itself does not occur in the Ḳurʾān. More general passages like II, 188, and V, 42, 62-3 (*suḥt*) were interpreted to include the prohibition of bribe-taking. The *ḥadīth*, however, makes the matter perfectly clear. One of the most explicit statements invokes the divine curse upon those who offer and who take bribes (*rāshī, murtashī*), sometimes adding the go-between (*rāʾish*) and the specification *fi 'l-ḥukm*.

Other words may refer to the process of bribery such as *djaʿāla/djuʿl* or, in the course of time, drift in that direction such as *itāwa* or *bakhshīsh* [*q.v.*], but none of them ever became as unambiguous and forceful as *rashwa*. An insignificant exception may possibly be *birṭīl*, if it is derived from Greek *proteleia* and the interpretation of *proteleia* as "previous payment, advance" (Liddell and Scott, 1524) in a 6th-century papyrus from Egypt is correct; in this case, Persian *partala* "gift" could be secondary or another derivation from the Greek (see S. Fraenkel, *Aram. Fremdwörter*, Leiden 1886, 84). A picturesque euphemism for bribing, "pouring oil in the lamp" or simply *ḳandala*, is listed by al-Thaʿālibī, *Kināya*, Beirut 1405/1984, 70; al-Rāghib, *Muḥāḍarāt*, Būlāḳ 1286-87, i, 128.

Nothwithstanding the legal prohibition, bribery was as common in Islam as in other large societies, although the degree of its prevalence no doubt widely varied. It was, therefore, necessary for jurists to define what distinguished it from allowable gifts [see HIBA] and to circumscribe its boundaries. In contrast to supposedly disinterested and unconditional gifts, bribes were stated to be what was given for a purpose. This left open the possibility of beneficial purposes such as attempts to prevent wrongdoing and injustice, see, e.g., *LA*, s.v. *r-sh-w*: "gifts that lead to obtaining a right or ward off a wrong," or al-Sharīshī, commenting on "death does not take bribes" in al-Ḥarīrī's twenty-first *maḳāma*: "a gift given for warding off the harm of someone who has power over you" (*Sharḥ al-Maḳāmāt*, Cairo 1306, i, 279). In the legal view, however, the beneficial purpose did not invalidate the general prohibition; while the briber may be within his rights in offering a bribe, it is illegal to accept it, since the intended recipient should do on his own volition what is required and proper. It was, however, recognised by some that any gift whatever was given for some purpose. Al-Ghazālī thus discusses hypothetical situations such as giving something to a ruler's officials or intimates in order to gain access to him, as well as other situations of gift-giving for expected services. The negative view mostly prevailed, but it is obvious that the very discussion opened up potential loopholes. Note that the alleged "first case of bribery in Islam" involves outstanding early Muslims and access to the caliph (Ibn Ḳutayba, *Maʿārif*, ed. ʿUkkāsha, 558, and the *awāʾil* collections).

The environment where unlawful bribing was seen as particularly at home was the twin realms of government and judiciary. On a widely discussed problem where the two clearly intertwined concerned the expenditure of money for an appointment to a judgeship, see, most concisely, al-Māwardī, *Adab al-ḳāḍī*, ed. M.H. Sarḥān, Baghdād 1391/1971, i, 151-2, and Tyan. While bribery on various governmental levels, internally as well as internationally, was discussed (see al-Subkī, *Faṣl al-maḳāl fī hadāyā al-ʿummāl*; Rosenthal, 137-8), the principal concern was with the judiciary, where the concept of bribery and its practical role were seen as most deeply embedded and unquestionably corruptive. In the case of judges, the acceptance of well-intentioned gifts even by relatives could constitute a problem calling for legal discussion. Gift-giving among ordinary individuals and, presumably, in business pursuits not involving officialdom was, it seems, not considered to incur the danger of developing into forbidden *rashwa*.

Someone found guilty of bribery could, of course, be dismissed. Legally, punishment was left to the decision of the judge (*taʿzīr*). The Ḥanafī Ibn Nudjaym appears to have considered public exposure as the most effective deterrent.

The attention paid to *rashwa* throughout the literature proves, if proof is needed, that bribery was an ever-present problem. Its social effects were no doubt considerable but cannot be accurately, or even approximately, quantified. It appears to have become institutionalised at certain periods and locations. From Ottoman times, an increase in monographs on the subject is noticeable. Political thinkers were much concerned with it and even ended up in almost despairing of finding a remedy for it (see Wright). Westerners often felt convinced that bribery was a way of life in the East. It may, however, be doubted whether detailed research will provide valid clues to a specific role of bribery in mediaeval Muslim civilisation as a whole, if, indeed, there was anything specific to it.

Bibliography: Some of the vast and scattered source material is cited by E. Tyan, *Histoire de l'organization judiciaire en pays d'Islam*, Paris 1938-43, i, 425-31, 2nd. ed., Leiden 1960, 289-92, and F. Rosenthal, *Gifts and bribes: the Muslim view*, in *Proceedings of the American Philosophical Society*, cviii (1964), 135-44, repr. in idem, *Muslim intellectual and social history*, Variorum Reprints, Aldershot 1990. See, for example, Wakīʿ, *Akhbār al-ḳuḍāt*, ed. ʿAbd al-ʿAzīz Muṣṭafā al-Marāghī, Cairo 1366-69/1947-50, i, 45-60; Ghazālī, *Iḥyāʾ*, book II, ch. 4 at end, tr. H. Bauer, *Erlaubtes und verbotenes Gut*, Halle 1922, 206-12, and Murtaḍā al-Zabīdī, *Itḥāf*, Cairo 1311, repr. Beirut, vi, 157-69; Dhahabī, *Kabāʾir*, ch. 32; Ibn Nudjaym, *Risāla mukhtaṣara fī bayān al-rashwa wa-aḳsāmihā*, in *Rasāʾil*, Beirut 1400/1980, 110-17; Ḥādjdjī Khalīfa, *The Balance of Truth*, tr. G.L. Lewis, 124-27; W.L. Wright, *Ottoman statecraft*, Princeton 1935, text, 38 ff., tr. 87-93; Ahmet Mumcu, *Osmanlı devletinde rüşvet* (Ankara 1969).

(F. Rosenthal)

RĀSIM [see AḤMAD RĀSIM].

RASM (A., pl. *rusūm*), the act of drawing, a drawing, is not always distinguished from painting; nor can it be. Drawing was performed both as a preliminary to painting and to produce works to stand alone. It might be representational [see TAṢWĪR] or decorative (historians of Islamic manuscripts confine the term illumination to decorative work). *Naḳḳāshī* covers drawing and painting, whether representational or decorative; *ṭarrāḥī* is designing, in the context of pictures, the production of the underdrawing. In addition to the illustration of manuscripts, drawing is an important element in the decoration of ceramics and other forms of applied art; draughtsmen might exercise their skill in several fields. Writing in the early 11th/17th century, Ḳāḍī Aḥmad distinguishes two sorts of *ḳalam*, the one from a plant and the other from an animal (see *Calligraphers and painters: a treatise by Qāḍī Aḥmad, son of Mīr-Munshī (circa A.H. 1015/A.D. 1606)*, tr. V. Minorsky, Washington, D.C. 1959, 50): these are the calligrapher's reed pen and the painter's brush, probably made with squirrel-hair. Ink [see MIDĀD] was prepared from soot, gallnut and alum, in a medium of gum arabic. Dilute ink (or a red pigment, perhaps minium) was used, usually with a brush, for the underdrawings of paintings. Either pen, brush, or a combination, was used for autonomous drawings; some drawings include small areas of ink wash, thin colour or details in gold. Training in the drawing of particular motifs might be carried out by pouncing, using a gazelle skin (Persian *čarba*). A draughtsman often worked with a drawing-board supported by his knee. The line generally reveals the influence of the calligraphy of its period, in its curves and rhythms. Ruler and compass were used in the basic layout of schemes of illumination, but many complex curved lines appear to be drawn freehand. There is occasional use of stencils from the 15th century onwards. The illuminator (*mu<u>dh</u>ahhib*) worked, among other things, with brush-gold, gold-leaf rubbed into moist or dry glue and diluted.

Early period

Surviving examples of drawing from the early Islamic period are mostly in the service of wall- or floor-paintings in Umayyad palaces (Ḳuṣayr ʿAmra [see ARCHITECTURE] or Ḳaṣr al-Ḥayr al-<u>Gh</u>arbī [*q.v.*]); there is an evident debt to late classical and Sāsānid art, and outlines are heavily marked (but have sometimes been exaggerated in excessive restoration). The earliest surviving book illustrations appear to be the highly formalised, coloured drawings of mosques and trees in an Umayyad Ḳurʾān, discovered in Ṣanʿāʾ (see H.-C. Graf von Bothmer, *Architekturbilder im Koran: eine Prachthandschrift der Umayyadenzeit aus Yemen*, in *Pantheon*, xlv [1987], 4-20). The earliest surviving drawings in which line is exploited for aesthetic effect are figures of the constellations in a manuscript of al-Ṣūfī's *Ṣuwar al-kawākib al-<u>th</u>ābita* (Bodleian Library, Oxford), whose text was copied in 400/1009-10, presumably in Ba<u>gh</u>dād. The wiry line describes the notional body with smooth contours and the clothing with exuberant bracketing folds; Sāsānid and Chinese influences are evident. Approximately contemporary is a Fāṭimid drawing of a nude female musician (Israel Museum, Jerusalem). Over a red underdrawing, the line is slightly more variable, but volume is chiefly conveyed by curves. In works of the Arab school of the 7th/13th and 8th/14th centuries, figures have large and expressive faces and eloquent gestures of the hand (fig. 1). The line is rapid and confident, sometimes to the point of carelessness. Drawing in the Sal<u>dj</u>ūḳ tradition at this period, as represented in *Warḳa u Gul<u>sh</u>āh* (Topkapı Sarayı Library, Istanbul) or on lustre ceramics, is more sober; faces are more oriental, and on the ceramics pattern is more pervasive.

Chinoiserie

A new mode of drawing begins in the late 7th/13th century as Chinese influence, mediated by various arts, introduces new motifs and softens the Islamic line. Finished ink drawings, exercises and designs for applied arts are preserved in Albums in the Topkapı Sarayı, Istanbul, and the Staatsbibliothek in Berlin [see MURAḲḲAʿ]. In general, these are datable to the 8th/14th and 9th/15th centuries, but more particular datings are a matter of debate; vigour tends to suggest the earlier century, and delicacy the later. Ink drawing was known at this period as *ḳalam-i siyāhī/siyāh ḳalam*; Dūst Muḥammad, who compiled one of th[e] Albums for the Ṣafawid Bahrām Mīrzā in 951/1544 mentions one Amīr Dawlat Yār, proficient in this fiel[d] in the 14th century (see W.M. Thackston, *A century [of] princes: sources on Timurid history and art*, Cambridge Mass. 1989, 345). Islamic arabesque ornament accepted new motifs, lotus leaves or flowers, Chines[e] clouds, ducks, peris, cloud-deer, dragons and *sīmur<u>gh</u>* (a Chinese form for the legendary Persian bird); car[touches] have "cloud-collar" edges (fig. 2). Som[e] studies draw on Buddhist mythology. In the 9th/15th century, chinoiserie is enriched by motifs from th[e] Islamic tradition, hunting felines, monkeys, peacocks and the *wāḳwāḳ* scroll (a scroll inhabited by faces named after the tree of talking heads encountered b[y] Iskandar in Firdawsī's *<u>Sh</u>āh-nāma*). By the 10th/16th century Persian illuminators execute chinoiseri[e] borders in brush-gold with subtle variations in density. Chinoiserie was carried to the Ottoman sphere where, in the 10th/16th century, draughtsmen mak[e] a speciality of ink drawings of the *sāz* motif, th[e] feather-like flower of the reed. From the late 10th/16th century, Mu<u>gh</u>al painters introduce into gol[d] chinoiserie borders figures which are increasingl[y] realistic and coloured.

Classical Persian and Mu<u>gh</u>al drawings

In classical Persian painting, produced from th[e] 1390s to 1540s, outline becomes much less visible tha[n] hitherto. A sketchy underdrawing indicates where on[e] block of colour is to abut on another, and the edge o[f] the colour-block assumes the greater part of the defining function. Lines applied over the colour blocks t[o] indicate features, folds, patterns or other details, ar[e] delicate. Chinese influence is evident in the convention of round, small-featured faces. Outlines are mor[e] evident in provincial styles. Drawings of narrativ[e] subjects are preserved in the Albums, and drawing predominates over painting in the illustrations to [a] *Ṣuwar al-kawākib al-<u>th</u>ābita* made for Ulu<u>gh</u> Beg [*q.v.*], presumably in the 1430s and at Samarḳand (Bibliothèque Nationale, Paris).

In Mu<u>gh</u>al painting of the late 10th/16th and early 11th/17th centuries [see MU<u>GH</u>ALS. 9], the Persian colour-block system is modified by traditions both linear and painterly. Line may be strongly marked, and is sometimes further emphasised by a surrounding shadow; at other times it is lost. For drawing *per se*, a fruitful source of inspiration was found in European prints (and probably also illustrations in *grisaille*). In the late 10th/16th century, Basāwan produced masterly drawings with adaptations of European style and European classical mythology. In the 11th/17th century, the Mu<u>gh</u>al interest in reportage fostered portrait drawings—including those of elephants—and drawing from the life [see MU<u>GH</u>ALS. 9]. Some drawings, usually of more traditional subjects, were accompanied with half-colour (*nīm ḳalam*). A class of *jeu d'esprit*, perhaps a development from metamorphic tendencies in Persian ornament with assistance from chinoiserie, is formed by drawings in which ridden elephants or camels are composed from subsidiary figures in the archimboldesque manner.

Later Persian drawing

With a growing taste for Albums in Persia in the later 10th/16th century [see MURAḲḲAʿ], the finished ink drawing gains in importance as an independent work. Subjects are often single figures of the upper classes, sitting or standing, by the 11th/17th century sometimes presented against a minimal landscape of hills, trees and cloud. Conversation pieces are also found, low-life or eccentric characters, and animals; in addition, there are a small number of studies of

Abū Zayd's son commends his father's sermon, *Maḳāmāt* of al-Ḥarīrī, 723/1323. Add. 7293, 285b. Courtesy of the British Library, London.

Chinoiserie cartouche, *ca*. 1410. Diez A Fol. 73, S. 54. Staatsbibliothek zu Berlin, Preussischer Kulturbesitz, Orientabteilung.

arlier manuscript illustrations. Line of strongly alligraphic quality and varying width is used, both or its descriptive and abstract value. Volumes are argely implied by fold lines; hatching is not mployed, but in some areas fold lines cluster ogether. Signatures, or attributions, and dates are not infrequent. Prominent draughtsmen of the 0th/16th and 11th/17th centuries are Ṣādiḳ, Riḍā-yi Abbāsī [*q.v.*] and the latter's pupil Muʿīn Muṣawwir.

The second half of the 19th century sees the acceptance of new means of graphic expression, the pencil with shading by hatching and smudging) and the ithograph. Influential in this was Abu 'l Ḥasan Ghafārī, Ṣāniʿ al-Mulk, first director of art in the *Dār al-Funūn* (Polytechnic) in Tehran, who died in 1866. Portraits in the new media have a cautious stillness, derived from photography; but drawing of a more traditional character may venture into caricature.

Bibliography: F.R. Martin, *The miniature painters of Persia, India and Turkey: from the 8th to the 18th century*, London 1912; R. Ettinghausen, *Arab painting*, Geneva 1962; M.Ş. İpşiroğlu, *Saray-Alben: Diez'sche Klebebände aus der Berliner Sammlungen*, Wiesbaden 1964; E. Atil, *The brush of the masters: drawings from Iran and India*, Washington, D.C. 1978; M.C. Beach, *The Grand Mogul: imperial painting in India 1600-1660*, Williamstown 1978; B. Gray (ed.), *The arts of the book in Central Asia*, Paris and London 1979; *Islamic Art*, i (1981); N.M. Titley, *Persian miniature painting*, London 1983; A. Nègre, A. Okada, F. Richard, *A la cour du Grand Moghol*, Paris 1986; Y. Porter, *Peinture et arts du livre*, Paris 1992.

(BARBARA BREND)

RASM. In ottoman Turkish usage [see RESM].

AL-**RASS**, the name in Arabic geographical writing for the Araxes River (Perso-Turkish form Aras, Armenian Eraskʿ, Georgian Rakhshī, modern Aras). It rises in what is now eastern Turkey near Erzurum and flows generally in an eastwards direction for 1,072 km/670 miles into the Caspian Sea. Its middle reaches, from a point near Mount Ararat, today form the boundary between the former Azerbaijan SSR and Persia, with the lower stretch receiving the Kur River and flowing through the Mūḳān [*q.v.*] steppes and what is now wholly Azerbaijani territory.

The early Arabic name al-Rass led the Muslim exegetes to connect it with the *Aṣḥāb al-Rass* [*q.v.*] of Ḳurʾān, XXV, 38, L. 12, mentioned as one of the unbelieving peoples destroyed for their impiety. The eastern and middle stretches of the Araxes came under Arab control when the Muslim invaders pushed through Ādharbāydjān towards eastern Caucasia in the later 1st/7th century, but for many centuries these remained frontier regions, open to attacks from the Alans [see OSSETES], the Khazars and the Rūs [*q.vv.*] from the north and from the Armenian princes and the Byzantines from the west.

The river valley was a very fertile area and formed a corridor for commerce connecting the Black Sea with the Caspian and northwestern Persia, so that urban centres like Dwīn [*q.v.*] or Dabīl, Ānī [*q.v.*] and Djulfa flourished greatly. In the Saldjūḳ period, migratory Turkmens passed along it heading for eastern Anatolia once the Byzantine defences there had collapsed after the battle of Malāzgird [*q.v.*] in 464/1071. In later times, independent or semi-independent local khānates like those of Ḳarabāgh, Nakhčiwān and Ordūbād [*q.vv.*] formed buffers between the Ṣafawids and Ottomans. By the early 19th century, Persia was compelled to relinquish control over the lands to the north of the Araxes and of its lower course, with the Treaty of Turkmančay of 1828 establishing the present boundary between Azerbaijan and Armenia on the one side and Persia on the other along the river's middle stretch.

Bibliography: Tomaschek, in *PW*, ii/1, cols. 402-4; *Ḥudūd al-ʿālam*, tr. Minorsky, 77, § 6.55; Abū Dulaf, *Second Risāla*, ed. and tr. Minorsky, Cairo 1955, § 16, tr. 36; Le Strange, *Lands of the Eastern Caliphate*, 166-8; *EIr* art. *Araxes* (W.B. Fisher and C.E. Bosworth).

(C.E. BOSWORTH)

AL-**RASS** [see AṢḤĀB AL-RASS].

AL-**RASSĪ**, AL-ḲĀSIM B. IBRĀHĪM b. Ismāʿīl b. Ibrāhīm b. al-Ḥasan b. al-Ḥasan b. ʿAlī b. Abī Ṭālib (169-246/785-860), Zaydī *imām* and founder of the legal and theological school later prevalent among the Zaydīs in the Yemen.

He grew up in Medina where he was taught basic Zaydī religious doctrine in his family and Medinan *ḥadīth*, and perhaps Ḳurʾān readings and Arabic language, by Abū Bakr ʿAbd al-Ḥamīd b. Abī Uways, a nephew of Mālik b. Anas. Before 199/815 he came to Egypt, probably al-Fusṭāṭ. It is doubtful whether he was, as reported by a late source, sent there by his brother Muḥammad who at that time was recognised as *imām* by the Kūfan Zaydīs. Al-Ḳāsim, in any case, later expressed reservations about Muḥammad's theological views. In Egypt he studied the Jewish and Christian scriptures and Christian theological and philosophical treatises and engaged in debates with Muslim and non-Muslim scholars. His refutations of a Manichaean treatise ascribed to Ibn al-Muḳaffaʿ [*q.v.*] (ed. M. Guidi, *La lotta tra l'islam e il manichéismo*, Rome 1927) and of the Christians (ed. I. Di Matteo in *RSO*, ix [1921-3], 301 ff.) were written there. Evidently under the influence of Christian writings he adopted some of his characteristic views on the divine attributes and upholding human free will which deviated from the earlier Zaydī tradition. Under suspicion of seditious activity by the authorities, he left Egypt soon after 211/826, returning to Medina. He bought an estate at al-Rass near Dhu 'l-Ḥulayfa and stayed there writing and teaching Zaydī visitors, especially from Kūfa and western Ṭabaristān, until his death. There is no sound evidence that he ever seriously attempted to lead a Zaydī revolt.

Al-Ḳāsim summed up his religious teaching in five principles (*uṣūl*) which only partly agreed with those of the Muʿtazila [*q.v.*].

1. In his sharply anti-anthropomorphist doctrine of the unity of God he stressed, in agreement with contemporary Christian theology, the total dissimilarity (*khilāf*) of God to all creation, while rejecting the corollary of an aspect of similarity upheld in the Christian doctrine. Under Christian theological influence he also placed the essential generosity (*djūd*) and goodness of God at the centre of his doctrine of divine attributes. He ignored the Muʿtazilī distinction between divine attributes of essence and of act.

2. Concerning divine justice he strictly dissociated God from evil acts and affirmed human free will. He rejected, however, the Muʿtazilī doctrine of compensation (*ʿiwaḍ*) owed by God for undeserved pain inflicted by Him and held, in accordance with Christian doctrine, that the blessings of God to children and others completely outweighed any pains. He also distanced himself from the Muʿtazilī interpretation of the predestinarian terms *ḳaḍāʾ* and *ḳadar* as meaning merely commandment and judgment. Here he clearly tried to avoid expressing condemnation of the traditional Zaydī position affirming predestination.

3. On the basis of his concept of divine justice he upheld the tenet of the divine "promise and threat"

(*waʿd wa-waʿīd*) entailing the unconditional punishment of the unrepentant sinner in the hereafter. Unlike the Muʿtazila, and in agreement with the early Zaydī view, he held that evil acts, in particular injustice, oppression and transgression (*ʿudwān*) constituted forms of unbelief (*kufr*), though not of unbelief in God or polytheism (*shirk*). Thus it was licit to make war on Muslim oppressors and their supporters.

4. The fourth principle stressed the overriding authority of the Ḳurʾān as a guide-line in all religious matters. Al-Ḳāsim affirmed that the Ḳurʾān as a whole is detailed, unambiguous and free of contradiction. He rejected Imāmī assertions that parts of it had been lost or tampered with. Although his theological principles implied the created nature of the Ḳurʾān, he refused to call it either created or uncreated, partly because of his veneration of the Holy Book and partly because the question was controversial among the contemporary Zaydīs, the majority considering the Ḳurʾān uncreated. Sharply reacting against the rising tide of Sunnī traditionalism, he affirmed that the *sunna* of the Prophet consisted only of what was mentioned or intended in the Ḳurʾān. He accused the Ḥashwiyya (Sunnī traditionalists) of massive forgery of *ḥadīth* and viewed them as the main supporters of the oppressors.

5. Al-Ḳāsim defined the lands dominated by the illegitimate Muslim rulers as an "abode of injustice (*dār al-ẓulm*)" where disposal over property, trade, and economic gain were not fully licit because of the prevalence of usurpation and extortion. Unable to resist the tyrants, the faithful were obliged to emigrate from there. The Ḳurʾānic duty of *hidjra*, imposed initially on the faithful in order that they should dissociate from the polytheists, was permanent and now applied to their dissociation from the unjust and oppressors.

Al-Ḳāsim's view on the imāmate agreed generally with the contemporary Zaydī position [see IMĀMA]. He stressed, however, superior religious knowledge as a prime requirement for the rightful imāmate and ignored the traditional Zaydī requirement of armed revolt. He considered ʿAlī the only legitimate successor of Muḥammad and rejected the caliphate of his three predecessors.

His legal doctrine was basically Medinan and lacked some characteristic Shīʿī elements like the formula *ḥayya ʿalā khayri ʾl-ʿamal* in the *adhān* [*q.v.*] and rights of non-agnates in inheritance. He recognised, however, the validity of the consensus of the Family of the Prophet and relied on reports about ʿAlī transmitted to him by Abū Bakr b. Abī Uways from Ḥusayn b. ʿAbd Allāh b. Ḍumayra with a family *isnād*. He accepted the fifth *imām* of the Imāmī Shīʿa, Muḥammad al-Bāḳir [*q.v.*], as a legal authority, but condemned the later Imāmī *imāms* as wordly exploiters of their pious followers. He is known, however, to have transmitted a book of traditions of Djaʿfar al-Ṣādiḳ [*q.v.*] from his father on the authority of Mūsā al-Kāẓim [*q.v.*] (al-Nadjāshī, *Ridjāl*, ed. Mūsā al-Zandjānī, Ḳumm 1407, 314).

Al-Ḳāsim's theological and legal teaching became basic in the Zaydī communities in western Ṭabaristān and the Yemen. It was, however, partly superseded by the Muʿtazilī and more strictly Shīʿī teaching of his grandson al-Hādī ila ʾl-Ḥaḳḳ [*q.v.* in Suppl.].

Bibliography: The basic biography of al-Ḳāsim is contained in Abu ʾl-ʿAbbās al-Ḥasanī, *al-Maṣābīḥ*, ms. Ambros. B 83; al-Nāṭiḳ bi ʾl-Ḥaḳḳ, *al-Ifāda*, ms. Berlin Glaser 37, partly edited and analysed by R. Strothmann, in *Isl.*, ii (1911), 49-52, 76-8; and al-Muḥallī, *al-Ḥadāʾiḳ al-wardiyya*, ms. B.L. Or. 3786, fols. 2b-15b. Of studies, see W. Madelung, *Der Imam al-Qāsim ibn Ibrāhīm und die Glaubenslehre der Zaiditen*, Berlin 1965; idem, *Imam al-Qāsim ibn Ibrāhīm and Muʿtazilism*, in *On both sides of Al-Mandab ... Studies presented to Oscar Löfgren* Stockholm 1989, 39-47; idem, *Al-Qāsim ibn Ibrāhīm and Christian theology*, forthcoming in *Aram*; B. Abrahamov, *al-Ḳāsim ibn Ibrāhīm's argument from design*, in *Oriens*, xxix-xxx (1986), 259-84; idem, *Al-Ḳāsim Ibn Ibrāhīm's theory of the imamate*, in *Arabica* xxxiv (1987), 80-105; idem, *Al-Ḳāsim b. Ibrāhīm on the proof of God's existence: Kitāb al-dalīl al-kabīr* Leiden 1990. (W. MADELUNG)

RASSIDS, a name sometimes used, most notably by Ibn Khaldūn (*ʿIbar*, iv, 111), of the Zaydī imāms of the Yemen [see ZAYDIYYA]. The term "Banu ʾl-Rassī" is not commonly used by the Yemeni Zaydī historians and may only have gained some currency in Europe after Kay's translation (*Yaman* 184 ff.) of the chapter in Ibn Khaldūn's *ʿIbar*. Perhaps also as a result of Kay's translation, the term Rassid imāms was used soon after in Lane-Poole's *Dynasties*, 102 and table, for the Zaydī imāms down to *ca.* 700/1300. The *nisba* is derived from a place in the Ḥidjāz, al-Rass, held by al-Ḳāsim b. Ibrāhīm Ṭabāṭabā al-Rassī [*q.v.*], the grandfather of al-Hādī ilā ʾl-Ḥaḳḳ Yaḥyā b. al-Ḥusayn [*q.v.*], the first Zaydī imām in the Yemen.

Bibliography: Ibn Khaldūn, *ʿIbar*; H.C. Kay, *Yaman, its early mediaeval history* ..., London 1892; S. Lane-Poole, *The Mohammadan dynasties–chronological and genealogical tables with historical introductions*, Westminster 1894; C.E. Bosworth, *The Islamic dynasties*, Edinburgh 1967, 71-3. (G.R. SMITH)

RASŪL (A., pl. *rusul*), messenger, apostle.

1. In the religious sense. According to the Ḳurʾān, there is a close relation between the apostle and his people (*umma* [*q.v.*]). To each *umma* God sends only one apostle (sūra X, 48, XVI, 38 cf. XXIII, 46, XL, 5). These statements are parallel to those which mention the witness whom God will take from each *umma* at the Day of Judgment (IV, 45, XXVIII, 75 and cf. the descriptions of the *rasūl* who will cross the bridge to the other world at the head of his *umma*: al-Bukhārī, *Adhān, bāb* 129; *Riḳāḳ, bāb* 52).

Muḥammad is sent to a people to whom Allāh has not yet sent an apostle (XXVIII, 46, XXXII, 2, XXXIV, 43). The other individuals to whom the Ḳurʾān accords the dignity of *rasūl* are Nūḥ, Lūṭ, Ismāʿīl, Mūsā, Shuʿayb, Hūd, Ṣāliḥ and ʿĪsā.

The list of the prophets [see NABĪ in *EI*[1] and NUBUWWA] is a longer one; it contains, besides the majority of the apostles, Biblical or quasi-Biblical characters like Ibrāhīm, Isḥāḳ, Yaʿḳūb, Hārūn, Dāwūd, Sulaymān, Ayyūb and Dhu ʾl-Nūn. Muḥammad in the Ḳurʾān is called sometimes *rasūl*, sometimes *nabī*. It seems that the prophets are those sent by God as preachers and *nadhīr* [*q.v.*] to their people, but are not the head of an *umma* like the *rasūl*. One is tempted to imagine a distinction between *rasūl* and *nabī* such as is found in Christian literature: the apostle is at the same time a prophet, but the prophet is not necessarily at the same time an apostle. But this is not absolutely certain, the doctrine at the basis of the Ḳurʾānic utterances not being always clear.

As to the close relation which exists between the *rasūl* and his *umma*, it may be compared with the doctrine of the *Acta apostolorum apocrypha*, according to which the twelve apostles divided the whole world among them so that each one had the task of preaching the Gospel to a certain people.

As regards the term *rasūl*, account must be taken of the use of the word apostle in Christianity, as well as of the use of the corresponding verb (*shalaḥ*) in connection with the prophets in the Old Testament (Exodus, iii, 13-14, iv, 13; Isaiah, vi, 8; Jeremiah, i, 7). The term *rasūl Allāh* is used in its Syriac form (*sheliḥeh d-allāhā*) *passim* in the aprocryphal Acts of St. Thomas.

Post Ḳurʾānic teaching has increased the number of apostles to 313 or 315 without giving the names of all of them (Ibn Saʿd, ed. Sachau, i/1, 10; *Fiḳh Akbar III*, art. 22; Reland, *De religione mohammedica*, 2nd ed., Utrecht 1717, 40).

The doctrine that they were free from mortal sin is part of the faith [see ʿIṣMA]. For the rest, the difference between *rasūl* and *nabī*—apart from the considerable difference in point of numbers—seems in later literature to disappear in the general teaching about the prophets. Thus in the *ʿAḳīda* of Abū Ḥafṣ ʿUmar al-Nasafī, the two categories are treated together and the author makes no difference between *rasūl* and *nabī*. Similarly, al-Īdjī deals with prophets in general, so far as can be seen, including in them the *rasūl*s. If one difference can be pointed out, it is that the *rasūl*, in contrast to the prophet, is a law-giver and provided with a book (commentary on the *Fiḳh Akbar II* by Abu 'l-Muntahā, Ḥaydarābād 1321, 4). According to the catechism published by Reland (40-4), the *rasūl* lawgivers were Ādam, Nūḥ, Ibrāhīm, Mūsā, ʿĪsā and Muḥammad.

In the catechism of Abū Ḥafṣ ʿUmar al-Nasafī, the sending of the apostles (*risāla*) is called an act of wisdom on the part of God. Al-Taftāzānī's commentary calls it *wādjib*, not in the sense of an obligation resting upon God but as a consequence arising from his wisdom. This semi-rationalist point of view is not, however, shared by all the scholastics: according to e.g. al-Sanūsī (cf. his *Umm al-barāhīn*), it is *djāʾiz* in itself but belief in it is obligatory.

Bibliography: A. Sprenger, *Das Leben und die Lehre des Moḥammed*, ii, 251 ff.; Snouck Hurgronje, *Verspreide Geschriften*, index, under "gezanten Gods"; J. Horovitz, *Koranische Untersuchungen*, Berlin-Leipzig 1926, 44 ff.; E. Pautz, *Muhammeds Lehre von der Offenbarung*, index; A.J. Wensinck, in *AO*, ii, 168 ff.; idem, *The Muslim creed*, Cambridge 1932, 203-4; al-Īdjī, *Mawāḳif*, ed. Soerensen, 169 ff.; A. Jeffery, *The Qurʾan as scripture*, in *MW*, xl (1950). See also the *Bibl.* to NUBUWWA.

(A.J. WENSINCK)

2. In the secular sense. For its meaning of "diplomatic envoy, ambassador", in later Arabic usage *safīr*, see ELČI and SAFĪR.

RASŪLIDS, name of a Sunnī dynasty of the Yemen. They took their name from a certain Muḥammad b. Hārūn who had earned for himself the nickname Rasūl ("messenger") under one of the ʿAbbāsid caliphs in the 6th/12th century because of his trustworthiness and efficiency as a confidential envoy. The family tree can be constructed as given below (the element *al-Malik* prefixed to the rulers' honorific titles is omitted here).

By the time the last sultan appeared on the scene, Rasūlid history was marked by serious family squabbles over the leadership.

1. History. The Rasūlid historians and genealogists all claim an Arab pedigree for the family and call them Ghassānids, a branch of al-Azd [*q.v.*]. They further claim that a distant ancestor in the time of the caliph ʿUmar b. al-Khaṭṭāb became a Christian and went to live in Byzantine territory. His children migrated into the lands of the Turkomans and settled among what is described as being the noblest of their tribes, Mandjik. It is probable that the Mendjik of the Oghuz Turks is meant. There they lost their Arab

Muḥammad b. Hārūn (Rasūl)
|
ʿAlī
|
al-Manṣūr ʿUmar (I) (626-47/1228-49)
|
al-Muẓaffar Yūsuf (II) (647-94/1249-95)
|
al-Ashraf ʿUmar (III) (694-6/1295-6) — al-Muʾayyad Dāwūd (IV) (696-721/1296-1322)
|
al-Mudjāhid ʿAlī (V) (721-64/1322-63)
|
al-Afḍal ʿAbbās (VI) (764-78/1363-77)
|
al-Ashraf Ismāʿīl (VII) (778-803/1377-1401)
|
al-Nāṣir Aḥmad (VIII) (803-27/1401-24)
|
al-Manṣūr ʿAbd Allāh (IX) (827-30/1424-7)
|
al-Ashraf Ismāʿīl (X) (830-1/1427-8)
|
al-Ẓāhir Yaḥyā (XI) (831-42/1428-38) — ʿUmar
|
al-Ashraf Ismāʿīl (XII) (842-5/1438-41) — al-Muẓaffar Yūsuf (XIII)

identity entirely and intermarried with the Turkomans and spoke their language. It was only about the time of Muḥammad b. Hārūn himself that the family moved to ʿIrāḳ and from there to Syria and finally to Egypt. There they came to the notice of the ruling Ayyūbid dynasty [*q.v.*]. In all probability, however, the family was originally of Mendjik, Oghuz Turkish origin.

It was either in the train of Tūrānshāh [*q.v.*], the first Ayyūbid sultan in the Yemen and the brother of Ṣalāḥ al-Dīn [*q.v.*], when he conquered the country from Egypt in 567/1173, or in that of his successor and brother, Ṭughtakīn, in 579/1183 that a number of Rasūlid *amīr*s first entered the country. Nūr al-Dīn ʿUmar b. ʿAlī was a fief-holder (*muḳtaʿ*) during the period of Ayyūbid control of the Yemen, and when the last Ayyūbid, al-Malik al-Masʿūd, left the Yemen to travel north to take up the governorship of Damascus in 626/1228-9, he could find no one other than Nūr al-Dīn ʿUmar to act as his deputy there. Al-Masʿūd died in Mecca on his way north. Although Nūr al-Dīn ʿUmar had been instructed to hold the Yemen for the Ayyūbid house until the arrival of a new Ayyūbid ruler, no other member of the family was ever to set foot in the Yemen again. Nūr al-Dīn ʿUmar showed outward allegiance to his Ayyūbid masters in Egypt until 632/1235, when he received an official diploma of authority from the ʿAbbāsid caliph al-Mustanṣir [*q.v.*]. This marks the real beginning of the independent Rasūlid state in Southern Arabia.

The Ayyūbids had made a thorough job of conquering and controlling Tihāma [*q.v.*], the Red Sea coastal plain, and the southern highlands as far north as Ṣanʿāʾ [*q.v.*]. This was the territory the Rasūlids inherited. The Zaydī *imāms* [see ZAYDIYYA] continued to hold much of the land north of Ṣanʿāʾ and the city itself was frequently disputed between them and the Sunnī Rasūlids.

The period after 632/1235, during which the Rasūlids held control of Tihāma and southern Yemen, was without doubt the most brilliant in the mediaeval history of the country. All the hard, pioneering work had been done by their predecessors, the Ayyūbids, with their vast armies, including numerous cavalry. Their conquests had been thorough. In addition, their skilled administrators trained in Syria and Egypt had established an effective administration in the Yemen. The Rasūlids were able to build on to these achievements. They, too, had efficient local civil servants and, what is more, the royal house was blessed with a plethora of gifted intellectuals who brought great scholarly effort to an already highly educated country (see below, 3. Monuments, and 5. Literature).

It is not possible to chronicle in detail the events of more than two centuries of Rasūlid rule in the Yemen. Until his death in 647/1249, al-Manṣūr ʿUmar, the first sultan, was kept busy with the internal affairs of the city of Ṣanʿāʾ. He had signed a peace treaty with the Zaydīs in 628/1230 which included a clause declaring the intention of excluding the Ayyūbid house from the region. Ṣanʿāʾ was granted as a fief to his nephew, Asad al-Dīn Muḥammad b. Ḥasan. He was to prove unreliable, if not actually treacherous, and this is what involved al-Manṣūr so much in the affairs of the city. Al-Manṣūr ʿUmar was murdered in al-Djanad [*q.v.*] near Taʿizz [*q.v.*] in 647/1249 by a gang of *mamlūks*, and al-Khazradjī [*q.v.*], the Rasūlid court historian, has no hesitation in pointing the finger at Asad al-Dīn Muḥammad.

Al-Manṣūr ʿUmar's preoccupation with problems in Ṣanʿāʾ had brought about the neglect of Tihāma and the south of the Yemen. The new sultan, his son, al-Muẓaffar Yūsuf, spent the early years of his rule re-establishing Rasūlid control over these areas. It is surprising that he retained Asad al-Dīn Muḥammad in charge of Ṣanʿāʾ, but the latter was removed in 658/1260 and ʿAlam al-Dīn al-Shaʿbī appointed over Ṣanʿāʾ in his stead. With this new appointment we enter into the zenith of Rasūlid power and achievement in southern Arabia. ʿAlam al-Dīn was a loyal and gifted servant of the Rasūlid house and, with his team of effective troubleshooters, he did much to reassert control over Ṣanʿāʾ and the north of the country.

Thus from his capital city Taʿizz, al-Muẓaffar Yūsuf presided over a Yemen, with the exclusion of the northern highlands north of Ṣanʿāʾ, of unparalleled peace, stability and brilliance. It was during his reign, until 694/1295, that Rasūlid territory reached its most extensive, for, apart from Tihāma and the southern highlands, the northern highlands including Ṣanʿāʾ can be reckoned within Rasūlid control, and also vast territories in the east, Ḥaḍramawt [*q.v.*] and Southern Arabia as far as the maritime settlement of Ẓafār [*q.v.*], present-day al-Balīd, near Ṣalāla in Oman. Here a branch of the family ruled independently or semi-independently for some time (see *Bibl.*, Porter and Smith, in *JRAS*).

Al-Muẓaffar's death in 694/1295 heralded the rule of a long line of his direct descendants. A number of these were extremely able rulers and they promoted the interests of the Rasūlid extremely effectively. It is however, of interest to note that after the death of ʿAlam al-Dīn al-Shaʿbī in 682/1283 Ṣanʿāʾ never again remained long in Rasūlid hands. One might say too that the dynasty never attained its former glory. Gifted as the successive Rasūlid rulers undoubtedly were, the house suffered greatly at the hands of unreliable and at times openly rebellious tribes and equally at the hands of envious and mutinous *mamlūks*.

When al-Nāṣir Aḥmad died in 827/1424, the Rasūlid dynasty crumbled fast. Al-Nāṣir had done much to revive the flagging fortunes of the house. He had made military gains within the Yemen and received rich gifts from as far away as China. Throughout the 830s and 840s/1420s and 1430s, sultans came and went, unable to hold the dynasty together. The *mamlūks* revolted time after time and, what is more, plague visited the land. The Rasūlid *amīrs* began to quarrel among themselves. With the fall of Aden [see ʿADAN] to the Ṭāhirids [*q.v.*] in 858/1454 and the surrender of the Rasūlid *amīr* there, the dynasty came to an end.

2. Coins and mints. A very large number of Rasūlid coins covering at least the period 634-*ca.* 842/1236-*ca.* 1438 minted by all the sultans from al-Manṣūr to al-Ẓāhir is extant. Their main mint towns were Aden, Taʿizz, Zabīd [*q.v.*] and al-Mahdjam, although coins are also known minted in al-Dumluwa, Ṣanʿāʾ, Ḥadjdja, al-Djāhilī, Ẓafār and Thaʿbāt (see below). An interesting feature of Rasūlid coins is the mint figure: for Aden, a fish; for Zabīd, a bird; for al-Mahdjam, a lion; and for Taʿizz and Thaʿbāt, a seated man. It is clear that between the years 735-*ca.* 777/1334-*ca.* 1376, during which coins were minted by the Rasūlids in their small mountain retreat, Thaʿbāt, very near Taʿizz, no coins during this period were minted in the latter place. Fairly recently Rasūlid coins minted in Mabyan have been published (see *Bibl.*, Porter).

3. Monuments. The Rasūlids were great builders also and the visitor today to the southern Yemeni city of Taʿizz can still see the remarkable design and craftsmanship of such buildings as the Djāmiʿ al-Muẓaffar, named after the second sultan, al-Malik al-Muẓaffar (647-94/1249-95) and the Ashrafiyya, named after al-Malik al-Ashraf II (764-78/1377-1401). Other monuments were built by the Rasūlid sultans in al-Djanad, Zabīd, Ibb and other parts of southern Yemen. The monuments show a clear dependence on outside influences, Egyptian, Syrian, etc., and mark an evident break with the early architectural tradition of the Yemen. This break should perhaps be more correctly assigned to the beginning of the Ayyūbid period (569-1173), but the number of Ayyūbid monuments still extant is small.

4. Trade and commerce. Political stability and an efficient administration provided an ideal background for thriving trade and commerce. With Aden as the main port, a remarkable range of goods flowed through, on their way to and from East Africa, Egypt and the Mediterranean, India, South-East Asia and China. Merchants were held in high esteem and were organised under a head of merchants, especially taken care of by the sultan himself. Usually the head of the merchants was in charge of the sultan's *matdjar al-sulṭānī*. Unfortunately, the two texts specifically providing details of this flourishing trade, *Mulakhkhaṣ al-fitan* (see *Bibl.*, Cahen and Serjeant, in *Arabica*) concerning Aden in 814/1411-12 and another from the time of al-Muẓaffar (647-94/1249-95), of which the correct title and author are unknown, remain un-

published. However, both are now providing information on Rasūlid trade and commerce which fully confirms how widespread, sophisticated and lucrative they were. Main imports coming into Aden were cloths, spices and perfumes from India, South-East Asia and China and slaves, ivory and pepper from East Africa. Main exports through Aden in Rasūlid times were textiles, lead and kohl going out to India from Egypt and North Africa. Although precise information is still scant, it can perhaps be noted that three main fees were payable on goods coming into, and going out from, the port of Aden in Rasūlid times. There were the *ʿus͟hūr*, customs dues only rarely in fact a "tenth", the *dilāla*, a commission fee, and the *s͟hawānī*, the latter literally meaning "galleys", a tax imposed from the time of the Ayyūbid al-Masʿūd (d. 626/1228) for the maintenance of the warships employed by the state in the protection of the merchant fleet.

5. Literature. Not surprisingly, the Rasūlid period saw a flowering of literature and a number of members of the royal house were themselves authors of some repute. Al-Muẓaffar Yūsuf (d. 694/1295) composed a selection of forty *ḥadīt͟hs*, a treatise on the movements of the heavenly bodies which is extant, a treatise on medicine (extant), a literary *Mufākahāt al-d͟jalīs* on entertainment and a volume in ten chapters on the pen, ink, gold and silver writing, etc. Al-As͟hraf ʿUmar (d. 696/1296) composed a treatise on astronomy entitled *al-Tabṣira fī ʿilm al-nud͟jūm*, as well as another on veterinary science, *al-Mug͟hnī fi 'l-bayṭara*. Al-Afḍal ʿAbbās (d. 778/1377) produced a miscellany of writings of practical utility, intellectual interest and entertainment entitled *Fuṣūl mad͟jmūʿa fi 'l-anwāʾ wa 'l-zurūʿ wa 'l-ḥiṣād*. The contents include astronomical and astrological data, the astrolabe, agriculture, animals and animal husbandry, warfare, the mangonel, geographical information, a brief polyglot dictionary, etc. Al-As͟hraf Ismāʿīl (d. 803/1401) was the author of a general history of the Yemen entitled *Fākihat al-zaman wa-mufākahat al-ādāb wa 'l-fitan fī ak͟hbār man malaka 'l-Yaman*. The section of this work on the Rasūlids themselves which continues almost to al-As͟hraf's death is particularly useful. This list is by no means exhaustive, and is meant merely to indicate some of the remarkable achievements of the Rasūlid monarchs in the field of literature in its broadest sense.

Bibliography: 1. History. al-As͟hraf Ismāʿīl b. al-ʿAbbās Ibn Rasūl, *Fākihat al-zaman wa-mufākahat al-ādāb wa 'l-fitan fī ak͟hbār man malaka 'l-Yaman*, John Rylands University Library of Manchester, Arabic ms. 19; ʿAlī b. al-Ḥasan al-K͟hazrad͟jī, *al-ʿUkūd al-luʾluʾiyya fī taʾrīk͟h al-dawla al-Rasūliyya, El-Khazreji's History of the Resúlí dynasty of Yemen*, with translation, introduction, annotations, index, tables and map by J.W. Redhouse, text edited by Muḥammad ʿAsal, G.M.S., III, Leiden and London 1906-18, 5 vols., G.R. Smith, *The Ayyubids and Rasulids—the transfer of power in 7th/13th century Yemen*, in *IC*, xliii (1969), 175-88; ʿAbd al-Raḥmān b. ʿAlī Ibn al-Daybaʿ, *Ḳurrat al-ʿuyūn bi-ak͟hbār al-Yaman al-maymūn*. ed. Muḥammad ʿAlī al-Akwaʿ, Cairo 1977, 2 vols.; Smith, *The Ayyubids and early Rasulids in the Yemen*, G.M.S., XXVI, London, 1974-8, 2 vols. (vol. i = the text of Ibn Ḥātim's *al-Simṭ al-g͟hālī al-t͟haman*); *Taʾrīk͟h al-dawla al-Rasūliyya*, ed. ʿAbdallāh Muḥammad al-Ḥibs͟hī, Ṣanʿāʾ 1984; Smith, *The political history of the Islamic Yemen down to the first Turkish invasion (1-945/622-1538)*, in W. Daum (ed.), *Yemen—3000 years of art and civilisation in Arabia Felix*, Innsbruck and Frankfurt/Main, n.d. [*ca.* 1988]; *The Rasulids in Dhofar in the viith-viiith/xiii-xivth centuries*, part I, *The historical background* by G. Rex Smith, part II, *Three Rasulid tombstones from Ẓafār* by Venetia Porter, in *JRAS* (1988), 26-44.

2. Coins and mints. W.F. Prideaux, *Coins of the Benee Rasool dynasty of South Arabia*, in *JBBRAS*, xvi (1885), 8-16; H. Nützel, *Münzen der Rasuliden*, Berlin 1891; idem, *Münzen der Rasuliden nebst einem Abriss der Geschichte dieser jemenischen Dynastie*, in *Zeitschrift für Numismatik*, xviii (1892), 127; E. von Zambaur, *Die Münzprägungen des Islams*, Wiesbaden 1968; Smith, *The Yemenite settlement of Thaʿbāt: historical, numismatic and epigraphic notes*, in *Arabian Studies*, i (1974), 119-34; idem, *Some medieval Yemenite numismatic problems—observations on some recently sold coins*, in *Arabian archaeology and epigraphy*, i (1990), 29-37; Porter, *The Rasulid Sultan al-Malik al-Manṣūr and the mint of Mabyan*, in *ibid.*, 38-45.

3. Monuments. R. Lewcock and G.R. Smith, *Three medieval mosques in the Yemen*, in *Oriental Art*, xx (1974), 75-86 and 192-203; Ismāʿīl b. ʿAlī al-Akwaʿ, *al-Madāris al-Islāmiyya fi 'l-Yaman*, Ṣanʿāʾ 1980; Lewcock, *The medieval architecture of Yemen*, in Daum, *Yemen*, 204-12; Porter, *The art of the Rasulids*, in *ibid.*, 232-54; Barbara Finster, *The architecture of the Rasulids*, in *ibid.*, 254-65.

4. Trade and commerce. Cl. Cahen and R.B. Serjeant, *A fiscal survey of medieval Yemen*, in *Arabica*, iv (1957), 23-33; Serjeant, *Early Islamic and mediaeval trade and commerce in the Yemen*, in Daum, *Yemen*, 163-7; D.M. Varisco, *Medieval agricultural texts from Rasulid Yemen*, in *Manuscripts of the Middle East*, iv (1989), 150-4.

5. Literature. Varisco, *op. cit.*; A. El-Shami and R.B. Serjeant, *Regional literature: the Yemen*, in Julia Ashtiany *et alii* (eds.), *The Cambridge history of Arabic literature. ʿAbbasid belles-lettres*, Cambridge 1990, 442-68. (G.R. Smith)

RATAN, Bābā, Ḥād͟jd͟jī, Abu 'l-Riḍā, a long-lived Indian saint, famous in almost all the lands of Islam, called Ratan b. Kirbāl b. Ratan al-Batrandī in the *Ḳāmūs* (Cairo 1330, iv, 226; see variants in *Iṣāba*, Calcutta, i, 1087; *Lisān al-mīzān*, ii, 450 ff.). The *nisba* (vocalised as al-Bitrandī in *Lisān al-mīzān*, and *Tād͟j al-ʿarūs*, ix, 212) is derived, according to al-Zabīdī, from al-Bitranda, "a city in India", where, as we learn from the *Āʾīn-i Akbarī* (ed. Sayyid Aḥmad K͟hān, ii, 207 = tr. Jarrett, iii, 360), Ratan was born and where he died. This place is now called Bhatinda, lies in 30° 13′ N. and 75° E., and is the headquarters of the Govindgarh *taḥṣīl* (in Anāhadgaṙh Niẓāmat) of what was the Patiāla State, hence now in the East Pand͟jāb state of the Indian Union [see bhattinda]. It is an important railway junction and its old name was probably Tabarhind (see *Punjab States Gazetteers*, xvii, A; *Phulkian States*, Lahore 1909, 188 ff.). Three miles from this town, at a place called Ḥād͟jd͟jī Ratan, exists the shrine of the saint, "a large building with a mosque and gateway, and surrounded by a wall on all sides" (*ibid.*, 80). The shrine, which seems to have been an important place of pilgrimage even in the 12th/18th century (see *Tād͟j al-ʿarūs*, *loc. cit.*), is visited now mostly by Muslims, but Hindus also frequent it, particularly at the *ʿurs* (annual fair) of the Ḥād͟jd͟jī, held from the 7th to the 10th D͟hu 'l-Ḥid͟jd͟ja, when a large number of Sādhūs also attend. For nearly five centuries the shrine has been held by Madārī *faḳīrs*, whose ancestor S͟hāh Čānd came from Makanpur in Oudh. These *gaddīnashīrs* let their hair grow and do not marry.

Who was this Ḥād͟jd͟jī Ratan? It appears from combining the extant narratives of over a dozen men who had visited him in his native place from various parts of the Muslim world, that, in the 7th/13th century, there lived at Bhatinda a man, Ratan by name, about whom "it was said that he was a long-lived individual, who had met the Prophet, was present with him at the Ditch (at the siege of Medina in A.H. 6), when the Prophet prayed for his long life, that he was present when Fāṭima was conducted as a bride to ʿAlī, may God be pleased with both of them, and who transmitted *ḥadīth*" (*Tādj al-ʿarūs, loc. cit.*).

We get the following particulars also from some of these narratives about his mode of life, personal appearance, etc. A merchant of Khurāsān, who had interviewed him, tells us that Ratan was living under a *fūfal* tree (peepal?—for *fūfal* or *Areca catechu* does not fit in with the context), that his teeth were small like those of a serpent, that his beard, whose hairs were mostly white, was like thorns, that he lifted his eyebrows, which reached down to his cheeks, with a hook, that he said he had never been married, and the length of the space occupied by him, when sitting, was three cubits (al-Djanadī, quoted in *Iṣāba*, i, 1099). Another merchant, from the same land, found him laid like the young one of a bird, in a large basket, stuffed with cotton, which was hanging from a branch of a huge tree outside the village, and was worked by means of a pulley. He spoke in Persian, his voice being like the humming of a bee. He referred to all the inhabitants of the big village as his children or grandchildren (*Iṣāba*, i, 1094; *Lisān al-mīzān*, ii, 452, quoting the *Tadhkira* of al-Ṣafadī, who, in his turn, is quoting the *Tadhkira* of al-Wadāʿī (d. 726/1326), see Brockelmann, II², 10, S II; Ḥādjdjī Khalīfa, ii, 264). Contrary to the first narrative, which tells us that he was never married, the second makes him say that he had a large progeny, and, in fact, Ibn Ḥadjar includes two of Ratan's sons, Maḥmūd and ʿAbd Allāh, among the transmitters of *ḥadīth* from him.

Some of these narratives represent him as having been first converted to Christianity and then to Islam (*Iṣāba*, i, 1097-8).

The date of his death is given variously, as A.H. 596, 608, 612, 632 (*Iṣāba*), 700, and even 709 (*Āʾīn-i Akbarī*; *Fawāt al-wafayāt*).

The sayings of the Prophet, which Ratan transmitted from him directly, called *al-Rataniyyāt* (cf. *Tādj al-ʿarūs, loc. cit.*), were collected in book form and a copy, containing about 300 *ḥadīth*, and dated A.H. 710, was seen by Ibn Ḥadjar. These were handed down from Ratan by Abu 'l-Fatḥ Mūsā b. Mudjallī al-Ṣūfī, and al-Dhahabī suspected that either he had forged them or that they had been forged for Mūsā by someone who had invented for him the story of Ratan (*Iṣāba*, i, 1090). An earlier collection of forty sayings was made, out of Mūsā's stock, by Tādj al-Dīn Muḥammad b. Aḥmad al-Khurāsānī. Some of these sayings, of which about eighteen are quoted in the *Iṣāba*, are preserved in manuscripts in Leiden, Berlin and Lucknow, and show "traces of both Shīʿite (or perhaps better ʿAlide) and Ṣūfic tendencies" (*Journal of the Panjab Historical Society*, ii, 112). Al-Fīrūzābādī had heard them from the companions of Ratan's companions (*Ḳāmūs, loc. cit.*).

The claims of Ratan widely attracted the attention of Muslims in the 7th/13th century, and caused a lot of differences of opinion in Muslim circles in subsequent centuries, as would be indicated by the following list of some outstanding personalities, who expressed themselves for or against his main claim, viz. of being a long-lived Companion of the Prophet.

For: 1. Shaykh Raḍiyy al-Dīn ʿAlī-yi Lālā al-Ghaznawī (d. 642/1244), who associated with Ratan in India and received from him a comb, with the transmission of which the Prophet had entrusted Ratan; 2. Rukn al-Dīn ʿAlāʾ al-Dawla al-Simnānī (d. 736/1336), whom the above-mentioned comb ultimately reached, along with a *khirḳa* received by ʿAlī-yi Lālā from Ratan. Rukn al-Dīn attested this in writing (see *Nafaḥāt al-uns*, Calcutta 1858, 50, with notes of Lārī on the passage); 3. ʿAbd al-Ghaffār b. Nūḥ al-Ḳūṣī (d. 708/1309), the author of the *Kitāb al-Waḥīd fī sulūk ahl al-tawḥīd*, for which see Ḥādjdjī Khalīfa, vi, 432, cf. Brockelmann, II², 142 (see *Iṣāba*, i, 1096); 4. al-Djanadī (d. 732/1332), the author of the *Taʾrīkh al-Yaman*; cf. Brockelmann, II², 234 (in *Iṣāba*, i, 1096-7); 5. Ṣalāḥ al-Dīn al-Ṣafadī (d. 764/1363); see above (previous col.); 6. Shams al-Dīn Muḥammad b. Ibrāhīm al-Djazarī (d. 739/1338-9), the author of *Ḥawādith al-zamān wa anbāʾihi* for which see Sarkīs, *Muʿdjam al-maṭbūʿāt*, col. 696, is also apparently to be added to this list; see *Iṣāba*, i, 1092; 7. Khʷādja Muḥammad Pārsā (d. 822/1419), see *Āʾīn-i Akbarī*, ii, 207 (= tr. Jarrett, iii, 360); 8. Nūr Allāh Shūshtarī (about 1010), who maintains that the Sunnī opposition to Ratan's claim was really due to (*a*) Ratan's being a Shīʿī, most of whose *ḥadīth* was in praise of the *Ahl al-Bayt* and their partisans, and to (*b*) the jealousy of the contemporary Sunnī *ʿulamāʾ*, who were thrown into shade by the *Ṣaḥābī*, who could transmit *ḥadīth* directly from the Prophet (*Madjālis al-muʾminīn*, Tehran 1299/1882, 309).

Against: 1. al-Dhahabī (673-748/1274-1348), who attacked Ratan violently in his *Tadjrīd* (quoted in *Iṣāba*, i, 1087), *Mīzān al-iʿtidāl*, i, 336, and *al-Mushtabih*, 215, and even wrote a monograph on the subject entitled *Kasr wathan Ratan* (quoted in *Iṣāba*, i, 1088-9), in which he insinuated that only those could admit his claim to Companionship of the Prophet who believed in the continued existence of Muḥammad (al-Muntaẓar) b. al-Ḥasan (the twelfth Imām), and the palingenesis (*radjʿa*) of ʿAlī (see *Iṣāba*, i, 1091; cf. *Lisān al-mīzān*, ii, 452); 2. ʿAlam al-Dīn al-Birzālī al-Shāfiʿī (d. 739/1339) (see *Fawāt al-wafayāt*, i, 163); 3. Burhān al-Dīn Ibn Djamāʿa (d. 790/1388, see Brockelmann, II², 136) (quoted in *Iṣāba*, i, 1101); 4. Madjd al-Dīn al-Fīrūzābādī, who was in India about A.H. 785-90 and had visited Bhatinda (in *Ḳāmūs, loc. cit.*; but cf. *Iṣāba*, i, 1102); 5. Ibn Ḥadjar al-ʿAsḳalānī (d. 852/1449), in *Iṣāba*, i, 1101-2, and in *Tabṣīr al-muntabih,* Rāmpūr ms., p. 79, also quoted in *Tādj al-ʿarūs*, ix, 212; 6. al-Zabīdī (d. 1205/1791), in *Tādj al-ʿarūs, loc. cit.*

Apart from the above literary tradition, the Muslims as well as the Hindus of Bhatinda, have preserved local versions of Ratan's story.

The earlier Muslim version represents him as the Minister of Vena Pāl, the Hindu Rādja of Bhatinda, at the time of Shihāb al-Dīn Muḥammad Ghūrī's invasion, when he betrayed the fortress to the Muslims. He was converted to Islam and performed the *hadjdj*. According to a fuller version, still current in Bhatinda, he was a Čawhān Rādjpūt, Ratanpāl by name. He knew by his knowledge of astrology that the Prophet would be born in Arabia and spread Islam. In order to be able to see him, he practiced restraining his breath. After the miracle of *shaḳḳ al-ḳamar* (splitting the moon into two), which he witnessed, Ratan set out for Mecca, was converted to Islam, and lived with the Prophet for thirty years. Then he returned to India and stayed where his shrine is now, continuing the practice of restraining his breath. Later, when Shihāb al-Dīn Ghūrī proceeded to Bhatinda to fight Prithī Rādj, the sultan visited the Ḥādjdjī, the saint performed a miracle and became instrumental in the conquest of the fort, shortly after which event he died, at the age of 700 years (*Journal of the Panjab Historical Society*, ii, 98; *Glossary of the tribes and castes of the Panjab and N.W.F. Province*, i, 551).

The Hindu version, also still current at Bhatinda, asserts that he was a much-travelled, miracle-working Hindu Sādhū, of the Nāth clan, and that his name was Ratan Nāth. He won the confidence of the Muslims by manifesting his miraculous powers in Mecca, which he had visited in his wanderings. He then came to Bhatinda, and lived and died there. He was buried and his *samādh* was built, which the Muslim replaced by a *khānkāh*, and called him Ḥādjdjī, on account of his visit to Mecca (see *JPHS*, ii, 100; it gives some other Hindu versions also).

For Ratan's connection with some versions of Gūga's legend, see *Glossary of the tribes and castes of the Panjab and N.W.F. Province*, i, 175, 179, 181.

Horovitz reconciled these divergent versions in a striking theory: "It may be that Ratan was originally a Yogī, who as such was believed to have been alive hundreds of years and who on becoming acquainted with the Muḥammadan aspects of longevity, used them to strengthen his position in the eyes of his Muḥammadan followers... The saint had two faces: he showed that of a long-lived Yogī to the Hindūs, that of a companion of the Prophet to the Muḥammadans" (*JPHS*, ii, 113-14).

Bibliography: J. Horovitz's article on *Bāba Ratan, the Saint of Bhatinda*, in *JPHS*, ii, 97 ff., gives the fullest information, with references, to which may be added: Ibn Ḥadjar, *Lisān al-mīzān*, Ḥaydarābād 1330, ii, 450 ff. (mostly repeats his own article in *Iṣāba*); Zabīdī, *Tādj al-ʿarūs*, ix, 212; H.A. Rose, *A glossary of the tribes and castes of the Punjab and North-West Frontier Province*, 1919, i, 152, 175, 179, 181. In an Arabic-Persian *Kitāb al-Arbaʿīn* (ms. in the Pandjāb University Library, defective at the beginning), a fuller version of the story given by Horovitz on p. 110 n. 1, occurs, with the name of Hārūn substituted for that of Sultan Maḥmūd.

(Moḥammad Shafīʿ)

RĀTIB (A., pl. *rawātib*), a word meaning what is fixed and hence applied to certain non-obligatory *ṣalāt*s or certain litanies. The term is not found in the Ḳurʾān nor as a technical term in *Ḥadīth*. On the first meaning, see NĀFILA. As to the second, it is applied to the *dhikr* [*q.v.*] which one recites alone, as well as to those which are recited in groups. We owe to Snouck Hurgronje a detailed description of the *rawātib* practised in Acheh [*q.v.*].

Bibliography: C. Snouck Hurgronje, *De Atjèhers*, Batavia-Leiden 1893-4, ii, 220. English tr. O'Sullivan, *The Achehnese*. Leiden 1906, ii, 216; Constance E. Padwick, *Muslim devotions*, London 1961, 22 (definition), 291 and 301 (lists of *rawātib* ascribed to well-known *shaykhs*).

(A.J. Wensinck)

RAṬL [see MAKĀYIL].

RAWĀḤA, Banū, a Shāfiʿī family originally from the town of Ḥamāt [*q.v.*], numerous members of which held public office in this town, as also in Damascus and Tripoli during the Ayyūbid period and in the early times of the Baḥriyya Mamlūks. The Banū Rawāḥa, of Medinan origin and belonging to the tribe of Khazradj, seem to have had an ancestor in the Companion of the Prophet ʿAbd Allāh b. Rawāḥa b. Imriʾ al-Ḳays, who distinguished himself in the majority of his military campaigns, became Muḥammad's accredited poet and died a martyr's death at Muʾta [*q.v.*] in 8/629; this would account for the fact that numerous members of this family are known to have born the name ʿAbd Allāh. (Ibn Saʿd, *Ṭabaḳāt*, ed. Sachau, iii/2, 79-82; al-Ṣafadī, *Wāfī*, xvii, 168-70; art. ʿABD ALLĀH B. RAWĀḤA).

Four members of a primary branch of the Banū Rawāḥa, linked by direct line of descent, are known to us:

(1) Abū Muḥammad ʿABD ALLĀH b. al-Ḥusayn, "*khaṭīb* Ḥamāt", died in 561/1166 (or 562/1167), aged 75. Official preacher of Ḥamāt and poet, he composed, while passing through Baghdād in the course of the Pilgrimage, numerous poems in praise of the caliph al-Muḳtafī (Sibṭ Ibn al-Djawzī, *Mirʾāt al-zamān*, viii/1, 263; *Wāfī*, xvii, 142-4).

(2) His son, Abū ʿAlī AL-ḤUSAYN (515-85/1121-89), *faḳīh* and poet; his surviving works include an ode honouring Ṣalāḥ al-Dīn and a few fragments of erotic poetry (al-ʿImād al-Iṣfahānī, *Kharīdat al-ḳaṣr (Shām)*, i, 484, and Yāḳūt, *Muʿdjam al-udabāʾ*, x, 46-56). His life was eventful; taken prisoner, he lived in Sicily, then on his release he spent some time in Alexandria, returned to Syria and died a martyr's death at the battle of Mardj ʿAkkā (*Wāfī*, xii, 413-14).

(3) The son of the above-named, ʿIzz al-Dīn Abu 'l-Ḳāsim ʿABD ALLĀH, born in Sicily in 560/1165, during the captivity of his father; in Alexandria, he had numerous audiences with the eminent traditionist al-Silafī, between 570/1175 and 575/1179, the date of the latter's death. A *muḥaddith* himself and a poet, he lived in Aleppo and in Ḥamāt, where he was buried in Djumādā II 646/July-August 1248 (al-Dhahabī, *Tārīkh*, ms. Bodl. Land 305, fol. 212; *Wāfī*, xvii, 144-5).

(4) His grandson, Nūr al-Dīn AḤMAD b. ʿAbd al-Raḥmān b. ʿAbd Allāh, known as "*al-khaṭīb*", held the post of *kātib al-inshāʾ* at Tripoli and in the occupied cities (*futūḥ*). He died in Ḥamāt in Shaʿbān 712/December 1312 (Ibn al-Ṣuḳāʿī, *Tālī al-wafayāt*, 45 (44 in the Arabic text) and 148; *Wāfī*, vi, 56-7).

From a collateral branch of the Banū Rawāḥa, another known individual is Zakī al-Dīn HIBAT ALLĀH b. Muḥammad b. ʿAbd al-Wāḥid b. Rawāḥa, apparently a first cousin to al-Ḥusayn (cf. no. 2, above), who lived in Damascus and died there in Radjab 623/June-July 1226. A wealthy merchant, poet and sworn witness (*muʿaddal*), enjoying much respect in Damascus, he founded two *madrasa*s for the teaching of Shāfiʿī *fiḳh*, one at Aleppo, the other in Damascus, this being the Rawāḥiyya, founded in 622/1225. No longer in existence, it was situated in the interior of the Bāb al-Farādīs, to the north of the Great Mosque. Its founder lived there until his death in an apartment to the east of the *madrasa*, opposite the opulent library which he had also founded. He had richly endowed this *madrasa*, thus enabling students of humble means to lodge there, including the eminent *muḥaddith* and *faḳīh* al-Nawawī (d. 676/1277 [*q.v.*]). He had laid down the following conditions for admission to this *madrasa*: "Neither Jew nor Christian nor anthropomorphist Ḥanbalī (*ḥashwī*) shall enter here." Before his death he had designated as superintendent (*nāẓir*) of the *madrasa* the great *faḳīh* Taḳī al-Dīn Ibn Ṣalāḥ al-Shahrazūrī (d. 643/1245); but after his death two individuals, the Ṣūfī Ibn ʿArabī and a grammarian named Khazʿal, who both lived close to the *madrasa* in question, accused Ibn Rawāḥa of having dismissed him.

Serious disruption ensued in the functioning of the *madrasa*, at least until the time of the death in 665/1267 of Abū Shāma, our principal source of information.

Bibliography: In addition to the references cited in the text, see Abū Shāma, *Tarādjim* (= *Dhayl al-*

Rawḍatayn), ed. Kawt͟harī, 149; cf. also D͟hahabī, *ʿIbar*, v, 92; Ṣafadī, *Wāfī*, ms. Bodl. 1,678, fol. 208; Ibn Kat͟hīr, *Bidāya*, xiii, 116, who dates his death to 622/1225, and especially, Nuʿaymī, *al-Dāris*, i, 266, 267; see also L. Pouzet, *Damas au VIIe/XIIIe siècle*, Beirut 1988, 155, 157, 170. (L. Pouzet)

RĀWALPINDI, the name of a city, district and division of the northern Pand͟jāb in Pākistān. The city lies in lat. 33° 40′ N. and long. 73° 08′ E. at an altitude of 530 m/1,750 feet. In British Indian times, it was one of the most important military stations of northern India, and is now the headquarters of the Pākistān Army, with extensive cantonments, as well as being an important commercial and industrial centre and the starting-point of the route into Kas͟hmīr. From 1959 to 1969 it was the capital of Pākistān before the removal of this to the new city of Islāmābād 14 km/9 miles to its northeast. The population of the city and of the surrounding district and division is almost wholly Muslim. In 1972 the city had an estimated population of 615,000.

Since Rāwalpindi lies in the path of invaders from the north-west, much of its history resembles that of the Pand͟jāb [*q.v.*]. The district formed part of Gandhāra and was included in the Persian empire of the Achaemenids. About ten miles to the north-west of the town lie the ruins of the ancient city of Taks͟haçila (Taxila) which was an important seat of learning in the 4th century B.C. The Muslim invaders experienced much trouble from the turbulent Gakkhar tribes of this area who are still the most important tribe socially in the district. In the days of Akbar [*q.v.*], the territories included in the modern district of Rāwalpindi formed part of the *sarkar* of Sind Sāgar Dōāb in the *ṣūba* of Lahore (*Āʾīn-i Akbarī*, tr. Jarrett, ii, 324).

Rāwalpindi grew in importance when a Sikh adventurer, Sardār Milka Singh, occupied it in 1765 and brought in colonists to it, but after 1849 it passed, with the rest of the Pand͟jāb, under British control.

Bibliography: In addition to the works cited in pand͟jāb, see *Imperial gazetteer of India*², xxi, 261-73; J.H. Marshall, *Archaeological discoveries at Taxila*, 1913; *Guide to Taxila*, 1918; *Rāwalpindi District Gazetteer*, 1907; H.A. Rose, *A glossary of the tribes and castes of the Punjab and North-West Frontier Province*, 1919, s.v. Gakkhars.

(C. Collin Davies-[C.E. Bosworth])

al-**RĀWANDĀN** (present-day [Turkish] Revanda Kalesi; Frankish Ravendel; Armenian Arevĕntan), a fortress of the north Syrian borderlands, situated south of Gaziantep (ʿAyn Tāb [see ʿaynṭāb]), and about 16 km/10 miles west of Kilis on the Turkish side of the modern frontier with Syria. It occupies the top of a conical hill overlooking the upper ʿAfrīn River. We first hear of the place in 490-1/1097, at the start of the Crusades, when it was seized by Baldwin of le Bourg from the Turks, who had taken it from the Armenians, apparently the first occupants. Baldwin restored it to the Armenians, but later retrieved it from them, giving it, in 495-6/1102, to Joscelin I. After a brief period of Byzantine control following on the capture of its Frankish ruler Joscelin II, Count of Courtenay, it was secured in 546/1151-2 by Nūr al-Dīn Maḥmūd b. Zangī [*q.v.*], passing in due course from Zangid to Ayyūbid hands. Subsequent rulers included al-Malik al-Ẓāhir, ruler of Aleppo, and S͟hihāb al-Dīn Ṭog͟hril, regent for al-Ẓāhir's infant heir al-Malik al-ʿAzīz. In 624/1226-7, Ṭog͟hril gave it to al-Malik al-Ṣāliḥ Aḥmad of ʿAyn Tāb. On the latter's death, the fortress passed to al-Ṣāliḥ's nephew, al-Malik al-Nāṣir Yūsuf II, the ruler of Aleppo. Thereafter, al-Rāwandān's fortunes shared those of the rest of northern Syria: the onslaught of the Mongols, followed by their retreat, and the establishment of Mamlūk rule under Baybars. Little remains today of the fortress except the entrance arrangements, and the principal salients of the walls.

Bibliography: Albert of Aix, *Historia Hierosolymitana*, iii/17-18, in *RHC, historiens occidentaux*, iv, 350-1; Ibn al-ʿAdīm, *Bughya*, ed. S. Zakkār, Damascus 1988, i, 324, 457; Ibn al-At͟hīr, *al-Dawla al-Atābakiyya*, in *RHC, historiens orientaux*, ii/2, 182-3; Ibn S͟haddād, *al-Aʿlāḳ*, i/2, ed. Y. ʿAbbāra, Damascus 1991, 94-7; William of Tyre, *Historia Rerum in partibus transmarinis gestarum*, x/24, in *RHC, historiens occidentaux*, i/1, 437; Yāḳūt, *Buldān*, Beirut 1979, iii, 19; Cahen, *La Syrie du Nord*, 117-18; H. Hellenkemper, *Burgen der Kreuzritterzeit*, Bonn 1976, 43-6; D. Morray, in *Anatolian Studies*, liii (1993) (on a visit by Ibn al-ʿAdīm to al-Rāwandān).

(D.W. Morray)

RĀWANDĪ, Muḥammad b. ʿAlī, Persian historian who flourished at the end of the Sald͟jūḳ period. Details of his life are known only from information in his sole surviving work, the *Rāḥat al-ṣudūr wa-āyat al-surūr*, a dynastic history of the Great Sald͟jūḳs [*q.v.*]. Rāwandī belonged to a scholarly family from Rāwand, near Kās͟hān. He studied Ḥanafī *fiḳh* in Hamad͟hān from 570/1174 to 580/1184 and became a skilled calligrapher and gilder. When sultan Ṭog͟hrïl III b. Arslan wanted a beautiful Ḳurʾān, Rāwandī, as a member of the team of craftsmen, gained favour at court. After Ṭog͟hrïl's imprisonment in 586/1190, Rāwandī found other patrons and one of them, a certain S͟hihāb al-Dīn al-Kās͟hānī, encouraged him to begin writing the *Rāḥat al-ṣudūr* in 599/1202.

Rāwandī would have doubtless liked to dedicate his work to a Sald͟jūḳ prince of Persia. After the dynasty's demise in Persia in 590/1194 and the advent of the K͟hʷārazms͟hāh, whose rule Rāwandī deplores (30-2), he sought patronage from Ḳonya, wanting his book to be in the "name of a Sald͟jūḳ sultan" (62). Indeed, he went there personally to present his work (64). Originally, he had dedicated it to sultan Sulaymān II (d. 600/1204), but he was obliged to re-address his panegyrics to Kayk͟husraw I [*q.v.*] after his accession that year (19-38). The re-orientation of Rāwandī's work towards Rūm is a clear indication that early 7th/13th century Persian scholars viewed the Anatolian Sald͟jūḳ dynasty as the new champions of Sunnī Islam, and Ḳonya as the centre for the continuation of Persian scholarly traditions.

For its account of Sald͟jūḳ history until Ṭog͟hrïl III, the *Rāḥat al-ṣudūr* is one of several Persian historical sources dependent on the *Sald͟jūḳ-nāma* of Nīs͟hāpūrī (d. *ca.* 582/1182 [*q.v.*]). Rāwandī's history is, however, an invaluable first-hand source for Ṭog͟hrïl's reign. The work is deeply permeated with the *Fürstenspiegel* ethos. Far from being a detailed history, it is a didactic essay on exemplary kingship in which a skeletal narrative framework is fleshed out with illustrative anecdotes, Arabic aphorisms (with accompanying Persian translations) and poetic quotations (notably from Niẓāmī and the *S͟hāh-nāma*, as well as lesser-known poets, including Rāwandī himself). The last section of the book discusses courtly accomplishments and is drawn from Ḥanafī legal works (418). Generally, Rāwandī's approach resembles that of Muḥammad Malaṭyawī in his *Barīd al-saʿādat*, dedicated to Kayk͟husraw's successor in Ḳonya, Kaykāwūs (cf. Fouchécour, 430).

Rāwandī's history was often used by later Persian

historians (especially Yazdī) and was translated into Turkish in the reign of sultan Murād II (cf. Barthold, 16; Storey, i, 257). Rāwandī also wrote a polemical work against the Rāfiḍīs [see RĀFIḌIYYA] and another on calligraphy (*Rāḥat al-ṣudūr*, 394, 445), which have apparently not survived.

Bibliography: Ch. Schefer, *Nouveaux mélanges orientaux*, Paris 1886, 3-47; E.G. Browne, *Account of a rare, if not unique, manuscript history of the Seljúqs*, in *JRAS* (1902), 567-610, 849-87; Muḥammad Yazdī, *al-ʿUrāḍa fi ʾl-ḥikāya al-saldjukiyya*, ed. K. Süssheim, Leiden 1909; Rāwandī, *Rāḥat al-ṣudūr*, ed. Muḥammad Iqbál, London 1921, Tkish. tr. Ahmed Ateş, Ankara 1957-60; Barthold, *Turkestan down to the Mongol invasion*[3], 29; Ẓahīr al-Dīn Nīshāpūrī, *Saldjūk-nāma*, Tehran 1332/1954; K.A. Luther, *The political transformation of the Seljuq sultanate of Iraq and Western Iran, 1152-1187*, Ph.D. diss., Princeton 1964, unpubl.; idem, *Rāvandī's report on the administrative changes of Muḥammad Jahān Pahlavān*, in C.E. Bosworth (ed.), *Iran and Islam, in memory of the late Vladimir Minorsky*, Edinburgh 1971, 393-406; Ch. de Fouchécour, *Moralia, les notions morales dans la littérature persane du 3e/9e au 7e/13e siècle*, Paris 1986; Storey, i, 256-7; Storey-Bregel, ii, 747-9.

(CAROLE HILLENBRAND)

AL-**RĀWANDIYYA**, a term referring to an extremist Shīʿī group which originated within the ʿAbbāsid movement in Khurāsān. The term was subsequently expanded to include at times the entire ʿAbbāsid *shīʿa*, but unless otherwise stated it will be used in this article in its original sense. It is said in some sources to derive from al-Ḳāsim b. Rāwand or from Abu ʾl-ʿAbbās al-Rāwandī, both of whom are otherwise unknown; other sources more plausibly derive it from ʿAbd Allāh al-Rāwandī, who appears in a list of propagandists (*duʿāt*) of Muḥammad b. ʿAlī b. ʿAbd Allāh b. al-ʿAbbās [*q.v.*] (see *Akhbār al-dawla al-ʿabbāsiyya*, ed. ʿAbd al-ʿAzīz al-Dūrī and ʿAbd al-Djabbār al-Muṭṭalibī, Beirut 1971, 222). Both ʿAbd Allāh's son Ḥarb (d. 147/764) and his grandson Naṣr b. Ḥarb were senior officers in the ʿAbbāsid army in ʿIrāḳ during al-Manṣūr's reign. Ḥarb who, like his son, is said to have been a member of the Rāwandiyya [see KAYSĀNIYYA], participated in the crushing of the revolt of the Ḥasanid Ibrāhīm b. ʿAbd Allāh [*q.v.*] before being killed in Armenia by Turkish rebels (al-Ṭabarī, iii, 296, 353); he was also given an estate in an area north of the Round City of Baghdād which became known after him as al-Ḥarbiyya (cf. *ibid.*, iii, 328).

Initially, the Rāwandiyya appear to have argued (in line with the bulk of the Hāshimiyya) that the imāmate had passed from ʿAlī via Muḥammad b. al-Ḥanafiyya to the latter's son Abū Hāshim ʿAbd Allāh and then, in accordance with Abū Hāshim's testament (*waṣiyya*), to Muḥammad b. ʿAlī b. ʿAbd Allāh b. al-ʿAbbās (al-Nawbakhtī, *Firaḳ*, 29-30; Saʿd b. ʿAbd Allāh, *Maḳālāt*, 39-40; al-Baghdādī, *Farḳ*, 40); they are therefore occasionally counted among the Kaysāniyya. Al-Nawbakhtī's source (evidently Hishām b. al-Ḥakam [*q.v.*]), referring to the group as *ghulāt al-rāwandiyya*, adds that the doctrines which they espoused included deification of the imāms, belief in their omniscience, and dispensation from the religious law for those who know the imāms; he notes that their strength increased when most of the followers of ʿAbd Allāh b. Muʿāwiya [*q.v.*] joined their ranks. Some further details are provided by al-Madāʾinī's [*q.v.*] father (as cited in al-Ṭabarī, iii, 418) when he describes the first recorded Rāwandī uprising, crushed by Asad b. ʿAbd Allāh al-Ḳasrī [*q.v.*] during his governorship of Khurāsān (116-19/734-7). A leper called al-Ablaḳ ("piebald"), who aspired to lead the Rāwandiyya at the time, upheld the doctrine of the periodic incarnation of the deity on earth by claiming that the spirit of Jesus had passed on to ʿAlī and then, successively, to each of the imāms up to Muḥammad b. ʿAlī's son Ibrāhīm [see IBRĀHĪM B. MUḤAMMAD]; he and his followers also sanctioned communal access to women.

Most sources agree that the Rāwandī doctrine of the imāmate underwent a significant shift after the ʿAbbāsid rise to power: the imāmate was no longer believed to have started with ʿAlī rather than with al-ʿAbbās, from whom it passed to his descendants. The Rāwandiyya based their belief in al-ʿAbbās's succession to the Prophet on the ancient inheritance laws whereby the paternal uncle excludes daughters, cousins and nephews; and they interpreted accordingly the Ḳurʾānic verse "Those related by blood are nearer to one another in the Book of God" (VIII, 75, XXXIII, 6). There are indications that this doctrine had its advocates in the ʿAbbāsid court some time before its emergence as an official tenet under al-Manṣūr and especially under al-Mahdī (cf. M. Sharon, *Black banners from the East*, Jerusalem and Leiden 1983, 82-99); it remains to be established whether it was first elaborated among the Rāwandiyya and was then adopted as the official ʿAbbāsid line or whether, in contrast, the Rāwandiyya mirrored the changing court ideology.

In a report from an unnamed source, Ibn al-Djawzī (viii, 29) describes the Rāwandiyya as a group (*ṭāʾifa*) of Bāṭinīs (i.e. Ismāʿīlīs) known as Sabʿiyya, who believed that the cycle (*dawr*) of the imāms which began with al-ʿAbbās ended with the seventh, al-Manṣūr. The reference to the Rāwandiyya as Bāṭinīs must be a back-projection; at the same time, if indeed they insisted on a line of seven imāms, this would make them the earliest "Sevener" Shīʿī group, predating the Wāḳifiyya who emerged after the death of Mūsā al-Kāẓim [*q.v.*].

The sources present a confused and sometimes contradictory picture of the relationship between the Rāwandiyya and other groups in the early ʿAbbāsid period. Some (such as Ps.-Nāshiʾ) identify them with the Hurayriyya (followers of Abū Hurayra al-Rāwandī or al-Dimashḳī), and regard the Rizāmiyya (followers of Rizām b. Sābiḳ) as an offshoot of the Rāwandiyya/Hurayriyya. Others (e.g. Abū Ḥātim al-Rāzī [*q.v.*]) maintain that both the Rāwandiyya and Hurayriyya upheld the pure ʿAbbāsid line, but that the Rāwandiyya also believed in the divinity of al-Manṣūr and the prophethood of Abū Muslim; the Rizāmiyya, in turn, held to the earlier line of imāms via Abū Hāshim, believing in addition that Abū Muslim had not died. In Abū Ḥātim al-Rāzī's *K. al-Zīna* these three groups are described as comprising the ʿAbbāsiyya (i.e. the ʿAbbāsid *shīʿa*). In contrast, al-Nawbakhtī's source identifies the Rāwandiyya with the ʿAbbāsid *shīʿa* as a whole and says that it consisted of three subgroups: the Abū Muslimiyya, for whom Abū Muslim was the living imām; the Rizāmiyya who, in addition to following the line of imāms via Abū Hāshim, secretly believed in Abū Muslim (presumably while acknowledging that he had died); and the Hurayriyya, described as "the pure ʿAbbāsids" (*al-ʿabbāsiyya al-khullaṣ*), who upheld the imāmate from al-ʿAbbās.

There are scattered references to disturbances involving Rāwandīs in the first ʿAbbāsid decade. In 135/752-3 a group from Ṭālaḳān, headed by Abū Isḥāḳ (perhaps Khālid b. ʿUthmān, an ʿAbbāsid *dāʿī* who had been commander of Abū Muslim's guard), attacked and killed one of Abū Muslim's officers before they themselves were slain (al-Ṭabarī, iii, 82). After this incident they were no longer heard of in Khurāsān, but they reappeared a few years later in the West. Here the most widely reported event is the riot sometimes referred to as *yawm al-rāwandiyya*. Its date is variously given as 136 or 137 (al-Ṭabarī, citing an anonymous source), 139 or the beginning of 140 (al-Balādhurī), 140 (Ibn al-ʿIbrī), 141 (al-Ṭabarī and others) and 142 (al-Dīnawarī), and it is said to have taken place in al-Hāshimiyya [*q.v.*] (or in Baṣra, according to al-Dīnawarī, whose version also differs in other details). The accounts in al-Balādhurī (iii, 235-6) and al-Ṭabarī (iii, 129-33) speak of 600 Rāwandīs who took part, all of whom were Khurāsānī followers of Abū Muslim who believed that Ādam's soul resided in ʿUthmān b. Nahīk (one of al-Manṣūr's security officers who was killed in the ensuing combat) and that al-Haytham b. Muʿāwiya (like ʿUthmān, an ʿAbbāsid *dāʿī*) was the angel Gabriel. They began to circumambulate al-Manṣūr's palace, hailing him as their God (*rabb*) who provided them with food and drink. At this point al-Manṣūr, who seems at first to have tolerated (or even welcomed) their excesses, drew the line. He had 200 of their leaders incarcerated and forbade the others to congregate; disregarding his order, they stormed the prison and released their colleagues. When they headed back towards the palace al-Manṣūr left on foot and was provided with a saddled horse outside. The Shaybānī leader Maʿn b. Zāʾida [*q.v.*], an erstwhile Umayyad general who had been in hiding from the ʿAbbāsids, came to the rescue and, in a display of courage which won al-Manṣūr's admiration, managed to beat off the attackers, virtually all of whom were killed. According to other reports, Abū Naṣr Mālik b. al-Haytham (who had been among the original *nuḳabāʾ*) personally guarded the palace gates, while the military commander Khāzim b. Khuzayma, together with the local populace, was instrumental in overcoming the Rāwandīs. One of the attackers, Rizām (founder of the Rizāmiyya?), was granted amnesty after he sought refuge with the caliph's son Djaʿfar. The reason given in the sources for the attackers turning against al-Manṣūr is their anger at the arrest of their leaders; it would seem that they were also bitterly disappointed with the caliph's unwillingness to come up to their expectations of him. That al-Manṣūr was in serious danger is confirmed by reports that he was almost killed by the rioters (e.g. Ibn al-Athīr, v, 502: *kādū yaḳtulūnahu*). The incident dramatically pointed up the caliph's vulnerability and contributed to his decision to look for a capital elsewhere, a decision which eventually led to the beginning of work on Baghdād.

Two reports concerning the riot are especially noteworthy. The first (al-Ṭabarī, iii, 418-9) describes some Rāwandīs as jumping to their deaths from the green dome of the palace (referred to as al-Khaḍrāʾ, which was also the name of the green dome of the Baghdād palace; cf. J. Lassner, *The topography of Baghdad in the early Middle Ages*, Detroit 1970, 135-6). That such behaviour was not atypical is suggested by an account concerning another group of Rāwandīs. These men revolted in Aleppo and Ḥarrān in 141/758-9; believing themselves to be in the same rank (*manzila*) as angels, they mounted a hill in Aleppo, put on silk clothes, jumped off and perished (Ibn al-ʿAdīm, *Zubdat al-ḥalab min taʾrīkh Ḥalab*, ed. Sāmī al-Dahhān, i, Damascus 1370/1951, 59-60). In the second report (al-Balādhurī, iii, 235) the Rāwandiyya state that, if al-Manṣūr wished, he could make the mountains move, and if he were to order them to turn their backs to Mecca during prayer they would comply. This formulation also appears in Ibn al-Muḳaffaʿ's [*q.v.*] *Risāla fī 'l-ṣaḥāba* which he composed for al-Manṣūr (probably between 136/754 and 142/759), when he describes the views of some over-zealous Khurāsānian troops (ed. Muḥammad Kurd ʿAlī, Cairo 1946, 120; cf. S.D. Goitein, *A turning point in the history of the Muslim state,* in his *Studies in Islamic history and institutions*, Leiden 1966, 156). It is thus possible that the troops against whom he warned the caliph were the Rāwandiyya.

Hardly anything is heard of this group after the death of al-Manṣūr, though some of them were involved in the struggle over his succession. The more extreme elements merged into other sects known collectively as Khurramiyya [*q.v.*]. The number of those who upheld al-ʿAbbās's designation as Muḥammad's successor appears also to have diminished sharply. Marwān b. Abi 'l-Djanūb [*q.v.*] still wrote for al-Mutawakkil a poem about the hereditary rights of the ʿAbbāsids (al-Ṭabarī, iii, 1465-6, cited in Goldziher, *Muslim studies*, ed. S.M. Stern, ii, London 1971, 100-1); yet by the time of al-Sharīf al-Murtaḍā (d. 436/1044) the last adherents of this doctrine had apparently disappeared (cf. *al-Shāfī fi 'l-imāma*, Tehran 1301/1884, 99).

Bibliography (in addition to the references given in the article): Ps.-Nāshiʾ, in J. van Ess, *Frühe muʿtazilitische Häresiographie*, Beirut 1971, Ar. text, 31-2, 35-6; Balādhurī, *Ansāb al-ashrāf*, iii, ed. ʿAbd al-ʿAzīz al-Dūrī, Beirut 1398/1978, 208, 210, 235, 236; Dīnawarī, *al-Akhbār al-ṭiwāl*, ed. V. Guirgass, Leiden 1888, 380; Nawbakhtī, *K. firaḳ al-shīʿa*, ed. H. Ritter, Istanbul 1931, 30, 35, 41-2, 46-7; Saʿd b. ʿAbd Allāh al-Ḳummī, *K. al-Maḳālāt wa 'l-firaḳ*, ed. Muḥammad Djawād Mashkūr, Tehran 1963, 40, 64, 69-70; Ashʿarī, *Maḳālāt*, ed. H. Ritter, 21-2, 462; idem, *al-Ibāna ʿan uṣūl al-diyāna*, Ḥaydarābād 1321, 94; Ṭabarī, index; Abū Ḥātim al-Rāzī, *K. al-Zīna*, iii, in ʿAbd Allāh S. al-Sāmarrāʾī, *al-Ghuluww wa 'l-firaḳ al-ghāliya fi 'l-ḥaḍāra al-islāmiyya*, Baghdād 1392/1972, 300, 305; Azdī, *Taʾrīkh al-Mawṣil*, ed. ʿA. Ḥabība, Cairo 1387/1967, 173; al-Maḳdisī, *al-Badʾ wa 'l-taʾrīkh*, ed. Cl. Huart, Paris 1899-1919, v, 124, 131-2, 133, vi, 83-4; Masʿūdī, *Murūdj*, ed. and tr. Pellat, index; al-Ḳāḍī al-Nuʿmān, *al-Urdjūza al-mukhtāra*, ed. I.K. Poonawala, Quebec 1970, 209-10; ʿAbd al-Djabbār, *al-Mughnī*, xx/i, Cairo n.d., 238, xx/ii, Cairo n.d., 177-8 (citing Abu 'l-Ḳāsim al-Balkhī); ʿAbd al-Ḳāhir al-Baghdādī, *al-Farḳ bayna 'l-firaḳ*, Beirut n.d., 40, 272-3; idem, *al-Milal wa 'l-niḥal*, ed. A. Nader, Beirut 1970, 54; Ibn Ḥazm, *al-Fiṣal*, ed. Muḥammad Ibrāhīm Nuṣayr and ʿAbd al-Raḥmān ʿUmayra, Beirut 1405/1985, v, 49; *al-ʿUyūn wa 'l-ḥadāʾiḳ*, ed. M.J. de Goeje and P. de Jong, Leiden 1871, 227-8; Nashwān b. Saʿīd al-Ḥimyarī, *al-Ḥūr al-ʿīn*, Cairo 1948, 153; Ibn al-Djawzī, *al-Muntaẓam*, ed. Muḥammad ʿAbd al-Ḳādir ʿAṭāʾ and Muṣṭafā ʿAbd al-Ḳādir ʿAṭāʾ, Beirut 1412/1992, viii, 29-30; Fakhr al-Dīn al-Rāzī, *Iʿtiḳādāt firaḳ al-muslimīn wa 'l-mushrikīn*, Cairo 1356/1938, 63; Ibn al-Athīr, *al-Kāmil fi 'l-taʾrīkh*, Beirut 1385-6/1965-6, v, 502-4; Abu 'l-Faradj Ibn al-ʿIbrī (Bar Hebraeus), *Mukhtaṣar taʾrīkh al-duwal*, Beirut n.d. [1978-9], 122; Ibn al-Ṭiḳṭaḳā, *al-Fakhrī*, ed. H. Derenbourg, Paris 1895, 216-17; Murtaḍā b. Dāʿī Rāzī, *Tabṣirat al-ʿawāmm*, ed. ʿAbbās Iḳbāl, Tehran 1313 Sh./1934, 33, 178-80, 208; Dhahabī, *Taʾrīkh al-islām*, ed. ʿUmar ʿAbd al-Salām Tadmurī, ix, Beirut 1408/1988, 5-7; Ibn Kathīr, *al-*

Bidāya wa 'l-nihāya, Cairo 1351-8/1932-9, x, 75-6; G. van Vloten, *Recherches sur la domination arabe* etc., Amsterdam 1894, 48-9; I. Friedlaender, *The heterodoxies of the Shiites*, New Haven 1909, i, 70, ii, 100-1, 121-4; idem, *Jewish-Arabic studies*, in *JQR*, N.S., ii (1911-2), 503-4; Gholam Hossein Sadighi, *Les mouvements religieux iraniens au IIe et au IIIe siècle de l'hégire*, Paris 1938, 180, 209-11; ʿAbd al-ʿAzīz al-Dūrī, *al-ʿAṣr al-ʿabbāsī al-awwal*, Bag͟hdād 1363/1943, 37-8, 88-90; S. Moscati, *Il testamento di Abū Hāšim*, in *RSO*, xxvii (1952), 28-46, at 33, 46; H. Laoust, *Les schismes dans l'Islam*, Paris 1965, 31, 55, 62; Farouk Omar, *The ʿAbbāsid caliphate*, Bag͟hdād 1969, 138, 163, 192-9; idem, *Buḥūt͟h fi 'l-taʾrīk͟h al-ʿabbāsī*, Beirut 1977, 68-9; T. Nagel, *Untersuchungen zur Entstehung des abbasidischen Kalifates*, Bonn 1972, 28, 53; idem, *Rechtleitung und Kalifat*, Bonn 1975, 118, 301-9, 415; W. Montgomery Watt, *The formative period of Islamic thought*, Edinburgh 1973, 155-6; Wadād al-Ḳāḍī, *The development of the term Ghulāt in Muslim literature with special reference to the Kaysāniyya*, in *Akten des VII. Kongresses für Arabistik und Islamwissenschaft*, ed. A. Dietrich, Göttingen 1976, 295-319, at 305; J. Lassner, *The shaping of ʿAbbāsid rule*, Princeton 1980, 109-11, 159-60, 182; H. Kennedy, *The early Abbasid caliphate*, London 1981, index; D. Gimaret and G. Monnot, *Livre des religions et des sectes*, i, Peeters/Unesco 1986, index; van Ess, *Theologie und Gesellschaft im 2. und 3. Jahrhundert Hidschra*, iii, Berlin and New York 1992, 10-19.

(E. Kohlberg)

RAWĀNDIZ, Ruwāndiz, a town of Kurdish ʿIrāḳ, the chef-lieu of a *ḳaḍāʾ* in the *liwāʾ* of Irbil. In *ca.* 1940 it had a population of 7,000. It lies in lat. 36° 37′ N. and long. 44° 33′ E. at an altitude of *ca.* 914 m/3,000 feet on a route which connects Mawṣil and Irbil [*q.vv.*] via the Garū S͟hinka pass (1,830 m/6,000 feet) with Mahābād/Sāwd͟j-Bulāḳ [*q.vv.*]. The route was described in early Islamic times only by Yāḳūt, enumerating seven stages from Mawṣil to Sāwd͟j-Bulāḳ.

History. It will be evident that Rawāndiz, situated at the intersection of the communications of Kurdistān as well as of roads leading farther afield, has always owed its importance to its position. It should also be remembered that in the period of prosperity of the Nestorian Church all this country played a great part, mainly on account of the influence of the Metropolitan see of Arbil. We may mention (cf. Hoffmann, *Auszüge*) the names of Dara, Hanitha, S͟haḳlāwa (from which came one of the mss. which enabled the Abbé Chabot to establish the text of the *Synodicon orientale*, Paris 1902), as well as the fact that there were many monasteries in these parts. According to the late Metropolitan Mar Ḥanānīs͟hōʿ, the *naḥall* of Barādost (not to be confused with the Barādost of the S͟hiḳāḳ Kurds to the north of Tergawar; see urmiya) before the First World War had still a few Christian communities. From the point of view of Kurdish history, the destinies of Rawāndiz have been frequently those of S͟hahrizūr, of which it formed part at certain times. The Persian historian Aḥmad Kasrawī Tabrīzī (*S͟hahriyārān-i gum-nām*, ii, *Rawādiyān*, Tehran 1308/1929) gives us some notes (125, 133-6) on Rawāndiz in the time of the Aḥmadīlī [*q.v.*] Atābeks (501-624/1106-1227) the last representative of whom, a woman, became the wife of D͟jalāl al-Dīn K͟hʷārazms͟hāh. A local history of the *wālī*s of Ardalān, a resumé of which was published by B. Nikitine, in *RMM*, xlix, 70 ff., also contains some information about the families ruling in Rawāndiz down to A.H. 1249.

In the early 19th century, one of these lords, the half-blind Muḥammad K͟hor ("the blind"), dominated the local tribes and established his power from 1826 onwards as far as the Little Zāb and Irbil and then in 1833 as far as ʿAmādiyya and Zak͟hō, and minted coins of his own as *al-Amīr al-Manṣūr Muḥammad Bīk*; but after his fall in 1836 and deportation by the Ottomans, Rawāndiz shrank once more to a place of minor significance only. During the First World War the Rawāndiz road was used in the winter of 1914-15 by K͟halīl Bey's troops advancing on Urmiya (contrary to H. Grothe, *Die Türken und ihre Gegner*, Frankfurt a.M. 1915) and later in July 1916 by the Russian Rybalčenko. After the armistice and during the period till December 1925, when the League of Nations made its decision on the *wilāyat* of Mawṣil, Rawāndiz was the focus for attempts at some form of autonomy or independence under the Kurdish chief S͟hayk͟h Maḥmūd Barzand͟jī, who in 1922 proclaimed himself in the *liwāʾ* of Sulaymāniyya "Pādis͟hāh of Kurdistān", and also for Turkish attempts at this time to retain the region within Turkey, with a Turkish *ḳāʾim-maḳām*, ʿAlī S͟hefīḳ, appointed to Rawāndiz in 1922. The town was, however, recovered for the new Kingdom of ʿIrāḳ government in April 1923 by a combined operation of the ʿIrāḳī army and local Assyrian Christian levies, and an administration installed there under Sayyid Ṭāhā of Neri as *ḳāʾim-maḳām*. In 1925 a League of Nations commission awarded the *wilāyet* of Mawṣil, including Rawāndiz, to ʿIrāḳ.

Language. Kurdish is the language spoken in this region, except by the town dwellers (Irbil, Altūn Köprü, Kirkuk, etc.) of Turkish origin. According to O. Mann (*Die Mundart der Mukri Kurden*, ii, 205), the dialect of Rawāndiz is very like that of S͟hamdīnān, but E.B. Soane did not share this opinion (*Kurdish grammar*, London 1913). F. Jardine's manual, *Bahdinan Kurmanji, a grammar of the Kurmanji of the Kurds of Mosul division and surrounding districts of Kurdistan*, London 1922, is more particularly devoted to this dialect.

Bibliography: M. Bittner, *Der Kurdengau Uschnûje und die Stadt Urûmije*, Vienna 1895; M. Streck, *Das Gebiet der heutigen Landschaften ... Kurdistân*, in *ZA*, xv (1900); S.H. Longrigg, *Four centuries of modern Iraq*, Oxford 1925; *Admiralty Handbooks. Iraq and the Persian Gulf*, London 1944, 548-50 and index; Longrigg, *ʿIraq 1900 to 1950, a political, social and economic history*, London 1953; B. Nikitine, *Les Kurdes, étude sociologique et historique*, Paris 1956; C.J. Edmonds, *Kurds, Turks and Arabs*, London 1957. See also kurds, kurdistān.

(B. Nikitine-[C.E. Bosworth])

RAWḌA (a.), literally "garden"; an island in the Nile in the southern part of Cairo about 3 km/2 miles long and with an average width of 500 m/1,640 ft. A narrow canal (al-K͟halīd͟j or Sayyālat al-Rawḍa) divides the eastern bank of the river from the island. Before the regulation of the river in the 19th century, the canal often dried out. From the time of the establishment of Arab rule until the early 19th century, the island was mostly connected by pontoon bridges with both banks of the river (the Fusṭāṭ as well as the D͟jīza shore). The island has been the place of a Nilometer (*Miḳyās* [*q.v.*]) since the early 2nd/8th century. Concerning the historical topography of Rawḍa, see miṣr. C. 2. ii.

As long as the annual rise of the Nile was celebrated, the island was of crucial importance in the social life of Cairo. Each year at this time, until the high crest was reached (*wafāʾ al-Nīl*), i.e. for about two months, people gathered in tents and pavilions on the island celebrating, while expecting the opening of the Cairo canal in early August. Their unbridled behaviour often led to their removal from the island and the burning down of their tents (see Ibn Iyās, *Badāʾiʿ al-zuhūr*, Cairo 1960-92, who reports this fact for later mediaeval times). In mediaeval times, the island was used, for strategic reasons, for fortifications and the naval arsenal [see MIṢR, *loc. cit.*]. Two rulers, Aḥmad b. Ṭūlūn (254-70/868-84 [*q.v.*]) and the Ayyūbid al-Malik al-Ṣāliḥ (636-47/1240-9) thought it worthwhile to build fortresses on the island; neither of these, however, lasted for long. Ibn Ṭūlūn's fortress was built as a place of retreat when he was threatened by the caliphal power, but it was never used and soon decayed. Al-Malik al-Ṣāliḥ was equally led to take advantage of the island. In order to secure his position he had begun to import Turkish Mamlūks, and it was more convenient to have them reside outside al-Ḳāhira. He may also have intended securing a retreat for himself in case of an attack by the Crusaders, but it seems more plausible to assume that he wanted to be able to deploy instantaneously his warships anchoring there in case of a Frankish attack on Egypt's Mediterranean ports. After al-Ṣāliḥ's death, the vast fortress—half of the island was encircled by walls—was abandoned. The Mamlūk ruler al-Ẓāhir Baybars (658-76/1260-77 [*q.v.*]) rebuilt the *ḳalʿa*; apparently he intended to use this Rawḍa citadel as his stronghold, but the advantages were not sufficient to replace in the long run the Ḳalʿat al-Djabal (see *EI*[1] art. *Rawḍa*, where it is falsely stated that the Baḥrī line of the Mamlūks reigned there). Thereafter, the materials of the Ḳalʿat al-Rawḍa were re-used by succeeding sultans for their own buildings.

From the 4th/10th century, Rawḍa was a place of recreation, due to its clement climatic conditions. Gardens and palaces, and a residential area were built. Muḥammad b. Ṭughdj al-Ikhshīd (323-34/935-46 [*q.v.*]) built a garden called al-Mukhtār, and the Fāṭimid vizier al-Afḍal b. Badr al-Djamālī (d. 515/1121 [*q.v.*]) laid out the garden, *rawḍa*, whence the name of the island. In the time before this and afterwards, the island was called Djazīrat Miṣr or simply al-Djazīra. In *ca.* 519/1125, the Fāṭimid caliph al-Āmir [*q.v.*] built a palace called Hawdadj. During these times, Rawḍa is said to have been a town in itself, and several Friday mosques were built, pointing to the growing population density on the island. The oldest mosque, the Djāmiʿ Ghayn, is attributed to the black eunuch Ghayn (d. 404/1013), a high Fāṭimid official.

About a century later, the above-mentioned al-Afḍal built the Djāmiʿ al-Miḳyās, which was later rebuilt by al-Malik al-Ṣāliḥ, became part of his *ḳalʿa* and was called Djāmiʿ al-Rawḍa. This mosque was destroyed and rebuilt by al-Muʾayyad Shaykh al-Maḥmūdī in 824/1421 (Ibn Duḳmāḳ, *K. al-Intiṣār*, i, Cairo 1310/1893, 115-16) and finally destroyed in the 19th century (ʿAlī Mubārak Pasha, *al-Khiṭaṭ al-djadīda*, xviii, 13). The erection of the huge *ḳalʿa* temporarily put an end to that situation because al-Malik al-Ṣāliḥ evacuated the island and destroyed the greater part of the buildings. But after al-Ṣāliḥ's death, the island apparently became more populated because the number of buildings round the Djāmiʿ Ghayn increased and the *khuṭba* was pronounced there again. Parts of the decayed *ḳalʿa* were used for private buildings, and a new Friday mosque was built in the early 8th/14th century (the Djāmiʿ Fakhr). This mosque was renovated a few decades later by the vizier al-Maḳsī, hence was called the Djāmiʿ al-Maḳsī. In 886/1481 the dilapidated mosque wa[s] demolished by Sultan Ḳāyitbāy and again rebuilt. Thereafter, it was called Djāmiʿ al-Sulṭān (or Djāmiʿ Ḳāyitbāy). This mosque existed until the 19th century (*al-Khiṭaṭ al-djadīda*, xviii, 13-14). In 896/1491 the still extant *madrasa* of Ḳāyitbāy was completed as well. There also existed after 770/1368 a Friday mosque called the Djāmiʿ al-Raʾīs, Ibn Duḳmāḳ mentions about 20 *masdjids* and several *zāwiyas* on the island a[t] the beginning of the 9th/15th century. According to Ibn Ẓahīra (= Abū Ḥāmid al-Ḳudsī), *al-Faḍāʾil al bāhira*, Cairo 1969, 202, in the late 9th/15th century the eastern shore of the island was densely built up and Felix Fabri, a European traveller who stayed there in 1483, even reports that the whole island wa[s] encircled by high buildings with people everywhere (*Le Voyage en Egypte de Félix Fabri 1483*, Cairo 1975, 3 vols., iii, 443-4); but he was also told that, just 1[5] years previously, no building was to be found there. His impression was that the arm of the Nile dividing Rawḍa and Cairo cut the town in half. Leo Africanu[s] in 1517 confirmed the crowdedness of the island; he counted 1,500 hearths and mentions a palace which the reigning sultan had built at the northern end of the island (*Description de l'Afrique*, tr. A. Épaulard, Paris 1956, 511-12). The Sultan al-Ghawrī is said to have ordered the building of a new Friday mosque near the Nilometer in 917/1511 (Ibn Iyās, iv, 175).

Several statements of travellers in the 16th and 17th centuries suggest that Rawḍa was used as a place fo[r] recreation by the local inhabitants and as a residential area, contrary to the assumption, expressed in *EI*[1] art. *Rawḍa*, that the island was abandoned in Ottoman times up to the early 19th century. In 159[8] Harant mentioned about 100 houses (*Le Voyage en Egypte de Christophe Harant*, Cairo 1972, 231). Half-a-century later, de Monconys reported that there were to be found buildings and an area with pavilions of the nobles which was like a town of its own (*Le Voyage en Egypte de Balthasar de Monconys*, Cairo 1973, 157-8). This is corroborated by Ewliyā Čelebi (1091/1680)—whose statements have to be taken critically—when he praises the island, mentioning numerous streets and buildings (*Seyāḥat-nāme*, Istanbul 1938, x, 321-2, 325-7). ʿAbd al-Ghanī al-Nābulusī spent some time on the island, and praised it for its beauty (*al-Ḥaḳīḳa wa 'l-madjāz*, Cairo 1986, 236-7). In 1806 ʿAlī Bey al-ʿAbbāsī found Rawḍa abandoned, having been formerly a little paradise; he praises the French for having formed the walk with rows of trees which traversed the island from south to north (*Travels*, London 1816, repr. 1970, ii, 22-3). In later Ottoman times, Rawḍa was likewise one of the favourite fields of military practice for the Mamlūks; in the fights between the rival Mamlūk groups, one of the factions used to resort to the island.

In the 19th century many gardens and palaces, and also mosques (sometimes used as funerary mosques), were built. A large garden (no longer extant), which is described as a kind of botanical and zoological garden, was founded in the northern part of the island (*al-Khiṭaṭ al-djadīda*, xviii, 11). In recent times, the island has become mainly a residential area.

It should be mentioned that poetry on Rawḍa is abundant, often as a part of anthologies on gardens (*rawḍiyyāt*); see e.g. Abū Djaʿfar al-Idrīsī, *Anwār ʿulwiyy al-adjrām*; al-Suyūṭī, *Kawkab al-Rawḍa* (Brockelmann, II[2], 202); Ibn Duḳmāḳ *op. cit.*, ch. on Rawḍa; and ʿAbd al-Ghanī al-Nābulusī, *op. cit.*

Bibliography: In addition to references in the article, see Suyūṭī, *Ḥusn al-muḥāḍara fī taʾrīkh Miṣr wa 'l-Ḳāhira*, ed. Muḥammad Abu 'l-Faḍl Ibrāhīm,

Cairo 1386/1968; Maḳrīzī, *Kitāb al-Mawāʿiẓ*; ʿAlī Mubārak Pas̲h̲a, *al-K̲h̲iṭaṭ al-d̲j̲adīda*, Cairo 1306/1888-9, xviii, 2-111. (O. Weintritt)

RAWḌA-K̲H̲ᵂĀNĪ, a S̲h̲īʿī Persian mourning ritual commemorating the suffering and martyrdom of Imām Ḥusayn, the grandson of the prophet Muḥammad and other S̲h̲īʿī martyrs. The name of this public lamentation is derived from the title of a literary masterpiece called *Rawḍat al-s̲h̲uhadāʾ* ("The Garden of the Martyrs"). This book, written in Persian but under an Arabic title, was composed by Ḥusayn Wāʿiẓ Kās̲h̲ifī [*q.v.*] in 908/1502-3 when S̲h̲īʿī Islam was being imposed as the state religion of Persia. *Rawḍa-k̲h̲ʷānī* literally means "recitation from the Garden [of the Martyrs]" and is popularly called just *rawḍa*. Originally, it was customary to recite or chant a chapter from *The Garden of the Martyrs* in public each day during the first ten days of the month of Muḥarram. Gradually, it was staged during the whole month of Muḥarram and the following month of Ṣafar, eventually to be performed all year round. Today, despite the fact that it is still called "the Garden Recitation", the original text has been almost abandoned as each *Rawḍa-k̲h̲ʷān* (person who does the recitation) tries his own creative skills in conjuring up the story.

All classes of society participate in the *Rawḍa-k̲h̲ʷānī*, which can be held anywhere from black tents set up for the occasion in the public square of a village or town, to a mosque or a courtyard of a private house, or even to special edifices built for the S̲h̲īʿī mourning rituals called *Ḥusayniyya* or *takiyya*. These buildings have been constructed in Persia from the end of the 18th century onwards.

Rawḍa-k̲h̲ʷānī belongs to the category of the stationary S̲h̲īʿī commemorative rituals which are collectively known at *mad̲j̲ālis al-ʿazāʾ*. It starts with the chants invoking the prophet Muḥammad and other saints and is followed by a *rawḍa-k̲h̲ʷān*, a master story-teller, who recites and sings the story of Ḥusayn and his family and followers at the bloody battle of Karbalāʾ while sitting on a *minbar* above the assembled crowd. His rapid chanting in a high-pitched voice alternates with sobbing and crying to arouse the audience to an intense state of emotion. The audience responds with weeping, chest beating, and body flagellation. The performance can last from a couple of hours to an entire day, well into the night as a succession of *rawḍa-k̲h̲ʷāns* are being used. The *rawḍa-k̲h̲ʷānī* ends with the congregational singing of *nawḥa* [see niyāḥa] (dirges).

The art of *rawḍa-k̲h̲ʷānī* depends on the ability of the *rawḍa-k̲h̲ʷān* to manipulate the assembled crowd, using his (or her, if the gathering is entirely female) choice of episodes of the tragedy as well as his or her use of body language and tonality. A successful *rawḍa-k̲h̲ʷān* is able to bring the audience to a state of frenzy in which the members of the audience identify with the suffering of Ḥusayn and other martyrs. According to popular belief, participation in *rawḍa-k̲h̲ʷānī* ensures participants of intercession by Ḥusayn on Judgement Day. Almost from its inception it has been a tradition that mixed the past with the contemporary, and *rawḍa-k̲h̲ʷāns* often make digressions into the political, social and moral issues of the day. This makes the *rawḍa-k̲h̲ʷānī* a very important political weapon.

Outside Persia, *rawḍa-k̲h̲ʷānī* had been used in India in its original form, but now exists in modified versions reflecting Indian cultural influences. In Baḥrayn, the Persian model is still followed. Other S̲h̲īʿa communities also observe this public lamentation for Ḥusayn and other martyrs according to local traditions. The intensity of feeling discharged in these rituals, no matter where, is universal.

Bibliography: Ḥusayn Wāʿiẓ Kās̲h̲ifī, *Rawḍat al-s̲h̲uhadāʾ*, Tehran 1341 *S̲h̲*.; Mahmoud Ayoub, *Redemptive suffering in Islam*, The Hague 1978; P.J. Chelkowski (ed.), *Taʿziyeh: ritual and drama in Iran*, New York-Tehran 1979; G.E. von Grunebaum, *Muhammadan festivals*, New York-London 1958; G. Thaiss, *Religious symbolism in social change. The drama of Husain*, in Nikki R. Keddie (ed.), *Scholars, saints, and Sufis*, Berkeley, etc. 1972. (P. Chelkowski)

RAWḤ b. ḤĀTIM b. Ḳabīṣa b. al-Muhallab b. Abī Ṣufra (d. 18 Ramaḍān 174/28 January 791) was the fourth governor from the Muhallabids [*q.v.*] of Ifrīḳiya, where there preceded him successively a distant cousin, ʿUmar b. Ḥafṣ b. ʿUt̲h̲mān b. Ḳabīṣa (151-4/768-71), his brother Yazīd (19 D̲j̲umādā II 155-18 Ramaḍān 170/27 May 772-13 March 787) and his nephew Dāwūd b. Yazīd who, on his father's death, took over in the interim until the arrival of his uncle Rawḥ on 1 Rad̲j̲ab 171/16 December 787.

Rawḥ had first served in the army before rejoining, in 159/776, the group of governors. He is mentioned for the first time in 132/749-50, at the siege of Wāsiṭ, in the army of Abu 'l-ʿAbbās al-Saffāḥ. Ten years later, in 142/759, he fought in Ṭabaristān in the service of al-Manṣūr, and is then found subsequently acting as chamberlain for the latter caliph.

In 159/776 he was made governor of Sind by al-Mahdī. From then onwards, with intervals of varying length when he was available for service, spent probably at court, he was appointed governor of Kūfa, Baṣra, Ṭabaristān, Armenia and Palestine, this being his last post in the east. In 166/782-3, when he was governor of Baṣra, his son Dāwūd was accused of *zandaḳa* and arrested, but freed once he had recanted. Recalled from Palestine, Rawḥ learnt in Bag̲h̲dād of the death of his brother Yazīd at Ḳayrawān. The new caliph Hārūn al-Ras̲h̲īd appointed him as Yazīd's successor.

He found a province left in a peaceful state by his brother, allowing him to govern there without incident. He had the good sense to make peace firm by establishing good relations with the Imām of Tāhart. By then he was very aged, and it often happened, we are told, that he went to sleep during meetings. The officer in charge of the *barīd* [*q.v.*] (postal and intelligence service) informed al-Ras̲h̲īd about this, who, in order to prepare for all eventualities, secretly appointed another Muhallabid, Naṣr b. Ḥabīb, to succeed Rawḥ on his death. Rawḥ, for his part, had left the power to his son Ḳabīṣa. In this way, probably with a deliberately theatrical gesture, during the investiture ceremony for Ḳabīṣa in the Great Mosque, the *ṣāḥib al-barīd* exhibited al-Ras̲h̲īd's diploma in favour of Naṣr. Those present acquiesced.

The evidence shows that the caliph was keeping a weather eye open, and did not want a dynastic tradition to become established in North Africa. After two years and three months, Naṣr was dismissed, and the interim authority entrusted to al-Muhallab b. Yazīd whilst the new governor, another son of Rawḥ, al-Faḍl, was awaited. Al-Faḍl entered Ḳayrawān in Muḥarram 177/April-May 793, the eighth and last Muhallabid governor in Ifrīḳiya. Trouble broke out immediately, and in S̲h̲aʿbān 178/November 794, al-Faḍl was killed in a revolt by the *d̲j̲und*.

With the Muhallabids, a dynastic tradition was appearing in the last province of the Mag̲h̲rib still in caliphal hands. It was, however, abortive. Another period of troubles had to arise in order to convince the caliphs to relax their control, and this was, in 184/800, to the profit of Ibrāhīm b. al-Aghlab, founder of the Aghlabid [*q.v.*] dynasty of governors.

Bibliography: 1. Sources. Ṭabarī, index; Yaʿḳūbī, *Taʾrīkh*, index; Ḳudāma b. Djaʿfar, *K. al-Kharādj*, Baghdād 1981, 320, 334, 348; Ps. al-Raḳīḳ, *Taʾrīkh*, Tunis 1967, 148-202; Ibn al-Athīr, index; *T. al-Ridda*, extracts from the *Iktifāʾ* of al-Kalaʿī al-Balansī, gathered together by Khurshid Ahmad Fariq, New Delhi 1970, 150; Ibn Taghrībirdī, *Nudjūm*, Cairo 1963, ii, 16, 77; Nuwayrī, *Nihāya*, Cairo 1984, xxii, 96, 100, xxiv, 79-92; Ibn ʿIdhārī, *Bayān*, Leiden 1948, i, 84-5; Ibn Khaldūn, *ʿIbar*, Beirut 1958, iv, 415; Ibn Khallikān, ed. ʿAbbās, ii, 305-7, tr. de Slane, i, 529-31; Nāṣirī, *Istiḳṣāʾ*, Casablanca 1954, i, 120-1; Mālikī, *Riyāḍ*, Beirut 1983, i, 168, 183, 221-2, 237; M. Talbi (ed.), *Biographies aghlabides extraites des* Madārik *du Cadi ʿIyāḍ*, Tunis 1968, 11, 25, 44-5; Dabbāgh and Tidjānī, *Maʿālim*, Cairo 1968, i, 225, 242, 291-2.

2. Studies. Ziriklī, *Aʿlām*³, iii, 63; Saʿd Zaghlūl, *T. al-Maghrib*, Cairo 1965, 320-48; M. Talbi, *L'émirat Aghlabide*, Paris 1966, 76-7, 134; Muḥammad Shīṭ Khaṭṭāb, *al-Muhallab b. Abī Ṣufra*, in *Madjallat Kulliyyat al-Ādāb*, Univ. of Baghdād, vii (April 1964), 324-83; A. Laroui, *L'histoire du Maghreb*, Paris 1970, 91, 106. See also AL-MUHALLAB and MUHALLABIDS. (M. TALBI)

RAWḤ b. **ZINBĀʿ** AL-DJUDHĀMĪ, an Arab tribal leader, especially prominent in upholding the Umayyad cause against the Zubayrids in the second civil war (64-72/683-92).

Son of a notable from the Banū Djudhām [*q.v.*], which had been settled in Palestine from before the Arab conquest of the region, Rawḥ is said to have incurred Muʿāwiya's suspicion in circumstances which are obscure. Later, we find him named as one of a group of Syrian *ashrāf* whom Yazīd b. Muʿāwiya [*q.v.*] sent to ʿAbd Allāh b. al-Zubayr [*q.v.*] in an attempt to obtain the latter's *bayʿa*, and, shortly afterwards, as one of the commanders of the army sent to the Ḥidjāz by Yazīd under Muslim b. ʿUḳba al-Murrī [*q.v.*] in 63/682-3.

Following the death of Yazīd and that of his short-lived son and successor Muʿāwiya (II) [*q.v.*] in 64/683-4, Ḥassān b. Mālik b. Baḥdal al-Kalbī, who was governing the *djund* of Filasṭīn for the Umayyads, was unable to maintain his position and withdrew. He left Rawḥ behind as his representative, but Rawḥ too had to abandon his post in the face of opposition from his rival for the leadership of Djudhām, Nātil b. Ḳays. The latter, who seems to have enjoyed seniority, proclaimed his allegiance to Ibn al-Zubayr in an attempt to secure his own position, while Rawḥ may have alienated many of his tribe by a reported maladroit attempt to attach Djudhām to the "northern" (Maʿaddī) descent group (eventually they were generally accepted as belonging to the "southern", Ḳaḥṭānī, group). However, Rawḥ's continuing support for the Umayyads in the person of Marwān b. al-Ḥakam [*q.v.*] (he is credited with a speech eulogising Marwān and calling for his succession in preference to other candidates) proved well judged. Following the victory of the Kalb at Mardj Rāhiṭ [*q.v.*] and the consequent extension of Marwān's authority over Syria, it was the turn of Nātil b. Ḳays to flee and Rawḥ again became governor of Palestine. When ʿAbd al-Malik followed his father Marwān as caliph (Ramaḍān 65/April 685), Rawḥ became one of his influential confidantes and advisors. In some of the literature he appears as a prototype of the later viziers.

Rawḥ is said to have died in 84/703. He is known as a transmitter of *ḥadīth* and is even counted by son *ḥadīth* authorities as a Companion of the Prophet. H descendants are referred to in reports about t disturbances in Syria towards the end of the Umayya period.

Bibliography: Ṭabarī, ii, 424, 468-69, 47 1164-5; Balādhurī, *Ansāb*, i, 36, iv a, 53-4, 70, 12 iv b, 20, 40, 46, 55, v, 128, 132, 134, 148, 149, 20 304, 356, 377; Yaʿḳūbī, *Taʾrīkh*, ii, 299, 301, 30 306, 321, 335; Masʿūdī, *Murūdj*, v, 191-92, 254-5 282-86, vi, 123-24; *Aghānī, Tables*, 351; Moḥan mad Shafīʿ, *Analytical indices to the Kitāb al-ʿIqd a Farīd of ... Ibn ʿAbd Rabbihi*, Calcutta 1935, 36 Djahshiyārī, *Kitāb al-Wuzarāʾ wa 'l-kuttāb*, Cair 1938, 35-7; Ibn ʿAsākir, *Taʾrīkh Madīnat Dimash* 19 vols. lithograph, Dār al-Bashīr, Amman n.d vii, 297-304; W. Caskel and G. Strenziok, *Ǧamhar an-nasab. Das genealogische Werk des Hišām b. Muḥan mad al-Kalbī*, 2 vols., Leiden 1966, index, s.v.; H Lammens, *Le califat de Yazîd 1er*, Beirut 192 301 ff. (= *MFOB*, v [1912], 620 ff.); P. Cron *Slaves on horses*, Cambridge 1980, 34-5, 99-100; G Rotter, *Die Umayyaden und der zweite Bürgerkrieg (68 692)*, Wiesbaden 1982, 130, 136-7, 144, 146, 150- 183, 212, 225; M. Gil, *A History of Palestine, 63 1099*, Cambridge 1992, 79-81; I. Hasson, *Le ch judhāmite Rawḥ ibn Zinbāʿ*, in *SI*, lxxvii (1993 95-122. (G.R. HAWTING)

RĀWĪ (A.), pl. *ruwāt*, reciter and transmitter o poetry, as also of narrative traditions (*akhbār*) an *ḥadīth* [*q.v.*]. The term is derived from *rawā* "to bring carry or convey water", and has been extended t "carrying" in a figurative sense, i.e. "to bear b memory, to transmit or recite" (cf. Lane, 1194 There is an intensive form *rāwiya*, explained a "copious transmitter" (*kathīr al-riwāya*), used i mediaeval sources as a synonym to *rāwī*. In moder research it is applied, as a rule, to the learned collec tors of Bedouin poetry in the 8th century.

The institution of the *rāwī* is the main basis for th preservation of pre-Islamic poetry. In the *Djāhiliyy* [*q.v.*] poets used to have one or more *rāwīs*, who learn ed their verses by heart, recited them in public especially at the annual fairs, where poetic contest took place, and transmitted them to the next genera tion. It often happened that a *rāwī* became a famou poet himself. Lists of poets and their *rāwīs* are know over several generations. A spectacular line, extend ing over two centuries, begins with Aws b. Ḥadja [*q.v.*], the stepfather of Zuhayr b. Abī Sulmā [*q.v.*] who was his *rāwī* (Ibn Ḳutayba, *Shiʿr*, 57). Zuhayr who also had his son Kaʿb [*q.v.*] for a *rāwī*, figures a the beginning of the following list (*Aghānī*¹, vii, 78) Zuhayr, al-Ḥuṭayʾa [*q.v.*], Hudba b. Khashram Djamīl [*q.v.*], Kuthayyir ʿAzza [*q.v.*], who died ir 105/723. He was "the last to combine the function o poet and *rāwī*" (*ākhir man idjtamaʿa lahu al-shiʿr wa 'l-riwāya, loc. cit.*). From the list and similar information it appears that transmission of poetry often took place in the same family or clan, but not necessarily, which implies that *rāwī* was an accepted profession or semi-profession.

The question whether transmission in the *Djāhiliyya* was exclusively oral, or whether poets and transmitters assisted their memory by writing, remains controversial. Whereas Sezgin (*GAS*, ii, 22-33) maintains the early use of writing in the process of transmission, other scholars have emphasised the oral character of pre-Islamic texts (M. Zwettler, *The oral character of classical Arabic poetry*, Columbus 1978, cf. 85-8). Since there is no conclusive evidence, one can only attempt to evaluate the known facts. In the *Djāhiliyya*, the use of writing, although well established for contracts, treaties or other official documents, could hardly have played a significant part in poetic transmission. It is possible that poets in contact with the courts of Ḥīra [*q.v.*] and Ghassān [*q.v.*] were able to write, but among Bedouins that knowledge cannot have been common. Furthermore, the corpus of pre-Islamic verses presents characteristic features of oral literature, e.g. a high percentage of formulaic expressions, semantic repetition and independence of detail, which later gave way to other stylistic features and modes of composition. Thus it is to be assumed that during the 6th century A.D. composition and transmission of poetry took place orally, which does not exclude the possibility of a *rāwī* noting down verses as a mnemonic aid.

In the course of the first Islamic century, the use of writing increased in various fields (cf. G. Schoeler, *Schreiben und Veröffentlichen. Zur Verwendung und Funktion der Schrift in den ersten islamischen Jahrhunderten*, in *Isl.*, lxix [1992], 1-43). The first collections of poetry were made in the early Umayyad period, e.g. the *Muʿallaḳāt* [*q.v.*] (cf. M.J. Kister, *The Seven Odes*, in *RSO*, xliv (1979) 27-36). The poet al-Farazdaḳ [*q.v.*] mentions in some of his verses that he possessed "books" with collected poetry of other poets (*The Naḳāʾiḍ of Jarīr and al-Farazdaḳ*, ed. A.A. Bevan, i-iii, Leiden 1905-12, i, 201, v. 57, 61). It is further reported that Djarīr [*q.v.*] and al-Farazdaḳ used to dictate to their *rāwīs* (*Naḳāʾiḍ*, i, 430, 12; ii, 908, 2). It seems therefore, that oral transmission was at first aided, and then gradually replaced, by writing.

In the final stage of poetic transmission, the early ʿAbbāsid period, Bedouin poetry was systematically collected by learned *rāwīs* like Khalaf al-Aḥmar, Ḥammād al-Rāwiya and al-Mufaḍḍal al-Ḍabbī [*q.vv.*]. There is ample evidence that they had written collections of poetry at their disposal, but they were still expected to know the texts by heart, and to recite them when requested (*Aghānī*[1], v, 174). In addition, they used to collect information from Bedouins and to verify their knowledge by questioning them. These Bedouin informants, who were also called "*rāwī*", are in part known by name (cf. Ch. Pellat, *Le milieu baṣrien et la formation de Ǧāḥiẓ*, Paris 1953, 137-8). Thus presumably the term *rāwī/rāwiya* was applied, as long as learning by heart and reciting of verses still played a part, even if a marginal one, in poetic transmission.

Another aspect is the exact function of the *rāwī* and his relation to the poet who employed him. Since a *rāwī* often became a poet himself, it has been assumed that he also served an apprenticeship with his poet, receiving a thorough training in metrics and the art of composition. This would imply that the institution of the *rāwī* not only assured the preservation of poetry, but also the continuity of technical knowledge, and of the vocabulary, style, and thematic range of an individual poet. The first to consider the possibility of establishing "schools" of poetry was Ṭāhā Ḥusayn, who with regard to the list of *rāwīs* mentioned above speaks of the "poetic school" (*madhhab shiʿrī*) of Aws b. Ḥadjar (*Fi 'l-adab al-djāhilī*, Cairo 1927, [16]1989, 270). The question has been studied with regard to the poetry of Hudhayl [*q.v.*] by E. Bräunlich (*Versuch einer literargeschichtlichen Betrachtungsweise altarabischer Poesien*, in *Isl.*, xxiv [1937], 201-69; cf. 221 ff.), as also by G.E. von Grunebaum (*Zur Chronologie der früharabischen Dichtung*, in *Orientalia*, N.S. viii [1939], 328-45), who established six "schools" of poetry in the pre-Islamic period.

The assumption that *rāwīs* received a thorough education, and reached a competence equal to that of the poets they served, is further evidenced by reports that a *rāwī* was expected to correct, to polish up or even to embellish the verses of his master. This seems to have been a common practice in the *Djāhiliyya* (cf. Goldziher, *Muh. St.*, ii, 8 [2]), as also in the Umayyad period. There is a story concerning Djarīr and al-Farazdaḳ, whose *rāwīs* were found to correct their metrical blunders (*Aghānī*[1], iv, 54). In view of this and similar reports, it is easy to appreciate the exclamation of al-Ḥuṭayʾa: "Woe to verses in the hand of a bad transmitter!" (*waylun li 'l-shiʿri min rāwiyat al-sūʾ*; *Aghānī*[1], ii, 59). It also underlines the difficulty, and sometimes the impossibility, for historians of literature to clearly differentiate between the work of a poet and that of his *rāwī*.

Bibliography: In addition to references in the article, see Blachère, *HLA*, i, 85-127, and in particular, Nāṣir al-Dīn Asad, *Maṣādir al-shiʿr al-djāhilī wa-ḳīmatuhā al-taʾrīkhiyya*, Cairo 1978, 222-54.

(RENATE JACOBI)

RAWK (Egyptian pronounciation: *rōk*), a word of non-Arabic origin, probably derived from Demotic *ruwkh*, "land distribution". From the noun is derived an Arabic verb *rāka, yarūku*.

In the language of Egyptian administration, *rawk* means a kind of cadastral survey which is followed by a redistribution of the arable land. The procedure comprises the surveying (*misāḥa* [*q.v.*]) of the fields, the ascertainment of their legal status (private property, endowment, crown land, grant, etc.), and the assessment of their prospective taxable capacity (*ʿibra*). Until the fall of the Fāṭimid dynasty the bulk of the arable land was bestowed on private tax farmers (*mutaḳabbil* or *ḍāmin*), whereas in the Ayyūbid and Mamlūk periods it was granted to officers and free soldiers as military grants (*iḳṭāʿ* [*q.v.*]).

Al-Maḳrīzī states that in early Islamic times a *rawk* had been carried out every thirty years, in order to synchronise the lunar (*hilālī*) and the fiscal (*kharādjī*) calendars (*Khiṭaṭ*, ed. Wiet, ii, 2), but this statement rather seems to reflect the ideal case. In fact, in the eight-and-a-half centuries between the Arabs' appearance and the Ottoman conquest, only six *rawks* are mentioned in the sources. The first is that which ʿUbayd Allāh b. al-Ḥabḥāb, director of the finances (*ʿāmil*) of Egypt, executed in the years 105-7/724-5 during the reign of the caliph Hishām. The result of the survey is said to have been an arable surface of 30,000,000 *faddān* (*ca.* 191,000 km^2); the fiscal register established in 107/725-6 recorded a yield of *kharādj* [*q.v.*] of 1,700,837 *dīnārs* for all Egypt, and that of 1,449,420.5 for Upper Egypt and 251, 416.5 for the Delta (al-Maḳrīzī, *op. cit.*, 62.)

The *rawk* of Aḥmad b. al-Mudabbir, *ʿāmil* of Egypt, accomplished around 253/867-8, just before the arrival of Aḥmad b. Ṭūlūn [*q.v.*], amounted to 24,000,000 *faddāns* or *ca.* 153,000 km^2 (al-Maḳrīzī, *op. cit.*, ii, 62-3, 69, 81).

The third *rawk*, called *al-Afḍalī*, was the only one carried out under Fāṭimid rule. His initiator was the general and future vizier Muḥammad b. Fātik "al-Maʾmūn" al-Baṭāʾiḥī, to whose son Mūsā we owe a detailed report (quoted by al-Maḳrīzī, *op. cit.*, ii, 5-6). At the suggestion of al-Baṭāʾiḥī, the vizier al-Afḍal b. Badr al-Djamālī in 501/1107-8 gave orders to perform a new survey in order to remedy grievances and to abolish unjustified privileges which had spread since the last *rawk*.

The *rawk al-Ṣalāḥī*, performed in the years 572-7/1176-81 by the eunuch Bahāʾ al-Dīn Ḳarāḳūsh (the builder of the Cairo citadel) on the orders of Sultan Ṣalāḥ al-Dīn al-Ayyūbī, laid the foundation of a completely new military system; it was closely linked to the introduction of the *iḳṭāʿ* system. The assessed *kharādj* yield of 3,670,500 *dīnār*s was split into *iḳṭāʿ*s for 111 officers (*amīr*), 6976 heavily-armed horsemen (*ṭawāshī*) and 1,553 light cavalrymen (*ḳarā-ghulām*) (al-Maḳrīzī, *op. cit.*, ii, 16-17). Ibn Mammātī in his book on the rules of administration (*Kitāb Ḳawānīn al-dawāwīn*) has preserved the complete list of all places of Egypt surveyed in the Ṣalāḥī *rawk* (ed. A.S. Atiya, Cairo 1943, 84-200).

The *rawk al-Ḥusāmī* was initiated by the Mamlūk sultan Ḥusām al-Dīn Lādjīn in 697/1298 in order to curtail the power of the great *amīr*s and to strengthen that of the sultan, but it completely failed, and the sultan was murdered by his officers (al-Maḳrīzī, *op. cit.*, ii, 21; idem, *Sulūk*, ed. Ziyāda, Cairo 1934-58, i/3, 841-4; Ibn Taghrībirdī, *Nudjūm*, ed. Cairo, viii, 90-5; Ibn Iyās, *Badāʾiʿ*, ed. M. Moṣṭafā, Wiesbaden 1975, i/1, 396-7). The list of place names surveyed by the Ḥusāmī *rawk* seems to be preserved in the anonymous *Tuḥfat al-irshād*, discovered by M. Ramzī in the library of the Azhar in 1932.

The last *rawk* was carried out by order of sultan al-Nāṣir Muḥammad b. Ḳalāwūn during his third reign. The Nāṣirī *rawk*, which combined a survey of some regions of Syria in 713/1313-14 with one of all Egypt in 715/1315, was a repetition of the failed Ḥusāmī *rawk*, and this time the sultan was successful in depriving the great *amīr*s of their power. The Nāṣirī *rawk* can be considered as a kind of coup d'état: the crown land (*khāṣṣ al-sulṭān*) was considerably increased; the whole province of al-Djīza was transformed into *khāṣṣ* land (al-Maḳrīzī, *Khiṭaṭ*, ii, 22-32; idem, *Sulūk*, ii/1, 146-57; *Tübinger Atlas des Vorderen Orients*, map B VIII 13). The registers set up in the Nāṣirī *rawk* have been copied by Ibn Duḳmāḳ, *K. al-Intiṣār* (ed. Vollers, Cairo 1893) and Ibn al-Djīʿān, *al-Tuḥfa al-saniyya* (ed. B. Moritz, Cairo 1898, repr. Cairo 1974).

Bibliography: C.H. Becker, *Beiträge zur Geschichte Ägyptens unter dem Islam*, Straßburg 1913, ii, 107-10, 140-8; H. Rabie, *The financial system of Egypt*, London 1972, 50-6; H. Halm, *Ägypten nach den mamlukischen Lehensregistern*, Wiesbaden 1979-82, i, 8-56. (H. Halm)

RAWSHANIYYA, a mystical and gnostic Islamic sect founded amongst the Afghāns of the North-West Frontier region, with centres at e.g. Kānīgurām and Tīrāh in Wazīristān, by Bāyazīd b. ʿAbd Allāh Anṣārī of Kānīgurām (*ca.* 931-80/*ca.* 1525-73). He claimed to be, if not actually a Mahdī, at least a *hādī* or guide towards *tawḥīd*, the Divine Unity, for his followers. He styled himself *pīr-i rawshan* "the divinely-illuminated *pīr* [*q.v.*]", although his orthodox enemies called him *pīr-i tārīkī* "the *pīr* of darkness" and his adherents *Tārīkiyān* "devotees of darkness". The movement had distinct elements of Afghān national consciousness within it, reacting against Mughal expansionism in the Frontier region and against Kābul, as well as a religious significance.

1. Bāyazīd Anṣārī's career. For this, the last years of which were spent in the warfare against the Mughals in which he eventually was killed, see the article s.v.

2. Later history of the movement. Bāyazīd's activities were resumed by the eldest of his five sons, ʿUmar, who attacked the Yūsufzāī, a tribe which had followed Bāyazīd but had reverted to orthodox Islam; in the battle which ensued ʿUmar was killed, as was also his brother Khayr al-Dīn; another brother, Nūr al-Dīn, was put to death by the Gudjars. The youngest son, Djalāl al-Dīn, was captured by the Yūsufzāī, who surrendered him to Akbar in 989/1581. Escaping from Akbar's court he returned to Tīrāh, where he assumed the role of sovereign of Afghānistān, and Akbar found it necessary to send an army against him in Ṣafar 994/January-February 1586. This army met with a serious defeat, which was repaired by a later expedition (995/1587). The numbers of the Rawshanīs are given on this occasion as 20,000 foot and 5,000 horse. A further expedition was sent in 1000/1591 (or 1001) which captured some 14,000 men (according to Badāʾūnī) with Djalāl al-Dīn's wives and children, but not apparently himself, since in 1007/1598-9 he took Ghaznī, but was unable to maintain himself there, and on retiring was attacked by the Hazāras [*q.v.* in Suppl.], wounded and put to death. This last affair is by some assigned to a son of his bearing the same name.

The next head of the community was Djalāl al-Dīn's son Iḥdād, who figures in the history of Djahāngīr. In 1020/1611 he surprised Kābul in the absence of its governor Khān Dawrān. The attack was beaten off with great loss to the raiders, yet in 1023/1614 Iḥdād was again in the field, but sustained a serious defeat at Pīsh Bulāgh. After a series of enterprises with varied success he was besieged in the fortress of Nuaghar, and killed by a musket-shot.

The historian of Shāh Djahān, Muḥammad Ṣāliḥ Kanbo, asserts that in the second year of his reign (1038/1628-9) that monarch took effective steps to suppress the heresy started by Bāyazīd; nevertheless, in the following year he records how the Afghān Kamāl al-Dīn was joined in the attack on Peshāwar by ʿAbd al-Ḳādir, son of Iḥdād, and Karīmdād, son of Djalāla (Djalāl al-Dīn). The place was relieved by Saʿīd Khān, and ʿAbd al-Ḳādir induced to submit; in 1043/1633-4 he was recommended by Ṣaʿīd Khān, "who had caused him to repent of his evil deeds" to Shāh Djahān, who gave him a command of 1,600 horse. Other members of Iḥdād's family received honours and rewards in 1047/1637-8. In the same year, Karīmdād, who had taken refuge in the Mohmand country, but had been recalled by the tribes of Bangash, was attacked, captured and executed by Ṣaʿīd Khān. It is asserted that some relics of the community still exist in this region. A branch of the sect, called ʿĪsawī, was founded at Swat by one Sayyid ʿĪsā of Peshāwar (T.C. Plowden, translation of the *Kālid-i Afghānī*, Lahore 1875).

3. Doctrines of the sect. According to the *Dabistān*, which is friendly to the sect, Bāyazīd's doctrine was extreme pantheism; "If I pray" he said, "I am a *mushrik*; if I pray not, I am a *kāfir*." He marked eight stages (*maḳām*) in religious progress: *sharīʿa, ṭarīḳa, ḥaḳīḳa, maʿrifa, ḳurba, wuṣla, waḥda, sukūn*; the four last are said to be technicalities of his system. The explanation of these stages, quoted from Bāyazīd's *Ḥāl-nāma*, inculcates lofty morality, e.g. to hurt no creature of God. The account which follows is inconsistent with this, as noxious persons were to be killed because they resembled wild creatures, and harmless persons who did not possess self-knowledge might be killed, because they resembled domestic animals. They might be regarded as dead, and their property might be seized by the "living". Further, he abrogated the direction of prayer and the preliminary ablution. Other details are furnished by a hostile writer, the historian of Shāh Djahān quoted above, copied in Khāfī Khān's *Muntakhab al-lubāb*. Marriage, he says, is without a contract, there being merely a feast at which a cow is slaughtered. Divorce is ratified by placing some pebbles in the wife's hand. The widow is deprived of inheritance, and indeed is at the disposal of the heirs, who may marry her themselves

r sell her to someone else. When a son is born to one f them, an incision is made in the ear of an ass, and ιe blood dripped on the infant's tongue. This is in rder to ensure that the infant shall be bloodthirsty ιnd have the mind of an ass. Any stranger who falls ιto their hands is enslaved and can be bought or sold.)aughters receive no share in the inheritance. They ιassacre whole tribes when they conquer them. Even ι the Day of Judgment their victims, though mar-yrs, will not hold them to account. According to thers, however, they recognised neither Paradise nor Iell.

4. Literature of the sect. Bāyazīd is said to have ʋritten much. For his own works, see BĀYAZĪD ANṢĀRĪ. Vorks composed by his opponents and in refutation f his doctrines include the orthodox Āk̲h̲ūnd Dar-ʋīza's *Mak̲h̲zan-i Afg̲h̲ānī* and *Tad̲h̲kirat al-abrār wa 'l-s̲h̲rār.* Such works composed at the Mug̲h̲al court as ʌbu 'l-Faḍl ʿAllāmī's *Akbar-nāma* (detailed account of he warfare with the Raws̲h̲aniyya), Badā'ūnī's *Mun-ιk̲h̲ab al-tawārīk̲h̲*, D̲j̲ahāngīr's *Tuzūk*, the *Ta'rīk̲h̲-i ʿirishta* and Muḥammad Ṣāliḥ Kanbo Lāhawrī's *Amal-i Ṣāliḥ*, were necessarily hostile; but Farīd 3ukhārī's *D̲h̲akhīrat al-k̲h̲awānīn* (biographical accounts f Mug̲h̲al nobles) gives a more sympathetic view of hem.

Bibliography: The account of the sect given by J. Leyden, in *Asiatic Researches*, xi, 363-428, London 1810, based on the *Dabistān al-mad̲h̲āhib* (= 247-253 in ed. Bombay 1292) and the Pas̲h̲to work *Mak̲h̲zan al-Islām* of Āk̲h̲ūnd Darwīza furnished the material for the account of the sect in Graf T.A. von Noer's *Kaiser Akbar*, Leiden 1885, ii, 179, and largely for that in *Glossary of the Punjab tribes and castes*, Lahore 1915, iii, 335 ff. Notices of the sect were also got from Indian historical works; from the *Akbar-nāma* (printed Calcutta 1881) in M. Elphinstone, *History of India*, London 1866, 517 etc.; from the *Ṭabaḳāt-i Akbarī* (lith., Lahore 1292), in H. Elliot, *History of India*, London 1873, v, 450; from the *Tuzūk-i Djahāngīrī*, tr. A. Rogers and H. Beveridge, London 1909, in Beni Prasad, *History of Jahangir*, Oxford 1922, who also used the *Iḳbāl-nāma-yi Djahāngīrī*, Calcutta 1865. For S̲h̲āh D̲j̲ahān's time, the *S̲h̲āh D̲j̲ahān-nāma*, called *ʿAmal-i Ṣāliḥ*, of Muḥammad Ṣāliḥ Kanbo, ed. Ghulam Yazdani, Calcutta 1923-7, is the chief authority. The printed text of ʿAbd al-Ḥamīd Lāhawrī's *Bādis̲h̲āh-nāma* (Calcutta 1867-8) which, according to the *Mun-tak̲h̲ab al-lubāb*, Calcutta 1869, should contain an exaggerated account of the atrocities of the sect, has very little about it.

See further H.G. Raverty, *Ethnographical notes on Afghanistan and part of Baluchistan*, London 1880-3; Sir Olaf Caroe, *The Pathans 550 B.C.-A.D. 1957*, London 1958, 199-204, 226-30; S.A.A. Rizvi, *Raws̲h̲aniyya movement*, in *Abr-Nahrain*, vi (1965-6), 63-91, vii (1967-8), 62-98; Annemarie Schimmel, *Islam in the Indian subcontinent*, HO, II.4.3, Leiden-Köln 1984, 87-8.

(D.S. Margoliouth-[C.E. Bosworth])

RAWTHER (Tamil *irauttur* meaning "horseman" ɔr "trooper", also known as Rowther, Ravuttan, Rayuttān), a community of Tamil-speaking Muslims located in the state of Tamilnadu, India, ɔne of four sub-divisions of the Tamil-speaking Muslim community, the others being Marakkayar, Kayalar and Labbai [*q.v.*]. Like the Labbai, the Rawther follow the S̲h̲āfiʿī school, whilst the others ιre Ḥanafīs. Unlike the other sub-divisions, the Rawther and Labbai are found in greatest numbers in he interior, where they are mostly petty merchants ιnd tradesmen.

Effectively endogamous like the other sub-divisions and historically located in particular districts (Madurai and Tiruchirapalli), there has nevertheless been a blurring of group boundaries. Migration to larger urban centres, some intermarriage and Islamic revival movements, have stressed their egalitarian outlook and weakened clan-based lineages with their focus on the shrines of particular saints.

The Rawther probably originated as cavalry militia, comprising indigenous converts to Islam, for Tamil Hindu rulers before pre-colonial Muslim rulers began similar recruitment in the late 17th century. During the 19th century Wahhābī missionaries began a process of Islamisation, attacking vestiges of Hindu ritual practices, stressing Sunnī orthodoxy and encouraging the use of Urdu as a symbol of "pure" Islam. Many Tamil Muslims were affected by this movement, and a considerable number of Labbai adopted the title of Rawther because they regarded any claim to martial ancestry as more orthodox and prestigious than simple Labbai status. Urdu, however, remained primarily the second language of a minority of Rawthers.

Bibliography: M. Mines, *Muslim social stratification in India: the basis for variation*, in *Southwestern Journal of Anthropology*, xxviii (1972), 333-49, and Susan Bayly, *Saints, Goddesses and Kings. Muslims and Christians in South Indian society, 1700-1900*, Cambridge 1989, are fundamental. See also W. Frances, *South Arcot District manual*, Madras 1906; idem, *Madura District gazetteer*, Madras 1920; F.R. Hemingway, *Trichinopoly District manual*, Madras 1907 (useful). For the Rawther in a broader historical context, see S.K. Aiyangar, *South India and her Muhammedan invaders*, Madras 1921; Qadir H. Khan, *South Indian Mussalmans*, Madras 1910; K. McPherson, *The political development of the Urdu- and Tamil-speaking Muslims of the Madras Presidency 1901 to 1937*, M.A. thesis, University of Western Australia 1968, unpubl. (K. McPherson)

RAWWĀDIDS or BANŪ RAWWĀD, a minor dynasty of northwestern Persia which flourished during the period which Minorsky characterised as the "Iranian intermezzo" between the decline of Arab power there and the incoming of Turkish peoples like the Saldjūks, essentially during the 4th-5th/10th-11th centuries.

Although the Daylamīs [see DAYLAM] were the most prominent in this upsurge of northern Persian mountain peoples, the part of other races like the Kurds was not negligible. The Rawwādids (the form "Rawād" later becomes common in the sources) were originally of Azdī Arab stock, but gradually became assimilated to their environment in Ād̲h̲arbaydjān (and especially, the area around Tabrīz) and became Kurdicised (cf. the similar process taking place in S̲h̲irwān [*q.v.*] or S̲h̲arwān, where the Yazīdī S̲h̲irwān-S̲h̲āhs became Iranised). In *ca.* 141/758-9 the caliph al-Manṣūr's governor of Ād̲h̲arbaydjān, Yazīd b. Ḥātim al-Muhallabī appointed al-Rawwād b. al-Mut̲h̲annā [*q.v.* in Suppl.] to secure the region between Tabrīz and al-Bad̲h̲d̲h̲ [*q.v.* in Suppl.]. Over the next two centuries, al-Rawwād's descendants became thoroughly Kurdicised, and Kurdish forms like "Mamlān" for Muḥammad and "Aḥmadīl" for Aḥmad begin to appear in their genealogy.

In the disturbed condition of Ād̲h̲arbaydjān during the mid-4th/10th century, consequent on the disappearance of the Sād̲j̲ids [*q.v.*] from there, the Rawwādid Abu 'l-Hayd̲j̲ā' Ḥusayn b. Muḥammad (344-78/955-88) succeeded to the heritage of the Kangarids or Musāfirids [*q.v.*]. During the next century, the outstanding member of the family was Abu

Manṣūr Wahsūdān b. Mamlān b. Abi 'l-Hayd̲j̲ā² (*ca.* 410-46/*ca.* 1019-54). He early faced the incursions of the so-called "ʿIrāḳī" Turkmens driven out of K̲h̲urāsān by Maḥmūd of G̲h̲azna and of independently-operating Turkish bands, but it was not until 446/1054 that the Sald̲j̲ūḳ leader T̲og̲h̲ril Beg [*q.v.*] resolved to bring Ād̲h̲arbayd̲j̲ān and Arrān under his control and to make the petty rulers of northwestern Persia and eastern Transcaucasia his vassals. Wahsūdān's eldest son Mamlān was confirmed in his father's territories by T̲og̲h̲ril in 450/1058, but the days of the dynasty as an autonomous power were numbered. The Ottoman historian Müned̲j̲d̲j̲im Bas̲h̲ī [*q.v.*], quoting earlier chronicles on the history of the region, states that, when the Sald̲j̲ūḳ sultan Alp Arslan returned in 463/1071 from his Anatolian campaign against the Byzantines, he deposed Mamlān. But a later member of the family, Aḥmadīl b. Ibrāhīm b. Wahsūdān, held Marāg̲h̲a [*q.v.*] and took part in warfare against the Crusaders in Syria, and his personal name was perpetuated by the line of his Turkish *g̲h̲ulāms*, the Aḥmadīlīs [*q.v.*], who ruled in Marāg̲h̲a as Atabegs during the 6th/13th century; survivors of the actual Rawwādid family can be traced up to Il-K̲h̲ānid times in the early 8th/14th century.

Bibliography: Aḥmad Kasrawī, *S̲h̲ahriyārān-i gum-nām*², Tehran 1335/1957, ii, 130-225, 251; V. Minorsky, *Studies in Caucasian history*, London 1953, 115-16, 164-9; W. Madelung, in *Cambridge history of Iran*, iv, 236-9; Bosworth, in *ibid.*, v, 32-4; idem, *The Islamic dynasties*, 88-9. See also TABRĪZ.

(C.E. BOSWORTH)

RAʾY [see Suppl.].

RĀYČŪR, a town and district of South India, now in the Gulbarga division of the Indian Union state of Karnataka, before 1947 in the Ḥaydarābād princely state of British India (lat. 16° 15′ N., long. 77° 20′ E.).

An ancient Hindu town formerly part of the kingdom of Warangal, it passed to the K̲h̲ald̲j̲ī Sultans of Dihlī in the 8th/14th century, then to the Bahmanīs and, after Awrangzīb's Deccan conquests, to the Mug̲h̲als. Rāyčūr has interesting Islamic monuments. The Bahmanī Ek mīnār kī masd̲j̲id has its minaret in the corner of the courtyard [see MANĀRA. 2. In India]. The fortifications and gateway were built by Ibrāhīm I ʿĀdil S̲h̲āh in the mid-10th/16th century, and the Djāmiʿ masd̲j̲id or Friday mosque stems from 1022/1618.

Bibliography: *Imperial gazetteer of India*², xxi, 34-45; *Annual report*, *Arch. Dept. Hyderabad*, 1339F; Elisabeth S. Merklinger, *Indian Islamic architecture: the Deccan 1347-1686*, Warminster, Wilts. 1981, 48, 51 and plan 28. (C.E. BOSWORTH)

RAYDA (Rīda, Rēda) is the name of a number of places in ʿAsīr, in the Yemen and in Ḥaḍramawt. The word *rayd* (pl. *aryād/ruyūd*) means a ledge of a mountain, resembling a wall, or a resting upon ledges of mountains (Lane, *Lexicon*, *s.v.*). At least in Ḥaḍramawt, it is the term for the centre of the territory of a Bedouin tribe, which is generally a depression in the rocky plateau (D. van der Meulen and H. von Wissmann, *Hadramaut, some of its mysteries unveiled*, Leiden 1932, 22, n. 1). There are several places of this name (*Rēda*) in Hadramawt: Raydat al-Ṣayʿar, Raydat Arḍayn, Raydat al-ʿIbād, Raydat al-Ḥar(a)miyya. In ʿAsīr, Muḥammad b. ʿĀʾid of the Āl ʿĀʾid [see ʿASĪR; ʿARAB, D̲J̲AZĪRAT AL-] was defeated in 1872 by the Ottomans, under Muḥammad Reḍīf Pas̲h̲a, at Raydat Banī Mufīd. The territory was annexed by King ʿAbd al-ʿAzīz after he had conquered

al-Ḥid̲j̲āz. The best-known place of this name is Raydat al-Bawn (Raydat S̲h̲ahīr) in the Yemen, a large village in the plain of Bawn (Hamdān), at lat. 15° 49′ N., long. 44° 2′ E. According to A. Sprenger, *Die alte Geographie Arabiens als Grundlage der Entwicklungsgeschichte des Semitismus*, repr. Amsterdam 1966, no. 293, its location corresponds with Μαγουλαυα of Ptolemy. Actually, Raydat al-Bawn is the chief place of the district (*nāḥiya*) of the same name, with a population (in 1979) of 1,637 inhabitants. The well-known Abū Muḥammad al-Ḥasan al-Hamdānī [*q.v.*] spent the greater part of his life in Raydat al-Bawn, where he probably died and was buried after 340/951-2. The place is also known for its pre-Islamic inscriptions.

Bibliography: Besides the works given in the text, see, for a full discussion of the sources for Raydat al-Bawn and its inscriptions (with photographs), Chr. Robin, *Les hautes-terres du Nord-Yemen avant l'Islam*. Leiden-Istanbul, 2 vols. 1982.

(ED.)

AL-RAYDĀNIYYA [see MAMLŪKS. i. e; SELIM I].

AL-RAYḤĀNĪ, AMĪN, Lebanese polygraph, of Maronite persuasion, born at Freika (al-Furayka) 24 November 1876 and died there 13 September 1940.

At twelve years old, he emigrated with his uncle to New York, where he dabbled in business, appeared on the stage and studied law for a while, but principally worked tirelessly to perfect his knowledge of English. Subsequently, he moved back and forth between the West and the East, studied Arabic authors and discovered al-Maʿarrī [*q.v.*], whose work he translated into English. Following the publication of an anti-clerical pamphlet, *al-Muḥālafa al-t̲h̲ulāt̲h̲iyya fi 'l-mamlaka al-ḥayawāniyya*, New York 1903, 138 pp., he was excommunicated. His vision of life is expressed in *The Book of Khalid*, New York 1911, 349 pp. During the First World War, he was a newspaper correspondent in Europe. In 1922, he embarked on a tour of the Arabian Peninsula, a journey which lasted a year and was to be the subject of a remarkable account, *Mulūk al-ʿArab*, Beirut 1924, 925 pp. He lived alone for most of his life, and his marriage to Bertha Case (1879-1970) did not last long. He maintained a literary salon and diffused his energy in countless conferences and articles.

His corpus comprises some forty works, including ten in English and eight published posthumously (fifteen have been edited in the USA). It was republished by his brother Albert in Beirut between 1980 and 1983. However, this last is not an accurate and complete edition: in a political context, where the author uses the word Syria this is often replaced by Lebanon, and in a religious context, certain criticisms aimed at the Maronite community are mitigated. Finally, the text of his will in which he insisted on a secular burial has been censored. A new, complete edition has subsequently appeared, under the patronage of his nephew Amīn, also in Beirut, at Dār al-D̲j̲īl (with a large print-run).

Unlike many Arab writers of his generation who sought a haven in the West, Amīn al-Rayḥānī undertook a return to the East, under the influence of Emerson and Carlyle. He regarded himself as a philosopher, while as a poet, he was one of the first to compose texts in free verse. In prose, his style is strongly influenced by the Ḳurʾān. He believed in God, but his religion tended towards the kind of naturalism favoured by Rousseau. He was a supporter of Darwinian theories of evolution. Motivated by sentiments of revolt against institutions (sectarianism in particular) and intolerance, he defended human liberty and fraternity with determination. A social reformer, he preached justice and the virtues of work. His political ideal was based on an Arab nationalism extending over an area considerably exceeding the boundaries of contemporary Lebanon; such an independent entity, he believed, would be capable of confronting the foreign intruder and guaranteeing the future of Palestine.

Bibliography: Brockelmann, S III, 399-414; Dāg͟hir, *Maṣādir*, 1956, ii, 404-11.

Monographs: T. al-Rāfiʿī, Cairo 1922; A. al-Rayḥānī, Beirut 1941; D̲j. D̲jabr, Beirut 1947; R. al-K̲h̲ūrī, Beirut 1948; M. ʿAbbūd, Cairo 1952; S. al-Kayālī, Cairo 1960; M.ʿA. Mūsā, Beirut 1961; M. Abū ʿAlī, Beirut 1963; ʿI.M. Ṣābā, Cairo 1968; F. Ayyūb, Beirut 1968; W. Bāḳī, Damascus 1968; H.S. al-K̲h̲aṭīb, Beirut 1970; M.N. Kanʿān, Beirut 1971; N.M. Zakka, University of Lille III, 1979, 271 pp.; N. Mūsā-ʿA. Ḥasan, Beirut 1982.

Anthologies: *al-Maks̲h̲ūf*, no. 271, 22 October 1940; Mad̲j̲lis al-Matn al-S̲h̲amālī li 'l-T̲h̲aḳāfa, *Amīn al-Rayḥānī baʿd rubʿ ḳarn*, Beirut 1966; Ittiḥād al-Kuttāb al-Lubnāniyyīn, *Amīn al-Rayḥānī rāʾid nahḍāwī min Lubnān*, Beirut 1988 (J. FONTAINE)

AL-**RAYY**, the ancient Rag͟hā, a city in the old Persian region of Media, during Islamic times in the province of D̲j̲ibāl [*q.v.*].

Its ruins may be seen about 5 miles south-south-east of Tehran [*q.v.*] to the south of a spur projecting from Elburz into the plain. The village and sanctuary of S̲h̲āh ʿAbd al-ʿAẓīm lie immediately south of the ruins. The geographical importance of the town lies in the fact that it was situated in the fertile zone which lies between the mountains and the desert, by which from time immemorial communication has taken place between the west and east of Persia. Several roads from Māzandarān [*q.v.*] converge on Rayy on the north side.

1. History.

In the Avesta, *Wīdēwdāt*, i, 15, Rag͟hā is mentioned as the twelfth sacred place created by Ahura-Mazda. In the Old Persian inscriptions (Behistun 2, 10-18), Ragā appears as the province of Media in which in the autumn of 521 B.C. the false king of Media Frawarish sought refuge in vain; from Rag͟hā also Darius sent reinforcements to his father Wis̲h̲tāspa when the latter was putting down the rebellion in Parthia (Behistun 3, 1-10).

Rag͟hā is also mentioned in the Apocrypha. Tobit sent his son Tobias from Niniveh to recover the silver deposited in Rag͟hā with Gabael, brother of Gabrias (Tobit, i, 14). The book of Judith (i, 15) puts near Ragau (if indeed it was Rag͟hā) the plain in which Nebuchadnezzar defeated the king of Media, Arphaxad (Phraortes?).

In the summer of 330 B.C., Alexander the Great, following Darius III took 11 days to go from Ecbatane to Rhagae (Arrian, 3, 20, 2). According to Strabo, xi, 9, 1 and xi, 13, 6, Seleucus Nicator (312-280) rebuilt Rhagae under the name of Eurōpos (in memory of his native town in Macedonia), and near Eurōpos the towns of Laodicea, Apamaea and Heraclea were peopled with Macedonians. After the coming of the Parthians the town was renamed Arsakia. It is, however, possible that all these towns, although situated in the same locality, occupied slightly different sites or they are mentioned side by side in the authorities. Rawlinson (*JGS*, x, 119) would put Eurōpos at Varāmīn [*q.v.*]. The Greek popular etymologies which explain the name Rag͟hā as alluding to earthquakes seem to reflect the frequency of this phenomenon in this region so close to Damāwand.

In the Sāsānid period, Yazdagird III in 641 issued from Rayy his last appeal to the nation before fleeing to K̲h̲urāsān. The sanctuary of Bībī S̲h̲ahr-Bānū situated on the south face of the already mentioned spur and accessible only to women is associated with the memory of the daughter of Yazdagird who, according to tradition, became the wife of al-Ḥusayn b. ʿAlī. In the years A.D. 486, 499, 553, Rayy is mentioned as the see of bishops of the Eastern Syrian church.

Arab conquest. The year of the conquest is variously given (18-24/639-44), and it is possible that the Arab power was consolidated gradually. As late as 25/646 a rebellion was suppressed in Rayy by Saʿd b. Abī Waḳḳāṣ. The Arabs seem to have profited by the dissensions among the noble Persian families. Rayy was the fief of the Mihrān family and, in consequence of the resistance of Siyāwak̲h̲s̲h̲ b. Mihrān b. Bahrām Čūbīn, Nuʿaym b. Muḳarrin had the old town destroyed and ordered Farruk̲h̲ān b. Zaynabī (Zaynadī?) b. Ḳūla [see MAṢMUG̲H̲ĀN] to build a new town (al-Ṭabarī, i, 2655). In 71/690, again, a king of the family of Farruk̲h̲ān is mentioned alongside of the Arab governor.

The passing of power from the Umayyads to the ʿAbbāsids took place at Rayy without incident but in 136/753 the "K̲h̲urramī" Sunbad̲h̲, one of Abū Muslim's stalwarts, seized the town for a short time. The new era for Rayy began with the appointment of the heir to the throne Muḥammad al-Mahdī to the governorship of the east (141-52/758-68). He rebuilt Rayy under the name of Muḥammadiyya and surrounded it by a ditch. The suburb of Mahdī-ābād̲h̲ was built for those of the inhabitants who had to give up their property in the old town. Hārūn al-Ras̲h̲īd, son of al-Mahdī, was born in Rayy and used often to recall with pleasure his native town and its principal street. In 195/810 al-Maʾmūn's general Ṭāhir b. Ḥusayn won a victory over al-Amīn's troops near Rayy. In 250/865 the struggle began in Rayy between the Zaydī ʿAlids of Ṭabaristān and first the Ṭāhirids and later the caliph's Turkish generals. It was not till 272/885 that Äd̲h̲gü-tegin of Ḳazwīn took the town from the ʿAlids. In 261/894 the caliph al-Muʿtamid, wishing to consolidate his position, appointed to Rayy his son, the future caliph al-Muktafī. Soon afterwards, the Sāmānids began to interfere in Rayy. Ismāʿīl b. Aḥmad seized Rayy in 289/912, and the fait accompli was confirmed by the caliph al-Muktafī. In 296/909 Aḥmad b. Ismāʿīl received investiture from al-Muḳtadir in Rayy (Gardīzī, ed. Nāẓim, 21-2).

In the 4th/10th century, Rayy is described in detail in the works of the contemporary Arab geographers. In spite of the interest which Bag͟hdād displayed in Rayy, the number of Arabs there was insignificant, and the population consisted of Persians of all classes (*ak̲h̲lāṭ*; al-Yaʿḳūbī, *Buldān*, Yaʿḳūbī, 276). Among the products of Rayy, Ibn al-Faḳīh, 253, mentions silks and other stuffs, articles of wood and "lustre dishes", an interesting detail in view of the celebrity enjoyed by the ceramics "of Rhages". All writers emphasise the very great importance of Rayy as a commercial centre. According to al-Iṣṭak̲h̲rī, 207, the town covered an area of 1½ by 1½ *farsak̲h̲*s, the buildings were of clay (*ṭīn*) but the use of bricks and plaster (*d̲j̲iṣṣ = gač*) was also known. The town had five great gates and eight large bazaars. Al-Muḳaddasī, 391, calls Rayy one of the glories of the lands of Islam, and among other things mentions its library in the Rūd̲h̲a quarter which was watered by the Sūrḳānī canal.

Daylamī period. In 304/916 the lord of Äd̲h̲arbāyd̲j̲ān Yūsuf b. Abi 'l-Sād̲j̲ [see SĀD̲J̲IDS] occupied

Rayy, out of which he drove the Daylamī Muḥammad b. ʿAlī Ṣuʿlūḳ who represented the Sāmānid Naṣr (Ibn al-Athīr, viii, 74). This occupation, commemorated in coins struck by Yūsuf at Muḥammadiyya (see Miles, *The numis-matic history of Rayy*, 140-2), was the beginning of a troubled period. Rayy passed successively into the hands of the Daylamī ʿAlī b. Wahsūdhān, Waṣīf Bektimūrī, the Daylamī Aḥmad b. ʿAlī and of Mufliḥ, slave of Yūsuf (in 313/925; cf. R. Vasmer, *O monetakh Sadjidov*, Baku 1927). Lastly, the Sāmānids, encouraged by the caliph, succeeded in bringing Rayy again within their sphere of influence but soon their general Asfār (a Daylamī) became independent in Rayy. In 318/930 Asfār was killed by his lieutenant Mardāwīdj [*q.v.*] (a native of Gīlān and one of the founders of the Ziyārid dynasty [see ZIYĀRIDS]) who took over his master's lands (Cl. Huart, *Les Ziyārides*, in *Mém. Acad. Inscrs. et Belles-Lettres*, xlii (1922), 363 [= 11]).

After the assassination of Mardāwidj (323/925), the Būyids established themselves in Rayy, which became the fief of the branch of Rukn al-Dawla [*q.v.*] which held out there for about 100 years. In 390/1000 the last Sāmānid al-Muntaṣir made an attempt to seize Rayy but failed. In 420/1027 the Būyid Madjd al-Dawla [*q.v.*] was ill-advised enough to invoke against the Daylamīs the help of Maḥmūd of Ghazna, who seized his lands (cf. Muḥammad Nāẓim, *The life and times of Sulṭān Maḥmūd*, Cambridge 1931, 80-5; C.E. Bosworth, in *Camb. hist. of Iran*, iv, 176-7). The brief rule of the Ghaznawids was marked by acts of obscurantism, like the destruction of books on philosophy and astrology and the atrocious persecutions of the Ḳarmaṭians and Muʿtazilīs (Gardīzī, 91; Ibn al-Athīr, ix, 262).

The Saldjūḳs. The Ghuzz laid Rayy waste in 427/1035, and in 434/1042 the town, where Madjd al-Dawla still held out in the fort of Ṭabarak (Ibn al-Athīr, ix, 347), fell into the power of the Saldjūḳs and became one of their principal cities. The last Būyid, al-Malik al-Raḥīm, died a prisoner in Ṭabarak in 450/1058 (or in 455/1063; cf. H. Bowen, in *JRAS* [1929], 238) and the new lord Ṭoghril [*q.v.*] also died at Rayy in 455/1063. Henceforth, Rayy is constantly mentioned in connection with events relating to the Great Saldjūḳs and their branch in Persian ʿIrāḳ.

From the reign of Ghiyāth al-Dīn Masʿūd (529-547/1133-52 [*q.v.*]), Rayy was ruled by the *amīr* Inandj whose daughter Inandj Khātūn became the wife of Pahlawān, son of the famous atābeg of Ādharbāydjān, Ildegiz [*q.v.*]. When the latter put on the throne sultan Arslān Shāh (whose mother he had married), Inandj opposed this nomination but was defeated in 555/1160. Inandj withdrew to Bisṭām, but with the help of the Khʷārazmshāh Il Arslān reoccupied Rayy. He was finally murdered at the instigation of Ildegiz, who gave Rayy as a fief to Pahlawān. Later, the town passed to Ḳutlugh Inandj b. Pahlawān who, like his maternal grandfather, brought about the intervention of the Khʷārazmshāh Tekish in the affairs of Persia (588/1192). Two years later, in a battle near Rayy, the last Saldjūḳ Ṭoghrīl III was killed by Ḳutlugh Inandj but the country remained with the Khʷārazmians. In 614/1217 the atābeg of Fārs Saʿd b. Zangī [see SALGHURIDS] succeeded in occupying Rayy, but was almost immediately driven out by the Khʷārazmshāh Djalāl al-Dīn (cf. Nasawī, ed. Houdas).

Civil strife. Al-Muḳaddasī, 391, 395-6, mentions the dissensions (*ʿaṣabiyyāt*) among the people of Rayy in matters of religion. Under 582/1186-7, Ibn al-Athīr, xi, 237, records the damage done in Rayy in the civil war between Sunnīs and Shīʿīs; the inhabitants were killed or scattered and the town left in ruins. Yāḳūt, who, fleeing before the Mongols, went through Rayy in 617/1220, gives the results of his enquiry about the three parties, the Ḥanafīs, the Shāfiʿīs, and the Shīʿīs, of which the two first began by wiping out the Shīʿīs who formed half the population of the town and the majority in the country. Later, the Shāfiʿīs triumphed over the Ḥanafīs. The result was that there only survived in Rayy the Shāfiʿī quarter which was the smallest. Yāḳūt describes the underground houses at Rayy and the dark streets difficult of access which reflected the care of the inhabitants to protect themselves against enemies.

The Mongols. The Mongols who occupied Rayy after Yāḳūt's visit dealt it the final blow. Ibn al-Athīr (xii, 184) goes so far as to say that all the population was massacred by the Mongols in 617/1220 and the survivors put to death in 621/1224. It is, however, possible that the historian, echoing the panic which seized the Muslim world, exaggerates the extent of the destruction. Djuwaynī (ed. Ḳazwīnī, i, 115, tr. Boyle, i, 147) only says that the Mongol leaders put many people to death at Khʷār Rayy (in the country inhabited by Shīʿīs?) but in Rayy they were met by the (Shāfiʿī?) *ḳāḍī* who submitted to the invaders (*īl shud*) after which the latter went on. Rashīd al-Dīn (ed. Bérézine, in *Trudy VO*, xv, 135 [tr. 89]) admits that the Mongols under Djebe and Sübetey killed and plundered (*kushish wa-ghārat*) at "Rayy", but he seems to make a distinction between Rayy and Ḳum, in which the inhabitants were completely (*ba-kullī*) massacred.

The fact that life was not completely extinguished at Rayy is evident from the dates of pottery which apparently continued to be made in Rayy (cf. R. Guest, *A dated Rayy bowl*, in *Burlington Magazine* [1931], 134-5: the painted bowl bears the date 640/1243). The citadel of Ṭabarak was rebuilt under Ghazan Khān (1295-1304) but certain economic reasons (irrigation?) if not political and religious reasons, must have been against the restoration of Rayy, and the centre of the new administrative Mongol division (the *tumān* of Rayy) became Warāmīn [*q.v.*] (cf. *Nuzhat al-ḳulūb*, ed. Le Strange, 55). After the end of the Il-Khānids, Rayy fell to the sphere of influence of Tughā-Tīmūr [*q.v.*] of Astarābād. In 1384, Tīmūr's troops occupied Rayy without striking a blow but this must mean the district and not the town of Rayy, for Clavijo (ed. Sreznevsky, 187), who passed through this country in 1404, confirms that Rayy (*Xaharíprey* = *Shahr-i Rayy*) was no longer inhabited (*agora deshabitada*). No importance is to be attached to the mention of "Rayy" in the time of Shāh Rukh (*Maṭlaʿ al-saʿdayn*, under the year 841/1437) or of Shāh Ismāʿīl, in *Ḥabīb al-siyar*.

Bibliography: Ancient history: Marquart, *Ērānšahr*, 122-4; A.V.W. Jackson, *Persia, loc. cit.*; idem, *Historical sketch of Ragha*, in *Spiegel memorial volume*, Bombay 1908, 237-45; idem, in *Essays in modern theology to Ch.A. Briggs*, New York 1911, 93-7; Weissbach, arts. *Arsakia, Europos* and *Raga*, in Pauly-Wissowa, *Real-Encyclopädie*; Herzfeld, *Archäolog. Mitteil. aus Iran*, ii (1930), 95-8.

Islamic history: A *Taʾrīkh al-Rayy* was written by Abū Saʿd Manṣūr b. Ḥusayn al-Ābī [= Āwaʾī]; the author was the vizier of the Būyid Madjd al-Dawla and had access to very good sources; Yāḳūt often cites this history (i, 57, s.v. *Āba*); another *Taʾrīkh al-Rayy* is attributed to the Persian scholar Muntadjab al-Dīn al-Ḳummī (d. 575/1179-8 [*q.v.*]), quoted in Ibn Hadjar al-ʿAskalānī's *Lisān al-mīzān*; Quatremère, *Histoire des Mongols*, 272-5 (many quotations from the *Mudjmal al-tawārīkh*); Barbier de Meynard, *Dict. géographique*, 1861 (quotations from the *Haft iḳlīm* of Aḥmad Rāzī); G. Le Strange, *The lands of the Eastern Caliphate*, 214-18; P. Schwarz, *Iran im Mittelalter*, 740-809 (very complete utilisation of the Arabic sources; complete list of the dependencies of Rayy); *Ḥudūd al-ʿālam*, tr. Minorsky, 132-3, comm. 384; G.C. Miles, *The numismatic history of Rayy*, New York 1938; Abū Dulaf, *Second Risāla*, ed. and tr. Minorsky, *Abū-Dulaf Misʿar ibn Muhalhil's travels in Iran (circa A.D. 950)*, Cairo 1955, text §§ 47-50, tr. 51-3; W. Barthold, *An historical geography of Iran*, Princeton 1984, 121-6. (V. MINORSKY)

2. Archaeology and monuments.

Olivier in 1797 sought the ruins of Rayy in vain and, it was Truilhier and Gardane who first discovered them. The earliest descriptions are by J. Morier, Ker Porter and Sir W. Ouseley. The first has preserved for us a sketch of a Sāsānid bas-relief which was later replaced by a sculpture of Fatḥ Alī Shāh. The description, and particularly the plan by Ker Porter (reproduced in Sarre and A.V.W. Jackson, *Persia*), are still of value because since his time the needs of agriculture and unsystematic digging have destroyed the walls and confused the strata. Large numbers of objects of archaeological interest, and particularly the celebrated pottery covered with paintings, have flooded the European and American markets as a result of the activity of the dealers. Scientific investigation was begun by the Joint Expedition to Rayy of the Museum of Fine Arts, Boston, and the Univ. of Pennsylvania, Philadelphia, in 1934 (cf. *The Illustrated London News* [22 June 1935], 1122-3; E.F. Schmidt, *The Persian expedition [Rayy]*, in *Bulletin of the University Museum*, Philadelphia, v [1935], 41-9, cf. 25-7), and was continued by Chahryar Adle from 1974 onwards. In the citadel hill, Dr. Erich Schmidt found a great variety of pottery and the remains of buildings among which the most interesting are the foundations of al-Mahdī's mosque (communication by A. Godard to the Congress of Persian Art at Leningrad in September 1935).

In an interesting passage, al-Muḳaddasī, 210, speaks of the high domes which the Būyids built over their tombs. The remains of three tomb towers are still visible at Rayy, including a twelve-sided one whose site accords with two buildings of the Būyid period mentioned in Niẓām al-Mulk's *Siyāsat-nāma*, ed. Darke, 211, tr. idem², 167, sc. a *dakhma* or Tower of Silence built by a Zoroastrian at Ṭabarak, later called the *dīda-yi sipāhsālārān* "vantage-point of the commanders", and the nearby "dome (*gunbadh*) of Fakhr al-Dawla", presumably the Būyid *amīr*'s tomb [see FAKHR AL-DAWLA], and also the so-called "Tomb of Ṭoghrīl", which had an iron plate on it with the date Radjab 534/March 1140 (see on this last, G.C. Miles, in *Ars Orientalis*, vi [1966], 45-6, and on the towers in general, R. Hillenbrand, *The tomb towers of Iran to 1550*, diss. Oxford University 1974, unpubl., ii, 68-9, 73-5, 82-8). A further tomb tower, circular in plan and probably originally having a conical cap like the Gunbadh-i Ḳābūs [*q.v.*] in Gurgān, was photographed by Curzon in 1890 (see his *Persia and the Persian question*, i, 351) but destroyed in *ca.* 1895 for use as building materials (the fate of so many of the buildings of Rayy in the 19th and early 20th centuries); its Kūfic inscription band probably bore the date 466/1073 or, less likely, 476/1083-4 (see Chahryar Adle, *Notes préliminaires sur la tour disparue de Ray (466/1073-74)*, in *Memorial vol. of the VIth Internat. Congress of Iranian Art and Archaeology, Oxford, September 11-16th 1972*, Tehran 1976, 1-12). The remains of several subterranean tombs and of what were above-ground tomb structures have also been discovered, see Adle, *Constructions funéraires à Ray circa Xe-XIIe siècle*, in *Archäologische Mitteilungen aus Iran, Ergänzungsband 6*, Berlin 1979 (= *Akten des VII. Internationalen Kongresses für Iranische Kunst und Archäologie, München 7.-10 September 1976*), 511-15.

The hill of Ṭabarak on which was the citadel (destroyed in 588/1192 by the Saldjūḳ sultan Ṭoghrīl III) was, according to Yāḳūt, situated to "the right" of the Khurāsān road, while the high mountain was to "the left" of this road. Ṭabarak therefore must have been on the top of the hill opposite the great spur (hill *G* in Ker Porter's plan: "fortress finely built of stone and on the summit of an immense rock which commands the open country to the south"); cf. the map in A.F. Stahl, *Die Umgegend von Teheran*, in *Pet. Mitt.* (1900).

Finally, one should note that a considerable number of silk fragments from the Būyid period, many of them with inscriptions on them, have ostensibly been found at Rayy, although not in a controlled archaeological context; their authenticity accordingly remains disputed, see Dorothy F. Shepherd, *Medieval Persian silks in fact and fancy*, in *Bull. de Liaison du Centre International d'Etude des textiles anciens*, no. 39-40, Lyons 1974.

Bibliography (in addition to references given in the article): Description of the ruins: J. Morier, *A Journey*, 1812, 232, 403; *Second Journey*, 1818, 190; Ker Porter, *Travels*, 1821, i, 357-64 (map); Ouseley, *Travels*, 1823, iii, 174-99, plate lxv; Ritter, *Erdkunde*, vi/1, 1838, 595-604; Curzon, *Persia*, i, 347-52; F. Sarre, *Denkmäler persischer Baukunst*, Berlin 1901, text, 55-58; A.V.W. Williams Jackson, *Persia past and present*, New York 1905, 428-41 (plan by Ker Porter).

Modern studies: Ḥusayn Karīmān, *Rayy-i bāstān*, Tehran 1345-9/1966-70, 2 vols., is the most detailed work here, but does not take account of the subsequent work by Adle, Y. Kossar and others; see, regarding this, Adle, *Notes sur les première et seconde campagnes archéologiques à Rey. Automne-hiver 1354-55/1976-7*, in *Mélanges Jean Perrot*, Paris 1990, 295-307, providing a resume of a 6-vol. report on these investigations deposited at the Centre iranien pour les recherches archéologiques. See also Sylvia A. Matheson, *Persia: an archaeological guide²*, London 1976, 46 ff., and the arts. ṬIHRĀN and WARĀMĪN.

(V. MINORSKY-[C.E. BOSWORTH])

RAYY [see MAʾ].

RAYYA, modern Spanish rendering REYYO (RAYYO), the name given in Muslim Spain to the administrative circle (*kūra*) comprising the south of the Peninsula, the capital of which was successively Archidona (Arabic *Urdjudhūna*) and Málaga. The usual Arabic orthography is ريّة: in particular, this is the form found in the *Muʿdjam al-buldān* of Yāḳūt; but some Spanish mss. give the orthography ريُّه, more in keeping with the local pronunciation Reyyo (Rayyu) attested by Ibn Ḥawḳal. It is probably, as Dozy thought, a transcription of the Latin *regio* (no doubt *Malacitana regio*); the suggestion put forward by Gayangos of a connection with the Persian town-name al-Rayy is of course untenable.

When the fiefs in the south of Spain were assigned to the former companions of Baldj b. Bishr [*q.v.*], the district of Reyyo was alloted to the *djund* of Jordan (*al-Urdunn*). During the Umayyad caliphate of Cordova, the *kūra* of Reyyo was bounded by those of Cabra and Algeciras in the west, by the Mediterranean in the south and by the *kūra* of Elvira in the east.

One should now add to the above a reference to J. Vallvé, *La división territorial de la España musulmana*, Madrid, Consejo Superior de Investigaciones Científicas 1986, of which pp. 328-31 are devoted to "la cora de Rayya". According to this author, one should read Rayya and not Rayyo, basing himself on the sole topographical trace of this name, *Campo de Zafarraya*, interpreted as *Faḥṣ Rayya*, and, above all, on certain poems which require this reading for their end rhymes. An origin of the name has also been suggested in Phoenician via Latin.

The main problem regarding this *kūra* is the exact situation of the fortress of Bobastro (Bubas̲h̲tr, Bubas̲h̲tur), the main refuge of the rebel ʿUmar b. Ḥafṣūn, which we know was held by him and for which several localisations have been proposed. The traditional identification, with the place called Las Mesas de Villaverde, was defended by F.J. Simonet (earlier works cited in M. Riu Riu, *Aportación de la arqueología al estudio de los Mozárabes de al-Andalus*, in *Tres estudios de historia medieval andaluza*, Cordova 1977, 85-112), but Vallvé has proposed an identification with the high ground of Marmuyas in the district of Comares, where several seasons of excavations "with interesting results" have taken place. See for a full discussion, BUBAS̲H̲TRU in Suppl. Vallvé further cites, in regard to Rayya, the passage describing it by Ibn G̲h̲ālib, published by him and translated in the above-mentioned work; he also translates the passage of al-Nubāhī (*K. al-Markaba al-ʿulyā*, published by Lévi-Provençal), written in the 8th/14th century and giving the earlier borders of the *kūra*.

Bibliography (in addition to references given in the article): Idrīsī, *Description de l'Afrique et de l'Espagne*, ed. and tr. Dozy and de Goeje, 174, 204 of the text, 209, 250 of the tr.; Yāḳūt, ii, 892 (cf. ii, 826); Ibn ʿAbd al-Muʿnim al-Ḥimyarī, *al-Rawḍ al-miʿṭār*, Spanish ed. 81; Dozy, *Recherches*[3], i, 317-20; Alemany Bolufer, *La geografía de la Península ibérica en los escritores árabes*, Granada 1921, 118; E. Lévi-Provençal, *L'Espagne musulmane au X*[ème] *siècle*, Paris 1932, 116-18; J. Vallvé, *De nuevo sobre Bobastro*, in *And.*, xxx (1965), 139-74; idem, *Notas de toponimia hispanoárabe. La Cora de Rayya (Malaga)*, in *Homenaje a Manuel Ocaña Jiménez*, Cordova 1990, 213-20.

(E. LÉVI-PROVENÇAL-[J.-P. MOLÉNAT])

AL-**RĀZĪ**, ABŪ BAKR MUḤAMMAD B. ZAKARIYYĀʾ, known to the Latins as Rhazes (*ca.* 250/854-313/925 or 323/935), physician, philosopher and alchemist.

The most free-thinking of the major philosophers of Islam, al-Rāzī was born in Rayy, where he was well trained in the Greek sciences. He was reputedly well versed in musical theory and performance before becoming a physician. His work in alchemy takes a new, more empirical and naturalistic approach than that of the Greeks or D̲j̲ābir, and he brought the same empirical spirit to medicine. Immersed in the Galenic tradition, and apparently even conversant with Greek (al-Bīrūnī ascribes to him translations and abridgements from the Greek and even a poem "in the Greek language"), al-Rāzī greatly profited from the Arabic translations of Greek medical and philosophical texts. He headed the hospital of Rayy before assuming the corresponding post in Bag̲h̲dād. His property in the vicinity seems to have brought him back often to Rayy, and he died there, somewhat embittered and alienated, partly by the loss of his eyesight. Like many of the great physicians of Islam, al-Rāzī was a courtier as well as a scholar, clinician and teacher. His medical handbook the *Manṣūrī*, translated into Latin by Gerard of Cremona in the 12th century, was dedicated to Manṣūr b. Isḥāḳ, the Sāmānid governor of Rayy; his *Mulūkī* or *Regius*, to ʿAlī b. Wāhsūd̲h̲ān of Ṭabaristān. The author of some two hundred books, al-Rāzī claims in his apologia, the *Sīra al-falsafiyya*, or "Philosophical Way of Life", that his has been a life of moderation, excessive only in his devotion to learning; he associated with princes never as a man at arms or an officer of state but always, and only, as a physician and a friend. He was constantly writing. In one year, he urges, he wrote over twenty thousand pages, "in a hand like an amulet maker's." Others remark on his generosity and compassion, seeing that the poor among his patients were properly fed and given adequate nursing care. Arriving patients first saw an outer circle of disciples, and then an inner circle, if these could not aid them, leaving al-Rāzī himself to treat the hardest cases. His medical research was similarly methodical, as revealed in his notebooks. These were edited, in some 25 volumes, as the *K. al-Ḥāwī fi 'l-ṭibb*, at the instance of Ibn al-ʿAmīd [*q.v.*], the vizier of Rukn al-Dawla [*q.v.*]. Translated as the *Continens* in 1279 by the Jewish physician Farad̲j̲ b. Sālim (known as Farraguth) for King Charles of Anjou, it was printed at Brescia in 1486 and repeatedly thereafter. The text (Ḥaydarābād 1955) contains al-Rāzī's extensive notes from a wide range of sources, organised anatomically, from head to toe. His own clinical observations, often at variance with received opinions, typically close the sections. Al-Rāzī mined these files for his numerous medical works, and several unfinished works can be discerned in the *Ḥāwī* in embryo. His magnum opus, the *Kitāb al-D̲j̲āmiʿ al-kabīr*, or "Great Medical Compendium", often confused with the *Ḥāwī*, was a work that al-Rāzī published, not the corpus of his private files. Among the most famous of his medical writings are those on *Stones in the kidney and bladder* (*K. al-Ḥaṣā fi 'l-kulā wa 'l-mat̲h̲āna*) and *Smallpox and measles* (*K. al-D̲j̲adarī wa 'l-ḥaṣba*). The latter was the first book on smallpox, and was translated over a dozen times into Latin and other European languages. Its lack of dogmatism and its Hippocratic reliance on clinical observation typify al-Rāzī's medical methods. His independent mind is strikingly revealed in his *S̲h̲ukūk ʿalā D̲j̲alīnūs* or "Doubts about Galen". Here al-Rāzī rejects claims of Galen's, from the alleged superiority of the Greek language to many of his cosmological and medical views. He places medicine within philosophy, inferring that sound practice demands independent thinking. His own clinical records, he reports, do not confirm Galen's descriptions of the course of a fever. And in some cases he finds that his clinical experience exceeds Galen's. He rejects the notion, central to the theory of humours, that the body is warmed or cooled only by warmer or cooler bodies; for a warm drink may heat the body to a degree much hotter than its own. Thus the drink must trigger a response rather than simply communicating its own warmth or coldness. This line of criticism has the potential, in time, to bring down the whole theory of humours and the scheme of the four elements, on which it was grounded. Al-Rāzī's alchemy, like his medical thinking, struggles within the cocoon of hylomorphism. It dismisses the idea of potions and dispenses with an appeal to magic, if magic means reliance on symbols as causes. But al-Rāzī does not reject the idea that there are wonders in the sense of unexplained phenomena in nature. His alchemical stockroom, accordingly, is enriched with the products of Persian mining and anufacture, and the Chinese discovery, sal amoniac. Still reliant on the idea of dominant forms or ssences and thus on the Neoplatonic conception of ausality as inherently intellectual rather than echanical, al-Rāzī's alchemy nonetheless brings to e fore such empiric qualities as salinity and flammability—the latter ascribed to "oiliness" and sulphuriousness". Such properties are not readily xplained by the traditional fire, water, earth and air hematism, as al-Ghazālī and other later comers, rimed by thoughts like al-Rāzī's, were quick to note.

Like Galen, al-Rāzī was speculatively interested in e art and profession of medicine. He wrote essays on ich subjects as "The reasons for people's preference inferior physicians," "A mistaken view of the funcon of the physician," "Why some people leave a hysician if he is intelligent," "That an intelligent hysician cannot heal all diseases, since that is not ossible," and "Why ignorant physicians, common lk, and women in the cities are more successful than ientists in treating certain diseases—and the physiian's excuse for this." He also shared Galen's inrest in philosophy and heeded his treatise, "That e outstanding physician must also be a philosoher." Al-Bīrūnī lists some eighty philosophical titles his al-Rāzī bibliography, and al-Nadīm lists dozens his works on logic, cosmology, theology, athematics and alchemy. Given the general epugnance toward al-Rāzī's philosophical ideas mong his contemporaries and medieval successors, w of these works were copied. But fragments survive quotations by later authors, as do the *Sīra allsafiyya* and the *Ṭibb al-rūḥānī*, the "Spiritual hysick" or "Psychological medicine," which emodies al-Rāzī's largely Epicurean ethical system. mong the writings of which we have mention are: commentary on Plato's *Timaeus*, perhaps based on e epitome of Galen, a rebuttal of Iamblichus' esponse to Porphyry's *Letter to Anebos* (that is, the *De ysteriis*), an appraisal of the Ḳurʾān, a critique of uʿtazilism, another on the infallible Ismāʿīlī Imām, work on how to measure intelligence, an introducon to and vindication of algebra, a defence of the inorporeality of the soul, a debate with a Manichaean, nd an explanation of the difficulty people have in acepting the sphericity of the earth when they are not ained in rigorous demonstration. Other works deal ith eros, coitus, nudity and clothing, the fatal effects f the Simoom (or simply, of poisons, *sumūm*, cf. ezgin, *GAS*, iii, 289 no. 32) on animal life, the easons of autumn and spring, the wisdom of the reator, and the reason for the creation of savage easts and reptiles. One work defends the proposition at God does not interfere with the actions of other gents. Another rebuts the claim that the earth evolves. Al-Rāzī discussed the innate or intrinsic haracter of motion, a sensitive point at the juncture etween Democritean and Aristotelian physics. He rote several treatments of the nature of matter, and ne on the unseen causes of motion. His exposé of the isks of ignoring the axioms of geometry may aim at *alām* defenders of dimensionless atoms; and his book n the diagonal of the square may have defended his wn atomism against the ancient charge, first levelled t Pythagoreanism, that atomism is refuted by the emonstrated incommensurability of a square's side ith its diagonal; for al-Rāzī's acceptance of the void nd rejection of Aristotle's doctrine of the relativity of pace disarms that charge, since al-Rāzī's absolute pace is a Euclidean continuum and need not, like his atter, be composed of discrete, indivisible quanta.

The *Ṭibb al-rūḥānī*, written for al-Manṣūr as a companion to the *Manṣūrī*, develops a moderately ascetic ideal of life from the premise that all pleasures presuppose a prior pain (or dislocation). This means that peace of mind or lack of perturbation is the optimum of pleasure, as al-Rāzī explains in his widely-cited lost work on pleasure. Pleasures cannot be amassed or hoarded, and what some hedonists might think of as "peak experiences" are reached only by traversing a corresponding valley. To feed an appetite, moreover, is only to enlarge it. So the attempt to maximise one's happiness by serving the appetites and passions is a self-defeating strategy, as Plato showed when he argued that such a life is comparable to trying to carry water in a sieve. Epicurus took that argument very much to heart when he sought to devise a hedonistic alternative to the sybaritic outlook of the Cyrenaic philosophers, and al-Rāzī does so as well. His ethical treatise follows al-Kindī's precedent in treating ethics as a kind of psychic medicine or clinical psychology, an approach later used by Ibn Gabirol and Maimonides. But the basis of the art in question, which is the Socratic tendance of the soul, is not primarily the Platonic "second voyage," the endeavour to flee to a higher world—although that theme is important to al-Rāzī. Expressing grave doubts about the demonstrability of immortality, he falls back on the less metaphysically demanding and more dialectically persuasive position that, if death is the ultimate end of our existence, it is nothing to be feared but only a surcease of our pains and troubles.

Wisdom, then, springs not from the thought of death, as many philosophers and pious teachers have supposed, but from overcoming that thought. For, even more than the appetites themselves, the fear of death is the goad of the passions that hamper human rationality and undermine human happiness. As al-Rāzī explains: "As long as the fear of death persists, one will incline away from reason and toward passion (*hawāʾ*)." The argument is Epicurean. The passions here, as in Epicurus, are thought of as neuroses, compulsions, pleasureless addictions, to use al-Rāzī's description (his word for an addict is *mudmin*). The glutton, the miser, even the sexual obsessive, are, by al-Rāzī's analysis, as much moved by the fear of death as by natural appetites. For natural needs, as Epicurus would explain, are always in measure. The unwholesome excess that makes vice a disease comes from the irrational and unselfconscious mental linking of natural pleasures and gratifications with security, that is, a sense of freedom from the fear of death. Ethics here becomes entirely prudential, as al-Rāzī's critics were not slow to note. If we knew that our ultimate state was immortality, and the return of the soul in us to her true home, our mad scrabbling after the surrogates of immortality would cease. But the fear of death "can never be banished altogether from the soul, unless one is certain that after death it shifts to a better state." And his conclusion is that it "would require very lengthy argumentation, if one sought proof rather than just allegations (*khabar*). There really is no method whatever for argument to adopt on this topic... The subject is too elevated and too broad as well as too long.... It would require examination of all faiths and rites that hold or imply beliefs about an afterlife and a verdict as to which are true and which are false"—a task al-Rāzī has no immediate or pressing intention of attempting. For practical purposes, then, he offers the Epicurean consolation that death is nothing to us, if the soul is really mortal. What scripture has to say on the subject is just another undemonstrated report, an unsubstantiated allegation.

In his debates with an Ismāʿīlī adversary, Abū Ḥātim al-Rāzī (d. 322/934 [*q.v.*]), chief lieutenant to the Ismāʿīlī *dāʿī* of Rayy, and later chief *dāʿī* himself, al-Rāzī faces a Muʿtazilī argument that harks back to Stoic sources: God's mercy would not deny humanity the guidance of leaders inspired with revealed knowledge of God's own will and His plan for human destiny. Al-Rāzī answers that God has provided what we need to know, not in the arbitrary and divisive gift of special revelation, which only foments bloodshed and contention, but in reason, which belongs equally to all. Prophets are impostors, at best misled by the demonic shades of restless and envious spirits. But ordinary men are fully capable of thinking for themselves and need no guidance from another. One can see their intelligence and ingenuity in the crafts and devices by which they get their living, for it is here that they apply their interest and their energy. Intellectuals who have not devoted their energies, say, to mechanical devices would be baffled by the skills and techniques of such men; but all human beings are capable of the independent thinking that is so critical to human destiny. It is only because the philosopher has applied himself to abstract speculations that he has attained some measure of understanding in intellectual matters.

Asked if a philosopher can follow a prophetically revealed religion, al-Rāzī openly retorts: "How can anyone think philosophically while committed to those old wives' tales, founded on contradictions, obdurate ignorance, and dogmatism (*muḳim ʿalā 'l-i<u>kh</u>tilāfat, muṣirr ʿalā 'l-<u>dj</u>ahl wa 'l-taḳlīd*)?" Al-Rāzī takes issue with ritualism for what he sees as its obsession with unseen and unseeable sources of impurity; but he also combats the natural tendency of his contemporaries to think of philosophy as a dogmatic school or even a sect, their expectation that a philosopher should believe and behave as Socrates or Plato did. Like many philosophers, he has difficulty explaining to others that philosophical disagreements and divergences of outlook are not a scandal but a source of vitality. A philosopher, he urges, does not slavishly follow the actions and ideas of some master. One learns from one's predecessors, to be sure, but the hope is to surpass them. Al-Rāzī admits that he will never be a Socrates, and cautions against anyone's expecting in short order to rival Socrates, Plato, Aristotle, Theophrastus, Eudemus, Chrysippus, Themistius or Alexander of Aphrodisias. But he also affirms a belief in progress, at least for individuals, and denies that one is trapped within the teachings of the great founders of traditions: "You must realise," he tells Abū Ḥātim, "that every later philosopher who commits himself creatively (*i<u>dj</u>tahada*), diligently, and persistently to philosophical inquiry where subtle difficulties have led his predecessors to disagree, will understand what they understood and retain it, having a quick mind and much experience of thought and inquiry in other areas. Rapidly mastering what his predecessors knew and grasping the lessons they afford, he readily surpasses them. For inquiry, thought and originality make progress and improvement inevitable." The smallest measure of original thought, even if it does not reach unrevisable truth, al-Rāzī insists, helps to free the soul from its thrall in this world and secure for us that immortality which was so wrongly described and so vainly promised by the prophets.

The Soul, al-Rāzī argues in such works as his *Kitāb al-ʿIlm al-ilāhī* or "Theology", and *On the five eternals*, both now lost, but well represented by fragments, paraphrases, descriptions and refutations, was one of five eternal things that antedate the cosmos. The other four were God, matter, time and space. Space is the void. It may or may not have atoms in it. Time, like space, is absolute, not relative to bodies in motion, as in Aristotle. Being absolute, time is eternal. Motion is not. For matter, in itself, is inert; its motion stems from the activity of soul. Soul, the world soul, initially stood apart from matter, in a spiritual realm of her own. She yearned, however, to be embodied. And God, like a wise father, understanding that Soul learns only by experience, allowed her to embroil herself here, as a king might allow his headstrong son into a tempting but in many ways noxious garden, not out of ignorance, unconcern, or even powerlessness or spite, but out of understanding that only through experience will the boy's restlessness abate. In the case of Soul's entry into materiality, chaos was the first result, as she set matter stirring in wild and disordered motion. God, in His grace, intervened, imparting intelligence of His own to the world that Soul's impetuous desire had formed. As an immanent principle, intelligence gave order to the world, stabilising its motions and rendering them comprehensible. But it also gave understanding to the Soul itself, allowing her to recognise her estrangement in this world and seek a return from exile. It is this striving for return that gives meaning to all human strivings in the realm of life.

Only by such a theory, al-Rāzī insists, can creationists hope to overcome the elenchus of the eternalists, who deny creation altogether. A quasi-gnostic quasi-Platonic *formatio mundi*, then, not *creatio ex nihilo* is the sole workable hypothesis which al-Rāzī can offer on behalf of the world's temporal origination, as opposed to its eternal, Plotinian emanation or its perpetual existence as a Democritean or Epicurean mechanism. Clearly the materialists, al-Rāzī reasons improperly ignore the life and intelligence that course through nature, giving directed and stable movement to otherwise inert and passive matter. As for the Neoplatonic Aristotelians, their theory of emanation leads them to fudge (as Aristotle had done) on the inertness of matter. For, by treating the natural order as eternal, they seem to make motion and ordering form inherent properties of matter, rather than imparted acts and powers, as Neoplatonic principles should require. Only the affirmation of a temporal origin which al-Rāzī unabashedly adopts from scripture and from the concurring authority of Plato's *Timaeus* seems to do justice to the fact that nature's order is not intrinsic but imparted; and only a temporal creation does justice to the unimpeded operation of the forces of nature and the self-governing actions of human intelligence and will. For these gifts were given long ago and are not, as in Neoplatonism, timelessly imparted without ever really departing from their Source.

But although creation involves a kind of gift, al-Rāzī cannot treat the act of creation as a sheer act of grace, as many of his contemporaries might wish to do. His view that in this life evils outweigh goods, endorsed by Epicurean concerns over the problem of evil, and by physiological arguments about the ultimate prevalence of pain and suffering over peace and pleasure in all sensate beings, press him toward the gnostic conclusion that creation is a tragedy or mistake. Stopping short of such condemnation, al-Rāzī treats creation as a qualified evil: Life as a whole and bodily existence in general represent a fall for the life-giving principle, the Soul. But the fall is broken by the gift of intelligence. The crypt of the gnostic image has a skylight, through which streams the light of day. There is an avenue of escape. And the Soul's fall, either devised nor forced by God, is ascribed to her spontaneity, not to God's will or wisdom. It was neither coerced and destined nor mandated by the very nature of intelligence, as though it were (as in Neoplatonism) a demand of logic, but it was foreseen and tolerated by an all-seeing wisdom. And the loss it brought about will be overcome.

Bibliography: 1. Works by al-Rāzī. A.J. Arberry (tr.), *The Spiritual Physick of Rhazes*, London 1950; W.A. Greenhill (tr.), *A treatise on the smallpox and measles*, London 1847; P. de Koning (tr.), *Traité sur le calcul dans les reins et dans la vessie*, Leiden 1896; P. Kraus (ed.), *Abi Mohammadi Filii Zachariae Raghensis (Razis) opera philosophica fragmentaque quae supersunt*, Cairo 1939, *Pars prior* (all that was published), repr. Beirut 1973; M. Meyerhof, *Thirty-three clinical observations by Rhazes [from the Ḥāwī]*, in *Isis*, xxiii (1935), 321-56, see also Aziz Pasha's synopses and discussions of the *Ḥāwī*, in *Bulletin of the Department of the History of Medicine*, Osmania Medical College, Ḥaydarābād, i (1963), 163-87, ii (1964), 23-32, iii (1965), 220-5, etc.; J. Ruska (tr.), *Al-Razī's Buch Geheimnis der Geheimnisse*, Berlin 1937; M. Vazquez (ed. and tr.), *Libro de la introducción al arte de la medicina*, Salamanca 1979.

2. Studies and sources. M. Azeez Pasha, *Biographies of Unani [Greek] physicians found in Al-Ḥāwī of Rhazes*, in *Bulletin of the Indian Institute of the History of Medicine*, vii (1977), 38-40; Bīrūnī, *Risāla fī Fihrist kutub M. b. Zakariyyāʾ al-Rāzī*, ed. P. Kraus, Paris 1936, ed. with Persian tr. M. Mohaghegh, Tehran 1984-5, partial German tr. Ruska in *Isis*, v (1922), 26-50; M. Fakhry, *A tenth-century Arabic interpretation of Plato's Cosmology*, in *Journal of the History of Philosophy*, vi (1968), 15-22; D. Gutas, *Notes and texts from Cairo mss. I. Addenda to P. Kraus' edition of Abū Bakr al-Rāzī's* Ṭibb al-Rūḥānī, in *Arabica*, xxiv (1977), 91-3; G. Hofmeister, *Rasis' Traumlehre*, in *Archiv für Kulturgeschichte*, li (1969), 137-59; Ibn al-Ḳifṭī, *Taʾrīkh al-Ḥukamāʾ*, ed. Lippert, 271-7; Ibn Abī Uṣaybiʿa, *ʿUyūn al-anbāʾ*, ed. Müller, i, 309-21; M. Gaudefroy-Demombynes, *Er-Rāzī philosophe, d'après des ouvrages récents*, in *RHR*, cxxiv (1941), 142-90; L.E. Goodman, *The Epicurean ethic of M. b. Zakariyāʾ ar-Rāzī*, in *SI*, xxxiv (1971), 5-26; idem, *Rāzī's myth of the fall of the soul: its function in his philosophy*, in G. Hourani (ed.), *Essays on Islamic philosophy and science*, Albany 1975, 25-40; idem, *Rāzī's psychology*, in *Philosophical Forum*, iv (1972), 26-48; G. Heym, *Al-Rāzī and alchemy*, in *Ambix*, i (1938), 184-91; A.Z. Iskandar, *The medical bibliography of al-Rāzī*, in G. Hourani (ed.), *op. cit.*, 41-6; Maimonides, *Guide to the perplexed*, ed. Munk, iii, 18; M. Mohaghegh, *Notes on the ''Spiritual Physick'' of al-Rāzī*, in *SI*, xxvi (1967), 5-22; idem, *Rāzī's* Kitāb al-ʿIlm al-Ilāhī *and the five eternals*, in *Abr-Nahrain*, xiii (1973), 16-23; Nadīm, *Fihrist*, ed. Flügel, 299-302, 358, tr. Bayard Dodge, New York 1970, 82, 377, 435, 599, 701-9; J.R. Partington, *The chemistry of Rāzī*, in *Ambix*, i (1938), 192-6; S. Pinès, *Razi, critique de Galien*, in *Actes du Septième Congrès International d'Histoire des Sciences*, Jerusalem 1953; 480-7; idem, art. *al-Rāzī*, in *Dictionary of Scientific Biography*; Abū Ḥātim al-Rāzī, *Aʿlām al-nubuwwa*, ed. Salah al-Sawy, with an English introd. S.H. Nasr, Tehran 1977, extracts tr. F. Brion, in *Bulletin de Philosophie Medievale*, xxviii (1986), 134-62; F. Rosenthal, *Ar-Razī on the hidden illness*, in *Bulletin of the History of Medicine*, lii (1978), 45-60; Ruska, *Al-Rāzī als Chemiker*, in *Zeitschrift für Chemie* (1922), 719-22; idem, in *Isl.*, xxii (1935), 281-319, xxv (1939), 1-34, 191-3; idem, *Al-Bīrūnī*

als Quelle für das Leben und die Schriften al-Rāzī's, in *Isis*, v (1923), 26-50; H. Said, *Razi and treatment through nutritive correction*, in *Hamdard Islamicus*, xix (1976), 113-20; Sezgin, *GAS*, iii, 274-94, iv, 275-82, v, 282, vi, 187-8, vii, 160, 271-2; O. Timkin, *A medieval translation of Rhazes' Clinical observations*, in *Bulletin of the History of Medicine*, xii (1942), 102-17.

(L.E. Goodman)

AL-RĀZĪ, Aḥmad b. ʿAbd Allāh, Yemenite historian whose full name is Abu 'l-ʿAbbās Aḥmad b. ʿAbd Allāh b. Muḥammad al-Rāzī. The date of his birth in Ṣanʿāʾ is unknown; he died there *ca.* 460/1068. The little that is known of this historian is owed to al-Djanadī (d. 732/1332) who, in his book *al-Sulūk* (ms.), indicates that he was a native of the capital of the Yemen, and that he was an *imām*, well-informed in matters of *fikh* and *ḥadīth*. Furthermore, it seems that he was a Sunnī, a fact to which his work alludes, and al-Djanadī attributes to him an ''extensive tradition'' and a ''perfect spirit''. The biographer believes that the author's family came originally from the town of Rayy (hence the *nisba*; on this point see Yākūt's list, *Muʿdjam*, iii, 120-2, in which his name does not however appear), but he gives no information as to when the family took up residence in the Yemen; it could have been with the Persian expedition of the 6th century A.D., in support of the Ḥimyarite dynasty, with Sayf b. Dhī Yazan (see R.G. Khoury, *Wahb b. Munabbih*, 189 ff.), or with the *Ṭabarāniyyūn*, who came from Ṭabaristān to the aid of the *imām* al-Hādī Yaḥyā b. al-Ḥusayn (220-98/835-911) (see e.g. *Sīrat al-Hādī*, ed. S. Zakkār, 116, 236; W. Madelung, *Der Imām al-Qāsim*, etc.), or later still, which seems less likely.

In his capacity as an author, al-Djanadī mentions his *Taʾrīkh Ṣanʿāʾ*, which he describes as having gained popular acclaim and which he must have used as a primary source in the writing of his own *al-Sulūk fī ṭabakāt al-ʿulamāʾ wa 'l-mulūk*. He gives no other information on this subject. Yet a version of the *Taʾrīkh* of al-Rāzī is currently available; it has been edited by Ḥusayn ʿAbd Allāh al-ʿAmrī and ʿAbd al-Djabbār Zakkār, under the title *Taʾrīkh madīnat Ṣanʿāʾ* (see *Bibl.*). The content of the book covers the period from the foundation of the city to the times in which the chronicler lived, i.e. the 5th/11th century; Brockelmann barely mentions this historian (*GAL*, SI, 570) and Sezgin not at all, although at least eight manuscript copies of the book existed in various libraries and were accessible to the editors.

The book comprises two major elements: a historical element which goes beyond the framework of history as such, and a bio-bibliographical element.

The historical section opens with general information concerning the Yemen, its capital and the villages surrounding it, the construction of this capital, the boundaries of which were established by Shem, under divine inspiration, and which attained its maximum level of development towards the end of the 3rd/9th century, a level which it had regained in the lifetime of the author, after its destruction. Details are also provided regarding the fortress of Ghumdān, the merits of the Yemen and of Ṣanʿāʾ, formerly called Azāl, and the numerous mosques of the city, the first of which was planned by the first Muslim governor, Wabar b. Yuḥannis, and constructed and enlarged by his successors. This section, the shorter of the two, contains beyond any doubt the most detailed of information concerning the history of the city, providing data which are precise and useful, up to a point (for example, regarding the mosques, the valleys, the quarters, etc.). However, as a whole the work is unsatisfactory, since it is rife with traditions traced back to various historical and religious sources and individuals, which have a single purpose: to promote the cause of the Yemen among the lands of God's Elect, and to extol the merits of the capital, as much in the Biblical tradition as in that of the Prophet Muḥammad. The conspicuous exaggerations are motivated by this purpose, as for example the claim that the first church of the town was built on the site where Jesus had prayed, or the latter's prophecy concerning the powerful individual who was to come forth from the town at the end of time; such items are to be found in all the chronicles of ancient Islamic cities.

The second elements of the book is bio-bibliographical. It begins with the Companions of the Prophet who came to the Yemen and some of whom were appointed governors of this land.

However the work becomes more systematic with its consideration of the élite of Yemenite scholars and ascetics, prominent among whom is the most illustrious figure of Ṣanʿāʾ, Wahb b. Munabbih (d. 110/728 or 114/732 [*q.v.*]), an ideal source of Biblical history for later Islamic historians, and thus for Ibn Isḥāḳ, whose universal Muslim history he had anticipated, and one of the principal sources of al-Rāzī. In the main his information is valuable, since many of these scholars are barely known or not at all. Details are provided here of their origin, their connections with the Yemen, the traditions attributed to them or concerning them, material such as is encountered in other Islamic books of the same genre. Unfortunately there are few dates, and, in the case of some of them, nothing more than one or a few trifling traditions. With the importance accorded to the bio-bibliographical element, it is evident that the interest in the work of al-Rāzī, as in that for example of the chroniclers al-Khaṭīb al-Baghdādī (392-463/1002-71) in his *Taʾrīkh Baghdād*, or Ibn ʿAsākir (499-571/1106-76), in *Taʾrīkh madīnat Dimashḳ*, can be explained by the fact that they were primarily historians and *muḥaddithūn*, for whom it was natural to employ the method of the *ahl al-ḥadīth*, albeit with particular nuances and the often considerable differences between these works (and others which are not mentioned here), to which the writer of this article has drawn attention elsewhere (see R.G. Khoury, *Zur Bedeutung des Aḥmad... al-Rāzī*, 93-6, 98, 100).

It is important to recognise that this book, in the terms of the literary production of its time, remains a relatively reliable and positive source, in particular for certain aspects of the history, geography and archaeology of the city and even of the country, not to mention his bio-bibliographical notices which supply the titles of a large number of books, most of them lost, which are the sources to which the author refers (see *ibid.*, 91 ff.).

Bibliography: Djanadī, *al-Sulūk fī ṭabaḳāt al-ʿulamāʾ wa l-mulūk* (ms., see Brockelmann, S II, 236); Yāḳūt, *Muʿdjam*, iii; al-Khaṭīb al-Baghdādī; Ibn ʿAsākir; W. Madelung, *Der Imām al-Qāsim ibn Ibrāhīm und die Glaubenslehre der Zaiditen*, Berlin 1965; R.G. Khoury, *Wahb b. Munabbih. Der Heidelberger Papyrus Heid. Arab. 23. Leben und Werk des Dichters*, Wiesbaden 1972; idem, *Zur Bedeuting des Aḥmad b. ʿAbdallah ar-Razi für die Geschichte des Jemen*, in *WI*, xx (1981), 87-103; *Sīrat al-Hādī ilā 'l-ḥaḳḳ Yaḥyā b. al-Ḥusayn*, ed. S. Zakkār, Beirut 1972; Rāzī, *Taʾrīkh madīnat Ṣanʿāʾ*, ed. H.ʿA.A. al-ʿAmrī and ʿA.Dj. Zakkār, Ṣanʿāʾ 1401/1981. (R.G. KHOURY)

RĀZĪ, AMĪN AḤMAD, a Persian biographer of the later 10th/16th and early 11th/17th centuries. Hardly anything is known of his life. He belonged t Rayy, where his father Khwādja Mīrzā Aḥmad wa celebrated for his wealth and benevolence. The latte was in high favour with Shāh Ṭahmāsp and was ap pointed by him *kalāntar* [*q.v.*] of his native town. Hi paternal uncle Khwādja Muḥammad Sharīf wa vizier of Khurāsān, Yazd and Iṣfahān, and his cousi Ghiyāth Beg a high official at the court of th Emperor Akbar. Amīn himself is said to have visite India. The work to which he owes his fame is the grea collection of biographies *Haft iḳlīm* (finished i 1002/1594). For many years he collected informatio about famous men, until finally he yielded to the en treaties of one of his friends and arranged his materia in book form. The final editing of it took six years The biographies are arranged geographically accord ing to the 7 climes. In each clime the biographical par is preceded by a short geographical and historical in troduction which is followed by notes on poets *ʿulamāʾ* famous *shaykhs*, etc. in chronological order. The wor is of special importance for the history of Persia literature, as the biographies of poets contai numerous specimens of their works, some of whic are very rare. It contains the following sections: Clim I: Yaman, Bilād al-Zandj, Nubia, China. Clime II Mecca, Medina, Yamāma, Hurmuz, Dekkān Aḥmadnagar, Dawlatābād, Golkonda, Aḥmadābād Sūrat, Bengal, Orissa and Kūsh. Clime III: ʿIrāḳ Baghdād, Kūfa, Nadjaf, Baṣra, Yazd, Fārs, Sīstān Ḳandahār, Ghaznīn, Lahawr, Dihlī, India from th oldest times down to Akbar, Syria, Egypt. Clime IV Khurāsān, Balkh, Harāt, Djām, Mashhad Nīshāpūr, Sabzawār, Isfarāʾīn, Iṣfahān, Kāshān Ḳum, Susa, Hamadhān, Rayy and Ṭihrān, Damā wand, Astarābād, Ṭabaristān, Māzandarān, Gīlān Ḳazwīn, Ādharbāydjān, Tabrīz, Ardabīl, Marāgha Clime V: Shīrwān, Gandja, Khwārazm, Mā warā al-Nahr, Samarḳand, Bukhārā, Farghāna. Clime VI Turkistān, Fārāb, Yārkand, Rūs, Constantinople Rūm. Clime VII: Bulghār, Ṣaḳlab, Yādjūdj Mādjūdj.

The Calcutta 1918-72 edition of E. Denison Ross ʿAbdul Muqtadir, A.H. Harley, etc., omits the fourt clime, over half the complete work; complete ed (poor) by Djawād Fāḍil, 3 vols., Tehran 1340/1961

Bibliography: H. Ethé, *Neupersische Literatur*, i *GrIPh*, ii, 213; Browne, *Lit. hist. of Persia*, iv, 448 Rypka, *Hist. of Iranian literature*, 452, 495; Storey, i 1169-71, 1365; M.U. Memon, *Amīn Aḥmad Rāzī*, i *EIr*, i, 939. (E. BERTHELS*)

AL-**RĀZĪ**, FAKHR AL-DĪN [see FAKHR AL-DĪ AL-RĀZĪ].

RAZĪN, BANŪ, the dynasty which ruled the pett state [see MULŪK AL-ṬAWĀʾIF] of al-Sahla [*q.v.*] (o Albarracín, derived from their name) in al-Andalu [*q.v.*] during the 5th/11th century.

Of Berber descent, but long settled in the penin sula, they remained loyal to the legitimist Umayya regime of Hishām II al-Muʾayyad at the time of th collapse of the caliphate, but finally switched to sup port of Sulaymān al-Mustaʿīn, who recognised the as governors of their local territory. They survived a independent or semi-independent rulers from *ca* 405/1014-15 (possibly as early as 403/1012-13) t Radjab 497/April 1104, when they were deposed b the Almoravids or al-Murābiṭūn [*q.v.*]. The list o their rulers is not entirely clear: the founder of th dynasty, Hudhayl b. Khalaf b. Lubb (the name ma point to intermarriage with local Christian families Ibn Razīn, seems to have ruled until 436/1044-5, an to have been succeeded by a son, Abū Marwān ʿAb al-Malik, Djabr al-Dawla. The latter, who reigned fo a remarkable sixty years, until 496/1103, is usually identified as Ḥusām al-Dawla in the sources, but the fragmentary text edited by Lévi-Provençal as an appendix to Ibn ʿIdhārī, vol. iii, reports that he used the title Ḥusām al-Dawla only before his accession and gives that title as a throne-name to this ruler's successor, Yaḥyā, who reigned for the last year of the dynasty's existence. The founder of the dynasty is generally described with the superlatives characteristic of mediaeval sources on the taifa rulers, although he is also said to have been directly involved in the murder of his own mother; the sources seem more impressed with the amounts he spent on the acquisition of singing-girls. A few lines of poetry by members of the dynasty are preserved. The survival of the dynasty, and of the state which it ruled, for so long seems to be the product of a combination of geographical isolation, overall unimportance and luck rather than of any particular skills possessed by the members of this family.

A. Vives y Escudero, *Monedas de las dinastías arábigo-españolas*, Madrid 1893, 206, no. 1266, assigns one coin (surviving in only a single specimen) to this dynasty, but there seems to be a confusion here with the rulers of Alpuente (al-Bunt [*q.v.*]) (the coin itself presents other difficulties); A. Prieto y Vives, *Los Reyes de Taifas, estudio histórico-numismático de los musulmanes españoles en el siglo V de la hégira (XI de J. C.)*, Madrid 1926, 107, suggests that some other coins (a total of four specimens of two types recorded by Vives, nos. 799-800 = Prieto, nos. 29-30) of the year 405/1014-15, struck in the name of Sulaymān al-Mustaʿīn and naming his son Muḥammad as heir, which bear also the name Ibn Khalaf, may be issues of the first member of this dynasty. The suggestion seems plausible.

Bibliography: in addition to that given above and in D. Wasserstein, *The rise and fall of the Party-Kings: politics and society in Islamic Spain, 1002-1086*, Princeton 1985, 93, see Ibn al-Khaṭīb, *Aʿmāl al-aʿlām*, ed. E. Lévi-Provençal, [2]Beirut 1956, 205-6, tr. W. Hoenerbach, *Islamische Geschichte Spaniens. Übersetzung der Aʿmāl al-Aʿlām und ergänzender Texte*, Zürich and Stuttgart 1970, 372, 389-93, and 596-97, notes 59-68 (with further references); A.R. Nykl, *Hispano-Arabic poetry and its relations with the Old Provençal troubadours*, Baltimore 1946, 206-8; and P. Guichard, *Structures sociales "orientales" et "occidentales" dans l'Espagne musulmane*, Paris-The Hague 1977, 270-2 (useful for the political behaviour of the family in the 4th/10th century).

(D.J. WASSERSTEIN)

RAZĪN B. MUʿĀWIYA, Abu 'l-Ḥasan b. ʿAmmār al-ʿAbdarī al-Saraḳusṭī (d. 524/1129 or 535/1140), Andalusian traditionist. Of unknown date of birth, his *nisba* indicates that he probably was born in Saragossa. The biographical works do not record any data about his life in al-Andalus. If he did live in Saragossa, he may have left it when the Almoravids captured the town in 503/1110, in which case he must have belonged to those who did not welcome the new lords of the Peninsula. Otherwise, he may have left the town after the Christian conquest of 512/1118. The 6th/12th century marks the beginning of the wave of Andalusians emigrating to safer lands. It may also be that Razīn b. Muʿāwiya's travel to the East was not motivated by either political or military reasons, but simply by the desire to perform the *riḥla fī ṭalab al-ʿilm* and the pilgrimage. He settled in Mecca, where he died at an advanced age. Nothing is known about his Andalusian teachers, but his teachers in Mecca were Abū ʿAbd Allāh al-Ḥusayn al-Ṭabarī, with whom he studied Muslim's *Ṣaḥīḥ*, and Abū Maktūm ʿĪsā b. Abī Dharr al-Harawī, with whom he studied al-Bukhārī's work. Abū Maktūm was the son of one of the most influential transmitters of al-Bukhārī's *Ṣaḥīḥ*, whose *riwāya* was well known in al-Andalus. Razīn b. Muʿāwiya wrote his two known works in Mecca: a history of Mecca, which seems to have included also information on Medina (*Kitāb fī akhbār Makka*, also called *Akhbār Makka wa 'l-Madīna wa-faḍlihimā*), and *al-Tadjrīd fī 'l-djamʿ bayn al-Ṣiḥāḥ al-sitta* or *Tadjrīd al-Ṣiḥāḥ*, a collection of the traditions common to the works of al-Bukhārī, Muslim, Abū Dāwūd, al-Tirmidhī, al-Nasāʾī and Mālik's *Muwaṭṭaʾ*. The inclusion of Mālik's work among the canonical collections of *ḥadīth* shows clearly the Western Islamic background of the author. The extant manuscripts (mentioned in *GAL*) remain unpublished. The *Tadjrīd* is one of the sources of Madjd al-Dīn Ibn al-Athīr's *Djāmiʿ al-uṣūl*, as Ibn al-Athīr himself (d. 606/1209) explains in his introduction. The interest of Razīn b. Muʿāwiya's work can be deduced from the following example. The controversial tradition which runs "whosoever spends liberally on his household on the day of ʿĀshūrāʾ, God will bestow plenty upon him throughout the remainder of the year" (*man wassaʿa ʿalā (nafsihi wa-)ahlihi/ʿiyālihi (fī 'l-nafaḳa) yawm ʿĀshūrāʾ wassaʿa Allāh ʿalayhi (wa-ʿalā ahlihi) sāʾir al-sana/ṭūla sanatihi*), mentioned among others by Sulaymān b. Aḥmad al-Ṭabarānī (d. 360/971) in his *al-Muʿdjam al-kabīr* (10 vols., Beirut 1983), x, 94, no. 10,007), is quoted by Ibn al-Athīr in his *Djāmiʿ al-uṣūl* in the chapter *fī faḍl al-nafaḳa* (ed. ʿAbd al-Ḳādir Arnāʾūṭ, 10 vols., n.p. 1969, ix, 527), stating that his source is Razīn b. Muʿāwiya's *Tadjrīd*. It would seem therefore that Razīn thought that the tradition was included either in the *Muwaṭṭaʾ* or in the other above-mentioned collections, but it is found in none of the extant versions of these works, according to the *Concordance*. Among others, al-Udjhūrī (d. 1066/1656) pointed out in his *Faḍāʾil yawm ʿĀshūrāʾ* (ms. B.N. Paris, no. 3244, fols. 153-75) that it was very strange that Ibn al-Athīr quotes the tradition on liberal spending on ʿĀshūrāʾ day in his *Djāmiʿ* and more strange still that Ibn al-Athīr's brother reiterates it in his *Ikhtiṣār Djāmiʿ al-uṣūl*, both stating that the tradition is to be found in al-Bukhārī's and Muslim's collections. It is in Razīn's work where an explanation for this "oddity" is to be found. Two possibilities can be taken into account. Either Razīn included it because he agreed with its contents, disregarding its absence in the canonical collections; or else he found the tradition in the version of one of those collections at his disposal. The latter possibility can be sustained by evidence on the circulation of different versions of al-Bukhārī's collection. Among Razīn b. Muʿāwiya's pupils the following are mentioned: the ascetic Aḥmad b. Muḥammad b. Ḳudāma (of the famous family of the Banū Ḳudāma), Ibn ʿAsākir and the judge of Mecca Abu 'l-Muẓaffar Muḥammad b. ʿAlī al-Ṭabarī, who wrote to Ibn Bashkuwāl informing him of Razīn's death.

Bibliography: 1. Sources. Ibn Bashkuwāl, no. 424 (ed. ʿI. al-Ḥusaynī, 2 vols., Cairo 1374/1955, no. 428); Ḍabbī, no. 741; Ibn Khayr, *Fahrasa*, ed. F. Codera and J. Ribera, 2 vols., Saragossa 1893, i, 123, 279, 451; Dhahabī, *Siyar aʿlām al-nubalāʾ*, 23 vols., Beirut 1985, xx, 204-6 (129); Ibn Farḥūn, *al-Dībādj al-mudhhab*, 2 vols., Cairo 1972, i, 366-7; Ḥādjdjī Khalīfa, ed. Flügel, ii, 192, no. 2445, and v, 175, no. 10638; Ibn al-ʿImād, *Shadharāt al-dhahab*, 4 vols., Beirut n.d., iv, 106; Makhlūf, *Shadjarat al-nūr*, Cairo 1950-2, i, 133, no. 395.

2. Studies. F. Pons Boigues, *Ensayo bio-bibliográfico sobre los historiadores y geógrafos arábigo-españoles*, Madrid 1898, 185, no. 153; Kaḥḥāla, iv, 155-6; Brockelmann, S I, 630; J. Mª Fórneas, *La primitiva* Sīra *de Ibn Ishāq en al-Andalus*, in *Homenaje ... Bosch Vilá*, Granada 1991, 167-8; Mª I. Fierro, *Obras y transmisiones de ḥadīt̲ (ss. V/XI-VII/XIII) en la* Takmila *de Ibn al-Abbār*, in *Ibn al-Abbar. Polític i escriptor àrab valencià (1199-1260)*, Valencia 1990, 205-22; M. Fierro, *The celebration of ᶜĀshūrāʾ in Sunnī Islam*, in *Procs. du XIVᵉ Congrès de l'Union Européenne des Arabisants et Islamisants*, Budapest 1988, forthcoming. (Maribel Fierro)

REDJĀʾĪ-ZĀDE Meḥmed Djelāl Bey (1254-1300/1838-82), Turkish writer and poet, and elder brother of Redjāʾī-zāde Maḥmūd Ekrem Bey [see ekrem bey]. He had a moderately successful administrative career, entering the Translation Office (*Terdjüme Odasī*) of the Sublime Porte in 1270/1853-4, being appointed in 1279/1862-3 chief clerk to the embassy in St. Petersburg, becoming assistant secretary (*mektūbī muᶜāwini*) under Aḥmed Djewdet Pasha [*q.v.*] in 1282-1865-6, when the latter became *wālī* of Aleppo, and finally chief secretary of the provinces of Kastamonu (in 1288/1871-2) and Aydın (in 1294/1877). In 1298/1881 he was dismissed from his last post.

His poetry has apparently never been published. Some specimens can be found in İnal (see Bibl.). He belonged for a while to the salon of ᶜĀrif Ḥikmet Bey [*q.v.*], the last great representative of the classical *dīwān* school, and his poetry seems unaffected by the new trends personified by his brother. His forte appears to have been *hezliyyāt* "jesting poems." His pen-name for these is Dhewḳī, while his serious *ghazels* are signed Djelāl. He also composed some poetry in Persian (a *mukhammas* in İnal, 203).

Bibliography: Ibnülemin Mahmud Kemal [İnal], *Son asır türk şairleri*, Istanbul 1930, 200-4; Ibrahim Alâettin Gövsa, *Türk meşhurları ansiklopedisi*, [Istanbul] n.d. [*ca.* 1945], 80. (Ed.)

REDJEB PASHA, Topal (d. 1041/1632), Ottoman Grand Vizier under Sultan Murād IV [*q.v.*]. Of Bosnian origin, he began his career in the *bostandjī* corps and attained the high office of *Bostandjī-bashī* [*q.v.*] in the reign of Aḥmed I [*q.v.*]. Although slightly invalid (a sufferer from gout, hence *topal*), he continued his career: a vizier since 1031/1622, he was appointed commander-in-chief in the Black Sea. With his squadron he defeated a Cossack fleet of 600 *shayḳas*. Redjeb Pasha was *Ḳapudān-pasha* 1032-5/1623-26. Commanding the fleet in Radjab-Ramaḍān 1033/May-July 1624 at the time of a revolt of the *Khān* of the Crimea Meḥmed Girāy III (second reign 1032-6/1623-7), he was able to hold Kefe [*q.v.*]. Next year, he again defeated a Cossack force of 350 *shayḳas* off Kara Harman (to the north of Köstendje/Constanța [*q.v.*]). In 1035/1626 he organised a revolt of Janissaries in the capital and gained the position of *ḳāʾim-maḳām* instead of Gürdjü Meḥmed Pasha [*q.v.*]. Provoked by the dismissal of the Grand Vizier Khosrew Pasha [*q.v.*], in 1041/1631 he incited another uprising of Janissaries and Sipāhīs of the Porte who were of Bosnian and Albanian origin (1042/1632). This violent episode led to the murder of Grand Vizier Ḥāfiẓ Aḥmed Pasha [*q.v.*] in front of Murād IV and the massacre of a number of the sultan's favourites, rivals to Redjeb's faction. In this way, he became Grand Vizier on 19 Radjab 1041/10 February 1632. Murād IV, however, soon made an end to this *zorba* régime and had Redjeb Pasha executed inside the seraglio on 28 Shawwāl 1041/18 May 1632 (von Hammer, following Pečewi, has 1‍ May); this execution meant the beginning of Murā‍ IV's personal rule. Redjeb Pasha was married t‍ Djewher Khān Sulṭān, a daughter of Aḥmed I an‍ earlier the widow of Dāmād Meḥmed Pasha Ökü‍ [*q.v.*] and Ḥāfiẓ Aḥmed Pasha. He had a daughte‍ born in 1040/1630.

Bibliography: Dispatches 1631-2 of Corneli‍ Haga, Dutch ambassador to the Porte, Genera‍ State Archives (ARA) SG 6901, partially publ. i‍ *Kronijk Historisch Genootschap* Utrecht 1867, 370-455 I. Dujcev, *Lettres d'information de la République d‍ Raguse (XVIIᵉ s.)* Sofia 1937, 29-31; Meḥme‍ Khalīfe, *Taʾrīkh-i Ghilmānī*, new (pop.) ed. K. Su‍ Istanbul 1976, 12-13; Ibrāhīm Pečewī, *Taʾrīkh* Istanbul 1283, ii, 420-6; Naᶜīmā, *Taʾrīkh*, Istanbu‍ 1283, ii, 208, 245, 332-41, 356-60, 394-5, 400, iii 75-112; Solāḳ-zāde, *Taʾrīkh*, new ed. V. Çabuk *Solakzade tarihi*, Ankara 1989, ii, 497, 519, 522 530 ff.; İ.H. Danişmend, *Osmanlı tarihi kronolojisi* Istanbul 1961, iii, 329, 333, 349-54; [M. Cezar *e‍ alii*] *Mufassal Osmanlı tarihi*, 6 vols., Istanbul 1957-63, iv, 1884-1904, 1978-9; Hammer-Purgstall *Histoire*, ix, 82-3, 168-83; A.D. Alderson, *The structure of the Ottoman dynasty*, Oxford 1956, tabl‍ XXXIV; A.H. de Groot, *The Ottoman Empire and th‍ Dutch Republic*, Leiden-Istanbul 1978, 172, 176. (A.H. de Groot)

REFĪᶜĪ, an Ottoman poet and Ḥurūfī [se‍ ḥurūfiyya]. Of Refīᶜī's life we only have a few hint‍ from himself; the Ottoman biographers and historian‍ do not seem to mention him at all. He himsel‍ describes how in his youth he studied many branche‍ of knowledge but did not know what he shoul‍ believe, and how sometimes he turned to the Sunna, sometimes to philosophy and sometimes t‍ materialism. He often travelled a great distance t‍ visit a particular scholar but always was disappointed The poet Nesīmī [*q.v.*] was the first to teach him th‍ grace of God and the truth, and ordered him to teac‍ this truth in his turn to the people of Rūm, and for thi‍ purpose he had to speak in Turkish. He therefor‍ wrote his *Beshāret-nāme*, "the message of joy", whic‍ he finished on the first Friday of Ramaḍān 811/18 January 1409. This work is not yet printed; it is quit‍ short and written in the same metre as ᶜĀshiḳ-pasha's *Gharīb-nāme*, a *remel* of six feet with irregular prosody. The Ḥurūfī teaching is expounded in a very prosai‍ style, the merits of the names and letters, the sacre‍ number 32, the prophets, the throne of God, the human countenance, the splitting of the moon, Faḍ‍ Allāh [*q.v.*], the founder of the Ḥurūfī sect—all this is dealt with from the usual Ḥurūfī point of view. As sources, an *ᶜArsh-nāme*, a *Djāwidān-nāme*, and a *Maḥabbet-nāme* are quoted, all three probably the works of the same names by Faḍl Allāh.

Another of Refīᶜī's works is the "Book o‍ Treasure" (*Gendj-nāme*), facs. edn. Istanbul 1946. Th‍ *Gendj-nāme* is better as poetry and on the whole les‍ Ḥurūfī than generally Ṣūfī in tone. Man from the Ḥurūfī and philosophic point of view, Faḍl Allāh and Aḥmad (= Muḥammad), the 72 sects, the greatest Name (*ism-i aᶜẓam*), the water of life, etc., are discussed in it.

Nesīmī and his pupil Refīᶜī seem to be the only Ottoman Ḥurūfī poets of importance, and while the sect, in spite of all persecutions, continued to exist long after and even had connections with the Bektāshiyya [*q.v.*], these two poets as such do not seem to have produced any school.

Bibliography: Gibb, *HOP*, i, 336, 341, 344, 351, 369-80; Meḥmed Fuʾād *Köprülü, Türk edebiyyātïnda ilk müteṣawwifler*, Istanbul 1918, 363, 388².—Mss. of the *Beshāret-nāme*: Vienna, Flügel, ii, 261-2, no. 1968 (incomplete) and 1970; London, British Museum, Rieu, 164-5. Add. 5986; of the *Gendj-nāme*: Vienna, Flügel, i, 720, no. 778, fols. 5a-8a; printed in the *Dīwān-i Nesīmī*, Istanbul 1260/1844, 9-14, also facs. edn., see above; both works in the Browne ms. A 43, Turkish, see E.G. Browne, *Further notes on the literature of the Ḥurúfís and their connection with the Bektáshí order of dervishes*, in *JRAS*, xxxix (1907), 556-8; R.A. Nicholson, *A descriptive catalogue of the Oriental mss. belonging to the late E.G. Browne*, Cambridge 1932, 45, 49; *İA*, art. *Refîî* (Günay Alpay). (W. Björkman)

REFIḲ KHĀLID KARAY [see KARAY, REFĪḲ KHĀLID].

REG, a form generally retained in European languages for the Arabic *riḳḳ* "dessicated terrain", in its Bedouin realisation (Sahara of the Maghrib) *reg*; cf. *LʿA. s.vv. riḳḳ, raḳḳ, raḳāḳ, ruḳāḳ*, with a common denominator meaning "terrain where water has disappeared, at least on the surface", and with varying connotations. See G. Boris, *Lexique du parler arabe des Marazig*, Paris 1958, 220: *rᵉgāg*, pl. *rᵉgāgāt*, "a wide expanse of desert terrain".

In French, the word has become a scientific term which may be used in reference to any part of the globe. As a stony flat or almost flat surface, commonly found in the deserts where deposits of sand are lacking, the reg corresponds to the removal of minute, fine materials by the winnowing effects of winds, which only leave a hard crust beneath which one may often find the finer material protected by the stones. A reg can be covered over: by shingle (alluvial and allochthonous, as in the regs of the ancient course of the Oued Ighagha to the south of the *ḥamāda* of Tinghert, towards 28° N, 6° E); by angular, autochthonous gravel (reg formed by the removal of the weathered surfaces of *ḥamādas*, such as those of the northern piedmont of the Saharan Atlas, forming a band running west-south-west to east-north-east some 100-150 km wide and 800 km long, from 31° N, 1° W to 33° N, 6° E); or by rounded material joined together and too large for the wind to move them (*sarīr* of the Libyan desert forming a paved-like or mosaic-like reg, like the Tibesti *sarīr* around 24° N, 17° E). The nomads sometimes use the term *mriyyé* "mirror" to describe certain regs which are particularly regular. The surfaces of regs are often very stable areas, where the fact that the elements composing them remain in the same place favours atmospheric actions, such as polishing by the wind, the formation of polished desert surfaces, and even of pebbles with wind-polished facets (dreikanters) in the regions characterised by continuous winds.

The regs cover extensive surfaces in the Saharan-Arabian and the Asiatic deserts of the Islamic world, whether on the plains or on the plateaux, since they form the surface pattern which is habitual in desert regions when the sand layer is insufficient to cover the soil. For example, in the central Sahara, the regs of the fringes of the Hoggar cover the greater part of the slopes and plains surrounding the mountain massifs. The regs constitute areas which are very unfavourable for the growth of vegetation, hence for human activity, except in times of rain. On the other hand, they are often, when the surface débris is not too large in size, stretches of terrain more easily adapted for moving about than the ergs (*ʿirḳ*), the mountain zones and the dissected plateaux of the *tassili* type, and they have been instrumental in siting the great caravan tracks in the desert regions and, later, roads for motor traffic.

Bibliography: J. Tricart and A. Cailleux, *Le modelé des régions sèches*, Paris 1969; R. Coque, *Géomorphologie*, Paris 1993. (Y. Callot)

REʾĪS ÜL-KÜTTĀB or Reʾīs Efendi (a., used in Turkey), properly "chief of the men of the pen", a high Ottoman dignitary, directly under the Grand Vizier, originally head of the chancery of the Imperial Dīwān (*dīwān-i hümāyūn*), later secretary of state or chancellor and Minister of Foreign Affairs. According to d'Herbelot, he was called also *reʾīs kitāb*.

This office, unlike many others, is purely Ottoman, at least as regards the particular line of development that it took. Establishing itself at the expense of the functions of the *nishāndjī* [*q.v.*], we may say that it owes nothing to the influence of the more or less Persianised Saldjūḳs nor to the Byzantines. In its origins it seems rather to be connected with a more general and more vague institution of the East, one which deserves more profound study: that of the secretaries of the *dīwān* or chiefs of the secretariat of the *dīwān*. This office is found in different Muslim countries under different names: *perwāne* among the Mongols of Persia, *dīwān begi* among the Tīmūrids and *munshī* in Persia (cf. Chardin, vi, 175; Ewliyā Čelebi, ii, 267). In the Ottoman provinces there was attached also to the *wālī* an important official known as the *dīwān efendi(si)*; in Egypt, under Muḥammad ʿAlī, the *dīwān efendi* became a kind of president of the council of ministers. The *reʾīs ül-küttāb* was in brief the *dīwān efendisi* of the capital. It is perhaps to this that we owe the use of the title *reʾīs efendi*, by which they were more commonly known. We know that the term *efendi* was generally applied to people of the pen. This connection seems to have already been noticed by E. Blochet (*Voyage en Orient de Carlier Pinon*, Paris 1920, 83).

Until the time of Süleymān the Magnificent, the title *reʾīs ül-küttāb* (or *reʾīs efendi*) was not used. At least, this is what we are told by Aḥmed Resmī, who quotes in this connection the *Bedāʾiʿ ül-weḳāʾiʿ* of the historian Ḳodja Ḥüseyn Efendi of Sarajevo (cf. Babinger, *GOW*, 186). The latter, who was himself *reʾīs ül-küttāb*, says that before Süleymān, the official correspondence was in the hands of the *emīn-i aḥkām* or "depository of the decisions (of the *Dīwān*)" along with the *nishāndjī*. This point of view has been adopted by other historians (von Hammer; cf. also the *Sālnāme-yi neẓāret-i khāridjiyye*).

There is, however, no agreement as to who was the first *reʾīs ül-küttāb*; it is usually said to have been Djalāl (Djelāl)-zāde Muṣṭafā Čelebi [*q.v.*] (see Babinger, *GOW*, 102). This well-known historian, whose genealogy is taken back to the legendary founder of Byzantium, Yanḳo b. Mādyān, was *reʾīs ül-küttāb* in 931/1524-5 before becoming *nishāndjī*, but the *Nukhbet ül-tewārīkh* of Meḥmed b. Meḥmed refers to the death in 930/1523-4 of a *reʾīs ül-küttāb* of the name of Ḥaydar Efendi. According to other indications, it would even appear that the office goes back to Meḥemmed II [see NISHĀNDJĪ].

The *riyāset* or office of *reʾīs efendi* lasted over three centuries, during which its holder changed 130 times, the average tenure of office being 2 years and 5 months, which reveals a remarkable lack of ministerial stability: some of the occupants held the office twice, thrice and even four times.

Duties of the *reʾīs efendi*. As secretary of state the *reʾīs* kept records of memoirs and reports (*telkhīṣ* and *taḳrīr*) presented to the sultan by the Grand Vizier acting as representative of the government and of the *Dīwān*. These documents which were prepared by the *āmedī-yi dīwān-i hümāyūn* or *āmeddjī* (referendar or reporter of the Imperial *Dīwān*) were brought in a bag (*kīse*) kept for the purpose to the ceremonial sittings of the *Dīwān* by the *re᾿īs* himself who handed them to the Grand Vizier. After being read, they were given to a special officer, the *telkhīṣdji*, whose duty it was to present them to the sultan.

As chancellor, the *re᾿īs* had a kind of jurisdiction over all the civil functionaries and was the immediate head of the department of the Imperial *Dīwān* (*dīwān-i hümāyūn ḳalemi*).

This chancellery was divided into three offices (*oda* or *ḳalem*):

1. the *beylik*, the most important, saw to the despatch of imperial rescripts (*firmān*), orders of the viziers, and in general all ordinances (*ewāmir*) other than those of the department of finance (*defterdār dā᾿iresi*). This office kept copies of them, as did the Grand Vizier also. Ordinances bearing on the back the signatures of the clerk, of the chief editor (*mümeyyiz*), and of the head of the office (*beylikdji*), were submitted by the latter to the *re᾿īs*, who placed his sign (*resīd*) upon them and, if it was a *firmān*, sent it to the *nishāndjī* for the *tughrā* [*q.v.*] to be placed upon it. The *beylik* in addition retained the originals of civil and military regulations (*ḳānūn* or *ḳānūn-nāme*) (usually elaborated by the *nishāndjī*), as well as of treaties and capitulations (*ʿahd-nāme*) with foreign powers. The *re᾿īs* had to consult these treaties, notably when certifying the *der-kenār* or "marginal" answers put by his subordinates on the requests or notes, known as verbal (*taḳrīr*), which the ambassadors addressed to the Grand Vizier. It is this side of his activity which, gradually becoming more and more important and absorbing, ended by making the *re᾿īs* a Minister of Foreign Affairs.

2. office of the *taḥwīl* or "annual renewal" of the diplomas of the governors of provinces (*berāt* [*q.v.*]), of the brevets of the *mollās* or judges in towns of the first class (*taḥwīl*), of the brevets of the timariots or holders of military fiefs (*ḍabṭ firmānī*).

3. office of the *ru᾿ūs* or "provisions" of different officials, as well as of the orders for pensions from the treasury (*sergi*) or from *waḳf*s (see for the details of the organisation of this office, Mouradgea d'Ohsson, vii, 161).

The *re᾿īs* accompanied the Grand Vizier to the audiences which the sultan gave him and to those which the Grand Vizier himself gave to ambassadors. He shared with his master the midday meal, as did the *čawush bashī* [see ČAWUSH] and the two *tezkeredjis*, except on Wednesdays when these two were replaced by the four judges of Istanbul.

In the official protocol, the *re᾿īs* had the same rank as the *čawush bashī*, with whom he walked in official processions, before the *defterdār*s (which showed he was of lower rank than the latter).

The *elḳāb* or epistolary formulae to which they were entitled are found in Ferīdūn, *Münshe᾿āt*, 10. They were the same as for the *agha*s of the stirrup [see RIKĀBDĀR] and the *defter emīni*. For the dress of the *re᾿īs*, see Brindesi, *Anciens costumes turcs*, pl. 2; Castellan, iv, 107.

According to Mouradgea d'Ohsson, the *re᾿īs* used to act as agent for the *khān*s of the Crimea.

Administrative career of the *re᾿īs*. The *re᾿īs*, like all Ottoman officials, were chosen by the sultan or Grand Vizier as they pleased, but, except in case of appointment by favour, they followed a fixed line of promotion (*ṭarīḳ*) in the administration. It was in the administrative offices, i.e. among the *khʷādjegān* (Persian pl. which was given as an honorific title to the principal clerks or *khʷadja*/*khodja* or *ḳalem ḍābiṭleri*), that this career was spent.

In examining the *Sefīnet ül-rü᾿esā᾿* of Aḥmed Resmī we find that, up to the *re᾿īs* Boyalī Meḥmed Efendi (Pasha) (d. 977/1569-70), there is no information available about the career of the *re᾿īs*, but starting with him we find that the *re᾿īs* were regularly chosen from among the former *tedhkeredjis* of the *wezīrs* or of the Grand Vizier. From Sheykh-zāde ʿAbdī Efendi (d. 1014/1605-6) onwards, the *re᾿īs* were mainly taken from the *wezīr mektūbdjisis* or private secretaries of the Grand Vizier. These secretaries were themselves at the head of an office (*oda*) which contained a very small number of officials (*khalīfe* or *kalfa*, pl. *khulefā᾿*); there were only two between the years 1090/1679 and 1100/1689. When the number increased (at a later date there were about 30), the career of the future *re᾿īs* was as follows: *khalīfe* in the office in question, called also *mektūbī-yi ṣadr-i ʿālī odasī*, then *ser-khalīfe* or *bash kalfa* "chief clerk", then *mektūbdji*. The post of *mektūbdji* was much sought after. It brought its holder into close contact with the Grand Vizier and it was then very easy to advance oneself. More rarely, the future *re᾿īs* rose through the similar but less important office of secretary to the lieutenant to the Grand Vizier or Kahya Bey (*ketkhüda kātibi odasī*).

The *riyāset* did not mark the end of a career, but gave access to still higher posts (see NISHĀNDJĪ for the old rules of promotion by which the *re᾿īs* became *nishāndjī*). It was one of what were known as the "six [principal] dignities", *menāṣib-i sitte*, namely, the *nishāndjī*, *defterdār*, *re᾿īs ül-küttāb*, *defter emīni*, *shikk-i thānī defterdārī*, *shikk-i thālith defterdārī* (Aḥmed Rāsim, *Ta᾿rīkh*, 756).

According to the *Naṣīḥat-nāme* (39-40 of the French translation), the *re᾿īs* was under the authority of the Grand Defterdār (for financial matters only?).

Increasing importance of the office of *re᾿īs*. The growing influence of the *re᾿īs* is explained by the increasing importance of foreign policy in Turkey (including the so-called "Eastern Question").

Down to the end of the 10th/16th century, the *nishāndjī*s were certainly superior to the *re᾿īs*; they controlled and even revised the orders and decisions of the *dīwān* (*aḥkām*), but from the 17th century onwards, *re᾿īs* like Oḳdju-zāde Meḥmed Shāh Efendi, Lām-ʿAlī Čelebi and Ḥükmī Efendi shed a certain lustre on their office. From 1060/1650 the incapacity of certain *nishāndjī*s precipitated the decline of their office in spite of the ephemeral efforts by Grand Viziers like Shehīd ʿAlī Pāshā and of the *nishāndjī*s appointed by him (Rāshid Efendi and Selīm Efendi). It was in this period that the office of *beylikdji* was created (see above).

The Ottoman protocol (*teshrīfāt*) was nevertheless still to retain for a long time traces of the originally rather subordinate position of the *re᾿īs*. For example, they did not sit in the office of the *Dīwān* itself, called *Dīwān-khāne* (in the Top Ḳapu Sarayī or "Old Serai"), but remained seated outside of the room in a place called *re᾿īs takhtasī*, "the bench of the *re᾿īs*", where there were also seats for certain other officials to wait upon. In the formal sittings, even in those like the distribution of pay (*ʿulūfe*) to the Janissaries which took place in the presence of foreign ambassadors, the part played by the *re᾿īs* was rather limited. He carried in, with slow step and the sleeves of his *üst* turned up, the bag containing the *telkhīṣ* (see above). He kissed the hem (*etek*) of the Grand Vizier's robe, placed the bag on his left, kissed the hem of his robe again and withdrew to his place. He came in again to open the bag, handed the documents to the Grand Vizier, took them back from him to fold them (*baghlamaḳ*), sealed them and gave them to the *telkhīṣdji*. If he was unable be present, the bag of the *telkhīṣ* was handed to the rand Vizier by the *büyük tezkeredji* (*Ḳanūn-nāme* of Abd ül-Raḥmān Pasha, 85, 123 etc.).

Lucas (*Second Voyage*, Paris 1712, 216) writes that uring the audience given by the Grand Vizier to the rench Ambassador "le Ray Affendy ou Grand hancelier demeura debout et appuïé contre la uraille".

Things were changed at the reform of the *Dīwān* efected at the beginning of his reign (1792) by Selīm II, desirous of limiting the power of the Grand Vizier. The old *Dīwān* consisted of six *wazīrs* of the ome (having only one consultative voice; see ḲUBBE VEZĪRI), of the *Muftī* (*Sheykh ül-Islām*) and the two *azaskers*. The new *Dīwān* was to consist of 10 members by right of office and others chosen in different ways (about 40 in all). The members by right f office were the Kahya Bey, the Reʾīs Efendi, the Grand Defterdār, the Čelebi Efendi, the Tersāne Emīni, the Čawush Bashî, etc. (Zinkeisen, *Geschichte*, ii, 1863, 321).

The office of *reʾīs* tended more and more to become he Ministry of Foreign Affairs of the Sublime Porte, arallel to the post of Kaḥya Bey (Interior).

Suppression of the dignity of *reʾīs*. The title of *reʾīs* was suppressed by the *khaṭṭ-i hümāyūn* of Sultan Maḥmūd II addressed on Friday 23 Dhu 'l-Ḳaʿda 1251/11 March 1836 to the Grand Vizier Meḥmed Emīn Pasha. The Turkish text will be found in the *Sālnāme* of the Turkish Ministry of Foreign Affairs; the French translation (or at least parts of it) was published in the *Moniteur Ottoman* of 23 April 1836 (according to A. Ubicini, *Lettres sur la Turquie*, 38, n. 1). This document at the same time created two new ministries (*neẓāret*), which in memory of their origin emained to the end in the same building as the grand vizierate [see BĀB-I ʿĀLĪ]: 1. the Ministry of the Interior (originally of civil affairs or *umūr-u mülkiyye*, ater *dākhiliyye*) replacing the department of the Kaḥya Bey; and 2. the Ministry of Foreign Affairs *khāridjiyye*) replacing that of the *reʾīs*. The preamble said that, abandoning the old regulations of the service, the sultan had thought it advisable to create real posts of *wezīr* (*wizāret*) and not honorary ones, but without its being necessary to give the new *wezīr* of foreign affairs the title of *pasha* [*q.v.*], "which is mainy a military one".

Bibliography: By far the most important source is the work known as *Sefīnet ül-rüʾesāʾ*, which consists of: 1. Aḥmad Resmī's work (Babinger, *GOR*, 309-10) which contains the biographies of 64 *reʾīs* down to Rāghib Meḥmed Efendi (1157/1744), and 2. its continuation by Süleymān Fāʾiḳ Efendi, which contains the biographies of 30 *reʾīs* down to Aḥmed Wāṣif Efendi at the beginning of the 19th century. According to the preface to Süleymān Fāʾiḳ's (not Fātik) continuation, Aḥmed Resmī had entitled his work *Ḥaḳīḳat ül-rüʾesāʾ*, in imitation of the *Ḥadīkat ül-wüzerāʾ* of ʿOthmān-zāde Tāʾib, but changed it at the suggestion of Rāghib Pasha to *Sefīnet ül-rüʾesāʾ* (the references in the Catalogue of Turkish mss. in the Bibliothèque Nationale by E. Blochet, ii, 158, should be corrected accordingly). The word *ḥalīḳat* apparently makes no sense; that of *khalīfat* which is usually found in other works (Flügel, *Cat.*, ii, 407, no. 1250; Babinger; Bursalî Meḥmed Ṭāhir, iii, 59 n.), does not seem correct either. One ought undoubtedly to read *khalīḳat* (which rhymes with the *ḥadīkat* of the prototype). The *Sefīnet ül-rüʾesāʾ* was published by the State Press in Istanbul in 1269/1853.

See also in addition to the references in the text: Mouradgea d'Ohsson, *Etat de l'Empire Othoman*, vii, 1824, index; J. von Hammer, *Des osmanischen Reichs Staatsverfassung und Staatsverwaltung*, Vienna 1815, ii, index; *Ḳanūn-nāme* of Tewḳīʿī (*nishāndjī*) ʿAbd ül-Raḥmān Pasha, written in 1087/1676-7 and ed. by F. Köprülü (*MTM*, 508); Esʿad Efendi, *Teshrifāt-î Dewlet-i ʿAliyye*, 85, 123, etc.; *Sālnāme-i neẓāret-i khāridjiyye*, 1 year, 1301/1885, Ebüzziya Press, Istanbul (contains in addition a historical resumé and a chronological list of all the grand viziers and all the *reʾīs*); C. Perry, *A View of the Levant, particularly of Constantinople*, etc., London 1743, 36; C.V. Findley, *Bureaucratic reform in the Ottoman empire: the Sublime Porte, 1789-1922*, Princeton 1980; idem, *Ottoman civil officialdom: a social history*, Princeton 1989; *İA*, art. s.v. (Halil İnalcık). On the *ṣāḥib al-dīwān* or *raʾīs* (!) *al-dīwān*, see Ḳalḳashandī, *Ṣubḥ al-aʿshā*, i, 101 ff.; vi, 14, 17-18, 50; H. Massé, *Code de la Chancellerie d'Etat... d'Ibn al-Ṣayrafī*, in *BIFC*, xi, 79 ff. Among the Saldjūḳs, the offices of *ṣāḥib al-dīwān* and *perwāne* were quite separate; cf. Ibn Bībī, in Houtsma, *Recueil d. textes .... Seldj.*, iii, 105.

(J. DENY)

REMBAU (Rumbow), a traditional district (*luak*) in Negri Sembilan, Malaysia. It is important in Islamic studies for two reasons.

First, the social structure of the Malay-Muslim population is based on matrilineal descent groups (*suku*), in which succession to office and inheritance of property descend in the female line. This has serious repercussions for Islam's rules of inheritance which are widely avoided, or at least compromised. The Malay population is otherwise devoutly Muslim. The obvious parallel is Minangkabau [*q.v.*] in Sumatra.

Second, while the Undang (*lawgiver*) of Rembau qualifies for his office by descent in the matrilineal line, he is also a component part of "The Ruler" of the State of Negri Sembilan along with three other "Ruling Chiefs" and the Yang di-Pentuan Besar. As such, he forms part of a single constitutional ruler for the State. One of the duties of the Ruler is to protect the religion of Islam, and this has difficult repercussions, given the realities of politics and the matrilineal element. Rembau is thus a classic case for the study of Islam and *adat* [see ʿĀDA], the social implications of religion in a peasant community and the politics of religion.

Bibliography: C.W.C. Parr and W.H. Mackray, *Rembau: its history, constitution and customs*, in *JRAS, Straits Branch*, lvi (1910), 1-157; P.E. de Josselin de Jong, *Islam versus adat in Negri Sembilan*, in *Bijdragen*, cxvi (1960), 158-203; M.B. Hooker, *Adat laws in modern Malaya*, Kuala Lumpur 1972, chs. 7 and 9. (M.B. HOOKER)

RESHĀD NŪRĪ (REŞAD NURİ GÜNTEKİN), late Ottoman and modern Turkish author, born in 1889 in Istanbul, died in 1956 in London. He was the son of a military doctor, Nūrī, and Luṭfiyye, the daughter of Yawer Pasha, governor of Erzurum. He attended Galatasaray Lycée in Istanbul and, later, the Frères High School in Izmir. After graduating from the Faculty of Letters of Istanbul University in 1912, he worked as a teacher and schoolmaster in Bursa and in several lycées in Istanbul (Vefa, Çamlıca, Kabataş, Galatasaray and Erenköy), teaching French, Turkish literature and philosophy. In 1927 he became an inspector for the Ministry of Education. In 1939 he was elected to the Parliament as Halk Partisi representative for Çanakkale. In 1943 he went back to the Civil Service, and in 1947 was promoted to Chief Inspector for schools in the Ministry for Education. He was sent to Paris to represent Turkey at UNESCO and as the Turkish educational attaché in France. He retired in 1954, and died in London on 7 December 1956, where he was receiving treatment for cancer.

Reshād Nūrī started his literary career by publishing unsigned poems. He attracted attention during the First World War with his articles on Turkish literature in *La Pensée Turque* and the newspaper *Zamān*. These were followed by his story *Eski aḥbāb*, published in *Diken* (1917), and a novel *Kharābeleriñ čičeghi* (1918), in *Zamān*, and his first play, *Ḥaḳīḳī ḳahramān* (1919). When his play *Istanbul ḳîzî* was not liked by the Istanbul theatres, Reshād Nūrī changed it into a novel and it was published as a serial with the title *Čalîḳushu* in *Waḳit* newspaper (1922); in this form, it was read so widely that he became famous. In 1936, his travel experience in literary form were published with the title *Anadolu notları*. During 1942, he wrote satire, using the pseudonyms "Fire-Fly" and "Cicada" for the journal *Kelebek* which he published with Mahmut Yesari, Münif Fehim and İbnürrefik Ahmed Nuri. In 1947 he started to publish a daily newspaper *Memleket* which aimed to defend and express the views of the Turkish republican régime, but it did not last long. Between the years 1918 and 1955 he not only published books but also wrote articles in numerous literary journals. Reşad Nuri is the most popular author of modern Turkish literature; his novel *Çalıkuşu* is still read widely, and he is often known simply as "the author of *Çalıkuşu*". This popularity is due to the fact that he was able to combine the eastern and western traditions of fiction in his works. The clash between the individual and the society is the most recurrent theme of his works, but he treated even the villains of his novels as human beings who need love and pity and compassion, so that the reader is left with the feeling that there are only "good people" and "not so good people" on earth. His works are all set in the late 19th century and the early days of the Republic, and are characterised by detailed and precise descriptions of events and people. However, he reflects the problems, beliefs, ideas, dreams, feelings of individuals from different sections of society without imposing an ideological framework on the reader. From the linguistic point of view, he used Turkish in a masterful fashion, blending spoken and literary languages, and the simple, sincere and natural style of his prose is easily recognised. He has accordingly become the symbol of the "New language" and "National literature" movements.

Bibliography: 1. His works (first editions). (a) Novels—*Çalıkuşu*, Istanbul 1922 (German tr. M. Schultz, *Zaunkönig, der Roman eines türkischen Mädchens*, Leipzig 1942; Eng. tr. Sir Wyndham Deede, *The autobiography of a Turkish girl*, London 1949); *Gizli el*, Istanbul 1924; *Damga*, Istanbul 1924; *Dudaktan kalbe*, Istanbul 1924; *Akşam güneşi*, Istanbul 1926; *Bir kadın düşmanı*, Istanbul 1927; *Yeşil gece*, 1928; *Yaprak dökümü*, Istanbul 1930; *Kızılcık dalları*, Istanbul 1932; *Gökyüzü*, Istanbul 1935; *Eski hastalık*, Istanbul 1938; *Ateş gecesi*, Istanbul, 1942; *Değirmen*, Istanbul 1944; *Miskinler tekkesi*, Istanbul 1946; *Harabelerin çiçeği* (as an independent book), Istanbul 1953; *Kavak yelleri*, Istanbul 1961; *Son sığınak*, Istanbul 1961; *Kan davası*, Istanbul 1962. (b) Short stories—*Recm, gençlik ve güzellik*, Istanbul 1919; *Roçild Bey*, Istanbul 1919; *Eski ahbab*, Istanbul n.d.; *Tanrı misafiri*, Istanbul 1927; *Sönmüş yıldızlar*, Istanbul 1928; *Leyla ile Mecnun*, Istanbul 1928; *Olağan işler*, Istanbul 1930. (c) Plays—*Hançer*, Istanbul 1920; *Eski rüya*, Istanbul 1922; *Ümidin güneşi*, Istanbul 1924; *Gazeteci düşmanı, Şemsiye hırsızı, Ihtiyar sereri* (three plays), Istanbul 1925; *Taş parçası*, Istanbul 1926; *Bir köy hocası*, Istanbul 1928; *Babur Şah'ın seccadesi*, Istanbul 1931; *Bir köy eğlencesi*, Istanbul 1931; *Ümit mektebinde*, Istanbul 1931; *Felaket karşısında, Gözdağı, Eski borç*, Istanbul 1931; *İstiklal*, Ankara 1933; *Vergi hırsızı*, Istanbul 1933; *Hülleci*, Istanbul 1933; *Bir yağmur gecesi*, Ankara 1943; *Yaprak dökümü*, Istanbul 1971; *Eski şarkı*, Istanbul 1971; *Balıkkesir muhasebecisi*, Istanbul 1971; *Tanrıdağı ziyafeti*, Istanbul 1971. (d) Travel notes—*Anadolu notları*, 2 vols., Istanbul 1936. Numerous articles and several translations, e.g. from French, were published in journals and newspapers.

2. Studies. O. Spies, *Die türkische Prosaliteratur der Gegenwart*, Leipzig 1943; Ibrahim Hilmi Yücebaş, *Bütün cepheleriyle Reşat Nuri*, Istanbul 1957; Türkan Poyraz-Muazzez Alpbek, *Reşat Nuri Güntekin, hayatı ve eserlerinin tam listesi*, Ankara 1957; Kenan Akyüz, in *PTF*, ii, 586 ff.; Muzaffer Uyguner, *Reşat Nuri Güntekin, hayatı, sanatı, eserleri*, Istanbul 1967; Zeki Burdurlu, *Reşat Nuri Güntekin*, Izmir 1974; Seyit Kemal Karaalioğlu, *Türk edebiyatı tarihi, iv.*, Istanbul 1982; Olcay Önertoy, *Reşat Nuri Güntekin*, Ankara 1983; Emin Birol, *Reşat Nuri Güntekin*, Ankara 1989.

(Çiğdem Balim)

RESHĪD PASHA, MUSṬAFĀ (1800-1858), Ottoman diplomat, statesman and reformer.

Reshīd was born, the son of a financial clerk in Istanbul, on 13 March 1800, but his family originally hailed from Kastamonu. His father died in 1810, after which he grew up under the protection of his uncle Ispartalî Seyyid Pasha. He studied at a *medrese*, but did not graduate (i.e. he did not get an *idjāza* [*q.v.*]). Thereafter, he was trained within the scribal institution. Reshīd took part in the campaign against the Greek insurgents in 1821, as seal-keeper of the commander-in-chief, Seyyid ʿAlī Pasha. During this campaign, he saw for himself the hopeless condition of the Ottoman army. When Seyyid ʿAlī Pasha was dismissed, his followers, among them Reshīd, according to the Ottoman tradition of *intisāb*, were also forced out of office. Reshīd had some trouble finding a new position, but after a while landed a job at the correspondence office of the Porte.

During the Ottoman-Russian war of 1828, Reshīd served as army clerk. The reports he sent to the capital in this capacity drew the attention of the sultan, Maḥmūd II [*q.v.*], who was looking for capable and reform-minded servants to implement his reforms. Reshīd was now taken into the *Āmedī Odasî*, the secretariat for incoming correspondence of the Porte. In 1829, he was attached as secretary to the Ottoman delegation to the peace negotiations with the Russians in Edirne. By now, he seems to have belonged to the circle of Pertew Pasha, the *Reʾīs ül-Küttāb* (Chief Scribe) and former *Āmedī* (Receiver, head of the incoming correspondence secretariat), whose pro-British policies and close relationship with the British ambassador Ponsonby may have influenced Reshīd in the same direction. He joined Pertew Pasha in July 1830 on his mission to Egypt for negotiations with Muḥammad ʿAlī Pasha [*q.v.*] and from then on gained a reputation as an expert in Egyptian affairs during the years when Muḥammad ʿAlī constituted the greatest threat to the continued existence of the Ottoman Empire. In March 1833 he was sent to Kütahya to negotiate with Muḥammad ʿAlī's son Ibrāhīm Pasha [*q.v.*], who had conquered Syria and defeated the Ottoman army near Konya. His decision to grant Ibrāhīm Pasha the position of tax collector for the district of Adana (besides the governorship of the provinces of Damascus and Aleppo) was very unpopular in Istanbul, but he managed to survive it both physically and politically.

In 1834 Res͟hīd was sent to Paris as special envoy with a mission to regain Algeria from the French. While he was bound to be unsuccessful in this, he did manage to loosen the ties between Paris and Muḥammad ʿAlī. He returned to Istanbul in March 1835, but was sent to Paris again three months later, now as a full ambassador. After a year in Paris he was transferred to London. There, his crucial achievement was to gain the unequivocal support of the British government in the conflict with Muḥammad ʿAlī Pas͟ha. From now on, Res͟hīd would work closely with the British government almost continually for the rest of his life. In July 1837 he was made a marshal (*müs͟hīr* [*q.v.*]) and given the position of Minister of Foreign Affairs. After a tour of factories in Britain, he returned to Istanbul to take up his new job. Early in 1838 he was made a Pas͟ha. Foreign affairs remained his preoccupation, but we now see Res͟hīd Pas͟ha initiating reforms in other spheres, too (such as the first attempts at a modern census). For the next thirty years, the Foreign Office would remain deeply involved in the wider programme of administrative, legal and educational reform in the Ottoman Empire. This reflected both the importance of European, notably British, diplomatic pressure in favour of reform and the fact that the Foreign Office was the greatest repository of knowledge about Europe and its ways.

In August 1838 Res͟hīd was sent to London once more, to try to conclude a defensive alliance with Britain against Egypt. The alliance did not materialise, but Res͟hīd did receive guarantees of British support. As part of the effort to gain British support, a commercial treaty opening the Ottoman market to British goods and promising the abolishing of state monopolies was concluded on 16 August 1838.

After the death of Sultan Maḥmūd II in the midst of the second Egyptian crisis on 1 July 1839, Res͟hīd returned to Istanbul. There he took a leading part in the promulgation of the Gülk͟hāne edict [see K͟HAṬṬ-Ī HUMĀYŪN], which promised the subjects of the Sultan security of life, honour and property; an orderly system of taxation and conscription; and—in somewhat ambiguous terms—equality before the law irrespective of their religion. Like the trade treaty of a year before, the edict was clearly meant as an attempt to gain foreign, and especially British, diplomatic support in the conflict with Egypt, but it also reflected the genuine concerns of the reformist circles around Res͟hīd. It is hard to say whether the edict was instrumental in convincing British policy makers, but the Egyptian crisis was solved in the Ottomans' favour when British military intervention forced the Egyptian troops to evacuate Syria in late 1840.

Muḥammad ʿAlī now clearly identified Res͟hīd as his main opponent, and he used bribes to have him removed from the post of Foreign Minister in March 1841. Res͟hīd was sent to Paris once more, but soon returned, ostensibly for health reasons. All his efforts to regain his position failed, however (he was only offered the post of governor of Edirne, which he refused), and he had to return to France in 1843. There he occupied himself primarily with negotiations on the Lebanon, where the situation had beome highly unstable after the retreat of the Egyptians and the attendant fall of the Druze Amīr Bas͟hīr II.

In 1845 Res͟hīd was restored as Foreign Minister, and in September 1846 he was made Grand Vizier for the first time. With a short interruption of less than four months in 1848, he remained Grand Vizier for the unusually long period of six years. These years were his most productive ones in terms of the modernising reforms introduced in the legal system (founding of mixed commercial courts in 1847, adoption of a new commercial code (copied from France) in 1850, prohibition of torture and slavery); in education (founding of secular secondary schools for boys between 10 and 15, the *Rüs͟hdiyye*s, of a separate Ministry of Education and, in 1851, of an Academy of Sciences, the *Endjümen-i Dānis͟h*); and in the administration (including, in 1846, a first attempt to organise a modern archive, the *K͟hazīne-yi Ewrāḳ*). In the reforms, as in his foreign policy, Res͟hīd closely collaborated with the British ambassador, Stratford Canning (or Lord Stratford de Redcliffe, as he would later become). His intimate relationship with the British ambassador made him suspect in the eyes of representatives of other foreign powers, including the French. In January 1852 Res͟hīd was deposed, but barely two months later he was reappointed, only to be deposed a second time in August, after a row between him and the commander of the Imperial Arsenal.

The conflict between France and Russia over the Holy Places in Palestine, which was to result in the Crimean War, reached crisis proportions when the Russians demanded the right to protect the Orthodox population of the Ottoman Empire on 5 May 1853. This crisis brought about the return of Res͟hīd Pas͟ha as Foreign Minister on 15 May. Closely collaborating with Stratford Canning once more, Res͟hīd played for time, while refusing the Russian demands. Once he knew that the Ottoman Empire was assured of a military alliance with Britain and France he supported the declaration of war (28 March 1854). During the war he was appointed Grand Vizier again (November 1854). During his six-month stay in office he instituted the *Medjlis-i ʿAlī-yi Tanẓīmat* (High Council for Reforms) which had the twin functions of preparing legislation and of keeping watch over the bureaucracy. His dismissal as Grand Vizier in May 1855 was due to his intriguing in order to prevent the granting of the concession for the Suez Canal. This upset the French, who saw Res͟hīd anyway as a British puppet and preferred to deal instead with his pupils ʿAlī Pas͟ha and Fuʾād Pas͟ha.

Res͟hīd's dismissal meant that he was left outside the work of the peace conference in Paris which ended the Crimean War and that he had no hand in the imperial reform edict (the *Iṣlāḥāt Fermānī*) of February 1856, which was drawn up by the British and French ambassadors together with ʿAlī Pas͟ha in order to forestall Russian demands for reforms. By now, Res͟hīd's relations with his former pupils, now competitors, had turned sour. Res͟hīd had a good eye for talent, and in the best Ottoman *intisāb* tradition he had always actively sought to further the careers of the members of his circle, but he was also extremely jealous when they evolved from clients to colleagues and equals.

It took Res͟hīd a year and a half to topple his rivals and to return to power. In November 1856 he was restored to the Grand Vizierate under British pressure. His stubborn resistance to French demands for eventual unification of the Principalities into a new Rumanian state led to his dismissal under French pressure at the end of July 1857. Three months later, he was back again, being appointed Grand Vizier for a sixth and last time on 22 October. On 7 January 1858 Muṣṭafā Res͟hīd Pas͟ha died of a heart attack. He was buried in a *türbe* on the Okčular Djaddesi in the Beyazīd area of Istanbul.

Res͟hīd Pas͟ha was married twice and had five

children, one son by his first wife and four by his second.

His legacy was a lasting one, even if intra-élite factionalism, lack of funds and qualified personnel, and the non-existence of broadly-based support in society, meant that the results of his reform programme were very patchy. On the one hand, the Gül<u>kh</u>āne edict which he introduced and the reforms which he and his circle launched in the 1840s and 1850s formed a crucial phase in the transition from a traditional and patrimonial system of government to a legal-rational system. During Re<u>sh</u>īd's lifetime, the clerks of the Porte evolved into a bureaucracy which formed the strongest force in the state. The edict and the reforms also marked the start of the legal emancipation of the non-Muslim communities of the Empire. At the same time, Re<u>sh</u>īd and his colleagues often seemed to be reduced to the position of pawns in the games of the Great Powers, with Re<u>sh</u>īd serving British policy objectives in particular. However, given the weakened state of the central Ottoman government, it is hard to see how that could have been otherwise.

Bibliography: The literature which appeared up to 1961 is both used and given in Ercüment Kuran's article *Mustafa Reşit Paşa* in *İA*, ix, 701-5, ²Istanbul 1971. Most important among the pre-1961 publications are Cavit Baysun's article *Mustafa Reşit Paşa*, in *Tanzimat*, Ankara 1940, 723-46, and Reşat Kaynar, *Mustafa Reşit Paşa ve Tanzimat*, Ankara 1954. In the last thirty years, no scholarly monographs on Re<u>sh</u>īd have appeared, but quite a few important works have appeared on the *Tanẓīmāt* [*q.v.*], the reform programme with which Re<u>sh</u>īd was so intimately associated. Among the ones that should be consulted are: C.V. Findley, *Bureaucratic reform in the Ottoman Empire. The Sublime Porte, 1789-1922*, Princeton 1980; idem, *Ottoman civil officialdom. A social history*, Princeton 1989; Şerif Mardın, *The genesis of Young Ottoman thought. A study in the modernization of Turkish political ideas*, Princeton 1962; İlber Ortaylı, *İmparatorluğun en uzun yüzyılı*, ²Istanbul 1987; R.H. Davison, *Reform in the Ottoman Empire 1856-1876*, New York 1973². Murat Belge (ed.), *Tanzimat'tan Cumhuriyet'e Türkiye Ansiklopedisi*, Istanbul 1986, 6 vols. represents the state of the art in Turkey at the time of writing, although the article on Muṣṭafā Re<u>sh</u>īd Pa<u>sh</u>a is an excerpt from Baysun's work. (E.J. Zürcher)

RESM. The Arabic word *rasm*, in Turkish *resm*, *resim*, means in Ottoman usage state practices and organisations as distinguished from those based on Islamic principles and traditions. Specifically, the word indicates taxes and dues introduced by the state called *rüsūm-i ʿurfiyye* [see ʿurf] as distinguished from the *<u>sh</u>arʿī* taxes which are called *ḥuḳūḳ-ı̊ <u>sh</u>erʿiyye*. In the Ottoman Empire, *resm* was sometimes called *ḥaḳḳ* in the sense of legal right, as in the term *ḥaḳḳ-ı̊ ḳarār*, a fee which *sipahī* or feudal cavalryman took when vacant *mīrī* [*q.v.*] land was assigned to a peasant.

The term *resm* is used synonymously with *ḳanūn* [*q.v.*], *teklīf* and *ʿādat*. A *resm* is usually called *ʿādat* whenever it originates from a locally-established custom, such as *ʿādat-i <u>kh</u>armān* (harvest custom). Also, pre-Ottoman state practices are occasionally called *ʿādat*, as in the example of *ʿādat-ı̊ Ḳāyitbāy*. Those *rüsūm* which were paid in cash were often called *aḳče*, as in the examples of *čift aḳčesi* and *bostān aḳčesi*. Most of the *rüsūm* originated from the tax system of the conquered lands.

Ottoman administration tried carefully to discover and incorporate into the Ottoman tax system the well-established pre-conquest taxes and dues under th[e] term *rüsūm*. Even the pig tax, *resm-i <u>kh</u>inzīr*, wa[s] adopted in the Balkan provinces. Although they wer[e] often called *bidʿat*, innovations against the religiou[s] law, such taxes were distinguished into *bidʿat-i maʿrūf[e]* those customarily recognised, or *bidʿat-i marfūʿe*, thos[e] abolished by the sultan's specific order. Exaction[s] taken illegally by local authorities are called *tekālīf-<u>sh</u>āḳḳa*, or onerous exactions and, when discovered, were prohibited by the sultan.

In adopting a local tax into the Ottoman system the administration made inquiries as to whether o[r] not it yielded a sufficient amount of revenue o[r] whether it caused discontent in the newly-conquere[d] areas. Then, the new tax with the estimated amoun[t] of yearly yield, was entered into the *muḳāṭaʿa* [*q.v.*] registers, thus becoming a regular state tax.

The commercial dues were variously called according to the regulations to which they are subject. Good[s] sold wholesale at the urban bazaars or fairs were liabl[e] to a *bād<u>j</u>* or *tam<u>gh</u>ā* per unit, bale, sack, cask, or cart whereas valuable goods were to be brought an[d] weighed at the public scales and taxed by weight, paying *resm-i ḳapan* (*ḳabbān*), *resm-i ḳanṭar* or *resm-i mīzān*. Goods paid also a *bād<u>j</u>-i ʿubūr* at fixed points on caravan route. Imported and exported goods pai[d] *gümrük* [*q.v.*] (from Greek *kommerkion*) at various rates according to the kind of the good or whether the im[-]porter or exporter was a *Muslim*, a *<u>Dh</u>immī* or a *Ḥarbī*.

Bidʿats, particularly those affecting the well-being o[f] the Muslims (such as *bād<u>j</u>* and *tam<u>gh</u>ā* imposed upo[n] necessities and causing prices to rise), were hated b[y] the public and denounced by the *ʿulemāʾ* as contrar[y] to the *<u>Sh</u>arīʿa*. At critical times, particularly at the tim[e] of accession to the throne, rulers abolished them an[d] inscribed their orders on the gates of mosques or for[-]tresses to show their concern for the public. However in all of the Islamic states, *rusūm* and *bidʿats* were [a] significant source of revenue cash for the stat[e] treasury, and those which had been abolished onc[e] were reintroduced before long.

Although *ʿawāriḍ-i dīwāniyye* [see ʿawāriḍ] o[r] *sal<u>gh</u>un*/*sal<u>gh</u>ïn*, emergency levies, which were collecte[d] by the state in kind, cash or services rendered, wer[e] denounced as an unjust burden on the peasantry, the[y] were frequently collected and over the course of tim[e] converted to a regular tax. In a crisis, such taxes wer[e] even legitimised by special *fatwās* [*q.v.*] as a *farḍ* religious duty for the defence of Islam. *Sal<u>gh</u>uns* wer[e] introduced by a commander in an emergency situa[-]tion, but were usually prohibited by the centra[l] government. A grain tax added to *aʿ<u>sh</u>ār*, called *sālārlïḳ* or *sālāriyye* (increasing the regular tithe to one-eight[h] of the produce) was introduced into the earlier ta[x] systems prior to the Ottoman period. The Ottoman[s] continued it, although the peasantry complaine[d] about this additional tithe. The *<u>Sh</u>ayk<u>h</u> al-Islām* Abu 'l-Suʿūd [*q.v.*] attempted to legitimise it by claiming tha[t] the lands conquered by the Ottomans were all of th[e] *<u>kh</u>arād<u>j</u>ī* type and thus subject to *<u>kh</u>arād<u>j</u>*, which coul[d] go up to one-fifth of the produce.

A widespread Byzantine/Balkan grain tax which survived into the Ottoman tax system was that of on[e] or two measures of barley and wheat delivered to th[e] feudal lord or the state. It corresponded to the Ottoman *ʿawāriḍ*.

A *resm* of particular importance was the *resm-i čift*, a one-gold coin tax per household or its equivalent in silver coins, imposed upon a peasant family in possession of a *čiftlik* [*q.v.*] and a pair of oxen. Traced back to the Roman *jugum-caput* and Byzantine *zeugaratikion*, this tax was probably the origin of the *čift-bā-<u>kh</u>āne*

·stem in the Ottoman empire. Its nature, combining hearth-tax and land-tax, confused bureaucrats as ·ell as scholars. It must be the origin of the *kharādj* ·nd the *djizya* in the early Islamic tax system. ·*eugaratikion* and the *čift-resmi* [*q.v.*] system gave the ·hole of rural society in Anatolia and the Balkans its ·articular social-fiscal organisation under the Byzan·ne and Ottoman Empires. The *resm-i čift* was a com·ound tax which included cash equivalents of various ·udal services (see İnalcık, *Osmanlilarda raiyyet rusûmu*, ·nd idem, *Village, peasant and empire*).

The *resm-i čift* system included *resm-i čift, resm-i nīm-·ft, resm-i bennāk, resm-i čiftlü bennāk, resm-i ekinlü ben-·āk, resm-i mudjarrad, resm-i ḳara, resm-i djabā, resm-i ·iwa, resm-i dönüm, resm-i duhān, resm-i zamīn, resm-i čift-·ozan, resm-i yaylaḳ* and *resm-i ḳishlaḳ*.

Ispendje or *ispenče*, from Slavic *yupanitsa*, a feudal ·easant household tax in the pre-Ottoman Balkans, ·as incorporated into the Ottoman tax system and ex·ended into eastern Anatolia from 1540 onwards. ·very non-Muslim peasant household or individual ·aid it at the rate of 25 *akčes*. Abu 'l-Suʿūd interpreted · as *kharādj-i muwaẓẓafa* or "fixed *kharādj*". In the ·540s, the Ottomans identified it with *resm-i ḳapu* or ·ate-tax in Hungary, raising its rate to fifty *akčes*, ·bout the value of one gold piece in Ottoman silver ·oins in the period. Collection of *resm-i čift, ispendje* ·nd *djizya* at the same time came to triple the original ·earth-tax. Such double taxing, due to the confusion ·bout the origin of the tax, often occured in the newly·stablished régimes.

The *resm-i filori* [*q.v.*], originally a one-gold piece ·ax applied to the Eflāķṣ, non-Muslim nomads of the Balkans, was another composite tax paid by household.

The *resm-i bād-i hawā*, evidently from the Byzantine *aerikon*, also called *ṭayyārāt*, was another composite tax which included occasional taxes such as *djerāʾim* or fines, *resm-i ʿarūsāne*, also called *resm-i cerdek*, marriage-tax, *resm-i dashtbāniyye*, field-guard fee, and *resm-i ṭapu* or fee on land transfers. The above-mentioned composit taxes of pre-Ottoman origin, namely *resm-i čift* and its derivatives, *ispendje* and *bād-i hawā*, were paid directly to the *sipahī* as part of his *timār* [*q.v.*].

The Ottoman tax system also allowed government agents to collect for themselves a small fee for their services. It was called *khidmet akčesi*, service-money or *maʿīshet*, livelihood. In later periods many such fees were returned to the treasury. However, in the 17th century when *timār* revenues drastically lost their value, government agents in the provinces invented a host of service fees (see Inalcik, *Military and fiscal transformation*).

The sultan's favour, which established privileges and benefits for persons, was thought to be reciprocated by payments. So, an important category of *rüsūm*, including the *resm-i berāt*, diploma fee, or *resm-i tedhkire*, certificate fee, brought to the treasury quite a sizeable revenue.

The sale of offices which became widespread from the end of the 16th century onwards, must be interpreted in the same way.

In the courts, *Ḳāḍīs* took several *resms* for their services. Their abuses caused widespread complaints, and from time to time Ottoman rulers issued regulations fixing the rates of court fees.

Fees at the Law Courts
(in *akčes*)

	ʿItāḳ-nāme (Manumission certificate)			*Nikāḥ resmi* (Marriage tax)			*Resm-i ḳismet* (Division of inheritances per thousand)			*Ḥudjdjet* (Certificates)			S	Rc	R
	Kd	H	KE	Kd	H	Kt	Kd	H	Kt	Kd	H	Kt			
Ḥukm dated H.884	30	1	1	20	5 for both		20	–		15	1		–	–	–
Ḥukm dated H.928	20	6	4	–			14	4	2	20	4		–	7	7
Ḥukm dated H.1054.......	50	10	6	20			15	–		20	5 for both		12	12	8

Abbreviations:
Kd : Ḳāḍī
KE : Kātib Emīn
Kt : Kātib
H : Hidjrī date
S : Signature
Rc : Record
R : Reportion

Bibliography: H. İnalcık, *Osmanlılarda raiyyet rusûm*, in *Belleten*, xxiii, 575-610; idem, *Military and fiscal transformation in the Ottoman empire, 1600-1700*, in *Archivum Ottomanicum*, vi, 283-337; idem, *Village, peasant and empire*, in *The Middle East and the Balkans under the Ottoman empire*, Bloomington, Ind. 1993, 136-60. (Halil İnalcık)

REWĀN, Eriwan, the capital city of Armenia, possibly identical with the town called Arran by the Arab geographers Ibn Rusta and Ibn Faḳīh, which in Armenian is called Hrastan and Rewān in Ottoman sources.

In Islamic times, the town seems to have become important from the mid-10th/16th century onward. The city is located close to the Armenian patriarchal seat of Echmiadzin, often referred to as Üčkilise "Three Churches" in Ottoman and European sources, even though there are actually four churches. In the 10th/16th century, the town formed part of Ṣafawid Persia, but was raided several times by Ottoman forces. In 990/1582 Rewān was conquered by the Ottoman *serdār* Ferhād Pasha, who ordered the construction of new fortifications. In the reign of Shāh ʿAbbās, Eriwan was taken back by the Ṣafawids and in 1025/1616 besieged by the Ottomans, who were however unable to take the city. In 1041-2/1632 the Ottoman Sultan Murād IV retook Rewān and had a famous *köšk*, the Rewān Köškü, added to the Ṭopḳapî Sarayî to commemorate the event. However Rewān was soon after reconquered by the Ṣafawids. According to the treaty of Ḳaṣr-i Shīrīn (1048-49/1639) the city thenceforth remained in Persian hands, apart from a brief Ottoman interlude which ended in 1159/1746.

From the 11th/17th century date the first extensive descriptions of Eriwan. Ewliyā Čelebi visited the place in 1057/1647, and describes the sieges and counter-sieges of the reign of Murād IV, who had taken a liking to the former *khān* of Rewān, Emīrgūn. Ewliyā felt that the walls of Rewān, consisting of but a single ring, were in no condition to resist a serious siege. At the time of his visit, those parts of the walls erected by Ferhād Pasha could still be distinguished from the higher sections built by the Persian governor Toḳmaḳ Khān. The city was entered by three strong gates, and well-stocked with weaponry. Among the officials present in Rewān Ewliyā mentions the *ḳāḍī*, along with a full complement of civilian and military officials. At certain times the city was governed by a *khān* of *khān*s.

Another extensive description was provided by the French jeweller and merchant J.-B. Tavernier, who visited Rewān in 1065-6/1655. He notes that the province was one of the richest in the Ṣafawid empire, both on account of transit trade and the fertility of the area, which permitted the cultivation of rice. Raw silk was here collected for export, and merchants enjoyed the privilege of paying a flat rate, without opening their bales. Tavernier claims that the old city had been ruined during the Ottoman-Ṣafawid wars, and a new one built on the boards of the river Zengi Çayı; this may be compared to Ewliyā's statement that the town had only been founded in the reign of Tīmūr Lenk. Tavernier refers to an active commercial suburb equally mentioned by Ewliyā Čelebi, where merchants and artisans, particularly Armenians, resided. He also describes a stone bridge with chambers underneath, where the *khān* sometimes spent the hottest hours of summer.

About a decade later, Rewān was described by J. Chardin, as a large city with numerous gardens and vineyards. The citadel contained about 800 houses, inhabited only by Persians, while Armenian shopowners left the enclosure in the evenings. The garrison amounted to 2,000 men. There was a second fortress, by the name of "Quetchy-kala", with a double wall and cannons, suitable for another 200 men. The core of the city was located at a cannon shot's distance from the citadel. It contained a *maydān* surrounded by trees, where parades and games were held. The principal mosque was located in the market area, and there were also several Armenian churches, built partly underground. Chardin praises the city's public baths and caravanserais, the most recent of which had been built by a governor; the gallery was filled with shops selling a variety of textiles, and there were 63 apartments along with stables and storage spaces. This building is probably identical to the Gorji (Georgian) *khān* of later times, where goods from Russia and Georgia were usually stored. In spite of the cold climate in winter, the area was famous for its grapes and wine, the Armenian peasants burying their vines at the approach of winter. In the summer of 1113/1701, Joseph Pitton de Tournefort also visited Rewān; however, his account of the city only repeats those of his predecessors.

After his appointment to the Caucasus in 1217-18/1803, General Tsitsianov attempted to force the *khān* of Rewān to abandon his Persian allegiance and submit to Russia; however a siege in 1219/1804 ended in failure. Between 1225/1810 and 1233-4/1818, the diplomat J. Morier visited Rewān and recorded the post-war atmosphere in the city; the houses in the citadel for the most part lay in ruins, and the citadel mosque had been converted into a storehouse. According to a register prepared at this time by Ḥasan Khān, brother of the current *sardār*, Rewān and its villages contained a total of 18,700 males between the ages of 15 and 50, which according to Morier's assumption, corresponded to a population of 74,800. A separate register recorded 5,000 Kurdish families, which brought the total up to about 100,000. Official revenues collected in the area amounted to 168,000 *tūmān*s, and consisted mainly of rural dues, customs duties yielded 12,000 *tūmān*s, and dues from the salt mines of Kolpi 6,000. In certain areas, one-third of rural produce apparently was collected as taxes. The *sardār* monopolised the cotton crop and sold it to Georgia, importing Georgian fabrics in return.

During another Russo-Persian war (1241-3/1826-7) Rewān was again besieged, and local notables arranged for a surrender to the forces of General Paskevich; Russian domination was confirmed by the treaty of Turkmānčāy in February 1828/Shaʿbān 1243. Extensive data on the urban resources and population of Rewān date from 1244-8/1829-32, when the new Russian administration conducted a detailed survey. According to this document, the city had 7,331 Muslim inhabitants of both sexes, along with 3,937 Armenians. Among the latter, 1,715 were recent immigrants from Persia. The total urban population amounted to 11,463 persons in 2,751 households, distributed over three large quarters encompassing 1,736 houses. Apart from the Muslims who had left the khānate after the Russian conquest, the newly-acquired Russian province contained a population of 115,152 persons in 20,932 households, of which 61,018 were males. The Turkish nomad population before the Russian conquest had numbered more than 20,000; about 10% must have left the area immediately following the war, as the Russian survey counted only 18,287.

At the time of the Russian takeover, there were 851 stores in Eriwan; 543 formed part of the bazaar, while 252 were attached to the city's seven caravanserais and another 32 located in the fortress. The three quarters making up the remainder of the city must therefore have been all but exclusively residential. There were eight mosques with attached *madrasas* (one of them, the Shehir Djāmiʿ, with its Turkish inscription of 1098/1687), and seven Armenian churches, while the ten public baths were mostly part of mosque or caravanserai complexes. Imports from Persia included silk, coffee, sugar, indigo, cotton, wool, dried fruit, raisins and condiments; while from the Ottoman empire came wool, cloth, butter, coffee, wine, fruit, nuts, wood and tobacco. Exports to Persia were limited to cloth and grain, while the Ottoman Empire bought raisins, indigo, silk and cotton. From Georgia, cloth, wine, tea, fruit and nuts as well as wood were imported, while wood and salt were conveyed there. Russian and other European imports were usually luxury products. Merchants were numerous both among the Muslim and the Armenian population; among the Armenian immigrants from Persia, there were 105 weavers and 64 carpenters established in the city proper. In addition, women weavers worked at home; the survey records almost 3,000 looms for the khānate in its entirety.

An impressionistic account of Rewān in the 1240s-1250s/1830s was published by F. Dubois de Montpéreux. He described the reception hall of the last Persian *sardār*, decorated with mirrors and wall paintings of Shāh ʿAbbās, Nādir Shāh, Fatḥ ʿAlī Shāh, the heir-apparent ʿAbbās Mīrzā, the *sardār* himself and various mythological figures. Dubois also has published sketches of several of these paintings. The *sardār*'s *ḥaram* at this time had been transformed into a barracks, but the traveller was able to see the canal providing water to this section of the palace as well as the four *ayvāns*, which at this time still retained their original decoration. One of the two mosques, with a façade richly decorated with tilework was still being used as an arsenal, while the other had been transformed into a Russian church. The business district was in poor condition, with many of the shops closed. This impression was confirmed by R. Wilbraham, who visited the city at about the same time and saw but a single public bath in working order; reportedly no repairs had been made as there were plans afoot to move the fortress to another, healthier site.

For 1310-16/1893-8 there exists an extensive description by H.F.B. Lynch, who records that the city now contained about 15,000 inhabitants, half of them Muslims and the other half Armenians. It was divided into two sections by the road to Tiflis and by a central park, the western part being inhabited by Armenians and the eastern part by Shī^c^ī Muslims speaking Ādherī Turkish. However, the Gök Djāmi^c^, the principal mosque, though located in the western section, was surrounded by a Muslim quarter; according to local informants, it had been built by Nādir Shāh. The mosque in the citadel, already in ruinous condition, was dated to the reign of Fatḥ ^c^Alī Shāh and called the ^c^Abbās Mīrzā Djāmi^c^; this was probably the structure seen by Morier and Dubois. Lynch briefly describes the churches, but considers that the most important monument in the city was the *köshk* of the Persian governors (*sardārs*) located close to the citadel at some distance from the city centre; from its decoration, it was probably built or at least restored in the 13th/19th century.

The extreme centralisation of the Russian Empire, along with policies probably intended to favour future Russian settlement, in Lynch's opinion inhibited the city's economic development. There was almost no transit trade with Persia, while raw cotton to the value of £400,000 was despatched to Russian manufactures by way of the Caspian Sea. While the cotton trade was monopolised by a few Russian firms, Armenians sold a limited quantity of local wine to Russia, while rice was exported to Erzurum. Well-to-do Armenian merchants invested in education, their schools competing with state-sponsored Russian establishments; Lynch comments on the small number of Muslim students in the latter. Wealthy Muslims were often landowners cultivating the fruit for which Rewān was locally famous; but Muslims were found also among the substantial shopkeepers, while the poor earned their livings as hucksters, irrigation workers and cart drivers.

After the fall of the Tsarist government (March 1917), Russian troops withdraw from the area, and in late November, an interim government was formed in Tiflis which attempted to negotiate on behalf of the entire region. This government dissolved after an Ottoman military advance in the Caucasus. A separate Republic of Armenia was formed, with its capital in Rewān/Yerevan, which the Ottoman Empire recognised by the Treaty of Batum (June 1918). In another war (September 1920), waged between the Republic of Armenia on one side and the Soviet Union and the Kemālist forces recently constituted in Anatolia on the other, the intervention of Red Army troops ensured the establishment of a Soviet Socialist Republic, again with its capital in Yerevan. By 1932, the city's population had grown to about 100,000. New town quarters had been built to accommodate a large number of new arrivals, many of them refugees from Anatolia. At this time, the city had acquired a university, a state library and other institutions of higher learning. Of the monuments from the Persian period, there remained the stone bridge over the river Zengi, the Gök Masdjid and the remains of the Sardār Mosque and Palace. After the dissolution of the Soviet Union at the end of 1991, Yerevan once more began to function as the capital of a state, now named the Republic of Armenia.

Bibliography: For an extensive bibl. of the work on Rewān in Armenian, Persian and Russian, see Bournoutian, *The Khanate of Erevan*, 285-323. Of other works, see Chardin, *Voyages de Mr le Chevalier Chardin en Perse et en autres lieux de l'Orient*..., Amsterdam 1711, ii, 218 ff.; Morier, *Second Voyage en Perse, en Arménie et dans l'Asie Mineure, fait de 1810 à 1816*, Paris 1818, 253-60; Dubois de Montpéreux, *Voyage autour du Caucase, chez les Tcherkesses et les Abkhases*..., Paris 1839, iii, 334 ff.; R. Wilbraham, *Travels in the Transcaucasian provinces of Russia and along the southern shore of the lakes of Van and Urumiah in the autumn and winter of 1837*, London 1839, 88-90; Muṣṭafā Na^c^īmā, *Rawḍat al-ḥüseyin*..., Istanbul 1281-3/1864-6, i, 339-40; Ewliyā Čelebi, *Seyāḥat-nāme*, Istanbul 1314/1896-7, ii, 284 ff.; Mirza Bala, *İA* art. *Erivan*; Bekir Kütükoğlu, *Osmanlı-İran siyâsî münâsebetleri*, i. *1578-1590*, Istanbul 1962, *passim*; Lynch, *Armenia, travels and studies*, repr. Beirut 1965, i, 200-27; U. Trumpener, *Germany and the Ottoman Empire, 1914-1918*, Princeton 1968, 257 ff.; Fahrettin Kırzıoğlu, *Osmanlılar'ın Kafkas-elleri'ni fethi (1451-1590)*, Ankara 1976, *passim*; Muriel Atkin, *Russia and Iran, 1780-1828*, Minneapolis 1980, 76-81, 158-9; Tavernier, *Les six voyages de Turquie et de Perse*, annotated by Stéphane Yérasimos, Paris 1981, i, 82-6; J. Pitton de Tournefort, *Voyage d'un botaniste*, ii. *La Turquie, la Géorgie, l'Arménie*, annotated by Stéphane Yérasimos, Paris 1982, 221-5; G. Bournoutian, *The Khanate of Erevan under Qajar rule 1795-1828*, Costa Mesa, Cal. and New York 1992.

(SURAIYA FAROQHI)

REWĀNĪ, an Ottoman poet. His real name was Ilyās Shudjā^c^ Čelebī, his father's name was ^c^Abd Allāh (^c^Abdullāh), and he was born *ca.* 1475 and educated in Edirne (Abdülkadir Karahan, art. *Revani İA*). Tradition has it that he took his pen-name of Rewānī from the river Tundja, which flowed (*rewān*) past his garden. He entered the service of Sultan Bāyezīd II (886-918/1481-1512) in Istanbul, and was sent by him as administrator of the *ṣurre* (the annual sum set aside for the poor of Mecca and Medina) to the Holy Cities in order to distribute the money. Accused by the Meccans of unjust distribution and/or embezzling a part of the money, however, he was dismissed (*ibid.*). A malady of the eyes, which affected Rewānī at this time, was described by a poet hostile to him as the just punishment of God, whereupon Rewānī answered him, also in verse, and calmly confessed: "He who has honey licks his fingers." He fled to the court of Prince Selīm, then governor of the province of Trabzon, and entered his service. Here too, however, he committed some indiscretion and his property was confiscated. Some sources put his appointment to the *ṣurre* at this date. Others say he determined to go to Egypt, but Selīm pardoned him and restored him to favour, Rewānī henceforth serving him all the more faithfully. Thus Rewānī was in Selīm's entourage when in 918/1512 the latter came to Istanbul to dethrone his father Bāyezīd, and is said at the last decisive council of war to have thrown his turban in the air with joy and to have praised the day. After Selīm's accession he was appointed superintendent of the kitchen (*maṭbakh emīni*), then entrusted with the administration of Aya Sofya and of the hot baths (*ḳablīdja*) in Bursa. With the wealth he accumulated, he built a mosque complex (no longer standing) in the Ḳîrḳ Česhme quarter of Istanbul. This mosque was named after him, and he was buried there on his death in 930/1524 during the reign of Süleymān the Magnificent. Rewānī left a *Dīwān*, dedicated to Selīm, and a *methnewī* entitled *ʿIshret-nāme* ("Book of the wine-feast"). There is an unpublished critical edition and transcription of the former (Samiye İnceoğlu, *Revani divanı edisyon kritik ve transkripsiyonu*, İstanbul Üniversitesi, Mezuniyet Tezi, 1961) and another study is in process (Ziya Avşar, *Revani divanı*, Ankara Üniversitesi, Yüksek Lisans Tezi). Critics consider that the real strength of Rewānī's *Dīwān* is in its *ghazel*s, in which he sings in a lively and easily flowing manner of both human and mystic love; many of these were set to music and quickly became popular in the coffee and winehouses (Karahan, *op. cit.*; Nihad Sâmi Banarlı, *Resimli türk edebiyatı*, Istanbul 1989, 478).

The *ʿIshret-nāme*, a *methnewī* of 694 *beyts* (Rıdvan Çanım, art. *Sâkînâme*, in *Türk dili ve edebiyatı ansiklopedisi* [1990] vii, 433-7) is undated but may have been written towards the end of the poet's life since he refers to his white hair and to his being in the autumn of life. In it, Rewānī relates legends concerning the origin of viniculture and the discovery of wine, and describes in realistic detail the etiquette of the drinking bouts of his time, the meal served before them, the wine, wineglass, flagon, candle, musical instruments, cupbearers, etc. Towards the end he suggests that the poem may be given a mystical interpretation, but this is to be considered as a safety-net against attacks from the devout, the contents really reflecting the existence of such activities in his day, and his own penchant for them; and although he is said to have renounced this in his old age, in general he left behind him a reputation for dishonesty and libertinism (see A. Bombaci, *La letteratura turca*, Milan 1969, 334).

Poems containing bacchic themes have a long history in the literature of the Arabs and Persians (see KHAMRIYYA, and Çanım, art. *Sâkînâme*, 434), the metaphor of wine also becoming an all-important feature of mystical poetry. Bacchic elements are found in the literature of the Turks in the 14th and 15th centuries (*ibid.*, 435), but Rewānī's *ʿIshret-nāme* is the first poem of its kind in Ottoman Turkish literature, and the *sāḳī-nāme* genre only became popular a century later. His work is, therefore considered original and his own invention, and it has been praised for its wit and its language, which is graceful and elegant, but at the same time simple and clear (Karahan, *loc. cit.*). Sehī states that the *ʿIshret-nāme* is only one part of a *Khamse-yi Rūm*, which Ṭāhir says includes a poem entitled *Djāmiʿ al-nasāʾiḥ*. Nothing further, however, seems to be known of this.

Bibliography: In addition to works mentioned in the article, for mss. and *tedhkere*s see the catalogues for Berlin, Gotha, Vienna, Cairo and Istanbul, and bibliographies in the arts. *Revani* in *İA* (Karahan) and *Büyük türk klâsikleri*, Istanbul [1986], iii, 226-9; Ẓiyā Pasha, *Kharābāt*, ii, 148; J. von Hammer-Purgstall, *GOR*, iii, 465; idem, *GOD*, i, 187-97; Gibb, *HOP*, ii, 317-46; K.J. Basmadjian, *Essai sur l'histoire de la littérature ottomane*, Paris and Constantinople 1910, 63-4; Rıdvan Çanım, *Sâkî-nâmeler ve Edirneli Revânî'nin İşretnâmesi*, Atatürk Üniversitesi, Yüksek Lisans Tezi, 1987; *Türk dili ve edebiyatı ansiklopedisi*, vii [1990] s.v. *Revanî* (Mustafa Kutlu) and *İşretname* (M. Şahidî Örnek). Examples of Rewānī's poems are given in Ali Nihad Tarlan, *Şi mecmualarında XVI ve XVII. asır divan şiiri*, seri i fasikül 4, Istanbul 1949, 5-22; Fahir İz, *Eski tür edebiyatında nazım*, Istanbul 1966-7, i, 223-4; an *Büyük türk klâsikleri*, Istanbul [1986], iii, 227-30.

(W. Björkman-[Kathleen Burrill])

RIAU (Dutch, Riouw), the name of the forme Malay kingdom of Johore Riau-Lingga, which wa regarded as the successor state to Melaka (Malacc [*q.v.*]) after it fell to the Portuguese in 1511. Th rulers of the Melakan line re-established their authority on the island of Bintan (also known as Riau), sout of Singapore, in the late 17th century, and after period of instability, during which Bugis adventurer entered the scene, a new more prosperous era began By the mid-18th century, an extensive trading network had developed around the main port of Ria which attracted merchants from the Middle East China and Europe as well as neighbouring areas o Southeast Asia. The Bugis adventurers married int the Malay royal line and were granted the title o Yang Dipertuan Muda, or Junior Ruler. They amassed fortunes in the opium and tin trades and i 1784 laid siege to the Dutch garrison in Melaka. Thi led to a Dutch reprisal which resulted in a permanen Dutch presence on Riau. The Malay Sultan movec his court to the island of Lingga to the south, and th kingdom became divided into two centres, the Dutc and Bugis in control of Riau, and the Malay Sulta and his court on Lingga. In 1818 Sir Thomas Stamford Raffles leased the island of Singapore, dependency of the kingdom of Johore Riau-Lingga from one of the hereditary chiefs of the Malay court and installed a member of the Malay royal family a Sultan. The economic decline of Riau began with th Anglo-Dutch Treaty of 1824, which demarcatec British and Dutch areas of influence. Singapor became a free port and attracted Riau's former trade In 1857 the Dutch demonstrated their political contro of Riau-Lingga by deposing the reigning Mala Sultan, and in 1913 they formally abolished th historic kingdom.

Since Indonesian Independence in 1945, Riau ha been a Sumatran Province, covering part of the central coast of East Sumatra and more than 3,20 islands between Sumatra and the South China Sea. The island of Bintan, Riau, remains the cultural heartland of the area and since the 1980s has experienced a cultural revival with renewed interest in all aspects of its past, including its status as an Islamic centre. Economic revival will probably follow, as Riau is closely linked to the new industrial and trade triangle of Johor-Singapore-Batam.

For the history of Islam in Southeast Asia, Riau is famous as a 19th century centre of Muslim scholarship and piety. European visitors of the time reported that the nobles vied to outdo each other in performing their religious obligations, and anything non-Islamic was regarded as anathema. A local text, *Tuḥfat al-nafīs*, composed in 1865 by Radjā ʿAlī Ḥādjdjī, one of the leading Muslim scholars, describes religious life in Riau. During the 19th century a series of Yang Dipertuan Mudas, inspired by the writings of al-Ghazālī [*q.v.*], especially his *Naṣīḥat al-mulūk*, strove to behave as ideal Muslim rulers and to establish conditions in Riau which would enable their subjects to fulfill all their religious obligations and lead a godly life. They invited religious scholars from the Middle East to stay on Riau and teach, and the *Tuḥfat al-nafīs* lists the works that were studied. They banned behaviour that was unseemly, enforced the daily prayers and sponsored the copying and composition of religious and didactic treatises. In the late 1880s a study group, the *Persekutuan Rushdiyyah*, was formed to discuss religious and literary matters and to publish texts written by its members using their own printing press. These works were disseminated to Singapore and Peninsular Malaysia. Early in the 19th century the Naḳshabandī *Tarikat* [see NAḲSHBANDIYYA] was introduced to Riau and became very popular. The *Tuḥfa* records that all the Riau princes studied mysticism and copies of the texts are still kept in the area. One of the Riau rulers bought a wide selection of books, mainly Islamic texts from India and the Middle East, and established a library which is still maintained in the mosque on Penyengat island. Students (such as Sayyid Shaykh al-Hādī), who received their initial training in Riau, went on to found religious journals and schools in Singapore and Penang and to influence the course of modernist Islam in the Malay speaking world.

The tradition of religious teaching was continued in Riau until the 1930s, and scholars from the Middle East, including an expert in astronomy from al-Azhar, regularly visited Riau to advise the local religious teachers. The Second World War disrupted this pattern, and the local population has declined since the early years of the century. However, Riau has maintained its reputation as a religious and literary centre which is respected both in Malaysia and in Indonesia.

Bibliography: L.Y. Andaya, *The kingdom of Johor 1641-1728*, Kuala Lumpur 1975; Barbara Watson Andaya and Virginia Matheson, *Islamic thought and Malay tradition: the writings of Raja Ali Haji of Riau (ca. 1809-ca. 1870)*, in *Perceptions of the past in Southeast Asia*, ed. A. Reid and D. Marr, Singapore 1979; Matheson and Andaya (eds. and translators), *The Precious Gift, Tuhfat al-nafis*, Kuala Lumpur 1982; Matheson, *Pulau Penyengat: nineteenth century Islamic centre of Riau*, in *Archipel*, xxxvii (1989), 153-72; Vivienne Wee, *Melayu: hierarchies of being in Riau*, Ph.D thesis, ANU Canberra 1985; eadem, *Material dependence and symbolic independence: constructions of Melayu ethnicity in Island Riau, Indonesia*, Working Paper 75, Dept. of Sociology, National University of Singapore 1986.

(VIRGINIA MATHESON HOOKER)

RIBĀ (A.), lit. increase, as a technical term, usury and interest, and in general any unjustified increase of capital for which no compensation is given. Derivatives from the same root are used in other Semitic languages to describe interest.

A. In classical Islamic law.

1. Transactions with a fixed time limit and payment of interest, as well as speculations of all kinds, formed an essential element in the highly developed trading system of Mecca (cf. Lammens, *La Mecque à la veille de l'hégire*, 139 ff., 155 ff., 213-14). Among the details given by the Muslim sources we may believe at least the statement that a debtor who could not repay the capital (money or goods) with the accumulated interest at the time it fell due, was given an extension of time in which to pay, but at the same time the sum due was doubled. This is clearly referred to in two passages in the Ḳurʾān (III, 130; XXX, 39) and is in keeping with a still usual practice. As early as sūra XXX, 39, of the third Meccan period (on the dating, cf. Nöldeke-Schwally, *Geschichte des Qorāns*, i), the Ḳurʾān contrasts *ribā* with the obligation to pay *zakāt* but without directly forbidding it: "Whatever ye give in usury to gain interest from men's substance shall not bear interest with Allāh, but what ye give as *zakāt* in seeking the face of Allāh, these shall gain double". The express prohibition follows in III, 130 (Medinan, obviously earlier than the following passage): "Believers, devour not the *ribā* with continual doubling; fear God, perhaps it will go with you". This prohibition had to be intensified in II, 275-80 (evidently of the earlier Medinan period, cf. the following passage): "Those who devour *ribā* shall only rise again as one whom Satan strikes with his touch; this because they say, 'selling is like usury'; but Allāh has permitted selling and forbidden usury. He therefore who receives a warning from his Lord and abstains shall have pardon for what is past and his affair is with Allāh; but they who relapse into usury are the people of Hell, and they shall remain in it for ever. Allāh abolishes usury and makes alms bring interest; Allāh loveth no sinful unbeliever... Believers, fear Allāh and remit the balance of the *ribā* if ye be believers. But if ye do not, be prepared for war from Allāh and his apostle. If ye repent, ye shall receive your capital without doing an injustice or suffering injustice. If any one is in difficulty, let there be a delay till he is able to pay, but it is better for you to remit if ye be wise". To evade the dogmatic difficulty of an eternal punishment for the sin of a believer, the passage in question (already presupposed in al-Ṭabarī) has been interpreted to mean that by relapse is meant the holding lawful and not the taking of interest; in any case the Ḳurʾān regards *ribā* as a practice of unbelievers and demands as a test of belief that it should be abandoned. It comes up again in sūra IV, 161 (of the period between the end of the year 3 and the end of the year 5; this also gives a clue to the date of the preceding passage), in a passage which sums up the reproaches levelled against the Jews: "and because they take *ribā*, while it was forbidden them, and devour uselessly the substance of the people". The fact that the principal passages against interest belong to the Medinan period and that the Jews are reproached with breaking the prohibition, suggests that the Muslim prohibition of *ribā* owes less to conditions in Mecca than to the Prophet's closer acquaintance with Jewish doctrine and practice in Medina. In the later development of the teaching on the subject as we find it in tradition, Jewish influence is in any case undeniable (cf. Juynboll, *Handleiding*, 286).

2. The traditions give varying answers to the question, what forms of business come under the Ḳurʾānic prohibition of *ribā*, none of which can be regarded as authentic. The ignorance of the correct interpretation is emphasised in a tendentious tradition, obviously put into circulation by interested individuals (the tradition is probably older than Lammens, *op. cit.*, 214, thinks); according to this view, the principal passage in sūra II is the latest in the whole Ḳurʾān, which the Prophet could not expound before his death. That the rigid prohibition of usury in Islamic law only developed gradually is clear from many traditions. Alongside of the view repeatedly expressed, but also challenged, that *ribā* consists only in (the increase of substance in) a business agreement with a fixed period (*nasīʾa, naẓīra, dayn*) we have the still more distinct statement that there is no *ribā* if the transfer of ownership takes place immediately (*yadan bi-yad*). But even in arrangements with a time limit, a number of traditions pre-suppose a general ignorance of the later restrictions; for example, we are told that in Baṣra under Ziyād b. Abīhi [*q.v.*] gold was sold on credit for silver (this may have an anti-Umayyad bias—cf. below on Muʿāwiya—but it is illuminating); but at a later date such forms of the traditions against *ribā* were to some extent dropped. What was generally understood in the earliest period as the *ribā* forbidden in the Ḳurʾān, seems only to have been interest on loans

mounts, with a view to battle. In this case, the term *ribāṭ* is used as a verbal noun, a *maṣdar*, and not as a substantive. The period immediately following the great conquests, which saw the establishment of Muslim powers in new territories, was to change the modalities of war. This was to become a war of position, during the intervals between continuing offensives. Dispositions of defence were constructed (or re-used in cases where there were previous constructions), on the coasts and on the land frontiers. This was done progressively, during the time of the caliphate at Medina, most notably under the caliph ʿUthmān, and was continued under the Umayyads, according to local requirements and conditions, although no unified doctrine was obligatorily applied.

It may be supposed that it was from this time onward that the word *ribāṭ* and the terms associated with it came to be applied to new objects. The ancient connotations did not disappear entirely, although they did require adaptation. It is not known whether it was during this period, or rather later, under the earlier ʿAbbāsids, that the term began to be used to denote a fortified edifice (from the simple observation tower, to the small fort, to the fortress, and to the caravanserai). These very diverse establishments would normally be situated in hazardous regions, on frontiers, on coasts, or on difficult internal routes. But this mutation of sense does not seem to have been general. The only elements of localisation are supplied by relatively late sources, which usually mention the fact without any indication which could be used in establishing a chronology. It seems that what is involved is the simple imposition of a noun, probably denoting the existence of danger and the need to take precautions against it, upon various pre-existing constructions, without any suggestion that there is, at the outset, such a thing as a unique type of edifice which could be called *ribāṭ*. It can thus be stated with confidence that to define it a "Muslim military monastery" is evidence of extrapolation and misinterpretation, and this applies, whatever the period and the region. It cannot be denied that the urban residences of Ṣūfīs were subsequently known as *ribāṭ*. In the east of the empire and in Egypt, they were more commonly known as *khānḳāh* [*q.v.*]. ʿIrāḳ supplies a notable exception in this zone, since until the middle of the 7th/13th century these establishments were known there exclusively by the name *ribāṭ*, possibly in preference to the use of a word with such strong connotations of origin (a purely Persian word and the Iranian provenance of the establishment). But, with very few exceptions, constructions of this type did not truly begin to develop until after the 6th/12th century, at the time of the burgeoning of the mystical fraternities of the Muslim *ṭarīḳas* (*q.v.* in *EI*[1]; on the other hand, the Karrāmī *khānḳāhs* [*q.v.*] are more ancient). These communal establishments for mystics (which often also accommodated travellers) had, in any case, nothing in common with the fortified constructions of the frontier which, in mediaeval Muslim representation, after a certain period, are reckoned to have welcomed "warriors of the faith". It will be observed that this last consideration, linked to a representation of *djihād* [*q.v.*]—often treated as evidence in itself—needs to be approached with caution. It could derive, to a great extent, from the ideology and imagery of belief, rather than from direct historical actuality (see the detailed examination by C.E. Bosworth of the term *ribāṭ* and its evolution, in *The city of Tarsus and the Arab-Byzantine frontiers*, in *Oriens*, xxxiii [1992], 284-6).

a. *Ribāṭ* as a verbal noun, from tribal Arabia to the frontiers of the empire.

The root *r-b-ṭ* gives the general sense of attaching or linking, in a concrete sense, and of strengthening (the heart), in a figurative sense (three Ḳurʾānic instances display this latter sense). The theme of linkage seems to have become specific in reference to the act of assembling and keeping together the horses which were to be used in the razzia. In tribal Arabia, according to traditional representation, horses were mounted when the attack was imminent, while camels were reserved for the advance to the site of the combat. Most of these horses would have been mares, which were considered, in tribal society, particularly valuable beasts (see the modern testimony of Ch. Doughty, *Travels in Arabia deserta*, 2nd ed. London 1921, and of A. Jaussen, *Les Arabes au pays de Moab*, Paris, new ed. 1948; for the use of the horse in pre-Islamic Arabia and subsequently, see FARAS; according to F. Viré, author of the article, this usage did not date back beyond the 4th century A.D.). The term *ribāṭ* is considered by mediaeval Arabic dictionaries as the plural of the singular *rabīṭ* (with a passive sense). The word is said to denote either "the group of horses which have been gathered together in anticipation of combat" (according to the *LʿA*, there should be at least five of them) or "the place where these mares were kept hobbled and where they were fed". In the desert, they were kept under the awnings of tents. But *ribāṭ* could, equally, perform the function of a *maṣdar* of the Form III verb *rābaṭa*. This supplies, in general, the notion of staying or of attachment to a place (or sometimes to a person). But it also applies very precisely to the act of "assembling horses with a view to preparing a razzia" or to the notion of "being ready for combat, having gathered the horses".

It is this specialised sense which seems appropriate to two of the five Ḳurʾānic instances where the root is employed. In both cases, the context is effectively that of preparation for war. In sūra VIII, 60, it is a matter of gathering "horses in sufficient number", *ribāṭ al-khayl*, to intimidate the adversary. The latter is called "enemy of God" and denoted by the periphrasis *alladhīna kafarū* "those who have been ungrateful", in other words—in the late Medinan context—those who have refused alliance with Medina and conversion. In III, 200, there is the final and isolated verse which closes the sūra with a triple exhortation: in order to prevail, there is a need to "show oneself personally resolute" (*aṣbirū*), to "confront the adversary" (not named in this instance) (*ṣabirū*) and to "make *ribāṭ*". The Ḳurʾānic text contains the imperative *rābiṭū*, which would signify, in the context, the act of taking measures consisting in "gathering the mares to show readiness for battle". In this passage, there is no suggestion of "going to the frontier". This meaning can only have emerged at a later stage, either in the period of conquests or in the period which followed it, that of the war of position, which was to see over several centuries the Muslim caliphate in confrontation with its Byzantine opponents, especially on the Cilician borders in the foothills of the Taurus mountains, in the region known as the *thughūr* [see *EI*[1], THAGHR, and also ʿAWĀṢIM and RŪM. 2. in *EI*[2]]. The Central Asian frontier, facing the Turkish world, was to be stabilised to a certain extent, in the mid-2nd/8th century. It was to be further pacified, from the 4th/10th century onward, by means of victorious Muslim incursions into Turkish territory, also by gradually becoming a zone of conversion, allowing a progressive infiltration of Turkish elements into the Muslim lands. However, the sources of the 4th/10th century continue to see it as a "region of *ribāṭs*", which poses a historical problem.

The tribal sense does not seem to have evolved uring the caliphate of Medina and the period of .tūḥ, the great extra-peninsular conquests. There ere certainly numerous opportunities for the prac- ce of *ribāṭ* in the traditional sense. Significant umbers of cavalry mounts were supplied under the *daḳa*, the obligatory contribution of allegiance and lidarity which was levied each year, in kind (i.e. vestock), on the allied tribes. The animals were athered in *ḥimās* [*q.v.*], special pastures under the ontrol of the caliphate. The horses were pastured on site known as *al-Naḳīʿ* (Yāḳūt, *Muʿdjam al-buldān*). ut while the camels were subsequently distributed mong those entitled to them, the caliph ʿUmar decid- d to keep all the horses for purposes of war, thus per- orming an act of *ribāṭ*. The term is not used, but the ccount is unequivocal and testifies to the persistence f the former situation (on this episode, see Abdallah heikh Moussa and Didier Gazagnadou, *Comment on crit l'histoire ... de l'islam!*, in *Arabica*, xl [1993], 208).

In the 3rd/9th and 4th/10th centuries, in exegetical, istoriographical, geographical or legal sources, there ppear some important divergences from this first tratum of meaning and the ancient status of the word *ibāṭ* (the earliest sources date back to the mid-2nd/8th entury; they are few in number and often are only reserved in later works). First to be noted is a ivergence which is less of sense than of purpose. In- reasingly often, the term comes to be associated with he ideology of *djihād* [*q.v.*] as it developed, probably nly after the ʿAbbāsid period. It did so, apparently n uneven fashion, possibly first among the tradi- ionists and historiographers, before passing into the ealm of the jurists. The first post-Ḳurʾānic usages of he representation of *djihād*, as war to the death, are onfused. They are sometimes taken to refer to sec- arian exclusions of the *takfīr* type (descriptive of lisbelief) practised by various ancient movements such as certain Khāridjite or Shīʿī tendencies against heir own co-religionists rather than against the external enemy. In the Ḳurʾān, while often invoked on the subject, it is the term *ḳifāl* and not *djihād* (e.g. IX, 29-35) which refers to conflict with the *Ahl al-Kitāb*.

An interesting perspective, regarding the probable chronology of the change in meaning of a term such as *ribāṭ*, may be found in comparing the most ancient eastern edition of the *Muwaṭṭaʾ* of Mālik b. Anas (d. 179/795 [*q.v.*]) by the Baghdādi Muḥammad al-Shaybānī (d. 189/804, a disciple of Abū Ḥanīfa who was also familiar with the teaching of Mālik), with the major compilations of prophetic traditions of the 3rd/9th century which were soon to be taken for the canonical sum-total of Sunnī Islam. The edition of the easterner al-Shaybani is also opposed to that of the Cordovan Mālikī Yaḥyā al-Maṣmūdī (d. 234/848), in that the content of the two editions is not identical (on these divergences, see Sezgin, *GAS*, i, 458-60). The Cordovan version contains a *Kitāb al-djihād* which does not appear in the text transmitted by al-Shaybani (opinion of Michael Bonner on the subject, in his *Some observations concerning the early development of Jihad on the Arab-Byzantine frontier*, in *SI*, lxxv [1992], 24-5).

The *Muwaṭṭaʾ* compiled by al-Shaybānī (ed. ʿAbd al-Wahhāb ʿAbd al-Laṭīf, Dār al-Taḥrīr, Cairo 1967) seems, curiously, to deny any endorsement of warfare on the frontier in a context of *djihād* (al-Shaybānī is, however, himself the author of a book of *Siyar*, Sezgin, i, 430; this text is preserved in the refutation of al-Shāfiʿī (d. 204/820), which is to be found in the *Kitāb al-Umm*, Beirut 1980, vii, 321-90; it deals with rules of conduct concerning war; this is the sense of the term *siyar* for jurists; it is neither an exhortative nor an apologetic treatise, and *djihād* is not evoked). A brief passage of the *Muwaṭṭaʾ, in the recension of al-*Shaybānī (included at the end of the chapters on prayer, *abwāb al-ṣalāt*) is incorrectly entitled by the editor *faḍl al-djihād* "the virtue attached to *djihād*", while all that appears, in the received tradition, is the Ḳurʾānic expression *al-mudjāhid fī sabīl Allāh*, which refers, probably, to a verse of the type of sūra IV, 95 (in this verse, the expression is in the plural; other Ḳurʾānic usages, II, 218, V, 54 etc., comprise a ver- bal periphrasis with *djāhada*). In this passage of the *Muwaṭṭāʾ*, there is a very brief mention of the Ḳurʾānic stereotype of "death in battle", *shahāda*, without which the word *djihād* is never used as a prop- er noun. This status of a proper noun is effectively non-Ḳurʾānic. It is thus possible to suppose that, in the mid-2nd/8th century, the Medinan scholar (or, at least, his Ḥanafī editor, a generation later) may have belonged to a tendency which was sceptical about war- fare on the frontier, particular with regard to the puri- ty of the intentions of the fighters (they were certainly not regarded as "warriors of faith"; certain traditions accuse them of having no object in mind but booty; see s.v. *maghnam* in Wensinck's *Les Concordances*). In the Cordovan recension (but not in that of al-Shaybānī) there is furthermore attributed to Mālik the transmission of a *ḥadīth*, according to which the most scrupulous piety (ablutions, attendance at the mosque, continual observance of prayer) would be "the true *ribāṭ*", *dhālikum al-ribāṭ* (in this text, the term *ribāṭ* evidently functions as a verbal noun; reference in Wensinck, *op. cit.*, under *ribāṭ*, ii, 212; re-examined, *in extenso*, by *LʿA*, under the root *r-b-ṭ*; also Ibn Ḥanbal's *Musnad*, ²Beirut 1398/1978, ii, 277). This does indeed seem to represent a position which would effec- tively have been professed by Mālik. It is further con- firmed by another passage (included in the chapter on "the virtues of mosques", *faḍl al-masādjid*, 55-6, no. 95, in the recension of al-Shaybānī), according to which "he who goes morning and evening to the mosque", *ghadā aw rāḥa*, without ulterior motive, *lā yurīdu ghayra-hu* ("not wanting anything else"), has the same status as the *mudjāhid*. It should certainly be understood, in this case, that the comparison is made with the Ḳurʾānic *mudjāhid* and not with the contem- porary soldiers of the *thughūr*.

It may be wondered whether these traditions do not allow the supposition of a conflict of representation between traditionists at the end of the 2nd/8th cen- tury. These indications could permit the fixing of the time when the ideology of *djihād*, professed by circles yet to be identified, began to stress the meritorious aspect of military service on the frontier, while in other circles there was manifest opposition to this new point of view (possibly from the peoples of Arabia, i.e. of ʿIrāḳ, against the Syrians, the Khurāsānians and the westerners, Maghribīs and Spaniards; thorough analysis by M. Bonner, *op. cit.*, but the problem of the opposition to this ideology is not addressed). If such was the case, it could be said that this conflict would, as if symbolically, have divided those who, of quietist tendency, aspired to make *mudjāwara* (the *mudjāwirūn* are "those who dwell close to the Kaʿba"; this is the ancient sense of the term, although subsequently the descriptive *mudjāwir* would be applied even to those dwelling in other places considered as sacred or as conferring blessing, including on the frontier), from those who aspired to make *ribāṭ* (the *murābiṭūn*, to be understood in the new sense would be "those who dwell on the frontier"). The latter would have profes- sed a new type of activism. Confirmation for this hypothesis could be found in the anecdote (true or fictitious, but significant as the expression of a point of view) which is put, by the *ʿUyūn al-a͟kh͟bār* of the *adīb* Ibn Ḳutayba (d. 276/889 [*q.v.*]), into the mouth of a major quietist figure of Islamic tradition of the late 2nd/8th century, Fuḍayl b. ʿIyāḍ (he allegedly died as a *mud͟jāwir*, in Mecca, in 187/803). The story related is that of a man who made great efforts to make his way to Ṭarsus, on the frontier and with the intention of making *ribāṭ*. But, following his capture by the Christians, he abjured Islam (*ʿUyūn*, ed. A.Z. al-ʿAdawī, Cairo 1925-30, ii, 365). In another anecdote reported ironically by the *ʿUyūn* (i, 219), an ascetic of al-Maṣṣīṣa [*q.v.*] (Mopsuestis, a city of the Cilician frontier zone) fasted so rigorously that he was driven to the verge of insanity. It is true that in the *Ṣifat al-ṣafwa* of Ibn al-D͟jawzī (d. 597/1200), Fuḍayl is introduced as an admirer of Ibn al-Mubārak (ed. M. Fāk͟hūrī, Aleppo 1393/1973-4, iv, 140-1); but it is his son, Muḥammad b. Fuḍayl, who deserves the credit for putting that person in a position of describing the merits "of *d͟jihād* and of *ribāṭ*" (*op. cit.*, iv, 147). This type of anecdote, which produces a face-to-face encounter between figures of importance, is often of symbolic significance and has little to do with factual history. Whatever the motives behind the ideological exploitation of these figures, the text of Ibn Ḳutayba shows that the representation of the merits of *d͟jihād* does not seem to have been evenly shared during the 3rd/9th century.

The contrast appears very striking, among traditionists, between the time of Mālik and that of the major figures of the following century: the Bag͟hdādī Ibn Ḥanbal [*q.v.*] (d. 241/855, numerous passages of the *Musnad*, see *Concordances*, under *d͟jihād* and *ribāṭ*); the Transoxianian al-Buk͟hārī (d. 256/870 [*q.v.*]), *Ṣaḥīḥ*; the work contains a *Bāb faḍl al-d͟jihād wa 'l-siyar*, iv, 17-128, *Maṭābiʿ al-s͟haʿb*, n.p. 1378/1958-9, 51 (certain traditions relate battles against Constantinople, "the city of Caesar" and against the Turks); the K͟hurāsānians Muslim (d. 261/875 [*q.v.*]), *Ṣaḥīḥ*, Beirut n.d. (passages are to be found in the *K. al-d͟jihād wa 'l-siyar*, v, 139-200, and in the *K. al-imāra*, vi, 2-55), Ibn Mād͟ja (d. 273/886 [*q.v.*]), *Sunan*, ii, *K. al-d͟jihād*, 920/61, ed. M.F. ʿAbd al-Bāḳī, Maṭbaʿat al-Ḥalabī, Cairo n.d.), Abū Dāwūd al-Sid͟jistānī (d. 275/888 [*q.v.*]), *Sunan*, iii, *K. al-d͟jihād*, 3-93, ed. M.M. ʿAbd al-Ḥamīd, n.p. n.d. (a passage on the merits involved in waging war successfully against the Byzantines, *Rūm*, 5), al-Tirmid͟hī (d. 279/892 [*q.v.*]), *Sunan*, iii, *K. abwāb faḍāʾil al-d͟jihād*, 88-131, ed. ʿA.R. Muḥammad ʿUt͟hmān, Cairo 1384/1964) and al-Nasāʾī (d. 303/915 [*q.v.*]), *Sunan*, vi, *K. al-d͟jihād*, 2-50, ed. Ḥ.M. al-Masʿūdī, Beirut n.d. All present special chapters, sometimes very long, in which the term *d͟jihād* is employed, without ambiguity, as a proper noun. The traditions related in these chapters stress the need to conduct, "in the way of God", *fī sabīl Allāh*, warfare on the frontier, whether this is in the East, facing the Turkish steppes, or in the Cilician border zone, confronting Byzantium. These traditionists do not deal with the West, where, nevertheless, the same ideology seems to have been put into effect in various ways, in the action of the autonomous province of the Ag͟hlabids, in Ifrīḳiya, or in that of the Umayyad caliphate of Spain (on the "existence of the *ribāṭ*" in al-Andalus, see references given by C.E. Bosworth, *art. cit.*, 276, 285; A. Castro, *The structure of Spanish history*, Princeton 1954, 88-9, 202). *D͟jihād* is presented as situated, in direct line, in the tradition of Muḥammad's conflict with the polytheists of Arabia. All these works include, in the context of *d͟jihād*, traditions concerning *ribāṭ*. The term seems to have gone beyond th second level of "assembling of mounts", arriving a the sole meaning of "prolonged presence on the fron tier" (*mulāzamat al-t͟hag͟hr*, according to *LʿA*). The term nevertheless continues to imply a presence "unde arms". Some special traditions dealt with *irtibāṭ*. Th second term continues to apply to the mounts them selves and to the need to keep them in good conditio (the combattants in frontier expeditions theoretical all being horsemen).

In all these texts of the 3rd/9th century, the ter *ribāṭ* and its derivatives thus revive, with modifica tions, the ancient tribal sense. It should be noted th on the Byzantine frontier there is never any questic of an edifice bearing the name *ribāṭ*. The fortification have different names, according to their nature. Th word *ḥiṣn* "fortress" seems to dominate. It is contair ed in a number of toponyms. Often these are cor structions prior to Islam which have been restored (o this zone, see for example the references concernin Tarsus/Ṭarsūs and Mopsuestis/al-Maṣṣīṣa, which ar ancient fortified towns; descriptions of the Cilicia plain and its cities in Cl. Cahen, *La Syrie du Nord l'époque des croisades*, Paris 1940, 148-52; on genuin and mythical history, C.E. Bosworth, *art. cit.*; on th absence of designation by the term *ribāṭ*, 285).

It should be noted, in particular, as regards thi zone (the point of departure for caliphal summer ex peditions, known as *ṣawāʾif* [see ṢĀʾIFA], description i the *K. al-K͟harād͟j* of Ḳudāma b. D͟jaʿfar, 259, se below), that, from a historical viewpoint, the ideolog of *d͟jihād* seems to correspond poorly with the realitie of frontier warfare, in the first and second Muslin centuries, and even later. The army consisted of pro fessional soldiers, receiving pay, the *ʿaṭāʾ* [*q.v.*], an groups of mercenary irregulars, often drawn fron tribal splinter-groups and led by their own chieftains These last receivd the *d͟juʿl* (A. Cheikh Moussa and D Gazagnadou, *op. cit.*, 224, nn. 153-4), a kind of con tract, regarded as degrading (other forms with the same meaning, *d͟jiʿāl, d͟jaʿāla, d͟jaʿīla*, etc.; the same term served to designate the sum, levied in advance as insurance against failure to participate in ar obligatory razzia). These quasi-autonomous troops pillaged on their own account and were excluded fron official booty, the *mag͟hnam*. They had thei equivalent, on the Byzantine side of the frontier. Unequivocal confirmation of the presence on the frontie of these irregular troops (who seem to have nothing to do with "battle for the faith") is to be found in the seventh chapter of the *K. al-K͟harād͟j*, which is devoted specifically to frontier zones, on the Muslim side as well as on that of its adversaries: *D͟hikr t͟hug͟hūr al-Islām wa 'l-umam wa 'l-ad͟jyāl al-muṭīfa bi-hā*, 252-66 (edition following the *Kitāb al-Masālik wa 'l-mamālik* of Ibn K͟hurradād͟hbih (d. 272/885 [*q.v.*], ed. De Goeje). The *K. al-K͟harād͟j*, preserved only in part, ostensibly had for its author a Bag͟hdādī secretary occupying a senior position in the caliphal administration, Ḳudāma b. D͟jaʿfar [*q.v.*], who died at the beginning of the 4th/10th century. In this text, the frontier garrisons are explicitly described as composed of "regular soldiers", *d͟jund*, and of *ṣaʿālīk*. It is known that this term (sing. *ṣuʿlūk*), denoted, in Arabia, the tribal outcasts and brigands who often joined together in bands (Barbier de Meynard translated this as "irregular troops", *op. cit.*, 193, 194, see also MUTAṬAWWIʿA). It is worth noting the totally a-religious tone of this secretary of the caliphal administration, who deploys a varied vocabulary to speak of the different defensive works of the frontiers (the word *ribāṭ* is never used to denote a building of ny kind). There is an unexpected and very significant verbal use of *rābaṭa* which is taken in its strictly military sense when speaking of the frontier of Daylam on which there is said to have been "stationed", *yurābiṭūn*, garrisons of Persian horsemen, *sāwira*. It is crucial to note that this situation is given s describing affairs "before Islam" (*op. cit.*, Arabic ext, 261, tr. 202). Finally, a tradition preented as Prophetal ostensibly discouraged attacks gainst the Turks, "who should be left alone as long s they leave you alone" (a play of words on the rabic root *t-r-k*, Arabic text, 262, tr. 204). What is erhaps nothing more than a pleasantry on the part of diplomatic secretary challenged the validity of the epresentation of a permanent *djihād* against the Turks of the steppes which is described by numerous uthors of this period (it is true that Ḳudāma seems o be speaking of the caliphal period or that of the Ṭāhirid governorate, and probably not that of the āmānids; but as will be seen, below, their overall olicy seems to have been of much the same nature). Another important passage regarding the composition f irregular troops is provided by the geographer Ibn Ḥawḳal (d. 367/977 [*q.v.*]), who compares with the ew Sāmānid armies of the 4th/10th century, composed of loyal and disciplined "Turkish slaves" (*al-atrāk l-mamlūkūn*), the "dregs of the tribes" (*shudhdhādh al-abā'il*), lacking any sense of faith or law, who in ormer times fought on the frontier (they are also alled *ṣa*ʿ*ālīk al-*ʿ*asākir, K. Ṣūrat al-arḍ*[2], 471, ch. on Transoxiana). Later, in the period of the Crusades, even if collective emotion sometimes inspired groups f volunteers nourished with the ideology of *djihād*, a ong-standing component of belief, it was not the 'warriors of faith'' who were to recapture the cities nd fortresses under Christian domination. Those who fought these battles were first the Saldjūḳ *amīrs* of Syria with their Turcoman contingents (N. Elisséeff, *Nūr al-dīn*, Damascus 1967, ii, 317; Sivan does not hare this writer's reservations, see his *L'Islam et les Croisades. Idéologie et propagande dans les réactions musulmanes aux Croisades*, Paris 1968), and then the professional Ayyūbid armies, well-trained and equipped. These armies were composed essentially of Turko-Kurdish elements [see AYYŪBIDS and also ḤAṬṬĪN, ḤIṬṬĪN, Ṣalāh al-Dīn's great victory near Tiberias n 583/1187].

However, the assumptions of the ideology of *djihād* are entirely different. It is "the Muslims" (a vague and sociological expression without any real significance) who are supposed to commit themselves as "volunteers", *muṭṭawwi*ʿ*a*, to play the role of *mudjāhidūn*, "those who perform *djihād*" or *murābiṭūn*, "those who perform *ribāṭ*" on the frontier. They are also said to have born the name of *ghāzī* [*q.v.*], pl. *ghuzāt*, which seems to originate from the frontier of Khurāsān and Transoxiana, a symbolic name which recalls the warriors of the mythologised *ghazwa* [*q.v.*] of the Prophet (the term is, however, used by Ḳudāma in a neutral fashion). In the sources of the 4th/10th century, the representation of *djihād* seems to be promulgated in two major directions. On the one hand, there is Ṣūfism, which tends to lay claim to an irreproachable past (J. Chabbi, *Réflexions sur le soufisme iranien primitif*, in *JA*, cclxvi [1978]). But it seems that certain minorities within Sunnism professed parallel ideas, advocating exterior activism and inner moralisation. The movement appears to have expanded during the 5th/11th century. In the East, works of theoretical law, like those of applied law, henceforth deal with the question (on the *Wadjīz* of al-Ghazālī (d. 505/111), see H. Laoust, *La politique de Gazālī*, Paris 1970, 264, 342-3). The same applies to numerous works of theology: the Ashʿarī Abū Manṣūr ʿAbd al-Ḳāhir al-Baghdādī (d. 429/1037), the great scourge of the lukewarm or the deviant in matters of religion, gives in his *Uṣūl al-dīn* an overtly activist interpretation of *djihād* in giving it the basis of "commandment of good and prohibition of evil" (ed. Madrasat al-ilāhiyyāt, Istanbul 1928, 193-4). As for the West, the *Risāla* of the Mālikī Ibn Abī Zayd al-Ḳayrawānī (d. 386/996), contains, in ch. xxx, a *Bāb fi 'l-djihād* (ed. J. Carbonel, Algiers 1945, 63-7: mention of the merit attached to performance of *ribāṭ* in a *thaghr*, 165). H. Laoust, who published numerous Ḥanbalī ʿ*aḳīdas*, declared that, in the most ancient ones, the term *ghazw* occurs more frequently than *djihād* (*La profession de foi d'Ibn Baṭṭa*, Damascus 1958, 47, 127). This is the case with the ʿ*Aḳīda* of Ibn Baṭṭa (d. 387/997). This could indicate that the principle of *djihād* is no longer an issue for theoretical speculation on the part of the author concerned. On the other hand, in the work of the later Ḥanbalī Ibn Ḳudāma (d. 620/1223), *djihād* is the only issue (H. Laoust, *Le précis de droit d'Ibn Kudāma*, Damascus 1950, 271-81, tr. and annotation of the ʿ*Umda*, which is a summary of the celebrated *Mughnī fi 'l-uṣūl*: a passage on the duration of residence of the *ribāṭ* type on the frontier, 272; *djihād* in the *Mughnī*, x, 364-97).

As a historical guide, it may be noted that the *Kitāb al-Umm* of al-Shāfiʿī (d. 204/820 [*q.v.*]), ed. Beirut 1980, followed by the *Mukhtaṣar* of al-Muzanī (d. 264/877), includes, on the one hand, traditional chapters of *siyar*, on the law of war, with a discussion, *radd*, on the ideas of Mālik (vii, 201-84) and of the treatise on *siyar* attributed to al-Awzāʿī (the text is given in the context of its refutation by the Ḥanbalī Abū Yūsuf (d. 182/798), vii, 352-89). The work contains, on the other hand, a theory of *djihād*, which is included in the *Kitāb al-djizya* (iv, 167-222, on *djihād*, esp. 170-80). In these passages, al-Shāfiʿī formulates, for the first time, the definition of *farḍ kifāya*, "collective obligation" in regard to external war (*K. al-Umm*, iv, 176, is opposed to individual duty, *farḍ* ʿ*ayn*, see DJIHĀD). He defines the obligations of the caliphate, as well as the precautions to be taken to ensure that the campaigns (at least annual, or biennial when this is possible) do not end in disaster, *mahlaka* (*K. al-Umm, tafrī*ʿ *farḍ al-djihād*, iv, 177-8). The defensive situation of the frontier, *thughur* (or *aṭrāf*, "the extremities") is evoked (the presence of fortresses, *ḥuṣūn*, and ditches and ramparts, *khanādiḳ*, is assumed). The frontiers should be manned with soldiers. Their status as warriors of the faith is given no particular emphasis. They are under the command of trusted, wise and courageous men. When an attack, *ghazwa*, has been launched and there is a risk of it failing, the soldiers must withdraw to their camp and to the *ribāṭ al-djihād*. This expression does not seem to denote a type of building which could be called *ribāṭ*. It appears rather to refer to the operational base where defensive measures could be taken. The phrase would simply signify that there should be no hesitation in returning to the camp or the fortress which is the point of departure, when an operation has been begun but its continuation appears hazardous. This passage would indicate that, at the beginning of the 3rd/9th century, there seems to be no question of the presence of warrior-monks, volunteers of the faith, on the frontier, at least in regard to that of Byzantium, which seems to be the only one under consideration here. It is even less likely that they would be gathered together in buildings of their own. It may be supposed that this representation of a warlike monasticism reflects, in

term *ribāṭ* which was to be used in the 4th/10th century, he uses the term *khān* [*q.v.*] to denote the caravanserai and *sikka* for the "relay" of the postal service *barīd* [*q.v.*] (association of the *khān* and the *sikka*, in certain isolated "stages", *manzil*, 209, 210), and this over the whole extent of the empire (however, it is generally supposed that it was the relays of the eastern post which were called *ribāṭ* [see BARĪD].). Even if local powers from time to time conducted a more offensive policy (without disruption of commerce, and in particular, the very lucrative trade in slaves, some of whom were to become caliphal soldiers from the 3rd/9th century onward, see GHULĀM), it may be noted that the Muslim rulers of Persia finally found themselves in a situation similar to that of the empires which had preceded them, confronted by nomads from the north and the east (a legendary evocation of relations between the Sāsānid Anūshirwān and the king of the Khazars, which led the former to build a wall of bricks, *ḥā'iṭ*, against the raids of the nomads, intractable subjects of the latter, Ḳudāma, 259-61).

A related question concerns, in particular, the representation of *djihād* on the eastern frontiers of Persia. It may be wondered whether what is presented, in the sources, as a generalised *djihād*, performed from the starting-point of thousands of *ribāṭs*, in fact reflects historical facts. Al-Muḳaddasī speaks of a thousand *ribāṭs* at Paykand, on the border of Bukhara (282). They are said to be "in ruins" or disused, *kharāb*, or "in active use", *ʿāmir*, although the respective proportion is not given. The same author states the presence (without specifying whether active or otherwise) of 1,700 *ribāṭs* at Isfīdjāb, on the right bank of the Syr Darya or Sayḥūn (273; Ibn Ḥawḳal also speaks of a thousand *ribāṭs* at Paykand, 489). These highly implausible figures are probably a reflection of hyperbole and mythic representation. In fact, the historical elements of the context (drawn from historiographical sources, as well as from certain passages of the geographers themselves), on the policy conducted by the local Muslim powers (the Ṭāhirid governors at first, later, the Sāmānid *amīrs*), during the 3rd/9th and 4th/10th centuries, confronted by the Turkish peoples of the steppe (Ghuzz, Ḳarluḳ [*q.vv.*], Arabic *Kharlūkh*), present a quite different picture. In both cases, it is a policy of defence (based on fortresses, *ḥiṣn* or *ḳuhandiz* (the Persian word), of towns encircled by walls, *muḥaṣṣana*, or by ditches and ramparts *khandaḳ*, especially in Khʷārazm, works of which many must have been pre-Islamic) and not of attack, which seems to have been practised once the conquests had reached the unclear, but traditional, frontier of the steppe. In response to raids by the Turkish nomads (who normally took the initiative), there appear to have been punitive Muslim expeditions, of which the best-known is that of the Sāmānid Ismāʿīl I (279-95/892-907 [*q.v.*]) against one of the Turkish centres of population, that of the Ḳarluḳ, the town of Ṭalas, in 280/893. This must have established calm on the frontier for most of the 4th/10th century. From this period, which is precisely contemporary with that of the geographer-travellers, the warfare would have been over. This was achieved, furthermore, by the progressive conversion of the Turkish border tribes. Information on these conversions is also found in the writings of the geographers themselves who, furthermore (without concern over contradictions or over anachronisms), continue to speak of the burgeoning activity of the *ribāṭs* and of the influx of volunteers. Al-Muḳaddasī tends to hark back to this theme, which had probably become, in part, mythic: on Ush in Farghāna, *muṭṭawwiʿa*, 272; the district Paykand, to the west of Bukhārā, *ghuzāt*, 282. H mentions, however, some precise examples whic seem more plausible. Such would be the case of th approaches to the mountain massif of the Ghūr [*q.v.* between Harāt and Bāmiyān. This region was not, i fact, to be conquered and converted until the 5th/11 century, by Maḥmūd of Ghazna (cf. al-Muḳaddas 306). In this region, it is furthermore not so much question of volunteers as of regular soldier "posted", *murattabūn*, there, and of "watchmen' *ḥurrās*. Similarly, in the description of a forward po in the district of Ustuwā, two places are mentione which are called *ribāṭ*, or rather pertaining to *ribāṭ* (i the capacity of a verbal noun), where there are st tioned "ardent and decisive men", *ridjāl shihām*, wel equiped with arms and with horses. It is impossible tell whether this refers to volunteers. They ai deployed, facing the sands, in three forts, *ḥiṣn*, "link ed together", *muttaṣila*, one of them being defende by a ditch and rampart, *khandaḳ* (al-Muḳaddasī, 320 The mode of expression is lyrical; it could refer to th reality of the previous century. On the other hanc Ibn Ḥawḳal provides a significant extract on the cor verted tribes installed on the pasture-lands of Shāsh the region of what is today Tashkent (511; a Muḳaddasī is decidedly more discreet, 274). Furthe more, it was soon to be the Muslim irregulars of th frontier who were causing problems. In the articl GHĀZĪ, Cl. Cahen defines them as companies c "mercenaries" and not as volunteers for the faith (may be recalled that Ḳudāma and Ibn Ḥawḳal spol of *saʿālīk* to denote these irregulars, see above). Fo want of external action, they seem to have found diversion in participating in various revolts, includin one in Sāmānid Bukhara, in 318/930 [see GHĀZĪ] Some reportedly sought in the mid-4th/10th centur to leave for the West (*Camb. hist. Iran*, iv, *Th Sāmānids*, ed. R.N. Frye, 155). Others were probabl employed by Maḥmūd the Ghaznawid in his expedi tions to the Pandjāb at the beginning of the 5th/11t century. It could almost be said that, it is only whe the mercenaries of the frontier have left the scene, tha the warriors of faith make their entrance, in a idealised representation of the past, in this region jus as in the Syrian marches.

From these first elements it can be seen that it is n longer possible to subscribe, in a global manner, t the definition of G. Marçais, who presents *ribāṭ* (in hi *EI*[1] article s.v.) as "a type of establishment, bot religious and military, which seems quite specificall Muslim" and which would have appeared "at an ear ly stage". It is no longer possible to retain as "cur rent" the interpretation of "fortified convent" (se above). Before drawing hasty conclusions, the mos prudent course is, without doubt, to analyse th sources and to identify the points where usage seem to indicate the presence of edifices called *ribāṭ*. Thi will not be sufficient to indicate whether it is th edifice itself which bears this name or it is the functio assigned to it which accounts for the name. In the firs case, there would effectively be a specific construc tion. In the second case, there would be a commo name denoting various types of edifice, according t the function attributed to them. Thus the full range c evolutionary senses of the verbal noun would be en countered, from preparation for combat, to vigilanc or to a protected halting-place (a use as verbal nou in the writings of al-Muḳaddasī, 303, with referenc to Badakhshān, in the mountains of the upper Oxu basin).

Furthermore, a careful reading of the texts reveal

at it is probably a mistake to attribute a military nction to certain *ribāṭs*; sometimes the reference ems to be to a simple hospice for travellers, especially in the case of an edifice situated at the gate of a city, unded by a specifically-named individual and maintained by the incomes of a *waḳf* or mortmain (see ʼAḲF, and Cahen, *Réflexions sur le waqf ancien*, in *Les uples musulmans dans l'histoire médiévale*, Damascus 977, 287-306). This would be the case of the four *bāṭs* of Isfīdjāb, each situated at the gates of the town nd not in the vicinity of the great mosque, as sugested by the unclear text of al-Muḳaddasī, 272-3; cf. on Ḥawḳal, 510, making possible a correction of Miuel, iv, 56), on an important route leading from the ajor regional metropolises. These hospice-*ribāṭs* em to have been specifically for the accommodation travellers who were natives of these cities (see the ase of the *ribāṭ* probably founded by Ḳaratigin, a āmānid military dignitary, who is buried there and ho converted into *waḳf* the revenues of a market; anther possible case, in the writings of al-Muḳaddasī, the *ribāṭ* of Mīrkī (?), the founder of which was a āmānid *amīr*; in this case, too, the establishment is in e environs of the town, 275). On the other hand, in e writings of Ibn Ḥawḳal passages are found which ndicate more clearly the purpose of the edifice: *ribāṭs* or travellers on internal routes maintained by the *akfs*, *manāzil wa-ribāṭāt mawḳūfa ʿalā sābilat al-ṭarīḳ* 401). As for the *ribāṭ* situated on the plain to the north f Usrūshana, facing the steppe which borders on the eft bank of the Sayḥūn, the foundation of which is atributed to the celebrated Afshīn [*q.v.*], the prince of his province who distinguished himself in far-flung ampaigns (before ultimately being imprisoned as a ebel, in Sāmarrā, in 226/841), it seems to be of istinctly military purpose (Ibn Ḥawḳal, 504-5; this nstitution was supported by the revenues of lands which had been constituted as *waḳf*). The verb *banā* learly denotes the effective construction of an edifice y this person. It is, however, not known whether it was originally intended as a *ribāṭ*. Clearly less ambiguous are the passages in the works of geographers oncerning the halting-places on internal routes called *ibāṭ*. They are generally denoted by a composite exression, "the *ribāṭ* of...", followed by a place or the ame of a founder (Miquel, iv, 55, n. 120, mentionng in particular Ibn Ḥawḳal, 454, with a commenary of the latter on the services provided by the *ribāṭ* s place of protection or accommodation; see also al-Mukaddasi, 291, a *ribāṭ* outside the town, near Bukhārā, founded and financed by a Sāmānid *amīr*). But these halting-places were also very often established in connection with the postal service, the *barīd* nd its relays, especially in eastern and central Persia. The term *ribāṭ* is applied to them specifically by al-Muḳaddasī (thus differing from Ḳudāma, see above), n his lists of itineraries in the east (372, 493; in western Khurāsān, with a description of the *ribāṭ* ounded by Ibn Sīmdjūr, the Sāmānid general.

It is, however, quite true that certain *ribāṭs* (which did not necessarily originate as military establishments; here too, each case must be analysed separately) seem to have been ultimately represented as *mashāhid* (mentioned by Miquel, iv, 51, n. 92), signifying both "[supposed] places of martyrdom" and "blessed places". A legendary tomb is often associated with them. It may appeal to a collective patronage, that of the "Companions of Muḥammad", on an itinerary of the region of Naysābūr, in Khurāsān (al-Muḳaddasī, 334). It may even claim identification with great mythical figures such as Dhu 'l-Ḳarnayn, the Ḳurʾānic Alexander and the mysterious prophet Dhu 'l-Kifl (Ḳurʾān, XXI, 85). These two figures are associated with two twin *ribāṭs*, each situated on a bank of the Oxus, one on the Hephthalite side, that of the *Hayṭal* [see HAYĀṬILA], and the other on the side of Khurāsān, downriver from Tirmidh (mentioned by Miquel, *loc. cit.*; list in al-Muḳaddasī, 291, 333). Also to be found (idem, 292), is the exceptional mention of *mudjāwirūn* in a *ribāṭ* (guard-post or halting-place?) which apparently served as a crossing-point of the Oxus. *Djiwār*, originally linked with residence in Mecca, is to be understood here in an extended sense, perhaps referring to non-combatant pietists, possibly preachers and evangelists. The movement of the Karrāmiyya [*q.v.*] could possibly have played a role of this type in the Turkish zone, under the Sāmānids and then under the Ghaznawids. This role is also attributed to the Ṣūfīs with whom the Karrāmiyya are often confused. It should be remembered, however, that Ṣūfīs did not appear in Persia until the mid-4th/10th century (see Chabbi, *op. cit.*, and eadem, *Remarques sur le développement historique des mouvements ascétiques et mystiques au Khurāsān* in *SI* [1977]). The facts of the sanctification of certain sites, called *ribāṭ* by certain authors, should, in this writer's opinion, be often considered (at least on the eastern border; the situation in the West is less clear, see below, in regard to Ifriḳiya), as phenomena adduced *a posteriori*, especially in the case of military posts which had lost their importance or fallen into disuse. It is clear that each passage needs to be examined in detail and compared with parallel sources, since each case seems to pose different questions, even when the same region is under discussion. In any case, the important question remains open: who is finally responsible for allocating the name *ribāṭ* to certain edifices—the founders, the actual users, or later authors describing events?

ii. *The central coastal zones and the western frontier*

According to Ḳudāma's formula, all the coasts from Syria to Egypt are *thaghrs* (253; details of the coastal cities, 255; a brief paragraph is devoted, at the end of the chapter, to the *thughūr al-gharb* which begin with Ifrīḳiya, 265-6). The geographers of the 4th/10th century are less synthetic in approach. They do not omit to mention all the fortified towns of the coast (*musawwara*, encircled by a *sūr*, wall, or *muḥaṣṣana*, defended like a *ḥiṣn*; these expressions are recurrent in their writings). It is therefore surprising, with regard to these coasts, that there are so few references to *ribāṭs*, except in the cases of Ifrīḳiya and of Sicily. Ibn Ḥawḳal confines himself to saying that Damascenes go to Beirut to perform *ribāṭ*, sc. *yurābiṭūn*, with the soldiers, when there is an appeal in case of danger (*istinfār* "call to arms, general mobilisation", 175; no site of the Near Eastern littoral is mentioned). Concerning the frontiers of the West, al-Muḳaddasī confines himself to very vague formulae: the Maghrib is in a state of permanent *djihād* (215, the same applying to Cordova, 233). The coasts of Sicily are "noble *thaghrs*" which contain "superb *ribāṭs*", *thughūr djalīla wa-ribāṭāt fāḍila* (or superb "places of *ribāṭ*"?) (15); as for Ibn Ḥawḳal, he goes into most detail when describing Ifrīḳiya and Sicily, see below. On the other hand, with regard to the coasts of the eastern Mediterranean, al-Muḳaddasī makes a double exception. This concerns, on the one hand, the whole of the coast-line controlled by Ramla, the "capital", *ḳaṣaba*, of the district of Palestine, a city some distance removed from the littoral, and on the other hand, the zone of Damietta, Dimyāṭ, in Egypt. There are said to have been, on the coast at Damietta, numerous *ribāṭ* (edifices or verbal noun denoting a place of *ribāṭ*?)

which are not otherwise adduced. They presumably had a "season" of activity, *mawsim*, during which there was an influx of *murābiṭūn*. The passage is fairly enigmatic (203). It is perhaps linked to maritime conditions, which rendered approach to the Egyptian coast extremely difficult for the greater part of the year. The *ribāṭ*s dependent on Ramla are even more surprising (177; Miquel has partially translated the passage, in *La géographie humaine*, iv, 55). The points on the coast identified as *ribāṭ* represent the totality of maritime cities of the Palestinian coast or their ports. The city itself may be somewhat removed from the coast, as is the case of Ghazza in relation to Mīmās in the south and of Azdūd and Yubnā in the central zone. The port of these two small cities is called *māḥūz* (a word normally meaning "space between two armies", which could be applied to a maritime forward post in relation to the city by which it is controlled). The other *ribāṭ*s are fortified cities situated directly on the seaboard, Ascalon or ʿAsḳalān (between Mīmās and Azdūd), Jaffa or Yāfā (considered to be the port of Ramla) and finally Arsūf, a fortified port situated further to the north (description of the defensive works of these cities, 174, with the exception of Azdūd and Yubnā, which are mentioned only in the above-mentioned passage, 177). Given this context, it is reasonable to assume that it is a question of places where *ribāṭ* was practised, rather than of edifices of a particular type. The latter are described, furthermore, by their customary names, whether it is a case of "fortresses", *ḥiṣn*, small forts with "observation towers", *maḥāris* (sing. *maḥras*; these were apparently especially numerous in the zone of Ascalon. The town is described as *kathīrat al-maḥāris*, 174). The *ribāṭ* which, according to al-Muḳaddasī, is practised in this zone is of a very particular type. It is not a question of combat but of *fidāʾ* [*q.v.* in Suppl.], "the ransoming of prisoners" (the principal source on this subject is al-Masʿūdī, *Tanbīh*, 189-96, who deals with official "campaigns" of ransom conducted by caliphal representatives; there is no mention of ransoms effected on the Palestinian coast). Miquel has good reason for wondering whether, in fact, it was not rather a matter of exchange (ii, 471). According to the procedure described by al-Muḳaddasī as regards the Palestinian coasts, as soon as the galleys and barques arriving from the Christian shores (their provenance is not specified) are sighted, the alarm is raised throughout the region. The inhabitants come to negotiate in the above-mentioned ports. Such activities are highly plausible, especially as it is unclear who, in the event, represented the Christian side (legitimate traders or pirates?) Besides, it would not be unreasonable to wonder whether, from a historical point of view, all actions on these coasts were motivated purely by faith, as the sources would have us piously believe.

Ifrīḳiya is reputed to have supplied the most ancient evidence of the existence of an establishment known as *ribāṭ*. The earliest foundations reportedly date back to the first half-century of the ʿAbbāsid period, shortly before the appearance of the hereditary Aghlabid governorate (established from 184/800 onward). The purpose would have been to reinforce the coastal defences against raids launched from the Christian shores of the north. The Aghlabids [*q.v.*] continued this policy, erecting numerous walls and fortresses. The first expeditions against Sicily were mounted in 211/187 and its capital, Palermo or Bālarm, was taken in 216/831. There is doubt as to which is the more ancient, the *ribāṭ* of Monastir or that of Sousse (see MONASTIR for this city and constructions in other near-by towns, Sousse and the region of Mahdiyya). Ib Ḥawḳal gives the most detailed account concernin the whole of this region, including Sicily. He seems t have been present in the area in 361/972. Concernin the fortress which is today considered as the *ribāṭ* Monastir (which is a fortress, *ḳaṣr*, to which simil works were to be added, at a later stage, by variou local powers, from the Fāṭimids to the Zīrīds, th whole constituting *ḳuṣūr*), the question is the same that posed in the East, whether the edifice was reall called, from the outset, a *ribāṭ* or is it a case of simpl extension of the verbal noun, denoting the "place *ribāṭ*"? Perusal of the text devoted to the city by Ib Ḥawḳal suggests that the second hypothesis is valid, least for the ancient period. The few lines dealing wit the shores of central Tunisia (73) include three uses the term. The first could indicate either an edifice, c a place of residence, *ribāṭ yaskunu-hu umma min al-nā* "a *ribāṭ* (a place of *ribāṭ*), where a significant numbe of people reside", *ʿalā 'l-ayyām wa 'l-sāʿāt*, "accordin to days and periods", *yuʿrafu bi-Munastīr*, "(plac which is known by the name of Munastīr". Th second use appears in an expression which makes *rib* a functional epithet (*ḳaṣr ribāṭ*, "a fortress having th function of *ribāṭ*"). The third use is a verbal noun "there are at the edge of the sea two large fortresses" *ḳaṣrān ʿaẓīmān, li 'l-ribāṭ wa 'l-ʿibāda*, "for *ribāṭ* an religious observance", *ʿalay-himā awḳāf kathīra b Ifrīḳiya*, "which are maintained by the benefits c numerous *waḳf*s situated in Ifrīḳiya", *wa 'l-ṣadaḳ taʾtī-hā min kulli arḍ* "and by alms which come fron everywhere".

There is no doubt that, at a later stage, when the military role had perhaps become less important, th fortresses of Monastir were considered as sanctifie sites, favoured by the nobility as places of intermen (see MONASTIR: the acts of piety related by the source are, however, perhaps interpreted a little too literall here). It could be considered that the text of Ib Ḥawḳal tends to idealise the situation on the coast c Africa (as also the case of Salé in Morocco, confron ting the Barghwāṭa Berbers, considered at the time t be unconverted, 81-2), while he castigates the vic prevalent in the Sicilian places of *ribāṭ* (121; partial tr A. Miquel, in *La géographie humaine*, iv, 55). Historica reality probably lies between the two extremes. How ever, there may well have been periods during whic zealous Muslims (or simply citizens anxious to par ticipate in the defence and security of their homes could have succeeded in transforming these fortresse into convents, as is postulated by numerous moder studies. If mystical movements were able at a late stage partially to occupy this type of edifice, they seen absolutely unrepresentative of the situations whicl could have arisen in more ancient times.

In Andalusia, three marches confronted the Christ ian kingdoms, including the famous Galician march *thaghr al-djalāliḳa*. The war which was waged agains the local Christians, "of quarrelsome and obstinat temperament", was, according to Ibn Ḥawḳal (who i manifestly prejudiced), a war characterised b trickery and ambushes which have little to do with th rules of chivalry, *furūsiyya*. No mention of *ribāṭ* is to b found in his text (111, 114; but the province of Spai appears to be little known; only a few pages deal wit it). In this respect, al-Muḳaddasī is equally vague; o the difficulties of documentation regarding Muslin Spain in the early period, see AL-ANDALUS. (iii "Outline of the historical geography of al-Andalus" on military history, very rich in varied vicissitudes (vi "General survey of the history of al-Andalus". I may, however, be wondered whether the lands of th

Muslim West genuinely link, to a greater extent than n the east, military action and guarding of the fron-ier to a sustained devotional practice (which is not to e confused with a mystical practice!) A critical study f the sources on this subject would unquestionably be a worthwhile project. The Sicilian counter-example which Ibn Ḥawḳal gives, with a view to denouncing t, and which describes the undesirable elements of the rontier, is very significant in this respect. On the ther hand, it is no doubt necessary to take account, as in continuity with ancient usages and not as a novelty, of the fact noted by G. Marçais [see RIBĀṬ in *EI*[1]], concerning the existence, in Spanish, of the word *rebato* to denote "an action performed by a troop of horsemen in conformity with Muslim tactics". Encountered in this definition is the precise basic sense of the verbal noun of the early caliphal period. It does not go as far as the original *ribāṭ*, on the banks of the Senegal river, which has long been reckoned the point of departure of the Almoravid Berbers, a fact which is not today held in doubt [see H.T. Norris, AL-MURĀBIṬŪN]. The Almoravid movement, which began in the Maghrib at the beginning of the 5th/11th century, passed into Spain during the final quarter of the same century (479/1086, victory of Yūsuf b. Tāshfīn at Zallāḳa, see P. Chalmeta, AL-MURĀBIṬŪN. iv. "The Almoravids in Spain") and dominates it politically, while unleashing war on the frontier, using both regular troops and mercenaries, exactly as in the East. In this context, there seems however to appear, as a specific case, the activity of certain splinter-groups of Mālikism from the Maghrib which preached an activist application of religious observance. This would be the case of the founder of the *Dār al-murābiṭīn* (mentioned by Norris, in *art. cit.*, and located in the Moroccan Sous) which apparently professed a blend of pietism and warfare. This movement could first have inspired the faith of the Saharan Almoravids, then that of the ideologues who followed them, and who were to be recruited into circles of jurists of the Mālikī persuasion. It is nevertheless important not to continue to confuse these modalities of active observance, perfectly identified (which could, in certain aspects, be compared, in the East, to Ḥanbalī activism and, much later, to Wahhābism) with the use which the Ṣūfīs and the mystical brotherhoods were to make of the institution of *ribāṭ*. On the contrary, the Almohad *ribāṭ*s of the 6th/12th century, mentioned by G. Marçais in his *EI*[1] article, seem, at first sight, to be of a far more classical nature, since their role is that of *ribāṭ Tāzā* [*q.v.* in *EI*[1]], the base of operations for anti-Almoravid action. As for the *ribāṭ al-fatḥ* [*q.v.*], it was the mustering point for men and materials awaiting transfer to Spain. Before becoming the site of the future city of Rabat, this area of coastal *ribāṭ* apparently served as a necropolis for the Marīnids (after the example of certain *ribāṭ*s of Ifrīḳiya, for the local dynasties: see RIBĀṬ in *EI*[1]). It should probably be born in mind that it would be impossible to continue to deal with the problem of *ribāṭ*, in general and without reference to the precise contexts in which the usages of this term have been forged and have evolved. The permanent confrontation which, from the moment of the launching of the *Reconquista*, opposed the lands of the Muslim West to the Christian kingdoms, makes it reasonable to suppose that very particular cases of utilisation of the ancient terminology are to be encountered. These specific usages probably involved not only the ideology of *djihād* and its associated terms, including the verbal noun *ribāṭ*, but also the emergence of practices of magical mysticism, thaumaturgy, and the liturgy of intercession which were to be a fundamental element of maraboutism (with various usages of the root *r-b-ṭ*; "marabout" evidently emanates from one of the late usages of the Arabic *murābiṭ*). G. Marçais noted, moreover, the multiplication of usage, in Muslim Spain, in a fairly late period (which he did not, however, specify), of the term *rābiṭa* to denote certain innovations which he supposes to be of a mystical nature (by analogy with the Maghribī usage defined by G. Colin in his translation of the *Maḳṣad... fī dhikr ṣulaḥā*ʾ *al-Rīf*, of Abū Muḥammad ʿAbd al-Ḥaḳḳ al-Bādīsī, d. 711/1312, in *Arch. Maroc.*, xxvii, Paris 1926, 240: "a hermitage which is the retreat of a saint and where he lived surrounded by his disciples and his religious servitors"; see also *EI*[1] art. ZĀWIYA; it would also definitely be useful to refer to the volumes of the *Nafḥ al-ṭīb* of al-Maḳḳarī [*q.v.*], which deal with al-Andalus). G. Marçais also claimed to have found a direct echo of the term *rābiṭa* in a number of Spanish toponyms such as *Rápita, Rávita* and *Rábida*.

iii. Ribāṭ, *as an establishment for mystics (relations with establishments of similar type*—khanḳāh, zāwiya, tekke)

It is not known at exactly which point in history the term *ribāṭ* and parallel terms, in particular *khanḳāh* in the East, *zāwiya* in the West, were first effectively and regularly applied to groups of mystics devoting themselves to practices of piety, *ʿibāda*, in a building to which they had rights of ownership. It can only be asserted that the phenomenon became established—at the earliest, but still in a very uneven manner—from the second half of the 5th/11th century, in the Saldjūḳ lands of Persia. Similar structures were apparently also in evidence among the Ghaznawids of north-eastern Persia, as far as the approaches to the Pandjāb. It subsequently spread very widely over the newly-conquered territories, arriving, from the 7th/13th century onward, in the Dihlī Sultanate [*q.v.*], when this region was settled by Persian élites fleeing from Mongol domination, henceforward established throughout Persia (K.A. Nizami, *Some aspects of khānqah life in medieval India*, in *SI*, viii [1957], 51-69). In the same manner, the progress of these establishments seems to have followed, in the West, the advance of the Saldjūḳs and their successors, first in Zangid Syria and then in Ayyūbid Egypt, as well as in Anatolia (which passed definitively under Muslim control after the victory won at Manzikert or Malāzgird [*q.v.*] by the second Great Saldjūḳ sultan, Alp Arslan [*q.v.*], in 463/1071). Subsequently the movement of founding these institutions continued to spread, in particular, as the result of the development of the mystical brotherhoods, *ṭuruḳ* (sing. *ṭarīḳa, q.v.* in *EI*[1]). The entire Muslim world was thus affected. Local particularities and significant disparities between establishments are to be noted, however, resulting from the circumstances of foundation (whether or not the initiative was sponsored by a dynasty or a powerful individual, and the level and permanence of the *waḳf*s intended for their support).

It should be noted, for example, that the genesis and evolution of mysticism in the Muslim West, Maghrib and Spain, seem to have been quite different from what took place in the East, possibly as a result of the quasi-exclusive domination of the Mālikī school of law, which was able to impose certain obstacles in matters of the spiritualisation and the practice of faith. In these regions, as was later to be the case in sub-Saharan Africa, the overwhelming mystical phenomenon was maraboutism (elements in E. Doutté, *Magie et religion dans l'Afrique du Nord*, Algiers 1908, repr. Paris 1983; G. Drague, *Esquisse d'histoire religieuse du Maroc: confréries et zaouias*, Paris 1951; E.

Dermenghem, *Le culte des Saints dans l'Islam maghrébin*, Paris 1954). However, the Ṣūfī brotherhood movement was ultimately to be established in the West also. There it took on some quite specific traits (on the mystical brotherhoods in general, see J.S. Trimingham, *The Sufi orders in Islam*, Oxford 1971, on the establishments and the phenomenon of *ziyāra*, "pious visiting [of a shrine or tomb]" see ch. vi, esp. 166-80). The thesis which continues to be propounded, in regard to the Muslim West, consists in saying, following E. Lévi-Provençal [see ZĀWIYA in *EI*¹] that the ancient local term was probably *rābiṭa* (see above), which applied to a "hermitage", while *zāwiya* was later to be systematically employed in the same sense, but only from the 7th/13th century onward. This thesis seems to require renewed discussion.

In the central and eastern regions (from the time of their submission to Sal<u>dj</u>ūḳ domination), the establishments for mystics (these latter being henceforward all denoted as Ṣūfīs, with the exception of the remnants of the Karrāmiyya, surviving in the <u>Gh</u>ūrid domain, see <u>GH</u>ŪRIDS), took either the name *<u>kh</u>anḳāh* [*q.v.*], which was the dominant usage in numerous regions, or *ribāṭ*. There is sometimes concurrence of the two terms in the same zone (Syria and Egypt). In lists of establishments compiled in a later period and applying to Egypt as well as Syria (see below), the appellation *zāwiya* is also found referring to urban establishments which seem to be of the same nature as *ribāṭ*s or *<u>kh</u>anḳāh*s. It is not known in what circumstances this third term (which is supposed, *a priori*, to be of western origin) is applied in these central regions. As for designation by the word *ribāṭ*, it is seldom an exclusive usage, except in ʿIrāḳ, in the region of Ba<u>gh</u>dād (but only until the Mongol period). It is, in fact, this declining caliphal metropolis which seems to have provided, for some time, the most important and probably the most ancient stratum of urban *ribāṭ*s (cf. the present writer's article on the pre-Mongol period of foundation of the Ba<u>gh</u>dādī *ribāṭ*s, see below). Elsewhere, it is the appellation of *<u>kh</u>anḳāh* which seems to have originally been prevalent, this applying to all the lands of the Muslim East or lands of the Levant, controlled, directly or indirectly, by powers of Sal<u>dj</u>ūḳ origin (Syria and Egypt). It is this, moreover, which seems to have impressed western travellers like Ibn <u>D</u>jubayr in the 6th/12th century and Ibn Baṭṭūṭa in the 8th/14th century (see below). The names given to these establishments, most of them founded between the 6th/12th and the 7th/13th centuries, were not subsequently to change, though the foundations could be of very different nature, in terms of their dimensions, their importance, their financial means, even their users, whether or not under the control of successive powers. The most important foundations often accommodated the tomb of the founder, even if the latter had no connection with mysticism (see ḲUBBA, where the primary concern is with tombs in *madrasas*; see also the term *turba/türbe*). This was to be the case especially in Mamlūk Egypt (see <u>KH</u>ANḲĀH). Lists of establishments are to be found in certain relatively late sources. For Egypt, they feature in the *<u>Kh</u>iṭaṭ* of al-Maḳrīzī (d. 845/1442 [*q.v.*]). According to this author, the city of Cairo is said to have contained 23 *<u>kh</u>anḳāh*s, 12 *ribāṭ*s and 26 *zāwiyas* (*op. cit.*, Būlāk 1270/1853, repr. offset, Ba<u>gh</u>dād n.d., ii, 414-36). These establishments evidently do not all belong to the same period. The chronology here is defective, needing to be restored before any analysis is attempted. Thus it is possible that the *<u>kh</u>anḳāh*s could be the most ancient, which would explain the astonishment of the Ma<u>gh</u>ribī travellers who passed through Cairo, between the 6th/12th and 8th/14th centuries (if the lists supplied in the sources are to be believed, there had, however, been *zāwiya*s since the 7th/13th century, in Syria and in Egypt). For Damascus, there is a list comparable to that of Cairo but of even later date. It is owed to ʿAbd al-Ḳādir al-Nuʿaymī (d. 927/1521, see Brockelmann, S II, 164 and feature in the *Tanbīh al-ṭālib wa-ir<u>sh</u>ād al-dāris* (2 vols., Damascus 1948; al-Nuʿaymī makes frequent references to Yūsuf Ibn Shaddād, d. 632/1235, for the more ancient establishments). The figures were reportedly as follows: 29 *<u>kh</u>anḳāh*s, 26 *zāwiya*s and 21 *ribāṭ*s (to this list should be added an indeterminate number of *tekke*s, from the Ottoman period [see DIMA<u>SH</u>Ḳ]. This Turkicised word denotes an establishment of the same type as those already mentioned, its Arabic form being *takkiya*). Here, too, the chronology is defective, and the dates of foundation of the establishments are not given systematically. Historical exploitation of these lists has yet to be undertaken.

In the Ma<u>gh</u>rib, it was to be the appellation *zāwiya* which was prevalent before the Ottomans. The latter were to build a certain number of *tekke*s, alongside older establishments, except in Morocco, which escaped their domination (given the conditions of local mysticism, the Ma<u>gh</u>ribī *zāwiya*s are not necessarily urban establishments, see Trimingham, *op. cit.*, index, 314). The observation of Ibn <u>D</u>jubayr (who was in the East at the end of the 6th/12th century, see below, *Riḥla*, 330) suggests that while *<u>kh</u>anḳāh* was probably unknown in the West, there were nevertheless usages of the term *ribāṭ*, taken in the sense of a generic term. It should be noted that, in another *Riḥla*, of two centuries later, Ibn Baṭṭūṭa, the great traveller and a native of Tangier (*q.v.*; he is said to have died in 779/1377 or a little earlier), for his part uses *zāwiya* as a term of reference to denote all kinds of establishments, from institutions for mystical brotherhoods to simple wayside hostelries. This uniformity of nomenclature does not seem to correspond to reality. It could be the product of extrapolation, deriving from a typically Ma<u>gh</u>ribī usage. In his accounts, often lively and spiced with anecdotes, this traveller-narrator would be unlikely to mention the terminology actually used in the regions of which he speaks. Furthermore, he abandons his procedure, at least once, in reference to Cairo when he declares, "as for *zāwiya*s, which are here called *<u>kh</u>anḳāh*s". The passage is included in a chapter devoted to the various establishments of Cairo (the mosque of ʿAmr, the *madrasa*s, the *māristān*s and the *zāwiya*s), see his *Riḥla*, Beirut 1967, 37). In pre-Ottoman Turkey, it is also *zāwiya*s which are attributed by him to the Turkoman organisations of the *a<u>kh</u>ī*s [*q.v.*], who were to revive, in Anatolia, the most ancient tradition of the *futuwwa* (*q.v.*; see also Cl. Cahen, *Pre-ottoman Turkey*, London 1968, 196-200). The word *ribāṭ* seems to be completely absent in the *Riḥla* of Ibn Baṭṭūṭa. There is a single isolated use of the term *rābiṭa*, apparently denoting an oratory regarded as a sacred site (placed under the mythic patronage of the prophet Ilyās and of <u>Kh</u>aḍir [*q.v.*], in the region of Sinope or Ṣinūb (*op. cit.*, 319-26).

Returning to the genesis of the process, it will be noted that the most distinguishing feature of these new kinds of establishment is that they are situated, in principle, in cities (except in the case of marabout edifices, many of which reflect the local configuration of places collectively recognised as "sacred") and not on a frontier or in an exposed place. Just like the *madrasa*s or colleges of law [*q.v.*], which also appear in towns, in the same places and during the same eriods, the urban establishments for Ṣūfīs were to be lmost exclusively financed by the system of *waḳfs* (see bove). These enabled them to continue in existence nd to survive, without too much damage, some articularly turbulent political phases. These were ometimes private *waḳfs* (especially as regards small nd ancient foundations, for the use of a single master nd his disciples). Later, in establishments of importance, these were to be public or semi-public foundaions, initiated by persons belonging to the higher chelons of the state or of the court. There are cases, or example, of foundations created by princesses and y the wives of caliphs and sultans (the position in Baghdād from the 5th/11th century to the 7th/13th entury is well-known through local chronicles such as he *Muntaẓam* of Ibn al-Djawzī [*q.v.*]; see J. Chabbi, *La fonction du ribat à Bagdad du Ve siècle au début du VIIe iècle*, in *REI*, xlii/1 [1974]).

But this phase of official foundations, which began n Persia with the first Saldjūḳs of the 5th/11th century, seems to have been preceded by a much more obscure period during which the transition was made rom the very overt tradition of the diffusion of knowledge, *ʿilm* (religious knowledge, in this case), which was normally dispensed in the mosques, *masdjid* [*q.v.*], or the great-mosques, *djāmiʿ* [see MASDJID], to nstruction conveyed in the enclosed space of the new nstitutions. The latter did not, however, cause the disappearance of the former. It is, yet again, in Persia that the process seems to have begun, probably on the basis of previous local models. The invention of the Muslim *khanḳāh* (a word in Persian undifferentiated in gender which has evolved into a feminine in Arabic) is probably the most ancient. It may be attributed to the ascetic preachers of the movement of the Karrāmiyya, on the basis of a model which is possibly Manichaean. The earliest foundations seem to have been established, in north-eastern Persia, between Transoxiana and Khurāsān, during the Sāmānid period, probably from the end of the 3rd/9th century onwards. Until around the middle of the following century, the *khanḳāh* seems to belong specifically to the movement represented by those whom al-Muḳaddasī calls *khānḳāʾī*, "man of the *khānḳāh*" (44; *khawāniḳ* is the Arabised plural of this word). It seems that the use of this kind of institution by Ṣūfism (established in Persia in the mid-4th/10th century, see above) came about in a later period and in conditions which have yet to be elucidated, from a historical point of view. There are pieces of evidence concerning Naysabūr [see NĪSHĀPŪR], the great metropolis of knowledge in Khurāsān, during the 4th/10th century. But these apply primarily to the foundation of *madrasas*, assigned to the various juristic rites. This seems, furthermore, to be a question of small institutions, of a private type, reserved for the teaching of a single master, for whom the establishment doubtless also served as a residence (R.W. Bulliet, *The patricians of Nishapur*, Cambridge, Mass. 1972, 249-55, gives a complete list of these pieces of evidence). Bulliet also speaks of the *khānḳāh*. But he does not seem to assess correctly its exclusive ancient relationship to the movement of the Karrāmiyya (for example, an erroneous substitution of terms, 229, n. 5). On the other hand, it is important to note that he makes no mention of the urban *ribāṭ* for Ṣūfīs in the sources that he has studied. For his part, F. Meier devotes an entire section of ch. 13 of his study of the (Persian-speaking) Khurāsānian Ṣūfī, Abū Saʿīd b. Abi 'l-Khayr (d. 440/1049), a native of Mayhana [*q.v.*] near Sarakhs; this Ṣūfī apparently maintained a personal *khānḳāh* in his town), to what he calls "convents", *Konvente*. He attempts to discover the most ancient attestations of the *ribāṭ* for Ṣūfīs as well as of *khānḳāh*. But his study lacks a thorough placing in the context of the citations (*Abū Saʿīd-i-Abū l-Ḫayr, Wirklichkeit und Legende*, in Acta Iranica, Ser. 3, vol. iv, Leiden 1976). It may, however, be supposed that the process probably developed during the 4th/10th century, at least in reference to Persia, and that it was definitively established in the following century. With the exception of one case, presented in a fairly obscure fashion, at Dabīl or Dvīn in Armenia, at 379, it should be noted that al-Muḳaddasī never links the *khānḳāh* to Ṣūfism. On the other hand, the association which he seems to establish, in several passages (412, 414, 415), between *ribāṭs* and Ṣūfism has been interpreted as suggesting that "convents" are to be envisaged. But an anecdote which he locates in Susiana and in which he is personally involved (he is mistaken for a Ṣūfī on account of the woollen gown which he wears), seems to show that this is not the case, 415; the Ṣūfīs have their circle, *madjlis* or "meeting place", in the great mosque of Susa; they seem to have an inclination to travel, they are considered as bearers of sanctity and they receive donations; the *ribāṭs* which they frequent are not their own property, but the small forts on the nearby coast in the region of Abbādān which, at the time, must still have been in a reasonable state of repair). The equivalence between the two terms *ribāṭ* and *khānḳāh*, which for Syria, and in the context of Ṣūfism, was to be established two centuries later by the traveller-pilgrim Ibn Djubayr [*q.v.*], seems to be far removed from current opinions (his *Riḥla* ed. Wright and De Goeje, *Travels of Ibn Jubayr*, GMS, V, 1907, tr. M. Gaudefroy-Demombynes, *Ibn Jobair, Voyages,* Paris 1949-65). This text is extremely valuable because it offers testimony *de visu*. The passages on the Ṣūfīs and their recognised establishments, all situated in urban surroundings, are exclusively concerned with the Syria of Ṣalāh al-Dīn (Ibn Djubayr was residing there in 580/1184). It is the terminology of the *khānḳāh* which seems to be asserted here first, in a spectacular fashion (see Cahen's remarks on the utilisation of Persian terminology in Ayyūbid Syria: *L'émigration persane des origines de l'Islam aux Mongols,* Communication, Rome 1970, repr., *Les peuples musulmans dans l'histoire médiévale*, Damascus 1977, on *khānḳāhs*, 448; on the pre-Ayyūbid period, see N. Elisséef, *Nur ad-Din, un grand prince musulman de Syrie au temps des croisades (511-569H/1118-1174)*, Damascus 1967, index). The very expression used by Ibn Djubayr suggests that he knew elsewhere of the *ribāṭ* for Ṣūfīs ("the *ribāṭs* which are here called *khānḳāh*", see below, tr. 330). The conditions of foundation, maintenance, as well as the magnificence of certain establishments, are the object of precise observations (the seminal passage with the exclamation, "the Ṣūfīs are the kings of this land!" (text 284, tr. 330-1; foundations by princesses, text 275, tr. 318; a case of double appellation, *khānḳāh* and *ribāṭ*, text 243, tr. 279-80).

It is for the moment impossible to detail the successive stages of evolution which led to the situation described, from the 6th/12th century onward, by concordant sources. Thus it is not known why it is the term *ribāṭ*, long associated—in the ambiguous conditions which have been described—with the history of the frontier, which comes to be established (in the Arabic version) as the designation of establishments *intra muros*, dedicated to the shelter of mystics. It could evidently be supposed that, by this means, the mystic establishment reverts to the old sense proposed by the contemporary traditionist who held that religious observance constituted the true *ribāṭ*. But it may further be supposed that the word is linked to the symbolic representation of *dj̲ihād*, which becomes the mystic *mudj̲āhada*, the *dj̲ihād* against oneself. It is this interpretation which is proposed, in ʿIrāḳ towards the end of the ʿAbbāsid caliphate, at the beginning of the 7th/13th century, by a major connoisseur of Bag̲h̲dādī establishments, the Ṣūfī author Abū Ḥafṣ ʿUmar al-Suhrawardī (d. 632/1234) in his compendium of Ṣūfism, the *Kitāb ʿAwārif al-maʿārif* (publ. as a supplement to the *Ihyā᾽ ʿulūm al-dīn* of al-G̲h̲azālī, Maktaba Tidj̲āriyya, Cairo n.d., chs. 13-18 of which are devoted to what could be called "the rules of *ribāṭ*"; the rules of *ribāṭ* are said to have been defined in Persian by the Ṣūfī Abū Saʿīd, at the beginning of the 5th/11th century). The proposed interpretation has the merit of coherence, but it supplies no historical justification. It has to be recognised that, for the moment, no explanation is available which could be supported by admissible historical evidence. Furthermore, there are certainly considerable differences, according to periods, regions, types of foundation, between the establishments which are quite simply called *ribāṭ, k̲h̲ānḳāh, zāwiya* or, later, *tekke*. Ibn Dj̲ubayr seems most astonished at finding in Syria establishments which resemble, according to him, palaces, *ḳuṣūr*. This indicates that the entire history of the word, in its mystical sense, remains to be written. All that is certain is that, once launched, in very disputable conditions, the movement was to be irreversible. It was all the more so in that it was soon to be supported by the mystical brotherhoods. But it could be that an even greater contribution was made by the untiring activities of the founders. It may be supposed that, over and above the pious work with which they associated their name (such establishments usually bore the name of their founder), aristocratic persons soon came to regard the establishments which they had initiated and financed as a not inconsiderable perquisite of power, albeit symbolic.

With more precise regard to *ribāṭ*, and as a way of concluding the account of the adventures of this word, it may be noted that it is the final evolution of the term which tends to cover, with its sense, all the ancient and intermediate stages of its itinerary, through the successive contexts of Muslim societies. It is no doubt as a result of this that there is regularly encountered, in translation, a misinterpretation which could be described as functional, that which, in defiance of all the ancient usages, makes of *ribāṭ* a "military convent"—one thing which it never was.

Bibliography: Given in the text. (J. Chabbi)

2. Architecture.

Ribāṭ architecture developed from notions of preparedness and defensibility and from models in conquered lands that could be appropriated for these purposes. Early *ribāṭ*s varied in size and complexity from isolated watchtowers to fortresses with cells for the *murābiṭūn*, a mosque, storehouses, stables, and towers. Examples of the former cannot be identified with any certainty, and only two verified examples of the latter survive in Tunisia. The first, heavily renovated and remodeled, is in Monastir [*q.v.*]. The second, the Ribāṭ of Sūsā on the Gulf of Gabès, is a fine representative of the full-fledged fortress-*ribāṭ*. Its core dates to the period 154-80/770-96, and its last stage of construction is attributed to the Ag̲h̲labid *amīr* Ziyādat Allāh (201-23/817-38). It consists of a fortified, square enclosure (approximately 39 m to the side) with a single, central, projecting entrance in the southern wall, four attached, round towers in the four corners, and three semi-round towers in the middle of the three other sides. The southeastern tower, much higher than the others and encased in a square base, doubles as a *manār*, both for the call to prayer and for watching and signaling. The courtyard is surrounded by vaulted porticoes, behind which run windowless cells on the east, north, and west sides. The second story contains similar cells, for which the porticoes serve as a continuous gallery. The southern side of the second floor is occupied by an arcaded mosque with a concave *miḥrāb* in its centre (for both *ribāṭ*s, see K.A.C. Creswell, *A short account of early Muslim architecture*, ed. J.W. Allan, Cairo 1989, 286-90, and A. Lézine, *Deux villes d'Ifriqiya*, Paris 1971, 82-8 for Sūsa and idem, *Architecture de l'Ifriqiya*, Paris 1966, 122-6 for Monastir).

This prototypical *ribāṭ* layout was adopted for a non-military building type that existed from the earliest Islamic period, sc. the *k̲h̲ān* [*q.v.*] or caravanserai. *K̲h̲ān*s, too, were fortified, well-guarded enclosures with a single entrance to a court surrounded by cells for travellers, stables for their mounts, a mosque, and in many instances a watchtower. Perhaps this is why many mediaeval caravanserais in Persia are called *ribāṭ*, as they all exhibit the same basic scheme as the one encountered in authentic *ribāṭ*s (see, for example, B. O'Kane, *Timurid architecture in Khorassan*. Malibu, Calif. 1987, 287-97 and figs 40-1; and cf. ribāṭ-i s̲h̲araf). But post-Seldj̲ūk sources use the term *ribāṭ* to designate quite another type of building, sc. houses for Ṣūfīs. This is probably a development out of the initial function of *ribāṭ*, where pious *murābiṭūn* spent their time in devotional exercises during peaceful periods and it does not reflect a continuation of the original layout. *Waḳf* descriptions of Mamlūk *ribāṭ*s, for example, show that they were a variation on *k̲h̲ānḳāhs* [*q.v.*] except perhaps that some of them accommodated non-Ṣūfīs (Laila Ibrahim and M.M. Amin, *Architectural terms in Mamluks documents*, Cairo 1990, 52; Leonor Fernandes, *The evolution of a Sufi institution in Mamluk Egypt; the* Khanqah, Berlin 1988, 10-13.

Bibliography: Given in the text.

(Nasser Rabbat)

RIBĀṬ al-FATḤ, Rabat, colloquially *er-Rbāṭ* (ethnic *Ribāṭī*, colloqu. *Rbāṭī*), a town in Morocco, situated on the south bank at the mouth of the Wādī Abū Raḳrāḳ (Wed Bou Regreg) opposite the town of Salé [see salā]. After the establishment of the French Protectorate, it became the administrative capital of the S̲h̲arīfian empire, the usual residence of the sultan of Morroco and the headquarters of the *mak̲h̲zen* [see mak̲h̲zan] and of the French authorities. The choice of Rabat as the administrative centre of Morroco brought to this town considerable development in place of its earlier somnolence.

When Morroco regained its independence (1956), Rabat became the official capital of the land, and the seat of political (Royal Palace, Parliament), administrative (government ministers, services of the state) and military power. All the diplomatic representatives were concentrated there. But the economic and commercial capital remained Casablanca (headquarters of large businesses, banks, export and import agencies, etc.). Morroco is thus the only North African state which has two capitals with specialised functions, 56 miles/90 km from each other, a fact which avoids, to some extent, too great a concentration of powers and functions in one dominating metropolis.

The foundation of Ribāṭ al-Fatḥ was the work of the Almohads [see al-muwaḥḥidūn]. The site of the "Two Banks" (*al-ʿIdwatān*) of the estuary of the Bou

Regreg had previously been the scene of Roman and pre-Roman settlements: the Punic, later Roman Sala was built on the left bank of the river higher up at the site of the royal Marīnid necropolis of Chella (S̲h̲ālla [q.v.]). The Muslim town of Salā on the right bank, from the beginning of the 4th/10th century, in order to protect it against the inroads of the Barg̲h̲awāṭa [q.v.] heretics at the time when it was the capital of a little Ifrānid kingdom, had fortified on the other side of the Bou Regreg a *ribāṭ* [q.v.], which was permanently manned by devout volunteers, who in this way desired to carry out their vow of *d̲j̲ihād* [q.v.]; the geographer Ibn Ḥawḳal is authority for its existence at this date (ed. de Goeje, 56). But we know very little of the part played by this *ribāṭ* in the course of the sanguinary wars later fought between the Barg̲h̲awāṭa and the Almoravids [see AL-MURĀBIṬŪN]. It is not even possible to point out its exact situation. It was perhaps the same fortified spot that is mentioned in the middle of the 6th/12th century under the name of Ḳaṣr Banī Targh by the geographer al-Fazārī.

The final and complete subjugation of the Barg̲h̲awāṭa meant that a different part was to be played by the *ribāṭ* on the estuary of the Bou Regreg. In 545/1150, the founder of the dynasty of the Muʾminid Almohads, ʿAbd al-Muʾmin, chose the fort and its vicinity as the place of mobilisation for the troops intended to carry the holy war into Spain. A permanent camp was established there and he provided for a supply of fresh water by bringing a conduit from a neighbouring source, ʿAyn G̲h̲abūla. The permanent establishments,—mosque, royal residence—formed a little town which received the name of al-Mahdiyya [q.v.] as a souvenir of the Mahdī Ibn Tūmart [q.v.]. On several occasions, very large bodies of men were concentrated around the *ribāṭ*, and it was here that ʿAbd al-Muʾmin died on the eve of his departure for Spain in 558/1163.

The development of the camp went on under ʿAbd al-Muʾmin's successor, Abū Yaʿḳūb Yūsuf (558-80/1163-84), but it was the following prince of the Muʾminid dynasty, Abū Yūsuf Yaʿḳūb al-Manṣūr, who at the beginning of his reign gave the orders and opened the treasuries necessary for its completion. In memory of the victory gained in 591/1195 by the Almohads over Alfonso VIII of Castile at Alarcos [see AL-ARAK], it was given the name of Ribāṭ al-Fatḥ. The camp was surrounded by a wall of earth flanked with square towers enclosing with the sea and the river an area of 450 ha. The wall is still standing for the most part, and is nearly four miles in length; two monumental gates, one now known as Bāb al-Ruwāḥ, the other which gives access to the *ḳaṣaba* (Kasba of the Udāya), date from this period. It was also Yaʿḳūb al-Manṣūr who ordered the building inside Ribāṭ al-Fatḥ of a colossal mosque which was never finished; rectangular in plan it measured 183 m/610 feet long by 139 m/470 feet broad; the only mosque in the Muslim world of greater area was that of Sāmarrā [q.v.]. It was entered by 16 doors and in addition to three courts had a hall of prayer, supported by over 200 columns. In spite of recent excavations more or less successfully conducted, this mosque still remains very much a puzzle from the architectural point of view. But the minaret, which also remained unfinished and was never given its upper lantern, still surprises the traveller by its unusual dimensions. It is now called the Tower of Ḥassān (*burd̲j̲ Ḥassān*). Built entirely of stones of uniform shape it is 44 m/160 feet high on a square base 16 m/55 feet square. Its walls are 2.5 m/8 feet thick. The upper platform is reached by a ramp 2 m/6 feet 8 ins. broad with a gentle slope. This tower in its proportions, its arrangement and decoration, is closely related to two Almohad minarets of the same period: that of the mosque of the Kutubiyya at Marrākus̲h̲ [q.v.] and that of the great mosque of Seville, the Giralda [see IS̲H̲BĪLIYYA].

Yaʿḳūb al-Manṣūr's great foundation never received the population which its area might have held and the town opposite, Salé, retained under the last Almohads and in the 7th-8th/13th-14th centuries all its political and commercial importance. Rabat and Salé in 1248 passed under the rule of the Marīnids, and it seems that Rabat in those days was simply a military station of no great importance, sharing the fortunes of its neighbour, which had gradually become a considerable port having busy commercial relations with the principal trading centres of the Mediterranean. But a chance circumstance was suddenly to give the town of the "Two Banks" a new aspect. The expulsion from Spain of the last Moriscos [q.v.] decided upon in 1610 by Philip III brought to Rabat and Salé an important colony of Andalusian refugees, who increased to a marked degree the number of their compatriots in these towns who had previously left Spain of their own free-will after the reconquest. While the population of the other Moroccan cities, Fās and Tetouan principally, in which the exiles took refuge, very quickly absorbed the new arrivals whom they had welcomed without distrust, the people of Rabat and Salé could not see without misgivings this colony from Spain settle beside them, for they lived apart, never mingled with the older inhabitants and devoted themselves to piracy and soon completely dominated the two towns and their hinterland. Rabat, known in Europe as "New Salé" in contrast to Salé ("Old Salé"), soon became the centre of a regular little maritime republic in the hands of the Spanish Moors who had either left of their own accord before 1610, the so-called "Hornachuelas", or had been expelled in 1610, the so-called "Moriscos", the former, however, being clearly in the majority. This republic, on the origin and life of which the documents from European archives published by H. de Castries and P. de Cenival threw new light, hardly recognised the suzerainty of the *s̲h̲arīf* who ruled over the rest of Morocco. While boasting of their *d̲j̲ihād* against the Christians, the Andalusians of the "Two Banks" really found their activity at sea a considerable source of revenue. They had retained the use of the Spanish language and the mode of life they had been used to in Spain. They thus raised Rabat from its decadence. Their descendants still form the essential part of the Muslim population of the town and they have Spanish patronymics like Bargās̲h̲ (Vargas), Palāmīno, Morēno, Lōpēz, Pērēz, Chiquīto, Dinya (Span. Dénia), Runda (Span. Ronda), Mūlīn (Molina), etc.

The spirit of independence and the wealth of the Spanish Moors in Rabat soon made the town a most desirable object in the eyes of the sultans of Morocco. Nevertheless, the little republic with periods of more or less unreal independence, was able to survive until the accession of the ʿAlawī sultan Sīdī Muḥammad b. ʿAbd Allāh in 1171/1757. This prince now endeavoured to organise for his own behalf the piracy hitherto practised by the sailors of the republic of the "Two Banks". He even ordered several ships of the line to be built. But the official character thus given to the pirates of Salé very soon resulted in the bombardment of Salé and Larache [see AL-ʿARĀʾIS̲H̲] by a French fleet in 1765. The successors of Muḥammad b. ʿAbd Allāh had very soon to renounce any further attempt to wage the "holy war" by sea. The result was a long period of decline for Salé which found expression not only in the gradual diminution of its trade but also in a very marked hatred of each town for the other. At the beginning of the 20th century, Rabat, like Salé, had completely lost its old importance. They were both occupied by French troops on 19 July 1911.

After the installation of the Protectorate, the demographical and spatial growth of Rabat was intensified. The population in 1912 was estimated at 24,283 (comprising 23,000 Moroccans and 1,283 Europeans), adjacent to Salé with 17,000 inhabitants, all Moroccans. In 1952, a few years before independence, the census of population gave 156,209 inhabitants for Rabat (114,709 Moroccans and 41,500 Europeans). In 1982, the date of the latest official census, valid until the present time, Rabat had a total of 526,100. But one should take into account not only the residents of the capital city but also those of Salé, closely linked with Rabat (316,700 inhabitants) and *ca.* 150,000 in the surrounding suburbs. Hence the whole agglomeration of Rabat-Salé has more than a million people, forming the second largest urban grouping of Morocco, after Casablanca, and spreading its buildings over more than 130 km^2.

The "bipartite urban settlement" which as grown out of the "Republic of the Two Banks" has thus become strongly dissymetrical, from all points of view. Together with its suburbs, Rabat holds three-fifths of the population of the agglomeration, the essential part of the tertiary sector jobs and even the industrial ones. The industrial concerns, estimated at 8,000 in 1986, make the capital the sixth of the industrial centres of Morocco, which hardly allows one to visualise it as a residential and official city. Rabat provides numerous jobs, distributes the resources to a multitude of officials but also to modest households existing in the shadow of the propertied classes (informal employment). As for Salé, it provides housing for employees and workers and appears as a "dormitory town" narrowly dependent on its powerful neighbour.

The urban structure of the two cities also differs. It is true that the two *madīna*s have always faced the mouth of the Bou Regreg and contain the historic memorials of the two cities (gate of Bab el-Alou and the ancient *mellāḥ* and Kasba of the Ūdāya at Rabat; and the gate of Bab Sabta, and the Marīnid Great Mosque and Medersa at Salé). But the Rabat *madīna* has been less densely packed than the Salé one, and its role in the agglomeration is secondary. On the other hand, the Salé *madīna* is overpopulated but in other respects is more attractive to the population on the right bank of the river.

The extensions *extra muros*, in effect the 20th century quarters, are of a very different nature on each side of the river.

In Rabat, these are large, well-spaced blocks, with wide roads and numerous green spaces, which have brought about, since the beginning of the "colonial city"—where the town planners Prost and Ecochard distinguished themselves—a relatively harmonious city (quarters of the Centre, the Residence, Tour Ḥassān, Orangers and Āgadāl). The sites laid out after independence (Amal Fath, university campus, enlargement of the quarter of the luxurious villas of Souissi and the spacious plots of Ryad) have perpetuated this tendency, even if some poverty belts have grown up in the southern suburbs. The expanse of these suburbs, which are either "spontaneous" or have been remodelled by the state, is incontestably more limited there than on the Salé bank of the river.

In Salé, beyond the *madīna*, there is a rabbit's warren of "refuge quarters" which have gradually grown up, biting into the old market gardens and throwing into relief the lower-class and dependent nature of this city, which is neither a rival nor a twin of Rabat but which has become simply an annexe of the capital city.

Strangely enough, although Rabat is the undisputed national capital, it is not a regional centre. Its hinterland is limited to the Zaër country to the south, an important region for stock-rearing, and to a string of bathing resorts along the Atlantic coast. Contrariwise, the economic hinterland of Salé is much more extensive and clearly dominated by the city of Salé itself, and comprises the regions of the Sehoul and the Zemmour. Thus Salé has retained an active role within the adjoining rural world, which is characteristic of traditional Islamic towns, whereas Rabat seems to have turned its back on the countryside, as befits a relatively new and probably still to some extent artificial town.

Bibliography: In the *Archives Marocaines* and in the periodical *Hespéris* there are many articles on Rabat, its monuments, its industries and dialectical topography. See also the important monograph *Villes et tribus du Maroc*, publication de la Mission scientifique du Maroc, *Rabat et sa région*, 3 vols., Paris 1918-20. The maritime life and the Arabic dialect of Rabat have been studied by L. Brunot, *La mer et les traditions indigènes à Rabat et Salé* (*PIHEM*, v, Paris 1920); idem, *Notes lexicologiques sur le vocabulaire maritime de Rabat et Salé* (*PIHEM*, vi, Paris 1920); idem, *Textes arabes de Rabat* (*PIHEM*, xx, Paris 1931). On the Jews of Rabat: J. Goulven, *Les Mellahs de Rabat-Salé*, Paris 1927. On the history of the seafaring republic of Rabat: H. de Castries, *Les Sources inédites de l'histoire du Maroc*, Paris 1905-27, index. On the monuments of Almohad Rabat: cf. Dieulafoy, *La mosquée d'Hassan*, in the *Mémoires de l'Académie des Inscriptions et Belles-Lettres*, xliii, 167; G. Marçais, *Manuel d'art musulman*, Paris 1926, i; H. Terrasse, *L'art hispano-mauresque des origines au XIIIème siècle* (*PIHEM*, xxv, Paris 1932). Also Jérôme and Jean Tharaud, *Rabat ou les heures marocaines*, Paris 1918; P. Champion, *Rabat et Marrakech* (collection *Les villes d'art célèbres*), Paris 1926; C. Mauclair, *Rabat et Salé*, Paris 1934; Léandre Vaillat, *Le visage français du Maroc*, Paris 1931. On the development of Rabat between the two Wars, see H. Prost, *L'urbanisme au Maroc*, in *Cahiers Nord-Africains*, 1932; F. Gendre, *Le plan de Rabat-Salé*, in *Revue de Géographie du Maroc* (4th trimester 1937); M. Ecochard, *Rapport de Présentation de l'esquisse de Rabat-Salé*, Dec. 1948; F. Mauret, *Le développement de l'agglomération de Rabat-Salé*, in *Bull. Économique et Social du Maroc* (4th trimester 1953). On the recent urban spread of Rabat, see Kingdom of Morocco, Ministry of the Interior, *Schéma directeur d'aménagement et d'urbanisme de l'agglomération Rabat-Salé*, Rabat n.d. [*ca.* 1972]; J.L. Abu Lughod, *Rabat, urban apartheid in Morocco*, Princeton 1980; R. Escallier, *Citadins et espaces urbains au Maroc*, in *ERA* 706, fasc. 8-9 (Univ. of Tours 1981); collective work, *Présent et avenir des médinas*, in *ERA* 106, fasc. 10-11 (Univ. of Tours 1982); M. Belfquih and A. Fadloullah, *Mécanismes et formes de croissance urbaine au Maroc. Le cas de l'agglomération de Rabat-Salé*, 3 vols., Al Maârif, Rabat 1986 (essential).

(E. Lévi-Provençal-[J.F. Troin])

RIBĀṬ-I SHARAF, a building in mediaeval Islamic Khurāsān, situated on the Nīshāpūr-Sarakhs

:aravan route, two stages from Sarakhs. It consists of wo four-*īwān* courtyards, each containing a mosque. The larger inner court is surrounded by extensive uites of rooms; the outer court served mainly for tabling.

On the *pīshṭāḳ* [*q.v.*] at the rear of the inner court is an inscription with a date in which the units ended in 3. The *īwān* behind it has a stucco inscription dated 549/1154-5 in the name of the Saldjūḳ sultan Sandjar [*q.v.*], crediting the work to his wife Turkān Khātūn. At this date, Sandjar was being held captive by the Ghuzz; A. Godard (*Khorāsān*, in *Āthār-i Īrān*, iv [1949], 7-68) suggested that Turkān Khātūn's work involved mostly decorative repairs, and that on stylistic grounds 508/1114-15 was the date of the original foundation.

Although the building was restored in the 1970s, leading to the find of a cache of 11-14th century metalware and pottery, a lacquer box and a Ṣafawid *firmān* under one of the floors (M.Y. Kiani, *Robat-e Sharaf*, Tehran 1981), there has been no systematic study of the building to confirm Godard's sometimes problematic hypotheses regarding attribution of the work to the original building period or to restoration. For instance, the stucco revetment of the squinch of the mosque, ascribed by Godard to 1154-5, is almost identical to that of the Yarti Gunbad in Turkmenistan dated 491/1098 (S. Blair, *The monumental inscriptions from early Islamic Iran and Transoxiana*, Leiden 1992, 180).

The stucco is extraordinarily varied, ranging from the multi-layered arabesques of the soffit of the axial *īwān* to archaic work (best published in A. Hutt, *Iran 1*, London 1977, Pl. 65) suggesting the involvement of the same team responsible for the stucco of the tomb of Sandjar at Marw. The range of brick decoration and vaulting techniques, as yet inadequately published, is equally impressive.

This sumptuousness, together with the royal restoration inscription, make it likely, as J.M. Rogers has pointed out (in J. Sourdel-Thomine and B. Spuler (eds.), *Die Kunst des Islam*, Berlin 1973, no. 242), that the building was as much a palace as a caravansaray. A monumental gateway with the fragmentary remains of a royal inscription at nearby Du Barār (W.M. Clevenger, *Some minor monuments in Khurāsān*, in *Iran*, vi [1968], 58) may have been the gateway to the caravansaray/palace or a surrounding *ḥayr*.

Bibliography: Given in the text.

(B. O'Kane)

RIḌĀ (A.), literally "the fact of being pleased or contented; contentment, approval" (see Lane, 1100), a term found in Ṣūfī mysticism and also in early Islamic history.

1. In mystical vocabulary. In the Ḳurʾān, the root *raḍiya* and its derivatives occur frequently in the general sense of "to be content", with nominal forms like *riḍwān* "God's grace, acceptance of man's submission" (e.g. III, 156/61, 168/174; IV, 13/12; IX, 73/72; LVII, 20, 27), although the actual form *riḍā* does not occur. In the writings of the proto-Ṣūfī al-Ḥasan al-Baṣrī [*q.v.*], it is a moral state, contentment with the divine precepts and decrees, and the reciprocal contentment of the soul and God (see L. Massignon, *Essai sur les origines du lexique technique de la mystique musulmane*, Paris 1954, index).

2. In early Islamic history. The term has a special role in the events leading up to the ʿAbbāsid Revolution of 128-32/746-50, when the anti-Umayyad *duʿāt* made their propaganda in the name of *al-riḍā* (? *al-raḍī*) *min āl Muḥammad* "a member of the House of the Prophet who shall be acceptable to everybody". This conveniently vague term enabled both the partisans of ʿAlī's family, the Shīʿa, and those of the Prophet's paternal uncle, al-ʿAbbās, to claim that they were the intended new leaders of the *umma* (see M. Sharon, *Black banners from the East. The establishment of the ʿAbbāsid state—incubation of a revolt*, Jerusalem 1983, 146-7, 158-9 n. 14, 172).

Subsequently, the term tended to be particularly identified with the Shīʿa; it was, for instance, the *laḳab* [*q.v.*] of the Eighth Imām, ʿAlī al-Riḍā b. Mūsā al-Kāẓim [*q.v.*].

Bibliography: Given in the article. (Ed.)

RIḌĀ, an Ottoman biographer of poets. Meḥmed Riḍā b. Meḥmed, called Zehir Mār-zāde, was born into a family living in Edirne. Of his life we know only that he was for a time, respectively, *müderris* with a salary of 40 *aḳčes*, *nāʾib* and *müftī*—he held this latter function at Uzun Köprü near Edirne—and that he died in his native town in 1082/1671-2. Besides a collection of poems (*Dīwān*) and a work with the title *Ḳawāʿid-i fārisiyye* (no manuscript of these works has yet been found), Riḍā wrote a *Tadhkirat al-shuʿarāʾ*, a biographical collection in which he dealt in alphabetical order with the poets who lived in the first half of the 9th century A.H., i.e. 1591-2 to 1640-1. In the introduction he discussed eleven sultans who wrote poetry. The book was completed in 1050/1640-1 as the *taʾrīkh* or chronogram shows. The few manuscripts which do exist (in libraries in Istanbul and Vienna) contain, apart from the introduction, sometimes 165 and sometimes as many as 260 short biographies illustrated with quotations in verse. The printed edition (by Aḥmed Djewdet, *Tedkire-yi Riḍā*, Istanbul 1316/1900-1) has 173 biographies.

Bibliography: J. von Hammer, *GOD*, iii, 486; *Sidjill-i ʿOthmānī*, ii, 397; *ʿOthmānlî müʾellifleri*, ii, 185-6; Babinger, *GOW*, 215-16; Ismāʿīl Pasha, *Īḍāḥ al-maknūn fī 'l-dhayl ʿalā Kashf al-ẓunūn*, i, 274; Günay Alpay, *İA* art. *Rizâ*.

(F. Babinger-[J. Schmidt])

RIḌĀ ʿABBĀSĪ, leading artist at the court of the Ṣafawid Shāh ʿAbbās I [*q.v.*]. In addition to 29 works dated between 1001/1591-2 and 1044/1634, the four main sources for Riḍā ʿAbbāsī's life are: (1) Ḳāḍī Aḥmad b. Mīr Munshī, *Gulistān-i hunar* (1005/1596 and 1015/1606), *Calligraphers and painters...*, tr. V. Minorsky, Washington, D.C. 1959, 192-3; (2) Iskandar Munshī, *Taʾrīkh-i ʿālam-ārā-yi ʿAbbāsī* (*ca.* 1025/1616 and 1038/1629), *History of Shah ʿAbbās*, i, tr. R.M. Savory, Boulder, Colo. 1978, 273, and T.W. Arnold, *Painting in Islam*, Oxford 1928, 143-4; (3) "The Robber, the poet and the dogs" (Keir Coll., Richmond, Surrey), a drawing which Riḍā began in 1028/1619 and his son Shafīʿ ʿAbbāsī completed in 1064/1654; and (4) Portrait of Riḍā ʿAbbāsī, by Muʿīn Muṣawwir (Princeton University Library, 96G), begun in 1045/1635, completed in 1087/1673.

Riḍā, the son of the Ṣafawid court artist ʿAlī Aṣghar, served Shāh ʿAbbās. Scholars have questioned whether "Riḍā" and "Āḳā Riḍā" were identical to "Riḍā ʿAbbāsī". "The Robber, the poet and the dogs" contains one inscription by Riḍā referring to himself as "Riḍā Muṣawwir [ʿAbbā]sī" and another by Shafīʿ ʿAbbāsī, calling him "Āḳā Riḍā". Likewise, Muʿīn Muṣawwir calls him "Riḍā-yi Muṣawwir ʿAbbāsī... also known as Riḍā-yi ʿAlī Aṣghar".

Riḍā's career consists of three periods. (1) *Ca.* 995-1013/1587-1604 his style developed away from the attenuated forms of the Ḳazwīn school of 1560-80. Extremely delicate brushwork characterises his paintings; his drawings introduce a calligraphic line of variable thickness used to define form and suggest movement. (2) *Ca.* 1013-1019/1604-10. After the move to the new capital, Iṣfahān, in 1006-7/1598 and the addition of the honorific "ᶜAbbāsī" to his name *ca.* 1011-12/1603, Riḍā rebelled, ceasing to portray courtly figures. His staccato style of draughtmanship fits the subject-matter of the period—lone, anguished men in the wilderness. (3) *Ca.* 1019-44/1610-35. Resuming court employment, Riḍā introduced a ponderous figural style, a palette of half-tones, and multi-figure compositions to his oeuvre. The single-page subjects include portraits of *shaykhs*, courtiers, Europeans, and drawings after originals by Bihzād [*q.v.*]. Riḍā's work strongly influenced contemporaries and followers throughout the 11th/17th century.

Bibliography: In addition to sources cited, see, I. Stchoukine, *Les Peintures des manuscrits de Shāh ᶜAbbās Ier*, Paris 1964, 85-133 and *passim*; A. Welch, *Artists for the Shah*, New Haven 1976, 100-49; S.R. Canby, *Age and time in the work of Riza*, in *Persian masters: five centuries of painting*, ed. Canby, Bombay 1990, 71-84; A. Soudavar, *Art of the Persian courts*, New York 1992, 261-85; Canby, *The rebellious reformer: Riza, painter of Isfahan*, London 1994.

(SHEILA R. CANBY)

RIḌĀ ḲULĪ KHĀN B. MUḤAMMAD HĀDĪ B. ISMĀᶜĪL KAMĀL, Persian scholar and man of letters, "l'un des hommes les plus spirituels et les plus aimables que j'aie rencontrés dans aucune partie du monde" (Gobineau). A descendant of the poet Kamāl Khudjandī [*q.v.*], the grandfather of Riḍā Ḳulī, chief of the notables of Čarda Kilāta (district of Dāmghān), was put to death by the partisans of Karīm Khān Zand against whom he supported the Ḳādjārs (cf. *Relation de l'ambassade au Kharezm*, tr. Schefer, 203). His father became one of the dignitaries of the court of the Ḳādjārs; in 1215/1800, while on a pilgrimage to Mashhad, he heard of the birth of a son in Tehran to whom he gave the name of the *imām*. Becoming an orphan in 1802, Riḍā Ḳulī spent his early years in Fārs; he was brought back from Fārs to Tehran, lived some time with relatives at Barfurush (Māzandarān), then returned to Fārs where he received his education; he then entered the service of the state under the patronage of the governor-general of Fārs. His earliest efforts in poetry were published under pseudonym of Čākir, which he soon changed to that of Hidāyat. In 1829, on the occasion of Fatḥ ᶜAlī Shāh's stay in Shīrāz, he composed a panegyric and other poems which gained him the royal favour; but a serious illness prevented him from leaving Shīrāz. In 1838 Muḥammad Shāh showed such esteem for him that he entrusted his son ᶜAbbās Mīrzā's education to him. The political troubles that followed the Shāh's death in 1848 sent Riḍā Ḳulī into retirement. In 1851 Nāṣir al-Dīn Shāh recalled him and sent him on an embassy to Khīwa. He was next appointed to the Ministry of Education, became Director of the Royal College (*dār al-funūn*), then fifteen years later, tutor (*lālā-bāshī*) to the crown prince Muẓaffar al-Dīn, whom he followed to Tarīz, where he spent several years. He returned to Tehran where he died in 1288/1871.

His very numerous works include e.g. some treatises on theology and letters (one may mention only the *Miftāḥ al-kunūz*, a commentary on difficult verses in Khāḳānī, and the *Nižād-nāme-yi salāṭīn-i ᶜadjam-nižād*, on early Persian dynasties: analysed in *JRAS* [1886], 198). His lyrical poetry (*Dīwān*) totals about 30,000 lines. Of his six *mathnawīs* (enumerated by himself, *Madjmaᶜ al-fuṣaḥāʾ*, ii, 582) only the epic entitled *Bektāsh-nāme* (or *Gulistān-i Iram*, lith. Tabrīz, 1270/1853) is published: it celebrates the tragic loves of the hero and the Persian poetess of Arab origin Rabīᶜa Ḳizdārī Balkhī, known as Zayn al-ᶜArab. His other works which are published are mainly of a documentary nature and therefore very important. The *Fihris al-tawārīkh* ("Repertory of chronicles" chronology, lith. in part at Tabrīz) was presented to Nāsir al-Dīn Shāh before the author's departure to Khʷārazm (1851); the *Adjmal al-tawarīkh* (lith. Tabrīz 1283) is a short précis of the history of Persia composed for the crown prince Muẓaffar al-Dīn; the *Rawḍat al-ṣafā-yi Nāṣirī*, continuation of the *Rawḍat al-ṣafā* of Mīr Khʷānd [*q.v.*] down to 1270/1853 (Tehran 1270, 3 vols. fol., also Tehran 1338-9/1959-60, 10 vols.), is a work of considerable size, based on eastern sources (of which several are still unpublished) and on official documents, most of which are reproduced in full; in addition to the record of political events the work contains much geographical, literary and artistic information. The *Riyāḍ al-ᶜārifīn* ("Gardens of the initiated"), biographies of mystical poets, with an excellent introduction on Ṣūfism, was prepared for Muḥammad Shāh (lith. 1305, Tehran, printed Tehran 1336-40/1957-61, 2 vols. in 6). It is closely connected with the *Madjmaᶜ al-fuṣaḥāʾ* ("Assembly of eloquent individuals"), of first importance for the history of Persian poetry (lith. Tehran 1294, 2 vols. fol.); this last work, the author's best, contains after a general introduction on the history of Persian poetry, biographies and select pieces from all the poets (the poet laureates form the first section); at the end is an autobiography and an anthology of the poems of Hidāyat (ii, 581-678; autobiography and a number of the verses reproduced by the author of the *Fārs-nāma-yi Nāṣirī*, ii, 125). The researches necessary for these last two works showed Hidāyat the inadequacy of the dictionaries at his disposal; he intended to remedy this by his *Farhang-i andjuman-ārā-yi Nāṣirī* (lith. Tehran 1288) which, preceded by a remarkable introduction, gives the different meanings of each Persian word, with quotations from the classical poets. The work entitled *Madāridj al-balāgha* (lith. 1331) is a glossary of rhetorical and poetical terms with many examples taken from different poets. Lastly, we owe to Hidāyat the first editions of the *Dīwān* of Manūčihrī (lith. Tehran 1297), of the *Ḳābūs-nāma* (*ibid.* 1275) and of the *Nafthat al-maṣdūr* (history of the fall of the Khʷārazmian empire) of Muḥammad Zaydarī (publ. posthumously, Tehran 1308). Its autobiographical character gives the attractive "Narrative of a Journey to Khʷārazm" (*Safar-nāma-yi Khʷārazm*, ed. and tr. Schefer, in *PEIOV*, Paris 1879) a special place among his works; he undertook this journey in 1851 as ambassador sent to settle the differences between the courts of Tehran and Khīwa. This journal is a valuable document for the history of the khānates and has been utilised by later Persian historians (notably Muḥammad Ḥasan Khān [*q.v.*]); besides valuable historical, archaeological and geographical matter, the book, which is written in a simple and natural style, is a contribution to the study of the manners and customs of the period (notably, conditions of travel); we find in it pretty pictures of native life and charming landscapes. Several of Hidāyat's descendants have taken a prominent part in literature, politics and administration.

Bibliography: In addition to works already mentioned: Rieu, *Cat. of Persian manuscripts in the British Museum*, Suppl., index; Edwards, *Persian printed books in the British Museum*; E.G. Browne, *LHP*, iv (index and portrait, 344); *GrIPh.*, ii, index; de Gobineau, *Trois ans en Asie* (ch. "Les caractères"); S. Churchill, in *JRAS* (1886), 196-204, (1887), 163;

A. Kégl, *Riza Kuli Xan als Dichter*, in *WZKM*, xi (1897), 63-74; Niẓāmī-i ʿArūḍī, *Čahār maḳāla*, ed. Browne, index, 320, s.v. Madjmaʿ ul-Fuṣaḥāʾ; Storey, i, 224, 239, 342-3, 906-13, 1246.

(H. Massé*)

RİḌĀ NŪR, Rizâ Nur (1879-8 September 1942), urkish medical doctor, politician, diplomat, an of letters and nationalist ideologue, born the Black Sea town of Sinop in 1879. After 'aduating from the military medical college he ught at the Faculty of Medicine, but abandoned edicine for politics after the constitution was stored in July 1908. Elected to the parliament from nop, Rīḍā Nūr joined the opposition Liberal party *ḥrār Fïrḳasï*) against the *Ittiḥād ve Teraḳḳī Djemʿiyyeti* .*v.*], the CUP. Suspected of playing a role in the ortive counter-revolution of April 1909, he fled to gypt but returned to continue his oppositional role gainst the CUP. On 19 July 1910 he was arrested for onspiring against the government but was acquitted r lack of evidence. He became a founding member the *Ḥürriyyet ve Iʾtilāf Fïrḳasï* [*q.v.*] in November 911, which attempted to unite all the opponents of e CUP. After the assassination of Maḥmūd hewkat Pasha [*q.v.*] in June 1913 he was exiled to urope.

Rīḍā Nūr returned to Istanbul after the armistice of ctober 1918 and was elected to the last Ottoman arliament, where he allied with the Islamists and ttoman patriots. But in April 1920 he joined the ationalists in Ankara, serving the movement in variıs capacities: as Minister of Education (May 1920); the delegation to Moscow (January 1921); Minister Health (December 1921-September 1922); and elegate to the Lausanne Conference (1922-23). As a pporter of the caliphate, he sided with the conseratives against Muṣṭafā Kemāl and was again forced go into exile. He published the *Revue de Turcologie* Paris and Alexandria between 1931 and 1937 and ft behind a number of manuscripts, including his emoirs, in the British Library, London. Rīḍā Nūr as allowed to return to Turkey in December 1938 ter Kemal Atatürk's death and again became active politics and the pan-Turkist press, writing in jourals like *Kopuz*. He founded *Tanrıdağ* in May 1942 nd died soon after in September, having led an dventurous and colourful life.

Bibliography: Rīḍā Nūr, *Medjlisī Mebʿūthānda firḳalar mesʾelesi*, Istanbul 1325; idem, *Djemʿiyyet-i khāfiye*. Istanbul 1330; idem, *Hürriyyet ve Iʾtilāf naṣïl doghdu, naṣïl öldü*, Istanbul 1334; idem, *Hayat ve hatıratım*, 4 vols., Istanbul 1967-8; T.Z. Tunaya, *Türkiye'de siyasi partiler 1859-1952*, Istanbul 1952; idem, *Türkiye'de siyasal partiler*, 3 vols., Istanbul 1984-9; Utkan Kocatürk, *Atatürk ve Türkiye Cumhuriyeti tarihi kronolojisi 1918-1938*, Ankara 1983; Sina Akşin, *31 Mart olayı*, Ankara 1970; idem, *Jön Türkler ve İttihat ve Terakki*, Istanbul 1987; Feroz Ahmad, *The Young Turks: the Committee of Union and Progress in Turkish politics 1908-1914*, Oxford 1969; Ergun Aybars, *İstiklâl mahkemeleri*, i-ii, Izmir 1989 (and earlier eds.); J. Landau, *Pan-Turkism in Turkey*, London 1981; Cemil Koçak, *Türkiye'de milli şef dönemi (1938-1945)*, Ankara 1986; Cavit Orhan Tütengil, *Doktor Rıza Nur üzerine, üç yazı-yankılar-belgeler*, Ankara 1965; idem, *Rıza Nur'un kişiliği*, in *Cumhuriyet*, 10 August 1964. (Feroz Ahmad)

RIḌĀ SHĀH (1295-1365/1878-1944), founder nd first ruler of the Pahlavī dynasty of Persia 344-99/1925-79). Riḍā Shāh replaced the deposed ḥmad Shāh Ḳādjār in 1925, having previously parcipated in the *coup d'état* of 1921, which eventually led to the ousting of the Ḳādjār dynasty. Between 1925 and 1941, he was the catalyst for the modernisation programme which gave Iran the infrastructure of a 20th-century nation-state. In 1941, he was forced to abdicate by the British and Soviets on account of his pro-Nazi leanings. He died in exile outside Johannesburg in 1944.

Riḍā Shāh's career falls into two distinct phases: his first forty-five years as a commoner, and the fifteen years of his rule as Shāh. As with other founders of dynasties, Riḍā Shāh's origins are comparatively obscure. The official date of his birth was 16 March 1878 and he was born in the village of Alasht in the Sawad Kūh of Māzandarān. His father, ʿAbbās ʿAlī Khān, who was an officer in the Ḳādjār army, died in the same year. His mother, from an emigrant family from Erivan, then took him to Tehran where, around 1893, he joined the Shāh's Cossack Brigade. This unit, established by Nāṣir al-Dīn Shāh in 1879 and officered by Russians, was at that time the most effective unit in the Iranian army. Riḍā enlisted as a common soldier, but was soon promoted successively to corporal, sergeant, and sergeant-major, and in 1911, having seen active service in the turbulent period which followed the constitutional movement of 1905-6, was commissioned as a second lieutenant, and a year later, promoted to lieutenant. After further experience campaigning against recalcitrant tribes, in 1915 he was promoted to the rank of major. He was regarded as a model officer, with a reputation for both bravery and conscientiousness. He also seems to have become politically *engagé* about this time as the result of neutral Iran's occupation by British, Russian, and Ottoman forces during the course of the First World War.

In 1916, he became a lieutenant-colonel, and a year later was appointed to command one of the Cossack regiments. It seems that Riḍā Khān felt increasingly bitter that the force in which he served, although regarded as the "crack" unit of the Iranian army, was an instrument of Russian influence in Persia. The outbreak of the Russian Revolution in 1917 shattered the Russian command-structure in the Cossack Brigade and in the course of the machinations which followed, Riḍā Khān was promoted rapidly to the rank of general officer. The First World War had now ended, the Anglo-Persian Agreement of 1919 had been drawn up, virtually reducing the country to the status of a British protectorate, and a British military mission, under Major-General W.E.R. Dickson, had arrived in Tehran. In May 1920, Bolshevik forces bombarded Enzelī, and the Djangalī movement under Kūčak Khān [*q.v.*] in Gīlān forced a response from the feeble central government, resulting in Riḍā Khān's participation in the fighting in Gīlān, in which, despite militarily inconclusive results, he returned to Tehran with an enhanced reputation for courage and resourcefulness.

Promoted to the rank of full general, he was now appointed to command the Cossack regiments stationed in Ḳazwīn, and it was probably here that he first made contact with the British. In October 1920, the British forces stationed in northwestern Persia (a holdover from the First World War) were placed under the command of General Edmund Ironside, who, along with other British officers, came to respect the morose giant as the outstanding figure among the Cossack officers of the Ḳazwīn garrison. Only a few months later, there occurred the *coup d'état* of February 1921, involving *inter alios* the pro-British journalist, Sayyid Ḍiyāʾ al-Dīn Ṭabāṭabāʾī, which provided the opportunity for Riḍā Khān's rise to power. For the

Sayyid needed military force to carry through his *coup*, and Riḍā Khān was the man to provide it, when his Cossacks advanced on Tehran from Ḳazwīn (18-21 February 1921). At the time, public opinion in Tehran assumed that the British must have been behind these events, a viewpoint later frowned upon during the Pahlavī period, when the coup was represented to have been a spontaneous act in which Riḍā Khān played the leading part. Recent publications (e.g. Zirinsky, *Imperial power and dictatorship*) point to local British military and diplomatic involvement, but not British government sponsorship.

Ḍiyāʾ, who became Prime Minister following the coup, sought to initiate a coherent programme of internal reform and to end the threat of further national disintegration and fragmentation, working within the framework of the Constitution of 1906-7, and with Aḥmad Shāh Ḳādjār (1327-42/1909-24) as a constitutional monarch. Although lacking political acumen, Ḍiyāʾ was a high-minded patriot of considerable ability and from the outset understood that reform had to include military reform. In the first proclamation of his new government (24 February 1921), he declared himself in favour of "An army before and above everything. Everything first for the army, and again for the army ... until our armed forces reach the highest stage of development" (Wilber, *Riza Shah Pahlavi*, 49). This was, no doubt, the *quid pro quo* between Ḍiyāʾ and Riḍā Khān which had led to their collaboration, for Riḍā Khān had long deplored the supine state of the country and its helplessness in the face of foreign aggression, which was the direct consequence of its military backwardness. Riḍā Khān was now appointed *Sardār-i Sipah* (Army Commander), subordinate to the Minister of War, a post which he was also to assume within a matter of months. He now undertook what was to be his most concrete achievement, the modernisation of Persia's armed forces, which coincided with the effective suppression of insurgency in Ādharbaydjān, Gīlān and Khurāsān, and among the Kurds, Lurs, Bakhtiyārīs and Ḳashḳāʾīs, a process which was to continue in the years following his accession to the throne. The two processes complemented each other. The army, reorganised, well-disciplined and equipped with modern weapons, became the agent for the forceful reassertion of the authority of the central government throughout the provinces, while its successes in the field reinforced its prestige and self-confidence, making the man who had willed it into existence—Riḍā Khān—indispensable to the politicians.

As *Sardār-i Sipah*, Riḍā Khān, semi-literate and unpolished compared with the old-style Persian aristocracy, found himself "odd man out" in a government in which his colleagues were mostly, and inevitably, scions of the old Ḳādjār ruling élite. Ḍiyāʾ himself did not last long—by May, he had resigned and gone into exile—and his replacement as prime minister was Ḳawām al-Salṭana, a former governor-general of Khurāsān recently imprisoned by Ḍiyāʾ, the brother of the former premier, Wuthūḳ al-Dawla (1918-20), and one of the greatest Persian statesmen of the 20th century. As Minister of War, Riḍā Khān's name continued to be in the forefront of affairs. In October 1921, the Djangalī revolt in Gīlān collapsed and Kūčak Khān died in that same month, and by the middle of the following year, the Kurdish rebels had been defeated and their leader, Ismāʿīl Khān "Simko", had fled into exile. These successes convinced the Madjlis (Parliament) of the value of Riḍā Khān's army reforms, and even if it did not trust him, it was prevailed upon to grant him additional revenues with which to provide for the further expa sion of the army. With regard to funds for the latte his appetite was insatiable. Meanwhile, the army w emerging as a new and, ultimately, the dominant fa tor in the Persian equation. In Avery's word "uniforms and extortion, heavy boots and the rif butt came to symbolise a new form of tyranny. In o forms there were always detachable elements and certain sense of community had existed betwee tyrants and the people. ... The nobility and the clerg for all their faults and shortcomings, had social virtu which from time to time were exercised for the benef of the society of which they formed a recognised an integrated part. They had nothing to do with the ho rors of the guardroom and military prison" (Avery *Modern Iran*, 259).

During the 1920s, the two great powers long a customed to deciding the fate of Persia, Russia an Great Britain, were both preoccupied elsewhere. Bri ain was war-weary and distracted by world-wid responsibilities, while the new Soviet Union was lock ed in civil strife, massive social dislocation, an economic experimentation. Under Diyāʾ, a Russ Persian treaty, which had been under negotiatio since the previous year, was signed on 26 Februar 1921, which, for the time being, satisfactorily redef ned relations between the two countries. On the sam day, the Sayyid repudiated the hated Anglo-Persia Agreement, leaving British policy in Persia in tempo rary limbo. Thus, the British would be forced t acquiesce in Riḍā Khān's pacification of the Bakh tiyārī, and his overthrow of Shaykh Khazʿal [*q.v.*] o Muḥammara in Khūzistān (November 1924-Januar 1925), both erstwhile clients of the Anglo-Persian O Company. As Minister of War, his authority grew a that of his colleagues declined, and on 28 Octobe 1923 the Shāh grudgingly appointed him Prim Minister prior to his own departure for Europe o health grounds. He never returned to Persia, dying i France four years later. On 13 March 1924, th Madjlis met and appointed a committee to conside the question of Persia becoming a republic, a mov which Riḍā Khān initially seemed to favour, and a bi was submitted to the Madjlis on 15 March. But i that same month, the Turkish Grand Nationa Assembly abolished the caliphate, confiscated *awḳā* (religious endowments) and brought religious educa tion under the jurisdiction of the Ministry of Educa tion. The Shīʿī *ʿulamāʾ* in Persia were naturally ap prehensive at these developments, which seemed t equate republicanism with secularism and sacrilege and Riḍā Khān heeded their fears and played o them, proclaiming on 1 April 1925, following a visi to Ḳum, that a republic would be better for the wel fare of the country. On 31 October 1925, the Madjli formally deposed Aḥmād Shāh and ended the rule o the Ḳādjār dynasty, although in a long dissentien speech, Dr. Muḥammad Muṣaddiḳ [*q.v.*] (formerly Muṣaddiḳ al-Salṭana), anticipating Riḍā Khān' imminent elevation to the throne, pointed out that whatever the good qualities of the Prime Minister ha been, as Shāh he would wield a power contrary to th Constitution. Finally, on 12 December 1925, th Madjlis voted for Riḍā Khān to become Shāh. Ther were some abstentions, but only four publicly oppose the vote: the veteran Constitutionalist Sayyid Ḥasa Taḳīzāda, Ḥusayn ʿAlā, Yaḥyā Dawlatābādī and Dr Muṣaddiḳ. Riḍā Khān had already assumed th family name of Pahlavī, redolent of ancient pre Islamic Iranian glories, and so the Pahlavī dynast was duly established by law.

Crowned Shāh in the old Gulistān Palace on 25

April 1926, Riḍā Shāh now embarked upon a brutal but effective programme of modernisation which left untouched almost no area of Iranian life. The overall social structure remained superficially the same, but military officers, bureaucrats, and well-connected entrepreneurs and contractors came into prominence, often becoming richer and certainly more influential than the former court nobility, landlords, clerics, and *bāzārīs*. Now, cronyism became the most direct road to wealth and power, and vast fortunes were dubiously acquired, that of Riḍā Shāh himself being of spectacular extent. The predominant characteristics of the new régime were centralisation and regulation, a despotism of licenses and permits, enforced by a horde of officials, police and, ultimately, the army. Most manifestations of free speech or opposition were ruthlessly stamped out, and the fiscal rapacity of the régime probably exceeded that of any of its predecessors. In this sense, Riḍā Shāh's rule strongly resembled the governing style of the other dictatorships which emerged during the 1920s and 1930s.

At the same time, enormous changes took place in the material life of the Iranian people. Roads were built (generally, with strategic considerations to the fore, especially in tribal territory), a Trans-Iranian railway linked the Persian Gulf to the Caspian Sea, and Iran was integrated with the rest of the world by air- and steamship-links. New industries were set up—textile mills, sugar refineries, cement works. There was an emphasis on the pre-Islamic components of Persian culture; language reform to eliminate Arabic elements; and a downplaying of Iran's historic links with the Arab lands of the Middle East. At the level of scholarship and archaeology, there was a remarkable revival of knowledge of Iran's early history, much of it due to European savants.

Yet despite the achievements of these fifteen years, Riḍā Shāh remained the quintessential dictator, suspicious of those around him, fearful lest anyone other than himself should earn public respect or admiration, and malignant toward those who opposed his will or offered alternative solutions. His vindictiveness was proverbial and his prisons were kept full. Former collaborators and helpmates such as Tīmūrtāsh, the Minister of Court, and Sardār Asʿad Bakhtiyārī, the Minister of War, died in prison under mysterious circumstances, as did his critic in the Madjlis, Sayyid Ḥasan Mudarris. ʿAlī Akbar Dāwar, the Minister of Justice, committed suicide. Writers and journalists were no less subject to persecution. The poet ʿIshḳī was murdered; the novelist Buzurg ʿAlawī was imprisoned, and there were others.

The style of Riḍā Shāh's government was despotic and militaristic, with the Shāh taking the important decisions, which were then carried out by his ministers, most of whom (Dāwar was an exception) were ciphers. In foreign policy, Riḍā Shāh's achievements were more positive in that, conscious of the past diplomatic history of his country, he was able to diminish the role of both Great Britain and the Soviet Union in its internal affairs, establishing an international persona for a country which had for so long seemed to be an Anglo-Russian protectorate. Iran (he had abandoned the Eurocentric name of Persia) was an early signatory of the League of Nations, thereafter widening its diplomatic representation overseas. Of particular significance were Riḍā Shāh's diplomatic forays into the Middle East. In 1934, he paid a state visit to Turkey, becoming personally acquainted with Atatürk, and in 1937, he engineered the regional Saʿdābād Pact with Afghānistān, ʿIrāḳ and Turkey. In that same year, Iran signed a treaty with ʿIrāḳ over the Shaṭṭ al-ʿArab. An Egyptian marriage for the Crown Prince, Muḥammad Riḍā [*q.v.*], established links with Egypt's ruling élite and did something to open up a court which had hitherto been drab and provincial. Riḍā Shāh had four wives: the first, Hamdām, had a daughter of the same name; the second, Tādj-i Malik, gave him Shams, the twins Muḥammad Riḍā and Ashraf, and ʿAlī Riḍā; the third, Turān, a Ḳādjār, gave him one son, Ghulām Riḍā; and by ʿIṣmat, also a Ḳādjār, he had four sons—ʿAbd al-Riḍā, Maḥmūd Riḍā, Aḥmad Riḍā and Ḥamīd Riḍā—and a daughter, Fāṭima.

In the years prior to the Second World War, Riḍā Shāh rashly assumed a pro-German stance, intended to reduce Iran's dependence on Great Britain and the Soviet Union, while the Nazis assiduously wooed and flattered him. With the outbreak of war, both Great Britain and the Soviet Union demanded that these German connections be severed. The Shāh, however, prevaricated, and he was forced to witness the invasion of his country by British and Soviet units, which began on 25 August 1941. Against these, his prized and pampered army performed abysmally. He abdicated on 16 September 1941, in order to ensure his son's succession, and was taken by the British first to Mauritius and then to the Transvaal in South Africa, where he died on 26 July 1944.

There is little disagreement about Riḍā Shāh's character and temperament. He had developed at an early age the soldierly virtues of personal courage, self-discipline and concentrated application, and these qualities were to stand him in good stead throughout his life. A man of limited formal education and little imagination, he seems to have been a remarkable example of the self-taught man of action who utilised his limited experience to maximum advantage as a head of state who was both usurper and revolutionary. In this sense, he was more reminiscent of Peter I of Russia or Muḥammad ʿAlī of Egypt than of Atatürk, the man with whom he is usually compared, who was at once a more complicated and a more cosmopolitan personality.

With his great height, commanding bearing, and raptorial glare, Riḍā Shāh's awe-inspiring presence reinforced an impression of ruthlessness and brutal strength. His son would write: "Those eyes could make a strong man shrivel up inside" (Mohammad Reza Pahlavi, *Mission for my country*, London 1961, 36). General Ḥasan Arfa, encountering him soon after his promotion to *Sardār-i Sipah*, noted: "His complexion was rather dark and his eyes of a strange golden hue were large with a searching look which it took courage to meet. He had a small black moustache slightly turned up at the ends, and altogether his appearance was extremely virile and soldierly" (*Under five Shahs*, 115-16). At his coronation, four years later, Vita Sackville-West described him as "... an alarming man, six feet three in height, with a sullen manner, a huge nose, grizzled hair, and a brutal jowl" (V. Sackville-West, *Passenger to Tehran*, London 1926, 103-4). Decades after his death, his principal wife, Tādj-i Malik, confessed that "she did her best to keep out of his way" (A. Alam, *The Shah and I*, New York 1992, 447), and his daughter Ashraf wrote that "Even as an adult I would weigh my words carefully before I brought up any subject that might provoke or displease him", while at the same time she admired "his stubbornness, his fierce pride, and his iron will" (Ashraf Pahlavi, *Faces in a mirror*, Englewood Cliffs 1980, 13-14). These were no doubt the qualities needed at that time to impose by sheer will-power from above the radical reorganisation of a profoundly conservative society, and it was just that which was to prove Riḍā Sh̲āh's lasting achievement.

Bibliography: Yaḥyā Dawlatābādī, Tārīkh-i muʿāṣir yā ḥayāt-i Yaḥyā, Tehran 1331/1952; Ḥusayn Makkī, Tārīkh-i bīst-sāla-yi Īrān, Tehran 1324/1945; Hassan Arfa, Under five Shahs, London 1964; Amin Banani, The modernization of Iran, Stanford 1961; P. Avery, Modern Iran, London 1965; D.N. Wilber, Riza Shah Pahlavi: the resurrection and reconstruction of Iran, New York 1975; L.P. Elwell-Sutton, Reza Shah the Great: founder of the Pahlavi dynasty, in Iran under the Pahlavis, ed. G. Lenczowski, Stanford 1978, 1-50; E. Abrahamian, Iran between two revolutions, Princeton 1982; M.P. Zirinsky, Blood, power, and hypocrisy: the murder of Robert Imbrie and American relations with Pahlavi Iran, 1924, in IJMES, xviii (1986), 275-92; Sussan Siavoshi, Liberal nationalism in Iran: the failure of a movement, Boulder 1990; G.R.G. Hambly, The Pahlavi autocracy: Riza Shah, 1921-1941, in The Cambridge History of Iran, vii, ed. Avery and Hambly, Cambridge 1991, 213-43; Zirinsky, Imperial power and dictatorship: Britain and the rise of Reza Shah, 1921-1926, in IJMES, xxiv (1992), 639-63.
(G.R.G. Hambly)

RIḌĀ TEWFĪḲ [see bölükbash̲ī, rīḍā tewfīḳ, in Suppl.].

RIḌĀʿ [see raḍāʿ].

RIḌĀʾĪ, Āḳā, Muḥammad D̲jahāngīrī or Harāwī, Persian painter in the service of the Mug̲h̲al prince Salīm or D̲jahāngīr in the late 10th-early 11th/late 16th-early 17th century. Mentioned in D̲jahāngīr's memoirs, Āḳā Riḍāʾī of Harāt or Marw joined Salīm's service before 997/1588-9, the year in which his son Abu 'l-Ḥasan was born at Salīm's court. On a portrait of Shāh D̲jahān of ca. 1050/1640, Abu 'l-Ḥasan refers to himself as "al-Mash̲hadī", a nisba repeated on a painting by his brother ʿĀbid. However, no direct connection between Āḳā Riḍāʾī and Mash̲had can be established. He may have emigrated to India as a result of the Uzbek invasion of Harāt and massacre of its inhabitants in 996/1587.

Āḳā Riḍāʾī's known work ranges in date between ca. 996-1018/1587-1609 and includes manuscript illustrations, album margins and single-page portraits. Stylistically, his oeuvre adheres closely to Persian models; his manuscript illustrations reflect a familiarity with the court painting of Sh̲āh Ṭahmāsp (r. 931-84/1524-76 [q.v.]), while his single-figure portraits rely on the Kh̲urāsān style of Muḥammadī Harawī (fl. 968-99/1560-90). Although Āḳā Riḍāʾī consistently preferred the two-dimensionality and decorative surface treatment of Persian painting, he did employ shading, especially on faces, a concession to Mug̲h̲al naturalism. Having worked for Salīm at Lahore, he continued in the service of the prince during his rebellion at Allāhābād from 1008/1599 to 1013/1604. As the leading artist at Salīm's Allāhābād court, Āḳā Riḍāʾī exerted a strong Persianate influence on the art of his fellow painters. Yet he also absorbed some elements of late Akbarī painting, enlarging the scale and reducing the number of figures in his manuscript illustrations. When Salīm acceded to the throne in 1014/1605 and took charge of the imperial artists' atelier, Āḳā Riḍāʾī was rapidly eclipsed by painters working in the fully synthesised Mug̲h̲al style.

His major works include: 1-4. Marginal illustrations of four folios of the Muraḳḳaʿ-i Gulshan, Gulistan Library, Tehran, fols. 29, 105, 145, 152. One, with vignettes based on European prints, is dated 28 Ramaḍān 1008/12 April 1600. 5-7. Two manuscript illustrations and one portrait of a prince kneeling before Sh̲aykh̲ Salīm Čisht̲ī, from the Muraḳḳaʿ-i Gulshan. The manuscript illustrations rely closely on Ṣafawid prototypes and may date from the late 990s/1580s. 8-12. Five illustrations to the Anwār-i Suhaylī, British Library, Add. 18,579, fols. 21a, 36a, 40b, 54b, and 331b, dated 1013-19/1604-10; 13. Seated Musician, late 990s/1580s, Museum of Fine Arts, Boston, 14.609; 14. Bustān of Saʿdī, dated 1014/1605-6, Agra, fol. 147a, Art and History Trust Collection, Houston; 15. Kulliyyāt of Saʿdī, Prince Sadruddin Aga Khan Collection, fol. 91a. Other attributed works are listed in Beach, The Grand Mogul, 94-5. Āḳā Riḍāʾī signed his paintings on rocks or near the main figures, referring to himself as murīd, g̲h̲ulām or banda ("disciple", "servant" or "slave") bā-ikhlāṣ (sincere) of Sh̲āh, Sultan or Pādish̲āh Salīm or D̲jahāngīr, depending on the date. Attributions are written near or in the margins.

Bibliography: Tūzuk-i D̲jahāngīrī, tr. Rogers and Beveridge, London 1914, ii, 20; The Lights of Canopus, Anvar-i Suhaili, described by J.V.S. Wilkinson, London, n.d., 15 and pls. iii, iv, v, vii, xxix; Binyon, Wilkinson, and Gray, Persian miniature painting, Oxford 1933, 149 (no 236), 160, 192 and pl. CIVa; M.C. Beach, The Grand Mogul, Williamston, Mass. 1978, 92-5, cat. no. 30. This contains a thorough list of attributions and bibliography; A. Welch and S.C. Welch, Arts of the Islamic book: the collection of Prince Sadruddin Aga Khan, 179-82, 191-7, cat. nos. 60, 64, fol. 91a; P.P. Soucek, art. Āqā Reżā Heravī", in EIr, ii, 180-2; A. Okada, Imperial Mughal painters, Paris 1992, 104-11; A. Soudavar, Art of the Persian courts, New York 1992, 348-9, cat. no. 137p, fol. 147r.
(R. Ettinghausen-[Sheila R. Canby])

AL-RIDDA [see Suppl.].

RIḌIYYA [see raḍiyya].

RIDJĀL (A.), pl. of rad̲jul, a common Arabic word for "man", used specifically in Arabic literature for transmitters of ḥadīth [q.v.], i.e. Muslim tradition. When in the course of the second half of the 1st century of the hid̲jra (the 690s) the isnād [q.v.], i.e. the chain of transmitters of a tradition, had been introduced as the semi-official authentification device for it to be accepted or rejected, rather than that authentification was achieved by weighing the matn, i.e. its actual contents, the need to identify ḥadīth transmitters and to obtain detailed information on them, gave rise to the so-called rid̲jāl books which, beginning with the late 2nd/8th century, eventually acquired gigantic proportions. Islam's multi-volume biographical dictionaries may be thought of as having grown out of the rid̲jāl lexicons. During the first three centuries of Islam, giving information on someone was tantamount to supplying details about his study and handling of ḥadīths. Only in a later stage did biographical dictionaries (e.g. those of Yāḳūt (d. 626/1229 [q.v.]) and Ibn Kh̲allikān (d. 681/1282 [q.v.]) gradually develop their own characteristics, being no longer confined within strictly ḥadīth-determined dimensions.

With the introduction under ʿUmar b. al-Kh̲aṭṭāb [q.v.] of the dīwān [q.v. at II, 323b], listing those entitled to an annual stipend from the treasury, the ancient Arab interest in tribal genealogy received a new impulse; with the emergence of isnāds half a century later this interest was deepened even more. The isnād requirement stipulated that, apart from simple identification of a transmitter within his lineage, information on his lifetime as well as that of his alleged ḥadīth masters and pupils be gathered, which was meant to facilitate the drawing of conclusions as to the feasibility of his actual having met with either. The science of ḥadīth criticism became inextricably intertwined with *ridjāl* expertise, which formed its major constituent. This science also goes by the name of *al-djarḥ wa 'l-ta*ʿ*dīl* [*q.v.*] (i.e. the science of disparaging and declaring trustworthy, sc. *ḥadīth* transmitters). For a survey of the mediaeval Muslim *ḥadīth* scholar's wielding of the technical terms and criteria used in *ridjāl* criticism, see AL-DJARḤ WA 'L-TAʿDĪL; for a modern appraisal of the same, see what follows, and also G.H.A. Juynboll, *Muslim tradition* etc., Cambridge 1983, chs. 4-5.

The classical period

The first *ḥadīth* expert whose name is linked to the science of "men" was Shuʿba b. al-Ḥadjdjādj (d. 160/776 [*q.v.*]) from Baṣra. He was soon followed in this by a string of other *ḥadīth* experts, e.g. Yaḥyā b. Saʿīd al-Ḳaṭṭān (d. 198/813), allegedly the first whose judgements were compiled in a book (cf. Ibn Ḥadjar, *Lisān al-mīzān*, i, 5), ʿAbd al-Raḥmān b. Mahdī (d. 198/813), Muḥammad b. ʿUmar al-Wāḳidī, the author of the *Maghāzī* (d. 207/822) and Abū Nuʿaym al-Faḍl b. Dukayn (d. 219/834) [*q.v.*]), but their collections of data have not been preserved except for occasional quotations in biographical lexicons compiled later. The oldest extant printed collection deserving the qualification *ridjāl* lexicon is the *Kitāb al-Ṭabaḳāt al-kabīr* by Ibn Saʿd [*q.v.*] (ed. E. Sachau *et alii*, Leiden 1905-17, 9 vols., with some 4250 entries), who died in 230/845. Muḥammad b. Saʿd used to be al-Wāḳidī's secretary, which permits the assumption that the data we find in his work may be at least partly al-Wāḳidī's. As its title indicates, Ibn Saʿd's *ṭabaḳāt* work is built upon the successive "generations" (literally: "layers") of *ḥadīth* transmitters from each major urban centre in the early Islamic domain. Ibn Saʿd preceded his *ridjāl* information by an extensive biography of the Prophet. Large numbers of the *ridjāl* dealt with are only mentioned by name, and their historicity—if any—is well-nigh impossible to establish.

From the beginning, *isnād* criticism comprised two main approaches, knowledge of *ridjāl* and that of *ʿilal* (the plural of *ʿilla*, usually rendered "hidden defects", sc. mostly in *isnāds*, highlighting links between certain pairs of transmitters which are subject to dispute). *Ridjāl* studies contain of necessity numerous references to *ʿilal*, while *ʿilal* studies are in fact *ridjāl* works analysing (the absence of) certain links among them. The earliest works after Ibn Saʿd's *Ṭabaḳāt* still reflect both approaches in their titles, such as the *Kitāb al-ʿIlal wa-maʿrifat al-ridjāl* of Aḥmad Ibn Ḥanbal (d. 241/855 [*q.v.*]), in which there is not yet discernible an alphabetical arrangement of the *ridjāl* treated (cf. the edition by T. Koçyiğit and İ. Cerrahoğlu, Ankara 1963, i). Later *ridjāl*-cum-*ʿilal* works often have the title *taʾrīkh*. In its earliest usage this term does not necessarily mean historiography *per se*, since the "men" surveyed in such works are not described in their political roles but are mostly assessed exclusively as to their merits or demerits in the transmission of *ḥadīth*. On the whole, the genres of *ṭabaḳāt, ʿilal* and *taʾrīkh* (the last-mentioned in the *ḥadīth*-technical sense of the term) show in many early works a considerable, if not total, overlap.

Khalīfa b. Khayyāṭ (d. 240/854 [see IBN KHAYYĀṬ AL-ʿUṢFURĪ]) separated his *ridjāl* material from his other information by producing a *ṭabaḳāt* work proper (cf. the edition of A.Ḍ. al-ʿUmarī, Baghdād 1967, with some 3,300 entries), next to a *Taʾrīkh*, the earliest published annalistic chronicle of Islam (cf. the editions of A.Ḍ. al-ʿUmarī, 2nd impr., Damascus-Beirut 1977, and Suhayl Zakkār, Damascus 1967, 2 vols.). Al-Ṭabarī's *Taʾrīkh*, Islam's best-known annalistic history compiled a little more than half a century later, is arranged like Khalīfa's, but is concluded by a *ridjāl* section entitled *Dhayl al-mudhayyal min taʾrīkh al-ṣaḥāba wa 'l-tābiʿīn* (ed. De Goeje, iii, 2296-2561). Furthermore, the title *taʾrīkh* was given to works of even more varied, almost encyclopaedic, contents: the *Taʾrīkh* of the Andalusian author ʿAbd al-Malik b. Ḥabīb (d. 238/853) contains only a relatively brief section on *ṭabaḳāt*, cf. the edition of J. Aguadé, Madrid 1991, 156-78. Many 3rd/9th century *ʿilal, ṭabaḳāt* and *taʾrīkh* works by authors contemporaneous with, and somewhat later than, Ibn Saʿd have not been preserved, but references to these can be found in *GAS*, i, title index, and Juynboll, *Muslim tradition*, 238-41. In the following, only some of those works that are presently extant in printed editions will be surveyed in roughly chronological order, together with their respective salient features and innovative approach (if any). In order to illustrate the ongoing updating at the hands of later compilers, resulting in constantly swelling numbers of transmitters described (for this phenomenon, see Juynboll, *Muslim tradition*, 23-30, 137-46), the number of entries will be included where that could be obtained from the editions or otherwise approximated.

Among the most critical early *isnād* experts is Yaḥyā b. Maʿīn (d. 233/847). Several of his *ridjāl* works in different redactions of pupils bearing various titles (cf. *GAS*, i, 107) have recently become available in print (editions by Aḥmad M. Nūr Sayf, Damascus-Beirut 1980). Quotations from his works in later collections are mostly introduced by *ḳāla* ... *ʿan Yaḥyā* ..., or *ḳāla Yaḥyā*....

Allegedly less severe, but as frequently quoted, is ʿAlī b. ʿAbd Allāh Ibn al-Madīnī (d. 234/849). His works acquired such fame that references to them mostly begin with the words: *ḳāla ʿAlī*... His *ʿIlal* (*al-ḥadīth wa-maʿrifat al-ridjāl*) was printed in Beirut, 1972 (ed. M.M. al-Aʿẓamī), and Aleppo 1980 (ed. ʿAbd al-Muʿṭī Amīn Ḳalʿadjī).

After Ibn Saʿd's *Ṭabaḳāt*, the first similarly extensive *ridjāl* lexicon is that of al-Bukhārī (d. 256/870 [*q.v.*]). As was the case with Ibn Saʿd, information on a great many individual transmitters in al-Bukhārī's *Taʾrīkh kabīr* (ed. Ḥaydarābād 1361-5, 8 vols.) is lacking or very brief and constitutes evidence of the as yet overall scantiness of biographical data in circulation. But the proliferation of single strand *isnāds* had become so widespread, also because of wide-scale imitation of Ibn Ḥanbal's skill in devising them, that many hundreds of transmitters populating these strands had to be accounted for in al-Bukhārī's lexicon, with its 12,791 entries. After all the persons called Muḥammad have been enumerated, a still loosely applied alphabetical order of names is observed: *isms*, and within each *ism* the patronymics, are arranged only on the basis of the first letter; within each new entry the frequency of *isms* is mostly the determining factor in the order observed, not the alphabet. Shortened versions of al-Bukhārī's *Taʾrīkh* are his *Taʾrīkh awsaṭ* and *T. ṣaghīr* (cf. the latter's edition by M.I. Zāyid, Aleppo 1976-7, 2 vols.). Al-Bukhārī has brought those, in his opinion, especially questionable transmitters together in a separate collection, the first of its kind, called *K. al-ḍuʿafāʾ al-ṣaghīr* with 418 entries (edited together with a similar work by al-Nasāʾī (d. 303/915) with 675 entries by M.I. Zāyid, Aleppo 1396).

The Syrian tradition scholar Ibrāhīm b. Yaʿḳūb al-Djūzadjānī (d. 259/873) compiled a very critical *ridjāl* lexicon with 388 entries entitled (*Shadjara fī*) *aḥwāl al-ridjāl*, ed. Ṣubḥī al-Badrī al-Sāmarrāʾī, Beirut 1985, in which he especially criticised ʿIrāḳī transmitters.

The compiler of Islam's second most revered canonical tradition collection, Muslim b. al-Ḥadjdjādj (d. 261/875 [*q.v.*]), devoted the middle part of the introduction to his *Ṣaḥīḥ* to *ridjāl*-critical remarks (cf. the Eng. tr. of this introduction in *JSAI*, v, 273-92). Difficulties in the identification of persons only known by their *kunyas* gave rise to the *kunya* genre, in which Muslim, following the example of Ibn Ḥanbal's *al-Asāmī wa 'l-kunā*, collected his *al-Kunā wa 'l-asmā'*, cf. the facs. edition of Damascus 1984; a similar work was compiled by M. b. A. al-Dūlābī (d. 310/923), cf. the edition of Ḥaydarābād 1904, 2 vols. For other *ridjāl*-related works of Muslim, cf. *GAS*, i, 143.

Aḥmad b. ʿAbd Allāh al-ʿIdjlī (d. 261/875) compiled a work called *Ta'rīkh al-Thiḳāt* which is, like its predecessors, remarkable for its ultra-brief information on most of the transmitters dealt with; the majority of *tardjamas* consists only of the qualification *thiḳa* accompanied by a *nisba* indicating his provenance or his generation. However, it is the most extensive early record of those transmitters defined as *ṣāḥib sunna* (for this technical term, cf. *JSAI*, x [1987], 112-6; moreover, it often indicates that the transmitter thus qualified was considered to have been responsible for certain *sunnas*—to be interpreted in this context as legal or ritual prescriptions—to have come into existence, an allegation confirmed by their frequently-observed position as "common link" in the *isnād* bundles of said *sunnas*). The work was edited in a strictly alphabetical arrangement of its 2,116 entries by ʿAbd al-Muʿṭī Ḳalʿadjī, Beirut 1984.

Abū Zurʿa ʿUbayd Allāh b. ʿAbd al-Karīm al-Rāzī (d. 264/878) compiled a collection of weak transmitters, *K. al-Ḍuʿafā'*, edited together with a similar work of Saʿīd b. ʿAmr al-Bardhaʿī (d. 292/905) by Saʿdī al-Hāshimī, Medina 1982, 3 vols.

Yaʿḳūb b. Sufyān al-Fasawī (d. 277/890) wrote a *K. al-Maʿrifa wa 'l-ta'rīkh* of which the first part is an annalistic history comprising early Islamic history up to the year 240/854, the second and third parts constituting a *ridjāl* lexicon, partly based upon *ṭabaḳāt*, with a host of original data not found in other such works. The annals covering the first 134 years are now lost; for the rest of the work, see the edition of A.Ḍ. al-ʿUmarī, Baghdād 1974, 3 vols.

Abū ʿĪsā Muḥammad b. ʿĪsā al-Tirmidhī (d. 279/892 [*q.v.*]), compiler of one of the six canonical collections, added to his *Djāmiʿ* a final chapter on *ʿilal*; this important *ʿilal* collection was rearranged by one Abū Ṭālib al-Ḳāḍī (d. ?) and edited by Ṣubḥī al-Sāmarrā'ī *et alii*, Beirut 1989. The Ḥanbalī Ibn Radjab (d. 795/1393) wrote an extensive commentary on this *ʿilal* chapter called *Sharḥ ʿilal al-Tirmidhī* (cf. the edition of Ṣubḥī Djāsim al-Ḥumaydī, Baghdād 1396). Beside being a *ridjāl*-cum-*ʿilal* book, Ibn Radjab's study is now recognised as one of the most important *ḥadīth*-theoretical monographs of the Middle Ages.

Abū Dāwūd (d. 275/889), the compiler of one of the canonical collections, had a pupil, Abū ʿUbayd al-Ādjurrī (*fl. ca.* 300/913) who collected his master's pronouncements on *ridjāl* entitled *Su'ālāt adjāba ʿanhā Abū Dāwūd* etc., see the edition of M.ʿA.Ḳ. al-ʿUmarī, Medina 1983.

Aḥmad b. Hārūn al-Bardīdjī (d. 301/914) compiled a *K. al-Ṭabaḳāt fi 'l-asmā' al-mufrada min asmā' al-ʿulamā' wa-aṣḥāb al-ḥadīth* which is available in two editions by S. Shihābī, Damascus 1987, and ʿAbduh ʿA. Kūshk, Damascus 1990.

Muḥammad b. ʿAmr al-ʿUḳaylī (d. 322/934) compiled a *K. al-Ḍuʿafā' wa 'l-matrūkīn*, ed. ʿAbd al-Muʿṭī A. Ḳalʿadjī in 4 vols. with 2,101 entries, Beirut 1984. Apart from the data which are also found in its predecessors in this genre, the book constitutes a major enlargement in that it contains numerous examples of prophetic traditions which the weak and rejected transmitters described are supposed to have brought into circulation.

ʿAbd al-Raḥmān b. Abī Ḥātim al-Rāzī (d. 327/938) produced a massive *ridjāl* lexicon entitled *K. al-Djarḥ wa 'l-taʿdīl*, which is almost wholly based on the data provided by his father, Abū Ḥātim Muḥammad b. Idrīs al-Rāzī (d. 277/890) and the latter's lifelong friend and fellow-tradition expert Abū Zurʿa al-Rāzī. For the transmission paths along which this *ridjāl* information reached Ibn Abī Ḥātim, see Juynboll, *Muslim tradition*, 243 f. In this lexicon, Ibn Abī Ḥātim applied a similar, loosely alphabetical, order in listing names as did al-Bukhārī in his *Ta'rīkh*, with which work it differs in that, with its 18,040 entries (over 5,000 more than al-Bukhārī's) it lists an even greater number of strictly unknown transmitters, the so-called *madjhūlūn*. He also wrote a separate study on *ʿilal*, see the edition (entitled *K. al-ʿilal*) of Cairo 1343-4, 2 vols. It is the first such work in which the traditions with their respective *ʿilal* are primarily arranged according to the order of chapters observed in tradition collections. To Ibn Abī Ḥatim we also owe a brief *ridjāl* work on the shortcomings of al-Bukhārī's *Ta'rīkh*, entitled *Bayān khaṭa' al-Bukhārī fī ta'rīkhihi*, Ḥaydarābād 1961.

Muḥammad b. Ḥibbān al-Bustī (d. 354/965 [see IBN ḤIBBĀN]) was the author of a large tradition collection but he also produced several major *ridjāl* works. One, his *K. al-Thiḳāt* (ed. Ḥaydarābād 1973-83, 9 vols.) is, like Ibn Saʿd's *Ṭabaḳāt*, preceded by an extensive biography of the Prophet. It is further organised on the basis of three *ṭabaḳāt*: that of the Successors and those of the following two generations. The technical term *thiḳāt* from the title is not to be taken in its literal sense of "reliable persons"; a sizeable percentage of *ridjāl* dealt with are *madjhūlūn*. For lack of more precise characteristics, they were labelled *thiḳa*. This term was often used especially in order to classify transmitters about whom little, if anything, was known. The traditions in whose *isnāds* they occurred, however, had a certain appeal, which prevented *ridjāl* experts from rejecting them altogether. While describing someone about whom (next to) nothing is known, later *ridjāl* experts frequently refer to Ibn Ḥibbān's lexicon using the term *waththaḳahu Ibn Ḥibbān*, or *dhakarahu Ibn Ḥibbān fi 'l-thiḳāt* ... or similar expressions, thereby indicating that that transmitter, as well as the mostly innocuous tradition(s) he is reported to have transmitted, may be preserved, be it merely for the sake of comparison. Furthermore, there is Ibn Ḥibbān's *Kitāb al-Madjrūḥīn (wa 'l-ḍuʿafā') min al-muḥaddithīn*, ed. ʿAzīz Bey al-Ḳādirī, Ḥaydarābād 1970, 2 vols., also listing often the traditions in whose proliferation the weak transmitters dealt with in the lexicon are alleged to have had a hand. Ibn Ḥibbān's *Mashāhīr ʿulamā' al-amṣār*, a lexicon with 1,602 entries built upon the *ṭabaḳāt* principle, was edited by M. Fleischhammer, Wiesbaden 1959.

By general agreement, the most extensive early lexicon of doubtful transmitters was that of ʿAbd Allāh b. ʿAdī (d. 365/976). What was said for al-ʿUḳaylī's lexicon is equally true for Ibn ʿAdī's *K. al-Kāmil fi (maʿrifat) ḍuʿafā' al-ridjāl (al-muḥaddithīn wa-ʿilal al-ḥadīth)* with approximately the same number of entries (more than 2,000). However, it surpasses al-ʿUḳaylī's in size, especially in numbers of doubtful traditions quoted in connection with their alleged originators. This lexicon is, furthermore, the first in which the Arabic term *madār* is occasionally used to indicate that

:ertain *matns*, or *matn* clusters, are due to one par- :icul ır transmitter who is held responsible for disseminating these to a number of pupils. The term *nadār*, first used in ʿAlī Ibn al-Madīnī's *ʿIlal*, is in Ibn ·Adī's usage a genuine technical term which comes :losest to the term "common link" coined by Schacht cf. *The origins of Muhammadan jurisprudence*, Oxford 1950, 171 ff.) and further elaborated in Juynboll, *Muslim tradition*, 206-17.

ʿUmar b. Aḥmad Ibn Shāhīn (d. 385/995) wrote a *Taʾrīkh Asmāʾ al-thiḳāt mimman nuḳila ʿanhum al-ʿilm*, cf. he edition of ʿAbd al-Muʿṭī A. Ḳalʿadjī, Beirut 1986, with 1,569 entries. Like the *thiḳa* collections of ʿIdjlī and Ibn Ḥibbān mentioned above, the transmitters are arranged in loosely alphabetical order and are not, contrary to what its title suggests, universally considered reliable.

ʿAlī b. ʿUmar al-Dāraḳuṭnī (d. 385/995) compiled a *Kitāb al-Ḍuʿafāʾ wa ʾl-matrūkīn*, ed. Ṣubḥī al-Badrī al-Sāmarrāʾī, Beirut 1986, with 632 entries.

The post-classical period

With the 4th/10th century, there begins, as Brockelmann defined it, the post-classical period, with initially relatively little activity in the compilation of *ridjāl* works. On the basis of a remark of ʿAbd al-Raḥmān b. ʿAlī Ibn al-Djawzī (d. 597/1200 [*q.v.*]), one could almost infer that, during the two centuries after al-Dāraḳuṭnī's lexicon, there do not seem to have been any basically new additions to the genre, for Ibn al-Djawzī enumerates in the introduction to his *Kitāb al-Ḍuʿafāʾ wa ʾl-matrūkīn* (see the edition with 4,018 alphabetical entries of Abu ʾl-Fidāʾ ʿAbd Allāh al-Ḳāḍī, Beirut 1986, i, 7) the sources from which he compiled his work: they are the same as all those listed hitherto, the last being the al-Dāraḳutnī work. After Ibn al-Djawzī, however, various major, and increasingly more-embracing, *ridjāl* lexicons did see the light which were constantly subject to expansion as well as abridgements at the hands of subsequent compilers.

At the centre of these activities stands Yūsuf b. al-Zakī ʿAbd al-Raḥmān al-Mizzī (d. 742/1341 [*q.v.*]), the author of a colossal biographical dictionary of transmitters occurring in the Six Books and a few minor collections entitled *Tahdhīb al-kamāl fī asmāʾ al-ridjāl*, which grew out of a work by ʿAbd al-Ghanī b. ʿAbd al-Wāḥid al-Djammāʿīlī (d. 600/1203, cf. Brockelmann, S I, 606). It is presently only partly available in the edition of Bashshār ʿAwwād Maʿrūf Beirut 1980–, 15 vols. with, at the time of writing, some 20 more to follow). Al-Mizzī's work, together with some lexicons of his pupil al-Dhahabī (cf. below), lie then again at the basis of arguably the most famous *ridjāl* work of all: the *Tahdhīb al-tahdhīb* of Ibn Ḥadjar al-ʿAskalānī (d. 852/1448 [*q.v.*]), with its *ca.* 7,300 *tardjamas* being a compendium of al-Mizzī's work but, because of its smaller size, less unwieldy. (For more on this lexicon, see Juynboll, *Muslim tradition*, 134-7, 138-41.) What makes al-Mizzī's original, however, even more useful than Ibn Ḥadjar's abridgement is that in each transmitter's *tardjama*, at the mention of each of his masters as well as of each of his pupils, symbols of tradition collections are sometimes inserted indicating in which of the Six Books material of the described transmitter can be found, whereas in Ibn Ḥadjar's lexicon—at least in the only available edition, that of Ḥaydarābād 1325-7— these symbols are solely listed preceding the name of each *muhaddith* treated. Al-Mizzī's arrangement of his material thus allows the drawing of inferences as to either the origins of certain transmitters' fictitiousness or doubtful personae, as well as other conclusions.

Beside al-Mizzī, his pupil al-Dhahabī (d. 748/1348) deserves separate mention. For a survey of his contributions to *taʾrīkh* and *ridjāl* works and how these are interdependent, see AL-DHAHABĪ. Moreover, mention should be made of a few major new editions of his specific *ridjāl* works: *al-Mughnī fi ʾl-ḍuʿafāʾ*, ed. Nūr al-Dīn ʿItr, Aleppo 1971, 2 vols.; *Siyar aʿlām al-nubalāʾ*, ed. Shuʿayb al-Arnaʾūṭ, Ḥusayn al-Asad *et alii*, Beirut 1981-4, 23 vols.; *Tadhkirat al-ḥuffāẓ*, several impr., Haydarābād 1955-70, 4 vols. (with *dhayls* by M. b. ʿA. al-Ḥusaynī, M. b. M. Ibn Fahd and al-Suyūṭī); *al-Kāshif fī maʿrifat man lahu riwāya fi ʾl-kutub al-sitta*, ed. ʿIzzat ʿAlī ʿĪd ʿAṭiyya and Mūsā M.ʿA. al-Mawshī, Cairo 1972, 3 vols, with more than 7,000 entries; and *Mīzān al-iʿtidāl*, ed. ʿA.M. al-Badjāwī, Cairo 1963, 4 vols., with 11,053 entries. In this last work he assembled not only all the weak transmitters he could find but also scores of at first sight blameless ones. This lexicon was revised and enlarged by Ibn Ḥadjar al-ʿAṣkalānī (d. 852/1449 [*q.v.*]), resulting in his *Lisān al-mīzān*, Haydarābād 1329, 6 or 7 vols., with *ca.* 15,000 entries. A large number of data concerning political, cultural and literary history as well as theological discussion can be gleaned from both lexicons. The *Lisān* is especially rich in examples of traditions which are deemed fabricated by the man in whose biography they are cited, allegations that could often be confirmed by modern *isnād* analysis, as was the case with the *ḍuʿafāʾ* lexicons of al-ʿUḳaylī and Ibn ʿAdī described above.

All the time, other types of *ridjāl* lexicons, too numerous to list all, had made their appearance. Some of these are described here by genre.

(1) The generation of Companions received special attention, something which was probably also stimulated by the establishment of their collective *taʿdīl*, a dogma that seems to have found its first formulation sometime in the course of the final decades of the 2nd/8th and the first decades of the 3rd/9th centuries (cf. Juynboll, *Muslim tradition*, 190-206). The earliest author credited with a lexicon exclusively devoted to Companions and their alleged roles in the transmission of prophetic traditions was Muḥammad b. ʿAbd Allāh b. Sulaymān al-Ḥaḍramī Muṭayyan (d. 297/909). No mss. of it are listed in *GAS*, i. Ibn Ḥibbān compiled a *Taʾrīkh al-Ṣaḥāba alladhīna ruwiya ʿanhum al-akhbār* (ed. Būrān al-Ḍannāwī, Beirut 1988, with 1,608 entries). This work is the first lexicon solely devoted to the subject and available in a printed edition. It was improved upon by, among others, the following: Ibn ʿAbd al-Barr (d. 463/1071 [*q.v.*]), *K. al-Istīʿāb fī asmāʾ al-aṣḥāb*, ed. ʿA.M. al-Badjāwī, Cairo 1960, 4 vols. with 4,225 entries; ʿIzz al-Dīn Ibn al-Athīr (d. 630/1233), *Usd al-ghāba fī maʿrifat al-ṣaḥāba*, ed. Cairo 1970, 7 vols. with 7,703 entries; al-Dhahabī, *Tadjrīd asmāʾ al-ṣaḥāba*, ed. ʿAbd al-Ḥakīm Sharaf al-Dīn, Bombay 1969-70, 2 vols. with 8,859 entries, and finally Ibn Ḥadjar, *K. al-Iṣāba fī tamyīz al-ṣaḥāba*, ed. ʿA.M. al-Badjāwī, Cairo 1970-2, 8 vols. with 12,290 entries. To be sure, in this last source not all persons paraded were Companions in the technical sense of the word; Ibn Ḥadjar added scores of borderline cases in his so-called second, third and fourth *ḳisms*.

(2) A specifically Muʿtazilī-influenced *ridjāl* work is *K. Ḳabūl al-akhbār wa-maʿrifat al-ridjāl* by Abu ʾl-Ḳāsim al-Kaʿbī al-Balkhī (d. 319/931 [*q.v.*], and Juynboll, *Muslim tradition*, index s.n.). An edition is in preparation in Leiden University Library.

(3) The first Shīʿī *ridjāl* work is that of Muḥammad b. ʿUmar al-Kashshī (d. *ca.* 340/951 [*q.v.*]), see the corrected redaction with 520 entries of Muḥammad b. al-Ḥasan al-Ṭūsī (d. 460/1068) in the edition of

Aḥmad al-Ḥusaynī, Karbalā 1963. The work is based on the *ṭabaḳāt* principle, describing the persons in the entourage of the respective *imāms*. The majority of people enumerated are assessed as to their political position in society, but the lexicon does give extensive *ḥadīth*-technical information. The other Shīʿī lexicons are perfectly ordinary *ḥadīth*-related, alphabetically arranged dictionaries of transmitters closely resembling their Sunnī counterparts. To the same al-Ṭūsī we owe a work called *Ridjāl al-Ṭūsī*, ed. M. Ṣādiḳ Āl Baḥr al-ʿUlūm, Nadjaf 1961, comprising some 8,900 transmitters. Al-Nadjāshī (d. 450/1058) wrote a *K. al-ridjāl*, ed. Djalāl al-Dīn al-ʿĀmilī, Tehran 1958. ʿInāyat al-Dīn ʿAlī al-Ḳuhpāʾī (*fl. ca.* 1016/1607) compiled a lexicon in which he incorporated five earlier major *ridjāl* lexicons, including the three just mentioned, entitled *Madjmaʿ al-ridjāl*, ed. Ḍiyāʾ al-Dīn al-Iṣfahānī, Iṣfahān 1384, 7 vols. Muḥammad b. ʿAlī al-Ardabīlī (*fl. ca.* 1100/1689, cf. Ziriklī, 4th impr., vi, 294-5) produced a *Djāmiʿ al-ruwāt*, Ḳumm *ca.* 1967, 2 vols. See further, ʿILM AL-RIDJĀL.

(4) Al-Bukhārī's and Muslim's collections were especially subjected to a sort of *isnād* scrutiny, resulting in *ridjāl* lexicons too numerous and too varied to enumerate all of them, in which in one way or another transmitters occurring in one collection are compared with those occurring in the other. Information on these *kutub ridjāliyya* can be found among the secondary works listed in *GAS*, i, derived from (commentaries on) the two *Ṣaḥīḥs*. But there is also a small and useful transmitters' lexicon on those of Mālik's *Muwaṭṭaʾ* by al-Suyūṭī (d. 911/1505 [*q.v.*]), *Isʿāf al-mubaṭṭaʾ bi-ridjāl al-Muwaṭṭaʾ*, ed. with the *Muwaṭṭaʾ* by Fārūḳ Saʿd, Beirut 1979.

(5) Another genre of *ridjāl* works is that of regional or city histories. Whereas Abū Zakariyyāʾ al-Azdī (d. 334/946) only occasionally touches on *ḥadīth* transmission in his *Taʾrīkh Mawṣil*, ed. ʿAlī Ḥabība, Cairo 1387, as does Aḥmad b. ʿAbd Allāh al-Rāzī (ed. 460/1068 [*q.v.*]) in his *Taʾrīkh Madīnat Ṣanʿāʾ*, ed. Ḥ.ʿA. al-ʿAmrī and ʿA.Dj. Zakkār, Ṣanʿāʾ 1401/1981, other works in this genre contain only very few purely historical data on the regions or cities dealt with and are in reality *ṭabaḳāt*-arranged or alphabetically ordered works, with all the trimmings of other *ridjāl* lexicons on *muḥaddithūn*, from all those who once lived in a particular region or city to those who merely passed through it. Some examples: Aslam b. Sahl Baḥshal (d. 292/905), *Taʾrīkh Wāsiṭ*, ed. Kūrkīs ʿAwwād, Baghdād 1967, a strictly *ḥadīth*-critical *ridjāl* work; Ḥamza b. Yūsuf al-Sahmī (d. 427/1036 [*q.v.*]), *Taʾrīkh Djurdjān aw kitāb maʿrifat ʿulamāʾ ahl Djurdjān*, ed. M. ʿAbd al-Muʿīd Khān, Ḥaydarābād 1950; Abū Nuʿaym al-Iṣbahānī (d. 430/1038 [*q.v.*]), *K. Dhikr akhbār Iṣbahān*, ed. S. Dedering, Leiden 1931-4, 2 vols.; the great tradition scholar al-Khaṭīb al-Baghdādī (d. 463/1071 [*q.v.*]) devoted his large *Taʾrīkh Baghdād*, cf. ed. Cairo 1931 + reprints, 14 vols., following a topographical introduction, almost wholly to *ḥadīth*-related characteristics of the 7,831 persons described in, again, a loosely alphabetical order; modelled on this lexicon but even more massive is the *Taʾrīkh Madīnat Dimashḳ* of ʿAlī b. al-Ḥasan Ibn ʿAsākir (d. 571/1176 [*q.v.*]), which is well on its way of being edited in complete form under the auspices of the Arab Academy of Damascus; for Spain we have Muḥammad b. Ḥārith al-Khushanī (d. 361/971 [*q.v.*]), *Akhbār al-fuḳahāʾ wa 'l-muḥaddithīn*, a specifically Andalusian lexicon with 527 entries, ed. Maria Luisa Ávila and Luis Molina, Madrid 1992. The *nisba* [*q.v.*] genre may be considered as an offshoot of city lexicons as well as genealogical works; under each *nisba* all the tradition experts and, occasionally, other religious scholars, are enumerated who were best known—or sometimes only known—by that *nisba*. The most famous compilation is the *K. al-Ansāb* of ʿAbd al-Karīm b. M. al-Samʿānī (d. 562/1166 [*q.v.*]), cf. the facs. ed. of Leiden-London 1912, and that of ʿAbd al-Raḥmān b. Y. al-Muʿallimī, Ḥaydarābād 1962-82, 13 vols.

(6) A special type is furthermore the so-called *aṭrāf* compilation, that is an alphabetically-arranged collection of the Companions' *musnads*, with every tradition ascribed to each of them shortened to its *ṭaraf* (i.e. gist or salient feature), accompanied by *all* the *isnād* strands supporting it which occur in the Six Books and a few other revered collections. The most famous representative of this type is the *Tuḥfat al-ashrāf bi-maʿrifat al-aṭrāf* by al-Mizzī; for a more detailed description, see AL-MIZZĪ. The work was imitated but never improved upon.

(7) In an attempt to solve onomastic difficulties around transmitters' identities, several lexicons were compiled listing ambiguous names with accompanying solutions as to their proper vocalisation and attribution. The best-known examples are the works entitled *Mūḍiḥ awhām al-djamʿ wa 'l-tafrīḳ*, Ḥaydarābād 1959-60, by al-Khaṭīb al-Baghdādī; *al-Ikmāl fī rafʿ al-irtiyāb ʿan al-muʾtalif wa 'l-mukhtalif min al-asmāʾ wa 'l-kunā wa 'l-ansāb* by ʿAlī b. Hibat Allāh Ibn Mākūlā (d. between 475/1082 and 487/1094), see the edition of ʿAbd al-Raḥmān b. Y. al-Muʿallimī and Nāyif al-ʿAbbās, Beirut 1962-7, 7 vols.; and al-Dhahabī's *K. al-Mushtabih (fī 'l-ridjāl)*, ed. P. de Jong, Leiden 1881, and ʿA.M. al-Badjāwī, Cairo 1962, 2 vols. See also IBN MĀKŪLĀ.

(8) Women *ḥadīth* transmitters are usually treated in the *ridjāl* lexicons at the very end after all the men have been dealt with, but one *nisāʾ* lexicon was made into a separate publication: ʿU.R. Kaḥḥāla, *Aʿlām al-nisāʾ fī ʿālamay al-ʿarab wa 'l-islām*, Damascus 1959-77, 5 vols. Its contents are exclusively based upon mediaeval sources. A large percentage of the women are described only as to their *ḥadīth* activities, but for the rest it is an ordinary biographical dictionary arranged in alphabetical order.

(9) There are quite a few lexicons arranged by year in which the *muḥaddithūn* and other religious scholars who died that year are enumerated, eventually with an admixture of purely historical data thrown in. Best-known in this genre is the *Shadharāt al-dhahab* of Ibn al-ʿImād (d. 1089/1678 [*q.v.*]), Beirut n.d., 8 vols.

(10) For the rich genre of lexicons in which lists of someone's *ḥadīth* masters are compiled, i.e. the so-called *mashyakha* works, see the comprehensive introduction of H. Schützinger's *Das Kitāb al-muʿǧam des Abū Bakr al-Ismāʿīlī* (= Abhandlungen für die Kunde des Morgenlandes, XLIII, 3), Wiesbaden 1978; and FAHRASA.

Biographical lexicons of Ḳurʾān reciters and exegetes, judges, governors, jurists, theologians, mystics, poets, grammarians, scientists and a host of other professions and shared characteristics (e.g. the blind and the longeval), although often containing *ḥadīth*-related data, do not really fall within the scope of the *ridjāl* genre in that they do not deal specifically with these categories' (de)merits in *ḥadīth* transmission. But they were doubtless modelled on the genuine *ridjāl* works.

Bibliography: Given in the article. Several recently published editions of the *ridjāl* lexicons mentioned contain in their introductions more or less adequate surveys of the genres on *thiḳāt* and *ḍuʿafāʾ*, especially the edition of Bashshār ʿAwwād

Maᶜrūf of Mizzī's *Tahdhīb*. For a general approach to the *ṭabaḳāt* genre, see I. Hafsi, *Recherches sur le genre Ṭabaqāt dans la littérature arabe*, in *Arabica*, xxiii (1976), 227-65, xxiv (1977), 1-41, 150-86; P. Auchterlonie, *Arabic biographical dictionaries: a summary guide and bibliography*, Durham 1987 (Middle East Libraries Committee research guides 2); for Shīᶜī *ridjāl* works, see the papers of B. Scarcia-Amoretti, A. Arioli and D. Amaldi in *Cahiers d'onomastique arabe*, i, Paris 1979, and ᶜILM AL-RIDJĀL. See further, Jacqueline Sublet, *Le voile du nom. Essai sur le nom propre arabe*, Paris 1991.

(G.H.A. JUYNBOLL)

RIḌWĀN, the guardian (*khāzin*) of Paradise, is bsent from the Ḳurʾān, early *tafsīr*, *ḥadīth* and lescriptions of Paradise. In Ibn Hishām, 268, this ngel is still called Ismāᶜīl. The proper name Riḍwān nay result from a personifying exegesis of the *riḍwān* = Allāh's favour) which believers will meet in the ereafter (Ḳurʾān, III, 15, etc.). In the anonymous th/10th century *Kitāb al-ᶜAẓama* (e.g. ms. Paris 4605, /atican 1480; ed. Raven, forthcoming) Riḍwān pens the gates of Paradise, dresses and serves the elievers, draws away the veils from the face of Allāh, tc. Slightly later he appears in the Shīᶜī legend about Alī and Fāṭima [*q.vv.*] and in Ismāᶜīlī cosmogony (H. Ialm, *Kosmologie und Heilslehre der frühen Ismāᶜīlīya*, Viesbaden 1978). He is an accepted figure in Arabic elles-lettres, at least from al-Maᶜarrī (*R. al-Ghufrān*) nwards, and in later Islamic literatures throughout.

(W. RAVEN)

RIḌWĀN or RUḌWĀN B. TUTUSH b. Alp Arslan, 'akhr al-Mulk (d. 507/1113), Saldjūḳ prince in leppo after the death of his father Tutush [*q.v.*] in afar 488/February 1095.

After assuming power in Aleppo, Riḍwān and his epfather, the Atabeg Djanāḥ al-Dawla Ḥusayn, imed at taking over Tutush's former capital)amascus and thus at controlling the whole of Syria nd Palestine not still in Fāṭimid hands. However, Riḍwān's brother Duḳāḳ and his Atabeg Ṭughtigin eld on to Damascus, and after Riḍwān broke with)janāḥ al-Dawla, the latter established himself in Iimṣ. For one month, in Ramaḍān-Shawwāl/ ugust-September 1097, Riḍwān acknowledged the 'āṭimid caliph al-Mustaᶜlī [*q.v.*] in the *khuṭba* at Alepo, but reverted to Sunnī allegiance and acknowledgement of the ᶜAbbāsid al-Mustaẓhir and the sultan erk-yaruḳ [*q.vv.*] when it became apparent that the 'āṭimids could not deliver any material help to him.

From Radjab 491/June 1098, Riḍwān had the rusader leader Bohemund, now Prince of Antioch, s his neighbour, and the ensuing years were filled vith warfare with Bohemund (and then with Tancred f Antioch and Edessa, Bohemund's successor) and lso with his Muslim rivals such as Djanāḥ al-Dawla intil the latter's death at the hands of the Assassins n Radjab 496/May 1103). It was around this time hat Riḍwān allied with the strong Ismāᶜīlī faction vithin Aleppo and used them as part of his tortuous olicies (which in 502/1108-9, e.g., allied him with 'ancred against the Muslim Čawli Saḳāw of Mawṣil), nd although he was unable to take Damascus, he had is name recognised in the *khuṭba* and *sikka* there by he young Tutush b. Duḳāḳ. When a Muslim army imed at the Crusaders appeared from Mawṣil before leppo, Riḍwān refused to admit it and defended his ity with Ismāᶜīlī help (Ṣafar 505/August-September 111). His standing with what was probably the marity Sunnī population of Aleppo was now understanably impaired. He allied with Ṭughtigin of amascus but secured peace in northern Syria by making payments to Tancred and (after November 1112) his son Roger. He substantially avoided taking part in a *djihād* against the Crusaders led by Ṭughtigin and Mawdūd b. Altuntash of Mawṣil, sending only a tiny token force, but died on 1 Rabīᶜ I 507/16 August 1113, to be succeeded briefly by his son Tādj al-Dawla Alp Arslan [see ḤALAB].

The Sunnī sources regard Riḍwān, from his use of the Syrian Ismāᶜīlīs, with disfavour, stigmatising him as *al-malᶜūn, sayyiʾ al-sīra*, etc. They even accuse him of having been converted to Ismāᶜīlism by the local leader in Aleppo, al-Ḥakīm al-Munadjdjim; it seems impossible to discern the truth here. He is further condemned for his miserliness, since he left a large treasury at his death. His diplomatic and political skills were, however, considerable, and within what was at that time a highly complex situation in Syria, he successfully maintained his power between the Crusaders and various Muslim rivals for nearly nineteen years.

Bibliography: 1. Sources. These include Ibn al-Ḳalānisī, *Dhayl Taʾrīkh Dimashḳ*, ed. Amedroz, tr. Gibb; Ibn al-ᶜAdīm, *Zubda*, ed. Dahhān; idem, *Bughya*, ed. Ali Sevim, Ankara 1976, biography of Riḍwān, no. XIV, Ar. text, 138-51, Tkish. résumé, 78-80; Ibn al-Athīr, x; Ibn Khallikān, ed. ᶜAbbās, i, 296, tr. de Slane, i, 274 (s.v. Tutush); Ṣafadī, *Wāfī*, xiv, ed. Dedering, 129-30 (biography of Riḍwān).

2. Studies. See the general histories of the Crusades by e.g. Grousset and Runciman, and Cahen's ch. *The Selchükids*, in Setton and Baldwin (eds.), *A history of the Crusades*, i. Also Cahen, *La Syrie du nord à l'époque des Croisades*, Paris 1940, index s.v. *Roḍwân*; M.G.S. Hodgson, *The order of Assassins*, The Hague 1955, 70, 89-92; R.W. Crawford, *Riḍwān the Maligned*, in J. Kritzeck and R.B. Winder (eds.), *The world of Islam, studies in honour of Philip K. Hitti*, London-New York 1959, 135-44; Farhad Daftary, *The Ismāᶜīlīs, their history and doctrines*, Cambridge 1990, 356 ff.

(C.E. BOSWORTH)

RIḌWĀN BEGOVIĆ ᶜAlī Pasha (in Serbo-Croat RIZVANBEGOVIĆ Ali-paša; *ca.* ?1783-1851), *wezīr* of Herzegovina from 1833 until his death by assassination in March 1851. He was an interesting individual, whose biography well illustrates the complex circumstances affecting this region of the Balkans in the closing stages of Ottoman domination.

He was descended from an old Muslim family. Towards the end of the 18th century his father, Dhu 'l-Fiḳār (Zulfikar), was governor (with the title of *mīr-i mīrān* (?), i.e. "provincial governor", or that of *ḳapudan* (?), a term rendered in Serbo-Croat by "kapetan") of the town of Stolac (in southern Herzegovina, to the south of Mostar [*q.v.*]) and its environs, hence his name of Stočević (or Rizvanbegović-Stočević) which is also encountered in the texts. ᶜAlī Pasha is said to have been born in this town *ca.* 1783 (considerably earlier, according to V. Ćorović, *ca.* 1761). Following a dispute with his father (over a trivial issue, according to S. Bašagić), he parted from his family while still a young man, only returning (and bringing with him a considerable sum of money, so it is alleged) after the death of his father, whereupon he engaged in conflict with his brothers, Muṣṭafā (Mustaj-Beg) and Hadžun (Ḥādjdjī Beg: some sources mention also the name of ᶜÖmer), for several months during the year 1222/1807, over the succession to the post of governor of Stolac and possession of the rich *aghalïḳ* of the village of Hutovo. This dispute was temporarily resolved the following year by a special envoy from Istanbul, in the course of negotiations which took place in Sarajevo, but it was subsequently revived, lasting many years and coming to an end only in 1229/1813-14, when ʿAlī Pasha finally succeeded his father in the capacity of governor of Stolac and the surrounding area, while Ḥādjdjī Beg obtained the *aghalïk* of Hutovo. With regard to these appointments, Ćorović comments, "ʿAlī Pasha and his brother Ḥādjdjī Beg were neither of them good masters or congenial neighbours, but Ḥādjdjī Beg was by far the worse". The relations maintained by ʿAlī Pasha with the powerful Muslim families of Bosnia-Herzegovina were variable; he was very close to the eminent Ismāʿīl Agha Čengić (an individual immortalised by the Croatian poet Ivan Mažuranić, 1814-90), but was in open conflict with his other neighbours, such as the Kapetanovićs of the town of Počitelj. It was in the course of a skirmish with Ismāʿīl Kapetanović and his supporters, during the siege of Počitelj in 1813, that he was wounded in the leg; as a result of this he was to be lame for the remainder of his life. By 1820 he was the most widely-known governor (*ḳapudan*) in the whole of Herzegovina, and an implacable foe of the *wezīrs* of Bosnia, based at Travnik. However, in 1831, at the time of the uprising of the Bosnian aristocracy, led by Ḥüseyn Beg Gradaščević (known as *Zmaj od Bosne*, "the dragon of Bosnia"), ʿAlī Pasha Rizvanbegović and Ismāʿīl Agha Čengić did not associate themselves with the rebels and sided ostensibly with the Ottoman sultan and the central authority. ʿAlī Pasha then took under his protection the ousted *wezīr* of Travnik, while his brother Ḥādjdjī Beg allied himself with the insurgents and met his death (27 February 1832) fighting alongside the troops of Gradaščević as the latter were laying siege to the town of Stolac. This fratricidal war claimed many other victims, on both sides; thus Ismāʿīl Agha Čengić ordered the assassination of one of his own relatives, Fejz Alaj-Beg Čengić. Following the failure of the rebel attacks on Nevesinje and Stolac, ʿAlī Pasha Rizvanbegović lent powerful support (with Ismāʿīl Agha Čengić and Bash Agha Redžepašić, ancestor of the eminent family of the Bašagić) to the troops of the *wezīr* Ḳara Maḥmūd Pasha in the course of the decisive battle which took place on the plain before Sarajevo on 17 May 1832, and which resulted in the total defeat of the supporters of Gradaščević.

ʿAlī Pasha subsequently participated, with an army raised in Bosnia-Herzegovina, in the expedition mounted by the Porte against Muḥammad ʿAlī [*q.v.*] of Egypt, during which he and his troops performed sterling service. He was rewarded in 1832 by the sultan Maḥmūd II [*q.v.*], who appointed him first *beylerbeyi*, then, in 1833, *wezīr* and *wālī* of Herzegovina, although this region was detached from the *wilāyet* of Bosnia.

He thus governed this region, in a quasi-independent fashion, for almost twenty years (living either at Mostar, or in his country residence on the river Buna), according to one of his celebrated maxims, *Evo vam Stanbul, Mostar; evo vam cara i u Mostaru* (according to another version, *Evo vam i cara u Mostaru*), which may be loosely translated as "Here you have an Istanbul, Mostar, and here you have an emperor, also at Mostar" (or, "and here you have also an emperor at Mostar"). He succeeded, in fact, at a very early stage in concentrating all power within his family and his circle of supporters, entrusting internal security to "gendarmes" commanded by *bölük bashīs* who were in his pay. He paid to the Porte an annual tribute of 87,000 florins, retaining the remainder of the funds raised by taxation, and took certain steps to improve agriculture and the economy. Thus he encouraged, for example, the populace to plant vegetables and fruits emanating from lands of the south, introducing the cultivation of olives, pomegranates, almonds, jasmine, tobacco, rice and even silk-worms.

His relations with the diverse populations of the region varied considerably, according to time and circumstances. Hence in the early stages he showed his gratitude to the local Serbs (who had given him strong support during the conflicts of 1831-2), authorising them in 1833 to rebuild the ancient Orthodox church of Mostar, and supporting the Serbian Orthodox clergy in its opposition to the appointment of Greek bishops to positions of authority in the church. Furthermore, he helped the Franciscans of Bosnia to acquire their own vicariate in 1846, and obtained for them in the same year a *firmān* permitting the foundation of a Catholic monastery at a place called Široki Brijeg. As for the Muslim community, he contributed substantial donations to various religious associations and had a number of building constructed at Mostar and elsewhere, including a mosque at Buna.

Regarding "external affairs", these were confined, as will be seen, to relations with Montenegro [see ḲARA DAGH] and with the Porte. This process began in 1836 with the battle of Grahovo, in the course of which Herzegovinan troops, commanded by ʿAlī Pasha and Ismāʿīl Agha Čengić, inflicted a heavy defeat on Montenegrin units, with the result that Grahovo became (temporarily) Ottoman territory. This defeat outraged the Montenegrins, who ultimately assassinated Ismāʿīl Agha Čengić in 1840. But in the meantime, the internal situation had changed considerably, and the rumour circulated among the Muslim circles of Herzegovina that the death of the aged Ismāʿīl Agha had been welcomed by Rizvanbegović, since for a considerable time previously Ismāʿīl Agha had been the leader of a party opposing Rizvanbegović, accusing him, on the one hand, of imposing increasingly draconian taxes on the population, and on the other, of brutally and shamelessly advancing the material interests of his own family. He had in fact undertaken a methodical redistribution of the former "capitanates" (rights of authority which had become hereditary within certain leading local families) into larger administrative units, which he then allocated to his sons and relatives. In spite of all this, to avenge the death of Ismāʿīl Agha and to silence the afore-mentioned rumours, Rizvanbegović in 1841 attacked the region of Drobnjak, slaughtering a number of its male inhabitants, while in 1842 rivalry over Grahovo resumed. With the aim of putting an end to the war, a meeting took place the same year at Dubrovnik between Rizvanbegović and the bishop of Montenegro, Peter II (the illustrious poet Petar II Petrović Njegoš), in the course of which the frontiers between the two countries were fixed. But the Porte was unwilling to recognise this accord, and negotiations continued for some time longer, until 28 October 1843, the date of the final signing at Kotor of a new accord which broadly stipulated a return to the frontiers as they had stood before the conflicts of 1836.

However, resentment against Rizvanbegović and his sons increased, to such an extent that even in Mostar an overt coalition against him was formed. Furthermore, ʿAlī Pasha had finally sided with the leading "feudal" Muslims of Bosnia, who were opposing, with weapons at the ready, the implementation of reforms introduced in Turkey by Maḥmūd II.

When, in 1850, the renowned "executioner" of the Bosnian Muslim nobility, ʿÖmer Pasha Latas, sent by the Porte to suppress the rebellion, set about methodically mopping up the pockets of resistance, his troops decisively defeated those of Rizvanbegović in a battle which took place near the town of Konjic. ʿAlī Pasha himself was taken prisoner on 5 February 1851, then displayed in Mostar, his capital, in a humiliating fashion (seated back to front on an ass, holding the animal's tail in his hands), then sent to the camp of ʿÖmer Pasha, who was based at this time near Banja Luka [see BANJALUKA]. But in the course of this transfer, on or about 20 March 1851, not far from this town, the elderly ʿAlī Pasha Rizvanbegović was "accidentally" killed by one of the soldiers escorting him. He left four sons: Ḥāfiẓ Pasha, Nāfidh Pasha, Rüstem Beg and Meḥmed ʿAlī Pasha. His daughter Ḥabība (1845-90) was a renowned poetess, a profession also followed by his grandson Ḥikmet (ʿĀrif Beg Rizvanbegović, 1839-1903).

Bibliography: Meḥmed Thüreyyā, *Sidjill-i ʿOthmānī*, Istanbul 1311/1893, iii, 569, s.v.; V. Ćorović, in *Narodna Enciklopedija*, Zagreb 1928, iii, 772-3, s.v.; S. Bašagić, *Znameniti Hrvati, Bošnjaci i Hercegovci u turskoj carevini*, Zagreb 1931, 11, s.v.; H. Kapidžić, in *Enciklopedija Jugoslavije*, Zagreb 1968, vii, 84, s.v.; S. Balić, in *Biographisches Lexikon zur Geschichte Südosteuropas*, ed. M. Bernath and K. Nehring, Munich 1980, iv, 52-3, s.v. See also J. Pamučina, in A. Giljferding, *Bosnija, Gercegovina i Staraja Serbija*, St. Petersburg 1859; Bašagić, *Kratka uputa u prošlost Bosne i Hercegovine*, Sarajevo 1900; Ćorović, *Mostar i njegovi književnici u prvoj polovini 19og veka*, Mostar 1907; P. Čokorilo, *Ljetopis hercegovacki 1831-1857*, in *Narod* (1908); idem, *Iz dnevnika P. Čokorila*, in *Glasnik Zemaljskog Muzeja*, xxv (Sarajevo 1913) 89 ff., 195 ff.; C. Patsch, *Aus Herzegowinas letzter Feudalzeit*, Vienna 1922; O. Knezović, *Ali-paša Rizvanbegović-Stočević, hercegovacki vezir 1832-1851*, in *Glasnik Zemaljskog Muzeja*, xl/2 (Sarajevo 1928), 11-53; H. Ćurić, *Ali-paša Rizvanbegović-Stočević*, in *Godišnjica Nikole Čupića*, xlvi (Belgrade 1937), 201-96; F. Šišić, *Bosna i Hercegovina za vreme vezirovanja Omer-paše Latasa (1850-1852). Isprave iz Bečkog Državnog Arhiva*, Belgrade-Subotica, 1938; H. Kapidžić, *Odnosi Ali-paše Rizvanbegovića i vladike Petra II Petrovića*, in *Istoriski Zapisi*, v/8 (Cetinje [Titograd] 1952), 69-98; idem, *Prilozi za istoriju Bosne i Hercegovine u XIX Vijeku*, Sarajevo 1956. (A. POPOVIC)

RIḌWĀN PASHA, a 10th/16th-century Ottoman *beylerbeyi* (governor) of Yemen largely responsible for the collapse of Ottoman authority there during 974-6/1566-8. He was the son of Muṣṭafā Pasha Ḳara Shāhīn [*q.v.*], a previous governor of Yemen (963-7/1556-60), and the brother of Bahrām Pasha, a later one (977-83/1570-5). When appointed to Yemen in Rabīʿ II 972/November 1564, he was *sandjaḳ beyi* of Ghazza.

Riḍwān, who reached Yemen in Ṣafar 973/September 1565, served only briefly before, on the recommendation of Maḥmūd Pasha [*q.v.*], his predecessor and the governor of Egypt after Radjab 973/February 1566, Yemen was divided, in Djumādā II 973/December 1565, into two provinces. Awarded the poorer and more demanding *beylerbeyilik* of Ṣanʿāʾ in the highlands, Riḍwān became resentful. His determination to widen his jurisdiction's sources of revenue and to amass personal wealth led him to violate the peace accord concluded with the Zaydīs in 959/1552 [see ÖZDEMIR PASHA]. The Zaydī leader al-Muṭahhar [*q.v.*] took the offensive and quickly succeeded in confining Riḍwān and his troops to the city of Ṣanʿāʾ (Radjab 974/January-February 1567).

Learning in Shawwāl 974/April 1567 of his dismissal, Riḍwān departed for Istanbul where, despite earlier efforts to defend his actions through dispatches, he was censured and imprisoned. His exoneration followed the assassination in Cairo during Djumādā I 975/November 1567 of Maḥmūd Pasha who, it was discovered, had concealed Riḍwān's alarming reports from Yemen. Riḍwān again became *sandjaḳ beyi* of Ghazza in 978/1570-1, and in Shawwāl 980/March 1573 was named *beylerbeyi* of Abyssinia (Ḥabesh [*q.v.*]), which appointment he held until after Rabīʿ II 982/July-August 1574. He is next mentioned only in 987/1579, serving in the Persian campaign. In late 990/1582 or early 991/1583 he was made *beylerbeyi* of Anadolu, in which office he died on 1 Rabīʿ II 993/2 April 1585.

Bibliography: Ms. sources include (in Arabic) the anonymous versified *al-Tīdjān al-wāfirat al-thaman*; Ibn Dāʿir, *Futūḥāt*; ʿĪsā b. Luṭfallāh, *Rawḥ al-rūḥ*; and (in Turkish) Luḳmān b. Sayyid Ḥusayn, *Mudjmal al-ṭūmār*.

Published materials: Nahrawālī, *al-Barḳ al-Yamānī = Ghazawāt al-Djarākisa*, ed. H. al-Djāsir, Riyāḍ 1967, 123 f., 131, 135, 137, 139, 157-9, 163-75, 197; Yaḥyā b. al-Ḥusayn, *Ghāyat al-amānī*, ed. S. ʿĀshūr, Cairo 1968, ii, 717, 722-8; Selānīkī, *Taʾrīkh*, Istanbul 1281/1864-5, 171, 189; Münedjdjim Bashī, iii, 242, 245-7, 249, 253; *Sidjill-i ʿOthmānī*, ii, 401-2, iv, 354; Rāshid, *Taʾrīkh-i Yemen*, Istanbul 1291/1874-5, i, 107, 111-18; F. Wüstenfeld, *Jemen*, Göttingen 1884, 10-12; İ.H. Danişmend, *Osmanlı tarihi kronolojisi*, Istanbul 1963, ii, 373, iii, 40, 43-4, 63; C. Orhonlu, *Habeş eyaleti*, Istanbul 1974, 54-5, 103-4, 112, 183, 192-203; J.R. Blackburn, *The collapse of Ottoman authority in Yemen*, in *WI*, xix (1980), 131-50; and H. Yavuz, *Yemen'de Osmanlı hâkimiyeti (1517-1571)*, Istanbul 1984, 74-8. (J.R. BLACKBURN)

RĪF (A.), "countryside".

I. As a geographical and territorial term.

1. One sense of this term early emerged from the Egyptian context, where an arid country is traversed by a river with food-producing fringes: the image is that of the fertile (and cultivated) banks of the Nile [see NĪL]. It includes two ideas, that of "fringe" (bank, littoral and, by extension, flank, limit) and that of "fertile countryside", "abundance" (as opposed to the desert; and, by extension, "countryside" as opposed to the town) (see the lexicon of Lane and Kazimirski).

2. In Morocco, where the natural environment is different, the sense of "fringe" is further found:

(a) Amongst certain groups of transhumant pastoralists, partly Arabophone, who call *rīf*, in the circle of tents, those which are on the periphery (Querleux, *Les Zemmour*, in *Archives Berbères*, ii [Rabat 1915-16], 127). By extension (?), certain Berberophone groups of the Middle Atlas use it to define a group of tents held together by a close relationship in the male line (the equivalent of the *ikhs* of other Berber speakers) (R. Montagne, *Les Berbères et le Makhzen dans le Sud du Maroc*, Paris 1930, 181 n. 1).

(b) In reference to the coastal chain, the Rīf, which extends from the Straits of Gibraltar to the approaches of Moulouya. Its presence here as a toponym, with a varying definition of extent, is probably due to the configuration of the geographical relief along the Mediterranean coast (however, this etymological version could be moderated by the fact that, in the western, Arabophone part of the Rīf, the villages sometimes call certain of their quarters *Rīf*).

The term appears as a neologism at the beginning

of the 7th/13th century to designate the ancient Mauretania Tingitana (H. Ferhat, *Sabta des origines jusqu'à 1306*, diss. Paris I, forthcoming). Ibn Saʿīd [*q.v.*] defines it as "littoral", known under the name of the "*Rīf* of the Ghumāra"; Ibn al-Abbār [*q.v.*], somewhat differently, describes it as "adjoining the Ghumāra"; and al-Bādisī, in the 8th/14th century, extends it from Sabta to Tlemcen.

History very early touched the Mediterranean shores of Morocco. The principality of Nakūr [*q.v.*], in the plain behind the bay of al-Ḥusayma [*q.v.* in Suppl.], was founded in 90/709 by a commander of the caliph in Damascus, Ṣāliḥ b. Manṣūr al-Ḥimyarī (the town was built some time around 143/761), thus preceeding the foundation of Fās. The town seems to have been subject to the same sort of hazards as the Idrīsid kingdom, squeezed between the Umayyads of Cordova and the Fāṭimids. It hardly survived, and was razed by the Almoravids (473-4/1080-1). The Idrīsids (and, in the first place, ʿUmar b. Idrīs, to whom the region fell) played a major role in the integration of the Rīf chain to the emergent nation. With Ḳalʿat Ḥadjar al-Nasr (within the tribe of the Sumāta), they even had an ephemeral capital there (4th/10th century), where they left behind a line which was rendered famous, in the 7th-8th/13th-14th centuries, in his hermitage on the Djabal al-ʿAlam (amongst the tribe of the Banī ʿArūṣ), by the *ḳuṭb* Mawlāy ʿAbd al-Salām Ibn Mashīsh, considered to have been the master of al-Shādhilī. It was the Almohads, masters of both shores, who really brought about the development of the littoral, with Sabta [*q.v.*], Bādis and a series of petty maritime settlements. The loss of al-Andalus, however, ruined it, and the consequent pressure was unceasing: the fall of its main ports (Sabta/Ceuta in 818/1415), the establishment of the Spanish *presidios* at several points on the coast, the "guerra de Africa" with the seizure of Tetouan (1859-60), and finally, the establishment of the Spanish Protectorate (1912). The disorders which accompanied or preceeded it (al-Raysūnī, Bū Ḥamāra) had hardly any long term effects, but it was a different matter with the resistance led by Bin ʿAbd al-Krīm al-Khaṭṭābī (1921-6), the first war of liberation in the 20th century; the victory of Anwāl (1921) had a deep effect on colonial peoples (see further, II. below).

Thus there are, in Morocco, three senses of the toponym Rīf:

(a) The Rīf of the chroniclers is a mountainous region bordering on the Mediterranean;

(b) The Rīf of the geologists is a region of folded strata from the Alpine period, about 360 km long and 80 km at its maximum width, laid down at a late date up against the Atlas region. Its altitude is not so great (Tidighine: 2,450 m), since it is deeply entrenched and forms a juxtaposition of mountainous compartments rather than a homogenous mountain chain (G. Maurer, *Les montagnes du Rif central. Etude géomorphologique*, Tangiers 1968); and

(c) The Rīf as understood by the population is exclusively formed from this eastern half of the chain together with the hills which prolong it as far as the mouth of the Moulouya, where the language spoken is *dhamazighth* (wrongly still called *dharifith*, Arabised into *tarifit*), belonging to the Zanātiya variety of the Berber tongues of Morocco. Its inhabitants are the only one bearing the name of Riyāfa (Rwāfa, Rīfiyyīn).

In their turn, the geographers distinguish a Rīf influenced by the Atlantic, humid and with good vegetation, and a sub-arid Rīf. The division is one of relief (the boundary passes where the limestone spine culminates, then through the central ridge of the Ṣanhādja Srayr, a little to the west of the meridian al-Ḥusayma-Taza); one of climate (it follows an isohyetal curve which begins at Djabha on the coast, bends eastwards, passes to the south of the Targuist basin and turns back southwards at the level of the above-mentioned meridian; see Maurer, *op. cit.*); and one of humans, since a series of linguistic and cultural pockets (Arabophone "Rīf" round the Banī Fraḥ; Ghmāra further to the west; Ṣanhādja further to the south, each with Berber islets of speech) extend along this fringe separating the Rīf, in the east, from the Djbāla, in the west.

In effect, although one cannot date its appearance, the word Djabal only later replaced, in the western part, the term Rīf and its inhabitants are called Djbāla (sing. Djablī). They form an arc which connects the Tingitana peninsula with the valley of the Wargha. They are the heirs of the ancient Ghumāra [*q.v.*] (an ethonym which has persisted only for the nine tribes, called Ghmāra, forming an enclave between the highest crest of the mountains and the sea). Ibn Khaldūn classed this group amongst the Maṣmūda family. Several traits remind one of the other great sub-group of the Maṣmūda, the mountain peoples of the Sūs (Swāsa). Thus we have a great number of learned men (*fuḳahāʾ*, *ʿulamāʾ* and *ṭulba*); the deserted settlements of the Rīf are traditionally attached to the Swāsa; and finally, although Arabised for many centuries, the speech of the Djbāla retains Berber intonations which connect it with *tashelḥit* rather than other varieties of Berber. On the other hand, certain traits connect the Djbāla territory with certain massifs of the Algerian and Tunisian Tells: an important vegetation cover, a great density of population, intensive labour and a great variety of production, large villages with thatched roofs, etc. One last peculiarity is the intensity of the urbanisation phenomenon; there is a real urbanisation belt around the Tingitana peninsula, often going back to Antiquity and in any case to the time when there were close communications with al-Andalus.

The Rīf and its maritime façade are probably the last great challenge which must face Morocco in order for its development to succeed: it is endeavouring to leave behind the accumulated backwardness (illustrated by the fragility of an over-exploited region, the monoculture of Indian hemp over a large area of the Rīf and the poverty of its infrastructures) and to close the dossier of the colonial period. Sabta/Ceuta, Melilla and a few islets remain occupied; the commercial domination of these two towns in respect of smuggling activities affects, notably, the regional structure of small and medium enterprises (see G.E.R.M., *Le Maroc méditerranéen. La troisième dimension*, Casablanca 1992).

Assets are not lacking: water, halieutic resources, sites for beaches and mountain resorts (cedar and pine plantations), banking facilities (Nador is the second most important financial centre after Casablanca) and, finally, the closeness of a key crossroads of the Mediterranean. From being on the periphery (more as a result of modern history than from geography, however), the Rīf—in its regional setting—is able to renew its age-old vocation of being a focus for economic activities and a bond of union between continents.

Bibliography (in addition to references in the article): H. Alfiguigui, *Muḳāwamat al-wudjūd al-ibīrī bi-thughūr al-shamāliyya al-muḥtalla (1415-1574)*, diss. Rabat 1991, unpubl.; E. Blanco-Izaga, *La vivienda rifeña*, Ceuta 1930; idem, *Las danzas rifeñas*, in *Africa* (Madrid 1946); G.S. Colin, *Le parler berbère des Gmāra*, in *Hespéris*, ix (Rabat 1929); A. Renisio, *Etude sur les dialects berbères des Beni Iznassen, du Rif et des Senhaja de Sfaïr*, Paris 1932; M. Chtatou, *Aspects of the phonology of a Berber dialect of the Rif*, diss. SOAS University of London 1982, unpubl.; P. Cressier, *Le développement urbain des côtes septentrionales du Maroc au Moyen-Age: frontière intérieure et frontière extérieure*, in *Castrum. 4. Frontière et peuplement dans le monde mediterranéen au Moyen-Age*, Madrid-Rome 1992; T. Garcia Figueras and R. de Roda Jimenez, *Economía social de Marruecos*, i, Madrid 1950; Groupe Pluridisciplinaire d'Etude sur les Jbala, *Jbala. Histoire et société. Etudes sur le Maroc du Nord-Ouest*, Casablanca-Paris 1991; D. Hart, *The Aith Waryaghar of the Moroccan Rif. An ethnography and history*, Tucson, Ariz. 1976; R. Jamous, *Honneur et baraka. Les structures sociales traditionelles dans le Rif*, Paris-Cambridge 1981; M. Mezzine, *Le temps des marabouts et des chorfa. Essai d'histoire sociale marocaine à travers les sources de jurisprudence religieuse. Le cas des Ghomara*, diss. Paris 1988, unpubl.; E. Michaux-Bellaire, *Quelques tribus de montagne de la région du Habt*, in *Arch. Marocaines* (1911).

(J. VIGNET-ZUNZ)

II. The Rīf War of the 1920s.

This frontier region of the Moroccan empire, protected by its geographical configuration, has always remained more or less rebellious against the central authority, e.g. since the time of the principality of Nakūr [*q.v.*], but especially, in recent times, against the authority of the *makhzan*. The rivalries which appeared amongst the European powers (above all, between Germany, France and Spain) from the 19th century soon precipitated disorders. The imprudent activities of sultan ʿAbd al-ʿAzīz led to the appearance in 1901 of a pretender, the *rūgi* Bū Ḥmāra, who from a base at Taza led a fierce rebellion during 1907-8. Agreements reached after great effort favoured the intervention as a pacifying influence, but one which was sometimes hazardous if not contradictory, of France and Spain. A chieftain of the Rīf rose to power thanks to German intrigues under cover of the First World War, Muḥammad b. ʿAbd al-Karīm, called Bin ʿAbd al-Krīm, and he managed to hold back the power of Spain thanks to the exactions of his rival Aḥmad b. Muḥammad al-Raysūlī/Raysūnī and to gain the resounding victory of Anwāl over the Spanish forces (1921). He came back again in 1925 against the forces of France under the Marshals Lyautey and then Pétain, and threatened Fās. The Rīf forces' offensive was definitively broken at the beginning of 1926 thanks to a combined offensive of the French and Spanish forces, and Bin ʿAbd al-Krīm was deported to the Isle de Réunion. Nevertheless, the last pockets of resistance did not surrender until the 1930s. Al-Raysūlī, the unfortunate rival of Bin ʿAbd al-Krīm, disappeared in 1925, after having, according to the flow of circumstances, at times assisted and at others hindered the efforts of Bin ʿAbd al-Krīm.

Bibliography: This is largely given in the arts. ʿALAWĪS and MAGHRIB, but see also Ch. Julien, *Histoire de l'Afrique du Nord*, Paris 1931; H. Terrasse, *Histoire du Maroc*, Paris 1949-50, ii, 239-41; A. Gaudio, *Rif, terre marocaine d'épopée et de légende*, Paris 1962; A. El-Bouayyachi, *Ḥarb al-Rīf al-taḥrīriyya wamarāḥil al-niḍāl*, Tangier 1974; D. Hart, *Emilio Blanco Izaga, Colonel in the Rif*, New Haven 1975; G. Ayache, *Les origines de la guerre du Rif*, Rabat-Paris 1981; C.R. Pennell, *A country with a government and a flag. The Rif War in Morocco 1921-1926*, Wisbech, Cambs. 1986.

(ED.)

RIFĀʿA BEY AL-ṬAHṬĀWĪ (1801-73), Egyptian educationist and author, who can, more than anyone else, be recognised as the initiator and symbol of the Egyptian "Awakening" (*nahḍa* [*q.v.*]) and considered the leading intellectual figure of his generation.

Abu 'l-ʿAzm Rifāʿa Rāfiʿ b. Badawī was born into a family of prominent *ʿulamāʾ* in the Upper Egyptian town of Ṭahṭā. In 1817 he came to Cairo and enrolled in al-Azhar. Of the professors there it was Ḥasan al-ʿAṭṭār (1766-1834) who had the greatest and most lasting influence on him. Al-ʿAṭṭār had come into contact with the French during their occupation of Egypt and become interested in Europe, its thought and sciences. Through the friendship with his teacher, Rifāʿa became acquainted with secular subjects not yet taught at al-Azhar as well as with some aspects of European thought while still studying at the university. Between 1822 and 1824 *shaykh* Rifāʿa occupied a teaching position at al-Azhar.

In 1824 al-ʿAṭṭār secured Rifāʿa's appointment as *wāʿiẓ* and *imām* of a regiment in the new Egyptian army, and when Muḥammad ʿAlī Pasha [*q.v.*] sent a mission of 44 students to France in 1826, *shaykh* Rifāʿa was chosen as one of the four *imāms* accompanying the mission, also on the recommendation of al-ʿAṭṭār.

In Paris, Rifāʿa, on his own initiative, studied French in order to be able to read works in that language, beginning with history and geography, later taking up philosophy and literature. His object was to translate the books he read into Arabic. During his stay he made friends with leading French orientalists, such as A.I. Silvestre de Sacy (1758-1838) and E.-F. Jomard (1777-1862), who also appreciated him as a learned Muslim scholar. Under their benevolent supervision, he became aware of the new discoveries of Egyptology and of western values and culture in general. On his return to Egypt at Muḥammad ʿAlī's request, he published his observations and impressions *Takhlīṣ al-ibrīz ilā talkhīṣ Bārīz* in 1834, a work which he had already written in Paris. This *riḥla* description became very well known and until the 1850s it remained the sole work in which Arabic-speaking readers were offered a description of a European country. J. Heyworth-Dunne has called it the only human document of the age by the only writer of this period to have produced anything readable.

After his return from Paris in 1831 and more especially after the death of al-ʿAṭṭār, Rifāʿa became Muḥammad ʿAlī's right-hand man among the *ʿulamāʾ*. Rifāʿa was an intellectual-cum-public servant acting as the main ideologue of the ruling family, a position of unquestioning adherence to the policy of the powers to be. Even when expressing his own opinions in writing, the limits were defined by others. Therefore, the final assessment of his contributions must also be an assessment of the endeavours of his patrons.

Between 1831 and 1834 Rifāʿa was employed as a translator first at the School of Medicine and then at the Artillery School. The real breakthrough came in 1836 in connection with the reorganisation of the Schools Administration when he was chosen as one of the permanent members—and the only Egyptian—of the Council. In 1837 Rifāʿa was made head of the newly-created School of Languages, where the European system was successfully adapted to the method employed by the *ʿulamāʾ*, and, in 1842, even entrusted with the editorship of the official newspaper *al-Waḳāʾiʿ al-Miṣriyya* for a time. But without question, his most important work was as a translator and supervisor of translators. He was rewarded in 1846 with the honorific title Bey.

All this came to an abrupt end with the death of Muḥammad ʿAlī; he was succeeded by his grandson ʿAbbās I [*q.v.*] who had Rifāʿa Bey sent to Khartūm in 1850 to what was, in fact, virtual exile. The translation movement came to an end, and the School of Languages was closed the following year. Only when Saʿīd [*q.v.*] succeeded ʿAbbās, who was assassinated, did Rifāʿa regain favour and was allowed to return to Cairo in 1854. He became head of a military school but when it was closed in 1861 he remained unemployed until the reign of Ismāʿīl [*q.v.*]. Ismāʿīl reopened the School of Languages in 1863 and appointed Rifāʿa as director; he was also one of the group that planned the new educational system. In 1870 Rifāʿa became the editor of *Rawḍat al-madāris*, a periodical for the Ministry of Education; he occupied this position until his death.

It is a moot question whether Rifāʿa owed most of what is regarded as European influence on him to his teacher at al-Azhar, Ḥasan al-ʿAṭṭār, or if he was a real innovator bringing back ideas from France. The main problem which he had to face as the ideologue of Muḥammad ʿAlī's innovations was how to have his countrymen partake in the modern world while remaining Muslim. In his writings he tried to answer this question. Though a prolific author, nothing Rifāʿa wrote after *Takhlīṣ* equalled it either in style or in significance. This is not to say that his writings were without impact; quite the contrary.

Although Rifāʿa himself was not a first-rate historian, it was he who laid the groundwork for later Egyptian achievements in historiography. A turning-point in the writing of history in Egypt as well as a turning-point in Egyptians' self-awareness as a nation occurred in 1868 when he published his *Anwār tawfīḳ al-djalīl fī akhbār Miṣr wa-tawthīḳ banī Ismāʿīl*. It was the first part of a history of Egypt planned to cover the period from the Deluge to his own time, although together with the posthumously (1874) published *sīra* of the Prophet *Nihāyat al-īdjāz fī sīrat sākin al-Ḥidjāz*, it was all that was published. *Anwār* included the ages of the ancient Egyptians, Alexander the Great, the Romans and the Byzantines, and it ended where Egyptian history written by Arabs had usually begun—the Arab conquest. Rifāʿa was the first writer who saw Egypt as something historically continuous, a distinct geographical unit, and he tried to explain this vision of an Egyptian nation in terms of Islamic thought.

Two other publications of Rifāʿa have to be mentioned here. They are a general book on Egyptian society *Manāhidj al-albāb al-miṣriyya fī mabāhidj al-ādāb al-ʿaṣriyya* (1869), and a book on education *al-Murshid al-amīn li'l-banāt wa'l-banīn* (1872). In the latter he advocated—albeit timidly—the necessity of extending general education to girls.

The pre-eminence which Rifāʿa Bey has come to hold, and deservedly so, reflects the intellectual mediocrity of the Muḥammad ʿAlī era.

Bibliography: Rifāʿa Bey's most important publications are mentioned in the article (1st editions); they have all gone through several editions often with alterations and omissions. Muḥammad ʿAmmāra (ed.), *al-Aʿmāl al-kāmila li-Rifāʿa Rāfiʿ al-Ṭahṭāwī*, i-iii, Beirut 1973; *Takhlīṣ al-ibrīz ilā talkhīṣ Bārīz* has been translated into German by K. Stowasser as *Ein Muslim entdeckt Europa*, Leipzig-Weimar 1988, and into French by A. Louca as *L'Or de Paris*, Paris 1988; Ṣāliḥ Madjdī, *Ḥilyat al-zaman bi-manāḳib khādim al-waṭan, Rifāʿa Bey Rāfiʿ al-Ṭahṭāwī*, Cairo 1958 (the author was a pupil and friend of Rifāʿa); J. Heyworth-Dunne, *Rifāʿah Badawī Rāfiʿ aṭ-Ṭahṭāwī: the Egyptian revivalist*, in *BSOS*, ix (1937-9), 961-7; x (1940), 399-415; Aḥmad Aḥmad Badawī, *Rifāʿa Rāfiʿ al-Ṭahṭāwī*, ²Cairo 1959; A. Hourani, *Arabic thought in the liberal age 1798-1939*, London 1962, ²1983, index; I. Abu-Lughod, *The Arab rediscovery of Europe*, Princeton 1963, 50-3 (partial listing of literary works translated into Arabic); A. Abdel-Malek, *Idéologie et renaissance nationale. L'Égypte moderne*, Paris 1969, *passim*; A. Louca, *Voyageurs et écrivains égyptiens en France au XIXᵉ siècle*, Paris 1970, 55-74; P. Gran, *Islamic roots of capitalism. Egypt, 1760-1840*, Austin-London 1979, index; G. Delanoue, *Moralistes et politiques musulmans dans l'Égypte du XIXᵉ siècle (1798-1882)*, Cairo 1982, *passim*; B. Lewis, *The Muslim discovery of Europe*, London 1982, 133, 219-20, 281-2, 191-3; J.A. Crabbs, Jr., *The writing of history in nineteenth-century Egypt*, Detroit 1984, 67-86; Y.M. Choueiri, *Arab history and the nation-state. A study in modern Arabic historiography 1820-1980*, London-New York 1989, 3-24, 197 f., 206; R.A. Hamed, *The Japanese and Egyptian enlightenment*, Tokyo 1990, *passim*; Lewis, *Islam and the West*, New York and Oxford 1993, 171-2.

(K. Öhrnberg)

AL-**RIFĀʿĪ**, Aḥmad b. ʿAlī, Abu 'l-ʿAbbas, Shāfiʿī *faḳīh* by training and founder of the Rifāʿiyya [*q.v.*] dervish order.

He was born in Muḥarram 500/September 1106 (or, according to other authorities, in Radjab 512/October-November 1118) at Ḳaryat Ḥasan, a village of the Baṭāʾiḥ or marshlands of lower ʿIrāḳ [see AL-BAṬĪḤA] between Baṣra and Wāsiṭ, whence the *nisba* sometimes given to him of al-Baṭāʾiḥī, and he died at Umm ʿUbayda in the same region on 22 Djumādā I 578/23 October 1182 (see Ibn Khallikān ed. ʿAbbās, i, 171-2, tr. de Slane, i, 152-3). The *nisba* al-Rifāʿī is usually explained as referring to an ancestor Rifāʿa, but by some is supposed to be a tribal name. This ancestor Rifāʿa is said to have migrated from Mecca to Seville in Spain in 317/929, whence Aḥmad's grandfather came to Baṣra in 450/1058. Hence he is also called al-Maghribī.

Ibn Khallikān's notice of him is meagre; more is given in al-Dhahabī's *Taʾrīkh al-Islām*, taken from a collection of his *Manāḳib* by Muḥyī 'l-Dīn Aḥmad b. Sulaymān al-Ḥammāmī recited by him to a disciple in 680/1281. This work does not appear in the lists of treatises on the same subject furnished by Abu 'l-Hudā Efendi al-Rāfiʿī al-Khālidī al-Ṣayyādī in his works *Tanwīr al-abṣār* (Cairo 1306) and *Ḳilādat al-djawāhir* (Beirut 1301), the latter of which is a copious biography, frequently citing *Tiryāḳ al-muḥibbīn* by Taḳī al-Dīn al-Wāsiṭī (see below), *Umm al-barāhīn* by Ḳāsim b. al-Ḥādjdj, *al-Nafḥa al-miskiyya* by ʿIzz al-Dīn al-Fārūthī (d. 694/1295), and others. Al-Ḥammāmī's statements are cited from one Yaʿḳūb b. Kurāz, who acted as *muʾadhdhin* for al-Rifāʿī. Great caution is required in the use of such materials.

Whereas according to some accounts he was a posthumous child, the majority date his father's death to 519/1125 in Baghdād, when Aḥmad was seven years old. He was then brought up by his maternal uncle Manṣūr al-Baṭāʾiḥī, resident at Nahr Daḳlā in the neighbourhood of Baṣra. This Manṣūr (of whom there is a notice in al-Shaʿrānī's *Lawāḳiḥ al-anwār*, i, 178) is represented as the head of a religious community, called by Aḥmad (if he is correctly reported by his grandson, *Ḳilāda*, 88) al-Rifāʿiyya; he sent his nephew to Wāsiṭ to study under a Shāfiʿī doctor Abu 'l-Faḍl ʿAlī al-Wāsiṭī and a maternal uncle Abū Bakr al-Wāsiṭī. His studies lasted till his twenty-seventh year, when he received an *idjāza* [*q.v.*] from Abu 'l-

Faḍl, and the khirḳa from his uncle Manṣūr, who bade him establish himself in Umm ʿUbayda, where (it would seem) his mother's family had property, and where her father Yaḥyā al-Nadjdjārī al-Anṣārī was buried. In the following year, 540/1145-6, Manṣūr died and bequeathed the headship of his community (mashyakha) to Aḥmad to the exclusion of his own son.

His activities appears to have been confined to Umm ʿUbayda and neighbouring villages, whose names are unknown to the geographers; even Umm Ubayda is not mentioned by Yāḳūt, though found in one copy of the Marāṣid al-iṭṭilāʿ. This fact renders incredible the huge figures cited by Abu 'l-Hudā for the number of his disciples (murīdīn) and even deputies (khulafāʾ), the princely style and the colossal buildings in which he entertained them. Sibṭ Ibn al-Djauzī in his Mirʾāt al-zamān, ed. Ḥaydarābād, viii, 370, says that one of their shaykhs told him he had seen some 100,000 persons with al-Rifāʿī on a night of Shaʿbān. In Ibn al-ʿImād's Shadharāt al-dhahab the experience is said to have been Sibṭ Ibn al-Djauzī's own, though his person was born in 581/1185, three years after al-Rifāʿī's death. In the Tanwīr al-abṣār (7, 8) his grandfather as well as himself is credited with the assertion.

His followers do not attribute to him any treatises, but Abu 'l-Hudā produces 1. two discourses (madjlis) delivered by him in 577/1181 and 578/1182-3 respectively; 2. a whole dīwān of odes; 3. a collection of prayers (adʿiya), devotional exercises (awrād), and incantations (aḥzāb); 4. a great number of casual utterances, sometimes nearly of the length of sermons, swollen by frequent repetitions. Since in 1, 2 and 4 he claims descent from ʿAlī and Fāṭima, and to be the substitute (nāʾib) for the Prophet on earth, whereas his biographers insist on his humility, and disclaiming such titles as ḳuṭb, ghawth, or even shaykh, the genuineness of these documents is questionable.

Various books were written on him by his followers and by subsequent members of the Rifāʿī ṭarīḳa, such as the Tiryāḳ al-muḥibbīn fī sīrat sulṭān al-ʿārifīn Aḥmad ʾbn al-Rifāʿī of Taḳī 'l-Dīn ʿAbd al-Raḥmān al-Wāsiṭī (d. 744/1343-4; see Brockelmann, S I, 781, S II, 214).

In Ibn al-ʿImād, op. cit., iv, 260, it is asserted that the marvellous performances associated with the Rifāʿīs, such as sitting in heated ovens, riding lions, etc. [see RIFĀ'IYYA] were unknown to the founder, and introduced after the Mongol invasion; in any case, they were no invention of his, since the like are recorded by al-Tanūkhī in the 4th/10th century. The anecdotes produced by al-Dhahabī (repeated by al-Subkī, Ṭabaḳāt al-Shāfiʿiyya al-kubrā, iv, 40) imply a doctrine similar to the Buddhist and Indian ahiṃsā, unwillingness to kill or give pain to living creatures, even lice and locusts. He is also said to have inculcated poverty, abstinence and non-resistance to injury. Thus Sibṭ Ibn al-Djawzī records how he allowed his wife to belabour him with a poker, though his friends collected 500 dīnārs to enable him to divorce her by returning her marriage gift. (The sum mentioned is inconsistent with his supposed poverty.)

Inconsistent accounts are given of his relations with his contemporary ʿAbd al-Ḳādir al-Djīlānī [q.v.]. In he Bahdjat al-asrār of Nūr al-Dīn al-Shaṭṭanawfī it is recorded by apparently faultless isnāds on the authority of two nephews of al-Rifāʿī, and a man who visited him at Umm ʿUbayda in 576/1180-1, that when ʿAbd al-Ḳādir in Baghdād declared that his foot was on the neck of every saint, al-Rifāʿī was heard to say at Umm Ubayda "and on mine". Hence some make him a disciple of ʿAbd al-Ḳādir. On the other hand, Abu 'l-Hudā's authorities make ʿAbd al-Ḳādir one of those who witnessed in Medina in the year 555/1160 the

unique miracle of the Prophet holding out his hand from the tomb for al-Rifāʿī to kiss; further, in the list of his predecessors in the discourse of 578/1182-3, al-Rifāʿī mentions Manṣūr but not ʿAbd al-Ḳādir. It is probable, therefore, that the two worked independently.

Details of his family are quoted from the work of al-Fārūthī, grandson of a disciple named ʿUmar. According to him, al-Rifāʿī married first Manṣūr's niece Khadīdja; after her death, her sister Rabīʿa; after her death Nafīsa, daughter of Muḥammad b. al-Ḳāsimiyya. There were many daughters; also three sons, who all died before their father. He was succeeded in the headship of his order by a sister's son, ʿAlī b. ʿUthmān.

Bibliography: In addition to references given in the article, see Shaʿrānī, Lawāḳiḥ al-anwār fī ṭabaḳāt al-akhyār, Cairo 1276/1859-60, i, 121-5; Ziriklī, Aʿlām, iii, 169; Muṣṭafā Kamāl Waṣfī, al-Imām al-Kabīr Aḥmad al-Rifāʿī, Cairo 1376/1957; J.S. Trimingham, The Sufi orders in Islam, Oxford 1971, 37 ff. and index; Brockelmann, S II, 780-1.

(D.S. MARGOLIOUTH*)

RIFĀ'IYYA, the name of one of the most prominent Ṣūfī orders from the period of the institutionalisation of the ṭarīḳas [q.v.], and one which came to be noted in pre-modern times for the extravagance of some of its practices.

It is unclear whether the founder, Aḥmad al-Rifāʿī [q.v.], was a mystic of the thaumaturgic, miracle-mongering type, but the order which he founded and which was developed by his kinsmen certainly acquired its extravagant reputation during the course of the 6th/12th century; it may not be without significance that the order grew up in the Lower ʿIrāḳ marshlands between Wāsiṭ and Baṣra where there was a mélange of faiths and beliefs, Muslim, Christian, Mandaean, etc., with many older survivals. Already, Ibn Khallikān [q.v.] (wrote ca. 654/1256) reported that the Rifāʿī dervishes rode on lions in the Baṭāʾiḥ and that eating live snakes and walking on hot coals were amongst their practices (ed. Iḥsān ʿAbbās, i, 172, tr. de Slane, i, 153).

Al-Rifāʿī's retreat in the marshlands was a focus for visiting dervishes, some of whom founded their own orders, such as the Badawiyya, Dasūḳiyya and Shādhiliyya, and it was the prototype for many zāwiyas which sprang up. Ibn Baṭṭūṭa [q.v.] frequently mentions the strange practices of their devotees. Thus when on Wāsiṭ in 727/1327, he visited Aḥmad al-Rifāʿī's shrine at Umm ʿUbayda, where he saw throngs of people and witnessed fire-walking and fire-swallowing (Riḥla, ii, 4-5, tr. Gibb, ii, 273-4); an eastern counterpart of these practices were those of the Ḳalandars [see ḲALANDARIYYA], dervishes of the Ḥaydariyya order, which he witnessed in India (Riḥla, ii, 6-7, iii, 79-9, tr. ii, 274-5, iii, 583).

The Rifāʿiyya spread rapidly into Egypt and Syria, possibly under the patronage of the Ayyūbids. In Syria, a key figure was Abū Muḥammad ʿAlī al-Ḥarīrī (d. 645/1268), so that this branch became known as the Ḥarīriyya; another Syrian branch which was later to become notorious for its extravagant practices, including that of the dawsa [q.v.] or trampling of adherents by the mounted shaykh of the order, was that of the Saʿdiyya [q.v.] or Djibāwiyya founded by Aḥmad al-Rifāʿī's grandson, ʿIzz al-Dīn Aḥmad al-Ṣayyād (d. 670/1271-2). In Egypt, the order became especially strong. ʿIzz al-Dīn al-Ṣayyād was teaching in Cairo in 638/1236 and married there an Ayyūbid descendant, the grand-daughter of Nūr al-Dīn al-Malik al-Afḍal. However, the great mosque of al-

Rifāᶜī, near the Cairo Citadel, was not begun till the later 19th century, and the tomb which it contains was thought by ᶜAlī Pasha Mubārak more likely to be that of one of Aḥmad al-Rifāᶜī's descendants or *khulafā*ʾ.

The Rifāᶜiyya order further became popular amongst the Turks in the course of the 7th-8th/13th-14th centuries, continuing so in Turkey up to the 20th century. Ibn Baṭṭūṭa, again, visited what he calls "Aḥmadī" *zāwiya*s in Anatolia, including at Amasya, Izmir and Bergama (*Riḥla*, ii, 292-3, 310, 315-16, tr. ii, 436, 445, 449); whilst at this same period, the Mewlewī Aflākī [*q.v.*] describes, with disapproval, the extravagances of fire-walking, snake-biting, etc., which could be seen at the *zāwiya* of "Sayyid Tādj al-Dīn Aḥmad al-Rifāᶜī" in Konya (*Manāḳib al-ᶜārifīn*, ed. and tr. Cl. Huart, Paris 1918-22, tr. ii, 203-4). From Anatolia, the order spread into the Balkans as far as Bosnia and across the Black Sea to the lands of the Golden Horde; Fuad Köprülü thought that the Rifāᶜiyya of the Turkish lands might have been additionally influenced by the semi-magical practices surviving from old Turkish shamanism (see Köprülüzade M. Fuad, *Influence du chamanisme turco-mongol sur les ordres mystiques musulmanes*, Istanbul 1929, 12-13; Gibb and Bowen, *Islamic society and the West*, i/2, 196-7).

In the Maghrib, the ecstatic practices of the Rifāᶜiyya or one of its offshoots were adopted by the ᶜĪsāwiyya or Isāwā [*q.v.*] founded by Muḥammad b. ᶜĪsā (d. 930/1524) after his travels in the central Islamic lands. Perhaps most distantly of all, Ibn Baṭṭūṭa even mentions Rifāᶜīs in the Maldive Islands [*q.v.*] (*Riḥla*, text, iv, 141).

The Rifāᶜiyya was thus the most widespread of all the *ṭuruḳ* until the 9th/15th century, when it was overtaken in popularity by the Ḳādiriyya [*q.v.*]. After this time, its greatest appeal was to be in the Arab lands, and especially in Egypt. In 18th century Cairo, the *mawlid* [*q.v.*] or birthday celebration of Aḥmad al-Rifāᶜī was celebrated on 12 Djumādā II at Rumayla. This order, and the associated one of the Badawiyya [see AḤMAD AL-BADAWĪ] were at this time widely recruited from the lower strata of society, compared with e.g. the Ḳādiriyya and Khalwatiyya [*q.v.*]; al-Djabartī stigmatises the Aḥmadiyya and Saᶜdiyya as popular amongst the *awbāsh* or lowest classes (see A. Raymond, *Artisans et commerçants au Caire au XVIIIe siècle*, Damascus 1973-4, ii, 435-6).

In the early 19th century, E.W. Lane gave a classic account of the grotesque practices of the Rifāᶜiyya "howling dervishes" and their offshoots the Saᶜdiyya and ᶜIlwāniyya, which included snake charming and the thrusting of iron spikes, glass, etc. into their bodies (*The manners and customs of the modern Egyptians*, chs. x, xx, xxv). By the middle years of the century, however, such popular excesses began to be deprecated by the Ottoman and Egyptian authorities, when the more progressive-minded of the ruling classes began to regard the *ṭuruḳ* as brakes on progress and as associations which were bringing the image of Islam into disrepute, in Western eyes. Hence in Egypt, the *dawsa* ceremony was prohibited by the Khedive Tawfīḳ on the basis of a *fatwā* from the Chief Muftī of Egypt, that it was a *bidᶜa ḳabīḥa* or reprehensible innovation. It continued, however, for some decades afterwards in Ottoman Syria, for the sultan ᶜAbd al-Ḥamīd II [*q.v.*] strongly favoured the dervish orders as part of his Pan-Islamic and pro-Islamic policies. The influence of the Rifāᶜī *shaykh* Abu 'l-Hudā Muḥammad al-Ṣayyād (1850-1909), of the Ṣayyādiyya branch of the Rifāᶜiyya in Aleppo, was particularly great at the Ottoman court, and this influence was much disapproved of by Islamic modernists and reformers of the stamp of Muḥamma[d] ᶜAbduh.

During the 20th century the Rifāᶜiyya have con[tinued] to be influential in Cairene life. A good pictur[e] of it as it was in the 1940s to 1960s, including the form of its *dhikr* [*q.v.*], is given by E. Bannerth in his *L[a] Rifaᶜiyya en Egypte*, in *MIDEO*, x (1970), 1-35. Bannerth noted that, at that time, the supreme head of th[e] order in Egypt was a descendant of the founder an[d] that the members of one section at least, th[e] ᶜAmriyya, included a good number of persons wit[h] secondary education and belonging to the middl[e] classes. The charismatic activities by members of th[e] order were played down, but in 1969 the author personally witnessed in the al-Rifāᶜī Mosque the piercin[g] of cheeks with sharpened iron skewers without an[y] resultant bleeding or visible wounds.

Bibliography (in addition to references given i[n] the article): J.W. McPherson, *The Moulids of Egyp[t]*, Cairo 1941, 283-4; J.S. Trimmingham, *The Su[fi] orders in Islam*, Oxford 1971, 37-40, 126-7, 247, 28[0]-1 (=Appx. H, list of Rifāᶜī *ṭāʾifa*s in the Ara[b] world); F. de Jong, *Ṭuruq and ṭuruq-linked institutio[ns] in nineteenth-century Egypt*, Leiden 1978, index.

(C.E. BOSWORTH)

RĪḤ (A.), wind. Arabic traditional knowledge o[f] the winds is gathered in ethno-astronomical an[d] meteorological treatises such as the *kutub al-anwāʾ* [se[e] ANWĀʾ] and other lexicographical treatises written b[y] Arabic philologists from the early 3rd/9th centuri[es] onwards. In these treatises, nearly one hundred word[s] depict different kinds of winds according to their e[f]fects, qualities and direction. Very little informatio[n] is given about their geographical location in the Ar[a]bian peninsula or the nature of the wind, if we excep[t] the fact that, in the *anwāʾ* system, the wind, especiall[y] hot ones (*bawāriḥ*), is seen as an effect of the star th[at] rises. In that tradition the compass rose is based o[n] four cardinal winds, the centre of which is the Kaᶜb[a]. The wind's direction is determined by the rising an[d] setting of the Sun and of certain stars [see MAṬLAᶜ an[d] KAᶜBA]. Al-Aṣmaᶜī and Abū ᶜUbayd say that the *Dab[ūr]* (west wind) comes from the back of the Kaᶜba, th[e] *Ḳabūl* (east wind) from its front; the *Shamāl* (nor[th] wind) from the Black Stone; the *Djanūb* from the op[]posite direction. According to Ibn al-Aᶜrābī, the *Dab[ūr]* blows between the *maṭlaᶜ* (rising-point) of Canop[us] and the *maṭlaᶜ* of the Pleiades; the *Ḳabūl* from th[e] *maṭlaᶜ* of the Pleiades to the *maṭlaᶜ* of the Great (?) Be[ar] (*Banāt Naᶜsh*); the *Shamāl* from the *maṭlaᶜ* of the Gre[at] (?) Bear (*Banāt Naᶜsh*) to the *maghrib* (setting point) [of] Altair: *Djanūb* from the *maghrib* of Altair to the *maṭl[aᶜ]* of Canopus [see the graphics in MAṬLAᶜ]. The win[ds] which blow between the cardinal ones are call[ed] *nakbāʾ*. Other compass roses with six winds, as well [as] synonyms of cardinal winds can be found in tho[se] sources. Information about local winds is contained [in] geographical treatises and calendars.

In the 3rd/9th century, an important developme[nt] in meteorology took place. It followed the classic[al] tradition of Aristotle's *Meteorology*, translated in[to] Arabic by Yaḥyā al-Biṭrīḳ (*Kitāb al-Āthār al-ᶜulwiyya*). Other classical sources were introduced, and amo[ng] the Arabic authors on this subject we can mention [al-]Kindī, Ḥunayn b. Isḥāḳ, Ibn al-Haytham, al-Bīrū[nī] and the Ikhwān al-Ṣafāʾ [*q.vv.*]. Aristotle conceiv[ed] the wind as an effect of dry and hot exhalations pr[o]duced by the Sun in the sphere of the air, but a mo[re] accurate explanation was furnished by al-Kindī, wh[o] stated that the wind is due to the movement of the a[ir] expanded by the heat of Sun towards colder plac[es] where the air is more contracted. Practical inform[ation]

tion about Greek winds is acquired by the translation of calendars such as Aratus of Soloi's *Phaenomena* or Ptolemy's *Phaseis* (translated by Sinān b. Th̲ābit b. Ḳurra and summarised by al-Bīrūnī in his *Kitāb al-Āth̲ār al-bāḳiya*).

Winds are particularly important in navigation treatises [see MILĀḤA and IBN MĀD̲J̲ID], in which we can find fairly detailed explanations about their causes, directions, effects in navigation, the monsoons and their seasons [see MAWSIM], coastal breezes and their causes, and the vocabulary of the sailors. The works of Ibn Mād̲j̲id (*fl.* 866-905/1462-1500) and Sulaymān al-Mahrī (*fl.* 917-60/1511-53) show that the sailors of the Indian Ocean also took into account the four cardinal winds. The most important were the *Ḳabūl*, called *Azyab* by the sailors, and the *Dabūr* or *Kaws*, because they were the prevailing winds of the three periods in which navigation was possible during the monsoons. The direction of the *Kaws* was determined by the setting of Sirius (*mag̲h̲īb al-Tīr*), while the direction of eastern winds was marked by the rising of a Boötis (*Simāk Rāmiḥ*).

Bibliography: 1. Arabic Sources: *Aristotle's Meteorology*, ed. C. Petraitis, Beirut 1967; Ibn Ḳutayba, *K. al-Anwāʾ*, ed. Ch. Pellat-M. Hamidullah, Ḥaydarābād 1956; Marzūḳī, *K. al-Azmina wa 'l-amkina*, Ḥaydarābād 1914; Ibn ʿĀṣim, *K. al-Anwāʾ*, Frankfurt 1985 (study and partial edition by M. Forcada in press); al-Bīrūnī, *K. al-Āth̲ār al-bāḳiya ʿan al-ḳurūn al-k̲h̲āliya*, ed. E. Sachau, Leipzig 1878; Ibn Sīduh, *Kitāb al-Muk̲h̲aṣṣaṣ*, Beirut n.d.; Abū Ḥāmid al-G̲h̲arnāṭī, *al-Mug̲h̲rib ʿan baʿḍ ʿad̲j̲āʾib al-Mag̲h̲rib*, ed. I. Bejarano, Madrid 1992; Ḳazwīnī, *K. ʿAd̲j̲āʾib al-mak̲h̲lūḳāt*, Cairo 1966; I. Khoury, *Arab nautical sciences, navigation texts and their analysis*. Part I, *Sulaymān al-Mahrī's work*, 3 vols., Damascus 1970-1, Part II, *Aḥmad b. Mād̲j̲id's work*, Damascus 1971; G.R. Tibbets, *Arabic navigation in the Indian Ocean before the coming of the Portuguese*, London 1971. 2. Secondary sources: F. Sezgin, *GAS*, vii (see the bibl. contained in it); J. Samsó and B. Rodríguez, *Las "Pháseis" de Ptolomeo y el Kitāb al-anwāʾ de Sinān b. T̲ābit*, in *And.*, xli (1976), 14-48; D.A. King, *Astronomy in the service of Islam*, London 1993.

(M. FORCADA)

RĪḤĀ, the name of two towns in the Levant.

1. The Arabs called the Jericho of the Bible Rīḥā or Arīḥā (Clermont-Ganneau, in *JA* [1877], i, 498). The town, which was 12 *mīls* east of Jerusalem, was reckoned sometimes to the *D̲j̲und* of Filasṭīn (e.g. Yāḳūt, *Muʿd̲j̲am*, iii, 913 and sometimes to the district of al-Balḳāʾ (al-Yaʿḳūbī, *Buldān*, 113); sometimes, however, it was called the capital of the province of Jordan (al-Urdunn) or of G̲h̲awr, the broad low-lying valley of the Jordan (Nahr al-Urdunn) from which it was 10 *mīl* distant (Yāḳūt, i, 227). As a result of its warm moist climate and the rich irrigation of its fields the country round the town produced a subtropical vegetation; among its products are mentioned, some already known in ancient times, dates and bananas, fragrant flowers, indigo (prepared from the *wasma* plant), sugar-cane, which yielded the best G̲h̲awr sugar. Not far from the town were the only sulphur mines in Palestine (Abu 'l-Fidāʾ, ed. Reinaud, 236). There were however many snakes and scorpions there and large numbers of fleas. From the flesh of the snakes called *tiryāḳiya* found there was made the antidote called "Jerusalem *tiryāḳ*" (θηριακὰ φάρμακα).

In the Ḳurʾān, Arīḥā is the town of the giants captured by Joshua; there was shown the tomb of Moses and the place where, according to the Christians, their Saviour was baptised. The eponymous founder of the town (Arīḥā) was said to have been a grandson of Arfak̲h̲s̲h̲ad/d̲h̲, grandson of Noah. The town was particularly prosperous during the Crusades but then began to decline and was in ruins in the 12th century. The modern Jericho in the Wādī el-Ḳelt (lat. 31° 52′ N., long. 35° 27′ E.) occupies the site of the town of the Crusaders; it is 250 m/820 feet below the level of the Mediterranean. Travellers of the 19th century expatiated on the squalor of Jericho, by then little more than a large village. It revived under the British Mandate of Palestine and after the West Bank's incorporation into Jordan in 1948, with a population of 6,830 in 1967; in that year, it passed under Israeli control.

Bibliography: On the Biblical Jericho, see Sir George Adam Smith, *Historical geography of the Holy Land*,[4] London 1897, 266 ff. On its archaeology (begun in the early 20th century by Sellin and then Garstang), see K.M. Kenyon and T.A. Holland, *Excavations at Jericho*, 5 vols., London 1960-83. On early Islamic Jericho, see Iṣṭak̲h̲rī, 56, 58; Ibn Ḥawḳal, 1st ed., 111, 113; Maḳdisī, 179-80; Yaʿḳūbī, *Taʾrīk̲h̲*, ed. Houtsma, 113; Yāḳūt, *Muʿd̲j̲am*, i, 200, 227, ii, 884, iii, 823, 913; Ṣafī al-Dīn, *Marāṣid al-iṭṭilāʿ*, ed. Juynboll, i, 52, 496, ii, 322, 362; Idrīsī, ed. Gildemeister, in *ZDPV*, viii, 3; Abu 'l-Fidāʾ, ed. Reinaud, 48, 236; G. Le Strange, *Palestine under the Moslems*, London 1890, 15, 18, 28-32, 53, 288, 381, 396-7; S. Marmardji, *Textes géographiques arabes sur la Palestine*, Paris 1951, 8-9. On the modern town, see Murray's handbooks, *Syria and Palestine*, new ed. London 1903, 163; Baedeker's *Palestine and Syria*[5], Leipzig 1912, 128-9; H.C. Luke and E. Keith-Roach, *The handbook of Palestine and Trans-Jordan*, London 1930, 127-9; Admiralty handbooks, *Palestine and Transjordan*, London 1943, 322-3 and index.

2. A little town in the district of Aleppo. According to Yāḳūt, it stood in a wooded, well watered area "on the slopes of the D̲j̲abal Lubnān". By this term the Arabs meant not only the Lebanon but also its northern continuation as far as the Orontes (Lammens, *Notes sur le Liban*, ii, 6; *MFOB*, i [1906], 271). But in the present case, the heights to the east of the Orontes are certainly wrongly included in the term. Rīḥā on the contrary is on the northern edge of the D̲j̲abal Banī ʿUlaym (Ibn al-S̲h̲iḥna, 102, 130), the modern D̲j̲ebel Arbaʿīn, a part of the D̲j̲ebel Rīḥā or D̲j̲ebel al-Zāwiyye (cf. the map D̲j̲ebel Rîḥā or D̲j̲ebel iz-Zâwiyeh by R. Garrett and F.A. Norris, in *Publics. of the Princeton Univ. Arch. Exp. to Syria*, div. ii, sect. B, part iii, Princeton 1909). The identification of Rīḥā with the *Rugia* or *Chastel Rouge* of the Franks is untenable, as Dussaud (*Topogr. de la Syrie*, 167, 174, 176, 213) rightly pointed out that this should rather be identified with al-Rūd̲j̲ of the Arabs.

There is a place noted for its ruins of antiquity called Ruwayḥa ("little Rīḥā") about 13 km/8 miles south-east of Rīḥā.

Rīḥā is very frequently mentioned in modern travel literature, as it was on the main road from Ḥalab to Ḥamā (Ritter, *Erdkunde*, xvii, 1502; Dussaud, *Topogr. de la Syrie*, 183), over which Nāṣir-i K̲h̲usraw (before 1047) and Ibn Baṭṭūṭa (1326) travelled in their day. The town is therefore mentioned by Belon du Mans (1548), Pietro Della Valle (1616), Wansleb (1671), Pococke (1737), Drummond (1754), C. Niebuhr (1778), Seetzen (1806-7), Burckhardt (1810-12) and many others.

Bibliography: Yāḳūt, *Muʿd̲j̲am*, ii, 885; Ṣafī al-Dīn, *Marāṣid al-iṭṭilāʿ*, i, 496; Ibn al-S̲h̲iḥna, *al-Durr al-muntak̲h̲ab fī taʾrīk̲h̲ Ḥalab*, Beirut 1909, 102, 130; R. Pococke, *Description of the East*, London 1745, ii,

rikāb already to the first Umayyad caliph of Spain (138-72/756-88; cf. *Analectes*, i, 605, reference given by Dozy). In Egypt at the court of the Fāṭimids, there were over 2,000 *rikābī* or *ṣibyān al-rikāb al-khāṣṣ*, so called "on account of their costume (*ziayy*)", whose duties were the same as those of the *silāḥdār* and *tabardār* of the time of al-Ḳalḳashandī (*Ṣubḥ*, iii, 482).

As to the Persian form *rikābdār*, it must have been in use among the Saldjūḳs for we have to admit by analogy that it was from them that the Ayyūbids and later the Mamlūks borrowed the term, like many others of the same kind.

In Persia itself, the term *rikābdār* was replaced by its (Turkish) synonym *üzengi* (or *zengü*) *ḳurčisi* (cf. Chardin, 1711 ed., vi, 112; Père Raph. du Mans, *Estat de la Perse*, 24). According to the *Burhān-i ḳāṭiʿ*, the *rikābdār* were replaced by the *djilawdār* (from *djilaw*, bridle), but it should be noted that the office of the latter was contemporary with and independent of that of *üzengi ḳurčisi*.

In Egypt, the *rikābdār*s of the Mamlūks, also called *rikābī*, were members of the *rikāb-khāna*, like the other "men of the sword" (*arbāb al-suyūf*), such as the *sandjaḳdār, mahmizdār, ḳara-ghulām* and *ghulām-mamlūk*. The *rikāb-khāna* (the *khizānat al-surūdj* of the Fāṭimids) was the depot for harness and in general for all the material required for horses and stables. The heads of this service were called *mihtar* (cf. the Ottoman *mehter* whose duties were different and humbler). The *rikābdār*s were under the command of the *amīr djāndār*, "Marshal of the Court" (cf. the *ḳapudjular kahyasî* of the Ottoman court). See al-Ḳalḳashandī, iv, 12, 20; Khalīl al-Ẓāhirī, 124; Gaudefroy-Demombynes, *Syrie*, pp. liii, lix.

The word *rikābdār* is found in the *1001 Nights*, where it is translated "palefrenier" by E. Gauttier, vi, 168, and "groom" by Burton, x, 365, n. 2. From the context we might also suggest "riding attendant". Bocthor gives (for Syria?) *r-k-bdār* under the French "écuyer (qui enseigne à monter à cheval)" and *r-kkīb al-khayl* under "groom (celui qui monte à cheval)". The synonymous expression *ṣāḥib al-rikāb*, in the sense of "good squire, one who mounts a horse well", is found in the romance of ʿAntara. In 19th and early 20th century Egyptian usage *rikib-dār* or *rakbdār* means "jockey, groom" (Spiro, Habeiche). (According to the *Burhān-i ḳāṭiʿ* [Turk. tr.], the *rikābdār* of Egypt was replaced by the *sarrādj* "saddler" mentioned by Volney and others.)

Turkish usage. In Turkey the office of *rikābdār* must have been taken over directly from the Saldjūḳs, but instead of becoming assimilated to that of humble grooms or *rikābī*s, as in Egypt, it became an important dignity at the sultan's court reserved for a single officer. It is in the reign of Orkhan (*ca*. 1324-62) that we find the first Ottoman *rikābdār*: he was called Ḳodja Ilyās Agha (*ʿAṭā tārīkhi*, i, 94). It was, however, only under Selīm I (1512-20) that the duties of the *rikābdār* were defined. According to the organisation at this time, the *rikābdār agha* was a *khāṣṣ odalî*, i.e. he was one of the *khāṣṣ oda* (and not *odasî*) or "company of the corps (Mouradgea d'Ohsson): chambrée suprême (Castillan); innerste Kammer (von Hammer)" which was the first of the six groups of officers of the household (*ič* or *enderūn*) of the Palace and consisted of the fixed number of 40 officers or pages, including in theory the sultan himself. It had been formed by Sultan Selīm to guard the relic of the Prophet's mantle (*khîrḳa-yî seʿādet*) brought back after the conquest of Egypt (ʿAṭā, i, 208; for details of the organisation, see *ibid.*, and Mouradgea d'Ohsson, vii, 34 ff.). The *rikābdār* was the third of these officers in order of precedence (following the *silihdār* and the *čohadār* and preceding the *dülbend aghasî*) and an officer passed in this order from one office to another. The four officers just mentioned were the only *khāṣṣ odalî* who had the right to wear the turban.

According to the usual definition repeated everywhere, the chief duty of the *rikābdār agha* was to hold the sultan's stirrup. It may have been so at first, but none of the documents available show the *rikābdār* performing this duty in practice. Indeed, we have seen [s.v. RIKĀB] who actually were the "*agha*s of the stirrup" entrusted with this duty. Now in spite of his name, the *rikābdār* was not one of these. The Arabic version of the *Āṣaf-nāme* (ed. Beirut, 9, n. 7) and the German translation (in *Türk. Bibl.*, no. 12, 1910, 17 n. 1) have therefore confused *rikābdār agha* and *rikāb aghasî*, which has given rise to an erroneous interpretation of the whole passage (see the corrected translation in RIKĀB).

On the other hand, Western writers of the 16th century mention as the third officer of the household (*ič oghlan*) after the *silihdār* and *čohadār* a "cup-bearer". Theodore Spandone (Spandouyn Cantacazin) calls him *sharābdār* (cf. Garzoni, 1573) and Leunclavius *küpdār* "bearer of the (water)-jar", a name also found in Lonicer (69). This water-carrier was given other names later. D'Ohsson (pl. 158) and the *ʿAṭā tārīkhi* (i, 282) speak of a *ḳoz-bekči* or "keeper of the *ḳoz*, probably for the Arabic-Persian *kūz(e)* or water-jar". Wearing a *berata*, he carried a ewer (*mashrapa*) of warm water at the end of a stick. Von Hammer calls this official *mataradji* or bearer of the gourd (*matara* for *maṭhara*). The use of warm water is easily explained by the fact that, as an author writing in 1631 tells us, the third gentleman of the sultan's chamber "carried him 'sherbet' to drink, and water to wash with" (de Stochove, *Voyage du Levant*, Brussels 1662, 84 *Ischioptar*, for *rikābdār*?; cf. Baudier who writes *rechioptar*).

On the other hand, there was an officer whose duty it was to carry a stool (*iskemle*) plated with silver which the sultan used in mounting his horse, when he did not prefer the assistance of a mute who went on his hands and knees on the ground (Castellan, *Mœurs*..., iii, 139; ʿAṭā, *loc. cit.*; d'Ohsson, pl. 157). He was the *iskemle aghasî* or *iskemledjiler bashi*, chosen from among the oldest grooms (*ḳapudju eskisi*). Wearing a *dolam* and a *keče*, he rode like the water-carrier on horseback in processions (*rikāb*). Probably through some confusion, Castellan calls him *rikābdār*, but adds that in his time the *rikābdār* was chosen not from among the *khāṣṣ odalî*, but from the *čawush* (mistake for *ḳapudju*?). Nor must we confuse, as Saineanu (*Influenţa orientala*, ii 104, s.v. *schemniaga*) does, the *iskemle* (or *iskemni*) *aghas* with the special commissioner of this name who was charged, along with the *sandjaḳ aghasî*, to install on the throne (*scamn*) the new *hospodar*s of Moldavia and Wallachia (cf. *Mélanges Iorga*, Paris 1933, 202). There were also *iskemle aghasî* similar to those of the sultan in certain provinces ([Rousseau], *Description du pachalik de Bagdad*, Paris 1809, 27).

Among the special duties of the *rikābdār*, one need only mention the custody and care of the harness, etc. of the sultan (as among the Mamlūks) and his *pabuč* or shoes and *čizme* or boots (*Ḳānūn-nāme* of Süleymān or *Naṣīḥat-nāme*, 132).

It should be noted that, according to the *ʿAṭā tārīkhi* (i, 208), the services of the *rikābdār*, like those of the *čohadār*s, were only required on gala days (*eiyyām-resmiyye*). This practice is said to have been introduced under Muṣṭafā III (1757-74) out of consideration for the age of these concerned, for they were generally over 60 and had spent 40 years in the service of the court (*odjak yolu*). According to the same source, these duties were reduced to very little. During the ceremonies (*selāmlik*) of the Prophet's birthday (*mewlid* or *mewlūd*), the two *bayrams* and at the *binish* or ceremonial appearances of the sultan, the *rikābdār* sat opposite the sultan in the imperial barge with the *silihdār*, *khāṣṣ oda bashi* and the two *čohadārs*.

From all this we may conclude that, if there really was a *rikābdār* in the time of Orkhan, he performed not only the duties of a squire but also those of a "cup-bearer", and we know that in Persian *rikābdār* means "cup-bearer" and *rikāb* means also "cup". In time, with the *rikābdār* becoming a more and more important personage, these duties were divided between two special officers: on the one hand, the *koz-bekči* and similar officers, and on the other, the *iskemle aghasi*.

The *rikābdār agha*, like the *čohadārs*, received a daily salary or *ʿulūfe* of 35 aspers (*akče*), while the *silihdār* drew 45 (Hezārfenn, ms. Bibliothèque Nationale, ancien fonds turc, fol. 18b). Like the *čohadārs*, they had in their service two *lalas* of the *khāṣṣ oda*, a *karakollukču*, a *baltadji* with tasselled caps (*zülüflü*), two *ṣofalis*, a *heybedji* and two *yedekčis*. The *rikābdārs* who did not attain the rank of *silihdār* were put on the retired list (became *čirak*) with a pension of 60-100,000 piastres. In the absence of the *čohadār*, the *rikābdār* performed the duties of the *silihdār*. On the quarters in the palace occupied by the *rikābdār*, see ʿAṭā, i, 312, 20.

The four chief officers of the *khāṣṣ oda*, including the *rikābdār*, were often called by the name—not official, however—of *koltuk wezīrleri* or "viziers of the armpit" because they had the privilege of touching the sultan, particularly of giving him their hand or taking him by the arm during a walk and they frequently attained the rank of *wezīr* (Cantemir, *Hist. Emp. Ott.*, Paris 1743, iv, 119-21). The *rikāb aghalari* [see RIKĀB] were also *koltuk wezīrleri*.

The same four officers were also called *ʿarḍ aghalari* because they had the right to present (*ʿarḍ*) to the sultan any petition which reached them, like the master of petitions (Rycaut, Bk. i, p. 97 of the French tr.; Castellan, iii, 185). According to Aḥmed Rāsim (ii, 639), in processions, the *iskemle aghasi* had the task of returning to those concerned petitions which were not granted.

The *rikābdārs* were abolished by Maḥmūd II, probably about the same time as the *koz bekči* (in 1248/1832-3; cf. Luṭfī, iv, 68) and the *silāḥdār* (in 1246; cf. Luṭfī, iv, 61); see von Hammer, *Hist.*, xvii, 191.

Bibliography: See the works already quoted above, of which the most important is the *ʿAṭā tārīkhi*. See also Aḥmed Rāsim, *Tārīkh*, i, 186, 479, ii, 526; von Hammer, *Hist.*, vii, 15, for references not used here; İ.H. Uzunçarşılı, *Osmanlı devleti teşkilâtına medhal*, Istanbul 1941, index.

(J. Deny)

RIKK [see RAKK].

RIND (P.), a word applied in Persian with a contemptuous connotation to "a knave, a rogue, a drunkard" or "a debauchee"; in the terminology of poets and mystics it acquired the positive meaning of "one whose exterior is liable to censure, but who at heart is sound" (Steingass, s.v., after the *Burhān-i kāṭiʿ*). The etymology of *rind* is unclear. It is not an Arabic loanword, in spite of the existence of the broken plural *runūd*, a learned form used next to the regular Persian plural *rindān*. The abstract noun *rindī* denotes the characteristic behaviour of a person thus qualified.

Mediaeval historians refer to *rinds* collectively as freebooters associated with the *ʿayyārūn* [*q.v.*] and the *awbāsh*. Locally they could be a political factor of some importance, as it appears from phrases like "the *rinds* of Baghdād" or "the *rinds* of Khʷārazm". Mention is also made of rural groups (*rindān-i rūstā*). They were further characters in popular literature. Bawdy tales about the *rinds* were considered to be unsuitable for a royal banquet (Ibn Isfandiyār, *Taʾrīkh-i Ṭabaristān*; see for these and other examples from historical sources, Dihkhudā, *Lughat-nāma* s.v. *rind*).

In the 5th/11th century, the Ismāʿīlī poet Nāṣir-i Khusraw [*q.v.*] still condemned their behaviour outright when he rebuked the world for "approving in its many children only that which results in bad behaviour and debauchery (*badfiʿlī-u rindī*)" (*Dīwān*, 493,-3). Even two centuries later, Saʿdī [*q.v.*] looked unfavourably upon their violent attacks on the Ṣūfīs and upon their sensuality (*Gulistān*, 107, 140).

Already at the beginning of the 6th/12th century, however, Sanāʾī [*q.v.*] gave ample evidence of a reversed appreciation. In his poetry, the word belongs to a cluster of terms and motifs peculiar to the *kalandariyyāt* [see KALANDARIYYA]. In this mystical genre, it came to denote the type of the antinomian mystic, like the cognate terms *kalandar* and *kallāsh*. The abandonment of all self-interest by the *rinds* is contrasted to the insincerity of ascetics (*zāhid*) and devout believers (*ʿābid*) whose piety is merely a mask for their selfishness.

After Sanāʾī, Farīd al-Dīn ʿAṭṭār [*q.v.*] further developed the genre in his *ghazals* and quatrains. The *rinds* are also frequently mentioned by Ḥāfiẓ [*q.v.*]. The "vices" he ascribes to them are being frantic lovers, ogling beautiful boys (*naẓarbāzī*), excessive drinking and gambling. They are beggars who have squandered all their earthly possessions (*muflis, pākbāz*) and have "set the world to fire" (*ʿālamsūz*). Willingly they destroy their good reputation, drinking the dregs of wine and suffering for the sake of love.

The reversal of terms like *rind* in the usage of the poets is related to the attitude of the *malāmatiyya* [*q.v.*], who from the 4th/10th century onwards dominated the spiritual atmosphere of Khurāsān. In a telling anecdote about Abū Saʿīd Mayhanī [*q.v.*] it is related that he learned the true meaning of *pākbāzī* from the *rindān* who honoured him as the "*amīr* of the gamblers" (Ritter, *Das Meer der Seele*, 202). Eventually, the term was adopted into standard mystical terminology. Shams al-Dīn Lāhidjī (d. 912/1506 [*q.v.*]), commenting on Maḥmūd Shabistarī's [*q.v.*] *Gulshan-i rāz*, defined the *rind* as someone who is completely detached from all qualities and conditions of the multitude of created being "having removed everything with the rasp (*randa*) of obliteration and effacement". Such a person would no longer be bound to anything, not even to the discipline of a spiritual teacher (*Mafātīḥ al-iʿdjāz*, 636).

The force of this imagery is not yet quite exhausted, though it has been used over and again by countless poets and mystics. In the present century, it could still serve Sir Muḥammad Iḳbāl [*q.v.*] as an item of his poetry which aimed at the revitalisation of Islam.

Bibliography: F. Steingass, *A comprehensive Persian-English Dictionary*, London 1892; Khalaf Tabrīzī, *Burhān-i kāṭiʿ*, ed. M. Muʿīn, Tehran 1331 sh./1952, ii, 963; ʿAlī-Akbar Dihkhudā, *Lughat-nāma*, Tehran 1325 sh./1946 ff., s.vv. *rind, rindī* and *runūd*; Nāṣir-i Khusraw, *Dīwān*, ed. Sayyid Naṣr Allāh Takawī, Tehran 1349 sh./1960; Saʿdī, *Gulistān*, ed. Gh.-Ḥ. Yūsufī, Tehran 1368 sh./1989; H. Ritter, *Das Meer der Seele*, Leiden 1955, 488-90; idem, *Philologika XV: Farīdaddīn ʿAṭṭār ... Der Dīwān*, in *Oriens*, xii (1959), 14-64; idem, *Philologika XVI: ... Muxtārnāme*, in *Oriens* xiii-xiv (1961), 219-22; J.T.P. de Bruijn, *The Qalandariyyāt in mystical poetry, from Sanāʾī onwards*, in *The legacy of mediaeval Persian Sufism*, ed. L. Lewisohn, London-New York 1992, 75-86; D.M. Correale, *The ghazals of Hafez. Concordance and vocabulary*, Rome 1988, 493; S͟hams al-Dīn Muḥammad Lāhid͟jī, *Mafātīḥ al-iʿd͟jāz fī s͟harḥ Guls͟han-i rāz*, ed. K. Samīʿī, Tehran 1337 s͟h./1958; J.C. Bürgel, *The Pious Rogue: a study in the meaning of qalandar and rend in the poetry of Muḥammad Iqbāl*, in *Edebiyât*, iv (1979), 43-64. (J.T.P. de Bruijn)

RISĀLA [see rasūl].

RISĀLA (a.), an Arabic term attested at a very early stage, in the ancient inscriptions of Arabia, with the meaning of message or of mission (G. Lankester Harding, *An index and concordance of pre-Islamic names and inscriptions*, Toronto 1971, 277).

In fact, *risāla* has many meanings; it has signified message, missive, letter, epistle and monograph; from the 5th/11th century onwards it could also be a synonym of maḳāma (see below, section on *Risāla* and *maḳāma*). The synonyms recorded are *kitāb* [*q.v.*], *k͟hiṭāb* (for Ps.-Ibn al-Mudabbir in the 3rd/9th century, *risāla* and *k͟hiṭāb* were synonyms, *Ṣafwat*, iv, 224; on numerous occasions, the Ṣāḥib Ibn ʿAbbād had recourse to the same term when speaking of his letters, *Dīwān rasāʾil al-Ṣāḥib Ibn ʿAbbād*, ms. B.N. arabe, 3411, fols. 152a, 176b, 186a, 189a, 194b; Saʿd b. Ḥaddād al-Munad͟jd͟jim, 3rd/9th century, did likewise, Yāḳūt, *Irs͟hād*, iv, 231, v, 381); *mīmar* (from Aramaic, attested in philosophy); *maḳāla* (Ḥād͟jd͟ji K͟halīfa, ii, 1781, l. 22; 1783, ll. 2, 7; the *risāla* of Ibn Sīnā, *Risālat al-Ḳuwā al-insāniyya wa-idrākātihā*, was also entitled by him *al-Maḳāla fī 'l-ḳuwā al-insāniyya*, see *ibid.*, 1783, l. 27); *lisān* (al-Ḥuṭayʾa, *Dīwān*, Beirut 1967, 71; al-Mufaḍḍaliyyāt, Oxford 1918, 482, l. 7; Aʿs͟hā Bāhila, *Gedichte von Abū Baṣīr Maimūn b. Ḳais al-Aʿshā*, London 1928, 266, iv, v. 4); *maʾluka* (al-K͟hansāʾ, *Dīwān*, ed. Cheikho, 188, l. 17; Suḥaym ʿAbd Banī al-Ḥasḥās, *Dīwān*, Cairo 1950, 19); *ṣaḥīfa* (al-D͟jāḥiẓ, *Ḥayawān*, iii, 48, l. 4; al-Ak͟hṭal, *Dīwān*, 387, l. 22); and *kalima* (*Ag͟hānī*³, xii, 246, l. 9; xiii, 345, l. 6).

1. In Arabic.

Maḳāla, lisān, kalima and *maʾluka* denoted an oral message. With the exception of the first, which was subsequently to denote a text (al-D͟jāḥiẓ, *Ḥayawān*, i, 12), the other terms retained their initial meaning. The etymology of these terms played a decisive role in this respect. The case of *kalima* and *lisān* requires no further explanation. For *maʾluka*, it is appropriate to note that, according to the lexicographers, the root *aluka* signifies "to champ the bit" when it is used in reference to a horse; it is thus closely related to speech (*al-Ag͟hānī*³, x, 222, l. 19, the poet ʿAlī b. al-D͟jahm; Abū Firās al-Ḥamdānī, *Dīwān*, Beirut 1944-5, iii, 354, v. 42). According to the lexicographer al-Layt͟h, "*alūk* is *risāla*; it is denoted thus because words are chewed by the mouth" (*LʿA*, s.v. *alaka*, ed. Ṣādir, Beirut, x, 292, ll. 7-8; *K. al-ʿAyn*, s.v.). (In reality, *maʾluka*, etc., is a metathesis of the root *l-ʾ-k*).

I. Evolution of the term

Risāla (pl. *rasāʾil, risālāt* being essentially Ḳurʾānic), denoted originally the oral transmission of a message. In pre-Islamic times, in the Ḳurʾān and throughout the Umayyad period, the term demonstrated a remarkable stability and remained closely linked to speech. It is the spoken message. In a tradition relating to al-Ḥārit͟h b. D͟jabala, it is stated specifically (*fa-ak͟hbarahu bi-risālati al-Ḥārit͟hi bni D͟jabalata fa-rakana ilā ḳawlihi*), sc. he reported to him (communicated to him orally) the message of al-Ḥārith b. D͟jabala, h relied entirely on his words (Ibn al-Anbārī, *Sharḥ al ḳaṣāʾid al-sabʿ al-ṭiwāl al-d͟jāhiliyyāt*, Cairo 1969, 480) Poetry confirms this state of affairs beyond all expec tation. The following structure is attested there "*ablig͟h* (followed by a name) *risālatᵃⁿ* (communicatec to (a certain person) the content of the followin message"; the text of the message follows, this clearl showing that it is a case of oral communicatio (*Ḥamāsa*, Bonn 1828, 186, l. 6, Riyāḥ b. Ẓāli al-Murrī; Zuhayr b. Abī Sulmā. ed. Ahlwardt, xvi, v 25; for the Umayyad period, al-Farazdaḳ, *Dīwān* Paris 1870, 68, v. 12; ʿUmar b. Abī Rabīʿa,. *Dīwān* Leipzig 1901-9, 117, v. 12). Furthermore, al-Kāsān (d. 587/1191), a highly original personality, has des cribed this situation well: *al-risālatu hiya an yursil rasūlᵃⁿ ilā rad͟julⁱⁿ ... fa d͟hahaba 'l-rasūlu wa-ballag͟ha 'l risālata li-anna 'l-rasūla safīrᵘⁿ wa muʿabbirᵘⁿ ʿan kalām 'l-mursili nāḳilᵘⁿ kalāmahu ilā 'l-mursali ilayhi* ("*risāl* consists in sending a messenger to a person... Th messenger goes and conveys the message, since th bearer is an envoy who expresses (through direc speech) and conveys the speech of the sender to th addressee" (al-Kāsānī, *K. Badāʾiʿ al-ṣanāʾi fī tartīb al s͟harāʾiʿ*, Cairo 1328/1910, v. 138).

The transference to written text takes place unde the reign of His͟hām b. ʿAbd al-Malik (105-23/724 43). It is associated with Sālim Abu 'l-ʿAlāʾ. Hi translation of the written correspondence betwee Alexander and his teacher includes in its title the ter *risāla: Risālat Arisṭāṭālīs ilā 'l-Iskandar fī siyāsat al-mudu* (M. Grignaschi, *Le roman épistolaire classique conser dans la version arabe de Sālim Abū l-ʿAlāʾ*, in *Le Muséon* lxxx [1967], 219, 223). In a eulogy addressed to al Saffāḥ, the first ʿAbbāsid caliph, the poet Ab Dulāma, for his part, evokes a *risāla* of the chieftain o the Banū Asad written (*tak͟huṭṭuhā*) by a female scrib (*Ag͟hānī*³, x, 266, ll. 12-13). Thus a significant muta tion is introduced into the genre; the former meanin disappears almost completely, except for a fe isolated vestiges encountered from time to time in th course of the texts (al-Ṣūlī, *K. al-Awrāḳ*, Cairo 1936 208; *Ag͟hānī*³, xx, 56; Yāḳūt, *Irshād*, ii, 4-5, vi, 106 166).

It is not unusual for the *risāla*, a written message, t adopt the form of a rhymed poem. It is attestec throughout the ʿAbbāsid period. Here however unlike in the *D͟jāhiliyya*, these notes are written. Th Arabic holdings of the Bibliothèque Nationale includ a manuscript intitled *Mad͟jmūʿ murāsalāt wa-tahān* (arabe, 3431); all the texts included are letters i poetic form. Furthermore, numerous stylists ha recourse to this process, notably Ibrāhīm b. Hilāl al Ṣābī and al-S͟harīf al-Raḍī, following the well-know pattern of poems adopting identical metres an rhymes (*Rasāʾil al-Ṣābī wa 'l-S͟harīf al-Raḍī*, Kuwai 1961, 7-62, section *al-mukātabāt bi 'l-s͟hiʿr*, comprisin eleven *ḳaṣīdas*).

This process of transference from oral usage to th written letter is, after all, quite natural. Constable an Hunger observe in this context that all ancien civilisations used the oral message exclusively at th outset (G. Constable, *Letters and letter-collection*, i *Typologie des sources du Moyen Age*, fasc. 17, Turnhou 1976, 48; H. Hunger, *Die hochsprachliche Literature de Byzantiner*, i, *Philosophie, Rhetorik, Epistolographie* Munich 1978, 199).

II. The poetry of the *Risāla*

In order to understand the transformation of thi structure, it is essential to take account of the crucia role of Greek letters. The scribes of Damascus wer familiar with the epistles of the Greeks, by way o

Hellenistic and Persian culture. As a result of the works of Mario Grignaschi, this influence has been established beyond doubt. In fact, one of the most illustrious representatives of this circle, Sālim Abu 'l-ʿAlāʾ (see above), the *mawlā* of Saʿīd b. ʿAbd al-Malik, in his translation of the letters of Aristotle to Alexander, included two chapters of great interest, *al-Siyāsa al-ʿāmma* and *al-Siyāsa fī tadbīr al-riʾāsa*: they contain, in effect, quotations and indications proving that he has followed "the outline of the Greek letter more closely than has sometimes been admitted" (*Les "Rasāʾil Arisṭāṭālīsa ilā l-Iskandar" de Salim Abu l-ʿAlāʾ et l'activité culturelle à l'époque umayyade*, in *BEO*, xix [1965-6], 9). Furthermore, ch. x, of classical origin, which has been published in an abridged version by Lippert under the title *Peri Basileas*, is identical in all respects to the Arabic ms. of Sālim (Köprülü 1608) except in one detail. The Arabic translation has added here two extracts from the *Testament d'Ardashīr*; Sālim has thus proceeded to an integration of the Greek foundation to the Sāsānid foundation (*ibid.*, 14).

Now, according to Ibn Khallikān, Sālim was the protector of ʿAbd al-Ḥamīd b. Yaḥyā al-Kātib and his master in the art of writing (*Wafayāt al-aʿyān*, Beirut 1397/1977, iii, 230), in other words the founder of the ʿAbbāsid *risāla* in all its variety (J.D. Latham, *The beginnings of Arabic prose: the epistolary genre*, in *The Cambridge history of Arabic literature*, Cambridge 1983, 155-79; Hannelore Schönig, *Das Sendschreiben des ʿAbd al-Ḥamīd b. Yaḥyā an den Kronprinzen ʿAbdallāh b. Marwān II*, Stuttgart 1985, introd. to the translation, 3-27).

The risāla *as monograph*

The transmission of knowledge under the first caliphs of the Marwānid branch was accomplished in the form of *risālas*. ʿAbd al-Malik b. Marwān, wishing to know more of the events which had accompanied the beginnings of Islam, addressed himself to ʿUrwa b. al-Zubayr, who replied to him with a written missive containing the information requested. These missives were preserved by al-Ṭabarī to constitute the basis of his documentation for the event in question (*Annales*, i, 1180-1, 1634-6, 1770, 1284-6). This framework offered numerous facilities and allowed the writer to lend to his work the tone of a direct conversation. As time passed, the addressee of the *risāla* was solicited and even invented by the writer himself with a view to exposing his ideas on a question which interested him particularly (A.F.L. Beeston, *The epistle on singing girls by Jāḥiẓ*, London 1980, § 3, 2-3; G. Lanson, *Choix de lettres du XVIIe siècle*, Paris 1913, p. xxv). This sub-genre was to enjoy lasting popularity. Numerous authors, from the time of ʿAbd al-Ḥamīd al-Kātib to the present day, have made frequent use of it.

Moreover, there was the opportunity of filling the letter-missive with personal ideas and nonconformist concepts which *adab* could not or would not accommodate, it being regulated by very strict rules. Knowledge (*ʿilm*), like literature, was considered the ultimate canonical genre; for the same reason, it was doomed to cantonisation in compilation; otherwise, there was the risk of impairment. Every *khabar* mentioned, real or fictitious, was endowed with an *isnād* which accentuated its status as a received text, rather than the product of independent thought. The *risāla*, the only remaining framework in prose, lent itself perfectly to the role of receptacle for personal thoughts, nonconformist ideas and texts based on analysis and not on quotation. This is why the most original texts were conceived as *risālas*. In politics, one of the most thorough analyses of religious, political and military institutions under the early ʿAbbāsids is supplied by the *Risāla fi 'l-ṣaḥāba* of Ibn al-Muḳaffaʿ (Ch. Pellat, *Ibn al-Muḳaffaʿ conseilleur du calife*, Paris 1976, 1, 4, 12). In literature, the *Risālat al-tarbīʿ wa 'l-tadwīr* by al-Djāḥiẓ and the *Risāla al-hazliyya* of Ibn Zaydūn presented the most successful examples of humorous texts (O. Rescher, *Excerpte und Übersetzungen aus der Schriften des... Jāḥiẓ*, Stuttgart 1931, 212-25; *al-Fikr*, xii/3, 54-60; T. Ḥusayn, *Min ḥadīth al-shiʿr wa 'l-nathr*, 88-99; H. Djād Ḥasan, *Ibn Zaydūn*, Cairo 1375/1955, 266-9, 274-5). More generally, *Risālat al-ghufrān* by Abu 'l-ʿAlāʾ al-Maʿarrī and *Risālat al-tawābiʿ wa 'l-zawābiʿ* by Ibn Shuhayd [*q.v.*] may be considered triumphs of classical Arabic literature. In poetry, the most penetrating analysis of the aesthetic rules governing poetry and the epistolary art, and also the most systematic, borrowed the same formal framework (A. Arazi, *Une épître d'Ibrāhīm b. Hilāl al-Ṣābī sur les genres littéraires*, in *Studies in Islamic history and civilization in honour of Professor David Ayalon*, Jerusalem and Leiden 1986, 473-505).

Indisputably, the *risāla* comprises, here, all the aspects which constitute the monograph or the essay. Henceforward, this framework was to play a role in all sectors of Arab culture: philosophy, grammar, lexicography and *fiḳh*—they all adopted it as a means of producing their finest achievements. The *Rasāʾil* of Djāḥiẓ dealt with a broad spectrum of theological, social, political and literary problems and count among the most profound analyses of the Baṣran thinker, perhaps of the whole of ʿAbbāsid literature. The format itself is a major contributor to this success: each title studies a single problem, which encourages reflection (Ch. Pellat, *The life and works of Jāḥiẓ*, London 1967, 14-26). It has even been written of some of them that they are psychological and moral studies in which the author is aware of producing original work; this is not a regular occurrence in the works of the 3rd/9th century (Ch. Vial, *Al-Djāḥiẓ, quatre essais*, IFAO, Cairo 1976, 3). The same phenomenon is attested in the work of a polygraph of the Mamlūk period, Djalal al-Dīn al-Suyūṭī (d. 911/1505 [*q.v.*]), whose principal claim to fame was his faculty for compilation. In his epistles, he attacked the abuses with which the society of his time was confronted, refraining from compiling for the pleasure of compiling.

However, it is in theology, in philosophy and in the domain of the sciences that this phenomenon seems to have taken on the broadest role. The translation, or perhaps the paraphrase, in Arabic, of the correspondence between Alexander and Aristotle, seems to have had an immediate impact on the framework and the format of Arabic religious writings relating to faith. Written texts were seen as indispensable for the formulation of all things concerning religious belief. Another external source, which was apparently to have a very profound influence on the *risāla*, was the translation into Arabic of the New Testament, which includes a very extensive section of epistles attributed to St. Paul and St. Peter. Systematically, they include in their titles the name of the region destined to receive them. It is interesting to note a similarity with the letters of certain *mutakallimūn* (see below).

Among the most ancient, a significant number of theological treatises are *risālas* attributed to historical figures (al-Ḥasan al-Baṣrī) and addressed to no less historical figures (the Umayyad caliphs). All these epistles have recently been the object of philological analysis by Michael Cook, *Early Muslim dogma*, Cambridge 1981 (with very comprehensive bibliography). The dating of these documents continues to be problematical, and expert opinion is divided as to their paternity; this last is accepted by van Ess, whilst others have not hesitated to draw attention to certain anachronisms featuring in these documents. Whatever the case, it seems very reasonable to place them at the end of the Umayyad dynasty or under the first ᶜAbbāsids. The authors, most of them *Tābiᶜūn* or Successors, chose this framework on account of its similarity to the letter, in other words, as a concrete message which would make their theological statements more easily understood. Later, numerous theologians made use of the epistle to propound their doctrines. Al-A<u>sh</u>ᶜarī had recourse to it in two instances: the first in the well-known *Vindication of the engagement in speculative theology* (R. MacCarthy, *The theology of al-Ashᶜarī*, Beirut 1953) and the second in *Risāla ilā ahl al-<u>th</u>a<u>gh</u>r*. The second in fact constitutes a brief exposition of the theology of the author (publ. in *Ilahiyat Fakültesi Mecmuası* (Istanbul), viii [1928]; on the two epistles, see D. Gimaret, *La doctrine d'al-A<u>sh</u>ᶜarī*, Paris 1990, 13-16). The *responsa* (*fatāwā, <u>dj</u>awābāt, a<u>dj</u>wiba, masāʾil*) constitute an ancient ramification of theological epistles. Numerous works belonging to this category have been attributed to Abū Hā<u>sh</u>im al-<u>Dj</u>ubbāʾī (d. 321/933), one of the most eminent Baṣran Muᶜtazilī thinkers; these also followed the previously-mentioned pattern, with a title bearing the name of the addressee and his country of residence. Worth mentioning, by way of example, are the *Ba<u>gh</u>dādiyyāt* and the *ᶜAskariyyāt* (Gimaret, *Matériaux pour une bibliographie des <u>Dj</u>ubbāʾī*, in *JA*, cclxiv [1976], 308, 321, and 286, a reply from his father Abū ᶜAlī to the inhabitants of <u>Kh</u>urāsān). Numerous collections, identical in every respect, were mentioned by the Muᶜtazilī *ḳāḍī* ᶜAbd al-<u>Dj</u>abbār (d. 416/1025), such as *al-Rāziyyāt, al-<u>Kh</u>ʷārazmiyyāt*, etc. (*al-Uṣūl al-<u>kh</u>amsa*, ed. ᶜA. U<u>th</u>mān, Cairo 1967, 21-3).

A similar process is in evidence in the epistles of Ibn Taymiyya (*Ma<u>dj</u>mūᶜat al-rasāʾil al-kubrā*, Beirut 1980, i-ii, repr. of the original edition). In addition to the usual framework, the introduction includes here the name of the questioner, the heading of the question and the mention of other circumstances which contribute to fix his *risāla* more firmly in reality. Thus the differences between *fatāwā* and epistles tend to become blurred. Another characteristic of theological *risāla*s, which could prove to be of great importance, since it is capable, possibly, of determining the character of the discussion, is the opportunity given to the author of providing a detailed account of his position on a point of doctrine. Such an opportunity was readily seized upon by the author, who expounded at length the subject which was being debated. These theological responses, thus enlarged, were transformed into veritable monographs; the question which is the point of departure then appears to arise from the incident (see below, on Judaeo-Arabic). The exposition of theological ideas, in the form of a monograph, in response to questions posed to an author, is known in Syriac sources (for example, in the work of Jacob of Edessa, late 7th-early 8th century), taking its inspiration, perhaps, from the Greek tradition through the intermediary of the Byzantines (Cook, *op. cit.*, 145-6). The most ancient manifestations of this framework in Christian theological literature written in Arabic are attested in the collection of *Mayāmir* attributed to the "Melkite" bishop Theodore Abū Ḳurra (d. 820, see G. Graf, *GCAL*, ii, 7-26; I. Dick, *Théodore Abū Ḳurra*, in *Proche-Orient Chrétien*, xii [1962], 209-23, xiii [1963], 114-29). It is appropriate to observe that the Aramaic *mīmar* (< *mīmrō* = *mēmrā*) might well have constituted the antecedent of the Arabic term *maḳāla* (J. Wansbrough, *The sectarian milieu*, Oxford 1978, 104-5, where he expresses the hypothesis of the existence of Christian theological treatises in Arabic in an earlier period).

Although numerous questions and uncertainties have been presented, with good reason, in the epistolary framework, many people have sought, and have succeeded, through its intermediacy, in preserving prolonged theological discussions owed to those who were unanimously recognised as authorities on the subject.

It should be noted that, at a very early stage, in various domains of the religious sciences, the term *risāla* was applied to numerous works, lists of which are to be found in various histories of Arabic literature. It is worth mentioning, for the sake of example, two of the most characteristic examples, these being the *Risāla* of al-<u>Sh</u>āfiᶜī (ed. A.M. <u>Sh</u>ākir, Cairo 1940) and the *Risāla* of Ibn Abī Zayd (d. 386/996), a compendium of Mālikī *fiḳh* (Sezgin, *GAS*, i, 478). In philosophy the *risāla* dates back to an early stage of the discipline. Al-Kindī, *faylasūf al-ᶜArab*, revealed the best aspects of his system (and of his scientific work) in the *Rasāʾil al-Kindī al-falsafiyya* (ed. M.ᶜA. Abū Rīda, Cairo 1950-3, i-ii). In any event, the resemblance of this work to the epistolary genre goes beyond the use of the epistolary formula attested in the introduction and the recourse to formal dedications (see e.g. the first lines of the epistle/article on metaphysics dedicated to the son of al-Muᶜtaṣim, tr. A. Ivry, *Al-Kindi's Metaphysics*, Albany 1974, 55, and notes to p. 115). The same applies to the philosophical works of Abū Bakr al-Rāzī (d. *ca.* 318/930 [*q.v.*]), wo used the *risāla* as a vehicle for his ideas.

During the 3rd/9th century, in philosophy as in other branches of learning, the epistle became the format habitually chosen by the authors of monographs. In fact, from the last quarter of the 3rd/9th century onwards, the equivalent terms *risāla* and *maḳāla* ("discourse, article") signify treatise or monograph. Hundreds, if not thousands of treatises on the different branches of science (medicine, mathematics, pharmacology, etc.) opt for this structure. Special mention should be made of a collection of epistle-monographs, on account of its scale but also on account of its importance, the *Rasāʾil I<u>kh</u>wān al-Ṣafāʾ* (numerous editions, e.g. 4 vols., Beirut 1957) which dealt with human knowledge classified into four major groups (mathematics, logic, natural sciences and metaphysics) and discussed these systematically in 52 letters. Adopting the form of letters written in the first person plural, they are addressed to a single addressee, to a single "brother". The format is that of a personal correspondence maintained with the addressee; also included, especially in the closing paragraphs, are various kinds of good wishes, advice regarding morals and other matters. This may be seen as an attempt to give a personal flavour to these theoretical discussions.

In this area, a special place belongs to the Andalusian philosopher Ibn Bā<u>dj</u><u>dj</u>a (d. 579/1183 [*q.v.*]), who seems to have displayed a marked predilection for the genre. His principal treatises are epistles (see *Rasāʾil Ibn Bā<u>dj</u><u>dj</u>a al-ilāhiyya*, Beirut 1968). The abridged commentaries of Ibn Ru<u>sh</u>d on the works of Aristotle (the *Epitomes*, Ar. *<u>Dj</u>awāmiᶜ*), in most cases bear in the manuscripts the title *rasāʾil* and the printed compilation of these extracts is intitled *Rasāʾil Ibn Ru<u>sh</u>d* (Ḥaydarābād 1947). On the other hand, this philosopher wrote numerous treatises which he called *maḳāla* (*Tal<u>kh</u>īṣ al-samāᶜ wa 'l-ᶜalāmāt*, Fez 1984, 32-4).

The term monograph should not mislead. It has not always denoted a short work; a *risāla* can extend over everal volumes (cf. the *Risāla* of Ibn Abī Zayd on Mālikī *fiḳh*; the *Risālat al-ṣadāḳa wa 'l-ṣadīḳ* covers more than 400 pages; etc.).

Writers of *risālas*, not being obliged to observe contraining conventions for fear of being considered at ault, as was the case with *adab*, were permitted to give ree rein to their creative spirit and express themselves vith total liberty. Furthermore, a cultural phenomenon comes into being: with the creation of new genres, in the absence of appropriate terminology, the vork receives the title of *risāla*. Thus the original title of the *riḥla* of Ibn Faḍlān is nothing other than *Risālat Ibn Faḍlān* (ed. Sāmī Dahān, Damascus 1379/1959), no doubt on account of its unedited nature and the impossibility of integrating it into one of the conventional literary categories.

Risāla *and autobiography*

A vital aspect of the literary *risāla* and of the personal letter, namely, its confessional nature, confers on this type of writing an autobiographical character which is unusual in classical Arabic texts. Ch. Vial has rightly stressed this aspect in the four epistles of al-Djāḥiẓ which he has studied (*Quatre essais*, 7). Abū Ḥayyan al-Tawḥīdī seems to have had a marked predilection for this genre of personal revelation. His *Risālat al-ṣadāḳa* contain numerous very intimate passages, of disconcerting candour. To an even greater extent, in his *Risāla fi 'l-ʿulūm*, which sets out a classification of sciences, the author unburdens himself, recounts intimate events, reveals his most ecret thoughts, informs the reader of his beliefs and akes the reader into his confidence in describing his tates of mind and justifying his behaviour (M. Bergé, *Risāla fi 'l-ʿulūm*, in *BEO*, xviii, 244-6; he does the ame thing at the beginning of the *Risālat al-ḥayāt*, Damascus 1951, 52-4). Any study of ancient autobiography must take into account the contribution of this thinker. In personal letters, this aspect has ometimes taken on a surprising intensity. The library of the University of Leiden possesses the third volume of the *Correspondence* of Abū Hilāl al-Ṣābī (ms. Or., 766, fols. 115a-118b). In a letter addressed to his son, al-Ṣābī, written at the age of 42, he feels that he is old and believes that he can detect in his dreams and in the incidents of daily life premonitions of death. Accordingly, he reviews the balance-sheet of his life, informs his son of the love that he holds for his wives, his fondness for animals and the bribes that he has handled; he declares his weariness and gives advice to his son.

Style

This type of correspondence and exchange of ideas greatly interested literary circles, stylists and amateur scholars among the aristocracy, and this led to the emergence of texts of a high literary standard. In fact, the very choice style verges on the precocious. The distilled language, laden with tropes, fine allusions, plays on words, verbal tricks and metalepses (*tawriya*), and is constantly rebarbative and not easily understood. Rhymed prose, almost of necessity, obliges the stylists to practise what are virtually verbal acrobatics. In a letter opposing the principle of fasting, al-ʿAmīd Abū Abd Allāh b. al-Ḥusayn b. Muḥammad employs rhymed periods of such precise equality that the editor of the *Yatīma* mistakes them for poetry and sets out the lines accordingly (al-Thaʿālibī, *Yatīmat al-dahr*, ed. Cairo, iii, 8). A similar process is evident in Byzantine culture (Hunger, 206). Such style, described by Karlsson as "ceremonial", can appear irritating. This cult of the form can only be understood in the light of the triumph of *badīʿ*; in the cultural environment, this means accepting the notion that educated literature submits of its own accord to a form of expression considered noble.

Undoubtedly, alongside such literary letters, there always existed letters of no literary pretension. These functional missives paid little regard to form; they were written in every-day language and discarded by the addressee once they have been read and their contents noted. In the opinion of scholars, such letters were not worth preserving. Having no literary merit, they were not considered "true" letters. Only a few score of them, written on papyrus, have survived, and these have been published by Y. Ragheb (*Marchands d'étoffes du Fayyoum d'après leurs archives* (*Actes et lettres*), i-iii, Cairo 1982-92). A vast gulf separates these brief texts, adopting the language of the vernacular, from the letters of scholars written in the purest literary Arabic.

III. The stylists

The extravagant elegance of style demands an unsurpassed mastery of the language. Gaining the status of an accredited epistolographer was the outcome of a long apprenticeship. The aspirant was obliged as a first step to familiarise himself with the most successful compositions of his predecessors (*rasāʾil al-mutaḳaddimīn*), with archaic poems, chronicles, biographies of eminent persons and amusing anecdotes, all of this leading to an enrichment and diversification of language. It was also necessary to study the *maḳāmāt*, the discourses and debates of the Ancients, the *maʿānī* of the *ʿadjam*, the maxims of the Persians (Ḍiyāʾ al-Dīn Ibn al-Athīr, *al-Mathal al-sāʾir fī adab al-kātib wa 'l-shāʿir*, Beirut 1411/1990, i, 87-148). Furthermore, the fact that their writings were read in public and their letters passed from hand to hand to be copied and annotated (Yāḳūt, *Irshād*, v, 329, 351, vi, 67-8), gave them a prominent position in society. It may be supposed that whole generations of preparation and training were required to produce the most illustrious of the stylists. The epistolary art underwent a process identical to that of poetry in the training of artists. The *dīwāns* of poets are matched by the *dīwāns* of *mutarassils* (Ibn al-Nadīm, *Fihrist*, Cairo n.d., 244, gives a list of 70 collections of letters attributed to epistolographers of the 2nd-3rd/8th-9th centuries. Through the good offices of Ibn al-Nadīm and his systematic approach, it is possible to trace the various stages, often spread over many decades, necessary to train a major stylist.

A good example is the family of the Banū Wahb, a veritable dynasty of *mutarassils*; its members were the descendents of Ḳanān b. Mattā, the eponymous ancestor. Immediately after the conquest of Syria, he held the post of *kātib* in the service of Yazīd b. Abī Sufyān; when he was appointed governor of Syria, Muʿāwiya retained him in the same post. He was "inherited" by Yazid b. Muʿawiya, and died during the latter's caliphate. His son Ḳays replaced him in his post, which he retained under ʿAbd al-Malik and Hishām. His grandson, al-Ḥuṣayn b. Ḳays b. Ḳanān b. Mattā, kept the same functions. He seems to have led an eventful life; after the assassination of Marwān II, he found a patron in Ibn Hubayra, then entered the service of al-Manṣūr and of his son al-Mahdī. The great-grandson, ʿAmr b. al-Ḥuṣayn b. Ḳays, followed the same course, subsequently serving Khālid b. Barmak. The fifth and sixth representatives, Saʿīd b. ʿAmr b. al-Ḥuṣayn and Wahb b. Saʿīd b. ʿAmr b. al-Ḥuṣayn served the Barmakids until their disgrace, subsequently supervising the correspondence of Ḥasan b. Sahl. The seventh link in the chain, Sulaymān b. Wahb b. Saʿīd b. ʿAmr b. al-Ḥuṣayn, enjoyed the status of a great stylist; in turn, starting at the age of 14 years, he supervised the correspondence of al-Maʾmūn, of Aytākh and of Ashnās before becoming the vizier of al-Muʿtamid. His letters were compiled in a *dīwān*. His brother, al-Ḥasan b. Wahb b. Saʿīd b. ʿAmr b. al-Ḥuṣayn b. Ḳays b. Ḳanān b. Mattā, voluntarily chose a literary career; in addition to his merit as *mutarassil*, he was considered an excellent poet. In addition, his letters were judged to be of superior quality and worthy of compilation in a *dīwān* (*Fihrist*, 177). This text provides a fascinating slice of history; veritable dynasties of stylists, experienced in the affairs of state, retaining their posts in spite of major changes and vicissitudes affecting the world of Islam. On the strictly literary level, this continuity encouraged the development of stable literary forms in the composition of letters. Furthermore, seven generations had to elapse before members of these families were enabled to compose collections of *risālas*. At the same time, it is possible to sense the genuine appreciation and respect felt by society towards the *risāla*.

IV. The *Risāla* and society

In ʿAbbāsid society, just as in ancient society (Constable, 11), letters were intended to be read by more than one person. The stylist was aware of this even before writing, and it was for this reason that he aspired to elegance rather than spontaneity and drew both the basis and the form of his letters from established formulae. Even an administrative letter should be composed according to artistic and literary criteria; in society's view, it belonged to the domain of the fine arts, and accordingly, the *kātib* was considered above all an artist (al-ʿAskarī, *K. al-Ṣināʿatayn*, Cairo 1372/1952, 69; al-Ḳalḳashandī, *Ṣubḥ al-aʿshā*, ii, 327).

At the same time, the people of that period tended to confuse the *risāla* genre with its practical and utilitarian functions. In their view, the epistolary art was a means of addressing the most important aspects of mediaeval Islamic society, such as the levying of land tax (*kharādj*), the fortification of frontier zones and the colonisation of distant regions; the *kātib* was called upon to soothe discord, to exhort to *djihād*, to engage in controversy with a particular sect and to congratulate the recipient of an honour or to offer condolences in the event of misfortune (Arazi, *Une épître sur les genres littéraires*, 490 and n. 64, 503).

Moreover, this was an idle and frequently bored society which looked to the letter as a means of distraction. Once a letter was received, and after numerous readings, the addressee invited his friends to a session at which the letter was read and re-read (*Madjmūʿ rasāʾil wa-maḳāmāt*, ms. B.N. Paris, arabe 3923, fols. 60b-61a; al-Thaʿālibī, *Yatīma*, iii, 312), and especially eloquent passages were admired (Yāḳūt, *Irshād*, v, 351; on reception of a letter from Ibn al-ʿAmīd, the meeting held to hear it resembled a veritable *madjlis*, complete with drinks and selected delicacies).

Such public reading was closely matched by the ceremonial of Byzantine letters. In fact, in Islamic territory, the practice was treated with rather less intensity. The Byzantine stylists of the middle and late period, such as Libanius, Synesius, Psellus and Nicephorus Gregorias, regarded the spectacle as a *theatron*, and the listeners as an audience (H. Hunger, *Die Hochsprachliche profane Literatur der Byzantiner. I. Philosophie, Rhetorik, Epistolographie, Geschichtsschreibung, Geographie*, Munich 1978, 210-11).

V. The letters

Various classifications have been suggested by modern theorists of the letter. Hunger proposes a distinction between the private letter; the literary letter (Hunger, 204); the didactic letter (Hunger, 205); the cliché letter (*Klischeebrief*), where all the correspondence is constructed according to accepted models dealing with immutable subjects; literary private letters (*literarischer Privatbriefe*), a median way between private and literary letters; and, finally, letters without any literary pretension (Hunger, 206, 212).

Constable, after discussing various methods of classification, suggests the adoption of that of the Ancients, to avoid the risks of casting aspersions on the ancient letter in all its variety (G. Constable, *Letters and letter-collections*, in *Typologie des sources du Moyen-Age occidental*, fasc. 17, Turnhout 1976, 25). This is a suitable method. For the classical Arabic *risāla*, there is a need to distinguish between *ikhwāniyya* and *dīwāniyya* in accordance with the ancient treatises; it is also necessary to study the monograph-*risāla*, which has not been studied by the above-mentioned critics, not being correspondence in the strict sense of the word.

The Risāla ikhwāniyya

The term derives from *ikhwān* "friends" and is correspondence between two friends. The exclusive subject of these letters is deep affection. It is a substitute for the absent friend; a friend who is in fact far away is evoked with nostalgia and the writer pines for him (*Ṣafwat*, iii, 114-5, a letter of Ghassān b. Ḥamīd, the *kātib* of Djaʿfar b. Sulaymān, period of al-Manṣūr; *Rasāʾil al-Ṣābī wa 'l-Sharīf al-Raḍī*, 104, 108-9, 112; Abū Bakr al-Khwārazmī, *Rasāʾil*, 26, 39, 42, 70, 81-2). The number of such notes written in this period is quite considerable. These protestations of friendship constitute the basis of the ceremonial of the letter, the conventional obstacle which needs to be overcome for the interpretation of the majority of these texts. These *risālas* evoke the minor events of daily life: congratulations on the birth of a son (Ṣafwat, iii, 57, Ibn al-Muḳaffaʿ; *Yatīma*, iv, 190, Badīʿ al-Zamān al-Hamadhānī), on the occasion of a marriage (Ṣafwat, iii, 120-1), accompanying a gift (al-Khwārazmī, *Rasāʾil*, 51-2), declarations of welcome (*Yatīma*, iv, 192), an invitation (*istizāra, Yatīma*, iii, 80-3) and condolences (*Yatīma*, iv, 191; Ṣafwat, iii, 122-4, numerous cases).

The most important question involves the precise meaning of *ikhwāniyya*. Abū Ḥayyān al-Tawḥīdī deserves the credit for providing a contemplation in depth of the issue, the *Risālat al-ṣadāḳa wa 'l-ṣadīḳ* (ed. Ibrāhīm Kaylānī, Damascus 1964). As in the majority of *risālas*, the analysis is systematic and the treatment of the subject carefully constructed. The concept of friendship seems to have been directly influenced by numerous factors, such as Greek thought, ambient cultures, Bedouin qualities, Islam and the current social situation. The *leitmotif* of the *ikhwāniyyat* may be defined by means of the following phrase: the attitude towards a friend is like the attitude towards oneself, the friend being an alternative self. The stylists proclaimed this in their letters, as did al-Tawḥīdī in his treatise (he said that he was quoting the opinions of the Greeks). No doubt he was referring to the translation of Aristotle's *Nichomachaean ethics* (in which books viii and ix deal with friendship) by Isḥaḳ b. Ḥunayn, the *K. al-Akhlāḳ*, which was universally known (M. Bergé, *Une anthologie sur l'amitié d'Abu Ḥayyan al-Tawḥīdī*, in *BEO*, xvi [1961], 15-59).

However, all these prolific letter-writers were obliged to face a contradiction inherent in the letter considered as an illustration of friendship. According to Aristotle, the vital first condition of friendship is the fact of living in close proximity: "if distance does not destroy friendship utterly, it puts an end to its free exercise. If an absence is prolonged, it makes a man forget his friendships" (tr. G. Karlsson, *Cérémonial et idéologie dans l'épistolographie byzantine*, Uppsala 1962, 22). In such a situation, according to the Arab letter-writers, the letter can represent the absent friend, giving the illusion of presence and preserving friendship, on condition that the memory of the friend is kept constantly alive; it is the *s͟hāhid al-ik͟hā*ʾ (testimony of friendship) in the words of a stylist of the early ʿAbbāsid period (Ṣafwat, iii, 136; al-K͟hʷārazmī, *Rasāʾil*, 39, 42, 63, 67, 81; *Mad͟jmūʿ rasāʾil wa-maḳāmāt*, B.N., arabe 3923, fol. 55b; the letter replaces the absent friend and the reading of it, his conversation).

Obviously, it is necessary to treat with caution this idealised conception of friendship. Cicero's *De amicitia*, the most wide-ranging treatise on friendship written in the Roman world (Constable, 32), elevates friendship to the status of a cult; however, it is based on mutual aid. P.A. Brunt has shown that sincere belief in this sentiment was accompanied by a cliquish spirit, with friends exchanging political, economic and personal services (*Amicitia in the Late Roman Republic*, in *Proceedings of the Cambridge Philological Society*, clxxxvi [1965], 4-6). This self-serving aspect constitutes an integral part of the *ik͟hwāniyya*; requests are made for help, money, a title, etc. The stylist appears in this context in the guise of a shameless petitioner (Ṣafwat, iii, 61, Ibn al-Muḳaffaʿ; *Kas͟hf al-maʿānī wa 'l-bayān ʿan rasāʾil Badīʿ al-Zamān*, Beirut 1890, 372-3, 431-2, 511).

The Arab *ars dictaminis* are not concerned with providing a list of the themes most frequently addressed by the *ik͟hwāniyyāt*; they confine themselves to mentioning *tahānī* (felicitations), *taʿāzī* (condolences) and *tahādī wa-mulāṭafāt* (mutual exchange of gifts and acts of benevolence). It is not until the time of al-Ḳalḳas͟handī (d. 821/1418) that a detailed list of themes is obtained. Those mentioned are: *al-s͟hafāʿāt* (intercessions), *al-ʿināyāt* (expressions of solicitude), *al-tas͟hawwuḳ* (nostalgia), *al-istizāra* (invitation), *al-mawadda* (friendship), *iftitāḥ al-mukātaba* (the beginnings of intercourse conducted by correspondence), *K͟hiṭbat al-nisāʾ* (request for marriage), *al-istirḍāʾ wa 'l-istiʿṭāf* (efforts to please and to arouse goodwill), *al-iʿtizār* (excuses), *al-s͟hakwā* (complaint), *istimāḥat al-ḥawāʾid͟j* (request for the fulfilment of one's needs), *al-s͟hukr* (gratitude), *al-ʿitāb* (disapproval), *al-ʿiyāda* (visiting the sick), *al-suʾāl ʿan ḥāl al-marīḍ* (request for news of a sick person), *al-d͟hamm* (lecturing), *al-ik͟hbār* (announcement) and *mudāʿaba* (pleasantry) (*Subḥ*, viii, 126).

The risāla dīwāniyya

This owes its name to the term *dīwān al-ins͟hāʾ* (Correspondence Bureau). Later, it was called *al-risāla al-ins͟hāʾiyya*, Evidently, this applies to official prose. It should be stressed that this correspondence differs fundamentally from the modern administrative letter, a very carefully considered text, documents in which every term is weighed and pondered. The *dīwāniyyas* belonged as much to the tradition of eloquent discourse as to that of administrative prose. In this respect, the works—and works is indeed the correct term—of Aḥmad b. Yūsūf al-Kātib, of Ibrahim b. Hilāl al-Ṣābī, of Ibn al-ʿAmīd, of al-Ṣāḥib b. ʿAbbād, and to a lesser degree, those of Ibn Nubāta and al-Ḳāḍī al-Fāḍil, attained and continued to attain the status of texts belonging to the domain of the fine arts, much appreciated by scholars (*Yatīma*, iii, 10-12; Ṣafwat, iv, 262, 364-5). Two lists citing the themes addressed by these letters are currently extant, that of Ibn al-Nadīm (*Fihrist*, 183) which includes 30 titles and that of al-Ḳalḳas͟handī (*Ṣubḥ*, i, 244-356), which comprises 22 titles, giving an impression of the wide variety of subjects. On the other hand, the existence of these lists threatened to classify the stylists in these categories and thus to constitute a classicism in the *dīwāniyyas*. Finally, the best specimens were preserved in the *dīwān* to serve as normative models. The stylist acted in the capacity of a memorialist, evoking, in his *risālas*, events and dealing with subjects neglected by ancient historiography. Furthermore, letters written in the name of the sovereign were intended to be read in public, and to be discussed and debated by a knowledgeable public. An enormous range of knowledge was required. At a very early stage, from the 3rd/9th century onward, voices were heard to lament the ignorance of these "pillars of the state" (G. Lecomte, *L'introduction au Kitāb adab al-kātib*, in *Mélanges Louis Massignon*, Damascus 1957, iii, 45-63).

In order to remedy this state of affairs and to put suitable tools at the disposal of stylists, *ars dictaminis* were compiled for their use, treatises in which advice was accompanied by model letters. These were essentially manuals, which never aspired to poetry. The authors confined themselves to mentioning formulas for opening and closing, some general advice regarding the necessity of brevity, of adapting the style to the nature of the addressee, the use of poetry and the need to abstain from poetry in letters addressed to princes. Another section included practical advise concerning ink, pens, dimensions of the page, etc. The manual concluded with the mention of the most characteristic *fuṣūl* (or sections) of the official letter, such as *ṣudūr* (openings), *taḥmīdāt* (doxology), etc.; model letters are cited in the collections.

In fact, this situation persisted until the 5th/11th century: anthologies, such as *al-manẓūm wa 'l-mant͟hūr* of Ibn Abī Ṭāhir Ṭayfūr (d. 280/893), constitute the best proof of this. The theoretical section is somewhat thin in his work, but he cites *fuṣūl* and model letters; this was undeniably a major asset for a *kātib* in search of a *taḥmīd*, for example. In a later period, from the mid-5th/11th century, with ʿAlī b. K͟halaf (d. 455/1063), the author of the *Mawadd al-bayān* (analysis of this work has been undertaken by S. al-Droubi, *A Critical edition of and study on Ibn Fadl Allāh's manual of secretaryship...*, Muʾta 1413/1992, 64-5), a degree of specialisation emerges. Collections of stylised pieces offer models drafted by functionaries of the past or of the present regarded as consumate specialists or stylists. On the other hand, manuals of formularies and instructions came into being (R. Vesely, in the introduction to Ibn Nāẓir al-D͟jays͟h, *Tat͟hḳif al-taʿrīf*, Cairo 1987, pp. i-iv). An exhaustive list of the *ars dictaminis* has been established, with a brief summary, by al-Droubi (*ibid.*, 60-79, section on *The genre of secretarial manuals down to al-ʿUmarī's time*).

The formulae employed are very old and date back, for the most part, to the second half of the 1st/7th century, since they are attested in the papyri of Ḳurra b. S͟harīk [*q.v.*], governor of Egypt in 90/709; people used, in effect, as 31 formulas, expressions which were dignified by usage, which means that they were well-respected in an even earlier period. The opening comprises the *basmala*, a very brief *taḥmīd* (*fa-innī aḥmadu Allāha 'l-lad͟hī lā ilāh illā huwa* "I praise God, there is no other god but He"), a formula of transition *ammā baʿdu* ("this is the gist of the subject"). The formula of salutation (*wa 'l-salāmu ʿalā man ittabaʿa 'l-hudā* "and greetings to those who follow the way of truth") closes the letter. The two last lines bear the name of the scribe and the date (C.H. Becker, *Papyri Schott Reinhardt*, i, Heidelberg 1906, 92-4, letter 10).

VI. *Risāla and maḳāma*

From the second half of the 5th/11th century, after

the publication of the *Maḳāmāt* of al-Hariri, numerous sources of the time confuse *risāla* and *maḳāma*, Ibn Ḥamdūn (d. 495/1102), in vol. vi of the *Tadhkira*, that devoted to the epistolary genre (*al-mukātabāt wa 'l-rasāʾil*), entitles a section of the book *Min rasāʾil Abi 'l-Faḍl Aḥmad b. al-Ḥusayn al-Hamadhānī 'l-maʿrūf b. Badīʿ al-Zamān al-Hamadhānī 'l-musammāt bi 'l-maḳāmāt* "(Choice) of the letters of Abū Faḍl Aḥmad b. al-Ḥusayn al-Hamadhānī, known by the name of Badīʿ al-Zamān al-Hamadhānī, which are called *al-maḳāmāt*" (ms. Reisülküttab Mustafa Efendi, no. 770, fol. 101b, ll. 10-12). In the 6th/12th century, this equivalence between the genres is attested on numerous occasions in the texts (numerous attestations have been gathered together by H. ʿAbbās, *Fann al-maḳāma fi 'l-ḳarn al-sādis*, Cairo 1986, 86, 97, 98-9, 120, 249, 320). Al-Zamakhsharī confuses *maḳāla* and *maḳāma* (Murtaḍā al-Shīrāzī, *al-Zamakhsharī lughawiyy^an^ wa-mufassir^an^*, Cairo 1977, 251). This tendency persisted in the manuscript of seven *risālas* of al-Suyūṭī copied in the 18th century; *al-Risāla al-sundusiyya* bears the following title, *Risālat al-maḳāma al-sundusiyya fi 'l-nisba al-muṣṭafawiyya* (cf. Ḥādjdjī Khalīfa, 1875, *maḳāmāt al-Suyūṭī wa-hiya tisʿūn wa-ishrūn risālat^an^*).

It is evident that what is encountered here is a cultural process which deserves study. As a result of the work of De la Granja (*Maḳāma y risālas andaluzas*, Madrid 1976, pp. xi-xiii), the various stages of this evolution can be traced. At the outset, the *risāla*, written in an artistic prose which had no well-established canons in the early stages, supplied the precious primal material from which the first writers of the *maḳama* derived their ideas. Here, as in the *risāla*, rhetoric and lexicography were pressed into the service of this original and entertaining creation. In the second half of the 5th/11th century, al-Ḥarīrī contributed to the launching of the *maḳāma* in new directions, with the appearance of the didactic *maḳāma*. The ingenious and eloquent beggar leaves the stage, to be replaced by medical, geographical, mystical and linguistic opuscules, in other words, *risāla*s. The distinction between the two genres no longer had any reason to exist, and this is why they were assimilated to each other.

However, a converse process seems to have come into play here. Certain *risāla*s, on account of their lofty literary qualities, were considered to be *maḳāma*s. Thus Ibn Sīnā, who seems to have shown an inclination towards artistic and rhythmic prose, composed numerous *rasāʾil* and poems (see *Tisʿ rasāʾil fi 'l-ḥikma wa 'l-ṭabīʿiyyāt*, Cairo 1908). The most interesting is that which borrows the methods of allegory, sc. *Ḥayy b. Yaḳẓān*. Rather than a *risāla*, as is specified by the title, this is in fact a *maḳāma*. A century later, the Andalusian philosopher Abū Bakr b. al-Ṭufayl [*q.v.*] composed a philosophical novel bearing the same title, even though the objects of the two works are different. Abraham b. ʿEzra (mid-12th century) composed an imitation of the allegory of Ibn Sīnā. In the introduction, written in Judaeo-Arabic, the mediaeval editor of the *Dīwān* (ms. Berlin, 186, section intitled *al-nathr al-masdjūʾ*) describes the letter as *risāla*, whereas the fragment of the same work preserved in the Geniza is intitled *maḳāma* (Cambridge T-S K. 16-70; see also the critical edition of Israel Levin, Tel Aviv 1983).

VII. THE *RISĀLA* IN JUDAEO-ARABIC

Quite naturally, letters in Judaeo-Arabic are similar in all respects to those composed in the mother culture. The Geniza of Cairo has preserved a large number of letters, differing considerably in style and in content. Qualitatively and quantitatively, these documents constitute a unique phenomenon in the annals of mediaeval Arab culture. However, on account of their Jewish provenance, they contained a considerable number of Hebrew terms, formulas and phrases. This applies principally to the polite formulae of opening the letter, to the glorification of God, to eulogies (*taḥmīdāt*) reserved for the addressee. Sometimes they adopt a precious style, an artistic Hebraic prose, often rhymed. Evidently, here also a close relationship existed between the style of the letter and the status of the writer and of the addressee, in the family and in society. In Judaeo-Arabic, the correspondence between local dignitaries and the communal functionaries belonging to institutions enjoying an "ecumenical" status has been preserved (M. Cohen, *Correspondence and social control in the Jewish communities of the Islamic world: a letter of the Nagid Joshua Maimonides*, in *Jewish History Quarterly*, i/2 [1986], 39-48; S.D. Goitein, *A Mediterranean society*, Berkeley and Los Angeles 1988, v, 422-4, see also i, 1967, 11-12). The development of artistic style in letters written in Judaeo-Arabic directly influenced the development of Hebraic prose among the Jewish writers of Christian Europe. Some highly significant examples are to be found in the letters written in Hebrew by Judah Ha-Levi (early decades of the 12th century, letters written from Lucena and from Narbonne published in his *Dīwān*, ed. H. Brody, Berlin 1893, i, letter 4; see also Goitein, *op. cit.*, v, 463-6, on the Arabic letters of Ha-Levi). The letters, emanating from the offices of certain senior rabbinical authorities, identical to the *dīwāniyya*s, reflect a little the personal style of the scribes, but to a greater extent the style of the *dīwān*s of correspondence, the fruit of numerous decades of maturation; a good example is provided by the letters featuring in the edition of S. Assaf, *A collection of letters by Samuel b. ʿElī*, Jerusalem 1930 (in Hebrew). These pieces, emanating from the offices of the Gaon (the Talmudic Academy) of Baghdād, are written in a very precious and ornate Judaeo-Arabic and are in no respect inferior to the letters of the ʿAbbāsid chancellery. Some, those addressed to East Kurdistan and to Persia, are written exclusively in Hebrew.

The poetry of the Judaeo-Arabic *risāla* does not differ in any respect from that of its Arabic parent; furthermore, the evolution of the two followed an identical course. It is thus that monograph-letters are attested in various branches of the culture of the Jews of the East; religious and scientific disciplines tally for the most part (M. Steinschneider, *Arabische Literatur der Juden*, index of Arabic titles, s.v. *maḳāla*, *risāla*). In the following lines, the principal aspects will be reviewed but only the cases which present special interest being examined.

One of the most ancient examples of the Judaeo-Arabic *risāla* is a treatise comparing Hebrew, Aramaic and Arabic attributed to Judah b. Ḳuraysh of Tāhart (Morocco, d. *ca.* 900; ed. D. Becker, Tel Aviv 1984). This work was addressed to the community of Fez, which had abandoned the custom of reciting the Aramaic translation of the Pentateuch (*Targum*). Still in the linguistic context, another monograph was intitled *risāla* by its author; this is the *Risālat al-Tanbīh* by Ibn Djanāḥ (Spain, first half of the 11th century, ed. J. and H. Derenbourg, Paris 1880).

Maimonides (1138-1205) composed numerous *risāla*s and *maḳāla*s in response to the questions and requests of the faithful. A large proportion of his work reflects the pre-occupations of an extremely gifted stylist, who was also an original thinker. This eminent authority on matters of religious law revealed his opinions on the problems and precepts of faith in meticulously-crafted *risālas*. Thus his philosophical work, *Dalālat al-ḥāʾirīn*, the well-known *Guide to the perplexed*, is described, in numerous passages of the book, as a *maḳāla*, in other words, as a letter. Furthermore, the prologue contains a personal letter addressed to his favourite disciple Joseph b. Judah (ed. Joel, 1931, 1; see also *The guide of the perplexed*, tr. S. Pines, 1963, 3-4). Some of these letters were written in Arabic, others in Judeao-Arabic, in accordance with the language of the addressee. The majority represent the type of enlarged *responsa* in which the author deals with problems in depth and beyond immediate circumstances. The best illustration of the profundity of his essays is supplied by *The Yemenite epistle* (ed. A.S. Halkin, the text of the medieval Hebrew tr.; English tr. B. Cohen, New York 1952), which was addressed to the Jews of the Yemen; it seems to have been motivated by serious incidents which had afflicted the community, in particular the appearance of a false Messiah; he deals in it with a number of problems, including that of prophecy and that of the status of the prophet Muḥammad in particular. The *risāla* contains a long prologue written in very ornate Hebrew rhymed prose. There is no doubt that, deriving from the genre, it conforms to the pattern of the Arabic epistle; on the other hand, it maintains in a direct line the traditional attitude of Jewish letters, stipulating that Hebrew alone is the language of poetry.

Bibliography (in addition to references given in the article): Aḥmad Zakī Ṣafwat, *D̲j̲amharat as̲h̲ʿār al-ʿArab fī ʾl-ʿuṣūr al-ʿarabiyya al-zāhira*, Cairo 1356-7/1937-8; M. Kurd ʿAlī, *Rasāʾil al-bulag̲h̲āʾ*, Damascus 1370/1950; idem, *Umarāʾ al-bayān al-ʿarabī*, Cairo 1367/1948; al-D̲j̲āḥiẓ, *Rasāʾil*, ed. Hārūn, Cairo 1399/1979; al-Ṣāḥib Ibn ʿAbbād, *Rasāʾil*, Cairo 1366/1947; al-Ṣābī, *Rasāʾil*, Bāʿabdā 1898. On modern theories about the letter: Karlsson; Hunger; Constable; Leclercq, *Le genre épistolaire au Moyen Age*, in *Revue du M.A. latin*, ii (1946), 63-78; idem, *L'amitié dans les lettres du Moyen Age*, in *ibid.*, i (1945), 391-410. For the study of the poetical history of the genre: Ibn al-Nadīm, *Fihrist*, 168-244 (indispensable); W. Marçais, *Les origines de la prose littéraire arabe*, in *R. Afr.*, cccxxx/1 (1927), 1-15; C.E. Bosworth, *A* maqāma *on secretaryship: al-Qalqashandī's* al-Kawākib al-durriyya fī manāqib al-badriyya, in *BSOAS*, xvii (1964), 291-8; S.A. Bonebakker, *A Fāṭimid manual for secretaries*, in *AIUON*, xvii (1977), 5-59; J.H. Escovitz, *Vocational patterns of the scribes of the Mamlūk chancery*, in *Arabica*, xxiii (1976), 42-62; Ḥ. Naṣṣār, *Nas̲h̲ʾat al-kitāba al-fanniyya*, Cairo 1966; M. Nabīh Ḥid̲j̲āb, *Balāg̲h̲at al-kuttāb fī ʾl-ʿaṣr al-ʿabbāsī*, Cairo 1385/1965; Ḥusnī Nāʿisa, *al-Kitāba al-fanniyya fī mas̲h̲riḳ al-dawla al-islāmiyya fī ʾl-ḳarn al-t̲h̲ālith al-hid̲j̲rī*, Beirut 1398/1978; S̲h̲awḳī Ḍayf, *al-Fann wa-mad̲h̲āhibuhu fī ʾl-nat̲h̲r al-ʿarabī*, Cairo 1960; Adūnīs, ʿAlī Aḥmad Saʿīd, *al-T̲h̲ābit wa ʾl-mutaḥawwil*, iii, Beirut 1983, 21-33.

(A. Arazi and H. Ben-S̲h̲ammay)

2. In Persian.

Risālas, or short treatises, composed in Persian, are numerous and varied. The majority of them may be classified under the following headings.

Religion. Among these, epistles connected with Ṣūfism are perhaps the most numerous. One of the earliest authors of such writings was K̲h̲ʷād̲j̲a ʿAbd Allāh Anṣārī (396-481/1006-89 [*q.v.*]), said to have composed the first *risālas* of their kind in rhymed prose. His treatises with a Ṣūfī message include *Dil u d̲j̲ān* "Heart and soul", *Kanz al-sālikīn* "Provisions of the travellers", *Ḳalandar-nāma* "Book of the mendicant" and *Maḥabbat-nāma* "Book of love". These writings, partly ethical, partly mystical, are distinguished by a mingling of prose and verse—a feature in which the author's pioneering efforts influenced many later writers.

A well-known treatise belonging to the early 6th/12th century is Aḥmad al-G̲h̲azālī's [*q.v.*] *Risālat al-sawāniḥ fī ʾl-ʿis̲h̲ḳ* "Treatise on ideas of love". The author was the younger brother of the famous ethical theologian Abū Ḥāmid Muḥammad G̲h̲azālī (d. 505/1111 [*q.v.*]). His work comprises 75 short chapters and seeks to give a Ṣūfī interpretation of the concept of love, lover and beloved. Its philosophical meaning is couched in a metaphorical language, and, like the works of ʿAbd Allāh Anṣārī cited above, it also uses the device of inserting short poems in its prose narrative. He was also the author of a *R. al-ṭuyūr* "T. on the birds", the theme of which constitutes a probable source of Farīd al-Dīn ʿAṭṭār's (d. 627/1299 [*q.v.*]) allegorical poem *Manṭiḳ al-ṭayr*.

A number of *risālas* were produced by individuals who were prominent in the Ṣūfī orders which emerged in Islam after the 6th-7th/12th-13th century. The founder of the Kubrāwī order, S̲h̲ayk̲h̲ Nad̲j̲m al-Dīn Kubrā (540-618/1145-1221 [*q.v.*]), was a prolific writer whose output included both Arabic and Persian works. In his epistle *al-Sāʾir al-ḥāʾir* "The bewildered traveller", the author outlines ten conditions for the novice to reach his goal. Nad̲j̲m al-Dīn Kubrā wrote this Persian treatise in response to a request by those of his disciples who were unacquainted with Arabic.

A disciple of Nad̲j̲m al-Dīn Kubrā was the noted Ṣūfī mystic and writer Nad̲j̲m al-Dīn Rāzī "Dāya" (d. 654/1256). His famous *R.-yi ʿis̲h̲ḳ u ʿaḳl* "T. on love and intellect", also named as *R.-yi miʿyār al-ṣidḳ fī miṣdāḳ al-ʿis̲h̲ḳ* "T. on the touchstone of truth to verify love", was written in answer to a question by one of the author's friends; it attempts to enquire into the relationship between love and reason, and shows a tendency towards philosophising.

Another prominent disciple of Nad̲j̲m al-Dīn Kubrā was Sayf al-Dīn Bāk̲h̲arzī (d. 659/1261), who continued to teach his master's way in Transoxiana after the latter's violent death at the hands of the Mongols. Primarily a poet known for his *rubāʿīs*, he was also the author of a prose *R.-yi ʿis̲h̲ḳ* "T. on love", which deals with an idealised view of human emotion and its psychological significance.

There are many *risālas* ascribed to Mīr Sayyid ʿAlī Hamadānī (713-86/1314-85), through whom the Kubrāwī order gained a foothold in Kas̲h̲mīr. Included in his works are the *R.-yi manāmiyya* "T. on dreams", *R.-yi wud̲j̲ūdiyya* "T. on existence", *R.-yi d̲h̲ikriyya* "T. on d̲h̲ikr", *R.-yi ʿaḳabāt* "T. on difficult paths" and *R.-yi darwīs̲h̲iyya* "T. on poverty".

Among the leaders of the Naḳs̲h̲bandī order, ʿAbd al-K̲h̲āliḳ G̲h̲ud̲j̲dawānī (d. 617/1220) was the author of the *R.-yi ṣāḥibiyya* "T. of the master", a manual describing the Ṣūfī stages advocated by his spiritual guide, Abū Yaʿḳūb Yūsuf b. Ayyūb Hamadānī (d. 535/1140). An important member of ʿAbd al-K̲h̲āliḳ G̲h̲ud̲j̲dawānī's chain of succession (*silsila*) was Bahāʾ al-Dīn Naḳs̲h̲band (d. 791/1389 [*q.v.*]), whose disciple, K̲h̲ʷād̲j̲a Abū Naṣr Pārsā (756-822/1355-1420), composed two major treatises on Ṣūfism, *R.-yi ḳudsiyya* "T. on sanctity" and *R.-yi kas̲h̲fiyya* "T. on revelation", both works presenting a Naḳs̲h̲bandī view of Ṣūfī thought. The first, based upon Bahāʾ al-Dīn Naḳs̲h̲band's lecture sessions, discusses twelve topics concerning Ṣūfī theory and practice; the second tries to explore the mystical states of inspiration, intuition and illumination.

The founder of the Niʿmat Allāhī order, S̲h̲āh

Ni^c^mat Allāh Walī (730-834/1330-1431 [see NI^c^MAT-ALLĀHIYYA]), was a prolific writer who contributed greatly to the exposition of Ṣūfism through his commentaries and interpretations. He is said to have produced over 500 works, of which an important number have survived. Some of his treatises are: the *R.-yi sulūk* "T. on the Ṣūfī pilgrimage", *R.-yi tawḥīd* "T. on the unity of God", *Naṣīḥat-nāma* "The book of counsels", *R.-yi nūriyya* "T. on light", *R.-yi ma^c^ārif* "T. on knowledge", *R.-yi tawwakkul* "T. on the trust in God", *R.-yi rūḥiyya* "T. on the soul", *R.-yi khalwat* "T. on retreat", *R.-yi ilhāmāt* "T. on divine revelations" and *R.-yi rumūz* "T. on mysteries".

An extreme offshoot of Ṣūfism was the Ḥurūfī or "Literalist" school which emerged in Persia in the 8th/14th century [see ḤURŪFIYYA]. Its founder was Faḍl Allāh Astarābādī (martyred in ? 796/1394), to whom Sa^c^īd Nafīsī ascribed the work named *R. dar uṣūl-i Ḥurūfiyya* "T. on the Ḥurūfī doctrine" (*Tārīkh-i naẓm u nathr dar Īrān*, ii, 791-2).

Ṣūfī literature was enriched by the *risālas* of some well-known literary figures such as the 7th/13th-century poet and mystic, Fakhr al-Dīn ^c^Irāḳī (d. 688/1289 [*q.v.*]), famed for his major work on Ṣūfism, the *Lama^c^āt* "Flashes". Apart from this work, he wrote a small *risāla* concerning Ṣūfī terminology and its symbolical meaning. The terms are arranged in three sections according to their association: the first section comprises the terms connected either with the beloved or the lover; the second contains names common to both the lover and the beloved; and the third consists of words identified more specifically with the lover and his mental states.

To ^c^Irāḳī's illustrious contemporary Sa^c^dī (d. 695/1295-6 [*q.v.*]) belong six *risālas*, two of which bear the impress of Ṣūfī thought. The first, entitled *^c^Aḳl u ^c^ishḳ* "Intellect and love", was written in response to a question asked by a certain Sa^c^d al-Dīn, and deals with the concept of attaining mystical knowledge of the Divine through emotion rather than by reason. It resembles the *Gulistān* in its style, and is written in a simple language. The second is named *Madjālis-i pandjgāna* "Five sessions"; it contains five sermons modelled after the discourses delivered by religious preachers and Ṣūfī divines in their services.

Maḥmūd Shabistarī (d. 720/1320-1 [*q.v.*]), the author of the famous *mathnawī* on Ṣūfī doctrine *Gulshan-i rāz* "Rose-garden of secrets", is credited with three prose writings, one of which is the *R.-yi ḥaḳḳ al-yaḳīn* "T. on certain truth", dealing with Ṣūfī theosophy. It contains eight chapters whose headings are mentioned by E.G. Browne in his account of the author (*LHP*, iii, 149-50). The work has been likened to ^c^Irāḳī's *Lama^c^āt*, but is inferior in merit (see Arberry, *Classical Persian literature*, 303).

The poet Ḳāsim Anwār (d. 837/1433-4), who was a major influence on the Ṣūfī movement of his time, was the author of two *risālas* reflecting his mystical leanings, the *R.-yi su^ʾ^āl u djawāb* "T. with questions and answers", an exchange on the topic of good and evil, and *R. dar bayān-i ^c^ilm* "T. explaining knowledge". Serious questions have been raised regarding the views of the author. He was suspected, during his lifetime, of complicity in the attempted assassination of Tīmūr's son, Shāh Rukh [*q.v.*], by a Ḥurūfī fanatic. More recently, it has been suggested that his poetry betrays Ḥurūfī tendencies although his writings show that he belonged to the mainstream of Ṣūfī thought.

The philosophical aspect of Sufism finds a vivid evidence in the *risālas* of Ṣā^ʾ^in al-Dīn Turka (d. *ca.* 836/1432), in whom the roles of the mystic and philosopher tend to coalesce. Like Ḳāsim Anwār, who was his contemporary, he was subjected to the allegation of being indirectly involved in the murder attempt on Shāh Rukh. His numerous writings in Arabic and Persian embrace a variety of mystical, theological and philosophical subjects, and include *R.-yi asrār-i ṣalāt* "T. on the secrets of prayer", a work interpreting the fundamentals of Muslim worship from a Ṣūfī perspective; *R.-yi shaḳḳ al-ḳamar wa sā^c^at* "T. on the splitting of the moon and the hour", on the Ḳur^ʾ^ānic verse "The hour drew nigh and the moon was rent in two" (LIV, 1); *R.-yi ḍaw^ʾ^ al-Lama^c^āt* "T. on the lustre of the Flashes", a commentary on ^c^Irāḳī's work *Lama^c^āt; R. dar bayān-i ma^c^nī-yi ^c^irfānī-yi ^c^ilm-i ṣarf* "T. explaining the gnostic meanings in morphology", on the relationship between mysticism and language; and *R.-yi ḥarf* (BL. Add. 23,983) "T. on the letters", sc. on the letters of the Arabic alphabet and their esoteric meanings.

Among the Persian treatises on Ṣūfism composed in India, mention may be made of the *R.-yi ḥaḳḳ-numā* "T. on the guide to truth", by Dārā Shikūh (1024-68/1615-58 [*q.v.*]), the eldest son of Emperor Shāh Djahān (*r.* 1037-70/1627-59 [*q.v.*]). Dārā Shikūh was the author of several works devoted to a synthesis of Hindu and Muslim thought, a movement initiated by his great-grandfather Akbar (*r.* 963-1014/1556-1605 [*q.v.*]). The *R.-yi ḥaḳḳ-numā*, completed in 1055/1645-6, comprises six parts dealing with the following topics: (1) world of humanity; (2) world of intelligible substances; (3) world of power; (4) world of divinity; (5) identification of the Lord of lords; and (6) unicity of being.

In addition to Ṣūfism, orthodox theology forms the subject-matter of various *risālas*. The poet Djāmī (817-98/1414-92 [*q.v.*]), whose large output extended over many topics, wrote on various theological and mystical matters which included the exegesis of the Ḳur^ʾ^ān, traditions of the Prophet and biographies of Muslim saints. His theological work *R.-yi arkān-i ḥadjdj* "T. on the pillars of the pilgrimage" describes the rules and ceremonies prescribed for the *ḥadjdj* and *^c^umra*.

One of the well-known theological treatises of the 9th/15th century is *al-R. al-^c^Aliyya fi 'l-aḥādīth al-nabawiyya* "The ^c^Alīd treatise on the traditions of the Prophet", by Ḥusayn b. ^c^Alī Wā^c^iẓ Kāshifī (d. 910/1504-5 [*q.v.*]), who is famous for his work on ethics the *Akhlāḳ-i Muḥsinī* as well as for his collection of fables the *Anwār-i Suhaylī* "The lights of Canopus". His theological *risāla*, mentioned above, contains forty traditions arranged in eight groups according to their themes.

Conspicuous among the theological writings dealing with the Ismā^c^īlī sect are two treatises by Naṣīr al-Dīn Ṭūsī (d. 672/1274 [*q.v.*]) namely *R. dar tawallā wa tabarrā* "T. on friendship and exoneration", and *R.-yi sayr u sulūk* "T. on travel and pilgrimage". The author was in the service of the Ismā^c^īlīs for a long time, and it is probably during this period that he wrote his two theological treatises in support of their doctrine.

From the 10th/16th century, theological works on Shī^c^ism found increasing currency in Persian. An interesting example of this type is the *R.-yi Ḥasaniyya* (BL. Egerton 1020) or *R.-yi Ḥusniyya* by Ibrahīm b. Walī Allāh Astarābādī, a writer of the 10th/16th century. It deals with Shī^c^ī doctrines, especially those relating to the prerogatives of ^c^Alī and his descendants. The treatise derives its title from the name of a slave-girl who is represented as debating the infallibility of the Shī^c^ī faith with learned scholars in the presence of the caliph Hārūn al-Rashīd. The author claims that his work was a translation from an Arabic original, supposedly composed by the 6th/12th-century commentator on the Ḳurʾān, Djamāl al-Dīn Abu 'l-Futūḥ Khuzāʿī Rāzī. He further states that the manuscript of the Arabic original came in his possession in Damascus, while he was on a Pilgrimage to Mecca, and that he translated it for the Ṣafawid monarch Shāh Ṭahmāsp I (*r.* 930-84/1524-76 [*q.v.*]).

Shīʿism found a vocal spokesman in the person of Nūr Allāh Shūshtarī (d. 1019/1610 [*q.v.*]), who went to India during Akbar's reign, and was appointed *ḳāḍī* of Lāhawr. During Djahāngīr's régime (1023-37/1605-27 [*q.v.*]), however, he became the target of Sunnī hostility and was executed by the orders of the Emperor. He is known primarily for his work *Madjālis al-muʾminīn* "Assemblies of believers", which contains the biographies of Shīʿī divines. He also composed the *R. dar taḥḳīḳ-i āya-yi Nūr* "T. containing an enquiry into the Light Verse" (Ḳurʾān, XXIV, 35), and *R. dar ḥurmat-i namāz-i djumʿa dar ayyām-i ghaybat* "T. on the sanctity of Friday prayer during the occultation of the Imām".

With the rise of the Ṣafawids in the 10th/16th century, there was an upsurge of hostile feeling towards the Ṣūfīs, encouraging the production of theological works concerned exclusively with the denunciation of Ṣūfī ideas and practices. One of these works was the *R.-yi khayrātiyya* (BL. Add. 24,411) "T. on charity", composed by Āḳā Muḥammad ʿAlī Bihbihānī (d. 1216/1801-2 [*q.v.* in Suppl.]) in 1211/1796-7; its appearance resulted in provoking violence against the Ṣūfīs that led to the murder of some of their leaders.

Philosophy. Early Persian treatises in philosophy are represented by some *risālas* attributed to Ibn Sīnā (d. 428/1037 [*q.v.*]). Among others, they include the *R.-yi ʿishḳ* "T. on love", and the manual on psychology *R.-yi nafs* "T. on the soul". However, frequent doubts have been expressed regarding the authenticity of their authorship, and it is only from a much later date that *risālas* of definite provenance become available.

The list of writers on philosophy after Ibn Sīnā is headed by Fakhr al-Dīn Rāzī (d. Harāt, 606/1209 [*q.v.*]) and Naṣīr al-Dīn Ṭūsī. Among the former's *risālas* is *al-R. al-kamāliyya fi 'l-ḥaḳāʾiḳ-i Ilāhiyya* "The perfect treatise on Divine truths", which comprises ten discourses concerning logic, divine philosophy and natural sciences.

Naṣīr al-Dīn Ṭūsī may be regarded as only second in importance to Ibn Sīnā for the influence which he exercised over philosophical trends in Persia. In his writings such as *R.-yi ithbāt-i wādjib al-wudjūd* "T. on proving the existence of the necessarily existing (i.e. God)", *R.-yi djabr u ḳadr* "T. on necessity and freewill" and *R. dar ḳismat-i mawdjūdāt u aḳsām-i ān* "T. on the division of created things and their varieties", he displays a keen intellectual insight in discussing some of the debatable religio-philosophical issues of his time.

One of his contemporaries, and reportedly his nephew, was Afḍal al-Dīn Kāshānī (d. 667/1268-9), author of several philosophical studies and a scholar influenced by Ibn Sīnā. He also translated some originally Greek works, obviously from Arabic. His *R.-yi nafs* "T. on the soul", is a Persian rendering of Aristotle's work on psychology. Another of his translations is the *R.-yi tuffāḥa* "The apple treatise", a pseudo-Aristotelian work called *De pomo et morte inclyte principis philosophorum Aristotelis*, which has been printed several times in Europe.

In logic, the writings of Athīr al-Dīn Mufaḍḍal Abharī (d. 663/1264-5) and Ḳuṭb al-Dīn Rāzī (d. 766/1364) have an important place; the former was a disciple of Fakhr al-Dīn Rāzī, and his *R. dar manṭiḳ* describes in brief some of the basic points of logic.

Among the learned men of the late Mongol period was Ḳuṭb al-Dīn Rāzī (d. 766/1364-5), a protégé of Ghiyāth al-Dīn Muḥammad (d. 736/1336), who was chief minister to the Īlkhānid ruler Abū Saʿīd (*r.* 716-36/1317-35 [*q.v.*]). Ḳuṭb al-Dīn Rāzī belonged to the group of writers who engaged themselves in preparing commentaries and textbooks for educational use, involving the writing of small treatises for the convenience of the students. His *risālas*, which were probably written with this purpose in mind, include *R. fī taḥḳīḳ al-kulliyyāt* "T. on the verification of universals", *R.-yi taḥḳīḳ-i taṣawwur u taṣdīḳ* "T. on the inquiry into concept and assent" and *R.-yi taḥḳīḳ-i maḥṣūrāt* "T. on the investigation into finitudes". It is most likely that Ḳuṭb al-Dīn Rāzī's approximate contemporary, Mīr Sayyid Sharīf Djurdjānī (d. 816/1413-14), also had an educational motive before him for writing some of his works; his writings on logic comprise the *R.-yi kubrā* "The major treatise", and the *R.-yi ṣughrā* "The minor treatise".

The Ṣafawid period witnessed some distinguished personalities in philosophy, the major exponents in this field being Ṣadr al-Dīn Muḥammad Shīrāzī (d. 1050/1640-1), popularly known as Mullā Ṣadra [*q.v.*], and Muḥammad Bāḳir of Astarābād (d. 1041/1631), commonly called Mīr Dāmād [see DĀMĀD]; but their contribution falls more appropriately within the realm of Arabic literature, since almost all their output is in Arabic. It is, therefore, difficult to find significant philosophical studies in Persian produced during the Ṣafawid period.

Science. Early scientific literature by Persian writers was produced mainly in Arabic, the language of learning and scholarship in Islam. However, from the 7th/13th century, works written in Persian became more frequent, and Naṣīr al-Dīn Ṭūsī wrote several *risālas* on astronomy, a field in which he was highly regarded for he was chosen by Hülegü to supervise the observatory established by the Mongol ruler at Marāgha. Probably his finest treatise on astronomy is the *R.-yi Muʿīniyya*, named after Muʿīn al-Dīn Abu 'l-Shams, son of the author's former patron, Nāṣir al-Dīn b. Abī Manṣūr (d. 655/1257-8), governor of Ḳuhistān.

In 824/1421 Ulugh Beg (d. 853/1449 [*q.v.*]), the talented son of Tīmūr, built an observatory at Samarḳand, and there brought together some of the leading scientific figures of his time, among whom was ʿAlāʾ al-Dīn ʿAlī b. Muḥammad Ḳūshdjī (d. 879/1474-5), commonly called ʿAlī Ḳūshdjī [*q.v.*]. Some time after the death of Ulugh Beg, the latter joined the service of the Ottoman sultan Meḥemmed II the Conqueror [*q.v.*], under whom he composed the *R. dar hayʾat* "T. on astronomy", otherwise known as *Fārsī hayʾat* "Persian astronomy", which enjoyed much popularity, and was used as a textbook for teaching astronomy in schools.

Among later works on astronomy is the *R. dar rubʿ-i mudjayyib* "T. on the astronomical quadrant", by Mīrem Čelebi (d. 931/1525), whose real name was Maḥmūd b. Muḥammad. A writer of the same period, Niẓām al-Dīn b. Muḥammad Ḥusayn Bīrdjandī (d. 934/1527), composed in 930/1523-4 the *R.-yi abʿād u adjrām* "T. on distances and bodies", which discusses, among other things, the measurements of the earth's surface and of the heavens and stars.

Interest in astronomical instruments gave rise to a number of treatises relating, more particularly, to the astrolabe. One of the best known is Naṣīr al-Dīn

Ṭūsī's *R.-yi bīst bāb dar maʿrifat-i asṭurlāb* "T. in twenty sections concerning the knowledge of the astrolabe", which found a host of commentators; this may have been an abridged version made by the author from one of his larger works on the subject.

G͟hiyāt͟h al-Dīn D͟jams͟hīd Kās͟hī (d. 832/1428-9 or 840/1436-7) worked on the staff of Ulug͟h Beg's observatory, and is the author of the *R. dar sāk͟ht-i asṭurlāb* "T. on the construction of the astrolabe", and the *R. dar s͟harḥ-i ālāt-i raṣad* "T. explaining astronomical instruments", the latter completed in 818/1416. Some other works which have a similar content include the *R. dar ṣifat-i kura-yi d͟jadīd,* "T. on the characteristic of a new sphere"; the *R.-yi asṭurlāb* "T. on the astrolabe"; and the *R. dar ālāt-i raṣadiyya* "T. on astronomical instruments". The first, which was written by ʿAlāʾ al-Dīn Kirmānī, was dedicated to the Ottoman sultan Bāyezīd I (*r.* 792-805/1389-1402) or to Bāyezīd II (*r.* 886-918/1481-1512), and deals with the construction and uses of a new armillary sphere; the second was completed in the 10th/16th century by Abu 'l-K͟hayr Fārsī; and the third was composed by ʿAbd al-Munʿim Āmulī in approximately 970/1562-3 on the orders of S͟hāh Ṭahmāsp I.

Hand in hand with the cultivation of astronomy went the study of meteorology. One of the earliest works dealing with this branch of knowledge is the *R.-yi āt͟hār-i ʿulwī* "T. on the celestial phenomena", by Abū Ḥātim Muẓaffar Isfizārī. Very little is known about the author except that he belonged to the town of Isfizār [*q.v.*], in present-day Afg͟hanistān. He dedicated his treatise to Fak͟hr al-Mulk, son of Malik S͟hāh's minister Niẓām al-Mulk. Since Fak͟hr al-Mulk met his death at the hands of the Assassins in 500/1106-7, the work may be dated to before that event. From the time of its composition, it continued to remain an important source utilised by other writers for their works.

Among the contributions on meteorology inspired by Isfizārī was the *R.-yi Sand͟jariyya fi 'l-kāʾināt al-ʿunṣuriyya* "T. for Sand͟jar [*q.v.*] concerning the world of elements", written for the Sald͟jūk ruler (*r.* 511-52/1118-57) by Zayn al-Dīn ʿUmar b. Sahlān Sāwī (Sāwad͟jī) who, as far as internal evidence is concerned, knew about Isfizārī's treatise. A more direct influence may be observed in S͟haraf al-Dīn Masʿūdī Marwazī's *R. dar bāra-yi āt͟hār-i ʿulwī* "T. concerning the celestial phenomena", which was completed in the middle of the 7th/13th century. Meteorology is also the subject of the *R.-yi kāʾināt-i d͟jaww* "T. on meteorology" by Muḥammad ʿAlī b. Abī Ṭālib Gīlānī, better known as Muḥammad ʿAlī Ḥazīn, who was born in Persia but spent a considerable portion of his life in India where he died in 1180/1766.

In the mathematical sciences, the first important epistle that may be mentioned is the *R. dar handasa* "T. on geometry", by Abū ʿUbayd ʿAbd al-Waḥīd b. Muḥammad D͟jūzd͟jānī, a pupil of Ibn Sīnā; his work represents a collection of his master's notes on geometry.

An early 7th/13th-century work is the *R. fī ṭarīḳ al-masāʾil al-ʿadadiyya* "T. on the handling of arithmetical problems", written by S͟haraf al-Dīn Ḥusayn b. Ḥasan Samarḳandī and completed in 632/1235. Contributions to mathematical studies were also made by certain scholars who had been active primarily in the field of astronomy. For instance, Naṣīr al-Dīn Ṭūsī wrote a *R. dar ḥisāb* "Treatise on arithmetic". This name also belongs to the work produced by Ṣalāḥ al-Dīn Mūsā, commonly known as Ḳāḍī-zāda Rūmī, who was attached to Ulug͟h Beg's observatory. His colleague, ʿAlī Ḳūs͟hd͟jī, mentioned earlier for his work on astronomy, was the author of a *R. dar ʿilm-i ḥisāb* "T. on the science of arithmetic", known alternatively as *Fārsī ḥisāb* "Persian arithmetic". The Tīmūrid historian S͟haraf al-Dīn Yazdī (d. 858/1454 [*q.v.*]), whose various learned activities included scientific work as well, has been credited with the authorship of a *R.-yi ḥisāb-i ʿiḳd-i anāmil* "T. on finger reckoning".

Medicine. The earliest Persian treatise in medicine is probably the so-called *R. dar nabḍ* "Treatise on the pulse", or *Rag-s͟hināsī* "Angiology", attributed to Ibn Sīnā. The number of medical *risālas* encountered after the 9th/15th century is comparatively large. Included among these is the *R. dar ʿilm-i ṭibb* "T. on medicine", by Uways al-Laṭīfī al-Ardabīlī (? *flor.* in the second half of the 9th/15th century). Another is the *R. dar muʿālad͟jāt-i badan* "T. on the treatments of the body" also known as *Ḳawānīn al-ʿilād͟j* "Canons of treatment" and *S͟hifāʾ al-amrāḍ* "Treatment of diseases" completed in 871/1466 by Muḥammad ʿAlāʾ al-Dīn Sabzawārī, popularly known as G͟hiyāt͟h Mutaṭabbib it comprises fourteen sections dealing with cures (BL Add. 23, 557).

The Ṣafawid period produced some noted physicians, one of whom was ʿImād al-Dīn Maḥmūd b. Masʿūd al-Ṭabīb, who lived towards the end of S͟hāh Ṭahmāsp I's reign. Besides his main contribution *Yanbūʿ fī ʿilm al-ṭibb* (BL. Add. 23, 560) "The source of medical science", he left several other *risālas*, such as *R.-yi afyūn* (BL. Add. 19, 619), "T. on opium", *R. dar bayān-i k͟hawāṣṣ u manfiʿat-i čūb-i čīnī* "T. on the properties and benefits of the Chinese root", and *R.-yi ātis͟hak* "Treatise on syphilis".

Among the distinguished writers on medicine who flourished in India under the Mug͟hals was Masīḥ al-Dīn Abu 'l-Fatḥ Gīlānī (d. 997/1589), Akbar's court physician and author of a *R.-yi ṭibb al-mud͟jarrabāt* "T. on tested remedies", a collection of cures tried by the author during the course of his profession.

Other specialised writings in this field include the *R. dar tas͟hrīḥ-i badan-i insān wa kayfiyyat-i awḍāʿ-i a*... "T. on the human anatomy and the nature of its bases", by Manṣūr b. Muḥammad, also called *Tas͟hrīḥ-i Manṣūrī* "Manṣūr's anatomy" and published under this title at Lucknow in 1264/1847-8. It gives a description of the limbs, organs, and other elements of the human body, and has been illustrated with anatomical diagrams. It was dedicated to Mīrzā Ḍiyāʾ al-Dīn Pīr Muḥammad Bahādur (d. 809/1406-7), a grandson of Tīmūr.

Studies on preventive medicine are represented by several works on hygiene such as the *R. dar ḥifẓ al-ṣiḥḥ*... "T. on hygiene" and *R. dar tadbīr-i ḥifẓ-i ṣiḥḥaṭ* "T. on the planning of hygiene" written respectively by two of S͟hāh Ṭahmāsp I's physicians, S͟haraf al-Dīn Bāfaḳī (d. 978/1570-1) and Kamāl al-Dīn Ḥusayn S͟hīrāzī. In addition, manuals which dealt with poisons and provided means to dispel their effects are also common, e.g. ʿImād al-Dīn Maḥmūd's handbooks *R.-yi sumūm* "T. on poisons", and *R.-yi pāzah* "T. on antidotes". Works on veterinary science include a *R. dar k͟hawāṣṣ al-ḥayawān* "T. on the characteristics of animals", by Muḥammad ʿAlī Ḥazīn. Most writings in this category deal with horses and were written in India. An example of this type of literature is the *risāla* entitled *Faras-nāma* "Book of horses" by this same author, who had been resident in India.

Poetics. Many authors wrote at length on prosody, rhetoric and rhyme. An early work in this field, whose authorship is attributed, in some manuscripts, to the poet Adīb Ṣābir (d. between 538-42/1143-8 [*q.v.*]

and, in others, to Rashīd al-Dīn Waṭwāṭ (d. 578/1182-3 [*q.v.*]) is a small treatise on metres. It has been published under the title *R.-yi dar bāb-i awzān-i shiʿr-i Arabī wa Fārsī* "T. concerning poetic metres in Arabic and Persian". The author of the *R.-yi ʿarūḍ-i Sayfī* "T. on prosody by Sayfī", Mullā Sayfī Bukhārī (d. probably 909/1503-4), served at the courts of sultan Abū Saʿīd and his successor in Harāt Ḥusayn Mīrzā; his work, completed in 896/1490-1, enjoys a respectable position among writings on Persian prosody. The contemporary Djāmī also composed a *risāla* on Persian prosody, but his better-known work is his treatise on rhyme named variously as *R.-yi ḳawāfī* and *R. dar fann-i ḳāfiya*, still a useful reference work for students of the technical aspects of Persian poetry.

During the 9th/15th and early 10th/16th centuries the acrostic verse (*muʿammā* [*q.v.*]) acquired much popularity, and was elevated to a respectable form of poetry. Prompted by its appeal, many works were written on composing the *muʿammā*, including three *risālas* by Djāmī. Similar treatises were produced by the historian Sharaf al-Dīn Yazdī and by Fuḍūlī (d. 963/1556 or after 988/1580 [*q.v.*]), the Turkish poet who also wrote in Persian, but the most distinguished work here was perhaps the *R. fi 'l-muʿammā* by Mīr Ḥusayn al-Ḥusaynī (d. 904/1499), called Muʿammāʾī, which gained an authoritative status, attracting commentaries in Persian and Turkish.

Miscellaneous. Mention may be made here of a few important *risālas* on miscellaneous topics, such as that of Farīdun b. Aḥmad Sipah-sālār, a biographical account of the leaders of the Mevlewī order and an important aid to the study of the history of Ṣūfism; its author was a high military commander who spent forty years as a disciple of Djalāl al-Dīn Rūmī (d. 672/1273 [*q.v.*]), and undertook the writing of his work soon after the death of his spiritual mentor.

In the field of music, Djamī's name is cited, as also that of Ṣadr al-Dīn Muḥammad (d. 903/1498), son of the astronomer Ghiyāth al-Dīn Manṣūr, who is said to have dedicated his *risāla* to the Tīmūrid prince Ḥusayn Mīrzā. Two other writers on music were Nadjm al-Dīn Kawākibī and Darwīsh ʿAlī, called Čangī-yi Khāḳānī; the former dedicated his *risāla* to the Shībānid ruler ʿAbd Allāh Khān (d. 1005/1597) and the latter to the Astrakhānid monarch Imām-ḳulī Khān (d. 1050/1640).

A work suggestive of social geography is the *R.-yi Rūḥī Anārdjānī*, named after an author who flourished in the second half of the 10th/16th century; composed probably in 992/1585 or 993/1586, it describes the beliefs and customs of the people of Tabrīz recorded by the author from personal observation.

Bibliography: *B.M. Cat. of Persian manuscripts*, London 1879-95; *Cat. of the Persian manuscripts in the library of the University of Cambridge*, Cambridge 1896; *India Office, Cat. of Persian manuscripts*, London 1903-37; *B.N. Paris, Catalogue des manuscrits Persans*, Paris 1905-12; *Descriptive cat. of the Arabic, Persian and Urdu manuscripts in the library of the University of Bombay*, Bombay 1935; *Fihrist-i nuskha-hā-yi khaṭṭī-yi kitābkhāna-yi Dānishkada-yi Adabiyyāt-i Tihrān*, Tehran 1339/1960; *Fihrist-i kitābkhāna-yi Dānishgāh-i Tihrān* (Mishkāt Collection), Tehran 1330-38/1951-9; H. Ethé, in *GI Ph*; Storey; Browne, *LHP*; Riḍāzāda Shafaḳ, *Tarīkh-i adabiyyāt-i Īrān*, Tehran 1321/1942; A.J. Arberry, *Classical Persian literature*, London 1958; Saʿīd Nafīsī, *Tārīkh-i naẓm u nathr dar Īrān wa dar zabān-i Fārsī*, repr. Tehran 1363/1984; idem, *Sarčashma-yi taṣawwuf dar Īrān*, Tehran 1345/1966; Dhabīḥ Allāh Ṣafā, *Tārīkh-i adabiyyāt dar Īrān*, repr. Tehran 1364/1985; idem, *Tārīkh-i ʿulūm-i ʿaḳlī dar tammaddun-i Islāmī*, i, Tehran 1331/1952-3; idem, *Muḳaddama-yi bar taṣawwuf*, Tehran 1974; Rypka *et alii*, *History of Iranian literature*; Ḳāsim Ghanī, *Baḥthī dar taṣawwuf*, Tehran 1340/1962; Annemarie Schimmel, *Mystical dimensions of Islam*, Chapel Hill N.C. 1975; ʿAbd Allāh Anṣārī, *Rasāʾil-i djāmiʿ*, ed. Sulṭān Ḥusayn Tābanda-yi Gunābādī, 3rd ed., Tehran 1347/1968; Muḥammad Djawād Sharīʿat, *Sukhanān-i Pīr-i Harāt*, Tehran 1358/1979; Aḥmad Ghazālī, *Madjmūʿa-yi āthār-i Fārsī*, Tehran 1370/1991; idem, *Sawāniḥ* (*Aphorismen über die Liebe*), ed. H. Ritter, Istanbul 1942; idem, *Risālat al-sawāniḥ fi 'l-ʿishḳ*, ed. Īradj Afshār, in *Madjalla-yi Dānishkada-yi Adabiyyāt, Dānishgāh-i Tihrān*, xiv (1346/1967); Nadjm al-Dīn Kubrā, *R. al-sāʾir al-ḥāʾir*, ed. Masʿūd Ḳāsimī, Tehran 1361/1982-3; Nadjm al-Dīn Rāzī, *R.-yi ʿishḳ u ʿaḳl*, ed. Taḳī Tafaḍḍulī (introd. Mudjtabā Mīnuwī), Tehran 1345/1966-7; Sayf al-Dīn Bākharzī, *Risāla-yi ʿishḳ*, ed. Afshār, in *Madjalla-yi Dānishkada-yi Adabiyyāt, Dānishgāh-i Tihrān*, viii/4 (1340/1961); Mīr Sayyid ʿAlī Hamadānī, *Aḥwāl u āthār u ashʿār* ... (*bā shish risāla az way*), ed. Muḥammad Riyāḍ, Islāmābād 1985; Muḥammad Akhtar Čīma, *Shakhṣiyyat-i ʿirfānī wa ʿilmī-yi Khwādja Muḥammad Pārsā-yi Naḳshbandī Bukhārī*, in *Madjalla-yi Dānishkada-yi Adabiyyāt u ʿUlūm-i Insānī, Dānishgāh-i Firdawsī*, x/3 (1353/1974); Shāh Niʿmat Allāh Walī, *Rasāʾil*, ed. Djawād Nūrbakhsh, ? 1340-51/1961-72, Fakhr al-Dīn ʿIrāḳī, *Kulliyyāt* (prose section), ed. Nafīsī, Tehran 1336/1957-8; Saʿdī, *Kulliyyāt* (prose section), ed. ʿAbbās Iḳbāl, Tehran 1340/1961; Ḳāsim Anwār, *Kulliyyāt* (prose section), ed. Nafīsī, Tehran 1337/1958; Ṣāʾin al-Dīn Turka, *Čahār-dah risāla-yi Fārsi*, ed. Sayyid ʿAlī Musawī Bihbihānī and Sayyid Ibrahīm Dībādjī, Tehran 1335/1956-7; Bihbihānī, *Iṭṭilāʿātī dar bāra-yi Ṣāʾin al-Dīn Iṣfahānī Khudjandī maʿrūf bi Turka*, in *Madjmūʿa-yi khiṭāba-hā-yi nukhustīn kungra-yi taḥḳīḳāt-i Īrānī (2), Dānishkada-yi Adabiyyāt u ʿUlūm-i Insānī, Dānishgāh-i Tihrān*, 1353/1975; Dārā Shikūh, *Muntakhabāt-i āthār*, ed. Sayyid Muḥammad Riḍā Djalālī Nāʾīnī, Tehran 1335/1956-7; Naṣīr al-Dīn Ṭūsī, *Madjmūʿa-yi rasāʾil*, ed. Muḥammad Mudarris Raḍawī, Tehran 1335/1956; idem, *R.-yi imāmat*, ed. Muḥammad Taḳī Dānish-pazhūh, Tehran 1335/1956; idem, *al-R. al-Muʿīniyya* (photocopy), publ. Dānish-pazhūh, Tehran 1335/1956; idem, *R.-yi ḥall-i mushkilāt-i Muʿīniyya* (photo-copy), publ. Dānish-puzhūh, Tehran 1335/1956; idem, *R.-yi bīst bāb dar maʿrifat-i asṭurlāb*, ed. Raḍawī, Tehran 1335/1956; idem, Muḥammad Muʿīn, *Naṣīr al-Dīn Ṭūsī wa zabān u adab-i Pārsī*, in *Madjalla-yi Dānishkada-yi Adabiyyāt, Dānishgāh-i Tihrān*, iii/4 (1335/1956); Ibn Sīnā, *R.-yi ʿishḳ*, ? n.d.; idem, *Rag-shināsī* (*R. dar nabḍ*), ed. Sayyid Muḥammad Mishkāt, Tehran 1330/1951; idem, *Tardjama-yi R.-yi aḳsām-i nufūs* (introd. and text), in *Madjalla-yi Dānishkada-yi Adabiyyāt, Dānishgāh-i Tihrān*, ii/1 (1333/1954); Fakhr al-Dīn Rāzī, *al-R. al-kamāliyya fi 'l-ḥaḳāʾiḳ-i Ilāhiyya*, ed. Muḥammad Bāḳir Sabzawārī, Tehran 1335/1956-7; Afḍal al-Dīn Kāshānī, *Muṣannafāt*, ed. Mīnuwī and Yaḥyā Mahdawī, Tehran 1366/1987; Athīr al-Dīn Mufaḍḍal Abharī, *R. dar manṭiḳ*, ed. Dānish-pazhūh, in *Madjalla-yi Dānishkada-yi Adabiyyāt u ʿUlūm-i Insānī, Dānishgāh-i Tihrān*, xvii/3-4 (1349/1970); Mīr Sayyid Sharīf Djurdjānī, *R. fī taḥḳīḳ al-wudjūd*, ed. Karāmat Raʿnā Ḥusaynī, in *ibid.*; Abū Ḥātim Muẓaffar Isfizārī, *R.-yi āthār-i ʿulwī*, ed. Raḍawī, Tehran 1977; Zayn al-Dīn ʿUmar b. Sahlān Sāwī (Sāwadjī), *R.-yi Sandjariyya fi 'l-kāʾināt al-ʿunṣuriyya*, in *Du risāla dar bāra-yi āthār-i ʿulwī*, ed. Dānishpazhūh, Tehran 1337/1958; Sharaf al-Dīn Muḥammad Masʿūdī Marwazī, *R.-yi āthār-i ʿulwī*, in *ibid.*; *R. dar bāb-i awzān-i shiʿr-i ʿArabī wa Fārsī*, ed. Minuwī, in *Madjalla-yi Dānishkada-yi Adabiyyāt, Dānishgāh-i Tihrān*, ix/3, 1341/1962; Parwīz Nātil Khānlarī, *Yād-dāshtī dar bāra-yi R.-yi ʿarūḍ mansūb bi Adīb Ṣābir yā Rashīd Waṭwāṭ*, in *ibid.*; H. Blochmann, *The prosody of the Persians* (*R.-yi ʿarūḍ-i Sayfī* and *R.-yi ḳāfiya-yi Djāmī*), repr. Calcutta 1972; *R.-yi Farīdūn b. Aḥmad Sipah-sālār*, ed. Nafīsī, Tehran 1325/1946; *R.-yi Rūḥī Anārdjānī*, ed. idem, in *Farhang-i Īrān-Zamīn*, ii (1333/1954). (Munibur Rahman)

3. In Ottoman Turkish.

In Ottoman Turkish, as well as the usual meanings in Arabic and Persian, *risāla* also denoted "a piece of cloth fixed to the front of a dervish's *tādj* or cap" and, by the 19th century, "a booklet or a weekly or monthly journal" (this last often called a *risāla-yi mawḳūta*) (see Redhouse, *Dictionary*, and Pakalın, s.v.).

Given such a strong Persian cultural influence on the Saldjūḳs of Rūm and their successors in Anatolia, it is not surprising that the first manuals for secretaries and collections of model letters written in Anatolia were in Persian, and it was not till the beginning of the 9th/15th century that such works began to appear in Turkish; see H.R. Roemer, *Staatsschreiben der Timuridenzeit*, Wiesbaden 1952, 2-7, and Yaḥyā b. Meḥmed ül-Kātib, *Menāhicü 'l-inşā*, ed. Şinasi Tekin, in *Sources of Oriental languages and literatures* 2, Cambridge, Mass. 1971, 9-11.

The constituent departments of the Ottoman chancery and their staff are examined in the articles DĪWĀN-I HÜMĀYŪN and REʾĪS ÜL-KÜTTĀB, whilst the official literature emanating from these offices is examined in INSHĀʾ. It is sufficient to note further here that a chancery style in Persian developed amongst the Saldjūḳs of Rūm at their court in Konya, from which we have examples of compilations of documents (see O. Turan, *Türkiye Selçukları hakkında resmi vesikalar*, Ankara 1958), and in the other *beylik*s of Anatolia during the 6th/12th and 7th/13th centuries. Ḥasan b. ʿAbd al-Muʾmin Khūyī composed in Persian for his patron the Čoban-oghlu ruler of Ḳastamonu, Muẓaffar al-Dīn Yuluḳ Arslan, and his son Maḥmūd two short works, the *Ghunyat al-kātib* and the *Rusūm al-rasāʾil* (see Turan, *op. cit.*; A.S. Erzi, *Selçukîler devrine âid inşâ eserleri. 1a. Ḥasān b. ʿAbdi 'l-Müʾmin el-Ḫōyī*, Ankara 1963). Hence by the time of the early Ottomans, there was a secretarial class at work for the sultans in their chanceries (see H. İnalcık, *İA*, art. Reîsülküttâb, at 672), and surviving documents seem to indicate that the Ottoman chancery had reached its developed form by the time of Murād II (d. 855/1451).

The secretaries working in the Ottoman chancery (*dīwān ḳalemi*) had to have a thorough education in all branches of literary composition for correspondence, including the correct forms of address for different ranks of persons, and in such skills as calligraphy, all these being part of what were termed the *fünūn-i kitābet we terassul*. Hence for such secretaries, various manuals of secretaryship were composed (for details, see İnalcık, *art. cit.*), including what might be called "quick reference works". These comprised works on epistolographic theory, with model or abstract examples of letters; collections of actual letters and administrative documents; and works which combined both a theoretical section with actual examples. The first type exists only in the Persian used amongst the Rūm Saldjūḳs (see Şinasi Tekin, *op. cit.*, 10), but the remaining two comprise various works written in Turkish.

We know of two chancery manuals in Turkish from the opening decades of the 9th/15th century, the court poet Aḥmed-i Dāʿī's *Terassul* (see İ.H. Ertaylan *Ahmed-i Da'i hayat ve eserleri*, Istanbul 1952, 157-60 with facsimile text 325-8; edition, tr. and annotation by W. Björkman, *Die Anfänge der türkische Briefsammlungen*, in *Orientalia Suecana*, v [1956, publ. 1957]) and Yaḥyā b. Meḥmed ül-Kātib's *Menāhidj ül-inshāʾ*, the oldest surviving copy of which (B.N. suppl. turc 660) dates from 883/1478 (ed. from this ms. by Tekin, *op. cit.*). Others follow in the early 10th/16th century such as the *Gülshan-i inshāʾ* of Maḥmūd b. Adham Amasyawī, composed during the reign of Selīm I (see Bursalî Meḥmed Ṭāhir, *ʿOthmānlî müʾellifleri*, i, 170 M. Ergin, *Bursa kitaplıklarındaki türkce yazmalar arasında*, in *Türk Dili ve Edebiyatı Dergisi*, iv/1-2 [1950], 107-32; Şinasi Tekin, *op. cit.*, 12), and the *Gül-i ṣad berg* by the poet Mesīḥī (d. 918/1512 [*q.v.*]), of which several mss. exist. According to İnalcık, Mesīḥī's collection forms the basis of the *Münsheʾāt* of Ferīdūn Beg (see below) (see İnalcık, *art. cit.*, at 678).

Collections of diplomatic and official documents form the *inshāʾ* or *münsheʾāt* collections, and these also include official and diplomatic *resāʾil* proper, i.e. letters to governors, rulers, etc., which may be in Arabic, Persian or Turkish. The oldest of this mixed type is a *Medjmūʿa-yi münsheʾāt* of Persian and Turkish letters belonging to the periods of Meḥemmed the Conqueror and Bāyezīd II (publ. by N. Lugal and A.S. Erzi, Istanbul 1956; see also Şinasi Tekin, *op. cit.*, 11-12). The celebrated *Münsheʾāt-i selāṭīn* of Ferīdūn Beg (d. 991/1583 [*q.v.*]) was early published (Istanbul 1274-5/1857-9), and an unknown contemporary of his further compiled a similar collection of Arabic, Persian and Ottoman Turkish documents ranging from the time of the Conqueror to that of Murād III, the latest document stemming from 986/1578 (see H. İlaydın and A.S. Erzi, *XVI. asra âit bir münşeât mecmuası*, in *Belleten*, xx, no. 82 [1957], 221-52). The genre continues in the 11th/17th century with the two collections of *münsheʿāt* by the famous *reʾīs ül-küttāb* Sarî ʿAbd Allāh (d. 1070/1660) and even goes up to the 19th century, when Ḥayret Efendi (d. 1241/1826) composed his *Inshāʾ-i Ḥayret*, containing letters and petitions to sultans, grand viziers, *sheykh ül Islāms*, etc. (printed Būlāḳ 1242/1826-7).

Finally, one may mention that the literary form of the *risāle* was also used by Ottoman writers in a more general fashion; one of the most famous of these is the *Risāle* of Ḳoči Beg [*q.v.*], written for sultan Murād IV in 1040/1630.

Bibliography: Given in the article.

(Gönül Alpay Tekin, shortened by the Editors)

RIWĀḲ (A.) or *ruwāḳ*, an Arabic architectural term with a great many meanings. The lexicographers derive it from the root *r-w-ḳ* which has two basic meanings (Ibn Fāris, *Muʿdjam maḳāyīs al lugha*, Cairo 1947-52, i, 460-1). The first one carries the idea of refinement or beauty and the second signifies the part that comes first in something, such as the bull's horns or youth, or the advanced battalion in an army (*rawḳ al-djaysh*), or the anterior section in a space (*rawḳ* or *riwāḳ al-bayt*); according to Ibn Fāris this last definition of the term was the original one from which the other functions developed. This may indicate that *riwāḳ* initially had a spatial connotation an observation that is further confirmed by the multiple uses of the word to designate either the space located forward in a tent or a room or a building, or the space above the first level, also called *samāwa* (which may have been derived from the word for sky *samāʾ*, though it was argued that it was not; cf. Ibn

Sīduh, *al-Mukhaṣṣaṣ*, Beirut, n.d., vi, 4), or, sometimes, an entire tent of a certain type similar to a *fusṭāṭ*, where the only support is a central post (*LA*, xi, 424-5; A. Dessus-Lamare, *Étude sur* Rawq, Riwāq, *et* Ruwāq *et leurs équivalents termes de construction, JA*, ccxxxviii [1950], 338-9). Despite the dicta of the Arabic lexicographers, the term is almost certainly Persian in origin.

Architecturally, the term was mainly applied to that part of a structure that forms its front. Depending on the type of structure, a *riwāḳ* could be a gallery, an ambulatory, a portico, a colonnade, a porch, or a balcony (ʿAbd al-Raḥīm Ghālib, *Mawsūʿat al-ʿimāra al-islāmiyya*, Beirut 1988, 207; H. Crane, *Risale-i-Miʿmariyye, an early seventeenth century Ottoman treatise on architecture*, Leiden 1987, 86). The word was also used to indicate a pre-Islamic architectural form, the Greek stoa, such as the stoa attributed to Aristotle in Alexandria (al-Maḳrīzī, *al-Mawāʿiẓ wa 'l-iʿtibār*, Būlāḳ 1856, i, 159-60). From this last usage was derived the Arabic term for the Stoics, *al-Riwāḳiyyūn* (Buṭrus al-Bustānī, *Muḥīṭ al-muḥīṭ*, Beirut 1867, 840; Dozy, *Suppl.*, i, 572). Dessus-Lamare (340) notes that one of the earliest appearances of *riwāḳ*, in the plural form *arwiḳa*, is in Ibn al-Faḳīh's description of the porticoes in the peristyle houses of Palmyra in the Syrian desert which date to the middle Roman period. A similar use of *riwāḳ* obtained in Islamic palaces and houses, where it also designated the arcades around the courtyard, as well as the specific portico with three doors fronting the T-shaped reception hall, known as *madjlis ḥīrī* after the city of al-Ḥīra [*q.v.*], which was common in ʿAbbāsid residences from Sāmarrā to Egypt (al-Maḳrīzī, *Khiṭaṭ*, i, 386-7; Ḥāzem Sayed, *The development of the Cairene Qāʿa: some considerations,* in *AI*, xxiii [1987], 32-9).

The word *riwāḳ* was also appropriated in religious architecture, especially in the Mashriḳ. The first mosque, the Mosque of the Prophet in Medina, founded in 1/622, originally had an empty courtyard and a simple, covered prayer hall, called *ẓulla*. Subsequent enlargements and alterations, beginning in the reigns of ʿUmar and ʿUthmān, resulted ultimately in surrounding the courtyard with arcades or colonnades, called *arwiḳa*, on all four sides. This development was probably inspired by the peristyle courts in the conquered lands [see MASDJID. I. D. 1]. Eventually, *riwāḳ* became the term most commonly used to designate all arcades in mosques, whether they constitute the porticoes around the courtyard or whether they form the transversal or longitudinal aisles inside the hypostyle prayer halls, such as in al-Muḳaddasī's description of the Umayyad Mosque in Damascus (157-8), and in al-Maḳrīzī's description of al-Azhar Mosque in Cairo (*Khiṭaṭ*, ii, 273-5). The word was also used to designate the entire covered area on one side of a mosque's courtyard, and, at the same time, one row of columns or pillars that carry the arches and make up one component of the covered area (Dessus-Lamare, 342-6). Moreover, a *riwāḳ* need not mean a straight arcade; it could be circular or octagonal in layout, such as the two ambulatories around the *Ḳubbat al-Ṣakhra* [*q.v.*] in Jerusalem, also called *arwiḳa* (al-Muḳaddasī, 169). In the Maghrib, however, *riwāḳ* in the sense of an arcade in a mosque was replaced by at least two other terms, *balāṭa* (pl. *balāṭ* or *balāṭāt*) and *saḳīfa* (pl. *saḳāʾif*) (Ibn Djubayr, *Riḥla*, Beirut 1964, 236-9; Dessus-Lamare, 352-60).

In the Mamlūk period in Egypt and Syria (648-922/1250-1517), *riwāḳ* maintained its meaning in religious architecture, but in residential architecture it gained a new spatial and formal significance (Van Berchem, *CIA*, *Egypt*, i, 43, n. 1; Laila Ibrāhīm and M.M. Amīn, *Architectural terms in Mamluk documents*, Cairo 1990, 57-8). The new application probably developed from one of the term's original definitions, as something akin to *samāwa*, or the upper part of a tent, but it acquired a specific contextual application to one of the particularities of Mamluk residential and palatial architecture. Thus in *waḳf* [*q.v.*] documents, *riwāḳ* was equated with a *ḳāʿa muʿallaḳa* or a raised hall, that is, a living unit located on the second floor (cf. Aḥmad Darrāg, *L'acte de waqf de Barsbay*, Cairo 1963, 16, 19, 35, 37). The plan of a *riwāḳ* was similar to that of a typical Mamlūk *ḳāʿa*, and was composed either of two opposing *īwāns* [*q.v.*] and a space in the middle called *durḳāʿa*, or of one *īwān* and a *durḳāʿa*, with or without dependencies, such as a latrine, cupboards and alcoves for sleeping (ʿAbd al-Laṭīf Ibrāhīm ʿAlī, *Wathīḳat al-Amīr Akhūr Kabīr Karāḳūdja al-Ḥasanī,* in *Madjallat Kulliyyat al-Ādāb* [Journal of the Faculty of Literature] xviii/2 [Dec., 1956], 231-2, n. 41; Mona Zakarya, *Deux palais du Caire médiéval, waqfs et architecture*, Marseilles 1983, 146). This residential application of the term survived into the Ottoman period (Nelly Hanna, *Habiter au Caire aux XVIIe et XVIIIe siècles*, Cairo 1991, 40, 44, 122), although new architectural elements appeared which had the same location and function but different names, such as the Turkish *oda* "room, chamber". Furthermore, another Mamlūk application of the term, which extended its meaning to encompass an entire structure, is still in use today. This is *riwāḳ* as residence hall, one usually reserved either for the members of a Ṣūfī order (al-Maḳrīzī, *Khiṭaṭ*, ii, 428; Dozy, *Suppl.*, i, 572), or for an ethnic or regional group of students, such as in al-Azhar Mosque where numerous *arwiḳa* were built at different times by various sponsors (lists in *EI*[1], Azhar. II and VI). Aside from that, the word is today confined to the domain of religious architecture and is equivalent to the English word gallery, with all its synonyms.

Bibliography: Given in the article.

(NASSER RABBAT)

RIWĀYA (A.), verbal noun of *rawā*, which originally means "to bear, to convey water" and hence signifies "to transmit, relate"; in classical Arabic the noun *riwāya* mostly applies to the technical meaning of transmission of poems, narratives, *ḥadīths*, and also applies to the authorised transmission of books (see below). *Riwāya* may sometimes appear synonymous with *ḥikāya* [*q.v.*], and is used in classical Persian in the sense of a *ḥadīth*; in modern Arabic usage it has become an equivalent of "story, novel, play".

The active participle *rāw^in*, having the general meaning of relater, is of particular significance for the poetry of pre-Islamic and early Islamic times, when the *rāwī* [*q.v.*], as a pupil and assistant of the poet, had to retain, recite and even arrange the verses of his master. This may have served as a model for the later activity and role of transmitters in other fields as well. The intensive form *rāwiya*, closely associated with the name of Ḥammād (d. 155/772) [*q.v.*], and others, such as Khalaf al-Aḥmar (d. *ca.* 180/796 [*q.v.*]), was reserved for the experts in collecting poetry and narrative traditions, who gathered their material from many different informants.

Riwāya generally means transmission through the spoken word, including purely oral retelling as well as recitation from notes and books. With the use of writing for the preservation of knowledge, *riwāya* came to mean, in practice, the transmission of a written text through oral expression. It is this function of *riwāya*, based on the great value attached to oral testimony, which is hard to understand for outsiders and which is most characteristic of Islamic scholarship.

Riwāya in Islamic scholarship. The development of *ʿulūm al-ḥadīth* fostered the methodology of the study of Tradition, describing a number of recognised methods by which traditions could be received (see ḤADĪTH. IV.). The very heart of these methods is the concept of an authorised transmission, as expressed by *idjāza* [*q.v.*], which was meant to guarantee the correctness of the text and its attribution. The *isnād* [*q.v.*] identifies the succession of real or supposed transmitters in the *riwāya* and thus supports the authority of a tradition or any text treated according to these rules. Manuscripts sometimes preserve, under the heading of *riwāya*, and with the confirmation of the *isnād* at the beginning of the text, the names of those who were responsible for the transmission of the whole text from generation to generation.

The reading of a text to a *shaykh* (*ḳirāʾa ʿalā*) was one of the most recommended ways to control the accuracy of a copy (*ʿarḍ*), and to obtain, by attending the session and listening to the reading, the authorisation for further transmission. This highly-formalised practice was widespread in medieval Islam and is documented on many manuscripts in the form of certificates of reading or hearing (*ḳirāʾa, samāʿ*; for a bibliography, see G. Vajda, *Transmission orale*). Few testimonies of this kind are preserved from the 4th/10th century (e.g. M. Muranyi, *Musnad ḥadīt*, 134-5; Y.M. al-Sawwās, *Fihris al-ʿUmariyya*, 691), but internal evidence, *isnād*s and traditions on *ʿilm*—as collected by al-Bukhārī and others—indicate that this method was an established practice even a century before. In any case, simple recitation, from memory or from notes, with the purpose of transmission, goes back to the beginning of the study of Tradition.

Formal transmission by *ḳirāʾa* was, although closely related to the study of Tradition, applied to other genres of literature as well and can be found in all those texts that were treated in academic sessions (*ḥalaḳāt, madjālis*) designed for that purpose. Among these we find, to give but a few examples, editions of and commentaries on the *dīwān*s of poets, such as Thaʿlab's (d. 291/904) *Sharḥ Dīwān Zuhayr b. Abī Sulmā* (Cairo 1363/1944) and Ibn al-Kalbī's (d. 204/819) *Dīwān Shiʿr Ḥātim al-Ṭāʾī wa-akhbāruhu* (ed. ʿĀdil Sulaymān Djamāl, Cairo 1411/1990), works on grammar, such as Sībawayhi's (d. *ca.* 180/796) *Kitāb* (ed. ʿAbd al-Salām M. Hārūn), and philology, such as al-Mubarrad's (d. 286/900) *al-Kāmil fi 'l-adab*, as well as works of *adab* literature, such as al-Muʿāfā b. Zakariyyāʾs (d. 390/1000) *al-Djalīs al-ṣāliḥ* (vol. i ed. Muḥammad Mursī al-Khūlī, Beirut 1981, 147-51).

Riwāya in the light of modern research. Principally, two sorts of inquiry, both indispensable for the study of early Arabic literature, deal with *riwāya*. A common procedure is to reconstruct hypothetically the sources of a work from the study of its *isnād*s, which include, among the *ruwāt* mentioned, earlier authors' names. This approach is to be complemented with the critical study of *riwāyāt* in the sense of transmissions of a work, given in manuscripts and by quotations in later collection-works. This implies the evaluation of variant readings that can be traced to particular transmitters, in contrast to variants produced by copyists. The analysis of *riwāyāt* is thus a principal tool for the study of the textual history of a text-unit or a book, and is equally important for the identification of the origin of a text from the peculiar forms of editing prevalent in early Arabic literature.

At a time when transmission was not yet generally based on complete written versions, that is to say, before 250/864, the "transmitter" could indeed be the writer of a book, editing the material that he had received from his teacher. This is demonstrated, for example, for *al-Kāmil* of al-Mubarrad [*q.v.*] the *Mufaḍḍaliyyāt* [*q.v.*], and several classical books on proverbs [see MATHAL, iii-iii, 5]. In this sense, *riwāya* implies redaction or recension. Closest to original authorship is the teacher's dictation (*imlāʾ*; J. Pedersen, *Book*, 23 ff.), next come the student's notes of the teachings (e.g. M. Muranyi, *Siyar*, 71, 77); a more independent operation is the quest for material apart from personal notes or memory, and even more of redactional work is implied, when the notes of the author are edited (S. Leder, *al-Haiṯam ibn ʿAdī*, 9, 12).

These procedures, and the fact that the methods of transmission were not yet firmly established or consistently practised, furthered the occurrence of divergency among the *riwāyāt* of a text. In so far as they concerned traditions, Islamic scholarship was eager to collect variants, as was done, for example, by Muslim b. al-Ḥadjdjādj in his *Ṣaḥīḥ*. In contrast, the study of variants in various transmissions of a work is an integral part of modern scholarship.

Divergence in *riwāyāt* is quite frequent for old, and even for not so very old texts (from the 3rd/9th century) of different genres (cf. R. Sellheim, *al-Qālī*, 366 f., 371 f.), and appears when a text rendered in quotations is compared to the *riwāya* of the original work (e.g. W. Werkmeister, *Quellenuntersuchungen*, 57-101, 130-1). Variant readings are, in part, due to retelling from memory, but they cannot be understood generally as indicators of oral transmission. As G. Schoeler has explained in detail, notes and notebooks played an important role in early Arabic literature. Books published by their authors in this way, or edited by transmitters on the basis of notes, have to be distinguished from works which were edited by the authors themselves in a completed form.

Variant *riwāyāt* may sometimes owe their existence to different versions given by the author himself during repeated lessons (e.g. Schoeler, *Frage*, 210-12), but in many cases the redactional interference of the editor-transmitters have to be taken into account (for details, see Leder, *op. cit.*, 10 f., ch. 3, 4, 6). Particularly in the case of collections of *isnād*-supported text-units, variants were also produced during the ongoing transmission, even after a work had been edited in a firmly-established form (idem, *Authorship*).

The study of *riwāyāt* may confirm their coherence or uncover divergency. In the latter case, and in particular when divergency is significant, we may become aware that we do not have an "original", but only several *riwāyāt* of a work, as in the case of the *Sīra* by Ibn Isḥāḳ (M. Muranyi, *Ibn Isḥāq's k. al-Maghāzī*). In this sense, *riwāyāt*, and not the authored works purported to be their origin, are the topics for textual criticism.

Bibliography (in addition to the *EI²* arts cited in the text): S. Leder, *Authorship and transmission in unauthored literature*, in *Oriens*, xxxi (1988), 67-81; idem, *Das Korpus al-Haiṯam ibn ʿAdī (st. 207/822), Herkunft, Überlieferung, Gestalt früher Texte der Aḫbār Literatur*, Frankfurt 1991; M. Muranyi, *Das Kitāb al-Siyar von Abū Isḥāq al-Fazārī*, in *JSAI*, vi (1985) 63-97; idem, *Das Kitāb Musnad ḥadīṯ Mālik ibn Anas* in *ZDMG*, cxxxviii (1988), 128-47; J. Pedersen, *The Arabic book*, Princeton 1984; Yāsīn M. al-Sawwās *Fihris madjāmiʿ al-Madrasa al-ʿUmariyya fī Dār al Kutub al-Ẓāhiriyya bi-Dimashk*, Kuwait 1407/1987; G Schoeler, *Die Frage der schriftlichen und mündlichen*

Überlieferung der Wissenschaften im Islam, in *Isl.*, lxii (1985), 201-30; idem, *Weiteres zur Frage der schriftlichen oder mündlichen Überlieferung der Wissenschaften im Islam*, in *Isl.*, lxvi (1989), 38-67; R. Sellheim, *Abū ʿAlī al-Qālī. Zum Problem mündlicher und schriftlicher Überlieferung am Beispiel von Sprichwörtersammlungen*, in *Studien zur Geschichte und Kultur des Vorderen Orients, Festschrift für Bertold Spuler*, ed. H.R. Roemer and A. Noth, Leiden 1981, 362-74; G. Vajda, *De la transmission orale du savoir dans l'Islam traditionel*, in *L'Arabisant*, iv (1975), 2-8, repr. in *La transmission du savoir en Islam (VIIe-XVIIe siècle)*, London, Variorum Reprints 1983; W. Werkmeister, *Quellenuntersuchungen zum Kitāb al-ʿIqd al-farīd des Andalusiers Ibn ʿAbdrabbih (246/860-328/940). Ein Beitrag zur arabischen Literaturgeschichte*, Berlin 1983 (Islamkundliche Untersuchungen 70).

For classical Arabic titles on the technical aspects of *riwāyā*, see ḤADĪTH, IV. In addition may be mentioned al-Rāmahurmuzī's (d. 360/971) *al-Muḥaddith al-fāṣil bayna 'l-rāwī wa 'l-wāʿī* ed. Muḥammad ʿAdjdjādj al-Khaṭīb, Beirut 1391/1971 and Ibn al-Ṣalāḥ's (d. 643/1245) *al-Muḳaddima*, ed. ʿĀʾisha ʿAbd al-Raḥmān Bint al-Shāṭiʾ, Cairo 1974, as well as the titles of al-Khaṭīb al-Baghdādī (d. 463/1071), *al-Kifāya fī ʿilm al-riwāya*, Ḥaydarābād 1357, and *Taḳyīd al-ʿilm*, ed. Youssef Eche, Damascus 1949. Further material concerning *riwāyāt* in Sellheim, *Materialien zur arabischen Literaturgeschichte*, 2 vols., Wiesbaden 1976-87, *Indices* vol. ii, 417; the beginnings of writing for the use of transmission are discussed by Schoeler also in his *Mündliche Thora und Ḥadīṯ, Überlieferung, Schreibverbot, Redaktion*, in *Isl.*, lxvi (1989), 213-51; the different functions of the *ruwāt* named in the *isnād*s are examined by S. Günther, *Quellenuntersuchungen zu den "Maqātil aṭ-Ṭālibiyyīn" des Abū l-Farağ al-Iṣfahānī (gest. 356/967)*, Hildesheim-Zürich-New York 1991 (Arabistische Texte und Studien Bd. 4); for *riwāya* in Ḳurʾān commentaries, see F. Leemhuis, *Origins and early development of the tafsīr tradition*, in A. Rippin (ed.), *Approaches to the history of the interpretation of the Qurʾān*, Oxford 1988, 13-30. (S. LEDER)

RIYĀʾ (A.), or RIʾĀʾ according to Ḳurʾānic orthography (thrice in the expression *riʾāʾ al-nās*, II, 264; IV, 38; VIII, 47), *maṣdar* or verbal noun of form III of *raʾā* "to see", with the meaning of ostentation or hypocrisy.

The concept of *riyāʾ* is made explicit and developed in Tradition; in Wensinck's *Concordance*, i/2, 202-3, there are to be found under *rāʾā* 23 distinct *ḥadīth*s. But the most complete source comes in the *Shuʿab al-īmān* of al-Bayhaḳī, in ch. 45, which deals with pious works devoted to God and the avoidance of ostentation (ed. Zaghlūl, 9 vols., Beirut 1990, v, 325-69, nos. 6805-6988). Al-Bayhaḳī cites other traditions than those listed in Wensinck; in addition, he mentions *logia* relative to *riyāʾ* pronounced by some fifty ascetics and spiritual masters, such as al-Ḥasan al-Baṣrī, Sufyān al-Thawrī, Fuḍayl b. ʿIyāḍ, Dhu 'l-Nūn al-Miṣrī (mentioned thirteen times in this chapter), Sarī al-Saḳaṭī, Sahl al-Tustārī, al-Djunayd, etc. One of the most frequently-used traditions is that *riyāʾ* is part of *shirk*, "associating other things with God", at times qualified as being *aṣghar*, minor, and at others as being *khafī*, hidden. *Riyāʾ* is contrasted with *ikhlāṣ*, which is purity of intention (*niyya*) and whole-hearted sincerity.

The first detailed analysis of *riyāʾ* is by al-Ḥārith b. Asad, better known under his by-name of al-Muḥāsibī (d. 243/857-8 [*q.v.*]), one of al-Djunayd's most senior masters. He devoted a whole book to it, bearing this title, published in *al-Riʿāya li-ḥuḳūḳ Allāh*, ed. ʿAbd al-Ḥalīm Maḥmūd and Ṭāhā ʿAbd al-Baḳī Surūr. This study by al-Muḥāsibī is divided into 43 chapters, supported by 79 traditions; it was to be taken over in complete form by al-Ghazālī (d. 505/1111 [*q.v.*]), but using a different order and adopting a clearer and more useable arrangement, in his *Iḥyāʾ*, in book xxviii, which deals with the reprehensibleness of honours (*djāh*) and ostentation (book viii, especially the second part, divided into 11 *bayān*s, new ed. Beirut in 5 vols., iii, 310-53). Al-Ghazālī cites al-Muḥāsibī here, iii, 325, explicitly, in regard to the controversial question, is a pious work voided when thoughts of ostentation become mixed with the initial purity of intention? (cf. al-Muḥāsibī, *K. al-Riyāʾ*, 193-4). He also cites him at iii, 332-3, on the various responses concerning the appropriate attitude towards the Devil in order to fend him off (cf. *K. al-Riyāʾ*, 160-3).

Al-Muḥāsibī (147-50) and al-Ghazālī (iii, 314-16) group under five categories the "objects of ostentation" (*al-murāʾā bihi*), which they list in the following order: the body; external appearance and dress; speech; action; and the company kept. Both of them being acute psychologists, they stigmatise fiercely the various manifestations of false piety. Some examples may be cited. Through emaciation and pallor, one may give the impression of being devoted to works of mortification and to spending the nights in vigil. One can lead people to believe that one is following Tradition and the example of holy men devoted to God by appearing with dishevelled hair, shorn-off moustache, bowed head when walking, slow and deliberate gestures, with marks of prostrations on the face, wearing coarse clothing such as woollen ones, hitching up one's garments to the calves, shortening the sleeves, wearing dirty and torn clothes and thus trying to pass as a Ṣūfī. Various pieces of hypocritical cant are also noted by them (cf. al-Muḥāsibī, 180-1, and al-Ghazālī, iii, 321), and they describe for us those who assume the appearance of mystics, full of humility, handing out words of wisdom, delivering sermons and exhorting their neighbours, in order to obtain the guilty favours of a woman or a young man (*wa-innamā ḳaṣduhu al-taḥabbub ilā marʾa aw ghulām li-adjl al-fudjūr*).

One should finally note that, if one of the possible senses of *riyāʾ* is seeking the exaggerated consideration of others, and if it can be combatted above all by the ecstatic mystics, the Ṣūfīs, the *ahl al-malāma* or "those incurring blame", attached the same importance to an exaggerated opinion of oneself (*ruʾyat al-nafs*), as al-Sulamī [*q.v.*] showed in his *Risālat al-Malāmatiyya* (tr. Deladrière as *La Lucidité implacable*, Paris 1991).

Bibliography: Given in the article.

(R. DELADRIÈRE)

AL-**RIYĀḌ** (A., pl. of *rawḍa* "garden"), the capital of Saudi Arabia (estimated population, 1993: 1.5 million).

1. *Natural setting*. Al-Riyāḍ is situated in the centre of the Arabian peninsula, in the region of Nadjd [*q.v.*], at 453 km/280 miles from Baḥrayn on the Gulf coast and 1,061 km/660 miles from Djudda [*q.v.*] on the Red Sea coast. The actual site is on a plateau with an average height of 600 m/1,968 ft. made up of sedimentary deposits, mainly calcareous, and of the Jurassic period. This plateau is intersected by valleys with scarped edges, notably that of the Wādī Ḥanīfa to the west, which forms a natural boundary to the region as a whole. A shallower valley, that of the Wādī Baṭḥa, running north-south, has determined the communications layout of the city centre before being covered over and transformed into a main road. To the east, the topography becomes more broken and

rocky hillocks hinder the growth of urbanisation. Like all Nadjd, al-Riyāḍ suffers from a hot desert climate: irregular rainfall, but less than 100 m per annum, average temperatures of 35° C in summer and 11° in winter, very low atmospheric humidity and a liability to violent winds raising sand storms which pose serious problems for traffic and the upkeep of public spaces.

2. *History*. The existence of underground water channels in the alluvial subsoil of the Wādīs Ḥanīfa and Baṭha allowed, well before the coming of Islam, the development of small human settlements, associated with date palm groves. The most notable seems to have been Hadjar, an oasis and market mentioned by Ibn Baṭṭūṭa *ca.* 732/1332 as a place of gardens and vegetation.

But it was only in the 12th/18th century that the name of al-Riyāḍ appears in history with the decline of Hadjar, ruined by local conflicts. The town of al-Dirᶜiyya [*q.v.*] was seized by the Āl Suᶜūd in 1187/1773 and chosen by them as their capital, as also once again after a period of eclipse in *ca.* 1238/1823 by Turkī b. ᶜAbd Allāh Ibn Suᶜūd, the restorer of Saudi power, who incorporated the Khardj [*q.v.*] in the newly-reconstituted state. The Āl Suᶜūd were thus able after this to resist incursions launched against them from the Ḥidjāz by the Egyptians, at the instigation of the Ottomans, in the 1840s. The dissensions after the death of Fayṣal b. Turkī in 1282/1865 ended in the conquest of al-Riyāḍ by the Āl Rashīd of Ḥāʾil [*q.vv.*]. The ensuing period of instability, characterised by revalries and conflicts between the "Turks" (in fact, the Egyptians), the Wahhābīs and the tribes, finally resulted in the recovery of al-Riyāḍ from its Rashīdī governor by ᶜAbd al-ᶜAzīz b. Suᶜūd b. Fayṣal in 1319/1902. After the submission of the Āl Rashīd and the reconquest of al-Ḥasā in 1331/1913, but above all with ᶜAbd al-ᶜAzīz's entry into Mecca on 6 Djumādā I 1343/13 December 1924, the Saudi state as then constituted comprised three-quarters of the peninsula. From then onwards, the evolution of al-Riyāḍ has been indissolubly linked with the political decision-making of the reigning dynasty and the decisions made to maximise the prodigious subterranean resources of the kingdom.

3. *Contemporary developments*. With a population of less than 30,000 in 1929, even in 1949 al-Riyāḍ was only a modest-sized town within fortified walls. In this year, the walls were demolished and the town grew to 83,000 people spread over 5 km². A continuous pattern of growth, strengthened by strong immigration currents, made the population pass the million point during the 1970s, to reach 1.5 million by 1993. At the same time, the surface extension of the agglomeration has reached around 600 km² today, whilst the development plan envisages an area of 1,781 km² including, at the present time, vast land reserves. This exceptional growth has taken place in parallel with the creation of a diversified base of various functions, generating numerous jobs. The industrial sector represents 20% of those employed, and the main zones of activity, whether public or private, lie on the eastern and southern peripheries of the city. But al-Riyāḍ has become above all a city of service enterprises, which has progressively concentrated, to the detriment of Djudda, all the centres of decision making, whether political or economic and financial, at the same time as it has been acquiring hospitals, as well as financial and university institutions, destined to exert an influence over the Arabic and Islamic world.

4. *Urban planning*. After a period of uncontrolled urbanisation, the Saudi authorities have opted for a highly-planned development of their metropolis. This is based on the Doxiadis Plan of 1968, actually put into practice in 1978 by SCET Inter, and contains all the main options for development to be realised in the following decades. These include: an extensive network of expressways which will complete a beltway around the city in order to assist traffic circulation, vital for a highly motorised population (600,000 private cars) which lives mainly in individual habitations. Furthermore, a general application of zoning has brought about the building of university complexes around the periphery, including an Islamic University and the King Saᶜūd University, as also a diplomatic quarter which includes all the diplomatic representatives and the royal and governmental quarter or KCOMMAS. On the southeastern periphery is likewise situated the extensive housing development of ᶜUraydja.

In distinction from other Arab capital cities, al-Riyāḍ has no historic centre and only a few preserved buildings bear witness to the former architectural traditions of Nadjd.

5. *The urban structure*. The administration of al-Riyāḍ is under the shared responsibility of the state and of a municipal administration, set up in 1936, whose powers were much increased in 1977. In 1951, al-Riyāḍ was linked to Dammām by a railway, but air travel remains the most used method of communications; the airport opened in 1952 to the north of the city, now judged inadequate, has been replaced since the 1980s by the King Khālid Airport which covers an area of 225 km². But the main preoccupation of the administration is the permanent challenge of a desert environment, against which it is setting up a double response: the systematic provision of green spaces for the whole agglomeration and an abundant provision of water. In order to satisfy a daily consumption of around 400 litres per head, the underground water levels of the region have been tapped and these resources are supplemented by the bringing in of desalinated water, whilst a growing proportion of the water used is being recycled for watering the numerous parks and gardens.

Bibliography: Ḥ. al-Djāsir, *Madīnat al-Riyāḍ ᶜabr aṭwār al-taʾrīkh*, al-Riyāḍ 1966; H. Pape, *Er Riad, Stadtgeographie und Stadtkartographie der Hauptstadt Saudi-Arabiens*, Bochumer Geographische Arbeiten, Sonderreihe 7, Paderborn 1977; A. Fares, *Mutation d'une ville du désert arabe*, diss. Univ. de Paris XII 1981, unpubl.; P. Bonnenfant, *Riyādh, métropole d'Arabie*, in *Bull. Soc. Languedocienne de Géogr.* (1986), 395-420; C. Chaline and A. Fares, *L'urbanisme contemporain et Riyad, réflexions sur l'aménagement urbain arabe et occidental*, Beirut 1986; Al-Ankary and El-S. Bushara (eds.), *Urban and rural profiles in Saudi Arabia*, Stuttgart 1989; W. Facey, *The Old City of Riyadh*, London 1991. See also AL-ᶜARAB, DJAZIRAT; AL-ḤASA; SUᶜUD, ĀL.

(C. CHALINE)

RIYĀḌĪ, an Ottoman biographer of poets. Mollā Meḥmed, known as Riyāḍī, was the son of a certain Muṣṭafā Efendi of Birge (to the south-east of İzmir) and was born in 980/1572. He was first of all employed as a *müderris*, later became *ḳāḍī* of Ḥaleb (Aleppo) and died on 9 Ṣafar 1054/17 April 1644 in Cairo. He was known as *al-Aṣamm*.

His chief work, *Riyaḍ al-shuᶜarāʾ*, is a biographical dictionary of poets. It is known to have been written by 1018/1609. According to F. Babinger and Niki Gamm, his *Tedhkire* contains 384 names, 8 Ottoman sultans as royal poets and 376 names of non-royal poets in 20 extant manuscripts (see Gamm, *Riyāżī's*

Tezkire as a source of information on Ottoman poets, in *JAOS*, xcix [1979], 643-44). But Namık Açıkgöz gives the number as 424, including royal poets and non-royal poets in 26 extant manuscripts (see his *Riyazü'ş-şu'ara*, AÜDTCF graduate/master's thesis Ankara 1982 unpubl.; idem, *Riyâzî divanı'ndan seçmeler*, Ankara 1990, 28-9; on the differences of the number of the poets in the *Tedhkire*, see Gönül Alpay [Tekin], art. *Riyâzi*, in *İA*, 2nd ed., 1970, 752.

As a *tedhkire* writer, Riyāḍī belongs to a group of writers who tried to cover the entire field of Ottoman poetry. Like them, he also selected such poets whose poetic abilities he valued as good, and he tried to justify his judgements, selecting appropriate examples from their work. From the information at the end of the *Tedhkire*, we understand that Riyāḍī completed his work and presented it to Sultan Aḥmed I in 1018/1609. Following the Introduction, which ends with a *ḳiṭʿa* and a *duʿā* (prayer) addressing Aḥmed I, it is divided into two sections (*rawḍas*). The first section contains information about the Ottoman sultan-poets Meḥemmed Fātiḥ, Bāyezīd II, Selīm I, Süleymān I, Selīm II, Murād III, Meḥemmed III and Aḥmed I. In this section, he gives basic information about the lives of the sultans, such as their father's name, their date of accession, their pen-names and their praisworthy deeds, and he quotes some verses both from their own poems and from those of other poets written about them.

In the second section, the biographical entries are given in alphabetical order by pen-name, and each poet is dealt with in a much more detailed way than in the first section. Here, he mentions the poet's birthplace, if known, and his date of birth and death; his full name; and information about his family, his education, his teachers, his profession; and whether he was a judge or a teacher, or whether he held a high official rank in the government. Occasionally, he refers to poets coming from the ranks of the army. Often he dwells on the unusual characteristics or witty nature of the poets, providing witty and sarcastic hints and anecdotes about their life. Then he makes an evaluation of the poet's poetical ability, giving some quotations from his poetry in order to prove the correctness of his judgement. Finally, he concludes by giving the poet's death date and place, and his burial ground. Sometimes he adds to this information a chronogram commemorating the death. He usually follows this pattern of information (*taʾrīkh*) as far as possible, and if he makes omissions, this stems from a lack of information.

Besides his *Tedhkire*, he compiled a *murattab Dīwān* consisting of 25 *ḳaṣīdas*, the *sāḳī-nāma*, 652 *ghazels*, 17 incomplete *ghazels*, 9 *ḳiṭʿas* (of which one is in Persian), 171 *rubāʿīs*, 89 *maṭlaʿs* and 11 *miyāna* couplets. *Ḳaṣīdas* are dedicated to *inter aliad* ʿOthmān II, Murād IV, the Grand Viziers ʿAlī Pasha and Ḥāfiẓ Aḥmed Pasha, and the Sheykh al-Islām Yaḥyā Efendī.

Riyāḍī's *Dīwān* is known in 30 extant mss., in scattered libraries all over the world. The *Sāḳī-nāma*, his other well-known work, was probably composed between 1011/1603 and 1012/1609, and was written in *mathnawī* form, consisting of 1054 couplets. Having embellished this *Sāḳī-nāma* with scattered *rubāʿīs* in appropriate places, Riyāḍī tries here to describe a drinking party which took place one night, and gives very lively descriptions of the tavern-keeper, the musicians and musical instruments, the wine-cups, the cupbearer, and the psychology of the drunkards. In addition to these, he describes very lively scenes taken from the real life of his time, sc. the beginning of the 11th/17th century.

His third work, the *Dustūr al-ʿamal*, is a Persian-Turkish encyclopaedic dictionary which was probably written *ca.* 1016/1607 and consists of 1050 phrases, expressions and some special usages of Persian phrases, with explanations of the grammatical issues. He also quotes Persian couplets in order to explain how these special usages and grammatical forms were used. Later, the author of the *Farhang-i Shuʿūrī*, Ḥasan Shuʿūrī, wrote an addendum to this work called the *Ḍurūb-i amthāl wa iṣṭilāḥāt* (*Topkapı Sarayı türkçe yazmalar kataloğu*, ii, 48).

Riyāḍī's *Lexicon* has not yet been published, but is accessible in a number of mss., a list of which is given by Babinger, *GOW*, no. 178; another one is in Süleymaniye, Lala İsmail no. 314. On a German translation of an extract from it by V. von Rosenzweig-Schwannau, see *ZDMG*, xx (1866), 439, no. 3.

Besides the above-mentioned works, there are other religious, historical and literary works of his recorded in the bibliographical works and in some historical sources, including 1. *Siyar*; 2. an abbreviated Turkish translation of Ibn Khallikān's *Wafayāt al-aʿyān*; 3. *Ṣaḥāʾif al-laṭāʾif fī anwāʿ al-ʿulūm wa 'l-maʿārif*; 4. *Kashf al-ḥidjāb ʿan wadjh al-ṣawāb*; and 5. *Risālat fī ʿilm al-bayān*.

Bibliography (in addition to references given in the article): Riḍā, *Tedhkire*, 38-9; Belīgh, *Güldeste-i riyāḍ-i ʿirfān ve wefeyāt-i dānish-warān-i nādirān*, 401; Sheykhī Meḥmed, *Wekāyiʿ al-fuḍalāʾ*, 133; ʿUshshāḳī-zāde Seyyid İbrāhīm, *Dheyl-i ʿUshshāḳī-zāde*, fol. 48a; *Sidjill-i ʿothmānī*, ii, 425; J. von Hammer, *GOD*, iii, 367; Bursalī Meḥmed Ṭāhir, *ʿOthmānlī müʾellifleri*, ii, 183-4 (with references); Babinger, *GOW*, 177-8; Namık Açıkgöz, *Divan edebiyatında mektup ve XVII. yüzyıl şâirlerinden Riyâzî'nin iki mektubu*, in *Fırat Üniversitesi Sosyal Bilimler Dergisi*, i/2 (Elâzığ 1987), 7-14; idem, *Riyâzî, hayatı, eserleri ve edebî kişiliği*, Ph.D diss., 3 vols., Fırat Üniversitesi, Elâzığ 1986, unpubl.

(Gönül Alpay Tekin)

AL-**RIYĀḌIYYĀT**, AL-RIYĀḌA (A.), mathematics.

Arabic mathematics are those cultivated by scholars of diverse ethnic origins and of diverse religions, over a period of at least seven centuries—from the 3rd/9th to the 10th/16th centuries—but who all wrote in Arabic and belonged to the civilisation of Islam in its widest sense. Other mathematical activities directly linked to these, in other languages, notably Persian, or those via translations of Arabic texts, e.g. in Latin or Hebrew, will not be treated here. Finally, given the limited space available and the vastness of mathematical activities in Arabic during this period, whose diversity and importance has been shown by recent research, not all the mathematical disciplines and the applied sciences can be treated. Also not considered are the important chapters like those on the projective methods (see R. Rashed, *Géométrie et dioptrique au Xe siècle. Ibn Sahl, al-Qūhī et Ibn al-Haytham*, Paris 1993, pp. CIII-CXXV), and fundamental applications in optics and in astronomy *inter alia*.

But, before tracing the history of these mathematical activities, let us look at the origins of its main traits, and, first, let us go back to Baghdād at the beginning of the 3rd/9th century. It was just at this period and in this milieu—that of the "House of Wisdom" [see BAYT AL-ḤIKMA] at Baghdād—that Muḥammad b. Mūsā al-Khwārazmī [*q.v.*] composed a book whose subject and style were new. It was in effect within these pages that, for the first time, algebra came forward as a distinct and independent mathematical discipline [see AL-DJABR WA 'L-MUḲĀBALA]. The event was crucial, and was seen as such by contemporaries, as much for the style of this mathematics as for the ontology of its object and, even more, the richness of the possibilities which it offered for the future. The style was at the same time algorithmic and demonstrative, and at that time and henceforth, with this algebra, the great potentiality which would suffuse mathematics from the 3rd/9th century onwards, may be glimpsed: the application of mathematical disciplines to each other. In other words, if algebra, through its style and the generality of its object, made these applications possible, the latter, by their number and the diversity of their nature, did not cease to modify the shape of mathematics after the 3rd/9th century.

Al-Khwārazmī's successors progressively undertook the application of arithmetic to algebra, of algebra to arithmetic, from each of these to trigonometry, from algebra to the Euclidian theory of numbers, from algebra to geometry and from geometry to algebra. These applications were always those laying the basic foundations for new disciplines or new chapters. Thus there saw light the algebra of polynomials, combinatorial analysis, numerical analysis, solving of numerical equations, the new elementary theory of numbers and the geometrical construction of equations. Other effects were to result from these multiple applications, such as the separation of the integer Diophantine analysis from rational Diophantine analysis, which became a complete, separate chapter of algebra under the title of "indeterminate analysis".

From the beginning of the 3rd/9th century, the mathematical landscape was no longer the same; it became transformed and its horizons widened. From the outset, we witness an extension of Hellenistic arithmetic and geometry: the theory of conics and that of parallels, projective studies, Archimedean methods for the measurement or curved areas and volumes, isoperimetric problems and geometrical transformations. All these domains became the objects of study for the most famous mathematicians—Thābit b. Ḳurra [*q.v.*] al-Ḳūhī [*q.v.* in Suppl.], Ibn Sahl and Ibn al-Haytham [*q.v.*], amongst others—who managed, through profound researches, to develop them in the same style as their predecessors or modified them when conditions required this. Furthermore, within these Hellenistic mathematical studies themselves, there was a movement towards non-Hellenistic areas.

It is this new landscape which we will now sketch out below in its main traits, without, however, let it be understood, any pretentions to exhaustiveness.

I. Algebra.

1. Al-Khwārazmī's book, which appeared between 197/813 and 215/830 in Baghdād, was the first book in which the term algebra appeared in a title (this was *K. al-Djabr wa 'l-muḳābala*). The two terms here denoted at the same time both the discipline and its operations. Thus for example

$x^2 + c - bx = d \quad$ with $c > d$

the algebra consists in transposing the subtractive expressions

$x^2 + c = bx + d$

and *al-muḳābala* in reducing the similar terms

$x^2 + (c - d) = bx.$

In this book, the author's aim is clear and never before envisaged: to elaborate a theory of equations which can be solved by roots, to which can be brought equally arithmetical and geometrical problems, and thus be of use in calculations, commercial operations, successions, mensuration of land, etc. In the first part of his book, the author begins by defining the basic terms of this theory, which, because of the requirement of resolution by radicals and because of his knowledge of the procedure in this domain, could only involve equations of the first two degrees. It is in fact a question of the unknown quantity, denoted indifferently by "root" and "thing", its square, positive rational numbers, the laws of arithmetic of $\pm$, $x/\div$, $\sqrt{}$, and of equality. The main concepts then introduced by al-Khwārazmī are the equation of the first degree, that of the second degree, associated binomials and trinomials, the normal form, algorithmic solutions and the demonstration of the formula for solutions. The concept of the equation appears in his book to denote an infinite class of problems and not, as with e.g. the Babylonians, in the course of the solution of one or other problem. On the other hand, equations are not presented in the course of the solution of problems to be solved, as amongst the Babylonians and Diophantus, but, from the outset, from the starting-point of primitive terms whose combinations are to yield all the possible forms. Thus, immediately after having given the basic terms, he gives the following six types:

$ax^2 = bx, \quad ax^2 = c, \quad bx = c, \quad ax^2 + bx = c,$
$ax^2 + c = bx, \quad ax^2 = bx + c.$

He then introduces the idea of normal form, and requires the reduction of each of the preceding equations to the normal corresponding form. From this there results, in particular, for the trinomial equations

$x^2 + px = q, \quad x^2 = px + q, \quad x^2 + q = px.$

He then passes to the determination of the algorithmic formulae for solutions.

He demonstrates equally the different formulae for solutions not algebraically but by means of the idea of the equality of areas. He was apparently inspired by a quite recent knowledge of Euclid's *Elements*, translated by his colleague in the "House of Wisdom", al-Ḥadjdjādj b. Maṭar.

Al-Khwārazmī then undertakes a brief study of some properties of the application of the elementary laws of arithmetic to the most simple algebraic expressions. Thus he studies products of the type

$(a \pm bx)(c \pm dx) \quad$ with $a, b, c, d \in \mathbb{Q}_+$.

In order to better grasp the idea which he made for himself of the new discipline, as well as its richness, one only needs to compare his book with the ancient mathematical works; it is equally necessary to examine the impact which he had on his contemporaries and his successors. It is only then that one can place him within his true historical dimension. Now, one of the features of his book, essential to our minds, is that he immediately stirred up a current of algebraic research. The bio-bibliographer of the 4th/10th century al-Nadīm [*q.v.*] already provides us with a long list of al-Khwārazmī's contemporaries and successors who followed his path of research. Amongst others, there figure Ibn Turk, Sind b. ʿAlī, al-Saydanānī, Thābit b. Ḳurra, Abū Kāmil, Sinān b. al-Fatḥ, al-Ḥubūbī and Abu 'l-Wafāʾ al-Būzadjānī [*q.v.*].

In this time and immediately after it, one witnesses essentially an extension of researches already dealt with by al-Khwārazmī: the theory of quadratic equations, algebraic calculus, the indeterminate analysis and application of algebra to the problems of successions, divisions of inheritances, etc. Research into the theory of equations was itself pursued along many paths. The first was that already blazed by al-Khwārazmī himself, but this time with an improvement of his proto-geometrical proofs; this is the way pursued by Ibn Turk, who without adding anything new, resumed a discussion of the proof which was nore closely-argued (see Aydin Sayili, *Logical ecessities in mixed equations by ʿAbd al-Ḥamīd ibn Turk and he algebra of his time*, Ankara 1962, 145 ff.). More im-ortant was the way taken a little later by Th̲ābit b. Ḳurra. This last went back in effect to the *Elements* of Euclid, in order at the same time to establish al-Kh̲ʷārazmī's proofs on more solid geometrical foun-ations and also to render geometrically the equations f the second degree. Th̲ābit was moreover the first to istinguish clearly between the two methods, lgebraic and geometrical, regarding which he tried to how that they both led in the end to the same result, .e. to the geometrical interpretation of algebraical rocedures.

But this geometrical rendering by Th̲ābit of al-Kh̲ʷārazmī's equations shows itself as particularly mportant, as will be seen, for the development of the heory of algebraic equations. Another rendering, ery different, took place at almost the same time, which was also to be fundamental for the development f this same theory: that of the problems of geometry n algebraic terms. Al-Māhānī, who was, in effect, a ontemporary of Th̲ābit's, only began by rendering ertain biquadratic problems of Book X of the *Elements* nto algebraic equations but also a solid problem, that iven in Archimedes' *The sphere and the cylinder*, as a ubic equation (see below).

One witnesses, moreover, following al-Kh̲ʷārazmī, he extension of algebraic calculation. This was, erhaps, the main theme of research and the one most hared together by the algebraists following him. Thus one began by extending the very terms of lgebra as far as the sixth power of the unknown, as nay be seen with Abū Kāmil and Sinān b. al-Fatḥ. The latter defined, furthermore, the powers nultiplicatively (see on the powers, in Sinān, Rashed, *Entre arithmétique et algèbre. Recherches sur l'histoire des nathématiques arabes*, Paris 1984, 21 n. 11), thus differ-ng from Abū Kāmil, who gave an additive definition. But it was the latter's work in the field of algebra which marks both the epoch and the history of algebra in his *K. al-D̲j̲abr wa 'l-muḳābala*). As well as the ex-ension of algebraic calculation, he brought within his ook a new chapter in algebra, indeterminate analysis r Diophantine rational analysis.

2. One would not be able to understand anything about the history of algebra if one did not underline he contributions of the two currents of research which leveloped in the period considered above. The first was concerned with the study of irrational quantities, whether on the occasion of a reading of Book X of the *Elements*, or, in some manner, independently. One nay mention, amongst many other mathematicians who participated in this work of research, the names of al-Māhānī, Sulaymān b. ʿIṣma, al-Kh̲āzin [*q.v.*], l-Ahwāzī, Yuḥannā b. Yūsuf and al-Hās̲h̲imī.

The second current was stimulated by the transla-ion into Arabic of the *Arithmetics* of Diophantus, and, notably, by the algebraical reading of this latter book. Now this *Arithmetics*, even if it was not a work of lgebra in al-Kh̲ʷārazmī's sense, nevertheless con-ained techniques of algebraic calculation, effective for he time: substitutions, eliminations, changes of variables, etc. It was the object of commentaries by nathematicians like Kusṭā b. Lūḳa [*q.v.*], its ranslator in the 3rd/9th century, and al-Būzad̲j̲ānī a entury later, but these texts are unfortunately lost.

Whatever may have been the case, this progress in lgebraic calculation, whether by its extension to ther domains or by the mass of technical results ob-ained, resulted finally in a renewal of the discipline tself. A century and a half after al-Kh̲ʷārazmī, the Bag̲h̲dād mathematician al-Karad̲j̲ī [*q.v.*] conceived another project of research: the application of arithmetic to algebra, i.e. the systematic study of the application of the laws of arithmetic and of certain of its algorithms to the algebraic expressions and, in particular, to polynomials. This is exactly this calculation on the algebraic expressions of the form

$$f(x) = \sum_{k=-m}^{n} a_k x^k \qquad m, n \in Z_+$$

which became the main object of algebra. The theory of algebraic equations is certainly always present, but occupies only a modest place amidst the preoccupations of the algebraists. One realises that, from this time onwards, the books about algebra undergo modifications not only in their content but also in their organisation.

Without going over here the history of six centuries of algebra let us illustrate this impact of al-Karad̲j̲ī's work by turning to another of his successors of the 6th/12th century, al-Samawʾal (d. 569/1174), who integrated within his book on algebra, *al-Bāhir*, the main writings of al-Karad̲j̲ī. Al-Samawʾal began by defining, quite generally, the idea of algebraic powers (he writes, after having noted in a table on both sides of x^o, the powers, "If the two powers are on one and the other side of the unity from one of them we count in the direction of the unity the number of elements of the table which separate the other power from the unity, and the number is on the same side as the unity. If the two powers are of the same side of the unity, we count in the direction opposite to the unity"; see *Al-Bāhir en algèbre d'al-Samawʾal*, ed., introd. and notes by S. Ahmad and R. Rashed, Damascus 1972), and, thanks to the definition $x^o = 1$, gives the rule equivalent to $x^m x^n = x^{m+n}$, m, n $\in$ Z. There then follows the study of the arithmetical operations on monomials and polynomials, notably those of the divisibility of polynomials, as also the approximation of the fractions by the elements of the ring of the polynomials. Thus one has, e.g.

$$\frac{f(x)}{g(x)} = \frac{20x^2 + 30x}{6x^2 + 12} \approx \frac{10}{3} + \frac{5}{x} - \frac{20}{3x^2} - \frac{10}{3x^2} + \frac{40}{x^3} + \frac{40}{3x^4} + \frac{20}{x^5} - \frac{80}{3x^6} - \frac{40}{x^7},$$

in which al-Samawʾal obtains a kind of limited development

$h(x) = \frac{f(x)}{g(x)}$, which is only valid for x when it is sufficiently great.

One then finds the extraction of the square root of a polynomial with rational coefficients. But, for all these calculations regarding polynomials, al-Karad̲j̲ī had devoted a work, at present lost but fortunately cited by al-Samawʾal, in which he exerts himself to establish the formula of the binomial development and the table of coefficients

$$(a+b)^n = \sum_{k=0}^{n} \binom{n}{k} a^{n-k} b^k \qquad n \in N.$$

It is on the occasion of the demonstration of this formula that one witnesses the appearance, in an archaic form, of the complete, finite induction as a procedure of the proof in mathematics. Amongst the means of auxiliary calculation, al-Samawʾal gives, following al-Karad̲j̲ī, the sum of the different arithmetical progressions, with their proof:

$$\sum_{k=1}^{n} k,\ \sum_{k=1}^{n} k^2,\ \left(\sum_{k=1}^{n} k\right)^2,\ \sum_{k=1}^{n} k\ (k+1),\ \ldots$$

There then follows the reply to the following question: "How can the multiplication, division, addition, subtraction and extraction of roots be used in regard to irrational quantities?" (see Ahmad and Rashed, *Al-Bāhir en algèbre* ... , 37). The reply to this question led al-Karadjī and his successors to read in an algebraic fashion and in a deliberate manner, Book X of the *Elements*, to extend to infinity the monomials and binomials given in that book and to propose rules for calculation, amongst which one finds explicitly formulated the one of al-Māhānī

$$\left(x^{\frac{1}{n}}\right)^{\frac{1}{m}} = \left(x^{\frac{1}{m}}\right)^{\frac{1}{n}} \quad \text{and} \quad x^{\frac{1}{m}} = (x^n)^{\frac{1}{mn}}$$

with others like the following

$$\left(x^{\frac{1}{m}} \pm y^{\frac{1}{m}}\right)^m = y\left(\left(\frac{x}{y}\right)^{\frac{1}{m}} \pm 1\right)^m.$$

There is also to be found an important chapter on rational diophantine analysis and another one on the resolution of systems of linear equations with several unknowns. Al-Samawʾal gives a system of 210 linear equations with ten unknowns.

Starting from the works of al-Karadjī, one sees a trend of research in algebra taking shape, a recognisable tradition regarding the content and organisation of each of the works.

At the heart of this trend, the chapter on the theory of algebraic equations, properly speaking, without being central had nevertheless made some progress. Al-Karadjī himself considered, like all his predecessors, quadratic equations. Certain of his successors tried, however, to study the solution of cubic equations and equations of the fourth degree. Thus al-Sulamī in the 6th/12th century concentrated on cubic equations in order to find a solution through radicals (*al-Muḳaddima al-kāfiya fī ḥisāb al-djabr wa 'l-muḳābala*, Collection Paul Sbāt, no. 5, ff. 92b-93a). This text of his bears witness to the interest of the mathematicians of his time, brought to bear on the solution by radicals of cubic equations.

3. The algebraists who were also arithmeticians concentrated on the solution by radicals of equations, and sought to justify the algorithm of the solution. One even encounters sometimes, in the same mathematician (e.g. Abū Kāmil), two justifications, one geometrical and the other algebraical. For the cubic equation, they lacked not only solutions by radicals but also the justification of the algorithm of solution, since the solution could not be constructed by means of a ruler and a compass. Recourse to conic sections, explicitly meant to resolve cubic equations, rapidly followed the first algebraic renderings of solid problems. We have mentioned, from the 3rd/9th century, al-Māhānī and Archimedes' lemma (see how al-Khayyām traced in this manner this story in his famous treatise of algebra, in *L'œuvre algébrique d'al-Khayyām*, Aleppo 1981, 11-12); other problems, such as, notably, the trisection of an angle, the two means and the regular heptagon, were very soon rendered in algebraic terms. But, on the other hand, confronted by the difficulty mentioned before, and thus by that in resolving cubic equations by means of radicals, the mathematicians of the 4th/10th century like al-Khāzin, Ibn ʿIrāḳ, Abu 'l-Djūd b. al-Layth and al-Shannī, were led to render this equation in the language of geometry (*op. cit.*, 82-4). They thus found themselves applying to the study of this equation a technique already at that time currently used for the examination of solid problems, i.e. the intersection of conic curves. It is precisely in this that there is found the main reason for the geometricisation of the theory of algebraic equations. This time, contrary to Thābit b. Ḳurra, people did not try to render geometrically algebraic equations in order to find the geometrical equivalent of the algebraic solution already obtained, but tried to determine, with the help of geometry, the positive roots of the equation which people had not been able to achieve otherwise. The attempts of al-Khāzin, al-Ḳūhī, Ibn al-Layth, al-Shannī, al-Bīrūnī, etc., are in this way partial contributions, up to the conception of the project by ʿUmar al-Khayyām (439-526/1048-1131 [*q.v.*]): the elaboration of a geometrical theory of equations of the third degree or less. For each of these types of equations, al-Khayyām found a construction of a positive root through the intersection of two conics. Thus e.g. in order to solve the equation "a cube is equal to a certain number of sides plus a number", i.e.

$$(*) \qquad x^3 = bx + c \qquad b, c > 0,$$

al-Khayyām only considered the positive root. In order to determine it, he proceeded by means of the intersection of a half-parabola and a branch of an equilateral hyperbola.

In order to elaborate upon this new theory, al-Khayyām saw himself as endeavouring the better to conceive and to formulate the new relationships between geometry and algebra. One needs to remember that, in this regard, the fundamental concept introduced by him was that of the unit of measurement which, suitably defined in relation to that of dimension, allowed the application of geometry to algebra. Now this application led al-Khayyām in two directions, which may seem at first view paradoxical: at a time when algebra was then identifying itself with the theory of algebraic equations, this last seemed henceforth, though still timidly, to be transcending the gap between algebra and geometry. The theory of equations was above all a place where algebra and geometry met, and, more and more, ways of reasoning and analytical methods. In his treatise, al-Khayyām arrived at two remarkable results which historians normally attribute to Descartes: a general solution for all equations of the third degree through the intersection of two conics, and, on the other hand, a geometrical calculation made possible by the choice of the unit of length, whilst nevertheless remaining, contrary to Descartes, faithful to the rule of homogenity.

One should note that al-Khayyām did not stop there, but tried to give an approximate numerical solution for the cubic equation. Thus in his work called *On the division of a quadrant of a circle* (*op. cit.*, 80), in which he announced a new project on the theory of equations, he got as far as an approximate numerical solution by means of trigonometrical tables.

4. Up to recently, it was thought that the contribution of the mathematicians of this time to the theory of algebraic equations was limited to al-Khayyām and his work. But in fact, it was nothing like this at all. Not only did al-Khayyām's work inaugurate a complete tradition, but, moreover, it became deeply transformed hardly half-a-century after his death.

Two generations after him, we come across one of the most important works of this current of ideas, Sharaf al-Dīn al-Ṭūsī's treatise *On equations* (see *Sharaf l-Dīn al-Ṭūsī. Oeuvres mathématiques. Algèbre et géométrie u XIIe siècle*, ed., tr. and comm. R. Rashed, Paris 986, 2 vols.). This treatise (*ca.* 565/1170) brings forvard some very important innovations in regard to he work of al-Khayyām. Contrasted with that of his redecessor, al-Ṭūsī's approach was not global and lgebraic but local and analytical. This radical hange, particularly important in the history of lassical mathematics, was able to construct a bridge etween classical algebra and the prehistory of initesimal methods (see *op. cit.*).

But al-Ṭūsī's example is sufficient to show that the heory of equations not only became transformed after he time of al-Khayyām, but never stopped getting urther and further away from the search for solutions y means of radicals; it thus finished by covering a ast domain, and included sectors which later were to elong to analytical geometry or simply to analysis.

I. Combinatorial analysis.

Combinatorial activity began by revealing itself as uch, but in a dispersed manner, amongst the inguists on one side and the algebraists on the other. t was only later that the meeting between the two curents was to take place and that combinatorial analysis vas to present itself as a mathematical tool applicable o the most various situation: linguistic, philosophical, nathematical, etc. It is then that one can speak of ombinatorial activity in Arabic. Already in the th/9th century, this activity can be found amongst he linguists and philosophers who set forth problems onnected with language, within three spheres in paricular: phonology, lexicography and, finally, crypography [see MU^cAMMĀ]. The name of al-Khalīl b. Aḥmad (99-169/718-86 [*q.v.*]) marks the history of hese three disciplines. He had explicit recourse, for is founding of Arabic lexicography, to a calculation f arrangements and combinations. For his lexicon, e began by calculating the number of combinations, vithout repeating, of the letters of the alphabet, taken to r, with r = 2, ..., 5, and then the number of pernutations in each group of r letters. In other terms, e calculated

$$A_n^r = r! \binom{n}{r}$$

being the number of letters of the alphabet, $1 < r \leq 5$.

Now this theory and method calculation used by al-Khalīl recurs later in the writings of most of the lexcographers. They further were utilised in crypography, developed from the 3rd/9th century onvards by al-Kindī and then, at the end of that same entury and the beginning of the next one, by nguists like Ibn Waḥshiyya [*q.v.*], Ibn Ṭabāṭabā, mongst several others. In the practice of their iscipline, the cryptographers had recourse to the honological analysis of al-Khalīl, calculation of letter equency in Arabic and that of permutations, ıbstitutions and combinations.

At the same time as this important activity in the eld of combination, the algebraists, as we have seen, ad put forward and demonstrated, at the end of the th/10th century, the rule for the formation of the rithmetical triangle for the calculation of binomial oefficients. Al-Karadjī (Ahmad and Rashed, *al-Bāhir algèbre d'al-Samaw'al*, 104 ff.) had in effect laid down e rule

$$(*) \qquad \binom{n}{r} = \binom{n-1}{r-1} + \binom{n-1}{r}$$

The algebraists applied the new rules in their calculations. E.g. al-Samaw'al (*ibid.*, Ar. text 232, introd. 77 ff.) set forth ten unknowns and searched for a system of linear equations with six unknowns. He then combined these ten figures, considered as symbols of these unknowns—today they would be called indices—six to six, and thus obtained his system of 210 equations. He likewise proceeded by means of these combinations to find the 504 conditions of compatibility within this system. All these combinatorial activities, these rules discovered in the course of linguistic research and algebraical studies, made up the concrete conditions for the emergence of this new chapter in mathematics. It remains, however, to note that the act of this chapter's birth consisted in the explicitly combinatorial interpretation of the arithmetical triangle, and of its law of formation, i.e. the rules given by al-Karadjī as tools of calculation. It would be excessive to think that the algebraists had not seized upon this interpretation fairly quickly. We are, on the contrary, more and more convinced that this interpretation had been noticed by the algebraists but that they had no stimulus for them to give an explicit formulation of it. The combinatorial interpretation is certainly there, very probably before the 7th/13th century, as we are now able to show thanks to a text of the mathematician and philosopher Naṣīr al-Dīn al-Ṭūsī (597-671/1201-73 [*q.v.*]), until the present time unknown. A reading of this text (see Rashed, *Métaphysique et combinatoire*, forthcoming) shows that he knew of this interpretation, that he put it forward in a totally natural fashion as something readily admitted and expressed it in a terminology which is to be found, either wholly or in part, in his successors. In the course of this study, he was led to calculate the number of combinations of n distinct objects taken k to k, with $1 \leq k \leq n$. Thus he calculated for n = 12

$$\sum_{k=1}^{n} \binom{n}{k}, \text{ and used in the course of his calculation}$$

the equality $\binom{n}{k} = \binom{n}{n-k}$.

One should now note that al-Ṭūsī had given in his book on arithmetic (*Djawāmi^c al-ḥisāb*, ed. A.S. Saidan, in *al-Abḥāth*, xx/2-3 [1967], 141-6) the arithmetical triangle and its law of formation. He calculated an expression equivalent to

$$\sum_{k=0}^{m} \binom{m}{k} \binom{n}{p-k} \quad \text{with } 1 \leq p \leq 16,\ n = 12.$$

After al-Ṭūsī at least, and very probably before him, one will continually come across the combinatorial interpretation of the arithmetical triangle and its law of formation, as well as the ensemble of elementary rules of combinatorial analysis. As we have shown, towards the end of this same century and at the beginning of the next, 8th/14th, Kamāl al-Dīn al-Fārisī (d. 719/1319 [*q.v.*]), in a treatise on the theory of numbers, returned to this interpretation and established the use of the arithmetical triangle for the numerical orders, i.e. the result which one normally attributed to Pascal. In effect, in order to form the represented numbers (see Rashed, *Matériaux pour l'histoire des nombres amiables et de l'analyse combinatoire*, in *Jnal. for the Hist. of Arabic Science*, vi [1982], 209-78; idem, *Nombres amiables, parties aliquotes et nombres figurés aux XIIIe et XIVe siècles*, in *Archive for Hist. of Exact Science*, xxviii [1983], 107-49, repr. in *Entre arithmétique et algèbre* ..., 259-99), al-Fārisī set up a relationship equivalent to

$$F_p^q = \sum_{k=1}^{p} F_k^{q-1} = \binom{p+q-1}{q}$$

with F_q^p the pth represented number of the order q, $F_1^q = 1$.

But at the same time as al-Fārisī was busy with his studies in Persia, Ibn al-Bannāʾ (cf. reference above) (d. 721/1321) was at work in Morocco on combinatorial analysis. In effect he went back to the combinatorial interpretation and took up the rules which were known before his time, notably those of the arrangement of n distinct objects, without repetition, r to r, of permutations and combinations without repetition:

$$(n)_r = n(n-1) \dots (n-r+1)$$

$$(n)_n = n\,!$$

$$\binom{n}{r} = \frac{(n)_r}{r!},$$

relations which were readily deducible from the expression (*) given by al-Karad̲j̲ī three centuries before.

Al-Fārisī and Ibn al-Bannāʾ not only followed after al-Ṭūsī but used the greater part of the technical lexicon already adopted by the latter. With these authors, combinatorial analysis no longer had as its domain algebraic or linguistic applications only, but the most varied domains, e.g. metaphysics, i.e. every domain in which scholars were concerned with the partition of a set of objects.

This concept and this chapter were to survive up the present time. Scholars were to continue to treat combinatorial analysis in different works of mathematics, and independent works were also to be devoted to it. Thus later mathematicians like al-Kās̲h̲ī (d. 840/1436-7 [*q.v.*]) (see his *Miftāḥ al-ḥisāb*, ed. A.S. al-Dimirdās̲h̲ and M.Ḥ. al-Ḥifnī, Cairo 1967, 73-4, where he gives the law for the composition of the arithmetical triangle), Ibn al-Malik al-Dimas̲h̲ḳī (*al-Isʿāf al-atamm*, ms. Dār al-Kutub, Cairo, Riyāḍa 182; he gives the arithmetical triangle and explains its formation at pp. 46-7; in the triangle, al-Dimas̲h̲ḳī places the names given as powers in abbreviation), al-Yazdī (*ʿUyūn al-ḥisāb*, ms. Süleymaniye, Istanbul, Hazine 1993; see the arithmetical triangle at fols. 1 and 20a-b) and Taḳī ʾl-Dīn Ibn Maʿrūf, to give only a few names, treat of it.

III. Numerical analysis.

Compared to Hellenistic mathematics, Arab mathematics offered a much more important number of numerical algorithms.

Algebra, in effect, did not just furnish the indispensable theoretic means for this development—even if this were only the study of polynomial expressions and the combinatorial rules—but also a vast domain of the application of these techniques: the methods developed for determining the positive roots of numerical equations. Research in astronomy, from another aspect, led mathematicians to take up the problems of the interpolation of certain trigonometric functions. Some of these methods, as will be seen, were applied in quantitative research in optics. The result, as may be already guessed, was an appreciable quantity of numerical techniques which it is impossible to describe here in a limited number of pages.

Yet more important than the number of numerical algorithms brought to light by the mathematicians was the discovery of new axes of research, such as the mathematical justification for algorithms, the comparison between the different algorithms with the aim of choosing the best one and, to sum it all up, conscious reflection on the nature and limit of approximations.

There remains now the task of going back to the main domains which divided up numerical analysis: the extraction of roots from an integer number and the resolution of numerical equations on one hand, and methods of interpolation on the other.

As far back as one can go in the history of mathematics, one meets algorithms meant for extracting square or cube roots, some of which are of Hellenistic origin, whilst other are probably of Indian origin, and, finally, yet others are owed to the Arab mathematicians themselves.

Thus amongst the formulae which circulated at the opening of the 4th/10th century, two should be particularly noted, each called "the conventional approximation":

$$\sqrt{N} = a + \frac{r}{2a+1} \text{ and } \sqrt[3]{N} = a + \frac{r}{3a^2+3a+1}.$$

At the end of this same century, the mathematicians possessed, according to all the evidence, the so-called Ruffini-Horner method. Kūs̲h̲iyār b. al-Labār [*q.v.*] applied this algorithm, in all appearance of Indian origin, in his Arithmetic (*Kūshyār ibn Labbān, principles of Hindu reckoning*, tr. M. Levey and M Petruck, Madison 1965; see the Arabic text established by A. Saidan, in *Rev. de l'Inst. de manuscrit. arabes*, Cairo [May 1967], 55-83). We know at present that Ibn al-Hayt̲h̲am (d. after 431/1040) not only knew of this algorithm but endeavoured himself to give a mathematical justification for it. It is his general approach which we will set forth here, but in a different language.

Let the polynomial with integer coefficients f(x) and the equation be

$$(*) \qquad f(x) = N$$

Let s be a positive root of this equation, and let us suppose (s_i) $i \geq 0$ (indice) to be a series of positive integers such that the partial sums are

$$\sum_{i=0}^{k} s_i \leq s;$$

one says that the s_i are parts of s.

It is evident that the equation

$$f_0(x) = f(x+s_0) - f(s_0) = N - f(s_0) = N_0$$

has as its roots those of equation (*) diminished by s_0.

For i > 0, let us form by recurrence the equation

$$f_i(x) = f(x + s_0 + \dots + s_i) - f(s_0 + \dots + s_i)$$
$$= [N - f(s_0 + \dots + s_{i-1})] - [f(s_0 + \dots + s_i) - f(s_0 + \dots + s_{i-1})]$$
$$= N_i;$$

thus. e.g. for i = 1, we have

$$f_1(x) = f(x + s_0 + s_1) - f(s_0 + s_1)$$
$$= [N - f(s_0)] - [f(s_0 + s_1) - f(s_0)]$$
$$= N_0 - [f(s_0 + s_1) - f(s_0)] = N_1.$$

The method used by Ibn al-Hayt̲h̲am and justified by him, which is found in Kūs̲h̲iyār and is called Ruffini-Horner, furnishes an algorithm which allows us to obtain the coefficients of the ist equation from the starting point of the coefficients of the (i − 1)^{t} equation. The principal idea behind this method lies here (see Rashed, *Les mathématiques infinitésimales entre le IXe et le XIe siècle*, ii, London 1994).

The ensemble of methods and of preceeding results gained at the beginning of the 5th/11th century, then comes up again not only in the contemporaries of these mathematicians but in the majority of the treatises on arithmetic, henceforth very numerous

.mongst many others, one may mention those of al-Iasawī, successor to Kūshiyār (see H. Suter, *Über das 'echenbuch des Alī ben Ahmed el-Nasawi*, in *Bibl. Mathematica*, 3. Folge, vii [1906-7], 113-19; see also *'asawī-nāma*, ed. Abu 'l-Ḳāsim Ghurbānī, Tehran 973, 65 ff. of the Pers. introd. to the edition, and ff. of the photocopy of the published Arabic text), of Iaṣīr al-Dīn al-Ṭūsī (*Djawāmiᶜ al-ḥisāb*, *op. cit.*, 44 ff., 266 ff.), of Ibn al-Khawwām al-Baghdādī (*al-'awāᵓid al-bahāᵓiyya fi 'l-ḳawāᶜid al-ḥisābiyya*, ms. B.L.)r. 5615, fols. 7b-8a), of Kamāl al-Dīn al-Fārisī (*Asās 'l-ḳawāᶜid*, ed. M. Mawaldi, diss. Univ. of Paris III, 989), etc.).

The mathematicians were in possession of the rithmetical triangle and the binomial formula from e end of the 4th/10th century onwards, and were not) meet any major difficulties for the generalisation of e preceeding methods and for the formulation of the lgorithm in the case of the root n^{th}. Similar at-mpts, unfortunately lost, already existed in the th/11th century with al-Bīrūnī and al-Khayyām. It as in his contribution of 568/1172-3 that al-amawᵓal (see above) not only applied the so-called uffini-Horner method for the extraction of the root th of a sexagesimal integer, but also formulated a ear concept of approximation. By "to approx-nate", the 6th/12th century mathematician meant:) know a real number by means of a series of known umbers with an approximation which the athematician could render as small as he wished. It then a case of measuring the divergence between the rational n^{th} root and a series of rational numbers. fter having defined the concept of approximation, l-Samawᵓal began by applying the so-called Ruffini-Iorner method for the example

$$f(x) = x^5 - Q = 0,$$

ith Q = 0; 0, 0, 2, 33, 43, 36, 48, 8, 16, 52, 30.

Now this method was to survive till the 6th/12th entury and was to be found in many other treatises n "Indian arithmetic", as they were called at that me. It was to be met yet later in the predecessors of l-Kāshī, in al-Kāshī himself and also in his suc-essors. To take only the example of al-Kāshī, in his *'ey to arithmetic* he resolves

$$f(x) = x^5 - N = 0,$$

ith N = 44 240 899 506 197.

If now we come to the extraction of the irrational th root from an integer, we encounter an analogous tuation. In his *Treatise on arithmetic*, al-Samawᵓal ives in effect a rule for approximating by means of actions the not integer part of the irrational root of n integer, and gives expressions equivalent to

$$x^n = N;$$

$$x' = x_0 + \frac{N - x_0^n}{\left[\sum_{k=1}^{n-1} \binom{n}{k} x_0^{n-k}\right] + 1},$$

e.

$$x' = x_0 + \frac{N - x_0^n}{(x_0 + 1)^n - x_0^n}.$$

It is thus a case of the generalisation of what athematicians have called "conventional approx-nation". We find it later amongst so many athematicians, such as al-Ṭūsī and al-Kāshī. It was, rthermore, with the aim of improving these approx-nations that there was conceived in an explicit man-er the decimal fractions, as the example of al-amawᵓal shows (see above).

It was in the course of the search for the extraction of the nth root and the problems of approximation that the first theory of decimal fractions was elaborated in the 6th/12th century. The first known exposition of these fractions was given by al-Samawᵓal in 569/1172-3, and it shows that the algebra of polynomials is essential to the invention of these fractions. These last survive in the work of al-Kāshī (*Miftāḥ al-ḥisāb*, 79, 121; P. Luckey, *Die Rechenkunst bei Ǧamšīd b. Masᶜūd al-Kāšī*, Wiesbaden 1951, 103. Cf. Rashed, *Entre arithmétique et algèbre*, 132 ff.), and appear again in the works of the mathematician and astronomer of the 10th/16th century Taḳī 'l-Dīn Ibn Maᶜrūf (*Bughyat al-ṭullāb*, fol. 131a ff.) and al-Yazdī (in his *ᶜUyūn al-ḥisāb* one cannot fail to discern a certain familiarity with decimal fractions, although he preferred to make calculations with sexagesimal fractions and ordinary ones, see e.g. fols. 9b, 49a-b) in the 11th/17th century. Several indications suggest that they were transmitted to the West before the middle of that century, and they are named in a Byzantine manuscript brought to Venice in 1562 as "Turkish" fractions (al-Kāshī introduced a vertical stroke which separated the fractional part; this representation is found amongst Western scholars like Rudolff, Apian and Cardan). The mathematician Mīzrahī (b. Constantinople 1455) used the same sign before Rudolff. As for the Byzantine ms., it reads, notably, "The Turks make multiplications and divisions of fractions by means of a special procedure for calculation. They introduced their fractions when they came to rule our land here". The example given by this writer leaves no possible doubt about the fact that he is speaking here of decimal fractions. Cf. H. Hunger and K. Vogel, *Ein byzantinisches Rechenbuch des 15. Jahrhundert*, Vienna 1963, 32 (problem no. 36).

Let us finally note that the methods of interpolation were already, long before this, applied by astronomers. From the 3rd/9th century onwards, they sought out methods for formulating and using astronomical and trigonometrical tables and, on this occasion, came back to methods of interpolation in order to improve them.

The numerousness of methods at the end of the 4th/10th century has set a new problem for research: how is one to compare these different methods amongst themselves, in order to be able to choose the most efficacious for the tabular function being studied? Al-Bīrūnī himself began to take this problem for his own consideration and to place side-by-side different methods for the case of the cotangent function, with its difficulties which are connected with the existence of the poles. In the next century, al-Samawᵓal was even more explicitly concerned with this task.

The mathematicians not only pursued their researches on these methods, but equally applied themselves to other disciplines like astronomy. Thus Kamāl al-Dīn al-Fārisī had recourse to one of them—called *ḳaws al-khilāf*, the arc of the difference—in order to establish the table of refractions. But this method called " the arc of the difference", applied by al-Fārisī at the opening of the 8th/14th century, goes back to al-Khāzin in the 4th/10th century, and was to be taken up again in the 9th/15th century by al-Kāshī in his *Zīdj Khāḳānī*. This last example shows well that, for this chapter, it is a case of stages in an identical tradition.

IV. Indeterminate analysis.

The emergence of indeterminate analysis or, as it is called today, Diophantine analysis, as a distinct chapter of algebra, goes back to al-Khʷārazmī's successors, notably Abū Kāmil, in his book written *ca.* 266/880.

Abū Kāmil aimed in his *Algebra* not at lingering any

longer over a diffuse exposition, but at giving a more systematic exposition in which would be highlighted, as well as the problems and algorithms for solution, the methods. He did, it is true, treat in the last part of his book of the 38 Diophantine problems of the second degree and of the systems of these equations, four systems of linear, indeterminate equations, other systems of linear, determinate equations, an ensemble of problems which led to arithmetical progressions and a study of these last (this part occupies fols. 79a-110b). This whole corresponds to the double aim fixed by Abū Kāmil: to resolve indeterminate problems, and on the other hand to resolve by means of algebra the problems treated at that time by arithmeticians. One should note that it is in his *Algebra* that one meets for the first time in history—to the present writer's knowledge—an explicit distinction between determinate problems and indeterminate one. Now the examination of these 38 Diophantine problems does not only reflect this distinction; it further shows that these problems do not follow each other haphazardly but according to an order meticulously indicated by Abū Kāmil. The first 25 thus belong to one and the same group, for which the author gives a necessary and sufficient condition in order to determine rational, positive solutions. Let us take just two examples. The first problem in this group (fols. 79a-b) may be set forth as

$$x^2 + 5 = y^2.$$

Abū Kāmil proposes to give two solutions amongst, as he himself proclaims, an infinity of rational solutions.

Another example of the same group is problem no. 19 (fols. 87a-b), which may be set forth as

$$8x - x^2 + 109 = y^2.$$

Abū Kāmil then considers the general formula

$$(1) \qquad ax - x^2 + b = y^2.$$

He then gives the sufficient condition for determining the rational, positive solutions of the preceding equation. This last may be expressed as

$$y^2 + \left(\frac{a}{2} - x\right)^2 = b + \left(\frac{a}{2}\right)^2;$$

let us now suppose that $x = \frac{a-t}{2}$, and one has

$$(2) \qquad y^2 + \left(\frac{t}{2}\right)^2 = b + \left(\frac{a}{2}\right)^2,$$

and the problem is thereby brought to dividing up a number, the sum of two squares, into two other squares: problem no. 12 of the same group, already resolved by Abū Kāmil. Let us suppose in effect that

$$b + \left(\frac{a}{2}\right)^2 = u^2 + v^2,$$

with u and v rational numbers. Abū Kāmil poses

$$y = u + \tau$$
$$t = 2(k\tau - v);$$

he substitutes in (2) and finds the values of y, t and finally x. Thus he knows that, if one of the variables can be expressed as a rational function of the other, or, in other terms, if one can have a rational parametrage, one has all the solutions; whereas, on the other hand, if the sum brings us to an expression whose root cannot be got round, one does not have any solution. In other terms, unknown to Abū Kāmil, a curve of the second degree of the genus 0 does not have any rational point, or is bi-rationally equivalent to a straight line.

The second group is made up of 13 problems—nos. 26-38—which do not allow a rational parametrage; or, this time again in a language unknown to Abū Kāmil, they define all curves of genus 1. Thus e.g. problem no. 31 (fol. 92b) may be set out as

$$x^2 + x = y^2,$$
$$x^2 + 1 = z^2,$$

which defines a skew quartic, a curve of $\mathbf{A}^3$ of genus 1.

The third group of indeterminate problems is made up of systems of linear equations, as e.g. in no. 3[?] (fols. 95a-b) which may be set out as

$$x + ay + az + at = u,$$
$$bx + y + bz + bt = u,$$
$$cx + cy + z + ct = u,$$
$$dx + dy + dz + t = u.$$

This interest brought to indeterminate analysis which led in the end to Abū Kāmil's contribution gave rise to another occurrence: the translation of Diophantus' *Arithmetic*.

In contrast to Diophantus, al-Karadjī does not give well set-out lists of problems and their solutions, but he organises his exposition in his *al-Badīʿ* around the number of terms which make up algebraic expressions and around the difference between their powers. E.g. he considers in successive paragraphs:

$$ax^{2n} \pm bx^{2n-1} = y^2, \quad ax^{2n} + bx^{2n-2} = y^2,$$
$$ax^2 + bx + c = y^2.$$

This principle of organisation was to be moreover borrowed by his successors. It is thus clear that al-Karadjī had as his aim the giving of a systematic exposition. On the other hand, he carried further the task begun by Abū Kāmil, which consisted in elucidating as far as possible the methods for each class of problems. In his *al-Fakhrī*, al-Karadjī brought forward only the principles of this analysis, indicating that it bore notably upon the equation

$$ax^2 + bx + c = y^2, \qquad a, b, c \in \mathbf{Z},$$

in which the trinomial in x is not a square, in order to pass finally to the different classes of problems, of which the greater part are indeterminate.

Al-Karadjī studied many other problems, notably *double equality*. Let us set simply forth the problem

$$(*) \qquad x^2 + a = y^2, \quad x^2 - b = z^2,$$

which defines a curve of the genus 1 in $\mathbf{A}^3$.

His successors did not merely comment upon his work, but endeavoured to advance further along the road traced out by him; thus in his *al-Bāhir*, al-Samawʾal commented on *al-Badīʿ* and studies equations of form:

$$y^3 = ax + b,$$

and considered then the equation

$$y^3 = ax^2 + bx.$$

We cannot here follow the works of al-Karadjī's successors on rational Diophantine analysis, but can only note that, in the future, this last was to form part of every algebraic treatise of any importance. Hence in the first half of the 6th/12th century, al-Zandjānī borrowed the greater part of al-Karadjī's problems and of the first four books of the Arabic translation of Diophantus. Ibn al-Khawwām set before himself certain Diophantine equations, including Fermat's equation for n = 3 [$(x^3 + y^3 = z^3)$], as also Kamāl al-Dīn al-Fārisī in his great commentary on the latter's work on algebra. This interest and these works on indeterminate analysis were followed unabatedly up to the 11th/17th century with al-Yazdī and, *contra* what the historians of this chapter say, it was not to end with al-Karadjī.

The translation of Diophantus' *Arithmetica* was not just essential to the development of rational Diophantine analysis as a chapter of algebra, but contribute[d] equally to the development of the integer Diophantine analysis as a chapter, not only of algebra but also of the theory of numbers. In the 4th/10th century, in effect, there took place for the first time the constituting of this chapter, probably thanks to algebra but also in opposition to it. In practice, the study of Diophantine problems was tackled by requiring on one side the obtaining of integer solutions, and on the other side the proceeding by proofs of the type of Euclid in the arithmetical books of the *Elements*. It is this combination, explicit for the first time in history—for the numerical domain, restricted to positive integer numbers interpreted as segments of straight lines, for algebraic techniques and for the requirement of giving a proof in the pure Euclidean style—which allowed the inauguration of this new Diophantine analysis. The translation of Diophantus' *Arithmetica* furnished these mathematicians, it will readily be understood, less with methods than with certain problems in the theory of numbers which were formulated there, which they did not hesitate to systematise and to examine for themselves, contrary to what can be seen in Diophantus. Such are e.g. the problems of the representation of a number as a sum of squares, congruent numbers, etc. In brief, one meets here the beginning of the new Diophantine analysis in the sense in which it was to be discovered and developed later by Bachet de Méziriac and Fermat (see Rashed, *L'analyse diophantienne au Xe siècle*, in *Rev. d'Histoire des Sciences*, xxxii/3 [1979], 193-222, repr. in *Entre arithmétique et algèbre*, 195-225).

Hence in an anonymous text of the 4th/10th century, after having introduced the basic concepts for studying Pythagorean triangles, the author posed questions about the integers which can be the hypotenuses of these triangles, i.e. the integers which one can represent as the sum of two squares. In particular, he announced that every element of the sequence of primitive Pythagorean triplets was such that the hypotenuse is of one or other form: 5 (mod 12) or 1 mod (12). However, he noted—like al-Khāzin after him—that certain numbers of this sequence—e.g. 49 and 77— are not hypotenuses of such triangles. This same author also knew that certain numbers of the form 1 (mod 4) could not be hypotenuses of primitive right-angled triangles.

Al-Khāzin later studied several problems involving numerical right-angled triangles, as well as the problems of congruent numbers, and set forth the following theorem:

if a *is a given natural integer, the following conditions are equivalent*

1. the system (*) admits of a solution;
2. there exist a pair of integers (m, n) such that $m^2 + n^2 = x^2$,
   $2\,mn = a$;

in these conditions, a has the form $2\,uv(u^2 - v^2)$.

It is in this tradition that scholars equally brought to bear the study of the representation of an integer as the sum of squares. Thus al-Khāzin devoted several propositions of his treatise to the study of this.

It was likewise these mathematicians who, as the first persons to do so, posed the question of impossible problems, such as the first case of Fermat's theorem. It has long been known that al-Khudjandī tried to prove that "the sum of two cubic numbers is not a cube". According to al-Khāzin (Rashed, *op. cit.*, 220), al-Khudjandī's proof was defective. A certain Abū Djaʿfar also tried to prove the same proposition. This is equally defective. Even if one has had to wait till Euler for the establishing of this proof, the problem never ceased, despite everything, to preoccupy the Arab mathematicians who, later, enunciated the impossibility of the case $x^4 + y^4 = z^4$.

Research on the integer Diophantine analysis, and notably, on numerical right-angled triangles, did not stop with its initiators of the first half of the 4th/10th century. Quite the opposite: their successors took it up again and in the same spirit, in the course of the second half of that century and at the beginning of the next one, as the examples of Abu 'l-Djūd Ibn al-Layth, al-Sidjzī and Ibn al-Haytham attest. Later on, others followed, in one manner or another, this line of research, such as Kamāl al-Dīn Ibn Yūnus.

V. The classical theory of numbers.

The contribution of the mathematicians of the time to the theory of numbers was not limited to integer Diophantine analysis. Two other currents of research, starting from two distinct points, led to the extension and renewal of the Hellenistic theory of numbers. The first current had as its source, but also as its model, the three arithmetical books of Euclid's *Elements*, whilst the second came within the line of Neo-Pythagorean arithmetic, as it appears in the *Arithmetical introduction* of Nicomachus of Gerasa. It is in Euclid's books that there is to be found a theory of parity and a theory of the multiplicative properties of integers: divisibility, prime numbers, etc. For Euclid, an integer is however represented by a segment of a line, a representation essential for the proof of the propositions. If the Neo-Pythagoreans shared this concept of the integers and were in a wide sense attached to the study of these same properties, or of properties derived from these last, there remains the fact that, by their methods and their aims, they were to be distinguished from Euclid. Whereas the latter proceeded by proofs, these others had as their only means that of induction. Moreover, for Euclid, arithmetic had no other aim beyond itself, whilst for Nicomachus it had philosophical goals and even psychological ones. This difference in method was clearly perceived by Arab mathematicians like Ibn al-Haytham. For those of the time, it was clearly a question thus of a difference between the methods of proof and not between the aims of arithmetic. From this time, it may be understood that, despite a marked preference for the Euclidean method, mathematicians, even those of Ibn al-Haytham's importance, reached the point of proceeding, in certain cases by induction, in accordance with the problem posed; it is thus that Ibn al-Haytham discusses the "Chinese remainder theorem" and Wilson's theorem. Furthermore, if the mathematicians of the first rank, and in accordance with certain philosophers like Avicenna, neglected the philosophical and psychological goals assigned to arithmetic by Nicomachus, other mathematicians of lower rank, philosophers, physicians, encyclopaedists, etc., interested themselves in this arithmetic. The history of this last is thus based on that of the culture of a scholar within Islamic society over the centuries, and goes well beyond the scope of the present article.

Research into the theory of numbers in the Euclidean and Pythagorean sense began early, before the end of the 3rd/9th century. It was contemporary with the translation of Nicomachus' book by Thābit b. Ḳurra (d. 288/901) and his revision of the translation of Euclid's *Elements*. It was in fact Thābit who set in motion this research into the theory of numbers, whilst elaborating the first theory of amicable numbers. This fact, known to historians since the last century thanks to the work of F. Woepcke (*Notice sur une théorie ajoutée par Thâbit Ben Qorrah à l'arithmétique spéculative des Grecs*, in *JA*, ser. 4, ii [1852], 420-9, in which the author gives a résumé of Thābit's opusculum), only had its full significance realised very recently, when the existence has been established of a complete tradition, begun by Thābit in the most pure of Euclidean styles, to end some centuries later in al-Fārisī (d. 719/1319), thanks to the application of algebra to the study of the first elementary arithmetical functions. This tradition is marked out by many names: al-Karābisī, al-Anṭākī, al-Ḳubaysī, Abu 'l-Wafā' al-Būzadjānī, al-Baghdādī, Ibn al-Haytham, Ibn Hūd, al-Karadjī, etc., to cite only a few of them. Clearly, one cannot in these few pages devoted to the theory, claim to give a detailed description. An attempt will simply be made to sketch this movement just mentioned.

At the end of Book IX of the *Elements*, Euclid gives a theory of perfect numbers and shows that the number $n = 2^p (2^{p+1} - 1)$ is a perfect one, i.e. equal to the sum of its own divisors, if $(2^{p+1} - 1)$ is a prime number. He does not mention the theory of amicable numbers, however. Thābit b. Ḳurra then decided to construct this theory. He set forth and proved, in pure Euclidean style, the most important theorem of amicable numbers up to this time, the one which bears his name today.

Let us note $\sigma_0(n)$ as the sum of the aliquot parts of the integer n, and $\sigma(n) = \sigma_0(n) + n$ as the sum of the divisors of n; and let us recall that two integers a and b are called amicable if $\sigma_0(a) = b$ and $\sigma_0(b) = a$.

Thābit b. Ḳurra's theorem:

For $n>1$, let $p_n = 3.2^n - 1$, $q_n = 9.2^{2n-1}-1$; if p_{n-1}, p_n, and q_n are prime numbers, then $a = 2^n p_{n-1} p_n$ and $b = 2^n q_n$ are amicable numbers.

It is with the algebraists, in particular, that the calculation of pairs of amicable numbers other than those given by Thābit was undertaken, i.e. (220, 284). Thus one finds in al-Fārisī in the East, in the milieu of Ibn al-Bannā' in the West, and in al-Tanūkhī and many other 7th/13th century mathematicians, the pair (17296, 18416), known under the name of Fermat's. Al-Yazdī was to calculate later the pair known as that of Descartes (9363584, 9437056).

The famous physicist and mathematician Kamāl al-Dīn al-Fārisī wrote a work in which he tried deliberately to prove Thābit's theorem in an algebraic fashion. This action obliged him to conceive the first arithmetical functions and to bring into being a complete preparation which led him to set forth for the first time the fundamental theorem of arithmetic. Al-Fārisī furthermore developed the combinatorial means required for this study, and thereby, a complete programme of research into figured numbers. In brief, it is a case this time of the elementary theory of numbers, just as one finds it later in the 11th/17th century.

Al-Fārisī examined the procedures of factorisation and the calculation of aliquot parts as functions of the number of prime factors. The most important result on this level was without any doubt the identification between the combinations and the figured numbers. Hence everything was then in place for the study of arithmetical functions. A first group of propositions concerned $\sigma(n)$. Even if al-Fārisī only in fact treated of $\sigma_0(n)$, it must be agreed that he recognised σ as a multiplicative function. Amongst the propositions of this group, one finds in particular:

(1) if $n = p_1 p_2$, with $(p_1,p_2) = 1$, then

$$\sigma_0(n) = p_1\sigma_0(p_2) + p_2\sigma_0(p_1) + \sigma_0(p_1)\sigma_0(p_2),$$

which shows that he knew the expression

(2) if $n = p_1 p_2$, with p_2 a prime number and $(p_1,p_2) = 1$, then

$$\sigma_0(n) = p_2\sigma_0(p_1) + \sigma_0(p_1) + (p_1),$$

(3) if $n = p^r$, p is a prime number, then

$$\sigma_0(n) = \sum_{k=0}^{r-1} p^k.$$

These three propositions have been until now attributed to Descartes.

(4) Finally, he tried, but without succeeding, as one may readily understand, to establish a formula valid for the case where $n = p_1 p_2$, with $(p_1, p_2) \neq 1$.

A second group includes several propositions bearing on the proposition $\tau(n)$: the number of divisors of n.

(5) if $n = p_1 p_2 \dots p_r$, with $p_1, \dots, p_r$ as distinct prime factors, then the number of parts of n denoted $\tau_0(n)$ is equal to

$$1 + \binom{r}{1} + \dots + \binom{r}{r-1},$$

a proposition attributed to the Abbé Deidier.

(6) if $n = p_1^{e_1} p_2^{e_2} \dots p_r^{e_r}$, with $p_1, p_2, \dots p_r$ as distinct prime factors, then

$$\tau(n) = \prod_{i=1}^{r} (e_i + 1)$$

and $\tau_0(n) = \tau(n) - 1$, a proposition attributed to John Keresy and to Montmort.

Al-Fārisī finally proved Thābit b. Ḳurra's theorem He had simply in effect to prove that

$$\sigma(2^n p_{n-1} p_n) = \sigma(2^n q_n) = 2^n[p_{n-1} p_n + q_n]$$
$$= 9.2^{2n-1}(2^{n+1}-1).$$

If, with the works on amicable numbers, the mathematicians sought also to characterise this class of integers, whilst studying perfect numbers, they followed the same goal. We know through al-Khāzin that in the 4th/10th century people were thinking about the existence of odd perfect numbers—a problem still unsolved (al-Khāzin wrote "This question is put to those who wonder to themselves [about abundant, deficient and perfect numbers] whether there exists a perfect number amongst the odd numbers or not"; cf. the Arabic text published by A. Anbouba, *Un traité d'Abū Jaʿfar al-Khāzin sur les triangles rectangles numériques*, in *Jnal. for Hist. of Arabic Science* iii/1 [1979], 134-78, see 157). At the end of the same century and at the beginning of the next one, al-Baghdādī obtained some results concerning these same numbers (see Rashed, *Nombres amiables* ..., 26 of repr.). Thus he gives

if $\sigma_0(2^n) = 2^n - 1$ is a prime number, then $1 + 2 + \dots + (2^n - 1)$ is a perfect number, a rule attributed to the 17th century mathematician J. Broscius. Al-Baghdādī's contemporary Ibn al-Haytham (see Rashed, *Ibn al-Haytham et les nombres parfaits*, in *Historia Mathematica*, xvi [1989], 343-52) tried, as the first, to characterise this class of even perfect numbers, by endeavouring to prove the following theorem:

if n is an even number, the following conditions are equivalent:

(1) if $n = 2^p(2^{p+1}-1)$, with $(2^{p+1}-1)$ a prime number then $\sigma_0(n) = n$;

(2) if $\sigma_0(n) = n$, then $n = 2^p(2^{p+1}-1)$, with $(2^{p+1}-1)$ a prime number.

It is known that (1) is none other than IX-36 of Euclid's *Elements*. Ibn al-Haytham then tried further to prove that every even perfect number is of Euclidean form, a theorem which was definitively to be e ıblished by Euler. It should be noted that Ibn al-Iaytham, no more than Thābit b. Ḳurra with regard ɔ amicable numbers, did not try, for perfect umbers, to calculate any other numbers beyond ıose known and handed down by tradition. This task f calculation was to be that of mathematicians of ›wer rank, closer to the tradition of Nicomachus of ;erasa, such as Ibn Fallus (d. 637/1240) and Ibn al-Aalik al-Dimashḳī (see Rashed, *op. cit.*), amongst ıany others. Their writings tell us that mathematiians knew at this time the first seven perfect umbers.

One of the axes of research into the theory of umbers was thus the characterisation of numbers: micable, equivalent (the numbers equivalent to a are ıe numbers defined by σ_0^{-1} (a)) and perfect. In these onditions, one should not be astonished that ıathematicians came back to the prime numbers in rder to move on to a similar task. This is exactly 'hat Ibn al-Haytham did in the course of his solution ɔ the problem called that of "the Chinese reıainder" (see Rashed, *Théorie des nombres et analyse ɔmbinatoire*, in *Entre arithmétique et algèbre*, 238). He 'ished in fact to solve the system of linear conruences

$$x \equiv 1 \pmod{m_i}$$
$$x \equiv 0 \pmod{m_p},$$

with p a prime number and $1 < m_i \leq p-1$.

In the course of this study, he gives a criterion for etermining prime numbers, the theorem called Vilson's:

if $n > 1$, the two following conditions are equialent:

(1) n is a prime number
(2) $(n - 1)! \equiv -1 \pmod{n}$.

The study of this system of congruences is partially ɔund once more in Ibn al-Haytham's successors in ıe 6th/12th century, e.g. al-Khilāṭī in Arabic and ibonacci in Latin (see Rashed, *op. cit.*).

One could add, to these areas of the theory of umbers in Arabic mathematics, a multitude of esults which can be classed within the line of Vicomachus' arithmetic, developed by arithmeticians r algebraists, or simply for the needs of other techiques such as the construction of magic squares or rithmetical games. One might note here the sums of owers of natural integers, polygonal numbers, roblems of linear congruence, etc. A considerable umber of results are involved there, which extend or rove what was known previously, but these cannot e detailed here (one only has to read the arithmetical 'orks of arithmeticians like al-Uḳlīdisī, al-Baghdādī, l-Umawī, etc., of algebraists like Abū Kāmil, al-ūzadjānī, al-Karadjī and al-Samawʾal, and of hilosophers like al-Kindī, Ibn Sīnā, al-Djūzdjānī, tc., amongst a hundred or so of others).

'I. Infinitesimal determinations.

The study of asymptotic behaviour and initesimal objects represents a substantial part of ıathematical research in Arabic. From the 3rd/9th entury onwards, mathematicians began work in hree main domains: the calculation of infinitesimal reas and volumes; the squaring of lunules, areas and olumes extrema at the time of examination of the soperimetric problem.

At the beginning of this same century, al-Ḥadjdjādj . Maṭar had translated Euclid's *Elements*. It was in Book X of this work that the mathematicians knew the ımous proposition for this calculation, which may be 'ritten: Let a and b be two known magnitudes, a > and b > 0, such that a<b; and let $(b_n)_{n \geq 1}$ a seuence such that, for every n, one has

$$b_n > \frac{1}{2}\left(b - \sum_{k=1}^{n-1} b_k\right),$$

then there exists n_0 such as, for $n > n_0$, one has

$$\left(b - \sum_{k=1}^{n} b_k\right) < a.$$

Two works of Archimedes were also translated into Arabic: the measuring of the circle, Κύκλου μέτρησις, and concerning the sphere and the cylinder, Περί σφαίρας καὶ κυλίνδρου. The translation of the first was known to al-Kindī and the Banū Mūsā (*q.v.* and see the art. s.v. in *Dict Scientific Biogr.*, 1970, i, 443-6; also the treatise of the Banū Mūsā cited below), whilst that of the second was revised by their collaborator Thābit b. Ḳurra. As for Archimedes' other books, i.e. on the spiral, on conoids and spheroids, on the squaring of a parabola, and on method, there is nothing to show that they were known to the Arab mathematicians. This last remark is especially important since Archimedes introduced into his book *On conoids and spheroids* the idea of lower and higher integral sums, which then completed the method of exhaustion.

The translation of Archimedes' two treatises, as well as of Eutocius' commentary (these texts were twice translated in the course of the 3rd/9th century, see Rashed, *Al-Kindī's Commentary on Archimedes'* The Measurement of the Circle, in *Arabic Science and Philosophy, a Historical Journal*, i, 3 no. 1, [1993], 7-53), and *Archimède dans les mathématiques arabes*, in I. Mueller (ed.), *Essays around the mathematical sciences of the Greeks*, Apeiron 1991), clearly correspond to the demands of al-Kindī, the Banū Mūsā and their school. The Banū Mūsā comprised three brothers, Muḥammad, Aḥmad and al-Ḥasan, who were all concerned with geometry—and notably, with conic sections—as much as with mechanics, music and astronomy. These three wrote at Baghdād in the first half of the century the first Arabic work in this sphere. Their treatise, called *On the measurement of plane and spherical figures*, did not merely launch Arabic research into the determination of areas and volumes but also remained the basic text for Latin science after it was translated in the 12th century by Gerard of Cremona. The treatise in fact falls into three sections. The first concerns the measurement of the circle; the second, the volume of the sphere; whilst the third deals with the classical problems of the two means and the trisection of the angle.

The brothers showed that the area of a circle is equal to S = r. c/2 (r being the radius and c the circumference). But in this proof, they did not compare S to S' > S and then to S" < S, but supposed that S = r. c/2 and compared c to a c' > c and to a c" < c, being thus content to compare the lengths.

The brothers then explained Archimedes' method for the approximate calculation of π, and brought out its general significance. They showed in effect that this method goes back to the construction of two adjacent sequences $(a_n)_n \geq 1$ and $(b_n)_n \geq 1$ — $a_n < b_n$ sequences for all n — and which converge towards the same limit 2rπ. This involves two sequences which can be set out as:

$$a_n = 2nr \sin \pi/n \qquad b_n = 2nr \operatorname{tg} \pi/n.$$

They remarked that "it is possible with the help of this method to attain any required degree of precision" (see Rashed, *op. cit.*). With a method analogous to that applied in the case of the area of a circle, they determined the area of the lateral surface of a sphere.

The contemporaries and successors of the Banū

Mūsā pursued research in this sphere very actively. Thus al-Māhānī did not only comment upon Archimedes' book *On the sphere and the cylinder*, but began on the determination of the segment of a parabola; this text of his has not, however, survived.

The brothers' collaborator, Thābit b. Ḳurra, contributed to this area of research on a large scale. He composed successively three treatises: one on the area of the segment of a parabola, one on the volume of a revolving paraboloid and one on sections of the cylinder and its lateral area. In the first treatise, on determining the area of a segment of a parabola, Thābit, who did not know of Archimedes' study on this subject, began by proving 21 propositions, 11 of these being arithmetical. Examination of these shows that Thābit knew perfectly and rigorously the concept of the upper limit of a set of square real numbers and the unicity of this upper limit. In effect, he used the following formula for characterising the upper limit:

let ABC be a segment of the parabola, AD its diameter corresponding to BC (Fig.). For all given $\varepsilon > 0$, one can make correspond to it the division A, G_1, G_2, ..., G_{n-1}, D, of the diameter AD, so that

area BAC - area of the polygon BE_{n-1} ... $E_2E_1AF_1F_2$ ...$F_{n-1}C < \varepsilon$,.

i.e. putting it another way, the area BAC is the upper limit of the area of these polygons.

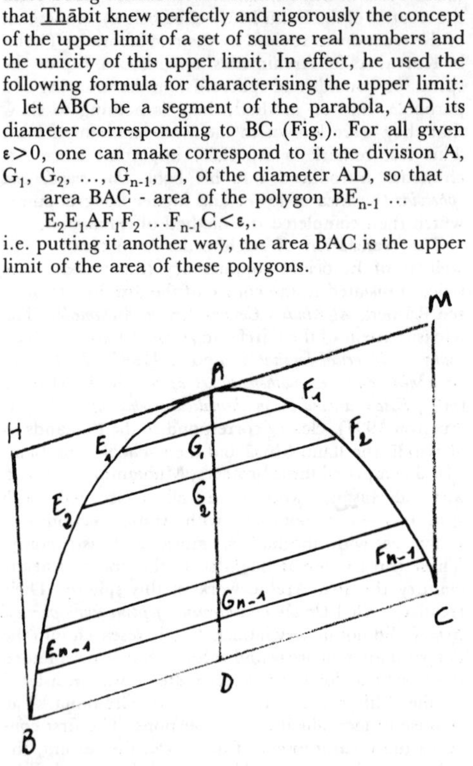

Thābit showed in quite a rigorous fashion that 2/3 of the area BHMC is the upper limit of the areas of the polygons already mentioned. He finally arrived at his theorem, thus formulated: "A parabola is infinite but the area of any one of its segments is equal to two-thirds of a parallelogram of the same base and the same height as that segment" (Cairo ms., Riyāḍa 40, fol. 180b).

One should note that his squaring, given the definition of a parabola, is equivalent to the calculation of the integral $\int_0^a \sqrt{px}\, dx$.

Thābit's contribution to this chapter did not, however, stop here. He undertook to determine the volume of a revolving paraboloid.

He finally undertook, in his treatise on *The sections of the cylinder and their surfaces*, a study of the different types of plane sections of an upright cylinder and an oblique one; he then determined the area of the ellipse and the area of elliptical segments; he discussed maximal and minimal sections of a cylinder and their axes; and determined the area of a part of the surface delimited by two plane sections.

It is impossible here to set forth the results and proofs of this rich and profound treatise, such as th proof by means of which Thābit showed that "the su face of an ellipse is equal to the surface of a circl whose square of the half-diameter is equal to th product of one of the two axes of this ellipse by th other", i.e. π ab, with a and b the two axes of th ellipse.

His contribution was to be actively followed by hi successors, such as his grandson Ibrāhīm b. Sinān This latter mathematician of genius only lived 3 years, and did not like, according to his own words "that al-Māhānī should have a study more advance than that of [my] grandfather, without one of us goin on further than him". Hence he wished to provide proof not only shorter than his grandfather's, whic needed 19 lemmata, as we have seen, but also tha that of al-Māhānī. The proposition on whic Ibrāhīm's proof was based and which he wa previously careful to set forth, was: *affine transformatio leaves the proportionality of the areas invariable.*

In the 4th/10th century, the mathematician al-ʿAlā b. Sahl (see Rashed, *Géometrie et dioptrique au Xe siècl* took up the study of the squaring of a parabola, bu his treatise has unfortunately not yet come to light. A for his contemporary al-Ḳūhī, by re-examining th determination of the volume of a revolvin paraboloid, he rediscovered the method of Ar chimedes.

The famed mathematician and physician Ibn al Haytham, successor to Ibn Sahl and al-Ḳūhī, took u the proof of the volume of a revolving paraboloid a well as that of the volume resulting from the rotatio of a parabola around its ordinate (see Rashed, *op. cit.* and *Ibn al-Haytham et la mesure du paraboloïde*, in *Jnal. f the Hist. of Arabic Science*, v [1982], 191-262). Let u rapidly examine this second type, more difficult tha the first one. In order to get to the determination c this volume, Ibn al-Haytham began by proving cer tain arithmetical lemmata: the sums of powers of successive integers, in order to establish a double ir equality, fundamental for his study. On this occasio he obtained results which mark a point in the histor of arithmetic, notably the sum of any integer power c n successive first integers

$$\sum_{k=1}^{n} k^i \quad , i = 1, 2, \ldots;$$

he then establishes the following inequality

$$(*) \qquad \sum_{k=1}^{n} [(n+1)^2 - k^2]^2 \leq \frac{8}{15}(n+1)(n+1)^4 \leq \sum_{k=0}^{n} [(n+1)^2 - k^2]^2 .$$

Let there now be a paraboloid generated by the rot tion of the part of the parabola ABC of the equatio $x = ky^2$ around the ordinate BC. Let $\sigma_n = (y_i)_{0 \leq i \leq 2^m}$ with $2^m = n$ a subdivision of the interval [0, b] of th step

$$h = \frac{b}{2^m} = \frac{b}{n}.$$

Let M_i be the points of a parabola of ordinates y_i ar of abscissae x_i respectively. Let us posit

$$r_i = c - x_i \qquad (0 \leq i \leq 2^m = n);$$

there results

$$r_i = k(b^2 - y_i^2) = kh^2(n^2 - i^2).$$

One has

$$I_n = \sum_{i=1}^{n-1} \pi k^2 h^5 (n^2 - i^2)^2$$

and

$$C_n = \sum_{i=0}^{n-1} \pi k^2 h^5 (n^2 - i^2)^2;$$

but, after the inequality (*), one obtains

$$I_n \leq \frac{8}{15} V \leq C_n,$$

where $V = \pi k^2 b^4 . b$ is the volume of the circumscribed cylinder. By using a different language from that of Ibn al-Hay<u>th</u>am:

As the function $g(y) = ky^2$ is continuous on $[0, b]$, Ibn al-Hay<u>th</u>am's calculation will be equivalent to the volume of the paraboloid

$$v(p) = \lim_{n\to\infty} \sum_{i=1}^{n} \pi k^2 h^5 (n^2 - i^2)^2$$

whence

$$v(p) = \lim_{n\to\infty} \sum_{i=1}^{n} \pi k^2 (b^4 - 2b^2y_i^2 + y_i^4) h,$$

whence

$$v(p) = \pi \int_0^b k^2 (b^4 - 2b^2y^2 + y^4) dy ,$$

whence

$$v(p) = \frac{8}{15} \pi k^2 b^5 = \frac{8}{15} V ,$$

V being the volume of the circumscribed cylinder.

Ibn al-Hay<u>th</u>am did not stop there; he turned afresh towards the small solids of framing in order to study their behaviour when the points of subdivision are increased indefinitely. This time we find ourselves in the presence of a clearly infinitesimalist, and in some ways functional, way of thinking, in so as the crux of the problem is explicitly the asymptotic behaviour of mathematical entities, the determination of whose variation is being sought.

Ibn al-Hay<u>th</u>am applied the same method to the determination of the volume of a sphere. There, equally, one notes that he gave an arithmetically inflected version of the method of exhaustion. In effect, in his researches, the role of explicit arithmetical calculation seems much more important than in the works of his predecessors.

In this study, one can see the development of the means and techniques of this chapter in Arabic mathematics. It has been seen that Ibn al-Hay<u>th</u>am, in his work on the paraboloid, obtained results which the historians have attributed to e.g. Kepler and Cavalieri. However, this chapter stops there, very probably because of the lack of a suitable symbolic means of expression.

VII. The squaring of lunules.

Amongst the problems of the determination of the areas of curved surfaces, the exact squaring of lunules—surfaces bounded by two arcs of circles—is one of the most ancient.

Ibn al-Hay<u>th</u>am's approach went back to the study of lunules bounded by any arcs, whilst seeking for the equivalents of surfaces. He introduced circles in general equivalent to sectors of the given circle in the problem, and expressed by a fraction of the latter. He justified the existence of the circles introduced, which he had to add or to subtract from polygonal surfaces, in order to obtain a surface equivalent to that of a lunule or the sum of two lunules.

Ibn al-Hay<u>th</u>am took back to its foundation the problem of the squaring of lunules, set it down on the plane of trigonometry, and tried to deduce the different cases as so many properties of a trigonometric function, one which would be recognised more precisely much later by Euler.

From the beginning of his treatise, Ibn al-Hay<u>th</u>am explicitly recognised that the calculation of the areas of lunules involved the sums and differences of the areas of sectors of the circle and of triangles, whose comparison in turn required the comparison of the relations of angles and the relations of segments. It was for this reason that he began by establishing four lemmata relating to the triangle ABC, right-angled at B in the first lemma, and with an obtuse angle in the other three, which was in future to show that the essential point of the study was taken back to a study of the function

$$f(x) = \frac{\sin^2 x}{x} \qquad 0 < x \leq \pi.$$

One can thus rewrite these lemmata:

1) If $0 < C < \frac{\pi}{4} < A < \frac{\pi}{2}$,

then $\frac{\sin^2 C}{C} < \frac{2}{\pi} < \frac{\sin^2 A}{A}$;

it is evident that if $C = A = \frac{\pi}{4}$,

then $\frac{\sin^2 C}{C} = \frac{\sin^2 A}{A} = \frac{2}{\pi}$.

2) Let $\pi - B = B_1$,

if $C < \frac{\pi}{4} < B_1 < \frac{\pi}{2}$, then $\frac{\sin^2 C}{C} = \frac{\sin^2 B_1}{B_1}$.

3) If $A \leq \frac{\pi}{4}$, then $\frac{\sin^2 A}{A} < \frac{\sin^2 B_1}{B_1}$.

4) Here Ibn al-Hay<u>th</u>am wished to study the case $A > \frac{\pi}{4}$; but the study is incomplete.

He showed that for a given A, one can find B_0 such that

$$B_1 \geq B_0 \Rightarrow \frac{\sin^2 A}{A} > \frac{\sin^2 B_1}{B_1}.$$

This incomplete study seems to have hidden from Ibn al-Hay<u>th</u>am's view the equality

$$\frac{\sin^2 A}{A} = \frac{\text{Sin}^2 B_1}{B_1}.$$

It may be remarked that these lemmata, since they link the problem of the squaring of lunules with trigonometry, changed its position, and allowed the unifying of the particular cases. But the incompleteness already mentioned masked the possibility of the existence of lunules capable of being squared.

Ibn al-Hay<u>th</u>am pursued his researches whilst solving important propositions which would take too long to set out here. He likewise contributed, following al-<u>Kh</u>āzin, to the study of isoperimetric and isepiphanic problems, which led him to pose important questions regarding the solid angle (see Rashed, *Les mathématiques infinitésimales entre le IXe et le XIe siècle*, ii).

We have just been present at the emergence of new researches into geometry, extensions of the Hellenistic heritage, or new chapters of which the Alexandrians never conceived: algebraic geometry in the sense of that used by al-Khayyām and Sharaf al-Dīn al-Ṭūsī. Other chapters on geometry, all of them important, saw the light, stimulated by the application of geometry to the other mathematical disciplines or to other fields, such as astronomy and optics. Thus the mathematicians developed the study of punctual geometrical transformations, notably in the course of their researches on infinitesimal determinations and in the course of their works on isoperimetric and isepiphanic problems. The analysis of the optical properties of conics developed thanks to catoptric and dioptric researches. The study of geometrical projections—conic and cylindrical—was brought into being through the needs of astronomy. To that may be added a whole tradition of research on the theory of parallels, on geometrical constructions and on practical geometry. Equally evident, for the first time in history, is the fact that trigonometry took shape as a branch of geometry. It is readily understandable that, within such a burgeoning, philosophers and mathematicians became interested in the philosophy of mathematics.

There exist so many other chapters which, for lack of space, we can only cite here but whose titles, added to those which we have already examined, allow us to realise the ramifications of mathematics and to place them within the history of this discipline.

Bibliography (in addition to references given in the article): arts. on individual mathematicians in *Dict. of scientific biogr.*; A. Youschkevitch, *Geschichte der Mathematik im Mittelalter*, Leipzig 1964, section on Arabic mathematics tr. into Fr. as *Les mathématiques arabes* (*VIIIe-XVe siècles*), Paris 1976; R. Rashed, *Entre arithmétique et algèbre. Recherches sur l'histoire des mathématiques arabes*, Les Belles Lettres Coll. Sciences et philosophie arabes. Études et reprises, Paris 1984, Ar. tr. Beirut 1989, Eng. tr. *The development of Arabic mathematics. Between arithmetic and algebra*, Kluwer 1994; idem, *Optique et mathématiques: recherches sur l'histoire de la pensée scientifique en arabe*, Variorum, London 1992. See also the *Bibl.* to ᶜILM AL-ḤISĀB.

(R. RASHED)

RIYĀFA (A.), from *rīf*, pl. *aryāf*, "cultivated and fertile region", generally designates the lands along a river or the sea and the fertile plains bordering the desert [see further RĪF]. The noun *riyāfa*, a recent formation on the model of *ḳiyāfa* (note that al-Djāḥiẓ, *K. al-Tarbīᶜ wa 'l-tadwīr*, ed. Pellat, 91-2, § 176, gives for *ḳiyāfa* [*q.v.*] the sense of the detection of paternity, the whereabouts of water, atmospheric phenomena and the earth), designates the water-diviner's art which estimates the depth of water under the earth through the smell of the earth, its vegetation and the instinctive reactions of certain creatures, in particular, the hoopoe (cf. Ḥādjdjī Khalīfa, iii, 523, who cites, at 1, 444, a *Mukhtaṣar* on this art by Badr al-Dīn Muḥammad al-Karkhī, d. 1006/1597, Brockelmann, II², 493, and who notes that the most important pieces of information on it are to be found in the *K. al-Filāḥa al-nabaṭiyya* (see ed. IFDEA, Damascus 1993, i, 54-111).

In effect, the *Nabataean agriculture* devotes a lengthy treatise to the discovery of water called *Bāb istinbāṭ al-miyāh wa-handasatihā*. This monograph, which can easily be detached from the rest of the work, has several chapters, with the following titles:

(1) Searching for water and the necessary technical knowledge for this; (2) How to dig wells and how t increase the flow of water by various proven device and techniques; (3) The drilling of wells; (4) device for increasing the water from wells; (5) How to get th water up from a very deep well; (6) How to increas the amount of water in the well and its sources; (7 How to change and improve the taste of the water and (8) Concerning the difference in the nature an the effect of the water according to the nearer or fur ther position of it in relation to the ecliptic.

The contents of this treatise on water have bee analysed by the present author, classifying thes under six headings: (1) Hydrology; (2) The search fo wells; (3) The drilling of wells; (4) Increasing the flo of the water of wells; (5) Hydrology, the modifyin and improving of the water's taste; (6) The differen natures and effects of the waters according to thei positions in relation to the ecliptic (see FAHD, *Un trai des eaux dans* al-Filāḥa l-nabaṭiyya: *hydrogéologie hydraulique agricole, hydrologie*, in *La Persia nel Medioevo* Accademia dei Lincei, Rome 1971, 277-326).

In the writings on *firāsa* [*q.v.*], the meaning of *riyāf* has been stretched to that of uncovering the presenc of metals underground: "l'accès à ces trésors enfoui procède de la connaissance des signes que recèlent ce montagnes et qui apparaissent aux yeux du con naisseur averti sous forme de veines ou filets dont il lu faut interpréter la nature, la disposition et la couleur" (Fahd, *La divination arabe*, 404). The seeker "doit con naître l'origine astrale du minéral qu'il recherche e savoir sous la domination de quelle planète il s trouve; car chaque métal a la couleur, la nature, le caractéristiques et les propriétés de la planète dont est censé être issu" (*ibid.*). Amongst the Ḥarrānians the following correspondences were to be found Gold-The Sun; Silver-The Moon, (Black) Lead Saturn; Tin-Jupiter; Copper-Venus; and Iron-Mar (see IBN AL-NADĪM, *Fihrist*, 411-12).

In general, it is a question of a natural gift whic "réside dans la connaissance de l'état des lieux san signes apparents, mais avec des pressentiments fondé sur des propriétés qu'il n'est pas donné à tout le monde de déceler; cela est généralement dû à l perfection des sens et à la force de l'imaginatio (Fahd, *op. cit.*, 403; Y. Mourad, *La physiognomie arab et le K. al-Firāsa de Fakhr al-Dīn al-Rāzī*, diss. Pari 1939, 137 n. 21, citing Zayn al-ᶜĀbidīn al-ᶜĀmirī).

Riyāfa, like *ḳiyāfa* (Fahd, *op. cit.*, 370-8), is classe among the physiognomic procedures since it involve "des déductions relatives à des choses cachées, pa tant de phénomènes apparents, par analogie avec le prévisions concernant l'aspect moral, basées su l'aspect physique" (*ibid.*). Further details on thes procedures in Mourad, *op. cit.*, 15 (the sciences con nected with *firāsa*).

Bibliography: In addition to the work c Mourad, see T. Fahd, *La divination arabe*, Pari 1967, 403-6; Zayn al-ᶜĀbidīn al-ᶜUmarī al-Shāfiᶜ (d. 970/1562), *K. al-Bahdja al-unsiyya fi 'l-firāsa al insāniyya wa 'l-ḥikamiyya* (mss. in Ankara, Istanbul Paris and Cairo, cf. Brockelmann, II², 440, S II 463, who reads for his *nisba* al-Ghumrī).

(T. FAHD)

RIYĀḤ, BANŪ, an Arab tribe, the most powerfu of those that, regarding themselves as descended fro Hilāl [*q.v.*], left Upper Egypt and invaded Barbary i the middle of the 5th/11th century. Their chief at tha time was Muᵓnis b. Yaḥyā of the family of Mirdās The Zīrid *amīr* al-Muᶜizz [*q.v.*], who did not forese the disastrous consequences of the entry of the Arab into Ifrīḳiya, tried to come to an arrangement wit him and to win over the Riyāḥ. The latter were th first to lay his country waste. But thanks to the protection of the chiefs of the Riyāḥ, to whom he had married his daughters, al-Muᶜizz himself succeeded in escaping from Ḳayrawān and reaching al-Mahdiyya [*q.v.*].

At the first partition of Ifrīḳiya which followed the invasion, the Riyāḥ were naturally the best served. They obtained the greater part of the plains, which the Berbers had abandoned to seek shelter among the mountains; they had thrust their relatives, the Athbidj, towards the east. They held Badja, which the Fāṭimid caliph in Cairo had allotted to them in anticipation. The people of Gabès [see ḲĀBIS] took the oath of loyalty to Muʾnis. "It was", says Ibn Khaldūn, "the first real conquest of the Arabs". The Djāmiᶜ, a family related to the Riyāḥ, made Gabès a regular little capital, which they adorned with their buildings. Lastly, a chief of the main tribe, Muḥriz b. Ziyād, made himself a fortress in al-Muᶜallaḳa (a Roman circus?), among the ruins of Carthage. The powerful lords of al-Muᶜallaḳa, however, supported the policy of the Zīrids of al-Mahdiyya, and joined them in their resistance to the Almohads.

This resistance did not long impede the expeditions sent by the Maghribīs against an Ifrīḳiya in anarchy. Defeated by ᶜAbd al-Muʾmin in 546/1152, 555/1160 and 583/1187, the Arabs were ordered to supply contingents for the holy war in Spain. ᶜAbd al-Muʾmin, leaving a section of the Riyāḥ in Ifrīḳiya under command of ᶜAsākir b. Sulṭān, took the others to the Maghrib with their chief, ᶜAsākir's brother Masᶜūd, known as *al-bulṭ* ("the axe"; cf. Dozy, *Supplément*, i, 111). He settled them in the Moroccan plains to the north of Bū Regreg. This control was little in keeping with the traditions of the Riyāḥ; Masᶜūd fled to Ifrīḳiya and there gave his support to the Banū Ghāniya [*q.v.*], who were trying to revive for their own advantage the Almoravid power.

It is known how the trouble stirred up by the Banū Ghāniya led to the Almohad caliph's appointing a governor of Ifrīḳiya invested with very extensive powers, Abū Muḥammad of the Ḥafṣid [*q.v.*] family. This governor naturally attacked the Riyāḥ, and, in order to be rid of them, encouraged the settlement in the country of the Sulaym Arabs [see SULAYM, BANŪ] hitherto quartered in Tripolitania. Under the pressure of the Sulaym, the Riyāḥ, the principal family of whom at this time was the Dawāwīda, migrated to the plains of Constantine where they were henceforth to remain.

In their new home, the position of the Riyāḥ remained a very strong one. They had rights over all the centre of the region of Constantine, approximately from the region of Guelma to that of Bougie. In the Zāb [*q.v.*] they were on terms—which were sometimes friendly but more often hostile— with the Banū Muznī of Biskra, who ruled this Ḥafṣid province. This is how the Banū Muznī had to fight against that curious movement, at once religious and social, stirred up by the Riyāḥid marabout Saᶜda. The Dawāwīda, and in particular their most powerful family, the Awlād Muḥammad, held winter pastures and enjoyed revenues paid by the people of the *ḳṣūr* in the Sahara region of the Wādī Rīgh.

During the whole of the 8th/14th century, the two chief branches of the main tribe, the Awlād Muḥammad and the Awlād Sibāᶜ, were actively engaged in the politics of the Ḥafṣid princes and the ᶜAbd al-Wādids of Tlemcen, in the enterprises of the pretenders who threatened their dynasties. The power of the Riyāḥ of central Barbary lasted till the 15th and 16th centuries. According to Bernardino of Mendoza, they had in 1536 10,000 horsemen and large numbers of foot. The 12th/18th century saw them assisting the Turkish Bey of Constantine, to whom they were connected by marriage and the independent sultans of Tuggurt. In 1844, Carette and Warnier noted that the name Dawāwīda was still synonymous with "noble Arabs".

Another group of the Riyāḥ played a notable part in the history of the Zanāta states. In the western Maghrib, bodies of them transported by the Almohads to the plains of the coast faithfully served this dynasty, by trying to check the advance of the Marīnids [*q.v.*]. Defeated near the Wādī Sbū in 614/1217, the Riyāḥ were mercilessly punished by the victorious Marīnids. Decimated and weakened, and driven northwards, they submitted to the humiliation of paying an annual tribute. Their name no longer figures on the map of modern Morocco except at a place near the road from al-Ḳsār to Tangiers.

Finally, at the other end of Barbary, in their first home, the name survives in the nomenclature of the tribes.

Bibliography: Ibn Khaldūn, *Histoire des Berbères*, ed. de Slane, i, 19 ff., tr. idem, i, 34 ff. and *passim*; Ibn ᶜIdhārī, *Bayān*, ed. Dozy, i, 300 ff., tr. E. Fagnan, i, 433 ff.; Ibn al-Athīr, ed Tornberg, ix, 387 ff., tr. Fagnan, *Annales du Maghreb et de l'Espagne*, 456 ff.; E. de la Primaudaie, *Documents inédits sur l'histoire de l'occupation espagnole en Afrique*, in *R. Afr.* (1877); Féraud, *Le Sahara de Constantine*, Algiers 1887; idem, *Histoire des villes de la province de Constantine, Bordj bou Arreridj*, in *Recueil de la Société archéologique de Constantine*, xv; Carette and Warnier, *Notice*, in *Établissements français*, 1844; Bouaziz ben Gana, *Le cheikh el-Arab*, Algiers 1930; Michaud-Bellaire et Salmon, *Tribus arabes de la vallée de l'Oued Lekkous*, in *Archives marocaines*, iv, 58-9; G. Marçais, *Les Arabes en Berbérie*, see index and genealogical table ii; R. Brunschwig, *Ḥafṣides*, index; H.R. Idris, *La Berbérie orientale sous les Zīrides*, Paris 1962, i-ii; H. Terrasse, *Histoire du Maroc*, Casablanca 1949-50, i. See also HILĀL. (G. MARÇAIS*)

RIYĀL, a name used for coins in a number of Islamic countries, derived from the silver *real* (*de plata*), first issued by Pedro the Cruel of Castile (1350-9), followed by Ferdinand of Portugal (1367-83). In Spain it continued until 1870 and in Portugal until 1910.

The relations of the Spanish and Portuguese currencies to those of the Near East belong to the monetary history of the Ottoman Empire and of Persia. From the early 16th century the eastern gold and silver currencies suffered frequent devaluation and debasement. Western merchants needed more stable monetary standards if they were not to incur loss, and so relied on imported currencies; they could make further profit by exporting them as bullion to India. Austria, Germany, Holland, Poland, Spain and Venice were the principal western sources; the Levant Company, of London, forbidden to export English currency, at first purchased Spanish *reals*, but turned later to Dutch coinage. Spanish and Mexican *reals* were greatly valued for their purity, but, being roughly struck, encouraged clipping; Austrian and Saxon issues became popular because they were minted with a collar, which defied clipping. Thus among Bedouin they have remained popular into the present century.

The term *riyāl* is first recorded in the east in Persia under Shāh ᶜAbbās I in 1609. With Fatḥ ᶜAlī Shāh's issue of 1797 it became the official name of the silver coinage, and this was retained in Riḍāʾ (Reza) Shāh's reforms of 1932. It was frequently devalued and debased, and bore no numismatic relationship to the Spanish and Portuguese issues. The earlier Persian term *lāri* [see LARIN] is recorded as the common currency at Mombasa, Kenya, in conjunction with "peeces 8/8", that is, "pieces-of-eight" or Spanish *reals*, by an English visitor in 1617.

In Yemen, while still under Ottoman sovereignty, Imām Yaḥyā b. Muḥammad al-Mutawakkil (1904-48) determined to defy the Ottoman right of *sikka*, that of issuing coinage. H.F. Jacob, then Political Agent for the Bombay Government in Aden, has left an account of how machinery ordered from England for a mint in Ṣanʿāʾ was passed through the Aden Customs manifested as something else. Ottoman troops sent to intercept it were outwitted by an escort of 500 Yemeni tribesmen. This mint operated from 1906-63. The Yemen still uses the term *riyāl* for its currency.

There were sporadic issues of *riyāls* elsewhere, at Ghurfa and two other mints in Ḥaḍramawt at the end of the 19th century, and in Zanzibar by Sultan Barghash b. Saʿīd, of silver in 1881, and of ½ and ¼ copper *riyāls* in 1882 and 1883. A curiosity of the pieces is that the ruler's given name is reversed with his patronymic, as Saʿīd b. Barghash. Slightly earlier, Charles Doughty, travelling down the Pilgrimage Route, found that the Maria Theresa *thaler* was the usual currency but that tribes further east preferred the *riyāl*.

In Saudi Arabia, the *riyāl* was instituted as local currency in 1935, in ʿUmān (Oman) in 1945, in the United Arab Emirates in 1966, and in Dubayy and Ḳaṭar (Qatar) since 1972. They all obtain their supply from the Royal Mint in Wales.

The history of the *riyāl* can only be traced in the works of foreign travellers. Official documentation is not available. F.W. Hasluck has printed extracts from travellers to the Ottoman Empire, and H.L. Rabino de Borgomale cites references to Persia. A detailed report, 1766, *Observations sur l'état actuel de l'Empire Ottoman*, by Henry Grenville, Ambassador to the Porte in 1762-65, and brother of George Grenville, Prime Minister of Great Britain 1763-65, gives an official account of the Ottoman economy and government. The Venetian *sequin* was the most favoured foreign currency, the Austrian *thaler* holding second place.

Bibliography: C.M. Almeida do Amaral, *Catálogo das moedas Portuguesas*, i, Lisbon 1875; R.H. Crofton, *Zanzibar affairs, 1914-33*, London 1953; C.M. Doughty, *Arabia Deserta*, London 1988; *Enciclopedia Universal Ilustrada Europeo-Americana*, Madrid, s.v. *real*; G.S.P. Freeman-Grenville (ed.), *The East African coast: select documents*, Oxford 1962; Henry Grenville, *Observations, etc.*, ed. A.S. Ehrenkreutz, Ann Arbor, Michigan 1965, 33-45; F.W. Hasluck, *The Levantine coinage*, in *NC*, 5th ser., vol. i (1921), 39-91; H.F. Jacob, *Kings of Arabia, the rise and set of the Turkish sovranty* [sic] *in the Arabian peninsula*, London 1923; C.L. Krause and C. Mishler with C.R. Bruce III, *Standard catalogue of world coins, 1750s through 1945*, Krause Publications, Iowa, Wisconsin 1961 edn.; H.L. Rabino di Borgomale, *Coins, medals and reals of the Shahs of Iran, 1500-1941*, 2 vols., Oxford 1945; R.B. Serjeant, *The Portuguese off the South Arabian coast*, Oxford 1963.

(G.S.P. FREEMAN-GRENVILLE)

RIYĀLA, RIYĀLE or RIYĀLA BEY, abbreviation of *riyala-yi hümāyūn kapudanī* "captain of the imperial [galley-] royal", from the Italian *riyale* (secondary form from *reale*, abbreviated from *galea reale*, "the royal galley"), a general officer of the Ottoman navy who commanded the galley of the same name, later "rear-admiral". There was also a popular pronunciation *īryāla* with the prosthetic *i* frequent in Turkish in loan-words with an initial *r* (cf. Hindoglou 113 under "contre-amiral" and 457 under "réale" the form *iryāla* is found as early as Ewliyā Čelebi, viii 466, 11). The Italian pronunciation *riyale* is attested in the *Itinéraire de Jérome Maurand d'Antibes à Constantinople* (1544), ed. L. Dorez, Paris 1901 (we also find there exceptionally *rialle, reale* and *realle*). For the pronunciation, we may compare the Turkish *riyāla* with the Turkish *riyāl*, Ar. *riyāl*, for the Spanish *real* (*del plata*) name of a coin [see RIYĀL]; cf. the French "gros royal", Turk. *grush, krush, gurush*, mod. *kuruş* "piastre, formerly écu". Here also we find the prosthetic form *iryāl* (Hindoglou, 200, s.v. "écu" Aucher gives *riyāl*, under "réal"). In the west, the Turkish word *riyāla* was sometimes transcribed *reala* no doubt regarded as more correct (Herbette, *Une Ambassade turque sous le Directoire*, Paris 1902, 238).

The rank of *riyāla*, as well as those of *ḳapudana* and *patrona* to be discussed later, was at first known among the Turks only as applied to officers of the navies of Christendom (see e.g. Ewliyā Čelebi and the Ottoman historians like Naʿīmā and others). These ranks came into use among the Turkish sailors, at first unofficially, in the time of Sultan Meḥemmed IV 1058-99/1648-87 (cf. below in connection with *patrona*). D'Ohsson, undoubtedly by confusion, says that they were used in the time of Meḥemmed II (855-86/1451-81). We do not, however, find these titles of foreign origin in the *Tuḥfet ül-kibār* of Ḥādjdjī Khalīfa (1066/1656) nor in Hezārfenn (d. 1102/1691). It was, it appears, under ʿAbd al-Ḥamīd I (1187-1203/1774-89) that they were officially adopted (Meḥmed Shükrī, *Esfār-ī baḥriyye-i ʿothmāniyye*, 1306/1890, i 145).

We are well informed about the hierarchy of the naval high command at this period, thanks to the *Teshrīfāt-ī ḳadīme*, a work of Ṣaḥḥāflar-Sheykhī-zāde Esʿad Meḥmed Efendi (d. 1848). On p. 102 ff. we have a list of the old establishment, which combined the non-sea-going officers, of which a list will be given here, and the sea-going officers, who will be dealt with in more detail because the *riyala* was one of them and bore, like them, a name taken from the Venetians.

a. General officers of the Admiralty (*tersāne-ʿāmire*).

(All three seem to have had, but perhaps only from the beginning of the 19th century, the right to the title of *pasha*.)

1. The *ḳapudan-pasha* [*q.v.*] having the rank of *wezīr* (*dewletlü*). He was the Capitan del Mar (*ḳapudan-deryā*) or, as was also said, the *ḳapudan* par excellence. The name *ḳapudan*, from the Venetian *capitan(o)* and its modernised form, probably under the influence of English, *ḳaptan*, was further applied to any commander of a ship, small or large, foreign or Turkish. (The vowel *u* in the second syllable is due to the influence of the neighbouring labial *p* and Trévoux's Dictionary gives the intermediate form "capoutan" under *capitan-bacha*; cf. also *Relation des 2 rebellions arrivées à Constantinople en 1730 et 1731*, The Hague 1737 23.)

2. *Tersāne(-i ʿāmire) emīni agha* (*seʿādetlü*) "Intendant de l'Arsenal" (d'Ohsson), Germ. "Intendant de Arsenals" (Hammer), Engl. "Intendant of the Marine" (Perry). He took the place of the Grand Admiral in his absence. From 1246/1830 onwards, he was called *müdīr*.

3. *Tersāne(-i ʿāmire) ketkhüdāsī* (*kahyasī*) *agha* "Intendant des galères", "Lieutenant of the Arsenal" "Sachwalter des Arsenals". He was particularly concerned with the police of the Admiralty.

b. Admirals with the title of *bey*.

Except the fourth, these officers were sea-going admirals and took the name, of Venetian origin, of the vessels they commanded. The name might have the addition of *hümāyūn* "imperial" in a Persian construction, whence the official barbarisms *bashtarda-yi hümāyūn*, *ḳapudana-yi hümāyūn*, etc. The full titles were in theory *bashtarda-yi hümāyūn ḳapudanī*, *ḳapudana-yi hümāyūn ḳapudanī*, etc.

1. *Bashtarda, bashtarda, basharda-(yi hümāyūn)*—Ital. *bastarda*, Fr. *bastarde* or *bâtardelle*. This was not the largest unit of the fleet. In Turkish as in Venetian usage, the bastarda was a galley larger than the *galea sensile* (Tk. *ḳadīrga* or *čektiri*), but smaller than the galeazza or galliass (Tk. *mauna*) and had a very rounded poop "like a water-melon" (*ḳarpuz ḳičli*). Among the Turks it contained 26-36 *oturaḳ*s or benches of 5-7 rowers. The one which had the Ḳapudan Pasha on board was called (*ḳapudan-*) *pasha bashtardasī* and had 26-36 *oturaḳ*s. It was distinguished by the three lanterns (*fener*) attached to the poop in addition to that on the main mast (*Tuḥfa*, fol. 69; *Djewdet Pasha tārīkhi*, 1309, 131). As it flew the flag of the Grand Admiral, it was sometimes (Meninski, *Thesaurus*, i, 663; Barbier de Meynard) called "Captain", but we shall see that among the Turks this name was given to another vessel. Chance has willed it that the first syllable in the word *bashtarda* means in Turkish "head, chief" but it is difficult to say that the Ottomans gave first place to this ship simply as a result of a popular etymology. The disappearance of the ship propelled by oars resulted in the abolition of the *bashtarda*. Officially disused in 1177/1764, according to d'Ohsson, it was still used from time to time on certain ceremonial occasions. The sailing-ship (*ḳalyun*, "galleon") which became the flagship of the *ḳapudan pasha*, was commanded by the "Flag Captain" who, according to d'Ohsson, was called in Turkish *süwari ḳapudanī* "captain of the ship commanders" and, according to von Hammer (*Staatsverf.*, ii, 493), *sandjaḳ ḳapudanī*, Germ. "Flaggenkapitän", cf. Eng. "flag captain". Esᶜad Meḥmed Efendi calls this officer, probably by an archaism, *bashtarda(-yi) hümāyūn-i pasha* "(commander of) the imperial *bashtarda* of the (*ḳapudan*) *pasha*.

2. *Ḳapudana bey*. *Ḳapudana* comes from the Venetian (*galea* or *nave*) *capitana* "galley or ship carrying the leader of a naval expedition, flag-ship" (Jal). In France it was called "la capitaine" or "capitainesse", but these terms disappeared in 1669 with the office of general of the galleys, and in the French navy pride of place was given to the Réale (see below). On the *ḳapudana* which took part in the naval battle of Česhme (1770), cf. Jaubert, *Grammaire*, appendice, 3. *Ḳapudana* and *ḳapudan* have often been confused (von Hammer, *Staatsverf.*, ii, 291; Blochet, *Voyage de Carlier de Pinon*, 128; Douin, *Navarin*, 250, 276, 295, 311). We find the full title of *ḳapudana-yi hümāyūn ḳapudanī*, e.g. in a letter from Muḥammad ᶜAlī Pasha [*q.v.*] (of Egypt) to the Grand Vizier of 29 Ramaḍān 1231/1 July 1821 register, no. 4, p. 71.

3. *Patrona bey*. *Patrona* comes from the Venetian (*galea* or *nave*) *patrona* or *padrona*, Fr. *la patronne* "galley carrying the lieutenant-general or the next in command to the chief of the squadron" (Jal). The earliest mention of an officer of this rank known to us is connected with the years 1676-85 (see *Sidjill-i ᶜothmānī*, i, 112, below. Patrona Khalīl [*q.v.*], a Janissary, and leader of the rebels who deposed Aḥmed III in 1143/1730, owed his epithet to the fact that he had been a *lewend* [*q.v.*] on board the *Patrona* (*Relation des 2 rebellions*, 8; Eng. tr. in Charles Perry, *A view of the Levant*, London 1743, 64). We also find the forms applied, it is true, to Christian ships: *patorna, patorona*,

batorna, and even *botrona* (Ewliyā Čelebi, viii, 579, 12; i, 104, 7; viii, 447, below; 446, 10; Ḥasan Agha, *Djewāhir al-tewārīkh*, ms. Bibl. Paris, S.T. 506, fols. 160b-161). All these pronunciations show that the word was already well known but that it was finding difficulty in being acclimatised in a correct form.

4. *Liman reʾīsi* "captain (admiral) of the port" of Istanbul, Ger. "Kapitän des Hafens". He was also commander of the midshipmen (*mandedji*).

5. *Riyāla bey*. *Riyāla* comes from the Venetian (*galea* or *nave*) *reale* "galley which carried the king or princes" (the same name was often also applied as an epithet to vessels beonging to the king, i.e to the state, in contrast to privately owned ships). For the lexicology of this borrowing from the Italian, see the beginning of the article.

At the battle of Lepanto, Don John of Austria, Captain of the League, sailed in a Reale. A Patrona Reale went astern of the Reale of the Prince and of the Capitana of the "General Capitan dell' Armata" of Venice. Except for these two ships, none of the 202 vessels of the allies was given the name of Reale (Contarini, *Historia delle cose .... della guerra mossa da Selim Ottomano a' Veneziani*, Venice 1572, fols. 36b ff.). In France, the Reale also went in front of the Patrone and was the first ship of the navy, intended to carry the king, princes, the admiral of France or in their absence the general of the galleys (Jal). At the conquest of Cyprus, in 1570, Contarini (Venice 1595) gives for 185 Christian ships 18 *capitana*, 7 *padrona* and 1 *bastardella* (no Reale); for the 276 Turkish ships 1 *real* (sic) and 29 *capitana* (these terms do not correspond exactly to those of Turkish usage of that time).

It is not explained how the title of Reale came to descend among the Turks until it was applied to the ship of the admiral of lowest rank. We may suppose that they were misled by the second meaning of the word Reale (see above), or that they confused him with the English "rear-admiral".

Marsigli (*Stato Militare...*, 1732, i, 146) mentions the Turkish "commandante nella Reale" as having a higher rank than the *gardyan bashi*, who was in turn superior to the captain of an ordinary galley. According to Esᶜad Efendi, the *riyale* came before the *ḳalyunlar kātibi*.

All the officers here mentioned, from the *ḳapudan pasha* to the *riyāla*, were *ṣāḥib deynek*, i.e. they had the right to carry, in imitation of their Venetian colleagues, a commander's baton or cane, *deynek*, also called *ṣadefkārī ᶜaṣā* (Esᶜad Efendi, 109, 7) because it was encrusted with mother of pearl of different colours (see below). It was what the Venetians called the *giannetta* or *cana (canna)*; from *canna d'India*, "Indian cane", often taken in the sense of "bamboo", from which we also have the English word "cane". They alone wore small turbans and fur-trimmed robes (cf. d'Ohsson, pl. 228).

When under ᶜAbd al-Ḥamīd I, or later under his successor Selīm III [*q.vv.*], the naval hierarchy was organised and to some extent modernised, three grades of admiral were instituted (independent of the *ḳapudan pasha*, who was the Grand Admiral or "amiralissimo"). They were:

1. The *ḳapudana bey* "Admiral". Meḥmed Shükrī regards his rank as equivalent to the more modern one of *shūrā-yi baḥriyye reʾīsi* "president of the Higher Council of the Navy". He had a fixed monthly salary of 4,500 piastres, and in addition received pay for 1,000 men (out of which he was liable to make various grants), but with the obligation to give to the *ḳapudan pasha* spices or *djāʾize* to the value of 4,000 piastres. He carried a green cane and had the right to have a pen-

non below the flag on the main mast (that of the *ḳapudan-pas̲h̲a* was above).

2. *Patrona bey* "vice-admiral" (Meḥmed S̲h̲ükrī), modern Turkish *vis amiral* but we also find the French equivalent of "guidon" (Sāmī Bey; Tinghir-Sinapian). Salary: 3,500 piastres. Pay of 800 men. *Dj̲āʾize* to the *ḳapudan pas̲h̲a* of 3,000 piastres. Blue cane. Flag on the fore-mast.

3. *Riyāla bey* "rear-admiral" (Meḥmed S̲h̲ükrī). Salary: 3,000 piastres. Pay of 700 men. *Dj̲āʾize* to the *ḳapudan pas̲h̲a*: 2,500 piastres. Blue cane. Flag on the mizzen-mast.

It may be noted that, in theory, there was only one officer of each of these ranks at one time.

All three took part in the battle of Navartino in 1827 (Douin, *Navarin*, 250 and *passim*). They were under the command of Ṭāhir Pas̲h̲a who had the rank of *mīrmīrān*. He was himself *patrona*, but this does not mean duplicating the office of the *patrona* who was subordinate to him, because the commanders-in-chief of the fleet (*ser-asker* or *bas̲h̲-bog̲h̲*) were chosen without regard to rank. K̲h̲iḍīr Ilyās (*Enderūn tārīk̲h̲i*, 481) mentions a *liman reʾīsi* with the rank of *patrona* in 1826.

The flag-commander of the *ḳapudan pas̲h̲a* retained his functions, but seems to have occupied a position on the edge of the hierarchy which the presence of the Grand Admiral on board sometimes made unenviable (von Hammer, *Staatsverf.*, ii, 293)

We do not know at what period these ranks were replaced by the more modern terms of *müs̲h̲īr*, *ferīḳ* and *liwā*. The equations of rank varied considerably. The *riyala* is regarded as *mīr afay, mīrmīrān, liwā ferīḳ* and even *birindj̲i ferīḳ*. It is probable that it was necessary to choose a grade between these. At Sebastopol in 1854, the Turkish fleet was commanded by a *patrona*, Aḥmed Pas̲h̲a (cf. Aḥmed Rāsim, *Tārīk̲h̲*, iv, 2015).

In Egypt under the K̲h̲edives, there was for a time a *riyala pas̲h̲a* in command of the fleet.

Bibliography: Only d'Ohsson gives definite information about the officers mentioned above, see his *Tableau de Empire Othoman*, vol. vii, bk. viii, 420-38, devoted to the Navy. See also Ubicini, *Lettres sur la Turquie*, 2nd ed., Paris 1853, i, 484 (important); Jouannin, *La Turquie*, 436; Pakalin, iii, s.v.; İ.H. Uzunçarşılı, *Osmanlı devletinin merkez ve bahriye teşkilâtı*, Ankara 1948, 434-5. See also BAḤRIYYA. iii, and ḲAPUDAN PAS̲H̲A. (J. DENY)

RIYĀM, BANŪ, also and perhaps originally Riʾām, a tribal grouping in ʿUmān [*q.v.*].

The tribe would appear to have originated in the coastal area of southern ʿUmān and in the 4th/10th century al-Hamdānī (*Ṣifa*, 52) refers to them as a *baṭn* of al-Ḳamar, which Ibn Manẓūr's *LA* (v, 115) states is a *baṭn* of Mahra b. Ḥaydān, not the main group of Mahra which remained in southern Arabia. Kaḥḥāla (*Muʿdj̲am*, ii, 458), relying on the 5th/11th century geographer, al-Bakrī, says Banū Riyām themselves are a *baṭn* of Mahra b. Ḥaydān b. ʿAmr b. al-Ḥāf, that they live in the coastal area of southern ʿUmān and that one of their fortresses is Raysūt (Wilkinson, *Imamate*, 75-6). The latter is the port of Ẓafār [*q.v.*], about 15 km/10 miles across the bay from the settlement. Al-Fīrūzābādī's *Ḳāmūs* (ii, 125) says that Banū Riyām are between Ẓafār and al-S̲h̲iḥr, the port of Ḥaḍramawt. Despite these early references placing Banū Riyām only in the south, their even earlier settlement pattern seems to have extended from the southern coastal area as far as the plateau of al-Dj̲abal al-Akhḍar, and their main centre was in Dj̲aʿlān, the area in the south-eastern corner of the Arabian Peninsula. The political importance of Banū Riyām in central ʿUmān, however, becomes clear at the end of the 3rd/9th century when they began to take over settlements at the foot of al-Dj̲abal al-Akhḍar on all sides (Wilkinson, *Settlement*, 245-6 and fig. 33). The area of al-Dj̲abal al-Akhḍar inhabited by Banū Riyām has become renowned for its cultivation of such fruits as pomegranates, grapes, peaches, figs and mulberries, as well as roses for making rose-water and walnuts (*ibid.*, 12-13).

Bibliography: Hamdānī; Ibn Manẓūr, *LA*, Beirut 1955-6; Fīrūzābādī, *al-Ḳāmūs al-muḥīṭ*, Cairo 1952; Caskel-Strenziok, *Ǧamharat an-nasab*, ii, table 328; ʿUmar Riḍā Kaḥḥāla, *Muʿdj̲am ḳabāʾil al-ʿArab*, Beirut 1982; J.C. Wilkinson, *Water and tribal settlement in South-East Arabia*, Oxford 1977; idem, *The Imamate tradition of Oman*, Cambridge 1987. (G.R. SMITH)

RIZE, a town on the northern, Black Sea coast of Asia Minor, in the eastern part of classical Pontus and in the later mediaeval Islamic Lazistān [see LAZ], now in the Turkish Republic (lat. 41° 03′ N., long. 40° 31′ E.).

In Byzantine times, Rhizus/Rhizaion was a place of some importance and was strongly fortified. With the Ottoman annexation of the Comneni empire of Trebizond in 865/1462 [see ṬARABZUN], it became part of the Ottoman empire. A list of Orthodox Church metropolitanates still in existence at the end of the 9th/15th century mentions the town, which formed part of the province of Trabzon, as a separate judicial district (*ḳaḍāʾ*). In the early years of Ḳānūnī Süleymān's reign, the town contained 215 Christian households, two further households recently converted to Islam and 41 men subject to the *bās̲h̲tīna* (landholding) tax. There also existed a monastery transcribed in the Ottoman register as Ayō Rāndōs. The town was protected by two fortresses, one of them guarded by 31 soldiers under the command of a *dizdār* and *ketk̲h̲udā*. A second *ketk̲h̲udā* was recorded for the "old fortress", which means that it was still in use. Two inhabitants of the town had been granted the privileges of *köprüdj̲üs*, that is, they were exempt from certain taxes while responsible for the construction and upkeep of a local bridge. After the conquest of Trabzon, Meḥemmed the Conquerer had resettled certain personages of the area in Rūmelī (*sürgüns*); this fact was still mentioned in the records of the early 10th/16th century. Among the town's residents there also were a few *sürgüns* from Bosnia and Morea. These were *timār*-holders and followers of a governor, that is, they had probably been people of distinction in their areas of origin.

In the rural district surrounding the town, there were at least 29 villages and 35 *maḥalle*s (quarters). This means that the non-nucleated settlement pattern, which is widespread in the area to the present day, existed in the 10th/16th century as well. The tax registers of the early 10th/16th century mention possessions of a Georgian power-holder (*Gürdj̲ü kāfir*) in the area, which had been turned into a *timār* after the Ottoman conquest. The total population of the *ḳaḍāʾ* of Rize was recorded as 6,152 households. The majority of the population was still Christian, and many villages bore Greek names.

In the 11th/17th century, Rize, similar to other settlements located on the Black Sea coast, was subject to raids both on the part of the Abaza, who attempted to capture slaves, and on the part of Cossacks from the northern shore of the Black Sea. Guard towers were therefore built in the vicinity, which were still standing when the Mekhitarist monk Minas Biz̲h̲is̲h̲kian visited them in the early 13th/19th century. He records only a single fortress in Rize, a port and some shops. At some point in the past, Persian Armenians seem to have settled in the town quarter of Ros̲h̲i and built a church; but it had apparently disappeared by the time of Biz̲h̲is̲h̲kian's visit. That the town went through difficult times in the 11th/17th century is probable; Ewliyāʾ Čelebi, who wrote a detailed description of Trabzon, merely mentions passing through or near Rize and does not supply any details.

Rize is mentioned in early 13th/19th century sources in connection with the Ṭuzd̲j̲u-og̲h̲ullarî, a local *aʿyān* family which rebelled against Sultan Maḥmūd II in 1229-32/1814-17 and again in 1234-7/1818-21 and 1248-50/1832-4. The Ṭuzd̲j̲u-og̲h̲ullarî had been influential in the area since at least the mid-12th/18th century. They engaged in trade and agriculture—Biz̲h̲is̲h̲kian praised the area's handsome orange and lemon groves, while maize by this date had already replaced millet as the principal food grain. Peasants unable to repay their debts to the Ṭuzd̲j̲u-og̲h̲ullarî had to hand over their land and work it as sharecroppers, a situation which entailed political loyalty toward this landholding *aʿyān* family. The latter paid the area's taxes as a lump sum (*maḳṭūʿ*), and at the height of their power, the central government's tax collectors could not enter the area. A handsome palace in Rize attested the power of the family. However, competition with another power-holder, who had succeeded in obtaining the governship of Trabzon, resulted in an uprising on the part of Memis̲h̲ Ag̲h̲a, the head of the Ṭuzd̲j̲u-og̲h̲ullarî. After recurrent revolts and considerable bloodshed, the principal members of the family surrendered and were banished to Ruse/Rusčuk and Varna.

In 1294-5/1877-8, Rize became part of the newly-established sub-province (*sand̲j̲aḳ*) of Lazistān and was promoted to the rank of provincial capital. *Ca.* 1307-8/1890, in addition to a covered market, the town possessed an administrative building (*ḳonaḳ*) and constituted the seat of a governor (*müteṣarrif*). At this time, the district contained a population of 160,000, of whom 138,820 were Muslims. Apart from agriculture, citrus growing and small-scale boat building, Rize was noted for a fine and high-quality striped linen, which was marketed as far as Bag̲h̲dād and Egypt. This fabric has had a long history; it is mentioned in records of the Comnenian period, and *ca.* 1245/1830, 75,000 pieces were produced every year; *ca.* 1308/1890, 150,000 pieces were being woven. However, Rize weavers were able to expand output only by lowering prices and profit margins, so that textile manufacturing relieved the poverty of the area only to a limited extent. Rize *pes̲h̲temāl* is being manufactured down to the present day.

Overpopulation in the course of the 13th/19th century caused many young men to emigrate. Some of them settled in Istanbul, while others found their way to Odessa. The migrants specialised in various crafts; many were pastry-cooks. After the Russian Revolution of 1917 and the following civil war, most migrants to Russia were obliged to return. The losses of World War I, the Allied occupation of Istanbul and the War of Independence, also made life impossible for many of those who had migrated to the capital. Therefore, the district of Rize lived through a period of acute overpopulation and crisis during the 1920s, particularly since the market for fruits and nuts, the principal export crops of the time, collapsed during the distress of these years.

In an attempt to find a new source of livelihood for the people of the area, state-supported experiments were begun with the cultivation of tea. Until after 1950, local interest remained limited, and the situation only changed when the government guaranteed prices and undertook to process and market the finished product; but given the high production costs, Rize tea has never been competitive with the major tea-growing areas of the outside world. Since the early 1980s, tea cultivation has slowed down, and emigration from the region to the industrial areas of Istanbul and northwestern Anatolia has continued.

Rize is now the chef-lieu of an *il* or province of that name. With a town population of 43,407 in 1980, Rize now possesses such public amenities as secondary schools and hospitals.

Bibliography: V. Cuinet, *La Turquie d'Asie*, Paris 1892, i, 119-22; W. Heyd, *Histoire du commerce du Levant au Moyen-âge*, ²Leipzig 1936, 94; M. Münir Aktepe, *Tuzcu oğulları isyanı*, in *Tarih Dergisi*, iii/5-6 (1951-2), 21-52; M. Tayyib Gökbilgin, *XVI yüzyıl başlarında Trabzon livası ve Doğu Karadeniz bölgesi*, in *Belleten*, xxvi/102 (1962), 293-337; P. Minas Bıjışkyan (Trabzonlu), *Karadeniz kıyıları tarih ve coğrafyası 1817-1819*, tr. and annotated Hrand Andreasyan, Istanbul 1969, 61-2; S. Vryonis, *The decline of medieval Hellenism in Asia Minor and the process of islamization from the eleventh through the fifteenth century*, Berkeley, Los Angeles and London 1971, 307, 395; M.E. Meeker, *The great family Aghas of Turkey: a study of a changing political culture*, in R. Antoun and I. Harik (eds.), *Rural politics and social change in the Middle East*, Bloomington 1972, 237-66; *Yurt Ansiklopedisi*, ix, Istanbul 1982-3, art. *Rize* (fundamental; extensive bibl.); C.M. Hann, *Second thoughts on smallholders: tea production, the state and social differentiation in the Rize region*, in *New perspectives on Turkey*, iv (1990), 57-80; idem, *Tea and the domestication of the Turkish state*, London 1990; D. Quataert, *Ottoman manufacturing in the age of the Industrial Revolution*, Cambridge 1993, 63-4; *Murray's handbook for Asia Minor, Transcaucasia, Persia, etc.*, London 1895, 209-10; *Baedekers Konstantinopel, Kleinasien, Balkanstaaten*², Leipzig 1914, 250-1. (Suraiya Faroqhi)

RIZḲ (A.), pl. *arzāḳ*, literally, "anything granted by someone to someone else as a benefit", hence "bounty, sustenance, nourishment".

1. As a theological concept.

Rizḳ, and the nominal and verbal forms derived from it, are very frequent in the Ḳurʾān, especially in reference to the *rizḳ Allāh*, God's provision and sustenance for mankind from the fruits of the earth and the animals upon it (e.g. II, 20/22, 23/25, 57/60, etc.) (see further, section 2. below). Hence one of God's most beautiful names [see al-asmāʾ al-ḥusnā] is *al-Razzāḳ*, the All-Provider. The ultimate origin of the Arabic word lies, according to Jeffery, *The foreign vocabulary of the Qurʾān*, 142-3, in Middle Persian *rōzīg* "daily bread" < *rōč* "day", New Persian *rūz*, borrowed into Arabic at an early date—since it occurs frequently in ancient poetry—via Syriac *rōzīḳā*.

The ancient Arabs seem to have regarded a man's *rizḳ*, sc. whether he would go hungry in life or not, as something settled by Fate, an obvious consequence of the harsh desert environment of Arabia, which could not be altered much by individual human effort. Under the new dispensation of Islam, the power to determine a man's sustenance and happiness in life was transferred to the All-Powerful God, as is expressed by Ḳurʾān, XI, 8, "There is not a beast in the earth but God is responsible for its sustenance; He knows its lair and its resting-place; everyone is in a clear book" (cf. W. Montgomery Watt, *Free will and predestination in early Islam*, London 1948, 16-17; idem, *Muhammad at Mecca*, Oxford 1953, 24-5, 77; idem, *The formative period of Islamic thought*, Edinburgh 1973, 89,

92). This Ḳurʾānic view was later strengthened by the *ḥadīth* which stated that God decrees (*ḳaḍā, ḳaddara*) every term of life, a man's labour and a man's sustenance, for the coming year, a tradition which also echoes the pre-Islamic concepts and which can be found in others of the older Near Eastern religions (see H. Ringgren, *Studies in Arabian fatalism*, Uppsala-Wiesbaden 1955, 13, 117 ff., 163, 176).

In later centuries, some of the Islamic theologians, and especially, the Muʿtazila, questioned whether it was right to say that God decreed things like a man's sustenance beforehand; what if a man were to live off stolen food? Hence the Muʿtazila concluded that God only provides for a man the sustenance to which he is lawfully entitled. On the other hand, orthodox theologians like al-Nadjdjār and al-Ashʿarī [*q.vv.*], faced with the proposition that God provided unlawful as well as lawful sustenance, made the distinction that, whilst God provides both lawful and unlawful sustenance, it was possible for Him to provide a thing without giving ownership of it (cf. Watt, *Free will and predestination*, 66-7, 146; idem, *The formative period of Islamic thought*, 201, 233). (C.E. Bosworth)

2. In the Ḳurʾān.

In the extensive Ḳurʾānic use of this *maṣdar* (55 occurrences) and its related verbal forms (68 occurrences), God is virtually always the subject or implied agent. XXX, 40, makes maintenance of human life the explicit correlate of God's creation of it. Like creation, the power to sustain belongs to God alone (cf. XVI, 73, XXIX, 17, XXXV, 3, LXVII, 21) and requires no reciprocal human offering (cf. XX, 132, LI, 57). Frequent repetition of the two phrases (and variants) "God provides/will provide for whom he wishes" and "God spreads (*yabsuṭu*) his provision generously for whom He wishes and sparingly [for whom He wishes]", conveys a sense of specific allotment and allowed the commentators to offer *ḥaẓẓ* (portion, lot) as a synonym for *rizḳ*. The believer is promised this divine allocation both in this life and the Hereafter, prompting him to continuous praise of this "Best of Providers" (*khayr al-rāziḳīn*; cf. V, 114, XXII, 58, etc.).

Ḳurʾānic specification of God's sustenance includes such general designators as "good things" (*ṭayyibāt*) and "a good, or generous, provision" (*rizḳ^an ḥasan^an/karīm^an*), as well as more explicit reference. The mention of fruit (*thamarāt, fawākih*) is associated particularly with Abraham's prayer and with the eschatological reward (cf. II, 25, 126, XIV, 37, XXVIII, 57), while livestock (*bahīmatu l-anʿām*) is specified as a provision for the *ḥadjdj* rituals (cf. XXII, 28, 34). Miraculous intervention marks the nourishment provided to Moses' people, i.e. manna and quail (cf. II, 67, VII, 160), and that supplied to Mary in her sanctuary (III, 37). Jesus prays for sustenance (V, 114) in the form of a table sent from heaven to be a feast and a sign from God. Occasional Ḳurʾānic designation of *rizḳ* as "lawful and good" (*ḥalāl^an wa-ṭayyib^an* generated an exegetical and legal debate about whether illicitly acquired elements could be reckoned as part of one's allotment (see section 1., above).

Although some Ṣūfī groups insisted that strict *tawakkul* [*q.v.*] precluded all efforts to secure one's livelihood, a more moderate view eventually prevailed. As recipient of God's beneficence, the human being incurs a consequent ethical and legal obligation. The frequent Ḳurʾānic approbation of those who "expend of what We have provided," often found linked with the injunctions to believe in God and to establish the ritual prayer, conveys a fundamental posture of orthopraxis. In one of the few uses of the verb where God is not the direct agent, the imperative (*wa-rzuḳūhum*) in IV, 5, 8, signals this responsibility for relatives and orphans and for the incompetent (*al-sufahāʾ*), while II, 233, mandates the provision of food and clothing for nursing mothers (*rizḳuhunna wa-kiswatuhunna*).

Bibliography: Within the commentary literature, see especially the excursus in Fakhr al-Dīn al-Rāzī, *al-Tafsīr al-kabīr*, on Ḳurʾān, II, 3; Ashʿarī, *Maḳālāt al-islāmiyyīn*, Istanbul 1930, 257, and *al-Ibāna*, tr. W. Klein, New Haven 1940, 117-19; Abū Ṭālib al-Makkī, *Ḳūt al-ḳulūb*, Cairo 1381, ii, 3-37; Bāḳillānī, *K. al-Tamhīd*, Beirut 1957, 328-9; ʿAbd al-Djabbār, *Mughnī*, Cairo 1385, ii, 27-55, and *Sharḥ al-uṣūl al-khamsa*, Cairo 1384, 784-8; Abū Yaʿlā Ibn al-Farrāʾ, *K. al-Muʿtamad*, Beirut 1974, 149-52; Djuwaynī, *K. al-Irshād*, Paris 1938, 208-9; L. Gardet, *Dieu et la destinée de l'homme*, Paris 1967, 132-4; B. Reinert, *Die Lehre vom tawakkul in der klassischen Sufik*, Berlin 1968, 35-43; D. Gimaret, *Les noms divins en Islam*, Paris 1988, 397-400.

(Jane D. McAuliffe)

3. In military terminology.

Rizḳ appears here for the regular payments, in cash and in kind, made to those soldiers registered on the *dīwān* of earliest Islamic times and, by the ʿAbbāsid period, on the more elaborate *dīwān al-djaysh*, hence equivalent to *ʿaṭāʾ* [*q.v.*, and also djaysh. 1. and djund] or *ṭamaʿ*. Such soldiers, the *murtaziḳa*, those drawing regular allowances, are contrasted with the *mutaṭawwiʿa* [*q.v.*], volunteers who served in the early Islamic armies without regular stipends but who shared in the plunder. A single pay allotment was termed a *razḳa*, pl. *razaḳāt*. A considerable amount of information can be gleaned from the sources on the pay procedures, the intervals between payments, etc., both of the central caliphate and also of its provincial successor dynasties; see, in particular, W. Hoenerbach, *Zur Heeresverwaltung der ʿAbbāsiden. Studie über Abulfarağ*: Dīwān al-ğaiš, in *Isl.*, xxix (1950), 278 ff., and C.E. Bosworth, *Abū ʿAbdallāh al-Khwārazmī on the technical terms of the secretary's art*, in *JESHO*, xii (1969), 144-6. (C.E. Bosworth)

RIẒWĀN BEGOWIĆ [see riḍwān begović].

RODOS, Turkish name (popular pronunciation also Rados) for Rhodes (Greek Rhodos, Latin Rhodus, both fem.), an island and port city near the southwestern corner of Turkey, since 1948 a Greek possession and administrative centre of the *nomos* of Dodekanesos [see on iki ada].

Rhodes stands out for its relatively large size (1,404 km^2; the second largest island of the eastern Aegean after Lesbos (see midilli); maximum length between capes Kumburnu and Praso, 80 km, maximum breadth between capes Lardos and Armenistis, 38 km), regular shape (an extended ellipse with a northeast-southwest axis), position at the southeastern extremity of the Aegean archipelago, and proximity to the Anatolian coast (18 km to the nearest point on Daraçya peninsula; 45 km separate the harbours of Rhodes and Marmaris). The interior is relatively mountainous (Attaviros, 1215 m/3,985 ft. is the highest peak) and has one of the last remaining forests that once covered the Aegean islands. Its warm but never extreme climate, beautiful scenery, and thriving vineyards and orchards, have since Antiquity elicited praise from poets, pilgrims and tourists.

In the past it was the island's strategic location on or near shipping lanes linking the eastern Mediterranean with the Aegean, Adriatic, and Black Seas that made it play a historic role in trade, war, piracy, and raffic of pilgrims to and from the shrines of the Near ;ast. Aside from the context of war with the Byzan-nes, the caliph Muʿāwiya may have foreseen some of ıese assets when in 52/672 he sent a fleet under Djunāda b. Abī Umayya al-Azdī to seize Rhodes after preliminary raid in 33/654 staged by him while still overnor of Syria; al-Balādhurī states that when 'azīd succeeded Muʿāwiya seven years later, he rdered Djunāda to destroy the fort built after the onquest and return to Syria. Byzantine reports im-ly, however, that the Arabs occupied the island inter-ıittently until definitive withdrawal in 717-18 caused y their failure to take Constantinople. According to Byzantine source, the Muslims sold during their rief presence the bronze statue of the Colossus, since 25 BC lying toppled by earthquake in the sea, to a ewish merchant of Edessa as scrap metal.

The next and most dramatic steps of Rhodos into slamic history began when the Knights of St. John of erusalem (the Hospitallers, after 1530 better known s Knights of Malta [see DĀWIYYA and ISBITĀRIYYA in uppl.]) acquired it as their new base and head-uarters. This military and charitable order, driven ut of Acre [see ʿAKKĀ], their last possession in alestine, in 1291 by the Mamlūks, first moved to yprus as guests of the Lusignan dynasty, but by 309 they established themselves in Rhodes as a com-lex theocratic, commercial, and naval power until ıeir defeat and expulsion by Süleymān the Magnifi-ent 213 years later. Besides adding various buildings f religious and utilitarian nature, the Knights kept renghtening the fortifications of the city and port to e point where it would take a supreme effort by the ttoman empire at the peak of its might to conquer . On the commercial and economic level, the Order, hich also possessed several other islands of the odecanese as well as the fortress of St. Peter (ancient alicarnassus; see BODRUM) and the small but impor-nt island of Meis (Castellorizo) by the Turkish oast, prospered through trade carried on by a osmopolitan lay community benefiting from the curity assured by the rulers, but also through crative piracy cloaked in the mantle of Holy War ıd practiced both by the Knights themselves and by rivateers welcomed under specific conditions. On the aritable level, the Order lived up to its original mis-on of caring for sick and needy pilgrims, for they uilt and ran a hospital described with admiration by any travellers; and on the military level, the Order, though initially new to maritime matters, created a nall but efficient fleet that became a thorn in the side the Muslim powers of the eastern Mediterranean, st the Mamlūks and then the Turks. Having iginated and functioned in Palestine as a byproduct the Crusades early in the 12th century, the ospitallers retained some of this attitude and par-cipated in several later Crusades; thus in 1344 they ayed a vital role in the league organised by Pope lement VI that captured Izmir from the *amīrs* of ydīn [*q.v.*]; placed in charge of the city, they ithstood all Turkish attempts to dislodge them until imūr [*q.v.*] stormed the place in 1403. In 1365, the ospitallers participated in the sack of Alexandria led the king of Cyprus Peter I. This attack provoked belated but vigorous response from the Mamlūks, ho in 1424-6 reduced Cyprus to vassalage, and who tween 1440 and 1444 made three attempts to con-ıer Rhodes. The second attempt (1443) ended with e seizure of Meis, but only the third attacked hodes itself; after a 40 days' long siege, however, unterattacks by the Knights forced the Mamlūks to sist and sail back to Damietta.

Despite the confrontations with the Mamlūks and, increasingly, the Turks, the Hospitallers also had intermittent diplomatic and commercial relations with the Muslims, not unlike those pursued by Venice and other merchant republics, except that their emphasis was on care for Christian pilgrims (consuls in Jerusalem, Ramla and Damietta). The Knights sent envoys with congratulations and presents on the occasion of Meḥemmed II's accession in 1451, and after the sultan's conquest of Constantinople, they proposed a commercial treaty. The new crusade projected by Pope Calixtus III did not materialise, but the plan forced the Knights to change their policy and to resume maritime depredations on Turkish shipping and coasts. As a result, punitive expeditions were sent in the course of the 1450s; none dared to attack the fortified port city itself, but the second under Ḥamza Bey raided Istanköy/Kos, the Knights' other largest and most important island possession, and the fortress of Archangelos on the northeastern coast of Rhodes. The subsequent accommodation stipulating a cessation of the Knights' depredations had limited effect, partly because war with Venice (1463-79) absorbed the Ottomans' naval resources; the *shehzāde* Djem [*q.v.*], as governor of Ḳaramān [*q.v.*], had the task of dealing with the vexing problem. The return of an envoy sent by him to plead with the Knights coincided with the conclusion of the war, and the sultan turned his main attention to Rhodes. An imperial fleet under Mesīḥ Pasha sailed in spring 1480, and the Turks besieged the port city for two months (May-July 1480), but the final assault on 28 July collapsed and they withdrew. The failure may have been partly caused by flaws in the vizier's leadership, but also by the absence of the sultan himself. Moreover, Meḥemmed II did not repeat the attempt the following year but threw the main force of the empire into a campaign that may have had Rome as its ultimate target; his own death in May 1481 caused the Turks to abandon their bridgehead at Otranto, and the subsequent fifteen years witnessed a paralysing contest between Djem and his brother, Sultan Bāyezīd II [*q.v.*], for the throne. The *shehzade*, defeated by his brother on the mainland, took refuge in Rhodes (July-August 1482), whence the Knights transferred him to the custody of their brethren in France; the threat which the pretender's existence posed to the sultan was held in check by payment of onerous indemnities, first to the Knights and then to the Pope, and it ceased only with Djem's death in 1495. Even more harmful, however, was the chronic threat posed by the powerful corsair Knights, whose port also functioned as an intelligence centre and a base for other Christian powers and pirates preying on "infidels", and the sultans' protracted neglect to resolve this problem. Ironically, however, the Hospitallers may have unwittingly assisted the birth of Ottoman power in North Africa, and the genesis of the greatest naval epic of the Islamic Mediterranean, when they turned the initially commerce-minded Barbarossa brothers into prodigiously successful Muslim corsairs by temporarily capturing and enslaving Khiḍir, the future Khayr al-Dīn [*q.v.*].

The overdue conquest of Rhodes was finally achieved by Süleymān the Magnificent after a five months' long siege (July-December 1522) whose magnitude, display of heroism by both sides, as well as mutual courtesy marking the two encounters between the Order's Grand Master Philippe Villiers de l'Isle Adam and the sultan, have secured it a choice place in the annals of Mediterranean history. Both adversaries were long aware of the inevitability of a final confrontation. Since the siege of 1480, the Knights had perfected the fortifications to the verge of impregnability. The sultan, however, eager to inaugurate his reign by succeeding where his illustrious ancestor had failed (at Belgrade [*q.v.*] and Rhodes), threw the formidable resources of the Ottoman empire against the daunting defences of the island fortress. The besiegers had at their disposal a war and logistical fleet estimated at up to 700 vessels; the sultan, who had come overland, embarked at Marmaris for the island. The operations themselves were revealing for the great strides the art of siege mining had made since the fall of Constantinople; it performed a role against the walls of Rhodes no less crucial than artillery had done against those of the Byzantine capital. The final surrender of the Hospitallers was facilitated by the generous terms which Süleyman the Magnificent accorded them; they included a safe departure of the Order as well as of all others wishing to leave. The Turks entered the fortress on Christmas Eve 1522; churches were turned into mosques on Christmas Day, and on St. Stephens' Day, a Friday, the sultan held a *dīwān*, at the end of which he received the Grand Master. The Order's evacuation, in its own ships, was completed by 1 January 1523, with Villiers de l'Isle Adam leaving on that day. The humaneness displayed by Süleymān at the conclusion of this triumph was marred by the arrest and execution of his uncle Murād, the son of D̲jem, who had remained in Rhodes and converted to Christianity, and of his son (his wife and two daughters were sent to Istanbul). Moreover, although the magnanimity of the sultan's treatment of the defeated Knights is indisputable, its wisdom is less certain: Süleymān underestimated the resiliency of the military order, which would become his nemesis at the conclusion of his life by repulsing a similar attempt to dislodge it from the island of Malta (1565), besides again becoming a thorn in the side of Muslim shipping.

After the conquest and for the rest of the Ottoman period (1522-1912), Rhodes lost much of its former prominence and strategic importance; this was due not only to the fact that it itself no longer threatened Turkish coasts and shipping but also because all of the eastern Mediterranean became part of the empire. Nevertheless, the port city could at times perform ancillary roles. Thus it served as a naval base during the conquest of Cyprus in 1571, and then again during that of Crete, 1645-69. Rhodes also began to play a role once Ottoman naval hegemony in the eastern Mediterranean was broken: in 1799, when it was the rallying point for the fleet sent to counter Napoleon's invasion of Egypt; and in 1824, when the Egyptian fleet joined the Ottoman one as part of the campaign launched to quell the uprising in the Morea [see MORA].

Meanwhile, Rhodes also declined as a commercial emporium, and the population of the port city shrank to a fraction of the size it is believed to have had during periods of prosperity from Antiquity to the Middle Ages. Ewliyā Čelebi, who stopped on the island in 1671 on his way to Mecca, describes the port city as containing, within the walls, 4,200 houses or 24 *maḥalle*s (neighbourhoods), of which 18 were inhabited by Muslims, 4 by Greeks, and 2 by Jews. Although the city acquired a predominantly Turkish population and a somewhat Ottoman touch, thanks to the minarets adorning its mosques, the countryside remained overwhelmingly Greek; it may also be that not all the dwellings of the Turkish quarters were occupied, as suggested by the figures arrived at by late 19th century censuses (data published by Cuinet, i, 370) which mention the island's population as 29,148 souls, of whom 6,825 were Muslims, 20,250 Gree[k] Orthodox, 1,513 Jews, 546 Catholics, and 14 Armenians; the port city itself was found to harbour 7,80[0] people, of whom 6,287 were Muslims and 1,513 Jew[s] within the walls, while 150 Muslims, 2,300 Greek Orthodox, 546 Catholics, and 14 Armenians live[d] outside the walls (the latter two groups were thu[s] limited to the capital's suburbs); in other words toward the end of the Ottoman period, most of it[s] Turkish population lived within the walls of the city o[f] Rhodes, whereas none of the Greeks did.

After the conquest, Rhodes became a *sand̲j̲aḳ in th[e]* *eyālet* of the archipelago (D̲jazāʾir-i Baḥr-i Safīd [*q.v.*]) under the command of the Ḳapudān Pas̲h̲a [*q.v.*]. With the 1283/1867 administrative reform of the empire, which established the *wilāyet* as the largest uni[t] consisting of *sand̲j̲aḳ*s and *ḳaḍā*ʾs, the new *wilāyet* use[d] the same name but was reduced to 4 *sand̲j̲aḳ*s (Chio[s] [see SAKĪZ], the administrative centre; Rhodes, Lesbo[s] [see MIDILLI], and Limni [*q.v.*] each with several adjacent islands). The administrative centre was moved t[o] Rhodes in 1283/1876, and from then on until 1912 th[e] two islands took turns to claim this primacy.

Rhodes left the *Dār al-Islām* in a manner that was a[s] antithetical to its glorious entry four centuries earlie[r] as the empire itself was to its former self. The Italia[n] conquest, a spin-off from the war over Tripolitania was little more than a formality when on 4 May 191[2] a 6,000 men strong force landed on the island an[d] marched the next day into the port city, abandoned b[y] the *wālī*, who had fled to the mainland, and by th[e] small garrison, which withdrew to the interior town o[f] Psinthos. The Italians reduced the latter by 1 June the casualties being 9 men on the invaders' side an[d] 100 on the defenders' one. This conquest wa[s] characteristic of the ease with which the coloni[al] powers of Europe usually overcame the resistance o[f] their non-European victims. The peace treaty o[f] Ouchy signed in October 1912 stipulated that Rhode[s] and other islands would be restored to the Ottomans but Italy then took advantage of Turkey's woes caused by the Balkan War and refused to honour th[e] pledge; moreover, Turkey's choice of the losing sid[e] in World War I and Italy's choice of the winning on[e] facilitated the latter's goal permanently to acquir[e] Rhodes with its dependent islands. This was th[e] genesis of the *Isole Italiane dell'Egeo*, a possession sanctioned by the peace treaty of Lausanne (24 July 1923). By then, however, not Turkey but Greece ha[d] become Italy's contender for the islands; but only th[e] effects of World War II made Greece's acquisition o[f] this archipelago possible (7 March 1948).

The four centuries of Ottoman rule in Rhodes le[ft] memories of historical as well as monuments of architectural interest. At the same time, the Turks allowed most of the island's earlier physiognomy to remain intact, so that Rhodes is now a treasure trove fo[r] scholars and tourists alike. A library founded i[n] 1208/1793 by Ḥāfiẓ Aḥmed Ag̲h̲a, a native of th[e] island, who had risen to the position of *rikābdār* *s̲h̲ehriyārī* at the court, was further enriched by his so[n] Ṭopk̲h̲āne Mus̲h̲īri Feth̲ī Pas̲h̲a, and is now one of th[e] source depositories for the history of Ottoman Rhode[s] (see Rossi in *Bibl.*). From among other buildings an[d] sites, the *külliyye* of Murād Reʾīs (d. 1018/1609) [is] especially noteworthy because the tombs of sever[al] notables retired or exiled to Rhodes (such as thre[e] khans of the Crimea) are in the courtyard of its *tekk[e]*.

Bibliography: (The pre-Islamic period as well a[s] non-Islamic aspects, outside the scope of this article, are covered by a literature whose volume an[d] quality dwarf that devoted to our topic; this is ex plained not only by the number and experience of scholars studying classical and mediaeval Rhodes but also by the relatively brief and superficial effect which the Muslims had on it. As basic treatment, the article *Rhodos* in Pauly-Wissowa's *Realenzyklopädie* can be cited; another example is the ten large volumes of *Clara Rhodos*, published between 1928 and 1941 by the Istituto Storico-archeologico di Rhodi.) Balādhurī, *The origins of the Islamic state*, tr. P.K. Hitti, New York 1916, repr. 1968, i, 375-6; H. Balducci, *Architettura turca in Rodi*, Milan 1932, and Turkish tr. C. Rodoslu, *Rodos'ta türk mimarisi*, Ankara 1945; C. Rodoslu, *Rodos ve İstanköy adalarında gömülü tarihî simalar*, Ankara 1945; A. Gabriel, *La cité de Rhodes*, Paris 1921; *Sālnāme* for Djezā'ir-i Bahr-i Sefīd, year 1303 (publ. 1311), 146 ff.; V. Cuinet, *La Turquie d'Asie*, Paris 1892, i, 345-97; Z. Çelikkol, *Rodos'taki türk eserleri ve tarihçe*, Ankara 1986; idem, *İstanköy'deki Türk eserleri ve tarihçe*, Ankara 1990; W.J. Eggeling, *Türkische Moscheen auf Rhodos*, in *Materialia Turcica*, vii-viii (1982); O. Aslanapa, *Rodos'ta Türk eserleri*, in *Türk Kültürü*, xlii (1966), 531-4; S. Turan, *Rodos'un zaptından Malta muhasarasına*, Ankara 1970; idem, *Rodos ve 12 Ada Türk hakimiyetinden çıkışı*, Ankara 1970; Michele Nicolas, *La Communauté musulmane de Grèce*, in *Turcica*, viii/1 (1976); M. Baştiyalı, *Osmanlı idaresinde Rodos* (unpubl. *mezuniyet tezi*, Ankara University 1970); C. Orhonlu, *On İki Ada meselesi*, in *Türk Kültürü*, xxiii (1964), 1-5; idem, *On İki Ada meselesi ve Türk nüfusü*, in *Türk Kültürü*, xxiv (1964), 29-34; Mustafa Čelebi Djelālzāde [Ḳodja Nishāndjī], *Ṭabaḳāt ul-memālik we deredjāt ul-mesālik*, ed. Petra Kappert, 1981, 55-9 (German summary), 65a-103b (facs. of the ms.); Ewliyā Čelebi, *Seyāḥat-nāme*, Istanbul 1935, ix, 233-57; Pīrī Re'īs, *Kitāb-i Baḥriyye*, Ankara 1935, 238-42, and new ed., Istanbul 1988, ii, 524-33; Kâtip Čelebi, *Tühfet ul-kibār fī esfār ul-biḥār*, Istanbul 1329, 16-17, 23-4; E. Rossi, *Assedio e conquista turca di Rodi nel 1522 secondo le relazioni edite e inedite dei Turchi; con un cenno sulla Biblioteca Hafiz di Rodi*, Rome 1927; idem, *Nuove ricerche sulle fonti turche relative all'assedio di Rodi nel 1522*, in *RSO*, xv (1934), 97-102; idem, *Storia della marina dell'Ordine di S. Giovanni di Gerusalemme, di Rodi e di Malta*, Rome-Milan 1926, esp. 12-31; V. Strumza, *Il "tecche" di Murad Reis a Rodi*, in *Rivista delle Colonie Italiane* (Jan. 1934), 3-9; Ziver Bey, *Radus ta'rīkhi*, Rhodes 1312; Michèle Nicolas, *Une communauté musulmane de Grèce* (*Rhodes et Kos*), in *Turcica*, viii (1976), 58-69; İ.H. Uzunçarşılı, *Osmanlı tarihi*, Ankara 1988, ii, *passim*; C.I. Papachristodoulou, *Istoria tis Rodou*, Athens 1972; E. Papaioannou, *Rhodes and modern texts*, 6 vols., Athens-Ioannina-Rhodes 1989-93 (in Grk.); C.E. Bosworth, *Arab attacks on Rhodes in the pre-Ottoman period*, forthcoming in *JRAS* (1995). See also the *Bibl.* to ON İKİ ADA. (S. Soucek)

RODOSTO [see TEKIRDAGH].

RŌH, the generic name, used by local western Pandjābīs and Balūč for the tract of northwestern India extending southwards from Swāt and Badjawr in the north and up to the Sulaymān Mountains in the west. It was significant in the history of the later 9th/15th century and early 10th/16th century as a region from which the Lōdī [*q.v.*] sultans of Dihlī drew many of their Afghān supporters.

Bibliography: Sir Olaf Caroe, *The Pathans 550 B.C.-A.D. 1957*, London 1958, index. See also ROHILKHAND. (Ed.)

ROHILKHAND, the "land of the Rohillas", is the historical appellation of an area of about 12,800 square miles between the Himalayas and the Ganges, including Katahr [*q.v.*] and the Mughal districts of Sambhal and Badā'ūn. It became current from about 1153/1740 onwards, when groups of Indo-Afghāns known as Rohīlas or, later, Rohillas, made their main settlement in India in the area thus denoted. *Rohilla* was simply an Indianised name for Afghān which developed in the 11th/17th century, but more specifically referred to the people from Rōh [*q.v.*], the term which in the 11th/17th-century Indian and Indo-Afghān works most often signified the area from Swāt to Badjawr in the north to Sībī and Bhakkar in Sind, and from Ḥasan Abdāl in the east to Kābul and Ḳandahār in the west. In the 12th/18th century Rohilla panegyric *Khulāṣat al-ansāb*, the extent of Rōh comes very close to that of present-day Afghānistān. Wendel wrote about the Rohillas in 1767: "Ils occupent seuls tout le païs au-dela du Gange, depuis le Gomaon jusqu'aux frontières du *soubah* d'Avat [Awadh], environ trois degrés en latitude, du 27° au 30°, et deux ou 2° 30 de longitude, de 94° au 96° et demi, prise du méridien de l'Isle-de-fer. Ce païs s'appelle, a notre tems, de leur nom et demeure *Rohél-Kand*" (Deleury, 156). The *Imperial Gazetteer of India* (1908), 304, says that "the name is often applied to the present Bareilly Division of the United Provinces; but it also denotes a definite historical tract nearly corresponding with that Division *plus* the Rāmpur and the Tarai *parganas* of Nainī Tāl District."

The successive Muslim rulers of Hindūstān have always attached great importance to the possession of this advantageously situated and fertile region. From early Islamic times onwards, the eastern part was known as Katahr, the home of the Katahriya Radjpūts, who, according to local traditions, may have arrived here in the 6th/12th and 8th/14th centuries, occupying first the country between the Rāmgangā and the Ganges, and subsequently spreading east of the former river. In 594/1197 Ḳuṭb al-Dīn Aybak [*q.v.*] conquered Badā'ūn [*q.v.*], probably from the Rāthor ruler Lakshmanapala. Badā'ūn was one of the earliest centres of Muslim culture in North India. Hundreds of Muslim martyrs lie buried there. The *iḳṭā'* of Badā'ūn was one of the most important assignments of governors already under the Mu'izzī Sultans of Dihlī and is mentioned frequently in the Indo-Muslim chronicles. Iltutmish [*q.v.*] came to the throne in 607/1211 while he held the *iḳṭā'* of Badā'ūn. In 633/1236 its governor Rukn al-Dīn became king of Dihlī. Some of the earliest Muslim architecture in the area dates back to these first governors. Badā'ūn held its position as the Muslim capital of Katahr for over four centuries, during which period numerous uprisings of the Katahriya *mawāsāt* ('brigands') are recorded. The importance of Badā'ūn decreased, and Bareilly became the capital, under Shāh Djahān, while Awrangzīb added the district of Sambhal (Western Rohilkhand) to the territory ruled over by the governor of Katahr.

The great majority of Afghān immigrants who, from the second half of the 11th/17th to the beginning of the 13th/19th century, settled in Katahr/Rohilkhand originated from the area of Peshāwar [*q.v.*] and belonged to the Yūsufzay tribe, mostly of the Mandanr subsection. At the beginning of the 12th/18th century, Mughal rule in the provinces of Sambhal and Badā'ūn was restricted to the vicinity of the larger cities of Bareilly, Murādābād and Badā'ūn, while there were already many Afghāns from the Peshāwar area in the local armies of the Katahr *rādjās*, and Katahr at large was dominated by rival Katahriya

Radjpūt, Djāt and Bandjara *zamīndārs*. Dāwūd Khān (*ca.* 1122-37/1710-25), founder of the Rohilla state, started his career as a petty horsetrader, and for some time was a military entrepreneur and cavalry officer in the service of one of the local *zamīndārs* of Katahr. The succeeding Rohilla leader, ʿAlī Muḥammad Khān (1137-62/1725-49), became increasingly involved in Mughal politics, assumed the title of *Nawwāb* [*q.v.*]—which was soon recognised by the emperor—and set up court at the new capital of Aonla. This happened in the wake of Nādir Shāh's invasion (1152/1739), when new waves of Yūsufzay immigrants from Rōh swelled the Rohilla ranks to around 100,000. In 1155/1742 a large campaign into the Terai and the northern hills was undertaken; Kumaon and Garhwal were reduced to tributary status. At the time of ʿAlī Muḥammad Khān's death, Mughal imperial influence in Rohilkhand had vanished. Ḳāʾim Khān, the Bangash *nawwāb* of the adjacent Afghān principality of Farrukhābād [*q.v.*], as the senior member of the Afghān nobility at the Dihlī court, now claimed the whole of Rohilkhand. He was killed, however, in the ensuing struggle with the Rohillas in 1161/1748-9, near Badāʾūn. Rohilkhand then became a confederacy of small principalities based on a dense and flourishing urban network. Another Rohilla parvenu, Nadjīb al-Dawla (1166-84/1753-70 [*q.v.*]), the main Indian ally of Aḥmad Shāh Durrānī and a supporter of the acting *wazīr* in Dihlī, ʿImād al-Mulk, against the Īrānī faction of the Awadh governor Ṣafdār Djang [*q.v.*], received Rohilkhand, next to Djalālābād [*q.v.* in Suppl.] and Sahāranpūr [*q.v.*] in *djāgīr*, with an imperial *manṣab* of 5,000. Nadjīb al-Dawla, a principal noble at the Dihlī court, became a strong champion of Sunnī revivalism, a patron of Shāh Walī Allah [*q.v.*], and Rohilkhand was turned into the ideological counterpart of Shīʿī Awadh. Having gained control of the entire Upper Miyān Doʾāb, Nadjīb al-Dawla founded a new capital which he called Nadjībābād [*q.v.*] and which was to become an important commercial centre for the control of the hill trade with Garhwal and Tibet and the east-west trade routes to Kashmīr and Peshāwar. Ṣafdār Djang, in the years 1161/1748 and 1165/1752, tried to oust the Afghāns from both Rohilkhand and Farrukhābād with the aid of the Marāthās [*q.v.*]. But Durrānī involvement in India in the 1160s/1750s and 1170s/1760s greatly boosted the power of the Rohillas. After Nadjīb al-Dawla's death in 1184/1770, again, Durrānī influence faded, while Marāthā incursions became more frequent. As a consequence of Durrānī withdrawal from India and increased British involvement, Rohilkhand was annexed to Awadh in 1188/1774.

In the subsequent period, until the British annexation of the area in 1216/1801, the *djamaʿ* figures for Rohilkhand declined sharply, as did the trading and important horse breeding activity in the area. In the 13th/19th century the Rohillas no longer played a dominant role, but are still encountered as mercenaries, local landlords and urban élites. Wendel, Tieffenthaler, Francklin, Forster, and Hardwick all describe the flourishing conditions of the Rohilla cities and the surrounding countryside in the 12th/18th century. Wendel mentions the Rohillas as the great producers of hemp, marijuana and opium of India. The population of Muslims in Rohilkhand was 28% of the total of near 6.2 million in 1908, about double that found in the Ceded Provinces as a whole.

Bibliography: A. Cunningham, *Report of tours in the Gangetic provinces from Badaon and Bihar in 1875-76 and 1877-78*, repr. Varanasi 1968, 1-11; G. Deleury, *Les Indes florissantes: anthologie des voyageurs français (1750-1820)*, Paris 1991, 109, 115, 155-9; *Imperial gazetteer of India*², xxi, 304-8; A. Wink, *Al-Hind. The making of the Indo-Islamic world, II. The Slave Kings and the Islamic conquest of India* (forthcoming); E.I. Brodkin, *Rohilkhand from conquest to revolt, 1774-1858: a study of the origins of the Indian Mutiny uprising*, Ph.D. diss. University of Cambridge 1968, unpubl.; J.J.L. Gommans, *Horse-traders, mercenaries and princes: the formation of the Indo-Afghan empire in eighteenth-century South and Central Asia*, Ph.D. diss., University of Leiden 1993, unpubl. (A. Wink)

ROHILLAS or Rohilas, the name given to Afghāns of various tribes who came from Rōh [*q.v.*] and settled in the 11th and 12th/17th and 18th centuries in Katahr [*q.v.*] (in the western part of modern Uttar Pradesh) called Rohilkhand [*q.v.*] after them.

Bahādur Khān Rohilla, a noble of Shāh Djahān (1037-68/1628-58) founded Shāhdjahānpur; and his brother Dilīr Khān founded Shāhābād (1664). The area began to attract Afghān immigrants, among them a mercenary Dāwūd Khān (killed in 1132/1720). Dāwūd Khān's adopted son ʿAlī Muḥammad Khān (d. 1160/1748) established himself at Aonla (near Bareilly) as a local chief, and it needed an expedition personally led by the Mughal Emperor Muḥammad Shāh (1157/1745 [*q.v.*]) to dislodge him from there. His son Nadjīb al-Dawla [*q.v.*] competed with the other Rohilla leaders Ḥāfiẓ Raḥmat Khān [*q.v.*] and Dūndī Khān, who took possession of his territory. In 1166/1753 Ḥāfiẓ Raḥmat Khān sided with the minister Ṣafdār Djang [*q.v.*], while Nadjīb al-Dawla aided the Emperor and was awarded a *manṣab* [*q.v.*] of 5,000. In 1169/1756 Nadjīb al-Dawla joined the Afghān ruler Aḥmad Shāh Durrānī or Abdālī [*q.v.*]. In 1170/1757 Nadjīb al-Dawla obtained appointment as Mīr Bakhshī. All the principal Rohilla chiefs allied themselves with Aḥmad Shāh Abdālī and played an important role in his victory over the Marāthās at Pānīpat [*q.v.*] in 1174/1761. As rewards extensive territories were assigned to them by the victor. But the Rohilla leaders could not consolidate their gains because of mutual jealousies. Nadjīb al-Dawla died in 1186/1772 and was succeeded by Ḍābiṭa Khān. Ḥāfiẓ Raḥmat Khān and his allies among the Rohilla chiefs were utterly overthrown by Shudjāʿ al-Dawla and the English in 1188/1774. Ḍābiṭa Khān (d. 1199/1785), who was not involved in this conflict maintained his position with difficulty; his son Ghulām Ḳādir became infamous by seizing Dihlī and blinding the Emperor Shāh ʿĀlam (1202/1788). He was killed soon afterwards, and Rohilla rule in the upper Doʾāb also disappeared; the Rāmpur State [*q.v.*] was the only Rohilla principality to survive.

The Rohillas obtained commendation from contemporary observers for their promotion of agriculture. As builders, their contributions were modest, though Nadjīb al-Dawla left a town named after him (Nadjībābād [*q.v.*]), where he built a fort and some other buildings. Nor did the Rohillas leave much of an imprint on art and literature. They do not appear to have promoted their own language, Pashto, in any notable way, and it soon disappeared. In the next century, the Rohillas under Khān Bahādur Khān, a grandson of Ḥāfiẓ Raḥmat Khān, joined the Sepoy Rebellion of 1857-8 and suffered the consequences of its failure.

Bibliography: Ghulām Ḥusayn, *Siyar al-mutaʾakhkhirīn*, Lucknow 1876; Ghulām ʿAlī Naḳwī *ʿImād al-saʿādat*, Lucknow 1897; W. Irvine, *The later Mughals*, ii, Calcutta 1922; Jadunath Sarkar, *Fall of the Mughal Empire*, iv, repr. Calcutta 1964; Sh. Abdur Rashid, *Najibud Daula, his life and times*, Aligarh 1952; Iqbal Husain, *The rise and decline of Rohila chieftains*, New Delhi 1993. (M. Athar Ali)

RŌHTĀS, a fortress in the Jhelum District of the Pandjāb province of Pākistān (lat. 32°55′ N., long. 73°48′ E.), 16 km/10 miles to the northwest of Jhelum town. It was built by Shīr Shāh Sūr [*q.v.*] in 949/1542 after his victory over the Mughal Humāyūn [*q.v.*] and named after Shēr Shāh's other fortress in Bihār, Rōhtāsgaṙh [*q.v.*].

Bibliography: *Imperial gazetteer of India*², xxi, 332. (Ed.)

RŌHTĀSGAṘH, a hill fortress and settlement in the Shāhābād District in the northeast of the state of Bihār in the Indian Union (lat. 24°37′ N., long. 83°55′ E.), some 50 km/30 miles south of the town of Sahsarām [*q.v.*]. There must have been a Hindu fort or settlement there previously, but the present fortifications date from its capture by Shīr Shāh Sūr [*q.v.*] in 946/1539. They were added to by Akbar's general Mān Singh [*q.v.*] when he was appointed governor of Bihār and Bengal. It was surrendered to the British army in Bengal soon after the battle of Baksar (Buxar [*q.v.*]) in 1764 through the efforts of Mīr Ḳāsim ᶜAlī's opponent Ghulām Ḥusayn Khān Ṭabāṭabāʾī [*q.vv.*].

Bibliography: *Imperial gazetteer of India*², xxi, 322-3. (Ed.)

RONDA [see runda].

ROSHANIYYA [see rawshaniyya].

al-**RUʾĀSĪ**, Ibn Akhī Muᶜādh al-Harrāʾ, Muḥammad [b. al-Ḥasan] b. Abī Sāra al-Nīlī al-Naḥwī, Abū Djaᶜfar, an Arab grammarian, regarded to be the legendary founder of the Kūfan school of grammar.

Very little is known about his life and grammatical views, which are rarely quoted by later grammarians. The legend about al-Ruʾāsī's founding the Kūfan school of grammar seems to have been invented by Thaᶜlab [*q.v.*] in his polemics with al-Mubarrad [*q.v.*]. Both grammarians quote the name of al-Ruʾāsī (this name from the largeness of his head) in a clearly polemical vein. Al-Ruʾāsī is said to be quoted by Sībawayhi as al-Kūfī "the Kufan", which is not corroborated by the text of *al-Kitāb*. Al-Ruʾāsī was a *mawlā* of Muḥammad b. Kaᶜb al-Ḳuraẓī, and probably a relative (according to Ibn al-Anbārī, his nephew) of the inventor of *taṣrīf* and Ḳurʾān reader Muᶜādh al-Harrāʾ, which might be inferred from his name Ibn Akhī Muᶜādh al-Harrāʾ. Later grammatical sources (e.g. al-Suyūṭī) confuse al-Ruʾāsī with his relative Muᶜādh al-Harrāʾ. In Kūfa, al-Ruʾāsī studied Ḳurʾānic recitation (*ḥurūf*) under al-Aᶜmash (d. 147/764); grammar he learned from ᶜĪsā b. ᶜUmar and Abū ᶜAmr b. al-ᶜAlāʾ. His disciples in Ḳurʾānic recitation were Khallād b. al-Minḳarī and ᶜAlī b. Muḥammad al-Kindī, and in grammar al-Kisāʾī and al-Farrāʾ, both famous grammarians from the Kūfan school. He is said to have visited Baṣra, but was never accepted there as a grammarian. Kūfa seems not to have been his favourite dwelling place; most of the time he spent in the neighbouring al-Nīl (whence his *nisba*), from where his wife originated. Judging from secondary evidence, al-Ruʾāsī lived in the second half of the 2nd/8th century; he was a contemporary of al-Khalīl b. Aḥmad [*q.v.*], with whom he maintained contacts. During the reign of Hārūn al-Rashīd he was said to have been very old (*ᶜummira*).

None of his works is extant. (1) His most frequently mentioned work on grammar is the treatise *al-Fayṣal* ("The Decisive"). The 3rd/9th century grammarian Ibn al-Sarrādj claimed to have read it (according to Yāḳūt). His other grammatical works are: (2) *al-Taṣghīr* on the diminutive; (3) *al-Ifrād wa 'l-djamᶜ* on the singular and plural. His main interest lay, however, in practical problems of Ḳurʾānic recitation. Quoted are the following works: (4) *Kitāb Maᶜānī al-Ḳurʾān*; (5) *al-Ikhtiyārāt fi 'l-ḳirāʾa*; (4) *Kitāb al-Waḳf wa 'l-ibtidāʾ al-kabīr*; (5) *K. al-Waḳf wa 'l-ibtidāʾ al-ṣaghīr*.

Bibliography: Ibn al-Nadīm, *Fihrist*, Cairo, 96-7; Abu 'l-Ṭayyib, *Marātib*, Cairo 1974, 48-9; Yāḳūt, *Muᶜdjam al-udabāʾ*, vi, 480-2; Ibn al-Anbārī, *Nuzhat al-alibbāʾ fī ṭabaḳāt al-udabāʾ*, Stockholm 1963, 32-3; Ḳifṭī, *Inbāh al-ruwāt fī anbāʾ al-nuḥāt*, Cairo, iv, 99-103; Suyūṭī, *Bughyat al-wuᶜāt*, i, 82-3 (no. 134), 109 (no. 180: another version of his biography); Sezgin, *GAS*, ix, 125-6. (J. Danecki)

al-**RUᶜAYNĪ**, Abu 'l-Ḥasan ᶜAlī b. Muḥammad b. ᶜAlī b. Muḥammad b. ᶜAbd al-Raḥmān b. Hayṣam (al-Ḥādjdj), scholar and *adīb* of Muslim Spain.

He belonged to a family, known as the Banu 'l-Ḥādjdj, established in Baṭsha (near Seville) and was also known as Ibn al-Fakhkhār, "the son of the potter", that being his father's occupation, which he refused to follow. Al-Ruᶜaynī was born in Seville in 592/1196 and died in Marrākush in 666/1267, where his funeral was widely attended. He studied the Ḳurʾānic sciences, grammar, *ḥadīth*, *fiḳh* and *adab*. Most of the details of his life we know through his own writing. He travelled widely in al-Andalus and in the Maghrib; he can be traced in Ḳabṭīl, Málaga, Jérez, Cordova, Murcia, Granada, Sabta, Tlemcen and Marrākush. At an early age (year 615/1218), he was *ḳāḍī* in Morón. However, his activities were soon concentrated in his work as *kātib* of the kings of al-Andalus and the Maghrib. By this it may be understood that he served not only the Almohads but probably also the various independent rulers who, taking advantage of the progressive weakness of the Almohad régime, appeared in al-Andalus and North Africa. In this, his career was similar to that of other contemporary *kuttāb* like Abu 'l-Muṭarrif Ibn ᶜAmīra [*q.v.*]. Al-Ruᶜaynī's exchange of letters with the famous *kātib* Abū ᶜAbd Allāh b. al-Djannān has been preserved by al-Marrākushī. Ibn al-Djannān having written a *Risāla ᶜayniyya*, al-Ruᶜaynī replied with two other letters using the same device, namely, employing words all of which contained the letter *ᶜayn*. He also exchanged letters with Ibn ᶜAmīra.

Al-Marrākushī has also recorded some of his poems, as well as the names of his teachers from al-Andalus and abroad, this information being more complete that the list found in al-Ruᶜaynī's own *barnāmadj*. This most important work, entitled *Kitāb al-Īrād li-nubdhat al-mustafād min al-riwāya wa 'l-isnād bi-liḳāʾ ḥamalat al-ᶜilm fi 'l-bilād ᶜalā ṭarīḳ al-iḳtiṣār wa 'l-iḳtiṣād*, is preserved in two mss. (Escorial, 1729 and private collection of Khayr al-Dīn al-Ziriklī). I. Shabbūḥ presented the text in an article which he published in 1959 and later edited in a book (Damascus 1962). The *barnāmadj* is organised according to the names of al-Ruᶜaynī's teachers and according to their teachings. Its methodology and value have been assessed by al-Ahwānī and Fórneas in their seminal work on Andalusian bibliographical literature. Al-Ruᶜaynī's *barnāmadj*, contrary to Ibn Khayr's *Fahrasa*, does not offer complete *riwāyāt* of the works mentioned and therefore is not of great use for the study of their introduction in al-Andalus. It is, however, of great value for the knowledge of which books were being written and transmitted in his lifetime and in those of his teachers. It contains abundant information on the teaching and transmission of the Ḳurʾānic sciences (especially *ḳirāʾāt*), *adab* works (like al-Ḥarīrī's *Maḳāmāt*) and poetry. Among the data which he offers, it is worth noting the transmission of the *Shiʿr fi 'l-ḥudjdja ʿalā ithbāt al-ḳadar* by al-Murādī, of the *Maḳāmiʿ al-ṣulbān* by al-Khazradjī, of other *barāmidj* (he quotes many *riwāyāt* by Ibn ʿUbayd Allāh al-Ḥadjarī, d. 591/1194, through Abu 'l-ʿAbbās al-ʿAzafī), of al-Suhrawardī's *K. ʿAwārif al-maʿārif* and ʿIyāḍ's *K. al-Shifāʾ*. He has recorded valuable information about his teachers and contemporaries, like Ibn Hishām al-Azdī (the author of *Mufīd li 'l-ḥukkām*), Ibn Kharūf al-Naḥwī (d. 609/1212), Ibn Zarḳūn (d. 622/1225), Ibn Khalfūn (d. 636/1238), Abu 'l-Rabīʿ al-Kalāʿī, Abu 'l-ʿAbbās al-ʿAzafī, Abū ʿĀmir b. Ubbā (author of several theological works) and Yaḥyā b. Ibrāhīm al-Khudhūdj al-Mursī, author of a work on chess. Also noteworthy is his wide use of the *idjāza*. Al-Ruʿaynī's leaning towards *adab* and poetry is shown in his *Djanā 'l-azāhir al-naḍīra wa-sanā 'l-zawāhir al-munīra fī ṣilat "al-Maṭmaḥ" wa 'l-"Dhakhīra" mimmā walladathu al-khawāṭir min al-maḥāsin fī hādhihi al-mudda al-akhīra*, a continuation of the works by Ibn Khāḳān and Ibn Bassām [*q.v.*]. He also wrote a work on *ḥadīth* entitled *Iḳtifāʾ al-sanan fī intiḳāʾ arbaʿīn min al-sunan*, and another on Ḳurʾānic readings, *Sharḥ al-Kāfī li-bn Shurayḥ*.

Bibliography: Marrākushī, *al-Dhayl wa 'l-takmila*, ed. Iḥsān ʿAbbās, Beirut n.d., v/1, 323-69, no. 636; Ibn al-Zubayr, *Ṣilat al-Ṣila*, ed. E. Lévi-Provençal, vii, Rabat 1938, 140, no. 283; F. Pons Boigues, *Ensayo bio-bibliográfico*, 301, no. 254; Ziriklī, iv, 333; ʿA. al-Ahwānī, *Kutub barāmidj al-ʿulamāʾ fī 'l-Andalus*, in *RIMA*, i (1955), 102-4; I. Shabbūḥ, *Barnāmadj shuyūkh Ibn al-Fakhkhār al-Ruʿaynī*, in *ibid.*, v (1959), 103-44; ed. idem, *Barnāmadj shuyūkh al-Ruʿaynī*, Damascus 1381/1962; J. Mª Fórneas, *Elencos bibliográficos arábigoandaluces. Estudio especial de la "Fahrasa" de Ibn ʿAṭiyya al-Ġarnāṭī (481-541/1088-1147)*, (Extracto de) Tesis Doctoral, Madrid, Facultad de Filosofía y Letras 1971 (Ruʿaynī's work is not mentioned in ʿA.Ḥ. al-Kattānī, *Fihris al-fahāris wa 'l-athbāt wa-muʿdjam al-maʿādjim wa 'l-mashyakhāt wa 'l-musalsalāt*, 2 vols., ²Beirut 1402/1982); M. b. Tāwīt, *Sabta al-muslima*, in *Al-Manāhil*, xxii (1982), 138, 142. The information contained in Ruʿaynī's work has been analysed by J. Mª Fórneas in the following articles: *Datos para un estudio de la* Mudawwana *de Saḥnūn en al-Andalus*, in *Actas IV. Coloquio hispano-tunecino/Palma de Mallorca, 1979*, Madrid 1983, 93-118; *La primitiva* Sīra *de Ibn Isḥāq en al-Andalus*, in *Homenaje Bosch Vilá*, Granada 1991, i, 169; *Recepción y difusión en al-Andalus de algunas obras de Ibn Abī Zayd al-Qayrawānī*, in *Homenaje al Prof. Darío Cabanelas Rodríguez, O.F.M. en su LXX aniversario*, i, Granada 1987, 315-44.

(Maribel Fierro)

RUBʿ (A.), literally, "quarter", in Islamic astronomical terminology, quadrant. The kind of large mural quadrant (*libna*) with a graduated altitude scale described by Ptolemy (see BAṬLAMIYŪS] was used by a series of Muslim astronomers over the centuries. Descriptions exist of *i.a.* those used in the Damascus observations in the early 3rd/9th century (*ca.* 5 m in radius), by the astronomer Ḥāmid b. Khiḍr al-Khudjandī at Rayy in the late 4th/10th century (called *al-suds al-Fakhrī*, radius *ca.* 20 m), and in the early 9th/15th century observatory of Ulugh Beg [*q.v.*] at Samarḳand (radius *ca.* 40 m!). The last-mentioned, actually a sextant rather than a quadrant, has been excavated and partially restored; those quadrants still to be seen in some of the stone observatories in India (early 18th century) are in the same tradition. With such instruments, astronomers could measure th meridian altitudes of the sun and stars, which the could then use to determine improved values of th local latitude, new values of the obliquity of the eclip tic [see MAYL and MINṬAḲA], and to check or improv stellar coordinates [see NUDJŪM].

In the 3rd/9th century, Muslim astronome developed three main varieties of smaller quadran (*rubʿ*) for timekeeping [see MĪḲĀT]. First, the horar quadrant (*rubʿ al-sāʿāt*), marked with a radial sola scale and curves for the hours. With this one coul simply hold the quadrant vertically and align th radial edge fitted with sights towards the sun; then th bead set at the appropriate solar longitude on a threa attached at the centre of the instrument would han over the hour curves, and from its position relative t these one could read the time (see Pls. XXXI XXXIII). Second, the trigonometric or sine quadran marked with a set of parallel horizontal lines (original ly for each 15° on the outer scale, representing hou lines). With this one could calculate the time of day in seasonal hours [see SĀʿA] from the observed sola altitude h and the meridian solar altitude H—th underlying formula was approximate, equivalent t the following in modern notation:

$$T = \frac{1}{15} \text{ arc sin} \left(\frac{\sin h}{\sin H} \right)$$

(Note that the boundary conditions when the sun is o the horizon (T = 0 when h = 0) and on the meridia (T = 6 when h = H) are satisfied; the formula is in fa accurate at the equinoxes). This approximate formul has the advantages that it is much simpler than the a curate formula, that it works for any terrestri latitude (within limits), and that it yields good resul for most practical purposes (if only for lower latitude and certainly not for latitudes in Northern Europe From this quadrant there developed in later centuri the sine quadrant (*rubʿ mudjayyab*) with marking resembling modern graph-paper; with this an problem of mediaeval trigonometry could be solve (see Pl. XXXV). Third, the universal horary qu drant (*rubʿ āfāḳī*), designed to solve the same trigo nometric formula as the second variety but qui different in appearance. The hour-curves are now set of circular arcs radiating from the centre to eac 15° on the outer scale (with a semicircle representin the sixth hour, that is, midday). Such markings we used by Muslim and European astronomers for ov a millennium, mainly on the backs of astrolabes [se ASṬURLĀB] and sometimes in combination, as show in Pl. XXXIII, and it can be assumed that few in late centuries (especially the Europeans) had any idea the underlying formula. This quadrant, then, is un versal (*āfāḳī*), and one enters simply with the sola meridian altitude, but it can be made specific b having a cursor marked with a solar or a calendric scale on the outer rim. A 3rd/9th-century treati from Baghdād describes such an instrument wi either a fixed cursor, serving a single latitude, or movable cursor, enabling the user to enter with th solar longitude. This instrument was known mediaeval Europe as *quadrans vetus* (see below).

Few early Islamic quadrants survive. But the sa markings—for performing trigonometric calculatio or for finding the hours—were added to the backs astrolabes, and it is there that we can trace the development in instrumentation.

In the 5th/11th or 6th/12th century, probably Egypt, an astronomer whose name is unknown to hit on the clever idea of using one-half of the markin on an astrolabe plate as a quadrant, replacing the re

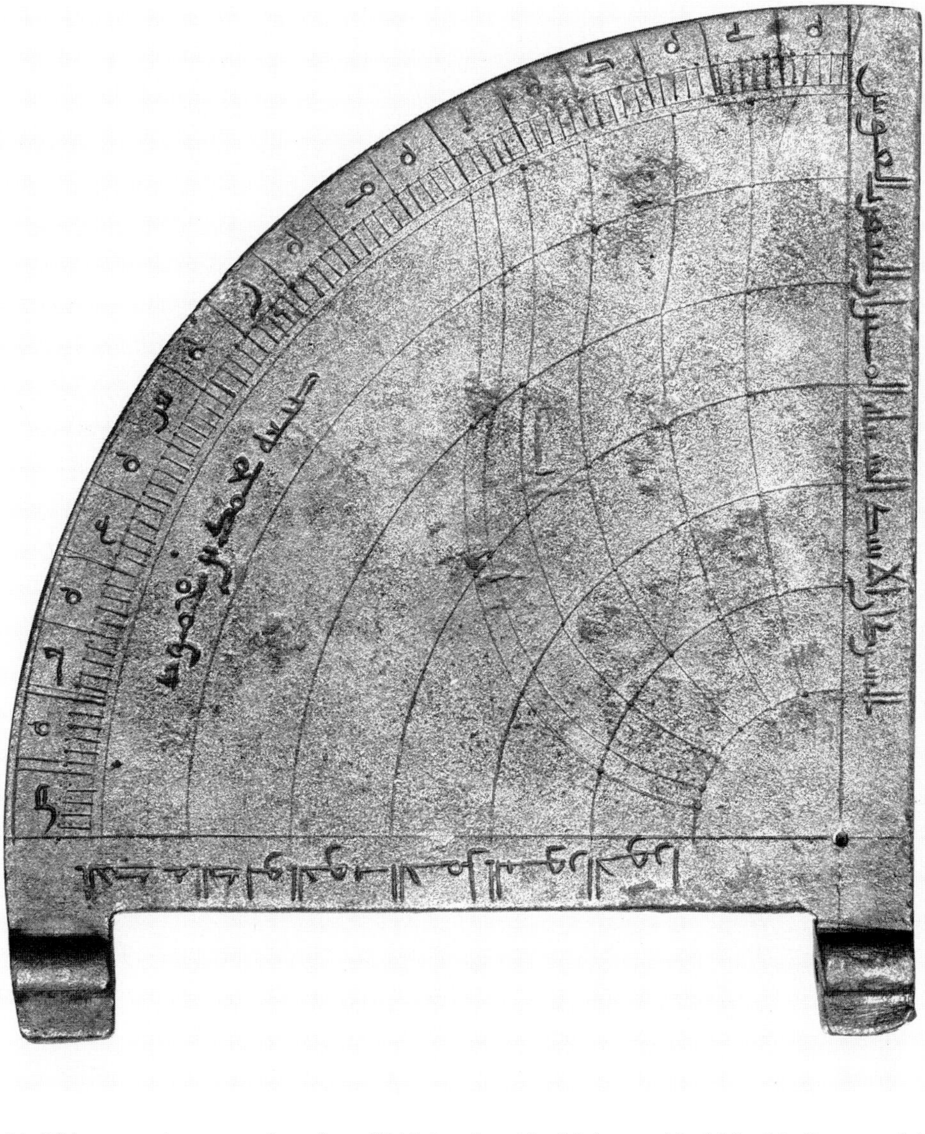

A 4th-/10th-century horary quadrant from Nīs͟hāpūr, signed by Muḥammad b. Maḥmūd. Courtesy of the Metropolitan Museum of Art, New York, N.Y. (inv. no. 36.20.54, radius 65 mm), Excavations of the Museum, 1935, purchase, Rogers Fund, 1936.

A trigonometric quadrant (upper left), horary quadrant for a specific latitude, in this case 41° serving Istanbul (upper right) and a universal horary quadrant (lower right) on an astrolabe dated 1125 AH [= 1713-14] signed by ʿAbdī. Courtesy of the Museum of the History of Science, Oxford (inv. no. 57-84/171A, diameter 131 mm).

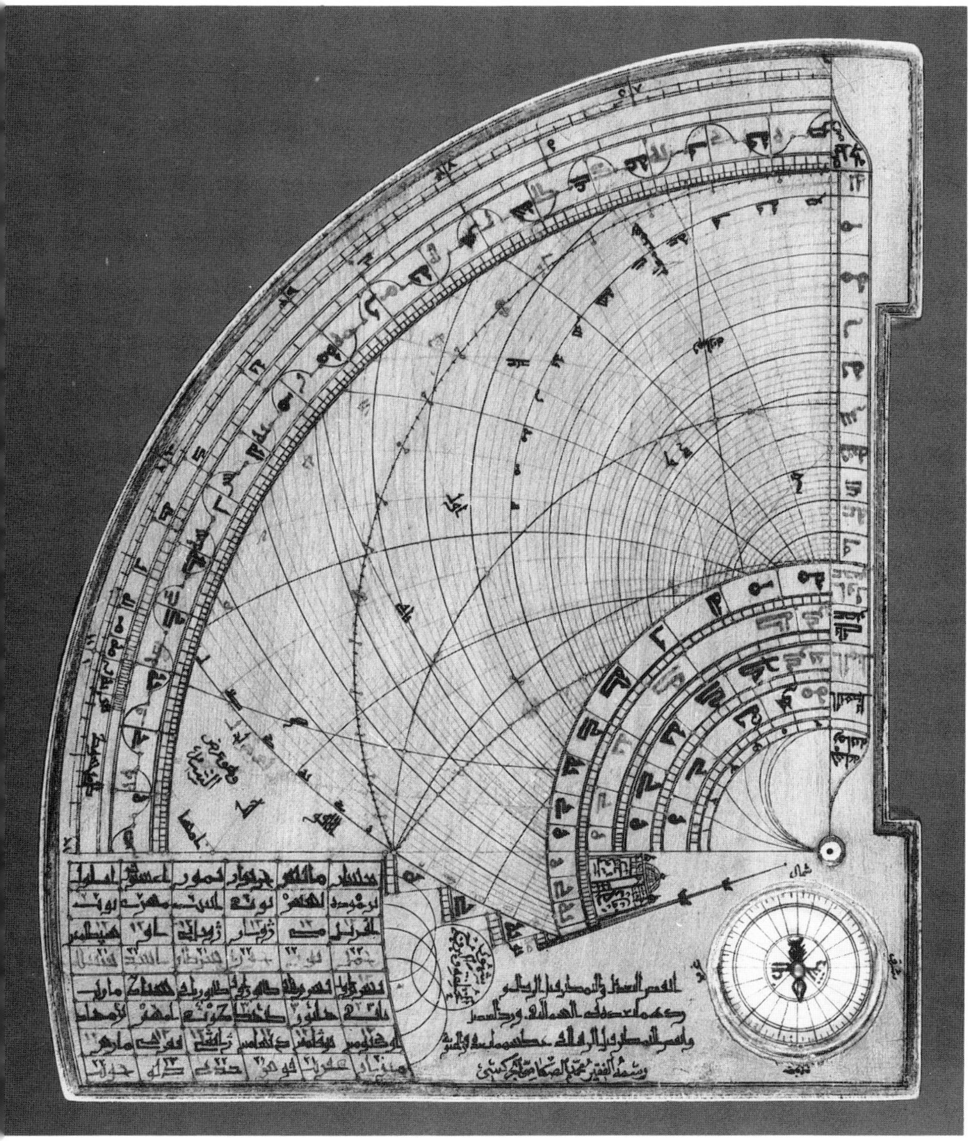

The astrolabic markings for latitude 33°30′, serving Damascus, on a quadrant signed by Muḥammad al-Ṣakāsī (?) al-Dj̲arkasī *ca.* 1800 (radii 134/110 mm). Private collection, courtesy of the owner, photographs (also Pl. XXXV) courtesy of Mr. Luis Marden, Washington, D.C.

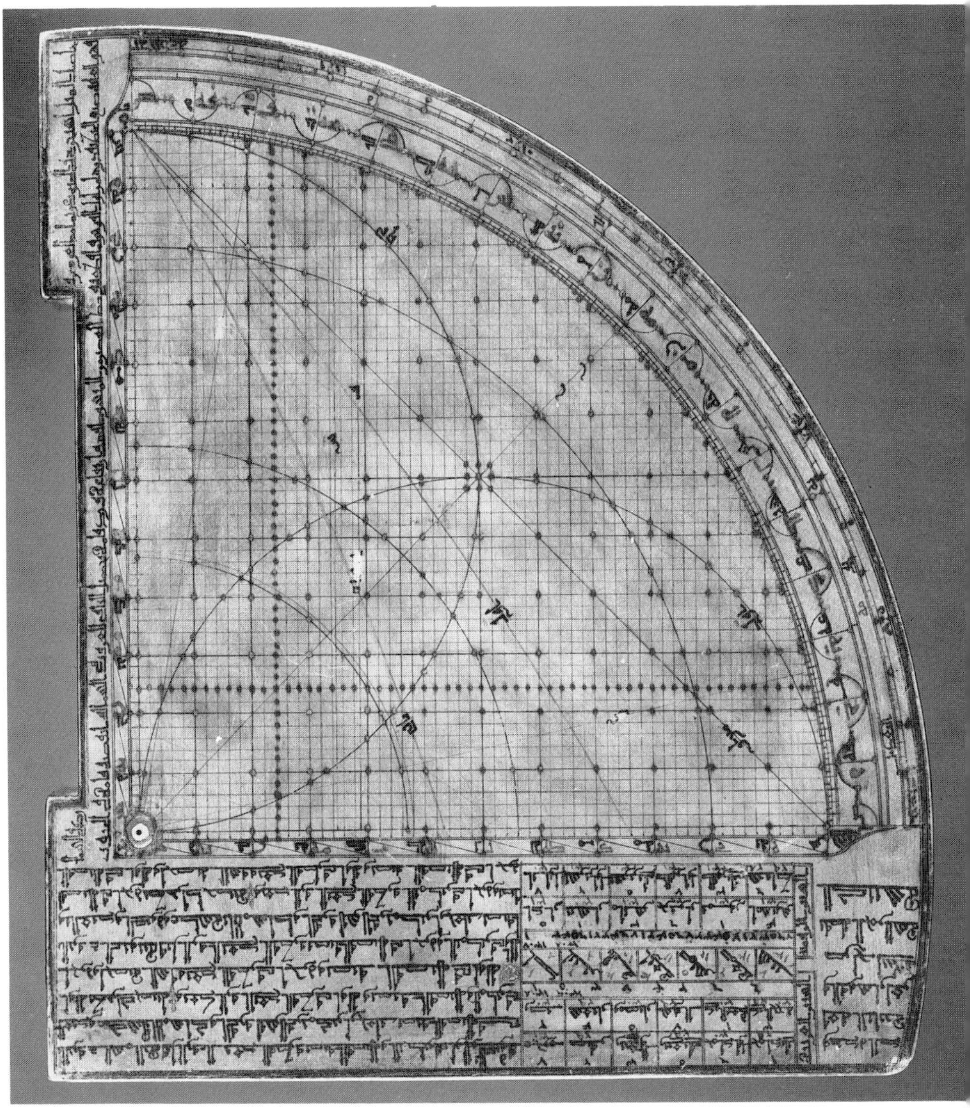

The trigonometrical markings on the back of the same instrument include all of the special lines and curves devised by Muslim astronomers over the centuries for solving specific problems of timekeeping.

with a thread with movable bead attached at the centre (*rubᶜ al-muḳanṭarāt*). The earliest surviving examples of this kind of astrolabic quadrant are by the early-8th/14th-century Damascus astronomer Muḥammad b. Aḥmad al-Mizzī. Such quadrants, with trigonometric markings on the back, were very popular in the Ottoman Empire and generally replaced the astrolabe in those regions. Dozens of late examples survive (see Pls. XXXIV, XXXV).

The writings of al-Marrākushī (*fl.* Cairo, *ca.* 680/1280 [*q.v.*]) and Ibn al-Sarrādj (*fl.* Aleppo, *ca.* 725/1325, unpublished, extant in ms. Dublin Chester Beatty 102, 2) illustrate the variety of other quadrants developed by Muslim astronomers. A minority of Ottoman quadrants are of unusual kinds described in these earlier sources. The numerous types of European quadrants are with few exceptions based on Islamic precursors. An exception appears to be the *quadrans novus* of Prophatius Judaeus (Provence, *ca.* 1290), an unhappy combination of the Islamic *quadrans vetus* (approximate) and astrolabic horizons (accurate). Meanwhile, Muslim astronomers had developed the more satisfactory astrolabic quadrant, which was unknown in Europe until a French instrument-maker hit on the idea about 1600.

Bibliography: (An asterisk indicates that the work in question is repr. in F. Sezgin *et al.*, eds., *Arabische Instrumente in orientalistischen Studien*, 6 vols., Frankfurt, Institut für Geschichte der Arabisch-Islamischen Wissenschaften, 1991.) On mural quadrants in Islamic observatories, see A. Sayılı, *The observatory in Islam*, Ankara 1960. For two examples, see H.J. Seeman, *Die Instrumente der Sternwarte zu Marâgha* ..., in *SBPMSE*, lx (1928), 15-126*, and art. *Ulugh Beg* in *The Dictionary of Scientific Biography*, New York 1960-80, xiii, 535-537. (The accounts of observational instruments in the Islamic sources, mainly published, let alone the archaeological findings, cry out for an overview to supplement Sayılı's pioneering work).

The standard work on smaller quadrants, based solely on textual sources, is P. Schmalzl, *Zur Geschichte des Quadranten bei den Arabern*, Munich 1929*, now very much outdated; see also H. Michel, *Traité de l'astrolabe*, Paris 1947, on the use of some of these. Useful studies of some quadrants by al-Mizzī and various late Ottoman instruments and texts are: W.H. Morley, *Description of an Arabic Quadrant*, in *JRAS*, xvii (1860), 322-30*; B. Dorn, *Drei in der Kaiserlichen Öffentlichen Bibliothek zu St. Petersburg befindliche astronomische Instrumente mit arabischen Inschriften*, in *Mémoires de l'Académie Impériale des Sciences de St. Pétersbourg*, 7ᵉ série, ix/1 (1865), 150 pp.*; J. Würschmidt, *Die Schriften Gedosis über die Höhenparallelen und über die Sinustafel (Zum Gebrauch des Quadranten im Islam)*, in *SBPMSE* (1928), 127-54*; and idem, *Ein türkisch-arabisches Quadrant-Astrolab*, in *Archiv für Geschichte der Naturwissenschaften und der Technik*, viii (1918), 167-81*. See also G. Fehérvári, *An eighth/fourteenth-century quadrant of the astrolabist al-Mizzī*, in *BSOAS*, xxxvi (1973), 115-17 and 2 plates; L. Janin and R. Rohr, *Deux astrolabes-quadrants turcs*, in *Centaurus*, xix (1975), 108-24; J. Mouliérac (ed.), *Syrie, mémoire et civilisation*, Paris, Institut du Monde Arabe 1993 (contains descriptions of two Syrian quadrants, including the one illustrated in Pl. XXXIII).

More recent studies include various articles reprinted in D.A. King, *Islamic astronomical instruments*, London, Variorum Reprints 1987, as well general remarks in idem, *Strumentazione astronomica nel mondo medievale islamico*, in G.L'E. Turner (ed.), *Gli strumenti*, Turin 1991, 154-89 and 581-5. Some of the earliest texts on the horary quadrant with cursor and the sine quadrant are discussed in idem, *A survey of the scientific manuscripts in the Egyptian National Library*, Winona Lake, Ind. 1986, 53 (no. B105), and idem, *al-Khwārizmī and new trends in mathematical astronomy in the ninth century*, in *Occasional Papers on the Near East* (Hagop Kevorkian Center for Near Eastern Studies, New York University), 2 (1983), esp. 28-31. On the universal horary quadrant, see especially J.D. North, *Astrolabes and the hour-line ritual*, and R.P. Lorch, *A note on the horary quadrant*, in *Journal for the History of Arabic Science*, v (1981), 113-14, and 115-120, and D.A. King (with D. Girke), *An approximate formula for astronomical timekeeping and its history over a millennium*, Institut für Geschichte der Naturwissenschaften, Frankfurt University, *Preprints Series*, 1 (1988).

(D.A. KING)

AL-**RUBᶜ** AL-**KHĀLĪ** (A.) (Empty Quarter), a vast and inhospitable sand-sea occupying much of the south and south-east of the Arabian Peninsula. It lies approximately between 45° E. and 57° E. and 17° N. and 23° N., encompassing some 200,000 sq. miles, consisting of tracts of aeolian sands with immense dunes rising over up to 60 m, areas of gravel and limestone known as *shukka* (pl. shiḳāḳ), and in the east, towards al-Liwāʾ (al-Djiwāʾ), *sabkha* [*q.v.*] at Umm al-Samīm and al-Kidan. It lies largely in Saudi Arabia, with its northwest limit roughly marked by the line of the Djabal Ṭuwayḳ escarpment. In the north and northeast the sands merge with the desert of Djafūra near the Djabrīn (or Yabrīn) oasis, and with the sands of al-Dahnāʾ [*q.v.*] in eastern Arabia. Al-Dahnāʾ in turn runs into the Nufūd [*q.v.*] sand sea in the north of Arabia. In the southwest and the south in Yemen, the Rubᶜ al-Khālī sands approach Mārib [*q.v.*] and Ḥaḍramawt [*q.v.*] respectively and in the east, they reach the Liwāʾ oasis in the United Arab Emirates and to the hinterland of ᶜUmān.

The aridity that characterises the desert today differs markedly from the environment of earlier times. In the late Miocene (6-7 million years BP [before present]), the climate was wetter with rivers flowing from the Rubᶜ al-Khālī into what is now the Arabian/Persian Gulf. Late Miocene elephant bones have been found in the UAE, while crocodile and turtle fossils indicate the presence of an ancient river system flowing from the Rubᶜ al-Khālī. Fresh-water lakes existed in the Rubᶜ al-Khālī between 9,700 BP and 6,390 BP, but desiccation followed thereafter, producing the harsh environment that constitutes the Rubᶜ al-Khālī today. In the east, the Wādī Idīma, Wādī Habawna and Wādī Nadjrān drain run-off from the ᶜAsīr highlands into the western Rubᶜ al-Khālī, where the waters run out in the sands. The broad bed of Sabkha Maṭṭī in western Abū Dhabī marks the course of a former river system that rose in the interior, with two major periods of flow in the period 80,000-70,000 BP and again 50,000 to 25,000 BP, and a lesser flow in the period 10,000 to 4,500 BP.

Some of the Rubᶜ al-Khālī sands may have blown in from the bed of the Arabian Gulf in the period before it was flooded as a result of sea level rises between about 18,000 BP and 8,000 BP, after the last Ice Age. A date of 23,000-17,000 BP has been given to the formation of sand dunes in the Liwāʾ oasis on the eastern side of the Rubᶜ al-Khālī.

The term Rubᶜ al-Khālī has attached itself to the entire sand-sea among Arabs and non-Arabs alike, although uncertainty exists over the origins of the name (Sir Percy Cox and D.G. Hogarth in R.E.

Cheesman, *The deserts of Jafura and Jabrin*, in *GJ*, lxv [Jan.-June 1925], 139). According to Cox, Bertram Thomas, Wilfred Thesiger and H.R.P. Dickson, the name Rubʿ al-Khālī was unknown to the indigenous people living around the desert perimeter and the only general term known to most modern travellers to describe the desert was "al-Ramal" or "al-Rimāl" (Thomas, 180; Thesiger, 37), although Cox also encountered the term Nufūd as well. Within the desert, specific tracts are identified by particular names, such as al-Ḳaʿāmiyyāt, Shuwaykla, Hawaya, Ramlat al-Kuthayyib, Shaḳḳat al-Kharīṭa and ʿUrūq al-Awārik.

By contrast, Philby (127-32) argued that the term Rubʿ al-Khālī was indeed known to the people with whom he travelled, including tribesmen from the sands. The terms al-Rimāl or al-Ramla were used to describe the areas occupied by pastoralists. Areas of briny water were known as Khirān; and areas of better water known as Sanam. Philby regarded the waterless district specifically as the Rubʿ al-Khālī, a term which he also equates with Rubʿ al-Kharab. More recently, D.P. Cole has noted that the Āl Murra used the term for the region as a whole, with lesser subdivisions given their own names.

The remoteness of the arduous terrain ensured that neither the Classical nor the Arab geographers had much detail to offer on the sands. Ptolemy gives the names of places, wells and mountains, but his knowledge of the interior is very limited. In the Arabic sources, part of the southern desert is termed al-Aḥḳāf, although its application varies. Al-Hamdānī, 87; see also 127, 216) uses al-Aḥḳāf for a valley between Ḥaḍramawt and Mahra. Al-Bakrī (76) associates al-Aḥḳāf with the region of Shiḥr [*q.v.*] in Ḥaḍramawt. Yāḳūt (ii, 78), on the authority of al-Aṣmaʿī, describes al-Aḥḳāf as a district of Arabia, placing it between Yemen and Sabā in the southwest and al-Yamāma, al-Shiḥr and ʿUmān in the southeast. Elsewhere, Yāḳūt associates al-Aḥḳāf with the pre-Islamic tribe of ʿĀd, iv, 1027, iii, 634), identifying it as a sandy district between ʿUmān, al-Shiḥr and Ḥaḍramawt. J. Halèvy in 1870 refers to the desert east of Nadjrān as al-Aḥḳāf, and von Wrede in 1843 (3, 22) marks it as the desert district immediately north of the Ḥaḍramawt (see also Hogarth, 333 ff.). Philby, however, declared that al-Aḥḳāf was a literary name for the sands and was not used by the local people he encountered.

Another place mentioned by the sources in the Rubʿ al-Khālī area is Wabar (or Ubar: see Thomas, 161) which Yāḳūt (iv, 896) locates between Yabrīn and Yemen. Wabar is said to have been cursed by Allāh when its people rejected the prophet Hūd, and the settlement was consumed by fire for the sins of its king, ʿĀd b. Kinad. Philby (168 ff.) visited a place pointed out to him as Wabar and known to his guides as al-Ḥadīda, but it proved to be a meteorite crater rather than a settlement. The iron-rich meteor is now in King Suʿūd University at al-Riyāḍ. Wabar has recently been associated with Shisur in Ẓufār by R. Fiennes and J. Zarins, but this view is not universally accepted.

A.R. al-Anṣāry has excavated a major archaeological site at Ḳaryat al-Fāw [see AL-FĀW], located on the southwestern edge of the Rubʿ al-Khālī at the point where there is a break in the Djabal Ṭuwayḳ escarpment. It was probably an important town before its decline in the early 4th c. A.D., with paintings and sculpture reflecting its diverse commercial and cultural contacts with Yemen, Egypt and elsewhere. To date, it is one of the better candidates to be related to Bedouin legends of ancient towns in the Rubʿ al-Khālī overwhelmed before Islam by sand o divine punishment.

The accounts by Thomas, Philby and Thesige show that in the heart of the Rubʿ al-Khālī, no tribe permanently inhabited the sands but rather, they liv ed a nomadic existence on its edges, occasionall entering the inner areas in pursuit of grazing or th oryx that formerly inhabited the remoter sands. Ma jor tribes around the Rubʿ al-Khālī include Āl Murr in the northeast, Banū Yās, Manāṣir, Rāshid an ʿAwāmir in the east, Rāshid, ʿAwāmir, Saʿar an Bayt Kathīr in the south, and Yām in the west. Th history of these camel-rearing tribes was formerly on of raiding and feud, with the seizure of camels as principal feature of their warfare. The inner areas o the Rubʿ al-Khālī provided a relatively secure retrea after raids on the desert margins.

The obstacle to travel formed by the Rubʿ al-Khā suggests to D.T. Potts that ancient routes avoided th sands, and he suggests that travellers followed easie routes between Yemen and Nadjd via al-Aflādj o from Nadjd through to Buraymī and ʿUmān. Never theless, there are persistent indications that route with seasonal pools exist between the southeaster coast and Yemen which are known to the tribes an are still used today.

The Rubʿ al-Khālī was the last part of the Penin sula to be explored, and ignorance of its vast inne areas endured until well into the 20th century Thomas (1930-1), Philby (1932) and Thesiger (1946 7, 1947-8) all conducted major journeys of exploratio in the sands, and in modern times, oil exploration an development have made it relatively more accessible Today, a number of international boundaries in th Rubʿ al-Khālī are disputed and the discovery of o has encouraged conflicting claims, several of which re main unresolved.

Bibliography: Bakrī, *Muʿdjam mā istaʿdjam*, ed F. Wüstenfeld, Göttingen and Paris 1877; Ham dānī, i; Yāḳūt, *Muʿdjam*; A.R. al-Anṣāry, *Qaryat al Fau. A portrait of pre-Islamic civilisation in Saudi Arabia* London 1981; R.A. Bramkamp *et al.*, *Geologic ma of the Southern Tuwayq quadrangle, Kingdom of Sau Arabia*, Miscellaneous Geologic Investigations, Ma 1-212 A, 1375/1956; eidem, *Geographic map of th western Rub al Khali quadrangle, Kingdom of Sau Arabia*, Miscellaneous Geologic Investigations, Ma 1-218 B, 1381/1962; C.S. Breed *et al.*, *Region studies of sand seas, using Landsat (ERTS) imagery*, i *A study of global sand seas*, Washington D.C. 1979 R.E. Cheesman, *In unknown Arabia*, London 1926 D. Cole, *Nomads of the nomads. The Āl Murrah bedoui of the Empty Quarter*, Chicago 1975; E.L. Elberg *al.*, *Geographic map of the eastern Rub al Kha quadrangle, Kingdom of Saudi Arabia*, Miscellaneou Geologic Investigations, Map 1-215 B, 1381/1962 H.R.P. Dickson, *The Arab of the desert*, Londo 1972, 287; J. Halévy, *Rapport sur une Mission Ar cheologique dans le Yemen*, in *JA* 6ᵉ série, xix (1872) 25; D.G. Hogarth, *The penetration of Arabia*, Beiru 1966; J.G. Lorimer, *Gazetteer of the Persian Gul ʾOmān and Central Arabia*, Calcutta 1908, IIB, 1594 H. St J. Philby, *The Empty Quarter, being a descriptio of the great southern desert of Arabia known as the Rubʿ a Khali*, London 1933; D.T. Potts, *The Arabian Gulf i antiquity*, Oxford 1990, ii, 323; L.F. Ramirez *et al. Geographic map of the southeastern Rub al-Kha quadrangle, Kingdom of Saudi Arabia*, Miscellaneou Geologic Investigations, Map 1-220 B, 1381/196 W. Thesiger, *Arabian sands*, London 1959, rep 1971; B. Thomas, *Arabia felix. Across the Empt Quarter of Arabia*, London 1932; G.A. Wallin, *Na rative of a journey from Cairo to Medina and Mecca, by Suez, Araba, Tawila, al-Jauf, Jubbe, Hail, and Nejd, in 1845*, in *JRGeog.S*, xxiv (1854), 169-170; A. von Wrede, *Reise in Hadhramaut*, Brunswick 1873.

(G.R.D. KING)

RUᵓBA B. AL-ᶜ**ADJDJĀDJ** AL-TAMĪMĪ, Abu 'l-Djahhāf (Abū Muḥammad also occurs), an Arab poet of the Umayyad and early ᶜAbbāsid era (d. 145/762), the greatest exponent of the *radjaz* [*q.v.*] *ḳaṣīda*. The name Ruᵓba, by which he was called after his grandfather, is attested seven times, and its diminutive Ruᵓayba eight times, in Ibn al-Kalbī's genealogy (see Caskel-Strenziok ii, 489b). There is no clear cluster of attestations in Eastern Arabia, which makes Krenkow's contention (see *EI*[1], s.n.) that the name is the Persian *rōbāh* "fox" less likely. Arabic philologists suggest several explanations of this peculiar name (Ibn Durayd, *al-Ishtiḳāḳ*, 260). Al-Āmidī (*al-Muᵓtalif*, 175-7) mentions three poets by that name, but only Ruᵓba b. al-ᶜAdjdjādj of the tribe of the Banū Mālik b. Saᶜd b. Zayd Manāt b. Tamīm became celebrated as a poet of *radjaz* verses, in which genre he surpassed both his father [see AL-ᶜADJDJĀDJ] and the latter's rival Abu 'l-Nadjm al-ᶜIdjlī [*q.v.*]. He and his father are sometimes jointly called al-ᶜAdjdjādjān[i] (dual *ᶜala 'l-taghlīb*).

Of his life very little is known. His birth date is unknown, but since he is said to have died at an advanced age, 65/685 is a likely guess. Like his father he spent most of his early life in the desert (*bādiya*). In his middle years he seems to have travelled widely in the Eastern parts of the empire (Khurāsān, Kirmān) as a panegyrist, but possibly also as a soldier and a merchant (he mentions the flourishing silk trade [*bayᶜ al-araḳ*, no. 12, l. 32] in Kirmān, though he himself is poverty-stricken). For the rest of his life he seems to have settled down in Basra (*min aᶜrāb al-Baṣra*), where he became *inter alia* an important linguistic informant for the nascent Baṣran circle of philologists.

Exact dates are hard to come by. In 97/716 he made the pilgrimage in the entourage of the caliph Sulaymān b. ᶜAbd al-Malik, which also included the poets Djarīr and al-Farazdaḳ (*Aghānī*, ed. Dār al-Kutub, xiv, 85). This may indicate the true beginning of his career as a panegyrist, as Blachère suggests (*HLA*, 526). His poem (no. 54) in praise of the general Maslama b. ᶜAbd al-Malik (d. 121/738 [*q.v.*]) alludes to the latter's victory over Yazīd b. al-Muhallab whom he killed in 102/720 [see MUHALLABIDS]; it clearly shows Ruᵓba's *ᶜaṣabiyya* against the Azd, though not necessarily against the Southerners in general (he praises, e.g., the Kalbī al-Ḥakam, see below). Other addressees of his poems include:

(1) Umayyad officials (*inter alios*):
Maslama b. ᶜAbd al-Malik (see above, also no. 10); Bilāl b. Abī Burda (*inter alia ḳāḍī* in Baṣra before 118, d. 126/744; nos. 6, 30, 42, and 57); ᶜAbd al-Malik b. Ḳays al-Dhiᵓbī (governor of Sind *c.* 105/723; no. 26); al-Ḥakam b. ᶜAwāna al-Kalbī (governor of Sind under Hishām, *Diiamben*, no. 13); Khālid b. ᶜAbd Allāh al-Ḳasrī (governor of Iraq, d. 126/743-4 [*q.v.*]; no. 18); Abān b. al-Walīd al-Badjalī (in 127/745 appointed chief of the guard by the caliph Marwān; nos. 15, 23, and 25); Naṣr b. Sayyār (last Umayyad governor of Khurāsān, d. 131/748 [*q.v.*]; nos. 19, 50); and al-Ḳāsim b. Muḥammad b. al-Ḳāsim al-Thaḳafī (Ahlwardt, *Dīwān*, lii, and Krenkow in *EI*[1] call him the conqueror of Sind, but that would be Muḥammad b. al-Ḳāsim [*q.v.*]; Ruᵓba addresses him as Ḳāsim and describes himself as old and bald, which he would not have been at the time of Muḥammad's death in 96/715, so al-Ḳāsim is possibly a son of the conqueror of Sind. Cf., however, al-Ṭabarī ii, 1256, where under the year 94 al-Ḳāsim b. Muḥammad is mentioned as the conqueror of *arḍ al-Hind*! No. 22).

(2) Umayyad caliphs:
Hishām (105-25/724-43; no. 2, where the introductory phrase wrongly states Maslama as the addressee, and *Diiamben*, no. 9); al-Walīd II b. Yazīd (125-6/743-4; no. 39); and Marwān II b. Muḥammad (127-32/744-50; no. 41).

As he had in his way shown his attachment to the Umayyads, it is no matter for surprise that Ruᵓba did not feel his life safe when he was summoned before Abū Muslim. Of the audience, we only know that Abū Muslim showed himself a connoisseur of Arabic. Two poems in praise of Abū Muslim are to be found in Geyer's *Diiamben*, nos. 4 and 6. Several other poems in praise of members of the new dynasty have survived; one of 400 lines (no. 55) is dedicated to Abū 'l-ᶜAbbās al-Saffāḥ and two to his uncle Sulaymān b. ᶜAlī (nos. 45 and 47), whom he appointed governor of Baṣra. The latest poems of Ruᵓba are in praise of al-Manṣūr, who succeeded his brother as caliph in 136/754 (no. 14 and *Diiamben*, no. 8). He was then an old man and is said to have died in 145/762.

All Ruᵓba's poems are in the *radjaz mashṭūr* metre; the few verses in other metres ascribed to him (nos. 104-8 of the *abyāt mufrada* in Ahlwardt's ed. of the *Dīwān*) are by other poets and wrongly attributed to him, with the possible exception of nos. 107 and 108, for which we have Abū ᶜUbayda's testimony that they constitute Ruᵓba's only non-*radjaz* output (see Ullmann, *Untersuchungen*, 31n.). He had learned the art from his father, whom he even accuses of taking credit for his poems when Ruᵓba began to write, and we actually have a poem by Ruᵓba in which he asserts himself against his father (no. 37). From his father he also inherited a fondness for unusual words and his poems are among the most difficult in the Arabic language, as they are full of words that are never or only very rarely found in other poets (cf. Ahlwardt's lexical-statistical proof of this phenomenon in *Dīwān*, xcviii-cxii, including both al-ᶜAdjdjādj and Ruᵓba). One even suspects that, for the sake of effect, the poet coined new words which did not previously exist. He certainly feels free to derive new words from existing roots and to bend roots and words to his liking. These are general features of *radjaz* (see Ullmann, *Untersuchungen*, chs. 3-8), but Ruᵓba may be particularly audacious in this violent handling of the language. He is also fonder than any other poet of accumulating a number of forms from the same verbal root in the same line (*tadjnīs ishtiḳāḳ* "figura etymologica"). The resulting style is rough, harsh, but forceful, at times willfully obscure, pronouncedly Bedouin-like, a *lingua rustica* (Ahlwardt, *Dīwān*, xii), which often borders on the grotesque and ironic and seems to acquire the character of a parody of the ancient *ḳaṣīda* (Ullmann, *Untersuchungen*, 37). However, Blachère has pointed out that Ruᵓba is quite capable of using simple language when the rhetorical exigencies of the situation require it (e.g. in no. 50, addressed to Naṣr b. Sayyār and warning him of Abū Muslim); it is Bedouin themes like the haunting desert descriptions that attract most of the *gharīb* vocabulary (*HLA*, 529).

As a rule, Ruᵓba's poems are remarkably long. The tripartite structure *nasīb-raḥīl-madīḥ* is often adhered to, but more complex structures are not uncommon, as Nallino (*Littérature*, 158) and Blachère (*HLA*, 528) have shown. One of the more interesting *fakhr* themes is pride in his own poetry (see the collection of *shawāhid* in Ahlwardt, *Dīwān*, lix-lxi). The *Dīwān* contains several monothematic pieces, in particular three desert descriptions (nos. 1, 34, and 40), which Ahlwardt considers to be incomplete poems. While this may be true, it should be noted that no. 40 (starting *wa-ḳātimi ʾl-aʿmāḳi khāwi ʾl-mukhtaraḳ*), which is the most famous of Ruʾba's poems, is unabashedly called a *ḳaṣīda* in the later literature and the quoted line its beginning.

Some important intellectual developments reflected in Ruʾba's poetry are the following: (1) In a poem in praise of Hishām (no. 2, l. 45), he speaks against the *ḳadariyyūn*, apparently in the less usual sense of people believing in predestination (this attestation to be added to the ones collected in ḲADARIYYA, vol. IV, 368b). (2) In no. 22, l. 139, the term *naḥwī* "language expert" is attested, in the context of a poetic *fakhr* asserting that the poet's command of the language is superior. (3) In several places, astrological notions are alluded to (Nallino, *Littérature*, 159). (4) Koranic themes and allusions are not infrequent. His eerie depiction of Jonah in the belly of the fish in the depth of the ocean is a most impressive example (no. 10, ll. 66-74). It is the final image in a poem of giving thanks to God for being delivered out of the hands of the Khāridjites; Jonah (referred to as *ṣāḥib al-ḥūt*, not *dhū ʾl-nūn*) is a model from the past for God's deliverance out of misery.

There are many reports that all the important early philologists of Baṣra and, less often, of Kūfa were in contact with him to increase their knowledge of the *lugha*, and this to such an extent that he became tired of them. He seems to have been an important link between the oral tradition of poetry and the nascent scholarship of the philologists. Due to the high percentage of *gharīb* in his poetry, he remained a favourite of the lexicographers; in the *LʿA* lines quoted from his poetry run into the thousands.

Ruʾba is also known as a *ḥadīth* transmitter (see, in particular, Ibn ʿAsākir, *Taʾrīkh*, vi, 284-92, and Ibn Ḥadjar, *Tahdhīb*, iii, 290-1).

He had two sons, ʿAbd Allāh, to whom two poems of remarkable tenderness are dedicated (nos. 20 and 56), and ʿUḳba who also wrote poems in the same metre as his father (*GAS*, ii, 369), though nothing survives.

Ruʾba's poems were collected by several scholars, among them his younger contemporaries Abū ʿAmr b. al-ʿAlāʾ, Abū ʿAmr al-Shaybānī and Ibn al-Aʿrābī [*q.vv.*] and the later al-Sukkarī [*q.v.*]. For details on the recensions and the mss. see *GAS*, ii, 368-9. On the basis of the Berlin ms. Landberg 826 (Ahlwardt 8155), a modern copy of the ms. Cairo *adab* 516, the *dīwān* has been edited by W. Ahlwardt (Berlin 1903, repr. Baghdād n.d.), unfortunately without the commentary by Muḥammad b. Ḥabīb (d. 245/860 [*q.v.*]) which is absolutely necessary for an understanding of the poems, and in the alphabetical order of the rhymes which makes it difficult to recognise the original arrangement of the collection. As this edition was incomplete, Geyer in 1908 published, in a collection of several *radjaz* poets entitled *Altarabische Diiamben*, twelve further poems with the commentary, basing himself on the different recension contained in the ms. Cairo *adab* 519. Ahlwardt had added to his edition a collection of verses which he had found in various works quoted as by Ruʾba. This collection was extended by Geyer in his *Beiträge zum Dīwān des Ruʾbah*, in *S.B. Ak. Wien*, clxiii (1910). Even then there remain lines attributed to Ruʾba which have escaped both editors. Confusion seems to have begun at quite an early date between the poems of Ruʾba and those of his father al-ʿAdjdjādj. Ahlwardt also published a complete German translation of the whole *Dīwān* in metre. The value of this translation is considered small by Krenkow in *EI*[1] for being only a paraphrase that does not help with the difficulties of the Arabic text. Ullmann gives a fairer and more positive evaluation (*Untersuchungen*, 30n.). The new edition by ʿAbd al-Ḥafīẓ al-Saṭlī, announced in *Akhbār al-turāth*, iii (1982), 15, has so far not yet appeared.

Bibliography: 1. Biographical notices on Ruʾba are found in Djumaḥī, *Ṭabaḳāt*, ed. M.M. Shākir, Cairo 1952, 579-81; Ibn Ḳutayba, *al-Shiʿr wa ʾl-shuʿarāʾ*, ed. de Goeje, 376-81, ed. A.M. Shākir, Cairo 1966, 594-601; Āmidī, *al-Muʾtalif wa ʾl-mukhtalif*, ed. ʿA.A. Farrādj, Cairo 1381/1961, 175-7; Marzubānī, *Muwashshah*, ed. M. al-Khaṭīb, Cairo [2]1395/[1965], 198 and index; *Kitāb al-Aghānī*, xxi, ed. R. Brünnow, 84-91, ed. Dār al-Kutub, xx, 345-55, ed. Beirut, xx, 312-25; Ibn ʿAsākir, *Taʾrīkh madīnat Dimashḳ*, facs. ed. M. b. Rizḳ b. al-Ṭarhūnī, n.p., n.d. (cf. Ibn Manẓūr, *Mukhtaṣar T. D.*, ed. M. al-Ṣāghirdjī, viii, 334-7, and Ibn Badrān, *Tahdhīb T. D.*, v, 331-5); Ibn Khallikān, ed. Iḥsān ʿAbbās, Beirut n.d., ii, 303-5; Yāḳūt, *Irshād*, ed. A.F. Rifāʿī, Cairo n.d., xi, 149-51; Suyūṭī, *al-Muzhir*, ed. M.A. Djād al-Mawlā *et alii*, Cairo n.d., i, 370-1; *Khizānat al-adab*, ed. ʿA.M. Hārūn, i, Cairo 1387/1967, 78-93.

2. Modern studies: the introductions to Ahlwardt's ed. and tr., R. Geyer, *Altarabische Diiamben*, Leipzig 1908; M.T. al-Bakrī, *K. Arādjīz al-ʿarab*, Cairo 1313/[1895-6]; Brockelmann, S I 90-1; Sezgin, *GAS*, ii, 367-9 and additions by R. Weipert in *ZGAIW*, ii (1985), 259, and *Oriens*, xxxi (1990), 355; C.-A. Nallino, *La littérature arabe des origines à l'époque de la dynastie umayyade*, Paris 1950, 156-62; R. Blachère, *Histoire de la littérature arabe*, iii, Paris 1966, 526-30; M. Ullmann, *Untersuchungen zur Rağazpoesie*, Wiesbaden 1966, 29-37; Kh.T. al-Hilālī: *Dirāsa lughawiyya fī arādjīz Ruʾba wa ʾl-ʿAdjdjādj*, 2 vols., Baghdād 1982 (vol. ii being a dictionary of the two *dīwāns*). (W.P. Heinrichs)

RUBĀʿĪ (pl. **RUBĀʿIYYĀT**), a verse form.

1. In Persian.

In Persian, this is the shortest type of formulaic poem; its long history, the strict rules governing its use and the richness of its expression make it one of the jewels of Persian literature. It is usually but inaccurately called "quatrain" (Arabic *rubāʿ*, "in fours, in foursomes"; *rubāʿī*, composed of four parts > "quadriliteral"). In the 7th/13th century, Shams Ḳays explained the Arabic appellation thus "because, in Arabic poetry, the *hazadj* metre is made up of four parts; thus, each *bayt* (in Persian) constructed on this metre forms two *bayts* in Arabic (Shams, 115, ll. 3-4). This reference to Arabic poetic technique in describing a specifically Persian form of poem has for a long time confused study of the quatrain.

Shams-i Ḳays, in his magisterial treatise on Persian poetic technique (completed after 630/1232), *al-Muʿdjam fī maʿāyīr ashʿār al-ʿadjam*, tells the story of an ancient Persian poet ("and I think that it was Rūdakī", 112, l. 4) who invented the metre of the quatrain on hearing a winsome child crying out in the course of a game: *ghaltān ghaltān hamī rawad tā bun-i g*[…] ("the ball is rolling, rolling to the bottom of the hole"), i.e. in quantitative metre: ––––∪–∪––∪∪–. On account of its rhythm and freshness, the poem thus invented was called *tarāna* ("young and fine") "it was also called *du baytī* (with two *bayt*)". This involved recourse to anecdote betrays awareness of the specifically Persian origin of the quatrain. But Sham[…]

no longer possessed the elements which would have enabled him to address correctly the study of the quatrain: this is a formal adaptation of Arabic technique to a poetic material of Iranian tradition.

The survey of the *rubāʿī* supplied by Shams-i Ḳays (112-27) is the most complete that is known. The numerous treatises subsequently composed are pedagogic adaptations of it. The studies in European languages by Fr. Gladwin, Garcin de Tassy, Fr. Rückert-W. Pertsch and H. Blochmann, are annotated translations of the latter. All give prominent place to the study of the *rubāʿī*, as does Shams-i Ḳays. In the first chapter of *al-Muʿdjam*, the first metre of which he analyses the constitution and usage is the *baḥr-i hazadj*, a metre of quantitative rhythm composed of a foot of one short and three longs (*mafāʿīlun*) repeated three times, hence four equal feet. Like his predecessors, Shams seeks to locate the *rubāʿī* among the realisations of the Arabic *hazadj* metre; but he finds it so original that he relegates study of it to a footnote at the end of his survey of this metre. He then has recourse to the authority of an *imām* of Khurāsān, Ḥasan Ḳaṭṭān (115, l. 19), who had constructed an overall diagram formed of two trees with twelve branches, designed to show all the opportunities for "changing the foot by excision of a syllable" (*ziḥāf*), available in Persian in the usage of *rubāʿī* and "which did not exist in Arabic" (115, l. 5), even though "today", he says, there are numerous *rubāʿiyyāt* in Arabic, imitations of the Persian. Case by case, over six pages, Shams subsequently brings his aesthetic appreciation to bear on the major realisations of *hazadj* metre in the *rubāʿī*; these are formed on the basis of two principal types of excision of a letter (or of a syllable) at the beginning of a foot, *kharb* or *kharm*. The specifically Persian *tarāna* was thus forced into a mould which was inappropriate for it and from which modern ingenuity has been unable to extricate it (M. Farzaad, *Persian poetic metres*, Leiden 1967, 99-123).

In order to escape from the impasse to which the false path of *hazadj* was leading, it has been necessary to undertake a philological study of the antecedents of this sophisticated *rubāʿī* and a statistical study of the reality of the usage of the metre of the Persian quatrain, setting all theories aside. It is undisputed that three elements characterise the *rubāʿī*: brevity, the use of a special metre and the use of a rhyme appropriate to its structure. In its classical form, it is the shortest of Persian poems. Each one begins in the same formal fashion. It is composed of two *bayts*; each *bayt* consists of two *miṣrāʿ*s or hemistiches; the four *miṣrāʿ*s have the same metre, or are arranged in pairs, with two variants of the metre. *Miṣrāʿ*s 1, 2 and 4 rhyme; in some cases *miṣrāʿ* 3 also rhymes with the others. In short, it is a form offering almost limitless possibilities for stylistic experiments.

It is not known when the quatrain first came into existence. Its emergence in literature can be pinpointed, but it is certainly of pre-Islamic origin, and of popular origin also: the *du baytī* remains a form of poetry widely practised throughout the Persian cultural sphere. Historically, the quatrain has followed the evolution of Persian poetry in general. Written evidence remains of pre-Islamic poetry based on a syllabic metre and an accentual verse with caesura; rhyme, admittedly irregular, appears in the early Islamic period, and is followed by the use of quantitative metre, irregular at first, ultimately becoming regular quantitative versification, with regular rhyme (Lazard 1975, 612-14). The appearance, under Arabic influence, of rhyme dictated by increasingly stringent rules is understandable; more singular is the subjection of the Iranian syllabic metre to Arabic quantitative prosody (Benveniste 1930, 224). There was imitation of the quantitative principle, but application took account of previous realities. It is for this reason that the Persian metre differs from the Arabic metre in the distribution of long sounds; this applies particularly to the quatrain. The Persian metre is a syllabic metre, but with syllables divided into long and short. Accents and caesuras had moulded the elementary distributions of syllables; the major Persian metres are moulded according to these distributions. The accent has ceased to be a factor in the distribution of syllables in the classical *bayt*. The reckoning of syllables, short and long, is what matters in Persian metrical systems, rather than the reckoning of letters, which are important only for the rhyme.

Various studies have been undertaken (Benveniste, Henning, Lazard and Shafīʿī Kadkanī) with the object of identifying, in fragments of verse in Pahlavi (of the *Bundahishn*) and in older Persian (before the 3rd/9th century), transmitted through texts in Arabic as well as in Manichaean fragments, what used to be known as the *tarāna*, a term of pre-Islamic origin which denoted songs intended for feasting and wine. Rūdakī (d. 329/940 [*q.v.*]) had, at the apogee of the Sāmānids of Bukhārā, a leading role, owed to a poetic genius which led to his acceptance as a master by all the poets of the 5th/11th century. Numerous quatrains were attributed to him (including, no doubt, some pseudepigrapha), and he was even credited with the invention of the genre. But among poets who preceded him, some by as much as a century, and among poets contemporary with him, examples are known of poems which conform to the characteristic traits of the *rubāʿī*. In Arabic, the *rubāʿī* did not appear until the end of the 4th/10th century, in Khurāsān and from the pen of a poet of Pūshang in the region of Harāt (Shafīʿī Kadkanī, 1988, 2331), evidently under Persian influence.

Another important feature in the history of the quatrain is its usage in Ṣūfī circles. The question was posed in the 4th/10th century: whether in the course of the spiritual observance and the dance which accompanies it (*samāʿ* [*q.v.*]), it is permitted to listen to *rubāʿiyyāt* (Abū Naṣr al-Sarrādj al-Ṭūsī (d. 378/988), *K. al-Lumaʿ*, 299, l. 3). A number of pieces of evidence emanating from Ṣūfī circles of Khurāsān, and also from Baghdād and elsewhere (thus al-Tanūkhī, in *Nishwār al-muḥāḍara*, written in 360/971), testify to the usage of the quatrain by the Persians, simple people expressing their love to the best of their ability; "it is the discourse of lovers and madmen", the master Djunayd (d. 298/910) is supposed to have said of it, according to Sulamī (d. 412/1021). According to the same, the *samāʿ al-rubāʿiyyāt* "is suitable only for strong and experienced men" (Shafīʿī Kadkanī, 2337, l. 22).

It is therefore not astonishing that in the 5th/11th century the quatrain was in use among all the Persian lyrical poets. Attempts have been made to establish Abū Saʿīd Abi 'l-Khayr (d. 440/1049 [*q.v.*]) as the inventor of the quatrain in Ṣūfism; like others before him, he practised it, but his eminent role in the history of Khurāsānian Ṣūfism gave added respectability to the *rubāʿī*, and poems attributed to him were considered to have been endorsed by his authority. In the same period, the Ḥanbalī Ṣūfī al-Anṣārī (d. 481/1088 [*q.v.*]) composed some fine quatrains, and the mountain-dwelling hermit Bābā Ṭāhir (d. in the middle of the same century [*q.v.*]) expressed the sum of his experience in *du baytī*s in which his Persian was blended with dialectal elements of Luristān. There are few poets who, over ten centuries, have not practised the quatrain; the modern period has seen the evolution of variants of the *rubāʿī* having 3 or 5 *miṣrāʿ*s. The most widely admired author of quatrains is ʿUmar K͟hayyam (d. before 530/1135 [*q.v.*]); his life, his work and his eminent position made him an easy target for pseudepigraphical artifice; it was not until a century after his death that a copy of a quatrain attributed to him was found, but the scholarly scepticism which is observed here corresponds closely to that which was denounced by the great mystic ʿAṭṭār (d. *ca.* 617/1220 [*q.v.*]), in regard to K͟hayyām precisely (*Ilāhī-nāma*, 215, ll. 5169-83). Thus was born a K͟hayyāmian tradition of quatrains, from the terrible century of the Mongols, the 7th/13th, onwards.

In his study of Persian metre based on statistical findings, P.N. K͟hānlari (K͟hānlarī 1966), has demonstrated once again that the metre of the *rubāʿī* followed rules exclusive to it. The basic structure of what he calls the *baḥr-i tarāna* consists, he asserts, of five feet; the first and the fourth, comprising two longs, never vary; feet 2 and 5, made up of two longs, may have as a variant: ⏑⏑–; foot 3, constructed thus: ⏑–⏑, can have two variants: –⏑⏑ and ––. Twelve principal realisations are identified by the author, emanating from the possibilities offered by these variants.

L.P. Elwell-Sutton (1976, 134-6), has set aside the division into feet and has sought to group the realisations of a sample of 400 lines or "hemistiches" (*miṣrāʿ*), under patterns capable of producing all the realisations. A group *a* corresponds to a basic pattern constructed thus:

––⏑⏑/–⏑–⏑––⏑⏑–

this is the most ancient, the most popular and the most frequent; group *b*:

––⏑⏑/––⏑⏑––⏑⏑–

For the two shorts in the penultimate position, it is quite common to substitute one long; the same substitution for the two shorts in the third position is exceptional, and this would be out of place in the middle of the line. These features are quite typical of Persian metre. The statistical survey has also enabled the author to state that lines of 12 and 11 syllables are the most frequent, and that there is no evidence to show that the rhyme pattern A A A A in the quatrain is older than the rhyme pattern A A B A, although the latter obtains in 70% of cases.

The quatrain is not restricted to a unique semantic field; it may be lyrical, satirical, mystical, philosophical, conveying aphoristic maxims or expressing states of mind. It should be dignified (*buland*), or delicate (*laṭīf*), or mordant (*tīz*). Its structure should be such that the first three *miṣrāʿ*s introduce the fourth, the first two sharing a certain unity, whence the ternary structure which is encountered in a number of quatrains (Bausani 1960, 532). While quatrains are to be found in almost all the Persian *dīwān*s, there are some *dīwān*s which are composed exclusively of quatrains.

There are numerous translations of Persian quatrians. The technical problems of translating the *rubāʿī* into European languages have only recently been the object of systematic consideration (Lazard 1991). The object must be to convey an impression of the form of the *rubāʿī*, a poem of such rigorous intensity that the rhythmic clash of words is constantly striking brilliant sparks of intelligence.

Bibliography: E. Benveniste, *Le texte du* Draxt Usūrīk *et la versification pehlevie*, in *JA*, ii (1930), 193-225; S͟hams al-Dīn Muḥammad b. Ḳays al-Rāzī, *al-Mud͟jam fī maʿāyīr as͟hʿār al-ʿad͟jam*, ed., introd. and notes Muḥammad Ḳazwīnī and Mudarris-i Raḍawī, Tehran 1314/1935, 374; A. Bausani, *La quartina*, in *Storia della letteratura persiana*, Milan 1960, 527-78; P.N. K͟hānlarī, *Wazn-i s͟hiʿr-i fārsī*, Tehran, 3rd ed. 1345/1966, 272-5; G. Lazard, āhu-ye kuhi... *Le chamois d'abu Hafs de Sogdiane et les origines du Robāi*, in *Henning memorial volume*, 1970, 238-44; L.P. Elwell-Sutton, *The* rubāʿī *in early Persian literature*, in *Camb. hist. of Iran*, iv, 633-57; idem, *The Persian metres*, Cambridge 1976; F. Thiessen, *A manual of classical Persian poetry*, Wiesbaden 1982, 166-73; B. Reinert, *Die prosodische Unterschiedlichkeit von persischem und arabischem Rubāʿī*, in R. Gramlich (ed.), *Islamwissenschaftliche Abhandlungen*, Wiesbaden 1974, 205-24; M.R. S͟hafīʿī Kadkanī, *Rūdakī wa rubāʿī*, in *Nāmwāra-i Duktur Maḥmūd Afs͟hār*, iv, Tehran 1367/1989, 2330-42; Lazard, *Comment traduire le robâî?*, in *Yād-Nāma. In memoria di Alessandro Bausani*, Rome 1991, 399-409.

(C.-H. de Fouchecour)

2. In Turkish.

It is impossible to deal with the problems of the Turkish *rubāʿī* without a suitable consideration of the corresponding Persian metre; the two civilisations have broadly amalgamated.

The word *rubāʿī* signifies here the distinct type described by Eilers, sc. an independent strophe of four lines, with the basic form ––⏑⏑––⏑⏑––⏑⏑–, the rhyme sequence *aaba* and a definite meaning sequence: introduction (the first two lines), surprising new motive (third line), pointe, return to the outset (last line). We may call this kind of quatrain the "perfect genuine *rubāʿī*" (abbreviated PGR).

In this rigid and narrow sense, the word *rubāʿī* is frequently employed in Turkish (and extra-Turkish) literature, for example in the following works: Kabaklı (i, 617-18, 678-9), Özkırımlı (996), *TDEA* (xxvii, 445), Dilçin (5, etc.). Karaalioğlu (605); Gibb (i, 88-90), Kowalski (161-3), Andrews (167-70). Nevertheless, the term is sometimes employed in a broader sense, namely as an equivalent of the Turkish *dörtlük*. That is, it signifies a quatrain: a strophe consisting of four lines (which we may abbreviate as FLS). Cf. Rypka, 694 ("the quatrain [*rubāʿī*]", by which term is meant the popular Persian strophe containing eleven syllables in each line), Köprülüzade, 113-22 (where the form is arranged into the general notion of *dörtlük*, e.g. some strophes of *Ḳutad͟hg͟hu bilig*, which are, nevertheless, *mutaḳārib maḥd͟hūf*), Bertel's, 88 (= Eastern Turkish *törtlük*), Eckmann, in *PTF*, ii, 299-300 (the quatrain quoted there as "*rubāʿī*" has the metre *fāʿilātun fāʿilātun fāʿilātun faʿūlun*, similar to *tuyug͟h*).

The origin of the PGR is controversial, since it is in *ʿarūḍ*, but not of the Arabic type. This diachronic problem must clearly be distinguished from the synchronic structure of the PRG, as it has been described above. See on this, Doerfer (Hungary, Sweden). Substantially, two opinions exist:

(a) The "*rubāʿī*" has a purely Persian origin, either as going back to Old Persian metres (Salemann, Gershevitch) or as having developed in an early New Persian epoch (Elwell-Sutton, Eilers, Meier, Andrews, Rypka). Most Turkish authors, too, support this thesis, under Köprülü's influence (Dilçin, 208; Kabaklı, 618, Özkırımlı, 996, *TDEA*, 350-1; Karaalioğlu, 605); cf. also *PTF*, ii, 104-5, 112-13, 256, 261. To be sure, "*rubāʿī*" is mainly confined here to the narrow sense of PGR.

(b) On the other hand, Köprülüzade remarks (113-22) that the *dörtlük* (= FLS) already existed in pre-Islamic Turkish literature. He says, furthermore, tha ɔr the "*rubāʿī*" (= PGR) neither a Turkish nor a Per-ːan origin can finally be proven (although PGR is ocumented in the Persian literature much earlier). ʌt any rate, the four-line strophe is popular both in 'urkish and Persian mediaeval and modern lyrics. 'he same differentiation is also expressed in Bertel's, 8, 107; the PGR has originated under the influence f the Turkish FLS, but it has assumed its ultimate hape in Persian literature.

The origin of the Persian PGR under the influence f the Turkish FLS has been underlined still more ex-ɪressively by Kowalski, 161-3: *Türk Ansiklopedisi*, 445; ;etin, in *İA*, 759-61; and Bausani, 527-78 (above all n 535, where Chinese parallels, also originating ınder Turkish influence, have been considered).

Indisputably, the first PGR metre has been ocumented much earlier in Persian poetry than in he Turkish. It is found as early as 333/944-5 in a oem by Abū Shakūr, whereas the first PGR metre in 'urkish language belongs to the second half of the th/12th century, see below. This fact proves that at ːast the d i r e c t origin of the PGR is Persian; and this imultaneously signifies that the hypothesis of an rigin from the Turkish FLS cannot in the strictest ɛnse be proven, particularly since the first Turkish oems belong to the 5th/11th century. On the other and, a diachronic investigation shows that an origin rom the Turkish FLS (or, at least, a certain influence ːom this side) can also not be excluded. The most fre-uent metre in Maḥmūd al-Kāshgharī's *Dīwān* is –∪–/–∪–. The *Dīwān* dates from 464-70/1072-8, ut derives from many earlier sources. But exactly his metre occurs, too, in the first *rubāʿī*-like poem in ɬew Persian literature, found in a satirical verse in al-'abarī under the year 108/726: *az Khuttalān āmadhīh / ī rū tabāh āmadhīh / āwār bāz āmadhīh / bē dil farāz madhīh*. The subsequent development of early Per-ian metrics gradually leads to the PGR. It should be oted that these metres are largely similar to al-Kāshgharī's eleven-syllable metre ––∪–/–∪–/––∪–. ;f. Ḥanẓala (250/864), ––∪–/∪––/∪––/–∪–; ⁄Iashriḳī (283/896), ––∪∪–/∪–∪–/–– (the same ıetre is found in a poem by Manūčihrī (432/1040-1); ʌbu 'l-Ḥusayn (311/923), ––∪∪–/–∪∪–/–∪–; hahīd (324/936), ––∪∪–/–∪∪–/–∪∪– (but only in two-line verse); and finally, in Abū Shakūr, –∪∪–/∪–∪–/–∪∪–. This last example is of par-cular interest, since it follows the PGR rhythm ex-ctly; however, it has a rhyme sequence *aaaa*. Both the hyme sequence *aaba* and the meaning sequence (see bove) have only gradually developed in Persian terature (see below), becoming a general norm from ıe 5th/11th century onwards. Since Bausani has ıown that a Turkish influence of the FLS both upon ıe East (China) and the West (Iran) is likely, the ypothesis of a Turkish FLS origin of the Persian GR may also be regarded as possible. But the efinitive shaping of PGR occurred on Persian soil, so ıat PGR is a witness to the Iranian spirit.

In other words, we may put forward the hypothesis ıat the Persians adopted models from both adjacent omadic societies: that west of Iran (the Arabic *ʿarūḍ*) nd that east of Iran (the Turkish FLS), but that they ːorganised these patterns into a genuine Persian ɪrm.

So much for metrics. The meaning sequence de-ːribed above is certainly of Persian origin and has een cultivated, above all, by ʿUmar Khayyām [*q.v.*], become an admired and frequently imitated model ot only for Persian, but also for Turkish poetry. The ɪirited and pointed rhyme sequence *aaba* has also een made a norm by ʿUmar Khayyām. It seems like-ly that *TDEA*, 350, is right in supposing that it was Mewlānā Djalāl al-Dīn Rūmī (604-72/1207-73 [*q.v.*]) who influenced Ottoman literature by his *Dīwān-i kabīr*, introducing the PGR in its perfect structure.

The rhyme sequence *aaba* occurs frequently in the Eastern Turkish literature of the 5th/11th century, e.g. in the *Ḳutadghu bilig* (196 verses) and in the *ʿAtabat al-ḥaḳāʾiḳ* (generally), cf. Köprülü, 341. To be sure, these verses are no PGR, but FLS in *mutaḳārib*, and resemble a collection of *ḳiṭaʿāt*. In MK's work, *aaba* is rare, if it exists at all, but it may be found in Stebleva's no. 44, which also follows the PGR-like metre ––∪–/–∪–/––∪̄–. This sequence is widespread in modern Turkish folk-poetry, not only in the Anatolian *māni* [*q.v.*] and in other regions of Western Turks, such as Persia, but also in Central Asia (Karakalpak, Kazakh, Uzbek and New Uyghur folklores). It is even found in South Siberia—above all in Tannu-Tuva—and this may be a hint at the archaic character of *aaba* in the Turkish world. On the other hand, in Iranian folk-poetry *aaba* is also well-documented. In Iranian educated literature, the older *rubāʿiyyāt* have mostly the rhyme sequence *aaaa*, cf. Elwell-Sutton, 639-44; seven Persian poets of the 5th/11th century offer 905 cases of *aaaa* (91%), against only 91 (9%) *aaba*. In ʿUmar Khayyām's work, on the contrary, *aaba* prevails over *aaaa* (70%: 30%), and this norm is still more valid in Ḥāfiẓ, where *aaaa* has become extremely rare (about 2.5%).

The Turkish development is almost a parallel of the Iranian one. However, extensive statistical investiga-tions of this topic are still lacking, and poets seem to behave very differently. Mīr ʿAlī Shīr Nawāʾī (845-906/1441-1501) favours *aaaa* both in his Čaghatay Turkish and Persian *rubāʿiyyāt* to about 88%. The last word is often identical in all four verses (then general-ly with a *radīf* [*q.v.*]). In poems of the Ādharbāydjānī poet Nesīmī (770-820/1369-1417), *aaaa* prevails over *aaba* (and *xaya*); 314 (86%) 52 : 1. But in the East Anatolian Ḳāḍī Burhān al-Dīn's (745-800/1345-98) poems we find *aaba* : *xaya* in a relation of 19 : 1; similarly in the Rumelian Yaḥyā Newʿī's (940-1007/1533-99) *rubāʿiyyāt*, *aaba* : *xaya* = 8 : 3; and in the Istanbulī Ḥāletī's (977-1040/1570-1631) poems (here, for example, the 16 poems quoted by Gibb, iii, 227-30, are *aaba* throughout). The same holds true of the Ādharbāydjānī Fuḍūlī's (d. 963/1556) work: *aaba* : *aaaa* = 65 : 7 (three *aaaa* with *radīf*), i.e. 90 : 10%. Generally speaking, the rhyme sequence *aaba* (which corresponds to that of the *māni*) found in-creased use in the course of time, particularly in the western area of Turkish literatures.

These and other hints at the Turkish origin of the FLS and PGR are remarkable, and may be due to a narrow Turkish-Iranian symbiosis. However, the PGR in its ideal form is owed to the Persians and above all to ʿUmar Khayyām. It remains (Eilers, 212) "ein wundervolles Zeugnis des persischen Genius". This PGR has been adopted by both Ottoman-Ādharbāydjānī and Čaghatay literature and plays an enormous role there. Kabaklı, 618, understates when he says that every *Dīwān* poet has written "one or two *rubāʿiyyāt*"; PGRs, sometimes in great number, are found in almost every important *dīwān*.

The earliest documented purely Turkish PGR was written by Mubārakshāh from Marw-i Rūd [*q.v.*] in eastern Khurāsān. It presumably belongs to the end of the 6th/12th century: *waʿdä berüsän näʾüčün kälmäs-sän / söz yalghanïnï mäning bilä ḳoymas-sän / yüzüng kün u sač tün ḳara körmäs-sän / ʿishḳingda ḳarārsïz äy ʿadjäb bilmäs-sän* "thou givest me a promise, (but) why doest thou not come? Thou abandonest neither lying nor me. Thou dost not see that thy face is (bright as) the sun and thy hairs are black (as) the night. Thou knowest, foresooth, that thou art unsteady in thy love". Furthermore, there are two macaronic *rubāʿiyyāt* dating from the same period, Badr al-Dīn al-Ḳawwāmī of the Rayy Oghuz (6th/12th century, with a rhyme sequence *aaaa*) and Ḳurashī from Transoxania (7th/13th century, rhyme sequence *aaba*), cf. Köprülüzade, *Türk dili ve edebiyatı hakkında avaştırmalav*, 118-20.

According to Köprülü (344, and in PTF, ii, 256) the PGR metre is not adapted for the Turkish language ("étranger au rhythme du mètre national turc et très difficile à adapter à la langue turque ... caprices individuels des poètes turcs possédant une solide connaissance de la métrique persane"). On the other hand, he explains (1934, 350) that the PGR was readily adaptable to Turkish prosody, since it is a four-line strophe. Indeed, the PGR has become a favoured genre in the Turkish literatures, at least those more or less influenced by Persian poetry. This preference lasted from the earliest period (e.g. Ḳāḍī Burhān al-Dīn until the modern era (e.g. Yaḥyā Kemāl Beyātlī, 1884-1958). *Rubāʿiyyāt* have been shaped not only in the Ottoman Empire and Turkey, but also in Ādharbāydjān (see above; Nesīmī, Fuḍūlī, and many others), in Turkmenia (Āzādī, 1700-60) and even in the successive regions of the Ulus Čaghatay (Nawāʾī; Shībānī, 855-916/1451-1510; Amānī, 945-1017/1538-1608; Bābur, 888-936/1483-1530; Kāmrān Mīrzā, 1825-99; Djahān Khatun, 19th century; cf. Eckmann, in *PTF*, ii, 304-402, and Hofman).

For the poets of the Ottoman Empire (and Turkey) cf. *PTF*, ii (index 952; references given by Björkman at 403-65); Kabaklı, 618; *Türk Ansiklopedisi*, 445; Dilçin, 168, 350, etc., Özkırımlı, 996, Karaalioğlu, 605; Necatigil. As well as those named above we may mention as the most outstanding *rubāʿī* poets: Ḳara Faḍlī (d. 1564), Rūḥī from Baghdād (d. 1014/1605); Fehīm (1036-58/1627-48); Djewrī (d. 1064/1654); Neshāṭī (d. 1085/1674); Thābit (1060-1124/1650-1712); Nābī (1052-1124/1642-1712); Nedīm (1092-1143/1681-1730); Sezāʾī (1080-1151/1669-1738); Naḥīfī (d. 1151/1738); Esrār Dede (d. 1210/1796); Sheykh Ghālib (1170-1214/1757-99); ʿAwnī from Yeñishehir (1826-83); Sabahattin Eyüboğlu (1908-73); Arif Nihat Asya (1904-75); and Cemal Yeşil (1900-77). The most famous and celebrated *rubāʿī* poet, however, is ʿAzmī-zāde Ḥāletī. Nedīm glorified him with the following verse: *Ḥāletī ewdj-i rubāʿīde učar ʿanḳā gibi* "Ḥāletī is like the *ʿanḳā* (bird), flying on the *rubāʿī*'s summit", cf. *PTF*, ii, 443; *TDEA*, 350. Muʿallim Nādjī, however, criticised him. As to his biography and literary creativity cf. *EI*[1] art. s.v. (Menzel), *İA*, v, 125-6 (Yöntem); *EI*[2] art, s.v. (İz), *Türk Ansiklopedisi*, xviii, Ankara 1970, 346-8. He wrote 2 *ʿarḍ-ı ḥāls*, 3 *ḳaṣīdas*, 2 *merthiyes*, 3 *ḳiṭʿa-yi kebīres*, 5 *tārīkhs*, 330 *beyts*, but 569 *rubāʿīs*. He was called *Üstād-i rubāʿī* "master of the *rubāʿī*" and *Khayyām-i Rūm*. (Gibb's and Kabaklı's opinion that Ḥāletī cannot equal Khayyām in respect of originality is disputed by Yöntem.)

In Turkish (Ottoman) *rubāʿiyyāt*, the *akhreb* pattern, whose first three syllables are ––⏑, is much more frequently employed than the *akhrem* pattern (–––), cf. *TDEA*, 350-1; the same holds true for Čaghatay literature (e.g. for Nawāʾī). This fact may be conditioned by the structure of the Turkish languages. The *rubāʿī* appears in 12 variants, of which Turkish poetry has made a certain selection; not only the *akhrem*, but also certain kinds of *akhreb* patterns occur less often. The following table shows the patterns and their frequency:

akhreb	1	––⏑/⏑–⏑–/⏑–––/–	frequent according to Kabaklı, *TDEA*, Dilçin; according to Andrews (along with 2) the most frequent pattern
	2	––⏑/⏑–⏑–/⏑––⏑/⏑–	frequent according to Kabaklı, *TDEA*, Dilçin; according to Andrews (along with 1) the most frequent pattern
	3	––⏑/⏑–––/–––/–	frequent only according to Kabaklı and *TDEA*
	4	––⏑/⏑–––/––⏑/⏑–	frequent only according to Kabaklı
	5	––⏑/⏑––⏑/⏑–––/–	frequent according to Kabaklı, *TDEA*, Dilçin
	6	––⏑/⏑––⏑/⏑––⏑/⏑–	frequent according to Kabaḳlı, *TDEA*, Dilçin
akhrem	7	–––/–⏑–/⏑–––/–	frequent only according to *TDEA*
	8	–––/–⏑–/⏑––⏑/⏑–	frequent only according to *TDEA*
	9	–––/–––/–––/–	rare
	10	–––/–––/–⏑⏑–/–	rare
	11	–––/––⏑⏑/–––/–	rare
	12	–––/––⏑⏑/––⏑⏑/–	rare

These statements can be corroborated. For example Newʿī's 11 *rubāʿiyyāt* and Ḳāḍī Burhān al-Dīn's 2(*rubāʿiyyāt* are all *akhreb*; in Fuḍūlī's 72 examples, onl one *akhrem* is to be found.

According to Dilçin, 207, a certain preference exist to employ two different variants in a *rubāʿī*, namely one for the verses 1,2,4 (which also rhyme with eacl other) and another for the third (in the *aaba* pattern unrhymed) verse; this is a frequent usage in Persiar poetry too, for example in ʿUmar Khayyām's poems This accentuation of the third verse, the underlying o its particular character is also known in the Turkis *māni*, where, to be sure, the same effect is produced b a change of caesura (e.g. *dam üstünde / duran ḳiz / bayram geldi / dolan ḳiz // ḳurbansiz / bayram olmaz // olan sana / ḳurban ḳiz* "girl standing on the roof; *bayram* ha come, walk around, girl; without victims there is n *bayram*; I may become a victim for you, girl": 4,3 4,3; 3,4; 4,3). In a more distant way, this underlinin of a verse resembles certain poems in al-Kāshgharī where, however, it is the last verse of the *aaab* patter which has a particular structure (e.g. in Stebleva 31.1, following the scheme ⏑––/⏑––//⏑––/⏑––//⏑––/⏑––//–⏑⏑–/–⏑–).

In whatever manner the problem of the genetic con nection of the Turkish and Persian folk poetries (o which the PRG is a sublimation) may be explained the symbiosis of these peoples and the similarity o their civilisations is undeniable.

Bibliography: W.G. Andrews, *An introduction t Ottoman poetry*, Minneapolis and Chicago 1976; A Pagliaro and A. Bausani, *Storia della letteratura persa* Milan 1960; E.É. Bertel's, *Istoriya persidsko tadžikskoi literaturî*, Moscow 1960; C. Dilçin *Örneklerle Türk şiiri bilgisi*, Ankara 1983; Doerfe (Hungary) = G. Doerfer, *Formen der älteren türkische Lyrik* (forthcoming); Doerfer (Sweden) = G Doerfer, *Gedanken zur Entstehung des* rubāʿī (forth coming); L.P. Elwell-Sutton, *The* rubāʿī *in early Persian literature*, in *Camb. hist. Iran*, v, Cambridge 1975, 633-57; W. Eilers, *Vierzeilendichtung, persisch und außerpersisch*, in *WZKM*, lxii (1969), 209-49; *PTF*, ii, ed. L. Bazin *et alii*, Wiesbaden 1964; *Fuzûlî, Türkçe divan*, ed. K. Akyüz *et alii*, Ankara 1958; E.J.W. Gibb, *HOP*; H.F. Hofman, *Turkish literature*, Utrecht 1969; A. Kabaklı, *Türk edebiyatı*, Istanbul 1985; S.Ḳ. Karaalioğlu, *Ansiklopedik edebiyat sözlüğü*, Istanbul 1969; F. Köprülü (= Köprülüzade), *Edebiyat araştırmaları*, Ankara 1966; idem, *Türk dili ve edebiyatı hakkında araştırmalar*, Istanbul 1934; T. Kowalski, *Ze studjów nad formą poezji ludów tureckich* ("Studies on the form of the poetry of the Turkish nations"), Kraków 1921; G. Lazard, *Les premiers poètes persans (IXe-Xe siècles)*, Tehran-Paris 1964; Maḥmūd al-Kāshgharī, *Dīwān lughāt al-turk*, according to Stebleva, q.v. (other editions by Brockelmann, Dankoff and Talât Tekin); F. Meier, *Die schöne Mahsatī*, Wiesbaden 1963; Mīr ʿAlī-Shīr Nawāʾī, *Dīwān*, ed. L.V. Dmitrieva, Moscow 1964; idem, *Divanlar*, ed. S.S. Levend, Ankara 1966; Necatigil = B. Necatigil, *Edebiyat ımızda isimler sözlüğü*, Istanbul 1991; Nesīmī = Imadäddin Näsimi, *Äsärläri*, i, ii, ed. Ḳährämanov, Baku 1973; Newʿī, *Dīwān*, ed. M. Tulum and M.A. Tanyeri, Istanbul 1977; A. Özkırımlı, *Türk edebiyat ansiklopedisi*, Istanbul 1987; Ḳāḍī Burhān al-Dīn, *Divan*, ed. M. Ergin, Istanbul 1980; J. Rypka, *History of Iranian literature*, Dordrecht 1968; I.V. Stebleva, *Razvitie tyurkskikh poètičeskikh form v XI veke*, Moscow 1971; *TDEA* = *Türk Dili ve Edebiyatı Ansiklopedisi*, vii, Istanbul 1990; *Türk Ansiklopedisi*, xxvii, Ankara 1978; ʿUmar Khayyām = A. Christensen, *Critical studies in the rubáiyát of ʿUmar-i-Khayyám*, Copenhagen 1927. (G. Doerfer)

3. In Arabic.

The *rubāʿiyya*, lit. "quadripartite entity", or quatrain occurs in Arabic literature both as an independent verse form and as an element of structure in longer compositions. It represents a comparatively late development of poetic form and its origins are not altogether clear.

The lines of the quatrain can either be lines in the sense of a *bayt* (two hemistichs with between 16 and 30 syllables and a caesura) or in the sense of a *miṣrāʿ* or *shaṭr* (a single hemistich so to speak, of 15 or less syllables). In the classical *ḳaṣīda* it is the *bayt* which represents the unit of structure, in *radjaz* poetry it is the *shaṭr*. In the *rubāʿiyya* either case can apply, leading to ambiguity in the usage of this term. However, more often than not, the *rubāʿiyya* denotes a quatrain whose lines have the length of half a *bayt*. This explains why expressions like *baytānⁱ* ("two *bayts*") or *dūbayt* (from Persian *du* "two"; also *dūbaytī*) are sometimes used as synonyms for *rubāʿiyya*.

Dūbayt, however, is more often used for a quatrain of a particular metre (*faʿlun mutafāʿilun faʿūlun faʿilun*) and rhyme scheme *aaba* (called *aʿradj*) or *aaaa*. Common metrical variations are: (a) ‒‒⏑⏑‒⏑‒⏑‒‒⏑⏑‒; (b) ‒‒⏑⏑‒‒⏑⏑‒‒⏑⏑‒; (c) ‒‒⏑⏑‒‒‒⏑‒‒⏑⏑‒. When used in this sense, *dūbayt* is the Arabic equivalent of the Persian *rubāʿī*. Its origins and its development are discussed extensively in the introductory essay of Kāmil Muṣṭafā al-Shaybī, *Dīwān al-dūbayt fi 'l-shiʿr al-ʿarabī (fī ʿasharat ḳurūn)*, Manshūrāt al-djāmiʿa 'l-Lībiyya, n.p. 1392/1972, 15-32. This book contains, arranged according to centuries, a collection of 808 poems in the *dūbayt* metre (mostly quatrains, but also some other forms, such as *muwashshaḥs*) by 168 poets from the 5th/11th century until the beginning of the 14th/20th century, together with 120 anonymous poems, of which 14 are in colloquial Arabic. Supplements have been published in *al-Mawrid* (1975), 153-72, and (1977), 49-108.

In most cases, only a few *dūbayt* quatrains of each author have been handed down in the literature. A more extensive collection is the *dūbayt dīwān Nukhbat al-shārib wa-ʿudjālat al-rākib*, by Niẓām al-Dīn al-Iṣfahānī (d. after 680/1281 or in 1278, Brockelmann, S I, 449), which contains some 500 quatrains arranged according to rhyme-letter in Arabic (predominantly), Persian and in a mixture of both languages (*mulammaʿ*). Eighty of the Arabic quatrains of this author are in al-Shaybī's book (*op. cit.*, 285-300). ʿImād al-Dīn al-Iṣfahānī (519-97/1125-1201 [*q.v.*]) and Ṣalāḥ al-Dīn al-Irbilī (572-631/1176-1234) are also said to have composed *dīwāns* of *dūbayt* quatrains (see al-Shaybī, *op. cit.* 74-5).

The rise of the *dūbayt* quatrain is placed by al-Shaybī among bilingual Persians in and around Ghazna, and the most easterly Iranian territories. As a date he suggests the 380s A.H., i.e. coinciding more or less with the beginnings of the Persian *rubāʿī*. The Persian origin is borne out by the occurrence of a *radīf* [*q.v.*] in three early Arabic *dūbayts* (al-Shaybī, *op. cit.*, nos. 2/1, 5/1 and 8/1).

The earliest textual examples of *dūbayt* quatrains go back to the first half of the 5th/11th century. They are preserved in the *Dumyat al-ḳaṣr* compiled by Abu 'l-Ḥasan ʿAlī al-Bākharzī (murdered in 467/1075 [*q.v.*]). In his comment on one of these quatrains, al-Bākharzī speaks of "pieces in the *rubāʿiyya* metre" (*ḳiṭaʿ ʿalā wazn al-rubāʿiyya*) and he remarks that he had not heard of this method (*ṭarīḳa*) until his father had recited quatrains in this manner (*rubāʿiyyāt ʿalā hādhā 'l-namaṭ*) (*Dumya*, ed. Muḥammad Rāghib al-Ṭabbākh, Aleppo 1349/1930, 174). Two early Arabic *dūbayts* are by the Persian mystic Abū Saʿīd b. Abi 'l-Khayr (357-440/967-1049 [*q.v.*]) famous for his more than 700 Persian quatrains.

References to quatrains of an earlier date do occur in the literature. Examples are Abū Naṣr al-Sarrādj (d. 378/988), *K. al-Lumaʿ fi 'l-taṣawwuf*, ed. R.A. Nicholson, London 1914, 299 (*Bāb fī man kariha 'l-samāʿ*); Abū ʿAlī al-Tanūkhī (329-84/939-94), *The table-talk of a Mesopotamian judge* (= *Nishwār al-Muḥāḍara*), ed. and tr. D.S. Margoliouth, London 1921-2, i, 54, ii, 59: "there was a Ṣūfī present, who was humming some *rubāʿiyyāt*"; Abū ʿAbd al-Raḥmān al-Sulamī (330-412/941-1021), *Ṭabaḳāt al-ṣūfiyya*, ed. Nūr al-Dīn Shurayba, Cairo 1953, 239, in a report in which Abu 'l-ʿAbbās Aḥmad b. Masrūḳ al-Ṭūsī (d. 298/911) is asked for his opinion on the permissibility of listening to musical performances of quatrains (*suʾila ʿan samāʿ al-rubāʿiyyāt*). All these texts suggest that these quatrains were popular in Baghdādī mystical circles. As the word *rubāʿiyya* is indefinite with regard to structural details, it is difficult to know if *dūbayt* quatrains are intended in any of these cases.

Another expression that may refer to the quatrain is *mathnāt*, mentioned in al-Djawharī, *Ṣiḥāḥ*, Cairo 1282, ii, 453 s.v. *th-n-y*, said to be equivalent to "what is called in Persian *dūbaytī*, which is singing (*al-ghināʾ*)" (see also *LA*, xiv, 119 s.v. *th-n-y*).

Quatrains or quatrain-like compositions may also be intended in a passage in *Aghānī*¹, xiii, 74 (= *Aghānī*³, xiv, 324) where *shiʿr muzāwidj baytaynⁱ baytaynⁱ* is attributed to Ḥammād ʿAdjrad (d. between 155/772 and 168/784 [*q.v.*]). See also G.E. von Grunebaum, in *JNES*, iii [1944], 10 and G. Vajda, *Les zindīqs en pays d'Islam au début de la période abbasside*, in *RSO*, xvii [1938], 205.

The 7th/13th century represents the Golden Age of the *dūbayt* quatrain, with many poets among mystics (such as Ibn al-Fāriḍ [*q.v.*] with over 30 quatrains and

Djalāl al-Dīn al-Rūmī [*q.v.*] with 19 Arabic *dūbayt*s in the *Kulliyyāt-i Shams*), princes, men of law, philosophers and physicians. There are experiments in form, e.g. the famous *dūbayt ḳaṣīda* by Bahāʾ al-Dīn Zuhayr (581-656/1186-1258 [*q.v.*]), *Dīwān*, ed. E.H. Palmer, Cambridge 1876, 202-4; the mixture of *dūbayt* and *muwashshah*, such as the example by Aḥmad al-Mawṣilī (603-56/1207-58) quoted in Ibn Shākir al-Kutubī, *Fawāt al-Wafayāt*, ed. Muḥammad Muḥyī al-Dīn ʿAbd al-Ḥamīd, Cairo [1951], ii, 510-11; as well as the many imitations (*muʿāraḍa* [*q.v.*]) which these innovations provoked.

In this century, the *dūbayt* also spread to the western part of the Muslim world. The Escorial ms. 288 contains four texts on the *dūbayt* written by Maghribī authors, Abu 'l-Ḥakam Mālik b. ʿAbd al-Raḥmān Ibn al-Muraḥḥal (604-99/1207-99), Abū Bakr al-Ḳalalūsī (d. 707/1307), Muḥammad b. ʿUmar al-Darrādj (authorship not certain) and Abu 'l-Ḥasan ʿAlī Ibn Barrī (d. 730/1330). Two of these texts have been published by Hilāl Nādjī, *Risālatān*[i] *farīdatān*[i] *fī ʿarūḍ al-dūbayt*, in *al-Mawrid*, iii (1974), 145-74. Ḥāzim al-Ḳarṭādjannī (608-84/1211-85 [*q.v.*]) finds the *dūbaytī* exquisite, in spite of its non-classical origin, and therefore approves of its being practised (*lā baʾs*[a] *bi 'l-ʿamal ʿalayhi fa-innahū mustaẓraf wa-waḍʿuhū mutanāsib*), see *Minhādj al-bulaghāʾ*, ed. M.H. Belkhodja, Tunis 1966, 243. After the 7th/13th century, the number of *dūbayt*-quatrains found in the literature dwindles, but there are examples in the work of authors such as Ṣafī al-Dīn al-Ḥillī (d. *ca.* 752/1351 [*q.v.*]), Ṣalāḥ al-Dīn al-Ṣafadī (d. 764/1363 [*q.v.*]), Ibn Ḥidjdja al-Ḥamawī (767-837/1366-1434 [*q.v.*]) and Ibn Ḥadjar al-ʿAsḳalānī (773-852/1372-1449 [*q.v.*]). Today, the *dūbayt* is said to be still in use in al-Kuwayt, al-Baḥrayn and ʿUmān.

In modern Arabic literature, the *rubāʿiyya* in the *dūbayt* metre is seldom found, but there are many instances of quatrains in original Khalīlian metres or modern derivatives. They represent one of the examples of the revival and development of strophic form in modern Arabic poetry (cf. S. Moreh, *Modern Arabic poetry 1800-1970*, Leiden 1976, and idem, *Technique and form in modern Arabic poetry up to World War II*, in *Studies in memory of Gaston Wiet*, ed. M. Rosen-Ayalon, Jerusalem 1977, 415-34 = Moreh, *Studies in modern Arabic prose and poetry*, Leiden 1988, 116-36).

The *dīwān* of Ibrāhīm Nādjī (1898-1953 [*q.v.*]), for example, contains, under the title *Rubāʿiyyāt*, a collection of 77 short-lined quatrains in the *sarīʿ* metre, partly in monorhyme *aaaa* and partly in cross rhyme *abab* (ed. Aḥmad Rāmī *et alii*, Cairo [1961], 225-34). In this *dīwān*, the short-lined quatrain is also used as a structural unit in 27 other poems, three of which are of the *murabbaʿ* type *aaaa, bbba, ccca* ... (see MUSAMMAṬ), most of the others showing cross rhyme (*abab cdcd efef* ...). The number of quatrains per poem varies between 4 and 35. Several metres are employed, especially *kāmil, ramal* and *sarīʿ*.

The long-lined quatrain (based on a *bayt* with two hemistichs) occurs in 11 poems. The rhyme scheme for most of these is *aa xa xa xa; xb xb xb xb; xc xc xc xc* (in which x represents unrhymed hemistichs). The number of quatrains varies between 4 and 33 per poem.

The Egyptian poet ʿAlī Maḥmūd Ṭāhā (1901-49) also employed both short-lined and long-lined quatrains in longer poems. His poem *Allāh wa 'l-shāʿir* consists of 108 short-lined quatrains in the *sarīʿ* metre with rhyme scheme *abab cdcd efef* ... (*al-Mallāḥ al-tāʾih*, Cairo 1943[3], 77-117).

Slightly longer is *Tardjamat shayṭān* by ʿAbbā[s] Maḥmūd al-ʿAḳḳād (1889-1964 [*q.v.*] in Suppl.), with the same rhyme scheme but in the *ramal* metr[e] (*Dīwān al-ʿAḳḳād*, Cairo 1346/1928, 238-54).

Djamīl Ṣidḳī al-Zahāwī (d. 1936 [*q.v.*]), has a *dīwā[n]* called *Rubāʿiyyāt*, Beirut 1924, containing 1,01[8] quatrains in different metres, all of them of the short-lined type.

Maḥmūd Darwīsh (b. 1942) publishes under th[e] title *Rubāʿiyyāt* 22 short-lined quatrains (*abab cdcd ef[ef]* rhyme) in *Awrāḳ al-zaytūn*, Beirut n.d. (original date o[f] publication 1964), 133-142. Eleven of these are i[n] *Dīwān Maḥmūd Darwīsh* i, Beirut 1979[6], 108-13. Hi[s] *Yawmiyyāt djurḥ filasṭīnī*, from *Ḥabībatī tanhaḍu mi[n] nawmihā*, is a poem of heterometric quatrains (mad[e] up of lines of differing lengths), with rhyme schem[e] *abab cdcd* and a *ramal*-type metre (*Dīwān* i, 542-62).

More traditional are the long-lined quatrains wit[h] rhyme scheme *xa xa xa xa* by the Mahdjar [*q.v.*] poet Ilyās Farḥāt (1893-1976) in *Rubāʿiyyāt Farḥāt*, Sã[o] Paulo 1954 ([1]1925), and Ilyās Ḳunṣul (1914-81), i[n] *Rubāʿiyyāt Ḳunṣul, al-Djuzʾ al-awwal*, Damascus 1956.

Ṣalāḥ Djāhīn (1931-86) published a collection o[f] quatrains in the *sarīʿ* metre in Egyptian Arabic unde[r] the title *Rubāʿiyyāt*, Cairo 1962; also in *Dawāwīn Ṣalā[ḥ] Djāhīn*, Cairo 1977, 205-61.

There is no uniformity with regard to th[e] nomenclature of the modern quatrains. The long lined quatrain is sometimes called *murabbaʿ*, the short lined quatrains with rhyme scheme *abab* are also re-ferred to as *muthannayāt* or *thunāʾiyyāt* (cf. Yūsuf Bak-kār, *Fi 'l-ʿarūḍ wa 'l-ḳāfiya*, Beirut 1990[2], 177-87).

The term *rubāʿiyyāt* is also used as a name fo[r] translations of Persian quatrains, such as those b[y] Ḥāfiẓ and Saʿdī, and, especially, ʿUmar Khayyā[m] [*q.vv.*]. Seldom have these quatrains been translate[d] in the original *rubāʿī* form, i.e. in the *dūbayt* metre there is one example of a quatrain by ʿUma[r] Khayyām translated as a *dūbayt* quatrain, in the wor[k] of the above-mentioned Niẓām al-Dīn al-Iṣfahānī (se[e] al-Shaybī, *op. cit.*, 287); there are six quatrains fro[m] the *Gulistān* of Saʿdī occurring in the Arabic transla-tion by Djabrāʾīl b. Yūsuf al-Mukhallaʿ (d. 1268/1851), ed. Cairo 1340/1921, 46, 137, 144, 151 168, 197; and some examples in the translation o[f] ʿUmar Khayyām's quatrains by Aḥmad al-Ṣāfī al-Nadjafī (1895-1978), ed. Damascus 1350/1931, e.g. nos. 24, 194, 243, 320. Aḥmad Zakī Abū Shād[ī] chooses the *khafīf* metre, following the example o[f] Djamīl Ṣidḳī al-Zahāwī, wrongly alleging that it coin-cides with the Persian original (*Rubāʿiyyāt ʿUmar a[l-] Khayyām*, Cairo 1931, 3). The translation made b[y] Aḥmad Rāmī ([1]1924), which is entirely in the *sar[īʿ]* metre, has become popular in its version sung by th[e] Egyptian singer Umm Kulthūm (d. 1975).

Apparently the first rendition in Arabic of a collec-tion of Khayyām's quatrains is the one published b[y] Wadīʿ al-Bustānī (1886-1954), Cairo 1912, which ha[s] the form of septets, a 7-line stanza with the rhym[e] scheme aaabbCD, brought together in two canto[s] (*nashīd*), in each of which the septets are linke[d] together throughout the canto by the common rhym[e] of the last two lines.

Muḥammad al-Sibāʿī (1881-1931) published in *ca.* 1918 his translation in three cantos of 44, 38 en[d] quintains cccAB, dddAB in an extended *muwashshah*-like fashion.

Structured along the same lines, but in Egyptia[n] Arabic, is the work of Ḥusayn Maẓlūm Riyāḍ *Rubāʿiyyāt al-Khayyām*, Ladjnat al-nashr li 'l-djāmiʿiyyīn, Cairo 1944.

A more recent translation in short-lined verse in th[e]

mutaḳārib metre is by the Baḥraynī poet Ibrāhīm ʿAbd al-Ḥusayn al-ʿUrayyiḍ (b. 1908), published as *Rubāʿiyyāt al-Khayyām*, Beirut 1966, 1984².

The term *rubāʿiyya* is also employed in the sense of a literary work in four parts, translating both tetralogy and quartet.

Bibliography (in addition to works already cited in the text): Muḥammad al-Sibāʿī, *Rubāʿiyyāt ʿUmar al-Khayyām*, Cairo n.d. [*ca.* 1918]; Aḥmad Zakī Abū Shādī (tr.), *Rubāʿiyyāt Ḥāfiẓ al-Shīrāzī*, Cairo 1931 (also in *al-Muḳtaṭaf* [1931]); idem, *Rubāʿiyyāt ʿUmar al-Khayyām*, Cairo 1931; Muṣṭafā Djawād, *al-Rubāʿiyyāt wa 'l-mathnayāt*, in *Madjallat madjmaʿ al-lugha al-ʿarabiyya bi-Dimashk*, xliv (1969), 982-9; B. Reinert, *Die prosodische Unterschiedlichkeit von persischem und arabischem Rubāʿī*, in R. Gramlich (ed.), *Islamwissenschaftliche Abhandlungen Fritz Meier zum sechzigsten Geburtstag*, Wiesbaden 1974, 205-25; W. Stoetzer, *Sur les quatrains arabes nommés "dūbayt"*, in *Quaderni di studi arabi*, v-vi (1987-8), 718-25; Yūsuf Bakkār, *al-Tardjamāt al-ʿarabiyya li-rubāʿiyyāt al-Khayyām*, Doha 1988 (not seen); Reinert, *Der Vierzeiler*, in W. Heinrichs (ed.), *Orientalisches Mittelalter* (= *Neues Handbuch der Literaturwissenschaft* Bd. V), 1990, 284-300. (W. Stoetzer)

RUBGHŪZĪ [see rabghūzī].

RUBIS [see yāḳūt].

RŪDAKĪ (properly Rōdhakī, arabicised as al-Rūdhakī) the leading Persian poet during the first half of the 4th/10th century and author of the earliest substantial surviving fragments of Persian verse. Al-Samʿānī gives his name as Abū ʿAbd Allāh Djaʿfar b. Muḥammad b. Ḥakīm b. ʿAbd al-Raḥmān b. Ādam al-Rūdhakī al-Shāʿir al-Samarḳandī, says that he was born in Rōdhak, a suburb of Samarḳand, and that he also died there in 329/940-1; there are, however, reasons to think that this date might be about a decade too early (see the discussion in Storey-de Blois). ʿAwfī says that Rūdakī was born blind and there are quite a few references to his blindness (though not to the fact that he was sightless from birth) in early Persian authors. The available biographical data all link him with the Sāmānid ruler of Bukhārā Naṣr II b. Aḥmad (301-31/914-43 [*q.v.*]) or with his minister Abu 'l-Faḍl al-Balʿamī [*q.v.*], and it was evidently under their patronage that he flourished.

Rūdakī left, as Asadī tells us, a *dīwān* of more than 180,000 verses. This was lost long ago. What have survived are a fairly large number of single verses quoted in the Persian dictionaries (notably in the oldest of them, Asadī's *Lughat-i Furs*) as well as a few complete poems quoted by anthologists and historians, the most important of the latter being a splendid *ḳaṣīda* of nearly 100 verses (beginning *mādar-i may*) which is preserved in the anonymous *Tārīkh-i Sīstān* and which, according to that source, Rūdakī sent from Naṣr's court in Bukhārā to the ruler of Sīstān, Aḥmad b. Muḥammad b. Khalaf. We also have (in chronological order of the authorities who cite them) five short poems, all of elegiac inspiration, quoted by the historian Abu 'l-Faḍl Bayhaḳī [*q.v.*], the verses beginning *bōy-i djōy-i Mūliyān* quoted by Niẓāmī ʿArūḍī in connection with an anecdote about Naṣr b. Aḥmad, a few short pieces quoted by ʿAwfī and Shams-i Ḳays and a description of spring quoted by the 8th/14th century anthologist Djādjarmī. The later anthologies add a few more poems, but the only one of these that can be ascribed more or less confidently to Rūdakī is a long ode, cited by Amīn Rāzī (1002/1593-4), in which the poet laments his old age and recalls the amorous adventures of his youth. This poem refers also the riches which the poet had formerly received from the Sāmānids, but also from "*mīr Mākān*" (evidently the Daylamī Mākān b. Kākī, d. 329/940-1 [*q.v.*]), and adds that "times have changed" and that the poet was now reduced to poverty.

The most famous of Rūdakī's works was evidently his versification of the book of *Kalīla wa-Dimna*. The *Shāh-nāma* of Firdawsī tells us how the *dastūr* Abu 'l-Faḍl (sc. Balʿamī) first had this book translated into Persian and how the *amīr* Naṣr subsequently appointed "interpreters" to read it out so that the blind Rūdakī could versify it. Horn noticed already that some of the rhymed couplets in *ramal* metre quoted from Rūdakī in Asadī's *Lughat-i Furs* clearly belong to the stories of *Kalīla wa-Dimna*, and the present author has been able to identify the location in those stories of about 50 verses. Moreover, Nöldeke (*apud* Horn) showed that some of the fragments in the same metre belong to the story of Sindbād and the Seven Ministers and that Rūdakī must consequently have versified that book as well.

From at least the 11th/17th century onwards the anthologists begin to ascribe to Rūdakī a number of poems that are in fact by Ḳaṭrān [*q.v.*], and these form the main content of the *dīwān* that is ascribed to Rūdakī in a number of manuscripts and which was lithographed in Persia in 1315/1897. It is now recognised that this *dīwān* is a forgery. The valuable collection of Rūdakī's fragments by Saʿīd Nafīsī (altogether 1,047 verses in the second edition) excises Ḳaṭrān's poems, but retains a number of other dubious verses from unreliable sources. Moreover, the collection includes a good number of pieces that the sources either quote anonymously or ascribe to a different poet, but which Nafīsī attributed to Rūdakī for stylistic reasons, as well as several "poems" that he patched together from single verses quoted in the lexica. The collection must therefore be used with caution.

Rūdakī's style is simple and direct, and consequently stands in stark contrast to the mannerism which dominated Persian poetry from the 6th/12th century onwards; it is thus hardly astonishing that his works, greatly admired though they were in his own time, soon seemed dreadfully old-fashioned and fell into oblivion. What he lacks in rhetorical ornament he makes up for in musical sonority; he is particularly fond of assonance and internal rhymes. Much of what remains of his poetry has a decidedly pessimistic tone, a lot of it along the usual lines of Islamic homiletic poetry (as represented, for example, by Abu 'l-ʿAtāhiya [*q.v.*]), but there is hardly anything overtly religious in his work and certainly no trace of Ṣūfism. "You ought not, O guests", he says in one poem, "to set your hearts for ever on this way-station, for you must slumber under the earth, even if now you sleep on silken brocade. What use to you is the companionship of others? The road into the grave must be taken alone and your companions under the ground will be ants and flies", etc. (Bayhaḳī, 188). Other poems are unashamedly hedonistic, though with a hedonism that is often shot through with melancholy. "Live merrily", he advises us, "amongst the black-eyed beauties, merrily, for the world is nought but wind and an idle tale. Be happy with what has come your way and give no heed to what has departed. Look rather at me in the company of a maiden with curly hair and the fragrance of fine musk, a face like the moon, of the race of the houris. ... This world is a breeze, a fleeting cloud, a jest. Bring the wine and let come what may." (ʿAwfī, ii, 9).

Bibliography: Firdawsī, *Shāh-nāma*, ed. Moscow

viii, *Nōshīn-ruwān* verses 3337-3470; Bayhaķī, *Tārīkh-i Masᶜūdī*, ed. Ghanī and Fayyāḍ, Tehran 1342 Sh./1945, 61, 188, 239, 366, 599; *Tārīkh-i Sīstān*, ed. M.T. Bahār, Tehran 1314 Sh./1935, 316-24; Asadī, *Lughat-i Furs, passim* (see the editions by Horn, Iķbāl and Mudjtabāʾī/Ṣādiķī, and also Horn's introd., 18-21); Rādūyānī, *Tardjumān al-balāgha*, ed. A. Ateş, Istanbul 1949, *passim* (and Ateş's notes, 90-2); Samᶜānī, fol. 262a-b = ed. Ḥaydarābād, vi, 192; Niẓāmī ᶜArūḍī, *Čahār maķāla*, ed. Ķazwīnī, London-Leiden 1910, 28, 31-4; ᶜAwfī, *Lubāb*, ii, 6-9; Shams-i Ķays, *al-Muᶜdjam fī maᶜāyīr ashᶜār al-ᶜadjam*, ed. Ķazwīnī, London 1909, *passim*; Muḥammad b. Badr al-Djādjarmī, *Muʾnis al-aḥrār fī daķāʾiķ al-ashᶜār*, ed. Ṭabībī, Tehran 1337-50 Sh./1959-79, ii, 453-4; Dawlatshāh, 31-3; Amīn Rāzī, *Haft iķlīm*, ed. Dj. Fāḍil, n.p. n.d., iii, 335-43; E.D. Ross, *Rudaki and Pseudo-Rudaki*, in *JRAS* (1924), 609-44; idem, *A Qasida by Rudaki*, in *JRAS* (1926), 213-37 (contains a critical edition of the ode *mādar i may*... by M. Ķazwīnī and a translation by Ross); S. Nafīsī, *Aḥwāl wa ashᶜār-i Rūdakī*, 3 vols., Tehran 1309-19 Sh./1930-40 (collection of the fragments in the last volume); revised ed. under the title *Muḥīṭ-i zindagī wa aḥwāl wa ashᶜār-i Rūdakī*, Tehran 1336 Sh./1958 and reprints; M. Dabīr-Siyāķī, *Rūdakī wa Sindbād-nāma*, in *Yaghmā*, viii (1334 Sh./1955), 218-23, 320-4, 413-6; *Osori Rūdakī*, ed. A. Mirzoyev, Stalin-abad 1958; Rudaki, *Stikhi*, ed. I.S. Braginskiy with Russian verse trs. by V.V. Levik and S.I. Lipkin, Moscow 1964; ᶜA.A. Ṣādiķī, *Ashᶜār-i tāza-yi Rūdakī*, in *Nashr-i Dānish*, ix/4 (1372 Sh./1993), 6-14; Storey-de Blois, v/1, 221-6 (with further literature).

(F.C. de Blois)

RŪDHBĀR, rūdbār, meaning literally in Persian, a district along a river or a district intersected by rivers, and a frequent toponym in Islamic Persia.

Yāķūt, *Buldān*, ed. Beirut, iii, 770-8, and al-Samᶜānī, *Ansāb*, ed. Ḥaydarābad, vi, 187-90, list Rūdhbārs at Iṣfahān, Ṭūs, Balkh, Marw, Hamadhān and Baghdād, and in the provinces of Shāsh and Daylam. As homes or places of origin of noted scholars, the most significant of these were the Rūdhbār by the gate of Ṭābarān, one of the two townships making up Ṭūs [*q.v.*]; the one near Baghdād; and the one near Hamadhān.

In the historical geography of Persia, the most significant Rūdhbārs have been:

1. On the left bank of the southernmost bend of the Helmand river in southwestern Afghānistān, now in the Nīmrōz province of modern Afghānistān (lat. 30°10′ N., long. 62°39′ E.), with the modern settlement there still preserving the mediaeval name as known e.g. in the periods of Arab and Ṣaffārid domination in Sīstan.

2. In Kirmān, a district along the present-day Mīnāb or Dozdān river which in mediaeval Islamic times lay on the road connecting Djīruft [*q.v.*] with the Persian Gulf at the Straits of Hormuz, the plain of Reobarles crossed by Marco Polo in the later 7th/13th century (see Yule and Cordier, *The Book of Ser Marco Polo*³, London 1903, i, 109, 113-14; Admiralty Handbooks, *Persia*, London 1945, 391).

3. In mediaeval Daylam [*q.v.*], with the name now surviving in the modern *bakhsh* or county of Rūdbār in Gīlān province and its chef-lieu of the same name in the valley of the Safīd Rūd [see ķizil-üzen] and on the Ķazwīn-Rasht road (lat. 36°49′ N., long. 49°29′ E.) (see Rāzmārā (ed.), *Farhang-i djughrāfiyā-yi Īrānzamīn*, ii, 133); the population of the *bakhsh* in *ca.* 1960 was *ca.* 60,000.

This is the most famous of the Rūdhbārs in Islamic history because the district was, from the late 5th/11th century to the 7th/13th century, a major centre for Ismāᶜīlī [see ismāᶜīliyya] activity. A century or so before the implantation of Ismāᶜīlism there, the Rūdhbār of Alamūt [*q.v.*], in the valley of the Shāh Rūd, the southern constituent stream of the Safīd Rūd, had been the residence of the Daylamī dynasty of the Djustānids (on whom see Sayyid Aḥmad Kasrawī, *Shahriyārān-i gum-nām*, Tehran 1307/1928, 22-34; W. Madelung, in *Camb. hist. of Iran*, iv, 223-4) and already a centre of Zaydī Shīᶜism. From Alamūt, Ḥasan-i Ṣabbāḥ [*q.v.*] furthered the Ismāᶜīlī *daᶜwa* by establishing garrisons in several other fortress in the Rūdhbār district towards the end of the 5th/11th century, such as Girdkūh, Lanbasar [*q.v.*] and Maymūndiz [*q.v.*]. These fortresses were held by the community until the operations in Daylam of Hülegü's Mongols in 651/1253, substantially completed with the reduction of most of the fortresses by 654/1256, although in the 1270s the local Ismāᶜīlīs seem to have re-occupied some of the Rūdhbār fortresses. See Freya Stark, *The valleys of the Assassins*, London 1936; P.J.E. Willey, *The castles of the Assassins*, London 1963; M.G.S. Hodgson, in *Camb. hist. of Iran*, v, 430-2; F. Daftary, *The Ismāᶜīlīs, their history and doctrines*, Cambridge 190, 344-8, 422 ff., 445, 448-9.

Bibliography: See also W. Barthold, *A historical geography of Iran*, Princeton 1983, 73, 141, 209, 232; D. Krawulsky, *Īrān—das Reich der Īlḫāne, eine topographisch-historische Studie*, Wiesbaden 1978, 57, 145.

(C.E. Bosworth)

RŪDHRĀWAR, a rural district (*rūstāķ, nāḥiya*) of the mediaeval Islamic province of Djibāl [*q.v.*], sc. western Persia. The geographers describe it as a fertile plain below the Kūh-i Alwand, containing 93 villages and producing high-quality saffron which was exported through the nearby towns of Hamadhān and Nihāwand. The chef-lieu of the district, in which was situated the *djāmiᶜ* and *minbar*, was known as Karadj-i Rūdhrāwar, characterised in the *Ḥudūd al-ᶜālam*, tr. 132, § 31.8-9, as prosperous and the resort of merchants. The site of this seems to have been distinct from the Karadj which had, in earlier ᶜAbbāsid times, been the seat of the Arab Dulafid family [see al-karadj] and which the author of the *Ḥudūd al-ᶜālam* states was in ruins by his own time (sc. late 4th/10th century), and it may be that Karadj-i Rūdhrāwar grew up on a new site to replace the old Dulafid capital.

Karadj-i Rūdhrāwar was still flourishing in the post-Mongol period, when Ḥamd Allāh Mustawfī described it as a town on which depended 70 villages, still famed for their saffron production and yielding a tax revenue of 23,500 dīnārs (*Nuzha*, 73, tr. 76). The present ruins known as Rūdīlāwar probably mark the site of Karadj-i Rūdhrāwar (J. de Morgan, *Mission scientifique en Perse*, Paris 1894-1904, ii, 136).

Bibliography: See also Samᶜānī, *Ansāb*, ed. Ḥaydarābād, vi, 190; Yāķūt, *Buldān*, ed. Beirut, iii, 78; Le Strange, *Lands of the Eastern Caliphate*, 197; Schwarz, *Iran im Mittelalter*, 504-5.

(C.E. Bosworth)

al-**RŪDHRĀWARĪ**, Abū Shudjāᶜ Muḥammad b. al-Ḥusayn, Ẓahīr al-Dīn, vizier to the ᶜAbbāsid caliphs and *adīb* (437-88/1045-95).

He was actually born at Kangāwar [see kinkiwar] in Djibāl, but his father, a member of the official classes, stemmed from the nearby district of Rūdhrāwar [*q.v.*]. Abū Shudjāᶜ Muḥammad served al-Muķtadī as vizier very briefly in 471/1078-8 after the dismissal of ᶜAmīd al-Dawla Ibn Djahīr [see djahīr,

ANŪ] and then for a longer period, Shaʿbān 476-afar or Rabīʿ I 484/December 1083 to January 1084-April or May 1091, after the second dismissal of Amīd al-Dawla Ibn Djahīr, until pressure on the aliph from the Saldjūḳ sultan Malik-Shāh [*q.v.*] pro-ured his dismissal. Hence in 478/1094 he left ʿIrāḳ or the Pilgrimage, and spent the last year of his life s a *mudjāwir* [*q.v.*] in Medina; he died in Djumādā II 88/June 1095 at the age of 51 and was buried in the aḳīʿ al-Gharḳad cemetery there.

Al-Rūdhrāwarī is said to have been a wise and umane vizier in Baghdād, who, amongst other hings, pursued a conciliatory policy regarding the unnīs and Shīʿīs and their rivalries in the city. The ources praise him both for his piety and his literary kills. He was the author of a poetic *dīwān*, of which ome 80 verses are extant in the literary and iographical sources, and of a *dhayl* or continuation to Miskawayh's [*q.v.*] history, the *Tadjārib al-umam*, overing the years 368-89/979-99 (ed. and Eng. tr. I.F. Amedroz and D.S. Margoliouth, in *Eclipse of the Abbasid caliphate*, iii, 9-332, tr. vi, 1-358; see Brockelmann, S I, 583, and Margoliouth, *Lectures on Arabic historians*, Calcutta 1930, 147).

Bibliography: ʿImād al-Dīn al-Iṣfahānī, *Kharīdat al-ḳaṣr, al-ḳism al-ʿirāḳī*, ed. M. Bahdjat al-Atharī and Djamīl Muʿabbar, Baghdād 1375/1955, part 1, 77-87; Ibn al-Djawzī, *Muntaẓam*, ix, 90-4 (lengthy death notice); Ibn al-Athīr, x, 39, 74-5, 78, 84, 94, 106, 111, 123-4, 156, 171, 221; Ibn Khallikān, ed. ʿAbbās, v, 134-7, tr. de Slane, iii, 288-90; Ibn al-Ṭiḳṭaḳā, *Fakhrī*, ed. Dérenbourg, 400-3, Eng. tr. Whitting, 287-9; Sayf al-Dīn ʿAḳīlī, *Āthār al-wuzarāʾ*, ed. Urmawī, Tehran 1337/1959.

(C.E. BOSWORTH)

RUDJŪʿ (A.), verbal noun from the verb *radjaʿa*, basically, "to return", and frequent in the Ḳurʾān n various senses, according to context. It is found e.g. n VII, 168, and XXX, 41, in the expression *laʿallahum yardjiʿūna* "perhaps they will return", which, explains al-Ḳurṭubī, has the sense "they will eturn from their unbelief" (*ʿan kufrihim*), or elsewhere given as the equivalent of *yatūbūna* ("they will epent of themselves"). *Rudjūʿ* would seem to be, in his sense, a synonym of *tawba*, and just as repentance s considered at the same time man's turning to God and God's turning to man, the verb *radjaʿa* is used both in the active and passive senses: man is said to eturn to God and be brought to God.

But the verb is employed in other contexts, and especially in verses like II, 28, "He makes you to die, and then He makes you to live, then you are brought o Him", or XXX, 11, "God begins the act of creaion, then He repeats it, then you are brought to Him". Al-Ḳurṭubī comments on the first of these verses thus: "that is to say, your return is towards His punishment (*ilā ʿadhābihi mardjiʿukum*) because of your unbelief; it is also said that it is towards life (sc. the esurrection after death) and the questioning *masʾala*), in such a way that their new beginning *iʿāda*) is like their beginning (*ibdāʾ*), and it is in this ense that one should understand *rudjūʿ*". This glossing seems to refer implicitly to the pre-eternal *mīthāḳ* *q.v.*] when God, creating mankind, asked them, 'Am I not your Lord? They replied, 'Yes' ". The interrogation at the end of time will pose the same question in order to know whether man has remained faithful to this first promise. The question is thus of a eturn to a primitive situation when, coming forth from the hands of God, man, at the very moment of his creation, can make no reply to his Creator but yes or no. Likewise, after death, at the moment of resurrection, "when the affair is decided" (*idh ḳuḍiya al-amr*), man is unable to plead his cause, and can only answer yes or no. This appears in Fakhr al-Dīn al-Rāzī's commentary on the second verse (XXX, 11), basing himself on the immediate sequel to this when it is a question of the Hour, whence of the Last Judgment. Having revealed, he says, that mankind will be brought back towards Him, "God explains what will take place at the moment of the return to Him (*waḳt al-rudjūʿ ilayhi*)", declaring, "those who are guilty will be thrown into despair (*yulbisu*)". Al-Rāzī explains the sense of this verb by citing the Baghdādī grammarian al-Zadjdjādjī (d. 311/923): the *mulbis* is the one who is silent (*al-sākit*) and who has his speech cut short in the course of his arguing (*al-munḳaṭiʿ fī ḥudjdjatihi*). This is how the return, in the commentaries on the verse in which the verb *radjaʿa* figures, is to be interpreted. The return to God, from this point of view, would appear to be essentially a summons to judgement at the time of the Last Judgement. It follows immediately after the resurrection, which, one might say, forms the first step. The question posed by the philosophers, that of knowing whether the soul alone, or even, the intellect alone, comes back to life, or whether there is also a resurrection of the body, is thus linked with that of *rudjūʿ*. In one sense, it is a question of faith; but belief in a spiritual return has obviously a special theological and philosophical interest.

For the *falāsifa*, such as Ibn Sīnā, the whole orientation of the human life—political, moral, intellectual and religious—is defined by two opposite poles, that of departing and that of arriving. At the departure, there is God in his oneness, God as the "First", from whom stem all the secondary beings; at the arrival, there is God as the "Last" (cf. Ḳurʾān, LVII, 3). Thus, in the political scheme of the *Shifāʾ*, Ibn Sīnā explains how the nature of the two notions of *tawḥīd* on one side, and *maʿād* [*q.v.*] on the other, must require every effort of reflection on the government of mankind. The *maʿād* as the place of return corresponds to the final cause which is, according to Ibn Sīnā, "the cause of the efficience of the efficient cause" (cf. his *Ishārāt*). The return accordingly has an ontological meaning, in so far as it is a constituent element of beings. At a first moment, starting from the First, who is a One, is seen the coming into being, by a descending process, of a multiplicity which ends up in the plurality of forms which the Agent Intellect, *wāhib al-ṣuwar*, gives, on the one hand, to the material elements and the things composed of them, and on the other, separated from all matter, to the human intelligence. From this moment onwards, there is a possible and progressive upwards motion towards unity, and it is this movement of return towards the One which, by rediscovering intelligible reality linked to unity, constitutes the return to God, without however prejudging what the outcome of this return will be. One might conceive of it from the viewpoint of a religious mystical phenomenon, or that of an intellectualist mystical phenomenon of the kind in Plotinus. For the Ikhwān al-Ṣafāʾ [*q.v.*], the particular souls, having accomplished their mission in regard to the bodies and having thus acquired the completeness (*tamām*) which they lacked, return to the universal soul. For them, to die is to pierce the covering of the body, just as, at birth, the embryo had pierced the enveloping membranes which surrounded it in the womb. (On all these questions, see the very interesting comments of L. Gardet, in his *Dieu et la destinée de l'homme*, Paris 1967, 267, 276, 279.)

The idea of a return to origins, which we have seen being sketched out in the commentaries on certain

Ḳurʾānic verses, easily takes on a mystical value. In the present life, men are separated from God by veils which their various faculties suspend between them and Him. Al-Djunayd accordingly used to teach that one should separate oneself from them by a purification of everything to which they cling in themselves, in order to lose oneself in the unique aim which is borne towards Him: this is *al-fanāʾ bi 'l-madhkūr*, the final aim of mystical experience, a return to the authentic origin of the creature in the divine creative act, *al-nihāya rudjūʿ ilā 'l-bidāya* (cf. al-Djunayd, *Enseignement spirituel*, tr. R. Deladrière, Paris 1983, 45-6). But this is a type of *rudjūʿ* which Ibn ʿArabī especially considered: the highest form of the mystical favour and gift is, not to arrive at the summit of the spiritual ascension but to be sent back amongst creatures in order to enlighten and guide them. Thus we have here a return to mankind. One should note that this is what happened to the Prophet: he was raised up at the time of the *miʿrādj* [*q.v.*], and he was sent back with the mission of announcing the good news and of adopting a watchful attitude (on this concept of return, see M. Chodkiewicz, *Le sceau des saints*, Paris 1986, 141, 185, 217). Finally, one should mention the idea of a return at the end of time: the return of the Messiah, of Muḥammad and of the Mahdī. This is totally bound up with the eschatological visions nurtured, above all, by various *ḥadīths*.

Bibliography: Given in the article.

(R. ARNALDEZ)

RŪFUS AL-AFSĪSĪ, Rufus of Ephesus, a Greek physician who lived at Ephesus [see AYA SOLŪK] around 100 A.D. Of his biography hardly anything is known. He was an important medical author, who wrote monographs on many questions concerning pathology and dietetics. Most of his writings, however, were lost during the Middle Ages since his work was overshadowed by that of Galen [see DJĀLĪNŪS] (cf. O. Temkin, *Galenism. Rise and decline of a medical philosophy*, Ithaca and London 1973). Consequently, only four of his works have survived in Greek: 1. On kidney and bladder diseases (ed. A. Sideras, *CMG* III, 1, Berlin 1977); 2. On satyriasmus and gonorrhea (ed. Daremberg and Ruelle, Paris 1879, 64-84); 3. On the names of the parts of the human body (ed. G. Kowalski, diss. Göttingen 1960), and 4. On questions put to patients by physicians (ed. H. Gärtner, *CMG*, Suppl. IV, Berlin 1962). Of all the other works by Rūfus, only fragments are known, transmitted by Byzantine compilers, mainly by Oribasius and Aetius of Amida. A work on the diseases of the joints was translated into Latin in the 6th century, and has thus been preserved (*De podagra*, ed. H. Mørland, Oslo 1933).

Under these circumstances, the Arabic tradition is of crucial importance. The translators, who in the 3rd/9th century rendered at Baghdād far more than one hundred books by Galen and other Greek physicians into Arabic, did not ignore Rūfus, whose works at that time had not yet been eclipsed by those of Galen. In his *Kitāb al-Ḥāwī*, Muḥammad b. Zakariyyāʾ al-Rāzī [*q.v.*] quotes a dozen works by Rūfus. In 377/987 Ibn al-Nadīm presents 42 titles of Rūfus (*Fihrist*, ed. Flügel, 291-2, ed. Tehran, 350), and this list was enlarged with 16 titles by Ibn Abī Uṣaybiʿa (d. 668/1270) (*ʿUyūn al-anbāʾ*, ed. A. Müller, i, 33-4). Both lists constitute an important guideline for the reconstruction of Rūfus's work.

Attention may in particular be called to the following works:

1. *Maḳāla fī Mā yanbaghī li 'l-ṭabīb an yasʾala ʿanhu 'l-ʿalīl* = Τί δεῖ τὸν ἰατρὸν ἐρωτᾶν τὸν νοσοῦντα (Ibn Abī Uṣaybiʿa, i, 34, 11-12). This work was used and copied out by Isḥāḳ b. ʿAlī al-Ruhāwī in his *K. Adab al-ṭabīb* (*The conduct of the physician by al-Ruhāwī*, facs. ed. Frankfurt a. M. 1985, 134-9).

2. *Maḳāla fī 'l-Yaraḳān* = Περὶ ἰκτέρου. Greek excerpts are preserved by Aetius of Amida (*Tetrabiblos* X, chs. 17-18). An epitome in Arabic is found in the codex Berolinensis (Ahlwardt 6232); there is also a 14th century Latin tr. by Nicolaus of Regium (Niccolò de Reggio) (ed. M. Ullmann, *Die Schrift des Rufus von Ephesos über die Gelbsucht in arabischer und lateinischer Übersetzung*, in *Abh. Akad. d. Wiss. Göttingen*, phil.-hist. Kl. III. Folge, no. 138, Göttingen 1983).

3. *Maḳāla fī 'l-Ḥifẓ* = Περὶ μνήμης ἀπολωλυίας. This work can partly be reconstructed from Greek excerpts in Aetius of Amida (*Tetrabiblos* VI, ch. 23) and from the Arabic transmission in al-Rāzī, *Ḥāwī*, i, 94-5).

4. *Maḳāla fī 'l-Mālankhūliyā* or *Kitāb al-Mirra al-sawdāʾ* = Περὶ μελαγχολίας. Next to excerpts found in Aetius, there are above all Arabic fragments available, preserved by al-Rāzī and by Isḥāḳ b. ʿImrān (*Abhandlung über die Melancholie und Constantini Africani Libri duo de Melancholia*, ed. K. Garbers, Hamburg 1977) (cf. H. Flashar, *Melancholie und Melancholiker in den medizinischen Theorien der Antike*, Berlin 1966, 84-104).

5. *Kitāb al-Tadbīr* = Περὶ διαίτης. This is a large work on dietetics, i.e. on a proper way of life, in which an harmonious balance is sought between work and leisure, movement and rest, food and drink, sexual intercourse and continence, sleep and vigil, joy and sorrow. Many fragments have been preserved in Oribasius as well as in Ḥunayn b. Isḥāḳ (*K. al-Aghdhiya*, ms. Bankipore, Khudābakhsh 2142), al-Rāzī, Ibn Samadjūn and Ibn al-Bayṭār.

6. *Kitāb al-Sharāb* = Περὶ οἴνου, translated into Arabic by Ḳusṭā b. Lūḳā [*q.v.*]. There are fragments in al-Rāzī, Isḥāḳ b. Sulaymān al-Isrāʾīlī and al-Raḳīḳ al-Nadīm al-Ḳayrawānī, *K. Ḳuṭb al-surūr fī awṣāf al-khumūr* (cf. Ullmann, *Neues zu den diätetischen Schriften des Rufus von Ephesos*, in *Medizinhistorisches Journal*, ix [1974], 30-7).

7. *Kitāb al-Laban* = Περὶ γάλακτος. From this work an excerpt was made by Aetius of Amida (*Tetrabiblos* II, chs. 86-103). A summary of the Arabic translation has been preserved in al-Rāzī, *Ḥāwī*, xxi, 440-7. It is a monograph in which all kinds of dairy products, milking and cheese are described from the most various points of view.

8. *Kitāb Tarbiyat al-aṭfāl* = Περὶ κομιδῆς παιδίων. This is a work on pediatrics and pediatric diseases, copied out by al-Rāzī in his *Ḥāwī* and by Aḥmad b. Muḥammad b. Yaḥyā al-Baladī (4th/10th century) in his *K. Tadbīr al-ḥabālā wa 'l-aṭfāl* (cf. Ullmann, *Die Schrift des Rufus "De infantium curatione" und das Problem der Autorenlemmata in den "Collectiones medicae" des Oreibasios*, in *Medizinhistorisches Journal*, x [1975], 165-90).

9. *Kitāb al-Adwiya al-ḳātila* (the Greek title has not been transmitted). This is a work on poisoning and its therapy, in which vegetable poisons and bites of insects, serpents and dogs are dealt with. Important fragments have been preserved by al-Rāzī, Ibn Sīnā (*Ḳānūn*) and al-Ḥusayn b. Abī Thaʿlab b. al-Mubārak, *K. al-Munḳidh min al-halaka* (ms. Chester Beatty 4525).

10. The so-called "Journals of sick persons" are a collection of 21 clinical reports which Sarābiyūn b. Ibrāhīm inserted in his *K. al-Fuṣūl al-muhimma fī ṭibb al-aʾimma* (ms. Oxford, Bodl., Hunt. 461). They deal with melancholy, frenzy, lethargy, epilepsy, paralysis, aches of the joints and angina. According to the title

they were noted down by "Rūfus and other ancient and modern physicians" (ed. Ullmann, *Rufus von Ephesos, Krankenjournale*, Wiesbaden 1978). The editor tried to prove that the 21 pieces form a unity and that no other physician than Rūfus can be considered as an author. F. Kudlien (in *Clio Medica*, xiv [1979], 148-9, and xv [1981], 137-42) is, however, of a different opinion.

All these writings show Rūfus as an all-round physician, who deals with many pathological questions and who attaches special importance to dietetic prescriptions. As can be inferred from many a remark which he interwove into his representations, he had strong cultural-historical interests. Like Galen he stood in the tradition of Hippocrates, but in contrast to the former he was not apparently interested in current philosophical questions. His attitude was less speculative, but rather, closer to the facts; yet the Middle Ages gave preference to Galen's system, which had a philosophical basis.

Bibliography: *Oeuvres de Rufus d'Éphèse*, publication commencée par Charles Daremberg, continuée et terminée par Charles-Émile Ruelle, Paris 1879 (repr. Amsterdam 1963); J. Ilberg, *Rufus von Ephesos, ein griechischer Arzt in trajanischer Zeit*, in *Abh. d. Sächsischen Akad. d. Wiss.*, phil-hist. Kl., xli (1930), no. 1, Leipzig 1930; Sezgin, *GAS*, iii, 64-8; M. Ullmann, *Die Medizin im Islam*, Leiden-Cologne 1970, 71-6; idem, *Die arabische Überlieferung der Schriften des Rufus von Ephesos*, in *Aufstieg und Niedergang der Römischen Welt*, ed. H. Temporini and W. Haase, Berlin, Teilband II, 37, 2 (forthcoming).

(M. ULLMANN)

RŪḤ [see NAFS].

RŪḤ B. **ḤĀTIM** [see RAWḤ B. ḤĀTIM].

RŪḤ ALLĀH [see KHUMAYNĪ in Suppl.].

AL-**RUHĀ** OR AL-RUHĀʾ, the Arabic name of a city which was in early Islamic times in the province of Diyār Muḍar [*q.v.*] but known in Western sources as EDESSA (Syriac Orhāy, Armenian Uṙhay). It is now in the province of Diyarbakır in the southeast of modern Turkey and is known as Urfa, a name for the city which is not clearly attested before the coming of the Turks to eastern Anatolia.

1. In pre-Islamic times.

The city is probably an ancient one, though efforts to identify it with the Babylonian Erech/Uruk or with Ur of the Chaldees cannot be taken seriously. Its site, at the junction of ancient highways from Armenia southwards and east-west from the fords across the Euphrates to Mesopotamia and Persia, must have made it strategically valuable when it was founded or re-founded by the Seleucids. Orhāy now received new names, such as "Antioch by the Callirrhoe", i.e. "by the beautiful, flowing [water]", a reference to its famed fish-ponds or to the river of Orhāy, and Edessa, originally the name of the Seleucids' own capital in Macedonia.

The names of the local rulers, called by the Greeks Phylarchs or Toparchs, are known. The early ones were vassals of the Parthians, in whose political and cultural sphere Edessa lay, but in the 2nd century A.D. it came sporadically under Roman rule, with its kings therefore as Roman vassals. These kings seem to have been of Arabic stock, although their regnal names included Iranian as well as Semitic ones. In the early 3rd century they are said to have adopted Christianity, and certainly, by the early 4th century the whole of the city was Christian and famed as the first kingdom officially to adopt Christianity as its state religion, a prominent role being assigned to King Abgar V, who was said to have acknowledged Jesus Christ as the Son of God before His crucifixion.

The monarchy in Edessa had ended *ca.* 242, affected adversely by the appearance on the scene in the Near East of the aggressive and expansionist Sāsānid Persian empire and the Roman withdrawal from much of the Mesopotamian countryside, although the Romans and the Byzantines retained dominion over the city until the Arab invasions. Edessa now became a major centre for Syriac-language literary activity and for Christian religious life, becoming, like most of Mesopotamia and Syria, Monophysite in theology during the course of the 6th century. When the Arabs appeared, there were in the city a small community of Nestorians, a Melkite hierarchy and community, and the two ethnic elements of Monophysites, the Syrian Jacobites (the majority in Edessa) and the Armenians.

2. The Islamic period up to the Ottomans.

Abū ʿUbayda in 16/637 sent ʿIyāḍ b. Ghanm to al-Djazīra. After the Greek governor Joannes Kateas, who had endeavoured to save the region of Osrhoëne by paying tribute, had been dismissed by the emperor Heraclius and the general Ptolemaius put in his place, al-Ruhāʾ (Edessa) had to surrender in 18/639 like the other towns of Mesopotamia (al-Balādhurī, 172-5; Ibn al-Athīr, ii, 414-17; Yāḳūt, s.v. *al-Djazīra*; Khʷārazmī, ed. Baethgen, *Fragmente syr. u. arab. Historiker*, Leipzig 1884, 16, 110 = *Abh. KM*, viii, no. 3; Theophanes, ed. de Boor, 517, 521). The town now lost its political and very soon also its religious significance and sank to the level of a second-rate provincial town. Its last bishop of note, Jacob of Edessa, spent only four years (684-7) and a later period again of four months in his office (708). The Maronite Theophilus of Edessa (d. 785) wrote a "Chronicle of the World" and translated into Syriac the "two Books of Homer about Ilion".

Al-Ruhāʾ, like al-Raḳḳa, Ḥarrān and Ḳarḳīsiya, was usually reckoned to Diyār Muḍar (Ibn al-Athīr, viii, 218; al-Yaʿḳūbī, i, 177; M. Hartmann, *Bohtān*, 88, no. 2 and 3 = *MVAG* [1897], i, 28; Canard, *Hʾamdanides*, 91-2). In 67/686-7 al-Ruhāʾ, Ḥarrān and Sumaysāṭ formed the governorship which Ibrāhīm b. al-Ashtar granted to Ḥātim b. al-Nuʿmān (Ibn al-Athīr, iv, 218).

The "old church" of the Christians was destroyed by two earthquakes (3 April 679 and 718). In 737 a Greek named Bashīr appeared in Ḥarrān and gave himself out to be "Tiberias the son of Constantine"; he was believed at first, but was later exposed and executed in al-Ruhāʾ (Barhebraeus, *Chron. syr.*, ed. Bedjan, 119). In 133/750-1 the town was the scene of fighting between Abū Djaʿfar, afterwards the caliph al-Manṣūr, and the followers of the Umayyads, Isḥāḳ b. Muslim al-ʿUḳaylī and his brother Bakkār, who only gave in after the death of Marwān (Ibn al-Athīr, v, 333-4). But continual revolts broke out again in al-Djazīra (Ibn al-Athīr, v, 370 ff.); in the reign of al-Manṣūr, for example, the governor of al-Ruhāʾ of the same name, the builder of Ḥiṣn Manṣūr, was executed in al-Raḳḳa in 141/758-9 (al-Balādhurī, 192). When Hārūn al-Rashīd passed through al-Ruhāʾ, an attempt was made to cast suspicion upon the Christians and it was said that the Byzantine emperor used to come to the city every year secretly in order to pray in their churches; but the caliph saw that these were slanders. The Gūmāyē (from al-Djūma, the valley of ʿAfrīn in Syria), who, with the Telmaḥrāyē and Ruṣāfāyē, were one of the leading families of al-Ruhāʾ, suffered a good deal, however, from his covetousness (Barhebraeus, *Chron. syr.*, 130). In 196/812 the Christians were only able to save the unprotected town from being plundered by the rebels Naṣr b. Shabath [*q.v.*] and ʿAmr by a heavy payment; Abū Shaykh therefore fortified al-Ruhāʾ at the expense of the citizens (Barhebraeus, 136-7). At the beginning of his reign, al-Maʾmūn sent his general Ṭāhir D̲h̲u 'l-Yamīnayn [q.v.] to al-Ruhāʾ, where his Persian soldiers were besieged by the two rebels, but offered a successful resistance supported by the inhabitants among whom was Mār Dionysius of Tellmaḥrē (Barhebraeus, 139). Ṭāhir, who himself had fled from his mutinous soldiers to Kallinikos, won the rebels over to his side and made ʿAbd al-Aʿlā governor of al-Ruhāʾ; he oppressed the town very much (ibid., 139-40). Muḥammad b. Ṭāhir, who governed al-D̲j̲azīra in 210/825, persecuted the Christians in al-Ruhāʾ, as did the governors under al-Muʿtaṣim and his successors.

In 331/942-3 the Byzantines occupied Diyārbakr, Arzan, Dārā and Rās al-ʿAyn, advanced on Naṣībīn and demanded from the people of al-Ruhāʾ the holy picture on linen of Christ called μανδύλιον (al-Īḳōna al-Mandīl); with the approval of the caliph al-Muttaḳī, it was handed over in return for the release of 200 Muslim prisoners and the promise to leave the town undisturbed in future (Yaḥyā b. Saʿīd al-Anṭākī, ed. Kračkovskiy-Vasilʾev, in Patrol. Orient., xviii, 730-2; T̲h̲ābit b. Sinān, ed. Baethgen, in op. cit., 90, 145). The picture reached Constantinople on 15 August 944, where it was brought with great ceremony into the Church of St. Sophia and the imperial palace (see in addition to Yaḥyā, loc. cit., al-Masʿūdī, Murūd̲j̲, ii, 331 = § 753; Ibn al-At̲h̲īr, viii, 302, and an oration ascribed to Constantine Porphyrogenitus on the εἰκὼν ἀχειροποίητος or De imagine Edessena, ed. Migne, Patrol. Graec., cxiii, col. 432, better ed. von Dobschütz, Christusbilder, in Texte u. Untersuch., xviii). But by 338/949-50 this treaty was broken by the Ḥamdānid Sayf al-Dawla, who, together with the inhabitants of al-Ruhāʾ, made a raid on al-Maṣṣīṣa (Yaḥyā, op. cit., 732). Under the Domesticus Leo the Byzantines in 348/959-60 entered Diyār Bakr and advanced on al-Ruhāʾ (Ibn al-At̲h̲īr, viii, 393). The emperor Nicephorus Phocas towards the end of 357/967-8 advanced on Diyār Muḍar, Mayyāfāriḳīn and Kafartūt̲h̲ā (Yaḥyā, 815). According to Ibn al-At̲h̲īr (viii, 454, below), al-Ruhāʾ was burned to the ground in Muḥarram 361/October-November 971 and troops left in al-D̲j̲azīra. One should rather read Muḥarram 362/October-November 972 and take the reference to be to the campaign of John Tzimisces, unless there is a confusion between Edessa and Emesa (Ḥimṣ) which was burned in 358/969 (Barhebraeus, Chron, syr., 190).

Ibn Ḥawḳal in ca. 367/978 refers to over 300 churches in al-Ruhāʾ, and al-Muḳaddasī reckons the cathedral, the ceilings of which were richly decorated with mosaics, among the four wonders of the world.

Down to 416/1025-6, the town belonged to the chief of the Banū Numayr, ʿUṭayr. The latter installed Aḥmad b. Muḥammad as nāʾib there, but afterwards had him assassinated. The inhabitants thereupon rebelled and offered the town to Naṣr al-Dawla the Marwānid of Diyārbakr (Greek Ἀπομερμάνης), who had it occupied by Zangī. After the murder of ʿUṭayr and the death of Zangī (418/1027), Naṣr al-Dawla gave ʿUṭayr's son one tower of al-Ruhāʾ and another to S̲h̲ibl's son (Ibn al-At̲h̲īr, ix, 244). The former (according to others, a Turk Salmān, Σαλαμάνης, appointed governor, who was hard pressed by ʿUṭayr's widow) then sold the fortress for 20,000 darics and four villages to the Byzantine Protospatharius Georgius Maniakes, son of Gudelius, who lived in Samosata; he appeared suddenly one night and occupied three towers. After a vain attempt by the Marwānid amīr of Mayyāfāriḳīn to drive him out again, in which the town, which was still inhabited by many Christians, was sacked and burned (winter of 1030-1). Maniakes again occupied the citadel and the town (Ibn al-At̲h̲īr, ix, 281 bis; Michael Syrus, ed. Chabot, iii, 147; Barhebraeus, Chron. syr., 214; Aristakēs Lastivertcʿi, c. 7, pp. 24-5; Matthew of Edessa, ed. 1898, c. 43, pp. 58-62 = tr. Dulaurier, 46-9; Cedrenus-Seylitzes, ed. Bonn, ii, 500; the accounts of the events preceding the surrender differ very much). Edessa under Maniakes seems to have enjoyed a certain amount of independence from Byzantium, as he sent an annual tribute thither (Cedrenus-Seylitzes, 502).

In Rad̲j̲ab 427/May 1036, the Patricius of Edessa became a prisoner of the Numayrī Ibn Waththāb and his many allies; the town was plundered but the fortress remained in the hands of the Greek garrison (Ibn al-At̲h̲īr, ix, 305; Barhebraeus, Chron. syr., 217). By the peace of 428/1037 the emperor again received complete possession of Edessa which was refortified (Ibn al-At̲h̲īr, ix, 313; Barhebraeus, 221).

According to the Armenian sources, Maniakes was followed by Apukʿap or Λέων Λεπενδρηνός, then by the Iberian Βαρασβατζέ as strategus of Edessa; in 1059 Ἰωάννης ὁ Δουκήτζης was catapanus of the town. In 1065-6 and 1066-7, the Turks under the K̲h̲urāsān Sālār attacked the town and the Sald̲j̲ūk Alp Arslān besieged it for fifty days in 462/1070; it was defended by Wasil (son of the Bulgar king Alōsian?). After the victory of Malāzgird [q.v.], Edessa was to be handed over to the sultan, but the defeated emperor Romanus Diogenes had no longer any authority over it, and its Catapanus Paulus went to his successor in Constantinople (Scylitzes, ed. Bonn, 702). In 1081-2 Edessa was again besieged by an amīr named K̲h̲usraw, but in vain. After the death of Wasil, the Armenian Smbat became lord of Edessa and six months later (2? September 1083) Philaretus Brachamius succeeded him. But he lost it in 1086-7 when, in his absence, his deputy was murdered and the town handed over to the Sald̲j̲ūk sultan Maliks̲h̲āh. The latter appointed the amīr Buzān governor of al-Ruhāʾ and Ḥarrān. When the latter had fallen in 487/1094 fighting against Tutus̲h̲ [q.v.], Tutus̲h̲'s general Alpyārūk̲ occupied the town, but it was not plundered by his army as he was poisoned by a Greek dancing-girl called Galī. Then the Armenian Kuropalates Tʿoros (Theodorus), son of Hetʿum, took the citadel. When in 1097-8 Count Baldwin of Bouillon captured Tel Bās̲h̲ir, Tʿoros asked him to come to al-Ruhāʾ to assist him against their joint enemies, and received him with joy, but was shortly afterwards treacherously murdered by him (Matthew of Edessa, ed. 1898, 260-2 = tr. Dulaurier, 218-21; Anonym. Syriac chronicle of 1203-1204, in Chabot, C.-R. Acad. Inscr. Lettr [1918], 431 ff.).

From 1098 the Latins ruled for half a century the "County of Edessa" to which also belonged Sumaysā and Sarūd̲j̲ (1098 Baldwin of Bouillon) I; 1100 Baldwin of Bourg II; 1119 Joscelin (de Courtenay) I 1131 the latter's son Joscelin II). The town suffered a great deal under them, and there was some justification for Matthew of Edessa's comment that Baldwin du Bourg "hated Christians more than Turks". Ecclesiastical disputes, for instance, on the vexed question of the date for celebrating Easter, divided the Christians, Latin versus Monophysites. Despite their private jealousies, the Crusaders managed to hold on to the county of Edessa, largely because of the divided counsels of the Muslim amīrs, but with the rise of the resolute and skilful Atabeg of Mawṣil, ʿImād al-Dīn Zangī—coinciding in 1143 with the deaths of two of the strongest figures in the Christian camp, the Byzantine emperor John II Comnenus and Fulk, king of Jerusalem—the days of Crusader control over Edessa were numbered.

On 25 Djumādā II 539/23 December 1144, ʿImād al-Dīn Zangī took it (a detailed description of these events in the *Anonymous Syriac chronicle of 1203-1204*, ed. Chabot, in *CSCO*, series iii, vol. xv, 118-26; tr. Chabot, *Une épisode de l'histoire des Croisades*, in *Mélanges Schlumberger*, i, Paris 1924, 171-9). Under Joscelin II and Baldwin of Kaysūm, the Franks again attempted to retake the town in October 1046 and succeeded in entering it by night, but six days later Nūr al-Dīn appeared with 10,000 Turks, and soon occupied and sacked it; the inhabitants were put to death or carried into slavery. Baldwin was killed and Joscelin escaped to Sumaysāṭ (Barhebraeus, 311-12). The fall of this eastern bulwark of the Crusaders aroused horror everywhere; in Europe it led to the Second Crusade. The Syrian Dionysius bar Ṣalībī as Diaconus wrote an "oration" and two poetic *mēmrē* about the destruction of the town. Three similar pieces were written by Basilius Abu 'l-Faradj b. Shummānā, the favourite of Zangī; he had also written a history of the town of Orhāy (Baumstark, *Gesch. d. syr. Lit.*, 293, 298).

After the death of Nūr al-Dīn, his nephew Sayf al-Dīn Ghāzī took the town in 1174; in 1182 it fell to the Ayyūbid Ṣalāḥ al-Dīn, who later handed it over to al-Malik al-Manṣūr. When al-Malik al-ʿĀdil died in 1218, his son al-Malik al-Ashraf Sharaf al-Dīn Mūsā became lord of al-Ruhāʾ, Ḥarrān and Khilāṭ. In June 1234 the town was taken by the army of the Rūm Saldjūḳ ʿAlāʾ al-Dīn Kayḳubād and its inhabitants deported to Asia Minor (Kamāl al-Dīn Ibn al-ʿAdīm, tr. Blochet, in *ROL*, v, 88; Barhebraeus, *Chron. syr.*, 468). But it was retaken within four months by al-Malik al-Kāmil. In 1244 the Mongols passed through the district of al-Ruhāʾ and in 1260 the troops of Hülegü. The people of al-Ruhāʾ and Ḥarrān surrendered voluntarily to him, but those of Sarūdj were all put to death (Barhebraeus, *Chron. syr.*, 509; *Chron. arab.*, ed. Beirut, 486).

In the time of Abu 'l-Fidāʾ, al-Ruhāʾ was in ruins. Ḥamd Allāh Mustawfī in *ca.* 740/1340 could still see isolated ruins of the main buildings. According to al-Ḳalḳashandī, the town had been rebuilt by his time (*ca.* 1400) and repopulated and was in a prosperous state. In connection with the campaigns of Tīmūr, who conquered al-Djazīra in 1393, al-Ruhāʾ is repeatedly mentioned in the *Ẓafar-nāma* of Sharaf al-Dīn ʿAlī Yazdī (written in 828/1425).

Bibliography: For older bibliography, see Honigmann's *EI*[1] art. *Orfa*. The information of the geographers is given in Le Strange, *Lands of the Eastern Caliphate*, 103-4, see also Naval Intelligence Division, Admiralty Handbooks, *Turkey*, London 1942-3, ii, 588-90. On history, see now Canard, *H'amdanides*, 91-2, 747-52; R. Grousset, *Histoire des Croisades*, Paris 1948, i, 382 ff., ii, 53-145, 169-209; S. Runciman, *A history of the Crusades*. ii. *The Kingdom of Jerusalem and the Frankish East 1100-1187*, Cambridge 1952, 107-39, 225-44; M.W. Baldwin (ed.), *A history of the Crusades*. i. *The first hundred years*, Philadelphia 1955; J.B. Segal, *Edessa 'The Blessed City'*, Oxford 1970.

(E. HONIGMANN-[C.E. BOSWORTH])

3. The Ottoman and modern periods.

Al-Ruhā was conquered by sultan Selīm I, probably in 923/1517. The first Ottoman tax register was compiled in 924/1518; the tax-paying population at that time consisted of 782 Muslim families and 75 bachelors, 300 Christian families and 42 bachelors, amounting to a total of 1,082 families and 117 bachelors, or an estimated population total of slightly over 5,500. This low figure was probably due to the upheavals of the Ottoman-Ṣafawid War, for only eight years later, in 932/1526, the tax-paying population had increased to 988 Muslim and 334 Christian families, along with 182 Muslim and 89 Christian bachelors. Moreover, 213 Ottoman military men had settled in the town, thus bringing total population to about 8,000 people. A further tax register from the last year of Süleyman the Magnificent (973/1566) records 1,704 Muslim and 866 Christian families, along with 705 Muslim and 221 Christian bachelors; these figures point to a total population of 13,000-14,000 inhabitants. The town consisted of five large *maḥalles* named after the five gates and must have possessed an active textile industry, for the dye houses of al-Ruhā and nearby Ḥarrān produced the impressive revenue of 100,000 *aḳčes*. A *bedestān* is also on record.

In the 10th/16th century, al-Ruhā formed part of the *beglerbeglik* of Diyārbekir, and was located on the caravan route from Mawṣil and Mārdīn to Aleppo. It was therefore visited by several European travellers, among them an anonymous merchant whose travel account was published in 971-2/1564. He mentions the principal features of the town which were to recur in European travel accounts throughout more than two centuries: the strong walls and impressive citadel, the sanctuary of Abraham/Ibrāhīm, venerated by Christians and particularly by Muslims, the fishpond next to the sanctuary, and, at a distance from the town, a well frequented by lepers and other sick people. A few years later, al-Ruhā was visited by the Augsburg physician and botanist Rauwolf (982/1575), who describes the town as handsome and well-built. The town possessed a lively trade in rugs and carpets, which were sometimes sold to Europe, and also served as a point of transit for goods from Damascus, Aleppo and Istanbul, which were sold in Persia and ʿIrāḳ.

The most detailed description of al-Ruhā/Urfa before the 13th/19th century is due to the Ottoman traveller Ewliyā Čelebi, who passed through the town (which he calls Urfa, as do all other visitors of this period) in 1056/1646. His interest in it may have been due to the fact that one of his relatives had served as a *ḳāḍī* there. He describes two fortresses, one the citadel on the hill and the other a fortified settlement (*wārōsh*). The citadel he links with King Nimrod, and the two Roman columns standing there Ewliyā interprets as a catapult with which this ruler supposedly had the prophet Ibrāhīm al-Khalīl (Abraham) thrown into the fire. Otherwise, the citadel contained 20 small houses inhabited by the commander (*dizdār*) and his 200 men, in addition to a mosque, an armoury, a barn and a number of cisterns. Ewliyā mentions only three gates, partly with names different from those recorded in the 10th/16th century tax register. He claims to have counted 2,600 houses in the fortified section. If his count was accurate and the area outside the fortifications remained uninhabited, the town must have stagnated since 973/1566. As Ewliyā's figures concerning houses are generally more generous than the household data found in late 10th/16th century tax registers, the upheavals of the Djelālī period, particularly the occupation by the forces of Ḳarā Yazīdjī in 1008/1599-1600, must have taken their toll. Houses were generally built of mud brick, but there were quite a few opulent residences with their own gardens and baths, belonging to pashas and more rarely to *ḳāḍīs*.

He also enumerates 22 mosques; the mosque

known as Ḳîzîl Djāmiʿ was considered to be of great age and a former monastery, converted into a mosque by Hārūn al-Rashīd. The minaret, undated, often has been regarded as the bell tower of the church which formerly stood on the mosque site, but according to Gabriel, it is an original minaret. Ewliyā has also picked up a legend of Jesus' visit to al-Ruhā and his stay in a local monastery. Ewliyā records three *medreses*; the *medreses* possessed no *waḳf* revenues, but the traveller comments on the multitude of Kurdish scholars, both in the *medreses* proper and in the local *dār al-ḥadīth* and *dār al-ḳurrāʾ*. There were also three *zāwiyes*. Among the public kitchens, the most notable was the *ʿimāret* of Ibrāhīm, supposedly built by the caliph al-Maʾmūn. Connected with the *ʿimāret* was al-Ruhā/Urfa's major sanctuary, dedicated to Ibrāhīm by Ṣalāḥ al-Dīn Ayyūbī's nephew al-Malik al-Ashraf (608/1211-12), and visited by pilgrims from all over the Islamic world.

Ewliyā was not much impressed with the shopping streets and markets of al-Ruhā/Urfa; but though the Küre Čarshîsî was not of imposing appearance, quantities of valuable goods were sold there. He records a total of 400 shops and a large number of mills, one of them named for a certain Ṭayyāroghlu Aḥmed Pasha. The town also possessed a tannery; here a superior quality of yellow maroquin leather was manufactured. According to the French merchant Tavernier, al-Ruhā/Urfa, along with Toḳāt and Diyārbekir, was the source of the finest maroquin leathers. In addition, the town was noted for its cotton fabrics, and there was also some silk production.

Ewliyā's account is confirmed by the description of Tavernier, who passed through the town in 1054/1644. On his sight-seeing tour, this merchant and traveller saw many houses poorly built or even totally in ruins; there were so many empty lots that Tavernier compared the town to a desert. He also observed rugs and carpets spread out by the side of the fish pond, and commented on the veneration Muslims felt for this site. A church in the midst of a cemetery supposedly had been selected by St. Alexis as a place of retreat; and not far from the town Tavernier was able to see the Armenian church and monastery of St Ephrem in the midst of a Christian necropolis. This monastery was partly located in grottoes cut into the living rock, a feature of the local landscape also noted by Ewliyā and many other travellers; in the early 13th/19th century they were used as habitations.

When Thévenot passed through al-Ruhā/Urfa in 1074/1664, the damages mentioned by Ewliyā and Tavernier were still clearly visible. A valuable record of al-Ruhā/Urfa's otherwise poorly documented 13th/18th century is found in the accounts of revenues and expenditures pertaining to the mosque of Ibrāhīm al-Khalīl and the then newly constructed Riḍwāniyye *medrese*. These survive for a few years beginning with 1151/1738-39 (Osmanlı Arşivi, Istanbul, Maliyeden Müdevver 2004). The register contains a listing of the shops, gardens, mills and public baths belonging to these foundations, along with information about tenants and rents. The foundations also received rent from the Aladja Khān, in addition to a mulberry orchard located in front of the *medrese*. These accounts document the existence of a flourishing *čarshı*, with relatively few properties untenanted. Apparently Urfa's recovery was under way by this time. Thévenot also commented on the large number of ruined houses, even though the walls were in good condition and the town populous.

The Danish traveller Niebuhr passed through the town in the spring of 1179-80/1766, and produced a sketch map of the built-up area, which shows the town as possessing four gates, but there must have been an entrance to the citadel, even though his sketch does not show any. Thus we can understand why most accounts mention only four gates, while the Ottoman tax registers and B. Poujoulat (before 1256/1840) record five. His account mentions twelve minarets, of which the mosque of Khalīl al-Raḥmān was the most notable, and also two Christian churches within the walls. The Armenian church was in a largely ruinous condition, but the surviving part richly decorated with Persian rugs; the congregation numbered about 500 families, while the Jacobite church served only about 150 persons. In Niebuhr's time, Turkish was the principal language spoken in al-Ruhā/Urfa, but merchants and mule drivers usually knew Arabic and Kurdish as well.

However, in socio-economic terms, the richest travel account between Ewliyā's time and the republican period is due to Buckingham. He visited the town in 1234/1816, and as Ottoman-Wahhābī warfare closed the roads, spent considerable time there. By his time, the name al-Ruhā had been almost completely supplanted by Urfa, the only people who still called the town by its old name being Christian Arabs. He estimated the town's population as 50,000 persons; 47,500 were Muslims, 2,000 Christians and 500 were Jews. However, Poujoulat, who was in Urfa before 1256/1840, claims that the population consisted of only about 15,000 (14,000 Muslims, 1,000 Armenians, 100 Jacobites). As in Aleppo, the town consisted of two factions, namely the Janissaries and the *sherīfs*, and Buckingham complained of the former's lack of discipline. Buckingham describes the houses as consisting of good masonry, and resembling those of Aleppo; many of the townsmen obviously lived more comfortably than their forefathers, who had made do with the mud brick seen by Ewliyā and his contemporaries. *Ḥarem* and *selāmlîḳ* were separated by a courtyard; the upper floors of the *selāmlîḳs* generally contained opulently furnished reception rooms. Because of the insecurity due to warfare, many of the bazaars were closed; but in more peaceful times, the townsmen were still known for their lively cotton trade. Buckingham was even able to observe cotton printers at work. In addition, rough woollen cloth and rugs, the latter of good quality, were manufactured in Urfa. Goods from India, Persia and Anatolia were ordinarily available. The traveller mentions mohair fabrics from Ankara, which he calls shalloons, and some cashmere shawls.

A slightly later description of Urfa is due to the Prussian officer von Moltke, who visited it in 1254/1838. He mentions a mosque which he does not name, and which must have been the Ḳîzîl Djāmiʿ, for the structure is described as a solidly-built tower of great antiquity. The author also visited a large foundation adjacent to the two fishponds, which he describes as a *medrese* and which must have been the foundation which Ṣalāḥ al-Dīn had added to the mosque of Ibrāhīm (587/1191). He also made a map of the town and recorded the presence of numerous orchards.

From 1307-8/1890 or slightly earlier dates the description by Cuinet. According to him, the town possessed a population of 55,000, of whom 40,835 were Muslims; about 1297/1880, Sachau had estimated the number of Urfa's inhabitants at minimally 50,000. However, these optimistic evaluations were contradicted by Djewdet Pasha's claim (1298/1881) that Urfa *ḳaḍā* consisted of only 2,380 households or families (1,337 Muslims, 1,003 Christians, 29 Jews).

f we compare the estimates by Buckingham and achau-Cuinet, it would seem that population growth n the 13th/19th century was just able to compensate or wartime population losses, and Urfa's population nust have been at a low ebb for several decades in the nid-century. Private houses in Cuinet's time were enerally built in rough or even regularly hewn stone. The streets possessed wide pavements, while a chanel in the centre served for the evacuation of water nd household waste. The city walls had deteriorated, ut the citadel apparently was in better condition. The town now possessed 18 *medreses* with 500 students, n addition to a *rüshdiyye*. There were also primary chools for the children of the various Christian churhes, so that a total of 2,464 students were receiving formal education.

At this time, Urfa was a flourishing centre of textile nanufacture. The cotton industry survived the cometition by factory-woven textiles, partly because nanufacturers switched to imported thread which was voven locally. However, to remain competitive, veavers were forced to accept very low wages. By the arly 20th century the ancient trade route linking orthern Mesopotamia with Aleppo had revived, and Jrfa's new prosperity permitted the construction of a own quarter *extra muros*. This development was, howver, cut short when, after the fall of the Ottoman mpire Syria became a French and ʿIrāḳa British nandate. British and later French troops occupied Jrfa in 1919-20. After severe fighting, which included local uprising, the Treaty of Lausanne determined he inclusion of Urfa into the newly-founded Republic f Turkey (1923).

Throughout the Republican period, it has not been ossible to re-establish Urfa's former trade links. This ituation has emphasised the agricultural character of he *vilayet*. Grain is the main crop; apart from wheat, arley and beans are also significant. Productivity is ften low, as much of the land is subject to erosion. A ignificant share of the grain grown is not intended for he market. Irrigation is a precondition for increasing roductivity, and the regulation of the Fırat Euphrates), the region's only important body of vater, is expected to expand the area amenable to irigation.

Limited opportunities in agriculture and the proress of mechanisation have diminished employment ere, so that there has been considerable migration of abour to e.g. Adana, Gaziantep and Diyarbekir in earch of work; female labour finds work cottonicking in the Çukorova. Low incomes have likewise mited the progress of education, and literacy rates re lower than the national average. Since 1980-2, owever, Urfa has been the site of a college of Dicle Jniversity at Diyarbekir, and the foundation of a ocal university is envisaged by the town's citizens.

Bibliography: G.B. Ramusio (ed.), *Secondo volume delle Navigationi et viaggi*... Venice 1564, 78; J.Ch. Tayfel, *Il viaggio del molto illustre signor Giovanni Christoforo Taifel*, Vienna 1598; J. Gassot, *Lettre ecritte d'Alep en Surie*... Bourges 1674, 1684; R. Fitch, *Aanmerklyke Reys na Ormus, Goa, Cambaya... 1583-91*, Leiden 1706; M. Poullet, *Nouvelles relations du Levant*, Paris 1668, ii, 441-3; J. Thévenot, *Suite du voyage de Mr de Thévenot au Levant*..., 2nd part, Paris 1689, 119 ff.; R. Pococke, *A Description of the East and some other Countries*, London 1745, ii/1, 159-61; M. Otter, *Voyages en Turquie et en Perse*, Paris 1748, i, 112-13; C. Niebuhr, *Reisebeschreibung nach Arabien und umliegenden Ländern*, Copenhagen 1778, ii, 406-10; J.S. Buckingham, *Travels to Mesopotamia, including a journey to Aleppo*, London 1827, 51-129; W. Ainsworth, *Researches in Assyria, Babylonia and Chaldea*... London 1838, 261-3 (geology of Urfa's site); B. Poujoulat, *Voyage dans l'Asie Mineure*..., Paris 1840, i, 407-19; Ainsworth, *Travels and researches in Asia Minor, Mesopotamia, Chaldea and Armenia*, London 1842, ii, 103; C. Ritter, *Die Erdkunde*, vii, *West-Asien*, Berlin 1844, 315-56; F. Chesney, *The expedition for the survey of the Rivers Euphrates and Tigris*, London 1850, i, 114, Pl. VII; Ch. Texier, *La ville et les monuments d'Edesse*, in *Revue américaine et orientale*, i (1859), 326-54; H. Petermann, *Reisen im Orient*, Leipzig 1861, ii, 351-6; E. Sachau, *Reise in Syrien und Mesopotamien*, Leipzig 1883, 190-210; V. Cuinet, *La Turquie d'Asie*, Paris 1891, ii, 249-63; H. von Moltke, *Briefe über Zustände und Begebenheiten in der Türkei aus den Jahren 1835 bis 1839*, 5th ed., Berlin 1891, 229-30; Ewliyā Čelebi, *Seyāḥat-nāme*, iii, Istanbul 1314/1896-7, 148-60; S. Guyer, *Reisen in Mesopotamien*, in *Petermanns Geographische Mitteilungen* (1916), 172-4; A. Baiao (ed.), *Itinerarios da India a Portugal por terra*, Coimbra 1923, 62, 240; A. Gabriel, *Voyages archéologiques dans la Turquie orientale*, Paris 1940, i, 277-86, 354 ff.; M. Akdağ, *Celâlî isyanları (1550-1603)*, Ankara 1963, 190-201; N. Göyünç, *XVI-yüzyılda Mardin sancağı*, Istanbul 1969, 34-5, 41-2, 66, 90, 134; L. Rauwolf, *Aigentliche Beschreibung der Raiss inn die Morgenlaender*, introd. D. Henze, Graz 1971, 258-62; *Urfa il yıllığı*, Ankara 1973; Göyünç, *XVI Yüzyılda güney-doğu Anadolu'nun ekonomik durumu: Kanunî Süleyman ve II. Selim devirleri*, in *Türkiye iktisat tarihi semineri*, ed. O. Okyar and Ü. Nalbantoğlu, Ankara 1975, 71-98; M. Köhbach, *Urfa und seine Legendentradition bei Evliya Çelebi*, in *Der Islam*, lvii (1980), 293-300; J.B. Tavernier, *Les six voyages de Turquie et de Perse*, notes by S. Yérasimos, Paris 1981, i, 244-6; Cevdet Paşa, *Tezâkir*, ed. Cavit Baysun, Ankara 1986, ii, 224, 235; İ. Şahin, *Evliya Çelebi'nin Urfa hakkında verdiği bilgilerin arşiv belgeleri ışığında değerlendirilmesi*, in *Türklük Araştırmaları dergisi*, iv (1989), 293-8; B. Masters, *The origins of western economic dominance in the Middle East*, New York 1988, 207; S. Yérasimos, *Les voyageurs dans l'Empire ottoman (XIVe-XVIe siècles)*, Ankara 1991, 156, 208, 271, 360, 394; *Yurt Ansiklopedisi, Türkiye, Il Il, Dünü, Bugünü, Yarını*, Istanbul 1982-4, art. *Urfa* (authors' names not given); *İA*, art. *Urfa* (Ottoman period by Göyünç; extensive bibl.)

(SURAIYA FAROQHI)

RŪḤĀNIYYA (A.), a term derived from the adjective *rūḥānī* according to a well-known mode for the formation of abstract nouns and generally translated by "spirituality" in modern dictionaries. In the ancient texts, however, its usual meaning is rather that of "spiritual being", except in cases where it refers to the *djinns* and the *shayāṭīn* which, like the *malāʾika*, evade the sensible perception of the majority of men, but are not of a "spiritual" nature. It is in fact in the vocabulary of angelology that it is most often encountered. Among the *falāsifa* and the Ṣūfīs, it denotes more specifically the *spiritus rector*, the angel who rules (*mudabbir*) each of the celestial spheres. It is in this sense that the Ikhwān al-Ṣafāʾ (*Rasāʾil*, Beirut 1957, xi, 215) speak of "angels which the *ḥukamāʾ* called *rūḥāniyyāt*". Similarly, ʿAbd al-Karīm al-Djīlī, in ch. lxii of his *K. al-Insān al-kāmil*, explains that each of the seven heavens is governed by an angel created *min rūḥāniyyati kawkab tilka 'l-samāʾ*. Among the Ishrāḳiyyūn or Illuminationists, and in particular in the work of al-Suhrawardī, *rūḥāniyya* is also used to denote the "angel of the species", the *rabb al-nawʿ* (see H. Corbin, *En Islam iranien*, Paris 1971, index s.v.).

This word appears frequently in literature relating

to magic. According to Ibn Khaldūn (*Muḳaddima*, iii, 127, tr. Rosethal, iii, 159), magic (*al-siḥr*) consists in "linking the superior natures with the inferior natures. The superior natures are the *rūḥāniyyāt al-kawākib*". This is a statement confirmed by ps.-Madjrīṭī (*Ghāyat al-ḥakīm*, ed. H. Ritter, Leipzig 1933, 182), who claims to reveal the techniques by which it is possible to convoke (*istidjlāb*) the *rūḥāniyya* of the celestial bodies.

While *rūḥāniyya* is currently used in Ṣūfī texts as a denomination of these "cosmic intelligences"—Ibn ʿArabī, for example, speaks in the *K. al-tadjalliyāt* (ed. O. Yahya, Tehran 1988, 317) of purified human spirits granted access to the contemplation of *rūḥāniyyāt mufāraḳa*, forthwith identified with the spirits (*arwāḥ*) of the celestial spheres—it also often denotes the "spiritual entity" of a prophet or of a deceased *walī* whose *murīd* receives supernatural assistance. Thus Ibn ʿArabī speaks (*al-Futūḥāt al-Makkiyya*, Būlāḳ 1329, iii, 43), of his *sulūk* with the *rūḥāniyya* of Jesus. This usage is associated with the notion of sainthood, *uwaysiyya*, which is characterised by the transmission of a *baraka* independently of any contact with a physically present *shaykh*. It is encountered frequently in the literature of the Naḳshbandī *ṭarīḳa*, where the *silsila* presents numerous cases of this type (e.g. that of Abu 'l-Ḥasan al-Kharaḳānī, d. 425/1033 [*q.v.*], who is directly linked with Abū Yazīd al-Bisṭāmī, d. 234/857 or 261/874 [*q.v.*]). On the doctrinal justification of these chronological anomalies, see ʿAbd al-Madjid al-Khānī, *al-Ḥadāʾiḳ al-wardiyya*, Damascus 1306, 9. In *al-Saʿāda al-abadiyya*, Damascus n.d., 27-8, the same author describes the rites which, at the time of *ziyārat al-ḳubūr*, allow the establishment of a connection with the *rūḥāniyya* of the *walī* whose body is interred in the tomb that is visited. (On this practice, see also the *Rashaḥātʿayn al-ḥayāt* of Fakhr al-Dīn ʿAlī Ṣafī, Tehran 1356/1977, ii, 468). Paul Fenton has drawn attention to an analogous Jewish practice, that of *yiḥūd*, which is also conducted over the tomb of a saint. On the beliefs associated with this meaning of *rūḥāniyya*, see M. Gaborieau, A. Popovic and T. Zarcone (eds.), *Naqshbandis. Cheminement et situation actuelle d'un ordre mystique musulman*, Istanbul-Paris 1990, index s.vv. *rūḥāniyya* and *uwaysiyya*. In *Imaginary Muslims*, London 1993, Julian Baldick has analysed a singular case of the exploitation of traditional data concerning this theme with the appearance in Central Asia, at the end of the 16th century, of a mythical "History of the Uwaysīs".

Bibliography: Given in the article.

(M. Chodkiewicz)

RŪḤĪ (d. after 917/1511), Ottoman historian. There is little definite information about this historian apart from his *makhlaṣ* Rūḥī. From ʿĀlī's [*q.v.*] reference to him in the *Künhü 'l-akhbār* as Edrenewī Mewlānā Rūḥī, it is probable that he was a member of the *ʿulamāʾ* and had a family or professional association with Edirne (J. Schmidt, *Muṣṭafā ʿĀlī's Künhü 'l-aḫbār and its preface according to the Leiden manuscript*, Istanbul 1987, 58). Any identification with Rūḥī Fāḍil Efendi (d. 927/1528), son of the *shaykh al-Islām* Zenbilli ʿAlī Efendi, remains hypothetical (Babinger, *GOW*, 42, and *EI*[1], art. *Rūḥī*). The format of his history and the declaration that he was commanded to write it by Bāyezīd II [*q.v.*] suggest that he may have been connected with the Ottoman court (cf. V.L. Ménage, *Edirneli Rûhî'ye atfedilen Osmanlı tarihinden iki parça*, in *İ.H. Uzunçarşılı'ya armağan*, Ankara 1976, 311-33).

Rūḥī's history, known either as *Tewārīkh-i Āl-i ʿOthmān* or as *Taʾrīkh-i Rūḥī*, narrates the history of the dynasty down to 917/1511. It is divided into tw parts: (i) *mebādī*, "beginnings", on general considera tions and the virtues of the Ottomans; and (ii) eigh *maṭālib*, "questions, researches", each of whic describes the reign of one sultan. It was cited as source by ʿĀlī and Münedjdjim-bashī, and may als have been used by Luṭfī Pasha [*q.v.*] in his *Taʾrīk* (M.K. Özergin, *İA*, art. *Rūḥī*, at ix, 765). It wa thought no longer to exist as an independent text un in 1925 J.H. Mordtmann identified several survivin manuscripts (*Rūḥī Edrenevī*, in *MOG*, ii [1925], 12 36). Of these, however, the "Oxford Anonymous (ms. Bodleian, Marsh 313) is probably not the wo of Rūḥī but an earlier history (covering events 889/1484 only) which was his main source (Ménag *Neshrī's History of the Ottomans*, London 1964, 11-13 The work remains unpublished (for manuscripts, s Babinger, *GOW*, 43).

Bibliography: In addition to the references give above, see the bibl. to M.K. Özergin, *İA*, art. *Rūḥ*

(F. Babinger-[Christine Woodhead])

RUHMĪ, a name given in early Islam geographical, travel and maritime literature to a eastern region of South Asia, most likely in th ancient Suhma region in the western part of Beng [see bangāla]. There is considerable confusion abo its location; readings vary from Ruhmī (al-Yaʿḳūb 106) to Rahma (Ibn al-Faḳīh, 15) and Dahum (*Shar al-Zamān Ṭāhir Marvazī on China, the Turks and Indi* ed. and tr. V. Minorsky, London 1942, text 35). O these, the closest to Bengali is Dharma (a spelling use by Sulaymān al-Tādjir), a possible reference to famous Bengali king Dharmapāla (769-801 A.D. Sulaymān al-Tādjir also noticed correctly Dha mapāla's non-aristocrat and humble origin. Accor ing to Ibn Khurradādhbih, 63-7, Ruhmī, a va kingdom, was bordered by Kāmrūn (Kamrup) not f from China, and was bountifully supplied wi elephants, buffaloes and Indian aloe woods. Its coas according to *Ḥudūd al-ʿālam*, tr. 87, included are such as Nimyās, Samandar, Andrās, Ūrshīn an Harkand (ancient Harikela near Čandradvīpa i South Bengal, from which comes Baḥr al-Harkan the early Arabic name for the Bay of Bengal). Th kingdom fought constantly with its neighbour Ballaharā (Radja Ballahrāya of the Rāṣṭrakūṭa dyna ty of the Deccan) and Djurz (Gurdjaras of Kanawdj It was particularly famous for its fine cotton clot later known as muslin. In addition to gold coin cowrie-shells were used for currency. Trade with th Arabs flourished in the port cities in the sout especially in Shāṭiʾ-djām (Chittagong [*q.v.*]) an Samandar. The recent dicovery of two ʿAbbāsid coi in Bangladesh, one from Paharpur dated 172/78 from the time of Hārūn al-Rashīd (170-208/786-80 and the other from Mainamati minted during th reign of al-Muntaṣir (247-8/861-2) attests to this ear Arab-Bengal trade link which undoubtedly speed up the Islamisation of the region.

Bibliography (in addition to references give above): Sulaymān al-Tādjir and Abū Zayd a Sīrāfī, *Akhbār al-Ṣīn wa 'l-Hind* (237/851), ed. an tr. J. Sauvaget, *Relation de la China et l'Inde*, Pa 1948, text 13-14. (M.Y. Siddiq)

RUḲAYYA, daughter of Muḥammad and h wife Khadīdja. She is sometimes said to have be the eldest of his four daughters, but this is unlikel She and her sister Umm Kulthūm were betrothed a married to two sons of Abū Lahab [*q.v.*], but the latt told his sons to divorce their wives when Muḥamm began his career as a prophet. The divorces could n have been, as sometimes stated, after the revelation sūra CXI, in which Abū Lahab is attacked, unless that was an early Meccan revelation. The statement in some sources that the divorces took place before the marriages had been consummated, is probably an invention to keep the holy family free from contamination with the family of Abū Lahab. After the divorce, Ruḳayya was married to ʿU͟thmān b. ʿAffān [*q.v.*], went with him and other Muslims to Abyssinia, and returned to Mecca before the *Hid͟jra*. She made the *Hid͟jra* to Medina with her husband, but died while Muḥammad was absent from Medina on the expedition to Badr [*q.v.*]. After several miscarriages she had a son, ʿAbd Allāh, but a few years after his mother's death a cock pecked his eye and he died.

Bibliography: Ibn Hi͟shām, see index; Wāḳidī, ed. Marsden Jones, London 1966, 101, 115, 154; Ibn Saʿd, viii, 24; Ibn al-Athīr, *Usd al-g͟hāba*, v, 456; Lammens, *Fāṭima et les filles de Mahomet*, Rome 1912, 3 ff. (W. Montgomery Watt)

RUK͟HĀM [see Suppl.].

al-**RUK͟HK͟H** (a.), a huge, ostrich-like bird (*Aepyornis maximus*), now extinct, probably existing well into historical times as a peculiar species in Madagascar, where it is mentioned by among others Marco Polo. Other aepyornitidae, such as the New Zealand Moa bird, which became extinct only around the 14th century, might have contributed to the genesis of the *ruk͟hk͟h*'s image. Though early Arab seafarers could conceivably have seen the bird face-to-face, Arabic tradition soon turned the *ruk͟hk͟h* into a fabulous creature embellishing it with all kinds of strange details.

While early references to al-D͟jāḥiẓ cannot be verified, the first mention of the *ruk͟hk͟h* is found in Buzurg b. S͟hahriyār's (4th/10th century) *ʿAd͟jāʾib al-Hind*. Further references are mostly contained in works belonging to the genre of *ʿad͟jāʾib* literature, such as Abū Ḥāmid al-G͟harnāṭī's (d. 565/1169-70 [*q.v.*]) *Tuḥfat al-albāb*, al-Dimas͟hḳī's (d. 727/1327 [*q.v.*]) *Nuk͟hbat al-dahr fī ʿad͟jāʾib al-barr wa 'l-baḥr* and Ibn al-Wardī's (d. 749/1349 [*q.v.*]) *K͟harīdat al-ʿad͟jāʾib*; later summaries are rendered by al-Damīrī (d. 808/1405 [*q.v.*]) and al-Ibs͟hīhī (9th/15th century [*q.v.*]). By way of its mention in the *Travels* of Sindbād the sailor, itself included in the widely-read *Arabian Nights* (Chauvin, *Bibliographie*, vi, 92-3, vii, 12), the *ruk͟hk͟h* became known and was discussed in Western sources.

According to the fabulous accounts of various Arabic authors, the *ruk͟hk͟h* is capable of carrying an elephant while airbound; each of its wings has 10,000 feathers of an enormous size, and it lays eggs as big as a mountain (cf. G. Thompson, *Motif-index*, B 31.1). These accounts obscured the opportunity to perceive the *ruk͟hk͟h* as a real creature and succeeded in relegating it to the realm of fantasy, similar to the Anḳāʾ [*q.v.*], and closely assimilated with the Sīmurg͟h [*q.v.*], with both of which the *ruk͟hk͟h* is in fact sometimes confused. On the other hand, already authors such as al-Ābī (d. 421/1030) in his *Nat͟hr al-durr*, vi, 532, qualify the alleged rejuvenating properties of his feathers (or beak) as a tall tale (*kad͟hib*).

Bibliography: J. Vernet, *Rujj = Aepyornis maximus*, in *Tamuda*, i (1953) 102-5; H. Eisenstein, *Einführung in die arabische Zoographie*, Berlin 1990, index s.v. *Vogel (ruḫḫ)*. (U. Marzolph)

al-**RUK͟HK͟HAD͟J** (in *Ḥudūd al-ʿālam*, tr. Minorsky, 111, 121, Ruk͟hud͟h; in al-Muḳaddasī, 50, 297, Ruk͟hūd, perhaps to be read as Ruk͟hwad͟h), the name given in early Islamic times to the region of south-eastern Afghanistan around the later city of Ḳandahār [*q.v.*] and occupying the lower basin of the Arg͟handāb river (see D. Balland, *EIr* art. *Arḡandāb*). The Islamic name preserves that of the classical Arachosia, through which Alexander the Great passed on his Indian expedition in 330 B.C. (see *PW*, ii/1, cols. 367-8 (W. Tomaschek)), which is itself a hellenisation of Old Pers. Harak͟huvatis͟h, Avestan Harak͟hvaiti. In Syriac it was rendered as Rok͟hwad, a region with a Nestorian Christian community, in the Acts of the Synod held at Ctesiphon in 544 A.D. (see Markwart-Messina, *A catalogue of the provincial capitals of Ērānshahr*, Rome 1931, 17, 84; C.E. Bosworth, *Sīstān under the Arabs, from the Islamic conquest to the rise of the Ṣaffārids (30-250/651-864)*, Rome 1968, 9).

The region was first raided by the Arab commander ʿAbd al-Raḥmān b. Samura in the caliphate of ʿU͟thmān, when Sīstān and Bust [*q.vv.*] were first attacked, but the Muslims were for long blocked in securing any permanent foothold beyond Bust by the implacable hostility of the local rulers of southeastern Afg͟hānistān, the Zunbīls, whose winter residence was in the *garmsīr* or hot region of al-Ruk͟hk͟had͟j and their summer one in the cooler *sardsīr* of the region of Zamīndāwar [*q.v.*] or Bilād al-Dāwar immediately to the north. These Zunbīls remained a hostile force till the second half of the 3rd/9th century, when the Ṣaffārid Yaʿḳūb b. al-Lay͟th engaged in warfare with them [see ṣaffārids], and it is only after this that the native dynasty disappears from historical mention and that the Islamic geographers were able to treat al-Ruk͟hk͟had͟j as part of the *Dār al-Islām*. Thus the *Ḥudūd al-ʿālam*, 111, describes it as a prosperous and pleasant district. These authors mention as two of its main towns Pand͟jwāy and Tigīnābād; for a discussion of the location of these, see ḳandahār at IV, 536b. Administratively, al-Ruk͟hk͟had͟j seems often to have been linked with Sīstān; Ibn Ḥawḳal², 425, tr. 412, gives a global figure for the revenues of these two provinces as 100,000 dīnārs plus 300,000 dirhams. After this time, the name al-Ruk͟hk͟had͟j falls out of use; the G͟haznawid historian Gardīzī (wrote in the mid-5th/11th century [*q.v.*]) seems to be the last author regularly to refer to Ruk͟hūd. Only the site of an Islamic settlement now called Tepe Aruk͟h preserves its name.

Since Arab raiders captured many slaves from the pagan region of al-Ruk͟hk͟had͟j, one occasionally meets the *nisba* al-Ruk͟hk͟had͟jī, e.g. for Hārūn al-Ras͟hīd's *mawlā* Abu 'l-Farad͟j, who became a very influential secretary and governor for the caliphs of the early 3rd/9th century; see Bosworth, *op. cit.*, 82-3; Patricia Crone, *Slaves on horses, the evolution of the Islamic polity*, Cambridge 1980, 190. Whether the vizier of the Būyid *amīr* in Bag͟hdād Mus͟harrif al-Dawla, Muʾayyid al-Mulk Abū ʿAlī al-Ḥusayn al-Ruk͟hk͟had͟jī (see H. Busse, *Chalif und Grosskönig, die Buyiden im Iraq (945-1055)*, Wiesbaden-Beirut 1969, 244), derived his *nisba* from Afg͟hānistān or from the village near Bag͟hdād of al-Ruk͟hk͟had͟jiyya (cf. Yāḳūt, *Buldān*, ed. Beirut, iii, 38—a settlement of persons transported from al-Ruk͟hk͟had͟j in Afg͟hānistān?), is unclear.

Bibliography (in addition to references given in the article): Marquart, *Ērānšahr*, 272 and index; Le Strange, *The Eastern lands of the Caliphate*, 345; Bosworth, *Sīstān under the Arabs*, 28-9, 35, 120-1 and index; idem, *The history of the Saffarids of Sistan and the Maliks of Nīmrūz (247/861 to 949/1542-3)*, Costa Mesa, Calif. 1994, index; see also ḳandahār.

(C.E. Bosworth)

RUKHṢA (a.), literally "permission", dispensation".

1. In law.

Here, *rukhṣa* is a legal ruling relaxing or suspending by way of exception under certain circumstances an injunction of a primary and general nature (*ʿazīma* [*q.v.*]).

The general obligation to fast during Ramaḍān is, by way of *rukhṣa*, suspended during the days of an illness or a journey, under condition that these days are made up after Ramaḍān. Similarly, the general prohibition to eat meat that has not been ritually slaughtered is suspended if a Muslim could only survive by violating it. As a rule, one has the choice whether or not to make use of the *rukhṣa*. However, if one fears that one may die if one does not avail oneself of the *rukhṣa*, following it is obligatory, except in the case that one is threatened to be killed if one does not renounce Islam, for then martyrdom is to be preferred. The circumstances permitting a dispensation of the strict rule are either the necessity to preserve one's life or the removal of hardship, such as in the permission for a physician to look at a woman's pudenda or the relaxation of the obligation to perform *ṣalāt* during a journey. The distinction between *rukhṣa* and *ʿazīma* does not have legal consequences, except that, according to the Ḥanafīs, tacit consensus (*idjmāʿ sukūtī*) can establish a *rukhṣa* but not a *ʿazīma*.

Bibliography: Mohammad Hashim Kamali, *Principles of Islamic jurisprudence*, rev. ed. Cambridge 1991, 339-40, 186; Muḥammad Abū Zahra, *Uṣūl al-fiḳh*, Cairo n.d., 49-52; Izmīrī, *Ḥāshiyat ʿalā Mirʾāt al-uṣūl sharḥ Mirḳāt al-wuṣūl li-Mollā Khosrew*, Istanbul 1309/1891-2, ii, 394-8; M.J. Kister, *On 'concessions' and conduct. A study in early Ḥadīth*, in G.H.A. Juynboll (ed.), *Studies in the first century of Islamic society*, Carbondale, Ill. 1982, 89-107.

(R. Peters)

2. In Ṣūfism.

The way in which the concepts of *rukhṣa* and its counterpart *ʿazīma* are used in Ṣūfism involves an extrapolation from a juridical to a much more ethical domain. Here they refer to two opposite and differently-valued patterns of behaviour. *ʿAzīma* denotes a way of life characterised by determination and firmness of purpose, and is consequently of a higher level than *rukhṣa*, which lacks these characteristics. These two words refer also, particularly in their plural form, to concrete deeds in which the two behavioural patterns manifest themselves. E.g. celibacy and *tawakkul* (trust in God to such an extent that one does not support oneself) are considered to be *ʿazāʾim*, whereas marriage and supporting oneself are seen as *rukhaṣ*. The depreciatory valuation of the latter is to be witnessed in the idea expressed e.g. by al-Makkī in his *Ḳūt al-ḳulūb* that *rukhaṣ* are (meant) for the weak, whereas the *ʿazāʾim* are characteristic of the strong. Also, al-Ḳushayrī makes it clear in his *Risāla* that, with these strong persons, the Ṣūfis are meant. On the other hand, in *Ḳūt al-ḳulūb* and also in the *Kitāb al-Lumaʿ* by Abū Naṣr al-Sarrādj, the tradition is quoted according to which God loves the use of both *rukhaṣ* and *ʿazāʾim* equally well, albeit that in the latter source this tradition is quoted primarily as a warning against denouncing people who avail themselves of *rukhaṣ*. Thus the overall picture painted by these sources is that in Ṣūfī circles a surplus value is attached to the *ʿazāʾim* (B. Reinert, *Die Lehre vom tawakkul in der klassischen Sufik*, Berlin 1968, 135-7; R. Gramlich, *Schlaglichter über das Sufitum. Abū Naṣr as-Sarrāǧs Kitāb al-lumaʿ eingeleitet, übersetzt und kommentiert*, Stuttgart 1990, 240; idem, *Das Sendschreiben al-Qušayris über das Sufitum*. Eingeleitet, übersetzt und kommentiert, Wiesbaden 1989, 538).

Naḳshbandī Ṣūfis even claim that their attitude of strictly confining themselves to *ʿazāʾim* and avoidin the use of *rukhaṣ* is one of the most distinctive charac teristics of their order. Yet even Naḳshbandīs hav had to take the above-mentioned tradition in con sideration, and therefore, according to a saying b Bahāʾ al-Dīn Naḳshband, this brotherhood, althoug abstaining from these practices, yet does not de nounce others who observe them (J. ter Haar, *Followe and heir of the Prophet. Shaykh Aḥmad Sirhindī (1564-1624 as mystic*, Leiden 1992, 80-1, 107). This strong em phasis on *ʿazīma* is partly a reaction to other Ṣūfis wh used the idea of *rukhṣa* in order to justify certain con troversial practices like *samāʿ* and *raḳṣ* [*q.vv.*] (L Massignon, *La passion d'al-Hallaj*, Paris 1922, ii, 779 81). A different and much more positive valuation c *rukhaṣ* is to be found in the *Kitāb Ādāb al-murīdīn* b Abu 'l-Nadjīb al-Suhrawardī, where they are con sidered to be an integral part of a special type of af filiation, viz. the affiliation of the *mutashabbihūn*, i.e the lay members affiliated to an order, a designatio which in this source at least has no pejorative connota tion. Their affiliation is admittedly of a lower leve compared to that of the Ṣūfis proper; nevertheless, i is a valuable one, since, according to a saying of th Prophet, "Whoever makes the effort to ressemble group of people is one of them" (M. Milson, *A Su rule for novices. Kitāb Ādāb al-Murīdīn of Abū al-Najīb al Suhrawardī*, Cambridge and London 1975, 17-21 72-81).

Bibliography: Given in the article.

(J.G.J. ter Haar)

RUKN (A.), pl. *arkān*, literally "corner (as in *a rukn al-yamānī* = the southeastern corner of the Kaʿba support, pillar". The singular *rukn* occurs twice in th Ḳurʾān, in XI, 82/80, when Lot seeks for support i a strong *rukn*, pillar, or, figuratively, a leader or chie and in LI, 39, where Pharaoh and his support, *rukn* i.e. retinue, reject Moses.

1. In religious and legal usage.

Here, it is commonly found in the expression *arkā al-dīn* or *arkān al-ʿibāda*, denoting the basic "pillars" c religion and religious observance. These so-calle "pillars of Islam" are usually enumerated as (1) th profession of faith, *shahāda*; (2) the pilgrimage, *ḥadjd* (3) the worship, *ṣalāt*; (4) fasting, *ṣawm*; and (5) alms giving, *zakāt*, *ṣadaḳa*. To these some authorities add sixth, perpetual warfare against infidels, *djihād*.

Bibliography: See almost all the general work on the Islamic faith, e.g. H.U.W. Stanton, *Th teaching of the Qur'an*, London 1919, 58 ff.; H.A.R Gibb, *Islam*, ch. 4; Gaudefroy-Demombyne: *Muslim institutions*, London 1954, ch. 6; A. Rippin *Muslims, their religious beliefs and practices. i. The fo mative period*, London and New York 1990, ch. 7 The teachings of ʿAbd al-Ḳāhir al-Baghdādī [*q.v* are translated in Rippin and J. Knappert (eds. *Textual sources for the study of Islam*, Manchester 1986 10-11, 89 ff. See also W.C. Smith, *Arkān*, in *Essay on Islamic civilization presented to Niyazi Berkes*, Leide 1976, 303-16, repr. in idem, *On understanding Islam* The Hague, etc. 1981, 162-73 (contends that *arkā* originally meant "parts of the body"). For greate detail, see the individual *EI* articles on thes "pillars" and also SHARĪʿA.

(Ed.)

2. In natural science and alchemy.

Here, it denotes "cardinal point", "part", "direc tion" and, in particular, "element".

In the *Sirr al-khalīḳa* attributed to Balīnās [se BALĪNŪS], a source that has played a fundamental rol in much of Islam's alchemical tradition, the word *ruk* appears in its literal sense of a corner, side or an ex tremity (see Lane, i/3, 1148-9). Yet it functions as

:chnical term in this text, since it is employed con-
sistently and exclusively in a cosmological context. 'hus in a discourse on winds (*riyāḥ* [see RĪḤ]), the author tells us that the *rukn* which faces the east *nuḳābil al-mas͟hriḳ*) is cold-moist, since it is here that ie cold-moist wind blows, stabilising and strengthening the *rukn* (*K. Sirr al-k͟halīḳa wa-ṣanʿat al-ṭabīʿa*, ed. U. Veisser, Aleppo 1979, 135). This cosmological idea of :rength appears to have subsequently been integrated ito the ordinary meaning of the word, for one of the ieanings of *rukn* found in the standard Arabic lex-.ons (e.g. *TʿA*) is the strongest side (*d̲j̲ānib*) of a thing see Lane, *loc. cit.*).

Again, in a discourse on the motion of celestial odies, the *Sirr*, 140, uses the term to designate each f the four geographical regions or sides of the hysical world—*rukn al-mas͟hriḳ, rukn al-g͟harbī*, etc. inally, in the course of an explication of the *ṭabāʾiʿ* natures) [see ṬABĪʿA], the term is employed strictly in conceptual sense, that of the four directions—*al-rukn l-s͟harḳī, al-rukn al-g͟harbī*, etc. (188). Here *rukn* is practically equivalent to *d̲j̲iha*.

But it is in the grand alchemical corpus attributed › D̲j̲ābir b. Ḥayyān [*q.v.*] that the term reaches its ıll technical maturity and sophistication. As in the *irr*, here too *rukn* appears in a cosmological context. 'hus, explicating variously his doctrine of the formaon and elemental structure of the physical world, the lchemist distinguishes between natural elements 'hich constitute gross physical bodies and artificial lements which are extracted out of these bodies ırough alchemical procedures; the former are esignated by the term *uṣṭuḳussāt* (sing. *uṣṭuḳuss*) or *ınāṣir* (sing. *ʿunṣur*), etc., and the latter by the term *rkān* (see e.g. *K. al-Lāhūt* and *K. al-Bāb*, ed. P. Lory,)amascus 1988, 12, 31; cf. P. Kraus, *Jābir ibn Ḥayyān*, ii, Cairo 1942, 6). In the *K. al-Ḥudūd, rukn* is nambiguously defined: it is that "compound" (see elow) which is produced by alchemical operations *ıl-mudabbara*) (ed. P. Kraus, Paris 1935, 481). This :ands in sharp contrast to the definition of Ibn Sīnā *ı.v.*], who explains *rukn* as a relative concept: it is any mple body (*d̲j̲ism basīṭ*), he tells us, that constitutes n essential part (*d̲j̲uzʾ d̲h̲ātī*) of the physical world. 'hus, according to Ibn Sīnā, an individual thing (*al-ayʾ*) is a *rukn* in relation to the world; in relation to hat is composed from it, it is an *uṣṭuḳuss*; and in relaon to what is generated from it, it is an *ʿunṣur* (Arabic :xt in A.M. Goichon, *Lexique de la langue philosophique 'Ibn Sīnā*, Paris 1938, 144).

There is in the *corpus D̲j̲ābirianum*, however, another istinct use of the term, something that manifests a rofoundly distinguishing philosophical feature of the osmological tradition which its author represents. 'hus *arkān* designates the four *ṭabāʾiʿ*, hot, cold, moist nd dry. Here, unlike the case practically with all ther philosophical traditions in Islam, the term *uwwa* (δύναμις) is never applied to the *ṭabāʾiʿ*; and *ayfiyya* (ποίοτης) extremely rarely (cf. P. Kraus, *Jābir n Ḥayyān*, ii, 147, 165; S.N. Haq, *Names, natures and ings*, Dordrecht and London 1993, 57-62). These j̲ābirian *arkān* were the primary material elements of ll things; they were the "first simple elements", as pposed to earth, water, air and fire which latter were e "second compound elements" (see e.g. *K. al-'aṣrīf* and *K. al-Mīzān al-ṣag͟hīr*, ed. Kraus, 412, 482).

In Abū Bakr al-Rāzī [*q.v.*], as much as we know of is writings, the term is used but rarely. In his *Sirr al-rār*, where *rukn* does make an appearance, it conveys e broad sense of an element, equivalent to the ristotelian στοιχεῖον (see tr. J. Ruska, Berlin 1937, 21). But, like D̲j̲ābir (Kraus, *Jābir ibn Ḥayyān*, i, Cairo 1943, no. 500), al-Rāzī too wrote a whole book on this subject, the lost *K. al-Arkān* (H.E. Stapleton, R.F. Azo and M.H. Ḥusain, *Chemistry in Iraq and Persia in the tenth century A.D.*, in *Memoirs of the Asiatic Society of Bengal*, viii [1927], 337). In general, it is in the specified Aristotelian sense that *rukn* is most frequently employed in the alchemical and cosmological writings of mediaeval Islam.

Bibliography: In addition to works cited in the text, see M. Berthelot and O. Houdas, *La chimie au Moyen Age*, iii, Paris 1893; E.J. Holmyard, *The Arabic works of Jābir ibn Ḥayyān*, Paris 1928; U. Weisser, *Das ,,Buch über das Geheimnis der Schöpfung" von Pseudo-Apollonius von Tyana*, Berlin and New York 1980. (S. NOMANUL HAQ)

RUKN AL-DAWLA, ABŪ ʿALĪ AL-ḤASAN B. BŪYA, second in age of the three brothers that founded the Būyid dynasty [see BUWAYHIDS]. His fortunes followed those of the elder brother ʿAlī (later ʿImād al-Dawla [*q.v.*]) up to the latter's occupation of Fārs in 322/934; Rukn al-Dawla was then given the governorship of Kāzarūn and other districts. But shortly afterwards he was forced by the ʿAbbāsid general Yāḳūt, at whose expense the Būyid conquest of Fārs had been made, to seek refuge with his brother; and when Yāḳūt was in turn defeated by the Ziyārid Mardāwīd̲j̲ [*q.v.*], the Būyids' former overlord, against whom they had revolted, ʿImād al-Dawla, who then found it advisable to conciliate Mardāwīd̲j̲, sent Rukn al-Dawla to him as a hostage. On Mardāwīd̲j̲'s assassination in the following year (323/935), Rukn al-Dawla escaped and rejoined ʿImād al-Dawla, by whom he was supplied with troops to dispute the possession of D̲j̲ibāl with Mardāwīd̲j̲'s brother and successor, Wus͟hmgīr. Rukn al-Dawla succeeded at the outset in taking Iṣfahān; but the first round of his contest with Wus͟hmgīr ended in Rukn al-Dawla's ejection from that city in 327/939, when he again fled to Fārs.

In the next year Rukn al-Dawla's help was sought by his younger brother al-Ḥusayn (later Muʿizz al-Dawla [*q.v.*]), who had meanwhile set himself up in K͟hūzistān, against the Barīdīs [*q.v.*]; whereupon Rukn al-Dawla, being now possessed of no territory, attempted to take Wāsiṭ but was obliged to retire when the caliph al-Rāḍī [*q.v.*] and the *amīr* Bad̲j̲kam [*q.v.*] opposed him. Almost immediately afterwards, however, he succeeded in recovering Iṣfahān, owing to Wus͟hmgīr's championship of Mākān b. Kākūya in a quarrel with the Sāmānid Naṣr b. Aḥmad [*q.v.*]; and when the latter ruler died in 331/943, Rukn al-Dawla, who had meanwhile supported the Sāmānid cause, was able to drive Wus͟hmgīr as well from al-Rayy, of which he had momentarily regained possession on the retirement of the Sāmānid general Abū ʿAlī Čag͟hānī.

With al-Rayy, Rukn al-Dawla gained control of the whole D̲j̲ibāl; and but for two short intervals (of about a year in each case) retained it for the rest of his days. Up to 344/955-6, however, his position was highly precarious. For not only Wus͟hmgīr but also the Sāmānids continued to challenge it. It was only by playing them off against each other and sowing dissensions between the Sāmānid princes and the commanders whom they sent against him that Rukn al-Dawla was able to maintain it. Even so (as indicated above) he was driven from al-Rayy, and his representatives were expelled from most parts of the province, once in 333/944-5 and again in 339/950-1, in each case by Sāmānid forces. Indeed, he was obliged in the end to become the Sāmānids' tributary (at least two agreements for the payment of tribute being recorded); it was on this basis that he first made peace with them in 344/955-6, as again in 361/971-2. In the course of his long contest with Wushmgīr, who, until he was killed in an accident in 357/968 never ceased to intrigue with the Sāmānids against him, Rukn al-Dawla on several occasions invaded Ṭabaristān and Gurgān, but was unable to incorporate these provinces permanently in his dominions. And though in 337/948-9, after he had defeated an attempt on al-Rayy made by the Musāfirid or Sallārid Marzubān b. Muḥammad, whom he took prisoner, he gained control of southern Ādharbāydjān, his ejection two years later from al-Rayy itself (see above) naturally cost him this as well.

Rukn al-Dawla received his *laḳab* simultaneously with his brothers in 334/945-6, on Muʿizz al-Dawla's entry into Baghdād; and on ʿImād al-Dawla's death in 338/949 succeeded him as head of the family and *amīr al-umarā*ʾ (though this title was also held by Muʿizz al-Dawla). The last two years of his life were rendered unhappy—so much so that he never recovered from the shock induced by the news—owing to the conduct of his son, ʿAḍud al-Dawla [*q.v.*], in taking advantage of an appeal for help sent by ʿIzz al-Dawla Bakhtiyār [*q.v.*] (son of Muʿizz al-Dawla and his successor in the rule of ʿIrāḳ), to imprison the latter, and, in conjunction with Rukn al-Dawla's own *wazīr* Abu 'l-Fatḥ Ibn al-ʿAmid [*q.v.*], who had been sent likewise with a force to Bakhtiyār's aid, to seize that province for himself. And though ʿAḍud al-Dawla obeyed his command to release Bakhtiyār and return to his government in Fārs, Rukn al-Dawla was only with difficulty persuaded to visit ʿAḍud al-Dawla in 365/975-6 at Iṣfahān, in order to ensure that by receiving a confirmation of his appointment as heir, he should succeed without dispute. Rukn al-Dawla died at al-Rayy in Muḥarram of the next year/September 976.

In the settlement arrangements made at Iṣfahān just before his death (see above), Rukn al-Dawla nominated his eldest son ʿAḍud al-Dawla, at this moment ruler in Fārs and subsequently in ʿIrāḳ also, as his successor, but provided that Rayy should go to his second son Fakhr al-Dawla [*q.v.*], and Hamadhān to the third son Muʾayyid al-Dawla [*q.v.*] as subordinate to ʿAḍud al-Dawla; in the event, Rayy passed under Muʾayyid al-Dawla's control, and Fakhr al-Dawla, who fled to the Ziyārids and Sāmānids, was only able to establish his claims there after Muʾayyid al-Dawla's death.

As shown above, Rukn al-Dawla faced considerable difficulties in setting the northern amirate of the Būyids on a firm basis, but what success he achieved was largely attributable to the firm backing and wise advice of his vizier, the famous Abu 'l-Faḍl Ibn al-ʿAmīd [*q.v.*], who served the Būyid for 32 lunar years (328-60/940-70) and was able to contain the violence and rapacity which were the normal attributes of a ruler like Rukn al-Dawla who had begun as a Daylamī robber chief. Nevertheless, Miskawayh, in *Eclipse of the ʿAbbasid caliphate*, ii, 279, tr. v, 298-9, lamented that Ibn al-ʿAmīd was prevented from establishing the rule of justice by his master's impetuosity and lack of inherited kingly authority. The circle of scholars and literary men which grew up around the vizier, one which at various times included such luminaries as Abū Ḥayyān al-Tawḥīdī [*q.v.*], the philosopher Abu 'l-Ḥasan al-ʿĀmirī [*q.v.* in Suppl.] and Miskawayh himself, as Ibn al-ʿAmīd's coadjutor, made Rayy at this time a dazzling centre of Arabic culture (see J.L. Kraemer, *Humanism in the renaissance of Islam. The cultural revival during the Buyid age*, Leiden 1986, 210-11, 223, 230, 241-6). It is less easy to estimate whether there was a specifically Persian element within Rukn al-Dawla's ethos of rulership, but he does seem to have conceived of himself as a monarch in the line of ancient Persia, possibly as an inheritance from his early life in the entourage of Mardāwīdj; a silver medal struck at Rayy in 351/962 depicts the *amīr* as a Persian emperor and has a legend in Pahlavi "May the glory of the king of kings increase!" (see G.C. Miles, *A portrait of the Buyid prince Rukn al-Dawlah*, ANS Museum Notes no. 11, New York 1964; Kraemer, *op. cit.*, 44).

Bibliography (in addition to references given in the article): 1. Sources. Miskawayh, in *Eclipse*, i-ii, tr. iv-v; Gardīzī, *Zayn al-akhbār*; Ibn al-Athīr, viii; Ibn Khallikān, ed. ʿAbbās, ii, 118-19 no. 176, tr. de Slane, i, 407-8; Mīrkhwānd, ed. and Ger. tr. F. Wilken, *Mirchonds Geschichte der Sultane aus dem Geschlechte Bujeh*, Berlin 1835. 2. Studies. Spuler, *Iran*, 94 ff.; H. Busse, *Chalif und Grosskönig, die Buyiden im Iraq (945-1055)*, Beirut-Wiesbaden 1969, index; idem, in *Camb. hist. Iran*, iv, 254, 262-9.

(H. Bowen-[C.E. Bosworth])

RUKN AL-DĪN [see ḲILĪDJ ARSLAN II and III].

RUKN AL-DĪN BĀRBAK SHĀH b. Nāṣir al-Dīn Maḥmūd Shāh, Bengal Sultan of the restored Ilyās Shāhī line, *r.* 864-79/1460-74.

Bārbak was one of the most powerful of the medieval rulers of Bengal, achieving a great reputation from his warfare against the Hindu rulers of Orissa and northern and eastern Bengal, regaining Silhet [*q.v.*] (Sylhet) and also Chittagong [*q.v.*] from the Arakanese. He recruited for his armies Ḥabashī military slaves and Arab mercenaries, and popular hagiographical tradition attributed many of Bārbak's conquest to one of this latter group, the warrior-saint Shāh Ismāʿīl Ghāzī ʿArabī, concerning whom a *Risālat al-Shuhadā*ʾ was composed in 1042/1633 by Pīr Muḥammad Shaṭṭārī, see Storey, i, 990. Bengal prospered under Bārbak; he undertook extensive building work on his palace at Gawr or Lakhnawtī [*q.v.*] and was a great patron of Bengali literature.

Bibliography: R.C. Majumdar (ed.), *The history and culture of the Indian people. VI. The Delhi Sultanate*, Bombay 1960, 212-13; K.A. Nizami and M. Habib (eds.), *A comprehensive history of India. V. The Delhi Sultanate (A.D. 1206-1526)*, Delhi etc. 1970, 1153-4.

(C.E. Bosworth)

RUKN AL-DĪN KHURSHĀH, Nizārī Ismāʿīlī *imām* and the last lord of Alamūt. The eldest son of ʿAlāʾ al-Dīn Muḥammad III (r. 618-53/1221-55), Rukn al-Dīn (al-Ḥasan), also known as Khurshāh was born in Rūdbār around the year 627/1230; and it was in his childhood that he was designated to succeed to the Nizārī imāmate. Rukn al-Dīn succeeded, as an *imām*, to the leadership of the Nizārī Ismāʿīlī community and state upon the assassination of his father on the last day of Shawwāl 653/1 December 1255. His very brief but eventful reign as the eighth and last lord of Alamūt coincided with the completion of the Mongol conquests in Persia and the final year in the history of the Persian Nizārī state of the Alamūt period.

By the time of Rukn al-Dīn's accession, the Persian Nizārīs of Ḳuhistān and Ḳūmis had already experienced a foretaste of the destructive powers of the Mongol hordes. But it remained for Hülegü or Hūlāgū [*q.v.*] or Hülegü himself, leading a major Mongol expedition to Persia, to uproot the Nizārī state centred in Rūdbār [see RŪDHBĀR] in the central Alburz mountains of northern Persia. The sources are generally ambiguous on Rukn al-Dīn's policy vis-à-vis the Mongol invaders. Vacillating between submis on and resistance, he eventually seems to have aim-d towards a compromise solution, perhaps hoping to vert at least the Mongol capture of the chief Nizārī rongholds in Rūdbār. But he did adopt a con-liatory policy towards the Sunnīs who had played a art in spurring the Mongols against the Nizārī smāʿīlīs. Be it as it may, Rukn al-Dīn was drawn into n intricate and ultimately futile web of negotiations ith the Mongols, from the time of Hūlāgū's arrival a Persia in Rabīʿ I 654/April 1256. The Nizārī ruler lso dispatched several embassies, headed variously y his vizier Shams al-Dīn Gīlakī and a number of his wn brothers, to Hūlāgū, who persistently demanded othing less than Rukn al-Dīn's total submission and is orders for the demolition of the Nizārī fortresses, ncluding Alamūt, the traditional seat of the Nizārī tate.

Having grown weary of Rukn al-Dīn's delaying actics, Hūlāgū soon decided to launch his assault on Nizārī Rūdbār, ordering the main Mongol armies to onverge on Maymūn-Diz [*q.v.*], where the Nizārī uler was then staying. On 18 Shawwāl 654/8 No-ember 1256, Hūlāgū himself encamped on a hilltop acing Maymūn-Diz. After the failure of a last round f Nizārī-Mongol negotiations followed by a few days f intense fighting, the Nizārī ruler was finally obliged o surrender. On 29 Shawwāl 654/19 November 256, Rukn al-Dīn Khurshāh, accompanied by a roup of Nizārī dignitaries and Naṣīr al-Dīn al-Ṭūsī, escended from Maymūn-Diz and presented himself efore the Mongol conqueror, marking the close of he Nizārī state of Persia; he had ruled for exactly one ear.

Subsequently, Rukn al-Dīn was treated hospitably y the Mongols whilst they still needed his coopera-on to persuade the remaining Nizārī strongholds to urrender. Rukn al-Dīn now issued a general order of urrender to the commandants of the Nizārī for-resses; about forty such fortresses in Rūdbār fell eadily into Mongol hands, and they were duly ismantled after their garrisons were taken into ustody. Alamūt did not surrender until the end of Dhu 'l-Ḳaʿda 654/December 1256, and Lanbasar *q.v.*] held out for another year while Girdkūh resisted s Mongol besiegers until 669/1270. The Persian istorian Djuwaynī, who took part in the truce egotiations between his master Hūlāgū and the Nizārīs and drew up Rukn al-Dīn's actual terms of urrender, has left a vivid description of Alamūt, efore the Mongols destroyed that impregnable for-ress and its famous library.

As the Nizārī *imām*'s usefulness to the Mongols ap-roached its end, Hūlāgū approved of Rukn al-Dīn's urious request to visit the Great Khān Möngke [*q.v.*] n Mongolia. On 1 Rabīʿ I 655/9 March 1257, Rukn l-Dīn set out on his fateful journey to Ḳaraḳorum, ccompanied by a group of companions and some Mongol escorts. Once in Ḳaraḳorum, or its vicinity, owever, Möngke refused to meet with the captive Nizārī *imām*, on the apparent pretext that he still had ot delivered Lanbasar and Girdkūh to the Mongols. By that time, Möngke had already sanctioned a eneral massacre of the Persian Nizārīs who were in Mongol custody. Rukn al-Dīn Khurshāh's own tragic nd occurred sometime in the late spring of 655/1257, hen he and his companions, then supposedly on the eturn journey to Persia, were put to the sword by heir Mongol guards somewhere along the edge of the Khangai mountains in central Mongolia.

Bibliography: Djuwaynī, iii, 106-42, 253-78; Djuwaynī-Boyle, ii, 618-40, 707-25; Rashīd al-Dīn Faḍl Allāh, *Djāmiʿ al-tawārīkh*, *ḳismat-i Ismāʿīliyān*, ed. M.T. Dānishpazhūh and M. Mudarrisī Zandjānī, Tehran 1338 *Sh*./1959, 182-95; idem, *Histoire des Mongols de la Perse*, ed. and tr. E. Quatremère, Paris 1836, 180-220; idem, *Djāmiʿ al-tawārīkh*, iii, ed. A.A. Alizade, Baku, 1957, 24 ff., 29-38; Abu 'l-Ḳāsim ʿAbd Allāh b. ʿAlī Kāshānī, *Zubdat al-tawārīkh, bakhsh-i Fāṭimiyān wa Nizāriyān*, ed. M.T. Dānishpazhūh, 2nd ed., Tehran 1366 *Sh*./1987, 219-20, 224-33; M.G.S. Hodgson, *The Order of Assassins*, The Hague 1955, 261-71; B. Lewis, *The Assassins*, London 1967, 91-6, French tr., *Les Assassins*, tr. A. Pélissier, Paris 1982, 132-7; J.A. Boyle, *The Ismāʿīlīs and the Mongol invasion*, in *Ismāʿīlī contributions to Islamic culture*, ed. S.H. Nasr, Tehran 1977, 7-22; F. Daftary, *The Ismāʿīlīs: Their history and doctrines*, Cambridge 1990, 421-9, 435, 444, 697-8 (containing further bibliographical references). (F. DAFTARY)

RUKNĀBĀD (or ĀB-I RUKNĪ, the water of Rukn al-Dawla), a subterranean canal (*ḳanāt*) which runs from a mountain (called Ḳulayʿa: P. Schwarz, *Iran im Mittelalter*, ii, 48, no. 7) about six miles from Shīrāz. Enlarged by a secondary canal, it follows for a part of the way the road from Iṣfahān to Shīrāz. Its waters reach as far as the vicinity of the town towards the cemetery in which the poet Ḥāfiẓ [*q.v.*] is buried, when they are not entirely absorbed for irrigation purposes. According to Ḥasan Fasāʾī (*Fārs-nāma-yi Nāṣirī*, part ii, 20), "all the waters of the plain of Shīrāz come by subterranean channels except the water from the spring of Djushk... The best waters are those of the Zangī and Ruknī canals.... The Ḳanāt-i Rukni (i.e. Ruknābād) was made in 338/949-50, one-and-a-half *farsakh*s to the northeast of Shīrāz by Rukn al-Dawla Ḥasan b. Būya [see BUWAYHIDS]; its waters rise in the ravine of Tang-i Allāh Akbar a mile north of Shīrāz; it waters the plain of al-Muṣallā". In the 8th/14th century, Ruknābād is mentioned by Ibn Baṭṭūṭa and by Ḥamd Allāh Mustawfī Ḳazwīnī (*Nuzhat al-ḳulūb*, tr. Le Strange, 113: "The water comes from subterranean canals and the best is that of Ruknābād"). But it is to the poets that this canal really owes its fame. In the 6th/12th century Saʿdī declares himself charmed by the land of Shīrāz and the waters of Ruknābād (*Kulliyyāt*, Calcutta 1791, fol. 299b, 1. 4). In the following century, ʿUbayd-i Zākānī sings: "The zephyr which blows from al-Muṣallā and the wave of Ruknābād remove from the stranger the memory of his native land" (text quoted by E.G. Browne, who finds in it an echo of Saʿdī, *LHP*, iii, 238). Ḥāfiẓ in particular immortalised Ruknābād in his verses: "Pour out, cup-bearer, the wine that is left, for in Paradise thou shalt find neither the stream of Ruknābād nor the promenade of al-Muṣallā" (ed. Khalkhālī, Tehran 1306/1927, no. 3, v. 2); "Shīrāz and the wave of Ruknī and the sweet breeze of the zephyr, blame them not, for they are the pride of the universe" (*ibid.*, no. 35, v. 7); "The zephyr which blows from al-Muṣallā and the wave of Ruknābād will never allow me to depart" (*ibid.*, no. 168, v. 9); "May God a hundred times preserve our Ruknābād, for its limpid waters give a life as long as that of Khiḍr" [*q.v.*] (*ibid.*, no. 277, v. 2), and in a piece which may be apocryphal (*ibid.*, part 2, no. 71): "The water of Ruknī, like sugar, rises in al-Tang (-i Allāh Akbar)". According to later writers, Ruknābād, which Ibn Baṭṭūṭa called a great water-course (*al-nahr al-kabīr*), gradually dried up. Among the notable travellers of the 17th century, Chardin, almost alone in mentioning it, saw only a large stream and gives Ruknābād the fanciful meaning "Ruknenabat, veine ou filet de sucre" (*Voyages*, ed. Langlès, viii, 241). At the end of the 18th century, W. Franklin praises the sweetness and clearness of the waters of this little stream to which the natives attribute medicinal qualities. At the beginning of the 19th century, Scott Waring notes that its breadth was nowhere more than six feet. Ker Porter observes that the canal has become choked up through neglect. The *Kulthūm-nāma* deplores the disappearance of the groves that surrounded it. At a later date we have the same observation by Gobineau ("Cette onde poétique ne m'apparut que sous l'aspect d'un trou bourbeux"), Curzon ("a tiny channel filled with running water") and Sykes ("a diminutive stream").

The *Fārs-nāma-yi Nāṣirī* mentions a second Ruknābād in Fārs: "The source of the warm stream of Ruknābād is part of the district of Bikha-yi Fāl (Lāristān); it is over a *farsakh* north of the village of Ruknābād; having a bad flavour and an unpleasant smell, it is of no use for agriculture; it cooks in a few minutes eggs put into it; one can only bathe in it at some distance from the spring" (ii, 318 middle, 288).

Bibliography: In addition to the references in the text, see Ibn Baṭṭūṭa, ii, 53, 87, tr. Gibb, ii, 299, 318; Abu 'l-ʿAbbās Aḥmad b. Abi 'l-Khayr Zarkūb Shīrāzī (8th/14th century), *Shīrāz-nāma*, Tehran 1305-10/1926-31, 23-4 (panegyric in a precious style); Zayn al-ʿĀbidīn Shirwānī (19th century), *Riyāḍ al-siyāḥa*, 336, ult. and *Būstān al-siyāḥa*, 326 middle (short notices); *Kitāb-i Kulthūm-nāma*, tr. Thonnelier, *Le livre des dames de la Perse*, Paris 1881, 120, tr. Atkinson, *Customs and manners of the women of Persia*, London 1832, 77; L. Dubeux, *La Perse*, Paris 1841, 34; W. Franklin, *Voyage du Bengal en Perse*, tr. Langlès, Paris, year VI, i, 107; Scott Waring, *A tour to Sheeraz*, London 1807, 40; Morier, *A second journey through Persia*, London 1818, 69; Ouseley, *Travels*, London 1819, i, 318, ii, 7; Porter, *Travels*, London 1821, i, 686/695; de Gobineau, *Trois ans en Asie*, Paris 1922, i, 199; H. Brugsch, *Reise... nach Persien*, Leipzig 1862, ii, 166; Curzon, *Persia*, London 1892, ii, 93, 96; E.G. Browne, *A year amongst the Persians*, London 1893, index; P.M. Sykes, *Ten thousand miles in Persia*, London 1902, 323; Le Strange, *The lands of the Eastern Caliphate*, Cambridge 1905, 250 (on the water supply of Shīrāz); A.V.W. Jackson, *Persia past and present*, New York 1906, 323; A.J. Arberry, *Shiraz*, Norman, Okla. 1960, index; W. Barthold, *An historical geography of Iran*, Princeton 1984, 156.

(H. Massé)

RUḲYA (A.), from the root *r - ḳ - y* meaning "to ascend" (cf. Ḳurʾān, XVII, 93, XXXVIII, 10; to this, LXXV, 27, adds the idea of "enchanter", "one who cures" and "magician" *rāḳin*, a term often found in the *Sīra*, in *Ḥadīth* and in the Sunna), "enchantment, magical spell". Since casting a spell was usually by means of a magical formula pronounced or written on an amulet of parchment or leather, *rāḳin* is to be connected with *ḳāriʾ* and *riḳḳ* [*q.v.*]. The term *tarāḳī* of the preceding verse, 26, from the root *r-ḳ-w/y*, variously understood by the commentators, means "collar bones" (see *TA* and Lane, s.v.; *Steingass, Persian-English dict.*, 291), and reminds one of the *Clavicules de Salomon*, a book of magic, printed in 1641 and reissued by Pierre Belfond, Paris n.d. It is known that Judaeo-Arabic tradition attributes various works of a magical nature (notably Solomon's seal) to Solomon, a mythic character of the Ḳurʾān who controls the winds, animals, spirits, named seventeen times in the Ḳurʾān (see esp., XXXVIII, 30-9, and cf. Ibn Saʿd, viii, 147; Ibn al-Athīr, i, 160-70; Ibn al-Mudjāwir, i, 103, ii, 164, 173, 180, etc.).

Ruḳya, corresponding to Latin *carmen*, magical chant, consists in the pronouncing of magical formulae for procuring an enchantment. It is one of the procedures of *siḥr* [*q.v.*], used by the Prophet himself and, because of this, permitted in exceptional cases on condition that it brings benefit to people and does not harm anyone. One may have recourse to it against poison, bites, fever, the evil eye, etc. (many refs. in A. Kovalenko, *Magie et Islam*, diss. Strasbourg 1979, reprod. by Minute S.A., Geneva 1981, pp. 721; cf. 113 and 247 (notes); see also G. Bousquet, *L'authentique tradition musulmane*, Paris 1964, 301 nos. 105-6, and 308 no. 130). According to Muslim, ii, 279, "charms are forbidden as soon as they touch upon, in one manner or another, polytheism".

The Prophet thought that beneficial *ruḳya* could modify the fate decreed by God and that it was in fact part of it (al-Tirmidhī, ii, 7). For him, "the evil eye definitely exists. If something could forestall destiny the [evil] eye would precede it" (Muslim, ii, 275). In this case, he recommended *ruḳya*. Faced with a slave whose colour had altered, he said to one of his wives "Have recourse to magical means, for he has been affected by some malevolent glance" (*ibid.*, ii, 277; Bousquet, *op. cit.*, 232-2 no. 104). He himself used *ruḳya* in order to cure a sick man; he placed his right hand on him and pronounced a conjuration formula (Muslim, ii, 276-7). When he was ill, he recited over himself magical formulae and spat. ʿĀʾisha used to do it for him when sorrow was particularly heavy upon him (*ibid.*, ii, 277). The angel Gabriel would sometimes come to him and apply a *ruḳya* (*ibid.*, ii, 274-5). There exists a complete literature called *al-Ṭibb al-nabawī* "Prophetic medicine", full of recipes and practices of this kind attributed to Muḥammad (see Ibn al-Athīr, *Usd al-ghāba*, ii, 258, 277 = ii, 289, 300; A. Perron, *La Médecine du Prophète*,; K. Opitz, *Die Medizin im Koran*, Stuttgart 1906; T. Fahd, *La divination arabe*, Paris 1967, 241-5; and art. KHAWĀṢṢ AL-ḲURʾĀN).

Starting from these Prophetic examples, *ruḳya* from then onwards multiplied enormously, and, especially, amongst the more backward milieux of society. The intellectual classes were unanimous in formally forbidding the practise of magic, but, in the absence of a definition of the idea of *siḥr* in the Ḳurʾān, as likewise in Islamic law, this prohibition was watered down by the Prophetic example. Al-Djuwaynī (d. 681/1283), an Ashʿarī jurist, wrote, "God has merely prohibited what is harmful and not that which is useful; if it is possible for you to be useful to your brother, then do it" (cited in Bousquet, *op. cit.*, 301 n. 104); whilst Ibn Khaldūn wrote, "The religious law makes no distinction between sorcery, talismans and prestidigitation. It puts them all into the same class of forbidden things" (*Muḳaddima*, tr. Rosenthal, iii, 169).

For al-Ghazālī, who provided Islamic theology with its definitive formulation, magic is based on a combined knowledge of the properties of certain terrestrial elements and of propitious astral risings. This knowledge is not in itself blameworthy, but it could only serve to injure others and to do evil (*Iḥyāʾ*, i, 49-50). The privileged place given to this knowledge is justified by words attributed to the Prophet, "The superiority of the believer who also possesses knowledge over the merely pious believer is that of 70 degrees" (cited in *ibid.*, i, 12).

Bibliography (in addition to references given in the text): I. Goldziher, *Zauberelemente im islamischen Gebiete*, in *Orientalistische Studien Th. Nöldeke gewidmet*, Giessen 1906, i, 303-29; E. Doutté, *Magie et religion dans l'Afrique du Nord*, Algiers 1909; W.B. Stevenson, *Some specimens of Moslem charms*, in *Studia semitica et orientalia* (J. Robertson vol.), Glasgow 1920, 84-114; G. Bousquet, *Fiqh et sorcellerie*, in *AIEO*, viii (1949-50), 230-4; H. Kriss-Heinrich, *Volksglaube im Bereich des Islam. II. Amulette und Beschwörungen*, Wiesbaden 1961 (with 104 pls.); T. Fahd, *Le monde du sorcier en Islam*, in *Le monde du sorcier* (= Sources orientales, 7), Paris 1966, 157-204; idem, art. *Magic in Islam*, in M. Eliade (ed.), *Encyclopaedia of religions*, New York 1987, repr. in L.E. Sullivan, *Hidden truths: magic, alchemy and the occult*, New York-London 1989, 122-30; Fahd, *La connaissance de l'inconnaissable et l'obtention de l'impossible dans la pensée mantique et magique de l'Islam*, in *BEO*, xliv (1993), 33-44; idem, *Sciences naturelles et magie dans* Ghāyat al-ḥakīm *du Ps.-Madjrīṭi*, in *Ciencias de la naturaleza en Al-Andalus. Textos y estudios*, i, ed. E. García Sanchez, Granada 1990, 11-21. (T. Fahd)

RŪM. 1. In Arabic literature.

Rūm occurs in Arabic literature with reference to the Romans, the Byzantines and the Christian Melkites interchangeably. This issue of nomenclature is the first problem that confronts the reader of Arabic literature. Most often, however, the reference is to the Byzantines, which is the meaning followed in this entry.

The sources for the pre-Islamic times include the important Namāra [*q.v.*] inscription. All the literary sources were written in later Islamic times, deriving from the historian Ibn al-Kalbī.

In the Islamic period, the first reference to Rūm occurs in the Ḳurʾān (*Sūrat al-Rūm*, XXX, 1-5): "The Rūm have been vanquished in the nearer part of the land..." Ḳurʾān exegesis contains several explanations for these verses and provides further information on the Byzantines (al-Ṭabarī, *Djāmiʿ al-bayān fī taʾwīl al-Ḳurʾān*, Cairo 1954, xviii, 17-19; al-Ālūsī, *Rūḥ al-maʿānī*; Ibn Kathīr, *Tafsīr al-Ḳurʾān al-ʿAẓīm*). Rūm also occurs in *ḥadīth* literature, where Constantinople, in particular, partakes in apocalyptic traditions. Such is the *ḥadīth* in al-Bukhārī stating that Umm Ḥaram had heard the Prophet saying "The first among my people to attack the city of Caesar will see their sins forgiven" (*Ṣaḥīḥ*, 56, ch. 93) or that found in Ibn Ḥanbal, "The Dadjdjāl will not appear until the Byzantines are vanquished" (*Musnad*, 178). The *Sīra* of Ibn Hishām includes several references to the Rūm in various contexts such as warfare, justice, trade and the diplomatic relations with Emperor Heraclius (*Sīrat al-Nabī*, ed. M. ʿAbd al-Ḥamīd, iv, 170). The conquest literature which chronicles the conflict between Byzantium and the Arab Islamic forces digresses into various other subjects as well such as Muḥammad al-Azdī's diversion into issues of Byzantine injustice (*K. Futūḥ al-Shām*, ed. Nassau Lees, Calcutta 157-8). Ibn al-Aʿtham al-Kūfī's references in his *K. al-Futūḥ*, Ḥaydarābād 1968, i, 151) are connected with scenes of Byzantine ceremonial, elegance and wealth.

In the main historical chronicles, in al-Ṭabarī's *Taʾrīkh al-Rusul wa 'l-mulūk*, for instance, references to Rūm are guaranteed at the end of each year; the account closes by mentioning Muslim raids into Byzantine territory. For Constantinople [see al-ḳusṭanṭīniyya], in particular, the last major siege led by Maslama in 98/716-17 is recounted in detail in the anonymous *Kitāb al-ʿUyūn*, ed. de Goeje, Leiden 1869, i, 23-33. The conflict between Byzantium and the Islamic state directed the orientation of the sources so that warfare holds a predominant place in the *Futūḥ*, chronicles and historical works.

The Rūm figure prominently in the Arabic geographical literature of the 3rd-5th/9th-11th centuries. The geographers of the early "ʿIrāḳī" school, Ibn Khurradādhbih, Ibn Rusta, Ibn al-Faḳīh and Ḳudāma b. Djaʿfar included in their respective works a chapter on the Byzantines. Ibn Khurradādhbih's *al-Masālik wa 'l-mamālik* provides information on fiscal revenues, itineraries, geographical boundaries, and the make-up of Byzantine population. Ibn Rusta's *al-Aʿlāḳ al-nafīsa* includes the most detailed Arabic description of Constantinople. Among the geographers of the "Balkhī" school, Ibn Ḥawḳal alone, in his *K. Ṣūrat al-arḍ*, provides a full-length chapter on the lands of Rūm. Foremost among all Arabic works are the two masterpieces of al-Masʿūdī, *K. al-Tanbīh wa 'l-ishrāf* and *Murūdj al-dhahab*, which include not only geographical material and anecdotes on the Rūm but also attempt at a systematic historical treatment of Byzantine history after the rise of Islam. See also Manuela Marin, *«Rūm» in the works of three Spanish Muslim geographers*, in *Graeco-Arabica*, iii (Athens 1984), 109-17.

The organisation of the Byzantine administration and the army is referred to in various texts such as Ḳudāma b. Djaʿfar's *K. al-Kharādj* (255-7) and the *Mafātīḥ al-ʿulūm* of al-Khʷārazmī (see for this last, C.E. Bosworth, *Al-Khʷārazmī on the secular and religious titles of the Byzantines and Christians*, in *CT*, xxxv, no. 139-40 [1987] (= *Mélanges Ch. Pellat*), 28-36). Descriptions of Byzantine ceremonial are found in Ibn Rusta, where the Muslim prisoner Hārūn b. Yaḥyā witnessed several ceremonials of the Byzantine court (123-5). Anecdotes concerning the court ceremonial are found in al-Masʿūdī (*Murūdj*, ii, 18) and Ibn al-Faḳīh (*Mukhtaṣar K. al-Buldān*, 137-8) and other works. Important references to Rūm are made in the context of embassies and diplomatic relations, hence the importance of Ibn al-Farrāʾ's *Taʾrīkh al-Rusul wa 'l-mulūk wa-man yaṣluḥ li 'l-sifāra* written in the 4th/10th century. Special works like the *K. al-Dhakhāʾir wa 'l-tuḥaf* of the Ḳāḍī Ibn al-Zubayr, ed. M. Ḥamīdullāh and S. Munadjdjid, Kuwayt 1959, from the 5th/11th century, deal mostly with exchange of gifts between Muslim and Byzantine rulers and include information on ceremonials.

In works typically referred to as *adab*, references to the Byzantines are most often scattered and anecdotal. Al-Djāḥiẓ has dispersed references in his *K. al-Ḥayawān*. He deals in a much more consistent way with the topic in his epistle *Risāla fī al-radd ʿalā 'l-Naṣārā* (ed. A. Hārūn, in *Rasāʾil*, iii) and in *al-Akhbār wa-kayfa taṣiḥḥ*, in *JA*, cclv [1967], 65-105). Some anecdotes are rather extensive, such as those mentioned by al-Tanūkhī (d. 384/945-6) concerning an Arab prisoner captured by the Byzantines (*al-Faradj baʿd al-shidda*, ed. A. al-Shāldjī, Beirut 1978, ii, 192-205) or the meeting between a Christian grandfather and a Muslim grandson (*ibid.*, ii, 29-31). The *K. al-Aghānī* includes information on the Byzantine Empress Irene (Būlāḳ, xvii, 44), anecdotes on the correspondence between the Umayyad caliph ʿUmar b. ʿAbd al-ʿAzīz and the Byzantine Emperor (viii, 157) as well as on the poet Imruʾ al-Ḳays, explaining how his death was related to a Byzantine princess (viii, 73). In a typical *adab* work such as Ibn Ḳutayba's *ʿUyūn al-akhbār*, references are mentioned in several books, depending on the context, whether war, food, morals, etc... In addition to anecdotes, some works of *adab* contain statements about the various civilised nations in the context of the Shuʿūbiyya [*q.v.*] controversy such as the *K. al-Imtāʿ wa 'l-muʾānasa* of Abū Ḥayyān al-Tawḥīdī (d. 414/1023). One should note also Ṣāʿid al-Andalusī's (d. 462/1070 [*q.v.*]) *Ṭabaḳāt al-umam*.

References to the Byzantine language and script imply some mutual knowledge of the rivals' respective language. Most of the information concerning the literary achievements of the Rūm appears within the intellectual discussion that accompanied the Shuʿūbī movement, notably by al-Djāḥiẓ in his *K. al-Bayān wa 'l-tabyīn*. The first section of the *Fihrist* of Ibn al-Nadīm describes the four different Greek scripts used by the Rūm in Baghdād.

In poetry, references are scattered in isolated verses. More significant poems are found in Abū Nuwās and Abu 'l-ʿAtāhiya as they sing the praises of Hārūn al-Rashīd, while Abū Tammām (*Dīwān*, ed. Shāhīn ʿAṭiyya, Beirut 1889, 289, verse 18 and 35, verses 6-10) and al-Buḥturī (*Dīwān*, Beirut, 1911, 24, verses 3-14) focus on the achievements of al-Maʾmūn and al-Muʿtaṣim. The capture of Amorium in 233/838 by al-Muʿtaṣim was the subject of a famous poem by Abū Tammām. The most notable Arab poet to deal at length with the Arab-Byzantine wars is al-Mutanabbī. As long as he remained at the court of the Ḥamdānid Sayf al-Dawla [*q.v.*] in Aleppo, Mutanabbī devoted poems to each of the Amīr's campaigns against the Byzantines, so that his poems are useful as topographical and historical sources.

Bibliography: This is enormous, since references to the Rūm can be found almost anywhere. One may single out, in addition to sources mentioned in the article, Ḳāḍī ʿAbd al-Djabbār's *Tathbīt dalāʾil al-nubuwwa*, Beirut 1966, which focuses on personal traits and morality of the Byzantines, and al-Ḳāḍī al-Nuʿmān's *K. al-Madjālis wa 'l-musāyarāt* which has the benefit of including the Fāṭimids in the picture. Irfan Shahid, *Byzantium and the Arabs in the fourth century*, Washington 1984, see also his *Byzantium and the Arabs in the fifth century*, Washington 1989, investigates very meticulously the pre-Islamic sources on the Byzantines. M. Canard, *Les éxpeditions des Arabes contre Constantinople dans l'histoire et la légende*, in *JA*, ccviii-ccix (1926), 61-121, provides a good introduction for the references to the Byzantines and, particularly, Constantinople in the genre of folkloric traditions. A. Miquel, *La geographie humaine du monde musulman jusqu'au milieu du XIème siècle*, Paris 1967-88, 4 vols., provides an excellent introduction to the Arab geographers' view of the world around them including the Rūm. Also valuable is Ahmad Shboul, *Byzantium and the Arabs: the image of the Byzantines as mirrored in Arabic Literature*, in *Proceedings of the First Australian Byzantine Studies Conference*, London 1979, and idem, *Al-Masʿūdī and his world*, London 1979, ch. 6, *The Byzantines*. See also AṢFAR, BANŪ 'L-.

(NADIA EL CHEIKH)

2. Relations between the Islamic powers and the Byzantines.

(a) *Military and political aspects of Arab-Byzantine relations*

The Muslims, first the Arabs and then, with the incursions of the Turkmens into Anatolia from the 5th/11th century onwards, the Turks, had close relations, often bellicose but at times on a more peaceful level, for a period of some eight centuries. This extended from the initial Arab conquests of Byzantine imperial territories in the Levant, Egypt and the Mediterranean islands until the final extinction of the remnants of the Byzantine empire, and also of Greek independence, by the falls of Constantinople (857/1453), the Despotate of Morea (864/1460) and the empire of Trebizond (865/1461).

The ambivalent relations of the two great world faiths and powers of the Near East and Eastern Europe were thus manifested in both the politico-military sphere and also the cultural one (see section (b) below). Constantinople was from the outset a goal of Muslim arms, as the supreme bastion of the rival faith of Christianity, and Arab raids were directed at the East Roman capital itself from the caliphate of ʿUthmān onwards, with the warriors' enthusiasm soon buttressed by apocalyptic traditions looking forward to the city's capture. Such traditions, e.g. the prophetal *ḥadīth* that Constantinople would fall to an Islamic ruler who bore the name of a prophet (in this case, of Solomon) seem to have been a motive behind the prolonged, but ultimately unsuccessful, onslaught on the Byzantine capital begun by Sulaymān b. ʿAbd al-Malik (97-99/716-18) (see R. Eisener, *Zwischen Faktum und Fiktion. Eine Studie zum Umayyadenkalifen Sulaimān b. ʿAbdalmalik und seinem Bild in den Quellen*, Wiesbaden 1987, 129-37; and see ḲUSṬANṬĪNIYYA).

When the new caliph ʿUmar (II) ʿAbd al-ʿAzīz abandoned the expansionist plans of his predecessors, the apocryphal and messianic motives decreased in vigour, and the last effort of the Arabs against Constantinople was that of the prince Hārūn, later the caliph al-Rashīd, who appeared at Scutari in 165/781-2 but was bought off by a timely offer of tribute from the Empress Irene. The real legacy of these Arab attacks was in the spheres of folklore and hagiography rather than a material one. Thus the tomb of the veteran Medinan Companion Abū Ayyūb al-Anṣārī [*q.v.*], who died during the siege of Constantinople by Yazīd b. Muʿāwiya in his father's caliphate, became regarded as a source of *baraka* or charisma for the Muslims, most recently by the Ottoman Meḥemmed II the Conqueror [*q.v.*], after his entry into Constantinople, who erected a splendid mosque, the present one of Eyüp, on the tomb's supposed site. The siege of Constantinople by Maslama b. ʿAbd al-Malik [*q.v.*] during Sulaymān's caliphate left behind, it was believed, a tangible memorial in the shape of a mosque, identified in the later popular mind with what is now called the Arab Camii in Karaköy (in fact, this building was given as a church to the Dominicans, as the Church of St. Paul or St. Dominic, in 1232, during the Latin occupation of Constantinople, and only became a mosque at the Ottoman conquest). Hārūn al-Rashīd's efforts, though in reality without issue, played a big part in later Ottoman Turkish folklore, and according to one story retailed by the 11th/17th century traveller Ewliyā Čelebi [*q.v.*], Hārūn avenged a massacre of Muslims within Constantinople by hanging the Emperor Nicephorus I in Santa Sophia (see M. Canard, *Les expéditions des Arabes contre Constantinople dans l'histoire et dans la légende*, in *JA*, ccviii [1926]. 87-106 = *Byzance et les Musulmanes du Proche Orient*, Variorum Reprints, London 1973, no. I; C.E. Bosworth, *Byzantium and the Arabs: war and peace between two world civilisations*, in *Jnal. of Oriental and African Studies*, iii-iv [Athens 1991-2], 1-4).

There was periodic naval warfare along the coasts of southern and western Anatolia and against Byzantine islands like Cyprus [see ḲUBRUS], Rhodes [see RODOS], Crete [see IḲRĪṬISH] and Sicily [see SIḲILLIYA], although the Byzantine navy generally managed to retain maritime control—with intervals of Muslim successes—over the first three of these islands and over the Aegean islands in general until the advent of Italian, Catalan and French adventurers there, above all, the Venetians and Genoese, in the 12th century A.D. (see, in general, E. Eickhoff, *Seekrieg und Seepolitik zwischen Islam und Abendland. Das Mittelmeer unter byzantinischer und arabische Hegemonie (650-1040)*,

Berlin 1966; H. Ahrweiler, *Byzance et la mer. La marine de guerre, la politique et les institutions maritime de Byzance aux VIIe-XVe siècles*, Paris 1966; and on one specific early naval battle, DHĀT AL-ṢAWĀRĪ, in Suppl.).

By land, warfare was intermittent between Greeks and Arabs in southeastern Anatolia and its marches for some four centuries. When not distracted by internal difficulties of the caliphate, the Muslims normally mounted summer raids (*ṣawāʾif*, sing. *ṣāʾifa* [*q.v.*]) and, occasionally, winter ones (*shawātī*, sing. *shātiya*), often under the leadership of Umayyad or ʿAbbāsid princes (e.g. Maslama, al-ʿAbbās b. al-Walīd b. ʿAbd al-Malik and ʿAbd al-Malik b. Ṣāliḥ b. ʿAlī) and other prominent commanders. Quite often, their raids penetrated deep into Byzantine territory, such as the famed sack by al-Muʿtaṣim of Amorion (ʿAmmūriya [*q.v.*]) in 223/838. But on the whole, there were no permanent, large-scale Arab annexations in Anatolia, and in the later 3rd/9th century, the advent to the throne in Byzantium of the vigorous Macedonian emperors set the Christians on the offensive in northern Syria and al-Djazīra, this impetus only being checked by the appearance of the Turkmens as a factor in the politics of the region and, behind them, the constituting of the Great Saldjūḳ sultanate [see SALDJŪḲS]. Only then, in the second half of the 5th/11th century, was the stage set for the gradual advance of the Turks into Anatolia after the Saldjūḳ sultan Alp Arslan [*q.v.*] had decisively defeated Romanus IV Diogenes at Mantzikert or Malāzgird [*q.v.*] in 463/1071, thereby gaining control over much of eastern Anatolia. During the next four centuries, Anatolia was to be completely taken over by Turkish dynasties, to be finally unified by the Ottomans [see OTHMĀNLĪ], with portentous changes in the ethnic and religious composition and the socio-economic make-up of Asia Minor (see section (c) below).

The interface of Byzantine-Arab land contact was essentially the region of southeastern Anatolia backed on the Muslim side by a line of "strongholds" (*ʿawāṣim* [*q.v.*]), a line of protective fortresses stretching in an arc from Antioch through the Anti-Taurus and the upper Euphrates region to Manbidj. Before this line of rear defences lay a stretch of debatable land, much fought over, the *ḍawāʾiḥ al-Rūm* or "exterior lands facing the Greeks", in which were situated the "gaps" or *thughūr* [*q.v.*], the forward strongholds, stretching from Tarsus on the Cilician coast to Malaṭya and the mountains of eastern Anatolia. For the general course of this frontier warfare, see the standard histories of Byzantine-Arab relations and of Byzantium, such as A.A. Vasiliev, H. Grégoire and M. Canard, *Byzance et les Arabes*, 4 vols., Brussels 1935-68 (incs. trs. by Canard of the relevant Arabic texts, and vol. iv, *Die Ostgrenze des byzantinische Reiches von 363 bis 1071* by E. Honigmann); Vasiliev, *History of the Byzantine empire*, Madison 1952, esp. vol. i; G. Ostrogorsky, *History of the Byzantine state*, Oxford 1956, ²Oxford 1969; R. Jenkins, *Byzantium, the imperial centuries A.D. 610-1071*, London 1966; J.M. Hussey (ed.), *The Cambridge medieval history*, iv, *The Byzantine empire*, esp. ch. XVII by Canard, *Byzantium and the Muslim world to the middle of the eleventh century*, and, more specifically from the Arab side, Bosworth, *The Byzantine defence system in Asia Minor and the first Arab incursions*, in *Procs. of the Fourth International Conference on the history of Bilād al-Shām*, i, ʿAmmān 1987, 116-24, and idem, *Byzantium and the Syrian frontier in the early Abbasid period*, in *Procs. of the Fifth International Conference on the History of Bilād al-Shām*, Eng. and Fr. section, ʿAmmān 1412/1991, 54-62.

A notable feature here is a certain symbiosis which takes place along the Byzantine-Arab borders, with the evolution of a frontier society differing from the more stable and peaceable communities of the hinterlands (see Bosworth, *The city of Tarsus and the Arab-Byzantine frontiers in early and middle ʿAbbāsid times*, in *Oriens*, xxxiii [1992], 276). Part of this society involved, from the Arab side, the activities of Islamic *ghāzīs* [*q.v.*] or fighters for the faith, motivated in varying proportions by a love of plunder and by a spirit of *djihād* [*q.v.*] or warfare for the extension of the *Dār al-Islām*, and from the Greek side, the activities of the *akritai* or frontier fighters. The Muslim *ghāzīs* based themselves in the frontier posts, variously called *ḥiṣn*, *maslaḥa ribāṭ*, etc., in the *ḍawaʾiḥ*, whilst their Greek counterparts sallied forth from cities and outposts on the Anatolian plateau and in the Taurus mountains, heavily fortified as part of the reshaping of the Byzantine empire, from the later 7th century A.D. onwards, into military themes perpetually organised for warfare (see R.-J. Lilie, *Die byzantinische Reaktion auf die Ausbreitung der Araber. Studien zur Strukturwandlung des byzantinisches Staates im 7. und 8. Jhd.*, Munich 1976; Bosworth, *The Byzantine defence system in Asia Minor and the first Arab incursions*, 119 ff.). A further feature of these frontier societies was the development of an epic literature there (although this was not necessarily contemporaneous with the events purported to be described in it), seen on the Greek side in the epic of Digenes Akrites and on the Arabic one in the stories of Sīdī Baṭṭāl [see AL-BAṬṬĀL, SAYYID GHĀZĪ] and Dhu 'l-Himma [*q.v.*], whilst, again on the Arab side, we know of an only partially-extant work, the *Siyar al-thughūr* "Ways of life, conduct, along the frontiers" by the 4th/10th century author al-Ṭarsūsī (himself a native of the *thaghr* of Tarsus [see ṬARSŪS], possession of which oscillated between the Greeks and Arabs until Nicephorus Phocas captured it in 354/965), which treated of life along the Muslim side of the frontier (see Bosworth, *The city of Tarsus and the Arab-Byzantine frontiers...*, 271-2, 280 ff.; idem, *Abū ʿAmr ʿUthmān al-Ṭarsūsī's* Siyar al-thughūr *and the last years of Arab rule in Tarsus (fourth/tenth century)*, in *Graeco-Arabica*, v [Athens 1993], 183-95).

The frontier warfare, and the territorial advances and withdrawals of each side, created in the *ḍawāḥī* something like a scorched-earth zone, and, at the human level, brought in plentiful supplies of slave captives for both sides. To make up depleted populations in the frontier territories, groups of peoples were often transplanted from the interiors of the Arab and Byzantine empires and settled there; thus there were to be found, on both sides of the frontier, members from the community of the Mardaites, brought from the Amanus region of northwestern Syria [see AL-DJARĀDJIMA, and also ZUṬṬ]. At intervals, exchanges of captives might be arranged, and these are enumerated in the Arabic sources as a series of *fidā's* [*q.v.* in Suppl.] or "ransomings", taking place during the 3rd/9th and 4th/10th centuries and usually on the banks of the Lamos or Lamas Su river near Seleucia or Silifke (see Bosworth, *Byzantium and the Arabs...*, 13-16, and LAMAS-ṢŪ).

(b) *Cultural and artistic relations of the Arabs and Byzantines*

One should not dwell exclusively on the military aspects of relations without noting that, interspersed between the frontier raiding and warfare, were long periods of peace (even if these last were, in strict Islamic law, periods of truce, *hudna*, rather than of *ṣulḥ*), during which diplomatic, cultural and commercial intercourse was possible. The two sides, the Arab-Muslim and the Greco-Byzantine, shared a common world-view, a teleological view of human existence as progressing from the divine act of Creation to the last things (these being, for the Muslims, the vanquishing of Satan or the Anti-Christ (*Dadjdjāl* [*q.v.*]), the Resurrection and the Judgement) and the end of human history; both had similar ethical standards, the pursuit of justice in this world and of individual salvation for the next one. Hence despite political rivalry and military clashes, there was the possibility of occasional co-operation in such spheres as artistic, cultural and scientific ventures.

This was favoured, in practice, by the fact that, although they were enemies of the Greeks from the religious point of view, the Arabs—in distinction from their view of the Franks or Western Europeans, whom they regarded with contempt as barbarians [see IFRANDJ]—considered Byzantium as a world power and world culture on a par with themselves. A passage in the *Kitāb. Ṭabaḳāt al-umam* of the Spanish Muslim *ḳāḍi* of Toledo, Ṣāʿid b. Aḥmad al-Ḳurṭubī (wrote 460/1068) divides the peoples of the world into those concerned with learning and the sciences and those not; in the first category are included peoples like the Indian, Persians, Chaldaeans, Greeks (as *Yūnān*, i.e. the ancient Greeks), the *Rūm* (i.e. the Byzantines), Egyptians, Arabs and Jews (Fr. tr. R. Blachère, *Livre des catégories des nations*, Paris 1935, 36-7, cited in B. Lewis, *The Muslim discovery of Europe*, London 1982, 68-9). For their part, the Byzantine emperors not infrequently accorded the representatives of their Muslim foes a higher rank at their court and among their society than those of the Western Europeans. In a famous passage of his *De ceremoniis aulae byzantinae*, Constantine VII Porphyrogenitus (913-59) gives "Saracen (lit. Hagarene) friends" precedence at the imperial table over the "Frankish friends", and amongst the Saracens in general, the eastern ones (*toi anatolikoi prokrinomenoi*) are accorded the best places (see Bosworth, *Byzantium and the Arabs*, 17).

When the Arabs overran the former territories of the Byzantine empire in the Near East, they saw numerous monuments to Christian architectural achievement. Above all, in Greater Syria, there were still some forested areas with timber as yet unfelled and plentiful supplies of fine building stone, together with a human tradition of building skills and fine craftmanship. The presence of these factors favoured the erection of imposing Islamic public buildings and private palaces in the region, of which the Umayyad Mosque in Damascus and the Mosque of ʿUmar and the Dome of the Rock in Jerusalem were conspicuous examples. Sir Hamilton Gibb suggested that, in Jerusalem, there was a conscious aim of emulating the Christian practice of cathedral building (*Arab-Byzantine relations under the Umayyad caliphate*, in *Studies on the civilization of Islam*, ed. S.J. Shaw and W.R. Polk, Boston 1962, 50 ff.). Moreover, there is a persistent tradition in later Islamic historians that the caliph al-Walīd (I) b. ʿAbd al-Malik sent to the Byzantine emperor (presumably Justinian II, 685-95, 705-11) requesting, and in fact obtaining, help for the adornment of the Umayyad Mosque in Damascus and the Prophet's Mosque in Medina, in which last place the governor ʿUmar b. ʿAbd al-ʿAzīz was building a fine new structure in place of the original, simple building [see ARCHITECTURE. I (2)]. The geographer al-Muḳaddasī (158, partial Fr. tr. A. Miquel, *La meilleure répartition pour la connaissance des provinces*, Damascus 1963, 170-1), describes how the Emperor sent precious metals, skilled artisans and mosaic cubes (*fasāfisa, fusayfisa* < Grk. *psēphos*), including some cubes retrieved from ancient cities, presumably in Anatolia (see Bosworth, *op. cit.*, 18-20, and FUSAYFISĀʾ). Such a request for the skills of artisans from Byzantium does, however, raise questions of the motivations behind the actions of both sides. It may be that the Emperor acceded to the caliph's request as an act of condescension, the bestowal of artistic expertise on benighted barbarians, and that al-Walīd thought that he was cunningly acquiring artistic and trade secrets, knowledge of which would in future make him independent of recourse to infidels. Oleg Grabar has discussed these questions, in an attempt *inter alia* to explain which mosaicists from Byzantium should be necessary when there were clearly, from the evidence of the workmanship of the new Islamic structures at Jerusalem, local artisans who were completely competent in such specialisations. (*Islamic art and Byzantium*, in *Dumbarton Oaks Papers*, xviii [1964], 69-88, esp. 82 ff. = *Studies in medieval Islamic art*, Variorum Reprints, London 1976, no. IV).

Recourse to Byzantium for artistic guidance, and for what would now be called technical aid, was made two-and-a-half centuries later by the Umayyad rulers of Muslim Spain, with whom Constantinople had intermittent diplomatic relations: both powers shared a common hostility to the ʿAbbāsids. In 839-40 the Emperor Theophilus (829-42) sent an embassy to ʿAbd al-Raḥmān II [*q.v.*] in his capital Cordova, seeking to get the *amīr* to use his influence among the band of Muslim adventurers from al-Andalus under Abū Ḥafṣ ʿUmar al-Ballūṭī, who had established themselves in the Byzantine posession of Crete and subjugated the Christian Greek population there. Then, a century later, the Umayyad caliph ʿAbd al-Raḥmān III [*q.v.*] looked to Constantinople for assistance and advice, regarding the Byzantine capital as the outstanding centre of cultural splendour in the Mediterranean basis, and possibly also in an endeavour to counterbalance the cultural impact in Spain of the Islamic East, and particularly of Baghdād. It seems that in the A.D. 950s ʿAbd al-Raḥmān sent the Mozarab bishop Recemundo or Rabīʿ b. Zayd [*q.v.*], who had already been employed on a mission to the Emperor Otto I, to Constantinople in order to acquire *objets d'art* for the decoration of the new palace, *al-Madīnat al-Zahrāʾ* [*q.v.*], which the Umayyad ruler was building outside Cordova. The later Moroccan historian Ibn ʿIdhārī records that, keeping up the tradition, ʿAbd al-Raḥmān's son al-Ḥakam I [*q.v.*] maintained these diplomatic relations with Byzantium, and sent to Nicephorus Phocas for a mosaicist and for materials to decorate the Great Mosque at Cordova (see E. Lévi-Provençal, *Un échange d'ambassades entre Cordoue et Byzance au IXᵉ siècle*, in *Byzantion*, xii [1937], 1-24; idem, *Hist. Esp. musulmane*, Paris-Leiden 1950, i, 251-4, ii, 146-53, cited in Bosworth, *op. cit.*, 20-1).

Canard, in his article *Le cérémonial fatimite et le cérémonial byzantin, essai de comparaison*, in *Byzantion*, xxi (1951), 355-420 = *Byzance et les Musulmanes du Proche Orient*, no. XIV, drew attention to similarities between the court practices of the Byzantine emperors (known to us in detail from Constantine Porphyrogenitus's *De ceremoniis*) and those of the Fāṭimid caliphs, and mooted the possibility (415 ff.) of cultural influences in Fāṭimid North Africa and Egypt emanating from Byzantium. He found it difficult to produce evidence of a deliberate policy of imitation on the part of the Fāṭimids, but did draw attention to the significant role in the early Fāṭimid caliphate of ethnic groups from various parts of the Byzantine empire, such as the Sicilian (or Dalmatian, or even Greek?)

Djawhar (d. 381/992 [*q.v.*]), in whose conquering army was certainly a corps of *Rūm*. I. Hrbek, discussing the role of the Ṣaḳāliba [*q.v.*] and Rūmīs in the Fāṭimid army, opined that the majority of these Rūmīs came from the Balkans, over which Byzantium claimed a general suzerainty, the Balkans being for long a great reservoir for slave manpower (*Die Slawen im Dienste der Fāṭimiden*, in *ArO*, xxi [1953], 543-81, esp. 567 ff.). We also have evidence of some direct diplomatic contact between Byzantium and the Fāṭimid caliph al-Muʿizz in the shape of an embassy from Constantinople to his palace at Manṣūriyya near Ḳayrawān in 346/957 seeking peace after naval clashes in the Mediterranean between ships of the Spanish Umayyads and their Byzantine allies on the one side and ships of the Fāṭimids on the other (S.M. Stern, *An embassy of the Byzantine emperor to the Fatimid caliph al-Muʿizz*, in *Byzantion*, xx [1950], 239-58 = *History and culture in the medieval Muslim world*, Variorum Reprints, London 1984, no. IX), but this seems to have been an isolated occurrence.

In addition to these sporadic artistic and cultural relations between Byzantines and Arabs, there were also odd cases of co-operation, and even, on one occasion, something like a joint expedition, for scientific purposes. The caliph al-Maʾmūn [*q.v.*] was known for his interest in science and learning, and he brought together various experts in his *Bayt al-Ḥikma* [*q.v.*] at Baghdād, with the aim of recovering and translating the ancient Greek scientific, medical and philosophical heritage. According to Ibn al-Nadīm's *Fihrist*, al-Maʾmūn sent to the Emperor in Constantinople for books on science, which the latter somewhat unwillingly sent, and he further endeavoured, but without success, to attract from the Byzantine capital to his own court the celebrated mathematician and philosopher Leo, subsequently Archbishop of Thessalonike. Al-Maʾmūn's son al-Wāthiḳ [*q.v.*] inherited his father's interests, and when he became caliph he sent to Ephesus in Rūm the astronomer and mathematician Muḥammad b. Mūsā al-Khwārazmī [*q.v.*], with the aim of getting information on the 'Companions of the Cave'', *Aṣḥāb al-Kahf* [*q.v.*]; for this quest, the Emperor Michael III (842-67) provided a guide (see Bosworth, *op. cit.*, 22-3).

After the 5th/10th century, the Byzantines and the Arabs tended to be separated from each other geographically by the intrusion of a new ethnic element, the Turks, as will be described in the next section, and diplomatic and cultural contacts were much reduced, although whilst ever the rulers in Constantinople controlled maritime traffic through the Straits and the Dardanelles, they had a continuing role in the slave trade between the Ḳïpčaḳ Steppe and South Russia which was such a vital factor in the replenishment of military personnel in the Mamlūk state [see MAMLŪK].

(c) *Byzantium and the Turks*

With the coming of the 5th/11th century, Muslim pressure on Byzantium passed from the hands of the Arabs into those of the Turks, in the shape of Turkmen begs or tribal leaders and the more organised Turkish principalities which arose in Anatolia towards the end of that century, such as that of the Dānishmandids [*q.v.*] in northern and eastern Anatolia and the branch of the Saldjūks in Konya. All these now became the spearhead of Islamic penetration of Anatolia and of the region's gradual subtraction from Byzantine control.

In later decades of the century, the Saldjūḳ adventurer Sulaymān b. Ḳutalmïsh b. Arslan Isrāʾīl and his raiding bands penetrated right across the length of Asia Minor, at a time when the Byzantine empire was weakened by succession disputes, so that for several years, until 490/1097, Sulaymān was able to make Nicaea or Iznik [*q.v.*], in the extreme northwest of Anatolia, his temporary capital.

Under the emperors of the Comneni dynasty, and with assistance from the Frankish Crusaders who passed through Asia Minor en route for the Holy Land, the Byzantine position was in the 6th/12th century generally re-established in western Anatolia and in the Black Sea and Mediterranean coastlands. But the defeat of Manuel I Comnenus at Myriocephalon in 572/1176 showed the rising strength of the Saldjūḳ sultanate of Rūm in Konya, and in the last two decades of the century the Byzantine frontier defences largely crumbled. Also, the Latin conquest of Constantinople in 1204 reduced the Byzantine hold over Asia Minor to its northwestern portion, ruled from their temporary capital of Nicaea for over half-a-century, and this meant that, even though the rule of the Palaeologi was restored in Constantinople, the next two centuries were ones of steady decline, with Byzantium as a vassal state of the Ottomans after the mid-8th/14th century.

These last Byzantine rulers formed merely one element, and that of decreasing authority, within a states-system of South-East Europe and Asia Minor which included rising powers in the Balkans like Serbia and Bulgaria, the Italian and other merchant adventurers in Greece and the Aegean isles, but, above all, the Turks of Anatolia. An indication of the Byzantine emperors' enfeeblement was that, whereas earlier monarchs had disdained to link themselves with lesser families, and certainly not with infidels, the Palaeologi had to seek allies where they could find them, and this not infrequently involved marriage alliances with Muslim ruling families. Michael VIII (1259-82) had diplomatic relations with the Mongol Golden Horde in South Russia and with the Il-Khānid of Persia, Hülegü, and gave his illegitimate daughter Euphrosyne in marriage to the Djočid *amīr* Noghay. The claimant to the throne in Constantinople John Cantacuzenus (1347-54) in 1346 allied with the Ottoman chief Orkhan during the course of a succession dispute within Byzantium, and gave his daughter Theodora in marriage to Orkhan. (C. Imber, *The Ottoman empire 1300-1481*, Istanbul 1990, 23). In the northeast of Anatolia, the empire of Trebizond, surrounded along its land frontiers with Turkish territory, only survived as long as it did by means of alliances and agreements with the Muslims. Thus the Bayandur Turkmen tribe pressed particularly hard on Trebizond until Ḳara ʿOthmān, founder of the Aḳ Ḳoyunlu [*q.v.*] or ''White Sheep'' Turkmen principality, married the princess Maria of Trebizond. Ḳara ʿOthmān's grandson Uzun Ḥasan married in *ca.* 862/1458 Despina, daughter of the Trebizond Emperor John IV Comnenus, and Despina's daughter Martha was to marry Shaykh Ḥaydar Ṣafawī of Ardabīl and become the mother of Shāh Ismāʿīl I of Persia [see UZUN ḤASAN, in *EI*[1]].

The history of the Turkish advance and the gradual take-over of Anatolia, may be followed in ANADOLU (iii), in ʿOTHMĀNLĪ, in SALDJŪḲ. III. 5, in the articles on the various *beyliks*, and in such standard works (which also discuss such contentious questions as the nature and pace of Islamisation and the relative contribution to Anatolian life and society by what eventually became the Greek and Armenian substratum) as Cl. Cahen, *Pre-Ottoman Turkey. A general survey of the material and spiritual culture and history c. 1071-1330*, London 1968; S. Vryonis, *The decline of medieval Hellenism in Asia Minor and the process of Islamization from the eleventh through the fifteenth century*, Berkeley, Los Angeles and London 1971; Osman Turan, *Selçuklar zamanında Türkiye. Siyâsi tarih Alp Arslan'dan Osman Gazi'ye 1071-1318*, Istanbul 1971; F. Taeschner's chs. *The Turks and the Byzantine empire to the end of the thirteenth century* and *The Ottoman Turks to 1453*, in *Camb. med. hist.*, iv/1, 737-75; A.G.C. Savvides, *Byzantium in the Near East: its relations with the Seljuk sultanate of Rum in Asia Minor, the Armenians of Cilicia and the Mongols A.D. c. 1192-1237*, Thessalonike 1981; etc.

Finally, it is interesting to note the vicissitudes of use of the actual ethnic/dynastic term *Rūm* during these later centuries of the empire's existence. Byzantine Greek sources refer to the empire as *Rhōmania* or *Rhōmaiōn/rhōmaikai chōrai* from the 9th century onwards. In more recent Islamic usage, *Rūm* had always had a geographical sense also (see above, (a)), designating the Greek lands of the Byzantine empire beyond the Taurus-upper Euphrates frontier zone. Hence when the Turks penetrated into these regions during the later 5th/11th century, it was natural that a line of begs like those of the Dānis͟hmandids [*q.v.*], who were originally based on the Sivas district, should style their territories Rūm, and we find Malik Muḥammad G͟hāzī (529-36/1134-42) styled on his Greek-legend coins "the Great King of Romania and Anatolia". The Anatolian Sald̲j̲ūḳs, whose principality was based on the region of Konya and southern Cappadocia—territories which were for long strongly Greek in ethnos and still in early Ottoman sources called *Yūnān wilāyeti* "province of the Greeks"—referred to their state, at least in informal usage, as that of Rūm and themselves as *Sald̲j̲ūḳiyān-i Rūm*, thereby in some measure conceiving of themselves as heirs to the Byzantines in south-central Anatolia (although *Rūm* continued also, as with regard to the Greeks who had lived within the Arab caliphate centuries before, to denote the Greek Christian population of Asia Minor; towards the middle of the 8th/14th century, the Moroccan traveller Ibn Baṭṭūṭa records sailing to Alanya in the Bilād al-Rūm, "called after the Rūm because it used to be their land in olden times, and from it came the ancient Rūm and the Yūnānīs. Later on it was conquered by the Muslims, but in it there are still large numbers of Christians under the protection of the Muslims, these latter being Turkmens", *Riḥla*, ii, 255, tr. Gibb, ii, 415).

The expansion of the Ottomans in the 8th/14th century eventually made them masters of the former Byzantine territories, *grosso modo* those of *Rhōmania*, in both Anatolia and the Greco-Balkan region. Since the territories of the Palaeologi were latterly mainly in Europe, this *Rhōmania* became for the Ottomans Rūm-eli [*q.v.*], or Rumelia, the land characterised by its predominantly Orthodox Christian population, the Rūm. The circumscribed remnant of the Byzantine empire was by now rarely in Ottoman sources styled *Rūm*, nor was its emperor styled Ḳayṣar, the latter office being more commonly referred to by the (originally Armenian) title *Tekfūr* "king". It was the Ottomans who took over for themselves, and especially from the times of Meḥemmed I and II [*q.vv.*], the title of *Sulṭān* (or *Pādis͟hāh* or *K͟hān*)-*i Rūm*, regarding themselves as being already, before the final capture of Constantinople, substantially the heirs to both the Byzantine empire and the Rūm Sald̲j̲ūḳ sultanate. Thus it was natural that the Tīmūrid historian Niẓām al-Dīn S͟hāmī [*q.v.*] should, in his *Ẓafar-nāma* (ed. F. Tauer, Prague 1937-56, i, 257), call the Ottomans of Bāyezīd I, whom Tīmūr crushed, the *Rūmiyān*, adducing at the same time the Ḳurʾānic reference to the Rūm and their defeat (XXX, 1, reading *g͟hulibat al-Rūm*). See in general on these questions, P. Wittek, *Le sultan de Roum*, in *Ann. de l'Inst. de Philologie et d'Hist. Or. et Slaves, Bruxelles*, vi = *Mélanges Emile Boisacq*, ii (1938), 361-90; Savvides, *A note on the terms Rūm and Anatolia in Seljuk and early Ottoman times*, in *Byzantinotourkika meletēmata. Anatypōse arthrōn 1981-1990*, Athens 1991, no. X [171]-[178].

Bibliography (in addition to references given in the article): G.E. von Grunebaum, *Medieval Islam. A study in cultural orientation*, Chicago 1946, 22 ff., 294 ff.; L. Massignon, *Le mirage byzantin dans le miroir bagdadien d'il y a mille ans*, in *AIPHOS*, x = *Mélanges Henri Grégoire*, iii (1950), 429-48; G.M. Miles, *Byzantium and the Arabs: relations in Crete and the Aegean area*, in *Dumbarton Oaks Papers*, xviii (1964), 1-32. (C.E. Bosworth)

RŪM ĶALʿESI, Ḳalʿat al-Rūm, a fortress in mediaeval northern Syria, which lay on the right bank of the Euphrates river where it takes its great westernmost bend, hence to the north-north-west of Bīred̲j̲ik [*q.v.*]. Its site accordingly comes within the modern Turkish province (*il*) of Gaziantep.

According to Arnold Nöldeke's description, it is situated "on a steeply sloping tongue of rock, lying along the right bank of the Euphrates, which bars the direct road to the Euphrates from the west for its tributary the Merziman as it breaks through the edge of the plateau, so that it is forced to make a curve northwards around this tongue. The connection between this tongue of rock, some 1,300 feet long and about half as broad, and the plateau which rises above it is broken by a ditch made by man about 100 feet deep. The walls of the citadel with towers and salients follow the outlines of the rock along its edge at an average height of 150 feet above the level of the Euphrates, while the ridge extending along the middle of the longer axis rises 100 to 120 feet higher" (A. Nöldeke, in *Petermanns Mitteil.* [1920], 53-4, where the main road up to the citadel, the buildings, etc., are also described).

The unusual position of the fortress on a high cliff suggests that it corresponds to the tower of S͟hītamrat "hovering like a cloud in the sky" which S͟halmaneser III took in 855 B.C. (E. Honigmann, art. *Syria*, in Pauly-Wissowa, iv, A, cols. 1569, 1592).

It seems probable (following e.g. Marmier, B. Moritz, F. Cumont, R. Dussaud, etc.) that Rūm Ḳalʿesi should be identified with Urima, Armenian Uremna, but later called in that language Hṛomklay and similar names. Urima was an Armenian bishopric, as is recorded up to the time of Matthew of Edessa, and it is likely that this was the place which Syriac historians like Michael the Syrian and Barhebraeus call Ḳalʿa Rōmaytā and Byzantine historians Rhōmaiōn Koula.

In the early 12th century, Rūm Ḳalʿesi came within the Frankish County of Edessa [see al-ruhā]. The Jacobite metropolitan Abu 'l-Farad̲j̲ Basīl bar S͟hummāna of Edessa, who escaped to Samosata after the second devastation of the town in 1146 by the Turks had been previously imprisoned in Rūm Ḳalʿesi by Joscelyn de Courtenay. In 1148 the Armenian Catholicos Grigor III Pahlavuni moved his residence to "the fortress of the Romans" (Arm. Hṛomklay) at the demand of the Franks of the former County of Edessa (whose capital had been since 1145 at Tell Bās͟hir). The Armenian Catholicos resided there until 1293, although Rūm Ḳalʿesi also contained many Jacobite as well as Armenian Christians. Until the later 13th century, events in Rūm Ḳalʿesi impinged little on the affairs of the Islamic lands, although when the Emperor Frederick Barbarossa passed through

Anatolia in 585/1189, it is recorded by Abū Shāma that the Armenian Catholicos of Ḳalʿat al-Rūm (sc. Grigor IV) sent a letter to the Ayyūbid sultan Ṣalāḥ al-Dīn [*q.v.*], and another in the following year, asking for help (*K. al-Rawḍatayn*, in *Rec. Hist. Or. des Croisades. Historiens arabes*, iv, 435-6, 453-6).

In 1260 the Mongol Il-Khan Hülegü [*q.v.*] crossed the Euphrates by bridges of boats at Malaṭya, Ḳalʿat al-Rūm, Bīra and Ḳarḳīsiyāʾ (Barhebraeus, *Mukhtaṣar T. al-Duwal*, Beirut 1890, 486; idem, *Chronography*, ed. Bedjan, 509). Then in the reign of the Mamlūk sultan al-Manṣūr Ḳalāwūn, an Egyptian army of 9,000 horse and 4,000 foot under Baysarī as well as Syrian forces under Ḥusām al-Dīn of ʿAyntāb came to Rūm Ḳalʿesi and laid siege to the fortress 19 May 1280. The sultan demanded that the Catholicos should surrender the fortress and move with his monks to Jerusalem, or if he preferred, to Cilicia. When the Catholicos refused to do so, the Egyptians laid waste the country around the town which was inhabited by Armenians, on the next day forced their way over a wall only recently built into the town, and set it on fire. The whole population fled into the citadel. After the Egyptians had ravaged and plundered the country round for five days, they retired.

In the reign of al-Ashraf Khalīl they undertook a new expedition against Rūm Ḳalʿesi in 691/1292, in which the prince of Ḥamā, al-Malik al-Muẓaffar, took part with Abu 'l-Fidāʾ in his retinue (Abu 'l-Fidāʾ, *Annales muslemici*, ed. Reiske-Adler, v, 102 ff.). On Tuesday, 8 Djumādā II, the Egyptians appeared before the town and erected 20 pieces of siege artillery. It fell after a siege of 33 days. On 11 Radjab/29 June 1292, it was plundered and a massacre carried out among the garrison of Armenians and Mongols. Among the 1,200 prisoners, who were mostly taken to the sultan's arsenal on 28 June (al-Nuwayrī, *Nihāya*, ms. Paris, fols. 100-1 cited in Quatremère, *Hist. des Sult. Mamlouks*, ii/1, 141, n. 30), was the Armenian Catholicos (Ar. "*Khalīfat al-Masīḥ*, whom they call *Kāthāghīkūs*", cf. Yāḳūt, iv, 164), Stephanos IV of Rūm Ḳalʿesi, with his monks; he died a prisoner in Damascus (Barhebraeus, *Chronography*, 579). According to the inscription of ownership in a Syrian manuscript (B.L. ms. Syr. no. 295), it belonged to a certain Rabban Barṣawmā of Ḳalʿa Rōmaytā, high priest of Raʿbān, who in a note refers to the harsh imprisonment which he suffered from the Egyptians; Armenian verses on the fall of the fortress are preserved on a relic casket (Wright, *Catal. syr. mss. Brit. Mus.*, i, 231b, Carrière, *Inscription d'un reliquaire arménien*, in *Mélanges orientaux*, Paris 1883, 210, n. 1; Pronis, *Mem. dell' accad. di Torino*, xxxv [1884], 125-30). The inscription on the great gate of the citadel, which was restored by al-Ashraf Khalīl, speaks of him as a victor who among other feats had put the Armenians to flight, an allusion to the capture of Rūm Ḳalʿesi (van Berchem, in *JA* [May-June 1902], 456; the inscription published by Sobernheim, in *Isl.*, xv [1926], 176). The sultan sent boastful bulletins of victory to the cities of Syria in which he proclaimed the capture of this impregnable citadel as an unprecedented feat of arms and concluded with the words: "After the capture of this fortress, the road is open to us to conquer the whole of the East, Asia Minor and ʿIrāḳ so that with God's will we shall become owners of all the lands from the rising of the sun to its setting" (al-Nuwayrī, ms. Leiden, fol. 58, tr. in Weil, *Gesch. d. Chalifen*, iv, 183-4).

The fortress of Ḳalʿat al-Rūm was rebuilt on orders of the sultan by the *nāʾib* of Syria, Sandjar al-Shudjāʿī, and given the name of Ḳalʿat al-Muslimīn; another part of the town was left in ruins, however (Quatremère, *Hist. des Sultans Mamlouks*, ii/1, 139-40).

The successor of the imprisoned Armenian patriarch Stephanos, Grigor VII of Anavarza (1293-1307), took up his residence in Sīs in Cilicia, which henceforth was the seat of the Catholicos. Rūm Ḳalʿesi, in spite of its restoration as a frontier fortress (cf. also Abu 'l-Fidāʾ, ed. Reinaud, 226; al-Dimishḳī, ed. Mehren, 214), under the Mamlūks never seems to have recovered from the blow. In 775/1373-4, much damage was done by floods in Ḳalʿat al-Muslimīn as well as in Aleppo, al-Ruhāʾ, al-Bīra and Baghdād (al-Ḥasan b. Habīb, *Durrat al-aslāk fī dawlat al-atrāk*, in Weijers, *Orientalia*, ii, Amsterdam 1846, 435).

In the spring of the year 881-2/1477 the Mamlūk sultan Ḳāʾitbay made a tour of inspection as far as Ḳalʿat al-Muslimīn (described by Abu 'l-Baḳāʾ Ibn al-Djīʿān, ed. R.V. Lanzone, *Viaggio in Palestina e Soria di Kaid Ba*, Turin 1878; tr. R.L. Devonshire, in *Bulletin IFAO*, xx [Cairo 1921], 1-43). After the battle of Mardj Dābiḳ [*q.v.*], the fortress became Ottoman, and under Ottoman rule came under the *pashalïḳ* of Aleppo (Ḥādjdjī Khalīfa, *Djihān-numā*, 598).

Only a few remnants of the fortress now remain, as well as of an Armenian monastery and a mosque (plans of the fortress in Moltke and following him in Humann and Puchstein, *Reisen...*, 175, and in A. Nöldeke, in *Peterm. Mitt.* [1920], pl. 3, map: *Plan von R.K. in 1:2000*; photographs in F. Frech, in *Geogr. Zeitschr.*, xxii [1916], pl. 1; Cumont, *Études syriennes*, 170, fig. 54; from the north: Humann and Puchstein, *op. cit.*, 176, fig. 25; from the east with the Euphrates: A. Nöldeke, *op. cit.*, pl. 13).

Bibliography: Yāḳūt, *Muʿdjam*, iv, 164; Ṣafī al-Dīn, *Marāṣid al-iṭṭilāʿ*, ed. Juynboll, ii, 442; Abu 'l-Fidāʾ, ed. Reinaud, 226, 279; Dimashḳī, ed. Mehren, 206, 214; Ibn al-Shiḥna, *al-Durr al-muntakhab fī taʾrīkh mamlakat Ḥalab*, Beirut 1909, 157, 238-9; R. Pococke, *Description of the East*, London 1754, ii, 155-7; Saint-Martin, *Mémoires sur l'Arménie*, i, Paris 1818, 196; K. Ritter, *Erdkunde*, x, 461 ff., 931-42; Quatremère, *Histoire des Sultans Mamlouks de l'Egypte*, ii/1, Paris 1842, 209, n. 2; Th. Nöldeke, in *NGW Gött.* (1876), 12, n. 2; G. Le Strange, *Palestine under the Moslems*, London 1890, 42, 475-6; Humann and Puchstein, *Reisen in Kleinasien und Nordsyrien*, Berlin 1890, 175-9 with pl. 1, 1; Marmier, *La route de Samosate au Zeugma*, in *Société de Géographie de l'Est, Bulletin trimestriel* (Nancy 1890), 531-4; M. van Berchem, in *CIA*, i, 503, n. 1, 504, n. 1; B. Moritz, in *MSOS As.*, i (1898), 131 ff.; P. Rohrbach, in *Preuss. Jahrbücher*, civ (1901), ii, 471; Papken C.W. Güleserean, *Cowkʿ, Tlukʿ und Hïom-Glay, eine historisch-topographische Studie*, Vienna 1904, 61-88; *Hist. orient. des croisad. Docum. armén.*, i, p. cxx; K.J. Basmadjian, in *ROC*, xix (1914), 361 (Catholicoi of Rūm Ḳalʿesi); R. Hartmann, in *ZDMG*, lxx (1916), 32, n. 10, 33; F. Frech, in *Geogr. Zeitschr.*, xxii (1916), 5; F. Cumont, *Études syriennes*, Paris 1917, 167-71, 203, 247, 293, 329; A. Nöldeke, in *Petermanns Mitteilungen* (1920), 53-4; M. Gaudefroy-Demombynes, *La Syrie à l'époque des Mamelouks*, Paris 1923, 86; R. Dussaud, *Topographie historique de la Syrie*, Paris 1927, 450, n. 2; Cl. Cahen, *La Syrie du nord a l'époque des Croisades*, Paris 1940, 122 and index; M. Canard, *Histoire de la dynastie des H'amdanides*, 277.

(E. Honigmann-[C.E. Bosworth])

RŪM SALDJŪḲS [see saldjūḳs].

RŪMELİ, originally Rūm-ili, the territory of the Rūm [*q.v.*], the geographical name given to the Balkan peninsula by the Ottomans; also the name of the Ottoman province which included this region. The Muslims knew the Byzantines as *Rūm*, and the Eastern Roman Empire as *Bilād al-Rūm* or *Mamlakat al-Rūm*, hence once Anatolia came under Turkish-Islamic rule, the designation Rūm survived as a geographic name to designate Asia Minor. Some Western travellers of the 13th century, however, referred to Anatolia under Turkish rule as *Turquemenie* or *Turquie* and used the name *Romania* for the area under Byzantine rule. Subsequently, this expression came to designate the Balkan peninsula where Greek Orthodoxy predominated.

Ottoman Turks borrowed the name *Rūm-ili* from the Greek *Rhōmania* and began to use it, in contradistinction to *Anadolu*, to refer to the lands they conquered from the Byzantines beyond the sea. The name *Rūm* by itself, retained its original meaning and remained as a geographical name designating the area under Saldjūḳ rule in Asia Minor (see further, RŪM. 2).

During the time of the Emperor Justinianus, the northern borders of the Byzantine Empire were the Danube and Drava. Ottoman sultans from Bāyezīd I [*q.v.*] onwards considered the peninsula extending to the south of the Danube as their area of sovereignty. Murād II was clearly following this notion when he obtained the commitment from Hungarians not to cross the Danube in the treaty he made with them in 1444 (H. Inalcik, *Fatih devri*, i, Ankara 1954, 22).

The first settlement of the Anatolian Turks in the Balkans is related to the incident of ʿIzz al-Dīn Kaykāwūs of the Saldjūḳs fleeing and taking refuge in Byzantium in 662/1264. The emperor Michael VIII Palaeologus allocated the steppes of the Dobrudja for him to settle there with his men. Following this, a group of 30 to 40 Turcoman clans (*oba*) who supported him, crossed to the Dobrudja in the company of Sarî Ṣaltuḳ Baba (see P. Wittek, *Yazîjîoghlu ʿAlī on the Christian Turks of the Dobruja*, in *BSOAS*, xiv [1952], 639-68). Ibn Baṭṭūṭa mentions Babadagh town around the 1330s (tr. H.A.R. Gibb, ii, 449). In the second half of the century, first the khan of the Golden Horde, Berke, and then the powerful *Amīr* Noghay, directly interfered in Balkan affairs and took the Muslim Turks in the Dobrudja under their protection. Around this time, Saḳdjî (Isaḳdjî) on the lower Danube is described as a Muslim city [see DOBRUDJA] and cited as the headquarters of Noghay (Baybars, *Zubdat al-fikra*, ed. W. Tiesenhausen, Tkish tr. *Altın-Ordu devleti tarihine ait metinler*, Istanbul 1941, 221).

Noghay, who converted to Islam, appears to have come under the influence of Sarî Ṣaltuḳ. After the fall of Noghay, Tokhtu, the pagan khan of the Golden Horde, appointed his son Tuḳal Bugha in Saḳdjî. Moreover, the Bulgarians having killed Noghay's son, Čeke began to harrass the Turks of the Dobrudja. In this situation, some of the Dobrudja Turks returned to Anatolia in 1307-11 (see Wittek, *op. cit.*, 651) and those who remained converted to Christianity. Most probably these Turks, together with the Christian Comans or Ḳumans, were established in the despotate of Dobrudja under the rule of Balîḳ and his brother Dobrotić shortly before the year 1366 [see DOBRUDJA]. Initially, the centre of this despotate was Ḳalliaḳra, but at the time when the Ottoman Turks arrived it was Varna.

In the first half of the 14th century, Turcoman *amīrs* of Aydîn, Ṣarukhān and Karasî, having conquered western Anatolia, crossed the Aegean Sea with their fleets and made raids into the Balkans. The most celebrated hero of these raids was Ghāzī Umur Bey [*q.v.*] of the Aydîn-oghlu.

The first Ottoman conquests in the Balkans.

Due to Umur's death in May 1348, the Ottomans assumed the leading role in the Turkish operations in Rūmeli. In 1345 when the Serbian king Stephen Dushan died and his empire in the Balkans disintegrated, the Ottoman leader Orkhan [*q.v.*] became an ally of John Cantacuzenus and married his daughter Theodora. In the second civil war that erupted in the Byzantine Empire, the Ottomans took sides with Cantacuzenus while the Serbians and Bulgarians supported John V. A contingent of 10,000 men sent by Orkhan under the command of his son Süleymān Pasha routed the Serbian-Greek forces supporting John V. This victory, won in the autumn of 1352, is the turning-point that made it possible for the Ottomans to settle in Rūmeli. Rūmeli had already become a field of operations for the *ghāzīs* from Anatolia. The *ghāzī* groups which had organised themselves independently, had already started crossing into Rūmeli, taking advantage of the Byzantine civil war and the struggle between Byzantium, the Serbs and Bulgarians.

Cantacuzenus notes Süleymān's reluctance to evacuate the various places which he occupied in Rūmeli, but he only mentions Tsympe (Djimbi or Djinbi) among these. Ottoman chronicles mention Aya Shiline or Aya Shilonya, Odköklek and Eksamilye among the fortresses which Süleymān occupied in the period 1352-4. The places which Cantacuzenus tried to have him evacuate must be these fortresses. Thus the first settlement of the Ottomans took place in the isthmus of Gallipoli in 1352 and the conquest of Gallipoli followed two years later. It was one of the sons of Asen, the *Tekfūr* of Gallipoli, who assisted the Ottomans to cross over to Rūmeli and settle there. He converted to Islam and took the name Melik. With his co-operation, a ship was built in Lapseki and Aḳča-Burgos on the opposite shore was taken, after which 3,000 men crossed to Ḳozlu-Dere and took Bolayîr. On 2 March 1354, hit by a violent earthquake, the city walls of Gallipoli unexpectedly collapsed and the *Tekfūr* of the fortress fled by ship and Süleymān Pasha captured the city.

According to the details given by Cantacuzenus, at the time when he was trying to recover the Tsympe fortress from Süleymān by promising him 10,000 pieces of gold, through "Divine Providence" a severe earthquake ruined almost all of the cities in Thrace and the people ran to take refuge in the cities whose walls were not affected. Süleymān conquered these cities, as well as Gallipoli, and placed there Turks whom he had brought from Anatolia. Ottoman settlements in Rūmeli created great agitation and anxiety in Constantinople, and Cantacuzenus, who was held responsible for this, was compelled to abdicate the throne.

Süleymān made Gallipoli the headquarters for his subsequent raids. His conquests in Rūmeli included Migalḳara (Malḳara), Ipsala, Vize, Tekfūr Daghî, Seyyid Ḳawaghî, Bolayîr and Gelibolu [*q.v.*] itself.

The Ottoman expansion in the Balkans.

Following their settlements in the towns of the Gallipoli isthmus and Gallipoli itself in the period 1352-4, the Ottomans established military posts or *udj*s, oriented in three directions. The first *udj* was used as the base for the raids along the shore in the direction of Tekfūr Daghî, Čorlu and Constantinople; the second in the middle was for the raids in the direction of Malkara, Hayrabolu and Vize through Ḳoñru-Dagh (today Kuru Dağ); and the third *udj* became the base for the raids along the River Maritsa, in the irection of Ipsala and Edirne. This *udj* system was naintained throughout the Ottoman conquest of ūmeli, and as the conquest advanced, the *udj* ettlements were moved farther ahead in the three lirections. Due to Süleymān's death in 1357 and Orhan's old age, there appears to have been a retreat. 'arious places conquered in Süleymān Pasha's time vere lost. During this time, Ḥadjdjī Ilbeyi and wrenos Bey had been active in the left-hand *udj*.)ver the course of time, this *udj* was transferred to Ipala, and then to Gümüldjine, Serez and Kara Ferye, nd from there on, splitting into two branches, it noved to Tirhala and Üsküp. As for the right-hand *dj*, it was first transferred to Yanbolu, Ḳarinova and 'ravadi, where it split into two, one moving to Tirova and Nikebolu and the other to the Dobrudja. The middle *udj* first moved to Čirmen, then to Zagra nd Filibe and then split into two, with one branch hifting to Sofia and Nish, and the other to Köstendil nd Üsküp. Conquests made in these three directions, onstituted the right, left and middle *sandjaks* of ūmeli. In the middle branch, the *sandjaks*, first of dirne then of Sofya, became the centres of the *eylerbeyi* or governor of Rūmeli. Turkish immigraion and settlement followed these frontier zones, tarting with Süleymān Pasha. The Ottomans in ūmeli dispatched successively Turcoman or Yörük lans in the *udjs*. As these frontier settlements moved orward, the earlier frontier centres which were left ehind flourished over the course of time as Turkish owns. Specifically, pious and commercial stablishments created by endowments [see WAḲF] layed an essential role in the development of these arly frontier towns. Edirne, Filibe, Serez, Üsküp, ofya, Silistre, Tirhala, Yeñi Shehir and Manastir inially developed in this manner, adorned by the enlowments of the *udj beyis*, and subsequently became he main towns of Rūmeli, maintaining their ignificance until the present time.

onditions at the Ottoman conquest.

In their conquests the Ottomans, along with the rontier raids, used the policy of *istimālet* or conciliaion towards the subject peoples, treating them in such way so as to win them over to their side. As noted y ʿAshiḳ Pasha-zāde (ed. Atsız, 123) "They did not njure the infidel population, perhaps they even ranted favours to them. They captured only those eading men among them". So "the infidels of Djinbi ecame allies with these *ghāzīs*". The Ottomans aithfully followed this policy in the conquest of ūmeli, with the state trying to win over the peasant opulation especially. The feudal lords were either liminated, or, if they did not resist, were integrated nto the Ottoman military cadres. Even during the imes of Murād II and Meḥemmed II [*q.vv.*], we find hristian military families kept as Ottoman *sipāhīs* enoying *tīmārs* (see Inalcik, *Ottoman methods of conquest*, in *I*, ii [1954], 103-29). Likewise, peasant soldiers alled *voyniḳ* or *voynuḳ* whom we find in the areas once nder the empire of Stephen Dushan, were, under the)ttomans, kept in the military cadres of the new state. n the 15th century, under the same name, they eached significant numbers in Macedonia, Thessaly nd Albania. Similarly, the Martolos [*q.v.*] in the foresses along the Danube and the Christian nomads of he military group called Eflāḳ [*q.v.*] (Vlachs) were adnitted into the Ottoman military cadres under the ommand of their own overlords. This policy, coupled vith the protection of the Church's organisation, acilitated Ottoman expansion in the Balkans. This ame at a time when the Byzantine Empire, the Bulgarian Tsardom and Dushan's empire had already disintegrated. Western feudal practices started to take hold in the Balkans, and due to the weakening of a central power, feudalism began to spread. The local feudal lords, called *tekfūr* by the Ottomans, strove to strengthen their control over land and peasant labour in the countryside. When the Ottomans arrived, they first ended the local feudal structures by placing agricultural lands exclusively under state control, as *mīrī* [*q.v.*]. They systematically abolished the corvées and replaced them with a fixed tax called *čift resmi* [*q.v.*]. The landlords, who could not secure the support of the peasants against Ottoman invasion, sought the aid of the Latins and Hungarians invading the Balkans under a Crusader banner. The Latins and Hungarians, of Roman Catholic faith, considered the native Greek Orthodox population as schismatics and had been trying to convert them to Catholicism by force. The Ottomans, on the other hand, not only offered recognition and protection to the Orthodox Church but they granted to its priests tax exemptions or even *tīmārs*, in order to turn them into employees of the state (see *Sûret-i defter-i sancak-i Arvanid*, ed. Inalcik, Ankara 1954, 58, 73).

The settlement of the Turks in the Balkans.

Mass immigration and settlement occurred especially in the 14th century. Later on, Tīmūr's occupation of Anatolia gave rise to a big wave of migration from Anatolia to Rūmeli. At that point, Edirne became the capital of the empire. As a result of these migrations, Thrace, eastern Bulgaria, the river valley of the Maritsa and then the Dobrudja became thickly populated by Turks. The evidence of the Ottoman population and tax registers reveals conclusively that, in these regions in the 16th century, Turks formed a large part of the population. Although spontaneous migration, continuing from the time of Orkhan, was by no means less important, the state's policy of deportation was largely responsible for this result. A classification of the place names found in the 15th century surveys indicates that settlements were associated with nomadic Yörük groups such as the Ḳayi, Salurlu, Türkmen and Aḳčaḳoyunlu, or with sedentary or nomadic groups associated with a place name in Anatolia, such as, Ṣarukhānli, Mentesheli, Simawli, Ḥamīdli and Eflughanli, or with the followers of famous military leaders, such as Dāwūdbegli and Turakhanli, or with members of the Ottoman military organisations such as *doghandji*, *čawush*, *damghadji*, *müderris*, *ḳāḍī* and *sekbān*, or with a *zāwiye* [see ZĀWIYA] or pious endowment. It should also be pointed out that dervish convents played a crucial role in the formation of Turkish villages. Turkish immigrants generally formed independent villages with Turkish names and did not generally mix with the local Christian populations. Even in the towns, Christian neighbourhoods were always separate. In the 14th-15th centuries, Islamisation appears to have been quite sporadic, occuring mostly on the successive military frontier zones on the Via Egnatia, Maritsa valley and eastern Balkan passes. According to the *djizye* registers of 893-6/1487-91, only 255 cases of conversion were identified over three years. Levies of Christian boys [see DEWSHIRME] are not included in the figure. The use of the native language can be taken as an indication of Islamisation. Bosnian and Albanian Muslims and Pomaks constitute the largest of such groups. Those Muslim groups who spoke exclusively Turkish or were bilingual, with Turkish as the mother tongue, were definitely of Anatolian Turkish origin. Turks or

Tatars of the northern Black Sea steppe, Turks of the Deli-Orman region, Dobrudja and Varna, as well as those of the Maritsa Valley, were of this category while there were also Noghays [q.v.] in the Dobrudj and in Budjak [q.v.] or Moldavia.

Population of Rūmeli, Ottoman census of 1894

Province	Muslim	Greek	Armenian	Bulgarian	Jewish
Edirne	434,366	267,220	16,642	102,245	13,721
Manastîr	630,000	228,121	29	—	5,072
Yanya	235,948	286,294	—	—	3,677
Ishkodra	330,728	5,913	—	—	2,797 Catholic
Girit	74,150	175,000	500	—	200
Adalar	30,809	226,590	83	2	2,956
Čataldja	18,701	35,848	585	5,586	966
Selānik	463,000	277,000	1,257	223,000	37,206 (2,311 Catholic)
Kosova	419,390	29,393	—	274,826	1,706 (5,588 Latin)

Source: K. Karpat, *Ottoman population*, Madison 1985, 155.

Quite numerous records (*ifrādāt*) about farms in the newly-opened up agricultural lands indicate the substantial expansion of arable lands in Rūmeli in the 16th century. It was coupled with a significant increase in population. It is estimated that shortly before 1535, the population of Rūmeli had risen to five millions. The Turks introduced or spread cotton and rice cultivation into the Balkans. The establishment of a large centre like Istanbul, with an estimated population of 400,000, in the 16th century, provided a great market for Thrace and Bulgaria and encouraged all sorts of agricultural production. In the Ottoman period, too, there was an increase in mining activities and new mineral workings were exploited. In Novobrdo, Kratovo, Rudnik, Trepče and Zaplanina in Serbia, copper, lead, gold, iron and, especially, silver were being produced. Sidre-Kapsa in Macedonia was the most important silver production centre. Silver and lead were being produced at various places in Bosnia-Herzegovina. The most important iron production sites were Samakov in Bulgaria, and Vlasina and Rudnik in Serbia.

The administrative organisation of Rūmeli.

In Gelibolu, Süleymān Pasha, bearing the official title of commander-in-chief of the main forces of the state, was in practice the *Beylerbeyi*. Murād I (1362-89) with his *Lala*, Shāhīn, conquered Adrianople in 1361. When he ascended the throne he apppointed Shāhīn to the middle *udj* to conquer territories in the direction of Filibe. The first chef-lieu was Adrianople or Edirne [q.v.]. Thus Rūmeli emerged as a separate military-administrative region under the rule of a *Beylerbeyi*. The fact that the empire was divided by the straits and the Sea of Marmara necessitated the *de facto* division of the realm into two large administrative regions, Rūmeli and Anadolu. The *beylerbeylik* of Rūmeli, the first such governorate in the Ottoman Empire, maintained its special position even after other *beylerbeyliks* were formed [see EYĀLET].

In the 14th and 15th centuries, the governor of Rūmeli mostly resided in the empire's capital city. Like the viziers, he bore the title of *pasha*, and participated in the government deliberations in the *diwān-i humāyūn*. Because the *Beylerbeyi* of Rūmeli commanded the most important army of the state, composed of *timār*-holding *sipāhīs* of Rūmeli, the Grand Viziers Maḥmūd Pasha and Ibrāhīm Pasha both held the position of *Beylerbeyi* of Rūmeli at the same time.

The areas conquered in the 15th century were added to the territory of the *Beylerbeyi* of Rūmeli; not only the area to the south of the Danube, but als Kilia and Aḳ Ḳermān beyond the Danube wer assigned to it in 1484. In 1541, however, with th establishment of the governorate of Budin, th number of Ottoman *beylerbeyliks* in Europe increased Bosnia became a *beylerbeylik* in the same year.

In a list of 1475 (Iacopo de Promontorio de Campis, ed. F. Babinger, *Die Aufzeichnungen*, Munic 1957), the following seventeen *sandjaḳ beys* are cited i Rūmeli: 1. Istanbul; 2. Gallipoli; 3. Adrianople; 4 Nikebolu/Nigbolu; 5. Vidin; 6. Sofia; 7. Serbia (Laz ili); 8. Serbia (Despot-ili); 9. Vardar (Ewrenos oghullarî); 10. Üsküp; 11. Arnawut-ili (that c Iskender Bey); 12. Arnawut-ili (that of Araniti); 13 Bosna (belonging to the king); 14. Bosna (that c Stephen); 15. Arta, Zituni and Athens; 16. Mora; an 17. Manastîr. The *Beylerbeyi* of Rūmeli would rais about 22,000 men from these seventeen *sandjaḳs*. I addition, there were 8,000 *aḳîndjîs* (skirmishers o raiders) and 6,000 *ʿazebs* (foot soldiers).

In an Ottoman document from the early years c Süleymān I's reign, the *sandjaḳs* or *liwās* of Rūmeli ar listed according to the rank of the beys in charge, wit each name of the *sandjaḳ* followed by the salary (i *akčes*) of the *sandjaḳ beyi*:

1. Pasha; 2. Bosna, 739,000; 3. Mora, 606,000; 4 Semendire, 622,000; 5. Vidin, 580,000; 6. Hersek 560,000; 7. Silistre, 560,000; 8. Okhri, 535,000; 9 Awlonya, 535,000; 10. Iskenderiyye, 512,000; 11 Yanya, 515,000; 12. Gelibolu, 500,000; 13. Köstendil, 500,000; 14. Nikebolu, 457,000; 15. Sofia 430,000; 16. Inebakhtî, 400,000; 17. Tîrhala 372,000; 18. Aladja Ḥiṣār, 360,000; 19. Vulčetrin 350,000; 20. Kefe, 300,000; 21. Prizren, 263,000; 22 Ḳarlî, 250,000; 23. Aghrîboz, 250,000; 24. Čirmen 250,000; 25. Vize, 230,000; 26. İzvornik, 264,000 27. Florina, 200,000; 28. Ilbasan, 200,000; 29 Čingene (Gypsies), 190,000; 30. Midilli, 170,000; 31 Ḳaradagh (Montenegro), 100,000; 32. *Müsellemān-Ḳîrḳ Kilise*, 81,000; and 33. *Voynuḳ*, 52,000.

Among these, Čingene, *Müsellem* and *Voynuḳ* wer not territorial *sandjaḳs* located in a particular place Each one of these scattered groups was put under *sandjaḳ-beyi*, whose main duty was to be the commander of the *sipāhīs* in his *sandjaḳ*. In a list compile *ca.* 1534 (Topkapı Palace Archives, D. 9578, se *Belleten*, no. 78, 250, 258), we find all the *sandjaḳ* mentioned above except Sofya, Inebakhtî an Florina. The *sandjaḳ* of Selānik is added. In general Selānik was included in the sultan's *khāṣṣ* [q.v.] o given to the viziers as a retirement pension. In thi period, Sofia was included in the sultan's _k̲h̲āṣṣ_, or else assigned independently to the administration of a _subas̲h̲ī_. The _sand̲j̲aḳ_ belonging to the _Beylerbeyi_ during the early years of Süleymān I included the cities of Üsküp, Pirlipe, Manastīr and Kesriye and was spread over a wide region. Afterwards, these towns became the centres for _sand̲j̲aḳ beyis_.

In the list given by ʿAynī ʿAlī shortly before 1018/1609 (_Ḳawānīn-i Āl-i ʿOt̲h̲mān_, published in _Taṣwīr-i Efkār_ [Istanbul 1280] 11-13), Sofya and Manastīr were included under the Pas̲h̲a _sand̲j̲aḳ_. This list includes additionally the _sand̲j̲aḳ_s of Selānik, Üsküp, Duḳagin, Ḳīrḳ Kilise and Aḳ Ḳermān (together with Bender). On the other hand, before 1609, some _sand̲j̲aḳ_s of Rūmeli were assigned to the newly-formed provinces of D̲j̲ezāʾir-i Baḥr-i Sefīd, Kefe and Bosna. _Sand̲j̲aḳ_s assigned to the D̲j̲ezāʾir-i Baḥr-i Sefīd were Gelibolu, Ag̲h̲rīboz, Inebak̲h̲tī, Ḳarlī ili and Midilli. Those assigned to the province of Bosna were Kilis, Hersek, Pojega, Izvornik, Začana (Začasna), Rahovid̲j̲a and Ḳīrḳa. The province of D̲j̲ezāʾir-i Baḥr-i Sefīd was created as a _beylerbeylik_ for Barbarossa K̲h̲ayr al-Dīn Pas̲h̲a [_q.v._], appointed grand admiral of the empire or _ḳapudan-i deryā_ in 1533 [see EYĀLET]. The _sand̲j̲aḳ_s of Silistre, Nikebolu/Nigbolu, Čirmen, Vize, Ḳīrḳ Kilise, Bender and Aḳ Ḳermān from Rūmeli were added to the province of Özi or Silistre. According to a _ruʾūs defteri_, official register of appointments of governors, written _ca._ 1644, the _sand̲j̲aḳ_s of Rūmeli were: 1. Köstendil, 2. Tīrhala, 3. Prizren, 4. Yanya, 5. Delvine, 6. Vulčetrin, 7. Üsküp, 8. Elbasan, 9. Awlonya, 10. Dukagin, 11. Iskenderiyye, 12. Ok̲h̲ri, 13. Alad̲j̲aḥiṣār, 14. Selānik, and 15. _sand̲j̲aḳ_ of the Voynuḳs. In the 18th century, Morea was separated from the _eyālet_ of Rūmeli to become an independent _eyālet_ under a _muḥaṣṣil_ [_q.v._].

During the period of the _Tanẓīmāt_ [_q.v._], in the 19th century, administrative divisions of Rūmeli underwent numerous changes, and smaller provinces were formed. Shortly before 1263/1847, the new _eyālet_s of Üsküp, Bosna, Yanya and Selānik were formed and the main _eyālet_ of Rūmeli included only the three _sand̲j̲aḳ_s of Iskenderiyye, Ok̲h̲ri and Kesriye (_Sāl-nāme_ of 1263/1847). In 1862, the first _wilāyet_ of Rūmeli was composed of the _liwā_s of Kesriye, Ok̲h̲ri and Is̲h̲ḳodra, with Manastīr as the centre of the _wilāyet_ (_Sāl-nāme_ of 1278/1862). Following the formation of the _wilāyet_ of Ṭuna in 1280/1864 with the _sand̲j̲aḳ_s of Rusčuk, Tulča, Vidin, Sofya, Tırnova, Nis̲h̲ and Varna, new _wilāyet_s were formed one after another, namely Bosna, Is̲h̲ḳodra, Yanya, Selānik and Edirne, thereby reducing Rūmeli to a mere geographical name. The new _wilāyet_ of Selānik included Manastīr, Serez, Drama and Üsküp. After Bulgaria seceded in 1312/1894, Rūmeli was divided into the _wilāyet_s of Edirne, Selānik, Ḳosova, Yanya, Is̲h̲ḳodra and Manastīr (_Sāl-name_ of 1312/1895).

Bibliography: N.V. Michoff, _Sources bibliographiques sur l'histoire de la Turquie et de la Bulgarie_, i-iv, Sofia 1914-34; idem, _Population de la Turquie et de la Bulgarie_, i-ii, 1915-24; L. Savadjian, _Bibliographie Balkanique_, Paris 1931; A. Boué, _La Turquie d'Europe_, i-iv, Paris 1840; J. Cvijić, _La Péninsule balkanique_, Paris 1918; Ph. Kanitz, _Donau-Bulgarien und der Balkan_, Leipzig 1875-9; G. Stadtmüller, _Geschichte Südosteuropas_, Munich 1950; C. Jireček, _Staat und Gesellschaft im mittelalterlichen Serbien_, Vienna 1912; idem, _Die Herrstrasse von Belgrad nach Constantinopel und die Balkanpässe_, Prague 1877; N. Jorga, _Une vingtaine de voyageurs dans l'Orient européen_, Paris 1928; Ö.L. Barkan, _XV. ve XVI ıncı asırlarda Osmanlı_

imparatorluğunda zirâi ekonominin hukuki ve mali esasları. _Kanunlar_, i, Istanbul 1943; Kātib Čelebi, _D̲j̲ihānnümā_, tr. J. von Hämmer, _Rumeli und Bosna_, Vienna 1812; T. Gökbilgin, _Kanunî Sultan Süleyman devri başlarında Rumeli eyâleti, livâları, şehir ve kasabaları_, in _Belleten_, xx, 247-86; _Kanun i Kanunnâme_ (_Zakonski Spomenici_, Ser. i/1, Orientalni Institut u Sarajevu, Sarajevo 1957, 1); H. Šabanović, _Bosanski Pašaluk_, Sarajevo 1959; Ewliyā Čelebi, _Seyāhat-nāme_, Istanbul 1898-1940; F.W. Hasluck, _Christianity and Islam under the Sultans_, Oxford 1929; C.H. Pouqueville, _Voyage dans la Grèce_, Paris 1820-1; Fr. Taeschner, _Die geographische Literatur der Osmanen_, in _ZDMG_, lxxvii (1923), 31-80; H. İnalcık, _Tanzimat ve Bulgar meselesi_, Ankara 1943; idem, _The Ottoman Turks and the Crusades_, in K.M. Setton (general ed.), _A history of the Crusades_, vi, ed. P. Zacour and H. Hazard, Madison 1989; idem (ed.), _Hicrî 835 Tarihli Defter-i Sancak-i Arvanid_, Ankara 1954; idem, _The Middle East and the Balkans under the Ottoman Empire_, in _Essays on economy and society_, Indiana University Turkish Studies, Bloomington 1993; idem _The Ottoman decline and its effects upon the Reaya_, in H. Birnbaum and S. Vryonis, eds., _Aspects of the Balkans: continuity and change_, The Hague 1972; N. Todorov, _The Balkan town, 1400-1900_, Seattle 1983; B. Şimşir, _Rumeli'de Türk göçleri_, Ankara 1989; B. McGowan, _Economic life in the Ottoman Empire_, Cambridge 1982; H. Kaleshi and H.-J. Kornrumpf, _Das Wilajet Prizren_, in _Südostforschungen_, xxvii (1967), 176-238; ʿAynī ʿAlī, _Ḳawānīn-i Āl-i ʿOt̲h̲mān_, Istanbul 1280/1872, 11-13; Ḳoči Bey, _Risāle_, ed. A.K. Aḳsüt; _Kemankeş Kara Mustafa Paşa lâyihası_, ed. F.R. Unat, in _TV_, vi, 462; Ö.L. Barkan, _Osmanlı imparatorluğunda iskân ve sürgünler_, in _IÜIFM_, xv, 209-37, map; idem, _894 (1488-1489) yılı cizye tahsilâtına ait muhasebe bilançoları_, in _Belgeler_, i, 1-117; R. Anhegger, _Beiträge zur Geschichte des Bergbaus im Osmanischen Reich_, Istanbul 1943; journals on the Balkans = _Etudes Balkaniques_, Sofia 1964-; _Balkan Studies_, Salonica 1959-; _Balkania_, Belgrade 1980; _Güney-doğu Avrupa Araştırmaları Dergisi_, Istanbul 1971-; F. Adanır, _Tradition and rural change in South-Eastern Europe during Ottoman rule_, in Chirot (ed.), _The origins of backwardness in Eastern Europe_, Berkeley 1989, 117-76; _Balkanlar: Ortadoğu ve Balkan incelemeleri vakfı_, Istanbul 1993; B. Jelavitch, _History of the Balkans_, Cambridge 1991; E. Hösch, _Geschichte der Balkanländer von der Frühzeit bis zur Gegenwart_, Munich 1988; O. Sander, _Balkan gelişmeleri ve Türkiye_, Ankara 1969; J.R. Lampe and M.R. Jackson, _Balkan economic history, 1550-1950_, Bloomington 1982; _Südosteuropa Bibliographie_, publ. Südostinstitut, Munich 1982. (H. İNALCIK)

RŪMELI ḤIṢĀRĪ, a fortress and village at the narrowest part of the Bosphorus which has at this point its strongest current (called Şeytan akıntısı). The castle served, together with Anadolu Ḥiṣārī [_q.v._], to control the maritime passage between the Euxine (Black Sea) and the Propontis (Sea of Marmara). In Ottoman sources it is also called Bog̲h̲azkesen and Rūmeli Orta Ḥiṣārī ḳalʿesi. Two existing Byzantine towers were taken in 1452 by Meḥemmed II and remodelled and enlarged in three months (oldest Ottoman inscription of Istanbul). The castle was completed in Rabīʿ II 856/June-July 1452, being the result of a division of labour between the sultan and his leading commanders (Sarud̲j̲a, K̲h̲alīl, Zag̲h̲anos), extensively described by Byzantine and Ottoman contemporaries. Only the Donjon of Coucy (Aisne) exceeded the three towers in size at this period. At the barbican (_ḥiṣār-pečče_), 18-20 guns were installed. Rūmeli Ḥiṣārī served as a prison and as a check-point for customs (see ISTANBUL, Plate VII; ʿOTHMĀNLĪ. v. ARCHITECTURE, Plate VI).

The village was already in Ewliyā's time a summer resort, frequented by members of the Ottoman ruling class (e.g. Köprülü-zāde ʿĀṣîm and Mekkī-zāde), who owned waterfront palaces (*yalî*). Rūmeli Ḥiṣārī preserved its predominantly Muslim character, with more than a dozen Friday mosques and *masdjids*, until the early 19th century. There were prominent dervish convents. The *sheykh* of the Bektāshī *tekke* of Shehīdler above the castle was an important figure in the Young Turk period. In 1863 Robert College, the forerunner of the modern Boğaziçi Üniversitesi, was opened by the American Presbyterian Christoph Rheinlander Robert. There was a small Armenian quarter in the vicinity of Surp Santukht (late 18th century).

Bibliography: Ewliyā Čelebi, *Seyāḥat-nāme*, 453; Ḥuseyin Aywānsarāyī, *Ḥadīḳat ul-djawāmiʿ*, ii, Meḥmed Rāʾif, *Mirʾat-i Istanbul*, 270-8; J. von Hammer, *Constantinopolis und der Bosporos*, 1822, ii, 220-7, G. Goodwin, *A history of Ottoman architecture*, London 1971; W. Müller-Wiener, *Bildlexikon zur Topographie Istanbuls*, Tübingen 1977, 335-7 (with further sources and literature); P. Tuğlacı, *İstanbul Ermeni kiliseleri/Armenian churches of Istanbul*, i, Istanbul 1991, 180-2. (K. KREISER)

RŪMĪ, a designation for the Turks from al-Rūm [*q.v.*], which was once under the Eastern Roman Empire. The name *Rūmī* was widespread in all eastern Islamic countries, including the Arab lands, Persia, Central Asia and Indonesia, from the 9th/15th century onwards. The Ottomans restricted the name *Rūm* to the provinces in the Amasya and Sivas areas. The *Rūmīs* were appreciated particularly for their tactical skills and for skills in the making of firearms. *Rūmī* mercenaries were employed by the Mamlūk sultans, the rulers of Arabia, ʿIrāḳ, and, thereafter, by the Indian and Indonesian rulers (J. Aubin, *Mare Luso-Indicum*, ii, 175-9).

While employment opportunities with high salaries attracted a great number of individual Anatolian soldiers, who had once been in the service of the Turcoman rulers, the Ottoman sultans also gave permission to friendly rulers to enlist volunteers from their territory. Such *Rūmī* mercenary groups equipped with muskets played in those countries a prominent part in the struggle against the Portuguese from the first decade of the 16th century. The Mamlūks and even local Arab chiefs in lower ʿIrāḳ took them into their service by the 1520s. *Rūmīs* who were sent by the Mamluk sultan to Yemen became a dominant military group in the internal power-struggle there until the Ottomans finally established their own firm control in the land *ca.* 1539. Already in 1513, Afonso de Albuquerque wrote to the king of Portugal that, unless *Rūmīs* were eliminated, there would be no security for the Portuguese in the Indian Ocean.

In Persia, *ustād-i Rūmīs*, Ottoman experts, founded guns in the *destūr-i Rūmī*, Ottoman style, for the first Ṣafawid rulers. In India, Bābur [*q.v.*] had in his service two *Rūmī* founders who founded guns and showed him how to use them tactically. In 1538 Ottoman soldiers from Süleymān Pasha's [*q.v.*] army entered the service of the sultan of Gudjarāt, who promised a salary ten times higher than that under the Ottomans. In 1567 two large ships carrying 500 Turks including gun-founders, gunners and engineers to build ships and fortresses, reached Atjeh [*q.v.*].

Not only Turkish soldiers, but also merchants known as *Rūmīs*, appeared on the western coasts of the Indian subcontinent and in Indonesia in the 10th/16th century, forming quite sizeable colonies in Diù, Calicut and Bantam. Joining earlier Arab traders, *Rūmīs* obtained a trading post at Pasai [*q.v.*] in Sumatra as early as 1540.

The term *Rūmī* also indicated a special motif in the form of a leaf or stylised animal designs in Ottoman art and in architectural ornamentation. For the *Rūmī* calendar, see TAʾRĪKH.

Bibliography: H. İnalcik (ed.), *An economic and social history of the Ottoman Empire*, Cambridge 1994. (HALIL İNALCIK)

RŪMIYA (wrongly Rūmiyya, cf. Yāḳūt, ii, 866-7), the name given to the city of Rome by the Arab geographers, with the exception of the western ones (al-Bakrī, al-Idrīsī and al-Ḥimyarī), who use the form Rūma, as also Ibn Khaldūn (only Ibn Rusta writes Rūmiyya, treating it as if it were a *nisba*).

Rome's fame, both as the seat of power of the Rūm [*q.v.*] and then as the centre of Christianity, could not fail to be noted by the mediaeval Arabs. In fact, the solicitude, if not critical sense, which they displayed in grasping at every item of information about the city, ended up in a host of pieces of information which is in striking contrast to their almost total ignorance, up to the time of al-Idrīsī, with regard to Christian Western Europe. Unfortunately, this involved only indirect information, with the unique exception of the narrative (in Ibn Rusta, 129-30) of the mysterious Hārūn b. Yaḥyā, who fell into the hands of the Byzantines and who visited Rome towards the end of the 9th century A.D. (furthermore, it is known that an event as sensational as the sacking of the Roman basilicas, in 846 A.D., has left no trace whatever in the Arabic texts). Again, the pieces of information are drawn from anonymous sources and, going beyond this fiction, from the domain of the imaginary and legendary, such as the largely factitious picture of mediaeval Rome fixed in the minds of the Arabs. It is as if they had seen its landscape, urban and rural, through the eyes of someone else, in other words, through the intermediacy of the Greco-Byzantine and Syriac tradition, as the analysis of texts (cf. I. Guidi, in *Bibl.*) has shown.

This procedure is indeed what is responsible, either through an ambiguous geographical representation, which goes back rather to Constantinople (presence of the sea on three sides, the golden gate and the gate "of the king", the situation of the great market); or through this fairy-like enchantment, marked by an unparalleled display of gold and precious stones (e.g. in regard to the altar of the Lateran church); or, finally, through exaggerated figures evoking a setting in which thousands of churches are crammed (with 120,000 bells...), as many as 23,000 monasteries, 22,000 markets and 660,000 baths! It should nevertheless be remarked that this attitude does not seem to be shared by all the authors. In so far as one can identify the different traditions, one may conclude that only Ibn Khurradādhbih [*q.v.*], on the one hand, followed by al-Idrīsī, al-ʿUmarī and (in part) Ibn Rusta, and on the other hand, Yāḳūt and al-Ḳazwīnī [*q.vv.*], following the version of Ibn al-Faḳīh (absent from the abridgment, which alone has survived), devote a considerable amount of space to the marvellous. In this context, one should particularly note the mention of the columns or talismanic statues, of which Yāḳūt and al-Ḳazwīnī preserve the most complete memory, connected with the legend of the *Salvatio Romae*, or indeed with that of the birds who bring olives to ensure a supply of oil for the lamps, or yet again, with the belief in the apotropaic power of certain images.

The edition which has recently appeared (see *Bibl.*)

of the *Masālik* of al-Bakrī [see ABŪ ʿUBAYD AL-BAKRĪ], comes opportunely to allow us to verify, at the same time as demonstrating the dependence of the *Rawḍ* of al-Ḥimyarī [see IBN ʿABD AL-MUNʿIM AL-ḤIMYARĪ], the existence, in regard to Rome, of a clearly different tradition, one in which an interest, which may be called "historical" in the wider sense, is dominant.

Instead of a topography with fabulous features, such as the enceinte with two walls separated by a paved-over river (or in some way covered over) with copper flags, side-by-side with a canal having the same paving with flags and running through the market, there appears here, within a natural setting which is much more realistic, nothing more than the name of the Tiber, at the side of that of Octavius (with the reminiscence of the age of bronze) and, on the other hand, that of Constantine. The sumptuous description of churches found elsewhere is here likewise reduced to that of St. Peter, not without some realistic details. A sequel to this absence, or near-absence, of the monumental and the fantastic, is the attention here to the human beings and to their nature (the Romans are the most cowardly people in the world!) and to their customs. If al-ʿUmarī himself knows a lot about the Pope, and if others (Yāḳūt, Ibn Rusta, etc.) underline the role, both spiritual and cultural (*sic*) of Rome, it is al-Bakrī and al-Ḥimyarī above all—and more than anyone else—who stop at the social and religious life of Rome's inhabitants, shown in a number of remarks: on Sunday and the celebration of the Eucharist, on monogamy and adultery, the laws of hereditary succession and fasting, oaths and the sacred texts. One would like to know the source from which they derived all this information. It is regrettable that, at the present stage of our knowledge, all one can say is to exclude any identification of this information with the *History* of Orosius (ed. Badawī, Beirut 1982), the sole work of Latin literature which was translated into Arabic.

Bibliography: I. Guidi, *La descrizione di Roma nei geografi arabi*, in *Archivio della Società Romana di Storia Patria*, i (1878), 173-218; M. Nallino, *Un'inèdita descrizione araba di Roma*, in *AIUON*, N.S. xiv (1964), 295-309, with references, to which should be added Abū ʿUbayd al-Bakrī, *K. al-Masālik wa 'l-mamālik*, ed. A.P. Van Leeuwen and A. Ferré, Tunis 1993; M. Nallino, *"Mirabilia" di Roma negli antichi geografi arabi*, in *Studi in onore di Italo Siciliano*, Florence 1966, 875-93. (R. TRAINI)

RŪMLI LEWEND [see LEWEND].

AL-**RUMMA** or RUMA, WĀDĪ, the main regional drainage system of north Arabia, running over 1,000 km/620 miles from the Ḥarrat Khaybar in the Ḥidjāz, to the north-east of Medina through al-Ḳaṣīm to run out in southern al-ʿIrāḳ. Al-Hamdānī (ed. Müller, i, 144) mentions Baṭn al-Rumma flowing between two mountain areas in the neighbourhood of the lands of the tribe of al-Ṭayyiʾ and the fertile land of al-Ḳaṣīm to the south. He also mentions (i, 145) Wādī Sarīr as being the name of the lower part of Wādī al-Rumma, in an area associated with the Banū ʿĀmir of Tamīm. Much the same is reported by Yāḳūt (i, 75) citing al-Aṣmaʿī: he also declares that the Wādī al-Rumma flows betweeen two mountains, the black Abān and the white Abān. Musil (*Northern Neǧd*, New York 1928, 224, also 130) knew of the two Abān mountains between which the Wādī al-Rumma ran its course. These distinctive ranges of rocky hills lie in western al-Ḳaṣīm beside the modern road to Medina under the names Abān al-Asmar (on the north side of the al-Rumma channel) and Abān al-Aḥmar (on the south bank) (R.A. Bramkamp, L.F. Ramirez, G.F. Brown and A.E. Pocock, *Geology of the Wadi ar Rimah quadrangle, Kingdom of Saudi Arabia*, in *Miscellaneous geologic investigations*, Map 1-206 A [1963/1383]).

Al-Bakrī, writing in the 5th/11th century, refers to it as a great valley (*ḳāʿ*) in Nadj into which a number of other wādīs flow (*Muʿdjam mā istaʿdjam*, ed. Wüstenfeld, Göttingen and Paris 1877, 410). Yāḳūt (ii, 635-6) refers to the Wādī as a valley that runs through north Arabia under a series of names. It was known as al-Rumma in the land of the Ghaṭafān, after which it was Baṭn al-Rumma on the road between Fayd [*q.v.* in Suppl.] (a Ḥadjdj halt on the Darb Zubayda) and Medina. The same watercourse then became Wādī 'l-Hādjir and in the lands of the Ṭayyiʾ it was known as Ḥāʾil. Among the Banū Taghlib the Wādī was called Suwā, while in the Banū Kalb land it was called Ḳurāḳir. It ran out at al-Nīl near al-Kūfa.

The great length of the Wādī led to the local changes of name recorded by al-Hamdānī and Yāḳūt and the same phenomenon is noted by modern authorities. From its head in the Ḥarrat Khaybar to al-Ḳaṣīm, it is called Wādī Rīsha (J.G. Lorimer, *Gazetteer of the Persian Gulf, ʾOmān and Central Arabia*, Calcutta 1908, IIA, 281-2, 597-8, IIB, 1591, 1601-2). By contrast, Musil, *op. cit.*, 220, refers to it merely as "al-Wādī" in al-Ḳasīm. Modern mapping describes the entire course in this area as Wādī al-Rumma (or al-Rimah) from its head in the Ḥarrat Khaybar as far as the point at which it reaches the Dahnāʾ [*q.v.*] sands to the north-east of al-Ḳaṣīm, and which form a great natural barrier. In the Dahnāʾ, the Rumma is known as Wādī al-Mustāwī (H.R.P. Dickson, *Kuwait and her neighbours*, London 1956, repr. 1968, 53), and beyond the Dahnāʾ it becomes Wādī al-Baṭn, whose course eventually marks Kuwait's western border with ʿIrāḳ. Wādī al-Baṭn runs out at the Ratk ridge towards Ḥawr al-Ḥammar, west of al-Basṛa.

The western reaches of the Wādī al-Rumma were first explored by C.M. Doughty (*Travels in Arabia Deserta*, Cambridge 1888, ii, 329, 391-3 and *passim*), who describes its shallowness, its salinity in al-Ḳaṣīm, and the sands blocking it to the east. C. Huber (*Journal d'un Voyage en Arabie, 1883-1884*, Paris 1891, ll. 13) also mapped its course around ʿUnayza. Musil, *op. cit.*, 38-9 describes the fertility of the alluvium that ran against the Dahnāʾ sands as they form a dam across the Wādī. In parts of al-Ḳaṣīm, the Wādī is virtually invisible and this is noted by several travellers. H.St.J. Philby (*Arabia of the Wahhabis*, London 1928, repr. 1977, 177 ff.) described wells and springs in the Wādī al-Rumma channel near to ʿUnayza, and the practice of establishing palm groves that tapped the brackish water beneath the saline *sabkha*. Doughty says that the Wādī had not flowed for some 40 years in his day, but Philby (*op. cit.*, 257) speaks of regular floods in the west of al-Ḳaṣīm before the early 20th century. These would transform the depression known as Zuḳaybiyya into a lake. In 1982, the present writer saw the entire country west of Uḳlat al-Ṣuḳūr on the western course of the Wādī al-Rumma turned by rainfall into a vast shallow lake which fed into the Rumma.

In the 19th century, the lower course, the Wādī al-Baṭn, provided a route from Kuwait into al-Ḳaṣīm (Doughty, ii, 392; D.G. Hogarth, *The penetration of Arabia*, repr. Beirut 1966, 277; Dickson, 60). Here there were wells, notably at Ḥafar and at Riḳāʿī, but in this lower stretch of its course, beyond the Dahnāʾ, the Wādī normally does not flow. By 1936 Ḥafar had a Saudi fortress, and today Ḥafar al-Baṭn has grown into a major Saudi military base.

Bibliography (in addition to references in the text): R.A. Bramkamp and L.F. Ramirez, *Geology of the Wadi al Batin quadrangle, Kingdom of Saudi Arabia*, in *Miscellaneous geologic investigations*, Map 1-203 A (1960/1379); Bramkamp and Ramirez, Geographic map of the Northern *Tuwayq quadrangle, Kingdom of Saudi Arabia*, in *Miscellaneous geologic investigations*, Map 1-207 B (1957/1377); G.F. Brown, N. Layne, G.H. Goudarzi, and W.H. Maclean, *Geology of the Northeastern Hijaz, quadrangle, Kingdom of Saudi Arabia*, in *Miscellaneous geologic investigations*, Map 1-205 A (1963/1383); G.A. Wallin, *Narrative of a journey from Cairo to Medina and Mecca, by Suez, Araba, Tawila, al-Jauf, Jubbe, Hail, and Nejd, in 1845*, in *JRGS*, xxiv (1854), 169-70; J.G. Wetzstein, *Nordarabien und die syrische Wüste nach den Angaben der Eingeboren*, in *Zeitschr. für allg. Erdkunde*, xviii, 408-98. (G.R.D. KING)

AL-**RUMMĀNĪ**, ABU 'L-ḤASAN ʿALĪ B. ʿĪSĀ b. ʿAlī b. ʿAbd Allāh (296-384/909-94). By profession a *warrāḳ* [*q.v.*], al-Rummānī (also known as al-Iḵẖsẖīdī, see below) was a seminal thinker in the Arab linguistic and literary sciences in 4th/10th century Baḡẖdād. He was born in Baḡẖdād and died there, having written, during the course of a long and active life, in excess of one hundred works on a wide but coherent range of topics (for a list of these works, see Mubārak, *Al-Rummānī*, 37-103). Much of his literary output was taken by dictation, and included works on grammar (*naḥw*), lexicography (*luḡẖa*), rhetoric (*balāḡẖa*), the Ḳurʾānic sciences (ʿ*ulūm al-Ḳurʾān*), and philosophical theology (*kalām*). Although he is widely quoted in later sources, only a handful of his works, or fragments thereof, appears to have survived. They are:

(1) *Ḳ al-Alfāẓ al-mutarādifa al-mutaḳāribat al-maʿnā* (ed. Fatḥ Allāh Ṣāliḥ ʿAlī al-Miṣrī, al-Mansūra 1407-1987). A short lexical work, it is divided into 142 *fuṣūl*, each *faṣl* containing a set of words (or phrases) that are synonymous. The work is representative of a technical genre common during this period.

(2) *K. al-Djāmiʿ fī ʿilm* (or *tafsīr*) *al-Ḳurʾān*. A work on Kurʾānic philology, it appears originally to have been very large, only parts of which have survived (as yet unedited). They are: Part 7—Paris, B.N. 6523; Part 10—Tashkent, Akademiya 3137; Part 12—Jerusalem, Masdjid al-Aḳṣā 29 (= Cairo, Maʿhad al-Makẖṭūṭāt, Microfilm Collection 18 (see *GAS*, viii, 113, and, for a discussion of the work, accompanied by citation of select passages, Mubārak, *Al-Rummānī*, 83-8).

(3) *K. al-Ḥudūd fī 'l-naḥw* (in *Rasāʾil fī 'l-naḥw wa 'l-luḡẖa*) ed. Muṣṭafā Djawād and Yaʿḳūb Maskūnī, *Silsilat kutub al-turāt̲ẖ̲*, 11, Baḡẖdād 1388/1989, 37-50). A short lexical work, it constitutes a small dictionary of 88 technical terms that commonly occur in Arab[ic] grammatical theory of the period.

(4) *K. Maʿāni 'l-ḥurūf* (ed. ʿAbd al-Fattāḥ Ismāʿīl S̲ẖ̲aldjī, Djudda 1404/1984). This is a systematic treatise on the categorical nature and function of the grammatical particles in Arabic. The work is representative of a technical genre that evolved, during this period, amidst debates over the nature of speech and the status of grammar in relation to logic.

(5) *K. Manāzil al-ḥurūf* (in *Rasāʾil fī 'l-naḥw wa 'l-luḡẖa*, 51-79). Although handed down as a separate work, it, in effect, constitutes, with some slight variation; the final 23 *abwāb* of the *K. Maʿāni 'l-ḥurūf*.

(6) *al-Nukat fī iʿdjāz al-Ḳurʾān* (in *T̲ẖ̲alāt̲ẖ̲ rasāʾil fī iʿdjāz al-Ḳurʾān*, ed. Muḥammad Kẖalafallāh and Muḥammad Zaghlūl Salām, *Dẖakẖāʾir al-ʿArab*, 18, Cairo 1955[1], 1988[2], 75-133[1] [= 89-104[2]]). This work

is a *risāla* that treats the subject of the uniqueness or inimitability of the Ḳurʾān. In structure, it constitutes a compilation of short paragraphs illustrating the author's teaching, but without any arguments (or counter-arguments), and with, sometimes, little contextual continuity. Without abandoning the traditional theological arguments that had been put forth on behalf of the Ḳurʾān's inimitability, al-Rummānī attempts to put the entire issue on firmer ground by logically subordinating the theological arguments to the notion of the Ḳurʾān's incomparable style, which rests squarely upon the quality of its eloquence (*balāḡẖa*). According to al-Rummānī, *balāḡẖa* is divisible into the following ten categories: (i) terseness (*īdjāz*), (ii) comparison (*tas̲ẖ̲bīh*), (iii) metaphor (*istiʿāra*), (iv) euphony (*talāʾum*), (v) end-rhymes [of the Ḳurʾānic verses] (*fawāṣil*), (vi) paronomasia (*tadjānus*), (vii) transformation of a root [into various awzān] (*taṣrīf*), (viii) implication (*taḍmīn*), (ix) emphasis (*mubālaḡẖa*), and (x) distinctiveness [of expression] (*ḥusn al-bayān*).

(7) The *S̲ẖ̲arḥ Kitāb Sībawayh*. This appears to have been a rather large work, only portions of which survive, for the most part unedited (see, however, E. Ambros (ed. and tr.), *Sieben Kapitel des S̲ẖ̲arḥ Kitāb Sībawaihi von ar-Rummānī in Edition und Übersetzung*, Vienna 1979; *Ḳism al-ṣarf, al-djuzʾ al-awwal*, ed. R.A. al-Damīrī, Cairo 1408/1988. They are: Istanbul Feyzullah Efendi 1984-7 (= vols. ii-v of the *S̲ẖ̲arḥ*); and Vienna, Akademie 2442 (= Part 3 of the *S̲ẖ̲arḥ*). This work has been the subject of a number of studies, the most comprehensive of which being Mubārak, *Al-Rummānī* (see also *GAS*, ix, 112, and *Bibl.* for further titles).

(8) *Tafsīr al-Ḳurʾān*. An apparently very large work, only a small portion of which has survived (as yet, unedited): Cairo, al-Kẖizāna al-Taymūriyya *tafsīr* 201 (*GAS*, viii, 270). It was highly regarded throughout the later mediaeval period (for a discussion of the work, with remarks about it from later authors, see Mubārak, *Al-Rummānī*, 96-9).

One thing that distinguishes Baṣran grammarians of this period, from their predecessors, is the patent and increasingly more refined awareness of the importance of distinguishing between purely syntactic phenomena and such stylistic alternatives as are available within the syntactic constraints of a given language (in this case, Arabic), when making judgements about acceptable and accepted usage. Al-Rummānī is representative of this trend.

Theologically, al-Rummānī belonged to the Iḵẖs̲ẖ̲īdiyya (Yāḳūt, *Irs̲ẖ̲ād*, V 280-1) after Ibn al-Iḵẖs̲ẖ̲īd, the eponymous founder of the school; whence al-Rummānī's auxillary *nisba*, al-Iḵẖs̲ẖ̲īdī), one of three competing Muʿtazilī schools of *kalām*, in Baḡẖdād, the other two being the Bā Hās̲ẖ̲imiyya and the so-called "old Baḡẖdād" school. As a young man, al-Rummānī had witnessed the legendary debate (320/932) between Abū Saʿīd al-Sīrāfī [*q.v.*] and Abū Bis̲ẖ̲r Mattā b. Yūnus over the relative merits of logic and grammar. He would serve as the main source for al-Tawḥīdī's recapitulation (*Imtāʿ*, i, 128) of the events (the other informant, albeit with less of a memory for the details, being al-Sīrāfī himself). As an expert in jurisprudence (*fiḳh*), as well as grammar and theology, al-Rummānī was appointed, along with al-Sīrāfī, to a judgeship over Baḡẖdād's East District, shortly after Abū Muḥammad Ibn Maʿrūf had been appointed chief judge of the city (Kraemer, *Philosophy*, 73; al-Hamad̲ẖ̲ānī, *Takmila*, 197; Ibn al-Djawzī, *Muntaẓam*, vii, 38, 54). Probably as Ibn Maʿrūf's official witness (*s̲ẖ̲āhid*), al-Rummānī was a member of

. self-appointed delegation of notables (many of them urisconsults) that appeared before ʿIzz al-Dawla Bakhtiyār to air the grievances of the populace (*Imtāʿ*, ii, 151-2).

Al-Rummānī studied under such influential figures as Ibn al-Sarrādj (d. 317/929), Ibn Durayd (d. 321/933), and al-Zadjdjādj (d. 311/923). Those who, at one time or other, had studied under al-Rummānī would prove themselves no less distinguished than his teachers. It is al-Rummānī who is credited with having dubbed one such student, Ibn Nuʿmān (d. 413/1022), with the epithet by which the precocious young *shaykh* would come better to be known, viz. *al-mufīd*, "the instructor", as a consequence of his having outwitted al-Rummānī in debate after having been present at, and posed a question during, one of the latter's widely attended lectures (Niʿma, *Falāsifat al-shīʿa*, 456). Among al-Rummānī's devoted disciples was the brilliant and irascible Abū Ḥayyān al-Tawḥīdī (d. 414/1023), the source for much of our knowledge about al-Rummānī. Al-Tawḥīdī adjudged al-Rummānī to be endowed with a capacity for eloquent expression tantamount to the legendary al-Djāḥiẓ (Yāḳūt, *Irshād*, v, 252, possibly the greatest praise he could lavish on anyone.) Other appraisals of al-Rummānī were less enthusiastic: "It used to be said", notes Yāḳūt (v, 281), "[that] 'the grammarians of the day are three: one whose speech is incomprehensible—that being al-Rummānī; one some of whose speech is comprehensible—that being Abū ʿAlī al-Fārisī; and [perhaps not without a tinge of irony] one all of whose speech is comprehensible without a teacher—that being al-Sīrāfī' "]. In another less than enthusiastic appraisal of al-Rummānī, apparently provoked by his somewhat controversial habit of integrating grammar and logic (*Nuzhat*, 157-8). It was the same Abū ʿAlī al-Fārisī who, on at least one occasion, made what he had to say completely understood, in no uncertain terms (Yāḳūt, v, 281), noting that "if grammar is what al-Rummānī says it is, then we have no part in it; and if grammar is what we say it is, then he has no part in it". If, by some estimates, perspicuity was the hallmark of eloquence, then, given some of al-Rummānī's notoriety for obfuscatory discourse, complicated by the fact that he treats the subject of eloquence, at some length, in the *Nukat fī iʿdjāz al-Ḳurʾān*, it is not entirely surprising to find at least one contemporary, Abū 'l-Ḥasan al-Badīhī (protégé of Yaḥyā b. ʿAdī, distinguished pupil of al-Fārābī), complaining that al-Rummānī was unaccustomed, with respect to eloquence, of practising what he so ardently preached (*Baṣāʾir*, i, 171-2). Al-Rummānī's definition of eloquence (*balāgha*) given in the *Nukat* (75) is preceded by two preliminary counter-definitions of what, in his opinion, eloquence is not, one of which, as if to respond to his critics, runs: "Eloquence is not the [act of] making a given meaning understood, because sometimes two speakers (*mutakallimān*) will make a given idea understood, one of whom is eloquent, the other incapable of expressing himself well" (*Nukat*, 75). His positive definition of eloquence, cited, with some slight variation, by Ibn Rashīḳ (*ʿUmda*, i, 246), yet ascribed not to al-Rummānī but to an unnamed *muḥdath* poet, runs as follows: *wa-innama 'l-balāgha īṣālu 'l-maʿnā ila 'l-ḳalbi fī aḥsani ṣūratⁱⁿ min(a) 'l-lafẓ*—"What eloquence in fact is, is the conveying of a given idea to the heart (= mind) in the most beautiful form of wording" (*Nukat*, 75; cf. *ʿUmda*, i, 246, wherein *ibdāʾ* replaces *īṣāl*). If, as Versteegh has attempted to show (*Greek elements*, 94, n. 20), al-Rummānī, like other Muʿtazilīs of the period, was operating under influences, either direct or indirect, that bear the stamp of stoicism, then his appeal to rhetoric is, in effect, an appeal to logic, under which the stoics, in contrast to the Aristotelians, subsumed rhetoric (along with dialectic).

In the context of his discussion of the incomparability of the Ḳurʾān's stylistic qualities, al-Rummānī introduces a number of innovations into the treatment of the tropical use of language, with e.g. his notion of the *aṣl al-lugha*, the basic or proper meaning of an expression, that would become pervasive throughout later literary theory. His treatment of metaphor (*istiʿāra*) and comparison (*tashbīh*) also exhibits a rather radical departure from previous theory (for a discussion of these topics, see Heinrichs, *Hand of the Northwind*). His approach to these and other matters would greatly influence other theorists, both contemporary and later, among them Abū Hilāl al-ʿAskarī (d. *ca.* 395/1004), al-Ḥātimī (d. 388/988), and Ibn Sinān al-Khafādjī (d. 455/1073-4), to name only a few, and signals the point at which Arab(ic) literary theory begins to emerge as a discipline independent of, for example, Ḳurʾānic hermeneutics, in the context of which much of the earlier theorising had taken place.

Bibliography: Extant works by al-Rummānī: see article, and Brockelmann, I, 113, S I, 175; *GAS*, viii, 112-14, 270, ix, 111-13, 314; Ziriklī, v, 134; Kaḥḥāla, vii, 102. Additional sources cited in the article: Hamadhānī, *Takmilat taʾrīkh al-Ṭabarī*, ed. A. Kanʿān, Beirut 1959; Ibn al-Anbārī, *Nuzhat al-alibbāʾ fī ṭabaḳāt al-udabāʾ*, ed. ʿA. Amer, Stockholm 1883; Ibn al-Djawzī, *Muntaẓam*; Ibn Rashīḳ, *ʿUmda*, 2 vols., ed. Muḥammad Muḥyiddīn ʿAbd al-Ḥamīd, Cairo 1383/1983: Tawḥīdī, *Akhlāḳ al-wazīrayn*, ed. M. al-Ṭandjī, Damascus 1955; idem, *al-Baṣāʾir wa 'l-dhakhāʾir*, 4 vols., ed. I. Kaylanī, Damascus 1984-8; Yāḳūt, *Irshād al-arīb*, 7 vols., ed. Margoliouth.—Studies cited in the article: W. Heinrichs, *The Hand of the Northwind*, Wiesbaden 1977; J. Kraemer, *Philosophy in the renaissance of Islam*, Leiden 1986; M. Mubārak, *Al-Rummānī al-naḥwī*, Damascus 1383/1983; ʿA. Niʿma, *Falāsifat al-shīʿa*, Beirut n.d.; C.H.M. Versteegh, *Greek elements in Arabic linguistic thinking*, Leiden 1977. Further studies of interest: Kraemer, *Humanism in the renaissance of Islam*, Leiden 1980; R.A. al-Damīrī, *Sharḥ Kitāb Sībawayh: al-Dirāsa*, Cairo 1308/1988; M. Carter, *Linguistic science and orthodoxy in conflict: the case of al-Rummānī*, in *ZGAIW*, i (1984), 212-32. (J. Flanagan)

RUNDA, Sp. Ronda, the chef-lieu of the district (*kūra*, sometimes *iḳlīm*) in mediaeval al-Andalus of Tākurunnā, situated to the north-west of Rayya [*q.v.*] (modern Malaga).

This is a very mountainous region, well watered by rivers and abundant rain, allowing the development of agriculture and stockrearing. The town of Runda is described in the Arabic sources as an impregnable fortress, and this fact, in addition to its geographical situation, has moulded its history. The northern part of the town is protected by a ravine (*tajo*) formed by the river, a kilometre long and 160 m deep. This natural defence was completed by a powerful fortress with triple walls. Outside the walls, urban expansion in the shape of suburbs (*rabaḍ*) only happened in the 13th and 14th centuries A.D. Traces of its Islamic past are visible today in its baths (situated below the town, on the river side), the *miḥrāb* of the great mosque, preserved in a church, a minaret and some *rābiṭas*. The so-called house of the Gigantes is the best example of civilian Islamic architecture there, since it has kept the greater part of its structure and décor.

One should also add the Almocabar (*al-maḳābir*) gate in the enceinte and a few other architectural remains preserved in the modern buildings. At the time of its conquest by the Christians (1485), the town had numerous mosques, dwelling houses (most of them on a modest scale) and 77 shops. The defensive value of Runda was reduced through the town's lack of a water supply, hence at some unknown date—but one during the Islamic period—a stairway was constructed in the rock down to the river, still in part preserved. The Arabic sources call the river the *nahr Runda*, but its Castilian name (Guadalevín) is clearly Arabic in origin. The usually accepted etymology (*wādī 'l-laban*) has been rejected by E. Terés, who suggests the local toponym *wādī 'l-liwā* as a possible alternative, even though it is not confirmed in the sources (the place name *al-liwā* is cited only once, in a *ḳaṣīda* by a poet of Runda).

The population of Runda and its hinterland comprised, as well as indigenous elements, a strong Berber presence, plus some Arab lineages. Among the Berbers, one notes the presence of the W.lhāsa (of Nafza [*q.v.*]), as well as the Banu 'l-Khalīʿ (see below) and the Banu 'l-Zadjdjālī. These last, of undistinguished origin, according to Ibn Ḥayyān, later installed themselves at Cordova and reached there a high position. The famous poet ʿAbbās b. Firnās (3rd/9th century) belonged to a Berber family settled in the Runda district (the very name of Tākurunnā is considered to be of Berber origin). The presence of Nafza Berbers is attested until a late date by the patronyms of persons like the poet Abu 'l-Baḳāʾ (7th/13th century) and the mystic Ibn ʿAbbād (8th/14th century), both born at Runda. The references to Arabic lineages are much less numerous. According to al-Rāzī, cited by Ibn al-Khaṭīb, a descendant of Saʿd b. ʿUbāda [*q.v.*] settled in the region of Tākurunnā. In the 5th/11th century the Banu 'l-Ḥakīm, an important Arab family of Seville, chose to reside at Runda and thereafter played an important role in the town's history. The Arabic *nisba*s borne by the natives of Runda are recorded in the biographical sources, but, as elsewhere in al-Andalus, this fact does not guarantee a genuine Arab origin. The existence of a small Jewish community is attested by the presence of a Jew as interpreter in the negotiations which led to the surrender of the town in 1485; and a Jewish physician of Runda is mentioned in the 6th/12th century.

In the Umayyad period, the Berbers of Runda and its district were often involved in rebellions against the *amīr*s of Cordova. However, the Banu 'l-Khalīʿ, who were clients of the Umayyads of Syria, had given their support to the youthful ʿAbd al-Raḥmān I when he had landed in the peninsula; the lord of the *kūra* of Tākurunnā, ʿAbd al-Aʿlā b. Awshadja, offered him his help and a body of 400 cavalrymen. In the reign of Hishām I, the Berbers of Tākurunnā rose in 178/795-6. This rising was severely suppressed by the *amīr*'s army, who killed a large part of the rebels; those who escaped took refuge in regions fairly distant from Runda (Talavera and Trujillo). This first Berber revolt resulted in a depopulation of Runda and its district, which has probably, however, been exaggerated by the Arabic sources. Other Berber revolts are recorded in the region in the reign of ʿAbd al-Raḥmān II, in 211/826 and 235/849; but it was above all in Muḥammad's reign (238-73/852-86) that the movement challenging the authority of the *amīr*s became widespread in the Runda district. At first revolt, led by Asad b. al-Ḥārith b. Rāfiʿ in 261/874, was soon extinguished. But in 265/878-9 the revolt reached the districts of Tākurunnā, Algeciras and Rayya, as a reaction against the tax exactions of the governors, and after this the Umayyad administration began building fortresses (*ḥuṣūn*) in order to overawe the region. Then in 267/880 broke out the great revolt of ʿUmar b. Ḥafṣūn [*q.v.*], himself a native of Runda. Under the *amīr* ʿAbd Allāh (275-300/888-912), this extended through the *kūra* of Rayya and adjacent regions, including Runda. In his struggle, ʿUmar sought help from Awshadja of the Banu 'l-Khalīʿ, who abandoned him, however, after his conversion to Christianity. ʿAbd al-Raḥmān III succeeded in re-establishing peace in the area, and after the fall of ʿUmar's capital Bobastro [see BUBASHTRU in Suppl.), all fortresses in the region were destroyed except for those necessary for exercising the central government's authority.

With the disintegration of caliphal power, Runda became one of the *taifa* principalities dominated by the Berbers, in this case by Zanāta members of the Banū Īfran, brought in as part of the armies of the *ḥādjib* Ibn Abī ʿĀmir al-Manṣūr [*q.v.*]. At first recognising the suzerainty of the Ḥammūdid ruler of Malaga, after 431/1039 Abū Nūr Hilāl al-Īfranī declared himself independent in Runda, as one of the belt of Berber principalities (Carmona, Morón, Arcos and Runda) surrounding the ʿAbbādid principality of Seville, and which were in fact absorbed by this latter power under al-Muʿtaḍid. Abū Nūr Hilāl was deposed by the ʿAbbādid, but his son Abū Naṣr Fatūḥ succeeded him in 449/1057 and ruled till 457/1064, when al-Muʿtaḍid finally incorporated Runda in his principality as the advance post of Sevillan authority expanding towards Malaga. Al-Muʿtamid entrusted it to his son al-Rāḍī [*q.v.*], and it was from him that the Almoravid commander Gharrūr took possession of the town in 484/1091.

In the last years of Almoravid power, local lords proclaimed their independence all through al-Andalus, and in 540/1145-6 the lord of Arcos, Jerez and Runda, Abu 'l-Ḳamar Ibn ʿAzzūn, recognised the authority of the Almohads immediately after they appeared at Cadiz. It was in this century that the armies of Castile attacked the region on several occasions, taking captives, burning crops and seizing fortresses. With the decay of the Almohads, Runda became a frontier post of the kingdom of Granada against the Christians, alternatively controlled by the Naṣrids and the Marīnids [*q.vv.*], although it seems also to have preserved a certain feeling of local solidarity and independence. This oscillation of control continued into the 8th/14th century, and during this period, especially under the Marīnid sultan Abu 'l-Ḥasan ʿAlī (731-49/1331-48), the fortifications of Runda were strengthened. However, Marīnid influence there declined after this, with Runda being frequently the seat of rivals for the Naṣrid throne in Granada. This role continued during the internal succession disputes of the Granadan rulers, but it remained also the advance position against Christian military pressure. Despite truces between Granada and Castile, frontier incidents were frequent, often only recorded in the Castilian chroniclers. Military activity intensified in the later part of the 9th/15th century. Thus the men of Runda were at the head of the important capture of Zahara, one of the last efforts undertaken against the Christians, when an army of 300 cavalry and 4,000 infantry seized the town in December 1481, under the command of Abrahem Alhaquine (thus according to Spanish sources; this Ibrāhīm al-Ḥakīm was probably a member of the family of the Banu 'l-Ḥakīm). But this success was short-lived, as the Catholic monarchs now began the final assault on the Granadian kingdom. In 1484 fresh Castilian advances isolated Runda more and more from the rest of the kingdom, and after a short siege (8-22 May 1485), the commander of Runda, Ibrāhīm al-Ḥakīm (the *alguacil mayor* of the Castilian chronicles) surrendered the town to the Marquis of Cadiz. This led to the loss of the whole surrounding region and that of Malaga and the Mediterranean shores. The population of Runda had to abandon the town to Christian settlers, although the people of the smaller rural settlements were allowed to remain as vassals of Castile.

Runda had never reached the cultural level of other towns in al-Andalus, but there was a certain intellectual development in the 7th/12th and 8th/14th centuries, when persons like Yūsuf b. Mūsā b. Sulaymān al-Muntas̲h̲āḳirī, a prolific author and the teacher of Ibn al-K̲h̲aṭīb [*q.v.*], emerged. But Runda's most famous sons were the poet Abu 'l-Baḳā' (601-84/1204-85), the author of a renowned *ḳaṣīda* on the loss of Cordova, Seville, Valencia and other towns of al-Andalus, and the mystic Ibn ʿAbbād [*q.v.*].

Bibliography: The Arabic and Castilian sources are cited, in the main, in the following works: A.M. al-ʿAbbādī, *El reino de Granada en la epoca de Muhammad V*, Madrid 1973; M. Acién Almansa, *Ronda y su serranía en tiempo de los Reyes Católicos*, Malaga 1979; idem and M.A. Martínez, *Catálogo de las inscripciones árabes del Museo de Málaga*, Madrid 1982; I.S. Allouche, *La revolte des Banū Aškīlūla contre le sultan naṣrīte Muḥammad II*, in *Hesperis*, xxv (1938), 1-11; R. Arié, *L'Espagne musulmane au temps des Naṣrides (1232-1492)*, Paris 1973; J. Bosch Vilá, *Los almorávides*, Granada 1990; J. de M. Carriazo, *Asiento de las cosas de Ronda. Conquista y repartimiento de la ciudad por los Reyes Católicos*, in *MEAH*, iii (1954), anejo, 1-134; ʿI. Dandas̲h̲, *al-Andalus fī nihāyat al-Murābiṭīn wa-mustahall al-Muwaḥḥidīn*, Beirut 1988; E. de Felipe Rodríguez, *Beréberes en al-Andalus: ss. II/VIII-IV/X*, diss. Univ. Complutense, Madrid 1991; F. de la Granja, *La venta de la esclava en el mercado en la obra de Abū l-Baqā' de Ronda*, in *RIEIM*, xiii (1965-6), 119-36; P. Guichard, *Al-Andalus. Estructura antropológica de una sociedad islámica en Occidente*, Barcelona 1976; L.P. Harvey, *Islamic Spain 1250 to 1500*, Chicago and London 1990; A. Huici Miranda, *Historia política del imperio almohade*, Tetouan 1956; E. Lévi-Provençal, *La "description de l'Espagne" d'Aḥmad al-Rāzī*, in *And.*, xviii (1953), 51-108; M.A. Manzano, *Apuntes sobre una institución representativa del sultanato nazarí: el* šayj al-guzāt, in *Al-Qanṭara*, xiii (1992), 305-22; idem, *La intervención de los benimerines en la Península Ibérica*, Madrid 1992; J. Oliver Asín, *Les tunisiens en Espagne, à travers la toponymie*, in *Les Cahiers de Tunisie*, lxix-lxx (1970), 15-20; B. Pavón Maldonado, *De nuevo sobre Ronda musulmana*, in *Awrāq*, iii (1980), 131-74; M.J. Rubiera, *El* d̲ū l-wizāratayn *Ibn al-Ḥakīm de Ronda*, in *And.*, xxxiv (1969), 105-21; C. Ruiz de Almodóvar Sel, *Notas para un estudio de la taifa beréber de Ronda: los Banū Īfran*, in *Andalucía islámica*, ii-iii (1981-2), 95-106; L. Seco de Lucena, *Los Ḥammūdíes, señores de Málaga y Algeciras*, Malaga 1955; E. Terés, *Materiales para el estudio de la toponimia hispanoárabe. Nómina fluvial*, Madrid 1986; L. Torres Balbás, *La acrópolis musulmana de Ronda*, in *And.*, ix (1944), 449-81; J. Vallvé, *La división territorial de la España musulmana*, Madrid 1986; M.J. Viguera, *Los reinos de Taifas y las invasiones magrebíes*, Madrid 1992; eadem, *Noticias dispersas sobre Ronda musulmana*, in *Actas del XII Congreso de la U.E.A.I. (Málaga 1984)*, Madrid 1986, 757-69.

(MANUELA MARÍN, shortened by the editors)

AL-**RUNDĪ**, Abū Khālid Yazīd b. Muḥammad al-Muʿtamid b. ʿAbbād, AL-RĀḌĪ BI-LLĀH, prince of Runda [*q.v.*] or Ronda in Spain (460-94/1068-91).

Yazīd, more generally known by his *laḳab* of al-Rāḍī, was one of the sons of the Taifa king of Seville, al-Muʿtamid [*q.v.*], born of his famous concubine Iʿtimād. Her master's love for her and his miserable end in the Almoravid's prisons, became a central feature of the ʿAbbādid poetic *dīwāns*, the most brilliant ones of the culture of al-Andalus. The fate of the children of this liaison seem likewise to have inherited some of the tragic poignancy.

Al-Rāḍī appears on the scene with the Almoravids [see AL-MURĀBIṬŪN]. In 479/1086 he was governor of Algeciras when the Berbers disembarked, summoned for help by the Taifa princes in face of the progress of the Christians. Distrustful of his new allies, Yūsuf b. Tās̲h̲ufīn, the Almoravid leader, decided to occupy the town. Al-Rāḍī had to cede the place at the orders of his father, and retired to Runda, where he was to remain permanently.

Averted for a while by the victory at Zallāḳa [*q.v.*], the danger from the Christians re-appeared two years later in the east. According to ʿAbd Allāh Ibn Zīrī, the ruler of Granada, al-Muʿtamid apparently saw the opportunity to re-assert his authority over Murcia, occupied but then relinquished a few years before, and to provide al-Rāḍī with an appanage worthy of him. He charged his son with attacking the Christians, who were devastating the region of Lorca, but the prince, more at home with his books than in battle, went down in defeat, and 3,000 of the troops of Seville were cut to pieces by 300 Christian cavalrymen. This inglorious rout drove al-Muʿtamid to make an irrevocable decision to call in fresh Almoravid intervention.

The Berbers' check at the siege of Aledo, for which Yūsuf b. Tās̲h̲ufīn blamed the Andalusian rulers, sealed the fate of the Taifas. After Granada and Malaga (483/1090), the Almoravid directed his blows towards the ʿAbbādids. Seville was taken by assault in Rad̲j̲ab 484/September 1091. Al-Muʿtamid was taken prisoner and compelled to order his sons to lay down their arms. Al-Rāḍī showed his reluctance. Runda, situated on a rocky outcrop, was practically impregnable, and the Almoravid forces, directed by G̲h̲arrūr, did not even dare to embark on the siege. In the end, al-Rāḍī gave in to the solicitations of his father, to which Iʿtimād is said to have joined her entreaties, and surrendered to the Berbers. As soon as he was in G̲h̲arrūr's hands, the latter, of whom ʿAbd Allāh Ibn Zīrī has left a distinctly unflattering portrait, had al-Rāḍī put to death in a corner of the ramparts.

Al-Rāḍī is, in sum, the most frequently-mentioned of al-Muʿtamid's sons, since he was, with his father, "the poet of the ʿAbbādids". An assiduous scholar, he leant towards Ibn Ḥazm's Ẓāhirī school. His father on several occasions reproached him for preferring the pen to the Arabs' lance, but other sources speak of his passion for horses. It is especially hard to grasp the reality of his character since the epic tale of the ʿAbbādids probably owes a lot to that of the Ḥamdānids. Both, as Arabs and as patrons, poets and warriors, fought against the Christians and against the mounting pressure of the "Barbarians" within Islam. These striking resemblances led posterity to assign the roles at Seville, as they had been at Aleppo, to the proud and brave al-Muʿtamid as Sayf al-Dawla, and his son al-Rāḍī, as a distant echo of Abū Firās, with whom he shared a love of poetry, a mediocre political sense and a miserable end.

Bibliography: The essential texts are gathered

together by R. Dozy in *Scriptorum arabum loci de Abbadidis*, Leiden 1852-63. To these may be added ʿAbd Allāh Ibn Zīrī, *al-Tibyān ʿan al-hāditha al-kāʾina bi-dawla Banī Zīrī fī Gharnāṭa*, ed. Lévi-Provençal, Cairo 1955, partial Fr. tr. idem, in *al-And*, iii-vi (1935-41), Span. tr. E. García Gómez, *El siglo XI en primera persona*, Madrid 1980, Eng. tr. Amin T. Tibi, *The Tibyān, memoirs of ʿAbd Allāh b. Buluggīn*, Leiden 1986; H. Pérès, *La poésie andalouse en arabe classique au XIᵉ siècle*, Paris 1953.

(G. Martinez Gros)

RŪNĪ, ABU 'L-FARADJ [see ABU 'L-FARADJ B. MASʿŪD RŪNĪ, in Suppl.].

RŪPIYYA, an Indian coin, a rupee. In the later 9th/15th and early 10th/16th centuries, the silver *tanka* [*q.v.*] of the sultans of Dihlī had become so debased that when Shīr Shāh (947-52/1540-5) reformed the coinage, the name could no longer be given to a silver coin. To his new silver coin, corresponding to the original fine silver *tanka*, he therefore gave the name *rūpiyya* = rupee, i.e. the silver coin (Sanskrit, *rūpya, rūpaka*), and *tanka* became a copper denomination. The weight of the rupee was 178 grains (11.53 gr) and it rapidly established itself in popular favour. Under the Mughals it was struck all over India at over 200 mints and with the decline of Mughal power continued to be struck by their successors, notably the English East India Company. In the 11th/17th century, Akbar and Djahāngīr struck many square rupees; on one coin of Akbar the name *rūpiyya* occurs. Djahāngīr for a short period struck a heavy rupee of 220 grains (14.259 gr), but, on the whole, the rupee showed little variation in weight. In the 19th century the British rupee gradually drove the local issues out of circulation, and with few exceptions, the local mints closed. Such native states as still issued their own rupees before 1947 struck them on the same standard as the Indian Government rupee.

Aḥmād Shāh Durrānī [*q.v.*] adopted the rupee as his monetary unit on becoming independent, and until the early 20th century it remained the standard coin of Afghānistān. The Hindu kings of Assam also struck the rupee. At present in South Asia, the rupee remains the currency of India, Pākistān, Nepal, Ceylon/Sri Lanka (since 1870) and Bhutan (there since the 1974 currency reform called the *ngultrum*) (see C.L. Krause, C. Mishler and C.R. Bruce II, *1991 Standard catalog of world coins*[17], Iola, Wisc. n.d. [1991], 197-201, 1347-68, 1593-6).

By the early years of the 20th century, the Indian rupee had become current along the Arabian shores of the Persian Gulf and along the East African coast, including the British and German possessions there. The rupee continued in use in East Africa until problems caused by the fluctuations of dual currency systems led to the rupee being suddenly demonitised there on 8 February 1921 in favour of local currencies (see V.T. Harlow *et alii*, *History of East Africa*, ii, Oxford 1965, 430).

In the Middle East, the Indian rupee had been brought to Mesopotamia by the British and Indian forces invading Ottoman territory there from the last months of 1914 onwards, and it became the established currency under the British post-war occupation of ʿIrāḳ and the Mandate until, just before the ending of the Mandate, it was displaced on 1 April 1932 by a national currency, the ʿIrāḳī dīnār (see Admiralty Handbooks, Naval Intelligence Division, *Iraq and the Persian Gulf*, London 1944, 478). Within eastern Arabia, the Indian rupee was counterstamped *Nadjd* in 1251/1835, 1256/1840 and 1278-93/1862-76. Kuwayt minted its own copper *bayzas* [see PAYSA] in 1304/1886-7, but no rupees, and inaugurated its own currency of *fulūs* and dīnārs in 1380/1961. In the Trucial Oman states, after 1971 the United Arab Emirates [see AL-IMĀRĀT AL-ʿARABIYYA AL-MUTTAḤIDA, in Suppl.], various emirates acquired their own currencies, based on the *riyāl*, in the 1960s and 1970s. In the Sultanate of Masḳaṭ and ʿUmān, until 1970 there was a dual currency of the rupee and the *riyāl*, the first made up of 64 *bayzas* and the second of 200 *baysas* (see RIYĀL and, in general, Krause *et alii*, *op. cit.*, 1194-5, 1409-13, 1533).

Bibliography (in addition to references given in the article): R. Chalmers, *The history of currency in the British colonies*, London 1893, 336-40; E. Thurston, *The coinage of the East India Company*, Madras 1890; Yule and Burnell, *Hobson-Jobson*[2], London 1903, 774-6. J. Allan-[C.E. Bosworth])

RŪS, occasionally *Rūsiya*, the Arabic rendering (and thence into other Islamic languages) of Eastern Slavic ***Poycь*** (*Rus'*). This was the designation of a people and land from which modern Russia, Ukraine and Belarus' derive.

The rapid ethnic, political and social evolution of this term and the people(s) which it denoted during the 3rd-4th/9th-10th centuries produced a series of temporally multi-layered, occasionally contradictory notices in the classical Islamic geographical literature. In contemporary Byzantine sources it appears as Ῥῶς (which may, indeed, be the source of the Arabic form, Barthold, *Arabskie isvestiya o rusakh*), cf. also Ῥωσσία, the name of the country derived from it and the infrequently noted form (pl.) Ῥούσιοι). Modern Russ. *Rossiya* ("Russia") is taken from the Byzantine ecclesiastical usage. Al-Idrīsī, 914, mentions "Outer Russia" (*bilād al-rūsiyya al-khāridjiyya*). It is not clear if this usage has any relationship to the ἔξω Ῥωσία noted by Constantine Porphyrogenitus, the geographical contours of which are equally uncertain. The form *Urus* and its variants, found in a number of Turkic languages (e.g. Ḳaračay-Balḳar *Orus*, Noghay, Ḳazaḳ *Orıs*, Čuvash *Vırăs*) goes back to the Arabic form. Mediaeval Latin sources record them as (*Annales Bertiniani*, s.a. 838-9) *Rhos*; (The Bavarian Geographer, 9th century) *Ruzzi*; (Liudprand of Cremona, mid-10th century) *Rusios*; (Thietmar of Merseburg, d. 1018) *Ruscia*; Old Germ. *Ruz, Riuz*; Old Swed. *Ryds*. Long-standing attempts to identify this ethnonym with the *Hrōs* mentioned in the 6th century Syriac ecclesiastical history of Pseudo-Zacharias Rhetor have generally (with the exception of some Soviet scholars) been rejected (see Łowmiański).

The origins of the Rūs

The origin and etymology of this term/ethnonym and thus, it is averred, the ethnic affiliations of the people or socio-mercantile group that first bore this name in the Islamic and other sources of the 3rd-4th/9th-10th century, are much debated. It has long been argued (cf. Thomsen) that *Rus'* is the Slavic rendering of the Baltic Finnic term for "Swede": Finn. *Ruotsi*, Est. *Roots*, Vot. *Rôtsi*, Liv. *R'uọt'š* (but cf. Volga Finnic: Mari *Ruš*, Udm. *Zuč*, Komi-Perm. *Roč* "Russian" and Samoyedic [Nenets] *Lūtsa, Lūsa* "Russian". There have been two centuries of occasionally heated discussion of this issue between "Normanists" (those favouring a Scandinavian origin of the Rus' and by extension the Rus' state) and their opponents, the "Anti-Normanists." The Classical Normanist position, from the philological perspective, posits: Slav. *Rus'* < Finn. *Routsi* < Old Norse *roþer, roþsmenn, roþskarlar* "rowers, seamen" associated with the coastal region of Sweden, Roslagen (see Łowmiański, and in Jenkins *et al.*, *Constantine Porphyrogenitus De administrando imperio. Commentary.* Historical evidence in support of the Scandinavian origin of the Rus' is adduced from the account in the *Annales Bertiniani*, s.a. 838-9, of an embassy from the "Rhos Chacanus" (Ḳag͟han of the Rus') to Constantinople. Unable to return to their homeland because of nomadic pressure in the Western Eurasian steppes, the embassy was diverted to the Frankish court at Ingelheim. There, to the consternation of the Franks, it was discovered that the mysterious Rhos were, indeed, Swedes. A century later, Liudprand of Cremona appears to confirm this ethnic identification in noting in his listing of the northern peoples the "Rusios whom we call by another name the Northmen" (*Rusios, quos alio nos nomine Nordmannos appellamus*). Elsewhere he further explains that there is a certain people established in the North whom, because of the characteristics of their physical appearance (*a qualitate corporis*) "the Greeks call Ρούσιος, Rusios, but we, however, because of their location call Northmen (*Nordmanni*)." On the basis of these and other connections made in contemporary sources with the Viking world, the formation of the Rus' state is thus seen as part of that outpouring of Viking energy aimed initially at gaining control of vital international trade routes and ending in some instances as conquest and colonisation. The name *Rūs* does, indeed, figure in some accounts of Viking raids on Muslim Spain. Al-Yaʿḳūbī, s.a. 229/843-4, tells of the attack of the "Mad͟jūs who are called Rūs" on Seville (Is͟hbīliyya). 'Mad͟jūs" [*q.v.*] was a term used rather broadly for pagans and more specifically for Zoroastrians and Norsemen. Al-Masʿūdī also mentions "a nation of the Mad͟jūs" who, before the year 300/912-3, had raided Andalus. He identified them with the Rūs and posited the Pontic region as their starting point. Ibn Ḥawḳal, in his account of the destruction of the K͟hazar cities at the hands of the Rūs in 358/968-9 (more probably several years earlier, this date represents the year in which Ibn Ḥawḳal first heard of these events), remarks that after their despoiling of K͟hazaria "they came at once to the land of Rūm and Andalus..." He then refers to earlier expeditions, commenting that they, the Rūs, "are the ones who of old went to Andalus and then to Bard͟haʿa." He also notes that "the ships of the Rūs and Pečeneg Turks" sometimes attack Spain. This alliance of Rus' and Pečenegs [*q.v.*], who were often at odds, while not unknown, is all the more remarkable in that it implies Pečeneg involvement in sea-borne expeditions. A most dramatic turn of events in Rūs activities in the Mediterranean occurred in 860, when the "Rhos" mounted an unsuccessful naval assault on Constantinople from which the Byzantines believed themselves to have been spared only through divine intercession. The Patriarch Photius (858-67, 878-86), an astute and well-informed statesman, referred to these invaders as an ἔθνος ἄγνωστον a hitherto "unknown people" (see Vasiliev). The Rūs who attacked the Byzantine capital appear to have come from Kiev (Vasiliev) rather than from Western or Northern Europe. Almost a century later, the Byzantine Emperor Constantine VII Porphyrogenitus (d. A.D. 959) in his *De administrando imperio*, written *ca.* 948-52, gives an account of how the Rus' merchants travel from Novgorod to Kiev and then down the Dnieper and into the Black Sea to trade with Constantinople. The names of the Dnieper rapids are reported in both Rhos (Ῥωσιστὶ) and Slavic (Σκλαβηνιστὶ). The "Rhos" forms are clearly Scandinavian.

G. Vernadsky proferred an Iranian origin: *Rus* < Alanic *Ruk͟hs-As* through a conjectured relationship of the Alans with the early (Eastern) Slavic tribal confederation of the Antes. The Varangians (Old Norse *Vaeringi*, pl. *Vaeringjar*, Rus'. ***Варяг*** (*Varąg*) Mod. Russ. ***Варяг*** (Varyag), Arab. *Warank*, Greek Βαράγγοι < *várar* "pledge, oath, guarantee" = "men of the pledge", he argues, who in the 8th-9th century became the dominant force here, merged with this grouping and assumed their name. This dilution of strict Normanism has found few adherents. Anti-Normanists have countered with a variety of theories, both philological and historical. Perhaps best grounded are the Slavist Anti-Normanists who point to the presence of toponyms and hydronyms with the element *rus-/ros-* in the Eastern Slavic lands. These, in turn, may be associated with the Slavic or Balto-Slavic **rud/*rus* "reddish, ruddy, blond" (e.g. Ukr. *rusïy* "blond", Lith.*raũsvas* "red", cf. Latin *russus* etc., see P. Rospond, Mavrodin). H. Paszkiewicz (*The origin of Russia*, 1954, repr. New York 1969, 143-4), a Normanist, suggested that this was the Slavic name of the Norsemen, so called because of their ruddy complexion.

Eastern Slavic sources do not help to clarify the situation. The later Kievan Rus' tradition associates "Rus'" with the south, i.e. the Middle Dnieper Kievan region (cf. Hrus͟hevs'kïy, i). The Primary Chronicle (also called the *Chronicle of Nestor*), however, in its introductory genealogical comments places the "Rus" among the peoples in Japheth's part of the world, in this case the northern, Finnic ethnic groupings. Further on, it includes them in a listing of the "Varangians, Swedes, Normans (*Ourmane*), Gotlanders, Angles, Galicians, Italians (*Volŭk͟hva*), Romans, Germans, etc. Clearly, they are associated with the Germanic North. The Chronicler, often evincing a Byzantinocentric viewpoint, comments (*PSRL*, i, 17) that the Rus' land began to be so-called at the time of the accession of the Emperor Michael III (852). In another passage (*PSRL*, i, 23) discussing Oleg's conquest of Kiev, traditionally dated to 882, the Rus' are again associated with the North: "he (sc. Oleg) had with him Varangians, Slovene (sc. a tribe associated with Novgorod) and the rest who are called Rus'." Elsewhere, however, the Chronicle (*PSRL*, i, 25-6), s.a. 898, notes the Polyane, the Eastern Slavic tribe most closely associated with Kiev, "who are now called Rus'" (*nïne zovomaya Rus'*). Still further on, the Chronicler attempts to explain these discrepancies thus (*PSRL*, i, 28): "the Slavic nation (*sloven'skïy yazïk*) and the Rus' (*rouskïy*) are one; for it was called Rus' from the Varangians (*ot Varyag bo prozvas͟hasya Rous'yu*), but first they were Slavs, although they were called Polyane, nonetheless, they were of Slavic speech..."

In addition to philological argumentation and to the ethnographic and ethnogenetic data offered by our sources, the Normanist position is based largely on the Primary Chronicle's "historical" account of the genesis of the Rus' state. According to it, in 859 (the dating, at best, is off by several years), the Varangians "from across the sea" levied tribute on the Finnic Čyud', the Novgorodian Slovene, the Finnic Merya and the Slavic Kriviči, while the Slavic Polyane, Severyane and Vyatiči to their south were tributaries of the K͟hazars. In 860-2, the Varangians were expelled, but the northern groupings proved unable to govern themselves. As a consequence, the Varangians, led by Ryurik, who settled in Novgorod, and his two brothers, Sineus and Truvor, were summoned to rule over them. Ryurik brought with him "the whole of Rus'." From "these Varangians it was called the land of Rus'" (*PSRL*, i, 19-20). Two Varangian subordinates of Ryurik, Askold and Dir, then came to the south, taking Kiev. Al-Masʿūdī (d. *ca.* 345/956-7) in his *Murūdj* (iii, 64 = § 908), mentions the "king al-Dīr [Dayr], first among the kings of the Ṣaḳāliba." The occasionally suggested identification of al-Dīr with the Varangian Dir is questionable. It is much more likely that, despite the similarity in names, al-Masʿūdī's al-Dīr was a Central European Slavic ruler and his contemporary. With Ryurik's death, sometime between 870-9, power was given to his kinsman, Oleg < *helgi*. Oleg is presented in the traditional narrative as the guardian of Ryurik's son, Igor'. In 880-2, Oleg took Kiev, killing Askold and Dir. Another Rus' tradition preserved in the Novgorodian First Chronicle (*NPL*, 107, 434), depicts Igor' as the conqueror of Kiev, with Oleg merely as his general. The charismatic Oleg, about whom legends imputing prophetic abilities developed, has also been identified with the הלגו *hlgw* of the Geniza Khazar Hebrew document, the so-called "Cambridge" or "Schechter" document. This *Helgu, the "king of Rusia", perished in the aftermath of an unsuccessful raid on Byzantium. According to the Primary Chronicle, Oleg, after taking Kiev then set about conquering the neighbouring Slavic tribes. In 907, he launched his first raid against Constantinople. Igor', according to the Chronicle, began to rule in 913. There are, indeed, serious problems of chronology and questions regarding the identity of the personages involved. Pritsak, for example, posits a conflation of several Helgi/Olegs, real and mythical. Nonetheless, it is generally accepted that the account has some underlying historical basis.

The Anti-Normanists minimise the importance of the non-autochthonous elements. They contend that in the 6th-7th century there existed in the Middle Dnieper region the Polyane tribal union which took the name *Ros* or *Rus* deriving from a toponym or hydronym. Some support for this may be found in the "Bavarian Geographer", an anonymous work composed before 821, which places the "Ruzzi" next to the "Caziri" (Khazars). The power of this Kiev-centred state, according to Soviet Anti-Normanists, grew as reflected in the 838-9 embassy to Constantinople. The Swedes noted here, they suggest, were merely Vikings in Rus' service. The tale of the summoning of the Varangians, they further argue, is mythical. Ryurik may have been a real figure, but his ethnic affiliation is unclear.

The Normanist vs. Anti-Normanist controversy cannot be resolved on the basis of the currently available written sources. Archaeological evidence, similarly, does not provide decisive proof. A recent assessment of the data from a Scandinavianist perspective concludes that the Rus' were Scandinavians, but constituted only one element in a mixed population. The Vikings called Rus' *svípjoð hian mikla* "Sweden the Great", indicating an almost proprietary sense in an area of economic expansion and opportunity. The other Old Norse term for the region was *Gǫrd/Gorðum* in the 10th-11th century and *Garðaríki*, "kingdom of (fortified) towns or steads", in the 12th-13th century.

The Islamic sources, while not providing the conclusive information needed to resolve these questions, shed some light on the early Rus'. Genealogical tradition, as reflected in the anonymous *Mudjmal al-tawārīkh*, dated 520/1126, presents the eponymous Rūs as the brother of Khazar and the son of Japheth. Dissatisfied with his own place of abode, Rūs wrote to his brother and "asked for a corner of his country." He obtained an island, difficult of access, with soggy soil and foul air. These and other themes are drawn from information that was part of the body of Islamic geographical literature of the 3rd-4th/9th-10th centuries (see below). Balʿamī, in his translation of al-Ṭabarī, s.a. 22/643, reports the words of Shahriyār, the ruler of Darband/Bāb al-Abwāb [*q.v.*], to the commander of the Arab advance forces, ʿAbd al-Raḥmān b. Rabīʿa, to the effect that he was "between two enemies the Khazar and the Rūs. These peoples are the enemies of the entire world and, in particular, of the Arabs." This seems very early, indeed, for a Rus' presence in this region. The Khazars, of course, were already an important factor in the North Caucasus. The pairing of the Rūs with them as enemies of the Islamic world has an anachronistic ring. Nonetheless, some scholars are willing to accept its historicity (cf. Lewicki, *Źródła arabskie do dziejów słowiańszczyzny*; Togan, *Ibn Faḍlān's Reisebericht*. Novosel'tsev cites several other references to the Rūs dating to the time of Khusraw I Anūshirwān (531-79), e.g. in al-Thaʿālibī, who built fortifications against the "Turks, Khazars and Rūs." These, too, are most probably anachronistic. The earliest reliable reference to Rūs in the Islamic sources is perhaps to be seen in the "mountain of the Rūs" from which the river *drws* flows, noted in al-Khʷārazmī's *Ṣūrat al-arḍ*; Novosel'tsev).

One of the earliest and most important notices is found in Ibn Khurradādhbih, writing probably *ca.* 272/885-6, on the "route of the Rūs merchants" who brought goods from Northern Europe/Northwestern Russia to Baghdād. It interrupts a notice on the route of the Rādhāniyya [*q.v.*], a Jewish merchant company, which appears to have been supplanted by the Rūs. Noonan has recently suggested that the latter may have initiated these contacts as early as A.D. 800. A hoard of coins found at Peterhof, near St. Petersburg, contains twenty coins (Sāsānid, Arabo-Sāsānid and Arab dirhams, the latest dated to 189/804-5) with graffitti in Arabic, Turkic (probably Khazar) runic, Greek and Scandinavian runic (more than half the total). This may be viewed as evidence for the existence of the route described in Ibn Khurradādhbih by the late 2nd/early 9th century (see T. Noonan, *When did Rūs/Rus' merchants first visit Khazaria and Baghdad?*). In Ibn Khurradādhbih's famous account, the Rūs are described as "a kind (*djins*) of the Ṣaḳāliba," a sentence that has often been taken to indicate that they are a Slavic tribe. The Arabic is much more imprecise. The primary meaning of *djins* is "kind, type, variety, species." The term Ṣaḳāliba (sing. Ṣaḳlabī < Gr. Σκλάβος) while often used to designate the Slavs, was also employed to denote the whole of the fair-haired, ruddy-complexioned population of Central, Eastern and North-eastern Europe. In mediaeval Greek and Latin, *sclavus* became synonymous with "slave" (the English word [< French *esclave*] deriving ultimately from the ethnic designation). Our source further notes that these Rūs merchants "transport beaver hides, the pelts of the black fox and swords from the farthest reaches of the Ṣaḳāliba to the Sea of Rūm. The ruler of Rūm takes a tithe of them. If they wish, they go to the (ms. Oxford, Bodleian, Huntington 433, fol. 74b نس, ms. Paris, Bibliothèque nationale 2213, fol. 49a بس, ms. Vienna, Nationalbibliothek 783, fol. 65a نيس, see also Golden, *Khazar studies*), تنيس **tnys* river (variously read/identified as the "Tanais" [Τάναϊς] i.e. the Don (so De Goeje), يتيل *yitil*, i.e. Itil (= Volga, see Lewicki, *Źródła*) or تين *Tīn* (= Don, see Marquart, or Siverskiĭ Donets', see Pritsak, *An Arabic text on the trade* *ute of the corporation of ar-Rūs in the second half of the ninth entury*), the River of the Ṣaḳāliba. They travel to Khamlīdj/Khamlīkh, the city of the Khazars whose uler takes a tithe of them. Then they betake themelves to the Sea of Djurdjān and they alight on whichever of its shores they wish .... Sometimes, they arry their goods from Djurdjān by camel to Baghdād. Ṣaḳlab slaves translate for them. They laim that they are Christians and pay the *djizya*." Much has also been made of the Rūs use of "Ṣaḳlab" ranslators, attesting, it is argued, a common Slavic ongue. Although we do not know with certainty what anguage was used, it may well have been Slavic, the most practical *lingua franca* in Central and Eastern Europe. Ibrāhīm b. Yaʿḳūb [*q.v.*], the 4rd/10th century Jewish traveller, who journeyed to Central Europe and the Western Slavic lands, remarked that 'the majority of the tribes of the North speak Ṣaḳlabī (most probably, here meaning Slavic) because of their ommingling with them. Among them are the Germans (Ṭudishkī), Hungarians (Unḳalī), Pečenegs, Rūs and Khazars." The *Ḥudūd*, has preserved the radition that among the Rūs "lives a group of Slavs who serve them" (see below). There is no doubt that he Rūs had very intimate ties with Slavic speakers and the Scandinavian-speaking element was certainly bilingual, if not completely slavicised by the late 10th entury. Igor's son, Svyatoslav (d. 972) already bears a Slavic name. There were, it might also be noted, Slavic colonies in caliphal territories that presumably could have also provided speakers fluent in Slavic and Arabic. A variant of Ibn Khurradādhbih's account, aken, perhaps, from a common source is found in Ibn al-Faḳīh. See also Pritsak, *An Arabic text*, and the earlier comments of Marquart, who suggest that the intellectual circle of Ibn al-Faḳīh's father in Hamadhān served as this common source. Here, the merchants in question are designated as Ṣaḳlab. After heir arrival at the Sea of Rūm (most probably the Black Sea is meant here) and their payment of the ithe, they go to "Samkarsh of the Jews" (cf. *Samkarṣ of the Khazar "Cambridge" document = Samkerč = Tmutorokan' /Ταμάταρχα /Φαναγουρία; see literature cited in Lewicki, *Źródła*). Then they turn towards the Ṣaḳāliba or they betake themselves from the Sea of the Ṣaḳāliba by this river, which is called the River of the Ṣaḳāliba, until they come to Khamlīkh..." Ultimately, their goods may go as far as Rayy. The identification of the various Ṣaḳlab waterways remains problematic. Al-Masʿūdī, *Murūdj*, remarks that the Rūs consist of "numerous peoples of diverse kinds. Among them are a kind (*djins*) called اللوذعانة *al-Lūdhʿāna* (or اللوذغانة **al-Lūdhghāna*) and they are the most numerous. They frequently visit, for the purpose of trade, the land of Spain [Andalus], Rome, Constantinople and the Khazars." The *Lūdhʿāna/Lūdhghana* have been identified with the Rūs grouping noted as الكوذكانة *al-Kūdhkāna* by al-Masʿūdī in his *Tanbīh*, 141. These, in turn, have been viewed as garblings of الاردمانة *al-Urdmāna* (cf. Marquart, who, while noting this possibility, preferred to view this as a corruption of *al-rāhdāniyya/al-rādhāniyya*; Minorsky, *Kuda ezdili drevnie rusi?*). Pritsak, following Kokovtsov, has suggested that the לוזניו *Lwznyw* of the "Cambridge" document, taken from an Arabic-script source لوزنيو (*lūznıyū*) is a corruption of لودمانى (*lūdmānī*, see Golb and Pritsak) = *Lo(r)dman* = *Nordman*. Pritsak has, moreover, put forward an interesting thesis in explication of the Ibn Khurradādhbih/Ibn al-Faḳīh notices. The Ṣaḳlab lands were primary sources for the slave trade (the "river of the Ṣaḳāliba" denoted the "river of Slaves" coming from the Khazar empire via the Volga and Don rivers). The two major companies involved in this trade on an international level were the Rādhāniyya/Rāhdāniyya (*ca.* 750) and the Rūs, who ultimately replaced them. Both were based in (southern) France (this is well-established for the Rādhāniyya, see Lewicki, *Źródła*, who associates the Rāhdāniyya mostly with trade in cloth). Kmietowicz, also places the Rādhāniyya "most probably in France, though they were equally connected with Spain." He derives the term for this trading diaspora from *raeda/rheda*, the name for a type of vehicle, > *veredarius* "messenger, courier, traveling merchant." The Rūs, according to Pritsak, were near Rodez: *Rutenicis* < Celto-Latin *Ruteni/Ruti* > Middle French *Rusi*, Middle Germ. *Rūzzi* (the source of Finnic *Routsi*). Unlike the Rādhāniyya, Pritsak argues, who as Jews enjoyed religious neutrality in the Mediterranean, the Rusi were obliged to seek a northern point of entry into Eastern Europe and the Baltic zone. They integrated themselves into the Frisian-Scandinavian world and by the late 8th century, developed a "Danish" type "society of nomads of the sea." Ryurik was the Frisian Danish king Rørik. The Slavic and "Rhos" (Scandinavian) languages noted by Constantine Porphyrogenitus were simply two of the *linguae francae* used by this trading diaspora (Pritsak, *Origin*). While it might be noted that neither of the two passages make any reference to the slave trade, Khazaria, as is well-known from the Arabic geographical literature, was a major source of slaves entering the eastern Islamic world and the Rūs were deeply involved in this trade.

The evidence is highly circumstantial at best. Given the complexities of their conjectured origins, it may, nonetheless, not be amiss to view the Rūs at this stage of their development, as they began to penetrate Eastern Europe, not as an ethnos, in the strict sense of the term, for this could shift as new ethnic elements were added, but rather as a commercial and political organisation. The term was certainly associated with maritime and riverine traders and merchant-mercenaries/pirates of "Ṣaḳāliba" stock (Northern and Eastern European, Scandinavian, Slavic and Finnic).

The Rūs Ḳaghanate

We have already noted that the *Annales Bertiniani* refer to the Rus' ruler as *Chacanus*. This is the Turkic title *Ḳaghan* "emperor". Kievan Rus' tradition, although overwhelmed by Byzantine models, occasionally made use of the title in literature of the Christian age: e.g. the references to "our ḳaghan Vladimir" (*kagan nash Vladimir*) and "our ḳaghan Georgii" (Yaroslav) in the mid-11th century religio-ideological tract "The sermon on Law and Grace" [*Slovo o zakone i blagodati*] of Metropolitan Ilarion (see *Des Metropoliten Ilarion Lobrede*) and the application of this title to several figures in the Igor' Tale (*Slovo o polku igoreve*). There is also the graffito in the Cathedral of St. Sophia in Kiev which reads "O Lord, save our ḳaghan" (*spasi gospodi kagana nashego*, Vîsotskiy). The Islamic geographers, based on traditions stemming from the 3rd/9th century, mention the *khāḳān rūs* (Ibn Rusta/*rūs-khāḳān* (*Ḥudūd*)/*khāḳān-i rūs* (Gardīzī, in Gardīzī/Barthold; *Mudjmal al-tawārīkh*). This title could only have come to the Rus', or more likely one grouping of them, through intimate contact (i.e. a marital tie) with one of the ruling, charismatic steppe dynasties. In all likelihood, this was the Khazar royal line. Such a tie is perhaps hinted at in the *Islendingabóc* with its references to "Yngve the King of the Turks" (see discussion in Golden, *The question of the*

Rus' Qağanate). The location of this Rūs ḳaghanate has been and remains the source of much speculation. Equally unclear are the inception point and ultimate fate of this polity. Pritsak, *Origin*, suggests that the Rūs ḳaghanate was founded by a Khazar ruler who fled to the Rus' *ca.* 830-40. He places the ḳaghanate in the Rostov-Yaroslav region of the Upper Volga. Smirnov, was of the opinion that it appeared only briefly, *ca.* 830, and was soon destroyed by the migration of the Ugro-Turkic tribal confederation that became the Hungarians in Danubian Europe. Since the latter were already on the Don by 838, cutting off the Rhos embassy from its return route from Constantinople and forcing its diversion to the Frankish lands, this would appear to have been a very short-lived political phenomenon. On the other hand, the sacral ruler described by Ibn Faḍlān in 309/921-2 (see below) certainly possessed many of the attributes of a holy Turkic Ḳaghan. The memory of this institution, in any event, endured into the Christian era of Rūs history, as we have seen, and could be summoned for ideological purposes.

The location of the Rūs lands

The tradition represented by Ibn Rusta, Gardīzī and others (cf. al-Maḳdisī, *Mudjmal*, Marwazī; al-Ḳazwīnī; Ibn Iyās, in Seippel; al-Bākuwī, see also discussion in Zakhoder, place the Rūs on an island of three days' journey in width in a lake (or a sea). It is densely wooded, damp, soggy and possessing foul, unhealthy air. Gardīzī (or rather his sources), followed by al-Maḳdisī, puts the island's population at 100,000. Ibn Iyās and al-Bākuwī comment that the island is a "fortress" that protects them from their enemies. Some scholars are inclined to place this island in the north. Novgorod, it might be remembered, in Scandinavian tradition was termed *Hólmgarðr* "Island-Garth" (Barthold, *Arab. izvest.*; Novosel'tsev). Other suggestions include Aldeigjuborg, North-east Rus', Kiev, Tmutorokan' and the Taman peninsula (see literature in Golden, *Question*). Fakhr al-Dīn Mubārakshāh, simply notes that they live on islands. This, however, may refer to a later time period. For example, al-Dimashḳī, says that they have islands in the "Sea of Māyuṭas" (text has the corrupted form "Mānīṭas" = Maeotis, the Sea of Azov). Al-Nuwayrī, terms the Black Sea the "Sea of the Rūs", adding that the Rūs "inhabit the islands in it". Al-Masʿūdī, who is uncertain of the geography involved and is perhaps referring to the situation in his day, comments regarding the Rūs who raided Spain that they "reach their country from a gulf (*khalīdj* "bay" ? "canal"?) which meets the Sea of Uḳyānus, (but) not through the gulf in which are the bronze lighthouses. In my opinion—but God knows best—this gulf is connected to the Sea of Māyuṭas and Bunṭas and this people is the Rūs..." A more northerly orientation can be assumed from Ibn Ḥawḳal's comment that the honey, wax and beaver furs brought to the Islamic world from Khazaria actually come from the region around Rūs and Bulghār. Indeed, some of the prized fur animals are only found "in these northern rivers which are near Bulghār, Rūs and Kūyāba" (see below). Al-Idrīsī, gives us some idea of the distances involved, informing us that "from Bulghār to the first border of Rūs is 10 days' journey. From Bulghār to Kūyāba it is about 20 days' journey." The anonymous author of the *Ḥudūd*, probably reporting the situation close to his own time (372/982) places the Rūs territory west of the "mountains of the Pečenegs." To its south is the river Rūtā (? Dūnā?), to the west are the Ṣaḳāliba and in the north are the "Uninhabited Lands." In contrast to the forbidding depiction of the island of the Rūs, the *Ḥudūd* views the Rūs habitat as "extremely favoured by nature with regard to all the necessities (of life)." Indeed, Ibn Rusta, seemingly contradicting his remarks about the Rus' island but obviously referring to a different grouping of Rūs and perhaps conflating earlier and later traditions, notes that they have many towns. The "island" theme, in any event, most probably referred to only one grouping of Rūs.

By the late 9th century, there were three urban-territorial units associated with the Rus'. The *Ḥudūd*, following the tradition also found in al-Iṣṭakhrī and Ibn Ḥawḳal (a mélange of these and other traditions are also recorded in al-Idrīsī), notes three subdivisions of the Rūs, each based on an urban centre: (1) *Kūyābā* (= Kiev, cf. the קייוב [Qiyōḇ] of the 10th century Khazar Kievan letter, Golb and Pritsak, the Κίοβα/Κίαβα noted by Const. Porph., who mentions that the city is also called Σαμβατάς, the meaning of which is unclear (Pritsak, *op. cit.*, 44, derives this term from Balkan Latin *sambata* "Saturday", the principal market day. He further suggests that Kiev is based on the name of the Khazarian vizierial family of Khʷārazmian origin Kūya (< **kaoya* "peculiar to the Iranian sacred ruling dynasty Kaway + *-āwa*"). This form arose in the late 9th century), and the *Cuiewa* of Western sources (Thietmar of Merseburg). Old Norse knew it as *Kœnugarðr* "Boat-Garth". This is the southernmost of the Rūs lands ("nearest to the Islamic lands"). It is also closest to and bigger than Bulghār. A Rūs king resides in Kūyābā. (2) *Ṣalāwiyya* (*Ṣalāba* in the *Ḥudūd*). Barely commented on by al-Iṣṭakhrī (who says that it is the farthest from them) and Ibn Ḥawḳal, the *Ḥudūd* remarks that it is a "pleasant town from which, whenever peace reigns, they go for trade to the districts of Bulghār." Only Ibn Ḥawḳal notes the presence of a king in it. Al-Idrīsī says that it is on the top of a mountain. The Ṣalāwiyya are clearly the Slovene of the Lake Il'men region and Novgorod. The latter was actually founded *ca.* 930, the earlier "Novgorod" is perhaps to be identified with the "Ryurikovo gorodishče", to the south which contains some Scandinavian finds (Clarke and Ambrosiani). It continued to have a strong trade orientation towards the Finno-Ugric forest peoples, competing here with Volga Bulgharia up to the Mongol conquest. (3) *Arthāniyya* (< *Rothania ? Ruthenia ?) whose city is *Ārthā(n)* (*Ḥudūd*: ارتاب *ʾrtāb*, recte ارثان) was noted for its secretiveness and inhospitality (killing all strangers who enter). Yet they actively engaged in trade bringing their goods to the outside world. According to al-Iṣṭakhrī and Ibn Ḥawḳal, they exported black sable, black fox, beaver pelts, lead and mercury (see also al-Idrīsī, 917-18). The *Ḥudūd* also ascribes to them the production of "very valuable blades and swords which can be bent in two, but as soon as the hand is removed they return to their former state." Al-Idrīsī locates it four days' travel from both Kūyāba and Ṣalāwa. Arthān(iyya) is probably to be located near the Volga or in the Volga-Oka mesopotamia (hence some efforts have been made to identify them with one or another Finno-Ugric people, cf. Swoboda). It might be noted in this connection that Arabo-Jewish documents refer to the Volga as *Arthā* and the furs imported from there were termed *arthī* (Goitein). It is unclear which, if any, of these centres may be identified with the Rūs Ḳaghanate.

Al-Idrīsī gives the names of a large number of cities in "Rūsiyya" and its immediate environs: Lūbasha (Lyubeč), Zāḳa (Sakov), Sklāhī, Ghalīsiyya (Galicia, Halič), Snūblī, Turūbī (Turov), Barazlāw

Pereyaslavl'), Qnw (Kanev ?), ʾIskī, Mūlsa, Kāw on the Danābrus/Dnieper = Kiev ?), Brzūla, Jsiyya, Brāsānsa, Lūdjgha, Armn, Mrtūrī, at the mouth of the river Danast/Dnestr (some of these are discussed in Lewicki, *Polska i kraje sąsiednie w świetle Księgi Rogera geografa arabskiego z xii w. al-Idrîsî'ego*, and Beylis.

Relations with neighbours

The Islamic sources paint a picture of largely bellicose relations with their neighbours. The *Ḥudūd* reports that "they war with all the infidels who live round them, and come out victorious." Ibn Rusta, Gardīzī and al-Maḳdisī, note the Ṣaḳāliba as the principal victims. The Rūs come by boat, capture them and send them off to the slave markets of Khazarān and Bulghār. They also take their foodstuffs since they have no cultivated fields of their own. Gardīzī adds that many Ṣaḳāliba agree to take service with the Rūs, working as servants (confirmed by the *Ḥudūd*, *loc. cit.*: "among them lives a group of Slavs who serve them"). It has often been assumed that these were the Ṣaḳlabī servants who functioned as translators for the Rūs merchants who came to Baghdād noted in Ibn Khurradādhbih (see above). How these translators acquired Arabic, if this was, in fact, the language to which they translated, is unclear. Ibrāhīm b. Yaʿḳūb remarks that the commerce of the Ṣaḳāliba "frequently comes by land and sea to the Rūs and Constantinople." The Ṣaḳāliba in question here are probably the Western Slavs. That same author, 5, reports that the Rūs also attack the Pruss (Burūs), crossing over to attack them in ships "from the West." These would appear to be Rūs operating in the Baltic. Prior to the 10th century Rūs and Ṣaḳāliba were to be found in the Khazar military service and as the servants of the Khāḳān, living in the Khazar capital. The Khazar judiciary made provisions for its ethnically variegated subject population. There were seven judges, two each for the Jews, Muslims and Christians and "one for the Ṣaḳāliba and Rūs who render judgment according to pagan judicial principles (*bi-ḥukm al-djāhiliyya*), the judgment of reason" (al-Masʿūdī, *Murūdj*; al-Iṣṭakhrī). Al-Masʿūdī, *Tanbīh*, mentions groups of Rūs, who like the Armenians, Bulgarians (Burghar) and Pečenegs, had entered the Byzantine military service. By the late 10th century, Rūs contingents, whose assistance, unlike the free-lance mercenaries already found in Byzantine service, had been requested by Constantinople, were used to suppress domestic rebellions in Anatolia (see below). Rūs-Pečeneg relations (the Pečenegs entered the Pontic steppe, driving out the Proto-Hungarian tribal union in the late 3rd/end of the 9th-beginning of the 10th century) were very complex. In 915, the first of a number of Rus'-Pečeneg "peaces" were arranged, but by 920, Igor' had launched a campaign against the nomads. Thereafter, the periods of hostility largely overshadowed the periods of more pacific interaction. As a consequence, Ibn Ḥawḳal's statement, that the Pečenegs are the "fighting power" (*shawka*) of the Rūs and their allies (*aḥlāf*)" seems quite remarkable, as does also his statement (see above) that Rūs and Pečeneg ships attacked Spain. Minorsky, *Kuda ezdili*, suggested a very different sense of this passage, translating *shawka* as "thorn" and emending *aḥlāf* to *akhlāf* "opponents." This seems closer to the general tenor of Rus'-Pečeneg relations. Although the Pečenegs had ceased to be a threat to the Kievan state and had largely been driven into the Byzantine borderlands by the Rūs and Ḳïpčaḳs by his day, al-Idrīsī made note of the warfare of these nomads on Rus' and Byzantium. He also was aware of the internecine strife that had become increasingly characteristic of Rus' domestic politics, commenting that the Rūs "have wars and constant dissension with their own kind (*maʿa djinsihim*) and with lands that are close to them" (904, 960). Allusions to similar problems may be seen in the statement of the *Mudjmal* that "they do not favour one another." Ibn Rusta and Gardīzī, however, using notices that go back to an earlier era, stress their unity, cf. Ibn Rusta: "if a people (*ṭāʾifa*) goes to war against them, they all go on campaign. They are not disunited, but are as one hand against their foes until they defeat them." He also comments that they are less fearless in combat when fighting on foot rather than from ships, their favoured mode of warfare. These two authors also note their use of "swords of Solomon" (*al-suyūf al-sulaymāniyya*), which were similar to "Frankish" blades, but less ornate. They appear to have been produced in the land of Salmān in Khurāsān (see Lewicki, *Źródła*).

Government

We have already noted the reports of the Muslim geographers regarding the Rūs Ḳaghan. Of our written sources, it is only Ibn Faḍlān, however, who appears to have actually encountered Rūs in Volga Bulgharia, during his sojourn there in 309/921-2. It is from him that we gain a detailed description of a Rūs ruler. It is not made clear if this ruler was the Ḳaghan; our source merely refers to him as the "king." According to Ibn Faḍlān, he resides in a castle, surrounded by his retinue of 400 select warriors who die when he dies. Each of them has a slave-girl to serve them. The king sits on a jewel-encrusted throne (al-Ḥanafī, in Seippel, *Fontes*, calls it a golden throne) along with 40 slave-girls, with whom he sometimes has public sexual intercourse. The king does not normally step down from the throne, even for the performance of natural functions. If he leaves the throne, his feet are not permitted to touch the ground. A horse is brought up to the throne and he mounts upon it from there. In addition, "he has a deputy who commands the armies, attacks the enemy and stands in his place before his subjects." This is clearly a description of a sacral king, in many respects similar to that of the Khazar Ḳaghanate (except for the sexual licentiousness), with its holy Ḳaghan and the *Shad/beg/yilig* who ran the actual affairs of government. If this notice is not a contamination from the notice on the Khazar Ḳaghan which immediately follows it in the text, it may be viewed as a significant piece of evidence in support of the thesis of the Khazar origins of the Rūs Ḳaghanate. Ibn Faḍlān, however, never refers to the Rūs ruler as "khāḳān." This special retinue or comitatus (perhaps the body referred to as "one group of them who practise chivalry" in the *Ḥudūd*), may be a variant of the Scandinavian *hirð* (Rus'. *grid'* "warrior, princely bodyguard", Fasmer; Jones).

The *Ḥudūd* remarks that a tithe is taken on their "booty and commercial profits." Gardīzī, however, states that their king collects this tax from merchants. Legal disputes are first brought to the "khāḳān" who renders a decision (Ibn Rusta; Gardīzī, see also al-Maḳdisī). If one of the disputants disagrees with the verdict, the king orders that they engage in a ceremonial sword fight. Whoever has the sharper sword and succeeds in chipping the blade of the other is declared the winner. Ibn Rusta adds, however, that "their companions come and stand armed. The two fight and whosoever of the two is more powerful than the other becomes the arbiter in his case as he wishes." A later report, from the 8th/14th century author Nadjm ad-Dīn al-Ḥarrānī (in Seippel, *Fontes*), states that "they do not obey a king or any law (*sharīʿa*)." There is a very distinct tradition found in al-Marwazī which is repeated and slightly mangled in ʿAwfī. The former remarks that the Rūs king is called Walādimīr (*bi-walādimīr*). In ʿAwfī this was transformed into "Būlādhmīr" (Kawerau; Barthold, *Novoe musul'manskoe izvestiye o russkikh*). This, of course, is a reference to Volodimir/Vladimir I (972-1015), who brought about the conversion of Rus' to Orthodox Christianity. Curiously, Ibn Khurradādhbih, who gives the titles of the various rulers of interest or importance (including those of the Ṣaḳāliba), makes no mention of the Rūs ruler.

Economy

The initial picture presented is that of mobile, urban-based traders/raiders. Ibn Rusta reports that the Rūs "possess no real estate property (*ʿaḳār*), nor villages, nor cultivated lands." He subsequently notes, however, that they have many towns. Rather than engaging in agrarian pursuits, "their profession is trade (*tidjāra*) in sable, grey squirrel and other such furs which they sell to purchasers. They take the value of the goods in gold and fasten it to their belts." This strong mercantile emphasis is noted by the other Muslim authors, who universally speak of their involvement in extensive trading relations with their immediate neighbours, the Khazar empire and Volga Bulgharia (through which their goods reached the Islamic lands), Byzantium, Spain and Central Europe (al-Iṣṭakhrī; al-Masʿūdī, *Murudj*). Ibrāhīm b. Yaḳūb reports that Rūs and Ṣaḳāliba traders come to "Farāgha [Prague] from Karākūʾ [Kraków]" for trade. Kiev's importance as a major commercial centre continued and is reflected in later Muslim sources. Thus al-Idrīsī comments that Muslim merchants from Armenia come to Kiev. This finds confirmation in contemporary Georgian sources (e.g. the journey of the "great merchant Zankan Zorababeli" of T'bilisi who was sent off to Rūs on a diplomatic-marital mission *ca.* 1184 "by relays of horses", *K'art'lis ts'khovreba*), using an already well-established route. The importance of this region for trade with the Islamic world would appear to be supported by considerable numismatic evidence (Islamic dirhams first begin to surface in what became Russia and the Baltic region *ca.* 800; on this see Noonan, *Why dirhams first reached Russia: the role of Arab-Khazar relations in the development of the earliest Islamic trade with Eastern Europe*). The volume of this trade seems to have exceeded that of their commercial relations with Byzantium. Although Sawyer (*Kings*, 123-6) cautions that the presence of these dirhams does not necessarily constitute evidence of a great volume of trade, nor need they have reached these areas solely by trade, Ibn Faḍlān (see below) gives direct evidence of goods being exchanged for Islamic coins. The Rūs, it may be concluded, at least in the early stages of their history, were largely merchant middlemen and on occasion pirates. They produced nothing of their own, but raided, extorted/collected tribute or traded for furs and other commodities of the Northern forest zone which they then brought to the Mediterranean or the Islamo-Central Asian world either directly or through yet other middlemen, Volga Bulgharia or Khazaria. However it was obtained, the volume of Islamic coinage entering Rus' declined in the late 10th century and had largely stopped by 1015. The causes of this change, much debated, remain unclear. Local sources of precious metals were not unknown. Thus, al-Masʿūdī (*Murūdj*) mentions silver mines in Rūs territory more or less equal to the silver sources in the Pandjhīr mountains in Khurāsān.

Personal appearance and clothing

Ibn Rusta describes the Rūs as possessed of "long bodies, a (good) visage and fearlessness." Our sources (Ibn Rusta, Gardīzī) stress their personal neatness; some are clean-shaven, others braid or plait their beard. Iṣṭakhrī and Ibn Ḥawḳal attribute this personal fastidiousness to their mercantile pursuits. Ibn Rusta further remarks that they treat their slaves well. This, too, could be viewed as an indication of a higher cultural level. Their clothing is made of linen (Gardīzī) and they wear arm bands/bracelets of gold. Their trousers, according to Ibn Rusta and the *Ḥudūd*, are made out of 100 cubits of (cotton) fabric, which they gather in at the knee and fasten there. They also wear "woollen bonnets with tails let down behind their necks" (*Ḥudūd*). Al-Iṣṭakhrī and Ibn Ḥawḳal report that they wear short coats. Ibn Faḍlān, however, who remarks that they are as tall as date palms, blond and ruddy, says that they do not wear short coats or caftans but a *kisāʾ* (a cloak, see Dozy, *Supplément*, ii, 476). He goes on to note that each of them carries an axe, a sword and a knife from which they are never parted. Their women are bedecked with various gold and silver ornaments in displays of ostentation commensurate with their husband's wealth.

Customs and religion

Our sources are impressed with the spirit of independence and enterprise inculcated among the Rūs from birth. Ibn Rusta, followed by Gardīzī, al-Maḳdisī and the *Mudjmal*, reports that "when a baby boy is born to one of them, he sets before the baby boy a drawn sword and places it between his hands and says to him 'I leave you no goods as inheritance. You have nothing except what you may acquire for yourself by this, your sword.'" Marwazī (in Kawerau) adds that the daughter receives her father's inheritance, while the son is given a sword and told "your father acquired his wealth by the sword, imitate and follow him." This same sense of rugged individualism was reflected in their treatment of the ill. Ibn Faḍlān remarks that "when one of them falls ill, they pitch a tent for him, in a secluded place away from them, and they cast him away there. They place with him quantities of bread and water" and leave him alone until he either recovers or dies. Transgressors were dealt with harshly. Thieves, this same source informs us, were hung by the neck from stout trees until dead and then left to rot.

This same author was quick to note their human frailties. He appears to contradict, at least in part, the report of their personal neatness noted above, declaring them the "dirtiest of God's creations" because of their lack of personal hygiene. To this failing were added inordinate suspicion and covetousness. Ibn Rusta and Gardīzī report as an example, in this regard, that they go out to perform their natural functions only when accompanied by several friends to stand guard. Otherwise, a man on his own would be killed. So great is their distrust and perfidy that if one acquires even a little wealth "his brothers and friends who are with him crave it, try to kill him and dispossess him of it" (Ibn Rusta). How much of this is accurate and how much travellers' tall tales highlighting the greed of the "barbarian" is difficult to gauge. It is highly doubtful, however, that the Rus' could have been as effective a commercial and military force as they were, given such a state of *bellum omnium*. Ibn Faḍlān was also shocked by their lack of modesty (engaging in sexual intercourse with their slave-girls while their friends looked on).

This same source has much to say about their beliefs. When ships arrive, he reports, they each come out bearing bread, meat, onions, milk and wine. They proceed to a long piece of wood planted in the ground on which has been carved the face of a man. It is surrounded by smaller idols and other long pieces of wood planted into the ground. They prostrate themselves before the large image, which they address as "Lord" and announce what goods they have brought. They conclude their devotions by saying "I want you to provide me with a merchant who has many dīnārs and dirhams, who will buy from me everything that I want him to buy, and he will not contradict me in what I say." If business is good, more offerings are made. In especially good circumstances, sheep and cattle are slaughtered, much of which are consumed, at night, by dogs. Ibn Faḍlān, occasionally adopting a mocking tone and anxious to display their ignorance to his readers, reports that nonetheless, he who made the offering says "my lord is satisfied with me and has eaten my gift".

According to the tradition preserved in the accounts of Ibn Rusta and Gardīzī, their shamans or "medicine men" (*aṭibbāʾ/ṭabībān*), enjoyed a very high status. They could pass judgment on the king and govern them. They could select as sacrifice to their gods whomsoever they pleased, human and animal. These unfortunates were hung by the neck until dead. The commandments of their "medicine men" must be carried out (Ibn Rusta; Gardīzī). We have relatively brief descriptions of their funerary customs in Ibn Rusta, Gardīzī and the *Ḥudūd*. Ibn Rusta reports that "when one of their important people (*dj̲alīl minhum*) dies, they dig him a grave, like a spacious house, and place him in it. Together with him, they place his personal clothing (*t̲h̲iyāb badanihi*), gold bracelets which he wore, much food, vessels with drink and gold money also. They bury with him in the grave the wife that he loved (best). She, after this (sc. his burial) is still alive. They seal up the door of the grave and she dies there." Al-Iṣṭak̲h̲rī and al-Masʿūdī, *Murūdj̲*, also note that they cremate their dead, together with their wife or slave-girl, horses and finery. Al-Masʿūdī further adds that "when the wife dies, the husband is not cremated. If one of the unmarried men dies, he is married after his demise, and the women request that they be cremated (with him) so that they may, according to their own thinking, enter among the souls of paradise." Ibn Faḍlān, however, provides us with one of the most extraordinary, ethnographically detailed depictions of the funeral of a Rūs chief. The customs were related and explained to him on a number of occasions ("they told me of the things they did with their chiefs at their death, the least of which is cremation"). He also appears to have witnessed one such spectacular funeral. The deceased was placed in a grave over which a roof was erected. He remained there for 10 days while new clothing was fashioned for him. When a great man dies they ask his household "who of you will die with him?" Those who answer in the affirmative are duty-bound to fulfill this commitment. The majority of those who agreed to do so were slave-girls. One of the slave-girls was then given this honour. The deceased was to be taken out of his grave and placed in a special structure on a boat which was taken out of the river and mounted on a kind of wooden holding frame. The corpse, because of the cold was remarkably well-preserved. An old woman called the "angel of death," was now put in charge. The deceased was placed in the special structure. Food (bread, meat, onions) was placed before him. A dog was sacrificed, cut in half and thrown on the boat. Two cows were also sacrificed (as well as other animals). The slave-girl who was to die with her master then had sexual intercourse with her master's relatives or boon companions and she was given copious amounts of wine so that she became dull-witted (*taballadat*). The men outside began to strike their shields with wooden sticks in order to drown her cries as she was strangled. A close relative of the deceased man, completely naked, set fire to the wood under the boat. The sacrificed slave-girl was placed beside her master. In response to Ibn Faḍlān's questions, one of the Rūs explains their views: "You Arabs are stupid. You take the most loved and distinguished among you and dump them in the earth. The earth consumes them (as do also) insects and worms. But we cremate them in fire, in the flick of an eye, and he enters Paradise immediately." A small burial mound was then set up on the site in which the boat was burned. A large piece of *k̲h̲adang* wood was placed on the spot and the deceased's name was written on it as well as that of the king of the Rūs. This *k̲h̲adang* wood was especially associated with the Rūs lands (see Ṭūsī, *ʿAdj̲āʾib al-mak̲h̲lūkāt*). The corpses of slaves were simply abandoned to dogs and birds of prey.

Although Art̲h̲a/Art̲h̲āniyya was famous for its inhospitality to strangers, killing all outsiders who came to it (al-Iṣṭak̲h̲rī and al-Ḥarrānī), the other areas of Rūs' were not. Ibn Rusta says that they were generous to their visitors. They were ferocious, however, in exacting revenge (*Mudj̲mal*).

The Rūs Caspian raids and the fall of K̲h̲azaria

It was undoubtedly the lucrative trade routes of the Volga that first drew the Rūs to Eastern Europe. The Rūs both traded with and raided the Islamic lands. As early as the era of the ʿAlid al-Ḥasan b. Zayd (250-70/864-84 [*q.v.*]), leader of the Zaydī S̲h̲īʿī principality in Ṭabaristān, the Rūs attempted to raid the region. A second raid took place in 297/909-10, aimed at Ābaskūn [*q.v.*]. A third raid took place in 299/911-12 and a fourth one, according to al-Masʿūdī "sometime after 300/312" (Dorn, Aliev, Minorsky; slightly different dates in Barthold and Pritsak). At the outset of this last raid the Rūs in return for being allowed passage through K̲h̲azar lands in order to raid the Caspian coasts, offered half of the spoils to the K̲h̲azar ruler. The raid caused much devastation, especially in the regions of Bard̲h̲aʿa, al-Rān, Baylakān, Ād̲h̲arbaydj̲ān, S̲h̲irwān and the city of Bākuh. The Rūs then returned to the Volga estuary. Here they were attacked, apparently with the acquiescence of the K̲h̲azar ruler, by K̲h̲azar Muslims (the Ursiyya and others), as well as some Christians, desirous of revenge. According to al-Masʿūdī, those that escaped were finished off by the Burṭās and Volga Bulg̲h̲ars. An even more ferocious eruption of the Rūs into the Caspian Islamic lands took place in 332/943-4. In that year Bard̲h̲aʿa [*q.v.*] was again a target. It was taken and the Rūs settled in, showing every intention of remaining for some time, but remained there only for some months. The K̲h̲azar-Byzantine entente by this time had come to an end. The Rūs now figured prominently in actions that were overtly hostile to K̲h̲azaria. According to the "Schechter" document, when the K̲h̲azar ruler Joseph, responding to Byzantine persecutions of Jews under the emperor Romanus I (920-44), "did away with many Christians" in his realm, Romanus retaliated by inciting "Helgu

[הלגו/Oleg, see above], king of Rusia'' against Khazaria. ''Helgu'' was forced to flee by sea where he and his men perished. The Letter of the Khazar ruler, Joseph, to Ḥasday b. Shaprut, the Jewish courtier of the Spanish Umayyads, reports, *ca.* 960, that the Khazars were continually at war with the Rūs. ''If I left them (in peace) for one hour, they would destroy the entire land of the Ishmaelites up to Bagdad'' (Kokovtsov). The main confrontation appears to have taken place in 354/965. The immediate causes for the Rūs assaults on Khazaria are not elucidated in our sources. Given the ongoing hostilities reported in the Letter of Joseph, however, Byzantine involvement in inciting revolts within the Khazar sphere of influence, the Rūs attempts to gain unrestricted passage through the Khazar-controlled Volga route to the Caspian, these may be easily conjectured. Khazaria was a fading power. The Rūs formed an alliance with the Oghuz Turks and together they advanced on Khazaria. The Primary Chronicle has a very laconic notice reporting only that in 6473/965 the Rūs ruler, Svyatoslav (d. 972) attacked the Khazars and ''took their city and Bela Veža'' (= Sarkel, a *var. lect.* says only that Bela Veža was captured). Al-Muḳaddasī reports two accounts that he ''heard.'' According to the first, Khazaria was attacked by al-Maʾmūn of Djurdjān who captured the Khazar ruler. He subsequently heard that ''an army from Rūm, called Rūs, conquered them and took possession of their land.'' Miskawayh writes that in 354/965 ''news came to the effect that the Turks had invaded the territory of the Khazars. The latter invoked the aid of the people of Khʷārazm, who declined saying: You are Jews; if you want us to help you, you must become Muslims. They all adopted Islam in consequence with the exception of their king.'' Ibn al-Athīr has, basically, the same report, adding, however, that after the Khʷārazmians drove off the Turks (the Oghuz), the Khazar ruler converted to Islam as well (see Golden, *The migrations of the Oğuz*, 77-80). Ibn Ḥawḳal, who learned of these events in 358/968-9, paints a picture of large-scale devastation. The dating of the events described in Ibn Ḥawḳal has been the subject of some debate, some scholars placing them in 358/968-969, the year in which our source first heard of the Rūs raid (Kalinina, *Svedeniya Ibn Khaukalya o pokhodakh Rusi vremeni Svyatoslava*, who, following Marquart and Barthold, *Arab. izvest.*, does not believe that Volga Bulgharia was affected by the raids). There is no reason, however, to doubt Ibn Ḥawḳal, who had first-hand information. In addition, the Rūs and their Oghuz allies followed a similar pattern 20 years later, in 985, when they attacked Volga Bulgharia, the first in boats, the second by land (*PSRL*, i, 84). A distant echo of these events is found in al-Idrīsī, writing in the mid-6th/12th century, who says of the Rūs who neighbour ''on the land of the Unkariyya (Hungarians) and Maḳadhuniyya; they have at present, at the time that we were writing this book, conquered the Burṭās, the Bulghār and Khazars, taken away control of their lands and nothing remains of these people except the name in (their former) lands.'' This, of course, is inaccurate for his day since the Burṭās and Volga Bulghars were still very much on the scene.

There are references to Rūs activities in Bāb al-Abwāb/Darband found in the *Taʾrīkh al-Bāb*. In 377/987, the *amīr* Maymūn called in the Rūs to help him against local chiefs. The Rūs came with 18 ships but uncertain of their reception, sent only one in to reconnoitre the situation. When these men were massacred by the local population, the Rūs went on to Masḳaṭ, which they looted. Rūs professional soldiers appear to have already been on the scene. Thus in 379/989, this same Maymūn is reported to have refused the demand of the Gīlānī preacher, Mūsā al-Ṭūzī, to turn over his Rūs ghulāms to him for either conversion to Islam or death. Maymūn's attempt to have a counterbalance (Rūs ghulāms) to the local population ultimately failed, for he was driven from the city and forced to surrender the ghulāms (Minorsky, *Sharvān*). He returned in 382/992. In 421/1030, the Rūs raided the Shirwān region, but were then induced, with ''much money,'' to aid the ruler of Gandja, Mūsā b. Faḍl, in suppressing a revolt in Baylaḳān. ''The Rūs then quitted Arrān for Rūm and thence proceeded to their own country'' (see *ibid.*). One of the variant mss. of this source (see idem, *Studies in Caucasian history*), using only the Top Kapı ms. 2951 of Münedjdjim-Bashī's *Djāmiʿ al-duwal*, which contains extracts from the *Taʾrīkh al-Bāb*, says that in 422/November 1031, the Rūs ''came a second time and Mūsā set forth and fought them near Bakūya. He killed a large number of their warriors and expelled them from his dominions.'' This was followed in 423/1032 by a Rūs raid into Shirwān, joined now by the Alans and Sarīr. They were defeated, in 424/1033, by local Muslims who ''wrought great havoc'' among them (Minorsky, *Studies*, and idem, *Sharvān*). It is unclear to which Rūs grouping these raiders may have belonged. Pritsak, *Origin*, suggests that they operated out of a base near the Terek estuary and had their principal home in Tmutorokan'. He also conjectures that shortly thereafter, the Rūs, operating in the Caspian, may have provided some military assistance to the Oghuz in a power struggle in Khʷārazm. Khāḳānī tells of a Rūs raid *ca.* 569/1173 or 570/1174. These Rūs appear to have been Volga pirates who came in 73 ships. At the same time, although it is unclear if their actions were coordinated, the Ḳîpčaḳs [*q.v.*] attacked Darband and went on to take Shābarān as well. The Shirwānshāh, Akhsitan/Aghsartan I turned to the Georgian king, Giorgi III (d. 1184), for aid. Together they defeated both the Rūs and the Ḳîpčaḳs. The Georgian sources, however, only mention attacks of the Khazars of Darband. Completely anachronistic, of course, is the tale of Alexander's wars against the Rūs found in Niẓāmī's *Iskandar-nāma*. The Rūs king, called Ḳnṭāl, is presented as the ruler of the Burṭās, Khazars, Alans and (W)īsū (Vepsi).

Later sources offer little new historical or ethnographical information regarding the Rūs, being largely compilations based on the earlier sources. We have a brief description of the Mongol conquest of Rus' in Djuwaynī, lacking in specific details. Other sources, e.g. Djūzdjānī, merely note them in passing.

There are occasional references to the ''Rūs'', here designating the Russians/Muscovites, in later Ottoman-Ṣafawid era Islamic sources, e.g. *kanāz Iwān* (Russ. *knyaz' Ivan* = Ivan IV ''the Terrible''), mentioned in a discussion of Russo-Crimean Tatar relations s.a. 980/1572-3, in Hasan Rūmlū, 584-5. The Crimean Tatars had raided and burned Moscow in 1571, but another raid the following year was repulsed. Ottoman materials for the history of the later Eastern Slavic peoples have been relatively little investigated (cf. Ewliyā Čelebī's comments on the *Rūs-ī menḥūs* ''inauspicious Rūs'' Ukrainian Cossacks).

The conversion of the Rūs

The Islamic and Arabic-writing Christian authors provide useful data on the conversion of the Rūs to

Orthodox Christianity. In 987, the Byzantine emperor Basil II (976-1025) was faced with the revolts of Bardas Sclerus and Bardas Phocas. The latter, having double-crossed Sclerus, with whom he briefly joined forces, proclaimed himself emperor on 17 Djumādā 377/14 Aylūl 1298/14 September 987, as we are informed by Yaḥyā of Antioch (d. *ca.* 1066). Basil, now desperate, sent to the Rūs, "even though they were enemies," for assistance. The Rūs ruler, Volodimir/Vladimir, agreed to send troops in return for a marital alliance. He was to marry Basil's sister. Volodimir also agreed to convert to Orthodoxy and, with him, his people, who were without any religion or religious law. Basil subsequently sent him a metropolitan and bishops. When the wedding arrangements were settled, the Rūs troops were sent and they helped to put down the revolt. Essentially similar accounts are given by Abu Shudjāʿ al-Rūdhrāwarī [*q.v.*] (d. 1095), al-Makīn, al-Dimashḳī and Ibn al-Athīr (see Rozen and Kawerau; Ibn al-Athīr dates these events to 375/985-6). Some of the 6,000 Rūs troops sent to aid Basil remained in Byzantine service, forming the nucleus of the famous "Varangian Guard" (see V.G. Vasil'evskiy). The Rus' tradition relates only that Volodimir, who had long been considering the adoption of a monotheistic religion and had examined Islam, Judaism and Christianity, was already inclining towards the latter in its Orthodox form. Islam he rejected because of its prohibition on alcohol, remarking that "for Rus', drinking is a joy, we cannot exist without it" (*PSRL*, i, 84 ff.). In 988 he marched on Byzantine Crimea, taking Chersones/Korsun'. With this he now forced Basil and his brother Constantine into a marital tie. Their sister Anna was sent to Volodimir, who in return agreed to convert himself and his people to Orthodoxy (*PSRL*, i, 109 ff.). The two accounts do not necessarily contradict each other. Volodimir may well have used his excursion to the Crimea to insure that he received his Byzantine princess.

Another Islamic tradition, however, depicts the Rūs as first converting to Christianity and somewhat later to Islam. Marwazī, who mentions that their ruler is called *Walādimīr* (see above) relates that after they "entered Christendom," their new faith "sheathed their swords" and prevented them from acquiring wealth by their customary means (warfare). They were reduced to poverty. They were then drawn to Islam, which allowed them to engage in holy war. They dispatched an embassy, consisting of four relatives of the king, to Khʷārazm. The Khʷārazm-shāh sent an Islamic scholar to instruct them and they converted to Islam (Kawerau, also found in ʿAwfī/Barthold, placing this event in 300/912).

Writing systems

Ibn Faḍlān speaks of wooden grave markers on which the Rūs inscribed the name of the deceased and that of the Rūs king. Similarly, al-Nadīm writes that one of his informants "believes that they have writing inscribed in wood, and he showed me a piece of white wood with an inscription on it." This may perhaps be a reference to writing on birchwood bark, well known in later Kievan Rus'. The Byzantine missionary Constantine (Cyril), before his famous mission to the Slavs of "Moravia" journeyed, *ca.* 860, to the Khazar empire. According to the *Vita Constantini*, in the Khersonese he found a Psalter and book of the Gospel written in the Rus' or Rush script (*ros'kî [rous'kîmi, roushkimi] pismenî pisano*). He also encountered someone who spoke this language and found that he could understand him. Indeed, he quickly began to read and speak this tongue (Grivec *et al.*; Istrin). Since, Constantine/Cyril was bilingual, in Greek and Slavic, it could only have been the latter tongue, whose writing system he was able to assimilate so quickly. Needless to say, there is much debate over the significance and indeed historicity of this passage. The existence of calendrical and other types of markings among the Eastern Slavs by the 2nd-4th centuries A.D. is posited by some Russian scholars (Rîbakov). The use of a "proto-Cyrillic" alphabet based on Greek, which was already employed in Danubian Bulgaria, is also suggested for Pre-Christian Rus' (Istrin). The oldest Cyrillic monument dates to 863 (from Preslav, Bulgaria). The earliest writings in Cyrillic in Rus' are dated to the early 10th century. There is still some debate over whether Constantine/Cyril invented the "Glagolitic" alphabet, itself perhaps derived from a Greek or Cyrillic base, but quite different in appearance from "Cyrillic", or the script that now bears his name.

Bibliography: 1. Primary sources (including translations).

Collections of Sources. S.D. Goitein, *Letters of Medieval Jewish traders*, Princeton 1973, 69; Labuda, *Źródła skandynawskie i anglosaskie do dziejów Słowiańszczyzny* ["Scandinavian and Anglo-Saxon sources for the history of the Slavs], Warszawa 1961,187; T. Lewicki, *Źródła arabskie do dziejów Słowiańszczyzny* ["Arab sources for the history of the Slavs], Wrocław-Kraków-Warszawa 1956, 1969, 1977, i, 127, 132-7, ii/1, 76-7, 82-3, ii/2,139; P. Kawerau, *Arabische Quellen zur Christianisierung Rußlands* (Marburger Abhandlungen zur Geschichte und Kultur Osteuropas, 7), Wiesbaden 1967, 14-41, 46-7; A.P. Novosel'tsev, *Vostočnîe istočniki o vostočnîkh slavyanakh* ["The eastern sources on the eastern Slavs"], in V.T. Pashuto, L.V. Čerepnin, *Drevnerusskoe gosudarstvo i ego meždunarodnoe značenie* ["The ancient Rus' state and its international significance"], Moscow 1965, 362-5, 373, 403; A. Seippel, *Rerum Normannicarum fontes arabici*, Oslo 1928, 108, 113; B.N. Zakhoder, *Kaspiyskiy svod svedeniy o vostočnoy evrope* ["The Caspian codex of information on Eastern Europe"], Moscow 1962-7, ii, 78-80.

Arabic Sources. Anon., *Taʾrīkh al-Bāb*, see excerpts in Minorsky, *Sharvān*, and *Studies*; Bākuwī, *Kitāb Talkhīṣ al-āthār wa-ʿadjāʾib al-Malik al-Ḳahhār*, ed. Z.M. Buniyatov, Moscow 1971, facs. 67a, Ru. tr. 104; Dimashḳī, *Cosmographie de Chems ad-Dīn Abou Abdallah Mohammed ed-Dimachqui*, ed. A.F. Mehren, St. Petersburg 1866, 263; Ibn al-Athīr, Beirut 1965-6, viii, 411-15, 565, ix, 43-4; Ibn Faḍlān: Z.V. Togan, *Ibn Faḍlān's Reisebericht (Abhandlungen für die Kunde des Morgenlandes*, Bd. xxiv/3, Leipzig 1939, 36-43/86-98; = ed. S. Dahhān, Damascus 1389/1959-60, 60, 149 ff., 152-66; *Kniga Akhmeda Ibn-Fadlana o ego puteshestvii na Volgu v 921-922gg.* ["The book of Aḥmad ibn Faḍlān about his journey to the Volga in 921-922"], facs. ed. and Russ. tr. A.P. Kovalevskiy, Khar'kov 1956; Ibn al-Faḳīh, ed. De Goeje, 270-1; Ibn Ḥawḳal, ed. Kramers, i, 15, ii, 92, 392-8; Ibn Khurradādhbih, ed. De Goeje 16-17, 154; Miskawayh, *Tadjārib al-umam*, ed. H.F. Amedroz, tr. D.S. Margoliouth, in *Eclipse of the ʿAbbasid caliphate*, Oxford 1914-21, ii, 62-7, 209, v, 67-74, 223; Ibn Rusta, ed. De Goeje, 145-6; Ibrāhīm b. Yaʿḳūb, T. Kowalski (ed. and tr.), *Relacja Ibrâhîma ibn Jaʿkûba z podróży do krajów słowiańskich w przekazie al-Bekrîego* (Pomniki dziejów Polski, seria II, t. 1), Kraków 1946, 3, 5, 7/52; al-Idrīsī, *Kitāb Nuzhat al-mushtāḳ fī ikhtirāḳ al-āfāḳ*: *Opus geographicum sive "Liber ad eorum delectationem qui terras peragrare studeant"*, ed. A. Bombaci *et al.*, Leiden 1970-84, 912-14, 917, 919-20, 955; Idrīsī: T. Lewicki, *Polska i kraje sąsiednie w świetle Księgi Rogera geografa arabskiego z xii w. al-Idrīsī'ego* ["Poland and neighbouring lands in light of the Book of Roger, an Arab geographer from the 12th century, al-Idrīsī"], Kraków 1945, Warsaw 1954; Iṣṭakhrī, ed. De Goeje, 225-6, 229; Ḳazwīnī, *Āthār al-bilād wa-akhbār al-ʿibād*, Beirut 1389/1969, 586; Khʷārazmī, *Das kitāb Ṣūrat al-Arḍ des abū Ga'far Muhammed ibn Musa al-Ḫuwārizmī*, ed. H. von Mžik (Bibliothek arabischer Historiker und Geographen, iii), Leipzig 1926, 136; Maḳdisī, *al-Badʾ wa 'l-taʾrīkh*, ed. Cl. Huart, Paris 1899-1919, iv, 66-7; Masʿūdī, *Murūdj al-dhahab*, ed. Barbier de Meynard and Pavet de Courteille, ed. and tr. Ch. Pellat, Beirut 1966-89, i, 354-5 = § 404, ii, 9 = § 449, 11 = § 451, 14-15 = §§ 454-5, 18-26 = §§ 458-61; idem, *Tanbīh*, ed. De Goeje, 140-1; Muḳaddasī, ed. De Goeje, 361, ed. M. Makhzūm, Beirut 1408/1987, 286; Nadīm, *Fihrist*, ed. M. al-Shuwaymī, Tunis 1406/1985, 105, tr. B. Dodge, New York-London 1970, i, 37; Nuwayrī, *Nihāyat al-arab*, Cairo 1342/1923, 247; Thaʿālibī, *Histoire des rois des perses*, ed. and tr. H. Zotenberg, Paris 1900, repr. Tehran 1963, 611; Yaʿḳūbī, *Buldān*, ed. De Goeje, 354; Yaḥyā al-Anṭakī: V.R. Rozen, ed. and tr., *Imperator Vasiliy Bolgaroboytsa. Izvlečeniya iz letopisi Yakh'i Antiokhiyskogo* ["The Emperor Basil the Bulgar-Slayer. Excerpts from the chronicle of Yaḥyā of Antioch"], St. Petersburg 1883, text 20-4, tr. 21-5, comm. 194 ff.

Armenian sources. Movsēs Dasxuranc̣i, *The History of the Caucasian Albanians*, tr. C.F.J. Dowsett, London 1961,224.

Byzantine Sources. Constantine Porphyrogenitus, *De administrando imperio*, ed. Gy. Moravcsik, Engl. tr. R.J.H. Jenkins (*Corpus fontium historiae Byzantinae*, vol. 1), Dumbarton Oaks, Washington, D.C. 1967, 56, 58.

Georgian Sources. K'art'lis Ts'khovreba ["History of Georgia"], ed. S. Ḳaukhch'ishvili, T'bilisi, 1955, 1959, ii, 17, 36-7.

Hebrew Sources. N. Golb, O. Pritsak, *Khazarian Hebrew documents of the tenth century*, Ithaca, N.Y. 1982, 114-21,129, 139-42; P.K. Kokovtsov, *Evreysko-Khazarskaya perepiska v X veke* ["The Jewish-Khazar correspondence in the 10th century"], Leningrad 1932, 122-3 n. 25.

Latin Sources. Annales Bertiniani, Annales de Saint-Bertin, ed. F. Grat, J. Vielliard and S. Clément, Paris 1964, 30; Liudprand of Cremona, *Antapodosis* in *Liudprandi Episcopi Cremonensis Opera*, 3rd ed. J. Becker, in *Scriptores Rerum Germanicarum in usum scholarium ex Monumentis Germanicae Historicis separatim editi*, Hanover-Leipzig 1915, repr. Hanover 1977, i, 11, v, 15.

Old Slavic Sources. F. Grivec *et al.* (eds.), *Constantinus et Methodius Thessalonicenses, fontes* (Radovi staroslavenskog instituta, iv), Zagreb 1960, 109; T. Lehr-Spławiński (ed. and tr.), *Żywoty Konstantyna i Metodego (obszerne)*, Poznań 1959.

Old Russian Sources. Des Metropoliten Ilarion Lobrede auf Vladimir den Heiligen und Glaubensbekenntnis, ed. L. Müller, Wiesbaden 1962, 13, 100, 103, 129, 143; *Novgorodskaya pervaya letopis' starshego i mladshego izvodov*, ed. A.N. Nasonov, Moscow-Leningrad 1950; *Polnoe sobranie russkikh letopisey*, St. Petersburg/Leningrad-Moscow 1846-; *Slovo o polku igoreve*, ed. D.S. Likhačev, Moscow 1982, 143; S.A. Vïsotskiy, *Drevnerusskie graffiti sofii kievskoy*, in *Numizmatika i epigrafika*, iii (1962).

Persian Sources. ʿAwfī, W. Barthold, *Novoe musul'manskoe izvestiye o russkikh* ["A new Muslim notice on the Russians"], in *Akademik V.V. Bartol'd Sočineniya*, Moscow 1963-73, ii/1, 805-9; Bayhaḳī, *Taʾrīkh-i Masʿūdī*, ed. ʿA.A. Fayyāḍ, Mashhad 1391/1971, 601; Abū ʿAlī Muḥammad Balʿamī, *Tardjuma-yi Tārīkh-i Ṭabarī*, ed. M.Dj. Mashkūr, Tehran 1337/1947-8, 336; Djuwaynī, ed. Ḳazwīnī, i, 224-5 tr. Boyle, Manchester 1958, i, 268-70; Djūzdjānī, *Ṭabaḳāt-i Nāṣirī*, ed. W.N. Lees, Calcutta 1864, 406, *Ṭabaḳât-i Nâṣirī*, tr. H.G. Raverty 1881, repr. New Delhi 1970, ii, 1169; Gardīzī/Barthold, V.V. Bartol'd, *Izvlečenie iz sočineniya Gardizi Zayn al-Akhbār* ["An excerpt from the work of Gardīzī, the *Zayn al-akhbār*"], in *Sočineniya*, viii, 23-62; Ḥasan-i Rūmlū, *Aḥsan al-tawārīkh*, ed. ʿAbd al-Ḥusayn Nawāʾī, Tehran 1357/1938, 584-5; anon., *Ḥudūd al-ʿālam*, tr. V.F. Minorsky, London 1937, repr. with additions 1970, 159, 181-2, 422, 432; Khāḳānī, *Dīwān-i Khāḳānī-yi Shirvānī*, ed. ʿAlī ʿAbd al-Rasūlī, Tehran 1316/1898-9; Fakhr al-Dīn Mubārakshāh, *Ta'rīkh-i Fakhruʾd-Dín Mubárakshāh*, ed. E. Denison Ross, London 1927, 42; anon., *Mudjmal at-Tawārīkh*, Tehran 1939, 101-2, 421; Muḥammad b. Maḥmūd Ṭūsī, *ʿAdjāʾib al-makhlūḳāt*, ed. M. Sutūda, Tehran 1386/1966, 312.

2. Secondary literature. S. Aliev, *O datirovke nabega rusov, upomyanutikh Ibn Isfandiyarom i Amoli* ["On the dating of the raid of the Rus' mentioned by Ibn Isfandiyār and Āmulī"), in A.S. Tveritinova (ed.), *Vostočnïe istočniki po istorii narodov yugo-vostočnoy i tsentral'noy evropy*, ii, Moscow 1969, 316-21; W. Barthold (V.V. Bartol'd), *Akademik V.V. Bartol'd, Sočineniya*, Moscow 1963-73, see his *Arabskie izvestiya o rusakh* ["Arabic notices on the Rus'"], ii/1, 810-58; idem, *Mesto prikaspiyskikh oblastey v istorii musul'manskogo mira* ["The place of the Caspian districts in the history of the Muslim world"], ii/1, 651-772; V.M. Beylis, *Al-Idrisi (XII v.) o vostočnom pričernomor'e i yugo-vostočnoy okraine russkikh zemel'* ["Al-Idrīsī (12th century) on the eastern Black Sea and southeastern borderland of the Russian lands"], in *Drevneyshie gosudarstva na territorii SSSR, 1982*, Moscow 1984, 208-28; I. Boba, *Nomads, Northmen and Slavs*, The Hague-Wiesbaden 1967; P.G. Bulgakov, *Kniga putey i gosudarstv Ibn Khurdadbekha (K izučeniyu i datirovke redaktsii)* ["The book of the routes and kingdoms of Ibn Khurdādhbih. Towards the study and dating of its redaction"], in *Palestinskiy Sbornik*, iii (lxvi) (1958), 127-36; H. Clarke and B. Ambrosiani, *Towns in the Viking age*, New York 1991; M. Fasmer (Vasmer), *Etimologičeskiy slovar' russkogo yazïka* ["Etymological dictionary of the Russian language"] tr. O.N. Trubačëv, 2nd ed., Moscow 1986-7, i, 458, iii, 522-3; B. Dorn, *Caspia. Über die Einfälle der alten Russen in Tabaristan, nebst Zugaben über andere von ihnen auf dem Kaspischen Meere und in den anliegenden Ländern ausgeführte Unternehmungen*, St. Petersburg 1875, 5-6; P.B. Golden, *The migrations of the Oğuz*, in *Archivum Ottomanicum*, iv (1972), 45-84; idem, *Khazar studies* (Bibliotheca Orientalis Hungarica, xxv), Budapest 1980; idem, *The question of the Rus' Qağanate*, in *Archivum Eurasiae Medii Aevi*, ii (1982), 77-97; idem, *Aspects of the nomadic factor in the economic development of Kievan Rus'*, in I.S. Koropeckyj (ed.), *Ukrainian economic history. Interpretive essays*, Cambridge, Mass. 1991, 58-101; H. Ḥasan, *Falakī-i Shirwānī: his times, life, and works*, London 1929, 36-9; M.S. Hrushevs'kïy, *Istoriya Ukraïnï-Rusï* ["History of Ukraine-Rus'"], i, 3rd ed., Kiev 1913, repr. Kiev 1991; V.I. Istrin, *1100 let slavyanskoy azbuki* ["1100 years of the Slavic alphabet"], 2nd ed., Moscow 1988,

19; R.J. Jenkins *et al.* (eds.), *Constantine Porphyrogenitus De administrando imperio.* Commentary, London 1962, 22-3; G. Jones, *A history of the Vikings*, rev. ed. Oxford 1984, 76 n. 1, 152-3, 211, 246-7, 248 n.3; T.M. Kalinina, *Svedeniya Ibn Khaukalya o pokhodakh Rusi vremeni Svyatoslava* ["The information of Ibn Ḥawḳal on the campaigns of the Rus' of the time of Svyatoslav"], *Drevneyshie gosudarstva na territorii SSSR. Materialī i issledovaniya 1975g.*, Moscow 1976, 90-101; F. Kmietowicz, *The term ar-Rādānīya in the work of Ibn Ḥurdādbeh*, in *Folia Orientalia*, xi (1969), 163-73; F. Kruze (Kruse), *O proiskhoždenii ryurika* ["On the origin of Ryurik"], in *Žurnal Ministerstva Narodnogo Prosvesheniya*, ix (1836), 47-73; E. Kválen, *The early Norwegian settlements on the Volga*, Vienna 1937; H. Łowmiański, *Zagadnienie roli normanów w genezie państw słowiańskich* ["The question of the role of the Normans in the genesis of the Slavic states"], Warsaw 1957, Russ. tr. *Rus' i normanny* ["'Rus' and the Normans"], Moscow 1985, 283; J. Marquart, *Osteuropäische und ostasiatische Streifzüge*, Leipzig 1903, 343-5, 350, 352, 355 ff., 385 ff., 474-5; V.V. Mavrodin, *Proiskhoždenie russkogo naroda* ["The origin of the Russian people"], Leningrad 1978; V.F. Minorsky, *Khāqānī and Andronicus Comnenus*, in *BSOAS*, xi (1945), 555-78; idem, *Studies in Caucasian history*, London 1953, 11-12, 76-7; idem, *A history of Sharvān and Darband*, Cambridge 1958, 9/31-2, 19/45, 21-47, 111; idem, *Kuda ezdili drevnie rusî?* ["Where did the ancient Rus' go?"], in *Vostočnîe istočniki po istorii narodov yugo-vostočnoy i tsenral'noy evropî*, ed. A.S. Tveritinova, Moscow 1964, 19-28; T.S. Noonan, *Ninth-century dirham hoards from European Russia: a preliminary analysis*, in A.R. Hands *et al.* (eds.), *Viking-age coinage in the northern lands*, Oxford 1981, 47-117; idem, *Why dirhams first reached Russia: the role of Arab-Khazar relations in the development of the earliest Islamic trade with Eastern Europe*, in *Archivum Eurasiae Medii Aevi*, iv (1984), 151-282; idem, *Khazaria as an intermediary between Islam and Eastern Europe in the second half of the ninth century: the numismatic perspective*, in *Archivum Eurasiae Medii Aevi*, v (1985), 179-204; idem, *When did Rūs/Rus' merchants first visit Khazaria and Baghdad?*, in *Archivum eurasiae medii aevi*, vii (1987-91), 213-19; N.V. Pigulëvskaya, *Imya "rus'" v siriyskom istočnike VI b. n.e.* ["The name 'Rus'" in a Syriac source of the 6th century A.D."], in *Akademiku B.D. Grekovu ko dnyu semidesyatiletiya*, Moscow 1952, 46-8; N.Ya. Polovoy, *O marshrute pokhoda Russkikh na Berdaa i Russko-Khazarskikh otnosheniyakh v 943 g.* ["On the route of the expedition of the Rus' against Bardhaʿa in 943"], in *Vizantiyskiy vremennik*, xxv (1961); O. Pritsak, *An Arabic text on the trade route of the corporation of ar-Rūs in the second half of the ninth century*, in *Folia Orientalia*, xii (1970), 241-59; idem, *The origin of Rus'*, Cambridge, Mass. 1981, 23-8, 44, 182, 442-4, 450-1; S. Rospond, *Pochodzenie nazwy Rus'* ["The origin of the name Rus'"], in *Rocznik Slawistyczny*, xxxviii/1 (1977), 35-50; A.V. Riasanovsky, *The Embassy of 838 revisited: some comments in connection with a "Normanist" source on early Russian history*, in *Jahrbücher für die Geschichte Osteuropas*, x/1 (1962), 1-12; B.A. Rîbakov, *Russkie zemli na karte Idrisi 1154g.* ["The Russian lands on the map of Idrisi of 1154"], in *Kratkie soobshčeniya instituta istorii material'noy kul'tury*, xliii (1953), 1-44; idem, *Kievskaya Rus' i Russkie knyažestva xii-xiii vv.* [Kievan Rus' and the Rus' principalities], Moscow 1982, 165 ff.; idem, *Yazičestvo drevney Rusi* ["The paganism of ancient Rus'"], Moscow 1987; P.H. Sawyer, *Kings and Vikings. Scandinavia and Europe A.D. 700-1100*, London-New York 1982, 123-6; A.A. Shakhmatov, *Drevneyshie sud'by russkogo plemeni* ["The ancientmost fortunes of the Russian tribe"], Petrograd 1919; P. Smirnov, *Volz'kîy shlyakh i starodavni Rusî* ["The Volga route and the ancient Rus'"], Kiev 1928, 132-45; A. Stender-Petersen, *Zur Rus-Frage*, in his *Varangica*, Aarhus 1953; W. Swoboda, *ʾArû-ʾArîsû-al-Artâniya*, in *Folia Orientalia*, xi (1969), 291-6; V. Thomsen, *The relations between ancient Russia and Scandinavia and the origin of the Russian state*, Oxford-London 1877; P.P. Toločko, *Drevnyaya Rus'* ["Ancient Rus'"], Kiev 1987, 15-20, 31-5; V.G. Vasil'evskiy, *Varyago-russkaya i varyago-angliyskaya družina v Konstantinopole xi i xii vekov*, in *Trudy V.G. Vasil'evskogo*, St. Petersburg 1908, repr. The Hague-Paris 1968, i, 176-401; A.A. Vasiliev, *The Russian attack on Constantinople in 860*, Cambridge, Mass. 1946; G. Vernadsky, *Ancient Russia*, New Haven 1943, 107,147,278; idem, *The origins of Russia*, Oxford 1959, 33, 53, 65, 78, 174-5; A.P. Vlasto, *The entry of the Slavs into Christendom*, Cambridge 1970.   (P.B. Golden)

AL-RUṢĀFA, the name of several places in the Islamic world, from Cordova in the west to Nīshāpūr in the east (see Yāḳūt, *Buldān*, ed. Beirut, iii, 46-50).

Amongst the Ruṣāfa settlements of ʿIrāḳ were:

1. Ruṣāfat Abi 'l-ʿAbbās (ʿAbd Allāh al-Saffāḥ), begun by the first ʿAbbāsid caliph in lower ʿIrāḳ on the banks of the Euphrates, near al-Anbār [*q.v.*], and probably identical with that town called al-Hāshimiyya.

Bibliography: Yaʿḳūbī, *Buldān*, 237, tr. Wiet, 9; Yāḳūt, *Buldān*, iii, 46.

2. al-Ruṣāfa, the name of a quarter of the city of Baghdād [*q.v.*] founded soon after the caliph al-Manṣūr [*q.v.*] built his Round City.

The quarter of al-Ruṣāfa (whose name refers to the paved, embanked causeway across the swampy ground enclosed by the bend of the Tigris within which the quarter was laid out) was, according to the historical accounts, built by al-Manṣūr on the eastern banks of the river, opposite the palace of al-Khuld and the Round City, for his son and heir al-Mahdī [*q.v.*] when the latter returned from Rayy in northern Persia in Shawwāl 151/October-November 768. It combined a palace complex, with protective rampart and moat, and an army encampment with a review ground (*maydān* [*q.v.*]) and with various estates granted out as *ḳaṭāʾiʿ* to members of the ʿAbbāsid family and to the great military commanders (see Yaʿḳūbī, *Buldān*, 249, 251, tr. 31-2, 35-6). From this last function as a military centre, it was originally known as ʿAskar al-Mahdī. Al-Ṭabarī (iii, 365-7, tr. H. Kennedy, *Al-Manṣūr and al-Mahdī*, Albany 1990, 56-9) plausibly explains that the caliph wished to separate his Arab supporting forces by the river which divided the two sides of Baghdād, so that if one section of the army rebelled, he could call upon the forces on the opposite bank.

The building of al-Ruṣāfa took seven years, and was not completed till 159/776, by which time al-Mahdī had (in 159/775) succeeded to the throne. The new quarter was connected to the western side of Baghdād by a bridge of boats, al-Djisr, whose obvious strategic importance was such that each end was guarded by a police post of the *shurṭa* [*q.v.*]. Lassner has suggested that al-Manṣūr began the construction in al-Ruṣāfa of a palace complex of such splendour in order to buttress his son's right to succeed to the caliphate against his nephew ʿĪsā b. Mūsā [*q.v.*], thereby asserting al-Mahdī's claims.

As caliph, al-Mahdī made al-Ruṣāfa his official

residence, but towards the end of his reign preferred to spend much of his time at a new palace and pleasure ground, that of ʿĪsābādh, also on the eastern side of the city but away from al-Ruṣāfa. His successors Hārūn al-Rashīd and al-Amīn [*q.vv.*] chose, however, to reside at al-Khuld on the western side; and eventually, al-Muʿtaṣim [*q.v.*] moved his seat to the new military centre of Sāmarrā [*q.v.*] some 100 km/60 miles upstream from Baghdād.

The foundation of al-Ruṣāfa was the starting-point for the expansion of Baghdād into such suburbs as Shammāsiyya to its north-east and Mukharrim to its south; in later times, the tombs of the ʿAbbāsid caliphs were located along the river bank above al-Ruṣāfa.

Bibliography: Le Strange, *Baghdad during the Abbasid caliphate*, Oxford 1900, 187-98; J. Lassner, *The topography of Baghdad in the early Middle Ages*, Detroit 1970, 64-5 (trs. the relevant section in the survey of the historical topography of Baghdād by al-Khaṭīb al-Baghdādī, 95 ff.). (C.E. Bosworth)

3. In Syria.

This place, distinguished as Ruṣāfat Hishām, Ruṣāfat al-Shām, is now a ruinous site 30 km/19 miles to the south of the Euphrates in a depression near the Djabal Bishrī, on the ancient desert route from Ḥimṣ-Salamiya to al-Raḳḳa or al-Raḥba, containing the pilgrimage place of the "Arab" Saint Sergius, martyred here in the early 4th century, after which it was officially named Sergiupolis in Byzantine times. Archaeological excavations have shown it to be a Roman site, which in the 6th century was embellished with four churches inside the impressive rectangular city walls; among them, the basilica of the Holy Cross, founded in 559 and housing the relics, shows by inscriptions a continuous building tradition until the 12th century. Also inside the city walls, three large cisterns and an ingenious system of supply and distribution of the spring rain water remained famous throughout mediaeval sources. It seems to be referred to in the *K. al-ʿUyūn wa 'l-ḥadāʾiḳ*: "It had been a Byzantine city of ancient foundation with cisterns and a 'water way' (*ṭarīḳ li 'l-māʾ*) from the margins of the desert" (in *Fragmenta*, 101). Outside the north gate a church or *praetorium* (?) is connected to the Ghassānid prince al-Mundhir b. al-Ḥārith (569-82) by an inscription, and literary sources point to the presence of the Ghassanids as well: al-Nuʿmān b. al-Ḥārith b. al-Ayham is mentioned as a governor there, and is said to have repaired the cisterns destroyed by a Lakhmid and to have constructed a large new one (Yāḳūt, ii, 955, 784 (according to the *Akhbār mulūk Ghassān*); Ḥamza al-Iṣfahānī, *Taʾrīkh*, Berlin 1340/1921-2, 79 (and quoted by Ibn al-ʿAdīm, *Bughya*, i, 114), as well as Abu 'l-Fidāʾ, *Mukhtaṣar*, Cairo 1325, i, 73, only mention the restoration).

Al-Aṣmaʿī mentions, besides the B. Djafna of Ghassān, the B. Ḥanīfa (of Bakr b. Wāʾil, Ibn al-Kalbī-Caskel, ii, 156; Kaḥḥāla, *Ḳabāʾil*, i, 312-13) as inhabitants (quoted by al-Bakrī, *Muʿdjam*, i, 441); it is he who gives a further name of this, *Ruṣāfa al-Zawrāʾ* (compare Bakrī with Yāḳūt, ii, 784, 955; Musil, *Palmyrena*, 267; the "Byzantine" name for al-Ruṣāfa, Ḳ.ṭāmīlā, supposed by Ibn al-ʿAdīm, i, 113, remains unexplained, cf. Ibn Khurradādhbih, 218, B.ṭ. lāmiyā, 35 *mīls* from it?). Earlier, the city was within the region of the Tanūkh (al-Balādhurī, *Futūḥ*, 145; I. Shahid, *Byzantium and the Arabs in the fourth century*, Washington 1984, 405, 465), and—after them?—of the Taghlib (al-Ṭabarī, i, 2072; Rotter, *Die Umayyaden und der zweite Bürgerkrieg*, Wiesbaden 1982, 131). This may have led to the occasional attribution of al-Ruṣāfa to Diyār Muḍar (e.g. al-Ṭabarī, iii, 2219). In the ʿAbbāsid period, it came under the control of the B. Khafādja b. ʿAmr, a branch of the (North Arabian) ʿUḳayl (al-Aṣmaʿī, in Yāḳūt, ii, 284; Caskel, ii, 338; Kaḥḥāla, *Ḳabāʾil*, i, 351); al-Bakrī alone connects this Ruṣāfa with a verse by al-Akhnas b. Shihāb al-Taghlibī on the extended animal-hunting of the (South Arabian) B. Bahrāʾ (? *sharakun lāḥibun*, 56; Yāḳūt, ii, 782). Ibn al-ʿAdīm mentions some B. Ṣāliḥ of Hāshim here at the time of Hārūn al-Rashīd (*Bughya*, iii, 1467-8, vii, 3446).

Administratively, al-Ruṣāfa belonged to Ḳinnasrīn or Aleppo in Umayyad and later ʿAbbāsid times (Ibn al-ʿAdīm, i, 113-14), under Hārūn al-Rashīd it was added to the *ʿawāṣim* province (Ibn al-Faḳīh, 111), but some transmitters were uncertain about its district (*Ruṣāfat al-Raḳḳa*, even *al-Ruṣāfa in the Djazīra*, Ibn al-ʿAdīm, v, 2103 with correction; Ibn ʿAsākir, iv, 259; Ibn Khurradādhbih mentions it twice, apparently with its closer neighbours, 74, and together with Bālis in the *ʿawāṣim*, 75). From Zangid until Mamlūk times it seems to have mostly been known as a Christian suburb or in the district of Ḳalʿat Djaʿbar, which was also called Kālōnīkōs/ Kallinikos—in this way a remark by Barhebraeus, *Chronography*, ed. Budge, 120, tr. ²111, could be understood: "Hishām died in Ruṣāfa of Kallinikos" (cf. *ibid.* tr. ²218; *Syriac Chronicle, ad a.* 1234, i, 215), and it would fit the reading of an Arabic inscription on the silver goblet from the Ruṣāfa treasury suggested by R. Degen, "This is what Zayn al-Dār, daughter of *ustādh* Abū Durra, bestowed to the church of the protected Ḳalʿat Djaʿba[r]," probably meaning al-Ruṣāfa (before 1243, in Ulbert, *Resafa*, iii, 72; for Ḳalʿat Djaʿbar as a district (*aʿmāl*), cf. Ibn al-Dawādārī, vii, 283, year 624/1227).

Nothing is reported on the Islamic conquest of al-Ruṣāfa, and the sources rather convey the impression of its lying in ruins until the building activities of Hishām (Ibn al-ʿAdīm, i, 113). But it is mentioned as being on the march of the Ḳaysī Djaḥḥāf b. Ḥakīm from the Djazīra against the B. Taghlib with their poet al-Akhṭal and their "day" at Djabal Bishrī in 73/692-3 (al-Balādhurī, *Ansāb*, v, 329; *Aghānī*, Būlāḳ, xi, 59; Ibn al-ʿAdīm, i, 431 ff.; *Khizānat al-adab*, Cairo, ix, 4); and also, before 724, a Bishop Abraham of al-Ruṣāfa is documented (Degen 70-1, quoting Wright, *Cat. of Syriac mss.*, ii, 796 ff.).

The main information on al-Ruṣāfa in Muslim sources pertains to the caliph Hishām (105-24/724-43), whose residence it became at least in summer and who was buried there. While these sources unanimously locate the residence in or next to this al-Ruṣāfa (e.g. Ibn Faḍl Allāh al-ʿUmarī, *Masālik*, Cairo 1342/1924, 332-3), some modern authors have doubted this and identified it with the ruins of Ḳaṣr al-Ḥayr al-Sharḳī [*q.v.*] (Sauvaget, *Remarques sur les monuments omeyyades*, in *JA* [1939], 1-13). This theory was finally rejected by O. Grabar (*City in the desert*, 1978, 1-2, 31). It is not very easy to recognise the original tradition within the several additions transmitted by the historians; the news of the death of his predecessor and the regalia were brought to Hishām at al-Zaytūna, where he possessed a small dwelling (*duwayra*), and he then rode from al-Ruṣāfa to Damascus (al-Ṭabarī, ii, 1467); perhaps because of the unexplained leap, later sources locate either the transmission of the news and the regalia to al-Ruṣāfa (*al-ʿUyūn wa 'l-ḥadāʾiḳ*, 82; Abu 'l-Fidāʾ, *Mukhtaṣar*, Cairo 1325, i, 203) or from al-Zaytūna to al-Ruṣāfa (Yāḳūt, ii, 784). While O. Grabar still thinks of an identification of al-Zaytūna with Ḳaṣr al-Ḥayr al-

S̲h̲arḳī (*City in the desert*, 13-14), a hint by Ibn Buṭlān [*q.v.*] possibly gives the clue to understanding the sequence of residences: His̲h̲ām was fleeing from the mosquitoes on the banks of the Euphrates to al-Ruṣāfa (in Yāḳūt, ii, 785)—this fits the surroundings of the straitened dimensions of his princely residence al-Zaytūna, perhaps in the vicinity of his further possessions near al-Raḳḳa. Another often-embellished story mentions him avoiding the Syrian cities in favour of al-Ruṣāfa because of the plague; like other Umayyads, he fled to the desert (e.g. al-Ṭabarī, ii, 1737; Ibn al-ʿAdīm, i, 113-14).

His̲h̲ām is reported to have reconstructed al-Ruṣāfa and erected two castles there (*ḳaṣrayn*, al-Ṭabarī, ii, 1738; *al-ʿUyūn wa 'l-ḥadāʾiḳ*, 101; Ibn Buṭlān, *ibid.*). Whether their descriptions as possessing a pool and olive yard (al-Ṭabarī, ii, 1813) or as being luxurious constructions with floral paintings (Ibn al-ʿAdīm, vii, 3044: *maṣāniʿ* here evidently not meaning the cisterns, as in *ibid.*, i, 113) go back to eye witnesses or are literary *topoi*, cannot be decided. Brief archaeological soundings and a survey showed several large Umayyad structures to the south of the city (Otto-Dorn, Ulbert, Sack). The court of His̲h̲ām was magnificent, and must have shown Persian traditions in several respects (cf. the analysis by R. Hamilton, *Walīd and his friends*, Oxford 1988, *passim*). Whoever was interested in Persian topics among the early ʿAbbāsid caliphs would also refer to accounts of His̲h̲ām's court (e.g. al-Manṣūr, al-Ṭabarī, iii, 412; al-Masʿūdī, iv, 47-8, 133-4 = §§ 2234, 2379). Even translations from the Persian seem to have originated from His̲h̲ām's secretaries in al-Ruṣāfa, Sālim b. ʿAbd al-Raḥmān or ʿAbd Allāh and his son D̲j̲abala (al-Ṭabarī, ii, 1750, 1649-50; al-Masʿūdī, *Tanbīh*, 106, 113; Ibn al-ʿAdīm, ix, 4143; M. Grignaschi, in *BEO*, xix [1967] 12-13, 24-5, 51-2). The Arab tradition at his court was upheld by the poets (see, besides the famous competition by al-Farazdāḳ, D̲j̲arīr and al-Ak̲h̲ṭal, descriptions by Ismāʿīl b. Yasār al-Nasāʾī, in *Ag̲h̲ānī*, iv, 125; K̲h̲ālid b. Ṣafwān al-Ahtam, in Ibn al-ʿAdīm, vii, 3044; Abu 'l-Nad̲j̲m, in *Ag̲h̲ānī*, ix, 78 ff., Ibn al-ʿAdīm, x, 4640). And in one respect he tried to surpass pre-Islamic customs: he himself built the greatest hippodrome (*ḥalba*) for 3,000 horses here, six bowshots long (*Ag̲h̲ānī*, x, 64; al-Masʿūdī, iv, 41 = § 2219; Ibn al-ʿAdīm, vi, 2858). Also, the biographies of traditionists at his court contain material on al-Ruṣāfa, most famous among them being al-Zuhrī (*GAS*, i, 280-3), Abū Manīʿ ʿUbayd Allāh b. Abī Ziyād and his grandson Abū Muḥammad al-Ḥad̲j̲d̲j̲ād̲j̲ b. Yūsuf (Ibn al-ʿAdīm, v, 2100 ff.; al-Samʿānī, vi, 135; Ibn ʿAsākir, x, 669-70, iv, 259-60), K̲h̲uṣayf b. ʿAbd al-Raḥmān or Ibn Yazīd al-Ḥarrānī (Ibn al-ʿAdīm, vii, esp. 3265-6). Out of His̲h̲ām's family, his son Sulaymān stayed in al-Ruṣāfa until his defeat by Marwān II (al-Ṭabarī, ii, 1908).

His̲h̲ām's tomb and body were desecrated under the first ʿAbbāsid (al-Ṭabarī, iii, 2498-9; al-Yaʿḳūbī, ii, 427-8). The town had an ʿAbbāsid governor in 137/754 (al-Ṭabarī, iii, 94-5); but apart from occasional visits of a caliph, only one event is mentioned, the sack by the Carmathians at the end of 289/December 902, when the mosque, adjoining the cathedral, was burnt and the ʿAbbāsid defender Sabk al-Daylamī killed (al-Ṭabarī, iii, 2219; Ibn al-ʿAdīm, ii, 946: better, S̲h̲ibl al-Daylamī; cf. the excavations by D. Sack).

Eyewitnesses are few, and are repeatedly quoted in geographical sources: al-Aṣmaʿī, who mentions merchants, rich and poor, travelling abroad and employing local Bedouins (*ʿarab*), a small *sūḳ* with ten shops and textile manufacturing (Yāḳūt, ii, 284-5; still in al-Idrīsī, ed. Rome, 649, Ibn al-ʿAdīm, i, 113-14, and Ḥād̲j̲d̲j̲ī K̲h̲alīfa, *D̲j̲ihān-numā*, 594, without any contemporary observations). Apart from the cisterns and the walls the city is especially famous for its Christian buildings, figuring in the mentioning of its *dayr*, listed separately by al-Bakrī, Yāḳūt, and al-Ḥimyarī. This gave rise to several *topoi* and anecdotes of nostalgia of the Umayyads and of the monasteries, which do not seem to correspond with reality, as already noticed by Musil (*Palmyrena*, 268; cf. the story connected to the visit of al-Mutawakkil in 244/858, al-Ṭabarī, iii, 1436; al-Ḥimyarī, *Rawḍ* (Beirut 1975), 253; Ibn al-ʿAdīm, i, 114, quoting the *K. al-Diyārāt* by al-S̲h̲ims̲h̲āṭī; for the cliché of the monastery, see L. Conrad, in *The quest for understanding*, ed. S. Seikaly *et alii*, Beirut 1991, 271-2). Only the Christian Ibn Buṭlān was interested in the great church, of which he describes the external gold mosaic in 440/1048-9 (cited in Yāḳūt, ii, 785). Judaeo-Arabic inscriptions in one building, dated 1102 and 1127, prove the presence of a Jewish community there (A. Caquot, in *Syria*, xxxii [1955], 70-4).

Ibn S̲h̲addād gives an account of the end of habitation in al-Ruṣāfa, added to a long quotation from Ibn al-ʿAdīm (ed. A.-M. Terrasse-Eddé, 394, tr. 21-2): the Mongols had spared the inhabitants on their march in 658/1260, and after the Mamlūk reconquest, a governor was left there until 668/1269-70, when the inhabitants left for Salamiya, Ḥamāt and other places, apparently because of the destruction, which is also archaeologically evident. Since then, the site has been deserted.

Bibliography: For the pre-Islamic and Christian history, see Pauly-Wissowa, *RE*, s.v. *Sergiupolis*, Honigmann in *EI*[1], and, especially, the excavation publications edited by Th. Ulbert, *Resafa*, i (1984 ff.), with detailed references; especially R. Degen, *ibid.* iii (1991), 65-76; D. Sack, *Die Große Moschee von Resafa/Ruṣāfat Hišām*, *ibid.* iv, with a ch. by B. Kellner-Heinkele on the sources (in course of publication); K. Otto-Dorn, in *Ars Orientalis*, ii (1957), 119-33. All Arabic text quotations from the standard editions (except where indicated), Ibn al-ʿAdīm, *Bug̲h̲yat al-ṭalab fī taʾrīk̲h̲ Ḥalab*, ed. S. Zakkār, Damascus 1408/1988; Ibn ʿAsākir, *Taʾrīk̲h̲ madīnat Dimas̲h̲ḳ*, facs. of the ms. Ẓāhiriyya, Damascus, *s.a.*; ʿAbd al-Malik b. Ḥabīb, *K. al-Taʾrīk̲h̲*, Madrid 1991, 133-5; Ibn S̲h̲addād, *al-Aʿlāḳ al-k̲h̲aṭīra*, ed. A.-M. Eddé-Terrasse, in *BEO*, xxxii-xxxiii, 394-393 [*sic*], tr. eadem, Damascus 1984, 19-22; Musil, *Palmyrena*, New York 1928, index; see also HIS̲H̲ĀM and ḲALʿAT D̲J̲AʿBAR.

(C.-P. HAASE)

4. In Muslim Spain.

Munyat al-Ruṣāfa, in Spanish Arrizafa, Arruzafa, is the name of the country residence founded by ʿAbd al-Raḥmān I (138-72/756-88 [*q.v.*]) to the north-west of Cordova and to which he gave the name of the Ruṣāfa in Syria (see 3. above) founded by his grandfather His̲h̲ām b. ʿAbd al-Malik.

The first Umayyad *amīr* of al-Andalus purchased lands which had belonged to a Berber chief of Ṭāriḳ's army, Razīn al-Burnusī, and built there a palace (*ḳaṣr*) and gardens. The Arabic sources class the Cordovan Ruṣāfa amongst the three most important constructions of ʿAbd al-Raḥmān I's reign (the other two being the Grand Mosque and the palace of Cordova). The *amīr* enjoyed living there very much and spent most of his time there. In the course of his residence at al-Ruṣāfa, he ordered the execution of three rebels: his nephew al-Mug̲h̲īra b. al-Walīd, Wahb Allāh b.

Maymūn and ʿAyshūn b. Sulaymān al-Aʿrābī. Their corpses were dragged as far as Cordova and gibbeted on the banks of the Guadalquivir. In his reign, it became, in some measure, the seat of power, since at the time of his death, his son Hishām, who happened to be at Mérida, hastened to arrive there before his brother Sulaymān (who was at Toledo and who was disputing with him the right of succession).

Moreover, ʿAbd al-Raḥmān I made the gardens at al-Ruṣāfa the first botanical gardens in the history of al-Andalus. He had planted in his grounds exotic plants, mainly brought from Syria, to which he sent envoys to contact his sisters. The most famous of these fruits imported from the East was the so-called *safarī* pomegranate, whose name is connected with Safr b. ʿUbayd al-Kilāʿī, from the *djund* of al-Urdunn. The latter is said to have cultivated this variety of pomegranate in the region of Rayya [*q.v.*], whence it was spread throughout al-Andalus. The origin of the date-palm groves in the Iberian Peninsula is equally attributed, with no real basis in truth, by some Arabic authors to a palm tree at al-Ruṣāfa. ʿAbd al-Raḥmān I's successors continued the tradition of periods of residence at al-Ruṣāfa. It was probably in the reign of ʿAbd al-Raḥmān II (206-38/822-52 [*q.v.*]) that the poet ʿAbbās b. Firnās tried, at al-Ruṣāfa, to imitate the flight of birds, dressed in a garment of silk covered with feathers and bearing wings. But above all, it was the *amīr* Muḥammad (238-73/852-86), known for his zeal as a builder, who enlarged and improved the buildings and the gardens of this residence, where he loved to take rest and where he organised hunting parties. The *amīr* transferred from Cordova to al-Ruṣāfa accompanied by his entourage of chamberlains and eunuchs, and thus surrounded by all the splendour of the Umayyad court. He charged his *wazīr* Hāshim b. ʿAbd al-ʿAzīz with the construction of a new *madjlis* at al-Ruṣāfa and provided him with 10,000 dīnārs for this. However, the *wazīr* had the *madjlis* built at his own expense. When the work of building was finished, Hāshim gave back to the *amīr* his 10,000 dīnārs and, as a further gesture, prepared for him a sumptuous banquet. The first Umayyad caliph, ʿAbd al-Raḥmān III al-Nāsir (300-50/912-61 [*q.v.*]), had accompanied, whilst he was still young, his grandfather the *amīr* ʿAbd Allāh during his pleasure sessions at al-Ruṣāfa. But his preferred country residence was the *munyat al-Nāʿūra*. During his reign, al-Ruṣāfa is mentioned as a residence for important visitors, such as the North African chief Ayyūb b. Abī Yazīd Makhlad b. Kaydād al-Īfranī in 335/946. Al-Nāṣir's son and successor al-Mustanṣir (350-66/962-76) preferred above all the *munyat Arḥāʾ Nāṣiḥ*.

Between the residential palace complex and the city of Cordova there developped a suburb (*rabaḍ*), equally called al-Ruṣāfa, and the *nisba* from this was borne by some Cordovan scholars, such as the father of al-Ḥumaydī [*q.v.*]. It was there that al-Manṣūr Ibn Abī ʿĀmir, al-Mustanṣir's *ḥādjib*, had his palace built, which he later abandoned for *al-munya al-ʿāmiriyya*, whose exact location is controversial. With the arrival of Berber troop contingents during the rule of al-Manṣūr, the suburb of al-Ruṣāfa became the residence of the Banū Māksan b. Zīrī and the Banū Zāwī b. Zīrī, whose houses were destroyed in the course of the troubles during the first reign of Muḥammad al-Mahdī. Like the other northern suburbs of Cordova, that of al-Ruṣāfa suffered the consequences of the *fitna* and its name disappears from the Arabic sources after the 4th/10th century.

As for the *munyat al-Ruṣāfa*, it was first of all despoiled by al-Mahdī in 400/1009 during his second reign. The caliph used the contents of the palace, like those of the *munyat al-Nāʿūra* and the royal palace in Cordova, in order to pay his troops and to support the costs of the fight against the rival army of the Berbers on which his rival Sulaymān al-Mustaʿīn depended. In the following year, and in order to ward off the Berber advance, al-Ruṣāfa was totally destroyed on the orders of Wāḍiḥ, the military chief of Cordova. He even had the trees in the famous gardens cut down, but shortly afterwards he realised the uselessness of his action from the point of view of the defence of Cordova. Only the name of the Umayyad princes' residence survived. After the Christian conquest, in 633/1236, the land involved was bestowed on the counts of Hornachuelos. Later, a monastery was established on the site.

The Ruṣāfa of Cordova early became a favoured subject of the court poets. Some very famous verses on its solitary palm tree are attributed to the founder, ʿAbd al-Raḥmān I (according to other version, its author is said to have been ʿAbd al-Malik b. Bishr b. ʿAbd al-Malik b. Marwān). A poem of ʿAbbās b. Firnās on al-Ruṣāfa, reproduced by Ibn Ḥayyān [*q.v.*], describes at length its buildings, streams, plants, birds, etc. After its destruction, Ruṣāfa became, like Cordova, a poetic subject for the expression of nostalgia for departed splendours (texts of Ibn Zaydūn and Ibn Burd, given by Ibn Bassām, Ibn Khāḳān and al-Maḳḳarī; this same Ibn Zaydūn mentions the existence of a garden of marguerites, *rawḍ al-uḳhuwān*). In Almohad times, poets still gathered before the site of al-Ruṣāfa in order to drink and to recite poetry. The poem of al-Ḳāsim b. ʿAbbūd al-Riyāḥī develops the theme of *ubi sunt*.

The second al-Ruṣāfa in al-Andalus was situated at Valencia, between the town and the sea (the place-name is still preserved under the form Ruzafa, a quarter of the modern town). There is no information on the foundation of this Valencian Ruṣāfa. E. Lévi-Provençal was the first to suggest the name of the Umayyad prince ʿAbd Allāh al-Balansī, son of ʿAbd al-Raḥmān I, as its possible founder, at the same time warning of the lack of documentary evidence. This hypothesis has nevertheless been commonly accepted by Spanish and Arab scholars. The Arabic sources stress above all the beauty of the grounds of al-Ruṣāfa, considered as the most attractive pleasure-ground in the vicinity of Valencia (together with the *munya* of Ibn Abī ʿĀmir). The poet Muḥammad b. Ghālib al-Ruṣāfī (d. 572/1177) was originally from there and devoted some poems to it. In 480/1087, Castilian troops commanded by Alvar Fáñez, giving aid to the prince al-Ḳādir, installed themselves at al-Ruṣāfa. It was likewise there that king James I of Aragon encamped with his army, besieged the town and conquered it in 636/1238. Like its Cordovan homonym, this Ruṣāfa became a literary subject in the poetical or rhymed prose texts written on the occasion of the loss of Valencia (texts of Ibn al-Abbār and Ibn ʿAmīra preserved by al-Ḥimyarī and al-Maḳḳarī).

Bibliography: 1. Sources. *Akhbār madjmūʿa*, ed. E. Lafuente Alcántara, Madrid 1867, 110, 115; *Dhikr bilād al-Andalus*, ed. L. Molina, Madrid 1983, i, 33; Ḥimyarī, *K. al-Rawḍ al-miʿṭār*, ed. I. ʿAbbās, Beirut 1975, s.v. *Balansiya* and *al-Ruṣāfa*; Ibn al-Abbār, *al-Ḥulla al-siyarāʾ*, ed. Ḥ. Muʾnis, Cairo 1963, i, 37, 39, 120; Ibn Bassām, *al-Dhakhīra*, ed. ʿAbbās, Beirut 1975-9, i, 422-3, 519; Ibn Ḥawḳal, 112-13; Ibn ʿIdhārī, ii, 57, 60, 51, 111, 214, 258, iii, 75, 99; Ibn Ḥayyān, *Muḳtabis*, ed. M. Makkī, Beirut 1973, 170, 226 ff., ed. Martínez Antuña,

Paris 1937, 23, 29; Ibn al-Kharrāṭ, *Ikhtiṣār iḳtibās al-anwār*, ed. Molina, Madrid 1990, 143; Ibn al-Kardabūs, *Iktifā*ᵓ, ed. A. al-ᶜAbbādī, Madrid 1971, 86; Ibn al-Khaṭīb, *Aᶜmāl al-aᶜlām*, ed. Lévi-Provençal, Rabat 1934, 10, 120, Ger. tr. W. Hoernerbach; Ibn al-Ḳūtiyya, *Iftitāḥ*, ed. J. Ribera, Madrid 1926, 84; Ibn Saᶜīd, *Mughrib*, ed. Sh. Ḍayf, Cairo 1953-5, ii, 126-7, 298, 311, 342; Maḳḳarī, *Nafḥ al-ṭib*, ed. ᶜAbbās, Beirut 1968, i, 179, 181, 466 ff., 545, 628-9, 678-9, iii, 54, 90, iv, 493, 497; ᶜUdhrī, *Tarṣīᶜ al-akhbār*, ed. ᶜA.ᶜA. al-Ahwānī, Madrid 1965, 122, Yāḳūt, *Buldān*, ed. Beirut, s.v. *al-Ruṣāfa*.

2. Studies. E. García Gómez, *Algunas precisiones sobre la ruina de la Córdoba omeya*, in *And.*, xii (1947), 267-93; T. Garulo, *Ar-Ruṣāfī de Valencia, poemas*, Madrid 1980; A. Huici Miranda, *Historia musulmana de Valencia y su región*, Valencia 1969, i, 118-27; Lévi-Provençal, *Hist. Esp. mus.*, i, 136; H. Pérès, *La poésie andalouse en arabe classique*, Paris 1937; idem, *Le palmier en Espagne. Notes d'après les textes arabes*, in *Mélanges Gaudefroy-Demombynes*, Cairo 1935-45, 225-39; M.J. Rubiera, *La conquista de València per Jaume I*, in *L'Aiguadolç*, vii (1988), 33-44; ᶜA.ᶜA. Sālim, *Maᶜālim Ḳurṭuba fī shiᶜr Ibn Zaydūn*, in *RIEEIM*, xxii (1983-4), 93-104; J. Samsó, *Ibn Hišām al-Lajmī y el primer jardín botánico de al-Andalus*, in *ibid.*, xxi (1981-2), 135-41; E. Terés, *ᶜAbbās ibn Firnās*, in *And.*, xxv (1960), 239-49; idem, *Sobre el "vuelo" de ᶜAbbās ibn Firnās*, in *ibid.*, xxix (1964), 365-69; idem, *Textos poéticos árabes sobre Valencia*, in *ibid.*, xxx (1965), 219-307; J. Zanón, *Topografía de Córdoba almohade a través de las fuentes árabes*, Madrid 1989. (Manuela Marín)

AL-**RUṢĀFĪ**, Abū ᶜAbd Allāh Muḥammad b. Ghālib, al-Balansī, Hispano-Arabic poet born at al-Ruṣāfa near Valencia, died in 572/1177.

Information on his life is very sparse. In his youth he left his native land, which he hymns in several poems suffused with nostalgia (*Dīwān*, no. 56 and, especially, no. 21). In 555/1160 he went, with several other poets, to Gibraltar in order to welcome and greet the Almohad caliph ᶜAbd al-Muᵓmin [*q.v.*], before whom he recited a long poem (no. 24), celebrating him as the restorer of orthodoxy. According to al-Marrākushī, al-Ruṣāfī was still not twenty years old at that point, which would place the date of his birth around 536/1140-1. On this reckoning, he must have died before the age of forty, a piece of information which one might have thought would have attracted the attention of the Arabic biographers, who are nevertheless silent on this question. This poem, like others dedicated to the Almohad rulers and notables, appears to have assured his career as a panegyrist of the new dynasty. However, al-Ruṣāfī prefered to live away from the court, for reasons which he explains (*Dīwān*, no. 23), and to make a living by practising his trade.

This trade of mending clothes (*raffā*ᵓ) and his living far away from Valencia led him to compare himself with al-Sarī al-Raffāᵓ [*q.v.*] of Mawṣil (*Dīwān*, no. 48), whilst the Hispano-Arabic anthologists compare him, on the basis of his descriptions, with Ibn al-Rūmī [*q.v.*]. He is the continuator of the poetic school of Ibn Khafādja [*q.v.*], sharing with Ibn Khafādja his independence with regard to authority, his taste for the classical form of the *ḳaṣīda* in face of the popular forms like the *muwashshaḥ* and the *zadjal* and the enthusiasm with which he hailed a new dynasty.

The *Dīwān* of al-Ruṣāfī, which was in circulation according to Ibn al-Abbār, is now lost. The one published by Ihsān ᶜAbbās in 1960, using the historical and literary sources, remains incomplete. There should be added to it the poems in the *Iḥāṭa* of Ibn al-Khaṭīb [*q.v.*] (Cairo 1974, ii, 505-15) and in the *Taᵓrīkh Mālaḳa* of Ibn ᶜAskar [*q.v.* in Suppl.]. Others may come to light, as has happened with the publication of the anthology of Ibn Bushrā (A. Jones, *The ᶜUddat al-jalīs of ᶜAlī ibn Bishrī. An anthology of Andalusian Arabic* Muwashshaḥāt, Cambridge 1992, 95-6).

Bibliography: Virtually all the bibliographical references can be found in *Dīwān al-Ruṣāfī al-Balansī, Abī ᶜAbd Allāh Muḥammad b. Ghālib, 572 h.*, ed. I. ᶜAbbās, Beirut 1960, which may be completed with *Ar-Ruṣāfī de Valencia. Poemas*, tr. and introd. T. Garulo, Madrid 1980, [2]1986. See also J.T. Monroe, *Hispano-Arabic poetry. A student anthology*, Berkeley and Los Angeles 1974; Garulo, *Una moaxaja de al-Ruṣāfī de Valencia*, in *Homenaje al Prof. Fórneas Besteiro*, Granada (in the press).

(Teresa Garulo)

AL-**RUṢĀFĪ, MAᶜRŪF** [see maᶜrūf al-ruṣāfī].

RUSČUK, an administrative district and a port on the Danube in Bulgaria (often wrongly called and written as Rushčuk), officially in Bulgarian Ruse (Русе). It is situated at the confluence of the Rusenski Lom (Tk. Ḳara Lom) and the Danube, which then reaches a width of 1,300 m/4,264 feet. It faces the Rumanian port of Giurgiu (Tk. Yer Köki) and spreads out along terraces of loess, above the level of flooding. It is the main port on the Danube and the fourth largest town of Bulgaria, being a rail and road hub (Bridge of Friendship over the river, built in 1954), as well as an industrial and cultural centre with a population of 200,000.

After the decay of the mediaeval Červen some 15 miles inland, which survived as the name of a Bulgarian eparchy and the ruins of which could still be seen in the 17th century (cf. Ḥādjdjī Khalīfa, *Rumeli und Bosna*, tr. J. von Hammer, Vienna 1812, 44), the new Ruse arose on the Danube half-a-day's journey away. The Turkish name Rusčuk, by which the town is still almost exclusively known outside of Bulgaria, is undoubtedly a diminutive from Ruse (Ruse = Rusčuḳ; cf. the name of the island of Rhodes, Turk. Rodos and Rodos-čiḳ for Rodosto), but only seems to have come into being in the first third of the 17th century. In the two treaties concluded between the Porte and Hungary on 20 August 1503 (cf. von Hammer, *GOR*, ii, 331-2, and the text on 618: *Rwcz* = Ruse) and 1 April 1519 (cf. Theiner, *Monumenta Hungarica*, ii, 624: *Kusly* for *Russy*) and in Mercator's map of 1584 the Bulgarian form still appears. The town must have already attained considerable prosperity in the 16th century. It quickly developed under Turkish rule and became an important centre of traffic, trade, industry and strategy in Danubian Bulgaria and surpassed the two fortified towns of Nicopolis [see nīkbūlī] and Silistria which played the leading part there at the beginning of Ottoman rule (cf. A. Iširkov, *Bulgarien, Land und Leute*, Leipzig 1917, ii, 102-3). The French traveller Pierre Lescalopier, who reached Rusčuk on 14 June 1576, in his valuable journal, which has only been published in part, describes *Rusci* as a populous town: *ceste ville est peuplé et y a quantité de marchandise de toutes sortes et des vivres en abondance et à bon pritz* (cf. *Revue de l'Histoire diplomatique*, xxxv [Paris 1921], 46). Shortly before, the famous Ottoman architect Sinān [*q.v.*] built a mosque there for the Grand Vizier Rustem Pasha [*q.v.*], still admired in the 17th century, presumably in the north at the water's edge. The figure given for the population, as for the mosques, varies; of the latter, Rusčuk had at one time a considerable number. The Franciscan Peter Bogdan

Bakšić, later Archbishop of Sofia, in 1640 found in *Ruhcich* 3,000 Turkish houses with 15,000 inhabitants and 10 mosques of stone (*fatte die pietra bianca*), and 200 Armenian houses with over 1,000 inhabitants and a citadel with five towers (cf. Eug. Fermendžin, *Acta Bulgariae ecclesiastica* = vol. xviii of the *Monumenta spectantia historiam Slavorum meridionalium*, Zagreb 1887, 74). In 1659 Filip Stanoslavov counted 6,000 Turkish wooden houses with over 30 mosques (*ibid.*, 263; cf. also 7, 10, 26, 31, 88, 137, 299 [*Russi o Ruhcich*: 1685], 300 with further particulars). Ewliyā Čelebi (*Seyāḥet-nāme*, iii, 313-14; cf. the Bulgarian tr. by D.G. Gadžanov, in *Periodičesko spisanie na bălgarskoto kniževno družestvo v' Sofija*, lxx, Plovdiv 1909, 654-5) about the same time mentions 2,200 houses of wood, also three Christian quarters, the mosque of Rustem Pasha, baths and three caravanserais in "Urusčuḳ". The only Jews, he says, were those who visited the place on their trading journeys. The people, whom he praises for their hospitality, lived by commerce and spoke Bulgarian as well as the "language of Wallachia and Moldavia". Ewliyā Čelebi says the melon (*ḳawun*) there was particularly good, 10 being sold for 1 *pen(e)z* (5 of which = 1 Vienna groschen or 3 kreuzers, 150 = 1 taler).

Rusčuk is regularly mentioned in the many records of travel on the Danube in the following centuries. References to the town in the 18th and first half of the 19th century are in general agreement. The inhabitants seem at all times to have conducted a busy trade in wool, cotton, silk, leather and tobacco, which at an earlier period was for a considerable part in the hands of Ragusan merchants, who had a settlement there from 1673 to 1755. The English clergyman R. Walsh (1827) estimated the population at 18-20,000 souls. The streets of the town, which was surrounded by walls on three sides after the manner of Turkish fortresses, as a rule sloped steeply to the Danube, which was partly undefended. Turks, Greeks, Bulgars and Armenians lived in some 7,000 houses and conducted a busy trade with Turkey (cf. R. Walsh, *Narrative of a journey from Constantinople to England*[2], London 1828, 207). Helmuth von Moltke who visited Rusčuk in 1835 and described it (cf. *Briefe über Zustände und Begebenheiten in der Türkei*[3], Berlin 1877, 11 ff., 132 ff., 424 ff.), was surprised that "this important Turkish fortress with its long, dominated and enfiladed lines without outer works, half armed and defectively planned" could offer the enemy such resistance.

As an important frontier fortress, Rusčuk was a military prize in the Russo-Turkish wars. Besieged in 1773, it was the site of a great battle on 4 July 1811. The fortunes of war favoured the Turks, led by the Grand Vizier Aḥmed Pasha, after which the Russians, commanded by Kutusov, constructed fortifications and fell back on to the other bank of the Danube after having reduced the town to cinders. During the Crimean War, Rusčuk served as the base for a diversionary manœuvre aimed at threatening Bucarest. During the War of 1877-8, Ottoman forces commanded by Ḳayṣerili Aḥmed Pasha had to surrender the town and its fortress to the Russians on 21 February 1878 after a long siege. Rusčuk was important in the history of the reform movement in the Ottoman empire. After the deposition of Selīm III [*q.v.*] (29 May 1807), the officers of the Niẓām-i Djedīd [*q.v.*] regrouped there around Muṣṭafā Bayraḳdār [*q.v.*] and launched the counter-revolution there which swept away Muṣṭafā IV. It was the seat of a *sandjaḳ bey*, and sometimes of a *pasha* (*ca.* 1840, when Danubian Bulgaria was divided into three *pashalïḳs*: Rusčuk, Vidin and Silistre); in 1864 the town became the administrative centre of the new *wilāyet* of the Danube (*Ṭūna wilāyeti*), whose first governor was the reformer Midḥat Pasha [*q.v.*]. Under his impulsion, it enjoyed an early process of Westernisation: urban reform, development of the docks, the first railway link (Rusčuk-Varna, 1866), the beginnings of industrialisation, the first hospital, etc.. A provincial printing press was set up, which published the bilingual newspaper *Tuna-Dunav* (14 March 1865-1 September 1877) and an annual *sālnāme* (*Ṭūna wilāyeti sālnāmesi*) which allows one to see the extent of these reforms.

Rusčuk was the birthplace of the Grand Vizier Čelebi-zāde Sherīf Ḥasan Pasha (d. 1205/1791), of the *kātib* Amānī Čelebi (d. 1000/1591 according to von Hammer, *GOD*, iii, 83), and of the famous Ottoman author Aḥmed Sherīf Ḥasan Midḥat Bey (1841-1912, cf. F. Babinger, *GOW*, 389-90), not forgetting the novelist of Sephardic Jewish origin and writer in German, Elias Canetti, the Nobel Prize-winner for literature in 1981.

The post-Ottoman history of Rusčuk, which became officially Ruse, begins in 1878. The Westernisation begun by Midḥat Pasha increased in momentum under Bulgarian rule. In accordance with the Treaty of Berlin, the fortifications were partly demolished, an urban plan transformed the main Muslim cemetery into a public garden, and numerous mosques disappeared (Kanitz numbered them at 29 in 1874; there were no more than seven in 1936). The eclectic architectural style of Central Europe triumphed. The Muslim population, despite being socially reduced in status and weakened by the exodus of its elites, nevertheless managed to maintain a certain cultural life. Thus eight journals in Turkish appeared up to 1910, essentially on account of the activity of Aḥmed Zekī. Turkish education remained active, with two secondary schools in 1921-2; from 1952 to 1957 there functioned in Rusčuk the sole Turkish lycée for girls in Bulgaria. After the 1960s, the policy of national assimilation pursued under the régime of Todor Živkov gradually stifled all signs of a specifically cultural and religious life. The town's population, which had risen from 26,000 in 1880 to 49,500 in 1934, grew rapidly with industrialisation, actively promoted by the Communist régime. The former Turkish element of the town disappeared under a massive influx of rural Bulgarians. In 1985 the town had 195,000 inhabitants; nevertheless, the villages of the administrative disitrict of Rusčuk have a 25% Turkish population.

Bibliography (in addition to references in the text): Carsten Niebuhr, *Reisebeschreibung nach Arabien*, iii, Hamburg 1837, 174; M.J. Quin, *A steam voyage down the Danube*[3], Paris 1836, 181; idem, *Voyage sur le Danube de Pest à Routchouk* (sic!), *par navire à vapeur*, i, Paris 1836, 276 ff.; Herrn Jenne's *Reisen nach St. Petersburg, nebst einem Reisejournal der Donaufahrt*, Pest 1788, 210-11; Gugomos, *Reise von Bucharest, der Hauptstadt in der Wallachai, über Giurgewo, Rustschuk, durch Oberbulgarien, bis gegen die Graenzen von Rumelien, und dann durch Unterbulgarien über Silistria wieder zurück, im Jahre 1789*, Landshut 1812; Ph. von Wussow, *Übersicht des Kriegsschauplatzes der europäischen Türkei*, Coblence 1828, 78-9; Ḥādjdjī Khalīfa, *Rumeli und Bosna*, tr. J. von Hammer, Vienna 1812, 43-4; M.F. Thielen, *Die europäische Türkey*, Vienna 1828, 238-9; C.W. Wutzer, *Reise in den Orient Europas und einen Theil Westasiens*, Elberfeld 1860, 209 ff.; von Hammer, *GOR*, viii, 144 ("Rusčuk stormed by rebels in 1751"); F. Kanitz, *Donau-Bulgarien und der Balkan*[2], i, Leipzig 1882, 123 ff.; C.J. Jireček, *Cesty po Bulharsku*, Prague 1888, 191-4; idem, *Das Fürstenthum Bulgarien*, Leipzig 1891, 410-11; A. Grisebach, *Reise durch Rumelien und nach Brussa*, i, Göttingen 1841, 23-4; C. Grübler, *Rustschuk, ein türkisches Städtebild*, in *Aus allen Welttheilen (Monatschrift für Länder- und Völkerkunde)*, year viii (1877), 70-5; H. von Moltke, *Der russisch-türkische Feldzug 1828 und 1829, dargestellt im Jahr 1845²*, Berlin 1877; M.K. Sarafov, *Über die Bevölkerung der Städte Rusčuk, Varna und Šumen* (Šumla), in *Periodičesko spisanie na bălgarskoto kniževno druženstvo*, year iii, Sofia 1882, 20; Karel Skorpil, *Opis na starinite po tečenieto na reka Rusenski Lom*, ii, Sofia 1914; Nikola G. Popov, *Opisanie na Rusčuk*, Ruse 1928 (contains an account of the state of Rusčuk in 1860-79); Mihajl Hadži Kostov, *Minaloto na Ruse*, Rusčuk 1929; the periodical, publ. in Rusčuk and now defunct, *Letopis* in its second year, nos. 4, 5, 7, 8 and 9 contained contributions to the history of the town; J. Gellert, *Rustschuk*, in *Mitteilungen des Vereins der Geographen an der Universität Leipzig*, Heft 14-15, Leipzig 1936; Sāmī Bey Frāsherī, *Ḳāmūs ül-aʿlām*, iii, 2323; S. Parmakov, *Ruse, včera i dnes*, Ruse 1936; A.F. Miller, *Mustafa Pasha Bayraktar*, Moscow-Leningrad 1947, Fr. tr. Bucharest 1975; *Izvestiya na narodniya muzey Ruse*, from 1964 onwards; D. Kazasov, *Ruse*, Sofia 1964; V. Doynov, *Ruse v nyakoi geografski karti, săčineniya i nadpisi*, in *Istoričeski Pregled*, i (1975); H.J. Kornrumpf, *Die Territorialverwaltung im östlichen Teil der europäischen Türkei*, Freiburg i. Br. 1978; S. Draganova, *Materiyali za Dunavskiya vilayet*, Sofia 1980; V. Doykov and I. Ivanov, *Ruse i negovite okolnosti. Pătevoditel*, Sofia 1983; V. Paskaleva, *Sredna Evropa i zemite po dolniya Dunav prez XVIII i XIX vek*, Sofia 1986; *Entsiklopediya Balgariya*, v, 839 ff.; B. Simsir, *The Turks of Bulgaria 1978-1985*, London 1988. (F. Babinger-[B. Lory])

AL-**RUSHĀṬĪ**, Abū Muḥammad ʿAbd Allāh b. ʿAlī b. ʿAbd Allāh b. ʿAlī b. Khalaf b. Aḥmad b. ʿUmar al-Lakhmī al-Marī al-Andalusī, traditionist and historian of Muslim Spain.

He was born in 466/1074 at Orihuela (Murcia). His *nisba* al-Rushāṭī is of Romance origin and refers to a physical characteristic. One of his ancestors had on his body a mole (*shāma*) of the type known as "rose" (*warda*) called by the Christians "*rūsha*"; the Romance-speaking servant (*khādim ʿadjamiyya*) who cared for him as a child called him "Rushaṭelo", from which the *nisba* of the family derived. When he was six years old, al-Rushāṭī's family moved to Almería, where he completed his studies and where later he taught. Having witnessed the conquest of the town by the Almoravids in 484/1091, he himself died a martyr when the Christians conquered Almería in 542/1147. His teachers were the two most famous traditionists of the time, Abū ʿAlī al-Ghassānī (d. 498/1104) and Abū ʿAlī al-Ṣadafī (d. 514/1120), the *mukriʾ* Abu 'l-Ḥasan Ibn Akhī 'l-Dūsh and his maternal uncle Abu 'l-Ḳāsim Ibn Fatḥūn (d. 505/1111), author of a *K. al-Wathāʾiḳ*. Al-Rushāṭī also obtained the *idjāza* from Abū ʿAbd Allāh al-Khawlānī (d. 508-1114), author of a *fahrasa*, and from his famous contemporary Abū Bakr b. al-ʿArabī (d. 543/1148 [*q.v.*]). Like many other scholars of his time, al-Rushāṭī did not perform the *riḥla fī ṭalab al-ʿilm* abroad. His most famous work is the *Iḳtibās al-anwār wa-iltimās al-azhār fī ansāb/asmāʾ al-ṣaḥāba wa-ruwāt al-āthār*, a book praised by Ibn Kathīr and one similar in methodology (*uslūb*) to the genealogical work by al-Samʿānī (d. 562/1167 [*q.v.*]). The only extant edition of this most important genealogical tract is the partial text by E. Molina López and J. Bosch-Vilá, restricted to the entries related to al-Andalus. According to Ḥ. al-Djāsir, ʿAbd al-Raḥmān al-ʿUthaymīn is preparing a complete edition of the preserved text. The *Iḳtibās* contained five parts, of which only parts one, three and five have reached us (the mss. are found in Tunis and Ḳarawiyyīn; their description can be found in Molina-Bosch Vilá's and al-Djāsir's works). Part of the missing contents can be restored by means of the preserved abridgements (a list in Molina, 541-3, and al-Djāsir, 623-38) written by later authors, among them, Ibn al-Kharrāṭ al-Ishbīlī (d. 581/1180) and Madjd al-Dīn Ismāʿīl b. Ibrāhīm al-Bilbīsī (d. 802/1399), in whose *talkhīṣ* he added what Ibn al-Athīr had added to the *Ansāb* of al-Samʿānī. The parts of Ibn al-Kharrāṭ's *Ikhtiṣār* dealing with al-Andalus have been incorporated by Molina-Bosch Vilá into their partial edition of al-Rushāṭī; they have also used material from al-Bilbīsī's abridgement.

Al-Rushāṭī's other works are the *Kitāb al-Iʿlām bi-mā fī Kitāb al-Mukhtalif wa 'l-muʾtalif li 'l-Dāraḳuṭnī min al-awhām* and a refutation of the famous *mufassir* ʿAbd al-Ḥaḳḳ b. ʿAṭiyya (d. 541-2/1146-7), who had criticised certain passages of his own genealogical work. Although he is remembered as an expert in *ansāb* and *ʿilm al-ridjāl*, al-Rushāṭī also studied grammar, *adab*, *fiḳh* and *ḥadīth*. In the last field, he transmitted the *K. ʿUlūm al-ḥadīth* by al-Ḥākim al-Nīsābūrī [*q.v.*]. Among his numerous pupils, we find especially traditionists (some with an interest in *ʿilm al-ridjāl* and history) like Abū Bakr b. Abī Djamra (d. 599/1202), Abu 'l-Walīd b. al-Dabbāgh (d. 546/1151), Ibn Bashkuwāl (d. 578/1182 [*q.v.*]), Ibn Ḳurḳūl (d. 569/1173), Ibn Ḥubaysh (d. 584/1188 [*q.v.*]), two authors of *fahāris*, Abū Muḥammad b. ʿUbayd Allāh (d. 591/1195) and Ibn Khayr (d. 575/1179 [*q.v.*]), as well as the grammarian Ibn Maḍāʾ [*q.v.*].

Bibliography: Ibn Bashkuwāl, no. 648 (ed. al-Ḥusaynī, Cairo, 1374/1955, no. 651); Ḍabbī, no. 943; Ibn al-Abbār, *Muʿdjam*, 217-22, no. 200; Ibn Khallikān, *Wafayāt*, iii, 106-7, no. 352; Dhahabī, *Siyar aʿlām al-nubalāʾ*, Beirut 1985, xx, 258-60, no. 175; Dhahabī, *Tadhkirat al-ḥuffāẓ*, Ḥaydarābād 1968-70, iv, 1307-8, no. 1084; Ṣafadī, *al-Wāfī bi l-wafayāt*, xvii, 326, no. 280; Ibn al-Zubayr, Ṣilat al-ṣila, ed. ʿA. Hārūn and S. Aʿrāb, Rabat 1993, no. 159; Ḥādjdjī Khalīfa, ed. Fluegel, i, 375, 456; Makhlūf, *Shadjarat al-nūr*, Cairo 1950-2, i, 135, no. 404; F. Pons Boigues, *Ensayo bio-bibliográfico*, 207, no. 169; Kaḥḥāla, vi, 90; Ziriklī, iv, 105; G. Vajda, *La transmission du savoir en Islam (VIIe-XVIIIe siècles)*, London 1983, no. IV ("La liste d'autorités (*Tuḥfat ahl al-ḥadīṯ fī īṣāl iğāzat al-qadīm bil-ḥadīṯ*) de Manṣūr ibn Salīm Wağīh ad-dīn al-Hamdānī), 376, no. 73; J. Bosch Vilá, *Una nueva fuente para la historia de al-Andalus: El* Kitāb Iqtibās al-anwār *de Abū Muḥammad al-Rušāṭī*, and E. Molina, *Almería islámica: Puerta de Oriente, objetivo militar. Nuevos datos para su estudio en el* Kitāb Iqtibās al-anwār *de Abū Muḥammad al-Rušāṭī*, both in *Actas XII Congreso U.E.A.I. (Málaga, 1984)*, Madrid 1986, 37-52 and 565-615; Mª L. Avila, *Las mujeres "sabias" en al-Andalus*, in *La mujer en al-Andalus*, ed. Mª J. Viguera, Seville 1989, 153, no. 13 (for the meaning of his *nisba*); E. Molina López, *El* Kitāb iḫtiṣār Iqtibās al-anwār *de Ibn al-Ḫarrāṭ. El autor y la obra. Análisis de las noticias históricas, geográficas y biográficas sobre al-Andalus*, in *Quaderni di Studi Arabi*, v-vi (1987-8), 541-60; *Abū Muḥammad al-Rušāṭī (m. 542/1147)/Ibn al-Jarrāṭ al-Išbīlī (m. 581/1186), Al-Andalus en el "Kitāb iqtibās al-anwār" y en el "Ijtiṣār Iqtibās al-anwār"*, ed. E. Molina López and J. Bosch Vilá, Madrid 1990

(*Fuentes Arábico-Hispanas*, 7); and see the corrections by Sh. al-Faḥḥām in *RAAD*, lxvii (1992), 318-335; Ḥ. al-Djāsir, *Ansāb al-Rushāṭī al-Andalusī wa-mukhtaṣarātu-hu*, in *ibid.*, lxvi (1991), 611-45.

(Maribel Fierro)

RUSTĀḲ, Arabised form of M. Pers. *rōstāg*, meaning "rural district, countryside", and given the broken pl. *rasātīḳ*.

(1) In the mediaeval Islamic usage of the Arabic and Persian geographers and of the Arabic writers on finance and taxation, *rustāḳ* is used both as a specific administrative term and in a more general sense. Thus, reflecting the more exact usage, in Sāsānid and early Islamic ʿIrāḳ, each *kūra* [*q.v.*] or province was divided into *ṭassūdjs* or sub-provinces, and these last were in turn divided into *rustāḳs*, districts or cantons, centred on a *madīna* or town. According to Hilāl al-Ṣābiʾ, *K. al-Wuzarāʾ*, a *ṭassūdj* might contain up to twelve *rustāḳs*, and a *rustāḳ* might contain up to twelve villages (cited in F. Løkkegaard, *Islamic taxation in the classic period,* Copenhagen 1950, 164-7). Al-Muḳaddasī's usage, however, is less neat and formal. Thus the *rasātīḳ* which he gives for the *iḳlīm* [*q.v.*] of Syria are extensive rural districts, such as the six ones of Damascus province (*kūra*): al-Ghūṭa, the Ḥawrān, al-Bathaniyya, al-Djawlān, al-Biḳāʿ and al-Ḥūla (text, 154, Fr. tr. A. Miquel, *Aḥsan at-aqāsīm* ... (*La meilleure répartition* ...), Damascus 1963, 160, cf. also 23 and n. 51). Likewise, the *Ḥudūd al-ʿālam* speaks of *rustāḳs* as administrative subdivisions, but in a vaguer sense (see tr. Minorsky, index at 524).

(2) In wider literary usage, the *rustāḳ/rustā* or countryside may be contrasted with the urban centres, and its populations regarded as country bumpkins compared with the more sophisticated town-dwellers, so that in Persian, *rustā-ṭabʿ* "having a rustic nature" was a contemptuous expression. Thus the Ṣūfī *shaykh* Abū Saʿīd Mayhanī [*q.v.*] had to be dissuaded from burying himself in the *rūstā*, in this case, the small country town of Mayhana [*q.v.*] in northern Khurāsān; cf. C.E. Bosworth, *The Ghaznavids*, 152.

Bibliography: Given in the article.

(C.E. Bosworth)

AL-**RUSTĀḲ**, the name of a town and area in ʿUmān [*q.v.*] which finds no place in the classical Arabic geographies. The town is situated about 112 km/70 miles west, as the crow flies, of the chief town of the Sultanate, Muscat [see MASḲAṬ], on the northern side of the range of al-Djabal al-Akhḍar. The district, according to Lorimer (*Gazetteer of the Persian Gulf*, Calcutta 1908, IIB, 1603-4), is the region of western Hadjar from al-Ḥazm with all the villages therein.

The word itself is universally defined as Arabised Persian (see the previous article) meaning "village", "market-town", "encampment of tents or huts", "rural area". The Arabic lexica invariably gloss it with the word *sawād* "rural district", "environs of town" (Fīrūzābādī, *al-Ḳāmūs al-muḥīṭ; LA*). The town was the centre of the interior during the pre-Islamic Sāsānid period, with Ṣuḥār [*q.v.*] as the port. The massive fort which can still be seen, and was known even in the 20th century as Ḳalʿat Ibn Sharwān (i.e. Anūshīrwān), had, one assumes, a pre-Islamic predecessor, though the present building dates in all probability from the times of the Yaʿāriba (11th-12th/17th-18th centuries). The early and late Yaʿāriba imāms, as well as the Āl Bū Saʿīd imāms [*q.v.*] (also 12th/18th century), regarded al-Rustāḳ as their capital.

The district today comprises 150 villages, including al-Ḥazm, and has an estimated population of 75,000. It is the centre of the Omani date industry and also produces limes, grapes, quinces and mangoes. Al-Rustāḳ has its own research apiary and is a centre for the production of honey in the Sultanate.

Bibliography (in addition to works mentioned in the text): J.C. Wilkinson, *Water and tribal settlement in South-East Arabia*, Oxford 1977, 131, 154; *Sultanate of Oman throughout 20 years: the promise and fulfilment*, Ministry of Information, Muscat n.d., 40-1.

(G.R. Smith)

RUSTAM, the principal hero of the Iranian epic, especially in the version of Firdawsī [*q.v.*].

1. In Iranian legend.

Neither his name nor that of his father Zāl occur in the Avesta. In the *Yashts*, Kərəsāspa (in Persian, Karshāsp or Garshāsp) is the most important heroic figure. Marquart conjectured that originally "Rustam" was no more than an epithet of Kərəsāspa, which only by chance was not attested in the extant Avestan texts. The exploits later attributed to Rustam would be the result of a blend of the legends of Kərəsāspa with historical memories of Gondophares, the ruler of the Indo-Parthian empire in the first century A.D. It is now generally accepted, however, that in the Avestan tradition Zāl and Rustam did not yet belong to the cyle of legends about the Kayanid kings. Some scholars (in particular Nöldeke) assumed that they had their origin in the legends of the original population of Drangiana and Arachosia; others assigned them to the traditions of the Saka people who came to the same lands (later known as Sīstān and Zābulistān) in the late 2nd century B.C. (cf. *Camb. hist. of Iran*, iii, 454-6).

The oldest form of the name known is the Middle Iranian Rōdstahm (in Pahlavi writing, *lwtsthm*), from which the Soghdian *rwstmy* was derived. It is likely that tales about Rustam were given a place already in the *Khwāday-nāmag*, the synthesis of various legendary cycles compiled in the late Sāsānid period. This lost source is reflected in the works of Muslim historians and writers of *adab* works, who already mention a few stories about Rustam, in particular his guardianship of Siyāwakhsh, his combat with Isfandiyār and his death. These stories are, however, far less elaborate than they are in the *Shāh-nāma*. Relatively close to the Persian epic is the chronicle of the kings of Iran by al-Thaʿālibī [*q.v.*], written in the early 5th/11th century, but also in this source many of the best known adventures are missing. Indications of Rustam's popularity in early Islamic times are the occurrence of his name in the 1st/7th century, both as that of a Sāsānid general and of Christian monks in Mesopotamia (cf. Nöldeke, 11). Fragments of his legends are to be found in the work of the Armenian Moses of Khoren (7th or 8th century A.D.) and in a Soghdian manuscript found at Turfan which relates Rustam's fights with the demon (see *Camb. hist. of Iran*, iii, 457, 1229, with further references).

Only Firdawsī's *Shāh-nāma* contains a continuous story of the hero. His ancestors were local rulers of Sīstān and Zābulistān, who were vassals to the kings of Iran. Among them Garshāsp and Narīmān are mentioned, but only his grandfather Sām is a figure of some epic content. Rustam's father Zāl, who especially in the Arabic sources is also called Dastān, married Rūdāba (Rūdhāwadh according to al-Thaʿālibī), the daughter of the king of Kābul who was descended from the "dragon-king" Ḍaḥḥāk. This indicates a demonic streak in Rustam. His body, commonly compared to that of an elephant, was already at the time of his birth so enormous that he could only be delivered with the help of the miraculous bird

Sīmurg̲h̲. When he grew up, he besought God to reduce his weight so that he could walk without sinking into the ground. In Arabic, a common epithet to his name is *al-s̲h̲adīd*; in Persian he is called *tahamtan* "the one with the mighty body". Rustam's steed Ra<u>k</u>h̲s̲h̲ is as formidable among horses as his master is among humans.

His earliest deeds are the killing of a white elephant escaped from his father's stables, and the conquest of the fortress of Sipand in revenge for his great-grandfather Narīmān. The philological evidence points out that these two narratives were later added to Firdawsī's text (cf. *S̲h̲āh-nāma*, i, 275-81). With the assignment to bring Kay Ḳubād down from the Alburz mountains, in order to become the king of Iran, begins his service to the Kayanid dynasty. He rescues Kay Kāwūs from the hands of the White Demon in Māzandarān and, another time, from his captivity with the Hamāwarān of Yaman. Conspicuous is his role in the wars with the arch-enemy Afrāsiyāb (Frāsiyāt in Arabic sources) of Tūrān. Major tales in the *S̲h̲āh-nāma* with Rustam as a prominent character are the revenge for prince Siyāwa<u>k</u>h̲s̲h̲ (or Siyāwu<u>s̲h̲</u>), his fight with the demon Akwān, the story of Bīz̲h̲an and Manīz̲h̲a and the duel with his son Suhrāb. The Herculean Seven Deeds (*haft k̲h̲wān*) of Rustam were in all likelihood copied from similar deeds ascribed to Isfandiyār.

The final episodes tell about a tragic controversy with the last Kayanid kings. According to the version of al-Dīnawarī, the cause of this conflict was Rustam's refusal to accept the new religion which king Gustās̲h̲p (Avestan Vistāspa; in Arabic, Bis̲h̲tāsb or Bis̲h̲tāsf), the protector of Zarathustra, had embraced. Other sources only mention Rustam's refusal to fulfill the duties of a vassal. Gustās̲h̲p sends his son Isfandiyār (Avestan Spəntō.dāta; called Isfandiyād̲h̲ by al-Dīnawarī) to capture the disobedient Rustam, who kills the prince in a man-to-man fight. Finally, the hero himself falls victim to the treachery of his own brother S̲h̲ag̲h̲ād, who lures him into a trap during a hunting-party. In a last effort before he dies, Rustam manages to kill his murderer by a miraculous shot from his bow. Isfandiyār's son Bahman takes revenge on Rustam's family and has his son Farāmurz executed.

Heroes modelled on Rustam appear many times over in Persian epics written after Firdawsī. The characters in those works often bear the names of his ancestors or descendants. In lyrical poetry, comparisons drawn with Rustam are particularly frequent in the panegyrics of Farru<u>k</u>h̲ī [*q.v.*], who himself came from Sīstān and was a near contemporary of Firdawsī. He was also used as an exemplum by mystical poets, notably by Sanā'ī and Djalāl al-Dīn Rūmī [*q.vv.*], especially in the latter's *Dīwān-i Kabīr*.

Bibliography: Justi, *Iranisches Namenbuch*; J. Marquart, *Beiträge zur Geschichte und Sage von Ērān*, in *ZDMG*, xlix (1895), 643-4; T̲h̲aʿālibī, *G̲h̲urar ak̲h̲bār mulūk al-furs wa-siyarihim*, ed. and tr. H. Zotenberg, Paris 1900; Th. Nöldeke, *Das iranische Nationalepos²*, Berlin-Leipzig 1920, 9-12; A. Christensen, *Les Kayanides*, Copenhagen 1931, 130-46 and *passim*; E. Yarshater, *Rustam dar zabān-i sug̲h̲dī*, in *Mihr*, vii (1331 s̲h̲./1952), 406 ff.; M. Molé, *L'épopée iranienne après Firdosi*, in *La Nouvelle Clio*, v (1953), 377-93; Dīnawarī, *al-Ak̲h̲bār al-ṭiwāl*, Cairo 1960, 25-6; D̲h̲abīḥ Allāh Ṣafā, *Ḥamāsa-sarāyī dar Īrān³*, Tehran 1352 s̲h̲./1973; C.-H. de Fouchécour, *Une lecture du Livre des Rois de Ferdowsi*, in *St. Ir.*, v (1976), 171-202; *Camb. hist. of Iran*, iii, *passim*, and esp. Yarshater's ch. *Iranian national history*, 373-77, 453-57;

M. Perlmann (tr.), *The History of al-Ṭabarī*, IV. *The Ancient kingdoms*, Albany 1987; Firdawsī, *S̲h̲āh-nāma*, ed. Dj. K̲h̲āliḳī-Muṭlaḳ, i-iii, Costa Mesa-New York 1988-93. (J.T.P. DE BRUIJN)

2. In Islamic art.

The earliest representation of Rustam in Islamic art is probably that in the Edinburgh University Library manuscript of Ras̲h̲īd al-Dīn's *Djāmiʿ al-tawārīk̲h̲* (1306; ms. Arab 20, fol. 6b). He is there represented seated before King Minūc̲h̲ihr, wearing a headcloth and tiger-skin over Mongol clothes, and grasping a mace; he is bearded and has long horizontal moustaches. In the celebrated Demotte *S̲h̲āh-nāma* (*ca.* 1330), Rustam wears Mongol dress or armour, but in the 14th century manuscripts of the epic produced at S̲h̲īrāz under the Indjū'id and Muẓaffarid rulers he is once more distinguished by a tiger-skin surcoat, and this convention, once established, persisted throughout Persian painting.

The next stage was the addition of a leopard's head or mask fixed over his helmet, and this originated under the patronage of Iskandar Sulṭān, its earliest appearances being in the British Library *Miscellany* of 1410-11 (Add. 27261, fol. 298b) and a fragment dated to 1413 in the Topkapı Sarayı Library (B. 411, fol. 161b). It seems not unlikely that this very effective addition to the hero's panoply was due to the initiative of the young prince himself; he could easily have seen, or been told of, classical or Hellenistic portrayals of Heracles in the skin of the Nemean lion with its mask on his head.

It took a little time for this complete panoply to be universally established. In Bāysung̲h̲ur's *S̲h̲āh-nāma* of 1430, Rustam always wears an ordinary helmet with his tiger-skin surcoat, but in the copy made a year or two later at S̲h̲īrāz for his brother Ibrāhīm Sulṭān (Bodleian Library, Ouseley Add. 176) the leopard's head appears in several miniatures. In the Royal Asiatic Society *S̲h̲āh-nāma* of Muḥammad Djūkī (ms. 239; Herat, *ca.* 1440) it appears in only one miniature (fol. 145b). *S̲h̲āh-nāma* manuscripts produced under Turkman patronage in the middle years of the 15th century also present the hero sometimes with, and sometimes without, the leopard's mask on his helmet. But in the numerous copies of the epic illustrated in the Commercial Turkman style, and issuing from S̲h̲īrāz during the last quarter of the century, the leopard's mask is invariable.

Thus by the beginning of the Ṣafawid dynasty, Rustam's full panoply is well established, and to this period (*ca.* 1505) belongs the most splendid portrayal of Rustam in the whole of Persian painting: "Rustam lassoing the King of S̲h̲ām" in the Kunstgewerbemuseum, Leipzig, in which the leopard's head helmet is topped by a magnificent seven-fold plume, and the hero's moustache and beard are red. This miniature is probably the work of Sulṭān Muḥammad in his young days. Later in the Ṣafawid period, attempts were made to represent Rustam as an old man in the latter stages of his career, but at the same time painters sometimes failed to show him as a child in his earliest exploits; thus, in depicting his killing the mad elephant, an artist may show him in full panoply with moustache and beard.

In the 17th century, the languid and slightly decadent style of Riḍā ʿAbbāsī [*q.v.*] was ill-suited to epic illustration, and Rustam sometimes presents an awkward and distinctly unheroic figure. His late appearances under the Ḳādjārs show him with the wasp waist and luxuriant black beard of Fatḥ ʿAlī S̲h̲āh [*q.v.*]. But the traditional panoply survives to the end.

Bibliography: B.W. Robinson, *Persian painting*

and the national epic, London 1983, and references there given. (B.W. Robinson)

RUSTAM b. FARRUKH HURMUZD (thus in al-Ṭabarī; in al-Masʿūdī, b. Farrukh-zād), Persian general and commander of the Sāsanid army at the battle of al-Ḳādisiyya [*q.v.*] fought against the Arabs in Muḥarram 15/February-March 536 or Muḥarram 16/February 637, the battle in which he was killed.

His father is described as the *ispabadh* [*q.v.*] of Khurāsān, for which province Rustam was deputy. In the lengthy account by al-Ṭabarī of the battle of al-Ḳādisiyya, derived mainly from Sayf b. ʿUmar, there is much folkloric material, doubtless derived from materials used by the *ḳuṣṣāṣ* [see ḳāṣṣ], in which the Persian Emperor Yazdagird III and Rustam try to dissuade the Muslims from battle by a use of verbal parables and a show of superior splendour and luxury; but these are of no avail, and Rustam leads his forces into battle and is killed by Hilāl b. ʿUllafa al-Taymī (See F.M. Donner, *The early Islamic conquests*, Princeton 1981, 397, for the various traditions concerning this episode).

Bibliography: Ṭabarī, i, 2243-4, 2247 ff.; 2261, 2265-85, 2335 ff., tr. Y. Friedmann, *The battle of al-Qādisiyyah and the conquest of Syria and Palestine*, Albany 1992; Balādhurī, *Futūḥ*, 254 ff.; Masʿūdī, *Murūdj*, iv, 207-8, 221-3 = §§ 1537-8, 1555-6; Nöldeke, *Geschichte der Perser und Araber*, 393-4; Justi, *Iranisches Namenbuch*, 263. See also al-ḳādisiyya. (Ed.)

RUSTAMIDS or Rustumids, an Ibāḍī dynasty, of Persian origin, which reigned from Tāhart (in what is now Algeria) 161-296/778-909.

The birth of the Ibāḍī principality of Tāhart is bound up with the great Berber rising begun by Maysara (called, as a tribute from his enemies, *al-Ḥaḳīr* "The Vile") in 122/740. As a result of this rising, the greater part of the Maghrib fell away definitively from the control of the caliphate in the East, with the exception of the principality of Ḳayrawān (Kairouan), which only achieved virtual independence with the coming of the Aghlabids [*q.v.*] in 184/800. The Ibāḍī chief Abu 'l-Khaṭṭāb al-Maʿāfirī [*q.v.*], once elected Imām, seized Tripoli and then, in 141/758, Kayrawān, from where he ejected the Ṣufrī Khāridjites and then entrusted its government to ʿAbd al-Raḥmān b. Rustam. It seemed that the whole of the Maghrib, now detached from the caliphate, was likely to fall to Khāridjism, with its two strands of Ibāḍism and Ṣufrism.

ʿAbd al-Raḥmān b. Rustam b. Bahrām, the founder of the Ibāḍī principality of Tāhart, was certainly of Persian origin, without one being able to connect him, with any certainty, to the Persian royal house, as certain sources suggest. Having arrived in Ḳayrawān, with his mother, as a child, he felt attracted towards Ibāḍism which, with other doctrines, was being taught in the Great Mosque there, until Saḥnūn [*q.v.*], appointed *ḳāḍī* in 234/848-9, "broke up the circles of innovators (*ahl al-bidaʿ*)" (M. Talbi, *Biographies Aghlabides* ..., Tunis 1968, 104), and forbade them to spread their "deviations" (*zayghahum*). In 135/752, like others, he took the high road towards the East (*riḥla*) in order to complete his education at Baṣra, at that time the spiritual centre of Ibāḍism, at the feet of Abū ʿUbayda Muslim b. Abī Karīma, the great authority of the age, who gave out instruction in which political theology necessarily played a large role, conformable to the general principles of Khāridjism which had itself arisen from of a succession to power crisis. Five years later, in 140/757, together with Abu 'l-Khaṭṭāb, he was one of five missionaries, the *ḥamalat al-ʿilm* (lit. "bearers of knowledge"), who set out for the Maghrib in order to pass on to the phase of the *khurūdj*, i.e. open insurrection, with the aim of installing a just Islamic régime conformable to the Ibāḍī ideas of an elective and equalitarian theocracy, considering that all the previous existing authorities had more or less betrayed true Islam since the time of the arbitration (*taḥkīm*) at Ṣiffīn (37/657) [see ibāḍiyya].

The conjunction of affairs was at that moment especially favourable. Khāridjite propaganda had been introduced into the Maghrib some four decades previously, and it found there its most fertile ground. The Ṣufrīs were the first to enter the lists and, thanks to some resounding victories, had founded three principalities: at Sidjilmāsa, at Tlemcen and in the region of Salé on the Atlantic shores. The Ibāḍīs had the ambition of assuming for themselves power over the eastern Maghrib, and nearly succeeded.

However, Baghdād was not yet disposed freely to relinquish control, and still had the means within its general framework of policy to achieve this. In 144/761 Ibn al-Ashʿath recaptured Ḳayrawān, and Ibn Rustam fled into the central Maghrib. He ended up at Old Tāhart, in a region where several Ibāḍī Berber tribes were solidly established. He was not immediately elected Imām in place of Abu 'l-Khaṭṭāb, killed in battle, but he continued his involvement in the warfare against the ʿAbbasids, and in 151/768 he besieged, without success, the chief town of the Zāb, Ṭubna, the ancient fortress of Tubunda, which had become an advance bastion protecting Ifrīḳiya.

The Ibāḍiyya in the end had to renounce the capture of Ḳayrawān, firmly held by a governor of first-rate competence, Yazīd b. Ḥātim al-Muhallabī, and then decided to found their own principality in the Tāhart region where ʿAbd al-Raḥmān b. Rustam had already found refuge. There, in 161/778, "on a slope which dominated, from a height of a thousand metres, the steppes and their pasture-grounds" (Ch.-A. Julien, *Histoire de l'Afrique du Nord*, ii, 34), and in a place where there was abundant water, they constructed their capital, New Tāhart or Tīhart (9 km/6 miles to the west of present-day Tihert, founded in 1863, the administrative centre of a *wilāya* or province in modern Algeria), around which was built a protective wall with four gates. The site offered advantages at the same time for sedentaries and nomads alike, and constituted a natural fortress.

After his return from Baṣra, ʿAbd al-Raḥmān b. Rustam had already been in charge of various responsibilities, whence the uncertainty of the sources regarding the date of his investiture as Imām. This probably did not take place officially till after the foundation of Tāhart, sc. in 162/779. Ibn Rustam evidently combined in himself the conditions of knowledge and piety required by the Ibāḍiyya for the election of their Imām. But the main reason which tipped the balance in his favour was that, if disputes should arise, he had "no tribe to bring him aid, and no clan to support him" (Ibn al-Ṣaghīr, *Akhbār* ..., in *CT*, nos. 91-2 [1975], 321-2).

Externally, Ibn Rustam practised a pacific policy with regard to his neighbours, the ʿAbbāsid governors in Ḳayrawān, the ʿAlid Idrīsids in Fās or Fez, and the Ṣufrī Midrārids in Sidjilmāsa. Internally, he devoted his efforts to strengthening his power and to furthering the economic prosperity of his principality, thanks, in particular, to financial support from the Ibāḍiyya of the East, to the impulse given to trans-Saharan trade, and to agricultural and urban development. Tāhart speedily became a rich and cosmopolitan metropolis, and the Sunnī Ibn al-Ṣaghīr observed a host of people there, people stemming from Baṣra, Kūfa, Ḳayrawān and other places, all attracted by the justice and order which prevailed there.

Before his death, which probably took place in 171/788, ʿAbd al-Raḥmān b. Rustam appointed a council to choose a new Imām. The choice fell on his son ʿAbd al-Wahhāb. Till the end of the kingdom of Tāhart, the succeeding Imāms all came from his line, but with a chronology more or less uncertain and with many troubles which often took on the character and tiresome nature of schisms. In a theocracy guided by the Ḳurʾān and Tradition, where the Imām had ideally to double as a pious theologian controlled by religious leaders no less pious than himself, in a theocracy which was in principle equalitarian, austere and puritanical—ʿAbd al-Raḥmān is depicted as perched on the roof of his modest house, finishing off its building with the help of a slave—such an evolution was inevitable. In Tāhart, wrote Julien, *op. cit.*, ii, 37, "people lived in a permanent state of religious exaltation". The following is the most likely succession of the Imāms, theoretically elected but in fact succeeding by virtue of the dynastic succession rule against a background of schisms and political crises:

ʿAbd al-Raḥmān b. Rustam, 161-71/778-88
ʿAbd al-Wahhāb b. ʿAbd al-Raḥmān, 171-208/788-824
Abū Saʿīd Aflaḥ b. ʿAbd al-Wahhāb, 208-58/824-72
Abū Bakr b. Aflaḥ, 258-60/872-4
Abu 'l-Yaḳẓān Muḥammad b. Aflaḥ, 260-81/874-94
Abū Ḥātim Yūsuf b. Muḥammad, first reign 281-2/894-5
Yaʿḳūb b. Aflaḥ, first reign 282-6/895-9
Abū Ḥātim Yūsuf b. Muḥammad, second reign 286-94/899-907
Yaʿḳūb b. Aflaḥ, second reign ?
Yaḳẓān b. Abi 'l-Yaḳẓān, 294-6/907-9

The first schism (*iftirāḳ*) broke out as soon as ʿAbd al-Wahhāb came to power, with his election contested by a splinter group of the Ibāḍiyya. It took shape as the Nukkāriyya [see AL-NUKKĀR], who had their hour of glory under the command of Abū Yazīd [*q.v.*], the "Man on the Donkey", who almost succeeded in putting an end to the Fāṭimid caliphate of Mahdiyya. Towards 195/811, a conflict broke out between the Ibāḍiyya of Tāhart and their Zanāta Berber neighbours, who professed Muʿtazilism in its Wāṣilī form. It is related that the controversy preceded the open conflict which was finally resolved in favour of Tāhart, thanks in particular to intellectual and military support from the Nafūsa [*q.v.*] Berbers of southern Tripolitania.

The second schism which broke out amongst the Ibāḍiyya was that of the Khalafiyya, from the name of Khalaf b. al-Samḥ, a grandson of the Imām Abu 'l-Khaṭṭāb, who succeeded his father as governor of the Djabal Nafūsa [*q.v.*] to the south of Tripoli but without the agreement of the Imām ʿAbd al-Wahhāb, who rightly feared that a new dynasty would become installed there. Khalaf's partisans, taking as a pretext the discontinuity of the kingdom of Tāhart, proclaimed Khalaf as an independent Imām. The secession of the Djabal Nafūsa continued during Aflaḥ's imāmate until at least 221/836—the date of a decisive defeat inflicted on Khalaf—and the Khalafiyya maintained their doctrinal stance until the very end of the Rustamids.

Aflaḥ's reign, an exceptionally long one, was the Golden Age of the Rustamid imāmate. Despite various shocks which rocked the eastern part of the principality, his reign was relatively peaceful. He was able, by a combination of pliant policies and largesse, to impose his autority on the nomadic tribes, which were quarrelsome by nature.

His successors were less fortunate or skilful. The Tāhart principality had fluid frontiers, more human than geographical ones. It was very little urbanised, and had no *limes* or frontier march supported by a line of powerful fortresses. The Imām's territory had no other frontiers except those of the tribes which considered themselves Ibāḍī, and consequently recognised his authority, and this ultimately on the spiritual rather than the temporal level. This was the case e.g. of the Ibāḍiyya within the Aghlabid principality. Moreover, the principality was a mosaic of very differing ethnic elements: Berber tribes, predominantly nomadic and having divergent interests, Persians who had got rich in the shadow of Rustamid power, and fractions of the Arab *djund*—through their profession, bellicose in nature—who had fled from Ifrīḳiya. Once the religious bond became relaxed, all these ingredients became a typically explosive mixture. Hence the internal history of the Rustamid state was full of ups and downs, especially after Aflaḥ's death.

Armed clashes forced Abū Bakr to yield his power to his brother Abu 'l-Yaḳẓān, who was supported by the Arabs. The latter was nevertheless not able to take up residence at Tāhart until 268/882, thanks to the support of the Lawāta and Nafūsa Berbers. Having learnt from these occurrences, he followed, it is recorded, a policy of justice, tolerance and balance, on an indispensable foundation of piety, austerity and erudition.

During his own lifetime, Abu 'l-Yaḳẓān appointed his son Abū Ḥātim to succeed himself, a procedure not at all, at least in principle, in accordance with Ibāḍi tradition. It is true that the make-up of Tāhart had, meanwhile, changed considerably. Henceforth, at the side of a cosmopolitan plebs or *ʿāmma*, there were all sorts of groups of people, including a great number of Mālikīs and Shīʿīs, whose weight began to be felt on the chequerboard of politics. In these conditions, an uncle of Abū Ḥātim, Yaʿḳūb b. Aflaḥ, preferred to leave the capital and settle amongst the Zuwāgha Berbers who formed part of the Khalafiyya. Civil warfare soon resumed. Abū Ḥātim was driven out of Tāhart and his uncle Yaʿḳūb took his place. But this was not for long, and political alliances, from now onwards no longer reserved for the Ibāḍī community, were made and unmade according to shifting interests. Yaʿḳūb, in turn, lost his capital, and Abū Ḥātim returned to power, supported by the *ʿāmma*, a mixture of both Ibāḍīs and non-Ibāḍīs. Disorder got worse and the central power became more relaxed. Abū Ḥātim was ruler only in name, and was assassinated by his nephews, which merely added to the disorders. Yaḳẓān b. Abi 'l-Yaḳẓān was on the throne when the troops of Abū ʿAbd Allāh al-Shīʿī came to extinguish the Rustamid principality; Tāhart offered no resistance.

Wedged between two hostile regimes, that of the ʿAlid Idrīsids on the west and that of the ʿAbbāsid governors, and then the Sunnī Aghlabids on the east, the Rustamids practised, by force of circumstances, a policy of rapprochement: to their south, with the Ṣufrī Midrārids of Sidjilmāsa, who, moreover, controlled the vital route by which gold came; and to their north, with the strongly Mālikī Umayyads of Cordova, disregarding, in the interests of practical politics, the fact that Mālik had condemned to death the Ibāḍī heretics (Saḥnūn, *Mudawwana*, Cairo 1323/1905, ii, 47).

To the east, after vain attempts to seize Tripoli

from the Aghlabids, the Imām ʿAbd al-Wahhāb, who had directed the battle in person, relinquished the town itself and the seas to the Aghlabids, and contented himself with the hinterland, having been neither conqueror not vanquished, and with a reversion to the *status quo ante*. In 239/853-4, the Aghlabid Abu 'l-ʿAbbās Muḥammad I built a town in the neighbourhood of Tāhart, which he provocatively called al-ʿAbbāsiyya in honour of his suzerains. The Imām Aflaḥ burnt it down and informed the caliph in Cordova of his action; the latter sent him 100,000 dirhams. Finally, in 283/896 Ibrāhīm II inflicted a severe defeat at Mānū, near the sea and to the south of Gabès, on the Nafūsa, the spear-head of Ibāḍī power. In the west, the Imām ʿAbd al-Wahhāb allowed Idrīs I to capture Tlemcen in 173/789 almost without any adverse reaction.

Across the seas, the Ibāḍī Imāms of Tāhart and the Mālikī *amīrs* of Cordova had extremely amicable relations, despite their doctrinal differences, united by a common political interest. In 207/822, ʿAbd al-Raḥmān II gave a warm welcome to three sons of the Imām ʿAbd al-Wahhāb arriving at Cordova on an embassy, probably to greet the *amīr* on his accession to power. In 229/844, "Cordova informed Tāhart officially of its victory over the Northmen" (Lévi-Provençal, *Hist. Esp. mus.*, i, 245), and in 239/853 Muḥammad I sent a sumptuous present to the Imām Aflaḥ on his accession. Furthermore, members of the Rustamid family, installed in Muslim Spain, held high offices in Cordova, up to the ranks of commander and vizier. Possibly one might think, as did Lévi-Provençal, of links of vassalage (*loc. cit.*).

At its apogee, the Rustamid capital was very prosperous. Al-Yaʿḳūbī describes it as "an important city, very famous and with a great influence, which people have termed the ʿIrāḳ of the Maghrib", adding that "a fortress on the coast serves as a port for the fleet of the principality of Tāhart; it is called Marsā Farūkh" (tr. Wiet, *Les Pays*, 216-17). Concerning the commercial routes by land, Ibn al-Ṣaghīr, *op. cit.*, 325, noted that there were roads connecting Tāhart with the land of Sūdān and with all the lands to the East and the West. It was probably in order to stimulate trade with Sub-Saharan Africa that Abū Bakr b. Aflaḥ sent an embassy headed by a rich merchant of Tāhart, Ibn ʿArafa, to the "king of the Sūdān" (*ibid.*, 340). A great tolerance reigned within the city, whose population included, amongst others, Christians (*ʿadjam*), who are described as being especially influential and rich (Julien, *op. cit.*, ii, 37). The people of Tāhart were fond of controversy and disputation, and the Imāms themselves were often scholars as well-versed in the profane sciences as the religious ones.

Bibliography: This is not extensive, but is limited here to the main sources and to modern works, which give more detailed references.

1. Sources. Ibn al-Ṣaghīr (Mālikī author contemporary with the events), *Akhbār al-aʾimma al-rustamiyyīn*, ed. and tr. Motylinsky, in *Actes du XIVe congrès international des orientalistes*, Paris 1908, 3-132, Ar. text republ. in *CT*, nos. 91-2 (1975), 315-68. Ibāḍī authors. Abū Zakariyyāʾ (d. 471/1078), *K. al-Sīra wa-akhbār al-aʾimma*, partial Fr. tr. E. Masqueray, Algiers 1878; new Fr. tr., 1st part, R. Le Tourneau, in *RAfr*, nos. 462-3 (1960), 99-176, nos. 464-5 (1960), 322-90, 2nd part H. R. Idris, in nos. 468-9 (1961), 323-74, nos. 470-1 (1962), 119-62; also ed. Algiers 1979, Tunis 1985; Dardjīnī (d. 670/1271), *Ṭabaḳāt al-mashāʾikh*, ed. Ibrāhīm Ṭallāy, Constantine n.d.; Shammākhī (d. 928/1522), *K. al-Siyar*, lith. Cairo 1301/1883. Sunnī authors: Ibn al-Athīr, ed. Beirut, v, 317-18, 599, vi, 270, 519, viii, 49-53; Ibn al-ʿIdhārī, *Bayān*, ed. Colin and Lévi-Provençal, i, 72, 75, 76, 153, 196-200; Ibn Khaldūn, *ʿIbar*, Beirut 1959, vi, index; Yaʿḳūbī, tr. Wiet, index; Ibn Ḥawḳal, Fr. tr. Kramers and Wiet, index; Bakrī, *Masālik*, ed. A.P. Van Leeuwen and A. Ferre, Tunis 1992, index, ed. and Fr. tr. de Slane, 137-41, Ar. text 66-9; Idrīsī, *Nuzha*, index.

2. Studies. G. Dangel, *L'Imamat ibâḍite de Tahert*, diss. Strasbourg 1977; W. Schwartz, *Die Anfänge der Ibaditen in Nordafrika*, Wiesbaden 1983; U. Rebstock, *Die Ibāḍiten im Maġrib, 2./8.-4./10. Jahrhundert. Die Geschichte einer Berber Bewegung im Gewand des Islam*, 1983; G. Marçais, *La Berbérie musulmane*, Paris 1946, 101-16; Ch.-A. Julien, *Histoire de l'Afrique du Nord*, Paris 1956, ii, 31-9; A. Bel, *La religion musulmane en Berbérie*, Paris 1938; P. Cuperly, *Professions de foi ibāḍites*, diss. Paris IV, 1982; M. Talbi, *La conversion des Berbères au Khāridjisme ibāḍito-ṣufrite*, in *Etudes d'histoire ifrīḳiyenne*, Tunis 1982, 13-81; idem, *L'emirat Aghlabide*, Paris 1966, index; S. al-Bārunī, *al-Azhār al-riyāḍiyya fī aʾimma wa-mulūk al-ibāḍiyya*, Cairo 1967; S.Z. ʿAbd al-Ḥamīd, *Taʾrīkh al-Maghrib al-arabī*, Cairo 1965, 367-98; M.I. ʿAbd al-Razzāḳ, *al-Khawāridj fī bilād al-Maghrib*, diss. Casablanca 1976, 144-234; Chikh Békri, *Le Khāridjisme berbère, quelques aspects du royaume rustumide*, in *AIEO Alger*, xv (1957), 55-109; S. Zakkār, *al-Dawla al-rustumiyya fī Tāhart*, in *Dirāsāt taʾrīkhiyya*, Damascus 1983, no. 12, 74-90; Ḥabīb Djanḥānī, *Tāhart, ʿāsimat al-dawla al-rustumiyya*, in *Rev. Tunis. des Scis. Soc.*, nos. 40-3 (1975), 7-54; Iḥsān ʿAbbās, *al-Mudjtamaʿ al-tāhartī fī ʿahd al-rustumiyyīn*, in *al-Aṣāla*, no. 45 (Algiers 1975), 20-36; Lévi-Provençal, *Hist. Esp. mus.*, index; ʿA.ʿA. Filālī, *al-ʿAlāḳāt al-siyāsiyya bayn al-dawla al-umawiyya fi 'l-Andalus wa-duwal al-Maghrib*, 2nd ed. Algiers 1983, 96-110; idem, in *CT*, nos. 155-6 (1991), 35-50; Muḥammad b. Tāwīt, *Dawlat al-rustumiyyīn aṣḥāb Tāhart*, in *Ṣaḥīfat Maʿhad al-Dirāsāt al-Islāmiyya*, v, Madrid 1957, 105-28; A.S. Ahmed and D.M. Hart (eds.), *Islam in tribal societies*, London 1984; C. Vanacker, *Géographie économique de l'Afrique du Nord*, in *Annales ESC* (1973), 659-80; J. Despois, *Le Djebel Nefousa*, Paris 1935. (M. Talbi)

RÜSTEM PASHA (906?-968/1500?-1561) Ottoman Grand Vizier.

Born *ca.* 1500 in a village near Sarajevo, Rüstem Pasha came of a family most probably of Bosnian origin (though some sources mention Croatian or possibly Albanian ancestry), whose pre-Muslim surname had been either Opukovič or Čigalič (cf. Albèri, *Relazioni degli ambasciatori veneti al senato*, ser. iii, vol. iii, 89; C. Truhelka, *Bosnische Post*, Sarajevo 1912, no. 80). A register from the *ḳāḍī*'s [*q.v.*] court at Sarajevo, dated 974/1557, records the sale of a house by Ḥādjdjī ʿAlī Beg b. Khayr al-Dīn, *mütewellī* of Rüstem Pasha's *bedesten* in the city, on behalf of one "Nefīsa Khanum, daughter of Muṣṭafā and sister of Rüstem Pasha". A brother, Sinān Pasha (d. 961/1554), was also in the service of the Ottoman government, rising to the rank of *Ḳapudan Pasha* [*q.v.*].

Educated in the palace school, Rüstem Pasha's first recorded post was as *silāḥdār* on the Mohács [*q.v.*] campaign, and then as *mīrākhūr-i ewwel*. The date of his appointment as *beglerbegi* [*q.v.*] of Diyār Bakr is unknown, but it was from this post that he was appointed *beglerbegi* of Anatolia in 945/1538 (Pečewī, *Taʾrīkh*, Istanbul 1281/1861, i, 206). The following year, he became third vizier and was married to

Mihrimāh, the daughter of Ḳānūnī Süleymān and Khurrem Sulṭān [*q.vv.*]. In 948/1541 he was promoted to second vizier, and in 951/1544 succeeded Khādim Süleymān Pasha [*q.v.*] as Grand Vizier. Dismissed in 960/1553 during the outcry caused by the execution of Süleymān's eldest son Muṣṭafā, Rüstem Pasha spent two years in retirement before being re-appointed Grand Vizier in 962/1555, following the execution (at which he is said to have connived) of Ḳara Aḥmed Pasha [*q.v.*], grand vizier since 960/1553. He then served in this post until his death, probably from dropsy, in 968/1561. He was buried in the *türbe* designed for him by the architect Sinān [*q.v.*] next to the Shehzāde mosque in Istanbul. (For further biographical details, see S. Altundağ and Ş. Turan, *İA*, art. *Rüstem Paşa*; F. Babinger, *EI*[1], art. *Rüstem Pasha*; *Sidjill-i ʿOthmānī*, ii, 377-8, iii, 106).

Rüstem Pasha was Süleymān's longest-serving Grand Vizier (a total of fourteen-and-a-half years in two periods of office), but one whose reputation, both contemporary and historical, was mixed. During his first period of office a major treaty was concluded with the Hapsburg Emperor (in 1547) stipulating the annual payment of 30,000 ducats' "tribute" by the latter. Internally, his tenure was marked throughout by his successful efforts to build up government finances, neglecting no possible sources of income, even, according to the Habsburg ambassador Busbecq, selling vegetables and flowers grown in the grounds of Ṭopḳapï Sarāyï [*q.v.*] (Ogier Ghiselin de Busbecq, *The Turkish letters*, tr. E.S. Forster, Oxford 1968, 30). On the other hand, Rüstem Pasha was held largely responsible for introducing the sale of government offices and for allowing imperial *khāṣṣ*s [*q.v.*] to be given out in tax farms, thus paving the way for the bribery and corruption detected by later Ottoman historians. He amassed an immense personal fortune (see the inventory of possessions on his death given by Pečewī, *Taʾrīkh*, i, 23, taken from ʿĀlī's [*q.v.*] *Künhü 'l-akhbār*), and was accused of greed and avarice both on his own behalf and that of the state (for several complaints against him, see M.T. Gökbilgin, *Rüstem Paşa ve hakkındaki ithamlar*, in *Tarih dergisi*, viii/11 [1955], 11-50).

Rüstem Pasha appears to have enjoyed the sultan's full confidence, due partly to his abilities and partly to the mutual agreement between himself, Mihrimāh Sulṭān and Khurrem Sulṭān. However, his positive achievements as Grand Vizier were overshadowed by his involvement in the conspiracy leading to the execution of the popular prince Muṣṭafā, which cleared the way for the eventual succession of one of Khurrem Sulṭān's two surviving sons, Selīm II [*q.v.*] (Gökbilgin, *op. cit.*, 20-4, 38-43). Rüstem's dismissal in 960/1553 may have been at his request, in order to forestall demands from supporters of Muṣṭafā for his own execution.

Busbecq's description of Rüstem Pasha as "a man of keen and far-seeing mind" is largely borne out by Ottoman sources, who attest his capable administration and loyal service, stressing his financial acumen and the fact that even where offices were sold these were only to worthy people who were never thereafter dismissed. Whereas to Busbecq he seemed "always gloomy and brutal" and ʿĀlī criticised his dislike of dervishes and poets, Pečewī stresses his correct manners, sobriety and piety (Busbecq, *Turkish letters*, 29, 190; J. Schmidt, *Pure water for thirsty Muslims: a study of Muṣṭafā ʿĀlī of Gallipoli's Künhü l-aḫbār*, Leiden 1991, 153, 89, 159; Pečewī, *Taʾrīkh*, i, 21-2). He was nevertheless a master of political intrigue and a controversial figure.

As a patron of architecture, Rüstem Pasha commissioned, in addition to his principal foundation in Istanbul, the Rüstem Pasha mosque, at least four *medrese*s and a number of other mosques, *ʿimārets*, *kerwānsarāys*, and other structures throughout Anatolia and Rumeli. Many of these were also designed by Sinān. However, it is now thought that the historical work *Tewārīkh-i Āl-i ʿOthmān* (or *Taʾrīkh-i Rüstem Pasha*) for long attributed to Rüstem Pasha's authorship, is in fact part of the *Djāmiʿ ul-tewārīkh* of Maṭrāḳčï Naṣūḥ [*q.v.*], compiled at Rüstem Pasha's request (L. Forrer, *Die Osmanische Chronik des Rustem Pascha,* Leipzig 1923; H.G. Yurdaydın, *An Ottoman historian of the XVIth century: Naṣūḥ al-Maṭrāḳī and his* Beyān-ı menāzil-i sefer-i ʿIrāḳayn *and its importance for some ʿIrāqī cities*, in *Turcica*, vii (1975), 180-2).

Bibliography: For further references in addition to those in the text, see the bibl. to S. Altundağ and Ş. Turan, *İA*, art. *Rüstem Paşa*.

(Christine Woodhead)

RUSWĀ, Mirzā Muḥammad Hādī, Urdu novelist, poet, translator and writer on scientific, philosophical and religious subjects. He was born in Lucknow most probably in 1858. His ancestors had migrated from Persia during the Mughal period. His great-grandfather, Mīrzā Dhu 'l-Faḳār ʿAlī Beg, took up permanent residence in Awadh [*q.v.*] during Āṣaf al-Dawla's time (1775-97), and became adjutant in the Nawāb's army. Ruswā received his early education from his father, Āghā Muḥammad Taḳī, who taught him Arabic, Persian and mathematics. For learning English, Ruswā went to La Martinière College, where he remained until the middle grade. By the time he was sixteen years of age both his parents died. Ruswā came into a large inheritance, but his maternal uncle, who was his guardian, appropriated most of it. What remained was squandered by Ruswā himself in self-indulgence and extravagant living. At this time, a friend of his father, by the name of Ḥaydar Bakhsh, who was a calligrapher by profession, came to Ruswā's aid, and helped him through his financial difficulties. Ruswā enrolled himself in Thomason Engineering School, Roorkee, and obtained an overseer's diploma in 1876. Thereafter, he worked first in Rae Bareli and, later, in the Quetta region of Balūčistān, where his duties were connected with the laying of railway tracks. Not long afterwards he resigned from his job, and took up employment as instructor of Persian in the Church Mission School, Lucknow. From there he passed his high school examination as a private candidate.

In 1888 Ruswā joined Christian College, Lucknow, to teach Arabic and Persian, and stayed there for over thirty years. In 1894 he passed his B.A. examination from Punjab University as a private student. Together with his full-time job in Christian College, he taught briefly in Isabella Thorburn College, an institution for women students. Towards the latter part of his life, he showed an open involvement with religion, which found expression in a number of religious tracts composed by him and in the publication of a journal entitled *al-Ḥakam*, which contained articles on religious matters written from a Shīʿī point of view. This journal continued to be published from 1902 to 1907. In 1919 Ruswā found employment in the Bureau of Translation, Osmania University, Ḥaydarābād (Deccan), where he spent the remaining years of his life. He died in Ḥaydarābād on 21 October 1931 and was buried there.

Ruswā was a man of varied talents. His intellectual preoccupations were not restricted only to literary pursuits, but extended to other fields as well, such as philosophy and science. For giving expression to his philosophical interest, he founded the bi-monthly *Ishrāk*, a journal devoted to the dissemination of philosophical ideas. It appeared for the first time on 5 May 1884, and was perhaps the first journal of its kind in Urdu. However, it was shortlived, and had to be discontinued after one and a half years due to a lack of enthusiasm on the part of Urdu readers. In addition to his original contributions, Ruswā published in this journal his Urdu translations of two of Plato's works, namely the *Apology* and *Crito*. At a later date, while working at Ḥaydarābād, he translated several works dealing with philosophy and psychology. He also took an interest in astronomy and chemistry, and composed some works on these subjects. Among his other accomplishments was his participation in the development of a system of Urdu shorthand and a keyboard for the Urdu typewriter.

In the literary field, Ruswā is known primarily for his novels. He was also a poet of a minor sort, writing conventional verses. His first poetical work, a *mathnawī* entitled *Naw bahār* ("Spring"), appeared in 1886. He also composed a verse drama, in the *mathnawī* form, under the title *Murakkaʿ-i Laylā Madjnūn* ("An album of Laylā and Madjnūn"), which was completed probably in 1887. He used the pen-name of "Mīrzā" for his poems, reserving the pseudonym "Ruswā" for his novels. In the beginning, his mentor in poetry was the respected contemporary poet of Lucknow, Dabīr (1803-75 [*q.v.*]). As a novelist, Ruswā was the author of five original works, namely *Afshā-yi rāz* ("Exposed secret"), *Umrāʾo Djān Adā*, *Dhāt-i sharīf* ("A perfect knave"), *Sharīf-zāda* ("Of good breed"), and *Akhtarī Begum*. *Afshā-yi rāz* (1896), of which only the first part seems to have been completed, represents Ruswā's earliest attempt at novel-writing. Its theme, dealing with the decadent society and culture of Lucknow during the latter part of the 19th century, was elaborated by the author in his next novel, *Umrāʾo Djān Adā* (1899), which tells the life story of a courtesan, on whose name the title of the novel is based. Ruswā's third novel, *Dhāt-i sharīf* (1900), has for its central theme the life of a gullible and degenerate aristocrat who succumbs to the deceptions and allurements of unscrupulous hangers-on, and brings destruction upon himself due to his indiscretions. In *Sharīf-zāda* (1900), the story revolves around a person of meagre means who, by virtue of his character, personal effort and hard work, finds success in life. Ruswā's last novel, *Akhtarī Begum* (1924), is a narrative of a middle class household, and contains a plot built upon misunderstandings. Of all the above-mentioned novels, *Umrāʾo Djān Adā* is decidedly a masterpiece, and contributes, for the most part, to Ruswā's literary fame. On its appearance, it was welcomed in literary circles and was so well-received by the reading public that it went through several editions during a short time. In this novel Ruswā gives a sensitive portrayal of the current state of society and provides an insight into the traditional culture representative of the Muslim upper class in Lucknow. Because of its realistic delineation of the theme, its successfully constructed plot, and its superb characterisation, *Umrāʾo Djān Adā* has come to be regarded by many critics as the first true novel in Urdu.

Bibliography: Mirzā Muḥammad Hādī Ruswā, *Umrāʾo Djān Adā*, ed. Ẓahīr Fatḥpūrī, Lahore 1963; idem, *Umrao Jan Ada (Courtesan of Lucknow)*, tr. Khushwant Singh and M.A. Husaini, Calcutta 1961; idem, *Afshā-yi rāz*, Lucknow 1896; idem, *Dhāt-i sharīf*, Lucknow 1965; idem, *Sharīf-zāda*, Allahabad 1968; idem, *Akhtarī Begum*, Karachi 1961; idem, *Naw bahār*, Lucknow 1886; idem, *Murakkaʿ-i Laylā Madjnūn*, Allahabad 1928; idem, *Mirzā Ruswā ke tanḳīdī murāsalāt*, ed. Muḥammad Ḥasan, Aligarh 1961; Maymūna Begum Anṣārī, *Mirzā Muḥammad Hādī Mirzā wa Ruswā: ḥayāt wa adabī kārnāme*, Lahore 1963; Ādam Shaykh, *Mirzā Ruswā: ḥayāt awr nāwil-nigārī*, Lucknow 1968; Ẓahīr Fatḥpūrī, *Ruswā kī nāwil-nigārī*, Rawalpindi 1970; Mirzā Muḥammad ʿAskarī (tr.), *Tārīkh-i adab-i Urdū*, repr. Lahore n.d.; ʿAlī ʿAbbās Ḥusaynī, art. *Mirzā Ruswā*, in *Nuḳūsh*, 47-8, Lahore 1955; Muhammad Sadiq, *A history of Urdu literature*, London 1964; T.W. Clark (ed.), *The novel in India*, Berkeley 1970; Fayyāḍ Maḥmūd and ʿIbādat Barelawī (eds.), *Tārīkh-i adabiyyāt-i Musalmānān-i Pākistān wa Hind*, iv, Lahore 1972; *Urdū dāʾira-yi maʿārif-i Islāmiyya*, x, Lahore 1973; Djaʿfar Ḥusayn, *Bīswīn ṣadī ke baʿd Lakhnawī adīb apne tahdhībī pas manẓar mēn*, Lucknow 1978; Salīm Akhtar, *Urdū adab kī mukhtaṣar-tarīn tārīkh*, Lahore 1981; Iʿdjāz Ḥusayn, *Mukhtaṣar tārīkh-i adab-i Urdū*, revised by Sayyid Muḥammad ʿAḳīl, Allahabad 1984; D.J. Matthews *et alii*, *Urdu literature*, London 1985.

(Munibur Rahman)

RUTBIL [see zunbil].

RUTUL, a people of Dāghistān in the eastern Caucasus.

Until the Soviet period the Rutuls lacked a common ethnic self-designation, but rather referred to themselves by village (*aul*) or as members of the *Rutul Magal*. The Rutul Magal was one of the numerous free societies or clan federations found in Dāghistān prior to the Soviet period. This is one of the few cases where all of the members of a given ethnic group belonged to the same free society. In addition to the Rutuls, who dominated this free society, a number of Tsakhur and Lezgin villages were also members of the Rutul Magal. The existence of this free society helped in the establishment of a distinct Rutul ethnic group during the Soviet period.

The Rutuls traditionally inhabited 20 villages in Rutul district in southern Dāghistān (18 of which are in the Samur valley and 2 others in the Akhtīčai valley) and 2 villages across the border in neighbouring Ādharbaydjān. The Rutuls lived under very strong Lezgin and Ādharbaydjānī influence, and until the Russian Revolution they were on the verge of total assimilation by these two other culturally more dominant peoples. The Rutul language belongs with Lezgin to the Samurian group of the northeast (Čečeno-Dāghistānī) division of the Caucasian language family. The Rutul language is only vernacular (i.e. it has no written form). Prior to the Russian Revolution, there was almost universal illiteracy among the Rutuls, and the few individuals who could write used classical Arabic. After the Revolution and until the 1930s, Lezgin and Azeri Turkish served as the literary language among the Rutuls. Since that time, Russian has been the primary literary language used by the Rutuls of Dāghistān, and Azeri by those of Ādharbaydjān.

The Rutuls were polytheistic until the appearance of Zoroastrianism in the northern Caucasus starting sometime around the 5th century B.C. Later Christian influences penetrated the Rutul region from the south (primarily by Armenians living in Ādharbaydjān prior to the appearance of the Ādharbaydjān Turks in the 11th century). According to Rutul legend, Islam was introduced by the Arabs in the 7th and 8th centuries, but was more likely spread from other areas in Dāghistān between the 10th-13th centuries. Although officially Muslim, Islam was practic ed among the Rutuls and other southern Dāghistānīs with many Christian, Zoroastrian, and polytheistic holdovers. During the 18th-19th centuries conservative Ṣūfī movements were active among the Rutuls and during this period many of the pre-Islamic cultural rituals and beliefs were eliminated. The Rutuls today are Sunnī Muslims. As among all other Dāghistānī peoples, and many other North Caucasians, pre-Islamic clan vendetta laws are still common among the Rutuls to this day.

Until the mid-20th century, patriarchal-clan endogamic marriage patterns prevailed among the Rutuls. Since that time traditional clan endogamy has been breaking down. In addition to clan exogamy, some ethnic intermarriage patterns with other Dāghistānī peoples is beginning to develop, and in particular in urban areas of Dāghistān.

The traditional economy among the Rutuls was based on transhumant pastoralism. Sheep and goats were the most common stock animals raised by the Rutuls for food, milk, and wool. As this is a dry and mountainous region, little agriculture was practised and animal husbandry predominated. Traditionally, women engaged in agriculture while the men tended the animals. Horses were also raised for transport as were some cattle. Rug weaving and ceramics were common crafts among the Rutuls, and the trade in these goods formed an important part of the Rutul traditional economy.

There was a long tradition of seasonal migration by the Rutul men to find winter employment in other parts of Dāghistān and northern Ādharbaydjān. As there are no urban areas within the Rutul region itself, a significant emigration to areas outside the Rutul region by young people developed during the Soviet period. Derbend and Makhač-kala in Dāghistān, and Bākū, Shekī, and Kuba in Ādharbaydjān are the main cities to which the Rutul migrate.

The Rutuls are one of the numerically small peoples of the Caucasus. According to the census returns of the USSR, there were 10,495 Rutuls in 1926; 6,732 in 1959; 12,071 in 1970; 15,032 in 1979; and 29,672 in 1989. The radical changes in population reflect the rapid rate of assimilation of the Rutuls by their neighbours during the 1930s, and then a reversal of that trend afterwards. The doubling of their population between 1979 and 1989 represents a rise in Rutul consciousness (i.e. redefinition by Rutuls who formerly called themselves Dāghistānīs, Lezgins or Ādharbaydjānīs).

Bibliography: *Narodî Dagestana,* Moscow 1955; *Narodî Kavkaza,* Moscow 1960; R. Wixman, *Language aspects of ethnic patterns and processes in the North Caucasus,* Chicago 1980; A. Bennigsen, *The problem of bilingualism and assimilation in the North Caucasus,* in *Central Asian Review,* xv/3 (1967), 205-11. (R. Wixman)

RUWALA (A., also Ruwayla, conventional renderings Eng., Roala, Rwala, Ruwalla, Ruweilah; German, frequently Ruala, Rualla, Ruola, also Rawalla and Erwalla; French, Rou'ala, Roualla), an important tribe in northern Arabia.

The Ruwala and other ʿAnaza [*q.v.*] say that the Ruwala are from the Ḍana Muslim group of ʿAnaza. An authoritative Ruwaylī genealogist, Fraywān b. Frayḥ al-Muʾabḥil al-Shaʿlān, opposes Djās to Bishr; Djās has, as descendants, Zayyid and Wahhāb; Zayyid has Rwayli (the Ruwala) and Mislim, who are the Swālma, Shadjaʿa and ʿAbdilla; the Wahhāb are opposed to Zayyid and the descendants of Wahhāb are the ʿAli (Wald ʿAli) and Mufarridj, who are the Ḥasana and Mesalīkh (Lancaster 1981, 25). Other authorities (e.g. Musil, 1928, quoting the then *amīr* Nūrī Shaʿlān) give the Ḍana Muslim as the Benī Wahhāb and the al-Djās: the Benī Wahhāb divide into the Ḥasana and the Wald ʿAlī; the Djās into the Miḥlef and the Ruwala. The names are similar, but their position in relation to each other is inconsistent.

The sections (*fukhūḍ*) of the Ruwala are: al-Murʾaẓ and al-Doghmān (who together are the Djumʿān), al-Ḳaʿādḳiʿa and al-Fraydja. The Kwātzba, now reckoned as part of the Ruwala, claim descent from Ḳaḥṭān [*q.v.*] and joined the Ruwala possibly in the 18th century (Musil, *Arabia deserta*, 1927, 14-6; Lancaster, 1981, 155-6). The shaikhly family is Ibn Shaʿlān of the Murʾaẓ section, who took over the shaykhdom from Ibn Ḳaʿḳāʿ of al-Ḳaʿādḳiʿa, possibly in the 16th century (Musil, 1928, 51; Lancaster, 1981, 126-7).

The areas used by the Ruwala in the present and past include Tayma and Khaybar, the Djubba, Wādī Sirḥān, al-Wudiyān, al-Labba, the Ḥamad and Ḥawrān. Numbers are difficult to establish, but the Ruwala say they were and are the largest and most powerful tribe in the northern Arabian desert. Shaykh Faysal b. Fawwāz Shaʿlān estimates there to be over half a million, most of whom are in northern Saudi Arabia, with a few in Syria and Jordan.

Inconsistencies, noticeable in the sources, in the precise relationships of the Ruwala to other parts of the Ḍana Muslim group, in their sections, locations and numbers, may be understood by reference to Ruwaylī concepts. The genealogy is seen as a way of talking about political and jural relationships of closeness and distance between constituent parts of the group, not actual descent. The shaikhly family often personifies the tribe in historical and political discussion; this encourages a shift in political focus to be seen as a migration from one area to another which is not justifiable when more detailed information is available. The Ruwala are, as they have always been, concerned with living their lives in their own terms; they see their *shaykh*s as ambassadors, or agents, between them and the agencies of other governments, rather than leaders as such. From this point of view, the movement northwards in the late 18th century is a political and economic shift on the part of the shaikhly family and those Ruwala who saw the shift as a useful option.

The Ruwala say they are from ʿAnaz, who was the brother of Maʿaz, the sons of Wāʾil. This ʿAnaz b. Wāʾil genealogy is not totally consistent with the information of Hishām b. Muḥammad al-Kalbi in his *Djamharat al-nasab* on ʿAnaza b. Asad, "alter Stamm, später zu Rabīʿa gerechnet" (tr. Caskel and Strenziok, Band ii, 189, and Band i, tables 141 and 172). The Rabīʿa and Bakr b. Wāʾil tribes dominate the recorded history of northern Arabia in the early and mediaeval periods. Yāḳūt, iii, 644, records the ʿAnaza in Khaybar, as does Abu 'l-Fidā, *Taḳwīm*, tr. Reinaud, 120. Sections of the Ruwala continue to own date gardens there and in Tayma (Lancaster, 1981, 128). The Djlās (identified with the Ruwala by Burckhardt, *Notes*, i, 6), and other ʿAnaza, are mentioned in Ottoman tax registers of 1558 as wintering around Ṣafad (A. Cohen and B. Lewis, *Population and revenue in 16th century Palestine*, Princeton 1979, 160). Abujabr (*Pioneers over Jordan*, London 1989, 166) mentions a family from a section of the Ruwala who left Tayma about 1600 and settled in al-Ḥusn, near Irbid in Jordan. Thus the Ruwala have been using the wider region for a long period, although political and economic shifts have caused them to be identified with, and to identify themselves with, different areas.

Musil, quoting other tribes in the region, says the Ruwala were the "most Bedu" tribe in northern Arabia. At this date (1908-16), "being Bedu" meant camel-herding. The camel herds provided subsistence and enabled the Ruwala to provide services of protection and restitution to those parts of the wider population unwilling or unable to protect themselves, to provide guides and protectors to caravans, and to sell camels in the markets of Syria and Egypt for meat, transport animals and for agricultural work. Camel herding, together with tribal political and jural processes, permitted a system of government (*ḥukūma*—based on mediation and consensus) that was an alternative to that of states. Raiding (*ghazu*) took a variety of forms (Lancaster 1981, 140-5), the purpose being the acquisition of booty and personal reputation.

Burckhardt, Wallin, Guarmani, the Blunts, and Musil provide a partial history of the tribe during the 19th century and up to the First World War. During this period the Ruwala became pre-eminent among the ʿAnaza tribes. Although opposing Wahhābī political ambitions, in 1809 they defeated a Turkish government army outside Baghdad in pursuit of the Wahhābī forces; thus the Ruwala achieved independence of both Ibn Suʿūd (who relieved them of the obligation to recognise his overlordship) and of the Turks (Lancaster, 1981, 128-9). Relationships with the Turkish government in Damascus were always ambivalent shifting between open hostility and uneasy compliance (Euting, 1896, i, 93; Musil, 1928). In 1909, Nawwāf b. Nūrī Shaʿlān, with his father's reluctant support (Musil 1927, 1928) retook Djawf from Ibn Rashīd of the Shammar, whose political fortunes were in decline [see RASHĪD, ĀL]. After the First World War, Nawwāf had plans for the Shaʿlān kingdom of northern Arabia, to which Nūrī was opposed. The rise of the power of Ibn Suʿūd, and the French and British mandates over Transjordan and Syria, together with the death of Nawwāf in 1921, ended any possibility of this, and *amīr* Nūrī handed over Djawf and the Wādī Sirḥān to Ibn Suʿūd in 1926, signing the Treaty of Hadda. *Amīr* Nūrī, according to one of his great-grandsons, Shaykh Fayṣal b. Fawwāz, was conscious of the contradictions inherent in the political role of a tribal *amīr* and an urban ruler. The present *amīr* Mitʿib b. Fawwāz, and his generation of Shaʿlān *shaykh*s, see their function as maintaining freedom of access for tribesmen to the economic and political resources of the various states in which the Ruwala live.

The increasing use of motor transport exacerbated a trend signalled by the opening of the Suez canal in 1870 and the Ḥidjāz Railway in 1908, to the point where there was little market for surplus camels, except for meat and some agricultural work. This was the real cause for the ending of raiding. The Ruwala had lost, between a declining market for camels, and the loss of services now provided by the Mandate governments or Ibn Saʿūd, a substantial part of their income. They managed, between the late 1920s until the 1950s, by having vastly increased herds, and employment in the Arab Legion, as Méharistes, and with Ibn Suʿūd. Some Ruwala became Ikhwān, and a few, under Firḥān al-Mashhūr, were involved in the Ikhwān revolt of Fayṣal al-Darwīsh of the Muṭayr (Glubb papers; Philby papers). There were also problems with the authorities of the French and British Mandates, and with Ibn Suʿūd, over whether the Ruwala were a Syrian or a Saudi tribe. As their *amīr* was based near Damascus, and many Ruwala used Syria in the summer, it was decided the Ruwala were a Syrian tribe, while those who stayed in Saudi Arabia in summer and paid taxes to Ibn Suʿūd were Saudi citizens. The Treaty of Hadda guaranteed the Ruwala their traditional markets and grazing areas. During the thirties, al-Awrens b. Ṭrād Shaʿlān based himself outside H4 (IPC pumping station) in eastern Jordan from where he advised the Iraq Petroleum Company and developed an extensive political network. The *amīr* Nūrī, and after 1936 his grandson *amīr* Fawwāz b. Nawwāf, were members of the Syrian Chamber of Deputies.

With the increase in oil wealth in Saudi Arabia, together with the drought of 1958-62, many Ruwala joined the newly-formed National Guard in Saudi Arabia or became employed in the oil companies. The rise of the Baʿth party to power in Syria in the 1960s, and the resulting political and economic difficulties for particular tribes, encouraged the Ruwala to concentrate on options in Saudi Arabia. At this date *amīr* Nāyif b. Nawwāf filled a position similar to that of Speaker of the House of Commons in Saudi Arabia. After the Shaʿlān lost their assets in Syria, many of them, under the leadership of Shaykh Nūrī b. Fawwāz, together with Ruwala tribesmen, collected at al-Rīsha in eastern Jordan and began smuggling from Saudi Arabia into Syria as a political action (Lancaster 1981). The antagonism to Syria was simultaneously expressed as active support for King Ḥusayn of Jordan in the troubles with the Palestinian *Fidāʾiyyīn*.

The smuggling ended with some reconciliation between the Shaʿlān and the Syrian authorities, together with pressure from the Jordanian government. The closing of the desert roads between Syria and Jordan by the Syrian authorities during the 1980s ended the viability of al-Rīsha as a base for trading (legitimate or otherwise) by the Ruwala and others. Profits from smuggling were invested in sheep herds, gardens, property and businesses, especially in Saudi Arabia but also in Jordan and in Syria. The Ruwala are an important group in the National Guard of Saudi Arabia, and are represented in the Army and Air Force; they play an active part in government, the professions and business in Saudi Arabia. Their political influence is apparent in Saudi Arabia, Jordan and Syria.

While they say they are no longer Bedouin, as they do not depend on the *bādiya* or desert as in the past, they maintain their strong tribal identity.

Bibliography: The chief authorities are A. Musil, particularly *The manners and customs of the Rwala bedouins*, New York 1928; *Arabia deserta*, New York 1927; and *Northern Nejd*, New York 1928. Raynaud and Martinet, *Les bedouins de la mouvance de Damas*, Beirut 1922; V.M.P. Mueller, *En Syrie avec les bedouins*, Paris 1931; and M. von Oppenheim, *Die Beduinen*, i, Leipzig 1939, continue Ruwala coverage. W. Lancaster, *The Rwala bedouin today*, Cambridge 1981, provides an anthropological analysis. Articles by Lancaster deal with detailed aspects: *The logic of the Rwala response to change in contemporary nomadic and pastoral peoples*, in *Asia and the North, studies in Third World societies*, viii (1982); *The concept of territoriality among the Rwala bedouin*, in *Nomadic Peoples*, xx (1986); and *Desert devices: the pastoral system of the Rwala bedouin,* in *A world of pastoralism; herding systems in comparative perspective*, ed. J.G. Galaty and D.L. Johnson, New York 1990.

Other important sources include; J.L. Burckhardt, *Notes on the Bedouins and Wahabys*, London 1831; G.A. Wallin, *Narrative of a journey from Cairo to Nejd*, in *JRGS*, xxiv (1854), 115-207; C. Doughty, *Travels in Arabia deserta*, London 1885; Lady Anne

Blunt, *Bedouin tribes of the Euphrates*, London 1879; C. Huber, *Voyage dans l'Arabie centrale 1878-82*, in *Bull. Soc. Geogr.*, vii/5 (1884); J. Euting, *Tagebuch einer Reise in Inner-Arabien*, 2 parts, Leiden 1896, 1914; C. Guarmani, *Northern Nejd*, London 1938; H.St.J. Philby, *Jauf and the northern Arabian desert*, in *GJ*, lxii/4 (1923) and *Arabia of the Wahabis*, London 1928 (but see Elizabeth Monroe, *Philby of Arabia*, London 1973); T.E. Lawrence, *Revolt in the desert*, London 1937; C.R. Raswan, *The black tents of Arabia*, London 1934 (for photographs); J.B. Glubb, *War in the desert*, London 1960; N. Lewis, *Nomads and settlers in Syria and Jordan 1800-1980*, Cambridge 1987; M. Meeker, *Literature and violence in northern Arabia*, Cambridge 1979 (a semiotic analysis of some Ruwala poetry, with which the Ruwala disagree on methods of analysis and interpretation). (W. and Fidelity Lancaster)

RUʾYĀ (a.), derived from the Semitic root *r-ʾ-y* which gives rise to formations expressing "sight" (*ruʾya(t)*) and "vision" (*ruʾyā*), one of the aspects of vision being nocturnal vision, the dream.

1. In the meaning of dream.

On relations between "seer" (*rōʾe* = Aram. *ḥōzē* = Ar. *ḥāzī*), "soothsayer" (*kāhin*, *ʿarrāf*, etc.) and "prophet" (*nabī*), see the articles kāhin, kihāna, nubuwwa.

The Semitic terminology of the dream and of the vision evolves in two fundamentally different semantic zones:

(1) The first is situated in the space extending between sleep and waking and is consequently expressed by the roots *y/w-sh-n* (cf. Akkadian *shittu* "sleep", and *shuttu* "dream", Hebr. *shēnā* "sleep", Ar. *sina* "sleep"), *n-w-m* (cf. Akk. *munattu* "dawn", "dream", Hebr. *tenūmā* "light sleep, dozing", Ar. *manām* "somnolence", "dream") and Akk. *b-r-y*, Aramaic *ḥ-z-y*, Hebr. and Ar. *r-ʾ-y* (whence, respectively, Akk. *tabrīt/mūshī*, Hebr. and Aram. *ḥēzion/layla*, Hebr. *marʾa/ha-layla*, Ar. *ruʾyā*, all denoting nocturnal vision or dream). Thus the first group expresses "deep sleep" and the second "light sleep", between sleeping and waking, an activity relating to the domain of waking, if not to waking itself. It is in this last group that is situated the point of concurrence between the nocturnal vision or dream and the prophetic vision (diurnal and nocturnal) or ecstasy (cf. Fahd, *La divination arabe*, 269, based on A.L. Oppenheim, *The interpretation of dreams in the Ancient Near East. With a translation of an Assyrian Dream-Book*, in *Transactions of the American Philosophical Society*, N.S., xlvi/3 [Philadelphia 1956], 179-373, cf. 225-6; E.L. Ehrlich, *Der Traum im Alten Testament*, Beihefte zur ZATW, lxxiii, Berlin 1953, 1-12; on the difficulty of establishing a line of demarcation between dream and vision, cf. A. Guillaume, *Prophétie et divination*, French tr. Paris 1941, 261-2).

(2) The second is situated in a specific period of life, sc. puberty, a period marked by the development of sexuality (*TʿA*, viii, 355). The dream is then expressed in all Semitic languages through the root *ḥ-l-m*, which indicates, in the adolescent, a degree of physical maturity (becoming fat, fleshy, expansion of the sexual organs, nocturnal pollution) and of intellectual maturity (acquiring good judgment, being kind and gentle, patient and master of oneself).

Concerned to distinguish the true dream, rendered by *ruʾyā*, from the false dream, resulting from the passions and preoccupations of the soul, or furthermore the dream inspired by God from that inspired by Satan, Muslim tradition adopted *ḥ-l-m* for the expression of the latter, on the basis of the following tradition: "The *ruʾyā* comes from God and the *ḥulm* from Satan" (cf. *Concordance*, i, 504; al-Bukhārī, ii, 324 = *Khalḳ*, 11; Ibn Khaldūn, *Muḳaddima*, iii, 8 ff., tr. Rosenthal, iii, 103 ff.; other references in Goldziher, *Abhandlungen zur arab. Philologie*, i, 110). However, the lexicographers continue to treat them as synonyms, as is the case with Ugaritic *ḥ-l-m*, Hebr. *ḥalōm*, Aram. *ḥelmā*/Syriac *ḥelmō*, etc., which refer to the prophetic dream as much as do the derivatives of *r-ʾ-y* and of *ḥ-z-y* (cf. Ehrlich, *op. cit.*, 1).

The Ḳurʾān seldom uses *ḥulm* in a pejorative sense with the meaning of dream; *aḥlām* appears twice, in XII, 44 and XXI, 5, preceded by *aḍghāth* "incoherent and confused dreams", and once unqualified in the former of these verses, in the expression *taʾwīl al-aḥlām*, "interpretation of dreams", while the innumerable verbal and nominal forms of *r-ʾ-y* are used to denote all kinds of vision, whether it be real, intellectual or metaphorical (see *Concordance*, s.v. *raʾā*). The verb *raʾā* and the substantive *ruʾyā* convey the dream of Joseph (XII, 4-5) as well as that of his fellow-prisoners (XII, 36) and that of the Pharaoh (XII, 43). The order communicated to Abraham to sacrifice his son (XXXVII, 102, 105) was given to him in a dream; Allāh fulfilled the dream (*ruʾyā*) of Muḥammad that he would return to Mecca (XLVIII, 27); the dream of the *isrāʾ* and of the *miʿrādj* which he had before the emigration to Medina, were given to him to test the faith of those who had followed him; this was, in a sense, "the Tree of Temptation in the Ḳurʾān" (XVII, 60).

After *ruʾyā* the Ḳurʾān uses *manām* (XXXVIII, 102), of which it makes a divine sign (XXX, 23) a summons before God, analogous to death (XXXIX, 42) and an instrument of divine direction, used by God to guide His Prophet and the believers step by step (VIII, 43-4). The *Sīra* and historiography relate a large number of dreams which marked the major events of the Prophet's life, those of his contemporaries and of his successors (cf. *La divination arabe*, 255 ff.).

Shortly before his death, the Prophet is supposed to have said: "Nothing remains of prophecy other than the good dream; the just man sees it or it makes itself seen by him" (Ibn Saʿd, *Ṭabaḳāt*, iii, 18). This gives an impression of the importance accorded by him to the dream in which he saw a divine intervention (on dream and prophecy, see nubuwwa).

As a result of the conduct of the Prophet, which consecrated a pre-Islamic usage, the study of dreams was developed considerably under Islam. The oneirocritics, of whom Abū Bakr, the first caliph was one, proliferated and Arab oneiromancy was born, nourished, at the outset, by the inexhaustible sources of the oral tradition, in which certain symbolic constants, certain techniques and even an oneirocritical style and clichés began to be established; they are to be found dispersed in the *Sīra*, the *Maghāzī*, in *Ḥadīth* and before long in the *Ṭabaḳāt* of Ibn Saʿd (d. 230/845), secretary of al-Wāḳidī (d. 207/823), where there is a list of dreams interpreted by Ibn al-Musayyab, who lived in the time of the Umayyad caliph ʿAbd al-Malik b. Marwān (65-86/685-705). This was the first attempt at the compilation of a literary genre which was to undergo a considerable expansion (*Ṭabaḳāt*, v, 91-3; list quoted in full in *La divination arabe*, 310-12).

Ibn al-Musayyab was succeeded by Ibn Sīrīn [*q.v.*], whose renown as an oneirocritic has survived to this day (cf. Abdel Daim, *L'oniromancie arabe d'après Ibn Sīrīn*, Damascus 1958; *La divination arabe*, 312 ff.; Fahd, *L'oniromancie orientale et ses répercussions sur l'oniromancie de l'Occident médiéval*, in *Oriente e Occidente nel Medioevo: Filosofia e Scienze*, Rome 1971, 347-74). His name figures among the ancestors of oneiromancy in the earliest treatise of *Taʿbīr* which is known, the *Dustūr fi 'l-taʿbīr* of Abū Isḥāḳ Ibrāhīm b. ʿAbd Allāh al-Kirmānī who lived under al-Mahdī (158-69/775-85), a treatise which has not survived, but the existence of which is confirmed by Abū Bakr al-Anbārī (d. 328/940); it served as the basis for numerous later works, in particular for *al-Is̲h̲āra ilā ʿilm al-ʿibāra* (cf. *La divination arabe*, 315, 345, 352).

At this stage, Arab oneiromancy lacked a method for the classification of dreams, according to precise categories, illustrated by concurrent examples which would make clearer the significance of symbolic constants in a secular spirit. The Arabic translation of the *Oneirocritica* of Artemidorus of Ephesus (cf. *Le Livre des Songes*, Arabic tr. by Ḥunayn b. Isḥāḳ, ed. Fahd, Damascus 1964), commissioned by al-Maʾmūn, and *al-Ḳādirī fi 'l-taʿbīr*, composed by Abū Saʿīd Naṣr b. Yaʿḳūb al-Dīnawarī for the caliph al-Ḳādir bi 'llāh (381-422/991-1031) in 397/1006, a work which makes systematic use of the former, filled this gap (cf. Fahd, *Ḥunayn Ibn Isḥāq est-il le traducteur des* Oneirocritica *d'Artémidore d'Ephèse?*, in *Arabica*, xxi [1975], 270-84).

Attributed to Ibn Ḳutayba is a *Taʿbīr al-ruʾyā* (cf. G. Lecomte, *Ibn Qutayba*, Damascus 1965, 157, no. 23), substantial extracts from which have been preserved by Abū ʿAlī al-Ḥusayn b. Ḥasan b. Ibrāhīm al-K̲h̲alīlī al-Dārī in his *al-Muntak̲h̲ab fī taʿbīr al-ruʾyā* (cf. *La divination arabe*, 316 ff., 335, no. 27; for the content of these extracts, *ibid.*, 317-26). If this attribution were to be proved authentic (see the indications of authenticity, *ibid.*, 326), "it would follow from this that Arab oneiromancy was, as early as the middle of the 3rd century of the Hid̲j̲ra, if not before, with al-Kirmānī, in possession of a coherent doctrine for the interpretation of dreams, with solid principles which were to serve as the basis for the development which it was later to undergo" (*ibid.*, 317).

This development is clearly illustrated in the inventory which the author of this article has compiled of oneirocritical treatises, in which 181 treatises have been identified and located (*La divination arabe*, 329-363). On the basis of the principal treatises it may be concluded that the symbolic constants of Arab oneiromancy, the origin of which is inseparable from that of the Arabs and which has developed and become enriched incessantly over the centuries, was supplemented, in the 3rd/9th century, by a written code of principles, laws, procedures, drawn from uninterrupted oral traditions, conveying the benefits of a long and rich experience of the past. The oneirocritical treatise always includes the following two sections, although in highly disproportionate volume: the first, a theoretical introduction revealing the general rules, the *modi procedendi* and the duties of the oneirocritic; the second, the symbolic, in the form of equations between realities of all kinds and symbols, often followed by justifications and examples. The internal organisation of the material takes the form of hierarchical lists of the beings or objects susceptible to being seen in dreams (the pattern of this may be found in *Les songes et leur interprétation en Islam*, in *Les songes et leur interprétation, Sources Orientales*, ii, Paris 1958, 132 f.).

But in practice, use of such lists can prove problematical. In an attempt to make consultation of such works easier, lists have come into being where oneirocritical themes are classified in alphabetical order. Such was the structure of the *Keys to dreams*, veritably encyclopaedic dictionaries of dreams, which held long and illustrious sway. Nevertheless, consultation is not always easy; dreams may be experienced in all kinds of circumstances where the work to be consulted is not within reach; and, since the dream is fleeting and may soon be forgotten, there is the risk of losing its benefit. This concern led to the versification of oneirocritical material, after the pattern of all materials of didactic vocation.

On the other hand, there exist monographs dealing with only one group of oneirocritical themes (see inventory: nos. 12, 43, 56, 81, 87, 95, 104). However, only the vision in dreams of the Prophet of Islam was the object of special monographs which were usually the result of a mystical experience (cf. nos. 3, 6, 16, 21, 22, 50, 51-4, 57, 74, 84, 111, 118, 119).

Finally, it is appropriate to provide a glimpse of the content of the typical theoretical introduction which is to be found in the major oneirocritical works. The most complete example is to be found in the introduction to *al-Ḳādirī fi 'l-taʿbīr* by Abū Saʿīd Naṣr b. Yaʿḳūb al-Dīnawarī (d. *ca.* 400/1009). It is the most ancient Arab oneirocritical treatise which has survived in its entirety, in spite of its substantial length. It exploited all the information from the *Book of Dreams* by Artemidorus that was susceptible of adaptation to its milieu.

The introduction to this treatise, composed of 30 chapters (*faṣls*), divided into 1396 *bābs*, comprises 15 *maḳālas* on the nature of sleep, the conduct to be followed by the dreamer, the modalities of the dream, the angel of the dream, the nature of the dream, the varieties of true and of false dream, the times and seasons of the dream, the definition of interpretation, the rules to be followed by the narrator of the dream and by the interpreter, the omens to be observed at the time of interpretation, interpretation and the days of the week and the types of oneirocritics (cf. *La divination arabe*, 336-7; for more detailed information, see *Les songes et leur interprétation en Islam*, 133-47).

Finally, it may be noted that incubation, practised by the ancient Semites (cf. Ehrlich, *op. cit.*, 13-55; Oppenheim, *loc. cit.*, index s.v. *Incubation dream*, 352; A. Haldar, *Associations of cult prophets among the ancient Semites*, Uppsala 1945, 81-2; *Sources orientales*, ii, 39-41 (Egypt), 80-1 (Assyro-Babylonia), has survived in *istik̲h̲āra* and the custom of sleeping in mosques (cf. ISTIK̲H̲ĀRA and *La divination arabe*, 363-6).

Bibliography: Most of the material contained in this article has been borrowed from the present author's *La divination arabe*, Paris 1987, and from his contribution to *Sources orientales*, ii, Paris 1959, 127-58, under the title *Les songes et leur interprétation en Islam*. Besides the references given in the text, see N. Vashide and H. Perron, *Le rêve prophétique dans la croyance et la philosophie des Arabes*, in *Bull. de la Société Anthropologique de Paris*, 5th series, iii (1902), 829-30; L. Massignon, *Thèmes archétypiques en onirocritique musulmane*, in *Eranos-Jahrbuch*, xii (1945) = *Festgabe für C.G. Jung*, 241-51; see also his lectures in *Annuaire du Collège de France*, 41st year (1940-1), 84-6; 42nd year (1941-2), 93-5; 51st year (1950-1), 179-83; P. Schwarz, *Traum und Traumdeutung nach ʿAbd al-G̲h̲anī an-Nābulsī*, in *ZDMG*, lxvii (1913), 473-93 (critique by A. Fischer, in *ibid.*, 681-3, and lxviii [1914], 275-325); Fahd, *Le rêve dans la société musulmane du Moyen âge*, in *Les rêves et les sociétés humaines*, ed. G.E. von Grunebaum and R. Caillois, Paris 1967, 335-65, Span. tr. Buenos Aires 1964, 193-230, Eng. tr. Berkeley and Los Angeles 1966, 351-79; idem, *Les corps de métiers au IVe/Xe siècle à Bag̲h̲dād d'après le ch. XII d'*al Qādirī fī t-taʿbīr *de Dīnawarī*, in *JESHO*, viii/1(1965), 186-212; F.

Krenkow, *The appearance of the Prophet in dreams*, in *JRAS* (1912), 77-9 (completed by I. Goldziher, in *ibid.*, 503-6); J. de Somoygi, *The interpretation of dreams in ad-Damīrī's* Ḥayāt al-Ḥayawān, in *ibid.* (1940), 1-20. (T. Fahd)

2. In its philosophical-mystical meaning.

In its philosophical-mystical meaning, the term, like *manām*, describes the dream as a means to transmit fictitious observations or, in the best instances, information and knowledge which convey another, higher reality. As such, this information has its origin in God or in persons near to God, such as prophets, holy men and Ṣūfīs. Starting points in this interpretation of dreams are found in the Ḳurʾān (sūras VIII, 43/45; XII, 43; XXXVII, 102/101; etc.) and in the tripartite subdivision of dreams, found in Islamic *ḥadīth* and in other cultures (see Gätje, *Traumlehren*, 258): true dreams, which have their origin in God and bear a prophetic character; false dreams, which come from Satan; and dreams connected with man's nature and therefore unable to predict anything about the future. In Ṣūfī literature, the dream mainly appears as a means for having a dialogue with deceased Ṣūfīs and holy men, or even with the Prophet, and to receive messages, warnings or pieces of advice (see the works by Schimmel and Smith, in *Bibl.*).

Islamic philosophy, going back to the Ḳurʾānic-mystical interpretation of the dream, considers it as a means to transmit the truth, its prophetical-divine origin serving as a criterion. This criterion, however, caused discussions about the postulates of dreams. Galen's explanation that they originate from a mixture of the fluids in the human body, and his localising (as against Aristotle) fantasy and thought in the brain and not in the heart, is often drawn into the argumentation. Beyond this, with reference to the Neoplatonic philosophy of the divine emanations as well as to the Aristotelian-Peripathetic doctrine of the soul and of the divine intellect, the dream is given an important part in the process of human perception. This development culminates in the precedence of divinely-inspired prophetic knowledge over human knowledge (see Daiber, *Abū Ḥātim*), defended by the Ismāʿīlī Abū Ḥātim al-Rāzī [*q.v.*] against Abū Bakr al-Rāzī [see al-rāzī, abū bakr], and in the transmission of this prophetic knowledge by way of portentous dreams, which owe their existence to the divine active intellect. The latter view is represented by Abū Naṣr al-Fārābī [*q.v.*].

The origin of this development can already be found in Abū Yūsuf al-Kindī [*q.v.*], who links up with Aristotle (*De anima*), but puts new accents, which he owes to the Alexandrian exegesis of Aristotle and which presuppose a Neoplatonic-hermetic concept of the soul (see Genequand, in *Bibl.*). In his *Fī Māhiyyat al-nawm wa 'l-ruʾyā* (= *Rasāʾil*, i, 293-311), which was translated into Latin by Gerhard of Cremona (ed. Baeumker, 12-27), and in his as yet unpublished treatise on the anamnesis of the soul (see Endress, *Al-Kindī's theory*), the soul appears in an intermediate position between the perception of matter and the eternal ideas of the divine intellect; in the process of its purification, and in its endeavour to return to its divine origin, the soul avails itself of the "shaping capacity" (*al-ḳuwwa al-muṣawwira*), i.e. of the fantasy, the carrier of the dreaming activity, which increasingly liberates itself from sensory perceptions. After that, the soul remembers more and more its originally divine situation i.e. the world of the intellect. In its most complete form, the dream is no longer confused dreams (*aḍghāth*), or mere opinion, but the remembrance of the shape of sensible objects, or of the genus and species of intelligible objects. Thus the soul is capable of anticipating the future in a dream (al-Kindī, *Rasāʾil*, i, 303).

Al-Kindī's doctrine of the dream is part of his doctrine of the intellect (see Jolivet, *L'intellect*, esp. 128 ff.), in which the cognitional constituent appears as being integrated in a Neoplatonic doctrine of anamnesis. This accentuation was not continued by al-Fārābī. In the latter's doctrine of the dream, the remembrance of intelligibles is not mentioned. On the contrary, in a newly created terminology al-Fārābī speaks of the "imitation" (*muḥākāt*) of perceptible particulars (*al-djuzʾiyyāt*) and of the "separating intelligibles" (*al-maʿḳūlāt al-mufāriḳa*) which ensue in a dream. The imaginative pictures in the dream are thus the result of a cooperation between perception, imitating imagination or fantasy, and the divine "active intellect". If this imitation is not limited to sensible phenomena, if it is not solely oriented towards the activities of nutrition and desire, and if it is not shaped by the constitution of the body (see Galen, *De dignotione ex insomniis*), then the dream represents "exalted objects" (*mawdjūdāt sharīfa*), i.e. the intelligibles of the divine "active intellect"; the point at issue then is prophecy, prophesying "divine things". From this al-Fārābī, while modifying Plato's doctrine of the philosopher-king, deduces his well-known thesis on the sovereign of the Ideal State, who should be both philosopher and prophet. His starting-points in literature are first of all Aristotle's works, in particular, *De anima*, the *Nicomachaean ethics* and the theory of the dream and divination in the *Parva naturalia*, and also the exegesis of Aristotle by Alexander of Aphrodisias. The parallel between al-Fārābī and the new accentuation of Aristotelian doctrines, found in the transmitted Arab version of the *Parva naturalia*, is remarkable. Deviating from the Greek text, the latter emphasises the divinity of the intellect, which causes the "images" (*ṣuwar*) which come into being in "true dreams" (see the Arabic ms. Raza Library, Rāmpūr, no. 1752, dating from the 11th/17th century, fols. 7a-54b, of which fols. 44b l. 11-fol. 47b l. 25 deal with the dream; cf. Davidson, 340 ff.; Pines; Ravitzky).

Above all, al-Fārābī is convinced that, as Aristotle said, the soul thinks in images, and for this needs perception; its imaginative power imitates reality and produces imitating images. The most perfect imitations of the particulars and intelligibles, which originate in the divine active intellect and are realised in a dream by the imaginative power, are made into statements about the future and into prophecies. They are then transmitted to mankind by the sovereign, either in the form of philosophical argumentations or in the form of prophetic "warnings". At this, al-Fārābī, in his thesis on the perfect "religion" as imitation of "philosophy", presupposes the reciprocal dependence of the two. Religion is an indispensable "instrument" of philosophy because, in the Ideal State (*al-madīna al-fāḍila*), it realises the practical part of the latter, namely ethics. In agreement with Aristotelian epistemology, according to which the soul does not think without the images of perception, religion is at the same time a perceptible image of philosophy and of the intelligibles, which experience their realisation in the most perfect form in the prophetical revelation (for further details, see Daiber, *Prophetie; Ruler*). And so prophetic revelation in a dream is not only a perceptive representation of what had been pre-existing in the mind, and what has been inspired by the active intellect; for by transmitting laws and prescriptions of "religion", this revelation also clears the way for realising the practical part of philosophy, namely the ethics of every single person in the Ideal State.

Later philosophers, above all Ibn Sīnā and Ibn Rus̲h̲d [*q.vv.*], were decisively influenced by al-Fārābī's doctrine of the divine active intellect as the cause of prophetic dreams. They took up al-Fārābī's Neoplatonic attachment of separate intellects to certain heavenly spheres, a doctrine which had further developed Aristotle's conception of the spirits of the spheres, as well as al-Kindī's doctrine of the intellect. In their works, the divine active intellect (*al-ʿaḳl al-faʿʿāl/al-fāʿil*), the tenth and last member of these intellects, appears as an emanation of the ninth intellect which rules the sphere of the moon. However, Ibn Sīnā and Ibn Rus̲h̲d did not adopt al-Fārābī's idea of religion as being the visualisation of philosophy. Contrary to Aristotle, but in consequent continuation of al-Kindī's Neoplatonism, they maintain that thinking does not need perception through the senses; the active intellect leads the thinking soul out of the stage of potentiality.

Ibn Sīnā's explanations in his *Kitāb al-S̲h̲ifāʾ* and in his *Risāla al-manāmiya* show that al-Fārābī's doctrine of dreams was modified. He gives more attention to the elements mentioned by Galen, and al-Fārābī's explanations are completed; in the common sense (*ḥiss mus̲h̲tarak*), the dream is the sensorial representation of the forms which have been abstracted from the matter. This representation has been realised by the preserving "forming power" (*muṣawwira*), together with the combining "fantasy" (*mutakhayyila*). The interpretation of dreams (*taʿbīr al-ruʾyā*) deals with the *maʿānī*, the *intentiones* of these abstractions, which belong to the realm of the perception, of the intellect or of the heavenly world. In Ibn Sīnā's work the function of the prophetic dream appears, in a modified form, as providence (*ʿināya*) of the "divine power", or of the "intellectual" and "heavenly angels"; the *ʿināya* becomes their tool, and is allotted to just rulers, to outstanding scholars and, beyond them, to all mankind; it is no longer a privilege of the prophet.

Ibn Rus̲h̲d, in his *Epitome of the Parva naturalia*, essentially follows Ibn Sīnā and does not bring any new element. The dream is a spiritual process and gets its bearings from the *maʿānī*, which are deposited in the faculty of memory (*ḥāfiẓa, d̲h̲ākira*), abstracted by the faculty of thought (*al-mufakkira*) from the individual perceptions, which at first have been united in the common sense, then preserved by the imaginative power (*muṣawwira, mutak̲h̲ayyila*). Beyond that, the prophetic dream is an activity of the active intellect; in as much as the sensorial representations and their *maʿānī* are already potentially present in the soul, the dream enables the actualisation of the potential intelligence of the human being, of his "material" intellect, that is, by the active eternal intellect. Certainly, the possibility of scientific knowledge through dreams, admitted by al-Fārābī and, to a certain extent, also by Ibn Sīnā, is limited by Ibn Rus̲h̲d (as already had been the case with Ibn Bād̲j̲d̲j̲a) (see Davidson, 342 ff.); the inspiration given by dreams is limited to what is useful or harmful, and to a few practical arts; it does not extend to theoretical science. Prophetic revelation recedes here into the background.

Instead, Ibn Rus̲h̲d propagates a connection between the form of the soul, understood as eternal potentiality of the "material" intellect, and the divine, eternal, active intellect. This connection is said to be the road to the most perfect form of human knowledge. For Ibn Rus̲h̲d, the universality of this general form of the soul excludes any individuality (and thus also the individual immortality of the soul). Here, too, can be detected a basic tenet of Islamic philosophical thinking, which had become apparent with al-Kindī and which could appeal to the Ḳurʾān, to mystics, and to the religious tradition of Islam, namely tracing human knowledge back to God, considering prophetical knowledge as superior to human knowledge, and dreams as the road along which God transmits knowledge to mankind. However, Ibn Rus̲h̲d limited the traditional appreciation of this road.

Bibliography: 1. Texts. *Rasāʾil al-Kindī al-falsafiyya*, ed. Muḥammad ʿAbd al-Hādī Abū Rīda, i-ii, Cairo 1950-3, partially new ed. 1978; partial Latin tr. Albino Nagy (ed.), *Die philosophischen Abhandlungen des Jaʿqūb Ben Iṣhāq Al-Kindī*, Münster 1897 (= Beiträge zur Geschichte der Philosophie des Mittelalters. Texte und Untersuchungen, ii/5); Fārābī, *Mabādiʾ ārāʾ ahl al-madīna al-fāḍila*, ed., and tr. R. Walzer, *al-Farabi on the Perfect State*, Oxford 1985; Ibn Sīnā, *al-S̲h̲ifāʾ, al-ṭabīʿiyyāt*, vi: *al-Nafs*, ed. G. Anawati and Saʿīd Zāyid, Cairo 1975; ed. F. Rahman, *Avicenna's De Anima (Arabic text) being the psychological part of Kitāb al-Shifāʾ*, Oxford 1959; idem, *al-Risāla al-manāmiyya*, ed. Muḥ. ʿAbd ul-Muʿīd K̲h̲ān, *A unique treatise on the interpretation of dreams*, in *Avicenna commemoration volume*, Calcutta 1956, 255-307; Eng. tr. idem, *Kitabu taʾbir-ir-ruya of Abu ʿAli b. Sina*, in *Indo-Iranica*, ix/3 (1956), 15-30; ix/4, 43-57; Ibn Rus̲h̲d, *Talk̲h̲īṣ Kitāb al-ḥiss wa 'l-maḥsūs*, ed. H. Gätje, Wiesbaden 1961; ed. H. Blumberg, Cambridge, Mass. 1972 (= Corpus commentariorum Averrois in Aristotelem [= CCAA], versio arabica, VII); Eng. tr. H. Blumberg, Cambridge, Mass. 1961 (= CCAA, versio anglica, VII).

2. Studies. D.P. Brewster, *Philosophical discussions of prophecy in medieval Islam*, diss. Oxford 1975, unpubl.; H. Daiber, *Abū Ḥātim ar-Rāzī (10th century A.D.) on the unity and diversity of religions*, in *Dialogue and syncretism. An interdisciplinary approach*, ed. J. Gort, H. Vroom *et alii*, Grand Rapids, Michigan 1989, 87-104; idem, *Die Autonomie der Philosophie im Islam*, in *Knowledge and the sciences in medieval philosophy*, ed. M. Asztalos, J.E. Murdoch, I. Niiniluoto, i (= Acta philosophica fennica, 48), 228-49; idem, *Naturwissenschaft bei den Arabern im 10. Jahrhundert n. Chr. Briefe des Abū l-Faḍl Ibn al-ʿAmīd (360/970) an ʿAḍudaddaula*, Leiden 1993 (= Islam. Philos., Theol. a Science, XIII), 150 ff. (Ibn al-ʿAmīd modifies al-Fārābīʾs doctrine of the dream); idem, *The ruler as philosopher. A new interpretation of al-Fārābī's view*, Amsterdam-Oxford-New York 1986 (= Mededelingen der Koninklijke Nederlandse Akademie van Wetenschappen, afd. Letterkunde, nr. 49/4); idem, *Prophetie und Ethik bei Fārābī (gest. 339/950)*, in *L'homme et son univers au moyen age*, ed. Chr. Wenin, ii (= Philosophes médiévaux, XXVII), 729-53; H.A. Davidson, *Alfarabi, Avicenna, and Averroes, on intellect*, New York-Oxford 1992; G. Endress, *Al-Kindī's theory of anamnesis*, in *Islām e arabismo na península ibérica. Actas do XI congresso da união europeia de arabistas e islamólogos*, ed. A. Sidarus, Évora 1986, 393-402; H. Gätje, *Die "inneren Sinne" bei Averroes*, in *ZDMG*, cxv (1965), 255-93; idem, *Philosophische Traumlehren im Islam*, in *ZDMG*, cix (1959), 258-85; idem, *Studien zur Überlieferung der aristotelischen Psychologie im Islam*, Heidelberg 1971, 81 ff. (on pp. 130 ff. cf. Daiber, *Prophetie*, 729, n. 1); Ch. Genequand, *Platonism and hermetism in Al-Kindīʾs Fī al-nafs*, in *ZGAIW*, iv, Frankfurt/M.

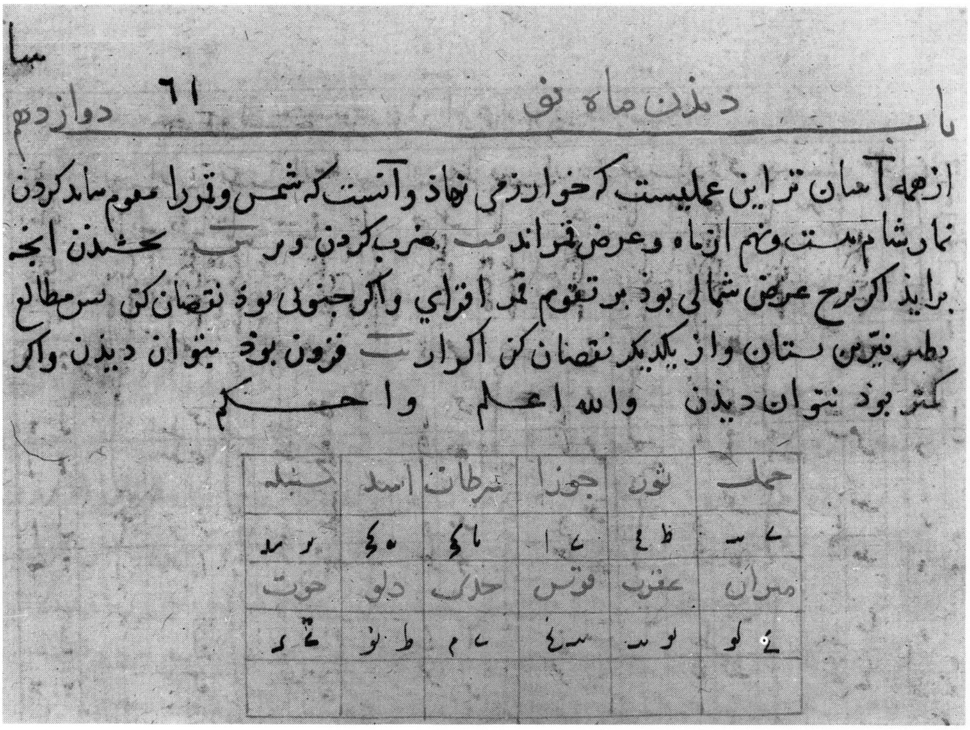

The crescent visibility theory of Abū Djaʿfar al-Khʷārazmī [*q.v.*] from the early 3rd/9th century. The table, which serves the latitude of Baghdād (taken by the author as 33°), displays the minimum distance between the sun and moon for each zodiacal sign. From ms. Cairo Ṭalʿat falak *fārisī* 11, fol. 61a, courtesy of the Egyptian National Library.

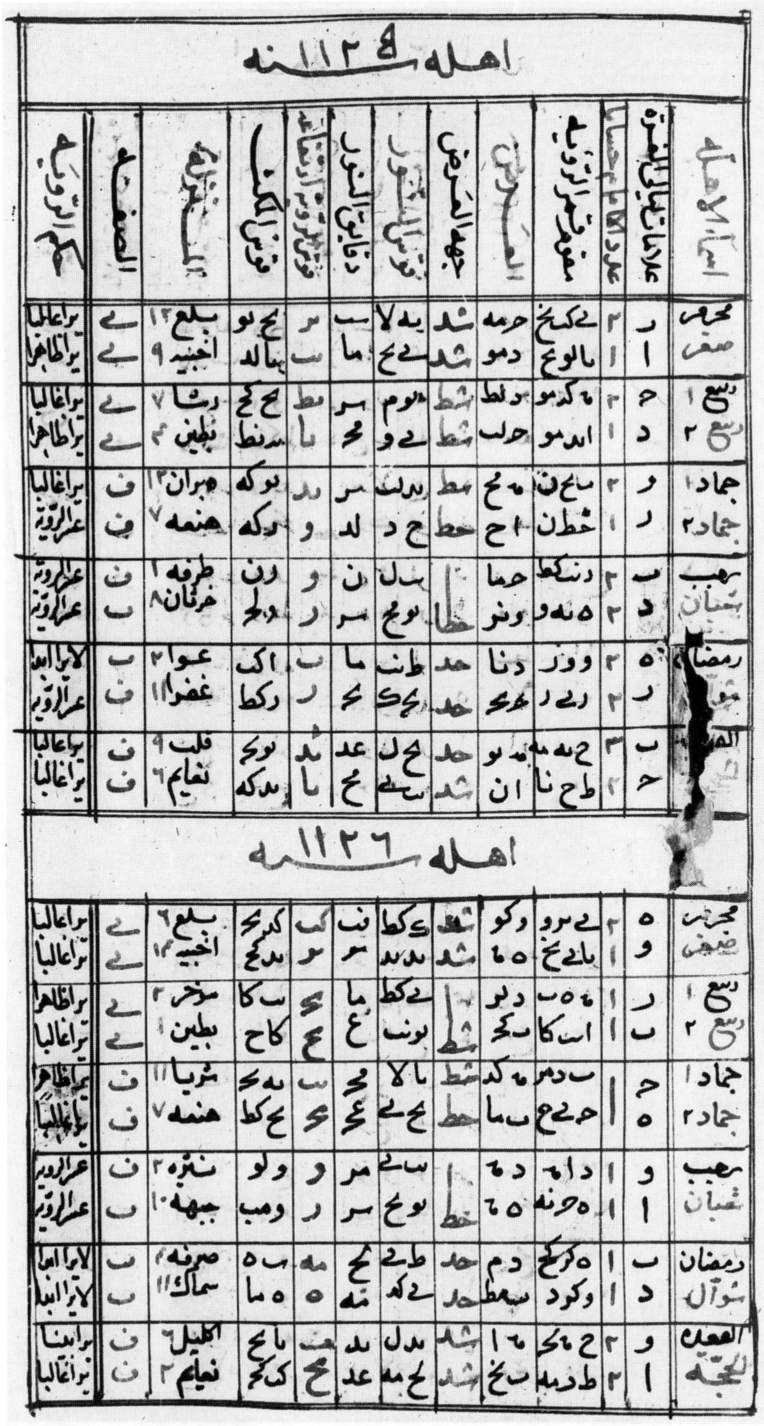

Calculations of the possibility of crescent visibility on the first day of the civil months of the year 1125 AH [= 1713-14]. The tables, part of a set for the years 1125-30 AH and serving Cairo, show the lunar longitude and latitude (but, alas, for the purposes of analysis not the solar longitude), the apparent distance between the sun and moon, the altitude of the moon, the difference in setting times of the two luminaries, and then at the end of each line a prediction. If the crescent cannot be seen, the new month will start on the next day. From ms. Cairo Dār al-Kutub *ṣināʿa* 166,2, fol. 40a, courtesy of the Egyptian National Library.

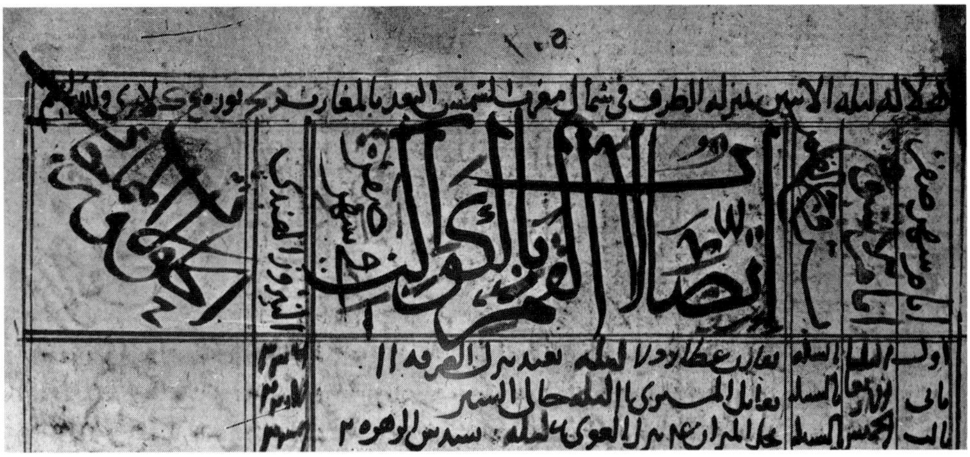

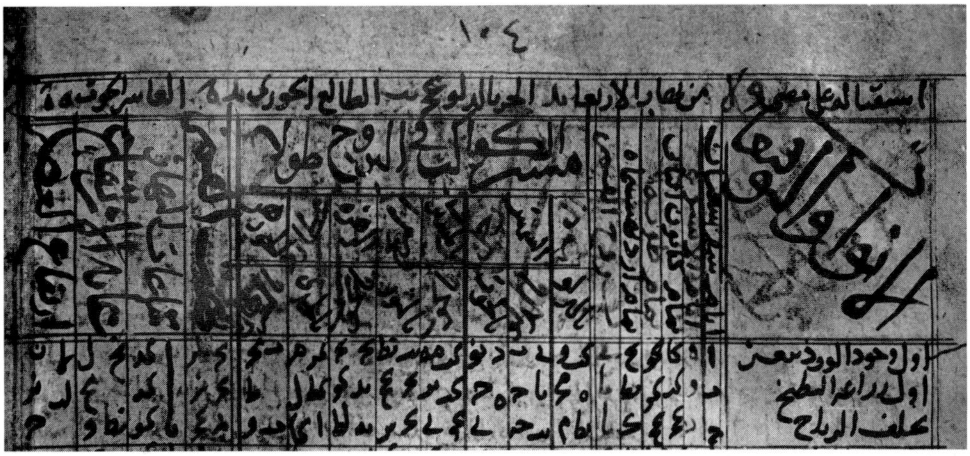

In these extracts from a Yemeni ephemeris for the year 808 AH [= 1405-6], the information at the top of the double-page for a specific civil month relates to the astrological implications of the full moon in the middle of that month and to the new moon on day one, for which the prediction is that it will not be seen (*lā yurā*). The main tables show the ecliptic positions of the sun, moon and five naked-eye planets, as well as the implications of the relative positions of the moon and the other celestial bodies, for each day of the month in question. From ms. Cairo Dār al-Kutub Taymūr *riyāḍa* 274, pp. 104-5, courtesy of the Egyptian National Library.

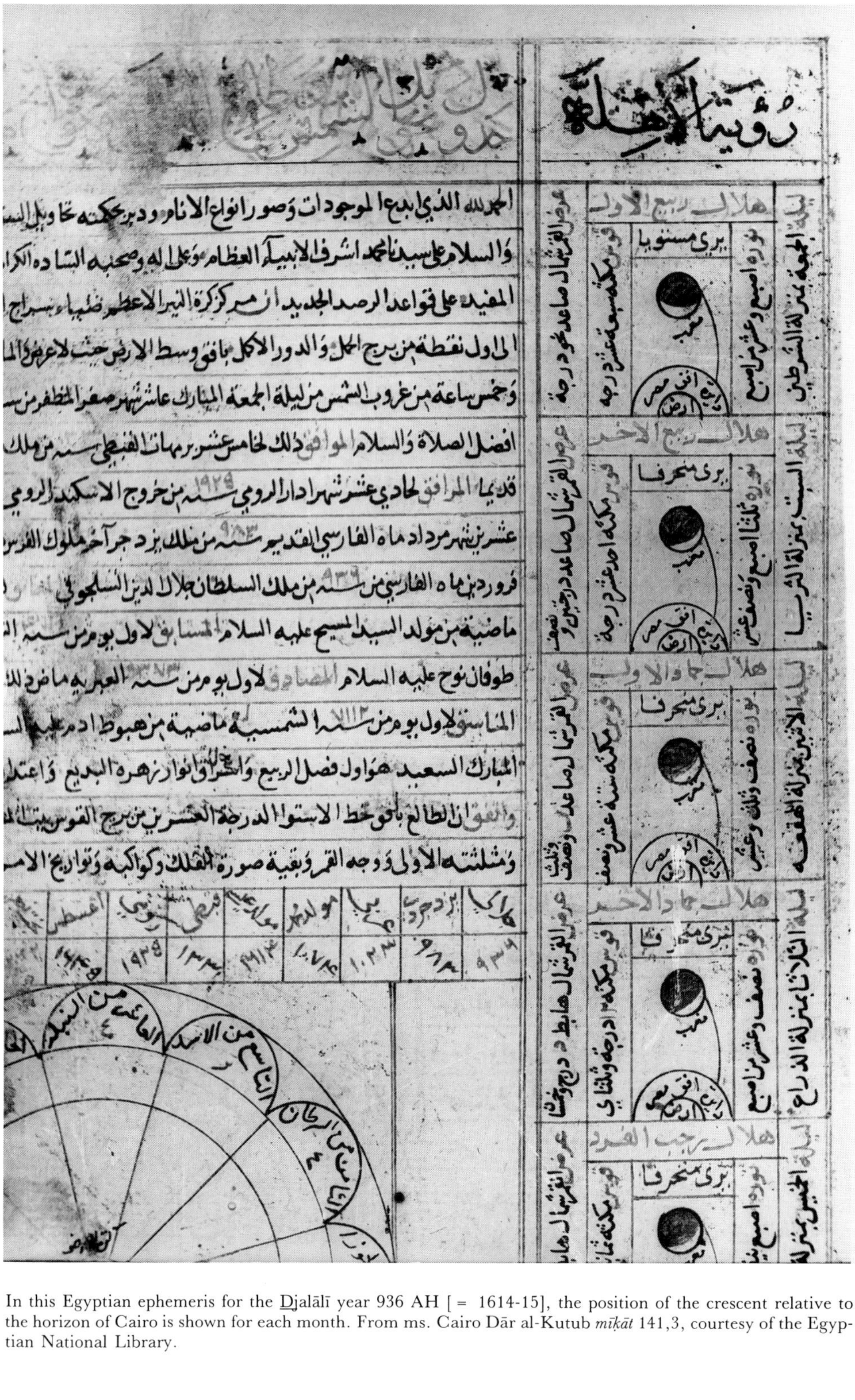

In this Egyptian ephemeris for the Djalālī year 936 AH [= 1614-15], the position of the crescent relative to the horizon of Cairo is shown for each month. From ms. Cairo Dār al-Kutub *mīḳāt* 141,3, courtesy of the Egyptian National Library.

(1987-9), 1-18; J. Jolivet, *L'intellect selon Kindī*, Leiden 1971 (cf. Endress, in *ZDMG*, cxxx [1980], 422-35); M.E. Marmura, *Avicenna's theory of prophecy in the light of Ashʿarite theology*, in *The seed of wisdom. Essays in honour of T.J. Meek*, ed. W.S. McCullough, Toronto 1964, 159-78; J.R. Michot, *La destinée de l'homme selon Avicenne*, Louvain 1986 (= Académie Royale de Belgique, Classe des Lettres, Fonds René Draguet, v), 104 ff.; A. Schimmel, *Mystische Dimensionen des Islam*, Cologne 1985; M. Smith, *Rabiʾa the mystic A.D. 717-801 and her fellow saints in Islam*, Cambridge 1928; Sh. Pines, *The Arabic recension of Parva Naturalia and the philosophical doctrine concerning veridical dreams according to al-Risāla al-Manāmiyya and other sources*, in *IOS*, iv (1974), 104-53; F. Rahman, *Prophecy in Islam*, London 1958; A. Ravitzky, *Hebrew quotations from the lost Arabic recension of Parva Naturalia*, in *JSAI*, iii (1981-2), 191-202; M. Wali Ur-Rahman, *Al-Fārābī and his theory of dreams*, in *IC*, x (1936), 137-51; R. Walzer, *Greek into Arabic*, Oxford ²1963, 206-19 (*Al-Fārābī's theory of prophecy and divination*). (H. DAIBER)

RUʾYAT ALLĀH, the vision of God. It is usually qualified by the phrase *bi 'l-abṣār*, "through perception", to distinguish it from a metaphorical concept, sometimes acknowledged, of vision "through the heart", cf. al-Ashʿarī, *Maḳālāt*, 157, ll. 10-13 and 216, ll. 10-13.

Whether it is or will be possible for men to see God with their own eyes is one of the questions which have deeply divided Muslim theologians. Sunnīs of all persuasions (Ḥanbalīs, Kullābiyya, Ashʿarīs, Karrāmiyya and Māturīdīs) maintain that it is so. The notion was absolutely refuted, on the other hand, by the Djahmiyya and then by the Muʿtazilīs, also, it is said, by the Khāridjīs, the Zaydīs, and the majority of the Murdjiʾīs (cf. *Maḳālāt*, 216, ll. 14-15; ʿAbd al-Djabbār, *al-Mughnī*, iv, 139, ll. 4-6; Abu 'l-Yusr al-Pazdawī, *Uṣūl*, 78, ll. 6-7). Among the Imāmī Shīʿīs, only the earliest theologians (Hishām b. al-Ḥakam, etc.), adherents of a "corporealist" conception of God, acknowledged His visibility; but early theologians such as al-Kulaynī and Ibn Bābawayh (thus, even before the "conversion" of the Imāmīs to Muʿtazilī *kalām*) adopted the contrary view (cf. Vajda, *Le problème*, in *Le Shīʿisme imâmite*, 33-46).

To say that God is "visible through perception" does not necessarily mean, for the adherents of this thesis, that He is so for all, and in all circumstances. The customary Sunnī position, as defined at an early stage in the profession of faith of the *aṣḥāb al-ḥadīth* articulated by al-Ashʿarī (*Maḳālāt*, 292, ll. 12-13) is that God will be seen only in the after-life and only by believers; infidels will be deprived of the sight of Him, in conformity with Ḳurʾān, LXXXIII, 15. In this world, on the other hand, God could be seen by nobody, with the exception of the Prophet Muḥammad (although this last point is controversial, on account, notably, of two contradictory statements attributed to Ibn ʿAbbās and ʿĀʾisha).

Here as elsewhere, the Ḳurʾān is invoked in support of both theories. The opponents of the notion of visibility invoke VI, 103: *lā tudrikuhu 'l-abṣāru*, "perceptions do not comprehend Him". In reply, the Sunnīs propose two interpretations. For some (such as al-Asharī), the implication of the verse is more specific; a qualification such as "in this world" is to be understood. Others, including Ibn Kullāb and later al-Māturīdī, distinguish between *idrāk* and *ruʾya*: God denies that perceptions "comprehend" Him, not that they "see" Him.

The Sunnīs, for their part, invoke LXXV, 22-3, where it is said that on the Day of Resurrection faces will be *ilā rabbihā nāẓira*, "their Lord regarding". To which the Muʿtazilīs reply that *naẓara* is equivalent here to *intaẓara*, and the expression is metonymical. It is the reward of their Lord which they "will wait for".

The Sunnīs also have recourse to VII, 143: since Moses, a prophet, asked to see God, it follows, they say, that God can be seen. To which the Muʿtazilīs reply, following al-Djubbāʾī, that it was not for himself that Moses made this request, but for his incredulous people, who demanded it of him.

The Sunnīs also base a major part of their argument on a well-known *ḥadīth* according to which the Prophet, on a night of full moon, is said to have promised his Companions "You shall see (*tarawna*) your Lord as you see this moon" (al-Bukhārī, *mawāḳīt*, 16 and 26; *tawḥīd*, 24, 1-3). For the Muʿtazilīs, either the *ḥadīth* is inauthentic or else *tarawna* is to be understood in a figurative sense, as a synonym of *taʿlamūna*.

In the realm of rational controversy, the Muʿtazilīs place the greatest emphasis on the argument that, in order to be seen, a thing must be either substance or accident, and God is neither one nor the other. The solution proposed by al-Ashʿarī (and also adopted by the Māturīdīs) is that visibility is not confined to substances and accidents; it is a necessary characteristic of all existing things—and God exists.

Bibliography: Ashʿarī, *Maḳālāt*, 2nd ed. Ritter, 213-17; idem, *al-Ibāna*, Damascus 1401/1981, 31-50; idem, *al-Lumaʿ*, ed. McCarthy, §§ 68-81; Māturīdī, *al-Tawḥīd*, ed. Kholeif, 77-85; Bāḳillānī, *al-Tamhīd*, ed. McCarthy, 266-79; idem, *al-Inṣāf*, Cairo 1382/1963, 176-93; Djuwaynī, *al-Irshād*, Cairo 1369/1950, 166-186; Pazdawī, *Uṣūl al-dīn*, ed. Linss, 77-88; Abu 'l-Muʿīn al-Nasafī, *Tabṣirat al-adilla*, Damascus 1990, 387-442; Abū Yaʿlā, *al-Muʿtamad*, Beirut 1974, §§ 147-53; ʿAbd al-Djabbār, *al-Mughnī*, iv, 33-240; Mānkdīm (*Taʿlīḳ*) *Sharḥ al-uṣūl al-khamsa*, ed. ʿA.K. ʿUthmān, 232-77; G. Vajda, *Le problème de la vision de Dieu* (ruʾya) *d'après quelques auteurs šīʿites duodécimains*, in T. Fahd (ed.) *Le Shīʿisme imâmite*, Paris 1970, 31-54 (repr. Variorum Reprints, London 1986); idem, *Le Problème de la vision de Dieu d'après Yūsuf al-Baṣīr*, in *Islamic philosophy and the Classical tradition* (Studies for R. Walzer), Oxford 1972, 473-89; A.K. Tuft, *The* ruʾyā (*sic*) *controversy and the interpretation of Qurʾān verse VII* (al-Aʿrāf): *143*, in *Hamdard Islamicus*, vi (1983), 3-41; D. Gimaret, *La Doctrine d'al-Ashʿarī*, Paris 1990, 329-44; J. van Ess, *Theologie und Gesellschaft im 2. und 3. Jahrhundert Hidschra*, iv, forthcoming. (D. GIMARET)

RUʾYAT AL-HILĀL (A.), a term in Islamic astronomy denoting the sighting of the lunar crescent. In this article, astronomical aspects are covered.

Muslim astronomers from the 2nd/8th century onwards performed calculations to predict the visibility of the lunar crescent, of particular importance for the fixing the beginning and end of Ramaḍān and the festivals [see HILĀL, i. In religious law; ʿĪD; RAMAḌĀN; ṢAWM; TAʾRĪKH]. Over the centuries, the techniques and visibility conditions that they used became more sophisticated. Even the simplest procedures involved a knowledge of the longitudes of the sun and moon at sunset on the night when visibility was in question and methods for finding the difference in setting times of the sun and moon [see MAṬĀLIʿ]. More complicated procedures involved the altitude of the moon above the horizon or the apparent velocity of the moon. These conditions are recorded in astronomical handbooks [see ZĪDJ] and treatises on astronomical timekeeping [see MĪḲĀT].

The earliest Muslim astronomers adopted a simple Indian visibility condition, namely, that the difference in setting times of the sun and moon be at least 12 equatorial degrees (or 48 minutes of time). Using this, they calculated tables displaying for a specific latitude and for different solar longitudes the minimum elongation between sun and moon necessary for visibility (see Pl. XXXVI). More complicated tables involved directly the lunar latitude or served a series of different latitudes. Some later astronomers used conditions so complex that they had to calculate by hand the various astronomical quantities involved and then investigate whether these satisfied their visibility conditions, not always explicitly stated (see Pl. XXXVII). The results of their labours were circulated in astronomical ephemerides [see TAKWĪM], in which for each day of a given year the positions of the sun, moon and planets would be tabulated and for each month the lunar visibility calculations and predictions, as well as astrological prognostications, would be recorded (see Pl. XXXVIII) and occasionally illustrated (see Pl. XXXIX). There are no known mediaeval records of conflicts with the *ʿulamāʾ*, who favoured actual sightings of the crescent (see HILĀL. i) and used simple arithmetical procedures (based on alternating months of 29 and 30 days) when adverse weather conditions prevailed.

This is a subject on which a great deal of work remains to be done. First, there are numerous astronomical discussions of the subject yet to be studied. Second, there are even more legal discussions awaiting study (see, for example, the volume by ʿAbd al-Wahhāb cited below). And third, there are references to actual practice scattered throughout the historical literature. Of particular historical interest are various S͟hīʿī treatises.

In the modern world, with instant communications between places where the crescent can be seen and others where it cannot, as well as less mutual understanding between religious scholars and scientists, there is occasionally some confusion about the beginning and end of Ramaḍān.

Bibliography: Several different mediaeval procedures and tables are analysed in the following articles: E.S. Kennedy, *The crescent visibility theory of Thābit bin Qurra*, in *Procs. of the Mathematical and Physical Society of the United Arab Republic* (1960), 71-4, idem and M. Janjanian, *The crescent visibility table in Al-Khwārizmī's* Zīj, in *Centaurus*, xi (1965), 73-8 (the table is Andalusian and unrelated to al-K͟hʷārazmī), and idem, *The lunar visibility theory of Yaʿqūb ibn Ṭāriq*, in *JNES*, xxvii (1968), 126-32, all three repr. in E.S. Kennedy *et al.*, *Studies in the exact sciences in Islam*, Beirut 1983; and D.A. King, *Some early Islamic tables for determining lunar crescent visibility*, in *Annals of the New York Academy of Sciences*, 500 (1986), 185-225, idem, *Ibn Yūnus on lunar crescent visibility*, *Jnal. of the History of Astronomy*, xix (1988), 155-68, and *idem*, *Lunar crescent visibility predictions in medieval Islamic ephemerides*, in S. Seikaly, R. Baalbaki, P. Dodd (eds.), *Quest for understanding. Arabic and Islamic studies in memory of Malcolm H. Kerr*, Beirut 1991, 233-51, all three repr. in King, *Astronomy in the service of Islam*, Aldershot, Variorum Reprints 1993; J.P. Hogendijk, *Three Islamic lunar crescent visibility tables*, in *Jnal. for the History of Astronomy*, xix (1988), 29-44, and idem, *New light on the lunar crescent visibility table of Yaqʿūb ibn Ṭāriq*, in *JNES*, xlvii (1988), 95-104. These works contain references to other technical literature on the subject (such as that in *zīd͟js*).

See also H.P.J. Renaud, *Sur les lunes du Ramadan*, in *Hespéris*, xxxii (1945), 51-68, unique of its genre, for the practice in Morocco. A large number of original sources from legal texts are collected in Muḥammad b. ʿAbd al-Wahhāb, *al-ʿAd͟hb al-zulāl fī mabāḥit͟h ruʾyat al-hilāl*, Ḳaṭar 1977.

On the problems associated with the Muslim calendar nowadays, see M. Ilyas, *A modern guide to the astronomical calculations of Islamic calendar, times & qibla*, Kuala Lumpur 1984, and Imad-ad-Dean Ahmad, *Signs in the heavens. A Muslim astronomer's perspective on religion and science*, Beltsville, Md. 1992.

(D.A. KING)

RŪYĀN, a district of the Caspian coastlands region of Persia comprising the western half of Māzandarān [*q.v.*].

Iranian tradition. According to Darmesteter, *Avesta*, ii, 416, Rūyān corresponds to the mountain called *Raodita* ("reddish") in *Yas͟ht*, 19, 2, and *Rōyis͟hnōmand* in *Bundahis͟hn*, xii, 2, 27 (tr. West, 34). Al-Bīrūnī, *Chronologie*, ed. Sachau, 220, makes Rūyān the scene of the exploits of the archer Āris͟h (cf. Ẓahīr al-Dīn Marʿas͟hī, *Taʾrīk͟h-i Ṭabaristān u Rūyān u Māzandarān*, ed. Dorn, 18 [*Yas͟ht* 8, 6, in this connection mentions the hill Aryō-xs͟hnθa]). In the letter addressed to the *mōbad* Tansar by king *Gus͟hnasps͟hāh (3rd century A.D.?), the latter claims to be lord of Ṭabaristān, Patis͟hk͟hʷār-gar, Gīlān, Daylamān, Rūyān and Damāwand.

Geography. According to Ibn Rusta, 150, and Ibn al-Faḳīh, 304 (the latter cites Balād͟hurī as authority, but the passage is lacking in the *Futūḥ al-buldān*), Rūyān was at first an independent *kūra* attached to Daylam. It was conquered by ʿUmar b. al-ʿAlāʾ (after 141/758), who built a town there with a *minbar* and attached it to Ṭabaristān. Rūyān comprised an extensive area the districts of which lay between two mountains (Ibn al-Faḳīh: "between the mountains of Rūyān and Daylam"); each township could supply from 400 to 1,000 soldiers (Ibn al-Faḳīh: in all 50,000). The *k͟harād͟j* levied on Rūyān by Hārūn al-Ras͟hīd was 400,050 dirhams. The town of Rūyān called Kad͟jd͟ja was the headquarters of the *wālī*. Rūyān was near the mountains of Rayy and was reached via Rayy. The text of the two authors above quoted suggests that, between Rūyān and unsubjected Daylam, was a region which formed the military zone from which operations were conducted against Daylam. To this zone belonged S͟hālūs or Čālūs, a town called *al-Kabīra* (situated opposite Kad͟jd͟ja), another (?) town called al-Muḥdat͟ha and lastly Muzn. (But on these frontiers, see the *Ḥudūd al-ʿālam* and Ẓahīr al-Dīn.)

Al-Iṣṭak͟hrī, 206, enumerates the mountains of "Daylam" (in the broad sense) as the following: D͟jibāl Ḳārin, D͟jibāl *Fād͟hūsbān and D͟jibāl al-Rūband͟j (according to Barthold, *al-Rūyand͟j = Rūyān). In these last-named highlands, there were formerly kingdoms (*mamālik*); in the part adjoining Ṭabaristān the kings were of Ṭabaristān, and in the part adjoining Rayy they were of Rayy.

According to the *Ḥudūd al-ʿālam* (written in 372/982), tr. Minorsky, 135, comm. 387, Nātil (according to Iṣṭak͟hrī, 217, one *marḥala* west of Āmul) Čālūs, Rūd͟hān (= Rūyān) and Kalār (west of Čālūs) formed a province of Ṭabaristān, but the authority there belonged to a king named Ustundār. Rūd͟hān produced red woollen materials for waterproofs and blue *gilīm* (a kind of carpet material).

Rustamdār. From the Mongol period we find the geographical term *Rustamdār*. According to Ḥamd Allāh Mustawfī, *Nuzhat al-ḳulūb*, ed. Le Strange, 161, the greater part of its territory was irrigated by the

[S]hāh-rūd (?!) and ʿAlī b. Shams al-Dīn Lāhīdjī, [T]aʾrīkh-i Khānī, ed. Dorn, 298, says that Ṭālaḳān (on [t]he upper Shāh-rūd) adjoined Rustamdār. On the [o]ther hand, Ẓahīr al-Dīn gives the term a larger con[n]otation and uses it sometimes as a synonym of [R]ūyān and sometimes with a special meaning. An ex[a]mination of the passages led R. Vasmer, *Die [E]roberung Ṭabaristāns*, 123-4, to the conclusion that [R]ustamdār in the proper sense was situated towards [K]udjūr and Kalār, while Rūyān primarily meant the [c]ountry between Rustamdār and Ḳasrān (i.e. the [c]ountry towards Rayy). According to Ẓahīr al-Dīn, [1]9-20, the eastern frontier of Rustamdār was original[l]y at Sī-sangān (near the mouth of the river of [K]udjūr), but in the time of the Saldjūḳ Sandjar was [b]rought back to Alīsha (near Āmul?); the western [f]rontier was at first at Malāṭ (near Langarūd in [G]īlān), but in 590/1193 was brought back to Sakh[s]asar (on the eastern frontier of Gīlān) and in [6]40/1242 at Namak-āwa-rūd (west of Kalārastāḳ). It [i]s curious that Ẓahīr al-Dīn, 17, seems to place the 'town of Rūyān'' (the Kadjdja of Ibn Rusta) at [K]udjūr, but the passage is not very explicit and the [l]egend of the foundation of the town given by Ẓahīr [a]l-Dīn may belong to a period before the appearance [o]f the term Rustamdār.

The princes of Rūyān. The title attested for the [d]ynasty is Ustundār (perhaps **Ustan-dār* < *Ōstān-dār*; [c]f. al-Ṭabarī, i, 2638). It is not clear if the dynasty [a]lso took the title of *pādhūspān* (< *pātgōspān*), which in [S]āsānid terminology was at first borne by the viceroys [o]f the four great divisions of the empire, the [p]rerogatives of which were lessened in time by the in[c]rease in power of the military commanders [(]*sipāhbadh*; cf. Christensen, *L'Iran sous les Sassanides*², [1]39, 352, 518 ff.). The fact is that in the passage in al-[I]ṣṭakhrī, 206, the mountain of *Fādhūsfān is men[t]ioned separately and, it seems, to the east of *Rūyāndj, but it is possible that the two names only [m]ean the two parts of "Rūyān" which at this time [w]ere under Ṭabaristān and Rayy respectively. In any [c]ase, in the genealogy of the Ustundārs (Ẓahīr al-Dīn, [1]46-54, 320-1), Pādūspān appears as the personal [n]ame of the eponymous founder and of certain [p]rinces only. The eponym Pādūspān (towards the end [o]f the 7th century?) was regarded as one of the three [s]ons of Gīl-Gawbāra, a descendant of the Sāsānid [D]jāmāsp (who reigned 497-9). Towards the begin[n]ing of the 4th/10th century (al-Iṣṭakhrī, 206, see [a]bove), the dynasty seems to have passed through a [c]risis which it survived. After the death of Djalāl al-[D]awla Kayūmarth b. Bīsutūn b. Gustahm in [8]57/1453, his possessions were divided between his [t]wo sons: the line of Kāwūs reigned in Nūr, in the [v]alley of the left bank tributary of the river of Āmul [(]Haraz-pay), and that of Iskandar at Kudjūr, on the [n]orthern slopes of the mountains of Nūr.

On the feudal wars in Māzandarān, see Ẓahīr al-[D]īn, ed. Dorn, also ed. ʿAbbās Shāyān, Tehran 1333 [S]h./1954, indices. The princes of Rustamdār retained [t]heir autonomy down to the time of the Ṣafawids. In [9]47/1540 the expedition of Shāh Ṭahmāsp against [M]alik Djahāngīr b. Malik Kāwūs, who had shut [h]imself up in the fortress of Lāridjān, was a failure (cf. Ḥasan Rūmlū, *Aḥsan al-tawārīkh*, ed. Seddon, 299). In [9]97/1589 the maliks Djahāngīr b. ʿAzīz of Nūr and Djahāngīr b. Muḥammad of Kudjūr came to pay [h]omage to Shāh ʿAbbās, but finally in 1003/1594 they [w]ere both dispossessed of their lands; the ruler of Nūr [s]ubmitted voluntarily, while he of Kudjūr was seized [b]y force (cf. Iskandar Munshī, *Taʾrīkh-i ʿĀlam-ārā*, [2]65, 334, 354-7).

Bibliography: See that to MĀZANDARĀN; F. Justi, *Iranisches Namenbuch*, s.v. *Patkōspān*, *Ustandār*, and 433-5; J. Marquart, *Ērānšahr*, 131, 135 (*Rvan*); G. Le Strange, *The lands of the Eastern Caliphate*, 373-4; R. Vasmer, *Die Eroberung Ṭabaristāns durch die Araber*, in *Islamica*, iii/1 (1927), 115-25 (a detailed analysis of the sources); H.L. Rabino, *Mázandarán and Astarábád*, London 1928, see index; idem, arts. listed in the *Bibl.* to MĀZANDARĀN; W. Barthold, *An historical geography of Iran*, Princeton 1984, 233-4.

(V. MINORSKY)

RŪZBIHĀN b. Abī Naṣr al-Fasāʾī al-Daylamī AL-BAḲLĪ AL-SHĪRĀZĪ, Ṣadr al-Dīn Abū Muḥammad (522-606/1128-1209), Persian Ṣūfī author. Rūzbihān was born into a family of Daylamī origin in the town of Fasāʾ (Pasāʾ) in Fārs and raised without religious guidance. From early youth, however, he was susceptible to dreams and powerful ecstasies, so that he soon abandoned his early trade as a grocer (whence his name Baḳlī), was initiated into a branch of the Kādharūnī *ṭarīḳa*, and travelled in search of religious knowledge. For 50 years he preached in the mosque of Shīrāz, and he established a *ribāṭ* [*q.v.*] there in 560/1165 that continued to be a centre of Ṣūfī training and activity under his descendants for several generations. His predilection for the outrageous ecstatic sayings (*shaṭhiyyāt*) of earlier Ṣūfīs earned him the sobriquet "Doctor Ecstaticus" (*shaykh-i shaṭṭāh*). He recorded his spiritual experiences with directness and power, using a prose style of great rhetorical density. Although the *ṭarīḳa Rūzbihāniyya* did not endure as an institution, his writings, particularly his mystical Ḳurʾān commentary, have been studied, preserved, and commented on by a select group of readers in the Ottoman regions (e.g. ʿAynī Sīmābī), in Central Asia (Djāmī [*q.v.*]), and in India (Dārā Shukōh [*q.v.*]), as well as in Persia proper, up to the present day.

Rūzbihān is the subject of two hagiographies written by his grandsons: *Tuḥfat ahl al-ʿirfān* by Sharaf al-Dīn Ibrāhīm b. Ṣadr al-Dīn Rūzbihān Thānī, completed in 700/1300 (ed. Dj. Nūrbakhsh, Tehran 1349/1970), and *Rūḥ al-djinān* by Shams al-Dīn ʿAbd al-Laṭīf b. Ṣadr al-Dīn Rūzbihān Thānī, which was dedicated to the Atābak Nuṣrat al-Dīn Aḥmad-i Lur (r. 696-733/1296-1333) (both texts ed. M.T. Dānish-Pazhūh, *Rūzbihān-nāma*, Tehran 1347/1969).

Among his chief extant writings on Ṣūfism are the following: (i) *Kashf al-asrār*, a spiritual autobiography in Arabic written in 577/1181-2 (partial editions by N. Hoca, Istanbul 1971, and P. Nwyia, in *al-Machriq*, lxiv [1970], 385-406); (ii) *ʿArāʾis al-bayān fī ḥaḳāʾiḳ al-Ḳurʾān* (several times lithographed in India), a voluminous Ṣūfī *tafsīr* in Arabic building on previous commentaries by al-Sulamī and al-Ḳushayrī [*q.vv.*]; (iii) *Manṭiḳ al-asrār*, an Arabic collection of ecstatic sayings (*shaṭhiyyāt*) with commentary and a lexicon of Ṣūfī terminology; (iv) *Sharḥ-i shaṭhiyyāt* (ed. H. Corbin, Tehran 1966), a Persian translation and expansion of the *Manṭiḳ al-asrār* (extracts tr. L. Massignon, in *Kitâb al ṭawâsîn*, Paris 1913, 79-108); (v) *ʿAbhar al-ʿāshiḳīn* (ed. with full bibliographic and biographic essays by H. Corbin and M. Muʿīn, Tehran 1958, also ed. Dj. Nūrbakhsh, Tehran 1349/1971), a Persian treatise on mystical love; (vi) *Mashrab al-arwāḥ* (ed. N. Hoca, Istanbul 1974), an Arabic treatise on 1,001 spiritual states (*aḥwāl*); (vii) *Risālat al-ḳuds* and (viii) *Ghalaṭāt al-sālikīn* (both ed. Dj. Nūrbakhsh, Tehran 1351/1972), Persian treatises for Ṣūfī novices; (ix) *al-Ighāna*, also known as *Sharḥ al-ḥujub wa 'l-astār fī maḳāmāt ahl al-anwār wa 'l-asrār* (lith. Ḥaydarābād 1333/1915), a commentary in Arabic on the veils that separate the soul from God. He also wrote poetry in

Arabic and Persian, plus numerous other works on standard religious subjects such as *ḥadīth*, exoteric Ḳurʾān commentary, and Shāfiʿī jurisprudence, some of which have only been preserved in excerpts in his biographies.

Bibliography: In addition to the texts mentioned in the article, see L. Massignon, *La vie et les œuvres de Ruzbehan Baqli*, in *Opera minora*, ed. Y. Moubarac, Beirut 1963, ii, 451-65; H. Corbin, *En islam iranien*, Paris 1972, iii, 9-146; C. Ernst, *Words of ecstasy in Sufism*, Albany 1985; idem, *The symbolism of birds and flight in the writings of Rūzbihān Baqlī*, in *Sufi*, xi (1991), 5-12; idem, *The stages of love in early Persian Sufism, from Rābiʿa to Rūzbihān*, in *Sufi*, xiv (1992), 16-23; A. Godlas, *The Qurʾanic hermeneutics of Rūzbihān al-Baqlī*, diss., University of California at Berkely 1991, unpubl. New editions and French translations of the *Kashf al-asrār, Risālat al-ḳuds, al-Ighāna*, and several minor theological texts are forthcoming from P. Ballanfat. (C. Ernst)

RŪZNĀMA (P.), literally "record of the day", hence acquiring meanings like "almanac, calendar, daily journal" etc.

1. As a mediaeval Islamic administrative term.

In the ʿAbbāsid caliphate's financial departments, the *rūznāmadj* was the day-book (*kitāb al-yawm*) in which all the financial transactions of the day—incoming taxation receipts, items of expenditure—were recorded before being transferred to the *awāradj*, the register showing the balance of taxation in hand. The form *rūznāmadj* points to an origin of this practice in Sāsānid administration. Later, in Fāṭimid and early Ayyūbid Egypt, *rūznāma* was used in a sense contrary to its etymological meaning and its usage in the eastern Islamic world, sc. for the rendering of accounts every ten days.

Bibliography: C.E. Bosworth, *Abū ʿAbdallāh al-Khwārazmī on the technical terms of the secretary's art*, in *JESHO*, xii (1969), 121-2. (C.E. Bosworth)

2. In the sense of almanac, calendar [see TAḲWĪM].

RŪZNĀMEDJI (P.-Tkish.), the Ottoman term for the keeper of a daybook (*rūznāme* or *rūznāmče*), referring principally to the official in charge of the register of daily income and expenditure of the central treasury, *khazīne*. From the diminutive form *rūznāmče*, this official was known alternatively as *rūznāmčedji*, a title often contracted to *rūznāmče* and identical with the name of the daybook itself. The *rūznāmedji* and his scribal staff formed part of the financial bureaucracy headed by the *bash defterdār* [*q.v.*]. The late-15th century *ḳānūnnāme* of Meḥmed II assigns a relatively high scribal status to the *rūznāmedji*. This, together with the essential nature of such a register, indicates that the post probably dates from the earliest period of Ottoman administration.

By the mid-10th/16th century, the *rūznāmedji*'s office was developing two relatively distinct branches. The *rūznāmedji-yi ewwel*, later *büyük rūznāmedji* (chief daybook keeper), was the senior official with overall responsibility for recording all kinds of income and expenditure; the *rūznāmedji-yi thānī*, later *küčük rūznāmedji* (second, or lesser, daybook keeper) became specifically concerned with recording expenditure on the wages and salaries of palace servants and lesser officials of the central administration.

The designation *rūznāmedji* was also applied generally to the daybook clerk(s) in various other offices of the central and provincial administration, e.g. keepers of *tīmār rūznāmeleri*, registers of appointments to *tīmār* and *zeʿāmet* [*q.vv.*] holdings.

During the 19th-century *Tanẓīmāt* [*q.v.*], the *khazīne* daybook was retitled synonymously *yewmiyye defteri*, and the *rūznāmedji* as *yewmiyye kātibi*.

Bibliography: Pakalın, iii, 60-2; İ.H. Uzunçarşılı, *Osmanlı devletinin merkez ve bahriye teşkilâtı*, Ankara 1984, 336-9 and passim; K. Röhrborn, *Untersuchungen zur osmanischen Verwaltungsgeschichte*, Berlin 1973, 36-9; H. Sahillioğlu, *Ruznamçe*, in [M. Kütükoğlu (ed.)], *Tarih boyunca paleografya ve diplomatik semineri, 30 nisan - 2 mayıs 1986: bildiriler*, Istanbul 1988, 113-39, 333-46. (Christine Woodhead)

AL-**RUZZ** (A., vars. *aruzz, uruzz*), the Arabic word for rice, *Oryza sativa* L., one of two major cultivated species, the other being the indigenous African variety *O. glaberrima*, both of which spring from perennial rice. Arabic agronomical manuals do not distinguish among the known varieties of wild rice, although several types may well have been employed in addition to the domesticated kind.

From its place(s) of origin in India or China *ca.* 3,000 BC., the use of rice spread to the Middle East, where it was also cultivated in pre-Islamic times, albeit in limited areas such as Mesopotamia and Jordan. Knowledge of rice spread slowly among the classical cultures of the Mediterranean; its diffusion westward as a cultivated crop is evident in Islamic times and references to its cultivation in al-Andalus from the 4th/10th century are numerous.

The 6th/12th century Andalusī author Ibn al-ʿAwwām, who cites (ii, 55-63), among others, his eastern predecessor Ibn Waḥshiyya [*q.v.*] (see ms. Bodleian, Hunt. 349, fol. 21), relates various methods of planting rice. These included the familiar (and recommended) submerging of the seedlings in water to drown their weed competitors; however, they were also planted in drier or drained areas which required careful weeding. Transplanting seedlings to the paddy field after they had swollen was the preferred technique, but non-transplanting was apparently also practiced. Milling techniques were basic; the plants were dried after harvesting and then placed in sacks and beaten with metal rods to remove the kernels. After winnowing, the kernels were placed in another bag and beaten to remove the husk. After a second winnowing, the milled, unpolished, white grains were stored in earthenware jars. There is no mention of subsequent polishing of the grains or of using the ancient Indian technique of parboiling the plant to preserve more of its nutrients, such as vitamin B1. Two crops a year were harvested, the summer crop being said to be better than the winter one.

Out of all the cereals known in the mediaeval Islamic world, rice did not seem to enjoy the widespread popularity that wheat, sorghum and barley did. Nevertheless, in areas where it was heavily cultivated, such as the southern parts of the Sawād of ʿIrāḳ and Khūzistān, rice bread was the staple of the poor (Ibn Ḳutayba, *ʿUyūn al-akhbār*, i, 221) and al-Djāḥiẓ reports that it was the favoured fare of misers, who offered it to their guests (*Kitāb al-Bukhalāʾ*, ed. van Vloten, 129; see also Ḥ. Zayyāt, *Khubz al-aruzz*, in *al-Machreq*, xxxv [1937], 377-80). The rice bread baker was called *khubz aruzzī* (the *nisba* of the popular poet of Baṣra Abu 'l-Ḳāsim Naṣr al-Khubzaʾ aruzzī [*q.v.*]. The physician al-Rāzī (d. 320/932) observed that rice bread was less digestible than wheat bread, hence it should be eaten with salty food or with a lot of fat or with milk or garlic in order to prevent ill side effects. In this connection, Canard (122) has remarked upon references to the consumption of rice and rice bread with fish in ʿIrāḳ. Ibn Zuhr (d. 557/1162) adds that rice bread produces thick humour, causes obstructions in the intestines and has an astringent effect upon the stomach.

The general medical view of rice itself was that it inclined towards the "cold" element by nature which, it was said, could be modified when cooked with milk or fat and eaten with sugar. When cooked with milk, oxymel was recommended to be drunk afterwards to counter obstructions in the stomach caused by it.

Food preparation with rice was not, however, confined only to bread among the lowest classes. The mediaeval Arabic culinary manuals, which reflect the urban ambience of a leisured class, contain recipes where rice is employed in a number of ways. The following is a representative selection taken from the anonymous work of probable Egyptian provenance of the 7/13 or 8/14 century (see anon., *Kanz*, index). These include rice as an alternative to cornstarch as a thickening agent in stews made with meat and vegetables, where the rice is added in the last stage of preparation. In another receipt, washed rice cooked in fresh milk and seasoned with mastic, camphor and cinnamon appears to be close to the modern popular rice pudding dish, *muḥallabiyya*. The mediaeval version of *muḥallabiyya*, by contrast, was made with meat or chicken, sweetened with honey and seasoned with spices to which saffron-coloured rice is added. Indeed, the most common way of using rice in a substantial dish was to cook meat and/or vegetables with it in the same pot. One variation called *al-labaniyya* containing meat and leeks or onion is cooked in milk (*laban*) together with a little powdered rice. A dish called *al-aruzziyya* contains meat and seasonings (pepper, dried coriander and dill), into which a small amount of powdered rice is added during cooking and washed (whole) rice towards the end of the preparation. A further use for rice is found in the well-known Egyptian spiced beverage *sūbiyya*, which could be made with either wheat or rice. And, as with certain other beverages, this could have been made in both an intoxicating and a legal, non-alcoholic, version. The method of preparing rice flour is given in one receipt for use in another preparation called *ushnān*, a perfumed (powdered, pasty?) mixture for washing and scenting the clothes and hands. Finally, rice was also used in making vinegar.

The remaining extant mediaeval Arabic cookbooks contain dishes similar in style to these just mentioned. One, *aruzz mufalfal*, which appears in several versions, was evidently very popular and ressembles a type of Turkish *pilaw*. Made with spiced meat and/or chick peas or pistachio nuts, the dish may contain rice coloured with saffron, white rice alone or a combination of both. A variation of this dish, called *al-mudjaddara*, made from lentils and plain rice, is similar to the modern preparation of the same name. Modern uses of rice which may not go back earlier than the 8th/14th century include rice presented alone as accompaniment to other dishes and as a filling for vegetables such as courgettes and the leaves of the cabbage and vine.

Bibliography: Ibn al-ʿAwwām, *Kitāb al-Filāḥa* (*Libro de Agricultura*), ed. and tr. J.A. Banqueri, 2 vols., Madrid 1802, repr. 1988; Abū Bakr al-Rāzī, *Manāfiʿ al-aghdhiyya wa-dafʿ maḍārrihā*, Cairo 1305; ʿAbd al-Mālik b. Zuhr, *Kitāb al-Aghdhiyya* (*Libro de los alimentos*), ed. and tr. E. Garcia Sanchez, Madrid 1992; Ibn al-ʿAdīm, *al-Wuṣla ilā 'l-ḥabīb fī waṣf al-ṭayyibāt wa 'l-ṭīb*, ed. S. Maḥjūb and D. al-Khaṭīb, Aleppo 1988; anon., *Kanz al-fawāʾid fī tanwīʿ al-mawāʾid*, ed. M. Marin and D. Waines, Wiesbaden 1993; Ibn Sayyār al-Warrāḳ, *Kitāb al-Ṭabīkh*, ed. K. Ohrnberg and S. Mroueh, Helsinki 1987; A. Watson, *Agricultural innovation in the early Islamic world*, Cambridge 1983; Ḥ. Zayyāt, *Kitāb al-Ṭabākha*, in *al-Machreq*, xxxv (1937), 370-6; M. Rodinson, *Recherches sur les documents arabes relatifs à la cuisine*, in *REI*, xvii (1949), 95-138; M. Canard, *Le riz dans le Proche Orient aux premiers siècles de l'Islam*, in *Arabica*, vi (1959), 113-131; E. Ashtor, *The diet of the salaried classes in the mediaeval Near East*, in *Jnal. of Asian History*, iv (1970), 1-24.

(D. WAINES)

RUZZĪK B. ṬALĀʾIʿ, Abū Shudjāʿ al-Malik al-ʿĀdil al-Nāṣir, Madjd al-Islām, vizier of the Fāṭimid caliph al-ʿĀḍid li-Dīn Allāh, d. 558/1163.

He succeeded his father, Abu 'l-Ghārāt Ṭalāʾiʿ b. Ruzzīk, al-Sayyid al-Adjall al-Malik al-Ṣāliḥ Fāris al-Islām, fatally wounded in Ramaḍān 556/September 1161. In order to avoid his father's fate, Ruzzīk, attacked in the doorway to his ministry, had a subterranean passage dug connecting the Dār Saʿīd al-Suʿadāʾ where he lived and the Dār al-Wizāra opposite to it. More relaxed than his father, who had wished to play in the Fāṭimid caliphate of Egypt the role which the Great Saldjūḳ sultans had played in the ʿAbbāsid caliphate a century previously (see al-Fāriḳī, cited in Ibn al-Ḳalānisī, *Dhayl Taʾrikh. Dimashḳ*, ed. Amedroz, Beirut 1909, 330, 360-1), Ruzzīk reduced the tax burden (on the meaning of *ḥusbānāt* in the passage of ʿUmāra of Yemen cited by Muḥammad Ḥamdī al-Mināwī, *al-Wizāra wa 'l-wuzarāʾ fī 'l-ʿaṣr al-fāṭimī*, Cairo 1970, 287, see Th. Bianquis, *Le fonctionnement des diwans financiers*, in *AA*, xxvi [1992], 57). He abolished the taxes levied on the pilgrims to the profit of ʿĪsā b. Abī Hishām, *amīr* of the Holy Cities. He summoned from Alexandria ʿAbd al-Raḥīm b. ʿAlī al-Baysānī, al-Ḳāḍī al-Fāḍil, who headed the *dīwān al-djaysh* and whose remarkable administrative career was to extend into the Ayyūbid period.

Ruzzīk did not have time properly to put into practice his reforms since he could not make firm his own power. Ṭalāʾiʿ b. Ruzzīk, on his death bed, had warned his son against the danger posed by the *amīr al-djuyūsh* Abū Shudjāʿ Shāwar b. Mudjīr al-Saʿdī, governor of the Ṣaʿīd or Upper Egypt, and had advised him not to provoke him unnecessarily. However, Ruzzīk wished to replace him at Ḳūṣ [*q.v.*] by the *amīr* Nāṣir al-Dīn Shaykh al-Dawla Ibn al-Rifʿa. Shāwar then marched on Cairo with his troops; repulsed towards the Oases, he returned back on to Tarūdja, to the west of the Delta, and finally occupied Cairo in Muḥarram 558/January 1163. Ruzzīk fled to one of the intimates of his sister, the wife of the caliph al-ʿĀḍid, Sulaymān, Yaʿḳūb or Munīl b. al-Fayḍ, al-Bīḍ, or al-Nayṣ al-Lakhmī, possibly a Christian, who betrayed him and handed him over to Ṭayy b. Shāwar. The later killed him in Ramaḍān 558/August 1163, putting an end to the attempt of this family, of Armenian origin, to assume supreme power in Egypt (its ancestor Ruzzīk had arrived in Egypt with Badr al-Djamālī [*q.v.*]). As a convert to Twelver Shīʿism, Ṭalāʾiʿ had been fiercely anti-Sunnī, and his son followed him in this.

Bibliography: The Arabic sources mentioning Ruzzīk are numerous but jejune and repetitive. See, above all, ʿUmāra al-Yamanī, *K. al-Nukat al-miṣriyya fī akhbār al-wuzarāʾ al-miṣriyya*, ed. Derenbourg, Paris 1897, 69-70; Ibn Ẓāfir, *Akhbār al-duwal al-munḳaṭiʿa*, ed. Ferré, Cairo 1972, 111-13, with rich annotation and bibl.; Maḳrīzī, *Ittiʿāẓ al-ḥunafāʾ*, iii, 242-63 and index. Further information on this vizierate and on the sources in Ayman Fuʾād Sayyid, *al-Dawla al-fāṭimiyya fī Miṣr, tafsīr djadīd*, Cairo 1413/1992, notes, 219-21. See also Ibn al-

Wardī, *Taʾrīkh*, n.p. n.d. [Cairo], ii, 66; J.-C. Garcin, *Remarques sur le plan topographique de la grande mosquée de Qûṣ*, in *AI*, ix (1970), 97-108; idem, *Un centre musulman de la Haute Egypte médiévale, Qûṣ*, Cairo 1976, indispensable for the period of the military vizierate. (Th. Bianquis)

RZEWUSKI, (Count) Wenceslas Severin (1785-1831?), the son of a Hetman or supreme general of Poland.

Born at Lemberg (Lvov), he was eight years old at the time of the Second Partition of Poland in 1793. Deeply moved by the dismemberment of his native land, Wenceslas' father voluntarily exiled himself to Austria and chose Vienna for his home. He established friendly relations with the Viennese aristocracy and the French emigrés, and it was in this Franco-Germanic milieu that the young Rzewuski was brought up. Under the influence of his uncle, Jan Potocki, he early acquired a great love for the Orient and avidly studied oriental languages. Together with the famous orientalist Josef von Hammer, he began in 1809 the publication of a periodical, *Die Fundgruben des Orients* "Treasures of the East".

Also, whilst applying himself to the study of Arabic, he set up his own stud farm, having conceived the extravagant idea of improving the European horse stocks by bringing in new blood from the Arabian desert. A journey to the East was now vital for him. In 1817, having made various preparations, he set out for Istanbul in order to realise his plan. His journey took two years and had no element of the merely pleasant jaunt. He explored Turkey and Syria; went into the mountains of Nadjd; ploughed through the desert with Bedouin tribes who proclaimed him *amīr*, joined up with, in their company, the escort providing the safety of the Pilgrimage Caravan and thus was able—although a non-Muslim—to get into Mecca, whose site and the rites there he describes briefly; had a long stay with Lady Hester Stanhope; took part, against his better judgement, in the rising at Aleppo of 1819 and returned to Europe with 140 horses chosen from amongst the best of the Nadjdī stock.

Once back home, he wrote in 1822 a work in two volumes, totalling some 800 pages, *Sur les chevaux orientaux et provenants* (sic) *de races orientales*. Vol. I is devoted to the Bedouins, their natural habitat, their customs and their tribes. It is thus a lively and vivid travel narrative, rich in anecdotes and descriptions of all kinds. Everything goes past in review: towns, notably Aleppo and Damascus, the countryside, the desert, famous historical sites (Palmyra, Baalbek), the Caravan to Mecca, eminent personalities (Lady Hester Stanhope and the explorer ʿAlī Bey, whose last moments he describes, dying, he affirms, in the Christian faith) and the main events, especially the great revolt at Aleppo, whose course is recorded day by day.

Bibliography: Rzewuski's book, unpublished, is in two volumes, richly illustrated with drawings in Indian ink, in the Warsaw Library, no. Tv. 6651; cf. L. Damoiseau, *Voyage en Syrie et dans le désert*, Paris 1833, 9, 67, 77, 114-15, 130, 140.

(J. Chelhod)

S

ṢĀʿ (a., masc. or fem.), a measure for grain "of the value of 4 *mudd* (*modius*) according to the custom of Medina" (*LʿA*; al-Khwārazmī, *Mafātīḥ al-ʿulūm*, ed. Van Vloten, 14). If the cubic contents of the *ṣāʿ*, like that of the *mudd*, varied with town and district as far as commercial transactions were concerned, the value of the *ṣāʿ* was from the canonical point of view fixed in religious law by the Prophet in the year 2/623-4 when he laid down the ritual details of the orthodox feast of *ʿīd al-fiṭr*, which carried with it the compulsory giving of alms called *zakāt al-fiṭr*, the value of which in grain was one *ṣāʿ* for each member of a family. It was, of course, the *ṣāʿ* of Medina that was chosen as the standard measure and the *mudd* of Medina henceforth was called *mudd al-nabī*.

This primitive *mudd* of orthodox Islam was standardised by Zayd b. Thābit; and it is from this standard that the *mudds* and *ṣāʿ*s made henceforth for religious use seem to have been copied more or less accurately. This is, at least, what has been proved for the Maghrib from various documents. According to these documents, the official capacity of the *mudd al-nabī* would be approximately 5 gills and that of the *ṣāʿ* 5 pints.

The Muslim jurists give the following estimates of this measure. For them the value of the *ṣāʿ* is 26 ²/₃ *riṭls* or *raṭls*, the *riṭl* being equivalent to 128 Meccan drams and the dram equivalent to 50 ²/₅ grains of barley. We see how lacking in precision this definition is. If there is no *mudd* or *ṣāʿ* available, the quantity of grain to be distributed for the *zakāt al-fiṭr* is measured with the hands held together, half open, with palms upwards.

Lastly, besides this use of the *ṣāʿ* and of the *mudd al nabī*, these measures are further used in certain measurements required by religious law: (1) to calculate the *zakāt*, and (2) to measure the minimum quantity of water necessary for an ordinary ablution (*wuḍūʾ*, a *mudd*) and for general ablution (*ghusl*, a *ṣāʿ*).

Bibliography: The Arabic dictionaries, especially the *Muḥīṭ al-muḥīṭ*, Beirut 1870, ii, 1221, col. 1; the treatises on Islamic law and the collections of Ḥadīth; A. Bel, *Note sur trois anciens vases en cuivre gravé, trouvés à Fès et servant à mesurer l'aumône légale du Fiṭr*, in *Bull. Archéolog.* (Paris 1917), 359-87, illustrated, where further references are given. See also makāyīl and the Bibl. there. (A. Bel)

SĀʿA (a.) "hour", hence "clock".

1. In technology.

Monumental water-clocks are described in detail in two Arabic treatises. Al-Djazarī [*q.v.* in Suppl.] in his book on mechanical contrivances completed in Diyār Bakr in 602/1206 describes two such machines. Riḍwān b. al-Sāʿātī, in a treatise dated 600/1203, describes the water-clock built by his father Muḥammad at the Djayrūn gate in Damascus (see E. Wiedemann and F. Hauser, *Über die Uhren in Bereich der Islamischen Kultur*, in *Nova Acta der Kaiserl. Leop. Deutschen Akad. der Naturforscher*, ciii [1918], 167-272). It fell into disrepair after Muḥammad's death and was restored to working condition under his son's supervision. It was a large construction, having a timber working face about 4.73 m wide by 2.78 m high, built into the front of a masonry structure. The clock had several design defects which undoubtedly caused the breakdown that Riḍwān undertook to repair. Moreover, Riḍwān himself was not an engineer and his description, though containing some valuable information, omits to deal with some important constructional details.

Al-Djazarī's two clocks, on the other hand, were manufactured and constructed in a very workmanlike manner. Although very similar in principle to al-Sāʿātī's, they did not incorporate any design defects. The first and larger of the two was described in such careful detail that it was possible to construct a full-size working facsimile from al-Djazarī's instructions and illustrations for the World of Islam Festival, in the South Kensington Science Museum, London, in 1976.

The working face of the clock consisted of a screen of bronze or wood about 225 cm high by 135 cm wide, set in the front wall of a roofless wooden house which contained the machinery. At the top of the screen was a Zodiac circle about 120 cm in diameter, its rim divided into the twelve "signs". It rotated at constant speed throughout the day. Below this circle were the time-signalling automata which were activated at each hour. (The clock worked on "unequal" hours, i.e. the hours of daylight or darkness were divided by twelve to give hours that varied in length from day to day.) These included doors that opened, falcons that dropped balls on to cymbals and the figures of five musicians—two drummers, two trumpeters and a cymbalist. The musicians were operated by the discharge of water from an orifice, whereas all the other automata were operated by a heavy float that descended at constant speed in a reservoir. A cord tied to a ring at the top of the float led to a system of pulleys that activated various tripping mechanisms.

The speed of descent of the float was controlled by very ingenious water machinery that included a feedback control system and a flow regulator, the latter for varying the rate of discharge daily in order to produce the "unequal" hours. The same system was used by Riḍwān, and both writers attribute its invention to Archimedes. There is a treatise that exists only in Arabic and is attributed to Archimedes (*On the construction of water-clocks*, ed. and tr. D.R. Hill, London 1976). The treatise almost certainly contains Hellenistic, Byzantine and Islamic material, but its first two chapters describe water machinery that is essentially the same as that used by Riḍwān and al-Djazarī. There is every likelihood that these chapters were indeed the work of Archimedes.

Al-Djazarī's book also contains descriptions of four other water-clocks, two of which embody the principle of the closed-loop, and four candle-clocks which on a small scale are as impressive from an engineering point of view as the water-clocks.

Other Arabic works add to our knowledge of Islamic hydraulic timekeeping. A certain Ibn Djalaf or Ibn Khalaf al-Murādī worked in al-Andalus in the 5th/11th century (D.R. Hill, *Arabic water-clocks*, Aleppo 1981, 36-46). Unfortunately, the unique manuscript of his treatise on machines is badly defaced, but it is possible to determine the essential details of the automata and water-clocks that are described in it. The most important feature that they incorporate is complex gear-trains, which include segmental gears (i.e. gears in which one of the wheels has teeth on only part of its perimeter, a device that makes intermittent action possible).

Al-Khāzinī's justly famous book on physics, *Kitāb Mīzān al-ḥikma* (ed. Hāshim al-Nadwa, Ḥaydarābād 1940) was completed in 515/1121-2. In the eighth treatise, two steelyard clepsydras are described. On the short arm of the beam was a vessel that discharged water at constant speed from a narrow orifice. Two sliding weights were suspended to the long arm, which was graduated into scales. At a given moment, the weights could be moved to bring the beam into balance and the time could then be read off from the scales (Hill, *Arabic water-clocks*, 47-62).

In 1276-7 a work entitled *Libros del saber de astronomia* was produced in Castilian under the sponsorship of Alfonso X of Castile (5 vols., ed. M. Rico y Sinobas, Madrid 1863). This consists of various works that are either translations or paraphrases of Arabic originals. It included five timepieces, one of which is of significance in the history of horology. This consisted of a large drum made of walnut or jujube wood tightly assembled and sealed with wax or resin. The interior of the drum was divided into twelve compartments, with small holes between the compartments through which mercury flowed. Enough mercury was enclosed to fill just half the compartments. The drum was mounted on the same axle as a large wheel powered by a weight-drive wound around the wheel. Also on the axle was a pinion with six teeth that meshed with 36 oaken teeth on the rim of an astrolabe dial. The mercury drum and pinion made a complete revolution every four hours, and the astrolabe dial made a complete revolution in 24 hours. This type of timepiece had been known in Islam since the 5th/11th century—at least 200 years before the first appearance of weight-driven clocks in the West (S.A. Bedini, *The compartmented cylindrical clepsydra*, in *Technology ad Culture*, iii [1963], 115-41).

The mechanical clock was invented in western Europe towards the end of the 13th century. Almost certainly its inventor came from the ranks of the makers of water-clocks. The verge escapement made the mechanical clock possible, but all its other features—weight-drive, automata, gear-trains and segmental gears—were present in Islamic water-clocks. It is highly probable that these ideas were transmitted from Islam to the European makers of water-clocks. An Islamic influence on the genesis of the mechanical clock may therefore be postulated.

Several of Taḳī al-Dīn's writings are concerned with timekeeping, and one of these, *The brightest stars for the construction of mechanical clocks*, written about 973/1565, has been edited with Turkish and English translations. (Sevim Tekeli, *The clocks in the Ottoman Empire*..., Ankara 1966). In this he described the construction of a weight-driven clock with verge-and-foliot escapement, a striking train of gears, an alarm and a representation of the moon's phases. He also described the manufacture of a spring-driven clock with a fusee escapement. He mentions several mechanisms invented by himself, including, for example, a new system for the striking train of a clock. He is known to have constructed an observatory clock and mentions elsewhere in his writings the use of the pocket watch in Turkey. Taḳī al-Dīn's descriptions are lucid, with clear illustrations, showing that he had mastered the art of horology. Clockmaking did not, however, become a viable indigenous industry, and Turkey was soon being supplied with cheap clocks from Europe. Taḳī al-Dīn himself commented on the low price of these European clocks, which entered Turkey, he said, from Holland, France, Hungary and Germany.

Bibliography: There is now an Arabic edition of al-Djazarī, *al-Djāmiʿ bayn al-ʿilm wa 'l-ʿamal al-nāfiʿa fī ṣināʿ at al-ḥiyal*, ed. Ahmad Y. al-Hassan, Institute for the History of Arabic Science, Aleppo; English tr. D.R. Hill, *The book of knowledge of ingenious mechanical devices*, Dordrecht 1974. Further bibliography given in the text. (D.R. Hill)

3. In eschatology.

Al-Sāʿa ("the Hour") is one of the most notable concepts of Ḳurʾānic eschatology, for which numerous parallels can be detected in Judaism and Christianity. *Al-Sāʿa* indicates throughout the scripture the time of the resurrection (XXII, 7) and of the Last Judgement (XXII, 55-7) [see BAʿTH; ḲIYĀMA]. When the *Sāʿa* comes, people will meet Allāh carrying their sins with them (VI, 31). Each soul will be given the reward due for its works (XX, 15); the believers will enter Paradise, whereas the idolaters will not be saved by their gods (XXX, 12-16). Those who disbelieve deny the *Sāʿa* (e.g. XXXIV, 3). The *Sāʿa* is inevitable (XL, 59), and expected to occur suddenly (XLVII, 18; XLIII, 66), and within a short time (e.g. XVI, 77; LIV, 1; XLII, 17; XXXIII, 63). It will be swift (LXXIX, 42-6). Its exact time is, however, known to Allāh alone (XLIII, 85).

The materialisation of the Ḳurʾānic *Sāʿa* will be preceded by a cataclysmic catastrophe. The moon will be split (LIV, 1), the earth will quake, and the people will be terrified (XXII, 1-2). The preceding signs (*as̲h̲rāṭ*) of the *Sāʿa* are already manifest (XLVII, 18). The Hour is already "heavy" in the heavens and in the earth (VII, 187).

In post-Ḳurʾānic *ḥadīt̲h̲*, the portents of the Hour became the subject of numerous traditions in which they were described as natural disasters. The sun will rise from the west (al-Buk̲h̲ārī, *Ṣaḥīḥ*, 81 [*Riḳāḳ*], 40), a "fire" [i.e. volcanic eruption] will thrust the people from the East to the West (Buk̲h̲ārī, 92 [*Fitan*], 24), or will burst out in the Ḥid̲j̲āz, and illuminate the necks of the camels in Syria (Muslim, 52 [*Fitan*]). Entire tribes will be swallowed up (*k̲h̲asf*, cf. Ḳurʾān LXVII, 16) by the earth (e.g. Aḥmad b. Ḥanbal, *Musnad*, Cairo 1313/1895, iii, 483, v, 31).

The statements about the portents of the *Sāʿa* are usually traced back to the Prophet himself; his knowledge about the coming events is taken to demonstrate his prophetic capability, for which reason the traditions containing his apocalyptic utterances concerning the *Sāʿa* sometimes appear in chapters about his miracles (e.g. al-Buk̲h̲ārī, 61 [*Manāḳib*], 25).

The most typical structure of Muḥammad's apocalyptic predictions is: "The Hour will not come until..."—*lā taḳūmu 'l-sāʿa ḥattā...* (for a thorough survey of the various traditions of this type, see Ibn Ḥad̲j̲ar al-ʿAsḳalānī, *Fatḥ al-bārī, s̲h̲arḥ Ṣaḥīḥ al-Buk̲h̲ārī*, Būlāḳ 1310/1892, repr. Beirut n.d., xiii, 72 f.).

Several traditions of the Prophet comply with the Ḳurʾānic tenet that the time of the Hour is known to Allāh alone (e.g. al-Buk̲h̲ārī, 2 [*Īmān*], 37). But other traditions stress that it is near at hand, and that Muḥammad was sent as a prophet at a distance of only two fingers away from it (e.g. ʿAbdallāh b. al-Mubārak (d. 181/797), *Musnad*, ed. al-Sāmarrāʾī, Riyāḍ 1987, no. 87). Sometimes a specific date was indicated for the Hour (e.g. at the turn of a century). After the date had elapsed while nothing happened, the traditions had to be reinterpreted, and new traditions shifting the end to a later date were put into circulation (see S. Bashear, *Muslim apocalypses and the Hour: a case-study in traditional reinterpretation*, in *IOS*, xiii [1993], 75-99).

The eschatological chaos which was to antedate the *Sāʿa* did not remain limited to natural disasters, but was also expanded in Muslim tradition to human society. Many traditions are based on the conviction that the *Sāʿa* will come when the orders of cultural and social structures are turned upside down; nomads will construct high buildings, masters will be born to slave-girls, the poor and naked will become leaders, etc. (e.g. al-Buk̲h̲ārī, 2 [*Īmān*], 37; Ibn Ḥanbal, i, 27, 51-2, 319). Religious and moral degeneration was turned into the most characteristic symptoms of the Hour: Knowledge will vanish, ignorance will prevail, fornication will become routine, and wine drinking will spread (*ibid.*, iii, 151). Spiritual values will give way to showy ambitions. The Hour will not come, says a tradition, till people start competing with each other in (erecting grandiose) mosques (e.g. Ibn Mād̲j̲a, 4 [*Masād̲j̲id*], 2). The most crucial signs of religious degeneration antedating the Hour are that the Arab tribes will revert to the idolatry of the *D̲j̲āhiliyya* (al-Buk̲h̲ārī, 92 [*Fitan*], 23), and that the pilgrimage to the Kaʿba will be renounced (*ibid.*, 25 [*Ḥad̲j̲d̲j̲*], 47). The decay of the Muslims before the Hour will eliminate the distinction between them and their non-Muslim predecessors. A tradition of the Prophet states that the Hour will not come until his community starts following in the footsteps of the previous communities (*ibid.*, 96 [*Iʿtiṣām*], 14; Ibn Ḥanbal, ii, 325, 336, 367).

Other traditions focus on specific Islamic groups whose decline is said to indicate the impending *Sāʿa*. A tradition says that the Hour will not occur as long as one Companion of Muḥammad is still alive (*ibid.*, i, 89, 93). Another tradition says that one of the portents of the Hour is the perdition of the Arabs (al-Tirmid̲h̲ī, 46 [*Manāḳib*], 69). Such statements indicate that, like many other topics, that of the *Sāʿa* was, too, used for advertising the virtues (*faḍāʾil*) of various groups and factions within the Islamic community.

The great bulk of the traditions about the *Sāʿa* are recorded in the *ḥadīt̲h̲* compilations in the sections entitled *Fitan* (sometimes also called *Malāḥim* [*q.v.*]), i.e. tribulations, civil strife and wars which started since the murder of ʿUt̲h̲mān [see FITNA]. These historical events were identified with the portents of the Hour, and they, too, appear in Muḥammad's apocalypses. They are often referred to in a cryptic manner. Once interpreted they can be used for dating the traditions (see L.I. Conrad, *Portents of the Hour: Ḥadīth and history in the first century A.H.* (forthcoming in *Isl.*). See also M. Cook, *Eschatology, history and the dating of traditions*, unpublished paper submitted to the third colloquium *From Jāhiliyya to Islam*, The Hebrew University, Jerusalem 1985).

The apocalyptic predictions of Muḥammad contain also messianic ideas: ʿĪsā b. Maryam [*q.v.*] will descend and restore peace, faith and justice, and will defeat the Dad̲j̲d̲j̲āl [*q.v.*] (e.g. Ibn Ḥanbal, ii, 406). This vision of eschatological combat with evil powers which will mark the beginning of a new golden era was incorporated into the symptoms of the Hour. The expected Descent of ʿĪsā and his clash with the Dad̲j̲d̲j̲āl appear amongst the portents of the Hour in the earliest *ḥadīt̲h̲* compilations. In the *D̲j̲āmiʿ* of Maʿmar b. Rās̲h̲id (d. 154/770) (preserved in the *Muṣannaf* of ʿAbd al-Razzāḳ (d. 211/827), x-xi, ed. Ḥabīb al-Raḥmān al-Aʿẓamī, Beirut 1970), a tradition is recorded in which ten symptoms of the Hour are counted (ʿAbd al-Razzāḳ, xi, no. 20792). Some of them reflect Ḳurʾānic imagery. The signs are: Three instances of people being swallowed up in the ground; the emergence of the Dad̲j̲d̲j̲āl; the Descent of ʿĪsā; the emergence of the Beast (*Dābba* [*q.v.*]; see Ḳurʾān, XXVII, 82); the Smoke (*Duk̲h̲ān*; see Ḳurʾān, XLIV, 10); the breaking loose of Yād̲j̲ūd̲j̲ and Mād̲j̲ūd̲j̲ (Gog and Magog; see Ḳurʾān, XXI, 96-7); a chilly wind which will take away the soul of every believer; and the rising of the sun from the west.

Historical enemies of the Muslims were turned into

the evil party of the eschatological wars. In the early *Ṣaḥīfa* of Hammām b. Munabbih (d. 132/749), they are the Turks. Battles with various Turkish tribes are said to mark the approaching Hour (Hammām b. Munabbih, *Ṣaḥīfa*, ed. Rifʿat Fawzī ʿAbd al-Muṭṭalib, Cairo 1985, no. 126). In the *Dj̲āmiʿ* of Maʿmar b. Rās̲h̲id, the Rūm, i.e. the Byzantines, appear as the eschatological rivals. The traditions about them reflect the greatest military ambition ever nurtured by the Muslims, namely the conquest of Constantinople [see KUSṬANṬĪNIYYA]. At the same time, they also reveal the Muslim apprehensions of the grand military power of the Byzantine empire. The expected battle for Constantinople is predicted in a clear eschatological context. It is stated in ʿAbd al-Razzāḳ (xi, no. 20812) that the Hour shall only come when the battle with the Byzantines breaks out. During the battle, Constantinople will fall, the Dad̲j̲d̲j̲āl will appear and the Muslims will die fighting him. But according to other traditions, the Dad̲j̲d̲j̲āl will soon be defeated by ʿĪsā (Ibn Ḥibbān, xv, no. 6813. See also W. Madelung, *Apocalyptic prophesies in Ḥimṣ in the Umayyad age*, *JSS*, xxxi [1986], 158 f.). In a tradition appearing in other *ḥadīt̲h̲* compilations (e.g. al-Buk̲h̲ārī, 58 [*Dj̲izya*], 15), the anticipated combat with the Byzantines is again set in an eschatological context, but this time, it is not the much-desired fall of Constantinople which is predicted but rather a massive Byzantine attack of which the Muslims seem to have been worried at the time when the tradition was first prompted. This attack is the last of six events which, according to Muḥammad's prophesy, will precede the Hour (for a detailed analysis of this tradition, see Conrad, *art. cit.*). The first five are well known from Islamic history: Muḥammad's own death; the conquest of Jerusalem; a frightful epidemic (interpreted by Muslim commentators as the plague of ʿAmwās [*q.v.*] in ʿUmar's days); abundance of wealth with which no one will be satisfied any longer (said to refer to spoils coming in from the occupied lands in the days of ʿUthmān); a devastating *fitna* (explained as the events which took place following the murder of ʿUthmān). The sixth sign is a truce with the Byzantines, which the latter will soon violate and then attack the Muslims with a mighty army. According to Muslim commentators, only the latter event is yet to come (see Ibn Ḥad̲j̲ar, *Fatḥ al-bārī*, vi, 199).

In less prevalent traditions, the expected eschatological wars include battles against other historical enemies of Islam, namely the Jews. Muslim tradition had turned them into the supporters of the Dad̲j̲d̲j̲āl. It is related that when the Hour occurs, inanimate objects will be able to talk, and each stone will surrender to the Muslims the Jew who hides behind it (e.g. al-Buk̲h̲ārī, 56 [*Dj̲ihād*], 94; Muslim, 52 [*Fitan*]; Ibn Ḥanbal, ii, 398, 417, 530).

The messianic expectations for salvation following the eschatological wars were not only focused on the Descent of ʿĪsā who would defeat the Dad̲j̲d̲j̲āl, but also on the appearance of the Mahdī [*q.v.*]. His exact identity was disputed between various political groups, and their disparate pretensions are often reflected in the traditions, including those referring to the Hour. In some of them, it is stated that the *Sāʿa* will not occur until a man from Muḥammad's family comes and fills the earth with justice (e.g. *ibid.*, iii, 17, 36). A more specific tradition attributes to Muḥammad the statement that the man's name will coincide with that of the Prophet (*ibid.*, i, 376). Such statements could confirm the claims of the ʿAlīds, who anticipated a Mahdī of Muḥammad's family. But other groups expected their own Mahdī. Muslims of Yamanī descent awaited the emergence of a South Arabian ("Ḳaḥṭānī"), i.e. non-Ḳuras̲h̲ī, leader, whose chief achievement would be the conquest of Constantinople (see Madelung, *Apocalyptic prophecies*, 149 f.). Some identified him with the prophet S̲h̲uʿayb b. Ṣāliḥ (Ibn Ḥad̲j̲ar, *Fatḥ al-bārī*, xiii, 67-8). Such expectations triggered off the reaction of those who believed that leadership should only be invested with members of Ḳurays̲h̲. The latter included the predicted advent of the Ḳaḥṭānī among the ominous portents of the *Sāʿa*. A tradition stating that the Hour will not come until the Ḳaḥṭānī leads the people was recorded by al-Buk̲h̲ārī under the derogatory heading (92 [*Fitan*], 23: "The change of time till idols are worshipped"). In other traditions with the same statement about the Ḳaḥṭānī, the hopes for the conquest of Constantinople are scorned (ʿAbd al-Razzāḳ, xi, no. 20816). Another tradition of the Prophet predicts the advent of a man from the *mawālī* whose name is Dj̲ahd̲j̲āh; he will lead the people at the end of days (al-Tirmid̲h̲ī, 31 [*Fitan*], 50; Ibn Ḥanbal, ii, 329). Some Muslim scholars identified him with the Ḳaḥṭānī (Ibn Ḥad̲j̲ar, *Fatḥ al-bārī*, vi, 397).

Bibliography (in addition to the references given in the article): Wensinck, *Handbook*, 100-1 (s.v. *Hour*). A variety of prophetic traditions with numerous kinds of *as̲h̲rāṭ al-sāʿa* may be found in the *Fitan* sections of the following *ḥadīt̲h̲* compilations: Ibn Abī S̲h̲ayba, *al-Muṣannaf fī 'l-aḥādīt̲h̲ wa 'l-āt̲h̲ār*, Bombay 1967, xv, 5 f.; Buk̲h̲ārī, *Ṣaḥīḥ*, *Kitāb* no. 92; Muslim, *Ṣaḥīḥ, Kitāb* no. 52; Abū Dāwūd, *Sunan, Kitāb* nos. 34, 36; Ibn Mād̲j̲a, *Sunan, Kitāb* no. 36; Tirmid̲h̲ī, *Ṣaḥīḥ, Kitāb* no. 31; Nūr al-Dīn al-Hayt̲h̲amī, *Kas̲h̲f al-astār ʿan zawāʾid al-Bazzār*, ed. Ḥabīb al-Raḥmān al-Aʿẓamī, Beirut 1979, iv, 88 f.; idem, *Mad̲j̲maʿ al-zawāʾid wa-manbaʿ al-fawāʾid*, repr. Beirut 1987, vii, 223 f., viii, 5 f.; Muḥammad b. Aḥmad Ibn Ḥibbān, *al-Iḥsān fī taḳrīb Ṣaḥīḥ Ibn Ḥibbān, tartīb ʿAlāʾ al-Dīn al-Fārisī*, ed. S̲h̲uʿayb al-Arnaʾūṭ, Beirut 1988, xv, 5 f.; al-Ḥākim al-Naysābūrī, *al-Mustadrak ʿalā 'l-Ṣaḥīḥayn*, Ḥaydarābād 1342/1923, iv, 418 f.; al-Ḥusayn b. Masʿūd al-Bag̲h̲awī, *Maṣābīḥ al-sunna*, Beirut 1987, iii, 465 f.; Ibn Ḥad̲j̲ar al-ʿAsḳalānī, *al-Maṭālib al-ʿāliya bi-zawāʾid al-masānīd al-t̲h̲amāniya*, ed. Ḥabīb al-Raḥmān al-Aʿẓamī, Beirut 1987, iv, 264 f.; al-Muttaḳī al-Hindī, *Kanz al-ʿummāl fī sunan al-aḳwāl wa 'l-afʿāl*, ed. Ṣafwat al-Saḳḳā, Bakrī al-Ḥayyānī, Beirut 1979, xi, 107 f.

Individual collections: Nuʿaym b. Ḥammād, *Kitāb al-fitan*, ed. S. Zakkār, Beirut 1993, 385-6; ʿAlī b. Mūsā Ibn Ṭāwūs, *al-Malāḥim wa 'l-fitan*, Beirut 1988. (U. RUBIN)

SAʿĀDA (A.), happiness, bliss, a central concept in Islamic philosophy to describe the highest aim of human striving, which can be reached through ethical perfection and increasing knowledge. In non-philosophical literature, the term (as opposed to *s̲h̲aḳāwa*, *s̲h̲aḳwa*, *s̲h̲aḳāʾ*, *s̲h̲aḳā*) describes either happy circumstances in life (see for instance Ibn Ḥanbal, *Musnad*, ed. Cairo 1313/1895-6, i, 168, 29-30, iii, 407, last section), the unexpected happiness of a long life (*Musnad*, iii, 332, 28), preservation from temptations (*ibid.*, i, 327, 9-10; Abū Dāwūd, *Sunan, Kitāb al-Fitan*, 2, Ḥimṣ 1973, iv, no. 4263), or the eternal stay in Paradise.

The last meaning is based on the Ḳurʾān (e.g. sūra XI, 105/107, 108/110), whose eschatological implications led to the newly-created term *yawm al-saʿāda* = "Day of Resurrection" (cf. Dozy, *Supplément*, i, 654). The Ḳurʾān, and occasionally *ḥadīt̲h̲* (e.g. al-Tirmid̲h̲ī, *Sunan, Tafsīr al-Ḳurʾān*, ed. Ḥimṣ, ix, no.

3341), already indicate that mankind, because of divine predestination, is divided into "happy" inhabitants of Paradise and "unhappy" dwellers in Hell. However, the impact of predestination is mitigated by utterances according to which an active effort of the human being is required. Next to human acceptance (*riḍā* [*q.v.*]) of what God has predestined, *Musnad*, i, 168, 26-7, also mentions the prayer to God for obtaining what is good (*istikhāra* [*q.v.*]) as a characteristic of *saʿāda*.

Under the influence of various classical doctrines (cf. Spaemann), namely of Platonic political philosophy, of Aristotelian ethics, of Neo-Platonism, and partly also of Islamic mysticism, the possibility for a human being to strive after *saʿāda* is often described in Islamic philosophy as the pursuit of "assimilation to God" (ὁμοίωεις θεῷ, Plato, *Theaet.*, 176 B), of nearness to God, and of knowledge of God through a virtuous life. At the beginning of Islamic philosophy, this interpretation is found in al-Kindī's works. His *Risāla fī ḥudūd al-ashyāʾ wa-rusūmihā* (ed. Abū Rīda, *Rasāʾil*, i, 177 ff. = *Cinq épîtres*, 37 ff.), his utterances transmitted in the *Muntakhab Ṣiwān al-ḥikma* of Abū Sulaymān al-Sidjistānī (ed. Dunlop, §§ 246-8), his *Risāla fī alfāẓ Suḳrāṭ* (ed. Fakhry, *Dirāsāt*, 45-60), his *Risāla fī Alkibiades wa-Suḳrāṭ* (cf. Atiyeh, 123 ff., Alon, 131 ff.; Butterworth, in *Political aspects*, 32 ff.) and his *Risāla fi 'l-ḥīla li-dafʿ al-aḥzān* (ed. Walzer-Ritter, 1938), which goes back to a lost Hellenistic treatise, describe a concept of virtue which is inspired by the Platonic cardinal virtues. Socrates is named as the ideal of moderation and of spiritual values, which are superior to wordly possessions. The person who turns his attention to intelligibles, and who in his doings keeps to the virtues, will "not be unhappy (*shaḳiyy*)" in the hereafter, will be near to his Creator and will know Him (*Muntakhab*, § 248, Eng. tr. Atiyeh 1966, 225). This image of Socrates was adopted, with some modifications, by Abū Bakr al-Rāzī [*q.v.*] in his *al-Sīra al-falsafiyya* (ed. Kraus, *Rasāʾil*, 99 ff.; tr. Arberry, *Aspects*, 120 ff; cf. Walker in *Political aspects*, 77 ff.). The person who leads a moderate life and who, as far as possible, restrains his passions, "assimilates himself to God as far as possible" (*Rasāʾil*, ed. Kraus, 108, 8 ff.). In his *Maḳāla fī amārāt al-iḳbāl wa 'l-dawla* (= "political success"), Abū Bakr al-Rāzī expresses this as follows (*Rasāʾil*, ed. Kraus, 145, 8): "progress (*tanaḳḳul*) and knowledge (*ʿilm*) belong to the symptoms of "happiness" (*iḳbāl*) and indicate that a person "is attentive to happiness" (*tayaḳḳuẓ al-saʿāda lahu*)." Knowledge and justice are named as the main aims of the human being.

This ideal of virtue was adopted by Abu Bakr's opponent, the Ismāʿīlī Abū Ḥātim al-Rāzī [*q.v.*], with one alteration: the bearer par excellence of the Platonic cardinal virtues and of the Aristotelian principle of the golden centre is the Prophet Muḥammad, who possesses knowledge revealed by God. He who follows him and does not rely upon his own intuition, is able to understand the religious laws and can be sure of salvation (*nadjāt*) (Abū Ḥātim, *Aʿlām*, ed. Al-Sawy, 77 ff., esp. 110, 9 ff.; cf. Daiber, 1989).

The high appreciation of reason as the guideline for a practical philosophy, understood as ethics in the first place, is characteristic of the philosophers mentioned so far, and culminates in al-Fārābī's [*q.v.*] thesis of the ideal sovereign as philosopher and prophet (cf. Daiber, *Ruler*). His knowledge, inspired by the divine active intellect, enables him to govern the Ideal State by ordering religious laws. Religion appears as the imitating picture ("imitation") and the "instrument" of philosophy, which is essentially understood here as practical philosophy and as ethics of the individual person in the State. In this way, philosophy, thus understood, realises itself through religion and becomes an ethical insight into "what is good and evil in the actions usually performed by human beings" (al-Farabi, *Mabādiʾ*, ed. Walzer, 204, 1-2). As was the case with Aristotle (*Nicomachean Ethics*, 1144a, 5-6), philosophy is not exclusively "scientific perception" or theoretical philosophy; rather, it provides a human being with an ultimate degree of happiness (*al-saʿāda al-ḳuṣwā* = *eudaimonía*; cf. Daiber, *Prophetie*, 733-4; Shahjahan) with the help of the above-mentioned ethical insight, i.e. practical philosophy. When al-Fārābī speaks of "political happiness" (see Galston, in *Political aspects*, 100 ff.), he has in mind the Aristotelian concept of the human being as ζῷον πολιτικόν (*Politics*, 1253a, 2), who needs the help of his fellow-citizen in an Ideal State, governed by a philosopher who possesses prophetical knowledge.

This "political happiness" is reflected in the practical aspect of al-Fārābī's concept of *saʿāda*. It is part of the ultimate happiness, namely that of the hereafter; the human being can reach this when his soul liberates itself from its corporeal existence, actualises its potential intellect and arrives at the level of the active intellect. But happiness, in its complete form, is at the same time practical perfection. For practical philosophy, on the one hand, shows the way to theoretical perfection, to contemplation; on the other, theoretical perfection is the signpost towards practical philosophy, the ethical insight into the Perfect State. The latter's sovereign, the prophet-philosopher, transmits it to his subjects, the state's citizens, in the form of religious laws, religion being the sum total of these laws.

In this way, theoretical philosophy develops into practical-ethical perfection through practical philosophy and through religion that is, through the guidance of religious prescriptions, transmitted by the philosopher-prophet. At the same time, practical-ethical perfection in the Ideal State, in society, is the prerequisite for theoretical perfection, i.e. contemplation. The theoretical and practical aspects of knowledge, of moral-ethical insight respectively, are thus inseparably united in al-Fārābī's concept of *saʿāda*.

This link between ethics and knowledge is also found in the *Epistles* (*Rasāʾil*) of the Ikhwān al-Ṣafāʾ [*q.v.*], possibly composed in A.D. 959-60. Their political philosophy betrays the influence of al-Fārābī (Enayat; Abouzeid), but they accentuate more strongly the Neo-Platonic elements and are eschatologically inspired. Through "purification" of his soul and reform of his character, the human being acquires increasing knowledge of "intelligibles" (*al-umūr al-ʿaḳliyya*), for it is only knowledge (*maʿrifa*) of God which leads to ultimate happiness and to salvation in the hereafter (*Rasāʾil*, iii, 241, 322-3; tr. and comm. Diwald, 203 ff., 419 ff.). For this, a human being needs as a preliminary step the fraternal society, a society which is aware of its solidarity in being obedient to the divine law (*nāmūs* [*q.v.*]), and jointly pursues "the good of the religion and of the world" (*ṣalāḥ al-dīn wa 'l-dunyā*) (*Rasāʾil*, i, 223, 16).

The stronger accentuation of individual ethics, already expressed by the Ikhwān al-Ṣafāʾ, led Miskawayh [*q.v.*], in his *Tahdhīb al-akhlāḳ*, to declare that a human being certainly does need the help of his fellow-citizen, and therefore must live with him in love (*maḥabba*) and friendship (*ṣadāḳa*), but also that inequality is the reason why everyone must strive after his own happiness by bringing his character to perfection (*al-kamāl al-khulkī*) (*Tahdhīb*, 72, 10 ff.). For the individual in society, he thus offers ethics which are inspired by the Platonic-Aristotelian doctrine of virtues (Fakhry, 1991, 107 ff.). Just and virtuous acts and increasing knowledge of the "spiritual things" (*Tahdhīb*, 83 at the end) purify the soul of the "physical things" (*al-umūr al-ṭabīᶜiyya*; see *Tahdhīb*, 91, 18; cf. Plotinus, *Enn.* I, 6), lead to "tranquility of the heart"(*Tahdhīb*, 40, 5) and to "nearness to God" (*djiwār rabb al-ᶜālamīn*; see *Tahdhīb*, 13 at the end). This is the state of perfect knowledge and of wisdom, in which the human being resembles the divine first principle, the divine intellect (*Tahdhīb*, 88-9); Miskawayh called it the ultimate happiness, which is preceded by several preliminary steps (*saᶜādāt*) (Miskawayh, *al-Saᶜāda*; Ansari 1963; Fakhry, 1991, 121 f.).

Among the Islamic thinkers who followed Miskawayh's ethics (Fakhry, 131 ff.), mention may be made here of al-Rāghib al-Iṣfahānī [*q.v.*]. In his *Kitāb al-Dharīᶜa ilā makārim al-sharīᶜa* he offers an original adaptation of Greek ethics as it was known to him through al-Fārābī, Miskawayh and the *Rasāʾil Ikhwān al-Ṣafāʾ*, to the statements of the Ḳurʾān (Daiber, *Griechische Ethik*). He replaces Miskawayh's Platonic-Neoplatonic concept of the assimilation to God by the Ḳurʾānic concept of *khilāfa* (sūra II, 30; VI, 165). As the "representative" (*khalīfa*) of God in this world, the human being imitates God as much as he is able to, by following the *sharīᶜa* and by concerning himself about his sustenance on this earth (cf. sūra XI, 61/64: *istaᶜmarakum*). Thus a human being acquires happiness in this world which, as in Miskawayh, is a preliminary to the "real happiness" in the hereafter (*al-Dharīᶜa*, 128, 4 ff.; cf. *Tafṣīl al-nashʾatayn*).

In al-Rāghib al-Iṣfahānī's ethics, by which al-Ghazālī [*q.v.*] was deeply impressed, a mystical tendency can be detected which was already visible in the *Rasāʾil Ikhwān al-Ṣafāʾ* and in Miskawayh's work. There is not so much concern about the rôle of the individual in society, but rather about striving after the happiness lying in the knowledge of, and the nearness to, God, which is a happiness of the hereafter. This corresponds to the Neoplatonic ἀπράγμων βίος ideal of the philosopher who withdraws from society (cf. Kraemer 1986, 128).

In accordance with this view, the prophet, for Ibn Sīnā, is a Ṣūfī who preaches the divine laws as a way to the mystical path, to the liberation of the soul from the body, to its intellectual perfection, and to the vision of God (Ibn Sīnā, *Risāla fi 'l-saᶜāda*; Ansari 1962-3; E.I.J. Rosenthal, 144 ff.). But for Ibn Sīnā too, life in society remains an indispensable preliminary to happiness in the hereafter. Obedience to the lawgiver, to the prophet, is a postulate, as is the fulfilment of duties towards God and towards the fellow man. According to Ibn Sīnā's view, which is clearly associated with that of al-Fārābī, the sovereign, who is a prophet and a Ṣūfī, unites in his person practical and theoretical wisdom (Morris, in *Political aspects*, 153 ff.). This union creates happiness (*al-Shifāʾ*, *al-Ilāhiyyāt*, ii, 455, 14), but is also a postulate for the sovereign, who combines it with prophetical qualities.

It was the Andalusian philosopher Ibn Bādjdja, and, above all, his younger contemporary Ibn Ṭufayl [*q.vv.*], who drew the final conclusion from the increasingly mystical-Neoplatonic orientation of the *saᶜāda* concept. Society is no longer a postulate for the individual to strive after happiness. On the contrary, it is only the isolated philosopher (*al-mutawaḥḥid*), the Ṣūfī, who, withdrawing from society, obtains ultimate happiness through his self-government (*tadbīr*) and his vision of the truth (Altmann; Daiber, *Autonomie*, 242 ff.; Harvey, in *Political aspects*, 199 ff.). For him, it is possible to achieve a mystical ascent to higher forms of knowledge, namely by liberating the soul from the matter and by the union (*ittiṣāl*) with the divine active intellect, which is an emanation from God. Society is only a place to meet (*liḳāʾ*, *iltiḳāʾ*), which may be useful for the individual and may stimulate his emulation in striving after intellectual perfection. In opposition to Plato's view, the citizen no longer serves society; at best, society can stimulate the individual in his striving after happiness, to be found in intellectual perfection.

In his philosophical novel *Ḥayy Ibn Yaḳẓān*, Ibn Ṭufayl (cf. Fradkin, in *Political aspects*, 234 ff.) consequently developed the thesis that the individual's philosophy and society's religion are not contradictory, but do not support each other either. Ibn Ṭufayl's compatriot Ibn Rushd, who was twenty years his junior did not share with him this radical turning-away from al-Fārābī (Daiber, *Autonomie*, 246-7). In his *Epistle on the possibility of conjunction with the active intellect*, he declares that in this life, too, it is possible to strive after happiness as long as this is not hampered by society. For this, theoretical study should be combined with acts (tr. Bland, 108-9). The aim of such a striving is the immortality of the soul, which is achieved when the soul increasingly unites its acquired knowledge with the active intellect. This union, which is the most perfect form of human cognition, is possible because the active intellect is the form of the *intellectus materialis*, which in its turn is the form of the soul, i.e. its eternal potentiality. It is not only remarkable that Ibn Rushd denies (against al-Ghazālī) the individual immortality, deriving this denial from the union of the soul with the eternal form of the active intellect; much more important is his conclusion that striving after philosophical knowledge, i.e. after happiness, is not a duty of individuals or of individual states, but a task of mankind. This philosophical knowledge is the most perfect form of the universal human knowledge of religious truth which is reflected in the *sharīᶜa*. Accordingly, the Ideal State, i.e. the Philosophical State, comprises all mankind; the best Islamic State, a State which only existed during the period of the first four caliphs, is at best an imitation of such a Philosophical State.

Ibn Khaldūn [*q.v.*], the last great Islamic thinker, incorporated into his philosophy of history Ibn Rushd's universalistic opinion, as well as al-Fārābī's and Ibn Sīnā's doctrines (Mahdi, 1957). He put new accents and, by introducing the term *ᶜaṣabiyya* [*q.v.*], he gave a new significance to the concept of society. The *polis*, the state, is indispensable for the entire human society, for its progress (*Muḳaddima*, iii, 54 at the end: *iṣlāḥ al-bashar*) and for its preservation. In his philosophy, which he preaches to mankind in the form of "political laws" (*aḥkām al-siyāsa*), the sovereign of the Ideal State, the prophetical lawgiver, deals with the well-being of the world (*maṣāliḥ al-dunyā*) and with the "salvation" of mankind "in the hereafter" (*ṣalāḥ ākhiratihim*) (*Muḳaddima*, i, 343). Philosophy, understood as ethics and politics, as well as religion and the society of the state, are seen here as indispensable materials for the well-being of all mankind in this world and for their happiness (*saᶜāda*: *Muḳaddima*, i, 343, 4) in the hereafter.

Bibliography: 1. Texts. *Rasāʾil al-Kindī al-falsafiyya*, ed. Muḥammad ᶜAbd al-Hādī Abū Rīda, i-ii, Cairo 1950-3, partially newly edited 1978, partial edition: *Cinq épitres*, Paris 1976; fragments in Abū Sulaymān al-Sidjistānī, *The Muntakhab Ṣiwān al-ḥikma*, ed. D.M. Dunlop, The Hague, etc. 1979, §§ 245 ff.; Abū Bakr al-Rāzī, *Rasā'il falsafiyya*, ed. P. Kraus, Cairo 1939; idem, *al-Sīra al-falsafiyya* (= ed. Kraus, 97-111), repr., with introd. and comm. Mehdi Mohaghegh, Tehran 1964; Abū Ḥātim al-Rāzī, *A^clām al-nubuwwa*, ed. with introd. and notes by Salah Al-Sawy, Tehran 1977; al-Fārābī, *Mabādi' ārā' ahl al-madīna al-fāḍila*, ed. and tr. R. Walzer, *al-Farabi on the Perfect State*, Oxford 1985; *Rasā'il Ikhwān al-Ṣafā'*, ed. Khayr al-Dīn al-Ziriklī, i-iv, Cairo 1347/1928; partial Ger. tr. S. Diwald, *Arabische Philosophie und Wissenschaft in der Enzyklopädie Kitāb Iḫwān aṣ-Ṣafā' (III). Die Lehre von Seele und Intellekt*, Wiesbaden 1975; Miskawayh, *Tahdhīb al-akhlāḳ*, ed. C.K. Zurayk, Beirut 1966 (Eng. tr. idem, *The refinement of character*, Beirut 1968); idem, *al-Sa^cāda*, ed. Maḥmūd ^cAlī Ṣubayḥ, Cairo 1346/1928 (also included, with identical pagination, in *al-Muntakhabāt al-adabiyya*, Cairo *ca.* 1928); al-Rāghib al-Iṣfahānī, *Kitāb al-Dharī^ca ilā makārim al-sharī^ca*, ed. Abu 'l-Yazīd al-^cAdjamī, Cairo [2]1987; idem, *Tafṣīl an-nash'atayn wa-taḥṣīl al-sa^cādatayn*, Cairo *ca.* 1920, new ed. ^cAbd al-Madjīd al-Nadjdjār, Beirut 1988; Ibn Sīnā, *al-Shifā', al-Ilāhiyyāt*, i-ii, ed. Muḥammad Yūsuf Mūsā, Sulaymān Dunyā, Sa^cīd Zāyid, Cairo 1960; idem, *Risāla fi 'l-sa^cāda wa 'l-ḥudjadj al-^cashara* [sic] ^calā anna 'l-nafs al-insāniyya *dhawhar*, Ḥaydarābād 1353/1934; idem, *al-Risāla al-aḍḥawiyya fī 'l-ma^cād*, ed. and tr. F. Lucchetta, *Epistola sulla vita futura*, Padua 1969, 200 ff. (cf. Lister, *Doctrine*, 168 ff.); Ibn Rushd, *The epistle on the possibility of conjunction with the active intellect by Ibn Rushd with the commentary of Moses Narboni*, ed. and tr. K.P. Bland, New York 1982; idem, *Averroes' commentary on Plato's Republic*, ed. with introd., tr. and notes E.I.J. Rosenthal, Cambridge 1956, repr. 1969, new English tr. R. Lerner, *Averroes on Plato's Republic*, Ithaca and London 1974; Ibn Khaldūn, *Muḳaddima*, ed. Quatremère, Eng. tr. F. Rosenthal, *Ibn Khaldūn. The Muqaddima*, London 1958, [2]1967.

2. Studies. O.A. Abouzeid, *A comparative study between the political theories of al-Fārābī and the Brethren of Purity*, diss. Toronto 1987, unpubl.; I. Alon, *Socrates in medieval Arabic literature*, Leiden-Jerusalem 1991 (= Isl. Philos., Theol. and Science, X); A. Altmann, *Ibn Bājja on man's ultimate felicity*, in idem, *Studies in religious philosophy and mysticism*, London 1969, 73-107 (also in *Harry Austryn Wolfson Jubilee volume*, English section, i, Jerusalem 1965, 335-55); M. Abdul Haq Ansari, *The conception of ultimate happiness in Muslim philosophy*, in *Studies in Islam*, i (New Delhi 1964), 165-73; idem, *Ibn Sīnā's Ethics*, in *Bulletin of the Institute of Islamic Studies*, vi-vii (Aligarh 1962-3), 72-82; idem, *Miskawayh's conception of Sa^cādah*, in *Islamic Studies*, ii (Karachi 1963), 317-35; A.J. Arberry, *Aspects of Islamic civilization*, London 1964; G.N. Atiyeh, *Al-Kindi, the philosopher of the Arabs*, Rawalpindi 1966, repr. 1984; ^cĀdil al-^cAwwā, *Madhāhib al-sa^cāda*, Damascus 1991; M. Burbach, *The theory of beatitude in Latin-Arabian philosophy and its initial impact on Christian thought*, diss. Toronto 1944, unpubl.; H. Daiber, *Abū Ḥātim al-Rāzī (10th century A.D.) on the unity and diversity of religions*, in *Dialogue and syncretism. An interdisciplinary approach*, ed. J. Gort *et alii*, Amsterdam 1989, 87-104; idem, *Die Autonomie der Philosophie im Islam*, in *Knowledge and the sciences in medieval philosophy*, ed. M. Asztalos, J.E. Murdoch, I. Niiniluoto I (= Acta philosophica fennica, 48), 228-49; idem, *Griechische Ethik in islamischem Gewande. Das Beispiel von Rāğib al-Iṣfahānī (11.Jh.)*, in *Historia philosophiae medii aevi. Studien zur Geschichte der Philosophie des Mittelalters*, hrsg.v. B. Mojsisch, Olaf Pluta, Amsterdam-Philadelphia 1991, 181-92; idem, *Islamic political philosophy*, in *The Routledge history of Islamic Philosophy*, London, in the press; idem, *Prophetie und Ethik bei Fārābī (st. 339/950)*, in *L'homme et son univers au moyen age*, ed. Chr. Wenin, ii (= Philosophes médiévaux, XXVII), 729-53; idem, *The ruler as philosopher. A new interpretation of al-Fārābī's view*, Amsterdam 1986 (= Mededelingen der Koninklijke Nederlandse Akademie van Wetenschappen, Afd. Letterkunde, no. 49/4); H. Enayat, *An outline of the political philosophy of the Rasā'il of the Ikhwān al-Ṣafā'*, in *Ismā^cīlī contributions to Islamic culture*, ed Seyyed Hossein Nasr, Tehran 1977, 23-49; M. Fakhry, *Dirāsāt fī 'l-fikr al-^carabī*, Beirut 1977; idem, *Ethical theories in Islam*, Leiden 1991 (= Isl. Philos., Theol. and Science, VIII); J. Kraemer, *Humanism in the renaissance of Islam*, Leiden 1986; Q. Lister, *The doctrine of Avicenna on the resurrection*, diss. Rome 1986, unpubl.; M. Mahdi, *Ibn Khaldūn's philosophy of history*, London 1957, [2]Chicago 1971; Sh. Pines, *La philosophie dans l'économie du genre humain selon Averroès; une réponse à al-Fārābī?* in *Multiple Averroès*, Paris 1978, 189-207; idem, *The societies providing for the bare necessities of life according to Ibn Khaldūn and to the philosophers*, in *SI*, xxxiv (1971), 125-38; *The political aspects of Islamic philosophy. Essays in honor of Muhsin S. Mahdi*, ed. Ch.E. Butterworth, Cambridge 1992; E.I.J. Rosenthal, *The concept of "Eudaimonia" in medieval Islamic and Jewish philosophy*, in idem, *Studia semitica*, ii, Cambridge 1971, 127-34; idem, *Griechisches Erbe in der jüdischen Religionsphilosophie des Mittelalters*, Stuttgart 1960, 27 ff.; idem, *Political thought in medieval Islam*, Cambridge [2]1962; M. Shahjahan, *An introduction to the ethics of al-Fārābī*, in *IC*, lix (1985), 45-52; R. Spaemann, art. *Glück* in *Historisches Wörterbuch der Philosophie*, ed. J. Ritter, iii, Darmstadt 1974, cols. 679-707; R. Walzer and H. Ritter, *Studi su Al-Kindī. II. Uno scritto morale inedito di Al-Kindī. Temistio peri alypias?*, in *Atti della Reale Accademia Nazionale dei Lincei. Memorie della Classe di Scienze morali, storiche e filologiche*, serie VI, vol. viii, Rome 1938-9, 5-63.

(H. Daiber)

SA^cĀDAT ^cALĪ KHĀN, Nawāb of Awadh or Oudh (regn. 1798-1814).

His brother Āṣaf al-Dawla had died in September 1797, but after a four months' interim, Āṣaf al-Dawla's putative son Wazīr ^cAlī Khān was set aside and the British governor-General Sir John Shore installed in his place Sa^cādat ^cAlī Khān, who had been living under British protection in Benares since 1776. His reign is noteworthy for the extension of British control over the Oudh territories. A treaty concluded with the late Nawāb in 1775 had placed these territories under the protection of the East India Company, which undertook to provide troops for their defence in return for an annual subsidy; in 1798, a fresh treaty increased the subsidy to 76 lakhs a year and transferred the fort of Allāhābād [*q.v.*] to the Company as an arsenal, the Company undertaking to maintain a body of 10,000 men for the defence of the Nawāb's dominions both against internal and external enemies. The mutinous behaviour of the Nawāb's troops prompted the new Governor-General, the Marquis Wellesley (1798-1805), to propose that this useless and dangerous force, which Sa^cādat ^cAlī Khān had himself declared would be useful only to the enemy, should be disbanded and replaced by the Company's troops. Alarmed by the dangers that threatened his person, Saᶜādat ᶜAlī Khān was at first eager for this reform, but afterwards refused his consent and also refused to abdicate, and only in 1801 yielded to pressure and signed the Treaty of Lucknow; this relieved him from all pecuniary obligations to the Company, by the cession of six districts yielding a revenue equal to the cost of the Company's troops, and the Nawāb undertook to introduce into his territories a system of administration conducive to the prosperity of his subjects and calculated to check the ruin that threatened the resources of his country.

Thus Wellesley's fears that the buffer state of Oudh might come under pressure from the west, in particular from the ruler of Afghānistān Zamān Shāh (who had already invaded the Pandjāb in 1797) in alliance with the Rohilla [*q.v.*] Afghāns, were set at rest. With the cession of the western part of Oudh and its lands along the Ganges and Djamnā rivers, only a rump of the state remained until its complete annexation in 1856. Europeans already controlled much of Oudh's economy by the early 19th century, especially the trade in fine cloths and raw cotton, and this commercial control now increased.

Saᶜādat ᶜAlī Khān's reign was an Indian summer of the Mughal culture of Hindūstān, with Lucknow especially flourishing as a centre of Shīᶜī culture [see LAKHNAW]. Saᶜādat ᶜAlī Khān died in 1814 and was succeeded by his second son Ghāzī al-Dīn Ḥaydar, who subsequently became the first king of Oudh [see AWADH].

Bibliography: Sayyid Ghulām ᶜAlī, *ᶜImād al-Saᶜādat*, Lucknow 1897, 169-74; Durgā Prasād, *Būstān-i-Awadh*, Lucknow 1892, 99-109 (with portrait); Sir C.U. Aitchison, *Collection of treaties relating to India*, i, Calcutta 1909, 118-37; Sir John Malcolm, *The political history of India from 1784 to 1823*, i, London 1826, 170-7, 273-83; *A selection from the despatches of the Marquess Wellesley*, ed. S.J. Owen, Oxford 1877, 188-207; H.C. Irwin, *The Garden of India, or chapters on Oudh history and affairs*, London 1880, 100-11; R.B. Barnett, *North India between empires. Awadh, the Mughals, and the British 1720-1801*, Berkeley etc. 1980, 233-8; C.A. Bayley, *Rulers, townsmen and bazaars: North India in the age of British expansion 1770-1870*, Cambridge 1983, 276; idem, *Indian society and the making of the British empire* (The New Cambridge History of India, ii/1), Cambridge 1988, 92.

(C.C. DAVIES-[C.E. BOSWORTH])

SAᶜADYĀ BEN YŌSĒF, SAᶜĪD (ABĪ) YAᶜḲŪB YŪSUF AL-FAYYŪMĪ (269-331/882-942), Jewish theologian, philosopher and philologist who wrote in Arabic, considered through his independence and breadth as the initiator of several Jewish intellectual disciplines, and a pioneer in mediaeval Jewish philosophy; he was one of the very few Jewish thinkers covered by the Arabic biographers (cf. Ibn al-Nadīm, *Fihrist*, i, 320).

1. *Life*

He was born at Dīlās in the province of Fayyūm in Egypt, but little is known of his youth except that his father, of humble origin, had the reputation of being a scholar. He probably received a solid education in the Biblical and Rabbinical spheres as well as in Arabic culture. Saᶜīd began his literary work at a precocious age, writing in 300/912-13 a Hebrew-Arabic dictionary called *ʾEgrōn* (Hebr. "Collection") (ed. N. Allony, Jerusalem 1969). If the title reminds one of the *K. al-Djāmiᶜ* of the grammarian ᶜĪsā b. ᶜUmar al-Thakafī (d. 149/766), its alphabetic arrangement according to the final letters "in order to facilitate the writing of verses" could have been the model for the *Ṣiḥāḥ* of al-Djawharī (d. 398/1007 [*q.v.*]). Of his *K. al-Lugha*, the oldest Hebrew grammar, also written at this time, only fragments exist. In the course of his period of education, he addressed to Isḥāḳ b. Sulaymān al-Isrāʾīlī (d. *ca.* 344/955) at Ḳayrawān, a physician at the Aghlabid court, a philosophical correspondence which did not, it seems, meet with the approbation of this Neoplatonist. In 303/915, he put together his defence of Rabbinical Judaism against the Karaites [*q.v.*], very numerous in Egypt.

In this same year, Saᶜīd left for Palestine, where, according to al-Masᶜūdī (*Tanbīh*, 113), he perfected his education at the feet of Abū Kathīr Yaḥyā al-Kātib al-Ṭabarānī (d. 320/932). The latter is also mentioned by Ibn Ḥazm in his *K. al-Fiṣlal wa 'l-niḥal*, iii, 171, as being, together with David al-Muḳammis and Saᶜīd himself, one of the *mutakallimūn* of the Jews.

In 309/921, very likely with the aim of getting to know the great Jewish academies of Mesopotamia, Saᶜīd left for Baghdād, stopping en route at Aleppo. In 310/922 he was the main protagonist in the controversy over the calendar, in which the heads of the Babylonian community were in opposition to Aharōn Ben Mēᶜīr, head of the Palestinian academy. Saᶜīd emerged victorious from this quarrel, which is mentioned even by the Syrian historian Elias of Nisibin (11th century) in his chronology. This victory had a determining influence on his career, since, in recognition of his services to the Rabbanite cause, Saᶜīd was elected *ᶜallūf* or master of the Babylonian academy of Pūm Peditha.

A Jewish society in full transition, becoming progressively Arabised and intellectually enriched by new philosophical and scientific disciplines, posed challenges, to which the creative genius of Saᶜīd was able to respond. Stopping up the breaches, he consolidated Rabbinical Judaism's authority, faced as it was with the twin threats of schismatic movements, in part inspired by Islamic heresies, and of Muslim polemics. According to Maimonides, "If it had not been for Saᶜadyā, the divine religion might well have almost disappeared, for he made clear its mysteries and strengthened its weak points by spreading it and supporting it by his word and pen" (*Epistle to the Yemen*, ed. A. Halkin, New York 1952, 64). In 316/928, despite his non-Babylonian origin, he was nominated as Gaʾōn or Chief Scholar of the academy at Sūraʾ (whence the name by which he is best known), and under his direction, this institution enjoyed a remarkable renaissance.

Through political intrigues in which the caliph al-Ḳāhir had to intervene, Saᶜīd Gaʾōn was deposed in 320/932, but was restored in 327/938 and functioned in the office till his death in 331/942. During the interim years of isolation, he had devoted himself to his literary work.

2. *Works*

H. Malter, Saᶜīd's biographer, listed over 200 titles, covering almost all the domains of learning cultivated at that time, such as exegesis, philosophy, philology, law, liturgy, polemics and chronology.

In the legal sphere, Saᶜīd was the first Jewish author to have composed his decisions in Arabic. He made the first attempts at codification, in the form of monographs whose structure is clearly inspired by the model of the Islamic *fatwās*.

His main work in philosophy, and the first systematic attempt at a synthesis between the philosophy of *kalām* and Jewish dogmas, was the *K. al-Amānāt wa 'l-iᶜtiḳādāt* (ed. in Arabic script S. Landauer, Leiden 1880, in Hebrew script, ed. Y. Kafih, Jerusalem 1970, Eng. tr. S. Rosenblatt, *The Book of beliefs and opinions*, New Haven 1948), written in 322/933. It had a deep influence on Jewish thought, above all in its Hebrew translation *Sefer ha-ʾemūnōt we-ha-deᶜōt*, made in 582/1186 by Yehūdāh Ibn Tibbon. Its importance only faded with the appearance of Maimonides' *Guide for the perplexed*. The arrangement of the work follows, without becoming dependent upon them in a servile fashion, the five principles (*uṣūl*) of Muᶜtazilī doctrine. Thus Saᶜīd adopted the proof of the existence of God by the contingency of the world, whilst he denied atomism, the rational basis of universal contingency according to *kalām*. His doctrine of the relations between reason and revelation and his rational justification for the dogmas of Judaism became the model for later Jewish philosophers. In it, he attacks, in particular, the Muslim theses concerning abrogation (*nas͟kh*) of the Mosaic revelation.

There are indications that Saᶜīd had presumably at his disposal the Arabic translation of the doxographical compilation *De placitis philosophorum* made by Ḳusṭā b. Lūḳā [*q.v.*]. He seems equally to have utilised the *K. al-Zahra* of his contemporary Ibn Dāwūd (d. 294/907). In his *Tafsīr Kitāb al-Mabādī* (Fr. tr. M. Lambert, *Commentaire sur le Sefer Yesira*, Paris 1891, written in 319/931, Saᶜīd, as a true *mutakallim*, was particularly interested in the problem of the origin of things.

Saᶜīd was also the author of the first translation of the Hebrew Bible into Arabic (*Tafsīr*). Each book was preceded by an Arabic preface, explaining its structure and contents. Faithful to the rationalist tendencies of the Muᶜtazila, Saᶜīd endeavoured to attenuate the anthropomorphisms. With the accompaniment of a commentary of a philosophical character, his translation became the Vulgate for Arabic-speaking Jews and served as a basis, too, for the Arabic version adopted by the Samaritans and by the Coptic Church. The first published edition, at Constantinople in 953/1546 within the polyglot Sorcino Pentateuch, was the first Arabic text to be printed in the East. The Arabic versions of the polyglot Pentateuch of Paris (1645), with the Latin translation of Gabriel Sionita, and of Walton (London 1654-7), were those of Saᶜīd.

Bibliography: I. Schwartstein, *Die arabische Interpretation des Pentateuchs von R. Saadia Hagaaon*, Frankfurt a. M. 1882; J. Guttmann, *Die Religionsphilosophie des Saadiah*, Göttingen 1882; H. and J. Dérenbourg, *Les œuvres complètes de R. Saadia*, 5 vols. (incomplete), Paris 1893-9; P. Kahle, *Die arabischen Bibelübersetzungen*, Leipzig 1904; H. Malter, *Saadia Gaon, his life and works*, Philadelphia 1921, repr. New York 1969 (exhaustive bibl.); idem, *Bibliography of the works of R. Saᶜadyah Gaʾōn*, in J.L. Fishman (ed.), *Rav Saᶜadyah Gaʾōn*, Jerusalem 1942, 571-643 + suppl. 644-57 (in Hebr.); M. Ventoura, *La philosophie de Saadia Gaon*, Paris 1934; E.I.J. Rosenthal, *Saadya studies*, Manchester 1943; *Saadiah anniversary volume*, American Acad. for Jewish Research, Texts and studies, II, New York 1943 (bibl. by A. Freimann); G. Vajda, *Etudes sur Saadia*, in *REJ*, cix (1948-9), 68-102; S. Skoss, *Saadia Gaon, the earliest Hebrew grammarian*, Philadelphia 1953; Vajda, *Saᶜadyā commentateur du "Livre de la Création"*, in *Annuaire de l'EPHE, Section des Sciences Religieuses*, Paris 1956-9; idem, *Autour de la théorie de la connaissance chez Saadia*, in *REJ*, cxxvi (1967), 135-89, 375-97; idem, in *Mélanges A. Abel*, Brussels, ii, 415-20; M. Zucker, *Rav Saadya Gaon's translation of the Torah*, New York 1959 (in Hebr., with Eng. summary); R. Ecker, *Die arabische Job Übersetzung des Gaon Saadja ben Josef*, Munich 1962; Zucker, *Saadya's commentary on Genesis*, New York 1984.

(P.-B. Fenton)

SABᶜ, SABᶜA (A.), seven, is a number of greatest importance in both the Semitic and the Iranian traditions as it combines the spiritual Three and the material Four. Its history probably begins in Babylon with the observation of four lunar phases of seven days each. The seven planets (including sun and moon) have reigned supreme in human thought since Antiquity. Each of them is connected with a specific colour, scent and character. Niẓāmī's (d. in the early 7th/13th century [*q.v.*]) Persian epic *Haft paykar* is the finest elaboration of these ideas. The imagined seven stations between the sublunar world and the transplanetary sphere served as models for the way of the seeker in almost all religions (the Mithras cult is a good example). In Islam, it found its best-known example in the seven valleys in ᶜAṭṭār's (d. in the early 7th/13th century [*q.v.*]) *Manṭiḳ al-ṭayr*. Before him, al-Nūrī (d. 294/907 [*q.v.*]) had spoken of the "city of the heart" with its seven walls. To this group of ideas belong also the 70,000 veils of light and darkness which, according to Ṣūfī thought, separate God and human beings. For the Ik͟hwān al-Ṣafāʾ [*q.v.*], divine creation reaches human kind in seven degrees through the First Intellect.

Seven was often connected with periodicity; the development of human life, especially, was thought to depend upon a seven-year rhythm. Here, the classical example is Ibn Ṭufayl's (d. 581/1185 [*q.v.*]) *Ḥayy Ibn Yaḳẓān*.

Seven plays a considerable role in early Islamic tradition: the Ḳurʾān often mentions the seven heavens, and heptads appear frequently in Sūrat Yūsuf. The *sabᶜ mat͟hānī* (sūra XV, 89) are often thought to point to the *Fātiḥa* with its seven sentences. The number of the *sawāḳiṭ al-Fātiḥa*, the letters not found in the *Fātiḥa* (which are used in magic) is again seven. Seven sūras begin with *ḥ-m*, which was later interpreted to mean *ḥabībī Muḥammad*, "My beloved Muḥammad", and the Ḳurʾān has not only seven *wud͟jūh* "aspects", but also seven canonical ways of recitation. During the *ḥad͟jd͟j* or Pilgrimage, the *ṭawāf* around the Kaᶜba has to be performed seven times, as has the running (*saᶜy*) between Ṣafā and Marwa, and Satan is stoned with three times seven stones.

Al-Buk͟hārī speaks of seven major sins, and many ritual acts, prayers and invocations should be repeated seven times in order to yield a positive result. But according to a *ḥadīt͟h*, the infidel eats "with seven stomachs."

The Seven Sleepers, mentioned in sūra XVIII, 22, may be the models for numerous groups of heptads, such as the *haft ᶜafīfa*, the seven virtuous women, who are venerated in Sind and the Pand͟jāb as a unit, or the seven protective saints in Marrakesh. In popular usage, one finds customs such as begging alms for a religious purpose from seven women called Fāṭima; in Pākistān, the material for the bridal dress is cut by seven happily-married women. In all these cases, seven points to completion, as it also does in book titles like *Haft iḳlīm* "The seven climes" or *Haft ḳulzum* "Seven oceans" (which, however, is a work on poetic rules).

Ṣūfism knows the seven *laṭāʾif*, fine spiritual points in the body, and seven major prophets are connected with them. Heptads appear in visions (see Rūmī, *Mat͟hnawī*, iii, ll. 1985 ff.). The mystical hierarchy has seven degrees, and in some Ṣūfī traditions, seven saints are sometimes called "the eyes of God." The Tīd͟jāniyya [*q.v.*] dervishes believe that the Prophet honours their meeting with his presence when a certain litany of blessings over him is repeated seven times.

In the Persian tradition, expressions with Seven abound. For Nawrūz [*q.v.*], *haft sīn* are prepared, that is 7 items (fruit, plants, etc.) whose names begin with *s*; heroic acts such as Rustam's *Haft kh^wān* appear sevenfold. Sindbād's seven journeys too belong in this category. The spheres are often called the "seven mills", Ursa Major appears as "seven thrones", *haft awrang*, and to ward off evil one may say "Be seven Ḳurʾāns (or seven mountains) between [the disaster and us]!" To do the work of seven mullās means "to achieve nothing."

Seven reigns the whole philosophy of the Ismāᶜīlīs, the Sevener Shīᶜīs [see ISMĀᶜĪLIYYA], who have developed a complicated system of heptads: seven prophets are the seven pillars of the House of Wisdom, the seventh imām in the succession of a prophet will bring the resurrection. From God's creative words "Be! and it becomes", with its seven Arabic letters (*k.n f.y.k.w.n*), are formed the principles out of which the seven primordial fountains flow. The seven prophets correspond to the seven spheres, the seven imāms in each prophetic cycle, to the seven earths. The heptagonal fountain in the Ismāᶜīlī Centre in London symbolises the structure underlying everything in Ismāᶜīlī thought in an artistic form.

Nevertheless, the number seven leads only to the goal at the end of the created universe, beyond which lies the Eight of eternal bliss—hence the *ḥadīth*, according to which Hell has seven gates, while Paradise has eight.

Bibliography: L.I. Conrad, *Seven and the* Tasbīᶜ. *On the implications of numerical symbolism for the study of medieval Islamic history*, in *JESHO*, xxxi (1988), 42-73; Hartmann-Schmitz, *Die Zahl 7 im sunnitischen Islam*, Frankfurt-Bern 1989; A. Schimmel, *The mystery of numbers*, New York 1993.

(ANNEMARIE SCHIMMEL)

SABAʾ or the Sabaeans (Greek Σαβαῖοι), the name of a folk who were bearers of a highly developed culture which flourished for over a millennium before Islam, together with three other folks, Maᶜīn, Ḳataban and Ḥaḍramawt [*q.vv.*]. The main Sabaean centre was at Maryab (later Mārib, see MAʾRIB) in Yemen with its fertile oasis on the western edge of the desert known to Arab geographers as Ṣayhad (modern Ramlat al-Sabᶜatayn). In early historical times there were also Sabaean settlements in the Wādī Adhana above the great dam which waters the oasis of Mārib, in some smaller oases to the north, and in parts of the Wādī Djawf or Wādī Madhāb. All these locations are approximately 1,000 m above sea level. The montane plains lying west of Mārib and having an average level of 2,000 m above sea level were the home of other folks who spoke the same language as the Sabaeans proper, and seem to have formed some kind of federation under the hegemony of Sabaʾ. Towards the end of the first millennium B.C., these highland folks became politically dominant in the Sabaean federation.

Our knowledge of the Sabaeans is derived principally from their own inscriptions. Modern scholarship was first made aware of these by Carsten Niebuhr, member of a Danish exploratory mission in the end of the 18th century. A sporadic number of inscriptions were published and studied during the earlier part of the 19th century, but it was Eduard Glaser's travels in the last decades of the century which produced a large number of copies (mostly squeezes) forming the real foundation of subsequent research. It must be admitted, however, that later 19th and early 20th century scholars indulged too freely in speculative deductions based on insufficient evidence. A turning point came in 1950; from then onwards, an ever more rapid archaeological activity resulting in the discovery of new texts has overturned not a few conclusions too confidently advanced by earlier researchers. At the time of writing, the flow of new material is still in full course, and it has to be anticipated that some of the presently current hypotheses may in their turn prove to be invalid. Any account that can be written at the moment must be taken as still tentative.

1. Script and language. The monumental inscriptions are drafted in a variety of South Semitic alphabet, the so-called *musnad* script [see MUSNAD. 1]. The Sabaic language, with the languages of Maᶜīn, Ḳataban and Ḥaḍramawt, forms an independent branch of Semitic, having in common one distinctive feature that is found nowhere else in Semitic: the use of suffixed *-ān* in the function of a "definite article" corresponding to the Arabic prefixed *al-*. Within this language group, Sabaic is distinguished from the other three by using *h* as prefix of the causative verb and as base of the 3rd person pronouns, where the others have a sibilant. On the southern borders of the Sabaean domain, the area between the Yisliḥ pass and Dhamār used Sabaic language, as did the non-Sabaean Radmān folk to the east thereof, in the Radāᶜ area. By the end of the 3rd century A.D. the other three languages had fallen into disuse, at least for epigraphic purposes, and the inscriptions throughout Yemen, now under Himyarite domination (see below), are in a late form of Sabaic; there are indications that the language may by this time have become a prestigious "learned" language, not in everyday use (this is comparable with the case in North Arabia, where the Nabataean inscriptions are in Aramaic, though the everyday language was probably Arabic).

The general consensus today is to assign the oldest substantial body of Sabaic inscriptions (apart from a handful of seemingly earlier examples) to the 8th century B.C. Yet it still remains not altogether easy to discount completely one point which led Pirenne to propose a dating a couple of centuries later. Inscriptions of this period have rigidly geometrical forms, subjected to strict canons of proportion, astonishingly like Greek inscriptions of the 6th-5th century, but wholly unlike any other Semitic script of that or any earlier dating. It is hard to envisage how this style can have evolved totally independently, with a time-lag of two centuries, in two adjacent cultures with ancient trade links between them. In the latter part of the first millennium B.C., the *musnad* script developed (as was the tendency in Greco-Roman inscriptions) more decorative embellishments, at first with the introduction of serifs at the ends of the strokes.

2. History. For the pre-history of Sabaʾ, that is, before the beginning of the epigraphic record, there is no evidence available as yet. Silt deposits in the Mārib oasis point to intensive agricultural exploitation by artificial irrigation going back to at least the early second millennium B.C.; but what, if any, connection there may have been between these ancient agriculturalists and the Sabaeans as we know them, is wholly obscure. Trade links between South Arabia and Mesopotamia there must have been, judging by Akkadian references to South Arabian products such as frankincense and myrrh; but the first specific mention of Sabaeans in Akkadian sources is in the 8th century B.C., when the governor of Suḫu (approximately ᶜĀna on the middle Euphrates) and Mari intercepted and plundered a caravan of folk from Taymāʾ and Sabaʾ ("whose home is far away"), seemingly for making a detour to evade transit dues in Suḫu (A.

Cavigneaux and B.K. Ismail, *Die Statthalter von Suḫu und Mari*, in *Baghdader Mitt.*, xxi [1990], 351). Two other texts, known to us for a long time and recording "gifts" made by Sabaeans to Assyrian rulers in *ca.* 715 and 685 B.C., have led some scholars to postulate a Sabaean group living close to Assyria, since "gifts" was interpreted as "tribute". In fact, it is now clear that the "gifts" were such as a trade mission would normally bring (and still do today) in order to smooth their path.

In this archaic phase, the Sabaean rulers used regnal names chosen from a total list of only six, but accompanied optionally by a cognomen chosen from a list of four; the use of these styles was exclusive to the rulers, hence a reference to an individual by these styles was sufficient to indicate ruler status. However, the inscriptions drafted as from the ruler himself commonly added the title "*mkrb* of Sabaʾ"; this term is now believed to have much the same signification as Arabic *mudjammiʿ* "unifier" (which was applied to Ḳuṣayy [*q.v.*]), possibly implying that he was head both of Sabaeans proper and of non-Sabaean elements in the federation. A few early inscriptions do contain references to "kings (*ʾmlk*) of Marib", as well as to "kings" of other small communities such as Haram, Nashḳ, etc. It remains uncertain whether or not a *mkrb* of Sabaʾ was simultaneously a "king" of Marib.

The archaic flowering of Sabaean culture lasted until some time after the middle of the first millennium B.C. The fact that through the fourth, third and second centuries B.C. the important frankincense trade was in the hands of the Maʿīn folk suggests some falling-off in Sabaean ascendancy.

The second great flowering of Sabaean culture was in the first three centuries A.D., by which time a very different political picture had emerged. The various folks of the 2,000 m highland zone played a much more dominant role; and some of their leaders, who traditionally bore the title *ḳwl* "prince" (in later Sabaic and in Arabic, *ḳayl*), founded dynasties who ruled as "king of Sabaʾ" or "king of Sabaʾ and *dhū* (lord of) Raydan". The dual title has been presumed to be the origin of the remark in the late first century A.D. Greek document known as the *Periplus* that a single ruler named Charibael was "king of two nations, Himyarites and Sabaeans", and had his residence at Ẓafār (near modern Yarim), of which the adjacent citadel is named Raydan (see ḤIMYAR). Throughout these three centuries there was a confused situation, with Sabaeans and Himyarites sometimes at war with each other, sometimes united under a single monarch as had been the case under Charibael; occasionally there appear to have been two rulers reigning simultaneously in Mārib and Ẓafār and both claiming the dual title "king of Sabaʾ and *dhu* Raydan". Somewhat oddly, the indigenous inscriptions of this period never speak of a "king" of the Himyarites; on one occasion when a king of Sabaʾ was at war with the Himyarites, he alludes to his antagonist simply as "the Raydanite" (much as a European might speak of "the Hapsburg").

In addition to the Sabaeo-Himyarite conflicts, there were wars waged by varying alliances among Sabaʾ, Ḳataban, Radman (see above) and Ḥaḍramawt, and also involving Abyssinians (Ḥabashat [*q.v.*]) settled in the Red Sea coastal region. But by the beginning of the 4th century A.D., Shammar Yurʿish, whom the Arab writers call "the first Tubbaʿ" [see TUBBAʿ] had put an end to these conflicts by eliminating Ḳataban and Ḥaḍramawt, and for the first time uniting the whole of what is today Yemen, employing the title "king of Sabaʾ and *dhu* Raydan and Ḥaḍramawt and the South (*Ymnt*)"; in the 5th century this title was further enlarged by the addition of "and their Arabs (i.e. Bedouin) in the highland and the Tihāma".

The 4th to 6th centuries A.D. are thus politically speaking a Himyarite period and do not properly belong to the history of Sabaʾ, despite the fact that what is called the Late Sabaic language continued to have great prestige value and to be employed for epigraphic purposes.

Mediaeval Arab writers have preserved for us from the Himyarite period a mass of oral traditions which contain much authentic material mingled with folklore motifs. But they knew practically nothing about the genuine history of Sabaʾ before the 4th century A.D., though they do mention the names of one or two of the most prominent individuals of the first-third centuries, notably king Ilīsharaḥ Yaḥḍib, whom they credit with the building of the famous palace of Ghumdān [*q.v.*] in Ṣanʿāʾ.

3. Religion. The religion of all four South Arabian folks down to the beginning of the 4th century A.D. was a polytheistic paganism. Though it is probable that this may have survived among the peasantry and in remoter parts of the kingdom through the 4th to the 6th centuries, the upper classes, who are the authors of our inscriptional material, went over to some form of monotheistic creed, a cult of "the Merciful (*Rḥmn-n*), the Lord of Heaven", which could perhaps best be described as "Ḥanafite" [see ḤANĪF] since it is devoid of explicit marks of either Judaism or Christianity. At the same time, already from the end of the 4th century, a few explicitly Jewish texts attest an influential Jewish presence, and in the 6th century under Abraha [*q.v.*] Christianity prevailed.

For the period down to the early 4th century A.D., few would now agree with the excessive reductionism of D. Nielsen, who in the 1920s held that all the many deities in the pagan pantheon were nothing more than varying manifestations of an astral triad of sun, moon and Venus-star; yet it is certainly the case that three deities tend to receive more frequent mention than the rest. The first, in the sense that his cult is found among all four of the South Arabian folks and that in invocations of several deities his name normally comes first, is ʿAthtar, a male counterpart of north Semitic Ishtar/ʿAshtoreth/Astarte. He is often qualified by the epithet "eastern" and occasionally by the complementary one "western", which tends to support the commonly accepted identification of him with the planet Venus, regarded as "morning star" and "evening star".

But just as the Greek local patron deities such as Athene in Athens, Artemis in Ephesus, etc., figure more prominently than the remoter and universal Zeus, so in South Arabia the most commonly invoked deity was a national one, who incorporated the sense of national identity. For the Sabaeans this was *ʾlmḳh* (with an occasional variant spelling *ʾlmḳhw*). A probable analysis of this name is as a compound of the old Semitic word *ʾl* "god" and a derivative of the root *ḳhw* meaning something like "fertility" (cf. Arabic *ḳahā* "flourish"); the *h* is certainly a root letter, and not, as some mediaeval writers seem to have imagined, a *tāʾ marbūṭa*, which in South Arabian is always spelt with *t*. The "federal" significance of this deity appears notably in the fact that at the shrine on Djabal Riyām (Arḥab) the worshippers of the local folk-deity Taʾlab were instructed that they must not omit to make an annual pilgrimage to *ʾlmḳh* in Mārib.

Many European scholars still refer to this deity in a simplicistic way as "the moon god", a notion stemming from the "triadic" hypothesis mentioned above;

yet Garbini has produced cogent arguments to show that the attributes of *ʾlmḳh* are rather those of a warrior-deity like Greek Herakles or a vegetation god like Dionysus. (The remarks made in the art. ḲATABĀN on this topic as it affects the situation in Ḳataban went to press before Garbini's article had appeared; they now need modifying in the light of that article.)

Nevertheless, the moon certainly had much religious significance. A very common symbol engraved on altars and religious buildings shows a crescent embracing a disc. It is presumably this symbol that the Muslim writers had in mind when they say that the first act of the day for an ancient Yemeni king was to "bow down to the images of the sun and moon". This is not to say, of course, that they were right in seeing the disc as representing the sun; some modern scholars have been inclined to think it represents the planet Venus.

The place occupied by the sun in the pantheon is not easy to assess. The Radman folk had as their national patron-deity *s²ms¹ ʿlyt* "Lofty Sun", and elsewhere there are mentions simply of "Sun" without qualification. But it is dubious whether the majority belief is justified, that numerous references to a feminine deity described simply as "She-who-is-possessed of (*dhāt*)" a certain quality, are necessarily to a solar goddess (too often, the interpretation proposed for the term describing the quality has been dictated by the preconception that it must be a quality of the sun).

Certain of the ancient religious practices have a special interests in that they have survived in some form or another until the present day. Worth mentioning are the communal pilgrimages (*ziyārāt*) on prescribed days; a code of ritual purity (see Ryckmans); and a ritualised hunting of the ibex, thought of as connected with the divine blessing of rain (Ryckmans and Serjeant).

4. Sabaʾ in Bible and Ḳurʾān. The visit of the Queen of Sheba to king Solomon, and the abundant accretions of legend around it [see BILḲĪS], have been too extensively discussed to need mention here, except for the remark that there is a possibility that such a visit might have been associated with a trade mission, like the missions to the Assyrian kings (see above). In the Ḳurʾānic allusion (XXVII, 27 ff.) the name Sabaʾ does not occur; she is simply "the queen of the south". But Sabaʾ does feature in a passage (XXXIV, 15-16) which is one of those where the fate of ancient peoples is mentioned as a warning against worldly pride. The prosperity of the Mārib oasis (situated on each side of the wadi bed, hence "the garden of the left" and "the garden of the right") had been dependent on the maintenance of the great dam in good order; after the death of king Abraha the political fabric that had made repairs possible crumbled, the irrigation system was destroyed and the oasis was devastated.

5. Sabaeans in Africa. Around the middle of the first millennium B.C., there were Sabaeans also in the Horn of Africa, in the area that later became the realm of Aksum (Eritrea). The evidence consists of only a scanty number of inscriptions, which, however, make it clear that we have to do with genuine Sabaeans, holding to the national cult of *ʾlmḳh*. They were mixed up with various non-Sabaean communities, and it is still much in dispute how one can envisage the actual demographic (and political) situation. There are five places in the Bible where the writer distinguishes Sheba (שבא) son of Yoḳṭan (who appears in the Arab genealogies as Ḳaḥṭān [*q.v.*]), i.e. the Yemenite Sabaeans, from Seba (סבא) son of Kush, implying an African habitat. This spelling differentiation, however, may be purely factitious; at all events the indigenous inscriptions make no such difference, and both Yemenite and African Sabaeans are there spelt in exactly the same way.

Bibliography: M.A. Bafaqih, *L'Unification du Yémen antique*, Paris 1990; A.F.L. Beeston, *Habashat and Ahabish*, in *Proc. Seminar for Arabian St.*, xvii (1987), 5-7; G. Garbini, *Il dio sabeo Almaqah*, in *RSO*, xlviii (1974), 15-22; *The Periplus Maris Erythraei*, text, tr. and comm. by L. Casson, Princeton 1989; J. Pirenne, *La Grèce et Saba*, in *Mém. Acad. des Inscr.*, xv, Paris 1955, 88-196; idem, *Paléographie des inscriptions sud-arabes*, in *Verh. van de koninklijke Vlaamse akademie, kl. der lett.*, xxvi, Brussel 1956; R.B. Serjeant, *The South Arabian hunt*, London 1976; J. Ryckmans, *Les confessions publiques sabéennes, le code sud-arabe de pureté rituelle*, in *AION*, xxxii (1972), 1-15; idem, *La chasse rituelle dans l'Arabie du sud ancienne*, in *Al-Bahit, Festschr. J. Henninger (Studia Inst. Anthropos, 28)*, St Augustin bei Bonn 1976, 259-308; C. Robin, *Les hautes terres du nord-Yémen avant l'Islam*, 2 vols. (*Uitg. van het nederl. hist.-arch. inst. te Istanbul*), Istanbul 1982; H. von Wissmann, *Zur Geschichte und Landeskunde von Alt-Südarabien,* in *Österr. Akad. d. Wiss., philos.-hist. Kl., Sitzungsber.* 246, Wien 1964; idem, *Geschichte von Saba II: das Grossreich der Sabäer*, in *ibid.* 402, Wien 1982.

(A.F.L. BEESTON)

ṢABĀ, FATḤ ʿALĪ KHĀN, Persian poet, was born in Kāshān, probably in 1179/1765, and died in 1238/1822-3. His people belonged originally to Ādharbaydjān, and came from the Dunbalī stock, a tribe of Kurds settled in the region of Khūy. Members of his family held jobs as governors and administrators under the Zand and Ḳādjār rulers. His father, Āḳā Muḥammad, was governor of Kāshān under the Zands, and his eldest brother, Muḥammad ʿAlī Khān, was minister to the Zand ruler Luṭf ʿAlī Khān (*r.* 1203-9/1789-94). Ṣabā also seems to have been identified with this monarch, and is reported to have composed poems in his praise. When Luṭf ʿAlī Khān fled from Kirmān in 1208/1794 from the Ḳādjārs, Ṣabā's brother was captured and put to death by the orders of Āghā Muḥammad Shāh (*r.* 1193-1212/1779-97 [*q.v.*]), founder of the Ḳādjār régime. Following this tragedy, the poet wandered from place to place in fear of his life until he was fortunate to find refuge with Fatḥ ʿAlī Khān (afterwards Fatḥ ʿAlī Shāh, *r.* 1212-50/1797-1834 [*q.v.*]), who was governor-general of Fārs at that time. Ṣabā transferred his allegiance to the Ḳādjārs, and reportedly destroyed the *dīwān* which contained poems composed by him in praise of his former patrons, the Zands.

In 1212/1797, on the occasion of Fatḥ ʿAlī Shāh's accession to the throne, Ṣabā presented a *ḳaṣīda* which was well received by the new ruler. His fortunes prospered until he was appointed poet-laureate at the court. For some time he was also governor of Ḳum and Kāshān, and held the honorary title of Iḥtisāb al-Mamālik ("Censor of the Provinces"). Eventually, however, he abandoned his administrative assignments to remain permanently at the court. He accompanied the monarch on his various travels and campaigns. It was during one of these campaigns in 1228/1813, involving Persia's hostilities with Russia, that Ṣabā, at the behest of the Shāh, undertook the composition of his long epic poem, *Shāhanshāh-nāma* ("Book of the King of Kings").

Ṣabā died in 1238/1822-3 in Tehran. His eldest son, Mīrzā Ḥusayn Khān (d. *ca.* 1264/1848), who used ᶜAndalīb as his pen-name, succeeded him as Fatḥ ᶜAlī Shāh's poet-laureate, and continued in that position during Muḥammad Shāh's reign (1250-64/1834-48 [*q.v.*]) as well. Ṣabā's family occupies a distinctive place in the history of 19th century Persian literature insofar as some of its members were leading literary figures of the Ḳādjār period. These included, in addition to Ḥusayn Khān ᶜAndalīb, Ṣabā's youngest son, Abu 'l-Ḳāsim Furūgh (d. 1290/1873), his nephew, Aḥmad Khan Ṣabūr (d. 1228/1813), and his grandson, Maḥmūd Khān (d. 1311/1893), the last-named being the poet-laureate of Nāṣir al-Dīn Shāh (*r.* 1264-1313/1848-96 [*q.v.*]).

Ṣabā was generous and helpful towards his fellow-writers. He often used his influence at the court to assist his literary colleagues in their professional needs. One of those benefiting from his good offices was the author Fāḍil Khān Garrūsī (b. 1196/1781-2, d. 1254/1838-9), who was officially commissioned, on Ṣabā's recommendation, to write a history of poets, later named by him as *Andjuman-i Khāḳān* ("Assembly of the Emperor").

Ṣabā was a prolific poet. In his youth he took his poetic training under Ḥādjdjī Sulaymān Ṣabāḥī (d. 1218/1803-4), who was his fellow-townsman. Ṣabā's verse output consists predominantly of *ḳaṣīdas* and *mathnawīs*. His poetic skill finds its characteristic expression in his panegyrics, of which those in praise of Fatḥ ᶜAlī Shāh and other dignitaries occupy a prominent place. Together with *Shāhanshāh-nāma*, cited earlier, his better-known *mathnawīs* include *Khudāwand-nāma* ("Book of the Lord"), *ᶜIbrat-nāma* ("Book of warning"), and *Gulshan-i Ṣabā* ("The rose-garden of Ṣabā"). *Shāhanshāh-nāma*, a poem containing some 40,000 couplets, which the poet claims to have composed in three years, is patterned after Firdawsī's *Shāh-nāma*, and describes chiefly the events of Fatḥ ᶜAlī Shāh's reign. *Khudāwand-nāma*, another lengthy poem of nearly 25,000 couplets, deals with the history and miracles of the Prophet Muḥammad and with the battles fought by his cousin and son-in-law, ᶜAlī. The third *mathnawī, ᶜIbrat-nāma*, is a poem denouncing some unnamed individuals, identified only as Jews, who were allegedly sowing mischief in the kingdom. The last-named *mathnawī, Gulshan-i Ṣabā*, contains counsels addressed to the author's son, Mīrzā Ḥusayn Khān ᶜAndalīb, and ends with a eulogy in praise of Fatḥ ᶜAlī Shāh and his family. Composed probably when Ṣabā was in his mid-forties, it represents one of the best works of the poet. In the simplicity of its expression, it presents a marked contrast to much of Ṣabā's poetry, which suffers from a frequent use of quaint and unfamiliar words and phrases.

Many contemporary and later writers have showered rich praise upon Ṣabā and his works. According to Riḍā-ḳulī Khān Hidāyat [*q.v.*], no poet equal to him had appeared in Persia for some seven hundred years. Comments such as these are of course a gross exaggeration of the truth, and do not merit serious consideration. The subject-matter of the poet is limited in its appeal and his style tends to be laboured and heavy. Ṣabā's chief contribution perhaps lies in the fact that he played a major role in the Persian poetic revival (*bāzgasht*), which began in the 12th/18th century and was directed towards a return to earlier native models in contrast to the Indian style (*sabk-i Hindī* [*q.v.*]) favoured by Persian poets of the preceding two centuries.

Bibliography: Fatḥ ᶜAlī Khān Ṣabā, *Dīwān-i ashᶜār-i Malik al-Shuᶜarāʾ Fatḥ ᶜAlī Khān Ṣabā*, ed. Muḥammad ᶜAlī Nadjātī, Tehran 1341/1962; Riḍā-ḳulī Khān Hidāyat, *Madjmaᶜ al-fuṣaḥāʾ*, ii/2, ed. Maẓāhir Muṣaffā, Tehran 1340/1961; idem, *Riyāḍ al-ᶜārifīn*, ed. Mihr ᶜAlī Gurgānī, Tehran 1344/1965; idem, Supplement to Mīr Khʷānd's *Rawḍat al-ṣafāʾ*, x, Ḳum 1339/1960; ᶜAbd al-Razzāḳ Dunbalī Maftūn, *Nigāristān-i Dārā*, i, ed. Khayyām-pūr, Tabrīz 1342/1963; Aḥmad b. Abi 'l-Ḥasan Shīrāzī (Dīwān Begī), *Ḥadīḳat al-shuᶜarāʾ*, ii, ed. ᶜAbd al-Ḥusayn Nawāʾī, Tehran 1365/1986; Muḥammad Taḳī Bahār, *Fatḥ ᶜAlī Khan Ṣabā*, in *Bahār wa adab-i Fārsī*, i, ed. Muḥammad Gulbun, Tehran 1351/1972; idem, *Lāmiyya-yi Fatḥ ᶜAlī Khān Ṣabā*, in *ibid.*; Browne, *LHP*, iv; *Fihrist-i Kitāb-khāna-yi Madjlis-i Shūrā-yi Millī*, iii, nos. 1013 and 1014, Tehran 1318-21/1939-42; Riḍā-zāda Shafaḳ, *Tārīkh-i adabiyyāt-i Īrān*, Tehran 1321/1942; Muḥammad ᶜAlī Tabrīzī (Mudarris), *Rayḥānat al-adab*, ii, Tabrīz 1327/1948; Muḥammad ᶜAlī Muᶜallim Ḥabībābādī, *Makārim al-āthār*, iv, Iṣfahān 1352/1973; Ḥādjdjī Ḥusayn Nakhdjawānī, *Zindaganī wa shakhṣiyyat-i Malik al-Shuᶜarā' Fatḥ ᶜAlī Khān Ṣabā*, in *Nashriyya-yi Dānishkada-yi Adabiyyāt-i Tabrīz*, iii (1329/1950); *Lughat-nāma-yi ᶜAlī Akbar Dihkhudā*, xvii/2, Tehran 1335/1956; Dhabīḥ Allāh Ṣafā, *Ḥamāsa-sarāyī dar Īrān*, Tehran 1363/1984; J. Rypka *et alii*, *History of Iranian literature*, Dordrecht 1968; Yaḥyā Āryanpūr, *Az Ṣabā tā Nīmā*, i, Tehran 1350/1971; Humā Nāṭiḳ, *Az Ṣabā tā Ḥādjdjī Bābā*, in *Az māst ki bar māst*, Tehran 1354/1975; ᶜAbd al-Rafīᶜ Ḥaḳīḳat (Rafīᶜ), *Farhang-i shāᶜirān-i zabān-i Pārsī*, Tehran 1368/1990. (MUNIBUR RAHMAN)

SABAB (A.), pl. *asbāb*, literally "rope" (*ḥabl*), the basic sense as given by the lexicographers (cf. *LᶜA*), coming to designate anything which binds or connects. It is "anything by means of which one gains an end (*maḳṣūd*; al-Djurdjānī) or an object sought" (*maṭlūb*; in the *Baḥr al-djawāhir*). One can mention *asbāb* with the sense of "bonds" in Ḳurʾān, II, 166: "When the bonds [which unite them] are broken...". Ibn ᶜAbbās interpreted this as friendship (*mawadda*); Mudjāhid, "alliance" (*tawāṣul*) in this context. The sense is also found of "a means of achieving s. th.". Ibn Manẓūr cites the expression "I made such a thing into a means of obtaining what I needed"; here, *sabab* is a synonym of *wadadj* "a means of arriving at s. th.". From this arises the sense of "way of access", found in the Ḳurʾān: the way which leads to the heavens (*asbāb al-samawāt*), and the use of the term in philosophy in the expression *asbāb al-ᶜilm* ("the ways of knowledge"; cf. Gardet and Anawati, *Introduction à la théologie musulmane*, 66, 375). From this same point of view, *asbāb* has assumed the sense of "means of subsistence".

1. In philosophy and medical science.

The *ḥukamāʾ* use the term as a synonym of *ᶜilla* (one may consult ᶜILLA, which deals with both terms in *falsafa* and *kalām*). Al-Tahānawī gives in his *Iṣṭilāḥāt*, following the *Baḥr al-djawāhir*, an interesting general presentation. The *sabab* is also called *mabdaʾ* "principle"; it is "that which a thing needs, whether in its quiddity or in its existence ... It is either complete (*tāmm*: this is the divine causality in its perfect unity) or else incomplete (*nāḳiṣ*), and is then divided into four types (these are the causes in the physical and metaphysical sense). The cause may be interior to the thing, and if the thing is with it potentially, it is the material cause (*sabab māddī*). If it is in activity, it is the formal cause (*sabab ṣūrī*). Or if it is not interior to the thing, then it has an effect on its existence; it is the efficient cause (*sabab fāᶜilī*). If it has an effect on the efficience of its efficient cause (*fī fāᶜiliyyat fāᶜilihi*), it is the final cause (*sabab ghāʾī*). One should note that this i he way Ibn Sīnā defines the final cause (cf. *Ishārāt*, d. Sulaymān Dunyā, iii, 444-5, with the comm. of Naṣīr al-Dīn Ṭūsī). If the efficacious action of the ause (*taʿaddī al-sabab*) is constant (*dāʾimī*) or present in he greater number of cases (*akthārī*, cf. Aristotle, τὸ πὶ τὸ πολύ), the cause is termed essential (*sabab dhātī*) nd the effect caused (*musabbab*) the essential end *ghāya dhātiyya*). If there is efficacity in the smallest umber of cases equal to that where it does not occur *taʿaddī aḳallī aw musāwī*), this cause is said to be acidental (*sabab ittifāḳī*), and the effect which is caused s termed the accidental end. It has been said that if ll the conditions of efficacity combine, the cause is ssential and the end essential. If not, the efficacity is mpossible and there is no accidental cause. To put it nother way, every cause, as such, has a necessary efect as soon as all the conditions for its action are rought together; if not, it has no action at all and the ower which essentially constitutes it as a cause renains without effect. Accordingly, there is no acidental cause.

One may reply to this that, amongst its conditions, verything which gives in reality its efficacity to the ction of the cause, is taken into account as part of the ause; but one must also take into account the factors vhich are not part of it, such as the absence of any bstacle (*intifāʾ al-māniʿ*) and the disposition of an obect to receive the action of a cause (*istiʿdād al-ḳābil*). Now when these two latter conditions can be equally ealised or not realised, the causality of the cause ecomes accidental there where it exerts its effect. Let s take an example. Fire burns by its essence; but it vill not burn a combustible matter which is damp here the dampness constitutes an obstacle) or an inombustible matter (which is incapable of receiving he action of fire). Consequently, if there are as many hances that the matter is or is not made up of dry vood, and if it happens that it is in fact dry wood, the ire burns, but accidentally, since it is accidental that lry wood is involved.

Physicians use the word *sabab* in a more particular ense than the philosophers. For them, it denoted iniquely the efficient cause, and even, not every effiient cause but exclusively those which have an effect vithin the human body, whether they produce illesses or restore health or preserve health. They are ither of a corporeal nature, and are then either ubstances like food or medicines, or they are acidents, such as heat and cold. They also distinguish he *asbāb* which are internal to the body, like the emperament and the humours; those which are exteral, like warm air; and those which are of a psychical ature (*min al-umūr al-nafsāniyya*), like anger.

Finally, in Ḳurʾānic exegesis one should undertand the expression *asbāb al-nuzūl* in a sense nalogical to its legal sense (see 2. below): the reasons r circumstances which explain the revelation of such r such a verse, and to which certain commentators ppeal in their quest for a rational form of exegesis see Gardet and Anawati, *op. cit.*, 29-30).

Bibliography: Given in the article.

(R. Arnaldez)

2. In law.

Here, *sabab* is defined as the designation given by he law maker for an injunction (*ḥukm*). The *sabab* tself may not be the actual cause but merely serves as mark (*ʿalāma*) to indicate that a certain *ḥukm* should pply. The classic example is found in the case of ravelling as permitting the breaking of fasting during Ramaḍān. The main difference between *sabab* and *illa*, when considering *ḳiyās*, is marginal in practice, ince *ʿilla* is merely a subdivision of *sabab*. *ʿIlla* is also termed *sabab munāsib*, a *sabab* which can be understood by human reasoning. Travelling is therefore described as both *ʿilla* and *sabab* in regard to permitting breaking of the fast during Ramaḍān since, by the application of reason, it is apparent that the objective is to reduce hardship. However, since there is no rational explanation why Ramaḍān has been prescribed for fasting, it is therefore *sabab* but not *ʿilla*.

The schools of *fiḳh* are divided in their opinions about *sabab*. The Shāfiʿī and Ḥanafī ones, like the modern Germanic school of law, concentrate on the apparent will. By contrast, the Mālikī and Ḥanbalī schools and the Shīʿa focus on the actual intention, a tendency similar to that in Roman law. In contemporary Islamic civil application, the importance of *sabab* can perhaps be well understood from the UAE Civil Code definition of it as "the direct purpose aimed at by the contract".

Bibliography: ʿAbd al-Razzāḳ al-Sanhūrī, *al-Wasīṭ fī sharḥ al-ḳānūn al-madanī*, Beirut 1952, i, 1314-15; Shāṭibī, *al-Muwāfaḳāt*, ed. A. Drāz, Beirut n.d., i, 187-262; Wahba al-Zuḥaylī, *al-Fiḳh al-islāmī wa-adillatuhu*, Damascus 1985, iv, 185-6; S.E. Rayner, *The theory of contracts in Islamic law*, London 1991, 132-3.

(M.Y. Izzi Dien)

3. In prosody [see also ʿarūḍ].

Here, *sabab*, lit. "tent rope", and *watid*, lit. "tent peg", denote the two smallest metrically meaningful elements which serve as building-blocks for the feet (*adjzāʾ*, sing. *djuzʾ*). Following the established tent-verse analogy of the *bayt*, the inventor of prosody, al-Khalīl [*q.v.*], coined these terms to characterise the variable (*sabab*) and the stable elements (*watid*) within each foot. The *sabab* consists of two letters/consonants (the *watid* of three), of which the second may be either vowelless or vowelled, resulting in the two subtypes of the *sabab khafīf*, "the light cord", and the *sabab thaḳīl*, "the heavy cord." Syllabically speaking, the light cord is one long syllable (e.g. *ḳad*), the heavy cord two short ones (e.g. *laka*). A foot consists of one *watid* and either one or two *sababs*. The "heavy cord" exists only in conjunction with a "light cord" to form the feet *mutafāʿilun* and *mufāʿalatun*, from which the metres *kāmil* and *wāfir* are constructed. The combination of "heavy cord" and "light cord" (*muta-fā-* and *-ʿalatun*, respectively, i.e. ◡◡–) is also covered by the metrical term *fāṣila* (more precisely *fāṣila ṣughrā*), which seems to go back to al-Khalīl also. Since neither this term nor the *fāṣila kubrā* (◡◡◡–) is useful for the system, because both can be interpreted in terms of *sabab* and *watid*, they are best seen as elements used in the analysis of the really existing metres (*awzān*) rather than the abstract ideal metres (*buḥūr*) of the system. Breaking the *fāṣila ṣughrā* up into two *sababs* allowed for a unified definition of the *ziḥāf* as a deviation from the ideal norm that befalls the second letter of a *sabab* (Stoetzer, 42-3). The *ziḥāfāt*, usually elisions, are characteristic of the *sabab*; they may change from one line to the next.

Some Persian prosodists introduce as a third type of *sabab* the *sabab-i mutawassiṭ*, consisting of an overlong syllable (e.g. *yār*) (Elwell-Sutton, 9; Khānlarī, 94, n. 2, quoting the *Durra-yi Nadjafī* of Nadjafḳulī Mīrzā Muʿizzī).

Bibliography: W. Stoetzer, *Theory and practice in Arabic metrics*, Leiden 1989, index; see also the bibliographies in ʿarūḍ, and in *Grundriss der Arabischen Philologie,* Bd. II, *Literaturwissenschaft*, Wiesbaden 1987, 205-7 (W. Heinrichs); and the additions in Bd. III, *Supplement*, Wiesbaden 1992, 276 (R. Weipert); for a clear presentation of the *ziḥāfāt* in the form of tables, see L.P. Elwell-Sutton, *The*

Persian metres, Cambridge 1976, 16-38; P.N. Khānlarī, *Wazn-i shiᶜr-i fārsī*, Tehran 1345 sh./1966.
(W.P. Heinrichs)

4. In grammar.

The term is used by Sībawayhi in his *Kitāb* 39 times (Troupeau, *Lexique-Index* s.v.) to denote a "semantic link" between words that brings about a change in the expected case ending. Thus alongside *zayd^{un} laḳītu akhāhu* we find *zayd^{an}laḳītu akhāhu*, where the dependent (*manṣūb*) form of *zayd^{an}* is acceptable because it is "semantically linked" with *akhāhu* (*min sababihi*, *Kitāb*, i, Der. 32/Būl. 43). In this way, Sībawayhi acounts for a variety of inflectional problems, particularly concord, the most familiar being the attraction of *ḥasan^{un}* to *ḥasan^{in}* in *marartu bi-radjul^{in} ḥasan^{in} abūhu* due to the *sabab* between *radjul^{in}* and *abūhu* (*ibid.*, i, 195/228). The "semantic link" is always realised by a bound pronoun, either suffixed (as in *akhāhu, abūhu*, above) or concealed, as in *anta fa-nẓur*, with *anta* assigned the same case as the concealed agent pronoun of *unẓur* because of the *sabab* between them (*ibid.*, i, 59/71). This pronoun is obligatory: in **mā zayd^{un} munṭaliḳ^{an} abū ᶜamrin* it is not enough to know that Abū ᶜAmr really is Zayd's father—without the pronoun this expression is disallowed, contrast *mā zayd^{un} munṭaliḳ^{an} abūhu* (*ibid.*, i, 24/31). In addition to the direct *sabab*, Sībawayhi recognised an indirect link which he calls *iltibās* "involvement", e.g. *marartu bi-radjul^{in} mukhāliṭihi dā^{ʾun}* (*ibid.*, i, 193/226; here the suffixed pronoun has moved from *dā^{ʾun}* to its predicate *mukhāliṭihi*) and, one stage more remote, "involvement with something semantically linked", e.g. *marartu bi-radjul^{in} mukhāliṭ^{in} abāhu dā^{ʾun}* (see Mosel, 297). Subsequently, *sabab* was largely dropped from grammatical theory and replaced by other explanations or synonyms. By the time of Ibn al-Sarrādj (d. 316/929, *Mūdjaz*, 62), it is virtually restricted to the adjectival structure *marartu bi radjul^{in} ḥasan^{in} abūhu*, later commonly termed the *naᶜt sababī*.

Bibliography: Sībawayhi, *Kitāb*, ed. H. Derenbourg, Paris 1881-9, ed. Būlāḳ, 1898-1900; Abū Bakr Muḥammad b. al-Sarrādj, *al-Mūdjaz fī 'l-naḥw*, ed. Moustafa El-Chouémi [Muṣṭafā 'l-Shuʾaymī] and Bensalem Damerdji [Bin Sālim al-Dāmirdjī], Beirut 1385/1965; U. Mosel, *Die syntaktische Terminologie bei Sībawaih*, diss. Univ. of Munich 1975; G. Troupeau, *Lexique-index du Kitāb de Sībawayhi*, Paris 1976; M. G. Carter, *The term* sabab *in Arabic grammar*, in *Zeitschr. für Arabische Linguistik*, xv (1985), 53-66. (M.G. Carter)

SABAH, a state consisting of over 29,000 square miles of territory on the northern coast of the island of Borneo and a constituent part of Malaysia since 1963. Formerly it was known as North Borneo (1877-8 to 1946) and was governed by the British North Borneo Company (incorporated by Royal Charter in 1881) by virtue of agreements between the Company and the Sultans of Brunei [*q.v.* in Suppl.] and Sulu [*q.v.*]. In July 1946 the Company transferred all its rights to Britain and the territory became a Crown Colony which lasted until 1963 when Sabah joined the Federation of Malaysia.

The Muslim population is a small percentage of the total (3%-4%), but increasing as a result of an aggressive *dakwah* programme. They are predominantly coastal dwellers (Bajaus and Bruneis), living in the major river towns where the language is Malay and Samal. Historically Islam has always had a presence in the area, at least from the 17th century, and the pre-modern history of Sabah is part of the history of Brunei and Sulu.

It is in the period from the late 19th century to the present that the historical record for Islam begins and it has three main features which, together, define the modern form of the religion.

First, the international aspect. The reference here is to the treaties between the Sultans of Brunei and Sulu with the British, as to the transfer of territory and sovereignty to the latter. They are examples of the late 19th century practice of international relations involving Muslim sovereigns and the modern European *imperium* in the East. Sovereignty was undoubtedly transferred from the European point of view but not necessarily from the Muslim. State practice on either side was not strictly comparable, and the misunderstandings of the 1880s continue to give rise to inter-state dispute in modern Southeast Asia, in this case between the Philippines and Malaysia.

Second, from the point of view of the colonial power, Islam was but one of a number of "native" religions and laws. From this perspective it had no status in state sovereignty or the definition of the state. The *sharīᶜa* came to be reduced in status and restricted to basic provisions on family matters and sexual misconduct. The line between *sharīᶜa* and *adat* or *ᶜāda* [*q.v.*] was typically blurred.

Third, from the transfer to the Federation of Malaysia in 1963, Islam gained an immediate political presence and its status was no longer that of "native belief" and law but instead became an important defining element in public and social life. Now, legislation has been introduced to implement the *sharīᶜa*, to encourage education in Islam, to distribute funds for religious purposes and, in general, to make Islam an essential element in the Malaysian polity.

Bibliography: S. Jayakumar, *The Philippine claim to Sabah and international law*, in *Malaya Law Review*, x (1968); L.R. Wright, *The origins of British Borneo*, Hong Kong 1970; J.P. Ongkili, *Pre-Western Brunei, Sarawak and Sabah*, in *Sarawak Museum Journal*, N.S. xx/40-1 (1972); M.B. Hooker, *Native law in Sabah and Sarawak*, Singapore 1980; Anwar Sullivan and Cecilia Leong (eds.), *Commemorative history of Sabah 1881-1981*, Sabah State Govt. 1981; M.B. Hooker, *Islamic law in South-East Asia*, Singapore 1984.
(Virginia Matheson Hooker)

ṢABĀḤ, ĀL, Arabian dynasty from the ᶜUtūb branch of the ᶜAnaza tribe, rulers of al-Kuwayt [*q.v.*] from *ca.* 1165/1752 until the present. They presided over its development from a small port dependent on pearling, fishing and the transit trade with India to its current position as an independent, oil-rich state.

Āl Ṣabāḥ originated in Nadjd and migrated with other members of the ᶜUtūb to Ḳaṭar [*q.v.*] in about 1085/1674 and then to al-Kuwayt early in the 12th/18th century. The rise to power of the founder of the dynasty, Ṣabāḥ I (*ca.* 1165-71/1752-6), remains obscure. His claim to authority was of a civil nature, not based on descent from the Prophet or any role as a religious leader, and he does not seem to have imposed it by force but by agreement with other sections of the ᶜUtbī community. During the late 12th-13th/18th-19th centuries, Āl Ṣabāḥ managed to maintain their political authority with the internal support of local tribesmen and merchants. They also succeeded for the most part in achieving a delicate balance in handling their relations with those external forces who could have swept them from power, namely the Ottomans, the British and the Suᶜūdī-led Wahhābīs. Moreover, the succession proceeded relatively smoothly, ensuring family cohesion and stability.

The exception to this pattern was the dynamic figure of Mubārak (1313-34/1896-1915), who came to power by assassinating two of his brothers, Muḥam ıad I (1310-13/1892-6) and Djarrāḥ. Despite Otɔman suspicions of British involvement in the coup nd Mubārak's concern to achieve British protection, : was not until 1316/1899 that an agreement was signɘd, excluding other foreign powers from acquiring ⁽uwaytī territory by lease or purchase and preventing heir representatives from being received in al-⁽uwayt without British approval. In an accompanyng letter, Mubārak was assured of "the good offices f the British Government". This close association ⁄ith Britain proved valuable in maintaining al-⁽uwayt's independence in the face of Ottoman ressures, especially during World War I, and it may ılso be seen as offering conditions promoting comnercial development and modernisation. However, it estricted Mubārak in his dealings with his Arabian eighbours, the Āl Rashīd [*q.v.*] of Djabal Shammar nd ᶜAbd al-ᶜAzīz b. Suᶜūd [*q.v.*], effectively preventng any Kuwaytī territorial expansion at their exense; early in the reign of Aḥmad I (1339-69/1921-0), it even led to territory being ceded to the Suᶜūdīs.

Following a period of recession with the decline of he pearling industry and economic warfare with Ibn ɔuᶜūd, al-Kuwayt won a reprieve with the discovery ɔf oil in 1356/1938. Exports began on 30 Radjab 365/30 June 1946, ushering in a new era of prosperty, especially after the accession of ᶜAbd Allāh III 1369-85/1950-65). ᶜAbd Allāh oversaw the creation ɔf al-Kuwayt's modern infrastructure, initiating amitious construction projects, a comprehensive welfare tate, extensive education and health facilities. He ılso ended the 1316/1899 Anglo-Kuwaytī agreement, which was increasingly resented, asserting al-Kuwayt's full independence as a sovereign state on 6 Muḥarram 1381/19 June 1961. Immediately, he was hreatened with invasion by al-ᶜIrāḳ, laying claim to sovereignty over al-Kuwayt, but on this occasion Briain's prompt action in sending forces to the border deterred the ᶜIrāḳīs from invading. The present ruler, Djābir III (1398-/1977-) was less fortunate when on 10 Muḥarram 1411/2 August 1990 he was faced with an actual ᶜIrāḳī invasion, resulting in the occupation ɔf his country and his exile in Suᶜūdī Arabia until after the liberation of al-Kuwayt in the Gulf War of Radjab-Shaᶜbān 1411/January-February 1991.

Bibliography: An authoritative genealogical study is A. Rush, *Al Sabah: history and genealogy of Kuwait's ruling family 1752-1987*, London and Atlantic Highlands 1987. See also B.C. Busch, *Britain and the Persian Gulf 1894-1914*, Berkeley 1967; G. Troeller, *The birth of Saudi Arabia: Britain and the rise of the house of Saᶜud*, London 1976; A.M. Abu-Hakima, *The modern history of Kuwait 1750-1965*, London 1983; Rosemary Said Zahlan, *The making of the modern Gulf states*, London 1989.

(Elizabeth M. Sirriyeh)

ṢABĀḤ al-DĪN ("Prens" Sabahattin) (1877-1948), late Ottoman political theorist. Ṣabāḥ al-Dīn was born in Istanbul, the elder son of *Dāmād* (imperial son-in-law) Maḥmūd Djelāl al-Dīn Pasha. His mother was Senīḥa Sulṭān, a younger sister of Sultan ᶜAbd al-Hamīd II. He was educated privately.

When his father fled to Paris in 1899, Ṣabāḥ al-Dīn and his younger brother Luṭf Allāh accompanied him. Ṣabāḥ al-Dīn came to the fore as one of the leading Young Turk emigré publicists and politicians. Backed by his father's wealth, he soon became a serious competitor of Aḥmed Riḍā for the leadership of the Young Turk movement. In 1902 he took the initiative in bringing together the first "Congress of Ottoman Liberals" in Paris, where his group, that of Aḥmed Riḍā, but also Armenian, Albanian and Arab delegations met. At the congress a split occurred between the centralist and nationalist Young Turk movement of Aḥmed Riḍā (the *Ittiḥād we Teraḳḳī Djemᶜiyyeti* [*q.v.*] or "Committee of Union and Progress") and the other groups over the question whether armed struggle, including foreign intervention, was acceptable as a means to depose the sultan. Together with the Armenians, Ṣabāḥ al-Dīn supported intervention and armed resistance (an abortive attempt at a military coup with the help of the garrison in Tripolitania was actually undertaken by his followers after the congress). Later in 1902, Ṣabāḥ al-Dīn united his followers in a separate organisation, the *ᶜAdem-i Merkeziyyet we Teshebbüs-ü Shakhsī Djemᶜiyyeti* ("Society for Decentralisation and Private Initiative").

The name of the society reflected Ṣabāḥ al-Dīn's ideological stance. He was a follower of Le Play and, especially, of Edmond Desmolins, whose *A quoi tient la supériorité des Anglo-Saxons* (1897) influenced him deeply. In Ṣabāḥ al-Dīn's eyes, society could only progress on the basis of the improvement of its smallest constituent parts, sc. the family and the individual. Unlike most other Young Turks, who saw the state as the only vehicle for the modernisation of society, he saw the secret in creating a strong "individualism" in the Ottoman Empire. Ṣabāḥ al-Dīn was a thinker and writer (from 1906 to 1908 he edited the Paris-based newspaper *Teraḳḳī* "Progress") but not a very astute politician. As a concrete political programme, his brand of sociology had little to offer in the way of solutions for the short-term problems of the Ottoman Empire.

In 1907, his group participated in the second "Congress of Ottoman Liberals" in Paris, which was organised by the Armenian Dashnaks. After the 1908 constitutional revolution, he returned to Istanbul, but, although he had many followers in the *Aḥrār Firḳasī* ("Liberal party", 1908-9) and the *Ḥürriyyet we Iᵓtilāf Firḳasī* ("Entente Liberale", 1912-13, 1919-22), he never joined any of these parties and he did not actively participate in the politics of the second constitutional period. He had to leave the Ottoman Empire when he was accused of involvement in the murder of the Grand Vizier Maḥmūd Shewket Pasha [*q.v.*] in 1913. After World War I he returned, but as a member of the Ottoman dynasty he was banned from Turkey again in 1924. Thereafter he lived in exile in Switzerland until his death in 1948.

Bibliography: Cavit Orhan Tütengil, *Prens Sabahattin*, Istanbul 1954; İbrahim Alaettin Gövsa, *Türk meşhurları ansiklopedisi*, Istanbul 1946 (?), 332; Şerif Mardin, *Jön Türklerin siyasî fikirleri 1895-1908*, Ankara 1964, 215-24; Ahmet Bedevi Kuran, *İnkılâp tarihimiz ve "Jön Türkler"*, Istanbul 1945; Ali Birinci, *Hürriyet ve İtilâf Fırkası*, Istanbul 1990.

(E.J. Zürcher)

SABAHATTİN ALİ (Ottoman orthography, Ṣabāḥ ul-Dīn ᶜAlī), Turkish novelist and short story writer, born in Komotini [see GÜMÜLDJINE, in Suppl.], eastern Thrace (now in Greece), on 12 February 1906 or 25 February 1907, died on 2 April 1948. His father was the army Captain Ali Salahaddin and he had his elementary education in Istanbul, Çanakkale, and Edremit. His childhood in Çanakkale during World War I was to leave deep emotional traces on him; later, when the family came to Edremit, the area was under invasion and they found themselves under dire financial circumstances, so that Sabahattin Ali had to work as a street seller. He continued his education at Balıkesir and Istanbul Teacher Training Colleges (1921-7). Upon graduation, he worked in Yozgat as a teacher for a year before he was sent to Germany in 1928 by the Ministry of Education to further his studies. He returned in 1930 and taught German in Aydın and Konya, but in 1932, because of his poem *Memleketten haberler*, he was sentenced to one year's imprisonment for disparaging Atatürk, being freed after 10 months under a general pardon. Between the years 1934 and 1945, he worked in the publications section of the Ministry of Education and later as a teacher in Ankara. He was highly criticised for his political activities and, in 1945, resigning from his duties, he moved to Istanbul, becoming a journalist. Because of an article which he published in the satirical magazine *Marko Paşa*, he was sentenced to three months in jail. In 1948, after he left prison, he began to work as a lorry driver and wrote in the journal *Zincirli Hürriyet*. He was under constant police surveillance, hence decided to run away to Bulgaria, but was killed on 2 April 1948, by the smuggler who was helping him to cross the frontier, possibly in an ambush.

Sabahattin Ali began to publish his sentimental poetry and short stories in journals during 1925-6. Later, he abandoned poetry and became known by his short stories and his novel *Kuyucaklı Yusuf*. His familiarity with the Anatolian villagers, which stemmed from his childhood memories, became clearer as he met more people in the prisons. The bulk of his later work is devoted to the village life and people; their struggle with nature, their social and economic conditions, and their mistrust for officials and intellectuals. Some of his stories are about workers, but these are not as detailed as the village stories. The middle-class people and the intellectuals are reflected as negative personalities who despise and mistreat the villagers; his administrators are corrupt and take sides with the rich. The women in his stories are pushed into prostitution by society. His characters are not well developed psychologically; the plot and the motivation of his characters are more important. His first novel *Kuyucaklı Yusuf (1937)* is his village novel. The events start in Aydın in 1903 and end in 1915 in Edremit. It is based on the oppositions of city: nature; corruption: naivety; lust: love. His second novel, *İçimizdeki şeytan*, takes place in İstanbul and is set among the young university students before World War II. *Kürk mantolu Madonna* is a love story about an intellectual, his problems with his family and his society. In all the three of his novels the heroes are men who are not in harmony with their communities.

Sabahattin Ali strove in his writings to be a social realist; he did not abstract art from society and believed that art and literature had a mission, which was to lead human beings towards the more beautiful and the just and to teach them about themselves and life. He began by employing an elaborate literary language, as in his early love stories, but shifted to using very plain, non-descriptive language, believing that the written language should reflect the spoken form.

Bibliography: 1. First editions of his works. (a) Poetry: *Dağlar ve rüzgâr,* Istanbul 1934. (b) Short story collections: *Değirmen*, Istanbul 1935; *Kağnı*, Istanbul 1936; *Ses*, Istanbul 1937; *Yeni dünya*, Istanbul 1943; *Sırça köşk*, Istanbul 1947. (c) Novels: *Kuyucaklı Yusuf*, Istanbul 1937 (in French: *Youssouf le Taciturne*, Paris 1977); *İçimizdeki şeytan*, Istanbul 1940; *Kürk mantolu Madonna*, Istanbul 1943.

2. Studies. Fethi Naci, *On Türk romanı*, Istanbul 1971; Mustafa Kutlu, *Sabahattin Ali*, Istanbul 1972; Asım Bezirci, *Sabahattin Ali: hayatı, hikayeleri, romanları*, Istanbul 1974; Kemal Bayram, *Sabahattin olayı*, Istanbul 1978; F.A. Laslo and Atilla Özkırımlı, *Sabahattin Ali*, Ankara 1979; Elisabeth Siedel, *Sabahattin Ali, Mystiker und Sozialist*, Berlin 1983; Olcay Önertoy, *Türk roman ve öyküsü*, Istanbul 1984; Berna Moran, *Türk romanına eleştirel bir bakış* ii, Istanbul 1990; Cevdet Kudret, *Türk edebiyatında hikaye ve roman,* iii, Istanbul 1990.

(Çiğdem Balim)

ŞABANDJA, modern Turkish Sapanca, a town in northwestern Anatolia, in the classical Bithynia situated on the southeastern bank of the freshwater lake of the same name and to the west of the Sakarya river (lat. 40°41′N., long. 30°15′E.).

Almost nothing is known of its pre-Islamic history although there are Byzantine remains; the name may be a popular transformation of Sophon. According to Ewliyā Čelebi, the town was founded by a certain Şabandjī Ḳodja, but this last must be merely an eponymous hero. It seems to appear in history only in the 10th/16th century, when Süleymān the Magnificent's Grand Vizier Ṣarī Rüstem Pasha [see RÜSTEM PASHA] is said to have founded there a mosque, a public bath and a caravanserai with 170 rooms. Ewliyā describes it a century later as having 1,000 houses, and Şabandja was at this time the centre of a *ḳaḍā*ʾ in the *liwā*ʾ of Ḳodja-eli [*q.v.*], connected administratively and financially with the *eyālet* of the Ḳapudan Pasha or Grand Admiral. Its main importance was as a staging-post on the road from the capital to the Anatolian interior, and then, in the early 20th century, as a station on the railway line from Üsküdar into Anatolia. During the Greco-Turkish warfare of 1921, it was occupied by the Greeks from 16 March to 21 June and damaged. It is now the chef-lieu of an *ilçe* or county in the *il* or province of Sakarya, with fruit-growing as an important local agricultural activity; in 1960 the town had a population of 5,788 and the *ilçe* one of 13,114.

The lake of Şabandja (15 km/9 miles by 5 km/3 miles) has been important for its fish since Antiquity; it is mentioned by Ammianus Marcellinus as *lacus sumonensis*, and in later Byzantine times the mountain by the lake was called Siphones. The project of connecting the lake by means of a canal with the Gulf of Izmit was mooted as far back as the Emperor Trajan's time, and in the Ottoman period, during the reigns of Muṣṭafā III and Murād III in the 10th/16th century, and after (see İ.H. Uzunçarşılı, *Sakarya nehrinin Izmit körfezine akıtılması ile Marmara ve Karadeniz'in birleştirilmesi hakkında vesîkalar ve tetkik raporu*, in *Belleten*, iv/14-15 [1940], 149-74).

Bibliography: Ewliyā Čelebi, *Seyāḥat-nāme*, Istanbul 1314-18/1896-1900, ii, 171-2, 459 ff., v, 74; Ḥādjdjī Khalīfa, *Djihān-numā*, 6560, 673; von Hammer, *GOR*, i, 72, 578, iv, 200; Sir W.M. Ramsay, *The historical geography of Asia Minor*, London 1890, 188; V. Cuinet, *La Turquie d'Asie*, Paris 1894, iv, 378; F. Taeschner, *Das anatolische Wegenetz*, Leipzig 1924, 93-4, 255; *İA*, art. *Sapanca* (Besim Darkot). For the European travellers in the area, see the *Bibl.* to F. Babinger's *EI*[1] art.

(C.E. Bosworth)

SABASṬIYYA, Sebasṭiyya, the Arabic name of various towns in the Near East.

1. The ancient Samaria, which Herod had changed to Σεβαστή in honour of Augustus. The form Σεβάστεια—as in the case of other towns of this name—was presumably also used, as the Arabic name (which is sometimes also written Sabaṣṭiyya) suggests. By the end of the classical period, the town, overshadowed by the neighbouring Neapolis (Sichem; Arabic, Nābulus), had sunk to be a small town (πολίχνιον) and played only an unimportant part in the Arab period. It was conquered by ʿAmr b. al-ʿĀṣ while Abū

ßakr was still caliph; the inhabitants were guaranteed heir lives and property on condition that they paid oll-tax and land-duties (al-Balādhurī, 138; Ibn al-Athīr, ii, 388). Al-Battānī is the first of the Arab geographers to mention it, but gives already much less ccurate figures for its position than Ptolemy had lone. In the later Arab geographers, Sabasṭiyya appears as a place in the Djund Filasṭīn. According to a radition found as early as Jerome, for example, the omb of John the Baptist was there (Ibn al-Athīr, *loc. it.*: Yaḥya b. Zakariyyā'; xi, 333); on its site there vas in Late Antiquity a basilica built and in the Crusading period (in the second half of the 6th/12th entury) a church of St. John; remains of the latter till survive. According to western sources, Sabasṭiyya vas again a bishopric at this time (Lequien, in *Oriens Christianus*, iii, 650 ff.). Usāma b. Munḳidh, about 534/1140, visited the town and its sanctuary. Ṣalāḥ al-Dīn advanced on Sabasṭiyya in 580/1184, but its bishop, by handing over 80 Muslim prisoners, saved he town from the terrible fate of Nābulus (Ibn al-Athīr, xi, 333; Abu 'l-Fidā', *Annales*, in *Recueil des hist. rient. des croisades*, i, 53; Ibn Shaddād, in *ibid.*, iii, 82; *Epistola Balduini*, in Röhricht, *Regesta regni Hierosol.*, no. 638). In the year 583/1187 it was finally taken from the Crusaders by Ḥusam al-Dīn ʿUmar b. Lādjīn; the church of St. John was turned into a mosque and the bishop brought to ʿAkkā (Ibn al-Athīr, xi, 357).

Bibliography: Battānī, *Kitāb Zīdj al-Ṣābī*, ed. Nallino, in the *Pubblicazioni d. Reale Osservat. di Brera in Milano*, xl/2, 39, no. 114; Ibn al-Faḳīh, 103; Ibn Khurradādhbih, 79; Yaʿḳūbī, *Buldān*, 329; Yāḳūt, *Buldān*, ed. Wüstenfeld, iii, 33; Derenbourg, *Vie d'Ousâma*, tr. 188-9, 486, Arabic text, 528, 617; V. Cuinet, *La Syrie*, 192; Thomsen, *Loca sancta*, i, 102; Schürer, *Gesch. d. jüd. Volkes im Zeitalter Christi*[4], ii, 195-8; R. Hartmann, *Palästina unter den Arabern* (*Das Land der Bibel*, i/4), 14; Baedeker, *Palästina u. Syrien*[6], Leipzig 1904, 195; Le Strange, *Palestine under the Moslems*, 28, 523; H.C. Luke and E. Keith-Roach, *The handbook of Palestine and Trans-Jordan*[2], London 1930, 130-1; A.-S. Marmardji, *Textes géographiques arabes sur la Palestine*, Paris 1951, 92.

2. A place in the Thughūr al-Shāmiyya, according to Ibn Khurradādhbih, 117, on the Cilician coast, 4 *mīls* from an otherwise unknown Iskandariyya, which again was 12 *mīls* from Ḳurāsiyya (Κοράσιον). It is the ancient 'Ελαιοῦσσα or Σεβαστή, the modern Ayaṣ.

Bibliography: Pauly-Wissowa, v, 2228, s.v. Elaiussa; ii/A, 952, s.v. Sebaste no. 5; Tomaschek, in *SB Ak. Wien* (1891), Abh. viii, 65; E. Herzfeld, in *Peterm. geogr. Mitteil.*, lv (1909), 29, col. 2.

3. A town in Asia Minor, which was taken by al-ʿAbbās b. al-Walīd in 93/711-12 along with al-Marzubānayn and Ṭūs (read Ṭarsūs!), whose situation is unknown. In some manuscripts of al-Ṭabarī and Ibn Taghrībirdī, the name is wrongly written Samasṭiyya (or something like that) which can hardly, as Brooks suggests, stand for the Byzantine Μίσθεια in Phrygia. The reference is rather to the Phrygian Σεβαστή (Pauly-Wissowa, ii/A, 951, no. 1).

Bibliography: Ibn al-Athīr, iv, 457; Ṭabarī, ii, 1236, with note *b.*; Ibn Taghrībirdī, *Nudjūm*, ed. Popper, i, 251; E.W. Brooks, in *Jnal. of Hellenic Studies*, xviii (1898), 193.

4. A town of this name said to be not far from Sumaysāṭ on the upper Euphrates is mentioned by Yāḳūt, iii, 33. It might be Juliopolis in Cappadocia (Ptolemy, v. 6. 25, ed. Müller, 893), which was presumably called after Augustus and perhaps may have also been called Sebasteia; but perhaps we should rather assume there has been some confusion with Sīwās on the Upper Nahr Ālis (Halys or Ḳizil Irmaḳ [*q.v.*]). (E. Honigmann*)

SABʿATU RIDJĀL, collective designation of seven patron saints venerated in certain Moroccan towns and tribal areas, as well as in some parts of Algeria. Probably the oldest group of this kind are the Seven of the Radjrādja (Regraga), a Berber maraboutic tribe (later: family) belonging to the Ḥāḥā (Maṣmūda) and composed of the descendants of 13 saints (the original seven plus six affiliates), whose tombs and *zāwiyas* are located west, east and on top of their holy mountain, Djabal al-Ḥadīd, between al-Sawīra (Mogador) and the Tansift in Shayāẓima (Chiadma) country.

According to local tradition, the Radjrādja had been Christians since the time of Christ, but when they heard of Muḥammad's call, seven of them travelled to Mecca, met the Prophet, embraced Islam and were commissioned to Islamise the Maghrib, which they did. The most conspicuous feature of their cult is the annual circular pilgrimage, *dawr*, which begins on 21 March (vernal equinox) and lasts 40 days. For a detailed description of its rites, symbolism and mythology by a *sawīrī* participant, see ʿA. Mana, *Les Regraga*, Casablanca 1988.

While the origins of the Seven Radjrādja are shrouded in myth, the Seven Saints of Marrakesh are historical persons who lived between the 6th/12th and 10th/16th centuries. They include men like the famous Ḳāḍī ʿIyāḍ [*q.v.*], and Muḥammad b. Sulaymān al-Djazūlī [*q.v.*], spiritual ancestor of most Moroccan Ṣūfī orders. H. de Castries, in his *Les sept patrons de Marrakech, les Sabʿatu Rijal*, in *Hespéris*, iv/3 (1924), 245-303, has shown that the circular pilgrimage to the Seven was established by the famous savant and mystic Abū ʿAlī al-Ḥasan al-Yūsī in 1688-9, at the demand of the Sultan Mawlāy Ismāʿīl [*q.v.*]. The latter took a dim view of Regraga influence, and tried to curb it by having the *ʿulamā'* of Fās issue a *fatwā* (1687-8) denying their title of Companions of the Prophet and by creating a rival pilgrimage centre at Marrakesh. The new *ziyāra* proved such a success that the term *sabʿatu ridjāl* became synonymous with the name of the city. In 1811 Mawlāy Sulaymān, under Wahhābī influence, condemned the Marrākushī infatuation with the Seven, but his successors respected it.

Other instances of the veneration of seven saints have been observed near Amizmiz, among the Barānis (northeastern Morocco), in Fās, in Shafshāwen and in other places in Northern Morocco, in Ifni and in Algeria (Kabylia, Awrās).

Bibliography (in addition to references in the article): A. Moulièras, *Le Maroc inconnu*, Oran-Paris 1899, ii, 171-8; H. Gaillard, *Une ville de l'Islam: Fès*, Paris 1905, 137; E. Doutté, *En tribu*, Paris 1914, 222, 360; R. Montagne, *Les Berbères et le Makhzen dans le Sud du Maroc*, Paris 1930, 27, 66, 67, 84, 87, 208; A. Domenech-Lafuente, *Del Territorio de Ifni*, etc., in *Cuadernos de Est. Afr.*, vii (1949), 9-21; E. Maldonado, *Sebaatu Riyal*, in *Africa*, vi/86 (1949), 55-9; E. Dermenghem, *Le Culte des saints dans l'Islam maghrébin*, Paris 1954, 47-9; J. Berque, *Structures sociales du Haut-Atlas*, Paris 1955, 66, 270, 296, 435; idem, *Al-Yousi*, Paris 1958; G. Deverdun, *Marrakech des origines à 1912*, Rabat 1959, i, 571-5; W. Hoenerbach and J. Kolenda, *Šefšāwen (Xauen)*, in *WI*, n.s. xiv (1973), 39. (P. Shinar)

ṢABBĀGH (A.), lit. dyer, is a technical term which was applied to a group of skilled craftsmen in Islamic Middle East and North Africa. In a polemical writing, the Arab writer al-Djāḥiẓ argued that the dyers, tanners, cuppers, etc. were exclusively Jewish in the early Islamic period, but historians like al-Khaṭīb al-Baghdādī and other writers have indicated names of Muslims bearing the name al-Ṣabbāgh which may indicate the involvement of Muslims in the dyer's profession at least during later Islamic centuries. A statement attributed to the Prophet Muḥammad said that "the most habitual liars were the dyers" (*akdhab al-nās al-ṣabbāghūn*); but, according to Abū ʿUbayd Ibn Sallām (d. 232/846), *al-ṣabbāgh* acquired a new shade of meaning and was applied to persons who were engaged in "forgery and embellishment of *ḥadīth*" (al-Khaṭīb, *Taʾrīkh Baghdād*, xiv, 216).

According to a tale in the *Alf layla wa-layla*, the dyer's trade tended to be hereditary. The dyers had a low status in society due to the foul odour associated with their work. The *ḥisba* manuals speak of the trickery of the dyers, who allegedly cheated their customers by applying non-permanent dye for their cloth. In the modern era, the Damascene dyers were well-known for providing the dye indigo (*al-nīl*), lapis lazuli (*lāuwardī*), dark blue dye (*kuḥlī*) and a variety of other shades for their customers' cloth (al-Ḳāsimī, *Ḳāmūs*, 267). The Yemeni dyers of the early 20th century have preserved some of the traditional skills of their trade. The biographer al-Ṣafadī (d. 764/1362) recorded the biographies of some notable Muslims affiliated to the dyers' families who had unusual names like ʿAbd al-Sayyid Muḥammad b. ʿAbd al-Wāḥid b. Djaʿfar al-Ṣabbāgh (d. 477/1084), who lectured on jurisprudence at the Niẓāmiyya college in Baghdād and wrote some books. His grandson ʿAbd al-Sayyid b. ʿAlī al-Ṣabbāgh (d. 563/1168) was also a man of some distinction.

Bibliography: Djāḥiẓ, *Thalāth rasāʾil*, ed. Finkel, Cairo 1926, 17; Thaʿālibī, *Thimār al-ḳulūb*, Cairo 1908, 193; Ibn Bassām al-Muḥtasib, *Nihāyat al-rutba fi-ṭalab al-ḥisba*, ed. H. al-Sāmarrāʾi, Baghdād 1968, 128; Ibn al-Ukhuwwa, *Maʿālim al-ḳurba*, ed. R. Levy, London 1938, 45; Ṣafadī, *al-Wāfī bi 'l-wafāyāt*, iv, 63, 152, viii, 118-19, xviii, 440-1, xix, 273; Subkī, *Ṭabaḳāt al-Shāfiʿiyya al-kubrā*, Cairo 1971, viii, 112; al-Ḳāḍī al-Ṭālaḳānī, *Risālat Amthāl al-baghdādiyya*, ms. Baghdād Museum n. 6929, 6; *Alf layla wa-layla*, ed. Hasan Djawhar *et alii*, Cairo 1952-4, part iv, 18-19; M.S. al-Ḳāsimī, *Ḳāmūs al-ṣināʿāt al-shāmiyya*, i-ii, Paris-The Hague 1960, 267-8; M.A.J. Beg, *Social mobility in Islamic civilization – the classical period*, Kuala Lumpur 1981, 64; R.B. Serjeant *et alii*, *Ṣanʿāʾ: an Arabian Islamic city*, Cambridge 1983, 265. (M.A.J. Beg)

ṢĀBIʾ (a.), or, with the usual weakening of final *hamza*, *Ṣābī*, plural *Ṣābiʾūn*, *Ṣābiʾa*, *Ṣāba*, in English "Sabian" (preferably not "Sabaean", which renders *Sabaʾ* [*q.v.*]), a name applied in Arabic to at least three entirely different religious communities:

(1) the *Ṣābiʾūn* who are mentioned three times in the Ḳurʾān (II 62, V 69, XXII 17) together with the Christians and Jews. Their identity, which has been much debated both by the Muslim commentators and by modern orientalists, was evidently uncertain already shortly after the time of Muḥammad and remains uncertain now. They were clearly not Mandaeans (as Chwolsohn and many others believed), and hardly Elchasaites (as proposed below, s.v. ṣābiʾa); there is indeed little reason to believe that Muḥammad and his compatriots could have had any knowledge of either of these communities. The present author has argued that they might possibly have been Manichaeans, i.e. what the Arab antiquaries refer to as the *zanādiḳa* among the Ḳuraysh.

(2) The *Ṣābat al-baṭāʾiḥ*, or *mughtasila*, of Southern ʿIrāḳ, the remnant of an ancient Jewish-Christian sect, the Elchasaites. They owed the designation "Sabians" evidently to the fact that some of the early Ḳurʾān commentators in Baṣra or Kūfa saw in them a possible candidate for identification with the Sabians of the holy book.

(3) The Sabians of Ḥarrān, a community following an old Semitic polytheistic religion, but with a strongly Hellenised elite, one of the last outposts of Late Antique paganism. These adopted the Ḳurʾānic name *Ṣābiʾa* during the 3rd/9th century so as to be able to claim the status of *ahl al-kitāb* and thus avoid persecution. (Arabic Muslim and Christian authors occasionally also apply the name *Ṣābiʾ*, by extension, to the pagans of ancient Greece and to other polytheists.) It is only with these last that Muslim authors of the ʿAbbāsid period were acquainted at first hand and except in discussions of the Ḳurʾān, the name *Ṣābiʾ* is normally applied either to Ḥarrānian pagans or else to their Muslim descendants (e.g. the astronomer al-Battānī [*q.v.*]). In particular, the name was applied, in effect as a *nisba*, to two distinguished families of scholars and secretaries of Ḥarrānian origin who flourished in Baghdād between the 3rd/9th and 5th/11th centuries, and it is with these that the present article is concerned.

The two families in question were related to each other by marriage, although the exact nature of their relationship has been the subject of much confusion. Ibn al-Ḳifṭī (*Taʾrīkh al-Ḥukamāʾ*, ed. A. Müller and J. Lippert, Leipzig 1902) says (twice on pp. 110-1) that Thābit b. Sinān (no. 4) was the maternal uncle (*khāl*) of the historian Hilāl b. al-Muḥassin (no. 9) and he says again (on p. 110) that Hilāl was "the son of his (i.e. Thābit's) sister"; this information is repeated by the sources dependent on Ibn al-Ḳifṭī (i.e. Ibn Abī Uṣaybiʿa and Ibn al-ʿIbrī) and has been accepted by modern authors. However, Yāḳūt (*Udabāʾ*, ii, 397) quotes a poem by Abū Isḥāḳ Ibrāhīm (no. 7) lamenting the death of "his maternal uncle" Thābit b. Sinān; i.e. Thābit was the maternal uncle not of Hilāl, but of his grandfather Ibrāhīm (similarly, al-Ṣafadī, x, 464, paraphrasing Yāḳūt, says of Ibrāhīm *wa huwa* <*ibn*> *ukht Thābit*; badly "emended" in the edition.) Yāḳūt's version is confirmed by Hilāl himself when he introduces one of the anecdotes in his *Rusūm dār al-khilāfa* (ed. ʿAwwād, Baghdād 1383/1964, 86) with the words: "My grandfather Ibrāhīm b. Hilāl told me about this matter saying: my grandfather Sinān b. Thābit told me saying: my father Thābit was", etc. It is thus clear that Sinān was the maternal grandfather of Ibrāhīm, not of Hilāl. To be sure, Hilāl refers elsewhere in the same book (p. 49) to Sinān b. Thābit as *djaddī*, but in the light of the just-quoted passage it is evident either that *djaddī* is a haplography for *djadd djaddī*, or else that it here means not "my grandfather" but "my ancestor".

Bibliography: The most complete study of the *Ṣābiʾūn* in general and of the two families outlined below remains D. Chwolsohn, *Die Ssabier und der Ssabismus*, 2 vols., St. Petersburg 1856. See also F. de Blois, *The "Sabians" (Ṣābiʾūn) in pre-Islamic Arabia* (forthcoming).

1. Abu 'l-Ḥasan Thābit b. Ḳurra b. Marwān b. Thābit [*q.v.*] (died 288/901), the celebrated mathematician, astronomer and translator of Greek books, was the first member of the Sabian community to come to the notice of Muslim intellectuals. He was born in Ḥarrān but spent most of his life in Baghdād where he enjoyed the especial patronage of the caliph al-Muʿtaḍid.

Genealogical table of the Ṣābiʾ families

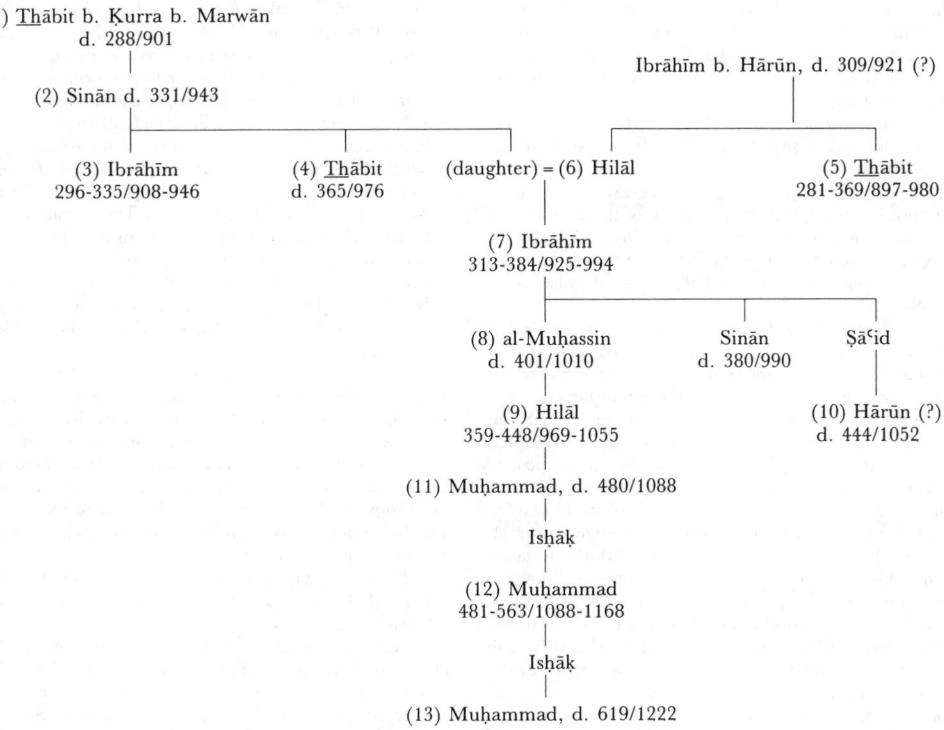

2. His son Abū Saʿīd Sinān served as personal physician of three successive caliphs: al-Muḳtadir, al-Ḳāhir and al-Rāḍī. Al-Ḳāhir forced him to convert to Islam, but his children apparently remained in the ancestral religion. Sinān was responsible for building hospitals and supervising the medical profession in Baghdād, and is credited with introducing a system of examining and licensing the practising doctors. The sources list various writings of his on history, mathematics and astronomy; strangely, they mention no medical titles. His only extant work seems to be a short treatise on ethics, *Siyāsat al-nufūs* (Brit. Mus. Cat., p. 205). He died (according to al-Ṣūlī and Yāḳūt) on 1 Dhu 'l-Ḳaʿda 331/943.

Bibliography: Ṣūlī, *Akhbār al-Rāḍī wa 'l-Muttaḳī*, ed. J. Heyworth Dunne, London 1935, 245; Masʿūdī, *Murūdj*, i, 19-20 = § 14; *Fihrist*, 272, 302; Bīrūnī, *al-Āthār al-bāḳiya*, 243-75 (detailed summary of Sinān's *Kitāb al-Anwāʾ*); Yāḳūt, *Udabāʾ*, iv, 257-8; Ibn al-Ḳifṭī, 190-5; Ibn Abī Uṣaybiʿa, i, 220-3; Chwolsohn, i, 569-77; Brockelmann, I², 244-5, S I, 386; Sezgin, v, 291, vii, 331; Y. Dold-Samplonius, *Sinān ibn Thābit*, in *Dictionary of scientific biography*, xii, 447-8; M. Ullmann, *Die Medizin im Islam*, Leiden 1970, 124.

3. His son Abū Isḥāḳ Ibrāhīm was an important astronomer and mathematician. He was born in 296/908-9 and died in Muḥarram 335/946 (according to Ibn Abī Uṣaybiʿa; the earlier authorities give no dates). A collection of six of his scientific writings has been published under the title *Rasāʾil ibn Sinān* (Ḥaydarābād 1366-7/1947-8).

Bibliography: Bīrūnī, *al-Āthār al-bāḳiya*, 326; *Fihrist*, 272; Ibn al-Ḳifṭī, 57-9; Ibn Abī Uṣaybiʿa, i, 226; Chwolsohn, i, 577-8; Brockelmann, I², 245, S I, 386; Sezgin, v, 292-5, vi, 193-5, vii, 274-5; R. Rashed, *Ibrāhīm ibn Sinān*, in *Dictionary of scientific biography*, vii, 2-3.

4. His brother Abu 'l-Ḥasan Thābit succeeded his father as physician to the caliph al-Rāḍī and served then in the same capacity under al-Muttaḳī, al-Mustakfī and al-Muṭīʿ. He died on 11 Dhu 'l-Ḳaʿda 365/976 (thus Ibn al-Nadīm and also Yāḳūt, quoting Hilāl; others differ). He was, however, best known as the author of a history of events from 295/908 (i.e. the ascension of al-Muḳtadir, with whose reign al-Ṭabarī's history breaks off) up to the year of his own death (according to Ibn al-Nadīm) or to the end of 363/974 (Ibn al-Athīr, viii, 476). Although this work is lost, it is quoted extensively not only in the surviving writings of Thābit's great-great nephew Hilāl (below, no. 9), but also by Miskawayh, al-Hamadhānī, Ibn al-Athīr, al-Dhahabī and others, and is thus indirectly doubtless one of the most important sources for the events of the period in question. As a court physician, Thābit was evidently especially well informed about the private affairs of his masters.

The *Taʾrīkh akhbār al-Ḳarāmiṭa* which has been published as the work of Thābit (ed. Suhayl Zakkār, Beirut 1391/1971) is, in the judgement of the present author, a clumsy forgery knocked together out of extracts from Ibn al-Athīr.

Bibliography: *Fihrist*, 302; Yāḳūt, *Udabāʾ*, ii, 397-8; Ibn al-Ḳifṭī, 109-11; Ibn Abī Uṣaybiʿa, i, 224-6; Ibn Khallikān, 127; Chwolsohn, i, 578-81; M.S. Khan, *Miskawaih and Ṯābit ibn Sinān*, in *ZDMG*, cxvii (1967), 303-17.

5. Abu 'l-Ḥasan Thābit b. Ibrāhim b. Hārūn (thus in Tadjaddud's edition of the *Fihrist*, 149, 360, and al-Thaʿālibī, *Yatīma*, ed. Damascus, ii, 23; most other sources have Zahrūn) was born in al-Raḳḳa in Dhu 'l-Ḳaʿda 283/897 and died in Baghdād in Shawwāl 369/980 (these dates according to Ibn al-Ḳifṭī, 115). He served as a physician to several important persons, among them the Būyid *amīr al-umarāʾ* ʿAḍud al-Dawla. His writings on medicine and his

translations of Greek medical books are not known to have survived. Ibn al-Ḳifṭī (76) surmised that his father might have been the Abū Isḥāḳ Ibrāhīm b. Zahrūn al-Ḥarrānī al-Manṭiḳī of whom T̲h̲ābit b. Sinān (as quoted by Ibn al-Ḳifṭī) says that he died in Ṣafar 309/921; however, the identification of the two is not certain.

Bibliography: Fihrist 272, 303; Ibn al-Ḳifṭī 111-5; Ibn Abī Uṣaybiʿa, i, 227-30; Chwolsohn, i, 584-5.

6. His brother Abu 'l-Ḥasan Hilāl, whose dates are not recorded, was the physician of the *amīr* Tūzūn at the same time that his brother-in-law T̲h̲ābit b. Sinān was looking after the health of the caliph.

Bibliography: Ibn al-Ḳifṭī 350; Chwolsohn, i, 587.

7. His son Abū Isḥāḳ Ibrāhīm was born on 5 Ramaḍān 313/925 and, though trained as a doctor and astronomer, he made his name as a secretary in the service of the Būyid *amīr* Muʿizz al-Dawla, who appointed him chief secretary (ṣāḥib dīwān al-inshāʾ) in 349/960. Although ʿIzz al-Dawla Bak̲h̲tiyār attempted to convert him to Islam and even offered the post of *wazīr* as a reward, Ibrāhīm remained true to the faith of his fathers. After the death of Muʿizz al-Dawla, Ibrāhīm got caught up in the rivalry between ʿIzz al-Dawla Bak̲h̲tiyār and his cousin ʿAḍud al-Dawla Fanā-K̲h̲usraw, and his attempts to serve two masters led to his being imprisoned by each of them in turn. The victorious ʿAḍud al-Dawla kept him under house arrest from 367/978 till 371/981 and ordered him to spend his enforced leisure composing a history of the Būyids, *al-Kitāb al-Tādjī fī ak̲h̲bār al-dawla al-daylamiyya*, the pages of which are reported to have been sent, as they were completed, to the *amīr*, who then returned them, corrected, to their imprisoned author. The often-repeated anecdote according to which Ibrāhīm provoked the anger of the *amīr* by confiding to an indiscreet friend that the history he was composing was nothing but a fabric of lies involves a number of chronological errors and cannot be taken at face value (see, in detail, the article by Madelung). The *Kitāb al-Tādjī* has not survived as such, though it is quoted (or plagiarised) by several later historians; moreover, a substantial extract from its first part was edited by an anonymous Zaydī author and has survived in a unique ms. in Ṣanʿāʾ (ed. Muḥammad Ḥusayn al-Zubaydī, Bag̲h̲dād 1977; also in W. Madelung, *Arabic texts concerning the history of the Zaydī imāms of Ṭabaristān, Daylamān and Gīlān*, Beirut 1987, 9-51).

Ibrāhīm returned to favour after the death of ʿAḍud al-Dawla (in 372/983) and enjoyed the friendship in particular of the celebrated Twelver S̲h̲īʿī poet al-S̲h̲arīf al-Raḍī [q.v.] with whom he corresponded in prose and verse (see *Rasāʾil al-Ṣābī wa 'l-S̲h̲arīf al-Raḍī*, ed. Muḥammad Yūsuf Nadjm, Kuwait 1961) and who lamented his death (on 12 S̲h̲awwāl 384/994) in a famous elegy. He also compiled a history of his own family (mentioned by Ibn al-Nadīm). His collected letters have survived in a number of manuscripts, but only a small selection has been printed (al-Muk̲h̲tār min rasāʾil Abī Isḥāḳ ... al-Ṣābī, al-djuzʾ al-awwal [apparently all published], ed. S̲h̲akīb Arslān, Bāʿabda 1898; repr. Beirut 1966). A good number of his poems are quoted by T̲h̲aʿālibī. Though he resisted to the end the temptation of conversion, Ibrāhīm was in all other regards a typically Muslim man of letters whose elegant Arabic epistles and poems were greatly admired by his contemporaries.

Bibliography: Fihrist, 134; al-T̲h̲aʿālibī, Yatīma, i, 14, 34, 69, 187-8, 190-1, 508, and especially ii,

23-86; idem, *Tatimmat al-yatīma*, ed. ʿA. Iḳbāl, i, 73; Yāḳūt, Udabāʾ, i, 324-58; Ibn al-At̲h̲īr, viii, 397; ix, 11, 74, 226; Ibn al-Ḳifṭī, 75-6; Chwolsohn, i, 588-604; Brockelmann, I², 95, S I, 153-4; J.Chr. Bürgel, *Die Hofkorrespondenz ʿAḍud ad-Daulas...*, Wiesbaden 1965, 112-21 and *passim* (contains summaries of many of his letters); Sezgin, ii, 592; v, 314; A. Arazi, *Une épître d'Ibrāhīm b. Hilāl al-Ṣābī sur les genres littéraires* [with an edition of his *Risāla fī 'l-farḳ bayn al-mutarassil wa 'l-s̲h̲āʿir*], in *Studies in Islamic history and civilisation in honour of Professor David Ayalon*, Jerusalem 1986, 473-505. The extract from *al-Kitāb al-Tādjī* has been studied in a series of articles by M.S. Khan, in *Arabica*, xii (1965), 27-44; xvii (1970), 151-60; xviii (1971), 194-201; in *Islamic Studies*, viii (1965), 247-52; and by W. Madelung, *Abū Isḥāḳ al-Ṣābī on the Alids of Ṭabaristān and Gīlān*, in *JNES*, xxvi (1967), 17-57.

8. His son Abū ʿAlī al-Muḥassin, called Ṣāḥib al-S̲h̲āma, died (according to Yāḳūt) on 8 Muḥarram 401/1010, like his father still a pagan. Ibn al-Ḳifṭī consulted an autograph of his containing bibliographies of the works of T̲h̲ābit b. Ḳurra and Sinān b. T̲h̲ābit. Yāḳūt quotes a few of his poems and mentions also his two brothers Abū Saʿīd Sinān (d. Radjab 380/990; see also his father's elegy on his death in al-T̲h̲aʿālibī, Yatīma, ii, 48-9) and Abu 'l-ʿAlāʾ Ṣāʿid.

Bibliography: Yāḳūt, Udabāʾ, vi, 244-9; Ibn al-Ḳifṭī, 114, 116, 119; Ibn Abī Uṣaybiʿa, i, 224-7; Chwolsohn, i, 604-5.

9. His son was the famous historian Abu 'l-Ḥusayn Hilāl [q.v.] (359-448/969-1055), a Muslim convert. His history (of which only a small part is extant) continues that of his ancestor T̲h̲ābit b. Sinān.

10. Abū Naṣr Hārūn b. Ṣāʿid "b. Hārūn" al-Ṣābiʾ, was (according to Ibn al-Ḳifṭī, 338) the chief physician in Bag̲h̲dād and died on 3 Ramaḍān 444/1052. He could well have been the son of Ṣāʿid b. Ibrāhīm (see no. 8).

11. Abu 'l-Ḥasan Muḥammad b. Hilāl, called G̲h̲ars al-Niʿma, served as a secretary at the time of the caliph al-Ḳāʾim. He inherited from his father a considerable fortune and was thus apparently able to retire from official service and devoted himself to literary and philanthropic activities. Of the latter, we know in particular of his endowment of a public library in Bag̲h̲dād with 1,000 books. He died in D̲h̲u 'l-Ḳaʿda 480/1088. His history, *D̲h̲ayl Taʾrīk̲h̲ Hilāl al-Ṣābī*, or *ʿUyūn al-tawārīk̲h̲*, which continued his father's chronicle down almost to the time of his own death, has not survived as such, but it was used extensively by al-K̲h̲aṭīb al-Bag̲h̲dādī, Ibn al-Djawzī and, in particular, by Sibṭ Ibn al-Djawzī, whose account of the events from 448-79/1055-86 seems to be almost entirely dependant on G̲h̲ars al-Niʿma. Extant is his *Kitāb al-Hafawāt al-nādira min al-muʿakkilīn al-malḥūzīn* (etc.), a collection of over 400 amusing anecdotes (ed. Ṣāliḥ al-As̲h̲tar, Damascus 1387/1967). Fragments survive of his *Kitāb al-Rabīʿ*, evidently also a compendium of anecdotes in the style of the *Nis̲h̲wār al-muḥāḍara* of al-Tanūk̲h̲ī.

Al-Ṣafadī (al-Wāfī bi 'l-wafayāt, ii, nos. 555, 570 following al-D̲h̲ahabī) gives the dates (reproduced in our table) of two of his descendants: his grandson Abu 'l-Ḥasan Muḥammad b. Abī Naṣr Isḥāḳ (no. 12) who was head of the *dīwān* of the caliph al-Muḳtadī and his great-great grandson al-S̲h̲ayk̲h̲ al-Ṣāliḥ Abu 'l-Ḥusayn Muḥammad b. Isḥāḳ (13), the last recorded member of this illustrious lineage.

Bibliography: Ibn al-Djawzī, *al-Muntaẓam* Ḥaydarābād 1357-9/1938-41, ix, 42-3; Ibn Khallikān, no. 785; Ibn Kat̲h̲īr, *al-Bidāya wa 'l nihāya*, Cairo 1351-8/1932-9, xii, 134; Ṣafadī, *Wāfī*, v, no. 2200; Brockelmann, I², 394-5; Sezgin, i, 327; I. ʿAbbās, *Shadharāt min kutub mafḳūda fī 'l-taʾrīkh*, Beirut 1988, 325-50, 329, 469-71; C.E. Bosworth, *Ghars al-Niʿma Hilāl al-Ṣābiʾ's Kitāb al-Hafawāt al-nādira and Būyid history*, in *Arabicus Felix, Luminosus Britannicus. Essays in honour of A.F.L. Beeston*, Reading 1991, 129-41. (F.C. de Blois)

ṢĀBIʾA (a.), the name of two rather mysterious groups in early Islamic times:

1. *Ṣābiʾat al-baṭāʾiḥ*.

The Mesopotamian dialectal pronunciation of *ṣābiʿa*, where the *ʿayn* has been transformed into *y* or *ī*, also occurs in Mandaean (cf. Lidzbarski, *Ginzā*; Nöldeke, *Mandäische Grammatik*; R. Macuch, *Handbook*, 94, l. 16: *ṣabuia*). This substantive, which became current in Mecca during the period of Ḳurʾānic preaching, irrespective of its etymology, derives from the Semitic root *ṣ-b-ʿ* (Aramaic, Hebrew, Syriac; Ethiopic *ṣabkha*), corresponding to *ṣ-b-gh* in Arabic. The verb signifies, in the first form, "to dye, to bathe, to immerse", whence, in the second form, "to baptise (by immersion)". Consequently, the noun denotes "baptists", named three times in the Ḳurʾān (II, 62; V, 69; XXII, 17), in the company of the Believers, the Jews and the Christians, with whom they share the title of "people of the Book" (*ahl al-kitāb*). In the last of these verses (XXII, 17), the *ṣābiʾūn* occupy the third place after the Believers and the Jews, and are followed by the Christians, the Zoroastrians and the polytheists; which would suggest a closer relationship between them and the Jews. A reference to baptism is to be found in sūra II, 138, where the context is that of the "imprint" (*ṣibgha*) of God on the Muslim, which is compared to Christian baptism (J. Penrice, *A Dictionary of the Koran*, repr. London 1970, 81; cf. al-Kulīnī, *Kāfī*, lith. Tehran 1307/1928, 152, where *ṭīna* "matter", is opposed to *ṣibgha* which "is Islam" (*hiya l-islām*); other references *apud* Kraus, *Jābir*, ii, 171, n. 1).

Given the indisputable monotheism of the *ṣābiʾūn* of the Ḳurʾān, this can only refer to a baptising religious community. There is a temptation to think immediately of the Mandaeans, who are dispersed, at the present day, on the banks of the Euphrates and of the Tigris in the south of ʿIrāḳ, and along the river Kārūn in Khūzistān. They are called by their Arab neighbours *ṣubba* or *ṣubbī* "baptisers"; they form two groups: the *mandāyē* (gnostics) and the *nāṣōrāyē* (observants). This is the thesis defended by D. Chwolsohn in *Die Ssabier und der Ssabismus*, dating from 1856. Although it has been severely criticised over certain of its conclusions, this work remains a basis for studies of the Sabians (cf. J. Hjärpe, *Analyse critique des traditions arabes sur les Sabéens Ḥarraniens*, Uppsala 1972, 1 ff.).

On the basis of a text of Ibn al-Nadīm (*Fihrist*, 340), where there is reference to a baptising sect called *al-mughtasila*, also known as *ṣābat al-baṭāʾih*, "the Sabaeans of the marshes", whose leader was called ' l.ḥ.s.y.ḥ (var. ' l.ḥ.s.ḥ and ' l.ḥ.s.dj), Chwolsohn identified the latter with Elchasai (i, 112 ff.), thus identifying Mandaeans and Elchasaites. He found evidence for this in information recorded by Hippolytus in *Refutatio omnium haeresium*, ix, 13 (ed. Wendland, 251), where it is said that Elchasai, founder of the sect, is supposed to have given a revealed book to a man named Sobai. Chwolsohn made of the last-named "a later personification of the name of a sect, this being that of the Sabaeans—the Mandaeans being called *al-ṣubba*" (Hjärpe, *op. cit.*, 11). On the basis of the etymological sense of *ṣābiʾa*, he considers that the term had been translated by *al-mughtasila*, "the baptisers" (i, 110). A year before the appearance of *Die Ssabier*, E. Renan had contributed a *Note sur l'identité de la secte gnostique des Elchasaïtes avec les Mandaïtes ou Sabiens*, in *JA*, vi (1855), 292-4.

Since then, researches into the Elchasaites have made it possible to correct this confusion (see, for example, A.J.W. Brandt, *Elchasai: ein Religionsstifter und sein Werk*, Leipzig 1912, and more recently, A.F.J. Klijn and G.J. Reinink, *Patristic evidence for Jewish-Christian Sects*, Leiden 1973 = *Suppl. to NT*, xxxvi; G.P. Luttikhuizen, *The revelation of Elchasai*, Tübingen 1985 = *Texte u. Studien zum antiken Judentum*, 8. It is thanks to the biography of Mānī, found in the *Codex Manichaicus Coloniensis* (cf. W. Sundermann, *Mitteliranische manichäische Texte kirchengeschichtlichen Inhalts* = Berliner Turfantexte, xi, East Berlin 1981, 19, text 2.1, tr. 3), that it is known that the Elchasaites were not identified with the Mandaeans. In fact, Mānī "grew up, lived, formed his system of thought and matured his vocation" between A.D. 219-20 and 240, in a community of sectaries called, in Greek and Coptic documents, *baptistai* ("baptisers, baptists"), by Arab authors, *al-mughtasila* ("those who purify themselves, who wash themselves") and, according to the Syriac tradition, the *mᵉnaqqᵉdē* ("those who purify themselves" or "are purified") and *ḥellē ḥewwārē* ("white vestments"). Cf. al-Ṭabarī, *Tafsīr*, xxviii, 55 f. on the *ḥawāriyyūn*, a term normally denoting the apostles of Jesus, but al-Ḍaḥḥāk sees here *al-ghassālūn* in Nabataean, since, as others specify "they cleaned their garments".

These "sectarians" are identical, as is declared by the Codex of Oxyrhyncus, not with the Mandaeans, which has been the general belief until now, but with the Elchasaites, disciples of the doctrine which spread in consequence of a vision experienced in "the land of the Parthians", around the year A.D. 100, by the prophet Elchasai (Alkhasaios) (H.-Ch. Puech, *Le manichéisme*, in *Histoire des Religions*, ii, Paris 1972 = *Encyclopedie de la Pléiade*). At twelve years old, then again at twenty-four years old, Mānī received from the Holy Spirit the command to leave this community and to show himself in public, vigorously proclaiming his doctrine. Excluded from his community for having deviated from the Law, in turning towards "Hellenism" and towards the "world", he left it accompanied by his father and by his two sole supporters. In his eyes, baptism was said to have been nothing more than a false religion, instigated by the "Spirit of Error" (*ibid.*, 532-3). In spite of this, he "claimed as his own a number of views borrowed from Elchasaism" (*ibid.*), while criticising "two of their principal practices: the habit of daily and frequently repeated ablutions; the prohibition concerning bread, fruit and vegetables of foreign provenance and of profane origin" (*ibid.*).

The Elchasaites are one of those sects which are described as "Judaeo-Christian", such as the Nazaraeans, the Ebionites and the Archontics. The Ebionites, established in Transjordania in the time of Trajan, formed one of the groups belonging to Palestinian Christianity; they were very close to Rabbinical Judaism and rejected all Greek doctrines, in particular the all-too-speculative Christology of St. Paul, in whom "they saw an Antichrist, responsible for the apostasy of so many brothers". In the eyes of the Hellenistic churches, they took on little by little "the appearance of a heretical sect, while in fact, they were the most direct heirs of the primitive Church, even if they no longer had the combative vitality". They adopted "a Gospel inspired by the synoptic

Gospels, but adapted to their doctrinal idiosyncrasies, the Gospels of the Ebionites, of which only a few fragments are known'' (cf. on this subject, E. Trocmé, *Le Christianisme des origines au Concile de Nicée*, in *Histoire des Religions*, ii, Paris 1972, 234-5).

These Ebionites drew the attention of a major theologian of the last century, A. von Harnack; he saw in their doctrine ''Christian parallels with Islam'' (*Christliche Parallelen zum Islam*, Vortrag im Leipziger akademischen Docentenverein, 1877-8, 18 ff.).

More recently, three scholars have taken an interest in this problem: P. Roncaglia, *Eléments ébionites et elkasaïtes dans le Coran*, in *Proche-Orient Chrétien*, xxi (1971), 101-26; M. Hamidullah, *Two christians of Pre-Islamic Mecca: ʿUthmān ibn al-Ḥuwairith and Waraqa ibn Naufal*, in *Jnal. of the Pakistan Historical Soc.*, vi (1958), 97-103, and Abū Mūsā 'l-Ḥarīrī (pseudonym of J. ʿAzzī), *Ḳiss wa-nabī. Baḥth fī nashʾat al-Islām* (''Priest and prophet. Research into the origin of Islam''), Jounieh-Kasslik 1979, pp. 223. This is a very methodical study of the Ḳurʾānic elements which make possible the construction of a thesis which has tempted many scholars in the past, sc. the Judaeo-Christian origin of Islam. Identifying ''Nazaraeans'' (*naṣārā*) with Ebionites, the author makes Waraḳa b. Nawfal, the cousin of Khadīdja, first wife of Muḥammad, the teacher and mentor of the latter, preparing him to succeed him at the head of the small Ebionite community of Mecca (on the Christians in Mecca on the eve of the Hidjra, cf. Lammens in *BIFAO*, xiv [1918], 191-230, and A. Jeffrey, *Christians at Mecca*, in *MW*, xix [1929], 24-35).

Having examined all the elements capable of having an origin in the Gospel of the Ebionites, known also by the name Gospel of the Hebrews, current according to St. Jerome among the Nazaraeans, in other words the Aramaic-speaking Judaeo-Christians of Palestine and Syria (cf. B. Altaner, *Précis de Patrologie*, tr. Grandcladon, Mulhouse-Tournai 1941, 53-4), the author considers that Muḥammad abandoned the path traced by Waraḳa when he left Mecca for Medina and founded the Islamic state, where the tradition of Arab political isolationism was revived. He sees the signs of this separation appearing in the contradictions arising between what he calls the ''Ḳurʾān of the priest and the prophet'' and the ''*muṣḥaf* of ʿUthmān''. The thesis in itself is fascinating, but its demonstration will remain based on assumptions which are not likely to be confirmed by new sources.

The ''baptismal imprint'', to which there is reference in sūra II, 138, quoted above, may apply to Ebionites/Nazaraeans as well as to Elchasaites/*mughtasila*. On the latter, see the interesting study written by F. de Blois, intitled *The Sabians* (Ṣābiʾūn) *in Pre-Islamic Arabia*, to appear in *JSS*, which includes an annotated translation of the text of the *Fihrist* concerning them. In this study the author proposes a new interpretation of the term *ṣābiʾūn* which he translates by ''converted'', on the basis of the root *ṣ-b-ʾ*, which will be considered further at a later stage. He sees in this term, applied to Muḥammad and his followers by their Meccan adversaries, a reference to the Manichaeans. On the basis of a possible equivalence between *ṣābiʾ* and *zindīḳ* in the sense of ''heretic'', ''infidel'', the author believes that, in the time of Muḥammad, the word *ṣābiʾ* signified ''Manichean'', being later replaced by *zindīḳ*. But Kister (*Arabica*, xv [1968], 144-5, quoted by de Blois, n. 39) supplies evidence for an equivalence *zindīḳ* = *mazdakī*.

Two texts seem ostensibly to support the view of F. de Blois:

The first refers to the caliph al-Walīd who, according to *Aghānī*, vi, 135-6, was a *zindīḳ* and followed the doctrine of Mānī, which was preached to him by a man of the Kalb. He had, in a basket covered by a silk veil (*ḥarīriyya*), an image (*ṣūra*) of a man, in the eyes of which mercury and sal-ammoniac had been placed. These eyes seemed to move and wink. The caliph is supposed to have said to his visitor, al-ʿAlāʾ al-Bandār, the narrator of this account: ''That is Mānī. God has sent no prophet either before him or after him!'' After leaving the caliph, the Kalbī was found strangled in the desert by a mysterious figure who descended from the sky. The Bedouins who witnessed the scene transported his body to the caliph.

The second text is a description of the *zandaḳa* by the ʿAbbāsid caliph al-Mahdī (cf. al-Ṭabarī, *Taʾrīkh*, iii, 588). A *zindīḳ* was brought before him who refused to repent; then he had him decapitated and crucified and said to his son al-Hādī: ''When you accede to the caliphate, devote yourself to the repression of this band (*ʿiṣba*), I mean the followers of Mānī. It is a sect (*firḳa*) which calls upon people to behave well, by avoiding the commission of turpitudes, by practising ascetism here on earth, by preparing for the life hereafter; then, it incites them to deny themselves the consumption of meat, the touching of pure water, to abstain from killing reptiles in order to avoid the commission of a sin; subsequently, it makes them worship two [entities]: the Light (*nūr*) and the Darkness (*ẓulma*); finally, it allows them marriage with sisters and daughters, ablution with urine, the seizure of children in the streets with the object of removing them from the Darkness and leading them towards the Lights. Raise before the followers of this sect the gibbet (*khashab*) and draw the sword from the scabbard, for the honour of Allāh, who has no partner''. And the caliph added: ''I have seen in a dream your grandfather al-ʿAbbās handing me two swords and commanding me to slay the dualists (*aṣḥāb al-ithnayn*)''.

Whatever the part played here by folkloric elements, these two texts reflect the opinion held by Muslims, in the Umayyad and ʿAbbāsid period, regarding the Manichaeans. However, there is no evidence to suggest that this opinion differed from that current in the time of Ḳurʾānic preaching. Therefore, it must be reckoned inconceivable that such Manichaeans could have been considered, in the Ḳurʾān, as forming part of the ''people of the Book''.

The Manichaeans had scriptures; but it is questionable to what extent these scriptures were known in Central Arabia at the beginning of the 7th century A.D. There are definitively some convergences to be observed between Ḳurʾānic and Manichaean concepts in matters of prophecy and revelation. But these convergences derive from ''an anonymous tendency of general thought'' (T. Andrae, *Mahomet*, 110), where are encountered ideas of the ''Messenger of God'', of the ''seal of the prophets'', of the Paraclete promised by Jesus, of ecumenism, of possession of total truth and absolute knowledge, the claim of accommodating previous revelations and of achieving ''a complete gnosis, a pure and perfect knowledge, of which the clarity and evidence are immediate and the scope infinite'' (Puech, *Histoire des litteratures*, i, 679).

It is important to bear in mind the fact that Central Arabia was (and remained) hermetically sealed to any religious mission emanating from Byzantium, from Persia, from Abyssinia. If Manichaeans succeeded in making their way to Mecca, it was only in the role of merchants or of slaves. The latter played a significant part in the penetration of certain Judaeo-Christian ideas into nascent Islam. An obvious example is that of Zayd b. Ḥāritha whom Muḥammad emancipated and then adopted. It was he who taught Muḥammad and ʿAlī to read and write. Attention may also be drawn to ʿAddās, a Christian slave and a native of Nineveh, who acknowledged the prophethood of Muḥammad, also to the seven djinns inhabiting Nisib who believed his message and went away to convey it to their fellows (Ḳurʾān XLVI, 29-32; LXXI, 1; etc.).

It may be noted, in conclusion, that the name Muḥammad was not widely known before the time of the Prophet. Among those who bore this name before Islam, Ibn Saʿd, *Ṭabaḳāt*, i, 1, 112, mentions Muḥammad b. Sufyān al-Tamīmī and describes him as a "bishop". This name corresponds to the Greek-Latin Εὐλόγιος/Eulogius. Did the adversaries of the Prophet see in this an indication of his belonging to a baptising community? Al-Ṭabarī, *Tafsīr*, i, 242, renders *ṣābiʾ* by *murtadd* "renegade", and adds that "The Arabs call *ṣābiʾ* anyone who abandons his religion for another". The polytheists said of the Prophet: *ḳad ṣabaʾa*, an expression which could be rendered by *ḳad taʿammada*, "he has had himself baptised" (cf. Ibn Saʿd, i/1, 123). In the same commentary, Ziyād b. Abīh (d. 53/673) and Ḳatāda (d. 117/735) supply the information that the *ṣābiʾūn* "worshipped the angels (*malāʾika*)", a fact attested by St. Hippolytus, ix, 13, 2-3, with regard to the Elchasaites; see also St. Epiphanius, xix, 4. 1-2; xxx, 17, 6; liii, 1, 9 (references given by de Blois, *loc. cit.*; cf. Marcel Simon, *Remarques sur l'angelolâtrie juive au début de l'ère chrétienne*, in *CRAI* [1971], 120-32). It may be noted, finally, that the *akwāl^un sabʿat^un*, "the seven words", which Ibn al-Nadīm attributes to the *mughtasila*, as they have been restored by I. Stern and M.A. Lewy (quoted by de Blois, *loc. cit.*), find an echo in sūra IV, 159, where, speaking of Jesus, the Ḳurʾān says: "On the day of Resurrection, he will testify against them (= those who are said to have believed in Him)".

2. *The Ṣābiʾat Ḥarrān.*

Thus far the discussion has been of baptising sects, whose nomenclature derives from the root *ṣ-b-ʿ*. Not being appropriate for the pagan gnostics of Ḥarrān, this root was replaced by the commentators by a root *ṣ-b-ʾ*, in the sense of "to bow down" before the celestial bodies, to worship the planets, which fitted the cults of the Ḥarrānians perfectly. In fact, bowing and prostration before the rising and setting planets formed part of their three daily prayers. Idolatry is often astrolatry. It was this last which was resisted by Abraham in Ḥarrān (Ḳurʾān, VI, 74-8; XXXVII, 83-8; etc.).

The astrolators of Ḥarrān sought to reach the "spiritual beings" (*rūḥāniyyāt*) with the aid of "celestial temples" (*al-hayākil al-ʿulwiyya*), the planets; these "temples" "rise and set" (Ḳurʾān, VI, 76-8); whence the necessity to have "figures and representations" (*ṣuwar wa-ashkhāṣ*) by which the "temples" may be reached and thereby the "spiritual beings", "because they bring us closer to God, they say" (Ḳurʾān, XXXIX, 4) and serve mankind as "mediators (*shufaʿāʾ*) before Him" (Ḳurʾān, X, 19). This information is to be found in the work of the Arab polygraphs and in al-Shahrastānī's *Milal*, the data from which have been collected and analysed by Hjärpe, *Les Sabéens Ḥarraniens*, cited in section 1. above. On the astral nature of Arab paganism, see T. Fahd, *Le panthéon de l'Arabie centrale à la veille de l'hégire*, Paris 1968, 18 ff.

The Arabic sources, and in particular Ibn al-Nadīm, who devoted to the Ḥarrānians copious pages which served as a point of departure for D. Chwolsohn, explain the designation of *ṣābiʾa*, claimed for themselves by the astrolators of Ḥarrān, as arising from an act of usurpation on their part, following a visit by the caliph al-Maʾmūn to the region. Called upon to explain their religious allegiance, they claimed to be *sābiʾa* and, consequently, "People of the Book", with the aim of evading the caliph's threats. For the same purpose, they declared themselves to be *ḥanīfs*, another Ḳurʾānic term for "monotheist" (vol. III, 60, 87-9, etc.; W. Montgomery Watt, art. ḤANĪF; Hjärpe, *op. cit.*).

The explanation is indeed plausible. Al-Maʾmūn had much respect for the Ḥarrānian scholars who were then present in large numbers in Baghdād. The most eminent of them was Thābit b. Ḳurra [*q.v.*]. Chwolsohn devotes a long chapter to biographies of the Sabian scholars (i, ch. 12); there he introduces some thirty of them: philosophers, doctors, astronomers and mathematicians.

The Sabians of Baghdād were, it seems, considered to be heterodox by the Sabians of Ḥarrān (Ibn Khallikān, *Wafayāt*, n. 127, tr. de Slane, i, 288). The threats of the caliph were to reveal support for the former, who had succeeded in gaining his favour as scholars and philosophers, against the latter whose paganism was even more manifest.

Thābit b. Ḳurra made known through numerous writings (Chwolsohn, ii, 1-6; Wiedemann, in *SPMSE* [1920-1]) the theology and the philosophy of the Ḥarrānians. He succeeded in forging amicable relations with the scholars of his time (Muslims, Jews and Christians) and was therefore capable of diffusing ideas which were to appear in the theologico-philosophical speculations of the subsequent period, at the time of the development of what has been called "Arab hermeticism" (cf. J. Doresse, *L'hermétisme égyptianisant*, in *Histoire des Religions*, ii, Paris 1972, 479-82), inspired by "Sabian" doctrines and "Indianised" hermeticist astrology, the expression of which is to be found in:

(1) *K. Sirr al-khalīḳa*, attributed to Bālīnūs [*q.v.*] Apollonius of Tyana (ed. and German tr. Ursula Weisser, Aleppo 1979 and Berlin-New York 1980), "drawn from a treatise of Hermes, *On the causes...*" "It offers two items of great interest, a study of the Creation and the famous account of the discovery of the *Emerald Table*" (cf. J. Ruska, *Tabula Smaragdina. Ein Beitrag zur Geschichte der hermetischen Literatur*, Heidelberg 1926).

(2) *Munāẓarat al-falāsifa* (*Turba philosophorum*), containing "fragments of the *Physica* and the *Mystica* of Democritus" (cf. Ruska, *Turba Philosophorum. Ein Beitrag zur Geschichte der Alchimie*, Berlin 1931).

(3) *Ghāyat al-ḥakīm* of Abu 'l-Ḳāsim Maslama b. Aḥmad al-Madjrīṭī, a manual of talismanic astrology nourished from Sabian sources, a factitious work of Hippocrates, translated into Latin under the title of *Picatrix* (cf. ed. H. Ritter, Teubner 1933; German tr. Ritter and M. Plessner, Leipzig-Berlin 1962; Ritter, *Picatrix, ein arabisches Handbuch hellenistischer Magie*, in Vorträge der Bibliothek Warburg, 1921-2, Leipzig-Berlin 1923, 94-124).

(4) *al-Filāḥa al-nabaṭiyya* (Damascus 1993), a geoponic compilation probably translated from the Syriac by Ibn Waḥshiyya [*q.v.*] at the end of the 9th and beginning of the 10th centuries A.D., containing "religious data" relating to a stellar theology based on "secrets" and on "revelations" made by the Sun, the Moon and Saturn to Adam, to Seth, his son, to Messus and to other leaders of rival gnostic sects in Babylonia. The author of the third recension of the book, Ḳūthāma, was the leader of the sect of the

Kūkaeans, known from Syriac authors; he relates, in long digressions, the echoes of their quarrels, the essential points of which are to be found in a brief survey published in *ZDMG*, suppl. iii/1, Wiesbaden 1977, 362 [see also NABAṬ. 2.].

In a very detailed study, Michel Tardieu sees the Ḥarrānians as Platonists (cf. *Ṣābiens coraniques et "Ṣābiens... de Ḥarran"*, in *JA*, cclxxiv [1986], 1-44), "in the academic sense of the term. Plato was the object of their study and the centre of the research activity of their school" (39). He refuses to describe them as "gnostics" since, according to him, "they were not philosophers by profession. But they utilised the philosophers, and Plato in particular" (*ibid.*). He bases his argument on a statement by al-Masʿūdī (*Murūḏj̲*, ed. Pellat, ii, Paris 1965, 536-7, § 1395; cf. also his *K. al-Tanbīh wa 'l-is̲h̲rāf*, 162, tr. 3-5), declaring that he "saw at Ḥarrān, on the knocker of the door of the meeting-place of the Ṣābians, an inscription in Syriac characters, drawn from Plato", which read as "He who knows his nature becomes a god" and "Man is a celestial plant. In fact, man resembles an upturned tree, the root being turned towards the sky and branches [sunk] in the ground" (Tardieu, 13 ff.). He sees, in the first "an echo of *Alcibiades*, 133.C" and, in the second, "a reminiscence" of *Timaeus*, 90 A.7-B.2 (cf. ref. 3, n. 8 and 14). It may be noted that echoes of these quotations are to be found in the literature of the "Sayings of the Sages" (*Placita philosophorum*) and that the quotation from the *Timaeus* occurs twice in the *Nabataean agriculture* (i, 360). There is no evidence to indicate that the Nabataeans of the region of Sūrā were Platonists; it has been observed that various currents of a gnostic tendency had developed there.

At the end of this extremely erudite survey, the author identifies the *ṣābiʾa* of the Ḳurʾān with the "Archontics" of Epiphanius (*Haer.*, xxix, 7, xl, 1, 5), known also by the name of "Stratiotics" (Epiphanius, *ibid.*, xxvi, 3, 7), followers of the "celestial bands", a Judaeo-Christian sect of gnostic character, formed in Palestine and known in Egypt (*ibid.*, xl, 1, 8) and in Arabia (*ibid.*, xl, 1, 5). The Ḳurʾānic term would be derived from the Hebrew *ṣābā*, "army" (an explanation already proposed by E. Pococke). Such an association leads the discussion back to Judaeo-Christian circles, among whom the Elchasaites/*mug̲h̲ü tasila* provide, in the present writer's opinion, the best explanation of the Ḳurʾānic *ṣābiʾa*.

Thus, whatever may be the origin of the name of the *ṣābiʾūn*, the latter are shown to belong to two distinct groups: on the one hand, the disciples of Judaeo-Christian baptising sects (Ebionites, Elchasaites, *mug̲h̲tasila*, Stratiotics) and, on the other, Ḥarrānian astrolators, the last representatives of decadent Greco-Roman paganism. Both groups may be described as gnostic: the first, Christian and the second, pagan. Hence the ambiguity of the term denoting them, and the diversity of commentaries relating to the three Ḳurʾānic verses which name them. A degree of corruption has occurred over the centuries, both in the terminology and the concepts, and this has greatly hindered the task of the historian of ideas and of religions.

Bibliography: Besides the references in the text, see, for studies and sources in general: D.A. Chwolsohn, *Die Ssabier und der Ssabismus*, i-ii, St. Petersburg 1856, where the bibliography of previous works is to be found; J. Hjärpe, *Analyse critique des traditions arabes sur les Sabéens Ḥarraniens*, typescript thesis, Uppsala 1972, pp. 187, including the remainder of the bibl. F. de Blois, cited in text,

has made a selection of important studies of the subject, of which the most recent are: C. Buck, *The identity of the Ṣābiʾūn: an historical quest*, in *MW*, lxxiv (1984), 172-86, and M. Tardieu, cited in text.

In addition to his study of Elchasai, cited in text, mention should be made of A.J.W. Brandt's *Die jüdischen Baptismen*, Giessen 1910; J. Thomas, *Le mouvement baptiste en Palestine et Syrie*, Gembloux 1935 (diss. theol. Louvain, ii, 28); M. Simon, *Sur deux points de contact entre le christianisme et l'Islam*, in *Iranica*, iii (1965), 20-7; H. Zimmern, *Nazoräer*, in *ZDMG*, lxxiv (1920), 429-38; B. Gärtner, *Die rätselhaften Termini Nazoräer und Iskariot*, Uppsala-Lund 1957 (*Horae Soederblomianae*); G. Widengren, *Réflexions sur le baptême dans la chrétienté syriaque*, in *Paganisme, Judaïsme, Christianisme* (= *Mél. M. Simon*), Paris 1978, 347-57; J.-D. Kaestli, *L'utilisation des actes apocryphes des Apôtres dans le manichéisme*, apud M. Krause (ed.), *Gnosis and gnosticism*, Leiden 1977, 207-16; see M. Tardieu, *Les livres sous le nom de Seth et les Séthiens de l'hérésiologie*, 204-10; M.J. Lagrange, *La gnose biblique et la tradition évangélique*, in *RB*, xxxvi (1927), 321-49; 481-515; 37/1928, 3-6; the same, *L'Evangile selon les Hébreux*, in *RB*, ii (1922), 161-81; 1923, 322-49; J. Daniélou, *Théologie du judéo-Christianisme*, Paris 1958; I. Goldziher, *Neuplatonische und gnostische Elemente im Ḥadīt̲*, in *ZA*, xxii (1909), 317-44.

Of the works of R. Macuch, the specialist on the Mandaeans, see his bibl. in *Histoire des Religions*, ii, Paris 1972, 520-2, and see K. Rudolph, ch. on the Mandaeans in *Die Religionen Altsyriens, Altarabiens und der Mandäer*, Stuttgart 1979, 403-62. On Manichaeism, see the excellent synthesis of H.-Ch. Puech, in *Histoire des Religions*, ii, 523-45 (bibl., 636-45); Seston, *Le roi sassanide Narsès, les Arabes et le manichéisme*, in *Mélanges R. Dussaud*, Paris 1939, 227-34 (= *BAH*, xxx); on *zandaḳa*, see the study by G. Vajda, *Les zindīqs en pays d'Islam au début de la période abbasside*, in *RSO*, xvii (1938), 173-229, supplemented by that of F. Gabrieli, *La "zandaḳa" au Iᵉʳ siècle abbaside*, in Cl. Cahen (ed.), *L'élaboration de l'Islam*, Symposium of Strasburg (12-14 June 1959), Paris 1961, 23-38; L. Massignon, *Inventaire de la littérature hermétique arabe*, appx. iii, *apud* Festugière, *La révélation d'Hermès Trismégiste*, i³, Paris 1950; Y. Marquet, *Sabéens et Ik̲h̲wān al-Ṣafāʾ*, in *SI*, xxiv (1966), 35 ff.; G. Monnot, *Sabéens et idolâtres selon ʿAbd al-Jabbār*, in *MIDEO*, xii (1974), 13-43; ʿAbd al-Razzāḳ al-Ḥasanī, *al-Ṣābiʾūn fī ḥāḏit̲hihim wa-māḏihim*, Ṣaydā 1955, Beirut 1958, 128 pp.

(T. FAHD)

AL-SĀBIḲŪN (A.), lit. "foregoers": a term occasionally applied in S̲h̲īʿism to the Prophet, Imāms, and Fāṭima in recognition of their status as pre-existent beings and the first of God's creatures to respond to the demand "Am I not your Lord?" (*a-lastu bi-rabbikum?*). The term derives primarily from Ḳurʾān, LVI, 10-11 (*wa 'l-sābiḳūn al-sābiḳūn ulāʾika 'l-muḳarribūn*); there are also examples of verbal usage (e.g. "how could we not be superior to the angels, since we preceded them (*sabaḳnāhum*) in knowledge of our Lord?" al-Kirmānī, *Mubīn*, i, 304). The S̲h̲īʿī concept of pre-existence closely parallels Ṣūfī theories concerning the Nūr Muḥammadī [*q.v.*] and the pre-eternal Covenant. Justification for the doctrine is found in numerous *ak̲h̲bār*, where a variety of details, many of them contradictory, are given concerning the series of events preceding the creation.

The theme of light is central to many of these traditions. Thus, "God created us from the light of his greatness" (al-Kulaynī, *Kitāb al-Ḥudj̲dj̲a*, bāb 94, p.

303); "God created me [Muḥammad] and ʿAlī and Fāṭima and Ḥasan and Ḥusayn and the (other) imāms from a light" (al-Kirmānī, *Mubīn*, i, 304); "I [Muḥammad] was created from the light of God; He created my family from my light and created those that love them from their light; the rest of mankind are in hell" (al-Kirmānī, *Faṣl*, 71); in one account, the Throne was created from the light of the Prophet, the angels from that of ʿAlī, the heavens and earth from that of Fāṭima, the sun and moon from that of Ḥasan, and heaven from that of Ḥusayn (*ibid.*, 75-6).

The term *sābiķūn* was also widely used in early Bābism, where it was applied with what seems deliberate ambiguity to the group of eighteen disciples who, with the Bāb, formed the primary cadre of the sect's hierarchy, the Letters of the Living (*ḥurūf al-ḥayy*). A faction which seems to have been broadly identical with the party centred on Ķurrat al-ʿAyn [*q.v.*] maintained that these early believers were *sābiķūn* in the double sense of having preceded the rest of mankind in recognition of the new cause and in being actual incarnations of the Prophet and Imāms. Thus Mullā Muḥammad Ḥusayn Bushrūʾī [*q.v.*] was identified as Muḥammad, Mullā ʿAlī Biṣṭāmī as ʿAlī and Ķurrat al-ʿAyn as Fāṭima. This doctrine received approval in several writings of the Bāb, notably in the early chapters of his Persian *Bayān*. Later, Bābism introduced numerous variations on this theme, and in the early period of Bahāʾī Bābism, several believers were given names of God, preceded by the title *Ism Allāh* (thus *Ism Allāh al-Aṣdaķ*).

Bibliography: Abū Dj̲aʿfar Muḥammad... b. Isḥāķ al-Kulaynī, *al-Uṣūl min al-Kāfī*, ed. Muḥammad Bāķir al-Bihbūdī and ʿAlī Akbar al-G̲h̲affārī, 4 vols., Tehran, 1392/1972, *Kitāb al-Ḥudjdja, bāb*s 94 and 111 (pp. 302-7, 434 ff.); Ḥādjdj Muḥammad K̲h̲ān Kirmānī, *al-Kitāb al-mubīn*, 2 vols., ²Kirmān 1354 S̲h̲./1975-6 (*bāb sabķ k̲h̲alķihim ʿalā malāʾikati 'llah; bāb innahum al-sābiķūn fī maʿrifat al-rabb...*, 304-5); idem, *Faṣl al-k̲h̲iṭāb*, ²Kirmān, 1392/1972, *Kitāb maʿrifat al-nubuwwa, bāb sabķ k̲h̲alķihi... ʿalā dj̲amīʿ al-kāʾināt, bāb inna dj̲amīʿ mā siwāhu min nūrihi...*, 71-2; *Kitāb maʿrifat al-imāma, bāb sabķ anwārihim ʿalā 'l-k̲h̲alķ bāb ṭīnatihim*, 75-6; Sayyid Kāẓim Ras̲h̲tī, *Uṣūl al-ʿakāʾid*, ms. pp. 57-8; Sayyid ʿAlī Muḥammad S̲h̲īrāzī, the Bāb, *Ķayyūm al-asmāʾ*, Cambridge University Library, Browne Or. ms. F. 11, fols. 37a, 45a, 132a, 161a, 162a, 182b; idem, *Bayān-i Fārsī*, n.p. [Tehran], n.d., i/2, pp. 6-7, i/3-19, pp. 8-10; D. MacEoin, *From Shaykhism to Babism: a study in charismatic renewal in Shīʿī Islam*, Ph.D. diss. Cambridge 1979, unpubl., 146 (and references), 205.

(D. MacEoin)

SABĪL (A.), pl. *subul*, literally "way, road, path", a word found frequently in the Ķurʾān and in Islamic religious usage.

1. As a religious concept.

Associated forms of the Arabic word are found in such Western Semitic languages as Hebrew and Aramaic, and also in Epigraphic South Arabian as *s¹bl* (see Joan C. Biella, *Dictionary of Old South Arabic, Sabaean dialect*, Cambridge, Mass. 1982, 326). A. Jeffery, following F. Schwally, in *ZDMG*, liii (1899), 197, surmised that *sabīl* was a loanword in Ķurʾānic usage, most likely taken from Syriac, where *s̲h̲ᵉbīlā* has both the literal sense of "road" and the figurative one of "way of life", just as in Arabic (*The foreign vocabulary of the Qurʾān*, Baroda 1938, 162).

Thus we find in the Ķurʾān its literal usage, as in III, 91/97, "whoever is able to make his way thither (sc. to the Kaʿba in Mecca)", etc. Figuratively, it has various senses, including (1) the idea of fighting in the way of God, *sabīl Allāh* (II, 149, etc.) [see DJIHĀD, MUDJĀHID]; (2) the true way of the Prophet, as in XXV, 29/27, "O would that I had taken, along with the Messenger, a way!"; (3) a means of achieving or acquiring an object, or finding a way out of a difficulty, as in IV, 19/15, "or [until] God appoints for them (i.e. women committing indecency) a way [of dealing with them]"; and (4) in the expression *ibn al-sabīl* "son of the road", later taken as "traveller, wayfarer" and therefore as a fit object of charity or compassion. Cf. II, 172/178 (which may however here refer to those early believers who had suffered in Mecca for their faith by displacement or forced emigration; see R. Bell, *Bell's commentary on the Qurʾān*, ed. C.E. Bosworth and M.E.J. Richardson, Manchester 1991, i, 35, and R. Paret, *Der Koran, Kommentar und Konkordanz*, Stuttgart etc. 1980, 38-9, with citation from G.-R. Puin, *Der Dīwān von ʿUmar ibn al-Ḫaṭṭāb*, Bonn 1970).

From the idea of doing something charitably or disinterestedly, *fī sabīl Allāh*, the word *sabīl* acquired in later Islamic times the specific meaning of "drinking fountain, public supply of water provided by someone's private munificence and charity", at the side of which is also found, less commonly, *sabbāla* "public fountain, drinking basin" (Dozy, *Supplement*, i, 630). For the social and architectural aspects of these, see 2. below.

Bibliography: Given in the article.

(C.E. Bosworth)

2. As an architectural term.

As noted above, the *sabīl* is used in mediaeval Islamic sources to designate water-houses which provided drinking water for free public use. In Egyptian *wakf* documents of the Mamlūk and Ottoman periods, the term *sabīl* is also used to designate other charitable objects, such as *ḥawḍ al-sabīl*, i.e. a drinking trough for the animals, or *maktab al-sabīl* which is a charitable elementary school for boys.

Although public water-supply is not specifically Islamic—it was a basic feature of Roman and Byzantine cities—the significance of the *sabīl* in Islamic cities is due to the repeated precept in the Ķurʾān to give water to the thirsty. However, the *sabīl* was not common in all Islamic cities, and in the cities where it was widespread its appearance does not seem to predate the 12th century. In some cities, such as Cairo, Fez or Istanbul, the *sabīl* is characterised by a distinctive architectural form. It is always richly decorated and thus meant to be an aesthetic element in the street.

1. Cairo. Mediaeval Cairo was at a distance from the Nile and, because of its hot and dry climate, the provision of drinking water was a matter of great importance. Drinking water was transported from the Nile in goats skins by camels and mules and sold in the street by ambulant water-carriers or in shops. However, providing water on a charitable basis gave the ruling establishment a good reason to demonstrate their piety.

As a charitable foundation, a *sabīl* was sustained by *wakf* endowments. The *wakf* documents of Mamlūk and Ottoman Cairo include a great deal of references to *sabīl*s, though the descriptions are generally brief. Some were attached to mosques, others were independent constructions. In the late 8th/14th century it became customary to combine the *sabīl* with a *maktab* or primary school for boys; the *maktab* was built above the *sabīl*.

The *sabīl* is usually built on two levels, an underground cistern (*ṣihrīdj*) and on the street level a room (*ḥānūt al-sabīl*) where the *muzammilātī*, or attendant of the *sabīl*, served the public. Through the window grills he issued the water in copper or ceramic cups to the passer-by. The openings at the lowest part of the grills have the shape of a row of arches which are large enough for the cups to be passed. A stone bench was built beneath the window to allow the user to stand at the level of the grill to receive the cup.

The intake of the *sabīl* was filled once a year during the season of the Nile flood in the summer; camels or mules carried the water from the Nile or the Khalīdj or Canal of Cairo in goat skins. The intake was filled in from an opening on the façade of the *sabīl*. It was made of brick and roofed with domes supported by piers and had an entrance for the maintenance staff. It was cleaned before the yearly refill and sprayed with incense; the water was perfumed with basil leaves.

Water from the intake was raised by means of buckets and filled into basins of stone or marble where the cups were replenished. A more sophisticated type of *sabīl*, such as that of Sultan al-Ghawrī, had a cistern located in a back room behind the *ḥānūt*. From this cistern a *shādirwān* was fed. The *shādirwān* in Cairene terminology is a fountain in the wall surmounted by a decorative niche, usually made of painted and gilded wood with *muḳarnas* [*q.v.*], and connected to a sloping marble panel (*salsabīl*) which led the water from the wall down into a stone or marble basin. The function of the *shādirwān*, which faced the *sabīl* window, was not only decorative but it served also to air the water coming from the cistern.

The floor of a *sabīl* was always paved with marble. Water was raised from the intake through a round opening surrounded by a marble balustrade (*kharaza*). The ceiling of the *sabīl*, which is visible to the public through the grills, was made of wood and as a rule richly painted and gilded. Cairene *sabīls* are usually adorned with the Ḳurʾānic inscription of *Sūrat al-insān* (LXXVI, 16-18) which refers to Paradise, where a heavenly ginger-flavoured water from a fountain called Salsabīl will be served.

The *maktab* of the *sabīl* is a room, similar to a loggia, open with a double or triple arch on each side. It was reached by its own staircase.

The *muzammilātī* was in charge of cleaning the premises of the *sabīl* and its utensils and of raising the water from the cistern and serving it to the thirsty. *Waḳf* documents usually stipulate that he should be clean, good-looking, free of infirmity and healthy; some documents stipulate that he should have good manners. The *muzammilātī* dwelt in an apartment attached to the *sabīl*.

Whereas Mamlūk *sabīls* were served by one person only, some Ottoman *sabīls* had more than one *muzammilātī*, such as that of ʿAbd al-Raḥmān Katkhudā, which had three. In the Ottoman period the *muzammilātī* was sometimes assisted by a person called the *sabīlī*.

The opening time of *sabīls* varied; some were open all day long, and during the month of Ramaḍān all night; others were open only at specific hours of the day, between the prayers of noon (*ẓuhr*) and afternoon (*ʿaṣr*); yet others were open only during summer.

Cairo has an important number of *sabīls* from the Mamlūk and Ottoman periods. The earliest extant *sabīl* is that of Sultan al-Nāṣir Muḥammad built in the early 8th/14th century. Today it is ruined and appears as an L-shaped portico on columns built along the corner of the *madrasa* of al-Nāṣir's father al-Manṣūr Ḳalāwūn. It was surmounted by a small dome decorated with faience mosaic on the base. The *sabīl* of Amīr Shaykhū (755/1354) is a very different type of building; it is hewn in the rock in the form of a vaulted room.

By the second half of the 8th/14th century, the standard location of the *sabīl* was at the corner of a religious building with a *maktab* on the upper floor. With two large iron-grilled windows, one on each façade, it was well ventilated. This device was maintained throughout the Mamlūk and Ottoman periods. Some mosques have more than one *sabīl-maktab*.

Sultan Ḳāʾit Bāy, who was a great builder, erected a number of separate *sabīls* all over the city. They had one or two apartments attached to them, sometimes also a shop. Some had a *miḥrāb* in the wall of the *ḥānūt*. The only extant free-standing *sabīl-maktab* of Ḳāʾit Bāy is at the Ṣalība street (884/1479); it has three façades and is one of the most lavishly decorated monuments of mediaeval Cairo, with polychrome inlaid marble, carvings, and inscriptions.

The *sabīl* of Sultan al-Ghawrī, attached to his religious-funerary complex (909/1504) in the centre of the old city of Cairo, is described in the *waḳf* document with more detail than usual. It projects from the street with three façades, each with a large window. Behind each window there was a marble basin connected to a *fawwāra*, a kind of water tap, which received water through lead tubes from the *shādirwān*. In summer the windows of the *sabīl* were protected with awnings against the sun.

The Ottomans founded fewer religious buildings than the Mamlūks, but they erected an important number of *sabīl-maktabs* in Cairo, some of which have a *miḥrāb* and were used also for prayer.

Until the 18th century the *sabīl-maktabs* continued to be built in the Mamlūk style. In the mid-18th century, a new trend for façade decoration in carved stone appears also in *sabīl* architecture. Amīr ʿAbd al-Raḥmān Katkhudā, a great patron of architecture who created a new style of façade decoration, sponsored in 1157/1744 one of the most handsome *sabīl-maktabs* of the old city of Cairo. Built at the bifurcation of the main street of al-Ḳāhira, it has three façades with marble carved in Turkish style and inlaid in Mamlūk style. The eastern façade has a trilobe *muḳarnas* portal. The interior is panelled with Turkish ceramic tiles. Two apartments for the staff are attached to the building. It has a *miḥrāb* in the shape of a painted niche in the ceramic tiles surmounted by a representation of Mecca.

In the late 18th century, the architectural style of the *sabīls* of Cairo shows Turkish influence. This can be seen at the curved semi-circular and faceted façades, the floral carvings, the inscribed cartouches with poems and chronograms, often in Turkish, and the elaborate window grills. However, the *sabīl* maintains its basic traditional features such as the *maktab* on the upper floor. The *sabīl* attached to the *madrasa* of Sultan Maḥmūd (1164/1750) has five facets and was used also for teaching; along with the *sabīls* of Ruḳayya Dūdū (1174/1761) and Nafīsa al-Bayḍāʾ (1211/1796), it is among the finest examples of the late Ottoman period. In the 19th century the Turco-Italian influence is even more pronounced, while the Islamic decorative repertoire tends to vanish. The *sabīls* of this period, unlike their contemporaries in Turkey, however, maintain the curved façades.

2. Fās. The city of Fās is often said to be built on water because of the abundance of the water which it receives from the river Fās and its tributaries, as well as from a multitude of springs. In the 5th/11th century an underground system of piped channels was built beneath the city to serve its mosques, houses and fountains.

Fās has preserved an important number of public fountains known popularly as *siḳāya* (from *saḳā* "to

The *sabīl* of ʿAbd al-Raḥmān Katkhudā in Cairo (1157/1744).

The fountain of al-Nadjdjārīn at Fās.

The *sabīl* of Sultan Aḥmed III in Istanbul (1141/1728).

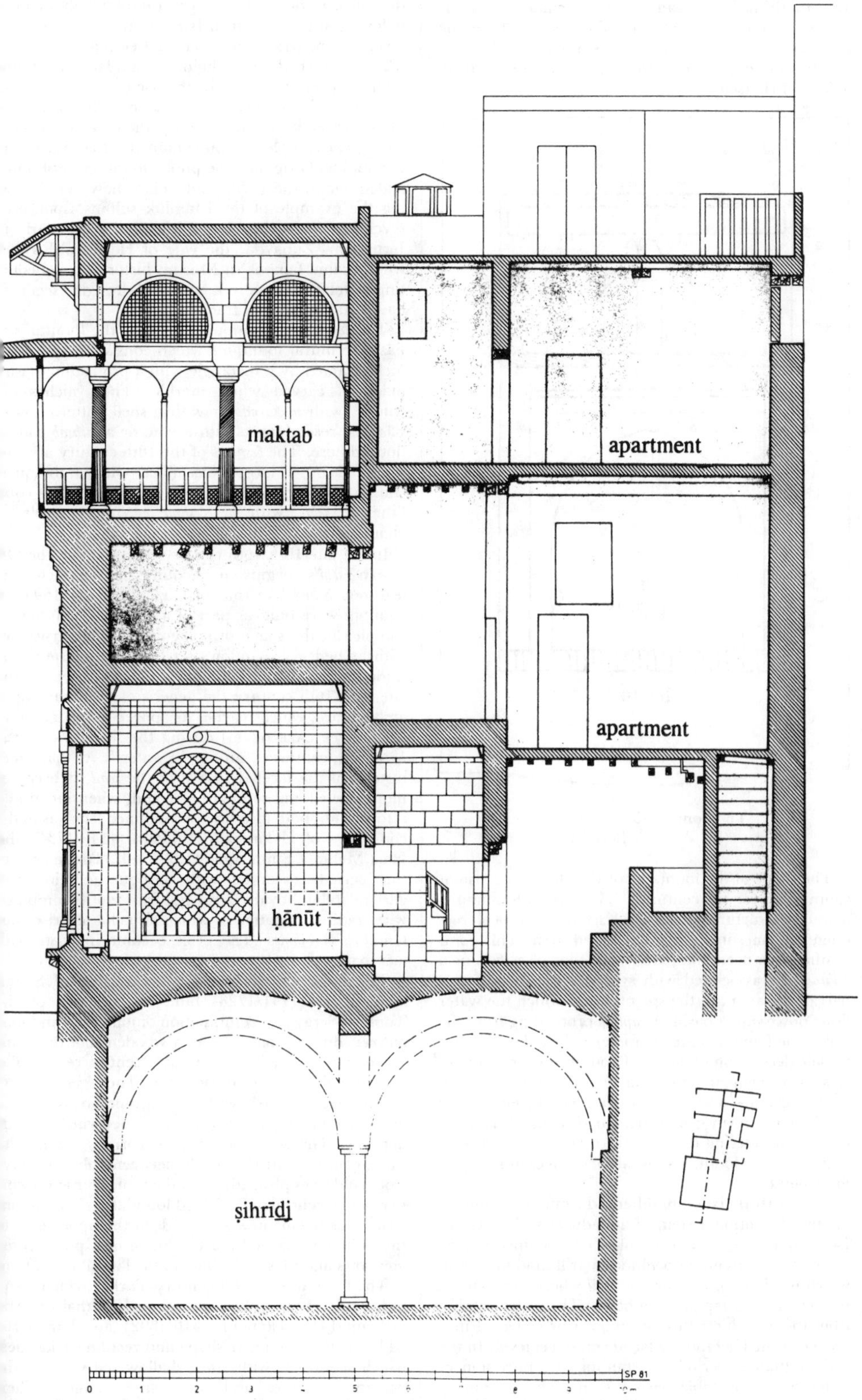

Fig. 1. The *sabīl* of ʿAbd al-Raḥmān Katkhudā in Cairo (1157/1744) (by Philip Speiser).

give to drink"). Already in the Almohad period, during the reign of al-Manṣūr, the city had 80 public fountains. Today 106 fountains survive, of which 93 are functioning. The earliest datable one is from 840/1436 (Betsch).

Fig. 2. The composition of a *sabīl* at Fās (by William Betsch).

The shape of the fountains of Fās show a persistent continuity over the centuries. The typical fountain is a mural structure which consists of a vertical rectangular panel including a recessed arch. This composition has been compared with that of a gate or a *miḥrāb* and associated with symbolism. At the lower part of the arch are the spigots from which the water flows down into a basin or *ṣundūḳ* protruding from the wall. The fountains are characterised by their faience mosaic decoration or *zallīdj*. Thousands of individually shaped elements cut from glazed ceramic tiles of several colours and cast into plaster or cement are combined to form geometric star designs of dazzling effect. Considering the white introverted architecture of the city, the fountains reveal themselves as aesthetic focal points.

3. Istanbul. Istanbul inherited from Constantinople the Byzantine system of aqueducts and pipes. In Istanbul there are two forms of *sabīl* fountains, the *sebīl* served by an attendant behind the grill, and the *česhme* which is a kind of self-service *sabīl* where the water is received from a tap above a basin. The water coming from the aqueducts through pipes was collected in a cistern located behind the façade on street level. In the early Ottoman period in Istanbul, the provision of water on a charitable basis was not very common, despite the widespread public kitchens. Public fountains were established only in the absence of alternative sources of water. J.M. Rogers has observed that the *waḳf* documents of great imperial foundation following the conquest of Istanbul did not include a a rule the provision of water for free public use. Th *siḳāyas* attached to religious foundations of th 10th/16th century were for the use of their own com munities only. References to *siḳāyas* with which mos ques were endowed indicate that their water was sold The great complex of Süleymān the Magnificent i Istanbul had originally no public fountain until Sinā added one in the 1570s. Süleyman, however, follow ing the example of the Mamlūk sultans, sponsore several *sabīls* in the Holy Cities and particularly i Jerusalem. Zubayda, the wife of Hārūn al-Rashīd who became famous in Muslim history for aqueduc ting water to Mecca in a period of drought, seems t have established this tradition.

The *česhmes* of Istanbul, similar to the fountains c Fās, are mural fountains which consist of a recesse niche framed by a rectangle with a protruding basin made of carved white marble. Their niches ar trilobe, with *muḳarnas* or with a shell pattern. As i Fās, the resemblance with a gate or a *miḥrāb* can b noticed here. The *česhmes* of the 18th century are sur mounted by a large crest filled with arabesques similar to that on manuscripts. Many fountains com bine a *sebīl* with a *česhme*. White marble i characteristic of Turkish water architecture.

In the late 10th/16th century, the shape of the Ot toman *sebīls* begins to acquire its characteristi features. *Sebīls* like that of Gazanfer Ağa (1599) i Istanbul were built as part of a religious or funerar complex in the shape of polygonal faceted structure with arched grill windows set between pilasters; th leaded domical roof had eaves. Goodwin sees in th late 10th/16th century the genesis of Ottoman wate architecture, which reaches its apogee in the late tuli period [see LALE DEVRI] during the first third of th 12th/18th century, "an age of water". At that time instead of the faceted façade of the *sebīl*, it become more curved and semi-circular and, when integrate into a tomb, both façades are combined, such as in th complexes of Hekimoğlu Ali Paşa (1147/1734) an Hacı Mehmet Emin Ağa (1152/1740). The marble c this period is carved with baroque foliation an garlands, flamboyant floral and fruit motifs combine with traditional patterns, which also characterise con temporary *česhmes*. The grills become intricate wit lacy patterns.

The most famous water-house is that of Sulta Aḥmed III (1141/1728) built at the gate of th Topkapı Seray as a combination of four *sebīls* and fou *česhmes*. Built of marble with a wooden roof that run down into eaves, it consists of a central rectangula cistern with a *česhme* on each side. The *česhmes* are se within arched panels with polychrome voussoirs an are flanked by a pair of *muḳarnas* niches which includ benches. The *sebīls* occupy the corners, each wit three concave intricate grills between columns. Fiv wooden domes protrude from the roof, four at the cor ners and a central one. Gilded foundation inscription written as poems in *nastaʿlīḳ* adorn the upper part c the building. Carved marble, paintings, polychrom voussoirs and tiles contribute to the lavish decoration

The fountains of 19th century Turkey which stan independently in public spaces, such as that of ʿAb ül-Ḥamīd II at Istanbul (1310/1892), are characteris ed by their rectangular shape and rectilinear façades which contrast with the shallow curves of th decorative arches and the volute designs. Thei decoration follows European tradition.

Bibliography: L.A. Mayer, *The buildings of Ḳāy bāy as described in his endowment deed*, London 1938

Abd al-Laṭīf Ibrāhīm ʿAlī, *Silsilat al-wat͟hāʾiḳ al-taʾrīk͟hiyya al-ḳawmiyya. mad͟jmūʿat al-wat͟hāʾiḳ al-mamlūkiyya*, in *Mad͟jallat kulliyyat al-ādāb—D͟jāmiʿat al-Ḳāhira*, xviii/2 (Dec. 1956), 183-250; R. Mantran, *Istanbul*, Paris 1962; G. Goodwin, *A history of Ottoman architecture*, London 1971; W. Betsch, *The fountains of Fez*, in *AARP*, xii (Dec. 1977), 33-46; A. Raymond, *Les fontaines publiques (Sabīl) du Caire à l'époque ottomane (1517-1798)*, in *AA*, xv (1979), 235-91; M.M. Amīn, *al-Awḳāf wa 'l-ḥayāt al-id͟jtimāʿiyya fī Miṣr (648-923/1250-1517)*, Cairo 1980; J.M. Rogers, *Innovation and continuity in Islamic urbanism*, in I. Sarageldin and S. el-Sadek (eds.), *The Arab city—its character and Islamic cultural heritage*, Medina (Arab Urban Development Institute) 1982, 53-9; Ph. Speiser, *Restaurierungsarbeiten in der islamischen Altstadt Kairos*, in *Mitteilungen des Deutschen Archäologischen Instituts Abteilung Kairo*, xxxviii (1982), 363-78; M.M. Amīn and L.A. Ibrāhīm, *al-Muṣṭalaḥāt al-miʿmāriyya fī 'l-wat͟hāʾiḳ al-mamlūkiyya*, Cairo 1990; M.Ḥ. al-Ḥusaynī, *al-Asbila 'l-ʿut͟hmāniyya bi-madīnat al-Ḳāhira (1517-1798)*, Cairo n.d.; S. Eyice, *İA*, art. *Çeşme* (incs. extensive bibl., mainly for Istanbul). See also H. İnalcik, art. ISTANBUL. (DORIS BEHRENS-ABOUSEIF)

ṢĀBIR B. ISMĀʿĪL AL-TIRMID͟HĪ, S͟hihāb al-Dīn, sually known as **ADĪB ṢĀBIR** a Persian poet of ıe first half of the 6th/12th century.

His *dīwān*, which has been published twice (ed. ʿAlī ̣awīm, Tehran 1331 *S͟h*./1952-3, and ed. M.ʿA. Nāṣiḥ, Tehran 1343 *S͟h*./1964), consists almost entire- of panegyrics praising the Sald͟jūḳ sultan Sand͟jar 511-52/1118-57), the K͟hʷārazms͟hāh Atsïz (521-8/1127-72) and various persons at their respective ourts, in particular Sand͟jar's *raʾīs-i K͟hurāsān*, Mad͟jd -Dīn ʿAlī b. D͟jaʿfar al-Musawī, the poet's principal atron. The rivalry between his two royal masters was ıe cause of his undoing. D͟juwaynī says that Ṣābir, hom Sand͟jar had sent to K͟hʷārazm with a message ır Atsïz, discovered that the K͟hʷārazms͟hāh had ispatched two men—D͟juwaynī says that they were *alāḥida* (i.e. Ismāʿīlīs)—to assassinate the sultan. ābir sent a secret message warning Sand͟jar of the lot and giving a description of the assassins, but Atsïz omehow found out about it and had Ṣābir drowned ı the Oxus. Although D͟juwaynī does not give the recise date of this incident, he does seem to imply ıat it was at some time between 538/1142-3 and 42/1147-8. Dawlats͟hāh (followed by others) repeats)juwaynī's story, but gives the date of Ṣābir's death s 546/1151-2, which seems too late.

The most noticeable feature of Ṣābir's poetry is his exterous use of artificial devices. ʿAwfī singles out a ontrived poem dedicated to Mad͟jd al-Dīn in which ābir uses the words *sarw* (cyprus) and *yāḳūt* ıyacinth) in every verse of the first (amatory) section nd then the words *āftāb* (sun) and *āsmān* (heaven) in very verse of the second (panegyric) section. He also omposed not one, but several long poems in which very verse enumerates three things ("one thing is A, second is B, a third is C") in its second *miṣrāʿ*, or gain, a *ḳaṣīda* in which he does without the letter *alif*. was for this sort of thing that he won the admiration f his contemporaries, for example that of the now uch more famous Anwarī [*q.v.*], who says in one of is verses: 'At least I am as good as Sanāʾī, even if I m not like Ṣābir'.

Bibliography: ʿAwfī, *Lubāb* ii, 117-25; D͟juwaynī ii, 8; Dawlats͟hāh, 92-3; Browne, *LHP*, ii, 333-5; S. Nafīsī, *Adīb Ṣābir-i Tirmid͟hī*, in *Armag͟hān*, iv (1920), 230-45, 294-306; Storey-de Blois, v, no. 276. (F.C. DE BLOIS)

ṢĀBIR, MĪRZĀ ʿALĪ AKBAR (b. 1862 in S͟hemākha, d. 1911 in Bākū), Azerbaijani satirical poet and journalist.

After the First Russian Revolution of 1905, a humorous and satirical literature grew up in Russian Ād͟harbayd͟jān, seen especially in the weekly journal *Mollā Naṣreddīn* founded at Tiflis in 1906 by D͟jelāl Meḥmed Ḳulī-zāde [see D͟JARĪDA. iv], which attacked the old literary forms, backwardness in education and religious fanaticism, achieving a circulation also in Turkey and Persian Ād͟harbayd͟jān. One of the writers in it was Ṣābir (who also sometimes used the pen-name Ag͟halar Güleyen, "he who laughs"), the most effective of the satirists on contemporary culture and political events, attacking *inter alia* both the Ottoman and Ḳād͟jār monarchies. After his death, his satirical poetry was collected in *Hop-hop-nāme* (Bākū 1912, repr. several times later).

Bibliography: Collected poetry in *S͟hiʿirler med͟jmūʿasi*, Bākū 1923, and subsequently in Cyrillic script in Moscow, Leningrad and Bākū. Of studies, see Ahmet Caferoğlu, in *PTF*, ii, 679-81, 690-6, 698, with specific studies on the poet noted in the bibl. there; J. Průšek (ed.), *Dict. of oriental literatures*. iii. *West Asia and North Africa*, London 1974, 163. (ED.)

SABʿIYYA, "Seveners", a designation for those S͟hīʿī sects which recognise a series of seven Imāms. Unlike the name *It͟hnā ʿas͟hariyya* or "Twelvers" the term *Sabʿiyya* does not occur in mediaeval Arabic texts; it seems to have been coined by modern scholars by analogy with the first term. The name is often used to designate the Ismāʿīliyya [*q.v.*], but this is not correct, because neither the Bohora nor the K͟hōd͟ja Ismāʿīlīs count seven Imāms. The term can be applied only to the earliest stage of the development of the Ismāʿīlī sect, during which the Ismāʿīlī propaganda proclaimed a line of seven Imāms, starting with al-Ḥasan b. ʿAlī b. Abī Ṭālib, and ending with Muḥammad b. Ismāʿīl b. D͟jaʿfar al-Ṣādiḳ whose return as the Mahdī was expected. The unity of the Ismāʿīlī movement was broken by the schism of the year 286/899 when the leader of *daʿwa*, the future Fāṭimid caliph al-Mahdī, claimed the ranks of *imām* and *mahdī*. His claim was rejected by the communities in ʿIrāḳ and al-Baḥrayn, which clung to the original doctrine, so that only these so-called Carmathian or "Ḳarmaṭī" communities preserved the old belief in a series of seven Imāms, whereas the "Fāṭimī" branch of the movement continued the line of Imāms beyond the seventh one; the actual leader of the K͟hōd͟ja branch of Ismāʿīlism, Āg͟hā K͟hān IV, is considered to be the 49th Imām. Given the inaccuracy of the artificial term, the name "Seveners" should best be avoided altogether.

Bibliography: See those for BOHORĀS; ISMĀʿĪLIYYA; ḲARMAṬĪ; K͟HŌD͟JA. (H. HALM)

SABK-I, HINDĪ (P.), the Indian style, is the third term of a classification of Persian literature into three stylistic periods. The other terms, *sabk-i K͟hurāsānī* (initially also called *sabk-i Turkistānī*) and *sabk-i ʿIrāḳī*, refer respectively to the eastern and the western parts of mediaeval Persia. The assumption underlying this geographical terminology is that the shifts of the centre of literary activity from one area to another, which took place repeatedly since the 4th/10th century, were paralleled by a stylistic development, especially in poetry. Broadly speaking, this amounted to a gradual change from the rather simple and harmonious poetical idiom of earlier times to a much more intricate manner of writing, often qualified as "baroque" [see further ĪRĀN. vii.

Literature, at vol. IV, 60a]. For a long time Persian critics have interpreted this development as a decline, which reached its lowest level during the period of the Indian style. The appellation "Indian style" was derived from the fact that the features usually associated with this style were most conspicuous in the works of poets and writers who were attached to Indian courts during the Mughal period. As the poets of the Ṣafawid court of Iṣfahān in the 17th and early 18th centuries wrote in a similar fashion, some modern Persian scholars have proposed to use the names *sabk-i Iṣfahānī* or *sabk-i Ṣafawī* instead.

Although a development of style as outlined by this classification cannot be denied, it is impossible to determine the chronological boundaries between the three periods with any precision. Only the end of the period of the Indian style can be dated approximately, and then only as far as Persia itself is concerned. In the middle of the 12th/18th century, poets in Iṣfahān and Shīrāz, notably Mushtāḳ, Maftūn and Luṭf-ʿAlī Beg [*q.v.*] Ādhar, began to criticise the excesses of the Indian style and to demand a return to what they regarded as the stylistic purety of early Persian poetry. This reaction, now known as the *bāzgasht-i adabī* (the "literary return"), initiated a neo-classicism which dominated the writing of poetry in Persia well into the present century. It also influenced the outlook of Persian critics on the Indian style. This outlook is reflected, for instance, in the introduction to Riḍā Ḳulī Khān Hidāyat's *Madjmaʿ al-fuṣaḥāʾ* (completed in 1288/1871), where the word *sabk* is already used in its modern sense although the geographical qualifications are not yet mentioned. Similar views were expressed in a letter on the subject written by Mīrzā Muḥammad Ḳazwīnī to E.G. Browne (*LHP*, iv, 26-8). This neo-classicist return did not affect, however, Persian poetry written in Afghanistan, Central Asia and, particularly, the Indian subcontinent, where the Indian style held its ground.

According to M.T. Bahār, the theory of the three styles came into being in the late 13th/19th century, when the question which one of the two early styles should be taken as a model for imitation was much debated. About 1880, literary critics at Mashhad, to which Bahār's father, the poet Ṣabūḥī, and the latter's teacher Nadīm Bāshī belonged, seem to have taken a leading part in these discussions (cf. *Sabk-shināsī*, i, pp. *y-yb*; see also *Armaghān*, xiii, 440 ff.).

It is less easy to determine the historical starting-point of the Indian style. Some modern scholars have maintained that its roots go back to the very beginnings of Indo-Persian poetry in the 7th/13th century; others have connected them to the rise of the Ṣafawid state in Persia (10th/16th century) and the exodus of Persian poets to the Indian courts which began in the course of the same century. Several names have been put forward as the initiators of these stylistic changes: among them are Fighānī [*q.v.*], who was attached to the courts of Harāt and Tabrīz during the transition between the Tīmūrid and the Ṣafawid dynasties, ʿUrfī [*q.v.*], a poet from Shīrāz who in the late 10th/16th century was one of the first Persians to make a career at the Mughal court, and his contemporary the Indian-born Fayḍī [*q.v.*]. Even much earlier poets have been mentioned occasionally as predecessors. The only statement which can be made with any degree of certainty is that the special traits of the Indian style are noticeable since the beginning of the 11th/17th century in all the countries where Persian poetry was cultivated. Eventually, it also made a strong impact on the poetry in the Persian manner which was written in Turkish, Urdu and other Indo-Aryan languages.

Several attempts have been made to define th distinctive traits of Indian style poetry and to explai its appearance. The Indian scholar Shiblī Nuʿmān [*q.v.*], in the third volume of his *Shiʿr al-ʿAdjam*, drew up a list of such features, which has been seminal fo subsequent research. Although the classification of th three regional styles was still unknown to him, he di acknowledge the innovations in the style of the poet of the 10th/16th-11th/17th centuries. The prominenc gained by the *ghazal* since the 7th/13th century (du mainly to the influence of Saʿdī, Amīr Khusraw Dihlawī and Ḥāfiẓ) was, according to Shiblī, o primary importance. An early new element was th addition of references to actual occurrences of a erotic nature to the usually abstract imagery of *ghaza* poetry, known as *wuḳūʿ-gūʾī*, "relating incidents". A remarkable example is the *Djalāliyya*, a cycle of *ghazal* written by Muḥtasham-i Kāshānī [*q.v.*] to celebrate a dancer he admired. The beloved was often identifie as a young craftsman in the bazaar (*maʿshūḳ-i bāzārī*) especially in *shahrāshūb* [*q.v.*] poetry, in which th beauty of the protagonist is described as "creatin havoc in the town". The rise of this genre betrays a tendency towards realism noticeable also in the use o images taken from real life and of elements fron popular speech, hitherto not regarded as suitable fo the poetic idiom.

A second major trend is the conceptual complexity affecting both imagery and themes, subsumed b Shiblī under the headings *khiyāl-bāfī* ("the weaving o the imagination") and *maḍmūn-sāzī* ("the creation o concepts"). His observations were further develope by A. Bausani, who pointed out that the novelty o Indian style poetry was caused by the increasin disregard of the rule of the harmonious an associative choice of images ("das Prinzip der har monischen oder beziehungsreichen Bildwahl", in th phrase of H. Ritter, cf. *Über die Bildersprache Nizāmīs* Berlin 1927, 25), which had disciplined the phantas of the classical poet. This greater freedom resulted i the combination of rather incongruous images withi the compass of a single verse as well as in a muc greater density of expression. The intricate play of th imagination these poets allowed themselves wen together with a pointed intellectualism. From the tim of ʿUrfī onwards, philosophical themes became a common element added to the Persian *ghazal*, whic was characterised already by its blend of anacreontism and mysticism. According to Bausani, th philosophical ideas expressed in this poetry wer rather superficial because the main emphasis was pu on the witticism of the expression itself. A cerebral at titude can also be observed in the frequent use of in finitives and abstract terms in a semi-allegorise mode. Shiblī mentioned the use of examples take from common speech as a kind of proverbia argumentation added to a poetic statemen (*mithāliyya*). The Persian poet Ṣāʾib [*q.v.*] was particu larly noted for this (see e.g. the specimens quoted b Browne, iv, 170-6).

Among the linguistic innovations, the formation o new compounds, a predilection for construction based on participles rather than on finite verbs, an the extension of the semantic spectrum of words ar particularly conspicuous (on this, see especially th monograph by W. Heinz). The syntax of the verse i not seldom unnatural, and this has become one of th most serious objections against the Indian style.

As a social factor promoting these changes, Shibl pointed to the rise, about the same time, of th *mushāʿaras* [*q.v.*], gatherings of poets where the poetic skills could be sharpened in competitive improvisations. This replaced the earlier tradition of imitating the works of older poets mainly accessible through written sources.

Explanations for the rise of these innovations have been sought in various directions: the political and religious revolution in Persia brought about by the establishment of the Ṣafawid state, the different cultural conditions in India as well as structural changes in Persian society. These theories were discussed, and nearly all refuted, by E. Yarshater (278 ff.), who himself proposed that the mannerism of the Indian style would signal the end of classical poetry as a living artistic tradition. In recent years, Persian critics have emphasised that a distinction should be made between an early, moderate phase, culminating in the works of Ṣāʾib (d. 1088/1677-8), and a more extreme stage of the same stylistic trends, as they are exemplified especially in the works of later poets who lived outside Persia, like Nāṣir ʿAlī Sirhindī [*q.v.*] (d. 1108/1697) and Bīdil [*q.v.*] (d. 1133/1720) in India and Shawkat of Bukhārā (d. 1107/1695-6) in Central Asia. This view led to a reappraisal of the artistic merits of Ṣafawid literature [*q.v.*].

Bibliography: Riḍā-Ḳulī Khān Hidāyat, *Madjmaʿ al-fuṣaḥāʾ*, Tehran 1295/1878, i, 1-5; Shiblī Nuʿmānī, *Shiʿr al-adjam*, Pers. tr. M.T. Fakhr-i Dāʿī Gīlānī, iii, Tehran 1335 *sh*./1956, 1 ff.; E.G. Browne, *LHP*, iv, Cambridge 1924; M.T. Bahār Malik al-Shuʿarāʾ, *Bāzgasht-i adabī*, in *Armaghān*, xiii (1311 *sh*./1932), 440 ff.; idem, *Sabkshināsī*, Tehran 1331 *sh*./1952, i, pp. *y-yb*; J.E. Bertel's, *K voprosu ob "Indiyskom stile" v persidskoy poezii*, in *Charisteria Orientalia*, ed. F. Tauer *et alii*, Prague 1956, 56-9; A. Bausani, *Contributo a una definizione dello "stile indiano" della poesia persiana*, in *AIUON*, N.S. vii (1958), 163-91; idem, *Storia della letteratura neopersiana*, Milan 1960, 478-93; idem, *Le letterature del Pakistan*, ²Milan 1968, 37-81; W. Heinz, *Der indische Stil in der persischen Literatur*, Wiesbaden 1973 (with *Literaturverzeichniss* at 115-18); Shafiʿi Kadkani, in *History of Persian literature from the beginning of the Islamic period to the present day*, ed. G. Morrison, Leiden 1981, 150-64; R. Zipoli, *Fra Ṣāʾeb e Ghāleb: Appunti per una storia filologica dell'estetica 'Indo-Persiana'*, in *La Bisaccia dello Sheikh*, Venice 1981, 275-89; idem, *Čirā sabk-i Hindī dar dunyā-yi gharb sabk-i bārūk khwānda mīshawad?*, Tehran 1363 *sh*./1985; Dh. Ṣafā, *Taʾrīkh-i adabiyyāt dar Īrān*, v/i, Tehran 1362 *sh*./1984, 521-75; Ehsan Yarshater, *The Indian or Safavid style: progress or decline?*, in *Persian literature*, ed. idem, Albany 1987, 249-88; Muḥammad Rasūl Daryāgasht, *Ṣāʾib wa sabk-i Hindī dar gustarā-yi taḥḳīḳāt-i adabī*, Tehran 1371 *sh*./1992.

(J.T.P. de Bruijn)

SABKHA (A.), pl. *sibākh*, the term used by the mediaeval Arabic geographers for salt marshes or lagoons and for the salt flats left by the evaporation of the water from such areas. Thus they employ it for describing the salt flats characteristic of parts of the Great Desert of central and eastern Persia (the present Dasht-i Kawīr and Dasht-i Lūṭ) and of the adjacent province of Sīstān (Ibn Ḥawḳal, ed. Kramers, 407, 415, tr. Kramers-Wiet, 397, 404; al-Muḳaddasī, 488; cf. A. Miquel, *La géographie humaine du monde musulman jusqu'au milieu du 11ᵉ siècle. iii. Le milieu naturelle*, Paris-The Hague 1980, 95).

In the Maghrib, the form *sebkha* is used to denote the salt lagoon, one of the characteristic features of the hydrography of North Africa and the Sahara, very common in the high plains, without communication with the sea. It is the terminus of a network of streams either above ground or subterranean, which have spread out and disappear in the ground; it is a shallow basin with well-marked contours sometimes delineated by steep sides. After rain, it is more or less completely filled with water impregnated with mineral substances which accumulate at the bottom of the basin. In periods of drought, the waters evaporate completely or partly and the floor is uncovered. The floor of the *sebkha* is covered with saline incrustations, sometimes traversed by crevasses in which the crystals gather. The salt deposit sometimes covers mud, quicksands and dangerous quagmires.

This definition and description of the features of the *sebkha* apply equally to the *shoṭṭ*. An attempt has been made to establish a distinction between the two, the former term being applied to hollows which always remain more or less moist, the second to those whose evaporation is greater than the access of subterranean water or to those the floor of which looks like a plain losing itself in the horizon. There is no real foundation for this distinction. The two terms are employed indifferently in the same district. For example, we have in Orania the *sebkha* of Oran and the *shoṭṭ* Gharliu and Sharḳī, in the Sahara the *sebkha* of Timimūn (Gurara), the *shoṭṭ* of Southern Tunisia, the *sebkha* of Wargla, of Siwa, etc.

Bibliography: See that to ṢAḤĀRĀ.

(G. Yver*)

ṢABR (A.), usually rendered "patience, endurance". The significance of this conception can hardly be conveyed in a West European language by a single word, as may be seen from the following. According to the Arabic lexicographers, the root *ṣ-b-r*, of which *ṣabr* is the *nomen actionis*, means to restrain or bind; thence *ḳatalahu ṣabran* "to bind and then slay someone". The slayer and the slain in this case are called *ṣābir* and *maṣbūr* respectively. The expression is applied, for example, to martyrs and prisoners of war put to death; in the *Ḥadīth* often to animals that—contrary to the Muslim prohibition—are tortured to death (e.g. al-Bukhārī, *Dhabāʾiḥ*, *bāb* 25; Muslim, *Ṣayd*, trad. 58; Aḥmad b. Ḥanbal, *Musnad*, iii, 171). The word has a special technical application in the expression *yamīnu ṣabrin*, by which is meant an oath imposed by the public authorities and therefore taken unwillingly (e.g. al-Bukhārī, *Manāḳib al-Anṣār*, *bāb* 27; *Aymān*, *bāb* 17; Muslim, *Īmān*, trad. 176).

In the Ḳurʾān, derivations from the root *ṣ-b-r* frequently occur, in the first place with the general meaning of being patient. Muḥammad is warned to be patient like the Apostles of God before him (XXXVIII, 16; XLVI, 34; "for Allāh's threats are fulfilled", is added in XXX, 60). A double reward is promised to the patient (XXXIII, 113; XXVIII, 54; cf. XXV, 75). In XXXIX, 16, it is even said that the *ṣābirūn* shall receive their reward without *ḥisāb* (which in this case is explained as measure or limitation).

The conception is given a special application to the holy war (e.g. III, 140; VIII, 66); in such connections it can be translated by "endurance, tenacity". Form VIII is also used in almost the same sense, e.g. XIX, 66, "Serve him and persevere in his service". The third stem is also found (III, 200; see below).

The word is next found with the meaning resignation, e.g. in the sūra of Joseph (XII, 18) where Jacob, on hearing of the death of his son, says "[My best course is] fitting resignation" (*fa-ṣabrun djamīlun*).

Sometimes *ṣabr* is associated with the *ṣalāt* (II, 42, 148). According to the commentators, it is in these passages synonymous with fasting, and they quote in support the name *shahr al-ṣabr* given to the month of Ramaḍān [*q.v.*].

As an adjective, we find *ṣabbār* in the Ḳurʾān,

associated with shakūr (XIV, 5 etc.); cf. thereon al-Ṭabarī, *Tafsīr*, "It is well with the man who is resigned when misfortune afflicts him, grateful when gifts of grace become his"; and Muslim, *Zuhd*, trad. 64, "Wonderful is the attitude of the believer; everything is for the best with him; if something pleasant happens to him, he is thankful and this proves for the best with him; and if misfortune meets him, he is resigned and this again is for the best with him." The ideas of *ṣabr* and *shukr* are also associated in al-Ghazālī, see below.

The later development of the conception is, of course, also reflected in the commentaries on the Ḳurʾān; it is difficult to say in how far these interpretations are already inherent in the language of the Ḳurʾān. In any case, the conception *ṣabr*, in all its shades of meaning, is essentially Hellenistic in so far as it includes the ἀταραξία of the Stoic, the patience of the Christian and the self-control and renunciation of the ascetic; cf. below. In place of many other explanations of the commentators, we will give here only that of Fakhr al-Dīn al-Rāzī (*Mafātīḥ al-ghayb*, Cairo 1278, on III, 200). He distinguishes four kinds of *ṣabr*: (1) endurance in the laborious intellectual task of dealing with matters of dogma, e.g. in the doctrine of *tawḥīd, ʿadl, nubuwwa, maʿād* and disputed points; (2) endurance in completing operations one is bound or recommended by law to do; (3) steadfastness in refraining from forbidden activities; and (4) resignation in calamity, etc. *Muṣābara* is, according to him, the application of *ṣabr* to one's fellow-creature (like neighbours, People of the Book), refraining from revenge, the *amr bi'l-maʿrūf wa'l-nahy ʿani 'l-munkar*, etc.

The high value laid upon *ṣabr* is also seen in the fact that al-Ṣabūr is included among the beautiful names of God. According to the *Lisān* (s.v. *ṣ-b-r*), Ṣabūr is a synonym of *ḥalīm*, with the difference that the sinner need not fear any retribution from al-Ḥalīm, but he is not sure of such leniency from al-Ṣabūr. God's *ṣabr* is in the *Ḥadīth* increased to the highest degree in the saying that no one is more patient than He towards that which wounds His hearing (al-Bukhārī, *Tawḥīd, bāb* 3).

In the *Ḥadīth*, *ṣabr* is, in the first place, found in general connections, like, to him who practises *ṣabr* God will grant *ṣabr*, for *ṣabr* is the greatest charisma (al-Bukhārī, *Zakāt, bāb* 50; *Riḳāḳ, bāb* 20; Aḥmad b. Ḥanbal, iii, 93); in the *Ḥadīth* also, *ṣabr* is applied to endurance in the holy war. A man asked Muḥammad: "If I take part in the *Djihād* with my life and my property and I am killed *ṣabr*^an^ and resigned, rushing forward without fleeing, shall I enter Paradise?" And Muḥammad answered: "Yes". (Aḥmad b. Ḥanbal, iii, 325). The word is found in other passages in the sense of enduring, e.g. towards the public authorities, "after my death ye shall suffer things, but exercise *ṣabr* until ye meet me at the heavenly pool" (*ḥawḍ*) (al-Bukhārī, *Riḳāḳ, bāb* 53; *Fitan, bāb* 2; cf. *Aḥkām, bāb* 4; Muslim, *Imāra*, trads. 53, 56, etc.). The word here usually has the meaning of resignation, as in the oft-recurring saying, "The (true) *ṣabr* is revealed at the first blow (*innamā 'l-ṣabr ʿinda 'l-ṣadmati 'l-ūlā*, or *awwali ṣadmatin* or *awwali 'l-ṣadmati*, al-Bukhārī, *Djanāʾiz, bāb* 32, 43; Muslim, *Djanāʾiz*, trad. 15; Abū Dāwūd, *Djanāʾiz, bāb* 22, etc.).

Significant, in other respects also, is the story of the epileptic woman who asked Muḥammad for his *duʿāʾ* for her healing; he replied to her that, if she refrained from her request and exercised *ṣabr*, paradise would be her portion (al-Bukhārī, *Marḍā, bāb* 6; Muslim, *al-Birr wa 'l-ṣila*, trad. 54). The word is often found in this connection associated with the proper word for resignation, viz. *iḥtisāb* (e.g. al-Bukhārī, *Aymān, bāb* [...] Muslim, *Djanāʾiz*, trad. 11); with this should be com[...]pared the following *ḥadīth ḳudsī*, "If my servant [...] deprived of the light of both his eyes, I grant hi[...] paradise in compensation" (al-Bukhārī, *Marḍā, b*[...] 67; Aḥmad b. Ḥanbal, iii, 283).

In conclusion, we may remark that in the canonic[...] *Ḥadīth* the meaning renunciation is exceeding[...] rare, a meaning which receives so great an impo[...]tance in ethico-ascetic mysticism (cf. what has alrea[...] been said above on sūra II, 42, 148). *Bāb* 20 of a[...] Bukhārī's *Kitāb al-Riḳāḳ* (which, like the chapter *zu*[...] in the other collections of traditions, represents th[...] oldest stage of this tendency in Islam) has in the *ta*[...]*djama*: ʿUmar said, "We have found the best of o[...] life in *ṣabr*." Here we already can trace the Hellenist[...] sphere of thought for which renunciation was the ki[...] of life fitting the true man, the wise man, the marty[...]

What the Ḳurʾān and *Ḥadīth* say about *ṣabr* recu[...] in part again in ethico-mystical literature; b[...] the word has here become, so to speak, a technic[...] term and to a very high degree, as *ṣabr* is the cardin[...] virtue in this school of thought. As with other fu[...]damental conceptions (see the series of definitions [...] Ṣūfī and Ṣūfism given by Nicholson in *JRAS* [1905][...] we find numerous definitions of *ṣabr*, definitio[...] which often point rather to fertility of imaginatio[...] than give an exhaustive exposition of the idea, but a[...] of great value for the light which they throw upon th[...] subject like lightning flashes. Al-Ḳushayrī in hi[...] *Risāla*, ed. ʿA.H. Maḥmūd and M. Ibn al-Sharī[...] Cairo 1385/1966, 397-404, gives the following colle[...]tion: "The gulping down of bitterness withou[...] making a wry face" (al-Djunayd); "the refrainin[...] from unpermitted things, silence in suffering blows [...] fate, showing oneself rich when poverty settles in th[...] courts of subsistence"; "steadfastness in fittin[...] behaviour (*Ḥusn al-adab*) under blows of fate" (Ib[...] ʿAṭāʾ); "bowing before the blow without a sound [...] complaint"; "the *ṣabbār* is he who has accustome[...] himself to suddenly meeting with forbidden things[...] (Abū ʿUthmān); "*ṣabr* consists in welcoming illness a[...] if it were health"; "steadfastness in God and meetin[...] His blows with a good countenance and equanimity[...] (ʿAmr b. ʿUthmān); "steadfastness in the ordinanc[...] of the Book and of the Sunna" (al-Khawwāṣ); "th[...] *ṣabr* of the mystics (literally, lovers) is more difficu[...] than that of the ascetics" (Yaḥyā b. Muʿādh[...] "refraining from complaint" (Ruwaym); "seekin[...] help with God" (Dhu 'l-Nūn); *ṣabr* is like its name i.e[...] [bitter] like aloes (*ṣabr*; see the next article) (Abū ʿA[...] al-Daḳḳāḳ); "there are three kinds of *ṣabr*, *ṣabr* of th[...] *mutaṣabbir*, of the *ṣābir* and of the *ṣabbār* (Abū ʿAb[...] Allāh b. Khafīf); "*ṣabr* is a steed that never stumbles[...] (ʿAlī b. Abī Ṭālib); and "*ṣabr* is not to distinguish be[...]tween the condition of grace and that of trial, in peac[...] of spirit in both; *taṣabbur* is calm under blows, whil[...] one feels the heavy trial" (Abū Muḥammad a[...] Djurayrī; cf. ἀταραξία).

Al-Ghazālī treats of *ṣabr* in Book II of the fourt[...] part of the *Iḥyāʾ*, which describes the virtues that mak[...] blessed. We have seen that, already in the Ḳurʾān[...] *ṣabr* and *shukr* are found in association. Al-Ghazā[...] discusses the two conceptions in the second boo[...] separately, but in reality in close connection. He base[...] the combination, not on the Ḳurʾānic phraseology but on the maxim "belief consists of two halves: th[...] one *ṣabr* and the other *shukr*". This again goes back t[...] the tradition "*ṣabr* is the half of belief" (cf. the tradi[...]tions given above which also associate *ṣabr* and *shukr*)

Al-Ghazālī comprises the treatment of *ṣabr* unde[...] the following heads: (1) the excellence of *ṣabr*; (2) it[...]

ature and conception; (3) *ṣabr*, the half of belief; (4) ynonyms with reference to the object of *ṣabr*; (5) kinds f *ṣabr* as regards strength and weakness; (6) opinions egarding the necessity of *ṣabr* and how man can never ispense with *ṣabr*; and (7) the healthfulness of *ṣabr* nd means of attaining it. This division is virtually dopted by Bar Hebraeus [see IBN AL-ʿIBRĪ] in his *thikon* for the *msaybrānūtā* (see A.J. Wensinck, *Bar Iebraeus' Book of the Dove*, Leiden 1919, pp. xvii-cxix).

Only the following out of these sections can be iven here. *Ṣabr*, like all religious *maḳāmāt*, consists of iree parts, *maʿrifa, ḥāl* and *ʿamal*. The *maʿārif* are like ie tree, the *aḥwāl* the branches and the *aʿmāl* the uits. Out of the three classes of beings, man alone iay possess *ṣabr*. For the animals are entirely gov- rned by their desires and impulses; the angels, on the ther hand, are completely filled by their longing for ie deity, so that no desire has power over them and s a result no *ṣabr* is necessary to overcome it. In man, n the contrary, two impulses (*bāʿith*) are fighting, the npulse of desires and the impulse of religion; the ormer is kindled by Satan and the latter by the ngels. *Ṣabr* means adherence to the religious as op- osed to the sensual impulse.

Ṣabr is of two kinds: (a) the physical, like the en- urance of physical ills, whether active, as in perform- ig difficult tasks, or passive, as in suffering blows, tc.; this kind is laudable; and (b) the spiritual, like enunciation in face of natural impulses. According to s different objects, it is called by synonyms like *ʿiffa, abṭ al-nafs, shadjāʿa, ḥilm, saʿat al-ṣadr, kitmān al-sirr, uhd* and *ḳanāʿa*. From this wide range of meanings, e can understand that Muḥammad, when asked, ould answer, "*īmān* is *ṣabr*". This kind is absolutely udable (*maḥmūd tāmm*).

As regards the greater or less strength of their *ṣabr*, iree classes of individuals are distinguishable: (a) the ery few in whom *ṣabr* has become a permanent condi- on; these are the *ṣiddīḳūn* and the *muḳarrabūn*; (b) iose in whom animal impulses predominate; and (c) iose in whom a continual struggle is going on be- veen the two impulses; these are the *mudjāhidūn*; erhaps Allāh will heed them. One of the gnostics ays al-Ghazālī) distinguishes three kinds of *ṣābirūn*: iose who renounce desires, these are the *tāʾibūn*; iose who submit to the divine decree, these are the *ihidūn*; and those who delight in whatever God allows come upon them, these are the *ṣiddīḳūn*.

In section VI, al-Ghazālī shows how the believer re- uires *ṣabr* under all circumstances; (a) in health and rosperity; here the close connection between *ṣabr* and ratitude is seen; and (b) in all that does not belong this category, as in the performance of legal obliga- ons, in refraining from forbidden things and in hatever happens to a man against his will, either om his fellow-men or by God's decree.

As *ṣabr* is an indication of the struggle between the vo impulses, its salutary effect consists in all that may rengthen the religious impulse and weaken the nimal one. The weakening of the animal impulse is rought about by asceticism, by avoiding whatever creases this impulse, e.g. by withdrawal (*ʿazla*), or y the practice of what is permitted, e.g. marriage. he strengthening of the religious impulse is brought bout (a) by the awakening of the desire for the fruits f *mudjāhada*, e.g. by means of the reading of the lives saints or prophets; and (b) by gradually accustom- ig this impulse to the struggle with its antagonist, so iat finally the consciousness of superiority becomes a elight.

Bibliography: Besides the references in the text, see Sprenger, *Dict. of the techn. terms*, i, 823 ff.; M. Asín Palacios, *La mystique d'al-Gazzali*, in *MFOB*, vii, 75 ff.; R. Hartmann, *al-Ḳuschairîs Darstellung des Ṣûfîtums*, Türk. Bibl., xviii, Berlin 1914, index; L. Massignon, *Al-Hallaj, martyr mystique de l'Islam*, Paris 1922, index; *Essai sur les origines du lexique technique de la mystique musulmane*, Paris 1954, index; ʿUmar al-Suhrawardī, *ʿAwārif al-maʿārif*, Beirut 1966, 480-1; Ibn Ḳayyim al-Djawziyya, *Madāridj al-sālikīn*, ed. al-Fīḳī, Beirut n.d., ii, 152-70; Ibn ʿArabī, *al-Futūḥāt al-makkiyya*, Cairo 1329, ii, 28-9, 206-8; P. Nwyia, *Exégèse coranique et langage mystique*, Beirut 1970, index; H. Ritter, *Das Meer der Seele*, Leiden 1978, 235-7: Annemarie Schimmel, *The Triumphal Sun. A study of the works of Jalaloddin Rumi*, London-The Hague 1980, 304-7; eadem. *Mystical dimensions of Islam*, Chapel Hill N.C. 1981, 124-5; R. Gramlich, *Das Sendschreiben al-Qušayrīs über das Sufitum*, Stuttgart 1989, 263-70; idem, *Schlaglichter über das Sufitum, Abū Naṣr al-Sarrāǧs Kitāb al-Lumaʿ*, Stuttgart 1990, 96-7, 258-61; Barbara R. von Schlegell (tr.), *Principles of Sufism by al-Qushayrī*, Berkeley and Los Angeles 1990, 147-56. On the divine name *al-Ṣabūr*, see D. Gimaret, *Les noms divins en Islam*, Paris 1988, 422.

(A.J. WENSINCK)

ṢABR (*ṣabir, ṣabur*) (A.) denotes the aloe, a species of the *Liliaceae*, which was widespread in the warm countries of the ancient world, mainly in Cyprus and on the mountains of Africa.

The leaves of many varieties provide fibres ("aloe-fibres") for spinning coarse cloths, and from the aloe's dark-brown wood a valued perfumery is won. Important was also the aloe drug, i.e. the juice pressed from the leaves, whose Greek name ἀλόη was borrowed by the Arab pharmacologists as *āluwī*. In the West, the name apparently was pronounced *ṣibar*, which survives in Spanish *acibar*. The most extensive descriptions of the plant and its drug are found in Ibn al-Bayṭār, *Djāmiʿ*, iii, 77-81 (tr. Leclerc no. 1388) and in al-Nuwayrī, *Nihāya*, xi, 304-7. According to them, the leaves of the plant resemble those of the sea onion (*ishkīl*), which are wide and thick, bent back, covered with a sticky liquid and whose ends are thorny. Among the numerous varieties of the aloe, three are generally mentioned: *suḳuṭrī*, *ʿarabī* (*ḥaḍramī*), and *simindjānī* (the latter reading is uncertain; it is perhaps derived from Simindjān in Ṭukhāristān). The first variety is considered to be the best and probably corresponds with the *Aloe Parryi* Baker, the *Aloe Socotrina*, which thrives in great quantities on the island of Socotra (Suḳuṭrā [*q.v.*]). The leaves, which are full of water, are squeezed, chopped up and pounded until the juice comes out. This is left to thicken, placed in a dish and exposed to the sun until it dries up. The juice resembles that of saffron, its scent that of myrh. The entire plant has a sharp odour and a very bitter taste. It has only one root. The drug was used above all as laxative, as an amarum or appetiser and as a choleretic; externally, it was applied on badly healing wounds, ulcers and burns; it was also used against inflamations of the eye, and as a means to improve bad breath.

Bibliography: A. Dietrich, *Dioscurides triumphans. Ein anonymer arabischer Kommentar (Ende 12. Jahrh. n. Chr.) zur Materia Medica*, no. III, 23, in *Abh. Ak. Göttingen*, Phil.-hist. Kl., Neue Folge, no. 173, Göttingen 1988.

(A. DIETRICH)

ṢABRA or SABRATHA, one of the three ancient cities (Leptis Magna = Lebda; Oea = Tripoli; and Sabratha or Sabrata = Ṣabra) which made up Tripolitania. Ṣabra Manṣūriyya [*q.v.*], another town

33 km/20 miles to the west of Tlemcen in Algeria bore (Ibn Khaldūn, *ʿIbar*, Beirut 1959, vii, 524), and still bears today, this same name, after having assumed that of Turenne in the colonial period. The homonomy here is fortuitous.

Ṣabrāṭa—now a tourist town and the centre of an archaeological zone along the littoral some 75 km/48 miles west of Tripoli and 35 km/20 miles west of Zuwāra—is a Tyrian foundation, or a Carthaginian one, dating from the 5th century B.C., of which imposing ruins remain.

In 22/642-3, ʿAmr b. al-ʿĀṣ, after having taken Tripoli, made a surprise attack on Sabratha, at that time in decline and inhabited by Berber Christians of the Nafūsa tribe [*q.v.*]. In 123/741, Ṣabra (or Sabrata according to the orthography of Ibn ʿAbd al-Ḥakam) was besieged by the Ṣufrī Berbers of the Zanāta tribe, and then relieved by the *amīr* of Tripoli. In 131/748-9, ʿAbd al-Raḥmān b. Ḥabīb, the master of Ḳayrawān, at that moment on bad terms with the caliphate, transferred the population and trade of Ṣabra to Nubāra, probably in consequence of a rebellion. This was almost certainly only a partial and temporary transfer. Towards the middle of the 3rd/9th century it was the "ancient statues in stone" which attracted al-Yaʿḳūbī's attention. Ibn Ḥawḳal noted that, at the time when he visited the Maghrib, in 340/951-2, a tax was levied on caravans which passed through the town. In the last quarter of the 4th/10th century, al-Muḳaddasī wrote that Ṣabra was a fortified town, surrounded by palm groves and orchards full of fig trees. In 403/1012-13 Ṣabra was at the centre of rebellions fomented by the Zanāta against the Zīrid *amīr* Bādīs. Towards the end of the 5th/11th century, al-Bakrī described it as a prosperous town, populated by Zuwāgha, who had taken the side of Ibn Khalaf against the last Rustamids [*q.v.*]. In the middle years of the 6th/12th century, al-Idrīsī merely mentions it, adding that it was, like all the other urban centres of the region, "a lifeless desert" (*khalāʾ balḳaʿ*), having been devastated by the Arabs of the Banū Hilāl and given over to pillage by the Mirdās and Riyāḥ, as confirmed by Ibn Khaldūn. In Ṣafar 707/August 1307, al-Tidjānī noted that the biggest populated unit of the region through which he was passing was Zuwāgha, and that in its environs, by the sea coast, were to be found "the ruins of an ancient city known as Ṣabra, which may also be sometimes written with a *sīn*". In the mid-10th/16th century, Leo Africanus/al-Ḥasan b. Muḥammad al-Zayyātī no longer mentions Ṣabra. He merely mentions Zuwāra, describing it as a small town in full decay. It was in the neighbourhood of this town that there was held, in a tent, the conference of March-September 1893 between France and the Ottomans which delimited the Tunisian-Libyan frontier.

Bibliography: 1. Sources. Ibn ʿAbd al-Ḥakam, *Futūḥ Ifrīḳiya* (= *Conquête de l'Afrique du Nord* ...), ed. and partial tr. A. Gateau, Algiers 1947, 34/35, 38/39, 126/127; Ibn Khurradādhbih, *Description du Maghreb*, ed. and partial tr. Hadj-Sadok, Algiers 1949, 4/5; Yaʿḳūbī, *Buldān*, tr. Wiet, 208; Ibn Ḥawḳal, tr. Kramers-Wiet, 60, 65; Muḳaddasī, *Description de l'Occident musulman*, ed. and partial tr. Ch. Pellat, Algiers 1950, 4/5, 12/13, 16/17; Bakrī, *Masālik*, Tunis 1992, ii, 665; Abū Zakariyyāʾ, *Sīra*, Tunis 1985, 146; Idrīsī, *Opus geographicum*, Naples-Rome 1984, iii, 276, 297; Ibn Khaldūn *ʿIbar*, Beirut 1959, ii, 1002-3, vi, 213, 230, vii, 87; Tidjānī, *Riḥla*, Tunis 1958, 211-12; Yāḳūt, *Buldān*, Beirut 1374-6/1955-7, v, 256; Leo Africanus, *Waṣf Ifrīḳiya*, 2nd ed. Beirut-Rabat 1983, ii, 96.

2. Studies. H. Fournel, *Les Berbères*, Paris 1875-81, i, 22-3; T. Lewicki, *Etudes Ibāḍites Nord Africaines*, Warsaw 1955, 52-4, 126; Ch.-A. Julien *Histoire de l'Afrique du Nord*, Paris 1956, i, 167, 173-5; H.R. Idris, *Zīrīdes*, Paris 1962, i, 105, ii, 460; A Martel, *Les confins Saharo-Tripolitains de la Tunisie (1881-1911)*, Paris 1965, 95, 538-66; P. Ward *Sabratha, a guide for visitors*, Stoughton, USA 1970 *Encycl. Britannica*, s.v. *Sabratha*. (M. TALBI)

ṢABRA or AL-**MANṢŪRIYYA**, or also MADĪNAT ʿIZZ AL-ISLĀM, a royal city founded between 334 and 336/945-8, at half-a-mile to the southeast of Ḳayrawān, by the Fāṭimid caliph al-Manṣūr—whence its name—in order to commemorate his victory over the rebel Abū Yazīd [*q.v.*], on the very spot so we are told, of a decisive battle.

The name. *Ṣabra* means "a very hard stone" (*LʿA* Beirut 1955, iv, 441, 442). Like *ṣakhr* "rock", the term is attested as a personal name (al-Ṭabarī, index al-Mālikī, *Riyāḍ*, Beirut 1983, i, 250) or as that of a clan (Kaḥḥāla, *Muʿdjam ḳabāʾil al-ʿArab*, Beirut 1968 ii, 631). As a toponym, Ṣabra probably designated a suburb or a stretch of land, in the proximity of Ḳayrawān, which derived its name from that of the occupiers of the place. The city founded on this spot or near it, was officially called al-Manṣūriyya "the Victorious City", and it is this name which, until 438/1046-7 (i.e. till the Zīrids' break with the Fāṭimids in Cairo), appears exclusively on coins. To symbolise the rupture in relations, the city officially changed its name from 439/1047-8 onwards. After then, there appears either the original name Ṣabra (which had never completely disappeared out of everyday usage) or that of Madīnat ʿIzz al-Islām "City of the Glory of Islam". The Ḳāḍī al-Nuʿmān [*q.v.*], the first judge of the city founded by al-Manṣūr, in his *K. al-Madjālis* (ed. Tunis 1978, index) never calls it by anything but its official name al-Manṣūriyya. Other authors call it indifferently by one or the other of its names. The derivation of the name Ṣabra from the root *ṣ-b-r* "to endure", with reference to the contradictory exhortations to resistance addressed to the Shīʿī troops by al-Mansūr (al Muḳaddasī, partial Fr. tr. Ch. Pellat, Algiers 1950, 16-17; Ibn Ḥammād, *Akhbār*, ed. and Fr. tr Vonderheyden, Algiers-Paris 1927, 23-41), or, per contra, to the Khāridjite troops by Abū Yazīd (Abū Zakariyyāʾ, *K. al-Sīra*, Tunis 1985), 175, is, so far as one can see, an imagined, *post eventum* explanation.

The city's evolution. On Tuesday 19 Shawwāl 337/1 May 949 al-Manṣūr transferred the seat of his government to al-Manṣūriyya (Ibn Ḥawḳal, *K. Ṣūrat al-arḍ* tr. Kramers-Wiet, 68). As with Baghdād, the city was round in plan—and this is confirmed by aerial photography—and the caliph's palace was in the centre. Its ramparts were pierced with four or five gates with iron fittings. The city had a copious supply of water and very soon developed greatly. Al-Manṣūr's successors in turn built numerous and luxurious palaces adorned with gardens and stretches of water palaces whose foundations have been partially revealed by excavations. The city had 300 *ḥammāms* which belonged largely to private houses. After al-Muʿizz's departure for Cairo, his lieutenant in the Maghrib, Buluggīn, installed himself on Thursday 11 Rabīʿ I 362/20 December 972 at al-Manṣūriyya, in the very palace which his sovereign had just left. This marked the beginning of the city's Zīrid period. Some decades later, in 405/1014-15, on the orders of Bādīs merchants and artisans were officially transplanted from Ḳayrawān to al-Manṣūriyya (Ibn ʿIdhārī *Bayān*, i, 261, see also i, 219-20, 241, 268, 276, 278

291, 293-4). The resultant dissatisfaction in Ḳayrawān, now deprived of its economic role, was not perhaps unconnected with the revolt which broke out there in 407/1016 at the coming of al-Muʿizz b. Bādīs [*q.v.*] and which spread to al-Manṣūriyya, which was badly damaged. Finally, in 449/1057, under pressure from the Banū Hilāl, al-Muʿizz fled to al-Mahdiyya. Al-Manṣūriyya was then totally devastated, and, unlike Ḳayrawān, never rose again from its ruins. Al-Idrīsī, in the middle of the 6th/12th century, depicts it as ruinous and deserted: "One no longer meets any living soul there" (*Opus geographicum*, Naples-Rome 1984, iii, 284).

Over the ensuing centuries, the site was pillaged, and the excavations, begun in 1921, have only yielded a few remains: paving materials, sculpted plaques, pottery with geometric or life-like decorations, etc.

Bibliography (in addition to references given in the article): 1. Sources. Bakrī, *Masālik*, Tunis 1992, §§ 1131-2, 1145, fr. tr. de Slane, 57-8, 68; Ibn al-Abbār, *Ḥulla*, Cairo 1963, ii, 21-2, 389; Ibn Khaldūn, *ʿIbar*, Beirut 1959, vi, 320; Tīdjānī, *Riḥla*, Tunis 1958, 328-9; Yāḳūt, *Buldān*, ed. Beirut, iii, 391-2.

2. Studies. Ḥ.Ḥ. ʿAbd al-Wahhāb, *Bisāṭ*, Tunis 1970, index; M. al-ʿAdjdjābī, *Ṣabra al-Manṣūriyya*, in *Encycl. de la Tunisie*, Tunis 1992, fasc. 3, 73-6; Brunschwig, *Ḥafṣides*, i, 304, 357, 363; F. Dachraoui, *Fatimides*, Tunis 1981, 187, 195, 260, 267; J. Farrugia de Candia, numismatic arts. in *RT* (1936), 341-3, 362-6 (1937), 132, 134-8 (1938), 90-2, 100-6, 110-25 (1948), 106, 112-16, 118-23, 126-9; H.W. Hazard, *The numismatic history of late medieval North Africa*, New York 1952, 14, 335, 345; H.R. Idris, *Zīrides*, ii, 425-7; Julien, *Hist. de l'Afrique du Nord*, Paris 1956, ii, 65, 68, 70, 107; G. Marçais, *L'architecture musulmane d'Occident*, Paris 1954, 66, 79-81; idem and L. Pinssot, *Objets kairouanais*, Tunis 1948-52, ii, 371; B. Roy and Poinssot, *Inscriptions arabes de Kairouan*, Paris 1950-8, i, 87-90; M. Solignac, *Recherches sur les installations hydrauliques de Kairouan ...*, Algiers 1953, 262-5, 268-72; S.M. Zbiss, *Mahdia et Sabra-Manṣoûriya ...*, in *JA* (1956), 79-93; H. Halm, *Das Reich des Mahdi. Der Aufstieg der Fatimiden*, Munich 1991, index. (M. TALBI)

SABT (A.), the sabbath, and thus (*yawm al-*) *sabt*, Saturday (technically, Friday evening to Saturday evening); it is also suggested to mean "a week", that is from *sabt* to *sabt*, as well as a more general sense of a long period of time. The word has been the common designator of the day which follows *yawm al-djumʿa* [see DJUMʿA] since early Islamic times at least [see ZAMĀN]. Clearly related to the Aramaic word *shabbᵉtā* and ultimately Hebrew *shabbāt*, the word was given an appropriately Islamic sense by the Ḳurʾān and later Muslim theological interpretation.

The Ḳurʾān associates Jews, the sabbath and not undertaking any work, in line with Jewish tradition. Ḳurʾān, IV, 154 indicates that the day of rest was imposed upon the Jews at Sinai. Muslim tradition elaborates this as a punishment for the Jewish refusal to worship on Friday, the appropriate holy day; Saturday would be accepted by God as long as the Jews ceased from any work on that day (see al-Ṭabarī, *Djāmiʿ al-bayān*, ed. Shākir, Cairo 1954-69, ii, 167-8). Opposing traditions are found (e.g. Muslim, *Ṣaḥīḥ*, *Djumʿa*, 22) which support all of Friday, Saturday and Sunday as legitimate days of worship, however. Ḳurʾān, XVI, 124, speaks of disputes over the observance of the Sabbath, perhaps a remnant of Jewish-Christian debates. The breaking of the law of the sabbath is the focus of three passages, II, 65, IV, 47, and VII, 163, in which the word *sabt* is used twice plus once verbally, *yasbitūna*; these passages, which provided significant occasions for exegetical elaboration, speak of those who transgressed the Sabbath being transformed into "despised apes", *ḳirada khāsiʾīn* (II, 65, VII, 166; also see V, 60). Opinion varied as to whether this was to be understood literally or metaphorically, for example as something which happened to Jewish hearts. Modern scholarship has not reached a consensus on the origins of this story.

Muslim exegetical reflection on these passages started out with statements associating the sabbath, *yawm al-sabt*, and "resting", and with knowledge of the justification of that idea—that God rested on the seventh day of creation. However, while the Ḳurʾān confirms that there were six days of creation (VII, 54, X, 3, XI, 7, etc.), it rejects the idea that God rested from creation: "Weariness did not touch us" (L, 38), God says of himself. Thus the exegetical problem arose of how to explain that the seventh day of the week was called *sabt* without that implying a sense of "rest". The answer was found through derivation of the word *sabt* from *sabata* which was said to be restricted in its meaning to senses of "ceasing" or "being still", without conveying an implication of "rest"; the word *subāt* was still seen to have that meaning, however, as was necessary in XXV, 47, and LXXVIII, 9.

Muslim-Jewish polemic often focussed upon the accusation that the Jews entertained an anthropomorphic concept of God because of the notion of his "resting" from creation on the sabbath. For Muslims, *yawm al-djumʿa*, while it contained aspects of a day of rest in its celebration (a facet which has become more pronounced in modern times), was generally not seen as a holiday from work, any more than *yawm al-sabt* was.

Bibliography: *Tafsīr* tradition, especially on Ḳurʾān, VII, 163-6; I. Goldziher, *Die Sabbathinstitution im Islam*, in M. Brann, F. Rosenthal (eds.), *Gedenkbuch zur Erinnerung an David Kaufmann*, Breslau 1900, 86-105 (including the Arabic text of al-Ṭabarī's *tafsīr* on Ḳurʾān L, 38) (partial French tr., G. Bousquet, *Etudes islamologiques d'Ignaz Goldziher*, in *Arabica*, vii (1960), 237-40; idem, *Islamisme et Parsisme*, in *Actes du premier Congrès international d'histoire de religions*, Paris 1900, 145-6 (= *RHR*, xliii [1901], 27-8 = Goldziher, *Gesammelte Schriften*, Hildesheim 1970, iv, 258-9) (Goldziher's suggestion that Ḳurʾānic ideas regarding creation and the sabbath came from Zoroastrianism have not gained much support in scholarship.) J. Horowitz, *Koranische Untersuchungen*, Berlin-Leipzig 1926, 96; H. Speyer, *Die biblischen Erzählungen im Qoran*, Gräfenhainichen 1931, 312-4, 340; I. Lichtenstadter, "*And become ye accursed apes*", in *JSAI*, xiv (1991), 153-75.

(A. RIPPIN)

SABTA, CEUTA, a town of northern Morocco. It is situated 16 km/10 miles to the south of Gibraltar on the Moroccan coast, 60 km/38 miles to the north-west of Tetouan and 210 km/130 miles from Fās. Sabta has the form of a peninsula, ending in a small mountain (the Djabal al-Minā or Mt. Hacho, 193 m/633 feet), which has played the double role of a natural acropolis and a watch point. The isthmus of the peninsula, 60 m/197 feet in height, is attached to the mainland by a narrow strip of land, easily defensible. The old town had its counterpart in the Marīnid town, the Āfrāg [*q.v.*].

Explanations of the placename's etymology abound. Thus it is said that Sabta derived from the Latin *Septem Fratres*, which denotes the seven nearby hills;

most of the Arabic chronicles attribute its foundation to one Sabt, a descendant of Noah and eponymous hero, whose tomb, in the form of a tumulus (*al-Ḳabr al-s͟hāṭṭ*) was still venerated at the beginning of the 9th/15th century. The Phoenician trading depot of Abyla and the Roman Iulia Traiecta have been situated there, but Rome does not seem to have attached much importance to the place (C. Posac Mon, *Estudios arqueología de Ceuta*, in *Actes du IXe Congrès*, Valladolid 1965). As successors to Rome, the Byzantines clashed with the Visigoths, who besieged Sabta in 534, but the Byzantines managed to occupy it, or to re-occupy it and, according to Procopius, "fortified, peopled and embellished it". The Emperor Justinian built it up into a strong fortress (F. Fita, *Ceuta wisigoda y byzantina durante el reino de Tuedes*, BRAH 1922).

The accounts of the conquest of al-Andalus bring into prominence Count Julian, the Visigothic governor, Byzantine Exarch or lord of the G͟humāra, according to the various chronicles (see Ibn ʿAbd al-Ḥakam, *Conquête de l'Afrique du Nord et de l'Espagne*, ed. and partial tr. A. Gateau, 2nd ed. Algiers 1947). It was a refuge for Arab forces during the K͟hārid͟jite rebellion, an Idrīsid principality (it was allegedly occupied by Idrīs I in 173/789-90), as the capital of the Banū ʿIṣām, who appear more as an independent dynasty than as Idrīsid governors, occupied by the Umayyads of Cordova in 319/931 and became a pawn in the struggle against the Fāṭimids. Al-Nāṣir proclaimed himself caliph and called himself "master of the two seas" after the conquest of the town. As a base for intervention in the Mag͟hrib, it had strong ramparts and could gather in the populations of towns threatened or ruined (Nakūr al-Baṣra, Tāhart, etc.). The decline of the caliphate allowed the Ḥammūdids [*q.v.*] to establish a principality which included Tangier, Ceuta, Algeciras and Malaga. The town's mint coined gold pieces, the *mancus ceptimus*, which became widely current. The Ḥammūdids' lieutenant, Saḳḳūt al-Barg͟hawāṭī, profited from the anarchy within al-Andalus to seize power and set up his own dynasty (al-Maḳḳarī, *Azhār*, i, 34; Ibn K͟haldūn, *Prolegomena*, tr. Rosenthal, ii, 220; Vallvé Bermejo, *Saqūt al-Barghawāṭī rey de Ceuta*, in *al-And.* [1962], 119); he recognised the ʿAbbāsid caliph and challenged the ʿAbbādids of Seville for control of the Straits. During his reign (453-75/1061-83), the town was prosperous and enjoyed a lively intellectual life. It resisted the Almoravids, who were held up before Sabta for six years before taking it in 475/1083.

As the native town of ʿAlī b. Yūsuf, Sabta was favoured by the Lamtūna and profited from the political unity established to develop economic links with sub-Saharan Africa and the lands on the northern fringes of the Mediterranean. Its powerful *ḳāḍī*s controlled activities, including the muezzins of the Great Mosque (H. Ferhat, *Un nouveau texte sur la mosquée de Sabta*, in *Hespéris*, forthcoming). When the Almohads arrived, the *ḳāḍī* ʿIyāḍ b. Mūsā [*q.v.*] led the resistance, but the town had to surrender and the *ḳāḍī* was exiled (M. Bencherifa, *al-Taʿrīf bi 'l-Ḳāḍī ʿIyāḍ*, Rabat 1974, 47). Sabta became one of the most important governorships of the empire; with its arsenal and anchorage for the fleet and its change of masters, the town was always given to a prince of the dynasty (*Sayyid*).

From 629/1231-2, Almohad unity began to break up, with the secession of Ibn Hūd in al-Andalus and also that of the Ḥafṣids [*q.v.*]. The governor of Sabta, the Sayyid Abū Mūsā, rebelled and assumed the title of al-Muʾayyad. Besieged by al-Maʾmūn, he negotiated the handing-over of the town to Ibn Hūd, who gave it to the admiral al-G͟hus͟htī. The latter was ejected by the populace, who handed power over to a rich merchant, Abu 'l-ʿAbbās al-Yanas͟htī, who now had to face a siege by the Genoese (Ibn al-ʿId͟hārī, *Bayān*, iii, 307; al-Ḥimyarī, *al-Rawḍ al-miʿṭār*, Beirut 1975, 622; Ch. Dufourcq, *La question de Ceuta au XIIIe siècle*, in *Hespéris* [1955], 67; Di Tucci, *Documenti inediti sulla spedizione e sulla Mahona di Genovesi a Ceuta*, Genoa 1935, 273-340). Irritated by al-Yanas͟htī, who aspired to personal power, the Sabtīs returned to the bosom of the Almohads and accepted Ibn K͟halāṣ, the caliph al-Ras͟hīd's envoy. Ḥafṣid intervention in the Straits led to occupation of the town, which recognised Abū Zakariyyāʾ. After the latter's death, a coup d'état expelled the agents of Tunis and gave power to Abu 'l-Ḳāsim al-ʿAzafī, whose dynasty was to last until 720/1320, including some temporary hiatuses (J.D. Latham, *The rise of the ʿAzafids of Ceuta*, in *IOS*, ii [1972], 263-87; idem, *The later ʿAzafids*, in *ROMM*, xv-xvi [1973], 109-25; idem, *The strategic position and defence of Ceuta in the later Muslim period*, in *IQ* [1971], 189-204; and see ʿAZAFI, BANU'L-, in Suppl.). The Banu 'l-ʿAzafī instituted a consultative régime (*al-s͟hūrā*) which preserved the town's autonomy whilst recognising the Almohad caliph.

As a bridge-head between the Saharan region and the Mediterranean, Sabta played a leading role in commercial exchanges and minted coins of excellent quality (J.J. Rodriguez-Lorente and T. b. Hafiz Ibrahim, *Numismatica de Ceuta musulmana*, Madrid 1987).

Taken by Granada in 705/1306, Sabta was sacked and its élites expelled. The inhabitants appealed to the Marīnids, who re-occupied it in 789/1387. Marīnid control, the loss of the Andalusian towns and a general regression in the region, weakened the town and its commerce; it was replaced regarding commerce into the interior by Genoese, Barcelonans and Majorcans established along the Atlantic coast of Morocco.

As the home of the geographer al-Idrīsī, of the *ḳāḍī* ʿIyāḍ and of Abu 'l-ʿAbbās al-Sabtī, Sabta played an important role as a centre of learning, and especially of *fiḳh*, *ḥadīt͟h*, grammar and medicine (H. al-Wariaghli, *S͟huyūk͟h al-ʿilm wa-mulūk al-dars fī Sabta*, Tetouan 1984; anon., *Bulg͟hat al-umniyya wa-maḳṣad al-labīb*, Rabat 1984). The mystical tendency was seen in Ibn al-ʿArīf and the school of Almeria. Abu 'l-Ḥasan al-S͟hārī founded there the first *madrasa* in the Mag͟hrib; al-ʿAzafī began there the *Mawlid*, a festival adopted officially by the Marīnids (*al-Durr al-Munaẓẓam*, ms.). If nothing now remains of the monuments of Sabta, Muḥammad al-Anṣārī describes at length the situation just after the town's fall (*Ik͟htiṣār al-ak͟hbār ʿammā kāna bi-t͟hag͟hr Sabta...*, tr. F.A. Turki, in *Hespéris-Tamuda* [1982], 83).

The Portuguese seized Sabta in D͟jumādā II 818/August 1415. It was abandoned, also the village of Balyūnas͟h, which had played a great role in its history, by its population. After the annexation of Portugal by Spain in 988/1580, Sabta was transferred to Spanish control, and despite numerous Moroccan attempts to regain it, Ceuta has always remained a Spanish *presidio* and a free zone.

After the Portuguese capture of Sabta in 818/1415, it was attacked by the *ḳāʾid* Ṣāliḥ, who led resistance in the district. Meanwhile, in 824/1421, a bishopric was created there. The quarters on the mainland were razed and the town, now reduced to the isthmus, provied with new fortifications. After the Portuguese check before Tangier in 860/1437, a treaty was sign-

·d, the return of Ceuta to Morocco was envisaged and Don Ferdinand sent as a hostage to guarantee the promise; but the Cortes refused to ratify it, and the prince died, as a martyr, at Fās in 847/1443. After the Battle of the Three Kings (986/1578), Spain seized Ceuta definitively. Nevertheless, the town was regularly attacked by neighbouring tribes and by the principality of Tetouan [see TIṬṬĀWĪN]. The siege decided upon by Mawlāy Ismāʿīl lasted from 1104/1693 to 1133/1721; that of 1180/1766 was ended by an ambiguous treaty, completed by the convention of 1188/1774 (J. Caillé, *Les accords de Sidi Mohammed Ben ʿAbdallah* (*1757-1790*), Paris 1960). Between 1196/1782 and 1214/1799, agreements conceded the territory to the Spanish, provoking the anger of the aggrieved tribes. Ceuta suffered from a lack of water and always coveted the Bullone (Balyūnash) hills; a series of disputes between Spain and Morocco led to the war of Tetouan (1860). In 1912 the Protectorate Treaty, awarding the north of Morocco to Spain, marked the revival of Ceuta, whose trade developed thanks to its double military and commercial role. When Morocco became independent (March 1956), Ceuta became a *presidio* and a free zone. Profiting from the ending of the international status of Tangier, the town received an influx of travellers and commerce, and an important smuggling activity developed, making a strong mark on the whole region's economy.

Bibliography (in addition to references given in the text): J. Marquez de Prado, *Historia de Ceuta*, Madrid 1859; E. Rouez de Card, *Les relations de l'Espagne et du Maroc pendant le XVIIIe et le XIXe siècles*, Paris 1905; R. Ricard, *Le Maroc septentrional au XVe siècle d'après les chroniques portugaises*, in *Hesp.*, xxii (1936), 89-143; V. Fernandez, *Description de la côte d'Afrique de Ceuta au Sénégal 1506-1507*, Paris 1938; *Chroniques de Gomes Eannes de Azurara*, Paris 1938; Ricard, *Etudes sur l'histoire des Portugais au Maroc*, Coimbra 1955; J. Caillé, *Le rôle des commerçants marseillais à Ceuta au XIIIe siècle*, in *Méls. d'Hist. et d'Archéol. de l'Occident musulman*, Algiers 1957; G. Ayyache, *Beliounech et le destin de Ceuta entre le Maroc et l'Espagne*, in *Hesp.-Tamuda* (1972); ʿIyāḍ, *al-Ghunya*, Tunis 1978; M.H. Ḥīla, *Rasāʾil dīwāniyya min Sabta fi 'l-ʿahd al-ʿAzafī*, Rabat 1979; Maḳḳarī, *Azhār al-riyāḍ fī akhbār ʿIyāḍ*, Rabat 1978-80; M. b. Tāwīt, *Taʾrīkh Sabta*, 1982; M. b. ʿIyāḍ, *Madhāhib al-ḥukkām*, Rabat 1990; H. Ferhat, *Sabta, état bibliographique*, in *Hesp.-Tamuda* (1990); eadem, *Sabta des origines au XIVe siècle*, Rabat, in press.

(HALIMA FERHAT)

AL-**SABTĪ**, AḤMAD B. DJAʿFAR al-Khazradjī, Abu 'l-ʿAbbās, renowned Moroccan saint, born at Sabta (Ceuta) in 524/1130, not to be confused, in the text of Ibn Khaldūn (*Muḳaddima*), with a homonym who lived in a later period and was the inventor of a circular divinatory table known as the *zāʾiradja al-ʿālam*.

Two accounts afford a glimpse of his career, which was contemporaneous with that of the great saint of Tlemcen Abū Madyan al-Andalusī (520-94/1126-97): that of the *ḳāḍī* al-Tādilī and that of Ibn Ḥāmawayh, which is more concise, recounted by al-Maḳḳarī. Born into a modest family, he lost his father at a very early age and became an apprentice to a trader in textiles (*bazzāz*) of Sabta, a town which was then enjoying a high level of commercial and cultural prosperity. His principal teacher was Abū ʿAbd Allāh al-Fakhkhār, himself a disciple of the *ḳāḍī* ʿIyāḍ, one of the most eminent representatives of the Hispano-Maghribī Mālikī school of the period. At about sixteen years old, he left Sabta with a companion and made his way to Mount Gillīz where the Almohad army was encamped, commanded by ʿAbd al-Muʾmin who was laying siege to Marrakesh (540/1146). After the capture of the city, he established himself there in a *funduḳ* known by the name of *funduḳ Muḳbil*. He then taught grammar and arithmetic, for which he received payment. He also apparently enjoyed an allowance in his capacity as a member of the *ṭalabat al-ḥaḍar* (a category of teachers supported financially by the Almohad authorities) and established a considerable household. He rapidly gained popularity as a result of his generosity. His doctrine was simple, according to al-Tādilī, who knew and visited him: every principle contained in religion (*sharʿ*) may be reduced to the deprival and to the bestowal of the goods which one possesses. He insists on the religious duty of *zakāt*. Charity (*ṣadaḳa*) is the essential theme of his sermons and of his injunctions. He denounces avarice (*al-bukhl*) and parsimony (*al-shuḥḥ*) and preaches generosity (*al-ʿaṭāʾ*, *al-djūd*), and beneficence (*al-iḥsān*, quoting Ḳurʾānic verses to illustrate his purpose (IX, 34; X, 88; LIII, 33; LXVIII, 17; XCII, 5-10). His symbolic interpretation of prayer and of its various manifestations illustrates his doctrine of asceticism, since it signifies the sharing and the abandonment of all goods.

Of presentable appearance, always carefully groomed, he was furthermore admired for his eloquence and his knowledge of dogma and for the ease with which he succeeded in convincing the most sceptical. His conduct earned him the reputation of a pious man, having no wish to publicise his virtues and willing to accept criticism (the Oriental mystical tradition of the Malāmatiyya). The philosopher Ibn Rushd sent an observer to study his ideas and, on his return, concluded that "the entire existence of Abu 'l-ʿAbbās is in interaction with charity" and that "his doctrine is that of a philosopher of antiquity". He then resolved to meet the man in person and travelled for this purpose to Marrakesh, where he died and was initially buried, before being transferred to Cordova. Abu 'l-ʿAbbās died soon afterwards, in 601/1205. He was interred outside Bāb Taghzūt.

Significant similarities of circumstances and events in the lives of Abu 'l-ʿAbbās and of Abū Madyan are evident: their modest origins; their beginnings as youthful apprentices in the textile trade, a substantial element in the economy of North Africa at the time; their theological training concurrent with the exercise of their profession; the departure and the journey (*siyāḥa*) in search of their path (a major Ṣūfī theme); their installation in an important city where they became known for their teaching and their piety; the themes, repeated in all circumstances, of humility, of submission to the divine will (*tawakkul*) and of the renunciation of material goods, a doctrine making a synthesis of Mālikī orthodoxy and of oriental mysticism and adapted to the Maghribī soul; the interest of the Almohad authorities in their knowledge and their popularity; and the policy of enticement and control of scholars which led to their installation at Marrakesh. Finally, each became the patron saint of the town in which he was buried. But the originality of Abu 'l-ʿAbbās consists in his withdrawal from political life and in the fact that he claimed allegiance to no school or great master. He did not found a school either. He devoted his life to the defence and promulgation of values which were promoted in North Africa principally by the Ṣūfīs and which exerted influence on the Christian culture of the Middle Ages, represented among others by one of the originators of the concept of chivalry, the Arabic-speaking Majorcan Ramon Lull. In the 20th century he still serves as a model for reformers (*muṣliḥūn*) who aspire towards moral rigour and social justice, such as Ibn al-Muwaḳḳit [*q.v.*].

Popular imagination has not been slow to transform the life of this pious individual into a legend, attended by an increasingly rich crop of miracles. His repute has extended throughout the Maghrib, benefiting initially by the unity imposed upon it by the Almohad empire. As an example of these miracles, he is supposed to have appeared at the side of the Muslim warriors at the time of the Battle of the Three Kings at al-Ḳaṣr al-Kabīr (Yawm al-Makhāzin), which ended with the defeat of the Portuguese, in 986/1578.

On the summit of Gillīz there is a *ḳubba* dedicated to him. In the same mountain there is a sacred cave in which he stayed during periods of meditation and which was approached by processions of townspeople appealing for rain. It was also in a cave that the Prophet took refuge, at the time of the emigration from Mecca to Medina, in the company of Abū Bakr (to whom the companion of Abu 'l-ʿAbbās, in the journey to Marrakesh, corresponds, Ḳurʾān, IX, 40), in the episode known as the *hidjra*.

Finally, while the sūra *al-Kahf* (XVIII), occupies an important place in Muslim liturgy, the cave represents, for the Ṣūfī who follows the sacred text of the Ḳurʾān to the letter, in a hostile world, the refuge of the sincere believer who awaits there the beneficence of the Lord (XVIII, 16).

Some well-known personalities have come, over the centuries, to invoke him or to seek protection or miraculous power associated with his sainthood (*baraka*): the illustrious Ibn al-Khaṭīb, Ibn Ḳunfudh of Constantine, the last king of Grenada Abū ʿAbd Allāh (Boabdil) and the writer from Timbuktu Aḥmad Bābā. At the beginning of the 17th century the Saʿdid sultan Abū Fāris Ibn Aḥmad al-Manṣūr ordered the restoration of his mausoleum and the building of a *madrasa* and the mosque which still exists. In the 18th century, his primacy was officially endorsed with the institution of the cycle of pilgrimage (*ziyāra*) to the seven patrons of Marrakesh (Sabʿatu ridjāl [*q.v.*]), as a counter-weight to that of the seven saints of Ragrāga, the latter probably being linked to the legend of the Seven Sleepers of Ephesus. The sultan Muḥammad b. ʿAbd Allāh (1171-1204/1757-90) had his *zāwiya* annexed to the town and constructed the mausoleum which still exists.

The peasant invokes him to make the rain fall or to protect a clutch of eggs. The farmer, to preserve his crop, makes a charitable gift of a portion of grain to the poor, in his name, in Morocco as in Algeria, or appeals to him to raise a wind from the west, which is advantageous for the winnowing of corn, or, like a seafarer, he asks for the quelling of a storm. In particular he is the patron of commerce in general, or travellers, of dealers in trimmings, of well-sinkers, of soap-makers, of operators of oil-presses and of healers of eyes. He is invoked at the time of a confinement. Charitable gifts of grain, fritters, fruit, meat or fish, made to the poor in his name, are often called *ʿabbāsiyya*. Similarly, in Algeria, the verb *ʿabbas* signifies "to go among the peasants to levy contributions of grain, butter, dried fruits etc...". A weekly pilgrimage takes place within his sanctuary (*ḥurm*), the majority of the participants being blind.

His radiant reputation in the Maghrib explains the presence of *ḳubbas* dedicated to him (Sidi Bel-Abbès, Ouargla, Djellida, etc.), as well as the formation and origin of certain family-names (Belabbas-Nabi, etc.), although the possibility of homonymy with local saints is not to be denied.

Bibliography: 1. Sources. Anon., *al-Dhakīra al-saniyya fī taʾrīkh al-dawla al-marīniyya*, Algiers 1921, 42; anon., *Manāḳib al-shaykh Abi 'l-ʿAbbās al-Sabtī*, ms. Rabat, Bibl. gen. 403; Aḥmad Bābā al-Timbuktī, *Nayl al-ibtihādj*, lith. Fās 1317/1899, 31; Ibn Farḥūn, *al-Dībādj al-mudhahhab fī maʿrifat aʿyān ʿulamāʾ al-madhhab*, Cairo 1351/1932 (appended to the previous work); Abū ʿAbd Allāh Muḥammad al-Ghālī, *Badāʾiʿ al-iḳtibās fi manāḳib Abi 'l-ʿAbbās*; ʿAlī b. Muḥammad al-Hawwārī, *Manāḳib Abi 'l-ʿAbbās al-Sabtī*, ms. Bibl. nat. Algiers 1713, 1; Muḥammad Ibn Abī Shanab, *Dictionnaire pratique arabe-français de M. Beaussier*, revised M. Bencheneb, repr. Paris 1958, 631, s.v. *ʿabbas*; Ibn Maryam, *al-Bustān fī dhikr al-awliyāʾ wa 'l-ʿulamāʾ*, Algiers 1326/1908, 189, tr. F. Provenzali, Algiers 1910, 217, 511 n. 805; Ibn al-Muwaḳḳit, *al-Saʿāda al-abadiyya fi 'l-taʿrīf bi-mashāhīr al-ḥadra al-Marrakūshiyya*, Fās 1917-18; idem. *Taʾthīr al-anfās fi 'l-taʿrīf bi 'l-shaykh Abi 'l-ʿAbbās*, Fās 1918; Ibn Khaldūn, *Muḳaddima*, tr. de Slane, i, 245-53, iii, 199-206, tr. Rosenthal, i, 238-45, iii, 182-8; Ibn Ḳunfudh al-Ḳusanṭīni, *Uns al-faḳīr*, Rabat 1965, 7-9; Maḳḳarī, *Nafḥ al-ṭīb*, Bulak 1885, iv, 355-61, ed. I. ʿAbbās, Beirut 1968, ii, 99-100, vii, 277; Marrakūshī, *K. al-Muʿdjib*, Casablanca n.d.; al-Nāṣirī al-Salāwī, *K. al-Istiḳṣāʾ*, iii (Almohads), tr. I. Hamet, Rabat 1927, 251-3, iv (Marinids), 355; Yūsuf b. Yaḥyā al-Shādhilī, *Manāḳib Abi 'l-ʿAbbās al-Sabtī*, ms. B.N. Paris, 2037; Ibn al-Zayyāt al-Tādilī, in Marrakūshi, *al-Iʿlām bi-man ḥalla Marrākush wa-Aghmāt min al-aʿlām*, Fās 1936, 240-65; Ibn al-Zayyāt, *Akhbār Abi 'l-ʿAbbās al-Sabtī* = a *dhayl* to his *al-Tashawwuf ilā ridjāl al-taṣawwuf*, ed. Aḥmad al-Tawfīḳ, Rabat 1404/1984, 451-77.

2. Studies. R. Basset, *Nedromah et les Traras*, in *Bull. de Correspondance Africaine* (1901), 206-7; M. Ben Cheneb, *Etude sur les personnages mentionnés dans l'idjaza du cheikh ʿAbd al-Qadir al-Fasi*, in *Actes du XIVe Congrès internat. des Orientalistes*, Paris 1907, iv §§ 102-3; idem, *EI*[1] art. *al-Sabtī*; H. des Castries *Sources inédites ... Dynastie saadienne*, iii, Paris 1911 213, 707, 733, and *Dynastie filalienne*, i, Paris 1922 640 and n. 4, ii, 201 and n. 6; idem, *Les sept patrons de Merrakech*, in *Hespéris*, iv (1924), 245-303; P. de Cenival, *EI*[1] art. *Marrakush*; E. Dermenghem, *Sidi Aboû 'l-ʿAbbâs, patron de Marrakech*, in *Recueil de travaux offerts à Clovis Brunel*, Paris 1955, i, 345-51 repr. in *Vie des saints musulmans*, Plan de la Tour 1981; G. Deverdun, *Marrakech*, Rabat 1959, i, 272-4; T. Fahd, *La divination arabe*, Leiden 1966; A. Faure, *Abū l-ʿAbbās as-Sabtī (524-601/1130-1204), la justice et la charité*, in *Hespéris*, xliii (1956), 448-56; H. Ferhat and H. Triki, *Abou Abbās Sebti, Saint Patron de Marrakech*, in *Mémorial du Maroc*, ii (1982), 276-83 eidem, *Hagiographie et religion au Maroc médiéval*, in *Hespéris-Tamuda*, xxiv (1986), 17-51; H. Ferhat, *Abū 'l-ʿAbbās: contestation et sainteté*, in *al-Qantara*, xiii (1992), 181-99; L. Massignon, *Enquête sur les corporations d'artisans et de commerçants au Maroc (1923-1924)*, Paris 1924, 15, 68-9, 147; Ch. Pellat, *EI*[2] art. *Manāḳib*; H.P.J. Renaud, *Divination et histoire nord africaine au temps d'Ibn-Khaldun*, in *Hespéris*, xxx (1943), 214; A. Sebti, *Hagiographie du voyage au Maroc médiéval*, in *al-Qantara*, xiii (1922), 167-79; D. Urvoy, *Penser l'Islam. Les présupposés islamiques de l'"art" de Lull*, Paris 1980, 162-3; E. Westermarck *Ritual and belief in Morocco*, i, 40, 62, 64-5, 90-1, 163 180-1, 188, 191, 56, ii, 231, 234, 238, 244, 253 268, 287.

There exist a large number of studies concerning, in detail or in general, the legends and the cul of this saint: L. Adoue, *La ville de Sidi Bel-Abbès*, Sidi Bel-Abbès 1927, 29-35; H. Basset, *Le cult des grottes au Maroc*, Algiers 1920, 72 (see also review by E. Laoust, in *Hesperis*, i [1921], 227); R. Brunel, *Le monachisme errant de l'Islam, Sidi Heddi et les Heddāwa*, Paris 1955, 37-8, 216, 227, 234, 268, 379; L. Brunot, *La mer dans les traditions et les industries indigènes à Rabat et Salé,* Paris 1920, 58-61; P. Champion, *Rabat et Marrakech*, Paris 1926, 116-17; E. Doutté, *Notes sur l'Islam maghrébin*, in *RHR*, xli (1900), 55-6; idem, *Merrakech*, Paris 1905, 211, 384; I. Goldziher, *Muh. Studien*, i, 238, Eng. tr. *Muslim studies*, i, 216-17; P.A. Koller, *Essai sur l'esprit du berbère marocain*, Fribourg 1949, 122, 342-3; Doctoresse Legey, *Essay sur le folklore marocain*, Paris 1926, 5, 92, 155, 158, 198; L. Massignon, *Les "Sept dormants" apocalypse de l'Islam*, in *Mél. Paul Peeters*, ii = *Analecta Bollandiana*, lxviii (1950), 245-60; idem, *Les Sept dormants d'Ephèse (ahl al-Kahf) en Islam et en chrétienté, recueil documentaire et iconographique*, in *REI*, xxii-xxx (1954-62); idem, *Le culte liturgique et populaire des VII Dormants Martyrs d'Ephèse*, in *Studia missionalia* (1961), repr. in *Opera minora*, ii, Paris 1969, 119-180; E. Montet, *Le culte des saints musulmans dans l'Afrique du Nord*, Geneva 1909, 53-6; A. Moulieras, *Le Maroc inconnu*, Paris 1895-9, 438-9, 702-3; M. de Périgny, *Au Maroc, Marrakech et les ports du Sud*, Paris 1918, 55, 165; G. Rohlfs, *Mein erster Aufenthalt in Marocco*, Bremen 1873, 392; H. Stumme, *Märchen der Schluh von Tazerwalt*, Leipzig 1895, 51-5, 166-73; E. Vaffier, *Visite à Sidi Bel-Abbès, cité des aveugles*, in *France-Maroc*, ix (1918), 270-3; J. Vernet, *La fecha de composicion de la zaʾirayat al-alam*, in *al-And.* (1969), 245-6.

(H. Bencheneb)

SABUKTIGĪN [see sebüktigin].

ṢĀBŪN (a.), soap.

Prodest et sapo, Gallorum hoc inventum rutilandis capillis; fit ex sebo et cinere ... duobus modis, spissus ac liquidus, uterque apud Germanos maiore in usu viris quam feminis (Pliny, *Hist. nat.* 28, 191). According to this passage, soap is a Gallic invention but the word itself is of German origin. The Romans borrowed it in the form of *sapo*, the Greeks from the latter as σάπων, which in its turn found its way into Arabic as *ṣābūn*. The word denotes a mixture of fat or tallow and vegetable ashes, used to dye the hair red; it was brought on the market in solid or liquid form. In Spain, *ṣābūn* also indicates the lye obtained by leaving the ashes soak in water (*la<u>kh</u><u>sh</u>iyya* < old Castilian *lexía* < Lat. *lixivium*, see Dietrich, *Dioscurides triumphans*, no. I, 109; and *Vocabulista*, ed. Schiaparelli, 460). Widely-spread substitutes for soap as a cleansing agent were natron [see naṭrūn], salt won from the ashes of alkaline plants (potash [see al-ḳily]), and also pastes made from ashes and argillaceous earth (cf. E. Schmauderer, in *Technikgeschichte*, xxxiv [Düsseldorf 1967], 300-10), and other materials. The Egyptians, for making soap, used oil from the radish (*fu<u>dj</u>l*), the rape (*sal<u>dj</u>am*) and the lettuce (*<u>kh</u>ass*); soap made from these plants was white, red, yellow or green (Abdallatif, *Relation de l'Egypte*, tr. S. de Sacy, 311). According to Ibn Biklāri<u>sh</u>, *Mustaʿīnī* (ms. Naples, Bibl. Naz. III, F. 65, fol. 84b), *al-raḳḳī* (after Raḳḳa) is named as a well-known kind of coarse soap, similar to date-palm paste (*al-marham al-na<u>kh</u>lī*), from which lozenges are made in Damascus. Other kinds of soap, such as those from ʿIrāḳ and the Ma<u>gh</u>rib, are mentioned by al-Anṭākī, *Ta<u>dh</u>kira*, Cairo 1371/1952, i, 221, who gives the most extensive details on soap altogether.

According to al-Anṭākī, *loc. cit.*, soap allegedly came into the Hermetic writings through a revelation, and is also said to be found in Hippocrates and Galen, partly among the compound drugs and partly among the simple ones. The best soap is said to be that made of clear olive oil, pure potash and good wax. In medicine, soap finds manifold applications, see e.g. Ibn al-Bayṭār, *<u>Dj</u>āmiʿ*, Būlāḳ 1291, iii, 36-7; Ibn Rasūl al-<u>Gh</u>assānī, *Muʿtamad*, ed. M. al-Saḳḳā, 280-1. Soap softens hard ulcers and ripens them; and it loosens colic pains and removes scabs and psoriasis if the affected spots are rubbed with a piece of cloth soaked in soap. Mixed with salt in equal parts, soap removes itching and festering scabies. Boiled up with attar of roses and rubbed on ulcers on children's heads, soap dries the fluids. If left for seven days as a compress on vesicular tumours (*al-ḳurūḥ al-<u>sh</u>ahdiyya*, see Dozy, *Suppl.*, i, 793) and then washed away with hot water, soap is revealed as an excellent medicine. Mixed with henna and applied as a compress on freckles, it removes them, etc.

Arab geographers frequently mention places where soap is fabricated: Aleppo (Ibn Ḥawḳal[1], 177), Bālis on the Euphrates (*ibid.*, 180), Bal<u>kh</u> and Tirmi<u>dh</u> (Muḳaddasī, 342), Arra<u>dj</u>ān (*ibid.*, 425), Bust (*Ḥudūd al-ʿālam*, 110). For the import of soap into Egypt, see Subhi Labib, *Handelsgeschichte Ägyptens im Spätmittelalter*, Wiesbaden 1965, 39, 206, 239, 346, and for special applications of soap in chemistry, see M. Berthelot, *La chimie au moyen âge*, Paris 1893, i, 165, 215, ii, 185, 330.

Bibliography (in addition to the works quoted in the article): Harawī, *Kitāb al-Abniya ʿan ḥaḳāʾiḳ al-adwiya*, ed. Bahmanyār, Tehran 1346, 213, tr. Achundow, Halle 1893, 228; Ibn Sīnā, *Ḳānūn*, Būlāḳ 1294, i, 415; Ibn Hubal, *Mu<u>kh</u>tārāt*, Ḥaydarābād 1362, 166; Maimonides, *<u>Sh</u>arḥ asmāʾ al-ʿuḳḳār*, ed. Meyerhof, no. 323; Ibn al-Ḳuff, *ʿUmda*, Ḥaydarābād 1356, i, 246, tr. Kircher, no. 156; *Tuḥfat al-aḥbāb*, ed. Renaud and Colin, Paris 1934, no. 295; E. Wiedemann, *Aufsätze zur arabischen Wissenschaftsgeschichte*, ii, 402-3; A. Dietrich, *Dioscurides triumphans. Ein anonymer arabischer Kommentar (Ende 12. Jahrh. n. Chr.) zur Materia Medica*, no. I, 109, in *Abh. Ak. Göttingen*, Phil.-hist. Kl., Neue Folge, no. 173, Göttingen 1988.

(A. Dietrich)

ṢĀBUN<u>DJ</u>Ī, Louis, a person of the second rank in the *Nahḍa* [*q.v.*], born at Dayrak on 20 April 1833, died in Los Angeles, 24 April 1931. With an original first name John, and born a Syrian Catholic, he attended the seminary at Charfé and then the Pontifical College for Propaganda at Rome, where he was ordained priest in 1863 (he renounced his priestly orders in 1899). He taught Latin at the Syrian Protestant College and founded the journal *al-Naḥla* ("The Bee"), which he took up again in London in 1877. He became a British representative in Cairo, accompanied ʿUrābī Pa<u>sh</u>a [*q.v.*] into exile in Ceylon, served the ruler of Zanzibar and then served the Ottoman sultan in Istanbul. From 1909 onwards, he lived in the United States. This traveller and adventurer (*al-Ṭawāf ḥawla kurat al-arḍ*, Istanbul 1896, pp. 84), eternal lover (*Dīwān al-naḥla al-manẓūm fī <u>kh</u>ilāl al-riḥla*, Alexandria 1901, pp. 584) and opportunist, often showed his sympathy for Islam in the form expounded by <u>Dj</u>amāl al-Dīn al-Af<u>gh</u>ānī [*q.v.*] (*K. al-Ikti<u>sh</u>āf al-<u>th</u>amīn li-iṭālat al-ʿumr miʾat min al-sinīn*, New York 1919, pp. 255). Ṣābun<u>dj</u>ī was a partisan of the naturalist school of evolutionism.

Bibliography: Y. Dā<u>gh</u>ir, *Maṣādir*, ii, 525-8; Ph. Ṭarrāzī, *Taʾrī<u>kh</u> al-Ṣaḥāfa*, passim; Ziriklī, *Aʿlām*, vi, 114; Kaḥḥāla, *Muʾallifīn*, viii, 161; Sarkīs, *Muʿ<u>dj</u>am*, 1177-8.

(J. Fontaine)

SĀBŪR B. **ARDASHĪR**, Abū Naṣr Bahāʾ al-Dīn (330-416/942-1025), official and vizier of the Buyids in Fārs. Beginning his career in high office as deputy to Sharaf al-Dawla's vizier Abū Manṣūr b. Ṣāliḥān, he subsequently became briefly vizier himself for the first time in 380/990 and for Sharaf al-Dawla's successor in Shīrāz, Bahāʾ al-Dawla [*q.v.* in Suppl.]. He was vizier again in Shīrāz in Djumādā I 386/May-June 996, this time for over three years, and in 390/1000 in Baghdād as deputy there for the vizier Abū ʿAlī al-Muwaffaḳ. Sābūr, although a native of Shīrāz, seems to have had estates or some power base in the Baṭāʾiḥ [see AL-BAṬĪḤA] or marshlands of Lower ʿIrāḳ, whither he frequently retired on his falls from office. His last years were spent in retirement, and he died in Baghdād aged 86 lunar years.

Sābūr had the reputation of being a taciturn and exacting functionary, adept at extracting money for his masters, but he also achieved a lasting fame as the patron of scholars and littérateurs, and al-Thaʿālibī has a section on the poets of Baghdād who praised him (al-Babbaghāʾ, Muḥammad b. Bulbul, Aḥmad b. ʿAlī al-Munadjdjim, etc.). He founded a *Dār al-ʿIlm* in the Bayn al-Sūrayn quarter of Baghdād which reportedly had a library of 10,000 volumes but which was largely destroyed in the fighting in Baghdād in 451/1059 between Arslan al-Basāsīrī and the Saldjūḳ Ṭoghrïl Beg [*q.vv.*]; Sābūr himself was a proponent of the Zaydī Shīʿa, and appointed several Muʿtazilī professors at his foundation.

Bibliography: Hilāl al-Ṣābiʾ, *Historical remains*, ed. H.F. Amedroz, Leiden 1904, index; Ibn al-Athīr, ix; Thaʿālibī, *Yatīma*², iii, 129-36; Ibn Khallikān, ed. ʿAbbās, ii, 354-6 no. 255, tr. de Slane, i, 554-5; Ṣafadī, *Wāfī*, xv, ed. B. Radtke, Wiesbaden 1979, 71-4; H. Busse, *Chalif und Grosskönig, die Buyiden im Iraq (945-1055)*, Beirut-Wiesbaden 1969, 240, 510-13, 525-7 and index; C.E. Bosworth, *Ghars al-Niʿma b. Hilāl al-Ṣābiʾ's* Kitāb al-Hafawāt al-nādira *and Būyid history*, in A. Jones (ed.), *Arabicus Felix, luminosus britannicus, essays in honour of A.F.L. Beeston on his eightieth birthday*, Reading 1991, 139-40. (C.E. BOSWORTH)

SĀBŪR B. **SAHL** B. SĀBŪR, Christian physician and pharmacologist (d. 21 Dhu 'l-Ḥidjdja 255/30 November 869).

Sābūr grew up in the Nestorian *milieu* of Khūzistān [*q.v.*]. He must have been educated at the "Academia Hippocratica" in Gondēshāpūr [*q.v.*], where he later held a position in the famous local hospital, and rose to be one of the leading physicians of his time. In Gondēshāpūr he practised medicine and pharmacology until he was appointed court physician by the ʿAbbāsid caliph al-Mutawakkil [*q.v.*] and his successors. Sābūr died "as a Christian" (*naṣrāniyyan*), perhaps in Sāmarrāʾ [*q.v.*].

Though some of Sābūr's writings are lost, two works on dietetics are preserved (i.e. *Ḳuwa 'l-aṭʿima; al-Ashriba*) and, more importantly, the small version of his main pharmacological work *al-Aḳrābādhīn* [*q.v.*] "The Dispensatory", a specialist's handbook on the preparation and application of compound drugs (*adwiya murakkaba*), which originally circulated in three different recensions. Together with ʿAlī b. Sahl Rabban al-Ṭabarī's [*q.v.*] *Firdaws al-ḥikma* and Yaʿḳūb b. Isḥāḳ al-Kindī's [*q.v.*] *al-Ikhtiyārāt*, Sābūr's dispensatory is a rare, hence important, witness of Arabic pharmacology in the 3rd/9th century.

Bibliography: *Fihrist*, 297; al-Ḳifṭī, *Taʾrīkh al-Ḥukamāʾ*, ed. J. Lippert, Leipzig 1320/1903, 207; Ibn al-ʿIbrī, *Taʾrīkh mukhtaṣar al-duwal*, ed. A. Ṣāliḥānī, Beirut ²1958, 147; Ibn Abī Uṣaybiʿa, *ʿUyūn al-anbāʾ*, ed. A. Müller, 2 vols., Cairo-Königsberg 1882-4, i, 161; cf. O. Kahl, *Sābūr ibn Sahl's (d. 255/869) Dispensatorium parvum [al-Aqrābādhīn al-ṣaghīr]*, diss. Manchester 1992, 28, 48 ff. (with additional bio-bibliographical literature). (O. KAHL)

SABZ ʿALĪ, RAMAḌĀN ʿALĪ, a Nizārī Ismāʿīlī *dāʿī* of the 20th century, and an emissary of the Imām of the time, Sulṭān Muḥammad Shāh Agha Khān III. He was born towards the end of the 19th century in Bombay into an established family of traders and was as a youth apprenticed with his uncle, a businessman in Gwādar. There he acquired an interest in learning more about Ismāʿīlī thought and began to deliver lectures on religious topics to members of the community.

He moved subsequently to Karachi to continue his business activities and became prominent in the community as a *wāʿiẓ* and a leader in social development programmes initiated by the Imām. He was also sent to promote the development of institutions in the newly settled Ismāʿīlī communities of Africa. His most noteworthy achievement was an extensive journey he undertook in 1923 as an emissary of the Imām to contact Central Asian Ismāʿīlī communities in the mountainous regions of the Pāmir (including parts of modern Afghānistān, Tādjīkistān and Sinkiang province in China), as well as the former principalities west of the Karakoram, Hunza and Čitrāl, in the northern areas of what is now Pākistān. He kept a diary in which he gave an account of his travels, sketching the hazardous terrain of the region, the location of various communities, often referring to the tumultuous changes affecting these areas after the 1917 Russian Revolution and the period of modernisation and European influence. After his return he continued to be an influential leader and a very effective preacher.

He died in 1938 and in recognition of his services was posthumously endowed with the title of *pīr* by the Imām.

Bibliography: An account of the journey based on Sabz ʿAlī's diary can be found in a Gudjarātī work, *Pīr Sabzāli ni Madhya Asianī mūsāfrī*, Bombay 1968. Biographical details are preserved in S. Abu Turabi, *Dharmnā dhwajdhārī*, Bombay 1981
(AZIM NANJI)

SABZAWĀR, the name for two towns of the eastern Iranian world.

1. Sabzawār in western Khurāsān was, together with Khusrūdjird, one of the two townships making up the administrative district of Bayhaḳ [*q.v.*], the name by which the whole district was generally known in mediaeval Islamic times. It lay in the cultivable zone on the northern rim of the Dasht-i Kawīr or Great Desert. Sabzawār itself is described in the *Ḥudūd al-ʿālam*, tr. 102, §23.2, as a small town and as the chef-lieu (*ḳaṣaba*) of a district; the Arabic geographers merely mention it as a stage along the roads of Khurāsān and as a *rūstāḳ* of Nīshāpūr. In Ḥamd Allāh Mustawfī's time (8th/14th century), Bayhaḳ was a flourishing district comprising 40 villages (*Nuzha*, 149-50, tr. 148). The Sabzawār district was in the middle years of that same century the centre of the Sarbadārids [*q.v.*], who dominated central Khurāsān during those years, and it is mentioned as the scene of fighting between the invading Özbegs and the Ṣafawids [*q.vv.*] in the later 10th/16th century.

The modern town of Sabzawār (lat. 36°13′ N., long. 52°38′ E.) lies on the highway connecting Tehran with Nīshāpūr and Mashhad, and is administratively the centre of a *bakhsh* or county within the province of Khurāsān; in *ca.* 1950 it had a population of 28,151 (Razmārā, *Farhang-i djughrāfiyā'-i Īrān-zamīn*, ix, 207-8), but 40 years later this had risen to 148,129 (*Preliminary results of the 1991 census*, Statistical Centre of Iran, Population Division).

Bibliography (in addition to references in the article): Le Strange, *The lands of the Eastern Caliphate*, 291; *EIr* art. *Bayhaq* (C.E. Bosworth); and see BAYHAḲ.

2. Sabzawār of Harāt (thus called to distinguish it from 1. above), the name by which the early medieval Islamic town of Isfizār or Asfizār in eastern Khurāsān was more recently called. It lay on the road connecting Sīstān with Harāt, and the mediaeval geographers connected it administratively as much with Sīstān as with Khurāsān. There were four small towns in the district of Isfizār; the region was agriculturally rich, with its lands irrigated by water from perennial streams running down from the mountains of Ghūr [*q.v.*] in central Afghānistān. The early historians mention it as the scene of violent Khāridjite activity, and the *Ḥudūd al-ʿālam* (372/982), tr. 104, § 23.29, comm. 327, describes the people of Isfizār as bellicose Khāridjites; however, by the time of Ḥamd Allāh Mustawfī, the region was strongly orthodox and Shāfiʿī.

Sabzawār of Harāt is now known as Shīndand, a town within the Farāh province of modern Afghānistān (lat. 33°18′ N., long. 62°08′ E.) and is on the modern highway connecting Harāt with Farāh and Ḳandahār.

Bibliography: Le Strange, *Lands*, 412; L.W. Adamec, *Historical and political gazetteer of Afghanistan*. ii. *Farah and southwestern Afghanistan*, Graz 1973, 277-8; *EIr* art. Asfezār (C.E. Bosworth).

(C.E. BOSWORTH)

SABZAWĀRĪ, ḤĀDJDJ MULLĀ HĀDĪ b. Ḥādjdj Mahdī (1212-95 or 1298/1797-1878 or 1881), Persian philosopher of the Ḳādjār period, best-known for his commentary on, and revival of the ideas of Ṣadr al-Dīn al-Shīrāzī, Mullā Ṣadrā (d. 1050/1640 [*q.v.*]).

Born in Sabzawār to a landowning merchant family, Mullā Hādī studied Arabic language and grammar in his home city and *fiḳh*, logic, mathematics and *ḥikma* in Mashhad. He then studied in Iṣfahān with such scholars as Mullā ʿAlī Nūrī (d. 1246/1830-1), the first of the Ḳādjār-period scholars of Ṣadrā, and Nūrī's student Mullā Ismāʿīl. Sabzawārī returned to Khurāsān, performed the pilgrimage and married in Kirmān on the homeward journey. He taught for some years in Mashhad and then returned to Sabzawār, where he taught until his death.

Among his most famous works are his *Ghurar al-farā'id* or *Sharḥ-i manẓūma*, an Arabic philosophical poem on which he wrote his own commentary (the first part of which, on metaphysics, was published by M. Mohaghegh and T. Izutzu, Tehran 1969); *Isrār al-ḥikam* (published by H.M. Farzād, Tehran 1361), written at the request of Nāṣir al-Dīn Shah (d. 1313/1896 [*q.v.*]); a Persian *dīwān* written under the pen-name of *Isrār*; and commentaries on Ṣadrā's *al-Asfār* and *al-Shawāhid al-rubūbiyya* (the latter published together with Ṣadrā's original by S. Djalāl al-Dīn Ashtiyānī, Mashhad 1346, 1360) and on Rūmī's *Mathnawī*.

Bibliography: In addition to references in the article, see also Cl. Huart, *Hādī Sabzewārī*, in *EI*[1]; Muḥsin al-Amīn al-Ḥusaynī al-ʿĀmilī, *Aʿyān al-shīʿa*, Damascus 1961, 1, 48-51; Mīrzā Muḥammad ʿAlī Mudarris, *Rayḥānat al-adab*, [2]Tabriz 1347/1968, ii, 422-7; S.H. Nasr, *Renaissance in Iran*, in M.M. Sharif (ed.), *A history of Muslim philosophy*, Wiesbaden 1966, ii, 1543-55; T. Izutsu, *The concept and reality of existence*, Tokyo 1971; idem and M. Mohaghegh, *The metaphysics of Sabzavārī*, Delmar, N.Y. 1977; S.H. Nasr, *The metaphysics of Sadr al-Din Shirazi and Islamic philosophy in Qajar Iran*, in E. Bosworth and C. Hillenbrand (eds.), *Qajar Iran, political, social and cultural change, 1800-1925*, Edinburgh 1983, 177-98.

(A.J. NEWMAN)

ṢĀD, the fourteenth letter of the Arabic alphabet, transcribed /ṣ/, with the numerical value of 90, according to the eastern order [see ABDJAD]. In the Maghribī order /ṣ/ takes the place of /s/ (thus 60) and /ḍ/ the place of /ṣ/. For an explanation of this fact, similarly attested in a Thamudic abecedary, see M.C.A. Macdonald (in *Bibl.*).

Definition: an alveolar sibilant, voiceless and velarised ("emphatic") in articulation. As a phoneme /ṣ/ is defined by the oppositions /*ṣ* -*s*/,/*ṣ* -*ṭ*/; it is thus velarised and sibilant.

In Ḳur'ānic recitation, or elevated style of recitation in general, the following assimilations occur: the /ṣ/ at the end of a word becomes assimilated to the /z/ at the beginning of the following word (-*ṣ z*-> -*z z*), but the velarisation may be retained (-*ṣ z*->-*ẓ ẓ*-). Within a word, the /ṣ/ is partially assimilated to /z/ before /d/ immediately following it (-*ṣd*- > -*zd*-), but the velarisation may also be retained (-*ṣd*-> -*ẓd*-). A /z/ at the end of a word becomes assimilated to a /ṣ/ at the beginning of the following word (-*z ṣ*->-*ṣ ṣ*-). In the 8th form of the verb the sequence /-ṣt-/ becomes /-ṣṭ-/ by assimilation, carried further by some to complete coalescence, i.e., -ṣṣ- (e.g. *muṣṭabir* and *muṣṣabir*). In analogy to this, initial /t/ of the perfect suffixes, when following /ṣ/, is pronounced /ṭ/ by some (e.g. *faḥaṣṭu*); according to Sībawayh, it is better Arabic not to do so, because the /t/ suffixes of the perfect are variables indicating the subject, while the /t/ infix of the 8th form is stable throughout the paradigm.

An /s/ may be velarised to /ṣ/ in pronunciation, when preceding a /gh/, /kh/, /ḳ/ or /ṭ/ in the same word (e.g. *ṣalakha* for *salakha*, *ṣāṭiʿ* for *sāṭiʿ*). This assimilation, though being only regressive and restricted to the four triggers, is nonetheless probably due to the spread of "emphasis" as a suprasegmental phonemic element throughout the word. That this phenomenon was more general than the orthoepists allow is shown by the spelling variants that are listed in the *ibdāl* works [*q.v.*], cf. pairs like *saʿūṭ*/*ṣaʿūṭ* and *sukhn*/*ṣukhn*, but also *ṭirs*/*ṭirṣ* and *khars*/*kharṣ* in Abu 'l-Ṭayyib al-Lughawī, *K. al-Ibdāl*, ii, 172-96.

For al-Khalīl, the *ṣād*, like the other sibilants (*sīn* and *zāy*), is pronounced with the point (*asala*) of the tongue, i.e., the tapering part (*mustadaḳḳ*) of its end (not the tip). The surviving fragments do not mention the other features of *ṣād* articulation. For Sībawayh, the sibilants (*ṣād, sīn,* and *zāy*) have their point of articulation "between the end (*ṭaraf*) of the tongue and a place slightly above (*fuwayḳ*) the incisors (*thanāyā*)." In addition, the *ṣād* is characterised as "muffled" (*mahmūs*), "soft" (*rikhw*), and "covered" (*muṭbaḳ*), which amounts to saying that it is "voiceless" (?), "non-occlusive", and "velarised". *Ṣād*, like all the sibilants, is characterised by a whistling sound (*ṣafīr*). Its "elevation" (*istiʿlā'*) prevents the vowel /a/ from inclining (*imāla*) towards /i/.

Sībawayh mentions two variants (*farʿ*) of *ṣād*: *ṣād* realised like *zāy* (*maṣdar*>*mazdar, yaṣduḳu*>*yazduḳu*) and *ṣād* realised like *sīn* (*ṣibgh*>*sibgh*), the first variation being the one which is alone considered to be good (*mustaḥsan*) in the recitation of the Ḳur'ān and poetry.

In modern Arabic dialects, *ṣād* seems to be mostly stable. Due to the common spread of velarisation over whole words, original /s/ often becomes /ṣ/ (for historical attestations of this phenomenon, see Blau, *Christian Arabic*, 111-113 and n. 163); in the Judaeo-Arabic of Tafilalt this occurs also with /sh/ (*shaʿr* > *ṣʿr*, see *ZAL*, ix [1982], 40). Sporadic develarisation of /ṣ/ to /s/ is not uncommon: *ṣadr* > *sder* (in certain Maghribi dialects, see *ibid.* and Cantineau, 48), *ṣadaḳa* > *sadaʾ* (and other, but not all, derivatives of this root in Egyptian, see Hinds-Badawi, *A dictionary of Egyptian Arabic*, Beirut 1986, s.v., and Blau, *op. cit.*, 109-10). This develarised /ṣ/ is further voiced in the word *zghīr/zghayyir* "small", common in several dialects. Unconditioned deviations are attested for Hadramaut (/ẓ/, see Landberg, *Ḥaḍramoût*, 239), and for parts of North Yemen (a monophonemic /st/ as in *stabrin* for *ṣabr*, see Behnstedt, 7-9, 184-85).

In borrowings from other languages, /ṣ/ renders Middle Persian /č/ (as in *ṣandj* < *čang* and in names like *al-Ṣīn* < *Čīn*) and sporadically Greek /s/ (as in *liṣṣ* < *lēstēs*, *ḳamīṣ* < *kamision* [Latin *camisia*], *ḳayṣar* < *kaisar*).

In *Persian* and *Turkish*, *ṣād* in Arabic loanwords is pronounced /s/. Some genuine Persian words show irregular spelling with the grapheme /ṣ/, such as *ṣad* "100" and *shaṣt* "60". In Ottoman Turkish, *ṣād* is used to render /s/ in the vicinity of back vowels, whereas *sīn* denotes /s/ in front vowel words, as in *ṣoḳmaḳ* vs. *sökmek*.

Bibliography: Sībawayh, *Kitāb*, ed. Dérenbourg, Paris 1889, ii, 452-5; al-Khalīl, *K. al-ʿAyn*, ed. Darwīsh, Baghdad 1967, 65; Ibn Yaʿīsh, *Sharḥ al-Mufaṣṣal*, ed. Cairo, x, 52-4, 123-31; J. Cantineau, *Etudes de linguistique arabe*, Paris 1960, 46-8, 170; H. Fleisch, *Traité de philologie arabe*, Beirut 1961, i, 57-9, 87; A. Roman, *Etude de la phonologie et de la morphologie de la koinè arabe*, Aix-Marseilles 1983, i, 52-65, 305-11; Abu 'l-Ṭayyib al-Lughawī, *K. al-Ibdāl*, ed. ʿI. al-Tanūkhī, 2 vols., Damascus 1379, 1; P. Behnstedt, *Die Dialekte der Gegend von Ṣaʿdah (Nord-Jemen)*, Wiesbaden 1987; C. de Landberg, *Ḥaḍramoût*, Leiden 1901; M.C.A. Macdonald, *ABCs and letter order in Ancient North Arabian*, in *Procs. of the Seminar for Arabian Studies*, xvi (1986), 101-68; idem, *On the placing of Ṣ in the Maghribi* Abjad *and the Khirbet al-Samrāʾ ABC*, in *JSS*, xxxvii (1992), 155-6.

(G. Troupeau, expanded by the Editors)

SAʿD b. ABĪ WAḲḲĀṢ (d. during Muʿāwiya's caliphate), a leading Companion of the Prophet and commander of the Arab armies during the conquest of ʿIrāḳ. His clan was the Banū Zuhra b. Kilāb of Ḳuraysh. His own *kunya* is given as Abū Isḥāḳ but he is also known as (and sometimes listed in biographical dictionaries under) Saʿd b. Mālik since his father's name was Mālik b. Wuhayb (or Uhayb) b. ʿAbd Manāf b. Zuhra. There does not seem to be any explanation why Mālik should have had the *kunya* Abū Waḳḳāṣ. A tradition says that Saʿd asked the Prophet who he was and received the answer, "You are Saʿd b. Mālik ... b. Zuhra and may the curse of God be upon whoever says otherwise". Since the Prophet's mother was also from the Banū Zuhra, the Prophet is said to have acknowledged Saʿd as his maternal uncle.

Saʿd is counted as one of the ten Companions to whom the Prophet promised entry into paradise. The entries devoted to him in the Sunnī biographical works consist largely of traditions reporting his early acceptance of Islam (he was the third, seventh or ninth to do so, at a time before prayer had become an obligation), his role regarding the revelation of certain Ḳurʾānic verses, his being the first to shed blood for Islam and the first to fire an arrow *fī sabīl Allah*, his guarding the Prophet during the night immediately after the *hidjra*, his participation in all of the battles of the Prophet, the fact that the Prophet said to him alone (or, according to another account, to him and to al-Zubayr), "May my mother and my father be a ransom for you", the Prophet's prayer to God that all of Saʿd's petitions would be granted, and other such details. In Shīʿī tradition, the Companions of the Prophet, including Saʿd, are generally viewed more negatively (see E. Kohlberg, *Some Zaydī views on the Companions of the Prophet*, in *BSOAS*, xxxix [1976], 91-98; idem, *Some Imāmī Shīʿī views on the ṣaḥāba*, in *JSAI*, v [1984], 143-75).

A group of traditions tells of the Prophet's visit to Saʿd, who was ill and apparently dying, in Mecca at a time after the *fatḥ* (the precise occasion is variantly given). These traditions focus partly on Saʿd's aversion to the prospect of death in a place from which he had made *hidjra* and partly upon a prophetic decision regarding the proportion of his estate which a Muslim may bequeath before death. For a detailed discussion, see R. Marsden Speight, *The will of Saʿd b. Abī Waqqāṣ: the growth of a tradition*, in *Isl.*, l (1973), 248-67; D.S. Powers, *The will of Saʿd b. Abī Waqqāṣ: a reassessment*, in *SI*, lviii (1983), 33-53.

Following the defeat of the Arabs at the battle of the Bridge, the caliph ʿUmar b. al-Khaṭṭāb [*q.v.*] is reported to have sent Saʿd in command of an army to central ʿIrāḳ. (Previously he had been ʿUmar's representative responsible for collecting the *ṣadaḳa* tax from the Hawāzin.) It was this army which defeated the Sāsānids at the battle of al-Ḳādisiyya [*q.v.*]. There is a report that Saʿd himself was ill at the time and took no part in the battle, and some sources cite verses critical of Saʿd which refer to his absence from the fighting. The victory of al-Ḳādisiyya led to the expulsion of the Sāsānids from ʿIrāḳ and the occupation by Saʿd of al-Madāʾin [*q.v.*], and was sealed by a further defeat inflicted on the Sāsānids at al-Djalūlāʾ [*q.v.*] by a force sent by Saʿd and commanded by his nephew Hāshim b. ʿUtba b. Abī Waḳḳāṣ. The chronology of these events is uncertain, but they are generally situated in the period 14-19/635-40 (for detailed discussion, see F.McG. Donner, *The early Islamic conquests*, Princeton 1981, 202-12).

The conquest of ʿIrāḳ was accompanied by the foundation of al-Kūfa [*q.v.*] as the garrison town for those forces which had been at al-Ḳādisiyya and subsequently quartered in al-Madāʾin. Although instructions for the founding of the new town are said to have come from the caliph ʿUmar himself, Saʿd is credited with responsibility for organising the settlement (*kawwafa al-Kūfa*), and he became its first governor. ʿUmar then removed him from office, apparently following complaints from the Kūfans. Prominent in the charges which are said to have been made against him was his failure to lead the prayer properly (*lā yuḥsinu 'l-ṣalāt*—some reports provide details), although accusations are also reported that he was unjust in his judgements, did not distribute spoils fairly, and failed to organise expeditions properly. Possibly also relevant here are reports about the undue elegance or luxury of Saʿd's residence in al-Kūfa, which ʿUmar is said to have found objectionable and caused to be burned. Some accounts indicate that Saʿd subsequently had further spells in authority over al-Kūfa under ʿUmar and possibly also ʿUthmān, but the details are uncertain.

In spite of his dismissal from the governorship of al-

Kūfa, it is widely reported that Saᶜd was named by ʿUmar as one of the group of six Companions (the *shūrā*) which he appointed to choose his successor as caliph in 23/644 (see, however, al-Balādhurī, *Ansāb*, v, 21, where Saᶜd's membership of the *shūrā* is explicitly denied on the authority of al-Wāḳidī ... Mūsā b. ᶜUḳba and of al-Zuhrī). At the time of appointing him to the *shūrā*, according to a report often cited, ʿUmar said that he had not removed Saᶜd from Kūfa because of any weakness or treachery, and that, if he was chosen as caliph, the choice should be accepted, and if not, then whoever was chosen should ask Saᶜd for advice.

The last important event in the early history of Islam in connexion with which Saᶜd is mentioned is the struggle between ᶜAlī b. Abī Ṭālib and Muᶜāwiya b. Abī Sufyān [*q.vv.*]. Saᶜd is said to have maintained a position of neutrality, in some reports responding to requests that he should take sides by saying, "Give me a sword which will distinguish between the *muʾmin* and the *kāfir*, and then I will do so". Sometimes this position of neutrality is presented as a sort of ascetic withdrawal. He is said to have refused to have put forward any claims to the caliphate for himself, although his status in Islam would have justified his doing so. There are contradictions within the sources as to whether he attended the "arbitration" court [see ADHRUḤ] or not. Some reports say that he did not give the *bayᶜa* to ᶜAlī following the murder of ᶜUthmān, and others that he eventually gave it to Muᶜāwiya after the end of the *fitna*, although he had earlier refused.

He is said to have spent the last period of his life in his residence (*ḳaṣr*) at al-ᶜAḳīḳ near Medina, and upon his death was carried from there to Medina to be buried in the cemetery of al-Baḳīᶜ. Marwān b. al-Ḥakam, the governor, prayed over him. Various dates between 50/670-1 and 58/677-8 are given for his death, and his age similarly varies from about 70 to over 80. It is likely that any memories of the historical Saᶜd b. Abī Waḳḳāṣ have been much elaborated and developed in the traditions, and the material on him probably reflects hagiographical, polemical, legal and other concerns, as well as the need for entertaining stories and speculation.

Bibliography: Material relating to Saᶜd, recycled, reworked and rearranged, is to be found in most of the forms of traditional Muslim literature, and only some of the more notable sources can be mentioned here. Among the biographical dictionaries, see Ibn Saᶜd, *Ṭabaḳāt*, iii/1, 97-105; Ibn ᶜAsākir, *Taʾrīkh Madīnat Dimashḳ*, lith., Dār al-Bashīr, ᶜAmmān n.d., vii, 132-80; Ibn Manẓūr, *Mukhtaṣar Taʾrīkh Dimashḳ liʾbni ᶜAsākir*, Damascus 1985, ix, 250-72; Dhahabī, *Siyar aᶜlām al-nubalāʾ*, Beirut 1401/1981, i, 92-124; Mizzī, *Tahdhīb al-kamāl*, Beirut 1408/1987, x, 309-14 (the bibliography provided by the editor, Bashshār ᶜAwwār Maᶜrūf, at 309 n. 2, is valuable). Of the biographical collections devoted to those who were promised paradise, see al-Muḥibb al-Ṭabarī, *al-Riyāḍ al-naḍira*, Beirut 1405/1984, iv, 319-35 (*bāb* 8). For references to Saᶜd in *sīra, taʾrīkh* and *futūḥ* works, see the indexes to, e.g., Ibn Hishām, *Sīra;* Wāḳidī, *Maghāzī*, ed. Marsden Jones, London 1966; Ibn Saᶜd, *Ṭabaḳāt*, i and ii; Ṭabarī, *Taʾrīkh*; Yaᶜḳūbī, *Taʾrīkh*; Balādhurī, *Futūḥ*. For Saᶜd's role as an "occasion of revelation", see the Ḳurʾānic commentaries to VI, 52, VIII, 1, and XXXI, 15, in particular. For references to Saᶜd in the standard collections of *ḥadīth*, see s.v. Saᶜd b. Abī Waḳḳāṣ in A.J. Wensinck *et alii*, *Concordance et indices de la tradition musulmane*, viii, Leiden 1988, and (in English) A.J. Wensinck, *Handbook*. For the genealogical tradition, see Ibn al-Kalbī, *Djamhara*, tr. W. Caskel and G. Strenziok, index s.v. Saᶜd b. Mālik. In addition to those studies mentioned in the article, see L. Caetani, *Annali dell'Islam*, index (vol. vi) to vols. iii, iv and v; M.G. Morony, *Iraq after the Muslim conquest*, Princeton 1984, index. (G.R. Hawting)

SAᶜD b. BAKR, Banū, a small Arab tribe, usually reckoned as part of the tribe or tribal group of Hawāzin [*q.v.*]. To a section of this tribe belonged Ḥalīma bint Abī Dhuʾayb, Muḥammad's wet-nurse. After the battle of Ḥunayn [*q.v.*] her daughter Shaymāʾ, who had been taken prisoner, obtained her release by proving to Muḥammad that she was his milk-sister [see also RAḌĀᶜ. 2]; and some of the men of the tribe, because they were Muḥammad's milk-brothers, were able to facilitate various negotiations. The tribe was apparently divided into several small sections. The group just mentioned fought against Muḥammad at Ḥunayn along with Hawāzin, but there were also others fighting on Muḥammad's side. Yet others supported him at the conquest of Mecca. The expedition to Fadak in 6/628 led by ᶜAlī against a group called only Banū Saᶜd was probably against the section of Saᶜd b. Bakr associated with Hawāzin; they were being punished for accepting Jewish bribes to give military help against Muḥammad.

Bibliography: W.M. Watt, *Muhammad at Medina*, Oxford 1956, 99 n. and index; Ibn Hishām, index; Wāḳidī, ed. Marsden Jones, London 1966, index. (W. Montgomery Watt)

SAᶜD b. MUᶜĀDH, chief of the clan of ᶜAbd al-Ashhal in Medina in succession to his father.

At the time of the *Hidjra* he seems to have been the strongest man in the tribe of al-Aws, of which his clan was a part. He had taken part in the fighting prior to the battle of Buᶜāth [*q.v.*] and been wounded. The leader of al-Aws at Buᶜāth, Ḥuḍayr b. Simāk, is reckoned to another clan, but his son, Usayd b. Ḥuḍayr, seems to have been second-in-command to Saᶜd in ᶜAbd al-Ashhal. Saᶜd and Usayd were both for a time opposed to Islam and wanted to stop its spread, but first Usayd and then Saᶜd were won over, and Saᶜd became probably the strongest supporter of Islam in Medina and made an important contribution to its wide acceptance. He did not, however, go with others to Mecca for the second meeting at al-ᶜAḳaba [*q.v.*], though he is said to have made the pilgrimage to Mecca on the first occasion after the *Hidjra*. He was the most prominent of the Anṣār to join Muḥammad in the expedition which led to the battle of Badr [*q.v.*], and encouraged many others to participate. In the course of the battle, he made special arrangements for Muḥammad's safety. Three years later, when the Meccans were besieging Medina (the battle of the Khandaḳ), the Jewish clan of Ḳurayẓa [*q.v.*] was in secret negotiations with the enemy, and after the Meccan withdrawal, Muḥammad attacked them and they were forced to surrender unconditionally. Saᶜd b. Muᶜādh had been seriously wounded by an arrow, but at this point he was entrusted with deciding the fate of Ḳurayẓa. This was because he was leader of al-Aws, and several sections of that tribe had been in alliance with Ḳurayẓa. Though these pressed for leniency, Saᶜd's decision was that all the men should be put to death and the women and children sold as slaves; he presumably realised that allegiance to the Islamic community must override all former tribal and clan allegiances. Shortly afterwards he died, and Muḥammad seems to have felt his loss deeply, since he had done more than any other of the Anṣār to ensure the growth of Islam.

Bibliography: Ibn Hishām, index; Wāḳidī, ed.

Marsden Jones, London 1966, index; Ibn al-Athīr, *Usd al-ghāba*, ii, 296-9; Ibn Saᶜd, iii/2, 2-13; W.M. Watt, *Muhammad at Medina*, Oxford 1956, index.

(W. MONTGOMERY WATT)

SAᶜD B. **MUḤAMMAD** [see ḤAYṢA BAYṢA].

SAᶜD B. **ᶜUBĀDA**, chief of the clan of Sāᶜida at Medina.

The clan appears to have been small since it is not mentioned in the fighting leading to the battle of Buᶜāth [*q.v.*], but it may have been more influential than its size warranted, perhaps because it was wealthy. Only two members of the clan were at the second meeting with Muḥammad at al-ᶜAḳaba [*q.v.*], but both were included among the *nuḳabāʾ* or representatives. One of these was Saᶜd b. ᶜUbāda, who had become a Muslim at an early date. Saᶜd was badly treated by some Meccans on his way back from al-ᶜAḳaba because they had heard something about "the pledge of war", but he eventually received the protection of other Meccans and was able to return to Medina. He appears to have been a wealthy man, because, when Muḥammad attacked the Jewish clan of al-Naḍīr [*q.v.*], he provided a tent and also a large quantity of dates for the army. On an expedition shortly before the conquest of Mecca, his son Ḳays is said to have purchased camels to be slaughtered as food for the army. Ibn Isḥāḳ says that Saᶜd was not at the battle of Badr [*q.v.*] because suffering from snake-bite, but al-Wāḳidī and others say he was present. The snake-bite was probably genuine and not an excuse, for Muḥammad seems to have trusted him fully. At this period, Saᶜd was probably the second most important man in the tribe of al-Khazradj after ᶜAbd Allāh b. Ubayy [*q.v.*], but the latter was never a whole-hearted supporter of Muḥammad, since before his arrival he had been hoping to become "king" of Medina. The struggle for power between Saᶜd and Ibn Ubayy led Saᶜd to give his fullest support to Muḥammad. In the "affair of the lie" against ᶜĀʾisha, shortly before the Khandaḳ attack on Medina, when Ibn Ubayy helped to spread the scandal, it eventually came to a showdown, with Muḥammad wanting to punish Ibn Ubayy. The tribe of al-Aws gave this full support, but Saᶜd opposed them on behalf of al-Khazradj and urged leniency. From this point onwards, Ibn Ubayy faded out and Saᶜd became leader of al-Khazradj, and after the death of Saᶜd b. Muᶜādh [*q.v.*] leader of the Anṣār as a whole. After the death of Muḥammad, the Anṣār met in the hall (*saḳīfa* [*q.v.*]) of his clan and might have made him Muḥammad's successor had not Abū Bakr and ᶜUmar intervened. He is then said to have settled in Syria, where he died a year or two later.

Bibliography: Ibn Hishām, index; Wāḳidī, ed. Marsden Jones, London 1966, index; Ibn al-Athīr, *Usd al-ghāba*, ii, 283-5; Ibn Saᶜd, iii/2, 142-5; W.M. Watt, *Muhammad at Medina*, Oxford 1956, index.

(W. MONTGOMERY WATT)

SAᶜD B. IBRĀHĪM **ZAGHLŪL**, Egyptian jurist and politician, from 1918 to his death in 1927 president of the Egyptian Wafd party and in 1924 Prime Minister.

Saᶜd Zaghlūl was born as the second son of Ibrāhīm Zaghlūl and his second wife Maryam in July 1858 (others say 1857, 1859 or 1860, discussed by Ramaḍān, *Mudhakkirāt*, i, 48 ff.). His father was a landowner in Abyāna near Fuwwa in the Lower Egyptian province of al-Gharbiyya. Besides the resident notable families Zayd and Ḥusām ad-Dīn, the Zaghālila belonged to the most prestigious and wealthy families of the village. Ibrāhīm Zaghlūl owned about 250 *faddāns* and acted as a village headman. He had inherited this position from his father Aḥmad, to whom the governor of the Buḥayra pr[o]vince, Muḥammad Fāḍil Pasha, had allocated abo[ut] 230 *faddāns* in around 1840. Although sever[al] rumours claimed that the Zaghālila were of Maghri[bi] origin and that they were originally Turks comin[g] from Algeria, the family presumably belonged [to] those "new Egyptian notables" (then called *abnāʾ a[l-] balad*) who gained fortunes and social power aft[er] 1750. It should be noted, however, that the Zaghālil[a] originally were Mālikīs and that only later did Saᶜ[d] Zaghlūl become a Shāfiᶜī. In contrast to this, man[y] national historians have tried to present Zaghlūl as [a] son of a local peasant family in order to stre[ss] Zaghlūl's "Egyptiannness" as a true "son of th[e] country". Saᶜd Zaghlūl also supported the mystific[a]tion around his origins when in 1883, after havin[g] been arrested by British military forces, he claime[d] that he was not an Egyptian but a Moroccan citize[n] with a Sharīfian genealogy. Ibrāhīm Zaghlūl's pos[i]tion in the agrarian society enabled him to mar[ry] Maryam, the daughter of Shaykh ᶜAbduh Barak[āt] from Minyat Murshid near Fuwwa, in 1851-2. Th[e] Barakāt family also belonged to the new agrarian éli[te] which came into power after having introduced th[e] growing of rice under the régime of Muḥammad ᶜAl[ī]. Ibrāhīm's first wife, Fāṭima, from a village famil[y] gave birth to two daughters and five sons. Maryam['s] sons were: Faradj (Allāh), who died after having bee[n] born, Saᶜd (Allāh) and (Aḥmad) Fatḥī (Fatḥ Allāh[,] born in 1863). Just after Fatḥī's birth, Ibrāhīm die[d] and Saᶜd was left in the hands of his elder brothe[r] Shināwī, who was a member of the local administr[a]tion. Like other family members, Saᶜd inherited a l[ot] of 20 *faddāns* from his father's estate.

As was a common practice among wealthy peasa[nt] families in those days, Saᶜd, being the eldest son [of] Maryam was sent to al-Azhar, whereas Fatḥī w[as] chosen to study at a *madrasa* to become a state officia[l]. Saᶜd went first to a local *kuttāb*, and after five year[s], in 1870, his half-brother Shināwī sent him to school i[n] the nearby provincial town Dasūḳ where he had bee[n] appointed as the head of the district administratio[n]. Saᶜd apparently stayed in Dasūḳ for about thre[e] years, mainly occupied in studying *tadjwīd* [*q.v.*]. F[or] a while, he joined his brother Fatḥī in Rashīd [or] Rosetta and took lessons from Shaykh Aḥmad Ab[ū] Rās, a specialist in law and grammar. In 1873, th[e] fifteen-years old Saᶜd moved to Cairo to live on h[is] own in the old city in order to pursue his studies at a[l-] Azhar. There is reason to believe that Saᶜd abrupt[ly] broke with his past, as he did not join a *riwāḳ* and onl[y] once revisited his native village during the next 4[...] years.

In Cairo, Saᶜd presented himself as an Islami[c] scholar and proudly carried the title and the outfit [of] a *shaykh*, although he never received an *ᶜālimiyya* fro[m] al-Azhar. Instead of studying at the University, Saᶜ[d] preferred to visit Djamāl ad-Dīn al-Afghānī's priva[te] salon, where he met Muḥammad ᶜAbduh, who wa[s] ten years older than he. Saᶜd became ᶜAbduh's *muri[d]* and regarded him as his true father and himself a[s] ᶜAbduh's disciple. Both tried to present their relation[]ship in the tradition of Ṣūfī brotherhood. For som[e] years Saᶜd's life was closely bound up with ᶜAbduh['s] destiny. In 1880, Saᶜd suddenly broke off his studie[s] at al-Azhar. Perhaps he hoped to get a position in th[e] state administration; but ᶜAbduh made him a sub[-]editor of the journal *al-Waḳāʾiᶜ al-miṣriyya* in Octobe[r] 1880. In May 1882, his ambitions for a governmen[t] career were satisfied. The *wakīl* of the Ministry of th[e] Interior, Ḥusayn al-Daramallī, made him a *bāsh mu*ᶜ*āwin* (secretary). A few days before the battle of a[l-]

Tall al-Kabīr (13 September 1882), Saᶜd accepted a position at the Law Court of Dj̲īza. This was his first opportunity to work as a jurist. Saᶜd could now change his outfit and become an Afandī. But in early October 1882 he resigned and was obviously considering following ᶜAbduh, who had left Egypt on 7 January 1883. But ᶜAbduh advised him to stay in Egypt; hence Saᶜd worked with his friend Ḥusayn Saḳar as a lawyer at the Dj̲īza court. As British officials suspected him to be a member of an obscure "society of revenge", Saᶜd was arrested on 20 June 1883; he was released four months later as the accusation proved to be false. Already in February 1884, he resumed his work as a lawyer and kept this position for the next eight years.

When Muḥammad ᶜAbduh returned to Egypt in 1888, Saᶜd Zag̲h̲lūl again had an intercessor within the intellectual and cultural urban élites. ᶜAbduh invited him to join the famous salon of Princess Nazlī Fāḍil, who had been an ardent supporter of Aḥmad ᶜUrābī. Now, however, the salon became a most important place of British-Egyptian private diplomacy. Here, Zag̲h̲lūl met for the first time the Consul-General Evelyn Baring, later the 1st Earl of Cromer, and many influential journalists and politicians. In 1890, he had already become a great name; as gossip concerning Zag̲h̲lūl's liaison with Princess Nazlī was spreading, he gained public recognition within colonial society. Wilfred Scawen Blunt even suggested him to Cromer as a possible minister in an "Egyptian government" which should oust the traditional élites from power. Two years later, Saᶜd's lobbying proved to be a success. He was appointed as a Deputy Chief Judge at the Court of Appeal on 27 June 1892. From now on, Zag̲h̲lūl had a well-established position in the Egyptian upper class; but this was only the beginning of his rapid career. From 1892 to 1897, he went several times to Europe in order to study languages and law, and in 1897, he got a diploma in law from the University of Paris. Obviously, he considered himself as a political personality, since he now started to keep a diary which recorded day-by-day summaries of events and cases at the law court and which was meant as an aide-mémoire for future activities. Only in 1903 did he begin to use the diaries for private reminiscences. Zag̲h̲lūl's integration into the upper class was crowned when in November 1895 he became engaged to Ṣafiyya, a daughter of Muṣṭafā Fahmī (1840-1914), who had just been appointed (for the third time) as Prime Minister. Now, Zag̲h̲lūl was also accepted by the old "Turco-Circassian" élites, as Fahmī himself was of a Turkish origin, his father having come from Algeria to Egypt in the early thirties of the 19th century.

By 1896, when he married Ṣafiyya, Zag̲h̲lūl was a rich man. He possessed everything which was important in those days to become a politician: a position, money, reputation, a good marriage and a good knowledge of French and a bit of German. In 1902, the couple moved into a new house in Cairo which would later become a national gathering place. In addition, Zag̲h̲lūl bought a large estate in the district of Damanhūr. At that time, the public considered Zag̲h̲lūl as a friend of the British, a protégé of the Khedive, a supporter of ᶜAlī Yūsuf (1863-1913) and his journal *al-Muʾayyad*, and as a member of the ruling class. Having been an Afandī in his twenties, Zag̲h̲lūl, now being 41 years old, turned into a Pas̲h̲a. But already at this stage, he was able to integrate within himself the three respective social codes of the Egyptian élites, presenting himself as the personification of an Egyptian identity.

The beginning of the colonial crisis in Egypt in 1905-6 deeply interfered with Saᶜd Zag̲h̲lūl's career. After the strike at the Law School in February 1906 and the famous Dins̲h̲awāy affair (13 June 1906), Cairo suddenly witnessed a growing public recognition of Muṣṭafā Kāmil's [*q.v.*] nationalist movement, which culminated in a gathering of the later members of the (third) National Party in Zag̲h̲lūl's house on 12 October 1906. The colonial consensus ended, and Saᶜd Zag̲h̲lūl had to choose either to join the ranks of the urban nationalists or to become a political member of the ruling élite. Cromer decided to promote an "Egyptianisation" of the cabinet by appointing Zag̲h̲lūl as the new Minister of Education on 28 October 1906. Obviously, however, Zag̲h̲lūl did not feel comfortable with his new position, as his ideas of reforming governmental institutions (here he proved to be more an Afandī than a Pas̲h̲a) provoked several severe conflicts even with the Khedive. After having decided not to join the urban nationalist movement, Zag̲h̲lūl was dragged into the foundation of a new "People's Party" (*ḥizb al-umma*, 21 September 1907) which was sponsored by landlords like ᶜAlī S̲h̲aᶜrāwī, Aḥmad Luṭfī as-Sayyid, Muḥammad Maḥmūd, Ḥamd al-Bāsil and Ṭalᶜaṭ Ḥarb. Zag̲h̲lūl, who openly declared his mistrust of the urban national movement, continued as Minister of Education in a new cabinet formed by Buṭrus G̲h̲ālī in 1908. As a minister, Zag̲h̲lūl had only little sucess. As he tried to fulfil his role as a reform-minded Afandī, he clashed with the palace and the traditional structures of governmental institutions; in early 1910, he thought of retiring from politics as he did not see any progress for the nationalist constitutional movement. In addition, urban nationalists heavily attacked him for promoting nepotism, and others even made propaganda for Fatḥī Zag̲h̲lūl, that he should replace his brother in office. Fearing to be excluded from the nationalist public, he dismissed the idea of resigning. When on 23 October 1910 he became Minister of Justice, he had to approve the policy that nationalist journalists were to be tried by special courts originally installed to deal with brigands; even more, he had to accept the imprisonment of the leader of the National Party, Muḥammad Farīd [*q.v.*] (23 January 1911). This difficult situation finally led him to retire from office in March 1912; he was then busy looking for new support in party politics. He succesfully rallied for a seat in the new Legislative Assembly, which made him its Vice-President in January 1914. Although his political programme contained only a few suggestions concerning the reforms of the judicial and educational system, Zag̲h̲lūl soon gained a reputation of being the most able Egyptian public orator. Being a convinced constitutionalist, Zag̲h̲lūl highly esteemed the role of the Assembly as the nation's only political representation. The Assembly met in June 1914 for the last time before the outbreak of the War and the proclamation which made Egypt a British Protectorate. As usual, Saᶜd Zag̲h̲lūl left to Europe for the summer; this time, however, he stressed that he wanted to use the break to rethink his political career. In spite of his earlier quarrels with the Khedive ᶜAbbās II Ḥilmī [*q.v.*], Zag̲h̲lūl now backed him after his deposition. Personal problems and a career crisis may have added to the fact that Zag̲h̲lūl gradually changed his political attitude towards British rule in Egypt. In his view, Britain had now become an opponent of a true constitutional order in Egypt. Being unemployed and showing symptoms of an addiction to gambling, he had lost most of his fortune and riches. He was highly in debt. In order to avoid the gambling salons of

Cairo, he retired to his newly-built house in Masdjid Waṣīf. His political ambition continued to aim at reinvesting the Legislative Assembly, which had been prorogued in late 1914, with power. After the death of Sultan Ḥusayn Kāmil, the new Sultan Fuʾād declared on the occasion of the New Year 1336 (18 October 1917), that the Assembly would "soon" resume its work. This, the parallel discussions on a new Constitution and Woodrow Wilson's declaration on 8 January 1918, encouraged Zaghlūl to revive his role in the Legislative Assembly as the true representative of the Egyptian nation, and consequently with his position as Vice-President, he regarded himself as its best advocate. Meanwhile, the Egyptian landlords openly protested against the rigid measures taken by the British authorities in order to secure the logistics and supply of the army. They pressed Zaghlūl to intervene, but he only carefully presented the complaints to the Sultan and the British officials. Both sides wished to neutralise Zaghlūl. Fuʾād even expressed his thanks to him by suggesting that he should become a minister again. At his house in Masdjid Waṣīf, Zaghlūl now wanted to take advantage of the wrangling over his political future, and he received the most prominent leaders of the nationalist movement. He accepted the idea which Prince Ṭūsūn had promoted of sending a delegation (*wafd*) of the Assembly to the British High Commissioner in order to get permission to travel to Paris and to present Egypt's demand for independence to the Peace Conference. The idea was also favoured by the government; but the Prime Minister Ḥusayn Rushdī (1863-1928) and ʿAdlī Yegen (1864-1933) disputed the right of Zaghlūl to speak in the name of the nation. On 13 October 1918, Zaghlūl was deputed to see the High Commissioner Wingate with his political friends ʿAlī Shaʿrāwī and ʿAbd al-ʿAzīz Fahmī and to present a demand for self-determination. The British, however, declared that Zaghlūl was unrepresentative of the Egyptian nation and cold-shouldered the three nationalists. Consequently, the small group started a campaign and issued a circular in which seven members of the Assembly, with Zaghlūl as their "president", were vested with the power to negotiate for the "complete independence" of Egypt, and which should be signed by the members of the Assembly and by the "Egyptian people". This campaign paved the way for the restoration of the national movement, and already in December 1918, the pro-Zaghlūl agitation had reduced other political factions to silence. Even the Prime Minister Rushdī had to accept Zaghlūl's new power position and finally resigned on 1 March 1919, as the British authorities continued to refuse the Wafd's permission to leave for the Peace Conference. On 8 March 1919, after Lord Curzon had accepted resolute action against the nationalists, Zaghlūl, Muḥammad Maḥmūd, Ismāʿīl Ṣidḳī and Ḥamd al-Bāsil were arrested and exiled to Malta.

From afar, Zaghlūl monitored the manifold unrest in Egypt which reached its peak in March-April 1919. In accordance with his nationalist world view, he considered the revolts to be a firm expression of the people's will to make him the true and only representative of the nation. Finally, the British authorities also implicitly accepted this view, as they wanted to act within the legal framework of a protectorate which required a functioning "indigenous" government. On 7 April 1919, after the Egyptian élites had openly condemned the rebellions, the Special High Commissioner General Allenby released the four exiles and allowed them to leave for Paris with 11 others. Two days later, Rushdī formed a new government; but he soon had to resign again, as he was not able to accept the demands of state officials to recognise Zaghlūl as the nation's sole representative. Meanwhile, since the Wafdists regarded themselves as the only true expression of the Egyptians' political will, Zaghlūl's compatriots started to build up an efficient nationwide organisation which should be the nucleus of a future Egyptian administration.

Zaghlūl spent the next two years in Europe. After the British Protectorate in Egypt was recognised by the Peace Treaty of Paris (28 June 1919), the 15 Wafdists tried to mobilise the public opinion in their favour, but had only a limited success. They also tried to control the boycott of the Milner Mission, which had been formed in order to investigate the spring revolts. Zaghlūl and his delegation stayed in Europe till the end of March 1921. Having reached Cairo on the demand of ʿAdlī, who wanted to shift the responsibility for the negotiations with the British officials on to the President of the Wafd, Zaghlūl started his famous campaign favouring the complete independence of Egypt. It tried to find a political position between ʿAdlī and the court faction on the one side and the urban nationalists' activists on the other side. The British warned him several times not to exploit the freedom of press and speech by attacking the government. Zaghlūl, however, did not give in. On 23 December 1921, he was again arrested together with five other leaders of the Wafd (Muṣṭafā an-Naḥḥās, Markam ʿUbayd, Sinōt Ḥannā, Fatḥ Allāh Barakāt and ʿĀṭif Barakāt) and sent to Aden. They arrived at the Seychelles six days before the unilateral British declaration of Egypt's independence (15 March 1922). In September 1922, Zaghlūl was sent to Gibraltar, where he was told that he was no more a prisoner but a guest of the British Government. In April 1923, he was allowed to leave Gibraltar for wherever he wanted; as usual, Zaghlūl first went to France (Aix-les-Bains) for a summer course of treatment. He finally returned to Cairo on 17 September 1923 and was welcomed by a large crowd. This embarassed the Liberals, who thought that, after the last elections which had given them a comfortable majority and the fact that Zaghlūl had not had any direct control of the negotiations with the British, the general sentiment in favour of Zaghlūl had cooled down. The Wafd Party, though it had radically criticised the new constitution promulgated on 13 April 1923, soon prepared to run for the next year's elections and tried to exploit the return of the "Nation's prophet" as Zaghlūl was often now called. He pulled out all the stops, toured in the country, invited notables and afandīs, and addressed all kinds of social groups in many public meetings. The poll of January 1924 gave the Wafd a 90% majority, and Zaghlūl was called to form a government which became known as "the people's cabinet". He soon began to centralise the complex decision-making procedures in his own hands and tried to negotiate with the British administration the still unsolved questions concerning the Sudan and the Suez Canal. But the more he exercised direct rule over the Egyptian administration, the more Fuʾād, now King of Egypt, and the British officials mistrusted him. In public, Zaghlūl even became a potential candidate for the presidency of an Egyptian republic. The murder of the *Sirdār* Sir Lee Stack (19 November 1924) provided British officials with a pretext to get rid of the troublemaker. Five days later, Zaghlūl had to resign. Though he continued to play an important public role in Parliament his deposition ruined his political career. He saw hi organisation turned into a political party accepting other parties as partners. Thus his hope of being the head of an organisation which should be the organic expression of the nation's will vanished. His contemporaries Atatürk and Riḍā Khān were to be more successful than he at becoming heads of state. In Egypt, however, the political public prevented an analogous development. In early summer 1927, his already shaken and poor health deteriorated, and on 23 August 1927 Zaghlūl died in Cairo of erysipelas.

Bibliography: Saᶜd Zaghlūl wrote very little. He published a booklet on Shāfiᶜī law, Cairo n.d. [*ca.* 1878]), a summary of Ibn Miskawayh on *inshā*ʾ and about 28 articles in Egyptian journals of the late seventies and early eighties of the 19th century. It is doubtful, however, whether he wrote them all personally or whether he edited articles of Muḥammad ᶜAbduh. The main sources of his political views are his diaries and some collections of his speeches. See his *Mudhakkirāt*, ed. ᶜAbd al-ᶜAẓīm Ramaḍān, i ff., Cairo 1987 ff. and collections of his speeches by Aḥmad Nasīb al-Sukkarī, Cairo 1923; Maḥmūd [Kāmil] Fuʾād, Cairo 1924; Muḥammad Ibrāhīm al-Djazīrī, Cairo 1927; and Maḥmūd Kāmil Fuʾād, Cairo 1927.

There are quite a lot of biographies in Arabic: by Muḥammad ᶜAbd al-Murshid Dāwūd, Cairo 1926; Aḥmad Fahmī Ḥāfiẓ, Cairo 1927; Karīm Thābit, Cairo 1929; ᶜAbduh Ḥasan al-Zayyāt, Cairo 1932; ᶜAbbās Maḥmūd al-ᶜAḳḳād, Cairo 1936; Ibrāhīm Rashād, Cairo 1937; Ḳadrī Ḳalᶜadjī, Beirut 1938; Yūsuf F. al-Naḥḥās, ᶜAbd al-ᶜAzīz Saᶜd, Cairo 1952; Ḥāmid al-Mulaydjī, Cairo 1954; Muḥammad Ibrāhīm al-Djazīrī, Cairo 1954; ᶜAbd al-Khāliḳ Lāshīn, Cairo 1974; idem, Beirut-Cairo 1975; Muḥammad Kāmil Salīm, Cairo 1975; idem, Cairo 1976; Ṭāriḳ al-Bishrī, Cairo 1977; Amīl Fahmī Shanūda, Cairo 1977; Muḥsin Muḥammad, Cairo 1983; ᶜAbbās Ḥāfiẓ, Cairo n.d.; Ḥamdān Sālim an-Naᶜnāᶜī, Damanhūr n.d.

Although there is a huge literature on the Egyptian nationalist movements in Western languages, there are hardly any biographies of Zaghlūl; cf. Fouad Yéghen, *Saad Zaghloul. Le "père du peuple" égyptien*, Paris 1927; for a short political account, see e.g. J.M. Ahmed, *The intellectual origins of Egyptian nationalism*, London 1960, 52-55, 113-17, and J. Berque, *L'Egypte. Impérialisme et révolution*, Paris 1967, 287-295. For his dealings with the British, see E. Kedourie, *Saᶜd Zaghlul and the British*, in idem, *The Chatham House version and other Middle Eastern studies*, London 1970, 82-159, shortened account in idem, *Politics in the Middle East*, Oxford 1992, 158-79. On Zaghlūl's role in the 1919 rebellions, see R. Schulze, *Die Rebellion der ägyptischen Fallahin 1919*, Berlin 1981. His place in the nationalist movements is discussed by *inter alii* I. Gershoni and J.P. Jankowski, *Egypt, Islam, and the Arabs. The search for Egyptian nationhood, 1900-1930*, New York 1986; M. Deeb, *Party politics in Egypt: the Wafd and its rivals, 1919-1939*, London 1979, and also within the frame of national historiography, ᶜAbd al-Raḥmān al-Rāfiᶜī, *Thawrat sana 1919*, 2 vols., Cairo 1946 and idem, *Fī aᶜḳāb al-thawra*, 3 vols., Cairo 1947-51.

(R. Schulze)

SAᶜD (I) b. ZANGĪ, Abū Shudjāᶜ ᶜIzz al-Dīn, Turkish Atabeg in Fārs of the Salghurid line [*q.v.*], reigned in Shīrāz from 599/1202-3 until most probably 623/1226.

On the death of his elder brother Takla/Tekele Degele, etc.?) b. Zangī in 594/1198, Saᶜd claimed power in Fārs, but his claim was contested by his cousin Ṭoghrīl, the son of his father's elder brother Sunḳur, who had founded the dynasty. Ṭoghrīl retained the royal title for nine years, but throughout that period warfare between him and his cousin continued without a decisive result for either, the country was wasted and depopulated, none would till the ground, and famine and pestilence smote the people. At length, in 599/1202-3, Saᶜd captured his cousin and ascended the throne of Fārs (according to Mīrkhʷānd this happened in 593/1197, after Ṭoghrīl had been defeated by Takla), but at the beginning of his reign famine was so sore in the land that the strong slew and ate the weak, and even when the famine had abated the pestilence remained; but Saᶜd gradually restored prosperity to his people, and, having completed this task, conquered Kirmān from the Shabānkāra Kurds. In 614/1217-18 he invaded ᶜIrāḳ, but was taken prisoner by the army of the Khʷārazm-Shāh ᶜAlāʾ al-Dīn Muḥammad [*q.v.*], and in order to regain his freedom was obliged to pay a ransom of two-thirds of a year's revenue of his kingdom, to surrender Iṣṭakhr and Ashkūrān, and to agree to pay tribute annually. On his return to Shīrāz, his son Abū Bakr, who had occupied the throne during his captivity, opposed his restoration, and a battle was fought between father and son, in which Saᶜd was wounded in the eye with an arrow, but the citizens admitted him into the city by night, and he seized and imprisoned his son. When the Khʷārazm-Shāh Djalāl al-Dīn Mingburnu [*q.v.*] passed through Fārs on his return from India in 621/1224, he interceded for Abū Bakr, and succeeded in persuading Saᶜd to release him.

According to the most reliable sources, Saᶜd died in Dhu 'l-Ḳaᶜda 623/November 1226 and after a reign of 29 years was succeeded by his son Abū Bakr. Amongst his building works was a celebrated Masdjid-i Naw or Masdjid-i Atabegī in Shīrāz, completed in 615/1218 (see W. Barthold, *An historical geography of Iran*, Princeton 1984, 156). However, the poet Saᶜdī [*q.v.*] derived his *takhalluṣ* or nom-de-plume not from this Saᶜd (I) but from his son Abī Bakr b. Saᶜd (I) and grandson Saᶜd (II) b. Abī Bakr.

Bibliography: 1. Sources. The main ones are Afḍal al-Dīn Kirmānī, *Simṭ al-ᶜulā* and *al-Muḍāf ilā Badāʾiᶜ al-zamān fī waḳāʾiᶜ Kirmān*; Nasawī; Djuwaynī; Rashīd al-Dīn; Ḥamd Allāh Mustawfī, *Guzīda*; and Mīrkhʷānd.

2. Studies. C.E. Bosworth, in *Camb. hist. of Iran*, v, 172-3; Erdoğan Merçil, *Fars atabegleri Salgurlular*, Ankara 1975, 62-82. See also Bosworth, *The Islamic dynasties*, 125-6.

(T.W. Haig-[C.E. Bosworth])

SAᶜD b. ZAYD MANĀT al-FIZR is the name by which a large section of the tribe of Tamīm is named.

The curious cognomen *Fizr* or (according to al-Aṣmaᶜī, *Fazr*) has received no satisfactory explanation, and the philologist Abū Manṣūr al-Azharī asserts that he never met any person who could explain it. Some lexicographers explain it as meaning "more than one", others as "goats", but we may assume that Ibn Durayd is correct when he derives it from the verb *fazara* with the meaning "to split" and that *fizr* means "a chip or fragment". The Arab genealogists give the name of the common ancestor as Saᶜd b. Zayd Manāt b. Tamīm and relate tales to account for the curious name, which amount to the following: Saᶜd had much cattle which he ordered his sons, by different mothers, to take to pasture; they refused and he invited the kindred tribesmen of Mālik b. Zayd Manāt to come and rob the camels. Then when only goats remained, he gave his sons the same order and they again refused to take them to pasturage. In his anger, he called Arabs of every tribe together (or, according to another version, took his animals to the fair of ᶜUkāẓ) and asked them to take each one goat as plunder (*intahaba*), but allowed no one to take more than one. Thus the goats were scattered all over the country, and this is said to be the origin of the proverb: "I shall not come to you till the goats of al-Fizr (are collected again into one herd)" (al-Maydānī, *Madjmaᶜ al-amthāl*, ed. ᶜAbd al-Ḥamīd, ²Cairo 1379/1959, ii, 212b = no 3496). The goats are probably imagined to have had the *wasm* or brand-mark of his clan. The underlying idea appears to be that the divisions of this tribe were found scattered over the whole of Eastern Arabia. The tribe of Tamīm [*q.v.*] is early mentioned, and the genealogies in their case are more fictitious than with other tribes; all they can serve is to show which of the clans shortly before and after the introduction of Islam felt itself as possessing a certain relationship. The poet al-Aḍbaṭ b. Ḳurayᶜ says: "In every wādī are Saᶜd" (Ibn Ḳutayba, *Shiᶜr*, ed. Shākir, Cairo 1966, 382), possibly pointing to their wide distribution. Of the many subdivisions mentioned by geneaologists, only those derived through his sons Kaᶜb and al-Ḥārith appear to have had a claim to pure descent, while the descendants of the other sons, ᶜAbd Shams, Djusham, ᶜAwf, ᶜUwāfa and Mālik, were called the *Abnāʾ*. There were doubts as to the purity of their descent; they were settled in Baḥrayn and had largely intermixed with the Persian settlers when this province was under Persian rule. They were, as regards numbers, perhaps the largest Arab tribe, and for this reason played an important part in the wars shortly before Islam and during the conquests, and many persons mentioned in the early times of Islam were members of the various clans of Saᶜd al-Fizr. They sided with ᶜAlī during the struggle for the caliphate and were most prominent during the unruly times in Khurāsān under the later Umayyads and appear to have settled in Persia in large numbers. Others emigrated to North Africa, and the Aghlabī rulers of Ifrīḳiya [see AGHLABIDS] claimed descent from them. The many subdivisions cannot be enumerated here, but it must be stated that the genealogists are far from unanimous in the affiliation of the various sections, and their names disappear early from history under the general name of Tamīm.

Importance may be attached to the tribe of Saᶜd al-Fizr and their nearest kindred clans for having spoken that Arabic which forms the basis of the classic Arabic of literature, as the earliest philologists seem to have framed the rules of Arabic grammar upon the dialect of Tamīm. This was no doubt on account of their widespread diffusion through which their dialect was understood in most parts of Arabia.

Bibliography: The Arabic lexica s.v. *Fizr*; Ibn Durayd, *Kitāb al-Ishtiḳāḳ*, ed. Wüstenfeld, 150 ff.; A.A. Bevan, *The Naḳāʾiḍ of Jarīr and al-Farazdaḳ*, Leiden 1905-12, passim; Ḳalḳashandī, *Nihāyat al-arab*, Baghdād, 236; Nuwayrī, *Nihāyat al-arab*, Cairo 1342, ii, 344-5; Ibn ᶜAbd Rabbihi, *al-ᶜIḳd al-farīd*, Cairo 1316, ii, 42; *Kitāb al-Aghānī*, passim; Ibn Ḥazm, *Djamharat ansāb al-ᶜArab*, ed. E. Lévi-Provençal, Cairo 1948, 204-11; Wüstenfeld, *Genealogische Tabellen*, L, and *Register*, 396; Ibn al-Kalbī-Caskel, i, Tafeln, no. 75, ii, Register, 497; S. Kazzarah, *Die Dichtung der Tamim in vorislamischer Zeit*, diss. Erlangen 1982, 145-6 (incs. those fragments of poetry attributed to Saᶜd al-Fizr).

(F. Krenkow*)

SAᶜD al-DAWLA b. al-Ṣafī b. Hibat Allāh b. Muhadhdhib al-Dawla al-Abharī, Jewish physician and *wazīr* of the Īlkhān Arghūn [see ĪLKHĀNS].

His tenure of office lasted from Djumādā II 688/June 1289 until his murder in Rabīᶜ I 690/March 1291. His *ism* and date of birth are unknown. His rise to power must be seen against the background of a radical change of the Mongol political élite in domestic and foreign policies; i.e. from the pro-Islamic policy of the Īlkhān Aḥmad (680-3/1282-4) back to the anti-Islamic policy of the Īlkhāns after the defeat at ᶜAyn Djālūt [*q.v.*] on 25 Ramaḍān 658/ 3 September 1260. This policy was aimed at a Mongol-Christian/European alliance against the Mamlūks [*q.v.*] of Egypt and Syria. Under Aḥmad, a convert to Islam, who strove for a peaceful agreement with the Mamlūks (al-Maḳrīzī, *Sulūk*, i/3, 707-8, 717, 722-3), the pro-Islamic Mongol élite, together with the *amīr* Buḳa, worked with the *wazīr* Shams al-Dīn al-Djuwaynī [*q.v.*]. After the murder of the Īlkhān Aḥmad and the enthronement of Arghūn, the *amīr* Buḳa, who had changed loyalties shortly before the coup d'état, became the most powerful *amīr* in the realm. He tried to preserve the status quo between Mongols and Muslims, even though he could not prevent the fall and murder of the *wazīr* Shams al-Dīn al-Djuwaynī. This situation changed abruptly when Buḳa fell from power and was murdered, and Saᶜd al-Dawla immediately after rose to power in Djumādā II 688/June 1289 (Rashīd al-Dīn, iii, 208-16, 217). One month later, on 3 Radjab 688/23 July 1289 the whole Djuwaynī family was liquidated (*ibid.*, 218-19). Arghūn issued an edict prohibiting the employment of Muslim secretaries (Bar Hebraeus, ed. Budge, i, 484-5). This edict was countered by the Mamlūks with an edict in Shaᶜbān 689/August 1290 prohibiting the employment of Jewish and Christian secretaries (al-Maḳrīzī, *Sulūk*, i/3, 753). Saᶜd al-Dawla gave all the key positions in the administration to his family, relatives and co-believers. His internal policy aimed at an increase in taxes and a redistribution of funds to fill the treasury. In foreign policy he, together with the Īlkhān, aimed at an alliance with Pope Nicolas IV and the Christian powers of Europe in order to oust the Mamlūks from Syria. A Crusade was planned and eventual possession of Jerusalem by the Pope was envisaged; but nothing came of these plans. Meanwhile, the Mamlūk sultan Ḳalāwūn [*q.v.*] and his son and successor al-Ashraf Khalīl had expelled the Crusaders from the Syrian coast. Their last stronghold, ᶜAkkā [*q.v.*], fell in Rabīᶜ II 690/March 1291. Shortly before this, on 7 Rabīᶜ II 690/10 March 1291, Arghūn died, and five days before his death Saᶜd al-Dawla was murdered by his Mongol enemies. A persecution of the Jews began that could only be forcibly suppressed by the government.

Regarding Saᶜd al-Dawla's earlier career, he appears for the first time in 682/1283, when Sharaf al-Dīn Hārūn, from the Djuwaynī family, became governor of Baghdād and Saᶜd al-Dawla was dismissed from the supervision of the endowments of the Māristān al-ᶜAḍudī [see BĪMĀRISTĀN] there. In 683/1284 he became deputy (*nāʾib*) of the *shiḥna* in Baghdād and in 686/1287 the financial administrator (*malik*) of Baghdād. Nāṣir al-Dīn Ḳutlugh Shāh, a *mamlūk* of the Djuwaynī family, complained about him to the Īlkhān. Saᶜd al-Dawla was sent to the camp of the Īlkhān in his capacity as a physician, and became the private one of Arghūn (Ibn al-Fuwaṭī, 428, 433, 450). He won the ruler's confidence and was twice sent to Baghdād to check the finances, being in Djumādā I 687/June 1288 made supervisor of finances (*mushrif*) there, and in the same year a group of Jews from Tiflis came to Baghdād to oversee the

charitable endowments of the Muslims. This brought about a revolt there, and the group had to resign (Ibn al-Fuwaṭī, 454-5). Then in Djumādā II 688/June 1289 he was made *ṣāḥib dīwān al-mamālik*, i.e. *wazīr*, by Arghūn; numerous sources confirm his administrative skill and abilities in general.

Bibliography: Rashīd al-Dīn, iii, ed. A.A. Alizade, Baku 1957, 208-10, 217-27; Ibn al-Fuwaṭī, *al-Ḥawādith al-djāmiᶜa fi 'l-miʾa al-sābiᶜa*, ed. Muṣṭafā Djawād, Baghdād 1351/1922, 457-64; Waṣṣāf, *Taʾrīkh*, Bombay 1269/1852-3, ii, 235-45; ᶜAbd al-Muḥammad Āyatī, *Taḥrīr-i taʾrīkh-i Waṣṣāf*, Tehran 1346/1967, 141-8; Bar Hebraeus, *Chronography*, ed. and tr. E.A. Wallis Budge, Oxford 1932, i, 484-91; Maḳrīzī, *Sulūk*, ed. M.M. Ziada, Cairo 1936-9; W.J. Fischel, *Jews in the economic and political life of mediaeval Islam*, New York 1969, 90-117; idem, *Azarbaijan in Jewish history*, in *Procs. of the American Academy for Jewish Research*, xxii (1953), 6-11; J. von Hammer-Purgstall, *Geschichte der Ilchane in Persien 1220-1350*, repr. Amsterdam 1974, i, 382-8, 392-3, 395-6; Spuler, *Mongolen*², 84-5, 246-7, 286, 349; J. Richard, *La papauté et les missions d'Orient au moyen age XIIIᵉ-XVᵉ siècles*, Rome 1977, 102-4.

(DOROTHEA KRAWULSKY)

SAᶜD AL-DAWLA [see ḤAMDĀNIDS].

SAᶜD AL-DĪN [see SAᶜDIYYA].

SAᶜD AL-DĪN AL-ḤAMMŪʾĪ (or al-Ḥamūʾī or al-Ḥamawī), MUḤAMMAD B. AL-MUʾAYYAD ... b. Ḥam(m)ūy(a) (or Ḥamawayh or Ḥamawiyya) AL-DJUWAYNĪ, famous Ṣūfī *shaykh* of the first half of the 7th/13th century; second cousin of the influential *Awlād al-Shaykh* [*q.v.*] and of another Saᶜd al-Dīn (b. Tādj al-Dīn, d. 674/1276); father of Ṣadr al-Dīn Ibrāhīm (644-722/1247-1322). Saᶜd al-Dīn b. al-Muʾayyad's contemporary Sibṭ Ibn al-Djawzī mentions (*Mirʾāt al-zamān*, Chicago 1907, 525) that news of the Shaykh's death in Khurāsān had reached him during the year 651, and that he is said to have died in 650 A.H. The latter year is accepted by many authorities, including Djāmī, who specifies that the Shaykh died on 10 Dhu 'l-Ḥidjdja 650/11 February 1253 aged 63 (*Nafaḥāt al-uns*, Tehran 1370 A.H.S., 431 ff.). However, according to the biography written around 750 A.H. by his great-grandson Ghiyāth al-Dīn (summarised by M.T. Dānishpazhūh in *Farhang-i Īrānzamīn*, xiii [1344 A.H.S.], 298-310), as well as Khʷāfī's *Mudjmal-i Faṣīḥī* (Mashhad 1340 A.H.S., 268-9, 319), the precise dates for the Shaykh's birth and death are 23 Dhu 'l-Ḥidjdja 586/12 January 1191 and 18 Dhu 'l-Ḥidjdja 649/3 March 1252, respectively. On the other hand, equally precise but different dates (15 Djumādā I 588 to 12 Dhu 'l-Ḥidjdja 649) are found in marginal notes of a manuscript dated 728 A.H. (Princeton, Garrett Collection, Mach no. 3753). Still other dates on record are mentioned by Köprülü-zāde Fuʾād, art. *Saᶜd al-Dīn al-Ḥamawī* in *IA*.

Saᶜd al-Dīn is primarily known in Ṣūfī history as a disciple of Nadjm al-Dīn al-Kubrā (d. 618/1221 in Khʷārazm). Kubrā wrote an *idjāza* for him, and is said to have "brothered" him with Sayf al-Dīn al-Bākharzī (d. 659/1261 or earlier in Bukhārā). A letter written to him by the latter may indeed indicate such ties with the then nascent Kubrawiyya; but hagiographic reports (such as *Manāḳib-i Awḥad al-Dīn-i Kirmānī*, Tehran 1347/1969, 96-105) suggesting similar ties to Kubrā's major disciple, Madjd al-Dīn al-Baghdādī (d. 3 Djumādā II 606/3 December 1209, for which date, see W. Shpall in *Folia Orientalia*, xxii [1981-4], 72), should be treated with caution. According to Ghiyāth al-Dīn's biography, Saᶜd al-Dīn had pursued theological studies in Khurāsān and, between 605 and 609 A.H., in Khʷārazm; but he joined Kubrā only in 616 or 617 A.H., having in the meantime (A.H. 616 according to the *Mudjmal-i Faṣīḥī*) travelled to Damascus, where he received his formal initiation into Ṣūfism from his father's cousin, the Shaykh al-Shuyūkh Ṣadr al-Dīn Abu 'l-Ḥasan Muḥammad (d. 617/1220), and to Mecca, where he met Abū Ḥafṣ ᶜUmar al-Suhrawardī (d. 632/1234). Saᶜd al-Dīn himself, as quoted by Ḥaydar al-Āmulī (*Kitāb Naṣṣ al-nuṣūṣ*, Tehran-Paris 1975, 220-1), traced his Ṣūfī affiliation in two ways to Muḥammad b. Ḥamūya (d. 530/1135-6): (a) through direct spiritual association (in the way Muḥammad b. Ḥamūya himself was a "disciple of al-Khiḍr"); (b) through transmission of the *khirḳa* along the line of descent of the Syrian branch of his family (i.e. through Ṣadr al-Dīn Muḥammad).

In any case, some time after the Mongol sack of Khʷārazm, Saᶜd al-Dīn turned, again, to the Middle East, staying now for longer periods in Mecca and Damascus, and travelling widely until 640. During one of his stays in Damascus, he was undoubtedly in touch with Ibn ᶜArabī (d. 638/1240) and his circle, although it would appear that his real contact was the disciple Ṣadr al-Dīn al-Ḳūnawī (d. 673/1274) rather than the master himself (cf. Saᶜīd al-Dīn-i Farghānī, *Mashāriḳ al-darārī*, Mashhad 1357/1398, 128). Unlike Ibn ᶜArabī, Saᶜd al-Dīn evidently favoured the Ṣūfī practice of "listening to music" (*samāᶜ*; cf. Muʾayyid al-Dīn al-Djandī, *Sharḥ Fuṣūṣ al-ḥikam*, Mashhad 1361/1982, 107). Sibṭ Ibn al-Djawzī (*loc. cit.*) mentions that he lived with his followers on Mount Ḳāsiyūn and describes him as a holy man who shunned the rich, even his own cousins, despite great poverty, but says also that he enjoyed later in Khurāsān the favours of the "kings of the Tatars". The same source also points out that he spent the last week of his life by the tomb of Muḥammad b. Ḥamūya in Baḥrābād (near Djuwayn), and that he was buried there. According to Ghiyāth al-Dīn, he spent the last eight years of his life mainly in Āmul and various places in Khurāsān, including Baḥrābād, where he died during one of his visits.

It must have been during this last period in Khurāsān that ᶜAzīz-i Nasafī (d. *ca.* 700/1300) became his disciple. The latter, a prolific Persian author, popularised some of his master's esoteric ideas, particularly those concerning the unity of Being (*waḥdat al-wudjūd*) and the special status of the "saint" (*walī*). "Monistic" trends in Saᶜd al-Dīn's thought were also noted by Dhahabī (*Al-ᶜIbar*, Kuwayt 1960, v, 206). His peculiar ideas about *walāya* bear a certain affinity to gnostic Shīᶜism, although he belonged, like the rest of his family, to the Shāfiᶜī *madhhab*.

Unlike Nasafī's, Saᶜd al-Dīn's works were reputedly "difficult" due to his penchant for "*ḥurūfī*" speculations. Nasafī, *Kashf al-ḥaḳāʾiḳ*, Tehran 1344 *Sh.*/1965, 4, credits him with a total of 400 books, whereas Ghiyāth al-Dīn lists the titles of 32 otherwise unrecorded writings but mentions none of the works generally attributed to him (see e.g. Brockelmann, S II, 803). Among the latter, the Persian *Risālat al-Miṣbāḥ* has been published in 1983 with a useful introduction by N.M. Hirawī as *al-Miṣbāḥ fi 'l-taṣawwuf* (Tehran 1362/1403).

Bibliography (in addition to references in the article): Saᶜīd-i Nafīsī, *Khānadān-i Saᶜd al-Dīn-i Ḥamūy. Kundjkāwīhā-yi ᶜilmī wa adabī*, Tehran 1329 A.H.S., 6-39; F. Meier, *Die Schriften des ᶜAzīz-i Nasafī*, in *WZKM*, lii (1953), 125-82; idem, *Die Fawāʾiḥ al-ǧamāl wa-fawātiḥ al-ǧalāl des Naǧm ad-dīn al-Kubrā*, Wiesbaden 1957, *Einleitung*; M. Molé, *Les Kubrawîya entre sunnisme et shiisme aux huitième et neuvième siècles de l'hégire*, in *REI* (1961) 61-142; idem, *ᶜAzizoddin Nasafi: le Livre de l'Homme Parfait*, Tehran-Paris 1962, Introd.; H. Landolt, *Nûruddîn-i Isfarâyinî: le Révélateur des Mystères*, Lagrasse 1986, *Etude préliminaire*; C. Addas, *Ibn ᶜArabī ou la quête du Soufre Rouge*, Paris 1989. (H. LANDOLT)

SAᶜD AL-DĪN KĀSHGHARĪ (d. 860/1456), *shaykh* of the Nakshbandī Ṣūfī order in Harāt, best known as the preceptor of the poet and mystic ᶜAbd al-Raḥmān Djāmī (d. 898/1492 [*q.v.*]).

Kāshgharī's piety first showed itself, it is said, during the journeys on which as a child he used to accompany his father, a merchant of Kāshghar with *sayyid* ancestry. Thus when he was twelve years of age, he wept uncontrollably after listening to his father and his associates passionately haggling over the price of some goods for a whole morning. After completing the *madrasa* curriculum (the sources do not tell us where), Kāshgharī conceived an inclination to the Ṣūfī path, and travelling to Bukhārā he joined the circle of Niẓām al-Dīn Khāmūsh, initiatic heir to Bahāʾ al-Dīn Nakshband (d. 791/1391) by one intermediary, ᶜAlāʾ al-Dīn ᶜAṭṭār (d. 802/1400). Several years later, Kāshgharī set out from Bukhārā on the *ḥadjdj*, but as his master had predicted he was unable to proceed beyond Khurāsān. In Harāt, he made the acquaintance of Shaykh Zayn al-Dīn Khʷāfī (d. 838/1435) who appears to have attempted to recruit him into his own following, as well as Sayyid Ḳāsim-i Tabrīzī; Shaykh Bahāʾ al-Dīn ᶜUmar; and Mawlānā Abū Yazīd Pūrānī. It may have been on this journey that Kāshgharī decided to settle in Harāt; the episodic and staccato nature of the sources leave the matter unclear. It was, in any event, in Harāt that Kāshgharī spent the most influential years of his life, making the city the third chief centre of the Nakshbandiyya after Bukhārā and Samarḳand.

Despite possessing considerable wealth (inherited, perhaps, from his merchant father), Kāshgharī took up residence in the Madrasa-yi Ghiyāthiyya in Harāt, near the Masdjid-i Djāmiᶜ, and it was in that mosque, which he compared in its sanctity to the Masdjid al-Ḥarām in Mecca, that he met and discoursed with his devotees. These came to include many members of the cultural and literary élite of Herat, above all Djāmī, who was moved to become Kāshgharī's disciple by a dream in which the *shaykh* liberated him from the pangs of a profane love. Djāmī expressed his devotion to Kāshgharī not only in the pages he allotted him in *Nafaḥāt al-uns* (ed. Maḥmūd ᶜAbidī, Tehran 1370 *sh*./1991, 408-10) but also through a number of references to him in his *mathnawīs* (see e.g. *Silsilat al-dhahab*, in *Haft Awrang*, ed. Murtaḍā Mudarris Gīlānī, 3rd ed., Tehran 1361 *sh*./1982, 164-6) and, most strikingly, the moving *tarkīb-band* in which he eulogised him (*Kullīyyāt*, ed. Shams Brelwī, repr. Tehran 1362 *sh*./1983, 526-9). Kāshgharī's circle was, however, by no means exclusively aristocratic in its composition; it also included artisans such as Mīr Rangraz "the dyer".

Like his master Khāmūsh, Kāshgharī is said to have been in a near-constant state of ecstatic rapture (*ghalaba*); this would frequently overtake him while he was discoursing and cause him to bow his head and fall silent, creating in the uninitiated the impression that he had fallen asleep. He is also reported—again like his master—to have had the ability to manifest the divine attribute of wrath (*ḳahr*); however, he succeeded in containing this dangerous power. He does not appear to have left any writings, but sixteen of his sayings and discourses are recorded in Fakhr al-Dī[n] Wāᶜiẓ Kāshifī's *Rashaḥāt ᶜayn al-ḥayāt* (ed. Muᶜīniyān i, 210-18). Some of these, aphoristic in nature, ar[e] reminiscent of utterances by Khʷādja ᶜAbd Allāh An[ṣ]ārī (d. 481/1089 [*q.v.*]), which may not be fortuitous given Kāshgharī's acknowledgement of Anṣārī as th[e] pre-eminent saint of Harāt. From other pro[]nouncements of Kāshgharī may be deduced [a] familiarity with the concepts and terminology of Ib[n] ᶜArabī, whom Kāshgharī greatly admired, like othe[r] early Nakshbandīs (Hamid Algar, *Reflections of Ib[n] ᶜArabî in early Naqshbandî tradition*, in *Journal of th[e] Muhyiddin Ibn ᶜArabi Society*, x [1991], 54-5).

Kāshgharī died while performing the midda[y] prayer on 7 Djumādā I 860/12 May 1456, and wa[s] buried in the Khiyābān suburb of Harāt. The sit[e] soon acquired great sanctity, and several of hi[s] disciples, including Djāmī, were buried nearby. Hi[s] tomb was nonetheless neglected during the disorder that came to mark the history of Harāt, and ultimatel[y] the headstone itself disappeared. The tomb wa[s] restored, and the headstone replaced, by Aḥmad Sha[h] Durrānī [*q.v.*], who also constructed an *īwān* nearby This *īwān* was rebuilt and provided with two minaret in the late 1950s by Muḥammad Ẓāhir Shāh, the las[t] king of Afghānistān.

One of the devotees of Kāshgharī is said to hav[e] been told by the Prophet in a dream that Kāshghar[ī] had advanced no fewer than thirty-two people to th[e] rank of saintship (*wilāyat*), but none of these appear to have been clearly nominated as his successor Djāmī was manifestly the most prominent o[f] Kāshgharī's disciples, but being temperamentall[y] averse to assuming the burdens of preceptorship, h[e] encouraged the followers of Kāshgharī to gather, afte[r] his death, around Mawlānā Shams al-Dīn Muḥam[]mad Rūdjī (d. 904-1499). Important, too, among th[e] disciples of Kāshgharī was Mawlānā ᶜAlāʾ al-Dī[n] Maktabdār (d. 892/1487), several of whose devotee[s] carried the Nakshbandiyya to places such as Ḳazwī[n] and Tabrīz in western Persia. In general, however the initiatic lines descending from Kāshgharī fade[d] out after two or three generations; it was his great con[]temporary, ᶜUbayd Allāh Aḥrār [*q.v.* in Suppl.] o[f] Samarḳand, who proved more significant for the long term transmission of the Nakshbandī order.

Bibliography: Aṣīl al-Dīn Harawī, *Mazārāt-Harāt*, ed. Fikrī Saldjūḳī, Kābul 1967, i, 98-9, ii 52-3; Djāmī, *Nafaḥāt al-uns*, ed. Mahmūd ᶜĀbidī Tehran 1370 *sh*./1971, 408-10; Fakhr al-Dīn ᶜAlī b Ḥusayn Wāᶜiẓ Kāshifī, *Rashaḥāt ᶜayn al-ḥayāt*, ed ᶜAlī Aṣghar Muᶜīniyān, Tehran 2536 Im[]perial/1977, i, 205-32; idem (Fakhr al-Dīn ᶜAl[ī] Ṣafī), *Laṭāʾif al-ṭawāʾif*, ed. Aḥmad Gulčīn-Maᶜānī, Tehran 1336 *sh*./1957, 231, 235; Muᶜīn al Dīn Isfizārī, *Rawḍāt al-djannāt fī awṣāf madīnat Harāt* ed. Mohammad Ishaque, Aligarh 1961, 26 Muḥammad b. Ḥusayn Ḳazwīnī, *Silsila-nāma-y khʷādjagān-i Nakshband*, ms. B.N., suppl. persa[n] 1418, fols. 14b-18a; Ghulām Sarwar Lāhūrī *Khazīnat al-aṣfiyāʾ*, Bombay 1290/1873, i, 573-6 ᶜAbd al-Ghafūr Lārī, *Takmila-yi Nafaḥāt al-uns*, ed Bashīr Harawī, Kābul 1343 *sh*./1964, 13-14; J Paul, *Die politische und soziale Bedeutung der Naqšban[]diyya in Mittelasien im 15. Jahrhundert* (Studien zu[r] Sprache, Geschichte und Kultur des islamischer Orients, N.S. XIII), Berlin and New York 1991 24, 47, 58, 87; ᶜAbd al-Wāsiᶜ Bākharzī, *Maḳāmāt-Djāmī*, ed. Nadjīb Māyil Harawī, Tehran 137[1] *Sh*./1992, 81, 87, 104, 110, 132, 194, 232. (HAMID ALGAR)

SAᶜD AL-DĪN KÖPEK b. Muḥammad, an im[-]

ortant court official of two Saldjūḳ sultans of Rūm, Kayḳubād I and Kaykhusraw II. Köpek's place nd date of birth are unknown. He is first mentioned s a *tardjumān* (Ibn Bībī, 146). Late in Kayḳubād's eign, Köpek had risen to become *amīr-i shikār* (master f the hunt) and *miᶜmār* (minister of works), entrusted vith overseeing the construction of Kayḳubād's new alace at Ḳubādābād [*q.v.*] (*ibid.*, 147). Köpek himself rected in 633/1235 a large caravanserai, known as he Zazadin or Sadeddin Han, between Konya and Aksaray. Two extant inscriptions on its portals record he name *Köpek (k.w.b.k.) b. Muḥammad.*

After Kayḳubād's death in 634/1237, Köpek wield-d considerable influence over his successor, Kaykhusraw II. Murders, aimed at consolidating Kaykhusraw's position, then followed. Köpek sud-lenly seized a Khwārazmian *amīr*, Kīrkhān, who died n prison (Bar Hebraeus, 403; Ibn Bībī, 201). Köpek hen organised the murders of Kaykhusraw's two alf-brothers and their mother (Ibn Bībī, 204). In 635/1238 Kaykhusraw sent Köpek to occupy Sumaysāṭ on his behalf. Returning home, Köpek illed off the last of the "old guard" state officials, Kaymarī and Kāmyār, who, like him, had served Kayḳubād (Ibn Bībī, 208). In 637/1240, Kaykhusraw liminated Köpek, because he was a dangerous rival, vho had "destroyed the pillars of the state, one by ne" (*ibid.*). According to Ibn Bībī, who remains the rincipal, and often the sole source, for these events, he malevolent Köpek remained true to form, even in leath: one of the spectators, assembled to gloat over Köpek's dismembered body, suspended in a cage rom a gallows, was killed by the cage falling on him *ibid.*, 209).

The blame for the murders in Kaykhusraw's reign ould, of course, be apportioned differently. After all, bn Bībī, the court chronicler of the Rūm Saldjūḳs, is een to exonerate Kaykhusraw from responsibility for ll the deaths, save Köpek's.

Bibliography: 1. Primary sources. Bar Hebraeus, *The chronography*, tr. E.A.W. Budge, London 1932, i, 402-3; Ibn Bībī, *Die Seltschukengeschichte des Ibn Bibi*, tr. H.W. Duda, Copenhagen 1959, 146-7, 187, 199-207.

2. Secondary Sources. C. Cahen, *Pre-Ottoman Turkey*, London 1968, 133-4, 222, 225; Köprülü Zāde Fuʾād, *EI*[1] art. SAᶜD AL-DĪN KÖPEK; K. Erdmann, *Das anatolische Karavansaray des 13. Jahrhunderts*, Berlin 1961, Pt. 1, 102-7; V. Gordlevski, *Gosudarstvo seldzhukidov malo i azii*, Moscow 1941, 54-5, 74-6, 78, 87-9, 97, 119, 138; J.M. Rogers, *Patronage in Seljuk Anatolia*, diss. Oxford 1972, unpubl., 311, 335, 338, 352, 372.

(CAROLE HILLENBRAND)

SAᶜD AL-DĪN TAFTĀZĀNĪ [see AL-TAFTĀZĀNĪ].

SAᶜD WA-NAḤS (A.), literally, "the fortunate nd the unfortunate".

These concepts are based on the influence exerted y the planets and the signs of the Zodiac on earthly vents. The astrologers describe the stars as being ither *saᶜd* or *naḥs*. Thus Jupiter, Venus and the Moon re said to be *saᶜd*, Saturn is *naḥs* and the Sun and Mercury are at times called one or the other. But this an vary as a function of their positions in the ecliptic nd of their conjunctions (cf. Abū Maslama Muḥammad al-Madjrīṭī, *Ghāyat al-ḥakīm*, ed. H. Ritter, Leipig 1933, 198 ff. = M. Plessner, *Picatrix*, London 962, 209 ff.; *L'agriculture nabatéenne*, i, Damascus 993, 10-12 et *passim*).

Starting out from these basic indications, the strologers [see MUNADJDJIM] divided their art into two ranches: natural astrology, consisting in the observation of the fortunate or unfortunate influence of the stars on the natural elements, whence arises meteorological divination [see ANWĀʾ and MALĀḤIM]; and judicial or apotelesmatic divination, consisting in the observation of the influence of the stars on human destiny, whence arise genethlialogy (*mawālīd*) or the art of drawing omens from the position of the stars at a person's birth [see NUDJŪM, AḤKĀM AL-, 1.] and hemerology and menology [see IKHTIYĀRĀT], which consist in establishing the calendar of what is fortunate and what is unfortunate [see NUDJŪM, AḤKĀM AL-, 2.].

One should note that the name *saᶜd*, followed by a noun, is given to some stars and constellations (cf. P. Kunitzsch, *Über eine anwāʾ-Tradition mit bisher unbekannten Sternnamen*, in *Beiträge zur Lexicographie des Klassischen Arabisch, Nr. 4*, in *Abh. der Bayerischen Akad. der Wiss.*, phil.-hist. Kl. (Munich 1983), Heft 5, 57; see this same author's arts. MANĀZIL and NUDJŪM]. This designation does not seem to have borne any divinatory significance.

Bibliography: Given in the article. On Saᶜd, the idol of the Banū Milkān, and Saᶜdān (τύχαι), see T. Fahd, *Le panthéon de l'Arabie Centrale à la veille de l'hégire*, Paris 1968, 147-50. (T. FAHD)

ṢAᶜDA, a town approximately 240 km/150 miles to the north of the chief town of the Yemen, Ṣanᶜāʾ [*q.v.*], situated on the southern edge of the Ṣaᶜda plain, and the administrative capital of the province (*muḥāfaẓa*) of the same name. The town is about 1,800 m/5,904 ft. above sea level and in the 1986 census in the Yemen had a reported population of 24,245 persons. The inhabitants of the province numbered 323,110.

Although al-Hamdānī, 67, informs us that the town was called Djumāᶜ in pre-Islamic times, certain Sabaic inscriptions mention *hgrn ṢᶜDTm*, "the town Ṣaᶜda", together with reference to the predominant tribe of the area, Khawlān [*q.v.*] (Ja 658/11-13, A. Jamme, *Sabaean inscriptions from Maḥram Bilqīs*, Baltimore 1962, 163; Sharaf al-Dīn, 31/14-5; A.G. Lundin, *Sabeyskiy činovnik i diplomat III v.n.e*, in *Palestinskiy Sbornik*, xxv/88 (1974), 97; Ja 2109/7, A.F.L. Beeston, *Corpus des inscriptions et antiquités sud-arabes*, ii/1, Louvain 1986, 49-50). Al-Hamdānī also tells the anecdote of the origin of the name Ṣaᶜda. A weary Ḥidjāzī stopped for the night in the town and lay on his back contemplating the decorated ceiling which pleased him. Twice he exclaimed, "[Someone] has indeed raised it up (*ṣaᶜᶜada-hu, ṣaᶜᶜada-hu*)!" The town's fame for the manufacture of arrowheads is also mentioned by the 4th/10th century Yemeni scholar, who refers specifically to *niṣāl ṣaᶜdiyya/ṣāᶜidiyya*. Iron implements, particularly agricultural, of all kinds seem also to have been made in the town.

The 7th/13th century traveller to the Arabian Peninsula from the east, Ibn al-Mudjāwir [*q.v.*], reports in his *Taʾrīkh al-Mustabṣir*, ed. O. Löfgren, Leiden 1951-4, 202-6, that the route north to Ṣaᶜda from Ṣanᶜāʾ, originally an important trade and later pilgrim route, was 20 parasangs (on p. 232, the return journey is 19). The town was built in the pre-Islamic era by Shem, the son of Noah, he adds. The old town, however, did not survive and in the time of al-Hādī ilā 'l-Ḥaḳḳ, the first Zaydī imām (d. 298/911) a wealthy merchant who would take no expenses built a mosque, perhaps the mosque bearing al-Hādī's name still found in Ṣaᶜda to this day. A whole new town followed with markets, residences etc. Ibn al-Mudjāwir then goes on to describe the wall (*darb*), towers (*burūdj*) and gates, and the 11th/16th century Istanbul ms. contains a plan of the town which is reproduced in

Löfgren's edition, at p. 205. There were four towers: Darb al-ᶜAtīḳ (E), Darb al-Ḳāḍī (N), Darb al-Ghuzz (?) (W), built in the time of the Ayyūbid Ṭughtakīn b. Ayyūb (d. 571/1175) and Darb al-Ḳāḍī Ibn Zaydān (S). The gates were Bāb ᶜAlī b. Ḳāsim, Bāb Darb al-Ghuzz (?), Bāb Darb al-Ḳāḍī Ibn Zaydān, Bāb Ḥūth, presumably also a southern gate leading to the town of Ḥūth between Ṣaᶜda and Ṣanᶜāʾ, and Bāb Darb al-Imām. The latter tower was built, according to Ibn al-Mudjāwir, by the Zaydī imām al-Manṣūr bi'llāh ᶜAbd Allāh b. Ḥamza (d. 613/1216). The town flourished, watered by rivers and springs, thus producing wheat and barley and abundant trees. Ibn al-Mudjāwir's final comment concerns the clothing of the local inhabitants; it is made of silk and cotton, he says, since the area is so hot.

The geographer Yāḳūt (d. 627/1229) refers (ed. Beirut, iii, 406) to Ṣaᶜda as a province (*mikhlāf* [*q.v.*]), 60 parasangs from Ṣanᶜāʾ. He continues that the town is a commercial centre, fertile, and in particular a centre of tanning, the latter facilitated by the abundance of acacia (*ḳaraẓ, Acacia Ehrenbergiana* Hayne) in the area, a plant used in the tanning process.

The town appears to have had very little significance in Islamic times prior to the arrival there in 284/897 of Yaḥyā b. al-Ḥusayn, the future first Zaydī imām al-Hādī ilā 'l-Ḥaḳḳ. However, isolated references are found in the chronicles prior to that date, e.g. the first mention of the town in Yaḥyā b. al-Ḥusayn's Zaydī chronicle, *Ghāyat al-amānī fī akhbār al-ḳuṭr al-Yamānī*, ed. Saᶜīd ᶜAbd al-Fattāḥ ᶜĀshūr, Cairo 1968, 125, is under the year 130/748. It seems that the Ziyādids (203-*ca.* 409/818-*ca.* 1018), the Yuᶜfirids (232-387/847-997) and the Ṣulayḥids (439-532/1047-1138) were all involved in the area, though never for lengthy periods. After 284/897, however, the town assumes major historical importance as the spiritual, and very frequently the political, capital of the Zaydī imāmate in the Yemen. It remains the spiritual capital to this day. When al-Hādī died in 298/910, he was buried in the mosque in Ṣaᶜda which bore his name, as were two of his sons after him, al-Murtaḍā Muḥammad (d. 310/922) and al-Nāṣir Aḥmad (d. 324/935). The tomb and the mosque became particularly sacred among the Zaydīs.

Nowadays, one can still see the mud wall going back to the days of the Imām al-Mutawakkil Yaḥyā Sharaf al-Dīn (912-65/1506-57) and the five gates: Bāb al-Yaman (S), Bāb Nadjrān (N), Bāb al-Manṣūra, Bāb Djuᶜrān and Bāb al-Salām. Caravanserais (sing. *samsara*), baths and irrigation works abound, and on a large tell in the town the citadel, called al-Ḳashla, is situated, built at the beginning of the second Ottoman occupation of the Yemen in the time of the Imām al-Manṣūr in the mid-13th/19th century. The major tribe in the area is Khawlān b. ᶜAmr b. al-Ḥāf b. Ḳuḍāᶜa and the province is divided into five sub-districts (sing. *nāḥiya*): Ṣuḥār, Djumāᶜa, Khawlān, Rāziḥ (all of Khawlān b. ᶜAmr) and Hamdān.

From the year 294/906 Ṣaᶜda became the most important Zaydī mint-town in the Yemen.

Bibliography: ᶜAlī b. Muḥammad al-ᶜAbbāsī al-ᶜAlawī, *Sīrat al-Hādī ilā 'l-Ḥaḳḳ Yaḥyā b. al-Ḥusayn*, ed. Suhayl Zakkār, Damascus 1972, *passim*; C. van Arendonk, *Les débuts de l'Imamat Zaïdite au Yémen*, tr. J. Ryckmans, Leiden 1960, *passim* (an excellent gloss of the *Sīra*); H.C. Kay, *Yaman: its early mediaeval history*, London 1892, esp. 5, 172, 251; ᶜAbd al-Wāsiᶜ b. Yaḥyā al-Wāsiᶜī, *Taʾrīkh al-Yaman*, Cairo 1346, *passim*; Muḥammad b. Aḥmad al-Ḥadjarī, *Madjmūᶜ buldān al-Yaman wa-ḳabāʾili-hā*, Ṣanᶜāʾ 1984, ii, 467-80; Ibrāhīm Aḥmad al-Maḳḥafī, *Muᶜdjam al-buldān wa 'l-ḳabāʾil al-Yamaniyya*, Ṣanᶜāʾ 1988, 381; W. Daum (ed.), *Yemen: 3000 years of art and civilisation in Arabia Felix*, Innsbruck and Frankfurt/Main n.d. [*ca.* 1988], 129-40, 263 (photograph of the Mosque of al-Hādī); Yūsuf Muḥammad ᶜAbd Allāh, in Aḥmad Djābir ᶜAfīf *et alii* (eds.), *al-Mawsūᶜa al-Yamaniyya (The Encyclopedia of Yemen)*, Ṣanᶜāʾ 1992, ii, 570-72; E. von Zambaur, *Die Münzprägung des Islams*, Wiesbaden 1968, 166; Ramzi J. Bikhazi, *Coins of al-Yaman, 132-569 AH*, in *al-Abḥāth*, xxiii (1970), 3-127, esp. 45 ff.

(G.R. Smith)

ṢADĀ (A.), a term with many meanings, including those of thirst, voice, echo, and screech-owl in the sense of *hāma*, which denotes a bird charged with taking shape in the skull of someone who has been murdered, etc. (see the lexica).

It is this latter sense which interests us here. In effect, the pre-Islamic Arabs believed that after death, above all after a violent death, out of the blood of the skull (*hāma*) and parts of the body there arose a bird called *hāma* (or *hām*, the male owl; see Yāḳūt, *Buldān*, iii, 376), which returned to the tomb of the dead man until vengeance was exacted. This idea was not peculiar to the Arabs; according to F. Cumont (*Lux perpetua*, Paris 1949, 293), "the idea was in ancient times widespread amongst all the peoples of the Mediterranean basin that the essence or the essential being which gave life to a man escaped from the corpse in the form of a bird, above all, in the form of a bird of prey" (other refs. in T. Fahd, *Le panthéon de l'Arabie Centrale*, 3 n. 1).

Allusions to this belief are frequent in ancient poetry. One may cite, e.g., Ṭarafa b. al-ᶜAbd, *Muᶜallaḳa*, v. 61; ᶜAbd Allāh b. Zayd al-Thaᶜlabī of Ghaṭafān, in al-Buḥturī, *Ḥamāsa*, iii, 2, no. 93, 585; Abū Duʾād al-Iyādī, in *Aghānī*, xvi, 39; Ḳays b. ᶜAṣim, in Ibn al-Athīr, i, 289-90; and Dhu 'l-Iṣbaᶜ al-ᶜAdwānī, in al-Nuwayrī, *Nihāya*, Cairo 1924, iii, 121. In general, these poets reproach the family of the murdered person for delaying avenging him, thus delaying the appeasing of his soul. Other poets refer to the echo (*ṣadā*) of a barking announcing a fire implying hospitality [see nār], as in the case of Murra b. Maḥkān, cited by al-Tibrīzī, in *Ḥamāsa*, 690; or else the echo indicating the way to someone lost, as in the case of ᶜUtayba b. Buḥayr al-Māzinī and Abū Muḳbil, cited in *ibid.*, 685.

As for the historical and lexicographical sources, they reproduce the same notion set forth above, with slight variants (see esp. al-Shahrastānī, *Milal*, in the margins of Ibn Ḥazm, iii, 221; Masᶜūdī, *Murūdj*, iii, 310-13 = §§ 1191-5; *Aghānī*, xvi, 96; al-Tibrīzī, in *Ḥamāsa*, 454; al-Damīrī, *Ḥayawān*, ii, 440, citing Mālik b. Anas).

The Prophet denied the existence of three things which formed part of the superstitions of the Djāhiliyya, saying, *lā ᶜadwā wa-lā hāma wa-lā ṣafar* "there is no contagion, no death owl and no intestinal worms". People subsequently personified these three things and made them responsible, e.g., for contagion with a camel in contact with another there arises leprosy, or digestive and nervous disorders caused by a tapeworm. It is God, he affirms, who afflicts mankind by means of these ills (see *Concordance*, s.vv. al-Tibrīzī, in *Ḥamāsa*, 454; al-Shahrastānī, *loc. cit.*, al-Masᶜūdī, *loc. cit.*; *LᶜA*, s.vv.; al-Nuwayrī, *Nihāya*, ii, 119).

Bibliography: In addition to references given in the article, see T. Fahd, *Le panthéon de l'Arabie Centrale à la veille de l'hégire*, Paris 1968, 3; idem, *La divination arabe*[2], Paris 1987, 513, s.v. *Hibou*.

(T. Fahd)

ṢADAF (A.) (sing. *ṣadafa*) denotes two classes of molluscs: 1. Mussels (*Lamellibranchiata*); 2. Snails (*Gastropoda*), both including the mother-of-pearl. Pearls [see AL-DURR; LUʾLUʾ], originating from the excrescences in the interior of the pearl mussel (*ṣadaf al-durr, al-ṣadaf al-luʾluʾī*), are of great economic importance. To the edible mussels belong the oysters (*aṣṭūrū* < ὄστρειον) and, as a popular foodstuff, the common mussel, *Mytilus edulis L., Gr.* μύακες, which, from the ancient pharmacology of Dioscurides, came into the Arabic pharmacopoeias as *miyāḳis*. The same applies to the flat mussel, *Tellina planata*, Gr. τελλῖναι, Ar. *dillīnas*. The juice of mussels known as χῆμαι, Ar. *khīmī* (probably *Chana Lazarus* L.) is said to get the digestion going.

Among the snails, the most important are several varieties of the Murex species of the family of the Purpura (*ṣadaf furfūrā* or *ṣadaf al-firfīr*, Gr. πορφύρα). The hypobranchial gland, situated in their mantle cavity, secretes the costly purple dye. Ibn Djuldjul relates that this snail is found in the Algarve [see GHARB AL-ANDALUS] and near Algeciras [see AL-DJAZĪRA AL-KHAḌRĀʾ], and that only the Byzantine Emperor is entitled to wear purple. The horny shells of various water-snails, among which the Gr. ὄνυξ, Ar. *ūniḳs*, are valued because of their aroma; with regard to their claw-shaped feet, they are also called *aẓfār al-ṭīb* "aromatic claws". The interior of the Purpura and of the trumpet-snail (*Tritonium nodiferum* L., Gr. κήρυκες, Ar. *ṣadaf ḳīrūkis*), known as Gr. κιόνια, Ar. *kiyūniyā*, "columella", used to be burned for its etching power. The general term for snail in Arabic is in general *ḥalazūn*; in addition to this, the κοχλίας of Dioscurides was taken over as *kukhliyās* and explained by way of *ḳawḳan*, the usual term in Hispano-Arabic. Referring to the *K. al-Riḥla* of Ibn al-Rūmiyya, Ibn al-Bayṭār, *Djāmiʿ*, iii, 82, mentions a *ṣadaf al-bawāsīr* which, according to its name, was appropriate for the treatment of hemorrhoids; it was indigenous to the Red Sea coast. Ibn Hubal, *Mukhtārāt*, Ḥaydarābād 1396, 166, mentions a Babylonian and a Red Sea snail (*ṣadaf bābilī/ḳulzumī*).

In pharmaco-zoology, all varieties of mussels and snails are grouped together as *Limnaces*. Since Dioscurides, the burnt shells of various land and sea snails, mussels and oysters have been in use. Burned with salt in a pan, the shells proved to be a good dentifrice. With the ashes, ulcers could be cleansed and the healing of fresh wounds be quickened. The meat of the trumpet snail is tasty and digestible. Common mussels, when burned and mixed with honey, soften swollen eye-lids, remove obscuration of the pupils, etc.

Finally, the mother-of-pearl, the innermost layer of the shell of mussels and snails, acquires on the inside, through incident light, the well-known soft, iridescent colour, which has made it suitable and coveted for inlaid work and for making jewellery. The mother-of-pearl is called, *ʿirḳ (ʿurūḳ) al-luʾluʾ* "the veins of the pearl". On this, al-Dimashḳī, *Nukhbat al-dahr*, ed. Mehren 78, 6-8, tr. 90, remarks: "From the layers of the pearl mussel are won plates (*ṣafāʾiḥ*), which are similar to pearls and are called *ʿurūḳ al-luʾluʾ*. Each pearl is said to contain one hundred different layers, veined on two sides, which have stimulated poets, mystics and philosophers to use them as images".

Bibliography: The Greek names, mentioned in the article, are all found in Dioscurides, *De materia medica*, ed. M. Wellmann, Lib. II, chs. 4-9 (pp. 122-5); their Arabic renderings are accordingly found in the translation by Stephanos-Ḥunayn: *La "Materia médica" de Dioscórides*, ii, ed. Dubler and Terés, 1952-7, 128-31, and in Ibn al-Bayṭār, *Djāmiʿ*, iii, 81-2, tr. Leclerc, no. 1393; A. Dietrich, *Dioscurides triumphans*, Göttingen 1988, ii, 198-202; idem, *Die Dioscurides-Erklärung des Ibn al-Bayṭār*, Göttingen 1991, 92-4. For pearls in general, see AL-DURR and LUʾLUʾ. (A. DIETRICH)

AL-**ṢADAFĪ**, ABŪ ʿALĪ ḤUSAYN B. MUḤAMMAD b. Fīrruh (from the Romance word *fiero*, i.e. *al-ḥadīd*) b. Muḥammad b. Ḥayyūn b. Sukkara/Sukkaruh al-Ṣadafī al-Saraḳusṭī, known commonly as Abū ʿAlī al-Ṣadafī or Ibn Sukkara, Muslim Spanish scholar and traditionist.

According to ʿIyāḍ, he was born in Saragossa around the year 454/1062. He studied in that town, among others, with Abu 'l-Walīd al-Bādjī [*q.v.*], in Valencia with al-ʿUdhrī and in Almería with Ibn Saʿdūn al-Ḳarawī and Ibn al-Murābiṭ. He travelled to the East on 1 Muḥarram 481/1088, performing the pilgrimage and searching for knowledge in Mahdiyya, Cairo, Mecca, Baṣra, Anbār, Wāsiṭ, Baghdād (where his stay lasted five years), Damascus (Ibn ʿAsākir mentioned him in his *Taʾrīkh Dimashḳ* because of his visit to the town), Alexandria and Tinnīs. Among his many teachers during his *riḥla*, two were Andalusians, Abū ʿAbd Allāh al-Ḥumaydī and al-Ṭurṭūshī [*q.v.*], as well as Ḥusayn b. ʿAlī al-Ṭabarī, Abū Yaʿlā al-Mālikī, Abu 'l-ʿAbbās al-Djurdjānī, Abu 'l-Faḍl Aḥmad b. al-Ḥasan b. Khayrūn, Abu 'l-Ṭāhir Aḥmad b. ʿAlī b. ʿUbayd Allāh b. Siwār (author of the *Kitāb al-Mustanīr fi 'l-ḳirāʾāt*), al-Mubārak b. ʿAbd al-Djabbār al-Ṣayrafī, Ṭirād b. Muḥammad al-Zaynabī and Aḥmad b. Yaḥyā b. al-Djārūd. With the Shāfiʿī Abū Bakr al-Shāshī he studied his *al-Taʿlīḳa al-kubrā fī masāʾil al-khilāf*. In Cairo, al-Ṣadafī obtained the *idjāza* from Abū Isḥāḳ al-Ḥabbāl, the most reputed traditionist of the time who had been forbidden to teach by the Fāṭimids. In Ṣafar 490/1096, al-Ṣadafī arrived in al-Andalus, settling in Murcia, where he taught in the *djāmiʿ* mosque, attracting students from all over the Peninsula. Although he was considered a competent expert in *ḳirāʾāt*, he excelled especially in the science of *ḥadīth*, not only because of the quality of his knowledge but also because of his "high" *isnāds* (i.e. the fact that his chains of transmission had very few links). His powerful memory apparently allowed him to learn by heart entire compilations of *ḥadīth*, remembering both *matn* and *isnād*. He himself copied some of those compilations, like al-Bukhārī's and Muslim's *Ṣaḥīḥ* which, together with al-Tirmidhī's *Muṣannaf*, constituted the basis of his teachings. It is said that the major part of the copies of al-Bukhārī's work in the Maghrib are either in the *riwāya* of al-Bādjī (from Abū Dharr), or in the *riwāya* of Ibn Sukkara (transmitted by Ibn Saʿāda). Al-Ṣadafī's own production was limited. Apart from a *Fahrasa*, it consists mainly of *ḥadīth* works: *Djuzʾ min ḥadīthihi ʿan shuyūkhihi al-baghdādiyyīn, Musalsalāt, Subāʿiyyāt* (collected by Abu 'l-Rabīʿ b. Sālim). Pons and al-Kattānī credit him with writing a work on the *shuyūkh* of his teacher Ibn al-Djārūd. But al-Ṣadafī was mostly a transmitter, and as such he plays an important role in ʿIyāḍ's *Ghunya* and in Ibn Khayr's *Fahrasa*. Apart from some works in the field of Ḳurʾānic sciences and ascetism, he transmitted mainly *ḥadīth* works by authors like Ibn Khayrūn, Abu 'l-Fawāris Ṭirād, Abū Bakr al-Barḳānī, Abū Nuʿaym, al-Ḥasan b. Sufyān al-Nasawī al-Shaybānī, Ibn Shāhīn, ʿAbd al-Ghanī al-Azdī, Abū ʿUbayd, al-Ḥasan b. ʿArafa, Abu 'l-Ḥusayn Ibn Bashrān, al-Ḥākim, al-Dāraḳuṭnī, al-Khaṭīb al-Baghdādī, Ibn al-Djārūd and Abū Bakr b. al-Anbārī. Many of these transmissions were of works on *ʿilm al-ridjāl* by authors like Ibn ʿAdī,

al-Bukhārī, al-Nasāʾī, al-Kalābādhī, Muslim, Abū Bakr al-Barḳānī and al-Bādjī, as well as *ḥadīth* collections. He is remembered as having recited some verses from Muḥammad b. ʿAlī al-Ṣūrī against those who attacked traditionists and *ʿilm al-ḥadīth*. As a Mālikī, he also transmitted *fiḳh* works of this school and some *fahāris* like those of Ibn Khayrūn, al-Bādjī, Ibn Saʿdūn and Ibn al-Ṭuyūrī. Al-Ṣadafī was one of the central figures of his generation in the transmission of *ʿilm*, as has been shown by Urvoy. Among his Andalusian pupils there were members of the Banū Saʿāda, his relatives by marriage (he was married to a daughter of Abū ʿImrān Mūsā b. Saʿāda) who inherited his books and documents. Al-Ṣadafī gave the *idjāza* to Ibn Bashkuwāl, Ibn ʿAṭiyya and Abu 'l-Ṭāhir al-Silafī. Another pupil of his was Ḳāḍī ʿIyāḍ [*q.v.*], who studied with him in Ceuta and who wrote al-Ṣadafī's *Mashyakha*. Another *Muʿdjam shuyūkh al-Ṣadafī* was written by Ibn al-Dabbāgh al-Undī (d. 543/1148 or 546/1151). For his part, Ibn al-Abbār wrote the *Muʿdjam* of al-Ṣadafī's pupils, edited by F. Codera.

Al-Ṣadafī's career as *ḳāḍī* in Murcia was short-lived on his own choice. Although both the people and the Almoravid ruler are depicted as desiring him to be judge and forcing him to accept the post in the year 505/1111, he did so reluctantly and soon decided to retire. His resignation was not accepted and he went into hiding in Almería, finally being allowed to devote himself to the propagation of *ʿilm* (see A.J. Wensinck, *The refused dignity*, in *A volume of oriental studies presented to E.G. Browne*, Cambridge 1922, 491 ff., on the recurrent motif of the scholars' refusal to be judges). The letter written by al-Ṣadafī to ʿAlī b. Yūsuf b. Tāshufīn explaining his refusal to be *ḳāḍī* has been preserved by Yāḳūt. He died a martyr in the battle of Cutanda in the frontier of al-Andalus in the year 514/1120, fighting as a volunteer against the Christians (see Noth's and Urvoy's articles on the meaning of the participation of scholars in *djihād*).

Bibliography: 1. Sources. Ḍabbī, *Bughyat al-multamis*, ed. Codera and Ribera, no. 655; Dhahabī, *al-Muʿīn fī ṭabaḳāt al-muḥaddithīn*, ʿAmmān 1984, 150, no. 1633; idem, *Siyar aʿlām al-nubalāʾ*, Beirut 1985, xix, 376-8, no. 218; idem, *Tadhkirat al-ḥuffāẓ*, Ḥaydarābād 1968-70, iv, 1253-5, no. 1059; Ibn al-Abbār, *al-Muʿdjam fī aṣḥāb al-ḳāḍī 'l-imām Abī ʿAlī al-Ṣadafī*, ed. Codera, Madrid 1886; Ibn ʿAṭiyya, *Fihris*, ed. M. Abu 'l-Adjfān and M. al-Zāhī, Beirut 1980, no. 7; Ibn Bashkuwāl, *al-Ṣila*, ed. Codera, Madrid 1882-3, no. 327 (ed. ʿI. al-Ḥusaynī, Cairo 1374/1955, no. 330); Ibn al-Djazarī, *Ghāyat al-nihāya*, ed. G. Bergsträsser, 2 vols., Cairo 1351-2/1932-3, i, 250-1, no. 1138; Ibn Farḥūn, *al-Dībādj al-mudhhab*, Cairo 1972, i, 330-2, no. 2; ʿIyāḍ, *al-Ghunya*, ed. M. Djarrār, Beirut 1982, 129-38, no. 47; Maḳḳarī, *Nafḥ al-ṭīb*, ed. I. ʿAbbās, Beirut 1968, index; idem, *Azhār al-riyāḍ*, Rabat 1978-80, i, 151, iii, 151-4; Ṣafadī, *Wāfī*, xiii, 43, no. 41; Yāḳūt, *Buldān*, ed. Beirut, iv, 310-11 (art. *Ḳutanda*); Ibn al-ʿImād, *Shadharāt*, iv, 43; Makhlūf, *Shadjarat al-nūr al-zakiyya fī ṭabaḳāt al-mālikiyya*, Cairo 1950-2, i, 128-9, no. 373

2. Studies. Pons Boigues, *Ensayo bio-bibliográfico*, 177-8, no. 143; M. Ben Cheneb, *Etude sur les personnages mentionnés dans l'Idjâza du Cheikh ʿAbd al-Qādir al-Fāsy*, Paris 1907, 141-3, no. 91; E. Lévi-Provençal, *Le Ṣaḥīḥ d'al-Bujārī. Réproduction en phototype des manuscrits originaux de la récension occidentale dite "Récension d'Ibn Saʿāda" établie à Murcie en 492 de l'Hégire* (*1099 de J.C.*), Paris 1928; J.W. Fück, *Beiträge zur Ueberlieferungsgeschichte von Buḫārī's Traditionssammlung*, in *ZDMG*, xlii (1938), 74, and 77, no. 30; Kaḥḥāla, *Muʿdjam al-muʾallifīn*, iv, 56; Ziriklī, ii, 255; ʿA.Ḥ. al-Kattānī, *Fihris al-fahāris*, 2nd ed., Beirut 1402/1982, ii, 705-9, no. 364; J. Mª Fórneas, *Elencos bibliográficos arábigoandaluces. Estudio especial de la "Fahrasa" de Ibn ʿAṭiyya al-Garnāṭī (481-541/1088-1147)*, Extracto de Tesis Doctoral, Madrid 1971, 18-19; V. Lagardère, *La haute judicature à l'époque almoravide en al-Andalus*, in *Al-Qanṭara*, vii (1986), 135-228, esp. 221-8 (to be read with caution); J. Robson, *The transmission of Tirmidhī's* Jāmiʿ, in *BSOAS*, xvi (1954), 258-70; D. Urvoy, *Sur l'evolution de la notion de ǧihād dans l'Espagne musulmane*, in *Mélanges de la Casa de Velázquez*, ix (1973), 335-71; idem, *Le monde des ulémas andalous du V/XI au VII/XIII*, Geneva 1978, 62-3, 70-8, 95-6, 99-104, 137-72; Mª I. Fierro, *Obras y transmisiones de* ḥadīṯ *(ss. V/XI-VII/XII) en la* Takmila *de Ibn al-Abbār*, in *Ibn al-Abbar. Polític i escriptor àrab valencià (1199-1260)*, Valencia 1990, 205-22; A. Noth, *Les* ʿulamāʾ *en qualité de guerriers*, in *Saber religioso y poder político en el Islam*, Madrid 1993 (forthcoming). (MARIBEL FIERRO)

ṢADĀḲ, the equivalent of *mahr* [*q.v.*], dowry. Lane gives *ṣadāḳ*, with the alternative *ṣidāḳ* (noting that the former is more common but the latter more "chaste"), plurals *ṣuduḳ*, *ṣudḳ*, and *aṣdiḳa* as "the *mahr* of a woman". Amongst the other alternative forms given by Lane the most commonly found is *ṣaduḳa* (pl. *ṣaduḳāt*) and the form IV verb of the same root, *aṣdaḳa*, means to name or give a *ṣadāḳ* upon taking a woman in marriage. Al-Djazīrī says that it is derived from *ṣidḳ* truth, honesty, sincerity as it is an indication of the husband's desire to marry by the giving of money; thus the literal meaning is the giving of money which indicates the desire to contract marriage. *Ṣadāḳ* is not found in this form in the Ḳurʾan, but only *ṣaduḳāt* (pl. of *ṣaduḳa*) in sūra IV, 4: "Give the women their *ṣaduḳāt* as a gift". Both *ṣadāḳ* and *ṣaduḳa* appear in *ḥadīth*. "Djābir says: the Prophet of God said: 'He who gives his wife in *ṣadāḳ* a handful of *sawīḳ* [*q.v.*] or dates shall be permitted' (i.e. the marriage shall be valid)." In the *Muwaṭṭaʾ*, Mālik uses *ṣadāḳ* rather than any of the synonyms.

Bibliography: *LʿA*; Lane; Mālik b. Anas, *Muwaṭṭaʾ*; al-Sayyid Muḥammad Ṣiddīḳ Ḥasan Khān Bahādur, *Ḥusn al-uswa*, Beirut, 243-6; Djazīri, *K. al-fiḳh ala 'l-madhāhib al-arbaʿa*, Beirut 1986, iv, 94; Abū Dāwūd al-Sidjistānī, *Sunan*, part 2, §§ 2105-8. (D.S. EL ALAMI)

ṢADAḲA (A.) has among its meanings that of voluntary alms, often referred to in Islamic literature as *ṣadaḳat al-taṭawwuʿ* "alms of spontaneity", or *ṣadaḳat al-nafl* "alms of supererogation", in distinction to obligatory alms, frequently also termed *ṣadaḳa*, but more commonly known as *zakāt* [*q.v.*]. Both *ṣadaḳa* and *zakāt* are considered by Muslim writers to be of purely Arabic derivation; alms being called *ṣadaḳa* as indicating the sincerity (*ṣidḳ*) of the almgiver's religious belief (e.g. Ibn al-ʿArabi, *Aḥkām al-Ḳurʾān*, ed. al-Bidjāwī, Cairo 1387/1967, ii, 946-7; al-Shirbīnī, *al-Iḳnāʿ*, Cairo i, 212; M. Hamidullah, *Introduction to Islam*, Paris 1388/1968, 68; Ibn ʿArabī, *al-Futūḥāt al-makkiyya*, Būlāk, repr. Beirut 1968, i, 548, followed by al-Zabīdī, *Itḥāf al-sāda al-muttaḳīn*, Cairo, iv, 163, derives it from *ṣadḳ*, as being hard on the soul), and *zakāt* with reference to the increase (*yazkū*) or purification (*zakī*) of the property from which they are given (e.g. Ibn Baṭṭāl al-Rakbī, *al-Naẓm al-mustaʿdhab*, on the margin of Abū Isḥāḳ al-Shīrāzī, *al-Muhadhdhab*, Cairo, i, 140). Modern critical scholarship, however, regards both words as

borrowings, probably directly from Jewish usage (A. Jeffery, *The foreign vocabulary of the Qur'ān*, Baroda 1938, 153, 194). *Ṣadaḳa* reflects the Hebrew *ṣ^e dāḳā*, which from its original meaning of righteousness developed the sense of alms given to the poor and is commonly used in this sense in Apocryphal and Rabbinic literature, if not already in the Hebrew Bible (cf. F. Rosenthal, *Sedaka, charity*, in *Hebrew Union College Annual*, xxiii/1 [1950-1], 411-414). *Zakāt* is derived from the Jewish Aramaic *zāk͟hūt͟hā*, not attested in classical Jewish sources in the sense of alms (Th. Nöldeke, *Neue Beiträge zur semitischen Sprachwissenschaft*, Strassburg 1910, 25, but see J. Horovitz, *Jewish proper names and derivatives in the Koran*, in *HUCA*, ii [1925], repr. Hildesheim 1964, 206 [62]), but which may have acquired this meaning through its common use as the Targumic rendering of *ṣ^e daḳa* (H.J. Kasovsky, *Oṣar les͟hōn targūm Onkelos* (*Concordance*), Jerusalem 1933-40, revised ed. 1986, i, 156) in Biblical passages understood by post-Biblical Jews to refer to alms, an evolution that would parallel that of the Greek *eleēmosynē* (H. Balz and Schneider (eds.), *Exegetical dictionary of the New Testament*, Grand Rapids Mich. 1990, i, 428-9; but cf. G. Levi Della Vida, in *RSO*, iv/4 [1911-12], 1067-9). Modern Muslims have tended to find the claim of borrowing unconvincing (e.g. Yūsuf al-Ḳarḍāwī, *Fiḳh al-zakāt*, Beirut 1397/1977, i, 38-9 referring to *EI*[1]). Borrowed in turn from Muslims, *ṣadaḳa* and its derivatives are found in the religious writings of Jews and Christians under Islam (e.g. Bak͟hya b. Paḳūdā, *al-Hidāya ilā farā'iḍ al-ḳulūb*, ed. Yahuda, Leiden 1912, 211 (*al-ṣadaḳa wa 'l-zakāt*); Severus b. al-Muḳaffaʿ, *Miṣbāḥ al-ʿaḳl*, ed. Ebied and Young, Louvain 1975, 19). *Ṣadaḳa* is found as a male personal name for Muslims, starting from the second generation (Ibn Ḥad͟jar al-ʿAsḳalānī, *Tahd͟hīb al-tahd͟hīb*, iv, 414-9; A. Schimmel, *Islamic names*, Edinburgh 1989, 41; Brockelmann, S III, 765 (Ṣadaḳat Allāh)), and Jews (S.D. Goitein, *A Mediterranean society*, Berkeley 1967-93, ii, 576 n. 21, vi, 103-4; M. Steinschneider, *Die arabische Literatur der Juden*, Frankfurt 1902, 329, 331 (Samaritans)) and more recently as a Christian surname (G. Graf, *Geschichte der christlichen arabischen Literatur*, The Vatican, v, 138).

1. Ṣadaḳa *in the Ḳur'ān*. *Ṣadaḳa* and its related verbal forms (*taṣaddaḳa* and the assimilated *iṣṣaddaḳa*) are used 24 times in the Ḳur'ān. All of the passages except XII, 88, stem from the Medinan period (noted by Horovitz, 212 [68]), but the appearance of the plural form in the sense of alms (not a Jewish usage), the existence of the denominative verb *taṣaddaḳa*, to give alms (cf. Rosenthal, 423), and its usage in the extended sense of relinquishing a right (II, 280, V, 45, XII, 88) suggest that the history of *ṣadaḳa* in Arabic is pre-Islamic (cf. J. Obermann, *Islamic origins*, in N.A. Faris, ed., *The Arab heritage*, Princeton 1944, 109-10), a supposition supported by *ḥadīt͟h* which depict the giving of *ṣadaḳa* as familiar to both Arabian Jews and pagans before Islam (al-ʿAynī, *ʿUmdat al-ḳārī*, Cairo 1308, viii, 302; A.J. Wensinck, *Muhammad and the Jews of Medina*, tr. W. Behn, Freiburg im Breisgau 1978, 101). *Ṣaduḳa*, which appears in Ḳur'ān, IV, 4, in the sense of the bride's payment, more commonly known as the *ṣadāḳ* or *mahr*, is of Arabic origin (J. Wellhausen, *Die Ehe bei den Arabern*, in *NGW Gott.*, xi [1893], 434; Rosenthal, 420-1; the variant *ṣadaḳa* is not well attested (cf. Abū Ḥayyān al-Andalusī, *al-Baḥr al-muḥīṭ*, Cairo 1329, iii, 166, not recorded) and appears to be a philologist's creation (cf. Ibn K͟hālawayh, *Muk͟htaṣar fī s͟hawād͟hd͟h al-Ḳur'ān*, ed. Bergsträsser, Leipzig 1934, 24)). In the Ḳur'ān, but not the *ḥadīt͟h*, *zakāt*, perhaps formed to rhyme with another Aramaic borrowing, *ṣalāt*, with which it is so frequently paired in the Ḳur'ān (A. Spitaler, *Die Schreibung des Typus ṣlwt im Koran*, in *WZKN*, lvi [1960], 217)), is used only in the singular, like the Hebrew *ṣedaḳa*, and has no denominative verb corresponding to its sense of giving alms (noted by W.M. Watt and A.T. Welch, *Der Islam*, Stuttgart 1980, i, 302, but cf. on the latter point Fr. Schulthess, in *ZA*, xxvi [1912], 153, and Horovitz, 206 [62]). *Zakāt* thus appears to have a shorter history as an Arabic word than *ṣadaḳa* and a more pronounced religious colouring, for only it, not *ṣadaḳa*, is used in the Kur'ān in connection with prophets before Muhammad (Watt and Welch, i, 302).

According to Arabic lexicographers *ṣadaḳa* is broader than *zakāt* and is used in the Ḳur'ān for both voluntary and obligatory alms. It thus happens that certain of the most important Ḳur'ānic provisions concerning *zakāt* are couched in terms of *ṣadaḳa* (e.g. IX, 60). In some cases, it is regarded as doubtful whether *ṣadaḳa* is being used to refer to voluntary alms or *zakāt* or both (e.g. II, 271). A similar uncertainty extends to verses which refer to "spending" (*infāḳ*) (e.g. II, 3) and "giving" (e.g. II, 177). To complicate matters, *zakāt* is on occasion, it is claimed, used to refer to voluntary alms (e.g. Ḳur'ān V, 55, al-Bayḍāwī, *Anwār al-tanzīl*, ed. Fleischer, Leipzig 1846-8, i, 263 (given by ʿAlī while praying); Ḳur'ān, XXX, 39; al-D͟jazā'irī, *Ḳalā'id al-durar*, al-Nad͟jaf n.d., i, 284).

It has been argued that the distinction between voluntary and obligatory *ṣadaḳa* is post-Ḳur'ānic (C. Snouck Hurgronje, *La Zakât*, in *Selected works*, ed. G.H. Bousquet and J. Schacht, Leiden 1957, 150-70 [*Verspr. Geschr.*, ii, 1-58]). But verses such as II, 177, which refers both to giving one's property to beggars, among others, and to the giving of *zakāt* and LVIII, 13, which enjoins those who have failed to give *ṣadaḳa* to give *zakāt*, indicate that the Kur'an does make a distinction between voluntary alms and *zakāt*, as does IX, 79, which speaks of "believers who give alms of their own accord (*muṭṭawwiʿīn*)" (cf. Ibn al-ʿArabī, *K. al-Ḳabas fī s͟harḥ Muwaṭṭa' Mālik*, ed. Walad Karīm, Beirut 1992, iii, 1191). According to the Islamic sources, voluntary almsgiving, already practiced in Mecca, predates *zakāt*, which was instituted in Medina (e.g. al-Bayḍāwī, *Anwār al-tanzīl*, on VI, 141; on the date of imposition of *zakāt*, see Hurgronje, *La Zakat*, 157; cf. ʿAlī al-Ḳārī, *Mirḳāt al-mafātīḥ*, Cairo 1309, ii, 409 (*zakāt* was imposed in Mecca and regulated in detail in Medina).

The Ḳur'ānic provisions understood to refer to *ṣadaḳa* in its sense of voluntary alms touch upon themes developed throughout the Islamic tradition. God is spoken of as accepting the alms of His servants (IX, 104). The giving of alms to the poor in secret is said to be preferable to giving openly (II, 271). The proper motivation and demeanour of the almsgiver are indispensable to the religious value of the act: "O believers, do not render your alms of no account by obligation and insult, like one who expends his property for the sake of appearance before the people while not believing in God and the Last Day" (II, 264). The expiatory function of almsgiving is already found in II, 196, which institutes fasting, almsgiving, and sacrifice as atonement for the pilgrim's premature shaving of the head, and more generally in II, 271. The "verse of *ṣadaḳa*" (*āyat al-ṣadaḳa*), IX, 103, taken by most interpreters to refer to *zakāt*, is understood by some to refer to the taking of alms as expiation from certain Anṣārī penitents. The "verse of audience" (*āyat al-munād͟jāt, āyat al-nad͟jwa*), LVIII, 12, enjoins,

or at least encourages, the giving of *ṣadaḳa* before an audience with the Prophet. It is believed to have been in effect only briefly before being abrogated by LVIII, 13 (al-Bayḍāwī, *Anwār al-tanzīl*, ii, 320, cf. al-Zamakhsharī, *al-Kashshāf*, Beirut, iv, 494).

Other Ḳurʾānic verses, although they do not use the term *ṣadaḳa*, figure prominently in later discussions. Several verses (II, 177, III, 92, LXXVI, 8) stress the significance of giving from what one loves. In II, 267, believers are told to give of the "good things" (*ṭayyibāt*) that they have acquired and not to seek out the bad things (*khabīth*) that they would not themselves gladly accept, a verse said to have been revealed when usurious income, now prohibited, was being given away as *ṣadaḳa*. The bountiful reward in store for one who gives "in the cause of God" (*fī sabīl Allāh*) (II, 261, seven-hundredfold) or "to seek God's pleasure" (*ibtighāʾ marḍāt Allāh*) (II, 265, twofold) is contrasted with the vanity of giving "in pursuit of the life of this world" (*al-ḥayāt al-dunyā*) (III, 117). "Who is it that will make God a goodly loan" (*ḳarḍ ḥasan*), so that He will increase it many times" (II, 245; cf. Proverbs, xix, 17) is said to have been revealed with reference to the Anṣārī Abu 'l-Daḥdāḥ, who gave an orchard of 600 palm trees as *ṣadaḳa* and was rewarded with one million orchards in the hereafter. Ḳurʾān LIX, 9 praises those "who prefer over themselves, even though they be in want," a passage understood to refer to the Medinan *Anṣār* who, setting an example of self-sacrifice (*īthār*), gave so generously to the *Muhādjirūn* (al-Baghawī, *Sharḥ al-sunna*, ed. al-Arnāʾūṭ, Damascus 1390/1400, repr. Beirut 1403/1983, vi, 181; al-Bayḍāwī, *Anwār al-tanzīl*, ii, 324). In other passages, however, the Ḳurʾān urges moderation in giving (VI, 141, cf. al-Bayḍāwī, *op. cit.*, i, 312; XXV, 67).

2. Ṣadaḳa *in* Ḥadīth. The subject of *ṣadaḳa* is dealt with in many *ḥadīth* (most easily accessible in ʿAlī al-Muttaḳī al-Hindī, *Kanz al-ʿummāl*, ed. Ḥayyānī and al-Saḳḳā, Aleppo 1391/1971, vi). Although *ṣadaḳa* is sometimes used for voluntary alms in explicit contrast to *zakāt*, its use in the sense of *zakāt* (found also in papyri (G. Khan, *Selected Arabic papyri*, Oxford 1992, i, 53)) remains frequent, with the result that in the classical collections of traditions, the *ḥadīth* dealing with voluntary almsgiving are often found in the chapters on *zakāt*. Mālik's *Muwaṭṭaʾ*, however, already has in addition a separate section on voluntary almsgiving (in the recension of Yaḥyā b. Yaḥyā al-Maṣmūdī, ed. Muḥammad Fuʾād ʿAbd al-Bāḳī, Cairo n.d., 615-18). In the interpretation of neither the *ḥadīth* nor the Ḳurʾān was agreement reached as to which sense of *ṣadaḳa* was to be presumed as intended in the absence of further evidence.

Beyond the ambiguity occasioned by the continued use of *ṣadaḳa* for *zakāt*, there is further uncertainty in the interpretation of some traditions created by the not infrequent use of *ṣadaḳa* in the sense of permanent alms (*ṣadaḳa djāriya*), i.e. the trust or *wakf* [*q.v.*] (on this use in papyri, see R.G. Khoury, *Chrestomathie de papyrologie arabe*, Leiden 1993, 132-3 (Christian)). Some even claimed that *ṣadaḳa* was used in the *ḥadīth* in the sense of the poll tax (*djizya*) [*q.v.*], a usage others rejected as confined to the Taghlib and other Christian Arab tribes (ʿ*Umdat al-ḳārī*, ix, 4-5).

The references to *ṣadaḳa* in the *ḥadīth* are often of a homiletic character, stressing the excellence of alms given under one or another circumstance, whether that of the giver, the recipient, the time and place of the giving, or the gift (cf. al-Djazāʾirī, *Ḳalāʾid*, i, 309). Thus when asked what *ṣadaḳa* was best, the Prophet is reported to have answered: "the *ṣadaḳa* you give when you are still healthy and tight-fisted, fearing poverty and hoping for wealth (*Sharḥ al-sunna*, vi, 172-3; al-Tibrīzī, *Mishkāt al-maṣābīḥ*, tr. J. Robson, Lahore 1975, i, 395 (cf. Ḳurʾān, LXIII, 10)). The merit of almsgiving thus lies in the degree of self-denial (*mudjāhadat al-nafs*) (*Itḥāf al-sāda*, iv, 168) a point made more explicitly in the tradition that states that the best *ṣadaḳa* is that which the person with little can manage to give (*djuhd al-muḳill*) (Wensinck, *Handbook,* 20; *Mishkāt*, i, 411 (cf. Ḳurʾān, IX, 79)). Because it is not the monetary value of what of what is given that is paramount, *ṣadaḳa* consisting of a dirham that constitutes half the almsgiver's property is more meritorious than 100,000 dirhams given by a person of great wealth (al-Nasāʾī, *Sunan*, Cairo 1383/1964, v, 44; ʿAlī al-Ḳārī, *Sharḥ ʿayn al-ʿilm*, Cairo, i, 157). Alms given to a nearer neighbour is better than that given to one more distant. Giving alms to a relative is particularly meritorious, since one earns the rewards both for *ṣadaḳa* and for cultivating family ties. The reward for *ṣadaḳa* given on Friday is double that on other days of the week. Other traditions identify the best *ṣadaḳa* as that given in Ramaḍān. The reward for giving voluntary alms in secret is seventy times that of giving it publicly (al-Bayḍāwī, *Anwār al-tanzīl*, i, 138, on II, 271; ʿ*Umdat al-ḳārī*, viii, 284). The place in which alms are given is also significant to its merit. A dirham given in Mecca, according to a Shīʿī tradition, merits a hundred-thousandfold reward, in Medina ten-thousandfold, in Kūfa one-thousandfold. "Whoever gives one dirham of *ṣadaḳa* in Jerusalem (*Bayt al-Maḳdis*) gains his ransom from hellfire, and whoever gives a loaf of bread there is like one who has given [the weight of] of the earth's mountains in gold" (al-Ḥasan al-Baṣrī). Of all that might be given as alms, water is pronounced to be best, and one who gives water to a thirsty Muslim will drink of the wine of Paradise.

The importance of giving *ṣadaḳa* to avert tribulations in this life and to avoid the punishment of hellfire in the hereafter is the topic of many *ḥadīth*s "Whoever can protect himself against hellfire should do so, even if it should be with half a date". An angel is said to pray that the almsgiver be rewarded, while another angel prays for the destruction of the property of the one who withholds alms. Angels in the form of beggars sometimes come to test a family (al-Ḳāḍī al-Nuʿmān, *Daʿāʾim al-Islām*, ed. Fayḍī, Cairo 1389/1969, ii, 333), and it was Jacob's failure to give alms to an unrecognised prophet in the guise of a beggar that led to the tragedy of Joseph (*ibid.*, ii, 333-4). Where one has nothing tangible to give, one can still utter a kindly word (cf. *Talmud Bavā Bathrā* 9b). Conduct meriting a reward is in fact frequently termed *ṣadaḳa* in the *ḥadīth*. Thus a man's lawful sexual intercourse is *ṣadaḳa*, as is giving assistance with the loading of a beast, and every step take toward prayer. Planting something from which a person, bird or animal later eats counts as *ṣadaḳa*. One who supports himself and his family is credited with *ṣadaḳa* (with proper intention; cf. *Kethubbōth*, 50a). In this extended sense, corresponding to a large degree with the Jewish *gemīlūth ḥasadīm*, "acts of loving kindness" (G.F. Moore, *Judaism*, Cambridge, Mass. 1927, ii, 171-4), even greeting another with a cheerful face is deemed *ṣadaḳa* (cf. *Avōth de-Rabbī Nathan*, xiii, 4). In short, every good deed is *ṣadaḳa* (*kullu maʿrūfin ṣadaḳa*). Not even affirmative action is required, for a Muslim whose property is stolen is credited with having given it as *ṣadaḳa*.

The continuity of Islamic teaching on *ṣadaḳa* with certain Jewish and Christian conceptions of almsgiv-

ing is evidenced by more than one tradition. "Alms averts a bad death (*mītat al-sūʾ*)" (*Kanz al-ʿummāl*, vi, 345, in many versions etc.; *maṣāriʿ al-sūʾ, Kanz al-ʿummāl*, vi, 406) reproduces Proverbs, x, 2, "righteousness (*ṣᵉdaḳa*) delivers from death," understood in the Talmud (*Bavā Bat͟hrā* 10a) to refer to almsgiving delivering one from an unnatural death (*mīt͟hā mes͟hunnā*; cf. Targum ad loc. *mōt͟hā bīs͟hā*). The depiction of the giver of alms as dressed in an expanding coat of mail is reminiscent of Isa., lix, 17, "He put on righteousness (*ṣᵉdaḳa*) as a breastplate" which is taken in the Talmud (*Bavā Bat͟hrā* 9b) as comparing the assembly of a coat of armour, chain by chain, with the growth of small acts of almsgiving to a considerable sum. Several *ḥadīt͟h*s which stress the merit of secret almsgiving have exact Biblical parallels. "*Ṣadaḳa* in secret extinguishes the wrath of the Lord" renders Proverbs, xxi, 14, "a gift given in secret soothes anger" as interpreted in *Bavā Bat͟hrā* 9b. Christ's exhortation "do not let your left hand know what your right hand is doing so that your giving may be in secret" (Matt., vi, 3,4) appears at the teaching of Muḥammad in several traditions (Wensinck, *Handbook*, 20; *Mis͟hkāt*, i, 407; noted by Goldziher, *Muh. St.*, ii, 384, and L. S͟hayk͟hū, *al-Naṣrāniyya wa ādābuhā bayna ʿarab al-d͟jāhiliyya*, Beirut 1923, ii/2, 319).

The model for generosity in almsgiving is provided by the Prophet Muḥammad, who is described in the *ḥadīt͟h* as "the most generous of men, bestowing more good than the loosed wind". He made it a point to give with his own hand and derived more joy from giving than the poor to whom he gave. When asked for anything, he never said no. If he had nothing to give, he remained silent (to elicit others to speak on behalf of the beggar). He is said never to have delivered a sermon without mentioning *ṣadaḳa*.

The Prophet's wives were also known for their almsgiving, notably Zaynab bint D͟jaḥs͟h, the "longest in arm" (*ʿUmdat al-ḳārī*, viii, 282-3, others apply the tradition to Sawda), Zaynab bint K͟huzayma al-Hilāliyya, already known before Islam as the "mother of the poor" (*umm al-masākīn*) for her almsgiving, and ʿĀʾisha (al-G͟hazālī, *Iḥyāʾ ʿulūm al-dīn*, Cairo 1387/1967, i, 298), who insisted on returning any blessing bestowed upon her by those she had assisted with alms, thus setting an example of purity of motive (*ik͟hlāṣ*) in giving. Extraordinary generosity was exhibited by ʿUmar b. al-K͟haṭṭāb, who, when the Prophet urged the giving of *ṣadaḳa*, hastened to give away half of what he owned, only to find that once again he was bested by Abū Bakr, who had given away all that he had. Another Companion, Abū D͟harr al-G͟hifārī [*q.v.*], popular among modern Muslims (M. Rodinson, *Islam and capitalism*, New York 1973, 25), is said to have regarded the best *ṣadaḳa* as the most unsparing. Abū D͟harr was exiled by the caliph ʿUt͟hmān upon the complaint of Muʿāwiya, then governor of Syria, for his controversial view that *zakāt* had not abrogated all other forms of obligatory *ṣadaḳa* and that the Ḳurʾānic condemnation of "those who hoard gold and silver and do not expend it in the way of God" (IX, 34) was not averted by the payment of *zakāt*.

According to the *ḥadīt͟h*, the Prophet, himself so generous in giving *ṣadaḳa*, was scrupulous in not taking it, while accepting gifts intended as tokens of esteem (*hadiyya*) (cf. Ibn al-ʿArabī, *Aḥkām al-Ḳurʾān*, iii, 1449-50). It is agreed that the Prophet was prohibited from receiving *zakāt*, which, by cleansing the property and persons of those who pay it, acquires a taint of impurity, but opinions differ as to why the Prophet would not accept voluntary *ṣadaḳa*. Most, including Abū Ḥanīfa, Abū Yūsuf and Muḥammad al-S͟haybānī, held that he was prohibited from taking it. Among the explanations offered for this prohibition are the indignity, inconsistent with the prophetic office, of accepting alms, the appearance of self-interest (*tuhma*) were the Prophet to accept *ṣadaḳa* while urging others to give it, and the meritoriousness of the Prophet's special deprivation. A minority of scholars, including al-S͟hāfiʿī (*al-Umm*, Cairo 1321-5, iii, 279), entertained the possibility that the Prophet was permitted to accept *ṣadaḳa* but refrained from doing so out of pious scruple. On either view, the Prophet would be free to use amenities, such as wells, dedicated to the use of public at large. The Prophet's declining to accept the *ṣadaḳa* is deemed to be one of the signs of his prophethood (*dalāʾil al-nubuwwa*), the recognition of which led Salmān al-Fārisī [*q.v.*] to embrace Islam. There is disagreement whether or not it constitutes a proof for other prophets as well.

Also characteristic of the Prophet, according to the majority of Muslims, but not Imāmī or Ismāʿīlī S͟hīʿīs, is that upon his death he left nothing to his heirs, all his property being *ṣadaḳa*, used here in a sense that includes the *waḳf* of his real property (Wensinck, *Handbook*, 162; cf. I. Hrbek, *Muḥammads Nachlass und die Aliden*, in *ArO*, xviii/3 [1950], 145-6). Here, too, the avoidance of an appearance of self-interest is cited in explanation (*ʿUmdat al-ḳārī*, xxiii, 232). According to most authorities, all other prophets were like Muḥammad in leaving no estate for their heirs, but al-Ḥasan al-Baṣrī argued on the basis of Ḳurʾān, XIX, 6, and XXVII, 16, that other prophets had left estates, and certain Baṣrans, including Ibn ʿUlayya (d. 218/833), understood the fact of Muhammad's having left no estate to represent one of the personal distinctions (*faḍīla*) granted him, rather than an incident of the prophetic office as such.

3. Ṣadaḳa *in Islamic law*. In addition to using *ṣadaḳa* for voluntary alms, Muslim jurists continue to use the word in a number of other meanings. As in the Ḳurʾān and *ḥadīt͟h*, *ṣadaḳa* and *zakāt* are often used interchangeably for obligatory alms in legal literature, with which should be included the editorial matter of the *ḥadīt͟h* collections (cf. the occasional doubling usage *al-zakāt wa 'l-ṣadaḳāt* in al-Ḳāḍī al-Nuʿmān, *Daʿāʾim al-Islām*, i, 251 and *Taʾwīl al-daʿāʾim*, ed. al-Aʿẓamī, Cairo, ii, 124, 128). However, against the view that saw them as entirely equivalent (e.g. al-Māwardī, *al-Aḥkām al-sulṭāniyya*, Cairo 1386/1966, 113), others attempted to draw a distinction based on Ḳurʾānic usage between *zakāt*, which is to be given to the authorities (*ītāʾ al-zakāt*), and *ṣadaḳa*, which the authorities are directed to take (Ḳurʾān, IX, 103). On this view, which corresponds to the distinction between *ẓāhir* and *bāṭin* property [see ZAKĀT], *ṣadaḳa* is applicable to lifestock and crops, while *zakāt*, a special kind of *ṣadaḳa*, applies to such personal property (*amwāl*) as gold and silver. This usage, identified as that of certain Ḥanafīs, has left its traces, and a preference for using *ṣadaḳa* to refer to the tax on livestock can be noted elsewhere as well (e.g. Mālik, *al-Muwaṭṭaʾ*, 167-87). Although *ṣadaḳa* continues to be used for *waḳf*, an effort to reduce ambiguity can be observed in such expressions as *al-ṣadaḳāt al-mawḳūfāt, al-ṣadaḳāt al-muḥarramāt* (*al-Umm*, iii, 280-1), *al-ṣadaḳāt al-musabbala* (Ibn Muẓaffar, *K. al-Bayān al-s͟hāfī*, Ṣanʿāʾ 1404/1984, i, 533 (Zaydī), and *ṣadaḳa muʾabbada* (Ibn al-Muṭahhar al-Ḥillī, *Īḍāḥ al-fawāʾid*, ed. al-Kirmanī, Ḳumm 1388, ii, 378). The use of *ṣadaḳa* to refer to expiatory penalties is also found (al-Tahānawī, *K. Kas͟hs͟hāf iṣṭilāḥāt al-funūn*, Calcutta 1862, i, 851).

Ṣadaḳa as a distinct juristic institution only partially

reflects the various forms of charitable giving known to Islam. For the jurist, *ṣadaḳa* falls under the general heading of charitable gifts (*birr*) or gratuitous transfers, *tabarruʿāt*. More specifically, it is treated as a species of gift, *hiba* "in the wider sense" (*bi 'l-maʿnā al-aʿamm*), that is, a gratuitous transfer of tangible property (also *ʿaṭiyya*). It is distinguished from other species of gift by the intention with which it is given, which must be to please God (*li-wadjh Allāh*) in the hope of a reward in the hereafter (*thawāb al-ākhira* (al-Sanʿānī..., Beirut 1405/1985. *Subul al-salām*, ii, 196) and not for any wordly purpose such as to acquire a gift from the donee, which would render it an ordinary gift (also termed *hiba*) or to honour the donee (*hadiyya*). It must, that is, constitute a *ḳurba*, an act performed as a means of coming closer to God. The significance of the donor's intention is evidenced by the Prophet's acceptance of gifts as *hadiyya* but not *ṣadaḳa*, a distinction also found in the form of an explicit prophetic tradition and reflected in the classification of gifts attributed to ʿAlī. Gifts of usufruct (*manfaʿa*) are by definition excluded from *ṣadaḳa*, and fall under the headings of license to consume (*ibāḥa, ḍiyāfa*), loan (*ʿāriya*) or trust (*waḳf*). The extent to which *ṣadaḳa* is separately treated in legal works varies from text to text, and even in those cases where there is a separate discussion of *ṣadaḳa*, some of the rules governing it are to be found in the chapters on gifts and *zakāt*, although it is not to be regarded as a recommended (*sunna*) form of *zakāt* (recommended *zakāt* is, however, known to Imāmī law, Abū Djaʿfar al-Ṭūsī, *al-Nihāya*, Beirut 1390/1970, 176).

Islamic law, by way of the *ḥadīth*, has preserved only a few of the distinct forms of gift giving known to the Arabs, e.g. the *minḥa* or *manīḥa*, said to be the best kind of *ṣadaḳa*. With Islam there came a radically simpler set of distinctions (even the difference between *hiba* and *hadiyya* is a terminological innovation), in which *ṣadaḳa*, defined by its religious intention, held a special place. Not surprisingly there was a discernible tendency for those giving gifts to prefer the label *ṣadaḳa*, with its connotation of a pious motive, for their transactions, sometimes to the consternation of jurists and with consequences, such as irrevocability, that the donors may not have contemplated. Thus in several Shīʿī traditions Djaʿfar al-Ṣādiḳ is reported to have complained of an erroneous extension, unknown in the Prophet's day, of the term *ṣadaḳa* to ordinary gifts (al-Baḥrānī, *al-Ḥadāʾiḳ al-nāḍira*, ed. al-Irwānī, Beirut 1405/1985, xxii, 262-5; al-Kulaynī, *al-Kāfī*, ed. al-Ghaffārī, Tehran 1388-91, vii, 31; al-Ṭūsī, *al-Istibṣār*, ed. al-Kharsān, Tehran 1390, iv, 110; but cf. al-Ṭaḥāwī, *Sharḥ maʿānī al-āthār*, ii, 3-4 (*hiba* labelled *ṣadaḳa* in the Prophet's time).

While the giving of ordinary gifts is recommended (*mandūb ilayhi*), to give *ṣadaḳa* is especially recommended, and, on the basis of the many Ḳurʾānic verses and traditions enjoining it, is classified by later Shāfiʿīs as "strongly recommended" (*sunna muʾakkada*). Under certain circumstances, however, it may be prohibited to give *ṣadaḳa*, as for instance, when doing so would prejudice discharging one's obligation to support family members or pay off creditors, or when the giver knows or suspects that the *ṣadaḳa* will be used for an illegal purpose (*maʿṣiya*).

Even in such cases, however, the preferred view is that the donee acquires a good title. It is debated to what extent *ṣadaḳa* to a person in dire need is to be deemed obligatory. It is recommended that the gift of *ṣadaḳa* be accompanied by a supplication to God for its acceptance.

The rules governing the enforceability of the contract (*ʿaḳd*) of *ṣadaḳa* are essentially the same as those governing an ordinary gift, including the full legal capacity of the donor to enter into gratuitous transactions and the limitation on death-bed transactions [see HIBA]. However, some relaxation of the rules of gifts in their application to *ṣadaḳa* is occasionally to be noted. Thus most Shāfiʿīs in the case of *ṣadaḳa* dispense with the offer and acceptance (*al-īdjāb wa 'l-ḳabūl*) required by them for the validity of a gift. Although most jurists regard the taking of possession (*ḳabḍ, iḥrāz*) as just as essential to the enforceability of *ṣadaḳa* as of gifts, Isḥāḳ b. Rāhawayh made an exception of *ṣadaḳa*, as did al-Shāfiʿī for a time, and this is also reported of a number of early jurists (al-Sarakhsī, *al-Mabsūṭ*, Cairo 1324-31, xii, 48). The Mālikīs, starting from the enforceability in principle of an agreement to make a gift (possession being required to perfect the rights of the donee), go furthest in this direction. The declaration of a firm present intention, or indeed the present intention alone (*al-tabtīl bi 'l-niyya*), to give a particular person *ṣadaḳa*, according to the accepted (*mashhūr*) teaching of Mālik, is enforceable against the donor, so that *ṣadaḳa*, like *ṣᵉdaḳa* in Jewish law (cf. Maimonides, *Mishne Torā, Hilkhōth Mattenōth ʿAniyyim*, 8:1), is to this extent analysed as in the nature of a vow, rather than a contract. Along similar lines, *ṣadaḳa* intended for a particular person who cannot be found, according to some early authorities, including al-Ḥasan al-Baṣrī, must be given as *ṣadaḳa* to another (cf. *Talmud ʿArakhīm* 6a).

There is disagreement as to what extent the donor of *ṣadaḳa* can bind the donee by conditions attached to the gift. The Shāfiʿīs give effect to such conditions and hold that it is prohibited for the donee to use the *ṣadaḳa* otherwise than according to the terms of the gift. Ḥanafī, Ḥanbalī, Ẓāhirī, Twelver Shīʿī and Zaydī teaching, to the contrary, invalidates all terms and conditions inconsistent with an outright gift of the *ṣadaḳa* property (on the different Mālikī views, see al-Ḥaṭṭāb, *Mawāhib al-djalīl*, Cairo 1329, vi, 50-1).

A vow (*nadhr*) to give *ṣadaḳa* is discouraged, since the maker of the vow may never discharge it or may do so grudgingly. A vow to give *ṣadaḳa* may be discharged before the time originally stated, and a vow to give a specific thing as *ṣadaḳa* may be discharged by giving its value. A vow to give *ṣadaḳa* to the wealthy is said to be invalid. Disagreement is reported as to the judicial enforceability of a vow such as "If I have sexual intercourse with my slave-girl, she is yours as *ṣadaḳa*," said by a husband to his wife, where the intention is clearly not charitable (*nadhr al-ladjādj*).

Unlike *zakāt*, in which the nature and value of the property due is fixed by law (*muḳaddar*), the giver of *ṣadaḳa* is free to determine what and how much he will give. The traditions encouraging the giving of even such trivial things as half a date as *ṣadaḳa* indicate that the object of *ṣadaḳa*, unlike an ordinary gift, need have no market value. It is, however, more meritorious to give *ṣadaḳa* from one's best property, the giving of property that is adulterated or of poor quality being regarded as reprehensible (*makrūh*), and the giving of unlawful (*ḥarām*) property prohibited. Nonetheless, *ṣadaḳa* has functioned as a means of dealing with unsaleable merchandise (Ibn Farḥūn, *Tabṣirat al-ḥukkām*, on the margin of ʿUlaysh. *Fatḥ al-ʿalī al-mālik*, Cairo, ii, 298 (adulterated milk and other substances; badly woven mantles to be shredded as rags for *ṣadaḳa* rather than burned) and the proceeds of illegal transactions (Ibn Hubayra, *al-Ifṣāḥ*, ed. al-Dabbās, Aleppo 1366/1947, 229 (a sale of grapes for winemaking); *Subul al-salām* iii, 14 (a prostitute's earnings); Ibn ʿAbd al-Barr, *al-Tamhīd*, repr. Lahore 1404/1983, ii,

23-4 (misappropriated booty); cf. Ibn Mufliḥ, *K. al-Furū*ᶜ, ed. Farrādj, Beirut 1388/1967, ii, 663-6 (difficult cases)). The solution of the Ṣūfī al-Fuḍayl b. ᶜIyāḍ (d. 187/803), who simply threw away questionable money that had come into his hands, was regarded as unsatisfactory (*Iḥyā*ᵓ, ii, 166-8). In modern times, Muslims receiving payments of bank interest and insurance proceeds have been encouraged to rid themselves of these by giving them as *ṣadaḳa* (e.g. Dār al-Iftāᵓ al-Miṣrī, *al-Fatāwā al-islāmiyya*, ix/28 [1403/1983], 3340, 3342).

Just as there is no minimum for *ṣadaḳa*, according to most jurists there is no maximum (al-Nawawī, *Sharḥ Muslim*, Cairo, vii, 125 quoting Ḳāḍī ᶜIyāḍ; but cf. Ibn Ḥazm, *al-Muḥallā*, ix, 138 for a list of early jurists who rejected this). A Muslim of sound mind and body who is able to accept poverty is encouraged to dispose of all his property as *ṣadaḳa*, beyond narrow exemptions. Although there are Ḳurᵓānic verses (VI, 41, XVII, 26, 29) and traditions calling for moderation in giving, other verses (II, 262, IX, 79, LIX, 9) and traditions set no such limit, and it was to these as well as to the practice of early Muslims, not to speak of the Prophet, that the majority of jurists looked. The tradition stating that the best *ṣadaḳa* was that which left a sufficiency (*ᶜan ẓahr ghinā*), which the Ẓāhirī Ibn Ḥazm took as the only criterion for how much one might give (*al-Muḥallā*, ix, 136-42) was widely interpreted to mean "self sufficiency" (*ghinā al-nafs*), i.e. contentment. It is thus permitted to reduce oneself and one's family to penury if those affected are capable of enduring it without becoming a burden on society and without complaint; otherwise it is reprehensible to give away all of one's property, and subsequently to regret one's *ṣadaḳa* deprives it of its reward.

A minority of jurists set down specific limits on how much one might properly give: one-half, more commonly one-third, the proportion set down by Mālik, the Syrian jurists Makḥūl (d. 112/730) and al-Awzāᶜī (d. 157/774), and the Zaydī Imām al-Hādī (d. 298/911) and recommended by al-Ṭabarī (d. 310/923), or one-fifth, one-seventh, or one-tenth (depending on wealth, attributed to Djābir b. Zayd (d. 93/712) (cf. one-fifth in *Talmud Kethubbōth* 50a).

Unlike *zakāt*, which is designated for specified classes of recipients, there are virtually no restrictions on those to whom *ṣadaḳa* may be given, and the giver is encouraged not to restrict his giving to one group, although the law, following the *ḥadīth*, does identify preferred donees such as relatives and neighbours (al-Nawawī, *al-Madjmū*ᶜ, Cairo, vi, 260: consensus that relatives are preferred to strangers). A mosque or other institution can be a recipient of *ṣadaḳa*, which is accepted on its behalf by its representative, who can be the donor himself.

Most jurists understand the prohibition against the receipt of *ṣadaḳa* by members of the family (*āl*) of Muḥammad (as variously defined) to apply only to obligatory *ṣadaḳa*, that is, *zakāt*, although the matter was much controverted, with Abū Ḥanīfa, Abū Yūsuf, and Muḥammad al-Shaybānī and Aḥmad b. Ḥanbal reported as having prohibited voluntary *ṣadaḳa* to them as well, which was also the view of Zayd b. ᶜAlī, Ibn Ḥazm and a number of later jurists.

Although in popular usage *ṣadaḳa* was understood to refer to gifts to the poor, as may be gathered from lexicographical works, both general (*LA*, s.v. *ṣadaḳa*) and juridical (al-Nawawī, *Tahdhīb al-asmāᵓ wa 'l-lughāt*, Cairo n.d., repr. Tehran, ii, 197, s.v. *hiba*; idem, *Taṣḥīḥ al-tarbih*, 93, s.v. *hiba*), the teaching of the jurists is unanimous that *ṣadaḳa*, unlike *zakāt* and the Jewish *ṣedaḳa*, may be given to the "wealthy" (*ghanī*) (as defined for *zakāt* or *zakāt al-fiṭra*). Traditions such as "give to one who asks even if he is mounted on a horse" (*al-Muwaṭṭa*ᵓ, 615), the practice of the early Muslims, and Ḳurᵓān, XII, 88, are all cited in support of this doctrine. Nonetheless, the reward for giving to the needy is said to be seventy times that of giving to one not in need, and the greater merit (eighteenfold), according to a tradition, of making a loan as compared to giving *ṣadaḳa* (tenfold) is explained by the evident need of the borrower (cf. *Talmud Shabbath* 63a, and Rashi, *ad loc.*). In this spirit, the Shāfiᶜī jurists distinguish between *ṣadaḳa* to the poor, which requires no intention of a heavenly reward on the part of the donor, and *ṣadaḳa* to the wealthy, which does.

A point of departure for a thorough-going distinction between *ṣadaḳa* to the poor and to the wealthy is found in the Ḥanafī tradition. Abū Ḥanīfa, who did not recognise the validity of gifts of an undivided share, did uphold a gift in the form of *ṣadaḳa* or *hiba* to two poor persons but not to two wealthy persons (al-Shaybānī, *al-Djāmi*ᶜ *al-ṣaghīr*, Karachi 1407/1987, 356). In the former case, it was explained, the poor donees represented the actual single recipient, God. Certain Ḥanafīs are reported to have generalised this teaching and to have recognised as *ṣadaḳa* only gifts to the poor, whether designated by the donor as *ṣadaḳa* or *hiba*, since the intention of giving to the poor can only be to gain a heavenly reward, unlike gifts to the wealthy, where a wordly motive is imputed, even when they are designated as *ṣadaḳa* (al-Sarakhsī, *al-Mabsūṭ*, xii, 92).

Ṣadaḳa, unlike *zakāt*, may be given to non-Muslims. The earlier prohibition, or popular sentiment of the early Muslims, against doing so is understood to have been abrogated by Ḳurᵓān, II, 272, and the Prophet frequently gave *ṣadaḳa* to non-Muslims to bring them closer to Islam (Abu 'l-Hudā al-Ṣayyādī, *Ḍawᵓ al-shams*, 1394/1974, ii, 94). The validity of such *ṣadaḳa* applies in the first instance to *dhimmīs*, Jews, Christians and Magians, but according to some jurists *ṣadaḳa* may also be given to enemy aliens (*ḥarbī*) who are related or allied to the Muslims or who are being held as prisoners or whose conversion is hoped for. Such *ṣadaḳa* is deemed meritorious. Non-Muslims are not, however, to be given portions of sacrificial animals (*uḍḥiyya*). Some Shīᶜī jurists opposed giving *ṣadaḳa* to any non-Muslims or at least argued that *ṣadaḳa* to non-Muslims be given only in cases of need and only to the extent of that need, and there are Imāmī traditions that oppose the giving of *ṣadaḳa* to Sunnīs and Zaydīs.

The chief practical difference between *ṣadaḳa* and an ordinary gift lies in the almost universal recognition that a gift in the form of *ṣadaḳa* is not subject to revocation (*rudjū*ᶜ, *irtidjā*ᶜ, *iᶜtiṣār*). While the jurists differ in the degree to which they recognise the revocability, however much disapproved, of ordinary gifts, they agree that *ṣadaḳa* is in principle irrevocable, although the Ḥanafīs regard the irrevocability of *ṣadaḳa* to a wealthy person, which they uphold, as contrary to strict legal reasoning (*istiḥsān*). Mālikī doctrine departs from this principle to the extent of upholding an express right of revocation reserved by a father or mother in a gift of *ṣadaḳa* to their children, a rule extended by some Mālikīs to *ṣadaḳa* between strangers, rendering the gift inalienable during the lifetime of the donor, and both al-Shāfiᶜī and Aḥmad b. Ḥanbal are reported to have held that a father has a right to revoke *ṣadaḳa* to his child. The view of the Imāmī Abū Djaᶜfar al-Ṭūsī (d. 459/1067) (*al-Mabsūṭ*, iii, 314) that *ṣadaḳa* and ordinary gifts were legally indistinguishable, even as regards revocability, was regarded as exceptional, and it was, in fact, argued by others that *ṣadaḳa*, being irrevocable, should not be classified as a species of gift (al-Tahānawī, *Kashshāf*, ii, 1449).

Various explanations are offered for the irrevocability of *ṣadaḳa*. One is that the donor's heavenly reward for *ṣadaḳa* provides moral consideration for the gift, and gifts for which consideration has been given are irrevocable. This explanation, characteristic of the Ḥanafīs (al-Sarakhsī, *al-Mabsūṭ*, xii, 58), for whom it is part of a general theory of irrevocability, is cited by others as well, but is open to criticism. It is also suggested that *ṣadaḳa* is irrevocable inasmuch as is given in the first instance to God, the obligation to whom is discharged by delivery to the poor person (al-Sarakhsī, *al-Mabsūṭ*, xii, 58; cf. al-Zurḳānī, *Sharḥ al-Muwaṭṭa*ʾ, iv, 47 (irrevocable because for the sake of God)). Where the nature of the gift is disputed, the donee resisting revocation has the burden of proving that it is *ṣadaḳa*. Significantly, the rule of irrevocability was applied to gifts to the poor which were designated by their donors as ordinary gifts and not *ṣadaḳa*, but which were treated by the jurists, who looked to the substance, not the form, of the transaction, as within the scope of *ṣadaḳa*.

Closely related to the question of the irrevocability of *ṣadaḳa* was that of the re-acquisition of property given as *ṣadaḳa*. In a tradition the Prophet is reported to have told ʿUmar not to purchase a horse that he had previously given as *ṣadaḳa* and to have compared the person who goes back to his *ṣadaḳa* to a dog that returns to its vomit. For most jurists, re-acquisition by a voluntary act of the donor, such as purchase, gift or *ṣadaḳa*, is disapproved, but not passive re-acquisition by inheritance or a wife's re-acquisition as support of what she gave her husband as *ṣadaḳa*. For the Mālikīs, but not the Shāfiʿīs, the disapproval of re-acquisition extends to cases in which the property has passed through one or more intervening owners prior to its re-acquisition. A minority of jurists, including the Ẓāhirīs, regarded all instances of re-acquisition, even by inheritance, as prohibited. The disapproval of re-acquisition extends to obligatory *ṣadaḳa*, that is *zakāt*, and property given as expiation (*kaffāra*) or in discharge of a vow (*nadhr*), and to the enjoyment of the usufruct of what has been given, but not to *ṣadaḳa* intended for the public such as water for a mosque. The rule against re-acquisition (at least by purchase) is variously explained. According to one explanation, the donee in selling the *ṣadaḳa* to the donor will not feel free to bargain at arms' length, and the lower purchase price, coming as a consequence of the *ṣadaḳa*, will vitiate the original gift. A second explanation regards re-acquisition as compromising the "form" (*ṣūra*) of the *ṣadaḳa*, which requires completely divesting oneself of the gift. The Imāmī Muḥammad b. Idrīs al-Ḥillī (d. 598/1202) rejected the rules against re-acquisition as inconsistent with the donee's full right of ownership (*K. al-Sarāʾir*, Ḳumm 1410, iii, 174).

The acceptance of *ṣadaḳa* is subject to its own rules. Most consider acceptance under ordinary circumstances to be a "recommended" (*sunna*) act, obligatory only when the recipient is in the most dire need (*muḍṭarr*), and in such cases, the reward for taking may well exceed that for giving. A minority, including Ibn Ḥazm, require that a gift of *ṣadaḳa* be accepted, if only to be at once returned to the giver (*al-Muḥallā*, ix, 152-4).

Apart from a limited number of exceptions, including that of utter want, begging is prohibited, and even then the poor are encouraged to accept their fate without soliciting alms (cf. *Iḥyā*ʾ i, 298), the poor who do so being preferred as recipients of *ṣadaḳa* to beggars (cf. Ḳurʾān, II, 273). In any case, if one is able, it is better to earn one's livelihood by the most menial tasks than to beg (to thus be able to give *ṣadaḳa*). Begging has its own etiquette. Importunate begging, begging in a mosque, and begging in the name of God are all disapproved, although in the latter case, according to some, the beggar invoking God's name should not be turned away empty-handed. It is forbidden for a person of sufficient means to beg as if in need and disapproved for him to put himself in the way of receiving alms. Otherwise, such a person may accept unsolicited alms.

4. *The practice of* ṣadaḳa. The giving of *ṣadaḳa* was and remains widespread among Muslims, encouraged as it is by many Ḳurʾānic verses and traditions. These indicate that the giving of *ṣadaḳa* serves a number of distinct functions. *Ṣadaḳa* acts, in the first place, as expiation for sins, and it is recommended that it be given immediately following any transgression (*maʿṣiya*) (*Iḥyā*ʾ, i, 298, the advice of the legendary sage Luḳmān), for example, after intercourse with a menstruating woman. Voluntary almsgiving can thus make good shortcomings in the past payment of *zakāt*.

Closely related to the expiatory function of *ṣadaḳa* is its special role in affording protection against all manner of evils. According to a tradition, the *ṣadaḳa* that a Muslim gives wards off afflictions in this world, questioning in the grave, and punishment on Judgement Day (Ismāʿīl Ḥaḳḳī, *Tafsīr rūḥ al-bayān*, Istanbul 1911-25, i, 418). Accordingly, it is recommended to give *ṣadaḳa* at the start of each day as insurance against personal troubles (cf. Ḳurʾān, II, 274). The constant giving of little is said to please God more than the occasional giving of much. Although giving *ṣadaḳa* is recommended at all times, it is especially appropriate to give it upon significant occasions such as going to war or on a journey, and the tradition stating that "it is better for a man to give a dirham in alms while he is alive and healthy than one hundred dirhams when he is dying" did not prevent al-Ḥasan al-Baṣrī from teaching that "the most appropriate time for a man to give *ṣadaḳa* is his last day in this world and his first in the next" (al-ʿAbbās b. Aḥmad al-Ṣanʿānī, *Tatimma al-rawḍ al-naḍīr*, with *al-Rawḍ al-naḍīr*, iv, 122-3).

The positive side of giving *ṣadaḳa* lies in the merit that accrues to the giver, greater according to some than that of *zakāt*. *Ṣadaḳa* is encouraged as a means of bringing down sustenance (*rizḳ*) from heaven. The giver of *ṣadaḳa* is promised a reward many times what he has given, from ten times for *ṣadaḳa* given to a healthy person, ninety for a blind or handicapped person, nine hundred times for a needy relative, one hundred thousand for parents, and nine hundred thousand for a scholar.

The merit of giving *ṣadaḳa* does not stop with the giver. "Cure your sick with *ṣadaḳa*," the Prophet is reported to have said. Nor is the benefit of *ṣadaḳa* limited to the living, for according to the *ḥadīth*, *ṣadaḳa* may be given in the name of deceased Muslims, especially by a child on behalf of a parent, and its reward will be presented to them on a platter of light (*ṭabaḳ min nūr*). Although the Muʿtazila are alleged to have denied the efficacy of alms in the name of the deceased, a consensus is claimed for it (al-Nawawī, *Sharḥ Muslim*, vii, 90; al-Zurḳānī, *Sharḥ al-Muwaṭṭa*ʾ, iv, 56). The deceased is credited with the merit of having given the *ṣadaḳa*, a reward that does not diminish that of the giver.

In the giving of *ṣadaḳa* Muslims have found also a

means of moral edification. According to the Mālikī jurist Ibn Rāshid al-Ḳafṣī (d. 736/1336), the rationale (*ḥikma*) of the law of gifts is to purify the soul from the malady of avarice (*bukhl*) (*K. Lubāb al-lubāb*, Tunis 1346, 243), and *ṣadaḳa* embodies the virtue of generosity (*djūd, sakhā*ʾ), a reflection of the generosity of God the "All-Giving" (*al-Wahhāb*). "The believer is obligated to instruct his child in generosity and charity just as he is obligated to instruct him in monotheistic doctrine and belief, for the love of this world is the source of all sin," according to Abū Manṣūr al-Māturīdī (Ibn Nudjaym ..., Cairo 1334/1915, *al-Baḥr al-rāʾiḳ*, vii, 284). The transformation of *ṣadaḳa* in the act of giving is depicted in a tradition in which *ṣadaḳa*, personified, addresses its giver: "I was little and you made me much, I was small and you made me great, I was your enemy and you made me your friend, I was perishable and you made me permanent, I was guarded and you made me your guard." On the other hand, the role of *ṣadaḳa* in the redistribution of wealth has tended to be neglected in the growing literature by modern Muslims on Islamic economics, which has understandably focused on *zakāt* (but cf. A. Qureshi, *The economic and social system of Islam*, Lahore 1979, 91-7).

The Ḳurʾān urges believers not to undo their charitable gifts with "obligation" (*mann*) and "insult" (*adhā*). "Kind speech and forgiveness," it teaches, "are better than *ṣadaḳa* followed by insult" (II, 263-4). The giver is forbidden to regard himself as having conferred a benefit on the taker, an attitude than can be exhibited in thought, word or conduct or to demean the taker in any fashion. *Mann* is deemed to be a grave sin (*kabīra*), although there is disagreement as to whether it entirely destroys the reward of the *ṣadaḳa* or merely diminishes it (on the Muʿtazilī teaching of the cancellation of good deeds by bad (*iḥbāṭ*), see M.J. McDermott, *The theology of al-Shaykh al-Mufīd*, Beirut 1978, 258-62). "Obligation" and "insult" can be avoided by giving one's *ṣadaḳa* in secret. The Ḳurʾānic recommendation of "kind speech" is respected by the use of stereotyped replies in turning down the requests of beggars (see e.g. M. Piamenta, *The Muslim conception of God and human welfare as reflected in everyday Arabic speech*, Leiden 1983, 65-6; C.A. Nallino, *L'Arabo parlato in Egitto*, Milan 1939, repr. 1978, 134), although some early Muslims, like the Prophet, are reported to have preferred silence.

5. Ṣadaḳa *in Ṣūfism and Shīʿī esotericism*. The giving and receiving of *ṣadaḳa* have a special place in Ṣūfism with its encouragement of self-imposed poverty. This had led Ṣūfīs to be distinguished as givers of *ṣadaḳa* and by virtue of their poverty as suitable recipients. There are reports of fabulous sums given away as *ṣadaḳa* by those seeking to elevate their spiritual state (Abū Naṣr al-Sarrādj, *Kitāb al-Lumaʿ*, ed. Nicholson, Leiden 1914, 158; Ibn al-Djawzī, *Talbīs Iblīs*, ed. al-Munīr, Cairo, 170). Such Ṣūfīs could claim the Prophet and Abū Bakr as their models. In the light of the prophetic tradition that the "upper hand [of the giver] is superior to the lower hand [of the recipient]", pious givers of *ṣadaḳa*, unwilling to assume an attitude of superiority, resorted to such devices as putting their hand below that of the poor person (*Iḥyāʾ*, i, 286) or throwing the gift on the ground (al-Ḳushayrī, *al-Risāla*, Cairo, 114).

Ṣūfīs differed in their attitudes toward the acceptance of *ṣadaḳa*. Some, not wishing to compete with the rest of the poor (being themselves spiritually wealthy) and to avoid being indebted to anyone other than God, studiously refrained from accepting *ṣadaḳa*. But Ibn Ḳutayba (d. 276/889) already critically notes a Ṣūfī interpretation that the upper hand in the prophetic tradition refers to the recipient (*Talbīs Iblīs*, 179). In accepting *ṣadaḳa* the poor Ṣūfīs were actually conferring a benefit on the giver (al-Hudjwīrī, *Kashf al-maḥdjūb*, tr. Nicholson, Leiden 1914, 316-17 (rejecting the interpretation of the literalist *ahl-i ḥashw*; cf. *Lev. Rabbā* 34:8), and the Ḳurʾānic reference to God accepting *ṣadaḳāt* (IX, 104) and the tradition that the All-Merciful accepts *ṣadaḳa* in His right hand encouraged the view that the actual giver of *ṣadaḳa* was God (*Kashf al-maḥdjūb*, 316-317; *Iḥyāʾ*, i, 285; anon., *K. Adab al-mulūk fī bayān ḥaḳāʾiḳ al-taṣawwuf*, ed. Radtke, Beirut 1991, 41), a view said to have been cited by wealthy Ṣūfīs in justification of their abusive amassing of fortunes from alms (*Talbīs Iblīs*, 179). Al-Djunayd (d. 298/910 [*q.v.*]), who was among those who regarded it as better to take *ṣadaḳa* than *zakāt* (*Iḥyāʾ*, i, 302), strongly approved the practice of preferring the poor Ṣūfīs as recipients. The humiliation of begging was, in addition, imposed by some Ṣūfī masters on their novices as a form of spiritual discipline.

The influential Andalusian Ṣūfī Ibn ʿArabī (d. 638/1240) offered novel interpretations, at once paradoxical and harmonising, of *ṣadaḳa*. The superiority of voluntary alms to the obligatory *zakāt* is expounded on the basis of a metaphysical analysis of obligation (*Futūḥāt*, i, 590-1), but from another point of view the superiority of *zakāt* is upheld (*ibid.*, i, 587). The "upper" and "lower" hands of the tradition are both the "hands" of God, understood as different divine attributes bestowing mercy. The virtues of secret and public giving, properly understood, are such that both should be practiced (they are same for the gnostic or *ʿārif*). But the high point of the influence of *ṣadaḳa* upon Ṣūfī thought probably came with his predecessor Abu 'l-ʿAbbās al-Sabtī (d. 601/1205), whose entire teaching revolved around *ṣadaḳa*, the other institutions of Islam and even the nature of existence being interpreted in its light (al-Tādilī, *Akhbār Abi 'l-ʿAbbās al-Sabtī*, with his *al-Tashawwuf ilā ridjāl al-taṣawwuf*, Rabat 1404/1984, 453-4; C. Addas, *The quest for the red sulphur*, Cambridge 1993, 176-7).

The Shīʿī tradition of esoteric interpretation (*taʾwīl*) did not ignore *ṣadaḳa*. The giving of *ṣadaḳa* is taken as representative of the various forms of assistance that could be offered to the Imām of the Twelver Shīʿīs and his followers. The givers of *ṣadaḳa* mentioned in the Ḳurʾān are the Imāms, who bestow guidance. For the Fāṭimid Chief Justice al-Nuʿmān b. Muhammad (d. 363/957), voluntary *ṣadaḳa* symbolises the volunteered esoteric knowledge, in the form of admonition and exhortation, that those of higher ranks bestow on those below them (*Taʾwīl al-daʿāʾim*, ii, 94, iii, 63).

Bibliography: In addition to references in the text, see N.B.E. Baillee, *Digest of Moohummudan law*, London 1869, 1875 (vol. i, 2nd ed.), repr. Lahore 1975, i, 554-6 (Ḥanafī), ii, 224-5 (Imāmī), Juynboll, *Handbuch*, 94-6, 112 (Shāfiʿī), D. Santillana, *Istituzioni di diritto musulmano malichita*, Rome 1938, ii, 411-2, Y. Linant de Bellefonds, *Traité de droit musulman comparé*, Paris 1973, iii, 317-19. Tanzil-Ur-Rahman, *A Code of muslim personal law*, Karachi 1980, ii, 96-8; Ghazāli, *The Mysteries of almsgiving*, tr. N.A. Faris, Beirut 1966 (from *Iḥyāʾ ʿulūm al-dīn*), M.U. Kandhalvi, *Fazaʾil-e sadaqaat*, Karachi 1991 (tr. from the Urdu of a modern *ḥadīth* scholar), i; W.M. Watt, *Muhammad at Mecca*, Oxford 1953, 165-9; idem, *Muhammad at Medina*, Oxford 1956, 369-72 (Ḳurʾānic usage); W.F. Madelung, *The Hāshimiyyat of al-Kumayt and Hāshimī Shiʿism*, in *SI*, lxx (1989), 5-26 (prohibition of *ṣadaḳa*); N.A. Stillman, *Charity and social service in medieval Islam*, in

Societas, v/2 (1975), 105-115 (charitable institutions). (T.H. Weir-[A. Zysow])

ṢADAḲA, Banū, a name sometimes given in the mediaeval Arabic sources to the princes of the Mazyadids or Banū Mazyad [*q.v.*] in central ʿIrāḳ. The name derives from the most famous member of the line, Ṣadaḳa (I) b. Manṣūr (479-501/1086-1108 [*q.v.*]).

Bibliography: See that to mazyad, banū.

(Ed.)

ṢADAḲA b. Manṣūr b. Dubays b. ʿAlī b. Mazyad, Sayf al-Dawla Abu 'l-Ḥasan al-Asadī, ruler of al-Ḥilla of the Arab line of Mazyadids [see mazyad, banū]. After the death of his father in 479/1086-7, Ṣadaḳa was recognised by the Saldjūḳ sultan Malik Shāh as lord of the territory on the left bank of the Tigris. During the fighting between sultan Berk-yaruḳ and his brother Muḥammad, Ṣadaḳa was at first on the side of the former, but when Berk-yaruḳ's vizier, al-Aʿazz Abu 'l-Maḥāsin al-Dihistānī, demanded a large sum of money from him in 494/1100-1 and finally threatened him with war, Ṣadaḳa abandoned Berk-yaruḳ and had the *khuṭba* read in the name of Muḥammad. The sultan then tried to win him back by peaceful means; but Ṣadaḳa demanded that the vizier should be handed over to him, and as Berk-yaruḳ could not grant this, the negotiations fell through. Instead of agreeing with Berk-yaruḳ, Ṣadaḳa drove the sultan's governor out of Kūfa and himself occupied the town. In the following year al-Ḥilla [*q.v.*] was founded; previously, the Banū Mazyad had lived in tents.

When Gümüshtekin al-Ḳayṣarī by Berk-yaruḳ's orders appeared in Baghdād in the middle of Rabīʿ I 496/end of December 1102, Īlghāzī b. Artuḳ, Muḥammad's governor there, made an alliance with Ṣadaḳa. In the meanwhile, the caliph al-Mustaẓhir had Berk-yaruḳ again proclaimed sultan; nevertheless, Ṣadaḳa still declined to acknowledge his suzerainty. Soon afterwards Berk-yaruḳ's name was again dropped from the *khuṭba* and the *imāms* confined themselves for the time being to praying for the caliph only without mentioning by name either of the two contending sultans. But the war continued; by Rabīʿ II 496/January 1103, Gümüshtekin had to evacuate Baghdād and, as he was unable to hold out in Wāsiṭ either, Muḥammad was again recognised as sultan in both cities. Ṣadaḳa then extended his power over a great part of the ʿIrāḳ; in the same year, he took the town of Hīt [*q.v.*] on the Euphrates, which Berk-yaruḳ had granted as a fief to one of his followers, and appointed his cousin Thābit b. Kāmil governor of it. In Shawwāl 497/June-July 1104, Wāsiṭ met the same fate and here Muhadhdhib al-Dawla al-Saʿīd b. Abi 'l-Khayr was appointed governor. Next came the turn of Baṣra, which had fallen into the hands of the Saldjūḳ Ismāʿīl b. Arslāndjīḳ during the war between Berk-yaruḳ and his brothers. It was not till after the death of Berk-yaruḳ that sultan Muḥammad was able to think of dislodging Ismāʿīl from it and in 499/1105-6 he asked Ṣadaḳa to fight him. In Djumādā I of the same year/January-February 1106, Ṣadaḳa took the field against Ismāʿīl, who was soon forced to surrender, whereupon Ṣadaḳa appointed one of his grandfather Dubays's *mamlūk*s named Altūntāsh to govern Baṣra. But as the latter was very soon surprised and captured by Bedouin bandits, the sultan himself appointed another governor in his place. In Ṣafar 500/October 1106, Kayḳubādh b. Hazārasp al-Daylamī, lord of Takrīt [*q.v.*], had also to yield. After the death of Berk-yaruḳ, Muḥammad had sent the *amīr* Aḳsunḳur al-Bursuḳī [*q.v.*] to Takrīt to occupy the town. As Kayḳubādh would not obey, he was besieged. After several months had passed, he saw the impossibility of holding out any longer, and sent to Ṣadaḳa and surrendered the city to him. Warrām b. Abī Firās was then appointed governor of Takrīt. But Muḥammad could not always look on quietly while Ṣadaḳa's power kept growing, especially as the latter never had any scruples about affording shelter to anyone who had fallen into disgrace with the sultan. When Abū Dulaf Surkhāb b. Kaykhusraw, lord of Sāwa [*q.v.*], took refuge with him and Ṣadaḳa refused to hand him over, long negotiations between Ṣadaḳa and the sultan only resulted in an open breach between suzerain and vassal. The sultan set out in person from Baghdād with a large army, and in the fierce battle which was fought (according to the most usual statement) in the latter half of Radjab 501/beginning of March 1108, Ṣadaḳa was killed at the age of fifty-nine. Like his ancestors, he bore the title *Malik al-ʿArab*; the highest praise is given him by Arab poets and historians for his virtues, notably his liberality and readiness to give assistance, and he is rightly described by A. Müller (*Der Islam im Morgen- und Abendland*, ii, 122) as "a true Bedouin, brave, stubborn and wily".

Bibliography: Ibn Khallikān, ed. ʿAbbās, ii, 490-1, tr. de Slane, i, 634; Ibn al-Athīr, x, passim; Abu 'l-Fidāʾ, *Annales*, ed. Reiske, iii, 264, 308, 344, 354, 358, 362; Bundārī, in Houtsma, *Recueil de textes rel. à l'hist. d. Seldjoucides*, ii, 76, 102, 259; *Recueil des hist. des croisades*, *Hist. or.*, i, 9, 247-52, iii, 487, 517, 531; Weil, *Geschichte der Chalifen*, iii, 156-9; M.F. Sanaullah, *The decline of the Saljūqid empire*, Calcutta 1938, index; C.E. Bosworth, in *Camb. hist. Iran*, v, 108, 115, 121; ʿAbd al-Djabbār Nādjī, *al-Imāra al-Mazyadiyya ... 387-558/997-1162*, Baṣra 1970, 96 ff. See also the *Bibl.* to mazyad, banū.

(K.V. Zettersteen)

al-**SAʿDĀN**[1], "the two lucky (planets)", a technical term in astrology referring to the two beneficent planets Jupiter and Venus. On the opposite, Saturn and Mars are *al-naḥsān*[i], "the two unlucky, maleficent (planets)"; cf. al-Khʷārazmī, *Mafātīḥ al-ʿulūm*, ed. van Vloten, 228-9. In more detail, al-Bīrūnī, *K. al-Tafhīm li-awāʾil ṣināʿat al-tandjīm*, ed. and tr. R.R. Wright, London 1934, §§ 381-2, in the explanation of the "natures" (*ṭibāʿ*) of the planets, describes Saturn as *al-naḥs al-akbar*, and Mars as *al-naḥs al-aṣghar*, i.e. the greater and the lesser evil, and, correspondingly, Jupiter as *al-saʿd al-akbar* and Venus as *al-saʿd al-aṣghar*, i.e. the greater and the lesser luck. This division goes back to Ptolemy, *Tetrabiblos* i, 5 (on the ἀγαθοποιοί, beneficent, and κακοποιοί, maleficent, planets, according to the teachings of "the ancients", οἱ παλαιοί), and is based on the mixture of the four humours—warm, cool, dry, humid—in each planet. Mercury, according to Ptolemy, is ambivalent; when associated with another planet, it reinforces its power, either beneficent or maleficent; al-Bīrūnī (*loc. cit.*) adds that Mercury, when standing alone, is inclined to beneficence. Cf. also A. Bouché-Leclerc, *L'astrologie grecque*, Paris 1899, 101; J. Ruska, al-saʿdān in *EI*[1].

Bibliography: Given in the article.

(P. Kunitzsch)

al-**SĀDĀT**, Anwar, Egyptian statesman (1918-81).

He was born into a poor family in the Egyptian village of Mīt Abū Kōm, 60 km/40 miles north of Cairo. His father was a civil servant who had to support his wife and thirteen children. Sādāt spent his first seven years in his village, where he was left in the care of his grandmother while his parents were working in Sūdān (his mother was Sudanese). He went to the village school and thoroughly enjoyed his life amongst the local peasants. He later claimed that his early experiences gave him a deep understanding of the Egyptian peasant's mentality and of his deep roots in the countryside. He considered the *fallāḥ* to be the foundation of society and the guardian of its traditions. When in power, he enjoyed return visits to his village in order to re-establish contact with ordinary people.

In 1925 he moved with his father to Cairo, where he went to secondary school in 1930. In 1936 he just managed to pass his General Certificate of Education. Perhaps more importantly, he was drawn into the political atmosphere of street demonstrations against the British presence and of calls for evacuation and independence. This was the background of a number of young Egyptians at the time, among them ʿAbd al-Nāṣir [*q.v.* in Suppl.], who were later to play an active role in politics. Like ʿAbd al-Nāṣir, al-Sādāt entered the Military Academy, newly-open to sons of lower class families and previously the preserve of the upper classes.

He graduated as an army officer in 1938 and was sent with ʿAbd al-Nāṣir to Manḳābād in Upper Egypt. The two of them, with one or two others, formed a group of disgruntled soldiers who were eventually to form the core of the Free Officers. Al-Sādāt was transferred to Cairo, where the circle of officers dedicated to the overthrow of the régime gradually expanded. ʿAbd al-Nāṣir was the real leader of the group, although al-Sādāt in his memoirs tended to exaggerate the centrality of his own role. In his *Revolt on the Nile* (London 1957) he glorified ʿAbd al-Nāṣir as the leader of the movement. In his autobiography *In search of identity* (London 1978), he put himself at the centre and was much more critical of ʿAbd al-Nāṣir. Unbiased accounts would place al-Sādāt very much in the secondary role.

During the second World War, al-Sādāt showed distinct pro-Nazi sympathies in the belief that Germany would be victorious and give Egypt her independence. He was arrested by the British for dubious activities, tried by an Anglo-Egyptian court and imprisoned until October 1944. He escaped from jail and was on the run until the end of the war.

After the war, he did not go back to the army but was active on the fringes of political violence and terrorism. He admitted to being implicated in the assassination of Amīn ʿU͟thmān, the former Minister of Finance, in January 1946. He was re-arrested and tried only in 1948, when he was released without conviction. He then drifted into business and journalism without any great success. Surprisingly, he did not take part, with ʿAbd al-Nāṣir and his comrades, in the 1948 war in Palestine which had such a deep effect on their thinking about the future of Egypt. However, al-Sādāt's lack of success in business led him to rejoin the army as a captain in 1950, when he met again ʿAbd al-Nāṣir and ʿAbd al-Ḥakīm ʿĀmir. They joined together in planning the 1952 coup, although ʿAbd al-Nāṣir did not quite trust al-Sādāt, who had suspect links with al-Ik͟hwān al-Muslimūn [*q.v.*] and even with the palace. He was thus not given a leading role in the coup. On 21 July 1952 he was chosen to read a prepared statement on the radio announcing the coup and the army takeover.

From then on until ʿAbd al-Nāṣir's death, al-Sādāt was a faithful son of the revolution; some would say, a trimmer. He certainly worked loyally in ʿAbd al-Nāṣir's shadow and was at times mocked for his assiduous, self-effacing sycophancy. Once again, al-Sādāt provided two versions of his life with ʿAbd al-Nāṣir. In *My son, this is your uncle Gamal* (Cairo n.d.), published during ʿAbd al-Nāṣir's lifetime, he provided an extravagantly eulogistic picture of his master who could do no wrong and who was the only person who could lead Egypt to a bright future. In his later autobiography, he blamed ʿAbd al-Nāṣir for his dictatorial attitude, his unwillingness to heed advice and for having led Egypt into numerous disastrous situations, the Suez crisis, the Yemen war and the 1967 Israeli defeat.

Al-Sādāt held a number of posts under ʿAbd al-Nāṣir none of any great significance. He edited the newspaper *al-D͟jumhūriyya*, where he was able to express his own rather extravagant views. In 1962 ʿAbd al-Nāṣir appointed him Secretary-General of the Constituent Assembly with the task of drafting the National Charter. Al-Sādāt was later to claim that this document was merely a front to show that, ostensibly, ʿAbd al-Nāṣir was interested in the common man.

Al-Sādāt's most important role was to lead Egypt into one of the greatest setbacks. In 1962 ʿAbd al-Nāṣir sent him to Yemen to advise on whether Egypt should intervene in the struggle between Royalists and Republicans. Al-Sādāt wrongly reported that the Royalists could soon be defeated and that Egypt should send troops to support the Republicans. ʿAbd al-Nāṣir allowed himself to be dragged into a quagmire of fighting until 1967. Al-Sādāt was discredited and receded into the background for a time.

ʿAbd al-Nāṣir's prestige fell to its lowest ebb with the defeat in 1967 in the Six-Day War against Israel. He stayed on as President, tired and ill, and in 1969 he appointed al-Sādāt his deputy in an ostensible attempt to share the responsibilities of office. To what al-Sādāt owed this elevation, other than his total loyalty to ʿAbd al-Nāṣir, is not clear. However, when ʿAbd al-Nāṣir died in September 1970, al-Sādāt was there, ready to take over.

Emerging from the shadows, he quickly showed himself to be his own man, with policies radically different from those of his predecessor. He especially chafed under three of ʿAbd al-Nāṣir's bequests—the close ties with the Soviet Union, socialism and the Israeli occupation of the Sinai. He immediately made moves to lessen the burdens of socialism with his "revolution of rectification" and by opening the economy to Western investment, the *infitāḥ*. His relationship with the Soviets was uneasy from the first, and he surprised the world when he ordered all Soviet military experts to leave the country in July 1972. He had, however, to replace Russian aid, and, against all previous wisdom, he turned to the West and, in particular, to the Americans. He became popular in the West, the moderate after ʿAbd al-Nāṣir, who seemed to forgive and to forget all his past criticism of Britain and the United States.

He then turned to the real enemy, Israel, and after months of careful military planning on the morning of 6 October 1973 he launched an attack across the Suez Canal against Israeli fortifications. The Israelis were taken completely by surprise, but after fierce battles they were able to cross the Canal and surround the Egyptian army. The battle ended in a stalemate, but al-Sādāt had shown that Egyptians could plan and fight successfully and it gave him a new basis on which to negotiate. It gave him popularity in Egypt, and he was able to bring the Americans into the search for peace. Henry Kissinger helped to bring about a disengagement; the Israelis moved back across the

Canal, which was reopened for the first time since 1967.

At home, al-Sādāt was facing severe economic problems. He wanted peace with Israel in order to pursue economic development in an atmosphere of stability and security which would encourage foreign investment. A big drain on the budget were the large subsidies on basic foodstuffs and other items. To try to obtain loans from the World Bank (which disliked subsidies), al-Sādāt agreed to withdraw subsidies from several items. The result was immediate and shocking. In January 1977 rioting broke out all over the country. There were many deaths and the army had to be brought in to restore order. Al-Sādāt was stunned. He restored the subsidies and looked around for scapegoats. He blamed the Left and the Marxists, and arrested hundreds of them. It was the beginning of a gradual decline in his popularity. He overreacted as he felt threatened, and introduced stricter censorship and declared a state of emergency.

He had to look abroad for ways of regaining some of his popularity. He felt the peace process was stalled again, and stunned the world by making a dramatic visit to Jerusalem in November 1977 to present his case to the enemy. In a speech to the Knesset he made clear his conditions for a stable peace. The Israelis made no commitments immediately, and it needed the intervention of President Jimmy Carter to bring the two sides closer together during meetings at Camp David in March 1979. A peace treaty was signed between Egypt and Israel by which Israel agreed to withdraw from Sinai, diplomatic and trade relations were to be established and Israeli ships were to be allowed to use the Suez Canal.

The rest of the Arab world believed that al-Sādāt had betrayed the Palestinian cause, since the Israeli Prime-Minister, Menachem Begin, had made no concessions at all to the Palestinians. Egypt was expelled from the Arab League and opposition to the treaty was widespread in Egypt itself. The more extreme Muslim religious groups were very bitter in their opposition. They also believed that al-Sādāt had sold the country to the West, and to the United States in particular. They preached revenge against the traitor, and one group, *D̲j̲ihād*, put its message into practice when they assassinated al-Sādāt in October 1981 during a parade to celebrate the October crossing of the Canal.

Al-Sādāt was in many ways a leader who had the courage to bring in radical new policies, but he allowed himself to be carried away with his popularity in the West. At the same time he was viewed with deepening indifference or hostility by his own people and hated by other Arabs. Corruption spread around him, while he retreated into an isolation of utter self-confidence and an unwillingness to tolerate any criticism or opposition. His killers claimed that they had complete justification in ridding Egypt of a corrupt tyrant.

Bibliography: Anwar Sadat, *Revolt on the Nile*, London 1957; idem, *Yā waladī hād̲h̲ā ᶜammuka D̲j̲amāl*, Cairo 1958; idem, *Egypt in search of an identity*, London 1978; R.W. Baker, *Egypt's uncertain revolution under Nasser and Sadat*, Cambridge, Mass. 1979; R. Israeli (ed. and tr.), *The public diary of President Sadat*, 3 vols., Leiden 1979; J. Waterbury, *The Egypt of Nasser and Sadat*, Princeton 1983.

(D. HOPWOOD)

SADD AL-**D̲H̲ARĀʾIᶜ** (A.), a term of Islamic law, literally, closing off the means that can lead to evil.

The concept is based on the S̲h̲arīᶜa's tendency to prevent evil (*darʾ al-mafāsid*) and a legal maxim states that it has preference over achieving good (*d̲j̲alb al-maṣāliḥ*). *Sadd al-d̲h̲arāʾiᶜ* is viewed as a continuation of *maṣlaḥa mursala* rather than an independent source. Despite this, *sadd al-d̲h̲arāʾiᶜ* is often included in the books of law as an alternative legal source. Said to be based on the Ḳurʾān and *sunna*, it represents a mechanism devised by Mālikī jurists to resolve loopholes in the law. The practical function of *sadd al-d̲h̲arāʾiᶜ* is to prevent improper usage of a legal means to achieve an illegal end. However, unlike *maṣlaḥa* and *ᶜurf*, *sadd al-d̲h̲arāʾiᶜ* is probably the only source of Islamic law to be presented in a negative form. Some scholars, including Muḥammad Abū Zahra, have attempted to study it from a positive angle by focusing on *d̲h̲arāʾiᶜ* alone. This, however, would appear to deprive the source of an essential dimension in favour of a preconceived proviso to prevent a prohibited action. As Ibn al-Ḳayyim states in his *Iᶜlām*, "when objectives cannot be reached without certain means, these means become a part of these objectives and are treated as the objectives themselves".

Sadd al-d̲h̲arāʾiᶜ does not target what is good, but what is evil or leads to evil. Muslim lawyers use the "likelihood" of an evil result to prohibit the action that could lead to it. They differentiate between three frequencies, rare, frequent and imminent, although imminent is only labelled as such by assuming the occurrence of the result on the basis of circumstance. An example of a rare (*nādir*) occurrence is planting vines. Although vines could be used to produce alcohol, planting them is not prohibited, since they have many advantages that outweigh the small chance of harm. Selling the grapes to a person known to make wine would be prohibited. In that case, the chance of a harmful result is *kat̲h̲īr* (frequent) and should be prevented. The third category is based on the intention of the person rather than the possible outcome. Due to the significance of the intention, the four schools vary in how often they refer to *sadd al-d̲h̲arāʾiᶜ*, with the Ḥanbalī and Mālikī schools referring to it most frequently. This is largely caused by their different methodology in establishing the intention of a person. The Imām al-S̲h̲afiᶜī did not give a share of the inheritance to a wife divorced during her husband's last illness. Al-S̲h̲afiᶜī argued that "there is no proof that her husband divorced her merely to prevent her inheriting". The Ḥanafī school, like the Malikī and Ḥanbalī, refers to the circumstances to find the proof. The fact that the man pronounced the divorce during his last illness is an indication that he did so to prevent his wife's inheriting. This unjust intention is thus blocked by giving her her share of the inheritance in spite of her divorce.

Bibliography: Ibn Ḳayyim al-D̲j̲awziyya, *Iᶜlām al-muwaḳḳiᶜīn*, Cairo n.d., iii, 111-20; Ibrāhīm al-S̲h̲āṭibī, *al-Muwafaḳāt*, ed. A. Draz, Beirut n.d., ii, 227-33, iv 194-201; Muḥammad Abū Zahra, *Uṣūl al-fiḳh*, Cairo 1958, 287-9; N.J. Coulson, *A history of Islamic law*, Edinburgh 1964, 141; A. Zaydān, *Al-Wad̲j̲īz fi uṣūl al-fiḳh*, Bag̲h̲dād 1987, 245-59; M.H. Kamali, *Principles of Islamic jurisprudence*, Cambridge 1991, 310-20.

(M.Y. IZZI DIEN)

AL-**SAᶜDĪ**, ᶜABD AL-RAḤMĀN B. ᶜABD ALLĀH b. ᶜImrān, chronicler of Timbuktu, b. 30 Ramaḍān 1004/28 May 1594, d. after 1065/1655-56. His father's male line was traced to the Banū Saᶜd, though the family had been settled in Timbuktu for several generations. Nothing is known of his youth, but in 1036/1626-7 he became *imām* of the Sankore mosque of Bena near Jenne. In mid-life he was employed by the administration of the Bās̲h̲alik of Timbuktu (an institution which owed its origins to the occupation of the area by the forces of the Saᶜdian sultan al-Manṣūr al-Dhahabī in 999/1591), especially in the administration of Jenne and the Masina region of the Inland Niger Delta. In 1056/1646 he became chief secretary to the Bāshalik in Timbuktu.

His chief claim to fame is his history of Timbuktu and the Middle Niger, simply entitled *Taʾrīkh al-Sūdān*. This work, in 35 chapters, is mainly concerned with the history of the Songhay empire from the mid-9th/15th century until 1591 and the history of the Bāshalik of Timbuktu from that date down to 1655. The latter period occupies about half of the work. The early chapters are devoted to brief histories of earlier Songhay dynasties, of imperial Mali and of the Tuareg, and to biographies of the scholars and saints of both Timbuktu and Jenne. His acknowledged sources are few. For the 11th/17th century, he relies mainly on personal knowledge, evidently supported by notes (there are several chapters of obituaries and noteworthy events), and on records of the Bāshalik; for earlier periods he rarely mentions his sources, other than "trustworthy persons" or "one of my colleagues". He does, however, cite Ibn Baṭṭūṭa, the anonymous *al-Ḥulal al-mawshiyya* and, for some of the biographies of Timbuktu scholars, the biographical dictionary of Aḥmad Bābā al-Tinbuktī (d. 1036/1627 [*q.v.*]), *Kifāyat al-muḥtādj* (a supplement to Ibn Farḥūn's *al-Dībādj al-mudhahhab*). The *Taʾrīkh al-Sūdān* is a prime source for the history of the Middle Niger from the mid-15th to the mid-17th century, our only other chronicle being the *Taʾrīkh al-fattāsh* of Ibn al-Mukhtār (based on Maḥmūd Kaᶜti) which effectively stops at 1001/1593.

Bibliography: *al-Ṭālib* Muḥammad b. Abī Bakr al-Burtulī, *Fatḥ al-Shakūr fī maᶜrifat aᶜyān ᶜulamāʾ al-Takrūr*, ed. Muḥ. Ibrāhīm al-Kattānī and Muḥ. Ḥadjdjī, Beirut 1401/1981, 176; Muḥammad b. Muḥammad Makhlūf, *Shadjarat al-nūr al-zakiyya*, Cairo 1341/1930-1, no. 1198; Brockelmann, S II, 717; J. Lippert, in *MSOS, Afr.*, ii (1899), 244-53; Ch. Monteil, *Notes sur le Tarikh Es-Soudan*, ed. V. Monteil, in *BIFAN*, xxvii (1965), 479-530. The *Taʾrīkh al-Sūdān* was ed. and tr. into French by O. Houdas, Paris 1898-1900, repr. 1966, and is the source for the little we know about al-Saᶜdī's life. An annotated English translation is being prepared by the writer of this article. (J.O. Hunwick)

SAᶜDĪ, Abū ᶜAbd Allāh Musharrif al-Dīn b. Muṣliḥ Saᶜdī, known as Shaykh Saᶜdi, poet and prose writer of the 7th/13th century, is one of the most renowned authors of Persia.

He was born in Shīrāz early in the 7th/13th century, probably between 610-15/1213-19, and died in the same city on 27 Dhu 'l-Ḥidjdja 691/9 December 1292. More perhaps than any other Persian writer who preceeded him, or of his own period, Saᶜdī refers to himself constantly and in highly specific terms throughout the course of his writings; from shortly after his death until the present century elaborate biographies of the poet have been inferred from these references (the fullest and best known being that of Henri Massé, Paris 1919). More recent scholarship on the period and a greater awareness of the sophistication of medieval authors' constructed authorial personae has called many of these details in doubt. The virtual certainty that some are poetic inventions (for example, his capture by Europeans and subsequent deliverance by ransom (*Gulistān*, Book 2, anecdote 32), his unmasking of a fraudulent Brahmin at the Hindu temple in Somnāth (*Bustān*, Book 8, anecdote 8), his claim to have seen someone "in the west" be borne across water on his prayer-mat (*Bustān*, Book 3, anecdote 15)), has caused the authenticity of the remainder to become questionable, with the result that few facts can be deduced with certainty about the poet's life. We are left with the paradoxical situation of knowing very little about an author whose life and personality are considered to be familiar to all students of Persian literature. Among the stories which Saᶜdī recounts about himself which may or may not be true are that he was orphaned at an early age, that he studied and subsequently taught at the Niẓāmiyya college in Baghdād, that al-Suhrawardī and Ibn al-Djawzī were his teachers, that he was married at least twice (once in the Yemen, once to the daughter of the individual who, he claimed, ransomed him from the Europeans), and that he travelled extensively throughout the *dār al-Islām* and beyond. His work reveals a mastery of traditional Islamic education and a general intellectual sophistication that could well have been gained in an institution such as the Baghdād Niẓāmiyya. One claim can be accepted with little doubt; his writings imply wide knowledge of the world beyond Persia, and extensive travels clearly played a part in his life (he frequently admonishes his audience to treat travellers well), though whether he ever ventured into either Hindu areas in the East or Christian areas in the West is more problematic. With characteristic humour, Saᶜdī cautions his audience not to believe travellers' tales (*Gulistān*, Book 1, anecdote 32) since they are often exaggerations or outright lies, and as his most insistently presented persona in his works is that of a traveller, this should be taken as a warning when considering the truth of many of his statements. As to his being orphaned at an early age, it is true that Saᶜdī does show strong sympathy for orphans in his works. As with the admonitions to treat travellers benignly, the sentiment could well have traditional Islamic, rather than personal, causes, but Saᶜdī's concern does seem unusually strong and is perhaps drawn from personal experience. The anecdotes about his marriages are both incidental to his making moral points; both are placed in relatively distant lands (Syria, the Yemen—it is noticeable that Saᶜdī's stories seem to become less reliable as their provenance gets further from Shīrāz) and are probably to be regarded as fictions. His sexual preferences would seem to have been for young males (Southgate 1984) (no doubt poetic convention played a role, but here too his concern is so insistently presented as to make it seem at least partly personal) and this too perhaps makes the stories of his two marriages slightly less probable, though marriage for reasons that had nothing to do with sexual preference was of course expected of adult Muslims. The reference to al-Suhrawardī does not occur in the earliest mss. of the *Bustān*, besides which Saᶜdī was, as G.M. Wickens has remarked (*Morals pointed and tales adorned*, Leiden 1974, 267) "a great name-dropper", which makes the statement dubious. Some authors, however, e.g. Zarrīnkūb (1988, 175) consider that the reference may have been a later addition to the *Bustān* by Saᶜdī himself, as he lived almost forty years after the poem was first completed, and that it records an authentic incident in the poet's life. His claim to have been a pupil of the theologian Ibn al-Djawzi (*Gulistān*, Book 2, anecdote 20) has been doubted on the compelling grounds that Ibn al-Djawzī was dead before Saᶜdī's birth, but the statement is more credible if we accept that it was al-Djawzī's less illustrious grandson who was Saᶜdī's teacher (Ṣafā, iii, 1987, 594). Saᶜdī was also said to have met his great contemporary the Ṣūfī poet Mawlānā Djalāl al-Dīn Rūmī [*q.v.*], and a passage in a perhaps apocryphal treatise (*risāla*) attributed to Saᶜdī suggests that he met the historian Djuwaynī (author of the *Taʾrīkh-i Djahān-gushāy*) and Djuwaynī's brother, chief of the Il-Khānid civil service in Persia. There seems no particular reason to credit these anecdotes (stories of meetings between well known contemporaries being a common invention); the meeting with the Djuwaynī brothers is the more likely as Saᶜdī wrote panegyrics to both of them, but this need not imply actual contact so much as a wish for patronage.

It is in examining the identity of Saᶜdī's patrons and dedicatees that the most reliable information about his life and the world in which he lived can be gained. At least fifteen historical personages were either the subject of panegyrics by Saᶜdī or had works by him dedicated to them. His first datable work, completed after his youthful travels and his return to Shirāz, was the *Bustān* (655/1257) which he dedicated to the local Salghurid atabeg Abū Bakr b. Saᶜd b. Zangī; the *Gulistān*, completed a year later, was dedicated to this ruler's son, Saᶜd b. Abī Bakr b. Saᶜd [see SALGHURIDS]. The poet's *takhalluṣ* or pen-name of Saᶜdī is taken either from the latter, or from his grandfather Saᶜd b. Zangī. (Both derivations present problems; the grandfather died in 623/1226 when Saᶜdī in all probability was still an adolescent; the grandson ruled for only twelve days. The adoption of the *takhalluṣ* may have been made in honour of the grandson while he was still heir presumptive.) Abū Bakr b. Saᶜd ruled as atabeg for over thirty years, and managed to persuade the Mongols, who were busy devastating the north of Persia and ᶜIrāḳ, to leave him and Shīrāz in relative peace. Though his son ruled for a mere twelve days (one of Saᶜdī's most affecting public poems is an elegy on his death in the strophic form known as *tardjīᶜ-band*), the succession stayed within the same ruling house until 662/1264, and Saᶜdī continued to write panegyrics to its members. In a sense, the control of Shīrāz may be said to have stayed for a little longer under the control of the house of Saᶜd, as a granddaughter of Abū Bakr b. Saᶜd married Mengütemür, a son of the Mongol conqueror Hülegü, and she assumed the governorship, at least nominally, of Fārs. The very complex and dangerous political allegiances of the time are reflected in the list of dedicatees of Saᶜdī's poems. On the one side we have an elegy by him on the death of the last ᶜAbbāsid caliph (killed by the Mongols during their sack of Baghdād in 656/1258; Abū Bakr b. Saᶜd immediately travelled to the Mongol court and offered his congratulations, probably as a means of keeping Hülegü away from Fārs), and panegyrics on Saldjūḳ Shāh, the last independent Salghurid ruler of Fārs; on the other there is a panegyric on the murderer of both men, Hülegü, as well as panegyrics on various Mongol appointees to the government of Fārs, and to Ābish Khātūn, granddaughter of Abū Bakr b. Saᶜd and wife of Hülegü's son Mengütemür. As Ābish Khātūn and Saᶜdī both certainly knew, survival at this period depended on accommodation, and Saᶜdī's multiple allegiances, as evidenced by his panegyrics, are but the literary equivalent to the political manoeuvrings of his masters. Saᶜdī has received some blame for his apparent readiness to praise whoever might be in power in Fārs, but the practice was expected and such expediency was both prudent and commonplace (the Djuwaynī brothers, and their brilliant civil, scholarly and literary work done under Mongol patronage, are another case in point). Further, some of his public poems (e.g. his elegy on the death of the last ᶜAbbāsid caliph) cannot have been written with the hope of gain and could have been construed as politically risky. Saᶜdī himself claimed it was indigence that drove him to write panegyrics, and it may also be pointed out that his works in this form frequently consist of moral advice rather than undiluted and incredible praise. Despite the censure sometimes accorded them, his panegyrics contain very fine passages (e.g. the verses to the Mongol *ṣāḥib dīwān* (head of the chancery) Djuwaynī, beginning *kudām bāgh bi-dīdar-i dūstān mānad*).

Saᶜdī's works include the long (*ca.* 4,100 couplets) poem in *mathnawī* form, the *Bustān*, the prosimetrum (*maḳāma*) the *Gulistān*, panegyrics (*ḳaṣāʾid*) on various prominent men of his time, a small number of panegyric elegies (*marthiyāt*), numerous lyric poems (*ghazaliyyāt*), a number of shorter epigrammatic poems (*ḳiṭᶜāt* and *rubāʾiyyāt*) and a small collection of obscene pieces (*khabīthāt/hazaliyyāt*). He also wrote a small number of poems (mainly *ḳaṣāʾid*) in Arabic. Six prose treatises (*risālāt*) are also attributed to Saᶜdī, though the attribution of at least some of these is doubtful. Of these treatises the most interesting is the fifth, the *Naṣīḥat-i mulūk*, a brief mirror for princes. A second *mathnawī*, the *Pand-nāma* ("Book of advice") is now regarded as spurious. Saᶜdī's writings were edited by one Bīsītūn within thirty years of his death, and the mss. tradition derives from Bīsītūn's work. The many modern editions (a number of which omit the obscene pieces) of his collected works (*kulliyyāt*) are based on the recension prepared by Muḥammad ᶜAlī Furūghī in the early 1950s.

Saᶜdī's fame rests chiefly on the *Bustān*, the *Gulistān* and his *ghazals*. The *Bustān* and the *Gulistān* are both collections of moralising anecdotes, arranged according to subject matter in books (ten in the case of the *Bustān*, eight in the case of the *Gulistān*). Since both works have been frequently imitated, their formal innovations may not at first be apparent. As a collection of moral tales in verse, rather than a continuous narrative, with a Ṣūfī tinge but without the explicit programmatic Ṣūfism of Sanāʾī's, ᶜAṭṭār's or Rūmī's works, the *Būstan* is unlike any significant previous poem in Persian literature. Similarly, the mixture of prose and verse presented in the *Gulistān*, if not the first instance of its kind in Persian (ᶜAbd Allāh Anṣārī's religious treatises, with their occasional interposed verses, are a previously existing example), immediately makes the genre central to Persian literary history and elevates it to a new level of sophistication.

In order to understand the social and political background against which the works were composed, it is only necessary to point out that the *Gulistān* was completed in the same year as the sack of Baghdād and the extinction of the ᶜAbbāsid caliphate by the Mongols. Accommodation with those in power, a preternatural awareness of the vicissitudes of fortune, an extreme wariness of personal and political enemies, the frequent necessity to mask one's true feelings, and the advice to be content with even indigent survival, far from centres of power and influence, are themes that are repeatedly stressed by the author. The epithet "Machiavellian" which has sometimes been applied to Saᶜdī as a reproach is in many ways a valid characterisation, in that both Machiavelli and Saᶜdī, writing in turbulent and potentially disastrous political circumstances, strove to provide advice that would ensure their audience's successful negotiation of an exceptionally risky and faction-ridden world. The crucial difference is that, whereas Machiavelli writes directly to and for a central actor in such political upheavals, Saᶜdī's intended audience, despite his dedication of both works to powerful if provincial rulers, would seem to be much more those on the sidelines of major events, hoping to survive by luck and their wits. Further, in Saᶜdī's case, to this "Machiavellian" preoccupation with survival must be added a strong sympathy for the vulnerable and weak, especially if they are in any way ill-treated (it is very noticeable for example how often children figure in Saᶜdī's anecdotes, more perhaps than in the writings of any comparable figure in Persian literature), and a constantly reiterated plea for tolerance, perhaps the result of the poet's travels (but see below), the most famous example of which is the poem beginning *banī ādam aᶜḍā-yi yak paykarand* ("the children of Adam are members of one body..." (*Gulistān*, Book 1, anecdote 10).

The moralising tenor of Saᶜdī's writing in the *Bustān* and *Gulistān* on the one hand, and the works' attention to sheer survival on the other, may appear to be contradictory elements. It is undeniable that there is occasionally a sense of strain between the two concerns, but the poet's attempts to integrate them constitute a significant part of the distinctive flavour of the two works, and their immense popularity may perhaps be traced largely to this combination of goals. Although Saᶜdī's extreme facility in the writing of metrical aphorisms has led to many of his lines passing into the common stock of proverbial moral exhortation, the cumulative effect of the anecdotes in both the *Bustān* and the *Gulistān* is not that of an inflexible, internally coherent and absolute ethical system. Occasionally, the moral with which a story closes seems to have little to do with the story itself; anecdotes that offer contradictory moral advice can appear in close proximity (e.g. anecdote 17 of Book 1 of the *Bustān* recommends honesty when dealing with oppressive rulers; anecdote 19 of the same book recommends dissembling prudence when dealing with oppressive rulers) and, similarly, contradictory moral aphorisms are not uncommon (e.g. anecdote 20 of Book 2 of the *Bustān* ends with the advice to return evil with good; anecdote 26 of the same book ends with the statement that oppression of an oppressor is appropriate justice). The dilemma of whether to treat well enemies who may later have it in their power to harm you is one that Saᶜdī very frequently refers to, and anecdotes can be found supportive of both: on the one hand, the wisdom of pre-emptive draconian punishment and, on the other, the meliorating effects of timely mercy. That this relativism is at least to some extent deliberate is suggested by the books' structure; in the seventh books of both the *Bustān* and the *Gulistān*, there are long passages that imply the impossibility of absolute standards when dealing with fallible humanity. In the *Bustān*, the passage in question is that on calumny (towards the end of Book 7), in which it is stated, with typical humorous exasperation on Saᶜdī's part, that no course of action can meet with universal approval. Relativism is even more apparent in the last very lengthy anecdote of Book 7 of the *Gulistān*; here Saᶜdī presents a debate between himself and a *darwīsh* on the relative merits of poverty and wealth; the debate is inconclusive and the two take their question to a religious judge, who admonishes each of them to take account of the truth of the other's arguments and to be reconciled to one another. This conclusion, that moral conclusions are elusive (and that mutual respect and tolerance are preferable to disruptive ethical absolutism) can be gleaned from both the *Gulistān* and *Bustān*, if the anecdotes are taken as balancing and even occasionally contradicting each other rather than singly.

Saᶜdī's innovations, or refinements and organisation of previously extant elements, are no less apparent in his *ghazals*. The form had existed at least since the time of Sanāʾī (i.e. for approximately a century) before being taken up by him [see GHAZAL, ii], but it is with Saᶜdī that it achieves its "classical" perfection (which was to be reshaped and even, in the terms Saᶜdī had established it, disintegrated by Saᶜdī's fellow townsman Ḥāfiẓ [*q.v.*] in the following century). In Saᶜdī's hands, the *ghazal* becomes a lyric unified by tone and subject matter and by his poetic trademark, the (relative) simplicity of his language and its extraordinarily mellifluous elegance. The convention of placing one's *takhalluṣ*, in the penultimate or last line of the *ghazal* became standard with Saᶜdī, though he did not originate the practice. In his hands the *ghazal* achieves its final emancipation from the language of the *ḳaṣīda* (from which it originated), in that the rhetoric no longer addresses itself to public praise with the concomitant expectations of remote allusiveness and arcane corruscation (as for example, in the *ḳaṣīda*s of Khāḳānī and Anwarī [*q.vv.*]); the emotional tenor has become inward and private rather than brilliant and public, and this inwardness is confirmed by the substitution of the poet's own *takhalluṣ* as the culminating moment of the poem, rather than a reference to the public object of praise as was conventional in the *ḳaṣīda*. The indeterminacy of the addressee (a beloved, God, or a patron) of the *ghazal*, again a feature of the form before Saᶜdī's time, is treated with increased subtlety. The inferiority of the speaker to the addressee, axiomatic in the *ḳaṣīda*, is transformed from a political statement into an avowed simplicity of heart which, while certainly conventional, opens the way to finely nuanced adumbrations of personal, private emotional experience (although the possibility that some of Saᶜdī's *ghazals* are political statements under the guise of personal erotic/mystical complaint has also been suggested). Saᶜdī's *ghazals* are divided into four groups: *ṭayyibāt* ("noble, pleasant"— this is by far the largest group); *badāyiᶜ* ("rarities"); *khawātīm* ("seals, final"); and *ḳadīm* ("ancient"). It is not known whether the groupings are the poet's own. Though the *Bustān* and *Gulistān* are profoundly admired in Persia, their fame is second to that of the *ghazals*, which are considered Saᶜdī's greatest achievement. Perhaps because of the relatively easier task presented by the translation of narrative as against lyric work, the *Bustān* and *Gulistān* have in general been admired more than the *ghazals* in the West.

The achievement of Saᶜdī is by any reckoning very great, and his work has been a major formative influence on subsequent writing in Persian. In his writings all trace of a sense of the marginality, or purely local preoccupations, of Persian culture vis-à-vis Islam as a whole has disappeared. This may in part be due to the profound shock of the Mongol invasions, which must at first have appeared to call in question the very survival of the *dār al-Islām* in the East; in the ensuing chaos, the culture of hitherto relatively peripheral areas flourished. One such area was Fārs, where Islamic culture continued more or less undisturbed. (The "coming of age" of Persian as a language of international Islamic culture at this time is also evidenced by Saᶜdī's contemporary Rūmī in Turkey and the slightly younger Amīr Khusraw [*q.v.*] in India.) It is also undoubtedly due to the breadth of Saᶜdī's own sympathies and knowledge. This breadth of sympathy is further apparent in the "democratisation" of Saᶜdī's subject matter; previous poets (e.g. ᶜAṭṭār), who had looked beyond the court for subject matter, had done so largely for Ṣūfī reasons; Saᶜdī seems to do so from pure human sympathy, from a sense of the validity of life at any social level in and for itself. On a par with this is the relative simplification, and thus greater accessibility for a more various audience, of his language when we compare it with that of many of the court poets who preceeded him. Such wide sympathies have led to Saᶜdī being seen as a kind of universal deist (Emerson) or a "humanist" by some western commentators (Yohannan 1987), but there are clear limits to Saᶜdī's sympathies and these should not be overlooked. They are defined with few exceptions by the boundaries of Islam, and are operative within the *sharīᶜa*, hardly beyond it. His writings contain disparaging references to Jews (especially), to Christians and to Hindus (the anecdote concerning the Hindu temple at Somnāth (*Bustān*, Book 8) is such a farrago of misinformation as to make one suspect that it is a deliberate joke, but even if this is so, the joke is hardly one that will appeal now). A notable exception to this tendency is the anecdote (*Bustān*, Book 2, anecdote 1) that has Abraham reproved by God for acting inhospitably to a Zoroastrian (this can, however, be seen as an example of a general unwillingness, discernible in the works of many mediaeval Persian authors, to disparage the customs and civilisation of pre-Islamic Persia, rather than as an indiscriminate tolerance of non-Muslims). Even within Islam, Saᶜdī's sympathies clearly stopped short of being extended to blacks, and certain of his remarks about women have been seen by some as verging on misogyny (the penultimate story of Book 1 of the *Gulistān* is evidence of an at least temporary violent contempt for both blacks and women). Much of this must undoubtedly be attributed to the time in which Saᶜdī was writing, in that he was merely repeating the common prejudices of his age and culture (and part of the shock registered at such moments in Saᶜdī is because he seems so sympathetic to the disadvantaged and/or unfamiliar elsewhere), but there were other Persian writers of his period, and previous periods, who did not indulge in such gratuitously disparaging language to the same extent. ᶜAṭṭār and, in general, Rūmī are examples. That these poets were exclusively Ṣūfī authors is significant; their sense of the illusoriness of the physical world, and therefore of the irrelevance of its categories for judging people's true worth, is not shared by Saᶜdī, whose world-view accepts the validity of common-sense categories within which the earth is considered as a place of tangible reality, happiness and suffering. Saᶜdī's Ṣūfism (he apparently ended his days as a member of a Ṣūfī foundation in Shīrāz) would seem to be close to the "practical" Ṣūfism of al-Ghazālī; that is, it is a way of living in and dealing with the world rather than of renouncing it. Ṣūfism for Saᶜdī is a means of surviving with dignity, and relatively uncompromised, in a dangerous and morally dubious environment. It is linked to notions of retirement from strife rather than the passionate search for transcendence which we find in Saᶜdī's contemporary Rūmī.

One of the most interesting aspects of Saᶜdī's writings is his insistence on his own persona as a presence in his works and thus in his audience's mind. This has led to him being one of the most "known" of Persian authors, in that his readers feel aware of his character to an extent that is true of hardly any other Persian writer from the middle ages. He presents himself as widely travelled, of such ready sympathy that he can be intimate with both the powerful and the weak, almost always ready to intercede on behalf of the disadvantaged, tolerant, a peacemaker and a man who hates slander, pious but not bigoted, simple-hearted with the simple but also canny enough to see through hypocrisy and deception. Occasional stories against himself lend verisimilitude, but they are always placed in his childhood or youth, with the implication that he has now learned better. He is also insistent on his own fame, recounting stories of how he has heard his works recited as far away as India. Much of this must surely be taken as the deliberate creation of an authorial persona. It is, for example, similar to the persona created by the English mediaeval writer Chaucer, and probably for the same reasons; both poets present themselves as charming raconteurs—wise, attractive, avuncular companions, men with broad sympathies who have seen the world but still basically share the plain man's "common sense" world-view. This cosmopolitan, compassionate, shrewd persona is to be regarded chiefly as an advertisement for the work. Significant here, too, is Saᶜdī's strong sense of humour and his previously-noted warning that travellers are liars; Saᶜdī's presentation of himself is a brilliant literary device that he undertakes with every sign of relish at his undoubted skill; it is perhaps the greatest of his literary triumphs.

Perhaps in part because of their self-consciously "international" and unprovincial interests, Saᶜdī's writings were highly influential as models not only in Persia itself but also in Turkey of the Saldjūḳs and the *beyliks* and subsequently in the Ottoman empire. Similarly, in Mughal India, his works quickly achieved great fame, and his *ghazal*s were imitated by Persian-speaking Indian poets within his own lifetime or shortly afterwards. Generally speaking, in countries that have at different periods looked to Persia as a cultural model, he is thought of as the archetypal Persian author, and his works have been a fundamental part of the educational curriculum of those wishing to become acquainted with Persian belle-lettres. His popularity in the Ottoman empire and Mughal India led to his name being known in the West at a relatively early period. French, German and Latin translations of parts of his oeuvre appeared in the mid-7th century, and Gentius brought out an edition of the *Gulistān*, with a Latin translation, in Amsterdam in 1651. The benevolence of Saᶜdī's usual sentiments and his frequent advocacy of irenic tolerance made him particularly attractive to Enlightenment authors, and Voltaire pretended, tongue in cheek, that his *Zadig* was a translation from Saᶜdī. In Germany Herder, and in England Sir William Jones, were both enthusiastic advocates of Saᶜdī's work. In America, Benjamin Franklin borrowed an anecdote from the *Bustān* (that of Abraham and the Zoroastrian) "on account of the importance of the moral, well worth being made known to all mankind", and Emerson saw the poet in more or less the same light—i.e. as an Oriental version of a pragmatic Enlightenment deist. By the mid-19th century, Saᶜdī had been more extensively translated into European languages than any other Persian author, with the possible exception of Ḥāfiẓ.

Bibliography: 1. General works. Browne *LHP*, ii, 525-39; A.J. Arberry, *Classical Persian literature*, London 1958, 186-213; J. Rypka *et alii History of Iranian literature*, Dordrecht 1968, 250-3; R. Levy, *An introduction to Persian literature*, New York and London 1969, 116-27; G. Morrison, in *History of Persian literature* ... (*H. der Or.*, Abt. 1, Bd 4, Abschnitt 2), Leiden-Köln 1981, 59-63; Dhabīḥ Allāh Ṣafā, *Taᵓrīkh-i adabiyyāt dar Irān*, iii, [5]Tehran 1988.

2. Studies. Saᶜīd Nafīsī, *Taᵓrīkh-i durust-i dar gudhasht-i Saᶜdī*, in *Madjalla-yi Dānishkada-y*

Adabiyyāt-i Tihrān, vi/1 (1959), 64-82; ᶜAlī Da<u>sh</u>tī, *Ḳalamrū-yi Saᶜdī*, Tehran 1966; Minoo Southgate, *Men, women and boys: love and sex in the works of Saᶜdī*, in *Jnal. of the Soc. for Iranian Studies*, xvii/4 (autumn 1984), 423-52; *<u>Dh</u>ikr-i <u>dj</u>amīl-i Saᶜdī* (Essays and verses in commemoration of the 800th anniversary of Saᶜdī's birth), 3 vols., Tehran 1986; J.D. Yohannan, *The poet Saᶜdī*, New York 1987; ᶜAbd al-Ḥusayn Zarrīnkūb, *<u>Dj</u>ustu<u>dj</u>ū dar taṣawwuf-i Īrān*, Tehran 1989. (R. Davis)

SAᶜDIDS, Saᶜdians, a <u>Sh</u>arīfian dynasty which ruled in Morocco from the mid-10th/16th century to *ca.* 1070/1659. The Saᶜdids or Saᶜdians or Banū Saᶜd, make their appearance in the history of Morocco at the beginning of the 10/16th century, at the time when the last ruling dynasty of Berber origin, the Banū Waṭṭās [see waṭṭāsids], was in decline. The Banū Saᶜd claimed to have come originally from Yanbuᶜ in the Tihāma of the Ḥi<u>dj</u>āz and to be descendants of the Prophet; whatever their origin, they bore the title of *<u>sh</u>arīf*.

Since the 8th/14th century, they had lived in the central valley of the Darᶜa, at Tagmaddart. In the following century they established themselves in the Sūs at Tidsi. The first of the Saᶜdids to play a role in the internal politics of Morocco was called Abū ᶜAbd Allāh Muḥammad b. ᶜAbd al-Raḥman al-Ḳāʾim bi-amr Allāh. He was a saintly man, a disciple of al-<u>Dj</u>azūlī [*q.v.*], who enjoyed genuine prestige among the neighbouring tribes. In 916/1510 he was appointed war-leader and campaigned against the Portuguese, formally established at Agadir [*q.v.*] since 919/1513 (in reality since 1505). In 917/1511, he had named his eldest son Aḥmad al-Aᶜra<u>dj</u> governor of the Sūs; two years later he appointed him his successor. On his death in 923/1517-18, at Afū<u>gh</u>āl in the Ḥāḥa, two of his sons shared the political power which he had built up: al-Aᶜra<u>dj</u> governed to the north of the Atlas, the younger, Maḥammad al-<u>Sh</u>ay<u>kh</u>, in the Sūs. These two *<u>sh</u>arīfs* were the real founders of the Saᶜdian dynasty, the first <u>Sh</u>arīfian dynasty to take power in Morocco.

The two principal objectives of these princes were the struggle against the Christians, in this case the Portuguese, and the conquest of northern Morocco, in other words the eviction of the Waṭṭāsids. In 929/1523 hostilities were declared between them and the *amīr* of Fās, Muḥammad al-Burtugālī. Then in 930/1524 the two *<u>sh</u>arīfs* took possession of Marrāku<u>sh</u>, assassinating the *amīr* of the Hintāṭa, al-Nāsir Bū <u>Sh</u>entūf, who was in occupation of the town, and al-Aᶜra<u>dj</u> became the head of the new state, established *de facto*, with Marrāku<u>sh</u> as its capital. The tomb of al-<u>Dj</u>azūlī, which had been at Afū<u>gh</u>āl, was transferred there; thus the city became a venerated site. On two occasions the successor of Muḥammad al-Burtugālī, Mawlāy Aḥmad al-Waṭṭāsī, attempted to attack Marrāku<u>sh</u>, but without success, and in 916/1530 Waṭṭāsids and Saᶜdians established a frontier between their two "kingdoms", running from Umm al-Rabīᶜ to Wād al-ᶜAbīd. Six years later, the Waṭṭāsid army was routed by that of the *<u>sh</u>arīfs* and in 1537, the latter took possession of Tafilālt, part of the territory belonging to the Waṭṭāsids.

The *<u>sh</u>arīfs* also pursued the struggle against the Portuguese, and in 948/1541 Agadir, or Santa-Cruz do Cap de Cúe, was taken by Mawlāy Maḥammad. This victory led to a rift between the two Saᶜdian brothers, when Mawlāy Maḥammad refused to share the booty seized from the Portuguese fortress. The younger imprisoned his elder brother, and then in 949/1542 an accord was signed between them. In spite of this apparent reconciliation, a violent quarrel took place between the two princes in 950/1543, and al-Aᶜra<u>dj</u> was exiled with his entire family to the Tafilālt; Mawlāy Maḥammad was thus able to occupy Marrāku<u>sh</u>.

Sole master of the Saᶜdian lands, Mawlāy Muḥammad renewed the struggle against the Banū Waṭṭās of Fās; in 1545, near *Wādī* Derna, he succeeded in taking prisoner Aḥmad al-Waṭṭāsī. Set free two years later, the latter ceded Miknās, the <u>Gh</u>arb and the Habṭ to the Saᶜdian. The same year, 953/1547, the *<u>sh</u>arīf* laid siege to Fās, a siege which lasted until January 1549, at which date Fās fell, and Mawlāy Maḥammad became the sole ruler of Morocco. As for Aḥmad al-Waṭṭāsi, he was sent to Marrāku<u>sh</u>. One of the first consequences of this defeat was the abandonment by the Portuguese of their fortresses at Arzila/Aṣīla and at al-Ḳaṣr al-ṣa<u>gh</u>īr.

At the same time that the Saᶜdids were undertaking the conquest of Morocco, the Ottoman power established at Algiers was attempted to advance towards the west. Between the two new powers in the Ma<u>gh</u>rib lay an ancient "kingdom", Tlemcen, ruled by an enfeebled dynasty, the Banū Zayyān or ᶜAbd al-Wādids [*q.v.*]: the conquest of Tlemcen seemed a necessity both to the Ottomans and to the Saᶜdians. On 23 <u>Dj</u>umādā I 957/9 June 1550, a <u>Sh</u>arīfian army commanded by one of the sons of Mawlāy Maḥammad, Mawlāy al-Ḥarrān, entered Tlemcen. It did not stay there long, since a large proportion of the Moroccan troops had to be transferred to the Tafilālt in order to fight against Aḥmad al-Aᶜra<u>dj</u>, who had rebelled against his younger brother. In the summer of the same year, when the Saᶜdian garrison, left in the Zayyānid capital under the command of two of the sons of al-<u>Sh</u>ay<u>kh</u>, was attacked by the Pa<u>sh</u>a of Algiers, it was unable to resist, and in February 1551 the Algerian army took possession of Tlemcen, which remained henceforward under Ottoman control, the Moulouya/Malwiyya serving as a frontier between Morocco and the Algerian regency.

However, the Waṭṭāsids had not lost hope of regaining power: an uncle of the prince defeated in 956/1549, Abū Ḥassūn, who had for some time found refuge in Spain, succeeded with the aid of the Algerians in defeating the <u>Sh</u>arīfians under the walls of Fās, which he entered on 14 Ṣafar 962/7 January 1554. He even allied himself to al-Aᶜra<u>dj</u> and to the latter's son, Zaydān, who had succeeded in making themselves masters of the Tafilālt. And if a message addressed by Abū Ḥassūn to his new ally had not been intercepted by Mawlāy Maḥammad al-<u>Sh</u>ay<u>kh</u>—with the result that the defeat of his son Mawlāy ᶜAbd Allāh was transformed into victory—the Waṭṭāsid would probably have been able to regain the Moroccan throne. But al-Aᶜra<u>dj</u> and Zaydān surrendered, and al-<u>Sh</u>ay<u>kh</u> was enabled to renew the offensive against Abū Ḥassūn, who succumbed to a fatal lance-blow at Musallama on 15 <u>Sh</u>awwāl 961/13 September 1554. On this occasion, the Saᶜdians became the undisputed masters of Morocco.

Three years later, on 29 <u>Dh</u>u 'l-Ḳaᶜda 964/23 October 1557, Mawlāy Maḥammad was assassinated by a member of his Turkish bodyguard, Ṣalāḥ b. Kyāhya. Shortly before this, the other *<u>sh</u>arīf*, al-Aᶜra<u>dj</u>, imprisoned in Marrāku<u>sh</u>, had been executed by the governor of the town, along with seven of his sons and grandsons. The senior branch of the Saᶜdids was thus eliminated and the succession of the *<u>sh</u>arīf* Mawlāy Maḥammad fell to his son, Mawlāy ᶜAbd Allāh al-<u>Gh</u>ālib bi'llāh. At the start of his reign, which was marked by an anti-Turkish policy, three of his brothers advanced as far as Algiers, and two of them even reached Istanbul. In 965/1558, the new sovereign succeeded in defeating the Turko-Ottomans of Algiers near Wādī 'l-Laban and invading the Regency. He attempted, without success, to forge an alliance with the king of Navarre, Antoine de Bourbon. On the other hand, he succeeded in establishing peaceful relations with Spain, which earned him the hostility of the marabouts whose influence was increasing throughout the Maghrib. He also sought to deprive the Portuguese of Mazagan, their last fortress, but failed. Mawlāy ᶜAbd Allāh died in 981/1574, and his son Mawlāy Maḥammad, already governor of Fās, was recognised as sovereign without hindrance. But another Saᶜdid prince was a pretender to the Moroccan throne, Mawlāy ᶜAbd al-Malik, one of the brothers of the late *sharīf*, who from 1557 onward was conspiring with the Ottoman Sultan to obtain military and financial support. Two years after the death of his brother, Mawlāy ᶜAbd al-Malik, with a Turko-Algerian force, supplemented by Arab contigents, defeated his nephew at al-Rukn and entered Fās on 10 Dhu 'l-Ḥidjdja 983/11 March 1576. As for Mawlāy Maḥammad, he reached Marrākush, and then, following a further defeat at the hands of his uncle, he took refuge in the Sūs. Subsequently, with the help of the king of Spain, he made his way to Peñon de Vélez.

While the uncle had been aided by the Ottomans, the nephew ultimately obtained the aid of the Christian princes, especially that of the king of Portugal, Don Sebastian, who dreamed of conquering Morocco. In Djumādā I 986/July 1578, a substantial Christian army set out in support of Mawlāy Maḥammad. The clash between this army and that of Mawlāy ᶜAbd al-Malik took place on 4 August near the Wādī Mekhāzen; the two Moroccan pretenders and the king of Portugal died in the combat. This battle, the so-called Battle of the Three Kings, had vast repercussions in Europe as in Morocco, where it aroused a veritable surge of national consciousness. The victor was another brother of Mawlāy ᶜAbd Allāh, Mawlāy Aḥmad, who became sultan. His reign was one of the most significant in the entire history of Morocco, as well as one of the longest, since it lasted until 1012/1603.

Having reorganised the country, Mawlāy Aḥmad established diplomatic relations with the Ottoman empire, as well as with Christian nations including Spain, Portugal and England; in 993/1585 English merchants founded the Barbary Company which enjoyed free and exclusive trade with Morocco for twelve years. But the major achievement of the reign was the conquest of the western Sūdān; contacts between the Songhay of the loop of the Niger and Morocco had begun in the 5th/11th century. In the 10th/16th century, the salt-pans of Tegheza, between Timbuktu and Marrākush, were coveted by the Moroccans, and in 986/1578 Mawlāy Aḥmad asked Askia Dāwūd, the ruler of the Songhay, to allow him the exploitation of these salt-pans for a year. Three years later, the Saᶜdian *sharīf* ordered the occupation of Touat and the Gourara, and in 992/1584 sent to the western Sūdān a first expedition, which was a disastrous failure. The conquest of Sūdān was decided upon and in 1591 the Pasha Djūdar, commanding the Sharīfian troops, entered first Gao and then Timbuktu. In 994/1596 the Moroccans occupied the loop of the Niger from Koukya to Djenna; the western Sūdān came under Saᶜdian domination, and every year, tribute of Sudanese gold was paid to Marrākush. Dissension between the sons of Mawlāy Aḥmad, henceforward to be known as al-Manṣūr al-Dhahabī, cast a cloud over the end of the reign of the *sharīf*, who died of the plague on 17 Rabīᶜ I/25 August 1603.

During his lifetime, Mawlāy Aḥmad had given some of his sons a degree of administrative responsibility. Following his death, the princes Zaydān and Abū Fāris had themselves declared sultans, at Fās and at Marrākush respectively. A third brother, Maḥammad al-Shaykh al-Maʾmūn, who had been imprisoned by his father for rebellion, succeeded in defeating his brother Zaydān at al-Mouata and being proclaimed in his turn as sovereign at Fās (1604), while Mawlāy Zaydān gained control of the Sūs; the fratricidal struggles which were to lead to the dissolution of the dynasty had begun.

A fourth prince soon claimed his share of the "kingdom", sc. Mawlāy ᶜAbd Allāh, a son of al-Maʾmūn who, in 1015/1606, succeeded in establishing himself at Marrākush. All these struggles devastated the country and destitution was rife. Al-Maʾmūn, whose power was gradually ebbing away, attempted to obtain the support of Tuscany, then appealed to Spain for help, where he was obliged to take refuge in March 1608 as Mawlāy Zaydān had regained power in Marrākush and was threatening Fās. The following year, in the hope of gaining the support of the government of Philip III, king of Spain, the *sharīf* al-Maʾmūn signed a treaty according to which he guaranteed, in exchange for military aid, to cede to him the port of Larache/al-ᶜArāʾish [*q.v.*], which Spain had long coveted, lest it be occupied by the Ottoman fleet. On 20 November 1610 Spanish troops commanded by the Marquis of San Germán took possession of Larache, the port and the town. But instead of helping Mawlāy Muḥammad al-Maʾmūn, this action lost him every chance of returning to his throne. He was assassinated in 1022/1613 at Fadjdj al-Fāras.

In 1018/1609, the above-mentioned prince Mawlāy ᶜAbd Allāh, had had his uncle Abū Fāris strangled. He was thus able to succeed his father at Fās, but the kingdom of Fās was no more than a much-reduced territory. Despite the agitations of one of his brothers, Mawlāy Zaghūda, and despite the total anarchy existing in Fās, the reign of Mawlāy ᶜAbd Allāh lasted until his death in 1032/1623. After him another of his brothers, Mawlāy ᶜAbd al-Malik, ruled nominally in Fās for four years, but the descendants of al-Maʾmūn were no longer in a position to exert real power.

After the cession of Larache to the Spanish, the only Saᶜdian prince considered to be a legitimate sovereign was Mawlāy Zaydān. While the descendants of Mawlāy Muḥammad al-Shaykh tried to maintain their position at Fās, Zaydān established his capital at Marrākush and was recognised by foreign powers as sultan of Morocco. In 1021/1612 he was subjected to the attacks of a religious leader, Abū Maḥallī [*q.v.* in Suppl.], who had declared holy war against the Saᶜdids, and who even succeeded in entering Marrākush. Mawlāy Zaydān was obliged to flee to Ṣāfī [*q.v.*], whence he attempted to leave Morocco with his retinue, and seventy-three cases of Arabic books. These cases were loaded on a French ship which was intercepted and impounded by the Spanish, who declared it to be legitimate war-booty; the Arabic volumes thus remained in the possession of the Spanish, and were later deposited in the Escurial.

The state of anarchy which pervaded the country enabled various religious chiefs or marabouts to make themselves more or less independent of the ailing central power. Those of the Sūs did not pose a real threat

Genealogical table of the Saᶜdid Shurafāʾ

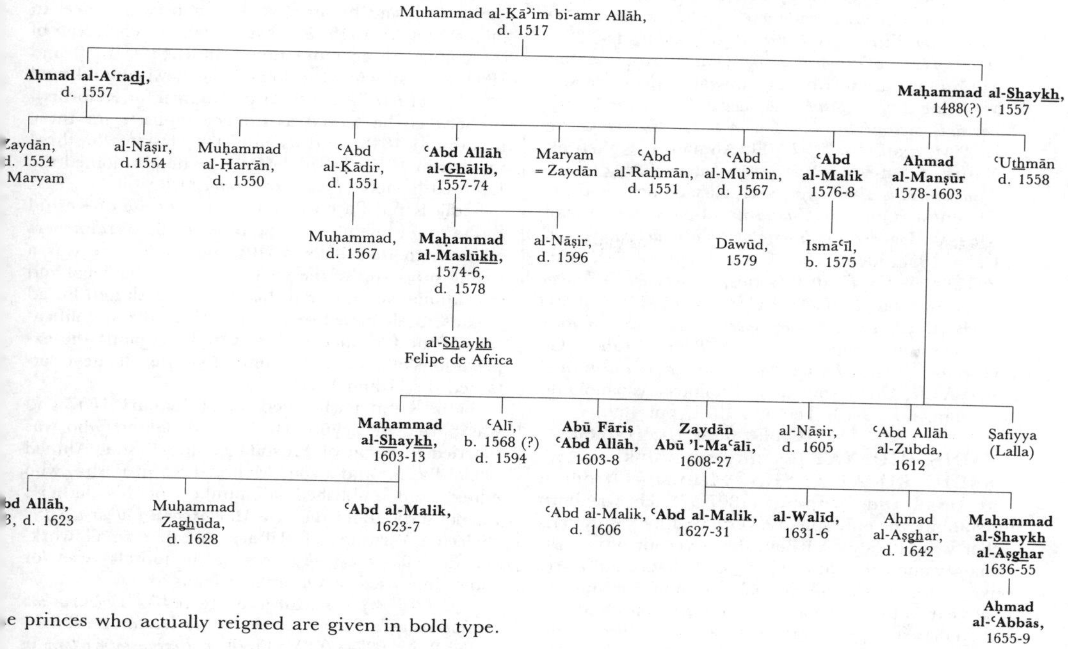

The princes who actually reigned are given in bold type.

to the dynasty, but those of northern Morocco put the government of the *sharīfs* in danger; the arrival of the Moriscos, especially following their expulsion from Spain (1609-10), and their occupation of Rabat which they declared an independent republic, as well as the agitation of a "marabout", al-ᶜAyyāshī, in the region of Salā and then at Salā itself, ultimately rendered Mawlāy Zaydān's authority purely theoretical in the north of Morocco.

The *sharīf* Zaydān died in 1036/1627, and his successor was his eldest son Mawlāy ᶜAbd al-Malik, who reigned only four years: he was assassinated on 6 Shaᶜbān 1040/10 March 1631. The treaty which he had negotiated with France was signed by his brother Muḥammad al-Walīd, on 20 Ṣafar 1041/17 September 1631. Al-Walīd, assassinated in turn, was succeeded by a third son of Mawlāy Zaydān, Mawlāy Maḥammad al-Shaykh al-Aṣghar. The latter succeeded in maintaining control over Morocco, or rather over the region of Marrākush, until 1065/1654; he faced opposition from another maraboutic power, the Dilāʾiyya of the central Atlas [see DILĀʾ in Suppl.]. The last Saᶜdian sovereign was the son of al-Shaykh, Aḥmad al-ᶜAbbās, who inherited a thoroughly decadent kingdom. After his assassination in 1069/1659, Morocco became the object of contention between the *shurafāʾ* of the Tafilālt, the ᶜAlawīs, and the Dilāʾiyya of the Atlas. The last-named were decisively defeated in 1079/1668, and the Saᶜdid *shurafāʾ* were succeeded by the ᶜAlawī *shurafāʾ* [see ᶜALAWĪS].

If the last Saᶜdid princes were characters without much depth, and were in many cases debauched, the first *sharīfs* were outstanding statesmen who encouraged the cultural and artistic life of the country. Although very little remains of the palace of Aḥmad al-Manṣūr, the Badīᶜ of Marrākush, various religious monuments from the Saᶜdian period have been preserved in this town: the great mosques of Bāb Dukkāla and of Mouassin, the tomb of al-Djazūlī, the Ben Yūsuf *madrasa*, and above all the mausoleums of the *sharīfs*, Ḳubūr al-Ashrāf. At Fās, the Saᶜdians built little, but to them are owed the two pavilions at the extremities of the court of the mosque of al-Ḳarawiyyīn, as well as the *basātīn*, the northern Burdj and the southern Burdj built by Aḥmad al-Manṣūr in 1582.

Until the death of this sultan, the economic situation was such that there were periods of considerable prosperity; the relations of Saᶜdian Morocco with European countries facilitated the export of various products such as textiles, horses, wheat, saltpetre, and especially sugar, principally to England (cultivation of the sugar-cane had appeared in Morocco in the 3rd/9th century, and disappeared shortly after the death of Aḥmad al-Manṣūr). It is also to the credit of the Saᶜdid *shurafāʾ* that they presided over the birth of a genuine feeling of national consciousness, which resisted any attempt at domination by Christians or Ottomans.

Bibliography: *Chronique anonyme de la dynastie saᶜdienne*, ed. G.S. Colin, in *Coll. de textes arabes* publ. by l'Institut des Hautes Études marocaines, Rabat 1934; Fr. tr. E. Fagnan, in *Extraits inédits relatifs au Maghreb*, Algiers 1924, 360-457; Abū Fāris ᶜAbd al-Azīz al-Fishtālī, *Manāhil al-ṣafāʾ fī akhbar al-mulūk al-shurafāʾ*, Rabat 1964; Muḥammad al-Ṣaghīr b. al-Hadjdj b. ᶜAbd Allāh al-Īfranī, *Nuzhat al-hādī. Histoire de la dynastie saadienne au Maroc (1511-1670)*, ed. and Fr. tr. O. Houdas, Paris 1888-9; D. de Torres, *Relación del origen y suceso de los xarifes y del estado de los reinos de Marruecos, Fez y Tarudante*, ed. y estudio de Mercedes Garcia Arenal, Madrid 1980; *Les sources inédites de l'histoire du Maroc, 1ère série, dynastie saᶜdienne*, France, i-iii; Spain, i-iii; England, i-iii; Netherlands, i-vi; Portugal, i-v, Paris 1905-61; A. Cour, *L'établissement des dynasties des Chérifs au Maroc*, Paris 1904; idem, *La dynastie marocaine des Beni Wattās*, Constantine 1920, 113-234; E. Lévi-Provençal, *Les historiens des Chorfa*, Paris 1922, 87-140; R. Le Tourneau, *Les débuts de la dynastie saᶜdienne jusqu'à la mort du sultan M'hammed ech-Cheikh*

(*1557*), Publ. de l'Institut d'études supérieures islamiques d'Alger, Algiers 1954; idem, *La décadence saʿdienne et l'anarchie marocaine au XVIIe siècle*, in *Annales de la Faculté des Lettres d'Aix*, xxxii, 187-225; idem, *Histoire de la dynastie saʿdide, extrait de* al-Turǧumān al-muʿrib ʿan duwal al-Mašriq wal Maǵrib *d'Abu al-Qāsim b. Aḥmad b. ʿAlī b. Ibrāhīm al-Zayyānī, presenté par L. Mougin et H. Hamburger*, in *ROMM*, xxiii (1983), 7-109; Aḥmad b. Khālid al-Nāṣirī, *K. al-Istiḳṣāʾ li-akhbār duwal al-Maghrib al-Aḳṣā, al-dawla al-saʿdiyya*, v-vi, Casablanca 1955; A. Guennun, *Cartas de historia de los Saadies*, Tetouan 1954; G. Deverdun, *Inscriptions arabes des Marrakech*, Rabat 1958; idem, *Marrakech des origines à 1912*, i-ii, Rabat 1959-66; H. de Castries, *La conquête du Soudan par al-Mansour (1591)*, in *Hespéris*, iv (1923), 433-88; P. Berthier, *Les anciennes sucreries du Maroc et leurs réseaux hydrauliques*, 2 vols., Rabat 1966; G. Gozalbes Busto, *La república andaluza de Rabat en el siglo XVII*, Cuadernos de la Biblioteca española de Tetuán, nos. 9-10, Tetouan 1974, pp. 469.

(Chantal de La Véronne)

ṢĀDIḲ HIDĀYAT [see hidāyat, ṣādiḳ].

ṢĀDİḲ RIFʿAT PASHA, Meḥmed, Ottoman statesman and diplomat (1807-57). He was born in Istanbul, the only son of a very wealthy family. His father was Ḥādjdjī ʿAlī Bey, the governor of the Ottoman cannon foundries (*Ṭopkhāne*). Ṣādiḳ Rifʿat received an education in the palace school, serving his final year in the *Enderūn-i Humāyūn Khazīne Odasi* (the imperial treasury). Thereafter, he was placed in the correspondence department (*Mektūbī Ḳalemi*) of the Grand Vizierate, as an assistant clerk. In 1824 he was promoted to the rank of *khwādja* (master) and in 1828 he became a junior clerk in the office of incoming correspondence.

He attracted the attention of Sulṭan Mahmūd II [*q.v.*] when accompanying the latter on his tour of Edirne and Gelibolu. He also joined the entourage of Pertew Pasha [*q.v.*], whose protégé he became, just like his more famous contemporary Muṣṭafā Reshīd [*q.v.*]. In 1834 he succeeded Reshid in the position of assistant-receiver (*Āmedī Wekīli*). Next year, Ṣādiḳ Rifʿat was appointed Ottoman ambassador to Vienna, where he gained the friendship of the Austrian chancellor Prince Metternich, but struck Joseph von Hammer as a novice in diplomacy. During his stay in Vienna, he wrote a memorandum on the "circumstances of Europe" (*Awrupā aḥwālīna dāʾir risāle*, 1837) in which he pointed out the importance of security of life and property and of rational bureaucratic practices, and advocated devoting more attention to trade and industry. According to Ṣādiḳ Rifʿat, the old Ottoman condescension towards people engaged in trade should end and productivity should be made a central aim of the Ottoman government. The ideas put forward in the memorandum resembled the provisions of the Anglo-Ottoman trade treaty of Balta Limānī of 1838 and of the famous Gülkhāne edict which issued in the *Tanẓīmāt* reforms in 1839.

In 1840, Ṣādiḳ Rifʿat, now under-secretary of state at the Foreign Office, led a mission to Egypt. Shortly after, he was appointed as under-secretary of state at the office of the Grand Vizier. In 1841, he was promoted to the rank of vizier and served as foreign secretary for nine months, the first of four separate tenures of that post (the others being in 1843-5, 1848 and 1853), always for short periods of time. In the same year he joined the *Medjlis-i Wālā-yi Aḥkām-i ʿAdliyye* (Exalted Council for Judicial Ordinances), the main consultative body of the early *Tanẓīmāt* era. After a second stint as ambassador to Austria (1842-3) and his second term as foreign secretary, he rejoined the council and became its chairman (with a seat in the cabinet) in 1845. He was to serve as chairman of the council three more times, in 1848-9, 1850 and 1853-4, after which he joined the newly established *Medjlis-i ʿĀlī-yi Tanẓīmāt* (High Council for Reforms). In between he served as finance minister for three months in 1848, and as minister of state for three months in 1850. In the latter year he also joined the Learned Society (*Endjümen-i Dānish*).

Ṣādiḳ Rifʿat Pasha was a close associate of Reshīd Pasha and a member of the inner circle of reformers all through the 1830s, 1840s and 1850s. He was a strong supporter of the secularisation of the legal and educational systems and, like Reshīd, ʿAlī and Fuʾād Pashas, both preached and practiced the simplification of the Ottoman chancery style. Against the expectations of many of his contemporaries, he never attained the Grand Vizierate.

Ṣādiḳ Rifʿat Pasha died on 11 January 1857 and was buried in Eyyūb. He left a daughter (who was married to a son of Muṣṭafā Reshīd Pasha, Aḥmed Djelāl Pasha) and a son, Meḥmed Raʾūf Pasha, who edited and published a number of his father's memoranda under the title *Muntakhabāt-i āthār-i Rifʿat* (Selected Writings of Rifʿat). Another small work, called *Risāle-yi akhlāḳ* (Treatise on morals) was for some time used in Ottoman schools.

Bibliography: Murat Belge (ed.), *Tanzimat'tan Cumhuriyet'e Türkiye ansiklopedisi*, Istanbul 1985, i, 250-2, iii, 622-3; C.V. Findley, *Bureaucratic reform in the Ottoman Empire. The Sublime Porte 1789-1922*, Princeton 1980, 136-8; İbrahim Alaettin Gövsa, *Türk meşhurları ansiklopedisi*, Istanbul 1946, 326; *Türk ansiklopedisi*, Ankara 1978, xxvii, 325.

(E.J. Zürcher)

ṢADĪḲĪ (the transcription often used by Indian numismatists of what should correctly be Ṣiddīḳī), the name given by Tīpū Sulṭān of Mysore [see mahisur] to a gold coin of the value of two pagodas (Port. *pardao*, the name of a gold coin long current in South India in pre-modern times and for which various etymologies have been propounded; see Yule-Burnell, *Hobson-Jobson, a glossary of Anglo-Indian colloquial words and phrases*, 652-7, 672-8), weighing 106 grains (= 6.87 gr). The name Ṣiddīḳī derives from the epithet borne by the first caliph Abū Bakr [*q.v.*] al-Ṣiddīḳ, in accordance with Tīpū's custom of naming the denominations of his coins after the first caliphs and the Shīʿī imāms.

Bibliography: J.R. Henderson, *The coins of Haidar Alī and Tīpū Sulṭān*, Madras 1921.

(J. Allan*)

al-ṢĀDIḲIYYA, al-Madrasa, in Tunisian Arabic eṣ-Ṣādḳiyya, in French, le Collège Sadiki, a prestigious educational establishment, founded by a decree of Muḥammad al-Ṣādiḳ Bey [*q.v.*] of Tunis on 5 Dhu 'l-Hidjdja 1291/13 January 1875 on the advice of the reforming minister Khayr al-Dīn [*q.v.*].

Its foundation marked the culmination of a period of reflection by the reforming élite in Tunisia which, from the middle of the 19th century, opened its eyes to the modern world, was disturbed at the social, cultural and economic backwardness of the country, and had the curiosity to make itself familiar with the sciences of the West. It took into account the fact that all reform, political or administrative, would necessarily involve the updating of teaching methods, the development of the programme of studies and its extension to as great a number as possible of pupils.

The foundation statue of the Ṣādiḳiyya envisaged a double objective: (1) conservation, "revivification" (*iḥyāʾ*) and renovation (*tad̲j̲dīd*) of the Arabo-Muslim cultural inheritance; and (2) an opening-up to the new world, in its various cultural forms: the mastery of foreign languages as a basic means of communication, and an initiation into the exact sciences and their manifold applications.

The foundation statue of the Ṣādiḳiyya

The College is meant for young Muslim Tunisians (art. 29); instruction there is free (art. 31). There are to be two categories of pupils (resident ones with bursaries, those with half-bursaries and those living externally). Three levels of instruction are envisaged: (1) Primary, in which is to be taught reading and writing, Ḳurʾān recitation, Prophetic tradition and the usual manuals of Islamic studies (*mutūn*); (2) Second level, in which the legal science of the *s̲h̲arīʿa* are to be taught; and (3) (and here are the innovations) the teaching of the exact and modern sciences (mathematics, inc. algebra, geometry, mensuration, engineering); cosmography; geography; natural sciences (the elements of medicine, vertinary science, botany, zoology, mineralogy, agriculture and chemistry); political science and legislation; and, in a word, "everything not prohibited by the *s̲h̲arʿ*, which it is necessary to make available to the Muslim community so that it may organise services of public value" (art. 25).

This third level was to take seven years. Art. 23 envisages the possibility for graduates of "continuing their studies" for a further seven years at the most. This last rule was in effect used in order to send certain pupils to France, Turkey and England; from 1878 to 1881 a dozen students followed courses at the Lycée Saint-Louis in Paris.

Installation of the Ṣādiḳiyya

The effective inauguration of the Ṣādiḳiyya took place on 20 Muḥarram 1292/27 February 1875. The "new school" was at that time installed in Tunis in a former barracks in the rue Ezzenaidya (*al-zanāʾidiyya* "the armourers"), baptised under the French Protectorate as the rue de l'Eglise, and is situated at the present in no. 55 in the rue D̲j̲āmiʿ al-Zaytūna. In 1897, the College was moved to a new building, in Arabo-Mag̲h̲ribī style, dominating the hill over the Ḳaṣba, and which gave place to the Administration of the Habous (*ḥubūs, awḳāf*) and then to an annexe of the National Library (Periodicals Service).

Financial arrangements

In order to provide the College with an assured and autonomous budget, K̲h̲ayr al-Dīn allotted to it the greater part of the properties of the former chief minister, Muṣṭafā K̲h̲aznadār [*q.v.*], confiscated by the state. These comprised enormous rural estates, olive groves, building plots in Tunis itself (Tunis-Marine) and in its outskirts (La Goulette, La Marsa, etc.), and houses and shops in the city centre. "By a decree of 10 March 1875, the properties forming the endowment of the Ṣādiḳi College were made into an habous (*ḥubus*) as property held in mainmort, of a religious nature and inalienable. Under the able administration of Muḥammad al-ʿĀrif, the College's finances rapidly prospered". These habous were valued in 1906 at about 20 million francs.

However, from the beginning of the Protectorate, the speculations of European colons, supported by the French administration, allowed, by means of a legal fiction or ruse (*ḥīla*), the disastrous exchange (*ʿiwaḍ*) of the rich properties of the North (*ca.* 4,000 ha) against rents "of enzel" (*inzāl* [*q.v.* in Suppl.]) or permanent lease), which could be subsequently bought out for the future payment of twenty annual payments.

Practical arrangements and their variations

A decree of 28 March 1906 (2 Ṣafar 1324) fixed the number of resident pupils of the College at 40, whilst that of the half-bursary holders was not to exceed 100.

These pupils were admitted after a competitive examination embracing the whole of Tunisia. A certificate of elementary primary studies was required of all candidates, whose age had to be (on the 31 December of the year of the competition) between 12 and 15. Between 1906 and 1929 the total number of pupils was 625. In comparison, one may note that in 1905, there were at the Lycée Carnot 846 pupils, including 44 Tunisian Muslims. It was not till the 1930s, under the direction of Gabriel Mérat, that numbers passed the peak of 160. But it was above all under the direction of a former pupil of the College, the first Tunisian who had surmounted the barrier of the competition for agregation in Arabic language and literature, Muḥammad ʿAṭiyya, that its evolution became spectacular. The number of pupils admitted to the entrance competition passed, in 1951, the maximum of 305. The effective total was multiplied by ten, and the prodigious efforts of the director were crowned by the building, on a plot of land belonging to the Crown demesnes, of an annexe to the College, the Lycée K̲h̲aznadār, to which the internal and part of the external students were transferred.

The syllabuses and their successive reform

It was political considerations which usually determined the changes in teaching programmes. Thus it was that, at the beginning of the Protectorate from 1882, the French Minister-Resident Paul Cambon understood the services which the College could render to the new administration. Under the direction of Delmas, in 1892, the secondary education syllabus was modified: kept at a level below that of the lycées, in the scientific field, instruction took on above all a practical and professional aspect. Special courses in literary, administrative and legal translation were introduced there in the light of the certificate and higher diploma in Arabic required for entry into the public service (decree of 1888). The first graduates of the Ṣādiḳiyya were caught up by the administration, which dangled before the eyes of the youth an assured position and treatment. The Ṣādiḳiyya ceased to be basically a place for shaping the learned education of Tunisian youth, but became a "nursery" for officials of the Protectorate administration, a "producer of white-collar workers".

After 1934, the director ʿAṭiyya, going back to the spirit of the College's founder and the letter of its foundation statue (respect for and preservation of the national heritage, with an opening on to the modern world), brought the syllabuses up to the scientific level required by the baccalauréat and assured Arabic language and literature of an adequate role. He diversified studies and, at the second level of instruction, increased the number of specialised sections corresponding to the different series of the baccalauréat:

Section A: classical literature (Latin and Greek introduced for the first time, whence, eventually, were formed cadres for the archaeological service and teachers of the history of ancient Tunisia).

Section B: Sciences plus languages (English, then Italian and German).

Section C: Latin plus sciences.

Section D (crowned by the sole Diploma of completed studies), an education on an administrative (legislative) and legal (elements of law and Islamic jurisprudence) basis.

An innovation should be noted. The director of the Ṣādiḳiyya could admit, as an option at the oral examination for the baccalauréat, questions on Arab-

Islamic philosophy (al-Fārābī, the I<u>kh</u>wān al-Ṣafāʾ, Ibn Sīnā, Ibn <u>Kh</u>aldūn, etc.).

The success of the Ṣādiḳiyya encouraged an increasing demand from Tunisians for it to be extended to other establishments. After 1944, the Direction of Public Instruction decided to create, on the same model, classes which were described as "Ṣādiḳian" and then "Tunisian" in a number of lycées and colleges: the College Aaloui, the Lycées of Sousse and Sfax and even, under pressure from the Union of Tunisian employees in Public Education, at the Lycée Carnot in Tunis and, for Muslim girls, at the Lycée Louis-René Millet in the rue du Pacha in Tunis.

In 1955, the numbers of participants in the "Tunisian" classes reached 6,000. Studies there were crowned by the "Diploma of Ṣādiḳian studies", which was replaced, after Independence in 1957, by that of the "Tunisian baccalauréat".

Finally, one should mention the indelible impact which the Ṣādiḳiyya has had on Tunisian society, quite apart from its role in the domain of education. "By bringing together on the same benches, in the same refectory and dormitory, children from all classes of this society, Sadiki went on to create the democratic education of youth ... Thanks to the possibility of boarding there, provincials and country-dwellers, hitherto disdained (as *āfāḳīs*) by the children of the capital, found themselves in contact with each other, and learned to know and love each other" (Ali Bach Hamba, 1906).

A mixing-together of youth from all social levels, a free comradeship and close solidarity of feeling, an atmosphere of hard work and a strong feeling of responsibility and duty, have characterised the atmosphere of the Ṣādiḳiyya right up to the present day.

Bibliography: *Foundation Statue of the Sadiki College*, decree of 5 <u>Dh</u>u 'l-Ḥi<u>dj</u><u>dj</u>a 1291, Official Tunisian Press; *Sadiki et les Sadikiens (1875-1975)*, Tunis 1975; L. Machuel (Director-General of Education in Tunisia), *L'enseignement public en Tunisie*, Tunis 1906, 29-42; Taoufik Bachrouch, *Les Sadikiens de la Première Heure ou la tentation de l'ouverture*, in *CT* (1st and 2nd tr. 1988), 167-82. (M. Souissi)

ṢĀDIN (A.), in early Arabia, the guardian of a shrine (abstract noun, *sidāna*).

The root *s - d - n* contains the sense of "veil, curtain", which puts *sādin* on a level with *ḥā<u>dj</u>ib*, the first term denoting the guardian of a shrine, and the second, the "door-keeper" of a palace, hence "chamberlain". The *ḥā<u>dj</u>ib* acts under the orders of someone else, whereas the *sādin* acts on his own initiative (*Lᶜ A*, xvii, 69, citing Ibn Barrī). However, the two terms may be found juxtaposed, e.g. in Ibn Hi<u>sh</u>ām, who says, "The Arabs possessed, as well as the Kaᶜba, *tawā<u>gh</u>īt* which were shrines (*buyūt*: cf. Fahd, *La divination arabe*, 132 ff.) which they used to venerate just as they venerated the Kaᶜba; these sanctuaries had *sadana* and *ḥu<u>dj</u><u>dj</u>āb*" (*Sīra*, 55, l. 10). According to him, the personnel of the cult could be reduced to the *sādin* and the *ḥā<u>dj</u>ib*. The site of the cult itself is called *bayt al-masdan* in a verse attributed to Ruʾba b. al-ᶜA<u>dj</u><u>dj</u>ā<u>dj</u> (*loc. cit.*, l. 11). For al-<u>Dj</u>āḥiẓ, *sādin* belongs to the <u>Dj</u>āhiliyya; it is replaced by *ḥā<u>dj</u>ib* (*Ḥayawān*, i, 160 ult.). Amongst the offices created by Ḳuṣayy [*q.v.*] figures that of the *ḥi<u>dj</u>āba* "guardianship of the Kaᶜba".

As well as his function as guardian of a shrine, the *sādin* watched over the offerings made to the divinities and practised belomancy [see AL-ISTIḲSĀM BI 'L-AZLĀM]. This was the situation regarding the custodian of the Kaᶜba; he shook up the divinatory arrows in the god Hubal's [*q.v.*] quiver.

The *sādin* appears thus in the sources concerning primitive Islam, when Arabian paganism was in full decadence. Going further back and placing him the context of the surrounding Semitic world, one notes that there was both a complementariness and a rivalry between the *sādin* and the *kāhin*. The first had a mantic and augural role, the second, an oracular and ecstatic one. But it often happened that the two were in rivalry and trespassed on each other's territory; also, the absence of one enabled the other to exercise both functions.

Bibliography: Full details in KĀHIN and in Fahd, *La divination arabe*², Paris 1987, 109-12. (T. Fahd)

SAᶜDIYYA, a Ṣūfi *ṭarīḳa* [*q.v.*] and family lineage particularly Syrian and <u>Sh</u>āfiᶜī in identity, still active today, that grew to prominence also in Ottoman Egypt, Turkey and the Balkans. Notable aspects of the Saᶜdiyya are their distinctive rituals and their role in the social history of Damascus. The eponymous founder is Saᶜd al-Dīn al-<u>Sh</u>aybānī al-<u>Dj</u>ibāwī (hereafter "Saᶜd"). His dates remain uncertain, but most probably fall in the 7-8th/13th-14th centuries. To the extent to which any *ṭarīḳa* may be characterised, the Saᶜdiyya is marked by the practice of *<u>kh</u>awāriḳ al-ᶜādāt* (deeds transcending the natural order, such as healing, spectacles involving body piercing, *ḍarb al-ṣilāḥ*, and, best known, the *dawsa* [*q.v.*], the *<u>shaykh</u>* riding horseback over a "living carpet" of men) and by wide appeal among the middle and lower classes. Few *ᶜulamāʾ* appear in the Saᶜdī *silsila* and the biographical compendia of notables and *ᶜulamāʾ* are ambivalent about Saᶜdī activities.

Through successful business and generous extension of their inherited *baraka*, many Damascene Saᶜdīs became extremely wealthy and offered a safe haven of hospitality for Ottoman dignitaries at their main *zāwiya* in the tempestuous Mīdān quarter. The order has been fraught with an unusually high level of competitive struggles over the *ma<u>sh</u>ay<u>kh</u>a* of the family, the Ṣūfī order and its *awḳāf*. Because the order by and large is hereditary in leadership, family connections predominate over acquired knowledge and training. The Saᶜdīs are a good example of the outcome of the combination of saintliness, Ṣūfī organisation and wealth in the Ottoman world.

The encyclopaedic Ṣūfī *silsila* collections of the 11-13/17-19th centuries do not feature the Saᶜdiyya prominently. Al-Ḳu<u>sh</u>ā<u>sh</u>ī (d. 1071/1661), al-ᶜU<u>dj</u>aymī (d. 1113/1702) and al-Sanūsī (d. 1276/1859) seem unconcerned with the order, but Murtaḍā al-Zabīdī (d. 1205/1790) received the Saᶜdī *ṭarīḳa* from the Damascene Aḥmad al-Manīnī (d. 1173/1759) and gives a second *sanad* following the familiar <u>Dj</u>unaydī/Imāmī line (*ᶜIḳd al-<u>dj</u>awhar fi 'l-<u>dh</u>ikr wa-ṭuruḳ al-ilbās wa 'l-talḳīn*, ms. Dār al-Kutub al-Miṣriyya, *taṣawwuf*, 3, 332, p. 58). Kamāl al-Dīn al-Ḥarīrī (d. 1299/1882) presents four *silsila*s, only one of which he received in a personal encounter (*Tibyān wasāʾil al-ḥaḳāʾiḳ fī bayān salāsil al-ṭarāʾiḳ*, ms. Fātiḥ Ibrāhīm 431, ii, fols. 129a-138a). This line, of his Aleppan *<u>shaykh</u>* Muḥammad b. Yāsīn (d. 1292/1875), can be collated with al-Muḥibbī and other sources to form a reasonably reliable *silsila* (*Tibyān*, ii, fols. 130b-131b; *<u>Kh</u>ulāṣa*, i, 34-5).

1. The founder. The hagiography of Saᶜd, eponym of the *ṭarīḳa*, serves a symbolic function for the order. Historical details about him are scant as is literary production by members of the *ṭarīḳa*. A 20th-century Saᶜdī *awrād* work puts his birth in Mecca in 460/1067 and his death in <u>Dj</u>ibā in the Ḥawrān (Golan, see al-Māliḥ, i, 144-5). The year 621, closer

to Margoliouth's 700/1300 reckoning (*EI*[1]), as a death date is more probable (al-Ḥarīrī, iii, 132, and al-Ziriklī, iii, 84-5) but, based on other members of the *silsila*, al-Nabhānī would place Saᶜd in the Mamlūk 8th/14th century (*Dj̲āmiᶜ karāmāt*, ii, 91). D'Ohsson gives the date of death as 736/1335 (*Tableau général*, iv, 623), which fits with al-Wāsiṭī's comments (see below). Along with al-Ḥarīrī's *ᶜĀbiḳ al-sādāt al-adabiyya fi ṭariḳ al-sādāt al-Saᶜdiyya* are two other *manāḳib* works, by Abū Ṭayyib al-ᶜIzzī, and S̲h̲ams al-Dīn Saᶜd al-Ḥalabī (see Ḥilmī, 269-70). Al-Muḥibbī's account of Saᶜd's transformation into a Ṣūfī *s̲h̲ayk̲h̲* is the earliest found (i, 153).

The father of Saᶜd al-Dīn, Yūnus al-S̲h̲aybānī, is traced genealogically by the Egyptians to Idrīs I, the conqueror of the Mag̲h̲rib, and, through him and Saᶜd's mother, Saᶜd is considered both Ḥasanī and Ḥusaynī (al-K̲h̲uḍarī, *al-Wafā᾽ bi 'l-ᶜahd*, 168-9). The Banū S̲h̲ayba [*q.v.*] have the right to drape the Kaᶜba, and in a poem attributed to Saᶜd he speaks of being from the "protectors of the Kaᶜba" (al-Ḥarīrī, ii, fol. 123b; Abāẓa and al-Ḥāfiẓ, n. 2, 505). He claims, as well, to be the "*s̲h̲ayk̲h̲* of each *ṭarīḳa*" as the direct *murīd* of the Prophet. This meeting with the Prophet is the climax of Saᶜd's conversion story. The young rebellious son of Yūnus had left Damascus for a life of highway robbery in the Ḥawrān. Either the Prophet alone, or with Abū Bakr and ᶜAlī, or with all the "ten promised Paradise" pose as victims of Saᶜd al-Dīn on the road. When the answer for Saᶜd's demand for goods and money is the first horseman's recital of Ḳur᾽ān, LVII, 16 "Has not the time come for the hearts of those who believe to turn humbly to the remembrance of God (*d̲h̲ikr Allāh*)?" Saᶜd goes into ecstasy and falls unconscious. The Prophet moistens some dates in his mouth and feeds them to a now-repentant Saᶜd. The leader of the *dj̲inn* is revealed, Saᶜd takes *ᶜahd* from him, returns obediently to his father and God and thence to Dj̲iba, where he dies after establishing a *ṭarīḳa* (al-Muḥibbī, i, 35; al-Witrī, in Bīṭār, i, 12-15; al-Ḥarīrī, ii, fol. 129b). Further *karāmāt* of Saᶜd are enumerated in *al-Wafā᾽*, 171-5.

2. *Ṭarīḳa* origins. European sources usually consider the Saᶜdiyya to be a Syrian branch of the Rifāᶜiyya (Le Chatelier, 214; Depont and Coppolani, 575; Bliss, 245; Gibb and Bowen, ii, 197). Trimingham makes the point by using al-Wāsiṭī's mention of the *k̲h̲irka Saᶜdiyya* in his work on the Rifāᶜīs, *Tiryāḳ al-muḥibbīn*, written *ca.* 720/1320 (*The Sūfi orders in Islam*, 73). In fact, al-Wāsiṭī simply lists the Saᶜdiyya along with five other Dj̲unaydī *ṭuruḳ* (*Tiryāḳ*, 48-9). Lane's note that the Saᶜdiyya is a "celebrated sect of the Rifāᶜees" reflects, perhaps, the similarity in practices between the two: loud *d̲h̲ikr*, *ḍarb al-ṣilāḥ*, power over snakes, and ingesting live coals and glass (*Manners and customs*..., 222). It is true that the two orders are popular in the same *milieus*. The connection between the orders, however, seems to be traceable to a careful manipulation of Saᶜd's spiritual lineage. The Syrian Rifāᶜī Abu 'l-Hudā al-Ṣayyādī, Sultan ᶜAbd al-Ḥamīd II's Ṣūfī advisor, championed his *ṭarīḳa*. In a work ascribed to his Bag̲h̲dādī Rifāᶜī *s̲h̲ayk̲h̲* Muḥammad al-Rawwās (see introd., al-Ṣayyādī, *al-Ṭarīḳa al-Rifāᶜiyya*), Saᶜd al-Dīn has a father named Mazīd, an intimate *k̲h̲alīfa* of Aḥmad al-Rifāᶜī [see RIFĀᶜIYYA] Yūnus al-S̲h̲aybānī is depicted as Saᶜd's pious grandfather, *Ṭayy al-sidj̲ill*, 384). He is said to have been initiated by the Rifāᶜī saint in 555/1160 outside Damascus. Aḥmad breathed into his mouth and declared "Mazīd, all that is ours is yours" (al-Witrī, cited by al-Bīṭār, i, 14). According to this version of Saᶜd's life, after his miraculous conversion, Mazīd clothed Saᶜd in his Rifāᶜī *k̲h̲irḳa*, the only one Saᶜd wore throughout his life. Several of the European accounts mention Abu 'l-Hudā as their source for *ṭarīḳa* backgrounds (e.g. Depont and Coppolani, where Saᶜd is "raised by" Aḥmad al-Rifāᶜī, 327, 330). If Abu 'l-Hudā had, indeed, worked to quash Arab nationalism and to have his brand of Arab Sufism the imperial favorite (Abu Manneh, 148 and *passim*), he was clever to subsume the popular Syrian *ḳuṭb* under his own, Rifāᶜī, banner. The Saᶜdīs, on their part, often have their *ṣāḥib al-ṭarīḳa* born long before Aḥmad al-Rifāᶜī (as noted by Le Chatelier in the late 19th century, 211). ᶜAlī Mubārak, writing around the same time as Abu 'l-Hudā, states that the Saᶜdiyya are independent of al-Rifāᶜī (*K̲h̲iṭaṭ*, iii, 129). Ḥarīrī, a devoted Rifāᶜī, does not link Saᶜd to al-Rifāᶜī. Any real ties between the two orders remain to be established.

3. History of the *Ṭarīḳa* in Syria. The first Saᶜdī for whom we have contemporary accounts is Ḥasan al-Dj̲ibāwī (d. 910 or 914), who came from the Ḥawrān to Damascus in the late Mamlūk period. "The women and most of the common folk believed he could cure insanity" by the thaumaturgic qualities of the *basmallah* (al-Nuᶜaymī, *al-Dāris*, ii, 221-2), attributed to Saᶜd's association with the *dj̲inn*. A *madj̲d̲h̲ūb* named K̲h̲amīs (or K̲h̲alīl, d. 912/1506) is reported by al-G̲h̲azzī as bringing Ḥasan to the Mīdān Fawḳānī district of Ḳubaybāt, where he roofed over the unfinished (and unoccupied) tomb of the *nā᾽ib* Īnāl al-Dj̲āḳmī for his residence and *zāwiya* (*Kawākib*, i, 191; Wulzinger, 101). From Ṣāliḥiyya ᶜAli b. Maymūn (d. 917/1511) took to criticising the obeisance K̲h̲amīs required of those who came into Ḥasan's presence, but was later chastened for his ill manners. Ḥasan's son and successor Ḥusayn (d. 926/1519) is the first to display what became a Saᶜdī trademark—he served both the spiritually needy and the worldly rulers of Damascus with lavish hospitality at the Saᶜdī home (al-G̲h̲azzī, citing Ibn Ṭūlūn [d. 953/1546], *Kawākib*, i, 185). Aḥmad b. Ḥusayn (d. 963/1555) continued the *ṭarīḳa* tradition by holding *ḥalaḳāt al-d̲h̲ikr* ("free of reprehensible acts and beardless boys"), writing amulets and treating all, *amīr* and *faḳīr*, to banquets at the *zāwiya* (*op. cit.*, ii, 103-4). Saᶜd al-Dīn "al-Aṣg̲h̲ar" (d. 986/1578) renovated the *zāwiya* in 964 and was one of only two *aᶜyān* mentioned at the inaugural *k̲h̲uṭba* at the Sulaymāniyya in 967 (iii, 157). It is worth noting that the Saᶜdīs never switched from the S̲h̲āfiᶜī to the Ottoman Ḥanafī *mad̲h̲hab*.

One of many inner-*ṭarīḳa* struggles occurred among the wealthy Aleppan Saᶜdīs, whose *zāwiya* stood outside Bāb al-Naṣr. They held a large *d̲h̲ikr*, mainly with *fallāḥī* participants, at the Umayyad Mosques of Aleppo. S̲h̲. Abu 'l-Wafā᾽ (d. 1010/1601) was reported to the Damascene S̲h̲. Saᶜd al-Dīn by a slighted Aleppan for being guilty of sexual misconduct. Saᶜd al-Dīn was convinced to strip the *k̲h̲ilāfa* from Abu 'l-Wafā᾽ and to confer it on one ᶜAbd al-Raḥīm in a written document, which neither Abu 'l-Wafā᾽ nor his disciples obeyed. Thus two competing circles of Saᶜdī *d̲h̲ikr* took place in the mosque. The scandal, according to al-Muḥibbī, was not Abu 'l-Wafā᾽'s violent temper or profligacy (Margoliouth, *EI*[1]) but the climate of *fitna* in the mosque as the two groups hurled abuse at each other during *d̲h̲ikr*, such that people came to hate both sides (*K̲h̲ulāṣa*, i, 152-4). Saᶜd al-Dīn's son Muḥammad came to Aleppo, bemoaned his father's involvement in the affair and ordered the two groups to separate places in the mosque. Abu 'l-Wafā᾽'s brother and successor Aḥmad (d. 1034/1624), a pious and humble man, avoided conflict with ᶜAbd al-Raḥīm's *fuḳarā*ᵓ (al-Muḥibbī, i, 298-9).

A bitter struggle between the brothers Ibrāhīm (d. 1008/1599) and Muḥammad b. Muḥammad (d. 1020/1611) led to the former's being ousted from heading the Saᶜdī *dhikr* at the Umayyad Mosque and from the family complex in Ḳubaybāt (al-Būrīnī, i, 305-6). Muḥammad held control of *mashyakhat Banī Saᶜd al-Dīn* and *sadjdjādat al-ṭarīḳ* for 35 years in Damascus. Holdings in agricultural and commercial properties, along with continuous gifts, made him one of the wealthiest men of his time (al-Muḥibbī, iv, 160-1). Ottoman rulers were frequent visitors at the *zāwiya*, and Muḥammad was invited to their homes. Guests describe the daily elaborate four-part ritual at the *zāwiya* of offering rare coffees, sweets, savories and perfumes (al-Ghazzī, *Luṭf al-samar*, 56-61). In a telling scene in 1118/1706, Ibn Kannān points out that while most of the great *ᶜulamā*ᵓ (including the three local *muftī*s) witnessed Muḥammad al-ᶜImādī's ceremonial first *dars* at the Sulaymāniyya, the Ottoman Ḳāḍī ᶜĀrif was absent that day; he was at the shrine of Sayyida Zaynab with a Saᶜdī *shaykh* in the company of a crowd of men and women (*Ḥawādith*, 104-5).

A second Saᶜdī *zāwiya*, in Shāghūr, was headed by Abu 'l-Wafāᵓ Ibrāhīm (d. 1170/1756). Received by three Ottoman sultans in Istanbul, he established *zāwiya*s and appointed *khalīfa*s, probably for the first time outside the hereditary line, in Anatolia, Egypt and Aleppo. The new order was the Saᶜdiyya-Wafāᵓiyya (Ḥilmī, 270, not to be confused with the Egyptian Shādhiliyya-Wafāᵓiyya). For years the *mutawallī* of the Umayyad Mosque *awḳāf*, this Abu 'l-Wafāᵓ appears faultless in the book of the Ḳubaybātī al-Budayrī (who calls him "our *shaykh*," *Ḥawādith*, 192-3; cf. Ibn Kannān, 430) but foppish in al-Murādī (for dragging his robes of state through the *sūḳ* and eating delicacies in common coffeehouses, *Silk*, i, 41-2). Abu 'l-Wafāᵓ is remembered for having turned over supervision of the Umayyad *awḳāf* to two Ottoman functionaries, who, after paying him a monthly stipend, spent the remaining vast income on themselves. In 1160/1747 Abu 'l-Wafāᵓ led supplicants to Sayyida Zaynab to pray for relief from the plague of locusts that year. The day culminated with his *dawsa* in front of the governor's palace (al-Budayrī, 91). The following year he intervened between imperial forces (*ḳabī ḳūl*) and a coalition of residents and local troops (*yerliyya*) in Mīdān. Treated with respect by the rebels, Abu 'l-Wafāᵓ nevertheless seems closer to the eventually victorious government powers (al-Budayrī 117-8, 131). The Shāghūr *zāwiya*, in Zaḳāḳ al-Shaykh, is today called "Masdjid al-Zāwiya" (al-ᶜUlabī, 419-20; cf. Aḥmad al-Saᶜdī's minaret inscription catalogued by Khālid Muᶜādh, dated 1187/1773-4).

Saᶜdī involvement in clashes between the central authorities and the Mīdān continued throughout the Ottoman era. Centred in the midst of this important commercial quarter, known for recalcitrance, the Ṣūfī family may, at times, have stood for localist sentiment (Schilcher, 18-9), but, more often than not, displayed a prudent pro-imperial stance. (It should be noted that Sultans Maḥmūd I, ᶜAbd al-Medjīd and ᶜAbd al-Ḥamīd II financed renovations at the Djibā Saᶜdī shrine; De Jong, *Les confréries ... Machreq arabe*, 212.)

ᶜAbd Allāh al-Čatadjī, who later was called "Conqueror of Damascus" by the Porte, began his term as governor in 1171/1757-8 by marshaling all non-Damascene soldiery, along with the Ḳābī Ḳūl, to crush the Yerliyya and the population of Mīdān (for his pilgrimage route victories, see al-Barzandjī, *al-Nafḥ al-farajī fī 'l-fatḥ al-djatadjī*, ms. Asas 8724). His troops looted over 20,000 homes and businesses, molested women and girls, killing young and old indiscriminately along their way to the southern end of Bāb Allāh. "The worst calamity since Tīmūr", proclaimed al-Budayrī (213-15), the people emerging after the call of 'All's well' "looking like the living dead" (Mikhāᵓīl al-Dimashḳī, n. 1, 215 of al-Budayrī). After ᶜAbd Allāh called off the plunder, he ordered the loot be deposited in sanctuary mosque sites. The most precious goods were put in the Saᶜdī *zāwiya* in Mīdān; they mysteriously disappeared (*ibid.*; Budayrī is ambiguous about the circumstances).

Under the Egyptian occupation (1831-9), the Saᶜdī compound clearly served as a refuge for resisting factions. To punish the Mīdānīs for sheltering a fugitive, an Egyptian contingent raided the *zāwiya* and captured twenty men for exile or execution (cf. *Mudhakkirāt ... ḥamlat Ibrāhīm Bāshā*, 64-5). The *shaykh* at the time could have been Khalīl al-Saᶜdī (d. 1264/1847), whom Turkish pilgrims sought (Bīṭār, i, 592; Shaṭṭī, 115-16) or Ibrāhīm b. Muṣṭafā al-Saᶜdī (d. 1282/1865, Bīṭār's father-in-law, *Ḥilya*, i, 12-15).

A Saᶜdī sub-order, the Taghlibiyya, is traced either to a brother (Hilāl, in Shaṭṭī, 301) or son (Muḥammad al-Sādis, in Ḥilmī, 270) of Saᶜd al-Dīn. Noted for the *dawsa* and other *karāmāt*, their most famous *shaykh* was ᶜAbd al-Ḳādir al-Taghlibī (d. 1135/1722). A great Ḥanbalī scholar, he took over Abu 'l-Mawāhib b. ᶜAbd al-Bāḳī's *fiḳh* lessons at the Umayyad mosque and was known for writing amulets for the ill (*Silk*, iii, 58; al-Shaṭṭī, 301). The Taghāliba use the *nisba* al-Shaybāni for their branch (cf. *Idjāza fī 'l-ṭarīḳa al-Shaybāniyya al-Saᶜdiyya*, ms. Asad 9485; al-Shaṭṭī, 218-19). *Dhikr* was held at the ᶜAmāra home (al-Ḥarīrī, i, 211; Bīṭār, ii, 1135). The Taghlibī house is now under the Ministry of Awḳāf, but a diminished *dhikr* takes place in a nearby location.

In addition to the Mīdān and Shāghūr centres, in 1282/1865 Muḥammad b. Amīn (d. 1285/1868) endowed his Ḳaymarī home as a Saᶜdī *zāwiya*. He then traveled to Istanbul to win control of all the Djibā *awḳāf*. His son Ibrāhīm held the *mashyakha* for 50 years, gathering *ᶜulamā*ᵓ and rulers to himself (al-Ḥiṣnī, 832; al-Shaṭṭī, 248-9). Disputes over revenues put this family at odds with the leadership at Djibā, where all residents are considered descendants of Saᶜd (De Jong, *op. cit.*, 213). A visitor still encounters ecstatic *ḥadra*s at the shrine, attached to a large modern mosque, with musical accompaniment and body piercing. Families camp out, hoping for a cure from the *walī* for mentally disturbed relatives.

The Ḳaymarī *zāwiya* received a hair of the Prophet from Sultan ᶜAbd al-Ḥamīd. The relic is still brought out on Miᶜrādj night as the Saᶜdī genealogy is presented to the President (or his representative) for his signature. Well into the 1960s, the Saᶜdiyya were hosts for the main Ramaḍān *dhikr* celebrations (Kayyāl, 107-9), but they no longer accept initiates in Damascus. De Jong notes active Saᶜdīs in Aleppo, Ḥamā, Ḥimṣ and the Ḥawrān (*op. cit.*, 212-13). The Saᶜdīs, as a native Syrian Ṣūfī family, continued to inspire reverence, especially in Mīdān. When the "fresh" corpse of Ḥasan al-Djibāwī was moved recently, witnesses saw crowds take away handfuls of the sweet-smelling soil from the grave. At contemporary Ḳādirī *dhikr*s in Damascus, Saᶜd is called upon as one of four great *ḳuṭb*s.

4. Egypt. According to Egyptian Saᶜdī accounts, the order came to Cairo with Yūnus, one of nine sons of Saᶜd al-Dīn, who is credited with beginning the *dawsa* (*al-Wafā*ᵓ, 170-1; cf. ᶜAlī Mubārak, ii, 71-2).

Saʿdī conflation between the elder, holy Yūnus al-Shaybānī and this son seems possible. The Fāṭimid dome over the Saʿdī shrine at Bāb al-Naṣr has been positively identified as that of Badr al-Djamālī, *amīr al-djuyūsh* under al-Mustanṣir (r. 427-87/1036-94; Raghib, *Le mausolee...*, 307), so the Saʿdīs in Cairo, also, are located in a pre-established tomb. Al-Maḳrīzī (d. 845/1441) does not mention Saʿdīs at the *turba* of al-Djamali; the propagator of the *ṭarīḳa* in Egypt would have been a much later descendant (*Khiṭaṭ*, i, 364). The first *shaykh* of the Damascene line to be buried at the Bāb al-Naṣr site, after Yūnus, is Aḥmad al-Saʿdī (d. 12th/18th century), but earlier generations emigrated from Syria and were buried elsewhere. Although ʿAbd al-Ghanī al-Nābulusī (d. 1143/1731) praised the Syrian Saʿdiyya in a poem (al-Ḥarīrī, ii, fols. 131a-b), he did not visit the Djibā tomb, and when he happened by chance upon a Saʿdī *dhikr* at the Ḥākim Mosque in Cairo, he participated without enthusiasm (in 1105/1693, *Ḥaḳīḳa*, 263, 423). Al-Djabartī, in describing events of the French invasion in 1218/1798, mentions the Saʿdiyya as joining with the ulema at al-Azhar to pray for deliverance (*ʿAdjāʾib*, iv, 291-2). The Cairene *mashyakha* passed two times to matrilineal descendants (to the Munzalāwīs, *khaṭībs* at the Ḥusayn Mosque, and to the Khuḍarīs).

The Saʿdīs, because of the *dawsa*, are central in the story of state regulation of Egyptian *ṭuruḳ*. Banned in 1881 by the Khedive Tawfīḳ, the prohibition seems to have been more the result of European than Muslim reformist pressure (its loss is bemoaned by McPherson, who blames secular modernism and "Americanism", *Moulids*, 26-8, 56, 264; see de Jong, *Ṭuruq*, 96-8). There is little doubt that the Saʿdīs' position weakened. In 1289/1872 they were at the head of ʿAlī al-Bakrī's convention of *mashāyikh*. In 1905, Saʿdiyya are placed last in the ranks of the official *ṭuruḳ* processions (*op. cit.*, 67, 214). In modern times, Sh. Ḥamūda al-Khuḍarī proclaimed that music in the *dhikr* is not allowed "in the houses of God" and that all dance and self-mutilation are not allowed. The current *shaykh*, ʿAlī b. Ḥamūda al-Khuḍarī, presides over mild *ḥaḍras* during the Saʿdī night in Ramaḍān at the Ḥusayn Mosque (under the aegis of Dr. Abu 'l-Wafāʾ al-Taftazānī, *shaykh mashāyikh al-ṭuruḳ*, see *Taṣawwuf al-Islāmī*, February 1994, 73). Sh. ʿAlī claims authority over the Saʿdīs "in all Islamic lands" from the Bāb al-Naṣr *zāwiya*. The *ṭarīḳa* is one of the most popular in Upper Egypt. In 1984 N. Biegman photographed Saʿdī *dawsas* in Abul Qumsan, where the chief of police, obeying instructions given him in a dream, allows all Ṣūfī practices (*Egypt*, 14, 160-4). The restraining influence of urban society has restricted Saʿdī practice both in Syria and Egypt.

5. Turkey. The earliest spread of the Saʿdiyya dates most likely from Abu 'l-Wafāʾ al-Shāghūrī's Turkish visits in the 12th/18th century. Gölpınarlı adds two other transmissions: by Sh. ʿAbd al-Salām (d. 1165/1751) and by Sh ʿOthmān from Kastamonu (*Mezhepler ve tarikatler*, 203-4). We have information about Saʿdī *tekkes* in Istanbul, but the fluidity of *ṭarīḳa* identity at *tekkes* should be kept in mind (Kreiser, *Dervish living*, 51). Of the 259 opportunities to attend different *dhikrs* each week in 19th-century Istanbul, 26 are Saʿdī (greater numbers of Khalwatī, Ḳādirī, Naḳshbandī and Rifāʿī gatherings are listed, *Tekkiye risalesi*, ms. Berlin or. 2792, 1-17). The last official survey of Istanbul *tekkes* mentions 25 Saʿdī *tekkes*, concentrated mainly along the Golden Horn (*Medjmūʿa-yi tekāyā*, publ. 1307/1889, cited in *İA*, art. *Istanbul*). S. Anderson and Brown come close to this figure for the turn of the 20th century (*Dervish orders*, 53-61, and *Dervishes*, 478-80, respectively). Dhākir Shükrī Ef.'s compilation of 1400 Ṣūfī *shaykhs* serving 159 Istanbul *tekkes* from the 10th-14th centuries A.H. includes only fourteen Saʿdīs (out of a total of 349 figures whose *ṭarīḳa* affiliation is stated, *Die Istanbuler Derwischkonvente*, 109-13). Evidence suggests that the Ottoman state attempted to institutionalise the orders in Turkey on the Mewlevī and Bektāshī "mother *zāwiya*" model. The same year in which Muḥammad ʿAlī gave Muḥammad al-Bakrī leadership over the Egyptian *ṭuruḳ* (1812), Sultan Maḥmūd II ordered all Saʿdī *tekkes* to recognise the ʿAbdül-Selām as their *āsitāne* (Kreiser, *Notes ... Turquie*, 56. For other regulating moves before the abolition of the *ṭuruḳ* in 1925, see Kara, *Tekkeler ve zaviyeler*, 255-84).

6. The Balkans. Depont and Coppolani noted Saʿdī centres in several Libyan locations and in the Ḥidjāz (*Les confreries religieuses*, 331-2), and de Jong mentions a Sudanese branch of the Egyptian Saʿdiyya (*Ṭuruq*, n. 218, 178) but the most important implantation of the order outside Syria, Egypt and Turkey occurred in the Balkans, where it continues today. A strong connection existed between local Saʿdī leaders there and the Damascene Saʿdīs, who issued *khilāfāt-nāmes* to the *āsitānes* in Djakovica and Prizren (Popovics, *Une texte...*, 339). Dates for their arrival are uncertain, but by the 18th century Saʿdī *tekkes* were established in Kosovo, Macedonia, Southern Serbia and in Belgrade (Popovic, *op. cit.*, 342). In 1947 they joined with eight other orders, representing between 60 and 100 *tekkes*, to form an organisation distinct from the official Sunnī community (known as ZIDRA, *Zajednica islamskih derviških redova Alije u SFRJ*, former Yugoslavia, cf. Popovic, *Contemporary situation*, 244-5).

A similar body was founded in Albania in 1936, called the "Divine Light" (*Drita Hyjnore, op. cit.*, n. 19, 250). The founder of the Saʿdiyya-ʿĀdjiziyya in Albania, Adjize Baba (from Bushat) was initiated into the order by Abu 'l-Wafāʾ al-Shāghūrī in Istanbul. He constructed the first Saʿdī *tekke* in Djakovica in 1111/1699 (Norton, *Islam...*, 245; Clayer, *L'Albanie*, 163-70). The order may have been introduced earlier, in Tepelen, by Demir Han, a semi-legendary figure from the Crimea. Claimed also by the Bektāshīs, he received the Saʿdī *ṭarīḳa* at the Djibā shrine in Syria. Ewliyā Čelebi does not mention a Saʿdī *tekke* on his visit to Tepelen in 1081/1670; Demir Han probably belongs to a later period (*ibid.*).

Finally, it may be noted that in the popular imagination the Saʿdiyya are linked with the Banū Saʿd, the tribe of the Prophet's wet-nurse Ḥalīma, whose milk was so abundant "she gave more than she could have hoped for" (*al-Wafāʾ*, 164-5). It is not surprising, then, that in addition to other healing talents, al-Murādī points out the Saʿdīs' ability to bolster poor milk supply by passing their hands over a mother's garments (*Silk*, iv, 221).

Bibliography: Manuscript sources are cited fully in the text. Other works: N. Abāẓa and M.M. al-Ḥāfiẓ, *Taʾrīkh ʿulamāʾ Dimashḳ fi 'l-ḳarn al-rābiʿ al-ʿashar*, Damascus 1986-91; B. Abu Manneh, *Sultan Abdulhamid II and Sh. Abulhuda Al-Sayyadi*, in *MEStudies*, v (1979), 131-53; S. Anderson, *Dervish orders of Constantinople*, in *MW*, xii (1922), 53-61; anon., *Mudhakkirāt tarīkhiyya ʿan ḥamlat Ibrāhīm Bāshā ʿalā Sūriya*, ed. A. Sabānū, Damascus 1980; N. Biegman, *Egypt: moulids, saints, Sufis*, The Hague 1990; ʿAbd al-Razzāḳ al-Bīṭār, *Ḥilyat al-bashar fī taʾrīkh al-ḳarn al-thālith ʿashar*, Damascus 1961-3; F.J.

Bliss, *The religions of modern Syria and Palestine*, New York 1912; J.P. Brown, *The dervishes*, London 1927; Aḥmad al-Budayrī, *Ḥawādith Dimashḳ al-yawmiyya*, Cairo 1959; Ḥasan al-Būrīnī, *Tarādjim al-aᶜyān min abnāʾ al-zamān*, Damascus 1963; A. le Chatelier, *Les confreries musulmanes du Hedjaz*, Paris 1887; N. Clayer, *L'Albanie, pays des derviches*, Berlin 1990; O. Depont and X. Coppolani, *Les confréries religieuses musulmanes*, Algiers 1897; Djabartī, *ᶜAdjāʾib al-āthār*, Cairo 1958; Ghazzī, *al-Kawākib al-sāʾira bi-aᶜyān al-miʾa al-ᶜāshira*, Beirut 1979; idem, *Luṭf al-samar wa-ḳaṭf al-thamar*, Damascus 1982; A. Gölpınarlı, *Turkiye'de mezhepler ve tarikatler*, Istanbul 1969; Aḥmad Ḥilmī, *Ḥadīḳat al-awliyāʾ* (mod. Turkish tr. Y. Necef Zade), Istanbul 1966; Taḳī al-Dīn al-Ḥiṣnī, *K. Muntakhabāt al-tawārīkh li-Dimashḳ*, Beirut 1979; Yūsuf b. ᶜAbd al-Hādī, *Thimār al-maḳāṣid fī dhikr al-masādjid*, ed. Asᶜad Ṭalas, Beirut 1975, *al-Dhayl*, 253; Muḥammad b. Kannān, *al-Ḥawādith al-yawmiyya min taʾrīkh iḥdā ᶜashar wa-alf wa-miʾa*, ed. Akram al-ᶜUlabī (forthcoming); F. de Jong, *Les confréries mystiques musulmanes au Machreq arabe*, in A. Popovic and G. Veinstein (eds.), *Les Ordres mystiques dans l'Islam*, Paris 1986, 205-44; idem, *Ṭuruq and ṭuruq-linked institutions in 19th century Egypt*, Leiden 1978; M. Kara, *Tekkeler ve zaviyeler*, Istanbul 1977; M. Kayyāl, *Ramaḍān wa-taḳālīduhu al-Dimāshḳiyya*, Damascus n.d.; Ḥamūda b. ᶜAlī al-Khuḍarī, *al-Wafāʾ bi 'l-ᶜahd*, Cairo 1383; K. Kreiser, *The dervish living*, in R. Lifshez (ed.), *The Dervish lodge: architecture, art, and Sufism in Ottoman Turkey*, Berkeley 1992, 49-56; idem, *Notes sur le présent et le passé des ordres mystiques en Turquie*, in Popovic and Veinstein (eds.), *op. cit.*, 49-62; Maḳrīzī, *al-Khiṭaṭ*, Būlāḳ 1853; M. al-Māliḥ, *Fihris makhṭūṭāt Dār al-Kutub al-Ẓāhiriyya: al-Taṣawwuf*, Damascus 1978; J.W. McPherson, *The moulids of Egypt*, Cairo 1941; ᶜAlī Mubārak, *al-Khiṭaṭ al-tawfiḳiyya*, Būlāḳ 1887; Muḥibbī, *Khulāsat al-āthār*, Cairo 1284; Murādī, *Silk al-durar*, Beirut 1988; Yūsuf al-Nabhāni, *Djāmiᶜ karāmāt al-awliyāʾ*, Beirut 1983; ᶜAbd al-Ghanī al-Nābulusī, *al-Ḥaḳīḳa wa 'l-madjāz fī riḥla ilā bilād al-Shām wa-Miṣr wa 'l-Ḥidjāz*, ed. A. Harīdī, Cairo 1986; H.T. Norton, *Islam in the Balkans*, Columbia, S.C. 1993; ᶜAbd al-Ḳādir al-Nuᶜaymī, *al-Dāris fī taʾrīkh al-madāris*, Cairo 1988; Mouradgea d'Ohsson, *Tableau général de l'Empire othman*; Paris 1788-1824; A. Popovic, *The contemporary situation of the muslim mystic orders in Yugoslavia*, in E. Gellner (ed.), *Islamic dilemmas: reformers, nationalists and industrialization*, Berlin 1985, 240-54; idem, *Un texte inédit de Hasan Kaleshi: l'ordre des Saᶜdīya en Yugoslavie*, in R. Dor and M. Nicolas (eds.), *Quand le crible était dans la paille*, Paris 1978, 335-48; Abdul Karim Rafeq, *The social and economic structure of Bāb-al-Muṣallā (al-Mīdān), Damascus, 1825-1875*, in G. Atiyeh and I. Oweiss (eds.), *Arab civilization: challenges and responses*, Albany, NY 1988, 272-311; Y. Raghib, *Le mausolée de Yūnus al-Saᶜdī, est-il celui de Badr al-Ǧamalī?*, in *Arabica*, xx (1973), 305-7; Muḥammad al-Rifāᶜī al-Rawwās, *Ṭayy al-sidjill*, Damascus 1391; Abu 'l-Hudā al-Ṣayyādī, *al-Ṭarīḳa al-Rifāᶜiyya*, n.p. 1969; Muḥammad al-Shaṭṭī, *Rawḍ al-bashar fī aᶜyān Dimashḳ*, Damascus 1946; J.S. Trimingham, *The Sufi orders in Islam*, London 1973; Akram al-ᶜUlabī, *Khiṭaṭ Dimashḳ*, Damascus 1989; Taḳī al-Dīn al-Wāsiṭī, *Tiryāḳ al-muḥibbīn fī ṭabaḳāt khirkat al-mashāyikh al-ᶜārifīn*, Cairo 1305; K. Wulzinger and C. Watzinger, *Damaskus, die islamische Stadt*, Berlin 1924; Dhākir Shukrī Ef., *Die Istanbuler Derwisch-Konvente und ihre Scheiche*, ed. Mehmet S. Tayşi and K. Kreiser, Freiburg 1980.

(Barbara von Schlegell)

SĀDJ (A.) (Aramaic *shāghā*, from Skr. *saka-*) is the teak tree, *Tectona grandis* L., of the family of the *Verbenaceae*.

This tree, indigenous to the Indian subcontinent and to South-East Asia, is above all coveted for its hard and extraordinarily durable wood and is of particular importance for ship-building and furniture industry. The tree and its qualities are described in detail by the Arabic authors. *Sādj* is the highest tree in the world; it towers high into the air (*yaᶜlū fi 'l-hawāʾ* [var. *'l-samāʾ*]) and has such a width that a multitude of people find a place in its shadow. The wood does not alter even in the advanced age of the tree; it does not decay, nor is it eaten by worms. Its leaves are the elephants' favourite food. They are longer and wider than those of the banana tree (*al-mawz*), and so people wrap themselves in a leaf for protection against the rain. The form of the leaves resembles that of Daylamī shields (*al-tirās al-daylamiyya*). The wood is of a red colour, occasionally turning to black, has a pleasant scent like that of the walnut tree (*al-djawz*) and is therefore used in ᶜIrāḳ, and especially in Baghdād, for house building. From its fruits, which have the size of areca nuts, a thick, blackish oil, the so-called teak oil (*duhn al-sādj*), is won. The secretion from the pouch of the musk deer [see MISK] is adulterated with teak oil by dribbling the latter into the pouch. The teak oil disappears completely in the musk and can no more be separated from it nor is it discernible any more; on the other hand, the teak oil increases the weight of the pouch. Only if the musk, when dried and pulverised, does not stick to the object with which it has been pulverised, is it unaltered; if it does stick, it has been adulterated with teak oil.

The most important healing powers ascribed to *sādj* are the following. If the wood, after burning, is extinguished with the juice of the horned poppy (*Glaucium corniculatum* L., *Papaveraceae*) and the remainder crushed and sieved, the powder thus obtained strengthens the pupils if rubbed on the eyes, and it helps against ulcers on the eyelids. If wood dust, obtained by abrading a piece of teak wood on a stone, is mixed with rose water, it heals the eyes and removes headaches. Mixed with water, the dust helps against purulent and bleeding ulcers and dissolves them. *Sādj* oil helps against fever and thirst, and, if taken with honey water, removes heat from the abdomen and stimulates hair growth.

Bibliography: A. Dietrich, *Die Ergänzung Ibn Ǧulǧul's zur Materia medica des Ibn al-Baiṭār*, no. 40, in *Abh. Ak. Göttingen*, Phil.-hist. Kl., Neue Folge, no. 202, with further literature. (A. Dietrich)

SADJᶜ (A.), originally, the formal expression of the oracular pronouncement.

1. As magical utterances in pre-Islamic Arabian usage.

Here, *sadjᶜ* was the rhythmical style practised by the Arab *kāhins* [*q.v.*] and *kāhinas* [see AL-KĀHINA], a style intermediate between that of the versified oracular utterances of the Sibylls and Pythians and that of the prose utterances of Apollo (see P. Amandry, *La mantique apollinienne à Delphes. Essai sur le fonctionnement de l'oracle*, diss. Paris 1950, 15). These utterances are "formulated in short, rhymed phrases, with rhythmical cadences and the use of an obscure, archaising, bizarre and cabalistic vocabulary" (Fahd *La divination arabe*, 152). Some have sought to see in them an imitation of the repeated, jerky and monotonous cooing of a pigeon or dove (*TᶜA*, v, 370 ll. 13 ff.) or the drawn-out and monotonous moaning of a camel (*ibid.*, ll. 10 ff.).

In origin, *sadjᶜ* denoted the *kāhin*'s entry into a trance, the oracular utterance issuing from this state and then the stylistic form of this utterance (details in Fahd, *op. cit.*, 152 ff.). "The fact that it was most often practised by the *kāhinas* (cf. *ibid.*, 98-102), that it was used in magical formulae of cursing, prayers of deprecation and charms, and that it was believed to be understood by the djinn and animals (Lammens, *Le culte des Bétyles et les processions religieuses chez les Arabes pré-islamites*, in *BIFAO*, xvii [1919-20], 50), shows that its usage goes back to far antiquity. A Sumerian origin for it is not excluded, since *shugītu*, fem. of *shegu* (Akk. and Hebr. *sh-g-ᶜ*, Ar. *s-dj-ᶜ*), borrowed from Sumerian, designates the hierodule (Bezold, *Babyl.-Assyr. Glossar*, 265), who had to act as oracle in the temple where she officiated" (Fahd, *op. cit.*, 152).

According to I. Goldziher, *sadjᶜ* formed the prehistory of Arabic poetic metre, since *radjaz* [*q.v.*], the oldest meter of Arabic prosody, is nothing but "ein rhythmisch discipliniertes *sağᶜ*" (*Abhandl. zur arab. Philologie*, i, 76; the same opinion by Wellhausen, *Reste*, ²135 n. 3), whilst Landberg (*La langue arabe et ses dialectes*, Leiden 1905, 7112) rejected this view and thought that *radjaz* and *sadjᶜ* were equally ancient (cf. A. Musil, *The manners and customs of the Rwala Bedouins*, New York 1928, 403 ff.). Concerning the connection of *radjaz* and its derivatives *r-dj-s* and *n-dj-s* with the pagan cult, see Fahd, *op. cit.*, 153 ff.

In origin, *sadjᶜ* and *radjaz* must have designated approximately the same idea, sc. the state of ecstasy, the oracular pronouncement which ensued and its formal expression. But gradually, *radjaz* took on a more specialised meaning, sc. that of the oracular utterance of war. Henceforth, *radjaz* was gradually removed from the functions of the *kāhin* and came to approach more closely those of the *shāᶜir* [*q.v.*], two functions primitively combined in one person (see Goldziher, *Die Ǧinnen der Dichter*, in *ZDMG*, xlv [1891], 685 ff.; and KĀHIN: Muḥammad considered as *kāhin* and *shāᶜir*), but progressively differentiated, since their respective sources of inspiration grew more diverse. It is in this sense that one can say that *radjaz* was the origin of secular poetry, whereas *sadjᶜ* remained the mode of expression of the diviner, who was always as conservative as the priest with whom he was often identified.

The sources for the first centuries of Islam have preserved for us a large number of oracular pronouncements in *sadjᶜ*, attributed by tradition to the pre-Islamic *kāhins* and *kāhinas*. They are generally considered by critics as "more or less successful pastiches" (R. Blachère, *Introd. au Coran*, 178 n. 242); however, they are taken as pieces of linguistic evidence. Blachère continues, "In effect, these are apocrypha, but capable of evoking compositions now disappeared for ever" (*HLA*, ii, 189-90). And further on, he adds that one might ask oneself whether these apocryphal oracular sayings do not reflect, more than one thinks, the ancient "prophecies" of the *kāhins*, addressing their tribe in a clumsy and unpolished language (192). Nöldeke avoided pronouncing on their ancientness, at the same time allowing this to emerge clearly (*G des Q*, i, 75 n. 1). Wellhausen wrote that the oldest sūras of the Ḳurʾān were the most important pieces of evidence for the style of the *kāhins* (*Reste*², 137 n. 4). Fück averred that the feature of rhyme in the ecstatic outpourings of the ancient diviners was above that of the common language, and this was the same for the Ḳurʾān (*ᶜArabīya*, Fr. tr. Paris 1955, 129-30).

References to these oracular sayings are collected together in Fahd, *op. cit.*, 159 1; their themes have been briefly enumerated by Wellhausen, *op. cit.*, 135, see also Nöldeke, *loc. cit.*). Wellhausen brings out the following features, often borrowed from procedures attested in the Ḳurʾān. The *kuhhān* have the custom of covering themselves at the time of their visions, whence the name Dhu 'l-Khimār "the man with the veiling" given to some of them. They use the poetic form *sadjᶜ*, short, parallel phrases, of which four to six are held together by a single rhyme. He wrote that "das *sağᶜ* ist ohne Zweifel die älteste Form der Poesie, entsprechend dem hebräischen Parallelismus der Glieder" (i, 135 n. 3). They are often themselves surprised in the face of their strange visions and utterances (*mā adrāka*), a formula cited 13 times in the Ḳurʾān but not attested in non-Ḳurʾānic oracular pronouncements. They begin with formulae of swearing, and swear by the sun (XCI, 1), the moon (CXI, 1; LXXIV, 32; LXXXIV, 18) and the stars (LIII, 1; LXXXVI, 1-2), by the evening (LXXXIV, 16; CIII, 1) and the morning (LXXXIX, 1; LXXIV, 34; XCI, 1; XCIII, 1), by the clouds (LI, 2 ?) and the winds (LI, 2; LXXVII, 1 ff. ?), by the mountains (XCV, 1 (Yāḳūt, *Buldān*, i, 911); XCV, 2; LII, 1) and the rivers (LI, 3 ?), by the plants (XC, 1) and animals (C, 1 ff. ?) by the woodpecker (?) and the pigeon (?), by the wolf and the frog (see al-Ṭabarī, i, 1933-4). Nöldeke only enumerates the sites and edges of the roads, animals (?) and birds (?), the day (XCI, 3; XCII, 2) and the night (CXXIV, 33; LXXXIV, 17; XCI, 4; XCII, 1-2), the light and the darkness, the sun, moon and stars, the heavens (LI, 7; LXXXV, 1; LXXXVI, 1, 11; XCI, 5) and the earth (LXXXVI, 12; XCI, 6).

The two authors give shape to the model of the Arabic oracular utterance on the basis of the ancient sūras of the Ḳurʾān, in so far as they are convinced that Muḥammad utilised the style of the inspired persons of Arabia, whose roots go back to the ancient Semitic past. It should, however, be noted that there are some Ḳurʾānic sayings which are marked by the cosmogonic, eschatological and prophetic ideas of monotheism, such as XXXVII, 1 ff.; LII, 1 ff. (cf. XXXVI, 1; XXXVIII, 1; XLIII, 2; XLIV, 2; L, 1); LXVIII, 1; LXXIV, 102; LXXXV, 2; XCI, 7; LI, 1 ff.; LXXVII, 1 ff.; LXXIX, 1 ff.; C, 1 ff.).

There was, consequently, an adaptation in the Ḳurʾān of the oracular saying to the exigencies of the new concepts which it had to express, a process of adaptation made all the more inevitable by the fact that the Prophet aimed at freeing himself from all the compromising forms of paganism in order to place in relief the originality of his own message and its transcendence.

From this fact, one can say that, although its vision of the created universe, whose witness it invokes solemnly, is expressed by the stylistic forms of divination, their spirit and terminology—which must have undergone substantial changes—do not permit us to discern the primitive model which must certainly have been much more sober and poorer in ideas; likewise, in the eyes of the nomads, the image of its inspirer must have been sketchy and the idea which they formed of themselves must have been feeble.

There is an analysis of some oracular utterances representative of the genre in *La divination arabe*, 162 ff.: one of ᶜAmr b. Luḥayy, two of Ṭarīfa, one of the *kāhina* of the Iyād, one of the *kāhin* of the B. Asad, one of the *kāhina* of the B. Ghanm, and those of the legendary Shiḳḳ and Saṭīḥ.

It should finally be noted that the oracular utterance which, in the preceding cases, is spoken through a human intermediary, supported implicitly or explicitly by a spirit, can also be heard without any such intermediary, either by a simple voice crying in the night—the case of the *hātif* [*q.v.*]—or through an idol—this is ventriloquism, cf. Fahd, *op. cit.*, 171-4—or by the summoning of the spirits of the dead—sc. necromancy [see ISTINZĀL]—or, finally, by the interpretation of the behaviour of living or inanimate objects—this is cleromancy [see FAʾL, ʿIYĀFA, ḲIYĀFA] oneiromancy [see RUʾYĀ] and all similar procedures [see DJAFR, FIRĀSA, ḤURŪF, IKHTILĀDJ, KAFF, KATIF, KHAṬṬ, ḲURʿA and MAYSIR]. All these forms arising out of the oracular utterances can be found attested in the traditional literature.

Bibliography: this article is essentially taken from Fahd, *op. cit.*, Paris 1987, 140-76, where can be found details and references. (T. FAHD)

2. Outside *kahāna* before Islam.

Other uses of rhymed sayings refer to weather phenomena. There are two genres. One is represented by a closed corpus of astrometeorological sayings of the Bedouins, the *nawʾ* adages [see ANWĀʾ], which form a kind of a farmer's calender. They relate the heliacal rising of a star, or group of stars, to certain weather changes and activities connected with them. Characteristically, they start with *idhā ṭalaʿa* [*ʾl-nadjm*], "when [the Pleiades] rise," and usually consist of between four and six cola rhyming with the name of the star(s). The oldest preserved book on the *anwāʾ* is Ibn Ḳutayba (d. 276/889 [*q.v.*]), *K. al-Anwāʾ*, ed. M. Ḥamīdullāh and Ch. Pellat, Ḥaydarābād-Deccan 1375/1956; here the sayings are introduced with *yaḳūlu sādjiʿu ʾl-ʿarab*, "the rhymer of the Arabs/Bedouins says," or, more freely, "a rhymed folk-saying is the following."

The other genre is descriptions of clouds and rain in what one might call Bedouin ornate prose. It is mostly characterised by "strophic" *sadjʿ*, i.e. a change of the rhyme after two, three, or four cola. Typical is also a liberal use of recherché archaic vocabulary. Ibn Durayd (d. 321/933 [*q.v.*]) says at the beginning of his *K. Waṣf al-maṭar wa ʾl-saḥāb*, ed. ʿIzz al-Dīn al-Tanūkhī, Damascus 1382/1963: "This is a book in which we have gathered together what the Bedouins (*ʿarab*) before and under Islam have said in the way of rain and cloud description." Some of the specimens collected in his book are clearly Islamic (e.g. at 30-1), others leave the impression of lexical études; but given the enormous importance of spotting rain and pasture, there is nothing inherently unlikely in stylised reports in somewhat hieratic language already before Islam.

Bibliography (in addition to references given in the article): C. Pellat, *Dictons rimés*, anwāʾ *et mansions lunaires chez les Arabes*, in *Arabica*, ii (1955), 17-41. (W.P. HEINRICHS)

3. In Arabic literature of the Islamic period.

Since pre-Islamic times, the word *sadjʿ* in the sense of "to recite or speak with assonances, using cadenced and elaborate language", has denoted a type of more or less rhythmical prose of which the principal characteristic is the use of rhythmic units which are generally quite short (from 4 to 10 syllables, on average), terminated by a clausula. These units are grouped sequentially on a common rhyme. The rhymed or assonanced clausula at the end of each rhythmic unit constitutes the essential element of *sadjʿ*, which is appropriately translated as "rhymed and rhythmic prose". It seems that this mode of expression pre-dates free prose and even metrical poetry, with which it has numerous aspects in common, but from which it is distinguished by the absence of metre and of a single rhyme. In the opinion of some scholars, this stylistic form could have been the origin of metrical and prosodic poetry.

A. *Principal phases in the evolution of* sadjʿ

The origins of sadjʿ *in literature*

Although no doubt apocryphal or corrupt, some examples of pre-Islamic rhymed and rhythmic prose have been preserved. They consist for the most part of proverbs, maxims, stories and legends (R. Blachère, *HLA*, ii, 190). Here there are also found formulas chanted communally on the occasion of the Pilgrimage to Mecca (see *EI*[1], TALBIYA; M. Gaudefroy-Demombynes, *Le pélerinage à la Mekke*, Paris 1923, 179-80). *Sadjʿ* had, furthermore, close links with magic; for these, see section 1, above. Also, the group of men who led the pre-Islamic Arab tribe often included among its members an eminent orator (*khaṭīb*), who should not be confused with the *kāhin,* although the same person might be both soothsayer and *khaṭīb*.

When he was not a poet himself, "the orator played a role analogous to that of the poet, in acting as the spokesman of the tribe in embassies, gatherings and fairs, also in arousing through his oratory the tribal sentiment of the members of his group" (Ch. Pellat, *Langue et littérature arabes*, 58). A semi-legendary individual, Ḳuss b. Sāʿida al-Iyādī [*q.v.*], was considered the greatest orator of the Djāhiliyya [*q.v.*] (al-Djāḥiẓ, *Bayān*, i, 52). His eloquence became proverbial, so that there were expressions such as *ablagh min Ḳuss* ("more eloquent than Ḳuss") (al-Maydānī, *Madjmaʿ*, i, 117-18). The Prophet Muḥammad, during his adolescence, is supposed to have encountered him delivering a sermon (*khuṭba*) while mounted on his camel at ʿUkāẓ. Then, some years later, the Prophet is said to have had occasion to recite in public a passage from this speech, which is no doubt apocryphal but is famous nonetheless, and which begins thus: *ayyuhā ʾl-nās / idjtamiʿū / wa-smaʿū / wa-ʿū /. Man ʿāsha māt / wa-man māta fāt / wa kullu mā huwa āt^in^ āt* (*Bayān,* i, 52, 308-9) ("O [good] people/gather [around me] / hear / and ponder / Every living being is mortal / he who dies belongs [for ever] to the past / and everything which [must] come to pass will [assuredly] come to pass").

Connections of sadjʿ *with the Ḳurʾān*

Form and stylistic refinement play a very important role in the Ḳurʾān, of which one of the principal characteristics is assonance. It is striking to ascertain to what extent this monument of the Arabic language is akin to rhymed and rhythmic prose which—without being used there systematically—nevertheless constitutes its most remarkable artistic peculiarity. The sūra "The Men" (*al-Nās,* CXIV), for example, consists of eight very short rhythmic units. By means of examples of this type, the Ḳurʾān fully legitimised *sadjʿ*.

However, instead of profiting from this providential legitimisation, of developing and expanding rhymed prose, contrary to all expectation, encountered a certain reticence on the part of a large number of the disciples of the new religion. Thus, in spite of this evident kinship and probably on account of it, *sadjʿ* was to experience a net decline and suffer a long eclipse. Although the reasons for this discredit are not entirely clear, it is possible to identify some of the factors responsible. It is known, first of all, that the Prophet Muḥammad was accused on numerous occasions by his adversaries of being a common soothsayer, and that some of them were intent on comparing the revealed text to the vaticinations of the *kuhhān* of the *Djāhiliyya*. On the other hand, the Muslims of the time dissociated themselves from this mode of expression which, in their view, was still too closely linked to magic and to certain practices belonging to paganism (al-Djāḥiẓ, *Bayān*, i, 289-90).

Furthermore, the decline of rhymed and rhythmic prose was a logical consequence of the dogma of the "inimitability" of the Ḳurʾānic text (*iʿdjaz al-Ḳurʾān*), a principle respected by the entire community. However, in spite of this suspicious attitude towards *sadjʿ*, the latter was never completely banned. It succeeded in surviving, for almost two centuries, especially in the oral form. Muḥammad's oration at the time of the Farewell Pilgrimage in 10/631 belongs within the framework of this oratorical genre which, subsequently, was to enjoy considerable success. After the death of the Prophet, the orators (*al-khuṭabāʾ*) spoke in *sadjʿ* before the first four caliphs without exposing themselves thereby to the least criticism (*Bayān*, i, 290) (but it should nevertheless be noted that, since at that time, many orators used *sadjʿ*-less prose, the authenticity of speeches in *sadjʿ* is very much in question).

Under the Umayyads, the multiplicity of politico-religious parties was a factor favourable to the development of the oratorical art, skilfully cultivated by political figures who knew how to make an impression on audiences who remained in spite of everything very partial to *sadjʿ*. Around the mosques, the tellers of edifying stories (*ḳuṣṣāṣ*, pl. of *ḳaṣṣ* [*q.v.*]) charmed the crowds, telling them edifying stories (*ḳiṣṣa* [*q.v.*]) in seductive language (Pellat, *Le milieu baṣrien*, 108 ff.).

Another resounding speech was that which was delivered by al-Ḥadjdjadj b. Yūsuf [*q.v.*], the new governor of ʿIrāḳ, on arriving in Kūfa in 75/694 (*Bayān*, ii, 138-40; M. Messadi, *Essai sur le rythme*, 117). Of untypical violence, the harangues of al-Ḥadjdjādj were full of threats designed to intimidate all those who opposed the central power of Damascus. In a general fashion, the expansion of Islam played a capital role in the development of the oratorical art.

Official and progressive rehabilitation of sadjʿ

Under the reign of the Umayyad caliph ʿAbd al-Malik (65-85/685-705), Arabic was finally established as the administrative language of the Arabo-Muslim empire. In gradual stages, a specialised bureaucracy came into being. Scribes distinguished themselves in the epistolary genre, official and private. The most eminent among them, ʿAbd al-Ḥamīd b. Yaḥyā, nicknamed al-Kātib (d. 133/750 [*q.v.*]), created the administrative style which was, at the outset, a sort of moderately rhymed and ornate prose. In a well-known epistle (*risāla* [*q.v.*]), he established the rules of the profession of the *kātib* [*q.v.*] and authorised to some extent a more or less discreet return to *sadjʿ*, which progressively becomes fashionable again through the expedients of the administration and of the chancellery.

Ibn al-Muḳaffaʿ (d. *ca.* 140/757 [*q.v.*]), a disciple of ʿAbd al-Ḥamīd, followed the latter's example in composing manuals to be used by scribes. Subsequently, he attempted to extend the use of this elegant but relatively sober style to texts of a more literary nature. This is what he did in his adaptation in Arabic of the Indian fables known by the title of *Kalīla wa-Dimna* [*q.v.*], which is considered one of the first books written in literary prose. The successful experiment was followed up and amplified by a number of authors of the 3rd/9th century and most notably by al-Djāḥiẓ. This author played a primary role in the rehabilitation of *sadjʿ*. He contributed to this by adopting attitudes in favour of rhymed and rhythmic prose, which he defended on numerous occasions in his work and in the *Bayān* in particular (i, 287-91, iii, 29). But the best homage which he rendered to *sadjʿ* consisted in the fact that he practised it himself "with the flexibility, the intelligence and the sense of proportion which appear in all his prose and which give it its subtle and rare quality" (Messadi, *Essai*, 159).

The defeat of the modernist trend and the appearance of the neo-classical movement, which engendered a certain lassitude with regard to ancient poetry, seem to have had the effect of impelling a large number of writers of the 3rd/9th century towards the more free and more varied rhythms of *sadjʿ*.

From the 4th/10th century onward, *sadjʿ* enjoyed immense success. Little by little, it invaded all domains of literature. "It would seem that the basis of this invasion is to be sought in the high respect accorded to the works of poets by the unanimous opinion of the educated classes. Becoming the substance of literature, a fully harmonious prose... represents, in the eyes of people in love with poetry, a Cinderella figure. Her simplicity seems to them like poverty, and in order to improve her condition, they reckon it appropriate to adorn her with at least one of the ornaments of her sister and rival, this being rhyme" (W. Marçais, *La langue arabe*).

In this period, the use of *sadjʿ* became generalised, in the first instance among the secretaries of the administration who adopted the habit of furnishing their texts with rhetorical artifices and literary reminiscencies.

The eminent vizier of the Būyid princes, al-Ṣāḥib Ibn ʿAbbad (326-85/938-95 [*q.v.*]), left a collection of letters of great value. The writer and philosopher Abū Ḥayyān al-Tawḥīdī (d. after 400/1009 [*q.v.*]) is often compared to al-Djāḥiẓ for his style, of which one of the essential characteristics was the use of a *sadjʿ* which was both erudite and simple. Badīʿ al-Zamān al-Hamadhānī (357-97/968-1007 [*q.v.*]) was one of the most illustrious epistolary stylists of the 4th/10th century. After being the protegé of al-Ṣāḥib Ibn ʿAbbād, he went to seek his fortune at Nishāpūr. A collection of his letters in artistic prose has been preserved. There was in fact a veritable explosion at this time of ornate prose, seen further in the *rasāʾil* (collections of which have also been preserved) by Abū Isḥāḳ Ibrāhīm b. Hilāl al-Ṣābiʾ, Abū Bakr al-Khʷārazmī, Ibn al-ʿAmīd and Ḳābūs b. Wushmagīr. It was even used for the writing of history, seen in al-ʿUtbī's *al-Taʾrīkh al-Yamīnī*. Another major name emerges from the host of letter-writers of the later centuries, this being al-Ḳāḍī al-Fāḍil (529-96/1135-1200 [*q.v.*]) who was for a long time the secretary of administration and then associate and vizier of Ṣalāḥ al-Dīn; and he had an equally illustrious "competitor" in Ḍiyāʾ al-Dīn Ibn al-Athīr and his collection of *rasāʾil*, likewise published. The few specimens of his official writings which have been preserved are characterised by the almost systematic use of rhyme, a highly-affected style which tends to be somewhat wearisome, an abundance of metaphors and of rhetorical devices. This style was to serve as a model in the chancelleries of later periods.

The maḳāma [*q.v.*]

Al-Hamadhānī's masterpiece is his collection of "sessions" which are stories characterised by the use of rhymed and rhythmic prose, sometimes blended with verse, and by the presence of two imaginary persons, the hero and the narrator. In his *maḳāmāt*, al-Hamadhānī did not use *sadjʿ* in a systematic manner. He resorted to free prose, for example, in the transitions or when he wanted to quicken the pace of the narrative. In any case, "he remains perfectly the master of his thought; the rhythmic units designed to convey the idea are constructed according to its terms, the idea is not at all dependent on them" (R. Blachère, *Séances*, 36).

The principal successor to al-Hamadhānī was a grammarian of Baṣra, al-Ḥarīrī (446-516/1054-1112 [*q.v.*]), who not only gave the "session" its classic and definitive form, but also, and more significantly, composed the finest monument of *sadj^c* which the Arabs possess. Al-Ḥarīrī is considered by many Arab critics an incomparable stylist. The interest and the originality of the narrative do not interest him greatly. His principal concern is the style, the rhetoric and the verbal acrobatics which often constitute an end in themselves. The work of al-Ḥarīrī notably includes two texts in which each word begins, in one with *s*, in the other with *sh*. Unlike al-Hamadhānī, al-Ḥarīrī excluded from his "sessions" any passages in free prose. In his work, the use of *sadj^c* was systematic. The rhythmic units, with subtle and complicated rhymes, were arranged in impeccable sequences.

This work immediately enjoyed an unparallelled and durable vogue (Yāḳūt, *Irshād*, xvi, 267). But the writers of later times were interested only in the artifices of rhetoric and verbal felicities. Furthermore, this literary genre, so original at the outset, was very soon diverted from its initial aim to serve the most diverse purposes. It ultimately came to be confused with the genre of the *risāla*, from which it was originally distinct. By gradual stages, the word *maḳāma* served "to denote any rhetorical exercise in rhymed prose and not in verse, whatever the motive which inspires it... Any motive whatsoever is considered valid, and this composition, laden to the point of asphyxia with all the sophistications of language, of erudition and of pedantry, such that it becomes indecipherable, is called indiscriminately *risāla* or *maḳāma*" (F. de la Granja, *Maqāmas y risālas andaluzas*, xiv).

Sadj^c *in the so-called period of decadence*

The use of *sadj^c* became obligatory. Whatever the subject addressed, history, geography or medicine, the prose-writers of the so-called period of decadence invariably resorted to this mode of expression, which offered them the advantage of concealing a poverty of ideas and, in any case, of enhancing the quality of a text.

The style of the chancellery remained indelibly marked by the method of the Ḳāḍī al-Fāḍil. The rhymed units were stretched and all the figures of *badī^c* [*q.v.*] pressed into service. Historians wrote their works in rhymed prose. For example, al-Khafādjī (979-1069/1571-1659), author of a collection of biographies, resorted to this mode which does not in principle spare any discipline. Numerous "sessions" composed after the manner of al-Ḥarīrī deal with subjects as diverse as love, wine, religion or Ṣūfism. The sonorous words, redundant forms and affectedness ultimately deprived these exercises in verbal acrobatics of any genuine literary worth.

Sadj^c *since the* Nahḍa [*q.v.*]

In the 19th century, in the period of the *Nahḍa* (renaissance), the attractions of *sadj^c* were as potent as ever. With the aim of serving the Arabic language, defending its purity and restoring its prestige, Nāṣīf al-Yāzidjī (1215-88/1800-71 [see AL-YĀZIDJĪ]) composed sixty *maḳāmāt*, with commentary by himself, collected under the title *Madjma^c al-baḥrayn* ("confluence of the two seas"). He chose this structure, with its long and distinguished pedigree, because it seemed to him ideal for his purpose. Other authors of the 19th century followed the example of al-Yāzidjī, but usually in a less systematic manner.

At the beginning of this century, Muḥammad al-Muwayliḥī (1868-1930 [*q.v.*]) tried, for his part, to revive the genre in his novel *Ḥadīth ^cĪsā b. Hishām*, where the name of the narrator is borrowed from the "sessions" of al-Hamadhānī (H. Pérès, *Les origines d'un roman célèbre de la littérature arabe*). This book, which is primarily a satire on contemporary morals, was composed in a very free rhymed and rhythmic prose. Consequently, this author's concern for form never obscured his concern for substance. Al-Muwayliḥī's approach proves clearly that he did not confine himself to imitating the "sessions" of al-Hamadhānī. The inspiration of the latter is undeniable, but it was used to create a work which is firmly located in the social and cultural reality of his time. Thus his *Ḥadīth ^cĪsā b. Hishām* represents a synthesis between the classical *maḳāma* and the modern novel.

Although this work is generally considered to be the first monument of the Arabic literature of the 20th century, and although it has inspired a number of imitations and has been the object of numerous studies, further proofs of its undeniable success, there is nonetheless a sense in which it arrived a little too late. It appeared at a time when rhymed prose was beginning to be considered obsolete and archaic, so that al-Muwayliḥī's novel is a kind of swansong of the genre.

However, it is important to avoid giving the impression that, even today, there has been a complete abandonment of *sadj^c*. It should not be forgotten that the latter is in current and constant use in the mosques. On the other hand, having learned by heart in their youth a certain amount of poetry, a few texts in artistic prose and, most important of all, the Ḳur^ɔān, partially or in total, Arab writers are unable to avoid submitting to an influence which is often unconscious. While generally expressing themselves in free prose, these authors rarely resist the temptation to adorn their style with Ḳur^ɔānic reminiscences, "with some clausulas, with some alliterations, which give the work a scent of archaism which is not at all disagreeable" (Ch. Pellat, *Langue et littérature arabes*, 205).

B. *The technique of* sadj^c

The structure of the Arabic language has without doubt favoured the emergence of *sadj^c* and its considerable development, from the *Djāhiliyya* to the present day. The great variety of morphological themes of the same syllabic structure and of identical or similar rhythm constitutes an inexhaustible supply of clausulas rich in rhyme for lovers of assonance and of verbal sonority. Thus the pattern *fi^cāl^{un}* is common to a singular such as *kitāb^{un}* ("book"), *^citāb^{un}* ("reproach") or to a plural such as *kilāb^{un}* ("dogs"). Similarly, the patterns *ḥamrā^ɔu* ("red") and *shu^carā^ɔu* ("poets") offer at the end identical cadences (Blachère, *HLA*, ii, 189).

I. *External characteristics of* sadj^c

(1) *The arithmetical rhythm*

A text written in *sadj^c* is articulated in members of a sentence, the length of which remains within the limit beyond which breath is exceeded. The exigencies of breath, in this context, are important since rhymed prose—like poetry—is intended to be recited before an audience, aloud and having regard to a form of delivery which should be neither too fast nor too slow. Nevertheless, the composer of artistic prose has a fairly wide margin of manoeuvre at his disposal. His rhythmic units can, in fact, be limited to two or three syllables, just as they can be extended to comprise 13 or 14. The hemistich, the rhythmic unit of verse, which like *sadj*ᶜ is subject to the requirements of breath, comprises from 8 to 15 syllables, according to the length of the metre in question. For this reason there is a tendency to recite the line, not in its entirety and in a single breath, which is difficult, but hemistich by hemistich (Messadi, *Essai*, 17).

In his *Mathal al-sā*ʾ*ir* (i, 257-8), Ibn al-Athīr distinguished between two types of *sadj*ᶜ: a short type and a long. The unit of measure which he used to determine the average length of each of these two types of *sadj*ᶜ is not the syllable but the word, which leads him draw very approximative conclusions. In fact, he defined the short *sadj*ᶜ as that where each rhythmic unit could comprise from two to a maximum of ten words. Beyond this limit, there begins the long *sadj*ᶜ, the members of which may be moderately long (11 to 15 words), long (15 to 20 words), and very long (20 words and more). Ibn al-Athīr stressed his own preference for the short *sadj*ᶜ, stating that the fewer words there are in each of the parts of the couplet, so much the better (*ibid.*, i, 257).

The rhythmic units being often coupled with clausulas on the same rhyme, the couplets thus constituted can be perfect or unequal. They are perfect when their two members are equal. Ibn al-Athīr considered this type of *sadj*ᶜ as that "which occupies the most noble rank, on account of the equilibrium which characterises it" (*ibid.*, i, 255). But too much equilibrium and regularity engender a monotony and lassitude, which often spoil the rhymed prose of al-Ḥarīrī but which al-Hamadhānī was able to avoid by means of the rhythmic variety of his style. On the other hand, to perfect couplets, Badīᶜ al-Zamān preferred unequal couplets, of which the first member is longer than the second. This category of couplet has the advantage of conforming to the requirements of breath, demanding less effort in the second, shorter member, than in the first, longer member. Ibn al-Athīr, on the other hand, had no regard for this latter type of combination; for, he explained, being shorter than the first, the second member "then resembles a thing so mutilated that the listener remains tense like one who stumbles, falling short of an objective which he seeks to attain" (*ibid.*, i, 257). This point of view is diametrically opposed to that of M. Messadi, which is hardly surprising, given that it was the *maḳāmāt* of al-Hamadhānī which served as the basic text for Messadi's study of *sadj*ᶜ and that, as mentioned above, al-Hamadhānī had a predilection for couplets in which the first member was longer than the second. The very rare exceptions to this rule, in the work of Badīᶜ al-Zamān, are generally justified by the sense (cf. Messadi, *Essai*, 23-4).

The third and final category of couplet is that where the second member is longer than the first. It seems that this is less common and less appreciated than the other two. In any case, couplets of this type are rare in the "sessions" of al-Hamadhānī who was, no doubt, obliged to avoid them because they contradicted the requirements of breathing. In this regard, Ibn al-Athīr adopted a more equivocal position. He reckoned, in fact, that unequal couplets with longer final member were acceptable so long as the latter was not "of such a length as to detract excessively from equilibrium" (*Mathal*, i, 255).

If, in *sadj*ᶜ, the couplet is the rule, often the rhythmic units are arranged in groups of three, four or more, on a single rhyme, and contain a perceptibly equal number of syllables. In many cases also, one or more free members, not linked by a single rhyme, succeed, for some reason or another, a series of coupled elements. Such an unexpected independent member, abruptly interrupting the cadence, can be refreshing. "It facilitates, by the relaxation thus obtained, the repetition of the cadence" (Messadi, *Essai*, 28).

While al-Hamadhānī resorted very frequently to free members, which represent approximately a quarter of his *sadj*ᶜ, al-Ḥarīrī avoided them, thus excluding free prose entirely from his *maḳāmāt* but thereby rendering his style rigid and monotonous.

(2) *The rhyme*

To avoid confusion between the rhyme of verse (*ḳāfiya* [*q.v.*]), and that of *sadj*ᶜ, the Arab rhetoricians refer to the latter by the name of *fāṣila, ḳarīna, sadj*ᶜ or *sadj*ᶜ*a*, which they define as "the correspondence of words in a position of rhyme through an identical [final] consonant" (al-ᶜAskarī, *Ṣināᶜatayn*, 262; Ibn al-Athīr, *Mathal*, i, 210). Rather more prolixly, Ibn Wahb al-Kātib gives the following definition: "The *sadj*ᶜ (rhyme) in prose is similar to the *ḳāfiya* (rhyme) in poetry" (*al-Burhān*, 208-9). Rhyme is one of the essential components of the rhythm of *sadj*ᶜ. It constitutes the most apparent phonetic link between two or more rhythmic units, and permits "the prominent setting of the periodicity which is the distinguishing mark of sonant rhythm" (Messadi, 29). It is this which "regulates the cadence and marks the measure", thus separating, like a frontier, the rhythmic members of a text in *sadj*ᶜ.

The richness of the rhyme can be very variable. It is sometimes reduced to the final consonant, then comprising only a single consonantal and a single vocalic element. But more complex combinations exist, formed of two or three corresponding consonantal and vocalic elements, or even more. In the "session" of the Fazāra of al-Hamadhānī, for example, there is a pair of consecutive clausulas in which *nadjībat*ᵃⁿ rhymes with *djanībat*ᵃⁿ. One might mention also that the rhyme in the pausal form in prose is in contradistinction from the rhyme in poetry (at least, in most cases) which has a vocalic element after the *rawī* (*ḳāfiya muṭlaḳa*), i.e. *kitāb* vs. *kitābū*.

Being the most striking external characteristic of *sadj*ᶜ, rhyme gradually comes to be seen as the fundamental element. Inferior composers of rhymed prose, especially from the 5th/11th century onward, tended to accord it too much importance, seeing it as identical with *sadj*ᶜ itself. However, despite appearances, rhyme plays a considerably more modest role. Admittedly, it brings to rhythmic prose the component of timbre and contributes to the regulation of the cadence of the *sadj*ᶜ by fixing the limit which separates the rhythmic groupings, but it has no influence at all over the formation and the structuring of the latter.

II. *Internal structures of* sadjᶜ

While the poet is subject to the double constraint of metre and of single rhyme, the writer in *sadj*ᶜ enjoys far greater freedom since, in principle, only rhyme is expected of him. Totally unforeseeable at the outset, the internal rhythm of the phrase depends on the talent of the writer himself. The first grouping of a couplet or of a series is always spontaneous and absolutely free, while the construction of the second is determined by that of the first, and should reflect it in a more or less faithful manner. Thus, unlike in poetry, the rhythmic unit in *sadj*ᶜ is the whole couplet and not the clausula alone, like the hemistich with regard to verse.

Sometimes the two members of the couplet present identical phonetic patterns. The symmetrical correspondences of long and of short syllables are then perfect. Here, for example, is a couplet with numerically equal panels:

yudhību 'l-shiʿra wa 'l-shiʿru yudhībuh // wa-yadʿu 'l-siḥra wa 'l-siḥru yudjību h

∪ – – – ∪ – – ∪ ∪ – – ∪ – – – ∪ – – ∪ ∪– –

"He (sc. the pre-Islamic poet Zuhayr b. Abī Sulmā) melts poetry and poetry melts him // He calls upon the enchantment and enchantment replies to him" (al-Hamadhānī, *Séance poétique*, i, 11). This rigorous type of correspondences is quite rare, partial correspondences being more common (Messadi, *Essai*, 47-51).

In order to improve or to consolidate the rhythmic quality of *sadjʿ*, recourse was often made to the resources of *badīʿ* and, in particular, to *djinās* or *tadjnīs* [*q.v.*], or alliteration, which can involve either the words placed in the interior of the clausula or the rhyming words. This latter category of *djinās* is the more common. It is in fact to be expected that, in the majority of cases, alliteration should appear only in rhyme "since *sadjʿ* is rhymed and by definition the rhyme is a reflection of timbre" (in this regard, the remarks made by Messadi concerning the *Maḳāmāt* of al-Hamadhānī apply most often to *sadjʿ* in general; see his *Essai*, 70-2).

The interplay of short and long syllables (open and closed) determines the rhythmic style of a text in *sadjʿ* or, indeed, in verse. In fact, "the predominance and/or a felicitous distribution of long open syllables (type *mā*) are the specific generators of a musical and singing style". On the other hand, when the themes addressed are those of threat, reprimand or military valour, and the style demanded is energetic and stern, the rhythm is then marked by a net predominance of long closed syllables (type *man*). When the proportion of short syllables is raised to the highest point, this signifies in principle that the style is amorphous and that the rhythm lacks contrast (*ibid.*, 97 ff.).

Besides phonetic coupling, another element engenders and regulates the rhythm also: this is semantic parallelism. The groupings which rhyme together are very often closely linked by a relationship of sense. Al-Djāḥiẓ, who did not seek out rhyme at any price, resorted on the contrary to the coupling of ideas as well as to parallel balance, as a way of improving the rhythm. In a passage of the *Kitāb al-Ḥayawān* (i, 41), he wrote, for example: *wa 'l-kitābu wiʿāʾun muliʾa ʿilman / wa-ẓarfun ḥushiya ẓurfan*... ("The book is a receptacle full of knowledge / a vessel replete with precious objects...").

Seeking to exploit to the maximum this rhythmic procedure, the writers of rhymed prose fell, little by little, into a sterile verbal automatism, consisting of repeating the same idea in different forms solely for the sake of balance. Showing himself very stern in this respect, Ibn al-Athīr condemned these unproductive repetitions, which he found too widespread in the works of eminent prosewriters, such as the Ṣāḥib Ibn ʿAbbād, al-Ḥarīrī and others besides (*al-Mathal al-sāʾir*, i, 214-15). Good *sadjʿ*, according to him, is that in which there is neither artifice (*takalluf*) nor violence (*taʿassuf*) done to the idea or to its expression for the requirements of the rhyme or of the rhythm (*ibid.*, i, 213).

Bibliography: Examples of *sadjʿ* are disseminated among the works of numerous authors, in particular Ibn Hishām, Ṭabarī, Masʿūdī, etc. See also Djāḥiẓ, *Bayān*, Cairo 1948, i, 21, 280, 284-306; ʿAskarī, *K. al-Ṣināʿatayn*, Cairo 1952, 260-5; Ibn Wahb al-Kātib, *al-Burhān fī wudjūh al-bayān*, ed. Aḥmad Maṭlūb and Khadīdja al-Ḥadīthī, Baghdād 1387/1967; Ibn al-Athīr, *al-Mathal al-sāʾir*, Cairo 1973, i, 210 ff.; Yāḳūt, *Irshād*, Cairo 1936, xvi, 267; *LʿA*, Beirut 1956, root *s-dj-ʿ*, viii, 150-1; W. Marçais, *La langue arabe*, in *BEA*, no. 21 (January-February 1945) (repr. in *Articles et conférences*, Paris 1961); H. Pérès, *Les origines d'un roman célèbre de la littérature arabe...*, in *BEO*, x (1943-4); Goldziher, *Der chaṭīb bei den Arabern*, in *WZKM*, iv, 97-102 (summarised by G.-H. Bousquet in *Arabica*, vii [1950], 16-18); Hamadhānī, *Maḳāmāt*, ed. Muḥammad ʿAbduh, Beirut 1889, 1924, 1958; S. de Sacy, *Chrestomathie arabe*, iii, 78 ff. (tr. of six sessions); idem, ed. of the *Maḳāmāt* of al-Ḥarīrī, 1822 (2nd ed. Reinaud and Derenbourg, Paris 1847-53); R. Blachère, *Etude sémantique sur le nom maqāma*, in *Machriq* (1953), 646-52 (repr. in *Analecta*, Damascus 1975, 61-7); idem, *HLA*, ii, 187 ff. and index; idem and P. Masnou, *Maqāmāt (Séances) choisies et traduites de l'arabe, avec une étude sur le genre*, Paris 1957; Z. Mubarak, *La prose arabe au IVe siècle de l'Hégire (Xe siècle)*, Paris 1931, index; idem, *al-Nathr al-fannī fi 'l-ḳarn al-rābiʿ*, Beirut 1975, index; M. Messadi, *Essai sur le rythme dans la prose rimée en arabe*, Tunis 1981, index; Ch. Pellat, *Le milieu baṣrien et la formation de Ǧāḥiẓ*, Paris 1953, 108 ff.; F. de la Granja, *Maqāmas y risālas andaluzas*, Madrid 1976; A. Kilito, *Les séances*, Paris 1983; *EI*[1], art. SADJʿ (F. Krenkow).

(AFIF BEN ABDESSELEM)

SADJĀḤ (i.e. Sadjāḥ[i]), Umm Ṣādir bint Aws b. Ḥiḳḳ b. Usāma, or bint al-Ḥārith b. Suwayd b. ʿUḳfān, prophetess and soothsayer, one of several prophets and tribal leaders who sprang up in Arabia shortly before and during the *Ridda* [*q.v.* in Suppl.], the risings undertaken after the Prophet's death to throw off the political and military supremacy in Arabia of Medina. The genealogy, which her history proves to be the true one, shows that she belonged to the Banū Tamīm. On her mother's side she was related to the Taghlib, a tribe which comprised many Christians. She was a Christian herself, or at least had learnt much concerning Christianity from her relatives. Next to nothing is known concerning the import of her revelations and doctrines; she delivered her messages from a *minbar*, in rhymed prose, and was attended by a *muʾadhdhin* and a *ḥādjib*. Her name, or one of her names, for God was "the Lord of the clouds" (*rabb al-saḥāb*).

Sadjāḥ came to the fore in 11/632-3, after Muḥammad's death. One account of her exploits describes her as a Taghlib upstart, who had arrived from Mesopotamia at the head of a band of followers belonging to Rabīʿa, Taghlib, the Banu 'l-Namir, the Banū Iyād and the Banū Shaybān; she found the Tamīm divided, in consequence of the Prophet's death, by deep internal strife between apostates, Muslims and those who wavered between revolt and allegiance to Medina, and succeeded in converting by her revelations and uniting under her command both branches of Ḥanẓala (the Banū Mālik and the Banū Yarbūʿ), which she intended to lead against Medina. The extent of her influence on the Tamīm seems, however, to have been much greater than this version, intended to minimise their share in the *Ridda*, would have us believe. The prophetess was no outsider, she really belonged to the Tamīm, as the end of her career implies, and had gained, probably for some time before Muḥammad's death, the support of her whole tribe, whose conversion to Islam had been mainly a matter of expediency, easily shaken off.

Sadjāḥ's forces began by attacking the confederation of the Ribāb, in obedience to one of her revelations, but were severely beaten. Repairing to al-Nibādj (in Yamāma) they suffered a second defeat at the hands of the Banū ᶜAmr, and Sadjāḥ had to promise that she would leave the territory of the Tamīm. Followed by the Yarbūᶜ, she decided to join the prophet Musaylima [*q.v.*], who still controlled most of Yamāma, in order to unite their fortunes or to restore her own. Their encounter happened at al-Amwāh or at Hadjr. Musaylima was menaced by the Muslim army, and the neighbouring tribes threatened to shake off his authority, so that the arrival of a vanquished, ambitious and desperate colleague, accompanied by many armed followers, proved a trying, indeed a dangerous visitation. There is no reliable account of the meeting: according to one version, the strange couple came to an understanding, recognised each other's mission and decided to unify their two religions and their worldly interests; they were actually married, and the prophetess stayed by Musaylima to the hour of his tragic death. Al-Ṭabarī preserves obscene and very probably fictitious details concerning this union, which must have been rather a political alliance than a lustful orgy; the wedding, according to these legends, was celebrated in the same walled garden where Musaylima was to meet his death.

Other accounts of the meeting are that Musaylima, after having married Sadjāḥ, cast her off, and that she returned to her people; a third version does not mention the marriage, and says that the prophet tried to persuade his rival and would-be ally to attack the Muslims, hoping thus to get rid of her; on her refusal he offered, if she consented to depart, half the year's crops of Yamāma; she declined to go unless he promised half of the next year's harvest as well, set off with the first part of the booty, and left her representatives with Musaylima to wait for the rest, repairing to her kinsfolk. The second part of the ransom was never collected, as Musaylima was vanquished and massacred by Khālid before the next harvest.

Whatever the outcome of Sadjāḥ's relations with Musaylima, her own career was either merged into his, or cut short by repulse, and we hear nothing more of her mission. According to all accounts, she went back to her native tribe, and lived obscurely amongst them. On Ibn al-Kalbī's authority we learn that she embraced Islam when her family decided to settle in Baṣra, which had become the principal centre of the Tamīm under the Umayyads, lived and died there a Muslim, and was buried with the customary prayers and ceremonies.

Bibliography: Ibn Ḳutayba, *Maᶜārif*, ed. ᶜUkkāsha, 405; Balādhurī, *Futūḥ*, 99-100; Ṭabarī, i, 1909-21, 1930, tr. F. McG. Donner, *The conquest of Arabia*, Albany 1993, 84-98, 106; *Aghānī*[1], xviii, 165; Ibn al-Athīr, ed. Beirut, ii, 353-7; Nuwayrī, *Nihāya*, xix, ed. Muḥ. Abu 'l-Faḍl Ibrāhīm, Cairo 1975, 75-82; Diyārbakrī, *T. al-Khamīs*, Cairo 1283/1866-7, ii, 158-9; Wellhausen, *Skizzen und Vorarbeiten*, vi, 13-15; Caetani, *Annali*, A.H. 11, §§ 160-4, 170-3, A.H. 12, §§ 92-3; Kaḥḥāla, *Aᶜlām al-nisāʾ*, ii, 177-80; E.H. Shoufani, *Al-Riddah and the Muslim conquest of Arabia*, Toronto 1972; Donner, *The early Islamic conquests*, Princeton 1981, 85, 183.

(V. Vacca*)

AL-**SADJĀWANDĪ**, Abū ᶜAbd Allāh (Abu 'l-Faḍl, Abū Djaᶜfar) Muḥammad (Aḥmad) b. Abī Yazīd Ṭayfūr al-Sadjāwandī al-Ghaznawī al-Muḳriʾ al-Mufassir al-Naḥwī al-Lughawī, an innovative Ḳurʾān reader and philologist, died 560/1165 (?).

He lived and worked in Sadj/g/kāwand, a small village half-way to the east of the route from Kābul to Ghaznī in the vicinity of Sayyidābād, dominated by a high-lying citadel, now in ruins, called Takht-i or Shār-i (Shahr-i) Djamshīd. On the foot of this mount is placed the mausoleum of Khwādja Aḥmad (Muḥammad). Here, even today, the Shaykh is revered as a great and popular Ḳurʾān reader. His system of five, or seven, kinds of pauses in recitation of the Ḳurʾān (1. *lāzim* = *m*, 2. *muṭlaḳ* = *ṭ*, 3. *djāʾiz* = *dj*, 4. *mudjawwaz li-wadjh^{in}* = *z*, 5. *murakhkhaṣ ḍarūrat^{an}* = *ḍ*, and 6. *ḳad ḳīla* = *ḳ*, 7. *lā* = *l*) has found broad acceptance not only in the East but it is also substantially adopted in the official Cairo edition of the Ḳurʾān (*Gesch. des Qor.*, iii, 236-7).

The manuscripts of his *K. al-Wuḳūf* or *al-Waḳf* or *al-Waḳf wa 'l-ibtidāʾ* are numerous. These are differentiated into: (a) a complete or "greater" book, (b) a brief or "shorter" book, often commented and glossed by others, and (c) compendia on this topic by later compilers who follow al-Sadjāwandī's system, also in verses (Garrett 2067, 1). The "greater" as well as the "shorter" *waḳf* book should have originated from his *K. ᶜAyn al-tafsīr*, which has not been discovered until today. According to the somewhat younger Ibn al-Ḳifṭī [*q.v.*] (*Inbāh*, iii, 153), al-Sadjāwandī in this commentary on the Ḳurʾān treated also *ḳirāʾāt, naḥw, lugha, shawāhid*, etc. His son Abū Naṣr (Abū Djaᶜfar ?) Aḥmad—father and son are sometimes confused—excerpted and presumably modified his father's work under the title *K. Insān al-ᶜayn*. Under several other titles attributed to the father dealing with specific themes seem to be hidden other excerpts and adaptations of his main work, for example on syntax and etymology, on strange words and morphology (e.g. Mashhad, Gawhar Shād, iii [1367/1988], 1617 no. 1161).

Bibliography: Brockelmann, I², 519, S I, 724; R. Sellheim, *Materialien zur arabischen Literaturgeschichte*, i-ii, Wiesbaden-Stuttgart, 1976-87, i, 10.14-20.104-8, ii, 98.105; Ziriklī, *al-Aᶜlām*⁴, Beirut 1979, vi, 179; Kaḥḥāla, *Muᶜdjam al-muʾallifīn*, Damascus 1380/1960, x, 112; M.ᶜA. Mudarris, *Rayḥānat al-adab*², Tabrīz 1347/1968, ii, 442-3; A.Kh. al-ᶜUmar, in *MMᶜIᶜI*, xxx, 4 (1400/1980), 170-3.

(R. Sellheim)

AL-**SADJĀWANDĪ**, Sirādj al-Dīn Abū Ṭāhir Muḥammad b. Muḥammad (Maḥmūd) b. ᶜAbd al-Rashīd, Ḥanafī jurist, *flor. ca.* 600/1023. Nothing is known about his life. His *K. al-Farāʾiḍ*, known as *al-Farāʾiḍ al-Sirādjiyya* or simply *al-Sirādjiyya*, on the law of inheritance, was and still is regarded as the standard work in this field. It has been commented upon, glossed, excerpted, shortened and augmented, also in Persian and Turkish, versified (most recently in Cairo 1386/1949; Mushār, 793), repeatedly printed, also in Eng. tr. (repr. New Delhi 1981). The author himself composed a detailed commentary on it. His *K. al-Tadjnīs fi 'l-ḥisāb* or *al-Tadjnīs fi 'l-masāʾil al-ḥisābiyya*, at first probably a part of his primary work, has also been glossed by others. How far his alleged *Kitāb fi 'l-Djabr wa 'l-muḳābala* (perhaps an enlarged version of his *Tadjnīs*?) has to be included here, is not certain (R. Şeşen, *Nawādir*, ii [1400/1980], 75-6).

Bibliography: Brockelmann, I², 470-1, S I, 650-1; R. Sellheim, *Materialien zur arabischen Literaturgeschichte*, i-ii, Wiesbaden-Stuttgart, 1976-87 i, 102. 104, 106-7, ii, 95. 105; Kaḥḥāla, *Muᶜdjam al-muʾallifīn*, Damascus 1380/1960, xi, 233; Ziriklī, *al-Aᶜlām*⁴, Beirut 1979, vii, 27 (here, as e.g. by Ismāᶜīl Pasha, *Hadiyyat al-ᶜārifīn*, Istanbul 1955, ii, 106, partially confused with al-Sadjāwandī, Abū ᶜAbd

Allāh [*q.v.*]); M.ᶜA. Mudarris, *Rayḥānat al-adab*², Tabrīz 1347/1968, ii, 443. (R. SELLHEIM)

SADJDA (A.) "bowing down", the name of two Ḳurʾānic sūras (XXXII, also called *tanzīl al-sadjda*, and XLI, more commonly called *fuṣṣilat* or *ḥā-mīm*) and within the technical phrase *sadjdat* (or *sidjdat*, or plural *sudjūd*) *al-tilāwa*, in reference to the 14 Ḳurʾānic passages (variant traditions suggest 16, 15, 11, 10, or 4 passages) which require a ritual of bowing to be performed at the end of their recitation. The passages are marked in the margin of the Ḳurʾān text, usually with the word *al-sadjda*. The practice is generally considered *wādjib* "required", in the Ḥanafī *madhhab*, and is declared *mustaḥabb* "desirable", in the other schools.

All but one of the Ḳurʾānic *sadjda* passages make direct reference to the act of bowing, although by no means has every possible passage become the focus of this attention (the root *s-dj-d* is used 64 times in the Ḳurʾān, not including the 28 times the word *masdjid*/*masādjid* is used). The passages vary in their suggestions regarding the practice. Some are direct commands to perform it: XXII, 77, "O you who believe, perform the prostration and bow down" (but it is primarily the Shāfiᶜī tradition which implements bowing here and sometimes omits it at XXII, 18, thus maintaining a total of 14 verses of *sudjūd*); XLI, 37-8, which indicates that God should be bowed down to, not the sun and the moon; LIII, 62, "So bow down to God and worship" (this verse is not included in some versions of the Mālikī tradition of *sudjūd*); and XCVI, 19, "Bow down and approach (God)" (not included in the Mālikī tradition). The command is expressed negatively in LXXXIV, 20-1, "What is with those who do not believe? When the Ḳurʾān is read to them, they do not bow down" (again, not included in the Mālikī tradition).

Less than commands but suggestive of Muslim practice are passages which speak of the past: XVII, 107-09, which speaks of those who "given the knowledge before you (Muḥammad), when it is recited to them, fall on their faces, bowing down"; XIX, 58, which describes the patriarchs who bowed when the signs/verses of the Merciful were recited; and XXXVIII, 24, "[David] asked forgiveness of his Lord and fell down in prostration and repented." In this one instance the word *sadjda* is not used in the verse but *rākiᶜ*; probably as a result, *sadjda* is not required for this verse according to some jurists especially in the Shāfiᶜī school (who do then, however, maintain a total of 14 *sudjūd* by including both XXII, 18 and XXII, 77).

Others passages invite a response, such that bowing may be interpreted as a prayerful affirmation, a statement which says "Yes, I do", or suggests affirmation of group membership by saying "I am one of those" or, indeed, "I am not one of those": VII, 206, "Those who are near to your Lord ... bow down to him"; XIII, 15, "All who are in the heavens and the earth bow down to God"; XVI, 49-50, "Everything in the heavens and everything on the earth ... bows down to God"; XXII, 18, "Do you not see that all who are in the heavens and all who are on the earth ... bow down to God?"; XXV, 60, "Shall we bow down to that which you command us?"; XXVII, 25-6, "They do not bow down to God, the one who brings out the hidden in the heavens and the earth"; and XXXII, 15, which suggests that those who bow down when they hear God's signs/verses gain paradise. Some variation in the precise verse ending at which the *sadjda* should be done is to be noted; performing a bowing at the end of *sūra* XV is also mentioned in some sources.

After any one of those passages is recited, whether in the context of *ṣalāt* or *tadjwīd* in general, the following ritual will be observed, although the precise details vary between the legal schools: the *takbīr* is pronounced, a prostration is performed such that the forehead touches the ground, words of praise or supplication appropriate to the verse in question are uttered, and the *takbīr* is uttered again upon rising. Performing these acts requires the state of ritual purity associated with prayer.

Among the oldest datable sources dealing with bowing during Ḳurʾān recitation is Abū ᶜUbayd (d. 224/838), *Faḍāʾil al-Ḳurʾān*, Beirut 1991, 66, where the practice in relationship to Ḳurʾān XIX, 58 (not XXXII, 15 as in the printed text) is mentioned; the emphasis of the chapter in this book, however, falls on weeping (*bukāʾ*) during recitation, a practice which in later texts (e.g. al-Nawawī (d. 676/1278 [*q.v.*]), *al-Tibyān*) tends to be overwhelmed by the more formalised bowing. In ᶜAbd Allāh b. Wahb (d. 197/812), *al-Djāmiᶜ*, ed. M. Muranyi, Wiesbaden 1992, 62-78, *sadjda* is treated fully, in a manner similar to later *ḥadīth* collections.

The *ḥadīth* books are replete with references to bowing in recitation and the practice of the bowings in the various passages may be established through their testimony. Much of the *ḥadīth* material reflects a debate over whether the practice was actually required or simply meritorious. Later jurists discussed many additional aspects of this practice, including what to do when one hears somebody else reciting a verse which requires *sadjda* and whether (and in which context) the *sadjda* could be delayed.

Bibliography: Wensinck, *Handbook*, s.v. "Prostration"; Shāfiᶜī, *K. al-Umm*, Beirut n.d., i, 133-9, esp. on the *sadjda* in sūra XXII; Muhammad Abul Quasem, *The recitation and interpretation of the Qurʾān: al-Ghazali's theory*, Kuala Lumpur 1979, 44-7 (a tr. of the eighth book from Ghazālī's *Iḥyāʾ ᶜulūm al-dīn*); Ḳurṭubī, *al-Djāmiᶜ li-aḥkām al-Ḳurʾān*, Cairo 1967, vii, 356-9 (*ad* Ḳurʾān, VII, 206); Nawawī, *al-Tibyān fī ādāb ḥamalat al-Ḳurʾān*, Cairo 1977, 95-108. (A. RIPPIN)

SADJDJĀD ḤUSAYN, SAYYID [see HIDJĀʾ. iv. Urdu].

SADJDJĀDA (A., pl. *sadjādjid, sadjādjīd, sawādjid*), the carpet on which the *ṣalāt* [*q.v.*] is performed. The word is found neither in the Ḳurʾān nor in the canonical Ḥadīth; the occasional use of a floor-covering of some kind was, however, known at quite an early period.

1. Early tradition. In the Ḥadīth [*q.v.*] we are often told how Muḥammad and his followers performed the *ṣalāt* on the floor of the mosque in Medina after a heavy shower of rain, so that their noses and heads came in contact with the mud (e.g. al-Bukhārī, *Adhān*, *bābs* 135, 151; Muslim, *Ṣiyām*, trads. 214-16, 218, etc.). At the time when such traditions arose, the use of some form of carpet was not so general that their origin can be dated so far back as the time of the Prophet. In a series of traditions, the saying is put into Muḥammad's mouth that it was his privilege, in contrast with the other prophets, that the earth was for him *masdjid wa-ṭahūr* (e.g. al-Bukhārī, *Tayammum, bāb* 1; *Ṣalāt, bāb* 56, etc.). Al-Tirmidhī, *Ṣalāt, bāb* 130, also tells us that some *faḳīhs* prefer the *ṣalāt* upon the bare earth.

The canonical Ḥadīth gives us the following picture: Muḥammad performs the *ṣalāt* on his own garment, protecting his arms against the heat of the soil during prostration with one of its sleeves, his knees with one end of his robes and his forehead with the *ᶜimāma* (turban) or the *ḳalansuwa* (cap) [see LIBĀS. (i)

Sadjdjāda. (*Namāzlîk*) (T.), from Gördes, Turkey, 18th century.
(*By courtesy of the Board of Trustees of the Victoria & Albert Museum*).

Sad̲j̲d̲j̲āda. (*D̲j̲ā-yi-namāz*) (P.), from Kirmān, Persia, 18th century.
(*By courtesy of the Board of Trustees of the Victoria & Albert Museum*).

The central and eastern Arab lands]; (al-Bukhārī, *Ṣalāt, bāb*s 22, 23; Muslim, *Masādjid*, trad. 191; Aḥmad b. Ḥanbal, *Musnad*, i, 320). Al-Bukhārī, *Ṣalāt, bāb* 22, tells us that Muḥammad performed the *ṣalāt* on his *firāsh* (quilt).

The Ḥadīth also informs us that the *ṣalāt* was performed on mats; e.g. al-Tirmidhī, *Ṣalāt, bāb* 131, where a *bisāṭ* [*q.v.* in Suppl.] is mentioned; also Ibn Mādja, *Iḳāmat al-ṣalawāt, bāb* 63; Aḥmad b. Ḥanbal, i, 232; iii, 160, 171, 184, 212; also a *ḥaṣīr* (a mat the length of a man), e.g. al-Bukhārī, *Ṣalāt, bāb* 20; Aḥmad b. Ḥanbal, iii, 52, 59, 130 ff., 145, 149, 164, 179, 184 ff., 190, 226, 291. This tradition is also found in Muslim, *Masādjid*, trad. 266. It is evident from Abu Dāwūd, *Ṣalāt, bāb* 91, that at the end of the 3rd/9th century, dressed skins of animals (*farwa maṣbūgha*) [see FARWA] were already being used.

We also frequently find it mentioned that Muḥammad performed the *ṣalāt* on a *khumra* (al-Bukhārī, *Ṣalāt, bāb* 21; Muslim, *Masādjid*, trad. 270; al-Tirmidhī, *Ṣalāt, bāb* 129; Aḥmad b. Ḥanbal, i, 269, 308 ff., 320, 358, ii, 91 ff., 98; al-Nasāʾī, *Masādjid, bāb* 43; Ibn Saʿd, i/2, 160). According to Muḥammad b. ʿAbd Allāh al-ʿAlawī's marginal glosses to Ibn Mādja, *Iḳāma, bāb*s 63, 64, the *khumra* afforded just sufficient room for the prostration (see above).

The word *sadjdjāda* is found a century after the conclusion of the canonical Ḥadīth literature. Al-Djawharī, *Ṣaḥāḥ*, explains it to be synonymous with *khumra*. Dozy, *Suppl.*, quotes passages from Ibn Baṭṭūṭa, who mentions among the customs of a certain *zāwiya* in Cairo that the whole congregation went to the mosque on a Friday, where a servant laid his *sadjdjāda* ready for each one (i, 73, cf. 72). The same traveller tells us something similar regarding Māllī (i.e. Mali [*q.v.*]) where everyone sends his servant with his *sadjdjāda* to the mosque, to lay it ready in his place. He adds that they were made out of the leaves of a palm-like tree (iv, 422).

Some early traditions survived until this century. In Mecca, everyone in the great mosque performs the *ṣalāt* on a *sadjdjāda*, usually a small carpet just large enough for the *sudjūd* [*q.v.*]. After use it is rolled up and carried off on the shoulder. In place of a carpet, a towel is sometimes used, for example the one used to dry oneself after the *wuḍūʾ* [*q.v.*].

In Morocco, the common people do not make any use of the *sadjdjāda*; the middle classes favour small felt carpets (*lăbda*), just large enough for performing the *sudjūd*. *Lăbda*s are especially used by *faḳīh*s and have almost become one of their distinctive marks. They fold them and bear them under their arm in an ostentatious way wherever they go; certain *faḳīh*s refuse to sit down on anything other than their *lăbda*. In Algeria, the *sadjdjāda* is rarely used, except among the heads of *ṭarīḳa*s and various marabouts; here, it usually consists of the skins of goats or gazelles. The common people ascribe miraculous powers to these skins.

In Egypt, *sadjdjāda*s used until the early 20th century to be imported from the carpet-weaving districts of Asia Minor, and were used only by the rich. Persons of the lower orders often perform the *ṣalāt* upon the bare ground; they seldom immediately wipe off the dust which adheres to the nose and forehead, regarding it as auspicious to retain traces of the *sudjūd*.

In the former Dutch East Indies (now Indonesia), long narrow mats and carpets were formerly placed on the floor of the mosque before the beginning of the services. After the service these were rolled up and laid aside (Snouke Hurgronje, *Verspr. Geschr.*, iv/2, 366).

The *sadjdjāda* has assumed special significance in the religious societies and in the dervish orders (see 3. below).

A whole series of mystical interpretations is associated with the *sadjdjāda* or *bisāṭ*. References are found to the *sadjdjāda* of the paths of salvation, and the profession of *tawḥīd* is called the *sadjdjāda* of the faith.

2. Surviving examples. The distinguishing iconography of the *sadjdjāda* as familiar today is the large central *miḥrāb* [*q.v.*], the arch of which is placed to one end of the rug; the field may be plain or decorated. The rug is surrounded by a series of decorative borders. When spread in a mosque, the *miḥrāb* is laid pointing towards the *ḳibla* [*q.v.*] wall; for private prayer in the home, the *miḥrāb* is similarly laid pointing in the direction of Mecca. In early *sadjdjāda*s, a representation of a mosque lamp is sometimes placed within the arch of the *miḥrāb*; by the early 13th/19th century, the lamp was often replaced by a bouquet of flowers. Sometimes a pair of candlesticks flank the *miḥrāb*; in later periods, two columns of flowers may be found. Sometimes a short text from the Ḳurʾān is woven at the head of the *miḥrāb*. For communal family prayers, a *ṣaff* (row), a long rug with a row of *miḥrāb*s side by side, may be used. In Turkey, the *sadjdjāda* was known as *namāzlīḳ* (T.); in Persia, as *djā-yi namāz* (P.)

A few rare *sadjdjāda*s in museum and private collections are attributed to the 10th-11th/16th-17th centuries, but the majority of "antique" *sadjdjāda*s date from the 12th-13th/18th-19th centuries. A few earlier representations of *sadjdjāda* survive in Persian miniatures. A manuscript of Balʿamī's translation of al-Ṭabarī's *Taʾrīkh*, painted in Shīrāz about the second quarter of the 8th/14th century, now in the Freer Gallery, Washington D.C., contains a miniature of Muḥammad seated upon a *sadjdjāda*, in conversation with Abū Bakr and ʿAlī. The *sadjdjāda* is here interpreted as a seat of honour, and a kind of spiritual throne. Similarly, a miniature in the *Miʿrādj-nāma* from Harāt, dated 840/1436, now in the Bibliothèque Nationale, Paris, depicts Muḥammad with an aureole around his head to indicate his spiritual authority, seated upon a *sadjdjāda*. To the left are Adam, Noah and David; to the right, Abraham, Moses and Jesus. Representations of the *ṣalāt* being performed are rare, but a Mughal miniature of the early 11th/17th century, in the Staatliche Museen, Berlin, depicts Djahāngīr and his son in prayer upon two *sadjdjāda*s; the courtiers share a large *bisāṭ*.

Turkey has for centuries been famous for the production of pile carpets. When weaving a *sadjdjāda*, the weaver uses the finest materials within his means, and his best workmanship. Turkey adheres to strict Islamic artistic tenets, wherein the representation of living creatures is forbidden. Turkish designs thus have a balanced formal structure, though the decoration is very rich, incorporating flowers with geometrical ornament. The most famous centres for the weaving of *sadjdjāda*s are Gördes (Ghiordes) and Kula.

The artistic tenets of Islam are less rigidly interpreted in Persia, where animals and birds often appear upon secular carpets. *Sadjdjāda*s are more graceful in style than in Turkey; but though the *miḥrāb* may have more naturalistic elegance, and the lamp and floral ornament more realism, when weaving a *sadjdjāda* the injunction against representing living creatures is observed. The *miḥrāb* is sometimes filled with the traditional "Tree of Life", or with a large flowering plant. A particularly rich *sadjdjāda* may be woven with warp and weft, or even pile, of silk.

In both Turkey and Persia, the rural people and the

nomadic tribes practise rug-weaving, including *sadjdjādas*. The designs are bold, colourful and often profusely ornamented with geometrical and stylised motifs. In addition to pile rugs, tapestry-woven rugs (*ḳilim*) are woven. The *miḥrāb* of the *sadjdjāda* is often very simply delineated, and usually of angular form.

The rugs and *sadjdjādas* of the Caucasus have been little known until the 13th/19th century. The *sadjdjādas* have distinctive geometrical ornament, and stylised motifs of local tradition; many *sadjdjādas* are *ḳilim*-woven.

The normal floor-mat in India is the *darī*, a flat-woven pile-less rug of thick cotton. In the hot season, a light floorspread of fine cotton, painted and printed, was practical. The art of pile-carpet weaving was not introduced until the reign of Akbar (963-1014/1556-1605) [see MUGHALS. 8. (a) Carpets]. Thereafter pile-woven carpets and *sadjdjādas* following closely the style of Eastern Persia were used only by the wealthy. Henry Cousens, examining the Djāmiʿ Masdjid at Bīdjāpūr [*q.v.*] for the ASI (Imperial Series of Reports, xxxvii [1916], 59 and plate XXIV), records several long mats with rows of *miḥrābs* for communal worship. Two or three are very simple and may be *darīs*. The rugs are undated, but may be 12th/18th or 13th/19th century. Other *darī*-woven *sadjdjādas*, of attractive simplicity, from the 13th/19th century, survive in museum collections.

A few rare cotton *sadjdjādas* survive, made in the region of Burhānpūr, Khāndesh, in the 12th/18th century. The design is restrained and dignified, the *miḥrāb* and the borders being ornamented with fine painted and printed floral meanders; a particularly Indian feature is the conventional representation of the domed minarets of a *masdjid* rising from the sides of the *miḥrāb* (Irwin and Hall [1971], 26 and plate 8). Printed cotton *sadjdjādas* made in the late 13th/19th century at Masulipatam, at very small cost for the ordinary people, survive in museum collections.

Bibliography: Part 1. Early tradition. In addition to the works cited in the text, see C. Snouck Hurgronje, *De Islam in Nederlandsch-Indie*, Baarn 1913; P. Kahle, *Zur Organisation der Derwischorden in Egypten*, in *Isl.*, vi (1916), 149 ff.

Part 2. Surviving examples. S.M. El Sadhi, *Antique prayer rugs from the Orient*, in *The Antiquarian*, xiii/3 (New York 1929), 32-5, 74; M. Mostafa, *Sadjādjid al-ṣalāt al-turkiyya*, Cairo, Museum of Islamic Art 1953; idem, *Turkish prayer rugs*, Cairo, Museum of Islamic Art 1953 (English ed.); R.E.G. Macey, *Oriental prayer rugs*, Leigh-on-Sea 1961; A. Hopf, *Tapis d'Orient: Anatolie, Transylvanie, Caucase, Perse, Turkestan*, Paris 1962 (col. plates pp. 2-6; 12; 14; 17; 20); J.V. McMullan, *Islamic carpets*, New York 1965 (col. plates pp. 4; 7; 30-32; 35-6; 90-1; 106); K.H. Turkhan, *Islamic rugs*, London 1968; Museum für Kunsthandwerk, *Islamische Teppiche: der Joseph V. McMullan Kollektion, New York* (exhibition catalogue), Frankfurt-am-Main 1968-9; J. Irwin and M. Hall, *Indian painted and printed fabrics*, Aḥmadābād 1971 (p. 26 and plate 8); Textile Museum, *Prayer rugs* (exhibition catalogue), Washington D.C. 1974; R. Bechirian, *Tapis: Perse, Turquie, Caucase, Asie centrale, Inde, Chine*, Paris 1976.

(A.J. WENSINCK-[MARGARET HALL])

3. In mysticism. Here, the meanings of this term are derivative from its principal function, i.e. a place upon which one prostrates him/herself in prayer. The peculiarity of its Ṣūfī usage is determined by its intimate association with such critical notions of Ṣūfism as "sainthood" (*wilāya* [*q.v.*]) and mystical "gnosis" (*maʿrifa* [*q.v.*]). In other words, if the praying person happens to be a holy and righteous "friend of God" (*walī* [*q.v.*]) or a gnostic possessed of God's sublime mysteries (*ʿārif*), the adherents of Ṣūfism often view him/her as imparting to the prayer mat some of his/her supernatural powers. It is out of the intricate alliance of all-Islamic and mystical beliefs that a distinctly mystical sense of this term has eventually crystallised.

As a symbol and attribute of piety, *sadjdjāda* was appropriated by the Ṣūfīs immediately after its introduction into the religious life of the Muslim community in the early 4th/10th (H. Landolt, *Gedanken zum islamischen Gebetsteppich*, in *Festschrift Alfred Bühler*, ed. C.A. Schmitz and R. Wildhaber, Basel 1965, 244, 247). A prayer mat, for instance, played an important role in an episode included in the collection of stories that depict the ordeal of al-Ḥallādj [*q.v.*], the celebrated Ṣūfī martyr of Baghdād (see *Akhbār al-Ḥallāj. Texte ancien relatif à la predication ... du mystique musulman al-Ḥosayn b. Manṣôur al-Ḥallāj*, ed., annot., and trans. by L. Massignon and P. Kraus, Paris 1936). In this episode, al-Ḥallādj's inadvertent discovery of the Supreme Name of God that was written on a piece of paper stuck under al-Djunayd's [*q.v.*] *sadjdjāda* led to an ominous encounter between the two Ṣūfī masters. In the course of the quarrel that ensued, al-Djunayd predicted the ghastly details of al-Ḥallādj's impending execution (Massignon, *Passion of al-Ḥallāj, mystic and martyr of Islam*, Princeton 1982, ii, 452). References to the prayer mat as a distinctive mark of the authentic Ṣūfī appear in the classic Ṣūfī manual of Abū Naṣr al-Sarrādj al-Ṭūsī [*q.v.*] and his contemporaries (*K. al-Lumaʿ fī 'l-taṣawwuf*, ed. R.A. Nicholson, London-Leiden 1914, 201; Landolt, *op. cit.*, 247). Somewhat later, in his "Rule for Ṣūfī novices" (*Ādāb al-murīdīn*, tr. F. Meier as *Ein Knigge für Sufis*, in *RSO*, xxxii [1957], 485-524) the noted Persian mystic Nadjm al-Dīn al-Kubrā [*q.v.*] listed the *sadjdjāda* among such recognisable Ṣūfī paraphernalia as the patched mantle (*muraḳḳaʿ* [*q.v.*]), the belt (*āstīn*), the staff (*ʿaṣā*), the turban (*dastār*), the leather bowl (*rakwa*), and, finally, the inevitable Ṣūfī robe (*khirḳa* [*q.v.*]). To each of these typical Ṣūfī items al-Kubrā attributes a symbolic meaning. Thus he describes the *sadjdjāda* as "the carpet of the proximity to God (*ḳurb*)" upon which His faithful servant "has set the foot of worship" (Meier, *op. cit.*, 508). In a passage based on the work of the earlier Ḥanbalī mystic ʿAbd Allāh al-Anṣārī [*q.v.*] of Harāt, al-Kubrā specifies the proper position to be assumed by a Ṣūfī beginner, when he installs himself on a *sadjdjāda*: he should sit with his hands and legs crossed, his face turned in the direction of Mecca; his thighs and private parts ought to be decently covered. While on his prayer carpet the Ṣūfī is not allowed to blow his nose, spit, or scratch himself. Nor should he converse loudly with those around him and gesticulate. Rather, he should focus his thoughts on God alone in an attempt to grasp what God expects him to do in each particular moment, and then act accordingly. All this, according to al-Kubrā, constitutes "the rules of the *sadjdjāda*." (Meier, *op. cit.*, 509-10). H. Landolt interprets al-Kubrā's instructions as an indication of the special significance that Ṣūfī theorists accorded to the prayer carpet. According to Landolt, it is more than a spot upon which the ritual prayer is performed; in the Ṣūfī tradition the *sadjdjāda* becomes a privileged spiritual space where direct contact with God is effected, i.e. an arena of mystical meditation *par excellence* (*op. cit.*, 247; cf. A. Ferrier, *Initiation au décor rituel du tapis de prière*, in *Connaissance des arts*, Paris [March 1959], 58, 61). This may be true. However, for all intents and purposes, the prayer rug has become neither an un-mistakeable sign nor an exclusive prerogative of the Ṣūfī _shaykh_. Rather, most Muslims considered it to be a symbol of righteousness and an important, albeit optional, condition of ritual purity not necessarily restricted to the realm of Islamic mysticism (see e.g. E.W. Lane, _Manners and customs of the modern Egyptians_, London-New York 1966, 73). This may explain why Ibn al-Djawzī [q.v.], the Ḥanbalī legist who under-took an exhaustive critique of contemporary Ṣūfī thought and practice, tellingly omits the prayer rug from his discussion of the Ṣūfī "excesses" and exotic "innovations" such as living in isolated lodges (_ribāṭ_ [q.v.]), donning exotic clothes (_muraḳḳaʿ_, _khirḳa_), making light of the ablutions and the prayer, en-couraging voluntary poverty and begging, indulging in disgraceful musical sessions and dances, etc. (_Talbīs Iblīs_, ed. Muḥammad ʿAlī Abū 'l-ʿAbbās, Cairo 1990, 145-340). This probably indicates that, in Ibn al-Djawzī's time at least, the _sadjdjāda_ was not regard-ed as an exclusive feature of Ṣūfī life style. In modern times, too, the prayer rug does not figure among the usual accessories of some contemporary mystical fraternities of Persia, i.e. the Dhahabiyya, Khāksār, Niʿmatullāhiyya, which have been meticulously des-cribed by R. Gramlich (_Die schitischen Derwischorden Persiens. Dritte Teil: Brauchtum und Riten_, Wiesbaden 1981, 3-12). Yet, the Ottoman traveller Ewliyā Čelebī (d. 1093/1682) in his description of a pilgrimage to the Bektāshī shrine at ʿUthmāndjīḳ (Anatolia) mentions that visitors (mostly members of the Bektāshī order) were given a _khirḳa_, a _sadjdjāda_, a standard, a drum, a staff, and a _tādj_ "as symbols of dervishship" (q. in J.R. Brown, _The dervishes, or Oriental mysticism_, ed. H.A. Rose, repr. London 1968, 214, 201; cf., how-ever, _idem_, 176-93, where the _sadjdjāda_ is not listed among the usual personal belongings of the Bektāshī dervish). Hence, as we can see, the status of the _sadjdjāda_ vis-à-vis Ṣūfism is somewhat tenuous. On some occasions it surely can be viewed as a hallmark of the Muslim mystic. Nonetheless, one cannot unreservedly link it to the Ṣūfī piety and way of living in contrast, for instance, to such distinct Ṣūfī ac-cesories as the _muraḳḳaʿ_ (and/or the _khirḳa_), the _tādj_ [q.v.], the rosary (_subha_) worn on the neck, the _kashkūl_ [q.v.], etc. (see Gramlich, _op. cit._, 3-12; cf. Brown, _op. cit._, 178-92).

This uncertainty notwithstanding, with the rise of organised Ṣūfism and the concomitant development of the notion of _wilāya_ from the 7/13th centuries on-wards, the mystical connotations of the _sadjdjāda_ became more strongly pronounced. In numerous oral and written accounts of Ṣūfī miracles (_karāmāt_ [q.v.]), which circulated widely among diverse Muslim au-diences, prayer carpets (or, sometimes, simple sheep and goat skins used for the same purposes) miraculously transport their holy owners, the Ṣūfī saints and marabouts, from one place to the other, a usual destination being Mecca. Again, the theme of "the flying carpet" was not confined exclusively to the mystical tradition. On the contrary, it has become a constantly recurring motif of Middle Eastern literature and folklore. According to one such legend, the last Baghdād caliph used a flying prayer mat in order to escape from the city besieged by the Mongols Ferrier, _op. cit._, 58). A person who, in the popular imagination, was closely bound with the motif of "the flying carpet" is the Ḳurʾānic Sulaymān. His magic silk carpet was delivered to him from Paradise (by either God or the Devil). With his throne installed on the carpet, Sulaymān was able to travel far and wide driven by winds which he controlled at will (Landolt,

op. cit., 252). Another Ḳurʾānic prophet, Adam, is said to be have received his _sadjdjāda_ from the angel Djībrīl, who had made it from the skins of the sheep of Paradise.

In contrast to popular lore that evinces particular fascination with the magic properties inherent in the _sadjdjāda_, Ṣūfī writers tend to emphasise that, whatever thaumaturgic qualities it may possess result from the sanctifying presence of the Ṣūfī _walī_, whose divinely given "grace" (_baraka_ [q.v.]) miraculously transforms everything around him. When a Ṣūfī saint spreads his shabby prayer rug above the waves (Lan-dolt, _op. cit._, 253) or performs his supererogatory prayers standing on the mat suspended in the air (Ibn ʿArabī, _al-Futūḥāt al-makkiyya_, Cairo 1329, i, 186; tr. in R.W.J. Austin, _Sufis of Andalusia_, Oxford 1971, 28-9), one realises that it is the saint, not his _sadjdjāda_, that makes such wondrous things possible. In the case of Ibn ʿArabī's narrative, the ordinariness of the prayer mat is intentionally stressed in order to throw into relief the supernatural powers that the presence of God's friend conveys to it. It is noteworthy that in both cases the flying rugs are brought into play with a view to persuading some sceptical, rationalist onlookers who doubted the reality of the miracles ascribed to the Ṣūfī saints.

In keeping with a widespread Ṣūfī belief that was shared by the generality of Muslims, the blessing and the beneficial grace of the _walī_ pervade all things and individuals that have come into direct contact with him/her. Such miracle-working grace does not cease with the _walī_'s death. It is thought to be inherited by his/her progeny. On the other hand, it is also immor-talised in the _walī_'s shrine as well as his/her personal effects. Both symbolise the saint's invisible presence among his/her relatives and followers. This helps to explain why such vestiges often become objects of veneration similar to that enjoyed by the relics of the Christian saints. It is against the background of this belief that one should view the concepts of the _shaykh_ [_walī_] _al-sadjdjāda_ and its Persian analogue _sadjdjāda-nishīn_, meaning "the prayer rug sitter" (see e.g. H.A.R. Gibb, _Muhammadanism: an historical survey_, ²Oxford 1968, 152). These terms were normally ap-plied to leaders of Ṣūfī communities or heads of holy lineages [see SHARĪF] who fell heir to the spiritual authority and blessing of a revered saintly founder (see F. Meier, _Abū Saʿīd-i Abū l-Ḥayr (357-440/967-1049). Wirklichkeit und Legende_, Leiden-Tehran-Liège 1976, 438-67, esp. 458). By extension, the entire mystical "path" initiated by a founding saint was regarded as his/her _sadjdjāda_. It can, therefore, be treated as another synonym of _ṭarīḳa_ [q.v.], _silsila_ [q.v.], and _khilāfa_ [q.v., section 3], i.e. of the terms ap-plied to various Ṣūfī organisations.

This usage became particularly prominent in Egypt and, to a lesser extent, in North Africa, whereas in the East it appears only sporadically, and does not carry the precise technical meaning ascribed to it in Western Islam (for such occasional usage, see e.g. H.R. Roemer, _Staatsschreiben der Timuridenzeit. Das Šaraf-nāma des ʿAbdallāh Marwarīd in kritischer Auswegung_, Wiesbaden 1952, 64, 158). In Egypt, the phrase _mashāyikh [shaykh] al-sadjdjāda_ (and its correlate _arbāb al-sadjādjīd_), as technical terms used in official documents, do not seem to have gained wide currency before the end of the 11th/17th century. Both terms were applied to the leaders of Egypt's major Ṣūfī _ṭuruḳ_ and _ṭuruḳ_-linked institutions, i.e. _zāwiya_ [q.v.], _takiyya_, and popular Ṣūfī shrines. The term _arbāb al-sadjādjīd_, however, seems to have been reserved for the four family-based mystical associations, namely those which traced themselves back to the Rightly-Guided Caliphs and the Companions. According to F. de Jong, these four were essentially family groups turned *ṭuruḳ*. They were: *al-Bakriyya* (descending from Abū Bakr al-Siddīḳ), *al-ʿInāniyya* (ʿUmar b. al-Khaṭṭāb), *al-Khudayriyya* (al-Zubayr b. al-ʿAwwām), and *al-Wafāʾiyya* (ʿAlī b. Abī Ṭālib) (*Ṭuruq and Ṭuruq-linked institutions in nineteenth century Egypt*, Leiden 1978, 13-14). Of the leaders of these family *ṭuruḳ*, the *shaykh al-sadjdjāda al-bakriyya* was to assume special importance when in 1227/1812, in a drive to secure better state control over the Egyptian religious establishment, the Viceroy of Egypt Muḥammad ʿAlī [*q.v.*] invested the holder of that office with authority over all mystical communities (*ṭawāʾif al-fuḳarāʾ al-ṣūfiyya*) as well as the Ṣūfī shrines and lodges of that country (al-Djabartī, *ʿAdjāʾib al-āthār*, Cairo 1297, iv, 165; for a tr. of Muḥammad ʿAlī's *firmān*, see de Jong, *op. cit.*, 192-3). For almost a century the holders of this office endeavoured, with varying success, to steer a middle course between the assertive temporal rulers and the restive leadership of Egyptian mystical associations who were anxious to preserve their independence vis-à-vis the Egyptian government (the policies pursued by the incumbents of the *al-sadjdjāda al-bakriyya* from 1227/1812 until 1321/1903 are analysed in de Jong, *op. cit.*). In the 19th and early 20th centuries, the leaders of the newly-founded Egyptian *ṭuruḳ* had to obtain the title of the *shaykh al-sadjdjāda* from the current holder of the Bakriyya "prayer mat", whose hereditary office was called *shaykh mashāyikh al-ṭuruḳ al-ṣufiyya*. Only after the latter's approval were they recognised by both the government and the Ṣūfī establishment of Egypt represented by the so-called "Ṣūfī Council" (*al-madjlis al-ṣūfī*). The latter, in turn, was always presided over by the *shaykh al-sadjdjāda al-bakriyya* (*ibid.*, 132-46, *et passim*; P. Kahle, *Zur Organisation der Derwischorden in Egypten*, in *Isl.*, vi [1916], 152-3; for a recent example of a newly-founded brotherhood seeking such an approval, see M. Gilsenan, *Saint and Sufi in modern Egypt*, Oxford 1973, 36, where the discussion centres on the rise and subsequent functioning of a modern *ṭarīḳa* called *al-ḥāmidiyya shādhiliyya*). In modern Egyptian usage, the central office of a Ṣūfī order, which today appears to be a rather bureaucratised and centralised institution, is called *bayt al-sadjdjāda* (dial. *beit al-siggāda*). It serves as the residence and the office of the order's *shaykh* or his senior aide (*wakīl*). These, in turn, are assisted by a group of the lesser officials known as *khulafāʾ* and *nuḳabāʾ al-sadjdjāda* (*ibid.*, 81). Deputies of the head of an order in a particular area (*khulafāʾ*), regularly send detailed reports on their activities to the *bayt al-sadjdjāda* with a view to keeping its leadership abreast of the developments at the lower levels of the brotherhood (Gilsenan, *op. cit.*, 82, 99, 101, etc.).

A *sadjdjāda* together with banners, drums, cymbals, staffs and a decorated litter are among the most valued regalia of the Egyptian brotherhood. Its guardianship is entrusted to one of the *shaykh's* closest associates, one named *naḳīb al-sadjdjāda par excellence*, in contradistinction to the ordinary *nuḳabāʾ* who run the brotherhood's regional cells on behalf of the regional deputy, i.e. *khalīfa*, a person appointed directly by the *shaykh al-sadjdjāda* (Kahle, *op. cit.*, 164). Yet, unlike the other items listed above, the prayer rug does not seem to play any role in the imposing annual festivities organised by each important Egyptian *ṭarīḳa* (sc. the *mawlid* [*q.v.*]). The *sadjdjāda*, however, comes to the fore in the elaborate ceremonies during which new *khulafāʾ* and *nuḳabāʾ* are introduced into the office respectively by the *shaykh al-sadjdjāda* and the *khalīfa* of a regional Ṣūfī lodge. After this ceremony, the new *khalīfa* buys a simple prayer rug that becomes a symbol of his changed status within the brotherhood (*ibid.*, 157).

The deputy's *sadjdjāda* is normally used in the famous ceremony of "ligature", or "binding the girdle" *shadd*, which was widely practiced by both Ṣūfī associations and some craft guilds (*aṣnāf*; sing. *ṣinf* [*q.v.*]) of the Muslim Middle East. The *shadd* ceremony normally takes place in a *bayt al-sadjdjāda*, a regional *zāwiya*, or, in the case of the *ṣinf*, in a guild's headquarters. The novice who seeks to join a guild or a *ṭarīka*—the same applies to the would-be *naḳīb*—enters the circle of dervishes or initiated artisans, where he is solemnly girdled by the *khalīfa* (or the guild's elder), while he is standing on the *sadjdjāda*. The latter on such occasions is referred to as "the carpet of the Truth" (*bisāṭ al-ḥaḳḳ*), or "the carpet of God" (*bisāṭ Allāh*), i.e. the terms indicative of divine presence. This formal initiation, which is seen by its participants as "binding" of a new member (*mashdūd*) to a mystical brotherhood or a fraternity of artisans, is followed by a repast shared by the brethren, who are sitting on the carpet of initiation (H. Thorning, *Beiträge zur Kenntnis des islamischen Vereinswesens auf Grund von "Basṭ madad et-taufīq"*, Berlin 1913, 101-64, 255-67, *et passim*; Kahle, *op. cit.*, 163-67; cf. Brown, *Dervishes*, 173-7; for similar practices in the modern Persian Ṣūfī associations, see Gramlich, *Die Schiitischen Derwischorden, passim*).

Similar initiatory rites are attested for the Ṣūfī *ṭuruḳ* of Anatolia and Persia. Here, however, a sheep-skin (Turk. *pūst, post*) normally replaces the *sadjdjāda* in the *shadd* and similar ceremonies. In Bektāshī lodges (*takiya*) the *posts*, which may be twelve in number but are usually four (J.K. Birge, *The Bektashi order of dervishes*, London-Hartford, Conn. 1937, 178-80; cf. Brown, *op. cit.*, 186-90), symbolise the perpetual presence of the *imāms* and the saints (mostly the order's founding fathers and outstanding *khulafāʾ*), who are especially revered by the Bektāshiyya [*q.v.*]. Among them are the sheep-skins that personify ʿAlī b. Abī Ṭālib, Sayyid ʿAlī Sulṭān, Hādjdjī Bektāsh, Ḳayghusuz Abdāl, Bālīm Sulṭān, al-Khaḍir, etc. In the course of the initiatory ceremony, both the head of the lodge (*bāba* [*q.v.*] or *murshid* [*q.v.*]) and the novice (*ṭālib*) prostrate themselves before these sheep-skins to show reverence to their invisible owners (Birge, *op. cit.*, 181-2). The Bektāshiyya go even further in treating the first four of the above-mentioned *posts* as seats of God and his angels. On the other hand, some Bektāshī theories interpreted these *posts* as symbols of the four major stages of the mystical path: *sharīʿa, ṭarīḳa, ḥaḳīḳa, maʿrifa* (Brown, *Dervishes*, 201-2; cf. Gramlich, *Die Schiitischen Derwischorden*, 83-4). The overriding importance of the *post* for this Turkish Ṣūfī order is further attested by a special Bektāshī prayer attached to it (Brown, *op. cit.*, 202). Characteristically, it revolves around the theme of the primordial covenant (*mīthāḳ* [*q.v.*]) between God and humankind, which is enshrined in the famous Ḳurʾānic phrase (VII, 172), "Am I not your Lord?" (*a-lastu bi-rabbikum*) (Gramlich, *op. cit.*, 95-6).

In the light of the foregoing, one may venture a guess that the ceremony of initiation into a brotherhood or a guild was deemed to replicate this pre-eternal event as described in the Ḳurʾān and refined in numerous mystical commentaries (see e.g. G. Böwering, *The mystical vision of existence in Classical Islam*, Berlin 1980, *passim*), only this time the novice, by repeating special oath-formulas, pledged allegiance not only to God but to his new spiritual family also.

Within the framework of this imposing pageant, the *sadjdjāda* or the *post* served as token representation of the highest witnesses to the novice's oath, i.e. God and his elect saints.

The sheep-skin belonging to the Ṣūfī leader plays a significant role in the exotic "spiritual concerts" of another Anatolian brotherhood, the Mawlawiyya [*q.v.*]. The Mawlawī dervishes treat it simultaneously as the seat of the spiritual pole of the universe (*ḳuṭb* [*q.v.*]), the throne of God, and a paradise on earth. It is not surprising therefore that this *post* enjoys special esteem among the members of this mystical association. Its centrality for the Mawlawī outlook is reflected in their colourful mystical performances as described by H. Ritter (*Der Reigen der "Tanzenden Derwische"*, in *Zeitschr. für vergleichende Musikwissenschaft*, Berlin, i/2 [1933], 28-40; M. Molé, *La danse extatique en Islam*, in *Sources orientales 6. Les danses sacrées*, Paris 1963, 247-50, 263, 268, etc.; cf. Landolt, *op. cit.*, 249).

Like their Turkish colleagues, modern Persian dervishes have used a *post* rather than a *sadjdjāda* in their initiatory rites, which otherwise follow the pattern of the Egyptian *ṭuruḳ* described above (Gramlich, *op. cit.*, 76-7 *et passim*). This fact, however, does not change the essence of the rite that logically flows from the mystical doctrine of *wilāya*. This doctrine, in turn, goes back to the pre-Islamic past (for an attempt to trace its origin to shamanism, Manicheanism and Buddhism, see Landolt, *op. cit.*, 249, 251-2).

Bibliography: Given in the article.

(A. Knysh)

SĀDJIDS, a line of military commanders who governed the northwestern provinces of the caliphate (Ādharbāydjān, Arrān and Armenia) in the later 3rd/9th and early 4th/10th centuries on behalf of the ʿAbbāsids.

The Sādjids were just some of several commanders, originally from the Iranian East and Central Asia, who came westwards to serve in the early ʿAbbāsid armies. The family seems to have originated in Ushrūsana [*q.v.*] on the middle Syr Darya in Transoxania, the region where the Afshīns [*q.v.*] were hereditary princes until at least the end of the 3rd/9th century, and was probably of Soghdian stock; by the time the family came to prominence in Islamic history, however, it had become culturally Arabicised to a considerable extent.

Abu 'l-Sādj Dēwdād (I) b. Yūsuf Dēwdasht fought in the Afshīn Ḥaydar's army against the anti-ʿAbbāsid rebel Bābak al-Khurramī [*q.v.*] (al-Ṭabarī, iii, 1222) and then with Ṭāhirid forces in Ṭabaristān against the rebel Māzyār [see ḲĀRINIDS] (*ibid.*, iii, 1276). Al-Muʿtazz later appointed him governor of Aleppo and Ḳinnasrīn, and as *ṣāḥib al-shurṭa* or police commander in Baghdād he was deeply involved in the strife involving the caliphs and their Turkish guards in Baghdād and Sāmarrā. In 261/875 he was appointed governor of Khūzistān, but when in the next year the Ṣaffārid Yaʿḳūb b. al-Layth [*q.v.*] prepared to march into ʿIrāḳ against the ʿAbbāsids, Abu 'l-Sādj Dēwdād joined Yaʿḳūb and took part in the battle near Dayr al-ʿĀḳūl [*q.v.*]; hence his estates and properties in ʿIrāḳ were confiscated by al-Muwaffaḳ. He nevertheless stayed faithful to the Ṣaffārids, and died at Djundīshābūr in the service of ʿAmr b. al-Layth [*q.v.*] in 266/879 (al-Ṭabarī, iii, 1937).

His two sons, Muḥammad and Yūsuf, remained, however, in the ʿAbbāsid service. Abū ʿUbayd Allāh or Abu 'l-Musāfir Muḥammad was active in the 880s in operations against rebels in the Ḥidjāz, and acted as the representative of the Ṣaffārid ʿAmr b. al-Layth [*q.v.*] in the Holy Cities. On the death of the governor of Egypt and Syria Aḥmad b. Ṭūlūn [*q.v.*] in 270/884, he accompanied the caliphal expedition against the latter's son Khumārawayh [*q.v.*] led by the general Isḥāḳ b. Kundādjik of Mawṣil, now appointed governor of Egypt and Syria, and took part in the tragicomic "Battle of the Mills". He subsequently quarrelled with Isḥāḳ and in the late 880s fought with him in the Mawṣil region. In 276/889-90, however, al-Muwaffaḳ appointed Muḥammad governor of Ādharbāydjān, the province which from this time onwards became the power-base of the Sādjid family. In 280/893 he acquired Marāgha [*q.v.*] from the local rebel ʿAbd Allāh b. al-Ḥasan al-Hamdānī, and was thus involved in warfare with the Armenian Bagratid ruler Smbat (in Arabic, Sunbāṭ) I, temporarily occupying Nakhčiwān and Dwīn [*q.vv.*]. He now felt strong enough to rebel against his ʿAbbāsid master, and it may have been at this point that he assumed the ancient Iranian title of Afshīn (see above), which appears on a dirham of his minted at Bardhaʿa [*q.v.*] in Arrān in 285/898. But he soon made peace again with al-Muʿtaḍid, was confirmed in his governorship and renewed operations against Smbat, penetrating to Ḳarṣ and Tiflis [*q.vv.*] and into Vaspurakan, then ruled by the Ardzrunid prince Sargis Ashot (Arabic, Ashūṭ) I. Muḥammad died of plague in Bardhaʿa in Rabīʿ I 288/March 901.

The army of Ādharbāydjān placed Muḥammad's son Dēwdād (II) in the governorship at Marāgha, but Dēwdād was soon forced out (Shaʿbān 288/July-August 901) by his uncle Abu 'l-Ḳāsim Yūsuf. Yūsuf transferred his capital to Ardabīl [*q.v.*]. He insisted on maintaining the direct Sādjid suzerainty over Smbat in Armenia, despite the latter's attempts to place himself directly under the caliph al-Muktafī in Baghdād and his seeking aid from the ʿAbbāsid against Yūsuf. However, on the accession of al-Muḳtadir Yūsuf's governorship of Ādharbāydjān, Arrān and Armenia was confirmed. Now with the authority of the caliph behind him, and with the powerful support within Baghdād of the vizier Ibn al-Furāt [*q.v.*], Yūsuf invaded Armenia and conducted a campaign of violence and devastation there, capturing Smbat and then in 301/914 executing him, but by *ca.* 304/917 recognising the rival Armenian dynasty of the Ardzrunids as his vassals in Dwīn.

Yūsuf now turned his attention to northern Persia and conquered Zandjān, Abhar, Ḳazwīn and Rayy from the governor on behalf of the Sāmānids Muḥammad b. ʿAlī Ṣuʿlūk, but his relations with al-Muḳtadir deteriorated and the caliph sent against his insubordinate servant an army under his commander-in-chief Muʾnis al-Muẓaffar [*q.v.*], who defeated Yūsuf in 307-919, capturing him and bringing him back to Baghdād for a spell of three years' imprisonment. On his release in 310/922, he was appointed governor of Ādharbāydjān, Rayy and northern Djibāl province, securing Ādharbāydjān and then Rayy and Hamadhān. In 314/926 the caliph recalled him and appointed him to command an army to be sent against the Ḳarāmiṭa [see ḲARMAṬĪ] in Lower ʿIrāḳ, but he was defeated near Kūfa by the Ḳarmaṭī leader Abū Ṭāhir al-Djannābī and killed (Dhu 'l-Ḥidjdja 315/February 928). It does not seem that it was at this point that some of Yūsuf's Turkish troops entered the caliphal service in Baghdād, to form there a special regiment of the Sādjiyya. This unit is mentioned previously (e.g. by Miskawayh, *Tadjārib al-umam*, in *Eclipse of the ʿAbbasid caliphate*, i, 116, tr. iv, 130, year 311/923-4), and Ibn Khallikān, ed. ʿAbbās, ii, 250-1, vi, 415, tr. de Slane, i, 500, iv, 315, cf. iv, 334 n. 11, expressly states that *al-adjnād al-Sādjiyya* in Baghdād were named after Abu 'l-Sādj Dēwdād (I), i.e. they were already in existence in the late 3rd/9th century (as noted by Canard, *Akhbâr ar-Râḍî billâh*, Algiers 1946, 49 n. 3).

After Yūsuf's death, his nephew Abu 'l-Musāfir Fatḥ b. Muḥammad Afshīn was made governor of Ādharbāydjān, but was in Shaʿbān 317/September 929 poisoned in Ardabīl by one of his slaves, so that the short line of Sādjid governors in northwestern Persia ended, and the province henceforth fell into the hands of various Kurdish and then Daylamī military adventurers. The Sādjid family did not die out totally; a son of Abu 'l-Musāfir Fatḥ's, Abu 'l-Faradj, was also a commander of the ʿAbbāsids in the mid-4th/10th century.

The Sādjid governorship over Arrān and Armenia was important for the extension of Arab control over the Armenian kingdoms there, particularly under Yūsuf b. Abi 'l-Sādj [see further, ARMĪNIYA, at I, 637]. But the Sādjids did not form an independent line of rulers in northwestern Persia, any more than did the Ṭāhirids in Khurāsān before them (even though the increasing enfeeblement of the caliphate after 295/908 made any bid for such independence more feasible), hence they are not to be equated with such an explicitly anti-ʿAbbāsid power as the Ṣaffārids on the eastern fringes of the caliphate; it was only after the end of Sādjid rule in Ādharbāydjān and eastern Transcaucasia that those regions came under native Iranian rather than Arab control. The dīnārs and dirhams minted by the Sādjids in Ādharbāydjān, Arrān, Armenia and, briefly, at Rayy (year 312/924-5, see G.C. Miles, *The numismatic history of Rayy*, New York 1938, 139-41) all acknowledge fully the ʿAbbāsid caliph as suzerain.

Genealogical table of the Sādjids

Yūsuf Dēwdasht

1. Abu 'l-Sādj Dēwdād (I)

2. Muḥammad — 4. Yūsuf

3. Dēwdād (II) — 5. Fatḥ

Bibliography: 1. Sources. Ṭabarī; ʿArīb; Muḥammad b. ʿAbd al-Malik al-Hamadhānī, *Takmilat taʾrīkh al-Ṭabarī*, Abū Bakr Muḥammad al-Ṣūlī, *Akhbār*, Masʿūdī, *Murūdj*, Ibn al-Athīr, viii.

2. Studies. C. Defrémery, *Mémoire sur la famille des Sadjides*, in *JA*, 4th ser., ix (1847), 409-16, x (1847), 396-436; M.J. de Goeje, *Mémoire sur les Carmathes du Bahraïn et les Fatimides*, Leiden 1886, 88-94; Zambaur, *Manuel*, 179; V. Minorsky, *Studies in Caucasian history*, London 1953, 110-11; W. Madelung, in *Camb. hist. Iran*, iv, 228-32. For Sādjid coins, see Miles in *ibid.*, 372.

(C.E. BOSWORTH)

ṢADR (A.), "chest, breast, bosom" (pl. *ṣudūr*), a peculiarly Arabic word, not attested in other Semitic languages, except as a borrowing from Arabic. Its semantic connection with other derivatives of the root *ṣ-d-r* within Arabic is unclear; it may be derived from the basic notion of the verb *ṣadara*, i.e. "to come up, move upward and outward, from the waterhole" (opposite: *warada*). Most concretely, it refers to the chest as part of the body, and as such is dealt with in the lexicographical monographs on the human body called *Khalḳ al-insān* (al-Aṣmaʿī, 214-18; Thābit b. Abī Thābit, 244-54; cf. also Ibn Sīdah, *al-Mukhaṣṣaṣ*, i, 19-24). *Ṣadr* may refer to the breast of all animals, or to that of humans only. In the latter case it is contrasted with e.g. the *kirkira* of the camel-stallion, the *labān* of the horse, the *zawr* of the lion, the *djuʾdjuʾ* of the bird, etc. (see al-Thaʿālibī, *Fiḳh al-lugha*, 109: *taḳsīm al-ṣudūr*), but the lexicographers are not unanimous in their definitions of these words (e.g. al-Aṣmaʿī, *Khalḳ al-insān*, 216, l. 12, equates *zawr* and *djuʾdjuʾ* with *ṣadr*). From the noun *ṣadr* the usual two body-part verbs may be derived: *ṣadara* "to hit, wound the chest" and *ṣudira* "to suffer from a chest ailment."

Bibliography: Aṣmaʿī, *K. Khalḳ al-insān*, ed. A. Haffner, in *Texte zur arabischen Lexikographie*, Leipzig 1905 [Arabic title page: Beirut 1903], 158-232; Thābit b. Abī Thābit, *Khalḳ al-insān*, ed. ʿA.A. Farrādj, Kuwait 1955; Ibn Sīdah, *al-Mukhaṣṣaṣ*, repr. Beirut n.d.; Thaʿālibī, *Fiḳh al-lugha*, ed. L. Cheikho, repr. Tripoli and Tunis 1981.

The *ṣadr*, like "bosom," is also the seat of emotions and convictions, and interestingly this is the only sense in which it occurs in the Ḳurʾān (with the possible exception of sūra XXII, 46; see, however, below). In the singular (but, strangely, never in the plural) it is consistently connected with the idea of "constriction" (root *ḍ-y-ḳ*, cf. XI 12; XV, 97; XXVI, 13; also root *ḥ-r-dj*, cf. VI, 125; VII, 2) or "dilatation" (root *sh-r-ḥ*, cf. VI, 125; XVI, 106; XX, 25; XXXIX, 22; XCIV, 1) to express anxiety, grief, and rejection vs. serenity, joy, and acceptance. The plural *ṣudūr* is mostly used in conjunction with the idea of thoughts and feelings that are hidden in them (roots *kh-f-y*, see III, 29; III, 118; XI, 5; XL, 19, and *k-n-n*, see XXVII, 74; XXVIII, 69), but which God knows nonetheless; this is particularly expressed in the refrain-like formula *inna 'llāha ʿalīmun bi-dhāti 'l-ṣudūr* "God knows well what ails [their] bosoms" [Arberry: "God knows the thoughts in their breasts"] (III, 119, among others). In two places the *ṣudūr* are closely connected with the *ḳulūb*, "hearts," (XXII, 46: *wa-lākin taʿmā l-ḳulūbu 'llatī fī 'l-ṣudūr* "but blind are the hearts within the breasts," and III, 154: *li-yabtaliya 'llāhu mā fī ṣudūrikum wa-li-yumaḥḥiṣa mā fī ḳulūbikum* "and that God might try what was in your breasts, and that he might prove what was in your hearts").

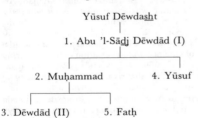

The early mystics, intent on formulating the internal stages of religious experience, availed themselves of some of these passages from the Ḳurʾān and defined *ṣadr* as one of the inner organs involved [see also ḲALB]. It is especially sūra XXXIX, 22 (*a-fa-man sharaḥa llāhu ṣadrahū li-l-islāmi* "Is he whose breast God has expanded unto Islam...") which prompted Abu 'l-Ḥusayn al-Nūrī (d. 295/907 [*q.v.*]) to establish a parallelism between *ṣadr* as the seat of *islām* and—moving inward and upward—between *ḳalb, fuʾād*, and *lubb*, all Ḳurʾānic terms, as the respective seats of *īmān, maʿrifa*, and *tawḥīd* (*Maḳāmāt al-ḳulūb*, 130, cf. P. Nwyia, *Exégèse coranique*, 321, who also points to a similar terminology in the *Tafsīr* attributed to Djaʿfar al-Ṣādiḳ (d. 148/765 [*q.v.*]), where the parallelisms are: *ṣadr* and submission (*taslīm*), *ḳalb* and certitude (*yaḳīn*), *fuʾād* and contemplation (*naẓar*), the *ḍamīr* and the secret (*sirr*), and the *nafs* as the refuge of all good and evil; *ḍamīr* not being Ḳurʾānic, al-Nūrī stays closer to the Ḳurʾān). A similar scheme is proposed by al-Ḥakīm al-Tirmidhī (d. after 318/930) in his *K. fī Bayān al-farḳ bayn al-ṣadr wa 'l-ḳalb wa 'l-fuʾād wa 'l-lubb*, 33-47, 79-83 (tr. 28-36, 244-5). He offers several analogies to characterise the relationship of the four parts of the heart (note that *ḳalb* has two meanings, one comprehensive and one specific), of which the following two may be quoted:

Heart	Almond	Sacred Precinct
ṣadr	outer shell	the *ḥaram*
ḳalb	inner shell	city of Mecca
fuʾād	kernel	Great Mosque
lubb	oil inside kernel	Kaʿba

The *ṣadr* is called thus, because it is the outer part (*ṣadr*) of the heart and its first station. In another work, al-Ḥakīm al-Tirmid͟hī uses an interpretation of the Light Verse (XXIV, 35) to explain the function of the heart and equates the *ṣadr* with the niche (*mis͟hkāt*; see *K. al-Aʿdāʾ wa ʾl-nafs*, 85).

Similar divisions remain popular with later writers, although the term *ṣadr* is not always included, while other terms may be added (relevant sections tr. and discussed by Sachiko Murata, *The Tao of Islam*, 292-9 and ff.). Al-Tirmid͟hī's scheme is taken up again, with certain alterations, in the Persian Ḳurʾānic commentary of Ras͟hīd al-Dīn Maybudī (wrote 520/1126 [*q.v.*]), who replaces the *lubb* by *s͟hag͟hāf* and, rather than *maʿrifa* and *tawḥīd*, assigns the two functions of *mus͟hāhadat-i Ḥaḳḳ* and *ʿis͟hḳ* to *fuʾād* and *s͟hag͟hāf* (*Kashf al-asrār*, viii, 411-12; cf. Murata, *op. cit.*, 296-7).

The *ṣadr* is described in a number of metaphorical ways as the place in which the internal dramas of good and evil are staged. According to one passage in al-Ḥakīm al-Tirmid͟hī, the heart is the home of faith, the soul is the home of passions. Between them is a wide space called *ṣadr*, from which emanate (*ṣadara*) the orders executed by external organs. Both heart and soul have an opening leading to that place. Through that of the heart the light of faith would shoot into the *ṣadr*, as the fire and smoke of passion would shoot into the breast through the opening of the *nafs*. Whichever triumphs over the other brings about obedience or disobedience. "Et telle est toute l'histoire du cœur et de l'âme" (P. Nwyia, *op. cit.*, 279, summarising a passage from the *Masāʾil*). For other descriptions, in al-Tirmid͟hī's work, of the struggle in the *ṣadr* between heart and soul, see *al-Furūḳ wa-manʿ al-tarāduf*, *apud* P. Nwyia, *op. cit.*, 122; *Bayān al-farḳ*, 40-7; *K͟hatm al-awliyāʾ*, 130-1; B. Radtke, *Al-Ḥakīm at-Tirmidī*, Freiburg 1980, 58-71 and index).

A strangely generalised use of the term *ṣadr* appears in *al-Futūḥāt al-Makkiyya* of Ibn al-ʿArabī (d. 638/1240 [*q.v.*]). Here the *ṣadr* is presented as a universal feature of creation; each thing can boast of one. Knowledge of it is among the loftiest knowledge on the Path, since the world and each genus is according to the shape of man (microcosm), who is the last created thing. Man alone is according to the Divine shape, externally and internally, and God has made for him a *ṣadr*. Between Him and man there are *ṣudūr* whose number only God knows (ii, 652). This is followed by an enumeration of twenty-seven *ṣudūr*, after which Ibn al-ʿArabī adds that every *ṣadr* has a *ḳalb* and, as long as the *ḳalb* remains in the *ṣadr*, it is blind (cf. sūra XXII, 46), because the *ṣadr* is a veil upon it. If God wills to make it seeing, it goes out from its *ṣadr* and thus sees. E.g. the causes (*asbāb*) are the *ṣudūr* of the existent things, and the existent things are like hearts. As long as an existent thing looks at its cause from which it emerges (*ṣadara*), it is blind to seeing God as the one who made it existent (ii, 652-3).

Bibliography: Abu ʾl-Ḥusayn al-Nūrī, *Maḳāmāt al-ḳulūb*, ed. P. Nwyia, in *MUSJ*, 44, 1968, 129-143; P. Nwyia, *Exégèse coranique et langage mystique*, Beirut 1970; al-Ḥakīm al-Tirmid͟hī, *K. al-Aʿdāʾ wa ʾl-nafs*, ed. Wad͟jīh Aḥmad ʿAbd Allāh, Alexandria 1991; idem, *K. fī Bayān al-farḳ bayn al-ṣadr wa ʾl-ḳalb wa ʾl-fuʾād wa ʾl-lubb*, ed. N. Heer, Cairo 1958 (tr. idem, in *MW*, li [1961], 25-36, 83-91, 163-72, 244-58); idem, *K͟hatm al-awliyāʾ*, ed. ʿUt͟hmān Yaḥyā, Beirut 1965; Sachiko Murata, *The Tao of Islam*, Albany 1992; Ras͟hīd al-Dīn Maybudī, *Kas͟hf al-asrār wa-ʿuddat al-abrār*, ed. ʿA.A. Ḥikmat, Tehran 1331-9/1952-60; Ibn al-ʿArabī, *al-Futūḥāt al-Makkiyya*, Cairo 1911.

In everyday life, the idea of the *ṣadr* being the container of something hidden is expressed in the proverb *ṣadruka awsaʿu li-sirrik(a)* "Your bosom is wide enough for your secret" admonishing a person to keep his secret to himself (al-Maydānī, *Mad͟jmaʿ al-amt͟hāl*, ed. Muḥammad Muḥyi ʾl-Dīn ʿAbd al-Ḥamīd, 2 vols., [2]Cairo 1379/1959, i, 396a).

In a figurative sense, *ṣadr* means any "first, front, or upper part" of a thing. A number of technical meanings result.

(a) In prosody *ṣadr* has two unrelated meanings. One refers to the first foot of a verse, as opposed to *ʿad͟juz*, the last foot. This latter is also known as *ḍarb*; this, however, defines it as the last foot of the second hemistich as opposed to the last foot of the first hemistich, the *ʿarūḍ*. The structure of a complete line in terms of characteristic elements (*arkān*) is the following: *ṣadr*–[*has͟hw*]–*ʿarūḍ*/*ibtidāʾ*–[*has͟hw*]–*ʿad͟juz* (*ḍarb*) (see al-Sakkākī, *Miftāḥ*, 523-4; Freytag, *Darstellung*, 117-120; Elwell-Sutton, *The Persian metres*, 40). *Ḥas͟hw* feet occur, of course, only if the hemistich consists of more than the initial and the final foot, i.e. in *musaddas* and *mut͟hamman* lines. The terms *ṣadr* and *ʿad͟juz* are often also loosely applied to the entire first and second hemistich, respectively (see Lane, s.v.). This has influenced their use in the technical term *radd al-ʿad͟juz ʿala ʾl-ṣadr*, referring to the rhetorical figure of anticipating the rhyme word in the first half (at times even the beginning of the second half) of the line (see G.E. von Grunebaum, who compares the *epanadiplosis* of classical rhetoric, *Tenth-century document*, 32 n. 247, 116; G. Kanazi, *Studies*, 56-7; note that, while *ʿad͟juz* is still used in its narrow sense of rhyme foot, *ṣadr* has acquired the broader meaning).

Bibliography: Sakkākī, *Miftāḥ al-ʿulūm*, ed. Nuʿaym Zarzūr, Beirut 1403/1983; G.W. Freytag, *Darstellung der arabischen Verskunst*, Bonn 1830; L.P. Elwell-Sutton, *The Persian metres*, Cambridge 1976; G.E. von Grunebaum, *A tenth-century document of Arab literary theory and criticism. The sections on poetry in al-Bâqillânî's Iʿjâz al-Qurʾân*, Chicago 1950, repr. 1974; G. Kanazi, *Studies in the Kitāb aṣ-Ṣināʿatayn of Abū Hilāl al-ʿAskarī*, Leiden 1989.

The other meaning of *ṣadr* in prosody occurs in the context of the phenomenon called *muʿāḳaba*, i.e. the obligatory alternation of the shortening of two adjacent cords [see SABAB]. Thus in the *ramal* metre, the foot *fāʿilātun* may have its first cord *fā-* shortened, thus *faʿilātun*, only if the last cord *-tun* of the preceding foot is not shortened; this case is called *ṣadr*. Or it may have the last cord *-tun* shortened, thus *fāʿilātu*, but only if the first cord *fā-* of the following foot is not shortened; this case is called *ʿad͟juz*. Or, finally, it may have both its first and its last cord shortened, thus *faʿilātu*, but only if the preceding and following cords are not shortened; this case is called *ṭarafān* or, more logically, *d͟hu ʾl-ṭarafayn* (the latter in al-Sakkākī, *Miftāḥ*, 527). These phenomena occur in the metres *madīd, ramal, k͟hafīf* and *mud͟jtat͟ht͟h* (Ibn Ras͟hīḳ, *al-ʿUmda*, i, 149). The apparent reason for their existence is to avoid a sequence of four moving letters.

Bibliography: Sakkākī (see above); Ibn Ras͟hīḳ,

al-ʿUmda fī ṣināʿat al-shiʿr wa-ādābih wa-naḳdih, ed. M.M. ʿAbd al-Ḥamīd, 2 vols., [3]Cairo 1383/1963-4; Freytag, *Darstellung* (see above), 108.

(b) In epistolography and the composing of texts in general, the term *ṣadr* refers to the introductory formulae of letters and prefaces in books (the latter also *taṣdīr*). For an extensive disquisition on *ṣudūr* in epistles, including the way one alludes to the main topic already in the *taḥmīd* and how one moves (*takhalluṣ*) from the *ṣadr* to the actual topic (*gharaḍ*), see al-Kalāʿī, *Iḥkām ṣanʿat al-kalām*, ed. Muḥ. Riḍwān al-Dāya, Beirut 1966, 58-72. *Ṣadr* is used in the "old translation" of Aristotle's Rhetoric as one of the terms to render προοίμιον, the exordium or proem, of a speech (see M.C. Lyons, *Aristotle's* Ars Rhetorica. *The Arabic version*, ii, *Glossary*, Cambridge 1982, 123-4, 226). This remains the rendition of choice with the later philosophers. Ibn Sīnā compares the proem which leads into the speech with clearing one's throat before the call to prayer and with warbling on a reed instrument before playing the actual piece (*al-Shifāʾ, al-Manṭiḳ*, 8. *al-Khaṭāba*, ed. M.S. Sālim, Cairo 1373/1954, 237, ll. 12-24). In books, the *ṣadr* may mean a non-technical "beginning, first part", but may also refer to preliminary remarks that precede the actual "introduction." Thus al-Ghazālī, in his *al-Mustaṣfā min ʿilm al-uṣūl*, Būlāḳ 1322, prefixes the following introductory materials to his book: 1. the *taḥmīd* (2-3); 2. the *khuṭba* (after *ammā baʿd*), mainly in *sadjʿ*, with general remarks about reason and knowledge, as well as some autobiographical indications, ending with the titling of the book (3-4); 3. the *ṣadr al-kitāb*, expressly so called, dealing with the definition, the hierarchical status, and the internal structure of *uṣūl al-fiḳh*, as also with the reason for the introduction (4-10); and 4. the *muḳaddima*, "introduction," again expressly so named, in which the author presents an outline of logic and epistemology (10-55). Derived from this *ṣadr* is the verb *ṣaddara kitābahū* (*LʿA*), cf. al-Fārābī's introductory epistle to his work on the Organon, the *Risāla ṣuddira bihā 'l-kitāb*, ed. Rafīḳ al-ʿAdjam, in *al-Manṭiḳ ʿind al-Fārābī*, Beirut 1985, i, 55-62. Again, this *ṣadr* contains general notions indicating the status of logic, such as logic vs. grammar, syllogistic vs. non-syllogistic crafts, review of the five syllogistic crafts, overview of Organon and of philosophy in general, and basic ideas about "concept," "proposition," and "definition."

Bibliography: Given in the text.

(c) From the expression *ṣadr al-madjlis*, the upper or front part of the assembly, i.e. "the place/seat of honour," the term *ṣadr* for an outstanding person is synecdochically derived (cf. *kāna ṣadr[an] fi 'l-farāʾiḍ wa 'l-ḥisāb*, "he was an eminent expert in inheritance computations and arithmetic," Dozy, s.v.). This has developed into an academic and an administrative sense. For the latter, i.e. the terms *ṣadr* and *ṣadr al-ṣudūr* for the head of the religious administration in post-Mongol Iran and *ṣadr-i aʿẓam* for the grand vizier in the Ottoman empire, see below. In the academic sense, it is mostly applied to a professor in *adab* and mostly in the derived forms *muṣaddar* and *mutaṣaddir*. The respective verbs, *ṣaddara* and *taṣaddara*, mean "to appoint s.o. a professor" and "to be appointed" or "to set o.s. up as a professor," the latter often with the implication of insufficient preparation (see G. Makdisi, *The rise of colleges*, Edinburgh 1981, 203-6, and, particularly, idem, *The rise of humanism*, Edinburgh 1990, 277-9).

Bibliography: Given in the text.

(W.P. Heinrichs)

ṢADR (a.), used in a personal sense, with an extended meaning from Arabic "breast" > "foremost, leading part of a thing", denotes an eminent or superior person or *primus inter pares*, whence its use for a chief, president or minister; cf. the Ottoman Turkish Grand Vizier's title *ṣadr-i aʿẓam* [*q.v.*]. The title was especially used in the Persian world for a high religious dignitary whose function (*ṣadārat, ṣidārat*) was concerned essentially with the administration of religious affairs. In the first mentions of the title and in the structural evolution of the office in the post-Il Khānid period, the titles and prerogatives of the *ṣadr* evolved considerably, and despite lacuna in our sources of information, their evolution can be traced chronologically, as described below.

(J. Calmard)

1. In Transoxania.
2. In the period from the Il-Khānids to the Tīmūrids.
3. The Tīmūrid and Turkmen periods.
4. In the Ṣafawid period.
5. In Mughal India.

1. In Transoxania.

In the cities and towns of Transoxania, the Islamic religious institution, by Ḳarakhānid and Saldjūḳ times predominantly Ḥanafī in *madhhab*, came to enjoy a special position of religious, social and often administrative power *vis-à-vis* the Ḳarakhānids [see ilek-khāns] and subsequent incoming Turkish dynasties. The members of this institution who held office as *imām* and *raʾīs* [*q.vv.*] also came to enjoy the title of *ṣadr*; such *ṣadr*s were to be found, e.g., in Samarḳand, Khudjand, Özkend, Almalīḳ, etc. They were especially influential in Bukhārā, where the Burhānī ones (see below) were further dignified by an intensive form of the title, that of *ṣadr al-ṣudūr*.

Already during the Sāmānid period there is mentioned (e.g. by the local historian Muḥammad b. Aḥmad al-Bukhārī al-Ghundjār, d. 412/1021, cf. Barthold, *Turkestan*[3], 15, and by al-Samʿānī, *Ansāb*, ed. Ḥaydarābād, i, 243-6) the family of the Ismāʿīlīs, who held religious and civic power in Bukhārā. After them there came in 5th/11th century the Ṣaffārīs. In addition to their religious and civic authority, such families were clearly economically powerful also, doubtless possessing urban property and/or rural estates; hence in the assertion of what they took to be their spiritual rights, and probably in defence of their property also, they frequently clashed with the temporal holders of power. Thus the Ḳarakhānid ruler Shams al-Mulk Naṣr b. Tamghač Khān Ibrāhīm in 461/1069 executed the *imām* and *ṣadr* Ismāʿīl b. Abī Naṣr al-Ṣaffār because he had, according to al-Samʿānī, exhorted the Khān to observe the ordinances of religion and to eschew forbidden things (*ibid.*, viii, 318; cf. Barthold, *op. cit.*, 316, 320).

This willingness to challenge the secular authorities and, if needs be, to suffer for it, was the mark of succeeding religious leaders in Bukhārā, above all, of the next, and particularly celebrated, line of *ṣadr*s, who now, as noted above, bore the more exalted title of *ṣadr al-ṣudūr*, sc. the family of Burhān; all but the founder appear in the sources with the additional designation of *al-Shahīd* "Martyr", having found death at the hands of the Ḳarakhānids or Ḳara Khitay [*q.v.*]. The Āl-i Burhān acquired its name from the fact that virtually all of them bore the *laḳab* or honorific title of Burhān al-Dīn "Proof of Religion" or Burhān al-Milla wa 'l-Dīn. The family traced its *nasab* back to the Arab tribes of Khurāsān in the Umayyad period, and seems always to have retained some connection with the city of Marw. Its history has, however, to be pieced together from scattered mentions in the historical sources for the Ḳarakhānid

Saldjūḳ and succeeding periods and from the *Kitāb-i Mullāzāda* or *K.-i Mazārāt-i Bukhārā* by the Tīmūrid author Muʿīn al-Fuḳarāʾ [see AḤMAD B. MUḤAMMAD, MUʿĪN AL-FUḲARĀʾ, in Suppl.]

When the Saldjūḳ sultan Sandjar [*q.v.*] came to Transoxania in 495/1102, he apparently deposed the reigning *raʾīs* and *imām* of Bukhārā, Abū Isḥāḳ Ibrāhīm al-Ṣaffārī, and replaced him by the Ḥanafī scholar ʿAbd al-ʿAzīz b. ʿUmar Māza, who assumed the title of *ṣadr*. There now began the period of dominance, lasting for nearly a century and a half, of the Āl-i Burhān. Linked to Sandjar by marriage, they became, like the Ḳarakhānids, immediate vassals of the Saldjūḳs, until ʿAbd al-ʿAzīz's son Ḥuṣām al-Dīn ʿUmar was killed by the pagan Ḳara Khitāy after Sandjar's disastrous defeat at the battle of the Ḳaṭwān Steppe in 536/1141. However, the Burhānīs made their peace with the Gur Khān and were acknowledged as representatives of the Ḳara Khitay in Bukhārā, collecting the land-tax there for the rulers. When the Khʷāram-Shāh Tekish appeared at Bukhārā in 578/1182, they likewise accommodated themselves to the new, in practice, temporary, régime. It was apparently to the *ṣadr* ʿAbd al-ʿAzīz (II) b. Muḥammad (d. 593/1196-7) that Muḥammad b. Ẓufar, the epitomiser of Narshakhī's *Taʾrīkh-i Bukhārā*, dedicated his local history. The Burhānīs continued to dominate civic life in Bukhārā under the restored Ḳarakhānids and Ḳara Khitay, and Muḥammad (II) b. Aḥmad (d. 616/1219) was renowned for his wealth and arrogance.'' We also know of eulogistic Persian poetry addressed to them by such authors as the satirist Sūzanī (d. ?569/1173-4 [*q.v.*]) and Shamsī-yi Aʿradj Bukhārī (*flor. ca.* 1200 AD) (see F. de Blois, *Persian literature*, v/2, 427, 432).

The end of Burhānī dominance came with the outbreak at Bukhārā of the popular movement led by the vendor of shields Maḥmūd Ṭārābī (636/1238-9), and the last Burhānī, Aḥmad (II) b. Muḥammad, was reduced by Ṭārābī to the status of *khalīfa* or deputy of a new *ṣadr al-ṣudūr*, hence preferred to flee and to take refuge with the Ḳara Khitay. But by now, these last were being hard pressed by the Mongols, and were not strong enough to replace Aḥmad in his former glory.

In his place, a new family took over the *ṣadāra* of Bukhārā. The Ḥanafī *faḳīh* Shams al-Dīn Muḥammad b. Aḥmad al-Maḥbūbī was Ṭārābī's candidate, and there now began a line of *ṣudūr* as long-lived and as influential as the Āl-i Burhān, that of the Āl-i Maḥbūb, who inherited from their predecessors the additional form of the title, *ṣadr-i djahān*. The Maḥbūbīs, like the Burhānīs, traced their ancestry back to the Arabs of the time of the Prophet, and they likewise at times employed the *laḳab* of Burhān al-Dīn. Already in the 6th/12th century they had produced notable Ḥanafī scholars, such as the theologian Aḥmad b. ʿUbayd Allāh al-Maḥbūbī (546-630/1151-1232), and in the next century or so members of the family continued to write many textbooks of Ḥanafī *fiḳh* which became standard. They are mentioned in the sources until the middle of the 8th/14th century, for Ibn Baṭṭūṭa met at Bukhārā in 733/1333 the Ṣadr al-Sharīʿa, probably ʿUbayd Allāh b. Masʿūd al-Maḥbūbī (*Riḥla*, iii, 28, tr. Gibb, iii, 554, apparently mis-identified in n. 56), who was famed as a legal scholar (see Brockelmann, I², 277-8, S II, 300-1); but thereafter, they fade from historical mention.

Bibliography: Barthold, *EI*¹ art. *Burhan* (outdated); C.E. Bosworth, *EIr* art. *Āl-e Borhān*; O. Pritsak, *Āl-i Burhān*, in *Isl.*, xxx (1952), 81-96 (incs. detailed bibliographical information and attempted chronologies of the Burhānī and Maḥbūbī families, with a genealogical table of the former).

(C.E. Bosworth)

2. In the period from the Il-Khānids to the Tīmūrids.

Apart from uses of *ṣadr* and its compounds in Transoxania, one finds that, under the Il-Khānids, the *laḳab* of *ṣadr-i djahān* was given to the vizier of Gaykhatu (690-4/1291-5), Ṣadr al-Dīn Aḥmad Khālidī Zandjānī, apparently as an honorific title (see Dihkhudā, *Lughat-nāma*, *s.v.*, citing Khʷāndamīr, *Ḥabīb al-siyar*, and the *Dastūr al-wuzarāʾ*). It was also the title of Mīr Ṣadr-i Djahān Pihānī, an envoy of the Mughals to ʿAbd Allāh Khān Özbeg (see Riazul Islam, *Indo-Persian relations* ..., Tehran 1970, 54; idem, *A Calendar of documents on Indo-Persian relations (1500-1750)*, Tehran and Karachi 1979-82, ii, 212, 214).

Since we have no precise indications on the function of the *ṣadārat* before the second half of the 8th/14th century, it has been incorrectly thought that it was a Tīmūrid creation (R.M. Savory, *The principal offices of the Ṣafawid state during the reign of Tahmāsp I (930-84/1524-76)*, in *BSOAS*, xxiv [1961], 103, also in his *Studies on the history of Ṣafawid Iran*, Variorum, London 1987) or even a Ṣafawid one (K. Röhrborn, *Provinzen und Zentralgewalt Persiens im 16. und 17. Jahrhundert*, Berlin 1966, 117; idem and H.R. Idris, *Regierung und Verwaltung des Vordern Orients in islamische Zeit*, Hb der Or. Leiden-Köln 1979, 46-7; criticisms by G. Herrmann, *Zur Entstehung des Ṣadr-Amtes*, in U. Haarmann and P. Bachmann, *Die islamische Welt zwischen Mittelalter und Neuzeit. Festschrift für Hans Robert Roemer*, Beirut-Wiesbaden 1979, 278, 282). A detailed study of the chancery literature (*inshāʾ*) and of official documents shows that there was no nomination of *ṣadrs* under the Djalāyirids [*q.v.*]. The highest magisterial function in Islam was at that time exercised by the *ḳāḍī 'l-ḳuḍāt*, with other religious affairs being the responsibility of the chief vizier or other officials like the *ḥākim-i dīwān-i awḳāf-i mamālik* (analysis of the *Dastūr al-kātib*; cf. Roemer, *Staatsschreiben der Timuridenzeit. Das Šaraf-nāmä des ʿAbdallāh Marwārīd in kritischer Auswertung*, Wiesbaden 1952, 142, and Herrmann, *op. cit.*, 284-5). Under the Muẓaffarids [*q.v.*], the highest religious dignitary was also still the *ḳāḍī 'l-ḳuḍāt*. The combination of the terms (but not of distinct functions) of *wizārat* and *ṣadārat* is attested under the Karts [*q.v.*] or Kurts of Harāt, with the bestowing of the *wizārat* on Shaykh Muʿīn al-Dīn Djāmī (J. Aubin, *Le khanat de Čaġatai et le Khorassan (1334-1380)*, in *Turcica*, viii [1976], 30; Herrmann, *op. cit.*, 294). The first document which we possess on the specific appointment to an office of *ṣadr* concerns Muʿīn al-Dīn's eldest son, Ḍiyāʾ al-Dīn Yūsuf (*manshūr* of Rabīʿ II 782/July-August 1380; see Aubin, *op. cit.*, 51; the document is ed., tr. and commented upon by Herrmann, *op. cit.*, 287 ff.). Tīmūr considered himself as a disciple of Ḍiyāʾ al-Dīn, who took part in the five-years' war and died at Tabrīz in 797/1394-5. His brother Shihāb al-Dīn ʿUmar was linked with Mīrān Shāh, the prince who held the appanage of Khurāsān (Aubin, *op. cit.*, 53). The office of *ṣadārat* attributed to Ḍiyāʾ al-Dīn encompassed the direction of affairs concerning all the religious dignitaries (*imāms*, *sayyids*, *shaykhs*, *ḳāḍīs*, *khaṭībs*, *muḥtasibs*, *amīns* ''and other religious authorities'') of the city of Harāt and its dependent districts. All decisions concerning judicial sentences, teaching, the leadership of the worship, the *khuṭba*, the supervision of weights and measures (*iḥtisāb*), the administration of the *awḳāf*, the inspectorship of finance (*ishrāf*) and activities of the treasury (*bayt al-māl*), as well as nominations, distributions, appointments and participations of all religious dignitaries and theological students, had to be submitted for his approval.

3. The Tīmūrid and Turkmen periods.

Despite Tīmūr's devotion to Ḍiyāʾ al-Dīn, the mention of three persons bearing the title of *ṣadr* (after their *ism*) in his reign does not clearly show that they occupied the actual functions of *ṣadārat* (Herrmann, *Zur Entstehung des Ṣadr-Amtes*, 293-4). This is, on the other hand, attested under his son Shāh Rukh (807-50/1405-47). The office is even attributed at one and the same time to several persons in Harāt (at the court's chancery) and in the provinces in the princes' appanages (*ibid.*, 280 ff.; on the provincial *ṣadrs* under Shāh Rukh, see Aubin, *Deux sayyids de Bam au XVe siècle. Contribution à l'histoire timouride*, in *Abh. der Akad. der Wiss. und der Lit. zu Mainz*, geistes- u. sozialwiss. Kl. [1956], no. 7, 398). This practice becomes the rule under Ḥusayn Bayḳara (875-912/1470-1506). During his reign, the revenues from *awḳāf* which, like other grants and favours enjoyed complete fiscal immunity, became so important that it was necessary to appoint several *ṣadrs* at the same time in order to supervise these revenues (Khʷāndamīr, Tehran 1333, iv, 321; cf. M. Subtelny, *Centralizing reform and its opponents in the late Timurid period*, in *Iranian Studies*, xxi/1-2 [1988], 126). However, in 910/1504-5, Ḥusayn Bayḳara appointed a *ṣadr* whose functions were especially attached to the ruler's service (*mansab-i ṣadārat-i khāṣṣayi humāyūn*, Khʷāndamīr, iv, 327; Hermann, *op. cit.*, 282). The fact that the office could be held by several dignitaries at the same time leads one to suppose that there was a hierarchy amongst the various *ṣadrs*. But the mention of a chief *ṣadr* (*ṣadr al-ṣudūr*) only appears once, in a late Tīmūrid document, which seems to indicate the provisional or exceptional character of the office (*ibid.*). The *ṣadr*'s department (*sarkār-i ṣadārat* or *dīwān-i ṣadārat*) occupied the third place in the Tīmūrid administration after the *dīwān-i tuwāčī* and the *dīwān-i māl*. The financial support for the *ṣadrs*, made up of allowances (*ʿulūfa*) and gratuities (*inʿām*) came from a specific tax (*rasm al-ṣadārat* or *sahm al-ṣadārat*) raised as a percentage on *waḳf* revenues (*ibid.*, 283-4).

As for the social origins of the *ṣadrs*, a strong tendency for the post to remain within one family, leading to hereditary control over the office, has been noted (Roemer, *Staatsschreiben der Timuridenzeit*, 143-6; Herrmann, *op. cit.*, 281). Although they were the superiors of the *sayyids*, it was only occasionally that they stemmed from this last group. Among the forty *ṣadrs* mentioned by Khʷāndamīr for Ḥusayn Bayḳara's reign, there are only three descendants of the Prophet (iv, 321-8; cf. Herrmann, *ibid.*). Some *ṣadrs* were accused of corruption during this reign. A dispute between the descendants of Aḥmad-i Djām and of ʿAbd Allāh Anṣārī provoked the intervention of the Naḳshbandī *shaykh* Khʷādja Aḥrār [*q.v.* in Suppl.] (J. Paul, *Die politische und soziale Bedeutung der Naqšbandiyya in Mittelasien im 15. Jahrhundert*, Berlin 1991, 57-8).

As well as the supervision of the religious leaders and of the *awḳāf* mentioned above for the Kart *ṣadr*, the Tīmūrid *ṣadr* was more explicitly charged with supervising and administering the application of the *Sharīʿa* as head of judicial authority in the state (Roemer, *op. cit.*, 143-6). This prerogative appears also in the Aḳ Ḳoyunlu state, in which one finds the *ṣadr al-sharīʿat* (J.E. Woods, *The Aqquyunlu. Clan, confederation, empire*, Minneapolis and Chicago 1976, 11). The reform-minded minister of the Aḳ Ḳonyunlu sultan Yaʿḳūb, the *Ḳāḍī* ʿĪsā Sāwadjī, held both the civil and religious functions with the rank of *ṣadr* (V. Minorsky, *Turkmenica II. The Aq-qoyunlu and land reform*, in *BSOAS*, xvii [1955], 451-8; Aubin, *Etudes safavides. I. Šāh Ismāʿīl et les notables de l'Iraq Persan*, in *JESHO*, ii [1959], 48-9; Woods, *op. cit.*, 156-7). In general, under the Turkmen Ḳara and Aḳ Ḳoyunlu the *ṣadr* held the highest religious office (Roemer, *op. cit.*, 14304).

Bibliography: 1. Sources. For the primary sources in Persian (chronicles, *tadhkirāt*, hagiographical-biographical works on the *ʿulamāʾ*, etc.) and in European languages, see the bibls. in the works cited above, and notably, in S.A. Arjomand, *The Shadow of God and the Hidden Imam*, Chicago-London 1984; Aubin, *opera cit.*, and *Etudes ṣafavides. III. L'évènement des Safavides reconsidéré*, in *Moyen Orient et Océan Indien*, v (1988); C.J. Beeson, *The origins of conflicts in the Ṣafawid religious institution*, diss. Princeton Univ. 1982, unpubl.; J. Calmard, *Les rituels chiites et le pouvoir. L'imposition du chiisme ṣafavide: eulogies et malédictions canoniques*, in idem (ed.), *Etudes ṣafavides*, Paris-Tehran 1993, 109-50; M.M. Mazzaoui, *The origins of the Ṣafavids. Shīʿism, Ṣūfism and the Ġulāt*, Wiesbaden 1972; Minorsky, *Tadhkirat al-mulūk. A manual of Ṣafavid administration*, GMS, London 1943; A.J. Newman, *The myth of the clerical migration to Ṣafawid Iran: Arab Shʿite opposite to ʿAlī al-Karakī and Ṣafawid Shiʿism*, in *WI*, xxxiii (1993), 66-112; R. Schimkoreit, *Regesten publizierter ṣafawidische Herrscherkunden*, Berlin 1982. On the Tīmūrid *ṣadrs*, see Roemer, text of the *Sharaf-nāma* and tr., 35-44 (for the *nishān-i ṣadārat* documents), comm. 143 ff., and Khʷāndamīr. For documents concerning the Ṣafawid *ṣadrs*, see Schimkoreit, *op. cit.*, index. Some documents issued by these *ṣadrs* or concerning them have been published by H. Mudarrisī Ṭabāṭabāʾī, *Mithāl-hā-yi ṣudūr-i ṣafawī*, Ḳum 1353/1974. (J. Calmard)

4. In the Ṣafawid period.

The complex of religious institutions inherited by the Ṣafawid administration consisted basically of mosques, religious colleges (*madrasa*), religious endowments (*awḳāf*), and the offices of *ḳāḍī* and *shaykh al-islām*. These were controlled by the state through the office of *ṣadr*, the most important religous position in the realm and one which, in pre-Ṣafawid Persia, had tended to be hereditary in nature (see 2. above). The main function of the *ṣadr* was to supervise and administer the *awḳāf* and the distribution of their revenues to students and scholars and also to charity, hence the full title *ṣadr al-mawḳūfāt*. However, with the advent of Shāh Ismāʿīl I (r. 907-30/1501-24 [*q.v.*]), the nature and function of the office of *ṣadr* changed considerably. Faced with the problem of how to reconcile the "men of the sword", the Turcoman military élite which had propelled him to power, with the "men of the pen", the Persian bureaucrats on whom he depended for the efficient functioning of his state, Ismāʿīl made the *ṣadr* a political appointee. In so far as this arrangement gave the *ṣadr* political influence, he built a bridge between the largely Persian ranks of the *ʿulamāʾ* and the political branch of the administration, dominated during the early Ṣafawid period by *Ḳizilbāsh* military commanders. Although the propagation of religious doctrine and the establishment of doctrinal conformity and uniformity were not the primary function of the *ṣadr*, some scholars believe that for a time he had also to supervise the imposition of Twelver Shīʿism and root out heresy and Sunnism. By the time of Ismāʿīl's death, however, doctrinal uniformity had been largely achieved, and the energies of the *ṣadr* were devoted once more to the preservation of the religious status quo, and especially to the administration of the *awḳāf*.

It is clear that although the Persian "clerical estate" from which the appointees to the *ṣadārat* were initially taken was essential to the smooth running of the nascent Ṣafawid administration, it was unable to provide the theological and legal backbone for the new Twelver Shīʿī establishment: of the ten *ṣadrs* under Shāh Ṭahmāsp I, for example, only one was versed in Twelver Shīʿī jurisprudence, while the Shīʿism of the other nine was open to question. Consequently, Shāh Ismāʿīl and his successors imported Twelver Shīʿī scholars from Baḥrayn, ʿIrāḳ and the Lebanon. The immigrant jurists, experts in Twelver *fiḳh* and *kalām*, began to fill the posts of *shaykh al-islām*, *ḳāḍī*, *ḥākim-i sharʿ* and *mudarris*, gradually, as the power of the Arab *mudjtahids* increased, the power of the *ṣadr* began to wane.

The position of the *ṣadr* was further weakened when, during the reign of Shāh Sulaymān, the *ṣadārat* was divided into a "crown" (*khāṣṣa*) and a "state" (*mamālik* or *ʿāmma*) branch. As the division suggests, the *ṣadr-i khāṣṣa* was responsible for the administration of the royal endowments, while the *ṣadr-i mamālik* was entrusted with the endowments of private persons.

The *ṣadr-i khāṣṣa*, who enjoyed a higher rank than his colleague, continued to oversee the religious institution in general; according to the *Tadhkirat al-mulūk*, one of the prerogatives of his post was "the leadership ... of all the [persons] called sayyid, ʿulamā, mudarris, Shaykh al-Islām, pīsh-namāz, qāḍī, mutavallī, ḥāfiẓ and the rest of the servants of the sacred tombs, schools, mosques and shrines" (tr. Minorsky, English text, 42). Sitting jointly with the Dīwān-begī, the *ṣadr-i khāṣṣa* would try the major crimes at a weekly tribunal held in the *keshīk-khāna*. Appointment of *sharīʿa* judges for the rest of the kingdom was also a function of the *ṣadārat*, and it is here that the sources on late Ṣafawid Persia are clear on the demarcation of duties between the *khāṣṣa* and the *mamālik* branches: the *ṣadr-i khāṣṣa* appointed the judges of provinces under the royal *khāṣṣa* and especially those lying in the neighbourhood of the capital Iṣfahān, while the *ṣadr-i mamālik* appointed the judges in the rest of the provinces, such as Khurāsān and Fārs.

The *ṣadr* was to remain one of the highest and most coveted positions in the Ṣafawid administrative hierarchy until the demise of the dynasty. At state functions, the *ṣadr-i khāṣṣa* would be seated at the king's left hand, and it was not uncommon for the incumbent to marry into royalty and build up vast estates and considerable wealth of his own. As a locus of religious and political power, however, by the reign of Shāh Sulaymān the *ṣadr* was a spent force, eclipsed by the *shaykh al-islām* and, during the reign of Sulaymān's successor, Shāh, Sulṭān Ḥusayn, by the *mullābāshī*.

Bibliography: Iskandar Beg, *ʿĀlam-ārā-yi ʿAbbāsī*, lith. Tehran 1314/1896-7; V. Minorsky, *Tadhkirat al-mulūk*, GMS, London 1943; R.M. Savory, *Iran under the Safavids*, Cambridge 1980. See also the *Bibl.* to the preceding section 2.

(C.P. TURNER)

5. In Mughal India.

Here the *ṣadr* was a provincial (*ṣūba*) level officer in charge of land-grants in the Mughal Empire. The *ṣadr al-ṣudūr* was a central minister, who was given this title when the Empire was divided into *ṣūbas* by Akbar in 988/1580. Besides controlling land-grants (*madad-i maʿāsh*) and cash-grants (*waẓīfa*), the *ṣadr al-ṣudūr* also recommended appointments of *ḳāḍīs* or judges and *muftīs*, or interpreters of law and customs, though he had himself no judicial functions. The provincial *ṣadrs* were his subordinates, and below them there were local *ṣadrs* (*ṣadr-i djuzw*) and *mutawallīs* (managers of land-grants). Like the *ṣadrs*, the *ṣadr al-ṣudūr* was usually a Muslim theologian, since most land-grants were conferred upon theologians and scholars. He could, however, be an officer in regular service (holder of *manṣab* [*q.v.*]) as well, receiving his own salary through the award of *manṣab*, rather than land-grant. From Akbar's time onwards, non-Muslim divines and religious institutions also began to receive land-grants, and a rigorous procedure of verification was established in which the *ṣadr al-ṣudūr*'s department played an important role. The *ṣadr al-ṣudūr*'s office was held, like that of other ministers, at the Emperor's pleasure, but tended to be of longer duration except during the last years of Akbar, when after the dismissal of the most powerful of these ministers, Shaykh ʿAbd al-Nabī, 987/1579-80, the incumbents changed quite frequently. Whereas Īrānīs dominated other ministerial offices in the Mughal Empire, the office of *ṣadr al-ṣudūr* remained largely (though not entirely) the preserve of Indian Muslims and Tūrānīs, possibly because a Sunnī religious orientation was generally expected here.

Bibliography: The bulk of our information comes from Mughal revenue-grant documents largely unpublished, for a calender of these see *Mughal documents (1526-1627)*, ed. S.A.I. Tirmizi, New Delhi 1989. The standard official statement on the office and its functioning is to be found in Abu 'l-Faḍl, *Āʾīn-i Akbarī*, ed. H. Blochmann, Calcutta 1867-77, i. See also Ibn Hasan, *The central structure of the Mughal Empire and its practical working up to the year 1657*, Oxford 1936; M. Athar Ali, *The apparatus of empire, awards of ranks, offices and titles to the Mughal nobility, 1574-1658*; Oxford 1985; Rafat M. Bilgrami, *Religious and quasi-religious departments of the Mughal period (1556-1707)*, New Delhi 1984.

(M. ATHAR ALI)

ṢADR-I AʿẒAM (T.) (commonly *ṣadr aʿẓam*), strictly "the greatest of the high dignitaries", that is, the Grand Vizier, a title which, in the Ottoman Empire, was used synonymously with *wezīr-i aʿẓam* from the mid-10th/16th century; its first use in this sense occurs in the *Āṣāf-nāme* of Lütfī Pasha [*q.v.*], himself a holder of the office 946-8/1539-41.

Earlier, in the late 8th/14th century, *ṣadr* had been used to refer to the highest official *ʿulemāʾ*, the *ḳāḍī ʿaskers* [*q.v.*], who were promoted to serve as viziers. Later, because the vizier came to operate as military commander in the absence of the sultan, he was appointed, early in the 9th/15th century, from the ranks of the commanders (*ümerāʾ*). Even then the term *ṣadr* continued to be employed in its original general sense of "prominent, high *ʿulemāʾ* dignitary" and, as such, was the common title of the two *ḳāḍī ʿaskers*, sc. the *ṣadr* of Rumeli and of Anatolia (*Rumeli ṣadrī*, *Anadolu ṣadrī*), and even, though less often, for the *sheykh ül-islām* as *ṣadr-ī fetwā*. Inasmuch as many of the *ümerāʾ*, and especially, a majority of the highest ranking *ümerāʾ* beys, were of slave and *dewshirme* [*q.v.*] origin, the functional shift in the vizierate from the *ʿulemāʾ* to the *ümerāʾ* also implied an ethnic shift away from the Turkish-Muslim-born to those of slave-*dewshirme* origin, especially (but not exclusively) from the imperial household. As such, this shift was a prominent feature in the exaltation of the sultan in the polity. When the number of viziers or *ümerāʾ* commanders to serve in the imperial council (*dīwān-ī humāyūn* [*q.v.*])

was increased first to three and later to five in the 9th/15th century, the chief vizier was distinguished from the others and called the "first" or "greatest" (*wezīr-i ewwel* or *ekber* or *aʿẓam*; see further, WAZĪR).

The *ṣadr aʿẓam*, upon appointment directly by the sultan as absolute deputy (*wekīl-i muṭlaḳ*), was given the sultan's golden signet (*ṭughra*) ring which he carried with him at all times worn around his neck on a silk cord; thus *ṣāḥib-i mühr* (holder of the seal) was another term used for him. However, the reference in the *ḳānūn-nāme* [*q.v.*] of Meḥemmed II [*q.v.*] specified the Grand Vizier as the "head of the *wüzerāʾ* and *ümerāʾ*", implying that his authority was limited to military-administrative matters (and did not extend to *ʿulemāʾ* affairs and appointments), in spite of the statement, practically in the same breath, that he is the "absolute deputy in all matters" (*djümle umūruñ wekīl-i muṭlaḳīdīr*). Neither was his position vs. the *defterdār* (chief of the treasury [*q.v.*]) clear-cut; the latter was independent in his own sphere in his capacity as the minister of the sultan's own treasury (*mālīmīn wekīli*, "the deputy for my treasury") although the Grand Vizier was named his *nāẓīr* or supervisor (*Ḳānūn-nāme-yi āl-i ʿOthmān*, ed. Meḥmed ʿĀrif, in *TOEM*, Suppl. [1330 A.H.], 10). Even in the late 10th/16th century, when the sultan's treasury had become, for all practical purposes, the state treasury, a *defterdār* accused of corruption was not tried by the imperial council on the grounds that he was directly responsible to the sultan.

From the time of Meḥemmed II, the sultan stopped routinely attending meetings of the imperial council and, from the mid-10th/16th century, he was hardly even present; he left it to the *ṣadr aʿẓam*, as the deputy, to chair the proceedings. After the council meeting, the *ṣadr aʿẓam* would report in person to the sultan by reading a *telkhīṣ* (précis) of the most important matters discussed. Sometime during the reign of Murād III [*q.v.*], instead of reading the *telkhīṣ* face-to-face with the sultan, the *ṣadr aʿẓam* was required to send in his *telkhīṣ* and await written instructions, especially on appointments (for examples of *telkhīṣ* and analysis of its significance, cf. Cengiz Orhonlu, *Telhisler*, Istanbul 1970 and Suraiya Faroqhi, *Das telḫīs, eine aktenkundlische Studie*, in *Isl.*, xlv [1969], 96-116).

This change allowed the inner circle of the palace, rather than the vizier, to have the sultan's ear and influence decisions. Consequently, in the first half of the 11th/17th century the *istiḳlāl* (independence) of the vizier, that is, independence of action free from undue influence of persons close to the ruler—his mother the dowager sultan (*wālide sulṭān*) or his consort (*khāṣṣeki*) or companions (*muṣāḥib*)—emerged as one of the most important political issues in the affairs of the empire. Naʿīmā [*q.v.*] claims that in 1066/1656, at a moment of internal and external crisis, Köprülü [*q.v.*] Meḥmed Pasha accepted the grand vizierate only after the young sultan Meḥemmed IV [*q.v.*] and his mother Turkhān Sulṭān agreed to his conditions of absolute independence in affairs of state (for an analysis of this appointment, cf. M. Kunt, *Naʾima, Köprülü, and the grand vezirate*, in *Boğaziçi Üniversitesi Dergisi—Hümaniter Bilimler*, i [1973], 57-63). The sultan and the dowager were so pleased with the old vizier's competent and wise service that, on his death five years later, he was succeeded in office by his son. Indeed, the Köprülü household supplied no less than seven Grand Viziers in the next half century, providing, after the Djandarlī [*q.v.*] family of the late 8th/14th to mid 9th/15th century, a second case of a vizierial dynasty (see also İ.H. Uzunçarşılı, *Çandarlı vezir ailesi*, Ankara 1974). It is in this period of restoration of vizierial authority that the *ḳānūn-nāme* of Tewḳi-ʿī ʿAbd ul-Raḥmān Pasha (1087/1676-7, published in *MTM*, i/3 [1331], 506 ff.) speaks of very comprehensive and far-reaching duties and powers of the office, without the limitations and the constraints of the two-centuries earlier *ḳānūn-nāme* of Meḥemmed II. Barely 20 years later, however, a particularly ambitious *sheykh ül-islām*, Feyḍ Allāh Efendi, with the full support of the reigning sultan, Muṣṭafa II [*q.v.*], attempted to dominate the Grand Vizier: this was one of the causes of the rebellion and constitutional crisis of 1115/1703.

In 1837, at the height of Maḥmūd II's [*q.v.*] programme of political restructuring, the title *ṣadr aʿẓam* was converted to *bashwekīl*, chief minister, while at the same time the deliberative function of the imperial council was divided among several new councils. These measures served to reduce both the position of the vizier as absolute deputy and the independence and centrality of government: the ruler and his palace once again became the focus of political as well as administrative life. Maḥmūd II died soon afterwards, in 1839, and the forceful Khüsrew Pasha took over power, restoring both the title and the authority of *ṣadr aʿẓam*, at the accession of the young and diffident ʿAbd al-Medjīd [*q.v.*]. In the early years of ʿAbd al-Ḥamīd II's [*q.v.*] reign, there were two more, equally unsuccessful, attempts to change the title to *bashwekīl*: this time, however, the impetus came not from the sultan but from reformist ministers, for the purpose of establishing the principle of a government sharing collective responsibility to parliament. In the event, even after the constitution was restored in 1908, *ṣadr aʿẓam* remained the title for the chief minister until the end of the sultanate, though now he was responsible to parliament (for an analysis of the grand vizier's position during the transformation of governmental and administrative institutions in the reform period, see C.V. Findley, *Bureaucratic reform in the Ottoman Empire*, Princeton 1980, 141, 153, 240 ff.).

Bibliography: In addition to items mentioned in the text, see Pakalın, s.vv. *Sadrazam* and *Vezir*, providing extensive details and comments; the most comprehensive discussion is in İ.H. Uzunçarşılı, *Osmanlı devletinin merkez ve bahriye teşkilâtı*, Ankara 1948, 111-79; both the *Osmanlı tarihi* sponsored by the Türk Tarih Kurumu (authors, Uzunçarşılı and E.Z. Karal), 7 vols., Ankara 1948-59, and İ.H. Danişmend's *İzahlı Osmanlı tarihi kronolojisi*, 4 vols., Istanbul 1947-55, include lists and brief biographical sketches of all grand viziers; Gibb and Bowen, especially i/1, 107-37, is still useful; for an excellent study of the palace of Süleymān the Magnificent's famous vizier Ibrāhīm Pasha [*q.v.*], see Nurhan Atasoy, *İbrahim Paşa Sarayı*, Istanbul 1972; the closest we have to a biographical study of a grand vizier is R. Dankoff's translation of relevant passages in Evliya Çelebi, *The intimate life of an Ottoman statesman, Melek Ahmed Pasha (1588-1662)*, New York 1991. (M. KUNT)

ṢADR AL-DĪN [see MULLĀ ṢADRĀ SHĪRĀZĪ].

ṢADR AL-DĪN ARDABĪLĪ (Shaykh Ṣadr al-Milla wa 'l-Dīn Mūsā), second son of Ṣafī al-Dīn Ardabīlī [*q.v.*], born 1 Shawwāl 704/26 April 1305 (Shaykh Ḥusayn b. Abdāl Zāhidī, *Silsilat al-nasab-i Ṣafawiyya*, Iranschähr Publications no. 6, Berlin 1924-5, 39). Designated by his father as his successor and vicegerent (*khalīfa wa nāʾib-munāb*), Ṣadr al-Dīn assumed the leadership of the Ṣafawid Order in 735/1334. He expanded the Ṣafawid mausoleum complex at Ardabīl, adding rooms for private meditation (*khalwat-khāna*), a residence for Ḳurʾān-readers (*dār al-ḥuffāẓ*), and a room (*čīnī-khāna*) which later housed

Sh̲āh̲ ʿAbbās I's *waḳf* of porcelain to the shrine (see J.A. Pope, *Chinese porcelains from the Ardebil Shrine*, Washington 1956).

Although the powerful Mongol *amīr* Čūbān [see ČŪBĀNIDS] had professed to be a disciple (*murīd*) of Sh̲aykh̲ Ṣafī al-Dīn (Sh̲araf al-Dīn Bidlīsī, *Sh̲araf-nāma*, éd. V. Véliaminov-Zernof, 2 vols., St. Petersburg 1860-2, ii, 132-3), Amīr Čūbān's son, Malik As̲h̲raf, possibly alarmed by Ṣadr al-Dīn's growing political influence, threw him into jail at Tabrīz. He released him after three months, but again tried to seize him; this time Ṣadr al-Dīn escaped to Gīlān. When D̲j̲ānī Beg Maḥmūd, ruler of the Blue Horde of Western Ḳipčāḳ (742-58/1341-57) [see BATUʾIDS] overthrew Malik As̲h̲raf and put him to death in 758/1357, Ṣadr al-Dīn returned to Ardabīl, but D̲j̲ānī Beg's promise to allot all Ṣafawid lands to the Sh̲aykh̲ in the form of a *soyūrg̲h̲āl* had not been enacted before D̲j̲ānī Beg's death (*Silsilat al-nasab*, 42-3); see also B. Spuler, *The Muslim world*, ii, *The Mongol period*, Leiden 1960, 54-5, and J.B. van Loon, *Taʾrīkh̲-i Sh̲aykh̲ Uways*, The Hague 1954, 11).

Ṣadr al-Dīn died in 794/1391-2, and was buried in the Ardabīl sanctuary (*Silsilat al-nasab*, 45). He left three sons: Kh̲wād̲j̲a ʿAlī (who succeeded him as head of the Ṣafawid Order); Sh̲ihāb al-Dīn and D̲j̲amāl al-Dīn (*ibid.*, 40).

Bibliography: Given in the text.

(R.M. Savory)

ṢADR AL-DĪN ʿAYNĪ, Russian form SADRIDDIN AYNI, one of the leading figures in the 20th century cultural life of Central Asia and in Tad̲j̲ik literature (1878-1954).

He began as a representative of the reform movement amongst the Muslims of Imperial Russia, that of the D̲j̲adīdīds [see D̲J̲ADĪD]. A formal education at the traditional *madrasa*s of Buk̲h̲ārā left him intellectually unsatisfied. In the early part of his career he was a talented poet in both Tad̲j̲ik and Uzbek, but after 1905 he became increasingly involved in the social and educational aspects of D̲j̲adīdism. In 1917 he espoused the cause of the revolutionary movements and, eventually, that of the Bolsheviks, and when in 1920 the Tad̲j̲ik S.S.R. was set up, he held leading positions in its cultural life, becoming the first President of the Tad̲j̲ik Academy of Sciences and retaining this office until his death. He now turned from poetry to prose-writing in a wide variety of fields—literary criticism, history and novels in both Tad̲j̲ik and Uzbek, culminating in his unfinished memoirs (*Yād-dāsht-hā/Yod-dosht-ho*, 4 vols., Stalinabad 1949-54). He is thus the dominant figure in the prose of socialist realism, as also in the moulding of modern Tad̲j̲ik literature in general.

Bibliography: J. Bečka, in Rypka *et alii, History of Iranian literatures*, Dordrecht 1968, 523-4, 535, 559-64; J. Prušek (general ed.), *Dictionary of oriental literatures. iii. Western Asia and North Africa*, London 1974, 24-5; Bečka, *Sadridin Ayni, father of modern Tajik culture*, Naples 1980; K. Hitchins, in E. Yarshater (ed.), *Persian literature*, Albany 1988, 457-60, 462-3, 467-8.

(Ed.)

ṢADR AL-DĪN MUḤAMMAD B. ISḤĀḲ B. MUḤAMMAD B. YŪNUS AL-ḲŪNAWĪ (b. 605/1207, d. 16 Muḥarram 673/22 July 1274), disciple of Ibn al-ʿArabī [*q.v.*] and author of influential works on theoretical Ṣūfism.

Ibn al-ʿArabī met Mad̲j̲d al-Dīn Isḥāḳ al-Rūmī, Ḳūnawī's father, in Mecca in 600/1203 and subsequently travelled with him to Anatolia. A source from the late 7th/13th century tells us that after Mad̲j̲d al-Dīn's death, Ibn al-ʿArabī married his widow and adopted his son Ṣadr al-Dīn (B. Furūzānfar, *Manāḳib-i Awḥad al-Dīn ... Kirmānī*, Tehran 1347/1968, 84); the fact that Ḳūnawī himself never mentions this is not surprising, given his extreme reticence concerning personal matters. The same source (85) tells us that Ibn al-ʿArabī entrusted Ṣadr al-Dīn for a time to the guidance of his friend Sh̲aykh̲ Awḥad al-Dīn Kirmānī (d. 635/1238), and this is confirmed by a manuscript letter in which Ḳūnawī says that he was Kirmānī's companion for two years, travelling with him as far as Sh̲īrāz (Chittick, *Faith and practice of Islam*, Albany 1992, 261). By the time he was twenty, Ḳūnawī appears among the listeners to Ibn al-ʿArabī's works in a *samāʿ* dated 626/1229 (O. Yahia, *Histoire et classification de l'œuvre d'Ibn ʿArabī*, Damascus 1964, 141). He seems to have remained with this *sh̲aykh̲* until the latter's death in 638/1240; his name is recorded in many *samāʿ*s deriving from this period. Presumably, the *fath̲ kullī*, or total unveiling of the invisible world, that he mentions as occurring in Damascus (*al-Nafaḥāt al-ilāhiyya*, 12) occurred at this time.

Ḳūnawī was teaching, probably in Konya, by the year 643/1245-6, when he led a group of scholars to Cairo and taught Ibn al-Fāriḍ's *Tāʾiyya* on the way [see SAʿĪD AL-DĪN FARG̲H̲ĀNĪ]. Little can be gleaned about his life from his works other than occasional references to instances in which he gained visionary knowledge. Thus, for example, on the night of 17 Sh̲awwāl 653/19 November 1255, Ibn al-ʿArabī appeared to him and confirmed that he was his preeminent disciple, even greater than his son Saʿd al-Dīn (*al-Nafaḥāt al-ilāhiyya*, 152-3; partial Persian tr. in D̲j̲āmī, *Nafaḥāt al-uns*, ed. Tawḥīdīpūr, Tehran 1336/1957, 556-7). Ḳūnawī reports that he did not receive oral explanation from Ibn al-ʿArabī concerning most of his works, but instead gained knowledge of them through God's effusion (*al-Fukūk*, ed. Kh̲wād̲j̲awī, 240). In his *Manāḳib al-ʿārifīn* (ed. T. Yazıcı, Ankara 1959), Aflākī recounts several anecdotes showing that Ḳūnawī had a highly favourable view of Rūmī, and he contrasts Rūmī's simplicity with the sumptuous scholarly trappings of Ḳūnawī's circle (e.g. 95-6). Among Ḳūnawī's important students were ʿAfīf al-Dīn al-Tilimsānī, Fak̲h̲r al-Dīn ʿIrāḳī, Saʿīd al-Dīn Farg̲h̲ānī [*q.vv.*], and Muʾayyid al-Dīn D̲j̲andī (d. *ca.* 700/1300), author of the most influential commentary on Ibn al-ʿArabī's *Fuṣūṣ al-ḥikam*. Farg̲h̲ānī is especially important because his *Mas̲h̲āriḳ al-darārī* represents summaries of Ḳūnawī's teachings far more detailed than any of Ḳūnawī's own works. The scientist and philosopher Ḳuṭb al-Dīn Sh̲īrāzī [*q.v.*] studied parts of D̲j̲āmiʿ *al-uṣūl fī aḥādīth̲ al-rasūl* by Mad̲j̲d al-Dīn Ibn al-Ath̲īr with him in the year 673 (H. Ritter, *Autographs in Turkish libraries*, in *Oriens*, vi [1953], 63-90).

The works ascribed to Ḳūnawī can be divided into those that are unquestionably authentic and those concerning which some doubts remain. The most important works in the first category are the following:

1. *Iʿd̲j̲āz al-bayān fī tafsīr umm al-ḳurʾān* or *Tafsīr al-fātiḥa* (published as *Iʿd̲j̲āz al-bayān*, Ḥaydarābād-Deccan 1949; and as *al-Tafsīr al-ṣūfī li 'l-Ḳurʾān*, ed. ʿA. Aḥmad ʿAṭāʾ, Cairo 1969). Both printed editions leave out the author's rather extensive marginal notes. This is Ḳūnawī's longest and perhaps most important work.

2. *Sh̲arḥ al-ḥadīth̲ al-arbaʿīn* (ed. H.K. Yılmaz, *Tasavvufī hadis şerhleri ve Konevînin kırk hadis şerhi*, Istanbul 1990). Ḳūnawī died after commenting on only 29 *ḥadīth̲*s. The commentary on *ḥadīth̲*s nos. 21-2 is extensive and provides important elucidations of Ḳūnawī's teachings on imagination and other matters.

3. *Sharḥ al-asmāʾ al-ḥusnā*. A relatively concise explanation of the ninety-nine names of God and their traces on the human level.

4. *al-Fukūk* or *Fakk al-khutūm* (ed. M. Khʷādjawī, Tehran 1413/1992; printed on the margin of Kāshānī, *Sharḥ manāzil al-sāʾirīn*, Tehran 1315/1897-8). A short commentary on the essential themes of Ibn al-ʿArabī's *Fuṣūṣ al-ḥikam*, focusing on the implications of the chapter headings.

5. *Miftāḥ al-ghayb* (published on the margin of Muḥammad al-Fanārī, *Miṣbāḥ al-ins bayn al-maʿḳūl wa 'l-mankūl fī sharḥ miftāḥ ghayb al-djamʿ wa 'l-wudjūd*, Tehran 1323/1905; partial ed. and French tr. S. Ruspoli, *La clé du monde suprasensible*, diss., Paris IV 1978). This has always been considered Ḳūnawī's key work; it was taught in Persian *madrasas* after students had mastered the most difficult texts in philosophy. At least nine commentaries have been written on it, mostly in Turkey. One of the more interesting is by 'Abd Allāh Mullā Ilāhī, written in Persian at the command of Meḥemmed II Fātiḥ; the author makes several asides to the ruler in the midst of the text, indicating that he was expecting him to read it (see Chittick, *Sultan Burhān al-Dīn's Sufi correspondence*, in *WZKM*, lxxiii [1981], 37-8).

6. *al-Nafaḥāt al-ilāhiyya* (Tehran 1316/1898), a series of about fifty "inspired breaths", along with other miscellaneous texts including at least 17 letters written to various friends and disciples. Many of the passages refer to Ḳūnawī's visionary experiences.

7. *al-Nuṣūṣ* (ed. S.Dj. Āshtiyānī, Tehran 1362/1983; appended to Kāshānī, *Sharḥ manāzil al-sāʾirīn, ed. cit.*; and appended to Ibn Turka, *Tamhīd al-ḳawāʿid*, Tehran 1315/1897-8). A collection of 21 texts that pertain exclusively to the "station of perfection"; the longest (no. 20), which is taken from the first section of *Miftāḥ al-ghayb*, is perhaps Ḳūnawī's most comprehensive exposition of the doctrine that later came to be known as *waḥdat al-wudjūd*.

8-9. *al-Mufāwaḍāt* (forthcoming critical ed. by Gudrun Schubert). A correspondence initiated by Ḳūnawī with Naṣīr al-Dīn Ṭūsī [*q.v.*]. Ḳūnawī's first treatise, *al-Mufṣiḥa ʿan muntahā 'l-afkār wa-sabab ikhtilāf al-umam*, addresses the weakness of human reason and poses a series of questions for Ṭūsī; a good portion of the introductory material is drawn from the beginning of *Iʿdjāz al-bayān*. His second treatise, *al-Hādiya*, responds to Ṭūsī's replies (for details on the contents, see Chittick, *Mysticism vs. philosophy in earlier Islamic history: the al-Ṭūsī, al-Qūnawī correspondence*, in *Religious Studies*, xvii [1981], 87-104).

Minor works include the following: 10. *al-Ilmāʿ bi-baʿḍ kulliyyāt asrār al-samāʾ*. A long letter to ʿAfīf al-Dīn al-Tilimsānī describing how, when Ḳūnawī was circumambulating the Kaʿba, the meaning of certain verses he had heard suddenly became clear to him. 11. *Nafthat al-maṣdūr wa-tuḥfat al-shakūr*, or *Rashḥ al-bāl bi-sharḥ al-ḥāl*, containing about 50 pages of intimate mystical prayers. This work was sent by mistake to Ṭūsī along with work no. 8, and he offered polite criticism of it in his response. 12. *al-Risāla al-hādiya al-murshidiyya*, also called *al-Risāla al-tawadjdjuhiyya* and *Risālat al-tawadjdjuh al-atamm*. This short work, of which a Persian translation was prepared during Ḳūnawī's lifetime, provides practical instructions concerning the remembrance of God (French tr. M. Valsan, *L'épître sur l'orientation parfaite*, in *Études traditionnelles*, lxvii [1966], 241-68). 13. *Waṣiyya*. A short last will, which mentions among other things Ḳūnawī's close relationship with Ibn al-ʿArabī and Awḥad al-Dīn Kirmānī. Ḳūnawī advises his disciples to avoid theoretical issues and concentrate on the practical instructions provided in work no. 12. His books on philosophy should be sold and the remaining books made into an endowment, and his own writings should be given to ʿAfīf al-Dīn. A second version adds the names of four people to whom money should be given and tells his daughter Sakīna that she should be careful to observe her ritual obligations (tr. of the first version in Chittick, *The Last Will and Testament of Ibn ʿArabī's foremost disciple and some notes on its author*, in *Sophia Perennis*, iv/1 [1978], 43-58; text of second in Ergin, *Sadraddīn al-Qunawi ve eserleri*, 82-3). Several letters and brief Persian treatises are also extant.

Works of questionable attribution include the following (for others of less likely authenticity, see Brockelmann, G I², 585-6, S I, 807-8): 1. *Mirʾāt al-ʿārifīn fī multamas Zayn al-ʿĀbidīn*. A relatively short discussion of cosmology in Ḳūnawī's characteristic style. Text and English tr. in S.H. Askari, *Reflection of the awakened*, London 1981. 2. *Taḥrīr al-bayān fī taḳrīr shuʿab al-īmān*. This and the following work, both relatively short, are attributed to Ḳūnawī in some manuscripts and reflect his style and concerns. 3. *Marātib al-taḳwā*. 4. *Kitāb al-Lumʿa al-nūrāniyya fī ḥall mushkilāt al-shadjarat al-nuʿmāniyya*. Commentary on a diagram that Ibn al-ʿArabī is said to have drawn up to illustrate the general direction of future events in Egypt [see MALḤAMA]. 5. *Tabṣirat al-mubtadī wa-tadhkirat al-muntahī*. A Persian work that is most likely by one Naṣīr or Nāṣir al-Dīn (tr. in Chittick, *Faith and practice of Islam*, Albany 1992; discussion of authorship at 255-62).

In contrast to Ibn al-ʿArabī, Ḳūnawī focuses on a relatively small number of issues, thereby singling them out as the most essential teachings of his master. His mode of exposition is in no way indebted to Ibn al-ʿArabī or to anyone else (a point he sometimes stresses e.g. *Iʿdjāz*, 147; *Nuṣūṣ*, 22). His major themes are perhaps best summarised in the last section of *Miftāḥ al-ghayb*, in which he proposes a series of questions that he then sets out to answer (282-3): What is the reality of the human being? From what, in what, and how did he come into existence? Who brought him into existence and why? What is the goal of his existence? Briefly, Ḳūnawī answers these questions by describing the modes in which *wudjūd* may and may not be known, the manner in which existent things are differentiated within *wudjūd* through the influence of the divine names, and the way in which the perfect human being (*al-insān al-kāmil*) brings *wudjūd* to full fruition. His essential point is that only the perfect human being manifests all divine names in perfect balance and equilibrium, thereby standing at the centre point of the circle of *wudjūd* and not coming under the influence of any specific attributes. Every other created thing manifests specific names of God and is dominated by either oneness or manyness. Although this theme is also found in Ibn al-ʿArabī's writings, it is not so clearly presented as the key doctrine. Ibn al-ʿArabī roots his teachings in the Ḳurʾān and the *Ḥadīth*, but Ḳūnawī employs a more abstract vocabulary that is much more reminiscent of texts on philosophy, and he highlights a number of technical terms that play no special role in Ibn al-ʿArabī's teachings, even though they become basic points of discussion in later works. These include *al-ḥaḍarā al-ilāhiyya al-khams, kamāl al-djalāʾ wa 'l-istidjlāʾ, iʿtidāl* and *taʿayyun* (for an outline of Ḳūnawī's teachings, see the introduction to Chittick and P.L. Wilson, *Fakhruddin ʿIrāqī: Divine flashes*, New York 1982). The key term *waḥdat al-wudjūd*, although found in at least one passage of Ḳūnawī's works, has no special technical significance for him. In the works of Farghānī based on Ḳūnawī's lectures, the term is used in a way that is not picked up by later authors (see Chittick, *Rūmī and* waḥdat al-wujūd, in *The heritage of Rumi*, ed. A. Banani and G. Sabagh, Cambridge, forthcoming).

Ḳūnawī's importance needs to be understood in light of Ibn al-ʿArabī's pervasive influence on the schools of theoretical Ṣūfism, philosophy and *kalām*. Djāmī had already recognised that Ḳūnawī was the primary interpreter of Ibn al-ʿArabī's teachings (*Nafaḥāt al-uns*, 556). In effect, the later intellectual tradition read Ibn al-ʿArabī's works according to the interpretation of Ḳūnawī and his immediate disciples. His role is symbolised by the correspondence he initiated with Ṭūsī. In the Persian letter that accompanies *al-Hādiya*, Ḳūnawī explains that he initiated the correspondence in order to combine the rational approach of the philosophers with the "unveiling" (*kashf*) of the Verifiers. In the correspondence, Ḳūnawī reveals himself as thoroughly familiar with Avicenna's writings and with Ṭūsī's commentary on Avicenna's *al-Ishārāt wa 'l-tanbīhāt*; his philosophical bent, in any case, is already obvious in other writings. Far more than Ibn al-ʿArabī, he employs clear and reasoned argumentation to demonstrate his conclusions, even if he also depends explicitly upon mystical intuition. Largely because of the themes that Ḳūnawī establishes in *al-Fukūk* and in the oral teachings that are reflected in the works of his students, the mainstream of Ibn al-ʿArabī's school of thought came to stress certain dimensions of the master's teachings that are not necessarily central to his own writings. This explains Michel Chodkiewicz's remark that Ḳūnawī "a donné à la doctrine de son maître une formulation philosophique sans doute nécessaire mais dont le systématisme a engendré bien des malentendus" (*Épître sur l'Unicité Absolue*, Paris 1982, 26).

Bibliography: C. Addas, *Quest for the Red Sulphur: the life of Ibn ʿArabī*, Cambridge 1993, *passim*; W.C. Chittick, *The circle of spiritual ascent according to al-Qūnawī*, in *Neoplatonism and Islamic thought*, ed. P. Morewedge, Albany 1992, 179-209; idem, *The five Divine Presences: from al-Qūnawī to al-Qayṣarī*, in *MW*, lxxii (1982), 107-28; idem, *Ṣadr al-Dīn Qūnawī on the oneness of being*, in *International Philosophical Quarterly*, xxi (1981), 171-84; Nihat Keklik, *Sadreddîn Konevî'nin felsefesinde. Allah-kâinât ve insan*, Istanbul 1967; *Selçuk Dergisi. Sadreddin Konevî özel sayısı*, iv (1989). On manuscripts of Ḳūnawī's works, see Osman Ergin, *Sadraddîn al-Qunawi ve eserleri*, in *Şarkiyat mecmuası*, ii (1957), 63-90; Khʷādjawī, introd. to Ḳūnawī, *al-Fukūk*, 32-9.

(W.C. Chittick)

ṢADR AL-DĪN MŪSĀ, the son and successor of Shaykh Ṣafī al-Dīn Ardabīlī [*q.v.*] and the founder at Ardabīl of the Ṣafawī order which stemmed from Shaykh Zāhid Gīlānī (d. 700/1301). Shaykh Ṣadr al-Dīn was born in 704/1305 from Ṣafī al-Dīn's second marriage with Bībī Fāṭima, daughter of Shaykh Zāhid, and died in 794/1391-2, according to the *Silsilat al-nasab-i ṣafawiyya*, hence dying aged 90 having directed the Ṣafawī order for 59 years. Although the hagio-biographical and historical sources concerning him have to be treated with caution, they allow us to trace the essential features of his long career as head of the order.

After the death of his eldest brother Muḥyī al-Dīn in 724/1324-5, Ṣadr al-Dīn replaced him in his function as *khalīfa*, and replaced his father, as his spiritual and material heir, when the latter fell ill before his death, although it seems that Ṣafī al-Dīn's sons were at odds with each other, above all regarding their father's material legacy. Being then 30, Ṣadr al-Dīn achieved the succession without any overt opposition, and at a point when, after the Il Khān Abū Saʿīd's death (736/1335), the Mongol clan of the Čopans/Čubāns of the Sulduz tribe were disputing over the succession with the Djalāyir tribe, and Ardabīl, the *dār al-irshād* of the Ṣafawiyya, changed hands several times. Originally favoured by the Čopanid Malik Ashraf, he fell out with him and had to flee from Ardabīl with his *khalīfas* and *murīds* to Gīlān; it was the protection of the Khān of Ḳīpčaḳ, Djānī Beg Maḥmūd, of the Golden Horde, who gave protection to Ṣadr al-Dīn and the Ṣafawiyya. When the Djalāyirids led by Uways secured control over Ādharbaydjān in 761/1361, the situation of the order improved. Uways allotted Ardabīl as a *soyurghal* [*q.v.*] to his son Aḥmad, and the latter confirmed and renewed in a *farmān* the established fiscal privileges and revenues of Ṣadr al-Dīn and the order (document of 773/1372 ed. by Massé, Ḳazwīnī, Bayānī, etc.). Despite the influence and respect which Ṣadr al-Dīn enjoyed, the hagio-biographical sources and the documents do not show that he claimed the title of *sayyid* or that he was considered as such during his lifetime, although there were later falsifications allegedly proving an ʿAlid descent for the Ṣafawids, one of the bases of their claim to dynastic legitimacy.

After his eldest brother's death, Ṣadr al-Dīn is presented as the closest and most favoured of Ṣafī al-Dīn's sons, with other sons relegated to the second rank. He was certainly influential on the material plane, and it is with him that the family's ambitions in acquiring extensive estates and other landed property take shape. Only a small part of these were constituted as *waḳf* proper, the remainder being acquired in full personal ownership (*milk*) or in the shape of family *waḳf* and transmissible to the family's descendants. These acquisitions were purchased from the *amīrs* or from other Turco-Mongol and Mongol nobles, and from other notables; sometimes they were obtained by questionable means, and this gave rise to litigation and conflicts, in particular between the Djuwaynī and Ṣafawī families. As well as the revenues accruing from his direction (*tawliya*) of these sources of wealth, Ṣadr al-Dīn must have had a substantial personal fortune, especially as his mother died soon after his father, as did his brother Abū Saʿīd and his two halfbrothers ʿAlāʾ al-Dīn and Sharaf al-Dīn. His properties in the region of Ardabīl included villages and shops, and some of these were acquired to the detriment of local notable families. His sons Shihāb al-Dīn and Ḍiyāʾ al-Dīn were equally active in amassing properties. Apparently through a sense of politics as much as by family sentiment, Ṣadr al-Dīn extended his care and control over the whole of the Ṣafawī family.

With these riches, Ṣadr al-Dīn contributed extensively to the growth of the Ardabīl shrine, which became a complex worthy of the order's prestige and importance. The construction of Ṣafī al-Dīn's tomb, completed towards 1344, is said to have taken ten years. The *Dār al-Ḥuffāẓ* was built on the site of a demolished *zāwiya*, and the building (or perhaps reconstruction?) of various buildings, whose original functions are uncertain, is attributed to him, including one called a *čīnī-khāna* in Shāh ʿAbbās I's time, a *čilla-khāna* and a *shahīd-gāh*.

With the respect behind him of the Mongol and Turkmen authorities, Ṣadr al-Dīn continued his father's work for the extension of the Ṣafawiyya order, in particular, by sending out *khalīfas* to places like Georgia. The most famous of these *khalīfas*, a controversial figure on account of his heterodox, Ḥurūfī doctrines [see ḤURŪFIYYA] was Shāh Ḳāsim al-Anwār [see ḲĀSIM-I ANWĀR], his envoy to Khurāsān, who also had links with Shāh Niʿmat Allāh [see NIʿMAT-ALLĀHIYYA]. According to an apparently late tradition, Ṣadr al-Dīn is said to have made the pilgrimage in 770/1368-9 and to have brought back from his visit to the Prophet's tomb in Medina a banner allegedly belonging to Fāṭima and two tambourines used ritually at Ardabīl. He is said to have asked the *Sharīf* of Mecca for his genealogical tree. But as with his father and other Ṣafawī *shaykhs*, he has left no work behind for us to get an idea of the range of his knowledge. Like his father, too, Ṣadr al-Dīn was a mediocre theologian but endowed with great charisma and famed for his Ṣūfī teaching. This fame seems to have gone beyond the Turco-Persian world, for his contemporary Ibn Khaldūn [*q.v.*] honours him with the title of *shaykh al-shuyūkh* (*ʿIbar*, Beirut 1951, v, 1171).

On his return from the Pilgrimage, Ṣadr al-Dīn is said to have appointed his eldest son Khwādja ʿAlī as his *khalīfa* and *nāʾib* and to have entrusted to him before his death the spiritual direction and teaching of his disciples (*sadjdjāda-yi irshād wa tarbiyat-i ʿibād*). It seems nevertheless that another son, Shihāb al-Dīn, acted as *shaykh* of the Ṣafawiyya for some time after his father's death, according to some documents. There may conceivably have been more division between *irshād* and *tawliyat*. Whatever the case, it was, according to the official Ṣafawid version, Khwādja ʿAlī who, probably because of his influence and "meetings" with Tīmūr, was considered as his father's successor after the latter's death in 794/1391-2. Ṣadr al-Dīn was buried at Ardabīl near his father.

Bibliography: This is given substantially in the article ṢAFĪ AL-DĪN ARDABĪLĪ, but see also J. Aubin, *La propriété foncière en Azerbaydjan sous les Mongols*, in *Le Monde iranien et l'Islam*, iv (1976-7), 79-132 (see genealogical table of the Ṣafawiyya at 86-7); idem, *Shaykh Ibrāhīm Zāhid Gīlānī (1218?-1301)*, in *Turcica*, xxi-xxiii (1991) (= *Mélanges Irène Melikoff*); idem, *De Kûhbanân à Bidar. La famille Niʿmatullahî*, in *StIr*, xx (1991-2), 233-61; H. Horst, *Tīmūr und Ḫoğa ʿAlī*, Wiesbaden 1958; A.H. Morton, *The Ardabil shrine in the reign of Shāh Ṭahmāsp I*, in *Iran*, *JBIPS*, xii (1974), 31-64, xiii (1975), 39-58; H. Sohrweide, *Der Sieg der Ṣafawiden in Persien und seine Rückwirkungen auf die Schiiten Anatoliens im 16. Jahrhundert*, in *Isl.*, xli (1965), 95-223; H. Zirke, *Ein hagiographisches Zeugnis zur persischen Geschichte aus der Mitte des 14. Jahrhunderts. Das achte Kapitel des Ṣafwat aṣ-ṣafā in kritischer Bearbeitung*, Berlin 1987. (J. CALMARD)

ṢADR AL-ṢUDŪR [see ṢADR].

SADRĀTA, a place in Algeria, founded in 296/908 at 8 km/5 miles to the south-west of Wardjilān (Ouargla) in the territory of the confederation of *ḳṣūr* of the Isedrāten, by the last Rustamid Imām, after the destruction of the principality of Tāhart [*q.v.*] by the Fāṭimids. Its fame is linked with the history of the Ibāḍī communities of the Maghrib. An Ibāḍī scholar, Abū Yaʿḳūb Yūsuf b. Ibrāhīm al-Sadrātī al-Wardjilānī (d. 570/1174-5) compiled there the *musnad* of al-Rabīʿ b. Ḥabīb, based essentially on the tradition of Abū ʿUbayda (ed. Masḳaṭ 1325/1908 under the title of *al-Djāmiʿ al-ṣaḥīḥ*).

The town was razed to the ground in 467/1074, and its people took refuge in Ouargla and in the Mzāb.

Bibliography: See those to IBĀḌIYYA, MZĀB, WARGLA, to which should be added ʿU.R. Kaḥḥāla, *Muʾallifīn*, xiii, 267; Ch. Pellat, *Le milieu baṣrien*, 214. (ED.)

AL-**ṢAFĀ** (A.), literally "hard, smooth stone", whence also "tract of stony ground".

1. Al-Ṣafā is the name of a mound at Mecca which now rises barely above the level of the ground and which, together with the slightly higher, similar eminence of al-Marwa, plays an important role in the ceremonies or *manāsik* of the Meccan Pilgrimage. The names al-Ṣafā and al-Marwa (this last also sometimes qualified, e.g. by the local historian al-Azraḳī [*q.v.*], as *al-Bayḍāʾ* "the white") both mean "the stone(s)" (see al-Ṭabarī, *Tafsīr*, *ad* sūra II, 153/158). The twin hillocks mark the beginning and conclusion of the course taken by the pilgrims (the *muʿtamir* performing the *ʿumra* and the *ḥādjdj* performing the *ḥadjdj*), sc. the *masʿā* or *masīl*, whose traversing forms the *saʿy* [*q.v.*], the prelude to the *ḥadjdj* proper.

According to tradition (see e.g. al-Bukhārī, *Anbiyāʾ*, *bāb* 9), the *saʿy* between the two hillocks commemorates the fact that Hādjar ran backwards and forwards seven times between these two eminences to look for a spring for her thirsty son. It is certain that cults were located at al-Ṣafā and al-Marwa, even in the pre-Islamic period. According to most traditions, there were two stone idols there, Isāf on al-Ṣafā and Nāʾila on al-Marwa, which the pagan Arabs on their *saʿy* used to touch. On the origin of these images, the following story is given in the commentary of al-Nīsābūrī on sūra II, 153/158, and al-Shāfiʿī gives his approval to it: Isāf and Nāʾila were guilty of indecent conduct in the Kaʿba and were therefore turned into stones, which were placed on the two pieces of raised ground al-Ṣafā and al-Marwa to be a warning to all. In course of time, the origin of the stone figures was forgotten and people began to pay them divine worship [see further, ISĀF WA-NĀʾILA]. According to another tradition, there were copper images there (cf. Snouck Hurgronje, *Het Mekkaansche Feest*, 26); according to a third story, demons lived on the two hills who shrieked at night (given in al-Ṭabarī, *Tafsīr*).

Bibliography: Yāḳūt, *Buldān*, iii, 397; Th.W. Juynboll, *Handbuch des islāmischen Gesetzes*, Leiden-Leipzig 1910, 136-7; C. Snouck Hurgronje, *Het Mekkaansche Feest*, Leiden 1880, 114 = *Verspr. Geschriften*, i, 76-7; J. Wellhausen, *Reste arabischen Heidentums*², Berlin 1897, 77; M. Gaudefroy-Demombynes, *Le pélerinage à la Mekke, étude d'histoire religieuse*, Paris 1923, 225-34; G.E. von Grunebaum, *Muhammadan festivals*, New York 1951, 30-1, 46; T. Fahd, *Le panthéon de l'Arabie centrale à la veille de l'Hégire*, Paris 1968, 105 ff., 165-6, 210. See also ḤADJDJ; MAKKA; SAʿY. (B. JOEL*)

2. It is further the name of a volcanic region of *ca.* 55 × 25 km to the south-east of Damascus. It is trapezoid and runs north-west/south-east, to the south of the Dīrat al-Tulūl and north-east of Djabal al-ʿArab (Djabal al-Durūz or Djabal Ḥawrān). It forms the southern and south-eastern borders respectively of Mardj Rāhiṭ and Mardj al-Ṣuffar [*q.vv.*], the scenes of several notable battles in the Islamic period.

The name has sometimes, incorrectly, been extended to cover the whole *ḥarra*, or basalt desert, east of Djabal al-ʿArab, particularly in connection with the misnamed "Safaitic" inscriptions [*q.v.*].

The Ṣafā proper is composed of three distinct volcanic cones, Tulūl Raghayla (873 m), Tulūl al-Ḍurs (or Ḍarāʾir or Ḍahīr) (860 m) and Tulūl al-Ṣafā (741 m), the first two being separated from the third by a depression, between one and five km wide known as Miftāḥ al-Ghayla.

The whole area is covered with the twisted and uneven lava flows from extensive volcanic eruptions in the Holocene, which have suffered very little erosion. Movement within the massif is consequently extremely difficult and there is only one track across it, all others running around its edges.

The lack of erosion means that there is very littl

soil, and vegetation is limited to a few small, scattered areas free of rocks. However, there is a forest of pistachio trees spread over a dozen km on the south-western edge of the Tulūl al-Ṣafā.

With the exception of the Miftāḥ al-G̲h̲ayla, the interior of the Ṣafā is too barren and too difficult of access to attract settlement, or even the attentions of nomads. However, it is bordered on all sides, except the north, by fertile silt-filled depressions, such as the Ruḥba, which are fed by the seasonal floods from Dj̲abal al-ʿArab. These depressions are known as *riḥāb* (sing. *raḥaba*) and are not, as some writers assume, *kiʿān* (sing. *kāʿ*), of which the soil is sterile. Some of the water from the winter floods passes into underground channels and some runs on to the *riḥāb*, forming lakes which can last for several months. This compensates to some extent for the low rainfall in this area (mean 100 mm p.a., with considerable variations).

The availability of water, together with the fertility of the soil, has attracted nomads to these *riḥāb* from the Epipalaeolithic onwards. Traces of prehistoric campsites, and graffiti by nomads of the Hellenistic and Roman periods [see SAFAITIC] have been found in large numbers near the *riḥāb* on the eastern and south-western edges of the Ṣafā, while, in the 19th century, Wetzstein (30-1) describes the G̲h̲ayāt̲h̲ section of the Ahl al-Dj̲abal sowing grain on the Ruḥba.

The semi-nomadic tribes known as ʿArab al-Ṣafā (Dussaud and Macler, 52-3) are not in fact resident in the Ṣafā but spend most of their time in the Ḥarra of Wādī Rādj̲il, the basalt desert to the south-east of it.

On present knowledge, sedentary occupation seems to have been restricted to the edges of the Ṣafā and to have occurred only in the Early Bronze Age (e.g. K̲h̲irbat al-Ḍabʿ), and the Byzantine/Umayyad period (e.g. K̲h̲irbat al-Baydāʾ [*q.v.*]).

Bibliography: J.G. Wetzstein, *Reisebericht über Hauran und die Trachonen*, Berlin 1860, 6-18, 30-2, 61-6 (still very useful); R. Dussaud and F. Macler, *Mission dans les régions désertiques de la Syrie moyenne*, Paris 1903, 49-52 (historical conclusions to be treated with caution); Dussaud, *Topographie historique de la Syrie antique et médiévale*, Paris 1927, 371-81; F. Huguet, *Aperçu géomorphologique sur les paysages volcaniques du Hauran (Syrie méridionale)*, in J.M. Dentzer (ed.), *Hauran. I*, Paris 1985, 5-17.

[F. BRAEMER and M.C.A. MACDONALD]

ṢAFAD, a small city surrounding the ruins of a once impressive fortress in the hilly region of northern Palestine, 40 km east of ʿAkkā [*q.v.*] and 20 km north of Ṭabariyya [*q.v.*]. The fortress is situated at the summit of a hill *ca.* 840 m high, and enjoys a fine view of the surrounding area, including the Sea of Galilee to the east. In the Crusader period, Ṣafad was an important Templar stronghold; in the Mamlūk period it served as the capital of a province (*mamlaka*), while under the Ottomans it was the centre of a *sandj̲ak* [*q.v.*]. Today it is the principal town of the upper Galilee region in the State of Israel, and is noted—as in the Middle Ages—for its mild and salubrious climate in the spring and summer (see al-ʿUt̲h̲mānī, ed. B. Lewis in *BSOAS*, xv [1954], 480).

The name Ṣafad derives from Hebr. Ṣefat < root *ṣ-f-h* "to look, observe, watch", appropriate for the splendid view afforded by its location. Ṣefat is not mentioned in the Old Testament, but has been identified with the Sepph or Seph of Josephus' *Jewish wars*, i, ch. 20, § 6. Its location is mentioned in the Jerusalem Talmud as one of the mountain tops on which bonfires were lit to announce the new moon and festivals.

Little is known of Ṣafad in the early Islamic period,

i.e. until the coming of the Frankish Crusaders in 1099. Yāḳūt, *Buldān*, ed. Beirut, iii, 412, has virtually no information about the town, and wrongly locates it in the mountains near Ḥimṣ, an indication of its relative obscurity even in the early 7th/13th century. According to Ibn S̲h̲addād, *Aʿlāḳ*, ed. Dahhān, 146, Ṣafad was originally a *tall* on which was found an inhabited village under Burdj̲ al-Yatīm, evidently referring to the future Frankish keep (or the main tower of the inner ward). The Arabic *nisba* al-Ṣafadī is found in a document from the Cairo Geniza, dating from the first half of the 5th/11th century, as is the Hebrew parallel Ha-Ṣefatī in another, almost contemporary document; whether this indicates a Jewish community in the town is a moot point (cf. M. Gil, *A history of Palestine, 634-1099*, Cambridge 1992, 213-14).

The Arab historians state that the Franks built the first fortress at Ṣafad in 495/1101-2, having taken the town in the initial conquest of the country. In 1140 it was apparently renovated (or perhaps built) by King Fulk, and served as a refuge for Baldwin in 1157 after his defeat north of the Sea of Galilee by Nūr al-Dīn [*q.v.*]; and eleven years later, it was transferred to the Knights Templar, since the local lord could no longer afford to keep it up (S. Runciman, *Hist. of the Crusades*, Cambridge 1954, ii, 343, 376; R.C. Smail, *Crusading warfare (1097-1193)*, Cambridge 1956, 102). After the Muslim victory of Ḥiṭṭīn [*q.v.*] in 583/1187, Ayyūbid troops kept the fortress under observation, but it was not till the next year that Ṣalāḥ al-Dīn was able to undertake the conquest of Ṣafad; it surrendered in S̲h̲awwāl 584/December 1187 after a fierce six weeks' siege, and the garrison received *amān* and departed for Tyre (M.C. Lyons and D.E.P. Jackson, *Saladin*, Cambridge 1982, 141, 145, 285-6, 291; J. Prawer, *Hist. du royaume latin de Jérusalem*, Paris 1969-70, i, 560, 562; J. Riley-Smith, in Ibn Furāt, *Ayyubids, Mamelukes and Crusaders*, tr. U. and M.C. Lyons, Cambridge 1971, ii, 213).

Ṣalāḥ al-Dīn initially gave Ṣafad and Ṭabariyya as an *iḳṭāʿ* [*q.v.*] to one of his commanders, but in the early years of the 7th/13th century, al-Malik al-ʿĀdil's son al-Malik al-Muʿaẓẓam ʿĪsā [*q.v.*] resumed control over these towns, and in 617/1219-20 razed the fortress, fearing an attack by the Franks, who had scored initial successes in Egypt. Then 638/1240 al-Malik al-Ṣāliḥ Ismāʿīl of Damascus, seeking a defensive alliance with the Crusaders against al-Malik al-Ṣāliḥ Ayyūb of Egypt, turned over to the Franks his possessions in Galilee and southern Lebanon, including Ṣafad, whose fortress the Templars now restored (see R.S. Humphreys, *From Saladin to the Mongols*, Albany 1977, 78, 142-3, 266-8; Prawer, *Histoire*, ii, 154-5, 166 and n., 279-80, 286). The restoration work was initiated by Benedict d'Alignan, bishop of Marseilles, and took two-and-a-half years at an immense cost; its annual upkeep was reportedly 40,000 bezants and its peacetime garrison 1,700, which in wartime swelled to 2,200.

The main strategic value of Ṣafad was that it offered the Crusaders an excellent observation point over the Ṭabariyya-Toron road, and more significantly, the Damascus-ʿAkkā road, particularly the important Jacob's Ford (Dj̲isr Banāt Yaʿḳūb [*q.v.*], Vadum Jacob) over the Jordan River, which is only 12 km away. Thus the fortress would gain early warning of approaching Muslim troops, be they raiders or invaders, and notify the other Frankish centres so that an appropriate response could be made. It is dubious whether the garrison of Ṣafad had any real control over these routes, particularly if the Muslims were out in any force, but it certainly served as a symbol of

Frankish power in the area. The fortress was the administrative and economic centre for the area, in which some 260 villages were supposed to be found; this figure would seem to be referring to the Galilee as a whole and not just the immediate hinterland of the town. In the 12th century, at least, there was located there a court of burgesses, indicating a large Frankish presence.

For the Muslims, Frankish Safad was a continual nuisance, and the Mamlūk sultan Baybars (658-76/1260-75 [*q.v.*]) soon set his sights on Ṣafad. In summer 664/1266 he began a six weeks' siege until the garrison, weakened by dissensions, surrendered under *amān*, which did not however allow them to take out arms and property; in fact, the sultan broke this *amān* and had almost the whole garrison killed (the Arabic sources are at pains to justify the sultan's evident rupture of the *amān*) (see P. Thorau, *The Lion of Egypt*, tr. P.M. Holt, London 1992, 168-70, 183-4 nn. 61-3; Prawer, *Histoire,* ii, 470-4). Baybars set about repairing the fortress, and Ṣafad was made the administrative centre of a new province, with new civilian buildings, including a mosque, markets, caravanserais and baths (see L.A. Mayer and J. Pinkerfeld, *Some principal Muslim religious buildings in Israel*, Jerusalem 1950, 44-6).

Geographers of the next century or so, including al-Dimas͟hḳī and al-ʿUmarī, describe Ṣafad as quite prosperous, although it was evidently something of a backwater intellectually. The chronicles give little information about events and conditions there, but like the province as a whole, it probably suffered decline from the time of the Black Death (*ca.* 749/1348) onwards. When the Ottomans took over Syria, the Mamlūk province of Ṣafad was transformed into a *sand͟jaḳ*, part of the larger *wilāyet/eyālet* or *beylerbeylik* of Damascus. Thanks to the relatively systematic tax registers of the Ottoman authorities in the first decades of their rule over Palestine, we have some idea of demographic and economic trends in the district and town. Ottoman rule brought more stability and a consequent prosperity and population increase to both the town and its rural hinterland; by 963/1555-6 there were about 280 villages, mainly Muslim but with a few Muslim-Christian and Muslim-Jewish ones, in the *sand͟jaḳ* (see H. Rhode, *The administration and population of the Sancak of Ṣafad in the sixteenth century*, diss. Columbia Univ. 1979, unpubl.; idem, *The geography of the sixteenth-century Sancak of Ṣafad*, in *Archivum Ottomanicum*, x [1985], 179-218; B. Lewis, in *BSOAS*, xvi [1954], 469-501; W.-D. Hütteroth and K. Abdulfattah, *Historical geography of Palestine, Transjordan and southern Syria in the late 16th century*, Erlangen 1977, 175-94). The town, in particular, prospered through the textile industry, having abundant water and accessibility to ports, hence to supplies of wool, and to markets, and also benefiting from an influx of Jewish craftsmen from the Iberian peninsula. There seems to have been a Jewish presence in Ṣafad since the 11th century, and eventually, the Sephardis and other newcomers outnumbered the indigenous "Arabised" (*mustaʿribūn*) Jews there. All this brought a rich spiritual life, so that in the 16th century Ṣafad was a major centre of Jewish mysticism, and the first printing shop of any kind in Syria originated in Ṣafad when a Hebrew printing press was established in 1563. There was some decline in the town's fortunes in the later 16th century, but in the 1670s Ewliyā Čelebi (*Seyāḥat-nāme*, ix, Istanbul 1935, 438-41, tr. in *QDAP*, iv [1935], 158-61) still found there three caravanserais, several mosques, seven *zāwiya*s and six public baths (see Lewis, *Notes and documents from the Turkish archives*, Jerusalem 1952, 5-7; Rhode, *op. cit.*, 167-9; A. Cohen and Lewis, *Population and revenue in the towns of Palestine in the sixteenth century*, Princeton 1978, 19-30).

By the early 17th century, Ṣafad had reverted to the status of a small town, and had come under the control of the Druze *amīr* Fak͟hr al-Dīn Maʿn [*q.v.*] of the Lebanon, with his rule subsequently recognised by the Ottoman authorities. In the later 18th century, Ṣafad revived somewhat, probably because of the relatively more stable government provided by the local leaders Ẓāhir (or Ḍāhir) al-ʿUmar (d. 1775) who hailed from Ṣafad, and Aḥmad al-D͟jazzār Pas͟ha (d. 1805 [*q.v.* in Suppl.]). , and some fresh Jewish immigration began to take place (see C.-F. Volney, *Travels through Syria and Egypt in the years 1783, 1784 and 1785,* 2nd ed. London 1788, ii, 230-1; P.M. Holt, *Egypt and the Fertile Crescent 1516-1922*, London 1966, 117, 124; Cohen, *Palestine in the 18th century*, Jerusalem 1973, passim, esp. 119-28). Under Ibrāhīm Pas͟ha's governorship of Syria (1831-40 [*q.v.*], Ṣafad became the commercial centre of Galilee, but suffered from natural disasters like earthquakes and pestilence until some prosperity began to return in the later 19th century. In 1880 Ṣafad became the seat of a *ḳaḍāʾ* in the *sand͟jaḳ* of ʿAkkā in the *wilāyet* of Beirut. S͟hems al-Dīn Sāmī, in his *Ḳāmūs al-ʿālam*, iv, Istanbul 1311/1894, gave the population for the *ḳaḍāʾ* of Ṣafad as 21,313, of whom 13,971 were Muslims, but a more reliable figure for the actual town is probably that of the 1922 census under the British Mandate (Ṣafad was captured by Allenby's forces in September 1918): 8,760, of whom 5,431 were Muslims, 2,986 Jews and 343 Christians. Under the Mandate, the population gradually grew; at the time of the 1948 war, the total population was 12,000, of whom some 2,000 were Jews. After fierce fighting, Jewish forces gained control of Ṣafad; the Arab populations, some of which had left during the fighting, almost completely abandoned the town (see B. Morris, *The birth of the Palestinian refugee problem 1947-8*, Cambridge 1987, 102-5). At the last census, in 1983, the town's population was 15,853, of whom 379 were Muslims.

Little now remains of the fortress of Ṣafad, already ruined in Ewliyā's time. It suffered much from earthquakes, and the remains were largely used as a quarry for building by the locals. Some excavations have been done by Israeli archaeologists, but the area is now covered with trees and is a park.

Bibliography (in addition to references in the article): Translations of Muslim sources: Gaudefroy-Demombynes, *La Syrie à l'époque des Mamelouks*, 118-24, 234-5; Marmardji, *Textes géographiques arabes sur la Palestine*, 116-17; Le Strange, *Palestine*, 524-5; R. Hartmann, *Politische Geographie des Mamlukenreichs,* in *ZDMG*, lxx (1916), 1-40, 477-511; idem, *Die geographischen Nachrichten unter Palästina und Syrien in Ḫalīl aẓ-Ẓāhiris Zubdat kašf al-mamālik*, diss. Tübingen 1907. 18th and 19th century descriptions : Volney; V. Guérin, *Descr. géographique, historique et archéologique de la Palestine*, Paris 1868-90, pt. III, vol. ii, 419-26; C.R. Conder and H. Kitchener, *The survey of Western Palestine, i, Galilee*, London 1881, 248-50, 255-6. General modern descriptions: M. Avi-Yonah *et alii, Safed*, in *Encycl. Judaica*, xiv, 626-36; E. Reiner *et alii, Sefat*, in *Encycl. Hebraica*, xxviii, 856-9; M.M. Dabbāg͟h, *Filasṭīn bilādunā*, Pt. 2, vol. vi, Beirut 1974, 74-139; N. Schur, *Hist. of Safed* (in Hebr.), Tel Aviv 1983. Studies of specific aspects: M.-L. Favreau-Lilie, *Landesbau und Burg ... Safad in Obergalilaea*, in *ZDPV*, xcvi (1980), 67-87;

D. Pringle, *Reconstructing the castle of Ṣafad*, in *PEQ*, cxvii (1975), 139-49; T. Th. Tarāwina, *Mamlakat Ṣafad fī ʿahd al-Mamālīk*, Beirut 1982.

(R. AMITAI-PREISS)

AL-**ṢAFADĪ**, AL-ḤASAN B. ABĪ MUḤAMMAD ʿABD ALLĀH AL-HĀSHIMĪ, appears to have been a minor government official during the early reign of the Egyptian Sulṭan al-Malik al-Nāṣir Muḥammad b. Ḳalāwūn [*q.v.*]. In any event, we know that in the year 694/1294-5 he was appointed by the *wazīr* Ibn al-Khalīlī to head a mission to al-Fāḳūs in Sharḳiyya province charged with cultivating the crown lands there. While on this mission, al-Ṣafadī reports on a grisly case of cannibalism that he observed at first hand during this famine year, a report which is characteristic of the anecdotal style of his only extant work. This book, *Nuzhat al-mālik wa 'l mamlūk fī mukhtaṣar sīrat man waliya Miṣr min al-mulūk* is a short history of Egypt that ends with the year 711/1311-12 or perhaps as late as 714/1314. From a statement in the British Library manuscript (Add. 233326), it appears that al-Ṣafadī composed the history in the year 716/1316. The earlier part of the work begins with the natural and other advantages of Egypt and gives a succinct account of the earlier rulers consisting mainly of anecdotes, but the chief interest lies in the portion which deals with the Turkish or Baḥrī sultans, in particular al-Malik al-Nāṣir Muḥammad. Even here, however, al-Ṣafadī records very little information which cannot be found in other sources. The B.L. ms., written for the Egyptian caliph al-Mutawakkil, proceeds to record events down to 795/1393, but these were obviously added later by another writer. Two other manuscripts of *Nuzhat al-mālik* are preserved in the B.N., Paris mss. 1706 and 1931, 22. The latter bears the erroneous title of *Faḍāʾil Miṣr*.

Bibliography: Brockelmann, S II, 34; D.P. Little, *An introduction to Mamlūk historiography*, Wiesbaden 1970, 38-9.

(F. KRENKOW-[D.P. LITTLE])

AL-**ṢAFADĪ**, ṢALĀḤ AL-DĪN KHALĪL B. AYBAK, Abu 'l-Ṣafāʾ al-Albakī (696-764/1297-1363), philologist, literary critic and littérateur, biographer, and all-round humanist.

Ṣafad was his family's home, and he was born there. His father, al-Amīr ʿIzz al-Dīn Aybak (b. ʿAbd Allāh!) was of Turkic origin; the *nisba* al-Albakī, after some *mamlūk amīr* named Albakī, seems to have belonged to him. From the apparent absence of any mention of him by his son, we may conclude that al-Ṣafadī considered him undistinguished. Relations with his father may also have been strained, if the statement known from Ibn Ḥadjar that his father showed no concern for his professional religious-legal studies until he was twenty was correctly transmitted. The additional indication that he previously studied on his own would seem confirmed by the impression that no early teachers of his are noted. However, he was obviously very gifted. When he went to Damascus as a young man aged twenty and had his first meeting with Ibn Taymiyya [*q.v.*] in 717/1317 or 718/1318, he displayed great knowledge as he proudly and repeatedly recalls (*Wāfī*, vii, 20-22; *Ghayth*, ii, 14; *Aʿyān*, i, 67); his choice of the controversial Ibn Taymiyya seems strange and may have been looked upon with disapproval by his family. He soon established ties, often of friendship, with the great scholars and writers of the age in Syria and Egypt such as Ibn Nubāta, Abū Ḥayyān al-Gharnāṭī, Ibn Sayyid al-Nās, and Ibn Faḍl Allāh al-ʿUmarī [*q.vv.*] among many others. His relationship, both professional and personal, with the older al-Dhahabī and the younger Tādj al-Dīn al-Subkī would appear to have been particularly close. Al-Subkī claims him as a Shāfiʿī, but in the cosmopolitan climate of Damascus and Cairo, it was natural for him to be acquainted with representatives of most Muslim and non-Muslim legal and religious groups of the time.

His abilities as a stylist and calligrapher opened up opportunities in government service. The positions he held, sometimes combined, depended on their importance for location; in roughly ascending order, they were *kātib al-dardj*, *al-dast*, *al-inshāʾ* and *al-sirr*, and also *wakīl al-khizāna*, which he was again at the time of his death. An occasional reference by contemporaries to him as *al-ḳāḍī* must have been merely honorary (Ibn Kathīr, *Bidāya*, xiv, 302; al-Subkī, ix, 160). In the 720s/1320s, his official duties brought him to his home town Ṣafad, to Aleppo (between 723/1323 and 726/1326), and, toward the end of the decade, also briefly to al-Raḥba (Raḥbat Mālik b. Tawḳ), but the capital cities of Damascus and Cairo were the centres of his activities. He shuttled back and forth between them, keeping up his intellectual contacts wherever he went and possibly spending more time on his scholarly work than his government employment. The year 755/1354 is attested as that of his pilgrimage undertaken together with the poet Muḥammad b. Yūsuf b. ʿAbd Allāh al-Khayyāṭ (*Aʿyān*, iii, 242); one of his works, *Ḥaḳīḳat al-madjāz ilā 'l-Ḥidjāz*, appears to have centred on it (listed in Ibn Taghrībirdī, *Manhal*, 244, l. 5, cf. the quotations in ʿAbd al-Ḳādir b. Muḥammad al-Djazīrī, *Durar al-fawāʾid*, 453 ff. [Cairo 1384], referred to by van Ess, in *Isl.*, liv, 250, n. 1). He also travelled widely in Syria on lecture tours which led him, for instance, to Aleppo in 759/1358 (*samāʿ* in *Taṣḥīḥ al-taṣḥīf*). Most of his time, however, was spent in Damascus where during one of the periodic outbreaks of the plague, his energetic activities came to an unexpected end in the night of Saturday to Sunday, 10 Shawwāl 764/23 July 1363.

He had a younger brother, Abū Isḥāḳ Djamāl al-Dīn Ibrāhīm, who died on 4 Djumādā II 742/15 November 1341. He devoted to him an emotional obituary notice that included many of his verses on his death (*Wāfī*, v, 330-7). From *samāʿ*s in his works, we know the names of two sons, both named Muḥammad (Abū ʿAbd Allāh and Abū Bakr), and two daughters, one of them named Fāṭima (Bonebakker, *Some early definitions*, 65 ff.; *Wāfī*, i, introd., p. *djīm*; al-Munadjdjid [ed.], *Umarāʾ Dimashḳ*, pl. 3; *Taṣḥīḥ al-taṣḥīf*, at end of first ms., etc.).

His numerous works provide an enormous amount of varied information. They are uniformly instructive and consistently entertaining. Moreover, they are characterised by sound scholarly method and, to all appearances, even a good measure of originality. He himself spoke of 300 volumes of his own composition (al-Subkī, x, 5) or, more plausibly, of 50 volumes and 500 volumes copied (Ibn al-ʿImād, *Shadharāt*). His copying activity is attested already from 718/1318 for a manuscript of Ibn Nubāta's *Khuṭab*, according to the Princeton *Catalogue of the Garrett collection*, no. 1907 (298B); his own copy of one of his sources, Ibn Khallikān, is preserved in ms. Gotha 1731 (Pertsch, iii, 319). An unusual number of autographs of his own works is preserved, as is often duly noted by scholars and editors, see e.g. H. Ritter, in *RSO*, xii (1929-30), 79-88, and R. Sellheim, *Materialien zur arabischen Literaturgeschichte*, Wiesbaden 1976-87, i, 200-1, pl. 30, ii, 111; they require comprehensive study, together with autograph *samāʿ*s and *idjāzas*. The preservation of so many autographs, the large number of preserved manuscripts, which still await a world-wide census, and the long chain of commentaries and imitations show the high esteem in which his work was held.

His concern with linguistic problems is evident throughout his literary production. It also led to the composition of long treatises such as *Taṣḥīḥ al-taṣḥīf wa-taḥrīr al-taḥrīf* on misspellings and misreadings (facs. of two mss. published in Frankfurt a/M 1985). The announced edition of *Ghawāmiḍ al-Ṣiḥāḥ* of al-Djawharī may not yet have appeared. Much more central is his seminal work on literary criticism, although by the nature of the enterprise, it is often debatable. Recognition as models of the genre was accorded to his commentaries on Ḍiyāʾ al-Dīn Ibn al-Athīr's *al-Mathal al-sāʾir*, entitled *Nuṣrat al-thāʾir*, a severely critical effort (ed. M.ʿA. Sulṭānī, Damascus 1972); on Ibn Zaydūn's *Risāla*, entitled *Tamām al-mutūn* (ed. M. Abu 'l-Faḍl Ibrāhīm, Cairo 1389/1969); and on al-Ṭughrāʾī's *Lāmiyyat al-ʿAdjam*, entitled *al-Ghayth al-musadjdjam* (sometimes *alladhi 'nsadjam*) (Cairo 1305 [cited here], Beirut 1395/1975, cf. Rosenthal, in *Oriens*, xxvii-xxviii [1981], 179-81). Individual rhetorical figures are treated in *Djinān al-djinās* (ed. Samīr Ḥusayn Ḥalabī, Beirut 1407/1987; although not an autograph, ms. Chester Beatty 3103 is dated in his lifetime [752/1351]) and *Faḍl al-khitām ʿan al-tawriya wa 'l-istikhdām* (ed. al-Muḥammadī ʿAbd al-ʿAzīz al-Ḥinnāwī, Cairo 1399/1979, see S.A. Bonebakker, *Some early definitions of the tawriya and Ṣafadī's Faḍḍ al-Xitām*, The Hague and Paris 1966).

His extensive poetical production is noted first for 718/1318 (*Ghayth*, ii, 4). His *muwashshaḥāt* make up part of his *Tawshīʿ al-tawshīḥ* (ed. Albert Ḥabīb Muṭlaḳ, Beirut? 1966. The title is correctly listed in Ibn Taghrībirdī, *Manhal*, but distorted to *Tawshīḥ al-tarshīḥ* in Ibn Ḥadjar). Epigrams were collected by him in *al-Rawḍ al-bāsim* and *al-Ḥusn al-ṣarīḥ fī miʾat malīḥ*. Explanations of old verses are said to be the subject of *Ikhtirāʿ al-khurāʿ*. A *maḳāma* on the pangs of love, *Lawʿat al-shākī wa-damʿat al-bākī*, has been printed frequently. His artistic prose in letters and documents appears to have been preserved in his *Munshaʾāt*, whose relationship, if any, to *Ikhtibār al-Ikhtiyār* in ms. Chester Beatty 5183, dated 753/1352, remains to be investigated. Further material of this sort in *Dīwān al-fuḳahāʾ* (ms. Vienna 389) and *Alḥān al-sawādjiʿ bayn al-bādiʾ wa 'l-murādjiʿ* (so correctly in Berlin Ahlwardt 8631 and Princeton Yahuda Collection, Mach 4368). Much of his poetry and artistic prose, both literary and official, is found dispersed throughout his works as well as some of the biographical literature.

Specialised treatises on subjects such as eyes, tears, riddles, and the valuable scholarly monograph on the numeral seven (70, 700, etc.), entitled *Ṭard al-sabʿ ʿan sard al-sabʿ*, which can also be read in al-Suyūṭī's commentary *ʿAyn al-nabʿ*, or the above-mentioned *Ḥaḳīḳat al-madjāz ilā 'l-Ḥidjāz*, probably inspired by the example of Ibn Faḍl Allāh al-ʿUmarī and containing much of his occasional poetry, fall basically in the *adab* category, and so does his vast *Tadhkira*, which will yield further information on his literary production and interests, cf. e.g. A.J. Arberry's description of the content of ms. Chester Beatty 3861 in *IQ*, vi (1961), 107-17.

His great biographical collections possess lasting usefulness and have remained indispensable for scholars. The publication of the massive *al-Wāfī bi 'l-wafayāt* has been due to the initiative of H. Ritter. The first volume appeared in his *Bibliotheca Islamica* in 1931 (repr. 1962). Publication was resumed in 1949, with twenty-two volumes edited by different scholars having appeared by 1993; its introduction was translated by É. Amar in *JA*, x/17-19 (1911-12). The *Wāfī* is alphabetically arranged according to the names of the biographees, as is *Aʿyān al-ʿaṣr wa-aʿwān al-naṣr* that deals *in extenso* with individuals from his own lifetime (3-vol. facs., Frankfurt a/M 1410/1990). For his sources, see Little and van Ess (in *Bibl.*). Specialised biographies of the blind and the one-eyed are, respectively, *Nakt al-himyān fī nukat al-ʿumyān* (ed. A. Zakī, Cairo 1329/1911, cf. F. Malti-Douglas, in *Cahiers d'onomastique arabe* [1979], 7-19, and eadem, in *The Islamic world. Essays in honor of Bernard Lewis*, Princeton 1989, 211-37), and the later and much shorter *al-Shuʿūr bi 'l-ʿūr* (ed. ʿAbd al-Razzāḳ Ḥusayn, ʿAmmān 1409/1988). His general historical knowledge was often put to good use by him, as e.g. in *Tamām al-mutūn*. His *Umarāʾ Dimashḳ* was published by Ṣalāḥ al-Dīn al-Munadjdjid from the *Tadhkira* (Damascus 1374/1955).

Expectedly, pseudo-attributions do exist and remain largely uninvestigated. Al-Ṣafadī could presumably have dealt with the theory and practice of music, but the *Risāla fī ʿilm al-mūsīḳā* published as his by ʿAbd al-Madjīd Diyāb and Ghaṭṭās ʿAbd al-Malik Khashaba (Cairo 1411/1991) is clearly not by him, cf. A. Shiloah, *The theory of music in Arabic writings*, Munich 1979, 276, 304-6. The even more striking attribution of a commentary on the *djafr* treatise *al-Shadjara al-Nuʿmāniyya fī 'l-dawla al-ʿUthmāniyya* supposedly by Ibn ʿArabī, which exists in numerous manuscripts, is only rarely marked by modern bibliographers as spurious, cf., for instance, ms. Berlin, Ahlwardt 4216, as against Princeton, Yahuda collection, Mach 5133; T. Fahd, *La divination arabe*, Strasbourg 1966, 226-7. A collection of stories and geographical data entitled *Madjmaʿ al-hisān wa-fawākih al-djinān* in ms. Yale Landberg 516 = Cat. Nemoy 469 is likewise wrongly ascribed to him.

Bibliography: While the autobiographical sketch mentioned by Ibn al-ʿImād has not yet been recovered, Ṣafadī's habit of frequently indicating the place and date of receiving information provides much biographical detail. This has been successfully exploited by D.P. Little, *al-Ṣafadī as biographer of his contemporaries*, in *Essays on Islamic civilization presented to Niyazi Berkes*, Leiden 1976, 109-20, mainly based on *Aʿyān*, and, in greater detail, J. van Ess, *Ṣafadī-Splitter*, in *Isl.*, liii (1976), 242-66, liv (1977), 77-108. Already his contemporaries, such as Dhahabī, in *al-Muʿdjam al-mukhtaṣṣ*, al-Ṭāʾif 1408/1988, 91-2, mentioned him as he did them, but the formal biographical notices are very limited as to the factual data they contain; if some are lengthy, this is due to ample quotations from his literary production. See, for instance, Muḥammad b. ʿAlī al-Ḥusaynī, *Dhayl al-ʿIbar*, iv, 203, in the Beirut 1405/1985 edition of Dhahabī, *ʿIbar*; Ibn Kathīr, *Bidāya*, xiv, 303; Ibn Rāfiʿ, *Wafayāt*, Beirut 1402/1982, ii, 268-270; Tādj al-Dīn al-Subkī, *Ṭabaḳāt al-Shāfiʿiyya*, x, 5-32; Ibn Ḥadjar, *Durar*, ii, 87-8; Ibn Ḳāḍī Shuhba, *Ṭabaḳāt al-Shāfiʿiyya*, ed. al-Ḥāfiẓ ʿAbd al-ʿAlīm Khān, Beirut 1407/1987, iii, 89-90; Ibn Taghrībirdī, *al-Manhal al-ṣāfī*, Cairo 1980—, v, 241-257, with a good list of titles of Ṣafadī's works, and idem, *Nudjūm*, Cairo, xi, 19-21; Ibn al-ʿImād, *Shadharāt*, vi, 200-1. See, further, Brockelmann, II², 39-41, S II, 27-9. F. Krenkow, in *EI*¹, s.v., and the introductions of modern editions are basically uncritical. Cf. also M. ʿA. Sulṭānī, *al-Naḳd al-adabī fī 'l-ḳarn al-thāmin al-hidjrī bayn al-Ṣafadī wa-muʿāṣirīh*, Damascus 1394/1974. For a reconsideration of his sources, see D. Krawulsky, in *wāfī*, xvii, 704-14.

(F. ROSENTHAL)

ṢAFAITIC is the modern name given to a group

of graffiti in a North Arabian language, expressed in a variety of the South Semitic script. They are found mainly on rocks in the deserts of southern Syria, north-eastern Jordan and northern Saudi Arabia, with isolated finds in ʿIrāḳ, Lebanon and at Pompeii (see M.C.A. Macdonald in *Syria*, lxx [1993], 304-5 for references), and their distribution and content show that they were written almost exclusively by nomads. They are conventionally dated between the 1st century B.C. and the 4th century A.D.

While the majority consist of the author's name and between one and 17 generations of his genealogy, a significant number also contain statements describing his actions or emotions, or events of which he was aware. Many also contain prayers to a variety of deities, and a considerable number refer to adjacent rock-drawings. This was the only period in which literacy has been widespread among the nomads of the Syro-Arabian desert—there are inscriptions by men, women and slaves [*fty*]—and these texts (and most of the Thamudic [*q.v.*] graffiti) are therefore the only surviving first-hand records of their way-of-life, before the pre-Islamic poetry. They are thus of considerable importance since they contain historical, linguistic and palaeo-ethnographic information which is not available from any other source. For a discussion of the phenomenon of literacy among these nomads, see Macdonald, *op. cit.*, 382-8.

The inscriptions were first discovered in 1857 near the eastern edge of the Ṣafā [*q.v.*] in southern Syria, and continue to be known by the 19th-century misnomer "Ṣafaitic", despite the fact that none have even been found within the Ṣafā itself (see *ibid.*, 305-10). More were discovered in 1860, and by 1901 the script had been deciphered. Throughout the 20th century a handful of expeditions have recorded vast numbers of these texts, and by the 1990s over 20,000 had been found in the limited number of areas which have been searched. There are clearly scores of thousands still awaiting discovery.

The Ṣafaitic alphabet belongs to the North Arabian branch of the South Semitic script. The palaeographical development, and the exact relationships within and between the North and South Arabian branches of this script are still disputed (see B. Sass, *Studia alphabetica*, Freiburg 1991, 28-93, and Macdonald in *Anchor Bible dictionary*, New York 1992, iii, 418-19 with script table). The Safaitic script appears to have been used solely for graffiti and to have been spread informally rather than in schools (idem, in *Syria*, lxx [1993], 382-8). Gemination of consonants is not represented, and, in contrast to Lihyanite [see LIḤYĀN], *matres lectionis* are not used, nor is there any notation of diphthongs (if they existed). Writing is continuous and without word-dividers and can be in any direction.

The language of the Ṣafaitic graffiti belongs to the group known as "North Arabian". Safaitic, together with Lihyanite/Dedanite, the different types of Thamudic, and Hasaitic, form a sub-group, known as "Frühnordarabisch", which is most obviously distinguished by its use of the definite article *h-/hn-*, in contrast to the other sub-group (which includes pre-Islamic and later Arabic), which uses *al-* (see W.W. Müller, in W. Fischer (ed.), *Grundriss der arabischen Philologie*, Wiesbaden 1982, i, 17-36). For descriptions of the grammar, see E. Littmann, *Safaïtic inscriptions*, Leiden 1943, pp. xii-xxiv, and Müller, in *Procs. of the Seminar for Arabian Studies*, x [1980] 68-72.

The nature and number of the Ṣafaitic inscriptions have produced an extraordinarily rich onomasticon (see Müller, *op. cit.*, 72-3 for a brief survey). Affiliation to a social group is expressed by taking the lineage back to the eponymous ancestor, or to one of his immediate descendants, or by use of the *nisba* (*h-ḍfy* "the Ḍayfite") or by use of the phrase *dh* *'l* at the end of the genealogy (*dhʾl ḍf* "of the tribe of Ḍayf"). However, the word *'l* (cf. Ar. *ʾāl*) is used of all social groups from immediate family to tribe, and even of peoples such as the Romans. On tribes, see Lankester Harding, in *al-Abḥāth*, xxii (1969), 3-25, and Macdonald, in *Syria*, lxx (1993), 352-67.

There is no trace of Christianity or Islam in the Ṣafaitic inscriptions. Prayers are offered to a number of deities among which the commonest are *Lt* (variants (?) *ʾlt* (as in Nabataean and Palmyrene), and in theophoric names *h-ʾlt*, presumably equivalent to the *hn-ʾlt* in the 5th century B.C. Aramaic inscriptions on bowls found at Tell al-Maskhūṭa in Egypt, one of which is by a king of Ḳēdār (Rabinowitz, in *JNES*, xv [1956] 1-9 and xviii [1959] 154-5), the *Alilat* of Herodotus 3:8, and Arabic al-Lāt [*q.v.*]); *Lh* (variants (?) *ʾlh* and *h-ʾlh*); *Rḍw/Rḍy*—apparently variants of the same name, for a deity of uncertain sex, but probably male and to be identified with *Ruldaiu* mentioned in the Assyrian Annals, *Orotalt* in Herodotus 3:8, *Arṣû* at Palmyra (see J.T. Milik, *Dédicaces faites par des dieux*, Paris 1972, 49) and *Ruḍan* of Ibn al-Kalbī, *K. al-Aṣnām*, Cairo 1914, 30-1; *Bʿls*^{1}*mn* (the great Aramaean sky god, whose name usually appears in Ṣafaitic as a direct loan from Aramaic *Baʿalshamīn*, though occasionally it is found as a calque in the form *Bʿls*^{1}*my*); *Ds*^{2}*r* (a loan from Nabataean *Dwshrʾ*, Dushara, but with variants *ds*^{2}*ry*, *dhs*^{2}*r*, and the etymologically correct *dhs*^{2}*ry* (cf. *Dhu 'l-Sharā* [*q.v.*]), which is, naturally, the common form in the Thamudic E texts of southern Jordan); *S*^{2}*ʿ-h-qm* (equivalent to Nabataean *Shyʿ-'l-qwm*) "the companion [or "succour", cf. Syriac *sûyāʿā*] of the group"; and *Ythʿ* (see Macdonald, in *Anchor Bible dictionary*, iii, 422). Invocations are also made to the *Gd* (i.e. *Tyche* or "Fortune") of the two major tribal groups, thus *Gd-Ḍf* and *Gd-ʿwdh*.

Any of these deities can be invoked singly or together and there is no discernible difference in the requests made to them. By far the commonest is for security (*s*^{1}*lm*), but there are numerous prayers for relief (*rwḥ*) from privation, freedom from want (*ghnyt*), booty (*ghnmt*), etc., as well as curses on those who damage the inscriptions or drawings and, less often, blessings on those who leave them intact. Other religious expressions include *ʿwdh b hʾlh* ("and he sought protection in *h-ʾlh*" (WH 3923, re-read by Macdonald in M. Ibrahim (ed.) *Arabian studies in honour of Mahmoud Ghul*, Wiesbaden 1989, 65-6) which is paralleled by *ʿwdh b rḍy* (WH 390). A number of other deities are attested in Ṣafaitic only in theophoric names, *Mnt* (cf. Nabataean *Mnwtw*, Arabic *Manāt* [*q.v.*]), *h-ʿzy* (cf. Nabataean *ʾl-ʿzʾ* and Arabic *al-ʿUzzā* [*q.v.*]), and, most common of all, *ʾl* (*ʾĪl*).

Of religious practice we have virtually no hint. The supposed Ṣafaitic evidence for pilgrimage to the temple of *Baʿalshamīn* (LP 350) is based on a misreading (see Macdonald, in *Syria*, lxx [1993], 315, n. 75 and 366, n. 414), though another text (CSNS 424) which refers to *Bʿls*^{1}*mn* as "the god of Sīʿʿ", suggests that the author knew of his famous temple at that place. Inscriptions mentioning sacrifice (*dhbḥ*) are usually found in groups, and seldom specify either the victim or the deity, though two texts (C 4358 and 4360) say their authors sacrificed to *Bʿls*^{1}*mn* and the authors of two others (unpublished) refer to a high place or altar (*ṣmd*) on which they sacrificed a camel (*dhbḥ gml ʿlh*).

Some texts record the building of a cairn (*rgm*) over

the dead (though cairns were often used for other purposes as well), a practice maintained by the modern inhabitants of the area, the Ahl al-D̲j̲abal (on "Ṣafaitic" cairns, see Macdonald, in Zaghloul *et alii*, *Studies in the history and archaeology of Jordan. IV*, Amman 1992, 303-7, and references there; on modern cairns, see W. and F. Lancaster in *Arabian Archaeology and Epigraphy*, iv [1993], 151-69). Some Ṣafaitic texts also refer to a *baliyya* [*q.v.*], or camel left to die at the grave of its master, a pre-Islamic practice described by Islamic writers, and which is also mentioned in an unpublished Nabataean inscription from southern Jordan, which was found associated with a burial of this type. Large numbers of texts are concerned with mourning (*wgm, ndm, wlh,* etc.) and a belief in a personified Death or Fate (*Manā/Mana*^{n}, *Manāyā*), paralleled in the pre-Islamic poetry, is suggested by the phrase "humbled by Fate" (*rg̲h̲m mny*), which is often used of the dead.

It is clear from these texts that their authors were aware of events beyond the desert. Herod the Great and his successors appear to be mentioned several times, as are (unspecified) Roman emperors (*ḳṣr*) and at least one Nabataean king (see Macdonald, in *Syria*, lxx [1993], 323-46, and in *Trade, contact, and the movement of peoples in the Eastern Mediterranean. Studies in honour of J. Basil Hennessy*, Sydney 1994) and there are a number of (mainly enigmatic) references to the Romans (*Rm*), the Nabataeans (*Nbṭ*), possibly the Ituraeans (*Yẓr*), and the Persians (*Md̲h̲y*). Unfortunately, in most cases it is impossible to identify the exact events referred to. There are also indications that some of the nomads were recruited into auxiliary units of the Roman army (see Macdonald, in *Syria*, lxx [1993], 368-77). The Ṣafaitic inscriptions provide no evidence of a "nomadic threat" to the Roman provinces of Syria and Arabia.

These graffiti provide a picture of the daily life of their authors which shows them to have been fully nomadic, rather than sedentaries or semi-nomads, as has sometimes been suggested (see discussion in Macdonald, in *op. cit.*, 311-22). They were mixed pastoralists, migrating annually with their herds, both of camels and of sheep and goats, between the *ḥarra* (or basalt desert) of southern Syria and north-eastern Jordan, and the *ḥamād* (which they called *mdbr*), in what is now western ʿIrāḳ and northern Saʿūdi Arabia (see Macdonald, in *JRAS*, 3rd series, vol. ii [1992], 1-11, and in *AAE*, iii [1992], 27-30). Many record returning to the same campsites [*dr*] year after year (*ʿm f ʿm*) and the sadness they felt on finding the traces (*ʾṯr*) of friends or relatives—a commonplace of nomadic life elevated to an artistic convention in pre-Islamic poetry. Relatively few mention raiding (*g̲h̲zz*), which is sometimes supposed to have taken up most of a nomad's time, but it clearly played a part in both the culture and the economy. There are rock drawings showing raids (Macdonald, in *AAE*, i [1990], 24-28) and many other activities, especially hunting and fighting both on horseback and on foot. It is clear from these drawings that these nomads used the North Arabian (*s̲h̲adād*) camel-saddle but, contrary to a common misapprehension, there is no evidence that these, or any other, North Arabian nomads ever fought from camel-back (see Macdonald in *Archaeology and the rise of Islam*, Special number of *Antiquity* [1995], and in *ZDPV*, cvii [1991], 103). Other entertainment was provided by singing and dancing girls (*ḳnt*, or simply *g̲h̲lmt*) who are also depicted in the drawings with bare breasts and swinging tasselled belts.

"*South Ṣafaitic*". E. Knauf has proposed that some of the texts labelled by Winnett "Thamudic E" (later, inappropriately, "Tabuki Thamudic") should be reclassified as "South Ṣafaitic" on the grounds that in style and onomastic content they had more in common with Ṣafaitic than with other forms of Thamudic (Knauf, in *Annual Dept. of Antiquities, Jordan*, xxvii [1983] 587-96). However, the fundamental work on these inscriptions by G.M.H. King has shown that they form a clearly definable group, related to, but distinct from, Ṣafaitic, and that they cannot be divided in the way Knauf suggests (see her *Early North Arabian Thamudic E*, diss. London 1990, in preparation for publication). It is therefore preferable to retain the old neutral label, "Thamudic E", rather than "Tabuki Thamudic" (only a small minority of the texts have been found near Tabuk) or "South Ṣafaitic", which blurs important distinctions. As would be expected, there are a handful of texts which seem to display features of both Ṣafaitic and Thamudic E and these are generally known as "Mixed texts" (see THAMUDIC and Macdonald, in *ADAJ*, xxiv [1980] 188).

Bibliography: In addition to works cited in the text, see for bibliographies, W.G. Oxtoby, *Some inscriptions of the Safaitic Bedouin*, New Haven 1968, and V.A. Clark, *A study of new Safaitic inscriptions from Jordan*, diss. available from University Microfilms International Ann Arbor 1979 [= CSNS].

General surveys: M.C.A. Macdonald, in *Anchor Bible dictionary*, New York 1992, iii, 418-23 (with script table and examples of texts) (N.B. the section on "South Ṣafaitic" should be corrected by reference to the present article), and W.W. Müller, in *PSAS* (1980), 67-74 and the works of Oxtoby and Clark mentioned above. For a detailed discussion of the historical content of the texts, see Macdonald in *Syria*, lxx (1993), 303-408.

Major collections: *Corpus inscriptionum semiticarum, pars v*, Paris 1950-1 [= C], E. Littmann, *Safaitic inscriptions*, Leiden 1943 [= LP] which contain texts mainly from Syria; F.V. Winnett, *Safaitic inscriptions from Jordan*, Toronto 1957, idem and G. Lankester Harding, *Inscriptions from Fifty Safaitic cairns*, Toronto 1978 [= WH], and the works of Oxtoby and Clark cited above, which contain texts from Jordan. Several thousand texts recorded in Jordan by Macdonald, King and Clark are in preparation. Safaitic inscriptions from northern Saudi Arabia are published by A. Jamme, in F. Altheim and R. Stiehl, *Christentum am Roten Meer*, Berlin 1971, i, 41-109, 611-37, and idem, in *Oriens Antiquus*, vi (1967), 189-213, and ix (1970), 129-32 (the interpretations in these three works should be treated with caution). Finally, G. Lankester Harding, *An index and concordance of pre-Islamic Arabian names and inscriptions*, Toronto 1971, is still an indispensable tool.

(M.C.A. MACDONALD)

SAFĀḲUS, conventional European form SFAX, a town of Tunisia, on the eastern coast to the north of the Gulf of Gabès.

The historical study of the towns of Tunisia poses a series of problems, the approaches to which are far from uniform, given the sparseness of information. The urban societies did not preserve the pieces of evidence, above all, the written ones, concerning their own past nor did they transmit them intact to us. Given these lacunae, stretching over a long period of centuries, historical information is necessarily laconic and disparate.

There was nothing which destined Sfax to become a great regional centre. In order to achieve this, the

Muslims did not mark down the site of Taenea, an important settlement some 12 km/7 miles to the south, despite the 83 ha extent of its site, but chose instead the obscure and modest Taparura for constructing their town. The reasons for this are not clear, although the strategic value of the site was not negligible, being on the sea-coast and at the meeting-point of the classical Africa Vetus and Byzacene, in effect, on the border between central Tunisia—studied by Jean Despois—and southern Tunisia. Hence from this position, Sfax was to play the role of a town situated at the crossroads of routes.

There was a general spurt of town-building in Ifrīḳiya as far back as the 3rd/9th century, in which Sfax played a part, but the processes of change and transition from Antiquity to the Middle Ages, are hidden from us, and archaeological excavations, hardly yet begun, have not provided any decisive information. Nevertheless, the orthagonal character of the Medina of Sfax and the alignments visible in its environs, lead one to recall the typical Roman layout. But one has to have recource to the information of the Arabic historical tradition, with all the attendant risks.

Origins.

An unusual fact, hence notable, is that, on the model of Tunis and Kairouan, Sfax had—if belatedly—its own historian, Maḥmūd b. Saʿīd Maḳdī<u>sh</u> al-Safāḳusī (d. at Kairouan in 1227/1813), author of the *Nuzhat al-anẓār fī ʿa<u>dj</u>āʾib al-tawārī<u>kh</u> wa 'l-a<u>kh</u>bār*, a compilation in which the author traces the history of his natal town from the Islamic conquest to the reign of Ḥammūda Pa<u>sh</u>a (1196-1229/1782-1814) (ed. Ali Zouari and M. Mahfoudh, Beirut 1988). It appears from the historical schema, which he reflects, that the original town had a military function but soon acquired a commercial one. The actual layout of the town and its buildings speedily reflected this process. It seems to have begun with a *ḳṣar* or *bur<u>dj</u>* or *maḥris*) called the *Bur<u>dj</u> al-aḥmar*, on the site of the modern casbah, and in the neighbourhood of the *zāwiya* of Sīdī <u>D</u>jabla. Did this begin as a simple *ribāṭ* or strong-point and then became a *ribāṭ-maḥris* surrounded by an agricultural-artisanal agglomeration? This particular *bur<u>dj</u>* was in fact merely one of several (Buṭriya, Lawza, In<u>sh</u>īla, Maḥris ʿAlī, etc.), numerous in the area and amongst which Ḳṣar Ziyād (35 km/20 miles to the north) was notable. Or was it a centre for fighters for the faith, an instructional centre for religious education, or a staging-post for the *barīd* [*q.v.*] before becoming a commercial centre? Whatever the case, the first nucleus of population was one of *murābiṭun*, to which two groups of fishermen (the *Aʿ<u>sh</u>ā<u>sh</u>* and the *Nwāwla*) were to join. The hinterland had a dense network of villages (*ḳurā*). The sources all agree that trade by land and by sea was the main cause for the evolution of the town.

Urban evolution.

As a mark of its success, Sfax seems to have acquired its first and last fortifications towards the time of Ibrāhīm Aḥmad b. al-A<u>gh</u>lab, between 246/860 and 249/863. The guiding spirit here was its future *ḳāḍī*, the *faḳīh* ʿAlī b. Sālim, a disciple of the Imām Saḥnūn [*q.v.*]. The space enclosed by these walls remained unchanged till the 12th/18th century. It took the form of a quadrilateral 600 m by 400 m, hence covering 24 ha (Sousse, 32 ha; Monastir, 28 ha). The fact that it was only slightly set back from the sea, with a shallow continental shelf there, provided, moreover, a good warning period in case of external attack. The great mosque presumably dated from that same period. It had numerous rebuildings and extensions (e.g. in 379/989 and 479/1086) and only assumed its final form, the one which we now know, in the years between 1183/1759 and 1197/1783. Restricted within its ramparts, the town soon became cramped, but it was not until 1189/1775 that the laying-out of a suburb, *rbāṭ*, near the eastern gate called the Bāb Bḥar, was allowed. It was also provided with a *funduḳ* (1778) and, a little later, a mosque (between 1779 and 1785). The population would have reached saturation point if it has not been for the epidemic of 1199/1785, claiming 15,000 victims, which checked the town's progress. The development process, over a millennium, of the internal lay-out of the town ended up, towards the mid-19th century, in a repertoire of buildings made up of 83 mosques and various oratories, 72 *zāwiyas*, 2,066 houses, 19 oil presses, 35 mills, as many ovens for bread-making, and 12 *bur<u>dj</u>s*. With such an array of buildings, Sfax took second place only after the capital Tunis, which had 8,000-9,000 houses. Water was scarce, hence streams had to be utilised, and three basins, as well as domestic and private cisterns, were constructed: the first, the Nāṣiriyya, goes back to the beginning of the 7th/13th century, and the other two date from 1188/1774.

Political history.

Although comparatively important, given the scale of the country, Sfax never assumed a political importance commensurate with its commercial one. Often coveted by outside powers, which often passed it by, it was never subject to any domination except a commercial one. Ḥammū b. Malīl assumed independent power there in 451/1059 when Zīrid power was in decline. After several fruitless attempts, Tamīm only managed to recover it in 493/1099-1100. It rebelled in 504/1110-11 against its Zīrid governor Abu 'l-Futūḥ. It took the side of the Almohad ʿAbd al-Muʾmin, the master of Ifrīḳiya, in 552/1160 before passing into the hands of the Majorcan Yaḥyā Ibn <u>Gh</u>āniya. It was seized for short periods by the rebels Ibn Abī ʿUmāra (681/1282) and the Banū Makkī (757/1356). It declared for the Ottoman Turks during the period of Ḥafṣid decline in the 10th/16th century, but only reluctantly. In effect autonomous, a *<u>dj</u>amāʿa* took the leading political role there. Even <u>Sh</u>ābbī Sīdī ʿArfa (948/1542) was unable to bring it within his control, though his warriors seized Dar<u>gh</u>ū<u>th</u>. When Kairouan fell to the latter in 964/1557, a *raʾīs* called Abū ʿAbd Allāh al-Makkānī was master of Sfax. It was attached to Tripoli and only restored to the *san<u>dj</u>aḳ* of Tunis in 996/1588.

However, the people of Sfax were not lacking in initiative when they managed to escape from the domination of their elites or acted in concert with them. Despite its trade, and perhaps connected with it, Sfax was none the less a corsair centre. For this reason, George of Antioch gave control of it to Roger II of Siciliy. Mastered in 538/1143 but occupied in 543/1148, it only broke free in 551/1156. It was caught up in the policies of Venice and Malta, and local tradition preserves the memory of a naval victory at Rās al-Ma<u>kh</u>biz in 1160/1747. Venetian attempts at an occupation (1200/1786 and 1205/1791) failed. Ships of Sfax asking permission to go out raiding represented 15% of all requests made between 1212/1797 and 1213/1798. These ships all belonged to the *ḳāʾid* of the town Maḥmūd <u>D</u>jallūlī. This involvement in the activism of the *<u>dj</u>ihād* gave the town an aptitude for resistance, seen at the time of the revolt of 1281/1864 and the insurrection of 1298/1881, although at the instigation of the neighbouring tribe of the Methelith.

Economic life.

The town's commerce flourished thanks to its inhabitants' spirit of enterprise, with a trade orientated towards the Levant. The establishment of the Protectorate dealt a blow to this, but the local people have been recovering their economic enterprise since Independence.

Cultivation of the olive has been known from the 3rd/9th century, and after a period of decline under the Hafsids, recovered in the 11th/17th century; a survey in 1852 enumerated 110,518 trees in the area to the north of the town. These were progressively replaced by almond trees from 1910 onwards. But olive cultivation in the whole of the Sfax region enjoyed an immense increase under the Protectorate, with a large injection of French capital, with 350,000 trees just after 1881, 5,159,829 in 1951 and 6,100.000 in 1972. This monoculture was not without its dangers, and potential difficulties were ony regulated by the creation in Sfax in 1930 of a special Office for Oil, which was to play a leading role in marketing and commerce. Whereas there were only 19 oil-pressing establishments in the mid-19th century, there were some 250 counted in 1972.

The economy of the town of Sfax itself rests on both artisanal production and on service industries (the latter comprising 37% of all enterprises in 1980). As well as the dominant position of olive production, their had been an industrial transformation from the phosphate production of the Gafsa basin. Trade, however, has been the traditional chief activity of the populace of Sfax; tourism has not taken root there. The local commercial mentality expresses itself in private capitalism, not unlike that of the people of D̲j̲arba [*q.v.*].

Population.

This is difficult to evaluate because of the diaspora, rural emigration and, above all, because of administrative boundary changes. The municipality, created in 1884, had 54,800 people in 1946. The Medina alone had 16,700 in 1954, compared with 130,000 for the rest of the agglomeration. The population tripled between 1936 and 1966, and reached 275,000 *ca* 1975. The town grew in consequence, at the expense of the Rbāt, the Frankish quarter, razed after the bombardments of 1943, of the surrounding *sabk̲h̲a*s and even of the nearby sea, whilst the surrounding orchards and gardens, *d̲j̲inān*s, have now completely disappeared. The urban area continues to grow in an anarchic and uncontrolled fashion. Even the medina has been affected by the invasiveness of commercial and artisanal activities spreading out from the *sūḳ*s and altering the ancient pattern of residential usage. There has also been threats of flooding and of atmospheric pollution. The safeguarding of the historic areas and rehabilitation of residential quarters will require official intervention, and is bound up with a public debate on the nature and characteristic of the towns of Tunisia, their pasts and their presents.

Bibliography: R. Brunschvig, *Ḥafṣides*; H.R. Idris, *Zīrīdes*; J. Despois, *La Tunisie orientale. Sahel et Basse Steppe. Etude géographique*, ²Paris 1955; G. Marçais and L. Golvin, *La Grande Mosquée de Sfax*, Tunis 1960; Golvin, *Notes sur le mot ribāt*, in *RDMM* (1969), 95-101; M. Fakhfakh, *La grande exploitation agricole dans la région sfaxienne*, Tunis; idem, *Croisance urbaine de l'agglomération sfaxienne*, in *Rev. Tunis, de Sciences Sociales*, no 25 (1971); idem, *Sfax et sa région: étude de géographie humaine et économique*, Tunis 1986; A. Zouari, *Correspondance de Ahmed al-Qlibi entre Tripoli et Sfax*, Tunis 1982; T. Bachrouch, *Le Sahel, essai de définition d'un espace citadin*, in *CT*, no. 137-8 (1986); idem, *Les cités de la Tunisie septentrionale au XIXᵉ siècle*, in *Annales de l'Univ. de Tunis, Mélanges Ahmed Abdesselam*, no. 30 (1989); idem, *Le Saint et le Prince en Tunisie*, Tunis 1989; Zouari, *Les relations commerciales entre Sfax et le Levant au XVIIIᵉ et XIXᵉ siècles*, Tunis 1990; M. Makdīs̲h̲, *La dynamique économique à Sfax entre le passé et le présent*, in *Actes du 1ᵉʳ colloque (28-30 novembre 1991)*, Sfax 1993, 170, 204. (T. Bachrouch)

SAFAR, (a.) "journey", "travel".

1. In law.

In Islamic law, travelling permits certain mitigations in the carrying out of ritual duties. This applies to three topics: 1. ritual purity: according to most schools, a traveller may extend the period during which he is allowed to perform the minor ritual ablution (*wuḍūʾ* [*q.v.*]) by rubbing his foot-covering instead of washing his feet, from one to three days; 2. ritual prayer (*ṣalāt* [*q.v.*]): a traveller is permitted to shorten (*ḳaṣr*) the *ṣalāt*s with four *rakʿa*s [*q.v.*], i.e. the *ṣalāt al-ẓuhr*, the *ṣalāt al-ʿaṣr*, and the *ṣalāt al-ʿis̲h̲āʾ*, to two *rakʿa*s, and, according to most schools, to combine (*d̲j̲amʿ*) the *ṣalāt al-ẓuhr* with the *ṣalāt al-ʿaṣr*, and the *ṣalāt al-mag̲h̲rib* with the *salāt al-ʿis̲h̲āʾ*; 3. fasting: a traveller is permitted, or according to some, obliged to break the fast of Ramaḍān, but must later make up for the days not fasted. A journey has to satisfy certain requirements in order to allow these mitigations. It has to be undertaken with the intention to cover a certain minimum distance (*masāfat al-ḳaṣr*). Most schools define it as 16 *farsak̲h̲*s, which modern jurists equate with *ca.* 82 km. The S̲h̲īʿīs mention a distance of 24 *mīl*s, i.e. *ca.* 48 km. According on the Ḥanafīs, this distance is three days' travelling with an average speed. The Ẓāhirīs, however, acting on the obvious meaning of the word *safar* in Ḳurʾān and *ḥadīth*, hold that any journey permits these mitigations. According to most schools, the aim of the journey is important. The Ḥanbalīs assert that only journeys with a religious purpose, such as performing the *ḥad̲j̲d̲j̲* or *d̲j̲ihād*, count in this respect, whereas the S̲h̲āfiʿīs, Mālikīs and S̲h̲īʿīs hold that the journey must have a lawful aim. According to the Ḥanafīs, the aim of the journey is irrelevant.

Bibliography: Ibn Rus̲h̲d, *Bidāyat al-mud̲j̲tahid*, Cairo 1965, i, 20-1, 166-74, 295-302; ʿAbd al-Raḥmān al-D̲j̲azīrī, *Kitāb al-fiḳh ʿalā al-mad̲h̲āhib al-arbaʿa*, ²Cairo n.d., i, 144-5, 471-87, 574-5; Ḥillī, *S̲h̲arāʾiʿ al-Islām fī masāʾil al-ḥalāl wa 'l-ḥarām*, Nad̲j̲af 1969, i, 132, 201-2. (R. Peters)

2. In Islamic life.

See for this, funduḳ; k̲h̲ān; riḥla; tid̲j̲āra. For envoys and ambassadors, see elči; safīr.2. For the pilgrims to Mecca, see ḥad̲j̲d̲j̲.iii.A. To the *Bibls.* of these articles, add I.R. Netton (ed.), *Golden roads. Migration, pilgrimage and travel in mediaeval and modern Islam*, London 1993.

ṢAFAR, name of the second month of the Islamic year, also called *Ṣ al-k̲h̲ayr* or *Ṣ al-muẓaffar* because of its being considered to be unlucky (C. Snouck Hurgronje, *The Atchehnese*, i, 206; idem, *Mekka*, ii, 56). The Muslim Tigrē tribes pronounce the name S̲h̲afar, the Achehnese Thapa. According to Wellhausen, in the old Arabian year, Ṣafar comprised a period of two months in which al-Muḥarram (which name, according to this scholar is a Muslim innovation) was included. As a matter of fact, tradition reports that the early Arabians called al-Muḥarram Ṣafar and considered an *ʿumra* during the months of the Ḥad̲j̲d̲j̲ as a practice of an extremely reprehensible nature. They embodied this view in the following saying: *Id̲h̲ā baraʾā 'l-dabar wa-ʿafā 'l-at̲h̲ar wa 'nsalak̲h̲a Ṣafar ḥallati 'l-ʿumra li-man iʿtamar*, i.e. "When the wounded backs of camels are healed and the vestiges [of the pilgrims] are obliterated and Ṣafar has passed, then the ʿUmra is allowed for those who undertake it."

Bibliography: E. Littmann, *Über die Ehrennamen und Neubenennungen der islamischen Monate*, in *Isl.*, viii (1918), 228 ff.; Snouck Hurgronje, *The Atchehnese*, i, 194-5; J. Wellhausen, *Reste arabischen Heidentums*², 95; Bukhārī, *Ḥadjdj*, *bāb* 34; *Manāḳib al-Anṣār, bāb* 26 and Ḳasṭallānī's commentary. See also AL-MUḤARRAM. (A.J. WENSINCK)

ṢAFAR (common spelling, Sfar), Muḥammad al-Bashīr a leading figure in the early Tunisian reformist ("evolutionist") and Young Tunisian movements, of Turkish parentage (1865-1917).

Born at Tūnis as the third son of Brigadier-General (*amīr liwāʾ*) Muṣṭafā Ṣafar, he received a strict education, attended first a Ḳurʾānic school and then the élitist Ṣādiḳī [*q.v.*] College from its inception (1875). His excellent record won him the favour of its founder, Khayr al-Dīn Pasha [*q.v.*] and a scholarship to Paris. Having lost it a year later owing to the diversion of the school's endowments by Khayr al-Dīn's successor, he entered government service (1882), where he rose in seven years to the position of head of the Accountancy department (*raʾīs ḳism al-muḥāsabāt*) of the General Administration, concurrently running and teaching a new Ṣādiḳī branch. More significant were his subseqent roles as (a) founder member of, and contributor to, the semi-official, moderately Islamic, Arabic weekly, *al-Ḥāḍira* ("the Capital", first issue 2 August 1888); (b) co-founder and president of the Khaldūniyya Association (opened 5 May 1897 [*q.v.*]), where he also gave courses in history which fostered national consciousness, won him a following among students of the Zaytūna [*q.v.*] and helped bring about a Ṣādiḳī-Zaytūnī alliance. One of his disciples was the future leader of the Algerian Salafiyya [*q.v.*], Ibn Bādīs [*q.v.*]; (c) president of the Beylical Ḥabūs Council (*djamʿiyyat al-aḥbās* or *al-awḳāf*, in the mid-1890s). In this capacity, he won particular popularity for the renovation of the Tūnis hospice (*takiyya*, 1905) and for his resistance to *colon* pressure for acquisition of *ḥabūs* lands (see INZĀL and B.D. Cannon, *The Beylical Habus Council and suburban development: Tunis, 1881-1914*, in *The Maghreb Review*, viii/5-6 [1983], 32-39 (important)], which made him obnoxious to the *colon* lobby and its chief, de Carnières; (d) co-founder and moving spirit of the "Ṣādiḳī Alumni Association", which became the main element of the Young Tunisian Party (1907). His ideology derived from a variety of sources: the Near Eastern *Nahḍa* [*q.v.*], Islamic modernism (Shaykh ʿAbduh) and reformism [see IṢLĀḤ], and Egyptian nationalism (Muṣṭafā Kāmil, Muḥammad Farīd [*q.vv.*]) on one hand, and French civilisation and liberalism on the other. After 1910 the Young Tunisians took on a marked Pan-Islamic (i.e. pro-Ottoman) colouring; al-Bashīr Ṣafar himself was regarded by the Resident-General Alapetite (in 1912) as "the agent of Pan-Islam in Tunisia" (A.H. Green, *The Tunisian Ulama, 1873-1915*, Leiden 1978, 203). Initially, his attitude regarding the Protectorate was that of close collaboration, but inasmuch as the latter yielded to *colon* pressure, it shifted to an oppositional stance, highlighted by his "*takiyya* speech" (24 March 1906) and his report on *ḥabūs* in Tunisia, presented to the North African Congress (Paris, 6-8 October 1908) (texts in C. Khairallah, *Le Mouvement jeune-tunisien*, Tunis 1957, 55-8, 110-17). Shortly before, in order to satisfy the *colons* without overtly antagonising the Tunisians, Ṣafar was appointed governor (*ḳāʾid*) of Sousse province (1908), which removed him from the capital, the control of the *ḥabūs* and the Khaldūniyya. It also precluded his involvement in Young-Tunisian militancy during the Zaytūna student strike (1910) and the tram boycott (1912). While other leaders (Bāsh-Ḥānba, al-Thaʿālibī, etc.) were arrested and exiled, al-Bashīr Ṣafar remained in his post until his death in 1917. Six months earlier, he sent to U. Blanc, Secretary-General of the Protectorate, a vibrant message of loyalty and appreciation of what France had done for the Tunisians (text in *Afrique française*, xxvii/6 [1917], 338B). Nevertheless, his lifelong dedication to the advancement of his people and the defence of its interests earned him a place of honour in the annals of the Tunisian national movement and the title "Father of the modern Tunisian renaissance" (*Abu 'l-nahḍa al-tūnusiyya al-ḥadītha*, H. Thāmir, *Hādhihi Tūnis*, Cairo 1948, 83).

Bibliography (in addition to references in the article): P. Lambert, *Dictionnaire illustré de la Tunisie*, Tunis 1912, 366; anon., *Béchir Sfar (1865-1917)*, in *IBLA*, xiv (1951), 101-8; J. Ganiage, *Les origines du Protectorat français en Tunisie (1861-1881)*, Paris 1959, 456, 481-2; Ch.-A. Julien, *Colons français et Jeunes tunisiens (1882-1912)*, in *Rev. fr. d'Histoire d'Outre-Mer*, liv (1967), 87-150; M.S. Zmerli, *Figures tunisiennes. Les successeurs*, Tunis 1967, 13-29; M.F. Ibn ʿĀshūr, *Tarādjim al-aʿlām*, Tunis 1970, 197-206; N. Sraieb, *Enseignement, élites et systèmes de valeur: le Collège Ṣadiki de Tunis*, in *Annuaire de l'Afr. du Nord*, x (1971), 122-35; idem, *Une institution scolaire: le Collège Sadiki de Tunis*, diss., Doct. d'État, Paris 1989, unpubl.; B. Tlili, *Rapports culturels et idéologiques ... en Tunisie au XIXe siècle (1830-1881)*, Tunis 1974, 651-65; idem, *Crises et mutations dans la Tunisie (1907-1912)*, Tunis 1978, i, 36-38, 428. (P. SHINAR)

ṢAFAWIDS, a dynasty which ruled in Persia as sovereigns 907-1135/1501-1722, as *fainéants* 1142-8/1729-36, and thereafter, existed as pretenders to the throne up to 1186/1773.

I. Dynastic, political and military history.
II. Economic and commercial history; trade relations with Europe.
III. Literature.
IV. Religion, philosophy and science.
V. Art and architecture. [see Suppl.]
VI. Numismatics.

I. Dynastic, political and military history.

The establishment of the Ṣafawid state in 907/1501 by Shāh Ismāʿīl I [*q.v.*] (initially ruler of Ādharbāydjān only) marks an important turning-point in Persian history. In the first place, the Ṣafawids restored Persian sovereignty over the whole of the area traditionally regarded as the heartlands of Persia for the first time since the Arab conquest of Persia eight and a half centuries previously. During the whole of that time, only once, during what Minorsky termed "the Iranian intermezzo" (334-447/945-1055), did a dynasty of Persian origin prevail over much of Iran [see BUWAYHIDS]; for the rest, Persia was ruled by a succession of Arab caliphs, and Turkish and Mongol sultans and khāns. Secondly, Shāh Ismāʿīl I declared that the Ithnā ʿAsharī form of Shīʿī Islam was to be the official religion of the new state. This was the first time in the history of Islam that a major Islamic state had taken this step. Ismāʿīl's motives in making this decision were probably a combination of religious conviction and the desire to provide the nascent Ṣafawid state with an ideology which would differentiate it from its powerful neighbour, the Sunnī Ottoman empire. At all events, the policy had far-reaching consequences, because it introduced into the Persian body politic the potential for conflict between "the turban and the crown", between the shahs, representing "secular" government, and the *mudjtahids*, whose dream was theocratic government. This conflict, always latent, emerged into the open from time to time during the Ḳādjār period, and finally burst forth with cataclysmic force in the Islamic Revolution of 1979.

(i) *The origins of the Ṣafawids.*

The origins of the Ṣafawid family are shrouded in some mystery, and the mystery is compounded by falsifications which were perpetrated, probably during the reign of Ismāʿīl I and certainly during that of Ṭahmāsp I [*q.v.*], in order to produce an "official" Ṣafawid genealogy [see ṢAFĪ AL-DĪN ARDABĪLĪ, *Bibliography*]. Petrushevskii thinks that the fabrication of the "official" Ṣafawid genealogy occurred even earlier, at the beginning of the 8th/14th century (see B. Nikitine, *Essai d'analyse du Ṣafvat al-ṣafā*, in *JA* [1957], 386). There seems now to be a consensus among scholars that the Ṣafawid family hailed from Persian Kurdistān, and later moved to Ādharbaydjān, finally settling in the 5th/11th century at Ardabīl. There, they lived an uneventful life, gradually acquiring a reputation for piety which attracted to them disciples (*murīd*), but it is only with the birth of Shaykh Ṣafī al-Dīn in 650/1252-3, the eponymous founder of the Ṣafawiyya or Ṣafawid order, that Ṣafawid history really begins.

(ii) *The development of the Ṣafawid order (700-907/1301-1501).*

In 700/1301, Ṣafī al-Dīn assumed the leadership of a local Ṣūfī order in Gīlān, and, under him and his successor, Ṣadr al-Dīn Mūsā [see ṢADR AL-DĪN ARDABĪLĪ], the order was transformed into a religious movement which conducted its propaganda (*daʿwa*) throughout Persia, Syria and Asia Minor. As yet there was no sign of the militant Shīʿism which became a feature of the movement later; indeed, Ṣafī al-Dīn himself was apparently a Sunnī of the Shāfiʿī school. However, the order was beginning to have a political impact, judging by the fact that it attracted the hostility of the Mongol *amīr* Malik Ashraf. We have few details of the development of the order under Khʷādja ʿAlī (794-832/1391-2 to 1429) and Ibrāhīm (832-51/1429-47). It is tempting to see the esoteric doctrine of the Ṣafawid order assuming a Shīʿī character under the leadership of Khʷādja ʿAlī (see, for example, W. Hinz, *Irans Aufstieg zum Nationalstaat im fünfzehnten Jahrhundert*, Berlin and Leipzig 1936, 23; and E.G. Browne, in *JRAS* [July 1921], 407, quoted in V. Minorsky's review of Hinz's book in *Deutsche Literaturzeitung*, xxiii [1937], 954). In the opinion of H.R. Roemer, however, although Shīʿī elements are always present in Folk Islam, "it cannot be proved conclusively that any of the ancestors of Ismāʿīl "had abjured the Sunna and turned Shīʿī" (*The Safavid period*, in *Camb. hist. Iran*, vi, Cambridge 1986, 196-7). At all events, there is no doubt that the Ṣafawid order, like many other religious movements that flourished in Anatolia from the 7th-10th/13th-16th centuries, was the direct beneficiary of the destruction by Hülegü of the Sunnī caliphate in 656/1258, and of the policy of the Mongol Īl-Khāns of tolerance toward all religious faiths, which facilitated the spread of heterodoxy generally. While not going as far as to endorse Henri Corbin's famous dictum that "True Shiʿism is the same as Taṣavvuf, and similarly, genuine and real Taṣavvuf cannot be anything other than Shiʿism" (quoted in M.M. Mazzaoui, *The origins of the Ṣafawids*, Wiesbaden 1972, 83 and n. 2), M.F. Köprülü seems correct in saying that, during that period, "Le Soufisme est en faveur, mais l'hétérodoxie recrute facilement des adepts" (L. Bouvat's tr., quoted in Mazzaoui, 57).

When Shaykh Djunayd [*q.v.*] assumed the leadership of the Ṣafawid order in 951/1447-8, the history of the Ṣafawid movement entered a new phase. Not only did he possess religious authority; he also sought material power (*salṭanat-i ṣūrī*) (Khʷūrshāh b. Ḳubād al-Ḥusaynī, *Tārīkh-i Īlčī-yi Niẓāmshāh*, B.L. ms. Add. 23,513, fol. 445b). The most powerful ruler in Persia at the time, the Ḳara Ḳoyunlu Djahānshāh [*q.v.*], felt threatened (Amīn b. Aḥmad Rāzī, *Haft iḳlīm*, B.L. ms. Add. 16,734, fol. 516a), and ordered Djunayd to disperse his forces and leave Ardabīl; otherwise, Ardabīl would be destroyed (B.L. ms. Or. 3248, fol. 19a). Djunayd fled, and eventually found asylum with Djahānshāh's rival, the Aḳ Ḳoyunlu *amīr* Uzun Ḥasan [see AḲ ḲOYUNLU] in Diyār Bakr. In 864/ 1460, Djunayd was killed during a foray into Shīrwān, and his son Ḥaydar [*q.v.*] succeeded him as head of the Ṣafawiyya. Initially, Ḥaydar continued the alliance with the Aḳ Ḳoyunlu and cemented it by marrying Uzun Ḥasan's daughter. After Uzun Ḥasan's death, however, his son Yaʿḳūb in his turn felt threatened by growing Ṣafawid power, and allied himself with the Shīrwānshāh to defeat and kill Ḥaydar in 893/1488. Ṣafawid supporters were now distinguished by the distinctive headgear (*tādj*) of twelve gores, denoting the twelve Ithnā ʿAsharī Imāms, surmounted by a red spike; this *tādj* is said to have been revealed to Ḥaydar in a dream by the Imām ʿAlī, and the wearing of it caused the Ottomans to dub Ṣafawid supporters *ḳîzîlbash* [*q.v.*] or "redheads"; this derisory appelation was adopted by the Ṣafawids as a mark of pride. Halil Inalcik has noted that, already in the 8th/14th century, Turcoman warriors wore a red cap known as *ḳîzîl börk*.

After the death of Ḥaydar, the Ṣūfīs of the Ṣafawid order gathered round his son ʿAlī at Ardabīl. The Aḳ Ḳoyunlu sultan Yaʿḳūb, now thoroughly alarmed, seized ʿAlī, his two younger brothers Ibrāhīm and Ismāʿīl, and their mother, and confined them in the fortress of Iṣṭakhr in Fārs. He is said to have spared the lives of the brothers only out of consideration for their mother, Ḥalīma Begī Āghā known as ʿĀlamshāh Begum, who was his own sister (B.L. ms. Or. 3248, fol. 24a). In the struggle for power which followed the death of Yaʿḳūb in 896/1490, one of the contenders, Rustam, released the Ṣafawid brothers from jail after four-and-a-half years (898/1493) and, with the assistance of their followers, defeated his main rival Bāysunḳur. He soon realised that the political aspirations of the Ṣafawids constituted a danger to himself; he re-arrested ʿAlī and his brothers, and planned to kill ʿAlī, and his followers at Tabrīz and Ardabīl. ʿAlī escaped from Rustam's camp, and made for Ardabīl, but was overtaken and killed by Aḳ Ḳoyunlu troops.

According to Ṣafawid "official history", ʿAlī, before he died, designated his younger brother, Ismāʿīl, to succeed him. However, A.H. Morton, in a paper given at the 2nd Safavid Round Table, held at Cambridge 8-11 September 1993, raised some important questions based on new evidence: why was Ismāʿīl given precedence over his elder brother Ibrāhīm, who might normally have been expected to succeed as leader of the Ṣafawid order? Did Ibrāhīm in fact succeed ʿAlī, and did Ibrāhīm's early death make it easier for Ṣafawid historians to "edit him out" of official Ṣafawid history? And, finally, does the passing over of Ibrāhīm in favour of Ismāʿīl mark a division in Ṣafawid ideology between Ibrāhīm, epresenting Ṣūfī quietism, and Ismāʿīl, representing nilitant Shīʿī *ghuluww* or extremism? At all events, smāʿīl made his way to Gīlān, where he was given anctuary at Lāhīdjān by the local ruler Kār Kiyā Mīrzā ʿAlī. Rustam prepared to invade Gīlān, but vas prevented from doing so by further dynastic feuds etween rival Aḳ Ḳoyunlu chiefs.

Prima facie, one might have expected that the afawid revolutionary movement, for such it had ecome, would have petered out after suffering what vould normally have been the devastating loss of not ne but three leaders within the space of 34 years. The act that it did not underlines the extraordinary effeciveness of the Ṣafawid *daʿwa*, particularly among the Turcoman tribesmen of eastern Anatolia and Syria. There were three principal elements which together nade up what Minorsky called the "dynamic deology of the Ṣafawid movement" (*Tadhkirat alnulūk*, translated and explained by V. Minorsky, .J.W. Gibb Memorial Series, N.S. XVI, London 943, 23). First, the Ṣūfī disciples (*murīds*) of the afawīd order owed unquestioning obedience to their *nurshid-i kāmil* [see MURSHID], the head of the order, vho was their spiritual director. Second, the potheosis of the Ṣafawid leader as a living emanation f the godhead. Already in the time of Djunayd the afawid *murīds* "openly called" their leader "God *ilāh*), and his son, Son of God (ibn Allāh) ... in his raise they said 'he is the Living One, there is no God ut he'" (Mazzaoui, *op. cit.*, 73). The poems of Shah smāʿīl, composed in the Ādharī dialect of Turkish nder the pen-name of Khaṭāʾī [see ISMĀʿĪL I. 2], are nequivocal on the subject of Ismāʿīl's divinity (see .M. Savory, *Some reflections on totalitarian tendencies n the Ṣafawid state*, in *Studies on the history of Ṣafawid ran*, Variorum Reprints, London 1987, X, 231-2). uch a deviant doctrine placed the Ṣafawids squarely n the camp of the *ghulāt* [*q.v.*], or Shīʿī extremists, uch as the Ahl-i Ḥaḳḳ [*q.v.*]. The third element of the afawid *daʿwa*, which assumed greater importance fter the establishment of the Ṣafawid dynasty as the hāhs strove to give legitimacy to their rule, was their laim to be the representatives on earth of the Twelfth mām or Mahdī of the Ithnā ʿAsharīs. In making this laim, they were of course usurping the traditional ole of the *mudhtahids*.

Taken together, these three elements of the Ṣafawid *aʿwa* produced a heady brew which could readily be ranslated into direct action, and, in the summer of 05/1499, Ismāʿīl left Lāhidjān for Ardabīl to make is bid for power. By the time he reached Ardabīl, ,500 followers from Syria and Anatolia had joined im (Ḥasan Rūmlū, *Aḥsan al-tawārīkh*, ed. G.N. Sedon, Baroda 1931, 25-6). From there, he sent heralds *djārčiyān*) and couriers (*musriʿān*) to summon more upporters from those areas and also from Ādharaydjān and ʿIrāḳ-i ʿAdjam [see DJIBĀL] to a rendezous at Arzindjān [see ERZINDJĀN], on the high road etween Aḳ Shehir and Erzerum [*q.v.*]. His choice of endezvous clearly indicates where the focal point of is support lay. By the summer of 906/1500, 7,000 *izilbāsh* had rallied to him; they came from the Jstādjlū, Shāmlū, Rūmlū, Takkalū, Dhu 'l-Ḳadar, fshār, Ḳādjār and Warsāḳ tribes. Leading his troops n a punitive expedition against the Shīrwānshāh *q.v.*], he exacted revenge for the deaths of his father Iaydar and his grand-father Djunayd in Shīrwān; smāʿīl then marched south into Ādharbāydjān. On he plain of Sharūr near Nakhčiwān, he decisively efeated a force of 30,000 Aḳ Ḳoyunlu under Alwand, nd shortly afterwards (summer of 906-7/1501; see rika Glassen, *Die frühen Safawiden nach Qāżī Aḥmad Qumī*, Freiburg i, Br. 1970, 85) entered Tabrīz. Coins were minted in his name; the *khuṭba* was read in the name of the Twelve Imāms, and the Imāmī rite was proclaimed the true religion (Khʷāndamīr, *Ḥabīb al-siyar*, Tehran n.d., iv, 467). Although masters initially only of Ādharbāydjān, and despite the fact that Alwand was mustering fresh forces; that another Aḳ Ḳoyunlu prince, Murād, was still in possession of Fārs and ʿIrāḳ-i ʿAdjam; and that the Tīmūrids still controlled Khurāsān, the Ṣafawids had in fact won the struggle for power in Persia which had been going on for nearly a century since the death of Tīmūr in 807/1405.

(iii). *The establishment of the Ṣafawid state.*

Since Ismāʿīl I was only seven years old in 900/1494 when his brother ʿAlī was killed in battle with Aḳ Ḳoyunlu troops, and was barely fourteen years old at the time of his accession, it is obvious that the momentum of the Ṣafawid revolutionary movement during that crucial decade was maintained by others. The sources term the men responsible the *ahl-i ikhtiṣāṣ*, a small group of about seven *ḳizilbāsh* chiefs who were singled out by their special devotion to their leader and who had a special relationship with him. They were charged not only with protecting the person of the young leader but also with planning the final stages of the Ṣafawid revolution.

The first decade of the 10th/16th century was spent by Shāh Ismāʿīl in extending Ṣafawid rule over the rest of Persia [see ISMĀʿĪL I], and also over Baghdād and the province of ʿIrāḳ-i ʿArab, which was wrested from Aḳ Ḳoyunlu control in 914/1508. In 917/1511 Ismāʿīl despatched a *ḳizilbāsh* expeditionary force to Transoxania to assist the Tīmūrid Ẓahīr al-Dīn Bābur [see BĀBUR] in recovering his ancestral dominions from the Shībānī Özbegs. The combined Ṣafawid and Timūrid force occupied Samarḳand, where Bābur made good his promise, in return for Ṣafawid help, to have Ismāʿīl's name inserted in the *khuṭba* and coins minted in his name (*Aḥsan al-tawārīkh*, 127), but "the numismatic evidence for this is equivocal" [see BĀBUR, and its *Bibliography*]. Bābur, having also occupied Bukhārā, sent the *ḳizilbāsh* troops home, whereupon the Özbegs promptly counter-attacked and drove him out of Bukhārā. Further Ṣafawid assistance from the governor of Balkh temporarily stabilised the situation, but in 918/1512 a Ṣafawid force under the *wakīl* Amīr Nadjm was annihilated by the Özbegs after many of the *ḳizilbāsh* had mutinied against their Persian commander (see Savory, *The political murder of Mīrzā Salmān*, in *Studies on the history of Ṣafawid Iran*, xv, 186-7). This defeat put an end to Ṣafawid aspirations to extend their influence into Transoxania, and, for most of the Ṣafawid period, the problem of the defence of the northeastern frontier against nomad invasions remained largely unsolved.

On the north-western frontier, Ṣafawid expansionism was a major factor in precipitating war with the Ottomans, a war which soon threatened the very existence of the nascent Ṣafawid state. Not surprisingly, the Sunnī Ottomans were alarmed by the vigorous propagation of the militantly Shīʿī Ṣafawid *daʿwa* in areas of eastern Anatolia and in the region of the Taurus mountains, which constituted an indeterminate frontier between the Ottoman empire and the Mamlūk state. Even more alarming for the Ottomans was the great success of this *daʿwa* among the Turcoman tribes, and the recruitment of significant numbers of these tribesmen into the Ṣafawid army. In 907-8/1502 the Ottoman sultan Bāyezīd II [*q.v.*] deported large numbers of Shīʿīs from Anatolia to the Morea, and he strengthened his garrisons on the eastern frontier after Ismāʿīl overran Diyār Bakr and large areas of Kurdistān in 913/1507-8. In 916/1510, after his great victory at Marw over the Özbegs, Ismāʿīl sent the head of the Özbeg leader, Muḥammad Shībānī Khān, to Bāyezīd III. The following year, 917/1511, when a major Shīʿī revolt broke out in Tekke, and at the same time civil war erupted between Bāyezīd and two of his sons, Selīm and Aḥmed, Shāh Ismāʿīl sought to turn the situation to his advantage. His scheme to mobilise support for Murād, son of Aḥmed, came to nothing, but a Ṣafawid force under Nūr ʿAlī Khalīfa Rūmlū carried fire and sword as far as Tūḳāt, where the *khuṭba* was read in the name of Ismāʿīl, and defeated a large Ottoman force under Sinān Pasha. Meanwhile, Bāyezīd II had been forced to abdicate in favour of his son Selīm on 7 Ṣafar 918/24 April 1512. At once, Selīm set about mustering a huge army of 200,000 men for the invasion of Persia, and, as an initial measure, "proscribed Shiʿism in his dominions and massacred all its adherents on whom he could lay hands" (H.A.R. Gibb and H. Bowen, *Islamic society and the West*, i/2, Oxford 1957, 189). Marching by easy stages across Anatolia into Ādharbāydjān, Selim reached Čāldirān [*q.v.*] on 1 Radjab 920/22 August 1514, where a battle was fought the following day (see M.J. McCaffrey, *Čālderān*, in *Encyclopaedia Iranica*, v, 656-8; Naṣr Allāh Falsafī, *Djang-i Čāldiran*, in *Madjalla-yi Dānishkada-yi Adabiyyāt-i Dānishgāh-i Tihrān*, i/2 [1953-4], 50-127). The Ṣafawid army was heavily defeated. Most sources say that the Ottomans outnumbered the Ṣafawid forces two to one, but the Ottoman artillery and handguns, of which as yet the Ṣafawids had little experience [see BĀRŪD. v], were the decisive factor. After their victory, the Ottomans entered Tabrīz, the Ṣafawid capital, but recalcitrant Janissaries thwarted Selīm's plan to winter there and complete the conquest of Persia the following year, and he withdrew eight days later, on 23 Radjab 920/13 September 1514.

The consequences of the defeat at Čāldirān were both material and psychological. In terms of territory, the result was the annexation by the Ottomans of the regions of Diyār Bakr, Marʿash and Albistān. In terms of casualties, many high-ranking *ḳizilbāsh amīrs*, and three prominent members of the *ʿulamāʾ*, were killed. Psychologically, the defeat destroyed Ismāʿīl's belief in his invincibility, based on his pretensions to divine status. During the last ten years of his life, despite serious losses on the eastern frontier (Balkh: 922/1516-17; Ḳandahār [*q.v.*]: 928/1522), and the near-loss of Harat in 927/1520 and 930/1523, Ismāʿīl never again took the field in person; furthermore, he gave less personal attention to state affairs. The defeat also fundamentally altered the relationship between Ismāʿīl as *murshid-i kāmil* and the *ḳizilbāsh*, his *murīds*. The habitual rivalries between the *ḳizilbāsh* tribes, which had been temporarily sublimated into the dynamic ideology of the Ṣafawid *daʿwa*, resurfaced in virulent form immediately after the death of Ismāʿīl, and led to ten years of civil war that rent the fabric of the Ṣafawid state (930-40/1524-33).

The administrative structure of the Ṣafawid state under Ismāʿīl I was essentially a Turco-Persian condominium. From the beginning there was tension (initially creative) between the *ḳizilbāsh* who, since their military prowess had achieved political power for the Ṣafawids, considered that the principal offices of state should be their perquisite, and the Persians, who in the main staffed the ranks of the bureaucracy and the religious establishment. Friction was inevitable because, as Minorsky put it, the *ḳizilbāsh* "were not party to the national Persian tradition. Like oil and water, the Turcomans and the Persians did not mix freely, and the dual character of the population profoundly affected both the military and civil administration" (*Tadhkirat al-mulūk*, 188). Each faction saw the other in terms of racial stereotypes (see Savory, *The Qizilbash, education and the arts*, in *Studies on the History of Ṣafawid Iran*, XVI, 168 ff.). The Persians saw the *ḳizilbāsh* as fighting men of only moderate intelligence. The *ḳizilbāsh* considered the Persians effete, and referred to them by the pejorative term "Tādjīk", i.e. non-Turk. Ismāʿīl attempted to reduce the friction by creating a new office of *wakīl-i nafs-nafīs-i humāyūn*, who was to be the *alter ego* of the Shāh [see DĪWĀN. iv], superior in rank both to the *wazīr*, the head of the bureaucracy, and the *amīr al-umarāʾ*, the commander-in-chief of the *ḳizilbāsh* forces (see *EIr* art. *Amīr al-Omarāʾ*. ii. Safavid usage). The weakness of this plan was that the appointee to the new office had to be either a Turk or a Tādjīk, and the antipathy between the two groups was, if anything, exacerbated rather than mitigated. The other administrative change made by Ismāʿīl I was to make the *ṣadr*, who had been the head of the religious institution in Aḳ Ḳoyunlu and Tīmūrid administrations, a political appointee. The idea was that the *ṣadr* would be answerable to the Shāh for the good behaviour of the *mudjtahids*, who resented the usurpation by the Shāh of their prerogative to be the representatives on earth of the Mahdī [*q.v.*], and who might feel inclined to challenge this presumption. This stratagem, too, was far from being an unqualified success.

(iv) *Internal discord and external enemies: the Ṣafawid state from 930/1524 to 996/1588.*

Ṭahmāsp, who succeeded in father Ismāʿīl I in 930/1524, was at the time ten years and three months old; he was the ward of a *ḳizilbāsh amīr* who saw himself as the *de facto* ruler of the state [see *EIr*, art. *Dīv Solṭān*]. For almost ten years rival *ḳizilbāsh* factions fought for control of the state (see Savory, *The principal offices of the Safawid state during the reign of Ṭahmāsp (930-84/1524-76)*, in *Studies on the history of Ṣafawid Iran*, V, 65-71). Eventually, Ṭahmāsp reasserted his authority to such good purpose that he ended up by reigning for 52 years, the longest reign in Persian history. Ṭahmāsp has been paid scant attention by historians. Perhaps his unattractive character has deterred them from making a major study of him. He is portrayed as a religious bigot (cf. e.g. the Jenkinson episode (Savory, *Iran under the Safavids*, 111-12), and the celebrated visit to Persia in 951/1544 of the fugitive Mughal Emperor Humāyūn [*q.v.*] (see also MUGHALS. 2. External relations, and Savory, *op. cit.*, 66); as avaricious (*Narrative of the Most Noble Vincentio d'Alessandri, ambassador to the King of Persia for the Most Illustrious Republic of Venice*, in *A narrative of Italian travels in Persia in the fifteenth and sixteenth centuries*, Hakluyt Society, London 1873, 217-19); *A chronicle of the Carmelites in Persia*, 2 vols., London 1939, i, 54); and as capable of ordering particularly sadistic punishments in an age in which cruel punishments were commonplace (see, for example, *Aḥsan al-tawārīkh*, 274, 285, 356). Apparently a debauchee in his youth, Ṭahmasp made a public act of repentance (*tawba*) at the age of twenty, and subsequently not only rigorously prohibited the drinking of wine and other alcoholic beverages, and the use of hashish, but placed severe restrictions on singing and the playing of musical instruments. Furthermore, he ordered that the considerable revenues accruing to the treasury from gambling casinos, taverns and brothels be expunged from the account-books (*ibid.*, 246, 489).

D'Alessandri's charge that Ṭahmāsp was "a man of very little courage" (*op. cit.*, 216) must be rejected (see Savory, *op. cit.*, 57-8). In the course of his reign, the Özbegs launched five major attacks on Khurāsān, and the Ottomans, under their most powerful sultan Süleyman II, made four major invasions of Persia. It is true that Persia lost territory (Baghdād in 942/1535), and that Ṭahmāsp was forced to move the Ṣafawid capital from Tabrīz to Ḳazwīn in 955/1548 (L. Lockhart, *Persian cities*, London 1960, 69; A.K.S. Lambton, in ḲAZWĪN, gives 962/1555), but, with the meagre resources available to him, he successfully fought a series of wars on two fronts (Savory, *op. cit.*, 58 ff.), and, in 962/1555, he was successful in negotiating with the Ottomans the Treaty of Amasya on terms not unfavourable to Persia; peace remained unbroken for the remainder of Ṭahmāsp's reign (see *EIr*, i, 928: AMASYA; N. Itzkowitz, *Ottoman empire and Islamic tradition*, New York 1972, 35-6; S.J. Shaw, *History of the Ottoman empire and modern Turkey*, 2 vols., Cambridge 1976, i, 109).

Although it was Shāh ʿAbbās I who accelerated the process of converting the Ṣafawid state from a Turco-Persian condominium into a multi-cultural society, it was Ṭahmāsp who began it by introducing new ethnic elements from the Caucasus region, namely, Armenians, Georgians and Circassians, and by recruiting members of these groups into Ṣafawid service. Such recruits were called *ghulāmān-i khāṣṣa-yi sharīfa* [see GHULĀM. ii, Persia], an obvious analogy with the Ottoman *ḳapi̊ ḳullari̊*. After the death of Ṭahmāsp in 984/1576, the struggle for a dominant position in the state was no longer only between the two "founding nations", Turcomans and Tādjīks, but was a three-cornered fight for power involving ambitious members of the new Caucasian factions. This fight was complicated greatly by the emergence of the *ḥaram* as an important source of political power, as Circassian and Georgian mothers of royal princes intrigued to secure the succession of their particular sons. From the time of Djunayd onwards, all Ṣafawid leaders had had Turcoman mothers. After the death of Ṭahmāsp, however, because neither of the "*ḳi̊zi̊lbāsh*" candidates, the mentally unstable Ismāʿīl and the purblind Sulṭān Muḥammad Khudābanda, was suitable as a ruler, one *ḳi̊zi̊lbāsh* tribe, the Ustādjlūs, threw its support behind Ṭahmāsp's third son, Ḥaydar, whose mother was a Georgian. The majority of the *ḳi̊zi̊lbāsh* saw the prospect of a ruler strongly supported by the Georgian faction as a threat to their own pre-eminence, and assassinated Ḥaydar; they then placed on the throne first, Ismāʿīl II (984-5/1576-7), and then Sulṭān Muḥammad Shāh (985-96/1578-88).

The history of the Ṣafawid state prior to the accession of ʿAbbās I (*q.v.*; see also *EIr*, art. *ʿAbbās I*) is an evolutionary phase, during which attempts were made to deal with certain basic problems posed by the establishment of the state. An attempt was made to incorporate the original Ṣūfī organisation of the Ṣafawid order in the state. An attempt was made to prevent the *ḳi̊zi̊lbāsh* from acquiring a dominant position in the state at the expense of the Tādjīks or Persians. Both failed. As a result of the first failure, there was a marked movement away from the theocratic form of government of the early Ṣafawid state toward a greater separation of spiritual and temporal powers. The second failure led to the introduction of elements which were neither Turcoman nor Persian, but Caucasian Christian, as a sort of "third force" to offset the influence of the other two.

The pre-ʿAbbās period was one in which the functions of the principal officers of state were not precisely defined, and the boundary between the political establishment and the religious establishment was not clearly demarcated. For example, one finds a military officer, the *amīr al-umarāʾ*, exercising a considerable measure of political authority, and one finds *ṣadr*s and other religious officials holding military rank and leading troops into battle; the *ṣadr* himself, as already noted, was a political appointee. One must beware, therefore, of using terms like "civil", "military", "religious", and the like, in any precise sense. By the end of the reign of Ṭahmāsp, the power of the *ṣadr* had declined. This was due in part to the division of the office into that of *ṣadr-i ʿāmma* and *ṣadr-i khāṣṣa*, and in part to the fact that one of the *ṣadr*'s important functions in the early Ṣafawid state, namely, the imposition of Ithnā ʿAsharī uniformity throughout Persia, had largely been achieved by the end of the reign of Ismāʿīl I. With the gradual abandonment of the concept of *wakīl* as the *alter ego* of the shāh, the importance of the *wazīr* as the head of the bureaucracy increased and, by the time of ʿAbbās I, the *wazīr* had emerged as one of the most powerful officers of state.

(v) *The Ṣafawid state at the height of its power under Shāh ʿAbbās I (996-1038/1588-1629).*

The *ḳi̊zi̊lbāsh* inter-tribal rivalry, the succession struggles, and the attempt by a Tādjīk faction to end *ḳi̊zi̊lbāsh* dominance, went on for eleven years after the death of Ṭahmāsp, and so weakened the ability of the state to resist its external enemies that the Ottomans made inroads in Ādharbāydjān and the Özbegs in Khurāsān: the citadel at Tabrīz had been in Ottoman hands since 993/1585; Harāt had fallen to the Özbegs in the spring of 996/1588. When ʿAbbās, the third son of Sulṭān Muḥammad Shāh, was placed on the throne in 996/1588, the prospects for the survival of the Ṣafawid state were as bleak as they had been in 920/1514 after the battle of Čāldirān. The events of ʿAbbās's youth had made him determined to make himself independent of the untrustworthy *ḳi̊zi̊lbāsh* tribes; yet he could not dispense entirely with their fighting qualities. His solution was to raise a standing army, itself an innovation in Persia, from the ranks of the *ghulāms*. The new regiments would be paid from the royal treasury, and would be loyal to him personally, and not to a tribal chief; they included regiments of musketeers [see BĀRŪD. v. The Ṣafawids]. The reorganisation of the army necessitated a reduction in the number of provinces under *ḳi̊zi̊lbāsh* administration (*mamālik*), in which the greater part of the revenue was consumed locally, and an increase in the number of provinces under direct royal administration (*khāṣṣa*), the revenues from which accrued to the royal treasury. *Ghulāms* were not only recruited for military service but were appointed to positions within the royal household and the *khāṣṣa* administration. These policies set in train a social and political revolution. Minorsky has calculated that, by the end of the reign of ʿAbbās I, about one-fifth of the high-ranking *amīrs* were *ghulāms* (*Tadhkirat al-mulūk*, 17-18); by 1007/1598, only ten years after the accession of ʿAbbās I, an Armenian from Georgia had risen to the position of commander-in-chief of all the Ṣafawid armed forces (see *EIr*, art. *Allāhverdī Khan*). The changed social and political basis of the Ṣafawid state was naturally reflected in its administrative structure. The offices of *wakīl* and *amīr al-umarāʾ*, relevant to the period of *ḳi̊zi̊lbāsh* domination, fell into disuse. The *ḳūrčībāshī*, or commander of the élite corps of *ḳūrčīs* [see ḲŪRČĪ] continued to be listed among the principal officers of state, but his importance, too, declined *pari passu* with the decline of the *ḳi̊zi̊lbāsh*. Instead, we hear of a new officer, the *sipāhsālār*, or commander-in-chief of all troops, *ḳizilbāsh* and non-*ḳizilbāsh*. The commanders of the two of the new regiments in the reorganised army, the *ḳullar-āḳāsi*, or commander of the *ghulāms*, and the *tufangčī-āḳāsi*, or commander of the musketeers, join the highest echelons of the administration. The growing centralisation of the bureaucracy resulted in the increased status of the *wazīr*, who now boasted such titles as *iʿtimād al-dawla* ("trusty support of the state") or *ṣadr-i aʿẓam* ("exalted seat of honour").

The new army could not be organised and trained overnight, and it was ten years before ʿAbbās felt ready to take the field. In the meantime, he had been forced to sign a treaty by which he ceded to the Ottomans large areas of Ṣafawid territory, including Ādharbāydjān, Ḳarabāgh, Gandja, Ḳarādja-dāgh, Georgia, and parts of Luristān and Kurdistān; in the east, the Özbegs overran the province of Sīstān, and in 998-9/1590 the Mughals recaptured Ḳandahār, which had been in Ṣafawid hands since 965/1558. The tide began to turn in 1007/1598, when ʿAbbās scored a signal victory over the Özbegs and recaptured Harāt, but the Özbegs remained a formidable enemy, and in 1011/1602 a Ṣafawid army was forced to retreat from Balkh with heavy losses. In 1012/1603 ʿAbbās launched a series of major offensives against the Ottomans in the north-west. Tabrīz was recaptured, and the Ottomans were pushed back behind the river Aras. By 1016/1607, the last Ottoman soldier had been expelled from Ṣafawid territory as defined by the Treaty of Amasya in 962/1555, and in 1033/1624 the Ṣafawids recaptured Baghdād.

The reputation of ʿAbbās I does not rest solely on his military and political achievements. His reign is notable for a remarkable flowering of the arts, both fine and applied. It is also notable for a major exercise in urban planning, when ʿAbbās I in 1007/1598 transferred the capital from Ḳazwīn to Iṣfahān, and proceeded to lay out an entirely new city cheek by jowl with the ancient one. The focus of the new city was the great Maydān-i Naḳsh-i Djahān, 507 m in length and 158 m in width; the Čahār Bāgh avenue (see *EIr*, art. *Č(ah)ār-bāġ-e Eṣfahān*) started at a point near the Maydān and ran south for more than two miles, crossed the Zāyanda-rūd by the Allāhverdī Khān bridge, and ended at the pleasure gardens known as Hazār-djarīb.

The economic prosperity of Persia also increased dramatically under ʿAbbās I. The new capital, Iṣfahān, became a thriving metropolis, and Western diplomatic representatives began to make their way to it. The primary objective of all European diplomats was the development of trade (see 2. Economic and commercial history). The secondary purpose of envoys from Roman Catholic countries was the furtherance of the interests of the various religious Orders operating in Persia: Dominicans, Franciscans, Augustinians, Carmelites, Jesuits and Capuchins. The first envoy who was not a member of a religious Order was Don García de Silva y Figueroa, ambassador from King Philip III of Spain, who arrived at Iṣfahān in 1025/1617; next, after ʿAbbās I had enlisted the aid of ships of the English East India Company to expel the Portuguese from Hormuz in 1031/1622, was the first official English ambassador to the Persian court, Sir Dodmore Cotton; finally, in 1076/1665, Louis XIV of France followed suit, and sent two envoys to Persia.

(vi) *The decline and fall of the Ṣafawids* (*1038-1135/1629-1722*).

Chardin's well-known dictum: "When this great prince (Shāh ʿAbbās I) ceased to live, Persia ceased to prosper!", though exaggerated, contains within it a kernel of truth. Shāh Ṣafī, the grandson and successor of ʿAbbās I (1038-52/1629-42), seemed intent only on maintaining his own position by putting to death or blinding possible rivals such as princes of the Ṣafawid house and powerful officers of state such as the *ḳūrčībāshī*. In 1047-8/1637-8 two important cities, Baghdād and Ḳandahār, were lost. Ṣafī's son and successor, ʿAbbās II (1052-77/1642-66), was a more able ruler, resembling his great-grandfather ʿAbbās I in his administrative skill and powers of military leadership. He was less able to withstand pressure from the religious leaders, however, and although Christians continued to enjoy considerable freedom of worship, ʿAbbās I's policy of religious tolerance was breached by ʿAbbās II's treatment of Jews. In fact, it was becoming clear that many of the policies put in place by ʿAbbās I could be maintained only by a ruler endowed with his outstanding abilities. It is the tragedy of the reign of ʿAbbās I that, by his own act, he made it unlikely that his successors would be of similar calibre. To begin with, he followed the traditional Ṣafawid practice of appointing the royal princes to provincial governorates, where they were placed in the care of a *ḳizilbāsh* chief who held the title of *lala* [*q.v.* in Suppl.] "guardian" or "tutor". The *lala* was responsible not only for his ward's physical well-being, but also for training him in statecraft. Thus in 999/1590-1 ʿAbbās I appointed his eldest son, Muḥammad Bāḳir Mīrzā, governor of Hamadān and *amīr al-umarāʾ* of the province (Iskandar Beg Munshī, *Tārīkh-i ʿĀlam-ārā-yi ʿAbbāsī*, text, ed. Īradj Afshār, 2 vols., Tehran 1334-5 *Sh*./1955-6, i, 440, tr. Savory, 2 vols., Boulder, Col. 1978, ii, 614). In 1024/1614, however, his son was murdered, probably with the Shāh's connivance, on suspicion of plotting against him (*ibid.*, text, ii, 883-4, tr., ii, 1098-9). From then on, the royal princes were closely confined in the *ḥaram*, where their only companions were their tutors, the court eunuchs, and the women of the *ḥaram*. The new policy bore obvious similarities to the Ottoman *ḳafes* ("cage") system, which was introduced slightly earlier, during the reign of Selīm II (974-82/1566-74) (see Shaw, *History of the Ottoman empire and modern Turkey*, i, 179). Shaw notes that the new system resulted in increased political power for the women of the harem, and introduced the "sultanate of the women", which lasted well into the 11th/17th century. In Ṣafawid Persia, there was a similar result. Chardin calls the *ḥaram* "un Conseil privé, qui l'emporte d'ordinaire par dessus tout, et qui donne la loi à tout" (*Voyages du Chevalier Chardin en Perse et autres lieux de l'Orient*, ed. Langlès, Paris 1811, 10 vols., v, 240). Moreover, the new policy failed in its essential purpose, namely, to prevent treasonable behaviour or the suspicion of treason on the part of the royal princes. On the contrary, once confined to the *ḥaram* they became the centre of intrigue to a far greater extent than had previously been the case. This led ʿAbbās to blind his sons Sulṭān Muḥammad Mīrzā in 1030/1620-1 (Iskandar Beg, text, ii, 965, tr., ii, 1187), and Imām Ḳulī Mīrzā in 1036/1626-7 (*ibid.*, text, ii, 1064, tr., ii, 1288); two other sons had died young of natural causes, and so ʿAbbas had left himself without an heir.

The third factor in the decline of the Ṣafawids was the inordinate extension of the policy, begun under ʿAbbās I and continued under his successors, of converting *mamālik* to *khāṣṣa* provinces. By the end of the reign of ʿAbbās I, only those frontier provinces in which an instant response to enemy invasion was essential, remained in the hands of *ḳizilbāsh* gover nors. This process had two undesirable effects: first, the military strength of the Ṣafawid state was weakened. Whether or not the *ghulām* troops were as good fighting material as their *ḳizilbāsh* predecessors is debatable, but, when the overall number of men in the army was allowed to decline, the consequences were predictable; second, the administration of the *khāṣṣa* provinces, by officials who were royal bailiffs or intendants and were little more than tax-farmers, was more oppressive than that of *ḳizilbāsh* governors of *mamālik* provinces. As Minorsky says, Chardin, "in his paragraph on the Khāṣṣa, ... has unmasked one of the basic evils of administration which contributed to the fall of the dynasty" (*Tadhkirat al-mulūk*, 26). The extent to which Ṣafawid military power had declined was dramatically demonstrated in 1135/1722, when a small band of marauding Afghāns succeeded in starving the Ṣafawid capital into surrender.

Under the last two Ṣafawid shāhs, Sulaymān (1077-1105/1666-94) and Sulṭān Ḥusayn (1105-35/1694-1722), the pace of decline accelerated. Both were weak and pliable rulers, products of the *ḥaram* system. Sulaymān, an alcoholic, had little interest in affairs of state. His son, Shāh Sulṭān Ḥusayn, was no better, and his derisive nickname "Mullā Ḥusayn" is significant. Unrestrained by the authority of the ruler, the "privy council" of the women of the *ḥaram* and the court eunuchs usurped power at the centre of the ruling institution. Equally serious was the emergence of the *mudjtahids* and other religious leaders as a powerful political force. The political role of the *ṣadr* was assumed first by the *shaykh al-islām*, and then, after the accession of Sulṭān Ḥusayn Mīrzā, by a new official called the *mullābāshī*. There was an outpouring of works on Ithnā ʿAsharī theology, jurisprudence and tradition and, as Shīʿī orthodoxy became more rigidly formalised, there was increasing persecution of heretics. Ṣūfīs, who had brought the Ṣafawids to power, were now a principal target of the *mudhtahids*, one of whom even acquired the soubriquet of *ṣūfī-kush* or "Ṣūfī-slayer" (see Browne, *LHP*, iv, 386 ff.). ʿAbbās I's policy of religious tolerance, which had been responsible for much of the economic prosperity of Persia during his reign, was abandoned. Not only did the usual targets, Christians and Jews, suffer as a result, but philosophers and non-conformist Muslims as well (D. Morgan, *Medieval Persia 1040-1797*, London and New York 1988, 149). The upsurge of religious intolerance resulting from the increased power of the *ʿulamāʾ* also had economic consequences (see section II), and this factor must be added to Minorsky's "more conspicuous factors" (*Tadhkirat al-mulūk*, 23) for Ṣafawid decline.

In 1121/1709 Mīr Ways, chief of the Ghalzay Afghāns [see GHALZAYS], hitherto a vassal of the Ṣafawids, rebelled and occupied Ḳandahar, and this was followed by the revolt of the Abdālī [*q.v.*] Afghāns. Mīr Ways's successor, Maḥmūd, subdued the Abdālīs and, in 1131/1719, led a force across the Dasht-i Lūṭ and entered Kirmān unopposed. Thus encouraged, he returned two years later with a larger force, and marched on Iṣfahān. Vacillation on the part of the Shāh, treachery within the ranks of Ṣafawid officials at Iṣfahān, and the pathetically weak state of the Ṣafawid army, enabled Maḥmūd to rout a mainly scratch Ṣafawid force at Gulnābād near Iṣfahān on 20 Djumādā I 1134/8 March 1722. Maḥmūd, his force too small to carry the city by storm, starved it into surrender six months later; on 1 Muḥarram 1135/12 October 1722 Sulṭān Ḥusayn Shāh surrendered unconditionally, and handed over the crown to Maḥmūd.

(vii) *The Afghān interregnum 1135-42/1722-29; Ṣafawid* rois-fainéants *(1135-48/1722-36); the end of the Ṣafawid dynasty.*

The third son of Shāh Sulṭān Ḥusayn, Ṭahmāsp Mīrzā, had escaped from Iṣfahān during the Afghān siege, and had proclaimed himself Shāh at Ḳazwīn on 30 Muḥarram 1135/10 November 1722 with the title of Ṭahmāsp II, but was driven out by the Afghāns and took refuge at Tabrīz. An uprising of the townspeople of Ḳazwīn against the Afghāns precipitated the slaughter by Maḥmūd at Iṣfahān of Persian government officials, members of the nobility, and about 3,000 *ḳizilbash* guards. In 1137/1725 a report that Shāh Sultān Ḥusayn's second son, Ṣafī Mīrzā, had escaped from Iṣfahān caused Maḥmūd to put to death at least eighteen members of the Ṣafawid royal family. Shortly afterwards, Maḥmūd was overthrown by his cousin Ashraf, who was proclaimed Shāh on 12 Shaʿbān 1137/26 April 1725. The Afghān writ only ran in central and south-eastern Persia, and Ashraf's efforts to seize Ṭahmāsp II failed. The strife in Persia tempted Tsar Peter the Great to occupy Darband and Bākū in 1135/1723, and in 1138-9/1726 the Ottomans also took advantage of the situation and once again invaded Ādharbāydjān; this invasion led Ashraf to execute Shāh Sulṭān Ḥusayn. In 1140/1727 Ashraf was forced to negotiate peace with the Ottomans and to recognise as Ottoman territory large areas of Persian Kurdistān, Ādharbāydjan, Ḳarabāgh and Georgia. In 1139/1726 Ṭahmāsp II was joined by Nādir Khān Afshār [see NĀDIR SHĀH AFSHĀR], who dubbed himself Ṭahmāsp Ḳulī Khān and claimed that his goal was the restoration of the Ṣafawid monarchy. After winning a number of victories over the rival Ḳādjārs and their Turcoman allies in Khurāsān, and over the Abdālīs, Nādir routed Ashraf, entered Iṣfahān on 16 Djumādā I 1142/7 December 1730, and placed Ṭahmāsp II on the throne.

After five years of campaigning (1142-48/1730-35), Nādir regained all Persian territory lost to the Ottomans (see Shaw, *op. cit.*, 238-9, 243), and peace was negotiated on the basis of a reversion to the frontiers laid down in the Treaty of Zuhāb in 1049/1639. Nādir's campaigns against the Russians were equally successful. By the terms of the Treaty of Rasht (4 Shaʿbān 1144/1 February 1732), Russia returned all Persian territory south of the river Kūra, and by the Treaty of Gandja (28 Dhu 'l-Ḥidjdja 1147/21 May 1735), Russia surrendered Bākū and Darband.

On 17 Rabīʿ I 1145/7 September 1732, Nādir deposed Ṭahmāsp II, and placed the latter's son on the throne with the title of ʿAbbās III. Four years later, Nādir abandoned the pretence of restoring the Ṣafawid monarchy, deposed ʿAbbās III, and had himself crowned Shāh on 24 Shawwāl 1148/8 March 1736 as the first ruler of the new Afshārid dynasty. During Nādir's absence in India, his son Riḍā Ḳulī Khān had Ṭahmāsp II and ʿAbbās III put to death in 1152/1740, together with ʿAbbās's younger brother Ismāʿīl (L. Lockhart, *Nadir Shah*, London 1938, 177-8, 180). The accession of Nādir Shāh brought to an end more than two centuries of Ṣafawid rule, which had existed in name only since 1135/1722, but Ṣafawid pretenders, who first made their appearance during the reign of the Afghān Ashraf, continued to manifest themselves as late as 1187/1773, under the Zands (see J.R. Perry, *The last Ṣafawids*, in *Iran JIBPS*, ix [1971], 59-69).

II. Economic and commercial history; trade relations with Europe.

(i) *European attempts to develop trade with Ṣafawid Persia.*

Trade has a way of ignoring national boundaries and the wishes of political leaders. Thus it was that, when the capture of Constantinople by the Ottomans in 857/1453 put an end to the trade of the Republic of Venice in the Black Sea, the Venetians found a temporary gap in the Ottoman defences in Ḳaramān, and continued to trade with the Aḳ Ḳoyunlu ruler Uzun Ḥasan via this route. The decisive defeat of Uzun Ḥasan by the Ottomans on the Upper Euphrates in 878/1473, and the final incorporation of Ḳaramān into the Ottoman empire in 880/1475, sealed off this line of communication with Iran. In 1488, however, the Portuguese sea-captain Bartolomeu Dias rounded the Cape of Good Hope, thus outflanking the Ottoman empire and also the Italian city-states of Venice and Genoa, and opening up the possibility of trade with Persia via the Persian Gulf. In 913/1507, less than a decade after Vasco da Gama had reached India, the Portuguese, under the command of Afonso de Albuquerque, arrived in the Persian Gulf. The Portuguese Viceroy at once saw the great strategic and commercial importance of Hormuz [see HURMŪZ], and in 921/1515 he returned and occupied the city, thus establishing the first European foothold on Ṣafawid territory. For the Portuguese, although the vassal (*titulado*) King of Hormuz had, by the Treaty of Mīnāb (929-30/1523) granted them *inter alia* a site for the construction of a factory, the most lucrative aspect of their occupation of Hormuz was control of the customs.

The English, conceding control of the Persian Gulf to the Portuguese for more than a century, attempted to turn the northern flank of the Ottoman empire by opening up a trade route to Russia and Persia via the hazardous sea route north of Scandinavia to Archangel. The first English joint-stock company formed for this purpose, in 1553, was called "The Mysterie and Companie of the Merchant Adventurers for the Discoverie of Regions, Dominions, Islands and Places unknown", and had Sebastian Cabot as its Governor. The Company was successively named "The Muscovy Company" and "The Russia Company". In 964-5/1557, Anthony Jenkinson and two other merchants reached Astrakhān, and crossed the Caspian Sea to Bukhārā. Four years later, Jenkinson returned, and this time crossed the Caspian and landed on Ṣafawid territory in Shīrwān. On 23 Rabīʿ I 970/20 November 1562, he was received in audience by Shāh Ṭahmāsp, and delivered to him a letter from Elizabeth I, in which the Queen desired "to treate of friendship, and free passage of our Merchants and people, to repaire and traffique within his dominions, for to bring in our commodities, and to carry away theirs to the honour of both princes, the mutual commoditie of both Realmes, and wealth of the Subjects" (Anthony Jenkinson, *Early voyages and travels to Russia and Persia*, Hakluyt Society, 1st Series, nos. lxxii-lxxiii, 2 vols., London 1886, i, 147). Although Shāh Ṭahmāsp dismissed Jenkinson with the remark "Oh thou unbeleever, we have no neede to have friendship with the unbelievers", the Shāh's brother-in-law, ʿAbd Allāh Khān Ustādjlū, governor of Shīrwān, granted important trading privileges to the Muscovy Company; but the dangers of the sea-route to the White Sea, and attacks by bandits in the Volga region, caused the Company to abandon this route in 988-9/1581.

In the same year, English merchants tried to gain access to the Persian market by the overland route from the eastern Mediterranean across Syria and Mesopotamia. John Newberie, having reached Hormuz on the Persian Gulf by this overland route, persuaded the merchants of the recently formed Levant Company to interest themselves in trade with Persia, and in 996-7/1583 he returned to Persia hoping to open a factory at Hormuz. He and his fellow-merchants were seized by the Portuguese commandant as heretics and spies, and sent to Goa to stand trial; they were subsequently released. In 1008-9/1600 John Mildenhall, a London merchant, again took the overland route to Persia, and went on to India, but English attempts to open up trade with Persia by the overland route from the Levant proved no more successful than their attempts to use the sea route north of Scandinavia.

By 988-9/1581, the Portuguese had fought off a challenge to their supremacy in the Persian Gulf from the Ottomans (see Savory, *The history of the Persian Gulf*, in A.J. Cottrell (ed.), *The Persian Gulf states*, Baltimore and London 1980, 23-4), but a new challenge faced them from the merchants of the English East India Company, founded in 1008-9/1600. On 12 Ramaḍān 1024/5 October 1615, two merchants of this Company, Richard Steele and John Crowther, obtained a *farmān* from Shāh ʿAbbās I which ordered the Shāh's subjects "to kindly receive and entertaine the English Frankes or Nation, at what time any of their ships or shipping shall arrive ate Jasques (Djāsk), or any other of the Ports in our Kingdome: to conduct them and their Merchandise to what place or places they themselves desire: and that you shall see them safely defended about our Coasts, from any other Frank or Franks whatsoever" (Samuel Purchas, *Hakluytus Posthumus or Purchas his pilgrim(e)s*, 20 vols., Glasgow 1905-71, iv, 279). The following year Edward Connock arrived at Djāsk to open a factory, and was cordially received by ʿAbbās I, who granted the Company further privileges. This second *farmān* does not appear to be extant, but the gist of it is probably contained in the *farmān* of Shāh Ṣafī dated 1038/1629, which *inter alia* gave English merchants the right to buy and sell freely in Persia; moreover, the English ambassador, when appointed, was empowered to appoint agents and factors in Persia (Sir Arnold T. Wilson, *The Persian Gulf: an historical sketch from the earliest times to the beginning of the twentieth century*, Oxford 1928, 139). In 1027-8/1618 ʿAbbās I agreed not to export any silk to Spain or Portugal, or to Europe via Ottoman territory. He also promised to supply the English East India Company with a quantity of silk annually at a fixed rate, and to allow this silk to be exported from Persia free of duty. Portugal did not give up its monopoly of Persian Gulf trade without a fight, but a strong Portuguese squadron under Ruy Freyre de Andrade was defeated in two naval battles off Djāsk in Muḥarram-Rabīʿ I 1030/December-January 1621. These victories paved the way for the combined operation in 1031/1622 in which Ṣafawid troops, transported by ships of the English East India Company, dislodged the Portuguese from Hormuz.

English ascendancy was short-lived. The formation of the Dutch East India Company in 1602 signalled the determination of the Dutch to challenge both England and Portugal for control of the East Indies spice and pepper trade, and within a few years they were challenging the position of England in the Persian Gulf as well. In 1031/1622, under the terms of the agreement with ʿAbbās I, the English East India Company was to receive one-half of all customs dues levied on merchandise passing through Bandar ʿAbbās, but the Dutch refused to pay. On the accession of Ṣafī I in 1038/1629, the Dutch outmanoeuvred the English and obtained important privileges from the Shāh. They founded a factory at Bandar ʿAbbās, and rapidly established a monopoly of the spice trade between Persia and the East Indies. In 1055/1645 they obtained from ʿAbbās II a licence to buy silk anywhere in Persia and export it free of customs duty. The English, who succeeded in getting their privileges renewed by Shāh Ṣafī only in 1042/1632, were fighting a losing battle. They started to move their factory from Bandar ʿAbbās to Baṣra, but a Dutch squadron sailed to Baṣra and destroyed it. In the second half of the 11th/17th century, the Dutch reigned supreme in the Persian Gulf. The third European East India Company, the French, came late to the field (1074-5/1664), but succeeded in obtaining from ʿAbbās II trading privileges similar to those already granted to the English and Dutch, including the right to open a factory at Bandar ʿAbbās. The overthrow of the Ṣafawids in 1135/1722 and the consequent insecurity in Persia militated against the operations of European merchants there, and at the same time the growth of piracy in the Persian Gulf threatened the safety of European vessels. By 1142-3/1730, most European countries trading with Persia were operating at a loss.

(ii) *Persia's domestic and foreign trade.*

The bases of the Ṣafawid domestic economy were agriculture and pastoralism, and, as formerly under the Saldjūḳs and the Mongols, there was a dichotomy between the settled rural life of the peasants and the semi-nomadic life of the pastoralists. In addition, there was an ethnic dichotomy. The Turcoman tribes "were cattle-breeders and lived apart from the surrounding population. They migrated from winter to summer quarters. They were organised in clans and obeyed their own chieftains" (A.K.S. Lambton, *Landlord and peasant in Persia*, Oxford 1953, 106). The Persian peasants tilled the land and were subject to a system of land-tenure which had changed little since Sāsānid times.

The Ṣafawid period saw the development of a money economy and the growth of economic prosperity which reached its highest point during the reign of ʿAbbās I and declined thereafter. ʿAbbās I, by his building of roads, and even more by the construction of numerous bridges and caravanserais along the main routes, provided the infrastructure essential to the development of trade. The stationing of road-guards (*rāhdārān*) at key points, besides providing useful revenue in the form of tolls, ensured, according to the testimony of European travellers, a degree of safety and security for travellers and caravans which exceeded that obtaining in neighbouring countries. Security declined under the weak Shāhs Sulaymān and Sulṭān Ḥusayn (J. Emerson, *Ex Oriente Lux: some European sources on the economic structure of Persia between about 1630 and 1690*, Cambridge Ph.D. thesis 1969, unpubl., 218).

An important feature of the domestic economy under ʿAbbās I was the royal workshops (*buyūtāt-i khāṣṣa-yi sharīfa*), which numbered 32 at the time of Chardin and 33 in 1138-9/1726 (*Tadhkirat al-mulūk*, 30), and employed some 5,000 skilled artisans and craftsmen. This system has been criticised as "state capitalism" (Banani, Keywānī), and ʿAbbās I's policy of making the silk trade a royal monopoly is said to have stifled the entrepreneurial spirit of Persian merchants. European travellers, however, attest to the flourishing state of the bazaars in Ḳazwīn, Iṣfahān and Shīrāz, and it is doubtful whether Persian merchants could have survived European competition in the silk trade without state support. Indeed, they lacked sufficient capital to sustain trade on a large scale at all (R.W. Ferrier, *Trade from mid-14th century to the end of the Safavid period*, in *Camb. hist. Iran*, vi, 484).

Domestic trade alone could not have raised the Ṣafawid state to the level of prosperity to which ʿAbbās I aspired, and he devoted much effort to the development of international trade. In this effort, Jews and Indians played an important role as brokers, and Armenians as providers of international credit. ʿAbbās I created a new suburb of Djulfā [*q.v.* in Suppl.] at Iṣfahān, and transferred there several thousand Armenian families from Djulfā in Ādharbāydjān. They were allowed to practise their Christian faith without harassment by the state (the Shāh even made a donation toward the cost of the Armenian cathedral), and ʿAbbās I, by granting them the privilege of being represented by an Armenian mayor (*kalāntar* [*q.v.*]), made them virtually an autonomous community (again, Ottoman parallels should be borne in mind [see MILLET]. The Armenian merchants prospered, and travelled throughout Europe in pursuit of commerce. Much of their wealth derived from the silk trade, the organisation of which "must be regarded as one of ʿAbbās's great organizational achievements" (N. Steensgaard, *The Asian trade revolution of the seventeenth century*, Chicago 1973, 381). English merchants who tried to force down the Shāh's price by buying silk on the free market found themselves unable to do so (*ibid.*, 377). Persian ambassadors accredited to European capitals were customarily required to include in their baggage some bales of silk; this rule applied even to ambassadors who were Europeans. With the accession of Shāh Ṣafī (1038/1629), the royal monopoly on silk was broken, and money was diverted from the royal coffers to the pockets of Armenian merchants. For a time, Dutch merchants who, unlike the English East India Company factors, were not reluctant to co-operate with the Armenians, turned a profit by buying silk privately. In desperation, the English East India Company offered the Armenians in 1099-1100/1688 the status of "honorary Englishmen" (Ferrier, *The Armenians and the East India Company in Persia in the seventeenth and early eighteenth century*, in *Economic History Review*, 2nd series, xxi [1973], 50), but it was too late; the Armenians preferred the security of the Aleppo route, in co-operation with the Levant Company, to the hazards of the sea-route from the Persian Gulf (hostilities between the Ottomans and the Ṣafawids had militated against the use of overland routes to Mediterranean ports, but the Treaty of Zuhāb (1049/1639) ushered in a long period of peace between the two, and the overland routes once more became attractive). The English East India Company was no longer able to compete in the silk trade, and stopped buying Persian silk after 1049-50/1640 when silk prices in Europe slumped (J. Foran, *Fragile resistance: social transformation in Iran from 1500 to the Revolution*, Westview Press 1993, 65). In any case, by about 1059-60/1650 Bengal silk had become a cheaper source of supply for the East India Companies. In general, however, the patterns of trade established with Europe in the 1620s were maintained until 1722. The average value of Persia's exports in the 11th/17th century, of which silk constituted a major part, was between £ 1-2 million sterling (*ibid.*, 69). Carpets never constituted a large part of Ṣafawid exports. Carpet workshops existed at Iṣfahān, Kāshān and Kirmān, and Shāh ʿAbbās I, like his grandfather Shāh Ṭahmāsp I, was personally interested in developing the carpet-weaving industry. It was quicker, easier and cheaper for Europeans to import carpets from Turkey than from Persia during the long periods when the Ottomans and Ṣafawids were at war. Ṣafawid carpets were exported to Mug̲h̲al India, to the Portuguese colony at Goa, and to Indonesia, mostly shipped by the Dutch East India Company; some of these found their way to the Netherlands and the London market. The Ṣafawids transformed a "simple produit artisanal des régions rurales" into "art digne de la cour et des palais princiers" (Nadereh Aram-Zanganeh, *Le tapis persan aux XVIᵉ et XVIIᵉ siècles: contribution à une sociologie de l'art persan*, Lausanne 1984, 12), but the luxury carpet trade, depending as it did on royal patronage, declined after the overthrow of the Ṣafawids (see Savory, in *EIr*, art. *Carpets*. i. Introductory survey, iv, 834-9).

Both internal and external factors contributed to the decline of the Persian economy after the time of ᶜAbbās II, and by the end of the 11th/17th century the balance of trade had turned against Persia. Silk production probably declined; and Persia began to import large quantities of cloth from India for which it had to pay cash. Furthermore, the Dutch drained large quantities of gold and silver from Persia as payment for spices (Foran, 67-9). The merchants with the greatest reserves of cash were the Armenians; the royal treasury tended to hoard the best coins, and in addition Indian moneylenders and Armenian merchants tended to take the better coins out of circulation or out of the country altogether. The result was a considerable degree of debasement of the currency. Nevertheless, there was little inflationary pressure on the economy until the Afg̲h̲ān occupation in 1135/1722, when it became a significant factor. Finally, the collapse of ᶜAbbās I's multicultural state with its policy of religious tolerance caused serious harm to the economy. The increased political influence of the *ᶜulamāʾ* in the last half-century of Ṣafawid rule (the persecution of Jews under ᶜAbbās II was an earlier portent of things to come) led to persecution of Armenian and Hindu merchants and the forcible conversion of Jews and Zoroastrians to Islam. Many Zoroastrians fled to the Kirmān area, where they welcomed the Afg̲h̲āns as "liberators". From 1131-2/1719 onwards, there were uprisings among non-S̲h̲īᶜī minorities in S̲h̲īrwān, Kurdistān, K̲h̲ūzistān and Balūčistān (Foran, 75 ff.). The dynastic struggles which followed the assassination of Nādir S̲h̲āh in 1160/1747 did still further damage to the economy, and, despite some improvement in trade in Fārs under the Zands, a Select Committee appointed by the Court of Directors of the English East India Company concluded in the 1780s that "the comparison between the past and present state of Persia, in every respect, will be found truly deplorable" (see C. Issawi (ed.), *The economic history of Iran 1800-1914*, Chicago 1971, 86).

Bibliography: In order to keep the bibliography within manageable limits, it has been restricted to a few selected works which are not cited in the text. Some recent publications have also been included. The works are listed under the various topics discussed in the text. (a) *Dynastic, political, administrative and military history*. ᶜAbd al-Ḥusayn Nawāʾī, *S̲h̲āh ᶜAbbās. Madjmūᶜa-yi asnād wa mukātabāt-i tārīk̲h̲ī hamrāh bā yāddās̲h̲thā-yi tafṣīlī*, 2 vols., Tehran 1352-3 S̲h̲./1973-4; Masashi Haneda, *Le Châh et les Qizilbāš. Le système militaire safavide*, Berlin 1987; R. Matthee, *Administrative stability and change in late-17th-century Iran: the case of S̲h̲ayk̲h̲ ᶜAlī K̲h̲ān Zanganeh (1669-89)*, in *IJMES*, xxvi (1994), 77-98; H. Busse, *Untersuchungen zum Islamischen Kanzleiwesen: an hand Turkmenischer und Safawidischer Urkunden*, Cairo 1959; Mīrzā Rafīᶜā (Mīrzā Rafīᶜ al-Dīn), *Dastūr al-mulūk*, ed. Muḥammad Taḳī Dānis̲h̲-paz̲h̲ūh, in *Madjalla-yi Dānis̲h̲kada-yi Adabiyyāt-i Dānis̲h̲gāh-i Tihrān*, xv (1346 S̲h̲./1967-8), 485-504, xvi (1347 S̲h̲./1968-9), 62-93, 298-322, 416-40, 540-64; Ḳāḍī Aḥmad b. S̲h̲araf al-Dīn al-Ḥusayn al-Ḥusaynī al-Ḳummī, *K̲h̲ulāṣat al-tawārīk̲h̲*, ed. E. Eshraghi, 2 vols., Tehran 1359-63 S̲h̲./1980-4; Muḥammad Yūsuf Wāla Iṣfahānī, *K̲h̲uld-i barīn*, ed. Mīr Hās̲h̲im Muḥaddit̲h̲, Tehran 1372 S̲h̲./1993; K.M. Röhrborn, *Provinzen und Zentralgewalt Persiens im 16. und 17. Jahrhundert*, Berlin 1966; Birgitt Hoffman, *Persische Geschichte 1694-1835, erlebt, erinnert und erfunden. Das* Rustam al-Tavārīk̲h̲ *in deutscher Bearbeitung*, 2 vols., Bamberg 1986; Renate Schimkoreit, *Regesten publizierter safawidischer Herrscherurkunden: Erlass und Staatsschreiben der frühen Neuzeit Irans*, Berlin 1982. (b) *It̲h̲nā ᶜAs̲h̲arī ideology and the role of the ᶜulamāʾ in the Ṣafawid state*. S.A. Arjumand, *The Turban for the Crown*, Oxford 1988; A.K.S. Lambton, *State and government in medieval Islam*, Oxford 1981, 219-87. (c) *Ottoman-Ṣafawid relations*. Adel Allouche, *The origins and development of the Ottoman-Safavid conflict 906-962/1500-1555*, Berlin 1983; J.-L. Bacqué-Grammont, *Les Ottomans, les Safavides et leurs voisins*, Istanbul 1987. (d) *The Safawid economy*. Amin Banani, *The social and economic structure of the Persian empire in its heyday*, paper submitted to the Harvard Colloquium on Tradition and Change in the Middle East, December 1967, unpubl.; B. Fragner, *Social and internal economic affairs*, in *Camb. hist. Iran*, vi, 491-567; Mehdi Keyvani, *Artisans and guild life in the later Safawid period: contributions to the socio-economic history of Persia* (Islamkundliche Untersuchungen 65), Berlin 1982, and review by Savory in *Amer. Hist. Review*, lxxxviii/5 (1983), 1302-3.

(R.M. Savory)

III. Literature.

It is still difficult to assess properly the effects of the Ṣafawid conquest on the cultural life of Persia. There can be no doubt about the importance of the Ṣafawid period to the history of Persian art. During the first half of the 16th century, the arts of the book flourished like never before. Calligraphy and book-painting benefited greatly from the patronage of the ruling dynasty and there was an equal interest in architecture, exemplified in particular by the magnificent buildings which were erected in Iṣfahān in the course of the 17th century. Philosophy also reached a high point of development in the works of Mullā Ṣadr al-Dīn al-S̲h̲īrāzī [*q.v.*] and other members of his school. Literature, however, fared less well, according to a generally held view. The founding of the Ṣafawid state, with all its momentous consequences for the social structure of the country and its religious life, allegedly brought the golden age of Persian literature to an end. From there on, a time of decline set in, which was not only poor in new heights of literary art but actually led to stagnation and a deterioration of style.

One of the factors which helped to create this negative view on Ṣafawid literature was the change of literary taste in Persia which occurred about the middle of the 18th century, shortly after the Ṣafawid period had come to a close. This brought about a strong condemnation of the excesses to which the Indian style [see SABK-I HINDĪ] in Persian poetry had led and a "return" (*bāzgas̲h̲t*) to the standards of earlier styles. As a result, a neo-classicist view of post-Tīmūrid literature was established which not only left its mark on Persian literary criticism until the present day, but also had a great impact on evaluations by Western scholars. Only recently a more positive appreciation of the Indian style is emerging. This seems however not yet to have led to a proper distinction between Ṣafawid literature and the Indian style, notwithstanding the fact that the latter did not have an effect on the poets of Persia until the second half of the rule of the Ṣafawids (see, for instance, E. Yarshater's essay *The Indian or Ṣafavid style: progress or decline?*). As a matter of fact, the 16th century constitutes a separate chapter in the history of Persian literature. The *tadhkira* writers of the period provide us with a lively picture of the literary scene in Ṣafawid Persia which is marked by a series of innovations quite distinct from those which later on became characteristic of the Indian style. Valuable collections of material on this period are available now in the works of Dh. Ṣafā and A. Gulčīn-i Maʿānī.

Furthermore, the impact on literature of the religious revolution brought about by the Ṣafawids tends to be overrated. The active support of the dynasty to the spread of Shīʿism in a country which was still overwhelmingly Sunnī, was even said to have caused a "Shiʿite standardisation of literature" (Rypka, 292). The well-known injunction of Shāh Ṭahmāsp I to the poet Muḥtasham [*q.v.*], to celebrate the Family of the Prophet in his poems rather than praise the secular ruler, is often quoted out of context. It has been given the significance of a radical turn from the traditions of court patronage by the Ṣafawid dynasty as a whole, whereas it probably only points to a personal change of heart of one monarch, which temporarily brought to an end a period of exceptionally lavish patronage to the arts during the first half of the 16th century. It is, on the other hand, evident that a very substantial part of the poems and prose works produced in this period could be labelled either secular or mystical, but do not carry specifically Shīʿī characteristics.

The Ṣafawids, both the shāhs and the other members of the royal house, were well-educated and often participated personally in artistic and literary pursuits. Already Ismāʿīl I (reigned 907-30/1501-24) resumed the traditional function of royal patronage, which had been fulfilled so brilliantly by two of his predecessors in the late 9th/15th century: the Tīmūrid Ḥusayn Baykārā (d. 912/1506) at Harāt and the Aḳ-Ḳoyunlu sultan Yaʿḳūb (d. 896/1490) at Tabrīz. In 917/1511, during his campaign in Khurāsān, Ismāʿīl took the time for a visit to Djām, where the aged poet Hātifī [*q.v.*] lived, to ask him to celebrate the Ṣafawid victory with an historical epic on the lines of his famous *Ẓafar-nāma* on the life of Tīmūr Lang. Although this poem remained unfinished, it set an example for similar *mathnawīs* in the heroic style of the *Shāh-nāma* written later on for the Ṣafawid Shāhs. Poems of this kind were composed, for instance, by Ḳāsimī Gunābādī (d. 982/1574?) for Ismāʿīl and Ṭahmāsp. The same poet also wrote a *Kār-nāma* on the former Shāh's performance as a polo player. The *ghazal* poet Ṣāʾib [*q.v.*] celebrated ʿAbbās II's conquest of Ḳandahār in 1059/1649-50 in an *ʿAbbās-nāma* (cf. Rieu, ii, 694).

Such martial panegyrics did not exhaust Ismāʿīl's interest in literature. Ahlī of Shīrāz (d. 942/1535), who had been a distinguished poet of the Aḳ-Ḳoyunlu, dedicated to him the romantic poem *Siḥr-i ḥalāl*, a work of great rhetorical artistry. Other officials and courtiers joined in this patronage, notably Ismāʿīl's *wakīl* Yār Aḥmad Khūzānī, better known as Nadjm-i Thānī (d. 918/1512). Among the poets attached to Ismāʿīl's court were Ummīdī (d. 925/1519 or 930/1523-4), who left a small number of panegyrics and religious *ḳaṣīdas*, Lisānī (d. 940/1533-4) and Wāḥidī (d. 942/1535). The Shāh himself, under the pen name Khaṭāʾī [see ISMĀʿĪL I. 2], wrote Turkish poetry, remarkable for its daring statements of extreme *ḳizilbāsh* doctrines.

More conspicuous yet was the interest Ṭahmāsp I (930-84/1524-76) took in literature and the arts during the first twenty years of his reign. His patronage was matched by the *wakīl* Ḳāḍī Djihān and the Shāh's brother Sām Mīrzā (923-74/1517-67 [*q.v.*]). The latter left the most valuable record of early Ṣafawid literature in a *tadhkira* entitled *Tuḥfa-yi Sāmī*. Prominent among the many court poets of his reign were the *wakīl*'s son Sharaf Djihān (d. 968/1560), the satirist Ḥayratī (d. 961/1553), Ḍamīrī (d. after 985/1578), and ʿAbdī Bēg Nawīdī (d. 988/1580). After Ṭahmāsp lost his interest in patronage, about 951/1544-5, the support of the central court to literature remained drastically reduced for several decades. This attitude had two noticeable consequences: the aforementioned emphasis on religious poetry, as exemplified in the works of Muḥtasham (d. 996/1587), and the beginning of the exodus of poets and artists to Indian courts.

This emigration of literary talent, in which also many artists and scholars took part, began in the late 16th century and continued up to the reign of the Mughal Emperor Awrangzīb (1068-1118/1658-1707), should be seen against the background of the internationalisation of Persian civilisation, which reached its height during this period. This phenomenon encompassed most of the Islamic lands in Asia, in particular the Indian subcontinent, Uzbek Central Asia and the Ottoman Empire, but India was by far the most important. A great demand for poets from Persia arose which could not be matched by the often wavering patronage of the Ṣafawids. As it appears from biographical sources, the motivations to travel to India were quite varied. Ghazālī of Mashhad (d. in Gudjārāt 980/1572), one of the first to leave Persia, fled from Shīrāz after he had been accused of heresy (*ilḥād*). Others had run into difficulties with their patrons at home, or were allured by the prospect of fame and riches to be won at the Indian courts.

Patronage in Ṣafawid Persia was not restricted to the court of the Shāh. Especially during the first century of Ṣafawid rule, the courts of provincial governors, usually also members of the royal house, made a significant contribution. At Hamādān, Ṭahmāsp's brother Bahrām Shāh supported his own circle of poets, whereas Mashhad unter the rule of the latter's son Ibrāhīm Mīrzā (964-76/1556-68) gained renown as an artistic centre compensating, temporarily at least, for the lack of interest at the Shāh's court. Here poets like Thanāʾī (d. Lahore 995 or 996/1586), Maylī of Harāt (d. in India 984/1576) and Walī Dasht-Bayāḍī (d. 1001/1592-3) flourished, as well as some of the most important painters and calligraphers. The more remote provincial court at Yazd under Mīr-Mīrān Ghiyāth al-Dīn patronised the poet Waḥshī [*q.v.*] of Bāfḳ (d. 991/1583). Outside the courts other cities were the scene of a lively pursuit of letters, e.g. Shīrāz, where ʿUrfī [*q.v.*] (d. in India 999/1590-1) spent his early years, and Kāshān, the hometown of Muḥtasham. It was not unusual for poets to stay away from the court while still writing panegyrics for the rulers. From Baghdād, Fuḍūlī (d. 970/1562-3 or 963/1556 [*q.v.*]), who is best known for his poems in Azeri Turkish, paid homage to the Ṣafawids until that city was taken over by the Ottomans. Muḥtasham sent his poems to Indian courts but never travelled there himself. Increasingly, it seems, poetry began to become a private matter, as for instance in the case of

Saḥābī of Astarābād (d. 1010/1601-2 [*q.v.*]), the master of the *rubāʿī* of this period, who lived for many years as a recluse near the shrine of Nadjaf.

Up to a certain extent, court poetry revived under ʿAbbās I (996-1038/1588-1629), first at Ḳazwīn, and since 1598 at Iṣfahān. The position of a *malik al-shuʿarāʾ* [*q.v.*] was filled by Ruknā Masīḥ (d. 1066/1655 or 1070/1659-60), and then by Shifāʾī (d. 1037/1627). They both also served the Shāh as physicians. In 1006/1597 Masīḥ went to India after he had been accused of giving too little attention to his patron's health. Discontent with the situation of the poets at the court of Iṣfahān was expressed by Kawtharī of Hamadān (d. after 1015/1606) when in a poem dedicated to Shāh ʿAbbās he made a reference to the lavish patronage offered at the courts of India (ʿAbdu'l Ghani, ii, 168-71). On the other hand, it is reported that the poet Shānī received his weight in gold as a reward for a single felicitous line in honour of the Imām ʿAlī (*ibid.*, ii, 163). Among the poets at ʿAbbās' court were further Fārigh (*fl. ca.* 1000/1591), Kamālī (d. 1020/1611-2), and Zulālī of Khʷānsār (d. 1024/1615).

A last period of great literary activity at the court of Iṣfahān were the reigns of Ṣafī I (1038-52/1629-42) and ʿAbbās's II (1052-77/1642-66). This was the time of Djalāl al-Dīn Asīr [*q.v.*] (d. 1049/1639-40), Ḳudsī (d. 1056/1646-7), Amānī of Māzandarān (d. 1061/1651) and Faṣīḥī (d. *ca.* 1080/1670), but above all of Ṣāʾib (d. 1088/1677-8 [*q.v.*]), the greatest poet of Ṣafawid literature.

The *ghazal* continued to be the principal poetic form, but the poets of the 16th century tried to renew its rather soulless and abstract features by developing a new style called already by contemporary writers *wuḳūʿ-gūʾī* or *zabān-i wuḳūʿ*. By this they meant the fashion to introduce references to actual experiences of love and incidents occurring in the relationship of lovers and their beloveds. Although the motives they used were usually conventional (most of them belonged to the tradition of *taghazzul* from the earliest period onwards), they succeeded in creating an elegant lyricism, written in a simple language, often close to everyday speech, and an unadorned style. Bābā Fighānī [*q.v.*] is frequently mentioned as a predecessor of his trend, one of the earliest representatives of which was Sharīf Djihān. The *wuḳūʿ* style generated a number of subsidiary genres, like the one called *wā-sūkht*, the theme of which was the lover's turning away from the beloved (cf. Gulčīn-i Maʿānī, *Wuḳūʿ*, 681-8), and *ḳaḍā wa ḳadar*, on erotic incidents which exhibit the workings of fate. Towards the end of the 16th century, a much more ingenious idiom began to develop: it was characterised by the search for new and unusual imagery and a sophisticated use of the traditional motifs. In the 17th century, Ṣāʾib brought the *ghazal* back to a more abstract level, without adding much to its stock of themes and motives. Recently, his poetry, marked by the frequent use of proverbial illustration (*irsāl-i mathal*), has been revalued by Persian critics as an acceptable form of the Indian style, to which the term "style of Iṣfahān" is applied.

The *ḳaṣīda* was still occasionally used for courtly panegyrics, but far more often as a medium for *manḳabat* poetry, i.e. hymns praising the Prophet and the Imāms. Stanzaic poems became extremely popular for Shīʿī elegies, like the famous *dawāzdah-band* of Muḥtasham. As a secular form of love poetry, expanded patterns known as *musaddas* and *murabbaʿ* were put into currency, especially by Waḥshī; some of these poems have survived as popular songs.

Mystical *rubāʿīs* were written in great numbers, as is evident from the anthologies compiled in this period. Intricate rhetorical artifices, which had come into fashion already during the Tīmūrid period, continued to be used in topical quatrains, especially in chronograms. The quatrain was also frequently used for poems featuring young craftsmen, known as *shahrangīz* [*q.v.*] or *shahrāshūb*. This genre was introduced at the court of Ṭahmāsp by Lisānī and Wāḥidī.

Many poets attempted to compose a *khamsa* [*q.v.*] after Niẓāmī's example, or even a *sabʿa* on the lines of Djāmī [*q.v.*]. Various new subjects for narrative poetry were introduced: they were either taken from ancient lore (eg. the love between Sultan Maḥmūd and his slave Ayāz), or they were newly invented as allegories. Outstanding *mathnawī* poets were ʿAbdī Bēg Nawīdī, who also wrote a work in imitation of Saʿdī's *Būstān*, Zulālī, whose *Maḥmūd wa Ayāz* became very popular, and Shifāʾī, the author of *Namakdān-i ḥaḳīḳat*, in the style of Sanāʾī. Short *mathnawīs* usually dealt with themes related to the *wuḳūʿ-gūʾī* as it was fashionable in *ghazals*. Most court poets produced a *Sāḳī-nāma*, based on motives derived from anacreontic verse, which could be either devoted to panegyrics or to mysticism.

Among the prose works written in Ṣafawid Persia, the *tadhkiras* took a prominent place. They were written according to the principles of this genre, which had been established in the late Tīmūrid period by Dawlatshāh and ʿAlī Shīr Nawāʾī [*q.vv.*]. The latter's work provided the model for *Madjmaʿ al-khawāṣṣ*, written in Čaghatāy Turkish by the painter and poet Ṣādiḳī Bēg [see further MUKHTĀRĀT. 2. In Persian literature]. The *tadhkiras* are also valuable sources of critical judgments on contemporary poetry. Among the historical works written under the Ṣafawids, Ḥasan Bēg Rūmlū's *Aḥsan al-tawārīkh* (985/1577) and Iskandar Munshī's [*q.v.*] *Taʾrīkh-i ʿālamārā-yi ʿAbbāsī* (1038/1628-9) deserve special mention. The *Tadhkira-yi Shāh Ṭahmāsp* is a contribution to historiography made by the Shāh himself on the basis of a speech delivered to Ottoman ambassadors at his court in 969/1562. In the religious sciences, including the flourishing school of Shīʿī philosophy, Arabic remained the common linguistic medium. However, several remarkable works were written in Persian as well, e.g. the *Djāmiʿ-i ʿAbbāsī* by Bahāʾ al-Dīn ʿĀmilī [*q.v.*], on religious law and various related subjects, and the theological treatise *Gawhar-i murād* by ʿMullā ʿAbd al-Razzāk Lāhīdjī [*q.v.*], one of the pupils of Mullā Ṣadrā, and a long series of theological writings by Muḥammad Bāḳir Madjlisī-yi Thānī [*q.v.*].

Persian literature of the Ṣafawid period has been dealt with also elsewhere in this Encyclopaedia: see Vol. IV, ĪRĀN. vii—Literature, 68a-69b, and, as far as contemporaneous Indo-Persian literature is concerned, Vol. VII, MUGHALS. 10. Literature, 340b-344a; on the most important stylistic trend of the period [see SABK-I HINDĪ].

Bibliography: E.G. Browne, *LHP*, iv, 161-77; Muhammad ʿAbdu'l Ghani, *A history of Persian language and literature at the Mughal court*, i-ii, Allahabad 1929; J. Rypka, *History of Iranian literature*, Dordrecht 1968, 291-304; Aḥmad Gulčīn-i Maʿānī, *Maktab-i wuḳūʿ dar shiʿr-i fārsī*, Tehrān 1348 Sh./1969-70; A. Welch, *Artists for the Shah*, New Haven-London 1976; Sh. Kadkanī, *The Safavid period*, in G. Morrison (ed.), *History of Persian literature*, H. der Or. Leiden-Köln 1981, 145-65; Dh. Ṣafā, *Tārīkh-i adabiyyāt dar Īrān*, v/1-2, Tehran 1363/1984, esp. 635-1420 (a list of 126 poets from this period, including poets at Indian courts); idem,

Persian literature in the Safavid period, in *Cambridge history of Iran*, vi, Cambridge 1986, 948-64; Ehsan Yarshater, *Persian poetry in the Timurid and Safavid periods*, in *ibid.*, 965-94; idem, *The Indian or Safavid style*, in E. Yarshater (ed.), *Persian literature*, Albany 1988, 249-88. (J.T.P. DE BRUIJN)

IV. Religion, philosophy and science.

As for all pre-modern societies so Ṣafawid-period developments in both "high"/"élite" and "low"/"popular" religious discourse, philosophical inquiry and certain areas of scientific theory and practice are most usefully understood in terms of the association of their practitioners with the patronage, 'lines of interest', links or influence of different segments of society. Because of a continuity with immediately preceding social formations, developments in the discourses of these disciplines tended to be enriched and enhanced rather than to suffer breaks with the pre-Ṣafawid heritage. More often than not the written legacy of these disciplines is dominated by the producers of "high"/"élite" discourse, i.e. the literate few, usually protégés of the socio-economic and political élite. So limited was their number that the same few names frequently appear as practitioners in different disciplines. "Popular" expression in these disciplines is also visible in this period, however, in the religious and medical realms in particular. Indeed, such was the extent of "popular" antipathy of various non-élite, social groups to some "high"/"élite" practitioners and their sponsors among the political and socio-economic élite, that only the continuous support of the latter insured the survival, if not the triumph, of their protégés and their contributions in their own time sufficient to provide some legacy for the future.

I. *Religious trends*

The importance of such links of association and the extent of "popular" animosity toward élite practitioners and their court patrons is particularly evident in the religious discourse of the period.

There had been Sẖīʿī communities scattered throughout Persia since the disappearance of the Twelfth Imām in 260/873-4. The establishment of Twelver Sẖīʿism by Sẖāh Ismāʿīl I [*q.v.*] in 907/1501-2, at the Ṣafawid capture of Tabrīz, portended a repeat of the short-lived conversion to the faith of the Il-Kẖānid Sultan Öldjeytu (d. 716/1316 [*q.v.*]) an "event" which must later have appeared to stem more from *Realpolitik* than from genuine conviction. Indeed, in the first century of the Ṣafawids, the court's identification with, and efforts to patronise and promulgate, the faith met with limited success in Ṣafawid territory and won little credibility within the Twelver community itself and, in fact, exacerbated existing differences between and among the Akẖbāriyya and the Uṣūliyya [*q.vv.*]

Ismāʿīl's interest in the faith had no basis in the history of the Ṣafawid Ṣūfī order. Initially, the order had comprised mainly Sẖāfiʿī Sunnīs, had maintained an attitude of political quietism and had claimed no special relationship to any member of the Prophet's family [see 1. above]. Following an influx of peasants and tribal nomads the order became a militantly messianic movement under Sẖaykh Ḥaydar (d. 851/1447) and Sẖaykh Djunayd (d. 893/1488) [*q.vv.*]. During Ismāʿīl's reign members of the Ḳizil-Bāsẖ [*q.v.*] élite evinced little interest in the details of the doctrines and practices of the newly established faith. Ṣafawid religious discourse simply appended extremist Twelver interpretations to similarly radical representations of other religious traditions in order to

legitimise the divine nature of the ruler and his mission: Ismāʿīl depicted himself variously as "Jesus, son of Mary", various pre-Islamic Persian epic figures, as well as *al-imām al-ʿādil al-kāmil* ("the just, the perfect Imām", the latter title being a reference both to a just secular ruler and, in Twelver terminology, to the Hidden Imām himself. Such allusions encouraged the reverence among the lower-ranking Ḳizil-Bāsẖ warriors required to fuel the constant struggle against such of the order's enemies as the Sunnī Özbegs and Ottomans, rival Sẖīʿī elements such as the Musẖaʿsẖaʿ [*q.v.*], and, throughout the period, competing Ṣūfī messianic movements, whose social origins and religious inclinations often approximated those of the Ṣafawids (Newman, *The myth*, 68-76).

If the Ṣafawids' commitment to orthodox Twelver Sẖīʿism seemed problematic, so was the existence of the Ṣafawid polity itself. The constant wars between the Ḳizil-Bāsẖ and their opponents and the Ṣafawids' repeated losses of territory to both the Özbegs and the Ottomans throughout this period, only underscored the fragility of the Ṣafawid experiment.

For Arab Twelver clerics resident outside Ṣafawid territory, a special, additional source of aggravation was the open association with and services rendered to Ṣafawid Sẖīʿism by ʿAlī b. al-Ḥusayn al-Karakī (d. 940/1534 [*q.v.*]) beginning soon after Ismāʿīl's profession of faith, as well as the compensation for these which al-Karakī received in land and cash.

In the Djabal ʿĀmil region of Lebanon, both well-established and such younger scholars as Sẖaykh Zayn al-Dīn b. ʿAlī, called al-Sẖahīd al-Thānī (the second martyr) (d. 965/1557), and his student and associate al-Ḥusayn b. ʿAbd al-Ṣamad (d. 984/1576) expressed their disapproval of Ṣafawid Sẖīʿism and of al-Karakī by shunning all Ṣafawid entanglements and territory, even though both al-Karakī and Sẖaykh Zayn al-Dīn were proponents of the Uṣūliyya tendency within Twelver Sẖīʿism.

By this period, owing expecially to the contributions of such scholars as Djaʿfar b. al-Ḥasan al-Muḥaḳḳiḳ al-Ḥillī (d. 676/1277) and al-Ḥasan b. Yūsuf al-ʿAllāma al-Ḥillī (d. 726/1325) [*q.vv.*] who had "converted" Öldjeytu, the Uṣūliyya had stressed the application of subjective disciplines and rationalist principles—including *idjtihād* [*q.v.*]—to the Twelver-accepted revelation, and the authorisation of *al-faḳīh al-djāmiʿ li-sẖarāʾiṭ al-iftāʾ* ("the legist whose study of those disciplines and principles permitted him to issue a *fatwā*") to undertake in the period of occultation (*gẖayba* [*q.v.*]) many practical activities reserved for the Imām during his presence, based on the Imām's designation of the *faḳīh* as his *nāʾib* (deputy). The Uṣūliyya also divided the community into the unschooled *ʿāmmī* (lay believer) and the *mudjtahid* [*q.v.*], requiring the former to practice *taḳlīd* [*q.v.*] of the latter's legal ruling and accept his authority over other matters of doctrine and practice within the community. In addition, the Uṣūliyya permitted the *faḳīh* a wide scope of interaction with the secular political establishment, especially insofar it might protect or further the interests of the community. Al-Karakī initially argued that his involvement with the court was permitted by virtue of his being *nāʾib* to *al-imām al-ʿādil*, an implicit acceptance of Ismāʿīl's claims to the imāmate. Criticised on this point, al-Karakī advanced the concept of *niyāba ʿāmma* ("general delegation of the Imām's authority"), identified *al-faḳīh al-djāmiʿ li ʾl-sẖarāʾiṭ* as *nāʾib ʿāmm* ("general deputy") of the Imām, and justified his involvement with the court as that permitted between the *nāʾib ʿāmm/faḳīh* and *al-djāʾir* (the tyrannous ruler) as leader of a non-Twelver political institution.

The open criticism of al-Karakī's association with the court by such clerics from the Gulf and the Shīʿī shrine cities in Arab ʿIrāḳ as Ibrāhīm b. Sulaymān al-Ḳaṭīfī (d. after 945/1539) pointed to the presence of anti-Uṣūlī, Akhbārī-style polemic in the community during the first Ṣafawid century. In exchanges with al-Karakī, al-Ḳaṭīfī, for example, promoted the definition of *al-djāʾir* of such earlier Akhbārīs as Muḥammad b. ʿAlī, al-Shaykh al-Ṣadūḳ (d. 381/991-2 [see IBN BĀBAWAYH]), as a false claimant to the imāmate—implicitly denouncing Ismāʿīl as such—and rejected the *niyāba* of the *faḳīh* and thereby the latter's role in such practical activities as the collection and distribution of *zakāt* and the leadership of Friday prayer. Where al-Karakī's support derived primarily from the court, elements of al-Ḳaṭīfī's critique clearly enjoyed the support of both certain Arab ʿIrāḳī Twelver clerics and of the local poor and artisanal sections of the ʿIrāḳī Shīʿa. The resentment of these "popular" classes derived at least partly from their having been taxed to pay for a tour of the area by Ismāʿīl, accompanied by al-Karakī, after the Ṣafawids' capture of Baghdād in 914/1508.

The widespread censure of al-Karakī forced his permanent relocation to the court. There the intra-Ḳizil-Bāsh civil war following Ismāʿīl's death encouraged factions at court to support the challenge of several Persian clerics and the *ṣadr* Niʿmat Allāh al-Ḥillī (d. 940/1533)—a student of al-Karakī and the first genuine Twelver cleric to hold the post—to the latter's ruling that the *faḳīh/nāʾib* might lead the Friday prayer, a challenge also supported by al-Ḳaṭīfī. Al-Ḥillī's co-*ṣadr* Ghiyāth al-Dīn Manṣūr b. Muḥammad al-Dashtakī (d. 948/1541) criticised specific instances of al-Karakī's exercise of power (see also below, subsections II and III. ii. on philosophy and astronomy).

Al-Karakī's triumph in these contests—al-Ḥillī was banished, al-Ḳaṭīfī admonished, al-Dashtakī dismissed, another student of al-Karakī was appointed *ṣadr*, and in 939/1532 a *firmān* was issued declaring al-Karakī *nāʾib al-Imām* and granting him authority over the polity's religious affairs and the faith's propagation—was, however, more apparent than real. Court support for al-Karakī owed more to the efforts of the ascendant Shamlū to hand over responsibility for the spiritual sphere to a cleric of proven loyalty, freeing themselves to consolidate their own position at the centre of the Ḳizil-Bāsh coalition; indeed, given the terminology of the *firmān*, al-Karakī was perhaps directed to compose the *firmān* himself. Beyond lip-service, the political élite paid little interest to the faith. Moreover, the *firmān*'s charge to al-Karakī to further promulgate the faith within the realm suggested that Twelver Shīʿism had failed to expand significantly the number of its adherents in Ṣafawid territory.

Indeed, internal and external forces opposed to al-Karakī, if not also Ṣafawid Shīʿism itself, only flourished. The former, as represented by al-Ḥillī, continued to grow stronger in such a way that, although a student of al-Karakī became *ṣadr* sometime after al-Karakī's death, Friday prayer services were discontinued in Ṣafawid territory. Within the larger Twelver community regionally, al-Ḳaṭīfī's sniping persisted, as did the Lebanese clerics' open boycott of Ṣafawid Shīʿism and disavowal of al-Karakī's association therewith. These clerics experienced little harassment from Sunnī Ottoman authorities. Zayn al-Dīn's sudden execution by the Ottomans in 965/1557—at which al-Ḥusayn fled to Ṣafawid territory with his young son, Shaykh Bahāʾī (d. 1030/1621) al-ʿĀmilī [*q.v.*, and see below, subsections II and III]—failed to spark any mass migration of Arab Twelver clerics from Ottoman to Ṣafawid territory. Al-Ḥusayn himself, though he accepted court positions and remuneration, later left Ṣafawid territory and disavowed his own Ṣafawid associations.

The continuing losses by the Ṣafawids of substantial territories to the Ottomans, beginning a year after al-Karakī's death in 941/1534 (including Baghdād and the shrine cities), the 962/1555 treaty formalising those losses, the chaos that further shook the "empire" at the death of Ṭahmāsp, and the effort to re-establish Sunnism under Ismāʿīl II (984/1576-7 [*q.v.*]) only pointed to the imminent demise of the Ṣafawid experiment and underlined the precarious position of the faith in Ṣafawid hands. Indeed, pockets of Persian Sunnism, e.g. in Ḳazwīn, remained viable over the entire period.

Prominent Twelver Uṣūlī scholars continued their boycott of Ṣafawid Shīʿism in the latter part of the century. Neither Zayn al-Dīn's son al-Ḥasan (d. 1011/1602-3), aged seven at his father's death, or his relative and associate Sayyid Muḥammad b. ʿAlī (d. 1009/1600)—authors of the important *Maʿālim al-dīn* and *Madārik al-aḥkām* respectively—were removed from Ottoman territory. Both studied with al-Ḥusayn b. ʿAbd al-Ṣamad in the Lebanon and in ʿIrāḳ with the Persian clerics ʿAbd Allāh al-Yazdī (d. 981/1573) and Aḥmad b. Muḥammad al-Ardabīlī (d. 993/1585, author of the influential *Madjmaʿ al-fāʾida* and *Zubdat al-bayān*), both of whom had abandoned Ṣafawid territory. Both also later forsook plans for a pilgrimage to Mashhad for fear ʿAbbās I [*q.v.*] would press them into his service.

The existence of significant Twelver communities located at and around the shrine cities of ʿIrāḳ, as well as the Gulf and the Lebanon, as alternative points of focus and independent bases for the community, facilitated both the Uṣūlī and Akhbārī critiques of Ṣafawid Shīʿism in general and the manner in which al-Karakī had cast his lot with Ṣafawid Shīʿism in particular.

In the 11th/17th century, however, in a gradually improving politico-military atmosphere, the patronage of the court and the Ṣafawid political and socio-economic élite was directed to the establishment of Twelver centres in Persia. The development of these as alternatives to the educational centres and shrines located in Ottoman territory, especially those of ʿIrāḳ—captured in 1033/1623-4 but lost to the Ottomans in 1048/1638 and never retaken—and Mecca and Medina, complemented Ṣafawid efforts to develop Persian centres of commerce and trade and stem the outflow of precious metals. Attention to economic considerations grew with rising expenditures and falling revenues over the century, particularly after the accession of ʿAbbās II in 1052/1642 (Matthee, *Politics and trade*, esp. 218-77, and 239, citing the 17th-century account of Tavernier; idem, *The career of Mohammed Beg*).

ʿAbbās I designated Iṣfahān as the new Ṣafawid capital and he, later shāhs, and associates of the court, made important additions to older buildings and founded new mosques and schools in the city; by late in the century, it contained more than 150 mosques and 48 religious schools. The court and its associates also contributed directly to the enhancement of Ḳum [*q.v.*], location of the tomb of Fāṭima, sister of the eighth Imām, as an educational centre and pilgrimage site; later shāhs were buried in precincts adjacent to the shrine itself. ʿAbbās I's famous walk from Iṣfahān to Mashhad, burial place of the eighth Imām, typified efforts made to enhance the fame of that city and its shrine.

Many individual clerics were often direct recipients of the patronage which these programmes involved. As part of his massive building programme in Iṣfahān, ʿAbbās built a school for ʿAbd Allāh al-Shushtarī (d. 1021/1612-13), who had come to Persia from Nadjaf, where he had studied with al-Ardabīlī. ʿAbbās built a mosque for Luṭf Allāh al-Maysī (d. 1032/1622-3), grandson of a Lebanese cleric who had avoided the court. Shaykh Bahāʾī, who had served as *Shaykh al-Islām* in Harāt and composed his *Zubdat al-uṣūl*, an important work of Uṣūlī jurisprudence, was appointed to the same post in Iṣfahān, took an active role in the capital's building programme and also undertook domestic political missions for ʿAbbās, managing the shāh's constitution of his estates as *wakf*.

As these clerics' close connection with the court paralleled that of al-Karakī, so many observed and built on his Uṣūlī pronouncements. All staunchly supported the conduct of Friday prayer service during the occultation, for example. Mīr Dāmād (d. 1040/1630-1 [see AL-DĀMĀD and below, subsections II and III. i])—whose father was son-in-law to al-Karakī, and who had studied under students of al-Shahīd al-Thānī, including the father of Shaykh Bahāʾī, and was a close associate of the courts of both ʿAbbās I and Ṣafī—using the concept of general delegation of authority, stated that the individual in possession of *al-niyāba al-ʿāmma* was to lead that prayer, and defined the latter as the *mudjtahid/faḳīh* who had attained *sharāʾiṭ al-iftāʾ*. Shaykh Bahāʾī supported an active role for the *faḳīh* in the collection and distribution of the *zakāt* and *khums*, following similar rulings by earlier Uṣūlī clerics. Their court connections affirmed these clerics' concomitant endorsement of the *faḳīh*'s associating with the established political institution, and legitimised the court's claim to a special, indeed exclusive, relationship with the faith itself.

These Persian centres and clerics increasingly became a focus for the region's Twelver community, attracting both Persian and Arab students and producing many of the most prominent scholars of the later 11th/17th century. Thus among Shaykh Bahāʾī's students were Ṣadr al-Dīn Muḥammad al-Shīrāzī (d. 1050/1640 [see MULLĀ ṢADRĀ, and also below]), Muḥammad Taḳī al-Madjlisī (d. 1070/1659 [*q.v.*]), Muḥammad Bāḳir al-Sabzawārī (d. 1090/1679), Muḥsin Fayḍ al-Kāshānī (d. 1091/1680 [*q.v.* and see below, subsections II and III. i]) and Mīrzā Rāfiʿ al-Dīn Nāʾinī (d. 1099/1688). Many of this generation of scholars also both supported, and enjoyed good relations with, the court and approved of the expanded role of the *faḳīh* during the occultation. Thus Sabzawārī—a proponent of *al-niyāba al-ʿāmma* and teacher at al-Shushtarī's school—officiated at, and Nāʾinī attended, the *djulūs* or accession ceremony of Shāh Sulayman. Muḥammad Taḳī al-Madjlisī was Friday prayer leader in Iṣfahān and his son the noted cleric Muḥammad Bāḳir (d. 1111/1699), following in the footsteps of his father's teacher Shaykh Bahāʾī, was appointed the capital's *Shaykh al-Islām* by Shāh Sulaymān; his famous, massive *ḥadīth* compilation, the *Biḥār al-anwār*, was assembled with court assistance (Kohlberg, *Beḥār al-Anwār*). Like the Madjlisī family, which included such later eminent Uṣūlī scholars as Muḥammad Bāḳir b. Muḥammad Akmal al-Bihbahānī, al-Waḥīd (d. 1205/1791 [*q.v.*]), the Marʿashī [*q.v.*] family, forebearers of the present-day Marʿashī-Nadjafī family, also had important court connections in this period. These included marriage with the family of ʿAbbās I, appointment to the position of *ṣadr*, and the designation by ʿAbbās II of one of their number, Khalīfa Sulṭān (d. 1065/1655), himself a noted cleric, to the vizierate.

The relations between this second-generation of Persian-based Twelver clerics and the court continued to legitimise the Ṣafawid's public, and exclusive, claim to a special association with the faith, although these claims were expressed in less extreme terms than in the previous century. Muḥammad Bāḳir al-Madjlisī, for example, in an essay reflective of the continued, but more restrained, nature of this affiliation, argued that Ismāʿīl's appearance portended the impending re-appearance of the Mahdī himself (Babayan, *The waning*, 182-5, 189-91). The same clerics were also actively involved in the domestic propagation of the faith. Al-Shushtarī's school was built in the heart of the bazaar, for example. Fayḍ al-Kāshānī, his associate and friend Muḥammad Taḳī al-Madjlisī, and his son Muḥammad Bāḳir, were among those who wrote numerous Persian-language tracts on the most basic doctrines and practices of the faith.

As the faith established and broadened its foothold in the country, so the disputes over matters of doctrine and practice, and the relation between the clergy and the state, found expression in Ṣafawid territory as well. The Uṣūliyya/Akhbāriyya dispute, which turned on this combination of arguments, was given new life in Persia following the accession of ʿAbbās I with the open association of such of the Uṣūlīs as Shaykh Bahāʾī and Mīr Dāmād with the court. By later in the century, the dispute had flourished to such an extent that among the ever-larger number of Twelver clerics resident in Persia factions within each tendency became discrete. Extreme Uṣūlīs asserted the falseness of the Ṣafawid association with the faith, and argued for direct clerical rule. The Uṣūlīs and the moderate Akhbārīs (*mudjtahid-muḥaddith*), however, agreed on the authority of the *faḳīh* as *djāmiʿ sharāʾiṭ al-idjtihād* over matters of doctrine and practice and permission for him to interact with the established political institution. This latter group included Muḥammad Amīn al-Astarābādī (d. 1030/1640) (often identified as the "founder" of the Akhbārī school, see Kohlberg, *Astarabadi*) and such higher-ranking, court-connected scholars at Iṣfahān and provincial centres as Muḥammad Taḳī al-Madjlisī, Khalīl al-Ḳazwīnī (d. 1088/1677), Fayḍ al-Kāshānī, Muḥammad Ṭāhir b. Muḥammad Ḥusayn al-Shīrāzī al-Ḳummī (d. 1098/1687, and *Shaykh al-Islām* in Ḳum during the reign of Shāh Sulaymān) and Muḥammad b. al-Ḥasan al-Ḥurr al-ʿĀmilī (d. 1104/1693 [*q.v.*]) (who came to Persia, settled in Mashhad, and was there appointed *Shaykh al-Islām*.

By contrast, the radical Akhbārīs (*muḥaddith*) were particularly a force in the provincial and smaller centres of the faith inside Ṣafawid Persia, such as Mashhad, and peripheral regions outside Ṣafawid territory, where they were more likely strong among lower-ranking urban clerics and recent immigrants to the cities. Unschooled in, and rejecting the validity of recourse to the rationalist legal sciences, these clerics relied solely on the *ḥadīth* of the Imāms in all matters of doctrine and practice; some rejected the Ḳurʾān itself as evidence (Newman, *The nature of the Akhbārī/Uṣūlī dispute*).

Religious orthodoxy did not always win the day among all segments of the "lay" community. "Popular" religious practices and customs, of which the court and its clerical protégés disapproved and tried to suppress or control, remained widespread.

Coffee-houses, for example, were a ubiquitous feature of the country, particularly in the second Ṣafawid century owing to the rapid urbanisation of such cities as Iṣfahān in this period [see ḲAHWA]. These were patronised by all classes of people, but especially by such of the "lower" orders as artists, poets, tellers of religious stories, scholars, musicians and Ṣūfīs. When the court perceived its interests were threatened, it enlisted the clergy to crack down on these and other "popular" pastimes and activities. The "purge" of 939/1523 coincided with the "victory" of al-Karakī over his opponents, for example (Rumlū, 113). In the second Ṣafawid century, as the economic hardships of the mid-century encouraged the court to develop indigenous religious centres, the court capitalised on clerical orthodoxy to check any coffee-house based dissent and to focus popular attention on minority merchants as prominent, subordinate, actors in the country's economic life. ʿAbbās I feared the overtly political nature of coffee-house conversations, and assigned clerics to monitor activities in coffee-houses and to preach sermons on Islamic law or lead prayers. ʿAbbās II's vizier K͟halīfa Sulṭān launched a widespread, if also temporary, suppression of certain coffee-house excesses, wine-drinking and prostitution, and a similarly shortlived effort to convert the country's Jews—like that undertaken by ʿAbbās I—and to restrict certain activities of Armenian merchants (Matthee, *Coffee in Safavid Iran*, esp. 26-30; idem, *The career of Muḥammed Beg*, 27-9; Āl-e Dāwūd, *Coffeehouse*, 1-2; Babayan, *The waning*, 255-6).

Also problematic were Ṣūfī influences rivalling the paramountcy of the Ṣafawid Ṣūfī order and the associated hegemonic position of the Uṣūlī clerical establishment. These challenges frequently involved elements of rural and urban *ṭarīḳa* Ṣūfism and became especially ominous when linked with messianic revivals among both rival and intra-Ḳïzïl-Bās͟h tribal movements. The various phases of the Nuḳṭawiyya [*q.v.*] "heresy" typified these connections and the resultant Ṣafawid concern, especially the Nuḳṭawī rebellion against ʿAbbās I in 1002/1593, in which both members of the Ḳïzïl-Bās͟h confederation and disaffected urban elements were implicated (Babayan, *op. cit.*, 46-7; Amoretti, *Religion*, 644-6). The *k͟hurūd͟j* of Darwīs͟h Riḍā in 1040/1631 was particularly threatening for its messianic overtones and the support the latter engendered among some Ṣafawid *oymaḳs* (Babayan, *op. cit.*, 103-4). The urbanisation trends of the second Ṣafawid century further encouraged the rise of urban-based lower-class/"popular" Ṣūfī movements.

The Uṣūlī/Ak͟hbārī polemic intersected with the broader concern with Ṣūfī influence. Members of each *mad͟hhab* denounced Ṣūfī orders and their "heretical" practices, but imputing "low" Ṣūfī tendencies especially became a device of the lower-ranking, or otherwise peripheralised, clerics with which to assault the small number of court-supported Uṣūlī and moderate Ak͟hbārī clerics and their associates. These were a small group, often conveniently related by ties of family and education, whose interests in aspects of élite/"high" philosophical or gnostic inquiry were as exclusivist and élitest in doctrine and practice as their jurisprudence. These denunciations were especially frequent during the second Ṣafawid century, coinciding with court efforts to combat such Ṣūfī-oriented movements as the Nuḳṭawīs and that of Darwīs͟h Riḍā, the still-strong Ṣūfī proclivities among the Ḳïzïl-Bās͟h and the Ṣūfī influence in the rapidly expanding urban centres, including e.g. Iṣfahān. Such criticism won sufficiently widespread appeal to help force the resignation of S͟hayk͟h Bahāʾī as *S͟hayk͟h al-Islām* in Iṣfahān. Bahāʾī's student Mullā Ṣadrā S͟hīrāzī was likewise charged with Ṣūfī inclinations; Rahman (*The philosophy of Mullā Ṣadrā*, 2-3) has suggested that Ṣadrā's disagreement with his teacher Mīr Dāmād and his subsequent repudiation of such concepts as *waḥdat al-wud͟jūd*, as in his *Ṭarḥ al-kawnayn*, can at least be partly explained as the result of such attacks. Ṣadrā's only Persian-language prose work, *Sih aṣl*, was a defence against allegations of Ṣūfī tendencies.

The interest of Fayḍ al-Kās͟hānī—a student of Bahāʾī, Mīr Dāmād, and Ṣadrā, and the latter's son-in-law—in Ak͟hbārism was at least partly defensive, stemming from a growing appreciation of the potential and real attacks against him for his court and family connections and his own philosophical interests. In fact, Fayḍ accepted enough of Uṣūlī doctrine—arguing that the command of the s͟hāh was sufficient justification for the performance of Friday prayer, leading Friday prayer in Iṣfahān and ruling that the *faḳīh*, based on *al-niyāba*, ought to oversee the collection and distribution of *al-k͟hums*—to qualify him as a *mud͟jtahid-muḥaddit͟h*; his philosophical proclivities similarly tended to the "high", exclusive gnosticism of his teachers. Sabzawārī was also attacked for his purported Ṣūfī tendencies.

Later in the century, Muḥammad Bāḳir al-Mad͟jlisī, another associate of the court and *S͟hayk͟h al-Islām* of the capital, was forced into a posthumous defence of his father Muḥammad Taḳī—like Fayḍ al-Kās͟hānī a *mud͟jtahid-muḥaddit͟h* with philosophical tendencies—against charges that the former was a Ṣūfī. His own disclaimer of interest in and his censure of Ṣūfism and philosophy, and also his work with Twelver *ḥadīt͟h*, at least partly stemmed from concern lest he be subjected to similar attacks from the same quarters. Nevertheless, al-Mad͟jlisī exhibited some interest in Islamic esoterica, and his essay on the Jews *Ṣawāʿiḳ al-Yahūd* is a balanced, if stern, discussion of the general duties enjoined on the *ahl al-d͟himma*, in which he stated that some prohibitions were without legal foundation and in which he permitted Muslim rulers a wide latitude in implementing any or all of them.

If widespread approval for anti-Uṣūlī polemics increased such "discretion" in Uṣūlī discourse, the court's backing for its clerical supporters nevertheless assured their dominance of key religious institutions, and thus the material wherewithal to continue their intellectual activity throughout the period. By later in the Ṣafawid period, the Persian centres of the faith were on a par with, if they had not eclipsed, the ʿIrāḳī shrines, and developments in the Uṣūlī and Ak͟hbārī traditions in this period enabled the faith to weather its disestablishment following the fall of the Ṣafawid house. Ak͟hbārīs fled to the ʿIrāḳī shrine cities at the time of the Afg͟hān invasion and were eventually defeated as a force within the community by al-Waḥīd al-Bihbahānī (Cole, *Shiʿi clerics*, esp. 15-23).

Crucial to and further cementing this Uṣūlī triumph, however, was the Ṣafawid-period articulation of concepts enhancing clerical authority within the community. The final formalisation of the concept of *al-mud͟jtahid al-muṭlaḳ*, for example, facilitated further differentiation in the clerical hierarchy and the subsequent evolution of such concepts as *mard͟jaʿ-i taḳlīd* (the source of emulation) [*q.v.*], the rankings of *ḥud͟jd͟jat al-islām* [see ḤUD͟JD͟JA] and *ayātullāh* [*q.v.* in Suppl.] and, eventually, the principle of government by an expert in jurisprudence, or *wilāyat-i faḳīh*. The Uṣūlīs' recovery of control over the Persian S͟hīʿī religious institution—the schools, shrines and mosques—and Ḳād͟jār patronage of the faith, on the

Ṣafawid model, provided the clergy with resources to maintain and eventually activate these concepts in spite of, if not also as much because of, the hostility of the various established political institutions and their ubiquitous foreign backers.

II. *Philosophy in the Ṣafawid period*

The written legacy of the practitioners of "high" philosophical and rationalist religious discussion identifies them as members of the same tiny, scholarly class who traditionally served and identified with the agenda of the established political institution. The conditional nature of court interest and support, the inherent tendency to restrict the scope for inquiry permitted the untrained, and the extent to which the scope and style of their inquiry was determined by the preceding discourse, were thus as much features of "high" philosophical inquiry as the "high" religious one. As leading Uṣūlī scholars, these philosophers also participated in the teaching and training of future generations of Shīʿī philosophers, thus enhancing the reputation of the Persian centres of education and study as well as creating a new class of clerics whose interests were linked with those of the political and socio-economic élite.

That the careers and scholarly agenda of the "high"/"élite" philosophers of the Ṣafawid and earlier periods were more similar than not, is evident from examining figures who lived through both. Djalāl al-Dīn Muḥammad Dawānī (830/1426-908/1502-03 [*q.v.*]), for example, was based in Shīrāz and studied with students of al-Sharīf al-Djurdjānī (d. 816/1413 [*q.v.*]) and teachers of Ibn Hadjar al-ʿAsḳalānī (d. 852/1449 [*q.v.*]). Dawānī enjoyed the patronage of and served the region's pre-Ṣafawid political establishments, including the Tīmūrid Abū Saʿīd (d. 873/1469 [*q.v.*]) and the Ottoman sultan Bāyezīd II (d. 918/1512 [*q.v.*]).

Although his philosophical contributions have yet to receive detailed, comparative attention, Dawānī appears to have been primarily a reviver of aspects of the Illuminationist tradition, while remaining loyal to the rationalist aspects of Ibn Sīnā's thought (Rahman, *The philosophy of Mullā Ṣadrā*, 9). Like Suhrawardī (d. 578/1191 [*q.v.*, and see also ISHRĀḲ and ISHRĀḲIYYŪN]), Dawānī maintained that existence had one reality and no multiplicity. Like Naṣīr al-Dīn al-Ṭūsī (d. 672/1274 [see AL-ṬŪSĪ]), Dawānī's cosmology involved the gradual unfolding of intellects, spheres, elements, and kingdoms. The active intellect—which he identified with the original essence of the Prophet—bridges the gap between heaven and earth. The revolutions of the spheres, by nature stationary but changeable in quality, control the material world and create new situations wherein the active intellect engendered a new form to reflect itself in the mirror of elemental matter. In this way, the intellect passes through the various states of matter and finally appears in man in the form of acquired intellect, eventually re-acquiring its original form of unity of collective potential. This circular process he termed *ḥarakat-i waḍāʿī*. The motions in the process are in fact the shadows of motion proceeding from God's desire for self-manifestation; the mystics term this the flashing of Self upon Self. In his metaphysical *al-Zawra*, Dawānī elevated mysticism above philosophy, even as he asserted both had the same goal, because mysticism benefitted from divine grace and so was free from doubt and uncertainty and thus nearer to prophethood.

At the same time, some of his works clearly reflect his other role as a royal scribe, the career for which he was probably as well, if not better, known at court. His works in this genre, written for royal benefactors, included a description of a military review in Fārs entitled *ʿArḍ-nāma*, and his contribution to the "mirror for princes" genre *Akhlāḳ-i djalālī*. Indeed, he also dedicated to his royal patrons his Ishrāḳī-style commentary *Shawākil al-nūr* on the *Hayākal al-nūr* of Suhrawardī.

Although later sources contend that he was a Shīʿī practising *taḳiyya* prior to the rise of Ismāʿīl, Dawānī's Sunnī proclivities were unequivocal in his early works. Even after the Ṣafawid occupation of Tabrīz, he is said to have rejected Ismāʿīl's messianic claims. The court functionary's traditional capacity for adjustment was evident, however, in Dawānī's almost perfunctorily Shīʿī work *Nūr al-hidāya*, probably composed as the Ṣafawids approached Shīrāz, where he died before the city's capture. Dawānī's student Djamāl al-Dīn al-Astarābādī (d. 931/1524-5) was the sixth Ṣafawid *ṣadr* but, like his teacher, was more comfortable with philosophical disputes than the tenets of the newly established faith (Newman, *The myth*, 75 n. 24).

Dawānī clashed with his contemporary Ṣadr al-Dīn Muḥammad Dashtakī (d. 903/1498), another "high" philosopher associated with both the Tīmūrid and Ṣafawid courts, both in treatises and also in glosses on works by al-Ṭūsī and Suhrawardī. Ṣadr al-Dīn's son Ghiyāth al-Dīn Manṣūr (see also the preceding section) continued the anti-Dawānī polemic after the death of the original protagonists. Although the details are still poorly understood, the disagreement involved points of debate well within the tradition of Islamic "high" philosophy to date. Dawānī, like Suhrawardī, argued e.g. that existence had but one, single reality, where Ghiyāth al-Dīn argued there was no existence at all.

Like Dawānī and his own father, Ghiyāth al-Dīn was as much a court protégé and functionary as other Shīrāzī philosophers in the tradition of Ḳutb al-Dīn al-Shīrāzī [*q.v.*; see also below, subsection III. ii], himself a student of al-Ṭūsī. Ghiyāth al-Dīn maintained good relations with Bāyezīd II, and served as vizier to the Tīmūrid Sultan Ḥusayn Bayḳara (r. 874-911/1469-1506 [*q.v.*]). Although for the Ṣafawids the religio-political proclivities of both Dashtakīs were less important than their status as court functionaries, later Ṣafawid and post-Ṣafawid biographers claimed that Ṣadr al-Dīn Muḥammad was the first openly Shīʿī member of the family. Shāh Ismāʿīl reportedly called on Ghiyāth al-Dīn to undertake repairs to al-Ṭūsī's observatory at Marāgha [*q.v.*] (see also below, subsection III. ii), and in 936/1529 Ṭahmāsp appointed him co-*ṣadr* with al-Ḥillī. Ghiyāth al-Dīn's challenge to al-Karakī coincided with, if it did not support, that of al-Ḥillī and certain tribal elements (see above). At his dismissal, Ghiyāth al-Dīn returned to Shīrāz's Manṣūriyya school.

Members of Nasr and Corbin's "Iṣfahān School of Philosophy"—Shaykh Bahāʾī, Mīr Dāmād, Mullā Ṣadrā, Fayḍ al-Kāshānī, Mīr Findiriskī (d. 1050/1640 [*q.v.* in Suppl.]) and ʿAbd al-Razzāḳ al-Lāhidjī (d. 1072/1662 [*q.v.*])—the "high" philosophers of the second Ṣafawid century, were similarly close associates of the court, but with clear-cut allegiance to the basic tenets of Uṣūlī Shīʿism. Like Ghiyāth al-Dīn, their fortunes varied with broader socio-religious and political trends. Like him also, they served the court also as scribes. However, spurred on by the interest of Nasr and Corbin, analysis has revealed they advanced important contributions to Islamic philosophy.

Nasr and Corbin distinguished Mīr Dāmād—student of both Shaykh Bahāʾī and the latter's father—as the outstanding figure of Ṣafawid-period philosophy. Subsequent Persian evaluations have only echoed this assessment, according him such titles as *Sayyid al-ḥukamā*ʾ ("Master of the wise men"), *Sayyid al-falāsifa* ("Master of the philosophers"), and *muʿallim-i thalāth* ("the third teacher", after Aristotle and al-Fārābī [*q.v.*]).

Mīr Dāmād's contribution to Uṣūlī doctrine and practice has been noted. His philosophical accomplishment was to build on the interpretations of Suhrawardī—whose notion of the principality of essence (*iṣālat al-māhiyya*) over existence (*wudjūd*) he accepted—and Dawānī and to revive Ibn Sīnā's metaphysics and transform it from a purely rational, abstract system of thought into a spiritual reality through the application of Ishrāḳī principles within a Shīʿī framework. His preoccupation with issues of time and the relation between the eternal (*ḳidam*) and the created (*ḥudūth*) produced his most famous philosophical contribution, the concept of *ḥudūth-i dahrī* ("origination, or creation, in perpetuity"). The latter distinguished three, separate and distinguishable levels of being and postulated a middle level (*dahr*) between the immutable world (*sarmad*) and the changing world (*zamān*), in which the two are related and through which the eternal, unchanging reality manifests itself in the world. Mīr Dāmād's merging of Avicennan philosophy with Suhrawardī's illuminationism within a Shīʿī construct informed the thought of later Ṣafawid-period philosophers, including that of his students Mullā Ṣadrā, Mīr Dāmād's son-in-law Sayyid Aḥmad ʿAlawī and Mullā Shamsā Gīlānī (d. 1098/1686-7). The latter, especially, continued Mīr Dāmād's efforts to harmonise aspects of the contributions of Ibn Sīnā and Suhrawardī.

Ṣadr al-Dīn Muḥammad Shīrāzī was born *ca.* 980/1571 to an aristocratic Shīrāzī family. In Iṣfahān he studied the Twelver Shīʿī religious sciences with Shaykh Bahāʾī and the rationalist, philosophical disciplines with Mīr Dāmād, spent more than a decade in Kahak near Ḳum, after which he was invited by ʿAbbās II to return to Shīrāz to teach. He spent the last thirty years of his life teaching at the city's Khān school—built for him by Allāhwardī Khān, the governor of Fārs—during which time he completed many of his best-known works.

Ṣadrā's thought built on that of Mīr Dāmād in order to integrate Ibn Sīnā's thought with Ishrāḳī interpretations through a Twelver Shīʿī framework. Initially, Ṣadrā agreed with Mīr Dāmād and Suhrawardī on the principality of essence, while existence was an unreal mental, phenomonological derivative. Eventually, however, as he made clear in his *magnum opus al-Asfār al-arbaʿa*, written when he was nearly sixty, he agreed with Ibn Sīnā's understanding of the principality of existence (*iṣālat al-wudjūd*) over essence, even as he accepted the notion that existence, while a single reality (thus following Dāwānī and Mīr Dāmād), manifested itself luminously in different degrees and stages (Rahman, *The philosophy*, 1-3; Nasr, *Three Muslim sages*, 67).

Ṣadrā also came to reject Mīr Dāmād's *ḥudūth-i dahrī*, on the grounds that the objects which become manifest in the *dahrī* level of existence are but individual forms and do not represent species as did Platonic forms. In this, he accepted aspects of Suhrawardī's doctrine of Lord of the Species (Rahman, *ibid.*, 47-8).

Ṣadrā's debt to Suhrawardī also manifested itself in his adherence to the notion of "trans-substantial motion" (*al-ḥaraka al-djawhariyya*). Ibn Sīnā had rejected this concept and denied the reality of "Platonic ideas". As Ṣadrā held that a single reality revealed itself in varying degrees and stages and upheld the notion of Platonic ideas of archetypes of things which became manifest in the world, *al-ḥaraka al-djawhariyya* became the means by which the substance of these changed and evolved to a stage where they achieved immutability. Likewise, man himself can achieve this state. Indeed, for Ṣadrā the goal of *ḥikma* is precisely the realisation of this status. Thus trans-substantial motion is for Ṣadrā both a point of metaphysics and of natural philosophy.

Ṣadrā's doctrines also included many of the basic principles of gnosis as formulated by Ibn al-ʿArabī [*q.v.*], as Ṣadrā understood the necessity for a relationship between mystical experience and logical thinking. In harmonising philosophy and gnosis, Mullā Ṣadrā was building on the work of Islamic thinkers from the 6th/12th to the 10th/16th century, including Ḳutb al-Dīn Shīrāzī, al-Djurdjānī, Ḥaydar Āmulī, Radjab Bursī, Ibn Turka Iṣfahānī, Ibn Abī Djumhūr Aḥsāʾī [*q.v.* in Suppl.] and Mīr Dāmād himself. However, unlike some of these earlier scholars, Ṣadrā grounded his reconciliation of these two traditions of inquiry firmly in the revelation of Twelver Shīʿism.

Of note is the fact that Ṣadrā composed nearly all of his works in Arabic, reflecting the fact that his intended audience was based in the exceedingly tiny class of highly sophisticated, mainly religious thinkers of the time. In his own time, the influence of Ṣadrā's thought was quite limited, though links to Akhbārī and Shaykhī thought have been suggested (Morris, *The wisdom*, 49). In the Ḳādjār period, Ṣadrā's contributions were re-activated by Mullā Hādī Sabzawārī (d. 1295/1878 or 1298/1880-1 [*q.v.*]).

Ṣadrā's students included his son-in-law Fayḍ al-Kāshānī and al-Lāhidjī, another son-in-law, who himself taught Muḥammad b. Saʿīd Ḳummī, Ḳāḍī Saʿīd Ḳummī (d. 1103/1691). In addition to being a judge, Ḳummī was also a physician and a gnostic, even as he, like the earlier generation of Iṣfahān School members, worked solidly within the framework of Twelver Shīʿism. Indeed, as summarised by Corbin, at the hands of Mīr Dāmād, Ṣadrā and Ḳāḍī Saʿīd Ḳummī "Ishrāḳī Avicennism became the Shīʿite philosophy" (*Creative imagination*, 23).

It has been suggested that Mīr Findiriskī was also a student of Mullā Ṣadrā. Mīr Findiriskī was a prominent figure both at court and among such of his contemporaries as Mīr Dāmād and Shaykh Bahāʾī, involved himself in some Ṣūfī practices, lived a simple, ascetic lifestyle, travelled to India several times and was familiar with aspects of Hinduism as well as with such of the occult sciences as alchemy. If he studied with Ṣadrā, his own "high" gnostic interests manifested themselves in a closer affiliation with Ibn Sīnā and included a denial of Ṣadrā's notion of trans-substantial motion. Among his students were Mullā Rāfiʿā Gīlānī (d. 1082/1671-2), the Uṣūlī jurisprudent Muḥammed Bāḳir Sabzawārī (see the preceding section), the jurisprudent and philosopher Āghā Ḥusayn Khʷānsārī (d. 1080/1669-70), and Radjab ʿAlī Tabrīzī (d. 1080/1669-70). The latter, also an opponent of trans-substantial motion, taught Ḳāḍī Saʿīd Ḳummī.

The prolonged attack against the "high" scholasticism practised by these philosophers and like-minded religious scholars in the second Ṣafawid century is discussed in the preceding section.

III. *Science and society in the Ṣafawid period*

As the patrons and practitioners of "high" philosophy and "high" religious discourse were drawn from the court and its small, learned coterie, so the legacy of Ṣafawid-period science, broadly construed, is initially understood with reference to the careers and contributions of those literate few who enjoyed the backing of both the central and provincial courts. Indeed, some of the small number of masters of "high" religious and philosophical inquiry attained proficiency in certain scientific disciplines. Evidence of "popular" theories and practices is available, however, especially, for example, in medicine.

i. Medicine in the Ṣafawid period

That Persian society as a whole was aware of and affected by issues of illness and wellness is amply attested. The court chronicles report plague (ṭāʿūn [q.v.]) in Ardabīl in 981/1573 (Ḳummī, i, 587), plague and cholera (wabāʾ) in Tabrīz in 988/1580 (ibid., ii, 713), plague in Ḳum and Ḵḥurāsān the next year (ibid., ii, 723), plague and cholera in Ḳazwīn in 1001/1592-3 (Munshī, ii, 631-2), and plague in Ādharbaydjān and then Ḳazwīn in 1033/1623-4 (ibid., ii, 1243). In 1095/1684 cholera struck Rasht and spread to Ardabīl the following year. In 1097/1686 cholera also struck Tabrīz and Māzandarān (Ḵḥātūnābādī, 538).

The court and its associates were themselves directly affected by illness in this period. Ismāʿīl died in 930/1524 from an illness which "skilful physicians" could not cure (Ḳummī, i, 153). Ṭahmāsp fell ill in 967/1559 for two months (Ḵḥātūnābādī, 481). Again, in 982/1574 he fell ill from a "burning fever" (tab-i muḥarraḳ), an event leading to a fitna at court (Ḳummī, i, 588). He was cured, but died of another illness two years later; in that instance one attending physician was executed for his treasonously unsuccessful efforts (ibid., i, 600). Muḥammad Ḵḥudābanda had an eye problem which Elgood put down to "corneal opacity" due to an attempt to blind him in his youth (Elgood, 61). ʿAbbās I fell ill on numerous occasions, from fever during a visit to Mashhad in 1008/1599-1600 (Munshī, ii, 783), in 1029/1619-20 from an illness which affected many at court (ibid., ii, 1176), and again in 1037/1628 from a fever which eventually killed him (ibid., ii, 1297-8). Illness felled ʿAbbās II.

Of the court literati, some of whose names have been mentioned above, Ḡḥiyāth al-Dīn Manṣūr Dashtakī had such a fear of syphilis (ātishak) that he refused to shake hands (Ḳummī, i, 296-7; Elgood, 24). The 1001/1592-3 plague and cholera which struck Ḳazwīn killed Ḥusayn al-Karakī al-ʿĀmilī, who had served as Ardabīl's Shaykh al-Islām and grandson of ʿAlī al-Karakī (Munshī, ii, 631-2). Mīr Dāmād was afflicted with scabies (djarab), and then "hectic fever" (ḥummā-yi diḳḳ) (Elgood, 40). This is not to mention the numerous instances of dysentery (which struck Muḥammad Ḵḥudābanda in his last days), smallpox, strokes and fevers, and unnamed illnesses which afflicted and killed those favoured by the court chroniclers.

The different medical theories and practices to which the court and its associates subscribed reveal the availability in society both of the traditional components of Islamic medicine—Galenic/humoural theory, prophetic medicine, and folk medicine and magic (Dols; Ṭibb al-aʾimma, vii-xxiii; Savage-Smith, Islamic medicine)—and other explanations of illness and wellness.

Many of the individual medical practitioners and medical families best-known in the contemporary and later sources were among the small number of associates of the central and provincial courts, and most were adherents of Galenic [see DJALĪNŪS] medicine. The early Ṣafawid-period physician Bahāʾ al-Dawla (d. ca. 912/1507), like Ḡḥiyāth al-Dīn Dashtakī, served the Tīmūrid Ḥusayn Baykara. Masʿūd b. Maḥmūd Kāshī (d. 946/1539), "the Galen of the time", was physician to Ṭahmāsp (Rumlū, 134; Ḳummī, i, 293). His medical "dynasty" included his two sons ʿImād al-Dīn and Kamāl al-Dīn Ḥusayn (d. 953/1546), the son of the latter, Nūr al-Dīn (d. 970/1562), who also served Ṭahmāsp, and the son of the former, Muḥammad Bāḳir, who served ʿAbbās I and wrote a well-known essay on ophthalmology. Both Shaykh Bahāʾī and Mīr Dāmād studied under and taught several court physicians. Bahāʾī, for example, taught Ḳāḍī b. Kāshif al-Dīn Ḥamawī (see also below, subsection ii), who had also studied with ʿImād al-Dīn and later sought and received a ruling from Bahāʾī to administer wine to Mīr Dāmād for his scabies and hectic fever, a cure which was successful. He wrote an essay on this point for ʿAbbās I, and another treatise for ʿAbbās II. Ḥamawī's father had come from Yazd to serve ʿAbbās I as a physician, and his son, also a physician, later emigrated to India. The surgeon Ḥakīm Muḥammad enjoyed the patronage of Shāh Ṣafī. Muḥammad Bāḳir ʿAlī Ḵḥān, author of a works on cardiac drugs, fevers and gynaecology, served Shāh Sulaymān and Sultan Ḥusayn. Mīr Muḥammad Zamān wrote the famous pharmocopoeia Tuḥfat al-muʾminīn for Sulaymān; his father had also served the court. Ḳāḍī Saʿīd Ḳummī (on whom see the preceding section) was also a physician (for a list of court-connected physicians, see Munshī, i, 263-6).

The medical writers in this tradition were familiar with the great medical compendia of the Islamic Galenic medical tradition, including those of al-Rāzī, Ibn Sīnā, al-Djurdjānī, and the late 8th/14th Shīrāzī medical writer Manṣūr b. Muḥammad, called Ibn Ilyās, but are perhaps better known for separate monographs on specific, practical medical issues, many of which were written for their royal patrons. Bahāʾ al-Dawla's magnum opus Khulāṣat al-tadjārib was arranged like al-Rāzī's al-Ḥāwī. ʿImād al-Dīn composed a general medical work in the style of the older books, but also an essay on the china root (čūb-i čīnī)—this being acknowledged as a universal cure, and which ʿImād stated cured infertility, opium addiction, baldness, rheumatism and haemorrhoids—and one on the bezoar stone. His essay on syphilis is said to have caused Ḡḥiyāth al-Dīn Dashtakī's fear of the illness (Elgood, 52-3, 24). In addition to his essay on alcohol, Ḥamawī also wrote an essay on the china root, tea and coffee for ʿAbbās II (Elgood, 39-40). Muḥammad Bāḳir b. ʿImād al-Dīn wrote an essay for ʿAbbās I on ophthalmology during the later's Tabrīz campaign; in fact, probably owing to the circumstances of its composition, it also covers wounds, ulcers and syphilis (Elgood, 69). Ḥakīm Muḥammad's work on surgery was dedicated to Shāh Ṣafī, and included chapters on pre- and post-operative procedures. This work suggests that most surgery was for accidents and wounds; the few operations of choice included castration and circumcision. The author devoted several pages to descriptions of surgical instruments, and a section to anaesthetics (Elgood, s.v., and esp. 153-4). A large number of pharmacopoeias [see AḲRĀBĀḎHĪN] were written in this period, including the Ṭibb-i shifāʾī of Muẓaffar b. Muḥammad al-Ḥusaynī al-Shifāʾī (d. 974/1556), the basis for the French work of 1681, the Pharmacopoeia persica of Father Angelus (Elgood, 33-4).

Although belonging to the Galenic tradition, these writers were not themselves unobservant or uncritical.

Elgood, himself a practising physician, credited Bahāʾ al-Dawla with the first accounts of whooping cough decades before the European account (Elgood, 279-80, xiv). He also commended Bahāʾ's awareness of raised blood pressure during pregnancy (270-1). The surgeon Ḥakīm Muḥammad stressed the necessity of cleaning surgical knives between uses, perhaps, so Elgood suggested, having observed the problem of implanting diseased cells from one patient to another (160). Ḥakīm Muḥammad also noted the tendency for cancer of the breast to reappear elsewhere in the body after a mastectomy (*ibid.*, 188, 231).

Indeed, women's illnesses and matters of pregnancy and fertility were frequently addressed in both medical textbooks and monographs. The latter included the essay of Murtaḍā Ḳulī Khān b. Ḥasan Shamlū—not a medical practitioner at all, but one-time civil governor of Ḳum—dedicated to Shāh Sulaymān and titled *Khirḳa-yi khānum dar ʿilm-i ṭibb* ("Women's rags on the science of medicine"), and that of Shāh Sulṭān Ḥusayn's court physician, *Mirʾāt al-djamāl* ("Mirror of beauty"). Such writings, some of whose material derived from earlier medical and religious writings, covered such matters as birth control and abortion, morning sickness, breast feeding and early childhood illnesses.

Given the occasional, spectacular lack of success of these court physicians with their most important patient/patron, and probably also due to the shāhs' tribal backgrounds, the court was also sympathetic to non-Galenic theories and practices.

Prophetic medicine was also a source of medical understanding. Among the Shīʿa, in particular, there was a tradition of medicine based on the *ḥadīth* of the Imāms and thus amenable to easy memorisation. As early as the 3rd/9th century collection *Ṭibb al-aʾimma*, this Shīʿī medical tradition included elements of the Galenic tradition, but also cited the Imāms' advice on preventive medicine, abstention from certain foods, cupping and cauterisation, the use of particular blends of herbs and spices, and statements involving "magic" and warnings about and prayers to counter the evil eye (*Ṭibb al-aʾimma*, Preface). In his anatomical treatise Ibn Ilyās, although not a Shīʿī, accorded equal weight to the prophetic and Galenic medical traditions. In the Ṣafawid period, ʿAlī Afḍal Ḳāṭiʿ included citations from earlier prophetic traditions in his *Ḳarābidīn* (Elgood, 36-8). Muḥammad Bāḳir al-Madjlisī devoted a portion of his *Biḥār al-anwār* to medicine, including a Galenic-style discussion of human anatomy followed by chapters of medical statements credited to the Imāms drawn from such early sources as *Ṭibb al-aʾimma*. As al-Madjlisī's compilation was the product of the Uṣūlī/court effort to promulgate its vision of orthodoxy throughout Ṣafawid territory, however, the inclusion of a medical section also suggests an effort to challenge less orthodox—perhaps especially, for example, Sunnī-based, or radical Akhbārī—prophetic medical traditions.

Evidence of other sources of medical theories and customs of the semi-literate and especially the illiterate classes (the bulk of the population in Ṣafawid Persia) can also be inferred. Pre-Ṣafawid medical texts often included citations of Persian-language medical verses on a variety of subjects. The anatomical treatise of Ibn Ilyās, *Tashrīḥ-i Manṣūrī*, cited verse often using the formal Arabic anatomical terminology similar to the medical verse of Ibn Sīnā, already available in Persian. In style, however, Ibn Ilyās's citations resemble the little-known Persian verse of the 3rd/9th century Persian physician Ḥakīm Maysarī (*Dānish-nāma dar ʿilm-i pazishkī*, ed. B. Zandjānī, Tehran 1344 *Sh.*/1987). The scanning and rhyming schemes of such verse facilitated its memorisation, and might have been especially useful for the semi-literate practitioners with whom the bulk of the population was most likely to come into contact.

Ṣafawid-period medical writers continued this tradition. In the early 10th/16th century, Yūsuf b. Muḥammad of Harāt composed several works of medical verse, including a versified discussion of illnesses which an individual far from any doctor might have to treat himself. ʿAlī Afḍal Ḳāṭiʿ, author of the pharmacopoeia *Ḳarābidīn*, quoted some medical verse (Elgood, 18, 113-15, 117). Ibn Ilyās's anatomy, with its medical verse, was also much copied in this period.

Other traditions of medical explanation were also available. Celestial events, including the appearance of a fiery comet in 1027/1617-18, for example, were blamed for subsequent wars and uprisings in Europe and the Ottoman empire, widespread pestilence in Gīlān and Māzandarān (predicted by astrologers after the comet's appearance), an earthquake in Khurāsān in 1028/1618-19, the death of many commoners and nobles, and, together with the terrible heat of Māzandarān, predicted by the same astrologers, the illness of ʿAbbās himself the next year (Munshī, ii, 1162-8, 1176). Shaykh Bahāʾī's death in 1030/1620-1 came after hearing a voice during prayers at the tomb of Bābā Rukn al-Dīn Iṣfahānī. After this incident he "prepared himself for death"; as he predicted, three months later he fell ill and died (Munshī, ii, 1189-90).

Aware of their own limitations and of the challenges of other traditions, the court-based medical practitioners did practice some medical pluralism. Bahāʾ al-Dawla prescribed certain incantations in the case of plague, and magic before surgery in the case of certain instances of the urethra being blocked (Elgood, 173-4, 179). Ḥakīm Muḥammad, although generally disavowing all sorts of magic, charms, and the evil eye, noted certain bone fractures required divine intervention (Elgood, xvi). The court's interest in astrology is also clear, as recounted above. Indeed, sometimes rulers consulted its practitioners about the suggestions of the Galenic practitioners (Minorsky, 57-8, 128).

The court was keenly aware of the importance of public welfare generally to the stability of the broader socio-political fabric. In response to the 910/1505 famine and inflation, for example, Ismāʿīl ordered the sale of grain, and eventually also the execution of the responsible official owing to his poor response to the crisis (Rumlū, 36). ʿAbbās I, following an earthquake that struck Shīrwān [*q.v.*] while he and his party were in the region, ordered court phlebotomists to bleed the injured after which, it was reported, they "revived a little" (Munshī, i, 928-9).

The court also took practical measures to secure the flow and quality control of health services in particular. In the second Ṣafawid century, "physicians, including druggists and perfume-sellers (*ʿaṭṭārān*)"—probably including such individuals as the opium seller, the seller of henna, and the seller of musk and perfume, and perhaps the surgeon (*djarrāḥ*), the stitcher (*bakhya-dūz*) (Keyvani, 263-4) and perhaps also the eye specialist (*kaḥḥāl*) (Elgood, 56, 63)—comprised one of the thirty-three main guilds in Iṣfahān, each of which would have been headed by a *bāshī* (Keyvani, 49-50). Some of these professions apparently had well defined ranks: the surgeon rank comprised the master surgeon (*ustād*), the bone-setter (*mudjabbir*), and the barber (*salmānī*) who, however, was considered of lower-status and did not have a shop in the bazaar

Na<u>sh</u>mī the Archer, signed by Riḍā and dated 1031/1622. Harvard University Art Museums.

Young Man in a Blue Cloak, signed by Riḍā, late 16th century. Harvard Art Museums.

Steel mirror, 17th century. Nelson-Atkins Gallery of Art.

"Shāh ʿAbbās" or "Polonaise" carpet, silk enriched with silver and gilt thread. Nelson-Atkins Gallery of Art.

Fragment of satin brocaded silk with silver thread. The Cleveland Museum of Art. Purchase from the J.H. Wade Fund.

Blue-and-white dish. Courtesy, Museum of Fine Arts, Boston.

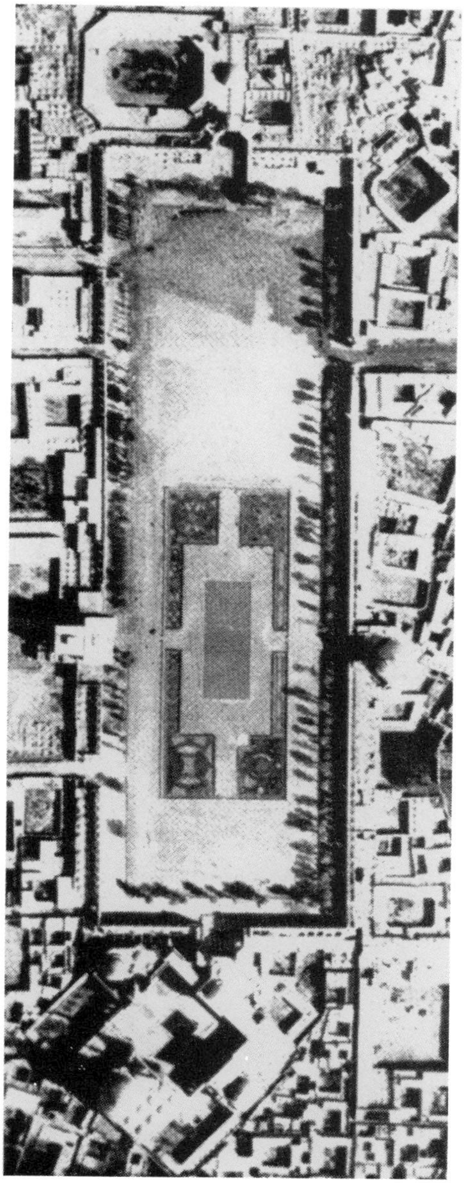

Maydān, Iṣfahān. Computer-enhanced aerial view from *Athār-e Īrān, Annales du Service archéologique de l'Īrān*, ii (1937), 104.

Bird, Butterflies, and Blossoms, signed by Shafīʿ ʿAbbāsī and dated 1062/1652. The Cleveland Museum of Art. Purchase, Andrew R. and Martha Holden Jennings Fund.

An Invocation for divine assistance and protection against evil. Calligraphy signed by Muḥammad Riḍā, late 17th century. Courtesy, Museum of Fine Arts, Boston.

Return from the flight into Egypt, 1100/1689, signed by Muḥammad Zamān and based on a print by Lucas Vosterman after Peter Paul Rubens. Harvard University Art Museums.

(Elgood, 56, 140-1, 145-6; Keyvani, 50-3). The barber could perform cupping as well as bleeding, and circumcision, which could also be done by a *mullā* or *ḳāḍī*. The richer the patient the more likely a professional was employed e.g. the master surgeon, for such tasks (Elgood, 126-8, 140, 146).

The court's purpose in maintaining an administrative apparatus for the guilds was both to maintain quality control and to organise these crafts for its own use. The court met its needs from the bazaar where some of these practitioners maintained stalls (Keyvani, 63-4, 240). To insure immediate access, however, the court also maintained sections within the royal workshops for such groups as "druggists and perfumers" (*ʿaṭṭār khāna*) (Keyvani, 169-70; Minorsky, 100, 128) and, when on the move, maintained its own band of phlebotomists. The shāh's private barber (*khāṣṣa-tarāsh*) oversaw such groups as bloodletters (*faṣṣādān*) and circumcisers (*khatna-kārān*) (Elgood, 143; Keyvani, 55-6). Some of these bazaar-based practitioners were probably among those who gravitated toward the growing urban-based Ṣūfī orders of the day (Keyvani, 205-11).

The Ṣafawids were more interested in and exercised greater control over guilds than had Tīmūrids (Keyvani, 63). Indeed, sometime in the 11th/17th century, the court established the post of *Ḥakīm-bāshī* ("chief doctor"), combining the position of the shāh's personal physician—in which he was assisted by the *ʿAṭṭār-bāshī* ("chief pharmacist")—with the position of chief of the entire profession. He also designated a physician for any member of the court requesting one (Minorsky, 57, 128).

Such earlier medical writers as al-Djurdjānī spoke with respect of the importance and role of midwives (Elgood, 205-7, 219-20, 227-8, 266-7, 281). Keyvani (177) noted the preponderance of Jews among Iṣfahān's midwives. He also cited the presence of Jewish druggists and observed that the Armenian community possessed an apparently parallel system of craft guilds, including medical practitioners (180-1).

The court also realised the importance of providing for the basic needs of the poorest urban elements, less able to afford access to the bazaar, especially during times of famine or economic crises. European visitors and Persian sources mention hospitals in such cities as Iṣfahān (Munshī, ii, 1295; Elgood, 29), Tabrīz (where Chardin saw three, Elgood, 29), Ardabīl (again seen by Chardin, Elgood, 29), Kazwīn (*ibid.*), and Yazd (*ibid.*), and the shrine at Mashhad (*ibid.*). The travellers' descriptions suggest, however, that some of these were either, or as much, a food distribution centre or else *sharbat-khāna* (dispensary), the latter like that headed by Ḥakīm Yār ʿAlī Ṭihrānī, and used especially to treat the poor and indigent, during the reign of Ṭahmāsp (Munshī, i, 265; Elgood, 32, Ḳummī, i, 605 n. 16).

The Ṣafawid élite also maintained the traditional interest in aspects of veterinary sciences, horses and falcons in particular, and the literati responded to this interest. Muṣliḥ al-Dīn Lārī (d. 980/1571), a student of Ghiyāth al-Dīn Dashtakī and later minister at the court in India of Humāyūn (d. 963/1556) and then guest of the Ottoman sultan Selīm II (d. 982/1574), composed an essay on *bayṭarī* (the veterinary sciences). The noted court-associate and *mudjtahid-muḥaddith* jurisprudent Fayḍ al-Kāshānī was among those who authored essays on horses, for example, his being entitled *Waṣf al-khayl* (Rumlū, 197; Ḳummī, 580; Sādjdjādī, *Dām-pazishkī*).

ii. *Astronomy and associated sciences*

The concern of the court, and indeed that of several segments of Persian society, with the divinatory sciences has already been noted. This interest manifested itself in support for "orthodox" and "less orthodox" practices and individuals.

Like their predecessors, the Ṣafawids paid the customary attention to *ʿilm al-hayʾa* [*q.v.*] or astronomy. The chief practitioners upon whom they called were drawn from the same small circle of scholars/court functionaries. Thus Ismāʿīl I summoned Ghiyāth al-Dīn Dashtakī from Shīrāz to undertake repairs to the observatory at Marāgha founded by Naṣīr al-Dīn al-Ṭūsī. The project, part of an extended effort to compile a set of star tables along the lines completed under earlier rulers, was envisioned as requiring a period of thirty years of observation, and so was abandoned, probably as a result of the same politico-military pressures which prompted the issuance of the *firmān* to al-Karakī. Dashtakī also wrote an essay *al-Safīr fī ʿilm al-hayʾa* ("The ambassador on the science of astronomy"), in which he both introduced and criticised aspects of Ptolemaic astronomy, including that practised by al-Ṭūsī (in particular, features of al-Ṭūsī's famous "Couple") and Ḳuṭb al-Dīn Shīrāzī, and referred to two other, still unlocated, studies of his own on the "reform" of this school of astronomy (Rumlū, 303-4; Ḳummī, i, 296; Newman, *Dashtakī, Ghiyāth al-Dīn*; Saliba, 93-4). Indeed, the nominal reason for his clash with al-Karakī was disagreement with the latter's calculations of the direction of the *ḳibla* [*q.v.*] in mosques throughout Ṣafawid territory. Later scholars opposed to al-Karakī's association with the court, including Shaykh Zayn al-Dīn and al-Ḥusayn b. ʿAbd al-Ṣamad, expressed their disapproval of that association by refusing to pray in the directions of the *ḳibla* specified by al-Karakī (Newman, *The myth*, 99-101, 105). Ṭahmāsp envisioned construction of an observatory at Iṣfahān as part of an effort to compile observational records (*zīdj*), but this project also never developed (Winter, 588).

Numerous astronomical manuals were written in this period. In the next century, for example, the jurisprudent/philosopher Shaykh Bahāʾī contributed to this tradition with his *Tashrīḥ al-aflāk*. Not surprisingly, opposition to Bahāʾī also manifested itself in this arena as well. *Tashrīḥ al-aflāk* contained a vigorous defence of the science of astronomy itself (Saliba, 95-6), suggesting that the forces conspiring against him as a representative of the court-supported traditions of Uṣūlī jurisprudence and "high" philosophical inquiry linked these with other "high" scientific disciplines. Indeed, his *al-Ḥabl al-matīn*, completed *ca.* 1007/1597, was at least partly written as a defence of astronomy generally, but also specifically of al-Karakī's *ḳibla* ruling of the previous century, to the point that Bahāʾī downplayed his own father's criticisms of al-Karakī's calculations (Newman, *Towards a reconsideration,* 180-5).

A contemporary commentator on Bahāʾī's *Tashrīḥ al-aflāk*, Muḥammad Ṣadr al-Dīn al-Ḥusaynī, also addressed issues in Ptolemaic astronomy and their solutions (Saliba, 97-8). Bahāʾī's student Ḳāḍī b. Kāshif al-Dīn Ḥamawī (see above, subsection i), a physician, also wrote an astronomical handbook (Winter, 592).

The court and its associates were also active patrons of makers of astrolabes [see ASṬURLĀB] and celestial globes. The traveller Chardin gave a detailed description of astrolabe construction in this period (Winter, 596-9; Savage-Smith, *Islamicate celestial globes,* 45-9, 74, 80). An early modern European celestial map brought to Ṣafawid Persia by Chardin's contemporary J.-B. Tavernier was probably the basis for astrolabe plates produced in Yazd which incorporated the latest European discoveries; the subsequent influence of these plates appears to have been negligible, however (Savage-Smith, *Celestial mapping*, 65-8). S͟hayk͟h Bahāʾī, again, dedicated a short essay on the astrolabe to a minister of ʿAbbās I (Winter, 592).

Divinatory methods considered less orthodox today also appear to have enjoyed official support. D̲j̲alāl al-Dīn Muḥammad b. ʿAbd Allāh Yazdī, author of the court chronicle *Tārīk͟h-i ʿAbbāsī* and chief astronomer to ʿAbbās I, also composed an essay on *raml* (geomancy) for K͟hān Aḥmad al-Ḥusaynī, ruler of Gīlān.

Related to the work in the astronomical sciences was that done in *ʿilm al-ḥiṣāb* [*q.v.*] or mathematics. Not surprisingly, perhaps, such close associates of the court as S͟hayk͟h Bahāʾī were among those who composed essays in this field.

iii. *Military technology*

Patterns of developments in military technology are similarly explicable in relation to the larger Persian social formation and the Ṣafawid politico-military achievement itself.

Firearms were available and used in Persia from the 9th/15th century and cannon were used by the Ṣafawid armies in their sieges of Anatolian cities of the Ottoman empire. The Ṣafawid interest in the new technology was spurred on by the Čāldirān defeat in 920/1514. Ṣafawid s͟hāhs received both firearms and cannon from the Tsars and requested both of these from Tuscany and the Pope. ʿAbbās I received arquebuses from Russia, Venice and England, the latter after the East Indian Company established relations with the court (Matthee, *Firearms*). There are frequent references to musketeers (*tufangčīs*) and artillery (*tūpk͟hāna*) in the late Ṣafawid administrative manual *Tad͟hkirat al-mulūk*, and one of the 33 main guilds of Iṣfahān was that of "armourers", comprising makers of bows and arrows as well as makers of rifle stocks, rifles and gunpowder (Keyvani, 50).

Nevertheless, muskets and arquebuses, cannon and siege artillery, never achieved widespread use in Ṣafawid armies. The mounted warriors of these armies spurned use of the former, "clumsy, cumbersome, and quite ineffective", noisy form of weaponry, the more so as the Ṣafawid infantry, the main employer of these weapons, was recruited from the peasantry and the poorer, probably urban, classes. Even the new *g͟hulām* [*q.v.*] corps, ostensibly introduced to undercut the power and prestige of the Ḳizil-Bās͟h forces, under-utilised these weapons, by contrast with such similar formations as the Ottoman Janisaries, and a similar Russian contingent, who were trained in and equipped with the latest technology (Matthee, *op. cit.*).

Especially in comparison with Persia's Ottoman and Mug͟hal neighbours, the general lack of wheeled transport and the Persian physical environment—e.g. the lack of navigable waterways—hindered the widespread incorporation of heavy field and siege artillery, although it was clearly available. The mining of ingredients crucial for the production of canon and gunpowder—sulphur, saltpetre, charcoal and such metals as iron, copper and tin—was extremely difficult in this period. Heavy artillery also was of little use to Persian military strategy, which was based on the ambush and a scorched earth policy and not on open confrontation with the enemy (*ibid.*).

Siege artillery was little used by the Ṣafawid armies for a variety of reasons. In this period, rulers left many cities unwalled or did not maintain city walls, devoting attention instead to the citadels within the cities. The extension of Ṣafawid power kept Persia's cities safe from internal threats and protected the interior ones from external threats. Moreover, the continued importance of the Ḳizil-Bās͟h in Persian society ensured that non-urbanised regions, the steppes in particular, were the subject of comparably greater attention.

Finally, the Ṣafawids' main enemies on the north and east, particularly the Özbegs, Afg͟hans and Balūč, utilised firearms less than the Ṣafawids themselves, thus providing little impetus for the Ṣafawids to change their military tactics. Unwieldy artillery was of little use in battles involving mounted cavalry. The Balūč and Afg͟hān advance into Ṣafawid territory, culminating in the capture of Iṣfahān in 1135/1722, was accomplished mainly without firearms. It was starvation which finally forced the city's surrender to the invaders, and not the few mounted guns which did appear there (Matthee, *Firearms*; and see further on the whole topic, BĀRŪD. v. The Ṣafawids).

Bibliography: I. Religious trends in the Ṣafawid period. ʿAlī Āl-i Dāwūd, *EIr*, art. *Coffeehouse*; B.S. Amoretti, *Religion in the Timurid and Safavid periods*, in *Camb. hist. of Iran*, vi, 610-55; K. Babayan, *The waning of the Qizilbash: the spiritual and the temporal in seventeenth century Iran*, Ph.D. thesis, Princeton University 1993, unpubl.; N. Calder, *Legitimacy and accomodation in Safavid Iran: the juristic theory of Muḥammad Bāqir al-Sabzawārī (d. 1090/1679)*, in *Iran*, xxv (1987), 91-105; idem, *Doubt and prerogative: the emergence of an Imami Shīʿī theory of Ijtihad*, in *SI*, lxx (1989), 57-78; idem, *Judicial authority in Imāmī Shīʿī jurisprudence*, in *Bull. British Society for Middle East Studies*, vi/2 (1979), 104-8; idem, *Zakāt in Imāmī Shīʿī jurisprudence, from the tenth to the sixteenth century, AD*, in *BSOAS*, xliv/3 (1981), 468-80; idem, *Khums in Imami Shii jurisprudence, from the tenth to the sixteenth century, AD*, in *BSOAS*, xlv/1 (1982), 39-47; J. Cole, *Shīʿī clerics in Iraq and Iran, 1722-1780: the Akhbārī-Uṣūlī conflict reconsidered*, in *Iranian Studies*, xviii/1 (1985), 3-34; R. D̲j̲aʿfariyān, *Dīn wa siyāsat dar dawra-yi Ṣafawī*, Ḳum 1370/1992; E. Kohlberg, *EIr*, arts. *Ak͟hbārīya*, *Bahāʾ al-Dīn al-ʿĀmilī*, *Beḥār al-Anwār*, *Astarābādī*, *Mollā Moḥammad Amīn*; idem, *Aspects of Ak͟hbārī thought in the seventeenth and eighteenth century*, in N. Levtzion and J. Voll (eds.), *Eighteenth-century renewal and reform in Islam*, Syracuse, N.Y. 1987, 133-60; W. Madelung, *Shīʿite discussions on the legality of the Kharaj*, in R. Peters (ed.), *Procs. of the Ninth Congress of the Union Européenne des Arabisants et Islamisants*, 1978, Leiden 1981, 193-202; R. Matthee, *Administrative change and stability in late 17th c. Iran: the case of Shaykh ʿAlī Khān Zangānah (1669-89)*, in *IJMES*, xxvi (1994), 77-98; idem, *Coffee in Safavid Iran: commerce and consumption*, in *JESHO*, xxxvii (1994), 1-32; idem, *Politics and trade in late Safavid Iran: commercial crisis and government reaction under Shāh Sulaymān (1666-1694)*, Ph.D. thesis, UCLA 1991, unpubl.; idem, *The career of Moḥammed Beg, Grand Vizier of Shah ʿAbbās II (r. 1642-1666)*, in *Iranian Studies*, xxiv/1-4 (1991), 17-36; V.B. Moreen, *Risāla-yi Ṣawāʿiq al-Yahūd (The treatise lightning bolts against the Jews) by Muḥammad Bāqir b. Muḥammad Taqī al-Majlisī (d. 1699)*, in *WI*, xxxii (1992), 177-95; A. Newman, *The myth of the clerical migration to Ṣafawid Iran: Arab Shīʿite opposition to ʿAlī al-Karakī and Safawid Shīʿism*, in *ibid.*, xxxiii (1993), 66-122; idem, *The nature of the Akhbārī/Uṣūlī dispute in late Ṣafawid Iran. Part 1: ʿAbdallāh al-Samāhijī's* Munyat al-mumārisīn, in *BSOAS*, lv/1 (1992), 22-51, *Part 2. The conflict reassessed*, in *ibid.*, lv/2 (1992), 250-61; idem, *Towards a reconsideration of the "Isfahān School of Philosophy": Shaykh Bahāʾī and the role of the Safawid* ᶜ*Ulamā*, in *SI*, xv/2 (1986), 165-99; D. Stewart, *A biographical note on Bahā al-Dīn al-ᶜĀmilī (d. 1030/1621)*, in *JAOS*, cxi/3 (1991), 563-71.

II. *Philosophy in the Ṣafawid period*. H. Corbin, *La place de Molla Sadra dans la philosophie Iranienne*, in *SI*, xviii (1963), 81-113; idem, *Confessions extatiques de Mīr Dāmād, maître de théologie à Ispahan (ob. 1041/1631-2)*, in *Mélanges Louis Massignon*, i, Damascus 1956, 331-78; idem, *Creative imagination in the Ṣūfism of Ibn ᶜArabī*, Princeton 1969; idem, *EIr*, art. *Aḥmad b. Zayn al-ᶜĀbedīn ᶜAlawī ᶜĀmilī Eṣfahānī, Sayyed*; J.W. Morris, *The Wisdom of the Throne, an introduction to the philosophy of Mulla Sadra*, Princeton 1981; S.H. Nasr, *Ṣadr al-Dīn Shīrāzī (Mullā Sadrā)*, in M.M. Sharif (ed.), *A history of Muslim philosophy*, Wiesbaden 1966, 932-61; idem, *Three Muslim sages, Avicenna-Suhrawardi-Ibn ᶜArabi*, Cambridge, Mass. 1964; idem, *The school of Ispahan*, in Sharif, *op. cit.*, 904-32; idem, *Spiritual movements, philosophy and theology in the Safavid period*, in *Camb. hist. of Iran*, vi, 656-97; idem, *Sadr al-Din Shirazi and his transcendant theosophy*, Tehran 1978; A. Newman, *EIr*, arts. *Gi̲ā̲t̲ al-Dīn Daštakī, Mīr Dāmād, Jalāl al-Dīn Davānī*; F. Rahman, *The philosophy of Mullā Ṣadrā*, Albany 1975; idem, *Mīr Dāmād's concept of Ḥudūth Dahrī: a contribution to the study of God-World relationship theories in Ṣafavid Iran*, in *JNES*, xxxix/2 (1980), 139-51; idem, *The God-World relationship in Mullā Ṣadrā*, in G.F. Hourani (ed.), *Essays on Islamic philosophy and science*, Albany 1975, 238 ff.; Bakhtiyar Husain Siddiqi, *Jalāl al-Dīn Dawwānī*, in Sharif, *op. cit.*, 883-888.

III. *Science and society in the Ṣafawid period*. i. *Medicine in the Ṣafawid period*. M.W. Dols, *Islam and medicine*, in *History of Science*, xxvi (1988); C. Elgood, *Safavid medical practice*, London 1970; Mehdi Keyvani, *Artisans and guild life in the later Safavid period*, Berlin 1992; V. Minorsky (tr.), *Tad̲h̲kirat al-mulūk*, London 1943; Iskandar Beg Muns̲h̲ī, *History of Shah ᶜAbbas the Great (Tārīk̲h̲i ᶜĀlamārā-yi ᶜAbbāsī)*, 2 vols., tr. R.M. Savory, Boulder, Colo. 1978; Ḳāḍī Aḥmad b. S̲h̲araf al-Dīn al-Ḥusayn al-Ḳummī, *K̲h̲ulāṣat al-tawārīk̲h̲*, ed. E. Eshraqi, 2 vols., Tehran 1359-63/1980-4; Ḥasan-i Rumlū, *Aḥsan al-tawārīk̲h̲*, tr. C.N. Seddon, Baroda 1934; Sayyid ᶜAbd al-Ḥusayn K̲h̲ātūnābādī, *Waḳāʾiᶜ al-sinīn*, Tehran 1352/1973-4; *Islamic medical wisdom, the Ṭibb al-aʾimma*, tr., B. Ispahany, ed. A. Newman, London 1991; Ṣādeq Sajjādī, *EIr*, arts. *Bīmārestān, Dām-Pazeškī, ii. In Islamic Persia*; E. Savage-Smith, *Islamic medicine*, forthcoming in *An encyclopedia of Arab science*, ed. R. Rashed, London.

ii. *Astronomy and associated sciences*. G. Saliba, *The astronomical tradition of Marāgha: a historical survey and prospects for future research,*, in *Arabic Sciences and Philosophy*, i (1991), 67-99; E. Savage-Smith and M. Smith, *Islamic geomancy and a thirteenth-century divinatory device*, Malibu, Calif. 1980; E. Savage-Smith, *Islamicate celestial globes, their history, construction and use*, Washington, D.C. 1985; eadem, *Celestial mapping*, in *The history of cartography*, Vol. ii, Book 1, *Cartography in the traditional Islamic and South Asian societies*, ed. J.B. Harley and D. Woodward, Chicago 1992, 12-70; H.J.J. Winter, *Persian science in Safavid times*, in *Camb. hist. of Iran*, vi, 581-609.

iii. *Military technology*. R. Matthee, *Unwalled cities and restless nomads: firearms and artillery in Safavid Iran*, forthcoming. (A.J. NEWMAN)

V. Arts and architecture.

The period of more than two centuries (907-1145/1501-1732) from the advent of S̲h̲āh Ismāᶜīl I to the demise of the last Ṣafawid rulers is marked by significant changes in Persian patronage, taste, and aesthetics and by the powerful role of political and religious ideology in shaping the arts. While royal patrons, like Ṭahmāsp I and ᶜAbbās I, who had long reigns in which to imprint their strong personal tastes on the arts, exerted great influence, there is abundant evidence documenting the increasing importance of sub-royal patronage and non-aristocratic patronage of the arts. As always, family ties were important in landing commissions and appointments at court, and intermarriage among artists' families was extensive: the 10th/16th-century calligrapher Muḥibb ᶜAlī, for instance, was the son of the royal scribe Rustam ᶜAlī and the grand-nephew of Bihzād [*q.v.*] and the cousin of the notable painter Muẓaffar ᶜAlī. Signed or reliably ascribed works of art and architecture became far more plentiful than in earlier times, as did overt displays of connoisseurship and proud references to impressive collections of precious books, not only illustrated manuscripts but also sumptuous albums (*muraḳḳaᶜ* [*q.v.*]) that included fragments of larger works, admired single-page calligraphies, paintings, and drawings, and occasional examples of the work of foreign artists: around 977/1570 prince Ibrāhīm assembled an album of paintings and drawings by Bihzād and several albums of calligraphies by Mīr ᶜAlī Harawī that were as much esteemed as a great illustrated manuscript. These changes imply a more pronounced artistic self-consciousmess and worldly appreciation of the arts than in Il-K̲h̲ānid or Tīmūrid Persia, as do the numerous lengthy accounts of the arts written by individuals like the painters Dūst Muḥammad and Ṣādiḳī Bek, the calligrapher Sulṭān ᶜAlī, and the art-loving officials Iskandar Muns̲h̲ī and Ḳāḍī Aḥmad. The latter writer takes special paints to establish a particularly Ṣafawid theoretical base for the visual arts that gives equal weight and propriety to painting and calligraphy: thus ᶜAlī b. Abī Ṭālib is credited with being the master of the two *ḳalams*, the reed of the scribe and the brush of the painter, so that ᶜAlī, as the first Muslim painter, ranks in importance with the renowned Mānī, the legendary pre-Islamic Iranian painter. The centrality of ᶜAlī is likewise evident in the earliest buildings constructed under Ṣafawid patronage and pervades the finest architectural inscriptions in Iṣfahān a century later: the state ideology that separated S̲h̲īᶜī Persia from rival Sunnī Ottoman, Uzbek and Mug̲h̲al domains pervades its arts. A profitable art trade brought European prints and printed books to Persia and took the work of some Ṣafawid painters to wealthy patrons in India, while Persian ceramics were purchased by European merchants for sale at home. The European presence in Ṣafawid Persia included not only diplomats, merchants, travellers and missionaries but also artists, and western European influence and an increasingly strong sense of naturalism are notable in the pictorial arts in the last century of Ṣafawid rule.

Ismāᶜīl I. Adherence to ᶜAlī and mystical S̲h̲īᶜism, early evident in the poetry of S̲h̲āh Ismāᶜīl, distinguished the régime from its western, northern, and eastern Sunnī neighbours and rivals and affected content and context of the visual arts. Architecture under this first Ṣafawid s̲h̲āh is little known: the two principal monuments are the 928-9/1521-2 Mas̲d̲jid-i ᶜAlī and the 918/1513 tomb of Hārūn-i Wilāyat, both in Iṣfahān's bazaar area and both reflecting in their names the strident adherence to ᶜAlī characteristic of Ismāᶜīl's reign. The tomb is justly celebrated for its portal, decorated in faience mosaic closer in style to the ornamentation of 9th/15th century Turcoman architecture of western Persia than to that of the

Tīmūrid east. Ismāʿīl's exposure to Turcoman styles is also evident in a painting attributed to the painter Sulṭān Muḥammad, *Sleeping Rustam defended from a lion by his horse Rakhsh* (reproduced in S.C. Welch, *A King's Book of Kings*, fig. 10), that most probably belonged to a *Shāh-nāma* begun and never completed for the first Ṣafawid ruler. The heir apparent, Ṭahmāsp Mīrzā, appointed governor of Harāt in 922/1516, returned to Tabrīz in 928/1522 at the age of nine, accompanied by the pre-eminent Tīmūrid painter, Bihzād, who was promptly appointed head of the royal *kitāb-khāna* (library and workshop). The convergence of the Turcoman and Tīmūrid artistic traditions during the first half of the 10th/16th century is the essential element in the development of mature Ṣafawid court styles in architecture and the arts.

Ṭahmāsp I. Too young to rule effectively in 930/1524, the young shāh turned his attention to the arts of the precious book and initiated the production of the greatest *Shāh-nāma* in Persian history. The *Shāh Ṭahmāsp Shāh-nāma* was a sumptuous creation, with 258 paintings, superb calligraphy and stunning illumination. The collaborative endeavour of dozens of different artists, it was successively under the direction of some Persia's foremost talents, like Āḳā Mīrak and Sulṭān Muḥammad, and its paintings delineate the evolution of Ṣafawid court style of Turcoman and Tīmūrid modes. Containing no colophon giving either the date of completion or the name of the scribe or scribes, the book occupied the talents of the royal atelier for some twenty years, and was complete when Dūst Muḥammad wrote his *Account of past and present painters* in 953/1546. As one of the important contributors to the *Shāh-nāma*, this painter, calligrapher, and chronicler of the arts knew it well and specifically singled out for great praise the painting of *The court of Gayūmarth* by Sulṭān Muḥammad (reproduced in Welch, *op. cit.*, 89). Other great projects of the shāh's patronage include the 946-50/1539-43 *Khamsa* of Niẓāmī now in the British Library. In keeping with the Tīmūrid princely tradition, the shāh's brothers Bahrām and Sām were also keenly interested in this most exclusive of court arts. The depiction of murals in illustrations of architectural interiors, as well as some surviving examples in extant buildings, indicate that wall painting was also an important activity for painters, and this tradition continued for the rest of the Ṣafawid era. In 955/1548 the shāh removed the seat of government from Tabrīz to Ḳazwīn. He came increasingly to favour orthodoxy, and his passion for the arts of the secular book waned, though a 959/1552 Ḳurʾān, almost certainly created for Ṭahmāsp, indicates that calligraphers and illuminators of the highest ability were still employed in the royal *kitāb-khāna* (reproduced in T. Falk (ed.), *Treasures of Islam*, 100-1). Many of his artists left the court in search of other patronage: some went to work for princes in provincial posts, like the shāh's gifted nephew Ibrāhīm (the patron of the great 963-72/1556-65 *Haft awrang* of Djāmī now in the Freer Gallery), while others, like Mīr Sayyid ʿAlī, moved further east to Mughal India, where they were instrumental in shaping classic Mughal court painting.

ʿAbbās I. Following a decade of instability after Ṭahmāsp I's death in 1576, ʿAbbās I brought great energy to his 42-year reign. Like his predecessors, he initiated a great *Shāh-nāma* project that re-established a large and productive royal atelier, and he took an active interest in the arts of the book. He particularly favoured the painters Ṣādiḳī Bek and Riḍā ʿAbbāsī [*q.v.*], supported the rival calligraphers ʿAlī Riḍā Tabrīzī and Mīr ʿImād, and even mediated disputes within the royal *kitābkhāna*. The dispersal of artistic talent during Shāh Ṭahmāsp's reign and the broader diffusion of wealth from ʿAbbās's economic reforms increased the numbers of patrons from the lesser aristocracy, official and military classes, professionals, and merchants. Many of these new patrons appear to have bought, rather than commissioned, works of art, so that the production of less expensive single-page drawings and paintings flourished. Virtuoso demonstrations more than collaborative endeavours, they took their subject matter from a variety of sources: images drawn from contemporary and mundane society that are often humorous or even sharply satirical (Pl. XLV); elegant courtiers, sometimes identified by name; wistful lovers and Riḍā's fashion-plate youths (Pl. XLVI), often accompanied by mystical verses, who presumably correspond to the divine beloved. Ṣafawid metalwork was also frequently adorned with mystical poetry that indicates how deeply and thoroughly Ṣūfism suffused the culture (Pl. XLVII).

But the shāh also recognised the importance of the arts in promoting the economic well-being of Persia. Some carpet manufacturing under royal patronage was profitably directed at commissions from European nobility (Pl. XLVIII), and the role of textiles in commerce, always significant in Islam's past, seems to have been especially enhanced. Ṣafawid silk textiles demonstrated diversity and virtuosity in technique, and they depended to a remarkable extent upon figural decoration; some royal painters worked as textile designers, and silk cloths were decorated with scenes of Ṣafawid victories over inveterate enemies like the Uzbeks, as well as with visiting Europeans, youthful lovers, and the beauties of gardens and nature (Pl. XLIX). Likewise, he encouraged ceramic production, and, in addition to more traditional lustre wares, Persian potters imitated Chinese blue-and-white ceramics for sale to European merchants in the China trade as well as to satisfy the substantial demand in Persia (Pl. L). Persian manuscripts and single-page works of art were even bought by merchants for sale outside Persia.

Foreign contacts and international trade were vital elements in ʿAbbās's strategy for his state, and, apart from the European and Indian diplomats and merchants who came to Persia, there were European scholars, missionaries, and independent travellers whose interests generally extended more broadly. They remained an important feature of Persian cultural and social life throughout the 11th/17th century, and their published reports not only stimulated contemporary interest in Persia but also serve as major sources of information for modern scholarship. Their attention was particular drawn to the city of Iṣfahān [*q.v.*], which ʿAbbās chose as his centre of government in 1006/1598 and where he undertook one of the greatest building programs in Islamic history. Blessed with year-round water from the Zayandeh River, the city appeared to visitors like a green forest accentuated by brilliant tiled domes. To the south across the river the shāh established the community of New Djulfā [*q.v.* in Suppl.] for Christian Armenians who provided most of the multilingual merchants involved in Persia's international commerce, and their richly decorated extant churches are a striking synthesis of 17th-century Persian and European art and archtitecture.

In order to promote safe commercial travel within Persia, ʿAbbās ordered the construction of dozens of *khāns* [*q.v.*] or caravanserais. Most of them also served as or were connected with bazaars, and they are among the most impressive examples of Ṣafawid architecture. The Ḳaysariyya bazaar in Iṣfahān is the best preserved and connected the city's old *d̲j̲āmiʿ* with ʿAbbās's new city centre, a large rectangular *maydān*, 2 km to the southwest (Pl. LI). It provided not only shops for manufacture and commerce but also access to immediately adjacent mosques, like the 1065/1654 Masd̲j̲id-i Ḥakīm, that served merchants and their customers. The Ḳaysariyya's entrance occupies the north end of the new *maydān*; 500 m distant at the south end is the entrance to the Masd̲j̲id-i Imām, a brilliant construction on the classic four-īwān plan completed in 1637. Both buildings dominate their respective sides and suggest the preoccupation with large size, showy opulence, glistening surfaces, and dramatic effects that are major components of the Ṣafawid aesthetic: the *maydān* itself was an open area for military parades, commerce, music, acrobatics, and other kinds of entertainment. Less dominant are the adjoining buildings—the single-domed S̲h̲ayk̲h̲ Luṭf Allāh mosque on the east side and, opposite it across the *maydān*, the ʿĀlī Ḳāpū or High Gate entrance to the s̲h̲āh's gardens and Čihil Sutūn palace that extend to the west. While the S̲h̲ayk̲h̲ Luṭf Allāh mosque's dome is decorated in traditional faience mosaic, the decorative programme of the Masd̲j̲id-i Imām is laid out in large glazed tiles, a technique demanding precise knowledge of the reaction of clays and glazes to firing, especially where the tiles were curved to cover the surface of domes and *mīnars*. Extensive use of this type of tile decoration must have required the employment of gifted potters and painters, and may partly account for the apparent decline in the sophistication of more traditional ceramics in the Ṣafawid period. Both mosques were provided with splendid inscriptions designed by ʿAlī Riḍā Tabrīzī that cite passages from both Ḳurʾān and *Ḥadīt̲h̲* underscoring and supporting the Ṣafawids' descent from ʿAlī and their special role as protectors of S̲h̲īʿī Islam in Persia. To the same end, ʿAbbās also made lavish gifts of carpets and ceramics to the dynastic shrine of S̲h̲ayk̲h̲ Ṣafī in Ardabīl.

The second level of the ʿĀlī Ḳāpū is dominated by its projecting *ṭālār*, a colonnaded verandah more usually associated with far more private dwellings, where it would provide an open and sheltered vista toward an enclosed garden, pool, or courtyard that served as the physical centre of domestic space. In the s̲h̲āh's palace, however, the *ṭālār* is no longer intimate but opens instead on to the *maydān*, as if that vast space were itself an inner court, enclosed by the arcades on all four sides and subject to the patriarch's focussed glance and discipline. The king could also ritually present himself to those assembled in the *maydān* below. It is an architectural simile for the increased power of the central administration and of the s̲h̲āh as both autocrat and head of the Ṣafawiyya Ṣūfī order. To the west, running roughly parallel to the *maydān*, was the *čahār bāg̲h̲*, an avenue and watercourse lined by the mansions and gardens of the wealthy and supplied by an elaborate hydraulic system with water from the river. While this part of Iṣfahān must have been a veritable garden city for the rich, its natural imagery does not seem to have permeated the imagery of painting, for the garden, which had served as the setting for many earlier illustrated scenes from Persian literature became a relatively infrequent backdrop in paintings by Iṣfahān's artists.

Later Ṣafawid art and architecture. In the century after S̲h̲āh ʿAbbās I, ceramics and sumptuous textiles continued to be important sources of revenue and were admired items of luxury trade in Europe and India. Traditional literary themes in the arts of the book were in part supplanted by often incisive depictions of actual, ordinary, and even outlandish individuals, of exotic persons from other lands, of implicit and occasionally fairly explicit eroticism, of carefully-observed nature (Pl. LII), and of actual events and formal portraits. Although the European technology of printing was ignored and traditional calligraphy continued to flourish in the hands of masters like Muḥammad Riḍā (Pl. LIII), the impact of European prints and the influence of European modes of representation increased, notably in the work of Muḥammad Zamān (Pl. LIV), and traditional styles began to take on a more international guise, while European travel accounts accorded Iṣfahān a reputation rivalling that of Istanbul, Dihlī, and Āgrā. Although there were no subsequent urban projects as grandiose as the *maydān*, architecture and the arts evinced similar aesthetic and cultural concerns. ʿAbbās II undertook major building and restoration programs at the Shrine of the Imām Riḍā in Mas̲h̲had [*q.v.*], and during the reign of Sultan Ḥusayn I an impressive *madrasa* and adjoining *k̲h̲ān* were built on the *čahār bāg̲h̲* in design and style making obeisance to the Masd̲j̲id-i Imām.

Bibliography: J. Sourdel-Thomine's article IṢFAHĀN. 2. Monuments. provides a list of publications essential to the study of Ṣafawid architecture. D.N. Wilber devotes part of his book, *Persian gardens and garden pavilions*, 1962, to the study of Ṣafawid gardens and pavilions. R. Holod (ed.), *Studies on Isfahan*, in *Iranian Studies, Journal of the Society for Iranian Studies*, vii, includes essential articles on architecture, urban planning, painting, metalwork, and ceramics by a number of scholars. Pioneering studies on all aspects of Ṣafawid art and architecture are to be found in *A Survey of Persian art*, 1939. A. Welch, *Shah ʿAbbas and the arts of Isfahan*, Asia Society, 1973, presents an overview of later Ṣafawid arts. The same author's *Artists for the Shah: late sixteenth century painting at the imperial court of Iran*, New Haven 1976, examines manuscript illustration during the reigns of Ṭahmāsp I, Ismāʿīl II, Muḥammad K̲h̲udābanda and ʿAbbās I. S.C. Welch and M.B. Dickson, *The Houghton Shahnameh*, Cambridge, Mass. 1981, is a magisterial study of the origins and development of early Ṣafawid painting and includes a translation of Ṣādiḳī Bek's treatise on painting, *Ḳānūn al-Ṣuwār*. Other major publications by S.C. Welch on early Ṣafawid painting are *A King's Book of Kings: the Shāhnāmeh of Shah Tahmasp*, Metropolitan Museum, New York 1972; *Persian painting: five royal Safavid manuscripts of the 16th century*, New York 1976; and *Wonders of the age*, Cambridge, Mass. 1979. T. Falk (ed.), *Treasures of Islam*, includes discussions of arts of the book by A. Welch, S.C. Welch, and Massumeh Farhad. I. Stchoukine, *Les peintures des manuscrits Safavis de 1502-1587*, Paris 1959, and *Les peintures des manuscrits de Shah ʿAbbas à la fin des Safavis*, Paris 1964, are basic sources for painting. A major primary source for arts of the book is Ḳāḍī Aḥmad, *Calligraphers and painters*, Washington 1959. One of the few studies of a calligrapher is M. Bayānī, *Mīr ʿImād*, Tehran 1951. The same author's *K̲h̲ūs̲h̲-niwīsān*, Tehran 1966, contains invaluable information about the works and careers of Ṣafawid calligraphers.

(A. WELCH)

VI. Numismatics.

The Ṣafawid coinage was introduced following the victories of S̲h̲āh Ismāʿīl I over the Aḳ Ḳoyunlu Turkmen in 907-8/1502, and continued without break until the deposition of S̲h̲āh ʿAbbās III by Nādir S̲h̲āh in 1148/1736. All the rulers, except for the ephemeral Sulṭān Ḥamza who administered the state in 994/1586, struck coinage in their own names, and one even struck it in two, first in that of Ṣafī II and then, after his re-enthronement, as Sulaymān. After Nādir S̲h̲āh's death in 1160/1747 coins were also occasionally issued in the names of Ṣafawid pretenders who claimed paternal, maternal or even entirely fictive royal descent until the death of the last claimant in 1200/1786. The examination of these coins, however, properly forms part of the later monetary history of Persia.

During the period of Ṣafawid rule, the Persian currency system was based on the tūmān, a unit of account whose value was fixed at the currently-established weight of 10,000 silver dīnārs. The weight of the tūmān was customarily expressed as a fixed number of mit̲h̲ḳāls or nuk̲h̲ūds of refined silver which could then be converted into coin with the value of 10,000 dīnārs. One mit̲h̲ḳāl, weighing approximately 4.60 gr, was equal to 24 nuk̲h̲ūds which each weighed about 0.192 gr.

Table 1 shows the extent of the Ṣafawid silver coinage, giving the name of the ruler, the weight(s) of the tūmān in nuk̲h̲ūds during his period of rule, and the names of the various silver coins, their individual value in dīnārs and their theoretical weight in grammes. It should be noted that weight standards were not always uniform and that local variations existed, particularly in the Caspian region and the eastern provinces. The heaviest coin was usually the most popular and most commonly struck. Under Ismāʿīl I the principal coin was the s̲h̲āhī valued at 50 dīnārs, 200 per tūmān. Then under Ṭahmāsb I came the double s̲h̲āhī, or 100 dīnārs, 100 per tūmān, which during the rule of Muḥammad K̲h̲udābanda was renamed the muḥammadī. ʿAbbās I introduced the four s̲h̲āhī, 200 dīnārs, 50 per tūmān, which he named the ʿabbāsī. The ʿabbāsī remained the normal Persian denomination for the remainder of the dynasty and for a time afterwards, except for a brief period between 1123 and 1129 under S̲h̲āh Sulṭān Ḥusayn when it was supplanted by the oblong-shaped five s̲h̲āhī (the ḥusaynī?). It should be noted that coins valued above five s̲h̲āhīs were produced especially for the ruler to distribute during the Nawrūz [q.v.] celebrations, and these usually quickly found their way to the jewellers for conversion into personal ornaments.

Table 2 summarises the Ṣafawid gold coinage. Gold played a much smaller rôle in the Persian currency system than did silver or copper. Indeed, in the century before the accession of S̲h̲āh Ismāʿīl I the Tīmūrids had struck no gold at all in their Persian mints. The Aḳ Ḳoyunlu, who succeeded the Tīmūrids in the west, introduced the striking of the gold as̲h̲rafī in Tabrīz during the last quarter of the 9th/15th century as a trade coin. In its weight, ca. 3.45 gr, dumpy fabric and epigraphy, it was copied so exactly on the Burdjī Mamlūk as̲h̲rafī popularised by al-As̲h̲raf Barsbāy that the name of the ruler in the legends often has to be read in order to distinguish one currency from another. The earliest gold coin of Ismāʿīl I was a copy of the Aḳ Ḳoyunlu/Burdjī Mamlūk as̲h̲rafī in both weight and design, but it was not long before the Persian artistic tradition reasserted itself as evidence of Ismāʿīl's determination to stage a Persian religious and cultural revival. Quite exceptionally in Islam, the Ṣafawids struck both their gold and silver coins from the same dies, and as none of them bore any mark of denomination it would have been easy for counterfeiters to gold-plate silver and

pass it off on the unwary had gold been in regular circulation. Contemporary travellers to Persia recorded that local gold was very rarely seen and little used in commerce.

Although all the gold coins were popularly called as̲h̲rafī, there were actually several different varieties to which this name was given, which were distinguished from one another by their weights rather than by their designs or legends. Ismāʿīl used two standards for his gold coinage—one based on the weight of the traditional Islamic mit̲h̲ḳāl or coinage dīnār of 24 nuk̲h̲ūds (approximately 4.60 gr), and the other, the true as̲h̲rafī, with its origin in the weight of the Venetian gold ducat, weighing 18 nuk̲h̲ūds (approximately 3.45 gr). The latter was theoretically exchangeable at par with European ducats, the Mamlūk as̲h̲rafī and the Ottoman sulṭānī. Halves and quarters were struck in both standards, and the latter became popular in eastern Persia where its use was linked to the quarter as̲h̲rafīs issued by the Mug̲h̲al rulers in the Badak̲h̲s̲h̲ān region of Afg̲h̲ānistān.

Under the Ṣafawids all gold coins were treated as a commodity with no fixed price against the silver tūmān. Their purchasing power fluctuated according to supply and demand, type of commodity, season of the year and the perceived reliability of the original issuing agent. Traders always preferred Venetian ducats, and generally held the Ṣafawid coinage in low esteem. In the 11th/17th century, local gold virtually vanished from the Middle East and Persia. Because both regions preferred silver to gold, the price of silver was relatively higher throughout these areas than it was in Europe, where gold was favoured. This gave European traders a perfect opportunity to import inexpensive silver from the New World which they sold locally for gold at great profit to themselves. In time, so much gold was siphoned out of Persia that it was said that the only gold coins to be struck by Ṣafī I, ʿAbbās II and Sulaymān were those that the rulers presented to their courtiers at the Nawrūz celebrations. Thus the custom arose of striking gold at the weight of the popular silver denominations, the ʿabbāsī, muḥammadī and s̲h̲āhī, and giving them a nominal value in dīnārs ten times that of their silver originals. These rare pieces, as well as the magnificent gold ten-mit̲h̲ḳāls and ten-as̲h̲rafīs modelled on the multiple ducats of Venice and the Holy Roman Empire, were pièces de plaisir, and were usually incorporated into jewellery as a sign of royal favour.

Copper coinage played a central rôle in the local economy of Ṣafawid Persia. While gold and silver were struck under royal license, copper fulūs were issued by the provincial governors. To avoid infringing upon the royal prerogative, the coins they struck did not bear the governors' names, but included easily-recognised figures of objects, often animals, birds or even humans on one face and the name of the mint and year of striking on the other. This made the fulūs easy to identify, which was important because it was the custom to recall the copper coinage not only annually but whenever the incumbent was replaced by a new appointee. The coinage was then recalled, restruck and sold to the people at a price which was said to yield a 50% profit on the value of the issue. To make this system feasible, only locally-struck copper coin was permitted to circulate, and only coins of the current governor and year were accepted at full value. Fulūs were occasionally given denominational names for example yek or dō dīnār were valued at one or two dīnārs, ḳaz or ḳazbak at five dīnārs and tanga at ten dīnārs. Because the lifespan of copper was so short very little care was taken in its manufacture, and

TABLE 1
ṢAFAWID SILVER COINAGE
Summary of weight standards and denominations

		bistī	*pūl*	*s̲h̲āhī*	*muḥammadī*	*ʿabbāsī*	5 *s̲h̲āhī*	donative coins						
Ruler and years	*Nuk̲h̲ūds* per *tūmān*	20 dīnār	25	50	100	200	250	300	400	500	750	800	1000	1500
Ismāʿīl I 906-23	9,600		4.60	9.20	18.40									
923-7	5,400		2.60	5.18	10.36									
928-30	4,050		1.94	3.88	7.77									
Ṭahmāsb I 930-8	4,050	1.55		3.88	7.77									
938-45	2,900	1.11		2.78	5.56									
(936-42)	2,800				5.18									
945-84	2,400		1.15	2.30	4.60									
Ismāʿīl II 984-5	2,400			2.30	4.60									
Muḥammad K̲h̲udābanda 985-95	2,400			2.30	4.60									
ʿAbbās I 995-1003	2,400		1.15	2.30	4.60	9.20								
1003-37	2,000	0.76		1.92	3.84	7.68								
Ṣafī I 1038-52	2,000	0.76		1.92	3.84	7.68	9.60							
ʿAbbās II 1052-77	1,925	0.74		1.84	3.69	7.39	9.24			18.48			36.96	
Ṣafī II Sulaymān 1077-1105	1,925	0.74		1.84	3.69	7.39				18.48			36.96	
Ḥusayn 1105-23	1,925	0.74		1.84	3.69	7.39				18.48			36.96	55.44
1123-9	1,800			1.73	3.45	6.91	8.64	10.36			26.88			
1129-35	1,400		0.67	1.34	2.68	5.37				13.44			26.88	
(1133-5)	1,200					4.60			9.20			18.40		
Ṭahmāsb III 1134-44	1,400	0.53		1.34	2.68	5.37				13.44			26.88	
ʿAbbās III 1144-8	1,400	0.53		1.34	2.68	5.37								

relatively few pieces have survived to find a place in museum coin cabinets.

As on other Islamic coinages, the coin legends used by the Ṣafawids fall into two main categories: the religious texts which are found on the obverse and the political on the reverse. The obverse for all rulers except S̲h̲āh Ismāʿīl II contains the S̲h̲īʿī profession of faith, *lā ilāh illā Allāh, Muḥammad rasūl* (or *nabī*) *Allāh,*

TABLE 2
ṢAFAWID GOLD COINAGE
Summary of weight standards and denominations

Ruler and years	*Mit͟hḳāl* or dīnār (24 *nuk͟hūd*) 1	½	¼(10)	*As͟hrafī* or ducat (18 *nuk͟hūd*) 1	½	¼(10)	2000 dīnārs, gold ʿAbbāsī	1000 dīnārs, gold Muḥammadī	500 dīnārs, gold S͟hāhī	Uncertain value	Remarks
Ismāʿīl I 906-30	4.60	2.30	1.15	3.45	1.73	0.86					gold plentiful, b standards in us
Ṭahmāsb I 930-84	4.60	2.30	1.15	3.45	?	0.86		29 *nuk͟hūd* 5.56			gold plentiful, b standards in us
Ismāʿīl II 984-5	4.60	?	?								coinage rare, *mit͟hḳāl* standard only
Muḥammad K͟hudābanda 985-95	4.60	2.30	?								gold plentiful, *mit͟hḳāl* standard only
ʿAbbās I 995-1003	4.60	2.30	1.15				48 *nuk͟hūd* 9.20 gr				gold plentiful, *mit͟hḳāl* standard only
1003-37							40 *nuk͟hūd* 7.68 gr	20 *nuk͟hūd* 3.84 gr	10 *nuk͟hūd* 1.92 gr		gold scarce; gol struck at weigh silver coinage
Ṣafī I 1038-52								20 *nuk͟hūd* 3.84 gr			gold rare; gold s at weight of sil coinage
ʿAbbās II 1052-77					1.73					14 *nuk͟hūd* 2.68 gr	gold rare, no f standard
Ṣafī II/ Sulaymān 1077-1105			46.00	3.45			38 *nuk͟hūd* 7.29 gr		9.5 *nuk͟hūd* 1.82 gr		gold rare, mix standards
Ḥusayn 1105-35				3.45			28 *nuk͟hūd* 5.37 gr.				gold scarce, du standard reviv
1133-5										15 *nuk͟hūd* 2.88 gr	emergency coinage
Ṭahmāsb II 1135-44				3.45		34.50	28 *nuk͟hūd* 5.37 gr.		7 *nuk͟hūd* 1.24 gr		gold plentiful, standard in us
ʿAbbās III 1144-8				3.45			28 *nuk͟hūd* 5.37 gr				gold plentiful, standard in us

ʿAlī walī Allāh with or without the names of the Twelve Imāms: *ʿAlī, Ḥasan, Ḥusayn, ʿAlī, Muḥammad, D̲j̲aʿfar, Mūsā, ʿAlī, Muḥammad, ʿAlī, Ḥasan* and *Muḥammad*. The names of the Twelve Imāms were first employed by the Ilk͟hān ruler Öld̲j̲eytü between 709 and 716 on his two S͟hīʿī coin types, and they then reappeared 200 years later when S͟hāh Ismāʿīl made Twelver S͟hīʿism the state faith of Persia. During his brief reign, S͟hāh Ismāʿīl II used a poetic distich in place of the *kalima* in order to prevent the holy words from falling into the hands of unbelievers. The religious legends were usually inscribed in *nask͟hī* script.

The reverse legends usually contain the name of the ruler, the mint names and the years of striking. The ruler's name usually lacks his patronymic, the exceptions being Ismāʿīl II and Muḥammad K͟hudābanda, who give that of their father *b. Ṭahmāsb*. Their titles are of two kinds, those that define the ruler's relationship to the people he ruled and those that define his relationship to the S͟hīʿī faith. The former are in Arabic, usually inscribed in *nask͟hī* script, and are more or less elaborate depending on the number of words which could be fitted on a die, e.g. *al-Sulṭān al-ʿĀdil, al-Kāmil, al-Hādī, al-Wālī, al-G͟hāzī fī Sabīl Allāh Abu 'l-Muẓaffar, S͟hāh.... Bahādur K͟hān, al-Ṣafawī al-Ḥusaynī, k͟hallada Allāh taʿālā mulkahu wa-sulṭānahu*. This form was used by Ismāʿīl I, Ṭahmāsb I, Ismāʿīl II, Muḥammad K͟hudābanda, ʿAbbās I and Ḥusayn. Ḥusayn also used *al-Sulṭān b. al-Sulṭān al-K͟hāḳān b. al-K͟hāḳān. Al-Ṣafawī al-Ḥusaynī* refers to S͟hayk͟h Ṣafī al

Dīn Ardabīlī [*q.v.*], the ancestor of the dynasty, who claimed descent from the third Imām Ḥusayn b. ʿAlī. This ancestral claim parallels that of the contemporary Ḥasanī Sharīfs of Morocco, who were then using *al-Ḥasanī* among their own titles. Perhaps both dynasties emphasised their illustrious descent in order to embarrass the Ottomans, who had no claim to such prestigious ancestry.

The legends which proclaim the ruler's Shīʿī allegiance are in Persian. The better known of these are *Ghulām-i Imām Mahdī ʿalayhi al-salām* and *Ghulām-i ʿAlī b. Abī Ṭālib ʿalayhi al-salām* used by Ṭahmāsb I and Muḥammad Khudābanda; *Banda-yi Shāh-i Wilāyat* used by ʿAbbās I, ʿAbbās II, Ṣafī II-Sulaymān and Ḥusayn, and *Ghulām-i Shāh-i Dīn* used by Ṭahmāsb II. Poetical distichs in Persian incorporating the name of the ruler within their texts were employed by ʿAbbās I, Ṣafī I, ʿAbbās II, Ṣafī II-Sulaymān, Ḥusayn, Ṭahmāsb II and ʿAbbās III. At the end of Ṣafawid power, when Ṭahmāsb Ḳulī Khān, the later Nādir Shāh [*q.v.*], controlled Ṭahmāsb II and ʿAbbās III, anonymous distichs were also inscribed in the name of the eighth Imam, ʿAlī b. Mūsā al-Riḍā. Such distichs were also used by the Zands and early Ḳādjārs, who avoided placing their own names on the coinage while a Ṣafawid pretender still existed. These secular legends are usualy inscribed in *nastaʿlīḳ*, the script in which poetry was usually written.

State control over the monetary system was exercised by the *Muʿayyir al-Mamālik*, the State Assayer, who reported directly to the ruler. Under him were the local chief assayers and *ḍarrābī bashī*, masters of the mint, who were jointly responsible for ensuring that the gold and silver were of the right alloy and that the manufacture of the blank flans and their striking into coin proceeded according to the regulations in force. The management of the mint was farmed out to local concessionaires who were responsible for collecting and remitting the seignorage, *wādjibī*, charged for refining metal, manufacturing gold and silver thread for weaving carpets and luxury cloth, and for striking coins. The raw metal was delivered to the mints in the form of bullion and foreign or obsolete coins. Seignorage varied widely from 2% to 20% of the metal value based on what local commercial and political circumstances could bear.

Under the Ṣafawids, the main state mints were located in Iṣfahān and Tabrīz, whenever the latter was not under Ottoman control. Other main urban centres that witnessed more or less continual minting activity were Hamadhān, Kāshān, Ḳazwīn, Shīrāz and Yazd, as well as those in the main shrine towns of Ardābil and Mashhad. The ports of Rasht in the north and Ḥuwayzā in the south were chiefly concerned with restriking foreign coin as it entered the Ṣafawid dominions, while the almost continuous wars were financed by the *Urdū* (army) mint as well as those located in the north-western fortress towns of Eriwān, Gandja, Nakhčiwān, Shamākhī and Tiflīs, whenever these were not held by the Ottomans. Besides these towns, both Ismāʿīl I and Ṭahmāsb I operated many local mints which varied greatly in their importance and in their production of coin. Initially they served to reinforce the ruler's authority throughout the country and to spread the observance of the Twelver Shīʿī doctrines to areas where they may have been only lightly observed before the Ṣafawid conquests. However, like the Ottomans, the Ṣafawids found that a large number of small and remote mints gave only a marginal return to the state treasury and were often wide open to local manipulation and malpractice. Thus during the economic hardships and inflation of the 11th/17th century most of them were closed down unless a locally powerful governor could maintain their existence either as a matter of local prestige or to meet exceptional local needs.

Although Ṣafawid coins have survived in large numbers, no systematic effort has been made to study them within their political and economic contexts. They are usually treated, quite correctly, as the first section of the modern coinage of the Shāhs of Persia. The standard works on the Ṣafawid coinage need to be updated because of the many discoveries that have been made since they were published.

Bibliography: S. Album, *A checklist of popular Islamic coins*, Santa Rosa, Calif. 1993; H. Farahbakhsh, *Iranian hammered coinage 1500-1879 A.D.*, Berlin 1975; R.S. Poole, *A catalogue of coins of the Shahs of Persia in the British Museum*, London 1887; H.L. Rabino di Borgomale, *Coins, medals and seals of the Shahs of Iran*, Hertford 1945; idem, *Album of coins, medals and seals of the Shahs of Iran*, Oxford 1951.

(R. Darley-Doran)

ṢAFDĀR DJANG, Mīrzā Muhammad Muḳīm Ṣafdār Djang ("the Lion in War") (1708-54) the second *Nawwāb* or ruler of the North Indian post-Mughal successor state of Awadh [*q.v.*] (Eng. Oudh) from 1739 until his death fifteen years later. Nephew, son-in-law, and successor to Saʿādat Khān Burhān al-Mulk, and like him an immigrant to India from Nīshāpūr, he expanded his territory in the Gangetic valley while retaining as much influence as possible within the declining Mughal Empire. This was an era of political fragmentation, regional state formation, and massive cultural revival that together help form modern South Asian identity, but the post-Mughal aristocracy still sought to restore the Empire, and Ṣafdār Djang was very prominent in the struggle.

The Niẓām of Ḥaydarābād, ruler of a larger successor state in the south, and *Wazīr* or deputy to the Mughal Emperor, wrote on his deathbed in 1748 to Ṣafdār Djang, "You are now the most promising of our current youth. Take that office [Imperial *Wazīr*] upon yourself, and exert yourself in recovering the affairs of the Empire." Ṣafdār Djang fought in a civil war in and around Dihlī in 1753 over the control of imperial offices, by then virtually powerless but invested with residual authority throughout India. This civil war marks the final breakaway of Awadh from the imperial system in India.

Although his reign marks the emergence of Awadh as an autonomous successor state in the mid-Gangetic plains, his tomb, a splendid example of late Mughal architecture, stands in what is now New Delhi.

Bibliography: Ghulām Ḥusayn Khān Ṭabāṭabāʾī, *Siyar al-mutaʾakhkhirīn*, 1797, tr. M. Raymond, Calcutta 1902; Harnām Singh "Nāmī", *Tārīkh-i Saʿādat-i Djāwīd*, 1806; Ghulām ʿAlī Khān Naḳawī, *ʿImād al-saʿādat*, Lucknow 1864, 1897; A.L. Srivastava, *The first two Nawabs of Awadh*, Lucknow 1933, [2]1954; Z.U. Malik, *The reign of Muhammad Shah, 1719-1748*, Delhi 1977. See also AWADH and MUḤAMMAD SHĀH B. DJAHĀN-SHĀH.

(R.B. Barnett)

ṢAFF (A.), pl. *ṣufūf*, literally "rank, row or line, company of men standing in a rank, row or line" (Lane, 1693 col. 3), a term with various usages.

1. In religious practice. Here, *ṣaff* is used for the lines of worshippers assembled in the mosque or elsewhere for the prescribed worship; see on this, ṢALĀT.

2. In military organisation. In the traditional formation of armies on the march or on the battlefield (*taʿbiya*), there was a classic five-fold division of a centre, its left and right wings, a vanguard and a

rearguard (whence the term *khamīs* for an army). In actual battle, such as the engagements of the Arabs with the imperial Sāsānid army in ʿIrāḳ in the 630s, the Arabs drew themselves up into *ṣufūf* or ranks. The Prophet is said to have straightened, with an arrow held in his hand, the *ṣufūf* of the Muslims before the battle of Badr [*q.v.*] in 2/624 (Ibn Hishām, *Sīra*, 443-4, tr. Guillaume, 300; al-Ṭabarī, i, 1319, tr. M.V. McDonald and W.M. Watt, *The History of al-Ṭabarī. VII. The foundations of the community*, Albany 1987, 53-4), and the Ḳurʾānic verse LXI, 4, "God loves those who fight in His way in ranks, as though they were a building well-compacted" was adduced in support of the *ṣaff* formation. Only in the later Umayyad period does the use come in of troops concentrated into small, compact blocks (*karādīs*, sing. *kardūs*, *kurdūs*), but the *ṣaff* formation continued after this as a standard deployment.

See further, ḤARB. ii. The Caliphate, and the *Bibl.* there, to which may be added C.E. Bosworth, *Armies of the Prophet*, in B. Lewis (ed.), *The world of Islam. Faith, people, culture*, London 1976, 202-4.

(C.E. BOSWORTH)

3. In North African social organisation. Here, *ṣaff* denotes in certain parts of the Maghrib, chiefly Algeria, Southern Tunisia and Libya, a league, alliance, faction or party. In Morocco, the term *leff* [*q.v.*] is used with the same meaning throughout. As such *ṣaff* is vocalised with a *ḍamma* instead of *fatḥa* (cf. Dozy, *Suppl.*, i, 834). French spellings vary from *çof* and *çoff* to *sof* and *soff* (pl. *sfouf*).

The term refers to a major form of rural sedentary and transhumant Berber and nomadic Arab political organisation, viz. a diffuse system of two (or more) mutually opposing or rivalling leagues, often of uncertain origin, dividing villages or desert towns *ḳṣūr* (sing, *ḳṣar*), clans and families, or comprising whole tribes. Parallels have been looked for in classical Greece (R. Montagne), archaic Rome (E. Masqueray), Albania and Corsica (J. Despois, L'*Afrique du Nord*, Paris 1949, 145) and in mediaeval Italy (e.g. Guelphs and Ghibellines). As a rule, neighbouring tribal units belonged to opposite alliances but a neighbour-but-one belonged to one's own alliance. The obligation of mutual assistance between league members was strict and might include cash, provisions, arms, volunteer labour, fighting, shelter and providing for a family whose head was killed in feud or battle. The stronger the solidarity of a given league, the less would an opposing neighbour feel tempted to attack or trespass on his neighbour lest he activate the entire league. Causes of conflict were never lacking at every tribal level, the most common being land, water, trees, grazing, pastures, livestock, harvests, women, honour or a personal vendetta.

In Greater Kabylia, where the *ṣaff* phenomenon was first observed by Europeans (Devaux, Hanoteau and Letourneux, Masqueray, see *Bibl.*), the basic political unit was the village. Divided into two moieties, its cohesion was due to its political organs: the village assembly (*djamāʿa*), its executive officer (*amīn*) and the customary law (*ḳānūn*). Its complex *ṣaff*-system, despite its dualistic and antagonistic character, managed, by some "strange and obscure ponderation" (P. Bourdieu, *Sociologie de l'Algérie*, Paris 1970², 20) to maintain an overall equilibrium. Until the end of the 18th century, the whole of Greater Kabylia was divided in two great leagues named the "upper" and the "lower" leagues (*soff ufella, soff bū ʿadda*). These were territorial, not personal alliances, and their disposition on the ground resembled that of a chequerboard—a pattern already apparent in the *ṣaff* map given by Devaux, 40, and later encountered in Morocco (Montagne 1930). By the end of the 19th century, this system was "overlaid" by four major alliances: Ait Iraten (comprising 12 tribes), Zwāwa (10 tribes), Ait Illilten (6 tribes) and Ait Djennād (7 tribes).

Further south, the Berber-speaking Shāwiya of the Awrās massif [*q.v.*] who lived in villages and hamlets like the Kabyles but were more dispersed and largely semi-nomadic, also retained, though more sketchily, their political organisation and *ṣaff* spirit; almost all groups rallied round the two great tribes, Awlād Dāwūd and Awlād ʿAbdī, and participated in their mutual quarrels. Of a more personal type were the *ṣaff*s of several Arab "feudal" families in the Constantinois, such as the clans of Bū ʿUkkāz and Ben Gāna.

Still further south, in the Ibāḍī confederation of the Mzāb [*q.v.*], despite the unity of its heterodox creed and religious leadership (*ḥalḳat al-ʿazzāba*), each of the seven walled settlements (*ḳṣūr*) had its own secular assembly (*djamāʿat al-ʿawāmm*), often conflicting interests and *ṣaff*s both within the *ḳṣar* and between the *ḳṣūr*. Here, too, causes for friction and conflict, sometimes sanguinary, were not lacking: first comes water shortage (after Ghardāya, the capital, had dammed off the wādī Mīzāb for her own use, creating endless disputes with the towns Mlīka and al-ʿAṭf). Ghardāya itself, in times of crisis, split in two hostile camps: Eastern (*ṣaff sharḳī*), led by Awlād b. Sulaymān and allied with the *ḳṣar* Bni Isgen, and Western (*ṣaff gharbī*), led by Awlād ʿAmmī ʿĪsā and in league with Mlīka. Even its Jewish quarter (*mallāḥ* [*q.v.*]) became infected by the *ṣaff* spirit; in 1893 it split in two parties, Sullam and Balouka, when the latter erected a separate synagogue. Other towns and oases in the High Plains and northern fringes of the Sahara so divided were Wargla (Wardjlān), where in addition to neighbourhood rivalries there was fierce enmity between it and nearby Ngusa since the end of the 14th century, when the latter concluded a defence pact with the nomadic Arab tribe of Saʿīd ʿUtba (Hilāl), posing as defenders of the Sunna against the largely Ibāḍī Warglīs (Lethielleux, *Ouargla*, Paris 1983, 173), and Laghouat (al-Aghwāṭ), where the two rivalling quarters—each with its own mosque and market—used to fight each other, but always outside the town, and on an appointed day. They, too, had their Arab nomad helpers, the Larbaa (*al-Arbaʿa*) confederation.

As a case *sui generis* can be seen the important maraboutic tribe of *Awlād Sīdī Shaykh* based on their *zāwiya* El Abiod, where Sharāḳa and Gharāba quarrelled over transfer of *baraka* and control of their alms, raiding in the process each other's flocks and involving in their rivalry the Turkish and Moroccan authorities. In 1838, Sī Ḥamza, leader of the Sharāḳa, rallied round the *amīr* ʿAbd al-Ḳādir [*q.v.*], but when their relations soured, Sī Shaykh, leader of the Gharāba, became ʿAbd al-Ḳādir's staunchest supporter. With the latter's defeat, Sī Shaykh was interned in Morocco, while Sī Ḥamza rose from underdog to victor: he was appointed *khalīfa* over the Sahara by the French. Even the oasis group of Tawāt [*q.v.*] (Touat) used to be divided into two opposing factions, the Yaḥmad and Sufyān. Though reconciled today, they still celebrate their annual *ziyāra* separately. The same goes for their "capital", the oasis of Tamentīt, divided in two opposing factions, the Mrabṭin and Dāreb (K. Suter, *Étude sur le Touat*, in *Rev. Geogr. alpine*, 1952/7, 449-50).

Tunisia, too, had its share in *ṣaff* formations. Traditionally, there existed two rivalling leagues in the south, with ramifications in the north, in Eastern

Algeria and Tripolitania, named S̲h̲addād and Yūsuf. The suggestion that these names reflect the opposition between Berbers and Arabs has been refuted by A. Martel (see *Bibl.*). Possibly they go back to the rivalries between the Hilāl and Sulaym [*q.vv.*], who invaded the Mag̲h̲rib in the 11th century and occupied there two distinct domains: the former, that of the West or Black Tents, the latter, that of the East or White Tents, with the partition line running along the meridian of Tripoli. Yet in the 13th century, the latter were encouraged by the Ḥafṣids to expand into Tunisia and push the Banū Riyāḥ (Hilāl) into the Constantinois and the Zāb, where the Ben Gāna, Tuggurt, Larbaʿa and Ḥanāns̲h̲a leaned on the *ṣaff* Yūsuf, while the Bū ʿUkkāẓ, Ṭrūd, S̲h̲aʿānba, Tamāsīn and al-Wād (El Oued) were supported by the *ṣaff* S̲h̲addād. In the east, the same leagues divided politically a number of tribes in the Fazzān and Greater Syrte (Martel, Cauneille, see *Bibl.*). Major issues on which they adopted opposite stances were: the Ottoman conquest, rule of the pas̲h̲as, the "national" beys, the revolt of ʿAlī Pas̲h̲a against his uncle Ḥusayn, founder of the Ḥusaynid dynasty, and the ensuing troubles (1729-56), which divided the tribes of the High and Low Steppes, as well as towns and villages in the coastal plain (*Sāḥil*), into two *ṣaff*s, the "Ḥusayniyya" and Bās̲h̲iyya (Despois, see *Bibl.*). In the south, the former were supported by *ṣaff* Yūsuf, the latter by S̲h̲addād.

Ṣaff/leff dynamics, as illustrated above, form one possible perspective on the structure and functioning of tribal society in North Africa and one way of explaining, how order, stability and cohesion are maintained in a stateless society, where central authority is lacking or ineffective. Another perspective and explanation is provided by the so-called segmentary theory, which uses the concept of "nesting" and "balanced opposition" of tribal segments at the same level of segmentation along the genealogical tree. This theory, to which the names of E. Durkheim, E.E. Evans-Pritchard, E. Gellner and D.M. Hart are chiefly attached, and which seems to dominate the field of social anthropology in North Africa today, falls outside the scope of this article.

Bibliography (in addition to references given in the article): C. Devaux, *Les Kabaïles du Djerdjera*. Paris 1859, 40 (carte des *ṣaff*s); Noëllat, *L'Algérie en 1882*, Paris 1882, 88-97; A. Hanoteau and A. Letourneux, *La Kabylie et les coutumes kabyles*, Paris 1872, ii, 11-20; E. Masqueray, *Formation des cités chez les population sédentaires de l'Algérie*, etc., Paris 1886, 139-42, 166-9; C. Amat, *Le Mzab et les Mzabites*, Paris 1888, 35-40; J. Huguet, *Les Sofs chez les Abadhites et notamment chez les Beni Mzab*, in *L'Anthropologie*, xxi (1910), 151-84, 313-20; R. Montagne, *Les Berbères et le Makhzen dans le Sud du Maroc*, Paris 1930, 196, 211-14; K. Suter, *Die Bedeutung der Sippen im Mzab*, in *Paideuma*, vi/8 (1958), 512-14; J. Despois, *Tunisie Orientale, Sahel et Basse Steppe*, Paris 1955², 184-5; A Cauneille, *Les Chaanba. Leur nomadisme*, Paris 1968, 21-6; P. von Sivers, *Alms and arms ... the Awlad Sidi Shaykh*, etc., in *The Maghreb Review*, viii/5-6 (1983), 113-23; H. Roberts, *Perspectives on Berber politics*, in *Moroccan Studies*, iii (1993), 1-19 (illuminating): A. Martel, art. *Ṣoff*, in *Encl. Berbère*, xiii (1994). 2031-5. (P. SHINAR)

AL-**ṢAFFĀḤ** [see ABU 'L-ʿABBĀS].

ṢAFFĀRIDS, a dynasty of mediaeval eastern Persia which ruled 247-393/861-1003 in the province of Sid̲j̲istān or Sīstān [*q.v.*], the region which now traddles the border between Iran and Afg̲h̲ānistān. The dynasty derived its name from the profession of coppersmith (*ṣaffār, rūygar*) of Yaʿḳūb b. al-Layth, founder of the dynasty. Sīstān, on the far eastern periphery of the caliphal lands, had begun to slip away from direct ʿAbbāsid rule at the end of the 8th century, when K̲h̲urāsān and Sīstān were caught up in the great K̲h̲āridjite rebellion, led by Ḥamza b. Ādharak (d. 213/828 [*q.v.*]), which took advantage of such factors as resentment against caliphal tax exactions. Thereafter, the *k̲h̲uṭba* was maintained in the capital of Sīstān, Zarand̲j̲ or Zarang, for the ʿAbbāsids; the caliphal governors of K̲h̲urāsān in Nīs̲h̲āpūr, the Ṭāhirids [*q.v.*], re-established the position in K̲h̲urāsān after Ḥamza's death, but were rarely able to collect revenue outside Zarang itself, and the surrounding countryside of Sīstān remained dominated by the K̲h̲āridjites. In this period of waning caliphal power in Sīstān, the orthodox elements in the towns there and in the town of Bust [*q.v.*] to the east, which depended administratively on Sīstān, were thrown back on their own resources. Hence they organised bodies of anti-K̲h̲āridjite vigilantes, *mutaṭawwiʿa* [*q.v.*], "volunteer fighters for the faith", a term which seems to have been largely co-terminous with that of the *ʿayyārūn* [*q.v.*], rowdy and bellicose urban elements, a feature of many of the eastern Persian and Transoxanian towns at this time (see C.E. Bosworth, *The Ghaznavids*, 167-71).

Yaʿḳūb b. al-Layth was one of four brothers, of plebeian origin, who arose out of one of these anti-K̲h̲āridjite *ʿayyār* bands. Displaying immediately leadership qualities, he was soon able to set aside the *ʿayyār* chiefs Ṣāliḥ b. al-Naḍr and Dirham b. Naṣr and assume power over Sīstān for himself (247/861). He then extended his authority eastwards into al-Rukhk̲h̲ad̲j̲ and Zamīndāwar [*q.vv.*] (in the east of modern Afg̲h̲ānistān), killing the local ruler there, the Zunbīl, in 251/865, and then penetrating into Zābulistān [*q.v.*], the district around G̲h̲azna and Gardīz [*q.v.*], and the Kābul-Bāmiyān region, where ruled the Kābul-S̲h̲āhs. He drew an extensive booty and slaves from these areas, and probably in some part paved the way for the gradual Islamisation in the next century of these fringes of the Indian cultural and religious world. The Ṭāhirid city of Harāt was attacked in 257/870-1, and Yaʿḳūb's operations in the Bād̲h̲g̲h̲īs [*q.v.*] region also led to the submission of substantial numbers of the local K̲h̲āridjites, some of whom entered the Ṣaffārid service and formed a special contingent within the army, the so-called D̲j̲ays̲h̲ al-S̲h̲urāt.

Yaʿḳūb now turned his attention to the much richer and more attractive lands to the west of Sīstān, and this of course meant more clashes with the representatives of caliphal power in such provinces as K̲h̲urāsān, Kirmān, Fārs and K̲h̲ūzistān. Kirmān was invaded in the early 250s/late 860s, so that the caliph was compelled to acknowledge Yaʿḳūb as governor there; and raids were made southwards into Makrān, the southern part of what is now Balūčistān, and westwards from Kirmān into Fārs, an especially rich province the loss of whose revenues was a serious blow to the ʿAbbāsids. In 259/873 Yaʿḳūb invaded K̲h̲urāsān, entered Nīs̲h̲āpūr without striking a blow and ended the rule there of the Ṭāhirid governors, afterwards pushing into the Caspian region against the local Iranian princes there but without achieving any permanent successes there. The caliph could not ignore the overthrow of his Ṭāhirid nominees, and al-Muʿtamid denounced publicly the unlawfulness of Yaʿḳūb's annexations. Yaʿḳūb's riposte was to march from K̲h̲ūzistān into ʿIrāḳ, but near Dayr al-ʿĀḳūl [*q.v.*] on the Tigris, only 50 miles from Bag̲h̲dād, he

Genealogical table of the Ṣaffārids

(a) The Laythids or "first line"

al-Layth
- 1. Yaʿḳūb
- 2. ʿAmr
  - Muḥammad
    - 3. Ṭāhir
    - Yaʿḳūb
      - 7. ʿAmr
    - Bānū = Muḥammad b. Khalaf, see (b)
- ʿAlī
  - 4. al-Layth
  - 5. al-Muʿaddal
  - 6. Muḥammad

(b) The Khalafids or "second line"

al-Layth
- Khalaf
  - Muḥammad = Bānū bt. Muḥammad b. ʿAmr, see (a)
    - 8. Abū Djaʿfar Aḥmad
      - 9. Khalaf

was defeated by caliphal forces (9 Radjab 262/8 April 876). Even so, he recovered Khūzistān and retained control of Fārs till his death three years later; Fārs remained thus, subtracted from ʿAbbāsid control and under the rule of the Ṣaffārids or of their commanders, until the time of the fifth Ṣaffārid *amīr*, Muḥammad b. ʿAlī b. al-Layth (298/910-11), when it was briefly recovered by the ʿAbbāsids, only to pass irrevocably from their hands into those of the Būyids or Buwayhids [*q.v.*] a quarter of a century later; we possess today more coins minted by the early Ṣaffārids in Fārs than from any other part of their empire.

Yaʿḳūb's brother ʿAmr [*q.v.*] succeeded to the command of the army, after a short trial of strength with his other brother ʿAlī, when the founder of Ṣaffārid fortunes died at Djundīshābūr in Shawwāl 265/June 879. Whilst tenaciously holding on to the Ṣaffārid conquests in Fārs and Khūzistān, ʿAmr in general adopted a somewhat more conciliatory policy towards the caliphate, at various times seeking formal investiture with the governorships of his various provinces; one effect of this new attitude was that the Regent al-Muwaffaḳ [*q.v.*] was now better able to concentrate on the suppression of the Zandj [*q.v.*] rebellion in Lower ʿIrāḳ and southern Khūzistān. Enjoying as he did—if only intermittently—some degree of caliphal approval, ʿAmr embarked on a protracted struggle to establish his authority in Khurāsān which, after Yaʿḳūb's capture of Nīshāpūr, had reverted to being controlled by various adventurers, former commanders of the Ṭāhirids (some of whom claimed to be aiming at restoring the Ṭāhirids, but all were in the long run forwarding their own personal interests), such as Aḥmad b. ʿAbd Allāh al-Khudjistānī [see KHUDJISTĀN] and Rāfiʿ b. Harthama [*q.v.*]. ʿAmr also continued his brother's policy of raiding into eastern Afghānistān towards the Indian borders at some point before 283/896, when rich presents of idols captured by him reached the caliph in Baghdād. Rāfiʿ was not finally subdued until 283/896, when ʿAmr was able to send his head to al-Muʿtaḍid. His prestige was now at its apogee, and the caliph invested him with all his existing territories, including now Khurāsān and Rayy. But ʿAmr's overweening pride now led him to claim, since he was legitimate governor of Khurāsān, suzerainty also in Transoxania, over the local dynasty there of the Sāmānids [*q.v.*], a pretension to which al-Muʿtaḍid assented. ʿAmr marched into Ṭukhāristān to assert these rights, but was defeated by Ismāʿīl b. Aḥmad (Rabīʿ I or II 287/March-May 900), who eventually sent him captive to Baghdād, where he was killed just after al-Muʿtaḍid's own death in 289/902.

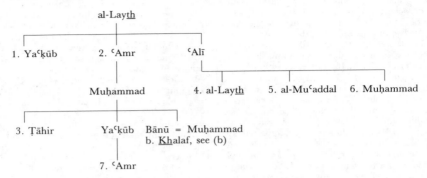

With ʿAmr's capture, the vast military empire which the two brothers had built up began to shrink somewhat. Khurāsān passed to the Sāmānids, and became an integral part of their dominions for nearly a century. But ʿAmr's successors and their Turkish commander Sebük-eri managed to hold on to Fārs and Kirmān, as well as the heartland of Sīstān itself, for another decade or so; suzerainty was exercised over the local rulers in Makrān, the Maʿdānids [see MAKRĀN], and for a while, it seems, across the Gulf of Oman in ʿUmān. The Ṣaffārid amirate was thus still far from negligible. ʿAmr was succeeded in Zarang by his grandson Ṭāhir b. Muḥammad b. ʿAmr, who ruled in effect jointly with his brother Yaʿḳūb, but there was a faction in Sīstān which favoured the claims of the sons of ʿAlī b. al-Layth, partly because ʿAlī had been Yaʿḳūb b. al-Laysh's original choice as successor but had been elbowed aside by ʿAmr (see above). Al-Layth b. ʿAlī prevailed militarily in 296/909, but had to face the continuing insubordination of Sebük-eri, who controlled Fārs and who in 297/910 defeated and dispossessed from Sīstān al-Layth. The latter's brother Muḥammad was hailed as *amīr* in Zarang (298/910), but at this point the caliph al-Muḳtadir invested the Sāmānid Aḥmad b. Ismāʿīl with the governorship of Sīstān and instructed him to end the rule of the Ṣaffārids for good. A Sāmānid invasion followed, with Zarang captured in Radjab 298/March 911, and Muḥammad and his brother al-Muʿaddal, who had also briefly held power in Zarang, were both captured and deported to Baghdād.

This marks the end of the first line of the Ṣaffārids, what might be termed the Laythids, sc. descendants of al-Layth, father of the four brothers. Yaʿḳūb and ʿAmr had been backed by a professional army of the type increasingly the norm in the central and eastern Islamic lands at this time. There was a nucleus of slave *ghulāms* [*q.v.*], comprising essentially Turks from the Central Asian steppes and Indians, plus troops of many other nations attracted by the prospects of plunder under the capable leadership of the two Ṣaffārid brothers. As a result of their conquests, the brothers amassed a full treasury, from which tribute was sent only intermittently, in the intervals of calm relations, to Baghdād. In fact, Yaʿḳūb especially was contemptuous of the ʿAbbāsids and of the aristocratic Arab political and social tradition which they and their governors like the Ṭāhirids represented and which had hitherto prevailed in the caliphal lands. As a self-made man of unpretentious background, he was concerned above all to promote his own family's interests and to cut loose his native province Sīstān from financial and other dependence on the ʿAbbāsids and their rapacious governors. Yaʿḳūb and ʿAmr therefore represent a new trend in the history of the Islamic lands at this time: a conscious repudiation of the "caliphal fiction" whereby all provincial rulers theoretically derived their authority from an act of delegation by the head of Sunnī Islam, and in this wise the constituting of their military empire marks a definite step in the decline of direct caliphal political authority and the corresponding rise of autonomous and later *de facto* independent provincial dynasties. It might also be noted that there formed round them, in later decades, a popular tradition in Sīstān which regarded them as upholders of the province's interests against predatory outsiders, a feeling that was to be a distinct factor in the failure of the Sāmānids permanently to establish their authority within Sīstān and the return of a parallel branch of the family to power (see below).

The twelve or thirteen years 298-311/911-23 form an interim during which the Sāmānids led two expeditions into Sīstān and during which what might be described as patriotic, perhaps even proto-nationalistic, reactions against them by the people of Sīstān took place. In the course of rebellion against the Sāmānids, a child great-grandson of ʿAmr b. al-Layth, Abū Ḥafṣ ʿAmr, was briefly raised to the throne (299-300/912-13) as a figure-head, but real power rested in the hands of several local commanders, such as Muḥammad b. Hurmuz, called Mawlā Ṣandalī, Kathīr b. Aḥmad and Aḥmad b. Ḳudām.

Disturbed conditions in Sīstān also allowed the local *ʿayyārs* to play a significant role during these years, and it was the *ʿayyārs* of Zarang who in 311/923 brought to power Abū Djaʿfar Aḥmad b. Muḥammad b. Khalaf, whose grandfather al-Layth (not identical with the al-Layth who was father of Yaʿḳūb and ʿAmr) had been a distant kinsman and associate of the two original Ṣaffārid brothers and whose father's wife had been a grand-daughter of ʿAmr's. Abū Djaʿfar thus inaugurates the second and last line of the Ṣaffārids, which may conveniently be styled the Khalafids, and he ruled for some 40 years (311-52/923-63). Abū Djaʿfar soon extended Ṣaffārid authority to Bust and into al-Rukhkhadj, and made Sīstān once more a force in the politics of the eastern Islamic world, with its *amīr* enjoying the prestige of an equal with that of the Sāmanids and without, it appears (e.g. on the evidence of coins) any sign of subordination to Bukhārā.

There seems to have been a growth of factionalism and internal opposition during the later part of Abū Djaʿfar's reign, leading to his murder by one of his Turkish *ghulāms* in Rabīʿ I 352/March 963. He was succeeded by his son Abū Aḥmad Khalaf (352-93/963-1003), last and more famous of the *amīrs* of this second line. Khalaf at first ruled in close partnership with a commander of Sīstān, Abu 'l-Ḥusayn Ṭāhir b. Muḥammad, who had Ṣaffārid blood in his veins on his mother's side, making Ṭāhir his regent when he departed for the pilgrimage. The not unpredictable result of this arrangement was that, when Khalaf returned to Sīstān in 358/969, Ṭāhir was unwilling to relinquish power and Khalaf had to secure military help from the Sāmānids to assert his claims, when Ṭāhir conveniently died in 359/970 and Khalaf could re-enter Zarang as *amīr*. The struggle was nevertheless carried on by Ṭāhir's son Ḥusayn, who in turn secured Sāmānid aid, this time against Khalaf. A period of civil warfare followed, with Ḥusayn generally supported by the Sāmānids and with Khalaf, so the sources imply, consequently refusing to send any tribute to Bukhārā. Only after 373/983, when Ḥusayn had been defeated and then died, was Khalaf's power firmly established, so that he was able to send expeditions into Kirmān to collect taxation there.

Meanwhile, a new power had arisen in eastern Afghānistān, that of Sebüktigin [*q.v.*] in Ghazna, the founder of Ghaznawid [*q.v.*] power there, who had in 367/977-8 occupied Bust and who in the 990s was asserting his power in Khurāsān also against the decaying Sāmānid authority. Khalaf tried to incite the Ḳarakhānids of Transoxania [see ILEK KHĀNS] against Sebüktigin and his son Maḥmūd, but once Maḥmūd was firmly on the throne in Ghazna (388/998), unrest and revolt within Sīstān allowed the Ghaznawid *amīr* to intervene there, and Khalaf was finally deposed in 393/1003, dying in captivity at Gardīz a few years later.

With Khalaf the Ṣaffārids end. Later in the 5th/11th century, a new line of local rulers emerges in Sīstān, under Saldjūḳ suzerainty, but these maliks of Nīmrūz, as they are often termed in the sources, had no demonstrable connection with the Ṣaffārids; for these maliks, see SĪSTĀN.

Although the careers of Yaʿḳūb and ʿAmr were filled with furious military activity, allowing little time for the arts of peace, the succeeding Khalafids had a distinctly significant part in the culture of their time. In fact, Yaʿḳūb, as a supremely successful commander, had already had his own circle of court panegyrists, one of whom, the secretary Muḥammad b. Waṣīf [*q.v.*], has a significance in the renaissance of New Persian literature by his having composed verses for the *amīr* in the only language he could understand, sc. Persian, rather than in the incomprehensible Arabic. Abū Djaʿfar Aḥmad assembled around himself a scintillating array of scholars who enjoyed his patronage, including the philosopher and logician Abū Sulaymān Muḥammad (d. *ca.* 375/985 [see ABŪ SULAYMĀN AL-MANṬIḲĪ], and he was the *mamdūḥ* of the Sāmānid poet Rūdakī [*q.v.*]. Khalaf's court in Zarang was visited by writers like Badīʿ al-Zamān al-

Hamadhānī [*q.v.*]; and the *amīr* secured lasting fame for himself by commissioning a 100-volume Ḳurʾān commentary, a summation of all previous knowledge on the Holy Book, the manuscript of which, however, did not survive the Mongol devastations of the cities of Khurāsān and their libraries.

Bibliography: 1. Sources. These include Yaʿḳūbī, *Taʾrīkh*; Ṭabarī; Masʿūdī, *Murūdj*; ʿUtbī; Gardīzī; Djūzdjānī; Ibn al-Athīr; Ibn Khallikān (biography of Yaʿḳūb and ʿAmr, ed. ʿAbbās, vi, 402-32 no. 828, tr. de Slane, iv, 301-35); ʿAwfī, *Djawāmiʿ al-ḥikāyāt*; but above all, the anonymous local history, the *Taʾrīkh-i Sīstān*, ed. M.S. Bahār, Tehran 1314/1935, Eng. tr. M. Gold, Rome 1976, Russian tr. L.P. Smirnova, Moscow 1971.

2. Studies. Th. Nöldeke, *Yakúb the Coppersmith and his dynasty*, in *Sketches from eastern history*, London and Edinburgh 1892, 176-206; W. Barthold, *Zur Geschichte der Ṣaffāriden*, in *Orientalische Studien Th. Nöldeke gewidmet*, Giessen 1906, i, 171-91; idem, *Turkestan*³, 215-26; R. Vasmer, *Über die Münzen der Ṣaffāriden und ihrer Gegner in Fārs und Ḫurāsān*, in *NZ*, N.S. lxiii (1930), 131-62; J. Walker, *The coinage of the second Saffarid dynasty in Sistan*, ANS Numismatic Notes and Monographs 72, New York 1936; Spuler, *Iran*, 69-81; C.E. Bosworth, *Sīstān under the Arabs, from the Islamic conquest to the rise of the Ṣaffārids (30-250/651-864)*, Rome 1968; idem, in *Camb. hist. of Iran*, iv, 106-35; S.M. Stern, *Yaʿqūb the Coppersmith and Persian national sentiment*, in Bosworth (ed.), *Iran and Islam, in memory of the late Vladimir Minorsky*, Edinburgh 1970, 535-55; Bosworth, *The history of the Ṣaffārids of Sistan and the Maliks of Nīmrūz (247/861 to 949/1542-3)*, Costa Mesa and New York 1994 (fully detailed history). (C.E. Bosworth)

al-**ṢĀFFĀT** (a.), the title of sūra XXXVII of the Ḳurʾān, and a word used three times in the text including at XXXVII, 1, where it is generally understood by the early *tafsīr* authorities to mean "(angels) standing in ranks" (and translated as "Celles qui sont en rangs" [R. Blachère], "Those who range themselves in ranks" [A. Yusuf Ali], and "Die in Reih und Glied stehen" [R. Paret]). The meaning is derived from the verb *ṣaffa* referring to camels (or military units) lined up in a row (for sacrifice, as in Ḳurʾān, XXII, 36, using the broken plural *ṣawāff*). The sense of the terse oath phrase *wa 'l-ṣāffāt*ⁱ *ṣaff*ᵃⁿ in XXXVII, 1, has been clarified through association with other Ḳurʾānic passages. The masculine plural form of the same word, *al-ṣāffūn*, is used in XXXVII, 165, to denote beings who "declare the glory of God", that being understood to be the function of angels as in II, 30, XXXIX, 75, XL, 7, XLI, 38 and XLII, 5; angels explicitly "stand in ranks", *ṣaff*ᵃⁿ, in LXXVIII, 38 and LXXXIX, 22.

In XXIV, 41, and LXVII, 19, however, the word *ṣāffāt* is frequently glossed as "outspread wings" of birds; this meaning derives from the contrast drawn in LXVII, 19, in which birds fly up above with "outspread wings", *al-ṭayr fawḳahum ṣāffāt*, and then "fold them in (when resting)" or "beat them (against their sides)", *yaḳbiḍna*; this is a more doubtful sense of the word, depending perhaps on an image of outstretched wings as being "in a line". Regardless, as a result, the passage in XXXVII, 1, is sometimes understood as a reference to birds rather than angels.

In interpreting these verses, a parallel is often drawn to Muslims standing in rows in the *ṣalāt*, the idea of being in rows linked thereby to images of the universe as worshipping God.

Bibliography: Lane, s.v.; the *tafsīr* tradition on the three verses, especially Ḳurṭubī, *al-Djāmiʿ li-aḥkām al-Ḳurʾān*, Cairo 1967, XV, 61-2 (*ad* Ḳurʾān, XXXVII, 1); R. Paret, *Der Koran. Kommentar und Konkordanz*, Stuttgart 1971, *ad* Ḳurʾān XXIV, 41.

(A. Rippin)

ṢAFĪ (pl. *ṣafāyā*), **ṢAWĀFĪ** (a.), two terms of mediaeval Islamic finance and land tenure. The first denotes special items consisting of immoveable property selected from booty by the leader [see fayʾ and ghanīma], while the second is the term for land which the Imām selects from the conquered territories for the treasury with the consent of those who had a share in the booty (al-Māwardī, *al-Aḥkām al-sulṭāniyya*, Cairo 1966, 192). In pre-Islamic Arabia the leader was also entitled to one-fourth (*rubʿ*) or one-fifth (*khums*) of the booty in addition to the *ṣafī*. The custom of *khums* was upheld by the prophet and given Ḳurʾānic sanction in sūra XLI. There was general agreement under the Rāshidūn caliphs that the caliph likewise might retain one-fifth of the booty. In the case of landed property, it became *ṣawāfī*, in effect crown land. In Sunnī theory, the right of the Prophet to select for himself moveable property from war booty terminated with his death, but in Shīʿī theory it passed to the Imāms.

In pre-Islamic Persia, crown lands were extensive; and the possessions of the Sāsānid royal household (*ōstān*) were scattered over the country. Their administration was under a special department called *dīwān ī ōstāndārīh* (A. Perekhanian, *Iran society and law*, in *Cambr. hist. Iran*, iii (2), 669). The accounts of the income from crown lands were kept in a separate register apart from the land tax. Prior to the reforms of the 6th century A.D., the Sāsānid land tax was assessed as a proportion of the crop, and varied from one-third to one-sixth of the crop, depending upon the amount of irrigation and the productivity of the land (A. Christensen, *L'Iran sous les Sassanides*, Copenhagen 1936, 118-119). Some crown lands were assigned to the royal family, as for example the crown district of Kaskar, which Khusraw Parwīz assigned to his cousin Narsah about the year A.D. 624; and some were granted as payments to supporters of the régime, such as the land grants made to the Banū Lakhm at Ḥīra to secure the desert frontier. Some royal property survived the Islamic conquest in the hands of those who had come to terms with the Muslims and some, in the confusion which followed the conquest, was appropriated by local *dahāḳīn* (M.G. Morony, *Landholding in seventh century Iraq*, in A.L. Udovitch (ed.), *The Islamic Middle East, 700-1900*, Princeton 1981, 148 ff.).

The legal theories developed by the *fuḳahāʾ* with regard to crown land, communal land and booty were based on the treatment of Sāsānid crown land, abandoned land and waste land in the Sawād [*q.v.*] after the Islamic conquest, and on the varying interpretations of incidents at the time of the conquest interpreted in terms of their own concept of communal ownership and the responsibilities of the caliph as Imām. M.G. Morony has drawn attention to a tendency on the part of both Islamic and Western scholars to describe the land settlement ascribed to ʿUmar I in terms of a conscious policy based on theories that only emerged later in the fully-developed Islamic law (*op. cit.*, 154. See also W. Schmucker, *Untersuchungen zu einigen wichtigen bodenrechtlichen Konsequenzen der islamischen Eroberungsbewegung*, Bonn 1972, 25-6 and *passim*).

It is difficult to disentangle the course of events during and after the conquest from the often conflicting traditions, in particular since many of the statements about what ʿUthmān did were elicited during the second civil war (Morony, 161). The measures adopted to deal with the administrative and other problems which arose were often of an *ad hoc* nature. It is generally accepted that ʿUmar I, after the defeat of the Sāsānids at the battle of Dj̲alūla (16/637), confiscated all lands belonging to the Persian royal house, property belonging to fire-temples, post-houses, and mills, drained marshes and swamps in Mesopotamia, exempted them from the *fayʾ* and declared them to be *ṣawāfī al-ustān* and, according to tradition, ordered four-fifths to be allotted to the army one-fifth to be reserved for the caliph for the community (*ibid.*, 155).

Al-Balād̲h̲urī states that ʿUmar established the peasants (*ahl al-sawād*) in their lands, levied *d̲j̲izya* on their heads and *ṭasḳ* on their lands (*Futūḥ*, 273; Morony, 159). This presumably refers to the practice in the Sawād generally, including those districts made into *ṣawāfī*. According to Ḳudāma's account, the *ṭasḳ* was levied in the *ṣawāfī al-ustān* at the rate of half the crop. It is not clear from Ḳudāma's account whether the Sawād, including the *ṣawāfī*, was originally assessed by measurement (*misāḥa*) or by *muḳāsama* [*q.vv.*], that is, by a proportion of the crop, or in some districts by *misāḥa* and in others by *muḳāsama*. He states that ʿUmar sent ʿUmar b. Ḥunayt̲h̲ to measure the Sawād (after the conquest) and that he imposed 10 dirhams *per d̲j̲arīb* on vines and trees, 5 dirhams on date palms, 6 dirhams on green sugar cane, 4 dirhams on wheat, and 2 dirhams on barley (or according to other traditions he assessed them at a higher rate). He then measured the cultivated land and all land to which water could be brought, so that it could be cultivated, and imposed on all this by way of tax one *ḳafīz* (of its produce) and one dirham. This was changed later by the *Imām*, taking into account the quantity of the crops and the expenses incurred in the transport of the grain and fruits to the market (*Taxation in Islam*, ii, *Qudāma b. Jaʿfar's Kitāb al-Kharāj, part seven*, tr. with introd. and notes by A. Ben Shemesh, Leiden 1965, 39, Arabic text, 121; Abū Yūsuf, *Le livre de l'impôt foncier*, tr. E. Fagnan, Paris 1921, 58 ff.). It seems probable that some at least of the land to which Ḳudāma refers, in particular that "to which water could be brought so that it could be cultivated", was or became *ṣawāfī*.

The revenue (*k̲h̲arād̲j̲*) from the territory of the Sawād which was made into *ṣawāfī* by ʿUmar is variously recorded. According to a tradition quoted by Yaḥyā b. Ādam, it was 7,000,000 dirhams (*Taxation in Islam*, i, *Yaḥyā ben Ādam's Kitāb al-kharāj*, ed. and tr. with introd. and notes by A. Ben Shemesh, Leiden 1967, 53). Abū Yūsuf quotes the same tradition; he also records that some of the elders of al-Madīna states that ʿUmar made *ḳaṭīʿa* grants from this land (Fagnan, 87, *Taxation in Islam*, iii, *Abū Yūsuf's Kitāb al-kharāj*, tr. with introd. by A. Ben Shemesh, Leiden 1969, 75). Ḳudāma similarly gives the figure of 7,000,000 dirhams (*Taxation in Islam*, ii, 35-6). Abū Yūsuf also quotes another tradition which gives the revenue of the *ṣawāfī al-ustān* as 4,000,000 dirhams (text, 86, tr., 75). Al-Māwardī, on the other hand, states that the revenue was 9,000,000 dirhams and that it was to be expended on the general interests of the Muslims. Contrary to the tradition quoted by Abū Yūsuf, he asserts that no *ḳaṭīʿa* grants were made on it (*al-Aḥkām al-sulṭāniyya*, Cairo 1966, 192-3).

Under ʿUt̲h̲mān changes began to occur in the theory of *ṣawāfī*. Gradually the concept emerged that property held by the Commander of the Faithful for the Islamic community was at his disposal, and the distinction between *fayʾ* land and *ṣawāfī* became blurred. ʿUt̲h̲mān made land grants (*ḳaṭāʾiʿ*) from *ṣawāfī* to tribal leaders at Kūfa. Among these were the grants to D̲j̲arīr b. ʿAbd Allāh al-Bad̲j̲alī on the banks of the Euphrates, to As̲h̲ʿat̲h̲ b. Ḳays al-Kindī at Tīzanābād̲h̲ near Ḳādisiyya, to Saʿd b. Mālik at the village of Hurmuzān and to ʿAbd Allāh b. Masʿūd in al-Nahrayn (Morony, 158; Balād̲h̲urī, *Futūḥ*, 273-4; al-Ṭabarī, i, 2376). In the last two cases, one-third and one-fourth of the produce was taken by way of rent (Abū Yūsuf, tr., 93), which suggests that by this time some or most of the *ṣawāfī* were assessed by *muḳāsama*. The village of Tīzanābād̲h̲, later called al-As̲h̲ʿat̲h̲, remained in the family of al-As̲h̲ʿat̲h̲ b. Ḳays at least until 74/693 (Morony, 173, 118 n.), which is evidence that some *ḳaṭīʿa* grants had by this time become hereditary.

ʿUt̲h̲mān also made *ḳaṭīʿa* grants of undeveloped land round Baṣra. One such was the grant of the swampy ground called S̲h̲aṭṭ ʿUt̲h̲mān across from Ubulla to ʿUt̲h̲mān b. Abi 'l-ʿĀṣ al-T̲h̲aḳafī in order to drain and reclaim it and to compensate him for the land the caliph had bought from him in Medina (*ibid.*, 158; al-Balād̲h̲urī, *Futūḥ*, 351). Ḳudāma and al-Māwardī interpret ʿUt̲h̲mān's actions in granting *ḳaṭāʾiʿ* as based on a belief that it was more beneficial for the Muslims that the *ṣawāfī* should be cultivated than left without cultivation and that he therefore granted them to whom he saw fit for the purpose of cultivation and so that the share (i.e. the rent or tax) due on them might be paid to the Muslims (*Taxation in Islam*, ii, 36; *al-Aḥkām al-sulṭāniyya*, 193). That revenue from *ṣawāfī* was said to have increased under ʿUt̲h̲mān to 50,000,000 dirhams (al-Māwardī, 192-3) is supporting evidence for Ḳudāma's interpretation. At the same time it would seem, ʿUt̲h̲mān's actions were also designed to reward his own followers. Morony considers that the result of ʿUmar's policy was to establish the nucleus of a Muslim Arab landed aristocracy in the Sawād, the property they held consisting of the same village estates that had been held by Sāsānid nobles from the crown before the conquest (*Landholding in seventh century Iraq*, 158). These grants to ʿUt̲h̲mān's supporters served, however, to alienate others of the Muslim community who disputed the conversion of the land round Kūfa into *ṣawāfī*, maintaining that it was *fayʾ* land, the revenue of which belonged to them. It was this dissatisfaction that was one of the causes of Kūfan support for the revolt which brought ʿUt̲h̲mān's caliphate to an end in 35/656 (*ibid.*).

In the reign of Muʿāwiya (41-60/661-80) there was a further increase in crown lands both in ʿIrāḳ and in the Ḥid̲j̲āz (Morony, 174; Schmucker, 135-6, 142). ʿAbd Allāh b. Darrād̲j̲, whom Muʿāwiya had put in charge of the *k̲h̲arād̲j̲* of Kūfa in 41/661, is said to have identified former Sāsānid crown lands on the basis of a supposed register of Sāsānid crown lands recovered from Ḥulwān where Yazdagird III is alleged to have left it, and to have cut down the reeds and built dams and thus reclaimed them from the swamps (*baṭāʾiḥ*) (al-Balād̲h̲urī, *Futūḥ*, 290, 295; al-Yaʿḳūbī, *Taʾrīk̲h̲*, ii, 258). A good deal of former Sāsānid crown land had apparently been lost to the swamps below Kaskar in A.D. 628, and it was there that Ibn Darrād̲j̲ began to reclaim land (Morony, 160). Grants, some of them very large, from this reclaimed land in Lower ʿIrāḳ were made to relatives and supporters of the Umayyads (*ibid.*, 161). In the revolt led by Ibn al-As̲h̲ʿat̲h̲ against al-Ḥad̲j̲d̲j̲ād̲j̲ in 82/701, the register of *ṣawāfī* land was burnt after the battle of Dayr al-D̲j̲amād̲j̲im and many *ṣawāfī* lands were seized by neighbouring landlords and others (Abū Yūsuf, tr.

Fagnan, 86-7; al-Māwardī, 193). However, the revolt was crushed, Wāsiṭ was founded and more land was reclaimed from the swamps of Lower ʿIrāḳ and turned over to the partisans of the Umayyads (Morony, 162). Further increases of *ṣawāfī* land occurred under ʿAbd al-Malik and Walīd I [see KHĀLIṢA], but ʿUmar II (99-101/717-20) forbade any further appropriations of state lands to individuals (H.A.R. Gibb, *The fiscal rescript of ʿUmar II*, in *Arabica*, ii [1955], 10).

Under the ʿAbbāsids it seems to have been tacitly assumed that the leader of the community, whether he was the caliph or a local ruler, might appropriate to himself extensive districts [see further KHĀLIṢA]. There was in any case a great increase in crown land in the ʿAbbāsid period. Increasingly from the reign of al-Mutawakkil (232-47/847-61), fiscal assignments were made on the land, and grants of land, including presumably *ṣawāfī*, were made to the troops and military officers and other officials of the caliph's administration. According to Miskawayh, al-Muḳtadir, after he was restored to the caliphate in 317/929, distributed largesse to the army, and when the available cash was exhausted he sold land to them and made it a condition in the documents of sale that the buyers should pay tax to the public treasury on what they had purchased at the rate levied on *ḳaṭīʿa* grants, which paid *ʿushr*. Thus the difference between what was paid on estates in *ustān* land (i.e. *ṣawāfī* land, the rent or tax of which might be as much as half the produce) and land given as *ḳaṭāʾiʿ* (which paid *ʿushr*) was contracted to the purchasers as a gift. These contracts made by ʿAlī b. ʿAbbās, whom al-Muḳtadir had appointed as his agent in the matter, were attested and the estates (*al-ḍiyāʿ wa 'l-amlāk*) were sold to the army for very low prices. Thābit b. Sinān relates that one day in the year 317/919-20 he was present in the office of the *wazīr* Ibn Muḳla [*q.v.*], who was "entirely occupied with the signing of sales of estates (*al-ḍiyāʿ*) to the troops and the assignation to them of the difference between the assessments as a gift. The officials in the bureaux were also kept at work hunting out the assessments of the lands which were being sold" (*Eclipse of the ʿAbbasid caliphate*, ed. and tr. Amedroz and Margoliouth, Arabic text, i, 200, iv, tr. 225). From this, it would seem that *ṣawāfī* land in ʿIrāḳ (whatever its origins) still paid a higher rate of taxation in the early 4th/10th century than land which had been granted as *ḳaṭāʾiʿ*.

In the early ʿAbbāsid period, Sunnī *fuḳahāʾ* belonging to the various schools assembled the traditions and legal prescriptions concerning the classification and taxation of land. Their theory concerning *ṣawāfī* was based primarily on ʿUmar's actions or supposed actions in the settlement of the Sawād. There are differences in matters of detail between them as a result of the different and sometimes contrary nature of the traditions, but the general consensus is that *ṣawafī* land derived from the principle which permitted the Imām to reserve one-fifth of the conquered land for the public treasury in the interests of the Muslims and that grants of *ṣawāfī* land did not carry full rights of ownership. In practice, there were frequent deviations from the theory of the early legal scholars. Nevertheless, later scholars maintained the theories put forward by their predecessors. There are, however, exceptions. Abū Bakr Aḥmad b. ʿAbd Allāh al-Kindī al-Samdī al-Nazwī (d. 557/1161-2) gives in the *Muṣannaf* different versions of the origin of *ṣawāfī*. One is to the effect that *ṣawāfī* were possessions that had been owned by people who had abandoned their lands because they had been treated iniquitously by unjust rulers. For this reason, al-Nazwī claims that legal scholars considered the *ṣawāfī* unlawful (*ḥarām*). Kister points out that this opinion reflects later perceptions (see his *Land, property and jihad*, in *JESHO*, xxxiv [1991], 308 ff.).

The Shīʿī theory of *ṣawāfī* differs from the Sunnī one and might cover both moveable or immoveable property. It is confused with *ṣafī* (see above). Whereas in Sunnī theory only one-fifth of the land of former kings was *ṣawāfī*, all the lands of former kings were considered to belong automatically to the Shīʿī Imām. They were regarded as part of the *anfāl*, which consisted of lands which were abandoned by their owners without fighting, dead lands, lands on mountain tops, plantations, mines and lands of former kings (*ḳaṭāʾiʿ al-mulūk*). *Anfāl* lands belonged to the imām, who could alienate them as he saw fit (Hossein Modarressi Tabatabaʾi, *Kharaj in Islamic law*, London 1983, 8 ff. See also A.K.S. Lambton, *State and government in medieval Islam*, Oxford 1981, 247, and KHĀLIṢA, at IV, 974).

Bibliography: (in addition to references given in the text): ʿAbd al-ʿAzīz Dūrī, *Niẓām al-ḍarāʾib fī ṣadr al-Islām*, in *Madjallat madjma al-lugha al-ʿarabiyya*, xliv/2 (1974), 44-60; M. van Berchem, *La proprieté territoriale et l'impot foncier sous les premiers califes*, Geneva 1886; P. Forand, *The status of the land and the inhabitants of the Sawād during the first two centuries of Islam*, in *JESHO*, xiv (1971), 25-37; A.K.S. Lambton, *Landlord and peasant in Persia*, Oxford 1953, repr. London and New York 1991 with new introd.; eadem, *State and government in medieval Islam*, Oxford 1981; F. Løkkegaard, *Islamic taxation in the classic period*, Copenhagen 1950; W. Madelung, *Land ownership and land tax in Northern Yemen and Najrān: 3rd-4th/9th-10th century*, in *Land tenure and social transformation in the Middle East*, ed. Tarif Khalidi, Beirut 1981, 189-207, also in idem, *Religious and ethnic movements in medieval Islam*, Variorum Reprints, Aldershot 1992; M.G. Morony, *Iraq after the Muslim conquest*, Princeton 1984; M.A. Shaban, *Islamic history, A.D. 600-750 (A.H. 132)*, Cambridge 1971; idem, *The ʿAbbāsid revolution*, Cambridge 1970. See also works quoted in the *Bibl.* to KHĀLIṢA.

(ANN K.S. LAMBTON)

ṢAFĪ, the by-name of FAKHR AL-DĪN ʿALĪ b. Ḥusayn Wāʿiẓ KĀSHIFĪ (b. 21 Djumādā I 867/11 February 1463, d. 939/1532-3), author, preache and prominent Naḳshbandī Ṣūfī, and son of the famous Kamāl al-Dīn Ḥusayn Wāʿiẓ [see KĀSHIFĪ].

Born in Sabzawār, he was brought up and educate in Harāt. His mother was the sister of Djāmī [*q.v.*] Among his early teachers were Djāmī and Raḍiyy al Dīn ʿAbd al-Ghafūr Lārī. He was early attracted by Naḳshbandī ideas, and travelled to Samarḳand in 889/1484 and again in 893/1487-8 to study with Khʷādja ʿUbayd Allāh Aḥrār [*q.v.* in Suppl.], chie of the Naḳshbandī order. In 904/1498-9 he marrie the daughter of Khʷādja Muḥammad Akbar b. Saʿ al-Dīn Kāshgharī. After the death of his father in 910/1504-5, Fakhr al-Dīn ʿAlī succeeded him a leading preacher in Harāt. In 938-9/1531-2 he wa confined for a year in Harāt when the city was besieg ed by the Özbegs. When the siege was broken by th forces of Shāh Ṭahmāsp in 939/1532-3, he took refug with Sayf al-Mulūk Shāh Muḥammad Sulṭān, the *shā* of GharDjistān [*q.v.*], but in the same year that are was attacked and he returned to Harāt, where he soo died and was buried in the city. Some have suggeste that he became a Shīʿī later in life, but nothin definite in this regard can be stated. His works are: (1 *Rashaḥāt-i ʿayn al-ḥayāt*, completed in 909/1503-4 (ed ʿA.A. Muʿīniyān, 2 vols., Tehran 2536/1977-8); (2

Laṭāʾif al-ṭawāʾif (ed. A. Gulčīn Maʿānī, Tehran 1367/1988-9); (3) *Ḥirz al-amānī min fitan al-zamān* (Lucknow 1290/1873); (4) *Kas͟hf al-asrār*, also called *Tuḥfa-yi k͟hānī* (Bodleian cat. 2749; Ivanow, cat. ASB [Curzon Coll.] 648); (5) a *mat͟hnawī* entitled *Maḥmūd wa Ayāz* (Ḥād͟jd͟jī K͟halīfa, iv, col. 445); (6) *Anīs al-ʿārifīn* (Ismāʿīl Pas͟ha Bag͟hdādlī, *Hadiyyat al-ʿārifīn*, ed. Bilge and İnal, Istanbul 1951-5, i, col. 743).

Bibliography: See that for KĀS͟HIFĪ.

(W.L. HANAWAY)

ṢAFĪ AL-DĪN ARDABĪLĪ, S͟hayk͟h Abu 'l-Fatḥ Isḥāḳ, son of Amīn al-Dīn D͟jibrāʾīl and Dawlatī, born 650/1252-3, died 12 Muḥarram 735/12 September 1334 at Ardabīl [*q.v.*], eponymous founder of the Ṣafawid Order of Ṣūfīs and hence of the Ṣafawid dynasty, rulers of Persia 907-1148/1501-1736 [see ṢAFAWIDS].

Traditional hagiographical accounts depict Ṣafī al-Dīn as being destined for future greatness from infancy. As a boy, he spent his time in religious exercises, experienced visions involving angelic beings, and was visited by the *abdāl* and *awtād* [*q.vv.*]. As he grew up, he could find no *murs͟hid* (spiritual director) at Ardabīl capable of satisfying his religious needs. When he was twenty years old (670/1271-2), he travelled to S͟hīrāz to meet S͟hayk͟h Nad͟jīb al-Dīn Buzg͟hūs͟h, who had been recommended to him as a *murs͟hid*. On his journey south, he continued to seek a spiritual director in the various towns through which he passed, but still without success, and, on his arrival at S͟hīrāz, he learned that S͟hayk͟h Nad͟jīb al-Dīn had just died. He was then advised that the only person capable of analysing his mystical state (*ḥāl wa aḥwāl*), his visions (*wāḳiʿāt*), and his spiritual stations (*maḳāmāt*) was a certain S͟hayk͟h Zāhid Gīlānī. Ṣafī al-Dīn eventually found S͟hayk͟h Zāhid at the village of Ḥilya Kirān on the Caspian in 675/1276-7, and at once realized that the S͟hayk͟h, then sixty years of age, was the *murs͟hid* he had been seeking.

S͟hayk͟h Zāhid treated Ṣafī al-Dīn with extraordinary favour. He gave his daughter Bībī Fāṭima in marriage to Ṣafī al-Dīn, and his son Ḥād͟jd͟jī S͟hams al-Dīn Muḥammad married Ṣafī al-Dīn's daughter. Ṣafī al-Dīn had three sons by Bībī Fāṭima: Muḥyī al-Dīn (died 724/1223-4); Ṣadr al-Milla wa 'l-Dīn, who succeeded him as head of the Ṣafawid order; and Abū Saʿīd. Before his death in Rad͟jab 700/March 1301, S͟hayk͟h Zāhid designated Ṣafī al-Dīn to succeed him as head of the Zāhidiyya order. This caused great resentment among some of S͟hayk͟h Zāhid's followers, and especially on the part of his elder son, D͟jamāl al-Dīn ʿAlī, and his family. S͟hayk͟h Zāhid's younger son, Ḥād͟jd͟jī S͟hams al-Dīn Muḥammad, who was in any case Ṣafī al-Dīn's son-in-law, was placated by grants of land and other property. There is evidence that Ṣafī al-Dīn connived at the expropriation by his son-in-law of certain *waḳf*s controlled by D͟jamāl al-Dīn's son, Badr al-Dīn D͟jamālān; the Mongol Īl-K͟hān Abū Saʿīd [*q.v.*] intervened in 720/1320 to restore the rights of Badr al-Dīn (V. Minorsky, *A Mongol decree of 720/1320 to the family of S͟hayk͟h Zāhid*, in *BSOAS*, xvi/3 [1954], 519-20). On the other hand, S͟hayk͟h Zāhid's descendants were not immune from the usurpations of Mongol *amīrs*.

Under Ṣafī al-Dīn's leadership, the Zāhidiyya order, under its new name Ṣafawiyya, was transformed from a Ṣūfī order of purely local significance into a religious movement, based on Ardabīl, whose religious propaganda (*daʿwa*) was disseminated throughout Persia, Syria and Asia Minor, and even as far away as Ceylon (H.R. Roemer, *The Safawid period*, in *Camb. Hist. Iran*, vi, 192). Even during his lifetime, Ṣafī al-Dīn wielded considerable political influence, and his designation of his son Ṣadr al-Dīn Mūsā to succeed him makes it clear that he was determined to keep this political power within the Ṣafawid family. After his death, his mausoleum at Ardabīl became an important place of pilgrimage (for an inventory of the contents of the shrine compiled in 1172/1758-9 by its *mutawallī* Sayyid Muḥammad Ḳāsim Beg Ṣafawī, see *Gand͟jīna-yi S͟hayk͟h Ṣafī*, Tabrīz 1348 S͟h./1969. See also M.E. Weaver, *The conservation of the shrine of Sheikh Safi at Ardabil, Second preliminary study, July-August 1971*, UNESCO, Paris 1971). Though he may be regarded as the founder of the Ṣafawid dynasty, which promulgated Ithnā ʿAs͟harī S͟hīʿism as the official religion of the state, Ṣafī al-Dīn himself was nominally a Sunnī of the S͟hāfiʿī *mad͟hhab*. However, given the syncretist religious climate of the period of Mongol rule in Persia, too much emphasis should not be placed on this.

Bibliography (in addition to sources referred to in the text): Darwīs͟h Tawakkulī b. Ismāʿīl Ibn Bazzāz, *Ṣafwat al-ṣafā*, written about 759/1357-8, some twenty-four years after the death of Ṣafī al-Dīn. It is a mainly hagiographical work. Because the whole question of Ṣafawid genealogy is extremely complex, and because later copies of the *Ṣafwat al-ṣafā* were tampered with during the reigns of S͟hāh Ismāʿīl I and S͟hāh Ṭahmāsp [*q.vv.*] to produce an "official version" of the origin of the Ṣafawids, the two copies of this ms. which antedate the establishment of the Ṣafawid state in 907/1501 are of particular importance: ms. Leiden 2639 (dated 890/1485), and Ayasofya 3099, dated 896/1491 (lith. text ed. Aḥmad al-Tibrīzī, Bombay 1329/1911). Study of these earlier mss. has led scholars to challenge the claim of the Ṣafawid family to *siyādat* and to descent from the Seventh Ithnā ʿAs͟harī Imām, Mūsā al-Kāẓim [*q.v.*]; see Sayyid Aḥmad Tabrīzī (Kasrawī) [*q.v.*], *Niz͟hād wa tabār-i Ṣafawiyya*, in *Āyanda*, ii (1927-8), 357-65; *Ṣafawiyya sayyid nabūda and*, in *ibid.*, 489-97; and *Bāz ham Ṣafawiyya*, in *ibid.*, 801-12 (a later publication, *S͟hayk͟h Ṣafī wa tabāras͟h*, [1]Tehran 1323 S͟h./1944, [2]Tehran 1342 S͟h./1963, is a rewritten and expanded version of these articles); Zeki Velidi Togan, *Sur l'origine des Safavides*, in *Mélanges Louis Massignon*, Damascus 1957, 345-57; M. Bina-Motlagh, *Scheich Safi von Ardabil*, diss. Göttingen 1969; Erika Glassen, *Die frühen Safawiden nach Qāżī Aḥmad Qumī*, Freiburg im Breisgau 1970; M. Mazzaoui, *The origins of the Safawids*, Freiburger Islamstudien, Band III, Wiesbaden 1972, 47 ff.; B. Nikitine, *Essai d'analyse du Ṣafwat al-Ṣafā*, in *JA* (1957), 385-394. On the history of S͟hayk͟h Ṣafī al-Dīn's time, see S͟hayk͟h Ḥusayn b. Abdāl Zāhidi, *Silsilat al-nasab-i Ṣafawiyya*, Iranschähr Publications no. 6, Berlin 1343/1924-5; Browne, *LHP*, iv, 3-44; W. Hinz, *Irans Aufstieg zum Nationalstaat im fünfzehnten Jahrhundert*, Berlin and Leipzig 1936, 12-14; R.M. Savory, *Iran under the Safavids*, Cambridge 1980, 5-9. On connections between the Ṣafawiyya and Anatolian dervish orders, see F. Babinger, *Schejch Bedr ed-Din*, Leipzig and Berlin 1921, 78 ff.; F. Babinger, *Marino Sanuto's Tagebücher als Quelle zur Geschichte der Ṣafawijja*, in *A volume of oriental studies presented to Edward G. Browne*, Cambridge 1922, 28-50; H.J. Kissling, *Zur Geschichte des Derwischordens der Bajrāmijje*, in *Südost-Forschungen*, Band XV, München 1956, 237-68.

(F. BABINGER-[R.M. SAVORY])

ṢAFĪ AL-DĪN ʿABD AL-ʿAZĪZ B. SARĀYĀ AL-**ḤILLĪ** al-Ṭāʾī al-Sinbisī, Abu 'l-Maḥāsin (b. 5 Rabīʿ II 677/26 August 1278 [according to al-Ṣafadī, *Wāfī*, xviii, 482, 6-7, and most other sources] or Djumādā II, 678/Oct.-Nov. 1279 [according to al-Birzālī (d. 739/1339; *q.v.*) who claims to have received this information from al-Ḥillī himself, see Ḥuwwar, 20], d. probably 749/1348), the most famous Arab poet of the 8th century A.H.

In spite of his fame, information about his life is rather scarce; even the year of his death is variously given (see Bosworth, *Underworld,* i, 138, n. 26). Born in al-Ḥilla [*q.v.*], a centre of Shīʿī learning, and a Shīʿī himself (see below), he left his native town in 701/1301-2 (see introd. to poems *Dīwān*, 70 and 94) to betake himself to the court of the Turkmen Artuḳids [*q.v.*] of Mārdīn. The reasons for this move were, on the one hand, the atmosphere of factionalism and vendetta in al-Ḥilla; he himself had taken revenge for one of his uncles, who had been murdered, and thus was in fear for his own life (al-Ṣafadī, *Wāfī*, xviii, 485 l. 1, mentions, from autopsy, the scars that Ṣafī al-Dīn had retained from the fight; see also Ṣafī al-Dīn's introd. to the *Dīwān*, 4, tr. Bosworth, *Underworld,* i, 137, and the ten poems devoted to the affair [*wāḳiʿa*] of his uncle in *Dīwān*, 9-18, 36-38, the introd. to the poem *Dīwān*, 11, dating the revenge to the same year 701/1301-2 in which he went to Mārdīn). On the other hand, the Artuḳid principality of Mārdīn, under Īlkhānid suzerainty, was a flourishing and relatively peaceful place. Ṣafī al-Dīn, who had already won some fame as a poet, was warmly received by al-Malik al-Manṣūr Nadjm al-Dīn Ghāzī (reigned 693-712/1294-1312) and most likely composed the *Durar al-nuḥūr fī madāʾiḥ al-Malik al-Manṣūr* (see below) to introduce himself to the prince. Henceforth, he considered Mārdīn his home town. He became a *nadīm* and court poet of al-Malik al-Manṣūr as well as of his son and successor (after the ephemeral ʿImād al-Dīn ʿAlī) al-Malik al-Ṣāliḥ Shams al-Dīn Ṣāliḥ (reigned 712-65/1312-64; the correct name is Ṣāliḥ rather than Maḥmūd given here vol. I, 663; see *Dīwān*, 5, where the name occurs as a *ḳarīna* in rhymed prose). However, his main source of income was trade. As a merchant he travelled widely, which also meant that a fair number of his praise poems were mailed to their addressees rather than recited in person. His travels also afforded him opportunities to present poems to other rulers and notables, thus the Ayyūbid lord of Ḥamāt (under Mamlūk suzerainty) and well-known historian and geographer al-Malik al-Muʾayyad Abu 'l-Fidāʾ Ismāʿīl (reigned 710-32/1310-31, see ABU 'L-FIDĀʾ; cf. *Dīwān*, 142-8) and his son and successor al-Malik al-Afḍal Muḥammad (reigned 732-42/1331-41, cf. *Dīwān*, 148-61, and al-Ṣafadī, *Aʿyān*, ii, 444). His most important sojourn outside Mārdīn, however, was his stay at the court of the Mamlūk sultan al-Nāṣir Muḥammad b. Ḳalāwūn [*q.v.*] in Cairo, following his pilgrimage in 723/1322 (see *Dīwān*, 62, l. 3, and for the date see 114, l. 10; al-Ṣafadī, *Aʿyān*, ii, 87, 21, and *Wāfī*, xviii, 482, ll. 7-8, dates his stay in Cairo "*ca.* 726/1326", but thinks that he may have visited Cairo twice). He was introduced to the sultan by the sultan's confidential secretary ʿAlāʾ al-Dīn Ibn al-Athīr (d. 730/1329), and he also met with important scholars, such as the *sīra* writer and poet Ibn Sayyid al-Nās (d. 734/1334 [*q.v.*]) and the grammarian Abū Ḥayyān al-Gharnāṭī (d. 745/1344 [*q.v.*]) (see al-Ṣafadī, *Aʿyān*, ii, 87, l. 23; *Wāfī*, xviii, 482, l. 9; Ibn Ḥadjar, *Durar*, ii, 370, l. 2). After some well-received panegyrics, the sultan suggested that Ṣafī al-Dīn collect his poetry into a thematically arranged diwan (see *Dīwān*, 5, for the story, and 62-9 for the poems). This is the existing *dīwān*. In 731/1331 al-Ṣafadī met Ṣafī al-Dīn near Aleppo, when the latter was petitioning the governor of Syria Sayf al-Dīn Tängiz, who was hunting in the area, to apprehend a thief who had stolen from him in Mārdīn. On that occasion al-Ṣafadī received a comprehensive *idjāza* from Ṣafī al-Dīn for all his past and future work and all works that he was permitted to transmit. In 747/1346-7 al-Fīrūzābādī (d. 817/1415 [*q.v.*]), then still a young man of seventeen, met Ṣafī al-Dīn in Baghdād, when the latter was about seventy years old; he says that it was hard to believe that this man had composed the poetry he was known for (quoted by al-Shushtarī, *Madjālis al-muʾminīn*, Tehran 1299/1881-2, 471).

As a man from al-Ḥilla, Ṣafī al-Dīn could hardly be anything but Shīʿī, and al-Ṣafadī says so explicitly, adding that being a Shīʿī was nothing "heretical" (*bidʿī*) in al-Ḥilla (*Aʿyān*, ii, 87, ll. 10-11). Ibn Ḥadjar felt that some of his poetry smelled of *rafḍ* (*Durar*, ii, 369, penult.), in the sense of an outright rejection and vituperation of the first caliphs, although al-Ḥillī himself—and Ibn Ḥadjar is aware of that—had expressed his esteem for the first caliphs, and the Companions in general, in his poetry (see e.g. *Dīwān*, 59, two poems). He could hardly have done otherwise in the strongly Sunnī world in which he moved.

Ṣafī al-Dīn's literary output includes the following works that are extant:

1. The *Dīwān*. Collected at the suggestion of al-Nāṣir b. Ḳalāwūn, probably in 723/1322 (see above), and arranged according to genres, this *Dīwān* is expressly called a selection. Moreover, poetry composed after completion of the *Dīwān* would *eo ipso* not be included; however, the *Dīwān* does contain a few poems referring to later events (see ʿAllūsh, 113-14, and Salīm, 38-9). Whether these were inserted by the poet himself or by later copyists is unclear. This means that a fair part of Ṣafī al-Dīn's total poetic production is not included in the *Dīwān*; the selections offered by al-Ṣafadī, both in the *Aʿyān* and the *Wāfī*, contain indeed a substantial number of items not to be found in the *Dīwān*. The same is true, though to a lesser extent, for the selections made by al-Kutubī. Brockelmann (II, 160, S II, 199-200) lists a number of poems that have been transmitted outside the *Dīwān*; no indication is given whether or not they are contained in the existing text.

The arrangement of the *Dīwān* is as follows (note that the chapter headings are composed in *sadjʿ* which accounts for some tautologies):

ch. 1: self-glorification, heroic songs, and incitation to assume leadership (*fī 'l-fakhr wa 'l-ḥamāsa wa 'l-taḥrīḍ ʿalā 'l-riʾāsa*);

ch. 2: encomium, praise, gratitude, and congratulation (*fī 'l-madḥ wa 'l-thanāʾ wa 'l-shukr wa 'l-hanāʾ*);

ch. 3: hunting poems and various descriptions (*fī 'l-ṭardiyyāt wa-anwāʿ al-ṣifāt*);

ch. 4: friendship poems and introductory poems in correspondences (*fī 'l-ikhwāniyyāt wa-ṣudūr al-murāsalāt*);

ch. 5: elegies on the great and condolences for friends (*fī marāthī 'l-aʿyān wa-taʿāzī 'l-ikhwān*)

ch. 6: flirtatious and elegiac love poetry and elegant amorous verse (*fī 'l-ghazal wa 'l-nasīb wa ẓarāʾif al-tashbīb*);

ch. 7: wine poems and select flower poems (*fī 'l-khamriyyāt wa 'l-nubadh al-zahriyyāt*);

ch. 8: complaint, reproof, calling in a promise and the answer (*fī 'l-shakwā wa 'l-ʿitāb wa-taḳāḍī 'l-waʿd wa 'l-djawāb*);

ch. 9: poems announcing presents, apologies, entreaties, and poems asking for forgiveness (*fī 'l-hadāyā wa 'l-iʿtidhār wa 'l-istiʿṭāf wa 'l-istighfār*);

ch. 10: tours-de-force, riddles, and mnemonic vers

(*fī 'l-ʿawīṣ wa 'l-alg͟hāz wa 'l-taḳyīd li 'l-īd͟jāz*);
ch. 11: jocular verse, satirical poems, and obscene poems (*fī 'l-mulaḥ wa 'l-ahād͟jī wa 'l-iḥmāḍ fī 'l-tanād͟jī*);
ch. 12: wise sayings, poems of renunciation, and remarkable odds and ends (*fī 'l-ādāb wa 'l-zuhdiyyāt wa-nawādir mukh͟talifāt*).

Al-Ḥillī clearly runs the whole gamut of existing genres and, in so doing, revives certain genres that had not been cultivated much for some time, such as the *k͟hamriyya* [*q.v.*] and the *ṭardiyya* [*q.v.*]. Others, such as *madḥ* and *hid͟jāʾ*, are comparatively under-represented, and for a reason: when al-Ḥillī embarked on his poetic career, he had the noble intention of not writing any panegyrics nor lampoons. Shunning the encomiastic genre was something he could not keep up, although it is remarkable that a number of poems addressed to the Artuḳids are an expression of gratitude rather than pure princely praise. As for the lampoons, he insists that he never wrote any for his own sake; the examples included in the pertinent chapter of the *Dīwān* are, so it is alleged, all ghost-written for friends. Unexpectedly, he includes even mnemonic verse in his *dīwān*, mainly containing lists of technical terms and the like in such diverse fields as music, rhyme theory, metrics, administration, ornithology, chess, and medicine.

The *Dīwān* contains only poems in the *fuṣḥā* language, except for two instances of a *k͟hard͟ja zad͟jaliyya* attached to a *muwas͟hs͟hah* (*Dīwān*, 321, 323); for al-Ḥillī's other dialect poetry see no. 4 below. He uses the full range of possible forms: *ḳaṣīda*, *ḳiṭʿa* (particularly also very short poems of an epigrammatic character as well as of the kind called "poetic snapshots" by G. von Grunebaum), *muwas͟hs͟haḥ* [*q.v.*] (in *Dīwān*, 144, he calls himself enamoured with this form), *musammaṭ* [*q.v.*] (in particular *mukh͟ammas*, including *takh͟mīsāt* of existing poems), and *dūbayt* (see RUBĀʿĪ).

Some conspicuous poems deserve special mention: (a) *al-Kāfiya al-badīʿiyya fi 'l-madāʾiḥ al-nabawiyya*, a poem in praise of the Prophet modeled on the *Burda* [*q.v.*] of al-Būṣīrī [*q.v.* in Suppl.], thus a *mīmiyya* in the metre *basīṭ*, 145 lines long, each line containing one, in some cases two or three, figures of speech, 151 altogether (*Dīwān*, 496-511). The names of the figures are explicitly given between the lines. The story of the poem's genesis is mentioned in a short prose introduction: how the poet intended to write a book on rhetorical figures, but was prevented from doing so by falling gravely ill; how in a dream he received a message from the Prophet enjoining him to praise the latter and promising speedy recovery; and how he combined his original intention with his new task by composing the *badīʿiyya*. It proved to be the starting-point of a new genre of poetry. For al-Ḥillī's own commentary see below no. 2.—(b) *al-Ḳaṣīda al-sāsāniyya*, a poem of 75 lines in the *ṭawīl* metre, written in the argot of the tramps, who called themselves the Banū Sāsān [*q.v.*] (*Dīwān*, 444-8). The poem was ghost-written for a friend who for some unspecified reason wanted to be accepted in the circles of the tramps. It is preceded by a *maḳāma*-like introduction. For a critical edition, translation, and study of the poem see C.E. Bosworth, *Underworld*, i, 132-49 (study); ii, 291-345 (tr. and comm.); 41-84 (ed., Arabic pagination). The above title of the poem does not occur in the *Dīwān*, where the argot is called *lug͟hat al-g͟hurabāʾ* ("language of the homeless"). Whether al-Ḥillī knew the work of his predecessors in the art of the argot *ḳaṣīda*, al-Aḥnaf al-ʿUkbarī and Abū Dulaf al-K͟hazrad͟jī, is not clear (see *ibid.*, i, 141-2); but given his wide-ranging literary interests, it stands to reason that he was aware of this poetic mini-genre. Comprehension of the poem is made possible by interlinear glosses in some of the manuscripts (see *ibid.*, i, 143).—(c) The *g͟harīb* poem, 15 lines in the *k͟hafīf* metre (*Dīwān*, 443-4), answering a criticism that his poetry, though good, suffered from a lack of rare (*g͟harīb*) vocabulary. Al-Ḥillī first gives four lines of cacophonous archaic words, then enters into a declaration of the unsuitability of such language for his own sophisticated age (cf. also I. Goldziher, *Abhandlungen zur arabischen Philologie*, Leiden 1896-99, i, 171-2; Bosworth, *Underworld*, i, 139-40).—(d) The Candle Cycle, a series of six poems of varying length, five in *kāmil*, one in *sarīʿ*, welcoming and describing the candles, when they were brought in and lit in the evening *mad͟jlis* at the court of al-Malik al-Ṣālih (*Dīwān*, 121-4). The first is said to have been improvised, with a promise to continue in the same way during the following nights.—(e) The Bacchic Cycle, a series of seven *k͟hamriyya*s addressed to al-Malik al-Ṣāliḥ, one for each day of the week, each seven lines long and rhyming with the name of the day, in various metres (*Dīwān*, 363-6).

For metrical peculiarities, one should mention a poem in a "long metre" (*wazn ṭawīl*) which, in the introduction, is said to have been used, if incorrectly, by earlier poets (*Dīwān*, 147). It seems to be a *munsariḥ* with a long syllable added at the beginning and end of each hemistich. Two further poems are characterised as being in Persian metres (*al-awzān al-aʿd͟jamiyya*); one is in the standard form of the *k͟hafīf musaddas makh͟būn maḥd͟hūf* (*Dīwān*, 293), the other in one of the most common Persian metres, the *muḍāriʿ mut͟hamman ak͟hrab makfūf maḥd͟hūf* (*Dīwān*, 307-8). A knowledge of Persian is not attested for al-Ḥillī, but it is not unlikely (cf. also his knowledge of the Persian musical terms *tarāna*, *awāza*, *awāzgas͟ht*, and *sarband*, in *ʿĀṭil*, 26, ll. 8-9).

2. *al-Natāʾid͟j al-ilāhiyya fī s͟harḥ al-Kāfiya al-badīʿiyya*, al-Ḥillī's own commentary on his *badīʿiyya*. In the introduction he gives a short overview of the history of "the science of *badīʿ*", and in an appendix at the end he lists the seventy *badīʿ* works that he read and used for his poem and commentary, adding that he owned copies of most of them.

3. *Durar al-nuḥūr fī madāʾiḥ* [var. *imtidāḥ*] *al-Malik al-Manṣūr*, also known as *al-Ḳaṣāʾid al-Artuḳiyyāt*, and referred to by the poet himself as *al-Maḥbūkāt* (*Dīwān*, 70, l. 2); the last title is actually a generic designation, more precisely *al-maḥbūkāt al-ṭarafayn* "those with two opposite ornamental seams" referring to their technical peculiarity as described below. This is a series of 29 odes, each of 29 lines (the version printed in the editions of the *Dīwān* has lacunae; the full text in ed. Cairo 1283/[1866] and in *Mad͟jmūʿ muzdawid͟jāt*, 95-134, which also contain the *sad͟jʿ* introduction missing from the *Dīwān* version). Each poem is characterised by a letter of the alphabet that serves (a) as the rhyme letter and (b) as the first letter of each line; the letters include *lām-alif* (preceding *yāʾ*), but there is no *maḳṣūra*. In the introduction, Ṣafī al-Dīn claims invention of this technique, but ʿAllūs͟h, 120-1, points out two earlier examples and one might add that the exact same organisational principle is used by Ibn al-ʿArabī (d. 638/1240 [*q.v.*]) in a series of ten-line poems in his *Dīwān* (Būlāḳ 1271/1855), 219-32. However, al-Ḥillī's work became the model for a mini-genre of poetry termed *rawḍa* "garden" (see ʿAllūs͟h, 121-2, for a list of later specimens).

4. *al-Kitāb al-ʿāṭil al-ḥālī wa 'l-murakh͟khaṣ al-g͟hālī*, the first poetics of Arabic dialect poetry. It deals with the

four genres of *zad̲j̲al* [*q.v.*], *mawāliyā* [*q.v.*], *kān wa-kān* [*q.v.*], and *ḳūmā* [*q.v.*]. The work is important not only as a—normative—description of the generic, prosodic, and linguistic properties of these types of popular poetry, but also as an anthology that has preserved much that would otherwise be lost. Ritter and Hoenerbach have exploited it for the contribution it makes to our knowledge of the work of the *zad̲j̲al* poets Ibn Ḳuzmān (d. 555/1160 [*q.v.*]) and Mudg̲h̲alīs (d. after 577/1181-2) (see *Bibl.*). In addition, Ṣafī al-Dīn also includes a goodly amount of his own production. He explicitly says that in his *Dīwān* he collected only his *muʿrab* poetry, i.e. *s̲h̲iʿr* (in the narrow sense), *muwas̲h̲s̲h̲aḥ*, and *dūbayt*, whereas his *malḥūn* poetry is relegated to the present work (*ʿĀṭil*, 6). In a way, then, the *ʿĀṭil* is an extension of his *Dīwān*.

5. *al-Durr al-nafīs fī ad̲j̲nās al-tad̲j̲nīs*, a treatise on one of the poet's favourite figures of speech, the paronomasia. Quoted in his *Dīwān* for a newly-invented type of *tad̲j̲nīs* used in the poem in question (*Dīwān*, 423-4), it is preserved in a defective ms in Cairo, Dār al-Kutub, 73 *mad̲j̲āmīʿ m* (five pages; see Ḥuwwar, 73).

6. *al-Ag̲h̲lāṭī*, an antibarbarus, preserved in ms. Escorial 123 (63 folios, see Ḥuwwar, 64).

7. There are five *Rasāʾil* printed in the *Dīwān*: (a) *Risālat al-Dār fī muḥāwarāt al-fār* (*Dīwān*, 484-91). This is a *maḳāma*-like story which, in an amusing style, addresses a complaint to al-Malik al-Ṣāliḥ. The narrator is al-Ḥillī's house in Mārdīn which describes to its neighbour, the citadel of the Artuḳid sultan, how the mice in the house complain to each other about the hard times on which the owner of the house has fallen, due to a large overdue loan given by him to a high governmental official.—(b) *al-Risāla al-muhmala* (*Dīwān*, 511-13). Addressed to al-Nāṣir b. Ḳalāwūn in 723/1323, it contains a complaint against the vizier Karīm al-Dīn [see IBN AL-SADĪD, KARĪM AL-DĪN]. As indicated by the title, the *risāla* is entirely composed of words with undotted letters.—(c) *al-Risāla al-tawʾamiyya* (*Dīwān*, 513-15). Written in 700/1300-1 in Mārdīn, it grew out of a discussion in the *mad̲j̲lis* of al-Malik al-Manṣūr about a poem by al-Ḥarīrī [*q.v.*] which displayed a technique that al-Ḥillī then imitates throughout the *risāla*, to wit: the text consists entirely of pairs of words that are identical in their *rasm* but different in their diacritics and/or vowels. The members of the *mad̲j̲lis* opined that none of their contemporaries would be able to imitate al-Ḥarīrī's tour-de-force. Ṣafī al-Dīn took up this challenge and produced a showcase of his talents, not least with the intention of gaining a secretarial position at the Artuḳid court. The date given seems to suggest that his stay in Mārdīn had an exploratory character and antedated his definitive move there. According to the author's introduction, the *risāla* is meant to inform al-Malik al-Manṣūr about the events in al-Ḥilla that forced the poet to flee.—(d) *Ḥall al-manẓūm* (*Dīwān*, 515-17). This is actually a report about a literary challenge, in which the author is asked to form a *risāla* out of all the letters, without addition or repetition, of the first seven lines of the *Muʿallaḳa* of Imraʾ al-Ḳays and then to reassemble them in a poem of the same metre and rhyme. Which, of course he does.—(e) An answer to the condolences sent by al-Malik al-Ḳāhir, lord of Arzan [Erzurum], to al-Malik al-Ṣāliḥ, lord of Mardin, on the occasion of the death of the latter's brother al-Malik Nāṣir al-Dīn (*Dīwān*, 517-18).—A fair number of *rasāʾil* must have been lost, as witnessed by the collection of short poems in the *Dīwān* that are said to have served as proems (*ṣudūr*) to the author's epistles (see above).

8. *al-Mat̲h̲ālit̲h̲ wa 'l-mat̲h̲ānī fi 'l-maʿālī wa 'l-maʿānī*, a selection of fragments of two or three lines from the *Dīwān* made at the behest of al-Malik al-Afḍal of Ḥamāt and arranged by topic in twenty chapters. The ms. preserved in Paris, BN 1553, was read before the author in 743/1342-3 (53 folios, see Ḥuwwar, 74-5; for a list of chapters which closely resembles that of the *Dīwān*, but adds to it, see Muḥammad Kurd ʿAlī, in *RAAD*, iv [1924], 210-20, here 214).

9. *al-Mīzān fī ʿilm al-adwār wa 'l-awzān*, a treatise on rhythmical cycles and metres in music, preserved in ms. Maʿhad al-Mak̲h̲ṭūṭāt 46 *mūsīḳī* (43 folios, see Ḥuwwar, 75).

10. *Fāʾida fī tawallud al-ang̲h̲ām baʿḍihā ʿan baʿḍ wa-tartībihā ʿala 'l-burūd̲j̲*, "an astrologico-musical treatise dealing with the connection of the notes of the musical scale with the heavenly bodies" (H.G. Farmer, *The sources of Arabian music*, Leiden 1965, no. 279).

11. *ʿIddat abḥur al-s̲h̲iʿr*, a short treatise on prosody, see Brockelmann, II, 160, no. 11.

12. *Kitāb fi 'l-Awzān al-mustaḥdat̲h̲a ka 'l-dūbayt*, see Brockelmann, S II, 200, no. 21.

As a poet, al-Ḥillī has enjoyed a rather uneven reputation. For his contemporaries he was "*the* poet of our time" (*s̲h̲āʿiru ʿaṣrinā ʿala 'l-iṭlāḳ, al-Ṣafadī, Wāfī*, xviii, 482, l. 1) and for some even unrivalled among all poets, ancient and modern (*lam yanẓim-i 'l-s̲h̲iʿra aḥad^un^ mit̲h̲luhu lā fi 'l-mutaḳaddimīna wa-lā fi 'l-mutak̲h̲k̲h̲irīna muṭlaḳ^an^*, S̲h̲ams al-Dīn ʿAbd al-Laṭīf [d. 731/1330, see al-Ṣafadī, *Aʿyān*, ii, 117-19], *apud* al-Ṣafadī, *Wāfī*, xviii, 482, ll. 10-12). His popularity in Arab lands has remained undiminished through the centuries (see personal note by Muḥammad Kurd ʿAlī, in *RAAD*, iv [1924], 212, bottom). Western evaluations have, at least in part, been less friendly. M. Hartmann (*Strophengedicht*, 79) und O. Rescher (*Beitraege*, 2) offer devastating judgements, but those are more or less foregone conclusions based on the preconception that as an epigone al-Ḥillī could not produce but empty chatter, made hardly more palatable by excessive wordplay. R. Nicholson is certainly more appreciative, stressing that "he combined subtlety of fancy with remarkable ease and sweetness of versification" (*Literary history*, 449), only to continue that "many of his pieces, however, are *jeux d'esprit*." More recently, W. Hoenerbach, in the introduction to his edition of *al-ʿĀṭil al-ḥālī*, has drawn attention to a *kān wa-kān* poem describing an erotic adventure where al-Ḥillī proves himself a master of lighthearted narrative poetry. A thorough literary study of al-Ḥillī's poetic works has yet to be undertaken, but the following preliminary characterisations can be made: (1) He was very conscious of being the heir to a long poetic tradition, and one of his goals, in this situation, was to cultivate each and every genre that existed, or ever had existed, in Arabic poetry, no matter whether this genre was defined by content, form, or language register. Typical in this respect is the remark he makes at the beginning of the *kān wa-kān* section in *al-ʿĀṭil al-ḥālī* (149, l. 4): "Among the things I composed in it [sc. *kān wa-kān*], so that my poetic output not be devoid of it ..." (*lī-allā yak̲h̲luwa naẓmī minhu*...). As already mentioned above, this pursuit of completeness resulted in the resuscitation of certain genres that had fallen by the wayside (e.g. *k̲h̲amriyya* and *ṭardiyya*) and also, where morally questionable poems like invectives were involved, in the use of the remarkable expedient that all these poems were ghost-written for friends.—(2) Likewise a reaction to the burden, or stimulus, of the tradition was his express use of intertextuality in the form of *tak̲h̲mīsāt* [see MUSAMMAṬ], especially of poems from the

Ḥamāsa of Abū Tammām [*q.v.*] (see *Dīwān*, 15-16, 22-6, 41-2), but also e.g. of the famous *nūniyya* of Ibn Zaydūn [*q.v.*] (see *Dīwān*, 349-53); or in the form of cento-like compositions (see *Dīwān*, 34-5, for a poem whose first hemistichs are taken from al-Ṭughrāʾī [*q.v.*], while the second hemistichs are borrowed from al-Mutanabbī [*q.v.*]). Less radical cases of "incorporation" (*taḍmīn*) are also to be found, and so are "counter-poems" (*muʿāraḍa*) and "answer-poems" (*idjāba*).—(3) The poetic productions just listed belong to an aspect of al-Ḥillī's art that might be called word games. This was an important, though perhaps to the contemporary Western mind somewhat unpoetic, activity in the *madjālis* of the *udabāʾ*. The characteristic terms, which one finds *passim* in the introductions to poems in the *Dīwān*, are *iḳtirāḥ* and *luzūm*. The first means the "suggestion" or the "challenge" that the members of a *madjlis* put to the poet, the second refers to any handicap that the *madjlis*, or the poet himself, may impose on the poet; it is, thus, more general than the rhyme scheme normally designated by this term (see LUZŪM MĀ LĀ YALZAM), of which there is also a number of examples in the *Dīwān*. Al-Ḥillī is so much in control of all aspects of the language that he masters the strangest impositions with staggering facility.—(4) Alongside these cerebral exercises, there is also poetry for the "heart". Ṣafī al-Dīn stresses several times that he aims at an accessible, easily comprehensible poetic language (even in his *Badīʿiyya*, see *Sharḥ*, 55). His *gharīb* poem (see above) is programmatic in this respect. Its beautiful last line reads: *innamā hādhihi 'l-ḳulūbu ḥadīd*^{un}*/wa-ladhīdhu 'l-alfāẓi maghnāṭīsu* which translates as: "These hearts [of ours] are iron and sweet words [their] magnet". Given his mostly pleasant and easy language, this line could serve as a motto for al-Ḥillī's poetry. Ibn Iyās (d. *ca.* 930/1524 [*q.v.*]) corroborates this by saying that double entendre (*tawriya*) was not al-Ḥillī's forte, since in his versification he preferred simple poetry (*wa-kāna yarḍā fī naẓmihi bi 'l-shiʿri 'l-sādhidj*, see *Badāʾiʿ al-zuhūr*, i/1, 526).

Bibliography: Works. (1) *Dīwān*, Damascus 1297/[1879]-1300/[1883] (*editio princeps*, used here for quotation, containing also the chapter on obscene poetry, suppressed in the two Beirut editions); the later editions Beirut 1893, al-Nadjaf 1956, and Beirut 1961 are mere reprints, the second Beirut edition with numerous omissions. All are uncritical and rather faulty. The claim on the title page of the al-Nadjaf edition that it is based on several mss. is untrue. A critical edition, including the poems preserved outside the *Dīwān*, has been prepared by Muḥammad Ibrāhīm Ḥuwwar (not seen; published?), see Ḥuwwar, 8.—(2) *Sharḥ al-Kāfiya al-badīʿiyya*, ed. Nasīb Nashāwī, Damascus 1402/1982.—(3) *Durar al-nuḥūr fī madāʾiḥ* [var. *imtidāḥ*] *al-Malik al-Manṣūr*, Cairo 1283/[1866]; also printed in *Dīwān*, 521-60 (with lacunae); and in *Madjmūʿ muzdawidjāt ... maʿa ḳaṣāʾid ẓarīfa ... minha 'l-Artuḳiyyāt*, ed. Ḥasan Aḥmad al-Ṭūkhī, lith. Cairo 1299/[1882], 95-134.—(4) *al-Kitāb al-ʿāṭil al-ḥālī wa-'l-murakhkhaṣ al-ghālī*, ed. W. Hoenerbach, *Die vulgärarabische Poetik al-Kitāb al-ʿāṭil al-ḥālī wal-muraḫḫaṣ al-ġālī des Ṣafīyaddīn Ḥillī*, Wiesbaden 1956 (used here for quotation); ed. Ḥusayn Naṣṣār, Cairo 1981.—Translations. *Szafieddini Hellensis ad Sulthanum Elmelik Aszszaleh Schemseddin Abulmekarem Ortokidam carmen*, ar. ed. interpret. et lat. et germ. annotationibusque illustr. G.H. Bernstein, Lipsiae 1816; F. Rückert, *Safi eddin von Hilla. Arabische Dichtung aus dem Nachlass*, ed. H. Bobzin, Wiesbaden 1988; G.W. Freytag, *Darstellung der arabischen Verskunst*, Bonn 1830, 405-8 (*takhmīs* of a *Ḥamāsa* poem by Ḳaṭarī b. al-Fudjāʾa [cf. *Dīwān*, 15-16], with German tr.); O. Rescher, *Beitraege zur Arabischen Poesie (Übersetzungen, Kritiken, Aufsätze)*, vi/1: *Qaçīden von Çafī eddīn el-Ḥillī, Ibn el-Wardī, el-Bustīy, el-Aʿṣā und Ferazdaq*, Stuttgart 1954-5, 1-49.—Sources. Ṣafadī, *al-Wāfī bi 'l-wafayāt*, xviii, ed. Ayman Fuʾād Sayyid, Stuttgart 1988, 481-512; idem, *Aʿyān al-ʿaṣr wa-aʿwān al-naṣr*, facs. ed. Fuat Sezgin, 3 vols., Frankfurt 1410/1990, ii, 86-98; Kutubī, *Fawāt al-wafayāt*, ed. Iḥsān ʿAbbās, Beirut 1973-8, ii, 335-50; Ibn Ḥadjar al-ʿAsḳalānī, *al-Durar al-kāmina*, Ḥaydarābād-Deccan 1349/[1930-1], ii, 369-71; Ibn Taghrībirdī, *al-Nudjūm al-zāhira*, Cairo n.d., x, 238-9; Ibn Iyās, *Badāʾiʿ al-zuhūr*, ed. Muḥ. Muṣṭafā, i/1, Wiesbaden 1395/1975, 526, 11 ff.—Studies. For an overview of critical writings in Arabic, see Ḥuwwar, 5-7; monographs: Djawād Aḥmad ʿAllūsh, *Shiʿr Ṣafī al-Dīn al-Ḥillī*, Baghdād 1379/1959; Maḥmūd Rizḳ Salīm, *Ṣafī al-Dīn al-Ḥillī*, Cairo 1960; Yāsīn al-Ayyūbī, *Ṣafī al-Dīn al-Ḥillī*, Beirut 1971; Muḥammad Ibrāhīm Ḥuwwar, *Ṣafī al-Dīn al-Ḥillī, ḥayātuh wa-āthāruh wa-shiʿruh*, ^{2}Damascus and Beirut 1410/1990.—C.E. Bosworth, *The Medieval Islamic underworld*, 2 vols., Leiden 1976, i, 132-49; ii, 291-345, Arabic pagination 43-84; M. Hartmann, *Das Arabische Strophengedicht. I. Das Muwaššaḥ*, Weimar 1897, 79-80; H. Ritter and W. Hoenerbach, *Neue Materialien zum Zacal. I. Ibn Quzmān* [&] *II. Mudġalīs*, in *Oriens*, iii (1950), 266-315; v (1952), 269-301 (mostly based on materials found in *al-ʿĀṭil*); W. Hoenerbach, introd. to *ʿĀṭil*.

(W.P. HEINRICHS)

ṢAFĪ AL-DĪN AL-URMAWĪ, ʿAbd al-Muʾmin b. Yūsuf b. Fākhir al-Urmawī al-Baghdādī (Ṣūfī al-Dīn in some Ottoman sources), renowned musician and writer on the theory of music, was born *ca.* 613/1216, probably in Urmiya. He died in Baghdād on 28 Ṣafar 693/28 January 1294, at the age of *ca.* 80 (Ibn al-Fuwaṭī, *al-Ḥawādith al-djāmiʿa*, 480).

The sources are silent about the ethnic origin of his family. He may have been of Persian descent (Ḳuṭb al-Dīn Shīrāzī [*q.v.*] calls him *afḍal-i Īrān*). In his youth, Ṣafī al-Dīn went to Baghdād. Well-educated in Arabic language, literature, history and penmanship, he made a name for himself as an excellent calligrapher and was appointed copyist at the new library built by the caliph al-Mustaʿṣim. Both Yāḳūt al-Mustaʿṣimī [*q.v.*] and Shams al-Dīn Aḥmad al-Suhrawardī (d. 741/1340) figure among his disciples in the art of calligraphy. After the fall of the caliphate, the governor of ʿIrāḳ, ʿAlāʾ al-Dīn ʿAṭā-Malik Djuwaynī [*q.v.*], and his brother, the *ṣāḥib-i dīwān* Shams al-Dīn Muḥammad Djuwaynī [*q.v.*], placed him in charge of the chancery (*dīwān al-inshāʾ*) of Baghdād. The honorific titles of *al-ṣadr al-kabīr*, *al-ʿālim al-fāḍil*, and *al-ʿallāma*, given to him in 676/1277 by the renowned littérateur and philologist Ibn al-Ṣayḳal (d. 701/1302), indicate his high literary and social status. He had also studied Shāfiʿī law and comparative law (*khilāf al-fiḳh*) at the Mustanṣiriyya *madrasa* (opened 631/1234). This qualified him to assume a post in al-Mustaʿṣim's juridical administration and, after 656/1258, to head the supervision of the foundations (*naẓariyyat al-waḳf*) in ʿIrāḳ until 665/1267, when Naṣīr al-Dīn al-Ṭūsī [*q.v.*] took over.

Only in the later days of al-Mustaʿṣim's reign did al-Urmawī become known as a musician and excellent lute player and accepted as a member of the private circle of boon companions, thanks to one of his music students, the caliph's favoured songstress Luḥāẓ. His additional salary of 5,000 dīnārs (= 60,000 dirhams at that time) from this activity allowed him to lead a luxurious life. It also helped him to survive the fall of Baghdād, namely, by generously accommodating one of Hülegü's officers who, in return, introduced him to the new ruler. Hülegü was impressed by his art and erudition, and doubled his income, if we can rely on the autobiographical data given by al-Urmawī to the historian ʿIzz al-Dīn al-Irbilī (d. 726/1326) when they met at Tabrīz in 689/1290. His musical career, however, seems to have been supported mainly by the Djuwaynī family, especially by Shams al-Dīn Muḥammad and his son Sharaf al-Dīn Hārūn (put to death in 685/1286). After the demise of his patrons, he fell into oblivion and poverty. Placed under arrest on account of a debt of 300 dīnārs, he died in the Shāfiʿī *Madrasat al-khall* in Baghdād. Two of his sons became secretaries in the capital. One was called Kamāl al-Dīn Aḥmad; the other, ʿIzz al-Dīn ʿAlī, died in 671/1272 and was buried in the *ribāṭ* of Ibn al-Sukrān (d. 667/1269), near Baghdād (see Ibn al-Fuwaṭī, *Madjmaʿ al-ādāb, sub* letters *ʿayn* and *kāf*). Another son, Djalāl al-Dīn Muḥammad, was a man of letters and in 676/1299 attended Ibn al-Ṣayḳal's interpretation of his *al-Maḳāmāt al-Zayniyya* in the Mustanṣiriyya (see G. ʿAwwād and Ḥ. ʿA. Maḥfūẓ, in *Madj. Kull. Ādāb, Baghdād*, iv [1963], 261).

As a composer, al-Urmawī cultivated the vocal forms of *ṣawt, ḳawl* and *nawba*. That the *ṣawt* was, in his days, a song of only a "few parts" (*ḳalīl al-adjzāʾ*), is explained by Mubārakshāh in his commentary on al-Urmawī's *Kitāb al-Adwār*. This is confirmed by two examples of *ṣawt* compositions that al-Urmawī has recorded in musical notation at the end of the *K. al-Adwār*, using letters for the pitch and numbers for the length of the notes. *Ḳawl* songs were more sophisticated compositions, as shown by a piece by al-Urmawī set down in a score by Ḳuṭb al-Dīn Shīrāzī at the end of the music chapter of his *Durrat al-tādj*. A *ḳawl* could also be one of the three (or four) parts of the vocal "suite" (*nawba* [*q.v.*]), a musical genre favoured in al-Urmawī's time. Ṣafī al-Dīn is reported to have composed no less than 130 pieces in the *nawba* form. Most of them were still known to the noted musician Kutayla (*fl.* 730/1330) who performed them at the courts of Mārdīn and Cairo. Al-Urmawī's students of the first and the second generation, among them Djamāl al-Dīn al-Wāsiṭī (born 661/1263) and Niẓām al-Dīn b. al-Ḥakīm (d. *ca.* 760/1358), disseminated his works in Persia, ʿIrāḳ, Syria and Egypt. Some of his song texts are transmitted with indications of the mode and the musical metre by Ibn Faḍl Allāh al-ʿUmarī [*q.v.*].

In the anonymous Persian *Kanz al-tuḥaf* (8th/14th cent.), al-Urmawī is credited with the invention of two stringed instruments, the *nuzha* and the *mughnī* (see H.G. Farmer, *Studies in oriental musical instruments*, First Series, London 1931). It is puzzling, however, that the musician and music theorist ʿAbd al-Ḳādir b. Ghaybī Marāghī [*q.v.*], who had a high regard for al-Urmawī and wrote a commentary on his *K. al-Adwār*, did not mention this when describing the *mughnī* in his own works.

Al-Urmawī owes his lasting fame to his two books on music theory, the *K. al-Adwār* and *al-Risāla al-Sharafiyya fi 'l-nisab al-taʾlīfiyya*. The former was written while he still worked in the library of al-Mustaʿṣim. The caliph was well-known for his addiction to music. Thus we can assume that this field was sufficiently represented in his library to provide al-Urmawī with the necessary source material. The earliest known manuscript of the *K. al-Adwār* was finished in 633/1236 (ms. Nuruosmaniye 3653), when the author was *ca.* 20 years old. Its ductus closely resembles Yāḳūt al-Mustaʿṣimī's handwriting, so it may well be a holograph. The *K. al-Adwār* is the first extant work on scientific music theory after the writings on music of Ibn Sīnā [*q.v.*]. It contains valuable information on the practice and theory of music in the Perso-ʿIrāḳī area, such as the factual establishment of the five-stringed lute (still an exception in Ibn Sīnā's time), the final stage in the division of the octave into 17 steps, the complete nomenclature and definition of the scales constituting the system of the twelve *maḳāms* (called *shudūd*) and the six *āwāz* modes (see O. Wright, below), precise depictions of contemporary musical metres, and the use of letters and numbers for the notation of melodies. All this occurs in the *K. al-Adwār* for the first time, making it a historical source of greatest value. By its conciseness it became the most popular and influential book on music for centuries. No other Arabic (Persian or Turkish) music treatise was so often copied, commented upon and translated into Oriental (and Western) languages. The *K. al-Adwār* was conceived as a compendium (*mukhtaṣar*) of the standard musical knowledge. However, owing both to its apparent uniqueness and to the fact that not a single authority or written source is quoted, the book was regarded as an original work with innovative contributions of its author, especially with regard to the division of the octave. Considering the youth of the author and the purely descriptive style of the book, which does not reveal any personal contribution, the original part of Ṣafī al-Dīn cannot be ascertained and may have been less than assumed. An analysis of the extant manuscripts, many of them transmitted anonymously, and of the differing redactions of the text, might help to clarify this question. The *K. al-Adwār* was translated several times into Persian. In addition to some anonymous translations, one was made in 746/1345 by ʿImād al-Dīn Yaḥyā b. Aḥmad Kāshānī for the ruler Abū Isḥāḳ Īndjū (see Munzawī, no. 40736). An enlarged version of the text was translated in 1296/1879 by Mīrzā Muḥammad Ismāʿīl b. Muḥammad Djaʿfar Iṣfahānī, and dedicated to Mīrzā Āḳā Khān Nūrī, the *ṣadr-i aʿẓam* of Nāṣir al-Dīn Shāh (printed, see below, cf. Munzawī, no. 40737). A Turkish translation was made by a certain Aḥmedoghlu Shükrüllāh (9th/15th cent.), and incorporated, as chapters 1-15, into his compilation called *Risāla min ʿamal al-adwār* (see Raʾūf Yektā, in *MTM*, ii/4 [1331/1913], 137; M. Bardakçı, in *Tarih ve toplum*, xiii [1990], 350-4). Several commentaries were composed during the 8th/14th century and at the beginning of the 9th/15th. The first of them, *Khulāṣat al-afkār fī maʿrifat al-Adwār*, was written in Persian on behalf of Sultan Uways [*q.v.*] by Shihāb al-Dīn ʿAbd Allāh al-Ṣayrafī (Munzawī, no. 40754). A most important Arabic commentary was composed in 777/1375 by a certain Mubārakshāh and dedicated to Shāh Shudjāʿ (French tr., see below; H.G. Farmer's identification of the author with ʿAlī b. Muḥammad al-Djurdjānī is not convincing). A Persian commentary was written in 798/1396 by Luṭf Allāh b. Muḥammad b. Maḥmūd Samarḳandī on behalf of a certain Amīrzāda Saydī (see Munzawī, nos. 40793-94). Another Persian commentary was written by ʿAbd al-Ḳādir b. Ghaybī Marāghī, supplemented by a lengthy *khātima*, called *Zawāʾid al-fawāʾid* (printed, see below). A passage from the *K. al-Adwār* was translated into French by F. Pétis de la Croix (d. 1713) on the request of Joseph Sauveur (d. 1716) who gave a first account of al-Urmawī's division of the octave (*Système général des intervalles de sons*, in *Mémoires de l'Acad. Royale* [Paris

1701], 328-30). A more complete French translation, based on the anonymous ms. Paris B.N. ar. 2865, was made by A.M.-F. Herbin (d. 1806) on behalf of G.-A. Villoteau. He printed part of it in his *De l'État actuel de l'art musical en Égypte* (in *Description de l'Égypte, État moderne*, xiv, Paris 1826, 47-110). The interpretations of both Villoteau and Fétis (*Histoire générale de la musique*, ii, Paris 1869, esp. 55), who erroneously detected one-third-tones in the scales described by al-Urmawī, were inferior to that of Sauveur, and even more so to the correct description already given by J.-B. De La Borde (*Essai sur la musique ancienne et moderne*, i, Paris 1780, 163-6). Al-Urmawī's division of the octave was much appreciated by European scholars from the late 19th century onwards.

Ṣafī al-Dīn's second book, *al-Risāla al-Sharafiyya*, was written around 665/1267. It is dedicated to his student and later patron, Sharaf al-Dīn Djuwaynī. In the scientific, literary and artistic circle of the Djuwaynī family, al-Urmawī was in contact with Naṣīr al-Dīn al-Ṭūsī. The eminent scholar (who left a short treatise on the proportions of musical intervals perceivable in the pulse) may have stimulated al-Urmawī's interest in Greek science. In fact, the *Sharafiyya*, though treating basically the same subject matter as the *K. al-Adwār*, is more indebted to Greek theory than the latter. It is also possible that al-Urmawī was inspired to write his second book after becoming acquainted with the *K. al-Mūsīḳī al-kabīr* of al-Fārābī [*q.v.*], in which ample use is made of Greek source material, and which he might not have known when he wrote the *K. al-Adwār*. In contrast to his first book, the teachings of his great predecessor al-Fārābī are quoted and discussed here. *Al-Risāla al-Sharafiyya*, although being the more extensive work, was, on the whole, less popular than the *K. al-Adwār*. In Ḳuṭb al-Dīn Shīrāzī's *Durrat al-tādj* and in the works of ʿAbd al-Ḳādir Marāghī, however, it was extensively used (partly criticised by Shīrāzī, but defended by Marāghī). The latter even refers to the *Durrat al-tādj* as a commentary on the *Sharafiyya* (see *Maḳāṣid al-alḥān*, Tehran 1344/1957, 58).

The supposed title *Fī ʿulūm al-ʿarūḍ wa 'l-ḳawāfī wa 'l-badīʿ* in ms. Oxford, Bodleian, Clark 21/1 (fols. 1-71, copied 758/1357, see *Cat.*, ii, 201-4, no. 247) is not the title of another book written by al-Urmawī (Brockelmann, S I, 907, no. 3, follows Farmer), but the subtitle of the *Miʿyār al-nuẓẓār fī ʿulūm al-ashʿār* by the philologist ʿIzz al-Dīn ʿAbd al-Wahhāb b. Ibrāhīm al-Zandjānī (Brockelmann, S I, 498, no. IV).

Bibliography (in addition to the sources quoted above): Biography. Ibn Faḍl Allāh al-ʿUmarī, *Masālik al-abṣār*, x, Frankfurt 1988, 309-15; Kutubī, *Fawāt al-wafayāt*, ii, Beirut 1974, 411-13; Ibn al-Ṭiḳṭaḳā, *Fakhrī*, Paris 1895, 74, 449-51; Ṣafadī, *Wāfī*, xix, Beirut 1993, 242-3; Ibn Taghrībirdī, *al-Manhal al-ṣāfī*, part IV, ms. Cairo 1113, fol. 356 (see G. Wiet, *Les biographies du Manhal Safi*, Cairo 1932, 216, no. 1482); Muḥīṭ Ṭabāṭabāʾī, in *Madjalla-yi mūsīḳī*, 3rd series, nos. 8-9 (1320 *sh.*/1941), 31-45, nos. 10-11 (1320 *sh.*/1942), 44-59 (fundamental); H.G. Farmer, in *EI*[1] Suppl.; idem, in Grove's *Dictionary of music and musicians*, 5th ed., vii, London 1954, 357-8.—Manuscripts. Brockelmann I[2], 653, S I, 906-7; Farmer, *The sources of Arabian music*, Leiden 1965, nos. 252, 253, commentaries, s. nos. 290, 295, 303; A. Shiloah, *The theory of music in Arabic writings*, Munich 1979, nos. 222, 224, commentaries, s. nos. 111, 329, 330; Aḥmad Munzawī, *Fihrist-i nuskhahā-yi khaṭṭī-yi fārisī*, v, Tehran 1349/1970, *passim*.—Editions, etc. *K. al-Adwār*, facsimile (of a ms. dated 870 A.H.), ed. Ḥusayn ʿAlī Maḥfūẓ, Baghdād 1961; ed. Hāshim Muḥammad al-Radjab, Baghdād 1980; facsimile (of ms. Istanbul Nuruosmaniye 3653), ed. E. Neubauer, Frankfurt 1984; ed. Ghaṭṭās ʿAbd al-Malik Khashaba, Maḥmūd Aḥmad al-Ḥifnī, Cairo 1986. Persian tr. by Mīrzā Muḥammad Ismāʿīl b. Muḥammad Djaʿfar Iṣfahānī, ed. Yaḥyā Dhakāʾī in *Madjalla-i mūsīḳī*, 3rd series, nos. 46-56 (Murdād 1339-Murdād 1340 *sh.*/July 1960-August 1961). French tr., together with the commentary of Mubārakshāh, by al-Manūbī al-Sanūsī in R. d'Erlanger, *La musique arabe*, iii, Paris 1938, 183-566. *Sharḥ-i Adwār* by ʿAbd al-Ḳādir Marāghī, ed. Taḳī Bīnish, Tehran 1370/1991. *Al-Risāla al-Sharafiyya*, ed. Hāshim Muḥammad al-Radjab, Baghdād 1982; facsimile (of ms. Istanbul Ahmet III, 3460), ed. Neubauer, Frankfurt 1984. Extensive Fr. résumé by Carra de Vaux, in *JA*, 8th ser., xviii (1891), 279-355; Fr. tr. in D'Erlanger, *op. cit.*, iii, 1-182.—Studies. J.P.L. Land, *Tonschriftversuche und Melodieproben aus dem muhammedanischen Mittelalter*, in *Sammelbände für vergleichende Musikwissenschaft*, i (1922), 77-85; I.R. Radjabov, *K istorii notnoy pis'mennosti na vostoke*, in *Uzbekistonda ishtimoij fanlar*, x (1962), 32-57; L. Manik, *Das arabische Tonsystem im Mittelalter*, Leiden 1969; V. Kubica, *Záhada hlavolamu*, in *Novy orient*, xxvii (1972), 142-3; Manik, *Zwei Fassungen einer von Ṣafī al-Dīn notierten Melodie*, in *Baessler-Archiv*, N.S. xxiii (1979), 145-51; O. Wright, *The modal system of Arab and Persian music A.D. 1250-1300*, Oxford 1978; B. Reinert, *Das Problem des pythagoräischen Kommas in der arabischen Musiktheorie*, in *Asiatische Studien*, xxxiii (1979), 199-217.

(E. Neubauer)

SAFĪD KŪH (p.), in Pashto Spīn Ghar ("The White Mountain"), the name of a mountain range falling mainly in eastern Afghānistān. According to Bābur, it derives its name from its perpetual covering of snow; from its northern slopes, nine rivers run down to the Kābul River (*Bābur-nāma*, tr. Beveridge, 209, cf. Appx. E, pp. xvii-xxiii).

The Safīd Kūh, with its outliers, runs from a point to the east of Ghazna [*q.v.*] in a northeasterly and then easterly direction almost to Attock [see atak] on the Indus (approx. between longs. 68° 40′ E. and 72° E.), in general separating the Kābul and Lōgar River valleys on its north and west from the Kurram River valley and the Afrīdī area of Tīrāh on its south. Its highest peak is Sikārām (4,761 m/15,620 ft.). The Khyber Pass [see khaybar] lies at its northeastern tip, and on its northern and eastern spurs are the passes between Kābul and Djalālābād which the British forces involved in Afghānistān during 1841-2 had to negotiate. The middle part of the range forms the present political boundary between the Nangrahār [*q.v.*] province of Afghānistān and the Khurram [*q.v.*] Tribal Area of Pākistān.

Bibliography: *Imperial gazetteer on India*[2], i, 28-9; J. Humlum *et alii*, *La géographie d'Afghanistan: étude d'un pays aride*, Copenhagen 1959, 28, 106.

(C.E. Bosworth)

SAFĪD RŪD (p.) "White River", a river system of northwestern Persia draining the southeastern part of Ādharbaydjān and what was, in mediaeval Islamic times, the region of Daylam [*q.v.*]. The geographers of the 4th/10th century already called it the Sabīd/Sapīdh Rūdh, and Ḥamd Allāh Mustawfī (8th/14th century) clearly applies it to the whole system.

In more recent times, however, the name tends to be restricted to that part of the system after it has been formed from the confluence at Mardjil of its two great affluents, the Ḳizil Üzen [*q.v.*] coming in from the left and the Shāh Rūd from the right. This stretch forces its way through a gap between the Alburz Mts. in the east and the Tālish Mts. to the north-west, and runs down to the Caspian Sea. Thus although its affluents are quite lengthy, the Safīd Rūd itself runs now for only some 110 km/60 miles. When it reaches the coastal plain of Gīlān [*q.v.*], the river divides into numerous channels, whose courses are continuously shifting, and flows out through the delta which the river's alluvia have pushed out into the Caspian. Parts of this delta region are thickly wooded, with a humid and unhealthy climate; here also, rice is cultivated. The gap beween the mountains through which the Safīd Rūd flows provides a means of communication from Gīlān to the plateau of the Persian interior, and at the present time carries the Rasht-Ḳazwīn-Tehran road.

Bibliography: Le Strange, *Lands of the Eastern caliphate*, 169-70; *Ḥudūd al-ʿālam*, tr. Minorsky, 77, 136-7, comm. 388-90; Admiralty Handbook, *Persia*, London 1945, 36-7, 146-8; *Camb. hist. Iran*, i, 11, 42, 269, 271. (C.E. Bosworth)

SAFĪNA (A. pls. *sufun, safāʾin, safīn*), a word used in Arabic from pre-Islamic times onwards for ship. Seamanship and navigation are in general dealt with in MILĀḤA, and the present article, after dealing with the question of knowledge of the sea and ships in Arabia at the time of the birth of Islam, not covered in MILĀḤA, will be confined to a consideration of sea and river craft.

1. In the pre-modern period.

(a) *Pre-Islamic and early Islamic aspects*.

The most general word for "ship" in early Arabic usage was *markab* "conveyance", used, however, in the first place for travel by land, with such specific meanings as "riding-beast", "conveyance drawn by animals". *Safīna* "ship" occurs only sparingly in the Ḳurʾān (three times, in connection with the boat used by Moses and al-Khiḍr and with Noah's Ark), and was early noted, e.g. by Guidi and Fraenkel, as a probable loan word from Syriac (with Hebrew and Akkadian forms), ultimately from the common Semitic root *s-p-n* "to cover in", cf. Akkad. *sapīnatu*, Hebr. *s^epīnah*, "ship", as in Jonah, i, 5; it probably entered Arabic via Syriac at an early date, since it occurs in pre-Islamic poetry (see S. Fraenkel, *Die aramäischen Fremdwörter im Arabischen*, Leiden 1886, 216-17; A. Jeffery, *The foreign vocabulary of the Qurʾān*, Baroda 1938, 171-2). Much more frequent in the Ḳurʾān is *fulk*, used *inter alia* of Noah's Ark and the ship from which Jonah was thrown, again clearly a loan word, but of less certain origin than *safīna*; Vollers suggested one from Greek *epholkion* "a dinghy towed after a boat", but also found in *The Periplus of the Erythraean Sea* to denote a larger vessel used in Red Sea waters (see Jeffery, *op. cit.*, 229-30).

The absence of a genuine Arabic word for "ship" is not surprising, given the Arabian peninsula's total lack of navigable rivers or lakes; the region thus contrasts sharply with the Nile valley of Egypt and with Mesopotamia, where traffic on its rivers early gave rise to a highly-developed vocabulary in Akkadian relating to ships and navigation (see A. Salonen, *Die Wasserfahrzeuge in Babylonien nach sumerisch-akkadischen Quellen* ..., Studia orientalia, Societas orientalia fennica, viii/4, Helsinki 1939), with a linguistic legacy which was handed down to Islamic times (see below).

The Arabian peninsula is, on the other hand, surrounded by seas on three sides, hence some of its inhabitants at least must have had some acquaintanceship with the sea and ships, even if the Arabs of the Ḥidjāz and Nadjd preferred travel by land, so that the original direction of Arab-Islamic expansion was northwards to Palestine, Syria and ʿIrāḳ rather than e.g. across the Bāb al-Mandab towards Ethiopia and the Horn of Africa. The use of ships was certainly familiar to the populations of the southern shores of the Persian Gulf, but the sailors involved were probably from the mixed Persian-Arab element of these coastlands; see further on this, G.F. Hourani, *Arab seafaring in the Indian Ocean in ancient and early medieval times*, Princeton 1951, ch. I, and MILĀḤA. 1.

A consideration of the sea in the Ḳurʾān and of Muḥammad's possible knowledge of it was undertaken by W. Barthold in a brief but suggestive article, *Der Koran und das Meer*, in *ZDMG*, lxxxiii (1929), 37-43. He asked, with justice, how the Holy Book could contain such vivid pictures of the sea and its storms. "This question", he says, "is of particular interest, because descriptions of the sea are in general foreign to Arab poetry, particularly pre-Islamic. Muḥammad's biography does not credit him with any sea voyages, not even with a journey along the coast". Nor does it make him visit any of the seaports of the time like Djudda [*q.v.*], Shuʿayba or Ghazza [*q.v.*]. Nöldeke went so far as to assume (*Isl.*, v [1914], 163, n. 3), where he was dealing with the trade of the Ḳuraysh with Abyssinia, that Muḥammad "may possibly himself have been there on one occasion, as sūras X, 23, XXIX, 65, XXIV, 40, sound as if he had personally experienced the terrors of seafaring". Fraenkel (*op. cit.*, 211) deduced from the Ḳurʾān, "that the early Arabs well appreciated that their land was washed by the sea on three sides. Seafaring was of great importance, at least among the commercial circles to which Muḥammad belonged", otherwise, he thought, Muḥammad would not have spoken in no less than 40 passages of the grace of God, who puts the sea at the service of mankind. Fraenkel even talked of "regular traffic" with Abyssinia, which is indicated among other things (e.g. Abyssinian slave-girls in Arabia at this time) by two traditions, according to one of which the wood of a ship stranded at Shuʿayba was used for building the Kaʿba (al-Ṭabarī, i, 1135), and, according to the other, the first *muhādjirūn* sailed on two merchant ships which were going to Abyssinia (al-Ṭabarī, i, 1182). But in the case of the stranded ship, it is definitely said to have been Byzantine, and in the second passage there is nothing to indicate that the ships were Arab (Lammens, *La Mecque à la veille de l'Hégire*, Beirut 1924, 380, thought that they were foreign). Everything indicates that it is much more probable that this connection between Arabia and the opposite coast was maintained by the Abyssinians, a suggestion made also by Barthold, *op. cit.*, 43, for quite different reasons. Lammens (*La Mecque*, 385) even spoke—not, however, without encountering contradiction—of an Abyssinian dominion of the seas and found in the Meccan chronicles no mention of an Arab ship trading with the kingdom of Aksum (idem, *Le berceau de l'Islam*, i, Rome 1914, 15). On the other hand, he had to acknowledge that the many references in the Ḳurʾān and *Sīra* to navigation suggest an intimate acquaintance with the sea. But no compatriot of Muḥammad or any Bedouin of the Tihāma is ever mentioned as a sailor; this is left to the foreigners on the Red Sea coast (idem, *La Mecque*, 379).

Among the references to sailing in the early poetry, that in l. 102 of ʿAmr b. Kulthūm's *Muʿallaḳa* is specially remarkable. He boasts of his Taghlibīs that they cover the surface of the sea with their ships. While Goldziher (*Das Schiff der Wüste*, in *ZDMG*, xliv [1890], 165-7), who held Fraenkel's point of view said that this line is undoubtedly of great importance Nöldeke, *Fünf Moʿallaqāt*, i, 49, was inclined to the view that "the Taghlib used sometimes to sail the Euphrates in boats" and that "there can be no question of seafaring in the proper sense". He takes *baḥr* here to mean the broad waters of the Euphrates. The whole context shows that we have here to deal simply with a poet's boasting (cf. also G. Jacob, *Altarabische Beduinenleben*², 149), which would have all the more effect as this kind of activity on water was quite unknown to other tribes and, indeed, they had a certain fear of it (see below). Apart from this isolated line, Goldziher, *op. cit.*, pointed out that, in the old poetry, the sea and various elements in navigation are frequently used in similes; the caravan on the march, for example, is frequently compared with ships sailing on the sea. These images, which are usually quite colourless, may, however, have originated on the coast and have wandered inland as clichés, without it being necessary to assume that the poet using them was personally acquainted with the sea. One recalls the stereotyped nature of the *nasīb* [*q.v.*].

Now, as the occasional references to navigation must have some basis in fact, and on the other hand, we know nothing of any enterprises by sea on any large scale, it is natural to assume that "the Arabs before Muḥammad never got beyond coastal traffic along the Red Sea and the Persian Gulf", as Wüstenfeld supposed in *NGW Gött.* (1880), 134. Lammens, *La Mecque*, 381, thought that there can only have been fishing on a very small scale not far from the shore and the occasional plundering of stranded ships (see above). With regard to the "foreign imports", which were already found at this date in Arabia, Jacob thought, *op. cit.*, 149, that "in any case foreign ships (especially Ethiopian and Indian) came to Arab ports more often than vice-versa". Imports are indicated by numerous foreign wares, while, as G.W. Freytag, *Einleitung in das Studium der Arabischen Sprache*, Bonn 1861, 276 ff., emphasised Arabia had few products likely to be exported by ship to foreign lands.

These remarks, however, hold primarily for the Ḥidjāz and adjoining lands and cannot be applied without question to the whole of Arabia. For this region, in particular, there were certain factors unfavourable for the development of shipping. The story of the stranded ship (see above) clearly shows the lack of wood in the neighbourhood of Mecca. There are no good or large harbours on the coast; certain old anchorages like Leukekome, al-Djār [*q.v.*] and Shuʿayba later became quite deserted [see ḤIDJĀZ]. The Red Sea itself was dreaded on account of its storms and reefs, particularly in the north (see BAḤR AL-ḲULZUM, and A. Mez, *Die Renaissance des Islâms*, Heidelberg 1922, 476, Eng. tr. 509). Arabia had, moreover, no navigable rivers which might have formed a training-ground for seafaring.

It is no wonder, then, if the true Badawī had a natural horror of the sea which for long prevented him from entrusting himself to the water. This attitude must have hampered the beginnings of Islamic seafaring, and can still be traced even to-day (see L. Brunot, *La mer dans les traditions ... à Rabat et Salé*, Paris 1920, 1, 3; W.G. Palgrave, *Narrative of a year's journey ...*, London 1865, i, 430, quotes "the most un-English words of the Ḥejazee camel-driver": "He who twice embarks on sea is a very infidel"). This dread finds expression in the Ḳurʾān, where we have references to "waves mountains high", "darkness on the wide deep sea, covered by the towering waves above which are clouds of darkness piled upon one another" etc. (sūras XI, 44, XXIV, 40, also X, 23, XI, 45, XXXI, 31; cf. also the humorous poem in Nöldeke, *Delectus*, 62). Perhaps it is for this reason that the Meccans left navigation to foreigners (see above); in addition, there was the contempt felt for certain trades (see Goldziher, in *Globus*, lxvi [1894], 203-5). As the Azdīs in ʿUmān were sailors and fishermen, they were scorned by the Tamīm as "sailors" (see Wellhausen, *Skizzen und Vorarbeiten*, vi, 25). We have also references to Nabataean and occasionally also to Jewish sailors (see Lyall, *The Dīwāns of ʿAbīd b. al-Abraṣ ...*, Leiden-London 1913, pp. viii, 5, 6).

It is therefore not surprising that in later times, when the value of shipping in peace and war was finally recognised, sayings were put into the mouth of the Prophet definitely permitting trade by sea and praising the merits of the martyr of the sea (see Wensinck, *Handbook*, s.v. *Barter* and *Martyr*(s); also Lammens, *Le berceau de l'Islam*, 15-16). But it was a long time before this view prevailed. Even at the time when Muḥammad was cutting the Ḳuraysh off from their markets in the north, they preferred a great detour through the desert to taking the sea route (Lammens, *La Mecque*, 381). The first caliphs were still against any enterprise at sea. ʿUmar was greatly impressed by a series of misfortunes in the Mediterranean and Red Sea (al-Ṭabarī, i, 2595, 2820; he is said to have forbidden sailing [or only for worldly purposes?], see Goldziher, *Das Schiff der Wüste, loc. cit.*). He even went so far as to punish the chief of the Badjīla tribe ʿArfadja b. Harthama al-Bāriḳī, whom he had ordered to invade ʿUmān, because he had done it by sea, even although he had been successful (Ibn Khaldūn, *ʿIbar*, i, 211). Yet within five years of Muḥammad's death (15/637) an Arab fleet from ʿUmān reached Tānah near Bombay and another expedition went to the Gulf of Daybul (al-Balādhurī, *Futūḥ*, 431-2). But it was Muʿāwiya who was the founder of the Arab navy. The creation of a fleet became more and more urgent during his wars against the Byzantines, in which the harbours of the Levant coasts and Egypt were often threatened. On this question, he had during his governorship to meet the resistance of the caliphs, but ʿUthmān finally consented. Alexandria, in particular, provided ships and sailors. It was not till a later date that Muʿāwiya is said to have established naval bases on the Palestine coast also (al-Balādhurī, 117). In spite of their dread of the sea, "the Arabs made the change from the desert and the camel to the sea and ship with astonishing rapidity" (so Wellhausen, in *NGW Gött.* [1901], 418). Bold and daring admirals soon arose among them, notably Busr b. Abī Arṭāt and Abu 'l-Aʿwar al-Sulamī [*q.vv.*].

We possess only very exiguous information on the actual vessels used in early times round the coasts of Arabia. These were probably simple craft, made of planks bound together with cords of palm fibre (such seems the most probably meaning of *dhāt alwāḥ wa-dusur* in Ḳurʾān, LIV, 13, a description of Noah's Ark): one of the *awāʾil* [*q.v.*] which the *udabāʾ* enumerated was that the Umayyad governor al-Ḥadjdjādj b. Yūsuf [*q.v.*] was the first to have had constructed ships of timber with the planks nailed and caulked (al-Djāḥiẓ, *Ḥayawān*, ed. A.S. Hārūn, Cairo n.d., i, 82-3). The so-called "sewn [with cord of fibre]" ships are mentioned at later dates, up to the 9th/15th century, as a feature of Indian Ocean ship building; a travellers' tale doubtless invented to explain the prevalence of this construction practice posited the existence of magnetic mountains or islands in the Red Sea or in Indian waters which drew the nails out of ships and caused them to sink [see MAGHNĀṬĪS. 1, at vol. V, 1168a].

(H. KINDERMANN-[C.E. BOSWORTH])

(b) *The Mediterranean.*

In Mediterranean waters, the Arab ships used against the Byzantines were crewed by the Greco-Semitic population of the Levantine and Egyptian coastlands and carried a fighting force, initially of the Arab *muḳātila* and then, at a later period, of professional soldiers, whose task was to hurl projectiles at the enemy, engage in hand-to-hand fighting when required and to disembark for land operations. Amongst various types of ship mentioned is the *shawna/shīnī/shīniyya/shānī*, pl. *shawānī*, a vessel of the galley type, i.e. with a crew of oarsmen, whose use is mentioned in the Arabic chronicles up to Mamlūk times; Ibn Ḥawḳal and al-Muḳaddasī (4th/10th century) apply it to the corresponding Byzantine vessels, of the *dromon* or war galley type (see H. Kindermann, *"Schiff" im Arabischen. Untersuchung über Vorkommen und Bedeutung der Termini*, Zwickau i. Sa. 1934, 53-4; Darwīsh al-Nukhaylī, *al-Sufun al-islāmiyya ʿalā ḥurūf al-muʿdjam*, Cairo 1974, 83-5; MILĀḤA. 1, at vol. VII, 44b). Another term, *khalī/khaliyya*, pl. *khalāyā*, is defined as a large ship; an attempt to see in this word the origin of Old Span. *galea/galera*, i.e. galley, was rightly dismissed by Kindermann, *op. cit.*, 25, as implausible. Frequently mentioned in accounts of the naval warfare between the Muslims and the Franks during Crusading and Mamlūk times is the large galley called *ghurāb*; thus the expedition launched from Būlāḳ by the Mamlūk sultan al-Malik al-Ẓāhir Čaḳmaḳ against the Knights Hospitaller in Rhodes in 844/1440 comprised fifteen *ghurābs* conveying a large force of royal *mamlūks* and volunteers (Ibn Taghrībirdī, *Nudjūm*, and al-Maḳrīzī, *Sulūk*, cited in C.E. Bosworth, *Arab attacks on Rhodes in the pre-Ottoman period*, forthcoming). The name *ghurāb* may derive, in the surmise of K. Vollers, from Span. *caraba* < Latin *carabus* < Grk. *karabos/karabion*, see Kindermann, 68-71, and al-Nukhaylī, 104-12 (in archaic Anglo-Indian usage, it yielded the term *grab*, a type of ship often mentioned, in the Indian Ocean context, from the arrival of the Portuguese to the 18th century, see Yule and Burnell, *Hobson-Jobson, a glossary of Anglo-Indian colloquial words and phrases*², London 1903, 391-2). (For information on the constituting and deployment of Muslim navies in the Mediterranean, see BAḤRIYYA. 1. The navy of the Arabs up to 1250, in Suppl., and 2. The navy of the Mamlūks.)

With the appearance of the Turks as a factor in naval warfare around the shores of Asia Minor and in the Aegean and eastern Mediterranean seas during the 9th/15th century, a new phase of ship construction began, based on the principal Ottoman dockyards at Gallipoli and at Ḳāsîm Pasha near Ghalaṭa [*q.v.* in Suppl.] in Istanbul [see TERSĀNE]. Until well into the 11th/17th century there persisted a general distinction between the heavy "round ships" used as merchantmen and the long galleys used as men-of-war, although the distinction was never absolute. But during the 9th/15th century significant advances in naval technology were made both in the Mediterranean and along the Atlantic seaboard of Europe. The clumsy, single-masted "cog" (Ital. *cocca*, Tkish. *köke*, see H. and R. Kahane and A. Tietze, *The lingua franca in the Levant. Turkish nautical terms of Italian and Greek origin*, Urbana, Ill. 1958, 171-3, no. 202), with a single square sail, gave way to three-masted vessels with more than one square sail on the mainmast and a lateen sail on the mizzen. These ships were far more manoeuvrable, and formed the basis of the world-wide naval ventures of the Portuguese and Spanish, and later, the English and Dutch. In the Mediterranean, both the Venetians and the Ottomans experimented with large round ships for use as warships; a galleon ordered by Mehemmed the Conqueror [*q.v.*], weighing 3,000 tons (*fūči* < Grk. *boutsi*, see Kahane and Tietze, 496-8, no. 752) and built in imitation of Italian and Spanish vessels, sank on launching; the mounting of heavy artillery on the upper decks posed obvious problems of stability.

But the armed long ship or galley (Tkish. *ḳadîrgha* < Grk. *katergon*, see Kahane and Tietze, 523-6, no. 785) remained the main, and at times, the only type of warship in the Ottoman fleets. This had the advantage of being swift and manoeuvrable, of having a shallow draught so that it could operate close inshore, and, since it had oars, could travel on calm days when the galleon which relied purely on sail was becalmed. However, the superior size and armament of the galleon made it more effective than the galley as a fighting ship, and this was seen in the Indian Ocean during the 10th/16th century when the Portuguese, with their carracks, could not be dislodged from Hurmuz and Goa by the Ottoman fleet's galleys. Within the Mediterranean, the galley fleets of both the Turks and the Christians had to operate in the comparatively storm-free spring and summer months, especially as such ships, with their cannon as well as their oarsmen and fighting troops, carried large crews in relationship to their size, hence could not operate for too long away from base.

The Venetians made an innovation in naval technology with their use of the galleass in their fleet at Lepanto [see AYNABAKHTĪ] in 979/1571; this ship tried to combine the advantages of the galleon, with the ability to fire cannon broadsides, and of the galley, with its hull and rigging. The Ottomans started building them (Tkish. *mawna*) in the next year, but it was not until the later 11th/17th century that the Ottomans began to employ galleons on a large scale. See in general, İ.H. Uzunçarşılı, *Osmanlı devletinin merkez ve bahriye teşkilâtı*, Ankara 1948; C.H. Imber, *The navy of Süleyman the Magnificent*, in *Archivum Ottomanicum*, vi (1980), 211-82, with a useful glossary of naval and administrative terms at 277-82; and BAḤRIYYA. 3. The Ottoman navy.

(c) *The Mesopotamian-Khūzistān river systems.*

Here, nautical traditions went back to ancient times (see Salonen, *op. cit.*). Some terminology from Sumerian and Akkadian was carried over into the Arabic vocabulary of sea and river navigation and of irrigation constructions and practices of Umayyad and ʿAbbāsid times (see Bosworth, ... *Some remarks on the terminology of irrigation practices and hydraulic constructions in the Eastern Arab and Iranian worlds in the third-fifth centuries A.H.*, in *Jnal. of Islamic Studies*, ii [1991], 78-85). Likewise, there must have been some continuity in the designing and building of boats suitable for use on the Euphrates, Tigris, Kārūn and their tributaries; this was certainly the case with the raft floated on inflatable goatskins called *kelek* [*q.v.*] (< Akk. *kalakku*, ultimately from Sumerian), and probably also with the similar raft of early ʿAbbāsid times, the *ṭawf*, although the etymology of this is obscure (see Bosworth, *op. cit.*, 84-5).

The historical and *adab* sources of the ʿAbbāsid period are replete with references to the various types of craft which conveyed both passengers and freight on these rivers, which were exceptionally favourable for navigation, especially as the slightly higher level of the Euphrates, compared with the Tigris, meant that the transverse canals from the former to the latter could be used for speedy transport eastwards. The Euphrates was navigable up to Samosata [see SUMAYSĀṬ], hence could be used for goods traffic between ʿIrāḳ and the Djazīra and northern Syria, whilst down the Tigris to Baghdād came goods from Armenia and Kurdistān. Amongst the large ships used especially for freight are mentioned the *kurkūr*, pl. *karākīr* (probably from Grk. *kerkouros*, Latin *cercurus*), known to the pre-Islamic poets who frequented the Lakhmid court at Ḥīra, including al-Nābigha al-Dhubyānī [*q.v.*], who speaks of the *kurkūrs* of the Nabaṭ on the Euphrates (Fraenkel, 217; Kindermann, 79-81; al-Nukhaylī, 120-5).

The types of craft for both passengers and goods were very numerous. The Baghdād parasite of the early 5th/11th century, Abu 'l-Ḳāsim [*q.v.*], recites in his *Ḥikāya* a list of nineteen of these, including the *kārib, zabzab, sumayrī, ḥarrāḳa, ṭayyāra* and *marākib ʿammāliyya* (*ʿammāla*) "freight craft" (ed. A. Mez, *Abulḳâsim, ein bagdâder Sittenbild*, Heidelberg 1902, 107). As in the last example, some names are clearly descriptive, e.g. *ṭayyāra* "flyer", a kind of skiff. *Ḥarrāḳa* "fire ship" presumably denoted in origin a warship from which fire could be hurled at the enemy, but was soon used for passenger-carrying craft in Mesopotamia and also on the Nile (Kindermann, 72-3; al-Nukhaylī, 32-7); the caliph al-Amīn had five luxury *ḥarrāḳāt* built as pleasure boats on the Tigris, each in the shape of a lion, elephant, eagle, serpent and horse (al-Tabarī, iii, 951-2). *Sumayriyyāt* are mentioned as troop-carrying craft in the historical accounts of the Zandj rebellion in the later 3rd/9th century, being used by both the caliphal forces and the rebels, whilst in 315/927 the general Muʾnis al-Muẓaffar [*q.v.*] sent 500 troops from Baghdād downstream in *sumayriyyāt* in order to prevent the Carmathians [see ḲARMAṬĪ] from crossing the Euphrates (Kindermann, 42-3).

Often mentioned as used by the caliphs and great men of state is the swift vessel called *zaww* (< Pers. *zūd* "speedy" or, more probably, Kindermann thought, from a Chinese word for "vessel", 36-7), which could be a luxuriously-appointed gondola. *Zawraḳ*, pl. *zawāriḳ* (a word of Persian origin?) denoted in the ʿIrāḳī context a skiff or dinghy, for local traffic (al-Iṣṭakhrī saw innumerable *zawraḳs* in the waterways around Baṣra); but what were obviously much larger, sea-going *zawraḳs* are recorded in the Mediterranean, including in fighting against the Crusaders off the Palestine coast and for transporting troops from Egypt for a further attack on Rhodes in 848/1444 (Kindermann, 37-8; al-Nukhaylī, 59-62; Ibn Taghrībirdī, cited in Bosworth, *Arab attacks on Rhodes in the pre-Ottoman period*). See for Mesopotamian river traffic in general, Mez, *Renaissance*, 455, Eng. tr. 485 ff.

(d) *The Arabian Sea and Indian Ocean shores.*

The characteristic features of the mediaeval Arabic ocean-going ships have been given by Hourani as, first, the sewing-together of the planks rather than nailing (see above) and, second, the fore-and-aft set of the sails. Ibn Djubayr observed large barques or *djalbas* (< Port.-Span. *gelba/gelva*, with another form *gallevat* which yielded Eng. "jolly-boat", cf. *Hobson-Jobson*, 361-3; in modern times, "jolly-boat" has been borrowed back into Arabic, since H. Ritter noted, in *Isl.*, ix [1919], 137, that the lifeboat of a steamer on the Tigris was called a *djālibōt*) being built at ʿAydhāb [*q.v.*] on the Red Sea coast which were stitched together with coir, i.e. coconut palm fibres (*ḳinbār*) (*Riḥla*, ed. Wright and de Goeje, 70). Only from the 9th/15th century did nailed construction begin to be used on the Malabar coast of South India, possibly in imitation of the Portuguese warships (Hourani, *Arab seafaring in the Indian Ocean*, 87 ff.).

A list of Arabic terms for ships used round the South Arabian coasts from later mediaeval times has been given by R.B. Serjeant in his *The Portuguese off the South Arabian coast. Ḥaḍramī chronicles*, Oxford 1963, repr. Beirut 1974, 132-7, Appx. II *Arabic terms for shipping*. Here are to be found terms used elsewhere in the Islamic world, such as *ghurāb* or grab; the *djal(a)ba*, pl. *djilāb*; and the *barsha*, according to Kindermann, 4-5, a long, covered boat, but also applied to large warships, as with the Ottoman *barčas* (< Ital. *bargia, barza*, see Kahane and Tietze, 98-9, n. 80) (cf. Imber, *The navy of Süleyman the Magnificent*, 212-13). Connected by observers of the early modern period with the Gulf of Oman and Indian waters was the *baghla*, lit. "mule", a large sailing ship (< Span.-Port. *bajel, baxel*, etc., yielding Anglo-Indian "buggalow" and possibly "budgerow", see *Hobson-Jobson*, 120, 123). Most characteristic, of course, of these waters, for western observers, was the dhow, which Kindermann, 26-7, noted under *dāw* or *dāwa*, suggesting a Persian or ultimately Indian etymology; see for the dhow, below, section 2. In modern times.

Bibliography: Given in the article. The works of Kindermann and al-Nukhaylī list the types of ship alphabetically. See also Suʿād Māhir, *al-Baḥriyya fī Miṣr al-islāmiyya wa-āthāruhā al-bāḳiya*, Cairo n.d. [1967], 147-238. (C.E. Bosworth)

2. In modern times.

See for this, MILĀḤA. 4. In modern times, to the *Bibl.* of which should be added H. Ritter, *Mesopotamische Studien. I. Arabische Flussfahrzeuge auf Euphrat und Tigris*, in *Isl.*, ix (1919), 121-43. (Ed.)

Finally, it should be noted that in astronomy, *Safīna* represents Argus, one of the eastern constellations made up of 45 stars, the brightest of which is *Suhayl* or Canopus. On the other hand, *Safīnat Nūḥ* denotes the Great Bear. (G. Oman)

SAFĪR (A., "ambassador", "messenger").

1. In Shīʿism.

Here, this is a term used to refer to the deputies of the twelfth imām during the Lesser Occultation (260-329/874-941) [see GHAYBA]; there were four such deputies.

The doctrine that the hidden imām is represented by a deputy appears to have taken shape in the circles of the Nawbakht family [*q.v.*], whose members played a prominent role in the ʿAbbāsid court in the early 4th/10th century. According to a recent study, it was Ibn Rawḥ (Rūḥ) al-Nawbakhtī [*q.v.*], regarded by the Twelver Shīʿīs as the third *safīr*, who first claimed to be such a deputy; the first and second *safīrs* were given this title posthumously in order to establish that the office of *sifāra* had come into being immediately following the occultation of the imām (V. Klemm, *Die vier sufarāʾ*, 140-1). The term *safīr* as referring to these deputies is first attested in the *K. al-Ghayba* of Muḥammad b. Ibrāhīm al-Nuʿmānī (d. *ca.* 345/956 or 360/971), though neither their names nor their number is given. The four are listed in Ibn Bābawayh's [*q.v.*] *Ikmāl al-dīn* (408-9); and the most detailed accounts of their activities are found in the *K. al-Ghayba* of Abū Djaʿfar al-Ṭūsī (d. 460/1067). These accounts are largely dependent on two works now lost, the *Akhbār Abī ʿAmr wa Abī Djaʿfar al-ʿAmriyyayn* of Abū Naṣr Hibat Allāh b. Aḥmad b. Muḥammad, known as Ibn Barniyya al-Kātib (*fl.* second half of 4th/10th century), and the *Akhbār al-wukalāʾ al-arbaʿa* of Aḥmad b. ʿAlī b. al-ʿAbbās b. Nūḥ al-Sīrāfī (d. *ca.* 413/1022).

The function of the *safīrs* as described in Twelver Shīʿī texts was to act as senior agents (*wakīls*) of the twelfth imām and to oversee the affairs of the community by coordinating the work of all other *wakīl*s in the ᶜAbbāsid empire, collecting the dues owed the imām and his family and transmitting his orders and responsa. According to Ibn Bābawayh and al-Ṭūsī (who are followed by later authors), the four *safīr*s were:

a. Abū ᶜAmr ᶜUṯẖmān b. Saᶜīd al-ᶜAmrī of the Banū Asad (d. before 267/880). When he was only eleven years old he already served the tenth imām ᶜAlī al-Hādī (d. 254/868) [see al-ᶜaskarī]; later he became a confidant of his son al-Ḥasan al-ᶜAskarī [*q.v.*]. Abū ᶜAmr traded in butter, and was therefore known as al-Sammān. His profession enabled him to conceal in butter receptacles the money collected from the S̲h̲īᶜīs and to transport it secretly to the imām. Before al-ᶜAskarī died he appointed Abū ᶜAmr as *safīr*, an appointment subsequently confirmed by the twelfth imām from his place of hiding.

b. Abū D̲j̲aᶜfar Muḥammad b. ᶜUṯẖmān al-ᶜAmrī (d. D̲j̲umādā I 304/916 or 305/917), son of the first *safīr*. He is said to have spent a total of some fifty years in the service of the tenth, eleventh and twelfth imāms.

c. Abu 'l-Ḳāsim al-Ḥusayn b. Rawḥ al-Nawbak̲h̲tī (d. 18 S̲h̲aᶜbān 326/20 June 938), author of a *K. al-Taʾdīb* and a close associate of the vizier family of Banu 'l-Furāt. Following the end of the second vizierate of ᶜAlī b. Muḥammad b. al-Furāt in 306/918 [see ibn al-furāt], Ibn Rawḥ was forced for reasons unknown to go into hiding; there he remained until Ibn al-Furāt's brief reinstallation in 311/923. During that time he appointed ᶜAlī b. Muḥammad al-S̲h̲almaghānī [*q.v.*] as his deputy, but then accused him of heresy. For five years (312-7/924-9) Ibn Rawḥ was imprisoned by the caliph al-Muḳtadir [*q.v.*], either for financial misconduct or because of his suspected links with the Ḳarmaṭīs. He was released by Muʾnis al-Muẓaffar [*q.v.*].

d. Abu 'l-Ḥasan ᶜAlī b. Muḥammad al-Simmarī (traditionally read al-Samarrī) (d. mid-S̲h̲aᶜbān 329/mid-May 941). Like his three predecessors, he lived and was buried in Bag̲h̲dād. His period in office was brief; a few days before his death he received a message from the twelfth imām announcing the onset of the Greater Occultation.

While the *safīr*s are regarded as inferior to the imāms, they are reported by most authorities to have been accorded some of the imāms' special powers, such as the ability to foretell future events and to perform miracles; this latter ability is said to have been conferred on them by the twelfth imām to serve as proof that they were his representatives (al-Ṭūsī, *K. al-G̲h̲ayba*, 256; cf. M.A. Amir-Moezzi, *Le guide divin dans le shīᶜisme originel*, Verdier 1992, 271-5). The Banū Nawbak̲h̲t, in contrast, argued like the Muᶜtazila that the *safīr*s could not perform miracles (al-Shayk̲h̲ al-Mufīd, *Awāʾil al-maḳālāt*, ed. Faḍl Allāh al-Zand̲j̲ānī, Tabriz 1371, 41).

In addition to the genuine *safīr*s, S̲h̲īᶜī authors mention various pretenders who claimed the title for themselves. Among them are Aḥmad b. Hilāl al-Kark̲h̲ī, Muḥammad b. Nuṣayr (the eponymous founder of the Nuṣayriyya) and al-S̲h̲almaghānī (E. Kohlberg, *Barāʾa in Shīᶜī doctrine*, in *JSAI*, vii [1986], 139-75, at 166-7).

Two further terms are used synonymously with *safīr*: (1) *bāb* (gate) [*q.v.*], a word which in the pre-*g̲h̲ayba* period referred *inter alia* to the personal attendant of the imām (Ibn S̲h̲ahrāshūb, *Manāḳib āl Abī Ṭālib*, Nad̲j̲af 1375-6/1956, iii, 232, 311, 340, 400, 438, 476, 487, 506, 525); (2) *nāʾib* (lieutenant) or *nāʾib k̲h̲āṣṣ*. The latter in particular was used by authors in the Ṣafawid period in contrast to the *nāʾib ᶜāmm* (the jurist) (N. Calder, *Zakāt in Imāmi Shīᶜī jurisprudence, from the tenth to the sixteenth century A.D.*, in *BSOAS*, xliv [1981], 468-80, at 479-80).

Bibliography (in addition to the references given in the article): Nuᶜmānī, *K. al-G̲h̲ayba*, Beirut 1403/1983, 113-5; Ibn Bābawayh, *Ikmāl al-dīn*, 1389/1970, 411, 415-7, 451-3, 466-76, 479-86; Muḥammad b. D̲j̲arīr b. Rustam al-Ṭabarī, *Dalāʾil al-imāma*, Beirut 1408/1988, 277-83; al-S̲h̲aykh al-Mufīd, *al-Irs̲h̲ād*, Beirut 1399/1979, 353, 355; idem, *al-Fuṣūl al-ᶜas̲h̲ara fi 'l-g̲h̲ayba*, Nad̲j̲af 1370/1951, 17-8, 28; Abū D̲j̲aᶜfar al-Ṭūsī, *K. al-G̲h̲ayba*, Nad̲j̲af 1385/1965, 76, 178-80, 183-8, 192-9, 209, 214-28, 236-58; idem, *Rid̲j̲āl*, ed. Muḥammad Ṣādiḳ Āl Baḥr al-ᶜUlūm, Nad̲j̲af 1381/1961, 420, 434; al-Faḍl b. al-Ḥasan al-Ṭabrisī, *Iᶜlām al-warā*, Nad̲j̲af 1390/1970, 443-54; Aḥmad al-Ṭabrisī, *al-Iḥtid̲j̲ād̲j̲*, Beirut 1410/1989, 469-81; Ibn al-Muṭahhar al-Ḥillī, *K̲h̲ulāṣat al-aḳwāl fī maᶜrifat al-rid̲j̲āl*, Tehran 1310, 62, 73; Muḥammad Bāḳir al-Mad̲j̲lisī, *Biḥār al-anwār*, li, Beirut 1403/1983, 343-81; ᶜAlī al-Yazdī al-Ḥāʾirī, *Ilzām al-nāṣib*, Beirut 1404/1984, i, 424-7; Māmaḳānī, *Tanḳīḥ al-maḳāl*, Nad̲j̲af 1349-52/1930-3, §§ 2806, 7783, 8476, 11051; D.M. Donaldson, *The Shiᶜite religion*, London 1933, 251-7; ᶜAbbās Iḳbāl, *K̲h̲āndān-i Nawbak̲h̲tī*, Tehran 1311 *s̲h̲*, 212-38; L. Massignon, *The passion of al-Ḥallāj*, tr. H. Mason, Princeton 1982, i, 315-20; Javad Ali, *Die beiden ersten Safīre des Zwölften Imāms*, in *Isl.*, xxv (1939), 197-227; D. Sourdel, *Le vizirat ᶜabbāside*, Damascus 1959-60, ii, 525; Muḥammad al-Ṣadr, *Taʾrīk̲h̲ al-g̲h̲ayba al-ṣug̲h̲rā*, Nad̲j̲af 1392/1972, 341-538, 609-55; A.A. Sachedina, *Islamic messianism*, Albany 1981, 85-99; idem, *The just ruler (al-sulṭān al-ᶜādil) in Shīᶜite Islam*, New York and Oxford 1988, 55-6, 60-1, 93; J.M. Hussain, *The role of the imāmite wikāla with special reference to the role of the first safīr*, in *Hamdard Islamicus*, v (1982), 25-52; idem, *The occultation of the Twelfth Imam*, London 1982, 79-142 and passim; V. Klemm, *Die vier sufarāʾ des Zwölften Imāms. Zur formativen Periode der Zwölferšīᶜa*, in *WO*, xv (1984), 126-43; M. Momen, *An introduction to Shiᶜi Islam*, New Haven and London 1985, 162-5; H. Halm, *Die Schia*, Darmstadt 1988, 41-5, 53-4 (tr. Janet Watson as *Shiism*, Edinburgh 1991, 35-9, 44); E. Kohlberg, *Belief and law in Imāmī Shīᶜism*, Variorum Reprints, Aldershot 1991, index, s.v.; H. Modarresi, *Crisis and consolidation in the formative period of Shīᶜite Islam*, Princeton 1993, part 1, *passim*.

(E. Kohlberg)

2. In diplomacy.

Here, *safīr*, pl. *sufarāʾ*, initially meaning envoy as well as mediator and conciliator, becomes ambassador or diplomatic agent (Turkish *sefīr*, but *elči* [*q.v.*] is more commonly used; Persian *safīr*).

(a) In the central and eastern Arab lands. Diplomacy by means of emissaries existed from the early days of Islam. The Prophet employed envoys in dealing with the towns of Ḥid̲j̲āz and Nad̲j̲d, dispatched messengers to Byzantium, Persia, Egypt and Ethiopia to invite them to join Islam, and received missions sent to him. Such diplomatic intercourse for military, political, and religious purposes continued under the Rās̲h̲idūn caliphs and the Umayyads, most prominently in negotiating war and truce with the Byzantines. Diplomacy became more organised with the stabilisation of the Islamic empire under the ᶜAbbāsids, who exchanged envoys with heads of other states near and far, in order to discuss issues of war, peace and international alliances, to deliver good-will messages and, invariably, to spy. A famous instance of these contacts (whose authenticity, however, is in some doubt) was the exchange of embassies between Charlemagne and Hārūn al-Rashīd, in which the former reportedly sought a coalition with the latter against Byzantium [see IFRANDJ]. Another line of dialogue developed through envoys between the caliph in Baghdād and provincial governors who had become autonomous, such as the Ayyūbids, and between the caliph and Islamic states not under his sovereignty, such as the Fāṭimids and Umayyads of Spain. With practice came the criteria for choosing state emissaries (prudence, courage, charm and, of course, dependability were prerequisite), patterns for conducting missions and modes of entertaining foreign envoys, as well as an elaborate diplomatic vocabulary. Al-Ḳalḳashandī's [*q.v.*] 9th/15th-century multi-volume manual for scribes in the Mamluk chancery, the *Ṣubḥ al-aʿshā*, is an impressive mirror of these sophisticated diplomatic standards.

The spread of European commerce brought European consuls to the Levant and North Africa from the 7th/13th century [see CONSUL], men who discharged a variety of diplomatic functions. In the 10th/16th century, as the Arab lands came under Ottoman rule, the region's locus of international diplomacy shifted to Istanbul [see ELČI]. Only Morocco, remaining an independent sultanate, continued to conduct international relations independently through correspondence and the occasional dispatch of emissaries. Until the late 18th century (when the Ottomans began setting up resident embassies abroad), official contacts with non-Muslim states took place mostly in the region itself, through foreign consuls and messengers. Muslim envoys were sent out quite infrequently, and then only on brief missions, often with limited objectives.

The establishment of new Arab states following the First World War marked a new stage in the region's diplomatic history. During the interwar period, relations among these states gradually assumed a formal nature, an emphatic sign—one among many—of their new status. This was so especially in the 1930s, with the attainment of greater or full independence from foreign control; the April 1936 Saudi-Iraqi Treaty of Friendship and its Saudi-Egyptian counterpart in May, both formalising diplomatic relations between the parties, were typical instances of this trend. Simultaneously, with the gradual departure of European powers from the region, their domination gave way to mutual diplomatic representation—as specified e.g. by the 1930 Anglo-Iraqi treaty and the 1936 Anglo-Egyptian treaty, both providing for a replacement of British High Commissioners by an exchange of ambassadors. Modern diplomatic protocol, terminology, and ranks, having been adopted by the Ottomans during the 19th century, were now readily applied. *Safīr* became the technical equivalent of ambassador (fem. *safīra,* ambassadress or an ambassador's wife), and came to be used for other functions in construct titles such as *safīr mufawwaḍ* (ambassador plenipotentiary), *safīr fawḳa 'l-ʿāda* (ambassador extraordinary), etc. More ranks and functions are represented by additional terms: *mabʿūth* (or *mandūb*), for envoy or minister, *mustashār* for counsellor, *sikratīr* for secretary, *mulḥaḳ* for attaché, and *ḳāʾim bi-aʿmāl* for chargé d'affaires.

Bibliography: Lane, s.v.; Ḳalḳashandī, *Ṣubḥ al-aʿshā*, vi, 15, 53; Muḥammad Ḥamīdullāh, *The Muslim conduct of state.* [6]Lahore 1973, 150-61; M. Khadduri, *War and peace in the law of Islam*, Baltimore 1955, 239-50; B. Lewis, *The Muslim discovery of Europe*, New York 1982, esp. ch. 4. For the usage of *safīr* and related terms in modern diplomacy, Mohammad Assaad Nafeh, *Nafeh's political encyclopaedia*, Cairo 1969, 735 ff. See also DIPLOMATIC; IMTIYĀZĀT. (A. AYALON)

(b) In Muslim Spain. In the Arabic sources of al-Andalus, we also find some words derived from the root *s-f-r*, meaning "to travel on mission on behalf of..."/"to be a negotiator, a mediator" (stem I) (as in al-Maḳḳarī, i, 645-6); "to make somebody travel", "to send somebody as an ambassador" (stem II); "to be sent on mission/embassy" (stem V); *safīr* (pl. *sufarāʾ*) "ambassador" (as in Ibn Ḳuzmān, 38/4/4; *Vocabulista*: "mediator", "nunciator"); *sifāra* (pl. *-āt*) "the charge of mediator", "embassy", "post or functions of ambassador". The usage of the words derived from the root *s-f-r* alternates—in a proportion and distribution not yet elucidated—with the words derived from the roots *r-s-l* ("to send a messenger", etc.) and *w-f-d* ("to go somewhere on behalf of somebody", etc.).

These words, and their contexts, throughout the history of al-Andalus, exhibit the fact that connections between individuals and groups were established by a "messenger", and that relations were engaged and accepted by all the Andalusī states; that means that more or less intensive and institutionalised diplomatic activities were established by an "ambassador" with the charge, the post, or rather the functions of representing the interests of a power, sporadical or continually, circumstantial or more specifically.

Although precise analysis on this aspect has not yet been done, we cannot deduce from the sources that the *sifāra* was an institutionalised charge, like a *wilāya* or *khuṭṭa*, but most probably was an "activity", in the sense that a person was *safīr* only while carrying out his mission. There is no indication in the sources on al-Andalus of the existence of permanent embassies.

Embassies were frequently assigned to those who knew another language in addition to Arabic, such as the *dhimmiyyūn*: the *naṣārā* (Christians of al-Andalus) and the Jews. Amongst the *naṣārā* were the Andalusian bishop sent by the caliph of Cordova ʿAbd al-Raḥmān III al-Nāṣir to Ramiro I of Leon (Ibn Ḥayyān, *Muḳtabas*, v, 350), and the bishop Recemundo, known as Rabīʿ b. Zayd [*q.v.*], sent by al-Nāṣir to Germany in 955-6. The Christians of al-Andalus [see MOZARABS] were also sent by the Christian kings of the North to the Islamic territories and, on some occasion, were alternate ambassadors, such as the *ḳūmis* Sisnando Davídiz, who was initially the messenger of al-Muʿtaḍid of Seville to the court of Leon and then became the ambassador of the Christian kings to the *mulūk al-ṭawāʾif*, for example to the *amīr* ʿAbd Allāh (*The Tibyān*, 226, n. 241).

Amongst the Jews were Ibn Shālib al-Yahūdī, ambassador of Alphonso VI of Castile to al-Muʿtamid of Seville [*q.v.*], who killed al-Yahūdī (it was a permanent risk for ambassadors); Ibrāhīm b. al-Fakhkhār al-Yahūdī, well-known poet in the Arabic language, was the ambassador of Castile to the Almohad court. Other Jews were also sent by the Andalusian kings, such as the powerful Cordovan Jew Ḥasdāy b. Shaprūṭ, who was the outstanding vizier of the caliph ʿAbd al-Raḥmān III al-Nāṣir, and was entrusted with missions to Barcelona (940), Leon (in 941 and 955) and Navarre. He was also assigned the task of receiving the Byzantine Constantine VIII's ambassadors in Cordova (944) and the Saxon emperor Otto I's ambassadors (956).

Some outstanding Muslim personalities in al-Andalus, renowned for their culture and eloquence, were also designated as ambassadors, such as the Cordovan poet al- G̲h̲azāl, sent by the amīr ʿAbd al-Raḥmān II to the Vikings (madj̲ūs), and to Constantinople; and the Granada vizier and polygraph Ibn al-K̲h̲aṭīb [q.v.], who went on three or four diplomatic missions to the Marīnids [q.v.] of Fās. Other personalities renowned for their religious prestige were also sent on missions. For example, the two Ibn al-ʿArabīs were entrusted with obtaining the recognition of the Almoravid amīr Yūsuf b. Tās̲h̲ufīn by the ʿAbbāsid court. Merchants sometimes played the role of ambassadors, such as the Granadan al-Bunyūlī, charged by the Naṣrid sultan to get help from the Mamlūk sultan al-Ẓāhir, in 845/1441.

It is useful to classify the Andalusian embassies according to their destination, whether within al-Andalus or outside it. The destinations of the external embassies are to be classified as either to Dār al-Islām (the other Muslim territories) or to Dār al-ḥarb (non-Muslim territories). The internal embassies were exchanged either amongst the different administrations or between the administration and the subjects, or vice-versa, such as those sent by the Almohad court in Marrākus̲h̲ to every part of its empire. The external embassies, well-known but not yet analysed, excepting those of the Umayyad period (Lévi-Provençal; el-Hajji), show that permanent relations between al-Andalus and the rest of the Muslim world existed as, for example, with the ʿAbbāsids, Egypt and finally with the Turks, but especially with the Mag̲h̲rib. There are many references to missions which were sent from al-Andalus to the Christian north of the Iberian Peninsula, to the Ifrandj̲a and other European parts, and especially to Byzantium.

Andalusian sources point out the luxury and ostentation of the receptions given by some Andalusian sovereigns for foreign ambassadors, with the purpose of political propaganda (Granja, Embajada).

Bibliography: ʿAbd Allāh, The Tibyān, tr. A.T. Tibi, Leiden 1986, 90, 226; Ibn Ḥayyān, Muktabas, v, ed. P. Chalmeta, F. Corriente, M. Subh et alii, Madrid 1979; tr. with notes by M.J. Viguera and F. Corriente, Madrid 1981, 344-57; Ibn Saʿīd, al-Mug̲h̲rib, esp. ii, 23; Ibn al-K̲h̲aṭīb, Rayḥānat al-kuttāb, ed. M.ʿA. ʿInān, El Cairo, 1980, 2 vols., tr. M. Gaspar Remiro, Correspondencia diplomática entre Granada y Fez (s. XIV), Granada 1911-16; Ibn Ḳuzmān, Dīwān (= F. Corriente, Léxico estándar y andalusí del Dīwān de Ibn Quzmān, Saragossa 1993, 76); Maḳḳarī, Nafḥ al-ṭīb = Analectes, ed. R. Dozy et alii, Leiden 1855-61, repr. Amsterdam 1967, 2 vols., i, 287, 645, ii, 354-5, 598, 677; F. Corriente, El léxico árabe andalusí según el "Vocabulista in arabico", Madrid 1989; M. Alarcón and R. García de Linares, Los documentos árabes diplomáticos del Archivo de la Corona de Aragón, Madrid-Granada 1940, esp. nos. 25, 55, 56, 66, 72, 73, 154; R. Arié, España musulmana (siglos VIII-XV), Barcelona 1982, 162-4; F. de la Granja, A propósito de una embajada cristiana en la corte de ʿAbd al-Raḥmān III, in al-And., xxxix (1974), 391-406; A.A. el-Hajji, Andalusian diplomatic relations with Western Europe during the Umayyad period, Beirut 1970; E. Lévi-Provençal, HEM, i, 239-54, ii, 65-98, 143-53, 184, 259; J. Lirola, El poder naval de al-Andalus en la época del Califato Omeya, Granada 1993, 117-36, 174-212, 232-6, 243-50, 267; ʿA.H. al-Tāzī, al-Taʾrīkh al-diblūmāsī li 'l-Mag̲h̲rib, Muḥammadiyya 1986-9, 10 vols.; M.J. Viguera, Los reinos de taifas y las invasiones magrebíes, Madrid 1992, 164, 173-4, 217, 294.　　　　　　　　　　　(M.J. Viguera)

3. In Muslim India.

Elaborate rules were laid down in mediaeval India regarding the qualifications and protocol duties of ambassadors. Fak̲h̲r-i Mudabbir quotes the following ḥadīth of the Prophet as the guiding principle: "When you send an ambassador to me, he should be of good reputation, handsome and of good voice." (Ādāb al-ḥarb wa 'l-s̲h̲adj̲āʿa, ed. A.S. K̲h̲wānsarī, Tehran 1346/1967, 142). The Dihlī Sultans received envoys in such awful atmosphere of dignity and grandeur that, according to Dj̲ūzdj̲ānī, many of them fainted in the darbār (Ṭabaḳāt-i Nāṣirī, Calcutta 1864, 316-19; Baranī, Tārīkh-i Fīrūz-S̲h̲āhī, Calcutta 1862, 30-3). Envoys were sent for different purposes—diplomatic, religious, economic, cultural etc.—and Abu 'l-Faḍl refers to the spiritual and temporal objectives of ambassadorial functions (Akbar-nāma, tr. Beveridge, ii, 262).

Envoys to and from the caliph. Envoys were sent to secure letters of investiture (mans̲h̲ūr) from the ʿAbbāsid caliphs. Iltutmis̲h̲ sent Ik̲h̲tiyār al-Mulk Ras̲h̲īd al-Dīn Abū Bakr Ḥabas̲h̲ to Bag̲h̲dād, and twice Raḍiyy al-Dīn Ḥasan al-Ṣag̲h̲ānī [q.v.] came to Iltutmis̲h̲ as envoy of the caliphs. When the caliph granted investiture to Iltutmis̲h̲, legalising the status of the Dihlī Sultanate, he celebrated the occasion with great éclat. On another occasion, the caliph sent an envoy, Ḳāḍī Dj̲alāl Urūs, with a copy of the Safinat al-k̲h̲ulafāʾ, allegedly containing an autographic inscription of the caliph al-Maʾmūn. With the fall of Bag̲h̲dād, contact with caliphal authority there came to an end, but after many enquiries, Muḥammad b. Tug̲h̲luḳ established contact with the fainéant ʿAbbāsids in Egypt. In 744/1343 he sent Ḥādj̲dj̲ī Radj̲ab Burḳuʿī to the caliph requesting a mans̲h̲ūr. When Ḥādj̲dj̲ī Saʿīd Ṣarṣarī, Sayyid Ziyād, Mubash-s̲h̲ir K̲h̲alwātī and Muḥammad Ṣūfī brought the investiture, the sultan went out barefoot to receive them. The caliph later sent S̲h̲ayk̲h̲ al-S̲h̲uyūk̲h̲ Rukn al-Dīn and Mak̲h̲dūm-zāda G̲h̲iyāth al-Dīn Muḥammad as his envoy to the sultan. As the Mak̲h̲dūm-zāda was the grandson of the caliph al-Mustanṣir bi'llāh, he was lodged at the palace of ʿAlāʾ al-Dīn K̲h̲aldj̲ī and 400,000 dīnārs were sent for washing his head (Ibn Baṭṭūṭa, iii, 261-2, tr. Gibb, iii, 680-1). In 754/1353 S̲h̲ayk̲h̲ S̲h̲ihāb al-Dīn Aḥmad Samīt brought an investiture patent for Fīrūz S̲h̲āh Tug̲h̲luḳ, and a new one arrived in 766/1364. The sultan sent to the caliph details of his benefactions, religious endowments and public works through Maḥmūd S̲h̲ams Kurd Ḳāḍī Nadj̲m al-Dīn Ḳuras̲h̲ī and K̲h̲wādj̲a Kāfūr K̲h̲alwatī, and Maḥmūd then brought back mandates from the caliph (Sīrat-i Fīrūz-S̲h̲āhī, ms. Bankipur). At a later date, the Mug̲h̲als did not recognise the Ottomans as caliphs, but in 1785 Tīpū Sulṭān [q.v.] sent his envoys to Istanbul to obtain an investiture from the Sultan-caliph.

The Mongol period. Both Čingiz K̲h̲ān and his rival the K̲h̲wārazm-S̲h̲āh sent their envoys to Iltutmis̲h̲ seeking his support. In 1246 when a Mongol commander attacked India, S̲h̲ayk̲h̲ Bahāʾ al-Dīn Zakariyyā of Multan, was sent to negotiate peace. Two years after the fall of Bag̲h̲dād, in 658/1260, emissaries from the Mongols visited India and were accorded a royal reception by sultan Nāṣir al-Dīn Maḥmūd (Tabaḳāt-i Nāṣirī, 317-18).

Envoys to and from the Il-K̲h̲ān. Arg̲h̲ūn G̲h̲azan and Muḥammad Öldjeytü K̲h̲udābanda sent their envoys to the Dihlī court, and the great vizier Ras̲h̲īd al-Dīn Faḍl Allāh [q.v.] came as an envoy to ʿAlāʾ al-Dīn K̲h̲aldj̲ī (Nizami, Rashid al-Din Fazl Allaʾ and India, in Proceedings of the Colloquium on Rashid-Al Din Fadl Allah, Tehran 1971, 36-53). Ras̲h̲īd al-Dīn came again as an envoy to the court of Mubāraḳ K̲h̲aldj̲ī (Āʾīn-i Akbarī, ed. Sir Sayyid Aḥmad K̲h̲ān ii, 200), and Muḥammad b. Tug͟hluḳ sent and received envoys from Sultan Abū Saʿīd.

Envoys to and from neighbouring countries. According to Baranī, ambassadors from distant lands came to the court of Balban. During the time of Muḥammad b. Tug͟hluḳ envoys came from ʿIrāḳ, Syria, China and K͟hʷārazm, and the Chinese ambassador, Tursi, came with a large retinue; in return, Muḥammad b. Tug͟hluḳ sent the Amīr Maḥmūd Harawī as his envoy to China.

Envoys to the Ottomans. Muḥammad S͟hāh Bahmanī III of the Deccan (867-87/1463-82) was the first Indian ruler to exchange envoys with the Ottomans, and Meḥemmed II Fātiḥ sent Mawlānā Afḍāl al-Dīn-og͟hlu Meḥmed Čelebi as his envoy. Maḥmūd S͟hāh Bahmanī (887-924/1482-1518) sent Mullā Niʿmat Allāh to Bāyezīd II as his emissary. The Muẓaffarids of Gud̲j̲arāt exchanged several embassies with Selīm I (918-26/1512-20), and Bahādur S͟hāh sent envoys to Istanbul seeking Ottoman help against the Mug͟hal Humāyūn. The Mug͟hals considered the Ottomans as their rivals and did not like to exchange envoys with them. Nevertheless, Turkish records say that Sīdī ʿAlī Reʾīs, the Ottoman admiral, carried a letter from Humāyūn to Süleymān the Magnificent in which Humāyūn addressed the Sultan as "the K͟halīfa of the highest qualities." The Ottoman documents used the terms *Hind elčisi* or *elčiye-i Hind* to denote Mug͟hal ambassadors, but no details are available in the Indian chronicles about these Mug͟hal envoys. The envoys of the Ottoman governor of Yemen were, however, treated with scant respect by Akbar (N.R. Faruqi, *Mughal-Ottoman relations*, Delhi 1989, 20 ff.).

Envoys to and from the Uzbeks. Akbar was afraid of Uzbek power and treated them with suspicion. However, in 979/1571 ʿAbd Allāh K͟hān Uzbek, ruler of Transoxiana, sent an embassy to Akbar.

Envoys to and from Tīmūrid and Ṣafawid Persia. The sultans of Golkonda, Bid̲j̲āpur and Aḥmadnagar sent ambassadors to the court of S͟hāh Ṭahmāsp I, whilst in 847/1443 S͟hāh Ruk͟h's ambassador ʿAbd al-Razzāḳ had been received by the Hindu ruler of Vijayanagar, King Devendra.

Humāyūn, who was beholden to the Ṣafawids for help, developed contact with them, and during the time of Akbar, many ambassadors came and went to Persia. In 1004/1596 the Emperor sent Mirza Ḍiyāʾ al-Dīn Kāsī and Abū Nāṣir Kāfī to S͟hāh ʿAbbās, and according to Iskandar Beg Muns͟hī, they were received with honour (tr. R.M. Savory, *History of Shah Abbas the Great*, Boulder, Col. 1978, ii, 705-6). Abu 'l-Faḍl's account of the reception of these envoys is silly and pedantic (*Akbar-nama*, tr. iii, 1112).

Several envoys were sent by S͟hāh ʿAbbās to D̲j̲ahāngīr. In 1020/1611 Yādgār ʿAlī Tālis͟h came to mourn Akbar's death and to congratulate D̲j̲ahāngīr on his accession. When Yādgār ʿAlī returned to Persia, D̲j̲ahāngīr's envoy K͟hān ʿAlam accompanied him. In 1024/1615 a second Persian embassy headed by Muṣṭafā Beg came to D̲j̲ahāngīr's court with huge presents, including European hounds which D̲j̲ahāngīr had asked for. In the following year Muḥammad Riḍā Beg came to D̲j̲ahāngīr to obtain monetary aid aginst Ottoman Turkey and to bring about an amicable settlement between D̲j̲ahāngīr and the Shīʿī states of the Deccan. For envoys to and from S͟hāh D̲j̲ahān, see Saksena, *History of Shahjahan*, Allahabad 1973, 210-32.

Queen Elizabeth's envoy to Akbar. Elizabeth of England sent an envoy to Akbar in 1583 with a letter which was "the earliest communication between the government of India and England" (V.A. Smith, *Akbar the Great Moghul*, Oxford 1919, 229).

Akbar's envoys to Europe. Akbar desired to send envoys to Philip II of Spain recommending universal peace and harmony; a diplomatic mission, consisting of Sayyid Muẓaffar, ʿAbd Allāh K͟hān and Father Monserrate was dispatched to Lisbon, but was unable to reach there.

Jesuit missions at Akbar's court. Akbar's interest in religious debates led to the arrival of several Jesuit Missions at Akbar's court in 1580 and after, and in return Akbar sent ʿAbd Allāh as his envoy to Portuguese Goa (see E. Maclagan, *The Jesuits and the Great Mogul*, London 1932).

British envoys at D̲j̲ahāngīr's court. D̲j̲ahāngīr welcomed William Hawkins and Sir Thomas Roe, but refused to conclude a commercial treaty with England. Hawkins was, however, persuaded to remain at the court as the resident ambassador.

Envoys of the Deccan states and provincial Indian states. Three types of envoys have been identified in regard to the Deccan of the 10th/16th century: (a) *ad hoc* envoys, called *rasūls*, who were sent to offer congratulations or condolences; (b) the *ḥād̲j̲ib-i muḳīm*, literally, attaché; originally assigned to the army of friendly powers; and (c) *wakīls* or permanent ambassadors accredited to certain foreign powers (H.K. Sherwani, *History of the Qutb Shahi dynasty*, Delhi 1974, 218-19). Provincial kingdoms like D̲j̲awnpūr, Bengal, Mālwā and Gud̲j̲arāt sent envoys within India with the limited objectives of winning support in their conflicts with the adjoining states, but it is only regarding the Deccan that one finds contact with outside powers. In Gud̲j̲arāt, the ambassadors were mainly concerned with the activities of the Portuguese.

Envoys to the West during the 18th and 19th centuries: Tīpū Sulṭān of Mysore sent his envoys to France and Turkey; Louis XVI received his envoy with honour, but refused to enter into any alliance against the British. One of the last Mug͟hal Emperors, Akbar S͟hāh II, sent Rad̲j̲a Rām Mohan Roy to London in 1827 to plead his case for an increase in his *pīs͟hkas͟h* or pension.

Bibliography (in addition to references given in the text): Ras͟hīd al-Dīn Faḍl Allāh, *Mukātabāt-i Ras͟hīdī*, ed. M. S͟hafīʿ, Lahore 1947; S͟hihāb al-Dīn al-ʿUmarī, *Masālik al-abṣār fī mamālik al-amṣār*, tr. O. Spies *et alii*, Lahore 1943; Abu 'l-Faḍl, *Maktūbāt-i ʿAllāmī*, Lucknow 1863; Maḥmūd Gāwan, *Riyāḍ al-ins͟hāʾ*, Ḥaydarābād 1948; S͟hāh Nawāz K͟hān, *Maʾāt͟hir al-umarāʾ*, Calcutta 1887-94; A. Monserrate, *Commentary on his journey to the Court of Akbar*, Cuttack 1922; Riazul Islam, *Indo-Persian relations*, Tehran 1957; I.H. Qureshi, *The administration of the Sultanate of Delhi*, Lahore 1944; *Studies in the foreign relations of India, Sherwani Felicitation Volume*, Ḥaydarābād 1975; A. Rahim, *Mughal relations with Persia and Central Asia*, in *IC*, viii-ix (1934-5); J. Aubin, *Les relations diplomatiques entre les Aq-qoyunlu et les Bahmanides*, in *Iran and Islam*, ed. C.E. Bosworth, Edinburgh 1971, 11-15. (K.A. Nizami)

ṢĀFĪT͟HA, a place in western Syria, situated in the D̲j̲abal Bahrāʾ region. This last becomes lower as it falls southwards, with a large gap commanded to the north by Ṣāfīt͟ha and Ḥiṣn al-Akrād [*q.v.*] and to the south by ʿAkkār and ʿIrḳa [*q.vv.*]. The mountains of the ʿAlawīs fall southwards into the Ṣāfīt͟ha depression.

Ṣāfīt͟ha was the 'Αργυρόκαστρων of Byzantine authors, Castrum Album or Chastel Blanc of the

Latin ones, and is the main place in the district, with its fortress called in Arabic texts Burd̲j̲ Ṣāfīt̲h̲a; this last lies to the east of the present village and dominates the foothills of the D̲j̲abal Nuṣayrī to the north. It commands two valleys at a point midway between Ḥiṣn al-Akrād and Ṭarṭūs and also a large gap, to the south of the D̲j̲abal Bahrāʾ, by means of which Ḥimṣ [q.v.] is connected with Ṭarābulus al-S̲h̲ām. From Antiquity, the castle of Ṣāfīt̲h̲a commanded the route connecting Ḥamāt [q.v.] and Ṭarṭūs on the coast, i.e. the passage from central Syria to the Mediterranean. Situated on a basalt peak at an altitude of over 400 m/1,312 feet, it protected the lands to the north in mediaeval times from the Nizārī Ismāʿīlīs. The region around Ṣāfīt̲h̲a was a fertile one, with olives grown there from classical times, and with vines, figs and white mulberry trees for silk worms grown there in mediaeval times.

The fortress of the mediaeval Christian town of Ṣāfīt̲h̲a was a strong rectangular donjon with rounded angles, originally protected by double defensive walls. The Order of the Temple was responsible for its construction, upkeep and manning. From 526/1132 onwards, the Franks built fortresses in the D̲j̲abal Anṣāriyya against the Ismāʿīlīs, who paid them a tribute in gold pieces and wheat. The Templars' aim was to control the gap between Ḥimṣ and Ṭarābulus in the hinterland of the Knights Hospitallers' territory. The plan of the castle resembled that of Markab [q.v.] in being elliptical, originally with a double wall, but later with a single wall with rectangular salients, as at Ṭarṭūs and ʿAt̲h̲līt̲h̲ [q.v.], and with a moat 15 m/49 feet deep and 13 m/42 feet wide. The stones were dovetailed together and linked by iron crampons sealed with lead. Some modifications to it were made by Louis IX (St. Louis) when he was staying in Syria (Ṣafar 548-Ṣafar 652/May 1252-end of April 1254), including an even more complex entry with a portcullis and four successive gates. The first protective wall, in the shape of an irregular polygon, had a glacis before it. The actual keep had its own water supply, kept in a vast subterranean cistern hewn out of the rock and replenished by rainfall brought through conduits, and could thus withstand a certain period of siege, and there was also an external cistern (birka) where mounts and other beasts could drink. The chapel of St. Michael within the castle resembled the Romanesque churches of the South of France of the late 12th century, and, like all similarly-placed chapels of the Templars and Hospitallers, was devoid of ornamentation. In the thickness of the walls, a staircase led to the Great Hall (palatium) and the armoury. The keep itself was 28 m/90 feet high and had two floors, reached by a staircase on the west side. Down below was a subterranean prison. The region, and Syria in general, was always liable to earthquakes, and the fortress of Ṣāfīt̲h̲a was damaged in 565/1170, 597/1201 and the following year, only the chapel of the fortress being unscathed. Communication between the strong points of the Franks was by means of smoke signals by day and fire ones by night, but the Crusaders learnt the use of carrier pigeons from the Muslims, and Jacques de Vitry, the envoy of Pope Honorius III, announced his arrival at Ṣāfīt̲h̲a in 614/1215 by this means. The garrison of the castle comprised over 700 knights and their squires, divided into 50-man sections, in addition to large numbers of artisans, such as blacksmiths and armourers, and also the prisoners. There were stores of supplies and provisions, and in times of threatened attack, the local villagers would seek refuge there also.

Of later history, it is recorded that in 1270/1854, a petty chieftain, Ismāʿīl Bey, seized Ṣāfīt̲h̲a and proclaimed himself mus̲h̲īr [q.v.] or governor acting as an "Old Man of the Mountain", which provoked a revolt of the Muslims of the region; four years later, he was murdered by a relative. After this, Ṣāfīt̲h̲a was integrated into the Ottoman empire.

The present-day village is situated on the site of the mediaeval fortress. In the early 19th century, the ḳaḍāʾ of Ṣāfīt̲h̲a was one of the constituents, with al-Markab, Tell Kalāk̲h̲, ʿUmrāniya and Ṭarṭūs, of the sand̲j̲aḳ of Ṭarṭūs. In 1916 it had 2,500 inhabitants, including 1,500 Nuṣayrīs [see NUṢAYRIYYA] and 850 Syrian Orthodox. In 1920 the administrative district of Ṣāfīt̲h̲a comprised 202 villages, with 41,500 people, including 20,000 Nuṣayrīs, 10,000 Muslims, 6,500 Greek Orthodox, 4,500 Maronites, 300 Greek Catholics and 200 Protestants. In this same year the ḳaḍāʾ of Ṣāfīt̲h̲a, with the town as its chef-lieu, was detached from the sand̲j̲aḳ of Ṭarābulus al-S̲h̲ām, and then made part of the State of the ʿAlawīs established in 1922 as part of the federation of Syria. In 1945 the ḳaḍāʾ became part of the muḥāfaẓa of the ʿAlawīs. After 1954, the local population, essentially peasant cultivators, supported the Parti Populaire Syrien. Local activities include carpet weaving and the cultivation of cotton and tobacco. The village now surrounds the castle and its dominating donjon, and its houses are essentially built from stones taken from the castle's enceinte. The chapel of St. Michael in the donjon is still used by the Greek Orthodox members of the population. In the 1960s Ṣāfīt̲h̲a became a tourist centre, for skiing in winter and with an open-air bathing pool.

Bibliography: 1. Arabic texts. Yāḳūt, *Muʿd̲j̲am al-buldān*, Beirut 1386/1957, iii, 389b-390a; Ibn Nāṣif, *Taʾrīk̲h̲ al-Manṣūrī*, facs. ed. Moscow 1960; Ibn al-ʿAdīm, *Zubda min taʾrīk̲h̲ Ḥalab*, ii, Damascus 1954, 324, 336, iii, Damascus 1968, 102, 180, Muḥyī 'l-Dīn ʿAbd al-Ẓāhir, *Tas̲h̲rīf al-ayyām wa 'l-ʿuṣūr fī sīrat al-Malik al-Manṣūr Ḳalāwūn*, Cairo 1971, 38, 83, 186, 210; Abū S̲h̲āma, *Kitāb al-Rawḍatayn*, i/1, Cairo 1956, 128; idem, *D̲h̲ayl ʿalā 'l-Rawḍatayn*, Cairo 1399/1947, 2nd part, 109, 126; Ibn S̲h̲addād, *al-Aʿlāḳ al-k̲h̲aṭīra*, Damascus 1963, 54; Maḳrīzī, *al-Sulūk li-maʿrifat al-mulūk*, ed. Ziyāda and ʿĀs̲h̲ūr, i/1, Cairo 1934, 100, 566, 590, 596, 638, 975, 987, ii/3, Cairo 1958, 596; idem, *Sulūk*, ed. Ziyāda, Cairo 1935, i, 238; Ibn Ṭūlūn, *al-Ḳalāʾid al-d̲j̲awhariyya*, Damascus 1368-75/1949-56, i, 168-9; M. Kurd ʿAlī, *K̲h̲iṭaṭ al-S̲h̲ām*, vi, Damascus 1928, 258-61.

2. Translations. Ibn al-Ḳalānisī, *The Damascus Chronicle of the Crusades* = *D̲h̲ayl taʾrīk̲h̲ Dimas̲h̲ḳ*, partial Eng. tr. H.A.R. Gibb, London 1932, 99-127, annotated Fr. tr. R. Le Tourneau, as *Damas de 1075 à 1154*, Damascus 1952, 116; Ibn al-At̲h̲īr, *Kāmil*, in *RHC, Hists. or.*, i, 584; ʿImād al-Dīn al-Iṣfahānī, *al-Fatḥ al-ḳussī fī 'l fatḥ al-ḳudsī*, tr. Massé, as *Conquête de la Syrie et de la Palestine par Saladin*, Paris 1972, 122, 284; Maḳrīzī, *Sulūk*, partial tr. Quatremère, as *Histoire des Sultans Mamlouks*, Paris 1837-45, i/2, 52; Usāma b. Munḳidh, *Iʿtibār*, tr. Miquel, *Des enseignements de la vie*, Paris 1983, 158-9, 204-5; Ibn D̲j̲ubayr, *Riḥla*, tr. Gaudefroy-Demombynes, Paris 1949-65, 286; Abū S̲h̲āma, *Rawḍatayn*, extracts and Fr. tr. Barbier de Meynard, in *RHC, hists. or.*, iv/5, Paris 1906, 155; Ibn al-Furāt, *Taʾrīk̲h̲ al-Duwal*, selection of texts tr. Lyons, Cambridge 1973, indices.

3. Studies. E.G. Rey, *Etude sur les monuments d l'architecture militaire des Croisés en Syrie ...*, Paris 1871

70, 84-92, 101-2 Pl. 9; E. Renan, *Mission en Phénicie*, Paris 1864-74, 105-6, 112-13 and atlas; R. Röhricht, in *ZDPV*, x (1887), 260 and n. 4; Le Strange, *Palestine under the Moslems*, 292; Clermont-Ganneau, *Recueil d'archéologie orientale*, ii, Paris 1897, bk. 16, 179-80, 239-40; R. Dussaud, *Hist. et religion des Nosaïris*, Paris 1900, 32-40; Gertrude Bell, *Syria, the desert and the sown*, London 1908, 210-11; Baedeker, *Palestine and Syria*, Leipzig 1912, 356; M. van Berchem, in *JA* (1912), i, 440; idem and E. Fatio, *Voyage en Syrie. Itinéraires du nord de la Syrie*, Cairo 1915; M. Gaudefroy-Demombynes, *La Syrie à l'époque des Mamelouks*, Paris 1923, 117 n. 2; Dussaud, *Topographie historique de la Syrie*, Paris 1927, 91, 96, 119-20, map V; P. Jacquot, *L'Etat des Alaouites*², Beirut 1931, 264; R. Dussaud, P. Deschamps and H. Seyrig, *La Syrie antique et médiévale illustrée*, Paris 1931, 9, 96; Deschamps, in *Syria*, xiii-xiv (1932), 369, 371; idem, in *La revue de l'Art*, lxii (Dec. 1932), 163; idem, *Le Crac des Chevaliers*, Paris 1934, index; Grousset, *Hist. des Croisades*, Paris 1934-6, indices; Cl. Cahen, *La Syrie du nord à l'époque des Croisades*, Damascus 1940, 170, 173-4, 176, 256, 329, 511, 514, 719; J. Weulersse, *Le pays des Alaouites*, Damascus 1940, i, 59, 62, 75, 78, 100, 103, 106, 115, 126, 315, 324, 332, 341-3, pls. LXXXVIII—XC; R. Fedden, *Syria*, London 1946, 182, 192 n. 1, 198, 201; J. Weulersse, *Paysans de Syrie et du Proche-Orient*, Paris 1946, 155 fig. 29, 158 figs. 29-30, 270; S. Runciman, *A hist. of the Crusades*, Cambridge 1952-4; E. de Vaumas, *L'Amanus et le Djebel Ansariyeh, étude morphologique*, in *Rev. de géogr. alpine* (1954), 111-42; K.M. Setton (general ed.), *A history of the Crusades*, Philadelphia, etc. 1954-85, indices; Deschamps, *Terre Sainte romane*, Paris 1964, 157-9; Hachette World Guides, *The Middle East. Lebanon, Syria, Jordan, Iraq, Iran*, Paris 1966, 438-9 and map at 440-1; B. Lewis, *The Assassins, a radical sect in Islam*, London 1967; N. Elisséeff, *Nūr ad-Dīn*, Damascus 1967, i, 239-40, ii, 424, 473 n. 3, 516 n. 2, 616, 654, 666; T.S.R. Boase, *Castles and churches of the Crusading kingdoms*, London 1967; Cahen, in *REI*, xxxiii (1970), 243-9; E. Wirth, *Syrien, eine geographische Ländeskunde*, Darmstadt 1971, 102, 296, 365, 370; Deschamps, *Les châteaux des Croisés en Terre Saint. iii. La défense du Comté de Tripoli et la Principauté d'Antioche*, Paris 1973, passim; R.C. Smail, *The Crusaders in Syria and the Holy Land*, London 1973, 26, 96, 98, 151, map fig. 3; H. Salamé-Sarkis, *Contribution à l'hist. de Tripoli et de sa région à l'époque des Croisades*, Paris 1980; T.E. Lawrence, *Crusader castles*, new ed. D. Pringle, Oxford 1990, passim. (N. Elisséeff)

ṢAFIYYA bt. Ḥuyayy b. Akhṭab, Muḥammad's eleventh wife, was born in Medina and belonged to the Jewish tribe of the Banu 'l-Naḍīr [see al-naḍīr]; her mother Barra bt. Samawʾal, the sister of Rifāʿa b. Samawʾal, was of the Banū Ḳurayẓa [*q.v.*]. Her father and her uncle Abū Yāsir were among the Prophet's most bitter enemies. When their tribe was expelled from Medina in 4 A.H., Ḥuyayy b. Akhṭab was one of those who settled in Khaybar [*q.v.*], together with Kināna b. al-Rabīʿ, to whom Ṣafiyya was married at the end of 6 or early in 7 A.H.; her age at this time was about 17. There is a tradition that she had formerly been the wife of Sallām b. Mashkam, who had divorced her.

When Khaybar fell, in Ṣafar 7/June-July 628, Ṣafiyya was captured, together with two of her cousins. In the division of the spoils she had been assigned, or actually given, to Diḥya b. Khalīfa al-Kalbī, but when Muḥammad saw her he was struck by her beauty, and threw his mantle over her as a sign that he had chosen her for himself. He redeemed her from Diḥya against seven head of cattle, and gave her the option of embracing Islam. Her husband was condemned to a cruel death by Muḥammad for having refused to give up the treasure of the Banu 'l-Naḍīr. The nuptials were celebrated with haste and with a modest wedding feast, either in Khaybar itself or on the way back to Medina. Ṣafiyya's dowry [see mahr] consisted of her emancipation. Her position as a wife, which was questioned, was established by the veil or *ḥidjāb* [*q.v.*] being imposed on her and her receiving a portion of Muḥammad's booty.

In Medina, Ṣafiyya received a cold welcome; ʿĀʾisha [*q.v.*] and Muḥammad's other wives showed their jealousy with slights upon her Jewish origin. She gave the Prophet's daughter Fāṭima [*q.v.*] gold from her earrings, which may indicate that the two were allies in the politics of Muḥammad's harem. Doubts about Ṣafiyya's commitment to Islam and the suspicion that she would avenge her slain kin are recurring themes in the numerous biographies of her composed through the centuries. In these stories, the Prophet (or ʿUmar) admonishes the doubters and re-affirms the quality of her Islam, despite her being a Jewish convert. During Muḥammad's last illness, Ṣafiyya expressed her devotion to him, and was criticised by the other wives.

Ṣafiyya's marriage to the Prophet was predicted in a dream while she was still married to Kināna, and her husband beat her for desiring another man. The miracle and her suffering for Islam and the Prophet, as well as her reputation for crying won her a place in Ṣūfī works. She appears in all the major books of *ḥadīths* and indices of transmitters, although she related relatively few traditions compared to ʿĀʾisha and Umm Salama [*q.v.*]. A number of events in her life serve as legal and customary precedents.

In 35/656, Ṣafiyya sided with ʿUthmān [*q.v.*]; while he was besieged in his house she made an unsuccessful attempt to reach him, and she used to bring him food and water by means of a plank placed between her dwelling and his. When ʿĀʾisha asked her to be present at ʿUthmān's last interview with ʿAlī, Ṭalḥa and al-Zubayr, which took place in her house, Ṣafiyya went, and tried to defend the unfortunate caliph.

She died in 50/670 or 52/672, during Muʿāwiya's caliphate, leaving a fortune of 100,000 dirhams in land and goods, one-third of which she bequeathed to her sister's son, who still followed the Jewish faith. Her dwelling in Medina was bought by Muʿāwiya for 180,000 dirhams.

Bibliography: Ibn Hishām, 354, 653, 762, 766; Ibn Saʿd, viii, 85-92; Ṭabarī, i, 173; Ibn Ḥibbān, *K. al-Thiḳāt*, Ḥaydarābād 1973-82, iii, 197; Abū Nuʿaym al-Iṣbahānī, *Ḥilyat al-awliyāʾ*, Cairo 1932-8, ii, no. 137; Ibn ʿAbd al-Barr, Cairo 1957-60, iv, no. 4005; Ibn al-Ḳaysarānī, *al-Djamʿ bayna kitābay Abī Naṣr al-Kalābādhī wa-Abī Bakr al-Iṣbahānī fī ridjāl al-Bukhārī wa-Muslim*, Haydarābād 1905, ii, no. 2373; Ibn al-Djawzī, *Ṣifat al-ṣafwa*, Ḥaydarābād 1936-8, ii, 27; Dhahabī, *Siyar aʿlām al-nubalāʾ*, Beirut 1981-8, ii, no. 26; Ibn Ḥadjar al-ʿAsḳalānī, *Iṣāba*, Cairo 1970-2, vii, no. 11401; Caetani, *Annali dell' Islam*, i, 379, 415; ii/1, 29-30, 34-6; viii, 223-4; N. Abbott, *Aishah, the beloved of Mohammed*, Chicago 1942, 39, 42-4, 51-2, 95, 122, 200; anon., *Ṣafiyya*, Cairo, Dar al-Maʿārif 1983.

(V. Vacca-[Ruth Roded])

ṢAFİYYE WĀLİDE SULṬĀN (Cecilia Baffo), Ottoman queen mother, born in Venice in 1550, died in 1014/1605.

The daughter of the Italian Baffo, governor of Corfu, when she was fourteen years old, while travelling between Venice and Corfu on the Adriatic Sea, she was captured by Ottoman pirates. On account of her beauty, she was taken to the palace of prince Murād, grandson of Süleymān and governor of the *sandjaḳ* of Manisa. In the Manisa palace, she became a Muslim, learned Turkish and was trained in palace manners. In 972/1565, she was presented to Murād. She gave birth in 973/1566 to prince Meḥemmed, who became the first great grandchild of Süleymān and was named by him, and subsequently to the princesses ʿĀʾis̲h̲e and Fāṭima. In 974/1566, after Süleymān's death, Murād's father took over the throne as Selīm II and Murād became the *welī ʿahd*. In 982/1574, following Selīm's death, Murād succeeded as Murād III. Ṣafiyye was now 25 years old and had already become the head *k̲h̲āṣṣekī* [*q.v.*]. During Murād's reign, she gained growing influence in the palace, taking great care that the relations between Venice and the Ottomans were amicable. She was 33 years old when her mother-in-law, Nūr Bānū Wālide Sulṭān [*q.v.*] died (991/1583), and Ṣafiyye became the first lady of the Ottoman Empire. Since she was constantly in conflict with her mother-in-law and with Süleymān's daughter Mihrimāh and her sisters-in-law Ismik̲h̲ān and Gewherk̲h̲ān, it was only after the deaths of these women that Ṣafiyye became very powerful. Murād III remained very much in love with her until his death in 1003/1595, when he was succeeded by Meḥemmed III. Ṣafiyye thus became queen mother at the age of 45, and exercised an extensive influence on the politics of the Empire. In 1012/1603 her son Meḥemmed III died, and her grandson Aḥmed I took over the throne. Repulsing his grandmother's influence on the Palace and on Ottoman politics, on S̲h̲aʿbān 1012/February 1604, 19 days after he was enthroned, he sent Ṣafiyye away from the Ṭopḳapī Palace to the old Palace in Bāyezīd; she died a year later in D̲j̲umādā II 1014/November 1605.

Ṣafiyye was the fifth of the queen mothers in the Ottoman palace. Her intelligence, beauty and the power which she exercised over the Empire became legendary, although it was alleged that she had managed to make herself a great fortune through bribery. She had started to build the *Yeñi D̲j̲āmiʿ* in Istanbul, but died before its completion.

Bibliography: *Türk ansiklopedisi*, xxviii, Ankara 1980, art. s.v.; Y. Yücel and A. Sevim, *Türkiye tarihi Osmanlı dönemi (1566-1730)*, Ankara 1992.

(Çiğdem Balim)

ṢAFḲA (A), a term of Islamic law meaning literally, "striking hands together". The parallel root *ṣ-f/p-ḳ* (and in other places, more correctly, *s-f/p-ḳ*) is found in Biblical Hebrew, cf. Isa. ii. 6 "they strike hands with foreigners". *Ṣafḳa* is a non-Ḳurʾānic word, but *taṣdiya* is found in sūra VIII, 35, with a comparable meaning.

Technically, *ṣafḳa* has come to mean the ratification of a commercial contract, a formal, symbolic act for concluding a contract which has been disregarded in practice by Islamic law. Striking hands together, although associated with sale (*bayʿ*), should be designated *ṣafḳ* rather than *bayʿ*, as stated by Schacht in art. BAYʿ. The concept of *ṣafḳa* remained unique in its usage since, unlike *bayʿ*, it contains the meaning of a bargain that is achieved swiftly and profitably. Evidently, striking the hands together can only be used as an expression of acceptance once an offer (*īd̲j̲āb*) is presented. Acceptance (*ḳabūl*), can according to most schools, excluding the S̲h̲āfiʿī, be delayed until the end of the meeting of the two parties (*mad̲j̲lis al-ʿaḳd*). The S̲h̲āfiʿīs, who require immediate accept-

ance, have made a provision that the two parties can cancel the contract providing they are still physically at the place where the deal was negotiated (*k̲h̲iyār al-mad̲j̲lis*); but once they leave, the deal is final. It is imperative to add that the expression of will, under these conditions, can be in any form, whether by striking the hands together or verbal affirmation, providing it conveys the clear intention.

Bibliography: *LʿA*, Beirut-Dār Ṣādir, n.d., x, 200; Ibrāhīm Anīs *et alii*, *al-Muʿd̲j̲am al-wasīṭ*, Cairo 1972, ii, 434; J. Schacht, *An introduction to Islamic law*, Oxford 1964, 8, 145-6; Wahba al-Zuḥaylī, *al-Fiḳh al-Islāmī wa-adillatuhu*, Damascus 1985, iv, 108, 366; see also BAYʿ.　　　(Mawil Izzi Dien)

ṢAFWĀN B. ṢAFWĀN AL-**ANṢĀRĪ**, Arab poet of the 2nd-3rd centuries A.H. known for his ideological poetry in support of the Muʿtazila [*q.v.*]. Al-D̲j̲āḥiẓ [*q.v.*] is the only source for the few bits of information on his life and the sparse samples from his poetry that we have. The biographical snippets show him in Multān at the court of the governor of Sind, Dāwūd b. Yazīd al-Muhallabī, who held this office from 184/800-205/820 [see MUHALLABIDS, toward the end]. In all of them he is al-D̲j̲āḥiẓ's authority on elephants, quoting poetry by the elephant expert Hārūn b. Mūsā al-Azdī *mawlāhum*; describing what kind of ruses this man used in fighting against war elephants; and indicating how the Indians trained these animals (*Ḥayawān*, vii, 76 [read, with Pellat, *zuwwār* for *ruwāt*], 77, 114-15). As for Ṣafwān's poetry the surviving pieces show strong support for Wāṣil b. ʿAṭāʾ, founder of the Muʿtazila (d. 131/748-9 [*q.v.*]), and other leaders of the movement and equally strong animosity against the poet Bas̲h̲s̲h̲ār b. Burd (d. 167 or 168/784-5 [*q.v.*]), after the latter had broken away from Wāṣil's circle. Since some of the lines in praise of Wāṣil seem to speak of a contemporary, Ṣafwān must have been of a ripe old age, when he joined the Multān governor, unless, of course, one assumes two different Ṣafwāns. However, in addition to his name, his apparent interest in natural history, which comes through in both the early poetry and the later reports, would be an argument for the identity of the two personages.

His most famous poem is the glorification of earth, a counter-poem against Bas̲h̲s̲h̲ār's apotheosis of fire, which also includes a pro-Muʿtazilī *fak̲h̲r* and a *hid̲j̲āʾ* against Bas̲h̲s̲h̲ār and his sect, the esoteric shadowy extremist Kāmiliyya S̲h̲īʿa (*Bayān*, i, 27-30; 33 lines, *ṭawīl*, rhyme -Cdi). Shortened versions of this poem, clearly quoted from al-D̲j̲āḥiẓ, appear also in al-Bag̲h̲dādī (d. 429/1037 [*q.v.*]), *al-Farḳ bayn al-firaḳ*, 39-42, in the section on the Kāmiliyya (20 lines), and in Abu 'l-Ḥasan ʿAlī b. Yūsuf al-Ḥakīm (8th/14th century), *al-Dawḥa al-mus̲h̲tabika*, 25-27, where it is quoted for the enumeration of minerals and ores it contains (13 lines). Of similar content is a shorter poem (*Bayān*, i, 32, 9 lines, *ṭawīl*, rhyme -Cdu). The earth-fire controversy has been seen as an early Muʿtazilī-S̲h̲īʿī polemics (Nyberg in *EI*[1], s.v. AL-MUʿTAZILA) as well as a S̲h̲uʿūbī attack by Bas̲h̲s̲h̲ār, defending the Zoroastrian holiness of fire, with a counter-attack upholding the claims of the earth. The context(s) in which this polemics became meaningful is none too clear. Another poem defending Wāṣil against Bas̲h̲s̲h̲ār's *hid̲j̲āʾ* also mentions the missionaries that Wāṣil sent out (*Bayān*, i, 25-6; 22 lines, *ṭawīl*, rhyme -3ri); this was interpreted by Nyberg, *loc. cit.*, as indicating the existence of a pro-Abbasid network of propagandists, but was probably not more than a religious undertaking [see AL-MUʿTAZILA, here vii, 783b-784a, and van Ess, ii, 386-7].

The remaining fragments are: two lines on the

date-palm (*Ḥayawān*, vii, 78; *mutaḳārib*, rhyme -2lu); one line characterising Wāṣil (*Bayān*, i, 22; *basīṭ*, rhyme -āḳi); one line in praise of Wāṣil's *zuhd* (*Bayān*, i, 27; *ṭawīl*, rhyme -3ʿuh); and two lines of *hid̲j̲āʾ* against Bas̲h̲s̲h̲ār and his brothers, addressed to his mother (*Bayān*, i, 31, *basīṭ*, rhyme -Cdi).

Bibliography : 1. Texts. D̲j̲āḥiẓ, *al-Bayān wa 'l-tabyīn*, ed. ʿAbd al-Salām Muḥammad Hārūn, 1367/1948; idem, *al-Ḥayawān*, ed. Hārūn, ²Cairo n.d.; Bag̲h̲dādī, *al-Farḳ bayn al-firaḳ*, ⁴Beirut 1400/1980; Abu 'l-Ḥasan ʿAlī b. Yūsuf al-Ḥakīm (8th/14th century), *al-Dawḥa al-mus̲h̲tabika fī ḍawābiṭ dār al-sikka*, ed. Ḥusayn Muʾnis, Madrid 1379/1960.

2. Studies. ʿAbd al-Ḥakīm Balbaʿ, *Adab al-Muʿtazila ilā nihāyat al-ḳarn al-rābiʿ al-hid̲j̲rī*, Cairo n.d. (preface dated 1959), 356-61, 390-6; Ch. Pellat, *Le Milieu baṣrien et la formation de Ǧāḥiẓ*, Paris 1955, 175-7; W.M. Watt, *Was Wāṣil a Khārijite?*, in R. Gramlich (ed.), *Islamwissenschaftliche Abhandlungen Fritz Meier zum sechzigsten Geburtstag*, Wiesbaden 1974, 306-11 (incs. a tr. of the "missionary" poem); Pellat, *Ṣafwān ibn Ṣafwān al-Anṣārī et Beshshār* [sic] *ibn Burd*, in R.M. Savory and D.A. Agius (eds.), *Logos Islamikos. Studia Islamica in honorem Georgii Michaelis Wickens*, Toronto 1984, 21-34 (includes tr. of the three long poems); J. van Ess, *Theologie und Gesellschaft im 2. und 3. Jahrhundert Hidschra*, ii, Berlin 1992, 382-7 (study of Ṣafwān with emphasis on the "missionary" poem), v, Berlin 1993, 183-92 (tr. of and comm. on the three long poems), see also ii, 5-14 (on Bas̲h̲s̲h̲ār), and i, Berlin 1991, 269-72 (on the Kāmiliyya).

(W.P. Heinrichs)

ṢAFWĀN b. **IDRĪS** b. Ibrāhīm b. ʿAbd al-Raḥmān b. ʿĪsā b. Idrīs al-Tud̲j̲ībī al-Mursī al-Kātib, Abū Baḥr (560-98/1164-1201), poet and scholar of Muslim Spain.

He was born in Murcia when the town was ruled by Ibn Mardanīs̲h̲ (d. 567/1172), but the major part of his life witnessed Almohad times (see the studies of Gaspar Remiro and Guichard about the history of Murcia under Almohad rule). He belonged to an important family of the town, the Banū Idrīs, some of whom were judges. Ṣafwān gives information on them in his *Zād al-musāfir* (152-7). He studied with his father and his relative, the *ḳāḍī* Abu 'l-Ḳāsim b. Idrīs, as well as with Abū Bakr b. Mug̲h̲āwir, Abu 'l-Ḥasan Ibn al-Ḳāsim, Abū Rid̲j̲āl b. G̲h̲albūn, Abū ʿAbd Allāh b. Ḥumayd, Abu 'l-ʿAbbās b. Maḍāʾ (who taught him Muslim's *Ṣaḥīḥ*), Abu 'l-Ḳāsim Ibn Ḥubays̲h̲, Ibn Bas̲h̲kuwāl (who gave him the *id̲j̲āza*), Abu 'l-Walīd b. Rus̲h̲d, Abū Muḥammad b. ʿUbayd Allāh al-Ḥad̲j̲arī, Abū Muḥammad b. Ḥawṭ Allāh and Ibn ʿAys̲h̲ūn. Ṣafwān b. Idrīs was one of the most important poets and *udabāʾ* of his time. His biographers record at length praises about him. He wrote: (1) *Badāhat al-mutaḥaffiz wa-ʿud̲j̲ālat al-mustawfiz*, a compilation of his prose and poetry; (2) *Kitāb al-Riḥla*; (3) *Zād al-musāfir wa-g̲h̲urrat muḥayyā 'l-adab al-sāfir*, a biographical compilation of Andalusian poets of the 6th/12th century, which supplements the works of Ibn K̲h̲āḳān (d. 529/1134) and Ibn al-Imām (d. *ca.* 550/1155). It was edited by ʿAbd al-Ḳādir Maḥdād, Beirut 1358/1939, repr. Beirut 1970. Ibn al-Abbār [*q.v.*] emulated it in his *Tuḥfat al-ḳādim*. It is one of the sources of Ibn Saʿīd al-Mag̲h̲ribī's *Rāyāt al-mubarrizīn*, which also includes a section devoted to Ṣafwān (see E. García Gómez, *El libro de las banderas de los campeones de Ibn Saʿīd al-Magribī*, Barcelona 1978, 138, 159, 195, 196, 239, 248, 253, and 243-4); (4) *Rasāʾil*, some of which have been preserved, like the letter he wrote congratulating the judge Abu 'l-Ḳāsim b. Baḳī (*Nafḥ al-ṭīb*, v, 68-9), another on *tag̲h̲āyur mudun al-Andalus* sent to the *amīr* ʿAbd al-Raḥmān b. Yūsuf b. ʿAbd al-Muʾmin b. ʿAlī (*Nafḥ al-ṭīb*, ii, 170-5; tr. F. de la Granja, *Geografía lírica de Andalucía musulmana, Historia de Andalucía*, Madrid 1981, v, 85-7), another entitled *Ṭirād al-d̲j̲iyād fi 'l-maydān wa-tanāzuʿ al-lad̲h̲d̲h̲āt wa 'l-ik̲h̲wān/al-ak̲h̲dān fī taḳdīm Mursiya ʿalā g̲h̲ayri-hā min al-buldān*; and (5) *Dīwān*. Some of his verses are recorded by his biographers. He is especially remembered for the elegies (*marāt̲h̲ī*) which he wrote in commemoration of al-Ḥusayn b. ʿAlī and the descendants of the Prophet (*taʾbīn al-Ḥusayn wa-bukāʾ ahl al-bayt*). In connection with this production, the sources record a story according to which Ṣafwān is said to have travelled to Marrākus̲h̲, where he tried to earn money by praising the rulers in his poems in order to pay for the trousseau of his daughter who had reached marriageable age. None of his attempts was successful. Disappointed, he decided to write panegyrics of the Prophet and his family. It was then that the Almohad al-Manṣūr Yaʿḳūb b. Yūsuf b. ʿAbd al-Muʾmin saw the Prophet in a dream interceding on Ṣafwān's behalf, and from then onwards Ṣafwān was never to have again financial problems. Ṣafwān corresponded with the poet Muḥammad b. Idrīs b. Mard̲j̲ al-Kuḥl (d. 634/1236) (*Nafḥ al-ṭīb*, v, 57-9). The most noted of Ṣafwān's pupils was Abu 'l-Rabīʿ b. Sālim al-Kalāʿī. Ṣafwān died young, aged 38, and his father recited the funeral prayer over him.

Bibliography: Ibn al-Abbār, *Takmila*, ed. Codera, no. 1231 (ed. ʿIzzat al-ʿAṭṭār al-Ḥusaynī, Cairo 1955, no. 1895); Balafīḳī, *al-Muḳtaḍab min Kitāb Tuḥfat al-ḳādim li-bn al-Abbār*, Cairo-Beirut 1982, 135-9; Yāḳūt, *Udabāʾ*, ed. Margoliouth, xii, 10-4, no. 3; Ibn Saʿīd, *al-Mug̲h̲rib fī ḥulā 'l-Mag̲h̲rib*, ed. Ṣ. Ḍayf, Cairo 1953-5, ii, 260-1, no. 533; Ibn al-Zubayr, *Ṣilat al-Ṣila*, ed. ʿA. Hārūn and S. Aʿrāb, Rabat 1993, no. 120 (the source is Ibn Furtūn's *D̲h̲ayl*); Ibn Saʿīd, *Rāyāt al-mubarrizīn*; Ibn ʿAbd al-Malik al-Marrākus̲h̲ī, *al-D̲h̲ayl wa 'l-takmila*, ed. I. ʿAbbās, Beirut n.d., iv, 140-3, no. 264; Ṣafadī, *Wāfī*, xvi, 321-4; Ibn al-K̲h̲aṭīb, *al-Iḥāṭa fī ak̲h̲bār G̲h̲arnāṭa*, ed. M.ʿA. ʿInān, Cairo 1973-7, iii, 349-59; Ibn S̲h̲ākir al-Kutubī, *Fawāt al-wafayāt*, ed. ʿAbbās, ii, 117, no. 198; Maḳḳarī, *Nafḥ al-ṭīb*, ed. ʿAbbās, Beirut 1968, v, 62-74 and index; Ḥad̲j̲d̲j̲ī K̲h̲alīfa, *Kas̲h̲f al-ẓunūn*, ii, 23 (no. 1694), ii, 236 (no. 2642), iii, 527 (no. 6769): Ibn Ibrāhīm, *al-Iʿlām bi-man ḥalla Marrākus̲h̲ wa-Ag̲h̲māt min al-aʿlām*, Rabat 1974-83, vii, 361-72, no. 1046; Mak̲h̲lūf, *S̲h̲ad̲j̲arat al-nūr*, Cairo 1950-2, i, 161, no. 496; Pons Boigues, *Ensayo bio-bibliográfico*, 256, no. 210; Brockelmann, I², 322, S I, 482; ʿU.R. Kaḥḥāla, *Muʿd̲j̲am al-muʾallifīn*, Damascus 1957-61, v, 19-20; A. González Palencia, *Historia de la literatura arábigo-española*, Barcelona 1928, 191; M. Gaspar Remiro, *Historia de Murcia musulmana*, Saragossa 1905, 259; P. Guichard, *Les musulmans de Valence et la reconquête (XIᵉ-XIIIᵉ siècles)*, Damascus 1990-1, esp. i, 127-32.

(Maribel Fierro)

ṢAFWĀN b. al-**MUʿAṬṬAL** (the *fatḥa* of the *ṭ* is confirmed in Ibn Durayd, *Is̲h̲tiḳāḳ*, ed. Hārūn, 310; occasionally wrongly al-Muʿaṭṭil), from the tribe of Sulaym, was a Companion of the Prophet Muḥammad. His year of birth does not seem to be recorded, and he is mentioned as having died a martyr's death during the Arabs' conquest of Armīniya in 17/638 (cf. Ṭabarī, i, 2506) or 19/640 (cf. Ibn Ḥad̲j̲ar, *Iṣāba*, iii, 441). Other reports have it that he met his death at a much later date in the year 59/679 (cf. K̲h̲alīfa, *Taʾrīk̲h̲*, ed. A.Ḍ. al-ʿUmarī, 226-7) or

60/680 in Shimshāṭ in the Djazīra (cf. Ibn al-Djawzī, *Muntaẓam*, iv, 282), where his grave was venerated.

He is said to have lived in Medina and to have embraced Islam shortly before the expedition to the well of al-Muraysīʿ of the Banu 'l-Muṣṭaliḳ. After that, he is reported to have participated in the Prophet's military campaigns, the first being the Battle of Khandaḳ or the Ditch. He owes his fame mostly to the role he is reported to have played in the *ifk* affair, i.e. the scandal around ʿĀʾisha [*q.v.*], the Prophet's favourite wife. An allegation had been brought into circulation, slanderous as it turned out, about ʿĀʾisha having had illicit relations with Ṣafwān on their joint return from the Prophet's expedition to the Banu 'l-Muṣṭaliḳ in the year 5/627, when, after having become separated from the main caravan, they sought to catch up with it on a solitary trek through the desert. For details of the affair, see Ibn Isḥāḳ's *Sīra*, ed. Muṣṭafā al-Saḳḳā *et alii*, iii, 309-18, ed. Wüstenfeld, 731-8 = al-Bukhārī, *Ṣaḥīḥ*, ed. Krehl, ii, 153-7, iii, 103-9. In the aftermath of the affair, ʿĀʾisha is said to have made a statement to the effect that Ṣafwān was impotent and had never touched a woman (also recorded in Ṣafwān's own words, al-Bukhārī, iii, 108, ult.). This allegation is contradicted in another report (cf. Abū Dāwūd, *Sunan*, ed. M. Muḥyī al-Dīn ʿAbd al-Ḥamīd, ii, 330, Ibn Ḥanbal, *Musnad*, iii, 80) in which it is alleged that someone presenting herself as Ṣafwān's wife once came to the Prophet in order to complain about her husband forcing his will upon her and hitting her, saying *ana radjul shābb fa-lā aṣbir* ... ; for an attempt at harmonisation, see Ibn Ḥadjar, *Iṣāba*, iii, 441.

During an exchange with the poet Ḥassān b. Thābit [*q.v.*], whom Ṣafwān blamed for having had a part in spreading the rumour about him and ʿĀʾisha, he is said to have struck him with his sword. Another story, extant in different versions, has it that he hit Ḥassān because of his denigrating verses directed at a group of *Muhādjirūn* who had sought out the Prophet to embrace his cause. Saʿd b. ʿUbāda [*q.v.*], a leading Anṣārī, induced Ḥassān in the presence of the Prophet to give up his claim for retaliation on Ṣafwān. Then Saʿd presented Ṣafwān with a mantle. The Prophet gave Ḥassān an Egyptian woman and/or a certain piece of property as appeasement, while Ṣafwān was ultimately left unpunished. The various versions of the story, complete with the verses supposedly recited by both, are recorded in many sources, most extensively in al-Wāḳidī, *Maghāzī*, ii, 436 ff., and *Aghānī*³, iv, 155-63. Whether or not they contain a kernel of historicity is hard to establish; they may be no more than background embellishments of Ṣafwān's role in the *ifk* affair, assuming then that the tale is historically tenable. (The story's plausibility has been recently evaluated anew in G.H.A. Juynboll, *Early Islamic society as reflected in its use of isnāds*, forthcoming in *Le Muséon* [1994].) According to Khalīfa b. Khayyāṭ, *Ṭabaḳāt*, 51, 181, he later settled in Baṣra and took up residence near the Mirbad [*q.v.*]. For other exploits of Ṣafwān, cf. al-Wāḳidī, index, s.n. For his participation in the conquest of al-Djazīra, see al-Balādhurī, *Futūḥ al-buldān*, 172-5, 184.

Bibliography: Given in the article. In general, see *Concordance et indices de la tradition musulmane*, viii, s.n.; Ibn Ḥanbal, *Musnad*, v, 312; Ibn Ḥadjar, *Iṣāba*, ed. Badjāwī, iii, 440-2; for the tribe of Sulaym, see M. Lecker, *The Banū Sulaym. A contribution to the study of early Islam*, Jerusalem 1989.

(G.H.A. Juynboll)

al-**ṢAGHĀNĪ**, ʿAbd al-Muʾmin b. Ḥasan, *adīb*, *floruit* during the 7th/13th century.

He is noted only for his poetic version of the animal fable collection, originally translated into Arabic by Ibn al-Muḳaffaʿ [*q.v.*], *Kalīla wa-Dimna* [*q.v.*]. This version he called *Durrat al-ḥikam fī amthāl al-Hunūd wa 'l-ʿAdjam*, and he completed it on 20 Djumādā 640/15 November 1242 (according to the Vienna ms.) or possibly some 25 years later (according to the other extant ms. of Munich); see Brockelmann, S I, 234-5.

Bibliography: Given in the article. (Ed.)

al-**ṢAGHĀNĪ**, Raḍiyy al-Dīn al-Ḥasan b. Muḥammad b. al-Ḥasan b. Ḥaydar b. ʿAlī b. Ismāʿīl al-Ḳurashī al-ʿAdawī al-ʿUmarī, lexicographer and *muḥaddith*, who owed his name to the upper Oxus province of Čaghāniyān [*q.v.*], Arabised form Ṣaghāniyān.

He was born in Lahore on 10 Ṣafar 577/25 June 1181 according to the most generally accepted report. He commenced his studies in Ghazna, first under his father who was a *mutakallim*, then under a number of scholars, most notable of whom was Niẓām al-Dīn al-Marghīnānī [*q.v.*]. In further pursuit of knowledge, he travelled—between the years 605/1208-9 and 615/1218-9—to Mecca, Medina, Aden and Maḳdishū. The notice by his contemporary, Yāḳūt [*q.v.*] (*Udabāʾ*, iii, 211-12), which ends in the year 613/1216-17, clearly shows that Ṣaghānī had by that early time acquired enough fame and respect to warrant his inclusion in a biographical dictionary. In Ṣafar 615/May 1218 he came to Baghdād for the first time (see his *al-ʿUbāb*, under the root *ḳ r ṭ*, in the editor's introd., 9), and two years later was sent to India by the caliph al-Nāṣir [*q.v.*], where he stayed for several years. He came back to Baghdād in 624/1226-7, only to be sent, in the same year, once more to India, this time by al-Mustanṣir [*q.v.*]. Impoverished there, he managed to get back to Aden in 630/1232-3 and then to Baghdād in 637/1239-40. In his later days he taught at the Marzubāniyya *ribāṭ*, but resigned his post in 640/1242-3 when he came to learn that the *shaykh* of this *ribāṭ* had to be a Shāfiʿī (Ibn al-Fuwaṭī, *al-Ḥawādith al-djāmiʿa*, Baghdād 1351/1932-3, 263); hence al-Mustaʿṣim entrusted him with the Ḥanafī Tutushiyya *madrasa*, and it is in this period that he wrote his *Mashāriḳ al-anwār* and *al-ʿUbāb*. His death is most widely reported to have been on 19 Shaʿbān 650/25 October 1252.

Al-Ṣaghānī's contribution was predominantly in the field of lexicography. By his time, it was deemed no longer possible for a lexicographer to investigate usage among the desert Arabs, due to the so-called loss of the earlier "purity" in their language. Al-Ṣaghānī, however, seems to have made up for this major handicap by concentrating on the shortcomings and errors of his predecessors in *riwāya*, *taṣḥīf*, attribution of poetry, etc. Aided by his vast knowledge (cf. his list of sources in *al-ʿUbāb*, i, 7-9), he produced three of his major works that can be seen in the light of the above. These are: (1) *al-Takmila wa 'l-dhayl wa 'l-ṣila* (ed. ʿA.ʿA. al-Ṭaḥāwī *et alii*, 6 vols., Cairo 1970-9), a supplement to al-Djawharī's *al-Ṣiḥāḥ*, which comprises linguistic usages overlooked by al-Djawharī and extensive corrections of his errors; (2) *Madjmaʿ al-baḥrayn* (Brockelmann, S I, 614; Sezgin, viii, 219), which incorporates *al-Ṣiḥāḥ*, *al-Takmila*, and al-Ṣaghānī's own *Ḥāshiya ʿalā 'l-Ṣiḥāḥ*, in which he amended still further errors of al-Djawharī, and (3) *al-ʿUbāb al-zākhir wa 'l-lubāb al-fākhir* (ed. Y.M. Ḥasan, i, Baghdād 1978, and ed. M.Ḥ. Āl Yāsīn, Baghdād 1397/1978 ff.) in which he only got as far as *b-k-m* before he died. This book, according to al-Suyūṭī (*Bughya*, Cairo 1964, i, 519) is the greatest linguistic treatise after the era of al-Djawharī, along with Ibn

Sīda's *al-Muḥkam*. It is indeed in this work that al-Ṣag͟hānī's mastery of the sources and his vast *riwāya* are most clearly manifested, and in his introduction (pp. 12-19) he lists but a few of the more glaring errors of al-Azharī in his *Tahd͟hīb al-lug͟ha* (over 1,000 in all), al-D̲j̲awharī in his *al-Ṣiḥāḥ* (over 2,000), and Ibn Fāris in his *al-Mud̲j̲mal* (over 500), and ridicules Ibn al-Sikkīt's *Iṣlāḥ al-manṭiḳ* as needing an *iṣlāḥ* of its own, and Ibn ʿAbbād's *al-Muḥīṭ* as having comprised (*aḥāṭa*) error and *taṣḥīf*.

Another obvious linguistic interest of al-Ṣag͟hānī is demonstrated by his work on patterns, as in his *K. yafʿūl* (ed. Ḥ. ʿAbd al-Wahhāb, Tunis 1939), *K. al-Infiʿāl* (ed. A. K͟hān, Islāmābād 1977), *K. al-Iftiʿāl* (Ḥad̲j̲d̲j̲ī K͟halīfa, v, 47), *Mā banat-hu 'l-ʿArab ʿalā faʿāli* (ed. ʿA. Ḥasan, Damascus 1964), and *Naḳʿat al-ṣadyān fīmā d̲j̲āʾa ʿalā wazn faʿlān* (Brockelmann, S I, 615). The published titles show that al-Ṣag͟hānī, despite being innovative in some of his subject matter, as in collecting the verbs of the *infaʿala* pattern (cf. *K. al-Infiʿāl*, 1), did not attempt to explore the meanings of each pattern or to establish general meanings with which constituent verbs can be identified; thus his books in this genre are merely lists of words from a certain pattern which any general lexicon would have, but listed alphabetically under their roots.

Some of al-Ṣag͟hānī's other lexicographical works include *al-S͟hawārid fi 'l-lug͟ha* (ed. ʿA.ʿA. al-Dūrī, Bag͟hdād 1983, and ed. M. Ḥid̲j̲āzī, Cairo 1983) of the *nawādir* genre; a *taws͟hīḥ* or *tasmīṭ* of Ibn Durayd's *maḳṣūra* called *S͟harḥ al-ḳilāda al-simṭiyya fī taws͟hīḥ al-Duraydiyya*, preserved in a *muk͟htaṣar* by Ibn al-Ḥād̲j̲ib (ed. S.M. al-ʿĀnī and Ḥ. Nād̲j̲ī, Bag͟hdād 1977); *K. al-Aḍdād* (ed. A. Haffner, Beirut 1912); and a number of thematic works the titles of which include *K. fī asmāʾ al-asad, K. fī asmāʾ al-d͟hiʾb wa-kunāhu, K. al-ʿāda fī asmāʾ al-g͟hāda*, and *K. K͟halḳ al-insān*.

To a lesser extent, Ṣag͟hānī contributed to the realm of *ḥadīt͟h*, and his main work here is *Mas͟hāriḳ al-anwār al-nabawiyya ʿalā ṣiḥāḥ al-ak͟hbār al-muṣṭafawiyya* (printed several times in Leipzig, Istanbul, and Beirut). The importance of this treatise, which integrates the two *ṣaḥīḥs* of Buk͟hārī and Muslim, lies in the fact that it is the earliest contribution of India to *ḥadīt͟h* literature (see HIND, in *EI*², at III, 435; and a list of its *s͟hurūḥ* in Ḥād̲j̲d̲j̲ī K͟halīfa, v, 548 ff.). Even here, al-Ṣag͟hānī's foremost linguistic interests emerge in his classification of the material, basically according to the particle (e.g. *in, id͟hā, mā, laysa, law, ḳad*, etc.) or morphological unit (e.g. elative, imperfect, imperative, etc.) with which the *ḥadīt͟h* begins. His other works include two *risālas* on apocryphal *ḥadīt͟h*, namely *al-Durr al-multaḳaṭ fī tabyīn al-g͟halaṭ* (ed. S.M. al-ʿĀnī, in *Mad̲j̲allat Kulliyyat al-Imām al-Aʿẓam*, i [1972], 139-42), and his *Risāla fī 'l-mawḍūʿāt min al-aḥādīt͟h* (published under the title *Mawḍūʿāt al-Ṣag͟hānī*, ed. N.ʿA. K͟halaf, Cairo 1980). Of the *rid̲j̲āl* genre are his *Naḳʿat al-ṣadyān fī man fī ṣuḥbatihim naẓar min al-ṣaḥāba* (ed. ʿA.K. Ḥasan, Beirut 1990) and *Asāmī s͟huyūk͟h al-Buk͟hārī* (Sezgin, i, 130).

Bibliography (further to that given in the text): Brockelmann, I², 443-4, S I, 613 ff.; Sezgin, *GAS*, viii, 327; Ḥād̲j̲d̲j̲ī K͟halīfa, ed. Flügel, vii, 1197, no. 7343; D͟hahabī, *Duwal al-Islām*, Ḥaydarābād 1337/1919, ii, 120; idem, *al-ʿIbar*, Kuwait 1960-6, v, 205; idem, *Siyar*, Beirut 1985, xxiii, 282; Ṣafadī, *al-Wāfī*, xii, Wiesbaden 1979, 240; Ibn S͟hākir, *Fawāt*, Beirut 1973, i, 358; Yāfiʿī, *Mirʾāt*, Ḥaydarābād 1339/1921, iv, 121; Sallāmī, *Tārīk͟h ʿUlamāʾ Bag͟hdād*, Bag͟hdād 1938, 48-9; Ibn Abī 'l-Wafāʾ, *al-D̲j̲awāhir al-muḍiyya*, Ḥaydarābād 1332/1914, i, 201-2; Ibn Rad̲j̲ab, *D͟hayl Ṭabaḳāt al-ḥanābila*, Cairo 1953, ii, 265; Fīrūzābādī, *al-Bulg͟ha*, Damascus 1972, 63; Makkī, *al-ʿIḳd al-t͟hamīn*, Cairo 1965, iv, 176-9; Maḳrīzī, *al-Sulūk*, Cairo 1956, i, 385; Ibn Tag͟hrībirdi, Cairo, vii, 26; Ibn Ḳuṭlūbug͟hā, *Tād̲j̲ al-tarād̲j̲im*, Bag͟hdād 1962, 24; Suyūṭī, *al-Muzhir*, ed. M.A. D̲j̲ād al-Mawlā *et alii*, Cairo n.d., ii, 421; Ibn Abī Mak͟hrama, *Taʾrīk͟h t͟hag͟hr ʿAdan*, ed. O. Löfgren, Leiden 1936, ii, 53; Ibn al-ʿImād, *S͟had͟harāt*, year 650; J.A. Haywood, *Arabic lexicography*, Leiden 1976, 67; J. Kraemer, *Studien zur altarabischen Lexikographie*, in *Oriens*, vi (1953), 228 ff.; Ḥusayn Naṣṣār, *al-Muʿd̲j̲am al-ʿArabī*, Cairo 1956, 530 ff.

(RAMZI BAALBAKI)

ṢAG͟HĪR (A.), infant, child, minor (opp. *bālig͟h* [*q.v.*]), one who has not attained to puberty (opp. *kabīr*). Minority ends with the onset of physical maturity, and the ability to control one's own affairs (see al-Wans͟harīsī, ii, 269). In the absence of signs of physical maturity, fifteen was generally regarded as the age that divided between majority and minority for males and females alike (see BĀLIG͟H and Goldziher, *Muh. Studien*, ii, 17, Eng. tr. *Muslim studies*, ii, 29). Entrusting a boy or a girl with their respective adult functions was the accepted way to examine mental maturity (*rus͟hd*) (see Ibn Ḳudāma, iv, 523). Physical maturity as coincident with the conclusion of formal-religious education and the start of work without parental supervision is reported also for contemporary Muslim societies (see e.g. Ammar, 183).

1. *Terminology*.

Arabic has a rich vocabulary to designate childhood and its subdivisions. Within high Islamic culture childhood is seen as a unique period which has its own gradual process of development, physically and psychologically different from other periods in human life. As such it finds clear expression in writings of various kinds, legal, theological, hygienic-medical, ethical and pedagogical as well as belles-lettres. At the same time, it remains difficult to know exactly how this and other (sometimes contradictory) concepts of childhood influenced the everyday life of children in Muslim societies.

While in its mother's womb, the child is called *d̲j̲anīn* (foetus). The general term for "child" is *walad*, and other terms have special shades of meaning, e.g. *nad̲j̲l* "progeny" and *faraṭ* "a child who dies before reaching maturity", lit. "dying before his/her parents". Other terms designate in addition a specific period within childhood. Among these are *ṣabiyy* ("a youth, boy, or male child... or one that has not yet been weaned... so called from the time of his birth"), *ṣabiyya* ("a young woman, girl, or female child", Lane), *salīl* ("a child or male offspring", Lane); "a child, specifically at the time of his birth and (from then) until its weaning" (Ibn Sīdah, *Muk͟haṣṣaṣ*, Būlāḳ 1316, 31); *ṭifl* ("... a child until he discriminates... after which he is called *ṣabiyy*..." or "a child from the time of his birth... until he attains to puberty...", Lane); ("at his birth the child is designated *ṣabiyy*, afterwards he is called *ṭifl* although I do not know how long...", Ibn Sīdah. 31): *ṭalā* (... "the youngling of any kind... an infant until a month old or more," Lane): *s͟hark͟h* ("a youth or young man... the offspring of a man...", Lane); *g͟hulām* ("a young man, youth, boy... or one from the time of his birth until he attains to the period termed *s͟habāb*, meaning young manhood...", Lane).

Terms for either a limited period within childhood or a specific phenomenon connected with a child's physical or mental development are *ṣadīg͟h* ("an epithet applied to a child... in the stage extending to his completion of seven days... because his temple becomes firm... only to this period'', Lane); *raḍīʿ* (''a child while it is a suckling'', Lane); the verb *taḍabbaba* (also *taḥallama*, Lane, and *ig͟htāla*, Ibn Sīdah, 32) (''he [a child] became fat...'', Lane); *itht͟hag͟hara* (''he [a boy] bred his central milk teeth... or... front teeth... or he bred his teeth after the former ones had fallen out'', Lane) (several terms refer to different stages of this process: *shakka, ṭalaʿa, nadjama, nasaʿa, intaḍat (al-sinn), adrama (al-ṣabiyy), aḥfara, abdaʾa* [Ibn Sīdah, 331]; *faṭīm* (''a child weaned or ablactated'', Lane); *dārid͟j* (*darad͟ja*: ''... said of a child: 'he walked a little, at his first beginning to walk' '', Lane); *d͟jafr* (*d͟jafara*: ''he, or it, became wide... or became inflated or swollen'', Lane; Ibn Sīdah, 33); *mustakris͟h* (*istakras͟ha* [also *tazakkara*, Lane] ''... he [a kid and a boy] became large in his stomach or became hard in his palate.. and began to eat''); *d͟jaḥwas͟h* (''the child who passed the stage of weaning becomes *d͟jaḥwas͟h*'', Ibn Sīdah, 33); *fāḳiʿ* (''he [a boy] became active, and grew...'', Lane); *ḥazawwar* (''a boy who has become strong... and has served... or one who has nearly attained the age of puberty...'', Lane); *mutaraʿriʿ* (also: *mulimm* [Ibn Sīdah, 34] ''... a boy... almost or quite past the age of ten years, or active'', Lane); *muṭabbik͟h* (''... a young man that is full [or plump]'', Lane); *yāfiʿ* (''a boy grown up... grown tall'', Lane); *k͟humāsiyy* (''a boy five spans [*as͟hbār*] in height... said of him who is increasing in height...'', Lane); *waṣīf* (*awṣafa* and *istawṣafa*: ''he [a boy] became of full stature and fit for service'', Lane); *g͟haydāḳ* (''... soft or tender; applied to a youth or young man... applied to a boy signifies 'that has not attained to puberty' '', Lane); *murāhiḳ* (also *kawkab*, Lane) (*rāhaḳa, arhaḳa*: ''... he [a boy] was, or became, near to attaining puberty or virility...'', Lane); *ak͟hlafa* (''the boy passed the time when he had nearly attained to puberty... he nearly attained to puberty; so that those who looked at him differed in opinion...'', Lane); *ḥālim* (''originally signifies *muḥtalim* [dreaming and particularly dreaming of copulation and experiencing an emission of the seminal fluid in dreaming]... hence used in a general sense... meaning one who has attained to puberty, or virility...'', Lane); *anbata* (''his [a boy's] hair of the pubes grew forth... he having nearly attained the age of puberty...'', Lane); *s͟habala* (''he [a boy...] became a youth or young man...'', Lane); *balag͟ha al-ḥint͟h* (''he [a boy] attained to the age when he was punishable for sin... or attained to the age when the pen [of the recording angels] began to register his acts of obedience and of disobedience...'', Lane); *as͟hhada* (''he [a boy] attained to puberty... and *as͟hhadat*: she [a girl] menstruated and attained to puberty''); *ḥāniṭ* (''a child who reached the age of reason'', Ibn Sīdah, 35). *TA* points to those terms which signify the main stages of childhood and arranges them according to the course of the child's development: ''a child when born is called *raḍīʿ* and *ṭifl*, then *faṭīm*, then *dārid͟j*, then *d͟jafr*, then *yāfiʿ*, then *s͟hadak͟h*, then *muṭabbik͟h* and then *kawkab*'' (see also Ibn Ḳayyim al-D͟jawziyya, 183).

The terms used in the Ḳurʾān to designate infants, children and young people are *ṭifl*, *ṣabiyy*, *walad* and *g͟hulām*, mentioned above, as well as *fatā* (a youth), *banūn* (male children), *d͟hurriyya* (offspring) and *yatīm* (a fatherless child) (O'Shaughnessy, 33-43).

2. Subdivisions of childhood.

Medical-hygienic writings contain detailed descriptions of the physical and mental characteristics of the various stages in childhood and relevant treatment instructions. Thus Ibn al-D͟jazzār al-Ḳayrawānī (d.? 395/1004), following Hippocrates, divides childhood into four periods: 1. infancy proper from birth to dentition (*sinn al-wildān*); 2. second infancy from dentition to the age of seven (*sinn al-ṣibyān*); 3. childhood from the age of seven to fourteen (*sinn ibn sabʿ sinīna*); 4. the age of transition from childhood to puberty starting at the age of fourteen (*Siyāsat al-ṣibyān*, 86-7). Another division is offered by ʿArīb b. Saʿd al-Ḳurṭubī [*q.v.*]: 1. from birth to forty days—a period characterised by drastic changes; 2. from forty days to the appearance of molar teeth, at seven months, a stage characterised, *inter alia*, by the beginning of the development of the senses as well as the imagination and the mental qualifications; 3. from dentition to the growth of the child's hair (the exact age is not mentioned), a stage characterised by further mental development as well as by weaning and the beginning of talking and walking, increase in the child's energy, and excellent memory (57-60, and also al-Baladī, 75).

Instructions for physical treatment as well as moral education of children on a more popular level, directed at parents and nurses, are based on the same concept of childhood as a unique period in human life with its own gradual development process (Ibn Ḳayyim al-D͟jawziyya, 137-44, and 183, where the author lists twelve terms which signify various periods in the child's life from birth to maturity).

In the context of children's mental development the appearance, at about the age of seven, of *tamyīz*, the faculty of ''discernment'', which enables the child to grasp abstract ideas and thus to distinguish between good and evil, is regarded by doctors and educators as a most important stage. Its obvious manifestation being a sense of shame, discernment rounds off the development of the senses, ushers in the ''stage of intellectual grasp'' and presages the perfection of mental and moral qualities in adolescence. (See e.g. al-G͟hazālī, *Iḥyāʾ*, iii, 22, 72, 92; Motzki, *Das Kind*, 421-3.) For the mental developments in the earliest period of a child's life, significant are the first smile, at the age of forty days, revealing the onset of the infant's self-awareness and mental development, and the first occurrence of dreams at the age of two months (Ibn Ḳayyim al-D͟jawziyya, 176). In socio-religious terms, important stages are: one week after birth, when the *ʿaḳīḳa* [*q.v.*] and *tasmiya* ceremonies (see below) take place; six years, when the child's (formal) education starts, nine years, when children are to be separated from each other in bed, thirteen years, when children should be beaten on neglecting prayer, sixteen years—the age of marriage (al-G͟hazālī, *Iḥyāʾ*, ii, 276).

3. Children and parents.

Certain branches of the Islamic religious literature frequently raise issues of child-rearing in the context of marital matters (see e.g. Ibn Bābawayh, iii, 274-7, 304-19; Ibn Ḳudāma, ix, 299-313). In Muslim societies the principal purpose of marriage was, and still is (see Ammar, 93), the bearing and rearing of children, its fulfillment an obligatory religious mission: to please God by contributing to the continued existence of the human race, using the means that God created for this goal, and to please the Prophet Muḥammad by enlarging the community of the faithful. This in addition to the personal advantages children bring: ''... the blessing of the righteous child's invocation after his father's death'' and ''... the intercession through the death of the young child should he precede his (father's) death'' (al-G͟hazālī, *Iḥyāʾ*, ii, 67-70; Farah, 53-4). Each child, particularly a good one (*al-walad al-ṣāliḥ*), is therefore regarded as one of God's blessings. On the other hand, contraception existed and was lawful in mediaeval Muslim societies for economic reasons, for the benefit of the woman and for the welfare of the existing children (Musallam, ch. 1).

Mediaeval Islamic sources abound in accounts of loving, tender relationships between parents and children including close physical contacts. The Prophet Muḥammad is often shown as one who knew how to treat children properly. For instance, once he hastened to wash the dirty face of a child and kiss him instead of ʿĀʾisha, who was unable to bring herself to do so, while on another occasion he remained prostrated in prayer longer than necessary so as not to disturb his grandson Ḥusayn who was riding on his back (al-Ghazālī, *Iḥyāʾ*, ii, 275-9). According to one of the most revealing traditions in this regard, a caring father who in the middle of the night gets up to warm his children with his own clothes is more virtuous than a fighter in a holy war (*ibid.*, ii, 41). No wonder, then, that Ṣalāḥ al-Dīn al-Ayyūbī [*q.v.*], the epitome of *djihād*, is also depicted as a loving father to his seventeen children (Ibn Shaddād, *Fī sīrat Ṣalāḥ al-Dīn*, n.p. n.d., 52, 59).

Children, especially when grown-up, are portrayed as arousing expectations in their parents, making them proud and others envious. They are expected to be energetic, brave and intelligent (al-Ḳaysī, fol. 171b). However, besides this type of parent-child relationships other, sometimes contradictory, types have always existed. On the whole, expressions of parental care for and love of their offspring refer to male children, with explicit observations reflecting discrimination against, even hatred of, females (see below). But even males were sometimes regarded as little other than property and a source of labour. Thus, while several Ḳurʾānic texts stress the strong love of parents for their children (e.g. XXVI, 17; XVII, 24; XXVIII, 9; XXXI, 33) the Ḳurʾān also depicts children (*banūn, awlād*), and possessions (*māl* or *amwāl*) as a temptation to disbelievers and believers alike (e.g. VIII, 28; LXIV, 15; LVII, 20; LXIII, 9; O'Shaughnessy, 38-9, 42). Side-by-side with the notion of the child's purity and innocence (for a comparison between children and saints, see al-Ghazālī, *Naṣīḥat al-mulūk*, Cairo 1317, 134) there existed an image of the child as an ignorant creature, full of desires and with a weak and vulnerable spirit. This image, and the concept behind it that childhood is no more than a "passage" leading to the "parlour" of adulthood, justified extensive, sometimes excessive, use, by parents and teachers, of corporal punishment in order to correct undesirable traits (although reservations and proposals for alternatives to physical punishment are also found in Muslim educational thought) (Giladi, *Children of Islam*, 61-6). Children also suffered from adult violence (verbal or physical) motivated by other than educational principles. On the other hand, child abandonment and infanticide, phenomena not unknown in mediaeval Muslim societies in spite of the unequivocal religious rejection Ḳurʾān LXXXI, 8; VI, 137, 140, 151; XVII, 31; LX, 12; XVI, 57-9), were not necessarily motivated always by feelings of hatred or contempt but may have served as a means of (post partum) birth control, particularly in times of want and economic duress Giladi, *ibid.*, 78-9, 101-15). Even in Islamic consolation treatises for bereaved parents (see below), one finds contradictory motivations: love and tenderness towards infants and children and strong emotional ties which made their death very difficult for parents to accept, on the one hand, and steadfastness in the face of children's death, even the readiness of parents to sacrifice their offspring for the sake of God, on the other (see Giladi, "*The child was small*", 367-86).

It has been suggested that in the traditional patrilineal Arabic-Islamic family the child "is a miniature adult, capable at most of childishness. His value lies in what he will be, not in what he is" and that "childhood is de-realised to such an extent that is deliberately ignored by the fathers who willingly hand over to the mothers responsibility for their sons for a large part of their childhood" (Bouhdiba, *Sexuality*, 219). The special emotional relationships between mothers and (particularly male) children and their long-term impact on the latter (Bianquis, 578; Bouhdiba, *The child and the mother*, 128, 132-5) can be explained against this background. Anthropological research among contemporary Muslim societies gives an even stronger impression than do historical sources of the complexity of parent-child relationships. Thus the centrality of children for their parents, adult awareness of the great responsibility involved in raising and educating children, the attention for children's needs, on the one hand, but limited and not very effective interactions between adults and children and a strong feeling that children are a heavy burden, on the other, together with differences in attitudes towards males and females, are some seemingly inconsistent and contradictory observations (Friedl, 195-7, 210-11; cf. Ammar, 53).

The Ḳurʾān, under Judaeo-Christian influence and as a response to the challenge of structural changes in tribal society, shows special sensitivity towards children. Rejecting the pre-Islamic concept of children as their fathers' property, it acknowledges their own right to live and regards their life as sacred (see e.g. XVII, 31; VI, 151). This principle the *Sharīʿa* extends even to foetuses: a special indemnity (*ghurra*) is to be paid for causing an abortion. An unborn child can inherit, receive a legacy and, if it is a slave, be manumitted (Schacht, 124, 186; Motzki, *Das Kind*, 409-10).

The child's right to an established paternity (*nasab*), crucial in patrilineal families, gives rise to mutual rights of inheritance, guardianship and maintenance (Nasir, 156-61). It should be emphasised that Islamic law placed very few difficulties in the way of recognising the legitimacy of children. By regulating *ʿidda* [*q.v.*], Ḳurʾānic law intended to help identify the biological father in cases of divorce or the father's death. As a rule, however, any child born in wedlock is regarded as legitimate (*al-walad li-ṣāḥib al-firāsh*... "the offspring belongs to the owner of the bed...", see Rubin, 5-26), provided that it is born not less than six months after the beginning of cohabitation, and not later than (according to the Ḥanafīs) two (according to the Shāfiʿīs and Mālikīs) four or even five years (al-Wansharīsī, iv, 477) after the last intercourse between husband and wife (see NIKĀḤ, at VIII, 28). This means, in fact, that any child born to a woman, from any intercourse, is to be considered the legal offspring of her husband or master. Formal paternity can be established also through acknowledgment (*iḳrār*), to be used only when the child's lineage is unknown and biological fathership is feasible, or through evidence (*bayyina*) involving the testimony of two men or a man and two women (Levy, 135-9; al-Barā, 11-20, 27). Only by *liʿān* [*q.v.*] can a husband challenge the legitimacy of a child and disown his paternity. Sunni jurists showed more leniency towards *awlad zinā* (offspring born out of wedlock) than Shīʿī-Imāmī ones in the contexts of purity, marriage and wet-nursing. But even among the Imāmī Shīʿīs, the argument that it remains impossible to know for certain whether or not someone is *walad al-zinā* played a role (Kohlberg, 237-66).

The Ḳurʾān abolished the pre-Islamic custom of adoption, whereby an adopted child could be assimilated in a legal sense into another family, and replaced it by the recommendation that believers treat children of unknown origin as their brothers in the faith and clients (XXXIII, 4-5, 37-40). Adoption was regarded by the *Sharīʿa* as a lie, as an artificial tie between adults and children, devoid of any real emotional relationship, as a cause of confusion where lineage was concerned and thus a possible source of problems regarding marriage between members of the same family and regarding inheritance (Fahd and Hammoudi, 334-6). However, the custom of adoption, rooted in local tradition, survived in some Muslim communities, e.g. those of North Bali (Wikan, 452).

Viewing children as vulnerable, dependent creatures, Islamic law supplies various rules for the protection of their body and property. In some cases more attention is given to the child's benefit (*manfaʿat al-walad*; see e.g. al-Sarakhsī, v, 207, vi, 169) than to the interests of its parents. Fathers, because of their discretion and compassion, retain the power of guardianship (*wilāya* [*q.v.*]) over the child which involves guardianship over property (*wilāyat al-māl*) and over the person (*wilāyat al-nafs*), including overall responsibility for physical care, socialisation and education. To these should be added the father's duty to marry his child off when the latter comes of age (*wilāyat al-tazwīdj*). Mothers, because of their pity and gentleness, are entrusted with the care and control of their children for the first few years of their life and, in case of dispute, have the right to custody during these years. If a mother dies, the responsibility falls on other female relatives, preferably in the mother's line (see ḤAḌĀNA, and Pearl, 92, 97-9).

Riḍāʿa (lactation) [see RAḌĀʿ] is the basic right of any infant at least during the first two years of its life (Ḳurʾān, II, 233; XXXI, 14; XLVI, 15). Moreover, it is the mother's obligation (which, according to some opinions, can be enforced on her, if necessary, even if this involves injury) unless the alternatives do not endanger the infant's life and are economically viable. At the same time, *riḍāʿa* is a mother's right, though it can be denied when she demands to be paid a certain sum for it and another woman is ready to suckle without or for lower pay. The father again is responsible for the infant's welfare in this regard, for covering the expenses involved (Ḳurʾān, *ibid.*, and LXV, 6), for finding a physically and morally suitable wet-nurse, if necessary, and for making sure she treats the infant well (Ibn Taymiyya, *Ikhtiyārāt*, 286; Ibn Ḳudāma, ix, 312; al-Sarakhsī, xv, 122; al-Barā, 31-5).

Cognisant of the infant's needs, and in the belief that character traits are transmitted through the mother's milk, Muslim jurists emphasise the preference of maternal suckling. Also, some jurists regard harmful for the nursling, and even forbid, sexual relations with a nursing woman (*ghīla*), in contrast to the authorisation given by a *ḥadīth* (Ibn Bābawayh, iii, 305; al-Djūghī, fol. 65a; Musallam, 15-16).

Feeding of children in general and breast-feeding in particular constitute a central theme in mediaeval medical-hygienic writings and in the child-rearing manuals that Muslim doctors compiled under the strong influence of Greek medicine. These writings deal with such key questions as maternal suckling versus wet-nursing, the recommended characteristics of wet-nurses, the frequency of breast-feeding, the weaning of the child and the like. This, in addition to instructions on how to treat the infant immediately after birth, how to prepare its cradle, to wash and swaddle it, advice on how to calm weeping children, on teething, on how to treat children when they start walking and talking and recommendations regarding entertainment and the company of other children. Together with observations on e.g. birth shock and the psychological development of the child, the authors discuss such theoretical issues as the relationships between innate dispositions and acquired characteristics, the changeability of natural dispositions, etc. It is clear that such 4th/10th-century authors of comprehensive medical compilations as al-Madjūsī [*q.v.*] and Ibn Sīnā [*q.v.*], but particularly the writers of gynaecological, embryological and paediatric treatises, like Ibn al-Djazzār, Muḥammad b. Yaḥyā al-Baladī and ʿArīb b. Saʿd al-Ḳurṭubī, attached perhaps even greater importance to paediatrics than their Greek predecessors. Moreover, their rich and diversified knowledge implied an understanding of some of the unique characteristics of children from physical as well as psychological points of view. Ibn al-Djazzār's *Siyāsat al-ṣibyān*, for instance, has fifteen chapters on infant diseases and methods of healing in addition to six chapters on the hygienic care of newborn infants. Part of the material included in these paediatric writings was later "Islamised", popularised and adapted for use by literate parents and nurses, for instance by Ibn Ḳayyim al-Djawziyya in his *Tuḥfat al-mawdūd* (Giladi, *Children of Islam*, 4-8, 19-34). Obviously, popular medicine and magic played an important role in the treatment of children among the common people (Ullmann, 2, 92).

The first stages of incorporating the new-born child into the larger human society, and particularly into the Muslim community, are symbolised by a series of childhood rites, most of them of tribal, pre-Islamic origin for whose performance the father has the responsibility. By reciting in his ears, immediately after birth, the formula used for the call to prayer (*adhān*) as well as the words chanted in the mosque at the beginning of the prayer (*iḳāma*), the infant was believed to acquire the basic principles of Islam. *Taḥnīk*, the rubbing of the infant's palate with a date, was another ceremony early Muslims performed soon after birth. It probably symbolised the curbing of the child's natural desires and the harnessing and directing of his energies, for it clearly parallels the practice of putting, for the first time, a rope in a horse's mouth. It might also signify the readiness of the community to share its food with the new-born child, accepting it as a member (Giladi, *Children of Islam*, 35-41; Motzki, *Das Kind*, 413). Other ceremonies, i.e. naming (*tasmiya*) (Schimmel, 14-24), the first haircut, which separates the child from its previous environment (Van Gennep, 50, 53-4), and the *ʿaḳīḳa* [*q.v.*], the slaughter of a sheep or a goat to redeem the child and to express gratitude for its birth, are delayed to the seventh day after birth when the prospects for the infant's life look brighter. By performing these rites, the father confirmed his fatherhood in public and thus his responsibility towards the child. Some Muslim scholars have suggested adding male circumcision (*khitān* [*q.v.*]), regarded as an act of purification and incorporation into the community of faithful (Van Gennep, 72), to the ceremonies of the seventh day. However, most say that circumcision should be performed later, at the age of seven (when the male child under his father's supervision, starts his systematic religious education) or ten or even thirteen years. In the latter case, it is probably designed to mark the beginning of adolescence and to prepare the child for marriage (Motzki, *ibid.*, 416-17). Female circumcision (*khafḍ* [*q.v.*]), explained as primarily a means of restraining a woman's sexual desire and maintaining chastity, is also practised when the girl is between six and thirteen years (on childhood rites, particularly male and female circumcision, in a contemporary Muslim community see Ammar, 116-23).

Ensuring that his children receive a good education is another of the father's duties. According to mediaeval Muslim thinkers, character training should start in early childhood, when the child's soul is still pure and impressionable and good character traits can be engraved upon it as upon a smooth stone. At this stage, protecting the child from harmful influences in its social environment is crucial. In writings inspired by Greek ethical thought, moral education is guided by the ideal of balancing the psychic forces of desire and anger. To be content with little, meekness and endurance are the traits the child should acquire through specific habits of eating, sleeping, dressing, and social conduct (see al-G͟hazālī, *Iḥyāʾ*, iii, 92-5). Recommendations concerning relaxing games and physical activity for children include the advice to teach them swimming and archery (Giladi, *Children of Islam*, 58-9). While the basic principles of faith should be inculcated as soon as the child starts talking, the age of *tamyīz* is generally perceived as the appropriate time to begin systematic education, primarily towards performing the religious commandments (see al-G͟hazālī, *ibid.*, al-Ṭabarsī/al-Ṭabrisī, 175), and for sending male children to the *kuttāb* [*q.v.*] (or *maktab*) for their elementary education. The popularity of this institution in Muslim countries might have delayed by some years the induction of children into the labour force. Female children were generally educated at home by their mothers to fulfill their religious duties and to carry out household work. Obedience to God, filial piety and good conduct are the basic aims of child education (see Ḳurʾān, IV, 36; XXXI, 13, 16-9), their accomplishment ensuring the child a happy life in this world and, more important, in the Hereafter (Motzki, *ibid.*, 35-48). After they had completed their elementary education, the father was expected to help his male children choose an occupation in accordance with their talents and inclinations and train them toward their vocation (Ibn Ḳayyim al-D̲j̲awziyya, 144-5).

Instructions for the rearing and education of children of the nobility and the upper classes are included in *waṣāyā* ("injunctions") which fathers formulated for tutors (many of which are scattered through *adab* compilations, see e.g. Ibn Ḳutayba, v, 166-8; al-D̲j̲āḥiẓ, ii, 75) and in the "Mirrors for Princes" literature. Thus al-Māwardī [*q.v.*] in his *Naṣīḥat al-mulūk* (fols. 106-10) makes the selection of a good woman as the future mother the starting point of his discussion. Special emphasis is laid on the moral and physical education of princes and on enriching the curriculum of their elementary education (usually consisting mainly of Ḳurʾān) with studies of language, history and poetry.

Parents were believed to be questioned (and accordingly rewarded in the Hereafter) as to how they had fulfilled their duties towards their offspring, particularly in the domain of education, since God regarded these as more important than the obligations children had towards their parents (Ibn Ḳayyim al-D̲j̲awziyya, 136; al-G͟hazālī, *Iḥyāʾ*, iii, 92).

Many parents in pre-modern Muslim societies experienced the loss of one or more children. The generally high rates of infant and child mortality rose even more drastically as a result of recurring epidemics of the Black Death, particularly from the 8th/14th century onwards. Juridical and theological writings deal with the ways in which deceased infants and children should be treated, and with their fate in the Hereafter. The focus of legalistic considerations is whether or not the child is to be regarded as a human being in the full sense of the word. The answer given by some well-known jurisconsults, like al-Sarak͟hsī (ii, 57), is in the affirmative. This means, for instance, that the coffin of a dead child is to be borne by people, not on the back of an animal, and that the washing of an infant's corpse and the prayer for him should be exactly the same as for a deceased adult. Ḳurʾān commentators, theologians and heresiographers discuss such issues as whether or not children are questioned in the grave, whether children of unbelievers are sent by God to Hell, whether God punishes children in the Hereafter, and the exact status of Muslim children in Paradise (Rosenthal, 9-15). Discussions of this sort, abstract as they were, mirror, in some cases, certain concepts of childhood and attitudes towards children.

Like *ḥadīt͟h* compilations, early Muslim sources contain much material on how to react to children's death, which later, against the background of the Black Death, were collected in special, apparently widely circulated, consolation treatises for bereaved parents (see e.g. al-Manbid̲j̲ī, al-Ḳaysī and al-Sak͟hāwī, all from the 8th-9th/14th-15th centuries). Their main task was not to deal with the theological problems involved in the death of innocent creatures but rather to help bereaved parents cope with outbursts of emotions and with the psychological difficulties they experienced. Most interesting in these treatises, as well as in a few lamentation poems written for or by bereaved fathers (see e.g. Ibn al-Rūmī, *Dīwān*, Cairo 1973-9, i, 244, ii, 625, 6; Ibn Nubāta, *Dīwān*, Cairo 1905, 156, 218, 347, 348, 546), are the tension between the emotional-spontaneous type of reaction, on the one hand, and the religious-"rational" one, on the other, and the efforts to harmonise them. They bring to light strong psychological attachments resulting in moving emotional reactions in case of death but also call for restraint and control and even point out the religious "advantages" of children's death. However, these efforts too of Muslim scholars to impose on the believers a certain cultural pattern for the emotional expression of grief often reveal a degree of understanding of basic psychological needs. Although lacking any precise information on mortality rates in pre-modern Muslim societies, consolation treatises can give us a clear idea of the dimensions of the problem and draw a partial picture of the circumstances of children's lives and causes of their deaths.

The burial of deceased infants as adults, strong psychological ties between parents and children expressed through intense, heart-rending grieving in cases of children's death, difficulties in comforting bereaved parents as well as opposite reactions of restraint and control are all part of contemporary Muslim communities. However, the link between them and Islamic ethics is not always unequivocal (Granqvist, 90-2; Wikan, 451-3).

4. Children in society.

Any child born to Muslim parents is regarded as Muslim. According to the rule, formulated by a *ḥadīt͟h*, that Islam "overcomes" other religions (*yaʿlū wa-lā yuʿlā*) (al-Buk͟hārī, *K. al-D̲j̲anāʾiz*, *bāb* 80) this is true also when only one parent is Muslim. Al-Sarak͟hsī (v, 210), on the other hand, maintains that the child follows his father's faith (*...al-walad... muslim bi-islām al-ab*).

According to some legal opinions, the fact that children lack responsibility (*takalluf*), that they are neither rewarded nor punished for their deeds (*marfūʿ al-ḳalam*), that they are not even addressed by religious preaching (*ghayr mukhāṭab bi 'l-islām*), makes their conversion to Islam (or their apostasy) invalid (al-Sarakhsī, x, 120, 122, 123). Other debatable questions are whether children should be obliged to pray, to fast during Ramaḍān, to pay legal alms, to make a pilgrimage, or even whether children may be allowed to serve as *imāms* in public prayer. Even though they are aware of the special religious status of children, there is no agreement between jurists on these questions. Thus for both Ibn Masʿūd and Ibn ʿAbbās a child could not lead in prayer since it is not one of the "people of perfection" (*ahl al-kamāl*) (Ibn Ḳudāma, ii, 54). A common argument is that the observance of religious commandments, particularly prayer and the fast of Ramaḍān, is for children of an educational rather than formal-religious significance.

The special legal status of the child is reflected also in spheres outside the purely ritual domain. Being subject to legal disability or interdiction (*ḥadjr*) children, like the insane (*madjnūn*) and the idiot (*maʿtūh*), do not have the capacity to contract and to dispose (*taṣarruf*), do not owe full obedience to criminal law and therefore cannot be punished as Muslims who are sane and come of age. Thus a minor may be guilty of deliberate homicide, but because legally he is not considered capable of forming a criminal intent, he is not subject to the death penalty (Coulson, 179). Still, Islamic law distinguishes between various stages of childhood: The infant (*ṭifl*), who is wholly incapable, can incur certain financial obligations. A minor (*ṣabiyy, ṣaghīr*) has in addition the capacity to conclude purely beneficial transactions and to accept donations and charitable gifts. An intelligent (*ṣabiyy yaʿḳilu*), discriminating (*mumayyiz*) minor, moreover, can adopt Islam, enter into a contract of manumission by *mukātaba*, if he is a slave, and carry out a procuration (Schacht, 124-5).

That Islamic law allows child marriage seems to contradict its general attitude of protection towards children. The *Sharīʿa* may have been following the social practice of the Islamic core countries in the 1st-4th/7th-10th centuries. Little is known about the frequency, the possibly differential regional distribution, manner of functioning and motives of child marriage, though the issue is raised, sometimes rather frequently, in pre-modern *fatāwā* collections from regions as far afield as Morocco (al-Wansharīsī, iii, 30, 90, 96, 130, 195, 281, 292, 378) and Palestine (Motzki, *Muslimische Kinderehen*, 82-90). Contemporary ethnological and sociological field studies have shown that in various regions and milieux of the Middle East there exists a practice of marriages in which either one or both partners are children. However, more recent family legislation in Islamic states prescribing a minimum age for social and demographic reasons has led to a marked decline in the number of child marriages [see NIKĀḤ]. From *al-Fatāwā al-Khayriyya* by the Ḥanafī jurisconsult Khayr al-Dīn al-Ramlī (993-1081/1585-1670), it emerges that the minors involved were predominantly girls, that marriage contracts were made up for them while their ages ranged anywhere between birth and sexual maturity, and that generally neither the wedding nor marital sexual intercourse were postponed until they had reached sexual maturity (Motzki, *ibid.*).

The sexuality of infants was deemed insignificant and males could be dressed, for instance, in silk clothes more typical of women (Ibn Ḳudāma, i, 629). This was no longer allowed for older children the moment adults noticed their budding sexuality (al-Ghazālī, *Iḥyāʾ*, iii, 93). *Ḥadīth* and *fiḳh* compilations recommend separating children in bed when they have reached the age of ten (according to one version, six), having adults avoid washing children of the other sex as soon as they are seven years, and even consider any form of physical contact between a mother and her six-year-old daughter a form of adultery (Ibn Bābawayh, iii, 275-6; Ibn Ḳudāma, ii, 313-4, 400; al-Djūghī, fol. 66a), thus reflecting the awareness of the latent sexuality of children approaching maturity. The popularity of child marriage renders this awareness even more obvious.

It is told of the Prophet that he did not allow the fourteen-year-old Ibn ʿUmar to join the Muslim fighters at Uḥud, but a year later agreed to include him among the warriors of the battle of Khandaḳ (al-Shāfiʿī, vi, 135). While reaffirming the age of fifteen as a criterion of majority, this *ḥadīth* reflects a general Islamic objection to the participation of children in war. The prohibition, attributed to the Prophet (see e.g. Mālik b. Anas, 163-4), against the killing of an enemy's children (and women) in time of war is also important here. In his explanation, Ibn Taymiyya (*Madjmūʿ fatāwā*, xvi, 80) bases himself on a threefold argument: (a) like Muslim children, the enemy's children, from the juridical point of view, are to be regarded as innocent and not responsible; (b) like women in the enemy's homeland, they are not a part of the fighting force; and (c) there is always the possibility for them to become Muslims.

The Ḳurʾān calls for a just treatment of a fatherless child (*yatīm*). Nineteen texts make mention of children of such status, the earliest speaking of God's providential care of Muḥammad. Several verses from the Meccan period forbid any harsh and oppressive treatment of fatherless children, urge kindness and justice towards them, particularly in the matter of property rights, and speak of feeding them as well as the poor. Exhortations to respect the property rights of children as well as to provide for their security by marrying them off are included in some of the Medinan *sūras* (O'Shaughnessy, 35-8) and echoed in later legal writings (see e.g. al-Sarakhsī, xv, 129; al-Djūghī fols. 66a-b). Orphanages and foundling homes were unknown in pre-modern Muslim societies (unlike their European counterparts), so that caring for these children and educating them was the responsibility of relatives. An abandoned child (*laḳīṭ* [*q.v.*], *manbūdh*) was also brought up within an individual family. That the practice of abandonment was known in mediaeval Muslim societies, probably as a means for regulating family size or as a device for disposing of illegitimate children, can be inferred from the juridical literature. Questions such as the status of the foundling and his religious identity, his maintenance, the management of his property, claiming abandoned children and the like are rather frequently dealt with (see e.g. Mālik b. Anas, 293; al-Shāfiʿī, vi, 263; al-Samarḳandī, i, 315-16).

A preference for males is typical of Muslim societies with a patrilineal family structure. The majority of the utterances in Arabic-Islamic sources that show understanding and sympathy for children refer to males. That females were discriminated against from birth is shown, *inter alia*, by the efforts religious scholars made to counteract this practice by praising fathers devoted to their daughters (Ibn al-Djawzī, 356-9) and denouncing the rejection of newborn females that sometimes led fathers to wish them dead (Ibn Ḳayyim al-Djawziyya, 10-13). It is against this background that differences in treating and educating male and female children and even female infanticide are to be explained. It should be emphasised, however, that infanticide was committed not only on females and that it was not necessarily always motivated by feelings of hatred or contempt for the victim (see above). Occasionally, jurists made attempts to close (or at least minimise) the gap between female and male children where religious status or education were concerned. Thus, while the common view was held that the urine of only female children was unclean, Ibn Ḳudāma (i, 734-5) claimed that the urine of children in general was impure. Statements, rare as they are, concerning the validity of the prayer of an intelligent female child, like that of her male counterpart (*ibid.*, i, 647), or regarding the obligatory status of female circumcision (Ibn al-Djawzī, 144) should also be mentioned in this context. Scholars urge Muslims to grant their daughters a basic religious and moral training, and there are testimonies to the effect that special institutions of elementary education for female children existed in mediaeval Muslim societies (Ibn al-Ukhuwwa, 171). Among the authors of consolation treatises for bereaved parents, Muḥammad b. ʿAbd al-Raḥmān al-Sakhāwī [*q.v.*] seems to have been particularly sensitive to the impact of female children's deaths and quotes an impressive number of narratives which pertain to bereaved mothers (Giladi, "*The child was small*"..., 382-5).

Contemporary Middle Eastern thinkers have drawn attention to the significance of Islamic as well as local-customary traditional attitudes towards children, of parent-child relations in patrilineal families and of the traditional methods of formal education in Islamic countries as influential factors in their societies (Bouhdiba, *The child and the mother*..., 126-41; Sharabi, 240-56). The growing awareness of the pschological and socio-cultural role of rearing and educating children and of their status in society is reflected in the relatively new inclination of authors of autobiographies to devote whole chapters, sometimes even entire works, to their childhood (see e.g. Ṭāhā Ḥusayn; Sayyid Ḳuṭb; Aḥmad Amīn; Ḥusayn Aḥmad Amīn).

Bibliography: Aḥmad Amīn, *Ḥayātī*, Cairo 1958; Ḥusayn Aḥmad Amīn, *Fī bayt Aḥmad Amīn*, Cairo 1985; Hamed Ammar, *Growing-up in an Egyptian village*, London 1966; Aḥmad al-Baladī, *K. Tadbīr al-ḥabālā wa 'l-aṭfāl wa 'l-ṣibyān wa-ḥifẓ ṣiḥḥatihim wa-mudāwāt al-amraḍ al-ʿāriḍa lahum*, ed. Maḥmūd al-Ḥādjdj Ḳāsim Muḥammad, Baghdād 1980; Zakariyyāʾ Aḥmad al-Barā, *Aḥkām al-awlād fi 'l-Islām*, Cairo 1963; Th. Bianquis, *La famille en Islam arabe*, in A. Burguière *et alii* (eds.), *Histoire de la famille*, Paris 1986; A. Bouhdiba, *Sexuality in Islam*, London 1985; idem, *The child and the mother in Arab Muslim society*, in L.C. Brown and N. Itzkowitz (eds.), *Psychological dimensions of Near Eastern studies*, Princeton 1977; Bukhārī, *al-Djāmiʿ al-ṣaḥīḥ*, ed. L. Krehl and Th.W. Juynboll, Leiden 1862-1908; N.J. Coulson, *Succession in the Muslim family*, Cambridge 1971; Djāḥiẓ, *al-Bayān wa 'l-tabyīn*, Cairo 1956; M. Farah, *Marriage and sexuality in Islam*, Salt Lake City 1984; Muḥammad al-Djūghī, *Shirʿat al-Islām ilā dār al-salām*, ms. Paris, B.N., Ar. 6576; T. Fahd and M. Hammoudi, *L'Enfant dans le droit islamique*, in *Recueils de la Société Jean Bodin pour l'Histoire Comparative des Institutions*, 35 (1975); E. Friedl, *Parents and children in a Village in Iran*, in A. Fathi (ed.), *Women and the family in Iran*, Leiden 1985; A. van Gennep, *The rites of passage*, London and Henley 1977; Ghazālī, *Iḥyāʾ ʿulūm al-dīn*, Cairo 1967; A. Giladi, *Children of Islam: concepts of childhood in medieval Muslim society*, Houndmill and London 1992; idem, "*The child was small... not so the grief for him*". *Sources, structure, and content of al-Sakhāwī's consolation treatise for bereaved parents*, in *Poetics Today*, xiv (1993); H. Granqvist, *Child problems among the Arabs*, Helsinki and Copenhagen 1950; Ṭāhā Ḥusayn, *al-Ayyām*, Cairo 1973; Ibn Bābawayh, *Man lā yaḥḍuruhu 'l-faḳīh*, Nadjaf 1378; Ibn al-Djazzār al-Ḳayrawānī, *Siyāsat al-ṣibyān*, Tunis 1968; Ibn al-Djawzī, *Aḥkām al-nisāʾ*, Beirut 1981; Ibn Ḳayyim al-Djawziyya, *Tuḥfat al-mawdūd fī aḥkām al-mawlūd*, Bombay 1961; Ibn Ḳudāma, *al-Mughnī*, Beirut 1972; Ibn Ḳutayba, *ʿUyūn al-akhbār*, Beirut 1925; Ibn Taymiyya, *al-Ikhtiyārāt al-fiḳhiyya min fatāwā Shaykh al-Islām Ibn Taymiyya*, Beirut n.d.; idem, *Madjmūʿ fatāwā*, Riyāḍ 1382; Nāṣir al-Dīn al-Ḳaysī, *Bard al-akbād ʿan faḳd al-awlād*, ms. Bodleian, Oxford, Marsh 583, printed ed. Cairo 1887; E. Kohlberg, *The position of the* Walad Zinā *in Imāmī Shīʿism*, in *BSOAS*, xlviii (1985); Ibn al-Ukhuwwa, *Maʿālim al-ḳurba fī aḥkām al-ḥisba*, ed. R. Levy, London 1938; ʿArīb b. Saʿd al-Ḳurṭubī, *K. Khalḳ al-djanīn wa-tadbīr al-ḥabālā wa 'l-mawlūdīn*, ed. H. Jahier and N. Abdelqader, Algiers 1965; Sayyid Ḳuṭb, *Ṭifl min al-ḳarya*, Djudda 1945; R. Levy, *The social structure of Islam*, Cambridge 1969; Y. Linant de Bellefonds, *Traité de droit musulman comparé*, Paris-The Hague 1965, iii; Mālik b. Anas, *al-Muwaṭṭaʾ*, ed. ʿAbd al-Bāḳī; Muḥammad al-Manbidjī, *Tasliyat ahl al-maṣāʾib fī mawt al-awlād wa 'l-aḳārib*, Medina 1960; Māwardī, *Naṣīḥat al-mulūk*, ms. B.N., Paris, Ar. 2447; H. Motzki, *Das Kind und seine Sozialisation in der islamischen Familie des Mittelalters*, in J. Martin and Nitschke (eds.), *Zur Sozialgeschichte der Kindheit*, Munich 1986; idem, *Muslimische Kinderehen in Palästina während des 17. Jahrhunderts.* Fatāwā *als Quellen zur Sozialgeschichte*, in *WI*, xxvii (1987); B. Musallam, *Sex and society in Islam*, Cambridge 1983; J.J. Nasir, *The Islamic law of personal status*, London 1990; Th.J. O'Shaughnessy, *The Qurʾānic view of youth and old age*, in *ZDMG*, cxli (1991); D. Pearl, *A textbook on Muslim personal law*, London 1987; F. Rosenthal, *Child psychology in Islam*, in *IC*, xxvi (1952); U. Rubin, "Al-Walad li-l-Firāsh": *on the Islamic campaign against* "Zinā", in *SI*, lxxviii, 1993; Sakhāwī, *Irtiyāḥ al-akbād bi-arbāḥ faḳd al-awlād*, ms. Chester Beatty, Ar. 3463; Abu 'l-Layth al-Samarḳandī, *Khizānat al-fiḳh*, Baghdād 1965; Sarakhsī, *K. al-Mabsūṭ*, Beirut 1980; J. Schacht, *An introduction to Islamic law*, Oxford 1966; A. Schimmel, *Islamic names*, Edinburgh 1989; al-Shāfiʿī, *K. al-Umm*, Bulak 1321; H. Sharabi, *Impact of class and culture on social behavior: the feudal-bourgeois family in Arab society*, in Brown and Itzkowitz (eds.), *op. cit.*; Thābit b. Abī Thābit, *Khalḳ al-insān*, Kuwayt 1965; Ṭabarsī/Ṭabrisī, *Makārim al-akhlāḳ*, Cairo n.d.; M. Ullmann, *Islamic medicine*, Edinburgh 1978; Aḥmad b. Yaḥyā al-Wansharīsī, *al-Miʿyār al-muʿrib wa 'l-djāmiʿ al-mughrib ʿan fatāwā ʿulamāʾ Ifrīḳiya wa 'l-Andalus wa 'l-Maghrib*, Beirut 1981; U. Wikan, *Bereavement and loss in two Muslim communities: Egypt and Bali compared*, in *Social Science and Medicine*, xxvii (1988).

(A. Giladi)

ṢAḤĀBA (A.), (pl., sing. *ṣaḥābī*, other plural forms are *aṣḥāb, ṣaḥb, ṣuḥbān*) are the Companions of the Prophet Muḥammad, who in many respects are key-figures in the early history of Islam. In the critical approach of tradition (*ʿilm al-ridjāl* [*q.v.*]), which is a section of *ḥadīth* literature, they are considered as reliable transmitters of statements, deeds and instructions of the Prophet. Their own deeds and statements, too, are worthy of imitation, particularly in the history of Islamic rites.

The first endeavours to define the *ṣaḥāba* as a distinct group of individuals, and to establish the most important criteria according to which someone might be given the title of *ṣaḥābī*, probably reach back to the outset of the 2nd/8th century. At the beginning of the *K. Faḍāʾil aṣḥāb al-nabī* of his *Ṣaḥīḥ*, al-Bukhārī [*q.v.*] gives a short definition of a *ṣaḥābī*, which, however, needs further interpretation. According to him, such an individual, while being a believing Muslim, must have accompanied (*ṣaḥiba, lahu ṣuḥba*) the Prophet or have seen him. It has always remained a point of discussion whether the simple fact of having seen (*ruʾya*) the Prophet is sufficient in this respect. In general, participation in a number of the Prophet's campaigns, adulthood (*bulūgh al-ḥulum*), and capability of transmitting directly from the Prophet were basic prerequisites. According to a passage in Ibn al-Athīr (*Usd al-ghāba*, ed. Tehran, n.d., i, 12), the division of the *ṣaḥāba* in classes was already common in the time of al-Wāḳidī (130-207/747-823 [*q.v.*]) at the latest. He clearly speaks of a classification of the *ṣaḥāba* according to their pre-eminence in Islam (*ʿalā ṭabaḳātihim wa-taḳaddumihim fi 'l-islām*). For this, the moment of conversion to Islam was evidently of particular importance. Ibn Saʿd (*al-Ṭabaḳāt al-kubrā*, ed. Sachau *et alii*, Leiden 1905-40) places the moment of conversion in a clearly defined historical context: certain individuals accepted Islam before the Prophet entered the house of al-Arḳam b. Abi 'l-Arḳam in the neighbourhood of Ṣafā (Ibn Saʿd, iii/1, 34, ll. 21-3; 59, ll. 10-11; 62, ll. 15-7; 88, ll. 2-4; 107, ll. 5-7; 116, ll. 21-3; 164, ll. 16-8, etc.; for further references, see M. Muranyi, *Die ersten Muslime von Mekka...* in *JSAI*, viii [1986], 28). This circle of early Muslims (*aslama ḳadīman/kāna ḳadīm al-islām*) is also designated as *al-sābiḳūn/al-sābiḳūn al-awwalūn* who, after ʿUmar b. al-Khaṭṭāb had entered al-Arḳam's house, counted 53 persons (see the list in al-Dhahabī, *Siyar aʿlām al-nubalāʾ*, ed. Shuʿayb al-Arnāʾūṭ and Ḥusayn al-Asad, Beirut 1990[7], i, 144-5).

The *sābiḳūn* are also mentioned in Ḳurʾān, IX, 100, and LVI, 10. Ḳurʾān exegesis (*tafsīr* [*q.v.*]) already defines them in the light of the historical events of Muḥammad's prophethood and considers as *sābiḳūn* those Muslims who prayed in both directions, viz. Jerusalem and Mecca, who emigrated with Muḥammad to Medina, and who took part in the battle of Badr [*q.v.*] and in the treaty of al-Ḥudaybiya [*q.v.*]. The latter are also called *aṣḥāb al-shadjara*, i.e. those who took the oath of allegiance to the Prophet (*bayʿat al-riḍwān*) under the tree in the oasis of al-Ḥudaybiya.

The élite of the Meccan Muslims are also designated as the (first) Emigrants (*al-muhādjirūn* (*al-awwalūn*)), i.e. those who had joined the Prophet by March 628 (al-Ḥudaybiya at the latest, or, according to another interpretation, by January 624 (the date of the change of the *ḳibla* [*q.v.*].

Members of Arab tribes, who settled at Medina after their conversion to Islam and thus renounced returning to their tribes, are also designated as *muhādjirūn*. However, in the endeavours of classification carried out by the following generations, these individuals do not appear among the "Emigrants" from Mecca, who emigrated with Muḥammad—or shortly afterwards—to Medina.

The above-mentioned classification cannot be established for the Medinan "Helpers" (*al-Anṣār* [*q.v.*]). Mentioned are only those representatives of the two main tribes of Yathrib [see MADĪNA]—the Aws and the Khazradj—who took part in the secret meetings which the Prophet held at al-ʿAḳaba [*q.v.*] in order to negotiate guarantees of protection for himself and for the Meccan emigrants at the eve of the Hidjra [*q.v.*]. The *Anṣār* did not take part in Muḥammad's campaigns before Badr (Ibn Saʿd, ii/1, 6, l. 16; al-Wāḳidī, *Kitāb al-Maghāzī*, ed. M. Jones, London 1966, i, 11, 48).

The moment of conversion to Islam and the participation in the campaigns of the Prophet were of particular importance for the economic and social position of the *ṣaḥāba* and of their descendants. These aspects seem to have been taken into consideration when, under ʿUmar b. al-Khaṭṭāb, the lists for endowments were established (see G.R. Puin, *Der Dīwān von ʿUmar b. al-Ḫaṭṭāb*, diss. Bonn 1970).

Early lists in the Maghāzī literature, among which is a papyrus fragment of the 2nd/8th century with the names of the fighters at Badr (A. Grohmann, *Arabic papyri from Ḫirbet al-Mird*, Louvain 1963, 82-4), confirm the keen interest of historiography in the above-mentioned endeavours of classification. Ibn Saʿd composed his *K. al-Ṭabaḳāt al-kubrā* on the basis of this principle of classification, and also from old lists given by the historiographers. In the first class (*ṭabaḳa*) are mentioned the *ahl al-sābiḳa*, the fighters at Badr from among the Meccan Emigrants and the *Anṣār*, the twelve *nuḳabāʾ* of al-ʿAḳaba and some Muslims whose participation in the battle of Badr cannot be proved beyond doubt. In the second class are found the Emigrants who were converted at an early date and had migrated to Abyssinia, and the fighters at Uḥud [*q.v.*]. A third class, only known to us through allusions by Ibn Ḥadjar al-ʿAskalānī [*q.v.*], comprises the participants in the "Battle of the Ditch" (*khandaḳ* [*q.v.*] (see *al-Iṣāba fī tamyīz al-ṣaḥāba*, ed. A. Sprenger, Calcutta 1853-4, i, 445 no. 1047). In still another class, Ibn Saʿd brings together the individuals who were converted before the conquest of Mecca. Another group of early Muslims, who accepted Islam during the Prophet's stay at Mecca, are the so-called *mustaḍʿafūn*, a term which W.M. Watt (*Muhammad at Mecca*, Oxford 1953, 88, 96) renders with "those who are considered weak". They represent the class of Meccans who were socio-economically weak and destitute, and who were prevented by their clans from participating in the Hidjra. According to Ḳurʾān exegesis, Sūra IV, 75, refers to this group of the oldest *ṣaḥāba*.

The good qualities and virtues of the *ṣaḥāba*, measured against their early merits for Islam (*manāḳib, faḍāʾil*), were a favourite theme already in the narrative art of the oldest historiographers of the early 2nd/8th century. The works of the 3rd/9th century known as *muṣannafāt* [*q.v.*] in their turn devote a special *kitāb* to this theme: *faḍāʾil aṣḥāb al-nabī, manāḳib al-anṣār*. In the meantime, specific collections were devoted to the ten Companions of the Prophet to whom he is said to have promised paradise (*al-mubashsharūn al-ʿashara*), namely the four "rightly guided" caliphs, Ṭalḥa b. ʿUbayd Allāh, al-Zubayr b. al-ʿAwwām, ʿAbd al-Raḥmān b. ʿAwf, Saʿd b. Mālik, Saʿīd b. Zayd and Abū ʿUbayda ʿĀmir b. al-Djarrāḥ [*q.vv.*] (see e.g. al-Muḥibb al-Ṭabarī, *al-Riyāḍ al-naḍira fī manāḳib al-ʿashara*, [2]Ṭanṭa 1953).

Due to the narrative art of the historiographers, the *ṣaḥāba* in later times gradually took on charismatic features. In Sunnī Islam, abuse of them (*sabb al-ṣaḥāba*) is considered as a sin and, according to many interpretations, is even to be punished by death. It is a duty to pronounce the *tarḍiya*, i.e. the eulogy *raḍiya 'llāhu ʿanhu*, when one mentions the name of a Companion of the Prophet.

Historiography, local history in particular, deals in detail with information which has been transmitted about the stay of *ṣaḥāba* in provincial towns. One-third of the *K. Futūḥ Miṣr wa-akhbāruhā* by the Egyptian author Ibn ʿAbd al-Ḥakam (d. 257/871) (ed. C.C. Torrey, New Haven 1922) consists of lists of those Companions who stayed in Egypt and whose traditions circulated there. Similar lists originated also in other localities: Aḥmad b. Muḥammad b. ʿĪsā (second half of the 3rd/9th century), *Kitāb Ṭabaḳāt ahl Ḥimṣ/Taʾrīkh al-Ḥimṣiyyīn*; Aslam b. Sahl b. Aslam b. Baḥshal, *Tasmiyat al-ḳarn al-awwal al-ḳādimīn madīnat Wāsiṭ min ṣaḥābat rasūl Allāh* (ed. Dj. ʿAwwād, Baghdād 1967, see W. Hoenerbach, *Über einige arabische Handschriften in Bagdad und Tetuan*, in *Oriens*, viii [1955], 103 ff.); Saʿīd b. ʿAbd al-Raḥmān al-Ḳushayrī (d. 334/946), *Taʾrīkh Raḳḳa wa-man nazalahā min aṣḥāb rasūl Allāh* (see *GAS*, i, 348). The *K. Taʾrīkh Dārayyā* by ʿAbd al-Djabbār b. ʿAbd Allāh b. Muḥammad al-Khawlānī (d. *ca.* 365-70/975-80, see *GAS*, i, 348) contains a chapter on the *ṣaḥāba* of the town: *dhikr man nazala Dārayyā min aṣḥāb rasūl Allāh...* (ms. Tunis, Aḥmadiyya, no. 15881, fols. 2b-4a; *GAS*, i, 348, is to be corrected accordingly). Many fragments from these works, and from others which have been lost, are found in Ibn Ḥadjar al-ʿAsḳalānī, *al-Iṣāba*, and in *Istīʿāb fī maʿrifat al-aṣḥāb* by the Cordovan Ibn ʿAbd al-Barr al-Namarī (d. 1070 [*q.v.*]) (ed. al-Bidjāwī, Cairo n.d.).

While Islamic historiography—apart from some controversial representations among Islamic sects—depicts almost without criticism the contribution of the *ṣaḥāba* to the early history of Islam and their historical role in it, *ḥadīth* literature and criticism of the late 2nd/8th and early 3rd/9th centuries apply other standards. It is true that they do not call into question the credibility of individual Companions of the Prophet as transmitters of his statements and as prime witnesses of his deeds, but an *isnād* [*q.v.*] with a specific *ṣaḥābī* as prime witness is nevertheless preferred to another one.

Bibliography: Besides the works quoted in the article, see Abū Nuʿaym al-Iṣfahānī, *Ḥilyat al-awliyāʾ wa-ṭabaḳāt al-aṣfiyāʾ*, repr. Beirut 1985; Abū Saʿd al-Khargūshī, *Sharaf al-Muṣṭafā*, ms. Leiden, Or. 3014; ʿAbd al-Raḥmān al-Khazradjī, *al-Durr al-munaẓẓam fī ziyārat al-Muḳaṭṭam*, ms. B.L. Or. 3049; E. Kohlberg, *Some Imāmī Shīʿī views on the Ṣaḥāba*, in *JSAI*, v (1984); M. Muranyi, *Die Prophetengenossen in der frühislamischen Geschichte*, Bonn 1973; W.M. Watt, *Muhammad at Medina*, Oxford 1956; R. Veselý, *Die Anṣār im ersten Bürgerkriege*, in *ArO*, xxvi (1958), 35-58. (M. Muranyi)

SAḤĀBĪ ASTARĀBĀDĪ, Kamāl al-Dīn, Persian poet of the 10th/16th century, born in Shushtar [*q.v.*]. He is known as Astarābādī after his father's place of origin, which was Astarābād, and also as Shūshtarī after his own place of birth. Some writers have called him Nadjafī since he lived for forty years at Nadjaf, where he went towards 970/1562-3 during the reign of the Ṣafawid ruler Ṭahmāsp I (930-84/1524-76). During his stay in that city, he studied and taught, as one of the jurists of his time, at the holy shrine attached to ʿAlī's tomb. The author of the *Haft iḳlīm*, Amīn Aḥmad Rāzī [*q.v.*], describes him as a man of austere habits whose pious living endeared him to people of all classes. He died at Nadjar in 1010/1601-2, and was buried there.

Saḥābī's poetical output consists chiefly of *ghazals* and *rubāʿīs*. He was also the author of a *mathnawī*, based upon a Ṣūfī theme and employing the same metrical form as that used by Niẓāmī for his *Bahrām-nāma* (*Haft paykar*). It comprises 343 couplets and was dedicated to Shāh ʿAbbās I (r. 996-1038/1588-1629). Saḥābī is remembered essentially for his *rubāʿīs*, the total number of which is most probably around 6,000. Some early writers, however, place the figures much higher, but the numbers quoted by them appear to be exaggerated. In his poetry, Saḥābī deals with mystical and moral themes. He was one of the chief poets of the Ṣafawid period whose verse, according to Shiblī Nuʿmānī, reflects a philosophical colour (cf. *Shiʿr al-ʿAdjam*, v, 3rd ed., Aʿẓamgaṛh 1942, 209). Besides poetry, Saḥābī also composed, in mixed prose and verse, a Ṣūfī treatise (*risāla*), entitled *ʿUrwat al-wuthḳā* ("The true faith").

Bibliography: Saḥābī Astarābādī, *Rubāʿiyyāt yā kulliyyāt-i Saḥābī Astarābādī*, in *Fihrist-i kutub-i khaṭṭī-yi Madjlis-i Shūrā-yi Millī*, iii, no. 1087; idem, *Muntakhab rubāʿiyyāt-i Saḥābī*, B.L. Or. 329; Rāzī, *Haft iḳlīm*, ed. Djawād Fāḍil, Tehran (?) n.d., iii; Luṭf ʿAlī Beg Ādhar, *Ātishkada*, ed. Ḥasan Sādāt Nāṣirī, Tehran 1338/1959, ii; Riḍā-ḳulī Khān Hidāyat, *Madjmaʿ al-fuṣaḥāʾ*, ed. Maẓāhir Muṣaffā, Tehran 1339/1961, ii/1; idem, *Riyāḍ al-ʿārifīn* Tehran 1344/1965; Shāhnawāz Khān Khʷāfī, *Bahāristān-i sukhan*, Madras 1958; Aḥmad ʿAlī Khān Sandīlawī, *Tadhkira-yi makhzan al-gharāʾib*, ed. Muḥammad Bāḳir, Lahore 1970, ii; Muḥammad Ḳudrat Allāh Gopāmawī, *Natāʾidj al-afkār*, Bombay 1336/1957; Muḥammad Muḥīṭ Ṭabāṭabāʾī, *Saḥābī Astarābādī*, in *Armaghān*, xiii/9 (November-December 1932); *Lughat-nāma-yi Dihkhudā*, xv/4; Browne, *LHP*, iv; Muḥammad ʿAlī Mudarris Tabrīzī, *Rayḥānat al-adab*, Tabrīz 1328/1949, ii; Saʿīd Nafīsī, *Tārīkh-i naẓm u nathr dar Īrān wa dar zabān-i Fārsī*, Tehran 1363/1984, i-ii; Dhabīh Allāh Ṣafā, *Tārīkh-i adabiyyāt dar Īrān*, Tehran 1367/1988, v/2; idem, *Gandj-i sukhan*[3], Tehran 1368/1989, iii; Rypka, *Hist. of Iranian literature*, Abū Ṭālib Raḍawī-nizhād, *Čahār-ṣad shāʿir-i barguzīda-yi Pārsī-gūy*, Tehran 1369/1990. (Munibur Rahman)

SAHARA [see al-ṢAḤRĀʾ].

SAHĀRANPŪR, a city of northern India in the uppermost part of the Ganges-Djamnā Doʾāb (lat. 29° 57′ N., long. 77° 33′ E.), now in the extreme northwestern tip of the Uttar Pradesh State of the Indian Union.

It was founded in *ca.* 740/1340, in the reign of Muḥammad b. Tughluḳ [*q.v.*] and was named after a local Muslim saint, Shāh Haran Čishtī. The city and district suffered severely during the invasion of Tīmūr; in 932/1526 Bābur traversed them on his way to Pānīpat, and some local Mughal colonies trace their origin to his followers. Muslim influence gained much by the proselytising zeal of ʿAbd al-Ḳuddūs, who ruled the district until the reign of Akbar. Under Akbar, it was the centre of a *sarkār* and important enough to be a mint place. In the reigns of Djahāngīr and Shāh Djahān, Sahāranpūr was a favourite summer resort of the court, owing to the coolness of its climate and the abundance of game in its neighbourhood. Nūr Djahān had a palace in the village of Nūrnagar, which perpetuates her name, and the royal hunting seat, Pādshāh Maḥall, was built for Shāh Djahān. After the death of Awrangzīb, the district suffered severely from the inroads of the Sikhs, who massacred Hindūs and Muslims indiscriminately, until, in 1716, they were temporarily crushed by the imperial Mughal authority. The upper Doʾāb then passed into the hands of the Sayyids of Bārha [*q.v.* in Suppl.], and on their fall in 1721 into those of several favourites. In 1754 Aḥmad Shāh Durrānī conferred it on the Rohilla, Nadjīb Khān [*q.v.*], as a reward for his services at the battle of Kotila. Before his death, in 1770, it was overrun by Sikhs and

Marāt́hās. His son Ḍābiṭ K͟hān revolted from Dihlī, but was reconciled, and his son G͟hulām Ḳādir, who succeeded him in 1785, established a strong government and dealt firmly with the Sikhs. He was a coarse and brutal chief, and in 1788 he blinded the emperor S͟hāh ʿĀlam, being subsequently justly mutilated and put to death by Sindhya. Sahāranpūr remained nominally in the hands of the Marāt́hās, but actually in those of the Sikhs, until its conquest and occupation by the British after the fall of ʿAlīgaŕh and the battle of Dihlī in 1803. Sahāranpūr was only slightly affected by the Sepoy Mutiny of 1857-8, even though this last broke out in the nearby city of Meerut [see MĪRAT́H], with order restored by a Gurkha force by the end of 1857.

It is now the administrative centre of a District of the same name, a meeting-place for roads and railways and a centre for agriculture and food processing. The population of the city was 225,700 in 1971; at the opening of the 20th century, a majority of this urban population was Muslim, but many of these migrated to Pakistan after 1947.

Bibliography: Abu 'l-Faḍl ʿAllāmī, *Āʾīn-i-Akbarī*, tr. Blochmann and Jarrett, Calcutta 1873-94; *Tūzuk-i-D͟jahāngīrī*, tr. Rogers and Beveridge, London 1909; ʿAbd al-Ḥamīd Lāhūrī, *Pād͟s͟hāh-nāma*, Calcutta 1867-8; W. Irvine, *The later Mug͟hals*, Calcutta 1922; *Imperial gazetteer of India*², xxi, 378-9.

(T.W. HAIG-[C.E. BOSWORTH])

AL-**SAHBĀʾ**, is the name of a wādī in the al-K͟hard͟j [*q.v.*] district of Nad͟jd [*q.v.* and see AL-ḤAWṬA], the central province of modern Saudi Arabia. The word itself is the feminine of an adjective of the form *afʿalu*, but it has no comparative or superlative signification (Wright, *Grammar*, i, 185A, cf. AL-ṢAḤRĀʾ). It is related to *sahb*, pl. *suhub* "desert, level country". The large valley runs eastwards into the Gulf basin across the sand desert of al-Dahnāʾ [*q.v.*] and, north of Yabrīn, of al-D͟jāfūra (see the map in AL-ʿARAB, D͟JAZĪRAT).

Bibliography: British Admiralty, *A handbook of Arabia*, London 1922; J.G. Lorimer, *Gazetteer of the Persian Gulf, ʾOman and Central Arabia*, Calcutta 1908-15, repr. Farnborough 1970; Central Office of Information, *The Arab states of the Persian Gulf and South-East Arabia*, London 1959; U.S. Geological Survey, *Western Persian Gulf*, Map I-208B (1958); R.E. Cheesman, *The deserts of Jafura and Jabrin*, in *GJ*, lxv, 112-41.

(E. VAN DONZEL)

SAḤBĀN WĀʾIL, the name given to an orator and poet of the tribe of Wāʾil, "whose seductive eloquence has passed into a proverb and who, it is said, whilst addressing an assembly for half-a-day, never used the same word twice" (Kazimirski, *Dictionnaire*, i, 1057; see *LʿA* and the other lexica). Speaking of the random effects of chance, whereby some person became a household word whereas others, equally meritorious, do not, al-D͟jāḥiẓ (*Ḥayawān*, ii, 104), cites Saḥbān Wāʾil, who was eclipsed by his contemporary Ibn al-Ḳirriyya, murdered by al-Ḥad͟jd͟jād͟j in 84/703 (*loc. cit.*, n. 5).

In his eulogy of the book (*al-kitāb*), the same al-D͟jāḥiẓ (*ibid.*, i, 39) says: "If you wish, it can be more eloquent for you than Saḥbān Wāʾil or more tongue-tied than Bāḳil" (an adolescent), echoing a proverb which figures in all the collections, where it is said "more convincing (*ablag͟h*) than Saḥbān Wāʾil, whereas one says "clearer (*afṣaḥ*) than Ḳuss b. Sāʿida [*q.v.*]" (cf. al-Nuwayrī, *Nihāya*, Cairo 1924, ii, 119).

Al-Ṭabarī, *Taʾrīk͟h*, ii, 1257, attributes to him seven verses in which he praises the courage of the army of Ḳutayba b. Muslim (49-96/669-715 [*q.v.*]) in the course of the conquest of Afg͟hānistān between 89/705 and 90/706, notably, at the time of the conquest of K͟hoḳand [*q.v.*], which would indicate that Saḥbān was still alive in the caliphate of al-Walīd I (86-96/705-15).

Bibliography: Given in the article.

(T. FAHD)

ṢĀḤIB (A.), "companion", a term with various senses in Islamic usage. Formally it is an active participle of the transitive verb *ṣaḥiba yaṣḥabu* "to associate with", but semantically a pure noun; it thus cannot govern an object in the accusative. The most common plural is *aṣḥāb*, of which the double plural (*d͟jamʿ al-d͟jamʿ*) *aṣāḥīb* is given in the dictionaries, while its "diminutive of the plural" (*taṣg͟hīr al-d͟jamʿ*) *uṣayḥāb* is attested (Wensinck, *Concordance*, s.v.). Other plurals include *ṣaḥb* (a collective noun), *ṣiḥāb* and *ṣuḥbān*, the verbal nouns *ṣuḥba* and *ṣaḥāba* are also employed as plurals (collectives). For the Companions of the Prophet one finds *ṣaḥb, aṣḥāb*, and specifically *ṣaḥāba* [*q.v.*], the last of which yields the designation of the individual, *ṣaḥābī*, by *nisba* formation (a procedure not uncommon with collective nouns). In the vocative the truncated form (*tark͟hīm*) *yā ṣāḥi* for *yā ṣāḥibī* "O my companion" is well attested. The fem. is *ṣāḥiba*, with the plural *ṣawāḥib* and the double plural *ṣawāḥibāt* (cf. Wensinck, *Concordance*, s.v.).

Ṣāḥib, in its various semantic transformations, has produced a considerable number of titles, allusive names, and some technical terms, mostly by being the first term in a genitive construct. The idea of "companion" is specialised in cases where one speaks of the *ṣāḥib* of a poet, soothsayer, or orator, meaning his *alter ego* among the *d͟jinn* from whom he receives (some of) his inspiration (also called *s͟hayṭān* [*q.v.*], *raʾī*, and *tābiʿ*); this is a pre-Islamic notion, but one that lives on in Islamic times as a literary fiction (e.g. in the *Risālat al-tawābiʿ wa 'l-zawābiʿ* of Ibn S͟huhayd [*q.v.*]). Still with the meaning "companion", the term has sometimes been used to refer to the counsellors of a ruler, thus in Ibn al-Muḳaffaʿ's *Risāla fī 'l-ṣaḥāba* (see Ch. Pellat, *Ibn al-Muqaffaʿ, mort vers 140/757, "conseilleur" du Calife* [Paris 1976], 88-9). The plural *aṣḥāb* followed by the name of a locality in the genitive serves to refer to people who are companions in that particular place; thus Ḳurʾānic phrases like *aṣḥāb al-d͟janna, aṣḥāb al-nār* and *aṣḥāb al-kahf*.

In a different specialisation *ṣāḥib* may acquire the meaning of "disciple", because the student is a constant companion of his master. Thus *al-Ṣāḥibān* in Ḥanafī sources refers to the "two disciples" of Abū Ḥanīfa [*q.v.*], i.e. Abū Yūsuf [*q.v.*] and Muḥammad al-S͟haybānī [see AL-S͟HAYBĀNĪ]. Specifically, this term is used in Ṣūfism to designate the "adept" as opposed to the *maṣḥūb*, the "master", their relationship being called *ṣuḥba* (see e.g. W.C. Chittick, *The Sufi path of knowledge*, Albany 1989, 270-4). The plural *aṣḥāb* followed by a personal name in the genitive is, alongside the *nisba* formation, the normal way of expressing the "adherents of so-and-so" or the "members of his school": *aṣḥāb Abī Ḥanīfa = al-Ḥanafiyya*. Al-Fayyūmī (d. 770/1368) considers this last usage figurative (*mad͟jāz*), presumably because the school members are mostly not contemporary with the founder (*al-Miṣbāḥ al-munīr*, Beirut 1398/1978, 394).

In one of its semantic developments, the term *ṣāḥib* becomes more general: "partner", "match" (sometimes "adversary"), and finally "someone (or something) endowed with s.th. or characterised by s.th." In this last sense it ends up being synonymous with *d͟hū* (cf. *ṣāḥib al-ḥāl = d͟hu 'l-ḥāl*, "the noun modified by a circumstantial accusative"). Here belong the rather popular allusive names, such as *ṣāḥib al-ḥūt* "the man with the fish = Jonah (see Sūra LXVIII, 48, and cf. the synonymous *dhu 'l-nūn* in Sūra XXI, 87); *ṣāḥib al-ḥimār* "the man with the donkey" = the Khāridjite rebel Abū Yazīd al-Nukkārī [*q.v.*] (cf. *dhu 'l-ḥimār*, nickname of the Yemeni pseudo-prophet Ayhaba at the time of the Prophet, and for the symbolism of riding a donkey, see C. Brockelmann, *Geschichte der islamischen Völker und Staaten*, Munich and Berlin ²1943, Eng. tr. *History of the Islamic peoples*, London 1949, 49); *ṣāḥib al-nāḳa* "the man with the she-camel" and *ṣāḥib al-shāma* "the man with the mole" = the two Ismāʿīlī agitators Yaḥyā b. Zikrawayh and al-Ḥusayn b. Zikrawayh (see F. Daftary, *The Ismāʿīlīs, their history and doctrine*, Cambridge 1990, 132). This type of cognomen seems to be particularly common with religious rebels and "liberators" and has the air of being a code and/or taboo name. This type may also occur in the plural: *aṣḥāb al-fīl* "those with the elephant" (Sūra CV, 2). In the same semantic category belongs the plural *aṣḥāb* followed by an abstract noun in the genitive to denote adherents of a specific concept: *aṣḥāb al-tanāsukh* "the believers in metempsychosis", *aṣḥāb al-raʾy* "the proponents of juridical discretion" as opposed to the *aṣḥāb al-ḥadīth* "the proponents of (the exclusive use) of Prophetic Tradition." The last example shows that, even with a concrete noun (*ḥadīth* being a corpus of texts), the resulting compound may still belong in this category, with "belief in", "defence of", or a similar notion being understood. Thus e.g. *ṣāḥib al-dīk* and *ṣāḥib al-kalb* "the advocate of the rooster" and "the advocate of the dog" (in al-Djāḥiẓ, *al-Ḥayawān*, passim); obviously, these expressions could also mean the "owners" of the rooster and the dog.

By narrowing the semantic field just mentioned one arrives at the notion of "possessor, owner, lord, chief." In the legal sense of ownership one finds it in *ṣāḥib al-bayt* "the owner of the house" and similarly in *ṣāḥib al-dayn* "debtor." In the sense of "chief" it forms part of the designation of a good many administrative offices: *ṣāḥib al-djaysh* "army chief", *ṣāḥib al-barīd* "chief of intelligence", *ṣāḥib al-shurṭa* "police chief", *ṣāḥib al-sūḳ* "market inspector" (= tr. of Grk. *agoranomos*, later on called *muḥtasib*, cf. J. Schacht, *An introduction to Islamic law*, Oxford 1964, 25), *ṣāḥib al-dīwān*, or Persian *ṣāḥib-dīwān* "chief financial administrator under the Īlkhāns, on a par with the vizier." Somewhat removed, but still in the same category, the author of a book may be called *ṣāḥib al-kitāb*. Used with the title of a famous book, this would again result in an allusive name: *ṣāḥib al-Kashshāf* "the author of the *Kashshāf*", i.e. al-Zamakhsharī, author of the Ḳurʾānic commentary of that title.

Bibliography: Given in the article.

(W.P. HEINRICHS)

ṢĀḤIB ATĀ OGHULLARÎ, the modern designation for the descendants of the Rūm Saldjūḳid vizier Fakhr al-Dīn ʿAlī (d. 687/1288), known as Ṣāḥib Atā. Literary sources record two sons of Fakhr al-Dīn, Tādj al-Dīn Ḥusayn, the eldest (Ibn Bībī, ed. M.Th. Houtsma, *Histoire des Seldjoucides d'Asie Mineure*, Leiden 1902, iii, 337) and Nuṣrat al-Dīn (Aḳsarāʾī, ed. Osman Turan, *Musāmarat al-akhbār*, Ankara 1944, 74). An anonymous *Tawārīkh-i āl-i Saldjūḳ* completed after 765/1363 also mentions a daughter (F.N. Uzluk, *Anadolu Selçukluları devleti tarihi*, Ankara 1952, *facs.* text 70). The enduring influence of the family in the western borderlands of the Rūm Saldjūḳid domains dates from the years following the accession of Rukn al-Dīn Ḳilič Arslan [see ḲÎLÎDJ ARSLAN IV] to the sultanate in 644/1246, when the principality of the March (*imārat-i wilāyat-i udj*) was bestowed on Tādj al-Dīn and Nuṣrat al-Dīn, with Kütahya [*q.v.*], Sanduḳlu, Ghurghurum and Aḳshehir as an appanage. (Aḳsarāʾī, 74). The brothers evidently did not retain these lands. However, in *ca.* 670/1271 they again jointly received the commandership (*serleshkerī* = *subashîlîḳ*) of Ladîḳ, Khonas and Ḳaraḥiṣār Devele (Ibn Bībī, *op. cit.*, iv, 308). The last of these is evidently the same as Afyūn Ḳaraḥiṣār [*q.v.*], which remained in the possession of the family into the following century.

In 676/1277 both brothers lost their lives at the battle of Altuntash against the rebel Djimri [see ḲARAMĀN-OGHULLARÎ) who, for a while, occupied Ḳaraḥiṣār Devele (Aḳsarāʾī, 151). However, after his defeat and death the town evidently returned to the possession of the family of Ṣāḥib Atā. The anonymous *Tawārīkh-i āl-i Saldjūḳ* refers to a victory in 686/1287 of the Germiyānids [see GERMIYĀN-OGHULLARÎ] over the lord of Ḳaraḥiṣār, the son of Ṣāḥib Atā's daughter (Uzluk, *loc. cit.*). In his list of Turkish principalities submitting to the *noyan* Čoban [*q.v.*] after the accession of the Ilkhānid Abū Saʿīd in 716/1316, Aḳsarāʾī, 311, mentions Ḳaraḥiṣār Devele as being in the possession of the "grandsons of Fakhr al-Dīn". Al-ʿUmarī too, in about 730/1330, notes that "Ḳarasār" belonged to "Ibn al-Ṣayib" (= al-Ṣāḥib) who possessed, in addition, a thousand villages and four thousand cavalrymen. To defend his possessions against Čoban's son, Timurtash, he had sought the protection of the lord of Germiyān through marriage to his daughter (*Masālik al-abṣār*, cited by Aḥmed Tewḥīd, in *TOEM*, 1st series, ii [1327/1909], 563 ff.). An inscription over the portal of the Ḳubbeli Djāmiʿ in Afyūn Ḳaraḥiṣār, bearing the date 731/1331, names the founder of the mosque as the "great lord" (*al-mawlā al-muʿaẓẓam*) Aḥmad b. Muḥammad, who was presumably the "Ibn al-Ṣāḥib" to whom al-ʿUmarī refers. An inscription dated 742/1341 on the Ulu Djāmiʿ in Afyūn Ḳaraḥiṣār refers to the same person as "Nuṣrat al-Dawla wa 'l-Dīn Aḥmad", describing him as "the progeny of the great viziers" (*sulālat al-wuzarāʾ al-ʿiẓām*) (Aḥmed Tewḥīd, in *TTEM*, 1st series, xi [1341/1923], 357). It is conceivable that this Aḥmad b. Muḥammad was the son of the "Shams al-Dīn Muḥammad son of (Nuṣrat al-Dīn?) Ḥasan son of (Fakhr al-Dīn) ʿAlī (Ṣāḥib Atā) son of Ḥusayn" who is buried in the Sahip Ata Mausoleum in Konya (Aḥmed Tewḥīd, *loc. cit.*).

Evidence of the family disappears in the second half of the 8th/14th century, but in the Ottoman period Afyūn Ḳaraḥiṣār continued to be known as Ṣāḥib'in Ḳaraḥiṣārî (Neshrī, ed. F.R. Unat and M.A. Köymen, *Kitāb-i Cihānnümā*, Ankara 1949, i, 65) or, from the 10th/16th century, as Ḳaraḥiṣār-i Ṣāḥib ("Ṣāḥib's Ḳaraḥiṣār").

Bibliography: Given in the article. See also İ.H. Uzunçarşılı, *Anadolu beylikleri*, Ankara 1969, 150-2; Cl. Cahen, *Pre-Ottoman Turkey*, London 1968.

(C. IMBER)

ṢĀḤIB AL-BĀB (A.), "high chamberlain", a title borne, in Fāṭimid Egypt, by a man of the sword counted amongst the first rank of *amīrs* ("*amīrs* bearing a collar", *al-umarāʾ al-muṭawwaḳūn*). This official ranked next after the vizier, and his office, or "lesser vizierate", was in fact the stepping-stone to the vizierate for Yānis al-Rūmī, Riḍwān al-Walakhshī and Abu 'l-Ashbāl Ḍirghām b. ʿĀmir. The greater part of our information on this official duties comes from Ibn al-Ṭuwayr: he was president of the tribunal considering petitions and requests when the vizier was not a "man of the sword", and he sat at the golden door of the palace in order to register complaints and pleas. When the vizier was a "man of the sword" and presided in person, the *ṣāḥib al-bāb*'s role as simple assistant was reminiscent of that of the *ḥādjib* amongst the Mamlūks.

The institution did not exist among the first Fāṭimids, and Ḥusām al-Mulk Aftakīn, in the time of the vizierate for al-Afḍal, was the first *ṣāḥib al-bāb* to be mentioned in the sources (beginning of the 6th/12th century). The *ṣāḥib al-bāb* was addressed as *al-Muʿaẓẓam*; the first to be thus called was the *amīr* Abu 'l-Muẓaffar Khumurtāsh al-Ḥāfiẓī in *ca.* 535/1141. His deputy, to whom he delegated the important office (called *al-niyāba al-sharīfa*) of assigning their places to envoys accredited to the court, was generally a legal figure or a religious dignitary, whom one addressed as ʿAdiyy al-Mulk. The *ṣāḥib al-bāb* occupied an important place in the processions forming part of the official ceremonies and the caliphal receptions of the later Fāṭimids [see MAWĀKIB. 1], a ceremonial occasion which Ibn al-Ṭuwayr [*q.v.*] describes in detail.

Bibliography: Ibn al-Ṭuwayr, *Nuzhat al-muklatayn fī akhbār al-dawlatayn*, ed. A.F. Sayyid, Beirut 1992, 120-8; Ibn al-Furāt, *Taʾrīkh*, ed. Ḥasan al-Shammāʿ, Baṣra 1967-70, iv/1, 136-7, 147; Ḳalḳashandī, *Ṣubḥ al-aʿshā*, iii, 478, 484; Maḳrīzī, *Khiṭaṭ*, i, 403, 461; idem, *Ittiʿāẓ al-ḥunafāʾ*, iii, 336, 342. (AYMAN F. SAYYID)

ṢĀḤIB GIRĀY KHĀN I, khān of the Crimea (939-58/1532-51) and khān of Ḳazan (927-30/1521-4), son of Mengli Girāy Khān I [*q.v.*] and his wife Nūr Dewlet, mother through an earlier marriage of Muḥammad Emīn (d. 925/1519), the last khān of Ḳazan [*q.v.*] in direct line from Ulugh Muḥammad, khān of the Golden Horde (1419-24, 1427-38). Half-brother of Meḥmed Girāy Khān I (920-9/1515-23 [*q.v.*]), Ṣāḥib Girāy was instrumental in this latter khān's new hostile policy against Muscovy, their father Mengli Girāy's traditional ally. In 927/1521, Ṣāḥib Girāy was able with the khān's help to drive away the Russian-backed candidate, Shāh ʿAlī, and to occupy the throne of Ḳazan, thus stressing the Girāy family's claims to the heritage of the Golden Horde. In concurrence with Meḥmed Girāy Khān I, he subsequently engaged in a struggle with Muscovy for the possession of the steppe region, which was to come to an end only 31 years later with Tsar Ivan IV's (1533-84) destruction of that khānate. In 929/1523, the brothers attacked the khānate of Astrakhān [*q.v.*], from where they ousted Ḥusayn Khān, Muscovy's candidate. In the same year, they launched a major campaign against Grand Prince Vasiliy III of Muscovy (1505-33). In the following year, as Vasiliy III prepared an expedition against Ḳazan, Ṣāḥib Girāy abdicated from the throne of Ḳazan, designated his nephew Ṣafā Girāy (first reign 930-7/1524-31) as his successor and took refuge with the Ottomans. The following eight years, Ṣāḥib Girāy stayed in Istanbul as a guest and trusted friend of sultan Süleymān Ḳānūnī (1520-66 [*q.v.*]). He not only participated in that sultan's campaigns, e.g. in Hungary in 1532, but he also became intimately acquainted with Ottoman institutions and culture.

After both the Ottoman-backed Seʿādet Girāy Khān I (1524-May 1532) and his nephew Islām Girāy Khān I (May-Sept. 1532 [*q.v.*]), who had found support with parts of the Crimean tribal aristocracy, had renounced the khānship, the Ottoman sultan confirmed with a *firmān* (reference to this is made in a document, the text and translation of which is given in *Khanat de Crimée*, 121-5; transcription in Gökbilgin 1973, 55-6) Ṣāḥib Girāy as the new khān and the former khān, Islām Girāy, as his *ḳalgha* [*q.v.*] or heir apparent. Accompanied by a large detachment of Ottoman troops (*ḳapï ḳulu*), among them 360 artillerymen (*topču* and *tüfenkčï*) and 1,000 Janissaries, the new khān received the homage of the representatives of the Crimean noble clans (*ḳaraču beys*) at the mouth of the Dnepr (Özü [see ÖZI]) river. He was the first Crimean khān to receive the *segbān aḳčesi* or accession money.

Obviously, the new khān had not been accepted by the entire Crimean noble families. An undated letter of a Crimean nobleman to the Ottoman sultan, probably written towards the end of 1533 or at the beginning of 1534 (See *Khanat de Crimée*, 125-7), accuses the khān of not respecting the customs and traditions of the past.

In the same letter, the sultan is asked to designate a new khān, arguing that the power struggle between Ṣāḥib Girāy Khān and his *ḳalgha* Islām Girāy, each supported by partisans from the noble clans, was threatening to ruin the country. Ṣāḥib Girāy's troubles with his nephew Islām Girāy continued until he succeeded, in 1537, in having him killed by Bāḳī Beg, one of the leaders of the eminent Crimean *ḳaraču* clan of the Manghïts and subsequently Ṣāḥib Girāy's most dangerous opponent. After this incident, the Crimean nobles who had been partisans of Islām Girāy paid allegiance to the khān.

Ṣāḥib Girāy Khān was now free to participate as a much-honoured ally in the Ottoman campaign against Moldavia (1538), which ended with the establishment of the *sandjaḳ* of Aḳkerman comprising the territories of Budjaḳ [*q.v.*], between the rivers Prut and Dnestr, and the neighbourhood of the former Tatar fortress of Özü/Očakov (cf. G. Veinstein, *L'occupation ottomane d'Očakov et le problème de la frontière lituano-tatare, 1538-1544*, in *Passé turco-tatar–Présent soviétique. Études offertes à A. Bennigsen*, Louvain-Paris 1986, 123-55). In the following year, the khān turned his attention towards his unruly Čerkes neighbours. Owing to the rugged terrain, however, the campaign was not successful, nor was another one in 1542.

In winter 1539/40, the khān sent an army of 30,000 men on a raid against Muscovy, under the command of the *ḳalgha*, his son Emīn Girāy. In winter 1541, Ṣāḥib Girāy in person led an—unsuccessful—campaign into Muscovite territory, but then finally managed to kill the Manghït Bāḳī Beg, associated with the Noghays [*q.v.*] of the steppe who represented the most imminent threat to the Crimean Tatars and their pasture lands outside the peninsula. In 1546, Ṣāḥib Girāy's firearms dealt a severe blow to the Noghays' pre-eminence in the steppe. In 1549, he went on a punitive campaign against the khān of Astrakhān in an effort to preserve Crimean political claims in that region.

In spite of his excellent relations with the Ottoman court, at least during the first half of his rule, Ṣāḥib Girāy proved to be more than a puppet ruler in the service of sultan Süleymān's power game in the Black Sea area, or, on a different level, the preservation of the sultan's peaceful policy towards Muscovy in view of his trade interests. The khān's main political objective remained the containment of his northern neighbour. In this aim, he made regular inroads into that territory.

Both the intervention of the Shīrīn bey on behalf of the powerful Crimean aristocracy and the suspicion of Ottoman court circles in regard to Ṣāḥib Girāy's independent political action led to the khān's final downfall. Under the pretext of investing Dewlet Girāy [*q.v.*], another "hostage" prince at the Sublime Porte, with the k͟hānship of Ḳazan, the Ottoman sultan sent Dewlet Girāy with an Ottoman detachment to the peninsula, where he was able to win general support (Ramaḍān 958/Sept. 1551). Ṣāḥib Girāy subsequently was murdered in the fortress of Ṭamān, together with his sons, by a partisan of his nephew and successor Dewlet Girāy, who was to become the most powerful k͟hān of the 16th century.

Ṣāḥib Girāy K͟hān was considered a courageous and resourceful, though harsh ruler, both by his contemporaries and by later chroniclers. In spite of his marked taste for Ottoman civilisation, he pursued Crimean political interests by strengthening the Čingizid steppe tradition—the k͟hān's power against that of the leaders of the tribal aristocracy (İnalcık, *passim*). It was most probably in the reign of Ṣāḥib Girāy K͟hān that the seat of power was transferred from Eski Ḳïrïm (Solg͟hat) to Bāg͟hče Sarāy [*q.v.*]. Diplomatic evidence seems to indicate that from 1533 onwards, Bāg͟hče Sarāy was the place where the k͟hāns had their palace and where they received foreign representatives (Fisher, *Crimean Tatars*, 29-30). ʿAbd ül-Ghaffār (*ʿUmdet ül-tewārīk͟h*, 101-2) mentions his building activities, a mosque, a medrese, palaces, a double bath and shops. The cultural life of the Crimean peninsula took a decisive turn towards Ottomanisation in the spheres of the military, of institutions and of the arts.

The most detailed source on both political and cultural life under Ṣāḥib Girāy K͟hān's reign is *Tārīk͟h-i Ṣāḥib Girāy K͟hān*, the first chronicle of Crimean Tatar history as such, completed in 960/1553, shortly after the k͟hān's death, by Ḳāysūnī-zāde Meḥmed Nidāʾī, known as Remmāl K͟hʷād͟ja, the k͟hān's physician and astrologer.

Bibliography: The best study on Ṣāḥib Girāy K͟hān is by H. İnalcık, *The Khan and the tribal aristocracy: the Crimean Khanate under Sahib Giray I*, in *Harvard Ukrainian Studies*, iii-iv (1979-80), 445-66, which is partly based on Remmāl K͟hʷād͟ja's work; the text was published by Ö. Gökbilgin, Ankara 1973; idem, *1532-1577 yılları arasında Kırım hanlığı'nın siyasi durumu*, Ankara 1973; Ḳïrïmī ʿAbd ül-G͟haffār used Remmāl's work in his *ʿUmdet ül-tewārīk͟h*, compl. in 1161/1748, ed. by Ned͟jīb ʿĀṣim, in *TOEM*, *ʿilāveler*, Istanbul 1343/1924, at 99-112; Ḥalīm Girāy, *Gülbün-i k͟hānān*, Istanbul 1287/1870, 14-18; missives from the reign of Ṣāḥib Girāy K͟hān were publ. in A. Bennigsen *et alii* (eds.), *Le khanat de Crimée dans les archives du musée du palais de Topkapı*, Paris 1978, 121-33, cf. also 328-30.

(B. Kellner-Heinkele)

ṢĀḤIB ḲIRĀN (A. and P.), a title meaning "Lord of the (auspicious) conjunction". *Ḳirān* means a conjunction of the planets, *ḳirān al-saʿdayn* [see AL-SAʿDĀN] a conjunction of the two auspicious planets (Jupiter and Venus), and *ḳirān al-naḥsayn* a conjunction of the two inauspicious planets (Saturn and Mars). In the title, the word refers, of course, to the former only. The Persian *i* of the *iḍāfa* is omitted, as in *ṣāḥib-dil*, by *fakk-i iḍāfa*. The title was first assumed by the Amīr Tīmūr, who is said to have been born under a fortunate conjunction, but with whom its assumption was, of course, an afterthought. After his death, poets and flatterers occasionally applied it to lesser sovereigns, even to so insignificant a ruler as the South Indian Burhān II Niẓām S͟hāh of Aḥmadnagar [see NIẒĀM S͟HĀHĪS], but it was officially assumed by Tīmūr's distant descendant, the Mug͟hal emperor S͟hāh D͟jahān [*q.v.*], who styled himself *Ṣāḥib Ḳirān-i-T͟hānī* "the second Lord of the Conjunction".

Ṣāḥib-Ḳirān was also, in Persia, where it has since been corrupted into *Ḳirān* or *Ḳrān*, the name of a coin of 1000 *dīnārs*, the tenth part of a *tūmān*.

Bibliography: S͟haraf al-Dīn ʿAlī Yazdī, *Ẓafar-nāma*, ed. F. Tauer, Prague 1937-50; Muḥammad Ḳāsim Firis͟hta, *Guls͟han-i Ibrāhīmī*, lith. Bombay 1832; ʿAbd al-Ḥamīd Lāhawrī, *Pāds͟hāh-nāma*, Bibliotheca Indica ed., Calcutta 1866-72; *Burhān-i-ḳāṭiʿ*, s.v. *ḳirān*.

(T.W. Haig)

ṢĀḤIB AL-MADĪNA (A.), an administrative function found in mediaeval Islamic Spain.

Documentation for this is almost exclusively found in regard to al-Andalus. The Granadan jurist Ibn Sahl [*q.v.*], in his *al-Aḥkām al-kubrā*, mentions it amongst the six traditional functions (*k͟huṭṭa* or "magistratures") which gave their holders the right to pronounce judgements (the *ḳāḍī*, the *ṣāḥib al-s͟hurṭa*, the *ṣ. al-maẓālim*, the *ṣ. al-radd*, the *ṣ. al-madīna* and the *ṣ. al-sūḳ*). According to the Valencian Ibn al-Abbār [*q.v.*], there existed until the 7th/13th century two distinct magistratures, sc. the *ṣāḥib al-madīna* and the *ṣ. al-s͟hurṭa*. In the 8th/14th century, Ibn Saʿīd [*q.v.*] (in the great, later compilation of Andalusian culture by al-Maḳḳarī, the *Nafḥ al-ṭīb*), and in the following one, Ibn K͟haldūn [*q.v.*], in his *Muḳaddima*, also mention the title of *ṣ. al-madīna*, but make it the designation of the chief of the police or *s͟hurṭa* in Muslim Spain. However, the Sevillan Ibn ʿAbdūn [*q.v.*], who in his treatise on *ḥisba*, written towards the end of the 5th/11th century, passes in review the administrative offices in the capital at the end of the period of the Taifas and that of the first Almoravids, does not mention it. Nor does it appear in the detailed list of functions given by the Mag͟hribī al-Wans͟harīsī [*q.v.*] in his *K. al-Wilāyāt*, even though this last is in part inspired by the Andalusian tradition.

Nevertheless, the Arabic sources on al-Andalus amply attest the existence of this "magistrature of the town" from the reign of the Umayyad *amīr* of Cordova ʿAbd al-Raḥmān II (206-38/822-52), who is said, according to Ibn Saʿīd, "to have separated the *wilāyat al-sūḳ* from the functions of the *s͟hurṭa* called *wilāyat al-madīna*", until the crisis of the caliphate in the early 5th/11th century. The names of a good number of its holders are known to us. Ibn Ḥayyān's [*q.v.*] *Muḳtabis*, which used the *Annals* of ʿĪsā b. Aḥmad al-Rāzī, an author contemporary with the caliphate, testifies to the existence of two *wilāyat al-madīnas*, one for Cordova and one for the new capital of Madīnat al-Zahrāʾ. The importance of the persons holding this first charge or dignity appears from the duties entrusted to them under the amīrate and the caliphate. These were diverse, and could involve policing and public order, justice, the levying of taxes and even leading armies, all of which leads one to think that there were no strictly determined duties but rather, on a basis difficult to determine for the city of Cordova, a nexus of functions varying in extent according to the confidence placed in the holder, especially as this last often piled up for himself other offices (was it as *ḳāʾid* or *wazīr*, or as *ṣāḥib al-madīna*, that such a person holding these offices at the same time might lead a military expedition?).

Under the caliph al-Ḥakam II, the detailed descriptions of the protocollary order of official ceremonies during the years 360-4/971-5 place the *wazīr*, *kātib* and *ṣāḥib al-madīna* of Cordova D͟jaʿfar b. ʿUt͟hmān al-Muṣḥafī immediately on the caliph's right; but since this concerns the "strong man" at this moment in the régime, it is hard to discern exactly under which title he held this preponderant role. It is nevertheless certain that the post was at this time a lofty one; on al-

Ḥakam's death in 366/976, al-Muṣḥafī designated the dead ruler's youngest son, Hishām II, as caliph, himself assumed the office of *ḥādjib* (which had not been filled for several years) and designated his own son *ṣāḥib al-madīna* of Cordova. A little later, in his brilliant ascension to the heights of power, Muhammad Ibn Abī ʿĀmir (the future al-Manṣūr), in the first place stripped the latter of his post in order to occupy it personally, and then eliminated al-Muṣḥafī himself and replaced him as *ḥādjib*. Afterwards, under the ʿĀmirid dictatorship, the function and title lost their importance. However, it is known that, at this time, a high personage, a cousin of al-Manṣūr's, held the title of *ṣāḥib al-madīnatayn* ("in charge of the two cities", i.e. Cordova and, it is thought, the official ʿĀmirid centre of al-Madīna al-Zāhira rather than the caliphal one of Madīnat al-Zahrāʾ, which had no importance in practice by this time).

The fact that the office seems to have existed only in al-Andalus poses a problem. It has been seen above that ʿAbd al-Raḥmān II is supposed to have created the office. J. Vallvé, in a detailed study of the history of this function under the Umayyads, has set forth the hypothesis that the *ṣāḥib al-madīna* could derive from the *comes civitatis* of the Roman and Visigothic period. The idea ought to be approached with prudence. Certainly, the sources bear witness to the existence, during the Umayyad amīrate, of an office of *ḳūmis* [*q.v.*] entrusted to a Christian, who originally had jurisdiction over the Mozarab community but who was at times the recipient of the sovereign's confidence and given various functions, including the command of the guard, the *kitāba* and the collection of taxes, even involving those from the Muslims. But the pieces of evidence adduced by Vallvé himself allow us to aver that, under ʿAbd al-Raḥmān II, there existed contemporaneously a *ḳūmis* of the Christians—for whom there are still some indications in the 4th/10th century—and a *ṣāḥib al-madīna*, and this makes the idea—in any case not very acceptable in the context of the Iberian peninsula under Islam—of a transformation pure and simple of the *comes civitatis* into the *ṣāḥib al-madīna* difficult to accept. Nevertheless, can one exclude the possibility that the change in numerical proportion between Christian and Muslim populations in Cordova in favour of the second group might, in the 3rd/9th century, have led to the transfer to a newly-created office/magistrature involving administrative and judicial functions which had been, in practice, and in the context of the capital city, exercised until then by the "count" of the Christians?

Vallvé's hypothesis endeavours to take into account an exceptional case in al-Andalus, which is complicated by the fact that, after the Reconquista, in Aragon and Navarre at the end of the 11th and beginning of the 12th centuries, the Christians gave to the municipal magistrate appointed by the king for administration and for rendering justice in the towns, the title of *justicia*, but also that of *zalmedina*, obviously a linguistic calque of the Arabic *ṣāḥib al-madīna*. The same state of affairs is attested in Christian Toledo, where there existed in the 12th century a *zafalmedina*. This leads one to suppose that, in the political capitals of principalities reconquered by the Christians at the end of the period of the Taifas, there still existed an official in the Umayyad tradition exercising the duties of *ṣāḥib al-madīna* or bearing the title.

Bibliography: 1. Arabic sources. Ibn al-Abbār, *al-Ḥulla al-siyarāʾ*, ed. Ḥ. Muʾnis, Cairo 1963, i, 277; Ibn ʿAbdūn, *R. fi 'l-ḳaḍāʾ wa 'l-ḥisba*, ed. E. Lévi-Provençal, in *JA* (April-June 1934), repr. in *Trois traités hispaniques de ḥisba*, Cairo 1955; Ibn Ḥayyān, *Muḳtabas*, ed. ʿA. al-R. al-Ḥadjdjī, Beirut 1965, 77; Ibn ʿIdhārī, *Bayān*, ed. Lévi-Provençal, iii, Paris 1930, 54; Ibn Khaldun, *ʿIbar*, ed. (with the *Muḳaddima* and *Taʿrīf*) Kh. Shihāda, 8 vols., Beirut ²1988; Ibn al-Ḳūtiyya, *T. Iftitāḥ al-Andalus*, ed. and tr. J. Ribera, Madrid 1926, 85/70; Ibn Sahl, *al-Aḥkām al-kubrā*, partial ed. M. ʿA. al-W. Khallāf, in *Wathāʾiḳ fī shuʾūn al-ḥisba fi 'l-Andalus*, Cairo 1985; Ibn Saʿīd, *Mughrib*, ed. Sh. Ḍayf, Cairo 1953-5, i, 46; Khushanī, *Ḳuḍāt Ḳurṭuba*, ed. and tr. Ribera, Madrid 1914, 104-6; Maḳḳarī, *Nafḥ al-ṭīb*, ed. Iḥsān ʿAbbās, Beirut 1968, ii, 218.

2. Studies. R. Arié, *L'Espagne musulmane au temps des Nasrids* (*1232-1492*), Paris 1973; M. Barceló, *El califa patente: el ceremonial de Córdoba o la escenificacion del poder*, in *Estructuras y formas del poder en la historia*, Salamanca 1991, 51-71; P. Guichard and D. Menjot, *Les emprunts aux vaincus. Les conséquences de la "reconquête" sur l'organisation institutionelle des Etats castillan et aragonais au Moyen Age*, in M. Balard (ed.), *Etat et colonisations au Moyen Age*, Lyons 1989, 379-96; M. ʿA. al-W. Khallāf, *Ṣāḥib al-madīna fi 'l-Andalus*, in *Madjallat Maʿhad al-Tarbiya li 'l-Muʿallimīn, al-Kuwayt*, i (1979), 53-63; E. Lévi-Provençal, *L'Espagne musulmane au Xᵉ siècle; institutions et vie sociale*, Paris 1932, 88-94; idem, *Hist. Esp. mus.*, i, 259, iii, 158-9; G. Martinez-Gros, *L'idéologie omeyyade. La construction de la légitimité du califat de Cordoue (Xᵉ-XIᵉ siècles)*, Madrid 1992; M. Meouak, *Les structures politiques et administratives de l'Etat andalou à l'époque umayyade (milieu IIᵉ/VIIIᵉ-fin IVᵉ/Xᵉ siècles)*, unpubl. diss., Lyons 1989; L.G. de Valdeavellano, *Curso de historia de las instituciones españolas de los origines al final de la Edad Media*, ²Madrid 1970; J. Vallvé, *El zalmedina de Córdoba*, in *Al-Qantara*, ii/1-2 (1981), 277-318.

(Mohamed Meouak and P. Guichard)

ṢAḤĪFA (A.), lit. "a flat object, a plaque, a leaf", whence "a surface or material on which one can write", applied especially to fragments of the Ḳurʾān or *ḥadīth* or any other document of a solemn nature, whence finally, the written texts themselves. The pl. *ṣuḥuf* is uncommon for feminine nouns (but cf. *madīna*, pl. *mudun* "town", *safīna* pl. *sufun* "ship").

1. Linguistic usage.

The term appears contemporaneously with the advent of Islam, but must evidently have existed before then. In Ḳurʾān, XLIII, 71, *ṣiḥāf* also appears as a pl. of *ṣaḥfa*, with the sense "plates, platters", but *ṣuḥuf* appears eight times in the sacred text. Sūras XX, 133, and LXXXVII, 18, refer to "the ancient scriptures", in LXXXVII, 19, and LIII, 36-7, described more narrowly as those of Abraham and Moses, always in the perspective of a continued revelation, from the Creation to Muḥammad, without naming the latter. But it is clearly Muḥammad who is referred to in LXXX "He frowned", and v. 13 mentions the *ṣuḥuf mukarrama* "honoured leaves". Slightly later, after the Hidjra of A.D. 622, there comes XCVIII, 2, *ṣuḥuf muṭahhara* "purified leaves". The Prophet's contemporaries, always hostile, would have liked some *ṣuḥuf munashshara* "leaves/scrolls spread out/unrolled", LXXIV, 52. Finally, to announce the end of the world, a series of utterances beginning with *idhā* "when..." describe apocalyptic events, including *wa-idhā 'l-ṣuḥuf nushirat* "when the leaves/scrolls will be spread out/unrolled" (LXXXI, 10), which could also mean the documents in which men's deeds are recorded.

Ṣaḥīfa and *muṣḥaf* and their plurals are attested in *Ḥadīth* 63 and 65 times respectively (Wensinck, *Con-*

cordance, iii, 360-1). As a leaf meant to receive a written text, the *saḥīfa* could be rolled up (*ṭawā*) or spread out/unrolled (*nas͟hara*), and might often be suspended (*ʿallaḳa*) e.g. from the hilt of a sword. It was meant to be read in public and put into effect like an edict or ordinance.

The Prophet, just before his death, asked for a *ṣaḥīfa* for writing upon at his dictation (Ibn Ḥanbal, iii, 346; Ibn Mād͟ja, *Zuhd*, 7). This must refer to a blank piece of writing material, a leaf of parchment or papyrus.

According to the *Sīra* (Ibn Isḥāḳ and Ibn His͟hām [*q.vv.*]), there will be a mysterious fire which will devour the unjust person but spare the one who has suffered injustice. Two priests will come forth publicly, with their *muṣḥaf*s round their necks, and walk through the fire. Idols and offerings will be consumed, but not the two *muṣḥaf*s (*Sīra*, Cairo 1937, i, 24). The first Muslim migrants to Ethiopia witnessed the bishops spreading out (*nas͟harū*) their *muṣḥaf*s (*ibid.*, i, 358). At the moment of ʿUmar's conversion, the latter found with his sister and brother-in-law a *ṣaḥīfa* (parchment? leaf?) on which was written the opening of sūra XX (*ibid.*, i, 364-6).

Correlatives of *ṣaḥīfa* include: *ḳirṭās* [*q.v.*], occurring once in the Ḳurʾān, as also its pl.; *kitāb* [*q.v.*], occurring 255 times, and its pl. six times; *lawḥ* [*q.v.*], once, and its pl. four times; *mawt͟hiḳ/mīt͟hāḳ* [*q.v.*], only to be connected with *ṣaḥīfa* under its aspect of pact, treaty, convention; *nusk͟ha* [*q.v.*], once only; *raḳḳ* [*q.v.*], once only; *ruḳʿa*, non Ḳurʾānic but with the sense of a piece of clothing or administrative document, or a sealed, personal message (*Sīra*, i, 26); *sifr*, non-Ḳurʾānic, but found there five times in its pl. *asfār*, with the sense of books, volumes; and *waraḳ(a)* [*q.v.*], three occurrences altogether, a leaf of a tree or of a ms. in *Ḥadīt͟h* (Ibn Mād͟ja). There are obvious links between all these terms designating materials meant to receive writing, with all the sacred connotations of this latter term. An impression is given that communication with the divine is perceived as taking place on three levels: (1) the *risāla*, or mission of God's messengers; (2) the *kutub*, the writings resulting from this mission; and (3) the *ṣuḥuf*, leaves in the form of archives, documents to which later reference is always possible.

2. Definition.

Ṣaḥīfa does not refer to a leaf, since we have the word *waraḳa* in both Ḳurʾān and *Ḥadīt͟h*, nor yet paper (only after *ca.* A.D. 750), but a flat, smooth surface specially prepared for writing, a document written on a page on a flat surface, not a stone, such as parchment or papyrus.

The *muṣḥaf* is a collection of written leaves placed between two covers (*ṣuḥuf bayn daffatayi/lawḥayi 'l-muṣḥaf*), or a collection of a complete assemblage of leaves, each leaf being called a *ṣaḥīfa*, or a collection of pieces, of documents, a corpus or vulgate. In his *LʿA*, ix, 186a-187a, Ibn Manẓūr defines a *ṣaḥīfa* as a surface of writing upon in the form of a leaf. It differs from a *ruḳʿa*, which is necessarily sealed, whilst a *ṣaḥīfa* can be opened out, fixed on a wall or attached to something. He mentions, in this connection, the anecdote about Ṭarafa and al-Mutalammis [*q.vv.*], both of them bearers of a *ṣaḥīfa*, an unsealed letter from the king ʿAmr b. Hind ordering their execution. By getting the letter deciphered by a youth, al-Mutalammis escaped death, whilst Ṭarafa perished.

A *ṣaḥīfa* could be a leaf on which was transcribed the text of a pact or treaty, meant to be read out to the people and fixed on the wall of the Kaʿba or public place, whilst the expression *ṣuḥuf muṭahhara/mukarrama* could mean the leaves on which the Divine Revelation was written.

3. History.

The conversion of ʿUmar was a shock for the Prophet's enemies and encouraged the first Muslims, who performed their worship at the Kaʿba itself. This conversion resulted from the discovery of a *ṣaḥīfa* (= page) of the Ḳurʾān which ʿUmar had read at his sister's house (see above). This gave rise to another *saḥīfa*, an agreement amongst the leading men of Ḳurays͟h, a kind of resolution voted upon by the people of Mecca and posted up inside the Kaʿba. (This edict recalls such documents amongst the ancient Romans, which were written on a leaf, read out to the people and publicly posted in the Forum.) (*Sīra*, i, 371, 397, 399; al-Ṭabarī, iii, 1189-98).

In A.D. 619, there had taken place the emigration of many of the Muslims from Mecca to Ethiopia [see HID͟JRA; MUHĀD͟JIRŪN], whilst those remaining in Mecca had protection from the young ʿUmar. But in a counter-stroke, the Meccan leaders produced from their deliberations a *ṣaḥīfa*, this event being the most important one in the history of Meccan-Muslim relations in the years immediately before the Hid͟jra. A social and economic boycott of the Muslims of the Banū Hās͟him and of al-Muṭṭalib was envisaged, involving a prohibition of marriages with them and avoidance of commercial contacts. These two Muslim clans took refuge in their *s͟hiʿb* or ravine, on the lands of Abū Ṭālib. The boycott lasted for two or three years, during which the *ṣaḥīfa* was posted up in the Kaʿba, but was not completely watertight. Certain citizens eventually banded together to denounce the pact, and five of them, Zuhayr b. Umayya, al-Muṭʿim b. ʿAdī, Abu 'l-Bak͟htarā b. His͟hām and Zamʿa b. al-Aswad, harangued the crowd in front of the Kaʿba and denounced the *ṣaḥīfa*; but the story goes that the words of it had all been eaten away by worms, with the exception of the opening words "In thy name, O Lord!" (*Sīra*, ed. Wüstenfeld, 247-51; W.M. Watt, *Muhammad at Mecca*, Oxford 1953, 121-2).

Bibliography: Given in the article.

(A. GHÉDIRA)

ṢAḤĪḤ (A.), literally, "sound, healthy".

1. As a technical term in the science of *ḥadīt͟h* [*q.v.*], i.e. Muslim tradition.

It did not come into use immediately with the onset of *isnād* criticism, for al-Rāmahurmuzī (d. 360/970 [*q.v.*]), who wrote the first systematic work on *ḥadīt͟h*, does not seem to have applied it yet. It is used by mediaeval as well as modern Muslim tradition experts (sometimes followed in this by some western scholars) to describe or qualify one particular prophetic tradition or a whole collection of such traditions. *Ṣaḥīḥ* traditions constitute one of the three major subdivisions of Muslim traditions, the other two being *ḥasan*, i.e. "fair", and *ḍaʿīf*, i.e. "weak". The commonest definition of a tradition which is declared *ṣaḥīḥ* is that it is supported by an *isnād* [*q.v.*] which is labelled as *ṣaḥīḥ*, namely, one which shows a chain of transmitters going back to the Prophet in an uninterrupted manner, i.e. each pair of two transmitters in that chain must both be considered *ʿadl*, i.e. "upright" or "honest" to the point that their testimonies are admissible in a court of law, and *ḍābiṭ*, i.e. "painstakingly accurate". Finally, they should be known to have met each other. In the case where a personal meeting of two transmitters is not recorded in so many words, it is imperative for an *isnād* in which these figure to be called *ṣaḥīḥ*, that their lifetimes should show a sufficient overlap (in Arabic: *muʿāṣara*) for a master-pupil relationship, or at least some transmission, to become feasible. Moreover, for a tradition to be *ṣaḥīḥ*, it should neither be *s͟hād͟hdh*, i.e. attested by a single *isnād* not found anywhere else, nor *muʿallal*, i.e. marred by a *ʿilla*, i.e. a (hidden) defect pertaining to one pair of transmitters in its *isnād*. In short, a *ḥadīth* that deserves to be labelled *ṣaḥīḥ* is one credited with the highest possible degree of acceptability.

Many different *isnād* strands received the qualification of being "the most *ṣaḥīḥ* strand of all" at the hands of various early tradition scholars, but none is more famous than al-Bukhārī's favourite strand: (al-Shāfiʿī [*q.v.*])-Mālik b. Anas [*q.v.*]-Nāfiʿ [*q.v.*]-ʿAbd Allāh b. ʿUmar [*q.v.*]-Prophet. This strand was used also to support untold numbers of doubtful traditions, as its very frequent occurrence in e.g. the *Lisān al-mīzān* of Ibn Ḥadjar [*q.v.*] testifies. For a survey of the other strands held to be particularly *ṣaḥīḥ*, see *Bibl.*

Tradition collections entitled *al-Djāmiʿ al-ṣaḥīḥ* are the canonical collections by al-Bukhārī (d. 256/870 [*q.v.*]), Muslim b. al-Ḥadjdjādj (d. 261/875 [*q.v.*]) and al-Tirmidhī (d. 279/892 [*q.v.*]). Those of al-Bukhārī and Muslim are, furthermore, generally referred to as "the two *Ṣaḥīḥs*". Besides, the post-canonical collection made by Ibn Ḥibbān al-Bustī (d. 354/965 [*q.v.*]) entitled *al-Musnad al-ṣaḥīḥ ʿalā 'l-taḳāsīm wa 'l-anwāʿ* is often abbreviated to *Ṣaḥīḥ Ibn Ḥibbān*, cf. the redaction of ʿAlāʾ al-Dīn ʿAlī b. Balbān al-Fārisī (d. 739/1339) called *al-Iḥsān bi-tartīb ṣaḥīḥ Ibn Ḥibbān*, ed. Kamāl Y. al-Ḥūt, Beirut 1987, 10 parts. Finally, there is the early, mainly Ibāḍī [see IBĀḌIYYA] collection of al-Rabīʿ b. Ḥabīb (d. *ca.* 170/785) which is sometimes called *al-Djāmiʿ al-ṣaḥīḥ*.

Bibliography: For a survey of definitions of, and gradations and sub-divisions within, the technical term, as well as the most *ṣaḥīḥ isnād* strands linked to various Companions and later key figures in *ḥadīth*, see al-Ḥākim al-Naysābūrī, *Maʿrifat ʿulūm al-ḥadīth*, ed. Muʿẓam Ḥusayn, Cairo-Ḥaydarābād 1937, 58-62; Nawawī, *Taḳrīb*, tr. by W. Marçais in *JA*, 9e série, XVI (1900), 480-97; Ibn al-Ṣalāḥ, *al-Muḳaddima* [*fī ʿulūm al-ḥadīth*], edited with *Maḥāsin al-iṣṭilāḥ* of Sirādj al-Dīn ʿUmar al-Bulḳīnī by ʿĀʾisha ʿAbd al-Raḥmān Bint al-Shāṭiʾ, Cairo 1974, 82-102; Djalāl al-Dīn al-Suyūṭī, *Tadrīb al-rāwī fī sharḥ taḳrīb al-Nawawī*, ed. ʿAbd al-Wahhāb ʿAbd al-Laṭīf, Cairo 1966, I, 62-152; Ṣubḥī al-Ṣāliḥ, *ʿUlūm al-ḥadīth wa-muṣṭalaḥuhu*, Damascus 1959, 141-57. (G.H.A. JUYNBOLL)

2. In law.

In Islamic law, a legal act is regarded as valid, i.e. having its desired legal effects, if all its essential elements (*rukn*, pl. *arkān*) are present and the necessary conditions (*sharṭ*, pl. *shurūṭ*) are fulfilled. If one or more of these elements or conditions are lacking, the act is null and void (*fāsid* or *bāṭil* [*q.v.*]), therefore does not exist and has no effect. This classification applies to acts of devotion (*ʿibādāt*) as well as to legal acts (*muʿāmalāt*). With regard to the former, the desired effect is being acquitted of an obligation, which will result in reward in the Hereafter. Thus an obligatory *ṣalāt* [*q.v.*] performed in compliance with the prescriptions, is valid, counts as the discharge of a duty and will be recompensed after one's death. Similarly, a repudiation duly pronounced according to the rules is valid and produces its legal effects such as the dissolution of the marriage and the beginning of the waiting period for the wife (*ʿidda* [*q.v.*]). Valid acts are not necessarily binding (*lāzim*). Most schools recognise as valid suspended (*mawḳūf*) acts, i.e. legal acts that have no obligatory effect until after their ratification by a third party, such as acts performed by an unauthorised agent (*fuḍūlī*) or a discerning minor (*mumayyiz*). In order to be binding they have to be approved by the principal or the guardian. They are classified as valid because, after ratification, they are regarded as having bound the principal or the minor from the moment the original act was performed.

Bibliography: Y. Linant de Bellefonds, *Traité de droit musulman comparé*, Paris 1965, i, 87-101; Muḥammad Abū Zahra, *Uṣūl al-fiḳh*, Cairo n.d., 62; Taftazānī, *Ḥāshiya ʿalā 'l-ʿAḍudiyya, sharḥ Mukhtaṣar al-muntahā al-uṣūlī li-Ibn Ḥādjib*, ed. Shaʿbān Muḥammad Ismāʿīl, Cairo 1974, ii, 7-8. (R. PETERS)

3. In grammar.

Here, *ṣaḥīḥ* usually refers to the "sound" letters, loosely the consonants of Arabic, defined by default as being neither "weak" letters, *muʿtalla*, viz. the semi-vowels *alif, wāw, yāʾ* [see ḤURŪF AL-HIDJĀʾ], nor vowels, viz. *fatḥa, kasra* and *ḍamma* [see ḤARAKA WA-SUKŪN, KASRA]. The criteria of soundness and weakness are purely phonetic and date at least to the 2nd/8th century; Sībawayhi (*flor.* 170/786 [*q.v.*]) and al-Khalīl b. Aḥmad (d. 175/791, e.g. *Kitāb al-ʿAyn*, i, 51, 57, 59) both use *ṣaḥīḥ* and *muʿtall*.

The soundness of a letter (sc. phoneme: *ḥarf* [*q.v.*] denotes grapheme and phoneme alike, which does not imply that the grammarians overlooked the distinction) lies in its stability in all vocalic environments, unlike the weak letters, which are unstable between and after vowels, and in its organic difference from the vowels, which are articulated without any interruption in the air stream, while the sound phonemes, continuant or plosive, always involve some constriction. The morphophonological implications of these articulatory features were minutely observed by the grammarians, who described in detail the various allophones and such sound-changes as assimilation (*idghām* [*q.v.*]), dissimilation, metathesis and substitution (*ibdāl* [*q.v.*], and see al-Nassir, Bakalla, Bohas and Guillaume).

On the morphological level, a verb stem containing no weak radicals is called a "sound verb" *fiʿl ṣaḥīḥ* (or *fiʿl sālim*), with much inconsistency regarding the place of *hamza* in this scheme, and the "sound" plural is likewise *al-djamʿ al-ṣaḥīḥ* as well as the more usual *al-djamʿ al-sālim*.

It has been noted that *ṣaḥīḥ* in later grammar may also denote a "correct" utterance (Versteegh, 34): a possible logical origin is hinted at, though the phrase *kalām ṣaḥīḥ* is already found in Sībawayhi, Derenbourg, i, 353, Būlāḳ, i, 400. More important than origins, however, is the still unexplored peculiarity that the same grammatical term may occur at different levels of analysis, indicating an approach to terminology fundamentally at variance with modern linguistic conventions.

Bibliography: The articles referred to above, especially ḤURŪF AL-HIDJĀʾ, contain extensive bibliographies, to which may now be added the following: G. Troupeau, *Lexique-index du Kitāb de Sībawayhi*, Paris 1976; M.H. Bakalla, *Ibn Jinnī: an early Arab Muslim phonetician. An interpretative study of his life and contribution to linguistics*, London-Taipei 1982; G. Bohas and J.-P. Guillaume, *Études des théories des grammairiens arabes. I, Morphologie et phonologie*, Damascus 1984; al-Khalīl, *K. al-ʿAyn*, ed. M. al-Makhzūmī and I. al-Samarrāʾī, Beirut 1988, i, 47-61; C.H.M. Versteegh, *Arabic grammar and Qurʾanic exegesis in early Islam*, Leiden 1993; A.A. al-Nassir, *Sibawayh the phonologist*, London 1993. (M.G. CARTER)

SĀḤIL (A.), European form Sahel, a geographical term meaning "edge, border zone". It is, grammatically, an active participle with a passive meaning (*fāʿil bi-maʿnā mafʿūl*, see e.g. *LʿA*, ed. Beirut

1375/1956, xi, 328a, "eaten away by the sea" whence "shore".

The term has various regional applications, in accordance with the meaning "fringe area, zone".

1. *In the Maghrib.*

(a) The Sāḥil of Tunisia (Sāḥil of Sousse, Sāḥil of Sfax). This is the coastal region of the low steppes of the north, around the towns of Sousse, Monastir and Mahdia, having a maritime climate and rainfall in excess of 300 mm per annum and characterised by the importance of its olive groves and the antiquity of its urban network.

(b) The Sāḥil of Algeria. This is applied to the coastal regions of Algeria, mainly those around Algiers and Oran.

2. *To the south of the Sahara.*

The Sāḥil (in the best known sense of the word) here is defined by the Arabic authors as a southern "shore" of the Sahara, here compared to a sea. The term was taken up in 1900 by the botanist Auguste Chevalier, who posited an opposition in West and Central Africa of increasingly humid zones called Saharan, Sahilian, Sudanian and Guinean.

The Sāḥil zone thus delimited includes several African states, from west to east: Senegal, Mauritania, Mali, Burkina Fasso (Upper Volta), Niger, the northeastern extremity of Nigeria, Chad and the Sudan, with an area of about 4 million km². The term is, however, used above all for the central and western part, from Tibesti to the Atlantic Ocean. The Sāḥil does not have any well-marked physical features. Like all the Sahara [see AL-ṢAḤRĀʾ], flat surfaces predominate, either in the form of plains resulting from the levelling of the ancient pre-Cambrian shield, making up the main part of the countryside and interrupted by rare *inselberg*s, or else in the form of essentially sandstone plateaux edged with abrupt slopes making up striking relief features, such as, from west to east, the Tagant and Assaba, the plateaux of Bandiagara and the Hombori, and the Ennedi massif. Really mountainous massifs are rare, apart from the volcanic one of the Djebel Marra in the Sudan, reaching 3,000 m/10,000 feet. Within this little-differentiated topography, the surface is often made up of *regs* [*q.v.*], but the dominant characteristic of the Sāḥil surfaces is the importance of the ergs (*ʿirḳ*). These great stretches of dunes, of which the great Saharan ergs often extend towards the southwest, are actually clothed with a herbaceous vegetation which stabilises the sands; they are made up of extended parallel bands of terrain (several dozen km), and increasingly flattened by water erosion as one travels southwards. Oriented ENE-WSW, and covered with reddish sands, these bands are separated by gullies between the dunes, e.g. the ergs of Trarza and Cayor in Mauritania, the Gourma to the south-east of Timbuctu, the Azaouak to the south-west of the Aïr, the Daza and Djourab to the north-east of Lake Chad and the Goz of Sudan. These ergs are the remnants of important climatic variations which have taken place over the last millennia, and have sometimes brought about an important advance of the desert southwards and the fixing of sand dunes, and at other times a retreat of the Sahara northwards accompanied by a considerable extension of Lake Chad and the overflowing of the Niger northwards, as was the case during the period 8,000-2,000 B.C., with the reversion to conditions identical with those of the present time having lasted hardly more than 3,000 years. Over the Sāḥil zone in general, there is shrubby steppeland in the south, becoming bushy in the north, with a weak vegetation covering index, and which is more and more open as one approaches the Sahara. Large, allogenous rivers—the Senegal, Niger, Chari and Nile—bring into the region waters which are often abundant.

The absence of topographical boundaries leads one to describe the Sāḥil as the zone of transition between the Sahara and the more humid regions of tropical Africa. Hence it can only be delimited by means of climatic characteristics, much discussed by writers; thus Ch. Toupet considers as Sāḥilian the band of terrain comprised between the annual mean isohyets of 100 mm in the north and 700 mm in the south, whilst Y. Péhaut limits it to the 150-200 mm band in the north and the 600 mm one in the south. This "climatic" definition is further complicated by the importance of variations in precipitation over the course of the years. The great droughts affecting the Sāḥil since 1967 have brought about displacements of the climatic zones towards the south by several hundred kilometres, and extensive changes for the worse in the natural habitat, worsened by the increases in population and their herds and by the fragility of the sandy soils of the ancient ergs; during years of greater rainfall, the Sahara-Sāḥil boundary retreats northwards, but the deterioration of the habitat is often irreversible and never completely restored. These droughts are due to the marginal position of the Sāḥil in relation to the inflow of rainfall. The Sāḥil in general is characterised by the alternation, in the course of each year, of a long dry season during which the northerly trade-winds (called *Harmattan* when they are continental) and a rainy season corresponding to the influx of humid air of the summer monsoons originating in the Atlantic Ocean (Gulf of Guinea). These monsoons, fairly abundant in the southern part of the Sāḥil, become more and more feeble and irregular as one approaches the Sahara.

The population of the Sāḥil is characterised by a marked decrease in density as one goes from south to north and by the mixture of "blacks" and "whites", more or less Islamised, with a distribution only explicable by what it has been possible to piece together of the history of the region and of the great empires which dominated it, poorly known for the central and western Sāḥil. The first empire, that of Ghāna [*q.v.*], which extended from the southern Sahara as far as Guinea, was described in 1068 by al-Bakrī in his description of West Africa. It was interrupted in the 5th/11th century by the arrival of the Almoravids [see AL-MURĀBIṬŪN], who came from southern Morocco and created an empire stretching from al-Andalus to the western Sāḥil; this did not last, but brought Islam and the Arabic language to the region. In the 7th/13th century, a new empire, that of Mali [*q.v.*], arose, from the Sāḥil to the tropical forest, in the bend of the Niger. After its apogee in the 8th/14th century, it was supplanted a century later by the Songhay empire, whose capital Gao was destroyed by an expedition sent from Morocco in 1591. At the same time, around Lake Chad, the dynasty of the Safawa reigned from the 3rd/9th to the 13th/19th century with various fortunes.

In all these regions, the penetration of Islam was achieved essentially in peaceful ways, favoured by the great empires based on commerce, and whose ruling classes showed themselves fairly tolerant. It was often the nobles and urban populations which became converts, whilst the rural populations, making up the mass of the people, remained animists. This penetration was equally the work of numerous Muslim traders involved in the trans-Saharan commerce, involving above all the export of gold, for which the

Sudan was the main world producer, to the Mediterranean countries, and the slave traffic, which had for long been important, to the lands of the Maghrib. It was likewise favoured by a general movement, since the Middle Ages, of the sedentary black populations, pushed southwards by nomads who were Muslims, and possibly by a deterioration in climate.

The present-day population of the Sāḥil shows a complex pattern of overlapping peoples, including societies often strongly hierarchical in social structure, which can be distinguished by their ways of life: the pure nomads, found especially in the northern Sāḥil, corresponding to the southwards extension of the great Saharan groups: Moors in the west, Touaregs in the centre and Tubus in the east. The semi-nomads, like the Kreda to the east of Lake Chad, regularly increase proportionately, and possess palm-groves or practise stock-rearing and an extensive agriculture at the same time, sometimes organising the transhumance of their herds under the care of herdsmen. The Peuls or Fulbe, a people whose origin is badly known, belong to this category, whilst practising stock-rearing of bovines which are more of a social value than one of food supply. Finally, the cultivators, mainly blacks, have great difficulty in practising dry farming in a climate with such feeble and irregular rainfall; the cultures utilising river water along the great waterways depend on the volume of the flood waters of those rivers, and irrigated systems of agriculture remain rare. Within these activities, formerly highly hierarchical, recent political changes have brought a reversal in the strength of forces; the nomadic Saharan tribes, which were formerly dominant through their razzias and through the slave traffic, have found themselves ruined by the drought, the disappearance of the great caravan traffic and the collapse of social structures, and are subordinate to a political authority in the hands of the sedentary black populations, more quickly susceptible to education.

The peoples of the Sāḥil have often been severely affected by the great droughts which have adversely affected their modes of life at a time when they have been demographically increasing—e.g. it has been estimated that the population of Senegal has increased from one million at the beginning of this century to one of *ca.* 7.5 millions in 1990—and the increase in herds has damaged the environment. Unfavourable economic conditions (decline in the value of primary products and of agricultural products for export), and the division of the Sāḥil into several states with scanty resources, have added to climatic deterioration to make the Sāḥil one of the regions of the globe in the greatest difficulties.

Bibliography: Y. Péhaut, art. *Le Sahel*, in *Encyclopaedia Universalis*, Paris 1989; Ch. Toupet, *Le Sahel*, Paris 1992. (Y. Callot)

SĀHIR, DJELĀL (Celal Sahir Erozan), Ottoman and early Republican Turkish poet and author, born in 1299/1883, died in 1935.

He was the son of Ismāʿīl Ḥaḳḳī Pasha of Yemen and Fehime Nüzhet of the Tatar Ḥādjī Dāwūd Khān family, herself an author and poet. Sāhir grew up with his mother in Istanbul, attended the Dāwūd Pasha Rūshdiyye and the Wefā Iʿdādī schools and took private French lessons. He began writing poetry at the age of 14, and his poems were first published in *Therwet-i fünūn* [*q.v.*], the journal of the literary group *Edebiyyāt-i djedīde*. When the group renewed itself under the name *Fedjr-i ātī* [*q.v.*], whose motto was art for art's sake, he became for a while the leader of the group. Although they were for the westernisation of Turkish literature, their language remained complex, with much use of the Persian and Arabic lexicons, the use of traditional love themes and writing in *ʿarūḍ*, i.e. the traditional metres of poetry. He left the Faculty of Law in Istanbul after two years and in 1903 was employed at the Foreign Office. After *Fedjr-i ātī* dissolved itself, Sāhir wrote for the journal *Genč ḳalemler* ("Young Pens") during 1911-12, this being the voice of the nationalist movement, advocating use of the national language and a national literature. During this time, Sāhir wrote with the syllabic folk metre of Turkish. He left the Foreign Office and first taught literature in high schools but later became a merchant. He acted chiefly as the founder or editor of various periodicals as well as writing in them (*Seyyāre, Demet, Kitāblar, Türk Yurdu, Bilgi, Khalḳa Doghru* and *Türk Sözü*). These journals were mostly devoted to the promotion of Turkish nationalism during the war years. *Kitāblar*, published in the 1920s, were monthly books containing poems, plays, short stories called *Birindji kitāb.... sekizindji kitāb*. He was appointed as a member of the Commission for Language Reform and became a member in the National Assembly for Zonguldak in 1928. In 1932 he was among the founding members of the *Türk Dili Tetkik Cemiyeti*. He died in 1935 in Istanbul, having married three times and having six children.

Bibliography: 1. First editions. *Ḳārdesh sesi*, 1908; *Beyāḍ gölgeler*, 1909; *Buḥrān*, 1909; *Siyāh kitāb*, 1912; *Istanbul ičin mebʿūth nāmzedlerim*, 1919; *Müntekhab čodjuḳ shiʿrleri*, 1918, 1919; *Ḳirāʾāt-i edebiyye*, 1919; *Imlā lughati*, 1929; *Simon* (translated from Eugène Brieux), 1919.

2. Selected studies. Mahir Ünlü and Ömer Özcan, *20.yy. Türk edebiyyatı*, Istanbul 1987; Nesrin Tağızade Karaca, *Celal Sahir Erozan*, Ankara 1992; Ataol Behramoğlu, *Büyük Türk şiiri antolojisi*, ii, Istanbul 1993; Kenan Akyüz, in *PTF*, ii, 525-6, 564-5, 571, 598-9. See also the *EI*[1] art. (T. Menzel) for older bibl. (Çiğdem Balim)

SAHL b. HĀRŪN b. RĀHAWAYH (or Rāhīyūn, Rāhyūn, Rāmnūy), Persian author, translator, and a poet of great repute who wrote in Arabic in the early ʿAbbāsid period and died in 215/830. He was born in Dast-i Maysān or in Maysān [*q.v.*] in south-eastern ʿIrāḳ. His family, originally from Nīshāpūr, had moved to the Maysān region and then to Baṣra, whence his *nisba* al-Baṣrī.

The period of his youth and early education remains in obscurity. He attracted public attention first as the secretary of Hārūn al-Rashīd's vizier Yaḥyā b. Khālid al-Barmakī (170-87/786-803). Under Yaḥyā, he was charged with the distribution of certain public payments (Ibn ʿAbd Rabbih, v, 58). He survived the fall of the Barmakids, became an intimate of al-Rashīd and acted as his *ṣāḥib al-dawāwīn* (Ibn al-Abbār, *Iʿtāb al-kuttāb*, Damascus 1961, 85-6). It is not known whether he held this office under al-Amīn, although during the pursuing civil war and fratricide which ravaged Baghdād, he remained in the capital and had contact with al-Amīn's vizier al-Faḍl b. al-Rabīʿ (al-Djāḥiẓ, *Bayān*, i, 346). Under al-Maʾmūn he was bound to al-Ḥasan b. Sahl [*q.v.*], and served primarily as the chief director of the House of Wisdom (*bayt al-ḥikma* [*q.v.*]).

Early literary tradition portrays Sahl as the foremost partisan of the Shuʿūbiyya [*q.v.*], though by religious preference he was a Shīʿī (al-Damīrī, *Ḥayāt al-ḥayawān*, Cairo 1887, i, 313). The story known as "Sahl's rooster", related by the zealous Shīʿī poet Diʿbil al-Khuzāʿī [*q.v.*], confirms his ties with the Shīʿīs (al-Djāḥiẓ, *Ḥayawān*, ii, 374-5). However, he seems to have favoured, as many learned men of his generation did, the Muᶜtazilī doctrine and is mentioned next to its leading mentors Abu 'l-Hudhayl, al-Naẓẓām and al-Djāḥiẓ (al-Djāḥiẓ, *Ḥayawān*, vii, 182, 206; al-Thaᶜālibī, *Thimār al-ḳulūb*, Cairo 1965, 172).

Sahl found an ardent admirer and friend in his younger contemporary al-Djāḥiẓ, who praised him as a trustworthy gentleman not shy in defending the truth even to his own loss; a superlative orator, master of rhetoric and style, author of many treatises and voluminous books (*Bayān*, i, 52, 89). Still more warmly Abu 'l-ᶜAynāʾ [*q.v.*] wrote of Sahl: "God enhanced the worth of the world by letting him be one of its residents!" (al-Tawḥīdī, *al-Baṣāʾir wa 'l-dhakhāʾir*, Damascus 1964, iii$_1$, 326 n. 1).

In his own time Sahl became outstanding in eloquence and learning, and wrote books in challenge of the Arabic classics (Ibn Nubāta, *Sarḥ al-ᶜuyūn*, Cairo 1964, 242). He had a refined taste for the creation of short, semi-lyrical exhortations, whose terse prose aroused the admiration of connoisseurs of the Arabic language. He was equally remarkable for the merit of his poetry. No *dīwān* or collection of poems survives from him. Ibn al-Nadīm (*Fihrist*, ed. Tadjaddud, 191) estimated his poems only at about fifty pages. Many of these, adorned with maxims and admonitory precepts, are extant in scattered *adab* works. By his wisdom and prudence and his literary aptitude, he acquired great celebrity and his name became proverbial. People would say: "Sahl b. Hārūn has composed your words!" (Ibn Nubāta, 242), or "You speak with the tongue of Sahl b. Hārūn!" (Ibn Bassām, *al-Dhakhīra fī maḥāsin ahl al-Djazīra*, Beirut 1978, ii/2, 729). More than five centuries afterwards, Ibn Khaldūn [*q.v.*], who considered Sahl's *Rasāʾil* as peerless examples of Arabic literary composition, recommended them to the intelligent critic and those with literary taste who desired to master the Arabic language and a high order of eloquence (*Muḳaddima*, tr. Rosenthal, iii, 393).

Together with Ibn al-Muḳaffaᶜ, Abān al-Lāḥiḳī [*q.vv.*], and ᶜAlī b. ᶜUbayda al-Rayḥānī, Sahl belongs to that community of authors and translators of Pahlavi literature who effected a prodigious place for Persian literary, political and cultural traditions among Muslims. The titles of his books clearly reveal his interest for the ancient heritage of Persia. The first field in which he relied heavily on Persian sources was the application of *andarz* or "wisdom" literature in his books of fable, told in the speech of humans, birds and animals (Ibn al-Nadīm, 197). He wrote a *Kitāb Thaᶜala wa-ᶜAfrāʾ*, and one *al-Namir wa 'l-Thaᶜlab* "the Panther and the Fox", in imitation of the revered Pahlavi fable *Kalīla wa-Dimna* [*q.v.*]. From the former only some brief excerpts are extant. The second survives in an abridged form, and has been published. This is told in a continuous narrative without the interjection of independent apologues characteristic of the *Kalīla*. In both books, Sahl creates situations for animals to convey ethical and didactic counsels to his readers, a literary device much favoured by Persians. From the published fragments it cannot be determined whether he translated these from Pahlavi originals or created them himself. Some mediaeval critics found these superior even to their prototype (al-Masᶜūdī, *Murūdj al-dhahab*, Beirut 1965-79, i, 89). A striking feature introduced for the first time into Arabic literature by Sahl is the application of an epistolary style in fables. Sahl's success in this field won him the honorable nickname "Buzurgmihr-i Islām", which not only put him in the same rank of Khusraw I Anūshirwān's (531-79) famed vizier Buzurgmihr, but also signified the role he had assumed in the Persianisation of al-Maʾmūn's court, that of the supreme wise man in politics and adviser to the caliph.

Sahl's famous encomium on avarice, *Risāla fi 'l-Bukhl*, whose authenticity is sometimes doubted, forms the beginning of al-Djāḥiẓ's *Kitāb al-Bukhalāʾ*, and is incorporated also by Ibn ᶜAbd Rabbih (vi, 200-4). Handling and exaltation of irreverent themes seems to have constituted a challenging arena for talented men to test their literary genius in this period. For the opponents of the Shuᶜūbiyya, however, it was easy to charge the author with frugality; and Sahl had to explain that his intention was the opposite (Ibn Nubāta, 244). This was recognised as an intellectual *coup de force* in exhibiting his literary puissance (al-Ḥuṣrī, 831).

Beside composing books of fable and belles-lettres, he also handled political subjects, as in his *Kitāb Tadbīr al-mulk wa 'l-siyāsa*, surely adopting his ideas from Persian political philosophy. Books on politics have left their greatest mark on the Arab-Islamic diplomatic practices. His description of the qualities of the chamberlain, *ḥādjib* [*q.v.*], was based perhaps as much on personal experience as on the lost Sāsānid book *Shāhī* or *Shāhīnī* (al-Djāḥiẓ, *Rasāʾil*, ii, 39). In *Sīrat al-Maʾmūn* (Ibn Nubāta, 242), Sahl treated topics common to *Siyar al-mulūk* which describe royal customs of the Persian kings, dignitaries and heroes. Al-Ṭabarī's long passages on the rise of rivalries between the two brothers al-Amīn and al-Maʾmūn, and anecdotes about al-Maʾmūn recorded on Sahl's authority in other sources, may have had their origin in this book. His treatise on jurisprudence and the function of the *ḳāḍī* [*q.v.*], *Risāla fi 'l-Ḳaḍāʾ*, addressed to the Persian jurist and judge of Baṣra ᶜĪsā b. Abān b. Ṣadaḳa b. ᶜAdī b. Mardānshāh of Fasā (in office from 211/826 until his death in 220/835), echoed his experience in judicial matters and legal interpretation.

Among Sahl's many translations was the romance *Wāmiḳ and ᶜAdhrāʾ* which was supposed to have been compiled at the time of Anūshirwān and presented to him. The famous verse on the wall of Ḳaṣr-i Shīrīn Palace, which pertains to the time of Khusraw Parwīz (590-628), is a direct reference to this romance (Rypka, *Iranische Literaturgeschichte*, Leipzig 1959, 132-3), but we have no indication whether Sahl's translation was in verse or in prose. Not knowing much about the content of this epic, one cannot determine its relationship to the poet ᶜUnṣurī's [*q.v.*] New Persian versification of the *Wāmiḳ u ᶜAdhrāʾ* romance, but the *Vorlage* of ᶜUnṣurī's version was clearly a Greek one and not any intermediate Pahlavi translation. Sahl's book *Adab Ashk b. Ashk*, apparently a compilation of political and wisdom literature attributed to the Arsacid King Ashk b. Ashk, displayed his interest in Parthian subjects. Sahl's books, amounting to some 20 titles—Ibn al-Nadīm listed only 13—were without doubt very popular and of great social value, but al-Djāḥiẓ's claim (*Rasāʾil*, i, 351) to have used Sahl's name to publicise some of his own works is more probably a fiction.

Bibliography (in addition to references given in the text): Sahl's only surviving book has been edited and translated by Abdelkader Mehiri, *An-Namir wa-t-taᶜlab (La Panthère et le Renard)*, Tunis 1973, also ed. Mundjī al-Kuᶜbī, Tunis 1980. For additional citations of Sahl's sentences and poems, see Ābī, *Nathr al-durr*, Cairo 1980-90, ii, 188, iii, 283, iv, 167, 191, 232-3, v, 113; al-Djāḥiẓ, *al-Bayān wa 'l-tabyīn*, Cairo 1968, i, 52, 58, 77, 89-91, 197, 238, 243, 332-3, 346, ii, 39, 43, 74, 104, 195, 196, iii, 29, 352, 373-4; idem, *Bukhalāʾ*, Cairo 1958, 9-16 (= *Risāla fi 'l-*

Bukhl), 1, 5, 21, 40, 43, 93, 106, 130, 154, 182, and the editor's notes 268-71, 279, 280, 288, 301, 357, 382; idem, *Ḥayawān*, Cairo 1947, ii, 374-75, iii, 66, 466, v, 603, vi, 388, 431; vii, 182, 201-2, 206; idem, *Rasāʾil*, Cairo 1964, ii, 38-39, 261-2, 303-4; al-Ḥuṣrī al-Ḳayrawānī, *Zahr al-ādāb*, Cairo 1969, 97, 109, 117, 151, 302, 365, 545, 576-8, 831, 949; Ibn ʿAbd Rabbih, *al-ʿIḳd al-farīd*, Cairo 1940-53, ii, 123, 136, 137, 207, 295, 338, iii, 7, 302, 311, iv, 179, 189, 198, v, 58-65, 69, 339, vi, 180, 196, 200-4; Ibn Ḥamdūn, *al-Tadhkira al-ḥamdūniyya*, Beirut 1983, i, 253, 299, 348, 374, 416-17, ii, 17, 325, 382. For studies, see ʿĪsā ʿĀkūb, *Taʾthīr al-ḥikam al-Fārisiyya fi ʾl-adab al-ʿArabī fī ʾl-ʿaṣr al-ʿAbbāsī al-awwal*, Damascus 1989, 183-8, 294-6; M.-G. Balty-Guesdon, *Le Bayt al-Ḥikma de Baghdād*, in *Arabica*, xxxix (1992), 131-50; J.H. Kramers, *EI*[1] art. s.v.; M. Kurd ʿAlī, *Sahl b. Hārūn*, in *Madjallat al-Madjmaʿ al-ʿIlmī al-ʿArabī*, vii (1927), 5-27, repr. in his *Umarāʾ al-bayān*, Cairo 1937, 159-90; Shawḳī Ḍayf, *Sahl b. Hārūn*, in his *al-ʿAṣr al-ʿAbbāsī al-awwal*, Cairo 1966, 526-40; A. Muhamed Yāgī, *Sahl ibn Hārūn. Edition des fragments avec traduction précédée d'une introduction sur cet auteur et ses œuvres*, diss. Paris, Sorbonne 1956, unpubl. (Mohsen Zakeri)

SAHL al-TUSTARĪ, Abū Muḥammad b. ʿAbd Allāh b. Yūnus b. ʿĪsā b. ʿAbd Allāh b. Rafīʿ, an influential Ṣūfī of mediaeval Islam, was probably born in 203/818 in Tustar, Khūzistān, and died in 283/896 in Baṣra. The essential course of his life can be reconstructed on the basis of fragmentary hagiographical accounts, included in the Ṣūfī primary sources, and incidental references of Islamic historical literature.

Until a short time after his pilgrimage to Mecca in 219/834, al-Tustarī received his basic education from his maternal uncle Muḥammad b. Sawwār (who transmitted *ḥadīth* on the authority of Sufyān al-Thawrī [*q.v.*]) and Ḥamza al-ʿAbbādānī, an obscure spiritual instructor residing at the *ribāṭ* of ʿAbbādān [*q.v.*], where al-Tustarī had a vision of God's supreme name (*ism Allāh al-aʿẓam*) written in the sky with green light from east to west (al-Tustarī, *Tafsīr*, 17, 24; Anṣārī, *Ṭabaḳāt*, 116). Al-Tustarī met his Ṣūfī forebear Dhu 'l-Nūn al-Miṣrī [*q.v.*] at least once in his life, but it is not certain whether he became his direct disciple. After spending some twenty-odd years in his hometown, engaged in austere practices, especially fasting, al-Tustarī emerged with a teaching of his own about the time of Dhu 'l-Nūn al-Miṣrī's death in 245/860 and gathered a group of disciples around himself. Prominent among his disciples were Abū ʿAbd Allāh Muḥammad b. Aḥmad b. Sālim al-Baṣrī (d. 297/909), said to have served al-Tustarī for sixty years, and al-Ḥallādj [*q.v.*] who stayed with him for about two years. About the time when the Zandj [*q.v.*] occupied Tustar for a short time in 263/877, al-Tustarī was summoned from Tustar to the camp of the Ṣaffārids to cure their ailing leader, Yaʿḳūb b. al-Layth [*q.v.*] (cf. Abū Nuʿaym, *Ḥilya*, x, 210), who had been wounded in his defeat by the caliphal regent al-Muwaffaḳ at Dayr al-ʿĀḳūl [*q.v.*] in 262/876. Expelled from his home town for political or doctrinal reasons (al-Sarrādj, *Lumaʿ*, 407, cf. Arberry, *Pages*, 9), al-Tustarī took up residence in Baṣra early in 263/877, though another strand of source evidence would suggest that he had settled there as early as 258/871 when the Zandj sacked the town (al-Makkī, *Ḳūt al-ḳulūb*, iii, 104). In Baṣra, al-Tustarī was welcomed by Abū Dāwūd al-Sidjistānī (d. 275/889 [*q.v.*]) but, because of his claim to be "the proof of God" (*ḥudjdjat Allāh*), became involved in religious controversy with Abū Yaḥyā Zakariyyāʾ al-Sādjī (d. 307/909) and Abū ʿAbd Allāh al-Zubayrī (d. 317/929), two leading Shāfiʿī scholars of the city (al-Shaʿrānī, *Ṭabaḳāt*, i, 67).

Shortly after his death in Baṣra, al-Tustarī's direct disciples split into two groups (cf. Böwering, *Mystical vision*, 75-99). One group selected Baghdād as the centre of activity, either joining the Ṣūfī circle of al-Djunayd [*q.v.*], as did Abū Muḥammad al-Djurayrī (d. 312/924) and Abu 'l-Ḥasan ʿAlī b. Muḥammad al-Muzayyin al-Tirmidhī (d. 328/939), or associating with the Ḥanbalīs in the Muḥawwal quarter of Baghdād, as did Abū Muḥammad al-Barbahārī (d. 329/941 [*q.v.*]) and two crucial transmitters of al-Tustarī's teachings, Abū Bakr Muḥammad b. al-Ashʿath al-Sidjzī and Abu 'l-Ḥasan ʿUmar b. Wāṣil al-ʿAnbarī (d. 312/924). The other group of al-Tustarī's disciples stayed on in Baṣra and found acceptance among the local Mālikīs. It formed the nucleus of a theological school, known as the Sālimiyya, that was organised by Abu 'l-Ḥasan Aḥmad b. Muḥammad b. Aḥmad b. Sālim al-Baṣrī (d. 356/967), who is frequently confused in the sources with his father, al-Tustarī's life-long associate. The most famous exponent of the Sālimiyya, however, was Abū Ṭālib al-Makkī (d. 386/996 [*q.v.*]) who, in his *Ḳūt al-ḳulūb*, frequently cites Abu 'l-Ḥasan Aḥmad b. Muḥammad b. Sālim as "our *shaykh*" and al-Tustarī as "our *imām*". The Sālimiyya, who also adopted ideas propagated by Abū Ḥulmān al-Fārisī al-Dimashḳī (d. *ca.* 340/951), became the target of a lost refutation (*ar-Radd ʿalā Ibn Sālim*) written by the Shāfiʿī (or Ẓāhirī) Ibn al-Khafīf (d. 371/981). Possibly on the basis of this refutation, a list of eighteen objectionable propositions was drawn up in Ḥanbalī circles by Ibn al-Farrāʾ (d. 458/1065 [*q.v.*]) in his *Muʿtamad* (217-21), of which ʿAbd al-Ḳādir al-Djīlānī [*q.v.*] copied and rejected twelve propositions in his *Ghunya* (i, 106-7). The last major exponents of the Ṣālimiyya were Abū ʿAlī al-Ḥasan b. ʿAlī al-Ahwāzī (d. 446/1055; cf. al-Dhahabī, *Siyar*, xviii, 13-8), Abū Shakūr Muḥammad b. ʿAbd al-Sayyid al-Sālimī (d. shortly after 470/1077; see *GAL*, I, 419; S I, 744) and Abū ʿAbd Allāh Muḥammad b. Yaḥyā al-Zabīdī (d. 555/1160; cf. al-Dhahabī, *Siyar*, xx, 316-9).

Beginning with Ibn al-Nadīm's *Fihrist*, 186, quite a number of treatises have been ascribed to al-Tustarī in Islamic bibliography. All of these appear to be lost under their titles, but two works attributed to al-Tustarī are extant. They are a Ḳurʾān commentary, *Kitāb Fahm al-Ḳurʾān* (published as *Tafsīr al-Ḳurʾān al-karīm*, Cairo 1326/1908 and 1329/1911), and a collection of al-Tustarī's sayings in three parts with the commentary of Abu 'l-Ḳāsim ʿAbd al-Raḥmān al-Ṣiḳillī (d. *ca.* 386/996), preserved in the collective ms. Köprülü 727 (one part of which, *al-Muʿāraḍa wa 'l-radd*, was published by M.K. Gaafer, Cairo 1980). Many fragments of al-Tustarī's commentary on Ḳurʾānic verses are cited in Sulamī's *Ḥaḳāʾiḳ al-tafsīr*, which is accessible only in manuscript (for a table of references and the parallel citations in Rūzbihān al-Baḳlī's *ʿArāʾis al-bayān*, see G. Böwering, *Mystical vision*, 113-24). Al-Tustarī's extant works are not his own writings, but were compiled by his followers who based themselves on the core of his teachings. The other tracts attributed to al-Tustarī (see *GAS*, i, 647) are marginal or spurious (for an annotated list of Tustarī's works, see Böwering, *op. cit.*, 11-18, and add *Tafsīr al-Ḳurʾān*, ms. Azhar, *Riwāḳ al-atrāk* 7, and the excerpts included in ms. Ẓāhiriyya 9595, fols. 35-43). The two works attributed to al-Tustarī and the considerable body of anecdotes and sayings quoted on his authority in the Ṣūfī primary sources give a fragmentary yet substantive picture of al-Tustarī's mystical theory and practice.

The central idea of al-Tustarī's mysticism is the Ṣūfī recollection of God (*dhikr* [*q.v.*]), which he put on a firm theoretical basis. All his life he observed the method of recollecting God by repeating a mental prayer, "God is my witness" (*Allāhu shāhidī*, cf. al-Ḳushayrī, *Risāla*, 83) and understanding it as his daily sustenance (*ḳūt*). He interpreted it experientially as the break-through to God, who effects His own recollection within the mystic's heart (*dhikr Allāh bi'llāh: al-dhikr bi 'l madhkūr*, cf. al-Tustarī, *Tafsīr al-Ḳur'ān*, 25-6, 80). Anchoring *dhikr* in the self-revelation of God at the primordial covenant in pre-existence (*a-lastu bi-rabbikum*, Ḳur'ān, VII, 172), al-Tustarī understood *dhikr* as anamnesis. The mystic rediscovers the primaeval moment before God in the inmost recesses of his soul (*sirr al-nafs*) when he listens to Pharaoh's blasphemous proclamation of his own lordship, "I am your Lord Most High" (*anā rabbukum al-aʿlā*, LXXIX, 24). Listening to God, the true speaker of the Ḳur'ān, the mystic ironically perceives the actual essence of belief flowing from the tongue of unbelief and remembers in his experience the moment when God, in pre-existence, affirmed His oneness and lordship before all humanity. There is only one who can truly say, "I am" (*anā*), God, giving expression to the secret of divine lordship (*sirr al-rubūbiyya*) captured by the mystic in the experience of *dhikr* (cf. Böwering, *Mystical vision*, 187-207). Al-Tustarī's practical Ṣūfī ideal was incessant repentance (*al-tawba farīḍa ʿalā 'l-ʿabd maʿa kulli nafas*, al-Sarrādj, *Lumaʿ*, 407, cf. Arberry, *Pages*, 9) and complete trust in God (*tawakkul*) which he understood as handing oneself over to God like the corpse in the hands of the undertaker (al-Ḳushayrī, *Risāla*, 368).

Al-Tustarī's thought is deeply intertwined with Ḳur'ānic exegesis. He proposed a pattern of Ḳur'ān interpretation that theoretically distinguished four meanings for each verse, literal (*ẓāhir*), allegorical (*bāṭin*), moral (*ḥadd*) and anagogical (*maṭlaʿ, muṭṭalaʿ*). In fact, however, he consistently employed only two levels of meaning, a literal and an allegorical sense, combining *ẓāhir* and *ḥadd* as opposed to *bāṭin* and *maṭlaʿ*. In his theology, al-Tustarī understood God under the symbol of light (*nūr*) on the background of the light verse (*āyat al-nūr*, XXIV, 35) and chose the phrase of "the light of Muḥammad" (*nūr Muḥammad*) to designate the primal man and prototypical mystic, apparently in vague association with logos speculations and Shīʿī terminology. In interpretation of II, 30, and LIII, 13-18, he conceived of Muḥammad as the column of light (*ʿamūd al-nūr*) standing in primordial adoration of God, the crystal which draws the divine light upon itself, absorbs it in its core (*ḳalb Muḥammad*) and projects it unto humanity in the Ḳur'ān.

In his psychology, al-Tustarī played on the double-entendre of *nafas* (breath; life-breath) and *nafs* (soul, self), and perceived the human soul as the theatre of a struggle between two antagonistic tendencies, that of the God-centred orientation of the human heart (*ḳalb*), his spiritual self (*nafs al-rūḥ*), and that of the self-centred inclination of the carnal soul (*al-nafs al-ammāra bi 'l-sū'*), his natural self (*nafs al-ṭabʿ*). Interpreting Ḳur'ān, XXXIX, 42, al-Tustarī traced the two selves to the notion of *tawaffī* (God's taking the souls unto Himself in death, sleep and mystic ascent) and understood each of them as a subtle substance (*laṭīf*), one luminous, the other coarse. Al-Tustarī's notion of faith (*īmān*) did not only include profession with the tongue (*ḳawl*), conformity of action (*ʿamal*) and intention (*niyya*) but also the light of certitude (*nūr al-yaḳīn*), by which the mystic is enabled to anticipate God's final self-revelation (*tadjallī*) experienced in the beatific vision. Al-Tustarī found the basis for his idea of *tadjallī* in Ḳur'ān, XLIII, 70-2, a reference to the people of paradise, rather than in the Ḳur'ānic reference to Moses, who was unable to bear the sight of God's revelation (VII, 143).

There are only fragmentary source texts illuminating al-Tustarī's resolution of the central problem of Muslim theology concerning the interrelation between divine omnipotence and human responsibility. Al-Tustarī's thought attempts to achieve a conjunction of opposites and foreshadows Ashʿarī themes. However, these themes may have been introduced into his *Tafsīr al-Ḳur'ān* by his disciples in the aftermath of al-Ashʿarī [*q.v.*]. God creates both good and evil and possesses two kinds of will, volition (*mashī'a*) and an express will (*irāda*). Since human action is caused by the divine agency, God has to possess divine foreknowledge (*ʿilm Allāh al-sābiḳ*) of it prior to its occurrence. God's providence (*tadbīr*), made explicit in His command (*amr*) and interdiction (*nahy*), runs parallel to God's guidance (*hidāya*), made explicit in His help (*maʿūna*, also termed *wilāya*) and protection (*ʿiṣma*). When man performs an action in conformity with the divine Command and Interdiction, he is granted the divine succour of God's *maʿūna*, i.e. divinely given success (*tawfīḳ*). Should he commit an action in opposition to the divine Command and Interdiction, man places himself outside the divine custody and is deserted by God, who withdraws His *ʿiṣma* and forsakes man (*khidhlān* [*q.v.*]). It is man's duty to turn to God with thanksgiving when he performs a good deed (*ḥasana*) and to seek God's succour through repentance when he commits an evil deed (*sayyi'a*). Whether man conforms to or opposes the divine Command and Interdiction, in each case the action comes from God although it is executed through man and by man (*minhu bihim wa-lahum*, see Böwering, *Mystical vision*, 175-84).

Bibliography: Tustarī, *Tafsīr al-Ḳur'ān al-karīm*, Cairo 1329/1911 (this edition cited); Sarrādj, *Kitāb al-Lumaʿ*, ed. R.A. Nicholson, Leiden 1914; Makkī, *Ḳūt al-ḳulūb fī muʿāmalāt al-maḥbūb*, 4 vols., Cairo 1351/1932; Sulamī, *Ṭabaḳāt al-ṣūfiyya*, ed. J. Pedersen, Leiden 1960, 199-205; Ḳushayrī, *al-Risāla al-ḳushayriyya*, Cairo 1385/1966; al-Anṣarī al-Harawī, *Ṭabaḳāt al-ṣūfiyya*, ed. ʿAbd al-Ḥayy Ḥabībī, Kābul 1341 *sh.*/1961; Abū Nuʿaym, *Ḥilyat al-awliyā' wa-ṭabaḳāt al-aṣfiyā'*, 10 vols., Cairo 1351-7/1932-9; Shaʿrānī, *al-Ṭabaḳāt al-kubrā*, 2 vols., Cairo 1315/1897; Ibn al-Farrā', *al-Muʿtamad fī uṣūl al-dīn*, Beirut 1974; ʿAbd al-Ḳādir al-Djīlānī, *al-Ghunya li-ṭālibī ṭarīḳ al-ḥaḳḳ*, 2 vols., Cairo 1322; A.J. Arberry, *Pages from the Kitāb al-lumaʿ*, London 1947; G. Böwering, *The mystical vision of existence in classical Islam*, Berlin-New York 1980; M.K. Gaafer, *Min al-turāth al-ṣūfī*, Cairo 1974; I. Goldziher, in *ZDMG*, xli (1907), 73-80; L. Massignon, *Essai sur les origines du lexique technique de la mystique musulmane*, Paris 1968; C. Tunc, *Sahl b. ʿAbd Allāh at-Tustarī und die Sālimīya*, Bonn 1970. (G. Böwering)

AL-**SAHM** (A.) "arrow". For the use of arrows in archery, see ḲAWS.

1. In science.

a. Geometrical term. If one erects a perpendicular *c b* in the middle of a chord of an arc, which reaches to the arc, this is called *al-sahm*, the versed sine (*al-djayb al-maʿkūs*) of the arc *a b*; the sine (*al-djayb al-mustawī*), which corresponds to our sine, is *a c* (see—in

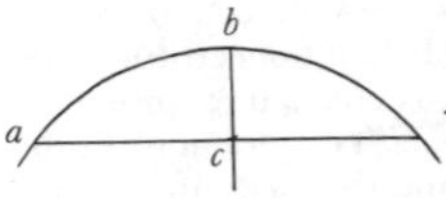

addition to many other passages—al-Khwārazmī, *Mafātīḥ al-ʿulūm* ed. van Vloten, 205). The versed sine played a much more important part in the older mathematics from the Hindus onwards than it does in modern mathematics (cf. e.g. A. von Braunmühl, *Geschichte der Trigonometrie*). Sine and versed sine are measured in the parts of the radius of the circle, the latter being taken as equal to 60 parts or = 1.

b. Astrological term. Ibn al-Ḳifṭī says that the expression *sahm al-ghayb* (the arrow, the hitting of the secret of the future , see *op. cit.*, 327, 338, 410) is astrological. (E. WIEDEMANN*)

c. Astronomical term. *Ṣūrat al-Rāmī*, constellation of Sagittarius, and also *al-Ḳaws*, bow of Sagittarius (cross-bow), is a southern constellation of the ecliptic, which, according to Ptolemy and the Arabs, consists of 31 stars mainly of southern latitude, which are almost all of the 3rd to 6th degrees of magnitude. Ptolemy gives only star 24 of Sagittarius (Arabic, *rukbat al-yad al-yusrā*, elbow of the left arm) the magnitude 2-3, while al-Bīrūnī (*al-Ḳānūn al-Masʿūdī*, Berl. ms. 275, fol. 205b) gives magnitude 2 for stars 24 and 23 (*kaʿb al-yad al-yusrā* = knuckle of the left hand); of Sagittarius in Ulugh Beg, however, except star 3 of Sagittarius (*ʿala ʾl-djānib al-djanūbī min al-ḳaws* = the one south of the bow), which, according to him, is 3-2 in magnitude, they are only of the 3rd or lower degrees of magnitude. This 20 ε Sagittarii is really of 1.9 magnitude (on *ʿUrkūb al-rāmī*, see C.A. Nallino, *Opus astronomicum*, ii, 163). The following stars of Sagittarius are also noteworthy: *Naṣl al-sahm* = point of the arrow, and the so-called "eye of the archer", *ʿAyn al-rāmī*, or, according to al-Bīrūnī, *op. cit.*, *al-Saḥāʾib al-muḍaʿʿafa ʿala ʾl-ʿayn* = the nebulous double-star which is in the eye. Neither in al-Bīrūnī nor in Ulugh Beg is there any mention of ostriches (the ostrich going to drink and coming back from drinking) which are mentioned by L. Ideler (see below).

Among the Greeks, Sagittarius was called ὁ τοξότης; among the Romans, Sagittarius, Sagittifer and Arcitenens. There is no evidence that the ancient Egyptians or Babylonians knew of *al-Ḳaws* as a bow-constellation. The bow-constellation of the latter was the bow-shaped group of stars ε δ τ Canis majoris + κ λ Puppis.

Bibliography: L. Ideler, *Untersuchungen über den Ursprung und die Bedeutung der Sternnamen*, Berlin 1809, 183-91; F.W.V. Lach, *Anleitung zur Kenntniss der Sternnahmen*, Leipzig 1796, 83; ʿAbd al-Raḥmān al-Ṣūfī, *Description des étoiles fixes composée au milieu du dixième siècle de notre ère par Abd al-Rahman al-Sûfi*, tr. H.C.F.C. Schjellerup, St. Petersburg 1874, 30; E.B. Knobel, *Ulugh Beg's catalogue of stars*, Washington 1917, 40, 105; P. Kunitzsch, *Arabische Sternnamen in Europa*, Wiesbaden 1959, 205.

(C. SCHOY*)

2. In law.

Here, *sahm*, pl. *ashum*, is found in two separate contexts. In *farāʾiḍ* [*q.v.*] (the allotted portions), it refers to the fixed share of an heir (*wārith*).

Sahm is also used in partnership (*sharika*) and profit-sharing (*muḍāraba*). As a term used in modern share companies (*sharikat al-ashum*), it is defined as a partial ownership of a large capital (*ḥuḳūḳ milkiyya djuzʾiyya*). The holder is called *musāhim*. *Sahm*, unlike the commercial bond *sanad*, is permitted in Islamic law because it contains no interest. According to al-Ḳarḍāwī, *zakāt* is only required on self-generating shares in companies that do not change the essence of their trading commodity, like import-export companies or dealers in crude oil. The shares in these examples are seen as the actual active capital, therefore they are liable to *zakāt*. *Zakāt* is not paid on shares which do not generate profit directly. An example of this is shares in companies that provide public services. However, Abū Zahra, ʿAbd al-Raḥmān Ḥasan and ʿAbd al-Wahhāb Khallāf maintain that all shares should be treated as ordinary capital. With regard to trading in *ashum*, it appears to be a *de facto* practice in most Muslim countries, including Saudi Arabia and the Gulf States. This is despite the fact that Islamic law views it with suspicion, likening it to gambling (*maysir* [*q.v.*]) and prohibited speculation.

Bibliography: J. Schacht. *An introduction to Islamic law*, Oxford 1964, 170; Yūsuf al-Ḳarḍāwī, *Fiḳh al-zakāt*, Beirut 1981, 524; W. Zuḥaylī, *al-Fiḳh al-Islāmī wa-adillatuhu*, Damascus 1985, ii, 773, viii, 247; M.N. Siddiqi, *Partnership and profit-sharing in Islamic law*, Leicester 1985, 9, 15-16; S.E. Ryner, *The theory of contracts in Islamic law*, London 1991, 302-3.

(MAWIL IZZI DIEN)

AL-**SAHMĪ**, ḤAMZA B. YŪSUF al-Ḳurashī al-Djurdjānī, Abu ʾl-Ḳāsim (b. at an unknown date towards the middle of the 4th/10th century, d. 427/1038 at Nīshāpūr), traditionist and legal scholar.

A native of Gurgān [*q.v.*] in the Caspian coastlands, where he was a *khaṭīb* and preacher, his major work, and apparently the sole surviving one, is his *Taʾrīkh Djurdjān* or *Kitāb Maʿrifat ʿulamāʾ ahl Djurdjān*, essentially a *ridjāl* [*q.v.*] work devoted to the scholars and *muḥaddithūn* of his native province, to which is prefixed (ed. Ḥaydarābād 1369/1950, 4-18) a brief historical introduction on the Arab conquest of Gurgān and its Arab governors. His information on the scholars of Gurgān was subsequently used by later writers such as al-Samʿānī, Ibn ʿAsākir, Yāḳūt, al-Dhahabī [*q.vv.*], etc. Ḥādjdjī Khalīfa also mentions of his work a *T. Astarābādh* and a *K. al-Arbaʿīn fī faḍāʾil al-ʿAbbās*, whilst his *Suʾālāt ʿan al-Ḥāfiẓ al-Dāraḳuṭnī* [*q.v.*] is quoted by later writers on *ḥadīth*.

Bibliography: See the introd. to the Ḥaydarābād edn. of the *T. Djurdjān* by ʿAbd Allāh b. Yaḥyā al-Yamānī; Ziriklī, *Aʿlām*, ii, 314; F. Rosenthal, *A history of Muslim historiography*², Leiden 1968, 446, 458, 465, 523; Brockelmann, I², 407-8; Sezgin, *GAS*, i, 209.

(C.E. BOSWORTH)

ṢAḤN-I THAMĀN or MEDĀRIS-I THAMĀNIYYE, the eight *medreses* or colleges [see MADRASA] founded by the Ottoman sultan Meḥemmed II [*q.v.*] as part of the ancillaries to his great Fātiḥ Mosque, the whole forming a *külliyye* [*q.v.*] or complex.

The *külliyye* was begun in 867/1463 and completed in 875/1471, and the architect responsible was one Sinān, called variously "the Elder", to distinguish him from the great architect of the following century, Ḳodja Sinān [see SINĀN], or *ʿĀtiḳ* or *Āzādli* "the freedman", implying that he had been of non-Turkish slave status. The eight *medreses* were situated to the east and west of the Mosque, the first group of higher *medreses* being called the Aḳdeñiz or "Mediterranean" group and the second one the Ḳaradeñiz or "Black Sea" group. There were further, lower (*Tetimme*) *medreses*, a hospital, an *ʿimāret* [*q.v.*], a *tābkhāne* or hospice, a library and the two tombs for the sultan himself and his wife Gülbahār Sulṭān, in the complex.

Each of the Ṣaḥn *medreses* had domed rooms (*hüdjres*) and a lecture room, with a total of 120 rooms for resident students who, according to the *wakfiyye* for the whole complex, had a stipend of two *aḳčes* a day; there were also day students, of which the 19th century historian Aḥmed Djewdet Pasha [*q.v.*] was one (*Tedhākir*, iv). The basic stipend of the *müderrisīn* was 30 *akčes* a day. Little definite is known about the organisation and curricula of the *Tetimme medreses*; their buildings have now disappeared, though those of the Ṣaḥn-i Thamān survive.

The Ṣaḥn-i Thamān produced a large number of scholars and jurists, some of whom played leading roles in the Ottoman state and society; like most of the surviving buildings in the complex, it was much restored and rebuilt over the centuries.

Bibliography: *Fatih Sultan Mehmed II vakfiyesi*, Istanbul 1938; Ö.L. Barkan, *Fatih Camii ve Imareti tesislerinin 1489-1490 yıllarına ait muhasebe bilâncoları*, in *İktisat Fakültesi Mecmuası*, xxiii/1-2, 297-341; A. Süheyl Ünver, *Fatih külliyesi ve zamani ilim hayatı*, Istanbul 1946; E. Mamboury, *The tourist's Istanbul*, Istanbul 1953, 405-7; İ.H. Uzunçarşılı, *Osmanlı devletinin ilmiye teşkilâtı*, Ankara 1965, 5-10; G. Goodwin, *A history of Ottoman architecture*, London 1971, 121-31 (with plans of the complex and its buildings at 128-9); Cahid Baltacı, *XV-XVI. asırda Osmanlı medreseleri, teşkilât-tarih*, Istanbul 1976, 350-407. (M. Ipsirli)

ṢAḤNA, a small town in the Zagros Mountains of western Persia on the highroad between Kangāwar and Bīsutūn at 61 km/38 miles from Kirmānshāh [*q.v.*]. The district of Ṣaḥna contains about 28 villages inhabited by settled Turks belonging to the tribe of Khodābandalū (of Hamadān). At Ṣaḥna there are a few Ahl-i-Ḥaḳḳ [*q.v.*], who are in touch with their spiritual superiors in Dīnawar [*q.v.*], a frontier district in the north. Ṣaḥna must not be confused with Sinna [*q.v.*] or Sanandadj [*q.v.*], the capital of the Persian province of Kurdistān, the former residence of the *Wālīs* of Ardalān [*q.v.*]. Quite near Ṣaḥna on the steep bank of the stream are two funerary chambers carved out of the rock and dating in all probability from the Achaemenid period. Yāḳūt, *Buldān*, ed. Beirut, iii, 195, spells Saḥna (with *sīn*), and further mentions another Saḥna near Anbār in ʿIrāḳ.

Modern Ṣaḥna is the chef-lieu of a *bakhsh* of the same name in the province of Kirmānshāh (long. 47° 33′ E., lat. 34° 29′ N., alt. 1,342 m/4,400 feet). In *ca.* 1950 the population of the *bakhsh* was 47,500; by 1991 the population of the town alone was 29,275 (*Preliminary results of the 1991 census*, Statistical Centre of Iran, Population Division).

Bibliography: E. Flandin, *Voyage en Perse*, Paris 1851, i, 413; Čirikov in the *Putevoï journal* of 1848-1852, St. Petersburg 1875, was the first to give a description of the two tombs; Rabino, *Kermanchah RMM*, vol. xxxviii, March 1920, p. 1-40; E. Herzfeld, *Am Tor von Asien*, Berlin 1920, p. 8 (detailed description of the principal tombs; Le Strange, *Lands of the eastern Caliphate*, 190, 220; Schwarz, *Iran im Mittelalter*, 497; Razmārā (ed.), *Farhang-i djughrāfiyā-yi Īrān-zamīn*, v, 285-6; Sylvia A. Matheson, *Persia, an archaeological guide*[2], London 1976, 124-5. (V. Minorsky*)

SAḤNŪN, Abū Saʿīd ʿAbd al-Salām b. Saʿīd b. Ḥabīb b. Ḥassān b. Hilāl b. Bakkār b. Rabīʿa al-Tanūkhī (160-Radjab 240/777-December 855) (nicknamed Saḥnūn, it is said, on account of his shrewdness, or from the name of a bird), a Kairouan *faḳīh* who played a decisive role in the conversion to the Mālikiyya [*q.v.*] of Muslim Spain and of the entire Maghrib where, even today, there exist only a few Ibāḍī pockets (the island of Djerba and Mzab), and a small number of Ḥanafīs.

The question as to whether Saḥnūn was an Arab by pedigree or by virtue of clientship was sometimes asked, and was resented by Saḥnūn; he was in no doubt as to the authenticity of his Arab genealogy. Although not common, the name Saḥnūn (cf., possibly, the diminutive of the form *faʿlūn*, which expresses affection, as in Khaldūn, Zaydūn, Saʿdūn and Ḥamdūn) is attested throughout the Muslim West, in Spain (Ibn Ḥayyān, *Muḳtabis*, Paris 1937, 79, 81, 113), in the central Maghrib (Brockelmann, S II, 715), and at Kairouan, where another *faḳīh* of the same period, Saḥnūn b. Aḥmad b. Yalūl, bore the same name (M. Talbi, *Biographies Aghlabides extraites des Madārik du Cadi ʿIyāḍ*, Tunis 1968, 202, 203). The form Suḥnūn, still in use today, is erroneous (Ibn Makkī al-Ṣiḳillī, *Tathḳīf al-Lisān*, Cairo 1966, 243).

Saʿīd, Saḥnūn's father and a native of Ḥimṣ [*q.v.*] in Syria, was probably a soldier in the army of Yazīd b. Ḥātim al-Muhallabī who, in 155/772, had brought Ifrīḳiya into the ʿAbbāsid orbit, and is said to have received, as a reward for his services, a modest allocation of land in the Sahel of Tunisia. Saḥnūn, who remained a farmer throughout his life, made considerable improvements to the fertility of the land and was thus enabled to exchange poverty for prosperity, allegedly without any change in his style of living. Even after becoming a prestigious *faḳīh* he would still go out, with his plough and his team, to work personally in his fields. Saḥnūn is described as "a man of average height, with light brown skin, a handsome beard, long hair, large eyes and broad shoulders" (Talbi, *op. cit.*, 95). He wore a string of beads around his neck; in the countryside he wore a woollen tunic, with a towel around his head; and in the town, in winter, he dressed in a black burnous. He is known to have had a daughter, Khadīdja, who remained a spinster and whom he held in the very highest of regard, and a son, Muḥammad, whom he educated with care and who became in his turn a brilliant *faḳīh*.

In the time of Saḥnūn, Kairouan was already a major metropolis in all respects: with its opulence, the diversity of its population, its expansionist policy in Sicily—an operation sponsored and directed by a *ḳāḍī*, Asad b. al-Furāt—and its numerous *faḳīhs*. All the trends of Muslim thought were represented there: Muʿtazilī, Murdjiʾī, Sunnī, Ibāḍī, Ḥanafī (then the majority trend) and Mālikī. In the mosques as well as in private dwellings, in the court or in the *ribāṭs*, discussions were animated, and relations often strained. There were mutual accusations of *kufr* (heresy), and copious exchanges of curses. It was in this environment that Saḥnūn was born and nurtured.

Many of the Kairouanese masters, including Asad b. al-Furāt who ultimately sided with the party of the Ḥanafīs, had studied directly under Mālik [*q.v.*], and it was with them that Saḥnūn served his first apprenticeship. Two of his masters exerted a particularly decisive influence on him: Buhlūl b. Rāshid (d. 183/799), who was more of an ascetic than a *faḳīh*, and most of all the Tunisian ʿAlī b. Ziyād (d. 183/799) who had been the first to introduce the *Muwaṭṭaʾ* of Mālik into Ifrīḳiya. All that remains of his version is a fragment recently edited by al-Shādhilī al-Nayfar (Beirut 1980, 1984).

Saḥnūn made his way to the East, for purposes of *riḥla*, to complete and perfect his education, either in 178/794 or in 188/804. The latter date is by far the more plausible. The list of his masters in the East includes 21 names; among these, the figure of the disciple of Mālik, the Egyptian Ibn al-Ḳāsim al-ʿAtakī (d. 191/807), stands out prominently. Asad b. al-Furāt (d. 212/827) had already preceded Saḥnūn in visiting Ibn al-Ḳāsim. From Saḥnūn's questions to the latter, starting from a Ḥanafī outline, and after discussion, the *Asadiyya* was born, the fruit of a compromise, of a kind of Ḥanafī-Mālikī syncretism. Almost from the moment of its completion, the *Asadiyya* wielded an enormous impact, first in Egypt, then in Ifrīḳiya. With it an era, that of *ḥadīth*, came to an end, and another began: that of *masāʾil*, of prepared solutions. It was a sort of code which responded to a pressing need and arrived at the right time.

Armed with a copy of this book, obtained by not the most scrupulous of means, Saḥnūn took the road to Fusṭāṭ in his turn. His *riḥla* was to last three years. Under the direction of Ibn al-Ḳāsim the *Asadiyya* was submitted to a new analysis, in a spirit of greater fidelity to the teaching of Mālik. Saḥnūn gave the text thus revised the title of *Mudawwana*, a name borrowed from another disciple of Mālik, As̲h̲hab (d. 204/819). Barely had it become known when the *Mudawwana*—the term is currently employed in Morocco with the meaning of code—eclipsed the *Asadiyya* completely. As evidence of this eclipse, only a few pages of the *Asadiyya* survive, while the *Mudawwana* has been the object of numerous commentaries and summaries [see MĀLIKIYYA, vol. VI, at 278b). Its influence was decisive in the crystallisation and diffusion of the *mad̲h̲hab* of Mālik throughout the Muslim West, as is proved by the fact that the Almohad caliph Abū Yūsuf [*q.v.*], in his attempt to eradicate Mālikism, consigned the work to the flames, thus paying it the ultimate tribute. The *Mudawwana* was edited in the name of Mālik, Saḥnūn's recension after Ibn al-Ḳāsim (Cairo 1323/1905-6).

Like Asad, Saḥnūn had begun his career teaching the Ḳurʾān to children in a building (*bayt*) rented for this purpose (ʿAbd al-Ḥamīd al-Munīf, *Ad̲j̲wibat Muḥammad b. Saḥnūn*, in *al-Nas̲h̲ra al-ʿilmiyya li 'l-Kulliyya al-Zaytūniyya*, Tunis 1982-3, vi, 239). On his return from the East in 191/807, henceforward enjoying the prestige conferred by the *riḥla*, he established himself as a teacher. He was then about thirty years old, with a long career in education, approximately half a century, ahead of him. Unlike Asad for example, he never seems to have taught in the Great Mosque of Kairouan. As opposed to primary education, higher education was offered free of charge. Saḥnūn gave his courses sometimes in Kairouan, at other times, according to the seasons, at his agricultural property, at Manzil Ṣiḳlāb in the Sahel. It was there that one of his most illustrious disciples, Yaḥyā b. ʿUmar (d. 289/902) first made his acquaintance. The students were received at his residence, according to the time of year, in a room set aside for the purpose, or in front of the main entrance. Armed with their books—they had previously made their own copies of the *Mudawwana*, and other works as well—and their ink-wells, they took their seats on the ground. Some brought mats. A student was nominated to read the text, and the master made comments, sometimes with angry vehemence. As the prestige of the master was consolidated, students flocked in from all directions, especially from Muslim Spain. The place was often crowded, and the students were of all ages and all classes. The future *ḳāḍī* Ibn Ṭālib (d. 275/888), of aristocratic family, began attending Saḥnūn's courses when he was barely an adolescent. Saḥnūn noticed him and urged him to wear "the scholarly habit". "When the next course began," Ibn Ṭālib relates, "I presented myself with shaved head, and dressed in the manner of scholars" (Talbi, *op. cit.*, 209). The throng which gathered around Saḥnūn was great, and somewhat bizarre. "His courses were attended by more pious people (*ʿubbād*) than genuine students" (Talbi, *op. cit.*, 119). Some slept openly. The master did not object, considering that even thus they were gaining the benefit of *samāʿ* (audition). The popularity of his courses is clearly illustrated by the fact that miraculous phenomena were associated with them; it is related in all seriousness that the *d̲j̲inn* themselves attended them.

In certain circumstances, prestige inevitably attracts controversy. Having become, with advancing age and after the death of Asad, the undisputed leader of Ifrīḳiyan Sunnism, Saḥnūn also became a legitimate target. In S̲h̲aʿbān 231/April 846, the old quarrel regarding the nature of the Ḳurʾān—created according to the Muʿtazilīs, uncreated according to the Sunnīs—became suddenly acrimonious. In Bag̲h̲dād, al-Wāt̲h̲iḳ declared his hostility towards the Sunnīs while in Kairouan, Abu D̲j̲aʿfar Aḥmad, who had usurped power at the expense of his brother, the *amīr* Muḥammad I, seized the opportunity to kill two birds with one stone, bringing his policy into line with that of the caliphate, as was traditional, and at the same time offering pledges to the Muʿtazilīs who had supported him in his confrontation with the Sunnīs. Aḥmad b. Naṣr, a fervent representative of the doctrine of the uncreated Ḳurʾān, was executed in Bag̲h̲dād by al-Wāt̲h̲iḳ personally in S̲h̲aʿbān 231/April 846. The following month, Saḥnūn, who had taken refuge in the *ribāṭ* of Kaṣr Ziyād in the Sahel, was arrested and transferred to Kairouan. A trial took place in the Palace in the course of which the Muʿtazilī *ḳāḍī* Ibn Abi 'l-D̲j̲awād, who had held this post for eighteen years and had sided with the usurper, demanded his execution. More fortunate than Aḥmad b. Naṣr, Saḥnūn was merely placed under house arrest. This did not last long; the following year the *amīr* Muḥammad I regained power, sent his brother into exile in the East, dismissed his *ḳāḍī* Ibn Abi 'l-D̲j̲awād and, in accordance with the movement which had begun in the East with the accession of al-Mutawakkil, practised a policy of reconciliation with the Sunnīs.

It was in these circumstances, and after protracted negotiations, that Saḥnūn was appointed *ḳāḍī*, with full powers (Monday, 4 Ramaḍān 234/1 April 849). He was then 74 years old. He was elevated to this post by a Sunnī consensus, and he was helped in particular by the support of the Ḥanafī *faḳīhs*, who were then broadly in the majority, and of their leader Sulaymān b. ʿImrān. As a means of consolidating the Sunnī consensus, Saḥnūn involved the latter in the exercise of his functions, and began taking important measures designed to strengthen Sunnism and to reinforce the power of the *ḳāḍī*. For audiences he set aside a special room to which only plaintiffs were admitted, having submitted a written application, in person and in turn, without the option of being represented by third parties, whatever the social rank of the applicant.

Released, as was to be expected, by the authorities, the Muʿtazilī Ibn Abi 'l-D̲j̲awād, son-in-law of Asad, was placed under arrest, officially on a charge of financial embezzlement, something which the accused persisted in denying until the end. Naturally, the underlying motive for the indictment was otherwise. In addition to personal motivations, Saḥnūn had decided to strike a blow against heresy. He was in fact, so it is related, very severe in his opposition to the innovators (*ahl al-bidaʿ*), of whom Ibn Abi 'l-D̲j̲awād was not one of the least. Day after day, with the object of extorting the desired confession from him, Saḥnūn had him flogged in the courtyard of the Great Mosque, until he died. This death, allegedly, weighed heavily on his conscience, but this did not deter him from pursuing energetically his policy of the repression of heresy, in other words the freedom of independent thought.

Hitherto, in the multiple circles of scholarship, representatives of all tendencies were able to express themselves freely in the Great Mosque of Kairouan. In a process amounting to a purging of the community of scholars there, Saḥnūn put an end to this "scandal". He dispersed the sects of the *ahl al-bidaʿ*; the leaders of heretical sects were paraded ignominiously, and some were compelled to recant in public. Saḥnūn was one of the greatest architects of the exclusive supremacy of Sunnism in its Mālikī form throughout the Muslim West.

Like all Sunnīs, he condemned recourse to the sword "even against the unjust *imāms*" (al-Mālikī, *Riyāḍ*, Beirut 1983, 368), which does not mean that the barometer of his relations with the authorities was set fair. From the outset he took the position of guarantor of an intransigent justice, upright and equal for all—including the entourage of the *amīr*—and of redresser of wrongs, which often led him into vehement confrontation with Muhammad I, in particular with his insistence on the release of numerous women unjustly condemned to slavery in the course of various operations aimed at the repression of insurrections. On numerous occasions he felt obliged to offer his resignation. Although he did not accept this resignation the *amīr*, tired of his criticisms and of the incessant complaints of his entourage, ultimately gave him an associate in the person of al-Ṭubnī, a *ḳāḍī* reputedly ignorant but complaisant. Some time later, in the morning of Sunday 7 Radjab 240/2 December 854, Saḥnūn died, depressed and embittered. As required by Tradition, he was buried in the afternoon of the same day. As a supreme tribute, or for reasons of political expediency, the *amīr* conducted the funeral prayers in person. His Muʿtazilī entourage was not so forgiving: "He accused us, and we accuse him, of heresy", they said (Talbi, *op. cit.*, 133). His mausoleum, in the outskirts of Kairouan, is the object of constant veneration.

The name of Saḥnūn remains associated with the definitive triumph of Mālikism throughout the Muslim West, a triumph which Ibn Khaldūn, as a sociologist, explains by reference to Bedouinism (*Muḳaddima*, Beirut 1956, 810-11). This explanation does not take account of the fact that it was Ḥanafism which enjoyed a broad majority at the outset. In the reversal of the situation, it is therefore necessary to stress the exceptional role played by Saḥnūn. At his initiative, and by means of his prestige, Kairouan became a major centre for the study and diffusion of Mālikī *fiḳh*. He left, it is said, some 700 disciples, all of them "truly shining lights in their respective towns" (Talbi, *op. cit.*, 120). Among them, we have recorded 57 in Muslim Spain.

But Saḥnūn was not only a great *faḳīh*. His knowledge was matched by his piety, and by a life which was austere to the point of asceticism. Although wealthy—at the end of his life he possessed 12,000 olive-trees (*ibid.*, 163)—he disposed of his income in the form of alms and continued to live a life of poverty. He was easily moved to tears, and frequently sought seclusion in the *ribāṭ* of Ḳaṣr Ziyād. Rather curiously, and in a manner contrary to much of tradition, he preached a version of monasticism: "If one can get by without a wife," he said, "it is preferable to renounce marriage" (al-Mālikī, *op. cit.*, 364). "In him there were qualities," wrote Abu 'l-ʿArab, "which were not to be found combined in any other: perfect knowledge of the law (*fiḳh*), sincere piety, rigour in the application of justice, contempt for temporal things, simple tastes in food and clothing, generosity and refusal to accept anything from princes" (*Ṭabaḳāt*, Algiers 1914, 101).

Saḥnūn was a great master of *fiḳh* and also a man of rigorous and demanding ethics. It is this which explains his success, and the constant veneration in which he is still held.

Bibliography: 1. Sources. Abu 'l-ʿArab, *Ṭabaḳāt*, Algiers 1914, index; Mālikī, *Riyāḍ*, Beirut 1983, i, 345-76 and index; M. Talbi, *Biographies Aghlabides extraites des Madārik du Cadi ʿIyāḍ*, Tunis 1968, 57-62, 86-136, and index; Ibn Farḥūn, *Dībādj*, Cairo 1351/1932-3, 160-6; Ghubrīnī, *ʿUnwān al-dirāya*, Algiers 1970, 124, 314; Dabbāgh/Ibn Nādjī, *Maʿālim*, Tunis 1320-5/1902-8, ii, 49-68, Cairo 1968-72, ii, 77-104; Ibn Khallikān, *Wafayāt*, ed. ʿAbbās, iii, 180-2; Shīrāzī, *Ṭabaḳāt*, Beirut 1970, 156-7; Ibn al-ʿImād al-Ḥanbalī, *Shadharāt*, Cairo 1350/1931-2, ii, 94; al-Wazīr al-Sarrādj, *Ḥulal*, Tunis 1970, i, fasc. 1, 285-8, fasc. 3, 769-807, index; Ibn al-Shabbāṭ, *Ṣila*, ms. BN Tunis (fonds Aḥmadiyya), no. 5065, fol. 120; Khushanī, *Ḳuḍāt Ḳurṭuba*, Cairo 1374/1954-5, 88, 93; Ibn al-Abbār, *Takmila*, Madrid 1888, nos. 783, 958; Ibn al-Faraḍī, *Taʾrīkh*, Madrid 1892, no. 967; Dhahabī, *ʿIbar*, Kuwait, 1966, i, 432-3; Dhahabī, *Duwal*, Ḥaydarābād 1337/1918-19, i, 113; Ibn Khayr, Fahrasa, Cairo-Beirut 1963, 240-1; Ibn al-Athīr, *Lubāb*, Beirut, Dār Ṣādir n.d., i, 79; Ibn Mākūlā, *Ikmāl*, Ḥaydarābād n.d., iv, 265-6; Samʿānī, *Ansāb*, Ḥaydarābād, i, 324; Ibn Ḥadjar al-ʿAsḳalānī, *Lisān*, Ḥaydarābād, iii, 8; Damīrī, *Ḥayāt al-ḥayawān*, Cairo 1311/1893-4, ii, 20; Yāfiʿī, *Mirʾāt*, Ḥaydarābād, ii, 131-2; Ibn Ḥayyān, *Muḳtabis*, Beirut 1973, index; al-Ḳāḍī al-Nuʿmān, *Iftitāḥ*, Beirut 1970, 82-4, Tunis 1975, 60-2; Marrākushī, *Muʿdjib*, Cairo 1963, 354-5; Ibn ʿIdhārī, *Bayān*, Leiden 1948, i, 107, 109-11, 120, 137, 139, 145, 154, 161, 162, 172, 180, 183, 187, 192, 203; Ibn Khaldūn, *Muḳaddima*, Beirut 1956, 812; *ʿIbar*, Beirut 1956, iv, 429.

2. Studies. Brockelmann, S I, 299-300; Makhlūf, *Shadjarat al-Nūr*, Cairo 1349/1930-1, 69-70; Ziriklī, *Aʿlām*, Beirut 1970, iv, 129; ʿU.R. Kaḥḥāla, *Muʾallifūn*, Damascus 1957-61, vi, 224; M. Talbi, *Emirat Aghlabide*, Paris 1967, index; *Etudes d'histoire Ifrīqienne*, Tunis 1982, 91-164, idem, *Kairouan et le Mālikisme espagnol*, in *Mél. Lévi-Provençal*, i, 317-37; F. Dachraoui, *Fāṭimides*, Tunis 1981, index; H.R. Idris, *Zīrides*, Paris 1962, index; R. Brunschvig, *Ḥafṣides*, Paris 1947, index; Muḥammad Zaynuhum Muḥammad ʿAzb, *Faḳīh Ifrīḳiya Abū Saʿīd ʿAbd al-Salām b. Saʿīd al-maʿrūf bi-Saḥnūn*, diss., Fac. of Letters, Cairo 1986; S. Ghrab, *Ibn ʿArafa*, Tunis 1993, index; A. al-Madjdūb, *al-Ṣirāʿ al-madhhabī bi-Ifrīḳiya*, Tunis, index; Ḥ.Ḥ. ʿAbd al-Wahhāb, *Kitāb al-ʿUmr*, Tunis 1990, ii, 585-7; A. Békir, *Histoire de l'Ecole Mālikite en Orient*, Tunis 1962, 31, 44-5, 75.

(M. Talbi)

AL-ṢAḤRĀʾ (A.), in English the Sahara, the name given to the desert in the northern part of Africa. *Ṣaḥrāʾ* is the feminine of the adjective *aṣḥar* "fawn, tawny coloured". It is applied by certain authors to an ensemble of stony terrain, steppelands and sands (cf. al-Idrīsī, ed. de Goeje, 37 n.), whilst the term *mudjdiba* designates more particularly terrain covered with moving sands and totally waterless (see Abu 'l-Fidāʾ, 137, tr. Reinaud, ii/2, 190). Leo Africanus uses it as a synonym for "desert" in general, see Schefer's ed., i/1, 5.

1. *History of the term.*

The Arabic authors provide only fragmentary and often vague items of information on the Sahara. The only region which they know with some precision is the northern zone, bordering on Ifrīḳiya and the Maghrib, the zone within which Ibn Khaldūn (*Hist. des Berbères*, ed. de Slane, i, 190) includes the Tafilalt, Touat, Gourara, Fezzan and even Ghadāmis. These authors further disagree on the boundaries of the Sahara. Thus al-Bakrī asserts that the sands mark the beginning of the "land of the blacks" (*Masālik*, Algiers 1911, 21, tr. de Slane, 49). Ibn Khaldūn, on the contrary, states that this land is separated from Barbary by a vast region formed from deserts "where one risks dying of thirst". One also finds here and there some information on the parts of the desert crossed by caravan routes (e.g. on the western Sahara; cf. the description of the desert called Nisar or Tisar by al-Idrīsī, Yusr by Abu 'l-Fidā᾽) or on certain trade centres like Tadmakka and Awdaghust [*q.v.*] (al-Bakrī, 339). Leo Africanus sums up the items of information given by his predecessors. He identifies the Sahara with the Libya of the ancients (i, 5) and attempts a regional division based on the peoples there. He distinguishes five parts to the Sahara: (1) the desert of the Zenaga from the Ocean to the salt workings of Tegaza; (2) the desert of Wanzigha, from the salt workings of Tegaza to the Aïr towards the east and the desert of Sidjilmāsa [*q.v.*] to the north; (3) the desert of Targa (Touareg), bounded in the west by Ighidi, to the north by Touat, Gourara and the Mzāb [*q.v.*] and to the south by the kingdom of Agades; (4) the desert of the Lamta [see LAMṬA], bounded on the north by the deserts of Ouargla and Ghadāmis, and on the south by the deserts which stretch as far as Kano; and (5) the desert of the Bardawa, that between the desert of the Lamta in the west, the desert of Awdjila in the east, Fezzan to the north and Bornu to the south (tr. Schefer, iii, 267 ff.).

2. *Boundaries.*

The present-day Sahara is bounded on the west by the Atlantic; on the north by the chains of the southern Atlas from the Moroccan High Atlas to the hills of Gafsa in Tunisia; then by the Mediterranean, then Libya (apart from some better-watered areas of Tripolitania and Cyrenaica) as far as Egypt; on the south by the Sāḥil [*q.v.*] and its extensions to the Sudan. To the east, some authors end it at the Nile valley, whilst others extend it as far as the Red Sea and include with it the deserts of Arabia, which in effect form part of the same, diagonal-running arid region extending from Mauritania to the deserts of China, in which the Red Sea is the only topographical interruption, though not climatically. The area of the Sahara may be estimated at between 8.5 million and 9.5 million km² according to the criteria adopted by various authors for its boundaries.

3. *Physical geography.*

(a) Climate and vegetation. The Sahara is characterised above all by its desert climate, linked to the great anticylones which often fix themselves there. The great scarcity and irregularity of rainfall, as well as its pronounced isolation, make the southern part of the region one of the hottest of the globe, where the average annual temperature can reach 30°. These two factors join together to make the air extremely dry and to bring about intense evaporation, even if there are notable differences between the central region of the desert and its fringes; on the periphery, rainfall, though feeble, arrives at least once a year, and the action of water running, favoured by the absence of vegetation cover, remains the predominant factor modifying the natural milieu in the semi-arid and aric areas, when these are not too pronounced; the steppe lands to the north, more complex in the Sāḥil [*q.v.*] t the south, mark the transition to wetter regions anc form milieux relatively more favourable to human activity and to pastoralism. It is only in the central par of the Sahara that the action of water becomes negligible in the areas which are completely arid and hyper arid; effective rainfall there is so rare, and separatec in time by several years, that the action o temperature and, above all, that of the wind, become the essential factor making for erosion of a virtuall fixed environment, such as can be observed in th great plains of Tanezrouft on the Algerian-Mali frontier and of Ténéré on the Algerian-Niger frontier, o in the *sarīr*s of southern Libya. In the desert proper vegetation is extremely sparse, apart from in certai wadi beds where some spiny trees manage to maintai themselves by deriving water from deep underground.

The abundance of prehistoric artefacts in the mos desolate regions of the Sahara point to the regio having undergone climatic modifications. Since th beginning of the Quaternary, it has been affected b alternate phases of humidity and dryness connecte above all with changes in the earth's orbit. The las humid phase, the better known, took place mainly be tween 6,000 and 2,000 B.C. It affected the whole c the Sahara, and conditions were clearly mor favourable, as shown by frequent traces of lake- dwelling sites which allowed the installation of Neolithi peoples throughout almost all the desert. Thes peoples covered the sandstone rock faces wit numerous carvings and paintings depicting the faun of wet zones.

(b) Relief. The mountainous massifs, even if times important, cover only a small part of th Sahara. They number three. The Tibesti (21° N, 18 E), the most extensive and the highest, reaching 3,40 m/10,300 feet; the Hoggar [see AHAGGAR] (23° N, 6 E), slightly lower at 3,000 m/9,000 feet; and the A (18° N, 8° E), only reaching 2,300 m/7,000 fee Other massifs, such as the Adrar of the Ifoghas an the Adrar of Atar [see ADRAR], are clearly of lesser in portance and are only remarkable in relation to th surrounding plains. In essence, the greater part of th Sahara is made up of vast flat regions, of divers origin and divisible into two groups. The vast erosic surfaces which have levelled the ancient shields of th African plate formation cover the greater part of th Sahara; they are often interrupted by residual relie with steep slopes, called in the Earth Sciences by Ge man terms, *inselberg*s when they are isolated, and *i selgebirge* when they form small mountainous massi covering a small part of the surface (e.g. the "massif of the Eglab on the Algerian-Mauritanian border The other surfaces are made up of sedimentary cove ings of the base, forming plateaux and called *ḥamād* when they are not too worn by erosion. These cove ings are sometimes ancient (sandstone *tassili*s arour the Hoggar and Tibesti massifs, often much dissect by erosion), and sometimes more recent (the gre Mesozoic *ḥamāda*s of the Tademaït plateaux to t north of In Salah, and the recently-formed *ḥamāda*s the southern piedmont region of the Saharan Atlas The greater part of these surfaces is covered by the [*q.v.*], occasionally covered by a thin sandy surfacin In effect, contrary to an idea frequently put forwar the sand dune massifs making up the *erg*s hardly cov more than one-sixth of the area of the Sahara, ev though they may at times make up very extensi ensembles like the Great Western Erg (*ca.* 80,0 km²) and the Great Eastern Erg in the north of the Algerian Sahara, and the Edeyen (a Berber term) of Murzouk in Libya, or the Great Erg of Bilma (Chad-Niger), at the point of contact between the Sahara and the Sāḥil. Watercourses (*wādīs*) are rare, above all in the hyper-arid central part; their valleys are often very wide and their beds, which are not commensurate with the current quantity of water transported, are favourable spots for human activity; they are the heritage of the more humid climatic variations of the Quaternary period.

Bibliography: E.F. Gautier, *Le Sahara*, Paris 1928; P. Rognon, *Biographie d'un désert*, Paris 1989; J. Dubief, *Le climat du Sahara*, Institut de Recherche Saharienne, Alger, 2 vols., Algiers 1959-63; R. Capot-Rey, *Le Sahara français*, Paris 1953; P. Rognon, *Un massif montagneux enrégion tropicale aride, l'Atakor. Relation entre le milieu naturel et le peuplement*, Montpellier 1971; J.-F. Troin (ed.), *Le Maghreb, hommes et espaces*, Paris 1987; *Montagnes du Sahara*, in *Rev. de Géogr. Alpine*, lxxix/1 (1991); Th. Monod, *Déserts*, Paris 1988.

(Y. Callot)

4. *Human geography and population*.

The ancient human population of the Sahara is complex, and has its roots in the distant past. One must in fact go back to the beginnings of the Neolithic period (*ca.* 8,000 B.C.) in order to see how, each time when the climate becomes more wet, the desert becomes repopulated on the its margins—Maghrib, Nile valley, the Sāḥil. The population was already varied, as is seen in the diversity of the axes of population. All through the Neolithic period, the ancestors of numerous present peoples of North Africa lived in the Sahara: Palaeoberbers, between North Africa, the Tropic of Cancer and the Nile, negroid Sudanese, and Nilotic peoples. Rock art shows this diversity: in the Tassili n'Ajjer, the Acacus, the Ahaggar, etc., are carved and, above all, painted scenes of hunting, livestock rearing and daily life which inevitably evoke the nomads of the Sahara and the northern Sāḥil—Moors, Touaregs, Tubus, Peuls or Fulanis, etc.

Growing desiccation led to, from 2,000 B.C. onwards and even earlier in the Egyptian Sahara, a retreat of human occupation; hunters, pastoralists and primary agriculturists had to follow southwards the retreat of the isohyets. In the eastern Sahara, numerous Palaeoberber groups (including the Lebu, who provided the ethonym "Libyan") were compelled, often with sucess, to penetrate into the Nile valley, where the Libyans or Tehennu played an important role in the birth and florescence of Pharaonic civilisation.

From the beginning of the present era, desiccation became general. Except for a few refuge areas, valleys or mountains, the Sahara henceforth made obligatory an economy and way of life which only certain human groups were ready to accept, and which was to allow them to control the Saharan expanses: Berbers (Lawāta, Sanhādja, Zanāta, Lamṭa, Hawāra, etc., ancestors more or less directly of the white-skinned nomads, Moors and Touaregs, of historical times), Tubus, Zaghāwa (between Fezzan, Tibesti, Lake Chad and Kordofan), etc.

The Romans, masters of Egypt and North Africa at this time, knew hardly anything of the Sahara. They were content with military campaigns of intimidation or of reconaissance, without any intention of colonisation, and with a simple, necessary belt of southern defences for controlling the nomads of the northern Sahara. Only Fezzan, under control of the Garamantes, to some extent vassals from A.D. 69 onwards, was frequented by the Romans, for reasons as much commercial as political, starting from the Libyan littoral and from the Nile valley.

The economy was based on stock rearing (goats and, above all, camels), the razzia and war, domination of the oases (where traces of the Neolithic period population survived) and the beginnings of caravan trade, initiated by the very rapid growth in the number of dromedaries.

At this time, the Sahara was already a barrier, as much climatic as cultural, between the Nile, North Africa and the Sāḥil. Each ensemble of territories now developed specific characteristics. Commerce and the advent of Islam, however, were to bring them together again, for, in future, the Sahara itself was only to be attractive because of the possibility of being out of sight there, as with the Khāridjites of Mzāb or of Sidjilmāsa, where were to be found certain Arab tribes which had been pushed back or were particularly adventurous.

Contrariwise, between the introduction of the dromedary and the lure of the rich markets of the Maghrib (from Fātimid times onwards) and of Europe, an economic system based on interchange developed progressively across the desert. From the 8th century onwards, bands of Arab traders coming from the Maghrib established themselves in the lands of the Sāḥil, which the Arab geographers and travellers describe (Ibn Ḥawḳal, al-Bakrī, Ibn Baṭṭūṭa, etc.). Towns either developed or were created (Awdaghust, Ghāna, Djenné, Gao, Tademekka, Agadès, etc.). From the 13th century, the Sāḥil profited extensively from the system, by controlling exports—and not only those of gold—across the desert.

The 14th century was the golden age for these trans-Saharan relations. The Meccan Pilgrimage of the king of Mali, Mansa Mūsā [*q.v.*], in 1324, was the apogee of this, so impressive was its richness. But from the end of the 15th century onwards, the more and more exigent presence of Europeans on the Atlantic coasts of Africa disturbed trans-Saharan relations and made human relations harder.

Around the 10th century, a period of climatic remission allowed a number of peoples of the Sāḥil—Soninke, Bambara, Soghaï, Mossi, Zarma, Hausa, Peul or Fulani, Kanuri, Kanemi, etc.—to re-establish themselves as far as the 20° latitude north, where they could now for the first time practise stock rearing and even, at times, agriculture. They also formed political entities, straddling the Sahara and Sāḥil, which were the first ones in that region and which clashed, towards the north, with those of the Berbers and Arabs.

Arab penetration was in fact an early one, along the tracks, which became the axes for human, commercial, intellectual and religious penetration. From the outset of their conquest of North Africa, they were attracted by the Sahara, in respect of gold and of slaves from its southern fringes. The first moves date from 666 (Fezzan and possibly Kawar), 682 (Sūs) and 734-5 (from Morocco towards Senegal). But during the 7th-8th centuries, the Arabs were still too much strangers to the Sahara for them to establish themselves there for any lengthy duration.

In the western Sahara, there was a strong current of contacts between Morocco and the Sāḥil, where the town of Awdaghust became important from before the 7th century. At the opening of the 11th one, Berbers of Mauritania—the Almoravids [see al-murābiṭūn]—launched themselves in an immense politico-religious movement of conquest, of which the Berber-Sudanese front was as important as the Moroccan-

Hispanic one. The region then fell once more into an indrawn state, troubled only by the progressive and irresistible movement, as far as the banks of the Senegal, of Arab tribes coming from Morocco, who gradually were to form, together with the Berber substratum, the basis of the Moorish peoples of the western Sahara.

In the Niger bend, Gao was already a powerful, and Muslim, town in the 8th century, frequented by the Massouf Berbers, living between Mauritania and Mali. Its relations with the Maghrib (Tāhart, Ghadāmis, Ghāt, Tunis and Tripoli) and with Egypt, and even with Spain, were close. Timbuctu [*q.v.*], founded in the 12th century, was another of these staging-post towns of the desert. The kingdom of Mali [*q.v.*] was a truly international power, which the Ottoman empire, the Ḥafṣids of Tunis and the Moroccan dynasties had to take into account. But the region was frequently devastated by the rivalries of the peoples of the Sāḥil (Soninke, Songhaï, Mossi, Peul or Fulani, etc.), the Touaregs (who definitively seized the Aïr from the Hausas in the 12th century) and, later, the Moroccans, who endeavoured, without great success, to establish their power in the Sāḥil in the 16th century by destroying the Songhaï empire (battle of Tondibi, 1591).

In the eastern Sahara, there were several large groupings, along axes to the Mediterranean, by means of two main routes, Aïr-Ahaggar and Kawar-Djado, with Fezzan as a staging-post. The kingdom of Bornu [*q.v.*] was the most important of these between the 16th and 18th centuries, in contact with the Ottomans, who controlled Cairo, Tripoli and Tunis, and who were above all interested in the slave traffic. The Tubus, long established between Fezzan, Djado, Ennedi and Lake Chad, resisted all pressures.

Yet further to the east, relations existed between the Chad basin and the Nile valley in the Sudan, via Ennedi and Dārfūr [*q.v.*].

The Europeans did not really appear until the 18th century. Previously, only the coastlands were known to them above all, to the Portuguese. The account of the Moroccan Leo Africanus [*q.v.*], who crossed the Sahara between 1510 and 1514, gave Europe access to knowledge which, alone amongst outsiders, was at that time accessible only to the Arabs. In the 19th century, the Europeans acquired for themselves the means for exploring the interior of Africa, for varying reasons, amongst which were prominent a desire to combat the places of origin for slavery and a search for new economic outlets. All through this century, numerous explorers laid down the ways for colonisation, which was often violent and which excited strong reactions, frequently led by the Muslim Ṣūfī orders of the Sāḥil, linked as they were with the Orient and the Maghrib. These last played an essential role in the definitive Islamisation of the Sāḥil. One may mention, amongst the main explorers, before they yielded place to military men, Mungo Park, Laing, Caillé, Barth, Duveyrier, Rohlfs and Nachtigal.

Bibliography: 1. Sources. Bakrī, *K. al-Masālik wa 'l-mamālik*, ed. de Slane, *Descr. de l'Afrique septentrionale,* Algiers 1857, tr. in *JA* (1857-8); Ibn Baṭṭūṭa, *Riḥla*; Leo Africanus, tr. Epaulard, Paris 1956; Maḥmūd Kātī, *Taʾrīkh al-Fattāsh*, Paris 1964; ʿAbd al-Raḥmān al-Saʿdī, *Taʾrīkh al-Sūdān*, ed. O. Houdas and E. Benoist, Paris 1898.

2. Studies. H. Lhote, *Le cheval et le chameau dans les peintures et gravures rupestres du Sahara*, in *Bull. IFAN*, xv/3 (1953), 1138-1228; T. Lewicki, *Traits d'histoire du commerce saharien: marchands et missionaires ibāḍites au Soudan occidental et central au cours des VIIe-IXe siècles*, in *Etnografia Polska*, viii (1964), 291-311; R. Mauny, *Les siècles obscurs de l'Afrique noire*, Paris 1970; S. and D. Robert and J. Devisse, *Tegdaoust. I. Recherches sur Aoudaghost*, Paris 1970; J.L. Triaud, *Islam et sociétés soudanaises au Moyen Age. Etude historique*, in *Recherches voltaïques*, no. 16, 1973; G. Camps, *Les civilisations préhistoriques de l'Afrique du Nord et du Sahara*, Paris 1974; J. Desanges, *L'Afrique noire et le monde meditérraneean dans l'Antiquité*, in *Rev. Fr. Hist. d'Outre-Mer*, no. 228 (1975), 391-414; D.T. Niane, *Le Soudan occidental au temps des grands empires, XIe-XVIe siècles*, Paris 1975; D. Lang, *Chronologie et histoire d'un royaume africain*, Paris 1977; M. Abitbol, *Tombouctou et les Arma (1591-1635)*, Paris 1979; Camps, *Berbères aux marges de l'histoire*, Toulouse 1980; P. Huard and J. Leclant, *La culture des chasseurs du Nil et du Sahara, Mém. Crape,* no. 29, Algiers 1980; P. Salama, *Le Sahara pendant l'Antiquité classique*, in *Hist. gén. de l'Afrique UNESCO*, ii, Paris 1980, 553-74; Desanges, *Les Protoberbères*, in *ibid.*, 453-74; T. Garrard, *Myth and metrology; the early trans-Saharan gold trade*, in *Jnal. Afr. Hist.*, xxiii (1982), 443-61; Lhote, *Les chars rupestres sahariens*, Toulouse 1982; idem, *Les Touaregs du Hoggar*, Paris 1984; J. Cuoq, *Histoire de l'islamisation de l'Afrique de l'Ouest,* Paris 1984; D. Porch, *The conquest of the Sahara*, London 1985; J. Devisse and S. Labib, *L'Afrique dans les relations intercontinentales*, in *Hist. gén. de l'Afrique UNESCO*, iv, Paris 1985, 693-730; D.M. Hamani, *Le sultanat touareg de l'Ayar*, Niamey 1989; *Libya antiqua, Symposium UNESCO janv. 1984*, Paris 1989; Devisse, *Commerce et routes du trafic en Afrique occidentale*, in *Hist. gén. de l'Afrique UNESCO*, iii, Paris 1990, 397-463; idem and J. Vancina, *L'Afrique du VIIIe au XIe: cinq siècles formateurs*, in *ibid.*, 797-842; I. Hrbek and Devisse, *Les Almoravides*, in *ibid.*, 365-95; J.M. Durou, *L'exploration du Sahara*, Arles 1993; G. Aumassip, *Entre Adrar des Ifoghas, Tassili et Aïr: les contacts du bassin du Niger avec le nord-est*, in *Vallées du Niger*, Paris, Réunion des Musées Nationaux 1993, 92-102; idem *et alii, Milieux, hommes et techniques du Sahara préhistorique. Problèmes actuels*, Paris 1994; Aumassip and R. Vernet, *Préhistoire du nord de l'Afrique*, forthcoming, Cl. Bataillon, *Le Souf, étude de géographie humaine* Algiers 1955; J. Bisson, *Le Gouara, étude de géographie humaine*, Algiers 1957; Bataillon (ed.), *Nomades et nomadisme au Sahara*, Paris 1963; M. Gast, *Alimentation des populations de l'Ahaggar*, Paris 1968; A. Cauneille, *Les Chaanba (leur nomadisme)*, CNRS Paris 1968; D. Champault, *Une oasis du Sahara nord-occidental, Tabelbala*, Paris 1969; Madeleine Rouvillois-Brigol, *Le pays d'Ouargla, Sahara algérien variations et organisation d'un espace rural en milieu désertique*, Paris-Sorbonne 1975; P.-R. Baduel, *Société et émigration temporaire au Nefzaoua*, Paris 1980; N. Marouf, *Lecture de l'espace oasien*, Paris 1980; A. Ravereau, *Le M'Zab, une leçon d'architecture*, Paris 1981; G. Aumassip, *Le bas Sahara dans la préhistoire* CNRS Paris 1986; Ch. Bousquet, *Les nouveaux citadins de Beni Isguen, M'Zab (Algérie)*, in *Petite ville et villes moyennes dans le Monde Arabe*, ii/17, CNRS (URBAMA) Tours 1986, 435-50; O. Bernezat *Hommes et montagnes du Hoggar*, Grenoble 1987; G. Bedoucha, *L'eau, l'amie du puissant, une communauté oasienne du Sud tunisien*, Paris 1987; Sophie Caratini *Les Rgaybat (1610-1934). I. Des chameliers à la conquête d'un territoire. II. Territoire et société*, Paris 1989 Aumassip, *Chronologies de l'art rupestre saharien et nord-africain*, Nice 1993. (R. Vernet)

5. *The contemporary Sahara.*

Insofar as agriculture has not been able to develo

in the desert except under the beneficent effect of irrigation (this marking the great difference between it and the countries of the Sāḥil, where one can speak of dry farming, under conditions of rainfall, as likewise in the lands bordering the northern edge of the Sahara), men have systematically colonised the more low-lying parts. These zones, on one hand, can benefit, all along the northern edge of the desert, from the flowing of streams whose waters can be diverted towards agricultural lands, and, on the other hand, they allow the underground water level to be reached more easily by means of wells from which water is raised by manpower, animal power or mechanical pumps. But since the end of the last century, the resources of the deep water table have been tapped through deep bore-holes, in this instance, artesian wells (water under pressure, hence spurting out) and provide a supplementary advantage. The most abundant resources are those of the so-called Albian water table (or the Intercalary Continental ones), utilised in the Algerian and Tunisian Sahara, which is also the origin of the Great Artificial river of Libya, an enormous aqueduct which transfers water towards the coastal zones. But inasmuch as the Intercalary Continental water table is made up of fossil water (the results of the last rainfall of the Quaternary period), the question must be posed, how long can this hydraulic source last? The question remains nonetheless pressing because it is these deep bore holes which are the basis for the spectacular development of the palm groves of the Algerian lower Sahara and the nearby Tunisian Sahara, comprising a commercial agriculture founded on the production of dates of exceptional quality (the "deglet nour") which has supplanted the self-subsistence agriculture which was for long the only one practiced in the oases. It is equally true that agriculture, even in regard to the date palm groves which best characterise the Saharan oasis and which furnish an important part of the food supply, has only, over the centuries, played a secondary role in the economy of the Sahara, and has never allowed the local peasants to become rich. For long, it has merely been the indispensable complement of urban development.

For the Sahara, the necessary means for passage between black Africa and the Mediterranean before maritime routes began to provide an alternative means of trade relations, has known quite a florescence of towns, mainly on its borders, the best known being Sid̲j̲ilmāsa (whose ruins lie near the town of Rissani in Morocco), Timbuctu (in modern Mali); in Algeria, Ouargla and Ghardaïa, and in Tunisia, Tozeur, were the termini for trans-Saharan caravans, whilst the towns of the Mauritanian Adrar (e.g. Atar) or of the Libyan desert (Ghat, G̲h̲adāmis) played the roles of staging-posts in the journey across the desert. These functions of the town, for long dormant after the disorganisation of traditional connections consequent on the partition of Africa by competing colonial powers, today enjoy a new vigour, but in a totally different context. This arises within the framework of new economic resources, utilising underground ones, notably hydrocarbons, above all in the Algerian and Libyan Saharas, and, much less, in Tunisia; also, there has been a diversification in employment, of which the towns have been the main beneficiaries, so that the pressure of urban populations weighs more and more heavily on the organisation of the Saharan region. Manufacturing and industrial activities, and administrative expansion—in order the better to control the Saharan region—and the growth of commerce, have all given a new vigour to the towns, whose populations have swollen enormously.

Because of this, the oasis societies have undergone deep changes, since the ways of urban consumption and ways of life have expanded rapidly, as much amongst the sedentaries as amongst the nomads. Many of the traditional modes inherited from the past, whose management has been perfectly mastered by the local populations, will probably continue to have their *raison d'être*. But the most spectacular evolution stems from the development of agriculture for the market, mainly based on the cultivation of out-of-season vegetables which the Sahara can produce, given its latitude and the length of sunshine there; the agricultural populations which have been best able to adapt to market demands are from those parts of the Sahara which are the best supplied with towns, with mercantile traditions, with the best food supplies and labour resources, and most easily linked to the great centres of consumption, i.e. the towns of the Mediterranean littoral and the export outlets. Furthermore, the Saharan expanses, by virtue of their rich hydraulic reserves, are more and more considered as reserves of land, immense regions to be colonised, whose value for intensive agriculture (mainly based on cereals, above all wheat) may possibly allow of a solution to the problem of finding food supplies (at least on the local scale; for the national scale, this is a utopian dream). Whence the increased number of deep bore-holes which supply the self-propelled sprinklers and which create a new landscape, that of agribusiness, whose real place in the desert will be determined in the future.

In this context, nomadism is only a residual, very much a minor, activity, despite the tenacious legend which sees the Sahara as essentially a land of nomads. Decades of unrestrained urbanisation have in fact radically modified the general picture, apart from the effects of the long periods of desiccation which have affected the fringes of the desert (where the most numerous groups of nomads live) and which have erased the complementary factors (climatic, whence vegetational) making up the support for nomadic life. A new complementarity, this time based on relationships with the town, has replaced these latter ones; the nomad may now raise livestock for slaughter on the account of his relatives who have become sedentarised, or he may now become an adjunct of tourism (guide or camel-driver accompanying excursionists), or yet again he may have become an agriculturist once more, often aided by the state, which endeavours to settle the nomads—unless these principal sources of income stem from what is regarded as a side-activity, the nomad himself having kept up a semi-way of life as a nomadic herdsman, with the family continuing to live in a tent. In sum, the abandonment of vast pastoral areas has as its corollary the end of a certain control over the expanses which the nomads enjoyed; the Saharan expanses have never been so empty, and the contrast between the towns where men and activities are now concentrated and the pasture lands which have now become useless, has never been so brutal.

Development policies applied to the Sahara all end up, whatever the political options chosen by the various states, in processes which inevitably converge on the same constant: a state-directed structure and a multiplication of relationships which bring about forms of association in the most varied fields. In practice, all of these work together to break up the isolation which was once the common lot of the Saharan peoples: a good network of roads, access to wage-earning employment, the developing role of the towns within the framework of a voluntarist policy and the generalising of a market economy. In sum, in a few decades only we have witnessed a process of integration in the sense used in politics, i.e. entry into a vast grouping which is transforming the life of the Saharan peoples by bringing them fully into the process of state-building.

That the Sahara is going to be, in the future, an expanse which not only retains its population but attracts people as well, is the tangible proof that it has become part of the development process. The attachment of these immense Saharan expanses to the Mediterranean province of each of the states involved constitutes a geopolitical factor of first-rank importance.

Bibliography: Ch. Bousquet, *Pérennité du centre ancien au M'Zab, le cas de Beni-Isguen*, in *Présent et avenir des médinas* (*de Marrakech à Alep*), CNRS (ERA 706) Tours 1982, 9-22; D. Retaille, *Le destin du pastoralisme nomade en Afrique*, in *Information géographique*, iii (1983), 103-13; A. Romey, *Les Saïd Atba de N'Goussa. Histoire et état actuel de leur nomadisme*, Paris 1983; J. Bisson, *L'industrie, la ville, la palmeraie: un quart de siècle d'évolution au Sahara algérien, in Maghreb-Machrek*, xcix (1983), 5-29; idem, *Les villes sahariennes: politique voluntariste et particulismes régionaux*, in *ibid.*, c (1983), 25-41; M. Jarir, *Exemple d'aménagement hydro-agricole de l'Etat dans le Présahara marocain, le périmètre du Tafīlalt*, in *L'homme et l'eau en Méditerranée et au Proche Orient. IV. L'eau dans l'agriculture*, Travaux de la Maison d'Orient 14, Lyons 1987, 191-208; Bisson and Jarir, *Ksour du Gourara et du Tafilelt, de l'ouverture de la société oasienne à la fermeture de la maison*, in *Habitat, Etat, Société au Maghreb*, CNRS (CRESM) Aix-en-Provence 1988, 329-45; M. Naciri, *Emigration et mutation spatiale dans l'oasis de Tinjdad*, in *ibid.*, 347-64; Bisson, *Développement et mutations au Sahara maghrébin*, Orleans 1993; idem, *Enjeux sahariens*, CNRS Aix-en-Provence 1984; idem, *Désert et montagne au Maghreb*, in *ROMM*, lxi-lxii (1986); idem, *Le nomade, l'oasis et la ville*, URBAMA, xx, Tours 1989; L. Blin, *L'Algérie du Sahara au Sahel*, Paris 1990; A. Bencherfia and H. Popp, *L'oasis de Figuig. Persistance et changement*, Univ. of Passau 1990; Bisson and Y. Callot, *Les hommes et la sécheresse autour du Grand Erg Occidental* (*Nord-Ouest du Sahara algérien*), in *Sécheresse*, ii (1990), 124-33; L. Ouhajou, *Les rapports sociaux liés aux droits d'eau, le cas de la vallée du Dra*, in *Espace rural*, Univ. Paul-Valéry, xxiv (1991), 87-100; Bisson, *Le Sahara dans le développement des Etats maghrébins*, in *Monde arabe, Maghreb-Machrek*, cxxxiv (1991), 3-27, cxxxv (1992), 79-106; D. Dubost, *Aridité, agriculture et développement, le cas des oasis algériennes*, in *Changements planétaires - Sécheresse*, ii (1992), 85-96; Bisson, *Les Foggaras du Sahara algérien, déclin ou renouveau?*, in *Les eaux cachées. Etude géographiques sur les galeries drainantes souterraines*, Paris-Sorbonne 1992, 7-26; Ch. Toupet, *Le Sahel*, Paris 1992; Bisson, *Développement et mutations au Sahara maghrébin*, Orleans 1993.

(J. BISSON)

SAHSARĀM, variously spelt as Sahasrām, Sasarām, Sassaram, Sasiram, a small town in the Shāhabād district of Bihār in India (lat. 24° 58′ N., long. 84° 01′ E.), associated with the name of Shīr Shāh Sūr (946-52/1539-45 [see DIHLĪ SULTANATE]), initially as his military *iḳṭāʿ* and subsequently as his burial place, this last considered to be "one of the grandest and most imaginative architectural conceptions in the whole of India" (P. Brown, *Indian architecture*, 84). Legend ascribes the name to "certain Asura or demon who had a thousand arms, each holding a separate plaything" (*Imperial Gazetteer of India*², xxii, 111). East of the town, near the summit of a spur of the Kaimur range is a Buddhist site where, in a small cave, there is an important Aśōka inscription. Here also stands the tomb of Pīr Čandan Shahīd. Abu 'l-Faḍl mentions Sahsarām as one of the 18 *maḥalls* of the *sarkār* of Rōhtās [*q.v.*] and refers to its revenues, climate, military contingents, etc.

The main attraction of Sahsarām is a group of royal tombs of Shīr Shāh, his father Ḥasan Sūr, his son Salīm Shāh and the architect ʿAlawal Khān, each of which has its own marked architectural character. Shīr Shāh's tomb is an "architectural masterpiece". It stands in a vast artificial lake with an octagonal hall surrounded by an arcade which forms a gallery. Its imposing structure rises in five stages to a total height of about 45.5 m. Spreading out to the water's edge is a continuous plinth of steps. The tomb chamber has inscriptions carved on the *ḳibla* wall. The roof is supported by four Gothic arches. Brown, *op. cit.*, 85, considers the tomb structure "an inspired achievement, a creation of sober and massive splendour of which any country would be proud."

Other buildings of Sahsarām worthy of mention are the *Ḳalʿa*, the *ʿIdgāh* and the *ḥammām* or Baths.

Bibliography: *Arch. Survey of India. Report for 1922-23*, 36-7; *Imperial gazetteer of India*², xxii, 111; L.S.S. O'Malley, *Shahabad*, revised ed. J.F.W. James, Patna 1924, 18, 62, 181-9; P. Brown, *Indian architecture* (*Islamic period*), Taraporewala, Bombay 1956, 84-6; S.H. Askari and Qeyamuddin (eds.), *Comprehensive history of Bihar*, ii/1, Patna 1983, 18, 262-3, 503 ff.

(K.A. NIZAMI)

AL-**SAḤŪL**, the name of both a town and a *wādī* in Yemen. The town lies on the road from Ibb [*q.v.*] to al-Makhādir near the ruins of Ẓafār al-Ashrāf, in ancient times the capital of the Ḥimyarite kingdom (see Smith, *Ayyūbids*, ii, 216). For Wādī Saḥūl, see *Eduard Glaser's Reise nach Mârib*, ed. D.H. Müller and N. Rhodokanakis, Vienna 1913, charts 2-3. Al-Saḥūl was called *Miṣr al-Yaman* on account of its wealth in corn, and was celebrated for the so-called Saḥūlī cloaks (*saḥūliyya*) made there of white cotton. The Prophet is said to have been shrouded (*kufina*) in two of them for burial. Al-Saḥūl is mentioned in connection with the journey made by Asad al-Dīn Muḥammad b. Badr al-Dīn Ḥasan from Djuwwa via Wuṣāb to Dhamār [*q.v.*] (see al-Khazradjī, i, 111; on Asad al-Dīn, see AL-MAHDĪ LI-DĪN ALLĀH AḤMAD, 1; RASŪLIDS, and Serjeant-Lewcock, *Ṣanʿāʾ*, 64-6).

Bibliography: Hamdānī, *Ṣifa*, ii, Index Geograficus, 57; partial tr. L. Forrer, *Südarabien nach al-Hamdani's "Beschreibung der arabischen Insel"*, Leipzig 1942; Ibn al-Mudjāwir, *Taʾrīkh al-Mustabṣir*, ed. Löfgren, ii, 175; Yāḳūt, *Muʿdjam*, i, 920, ii, 885, iii, 50, v, 21; Bakrī, *Muʿdjam*, ed. Wüstenfeld, ii, 767, ed. Cairo, iii, 727; Muḳaddasī 98; Masʿūdī, *Tanbīh*, 281; Khazradjī, *al-ʿUḳūd al-luʾluʾiyya*, ed. and tr. Redhouse, 61, 353; G.R. Smith, *The Ayyūbids and early Rasūlids in the Yemen*, London 1978, ii, 197; C. Niebuhr, *Beschreibung von Arabien*, Copenhagen 1772, 235; A. Sprenger, *Die alte Geographie Arabiens als Grundlage der Entwicklungsgeschichte des Semitismus*, Bern 1875, repr. Amsterdam 1966, 73, 184; idem, *Die Post- und Reiserouten des Orients*, Leipzig 1864, repr. Amsterdam 1962, 109, 147, 154; A.J. Wensinck, *A handbook of early Muhammadan tradition*, Leiden 1960 s.v. "shroud" (A. *kafan*), 214; *EI*¹ art. (A. Grohmann).

(E. VAN DONZEL)

ṢAHYŪN (present-day (Arabic) ṢALĀḤ AL-DĪN; Greek SIGON; Frankish SAÔNE), a stronghold of the Djabal al-ʿAlawiyyīn (Nuṣayrī Mountains), situated about 25 km/15 miles north-east of the Syrian port of al-Lād̲h̲iḳiyya (Latakia), near the town of al-Ḥaffeh. The castle occupies a narrow, east-west running spur, isolated by a rock-hewn fosse on the east, and protected by deep ravines on the north and south. The principal extant constructions are the remains of a Byzantine citadel on the highest, middle point of the site; extensive and better-preserved Frankish fortifications, including a massive keep, walls and bastions at the eastern end; and a mosque and a *ḥammām* bearing the name of the Mamlūk ruler Ḳalāwūn.

The earliest attested occupier was a dependant of Sayf al-Dawla [*q.v.*] the Ḥamdānid ruler of Aleppo. In 975/364-5, he surrendered the castle to the Byzantine Emperor John Tzimisces. The site remained in Byzantine hands until the beginning of the Crusades. By 513/1119, the castle was in the possession of the Frankish Count Robert the Leper, from whose descendants Ṣalāḥ al-Dīn wrested it in 584/1188. The Ayyūbid ruler gave the place to his lieutenant Mankurūs b. K̲h̲umārtigin. The latter's heirs ruled it until 671/1272, when it was handed over to the Mamlūk al-Ẓāhir Baybars. The castle subsequently became the refuge of Sunḳur al-As̲h̲ḳar, an *amīr* of Baybars' successor Ḳalāwūn, in al-As̲h̲ḳar's rebellions against Ḳalāwūn, until their dispute was resolved in 685-6/1287. For at least the next century under the Mamlūks, Ṣahyūn seems to have flourished. Abu 'l-Fidāʾ reports a town as having grown up next to the castle. Traces of extensive settlement are still visible to the east of the fosse. Later, however, the entire site was abandoned.

Bibliography: Ibn ʿAbd al-Ẓāhir, *Tas̲h̲rīf al-ayyām*, Cairo 1961, 102, 103, 148, 150; Ibn Baṭṭūṭa, *Riḥla*, Beirut 1960, 75, 76; Bahāʾ al-Dīn Ibn S̲h̲addād, *al-Nawādir al-sulṭāniyya*, Cairo 1903, 60; Abu 'l-Fidāʾ, *Taḳwīm al-buldān*, Paris 1840, 256, 257; Ibn al-Furāt, *Taʾrīk̲h̲*, vii, Beirut 1942, 162, 167, 168, 170, 172, 173, 185, 186, 214, 215, 217, 220, 221, viii, 49, 50; ʿImād al-Dīn al-Iṣfahānī, *al-Fatḥ al-Ḳussī*, Leiden 1888, 143-145; ʿIzz al-Dīn Ibn S̲h̲addād, *Sīrat al-Ẓāhir Baybars*, Wiesbaden 1983, 54; Ibn al-Ḳalānisī, *D̲h̲ayl taʾrīk̲h̲ Dimas̲h̲ḳ*, Beirut 1909, 27; Yaḥyā al-Anṭākī, *Extracts* (in Russian), St. Petersburg 1883, 87; Cahen, *La Syrie du Nord*, Paris 1940, see index; Deschamps, *La défense du comté de Tripoli et de la principauté d'Antioche*, Paris 1977, 217-47; Saʿāda, *Taʾrīk̲h̲ ḳalʿat Ṣalāḥ al-Dīn*, in *Mad̲j̲allat al-ḥawliyyāt al-at̲h̲ariyya al-Sūriyya*, xvii (1967), 59-81; Van Berchem and Fatio, *Voyage en Syrie*, Cairo 1913-5, i, 269, 276, 278, 279.

(D.W. Morray)

ṢĀʾIB, Mīrzā Muḥammad ʿAlī, Persian poet of the 11th/17th century.

The precise date of his birth is not known, but it is presumed that he was born around 1010/1601-2. His father, Mīrzā ʿAbd al-Raḥīm, was a leading merchant of Tabrīz. When S̲h̲āh ʿAbbās I (r. 985-1038/1587-1629) made Iṣfahān his capital he caused many merchants from Tabrīz to settle there, in the quarter named ʿAbbāsābād. At this time Ṣāʾib's father moved to Iṣfahān, where the poet is said to have been born. In his verses, however, Ṣāʾib often invokes his connection with Tabrīz, and consequently he is referred to both as Iṣfahānī and as Tabrīzī.

Ṣāʾib's early upbringing took place in Iṣfahān. He obtained his education at home, and became involved in poetical exercises at a young age. He is reported to have received his training in poetry from Ruknā Masīḥ of Kās̲h̲ān (d. 1066/1655 or 1070/1659-60) and from S̲h̲araf al-Dīn S̲h̲ifāʾī (d. 1037/1628), although this is discounted by some recent authorities. During his youth he made a pilgrimage to Mecca and also visited the shrine of ʿAlī al-Riḍā in Mas̲h̲had.

Towards 1034/1624-5, Ṣāʾib set out for India. His decision was, allegedly, in reaction to the conduct of some self-seeking individuals who were engaged in poisoning the ears of S̲h̲āh ʿAbbās I against him. It is also possible that, like other Persian poets of his age, he was drawn to the Mug̲h̲al court in expectation of rich rewards. His journey took him through Harāt and Kābul, where in the latter place he found access to Muḥammad Riḍā Aḥsan Allāh, popularly known as Ẓafar K̲h̲ān (1013-73/1604-63), who served as administrator on behalf of his father K̲h̲ʷād̲j̲a Abu 'l-Ḥasan Turbatī (d. 1042/1633), a distinguished Mug̲h̲al nobleman. Ṣāʾib benefited from the generosity of Ẓafar K̲h̲ān, and the two men struck up a friendship which seems to have continued even after the poet's return to Persia.

At the beginning of S̲h̲āh D̲j̲ahān's reign (1037-69/1627-58), Zafar K̲h̲ān was called back from Kābul to the royal court, and Ṣāʾib accompanied his patron to India. It is said that the Emperor bestowed upon the poet the title of Mustaʿidd K̲h̲ān and appointed him to the command of 1,000 horsemen, which carried with it an award of 20,000 rupees. In the middle of Rabīʿ II/November 1629, Ẓafar K̲h̲ān was sent to the Deccan, and Ṣāʾib accompanied him. While the poet was staying in Burhānpūr [*q.v.*], he received the news that his father had arrived in Āgra from Iṣfahān with the intention of inducing his son to return home. Upon hearing this, Ṣāʾib composed a *ḳaṣīda* in which he expressed the wish to return to Persia. In 1042/1632, Ẓafar K̲h̲ān was made governor of Kas̲h̲mīr, and he took Ṣāʾib with him. The poet visited Kas̲h̲mīr, and thence proceeded to Persia with his father.

Ṣāʾib's stay in India lasted for some seven years. His verses show that he missed his homeland and longed to go back; thereafter, he did not make any other long journey. He would sometimes visit places inside Persia, but only to meet poets and learned men in connection with his literary activities. His fame kept growing, and his works were in demand from rulers and dignitaries. He was appointed by S̲h̲āh ʿAbbās II (r. 1052-77/1642-66) as his poet-laureate—a position in which he reportedly enjoyed almost the same privileges as any minister. In his old age, he never set foot outside Iṣfahān, and was later buried in the same retreat where he stayed. Opinions differ regarding the date of his death, which is placed variously between 1080/1669-70 and 1088/1677-8.

Ṣāʾib is described as a devoutly religious man. According to the *K̲h̲izāna-yi ʿāmira*, he was a Sunnī. Despite his religious affiliation, he was well-liked by all classes of Persians, who were chiefly S̲h̲īʿī, because of his discretion as regards religious beliefs. Unlike many poets, he was free from greed, rivalry and malice. He often chose the works of other poets as a model for his own poems, acknowledging his source by name as a mark of appreciation.

The poetical output of Ṣāʾib is extremely voluminous. The total number of verses ascribed to him varies from 80,000 to 125,000. Likewise, estimates also differ regarding the size of his *mat̲h̲nawī Ḳandahār-nāma* ("The book of Ḳandahār"), which he composed to commemorate the capture of the Afg̲h̲ān province by the Persians from the Mug̲h̲als in 1059/1649. These estimates range from 35,000 to 135,000 couplets. To be sure, the above figures are an exaggeration, but, as S̲h̲iblī Nuʿmānī has pointed out, there can be no doubt that Ṣāʾib was the most prolific of the latter-day poets. It is reported that he prepared some collections of his verses according to their subject-matter. One of them, named *Mirʾāt al-d̲j̲amāl* ("The mirror of beauty"), contained verses relating to the physical features of the beloved; another, called *Mirʾāt al-khayāl* ("The mirror of thought"), included in its contents allusions to mirror and comb; and yet another, entitled *Maykhāna* ("Tavern"), devoted itself to examples of verses mentioning wine and tavern. In addition, Ṣāʾib put together a selection of the opening couplets from his poems and other verses in a volume which he called *Wādjib al-ḥifẓ* ("Worthy of keeping"). He also compiled an anthology, entitled *Bayāḍ*, which contained a selection of his own verses as well as those of other poets, both old and new.

Ṣāʾib was well-versed in the art of calligraphy, a family legacy which may be traced to his uncle, Shams al-Dīn Tabrīzī (d. 940/1533-4), titled Shīrīn-ḳalam ("Of sweet pen"), who was a master calligrapher of his time. There exist several manuscripts of Ṣāʾib's works in his own handwriting, indicating the poet's skill in the *nastaʿlīḳ* form of calligraphy.

Among the verse forms employed by Ṣāʾib, the predominant one was the *ghazal*. His collection contains some *ḳaṣīdas* and *mathnawīs*, but these constitute an insignificant part of his huge output. It is the quantity and quality of Ṣāʾib's *ghazals* that lend stature to his poetry. The poet sought to change the direction of the *ghazal* by investing it with a new imagery and a refreshing thought pattern. He was careful to avoid stereotypes. Even when presenting a conventional theme, his aim was to transform it so as to convey an impression of novelty. One of the devices he employed very successfully was the *irsāl-i mathal*, in which the poet makes a statement in the first line of the couplet and reinforces it by an example in the second line. With Ṣāʾib, this mode of expression, which could easily become contrived when employed by lesser poets, retained its spontaneity because of his skilful handling.

Ṣāʾib was a leading exponent of the Indian style of Persian poetry (*sabk-i Hindī* [*q.v.*]). He remained a towering figure in the literary world of Persia until his fame suffered a decline in the 18th and 19th centuries when the style which he represented lost its appeal with the local poets and arbiters of taste. This change is reflected in the views expressed by such later writers as Luṭf ʿAlī Beg Ādhar (d. 1195/1781) and Riḍā-ḳulī Khan Hidāyat (d. 1280/1871). Ādhar accuses Ṣāʾib of initiating "a novel and disagreeable style", following which poetical standards underwent progressive deterioration; and Hidāyat declares that the trend which the poet chose for himself was not admired during the author's time. While Ṣāʾib's popularity diminished in his own country, the esteem enjoyed by him in the Indian sub-continent among students of Persian literature has continued unabated over the ages. Lately, the literary scene in Persia has also witnessed a revival of interest in Ṣāʾib, as shown by the successive publication of his poetical works and the appearance of numerous articles about his poetry.

Bibliography: *Dīwān-i Ṣāʾib* (introd. by Amīrī Fīrūzkūhī), Tehran 1345/1966; *ibid.*, (introd. by Mumtāz Ḥasan), Lahore-Karachi 1977; Muḥammad Ṭāhir Naṣrābādī, *Tadhkira-yi Naṣrābādī*, ed. Waḥīd Dastgardī, Tehran 1352/1973; Luṭf ʿAlī Beg Ādhar, *Ātishkada-yi Ādhar*, ed. Ḥasan Sādāt Nāṣirī, Tehran 1336/1957, i; ʿAlī-ḳulī Khān Wālih Dāghistānī, *Riyāḍ al-shuʿarā*, B.L. Add. 16,729; Ghulām ʿAlī Āzād Bilgrāmī, *Sarw-i Āzād*, Ḥaydarābād (Deccan) 1913; idem, *Khizāna-yi ʿāmira*, Kānpūr 1871; Riḍā-ḳulī Khān Hidāyat, *Madjmaʿ al-fuṣaḥāʾ*, Tehran 1339/1960, ii/1; Muḥammad Ḳudrat Allāh Gopāmawī, *Natāʾidj al-afkār*, Bombay 1336/1957; Lačhmī Narayān Shafīḳ, *Shām-i gharībān*, ed. Akbar al-Dīn Ṣiddīḳī, Karachi 1977; Muḥammad Afḍal Sarkhush, *Kalimāt al-shuʿarāʾ*, ed. Ṣādiḳ ʿAlī Dilāwarī, Lahore 1942; Sirādj al-Dīn Khān Ārzū, *Madjmaʿ al-nafāʾis*, Bankipore ms., *Catalogue*, viii; Shems al-Dīn Sāmī, *Ḳāmūs al-aʿlām*, Istanbul 1889, iv; Mīrzā Muḥammad ʿAlī Khān Tarbiyat, *Dānishmandān-i Ādharbāydjān*, Tehran 1314/1935; idem, *Yak ṣafḥa-yi mukhtaṣar az risāla-yi hādī ʿashar*, in *Armaghān*, xiii/5-6 (1311/1932); Shiblī Nuʿmānī, *Shiʿr al-ʿAdjam*[4], Aʿẓamgaṙh 1945, iii; Browne, *LHP*, iv; Riḍā-zāda Shafaḳ, *Tārīkh-i adabiyyāt-i Īrān*, Tehran 1321/1942; Dhabīḥ Allāh Ṣafā, *Tārīkh-i adabiyyāt dar Īrān*[2], Tehran 1367/1988, v/2; idem, *Gandj-i sukhan*[3], 1368/1989, iii; Mahdī Mudjtahidī, *Sukhanī dar bāra-yi Ṣāʾib*, in *Mihr*, viii/4 (1331/1952); *Lughat-nāma-yi Dihkhudā*, xvii-xviii, Tehran 1333/1954; Ḥādjdj Ḥusayn Nakhdjawānī, *Āthār-i nathrī az natāyidj-i afkār-i Ṣāʾib Tabrīzī*, in *Nashriyya-yi Dānishkada-yi Adabiyyāt-i Tabrīz*, vi/3 (1333/1954); idem, *Munāẓaʿa-yi Ṣāʾib Tabrīzī bā Kalīm Hamadānī*, in *ibid.*, vii/2 (1334/1956); ʿAbd al-ʿAlī Dastghayb, *Ṣāʾib-i afsūngar wa ṭarz-i sukhan-i ū*, in *Payām-i nuwīn*, v/1 (1341/1962); Amīr Ḥasan ʿĀbidī, *Ṣāʾib Tabrīzī Iṣfahānī*, in *Indo-Iranica*, xviii/4 (1965); Rypka, *Hist. of Iranian literature*; Ḥusām al-Dīn Rāshidī, *Tadhkira-yi shuʿarā-yi Kashmīr*, Karachi 1968, ii; Maẓāhir Muṣaffā, *Ārāmgāh-i Ṣāʾib dar Iṣfahān*, in *Yaghmā*, xxi/7 (1347/1968); Yūnus Djaʿfarī, *Abyāt-i parākanda-yi Ṣāʾib* (introd. and poems), in *Armaghān*, xxxvii/7-9 (1347/1968); Aḥmad Gulčīn Maʿānī, *Mawlānā Ṣāʾib dar naẓar-i buzurgān-i zamān-i khud*, in *Madjalla-yi Dānishkada-yi Adabiyyāt wa ʿUlūm-i Insānī*, Mashhad, v/3 (1348/1969); idem, *Kārwān-i Hind*, Mashhad 1369/1990-1, i; Muḥammad Taḳī Bahār, *Ṣāʾib wa shīwa-yi ū*, in *Yaghmā*, xxiii/5 (1349/1970); M.L. Rahman, *Persian literature in India during the time of Jahangir and Shah Jahan*, Baroda 1970; Punjab University, *Urdū dāʾira-yi maʿārif-i Islāmiyya*, xii, Lahore 1973; ʿAzīz Dawlatābādī, *Sukhanwarān-i Ādharbāydjān*, Tabrīz 1355/1976; ʿAli Dashtī, *Nigāhī bi Ṣāʾib*, Tehran 1355/1976; Muḥammad Rasūl Daryāgasht (ed.), *Ṣāʾib wa sabk-i Hindī*, Tehran 1354/1976; Muḥammad Dayhīm, *Tadhkira-yi shuʿarā-yi Ādharbāydjan*, Tabrīz 1367/1988, ii.

(MUNIBUR RAHMAN)

SĀʾIB KHĀTHIR, influential musician of the early Umayyad period, d. 63/683.

According to the *Kitāb al-Aghānī*, the source for what information we have on him, Abū Djaʿfar Sāʾib Khāthir was a *mawlā* of Persian origin. By trade a food or, possibly, wheat (*ṭaʿām*) merchant in Medina, he became well-known as a singer and was attached to an important patron, ʿAbd Allāh b. Djaʿfar [*q.v.*]. He is also said to have sung, during the caliphate of Muʿāwiya (41-60/661-80), for his son Yazīd and, at the instigation of ʿAbd Allāh b. Djaʿfar, before Muʿāwiya himself. He was killed during the battle of al-Ḥarra, in 63/683.

The Ḥidjāz, and Medina in particular, was a centre of musical innovation during the 1st/7th century, and Sāʾib Khāthir is identified as one of the key figures in this process. He is portrayed in one account as having performed in traditional fashion, singing improvised (*murtadjil*) airs to the accompaniment of a percussion stick (*ḳaḍīb*). But in another, conforming to a standard narrative formula used in the *Aghānī* to encapsulate change, he is said to have been the first musician in Medina to introduce what would become the standard practice of the singer accompanying himself on the lute (*ʿūd*). With Sāʾib Khāthir, too, is associated the absorption and integration of Persian elements, for in reaction to the impression made on ʿAbd Allāh b.

Djaʿfar by the Persian songs of Nas͟hīṭ [*q.v.*], he is said to have set Arabic verse in the same style. It is such developments that were to lead to the elaboration of the sophisticated court-music tradition eventually codified by Isḥāḳ al-Mawṣilī (150-235/767-850 [*q.v.*]) and it is, indeed, Sāʾib K͟hāt͟hir's song *li-mani l-diyāru rusūmuhā ḳafru* that is claimed to initiate the stylistic prototype or first stage of that tradition, the early Umayyad *g͟hināʾ mutḳan*. Alternatively, this piece is perceived as the earliest instance in Arabic of *g͟hināʾ t͟haḳīl*, pointing towards the emergence of a "heavy" vs. "light" (*k͟hafīf*) divide with which will later be associated notions of an Arab vs. Persian stylistic cleavage. That Sāʾib K͟hāt͟hir was considered to be a major figure in this early period of radical change is also indicated by the roll-call of great Umayyad singers who are said to have learned from him (even if the extent of their indebtedness is impossible to define): Ibn Suraydj, Djamīla, ʿAzza al-Maylāʾ and, in particular, Maʿbad [*q.v.*], to whom, it is alleged, some of Sāʾib K͟hāt͟hir's own compositions were later attributed.

Bibliography: *Ag͟hānī*³, viii, 321-6; H.G. Farmer, *A history of Arabian music to the XIIIth century*, London 1929, repr. 1973, 53-4 and *passim;* S͟hawḳī Ḍayf, *al-S͟hiʿr wa 'l-g͟hināʾ fi 'l-Madīna wa-Makka li-ʿaṣr Banī Umayya*, Cairo n.d., 58.

(O. Wright)

SAʿĪD B. **ABĪ ARŪBA**, Mihrān Abu 'l-Naḍr al-ʿAdawī al-Baṣrī (born *ca.* 70/689, d. between 155 and 159/771-6), traditionist in Baṣra, *mawlā* of the Banū ʿAdī b. Yas͟hkur. Saʿīd is mentioned among the first who compiled systematic *ḥadīt͟h* collections of the *muṣannaf* [*q.v.*] type (see IBN DJURAYDJ; Juynboll, 22; Van Ess, 63). Among his works were a *K. al-Sunan* and a *K. al-Ṭalāḳ*; none of them is extant. His repute as a traditionist is equivocal; he is generally considered reliable until he became "confused" some ten years before his death. Aḥmad b. Ḥanbal is said to have accused him of tampering (*tadlīs* [*q.v.*]) with *isnāds* [*q.v.*] (al-D͟hahabī, *Mīzān al-iʿtidāl fī naḳd al-ridjāl*, ed. al-Badjāwī, Cairo 1963, ii, 152). Probably his reputation was impaired because he adhered to the doctrine of the free will [see ḲADARIYYA]. Saʿīd is known best as transmitter of al-Ḥasan al-Baṣrī [*q.v.*], and of his teacher Ḳatāda b. Diʿāma [*q.v.*], whose *K. al-Manāsik* he edited (Sezgin, *GAS*, i, 32; Van Ess, 143). Via Ḳatāda, he also transmitted Ḳurʾānic exegesis and stories about the prophets (see Khoury, *passim*). A number of people transmitted *ḥadīt͟h* or other materials from Saʿīd, notably ʿAbd al-Aʿlā b. ʿAbd al-Aʿlā al-Sāmī (d. 189/805; Van Ess, 73).

Bibliography: Sezgin, *GAS*, i, 91-2; J. van Ess, *Theologie und Gesellschaft im 2. und 3. Jahrhundert Hidschra. Eine Geschichte des religiösen Denkens im frühen Islam*, ii, Berlin-New York 1992, 62-5, 72-8; G.H.A. Juynboll, *Muslim Tradition. Studies in chronology, provenance and authorship of early* ḥadīth, Cambridge 1983, 22, 164; R.G. Khoury, *Les légendes prophétiques dans l'Islam*, Wiesbaden 1978.

(W. Raven)

SAʿĪD B. AL-**ʿĀṢ** B. UMAYYA, a member of the Aʿyāṣ [*q.v.* in Suppl.] component group of the Umayyad clan in Mecca and, later, governor of Kufa and Medina, died in 59/678-9, according to the majority of authorities.

His father had fallen, a pagan, fighting the Muslims at the battle of Badr [*q.v.*] on 2/624 when Saʿīd, his only son, can only have been an infant. He nevertheless speedily achieved great prestige in Islam not only as the leader of an aristocratic family group but also for his liberality, eloquence and learning. He was in especially high favour with ʿUt͟hmān, and was appointed by that caliph, together with the other Ḳuras͟hīs ʿAbd Allāh b. al-Zubayr [*q.v.*], ʿAbd al-Raḥmān b. al-Ḥārit͟h and the Medinan Zayd b. T͟hābit [*q.v.*], to prepare a Ḳurʾān vulgate text on the basis of the *muṣḥaf* [*q.v.*] of Ḥafṣa, probably in 32-3/652-4 (see Nöldeke-Schwally, *G des Q*, ii, 48, 50-2, 56). He married two of ʿUt͟hmān's daughters, Maryam and Umm ʿAmr, and also had links with the Marwānid branch of the clan through his marriage to Umm al-Banīn, daughter of Marwān b. al-Ḥakam [*q.v.*].

In 29/649-50 he was appointed governor of Kūfa in succession to al-Walīd b. ʿUḳba, achieving a reputation as a military commander by leading expeditions into Ād͟harbaydjān and the Caspian provinces. But he incurred unpopularity in unruly Kūfa—to him is attributed the saying that the Sawād [*q.v.*] of ʿIrāḳ was the garden of Ḳuraysh, i.e. meant to be exploited by the Meccans—and his return to his post from Medina at the end of 34/655 was blocked by the *ḳurrāʾ* and other agitators in Kūfa under Yazīd b. Ḳays al-Arḥabī and Mālik al-As͟htar, who proclaimed Abū Mūsā al-As͟hʿarī [*q.v.*] governor in the city. Saʿīd fought in defence of ʿUt͟hmān's *dār* in Medina when it was attacked by the rebels of the Egyptian army and was wounded protecting the caliph; but, after at first inclining to the cause of Ṭalḥa, al-Zubayr and ʿĀʾis͟ha, he declined to participate in the Battle of the Camel, and settled in Mecca. He did not participate in the events of Ṣiffīn [*q.v.*] either, but Muʿāwiya in 49/669 appointed him governor of Medina in place of Marwān b. al-Ḥakam, and he remained in office till replaced by the latter in 54/674.

He finally returned to his estates in the Wādī 'l-ʿAḳīḳ at Medina, and died at al-ʿArṣa, most probably in 59/678-9. The leadership of his family then devolved on his son (as many as 14 sons of his are enumerated in the *nasab* literature, e.g. in al-Balād͟hurī, *Ansāb*, ivb, 136-49) by Marwān's daughter, ʿAmr al-As͟hdaḳ [*q.v.*].

Although an Umayyad, Saʿīd had close relations with some members of the Hās͟himī family, and it was recalled by them that he had taken no part against ʿAlī in the First Civil War (see Lammens, *Moʿâwia Ier*, in *MFOB*, i [1906], 27-9); early Islamic historical writing is, accordingly, rather favourable to his image.

Bibliography (in addition to references in the article): 1. Sources. Zubayrī, *Nasab Ḳuraysh*, 176-8; Ibn Saʿd, v, 19-24; Balād͟hurī, *Futūḥ*, 119, 198, 280, 322, 328-9, 334, 336; idem, *Ansāb al-as͟hrāf*, ivb, ed. Schloessinger, 130-6; Yaʿḳūbī, *Taʾrīk͟h*, ii, 152, 190, 192, 207, 267, 283-4; Ṭabarī, i, index; Ibn al-At͟hīr, *Usd*, ii, 309 ff.; idem, *Kāmil*, iii and iv, index; Ibn Ḥadjar, *Iṣāba*, no. 5059; Nawawī, *Tahd͟hīb al-asmāʾ*, ed. Wüstenfeld, 281-2.

2. Studies. Wellhausen, *Skizzen und Vorarbeiten*, vi, 117-21; G. Rotter, *Die Umayyaden und der Zweite Bürgerkrieg (680-692)*, Wiesbaden 1982, 114-15, 117-18; Hichem Djaït, *La grande discorde. Religion et politique dans l'Islam des origines*, Paris 1989, 119, 122-5.

(C.E. Bosworth)

SAʿĪD B. AL-**BIṬRĪḲ** (not Baṭrīḳ) or Eutychius (263-328/877-940), Melkite patriarch of Alexandria, author of works of medicine, history and apologetics, and one of the most important figures in the Melkite literature of his period.

The only known biographical elements derive from the author himself (ed. Cheikho, ii, 69-70, 86-7, 88) and from his continuator (Yaḥyā, in *PO*, xviii, 713-19); they are repeated, without additional information, in Ibn Abī Uṣaybiʿa. Born at Fusṭāṭ on 27 D͟hu 'l-Ḥidjdja 263/10 September 877, Saʿīd b. al-Biṭrīḳ studied medicine and distinguished himself as a practitioner; he was elected patriarch of Alexandria on 8 Ṣafar 321/7 February 933, at the age of sixty, and then received the name Eutychius. To resolve the contradiction between the two items of information—the age and the year—M. Breydy (*Études*, 5 ff.) proposes fixing the accession of Saʿīd to the see of Alexandria on 13 Ṣafar 323/22 January 935 (according to the version given in two manuscripts). His patriarchate was controversial, and darkened by the division of the Melkite community of Egypt into two rival factions and by the spoliations which ensued. Saʿīd died on Monday, 30 Radjab 328/11 May 940 in Alexandria.

(a) *Medicine*.

Saʿīd b. al-Biṭrīḳ is the author of a medical treatise, *K. fi 'l-Ṭibb* or *Kunnāsh* (mentioned by Ibn Abī Uṣaybiʿa), of which a manuscript has been preserved in the Manādīlī collection at Aleppo (cf. P. Sbath, *al-Fihris*, i, 9, no. 23).

(b) *History*.

Saʿīd b. al-Biṭrīḳ is best known for his universal history dedicated to his fellow-physician ʿĪsā b. al-Biṭrīḳ, *K. al-Taʾrīkh al-madjmūʿ ʿalā 'l-taḥḳīḳ wa 'l-taṣdīḳ*, also called by the copyists *Naẓm al-djawhar*, and generally known, since its edition by Pococke, under the title of *Annales*, although this is not strictly speaking a case of annals but of a universal history in which the material is divided chronologically according to the reigns of sovereigns. With this first Christian history in the Arabic language, dealing simultaneously with religious and secular events, Saʿīd intended to offer to the Melkite community a history which would enable it to assert its identity vis-à-vis the other Christian communities, and vis-à-vis the Byzantine and Arab empires.

It begins with the creation of Adam and deals with Biblical history until the Babylonian exile, then expands into a history of the Near East until the birth of Christ, devotes substantial treatment to the beginnings of the Church, to heresies and to councils, to monasticism in Palestine, without, however, neglecting the reigns of Byzantine and Sāsānid sovereigns, and concludes with Arabo-Muslim history, pursued until the fifth year of the caliphate of al-Rāḍī (326/937-8). As he himself explains in the introduction, Saʿīd sets out to make a work of compilation on the basis of various sources which he does not mention, but the most important of which can be identified (cf. Breydy, *Études*, ch. ii): an Arabic version of the Bible, the *Cave of treasures*, the *Alexander Romance*, the history of the Sāsānid kings translated by Ibn al-Muḳaffaʿ [*q.v.*], hagiographical writings (St. Epiphanus of Cyprus, St. Euthymus, St. Sabas, St. John the Almoner, etc.), popular legends (including the Seven Sleepers of Ephesus), and Muslim traditionists such as ʿUthmān b. Ṣāliḥ (cf. Breydy, *La conquête arabe*. Cf. also G. Levi Della Vida, *Two fragments of Galen in Arabic translation*, in *JAOS*, lxx [1950], 182-7). Saʿīd b. al-Biṭrīḳ makes every effort to insert the information thus assembled into a chronological frame supplied successively by the history of the Bible, by the reigns of the kings of Persia, of Alexander, of the kings of Egypt, of Roman emperors, of Sāsānid sovereigns, of Byzantine emperors, and finally, from the time of the Arab conquest, of caliphs. Saʿīd situates the Incarnation in the year 5500, thereby following not the calculations of Byzantine chronographers but the era of Africanus, still used by those whom Grumel dubs "adherents of the mystical 5500" (*La chronologie*, 22 ff., 157).

The *Taʾrīkh* was continued at the beginning of the 5th/11th century by Yaḥyā al-Anṭākī [*q.v.*], who gives interesting details regarding the manuscripts which he has been able to consult: "I have examined a certain number of manuscripts of the book of Saʿīd b. al-Biṭrīḳ, and found that some of them contained history up until the beginning of the caliphate of al-Ḳāhir, in other words, until the year in which Saʿīd b. al-Biṭrīḳ was appointed Patriarch of Alexandria; on the other hand, other manuscripts had been supplemented for some reason by additions on the part of the continuator of the book, which were not to be found in the authentic manuscript. I have seen the authentic manuscript and, besides this, other manuscripts where [the history] reaches the point of the caliphate of al-Rāḍī, that is year 326 of the Hidjra. It is principally on the basis of this manuscript that I have composed this book, because this manuscript is the most complete in exposition and the closest to the period [of the author]. I believe that the reason for the incompleteness at the end of certain of these manuscripts, and for the fact that their account is abridged in relation to what appears in the authentic manuscript, is that the book was copied in the lifetime of the author at different times; the copies of this book becoming known to people, each copy contained in its entirety history up until the moment when [the copy] had been written" (*PO*, viii/5, 709-10).

Today, some thirty manuscripts of Saʿīd's *Taʾrīkh* have been counted (cf. Graf, *GCAL*, 34-5; Breydy, *Études*, ch. iv; J. Nasrallah, *Histoire du mouvement littéraire*, 26-7), which is indicative of the book's success. It was known in the West from the 17th century onwards. In 1642, John Selden edited, translated and commented on a brief extract concerning the preaching of St. Mark and the origins of the Church of Alexandria; in 1661, A. Ecchelensis refuted Selden by producing a new translation of the same passage; in 1658-9, E. Pococke published the complete text of the *Taʾrīkh* on the basis of the manuscripts obtained by Selden (all three copied in Aleppo in the 17th century), accompanied by a Latin translation and index. This translation was reproduced, as were those of Selden and of Ecchelensis, in the *Patrologia* of Migne. In 1906-9, L. Cheikho, alone for the first part, in collaboration with Ḥ. Zayyāt and B. Carra de Vaux for the second, re-edited the Arabic text on the basis of the manuscript of the Zayyāt collection while giving the variants according to the Pococke edition, to which B. Carra de Vaux added a collation with two manuscripts of the Bibliothèque Nationale de Paris; this edition also contains the continuation owed to Yaḥyā al-Anṭākī. In 1987, B. Pirone produced an annotated translation into Italian, according to Cheikho's text.

The manuscripts, even though they differ on the date of the end of the chronicle and contain more or less significant variants, represent the same recension of the text. Nevertheless, one manuscript stands out from the others: the ms. Sin. Arab. 580 (582) of Saint Catherine's Monastery in the Sinai, considered an anonymous chronicle (the manuscript is mutilated at the beginning and at the end) until Breydy claimed to have identified it as the original, and even autographical, recension of the *Taʾrīkh* of Saʿīd b. al-Biṭrīḳ, henceforward regarding all the other manuscripts as bearers of a version adapted and amplified in Antiochian circles in the 11th century, perhaps by Yaḥyā himself. Breydy bases his conclusion on three arguments: (1) The script of Sin. Arab 580 (582) makes it possible to date this manuscript at the beginning of the 10th century (a cursive Kūfic, sometimes poorly deciphered by the authors of the later recension, examples in *Mamila ou Maqella?*, 73-4, and in *Études*, 33-4); (2) The statement by Yaḥyā himself (*PO*, xviii/5, 708-9) that after his arrival in Antioch he had revised his own work with the aid of chronicles which then became available to him, and that he had intended to correct in the same manner the *Taʾrīkh* of Saᶜīd which he considered flawed and incomplete. Although he adds that he abandoned this project, Breydy thinks that he, or others, did not resist the temptation; (3) The fact that all the manuscripts of the *Annales* belong to the Antiochene Melkite circle, and the late date of a number of copies (the earliest do not date back beyond the 13th-14th centuries). Comparison between the so-called Alexandrian recension of Sin. Arab. 580 (582) and the so-called Antiochene recension of the Pococke and Cheikho editions, outlined in *Études*, ch. v., has not been made in detail by Breydy except with regard to the taking of Jerusalem by the Persians and its reconquest by Heraclius (in *Mamila ou Maqella?*); it permits him to establish the Arabo-Jacobite origin of the first version, while the additions and glosses of the second would seemingly derive from Byzantine sources found at Antioch. Only a critical edition taking account of the entirety of the manuscript tradition, comparison between the two versions, and precise study of the origin of the additions, could definitively confirm, or refute, the conclusions of Breydy.

The vehement opposition displayed by Saᶜīd b. al-Biṭrīḳ towards other Christian persuasions led to ripostes, among others, from the Copt Sāwīrus (Severus) Ibn al-Muḳaffaᶜ [*q.v.*] in his *Kitāb al-Madjāmiᶜ* (P. Chebli, *Réfutation de Saᶜīd ibn Batrīq (Eutychius). Le livre des conciles*, in *PO*, iii [1905], 121-242) and from the Nestorian Elias of Nisibis (L. Horst, *Das Metropoliten Elias von Nisibis Buch vom Beweis der Wahrheit des Glaubens*, Colmar 1886, 23, 56 ff.). The few lines in which Saᶜīd denies the perpetual orthodoxy of the Maronites (ed. Cheikho, i. 210), repeated by William of Tyre (*History*, ed. R.B.C. Huygens, 1018, cf. R.W. Crawford, *William of Tyre and the Maronites*, in *Speculum*, xxx [1955], 222-8), drew down upon Saᶜīd the fury of the Maronites, from Echelensis to historians of the present day. A rigorist Muslim, Ibn Taymiyya [*q.v.*], refuted in his turn the Chalcedonian views espoused by Saᶜīd, not out of affection for Nestorian or Monophysite doctrines but to show the contradictions of the Melkite doctrine (G. Troupeau, *Ibn Taymiyya et sa réfutation d'Eutychius*, in *BEO*, xxx [1978], 209-20). Numerous later authors made use of Saᶜīd's *Taʾrīkh*, among others al-Masᶜūdī [*q.v.*] who met him in Fusṭāṭ (*Tanbīh*, ed. De Goeje, 154, tr. B. Carra de Vaux, *Le Livre de l'avertissement*, 212; cf. also idem, *Murūdj*, tr. Ch. Pellat, ii, 493), George the Friar (cf. P. Schreiner, *Fragment d'une paraphrase grecque des Annales d'Eutychès d'Alexandrie*, in *Orientalia Christiana Periodica*, xxxvii [1971], 384-390), William of Tyre for his chronicle of Arab sovereigns (a work which is lost, but mentioned in the prologue to his *History*, ed. Huygens, 100; cf. H. Möhring, *Zu der Geschichte der orientalischen Herrscher des Wilhelm von Tyrus. Die Frage der Quellenabhängigkeiten*, in *Mittellateinisches Jahrbuch*, xix [1984], 170-83), not to mention Ṣalība b. Yūḥannā, al-Makīn [*q.v.*] and al-Maḳrīzī [*q.v.*].

Furthermore, it has been established that the account of events in Sicily for the years 827-965, which follows the *Annales* of Saᶜīd b. al-Biṭrīḳ in the Cambridge manuscript and is for this reason generally known as the *Cambridge chronicle* (for editions and translations of this text, see Brockelmann, I², 155), is to be attributed not to Saᶜīd but to an Arab compiler of the 11th century who followed a Greek text (cf. Vasiliev, *Byzance et les Arabes*, i, 342-6, ii, 2, 99-106). Nasrallah possessed in his personal library another manuscript of the *Annales* with this same addition (*Histoire du mouvement littéraire*, 27, 54). Similarly, a letter edited in Paris in 1642 and on numerous subsequent occasions should not be attributed to Saᶜīd (contrary to the affirmation of Brockelmann, I², 154) but to Eutychius, patriarch of Constantinople (552-65) who was in correspondence with Pope Vigilius.

(c) *Apologetics*.

Saᶜīd b. al-Biṭrīḳ undertook the defence of the Chalcedonian faith not only in his *Taʾrīkh* but also in a work of apologetics which has not been preserved: *K. al-Djadal bayn al-mukhālif wa 'l-naṣrānī* (mentioned by Saᶜīd himself, *Annales*, ed. Cheikho, i, 176, and by Ibn Abī Uṣaybiᶜa). Nasrallah (*op. cit.*, 31) has advanced the hypothesis that the three long refutations of the Nestorians and the Jacobites (ed. Cheikho, i, 159-61, 161-75, 196-7), which interrupt the narration and are introduced by the expression *ḳāla Saᶜīd b. al-Biṭrīḳ al-mutaṭabbib*, were inserted at a later stage, and that the first and the third of these passages are borrowings from the *K. al-Djadal*; as for the second of these passages, on account of its similarity to another work of apologetics, the *K. al-Burhān*, it poses a new problem, that of the attribution of this work to Saᶜīd. On the basis of the presence of the same passage in both books—the *Taʾrīkh* and the *K. al-Burhān*—G. Graf (*Ein bisher unbekanntes Werk*, and *GCAL*, ii, 37) considered that Saᶜīd was the author of the *K. al-Burhān*. While it is certain that this treatise was composed in Arabic by a Chalcedonian before 944 (since it situates in Edessa the mandilium which was transferred to Constantinople in that year, which is confirmed by a note to Sin. Arab. 75, composed in 982, declaring that its author inherited this manuscript from his grandfather, cf. Nasrallah, *op. cit.*, 32-3), the attribution to Saᶜīd is today not considered valid (criticism of Graf's hypothesis, notably from F. Tautil, in *al-Mashrik*, xxvii [1929], 914-19, and Nasrallah, *op. cit.*, 31 ff.).

Bibliography: Ed. and tr. of the whole *K. al-Taʾrīkh*: E. Pococke, *Contextio Gemmarum, sive Eutychii Patriarchae Alexandrini Annales*, 2 vols., Oxford 1658-9. Tr. only, re-edited by Migne in *PG*, cxi, cols. 889-1231. L. Cheikho, B. Carra de Vaux and H. Zayyat, *Eutychii Patriarchae Alexandrini Annales*, 2 vols., Louvain 1906-9 (*CSCO*, vols. l and li, *Scriptores arabici*, ser. 3, vi, vii). Ed. and German tr. of Sin. Arab. 580 (582), M. Breydy, *Das Annalenwerk des Eutychios von Alexandrien. Ausgewählte Geschichten und Legenden kompiliert von Saᶜīd ibn Baṭrīq um 935 A.D.*, Louvain 1985 (*CSCO*, 471-2, *Scriptores arabici*, 44-5). Annotated Italian tr. by B. Pirone, *Eutichio. Gli Annali*, Cairo, Franciscan Centre of Christian Oriental Studies, 1987 (*Studia Orientalia Christiana Monographiae*, i). Ed. by P. Cachia and English tr. by W. Montgomery Watt of the *K. al-Burhān*: *The Book of the Demonstration*, 4 vols., Louvain 1960-1 (*CSCO*, 192-3, 209-10, *Scriptores arabici*, 20-3).

Sources and studies of Saᶜīd: *Histoire de Yaḥyā-Ibn-Saᶜīd d'Antioche, continuateur de Saᶜīd-Ibn-Biṭrīq*, ed. and tr. J. Kratchkowsky and A. Vasiliev, in *PO*, xviii/5, xxiii/3; Ibn Abī Uṣaybiᶜa, ed. Müller, ii, 86-7, ed. Beirut, 545-6; L. Leclerc, *Histoire de la médecine arabe*, i, 404-5; G. Graf, *Ein bisher unbekanntes Werk des Patriarchen Eutychius von Alexandrien*, in *Oriens christianus*, N.S. i (1911), 227-44; F. Nau, *Eutychius*, in *DTC*, ii, cols. 1609-11; Brockelmann, I², 154-5, S I, 228; Graf, *GCAL*, ii, 32-8; Sezgin,

GAS, iii, 297; M. Breydy, *La conquête arabe de l'Égypte. Un fragment du traditionniste Uthman ibn Salih (144-219 A.H. = 761-834 A.D.), identifié dans les Annales d'Eutychios d'Alexandrie (877-940 A.D.)*, in *Parole de l'Orient*, viii (1977-8), 379-96; idem, *Mamila ou Maqella? La prise de Jérusalem et ses conséquences (614 AD) selon la recension* alexandrine *des Annales d'Eutychès*, in *Oriens christianus*, lxv (1981), 62-86; idem, *Études sur Saʿīd Ibn Baṭrīq et ses sources*, Louvain 1983 (*CSCO*, 450, *Subsidia*, lxix); J. Nasrallah, *Histoire du mouvement littéraire dans l'Eglise melchite du Vᵉ au XXᵉ siècle*, ii/2, Louvain 1988, 23-34.

(Françoise Micheau)

SAʿĪD b. **ḤUMAYD** b. Saʿīd al-Kātib, Abū ʿUthmān, ʿAbbāsid scribe, epistolographer and poet. His exact dates are unknown, but he was probably born in the last years of the 3rd century A.H. and died after 257/871 (or 260/874), the year of Faḍl al-Shāʿira's death [*q.v.* in Suppl.]. His family came from the lower Persian nobility—he himself is sometimes called *al-dihḳān*—and he claimed royal Persian descent. He seems to have held various lower provincial offices, before stepping into the limelight as the *kātib* of Aḥmad b. al-Khaṣīb, vizier to al-Muntaṣir (r. 247-8/861-2 [*q.v.*]), for whom he drew up the *bayʿa* declaration (preserved by al-Ṭabarī, *Taʾrīkh*, ix, 235, tr. J. Kraemer, 199-202; al-Sāmarrāʾī, 74-8). Under the latter's successor, al-Mustaʿīn (r. 248-52/862-6 [*q.v.*]), he headed the *dīwān al-rasāʾil* (al-Ṭabarī, ix, 264, tr. G. Saliba, 13).

He was, however, less of a career administrator, comparing, as he did, the government service with a bath-house: if you are inside, you want to get out, and if you are outside, you want to get in (Ibn Abī ʿAwn, *al-Tashbīhāt*, ed. Muḥ. ʿAbd al-Muʿīd Khān, Cambridge 1950, 316); his favourite ambience was the literary salons of his time, especially that of the famous poetess, songstress, and lute-player, Faḍl al-Shāʿira. With her he had a stormy love relationship, which occasioned a fair amount of poetry on both sides. But his love poetry and, if we can trust the anecdotes, his love life, was by no means restricted to females.

Ibn al-Nadīm lists a collection of his poetry (*Fihrist* 123^{23}; 166^{18-19} [50 folios]) and a collection of his letters (*ibid.* 123^{23}). Neither has been preserved, but the specimens and fragments transmitted in secondary sources have been collected by al-Sāmarrāʾī (see *Bibl.*). He lists 43 pieces of prose, many of which are short sayings, while only two are lengthy documents. One is the *bayʿa* for al-Muntaṣir (see above), the other presents a description of a battle during the civil war between al-Mustaʿīn and al-Muʿtazz [*q.v.*], written on 24 Ṣafar 251/25 March 865 (reading *baḳīna* for *khalawna* in the text) at the behest of the governor of Baghdād, Muḥammad b. ʿAbdallāh b. Ṭāhir, to be read in the Friday mosque (al-Ṭabarī, *Taʾrīkh*, ix, 296-303, tr. Saliba, 50-8; al-Sāmarrāʾī, 105-17). The collected poems and fragments of such run into 73 (plus 17 doubtful) items; the longest has thirteen lines. Ibn Abī Ṭāhir Ṭayfūr (d. 280/893 [*q.v.*]) presents Saʿīd b. Ḥumayd as a very able plagiariser (*Fihrist*, 123^{20-1}), remarking that, if one were to say to his prose and poetry "Return to your originators", nothing would stay with him. This is, however, not an original critique, either. According to the anecdotes, he was a facile improviser, and his poetry cannot be expected to be highly innovative. Most of the preserved pieces are in the *ghazal* genre; they are smooth and elegant.

His *shuʿūbī* attitude [see shuʿūbiyya] emerges from the title of another book, now lost, that reads *K. Intiṣāf al-ʿadjam min al-ʿarab*, "Demanding justice for the Persians from the Arabs", also known as *al-Taswiya* "The equalising" (*Fihrist*, 123^{22-3}). The choice of words here shows him to be a moderate who did not claim superiority for the Persians.

Saʿīd b. Ḥumayd had a number of namesakes—al-Sāmarrāʾī enumerates five of them (*op. cit.*, 32-4)—of which Abū ʿUthmān Saʿīd b. Ḥumayd b. al-Bakhtakān (*Fihrist*, 123^{27-30}) was easily confused with our man due to the similarity in name as well as in *shuʿūbī* conviction.

Bibliography: The main sources for his life and his works are Ṭabarī, tr. J. Kraemer, *The History of al-Ṭabarī*, xxxiv, *Incipient decline*, Albany 1989, tr. G. Saliba, xxxv, *The crisis of the ʿAbbāsid caliphate*, Albany 1985, index; and Iṣbahānī, *Aghānī*, ed. ʿA.A. Farrādj, xviii, Beirut 1959, 90-102 (on Saʿīd b. Ḥumayd), xix, Beirut 1960, 257-71 (on Faḍl al-Shāʿira). For other sources, see *GAS*, ii, 583. Study and collection of works by Yūnus Aḥmad al-Sāmarrāʾī, *Rasāʾil Saʿīd b. Ḥumayd wa-ashʿāruh*, Baghdād 1971.

(W.P. Heinrichs)

SAʿĪD b. **SULṬĀN** b. Aḥmad b. Saʿīd Āl Bū Saʿīdī, ruler of ʿUmān and Zanzibar (b. Muscat 1791, d. at sea on 19 Oct. 1856). He and his brother Sālim succeeded jointly in 1806, but shortly were usurped by their cousin Badr, whom Saʿīd assassinated. Sālim had the title Imām, but was a nonentity; the effective power was in Saʿīd's hands. When Sālim d. Saʿīd was not elected to the imāmate, he preferred using the title Sayyid, used without distinction by all the princes of the family. Nevertheless, European sources frequently refer to Saʿīd as Imām. He never used the title Sulṭān.

The fissiparous ʿUmānī tribal system, family quarrels, Wahhābī expansionism in central Arabia, and disputes with other Gulf states, together with Anglo-French rivalry, complicated the earlier part of his reign. Muscat, nevertheless, was pivotal in the western Indian Ocean in a lively commerce which had attracted resident Indian merchant houses. Saʿīd developed an army with Balūčī and other mercenaries, and also a fleet which could also serve mercantile ends. The grandson of its commander, Abdalla Saleh Farsy, was Saʿīd's Swahili biographer.

In 1698 the preceding Yaʿrubī dynasty had acquired the eastern African coast from Mogadishu to Tungi in northern Mozambique. Control was little more than nominal. In Mombasa [*q.v.*] the Mazarʿi *liwali*s had made themselves virtually independent, as had the Sultans of Pate and Kilwa [*q.vv.*], and petty rulers in Pemba, Tumbatu and Zanzibar, save for the occasional payment of tribute. In 1822 the Mazarʿi had seized Pemba [*q.v.*], and Saʿīd sent an expedition against them. In 1827 he came to enforce his authority over the Mazarʿi in person; in 1824-6 they had attempted independence under British protection, which was disowned by Whitehall.

By 1834 Saʿīd had determined to move his capital to Zanzibar, which he had first visited in 1828. He now divided his time between Muscat and Zanzibar almost equally, only finally settling in Zanzibar in 1840. Apart from tax revenue, his move was primarily commercial. After 1839 Indian caravans, that is, caravans funded by the Indian merchant houses, went inland, for ivory, slaves and other products of the interior. The caravans were armed, for Saʿīd had no ambitions for an interior empire. The changes were formalised by the establishment of consulates: United States (1837), Britain (1841), France (1844), whose countries, with Germany, became the principal buyers. Commerce was his principal preoccupation, and his own ships exported goods to India and

Arabia, and occasionally to Europe and to China. The range of his interests is exemplified in 1845, when he sent an Arab horse as a present to the American President, and himself received an Imperial dinner set of sixty-four pieces from the Chinese Emperor, of a kind of porcelain reserved for the Imperial Family alone.

From 1822 he was under pressure to end the slave trade, when he was forced to forbid the sale of slaves to Christian powers. In 1845 he was persuaded into a further treaty prohibiting both import and export of slaves from his African dominions. Since he had no control inland it was not difficult to evade these provisions.

The prosperity of Zanzibar, and in particular the wealth that accrued from the clove trade, in which Zanzibar now led the world, was to a great extent dependent on Saʿīd's patriarchal administration. He developed no constitutional or commercial system. He sat publicly daily to hear cases like any desert chieftain. Commercially, he was dependent on the ability and good will of the Indian merchants, whose immigration he encouraged. Mosques, palaces in the town and the countryside, and the packed houses in Zanzibar town spoke of the success of his regime.

His only existing portrait, painted from memory after an audience by an American naval officer, can be seen in the Peabody Museum, Salem, Massachusetts. An intimate portrait of his private life is given in the *Memoirs of an Arabian Princess* by his daughter Salme (so she pronounced Sālima), written in 1886. He had no children by his legal wives, but of his *surias*, chiefly Circassians, with some Georgians, Assyrians and Ethiopians, some seventy in all, twenty-five sons were born and an unknown number of daughters. Strict in his observance of the daily prayers, he delighted in lavish generosity at the great festivals; his personal life was of the simplest. He was an accomplished horseman and practical seaman. Saʿīd, wrote a British consul, was "most truly every man's friend; he wishes to do good to all."

Bibliography: Sources listed by C.F. Beckingham, art. BŪ SAʿĪD, are not repeated here. N.R. Bennett, *A history of the Arab State of Zanzibar*, London 1978; Mohmed Reza Bhacker, *Trade and empire in Muscat and Zanzibar*, London 1993, contains a very detailed bibl.; R.F. Burton, *Zanzibar, City, Island and Coast*, 2 vols., London 1972; E. van Donzel (ed.), Sayyida Salme/Emily Ruete, *An Arabian princess between two Worlds*, Leiden 1993; Abdalla Saleh Farsy, *Seyyid Said bin Sultan*, Mwongozi Press, Zanzibar 1942; J.R. Gray and D. Birmingham (eds.), *Pre-colonial African trade*, Oxford 1970; G.S.P. Freeman-Grenville (ed.), *Memoirs of an Arabian princess*, London 1981, 1993; Mbarak Ali Hinawi, *al-Akida and Fort Jesus*, London 1950; J. Middleton, *The world of the Swahili*, Yale 1992; H. Montgomery-Massingberd, *Burke's peerage. Royal families of the world*, ii, *Africa and Asia*, London 1980, C.S. Nicholls, *The Swahili coast: politics, diplomacy and trade on the East African littoral, 1798-1856*, London 1971; J.McL. Ritchie (ed. and tr.), Shaykh al-Amin b. ʿAlī al-Mazrui, *Akhbar Al al-Mazar'i: the history of the Mazrui*, British Academy, *Fontes Historiae Africanae, Series Arabica*, forthcoming.

(G.S.P. FREEMAN-GRENVILLE)

SAʿĪD B. ZAYD b. ʿAmr b. Nufayl ... b. ʿAdī b. Kaʿb b. Luʾayy, a Companion of the Prophet from the tribe of Ḳuraysh [*q.v.*] and one of Muḥammad's earliest converts.

His mother was Fāṭima bint Baʿdja b. Umayya of the clan of Khuzāʿa. His *kunya* was Abu 'l-Aʿwar or Abū Thawr. He was one of ʿUmar b. al-Khaṭṭāb's cousins and at the same time his brother-in-law through his wife, who was ʿUmar's sister, as well as through ʿUmar's wife who was his sister. He assumed Islam before Muḥammad entered the house of Zayd b. al-Arḳam and ʿUmar's conversion is said to have taken place under the influence of Saʿīd and his family.

His father, Zayd b. ʿAmr, was one of the *ḥanīfs*; he was much interested in monotheism, refused to worship idols, warned his contemporaries against idolatry and confessed the "religion of Abraham" [see ZAYD B. ʿAMR]. It is said that he died in the year when the Kaʿba was rebuilt, an event in which also Muḥammad is said to have taken part.

Saʿīd migrated with the Muslims to Medina, where Muḥammad "brothered" him with Rāfiʿ b. Mālik al-Zuraḳī, or, according to others, with Ubayy b. Kaʿb.

When the rumour of the return of the Ḳuraysh caravan from Syria reached Medina, Saʿīd, together with Ṭalḥa b. ʿUbayd Allāh, was sent on scouting service. They met the caravan at al-Ḥawrāʾ and hurried back to Medina to report the news. But Muḥammad was already on his way to Badr, and the battle took place without their taking part in it. They nevertheless obtained their portion from the booty. Saʿīd was present at all the other *mashāhid* and distinguished himself in the battle of Adjnādayn [*q.v.*] (13/634), where he was at the head of the cavalry in the battle of Fiḥl [see FAḤL] (13/634), where the infantry was under his command, and in the battle of the Yarmūk [*q.v.*] (15/636).

At ʿUmar's death, Saʿīd belonged to those who promoted ʿUthmān's election as caliph. Yet he was not content with his government, though he did not join the ʿAlid party.

He died in 50 or 51/670-1 in ʿAḳīḳ near Medina, where he was buried. It is said that he reached the age of over 70 years. According to others, he died as governor of al-Kūfa under Muʿāwiya.

Saʿīd never played a significant role in the Muslim community. He was honoured because of his early conversion and belongs to the ten who were promised Paradise (*al-ʿashara al-mubashshara*). Muḥammad is sometimes (Aḥmad b. Ḥanbal, *Musnad*, i, 187-8) represented as ascending mount Ḥirāʾ or Uḥud with some of his Companions. As the mountain begins to tremble, he says: "Stand fast, O mountain, for on thee walk a prophet, a *ṣiddīḳ* and witnesses." Then he proceeds to beatify his Companions, among whom Saʿīd mentions himself in a veiled manner in some traditions. Some of the forms of this report may remind us of Jesus' transfiguration on the mountain (Matt. xvii).

Saʿīd belonged to those whose curse (*duʿāʾ*) was efficacious. This is illustrated in the story of a woman who, being cursed by him, became blind and was drowned in a well into which she happened to fall because of her blindness.

Saʿīd's *musnad*, i.e. the traditions handed down on his authority, is to be found in Aḥmad b. Ḥanbal's *Musnad*, i, 187-90.

Bibliography: Ibn Saʿd, iii/1, 275-81; Ibn Ḥadjar, *Iṣāba*, ed. Badjawī, iii, 103-5; Ibn al-Athīr, *Usd* s.v.; Ibn Hishām, *Sīra*, index; Abū Nuʿaym, *Ḥilya*, i, 95-7; Ṭabarī, *Indices*, s.v.; Caetani, *Annali dell'Islām*, Indices, s.v.

(A.J. WENSINCK-[G.H.A. JUYNBOLL])

SAʿĪD (ABĪ) YAʿḲŪB YŪSUF AL-FAYYŪMĪ [see SAʿADYĀ BEN YŌSĒF].

SAʿĪD ABŪ BAKR (1317-67/1899-1948), Tunisian man of letters, who had an original and rich career as a self-taught poet, writer and journalist, all at the same time.

He was born at Moknine in the Tunisian Sāḥil on

28 October 1899 into a modest family of rural origin. His first studies were at the local Ḳurʾānic school of the town, where he speedily revealed himself to his teachers as one possessing a lively intelligence and, in particular, a precocious poetic talent. He composed his first verses at the age of eleven, and an anecdote is retailed about this, generally reported and related by those who had known him: he dealt with his subject of school composition in verse, at the same time preventing his masters from making the slightest correction. For financial reasons, he was unable to proceed to secondary studies, and it was from a lawyer and literary man from the Sāḥil region, one Rād̲j̲iḥ Ibrāhīm, who practiced at Sousse, that he found encouragement, both moral and material. This last made Saᶜīd his secretary and placed his personal library at his disposal. Saᶜīd profited from this to complete his education, as a genuine autodidact. Soon afterwards, he made contact with certain organs of the press in the capital Tunis, becoming a correspondent for them. Having mastered Arabic and French, and even Hebrew, with the encouragement of his patron Rād̲j̲iḥ Ibrāhīm, he went to Tunis and established himself there permanently, working as an editor for various newspapers and journals, such as *al-Fad̲j̲r, al-Badr, al-ᶜArab, Lisān al-S̲h̲aᶜb, al-Nadīm, al-Wazīr* and *al-Ṣawāb*, in the last of which he published his first poem, on 21 May 1920. This made him famous on account of its subject, the rights of the Tunisian woman (whose interests he hymned in several of his poems) to liberty, education, culture and total emancipation, thereby recalling Ṭāhir al-Ḥaddād, another contemporary man of letters who was, like Saᶜīd Abū Bakr, a strong defender of the rights of women.

But it was in *al-Nahḍa* that he made his career, and it was there that he came to prominence through his rich and colourful style, publishing there a long article on the sessions of the First Constituitive Congress of the Néo-Destour Party held at Ksar-Hellal on 2 March 1934. It was there also, as in *al-Nadīm* too, that he began and continued regularly to publish his poems of a social and political character, in particular, summoning the people to "awake from their torpor" and their miserable circumstances, and employing a revolutionary emphasis and an innovative style. Saᶜīd had little regard for the rigorous rules of prosody, and he appeared as an avant-garde poet for whom the restraints of metrics and rhyme were not to constitute a barrier to expression of basic feelings ideas and thought. This appeared quite clearly in his two poetic collections: *al-Saᶜīdiyyāt*, published in 1927 in one volume (2nd ed. 1981) and *al-Zaharāt*, published at an unspecified date.

On another level, one should mention that Saᶜīd brought out, from the 1930s to the beginning of the Second World War, an illustrated journal called *al-ᶜĀlam al-muṣawwara*, which became, for a time, *al-ᶜĀlam al-adabī*, and then, after October 1940, in an illustrated form, *Tūnis al-muṣawwara*, this being the main means whereby he earned his livelihood. After a long gap due to the Second World War, this journal re-appeared in July 1947. As a great lover of art, Saᶜīd assiduously frequented not only the men of letters but also the artistic circles in the capital, where he learnt to play the violin and got to know a girl of the Tunis petite bourgeoisie, whom he married.

He was equally fond of travelling, and visited, as well as France, Algeria (in particular, the Constantine region), Morocco and Spain, especially Andalusia, with its main cities (Granada, Cordova and Seville). With regard to this last region, "melting-pot of Arab-Islamic civilisation", he wrote a travel narrative, in the fashion of an Ibn Baṭṭūṭa, with the title *al-Andalus ka-annaka tarāhā* (1931).

On 29 January 1948 he died, and was buried at Tunis. After the achievement of Independence, his remains were moved to the Mausoleum of Martyrs in his native town of Moknine, and this last has, for several years, and in homage to the person and his work, organised regularly a cultural and artistic festival in his memory. His name has been given to one of the main streets of the capital as well as in towns of the interior.

Bibliography: Ḥ.Ḥ. ᶜAbd al-Wahhāb, *Mud̲j̲mal taʾrīk̲h̲ al-adab al-tūnisī*, Tunis 1968, 316-27; *Biblīyūg̲h̲rāfiyā Saᶜīd Abī Bakr*, Dār al-Kutub al-Waṭaniyya, Tunis 1973; H. Chaouch, *Adab al-riḥla fī turāt̲h̲ Saᶜīd Abī Bakr*, in *al-Fikr*, xxviii, no. 6 (March 1983), 14-25; R. D̲h̲awādī, *Udabāʾ tūnisiyyūn*, Dār al-Mag̲h̲rib al-ᶜArabī 1972, 28-45; K̲h̲ālid Aḥmad, *S̲h̲ak̲h̲ṣiyyāt wa-ṭayyārāt*, Tunis 1976, 65-97, 2nd ed. Tunis 1982, 76-135; idem, *Ṭāhir al-Ḥaddād wa 'l-bīʾa al-tūnisiyya fī 'l-t̲h̲ulut̲h̲ al-awwal min al-ḳarn al-ᶜis̲h̲rīn*, Tunis 1967, 274-9; M. Maḥfūẓ, *Tarād̲j̲im al-muʾallifīn al-tūnisiyyīn*, Beirut 1982, 146-61; *Muk̲h̲tārāt min al-adab al-tūnisī al-muᶜāṣir*, 2 vols., Tunis 1985, i, 247-51; *al-D̲h̲ikrā al-t̲h̲alāt̲h̲ūn li-wafāt al-s̲h̲āᶜir Saᶜīd Abī Bakr*, Ministry of Cultural Affairs, Tunis 1978; M. Rad̲j̲ab, *S̲h̲āᶜirān* (coll. Kitāb al-Baᶜt̲h̲, no. 14), Tunis 1957, 5-52; Z. al-Sanūsī, *al-Adab al-tūnisī fī 'l-ḳarn al-rābiᶜ ᶜas̲h̲ar*, Tunis 1979, 121-65; Ziriklī, *Aᶜlām*, 3rd ed. Beirut 1969, iii, 145.

(H. Chaouch)

SAᶜĪD b. Yaᶜḳūb al-**DIMAS̲H̲ḲĪ**, Abū ᶜUt̲h̲mān, physician and translator of Greek scientific works into Arabic. As one of the leading physicians of his time, he enjoyed the favours of the vizier ᶜAlī b. ᶜĪsā (d. 334/946 [*q.v.*]). When the latter endowed a hospital in the Ḥarbiyya quarter of Bag̲h̲dād in 302/914-15, he appointed Abū ᶜUt̲h̲mān as chief physician with the joint responsibility of supervising the hospitals of Bag̲h̲dād, Mecca and Medina (Ibn Abī Uṣaybiᶜa, i, 234, ll. 8-10, according to T̲h̲ābit b. Sinān; cf. Ibn al-D̲j̲awzī, *al-Muntaẓam*, vi, 128; on the vizier's measures for public health, see *ibid.*, 221-2, and al-Ḳifṭī, *Ḥukamāʾ*, 193-4).

As a translator, he served not only the demands of the medical profession but showed equal competence in mathematics and philosophy. Together with Isḥāḳ b. Ḥunayn and T̲h̲ābit b. Ḳurra [*q.vv.*], the most eminent transmitters of Hellenistic science in his generation, he was close to the Shīᶜī *mutakallim* and heresiographer al-Ḥasan b. Mūsā al-Nawbak̲h̲tī (*q.v.*; and see Ibn al-Nadīm, *al-Fihrist*, 177).

Of his medical works, versions of Galen's *De pulsibus ad tirones* (with a commentary ascribed to Johannes Philoponus) and *De nervorum dissectione*, and of *De urinis* by Magnus of Emesa, are extant in manuscript; his own tabular compendium of *De pulsibus* is lost (see Sezgin, *GAS*, iii, 82, 90, 159; M. Ullmann, *Die Medizin im Islam*, Leiden 1970, 81, 90). His translation of the commentary of Pappus on Euclid's *Elements*, book X (on commensurable and incommensurable magnitudes [irrationalities]) has preserved a valuable document, lost in the original Greek, of the late Alexandrian tradition of mathematics (see Sezgin, *GAS*, v, 175; ed. W. Thomson, with G. Junge, *The commentary of Pappus on book X of Euclid's Elements*, Cambridge, Mass. 1930; German tr. H. Suter, *Beiträge zur Geschichte der Mathematik bei den Griechen und Arabern*, Erlangen 1922, 9-78).

His lasting importance as a translator lies in his philosophical work, where his scope went far beyond the ethical Platonism and Galenism of the medical tradition, as attested in his own *masāʾil* on Galen's *De moribus* (lost, see Ibn Abī Uṣaybiʿa, i, 234) and a chapter of sayings in the *Ṣiwān al-ḥikma* (ed. Dunlop, 125-6). An ethical treatise *Faḍāʾil al-nafs*, attributed to Aristotle and otherwise unknown, is quoted by Miskawayh in Abū ʿUthmān's version (*Tahdhīb al-akhlāḳ*; ed. Ḳ. Zurayk, Beirut 1966, 86-91; see S. Pines, *Un texte inconnu d'Aristote en version arabe*, in *Archives d'histoire doctrinale et littéraire du moyen-âge*, xxiii [ann. 31: 1956], 5-43, esp. 16). His translation of Aristotle's *Topica*, books I-VII, became the definitive version of this fundamental textbook of logical reasoning (ed. ʿAbd-al-Raḥmān Badawī, *Manṭiḳ Arisṭū*, Cairo 1948-52, 467-689 = ²Kuwayt 1980, 487-725), finished before 298/910-11, the date of a copy taken from Abū ʿUthmān's exemplar (see *ibid.*, ¹532). Even more widely read was his rendering of Porphyry's introduction (*Isagoge*) to Aristotle's *Categories* (ed. Badawī, *Manṭiḳ Arisṭū*, ¹1019-68 = ²1055-1104). A partial translation of Aristotle's *Physics*, comprising at least books IV (with the commentary of Alexander of Aphrodisias, Ibn al-Nadīm, *Fihrist*, 250.14) and VII is quoted by the Arab commentators (ed. Badawī, Arisṭūṭālīs, *al-Ṭabīʿa*, Cairo 1962, 318 l. 2, 754-5). His version of Aristotle's *De generatione et corruptione* (*Fihrist*, 251 l. 3) may have formed the basis of a compendium written by his patron, al-Nawbakhtī (mentioned in the *Fihrist*, 177).

Of particular interest, and indicative of his philosophical leanings, is a number of treatises by (and attributed to) Alexander of Aphrodisias; some of these were translated by himself, but others were collected by him from earlier work done by a circle of translators around al-Kindī [*q.v.*], and transmitted as al-Dimashḳī's work in later copies. In view of Alexander's rôle as a mediator between Peripatetic and Neoplatonic thought, and due to the inclusion of excerpts from the *Elements of theology* by Proclus into the Arabic *Theology of Aristotle* drawn upon by al-Dimashḳī, he contributed to the integration of Hellenistic philosophy in the Aristotelianism of the *falāsifa*. (See J. van Ess, *Über einige neue Fragmente des Alexander von Aphrodisias und des Proklos in arabischer Übersetzung*, in *Isl.*, xlii [1966], 148-68; G. Endress, *Proclus Arabus*, Beirut-Wiesbaden 1973, 35-38, 58-61, 75-6; F.W. Zimmermann, *The origins of the so-called Theology of Aristotle*, in *Pseudo-Aristotle in the Middle Ages*, London 1986, 110-295, esp. 130, 184 ff.).

Bibliography (in addition to references given in the article): 1. Texts. Ibn al-Nadīm, *al-Fihrist*, ed. Flügel, i, 298; *Muntakhab Ṣiwān al-ḥikma* [ascribed to Abū Sulaymān al-Sidjistānī], ed. D.M. Dunlop. The Hague etc. 1979, 125-6; Ḳifṭī, *Taʾrīkh al-ḥukamāʾ*, ed. A. Müller and J. Lippert, index *s.n.*; Ibn Abī Uṣaybiʿa, *ʿUyūn al-anbāʾ fī ṭabaqāt al-aṭibbāʾ*, ed. Müller, Cairo-Königsberg 1882-4, i, 234 ll. 7-13.

2. Studies. A.G. Kapp, *Arabische Übersetzer und Kommentatoren Euklids ... auf Grund des Taʾrīkh al-Ḥukamāʾ des Ibn al-Qifṭī*, in *Isis*, xxiii (1935), 81-2; M. Meyerhof, *Von Alexandrien nach Bagdad*, in *SB Preuss. Akad. der Wiss.*, Phil.-hist. Kl., no. 23, Berlin 1930, 38; H. Suter, *Die Mathematiker und Astronomen der Araber und ihre Werke*, Leipzig 1900, 49 (no. 98); R. Walzer, *Greek into Arabic*, Oxford 1962, 67 (and index); S. Pines, *La doctrine de l'intellect selon Bakr al-Mawṣilī*, in *Studi orientalistici in onore di G. Levi Della Vida*, Rome 1956, ii, 350 ff. (on a treatise dedicated to Saʿīd).

(G. Endress)

SAʿĪD EFENDI, later **PASHA**, Meḥmed Čelebi-zāde, Ottoman Turkish official and Grand Vizier, born in Istanbul at an unknown date, died in 1174/1761. He was the son of the statesman and diplomat Mehmed Yirmisekiz Čelebi Efendi [*q.v.*], and accompanied his father on his diplomatic mission to France in 1132/1720-1. After a career as a secretary in the *Dīwān-i Humāyūn*, he himself was sent on embassies to Sweden and to France (1154-5/1741-2), and in 1169/1756 became Grand Vizier to ʿOthmān III [*q.v.*] for five-and-a-half months. He finished his career as governor of Egypt and then of Adana and Marʿash, dying in the latter place.

He was the author of *inter alia* a collection of poetry and a dictionary of materia medica, the *Fewāʾid ül-müfredāt*, but a particular claim of his to fame was his association with Ibrāhīm Müteferriḳa [*q.v.*], the pioneer printer of Islamic Turkish books in Turkey, being with Ibrāhīm the joint grantee of the original *firmān* issued by Aḥmed III for the establishment of a printing press in 1139/1727 [see maṭbaʿa. 2. In Turkey].

Bibliography: See that to meḥmed yirmisekiz čelebi; also Alaettin Gövsa, *Türk meşhurları ansiklopedisi*, s.v.; *Türk dili ve edebiyatı ansiklopedisi*, ii, 128-9.

(Ed.)

SAʿĪD PASHA, Muḥammad, youngest son of Muḥammad ʿAlī Pasha [*q.v.*] and hereditary viceroy of Egypt, theoretically under Ottoman suzerainty, 1854-63. He was styled Pasha, but was already known in informal and unofficial usage as Khedive before this latter title was formally adopted after his death [see khidīw].

Born in 1822, his father had had a high opinion of his capabilities and had sent him at the age of only nineteen to Istanbul for negotiations over the tribute payable by Egypt to the Porte. Saʿīd's uncle and predecessor in the governorship of Egypt, ʿAbbās Ḥilmī I b. Aḥmad Ṭūsūn [*q.v.*], had endeavoured to change the succcession arrangements in the Ottoman *firmān* of 1841, providing that the succession should go to the eldest living descendant of Muḥammad ʿAlī's line, in favour of his own progeny, hoping that his son Ilhāmī Pasha would succeed him. ʿAbbās's death was briefly concealed, but Saʿīd nevertheless managed to succeed without difficulty in July 1854.

ʿAbbās Ḥilmī had been both zealous in guarding his rights *vis-à-vis* the Ottoman sultan and also suspicious of European pressures on Egypt and of foreigners in general. Saʿīd, however, was less mistrustful of the West and its new techniques, having had several European tutors, and had an especial fondness for French culture; he appeared as a mild and benevolent ruler, more popular than his secretive, traditionalist predecessor. But he was also somewhat weak and susceptible to advice from interested parties, so that he succumbed to the charm of Ferdinand de Lesseps and granted to him the famous Suez Canal concession (see below).

Possibly influenced by outside advisers, Saʿīd revived many of his father's economic, social and legal policies, whilst relaxing the extreme centralisation of Muḥammad ʿAlī's time. He promulgated the first comprehensive law in Egypt on private landed and immoveable property, granting the right freely to dispose of this, and abolished the state monopoly over agricultural products (1858) (see G. Baer, *A history of landownership in modern Egypt 1800-1950*, London 1962, 7-10); these measures paralleled similar reforms in Turkey under the *Tanẓīmāt* [*q.v.*]. Saʿīd was interested in railways and other forms of communication. The railway between Cairo and Alexandria was finished and a concession granted to the Eastern Telegraph Co. In 1854 the first River Navigation and Transport Co. in Egypt was founded, and in 1857 a commercial

Navigation Co. to help foreign trade. Above all, in 1854 de Lesseps received his first Suez Canal concession, confirmed by the Pas͟ha in 1856. The European powers, including both France at the outset and Britian, tried by diplomacy to hinder the project, but work was begun in 1859 by peasant corvee labour and continued for a decade; the seaport at the northern end of the Canal was named Port Saʿīd [*q.v.*] after the Pas͟ha (see D.S. Landes, *Bankers and Pashas. International finance and economic imperialism in Egypt*, London 1958, 69 ff., 173 ff.; D.A. Farnie, *East and West of Suez. The Suez Canal in history 1854-1956*, Oxford 1969, 32 ff.).

In the financial sphere, the Bank of Egypt was founded in 1854 and the process began during Saʿīd's reign whereby European financial and commercial influence became pervasive. The Pas͟ha's financial needs for his military ventures (see below) and his public works led him to seek a £ 3 million loan from a London banking house, a harbinger of the disastrous financial policies which were to drag down his successor Ismāʿīl [*q.v.*] (see Landes, *op. cit.*, 62 ff.).

Saʿīd did not favour an expansionist policy in the Sudan, and left its governorship to Prince Ḥalīm; on the occasion of a visit to K͟harṭūm [*q.v.*] in 1857, he made the first attempts to abolish the traffic there in black slaves. He did, however, continue the Egyptian contingent of 8,000 men which ʿAbbās Ḥilmī had sent to the Ottomans' side when the Crimean War broke out, and he also sent a regiment to assist the Emperor Napoleon III in his endeavour to maintain the Archduke Maximilian on his throne in Mexico.

Saʿīd died in Alexandria on 17 January 1863 and was buried there. His nephew Ismāʿīl b. Ibrāhīm Pas͟ha [*q.v.*], who had already been prominent during Saʿīd's reign on diplomatic missions, including to Paris in 1855, as regent within Egypt and as *Sirdār* or Commander-in-Chief of the Egyptian Army in 1861, succeeded him without difficulty.

Bibliography: For older works, see the *EI*[1] art. Of modern references, in addition to those in the article, see P.M. Holt, *Egypt and the Fertile Crescent 1516-1922, a political history*, Ithaca 1966, 195-6; P.J. Vatikiotis, *The history of Egypt from Muhammad Ali to Sadat*[2], London 1980, 72-3; E.R. Toledano, *State and society in mid-nineteenth century Egypt*, Cambridge 1990, index s.n. *Sait Paşa*.

(C.E. Bosworth)

SAʿĪD AL-DĪN Muḥammad b. Aḥmad **FARG͟HĀNĪ**, often called Saʿīd-i Farg͟hānī, author of important Ṣūfī works pertaining to the school of Ibn al-ʿArabī. Sometimes the form Saʿd al-Dīn is found, but this seems to be a copyist's correction of the unusual form. On a manuscript of his *Mas͟hāriḳ al-darārī* dated 678/1279-80 (Esad Ef. 1511), the name is given as in the title of this entry, with "Kādānī" added after the *nisba* Farg͟hānī. Ḥād͟jd͟jī K͟halīfa gives death dates of 691/1292 and *ca.* 700/1300-1 (ed. Flügel, no. 365); Osman Yahia prefers 695/1296 (introd. to Sayyid Ḥaydar Āmulī, *Kitāb Naṣṣ al-nuṣūṣ*, Tehran 1975, 18); Brockelmann has 699/1299 (S I, 812).

Little is known of Saʿīd al-Dīn's life. In his *Manāhid͟j al-ʿibād* (Istanbul 1988, 184) he tells us that he entered Ṣūfism at the hand of S͟hayk͟h Nad͟jīb al-Dīn ʿAlī b. Buzg͟hus͟h of Shīrāz (d. 678/1279), a disciple of Shaykh S͟hihāb al-Dīn ʿUmar Suhrawardī. Later, he benefited from Shaykh Ṣadr al-Dīn Ḳūnawī (d. 673/1274), and then from S͟hayk͟h Muḥammad b. al-Sukrān al-Bag͟hdādī and "others." Ḳūnawī tells us that Farg͟hānī and several other scholars were his companions when he travelled in the year 643/1245-6 to Egypt and began teaching Ibn al-Fāriḍ's famous *ḳaṣīda, Naẓm al-sulūk* (also known as *al-Tāʾiyya*). Several people took notes with the aim of composing books, but only Farg͟hānī was successful (letter of approval to Farg͟hānī, *Mas͟hārik al-darārī*, ed. S.D͟j. Ās͟htiyānī, Mas͟hhad 1398/1978, 5-6, 77-8). Sibṭ Ibn al-Fāriḍ quotes S͟hams al-Dīn Ikī (d. 697/1298), a disciple of Ḳūnawī's and *s͟hayk͟h al-s͟huyūk͟h* in Cairo, to the effect that after lecturing on *ḥadīt͟h* in Arabic, Ḳūnawī would recite one verse of *Naẓm al-sulūk* and explain its meaning in Persian, and it was these explanations that Saʿīd al-Dīn recorded (Th.E. Homerin, *From Arab poet to Muslim saint*, Columbia, S.C. 1994, 29; cf. D͟jāmī, *Nafaḥāt al-uns*, ed. M. Tawḥīdīpūr, Tehran 1336/1957, 542).

Farg͟hānī is best known for his Persian and Arabic commentaries on *Naẓm al-sulūk*. The full name of the first is *Mas͟hāriḳ al-darārī al-zuhar fī kas͟hf ḥaḳāʾiḳ naẓm al-durar*, while the second is called *Muntahā 'l-madārik wa-mus͟htahā lubb kull kāmil aw ʿārif wa-sālik* (2 vols., Cairo 1293/1876). Ḳūnawī's just-cited letter of approval is appended to the end of the introduction to the Persian text. The Arabic commentary is half again as long as the Persian and includes a much expanded introduction, without Ḳūnawī's letter; it was being read in Cairo as early as 670/1271 (Massignon, *The Passion of al-Ḥallāj*, Eng. tr. Princeton 1982, i, 44). Both works were widely cited as authoritative expositions of the teachings of Ḳūnawī. D͟jāmī was particularly fond of *Muntahā 'l-madārik* and called its introduction an unparalleled exposition of "the science of reality" (*Nafaḥāt*, 559).

Farg͟hānī's third work, the Persian *Manāhid͟j al-ʿibād ilā 'l-maʿād*, outlines the five pillars of Islam along with basic Ṣūfī *ādāb*. It was not as widely read as the other two, but it gained more readership than it might have because Ḳutb al-Dīn S͟hīrāzī (d. 710/1311 [*q.v.*]), who studied *ḥadīt͟h* with Ḳūnawī, incorporated it into his philosophical encyclopedia, the *Durrat al-tād͟j*, as the last and "most important" part of the book (see J. Walbridge, *A Sufi scientist of the thirteenth century: the mystical ideas and practices of Quṭb al-Dīn Shīrāzī*, in L. Lewisohn (ed.), *The legacy of mediaeval Persian Sufism*, London 1992, 323-40; idem, *The science of mystic lights. Quṭb al-Dīn Shīrāzī and the Illuminationist tradition in Islamic philosophy*, Cambridge, Mass. 13, 176-8). According to Ḥād͟jd͟jī K͟halīfa, the *Manāhid͟j* was translated into Arabic with the title *Madārid͟j al-i ʿtiḳād* by Abu 'l-Faḍl Muḥammad b. Idrīs al-Bidlīsī. Ḥād͟jd͟jī K͟halīfa (no. 1263) also attributes a commentary on Ibn al-ʿArabī's *Fuṣūṣ al-ḥikam* to Saʿīd al-Dīn, but the ascription is unlikely. Another book that is often attributed to Farg͟hānī is the important unedited compendium of *Ṣūfī* technical terms, *Laṭāʾif al-i ʿlām fī is͟hārāt ahl al-ilhām*; some of the definitions are indeed taken from *Muntahā 'l-madārik*. However, neither the style of the work nor what the author says about himself allows for this attribution; he speaks of his own works on *kalām* (under the definition of *al-rūḥ*) and mentions (under *al-ʿilm al-ladunī*) that he was a disciple of ʿAlāʾ al-Dawla Simnānī (659-736/1261-1336 [*q.v.*]).

The *Mas͟hāriḳ al-darārī* and *Muntahā 'l-madārik* are important as two of the earliest commentaries on Ibn al-Fāriḍ's poem, but their main significance lies in their formative influence on the way in which the teachings of Ibn al-ʿArabī were developed. Like Ḳūnawī, Farg͟hānī singled out certain of Ibn al-ʿArabī's discussions and technical terms for emphasis. The net result was that Ibn al-ʿArabī's well-known followers were drawn much closer to the philosophical mode of expressing Islamic teachings than was the Shaykh al-Akbar himself. Farghānī's introduction to *Muntahā 'l-madārik* is an especially good example of a dense philosophical and relatively systematic exposition of Ibn al-ᶜArabī's teachings. It provides a better survey of the technical terms and discussions that were to play major roles in theoretical Ṣūfism in the coming centuries than does Ibn al-ᶜArabī's own *Fuṣūṣ al-ḥikam*, which was to be the object of over one hundred commentaries.

Bibliography: See also W.C. Chittick, *Spectrums of Islamic thought: Saᶜīd al-Dīn Farghānī on the implications of oneness and manyness*, in Lewisohn, *op. cit.*, 203-17.

(W.C. CHITTICK)

SAᶜĪD AL-SUᶜADĀᵓ, the name of a *khānḳāh* or establishment for Ṣūfīs at Cairo founded during the Ayyūbid period in a former Fāṭimid house within al-Ḳāhira, now in the modern Djamāliyya street (*Index des monuments historiques*, no. 480).

In Fāṭimid times it was a dwelling facing the *Dār al-wizāra*, at that period the ministry of justice. Some famous persons dwelt there, such as the vizier Ṭalāᵓiᶜ b. Ruzzīk [*q.v.*], who had a tunnel dug to connect it with the *Dār al-wizāra*. It was at this point that it acquired its name of Saᶜīd al-Suᶜadāᵓ "the Supremely-happy one", from the name of the person thus styled, the *ustādh* Ḳanbar (or ᶜAnbar), an instructor at the great palace under al-Mustanṣir [*q.v.*] (al-Maḳrīzī, *Khiṭaṭ*, ii, 415).

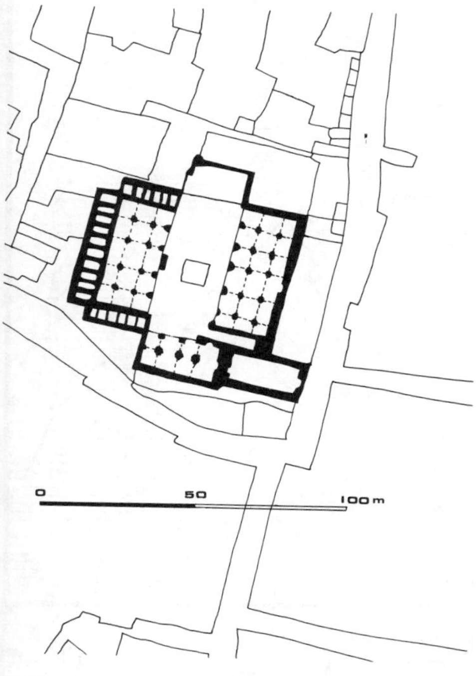

Khānḳāh Saᶜīd al-Suᶜadāᵓ: plan as it was in 1987 (CEAA, Versailles).

With the change of dynasties, the Fāṭimid palaces were destroyed, but this one was spared. At an early date, Ṣalāḥ al-Dīn installed there the Kurdish *amīrs* of his government and then, in the framework of his policy for the restoration of the Sunna (in which he founded not only *madrasas* but also *khānḳāhs*), he made it over to Ṣūfī *fuḳarāᵓ* who had come from a distance. He appointed over it a *shaykh* with a salary, whilst the Ṣūfīs themselves received a daily allowance of bread, meat and provisions from the revenues of the *waḳf* instituted in 569/1173-4. These properties comprised a garden in the district of Birkat al-Fīl and Ḳaysariyyat al-Sarrāb in Cairo, and part of Dahmur in al-Bahnasiyya. Saladin also built nearby a *ḥammām* for the Ṣūfīs (still functioning in the 19th century and called the "Ḥammām al-Djamāliyya", used by men and women, see ᶜAlī Pasha Mubārak, *Khiṭaṭ djadīda*, ii, 218).

This was the first *khānḳāh* in Egypt, and its head was appointed *shaykh al-shuyūkh*—this until this post reverted to the *shaykh* of the *khānḳāh* of Siryāḳūs in 724/1324—so that it was thus at the head of "official" Ṣūfism. From this time onwards, this place acquired the name of Duwayrat al-Ṣūfiyya, little house of the Ṣūfīs. It also sheltered Muslim travellers requiring shelter, religious hospitality being one of the basic duties in the Muslim world at this period. Since it was a *khānḳāh*, the *khuṭba* was not given there, and on Fridays the Ṣūfīs went to pray in the mosque of al-Ḥākim; later, when the mosque of al-Aḳmar had been restored, they went there for their worship. The Ṣūfīs of this *khānḳāh* were so famed that the people, in order to acquire their *baraka*, came each Friday from al-Fusṭāṭ and al-Ḳāhira to join with them in their procession to the mosque of al-Ḥākim. Al-Maḳrīzī (*Khiṭaṭ*, ii, 416) says that 300 Ṣūfīs were accommodated there. In addition to their daily bread and meat, they received confectionery, soap and a wardrobe (eight sets of clothing a year); in 708/1309 their emoluments were increased (idem, *Sulūk*, ii, 50). This prosperity lasted until the crises of 806/1403-4, when the kitchens had to be closed (idem, *Khiṭaṭ*, ii, 416). From the second half of the 9th/15th century onwards, the *khānḳāhs*, closely linked to the secular power, lost some of their prestige, and, with the decline of their *waḳfs*, some of their revenues. Saᶜīd al-Suᶜadāᵓ did not escape this process.

From the architectural viewpoint, this monument, rebuilt in the Mamlūk period (Fernandez, 22), displays a plan with a central court surrounded by four *īwāns*, the eastern one being the prayer room, and there are cells for the residents. A minaret was built at a late date, in the 780s/1380s, by the *shaykh* Shihāb al-Dīn Aḥmad al-Anṣārī (al-Maḳrīzī, *Khiṭaṭ*, ii, 416). This monument was classified by the Committee for the Preservation of Islamic Monuments in 1931.

Bibliography: There is a notice entitled *al-khānḳāh al-Ṣāliḥiyya dār Saᶜīd al-Suᶜadāᵓ duwayrat al-ṣūfiyya*, in Maḳrīzī, *Khiṭaṭ*, ii, 415-6, and another, *Djāmiᶜ al-khānḳāh* in ᶜAlī Pasha Mubārak, *al-Khiṭaṭ al-Tawfīḳiyya*, Cairo 1981, ii, 218. For the institution and its role in society, see L. Fernandez, *The evolution of a Sufi institution in Mamluk Egypt: the* khanqah, Berlin 1988. On Ṣūfism in mediaeval Egypt: E. Geoffroy, *Le soufisme en Egypte et en Syrie (fin époque mamlouke-début époque ottomane)*, IFEAD, Damascus, forthcoming; J. Berkey, *The transmission of knowledge in mediaeval Cairo, a social history of Islamic education*, Princeton 1992; J.S. Trimingham, *The Sufi orders in Islam*, Oxford 1971. For the topography of Cairo at this time, see N.D. MacKenzie, *Ayyubid Cairo, a topographical study*, Cairo 1992, and for the architecture of this *khānḳāh*, *Bull. du Comité de Conservation des Monuments Islamiques*, xxvii (1911), 192, and xxxvi (1936), 33.

(SYLVIE DENOIX)

AL-ṢAᶜĪD or ṢAᶜĪD MIṢR, the term which in Arabic denotes Upper Egypt, this being, in the strict sense of the term, the serviceable section of the Valley of the Nile (from 5 to 10 km in breadth by some 900 km in

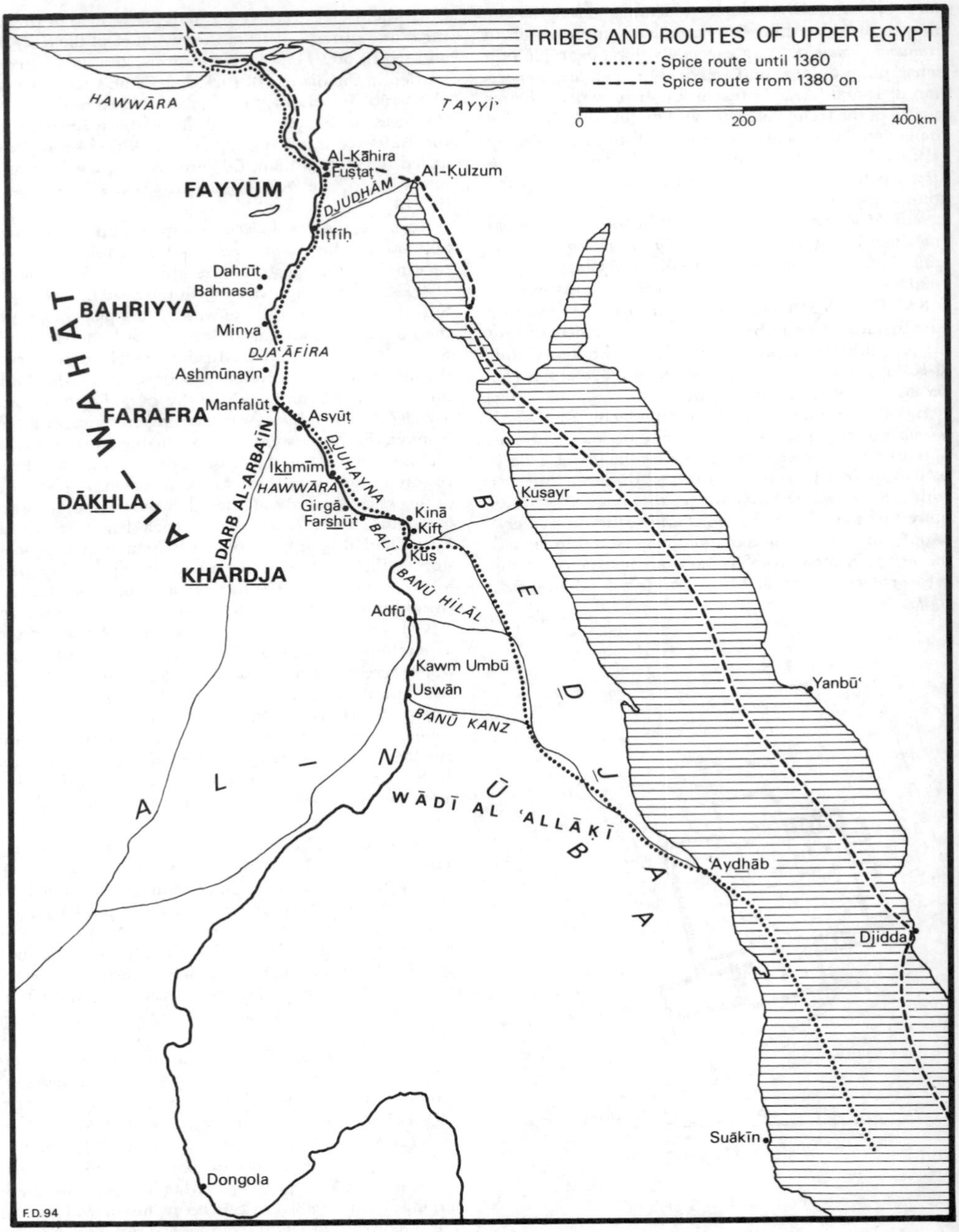

length), situated between Cairo and Aswān [*q.v.*]; to this should be added the Fayyūm [*q.v.*], considered one of the provinces of Upper Egypt, and the nearby oases in the western desert (al-Wāḥāt: Baḥriyya, Farāfra, Dākhla, Khārdja [*q.vv.*]), over which the authorities of the Valley have been obliged to exercise supervision; finally, to the east, the security of the tracks crossing the mountainous region between the Nile and the Red Sea has also been the responsibility of these authorities. The history of the Ṣaʿīd cannot be understood without consideration of these routes and of the populations which made use of them at different times; measures taken to control them were often the basis of the importance successively attained by different towns in the Valley.

1. History.

According to Ibn ʿAbd al-Ḥakam (*Futūḥ Miṣr*, 169) the Arab troops arriving from the north, in the year 20/641 or shortly thereafter, at first ignored the existence of the Fayyūm and proceeded along the Valley under the leadership of ʿAbd Allāh b. Saʿd, to whom control of Upper Egypt had been entrusted from the outset, until they encountered the forces of the kingdom of Nubia [see NŪBA]. An official treaty or *baḳ*[*q.v.*], a revival of the Graeco-Roman *pactum*, was established with the Nubians from 31/652 onwards. But in the interests of maintaining a recognised border, it was logical that the principal garrison of Upper Egypt should be established at Aswān, while in the Valley there were located only a few Arab military installations ranged along the Nile, quite isolated among the Coptic populations, which sometimes comprised large conurbations such as As͟hmūnayn and Ak͟hmīm (al-Balād͟hurī, *Futūḥ al-buldān*, 217). From the outset, Upper Egypt seems to have had its own governor, distinct from the governor of Fusṭāṭ (al-Kindī, *Wulāt*, 11; Ibn ʿAbd al-Ḥakam, *Futūḥ Miṣr*, 173), but this may have applied only in the context of the maintenance of order; the governor of Fusṭāṭ spent six months in Upper Egypt in 112/730 with the object of establishing there the basis of a taxation system. Anti-fiscal revolts seem to have erupted from the end of the 1st/7th century onward, before the great revolt of 121/739, which was suppressed with severity (al-Kindī, *Wulāt*, 81). Subsequently, Upper Egypt does not seem to have been involved in the other revolts occurring in the Delta.

Onomastic analysis of the funeral inscriptions of the cemetery of Aswān, which are known to this day, shows that conversions must have begun at a fairly early stage around the southern garrison. Furthermore, an Arab immigration, apparently with a Ḳaysī majority, took place directly from the Ḥid͟jāz, across the Red Sea. Overall, the Arab population of Upper Egypt increased considerably in the course of the 3rd/9th century. On the one hand, possibly following measures taken under al-Muʿtaṣim in 218/831 to remove Arabs from the army, two substantial Yemenī groups moved from the region of Fusṭāṭ towards Upper Egypt, the D͟juhayna towards the region of As͟hmūnayn and the Balī towards Ak͟hmīm, and there were others who moved further to the south between the Nile and the Red Sea. On the other hand, during the caliphate of al-Mutawakkil (232-47/847-61), an important Ḳaysī group of Rabīʿa (of the Banū Ḥanīfa of Yamāma) crossed the Red Sea and established itself in the Wādī ʿAllāḳī [*q.v.*] in the mountains to the south of Aswān, to extract gold there, setting negro slaves to work in the mines. It was probably this influx of Arab groups which provoked the reaction of the Bed͟ja [*q.v.*], populations of Hamitic language, partially converted to Christianity, living between the Nile and the Red Sea, who used to frequent the Valley for purposes of trade. Efforts were made to establish a *modus vivendi* with them, in order to facilitate trade and prevent incidents at the times of their visits to the Valley. In the 3rd/9th century they carried out raids on Aswān, Ḳūṣ [*q.v.*] and Ḳifṭ [*q.v.*], where defensive measures had to be taken. An initial military action aimed at pacification, led by a caliphal governor with authority over the lands of the Red Sea from the Gulf of Suez to Aswān (*ca.* 232/847), was compromised by the arrival of Arab gold prospectors in territory belonging to the Bed͟ja. Fresh military operations were necessary, as well as reinforcement of the Arab groups. The situation did not begin to stabilise until *ca.* 255/870, when a certain ʿAbd al-Raḥmān al-ʿUmarī, who claimed to be an ʿAlid, detached for himself an autonomous enclave in the region of the mines and beyond, relying on the support of groups of Rabīʿa and D͟juhayna in his conflict with the Bed͟ja and the Nubians. Subsequently, the Rabīʿa joined forces with the Bed͟ja to drive out the D͟juhayna, who probably emigrated towards Sawākin [*q.v.*]. The Bed͟ja thus entered into Arab tribal alliances, were gradually converted to Islam and became useful auxiliaries against the Nubians. This activity in the region of the mines, with its port on the Red Sea, ʿAyd͟hāb [*q.v.*], beginning at this time to engage in commerce beyond the simple provisioning of the mines, made of Aswān, which was trading on equal terms with Nubia, a vigorous city, the only Muslim city of Upper Egypt (even if all its inhabitants were not Muslims). The proximity of the Ḥid͟jāz accounts for the cultural activity of the place, especially in the realms of *ḥadīt͟h* and of *fiḳh*. The city attained the zenith of its prosperity in the 3rd/9th and 4th/10th centuries.

During these two centuries, certain characteristics of Muslim Upper Egypt became evident. With the numbers of Muslims in Egypt increasing, and the importance of Fusṭāṭ to the north recognised, Upper Egypt, poorly controlled by distant Aswān (which still had its own governor), was a natural refuge for any revolt against the power of the north, which was not always successful in its pursuit of a rebel towards the south: such was the case for example with the troops of Ahmad b. Ṭūlūn [*q.v.*], beaten to the north of Ḳūṣ in 256/870 before defeating, near Ak͟hmīm, Ibn al-Ṣūfī, an ʿAlid who ultimately escaped by way of ʿAyd͟hāb (al-Kindī, *Wulāt*, 213). Furthermore, since the Mag͟hrib had also become a country with a large Muslim population, and was above all an operational base for Fāṭimid ambitions, pressure was exerted on Upper Egypt by way of the western routes, controlled by Berber populations which also dominated the oases. In 307-9/919-21, Fāṭimid troops succeeded in reaching Upper Egypt, and in 323/935, a pro-Mag͟hribi armed group briefly controlled the Fayyūm before being obliged to withdraw westward via Alexandria and Cyrenaica. The Valley of the Nile, in spite of the multiplicity of communications between north and south, had still not yet acquired a solid unitary organisation in the context of a strong Muslim state. Shortly after the installation of the Fāṭimids in Cairo, in 361/973 a *s͟hayk͟h* of the Banū Kilāb (Ḳaysīs), rebelled in Middle Egypt in the name of the ʿAbbāsids, and from 362/973 to 364/975, the region between Ak͟hmīm and Asyūṭ [*q.v.*] was held by elements favourable to the Carmathians [see ḲARMAṬĪ]. Gradually, the Fāṭimid power was able to unify the Valley firmly and to impose between Arab groups a functional equilibrium, which was the foundation for the flowering of mediaeval Upper Egypt. Thus the caliph al-ʿAzīz (365-86/976-96 [*q.v.*]), installed in the southern part of Upper Egypt the Banū Hilāl [*q.v.*] and the Banū Sulaym (Ḳaysīs), some of whose members seem already to have moved into the region of the mines (it is known that the Banū Sulaym worked mines in Arabia), if not into the oases of the west. They should be distinguished from their fellow-tribesmen of the Delta, previously installed, whom the caliphs were to expel to the Mag͟hrib in the 5th/11th century on account of their frequent revolts. In Upper Egypt the Banū Hilāl were loyal supporters of the ruling power, and to the south, the Cairo government also relied on the Rabīʿa (Ḳaysīs) to protect the Nubian frontier: it was at the beginning of the 5th/11th century that the title *Kanz al-Dawla* appeared for the first time, bestowed by the caliph on the *s͟hayk͟h* of the Rabīʿa. Subsequently, the name Banū Kanz came to be applied to this composite tribal group (Rabīʿa and Bed͟ja), the ancestors of the present-day Kenouz. Thus the Cairo government preferred to rely in the south on the dominant Ḳaysī groups (Banū Hilāl, Rabīʿa), while in the north the Yemenī groups (Balī, D͟juhayna) were considered less dependable. First installed in the region of As͟hmūnayn, the D͟juhayna had been forced to move towards Asyūṭ, since the Fāṭimids had installed in their place members of the D͟jaʿāfira (from

Ḳuraysh), to contain them towards the north. Ḳaysī groups thus played an official role, also controlling the most important routes linking the Valley of the Nile with ᶜAydhāb, which was initially the point of access to the Ḥidjāz, which the Fāṭimids hoped to dominate, later a centre for the importation of spices which were transported towards Cairo and Alexandria.

In the 5th/11th century, the unification of the Valley of the Nile from Fusṭāṭ to Aswān, promoted by Fāṭimid policy, ultimately found expression in major changes, essentially resulting from the crisis which destabilised the caliphate in the 460s/1070s. Between 459/1067 and 466/1074, it is known that negro troops, in conflict with other elements of the army, expelled from the Delta and from Cairo, arrived and established themselves in the region of Aswān, and that all the Bedouin groups of Upper Egypt, from the Djaᶜāfira in the north to the Banū Kanz in the south (evidently including the Yemenī groups), withdrew from obedience to the government. When normality was restored in 469/1077 by Badr al-Djamalī [*q.v.*], it was announced that the authorities had decided (perhaps because the Banū Hilāl had remained loyal), to establish a new centre for the maintenance of order in Upper Egypt at Ḳūṣ, at the limit of their zone of settlement, in a locality hitherto essentially Coptic. In 467/1075, the expressions Upper Ṣaᶜīd and Lower Ṣaᶜīd are encountered for the first time (*Sidjillāt mustanṣiriyya*, 185): Ḳūṣ became the capital of Upper Ṣaᶜīd. Its importance grew gradually: following its selection by the authorities, the track from Ḳūṣ to ᶜAydhāb became the principal caravan route towards the Red Sea; in 516/1122 a mint was established there, which no doubt continued to function until the arrival of the Ayyūbids. From the 530s/1130s onward, the governors of Upper Ṣaᶜīd acquired, on account of their resources and the troops at their disposal, such status in the Fāṭimid realm that they intervened directly in the crises which marked the end of the caliphate. The result was evidently the laying of the foundations of a Muslim city at Ḳūṣ. The authority of the governor often extended to the north as far as Akhmīm. In Lower Ṣaᶜīd, the importance of Asyūṭ also grew, while in the north again, Minya, the object of concern on the part of the authorities (as evidenced by the foundation of its mosque by Ṭalāʾiᶜ, before 549/1154) gradually gained ascendancy over Ashmūnayn. In the far south, Aswān, although deprived of a major part of its administrative and economic role, nevertheless remained in the 5th/11th century the single major Muslim conurbation of Upper Egypt (the majority of the mausolea which have survived into the present date from this period), and the only true centre of culture and of the diffusion of Shīᶜism.

The transition from the Fāṭimids to the Ayyūbids was a difficult period for Upper Egypt, precisely because Shīᶜism had spread there and because the new arrivals, the Ghuzz as they were called in Egypt, immediately set about imposing the system of *iḳṭāᶜs* [*q.v.*], which was not to the liking of the Arab groups. In 570/1175 the whole of Upper Ṣaᶜīd rose in revolt with the object of restoring the Fāṭimids; the failure of the revolt did not discourage the Shīᶜīs of Ḳifṭ, who in 572/1177 were subjected to harsh repression; arrests continued to take place for a long time, and Shīᶜī groups survived in the south of Upper Egypt, towards Edfou, until the Mamlūk period. The reconquest of Upper Egypt by Sunnism was, however, encouraged by the fact that, since the end of the 5th/11th century and the installation of the Crusaders in Palestine, all the Pilgrims from the Muslim West, which had remained Sunnī, were obliged to utilise the routes of Upper Egypt towards ᶜAydhāb and the Ḥidjāz, which led sometimes to the implantation of Maghribī communities in the cities of the Valley, even to the creation of small localities with a Maghribī majority (such as Damāmīn, to the north of Ḳūṣ) and to the installation of fervent Sunnīs, zealots of the Sunnī counter-reformation, at Minya, at Asyūṭ and at Ḳenā [*q.v.*] in particular (ᶜAbd al-Raḥīm al-Ḳināʾī, d. 592/1195) and in its surrounding region, which became the most important departure-point for Pilgrims leaving the Valley for the Ḥidjāz. Even after Saladin had succeeded in overthrowing the kingdom of Jerusalem, Maghribī pilgrims continued to pass in large numbers through Upper Egypt, in the footsteps of their elders. It was in part as a result of their activities, and the use of their *ribāṭs*, that Sunnism was enabled to recapture the territory: Aswān had its *madrasa* before the end of the 7th/13th century and the first *madrasa* of Ḳūṣ was founded in 607/1210. For Upper Egypt, the first half of the 7th/13th century was a period of peace and prosperity, of agricultural progress (sugar-cane) and commercial activity instigated by the Kārimī [*q.v.*] merchants, and of urban growth.

The fall of the Ayyūbids was marked in Upper Egypt by a major Bedouin revolt, possibly beginning after the arrival of Louis IX at Damietta in 647/1250 (which had drawn the majority of the troops towards the north). It was led by the *Sharīf* Ḥiṣn al-Dīn Thaᶜlab, of the Djaᶜāfira, to the north of Asyūṭ, against the military régime which, even before the accession to power of the Mamlūks, had been felt to be increasingly oppressive. The revolt was finally crushed in 653/1255, but it was only the first manifestation of refusal on the part of the Arab groups to accept the military régime. In the Valley, order was firmly restored. The system of *iḳṭāᶜs* once more functioned regularly (stockbreeding no doubt contributed substantially to the burgeoning revenues), and following the reforms of 727/1327 there was a privatised system for administration of *iḳṭāᶜs*, which gave to the clerks, most of them Copts, a role which could only contribute to the prosperity of their community. But on the other hand, the movement towards the creation of Muslim élites in the *madrasas* of Upper Ṣaᶜīd (it is known that 16 *madrasas* existed at Ḳūṣ, and there were others in other localities), renewing the activity previously exercised by Aswān, let to a more thorough Islamisation of this region, while Middle Egypt remained sparsely Islamised. The Arabs were kept under strict supervision, and the authorities continued to rely on the same tribal groups. When in 671/1272 sultan Baybars [*q.v.*] inflicted the first blows against the Nubian kingdom, the Banū Kanz offered their assistance; it is known that this led to the installation at Dongola of a Muslim prince in 716/1316, and to the control, at least temporary, of the Banū Kanz over Nubia; but this was also the end of a sedentary power whose presence hitherto had played an important role in denying access to the Bedouin tribes, to the east of the Nile, but also to the west. Meanwhile, in Upper Egypt, Balī and Djuhayna (Yemenīs) remained hostile, taking advantage of all the opportunities offered by political troubles in Cairo, or by Mongol aggression, to rebel in the region of Asyūṭ and of Manfalūṭ, or to cause disruption on the routes between the Nile and the Red Sea. The definitive accession to power of al-Malik al-Nāṣir Muḥammad [*q.v.*], which owed much to the Bedouin of Syria, seemed to mark an improvement in relations between the Mamlūk power and the Arab groups; it was manifested especially by a relaxation of the strict supervision hitherto exercised over the tribes. Groups of Ṭayyiʾ and of Djudhām [*q.vv.*, Yemenīs] thus came from Syria to join the Yemenī groups of Middle Egypt, and by way of the *darb al-arbaʿīn*, their advance towards Central Africa, which was quite unhindered, began from Manfalūṭ. From 721/1321-2 onward, Manfalūṭ (already a royal *iḳṭāʿ*), became a famed slave market (al-Udfūwī, *Ṭāliʿ*, 427). The result of these developments appeared after the death of the great sultan: the Yemenī groups (under the leadership of the ʿArak, from the Djudhām rather than the Djuhayna), more numerous and enriched by their new activities, became uncontrollable, provoking ever more violent incidents (745-55/1345-55), to the point where the ruling power was forced to make concessions, agreeing to rely henceforward on the support of these Arab groups which had hitherto been hostile, entrusting to them responsibility for the maintenance of order and some *iḳṭāʿ*s.

The consequences of this evolution were significant in an Upper Egypt where epidemics, from the mid-8th/14th century onward, rendered more precarious the sedentary structures confronting the nomads. The Yemenī groups, which had outflanked the Banū Kanz by way of the south, forced them to withdraw towards Aswān, and from 767/1365-6 onward the latter, turning hostile, made the route to ʿAydhāb impassable (al-Maḳrīzī, *Khiṭaṭ*, ed. Wiet, iii, 300; from this date, the port ceased to be a centre for major commerce, and there are no grounds for suspecting deliberate destruction on the part of a Mamlūk sultan). The transport of spices was for some time conducted by way of Ḳuṣayr [*q.v.*], and then, as the extortions practised by the Mamlūk authorities in Upper Egypt proved a greater threat to the merchants than the aggression of the Bedouin, the merchants preferred to tackle the difficulties of navigating in the Red Sea, unloading the precious merchandise at Ṭōr, at the foot of the Sinai peninsula, where a port and a market were being developed (Ibn Duḳmāḳ, *Kitāb al-Intiṣār*, 54); from here, spices were transported directly to Cairo and no longer passed through Upper Egypt. The cessation of this traffic had the effect that Upper Egypt, increasingly difficult to control, lost much of its interest for the Mamlūk authorities and its development stagnated, although efforts were made for some time to protect Aswān, encircled at it was by the Banū Kanz. In the north, it was also necessary to forestall trouble. In 780/1378, a post of *nāʾib al-salṭana* (a sort of Prefect of Upper Egypt) was created and inaugurated at Asyūṭ. The centre of gravity of Muslim Upper Egypt was thus relocated: the regions of Asyūṭ and Akhmīm, still used for access to the Ḥidjāz by way of Ḳuṣayr, seemed at this stage more buoyant than the south. But the sultanate was no longer able to maintain in the country sufficient forces to impose its authority. In 782/1380, the grand *amīr* Barḳūḳ [*q.v.*], soon to be sultan, took the decision to install in the region a group of Hawwāra [*q.v.*] Berbers, hitherto in Behera, where pressure from the Bedouin was proving too strong (al-Maḳrīzī, *Bayān*, 60). They became the new supporters of the authorities against the Arab groups, more efficacious than the *nāʾib* of Asyūṭ (a function which seems not to have lasted long); the time of Asyūṭ was yet to come. The control of the Bedouin was now the principal problem in Upper Egypt. It was handled to an increasing extent by the annual dispatch of *amīrs* from Cairo, in missions known as *kashf*, which had hitherto consisted in guaranteeing security during harvests (Upper Egypt paid taxes in kind), and in inspecting the condition of the canals. From 784/1382 onward, an *amīr* of the *kashf*, whose powers extended to Bahnasā and Aṭfīḥ [*q.vv.*], was installed in the Fayyūm, no doubt to prevent too many Bedouin groups from following the Hawwāra towards the south. The latter were installed at Girgā [*q.v.*]. They supported Barḳūḳ loyally in his efforts to maintain himself in power in Cairo (in 791/1389) as well as against the Banū Kanz of the south, now in full revolt. In fact, other Bedouin had already succeeded in bypassing the barrier of the Fayyūm: other Hawwāra, hostile, who had installed themselves near Dahrūt, to the north of the ʿArak, as well as Fazāra (Dhubyān, Ḳaysīs) who had settled near Minya and were perhaps the originators of the links which were established from the 9th/15th century between this town and central Africa. New arrivals also came from the east, including the Aḥmadī, who, according to Ibn Ḥadjar, were Balī from the region of Yanbūʿ, coming from Arabia to rejoin their displaced fellow-tribesmen to the north of Ḳūṣ.

Upper Egypt at the end of the 8th/14th century was thus traversed by Bedouin groups, the most submissive of which could only be obedient to a stable power. At the time of the second Mongol invasion, political disorders and then a plague provoked a crisis at the beginning of the 9th/15th century in which the Mamlūk state narrowly avoided total dissolution. There can be no doubt that the insurrection was general; in 804/1401, the *nāʾib al-salṭana* of Asyūṭ and the governor of Manfalūṭ were both killed by Bedouin. Subsequently, nothing is known of events in Upper Egypt until 816/1413, at which date the sultan's *ustādār* brought from Upper Egypt to Cairo horses, camels, cattle, sheep, cereals, weapons, slaves, gold and jewellery seized forcibly as compensation for taxes which had not been paid during the crisis. It was not until the sultanate of Barsbāy [*q.v.*] that the administration of Upper Egypt regained a more regular aspect, less suggestive of official pillage of the land. At Girgā, the Hawwāra had become respectable landowners; the *amīr* Muḥammad b. ʿUmar b. ʿAbd al-ʿAzīz had founded the old mosque of the town; his successors, some of whom absorbed good Islamic culture and were regarded as saintly men, were now accepted by the Muslim élite of the region; agricultural land was exploited and the production of sugar cane kept the presses supplied. The sultan, whose authority no longer extended as far as Aswān (the land of the Banū Kanz began at Kom Ombo) was obliged to reckon with the *amīrs* of Girgā to the south, while to the north, two *kāshifs* (the term is still in use) were installed at Asyūṭ (where there was no longer a *nāʾib*) and in Middle Egypt, overriding the authority of the governors. Beginning with the decade of the sixties of the 9th/15th century, the sultans attempted to restore their authority overall, including over the *amīrs* of Girgā, but difficulties encountered anew by the régime in the second phase of the sultanate of Ḳāyitbāy [*q.v.*], foiled these aspirations. After the death of this sultan there was even a resumption of large-scale fiscal expeditions to Upper Egypt, these being the only means of collecting taxes, conducted this time by royal *dawādārs*. The Bedouin had clearly decided to exploit the opportunities provided by the confrontation with the Ottomans. After the defeat of the Egyptian army (922/1517), Ṭūmānbāy, the last sultan, attempted to go and regroup his forces in Upper Egypt, but was unable to move beyond Girgā. The *amīr* of the Hawwāra responded to his appeal for help with a declaration of loyalty to the Ottoman sultan Selīm. The latter, once installed in Cairo, awarded him direct authority over the whole of Upper Egypt, while the powers of the governor of Cairo were limited to the city and to the Delta.

The Ottoman state officially recognised the authority of the Banū ᶜUmar b. ᶜAbd al-ᶜAzīz until the beginning of the 11th/17th century; from 980/1570 onward, advantage was taken of familial tensions among the Banū ᶜUmar to install at Girgā an Ottoman detachment under the orders of a *sandjaḳ*, who exercised authority in conjunction with the *amīr*. In 1019/1610 or later, the power of the Hawwāra *amīrs* came to an end, and the *sandjaḳs* were replaced by beys. Ottoman administration was thus ultimately established in Upper Egypt and the land was divided into *kāshifliks*. The beys succeeded for some time in controlling the Bedouin and endowed Girgā with new monuments. The wealth of Upper Egypt made them important personnages, who intervened in the political struggles of Cairo. But from the 1660s onward, the succession of beys at Girgā proceeded at a more rapid rate, and there was a resurgence of Bedouin power, especially at Akhmīm and Farshūṭ. Pursuing the old Bedouin policy of infiltration of the state, the Bedouin *amīrs* allied themselves with the main body of the army, as Janissaries and *ᶜazabs*, and obtained by this means fallow land which they restored to fertility; and commerce with the lands of Black Africa brought them additional resources. They intervened thereafter in the nomination of the beys at Girgā, and the 12th/18th century was once more for Upper Egypt a period of Bedouin hegemony; the beys and the *kāshifs* were less powerful than them and were regarded as strangers in the land. Out of the conflicts between the numerous candidates for power among the Bedouin, from the 1150s/1740s onwards, another major Hawwāra family emerged, the Banū Hummām of Farshūṭ, who succeeded in imposing their authority until the intervention of the Cairo authorities in 1183/1769. Under their domination, the south of Upper Egypt enjoyed a degree of prosperity; the commerce of Ḳuṣayr increased, leading to the resurgence of Ḳenā, and caravans of slaves arrived from the sultanate of Fundj [*q.v.*] under the protection of ᶜAbābda Arabs (the heirs of the Banū Hilāl, competing for control of the routes with the heirs of the Yemenī groups, Banū Wāṣil and Maᶜazza). But further to the west of the Nile, the route of the *darb al-arbaᶜīn* under the protection of the Banū ᶜAdī (belonging to the Yemenī group of the Lakhm), evaded the control of the Hawwāra *shaykhs* and gave Asyūṭ its opportunity. When at the end of the 12th/18th century the Hawwāra were decisively defeated, Girgā lost its pre-eminence and Asyūṭ finally replaced it; commerce with the Negro lands was to bring it to its zenith in the 19th century. In the context of the revival of the state, Upper Egypt was to lose some of its specific nature. After it had offered a means of strategic retreat to the opponents of Muḥammad ᶜAlī, the victory over the beys in Ṣafar 1226/February 1811, between Ḳūṣ and Ḳenā, gave the signal for the massacre of the Mamlūks in the Citadel of Cairo, and one of the ancient roles of Upper Egypt came to an end. In 1227/1812, a new survey of territories definitively shattered the power of the Bedouin.

The influx of these populations has conditioned the history of Upper Egypt. The census of 1898 indicates the strongest Bedouin concentrations in the zones of access to the Valley in the north (they represent more than 10% of the population in the province of Beni Suef, the former governorate of Aṭfīḥ, and more than 16% in the Fayyūm) and in the zones of egress to the south (in Nubia, where Aswān is still situated they also account for more than 10%), in contrast to the centre (Minya: 6.6%; Asyūt: 3.7%; Girgā: 1.5%; Ḳenā: 4.4%), where their role has, however, been considerable. When the epidemics of the second half of the 8th/14th century had enfeebled the Mamlūk authorities, who reacted to the crisis with brutality alone, and when in consequence major commerce was diverted from Upper Egypt, depriving it of an important factor of development, the Bedouin influx had the effect that neither Asyūṭ nor Girgā was able to carry on establishing the productive works of the Muslim élites, begun by Aswān (9th-10th centuries) and Ḳūṣ (12th-14th). This explains the presence of the significant Christian minority in Middle Egypt, a part of the Valley the history of which has yet to be written.

Bibliography: Besides the references cited in the course of the article, see J. Maspero and G. Wiet, *Matériaux pour servir à la géographie de l'Égypte*, Cairo 1919; J.-C. Garcin, *Un centre musulman de la Haute Egypt médiévale: Qūṣ*, IFAO, Cairo 1976; T. Walz, *Trade between Egypt and Bilād as-Sūdān, 1700-1820*, IFAO, Cairo 1976. (J.-C. GARCIN)

2. Dialects.

In a broader sense, the Arabic dialects of the Ṣaᶜīd are those of the peasants and the Bedouins who dwell in the Nile valley, the oases of the Western Desert and the Eastern Desert. In a narrower sense, the dialects of the Ṣaᶜīd are those of the peasants, as they are spoken in the Nile Valley from al-Djīza in the north to Aswān in the south where the domain of the Nubian language begins. There are super-regional varieties used in popular songs, ballads etc., and poetry by ᶜAbd ar-Raḥmān al-Abnūdī is available in printed form.

These peasant dialects are relatively well known through the data collected for the Egyptian dialect atlas and other, more detailed studies (see *Bibl.*).

Some principal isoglosses which distinguish these Ṣaᶜīdī dialects from those of peasants in the north (in brackets) are:

(1) preservation of long vowels before consonant clusters: *māska* (*maska*)
(2) the closed antepenultima receives stress: *mádrasa* (*madrása*)
(3) no stress on the *-it/-at* of the 3.f.s. perfect: *ḍárabitu, ḍarábitu, ḍúrubta* etc. (*ḍarabítu*)
(4) l.s. perfect *gīt* "I came" (*gēt*)
(5) plural forms as *bibān* "doors", *fisān* "axes" (*ibwāb, fūs*), and *dukūṛa* "males", *sibūᶜa* "lions" (*dukúṛa, sibúᶜa*)
(6) numerous lexical items: *ṭūrya* "hoe" (*fās*), *fās* "axe" (*balṭa*), *zaᶜaf* "palm leaves" (*xūṣ*), *faṛṛūga* ~ *faṛrūga* "chicken" (*farxa*), *baḥḥa* ~ *biḥḥa* ~ *buḥḥa* "duck" (*baṭṭa*), *ḥawš* ~ *ḥōš* "stable, cow shed" (*zirība* ~ *zirbiyya*)

Two major groups of dialects can be distinguished within the Ṣaᶜīd: Middle Egyptian (ME) from the outskirts of al-Djīza to Abū Tīdj (some 25 km south of Asyūṭ) and Upper Egyptian (UE) proper from Abū Tīdj to Aswān. Whereas ME has basically the same rules of elison and insertion of /i/ as the Delta dialects, excluding those of the Sharḳiyya province, UE is strongly influenced by Bedouins, apparently of western origin, who settled there in the past and intermingled with the local population. Therefore, in ME there is no elision of /i/ after -CC *yíktibu* "they write" and insertion takes place after -CC *ibnə kalb* "son of a dog", in contrast to UE *yíktbu* ~ *yíkətbu* and *ibən kalb*, except UE 2 (see below) which resembles Southern ME (SME) not only in this respect. Further, all UE dialects show glottalised /ṭ/ [ṭ̕] like the Awlād ᶜAlī at the Mediterranean littoral, a verbal noun of the IInd stem of the type *xaṭṭīṭ* ~ *ziṭṭīṭ* "furrowing" (*taxṭīṭ*) and the plural types *fᶜilla, fiᶜᶜēl, fuᶜᶜūl* as in *ḥṣinna* "horses", *biṭṭēš* ~ *buṭṭūš* "buffalo calves". The dialectological distinction between ME and UE is consistent with differences in the material culture of the peasants, see Winkler, 1936, 455. ME and to some extent UE 2 seem to represent an older type of Ṣaʿīdi Arabic less influenced by Bedouins.

Other isoglosses permit further subdivision of the two groups: Northern ME with two subgroups: NME 1 (south of al-Dj̲īza, northern Banī Swayf province and al-Fayyūm), NME 2 (southern Banī Swayf from al-Fas̲h̲n to al-Minyā), SME (to Abū Tīdj̲), UE 1 (approximatively to Nadj̲ʿ Ḥammādi, on the east bank from Ḳūṣ farther south to the altitude of Armant, on the west bank from al-Ballāṣ to al-Ḳurna), UE 2 (the Ḳenà bow on the east bank approximatively from Nadj̲ʿ Ḥammādi to Ḳūṣ and on the west bank to al-Ballāṣ), UE 3 (on the west bank from al-Ḳurna (al-Baʿīrāt) to Esna), UE 4 (on the west bank from Esna to G̲h̲arb Aswān, on the east bank from the latitude of Armant to Aswān). Linguistic borders in UE tend to be somewhat blurred and the dialects may differ from village to village. The distinctive features of these dialect groups include:

(7) preservation of /i/ after -vC: *misikit* "she took" in NME, a feature which sets NME apart from SME and links it to the western and northern parts of the Delta and the oases

(8) insertion of /a/ in a cluster -Cr-: *bukaṛa* "tomorrow" in NME 1 which separates NME 1 from NME 2 with the borderline near al-Fas̲h̲n; /g,ğ for /*ḳ/ and /*ğ/ instead of /ʾ,g/ beginning from NME 2 to the south

(9) /g,ğ/ for /*ḳ/ and /*ğ/ instead of /ʾ,g/ beginning from NME 2 to the south

(10) preservation of diphthongs /aw/ and /ay/ in NME 1: *hawn* "mortar", *bayt* "house" (*hōn, bēt* elsewhere)

(11) allomorphy of the IInd and IIId stems: one allomorph for perfect and imperfect in NME: *kallam - yikallam* (NME 1), *killim - yikillim, ʿallim - yiʿallim* (NME 2), in contrast to two allomorphs with morphological distribution in SME and UE: *kallam - yikallim*

(12) preservation of /a/ in *katīr* "much" and *yitmasik* "he was seized" in SME and UE 2 (*kitīr, yitmisik* elsewhere)

(13) paradigmatic levelling in the imperfect, either complete, such as *niktib - nikətbu* in UE 1 and UE 3, or incomplete, such as *aktib - niktibu* in UE 2. There is no such levelling in ME and UE 4.

(14) genitive exponent: *s̲h̲uġl* in UE 1, *hinīn* in UE 2, *ihnīn* in UE 3, 4, *allīl* ~ *allēl* in UE 4

(15) Ist stem perfect i-type: *kíbir* in ME and UE 2, UE 4, *kbír* in UE 1, *íkbir* in UE 3

(16) *ba*-prefix for present tense in UE 2 and UE 4

(17) *gáhawa*-syndrome in UE 1 and UE 3: *aḥamaṛ* "red"

(18) stress on the final syllable of words like *s̲h̲tā* "winter" in UE 1 and UE 3 (*šíta* elsewhere)

(19) vowel alternations a > i,u in UE 3: *masak* "he took" - *misikat* "she took", *bagaṛ* "cows" - *buguṛa* "a cow"

(20) /a/ in word-initial position instead of /i/ in UE 4: *anta* "you m.", *aḥna* "we", *alli* "which", *al-* "the", *atfaḍḍal* "please", *ambāriḥ* "yesterday", *amm* "mother" etc. a feature shared with Central Sudan.

Fem.pl. forms, a Bedouin feature, such as *yíkətban* "they write" occur in UE 3 and 4. For historical aspects, see Woidich, 1994; for Coptic remnants in the lexicon, see Behnstedt, 1981.

Very little is known about the speech of Bedouins found mostly at the fringes of the Nile valley, the Oases and in the Eastern Desert. The dialects of the four Western Oases are closely related to ME by syllable structure, but deviate in many other respects (see Behnstedt-Woidich, 1982). The ʿAbābida in the Eastern desert (Bīr Umm ilFawaxīr) seem to speak a Sudanese type of dialect, with *riğílha* "her leg" and with a stressed final vowel in *ḥablī* "my rope" and *ḥamṛā* f. "red".

Bibliography: P. Behnstedt, *Weitere koptische Lehnwörter im Ägyptisch-Arabischen*, in *Die Welt des Orients*, xii (1981), 82-98; Behnstedt and M. Woidich, *Die ägyptischen Oasen - ein dialektologischer Vorbericht*, in ZAL, viii (1982), 39-71; eidem, *Ägyptischer Dialektatlas*. Band 1-2, Wiesbaden 1985. Band 3. *Texte*. Teil 2. *Niltal und Oasen*, Wiesbaden 1988; Abdelghany A. Khalafallah, *A descriptive grammar of Ṣaʿīdi Egyptian Arabic*, The Hague 1969; W. Vycichl, *Zur Sprache und Volkskunde der ʿAbbādi*, in *Anzeiger der Österreichischen Akademie der Wissenschaften*, Phil.-Hist. Kl. (1953), 177-84; H.A. Winkler, *Ägyptische Volkskunde*, Stuttgart 1936; M. Woidich, *Ein arabischer Bauerndialekt aus dem südlichen Oberägypten*, in *ZDMG*, cxxiv (1974), 42-58; idem, *Upper Egyptian Arabic and dialect mixing in historical perspective*, in *Festschrift Georg Krotkoff*, 1994.

(M. Woidich)

ṢĀʿID AL-ANDALUSĪ, Abu 'l-Ḳāsim Ṣāʿid b. Aḥmad b. ʿAbd al-Raḥmān al-Tag̲h̲libī, called al-Ḳāḍī Ṣāʿid (420-62/1029-70), Spanish Muslim author.

He was born at Alméria, where his parents had taken refuge during the civil wars which devastated Cordova, their place of origin, and his grandfather had been *ḳāḍī* of Sidonia. His father died as judge of Toledo in 449/1057, and Ṣāʿid was to succeed him there in 460/1068 till his death there in 462/1070. The sweep of his life reflected these circumstances. Born of a line of legal officials, he received a solid legal education at Alméria and then Cordova, following, according to Ibn Bas̲h̲kuwāl, Ibn Ḥazm's teaching. But the formation of the Taifas, the relative decline of the caliphal capital compared with the new provincial ones, the search for knowledge and for patrons, all led him to Toledo. There, in the reign of al-Maʾmūn b. D̲h̲i 'l-Nūn (429-67/1038-75), the "philosophical" sciences—mathematics, astronomy, logic and medicine—were enjoying a renaissance, and he was henceforth to devote himself to these.

Three works are attributed to Ṣāʿid: a *K. fī Iṣlāḥ ḥarakāt al-nudj̲ūm*, on the correction of earlier astronomical tables; a *D̲j̲awāmiʿ ak̲h̲bār al-umam min al-ʿArab wa 'l-ʿAd̲j̲am*, a universal history; and finally, his *Ṭabaḳāt al-umam*, a classification of the sciences and of the nations. Only this last work survives.

Its translator, R. Blachère, was astonished at the authority attributed to it already by the eastern scientific encyclopaedists, like Ibn al-Ḳifṭī and Ibn Abī Uṣaybiʿa. Ostensibly, the 80 pp. of the *Ṭabaḳāt* hardly merit so much honour. Their main point revolves round distinguishing at the outset, amongst the peoples of the world, those who do not know "philosophy"—Turks, Chinese, Berbers, etc.—from those who have achieved merit in them—Indians, Persians, Chaldaeans, Egyptians, Greeks and *Rūm*, Arabs and Jews. In all, there are thus eight nations for whom Ṣāʿid briefly cites, when he knows of them, their scholars and chosen disciplines.

The catalogue is rudimentary, but has a certain guiding thread. Science goes from East to West, from India to Spain, which holds its last living embodiment. Above all, these eight peoples have handed down the sciences according to the strict historical continuity—or geographical contiguousness—required by the *isnād* in the religious sciences, i.e. the chain of guarantors for a fact which one wishes to carry back, generation by generation, to the Prophet or his Companions. The success of Ṣāʿid's little work may well have stemmed from this trait, as set out in its title, *Ṭabaḳāt al-umam* "The generations of the nations". The *ḳāḍī* of Toledo thereby inserts within the classification of the philosophical sciences a principle directly inherited from the religious science disciplines, much more familiar to the immense majority of his readers. He established the truths of mathematics or astronomy as one would do for *ḥadīth*, by an irreproachable *isnād* which attests their exact transmission and preserved integralness, right from their origins.

From this point onwards, a question arises. Should one see in Ṣāʿid, in accordance with M.-G. Balty-Guesdon, one of those philosophers of which al-Andalus offers examples in the 6th/12th century, one of those who aimed at tracing the crucial frontier between rational knowledge and revealed religious dogma? Or should one, on the contrary, see in him the conciliator of two classes of the sciences which he knew well, as a judge by day and an astronomer by night? The plan and the guiding thread of the *Ṭabaḳāt*, as also the discrete reference to prophetic sources for all knowledge—the Semitic origin ascribed to Greek philosophy, the privileged place of the Jews at the end of the chain of nations—incline one rather to the second view.

Bibliography: *Ṭabaḳāt al-umam*, ed. L. Cheikho, Beirut 1913, new ed. H. Bū ʿAlwān, Beirut 1985, Fr. tr. R. Blachère, *Catégories des nations*, Paris 1935. See also M.-G. Balty-Guesdon, *Médecins et hommes de science en Espagne musulmane*, diss. Univ. of Paris III 1992, 3 vols.; idem, *Al-Andalus et l'héritage grec d'après les Ṭabaḳāt al-umam*, in *Perspectives sur la science et la philosophe grecque*, Paris 1993; G. Martinez-Gros, *Classification des sciences et classification des nations, trois exemples andalous du Vᵉ/XIᵉ siècle*, in *Mélanges de la Casa de Velasquez*, xx (1984), 83-114; idem, *La première histoire andalouse des sciences*, in *Autrement, Tolède XIIᵉ-XIIIᵉ siècles* (Feb. 1991), 200-17.
(G. MARTINEZ-GROS)

ṢĀʿID AL-BAGHDĀDĪ, ABU 'L-ʿALĀʾ ṢĀʿID B. AL-ḤASAN al-Rabaʿī al-Lughawī, poet and grammarian in Muslim Spain (*ca.* 339-417/*ca.* 950-1026).

Born at Mawṣil or in its region, educated in poetry and the linguistic sciences at Baghdād, Ṣāʿid arrived *ca.* 380/990 in Spain, probably attracted by the news of the largesse lavished by its princes on scholars who came to them from the East. All the sources agree in describing him as a facile poet, with an untidy appearance, an incorrigible drunkard and a perpetual spendthrift. But he knew how to ask for money with the same lightness of touch that he employed in spending it. Al-Andalus was at the peak of its might under the rule of the *ḥādjib* al-Manṣūr [*q.v.*], who had relegated the Umayyad caliph to the background. It was to the presence of this all-powerful minister that Ṣāʿid was admitted, and recompensed on a princely scale for his talents. One day, when he was short of cash, he made a shirt out of all the purses which he had received and, according to the source, dressed himself in it or dressed his slave Kāfūr in it. He appeared thus before the *ḥādjib*, whilst praising him for having given enough to cover a man with a tunic but which unfortunately revealed the bottoms, open to view and empty, of his money bags. Al-Manṣūr laughed, and opened up his coffers.

The minister's favour had, however, a more profound effect. As the seat of a caliphate since 317/929, Cordova intended to surpass Baghdād, and held mastery of the Arabic language as one of the stakes in this contest. The Andalusians freely admitted the fluency of the Easterners, but they stressed the solecisms which these Arabs, over-confident in their own natural speech, inflicted on the language of the ancient poets. The grammarians al-Ḳālī [*q.v.*], who came from Baghdād, and al-Zubaydī had thrown lustre on the reigns of the caliphs ʿAbd al-Raḥmān III (d. 350/961) and al-Ḥakam II (d. 365/976). Al-Manṣūr's usurpation added a question to the debate. The minister had in his turn to overshadow, by his merits, the glory of his masters, as they themselves had claimed to throw the star of Baghdād into the shade. Ṣāʿid was openly welcomed as the al-Ḳālī of al-Manṣūr. His major work *Fuṣūṣ fi 'l-ādāb wa 'l-ashʿār wa 'l-akhbār*, written in 385/995, prided itself on thrusting the *Nawādir* of the old master into oblivion without borrowing the least example from that work.

In practice, Ṣāʿid's preferences were for lexicography (*lugha*) rather than for grammar, and for the poetry which constituted its treasury. Put to the test when he first came to court, Ṣāʿid became worried over the grammatical obscurities which were hurled at him, but triumphed in the explanation of a verse by Imruʾ al-Ḳays. He could not have done anything better to please the *ḥādjib*, who on every occasion cultivated the purest of the Arabic values upon which the Cordovan caliphate aimed to base itself. The only other work of Ṣāʿid's which is mentioned was precisely a "story" in the Bedouin taste which he wrote for his master.

Altogether, the opinion of posterity in al-Andalus remained a guarded one. The Easterner was reproached for his boastfulness, and in this there may perhaps have been a discreet condemnation of the regime which he served. According to al-Makkarī, the Arab Ṣāʿid came out worst in a linguistic dispute with a knowledgeable young slave boy. Above all, Ibn al-ʿArīf [*q.v.*], the tutor of al-Manṣūr's children, after having failed in convincing the latter of Ṣāʿid's plagiarism, ridiculed Ṣāʿid by inventing a factitious book and author whom Ṣāʿid soon claimed to have read. Al-Manṣūr was furious, and had the *Fuṣūṣ* thrown into the river, before pardoning him. The world of scholarship was less indulgent.

After al-Manṣūr's death (392/1002), Ṣāʿid was less often seen in the entourage of his son al-Muẓaffar [*q.v.*]. Ibn Ḥazm, then aged 12, saw him, however, still declaiming one of his poems. The civil warfare (399-422/1009-31) caused him to move to Dénia, and then to Sicily, where he died, in 417/1026 according to Ibn Ḥazm.

Bibliography: R. Blachère, *Un pionnier de la culture arabe orientale en Espagne au Xᵉ siècle: Ṣâʿid de Bagdad*, in *Hesperis*, x (1930), 15-36, where a list of the relevant texts can be found, in particular, Maḳḳarī, i, 382-4, ii, 52-8; Ibn Bashkuwāl, no. 536; Ḥumaydī, no. 509. See also E. García Gómez, *La entrada de Ibn Ḥazm en el mundo official*, in al-And., xviii (1953), 437-8.
(G. MARTINEZ-GROS)

SAÏDA [see SAʿĪDA].

SAʿĪDA (French form, SAÏDA), a town of Algeria, the chef-lieu of the department (*wilāya*) of the same name, situated 175 km/108 miles from Oran (Wahrān [*q.v.*]) and 95 km/59 miles from Mascara (al-Muʿaskar [*q.v.*]), at an altitude of 900 m/2,950 feet. It is on the wādī Saʿīda, in touch with the Causse of Oran (hills of Saïda) and the High Plains, limestone plateaux which form part of the Atlas of the Tells, to the east of the hills of Ouarsenis (Wansharīs). The town had about 30,000 inhabitants and the department about 200,000 in 1987. The region is suitable for raising cereal crops and for sheep rearing.

The recurrent strategic position which the site has retained through history, ever since it was occupied by a Roman settlement, was highlighted in modern times when it became one of the headquarters of the *amīr* ᶜAbd al-Ḳādir [*q.v.*], who built a fort there but dismantled it in 1841 on the approach of French troops under General Bugeaud. In 1844, General Lamoricière constructed from it another fort slightly to the north, which became the nucleus of the present town.

Bibliography: See those to ᶜABD AL-ḲĀDIR B. MUḤYĪ ʾL-DĪN and AL-MUᶜASKAR. (ED.)

SAᶜĪDĀ GĪLĀNĪ, Indo-Persian poet of the 11th/17th century.

Details are lacking regarding his early life. He went to India from his native Persia during Djahāngīr's reign (1014-37/1605-27), and lived on to serve under his successor Shāh Djahān (1037-68/1628-58). Apart from poetry, he was skilled in calligraphy, engraving and assaying of precious stones. Djahāngīr gave him the title of Bēbadal Khān, perhaps as an appreciation of his talent since *bēbadal* means "matchless". In addition, he was appointed officer-in-charge of the royal jewellery, a position which he continued to hold during Shāh Djahān's reign. Under the latter ruler, he also received the command of 800 infantry and 100 cavalry.

In 1037/1628, soon after becoming emperor, Shāh Djahān decided that a lavish throne, inlaid with gems, should be constructed for his personal use. The charge of this enterprise, which later materialised in the celebrated Peacock Throne (*Takht-i Ṭāwūs*), was entrusted to Saᶜīdā Gīlānī, who supervised the project. It took seven years for the completion of the throne, which was inaugurated on Nawrūz 1044/23 March 1635. To commemorate this event, Saᶜīdā Gīlānī composed a *ḳaṣīda* of which only remnants have survived. The *ḳaṣīda* is said to have contained 134 couplets, each line of which carried a chronogram. Some of the chronograms were related to Shāh Djahān's birth (1000/1592), some to his coronation (1037/1628) and the majority to his gracing the Peacock Throne for the first time.

There is no information as to when or where Saᶜīdā Gīlānī died. That he was still living in 1047/1637-8 is confirmed by one of his chronograms of that date commemorating the completion of a mosque built by Shāh Djahān in Adjmēr.

Very little can be said about Saᶜīdā Gīlānī as a poet, since his extant writings are limited to a handful of pieces scattered in the historical accounts of the period. He is reported to have composed a *mathnawī* of some 5,000 couplets dealing with Djahāngīr's reign. His poetry earned for him royal recognition. On 14 Shahrīwar 1027/26 August 1618 he was rewarded handsomely by Djahāngīr for a *ḳaṣīda* composed by him for the emperor, and in 1042/1633 he received a similar treatment from Shāh Djahān for composing a poem which described the courage of Prince (afterwards Emperor) Awrangzīb in an elephant combat. Saᶜīdā Gīlānī's special skill lay perhaps in the making of chronograms. Apart from those mentioned earlier, he composed them on such events as Djahāngīr's conquest of the fort Kāngra (1029/1620), his building a mosque there (1031/1621-2) and the death of his wife Mumtāz Maḥall (1040/1631 [*q.v.*]).

Bibliography: *Tūzuk-i-Djahāngīrī*, ii, tr. A. Rogers, 2nd ed., Delhi 1968; Muḥammad Ṣāliḥ Kanbū, *ᶜAmal-i Ṣāliḥ* (*Shāh Djahān-nāma*), ed. Ghulām Yazdānī and Waḥīd Ḳurayshī, Lahore 1967-72; ᶜAbd al-Ḥamīd Lāhawrī, *Bādshāh-nāma*, i, ed. Kabīr al-Dīn Aḥmad and ᶜAbd al-Raḥīm, Calcutta 1867; Ṣamṣām al-Dawla Shāh Nawāz Khān, *Maʾāthir al-umarā*, i, tr. H. Beveridge, Calcutta 1941; Lačhmī Narāyan Shafīḳ, *Shām-i gharībān*, ed. Muḥammad Akbar al-Dīn Ṣiddīḳī, Karachi 1977; Hādī Ḥasan, *Mughal poetry*, Ḥaydarābād (Deccan) 1952 (?); idem, *Researches in Persian literature*, Ḥaydarābād (Deccan) 1958; Ḥādjdj Ḥusayn Nakhdjawānī, *Saᶜīdā-yi Gīlānī wa Takht-i Ṭāwūs*, in *Nashriyya-yi Dānishkada-yi Adabiyyāt-i Tabrīz*, ix/4 [1336/1957-8]; Ḥusām al-Dīn Rāshidī, *Tadhkira-yi shuᶜarā-yi Kashmīr*, i, Karachi 1967; M.L. Rahman, *Persian literature in India during the time of Jahangir and Shah Jahan*, Baroda 1970; ᶜAbd al-Ḥusayn Nawāʾī, *Shāh ᶜAbbās*, iii, Tehran 1368/1989; Aḥmad Gulčīn-Maᶜānī, *Kārwān-i Hind*, i, Mashhad 1369/1990-1.

(MUNIBUR RAHMAN)

ṢĀʾIFA (A.), pl. *ṣawāʾif* (<*ṣayf* "summer"), summer raid or military expedition (see Lane, 1756; Dozy, *Supplément*, i, 857).

1. In the Arab-Byzantine warfare.

The term is used by the early Islamic historians to denote the raids of the Arabs into Byzantine Anatolia. These were normally mounted annually, over a period of some two centuries, beginning during the governorship in Syria of Muᶜāwiya b. Abī Sufyān [*q.v.*], i.e. from *ca.* 640 onwards. They tailed off in the 3rd/9th century as the ᶜAbbāsid caliphate became racked by internal discord and as the Macedonian emperors in general turned the tables and took the offensive against the Arabs.

These expeditions were launched during the summer months, in order to avoid the harsh wintry conditions of the Anatolian plateau, from bases in the *thughūr* or frontier zones of northern Syria and northern Mesopotamia. The ways of entry through the Taurus and Anti-Taurus mountains included the Cilician Gates [see CILICIA], approached from bases like al-Maṣṣīṣa and Ṭarsūs [*q.vv.*], and the famous pass (*darb*) of al-Ḥadath [*q.v.*] between Marᶜash and Malaṭiya [*q.vv.*]. Such historical sources as al-Yaᶜḳūbī, Khalīfa b. al-Khayyāṭ and al-Ṭabarī are normally careful to list for each year the *amīr* who led the summer raid. This command was of premier importance. Sometimes caliphs like Muᶜāwiya, Sulaymān b. ᶜAbd al-Malik, Hārūn al-Rashīd or al-Muᶜtaṣim personally led their armies, or else the command would be held by some member of the ruling family, such as the Umayyad prince Maslama b. ᶜAbd al-Malik [*q.v.*] or the ᶜAbbāsid ones Ṣāliḥ b. ᶜAlī b. ᶜAbd Allāh b. al-ᶜAbbās and his son ᶜAbd al-Malik.

Bibliography: For the history of the campaigns, see the standard studies on Byzantine-Arab relations of Bury, *A history of the Eastern Roman empire*; Ostrogorsky; Vasiliev; Honigmann; Canard, in *Camb. med. hist.*, iv, *The Byzantine empire*, pt. i, *Byzantium and its neighbours*; and now W.E. Kaegi, *Byzantium and the early Arab conquests*, Cambridge 1992. Also C.E. Bosworth, *The Byzantine defence system in Asia Minor and the first Arab incursions*, in *The fourth international conference on the history of Bilād al-Shām*, Eng. and Fr. papers, vol. i, ᶜAmmān 1987, 116-24, and idem, *Byzantium and the Syrian frontier in the early Abbasid period*, in *The fifth international conference on the history of Bilād al-Shām*, Eng. and Fr. section, ᶜAmmān 1412/1991, 54-62. See further ᶜAWĀṢIM; GHĀZĪ; and THUGHŪR.

(C.E. BOSWORTH)

2. In Muslim-Christian warfare in Spain.

Given that Muslim Spain (al-Andalus) was geographically a European entity with Marches (see below), beyond which there was at all times an independent Christian presence to be reckoned with, the appearance of the *ṣāʾifa* in Umayyad Spain is not surprising. Of the importance it came to assume in Iberian Peninsular history one clear indication is the passage of *al-ṣāʾifa* into Castilian as *aceifa* (whence, for instance, *salir en campaña de aceifa* "go on a summer campaign"). Although in Arabic chronicles such expressions as *g͟hazā/ag͟hzā bi 'l-ṣāʾifa* "lead/send (s.o.) to lead the *ṣāʾifa*" occur mainly in the context of expeditions against the Christian north of the Peninsula, they occur also in the context of campaigns within al-Andalus itself against centres of rebellion or Viking raiders [see AL-MAD͟JŪS]. Thus it was not with the identity and location of the enemy that *ṣāʾifa* was primarily and originally associated, but with the time of year at which an expedition was launched—which could be as early as 1 May or as late as the end of July, though the norm would seem to have been at a time midway between these two extremes. When necessary, expedient or limited in scope, campaigns were conducted outside the summer season and likewise took their name from the time of the launch. Hence one in winter was a *s͟hātiya*, one in spring a *rabīʿiyya* and one in autumn a *k͟harīfiyya* (on these last two in the time of the ʿĀmirid al-Manṣūr (below, para. 4), see al-ʿUd͟hrī, in *Bibl.* below, 79, 80).

By the end of the reign of Alfonso I, king of Asturias (739-57) and conqueror of much of north-west Spain and Portugal, perhaps as much as a quarter of the Peninsula formed no part of al-Andalus, and of that proportion a fair share was an uninhabited *limes* known as the Marches (*al-t͟hug͟hūr*). Of these there were originally three: the Upper (*al-aʿlā*), the Middle (*al-awsaṭ*), and the Lower (*al-adnā*). Each was controlled, not by a civil governor, but by a military commander (*ḳāʾid*) based at Saragossa, Toledo and Mérida, respectively. Such was the position during the Emirate of the 3rd/9th century, though with the gradual contraction of al-Andalus changes had already begun to take place that in the long run were to result in the reduction of the *t͟hug͟hūr* to two: the Upper, or Farther (*al-aḳṣā*), still based on Saragossa and covering Navarre and the North-East, and the Middle, or Hither (*al-adnā*), covering Castile and the Kingdom of Léon, not from the increasingly remote Toledo, but from Medinaceli (Madīnat Sālim [*q.v.*]), which on the orders of the caliph ʿAbd al-Raḥmān III al-Nāṣir [*q.v.*] in 335/946 had been made into a heavily fortified base from which to launch *ṣawāʾif* against Christian positions in the upper and middle reaches of the Douro valley. The *t͟hug͟hūr* so constituted did not of course survive indefinitely: in time, frontiers inevitably changed as Islam retreated before advancing Christendom, and, as circumstances changed, the *ṣāʾifa* underwent changes of scale, form and style. This being so, attention here will be focused almost exclusively on a limited number of aspects drawn from data relating to *ṣawāʾif* against the Christian north during the Umayyad period (138-42/756-1031)—data which cannot of course be taken as valid for all Umayyad *ṣawāʾif* conducted by different leaders on different occasions over so long a span of time.

The conduct, scale, regularity and success of such *ṣawāʾif* depended on the central government's willingness, readiness and ability to launch them, all of which factors depended, in turn, on a ruler's strength of governance and purpose, internal peace and stability, the availability of reliable troops and loyal and able commanders, and so on. An early example of a ruler moved by religious zeal and bent on seizing opportunities open to him was His͟hām I (172-80/788-96 [*q.v.*]), whose generals led *ṣawāʾif* in almost every year of his reign—several against Alava and Old Castile in the north, several to the Asturias in the North-West and one, reaping a particularly rich harvest of booty, against Gerona and Narbonne in the North-East. For his son al-Ḥakam I (180-206/796-822 [*q.v.*]), obliged for much of his long reign to quell insurrections from the Marches down to Cordova itself, *ṣawāʾif* were anything but the annual events they became under his son ʿAbd al-Raḥmān II (206-38/796-822 [*q.v.*]), who, despite some early internal upheavals, personally led or dispatched *ṣawāʾif* almost every year of his reign against the Asturio-Leonese kingdom. In operations against the Franks in what is now Catalonia he entrusted command in 212/828 to his Umayyad kinsman ʿUbayd Allāh b. ʿAbd Allāh al-Balansī ("of Valencia"), a man whose Arabic designation *ṣāḥib al-ṣawāʾif* is worth noting here if only because it seems *not*, as may be thought, to have derived from any special office or rank he held, but was, rather, an *ad hominem* style acquired through the long and distinguished services he rendered as an organiser and leader of *ṣawāʾif*.

From among the constants and many variables of the Umayyad *ṣawāʾif*—under which those of the ʿĀmirid *ḥād͟jib* [*q.v.*] al-Manṣūr (Almanzor) [*q.v.*, at vol. VI, 430 ff.] are to be subsumed—only one or two can be touched on here. Of constants, the most important was the need, imposed by Cordova's remoteness from the far north, to ensure the smooth progress of troops towards a distant base from which, once rested and marshalled, they would take the field. To delay till the last moment disclosure of the chosen route was one factor offering Cordova the best prospect of success for the outward journey. By far the most crucial factor, however, was its need to provision its men on the march. As it was normal to have the army live off the land in areas to be crossed, ascertainment of the state of crops and harvests was a precondition of the launch of a *ṣāʾifa*, for drought could lead to the cancellation of a *ṣāʾifa* and the frustration of plans such as even ʿAbd al-Raḥmān III [*q.v.*] had to suffer, for example, in 303/915. Years later Ibn Abī ʿĀmir (al-Manṣūr from 371/981) was to provide against any similar setback by creating, notably in Cordova and strategic forward positions, vast stockpiles of grain, which lasted over several lean years from 378/988.

The recruitment, composition, organisation, funding and equipment of troops for Umayyad *ṣawāʾif* are, like their precise aims and *modus operandi*, beyond the scope of this article. What should be said, however, is that the *ḥus͟hūd* of our sources' expression *al-d͟junūd wa 'l-ḥus͟hūd* were provincial recruits enlisted for a *ṣāʾifa* to swell the regular army. Instructions for their recruitment went out as early as February, and after mobilisation (*istinfār*) in the summer they would converge on the outskirts of Cordova. Around the same time, commanders in the Marches would be ordered to prepare their contingents to join the Cordovan forces on arrival. Whether or not the ruler was to lead a *ṣāʾifa* in person, he would normally oversee preparations, which could last up to 30-40 days. From his palace he would process, amid popular acclaim, with his guard and entourage to royal quarters within his troops' encampment on the great Faḥṣ al-Surādiḳ ("pavilion plain"), north of Cordova. One notable ceremony to follow much later was the solemn fastening of banners (*ʿaḳd al-alwiya*) to commanders' lances in Cordova's Great Mosque on the Friday before the troops departed. Upon their return the banners would be replaced on the walls of the mosque.

Whatever profit the Umayyads may have derived

from even the most successful of their *ṣawāʾif*, it was certainly not any lasting extension of the boundaries of al-Andalus. That such was not the basic aim of the *ṣāʾifa* (Lévi-Provençal, *Hist. Esp. Mus.*, iii, 103 ff.) may well be true. What seems no less true is that in al-Manṣūr's hands the *ṣāʾifa* became less of a routine response to Christian initiatives than an assault of unexpected and unprecedented ferocity as it was drawn into the ʿĀmirid's military policy, which, however rewarding and morale-boosting in the short term, was ultimately to prove wholly counter-productive for Islam in Spain (on which see Chalmeta, at vol. VI, 432).

Bibliography: E. Lévi-Provençal, *Hist. Esp. Mus.*, ii, index *svv. ṣāʾifa* (to which add p. 145), *ṣāḥib al-ṣawāʾif*; iii, 18, 41, 55-112 (for all aspects of military organisation, many relevant to the *ṣāʾifa*, but see esp. 85-90, 92 n. 3, 101-6), 291, 465. For the Umayyad period, Lévi-Provençal used all the sources available to him. Although these remain very much the same, some, most notably important parts of the *Muķtabis* of Ibn Ḥayyān [*q.v.*], were not generally available either in the Arabic or in translation. The situation has since improved with the appearance of *Muķtabis* texts edited by ʿA. ʿAlī al-Ḥadjdjī, Beirut 1965, M. ʿAlī Makkī, Cairo 1971, P. Chalmeta, F. Corriente, M. Ṣubḥ, Madrid-Rabat 1979, and translations by E. García Gómez, *Anales palatinos del califa...Al-Ḥakam II*, Madrid 1969 (corresponding to Ḥadjdjī text), and Mª J. Viguera and F. Corriente, *Crónica del califa ʿAbdarraḥman III*, Saragossa 1981 (corresponding to Chalmeta text), etc. An important text for Almanzor is al-ʿUdhrī, *Nuṣūṣ ʿan al-Andalus/Fragmentos geográfico-históricos de al-Masālik*, ed. ʿA. al-Ahwānī, Madrid 1965, 74-80, and important studies are: L. Seco de Lucena, *Acerca de las campañas militares de Almanzor*, in *MEAH*, xiv-xv (1965-6), 7-29 (cf. idem, *New light on the military campaigns of Almanzor*, in *IQ*, xiv [1970], 126-42); J.M. Ruíz Asensio, *Campañas de Almanzor contra el reino de León (981-86)*, in *An. Est. Med.*, v (1965), 31-64. No attempt is made here to handle material for the post-Umayyad periods.

(J.D. LATHAM)

ṢĀʾIGH (A.), pl. *ṣāgha* and *ṣawwāghūn*, goldsmith, denotes a group of skilled craftsmen in Islamic society. In the early centuries of Islam, according to al-Djāḥiẓ and al-Khuzāʿī, the goldsmiths were mainly artisans of Jewish and Christian faith, but some Arab writers also recognised the existence of Muslim goldsmiths.

The earliest recorded goldsmiths known to Islamic history, according to Kattānī, belonged to the Jewish tribe of Banū Ķaynuķāʿ [*q.v.*] of Medina during the Prophet's time. Their skill was highly rated in society, yet the mediaeval Arabs thought that it was a demeaning skill which caused the loss of manliness (*murūwwa*). On the whole, public opinion was critical towards the goldsmith's profession, and they were allegedly censured by the Prophet Muḥammad in these harsh words: "The worst liars of mankind are the dyers (*ṣabbāghūn*) and the goldsmiths (*ṣawwāghūn*)" (al-Kattānī, *Tarātib*, ii, 91); in other words, he said, "The worst liars of my *umma* are the dyers and goldsmiths" (cf. al-Ibshīhī, *Mustaṭraf*, ii, 53). A similar attitude towards the *ṣāgha* was attributed to the caliph ʿUmar b. al-Khaṭṭāb, who doubted their reliability with customers (al-Kattānī, *Tarātib*, ii, 64). Aḥmad b. Ḥanbal and other scholars of the ʿAbbāsid period were said to have warned of evil moral consequences resulting frequent public visits to goldsmiths' shops (cf. al-Lubūdī, *Faḍl al-iktisāb*, fol. 58b). The *ḥisba* manuals are critical of their fraudulent alloying of gold with other cheaper metals like silver or copper, and their usurious transactions.

Among Arab bellelettrists, al-Djāḥiẓ cited an Arab woman's name as Salma bint al-Ṣāʾigh (cf. *Ḥayawān*, iv, 377) who belonged to the Syrian *Anbāṭ* (pl. of *Nabaṭ*, referring to the remnants of the Aramaic-speaking indigenous population of Syria and ʿIrāķ during the early ʿAbbāsid period). Moreover, Ibn al-Athīr and al-Samʿānī noted the usage of *al-Ṣāʾigh* as a *nisba* among Muslims from the 2nd/8th to 4th/10th century. Some of these persons were cited among expert transmitters of *ḥadīth* in the mediaeval Islamic world, and at least one of them was a well-known Arab writer called Ibn al-Ṣāʾigh ("goldsmith's son"). Besides being reliable transmitters of religious knowledge (*ʿilm*), some goldsmiths had attained upward social mobility. The customary law of *kafāʾa* was leniently applied to the goldsmiths, who could marry outside their own social group into the wealthy and respectable groups of the bourgeoisie such as the cloth-merchants (*bazzāz*) and perfumers (*ʿaṭṭār*).

Early Islamic cities such as Fusṭāṭ, Baghdād, Cairo, Damascus, Tunis, and so on had separate goldsmiths' markets (*sūķ al-ṣāgha*). Al-Ibshīhī, writing a rare tale about a goldsmith, illustrates the goldsmith's guild wherein the master-craftsman (*muʿallim*) employed and trained journeymen (*ṣāniʿ*, pl. *ṣunnāʿ*) in workshops and earned handsome wages. Literary sources provide evidence regarding the existence of goldsmith's guilds over the centuries in many Islamic cities of the Middle East until modern times.

Bibliography: Djāḥiẓ, *Ḥayawān*, iv, 377-9; idem, *al-Radd ʿalā 'l-Naṣāra*, in *Thalāth rasāʾil*, ed. Finkel, Cairo 1926, 17; Khuzāʿī, *Takhrīdj al-dalālāt*, Tunis n.d., ix, 460; Thaʿālibī, *Thimār al-ķulūb*, Cairo 1908, 195; Ibn al-Athīr, *al-Lubāb*, Baghdād n.d., ii, 232-3; Ibn al-Fuwāṭī, *al-Ḥawādith al-djāmiʿa* ed. M. Djawād, Baghdād 1932, 67; Samʿānī, *Ansāb*, Ḥaydarābād-Deccan 1977, viii, 266-71; Yāķūt, iv, 869; Dhahabī, *al-ʿIbar fī khabar man ghabar*, ed. Ṣ. al-Munadjdjid, Kuwait 1966, v, 344, 373; Ibn Kathīr, *Bidāya*, xiv, 98; al-Khaṭīb al-Baghdādī, *Taʾrīkh Baghdād*, Cairo 1931, xiv, 21; Kāsānī, *Badāʾiʿ al-ṣanāʾiʿ*, Cairo 1327/1909, ii, 320; Ibshīhī, *al-Mustaṭraf*, Cairo 1890, ii, 232-3; ʿAlāʾ al-Dīn al-Lubūdī, *Kitāb Faḍl al-iktisāb*, Chester Beatty ms. no. 4791, fol. 58b; ʿAbd al-Raḥmān al-Shayzarī, *Nihāyat al-rutba fi-ṭalab al-ḥisba* ed. al-Baz al-ʿArīnī, Cairo 1946, 77-8; Ibn Bassām al-Muḥtasib, *Nihāyat al-rutba fi-ṭalab al-ḥisba*, ed. Ḥusām al-Dīn al-Sāmarrāʾī, Baghdād 1968, 106-7; Ibn al-Ukhuwwa, *Maʿālim al-ķurba*, ed. R. Levy, London 1938, 144-7; Ibn al-Djawzī, *Manāķib Baghdād*, Baghdād 1924, 26; idem, *al-Muntaẓam*, Ḥaydarābād-Deccan, 1938-40, ix, 61; Ziriklī, *Aʿlām*, Cairo 1928, iii, 843-4; W.J. Fischel, *Jews in the economic and political life of mediaeval Islam*, London 1968, 74 ff.; M.S. Ķāsimī, *Ķāmūs al-ṣināʿāt al-shāmiyya*, Paris 1960, 264-5; Rafāʾīl Bābū Isḥāk, *Aḥwāl Naṣārā Baghdād fi ʿahd al-khilāfa al-ʿAbbāsiyya* ("The situation of the Christians of Baghdād during the ʿAbbāsid period"), Baghdād 1960, 64; ʿAbd al-Ḥayy al-Kattānī, *Tarātib al-idāriyya*, Beirut n.d., ii, 64, 91; G. Baer, *Egyptian guilds in modern times*, Jerusalem 1964, 155-69; idem, *Guilds in Middle Eastern history*, in *Studies in the economic history of the Middle East*, ed. M.A. Cook, London 1970, 11-30; M.A.J. Beg, *Social mobility in Islamic civilization—the classical period*, Kuala Lumpur, Malaysia, 1981, 62; S.D. Goitein, *A Mediterranean society*, iv, London 1983, 200-25.

(M.A.J. BEG)

ṢĀʾĪN ĶALʿA, a little town and district in

southern Ādharbaydjān, on the right bank of the Djaghātū, the modern town of Shāhīn Dizh. In the south the boundary runs a little over the river Sāruḳ, a tributary on the right bank of the Djaghātū. In the north it is bounded by the district of ʿAdjarī, in the east by the province of Khamse. The name is derived from the Mongol *sayin* "good".

The local Turkish Afshar tribe, of which a part had to emigrate to Urmiya to make room for the Čārdawrī (Čārdowlī) tribe of Lur origin (the district of Čardawr on the Saymara), were brought by Fatḥ ʿAlī Shāh from Shīrāz at the beginning of the 19th century. The chief of the Čārdowlī lived at Maḥmūddjiḳ and commanded about 5,000 men. In 1830 Ṣāʾīn Ḳalʿa was destroyed by a Kurdish invasion under Shaykh ʿUbayd Allāh. Ṣāʾīn Ḳalʿa, formerly occupied by a Persian garrison, guarded the entrance to Ādharbaydjān through the Djaghātū valley. The caves of Kereftū with a Greek inscription, described by Ker Porter (*Travels*, ii, 538-52; Ritter, ix, 816), as well as the site of Takht-i Sulaymān (the ancient Gazaka, al-Shīz of the Arabs; cf. Marquart, *Ērānšahr*, 108), are in the territory of the Afshars of Ṣāʾīn-Ḳalʿa. The lake of Čamli Göl (near the village of Bādarlī) with a floating island is likewise well known. A section of the Afshars belong to the Ahl-i Ḥaḳḳ sect [*q.v.*], the local chiefs of whom in Bent's time lived at Nazar-bābā and Gandjābād (cf. V. Minorsky, *Notes sur la secte des Ahl-i Ḥaḳḳ*, in *RMM*, xl-xli [1920], 19-97; *RMM* [1922], 53, 76).

The modern town of Shāhīn Dizh (long. 46° 35′ E., lat. 36° 43′ N., alt. 1,350 m/4,428 ft.) is the chef-lieu of a *bakhsh* of the same name in the province (*ustān*) of West Ādharbāydjān; in *ca.* 1950 it had a population of 3,170 (Razmārā, *Farhang-i djughrāfiyā-yi Īrān-zamīn*, iv, 295), which by 1991 had risen to 25,050 (Preliminary results of the 1991 census, Statistical Centre of Iran, Population Division).

Another fortress called Ṣāʾīn-Ḳalʿa on the river Abhar, to the east of Sulṭāniyya [*q.v.*] and mentioned by Ḥamd Allāh Mustawfī (see Le Strange, *Lands of the eastern Caliphate*, 222), should not be confused with this Ṣāʾīn Ḳalʿa.

Bibliography: Sir H. Rawlinson, in *JRGS*, x (1841), 40; H. Schindler, in *ZGEB*, xviii (1883), 327; T. Bent, in *Scotch Geogr. Magazine* (1890), 91; A.F. Stahl, in *Petermann's Mitteilungen* (1905), 33 (with a map of the district and indications of its mineral wealth); A.V.W. Jackson, *Persia past and present*, New York 1906, 121 ff.

(V. Minorsky*)

SAʿĪR (A.), one of the various words used in the Ḳurʾān for Hell Fire. *Saʿīr* seems to be a native Arabic formation (unlike Djahannam and possibly Ṣaḳar [*q.v.*]) with the meaning "[place of] fiercely kindled flame". It occurs 16 times in the Holy Book (IV, 11/10, 58/55, XXII, 4, etc.), most frequently in third Meccan period and Medinan sūras.

Bibliography: Nöldeke-Schwally, *G des Q*, i, 89; T. O'Shaughnessy, *The seven names for Hell in the Qur'ān*, in *BSOAS*, xxiv (1961), 455-7. (Ed.)

al-**SĀḲ** (A.), lit. "leg" or "thigh", used in various senses in Islamic mathematics and astronomy. Thus, for example, *sāḳ* means the foot of a compass, the perpendicular of a right-angled triangle with horizontal base, or the equal sides of an isosceles triangle. Another term for the foot of a compass is *ridjl*, and *dilʿ* is also used for any side of any triangle. (See further ʿilm al-handasa, in Suppl.).

In astronomy [see nudjūm] *sāḳ* may refer to a star that is in a leg of a constellation figure representing a person or an animal, as in *sāḳ al-asad* or *sāḳā 'l-asad* (dual) for either or both of α Bootis and α Virginis, regarded in Arab tradition as the hind legs of Leo. The word *sāḳ* in the name of the star *sāḳ sākib al-māʾ*, the leg of the water-carrier, δ Aquarii, was corrupted by Europeans in the Middle Ages to Scheat. The same star with its name half-Persianised as *sāḳ-i sākib-i māʾ* is represented on the retes of numerous Indo-Persian astrolabes [see asṭurlāb].

Sāḳ al-djarāda, lit. "the locust's leg", is the name given to a variety of vertical sundial [see mizwala] in which the horizontal gnomon is moved along a groove at the top of the rectangular sundial according to the season (since the shadow-lengths at the hours depend on the solar longitude). An example from Syria, made for the Ayyūbid sultan Nūr al-Dīn in 554/1159, with markings serving the latitudes of Damascus and Aleppo on either side, survives virtually intact (the gnomon is missing). The name of the device derives, with some stretching of the imagination, from the form and shape of the main astronomical markings.

Bibliography: On the use of *sāḳ* in simple geometry see, for example, Mohamed Souisi, *La langue des mathématiques en arabe*, Tunis 1968, 206-7 (*sub s-w-q*). On the star(s) *sāḳ al-asad*, see P. Kunitzsch, *Untersuchungen zur Sternnomenklatur der Araber*, Wiesbaden 1961, 104. On the star Scheat, see idem, *Arabische Sternnamen in Europa*, Wiesbaden 1959, 203. On the instrument called *sāḳ al-djarāda*, see P. Casanova, *La montre du sultan Noûr ad Dîn*, in *Syria*, iv (1923), 282-99, and S. Cluzan, J. Mouliérac and E. Delpont (eds.), *Syrie – Mémoire et civilisation*, Paris 1993, 436-7. (D.A. King)

al-**ṢAḲĀLIBA**, sing. Ṣaḳlabī, Ṣiḳlabī, the designation in mediaeval Islamic sources for the Slavs and other fair-haired, ruddy-complexioned peoples of Northern Europe (see A.Z. Velidi Togan, *Die Schwerter der Germanen*, 19-38).

1. The Ṣaḳāliba of Northern and Eastern Europe.

The actual name was a borrowing from Middle Greek Σλάβος, "Slav." This, in turn, is to be connected with the self-designation of the Slavs, *Slověne* (cf. the Rus' usage *Slověne, Slovyane, Sloven'skiy yazik* "Slavs", "Slavic nation" in the *Povest' vremyannikh let*, in *PSRL*, i, 5-6, 28, Mod. Russ. *Slavyane*, Ukr. *Slov'yani*, Pol. *Słowianie*, Czech. *Slované*, Bulg. *Slavyani*, etc.). This latter form is reflected in the Σκλαβηνοί, Σκλαυηνοί/*Sclaveni* (sing. Σκλαβηνός: **Slavěn-in* < **Slověn-in*), the Byzantino-Latin rendering of this collective name of the Slavs. It also was used to denote the central-southern grouping of Slavic tribes by 6th-7th century Byzantine (e.g. Procopius and Theophylactus of Simocatta) and Latinophone authors (e.g. Jordanes).

Due to the large numbers of slaves that came to Western Europe from the Slavic lands, the ethnonym "Slav" came to denote "slave" (< M. Eng. *sclave*, cf French *esclave*, Ital. *schiavo*, Germ. *Sklave*, Mod. Greek Σκλάβος) in a number of European languages (see comments of Menges, *Outline*, 11-12; Kupfer and Lewicki, *Źródła hebrajskie*, 29, n. 2). A reflection of this semantic development can be seen in the Hispano Arabic use of this term to designate, at first, Slavic slaves brought to Spain (where their role was analogous to that of the Turkic *ghilmān* of the rival ʿAbbāsids) and subsequently all foreign slaves in Spanish Umayyad service [see 3. below].

Although there was some ambiguity in the Arabic usage of this term, its initial meaning was undoubtedly "Slav." Early on, however, it spread to neighbouring peoples as well. Thus the early 3rd/9th century polymath al-Khʷārazmī (*Ṣūrat al-arḍ*, ed. Mžik, 105 speaks of the "country of G͟harmāniyā, which is the land of the Ṣaḳāliba." Ibn Faḍlān, who journeyed to Volga Bulg͟haria in 309-10/921-2 (the subject population of which included, in addition to various Turkic groups, Finno-Ugrian and other northern peoples), termed the Bulg͟hār ruler "King of the Ṣaḳāliba" (see Togan, *Ibn Faḍlān's Reisebericht*).

The Arab accounts derive the eponymous Ṣaḳlab from Mād͟hāy b. Yāfit͟h (al-Masʿūdī, Ibrāhīm b. Yaʿḳūb) or ʿŪd͟jān b. Yāfit͟h. Al-Ḳazwīnī (*Āt͟hār*, 614), however, derives him from the descendants of Līṭ b. Kalīk͟hīm b. Yūnān b. Yāfit͟h and presents him as the brother of Rūm, Arman and Firand͟j. According to the tale preserved in the anonymous *Mud͟jmal al-tawārīk͟h*, 103-4, Ṣaḳlab's father, whose mother died immediately after his birth, was raised on dog milk and developed a canine disposition. His son was called "Ṣaḳlab" (hence the popular etymology found in Gardīzī who derives this name from *Sag-lābī* < Pers. *sag* "dog"). Later, as each of Yāfit͟h's children acquired a land of their own, Ṣaḳlab struggled with Rūs, Kimārī and K͟hazar for possession of a territory, but was defeated. He was thus obliged to make his home in the north. This homeland of the Ṣaḳāliba is described as very cold, with homes built underground and heated by steam, a theme found in a number of the detailed descriptions in the Islamic geographical literature dealing with the Ṣaḳāliba lands. Gardīzī, in his tale of Ḳirg͟hīz (K͟hirk͟hīz) origins, relates that the leader of the K͟hirk͟hīz "was from the mass of the Saḳlābs." Having killed a Byzantine envoy, he was forced to flee to the K͟hazars, Bas͟hd͟jirts and Toḳuz Og͟huz. There he was joined by other Ṣaḳāliba. Gardīzī concludes that this is why "the features and traits of the Saḳlābs are to be found among the K͟hirk͟hīz (such as) reddishness of hair and whiteness of skin" (tr. Martinez, 124-6, ed. Barthold, 28-9). This constitutes one of several indications of the presence of an ancient Europoid strain among the Ḳirg͟hīz. It also shows the close association, in the Islamic geographical literature, of a certain fair-haired, ruddy complexioned population type of Eurasia with the Slavs.

The later Perso-Islamic historical tradition, in a notice of dubious historicity, mentions a "pass of the K͟hazars and Ṣaḳāliba" in connection with the activities of the Sāsānid D͟jāmāsp, who briefly ruled Persia 496-8. These and other notices purporting to record their presence in the north Caucasian zone in the early decades of Islam (e.g. Balʿamī) are almost certainly anachronistic. Paradoxically, we are probably on surer ground with references to Slavs that had been transplanted to Asia Minor or were serving in Byzantine forces that might have had contact with the Arabs as early as the decades preceding the advent of Islam. The earliest evidence for Arabo-Slavic contacts is found in the Byzantine sources. The 10th century chronographer Theophanes, ed. de Boor, i, 348, notes that *s.a.* 6156/664-5, some 5,000 Σκλαυινοί living on "Roman" territory defected to the Umayyad commander ʿAbd al-Raḥmān b. K͟hālid (ὁ Ἀβδεραχμάν ὁ τοῦ Χαλέδου), going with him to Syria and settling in the village of Seleucobolus in the region of Apamea. During the caliphate of ʿAbd al-Malik (Ἀβιμέλεχ), *s.a.* 6184/692-3, Νέβουλος, the commander of a force of 30,000 men that had been recruited from the Slavs settled in Asia Minor, was bribed by the Arabs and together with 20,000 of his men came over to the Arab side. The Byzantine Emperor Justinian II (685-95, 705-11) slaughtered the remaining Slavs at Leucate (Theophanes, i, 365-6).

The oldest reference in Arab writings, however, is found in the works of al-Ak͟hṭal (d. 91/710 [*q.v.*]), a Christian poet of the Tag͟hlib tribe who was one of the favourites of ʿAbd al-Malik. In one of his poems he makes a brief reference to the "throng of reddish Ṣaḳāliba" *d͟jamʿat al-Ṣaḳāliba al-ṣuhb*, see text and discussion in Lewicki, *Źródła arabskie*, i, 6 ff., and also his *Świat*, 339). Mention is made of the Saḳāliba by Yazīd b. al-Muhallab, a one-time governor of K͟hurāsān and then rebel against caliphal authority [see MUHALLABIDS], in a speech given on the eve of his final and fatal encounter with the Umayyads. This took place in 102/720, and his remarks were preserved in a collection of notable addresses by Ibn ʿAbd Rabbihi (see Lewicki, *Un temoignage arabe*, 319-31). The Saḳāliba noted here were, in all likelihood, one or another of the diasporan Slavic groupings that were either serving in the Byzantine forces or living as transplanted colonists in Asia Minor. This notice is important in that it comes directly from a contemporary. Direct contact with the Slavic lands, however, took place only after the Arabs had secured K͟hʷārazm in the early 8th century (see Lewicki, *Świat*, 326-7), and it became one of the principal entrepôts for commerce with eastern and northern Europe.

The later historian al-Yaʿḳūbī, *Taʾrīk͟h*, ii, 359, 360, mentions a "city of the Ṣaḳāliba" s.a. 96/714-5 and 98/716-7 which Maslama b. ʿAbd al-Malik [*q.v.*] conquered in 98/716-7 in his campaign against Constantinople. It is unclear whether this Slavic urban settlement is to be sought in Asia Minor or in the Balkans, although the former seems more likely. Several decades later, in a different theatre of operations, the Umayyad commander and future caliph Marwān b. Muḥammad, in 120/737 made a daring advance into K͟hazar territory, capturing the city of al-Bayḍāʾ (probably Sarkel on the Don). Proceeding further, as we learn from the account of Ibn Aʿt͟ham al-Kūfī (viii, 71-2, see also Togan, *Reisebericht*, 295 ff.), he "attacked the Ṣaḳāliba and the various infidels who lived beyond them", taking prisoner some 20,000 families. Marwān continued his advance and made camp on the "River of the Slavs" (*nahr al-Ṣaḳāliba*). In this region, he succeeded in capturing the K͟hazar Ḳag͟han and compelled him to embrace Islam. Al-Balād͟hurī, *Futūḥ*, 207-8, has a brief notice on this campaign, noting that the 20,000 captive Ṣaḳāliba who were settled in K͟hāk͟hīṭ (Kak͟het'i in Georgia) later revolted, and Marwān "attacked and killed them." The location of this *nahr al-Ṣaḳāliba* remains controversial. It has often been identified with the Volga (Togan, *Reisebericht*, 305). Another view (*ibid.*, 307), however, identifies these Ṣaḳāliba with the Burṭās, Suwār, Asgil and other Turkic and Finnic peoples of Volga Bulg͟haria. A passage in al-Masʿūdī's *Tanbīh*, 67, however, brings us southward to the Don. He remarks that "many settlements of the Ṣaḳāliba and other nations who penetrated deep into the north" are on a great river called *ṭnāys* (Tanais). The *Ḥudūd*, tr. Minorsky, 75, 216, reflects the confusion of the mediaeval Muslim historians and geographers regarding the rivers of the Ṣaḳāliba and Rūs lands, presenting us with a conflation of the information on the Don and Volga. It notes that the river of the Rūs "rises from the interior of the Ṣaḳlāb country ... skirts the confines" of the three Rūs urban centres and the Ḳīpčaḳ land and "empties itself into the river Ātil." With later authors the situation is not significantly clearer. Abū Ḥāmid al-G͟harnāṭī (473-565/1080-1170 [*q.v.*]), a native of Muslim Spain who spent much of his adult life in the Volga region (from 525/1131 largely in Ṣāḳṣīn/Sāk͟hsīn), passed through the lands of the Ṣaḳāliba (actually the Rūs region) on a journey that eventually brought him to Hungary *ca.* 1150. He reports that he left Bulg̲h̲ār by ship on the "river of the Ṣaḳāliba", by which he appears to have designated the Oka (ed. and tr. Dubler, 22/61, 196-9). His contemporary, al-Idrīsī (ed. Bombaci *et al.*, viii, 909-10), but without al-G̲h̲arnāṭī's first-hand knowledge, designates the Don as the *nahr rūsiyya*.

With regard to other riverine centres, al-Masʿūdī (*Tanbīh*, 67, 183) also mentions the *Danuba/*Danābī (Danube) and Malāwa (Morava) rivers on which Ṣaḳāliba settlements are to be found. Around the Malāwa, in particular, were the habitats of the *Nāmd̲j̲īn* (< Slav. *Nemčin* "German") and *Murāwāt* (Moravians, see below).

The same Marwān who led the successful 120/737 campaign, when he became caliph, placed Ṣaḳāliba colonies along the borders with Byzantium in Cilicia (at al-K̲h̲uṣūṣ), northern Syria (at Salmān, near Ḳūrus/Cyrrhus) and the upper Euphrates (Ḥiṣn Ziyād/Arm. K̲h̲artabirt, on the border zone). The second ʿAbbāsid caliph, al-Manṣūr, in 140/757-8 sent his son to raid the Ṣaḳāliba (al-Yaʿḳūbī, *Buldān*, 237). In that same year, according to al-Balād̲h̲urī, 166, the caliph rebuilt al-Maṣṣīṣa (Mopsuestia) and transplanted thither Ṣaḳāliba, Persians and Christian Nabataeans from al-K̲h̲uṣūṣ. Some of these Ṣaḳāliba may have been involved in the disturbances reported by al-Yaʿḳūbī (Lewicki, *Osadnictwo*, 488, and discussion in his *Źródła arabskie*, i, 265-6). Evidence for Slavo-Muslim co-operation against Byzantium can be seen in the notice found in Constantine Porphyrogenitus (*DAI*, 228/229) which tells of a raid on Patras in the Peoloponnesus *ca.* 805-7 by Slavs coming from that region who were assisted by "African Saracens." The antecedents of this alliance are obscure. Still more murky is the report in al-Yaʿḳūbī (*Taʾrīk̲h̲*, ii, 598-9), s.a. 239/853-5 or 240/854-5, regarding an unnamed "ruler (*ṣāḥib*)" of the Ṣaḳāliba, to whom the Georgian mountaineers, the Ṣanāriyya (Ts'anar), appealed (along with similar entreaties to the Byzantine Emperor and K̲h̲azar Ḳag̲h̲an) for aid against the caliphal forces led by the Turkic general Bug̲h̲a the Elder [*q.v.*].

The Slavic polities that took shape in the Balkans were, of course, oriented, in peace and war, towards Constantinople. Although the Muslim sources largely ignore the ferocious Byzantino-Bulg̲h̲ar wars of the 8th-9th centuries, al-Ṭabarī (iii, 2152-3) knows of a "king of the Ṣaḳāliba" who, in 283/896-7, attacked the Imperial capital. This was the now Slavicised Bulgarian king Symeon (*reg.* 893-927), whose attempt on Constantinople had actually begun in 894 and came to an end in 897 (on Symeon and Byzantium, see Fine, *The early medieval Balkans*, 137-58). According to al-Ṭabarī, the Emperor defeated him only with the aid of Muslim troops which he recruited from the Muslims who were in his territory, but Byzantine sources make no mention of such assistance.

Well before this time, however, the Muslim world was already gaining more direct access to the lands of the Ṣaḳāliba and incorporating the knowledge acquired thereby into geographical schemes derived from the Graeco-Roman tradition. Thus the *Kitāb al-Zīd̲j̲* written *ca.* 156/772-3 by al-Fazārī, typical of the mathematical geography of this era (the pertinent fragment from which is preserved in al-Masʿūdī, *Murūd̲j̲*, ed. Pellat, ii, 377), placed the Ṣaḳāliba at the end of a quite realistic listing of peoples that included the Tog̲h̲uzg̲h̲uz, the "Turks of the K̲h̲āḳān", the K̲h̲azars, al-Lān (Alans) and Burd̲j̲ān (Danubian-Balkan Bulg̲h̲ars), and presented them as occupying a region extending 3,500 *farsak̲h̲*s in length and 700 *farsak̲h̲*s in width. Al-K̲h̲ʷārazmī (105), however, equated the country of the Ṣaḳāliba with "G̲h̲armāniyā" (the "Germania" of the Latin tradition), i.e. Central Europe. In keeping with this scheme, the country of "Sarmāṭiyya" (Sarmatia) was identified with the territories of the Burd̲j̲ān and al-Lān (Alans). Ibn K̲h̲urradād̲h̲bih, 92, 155, with Ibn al-Faḳīh, 6-7, 83, following him, divides Europe (*Arūfā*) into "al-Andalus, al-Ṣaḳāliba, al-Rūm and Firanja." The Ṣaḳāliba are placed north of al-Andalus, alongside of the Burd̲j̲ān and Abar (Avars). In another passage, Ibn K̲h̲urradād̲h̲bih, 119, notes the K̲h̲azar, Alans, Ṣaḳāliba and Abar in a listing reflecting the disposition of the larger, politically more important peoples extending from the Volga to Central Europe (Ibn Rusta, 98 has a similar listing).

The location of the Ṣaḳāliba lands

By the 3rd-4th/9th-10th centuries, the material deriving from first-hand sources, i.e. travellers, merchants (Jewish and Muslim), Muslims who had spent time in Byzantium and Eastern Europe (e.g. Muslim b. Abī Muslim al-D̲j̲armī and the sources that came to comprise the "Caspian Codex", see Zak̲h̲oder, *Kaspiyskiy svod*) and had direct experience of the region, had substantially increased. As a consequence, the information available to the Muslim world, although not without serious lacunae (cf. the confusion noted above with regard to the "river of the Ṣaḳāliba"), became more expansive and richer in detail. Our 4th/10th century sources are unanimous that the Ṣaḳāliba occupied a heavily forested, "vast country" subject to ferocious frosts. The borders of this "country of the Ṣaḳāliba", however, are not precisely delineated. According to the *Ḥudūd*, tr. 158, to the east lay the Inner Bulg̲h̲ārs and some of the Rūs, to the south were some parts of the Gurz Sea (usually the Caspian but here designating (see 53) the Black Sea) and some parts of Rūm. To the west (actually north-west) and north were the "Uninhabited lands." The Sea of Azov (the Maeotis, *Māwṭs* in the *Ḥudūd*, 54) is noted as the "extreme limit of the Ṣaḳlābs towards the north." Al-Ḳazwīnī (*Āt̲h̲ār*, 614), writing in 674/1275-6, but largely using older data, places the Saḳlāb country in the west of the sixth and seventh climes, adjoining the K̲h̲azar realm and the mountains of Rūm.

The Slavic primary habitat and migrations

The imprecision of our sources with regard to Ṣaḳāliba borders is understandable. These lands, although very important for trade, were distant, dangerous and difficult of access. Moreover, from the 5th-9th centuries the Slavs had been undergoing a series of migrations out of their ancient habitat. Gothic, followed by Hunnic, pressures provided the catalyst for the breakup of Proto-Slavic "unity" and the migrations of elements of the Slavs southwards towards the Danube and across it to the Balkans and westward into Germanic and (earlier) Celtic lands. By 527, the Antes and Sclaveni were raiding the Byzantine Balkan holdings. This pressure increased with the advent of the Avars in the Western Eurasian steppes *ca.* 558. By the early 7th century, the Slavs were swarming over many parts of the Balkans, penetrating as far as Greece. Slavo-Avar pressure increased during the reign of Heraclius (610-41), who successfully defended Constantinople against a joint Avaro-Slav-Persian land and sea assault in 626. According to Constantine Porphyrogenitus (*DAI*, 146/147-148/149, 152/153), the Serbs and Croats took possession of the lands that now bear their names during the reign of Heraclius.

Although our Muslim sources came into direct contact with the Slavs after the great migrations were completed, the various Slavic groupings, extending from the Elbe and Baltic to the Pontic zone and Balkans, were still in the process of defining themselves as political entities. The Islamic authors of the ʿAbbāsid era were aware of them, collectively, as a distinct ethnolinguistic and cultural grouping consisting of various branches. Some of these subgroupings, in certain of our accounts, were already emerging as more clearly defined polities with their own identifying characteristics. Others, unaccountably, remained a liminal presence. Nonetheless, we have a number of remarkable accounts of the Ṣaḳāliba, with an occasional wealth of detail. These accounts are associated with three historico-geographical traditions (to some degree interrelated) that are represented by Ibn Rusta and Gardīzī; al-Masʿūdī; and Ibrāhīm b. Yaʿḳūb.

The Ṣaḳāliba lands

The Ibn Rusta-Gardīzī tradition (Ibn Rusta, 143-5; Gardīzī, ed. Barthold, 38-9, tr. Martinez, 162-6, elements of which are also preserved in the *Ḥudūd*, 158-9, and Marwazī) is largely ethnographic and derives primarily from sources belonging to the 3rd/9th century. It begins by noting that the Ṣaḳāliba lands were only 10 days' travel from those of the Pečenegs [*q.v.*]. The Ṣaḳāliba country was located beyond the steppe in dense forests. According to al-Masʿūdī (*Murūdj*, i, 142) "their residences are in the north towards where it joins the west." Ibrāhīm b. Yaʿḳūb (ed. Kowalski, *Relacja*, 1, 56), writing in the 960s, however, has them stretching from the Syrian Sea (*Baḥr al-Shāmī*, i.e. Eastern Mediterranean) to the "Ocean" (the Baltic being meant here). Ibn al-Faḳīh, 295, in a reference, perhaps, to an Eastern Slavic grouping located near the north Caucasus, remarks that the Caucasus is connected to the land of the Ṣaḳāliba and "in it there is also a tribe of the Ṣaḳāliba".

Tribes, political organisation and urban centres

Ibrāhīm b. Yaʿḳūb (7) describes the Ṣaḳāliba, in general, as possessing formidable military might. Indeed, if not for their excessive divisions, "no nation could stand up to them in power."

We have a variety of notices on the titles and leaders of the Ṣaḳāliba. Ibn Khurradādhbih, 17, and al-Bīrūnī, *Āthār*, 102, mention that the "king of the Ṣaḳāliba" has the title **ḳnāz* (al-Bīrūnī has قبّار *ḳbbār* = قناز cf. Russ. *knyaz'* "prince", a title ultimately of Germanic origin). Al-Masʿūdī (*Murūdj*, ii, 142-5) has an important notice on the Ṣaḳāliba tribal polities known to him. He remarks that they have kings, are divided along tribal lines ("they [comprise] many tribes and a vast [number] of types") and often war among themselves. He makes reference to a tribe among them "in which the kingdom (*al-mulk*) was of old", implying the earlier existence of some all-encompassing Slavic political union. "Their king was called *Mādjak* and his tribe is called *Walītāba*. The tribes of the Ṣaḳāliba followed this tribe in other times past...". He further comments that the *Walītāba* were the "purest of lineage, ... the greatest of their tribes and the foremost among them... Then the authority between these tribes was disputed and their (political) organisation (*niẓām*) came to an end. Their tribes formed different groups. Each tribe placed a king over itself...". Ibrāhīm b. Yaʿḳūb (1-2), who gives the name/title of this king as *Mākhā*, largely repeats al-Masʿūdī's information, adding that in his day, the "tribes of the north have gained ascendency over some of them and inhabit" some of their lands (probably a reference to the growing power of the Germanic Holy Roman Emperors in the western Slavic territories).

Elsewhere, al-Masʿūdī, *Murūdj*, ii, 144, perhaps referring to the situation in his own day, mentions *ʾldyr* as the leading king of the Ṣaḳāliba, a ruler possessing many towns, cultivated fields, large armies and to whose territory Muslim merchants were wont to travel for trade. Beyond his lands lay those of the "king of al-Afragh" (Prague, see below). The identity of this figure is also unknown. Russian and Ukrainian historians (e.g. Hrushevs'kiy, i, 408) suggested that *ʾldyr* was al-Dirr = the Varangian Dir of the Rus' chronicles, who briefly held Kiev in the mid-9th century. Given the context, this seems unlikely. Lewicki (*Świat*, 356) reads this name as **Aldayr* and proposes him as a ruler of White Croatia. This is not impossible, but it lacks corroborating evidence.

The Ibn Rusta-Gardīzī tradition, reflected also in the brief notices in the *Ḥudūd*, 159, and *Mudjmal*, 421, reports that their chief, whom all obey, wears a crown. Their chief of chiefs is named **swyyt blk* and his deputy is called **swbndj* (**shwbandj*). The first name appears to be a rendering of *Svętoplok/Světoplok (cf. Constantine Porphyrogenitus, *DAI*, 64/65, 176/177, 180/181, Σφενδοπλόκος), the king (*reg.* 870-94) of Moravia before it was overrun by the Hungarians.

The second name/title noted by our sources is viewed as an attempt to render a Slavic **zhupanets* < *zhupan* (an Old Slavic title of possible Avar or Turkic origin).

Ibrāhīm b. Yaʿḳūb (1) reports that in his day, the Ṣaḳāliba had four kings: an unnamed ruler of the Bulgarians (*Bulḳārīn*), *Bwyṣlāw* (*Boyeslav, probably Boleslav I, 935-67, the Bohemian ruler, see Kowalski, *Relacja*, 60), the "king of Frāgha (Prague), *Bwyma* (*Boyma = Bohemia) and *Krkwʾ* (Krakow, a reference to Boleslav I's control of White Croatia), *Mashka*, king of the North (a reference to Mieszko I of Poland) and *Nāḳwn* (Nakon) in the far west." Nakon was the ruler of the Obodriti/Obodriči, the most politically advanced grouping of the Polabian Slavs in the mid-10th century (see Leciejewicz, *Słowianie zachodni*, 157; Salivon, *Samosoznanie*, 131-40). Ibrāhīm, who journeyed to this land, has left us a detailed description of these kingdoms. Nakon's realm, in the west, was bordered by the Saxons (*Sakswn*) and the *Murmān* (Normans, probably Danes; see Kowalski, *Relacja*, 63); to the east were the Veleti/Vilci/Ljutiči; and in the south were the Lusatian Sorbs/White Serbs (see Salivon, *Samosoznanie*, 132). King Boyeslav/*Boleslav's realm extended from Prague to Krakow, requiring some three weeks' journey. Prague, our source notes, was constructed of stone and lime. This land, according to Ibrāhīm, who reports the prices for wheat, barley and fowl there, was deeply involved in commerce. Ṣaḳāliba, Rūs, Hungarians, Muslims and Jews came to trade, bringing out slaves, tin and furs. Ibrāhīm reckons among the remarkable characteristics of the people of Bohemia, given the stereotypical image of the Saḳāliba in the Islamic lands, the relative absence of blondness among them. Most, he reports, have dark brown hair.

The land of the king *Mashka* (Mieszko I) is described by Ibrāhīm 4-5) as the most extensive of the Saḳāliba domains, with fertile soil and an abundance of foodstuffs, meat and honey. The king supported his army of 3,000 armoured men, 100 of whom are equal to 1,000 of others, from the taxes levied on the markets. The king also provided for the children, male and female, of his army, including dowry and bride-price payments. Mas͟hḳa's neighbours are the Rūs in the east and the Baltic Pruss (*Brūs*) in the north. Our source then passes on to an account of the (now) Slavicised Bulgarians (*Bulḳārīn*), whose land he did not personally visit, but whose emissaries he met in Magdeburg (*Mād͟hīburg͟h*) at the court of Otto I. He reports that they had more than a rudimentary governmental apparatus and had men who were familiar with foreign languages.

Of the other tribes and their rulers, almost all of whom are to be found in the Central European Slavic lands, al-Masʿūdī (*Murūd͟j*, ii, 142-3) first mentions the **Usṭutrāna*. This name is also cited by Ibrāhīm b. Yaʿḳūb, 9, 120 ff.) who has the corrupted form *Ṣbrāba* (var. lect. *ʾṣṭbrāna, ʾṣṭrāna, ʾṣṭrāʾa, ʾṣṭbwāna*). These are the Stodorane of Brandenburg, the Heveldi of the German chroniclers (see Marquart, *Streifzüge*, 104). The king of these *Usṭutrāna* is recorded as *Baṣḳlabīd͟j*. Next are the *Dūlāba* whose king "at the present time is called *Wānd͟j ṣlāf*." These are the Dudlebi/Dulebî, an Eastern Slavic tribal grouping, much oppressed, according to Slavic historical tradition, by the Avars (*PSRL*, i, 11-12) whose territory extended into Western and Southern Slavic regions. The name of their ruler *Wānd͟j ṣlāf* is undoubtedly Vęceslav (Wenceslas), whom Marquart, *Streifzüge*, 103, identifies with Wenceslas I of Bohemia (920-9), for which there is no evidence other than a similarity of names. Our sources place them alongside the *Nāmd͟jīn* (<Slav. *nemčin, nemets* "German", see above), whose king is called *G͟harānd* and who are described as "the bravest of the tribes of the Ṣaḳāliba and the most chivalrous." These are the Germans of Conrad of Franconia (d. 919). Clearly, the use of the Slavic **Nemčin* probably points to a Slavic source for this ethnonym in the Muslim world (cf. also the K͟hazar Hebrew Correspondence; Ottoman Turkish [*q.v.*] *Nemče* "German, Austrian" is most probably a later, independent borrowing). Next to them is the unidentified tribe called *Mnābīn* (omitted in Ibrāhīm b. Yaʿḳūb) led by **Ratīmīr*. This grouping is followed by the *Sarbīn*, the Serbs, of whom al-Masʿūdī remarks that they are "awe-inspiring" (*muhīb*). Marquart, *Streifzüge*, 106-9, who conjectures that al-Masʿūdī's notice stemmed from the first third of the 9th century, identified them with the Lusatian Sorbs, the "White" or "unbaptised" Serbs noted by Constantine Porphyrogenitus (*DAI*, 152/153), as living beyond the Hungarians in a region called Βοϊκι, bordering also on the Franks and Great Croatia. Given the Central and Eastern European thrust of our source's information, which does not really touch on the South Slavs, this is probably correct.

Next are the *Murāwat*, the Morava or Moravians (most probably of the former Great Moravia, see Lewicki, *Znajomość*, 98-9). Gardīzī, tr. Martinez, 161, ed. Barthold, 38 (ms. *mrdāt* = *mrwāt*) places them 10 days' north of the "Nandur" (the Danubian Bulg͟hars), beyond the "great mountain range" (the Carpathians). They are described as numerous (greater than the Byzantines) and wearing clothing resembling that of the Arabs (turban, shirt and waistcoat). They practise agriculture and viniculture due to the abundance of water which is not channelled into ditches or canals, but follows its own course over the ground. They consist of two distinct communities (regrettably not further defined). Most of their trade is with the West (ms. *ʿrb* for *g͟hrb*, thus Barthold, 59, translates this as "they carry on their trade predominantly with the Arabs"). There is a rather confusing version of this notice in the *Ḥudūd*, 160, in its section on the "*Mirvāt*." Here, their eastern neighbours are given as some of the K͟hazarian Pečenegs and portions of an unnamed mountain range. To their south are other K͟hazarian Pečenegs and the Gurz Sea (the Black Sea). In the west are some parts of the Gurz sea (?!) and the Inner Bulg͟hārs. To the north are some Bulg͟hārs and the *Wnndr* mountains. The *Ḥudūd* further comments that they are Christians who speak Arabic (*Tāzī*) and *Rūmī*. Their dress is like that of the Arabs and they live in tents and felt huts. All of these details, in particular their linguistic affiliations, seem highly improbable (see Minorsky's comments, 442). They are portrayed, in the *Ḥudūd*, as being "on friendly terms with the Turks" (the Hungarians, who conquered them and destroyed their state in the late 9th century) and the Byzantines. This would appear to date this notice to the mid-9th century. Their neighbours, in al-Masʿūdī's narrative, are the *K͟hurwātīn* (the White Croatians are meant here, see above), the *Ṣāṣīn* (perhaps to be emended, as Marquart, *Streifzüge*, 122, suggests, to **Ṣāk͟hīn* "Ček͟hs") and the unidentified *Ḥs͟hyābīn, K͟has͟hānīn* in Ibrāhīm b. Yaʿḳūb. Marquart, *Streifzüge*, 140-1, would see in them the Guduscani (**D͟jus͟hs͟hānīn*), a Slavic tribe noted together with the Obodriti and Timočane in Frankish sources, who sent embassies to the Frankish court in the early 9th century. The last tribe in Ibrāhīm's variant of al-Masʿūdī's listing is the *Brānd͟jābīn*, in whom Marquart, *Streifzüge*, 107, would see *Braničevin.

Beyond the domain of *ʾldyr* (see above), the foremost king of the Ṣaḳāliba, according to al-Masʿūdī, *Murūd͟j*, ii, 144, is the king of al-Afrag͟h (Prague) who has "mines of gold, cities, vast, cultivated fields, many armies and great numbers (of people)." He conducts wars with the surrounding states of Rūm, the Franks (*al-Firand͟j*) and the Langobards (*lbzkrd*, recte *lnwkbrd* for *lnkwbrd*) with "alternating success (*sid͟jāl*). Beyond him is the "king of the Turks" (Hungarians), whose people are "the most handsome in appearance of the Ṣaḳāliba, the greatest in number and the most ferocious."

Near the eastern border of the Ṣaḳāliba is the town *Wāntīt (Ibn Rusta, 143, Gardīzī, ed. Barthold, 38, tr. Martinez, 162; *Ḥudūd*, 159: Wābnīt, cf. the *Wnntīt* of the K͟hazar Hebrew correspondence (Kokovtsov, 31, 88-9 n. 4)), some of whose inhabitants, according to the *Ḥudūd*, "resemble the Rūs." It has long been suggested that *Wāntīt* rendered **Vętič(i)*, the name of an Eastern Slavic tribe, the Vyatiči.

Although some elements of the accounts of the Muslim historians and geographers touch on the Eastern Slavic groupings, most of our information on the latter is inextricably tied to the Rūs theme [see RŪS]. Abū Ḥāmid (ed. Dubler, 25-6/64, tr. Bol's͟hakov, 37), however, makes no distinction, for in his day, the Rūs, whatever their origins, were fully Slavicised. He reports that he went to a city of the Ṣaḳāliba called *G͟hūr Karmān* (Dubler: G͟hūr Kūmān, cf. also Bol's͟hakov, who attempts to interpret "Kuyav" = Kiev from this form). "In it are thousands of Mag͟hribians, with the appearance of Turks. They speak Turkic and shoot arrows like the Turks. They are known in this country as the *Bad͟jna*" (= Pečeneg). In this connection we might recall that Ras͟hīd al-Dīn (ed. Karīmī, i, 482) refers to Kiev by its Turkic name *Men Kermen*. *Kermen* is a Ḳîpčak Turkic word meaning "fort, city." It was borrowed into 14th century Russian as well. Ras͟hīd al-Dīn further notes the presence there of the *ḳawm-i kulāh-i siyāhān*, the *Černii Kloboutsi* (Mod. Russ. *Černie Klobuki* "[people] of the black cowls") of the Rus' sources. These were Turkic tribesmen who had taken service with the Rus' princes of Kiev. One of the constituent elements of the Černii Kloboutsi were remnants of the Pečeneg tribal union. The confusion of these Turks with "Maghribians" probably stems from some element of their dress. Some of them seem to have been Muslims, for Abū Ḥāmid, who was departing for Hungary (*Bāshghird, Unkūriyya*), left behind some of his students to care for their needs. *Ghūr Karmān*, then, would appear to be a Turkic name for Kiev; see Pritsak, *Eine altaische Bezeichnung*, 1-13. In Hungary, Abū Ḥāmid also encountered Muslim "Maghribians", in all likelihood, Pečenegs (Hung. *Besenyő*) who were in the service of the Hungarian kings (see comments of Bol'shakov, 75).

The slave trade

The Ṣaḳāliba lands and peoples were intimately associated, as we have noted, with the slave trade, so much so that their name became synonymous with it. Slaving raids aimed at the Ṣaḳāliba were largely carried out by the Hungarians and the Rūs. Ibn Rusta, 142, has a particularly full notice. He reports that the "Madjghariyya" rule over their Ṣaḳāliba neighbours. "They require of them raw materials (*muʾan ghalīẓa*) (as tribute)" and treat them like prisoners of war. They raid them regularly and take their captives to "Kardj" (Kerč) in the Crimea. This, presumably, was their point of entry into the Byzantine world. The Rūs engaged in similar slaving raids, taking their captives to Khazaria and Volga Bulgharia, where they were sold. Some Ṣaḳāliba, according to Gardīzī (tr. Martinez, 166, 167, 169, ed. Barthold, 39), voluntarily worked for the Rūs as bond servants in order to be "free of [further obligations of] service." This same source, however, notes that the Ṣaḳāliba themselves have "many captured slaves." Al-Iṣṭakhrī, 305, reports that most of the Ṣaḳlabī, Khazar and Turkic slaves came to Khwārazm, along with the furs, etc. of the northern forests. Ibn Ḥawḳal, ed. Kramers, ii, 339, 340, 392, presents Khwārazm as not merely a passive recipient of this bounty. The Khwārazmians themselves engaged in slaving expeditions to Bulghār and the northern lands. In addition to Khwārazm and the Sāmānid orbit, Muslim Spain via the Maghrib, according to Ibn Ḥawḳal (i, 97, 110; see also Lewicki, *Świat*, 365), was one of the entry points of Ṣaḳāliba slaves into the Islamic world. Another market was Ādharbaydjān in Trancaucasia, whither Ṣaḳlābī, Greek, Armenian, Pečeneg and Khazar slaves were also brought (*Ḥudūd*, 142).

Religion

In his account of Khazaria, al-Masʿūdī, *Murūdj*, i, 213-14, portrays the Ṣaḳāliba and Rūs as the principal pagans of the country. In contrast to the Muslims, Christians and Jews, who each have two judges for their respective communities, the pagans were accorded only one "who renders judgment according to pagan practice (*bi-ḥukm al-djāhiliyya*), the judgment of reason." The tradition represented by Ibn Rusta, 144, Gardīzī, tr. Martinez, 164, ed. Barthold, 38, and the *Ḥudūd*, 158, states that they are all fire-worshippers. Clearly, this notice stems from material that had been gathered before elements of the Slavs were converted to Christianity in the mid-late 9th century. Worship of the hearth fire and of the sun among the pagan Slavs, bespeaking strong ancient Iranian influences, is well-established in the scholarly literature.

Ibn Rusta, 127, is aware, however, that Christianity had already been adopted by Balkan Slavs during the reign of the Byzantine emperor Basil I (867-87). In reality, Christianity had already begun to make headway among the Balkan Slavic peoples before the era of Basil I. Events came to a head in the latter years of the reign of Basil's predecessor, Michael III (842-67). In the course of an extraordinary concatenation of diplomatic and military initiatives undertaken by the Franks, Great Moravia, the Balkan (Turkic) Bulgharian realm and Byzantium, the Bulghar ruler, Boris, converted to Orthodox Christianity in 864 (on the Cyrillo-Methodian mission, which forms the backdrop to these events, see F. Dvornik, *Byzantine missions among the Slavs*, and Vlasto, *The entry of the Slavs*, 155 ff.). The Slavic subjects of the Bulghars were already moving towards Christianity. The conversion, at first resisted by some elements of the Turkic Bulghar aristocracy, ultimately contributed to their complete Slavicisation. The Slavs to which Ibn Rusta referred are generally believed to be elements of the southern Serbian tribes converted in 877 (Marquart, *Streifzüge*, 239-42). Vlasto, 208, has concluded that the bulk of the Serbs were Christian from about 870. Fine, *The early medieval Balkans*, 139-40, however, views them as still essentially pagan at this time. The comment by Ibn al-Faḳīh, 77, that the "Ṣaḳāliba have crosses" is, in all likelihood, a reference to the Balkan Slavs (Lewicki, *Źródła arabskie*, ii/1, 56). Similarly, the report in *Ḥudūd*, 157, regarding "Christianised Ṣaḳāliba" in a "province of Rūm" who pay taxes to the emperor points further to the South Slav area. Al-Masʿūdī, *Tanbīh*, 181-2, perhaps alluding to the struggle between Rome and Constantinople in the 9th century for the confessional loyalty of the newly-emerging Slavic Christian communities, notes that "the majority of the Ṣaḳāliba, the Burghar and other nations which are devoted to Christianity obey the ruler of "Rūmiyya." This must refer to the Byzantine emperor rather than the Pope of Rome.

Furs among the Ṣaḳāliba

According to Abū Ḥāmid (ed. Dubler, 22-3/61-2, tr. Bol'shakov, 35), the "River of the Ṣaḳāliba" has in it an animal with a black pelt that looks like a small cat. It is called a "water sable" and its hides are exported to Bulghār and Sakhsīn [see ṢAḲṢĪN]. They conduct their business affairs using fur-less, old squirrels pelts (as currency). If the head and claws are intact, 17 of these are worth one silver dirham. They tie them up in a bundle and call it a *djuḳn*. Furs, as we know from indigenous sources, served as currency in Rus', indeed a small unit of currency was the *kuna* (cf. Mod. Russ. *kunitsa* "marten"). Dubler (348) saw *djuḳn* as a possible garbling of *kuna*. Bol'shakov (73-4) preferred a reconstruction of the Arabic form as **djrfn* for Old Russ. *grivna*, a unit of currency larger than the *kuna*. Abū Ḥāmid then goes on to describe the use of these furs, with the ruler's seal on them, as currency.

Later references

There are some, anachronistic, references to the Saḳāliba in the later Muslim sources, which repeat information stemming from the 9th-10th centuries. Most of these, however, no longer deal with them as a specific ethno-linguistic unit, but rather as distinct countries, cf. al-Idrīsī's extensive treatment of "Buʾāmiyya" (Bohemia), "Buluniyya" (Poland) and "Rūsiyya (see Lewicki, *Polska*). Thus al-Dimashḳī (261-2) largely cites the information of al-Masʿūdī, al-Bakrī (who preserved Ibrāhīm b. Yaʿḳūb's account for us), al-Idrīsī and the historian Ibn al-Athīr (tale of the Rūs conversion). An interesting mix of old and more recent data is found in Abu 'l-Fidā's *Taḳwīm al-buldān*. For example, he reports the more current hydronyms: *Ṭunā* (Danube), *ʾzw* (Turk. Özü = the Dnepr), *Tān* (Don) (ed. Reinaud, 63-4). Following Ibn Saʿīd, he makes note of the city of *Lūyāniyya* which belonged to the greatest of the Ṣaḳāliba kings (206). It is described as one of the most important ports on the Baltic. Near it, towards the east, is the (city of ?) *Ṣāṣīn* (perhaps *Ṣādjīn*) (Lewicki, *Świat,* 328, suggests that the two Baltic Slavic centres noted here are Wolyń Pomorski and Szczecin). In the Balkans, he mentions the mountains of Croatia (Djabal *Khurwāsiyā) and Slavonia (*Ishkafūniyya*) (202). The latter is placed (211) on the shore of the "Sea of Venice" (the Adriatic). By the Mongol era, however, many of the themes of the classical Islamic geographers were repeated uncritically and occasionally incorrectly. Thus al-Ḳazwīnī, *Āthār*, 616-17, sees in Mashḳa (Mieszko, see above) the name of a "broad city in the country of the Ṣaḳāliba at the coast of the sea" as well as the name of its ruler. Moreover, his customs are contrasted with those of the "other Turks", blurring thus the Ṣaḳāliba, the Turks and others of the Northern peoples.

Bibliography: 1. Sources. Collections: (a) Arabic: T. Lewicki, *Źródła arabskie do dziejów Słowiańszczyzny* ["Arab sources for the history of the Slavs"], Wrocław-Krakow-Warszawa 1956-77; B.N. Zakhoder, *Kaspijskiy svod svedeniy o vostočnoy evrope* ["The Caspian Codex of information on Eastern Europe"], Moscow 1962-7. (b) Hebrew. F. Kupfer and T. Lewicki, *Źródłla hebrajskie do dziejów Słowian i niektórych innych ludów Środkowej i Wschodniej Europy* ["Hebrew sources for the history of the Slavs and several other peoples of Central and Eastern Europe"], Wrocław-Warszawa 1956.

Arabic Sources: Balādhurī, *Futūḥ al-buldān*, ed. de Goeje; Bīrūnī, *al-Āthār al-bāḳiya*, ed. Sachau; Dimashḳī, *Cosmographie*, ed. Mehren; Abu 'l-Fidā, *Taḳwīm al-buldān*, ed. Reinaud and de Slane; Abū Ḥāmid al-Gharnāṭī, *Abū Ḥamid el granadino y su relación de viaje por tierras eurasiáticas*, ed. and tr. C.E. Dubler, Madrid 1953; idem, *Puteshestvie Abu Khamida al-Garnati v vostočnuyu i tsentral'nuyu Evropu (1131-1153)*, tr. and comm. O.G. Bol'shakov and A.L. Mongayt, Moscow 1971; Ibn Aʿtham al-Kūfī, *Kitāb al-Futūḥ*, Ḥaydarābād 1388-95/1968-75; Ibn Faḍlān and Z.V. Togan, *Ibn Faḍlān's Reisebericht (Abhandlungen für die Kunde des Morgenlandes*, 24/3), Leipzig 1939; Ibn al-Faḳīh, ed. de Goeje; Ibn Ḥawḳal, ed. J.H. Kramers, Leiden 1938-9; Ibn Khurradādhbih, ed. de Goeje; Ibn Rusta, ed. de Goeje; Ibrāhīm b. Yaʿḳūb, *Relacja Ibrāhīma ibn Jaʿḳūba z podróży do krajów słowiańskich w przekazie al-Bekrīego* ["The account of Ibrāhīm ibn Yaʿḳūb about his journey to the lands of the Slavs as transmitted by al-Bakri"], ed. T. Kowalski, Krakow 1946; Idrīsī, *Nuzhat al-mushtāḳ*, ed. A. Bombaci *et al.*, Leiden 1970-84; Iṣṭakhrī, ed. de Goeje; Ḳazwīnī, *Āthār al-bilād*, Beirut 1389/1969; Khʷārazmī, *Das Kitāb Ṣūrat al-Arḍ des Abū Ǧaʿfar Muhammed ibn Musa al-Ḫuwārizmī*, H. von Mžik, Leipzig 1926; Masʿūdī, *Murūdj al-dhahab*, ed. Pellat, Beirut 1966-74; idem, *Tanbīh*, ed. de Goeje; Yaʿḳūbī, *Taʾrikh*, ed. Houtsma; idem, *Buldān*, ed. de Goeje.

Persian Sources: *Ḥudūd al-ʿālam*, tr. Minorsky; Gardīzī, ed. Barthold, *Izvlečenie iz sočineniya Gardizi Zayn al-akhbār* ["An extract from the work of Gardīzī, *Zayn al-Akhbār*"], in *Sočineniya*, Moscow 1963-73, viii, 23-62; tr. P. Martinez, *Gardīzī's two chapters on the Turks*, in *Archivum Eurasiae Medii Aevi*, ii (1982), 109-217; *Mudjmal al-tawārīkh*, ed. M.S. Bahār, Tehran 1939; Rashīd al-Dīn, *Djāmiʿ al-tawārīkh*, ed. B. Karīmī, Tehran 1338/1959.

Greek sources: Constantine Porphyrogenitus, *De administrando imperio*, ed. Gy. Moravcsik, Eng. tr. R.J.H. Jenkins (Corpus Fontium Historiae Byzantinae, 1), Dumbarton Oaks, Washington, D.C. 1967; Theophanes, *Chronographia*, ed. C. de Boor, Leipzig 1883.

Slavic sources: *Povest' vremyannīkh let* ["The tale of bygone years"], in *Polnoe sobranie russkikh letopisei* [= *PSRL*], St. Petersburg-Leningrad-Moscow 1846-.

2. Studies. F. Dvornik, *Byzantine missions among the Slavs*, New Brunswick 1970; J.V.A. Fine Jr., *The early medieval Balkans*, Ann Arbor 1983; M. Hrushevs'kīy, *Istoriya Ukrayinī-Rusī* ["The history of Ukraine-Rus'"], 3rd ed. Kiev 1913, repr. Kiev 1991; L. Leciejewicz, *Słowianie zachodni* ["The western Slavs"], Wrocław-Warsaw-Krakow 1989; T. Lewicki, *Osadnictwo słowiańskie w krajach muzułmańskich w świetle opisów średniowiecznych pisarzy arabskich* ["Slavic settlement in the Muslim lands in light of the accounts of the early mediaeval Arabic writers"], in *Sprawozdania Polskiej Akademii Umiejętności*, xlix (1948), 487-90; idem, *Świat słowiański w oczach pisarzy arabskich* ["The Slavic world in the eyes of the Arabic writers"], in *Slavia Antiqua*, ii (1949), 321-88; idem, *Znajomość krajów i ludów Europy u pisarzy arabskich IX-X w.* ["Familiarity with the lands and peoples of Europe on the part of the Arabic writers of the 9th-10th centuries"], in *Slavia Antiqua*, viii (1961); idem, *Un temoignage arabe inconnu sur les slaves de l'an 720*, in *Folia Orientalia*, iv (1962), 319-31; J. Marquart, *Osteuropäische und ostasiatische Streifzüge*, Leipzig 1903; K.H. Menges, *An outline of the early history and migrations of the Slavs*, New York 1953; O. Pritsak, *Eine altaische Bezeichnung für Kiew*, in *Isl.*, xxxii (1955), 1-13; A.N. Salivon, *Samosoznanie obodritov (k voprosu ob obrazovanii obodritskoy rannefeodal'noy narodnosti* ["Self-consciousness among the Obodrity. On the question of the formation of the Obodrite early feudal nationality"], in L.V. Zaborovskiy (ed.), *Formirovanie rannefeodal'nīkh slavyanskikh narodnostey* ["The formation of early feudal Slavic nationalities"], Moscow 1981, 130-51; A.Z. Validi Togan, *Die Schwerter der Germanen, nach arabischen Berichten des 9-11 Jahrhunderts*, in *ZDMG*, xc (1936), 19-38; A.P. Vlasto, *The entry of the Slavs into Christendom*, Cambridge 1970.

(P.B. Golden)

2. In the central lands of the caliphate.

The white slaves in the armies of the ʿAbbāsids when the caliphate underwent its military transformation during the 3rd/9th century [see DJAYSH and GHULĀM. 1], were predominantly Turks and Rūm, the latter probably in majority Greeks and Armenians. But by the opening of the 4th/10th century, a certain number of Ṣaḳāliba, here to be interpreted as Slavs from Central and Eastern Europe and possibly as some of the Ugrian peoples of Eastern Russia [see BURṬĀS], appear within the ʿAbbāsid caliphate, though only as a subordinate element of the slave troops there, given the easy availability to the ʿAbbāsids of Turks from Central Asia and the South Russian steppes.

It is with the Fāṭimids that we really find a significant Slav military element. Ṣaḳlabī commanders are known in the army of the Aghlabids of Tunisia, but the early Fāṭimids had a prominent commander and admiral, Ṣābir, a freedman of the governor of Sicily Ibn Ḳurhub, and Ṣābir's Slav seamen and troops har ried the coasts of southern Italy as far as Salerno and Naples. The geographer and traveller Ibn Ḥawḳal (378/988) noted that the most populous quarter in Palermo was the *ḥārat al-Ṣaḳāliba* (ed. Kramers, 119, tr. Kramers and Wiet, 118). But it was under the caliph al-Ḳāʾim (322-34/943-46 [*q.v.*]) that the Slav element in the Fāṭimid forces really increased, especially after the revolt of Abū Yazīd [*q.v.*] and his Berber Khāridjite supporters showed the need for reliable professional troops. Hence several Ṣaḳlabī commanders, with typical slave names like Maysūr, Marām and Bushrā, begin to be mentioned in the historical texts. Earlier authorities, such as Amari and his reviser Nallino, interpreted the consonant ductus الصقلي/الصقل of the sources as *al-Ṣiḳillī* "the Sicilian", but I. Hrbek has pointed out that it is unlikely that native Sicilians (for whom the plural form is normally *al-Ṣiḳilliyyūn*), enjoying protected *dhimmī* status, would be enslaved.

The real origin of these Ṣaḳāliba must have been the Slav peoples of Central Europe and the Balkans, then in considerable turmoil from the warfare of the Byzantines and local Croat, Serb and Bulghar rulers and from expansionist pressures against the Slavs from the Germanic *Ostmark*. Prague was a centre of the slave trade, and St. Adalbert relinquished the bishopric of Prague in A.D. 987 because he could not ransom all the Christian slaves which Jewish merchants brought thither. Captives of war were shipped as slaves, almost certainly by the Venetians, through the ports of Dalmatia [*q.v.* in Suppl.], with the Muslim potentates as their purchasers, and, despite Papal and Imperial anathemas, this traffic continued well into the 5th/11th century; in 1076 Pope Gregory VII made King Zvonimir swear as part of his coronation oath not to allow the slave trade in Croatia and Dalmatia.

Within the Fāṭimid caliphate, the Slavs continued to play a conspicuous role in the reign of al-Muʿizz (341-65/953-75 [*q.v.*]), and al-Maḳrīzī states that the caliph learnt the languages of his servants and retainers, sc. Berber, Rūmiyya (according to Hrbek, probably the Sicilian dialect of Italian), Sūdāniyya and Ṣaḳlabiyya. Two of his prominent commanders, the eunuch Ḳayṣar and Muẓaffar, were Slavs, but the most celebrated of all was the conqueror of Egypt for the caliph, Djawhar [see DJAWHAR AL-ṢIḲILLĪ], whose ambiguous *nisba* is probably to be interpreted as al-Ṣaḳlabī, as is possibly that of the eunuch commander Djawdhar [*q.v.*]. Djawhar's career, together with those of his son al-Ḥasan and, probably, of the eunuch Bardjawān [*q.v.*] in the reign of al-Ḥākim (386-411/996-1021 [*q.v.*]), mark the apogee of Slav influence in the Fāṭimid state. During the course of the 5th/11th century, Slavs became less prominent in the army as the share of the Turks increased and as conditions in the Balkans became more peaceable, with the formation of stronger nation states there. They nevertheless continued to be the favoured bearers of the ceremonial parasol or *miẓalla* [*q.v.*] (this office coming fourth in the administrative-military hierarchy after the vizier, the head chamberlain or *ṣāḥib al-bāb*, and the commander-in-chief or *isfahsālār*), and they left a mark on the topography of Fāṭimid Cairo, according to al-Maḳrīzī, *Khiṭaṭ*, Cairo 1324/1906, iii, 68, in the shape of the *darb al-Ṣaḳāliba* in the Zuwayla quarter of the city.

Bibliography: In addition to references in the article, see A. Mez, *Die Renaissance des Islams*, Heidelberg 1922, 155-6, Eng. tr. 159-60; I. Hrbek, *Die Slawen im Dienste der Fāṭimiden*, in *ArO*, XXI (1953), 543-81; J.L. Bacharach, *African military slaves in the medieval Middle East: the case of Iraq (869-955) and Egypt (848-1171)*, in *IJMES*, xiii (1984), 471-95.

(C.E. BOSWORTH)

3. In the Muslim West.

As noted in section 1 above, the Arabic geographers of the 3rd-4th/9th-10th centuries gave the name *Ṣaḳāliba* to the peoples of the centre and north-east of Europe occupying territories which stretched from north of the Byzantine empire to the lands of the Khazars and Bulghārs in the east to those of the Franks and Lombards in the west, corresponding, it appears, to the lands of the Slavs.

Since Umayyad times, slaves of such origin in the Islamic world had reached appreciable numbers, used as domestic slaves and as soldiers, in particular in caliphal service (see above, section 2). It seems that in the west, these Ṣaḳāliba came mainly from the commerce which had developed in the 8th and 9th centuries between the *Dār al-Islām* and the lands of the Carolingian West. Western sources, and to a small extent, Arabic ones, attest the fact that these slaves, the product of war and, probably also, of raids mounted from Christian Germany into the Slav lands, were forwarded to Spain, and probably also the Maghrib, by merchants from marginal ethno-cultural groups acting as intermediaries between the Christian and Islamic worlds: "Greeks" of Italy (Neapolitans, Amalfitans and, very likely also, Venetians), and above all, the Jews of Spain and Septimania.

It appears also that, very soon, the Ṣaḳāliba sold in Spain had previously, on reaching Muslim territory, undergone castration, evidently to increase their value on a market where the demand for eunuchs was strong, given the need for male staff for the running of harems. These facts doubtless explain why the term Ṣaḳāliba soon acquired the specialised meaning of "a white eunuch", in opposition to the *ʿabīd*, black slaves. In the 4th/10th century, this trade was very important and seems to have been the main cause for the rise of the great port of Almeria, from which these slaves were re-exported to other Muslim lands of the Mediterranean basin. Thus the castration was done in al-Andalus, in connection with an important Jewish group attested in the town of Lucena. Those Ṣaḳāliba brought to Khʷārazm or Khurāsān from the eastern part of the Slav world do not appear to have been the object of the same treatment, but little is known about this question apart from what is mentioned exiguously in the geographers.

In an important article, David Ayalon has considered afresh the question of the true origin of these Ṣaḳāliba, which most authors, following Dozy, considered as stemming from wars and raids of the Muslims of al-Andalus against the southern fringes of the Christian West (northern Spain, southern France, the coasts and islands of the Tyrrhenian Sea) rather than from the actual Slav lands. According to Ayalon, the text of Ibn Ḥawḳal adduced by Dozy, Lévy-Provençal, Ashtor, etc., has been wrongly interpreted. He holds that the Arabic geographers of the 3rd-4th/9th-10th centuries made a clear distinction between the Galicians, Franks and Lombards on one hand, and the Ṣaḳāliba or Slavs on the other. Hence it could be said that, given the fact that many of the Ṣaḳāliba were supposed to come from the Carolingian empire and not from the Slav lands, the military importance of slaves of Christian origin in the mediaeval Islamic world has been exaggerated. Ayalon's thesis is that, in the main centres of Muslim power, and even in al-Andalus, for long, pagan soldiers with white skins from the *Dār al-Ḥarb* were preferred to Christians from Europe, who appear in this role relatively late.

This reconsideration, and the interpretation of Ibn Ḥawḳal's text, should be approached with prudence. Ayalon virtually leaves out the Western documentation, in Arabic and Latin, which should be carefully re-examined before reaching the conclusion which he proposes. In principle, and from the ethno-geographical viewpoint, Ibn Ḥawḳal may not be confusing the Ṣaḳāliba with the Franks and other peoples of the West. But in the same passage he says that the people of al-Andalus "attack the Slav lands in the directions of Galicia, the Frankish lands, Lombardy and Calabria and take prisoners there", which is hardly comprehensible unless one admits that the human product of Saracen piracy on the Western European coasts was considered as belonging to the general group of Ṣaḳāliba. This point mignt be verifiable in certain particular cases, such as that of the "Slav" ruler of the Denia *ṭāʾifa* in the 5th/11th century, Mudjāhid, whose origin was, there is reason to think, Italian.

In the East, some Ṣaḳāliba—it is difficult to know whether these were eunuchs or not—were used as soldiers by the Umayyads of Damascus, perhaps in imitation of the Byzantines, who had corps of Slav troops. The ʿAbbāsids favoured the use of Turks, and the Slavs played only a minimal role in Baghdād. But in al-Andalus, the Cordovan Umayyads seem to have prolonged, in this sphere as in others, the Damascus tradition. Servants of Ṣaḳlabī origin are attested in the 3rd/9th century under the amīrate, but it was under the caliphate that their increase in numbers became spectacular. At the end of ʿAbd al-Raḥmān III's reign (350/961), there are said to have been almost 14,000 Ṣaḳāliba at Cordova.

These persons, who had come as children into the service of the state, received a good "technical" and intellectual education, and were used as domestic attendants, court officials, soldiers and administrators, reaching the highest levels in all these spheres. Already under the *amīr* ʿAbd Allāh, at the end of the 9th and opening of the 10th centuries, the most influential of the viziers was Badr al-Ṣaḳlabī. Under al-Ḥakam II, the influence of high Ṣaḳlābī officers rose still further. At his death in 365/976, two of them, Fāʾiḳ al-Niẓāmī and Djawdhar, director of the *ṭirāz* and court jewelry manufacture, and chief falconer, respectively, but also commanders of the Ṣaḳlabī guard, who had both enjoyed the trust of the dead ruler, wished to set aside his son and official heir, Hishām, who was not yet twelve years old, and enthrone in his place al-Mughīra, one of al-Ḥakam II's brothers. But their plans were frustrated by the ministers al-Muṣḥafī and Ibn Abī ʿĀmir, the future al-Mansūr, the first of Berber and the second of Arab origin, who took advantage of the disquiet amongst ruling circles concerning the increased power of the Ṣaḳāliba.

In Hishām's reign, power was speedily appropriated by al-Manṣūr, who in his turn relied on numerous Ṣaḳlabī elements faithful to him, as did likewise his two sons after him. During the crisis which followed the "Cordovan revolution" of 399/1009 and the fall of the ʿĀmirids, and until the demise of the caliphate in 422/1031, several chiefs from the ʿĀmirid Ṣaḳāliba played a major role in the politico-military manoeuvrings which accompanied tye breakdown of the Umayyad central administration. The main ones here were Wāḍiḥ, commander of the Medinaceli march, and head of the "Ṣaḳlabī-Andalusian" party which, with the caliph al-Mahdī, disputed control of Cordova with the Berbers of the caliphal army and their concurrent caliph al-Mustaʿīn until his death in 402/101. Two other chiefs, Khayrān and Mudjāhid, then played a comparable role, but based respectively on Almeria and Denia, where they had built up practically autonomous powers which were transformed into *ṭāʾifa*s once the central government disappeared completely.

Two other "Slav" *ṭāʾifa*s took shape at the same time on the eastern coast of al-Andalus, those of Tortosa and Valencia, without one knowing properly how the Ṣaḳlabī elements managed to achieve the upper hand in this region. The most brilliant of these rulers was incontrovertibly Mudjāhid of Denia (403-36/1012-45), famed for his ambitious, but unfortunate, enterprise against Sardinia [see SARDĀNIYA] and, above all, by his maecenate which made Denia for a while one of the cultural capitals of the Mediterranean West, especially in regard to lexicography and the Ḳurʾānic readings. It was at his court or that of his son ʿAlī (436-68/1045-75) that the *Risāla* of Ibn Garcia [see IBN GHARSIYA] was written, the only important Andalusian work belonging to the anti-Arab—although perfectly Arabised culturally—movement of the Shuʿūbiyya [*q.v.*]. The Slav *ṭāʾifa* of Denia is the one which lasted longest, the others having disappeared towards the middle of the 5th/11th century (the supply of Slavs hardly continued, it would appear, after the end of the caliphate).

The Ṣaḳāliba phenomenon in al-Andalus must be considered in company with the acquisition of power by Turkish elements in the ʿAbbāsid caliphate or by other military elements of servile origin in various parts of the Muslim world during the history of *mamlūk*s in Egypt and blacks in 11th/17th-century Morocco. In the though-provoking works on this problem of Patricia Crone and Daniel Pipes, neither have fully taken into account the Ṣaḳāliba of Spain and, more generally, of the Muslim West, although these would have merited consideration. Elements of this origin played a role, probably less important and under the political control of the régimes they served, in Ifrīḳiya from the Aghlabid period to the Zīrid one, above all in the Fāṭimid caliphate there and then in Cairo (see above, section 2). Al-Bakrī mentions contingents of Ṣaḳāliba in the little state of Nakūr [*q.v.*] in the 4th/10th century, but it is true that this principality lived in the shadow of al-Andalus. A quarter of Palermo is mentioned by Ibn Ḥawḳal as the *ḥārat al-Ṣaḳāliba*, and during the Arabo-Norman period, the kings of Sicily had in their service Muslim eunuchs who can probably be considered as Ṣaḳāliba.

Bibliography: A.M.ʿA.F. al-ʿAbbādī, *Los esclavos en España. Ojeada sobre su origen, desarollo y relación con el movimiento de la Šuʿūbiyya*, Madrid 1953; D. Ayalon, *On the eunuchs in Islam*, in *JSAI*, i (1979), 67-124; G.-H. Bousquet, *Les Çaqāliba chez Ibn Khaldoun*, in *RSO*, xl (1965), 139-41; P. Crone, *Slaves on horses*, Cambridge 1980; F. Dachraoui, *Le califat fatimide au Maghreb 296-362/909-973*, Tunis 1981; R. Doehaerd, *Le haut Moyen Age occidental. Economies et sociétés*, Paris 1971; P. Guichard, *Animation maritime et développement urbain des côtes de l'Espagne orientale et du Languedoc au Xᵉ siècle*, in *Occident et Orient au Xᵉ siècle. Actes du IXᵉ congrès de la Société des Médiévistes*, Paris 1979, 187-201; J.F.P. Hopkins, *Medieval Muslim government in Barbary*, London 1955; E. Lévi-Provençal, *Hist. Esp. mus.*; T. Lewicki, *L'apport des sources arabes médiévales (Xᵉ-XIᵉ siècles)*, in *Settimani di Studio del Centro Italiano di Studi sull'Alto Medioevo di Spoleto*, xii, 1965, 461-85; M. al Manūnī, *Thaḳāfat al-Ṣaḳāliba bi 'l-Andalus*, in *Awrāḳ ʿĀmirī*, Cairo 1961; Peter C. Seales, *The fall of the caliphate of Córdoba. Berbers and Andalusis in conflict*, Leiden 1994; D. Wasserstein, *The rise and fall of* (*milieu IIe/VIIIe-début V^e/XIe siècles*), in *Estudios onomástico-biográficos de al-Andalus* (*Homenaje a Jose Mª Fórneas*), Madrid 1994, 305-36; J.T. Monroe, *The Shu^cūbiyya in al-Andalus. The* Risāla *of Ibn Garcia and five refutations*, tr. introd. and notes, Berkeley, etc. 1970; D. Pipes, *Slave soldiers and Islam*, New Haven-London 1981; A. de Premare and P. Guichard, *Croissance urbaine et société rurale à Valence au début de l'époque des royaumes de taifas. Trad. et comm. d'un texte d'Ibn Ḥayyan*, in *ROMM*, xxxi (1981), 15-29; A. Prieto y Vives, *Los reyes de Taifas*, Madrid 1926; M.J. Rubiera Mata, *La taifa de Denia*, Alicante 1985; C. Sarnelli Cerqua, *Mudjāhid al-^cĀmirī*, Cairo 1961; Peter C. Scales, *The fall of the caliphate of Córdoba. Berbers and Andalusis in conflict*, Leiden 1994; D. Wasserstein, *The rise and fall of the Party-Kings*, Princeton 1985; idem, *The caliphate in the West, an Islamic political institution in the Iberian peninsula*, Oxford 1993.

(P. GUICHARD and MOHAMED MEOUAK)

SAḲAR (A.), one of the terms employed in the Ḳur'ān (LIV, 48; LXXIV, 26-7, 42) to denote Hell or, more precisely, according to certain authorities, one of the gates of Hell (see e.g. al-Ṭabarī, on LIV, 48) or else one of the "stages" (*daraka, ṭabaḳa*, see al-Ṭabarī and al-Rāzī on LXXIV, 26). There is uncertainty amongst the lexicographers as to whether the word was of foreign origin (like *djahannam*) or whether it was derived from the Arabic root *s-ḳ-r*/*ṣ-ḳ-r*, meaning the extreme heat of the sun (see *L^cA*, s.r. *ṣ-ḳ-r*; one should note that Jeffery, for his part, does not mention it in his *Foreign vocabulary of the Qur'ān*). See also SA^cĪR.

Bibliography: See also T. O'Shaughnessy, *The seven names of Hell in the Qur'ān*, in *BSOAS*, xxiv (1961), 462-3.

(D. GIMARET)

SAKARYA (Ottoman orthography Saḳārya or Ṣaḳārya, modern Turkish Sakarya), a river in Turkey. It rises near Bayāt in the northeast of Āfyūn Ḳara Hiṣār. In its eastward course it enters the *wilāyet* or *il* of Ankara, through which it runs to a point above Čaḳmaḳ after receiving on its left bank the Sayyid Ghāzī Ṣū and several other tributaries on the same side. It then turns northwards describing a curve round Siwri Ḥiṣār. Here it receives on the right bank the Engürü Sūyu from Ankara and near this confluence the Porsuk on the opposite bank. A little to the south of this point is the bridge of the Eski-shehir-Ankara railway. Farther on, towards the north, the Sakarya receives on its right bank the Kirmir Ṣū, and then taking a sudden turn, it runs westwards to Lefke, traversing the former *wilāyet*s of Kütahya and Khudāwendigār. At Lefke the Sakarya is joined on the left by the Gök Ṣū from Bursa. After Lefke it turns sharply to the north, entering the district of Izmid near Mekedje, having now run 400 km/250 miles. The most flourishing part of its course now begins, and there are fine crops of cotton, wheat, vegetables, besides vineyards and the rearing of silkworms. It now runs in a north-easterly direction through the districts of Geiwe, Ada Pazārī and Ḳandīra, to enter the Black Sea near Indjirli. The stretch of its course in the district of Izmid is 112 km/70 miles; near Ada Pazārī it receives the waters of the Mudirni Ṣū from Kastamūni on the right bank and of the Čarkh Ṣū from lake Ṣabandja [*q.v.*]; on the left, 2 km/1¼ miles north of Geiwe is a bridge of six arches built by Sultan Bāyezīd I and at Lefke, Ewliyā Čelebi (iii, 11) also mentions a fine bridge of wood. The railway crosses the river four times between Izmid and Biledjik.

The Sakarya is the ancient Sangarius (see Pauly-Wissowa, Ser. 2, i, col. 2269, and J. Tischler, *Kleinasiatische Hydronymie*, Wiesbaden 1977, 129, where the name, including Hittite parallels, is discussed). It has changed its course since the Byzantine period, as is shown by the great bridge built by Justinian over it in 561, which is now 3 km/2 miles from Ada Pazārī. This bridge is now called *Besh Köprü* (in classical times Pentegephyra or Pontogephyra; see Ramsay, *The historical geography of Asia Minor*, London 1890, 214, 215), but at the present day the river no longer runs below its arches.

The Sakarya is not navigable; its lower course is only used for transporting to the Black Sea the wood from the thick forests of the neighbourhood. In prehistoric times, the river ran westwards into the Sea of Marmara; the lake of Ṣabandja [*q.v.*] and the Gulf of Izmid mark the track of its ancient course. In 909/1503 Sultan Selīm I conceived the idea of re-establishing communication between the Sakarya, the lake (the level of which is above that of the river) and the gulf in order to bring more easily to his capital the wood required for the building of his fleet. Being convinced of the feasibility of the project by the report of experts, he gave orders for its execution, but the opponents of the scheme were able to frustrate it by the argument of the *rishwet* (Ḥādjdjī Khalīfa, *Djihān-numā*, Constantinople 1145, 660; see further, ṢABANDJA).

For a period, in the reign of ^cOthmān I [*q.v.*], the Sakarya formed the frontier of his territory on the west and south, and for his conquests he had to cross the river (e.g. for the capture of Aḳ Ḥiṣār in 1308; see ^cĀshiḳ-pasha-zāde, *Ta'rīkh*, Istanbul 1332/1914, 12, 24), After then, the Sakarya did not play an important part in Ottoman history until the famous battle on the Sakarya from 24 August to 10 September 1921, when the Greek army was defeated in a last great effort to reach Ankara. By the counter-offensive of 10 September, the Greeks were thrown back to the west of the Sakarya and forced to take up the line Eski shehir-Afyūn Ḳara Ḥiṣār. In August 1922, the Turkish army was victorious for a second time near the Sakarya; this was the beginning of the Turkish offensive which ended in the complete reconquest of Anatolia and the hurling of the Greek armies into the sea at Izmir (see S.J. and E.K. Shaw, *History of the Ottoman empire and modern Turkey*, Cambridge 1976-7, ii, 360-3).

Sakarya is now the name of an *il* or province of modern Turkey, with its chef-lieu at Adapazarı [see ADA PĀZĀRĪ].

Bibliography: V. Cuinet, *La Turquie d'Asie*, iv, Paris 1894, 329 ff.; Sāmī, *Ḳāmūs al-a^clām*, iv, 2584; E. Banse, *Die Türkei*³, Brunswick 1919, 77, 79; Ch. Texier, *Description de l'Asie Mineure*, Paris 1849, i, 56 ff.; Berthe Georges Gaulis, *Angora-Constantinople-Londres*, Paris 1922, 89-98; for the geographical bibl., see Pauly-Wissowa, *loc. cit.*

(J.H. KRAMERS*)

AL-**SAKHĀWĪ**, Shams al-Dīn Abu 'l-Khayr Muḥammad b. ^cAbd al-Raḥmān al-Shāfi^cī, Egyptian *Ḥadīth* scholar and prosopographer (b. Rabī^c I 830/January 1427, d. Sha^cbān 902/April 1497).

He belonged to a prominent family of *^culamā'* who had settled in a quarter of the old Fāṭimid district of Cairo after migrating from the central Delta town of Sakhā two generations previously. Al-Sakhāwī excelled in his formal education, his performance typical for a student who planned to teach the Islamic sciences. Introduced to advanced studies in Prophetic traditions by the famous *shaykh* Ibn Ḥadjar al-^cAsḳalānī [*q.v.*], al-Sakhāwī soon acquired renown for his own mastery of *Ḥadīth*-related disciplines. Revering Ibn Ḥadjar as a paragon of erudition and piety, al-Sakhāwī dedicated his career to augmenting his mentor's accomplishments. But in fact, al-Sakhāwī's aptitudes inclined him toward the production of works remarkable more for their encyclopaedic scope than for their originality of method. Al-Sakhāwī's most noteworthy achievement was his massive biographical dictionary of 9th/15th-century notables, *al-Ḍaw᾽ al-lāmiᶜ fī aᶜyān al-ḳarn al-tāsiᶜ* (ed. Ḥusām al-Dīn al-Ḳudsī, 12 vols., Cairo 1353-5/1934-6). While the range and diversity of individuals included (the final volume dwells exclusively on women) render the *Ḍaw᾽* one of the foremost primary sources for research on the *ᶜulamā᾽* of the central Islamic lands in pre-modern times, the organisation of data in its myriad entries highlights those qualities most esteemed by the scholastic élite when they evaluated their own peers.

Al-Sakhāwī held several appointments as *Shaykh al-Ḥadīth* in distinguished religio-academic institutions of Cairo. He also travelled to the Syrian districts of the Mamlūk empire, witnessing recitations of *Ḥadīth*s by candidates for *idjāza* certificates and debating controversial texts with colleagues on numerous occasions in the provincial capitals. Al-Sakhāwī made his first pilgrimage in 870/July-August 1466 and returned to the Ḥidjāz on the Ḥadjdj twice again, spending subsequent years in scholarly residence there. He relished his sojourns in the holy cities as a signal opportunity to interact with scholars from the eastern Muslim world. In Cairo, he had provoked the ire of several rivals, notably the other eminent polymath of his age, al-Suyūṭī [*q.v.*], for his outspoken criticism of their compositions. Al-Sakhāwī decried the state of contemporary studies in Prophetic traditions, convinced they were declining in accuracy for three reasons: mediocre training in appropriate methods of transmission, limited knowledge of history and its applications to related disciplines, and parochial deviation from orthodox curricular norms. He summarised these views in a treatise on historical methods, *al-Iᶜlān bi 'l-tawbīkh li-man dhamma ahl al-ta᾽rīkh* (publ. Damascus 1349/1930-1, tr. F. Rosenthal as *The open denunciation of the adverse critics of the historians*, in *A history of Muslim historiography*, ²Leiden 1968, 263-529). Although significant in its own right as an inventory of technical definitions and applications of scholastic terminology, the *Iᶜlān* is perhaps al-Sakhāwī's outstanding theoretical achievement because its author insightfully portrayed the historian's craft and objectives, learned and religious, as they evolved from the classical period of Islam to his own day.

Although justifiably respected as a prominent figure of late mediaeval scholasticism, al-Sakhāwī disguised a propensity for personal vindictiveness against his adversaries and those of his associates under the guise of a pious wish to evaluate his contemporaries' moral probity in order to assess the validity of their opinions, both for interpretation of the *Sharīᶜa* and the giving of historical details. While often captivating, al-Sakhāwī's caustic opinions of his colleagues and derogatory remarks about their shortcomings must be weighed with caution. By contrast, his factual information is reliable due to its centrality in his encyclopaedic approach and to his keen awareness that opponents would expose any errors or distortions he committed in return for his denunciation of them and their works.

In his final years, al-Sakhāwī returned to the Ḥidjāz where he devoted his remaining energies to the completion or refinement of several texts and the training of students in *Ḥadīth* transmissions. He died in Medina.

Bibliography: Inventory of works: Brockelmann, II², 43-4, S II, 31-3, of which no. 3, *Dhayl duwal al-Islām* by al-Ṣafadī, is noteworthy for its details on events in the Ḥidjāz. See also al-Sakhāwī's autobiographical entry in his *Ḍaw᾽*, viii, 2-32, and his treatment by Ibn al-ᶜImād in *Shadharāt al-dhahab fī akhbār man dhahab*, Cairo 1340/1931-2, viii, 15-17. Secondary studies (in addition to Rosenthal cited above): A.J. Arberry, *Sakhawiana, a study based on the Chester Beatty Ms. Arab. 733*, Chester Beatty Monographs, no. 1, London 1951, which focuses on an *idjāza* written by al-Sakhāwī for the Ḥalabī scholar Ibn al-Ḥīshī appended to the latter's *K. al-Buldāniyyāt*; R.S. Humphreys, *Islamic history, a framework for inquiry*, rev. ed. Princeton 1991, ch. 8; Huda Lutfi, *Al-Sakhāwī's* Kitāb al-Nisā᾽ *as a source for the social and economic history of Muslim women during the fifteenth century A.D.*, in *MW*, lxxi (1981), 104-24; Bernadette Martel-Thoumian, *Les civils et l'administration dans l'état militaire mamlūk (ixᵉ/xvᵉ siècle)*, Damascus 1991, 15-24; C.F. Petry, *The civilian elite of Cairo in the later middle ages*, Princeton 1981, 5-14; W. Popper, *Sakhāwī's criticism of Ibn Taghrī Birdī*, in *Studi orientalistici in onore di Giorgio Levi della Vida*, Rome 1956, ii, 371-89. (C.F. Petry)

ṢAKHR, Banū, an Arab tribe in what is now Jordan.

The Mamlūk encyclopaedists Ibn Faḍl Allāh al-ᶜUmarī (d. 723/1341) and al-Ḳalḳashandī (d. 821/1418) mention this Djudhāmī-Ḳaḥṭānī tribe as living in the eastern plateau of the Mamlūk province of al-Karak [*q.v.*]. The tribe comprised the following six clans: al-Daᶜdjiyyūn, Banū Shadjāᶜ, al-Ḍabiyyūn, al-ᶜAtwiyyūn, Banū Wahrān, and Banū Hūbir.

The Ottoman *tapu defters* mention about 12 groups (*djemāᶜāt*). Each *djemāᶜa* is listed under its own *shaykh*, with the total number of tribesmen about 643 households plus 36 bachelors. The Ottoman state levied *ᶜādat* from them and the tribe of Karīm, which amounted to 38,000 *aḳčes*. Records from the 17th and 18th centuries provide no more information, while 19th-century and early 20th-century sources report on the tribe in detail, especially in the accounts of European travellers such as Musil. The clan names of the earliest records do not match those in the later ones.

In modern-day oral tradition, the Banū Ṣakhr are in origin an 18th-century tribe that came to Transjordan from the Ḥidjāz in the early 19th century. They first settled in southern Jordan and then moved north; thus they claim that their territory extended from the Ḥawrān in the north to the south of modern Jordan. Part of the tribe settled in the northern villages of the *sandjaḳ* of ᶜAdjlūn while others, the Ṣukhūr al-Ghūr (the Jordan Valley Ṣukhūr), settled in the fertile northern regions of the Jordan Valley.

The Banū Ṣakhr tribe played a significant role in the Transjordanian steppe (*bādiya*) because the Pilgrimage route between Damascus and the Ḥidjāz passed through their territory. The Ottoman state paid them a subsidy or *al-ṣurra* annually, but during periods of Ottoman weakness, or when they suspended payment of the annual allocations, the tribesmen would violate their commitments and loot the Pilgrimage caravan as it passed through their territory. One of many such cases was in 1753, when Shaykh Ḳaᶜdān al-Fāyiz looted the caravan, amongst whose members was the sister of the Ottoman sultan.

The tribe also levied their own taxes as *khāwa* from the neighbouring villages, particularly those in the *sandjaḳ* of ᶜAdjlūn. More often they simply raided the villagers' fields. Arabic press accounts provide plenty of information on looting and attacks against the villages of the *sandjaḳ* of ᶜAdjlūn, particularly Ramthā in the late 19th and early 20th centuries. They also rented out their camels as transport animals for the pilgrimage caravan, merchants and travellers. With the construction of the Ḥidjāz Railway [*q.v.*] in 1906, their role diminished and they shifted away from camel herding to raising sheep and goats.

After the Ottoman *Tanẓīmāt* reforms, the Banū Ṣakhr began to settle near abandoned sites with wells or reservoirs constructed by the Romans and later mantained and repaired by the Mamlūks and Ottomans. To encourage this process, the Ottomans treated some of the tribal *shaykhs* with dignity and gave them honorific titles. This put the *shaykhs* in a privileged position to register the lands within their territory under their own names.

The relations between the Banū Ṣakhr and the other tribes, such as the Ḥuwayiṭāt, the Banū ʿAtiyya, and the Sardiyya, were almost hostile and they often raided each other. But these tribes, especially the Banū Ṣakhr and Sardiyya, formed an alliance, fostered by intermarriage, known as *ʿArab al-Shimāl* ("Bedouin of the North") to face the invading ʿAnaza tribe and its clients. As in other tribes, there were continuous struggles for leadership among the prominent members of the tribe. This was very evident in the paramount house of al-Fāyiz.

With the establishment of the modern state of Jordan, law and order gradually prevailed. The late King ʿAbd Allāh adopted a new pacification policy and took steps to assimilate as many members of this tribe and other tribes as possible into the armed forces, especially in the Desert Patrol Forces. The Banū Ṣakhr now have their own elective constituency and since the establishment of the first legislative house in Jordan in 1928 they have had their own representation. They are now almost totally integrated into the fabric of the state. With the spread of education, a growing portion of this tribe is opting for agriculture and business and deserting their old way of life, so that nomadism among them has almost come to an end.

Bibliography: 1. Primary sources. Ibn Faḍl Allāh al-ʿUmarī, *Masālik al-abṣār fī mamālik al-amṣār*, University of Frankfurt, Institute for Arabic and Islamic Sciences 1988, iv, 134; Ḳalḳashandī, *Nihāyat al-adab fī maʿrifat ansāb al-ʿArab*, ed. Ibrāhīm al-Abyārī, Cairo 1959, 132; idem, *Ṣubḥ al-aʿshā*, xiv, 42, 243; Muhammad Adnan Bakhit and Noufan Raja Hmoud (eds.), *The Detailed Defter of Liwāʾ ʿAjlūn (the District of ʿAjlūn) Tapu Defteri no. 970, Istanbul*, ʿAmmān 1989, 130-6; eidem (eds.), *The Detailed Defter of Liwāʾ ʿAjlūn (the District of ʿAjlūn) Tapu Defteri no. 185, Ankara 1005 A.H./1596 A.D.*, ʿAmmān 1991, 260-70; Aḥmad al-Budayrī al-Ḥallāḳ (d. 1175/1761), *Ḥawādith Dimashḳ al-yawmiyya 1154-1175*, ed. Aḥmad ʿIzzat ʿAbd al-Karīm, Cairo 1959, 203-4; *al-Muḳtabas*, nos. 85, 313, 345 (Damascus 1910); Muḥammad Khalīl al-Murādī (d. 1206/1791), *Silk al-durar fī aʿyān al-ḳarn al-thānī ʿashar*, Baghdād n.d., ii, 60-2; *al-Sharḳ al-ʿArabī*, no. 133 (ʿAmmān 1926), no. 198 (1928).

2. Arabic secondary studies. Hind Ghassān Abū al-Shaʿr, *Irbid wa-djiwāruhā (Nāḥiyat Banī ʿUbayd) 1850-1928*, Ph.D. diss., University of Jordan 1994, unpubl.; Muḥammad ʿAdnān al-Bakhīt, *Mamlakat al-Karak fī 'l-ahd al-Mamlūkī*, ʿAmmān 1976, 23, 42; *Banū Sakhr: min Ṭayyiʾ*, in *Madjallat al-ʿArab*, i/1, year 12 (1397/1977), 415-18; Nūfān Radjā al-Ḥumūd, *ʿAmmān wa-djiwāruhā khilāl al-fatra 1281 h./1864 m.-1340 h./1921 m.*, Ph.D. diss., University of Jordan 1994, unpubl., 144-57; F. Peake, *Tārīkh sharḳī al-Urdunn wa-ḳabāʾiluhā*, tr. Bahāʾ al-Dīn Tūḳān, Jerusalem, 214-21; George Farīd Ṭarīf Dāwūd, *Madīnat al-Salṭ wa-djiwāruhā khilāl al-fatra 1281*/1864-1340/1921, Ph.D. diss., University of Jordan 1994, unpubl., 120, 195, 198-9, 200-1, 231, 272, 310-11, 314, 319.

3. Western secondary studies. G. Schumacher, *Abila, Petra and northern Ajlun*, 20, 30; E. Littmann, *Eine ämtliche Liste der Beduinenstämme des Ostjordanlandes*, in *ZDPV*, xxiv (1901), 26-31; A. Musil, *Arabia Petraea*, repr. Vienna 1989, 112-29; *A collection of First World War military handbooks of Arabia 1913-1917*, iv, *A handbook of Arabia. 1. General* (*1916*), Archive Editions 1988, 55-8; Max Freiherr von Oppenheim, *Die Beduinen*. ii. *Die Beduinenstämme in Palästina, Transjordanien Sinai, Hedjaz*, Leipzig 1943, 232-49; M.A. Bakhit, *The Ottoman province of Damascus in the sixteenth century*, Beirut 1982, 195, 209, 220.

(MOHAMMAD AL-BAKHIT)

SĀḲĪ (A.), cup-bearer, the person charged with pouring wine, to be distinguished from the chief butler or sommelier (*sharābī* or *ṣāḥib al-sharāb*). The chief butler, an important official of the ʿAbbāsid court and the great houses of the highest classes (M.M. Ahsan, *Social life under the ʿAbbāsids*, London 1979, 156), is not unreminiscent of the *sār ha-mashkīm* of the Pharaohs' court (Gen. xl, 1) and the Sāsānid *maybadh* (A. Christensen, *L'Iran sous les Sassanides*[2], Copenhagen 1944, 21-3, 389).

1. In Arabic usage.

During the *Djāhiliyya*, *sāḳī* had a double connotation: on one hand, it denoted the generous man who gave water to thirsty persons when water was scarce, and as such, deserved high praise (al-Aʿshā, 273 ll. 5-6, poet Aʿshā Tamīm; Muḥammad b. Ḥabīb, *al-Munammaḳ*, 279; al-Khansāʾ, *Dīwān*, ed. Cheikho, 136 l. 12); on the other hand, it meant the person who gave out wine. The first sense was rapidly eclipsed, and only the second one remained, the subject of this article. *Sāḳī* meaning cup-bearer seems to have been in current usage in pre-Islamic and Umayyad poetry (*al-Aṣmaʿiyyāt*, ed. Ahlwardt, 8 l. 8; Salāma b. Djandal, *Dīwān*, ed. Cheikho, 14 l. 2; *Ḥamāsa*, 400 l. 11). Synonyms or quasi-synonyms are attested: *mudīr* (noun of agent from *adāra* "to circulate", Ibn al-Muʿtazz, *K. Fuṣūl al-tamāthīl*, 133, poet Muslim b. al-Walīd; Ibn Sanāʾ al-Mulk, *Dīwān*, Ḥaydarābād 1377/1958, 319); *khādim*, from the later Umayyad period (al-Walīd b. Yazīd, *Dīwān*, Beirut 1967, 29; al-Shābushtī, *Diyārāt*, 60, 70); and the paraphrase *dhū zudjādjāt* (the one who holds the glasses, al-Aʿshā, 45 v. 41). Essentially, the *Djāhilī* poets attached to the court of al-Ḥīra [*q.v.*], such as al-Aʿshā, ʿAdī b. Zayd, and at Djilliḳ, Ḥassān b. Thābit, had variations on this theme for many decades. Al-Aʿshā describes the *sāḳī* dressed in a *sirbāl* or tunic which he hitched up in order to be able to move more freely, and he protected his mouth by a piece of linen cloth (*fidām*), following the usage of Zoroastrian priests, which served as a filter for tasting the drink and also so that he could know the precise taste; the adjective *mufaddam* is used to denote such a *sāḳī*. Also, he had two pearls hanging from his ears (*nuṭaf, luʾluʾ, tūma, mutawwam*), and he smeared his hands with red *farsīd* (al-Aʿshā, 45 v. 41, 52 v. 21, 178 vv. 34-5, 200 vv. 6-7, 214 v. 24). In pre-Islamic times, at al-Ḥīra, drinking was done in the Persian fashion, as the terms employed for such proceedings, including those concerning the *sāḳī*, readily attest.

We are poorly informed about the social origins of these servants, but it is very likely that, outside the Syrian and ʿIrāḳī centres, they came with the *tudjdjār* or peripatetic wine-suppliers. However, references to female *sāḳiyas* indicate that this service was reserved for captives in war or in raids, hence it was a degrading task (Djarīr and al-Farazdaḳ, *Naḳāʾiḍ*, Leiden 1905-12, 1068).

In fact, the cup-bearer had to work hard, since he had various tasks to fulfil during the time which the drinking-session lasted. He filled cups and presented them to the participants, decanted the wine after broaching (*bazala*) the jars (*dinān*), mixed the wine with water (*ḳatal*), filtered it and even aged it (*ṣahbāʾu ʿattaḳahā li-sharb^in sāḳi*, al-Azharī, *Tahdhīb al-lugha*, i, 6 l. 4, poet Salāma b. Djandal; ʿUmar b. Abi 'l-Rabīʿa, *Dīwān*, Leipzig 1902, 47 l.10; *Simṭ al-laʾālī*, i, 554 l. 6, ii, 888 l. 9; al-Akhṭal, *Dīwān*, Beirut 1891, 3 l. 6, 321 l. 8; *LʿA*, vii, 7 l. 13). Under the ʿAbbāsids, the evolution of taverns meant for the cup-bearer an increased amount of work; the *khammāra* or *ḥānūt* could extend over two or even three storeys, entailing new procedures. A miniature of Sulṭān Muḥammad, illustrating a poem of Ḥāfiẓ, allows us to follow the *sāḳī*'s work: on the ground floor, a young, beardless cup-bearer takes up a full jar, and attaches it to a cord drawn by a colleague in order to serve the drinkers; on the second storey, another *sāḳī* empties a *dann* and pours the drink into a goblet (S.C. Welch, *Wonders of the age. Masterpieces of early Safavid painting*, Cambridge, Mass. 1979, no. 44, 128-9). Very often, even during the Djāhiliyya, a single server was not enough; this explains the need for two servers (*al-sāḳiyān^i*) for one *madjlis* or session (al-Ḥuṭayʾa, *Dīwān*, in *ZDMG*, xlvii, 78 l. 17; al-Azharī, ii, 259; Dhu 'l-Rumma, *Dīwān*, Cambridge 1919, 609, v. 45). On the other hand, girls were not good for this work. The *sāḳiya* is rarely found in the older period, but more frequently under the ʿAbbāsids (ʿAmr b. Ḳamīʾa, *Dīwān*, 29 l. 1; *Djamharat nasab Ḳuraysh*, i, 233; al-Aʿshā, 36 l. 1, evokes a young serving girl called al-Rabāb; for the ʿAbbāsids, see *Aghānī*³, xiii, 78, Ḥammād ʿAdjrad; Ibn al-Muʿtazz, *Ṭabaḳāt al-shuʿarāʾ*, Cairo 1968, 79, 85-6, poet Abu 'l-Shīṣ; al-Sarī al-Raffāʾ, *Dīwān*, 712, vv. 6-13). Finally, the anonymous poet cited by al-Djāḥiẓ affirms that the ideal *sāḳiya* should be a young girl between puberty and being nubile (*Rasāʾil*, Cairo, ii, 96). The sexual connotations need to be taken into account here, especially with the appearance of *ghulāmiyyāt* at the time of al-Amīn, who distributed the wine to the topers in the most private *madjālis*; their use is said to have been thought up by Umm Djaʿfar to distract the caliph's pronounced taste for catamites (al-Masʿūdī, *Murūdj*, Beirut 1974, v, 213-14 = §§ 3451-2). However, one should note in this connection that ʿAdī b. Zayd al-ʿIbādī, describing sessions amongst the Lakhmids (*Dīwān*, Baghdād 1385/1965, 78-9 vv. 13-17), and Ḥassān, mentioning another one amongst the Ghassānids (*Dīwān*, London 1971, 91), evoke the *ḳaynas* [*q.v.*] as fulfilling the function of cup-bearer. This second author states that this was only for a short period of time. They could, thus, be used in such milieux, and there were no obstacles to their undertaking this task.

The theme preserves a remarkable stability up to the beginning of the ʿAbbāsid period. Authors are content to describe the dress and deportment of the cup-bearer and to recount the various obligations which he had to fulfil. Libertines like Muṭīʿ b. Iyās and Ḥammād ʿAdjrad, and inveterate topers like Abu 'l-Hindī, display a rather surprising conservatism with regard to the *sāḳī*; everyone is happy to repeat al-Aʿshā and other *Djāhilī* poets. The extensive changes introduced into the world of wine with regard to the places of drinking, the distributor of the drinks and the social surroundings of the drinkers, are hardly mentioned. It is only with Wāliba b. al-Ḥubāb, the master of Abū Nuwās, that the essential step forward was made; he asked sexual favours of his *sāḳī* (*Aghānī*, Cairo 1390/1970, xviii, 100). Henceforward, the correspondence between the Ganymede and the cup-bearer is perfect. This personage of Greek mythology served as the cup-bearer, and, according to some, as the sexual companion of Zeus. Under the Romans, Ganymede assumed the role of cup-bearer and mignon (Pauly-Wissowa, i/13, 739, section *Hellenistisch-römische Zeit*). Moreover, in mediaeval Latin poetry the one who hands round the wine bestows his favours also on the drinkers.

Nevertheless, it is with Abū Nuwās [*q.v.*] that this personage assumes firm shape and becomes one of the main protagonists in Bacchic poetry. The effeminate character of the *sāḳī* takes shape and, indeed, assumes its definitive form. This involves a young boy, graceful and coquettish like a girl. His swaying bearing reveals his well-endowed hindquarters; he smears his eyes with collyrium, perfumes his hair and adorns his forehead and temples with a kiss-curl in the form of scorpions or of an elongated letter *nūn*. His voice and pronunciation are identical with those of women. He is clearly submissive and ready to consent to the advances of the topers. He is at one and the same time a cup-bearer, a mignon and a singer with an agreable voice. The poets have no compunction in adopting here the most frank modes of expression, especially as these mignons-servers were Christian *dhimmīs* wearing the distinguishing girdle or *zunnār* (J. Bencheikh, *Poésies bachiques d'Abū Nuwās, thèmes et personnages*, in *BEO*, xviii [1963-4], 62-3). Finally, this same poet transformed the *sāḳī* into a symbol of love in the manner of city-dwellers. By his intervention, he was able to give full rein to his hostility towards the Bedouins. In his *khamriyyāt*, he contrasts the happiness arising from possession of a cup-bearer and the perpetual unsatisfied yearning of the lover of Hind, Asmāʾ and Zaynab (A. Arazi, *Abū Nuwās, fut-il shuʿūbite?*, in *Arabica*, xxvi [1979], 14-15). From the 3rd/9th century onwards, this theme becomes a conventional one. The poets have no other way of treating this protagonist of Bacchic poetry in his double role of cup-bearer and mignon dispensing carnal favours. He becomes a stereotype; the same motifs, encounters, and even metaphors, recur amongst the poets over the centuries. Furthermore, he comes into relief, from this time onwards, in *adab* literature; the various anthologies devote chapters to him which go over the same material (see *Bibl.*).

The neighbouring Jewish and Persian cultures adopted the personage and the relevant motifs. The term, in its Arab form, is found in each one equally (H. Brody and J. Schirmann, *Secular poems*, Jerusalem 1974, dedicatee of poem, p. 24; Masʿūd-i Saʿd-i Salmān, *Dīwān*, ed. Yāsimī, 639). Hebrew poetry, with Samuel ha-Nagid (993-1056) (*Divan*, Jerusalem 1966, 88, 284, 286, 290, 294), Saloman ibn Gabirol (1020-57) (*Secular poems*, Jerusalem 1974, 24, 82) and Moshe ibn Ezra (1055-1135), imitate in every point the Arabic one (see Schirmann, *La poésie hébraïque en Espagne et en Provence*, Jerusalem-Tel Aviv 1959, 373, 391; idem, *The ephebe in medieval Hebrew poetry*, in *Sefarad*, xv [1955], 55-68; Y. Ratzabi, *The drinking songs of Samuel ha-Nagid*, in *Annual of Bar-Ilan Univ. in Judaica and the Humanities*, Ramat-Gan 1972, 423-74).

For Persian literature, see the following section.

Bibliography: In addition to references given in the text, see al-Aʿshā, *Dīwān*, ed. Geyer, London 1928, 36, 45, 52, 178, 200, 214, 273; Ibn al-Muʿtazz, *K. Fuṣūl al-tamāthīl fi tabāshīr al-surūr*, Damascus 1414/1989, 141-6; al-Sarī al-Raffāʾ,

Dīwān, Bag̲h̲dād 1981, i, 341, 404, 409, ii, 134, 205-6, 244-5, 290, 474, 582-3, 591-2, 712, 716-17, 732; idem, *al-Muḥibb wa 'l-maḥbūb wa 'l-mas̲h̲mūm wa 'l-mas̲h̲rūb*, Damascus 1407/1986, 259-72; Ibn S̲h̲uhayd, *Dīwān*, ed. Pellat, Beirut, 28, 39, 77-8, 81-3, 134; S̲h̲ābus̲h̲tī, *Diyārāt*, Bag̲h̲dād 1386/1966, 13, 58, 60, 65, 70-1, 167, 208, 211, 224, 229, 262, 287-8, 290, 292, 338; Kus̲h̲ād̲j̲im, *Adab al-nadīm*, Bag̲h̲dād 1990, passim; Nawād̲j̲ī, *Ḥalbat al-kumayt*, Cairo 1357/1938, 145-66; Nuwayrī, *Nihāyat al-arab*, vi, 149-52; A. Mez, *Die Renaissance des Islams*, Heidelberg 1922, Eng. tr. 357 ff.; H. Pérès, *La poésie andalouse en arabe classique au XIe siècle*, Paris 1953, 364-72; D.S. Rice, *Deacon or drink: some paintings from Sāmarrā re-examined*, in *Arabica*, v (1958), 15-33; D̲j̲amīl Saʿīd, *Taṭawwur al-k̲h̲amriyyāt fī 'l-s̲h̲iʿr al-ʿarabī min al-D̲j̲āhiliyya ilā Abī Nuwās*, Cairo 1945, 44-5, 63; ʿAlī S̲h̲alak, *G̲h̲azal Abī Nuwās*, Beirut 1954, 87-95; Muḥammad Muḥammad Ḥusayn, *Aṣālīb al-ṣināʿa fī s̲h̲iʿr al-k̲h̲amr wa 'l-nāḳa*, Alexandria 1960, 7-8, 15 ff. (A. ARAZI)

2. In Persian usage.

The *sāḳī* appears in New Persian literature as early as the 3rd/9th century in the poetry of Abū S̲h̲akūr of Balk̲h̲ (G. Lazard, *Les premiers poètes persans*, 2 vols., Paris 1964, i, 80, ii, 95). Niẓām al-Mulk (*Siyāsat-nāma*, ed. H. Darke, Tehran 1340/1962, 132-3) describes how Turkish slaves were trained during the Sāmānid period, though no longer in his own times. In the sixth year of an eight-year cycle in which the slave was trained for both military and domestic service, he could be made a cup bearer. The *sāḳī*s were considered part of the private staff of a ruler and they would stand near or around the throne (*ibid.*, 55). In the G̲h̲aznavid court they could also act as food tasters (Abu 'l-Faḍl Bayhaḳī, *Tārīk̲h̲*, ed. ʿA.A. Fayyāḍ, Mas̲h̲had 1350/1971, 527-9). At the court of Maḥmūd of G̲h̲azna, the *sāḳī*s were as close to the ruler as were the *nadīm*s (*ibid.*, 4). Physical beauty was important in the choice of individuals to be wine servers. Bayhaḳī (329-30, 527-9) describes festive occasions when the *sāḳī*s, whom he calls *māhrūyān* "moon-faced", would appear splendidly attired and attract the amorous glances of courtiers. These characteristics of the *sāḳī*, sc. being a Turk, military training, exceptional beauty, and closeness to the ruler, help explain the image of the *sāḳī* as it developed in poetry after the 5th/11th century.

As the influence of mystical thought became more widespread in Persia, the *sāḳī* developed into a "type" and became an important character among the *dramatis personae* of Persian lyric poetry. He is generally identified with the object of love and the same epithets are applied to him as to the earthly beloved. The two genres in which the *sāḳī* appears most prominently are the *g̲h̲azal* and the *sāḳī-nāma*. The mystical imagery of wine-drinking was well developed by the 8th/14th century, and two examples will be mentioned that show something of the nature of the *sāḳī* in this context. K̲h̲ʷād̲j̲ū Kirmānī (679-753 or 762/1281-1352 or 61), an older contemporary of Ḥāfiẓ, has a *g̲h̲azal* (*Dīwān*, ed. A. Suhaylī K̲h̲ʷānsārī, Tehran 336/1957, 331-2, no. 325) addressed to the *sāḳī* in which the wine server is intoxicatingly beautiful (with the conventional attributes of physical beauty), an idol, the K̲h̲iḍr of the age, the physician for the pain of separation, the ever-shining sun, and the never-waning moon that lights the sun. He serves the water of eternal life and the wine of union.

The *sāḳī-nāma* developed from a two-verse apostrophe beginning *biyā sāḳī* "Come, Sāḳī", the first known example being from a *mathnawī* in the mutaḳārib metre by Fak̲h̲r al-Dīn Gurgānī (*fl. ca.* 442/1050). Niẓāmī used it throughout his *S̲h̲araf-nāma*, as did his imitators in their romances of Alexander, and this apostrophe came to be called a *sāḳī-nāma*. Ḥāfiẓ wrote a *mathnawī* in *mutaḳārib* beginning *biyā sāḳī...*, and on this model there gradually developed a separate genre in the same metre and form wherein the speaker calls to the *sāḳī* for wine and complains of the instability of the world, the fickleness of destiny, and the inconstancy of his beloved. A recent example of the genre by G̲h̲. Raʿdī Ād̲h̲arak̲h̲s̲h̲ī is entitled *Biraw sāḳī...* "Go, Sāḳī" (*Āyanda*, v [1358/1979], 1-4).

Bibliography: G. Jacob, *Das Weinhaus nebst Zubehör nach den Ġazelen des Ḥāfiẓ*, in *Orientalische Studien Theodor Nöldeke ... gewidmet*, ed. C. Bezold, 2 vols., Giessen 1906, ii, 1055-76; E. Yarshater, *The theme of wine drinking and the concept of the beloved in early Persian poetry*, in *SI*, xix (1960), 43-53; M.D̲j̲. Maḥd̲j̲ūb, *Sāḳī nāma—mug̲h̲annī nāma*, in *Suk̲h̲an*, xiii (1339-40/1960-1), 69-79; A. Gulčīn Maʿānī, *Tad̲h̲kira-yi paymāna*, Mas̲h̲had 1359/1980; ʿAbd al-Nabī Fak̲h̲r al-Zamānī Ḳazwīnī, *Tad̲h̲kira-yi maykhāna*, ed. A. Gulčīn Maʿānī, Tehran 1363/1984. (W.L. HANAWAY)

3. Representations in Islamic art.

The fluctuating prominence of the *sāḳī* (m.) and the *sāḳiya* (f.) as a pictorial theme reflects phases of artistic development as well as variations in customs, etiquette and social status. *Sāḳī*s are portrayed in a variety of circumstances, from attendants at a court to servants in a tavern or as participants in drinking parties in which distinctions between the server and the served are often moot. During the 2nd/8th to 6th/12th centuries rulers and princely figures, although often portrayed cup in hand, are only rarely shown in the company of a *sāḳī*; the rulers' rigid frontal posture gives such images a formulaic quality (Mirjam Gelfer-Jørgenson, *The Islamic paintings in Cefalù Cathedral, Sicily*, in *Hafnia* [1978], 131-41).

Despite their rarity, early Islamic depictions of the *sāḳī* have historical importance. Both Sāsānid court protocol and themes drawn from Dionysiac imagery are reflected in early Islamic representations. The scene of wine-drinking depicted on a silver platter, attributed to 2nd/8th-century Persia, and now in the Hermitage Museum, St. Petersburg, shows various facets of the *sāḳī*'s role. The focal point of its composition is a princely figure, surrounded by attendants, reclining on a couch while holding a wine bowl in one hand and a flower stalk in the other hand. The foreground is occupied by a much smaller figure who appears to be a *sāḳī*. He stands with crossed hands resting on his chest and his mouth is covered by a protective mask similar to that worn by Zoroastrian priests, probably to avoid polluting the cup with his breath or saliva, a custom mentioned by the pre-Islamic poet al-Aʿs̲h̲ā (see above, section 1; J.K. Choksy, *Purity and pollution in Zoroastrianism*, Austin 1989, 84-6, fig. 12). The tools of his trade appear to the right—a ewer and a tripod supporting a sieve through which wine is being filtered into a two-handled jug. Judging by his small size, this *sāḳī* was a relatively humble servant. A larger attendant stands behind the reclining drinker while two seated musicians face the latter (V.G. Lukonin, *Iskusstvo drevnego Irana*, Moscow 1977, 169).

A fragmentary wall painting discovered in the ruins of an ʿAbbāsid palace at Sāmarrā [*q.v.*] depicts two *sāḳiya*s, with a flask in one hand and a bowl in the other. Each pours wine into the other's bowl, which hints at other ceremonial aspects of winedrinking (E. Herzfeld, *Die Malereien von Samarra*, Berlin 1927, 9-13, pls. I-III; Janine Sourdel-Thomine, B. Spuler *et alii*, *Die Kunst des Islam*, Berlin 1973, 223, pl. XXIII). Their dancing posture and interlocked arms suggest that they were mixing wine to a musical accompaniment. R. Ettinghausen has linked this painting with a Sāsānid adaptation of Dionysiac themes, such as the scantily clad women who dance or play musical instruments depicted on Sasanian silver vessels (*Dionysiac motifs*, in *From Byzantium to Sasanian Iran and the Islamic world*, Leiden 1972, 4-5, 9). The ʿAbbāsid poet Abu 'l-ʿAbbās al-Nā<u>sh</u>ī describes a wine bowl adorned with bending and coquettish women, and Abū Nuwās mentions a *sāḳiya* who performs a pagan ritual as she mixes wine and water (I.<u>Yu</u> Kračkovskiy, *Sasanidskaya ča<u>sh</u>a v sti<u>kh</u>a<u>kh</u> Abū Nuvāsa*, in *Izbrannye sočineniya*, Moscow 1956, 340; idem, *Abū Nuvās o Sasanidskoy ča<u>sh</u>e*, in *ibid.*, 389-91).

Both *sāḳīs* and *sāḳiyas* appear in depictions of Islamic princes or rulers in various media. Four female attendants, including two musicians and a *sāḳiya*, are shown in attendance around the seated ruler who is depicted on a silver platter, which has been attributed to early 3rd/9th-century Marw, now in the Hermitage Museum. The *sāḳiya* standing to the ruler's left holds a ewer in one hand and a piece of fruit in the other (B. Marschak, *Silberschätze des Orients*, Leipzig 1986, 76-7, figs. 30, 32). More commonly shown, however, are *sāḳīs*. One is depicted in a vignette from the ceiling of the Capella Palatina in Palermo, built in 1140, where he holds both a cup and a flask (R. Ettinghausen, *Arab painting*, Geneva 1962, 44-5). The Hermitage owns a silver vessel, attributed to <u>Kh</u>urāsān *ca.* 90/1000, which depicts a seated prince flanked by two youths in Turkish attire; one holds a flower, the other a ewer and cup (Marschak, *op. cit.*, 77-8, fig. 33).

Literary references suggest that by the 4th/10th century a Turkish youth was considered the ideal *sāḳī*. When the vizier al-Muhallabī was offered a drink of water at the palace of the caliph al-Muṭīʿ (334-63/946-74 [*q.v.*]), he was allowed to keep not only the service, a golden tray and a crystal jug covered with a piece of silk-brocade, but also the server, "a Turkish *<u>gh</u>ulām* with an unblemished visage and beautiful clothes" (Hilāl al-Ṣābī, *Rusūm dār al-<u>kh</u>ilāfa*, ed. M. ʿAwwād, Ba<u>gh</u>dād 1383/1964, 69). The mechanical *sāḳī* described by al-<u>Dj</u>azarī [*q.v.* in Suppl.] in his book on mechanical devices is characterised as a "ten-year old slave" who wears a short tunic and cap. He holds a glass cup in his right hand and a fish in his left. At prescribed intervals wine flows through the fish into the glass. The glass can be removed and the wine drunk. After the glass is returned to the *sāḳī*'s hand the process is repeated. A youthful *sāḳī* holding a ewer and cup also stands by the ruler's side in a mechanical boat filled with drinking figures which can be floated on a basin during festivities (*The Book of knowledge of ingenious mechanical devices*, tr. D.R. Hill, Dordrecht 1974, 107, 118, pls. XIV, XVII).

During the rule of slave dynasties such as the Atabegs in Syria or the Mamlūks of Egypt and Syria, youthful slaves chosen as an *amīr*'s or sultan's personal servants, including his *sāḳī*, acquired an increased importance and often rose to high rank in later life. *Sāḳīs* are depicted along with weapon-bearers clustered around seated rulers in paintings and on inlaid metalwork produced in ʿIrāḳ and Syria during the 6th/12th to 8th/14th centuries (Estelle Whelan, *The Khāṣṣakīyah and the origins of Mamluk emblems*, in *Content and context of visual arts in the Islamic world*, ed. Priscilla Soucek, University Park 1988, 220-4). A *sāḳī* standing with a cup in his right hand and a flask in his left is shown among other courtiers on the Mamlūk basin inlaid by Muḥammad Ibn al-Zayn now in the Louvre and often referred to as the "Baptistère de St. Louis" (Esin Atil, *Renaissance of Islam: art of the Mamluks*, Washington, D.C. 1981, 21-2). Among the Mamlūks, in particular, the *sāḳī*'s goblet was transformed from a token of servitude to an indicator that its bearer belonged to a privileged élite. Schematic drawings of a footed goblet appear on objects or structures belonging to *sāḳīs* or former *sāḳīs*. It was used as such by Sultan Kitbu<u>gh</u>ā both before and after his accession to the throne (Whelan, *op. cit.*, 230, 234; L.A. Mayer, *Saracenic heraldry*, Oxford 1933, 5, 10-11 and *passim*).

The world of the *sāḳī* was not restricted to the courts of rulers or their *amīrs*, for they were also employed in public taverns. The range of tasks they performed there is vividly illustrated in a painting from a manuscript of al-Ḥarīrī's *Maḳāmāt* dated to 634/1237. It shows the entire cycle of wine production and consumption in a two-storey tavern. On the lower level, grape juice flows out of a basin in which a youth tramples grapes, and another youth strains the juice through a cloth-covered vessel supported on a tripod. Two youths pass a wine jug from the first to second floor. Nearby, two men seated at a table drink wine from cups (Paris, B.N., ms. ar. 5847 fol. 33a; D. and Janine Sourdel, *La civilisation de l'Islam classique*, Paris 1968, 432, fig. 169). This condensed depiction may suggest that the beverage being consumed was only slightly fermented (J. Sadan, *Vin – fait de civilisation*, in *Studies in memory of Gaston Wiet*, ed. Miriam Rosen-Ayalon, Jerusalem 1977, 132-3).

The most significant transformations of the *sāḳī*'s visual role, however, occurred in post-Mongol Persia. The Mongols and their successors, particularly the Tīmūrids, were dynasties whose appetite for alcoholic beverages often reached epic proportions, and painters frequently depict both the serving and drinking of intoxicants in court settings. Under the Mongols, a form of official court portraiture existed in which a ruler and his consort were portrayed on a throne surrounded by their attendants, officials and relatives. Typically, the ruler and his consort appear to be drinking wine from shallow cups. One or more *sāḳīs* kneel before their throne holding a golden tray ready to replenish their cups from flasks standing on a nearby table (Filiz Çağman and Zeren Tanındı, *The Topkapı Saray Museum: the albums and illustrated manuscripts*, tr. J.M. Rogers, Boston 1986, 69, pls. 43, 44).

During the 8th/14th and 9th/15th centuries, features of these Mongol paintings—the table loaded with flasks, the kneeling *sāḳī*, and drinkers in a more naturalistic pose—are echoed in many subsequent depictions, even those produced for anonymous patrons which illustrate literary texts such as the *Shāhnāma* of Firdawsī or the *<u>Kh</u>amsas* of Niẓāmī and <u>Kh</u>usraw Dihlawī (*ibid.*, 89, pl. 56; T.W. Lentz and G.D. Lowry, *Timur and the princely vision*, Los Angeles 1989, cat. no. 21, p. 66, 110-11). Tīmūr's grandson Bāysun<u>gh</u>ur b. <u>Sh</u>āh Ru<u>kh</u> is even shown with a wine cup in hand and attended by *sāḳīs*, one of whom kneels, while on horseback at a hunt (*ibid.*, 132, fig. 132).

The most detailed presentation of the *sāḳī*'s role in Tīmūrid court life comes in the frontispiece of a *Bustān* of Saʿdī, now in Cairo, made for Sultan Ḥusayn Bāyḳarā and dated to 893/1488. This double-page painting executed by Bihzād shows a drinking party in progress. Even though several participants have already succumbed to the effects of alcohol, five *sāḳīs* on the right page prepare another round of drinks.

Two decant wine from an unglazed jug into flasks while another pair pours an unidentified liquid from a smaller silver flask through a funnel into a gold one. The fifth *sāḳī*, holding a spouted ewer, stands waiting, perhaps to mix water with the wine. Below them, a servant carrying a twohandled jug rushes toward the royal party. On the far left of the left-hand page, two more *sāḳīs* stand with tray and flask ready to fill any empty cups. This painting also hints at the court production of alcoholic beverages. In the upper right, above the five *sāḳīs*, is a building containing a large earthenware vessel which may be a wine-cellar. In front of this structure, two Indians sit near a distilling apparatus, possibly producing distilled spirits (*ibid.*, cat. no. 146, 260-61, 286).

A true fusion between the *sāḳī*'s practical and literary roles comes only in Ṣafawid paintings, which combine the relaxed and informal mood of the Tīmūrid drinking party with literary allusions. The best examples of this juxtaposition of the mundane and the mystical illustrate the poetry of Ḥāfiẓ. Two such paintings belong to a *dīwān* of Ḥāfiẓ made for Sām Mīrzā, the younger brother of S̲h̲āh Ṭahmāsp I; one depicts a prince and his courtiers celebrating the end of Ramaḍān, the other shows a drinking party in a tavern attended by both dervishes and angels. In the festival scene it is the s̲h̲āh, not the *sāḳī*, whom Ḥāfiẓ compares to the moon, and his appearance becomes a signal for the serving of wine to celebrate the end of Ramaḍān. As a *sāḳī* hands the prince a golden wine-cup, a veritable parade of attendants carrying golden flasks on silver trays prepare to serve his guests, and two of them distribute bottles among the celebrants. Another painting from this manuscript explores the metaphor of intoxication as path to salvation and divine union. Even the ''angel of mercy'' shown on the building's roof offers other angels a cup of wine. In the building and its surroundings, several *sāḳīs* ply their trade. One reaches deep into a large jar to fill the flask of a celebrant who brandishes a book in one hand as if trying to exchange it for wine, while others hold wine cups or wine jugs. The link between intoxication and poetic inspiration is alluded to by a white-bearded man, who tries to read in an inebriated state (S.C. Welch, *Persian painting*, New York 1976, 66-9, pls. 17, 18; Priscilla Soucek, *Sultan Muhammad Tabrizi: painter at the Safavid court*, in *Persian masters: five centuries of painting*, ed. Sheila Canby, Bombay 1990, 58-61).

Few paintings rival these in the subtlety and complexity of their interplay of visual and verbal conventions, but it is in the later 10th/16th and 11th/17th centuries that the *sāḳī or sāḳiya* emerges as an independent artistic theme in drawings or paintings designed to be mounted in albums. These *sāḳīs* or *sāḳiyas* stand in coquettish poses or project a langorous and often androgynous sensuality, attributes of the cup-bearer long stressed in the literary tradition (A. Welch, *Shah Abbas and the arts of Isfahan*, New York 1973, 32, 65, 72, 82, nos. 11, 50; I. Stchoukine, *Les peintures des manuscrits de Shah ʿAbbas Ier*, Paris 1954, 189, 193, pls. XXV-XXVI, XXX-XXXIII, LXXV, LXXVII-LXXIX; Marie Lukens Swietochowski and Sussan Babaie, *Persian drawings in the Metropolitan Museum of Art*, New York 1989, nos. 58-9, 74-7, nos. 24, 32-3). Remnants of similar paintings have been uncovered in the walls of Ṣafawid palaces such as the Čihil Sutūn and ʿĀlī Ḳapu and particularly in their private inner chambers (Babaie, *Safavid palaces at Isfahan: continuity and change (1590-1666)*, Ph.D. diss. New York University 1993, unpubl., 171-4, 183, 188-9, figs. 160-2, 169-72, 175-7).

The pairing of youthful *sāḳīs* with bearded men was evidently considered particularly appropriate to the poetry of Ḥāfiẓ. Two mid-11th/17th-century Ḥāfiẓ manuscripts, one in Dublin, Chester Beatty, ms. P. 299, the other in Istanbul, Topkapı Sarayı, H. 1010, are virtual albums (A.J. Arberry, B.W. Robinson *et alii*, *The Chester Beatty Library: a catalogue of the Persian manuscripts and miniatures*, Dublin 1962, 68; F.E. Karatay, *Farsça yazmalar kataloğu*, Istanbul 1962, 221, no. 645). The Dublin manuscript has 450 tinted drawings on 500 folios, and the Istanbul one 555 on 578 folios. Most of them juxtapose a youthful *sāḳī* and an older man.

Depictions of the *sāḳī* and *sāḳiya* in Islamic art have strong parallels with the descriptions of these figures in the literary tradition. Despite their initial role as servants, some came to embody an ideal of beauty which inspired poets and painters alike. This evolution, apparent in literature as early as in the 4th-5th/9th-10th centuries, became prominent in painting only later, especially under the Ṣafawids.

Bibliography: Given in the article.

(PRISCILLA P. SOUCEK)

AL-**SAḲĪFA**, SAḲĪFAT BANĪ SĀʿIDA. The word *saḳīfa* (*LʿA*, s.v.), an approximate synonym of *ṣuffa* (*LʿA*, s.v.: *bahw, mawḍiʿ muẓallal*), denotes in Arabic a covered communal place appropriate for conversation and discussion. While the word *ṣuffa* seems rather to be applied to the space covered with palm foliage which constituted the primitive mosque (see MASD̲J̲ID. I, 2), *saḳīfa* appears to denote any type of forum or public courtyard, covered in accordance with the same traditional procedures.

In historical texts, the term is applied virtually exclusively to the prolonged and acerbic negotiations which preceded the nomination of Abū Bakr as successor to the Prophet Muḥammad in the leadership of the nascent community. These took place at Medina in the summer of 11/632, on the territory of the Banū Sāʿida, a K̲h̲azrad̲j̲ī clan of the Anṣār [*q.v.*]. The expression *saḳīfat Banī Sāʿida*, usually shortened to *al-saḳīfa* or *yawm al-saḳīfa* in the texts, is furthermore invariably applied to this specific historical episode.

The texture of the narrative, which figures in practically all accounts of the beginnings of the community, presented in the earliest times not as a continuous narration but in the form of *ḥadīt̲h̲*, as a result of which it has become an article of faith in Sunni Islam, generally comprises the following elements:

(1) Respective merits of Abū Bakr and of ʿUmar. The Prophet had always shown a certain preference for his two original Companions, but possibly with a bias in favour of ʿUmar. The influence of ʿĀʾis̲h̲a [*q.v.*], who openly admired the latter, is perhaps not irrelevant in this context. The Prophet's explicit appointment of Abū Bakr to lead the Prayer in his place, which is often evoked, remains inconclusive in that it does not relate formally to the political leadership of the community. Always present in this narrative, ʿUmar was furthermore to play the role of elder statesman to Abū Bakr, himself a somewhat colourless personality, until his own accession to the caliphate.

(2) Account of the *saḳīfa* proper, with the following significant features.

The resistance of the Anṣār to the appointment of a Muhād̲j̲ir [see AL-MUHĀD̲J̲IRŪN] is first shown by the reluctance of one of their chieftains, named Bas̲h̲īr b. Saʿd b. T̲h̲aʿlaba [*q.v.*], who nevertheless was soon to pledge allegiance. But he was replaced by another, the rather more formidable Saʿd b. ʿUbāda [*q.v.*], who remained defiant until his death. The adherence of the Anṣār was ultimately obtained—by force where certain elements among them were concerned. The Banū Umayya, for their part, would yield only to the decisive injunctions of ʿUmar. The same applied to other individuals and groups whose adherence Abū Bakr and ʿUmar, supported by Abū ʿUbayda b. al-Djarrāḥ [*q.v.*], successively obtained. The list of these groups, and the chronology of their adherence, suggest the more or less deliberate appropriation of an undoubtedly authentic historical basis. Thus it is possible to observe successively the adherence of ʿUthmān and of the Banū Umayya, of Saʿd and ʿAbd al-Raḥmān b. ʿAwf, of the Banū Zuhra, of al-Zubayr b. al-ʿAwwām, and finally of ʿAlī [*q.vv.*].

In the account of Ibn Saʿd (d. 230/845), which is one of the most ancient known, the figures of ʿAlī, of Fāṭima, and subordinately, of al-ʿAbbās, are totally absent. They feature strongly, however, in that of al-Ṭabarī (d. 310/923), where ʿAlī is highlighted in his role of an opponent, supported by a faction of the Anṣār. Following on this, a special chapter is very often devoted to the oppositional attitude of ʿAlī and of his entourage, where all the evidence suggests that Fāṭima plays the central role. Being advised of the lukewarm opinions of the Anṣār, she is said then to have persuaded her husband to undertake a campaign of inducement aimed at them. Some weeks after the death of the Prophet she rather conveniently died, while ʿAlī remained apparently the last opponent. He was to come round in his turn, bringing with him the "Banū Hāshim". Al-ʿAbbās, who sometimes appears as an adviser of ʿAlī on behalf of the *ahl al-bayt* [*q.v.*], and who maintained strong reservations regarding Abū Bakr and ʿUmar, withdrew from the game, no doubt with an eye to the future.

A final chapter comprises the "*khuṭba* of Abū Bakr", a fragment of pious anthology of no great importance retained in the same terms by historians as well as by authors of *adab*.

The account of the *saḳīfa* is followed by that of the *ridda* [*q.v.* in Suppl.] and of the incomparable support which Abū Bakr received from ʿUmar in these circumstances.

The evolution of the form of the account, worthy of the ancient theatre, is very revealing. ʿAbbāsid propaganda, after the wavering of the Muʿtazilī era, was obliged to give prominence to the personalities of the first two caliphs, whose posterity never represented a political danger, in contradistinction to that of their two successors who, in various guises, remained the symbols of two oppositional dynastic tendencies.

It is no less important to show how the Umayyads, initially outsiders, were among the first to return to the fold, without a blow being struck. It is known that the tendency which become dominant from the 3rd/9th century onward is aimed at the rehabilitation of the "Umayyad century", with the object of forming a common front in opposition to the activities of the Shīʿīs.

The account of the oppositional intrigues of Fāṭima, perhaps superimposed, shows incontrovertibly the permanent distrust by Sunnism in regard to ʿAlid dynastic aspirations, claiming descent from the Prophet's daughter. But it is skilfully tempered by the account of the attitude of ʿAlī, who submitted without a murmur after the demise of his troublesome wife, earning his accession to the caliphate and the respect of future generations.

Bibliography: Ibn Hishām, *Sīra*, Cairo 1346, ii, 127-31; Ibn Saʿd, *Ṭabaḳāt*, Leiden 1904-40, iii/1, 126-33; Ps.-Ibn Ḳutayba, *K. al-Imāma wa 'l-siyāsa*, Cairo 1377/1957, 1-17; Ṭabarī, *Taʾrīkh*, i, 1815-30; Wāḳidī, *Maghāzī*, Oxford 1966, ii, 723-6, 727-31; Ibn Abi 'l-Ḥadīd, *Sharḥ Nahdj al-balāgha*, Cairo 1378/1958, i, 128; Ibn al-Athīr, *Kāmil*, Cairo 1303, ii, 122-5; G. Lecomte, *Sur une relation de la Saqīfa attribuée à Ibn Qutayba*, in *SI*, xxxi (1970), 171-83. See also the *Bibl.* of ABŪ BAKR, as well as articles devoted to the other major protagonists mentioned in the text.

(G. LECOMTE)

SAKĪNA (A.), a term of the Ḳurʾān and of Islamic religion. The root *sh-k-n* (Akkadian, Hebrew, Aramaic) or *s-k-n* (Arabic) means basically "to go down, rest, be quiescent, inhabit", and the corresponding Later Hebrew form to Arabic *sakīna* is *shᵉkhīnā* and the Jewish Palestinian Aramaic one *shᵉkhīnā*, Syriac *shᵉkīntā*. Cf. Hebr. *ham-mishkan, mishkan Yhwh*, Syr. *mashkan zabhnā/zabhnō*, Ar. *ḳubbat al-zamān* (al-Ḳardāḥī, *Lubāb*, Beirut 1887, ii, 546-7), referring to Moses' tent sanctuary, Exod. xxv. 22). The Hebrew usage is generally considered (though not by the native Arabic scholars) as the source of Ar. *sakīna*. Derived from the idea of "dwelling within s.th. or s.o." is Ar. *maskūn* "possessed by a spirit, demon, Iblīs", cf. Syr. *sheknō*, pl. *sheknē*, " the demon within a person". Not in fact connected with this Arabic term, but deriving from a different root in Akkadian, via Hebrew and Aramaic, is Ar. *miskīn*, "destitute, poor, wretched"; for this, see MISKĪN.

The Ḳurʾān has a large number of words derived from the root *s-k-n*. Apart from the basic meanings of "habitation, residence, hearth, shelter for the night, place where spouses meet", there are also "to subdue (the winds)" (XLII, 33), "to cause the water to settle on the earth (XXIII, 18), "to halt the shadow" (XXV, 45), etc. What interests us here is the allegorical sense assumed by the term *sakīna* in six verses of the Ḳurʾān, beginning with II, 248, where it refers to Biblical history. The Israelites, refusing to acknowledge the authority of Saul, God's Chosen One, to reign over them (cf. I Sam. x, 26 ff.), hear their prophet (*nabiyyuhum* = Samuel) say, "The sign of his kingship will be that the Ark (*tābūt*, which had been carried off by the Philistines, I Sam. v, 1 ff.) will come to you. [In this Ark] there is a *sakīna* from your Lord and a relic (*baḳiyya*, the heritage of the prophets, sc. Moses' staff and Aaron's yellow turban, according to Ibn Sīdah, in *LʿA*, ed. Beirut, ii, 174-5) of what was left by the family of Moses and the family of Aaron, and it (sc. the Ark) will be carried by the angels".

According to Exod. xl, 34-5, in the Ark there was "the glory (*kābōd*) of Yahweh. Now, according to G. Vajda, the term *shᵉkhīnā*, absent from the Bible, assumed "in some way a consequential meaning to the Biblical word *kābōd*. It implies something of God, without being taken, in the majority of its attestations, as being identical with God. His translation of "presence" is a step towards abstraction, its spiritualisation, if one wishes to express it thus, without bringing us much knowledge of the object signified (cf. the review of Goldberg [see *Bibl.*], in *REJ*, cxxviii [1969, publ. 1970], 280-2). In essence, Goldberg's opinion, 455, is that, in Vajda's formulation, the term *shᵉkhīnā* was expressly created to denote the act of inhabitation, and then the divinity which "inhabits". Originally, and above all, the term thus denoted the divinity present in the sanctuary; it was accordingly first of all limited to the type of *shᵉkhīnā* involving a presence and only understood secondarily in the sense of manifestations of the divinity (*ibid.*, 281).

This "presence" of God was equally displayed outside the Ark by a cloud which enveloped it. Its presence marked a halt in the march and its disappearance the resumption of the march (Exod. xl 36-8).

It is this presence of God which the term *sakīna* ex

presses in the other Ḳurʾānic citations, a presence shown in the divine aid vouchsafed to the Prophet and the believers in battle, giving them the victory. Hence at the encounter of al-Ḥudaybiya [*q.v.*] in the year 6/628, on the way to Mecca, "God was satisfied with the believers when they were swearing allegiance to you under the tree, and He knew what was in their hearts, and He sent down upon them the *sakīna* and He recompensed them with a victory near at hand" (xlviii, 18). At the time of the conquest of Mecca, "It is He who sent down the *sakīna* in the hearts of the believers, in order that they might add faith to their (existing) faith" (xlviii, 4). Confronting the unbelievers whose hearts were still animated by the fierceness of the *Dj̲āhiliyya*, "God sent down His *sakīna* upon His messenger and upon the believers, and caused them to cleave to the word of piety" (xlviii, 26). Already, fleeing from Mecca in the company of Abū Bakr, "God sent down His *sakīna* upon him (sc. in the Cave) and supported him with hosts whom you did not see" (ix, 40).

We are thus in a context of warfare, as were the Israelites in the time of Saul who asked God to give them a leader capable of leading them to victory (cf. Ḳurʾān, II, 246).

This divine aid, bestowed on the Prophet at Badr (III, 123 ff.), is vouchsafed by an innumerable, invisible army, which appears in the shape of a "transparent, waterless cloud" (or in the form of a mythical bird), called by Tradition *ṣarad, ṣurad* or *ṣurrad*. Mud̲j̲āhid [*q.v.*] relates that "the *sakīna*, the *ṣarad* and Gabriel came with Abraham from the north (*al-S̲h̲ām*)" (cf. his *Tafsīr*, ed. ʿAbd al-Raḥmān al-Ṭāhir b. Muḥammad al-Sūratī, Dōḥa, Ḳaṭar 1396/1976, 114). Al-Azraḳī, *Ak̲h̲bār Makka*, 27 ff., cf. also *LʿA*, *loc. cit.*, likewise relates that it was with Abraham (cf. Goldberg, 300 ff.) that the *sakīna* came to Mecca. It had a head like that of a she-cat and two wings (on the *sakīna* as a supernatural force in animal form, see Goldziher, *Abhandlungen zur arabischen Philologie*, Leiden 1896-9, i, 198, and Scholem [see *Bibl.*], 53), and it came down "like a cloud (*g̲h̲amāma*) or a mist (*ḍabāba*), having in its centre something like a head which could talk" (27). Later on (30), "Ibrāhīm came from Armenia on Burāḳ [*q.v.*] with the *sakīna*, which had a face which could talk; it whistled like a light breeze". When Abraham wished to build the Kaʿba, the *sakīna* unfolded itself like a snake on the first foundations and told him, "Build on top of me", "and so he built; hence every Bedouin in flight and every powerful person inevitably circumambulates the sanctuary under the *sakīna*'s protection" (31).

All these traditions connect the *sakīna* with the sanctuary, as it is in Ḳurʾān, II, 248, and link it with the Prophet's battles, with the idea of his being victorious, as in the other citations involving God's aid in the form of an invisible army. In a study on the *Ḥanīfs*, in *REJ*, cxxx (1971), 165-82, J.-Cl. Vadet brought forward an argument giving credence to this view of things. He explains the Ḳurʾānic hapax *ribbiyūn*, in III, 146, by the Biblical hapax *mē-ribh̲ᵉbh̲ōt ḳōdes̲h̲* (mostly amended to *mrībh̲ath̲ ḳādes̲h̲*) (Deut. xxxiii, 2, cf. v. 17, *rebᵉbōt̲h̲* "hosts" of Ephraim), to be translated as "the saintly hosts". Moses, "the man of God, blessed the Children of Israel before he died, saying Yahweh has come down from Sinai; He raised himself up for those of Seʿīr; He shone forth from the mountain of Pharan; and He came forth from the saintly hosts". Envisaging his approaching end, Muḥammad asks his devotees what they would do after his death, "Would you go back to your errors?", and he continues, "How many a prophet has there been who has fought at the head (or: accompanied by) numerous armies (*ribbiyyūn kat̲h̲īrᵘⁿ*), and they did not become discouraged because of what befell them in the way of God, nor grew weak nor became quiescent (*istakānū*)? God loves those who endure" (III, 146).

Placed in a context like that of Deut. xxxiii, 2, sc. Moses' farewell speech to his community, this verse takes on a quite different meaning. It is thus a case of innumerable, invisible armies by means of which God sustains His prophets in the accomplishment of their missions, i.e. of the *sakīna* being identified with the Ark and signifying its Presence, and of *ribbiyyūn/ṣarad* denoting the numberless army of angels, the saintly hosts, who appear in the form of a cloud. *Sakīna* and *ṣarad* represent two of the many forms of theophany.

Beyond this prophetic context just noted, the *sakīna* assumes in Ḥadīt̲h̲ (see *Concordance*, ii, 494-5), as in rabbinical tradition (see Goldberg), a spiritual and moral signification. It "enveloped" the Prophet (*g̲h̲as̲h̲iyat-hu*) at the moment of revelation (*waḥy*), came down (*nazalat*) on the Kurʾān ("We have brought down the Kurʾān in a discontinuous form (*faṣlᵃⁿ*) and the *sakīna* in a continuous one (*ṣabrᵃⁿ*)"), hovered above the Prophet when he left ʿArafa and above the believers, and spoke with the tongue (*lisān*) of ʿUmar (b. al-K̲h̲aṭṭāb). It is identified with a collection of moral attitudes and virtues—gravity, bearing, modesty, dignity, calmness, patience, magnanimity, clemency and everything which characterises a pious person. In Islamic mysticism, it becomes an "interior illumination" (*nūr fi 'l-ḳalb*), after the manner of gnosis and the Kabbala, which make it into a "light emanating from the primaeval light" (*Urlicht*) which is none other than God Himself (cf. Scholem, 78 ff.).

Bibliography: See especially, for the term in its Rabbinical context, A.M. Goldberg, *Untersuchungen über die Vorstellung von der Schekhinah in der frühen rabbinischen Literatur*, Studia Judaica, V, Berlin 1969, in which, with a little patience, one can find the origin of the Ḳurʾānic and Ḥadīt̲h̲ conception from the collection there of Islamic data. See also Goldziher, *La notion de la Sakîna chez les Mahométans*, in *RHR*, xxviii (1893), 1-13, and idem, *Abhandlungen*, i, 177-212. On the evolution of the notion of the *s̲h̲ᵉk̲h̲īnā*, see G. Scholem, *Zur Entwicklungsgeschichte der kabbalistischen Konzeption der Schechinah*, in *Eranos-Jahrbücher*, xxi (1953), 45-107.

(T. Fahd)

ṢAḲİZ (the Ottoman Turkish name for Chios, the Greek name of this island and of its capital; *ṣaḳiz* means "gum mastic", a testimony to the product for which Chios was famous), an island in the eastern Aegean alongside the Turkish coast, from which only 8 km/5 miles separate it at the narrowest point of the strait of Chios (*Ṣaḳiz bog̲h̲azî*); the large peninsula of Karaburun on the mainland, jutting north, separates the island's northern half from the gulf and port of Smyrna [see izmir in Suppl.].

With an area of 841 km², it is the fifth largest island of the Aegean after Crete [see iḳrītis̲h̲], Euboea [see eğriboz], Lesbos [see midilli], and Rhodes [see rodos]. Administratively, Chios forms one of Greece's 52 *nomoi*; its *nomos* also includes two other important features: the islands of Psara and Antipsara some 20 km/12 miles to the west, and the Oinousses islets (Koyun adaları in Turkish, Spalmadori in Italian; the last-named form is customarily used in western scholarly literature) between it and the Karaburun peninsula. The capital and main port city is situated on the island's eastern coast near the strait's narrowest point opposite the Turkish harbour of Çeşme [see česhme].

The importance of Chios, which it owed to several factors, rose to a peak between the 14th and 16th centuries but continued until the early 19th. The factors were its crossroads position on maritime and continental trading routes, the uniqueness of the much-prized gun mastic produced nowhere else (lentisk shrubs grow in other parts of the Mediterranean too, but only the soil of southern Chios gives to the gum which their bark exudes the desired quality), and the acumen of the Genoese (masters of the island between 1304 and 1566), who used the port, in tandem with Galata, as the hub of their commercial empire; in fact, most of these aspects continued even after the Ottoman conquest of 1566 or re-emerged in other forms (such as the enterprising spirit of its Greek population). The island's role in the Middle Ages must be linked with that of the two Phokaias from where the Genoese exported alum, and with the port of Çeşme from where goods other than alum brought from or through Anatolia were ferried to Chios for long-distance shipment. The last-named aspect continued well into the Ottoman period until it was definitively eclipsed by the dramatic rise of Smyrna in the 17th century.

No known evidence suggests that Chios would have attracted much attention of the Arabs in the early centuries of Islam, but its proximity to the mainland exposed this Byzantine possession to Muslim raids once the Turks penetrated Anatolia by the end of the 11th century. The maritime principality (1089-92) of the Saldjūḳ prince Čaka or Čakan, with Smyrna as its base, included Chios. Repetition of a similar conquest by the principality of Aydïn [see AYDÏN-OGHLU], especially by its dynamic prince Umur Beg [see UMUR PASHA] in the first half of the 14th century, was staved off by combinations of multinational and multiconfessional alliances, rivalries and military and naval campaigns, and even a Crusade. By itself, Byzantium appeared unable to defend Chios and the nearby coastal places against the Turks, and had to accept help from such naval powers as the Venetians, Catalans, Hospitallers of Rhodes, Genoese, or more general leagues of western Christendom, ceaselessly urged on by the Popes. The high price, both spiritual and economic, of western help and presence sometimes made such Byzantine emperors or contenders for the throne as Andronicus III (1329-41) or John Cantacuzenus prefer a Turkish alliance. Chios came by 1304 under the control of the Genoese family of Zaccaria; meanwhile, they or their other countrymen also laid hands on the two Phokaias (Old and New, Eski Foça and Yeni Foça in Turkish) near the northern entrance to the Gulf of Smyrna. Although their hold on Chios was interrupted by Andronicus, who with the help of Umur Beg reclaimed Byzantine control of some of these places (this help, however, could receive a different interpretation in the Turks' eyes: the Ottoman historian Eflākī mentions a raid on the island by Umur, who carried off much mastic as booty and subjected the island to the *kharādj* [*q.v.*], thus incorporating Chios into the *Dār al-Islām*; see İnalcık, in *Bibl.*).

The Crusade of 1344, which captured Smyrna from the Turks, set in motion a chain of events that indirectly led to a Genoese reconquest of Chios (1346). This time it was not a family but a company of shareholders who acquired control of the island and kept it until the Ottoman conquest of 1566. This company was known as the Maona of Chios, and secondarily, from 1362 when its definitive charter was established, as the Giustinianis; "Maona" is believed to be a term of Arabic origin (*maʿūna* "help, solidarity", hence commercial company; see *Bibl.* and MAʿŪNA). The Giustinianis were a family whose house in Genoa was acquired by the company as its headquarters there. A *podestà* sent by the government of Genoa was the titular governor of Chios (as were the two *podestàs* of Old and New Phokaia respectively), but otherwise, the company was virtually autonomous on the island. Initially, a vague kind of suzerainty was also conceded to the Byzantine emperor, and an annual sum was sent to him; gradually, however, the tribute paid to the Turks became more significant. At first given to those of Aydïn (by the Byzantine governor in Andronicus's time), eventually this sum became an important annual tribute sent to the Ottoman sultan, and kept increasing until it reached 14,000 ducats in Süleymān II's [*q.v.*] time (still bearable, if the reported revenue of 30,000 ducats did not falter). It was the Maona's inability to carry out this obligation during the last three years of their rule that by 1566 contributed to the Ottoman decision to seize the island.

Genoese rule in Chios was remarkable for its long duration in the face of Ottoman expansion, for the economic role the island played as a source of gum mastic, as a transit port in international shipping, and for the co-existence of a Greek Orthodox population with a ruling Latin Catholic élite. Luck (a grain blockade and then a devastating raid by Bāyezīd I [*q.v.*] with 60 ships, in or soon after 1397, might have been followed by conquest if Tīmūr [*q.v.*] had not eliminated the dynamic sultan). Diplomacy, economic strength and care not to provoke the Ottomans, rather than military or naval strength, ensured its long survival, in contrast to Hospitaller Rhodes, for example. This contrast, however, also showed the arrangement's ultimate fragility when we compare the Ottoman conquest of Rhodes (1522) with that of Chios. Frustrated by the failure to conquer Malta (1565), Süleymān sent the imperial fleet under the *ḳapudān pasha* Piyāle Pasha [*q.v.*], the conqueror of Djarba [*q.v.*] in 1560) in the spring of 1566 on a campaign whose goal, contrary to Europe's fears, was not a renewed attempt against Malta but against Chios: the conquest consisted of an arrest of the Maona's governing body whose twelve members had come with presents on board the commander's ship, and an unopposed occupation of the island.

Some of the contradictions and special features that marked the history of mediaeval Chios continued during its Ottoman period. Until the tragedy of 1822, the island enjoyed a unique status that made it stand out as a prosperous and happy place where all the three main communities—Orthodox Greek, Catholic Latin, and Muslim Ottoman—lived in relative harmony. Like other large islands and conquered provinces, Chios became a *sandjaḳ* [*q.v.*] (in this case, part of the *eyālet* [*q.v.*] of *Djazāʾir-i Baḥr-i Safīd* [*q.v.*]), governed by an administrative body of the standard type and secured by a garrison of at most 2,000 troops quartered chiefly in the capital's citadel; aside from these representatives of the Porte, there were almost no other Turks on the island, and the population had virtual autonomy in its internal affairs. Some of the mostly Genoese, Catholic élite stayed on after the conquest, and they did not lose all their privileges forthwith. These last survived even the 1599 attempt by the Florentines to conquer the island, but the Venetian conquest and brief possession in 1694-5 did deal them a serious blow which, however, further strengthened the position of the Orthodox majority governed by an enlightened oligarchy: the Catholic élite, accused of collaborating with the invader, definitively lost their privileges to the Greeks. The Venetian attack, undertaken during the Ottoman-Hapsburg war of 1683-99, provoked a naval response from the Turks, whose ultimate victory revealed the successful modernisation of the imperial fleet under the able leadership of Mezemorta Hüseyin Pas̲h̲a [see ḤUSAYN PAS̲H̲A, MEZZOMORTO]. For the reasons stated above, Turkish victory ushered in what may have been the happiest period in the history of Chios and which lasted until 1822. The island continued to export gum mastic (partly to Istanbul, where the ladies of the Harem were among the principal consumers), but it also participated in the dramatic surge of Ottoman Greek maritime trade and merchant marine during the 18th century. Enterprising families developed business ties with Europe, and participated in the intellectual and scientific rise of the West, some of which they in turn propagated in Ottoman society where they frequently enjoyed the status of high officials and the sultan's physicians. Alexander Mavrocordato (1637-1719), who had studied medicine in Padua, wrote a Latin treatise on the circulation of the blood, and became prominent as the chief dragoman of the Porte during the negotiations that led to the Treaty of Karlowitz in 1699 [see ḲARLOFČA].

The waters off Chios were visited by the Russians in the summer of 1770, an operation undertaken in the framework of the Russo-Turkish war of 1768-74. A clash between the Russian fleet under Admiral A.G. Orlov and the Ottoman one under Ḥusām ul-Dīn Pas̲h̲a ended in a draw, but it was highlighted by the exploits of the *ḳapudān-i humāyūn* Ḥasan Beg (later Pas̲h̲a; see D̲J̲EZĀʾIRLI G̲H̲ĀZĪ ḤASAN PAS̲H̲A) against the ship of Admiral G.A. Spiridov. The Turks withdrew to Çeşme, which by then served as a naval base; the result was the notorious destruction of the entire Ottoman fleet by fire ships with which the Russians managed to attack the crowded harbour in the night of 7 July. The subsequent attempt to seize the port of Chios was repulsed by the Turkish garrison, or was given up due to reports of the plague on the island. While the triumph at Çeşme earned Orlov the honorific title "Česmenskiy" conferred on him by Catherine II, Ḥasan Beg's heroism was noticed by Istanbul, which aptly entrusted to him the defence of the Dardanelles and the rescue of Lemnos from the Russians and eventually raised him to the post of *ḳapudān pas̲h̲a*.

The peace and prosperity of Chios abruptly ended in 1822, when revolutionary Greeks from other places, especially from the island of Samos [see SISAM], landed on Chios and incited some of its inhabitants to second the uprising which was agitating the mainland. The besieged Turkish garrison in the capital's citadel held out until the imperial fleet brought relief. The subsequent repression carried out on the orders of the governor, Waḥīd Pas̲h̲a, against the objections of the fleet's commander, the *ḳapudān pas̲h̲a* Naṣūḥ-zāde ʿAlī Pas̲h̲a, crippled the island (which lost over one-half of its population—estimated at some 80,000 souls—in the slaughter and deportation to the slave market in Smyrna), and may have indirectly spurred Europe to increase its support for Greece's independence. Like most conflicts involving Chios, this one too had a markedly naval dimension, and although the Ottoman fleet prevailed, the Greek side scored a well-remembered triumph when on 18 June Konstantin Kanaris sank the Turkish flagship in the harbour of Chios; while the *ḳapudān pas̲h̲a* with most hands perished, the Greek native of Psara thus launched his own career that would propel him to the pinnacle of Greek politics. Both Mezemorta Ḥüseyin Pas̲h̲a and Naṣūḥ-zāde ʿAlī Pas̲h̲a are buried in Chios.

Nevertheless, Chios displayed remarkable resilience even after this tragedy, and benefited once more from the benign Ottoman rule which by 1832 allowed the Greek population to re-establish much of its internal autonomy; this was underscored by the respect which the sultan ʿAbd al-Med̲j̲īd I [*q.v.*] showed the island's ruling elite during his 1856 visit. On the formal level, the Chiotes' self-rule ended in 1283/1866 as a result of the restructuring of the Ottoman empire, which replaced the *eyālet* structure with that of the much more uniform *wilāyat* [*q.v.*] system; the administrative centre of the new *wilāyat* of *D̲j̲azāʾir-i Baḥr-i Safīd*, usually in Rhodes, sometimes moved to Chios. The governor of the island (called *müteṣarrif* in this period) was from 1887 until his death in 1888 the Ottoman writer and reformist Nāmiḳ Kemāl [see KEMĀL, MEḤMED NĀMIḲ]. The recovery of Chios, well under way during this final stage of Ottoman rule, was dealt a serious blow by a devastating earthquake in 1881.

Ottoman rule in Chios ended in the same manner as in Lesbos but slightly later (December 1912/January 1913), and Greek sovereignty was ratified by the same two treaties (London 1913 and Lausanne 1923).

Bibliography: J.H. Mordtmann and B. Darkot, *İA*, s.v. *Sakız*; *Pauly-Wissowa*, iii/2 (1899), cols. 2286-2301 s.v. *Chios*, with a historical map of the Kastron and Chora (citadel and town) on col. 2299; *Megale Ellenike Enkyklopaideia*, xxviii (1957), s.v. *Chios*; *Enciclopedia Italiana*, xxxi (1936), s.v. *Scio*; S̲h̲. Sāmī, *Ḳāmūs al-aʿlām*, Istanbul 1894, iv, 2485-6; several official yearbooks (*sālnāmes*) for the *wilāyet*: *D̲j̲azāʾir-i Baḥr-i Sefīd sālnāmesi*, each with a section on Chios; V. Cuinet, *La Turquie d'Asie*, Paris 1894, i, 406-29; Ph.P. Argenti, *Bibliography of Chios from classical times to 1936*, London 1940; idem, *Chius vincta*, Cambridge 1941 (history of Chios in the Turkish period; and several other books and sources written or published by this author, member of a prominent Chiote family; the large 3-volume edition of travellers' accounts, in the original language with a facing Greek tr., deserves special mention: *E Chios para tois geografois kai periegetais...*, Athens 1946); A.M. Vlastos, *A history of the island of Chios*, London 1913 (tr. of his *Chiaka*, Hermupolis 1840); Pīrī Reʾīs, *Kitāb-i Baḥriyye*, Istanbul 1935, 164-71; idem, *Kitab-i Bahriye*, Istanbul 1988, i [356-70; includes Eng. tr.]; both these editions are those of the second (1526) version; idem, German tr. of the first (1521) version by P. Kahle, *Bahrije. ii. Übersetzung*, Berlin 1926, 48-52; Ewliyā Čelebi, *Seyāḥat-nāme*, Istanbul 1935, ix, 109-28; E. Armao, *In Giro per il Mar Egeo con Vincenzo Coronelli*, Florence 1951, 131-42; R. Dozy, *Supplément*, ii, 565-6; idem, *Glossaire des mots espagnols et portugais dérivés de l'arabe*², Leiden 1869, 179; M. Amari, *Storia degli Arabi in Sicilia*², Catania 1939, iii, 913 (all three *re* the etymology of *maʿūna*); H. Akın, *Aydinoğulları tarihi hakkında bir araştırma*², Ankara 1968; D. Goffman, *Izmir and the Levantine world, 1550-1650*, Seattle-London 1990, 61-4 and *passim* (see index); C. Hopf, *Les Giustiniani, dynastes de Chios*, Paris 1888; H. İnalcık, *The rise of the Turcoman maritime principalities in Anatolia, Byzantium, and the Crusades*, in *Byzantinische Forschungen*, ix (1985), 179-217; A.N. Kurat, *Çaka Bey*, Ankara 1966; P. Lemerle, *L'Emirat d'Aydin, Byzance et l'Occident*, Paris 1957; Susan Skilliter, *William Harborne and the trade with Turkey, 1578-1582*, Oxford 1977, 5, 9-10; eadem, *Una vicenda d'intoleranza religiosa nella Chio ottomana: il matrimonio del console Osborne*, in *Il Veltro*, xxiii (1979), 327-36; A.C. Wood, *A history of the Le-*

vant Company, Oxford 1935; Elizabeth A. Zachariadou, *Trade and crusade: Venetian Crete and the emirates of Menteshe and Aydin* (*1300-1415*), Venice 1983; S. Turan, *Sakız'ın türk hakimiyeti altına alınması*, in *Tarih Araştırmaları Dergisi*, iv (1966), 173-84; idem, *Türkiye-Italya ilişkileri. I. Selçuklulardan Bizans'ın sona erişine*, Istanbul 1990, index s.v. Sakız and Foça; Ṣafwet, *Ḳoyun adalarî önündeki deñiz ḥarbi we Ṣaḳîz'în ḳurtulus͟hu*, in *TOEM* (1326), 150-77 (the 1694-5 events); A. D̲j̲ewdet, *Taʾrīk̲h̲*, xii [Istanbul] 1309, 40-8 (the 1822 events); *Taʾrīk̲h̲-i weḳʿa-yi Ṣaḳîz*, Istanbul 1290/1873 (the 1822 events); R.C. Anderson, *Naval wars in the Levant, 1559-1853*, Liverpool 1952, 65-6, 193, 214-22, 286-92, 486-9; *Russkie i sovetskie moryaki na Sredizemnom more*, Moscow 1978, 36-43 (the 1770 events); E.V. Tarle, *Česmenskiy boy i pervaya russkaya ekspeditsiya v Arkhipelag*, Moscow-Leningrad 1945; *The Greek Merchant Marine, 1453-1850*, Athens 1972, *passim* (see index s.v. Chios). See also the articles LIMNI, MIDILLI, and RODOS, and their *Bibls*.

(S. SOUCEK)

SAḲḲĀʾ (A.), lit. water-carrier, was a term denoting manual workers who carried water in a leather-bottle (*ḳirba*) or jar (*kūz*) on their shoulders or on a mule (and even on a camel in rare circumstances) in pre-modern towns and large villages as well as pilgrimage centres throughout the Middle East and North Africa. A leather bottle during the early Islamic period reportedly cost a modest sum of about 3 dirhams. The necessity for supplying drinking water to the thirsty and the poor members of the community was regarded, according to a tradition (*ḥadīt̲h̲*), as a work of excellent charity (*ṣadaḳa*). On the other hand, refusal to supply water to a thirsty person is an act of great sin (al-D̲h̲ahabī, *Kabāʾir*, 362). It was therefore recommended to wealthy Muslims to build water-fountains (*sabīl* [*q.v.*]) and dig wells for charitable purposes. The habit of selling water from a well (*biʾr*) to the people of Medina, after the Hid̲j̲ra of the Prophet Muḥammad, led the companion ʿUt̲h̲mān b. ʿAffān to buy the well-known Biʾr Rūma for supplying water free of cost to many inhabitants of the oasis town. An engraving on a public fountain in Cairo proclaims the tradition that the offering of drinking water is an action of spiritual merit.

The virtue of carrying water extolled in an Islamic tradition inspired many pious Muslims to accept this profession. Such were the notable instances of the Arab poet Abū Tammām (d. 232/846), the Persian poet S̲h̲ayk̲h̲ Saʿdī (d. 682/1283) and the mystic Ibrāhīm b. Adham, who were water-carriers for various lengths of time in their life. The historian al-D̲h̲ahabī illustrates a typical water-carrier in the career of Muḥammad b. ʿAlī b. Muḥammad al-Muḳriʾ Abū ʿAbd Allāh Ibn al-Saḳḳāʾ (d. 572/1176) who regularly earned a livelihood as a water-carrier supplying water manually to the houses of the public. Ibn al-Saḳḳāʾ was also a recounter of Islamic traditions. Many Arab historians and writers of the ʿAbbāsid epoch quote D̲h̲u 'l-Nūn al-Miṣrī's (d. 245/859) frequent reference to a case of the virtue (*murūʾa*) in the life of a well-dressed Bag̲h̲dādī itinerant water-carrier (*saḳḳāʾ*) who refused to accept payment of a dīnār as the price of a drink of fresh water from a foreigner.

In spite of their good reputation, however, the water-carriers, according to al-D̲j̲āḥiẓ, could never become wealthy and prosperous during the heyday of the ʿAbbāsid caliphate; their poor economic condition was comparable to that of the brick-layers, potters, ploughmen and groups of other minor craftsmen and workers. The carriers of the essential commodity of water enjoyed probably the highest prestige among pre-industrial workers in Islamic society. Ibn Sīrīn (d. 110/729) affirmed the favourable status of the water-carrier in his interpretation of dreams. Also, the writers of the *ḥisba* manuals insisted on cleanliness and the hygienic condition of the jars, cups and leather bottles of the water-carriers in the interest of public health. The encyclopaedic Arab biographer al-Ṣafadī (d. 764/1362) noted that *al-Saḳḳāʾ* was an established *nisba* among his contemporaries, who included some teachers of *ḥadīt̲h̲* and learned men.

Bibliography: D̲j̲āḥiẓ, *al-Ḥayawān* ed. Hārūn, iv, 435; T̲h̲aʿālibī, *Bard al-akbād fi 'l-aʿdād*, in *K̲h̲ams rasāʾil*, Constantinople 1301/1883, 129; Ibn al-D̲j̲awzī, *Ak̲h̲bār al-ẓirāf*, Damascus 1928, 31; idem, *Manāḳib Bag̲h̲dād*, Bag̲h̲dād 1924, 31; Aḥmad b. Ḥanbal, *Musnad*, Cairo 1951, i, 203, xiii, 44, 180; Ibn Mād̲j̲a, *Sunan*, ii, Cairo 1953, 1214; Ibn al-At̲h̲īr, *al-Lubāb*, Cairo 1938, i, 547-8; Ibn al-Ḳifṭī, *Taʾrīk̲h̲ al-Ḥukamāʾ*, Leipzig 1903, 30-3; Iṣfahānī, *Maḳātil al-Ṭālibiyyīn*, Cairo 1949, 407; Ibn Bassām al-Muḥtasib, *Nihāyat al-rutba fi ṭalab al-ḥisba*, Bag̲h̲dād 1968, 25-6; Ibn al-Uk̲h̲uwwa, *Maʿālim al-ḳurba*, ed. R. Levy, London 1938, 96-7; al-K̲h̲aṭīb al-Bag̲h̲dādī, *Taʾrīk̲h̲ Bag̲h̲dād*, Cairo 1931, i, 50; Ḳus̲h̲ayrī, *Risāla*, i, Cairo n.d., 476; Ṣafadī *Wāfi*, i, 31, xxii, 74, 85; D̲h̲ahabī, *Kitāb al-Kabāʾir*, ed. A.R. Fak̲h̲ūrī, Aleppo 1978, 362; Ibs̲h̲īhī, *al-Mustaṭraf*, Cairo 1952, ii, 62; D̲j̲abartī, *ʿAd̲j̲āʾib al-āt̲h̲ar*, Cairo 1967, vii, 313-14; N. Élisséeff *et al.*, in *RCEA*, xvi, Cairo 1964, 145; M.A.J. Beg, *A contribution to the economic history of the Caliphate: a study of the cost of living and the economic status of artisans in ʿAbbāsid Iraq*, in *IQ*, xvi (1972), 140-67; idem, *Water-carriers in early Islamic civilization*, in *IC* (1984), 75-8; Ibn Seerin's *Dictionary of dreams*, translated from the Arabic by Muhammad M. al-Akili, Pennsylvania 1992, 469.

(M.A.J. BEG)

SAKKĀKĪ, one of the early poets in Čag̲h̲atay Turkish ("early" meaning, before Mīr ʿAlī S̲h̲īr Nawāʾī's [*q.v.*] time). He lived around 802/1400, presumably in Samarḳand, but certainly all his lifetime in Transoxania. As we can infer from the dedications of his *ḳaṣīdas*, his patrons included K̲h̲alīl Sulṭān (ruler in Samarḳand 807-12/1405-9), Ulug̲h̲ Beg (812-53/1409-49) and Arslan K̲h̲ʷād̲j̲a Tark̲h̲an. Almost all the information about his person is gained from remarks made about him by Nawāʾī in his *Mad̲j̲ālis an-nafāʾis* and in the *Muḥākamat al-lug̲h̲atayn*. Although he was popular in Samarḳand during his lifetime, Nawāʾī is relatively depreciative of Sakkākī's talent, a judgement apparently shared by others; apart from one *bayt* quoted by Nawāʾī, the only known reference to his work by another poet is the quotation of one *bayt* in the collective manuscript in which Sakkākī's *dīwān* is preserved. The following statement by Nawāʾī is well-known: he says that he heard people in Samarḳand claim that "all good poems by Luṭfī belong to him (Sakkākī); he (Luṭfī) has stolen them and has attached his name to them." Nawāʾī goes on to comment that "this is the kind of silly boast which is widespread in Transoxania". (The statement is usually wrongly interpreted the other way round by Turkish scholars as meaning that Sakkākī was rumoured to have done the stealing.) Indeed, Nawāʾī may just betray a shade of southern chauvinism here quite apart from the fact that a certain amount of local pride on the part of the Transoxanians may be expected for a time in which the focus of literary activity only just has been shifting southwards to Harāt. In any case, it is clear that the work of Sakkākī is directly interrelated with Luṭfī's poetry (Eckmann 1959) and that of others (Hofman 1969).

Both the language and poetics of Sakkākī highlight the arbitary nature of his classification as a "Čaghatay" poet; at least in the early stage, this designation at one and the same time refers to a person being a Persian-style court poet and to the political context (i.e. he worked at a Tīmūrid court). But his language has preserved some typical Khwārazmian Turkish traits, e.g. the rendering of *δ as z ~ y (e.g. *azaḳ* ~ *ayaḳ* "foot"); this tendency is probably enhanced by the fact that he was from Transoxania and may thus prove helpful in solving the problem of the relationship of his poetry with other contemporary poets (most notably: Luṭfī). The rules of *ʿarūḍ* metrics applied by Sakkākī also definitely reflect the late Khwārazmian Turkish stage. It is the same as is found in Khwārazmī's *Maḥabbat-nāma*: etymologically long vowels are still frequently metrically long, whereas a first stage of Persification of the metre is noticeable in the regular occurrence of *imāla* (only in Arabo-Persian loan words). Characteristic is the variable rendering of the words *birlä* ~ *bilä* "with" and *ermäs* ~ *emäs* to fit the exigences of the metre. The extended *radīf* is a feature also found in e.g. Luṭfī's poetry. The preponderance of the genres of the *ghazal* and the *ḳaṣīda* are to be expected with a court poet; they carry with them a larger range of metres and new Persian style imagery of the kind which is usually associated with Sakkākī's near-contemporary Ḥāfiẓ [*q.v.*]. However, considering the general context in which the poetry of Ḥāfiẓ arose, one should be careful when attributing similarities in any contemporary poet to Ḥāfiẓ's style to direct influence. Another commonplace statement about Sakkākī introducing elements of traditional oral poetry in his verses must also be viewed with caution: occasional sequences of alliteration are already encountered in Rabghūzī's [*q.v.*] *Ḳiṣaṣ al-anbiyāʾ* (710/1310). And after all, relatively simple language and inclusion of folksy elements are a common characteristic of *ghazal* writing (both Persian and Turkish) of his age.

These philological, linguistic and literary problems still await thorough treatment; even a critical edition of Sakkākī's poems is lacking. The only version of Sakkākī's *dīwān* extant is contained in 31 folia of a British Library manuscript, Or. 2079, and even that is incomplete. It contains one *munādjāt*, one *naʿt*, 12 *ḳaṣīdas* (plus one defective one) and 57 *ghazals* (*ghazals* with end rhymes from *bāʾ* to *nūn* are lacking). Three more *ghazals* (parallel in Uyghur and Arabic script) were found in a manuscript of the Ayasofya Library, Istanbul, 4757. One *bayt* is quoted by Nawāʾī, and one *bayt* by Yaḳīnī (ms. B.L. Or. 2079, fol. 319b).

Bibliography: 1. Edition. *Sakkākiy, Tanlangan asarlar*, Tashkent 1958 (in transliteration). Partial editions. J. Eckmann, *Çağatay dili örnekleri. III. Sekkâki divanından parçalar*, in *Türk Dili ve Edebiyatı Dergisi*, xx (1959), 157-74 (2 *ḳaṣīdas*, 14 *ghazals*); K. Eraslan, *Çağatay şiiri ~ Sekkâkí*, in *Türk Dili* (1986), 569-79 (in transliteraton; *munādjāt*, 1 *ḳaṣīda*, 4 *ghazals*); art. *Säkkaki* in *Uyghur kilassik ädibiyatidin nämunilär*, ed. T. Eliyop and R. Jari, Sindjan Khälq Näshriyati 1981, 189-225 (17 *ghazals* in modern Uyghur spelling).

2. Studies. J. Eckmann, *Die tschagataische Literatur*, in *PTF*, ii, Wiesbaden 1964, 306-8; H.F. Hofman, *Turkish literature*, Section 3, Pt. 1, Utrecht 1969, v, 153-7 (and further references there); E. Rustamov, *Uzbekskaya poeziya v pervoy polovine XV veka*, Moscow 1963; Ye.E. Bertel's, *Navoi. Opït tvorčeskoy biografii*, Moscow-Leningrad 1948, 54-8.

(H. Boeschoten)

AL-SAKKĀKĪ, Abū Yaʿḳūb Yūsuf b. Abī Bakr b. Muḥammad al-Khwārazmī Sirādj al-Dīn, influential rhetorician writing in Arabic. He was born in Khwārazm on 3 Djumādā I, 555/11 May 1160 according to most sources, or in the year 554, according to his contemporary Yāḳūt (*Irshād*, ed. Rifāʿī, xx, 59). He died toward the end of Radjab 626/mid-June 1229 in Ḳaryat al-Kindī near Almāligh in Farghāna. In spite of his fame already during his lifetime, the circumstances of his life are shrouded in obscurity—a fact most likely attributable to the upheavals of the Mongol conquest. Very brief notices on him appear in the Ḥanafī biographical dictionaries (Ibn Ḳuṭlūbughā, *Tādj al-tarādjim*, Baghdād 1962, 81-2; Ibn Abi 'l-Wafāʾ al-Ḳurashī, *al-Djawāhir al-muḍiyya*, Ḥaydarābād 1332, ii, 225-6; and ʿAbd al-Ḥayy al-Laknawī, *al-Fawāʾid al-bahiyya*, ed. B.A. al-Naʿsānī, Cairo 1324/1906, s.n.) as well as in al-Suyūṭī's dictionary of language scholars (*Bughyat al-wuʿāt*, ed. M.A. Ibrāhīm, Cairo 1384/1964-5, ii, 364), while some legendary anecdotal accounts have been transmitted in the Eastern tradition (prominently in al-Khwānsārī, *Rawḍāt al-djannāt*, ed. M.ʿA. al-Rawḍātī, n.p. 1367, 745-6). The edifying story that al-Khwānsārī recounts on the authority of the *Zīnat al-madjālis* of Madjd al-Dīn Muḥammad al-Ḥusaynī al-Madjdī (a contemporary of Bahāʾ al-Dīn al-ʿĀmilī, who died in 1030/1621), the gist of which is that al-Sakkākī started out as an accomplished craftsman (a smith) and began the career of a scholar rather late at the age of thirty, is very likely a transposition of a similar *curriculum vitae* told about the Shāfiʿī scholar al-Ḳaffāl ("the Locksmith") al-Marwazī (Ibn Khallikān, ed. I. ʿAbbās, Beirut n.d., iii, 46; al-Subkī, *Ṭabaḳāt al-Shāfiʿiyya*, Cairo n.d., iii, 199). Al-Khwānsārī hints at this possibility (*Rawḍāt*, 745, ll. 33-4), and the fact that, in the story, the teacher of al-Sakkākī is portrayed as a Shāfiʿī corroborates the borrowing. Nevertheless, a certain similarity in their life curves may have prompted the transposition of the story. However, whether al-Sakkākī himself or, more likely, one of his forebears was a die-cutter (*sakkāk*) or whether his *nisba* is derived from an otherwise unattested place-name Sakkāka is a moot point in the sources. Other stories depict al-Sakkākī as an expert in magic and occult sciences (al-Khwānsārī, *Rawḍāt*, 746; al-Laknawī, *Fawāʾid*, 301); as al-Nasawī's biography of the Khwārazmshāh Djalāl al-Dīn Mingburnu (*r.* 617-28/1220-31) shows, al-Sakkākī's fame in this field was already well established during his lifetime (*Sīra*, ed. O. Houdas, Paris 1891, 150-1; tr. idem, Paris 1895, 249-50; ed. Ḥ.A. Ḥamdī, Cairo 1953, 253-4). He seems to have made the transition from the Khwārazmshāhs to the Mongols quite successfully, since one of the stories that feature al-Sakkākī's magical powers put him in the entourage of Čaghatay Khān [*q.v.*] at Almāligh. However, calumnies on the part of the latter's vizier Ḳuṭb al-Dīn Ḥabash ʿAmīd resulted in al-Sakkākī's incarceration, and he is said to have died after three years in jail.

The Ḥanafī biographical dictionaries mention a few of his teachers in law, among whom Sadīd b. Muḥammad al-Khayyāṭī deserves mention, because in the chain of scholarship he was the link between al-Sakkākī and al-Zamakhsharī (d. 538/1144 [*q.v.*]). Like the latter, al-Sakkākī was a Muʿtazilī. As for the linguistic disciplines, he himself refers with great veneration to his teacher al-Ḥātimī who, however, cannot be otherwise identified (for references to quotations, see Simon, *Sprachbetrachtung*, 77-8, n. 38). The only known disciple of al-Sakkākī is Mukhtār b. Muḥammad al-Zāhidī (d. 658/1260) who is said to have studied *kalām* with him; Mukhtār is the author of the *fiḳh* work *Ḳunyat al-munya* which has acquired a certain fame for being one of the few sources for the old Khwārazmian language, containing, as it does, phrases in that language that have some legal import (see KHWĀRAZM, at vol. IV, 1062). It is not unlikely that al-Sakkākī was quadrilingual in Khwārazmian, Khwārazm Turkic, Persian and Arabic.

In spite of a number of lost or doubtful works that have been ascribed to him, al-Sakkākī is really a man of one book, the *Miftāḥ al-ʿulūm*. This "Key to the Sciences" is not, as imprecise formulations in secondary sources can lead one to believe, a work of rhetoric. Rather, the author intended to cover all linguistic disciplines, with the exception of *lugha* "lexicon, lexicography". The work is divided into three major parts dedicated respectively to *ʿilm al-ṣarf* "morphology", *ʿilm al-naḥw* "syntax", and *ʿilm al-maʿānī wa 'l-bayān* "stylistics and theory of imagery". The first part contains at its beginning also a brief section on phonetics (*makhāridj al-ḥurūf*) and a discussion of root formation and semantic derivation (*ishtiḳāḳ*), while the third part has the following supplements: (1) a brief section on rhetorical figures (*wudjūh ... li-ḳaṣd taḥsīn al-kalām*); (2) a *takmila* on *ḥadd* "definition", and (3) one on *istidlāl* "argumentation"; and (4) and (5) a *tatimma* on poetry dealing with *ʿilm al-ʿarūḍ* "metrics" and *ʿilm al-ḳāfiya* "rhyme theory". Finally, in the *khātima* the author wards off attacks on the linguistic correctness of the Ḳurʾān. A complete count of all the topics, whether dealt with in the main parts or in appendices, results in the number of "twelve Arab sciences (i.e. language sciences)" that later authors have detected in al-Sakkākī's work (see e.g. al-Khwānsārī, 745, l. 32). It is clear that the author wanted to cover all aspects of language, from the sounds to various shapes and styles of meaningful language.

Historically, the most important part of the work was its third chapter, on stylistics and imagery. It was the root from which most of the later *madrasa* literature on *ʿilm al-balāgha* "rhetoric" sprang (this term is not yet technically used in al-Sakkākī, as might appear from the art. BALĀGHA). Al-Sakkākī's main sources here were, for the "science of *maʿānī*" (i.e., *maʿānī al-naḥw* "semantics of syntactical relations"), the *Dalāʾil al-iʿdjāz* of ʿAbd al-Ḳāhir al-Djurdjānī (see AL-DJURDJĀNĪ in Suppl.) and, for the "science of *bayān*" (i.e., lit. "elucidating discourse" = "indirect presentation by way of images"), the same author's *Asrār al-balāgha*. In addition, he is influenced by Fakhr al-Dīn al-Rāzī's (d. 606/1209 [*q.v.*]) *Nihāyat al-īdjāz fī dirāyat al-iʿdjāz*. The latter is a precursor of al-Sakkākī in the sense that he, too, tried to harness the fertile but groping thought of al-Djurdjānī into a strict and logical system, though the outcome differs considerably from al-Sakkākī's.

The third chapter of the *Miftāḥ* was influential for Badr al-Dīn Ibn Mālik (d. 686/1287) in his *al-Miṣbāḥ fi 'l-maʿānī wa 'l-bayān*, although the extent of his dependence needs further study (see Sellheim, *Materialien*, i, 299 ff.). Historically more important by far are the two works of al-Khaṭīb al-Ḳazwīnī (d. 739/1338), the *Talkhīṣ al-Miftāḥ* and, less so, its expanded version, *al-Īḍāḥ*. Al-Ḳazwīnī was not averse to criticising al-Sakkākī on certain points and making a number of adjustments that prove his independent mind. Both Ibn Mālik and al-Ḳazwīnī raise al-Sakkākī's appendix on the rhetorical figures to the status of a separate discipline, the *ʿilm al-badīʿ*. Thus the "science of eloquence" (*ʿilm al-balāgha*) with its three branches of *maʿānī, bayān* and *badīʿ* takes its final shape and, as presented in the *Talkhīṣ al-Miftāḥ* of al-Ḳazwīnī, henceforth dominates scholastic rhetoric.

Bibliography: Editions. *Miftāḥ al-ʿulūm*, Cairo 1317 (with al-Suyūṭī, *Itmām al-dirāya li-ḳurrāʾ al-Nuḳāya*, on the margin; this combination was apparently repr. twice, Cairo 1318, 1348); Cairo 1356/1937; ed. Nuʿaym Zarzūr, Beirut 1403/1983. The old eds. offer a reasonable text; the Beirut ed. is well laid out, but rather faulty and defective. A critical ed. is a desideratum. For mss. see Brockelmann, I, 294; S I, 515; and Maṭlūb, *al-Sakkākī*, 61-3. Tr. of ch. on *ʿilm al-maʿānī* by U.G. Simon, *Mittelalterliche arabische Sprachbetrachtung zwischen Grammatik und Rhetorik*—ʿilm al-maʿānī *bei as-Sakkākī*, Heidelberg 1993.

Studies of the *Miftāḥ*. A. Maṭlūb, *al-Balāgha ʿind al-Sakkākī*, Baghdād 1384/1964; W. Smyth, *Persian and Arabic theories of literature: a comparative study of al-Sakkākī's Miftāḥ al-ulūm and Shams-i Qays' al-Muʿjam fī maʿāyīr ashʿār al-ʿajam*, unpubl. Ph.D. thesis, New York University 1986; idem, *Some quick rules* ut pictura poesis: *the rules for simile in* Miftāḥ al-ʿulūm, in *Oriens*, xxxiii (1992), 215-29; idem, *The making of a textbook*, in *SI*, lxxviii (1993), 99-115. For the commentary literature based on the *Miftāḥ*, see A. Maṭlūb, *al-Ḳazwīnī wa-shurūḥ al-Talkhīṣ*, Baghdād 1387/1967, and R. Sellheim, *Materialien zur arabischen Literaturgeschichte*, Teil I, Wiesbaden 1976, 299-334, Teil II, Wiesbaden 1987, 60-84.

(W.P. HEINRICHS)

SAḲḲĀRA, a village in the Egyptian province of al-Djīza, on the western bank of the Nile, near the mountain ridge that separates the fertile lands of the Nile Valley from the desert, approximately 20 km to the south of Cairo. In the 9th/15th century this locality seems to have been better known under the name of Arḍ al-Sidra (cf. Ibn al-Djīʿān, *Tuḥfa*, 139, l. 18; S. de Sacy, *Relation de l'Égypte par Abd Allatif, médecin arabe de Bagdad*, Paris 1810, 671; cf. also Ramzī, *al-Ḳāmūs al-djughrāfī li 'l-bilād al-miṣriyya*, ii/3, 45; Halm, *Ägypten nach den mamlukischen Lehensregistern*, i, 209), because it belonged to Būṣīr = (A)Bū Ṣīr al-Sidr, the neighbouring village to the north that was equally well known for its Pharaonic remains (see e.g. Ibn Mammātī, *Ḳawānīn al-dawāwīn*, 117: Bū Ṣīr Radjab = Bū Ṣīr al-Sidr). In the year 777/1376 (the date to which our source, Ibn al-Djīʿān's 15th-century cadastral survey, here refers), this village had an arable area of 240 *faddāns* and was in the hands of the sons of the governor Arghūn Shāh (d. 731/1331; cf. Ibn Taghrībirdī, *al-Manhal al-ṣāfī*, ii, 306-8, no. 367); ʿUmar b. Arghūn Shāh in particular was a key figure in Mamluk politics in the sixties of the 8th/14th century (al-Maḳrīzī, *Sulūk*, iii, 63, l. 2).

Originally, the name Saḳḳāra (one also finds Ṣaḳḳāra) seems to have referred to another village (in the Ṭammūh/Ṭamwayh district further north) with a tax yield of 10,000 army dīnārs and a cultivated territory of 790 *faddāns*. It formed, like most of the taxable settlements in al-Djīziyya province in Mamlūk times, part of the Royal domains, *al-dīwān al-sulṭānī* (cf. Ibn Mammātī, *Ḳawānīn al-dawāwīn*, 150; Ibn al-Duḳmāḳ, *al-Intiṣār*, iv, 132 [not 133, as in *EI*¹]; Ibn al-Djīʿān, *Tuḥfa*, 144, l. 25; de Sacy, 675). When this settlement was eventually given up, evidently well prior to the end of the Mamlūk sultanate, its name was transferred to "modern" Saḳḳāra.

Saḳḳāra is famous for the huge cemeteries of Pharaonic times (see the charts and tables in the article "Saqqara, Nekropolen", in *Lexikon der Ägyptologie*, v, 387-428, esp. 398-400, 401-2, 415) located on the slope of the Gebel and the adjacent elevated terrain, always in visual connection with Memphis (Manf [*q.v.*]), the capital of the Egyptian Old Kingdom, to which this city of the dead belonged. The modern Arabic name of the village is derived from Sokar/Socharis, "the coffined one", i.e. the King of the Dead, whose cave is supposed to have been in the vicinity. The famous necropolis of Saḳḳāra which developed, during the first three dynasties of the Old Kingdom, from north to south along the mountain range and then westward into the desert, contains royal tombs (pyramids, mastabas) of the three first dynasties (including the famous step pyramid (*al-haram al-mudarradj*) of King Djoser of the Third Dynasty), private tombs especially from the Fourth to Sixth Dynasties, free-standing chapels from the first intermediate period and the Middle Kingdom, and, last but not least, the burial sites from the Saitic era, when Memphis re-emerged, after the Assyrian yoke had been shaken off, as a major centre of the country. In this late period, the pristine Egyptian cults were consciously resuscitated, both on religious and economic grounds. New cemeteries were opened in Saḳḳāra—as it were, on sacred ground—for all strata of the population. And it was during this final period of Egyptian independence (21st Dynasty onwards) that the famous burial catacombs and mortuary-cult temples for the Sacred Animals of Memphis, notably the Serapaeum for the Apis Bulls, were erected within the Saḳḳāra necropolis. To the mediaeval Muslims the mummified animals that were found here were particularly fascinating (not the least because they were so reprehensible on dogmatic grounds) (cf. e.g. al-Maḳrīzī's report on the dead "hoopoe", *hudhud* = ibis, *Das Pyramidenkapitel in al-Maḳrîzî's "Ḫiṭaṭ"*, ed. and tr. E. Graefe, Leipzig 1911, Arabic text 21, l. 4, German tr. 67).

Saḳḳāra's importance for Egyptology was further enhanced by the discovery, in 1824, of the first two papyri, contained in sealed pottery, in a tomb (or well) in the funerary precinct.

The Arabic toponym that, during the Islamic Middle Ages, seems to have customarily denoted the necropolis of Saḳḳāra with its awe-inspiring and vast Pharaonic architectural vestiges, was, however, not Saḳḳāra, but rather, by way of metonymy, "Dayr (A)Bū Hirmīs", the monastery of Apa Jeremias (should one rather read: Dayr Hirimyas?, cf. Maspéro-Wiet, *Matériaux*, 95-6). In his list of the 54 villages surrounding the great pyramids of Djīza, Abū Djaʿfar al-Idrīsī (d. 649/1251) omits Saḳḳāra, yet names, as no. 14 and no. 16, both Bū Hirmīs and Shubrā Bū Hirmīs (*Anwār ʿulwiyy al-adjrām fi 'l-kashf ʿan asrār al-ahrām*, 50, ll. 7 and 8; we also find Bū Ṣīr Bū Radjab and Bū Ṣīr al-ahrām, 50, ll. 8 and 9). Apa Jeremias' monastery (whose remains were rediscovered only at the beginning of the 20th century and where excavations continue to be carried out) stood within the precinct of the Saḳḳāra necropolis. The historian and traditionist Ḳāḍī Muḥammad b. Salāma al-Ḳuḍāʿī (d. in Fusṭāṭ in 454/1062), reporting from the well-known Egyptian authority Yaḥyā b. ʿUthmān b. Ṣāliḥ (d. 282/895), relates the story of a denizen of the Upper Egyptian Koptos/Ḳifṭ and how a corpse was discovered in this monastery when a grave was dug. On the chest of the dead man, a papyrus scroll from the aegis of the Roman emperor Diocletian was found, written in "oldest Coptic" script, which informed of the otherwise inaccessible antediluvian Egyptian history (cf. Abū Djaʿfar al-Idrīsī, *Anwār*, 100, l. 3-102, l. 4; al-Maḳrīzī, *Khiṭaṭ*, in *Pyramidenkapitel*, 21, ll. 13 ff., German tr. 67 ff., cites the same report, probably on al-Idrīsī's authority).

The region of Apa Jeremias, i.e. Saḳḳāra, was correctly identified as the heartland of the most ancient history of Egypt. The Sharīf Tādj al-Sharaf Muḥammad al-Ḥusaynī al-Ḥalabī al-ʿUbaydalī (d. 666/1267), an avid student of Pharaonic architecture in his time, placed the cradle of the oldest Egyptian people in this very region (*nawāḥī Bū Ṣīr wa-Bū Hirmīs*, cf. *Anwār*, 107, l. 12), and, incidentally, even considered as conceivable a pre-Adamite (not just antediluvian) date for their impressive activities. From the testimony of stones found in St. Jeremias' monastery that bore hieroglyphic inscriptions not—or not only—on the visible front side, but also inside, where they were connected with neighbouring slabs, he inferred the existence of different historical layers in the history and architecture of Old Egypt.

The step pyramid in the immediate neighbourhood of Apa Jeremias' monastery is portrayed as the tomb of the legendary Egyptian knight (*fāris ahl Miṣr*) Ḳaryās, who had the valour and strength of one thousand fighters, whereas the huge pyramid to the north of the monastery, also built in steps, is said to have become the resting place of Ḳaryās' sovereign (cf. *Anwār*, 118, ll. 8 ff.; al-Maḳrīzī, *Pyramidenkapitel*, 27, ll. 3 ff., German tr. 72). Also, Yāḳūt speaks, in his geographical repertory (s.v. *Dayr Hirmis*), of the pyramid by the monastery of Apa Jeremias. Other authors, such as Abū Ṣāliḥ al-Armanī (*Churches and monasteries*, fol. 65a), only summarily refer to the "flourishing and populous" monasteries in the al-Djīziyya province.

Like all the spectacular Pharaonic sites, the mastabas of Saḳḳāra have also been identified with localities of the Muslim *ḳiṣaṣ al-anbiyāʾ* [*q.v.*]. Whereas the great pyramids of Djīza were seen, by some authors, as Joseph's granary, his prison (*sidjn Yūsuf*) tended to be localised in Saḳḳāra (see e.g. al-Ḳalḳashandī, *Ṣubḥ al-aʿshā*, iii, 317, l. 11; see also the reference given by J. Walker in the *EI*[1] art.).

Bibliography: A lengthy bibl. of mediaeval Islamic Pharaonica is to be found in U. Haarmann, *Das Pyramidenbuch des Abū Ǧaʿfar al-Idrīsī*, Beirut 1991, Arabic 272-83. On the apocryphal tradition associated with Old Egypt in mediaeval Islam, see now also U. Sezgin, *al-Masʿūdī, Ibrāhīm b. Waṣīfšāh und das* Kitāb al-ʿAǧāʾib. *Aigyptiaca in arabischen Texten des 10. Jahrhunderts n.Chr.*, in *ZGAIW*, viii (1993), 1-70.

(U. Haarmann)

SAḲḲIZ, a small town of Persian Kurdistan, now the chef-lieu of a *shahrastān* or county in the province of Kurdistan (lat. 36° 14′ N., long. 46° 15′ E.). It lies on the western side of the upper Djaghatū Čay valley some 77 km/50 miles to the southeast of Mahābād [*q.v.*] and on the road southwards to Sanandadj and Kirmānshāh [*q.vv.*].

The Kurdish population are from the Mukrī tribe, Shāfiʿī Sunnīs and with the Naḳshbandī Ṣūfī order influential amongst them. In the early 20th century, the local khān was a relative of the *wālī*s of Ardalān and Sanandadj. In *ca.* 1950 Saḳḳiz town had a population of 9,900, but by 1991 this had risen to 99,048 (*Preliminary results of the 1991 census*, Statistical Centre of Iran, Population Division). Until recently, it had a small community of Neo-Aramaic-speaking Jews, but these have now probably all emigrated to Israel.

Bibliography: Razmārā (ed.), *Farhang-i djughrāfiyā-yi Īrān-zamīn*, v, 241-2.

(C.E. Bosworth)

SAḲSĪN, the name of one or more cities in Western Eurasia.

The location of this city (or cities) is still unclear. It is unrecorded in the classical Islamic geographies. Maḥmūd al-Kāshgharī (tr. R. Dankoff and J. Kelly

Cambridge, Mass. 1982-5, i, 330), who finished writing his *Dīwān lug̲h̲at al-Turk* in *ca.* 469/1077, notes it as "a city near Bulg̲h̲ār. It is Suwār." The latter was a tribal name (*Saviri*/Σαβίροι of the Latin and Byzantine sources) of one of the constituent elements of the Volga Bulg̲h̲ārs. In this regard, Togan (*Ibn Faḍlān's Reisebericht*, 203-4, cites the theologian Sulaymān b. Dāwūd with the *nisba* al-Suwārī or al-Saḳsīnī. It seems unlikely that this is the Volga Bulg̲h̲arian city of Suwār, which was within the Bulg̲h̲ār core lands. Rather, it probably points to the presence of a substantial Suwār population in Saḳsīn which is confirmed by Abū Ḥāmid al-G̲h̲arnāṭī (see below). Mustawfī (*Nuzhat al-ḳulūb*, 259, 252; Togan, *op. cit.*, 204), pairs Saḳsīn and Bulg̲h̲ār as "two small cities of the sixth clime", much land belongs to them and they export furs. He places them at 32° = 750 farsak̲h̲s distant from Mecca (10/10) and remarks (21/23) that the eastern frontier of Iran, which begins in Sindh, runs to the frontier of Saḳsīn and Bulg̲h̲ār. The Islamic historians of the Mongol era invariably pair Saḳsīn and Bulg̲h̲ār. Thus D̲j̲ūzd̲j̲ānī, ed. Lees, 446, 451, tr. Raverty, ii, 1283, 1292, notes that Berke K̲h̲ān was born at the time that his father, Tūs̲h̲ī (D̲j̲oči) was invading the territory of Saḳsīn, Bulg̲h̲ār and Saḳlāb. Similarly, D̲j̲uwaynī, ed. Ḳazwīnī, i, 31, 150, 205, iii, 15, tr. Boyle, i, 42, 190, 249, ii, 557, and Ras̲h̲īd al-Dīn, *D̲j̲āmiʿ al-tawārīk̲h̲*, ed. Karīmī, i, 455, tr. Boyle, *Successors,* 33, place Saḳsīn and Bulg̲h̲ār in apparent close propinquity to one another and to the Ḳîpčaḳ country (see also Waṣṣāf and Aḥmad G̲h̲affārī (d. 975/1567-8) in Tiesenhausen, *Sbornik*, 82, 84, 86, 211/270). Indeed, D̲j̲uwaynī places the *ordu* of Batu in the "Bulg̲h̲ār and Saḳsīn country." Al-Bakūwī (ed. Buniyatov, fol. 69b/p. 107), a geographer of the early 9th/15th century, says that by his day Saḳsīn had been inundated and had vanished without a trace, but he appears to place the later Saray Berke at or near Saḳsīn. A broad over-view of the relationship of Saḳsīn to the other cities of the Mongol era is seen in al-ʿUmarī, ed. and tr. Lech, Arabic text, 85/142, who outlines the borders of the K̲h̲ānate of Ḳîpčaḳ (= the Ulus of D̲j̲oči) as: "the Amu Daryā, K̲h̲ʷārazm, Sig̲h̲nāḳ, Sawrān, Barkand, D̲j̲and, Sarāy, Mād̲j̲ar, Azāḳ, Aḳča Karmān, Kaffa, Sudāḳ, Saḳsīn, Ukak and Bulg̲h̲ār," placing Saḳsīn, it would appear, in the southern section of the Volga lands, east of the Crimean centre of Sudāḳ. This city also figures in an interesting listing of the lands and peoples given to D̲j̲oči as his appanage: K̲h̲ʷārazm, the Das̲h̲t-i K̲h̲azar, Bulg̲h̲ār, Saḳsīn, the Alans, the Ās, the Rūs, Mikes (?) and the Bas̲h̲kird (see Mustawfī, *Tārīk̲h̲-i guzīda*, in Tiesenhausen, *Sbornik,* ii, 91/Pers. text 219, see a similar listing in the anonymous *S̲h̲ad̲j̲arat al-Atrāk*, in *ibid.*, ii, 204/Pers. text 264).

According to the rendering of Ibn Saʿīd found in Abu 'l-Fidā, *Taḳwīm al-buldān*, ed. Reinaud and de Slane, Paris 1840, 204-5, it was a famous city, in which in his day a son of Berke resided. It was located in the north of the *Krmāniyya* (probably *Kūmāniyya*, i.e. Cumania) lands on the river *Ṭanābrus*. The latter hydronym normally renders the Dniepr, but in this instance most certainly designates some more easterly river. The text of Ibn Saʿīd, ed. ʿArabī, 203-4, sets it within the context of a discussion of the lands of the Ponto-Caspian region, following a discussion of Maṭark̲h̲ā (Ταμάταρχα of the Byzantine sources, Tmutorokan' of the Rus'). Abu 'l-Fidā goes on to place it at the 67° E. long, and 53° N. lat. and to the west of the city of *Swh* (ms. also *mwh*). To its east, according to Ibn Saʿīd, 204, was the city of *Ḳrāg̲h̲t*. Abu 'l-Fidā, subsequently in his narrative, citing the *Kitāb al-Aṭwāl*, notes the city *Sḳsn*, spelled without *yā*ʾ, which is placed at 162° 30′ E. long. and 40° 50′ N. lat., although he suspected that this might be another city. According to Yāḳūt, *Muʿd̲j̲am*, iv, 670, the fortress of Manḳis̲h̲lāg̲h̲ is between K̲h̲ʷārazm and Saḳsīn and the lands of the Rūs near the sea of Ṭabaristān (Caspian Sea). Al-Yazdādī, in Ibn Isfandiyār (tr. Browne, 33-4, ed. ʿAbbās Iḳbāl, Tehran 1320/1941, 80-1) says that in his time Āmul was the market for the wares of Saḳsīn and Bulg̲h̲ār. Merchants from ʿIrāḳ, Syria, K̲h̲urāsān and India came to Āmul to purchase goods there. The merchants of Ṭabaristān went to Bulg̲h̲ār and Saḳsīn which is "located on the shore of the sea opposite Āmul." This would appear to place this Saḳsīn in the lower Volga. Our source further adds that the voyage by boat from Āmul to Saḳsīn took three months, but the return journey was only one week because the former was upstream and the latter down (Pelliot, *Notes sur l'histoire de la Horde d'Or*, 170, views "Āmul" as a possible error for "Ātil" occasionally confused in the sources).

Modern scholars have placed Saḳsīn on the Yayîḳ/Ural rivers (Dorn, *Caspia*, 116) or with greater probability on the Volga, see Marquart, in *Osttürkische Dialektstudien*, 56, Barthold, *Očerk istorii turkmen. naroda*, in his *Sočineniya,* ii/1, 588. In other works e.g. *Mesto prikaspiyskik̲h̲ oblastey v istorii musul'manskogo mira*, in *ibid.*, ii/1, 690, Barthold also opted for the Ural River. Pelliot, *Notes sur la Horde d'Or*, 168, 170-2, however, was willing to accept either one. Moreover, he suggested that there were two Saḳsīns, confused in sources such as al-Ḳazwīnī, one the old K̲h̲azar city, the other dominated by Og̲h̲uz tribes (and a Bulg̲h̲ār official, see below). Following Ibn Saʿīd, he concluded that Saḳsīn, during the time of Berke (d. 1266) must have been the principal city of the D̲j̲očids. Polyak, *Noviе arabskie*, 46, suggested that Saḳsīn denoted the pre-Mongol era city, the k̲h̲ān's headquarters which later became Saray Berke as well as the whole region around it. He locates this on the Ak̲h̲tuba, an eastern tributary of the Volga. Minorsky, *Ḥudūd*, 453, was prepared to see in Saḳsīn the earlier K̲h̲azar city of Sarîg̲h̲s̲h̲în on the lower Volga. Dunlop, *History*, 248, was similarly inclined. Artamonov, *Ist. K̲h̲azar*, 445 (following yet another suggestion of Barthold, *Kavkaz, Turkestan, Volga*, in *Sočineniya*, ii/1, 794, and Westberg, *K analizu*, 37 ff.), viewed it as the revived Itil, the old K̲h̲azar capital in the Volga delta. The Mongol era information, in any event, appears to point in the direction of the lower Volga region.

Our most thorough account comes from Abū Ḥāmid al-G̲h̲arnāṭī (473-565/1080-1170 [*q.v.*]), a Spanish Muslim who spent a good part of his adult life in the Volga region (from 525/1131 onwards largely in Ṣaḳsīn). In his account (ed. Dubler, 5-9, Russ. tr. Bol's̲h̲akov, 27-30, considerable elements of which are repeated by al-Ḳazwīnī, *Āt̲h̲ār,* Beirut 1389/1969, 599), he places the city at some 40 days travel from Bulg̲h̲ār in the "country of the K̲h̲azars", which would again point to the lower Volga region. His reference to the K̲h̲azars and to Muslim communities from that people in the city, may be more consistent with the geographical nomenclature that he has adopted than with the ethnic realities, although it is certainly possible that Muslims of K̲h̲azar origin were still resident in the region. More concretely, he writes that there were 40 Og̲h̲uz tribes in the city, each led by its own *amīr*. Saḳsīn, however, appeared to be under Volga Bulg̲h̲ar overlordship for an *amīr* representing that powerful mercantile state resided in the centre of the city. The Bulg̲h̲ars also lived around a large Friday mosque. There was another Friday mosque for the Suwārs, who were "also numerous." The private residences seem to have largely been the tents of the nomads or log cabins made of pine wood. In this respect, Saksīn was much like the old Khazar capital and the Volga Bulghar cities. Similarly, the city was filled with foreign merchants, some, like our source, coming from the western regions of the Islamic world. In Abū Ḥāmid's account, the city has a strong Muslim character. Each of its various groups had its own judges, jurisconsults and preachers. With the exception of the Maghribīs of the Mālikī *madhhab* or other foreigners who followed the Shāfiʿī school, the natives of the city were Ḥanafīs.

In addition to the ferocious cold of the region, Abū Ḥāmid, in discussing the local peculiarities that might be of interest, mentions the enormous size and weight of certain types of fish caught in "the river" that are unique to that region. One such fish could only be carried by a powerful camel. Another type of fish is described as boneless, and it "is like the tail of a lamb roasted with chicken meat. It is even better than the meat of a plump lamb." Lamp oil can be extracted from this fish as well as isinglass. Its meat could also be cured and became "the best of all the dried meats in the world." The currency there is made of lead, of which eight Baghdād *mann* = 1 dīnār. Sheep cost ½ *dānaḳ* each, rams ¼ *tassūdj*; there is also much fruit.

Of Saksīn's actual history, we know little. Djūzdjānī, tr. Raverty, i, 234, says the early ruler of the Khwārazmshāh state, Ḳuṭb al-Dunyā wa 'l-Dīn Aybak (= Ḳuṭb al-Dīn Muḥammad? *regn.* 490-521/1097-1121) "guarded the frontiers of Khwārazm Shāh from the infidels of Saksīn, Bulghār and Ḳifčaḳ." Such "infidels" would almost certainly have been the Ḳïpčaḳ-Ḳanglï tribes [*q.vv.*] of the region. More concrete, but still infrequent references appear in the sources relating the events of the Mongol invasions. Ibn al-Athīr (ed. Beirut, xii, 388), notes that in late 620/1224, following their defeat at the hands of the Volga Bulghārs, the Tatars "came to Saksīn on the return route to their king Djankīz Khān and the land of the Ḳïpčaḳ was free of them." There are other scattered references to Saksīn in the accounts of the conquest of the lands of the Ḳïpčaḳ, Volga Bulghāria and Rūs (cf. also *Taʾrīkh-i Guzīda*, ed. Browne, 572; Yāḳūt, *Muʿdjam*, i, 255). After the conquest of Khwārazm, the Mongols, probably later in 1221 or 1222, invaded Saksīn, Volga Bulghāria and the "Slav" lands (Djūzdjānī). Another campaign was launched against them in 1229 (Djuwaynī, i, 150, tr. Boyle, i, 190). The Russian Chronicles (*PSRL*, i, 453) report that the "Saksini" and Cumans fled from the lowlands to the Volga Bulghārs. But, the Tatars defeated the Bulghār guards near the Ural river. Latin sources (Carpini, ed. Menestò, 290-1, and the *Tatar relation*, 100/101) indicate that the "Saxi" (for *Saxini? Benedict the Pole, who took part in this mission, remarks that the "Saxi", whom he took to be Goths, like their immediate neighbours, the "Alani" and "Gazari" were Christians, see Wyngaert, *Sinica Franciscana*, i, 137) in one of their cities resisted until the Tatars dug an underground passage into their city. In any event, by 1236 the whole region had been subjugated by the Mongols. William of Rubruck (tr. P. Jackson, London 1990, 257) mentions the city of "Summerkent", a city of the Saksīn region or a dependency of it, located on an island in the Volga, which resisted for some 8 more years before succumbing to the Tatars (on Mongol military operations here, see Allsen, *Prelude*, 12-16). Saksīn as a city survived the devastation of the Mongol conquest to enjoy a brief period of prominence, in association with the Mongol ruling line. Thus al-Dhahabī (in Tiesenhausen, *Sbornik*, i, 202/205) mentions it, sometime in the 640s/1240s, as the city from which Berke Khān went to Bukhārā to visit Shaykh Sayf al-Dīn al-Bākharzī [*q.v.*] who played a role in his conversion to Islam. As we have already noted, it was subsequently the residence of one of Berke's offspring.

Bibliography (in addition to references given in the article): 1. Sources. (a) *Collections*. C. Dawson (ed.), *The mission to Asia*, London 1955; V.G. Tiesenhausen (Tizengauzen), *Sbornik materialov otnosyashčikhsya k istorii Zolotoy Ordy*, St. Petersburg 1884, Moscow-Leningrad 1941. (b) *Arabic and Persian*. Abu 'l-Fidā, *Taḳwīm al-buldān*; Abū Ḥāmid al-Gharnāṭī, *Abū Ḥāmid el Granadino y su Relación de Viaje por Tierras eurasiáticas*, ed. C.E. Dubler, Madrid 1953; idem, *Puteshestvie Abu Khamida al-Garnati v Vostočnuyu i tsentral'nuyu evropu (1131-1153 gg.)*, Russ. tr. O.G. Bol'shakov, comm. A.L. Mongayt, Moscow 1971; Bakūwī, *Kitāb Talkhīṣ al-āthār wa ʿadjāʾib al-Malik al-Ḳahhār*, ed. Z.M. Buniyatov, Moscow 1971; Djuwaynī, *Taʾrīkh-i Djihān-gushā*, ed. Muḥammad Ḳazwīnī, Leiden 1906-37, tr. Boyle, Manchester 1958; Djūzdjānī, *Ṭabaḳāt-i Nāṣirī*, ed. W.N. Lees, Calcutta 1864, tr. H.G. Raverty, London 1881; Ḥamd Allāh Mustawfī al-Ḳazwīnī, *Nuzhat al-ḳulūb*, ed. G. Le Strange, Leiden 1913-19; idem, *Tārīkh-i guzīda*, in Tiesenhausen, *Sbornik*, tr. Browne, Leiden-London 1914; K. Lech, *Das Mongolische Weltreich. Al-ʿUmarī's Darstellung des mongolischen Reiche in seinem Werk Masālik al-abṣār fī mamālik al-amṣār*, Wiesbaden 1968; Rashīd al-Dīn, *Djāmiʿ al-tawārīkh*, ed. B. Karīmī, Tehran 1338/1959, partial tr. J.A. Boyle, *The successors of Genghis Khan*, New York 1971; A.Z.W. Togan, *Ibn Faḍlān's Reisebericht*, Abhandlungen für die Kunde des Morgenlandes, xxiv/3, Leipzig 1938. (c) *Latin*. Benedict the Pole, in P.A. van den Wyngaert, *Sinica Franciscana*, i, Florence 1929; Giovanni da Pian del Carpine, *Storia dei mongoli*, ed. E. Menestò, Ital. tr. M.C. Lungarotti, notes by P. Daffinà, Spoleto 1989, also in Wyngaert, *Sinica Franciscana*, i; Julianus = *Julianus barát és napkelet földezése*, tr. Gy. Györffy *et al.*, Budapest 1986; *The Vinland map and the Tatar relation*, ed. R.A. Skelton *et al.*, New Haven 1965; (d) *Russian*. *PSRL* = *Polnoe sobranie russkikh letopisey*, St. Petersburg/Leningrad-Moscow 1841-.

2. Studies. T. Allsen, *Prelude to the western campaigns: Mongol military operations in the Volga-Ural Region, 1217-1237*, in *Archivum Eurasiae Medii Aevi*, iii (1985), 5-24; M.I. Artamonov, *Istoriya Khazar* ["The history of the Khazars"], Leningrad 1962; W. Barthold (V.V. Bartol'd), *Očerk istorii turkmenskogo naroda* ["An outline of the history of the Turkmen people"], in his *Sočineniya*, Moscow 1963-73, ii/1, 545-623; idem, *Mesto prikaspiyskikh oblastey v istorii musul'manskogo mira* ["The place of the Caspian districts in the history of the Muslim world"], in *ibid.*, ii/1, 651-772; idem, *Kavkaz, Turkestan, Volga* ["The Caucasus, Turkestan, the Volga"], in *ibid.*, ii/1, 789-96; B. Dorn, *Caspia*, St. Petersburg 1875; D.M. Dunlop, *The history of the Jewish Khazars*, Princeton 1954; J. Marquart, *Über das Volkstum der Komanen*, in W. Bang and J. Marquart, *Osttürkische Dialektstudien*, Abh. Akad. Wiss. Göttingen, phil.-hist. Kl., N.F. XIII/1 (Berlin 1914), 25-238; P. Pelliot, *Notes sur l'histoire de la Horde d'Or, suivies de Quelques noms turcs d'hommes et de peuple finissant en "ar"*, in *Oeuvres posthumes de Paul Pelliot*, ii, Paris 1949; A.N. Polyak, *Novïe arabskie materialï pozdnego srednevekov'ya o Vostočnoy i Tsentral'noy Evrope* ["New

Arabic materials of the late Middle Ages on Eastern and Central Europe''], in A.S. Tveritinova (ed.), *Vostočnïe istočniki po istorii narodov Yugo-vostočnoy i Tsentral'noy Evrope* [''Oriental sources on the history of the peoples of South-Eastern and Central Europe''], Moscow 1964; B. Spuler, *Die Goldene Horde*, 2nd rev. ed., Wiesbaden 1965; F. Westberg (Vestberg), *K analizu vostočnïkh istočnikov o Vostočnoy Evrope* [''Towards an analysis of the oriental sources on Eastern Europe''], in *Žurnal ministerstva narodnogo prosveshčeniya*, xiii, xiv (1908).

(V.F. Büchner-[P.B. Golden])

SĀL-NĀME (t.), a term of Ottoman Turkish administration:

1. Official yearbooks issued by the Ottoman central government, by provincial authorities and a number of civil (ministries) and military (army, fleet) institutions, appearing between 1263/1847 and the end of the Empire (1918).

They unite characteristics of European handbooks (*Almanach de Gotha*, French *Annuaires Officiels*), a synoptic calendar and traditional Ottoman historical and bureaucratic materials (condensed history of the dynasty, itineraries, *defter*/registers such as budgets). The *sāl-nāmes* are reliable instruments with almost all details on state officials (at the supervisory level), administrative organisation, toponomy, communications, laws and regulations, although one should refer to the *Taḳwīm-i Weḳāʾiʿ* for up-to-date information. The Imperial *sāl-nāmes* give summary population data; the provincial editions often provided information on male and female population down to the *ḳaḍā* level, data on migration, numbers of household, births and deaths in urban areas, population by *millet*, and city and even village size, though the depth and quality of information varied according to geographic area (J. McCarthy, *Muslims and minorities. The population of Ottoman Anatolia and the end of the Empire*, New York 1983).

The first imperial *sāl-nāmes* were modest, lithographically-produced booklets, but their size and quality improved gradually (for the content of the first state year book, compare *Sâlnâme. Le premier annuaire de l'Empire ottoman ou tableau de l'état politique civil, militaire, judiciaire et administratif de la Turquie depuis l'introduction des réformes opérées dans ce pays par les sultans Mahmoud II et Abdul-Medjid, actuellement regnant; traduit du Turc et accompagné des notes explicatives par T[homas] X[avier] Bianchi*, Paris 1848 = *JA*, Sér. 4, x [1847], xi [1848]). After 1888, the Personal Records Administration (*Sidjill-i Aḥwāl-i Meʾmūrīn Idāresi*) was responsible for the governmental almanacs. In the provinces, the first almanacs appeared in Sarajevo (*Sāl-nāme-yi Wilāyet-i Bosna*, 1283/1866), Aleppo (Ḥaleb), Konya, Sūriye, and the Danube province (Ṭuna). Like the official provincial newspapers, they were the responsibility of the *mektūbdju-yi wilāyet*. Some provincial year-books appeared with Arabic, Greek and ''Bosnian'' translations. Many included illustrations and tables. They were an instrument to demonstrate progress made by the government and to encourage competition between administrators.

2. Semi-official and non-governmental annuals. Some of these were annual reports of welfare organisations (e.g. *ʿOthmānlï Hilāl-i Aḥmer Djemʿiyyeti*, 1329/1331; *Djemʿiyyet-i tedrīsiyye-i İslāmiyye*, 1332/1913). Ebu 'l-Ḍiyāʾ (Ebūżżiyā) Tewfiḳ [*q.v.*] was the publisher of the most successful almanacs for a vast reading public. The first appeared under the name *Sāl-nāme-yi Ḥadīḳa* (1873). Later, it was published under different names such as *Sāl-nāme-yi Ebu 'l-Ḍiyāʾ* (the first edition was destroyed in the printing press by order of the sultan) and *Newsāl-i Maʿrıfet*.

3. Republican Turkey published a series of *Türkiye Djumhūriyeti Dewlet Sāl-nāmesi* (first 3 vols. 1925-6 to 1927-8 in Arabic script; 1928-9 under the title *Türkiye Cumhuriyeti Devlet Yıllığı*). There were several attempts to revitalise the provincial almanacs under the name of *İl yıllıkları* (1967 and 1973).

Bibliography: Hasan Duman, *Ottoman year-books [Salname and Nevsal]. A bibliography and a union catalogue with reference to Istanbul libraries*, Istanbul 1982; A. Ubicini and Pavet de Courteille, *État présent de l'Empire ottoman. Statistique, gouvernement, administration, finances, armée, communautés non musulmanes etc. etc. d'après le Salnâméh (annuaire impérial) pour l'année 1293 de l'hégire (1875-76) et les documents officiels le plus récents*, Paris 1876; M. Hartmann, *Das erste Jahrbuch der geistlichen Behörden des Osmanischen Reiches*, in *WI*, iv (1916-17), 26-32; K. Kreiser, *Quellen zur Landeskunde und Geschichte des Jemen in türkischer Sprache*, in *Resultate aktueller Jemen-Forschung, eine Zwischenbilanz* (Bamberger Geographische Schriften, 1), Bamberg 1978, 93-122; J. McCarthy and J.D. Hyde, *Ottoman imperial and provincial Salnames*, in *IJMES* (1978); C.V. Findley, *Ottoman civil officialdom. A social history*, Princeton 1989. Many official and private *sāl-nāmes* are available in microfiche (Ottoman Microform Project. The University of Chicago/Middle East Documentation Center).

(K. Kreiser)

SALĀ, dialectically Sla, current French anc English form Salé, a town of Morocco on the Atlantic coast at the mouth of the Būragrag (olde Asmir), situated on a flat, sandy stretch of land. Pre-18th century sources often mix up Shalla, Salé anc Rabat. *Selā would mean ''crag, cliff'' in Puni (though not in fact attested in extant Punic texts) bu a Phoenician past for the town is based only o hypothesis.

Ibn Ḥawḳal, tr. Kramers-Wiet, 78, mentions a town and some *ribāṭ*s on the river of Salā, whilst al Bakrī states that ʿĪsā, the son of Idrīs II, was the rule of the town. But this could also refer to Shalla rathe than Salé proper. The town was probably founded b the Banū ʿAshara during the 5th/11th century. A first the Banū ʿAshara were at Shalla, but left it for th right bank of the river where they built palaces an held a court which rivalled those of the Spanish Taifa (M. Bencherifa, *Usrat Banī ʿAshara*, in *al-Baḥth al-ʿIlm* [Rabat 1967], 177-219). Under the Almoravids, th Banū ʿAshara retained their prestige in the town whose agricultural and commercial prosperity is des cribed by al-Idrīsī. Salé's resistance to the Almohad provoked the destruction of its ramparts and th elimination of the Banū ʿAshara, whose palace ʿAb al-Muʾmin requisitioned. The town became a roy encampment, although if the army stopped in th region on its way to al-Andalus, it was, rather, fro the Mediterranean ports that it embarked.

The re-foundation of Rabat [see ribāṭ al-fatḥ] does not seem to have harmed Salé, whose role co tinued to be important; the caliphs often stayed the and undertook important building works: the prov sion of water (*sūr al-aḳwās* or wall of the arches), an construction or restoration of the Great Mosqu Masdjid al-Ṭāliʿa, which has always occupied th same place. The Marīnid conquest was marked by th seizure and sack of the town by the Castilians 658/1260; goods were pillaged and burnt and substantial part of the population massacre Amongst the inhabitants carried off as slaves was th *ḳāḍī*, who was a descendant of the Banū ʿAshara. Th Marīnid Abū Yūsuf (656-85/1258-86) came to th help of the town and took part in rebuilding tho walls which had not been rebuilt by the Almoha

Salā. Court of the Marīnīd *medersa*.

(Ibn ʿIdhārī, *Bayān*, section on the Almohads, Rabat 1985, 418-25; A. Huici Miranda, *La toma de Salé por la escuada de Alfons X*, in *Hespéris* [1952]).

Between the 5th/11th and 8th/14th centuries Salé enjoyed real prosperity. The agricultural richness of the region, and commercial and artisanal activity, are attested in the sources, and despite the mediocre standard of the port (al-Idrīsī, *Maghrib* , 85), commercial traffic was important. Oil was imported from Seville, and corn, bees'- wax, hides, wool and indigo were exported (F.B. Peglotti, *La pratica della mercatura*, Cambridge, Mass. 1936). Ibn al-Khaṭīb, who spent three years there (760-3/1359-61) states that it was the "capital for cotton and linen" (*Miʿyār al-ikhtiyār*, Rabat 1977, 74). Fishing was especially flourishing. To the Almohad foundations, the Marīnids added a series of monuments, including two *madrasas*, a *māristān* and the Zāwiyat al-Nussāk. The arsenal, arranged within the interior of the walls, has not held out against the encroaching sands (H. Terrasse, *Les portes de l'arsenal de Salé*, in *Hespéris* [1922], 111). In the course of the 8th/14th century, Ibn ʿĀshir [*q.v.*], one of the two patron saints of the city, attracted thither an important group of Ṣūfīs, including Ibn ʿAbbād of Runda (M. al-Ḥaḍramī, *al-Salsal al-ʿadhb*, Salé 1988).

After the Iberian attacks on the Moroccan coasts, Salé remained one of the few ports which were not occupied and which the Saʿdians tried to utilise; the presence of an important Genoese colony attests commercial activity there. If the expelled Moriscos took refuge there, the so-called "corsairs of Salé" were in reality installed in the double city of Rabat (R. Coindreau, *Les corsaires de Salé*, Paris 1948). The town was an important stake in the struggle for power between the *zāwiya* of al-Dilā [*q.v.* in Suppl.] and the famous marabout al-ʿAyyāshī, murdered in 1051/1641 by the Khloṭs [see KHULṬ] (M. Ḥādjdjī, *al-Zāwiya al-Dilāʾiyya*, Rabat 1964). Rabat and Salé called in al-Khaḍir Ghaylān to expel the Dilāʾīs; the town suffered the effects of the general anarchy, and its history was very eventful. But the arrival in power of the ʿAlawīs [*q.v.*] was favourable for it. The system of defences was reinforced by a series of keeps and a girdle of walls, mosques were built, as well as a *madrasa*, al-Madrasa al-ʿAdjība; the Great Mosque was enlarged and provided with a new minaret. However, from the 18th century onwards, Salé's activities as a port began to decline; the harbour silted up and was unable to admit boats above a certain tonnage. The prohibition of corsair activity by the sultan Sīdī Muḥammad b. ʿAbd Allāh and the founding of the town of al-Sawīra (Mogador), which attracted European commerce, dealt a severe blow to its maritime role. Salé was, moreover, several times bombarded by the French (in 1844 and 1851).

Internal trade remained active and intellectual life relatively important up to the opening of the present century. The artisans of Salé, organised into guilds, were busy with leatherwork and pottery, and produced carpets, mats and embroidery. The immediately surrounding region provided the necessary cotton and linen; fishing for shad, which went back to mediaeval times, furnished substantial revenues for the habours. The town notables, interested in agriculture, invested in the Gharb [*q.v.*]. The opening up of the Moroccan market to European manufactures led to the collapse of these artisan activities, with the textile workers, tanners and sandalmakers particularly affected.

The establishment of the Protectorate had a threefold effect. The town became detached from its hinterland; its artisanal production collapsed; and it became a satellite town of the new capital, Rabat. Salé received a substantial influx of rural immigrants; its population leapt from 17,000 in 1918 to *ca.* 600,000 in 1992. The market-garden zone, which had been covered with orchards and *sāniyas*, was gobbled up by uncontrolled construction development.

Present-day industry makes use of an important manpower element (mainly female) for textiles; Salé continues to produce carpets, mats, embroidery and pottery, and supplies the countryside. Despite its aspect as a dormitory town and its numerous bidonvilles, the *médina* retains its traditional character and celebrates the Mawlid [*q.v.*] by an important ceremony which goes back to Saʿdian times (V. Loubignac, *La procession des cierges à Salé*, in *Hespéris* [1946], 5-30).

Bibliography (in addition to references given in the article): L. Brunot, *La mer dans les traditions et les industries indigènes de Rabat et Salé*, Paris 1920; *Villes et tribus du Maroc. Rabat et sa région*, Paris 1921; J. Goulven, *Les Mellahs de Rabat-Salé*, Rabat 1927; J. Couste, *Les grandes familles indigènes à Salé*, Rabat 1931; Leo Africanus, *Descr. de l'Afrique*, tr. A. Epaulard, Paris 1956; J. Meunié, *La Zaouya an Noussak*, in *Mél. d'Hist. et d'Archéol. de l'Occident musulmane, Alger*, ii (1957), 129-45; R. Thouvenot, *Les vestiges de la route romaine de Salé à l'oued Beth*, in *Hespéris* (1957), 73; Bakrī, *Descr. de l'Afrique Septentrionale*, Paris 1963; M. Naciri, *Salé, étude de géographie urbaine*, in *Revue de Geogr. du Maroc* (1963); K. Brown, *An urban view of Moroccan history: Salé, 1000-1888*, in *Hespéris-Tamuda*, xii (1971); Ḥimyarī, *al-Rawḍ al-miʿṭār*, ed. Iḥsān ʿAbbās, Beirut 1975; Brown, *People of Salé, tradition and change in a Moroccan city 1830-1930*, Manchester 1976; Benali Doukkali, *al-Itḥāf al-wadjīz*, Salé 1986; J. Bassar-Benslimane, *Le passé de la ville de Salé dans tous ses états*, Paris 1992. (HALIMA FERHAT)

SALADIN [see ṢALĀḤ AL-DĪN].

SALAF, a term of Islamic law and financial practice. As a noun doing duty for the verbal noun of *aslafa*, it is accorded a long entry in Lane (1403, col. 3), from which it can be seen that it is a word with a range of meanings relating to financial transactions of which the basic feature is a prepayment or a loan. A point that is not made in this entry, but which Lane would have done well to make for the benefit of the general, as opposed to the specialist, user of his lexicon is the essentially legal nature of the material utilised by his authorities for the various explanations of the word.

In works of classical jurisprudence *salaf* occurs in two main senses. Of these, one, when reduced to bare essentials, denotes a purchaser's prepayment for goods due for delivery by the recipient of such payment at the end of a specified period. In this sense, the term is held to be synonymous with *salam* [*q.v.*], the main aspects of which are dealt with under that head. The second of the two senses referred to is that attaching also to the term *ḳarḍ* or "loan", of a type recognised by the *Sharīʿa* as lawful and involving "the loan of fungible commodities, that is, goods which may be estimated and replaced according to weight, measure, and number" (Udovitch, 106; see *Bibl.* below). In this kind of loan "the borrower undertakes to return the equivalent or likes of that which he has received, but without any premium on the property, which would, of course, be construed as interest. The most likely object of a *ḳarḍ* loan would be currency or some other standard means of exchange" (*ibid.*, 106-7). Known also as *ḳarḍ ḥasan*, this type of loan must not only attract no interest, i.e. not be a *salaf bi-ziyāda*:

t must also be such as to allow no advantage (*manfaᶜa*) to accrue to the lender from his loan—though what constitutes "advantage" in what circumstances is, in fact, not a matter on which there is a consensus of juristic opinion (Saleh, 41 ff., 99; see *Bibl.* below).

For the sake of completeness and, more importantly, to dispel any confusion or misunderstanding that may arise in readers' minds, it should be noted that the *ḳarḍ* is but one of two types of loan recognised by the *S̲h̲arīᶜa*. The other is the *ᶜāriya* (or *ᶜāriyya*, the alternative preferred by Udovitch) "a loan for use which transfers the usufruct of property gratis to the borrower" (Udovitch, 106). Here the borrower's free use of the object of the loan, of which the lender retains ownership, lasts until and unless the contract is rescinded at will by either of the two parties to the agreement. To this type of loan the term *salaf* is, in Islamic law, technically inapplicable.

Bibliography: Lane, *loc. cit.* above (best consulted in conjunction with the present article and SALAM); A.L. Udovitch, *Partnership and profit in medieval Islam*, Princeton 1970; N.A. Saleh, *Unlawful gain and legitimate profit in Islamic law*, Cambridge 1986 (see esp. 35-48, 99-100). For primary sources, see the bibliographies contained in each of the last-named works. Particularly useful in certain respects for Mālikī law is O. Pesle, *La vente dans la doctrine malékite*, Rabat 1940 (see esp. 11 ff., 181, 197, 209), but the work suffers from the lack of a bibliography. To no small extent D. Santillana's monumental *Istituzioni di diritto musulmano malichita con riguardo anche al sistema sciafiita*, 2 vols., Rome 1925-38, will compensate readers for this deficiency. (J.D. LATHAM)

AL-**SALAF** WA 'L-**K̲H̲ALAF** (A.), lit. "the predecessors and the successors", names given to the first three generations and to the following generations of the Muslim community respectively.

It was the *Sunna* [*q.v.*] rather than the Ḳurʾān which instituted one of the most characteristic traits of the Islamic vision of history by imposing the idea a priori that this history was said to have begun with a golden age, which was said to have been inevitably followed by a period of relaxation of standards, deviation and finally of division. A saying of the Prophet—of which there exist various versions transmitted by different authorities—is accordingly very frequently cited in Islamic literature of all periods and in all sorts of disciplines mixed together: "The best of you are those of my own epoch (*ḳarnī*), then those who follow on, then those who follow them..." (the version of al-Buk̲h̲ārī, from ᶜImrān b. Ḥusayn, in *Ṣaḥīḥ, k. al-shahādāt, bāb lā yashhadu ᶜalā shahāda*...; for other versions, see *Concordance*, v, 372).

The word *ḳarn* "epoch, age" figuring in this *ḥadīth*, being most commonly, though not invariably, taken as a synonym of *ᶜaṣr* (cf. Fak̲h̲r al-Dīn al-Rāzī, *Mafātīḥ al-g̲h̲ayb*, Beirut 1411/1990, xii, 131), it is the three first "generations"—those of the Companions or *ṣaḥāba* [*q.v.*], of the Successors or *tābiᶜūn* [*q.v.*] and those of the Successors of the Successors or *atbāᶜ al-tābiᶜīn*—which are distinguished from the rest of the Islamic community, and it is in them that the community is to recognise the "Pious Predecessors" (*al-salaf al-ṣāliḥ*), its norms and its models. According to Ibn Taymiyya [*q.v.*] (see his *Madjmūᶜ al-fatāwā*, Rabat 1401/1981, x, 357), this privileged period of the community ended around 132/750 (hence it ran until the end of the Umayyad caliphate), but al-Rāzī, who refused to give precise dates, mentioned that certain authorities counted a *ḳarn* as comprising 60, 70 or even 80 lunar years.

In this way, each of the qualities given prominence by Islamic ethics is personified in one or other of the *salaf* (ᶜAlī typifies courage and bravery, ᶜAbd Allāh b. al-ᶜAbbās learning, etc.). Moreover, each particular intellectual discipline, and each particular trend of that discipline, whether appealing to the letter or the spirit, was to search for a precursor amongst the *salaf*, a person reputed to be its initiator hence embodying thereby the role of guarantor of the legitimacy of the discipline in question.

In practice, the precedence of the *salaf* is only fully displayed in regard to the generation of the Prophet's Companions. On one hand, for the majority of scholars, their quality of being reliable transmitters (*t̲h̲iḳa*) of the Prophet's *Sunna* was incontestable and so did not require the testing and verification procedure (*taᶜdīl*), traditionally required at the outset of all transmitters (see e.g. al-D̲j̲uwaynī, *al-Burhān fī uṣūl al-fiḳh*, Cairo 1400/1980, i, 625-32). On the other hand, only a minority of scholars were to go so far as to uphold the view that "the word of just one Companion" (*ḳawl al-wāḥid min al-ṣaḥāba*) constituted, after the manner of the Prophet's Sunna, a proof (*ḥud̲j̲d̲j̲a*) which could establish a legal prescription binding the Community in general: this leads back to a consideration of the Companions' sayings as one of the sources quite separate from *fiḳh* (see e.g. Ibn Ḳayyim al-D̲j̲awziyya, *Iᶜlām al-muwaḳḳiᶜīn*, Beirut 1991, iv, 90-117).

In a more general fashion, if the conception that the past model for the community is situated at some point beyond the present time is an invariable element within the Islamic conscience, its interpretation has nevertheless varied and has taken shape as two attitudes which are really antithetical to each other. The first may be described as a "confident reliance on the past", a genuine traditionalism which tends to neutralise the evolutionary effects linked with the tension created by the gap between an ideal past and a present always on this side of the ideal past. The second attitude, that of the *salafiyya* [*q.v.*], ancient and modern, on the contrary continually endeavours to update the changes—conceived as necessary alterations in relation to deviations and innovations, *bidᶜas*—believed to be necessary in view of the restoration in all respects of the ideal past (more or less freely defined in relation to the demands of each particular period) of the *salaf*.

Bibliography: Given in the article. Remarkably enough, there does not exist any special monograph on the theme of *al-salaf wa 'l-k̲h̲alaf* as such. Cf., however, R. Gramlich, *Vom islamischen Glauben an die "gute alte Zeit"*, in idem (ed.), *Islamwissenschaftliche Abhandlungen Fritz Meier zum 60. Geburtstag*, Wiesbaden 1974, 110-17.

(E. CHAUMONT)

SALAFIYYA, a neo-orthodox brand of Islamic reformism, originating in the late 19th century and centred on Egypt, aiming to regenerate Islam by a return to the tradition represented by the "pious forefathers" (*al-salaf al-ṣāliḥ*, hence its name) of the Primitive Faith. For definition, background, origins, doctrines and general aspects see IṢLĀḤ; MUḤAMMAD ᶜABDUH; RAS̲H̲ĪD RIḌĀ.

1. In North Africa.

(a) Tunisia. Tunisia was the first Mag̲h̲rib country to receive a reformist (though not purely *salafī*) message from the East. Muḥammad ᶜAbduh visited Tunis (December-January 1885) with a view to establish there a branch of al-ᶜUrwa al-Wut̲h̲ḳā secret society. He was received with some reserve by the older Zaytūna S̲h̲ayk̲h̲s of the Mālikī school, but found support among the junior Mālikī *ʿulamāʾ* and the Ḥanafīs. ʿAbduh's second visit to Tunis (September 1903) did not improve his relations with the Zaytūna conservatives, although he appeared with the prestige of Chief Muftī of Egypt. Facts that did not endear him to them included his insistence on the need to acquire secular knowledge beside the religious sciences and his condemnation of Ṣūfī quietism, fatalism and *tawakkul* [*q.v.*]; his "Transvaal *Fatwā*" (which permitted Muslims in a Christian country to wear a European hat and eat meat slaughtered by a *kitābī*); his clash with the Zaytūnī *ʿālim* Ṣāliḥ al-Sharīf, who accused him of Wahhābism (because of his sympathy with the Wahhābī drive against saint-worship); the appearance of the foremost Salafī journal *al-Manār* [*q.v.*], which a group of ultras, following ʿAbduh's visit, petitioned the Prime Minister to ban from entry to Tunisia; the uproar created in maraboutic circles by two young Salafīs, outspoken critics of saint worship, Muḥ. Shākir and ʿAbd al-ʿAzīz al-Thaʿālibī [*q.v.*]. The former, influenced by al-*Manār*, publicly condemned maraboutism as a form of paganism, for which he was dismissed from his teaching post in Sfax (1902). The latter, a Zaytūna student, had launched upon his return from a two-year stay in Egypt and the East, a violent campaign against the marabouts and pleaded for a rationalist interpretation of the Ḳurʾān. He was summoned before a *sharīʿa* court on a charge of blasphemy, but thanks to French intervention, got away with a light prison sentence (1904) (according to one version). The solid support lent to the attacked marabouts by the Mālikī *ʿulamāʾ* showed that the traditional accommodation between the two main components of the religious institution was still a reality and deterred other Salafī sympathisers among the *ʿulamāʾ*.

After ʿAbduh's death (1905), the contacts between the Zaytūna and the Cairene Salafiyya continued under his successor, Rashīd Riḍā, the latter's conservative bent being more to the liking of the former. Yet while they agreed on several issues such as opposition to the French Protectorate and the need of reform of the Zaytūna, they differed on points of Ḳurʾānic exegesis and on major political issues: the Young Turks (Riḍā was against them, the Tunisians in favour), the Arab Congress in Paris, the Great War and the Arab Revolt (the Tunisians sided with the Ottomans, Riḍā with the Arabs). Meanwhile, the Young Tunisian Party was founded (1907), based on an alliance of secular modernists and Salafī reformists and headed by ʿAlī Bāsh Ḥānba and al-Thaʿālibī, respectively. Their involvement in the Zaytūna student strike (1911) and the tram boycott (1912) resulted in a ban of their party and the expulsion of its leaders. In 1920, a similar alliance of secular and liberal nationalists with ʿAbduhists and Salafīs produced the Liberal Constitutional Party ("Destour") led by al-Thaʿālibī, whose anonymously printed publication *La Tunisie martyre* (1920), a nationalist manifesto and indictment sheet of French policy, formed the basis of its programme. After his departure for the East (1923) the Party stagnated until it was joined (since 1927) by a group of graduates of French universities, led by Dr. Materia and H. Bourguiba. The divergent tendencies of the oldtimers and newcomers inevitably led to a split (1934), after which the latter, henceforward known as the "Neo-Destour", spearheaded the nationalist struggle, while the former, dubbed by their opponents "Old Destour", persisted in an intransigent but ineffectual stance. In 1937, al-Thaʿālibī, back in Tunis from his long self-imposed exile, attempted to reunite the two parties under his leadership, but was defeated by Bourguiba and withdrew from politics.

Salafism, however, made itself felt in other domains: (a) the Free Schools; (b) the Arabic periodical press, most of which was permeated in the 1930s by a puritanical, "Wahhābī" spirit, extolling classical Arabic and its cultural heritage, emphasising Tunisia's ties with the Arab East, castigating social ills and vices (esp. alcoholism and prostitution), satirising imitation of Europe and feminism, condemning naturalisation and Christian missionary activities; (c) associations such as the Khaldūniyya [*q.v.*], Young Men's Muslim Association (YMMA) and the very popular but shortlived Society for the Preservation and Teaching of the Ḳurʾān (for adults). Yet the Tunisian Salafīs, unlike their Algerian counterparts, did not succeed in creating a durable organisation with a recognised leadership and action programme. They showed the people a middle road between the mediaeval synthesis and westernisation, but had no answer for Tunisia's social and economic problems, nor a practical means to recover its independence. Small wonder then that the Salafiyya did not find its place in independent Tunisia and kept silent, especially after the sweeping secularisation programme carried through legislature by the will of Bourguiba. Whether the current fundamentalist (or "Islamist") movement (MTI), which traces its roots back to the Ḳurʾānic Preservation Society (formed at the Zaytūna in 1970, cf. S. Waltz, *Islamist appeal in Tunisia*, in *MEJ*, xl [1986], 652), should be regarded as an avatar of the Salafiyya has not yet been definitely established.

Bibliography: G. Zawadowski, *Index de la presse indigène de Tunisie,* in *REI*, 1937/4, 355-89; idem, *Situation de l'Islam dans la Tunisie d'entre deux guerres*, in *En Terre d'Islam*, xviii, 22 (1943/2), 78-100; P. Shinar, *Origins of Arab nationalism in North-West Africa*, unpubl. thesis, Jerusalem 1957 (in Hebr.), 9-21 (reformism in Tunisia), 22-91 (in Algeria), 92-118 (in Morocco), 119-35 (revolt of ʿAbd al-Krīm); M.F. Ibn ʿĀshūr, *Arkān al-nahḍa al-adabiyya bi-Tūnis*, Tunis 1965; M. al-Shannūfī, *ʿAlāʾiḳ Rashīd Riḍā ... maʿa al-tūnisiyyīn*, in *Ḥawliyyāt al-Djāmiʿa al-Tūnisiyya*, iv (1967), 121-51; M. Chenoufi, *Les deux séjours de M. Abduh en Tunisie et leurs incidences sur le réformisme musulman tunisien* (*6 déc. 1884-4 janv. 1885 et 9-24 sept. 1903*), in *CT*, xvi (1968), 57-96; J. Berque, *Ulémas tunisois de jadis et de naguère*, etc. in *CT*, xx (1972/1-2), 87-128; A. Bouhdiba, *A la recherche des normes perdues*, Tunis 1973, 157-70 (L'Islam en Tunisie); M. Kraiem, *Au sujet des incidences des deux séjours de M. ʿAbduh en Tunisie*, in *Rev. d'Hist. maghrébine*, i (janv. 1974), 91-4; J. Damis, *The Free-School phenomenon: the cases of Tunisia and Algeria*, in *IJMES*, x (1974), 434-49; A.H. Green, *The Tunisian ʿUlama 1873-1915*, Leiden 1978, index, s.v. "Salafiya"; P. Shinar, *Orthodox reformism in Tunisia* (*1882-1939*), in *Hamizrāḥ Heḥādāsh*, xxxi (1986), 71-103 (in Hebr.).

(b) Algeria. Of all the Maghrib countries, it was Algeria where Salafī reformism found its fullest and most effective expression and response. Perhaps the main reasons of its success, apart from the quality of its leadership were that it was here that the danger to Algerian national identity, personality and "soul", to Islamic religion, ethics and way of life, and to classical Arabic language and culture was felt to be the greatest. This threefold threat was implicit in Algeria's colonial situation—her ambiguous status of being legally part of France but in fact a colony of massive European settlement which uprooted and proletarianised its native peasantry, forcing large numbers to emigrate to France, transforming its economy and creating a thin layer of gallicised *évolués* who were taught "nos ancêtres les Gaulois" and aspired to complete political and cultural (but not religious) identification with France.

The emergence of the Salafiyya in Algeria is usually seen as a consequence of ʿAbduh's visit to Algiers (and Constantine), August-September 1903. According to R. Bencheneb, the persons who met him represented three trends of the Algerian élite: the conservatives, the modernists and those of French civil status.

Prominent among the first-named were three professors of official *madrasas*, ʿAbd al-Ḳādir al-Madjdjāwī, who taught Arabic and Islamic Law at Algiers, was active in the Algerian *nahḍa* and wrote against social ills, superstitions and old customs; ʿAbd al-Ḥalīm b. Smāya, noted advocate of "Islamic nationalism" (*ḳawmiyya islāmiyya*), in close touch with Cairo and Istanbul, host of ʿAbduh's visit in Algiers and campaigner in 1911 against conscription into the French army; and Muḥ. Saʿīd b. Aḥmad al-Zawāwī, surnamed "Ibnu Zekri", a *zāwiya*-bred Kabyle scholar and *imām* of a mosque, who published in 1904 a pamphlet insisting on the need of *zāwiya* reform in Kabylia and denouncing customary laws that disadvantaged the Kabyle woman. To the same trend belonged two Constantine *ʿālims*, Ḥamdān al-Wanīsī, teacher and mentor of Ibn Bādīs [*q.v.*], and Mawlūd b. Mawhūb al-Ḥāfiẓī, real leader of the conservatives, long-time *Muftī* of Constantine, partisan of progress and reform, open to modern science and European ideas. For Merad (1967, 126), his reformism consisted in improvement of the moral and intellectual condition of Algerian Muslims without judging them for their beliefs, whether maraboutic or other. The French-assimilated modernists dismissed the conservatives as "old turbans", arrogant bourgeois, great feudals, selfish, lazy and corrupt, whose attachment to tradition impeded progress and merger.

ʿAbduh's visit, though brief, made a strong and lasting impression. He appeared as an educator and missionary of faith, hope and effort, he showed the Algerian intelligentsia what it was looking for: the possibility of reconciling religion and progress, tradition and renewal, while safeguarding their national identity. Whether he also conveyed a political message has been both suggested (Merad, 1964) and denied (Bencheneb 1981, 131). It took, however, a decade for the fruits of ʿAbduh's visit to become visible. In 1913 there appeared at Algiers two Arabic weeklies, *al-Fārūḳ* and *Dhu 'l-Faḳār*, both of expressly ʿAbduhist inspiration and non-political. Their aim was twofold: to publicise ʿAbduh's teachings and to criticise the religious situation in Algeria, chiefly the Ṣūfī orders and marabouts, popular superstitions and vices. A special target was the economic rôle of the local Jews. Both were suspended by 1915, but *al-Fārūḳ* reappeared in 1921.

A decade later, the diffuse Salafī trends begin to take shape again with the publication of *al-Muntaḳid* (July 1925), suspended and replaced shortly after by *al-Shihāb* (December 1925, first weekly, then monthly). Thanks to the extraordinary personality of its founder and editor, the Constantine *ʿālim* ʿAbd al-Ḥamīd Ibn Bādīs [*q.v.*, and see IṢLĀḤ], as well as the qualities of his collaborators, it became in the 1930s the most prestigious tribune of the Maghribī Salafiyya (it was dubbed "the *Manār* of the Maghrib"), until its cessation by the end of 1939.

The team assembled by Ibn Bādīs comprised a number of persons, most of whom shared a common "homeground"—the Province of Constantine—a period of study at the Zaytūna and (some of them) a stay of up to 10 years in the East, but they differed greatly in background, skills and temperament (see on these persons, Merad, 1967, 79-118). Six years later, this team became the nucleus of the Association of Algerian Muslim *ʿulamāʾ* (*Djamʿiyyat al-ʿulamāʾ al-muslimīn al-djazāʾiriyyīn* = AUMA) (1931). Its aims, as stated in the statutes, were to be purely religious, moral and cultural; all political discussion or interference in any political question were strictly forbidden. There ensued a struggle for dominance between the Salafīs and marabouts in which the former prevailed, but the latter, led by Ḥāfiẓī, set up a rival anti-reformist organisation which they called *Djamʿiyyat ʿulamāʾ al-sunna al-djazāʾiriyyīn* = AUSA (1932), the addition of the word *sunna* implying that their adversaries had become tainted by heresy in co-opting to their committee a representative of the Ibāḍiyya [*q.v.*], Ibrāhīm Bayyūd. There followed a year of bitter polemics between the two camps, which exposed the intrinsic weakness of the marabouts, their intellectual poverty, their moral decay and inability to evolve and meet the challenge of the times. They were on the whole unable, in spite of their numbers, well-knit framework, widespread ramifications, monastic discipline and economic strength, to devise effective long-range counter-measures to withstand the Salafī onslaught, and had to depend on the initiative, support and guidance of the French Administration, which did not enhance their prestige.

A secondary target of the Salafī reformists was the class of official ministers of the cult, or Muslim "clergy". In 1934-5 they numbered 385 (22 *muftīs*, 159 *imāms* and 204 others. Merad, 1967, 418). Since political dependability (i.e. loyalty and docility) were often given precedence over professional aptitude and moral integrity, the religious civil service as a whole lost in the course of time most of its credit in the public eye. Both sides, however, refrained as a rule from direct attacks on each other. The two major charges which the official "clergy" proffered against the Salafiyya were separatism (from France) and Wahhābism.

Apart from the upper hand gained by the Reformists over the marabouts, a number of events facilitated or marked the progress of the former during the 1930s: (a) Muslim resentment over the triumphant centennial celebrations of the French conquest of Algiers (1930); (b) the initially benevolent attitude of the anti-maraboutic director of Native Affairs, Jean Mirante, towards the Reformists. (c) the AUMA-Administration crisis of 1933-4 following the ban on unlicensed (i.e. Reformist) preaching in the official mosques and on Reformist teaching in a number of free schools, further widened popular support for the Reformists; (d) the paradoxical alliance of the Reformists with the assimilationist Fédération des Élus, led by Dr. Bendjelloul and Farḥāt ʿAbbās, for electoral purposes; (e) the bloody anti-Jewish riots of Constantine (3-5 August 1934); the fact that these riots occurred in the very centre of Salafī reformism and home town of Ibn Bādīs, cast a strong suspicion on the latter but redounded to his advantage thanks to his rôle as a restorer of intercommunal peace; (f) the first Reformist congress, held at Algiers in September 1935, enabled the AUMA to take stock and appear as a political and national force in Algerian public; (g) the central rôle played by the Reformists in the preparation and conduct of the Islamic Congress of Algiers (June 1936), convened with a view to adopt and present to the Popular Front Government the combined demands of the three main participants: *Élus*, Reformists and Communists (Marabouts and official ministers of the cult were not invited; a dissident participant was Aḥmad Meṣṣālī Ḥādjdj, leader of the Paris-based proletarian and separatist North African Star (since 1937 renamed Algerian People's Party = PPA), was not invited, but he attended nevertheless). The demands of the Reformists included: preservation of the Muslim personal status, reorganisation of the judicial systems, separation of Religion and State (i.e. independence of the Muslim cult), restitution of all religious buildings and control of *waḳf* revenues, and abolition of all discrimination regarding the Arabic language.

The congress delegation was well received in Paris, but a telegram disavowing it, sent by the Mālikī vice-Grand Muftī of Algiers, Maḥmūd Ben Dālī (dubbed Kaḥḥūl) and others to the Premier Léon Blum, had serious consequences: on 2 August the Muftī was murdered and the assassin pointed to the Reformist leader ʿUḳbī as the man who had hired him, although ʿUḳbī was finally exonerated in 1939.

ʿUḳbī's defenders after his arrest, who included also some Jewish civic leaders, presented the matter as a new Dreyfus affair, staged by the Administration in order to discredit the Reformists. From this joint effort to clear ʿUḳbī's name was born the "Union des Croyants Monothéistes", whose principal members on the Muslim side were Ibn Bādīs and ʿUḳbī. The exertions of this group are believed to account to some extent for the correct attitude observed by the Algerian Muslims towards the Jews during the Vichy régime, though incitements against the Jews were not lacking (see M. Ansky, *Les Juifs d'Algérie*, etc., Paris 1950, 81).

On the other hand, the ʿUḳbī affair sowed discord and confusion in the Muslim camp itself. A major event, that was seen by many as a turning-point in Franco-Algerian relations, was the failure of the so-called Projet Blum-Viollette, a bill of law that would have granted certain categories of *évolués* (*ca.* 21,000 persons) the political rights of a French citizen without loss of their Muslim personal status. Owing to opposition of the *colons* and their lobby in Paris, the bill never came up for discussion in the Chamber of Deputies.

A year later (July 1938) the *Élus* split, when each of their two leaders, Bendjelloul and F. ʿAbbās, tried to create a camp of his own. Lastly, the AUMA itself suffered breakaways. At its annual convention (September 1938), ʿUḳbī strongly criticised Ibn Bādīs' group for excessive involvement in politics and lack of support for France. A year later he founded a group and a paper of his own, *al-Iṣlāḥ al-islāmī*, forsook politics for free education and religious and moral reform, appealed to the Algerians to stand by France in her hour of need, and put a damper on his anti-maraboutic zeal.

ʿUḳbī's secession, more than anything else, underlined the AUMA's (chiefly, Ibn Bādīs' and Ibrāhīmī's) animosity against France. It became evident, already in 1936, in Ibn Bādīs' famous rejoinder to F. ʿAbbās, affirming that "... this nation is not France, cannot be France and does not want to be France" (*Shihāb*, April 1936). The crucial factor came after the outbreak of World War II, when the AUMA abstained from declaring its loyalty to France. During the War, the AUMA, classed as hostile to France, was practically dormant. In February 1945 it formed with the *Élus* and the PPA a nationalist front, headed by Abbās. Their campaigns against French dominance are believed to have had a share in creating the atmosphere that made possible the uprising in the Constantinois on V-Day (8 May 1945), in which a hundred Europeans and thousands of Algerians lost their lives. The deep rift opened between the French and the Algerians by this event was never bridged. The new hopes raised by the *Statut organique*, granted to Algeria by the law of 20 September 1947, were soon dashed. Its centrepiece, an elected Algerian Assembly, was to apply, *inter alia*, the principles of independence of the religious institution and of the equal status of the Arabic language, demanded by the AUMA from its inception. After 1950, with the opening of political crises in Tunisia and Morocco, it became increasingly clear that Algeria, too, was heading for a confrontation.

During the War of Liberation (1954-62), Islam played an important rôle as a diffuse but effective mobiliser of the masses, quite apart from the AUMA which, though morally supportive, was rather slow in joining hands with the FLN (manifesto of January 1956). According to A. Nadir (1975), this cautious stance was due to the aversion of the *ʿulamāʾ* from violence and to their bourgeois origin and culture. It also enabled the AUMA to keep its reserves intact. The FLN, on the other hand, could not dispense with the AUMA, owing to their ideological indigence and the inability of secularism and socialism to attract the masses. They made A.T. Madanī, historian and Secretary-General of the AUMA, the spokesman of the Provisional Algerian Government (GPRA, 1958) and entrusted him later (September 1962) with the Ministry of *Waḳf*s and Culture.

While Salafī reformism ceased to exist as a party in independent Algeria, it informed government policy in the religious field. By contrast, maraboutism, its old *bête noire*, is lying low. Government and the Reformists barely tolerate saint worship, but combat the religious charlatans and exorcists. It could thus be said, as late as 1977, that the regime "completely controlled the religious field" (B. Etienne, *L'Algérie, cultures et révolution*, Paris 1977, 118-43). Fifteen years later, this statement seems no longer true. The influence of the Islamic revolution in Iran and elsewhere, the ever-deepening economic and social crisis in Algeria, with a one-party army-controlled régime unable to cope with it effectively, and a belated attempt at democratisation made by President Ben-Djedīd—all these factors combined (coming on top of nearly seventy years of exposure to Salafī reformism) may explain the landslide victory of the fundamentalist Islamic Front of Salvation (FIS) and its allies in the first round of the general elections (January 1992). The refusal of the army to accept the verdict of the polls, and its resolve to use force instead of accommodation, have created a sanguinary confrontation whose outcome still lies in the future.

Apart from the record of Salafī reformism in politics, it achieved quite remarkable results in its proper spheres of activity, sc. religion, culture and ethics, which provided the spiritual foundation of Algerian nationalism. By 1958 the AUMA had an estimated 10,000 active members, and 100,000 (?) sympathisers, divided in 126 sections, 34 *cercle*s and 70 *communautés cultuelles*. It enjoyed wide support in the representative bodies of Algeria down to village *djamāʿa*s and even more in the Association of North African Muslim Students (AEMNA), had made converts among the graduates of official *madrasa*s and French schools, even among *muḳaddam*s of certain *zāwiya*s, had penetrated the Awrās massif, stronghold of maraboutism, the Summām valley and the Saharan fringes (Laghouat, Sūf). The principal means of

Salafī-Reformist indoctrination were the free school, the mosque and the press. The number of free schools grew steadily since 1925, especially in the province of Constantine, the "home-ground" of Ibn Bādīs and his team. For the year 1934-5 Merad (1967: 338) gives the figure of 70 schools, each consisting of one or two classes, totalling a hundred classes with 30,000 pupils of both sexes. According to a later estimate, there were by 1958 181 schools with 40,000 pupils, of which 123 were Reformist Ḳurʾānic schools and 58 free *madrasas* dispensing a primary education to 11,000 pupils. Classes were held 272 days annually (as against 157 days in French schools). In addition there was the Ben-Bādīs Institute (secondary school level, opened in 1947) with 700 students. Most schools served also as local branches of the AUMA and clubs for Reformist youth. In their curricula the emphasis was heavily on classical Arabic (spoken Arabic and Berber were banned), Ḳurʾān with relevant commentary, some *ḥadīth*, some *fiḳh*, history of the Arabs (chiefly the period of the Prophet and the *Rāshidūn* caliphs) and of Algeria, with a view to foster national pride and an aspiration to renew their pristine glories. Important items were Algerian patriotic songs and the formula-creed: Islam is my religion, Arabic is my langage, Algeria is my fatherland (*waṭanī*).

Next to teaching, the Salafī *ʿulamāʾ* tried to infuse new life into the preacher's art, which had become a purely mechanical affair, divorced from reality and the needs of the people. Three of them stand out as orators: Ibn Bādīs, Ibrāhīmī and ʿUḳbī, who greatly differed in style, but they all captivated their audiences by their excellent command of classical Arabic, their missionary zeal and the novelty of their message.

As to the press, the Algerian Arabic papers, like their Middle Eastern *confrères* [see DJARĪDA], suffered from a number of handicaps and shortcomings: they were published by amateurs, their financial resources were precarious, their technical equipment rudimentary, their readership restricted owing to high illiteracy, their very existence in constant danger of suspension. Few had a lifespan of more than 10 years. They were the veteran conservative *Nadjāḥ*, the Salafī *Shihāb*, *Iṣlāḥ* and *Baṣāʾir*, the ʿAlīwī *Balāgh* and the neo-Ibāḍī *Wādī-Mīzāb*. Despite the above drawbacks, the Salafī organs could attain their goal, as theirs was a press of opinion, not of information. Apart from Islam, Arabic and Algerian national identity, two themes were of major concern to them: (1) Salafī ethics, or "moral rearmament"; and (2) the "struggle for the past" or their vision of history.

The re-evaluation of Islamic ethics by the Algerian reformists, like that of the eastern Salafīs, stemmed from a poignant realisation of the contrast between the present state of subjection to an infidel power and Arab might and glory in the days of the *Salaf*. The call was therefore for a revival of those vital moral forces that had led the Arabs to greatness but had lain dormant for centuries under the influence of Ṣūfī ethics, with its emphasis on contempt of the *dunyā*, unconcern with the morrow and future, fatalism, quietism and passive acceptance of things as they were. In order for a change to occur, the Muslim must return to a pure, strictly unitarian belief in God and trust in destiny, the fruit of a scrupulous observance of ritual, which in turn foster vitality, energy, willpower, self-reliance, activity, work, movement and speed (value of time), resolve, effort, perseverance and constancy, ambition, quest of fame, hope—all of which become key-words in the Reformist lexicon.

In the domain of social ethics, the Reformist efforts did not extend beyond the fostering of qualities making for social cohesion and the combatting of certain vices, such as prostitution, alcoholism and gambling—made doubly hateful because of the Ḳurʾānic ban and the influence of the Europeans on their spreading. They also campaigned against customs proscribed by Wahhābī-Salafī puritanism, such as ruinous spending on weddings and other celebrations, noisy funerals and popular *bidʿas* relating to saint-worship. Social reform in the modern acceptation was none of their concern. They preferred to leave it to the politicians and labour leaders when they did not actually oppose it, as they did in all major questions relating to women's liberation, such as the veil, polygamy, divorce and inheritance (as did Rashīd Riḍā). This cautious stance may be explained by the strong conservatism of Maghribī society, the bourgeois background of Ibn Bādīs, the conviction that social justice was provided by the Ḳurʾān and the *Sharīʿa*, the desire to safeguard the traditional structure of the Algerian family as the last bulwark of Islam against the disruptive influences of the West and last, but perhaps not least, dependence for financial support on the well-to-do classes (as suggested by Merad, 1967, 304).

Reformist history writing (Mīlī, Madanī, Fāsī; see Shinar, 1971) was guided by several basic assumptions: there have existed a polarity and a dichotomy between East and West since the dawn of history; the East is superior to the West in spiritual values, ethics and original culture; the ways of the West, spearheaded by Rome and the Latin heirs of her imperial traditions, are domination, oppression and exploitation; the Maghrib is part of the Semitic East by origins, spirit and culture; the Berbers, already Semiticised by the Phoenicians, merged with the Arabs into one nation through Islam and the Arabic language, stood up to every conqueror and proved their capacity to establish one of the greatest states in the world; Algeria had and still has her own national identity and history, despite Western efforts to dilute and obliterate them. Her history is illustrated by the following figures and dynasties: Jugurtha the Numidian, Rome's greatest foe (see M.-Ch. Sahli, *Le message de Yougourtha*, Algiers 1947); ʿUḳba b. Nāfiʿ, Arab conqueror of the Maghrib for Islam, buried in Algerian soil; the Rustamid [*q.v.*] imāmate of Tāhart (despite its being heretical Khāridjite); ʿAbd al-Muʾmin the Algerian [*q.v.*], the real founder of the Almohad caliphate; and the ʿAbd al-Wādid [*q.v.*] dynasty of Tilimsān (Tlemcen). Even the Banū Hilāl [*q.v.*], whose invasion of the Maghrib had been described since Ibn Khaldūn as the greatest catastrophe to befall the region in the Middle Ages, is seen by the Reformists as a blessing in disguise, because it permanently fixed its Arab character. The latest hero has been ʿAbd al-Ḳādir b. Muḥyī al-Dīn [*q.v.*], champion of Algerian resistance to the French.

Bibliography: S. Zawāwī, *al-Islām al-Ṣaḥīḥ*, Cairo 1927; J. Desparmet, *Contribution ... la politique des Oulémas algériens (1911-1937)*, in *Bull. Com. Afr. fr.*, xlvii (1937), 352-8, 423-8, 523-7, 557-61; H. Pérès, *Le mouvement réformiste en Algérie et l'influence de l'Orient*, in *Entretiens sur l'évolution des pays de civilisation arabe*, i (1936), 49-59; M.A.D., *Le progrès du réformisme musulman dans l'Aurès*, in *France médit. et afr.*, i/1 (1938), 87-98; P.E. Sarrasin, *Crise algérienne*, Paris 1949, 105-21; A. Berque, *Les capteurs du divin. II. Les Ulémas*, in *Rev. de la Méditerranée*, ii, no. 44 (1951), 417-29; F. Wartalānī, *al-Djazāʾir al-thāʾira*, Beirut 1956; P. Shinar—see *Bibl.* of part (a); J. Carret, *L'Association des Oulama Réformistes d'Algérie*, in *Afr. et Asie*, no. 43 (1958/3), 23-44; Shinar, *Ibāḍiyya and orthodox Reformism in modern Algeria*, in *Scripta Hierosolymitana*, ix (1961), 97-120; R. Le Tourneau, *Évolution politique de l'Afrique du Nord musulmane 1920-1961*, Paris 1962, 317-9, 321-2, 330-1, 344-6, 369-71 *et passim*, see index; A. Merad, *L'enseignement politique de Muḥammad ʿAbduh aux Algériens (1903)*, in *Orient*, vii (1963), 75-123; L.C. Brown, *The Islamic reform movement in North Africa*, in *J. of Modern Afr. Stud.*, ii/1 (March 1964), 55-65; M. Bennabi, *Mémoires d'un témoin du siècle*, i, Algiers 1965; ʿA. Ṭālibī, *Kitāb āthār Ibn Bādīs*, 4 vols., Algiers 1966; A. Merad, *Réformisme*, 1967—see IṢLĀḤ, *Bibl.*; R. Turkī, *al-Shaykh ʿAbd al-Ḥamīd b. Bādīs. Falsafatuhu wa-djuhūduhu fī 'l-tarbiya wa 'l-taʿlīm*, Algiers 1969, ²1974; M.T. Fuḍalāʾ, *al-Imām al-rāʾid al-shaykh Muḥ. al-Bashīr al-Ibrāhīmī fī dhikrāhu al-ūlā*, Constantine 1967; A. Nādir, *Le mouvement réformiste algérien. Son rôle dans la formation de l'idéologie nationale*, unpubl. thesis, Paris 1968; M. Ḳāsim, *al-Imām ʿAbd al-Ḥamīd ibn Bādīs al-zaʿīm al-rūḥī li-ḥarb al-taḥrīr al-djazāʾiri*, Cairo 1968; Shinar, *The historical approach of the Reformist ʿUlamāʾ*, etc., in *As. and Afr. Stud.*, vii (1971), 181-210; J. Damis, *The Free-School phenomenon: the cases of Tunisia and Algeria*, in *IJMES*, v (1974), 434-49; Shinar, *Some observations on the ethical teachings of Orthodox Reformism in Algeria*, in *As. and Afr. Stud.*, viii (1972), 63-89; A. Taleb-Bendiab, *Le Congrès Musulman algérien (1935-35)* etc., Algiers 1973; A. Nadir, *Le parti réformiste algérien et la guerre de libération nationale*, in *Rev. d'hist. maghrébine*, iii (1975), 174-83; A.K. Saʿd Allāh, *Muḥammad al-ʿĪd*, etc. Cairo 1960, ²1975; A.T. al-Madani, *Ḥayāt kifāḥ. Mudhakkirāt*, 2 vols., Algiers 1976-7; F. Colonna, *L'Islam en milieu paysan: le cas de l'Aurès 1936-1938*, in *Rev. alg. des sc. jur. écon. et pol.*, xiv, no. 2 (juin 1977), 277-87; Shinar, *Traditional and Reformist Mawlid celebrations in the Maghrib*, in M. Rosen-Ayalon (ed.), *Studies in memory of Gaston Wiet*, Jerusalem 1977, 371-413; Saʿd Allāh, *al-Ḥaraka al-waṭaniyya al-djazāʾiriyya*, 2 vols., Algiers 1977, i, 428-54, 481-5, ii, 87-122, 159-81; C. Collot and J.-R. Henry, *Le mouvement national algérien. Textes, 1912-1954*, Paris 1978, 44-7, 64-115, 126-30, 177-83, 272-9; R. Bencheneb, *Le séjour du Šayh ʿAbduh en Algérie*, in *SI*, liii (1981), 121-35; Shinar, *A controversial exponent of the Algerian Salafiyya: Abū Yaʿlā al-Zawāwī*, in M. Sharon (ed.), *Stud. in Isl. history and civilization*, Jerusalem-Leiden 1986, 267-90; A. Lamchiohi, *Islam et contestation au Maghrib*, Paris 1989; M. al-Ahnaf, B. Botiveau and F. Frégosi, *L'Algérie par ses islamistes*, Paris 1991.

(c) Morocco. Like the Tunisian Salafiyya, its Moroccan counterpart cannot compare with that of Algeria as regards scope, duration and political significance. Nor did it create a centralised organisation, collective leadership and a common action programme. It was the first manifestation of an awakened national-Islamic consciousness, a transitional phase between armed Berber resistance against the French and Spanish occupiers and the emergence of a political movement, the Young Moroccan Party, which was stimulated by the Rīf War and triggered by the notorious Berber Dahir (1930). It absorbed the Salafī ideology and its agents, but went far beyond it. Yet, though brief, Salafism proved remarkably effective, winning support and sympathy in high quarters including sultans, *makhzen*, *ʿulamāʾ* of the Ḳarawiyyīn and the high bourgeoisie, but was seen by the French as a potential threat to their protectorate. Unlike the Algerian reformists, the Salafīs of Morocco did not have to create a separate national history and identity; existence of the latter was a historic fact, so they could dedicate themselves to the other major goals of Salafī reformism: the eradication of saint worship, especially the pilgrimages to saints' tombs with their attendant *bidʿas*, including the anthropolatrous and "naturistic" beliefs and practices of the lower Ṣūfī orders, and the reform of the traditional educational system in ʿAbduh's spirit. In addition, they campaigned against extravagant and ruinous wedding celebrations. A theme that came last to the fore, but then with dramatic effect, was France's Berber policy. In their drive against maraboutism, the Salafīs were preceded by two Wahhābī-inspired sultans, Sīdī Muḥammad b. ʿAbd Allāh and his son Mawlāy Sulaymān [see ʿALAWĪS]. The latter's anti-maraboutic "pastoral letter" (1811) involved him in a military struggle with the maraboutic establishment that nearly swept away the dynasty (1822). His immediate successors adopted a more cautious policy, but in May 1909 Mawlāy ʿAbd al-Ḥafīẓ, a strong Salafī sympathiser (he wrote a refutation of Tidjānī claims) put to death, and closed the *zāwiyas* of, the Idrīsī *sharīf* Muḥammad al-Kabīr b. ʿAbd al-Wahhāb al-Kattānī, chief of the Kattāniyya order and leader of the clerical opposition to the French. Al-Kattānī was suspected of plotting to overthrow the reigning dynasty and restore the Idrīsid one (E. Michaux-Bellaire, in *RMM*, v [1908], 393-423, and Laroui 1980, 405). The next sultan, Mawlāy Yūsuf, continued the same line. In 1924 the Council of *ʿUlamāʾ*, at his behest, decided to burn all writings of the Tidjānī writer Muḥammad al-Nadhīfī. In 1933, his son and successor Sīdī Muḥammad b. Yūsuf banned all manifestations of the ʿĪsāwa order, and in 1946 he prohibited the founding of new orders or opening of new *zāwiyas* without prior permission.

Even Muḥammad b. ʿAbd al-Karīm, leader of the Rīf War (1921-6) espoused the Salafī ideology and tried to spread it in the Rīf [*q.v.*] in order to bolster Rīfī morale and counteract the defeatist propaganda of some Ṣūfī orders, burning, as a reprisal, two of their *zāwiyas* (Shinar 1965, 169 ff.). This attitude of the orders was branded as treason by the Young Moroccans and deepened their enmity towards the entire Ṣūfī establishment. After the Rīf War, their chief maraboutic target became the new head of the Kattāniyya, al-Ḥādjdj ʿAbd al-Ḥayy al-Kattānī. First signs of an anti-maraboutic trend among Moroccan intellectuals appear in the second half of the 19th century: the historian Aḥmad b. Khālid al-Nāṣirī al-Salāwī (d. 1897 [*q.v.*]), who declared himself an enemy of pilgrimages to saints' tombs (*mawsims*) (E. Lévi-Provençal, *Hist. des Chorfa*, Paris 1922, 368), and ʿAbd Allāh b. Idrīs al-Sanūsī, *ʿālim* of the Ḳarawiyyīn and member of the Royal Council under Mawlāy Ḥasan (1873-1894), who brought back some Salafī ideas from his travels in the East and tried to propagate them in Morocco, but with little success.

Far more effective was the action led by Abū Shuʿayb b. ʿAbd al-Raḥmān al-Dukkālī, dubbed "the Moroccan ʿAbduh" (1878-1937). He studied at the Azhar around 1900, became Vizier of Justice, taught ʿAbduh's doctrine at the Ḳarawiyyīn and in Rabāṭ, left again for the East after 1912, expounded ʿAbduh's teachings at Mecca and befriended Rashīd Riḍā and his *Manār* group, as well as the "Father of Pan-Arabism", the Druze *amīr* Shakīb Arslān. After the First World War, he returned to Morocco and toured the country with a group of followers, preaching, felling sacred trees and smashing sacred stones. His eloquence and charisma earned him a wide following. Among his disciples the most militant were (a) Muḥammad Ghāzī, a native of Miknās (Meknès) who clashed with ʿAbd al-Ḥayy al-Kattānī (see above) in 1920, was expelled from the Ḳarawiyyīn in 1923 and founded a "free school" in 1926. He was noted as a nationalist poet and *faḳīh*; and (b) ʿAllāl al-Fāsī (1907-74 [*q.v.* in Suppl.]), *ʿālim*, of the Ḳarawiyyīn, fervent patriot, poet and teacher, became the foremost nationalist leader from 1929 onwards, thus embodying in his person the transition from Salafiyya to nationalism. The philosopher M.ʿA. Lahbabi (*Du clos à l'ouvert*, Casablanca 1961, 65) calls him the "theorist of the Salafiyya", by virtue of his book, *Self-criticism* (*al-Naḳd al-dhātī*, Cairo 1952).

Similar groups to those of Rabat and Fās were formed at Marrākush, Tiṭṭāwīn and Ṭandja. In the two latter towns, Salafī activity centred around Muḥammad Dāwūd, historian of Tiṭṭāwīn, and the Bennūna family, whose head, al-Ḥādjdj ʿAbd al-Salām, ex-Vizier of Justice, was dubbed "Father of Moroccan nationalism".

Finally, there must be mentioned the Islamic activist Muḥammad Makkī al-Nāṣirī, scion of a noted Rabāṭī family (b. 1904). He studied in Cairo, returned to Morocco in 1927, was expelled in 1930 following his campaign against the Berber Dahir and presented an indictment sheet against France's Berber policy to the pan-Islamic congress of Jerusalem (December 1931). In 1937 he founded and led the Moroccan Unity Party (PUM). For his early reformist thinking we have his pamphlet, entitled *Iẓhār al-ḥaḳīḳa wa-iblāgh al-khalīḳa*, which called for a reform of Muslim society by a return to true Ṣufism based on practical ethics (see L. Massignon, in *REI*, i [1927], 33).

The other major field of Salafī activity was the reform of the educational system, more especially the establishment of "free schools" (*madāris ḥurra*), also called "renovated Ḳurʾānic schools". The Salafīs were neither the first nor the only ones to create them. J. Damis distinguishes four categories among the "founding fathers" and patronage committees: merchants, Salafīs, *ʿulamāʾ*/*fuḳahāʾ* and members of some Ṣūfī orders. They shared an awareness of the backwardness of the traditional Ḳurʾānic school (*msīd*), the example of reformed schools in the East (Egypt and Syria), a cultural nationalism and a moral reservation with regards to the public school with its emphasis on French and modern subjects and its secular atmosphere, at the expense of Arabic, Ḳurʾān and Islam. Yet they were influenced by the public school in matters of organisation, management, methodology and equipment. The first free schools opened in 1919 in Rabāṭ, Fās and Tiṭṭāwīn. By the late 1940s there were 121 free schools with 14 annexes and 26,800 students. The teaching staff came mostly from the Ḳarawiyyīn and the pupils from the urban middle class. Their curricula varied. Thus the Bū-Hlāl school (Rabāṭ 1918) claimed to offer courses in modern sciences, history, geography, French and gymnastics, while the Marrākush school (1952) taught mainly Ḳurʾān, Arabic grammar, some *fiḳh*, arithmetic and French. The overall effect of the free school in Morocco was that it served as a reactor against French culture, a vehicle of modern Arabic culture, a precursor and (later) auxiliary of Moroccan nationalism, and a promoter of, and (later) brake on, social mobility and mutation.

The importance of the Salafiyya in Morocco has been variously assessed. E. Dermenghem, a keen and sympathetic observer of Maghribī Islam, marvelled in 1933 at the speed with which the Salafiyya had succeeded in drastically reducing the influence of the marabouts (al-Fāsī, 1948, 155). ʿA. Laroui, the Moroccan cultural historian, holds that from 1912 to 1925, Salafism had become the common ideology of the sultan, the central *makhzen*, the Fāsī *ʿulamāʾ* and the bourgeoisie, had rendered exclusive the sultan's religious authority, had inspired Bin ʿAbd al-Karīm's reform drive against local Berber custom (yet failed to win the support of the marabouts), with its methodology serving all schools of thought and all interest groups (Laroui 1980, 428-9). The Moroccan philosopher M.A. Lahbabi (al-Ḥabābī), on the other hand, finds that despite all its efforts and successes, the results of Salafī action were disappointing, owing to the upheavals engendered by the industrialisation of the modern Moroccan cities (*Du clos à l'ouvert*, Casablanca 1961, 65).

Bibliography: P. Marty, *Le Maroc de demain*, Paris 1925, 133-41 (Free Schools); E. Michaux-Bellaire, *Le Wahhabisme au Maroc*, in *Rens. Col. de l'Afr. fr.*, xxxviii/7 (juil. 1928), 489-92; E. Girardière, *L'école coranique et la politique nationaliste au Maroc*, in *France médit. et africaine*, i/1 (1938), 99-109; ʿA. al-Fāsī, *Taʾrīkh al-ḥarakāt al-istiḳlāliyya fi 'l-maghrib al-ʿarabī*, Cairo 1948, 153-9 (Salafiyya); M.I. b. Aḥmad al-Kattānī, *Abū Shuʿayb wa 'l-salafiyya* (quoted in ʿA.S. Ibn Sūda, *Dalīl muʾarrikh al-Maghrib al-Aḳṣā*, Tiṭṭāwīn 1309/1950, 207); R. Rézette, *Les partis politiques marocains*, Paris 1955 (on the Salafiyya press, see index); P. Shinar—see *Bibl.* of section (a), Tunisia; Dj. Abun Nasr, *The Salafiyya movement in Morocco*, in *St. Antony's Papers* (London), xvi (1963), 90-105; R.M. Speight, *Islamic reform in Morocco*, in *MW,* liii/1 (Jan. 1963), 41-9; J.P. Halstead, *The changing character of Moroccan Reformism 1921-1934*, in *J. of Afr. History*, v (1964), 435-47; ʿA.K. al-Ṣaḥrāwī, *Shaykh al-Islām Muḥammad al-ʿArabī al-ʿAlawī*, Casablanca 1965; Shinar, *ʿAbd al-Qādir and ʿAbd al-Krīm. Religious influences on their thought and action*, in *As. and Afr. Studies*, i (1965), 160-74 (on ʿAbd al-Krīm); A. Cohen, *ʿAllāl al-Fāsī: his ideas and his contribution towards Morocco's independence*, in *ibid.*, iii (1967), 121-64; J.J. Damis, *The Free School movement in Morocco, 1919-1970*, unpubl. thesis, Tufts Univ., Medford 1970; idem, *Early Moroccan reactions to the French Protectorate: the cultural dimension*, in *Humaniora Islamica*, i (1973), 15-31; A. Laroui, *Origines sociales et culturelles du nationalisme marocain* (*1830-1912*), Paris 1980. (P. Shinar)

2. In Egypt and Syria.

The early history of the Salafiyya in both Egypt and Syria (in the sense of *Bilād al-Shām*, Greater Syria) is closely connected. Muḥammad ʿAbduh's [*q.v.*] stay in Beirut (1882-8, with lengthy interruptions) gave him the opportunity to make some of the *ʿulamāʾ*, civil servants and intellectuals there familiar with his own and with al-Afghānī's [*q.v.*] ideas about the necessity and the contents of a reform of Islam [see IṢLĀḤ, and also Delanoue, in *Bibl.*].

Some years later, a considerable number of Syrian adherents and spokesmen of the Salafiyya, among them Ṭāhir al-Djazāʾirī and Djamāl al-Dīn al-Ḳāsimī (see below), travelled to Egypt. Some of them stayed there for a considerable length of time, some even taking up domicile in Egypt permanently and influencing, by their activities as publicists and in other ways, the discussion of Islamic reform, even far beyond Syria and Egypt.

Notwithstanding this mutual influence between Syrian and Egyptian Salafīs, manifesting itself, among other things, by lively correspondence, reciprocal visits, lecture tours, letters to the editor and book reviews, encounters at Pan-Islamic congresses [see MUʾTAMAR] etc., the Salafiyya attained in each region a certain degree of distinct and independent development. This was the case e.g. regarding some differences in emphasis within the intended reform concerning the perception of certain phases of Islamic history, and also with regard to the historical role of the *madhāhib*. With individual authors, these differences might reach from nuances to clear divergences. But the basic positions of the Salafiyya in Egypt and in Syria are to a large extent the same [see IṢLĀḤ, esp. C. *The principal doctrinal positions*].

(a) Egypt. The origin and early development of the Salafiyya in this country is above all connected with the names of al-Afghānī, ʿAbduh, al-Kawākibī and Rashīd Riḍā [*q.vv.*]. With *al-Manār* [*q.v.*], the last mentioned created in Cairo in 1898 the most influential organ of the Salafiyya. From 1926 onwards, *al-Manār* was joined by *al-Fatḥ* (Cairo), a periodical of similar tendency which, after the death of Rashīd Riḍā and the cessation of *al-Manār* in 1935, was considered until 1948 the most important (though not the only) journalistic forum of the Salafiyya in Egypt (see al-Djundī, *Taʾrīkh*, ii). Its editor and main author, Muḥibb al-Dīn al-Khaṭīb [*q.v.* in Suppl.], had founded, together with his Syrian compatriot ʿAbd al-Fattāḥ Ḳatlān (d. 1931), the *Maṭbaʿa Salafiyya* (including a bookshop), a printing press whose production reflects all the essential desiderata of the movement (see *Fihrist al-Maktaba al-Salafiyya*, ed. Ḳuṣayy Muḥibb al-Dīn al-Khaṭīb, Cairo 1399/1978-9).

In the years 1927-8 the development of the Salafiyya in Egypt entered a new phase. In this context, one may speak of the rise of a Neo-Salafiyya (Schulze, 90 ff., see Index, 499). With the *Djamʿiyyat al-shubbān al-muslimīn* and the Muslim Brotherhood [see AL-IKHWĀN AL-MUSLIMŪN] there now came into being for the first time organisations that wanted to bring the goals of the Salafiyya down from the level of an intellectual discourse to be spread among the masses of the people by way of the *daʿwa* [*q.v.*].

Characteristic for these and many other organisations of a later date, some of them radical and militant, are their relatively strict internal structure—often reminiscent of the tradition of the *ṭuruḳ* [see ṬARĪḲA]—, the authority of an *imām* or a *murshid* [*q.vv.*], and the emphasis on preserving a distance from the religious establishment and (even more so) from the government. In some cases the creation of secretly operating armed groups can be added to the list. The latter in particular consider themselves as a kind of avant-garde of the true *umma*; they justify their actions (including assaults against politicians and other presumed or real opponents) as *djihād* [*q.v.*; see also MUDJĀHID. 3. In modern Arab usage]. However, it is not only these, but also—and rightly so—other 'moderate' Islamic movements, intellectual circles and individual authors in Egypt that claim the spiritual heritage of the Salafiyya.

Central topics in the Salafiyya literature in Egypt were the necessity of a reform of Islam on the one hand and resistance to secularisation on the other. In the light of these two problems, the authors of the Salafiyya treated a number of specific questions, such as western imperialism, the role of the Christian missions and of Orientalism [see MUSTASHRIḲŪN], Zionism and Freemasonry [see FAR-MĀSŪNIYYA in Suppl.], foreign educational institutions and the westernisation of Egyptian culture, state universities, the Azhar [*q.v.*] and the necessity of its reform, the role played by the Ṣūfī orders (in the eyes of the Salafiyya a negative one), the question of the caliphate [see KHALĪFA] and the danger of importing the ideas of Kemālism [see ATATÜRK].

Some authors made it their aim to attack incessantly certain writers whom they considered as particularly dangerous representatives of secularisation and westernisation. A favourite target of their criticism was Ṭāhā Ḥusayn [*q.v.*] and his role as a man of letters, literary critic, historian of early Islam and cultural policy-maker (see e.g. Muṣṭafā Ṣādiḳ al-Rāfiʿī, *Taḥta rāyat al-Ḳurʾān*, [1]Cairo 1926, [7]1974; Anwar al-Djundī, *Ṭāhā Ḥusayn, ḥayātuhu wa-fikruhu fī mīzān al-islām*, [2]Cairo 1977). In the discussion about the authenticity of *ḥadīth* literature, which had flared up because of the influx of orientalist writings, the authors of the Salafiyya also took sides fervently (see G.H.A. Juynboll, *The authenticity of the Tradition literature. Discussions in modern Egypt*, Leiden 1969).

In principle, the Salafiyya in Egypt was and has remained oriented towards Pan-Islamism [*q.v.*]. On the other hand, some of its authors showed already in the 1920s, and even more so during the following two decades, a tendency towards blending Islam and Arab nationalism [see ḲAWMIYYA. i]. Muḥibb al-Dīn al-Khaṭīb and others increasingly emphasised in their writings the close relation between *ʿurūba* and Islam and the particular role of the Arabs in Islamic history. They described the Arab fatherland as a bastion of Islam and the Arab nation as an instrument of its political salvation in the present time. Thus Pan-Arab unity [see PAN-ARABISM] is the prerequisite for the union of all Muslims and therefore the immediate goal. Many authors of the Salafiyya ascribed to Egypt the leading role for achieving Arab unity, and therefore fought strongly against an Egyptian nationalism which limited itself to the valley of the Nile. Unintentionally, they encouraged in the 1930s and 1940s the rise of an essentially secular Arab nationalism, whose spokesmen up to Djamāl ʿAbd al-Nāṣir [*q.v.* in Suppl.] made selective use of certain arguments of the Egyptian Salafiyya (see Gershoni in *Bibl.*).

During the first two years after the "Free Officers" had seized power in 1952, the Salafiyya in Egypt had relatively favourable possibilities to develop. However, already at that time internal differences of opinion about specific questions became visible, for instance in the appraisal of hereditary monarchy and its role in the history of Islam (Ende, 99-103). After the Muslim Brotherhood had been banned in 1954, the public influence of the Salafiyya declined and many of its followers left the country (mainly to Saudi Arabia and Kuwayt). However, individual Salafīs such as Shaykh Muḥammad al-Ghazālī and Maḥmūd Muḥammad Shākir occasionally found the opportunity to express themselves in books or journals (e.g. in *al-Risāla*), for instance, in connection with the repeated campaigns of the government against the Marxist Left. Many writings of earlier or contemporary Salafiyya authors also appeared to be appropriate for providing a religious-legal justification for "Arab socialism" which was propagated by the State [see ISHTIRĀKIYYA]. For this reason, a description of Islamic socialism by the leader of the Syrian Muslim Brotherhood, Muṣṭafā al-Sibāʿī (d. 1964) could also be published in Cairo (*Ishtirākiyyat al-islām*, [1]Damascus 1959, [2]Damascus and Cairo 1960, [3]Cairo n.d., in the series *Ikhtarnā laka*; see for this, Sami A. Hanna and G.H. Gardner, *Arab socialism,* Leiden 1969, esp. 149-71).

However, the limits of a political activity in the sense of the (Neo-)Salafiyya, apart from the "Arab Socialist Union", were very narrowly prescribed. The government reacted very harshly indeed at alleged or real conspiracies, as was clearly shown by the execution of Sayyid Ḳuṭb [*q.v.*] in 1966.

After the war of June 1967, and even more so after the death of Djamāl ʿAbd al-Nāṣir in 1970, the ideas of the Salafiyya or of the Neo-Salafiyya (see above) saw a new boost in connection with the revival of ancient militant organisations and the emergence of new ones (see the studies by Carré, Jansen and Kepel, mentioned in the *Bibl.*).

(b) Syria. The origins of the Salafiyya in Syria are connected with the names of Ṭāhir al-Djazāʾirī and Djamāl al-Dīn al-Ḳāsimī in the first place. The circle of friends and disciples which formed around al-Djazāʾirī directly or indirectly influenced almost all the Sunni Muslim intellectuals who after the First World War became prominent in Syria. Having sought the support of the Ottoman Turkish reformers and, from 1908 onwards, of the Young Turks in particular, most of the Syrian Salafīs, already from 1909-10 onwards turned to Arab nationalism (see Commins, 124 ff.). Many of them played a role in the Arab clubs and movements of the time (including the secret organisations), and some of them, like ʿAbd al-Ḥamīd al-Zahrāwī (executed in 1916), are counted among the martyrs of the national movement against Ottoman Turkish domination (Adham al-Djundī, *Shuhadāʾ al-ḥarb al-ʿālamiyya al-kubrā*, Damascus 1960; E. Tauber, *The emergence of the Arab movements*, and idem, *The Arab movements in World War I*, both London 1993).

Ṭāhir al-Djazāʾirī, born in Damascus in 1852, was the son of a religious scholar who had emigrated from Algiers to Syria in 1846-7. Under him and under the Ḥanafī scholar Shaykh ʿAbd al-Ghanī al-Maydānī (d. 1881), Ṭāhir acquired a solid education in the religious sciences, but—already early on—he also developed an interest in the modern natural sciences. Supported by Midḥat Pasha [*q.v.*], he was, from 1877 onwards, engaged in building up a modern educational system in Syria (between 1879-83 as general supervisor for the elementary schools). From 1880 onwards, the above-mentioned circle of friends and disciples (*ḥalḳa*) began to form around him. Between 1907-19 Shaykh Ṭāhir lived in exile in Egypt. He died in Damascus in January 1920. Among his achievements are counted, among other things, the foundation (or new arrangement) of the Ẓāhiriyya library in Damascus and of the Khālidiyya library in Jerusalem.

Shaykh Ṭāhir's publications consist mainly of textbooks for the state schools. They reflect his religious-reformist ideas only indirectly. He preferred to expound and discuss his thoughts in his *ḥalḳa*. Djamāl al-Dīn al-Ḳāsimī (1866-1914), with whom Ṭāhir was in close contact, especially in the years 1906-7, proceeded differently. In most of his works (several of them have been published only posthumously) we meet al-Ḳāsimī as a resolute reformer (see the list of his writings, with commentary, in Ẓāfir al-Ḳāsimī, 632-88). His repeated criticism of *taḳlīd* and of the rigid adherence to the four Sunnī schools of law (*al-taʿaṣṣub li 'l-madhāhib*) laid him open to the accusation that he wished to found his own *madhhab*. The discussion he triggered on the advantages or dangers of *lā-madhhabiyya* is going on in Syria until the present day (Wild, *Muslim und Madhhab*; cf. Muḥammad Saʿīd Ramaḍān al-Būṭī, *al-Salafiyya, marḥala zamaniyya mubāraka, lā madhhab islāmī*, Damascus 1988).

From its beginning, the Syrian Salafiyya has never formed an ideologically homogeneous bloc. Rather, one recognises in individual representatives of the movement quite different positions about particular questions. However, their criticism of many forms of *taṣawwuf*, as well as of many popular religious customs and notions, inspired by Ibn Taymiyya [*q.v.*] and his school, is more or less uniform. Examples are ʿAbd al-Ḥamīd al-Zahrāwī's *al-Fiḳh wa 'l-taṣawwuf* (Cairo 1901) and al-Ḳāsimī's *Iṣlāḥ al-masādjid min al-bidaʿ wa 'l-ʿawāʾid* (Cairo 1923, [2]Beirut 1970). Likewise in the tradition of Ibn Taymiyya and the neo-Ḥanbalī school and in agreement with the sympathies of the Salafiyya for the Wahhābiyya is the generally critical appraisal of the Shīʿa and its role in Islamic history, though not all Syrian Salafīs are uniformly severe in their judgment (Laoust, *Essai*, index, 729; Ende, 59-75; Commins, 84-5). In the same context belongs the endeavour of some early Salafiyya authors in Syria and their disciples to glorify the empire of the Umayyads of Damascus as a truly *Arab* one, and to defend it against accusations by many historians and other authors of the past (Ende, esp. 64-75, 91 ff.). It was above all Muḥammad Kurd ʿAlī [see KURD ʿALĪ] who distinguished himself in this respect and who made it possible that this and other positions of the Salafiyya could be represented in the publications of the Arab Academy of Damascus, founded and directed by him for many years [see MADJMAʿ ʿILMĪ. 2a. *Syria*] (Hermann, esp. 207 ff.).

The "Arabisation of Islam", which can be observed later in the Egyptian Salafiyya (see above), is in part characterised by arguments which, already before the First World War, were discussed by members of the Syrian Salafiyya and have been propagated in Egypt by such authors as Muḥibb al-Dīn al-Khaṭīb, a disciple of Ṭāhir al-Djazāʾirī.

As in Egypt, the ideas of the Salafiyya have been taken up and converted into political action by radical Muslim organisations also in Syria. This holds true in the first place for the Muslim Brotherhood which in the middle of the 1940s emerged from the fusion of several Islamic societies. The leaders of the Brotherhood, above all Muṣṭafā al-Sibāʿī, Maʿrūf al-Dawālībī and Muḥammad al-Mubārak, found over several years the opportunity to make their ideas public in journals such as *al-Muslimūn* and *al-Tamaddun al-islāmī*. Having been banned for the first time in 1952, the Muslim Brotherhood and similar organisations of the militant Neo-Salafiyya of Syria have been suppressed in various degrees and at times persecuted with great harshness. Many of their members went into exile to such countries as Jordan and Saudi Arabia (see Reissner, Carré-Michaud and Abdallah).

Bibliography (in addition to references given in the article):

1. On the Salafiyya in Egypt. C.C. Adams, *Islam and modernism in Egypt*, New York 1933; H. Laoust, *Le réformisme orthodoxe des "salafiyya"*, in *REI*, vi (1933), 175-224; J. Heyworth-Dunne, *Religious and political trends in Modern Egypt*, Washington, D.C. 1950; R.P. Mitchell, *The society of the Muslim Brothers*, London 1969; I. Gershoni, *Arabization of Islam. The Egyptian Salafiyya and the rise of Arabism in pre-revolutionary Egypt*, in *Asian and African Studies*, xiii (1979), 22-57; Z.S. Bayyūmī, *al-Ikhwān al-muslimūn wa 'l-djamāʿāt al-islāmiyya fi 'l-ḥayāt al-siyāsiyya, 1928-1948*, Cairo 1979; O. Carré, *Mystique et politique. Lecture révolutionnaire du Coran par Sayyid Ḳuṭb, frère musulman radical*, Paris 1984; G. Kepel, *Le Prophète et Pharaon. Les mouvements islamistes dans l'Egypte contemporaine*, Paris 1984; J.J.G. Jansen, *The neglected duty: the creed of Sadat's assassins and Islamic resurgence in the Middle East*, London-New York 1986; Anwar al-Djundī, *Taʾrīkh al-ṣiḥāfa al-islāmiyya, ii. al-Fatḥ, Muḥibb al-Dīn al-Khaṭīb, 1926-1948*, Cairo n.d. [1986]; and idem, *al-Musādjalāt wa*

'l-maʿārik al-adabiyya, Cairo 1972; R. Schulze, *Islamischer Internationalismus im 20. Jahrhundert*, Leiden 1990.

2. On the Salafiyya in Syria. H. Laoust, *Essai sur les doctrines sociales et politiques de Taḳī-d-dīn Aḥmad b. Taimīya*, Cairo 1939; Ẓāfir al-Ḳāsimī, *Djamāl al-Dīn al-Ḳāsimī wa-ʿaṣruhu*, Damascus 1965; ʿAdnān al-Khaṭīb, *al-Shaykh Ṭāhir al-Djazāʾirī, rāʾid al-nahḍa al-ʿilmiyya fī bilād al-Shām wa-aʿlām min khirrīdjī madrasatihi*, Cairo 1971; G. Delanoue, *Endoctrinement religieux et idéologie ottomane: l'adresse de Muḥammad ʿAbduh au Cheikh al-Islam, Beyrouth, 1887*, in *ROMM*, xiii-xiv (1973), 293-312; W. Ende, *Arabische Nation und islamische Geschichte*, Beirut-Wiesbaden 1977; S. Wild, *Muslim und Madhhab*, in U. Haarmann and P. Bachmann (eds.), *Die islamische Welt zwischen Mittelalter und Neuzeit* (Festschrift H.R. Roemer), Beirut-Wiesbaden 1979, 674-89; J. Reissner, *Ideologie und Politik der Muslimbrüder Syriens*, Freiburg i.Br. 1980; O. Carré and G. Michaud, *Les Frères musulmans (1928-1982), Egypte et Syrie*, Paris 1983; U.F. Abdallah, *The Islamic struggle in Syria*, Berkeley 1983; J.H. Escovitz, *"He was the Muḥammad ʿAbduh of Syria". A study of Ṭāhir al-Jazāʾirī and his influence*, in *IJMES*, xviii (1986), 293-310; D.D. Commins, *Islamic reform. Politics and social change in late Ottoman Syria*, New York-Oxford 1990; R. Hermann, *Kulturkrise und konservative Erneuerung: Muḥammad Kurd ʿAlī (1876-1953) und das geistige Leben in Damaskus zu Beginn des 20. Jahrhunderts*, Frankfurt a.M. 1990; R. Deguilhem, *Le café à Damas et le traité du Shaykh Djamāl al-Dīn al-Ḳāṣimī*, in *BEO*, XLV (1993), 20-32.

(W. Ende)

ṢALĀḤ ʿABD AL-ṢABŪR (1931-81), leading Egyptian poet, critic, playwright, translator and journalist. He was born in al-Zaḳāzīḳ in the Delta; in his early youth he learnt the Ḳurʾān by heart and read the classical poets and the modern romantics such as Ibrāhīm Nādjī and Maḥmūd Ḥasan Ismaʿīl. Later on, during the 1940s he joined the Ikhwān al-Muslimūn [*q.v.*], but soon became disenchanted with their ideology and became interested in secular social realism, a view which he expressed in his *al-Nās fī bilādī* ("The people in my country").

Ṣalāḥ graduated from Cairo University in 1951 and worked at the Ministry of Education, but left it for journalism. He was an editor at the *Rūz al-Yūsuf* weekly journal and assistant literary editor of the Literary Supplement of *al-Ahrām*. He published in various leading Arabic newspapers, and also served in government positions, being director of *al-Hayʾa al-Miṣriyya al-ʿĀmma li 'l-Kitāb* until his premature death.

Ṣalāḥ acquired a great enthusiasm for Western literature. He read Shakespeare's plays and the romantic poets, followed by T.S. Eliot and Yeats, these last two poets making the deepest influence on his poetry, and versified dramas and criticism. He was one of the first Egyptian poets who adopted *vers irregulier* (1951), which the ʿIrāḳī poets termed "free verse", a method of versification which is based upon an irregular number of feet (*tafʿīl*) and an irregular rhyme scheme.

In Ṣalāḥ's poetry, sadness and melancholy prevail. His first anthology, *al-Nās fī bilādī*, bears clear influences of social realism, using simple diction similar to ordinary speech, as well as the poetic technique and ideas of T.S. Eliot. He depicted popular daily life and the emptiness, hard life and poverty of the ordinary urban and country Egyptians. Moreover, he was among the few Arab poets who were able to present Arabic poetry with a successful example of a poem written in blank verse (*shiʿr mursal*) entitled *Abī* ("My father") (*al-Nās*, 55-8). This is because he was aware of the importance of using enjambement (*tatmīm*) between the verses, a poetic technique which was considered a fault (*ʿayb*) in classical poetry. However, there are also clear influences in the motives and images, and even in wording, from Eliot's *The waste land, The hollow men, Ash Wednesday*, and *The love song of J. Alfred Prufrock*, upon Ṣalāḥ's poetry, which was published in several other anthologies.

In drama, Ṣalāḥ was among the leading Arab writers of plays in blank verse. He was acquainted with dramatic literature through reading the plays of Tawfīḳ al-Ḥakīm and ʿAlī Aḥmad Bākathīr in Arabic, and of Shakespeare, Oscar Wilde and Bernard Shaw and Greek drama in English, though he did not see any play performed on stage till he came to Cairo at the age of twenty.

His dramas deal with the tyranny and oppression exercised by the authorities and the responsibility of art and literature towards social institutions. His characters are engaged tragic heroes or cowardly conspirators who betray their values and join forces with the authorities. However, being a talented poet, his poetic style and images save him from direct and prosaic expression. His first drama, *Maʾsāt al-Ḥallādj* ("The tragedy of al-Ḥallādj") (1964), bears the influence of Greek tragedy. The play deals with the engagement of the intellectual in a historical frame, putting forward the view that al-Ḥallādj [*q.v.*] was crucified in consequence of what were considered revolutionary action, blasphemous ideas and utterances, as in the cases of Socrates and Jesus. There are clear influences from Eliot's *Murder in the Cathedral* upon this play, especially in the motives of martyrdom, justice, and the struggle between the state and the religious authorities.

The second play by Ṣalāḥ ʿAbd al-Ṣabūr is *Musāfir layl* ("Traveller at night") (1969), in which he depicted the role of social and political institutions in destroying the individual. In his third play, *al-Amīra tantaẓir* ("The Princess is waiting") (1969), he dealt with the idolising of leaders; while in his fourth play, *Laylā wa 'l-madjnūn* ("Layla and the madman") (1970), he was concerned with poverty, the oppression of women and the spiritual emptiness and impotency of intellectuals in Egypt before the revolution of 1952, which encouraged political corruption. In his mythological play *Baʿda an yamūt al-malik* ("After the death of the King") (Beirut-Cairo 1973), he considered the political conditions in Egypt in the seventies, calling for a revival of life through death.

In his youth, Ṣalāḥ was influenced by the poets of the Mahdjar [*q.v.*]. In his spiritual autobiography *Ḥayātī fi 'l-shiʿr* ("My life in poetry") he revealed his theory of poetics which was developed under the influence of Plato, Aristotle and Nietzsche, giving them his own interpretation; thus he claimed that Aristotle's catharsis takes place at the time of the creative process and that it does not only purify the soul from fear and pity but also from the emotion of revenge.

Ṣalāḥ ʿAbd al-Ṣabūr wrote, beside his four translations of books by Ibsen, Eliot and Lorca, several collections of articles in which he discussed his ideas and theories on literature, politics, society and arts, as well as European and American theatre and literature, all presented in a clear and elegant style, in such collections as *Aṣwāt al-ʿaṣr* ("The voices of the age") (1961) (on European and American literature and theatre); *Mādhā yabḳā minhum li 'l-tārīkh* ("Which memory will they leave after their death?") (1962) (studies on the achievements of Ṭāhā Ḥusayn, al-ʿAḳḳād, Tawfīḳ al-Ḥakīm and al-Māzinī); and several others.

Bibliography: Special issue of *Fuṣūl, Madjallat al-*

Naḳd al-Adabī, Cairo, entitled "al-S̲h̲āʿir wa 'l-Kalima", ii/1 (October, 1981) dedicated to Ṣalāḥ ʿAbd al-Ṣabūr with a comprehensive bibl. on the author by Ḥamdī al-Sakkūt and M. Jones; Badr al-Dīb, introd. to Ṣalāḥ, *al-Nās fī bilādī*, Beirut 1957, 5-36; idem, *Ḥayātī fi 'l-s̲h̲iʿr*, Beirut 1969; idem, *Murder in Baghdad* (= "The tragedy of al-Ḥallād̲j̲"), tr. Khalil I. Semaan, Leiden 1972; idem, *The Princess waits*, tr. S. Megally, Cairo 1975; idem, *Night traveller*, tr. M. Enani, Cairo 1980; Māhir S̲h̲afīḳ Farīd, *At̲h̲ar T.S. Eliot fī 'l-adab al-ʿarabī al-ḥadīt̲h̲*, in *Fuṣūl*, i/4 (July 1981), 173-92; Ibrāhīm ʿAbd al-Ḥamīd, *D̲j̲arīmat ḳatl bayna Eliot wa-ʿAbd al-Ṣabūr*, in *Fuṣūl*, iii/4 (July-August-September 1983), 193-203; Arieh Loya, *Al-Sayyāb and the influence of T.S. Eliot*, in *MW*, lxi (1971), 187-201; S. Moreh, *Modern Arabic poetry 1800-1970*, Leiden 1976; Khalil I. Semaan, *T.S. Eliot's influence on Arabic poetry and theatre*, in *Comparative Literature Studies*, iv (1969), 472-89; Reuven Snir, *The poetic creative process according to Ṣalāḥ ʿAbd al-Ṣabūr*, in Ami Elad (ed.), *Writer, culture, text: studies in modern Arabic literature*, Fredericton 1993, 74-88; idem, *Ṣūfiyya bi-lā taṣawwuf, ḳirāʾa d̲j̲adīda fī ḳaṣīdat Ṣalāḥ ʿAbd al-Ṣabūr: al-ilāh al-ṣaghīr*, in *al-Karmil* (Haifa), no. 6 (1985), 129-46; L. Tremaine, *Witnesses to the event in* Maʾsāt al-Ḥallāj *and* Murder in the Cathedral, in *MW*, lxvii (1977), 33-46. (S. MOREH)

ṢALĀḤ AL-DĪN, AL-MALIK AL-NĀṢIR ABU 'L-MUẒAFFAR YŪSUF B. AYYŪB (SALADIN), the founder of the dynasty of the Ayyūbids [*q.v.*], and the champion of the *d̲j̲ihād* against the Crusaders (born 532/1138, died 589/1193).

Ṣalāḥ al-Dīn, or Saladin as he is normally known in Europe, was a Kurd, whose family originated from Dvīn in Armenia. His father Ayyūb and his uncle S̲h̲īrkūh [*q.v.*] found service in the Sald̲j̲ūḳ state, and Saladin was born at Takrīt on the Tigris above Bag̲h̲dād while Ayyūb was acting as governor there. The family transferred its services to Zangī [*q.v.*] and then to his son and successor in Aleppo, and later also ruler of Damascus, Nūr al-Dīn Maḥmūd [*q.v.*]. In Saladin's early manhood (the precise date is doubtful), he followed his elder brother Tūrāns̲h̲āh in the post of prefect (*s̲h̲iḥna*) at Damascus. S̲h̲īrkūh persuaded Nūr al-Dīn to sanction a series of interventionary expeditions to Egypt, where the Fāṭimid caliphate was threatened by the forces of the kingdom of Jerusalem. On three occasions Zangid armies entered Egypt, in 559/1164, 562/1167 and 564/1169, the last occasion resulting in S̲h̲īrkūh's taking power as Fāṭimid vizier. During these expeditions Saladin, though generally unwilling to go, played a significant role, particularly in defending Alexandria besieged during the second campaign.

S̲h̲īrkūh soon died (22 D̲j̲umādā II 564/23 March 1169) and within a short while, by a combination of pressure and largesse, Saladin emerged to follow him as commander of the Syrian force and as vizier appointed by the palace. It is with this appointment that, in the style of Fāṭimid viziers, he adopted the title al-Malik al-Nāṣir. It is said that Saladin won supporters by being generous "as though they were his kin", a revealing phrase. Extravagant generosity was to remain an instrument of his policy, though not one that passed without criticism from his hard-pressed administrators, such as al-Ḳāḍī al-Fāḍil [*q.v.*]. Some early sources suggest that before this juncture in his life Saladin was lax in his religious observance and lacking in moral seriousness, but that, with his new responsibilities, he professed "repentence" (*tawba*) and developed a sense of purpose. This has all the hallmarks of a stock theme.

The next few years were spent securing his position in Egypt against the residual forces of the Fāṭimid caliphate (e.g. by crushing the Sudanese regiments in 564/1168), and against external attacks on Egypt (by defeating the joint Crusader-Byzantine attempt on Damietta in 565/1169). Nūr al-Dīn's demands for more active military support and for substantial financial contributions towards his plans of reconquest from the Franks were not answered by Saladin. The contradictions inherent in Saladin's position were clear. Whether or not he was loath to suppress the Fāṭimid caliphate because his position as Fāṭimid vizier gave him independent authority, that step, demanded by Nūr al-Dīn, was finally taken in 567/1171 with little or no public disturbance, and Egypt became officially Sunnī and returned to ʿAbbāsid allegiance. The title *Muḥyī dawlat amīr al-muʾminīn* ("Reviver of the empire of the Commander of the Faithful") was to be frequently employed in Saladin's inscriptions.

Nūr al-Dīn without doubt remained discontented with the situation. He sent Ibn al-Kaysarānī in 569/1174 to audit the finances of Egypt, which, if one believes Ibn Abī Ṭayy, almost led to an open breach, and Nūr al-Dīn was perhaps contemplating a military expedition to impose his authority directly, when in S̲h̲awwāl/May of that same year he died. The nature of any difference between Saladin and Nūr al-Dīn is difficult to gauge, granted the partiality and *ex post facto* nature of our sources.

Nūr al-Dīn's successor, Ismāʿīl, was young and inexperienced. Damascus and Aleppo fell to opposing cliques, willing to make concessions to the Franks to win their support or divert their attacks, and the branch of the Zangid house that ruled at Mawṣil showed expansionist ambitions. At this juncture Saladin took the important step that marked out the rest of his life. He responded to the invitation of the *amīr* Ibn al-Muḳaddam and took over Damascus (Rabīʿ II 570/October 1174). He presented himself as the true moral heir of Nūr al-Dīn and the most fit and disinterested protector of his successor, Ismāʿīl. Pro-Zangid sources attacked him as an adventurer and usurper, a self-seeking upstart Kurd who would thrust aside the descendants of his former master. The question of motives, possibly irrelevant in the last resort, cannot be satisfactorily answered. Ambition and a consciousness of personal worth and fitness for a task are not incompatible with a high moral purpose.

If the Franks were ever to be expelled, it was necessary to unite large Muslim forces. As at least one Shāfiʿī *faḳīh* recognised soon after the establishment of the Crusader states, the union of the forces of Egypt, Syria and the D̲j̲azīra was likely to be needed (E. Sivan, *Genèse de la contre-croisade, un traité damasquin du début du xiie siècle*, in *JA*, ccliv [1966], 213). To create such a union necessarily involved whoever sought to do that in a policy of expansion, as it had involved Nūr al-Dīn. The problem for Saladin, which had also existed for Nūr al-Dīn, was that in order to pursue such a union he had to wage war on Muslims to compel their submission if they rejected the call to perform their duty in the *d̲j̲ihād*, and he had either to conclude agreements with the Franks to secure himself on that front during his campaigning absences in the D̲j̲azīra or risk their damaging raids, in both cases leaving himself open to criticisms of neglecting the *d̲j̲ihād*.

With Damascus gained, Ḥims, Ḥamāt and Baʿlabakk came quickly under Saladin's control, but in Rad̲j̲ab 570/January 1175 he withdrew from a short siege of Aleppo when faced by combined Zangid counter-moves. Having first offered to give up all but Damascus and to accept the nominal suzerainty of

Ismāʿīl, Saladin gained a victory over the Zangid forces at the Horns of Ḥamāt in Ramaḍān 570/April 1175, after which a peace was made, and Saladin also received a diploma from the caliph, granting him delegated authority over Egypt and Syria, except for Aleppo and its dependencies. In Shawwāl 571/April 1176 the combined Zangid armies, having taken the offensive despite the treaty of the previous year, were defeated for the second time at Tall al-Sulṭān, near Aleppo, but Saladin was still unable to force the city's surrender. Saladin's gains, including some north of Aleppo, were confirmed by a new treaty in Muḥarram 572/July 1176. However, the ruling junta around al-Ṣāliḥ Ismāʿīl in Aleppo, and the other Zangid princes, remained impervious to Saladin's propaganda and suspicious of his aims.

During these campaigns Saladin suffered two attacks by Rashīd al-Dīn Sinān's [*q.v.*] Ismāʿīlī Assassins, prompted by his Aleppan enemies, but subsequently, after some show of force in Assassin territory, he seems to have established a *modus vivendi* with them (see B. Lewis, *Saladin and the Assassins*, in *BSOAS*, xv [1953], 239-45).

His campaigning against the Franks was limited at this time and included the overconfident raid into Palestine that ended in defeat between Ascalon and Ramla at the unidentified "Mons Gisardi" in Djumādā 573/November 1177. This lesson was taken to heart, but it was an inauspicious beginning to any plan of making good his claim to be Nūr al-Dīn's successor in the prosecution of the *djihād*. Better success followed in Muḥarram 575/June 1179 with the defeat of King Baldwin at Mardj ʿUyūn and the destruction of Bayt al-Aḥzān or Jacob's Castle in Rabīʿ I/August of that year.

During the next five or six years, Saladin was mostly involved in Mesopotamian affairs, which were of great complexity and are too complicated to be treated exhaustively here. On several occasions Saladin was able to make gains on being invited to intervene in disputes or after appeals for assistance. In 576/1180 the Artuḳid ruler of Ḥisn Kayfā, Nūr al-Dīn Muḥammad b. Ḳara Arslan, appealed to him for help in a dispute with Ḳilidj Arslan [*q.v.*], the Rūm Saldjūḳid, whose advance against Raʿbān had been checked the year before by Saladin's nephew, Taḳī 'l-Dīn ʿUmar. Saladin also intervened in Zangid politics after the death of Sayf al-Dīn Ghāzī, the ruler of Mawṣil, in Ṣafar 576/June 1180, and refused to acknowledge the succession of his brother, ʿIzz al-Dīn, arguing that he was acting with the authority granted him by the caliph. In Aleppo al-Ṣāliḥ Ismāʿīl died during Radjab 577/December 1181. Saladin was anxious that Aleppo and Mawṣil should not be combined in hostile hands. In Muḥarram 578/May 1182 he marched from Cairo, never to return again. His main preoccupation was Aleppo, which in the meantime ʿIzz al-Dīn had exchanged for Sindjār [*q.v.*] with his brother, ʿImād al-Dīn Ghāzī. After some operations against the Franks, including a major but inconclusive battle near Baysān and an opportunistic assault on Beirut, Saladin arrived at Aleppo in Muḥarram 579/September 1182. He embarked on negotiations rather than active military measures. However, he was then invited by sympathisers, chiefly Gökburi of Ḥarrān, to cross the Euphrates, where he accepted the alliance, or received the surrender, of Begteginid, Artuḳid and Zangid possessions, Sarūdj, Edessa, Raḳḳa, al-Khābūr, and Nisibis. Mawṣil itself was then besieged, perhaps more in the hope of exerting pressure on ʿIzz al-Dīn in the continuing diplomatic and propaganda war than of reducing the city. Withdrawing from Mawṣil, Saladin captured Sindjār from ʿIzz al-Dīn before going into winter quarters at Ḥarrān.

In the following spring, Reynald de Chatillon launched his disturbing but ultimately unsuccessful naval raid into the Red Sea. The countering of this threat to the Ḥidjāz gave Saladin further propaganda opportunities. Beyond the Euphrates he resolutely confronted a force gathered from Mawṣil and its northern neighbours, Khilāt, Bitlīs and Mārdīn, which disbanded ineffectually. This was followed by Saladin's capture with caliphal sanction of the powerful fortress of ʿĀmid (Dhu 'l-Ḥidjdja 578/April 1183), which he gave, as promised, to his vassal Nūr al-Dīn Muḥammad. This constituted a great moral and propaganda coup. As a result of this the other Artuḳid cities of Mayyafāriḳīn and Mārdīn submitted to Saladin.

Aleppo, more isolated then ever, was once more put under pressure, and in Ṣafar 579/June 1183 ʿImād al-Dīn, rather against the will of his *amīrs* and the populace, agreed to surrender the city and receive back Sindjār along with other towns in addition. He also agreed to provide troops for Saladin's campaigns.

Having achieved this important goal, Saladin led large forces, gathered as a result of the recent extensions of his authority, into the territory of the kingdom of Jerusalem during the remainder of 579/1183, but provoked no decisive field engagement. There was also an unsuccessful attack on al-Karak [*q.v.*], followed by a second attack in Djumādā I-II 580/August-September 1184. Apart from the wish to punish Reynald, the lord of Transjordan, for his raids, the capture of al-Karak would mean an improvement in communications between Egypt and Damascus.

Saladin found another opportunity to move against Mawṣil when Zayn al-Dīn Yūsuf of Irbil called upon him for help against ʿIzz al-Dīn and the latter's new ally, Ḳizil Arslān, the Atabeg of Ādharbaydjān. Saladin arrived before Mawṣil in Rabīʿ II 581/July 1185 to besiege it for the second time. This same summer, some of the northern princes, Shāh Arman b. Sukmān of Khilāt and Nūr al-Dīn Muḥammad, the lord of ʿĀmid, died, and attempts to make a satisfactory settlement of their affairs deflected his efforts for a while. After returning to Mawṣil, negotiations were set afoot, but Saladin himself fell ill and withdrew his forces in Ramaḍān 581/December 1185. However, exhaustion and a lack of effective allies led Mawṣil to sue for a lasting peace. An embassy, in which the future biographer Bahāʾ al-Dīn Ibn Shaddād [*q.v.*], took part, came to Saladin at Ḥarrān in Dhu 'l-Ḥidjdja 581/February 1186 and reached satisfactory conclusions, accepting the crucial obligation to provide troops for the *djihād*, and so Saladin's overlordship was finally recognised.

After a year of recuperation and internal reorganisation, the long-awaited campaign was launched at the beginning of 583/spring 1187. Saladin's allies were summoned from all quarters, and the full forces of the Crusader states (except for Antioch with which a truce had been made) were brought to battle at the Horns of Ḥaṭṭīn, on the heights to the west of Tiberias, on Saturday, 24 Rabīʿ II 583/4 July 1187. It ended in an annihilating defeat for the Crusaders. Demoralised and with reduced garrisons, many towns and strongplaces surrendered or fell quickly. Acre surrendered on 1 Djumādā I/9 July and Saladin sent out his forces in various directions. By the middle of Djumādā II/early September, all the coast from Gaza to Djubayl was in Saladin's hands, apart from Tyre. At this point Saladin moved to Jerusalem, the symbolic goal of the *d̲j̲ihād*. The city surrendered, after nearly two weeks of siege and some spirited resistance, on 27 Rad̲j̲ab/2 October and Saladin solemnly installed in the Aḳṣā Mosque the *minbar* that Nūr al-Dīn had prepared for this moment.

Saladin has been criticised for his failure to give high priority to the capture of Tyre. This and the other ports would clearly be crucial for any eventual rescue expedition from Europe, but Saladin was not to know that Conrad de Montferrat would arrive just when he did to stiffen its defence. It was also strategically important to reduce the *points d'appui* represented by the inland castles, and the terms that Saladin offered, backed by the confidence that people had in his word, accelerated the surrender of many places. Although Saladin has been described as only a moderately good strategist and tactician, there is also a more positive judgement on his strategy at this stage in his operations, understood in the light of its possible relationship with the theoretical work of al-Harawī, *al-Tad̲h̲kirat al-harawiyya fī 'l-ḥiyal al-ḥarbiyya* (see W.J. Hamblin, *Saladin and Muslim military theory*, in *The Horns of Hattin*, ed. B.Z. Kedar, Jerusalem 1992, 228-38). Many refugees from the interior assembled in Tyre. A siege of the city that began in Ramaḍān 583/November 1187 proved fruitless, and the majority of the Muslim armies disbanded in Dhu 'l-Ḳaʿda 583/January 1188.

When campaigning began again during 584/1188, Saladin made further conquests in northern Syria, taking Ṭarṭūs, D̲j̲abala, Lād̲h̲aḳiyya, Ṣahyūn and Balāṭunus but not attempting Tripoli. He also took the outlying fortresses of the principality of Antioch, but then made a truce without any attack on Antioch itself. In S̲h̲awwāl 584/December 1188, having moved south *via* Damascus, Saladin forced the surrender of Ṣafad [*q.v.*], and Kawkab (Belvoir) fell in Dhu 'l-Ḳaʿda 584/January 1189. Further south, al-Karak finally succumbed to al-ʿĀdil's [*q.v.*] siege, and S̲h̲awbak [*q.v.*] followed several months later.

The regular arrival of the forces of the Third Crusade led to their investment of Acre and the besieging of the besiegers for a period of almost two years. Saladin looked far and wide for assistance, fostering relations with the Byzantines (see C.M. Brand, *The Byzantines and Saladin, 1185-1192: opponents of the Third Crusade*, in *Speculum*, xxxvii [1962], 167-81) and courting (unsuccessfully) the Almohads of North Africa for naval help (see M. Gaudefroy-Demombynes, *Une lettre de Saladin au Calife almohade*, in *Mélanges René Basset*, Paris 1925, ii, 279-304). Acre fell to the Franks in D̲j̲umādā II 587/July 1191. For a little more than a year after this military operations on the Palestine plain, led by Richard I of England, continued indecisively, and a Frankish attempt to march inland against Jerusalem had to be abandoned. Long and involved negotiations ended in S̲h̲aʿbān 588/September 1192 with the agreement to a general peace for three years and eight months and a recognition of Frankish coastal gains from Acre to Jaffa.

Saladin made various visits of inspection and organisation in the reconquered lands, again put off a proposed journey to the Ḥid̲j̲āz to perform the *Ḥad̲j̲d̲j̲*, and returned to Damascus, where he fell ill. After about two weeks of steady decline, movingly described by his confidant, Bahāʾ al-Dīn Ibn S̲h̲addād, he died on Wednesday, 27 Ṣafar 589/3 March 1193. He was buried initially within the Damascus citadel, but during Muḥarram 592/December 1195 his body was transferred to a newly-built tomb (*turba*) north of the Umayyad Mosque (Abū S̲h̲āma, *al-D̲h̲ayl ʿalā 'l-Rawḍatayn*, ed. al-Kawt̲h̲arī, Damascus 1947, 8, and Ibn K̲h̲allikān, ed. ʿAbbās, vii, 206).

Saladin's death occurred only a few months after the peace had been made. Bahāʾ al-Dīn Ibn S̲h̲addād claimed that Saladin had earlier contemplated the rejection of any peace proposals and wished to carry on the fight until every last Frank had been driven out of the Levant. The fact that the peace had been signed and a period of respite guaranteed was subsequently seen as a blessing, as his death while hostilities were still continuing would have produced a situation full of danger.

The cohesion of Saladin's empire was tested to the full by the events of the Third Crusade. The hardships and expense of this long campaigning, the reverses and the slow decline in morale, meant that some northern allies, also faced by their own local problems and rivalries, failed to send their troops. Saladin's nephew, Taḳī 'l-Dīn, also withdrew to follow his own ambitions at Mayyāfāriḳīn and added to that region's complications. However, the point has been fairly made by Gibb that many of Saladin's vassals, including the Zangids of Mawṣil and Sind̲j̲ār, although initially constrained to accept his suzerainty, continued to rally to his standard with their contingents throughout this period. Had they refused, it would have been difficult indeed to spare troops to force them. This suggests that by this stage Saladin's cause had to some extent been accepted as the cause of Islam and of the *d̲j̲ihād*.

Saladin's desire to win the wider acceptance and cooperation of ruling and religious circles are themes that informed his propaganda addressed to Bag̲h̲dād and elsewhere. The ways in which the ideals of the *d̲j̲ihād* were fostered and the message spread through society under Saladin have been studied exhaustively by E. Sivan (*L'Islam et la Croisade. Idéologie et propagande dans les réactions musulmanes aux Croisades*, Paris 1968, ch. 4). Saladin's public statements maintained that the ultimate aims of *d̲j̲ihād*, the duty of Muslim princes to participate, and also the delegated authority he had been given by the caliph, justified his compulsion of those unwilling to join the common cause. How much weight the pronouncements of the caliph and his granting of supporting diplomas had in the battle for mens' minds and allegiance over against considerations of temporal interest it is difficult to say. Saladin clearly thought it worth while to keep up a barrage of letters to Bag̲h̲dād seeking formal delegation of ever-widening authority and sanction for his politics and military moves. It is doubtful, however, whether the rhetoric in letters written by such persons as al-Ḳāḍī al-Fāḍil really amounted to the expression on Saladin's part of a desire to restore the caliphate as the active centre of a renewed Islamic political entity, as Gibb has suggested. Even he has admitted that "propaganda points may be difficult to disentangle from religious zeal." Indeed, it seems that the nearer the frontiers of Saladin's empire came to Bag̲h̲dād, the more troubled were his relations with the caliphate which itself was attempting to expand its temporal influence and areas of control. Symptomatic was the brawl over precedence between ʿIrāḳī and Syrian pilgrims during the *Ḥad̲j̲d̲j̲* of 583/February 1188, which ended in the death of Saladin's long-time supporter, the *amīr* Ibn al-Muḳaddam.

Saladin spent most of his life in Syria, and Damascus was always his preferred place of residence Egypt and her resources supplied the means for his expansionist policy and his victories. For long periods he entrusted its government to his brother al-ʿĀdil, and to his chief civilian administrator, al-Ḳāḍī al-Fāḍil There are signs that the economic strain of the constant campaigning affected Egypt and Syria too and that social unrest was growing. Serious financia problems arose, partly because of the exhaustion of the Upper Egyptian gold-mines but mainly from the demanding military expenditure. This led to the debasement of the dīnār, the end of the stability which the Fāṭimid currency had known (A. Ehrenkreutz, *The crisis of the* dīnār *in the Egypt of Saladin*, in *JAOS*, lxxvi [1956], 178-84). It is interesting to note that the addition of Yemen to the empire, which had been conquered for the Ayyūbids by Saladin's brother Tūrān-shāh, and later ruled by another brother, Ṭughtakīn, clearly created hopes that it would be a source of treasure, and that Saladin's complaints, when that was not satisfactorily forthcoming, mirror Nūr al-Dīn's earlier complaints about the insufficient aid he had received from Egypt.

Saladin's lands were administered by a decentralised bureaucracy, the details of which will probably always remain obscure. As for Egypt itself, we possess a work on the land tax, in an imperfect version, revised about 581/1185 (see ʿAlī b. ʿUthmān al-Makhzūmī, *Kitāb al-minhādj fī ʿilm al-kharādj*, ed. Cl. Cahen and Y. Ragheb, Cairo 1983, and also Cahen, *Makhzūmiyyāt. Études sur l'histoire économique et financière de l'Égypte médiévale,* Leiden 1977), and there is also extant a wider examination of the bureaucracy by Ibn Mammātī (d. 606/1209) entitled *Kitāb Ḳawānīn al-dawāwīn* (ed. A.S. Atiya, Cairo 1943). At various times during his life he delegated the control of parts of his empire to the growing number of family members and to trusted officers of the army, relying on family and personal loyalties and on a balance of interests to preserve the whole. The last arrangement he made for the division of power in his empire did not, however, endure long after his death. Saladin may or may not have been personally indifferent to wealth and possessions. In general, however, he recognised and forwarded the interests of his family and was eager to protect their dynastic future, although at times the wishes and ambitions of members of his family, especially his brothers Tūrān-shāh and Ṭughtakīn, caused him difficulties. He was nevertheless capable of arguing against claims of hereditary expectations on the occasions when the Zangids advanced them. Ultimately, the dominant role passed to a collateral branch of the Ayyūbid family, to his brother al-ʿĀdil and his descendants, and for most of the dynasty's history Saladin's direct descendants ruled only in Aleppo.

Fundamentally his position depended on the army, the core of which was his personal guard, the *ḥalḳa* [*q.v.*]. Apart from the dominant contribution of Egypt, each urban centre in greater Syria and the Djazīra maintained an *ʿaskar* commensurate with its resources. The whole army, which was paid by *iḳṭāʿ* [*q.v.*] or by monthly salary (*djāmakiyya*) was still largely free-born, although the sultan, princes and *amīrs* had their personal *mamlūk* contingents (see H.A.R. Gibb, *The armies of Saladin*, in S.J. Shaw and W.R. Polk (eds.), *Studies on the civilization of Islam*, Boston 1962, 74-90). Because of the domination of the Mediterranean by the Italian states both for trade and for the movement of troops, Saladin made attempts to revive Fāṭimid naval power, and his ships made some useful contributions to his operations, but ultimately lost control of the sea during the Third Crusade (see Ehrenkreutz, *The place of Saladin in the naval history of the Mediterranean Sea in the Middle Ages*, in *JAOS*, lxxv [1955], 100-16).

Unlike his mentor, Nūr al-Dīn, who was a Ḥanafī, Saladin adhered to the Shāfiʿī *madhhab*, in which he was followed by practically all the members of his dynasty. In his theology he was of the Ashʿarī persuasion. In the reported wording of the *waḳfiyya* for the *khānḳāh* which he founded in Cairo (see al-Maḳrīzī, *Khiṭaṭ*, ii, 415-16), the residual beneficiaries of the *waḳf* income are "poor Shāfiʿī or Mālikī *fuḳahāʾ*, who are of the Ashʿarī creed." In the construction inscription for the *madrasa* which he founded at the tomb of al-Shāfiʿī, in which unusually Saladin's name and titles have no mention but only the initiative of the *shaykh* al-Khabūshānī is stressed, the Ashʿarī anti-Ḥashwiyya nature of the foundation is made explicit. In many respects, in the public image at least, his régime followed that of Nūr al-Dīn in striving to suppress non-Islamic elements in society and administration and in promoting Sharīʿa norms. There is little evidence of specifically anti-Ismāʿīlī activity. Once the Fāṭimid court and the ruling establishment had been scattered and the ineffectual attempts at counter-coups dealt with, the underlying Sunnī nature of Egyptian society could assert itself. As for intellectual pursuits, he studied *Ḥadīth* and was fond of poetry, ʿUsāma b. Munḳidh being an especial favourite.

As regards his building activity, he was responsible for much military work throughout his lands. The grand design to enclose Cairo and Fusṭāṭ with a defensive wall was begun on his behalf by Bahāʾ al-Dīn Ḳarāḳūsh [*q.v.*] but never completed. The citadel at Cairo was also conceived by Saladin and started in 572/1176-7, but finished after his reign and subjected to many later changes. Adjacent to the Imām al-Shāfiʿī's tomb he constructed a *madrasa* for the Shāfiʿīs (see above) and near the mosque of ʿAmr b. al-ʿĀṣ a *madrasa* for the Mālikīs, which came to be known as al-Ḳumḥiyya. The latter was begun in Muḥarram 566/September 1170. In Cairo proper he converted the former residence (*dār*) of the Fāṭimid vizier al-Maʾmūn into a *madrasa* for the Ḥanafīs (*waḳfiyya* dated Shaʿbān 572/March 1177) and built a *khānḳāh* (*waḳfiyya* dated 569/1173-4). These were the earliest examples of such institutions to be founded in Egypt. He also converted part of the Fāṭimid palace into a hospital (*bīmāristān*) during 577/1182. After the reconquest, Jerusalem received much of his attention, in the restoration of the Dome of the Rock and the Aḳṣā Mosque to make them fit for Muslim worship, and also in the conversion of the Latin Patriarch's residence into a Ṣūfī *khānḳah* (endowed in 585/1189), the conversion of the church of St Anne into the Ṣalāḥiyya, a *madrasa* for the Shāfiʿīs (also endowed in 585/1189), and in the provision of a hospital (begun 588/1192).

Saladin's personality is somewhat hidden behind the image-making of his admirers. One thing beyond doubt is that he could inspire devotion in his followers. His generosity, fidelity and compassion are vividly portrayed, but he could also be ruthless. He was impatient of details of administration. The generally pro-Zangid Ibn al-Athīr [*q.v.*], who frequently skews his historical account to Saladin's disadvantage, in his final summary of Saladin's life and career nevertheless gives a more positive assessment, when he writes, "He was a man of religious knowledge and culture, a *Ḥadīth* scholar. In short he was a man of rare qualities in his time, much given to generosity and fine deeds, a mighty warrior of the *djihād* against the infidels." The contemporary historian William of Tyre, whose record of events ends at 1183, portrays him as a generous, energetic and ambitious ruler, whose policies present a real threat to the Crusader states. In due course, in mediaeval European literature the historical Saladin was lost sight of and he became a mythic figure of chivalry. A romanticised view of him continued into

19th-century literature, most notably in Sir Walter Scott's historical novel, *Ivanhoe*.

Bibliography: The fundamental sources are ʿImād al-Dīn al-Isfahānī, *al-Barḳ al-Shāmī*, lost except for two parts, part 3 (years 573-5/1177-80) ed. M. al-Ḥayyārī, ʿAmmān 1987, and part 5 (years 578-9/1182-4) ed. R. Şeşen, Istanbul 1971, and M. al-Ḥayyārī, ʿAmmān 1987; the epitome of this work by al-Bundarī, *Sanāʾ al-Barḳ al-Shāmī*, ed. R. Şeşen, Beirut 1971 (up to 576/1180), and ed. Fatḥiyya al-Nabarāwī, Cairo 1979 (up to 583/1188); ʿImād al-Dīn al-Isfahānī, *al-Fatḥ al-Ḳussī fī 'l-Fatḥ al-Ḳudsī*, ed. C. de Landberg, Leiden 1888 (tr. H. Massé, *Conquête de la Syrie et de la Palestine par Saladin*, Paris 1972); Bahāʾ al-Dīn Ibn Shaddād, *al-Nawādir al-sulṭaniyya wa 'l-maḥāsin al-Yūsufiyya* or *Sīrat Ṣalāḥ al-Dīn*, ed. al-Shayyal, Cairo 1964 (tr. C.W. Wilson, *The life of Saladin*, in *Palestine Pilgrims' Text Society*, xiii, London 1897, repr. New York 1971); Ibn Abī Ṭayy, quoted in Abū Shāma (see below); the private and official documents of al-Ḳāḍī al-Fāḍil, see A.H. Helbig, *al-Qāḍī al-Fāḍil, der Wezir Saladins*, Leipzig 1908, and various ms. collections; Ibn al-Athīr, *al-Kāmil fī 'l-taʾrīkh*, Dār Ṣādir ed., xi-xii, Beirut 1966; idem, *al-Taʾrīkh al-bāhir fī 'l-dawla al-atābakiyya*, ed. A.A. Tolaymat, Cairo and Baghdād [1963].

Consult also the later syntheses, Abū Shāma, *Kitāb al-Rawḍatayn fī akhbār al-dawlatayn*, Būlāḳ 1287-8/1870-2 (repr. Beirut n.d.), i-ii, and ed. M.H.A. Aḥmad, Cairo 1956-62, i/1-2; Ibn Wāṣil, *Mufarridj al-kurūb fī akhbār Banī Ayyūb*, ed. al-Shayyal, Cairo 1953-7, i-ii; Ibn al-Furāt, *Taʾrīkh*, ed. H. al-Shammā, Baṣra 1967-9, iv, parts 1-2; and the biographical notice in Ibn Khallikān, *Wafayāt al-aʿyān wa-anbāʾ abnāʾ al-zamān*, ed. I. ʿAbbās, Beirut n.d., vii, 139-212.

For studies of the sources, see H.A.R. Gibb, *The Arabic sources for the life of Saladin*, in *Speculum*, xxv (1950), 58-72; D.S. Richards, *A consideration of two sources for the life of Saladin*, in *JSS*, xxv (1980), 46-65; P.M. Holt, *Saladin and his admirers: a biographical reassessment*, in *BSOAS*, xlvi (1983), 235-9; M. Ripke, *Saladin und sein Biograph Baha addin b. Shaddad*, Bonn 1988.

As general studies, Gibb, *The achievement of Saladin*, in S.J. Shaw and W.R. Polk (eds.), *Studies on the civilization of Islam*, Boston 1962, 91-107; idem, *The life of Saladin* etc., Oxford 1973; A.S. Ehrenkreutz, *Saladin*, Albany 1972; M.C. Lyons and D.E.P. Jackson, *Saladin: the politics of the Holy War*, Cambridge 1982. For the family background and particular stages of his career, see V. Minorsky, *The pre-history of Saladin*, in *Studies in Caucasian history*, London 1953; Richards, *The early history of Saladin*, in *IQ*, xvii, 140-59; H. Möhring, *Saladin und die dritte Kreuzzug*, Wiesbaden 1980. For the battle of Ḥaṭṭīn and the subsequent campaign, see J. Prawer, *La bataille de Hattin*, in *Israel Exploration Journal*, xiv (1964), 160-79; B.Z. Kedar, *The battle of Hattin revisited*, in *The Horns of Hattin*, ed. idem, Jerusalem 1992, 190-207; R.B.C. Huygens, *La campagne de Saladin en Syrie du Nord* (*1188*), in *Apamée de Syrie. Bilan des recherches archéologiques 1969-1971*, Brussels 1972, 273-83.

For his building works in Egypt, see Maḳrīzī, *Khiṭaṭ*, Būlāḳ ed., ii, 202-3, 364, 365-6, 407; K.A.C. Creswell, *The Muslim architecture of Egypt. II. Ayyubid and early Bahrite Mamluks A.D. 1171-1326*, Oxford 1959, 1-40 (the citadel), 41-63 (the walls), 64 (the tomb of the Imām al-Shāfiʿī). For his Jerusalem foundations, see M. van Berchem, *CIA, Syrie du Sud, i. Jérusalem "Ville"*, *MIFAO*, xliii, Cairo 1922, 87-90, 90-9, 108-19; and K.Dj. al-ʿAsalī, *Maʿāhid al-ʿilm fī Bayt al-Maḳdis*, ʿAmmān 1981, 54-94, 294-7, 330-8.

For inscriptions, see G. Wiet, *Les inscriptions de Saladin*, in *Syria*, iii (1922), 307-28, and *RCEA*, ix, nos. 3334-5, 3339, 3343-4, 3359, 3368, 3374, 3380, 3399, 3402, 3420-3, 3438, 3447, 3449-50, 3453, 3471; M.H. Burgoyne and A. Abul-Hajj, *Twenty-four mediaeval Arabic inscriptions from Jerusalem*, in *Levant*, xi (1979), 112-37, nos. xv, xvi, xviii. For a study of Saladin's coinage, see P. Balog, *The coinage of the Ayyūbids*, London 1980, 3-5, 58-103.

For Saladin in European literature, see G. Paris, *La légende de Saladin*, in *Journal des Savants* (1893), 284-99, 354-65, 428-38, 486-98; A. Thomas, *La légende de Saladin en Poitou*, in *Journal des Savants* (1908), 467-71; R.-F. Cook and L.S. Crist, *Le deuxième cycle de la croisade: Deux études sur son développement*, Geneva 1972, 160-71.

(D.S. RICHARDS)

ṢALĀLA, the name of the administrative capital of the Southern Region (Ẓafār [*q.v.*], Dhofar, also Djanūbiyya) of the Sultanate of Oman [see ʿUMĀN) and of the plain in which the town is situated. The town stands on the shore of the Indian Ocean and is 850 km/528 miles as the crow flies south-west of the capital of the Sultanate, Muscat [see MASḲAṬ] and about 120 km/75 miles from the present border with the Republic of Yemen. The town is the seat of the Minister of State and the Wālī of Dhofar.

The town is a modern one which has developed from a small market town only in the post-1970 period. There is a plentiful supply of water from both wells and streams, and the town is the centre of a rich agricultural area which produces grain, papayas, bananas, sugarcane, fruit and vegetables. There are no dates in the area and the thousands of palms produce coconuts. Much of the produce is produced in Ṣalāla itself, and there is a green band of agricultural lands and gardens which stretches through the centre of the rectangular town and which can be seen clearly from the air when flying over the town. In the north and south of the town lie built-up areas, with the extremely prominent royal palace and its complex, called al-Ḥuṣn, in the south on the sea shore.

In the extreme east of the town lie the ruins of al-Balīd (a modern Djibbāli rather than an Arabic name). These undoubtedly mark the important mediaeval settlement of Ẓafār. The port of mediaeval Ẓafār and of modern Ṣalāla was and remains Raysūt, with its perfect natural harbour some 15 km/9 miles across the bay to the south-west.

Bibliography: There is little information on the town, but three books produced by the Ministry of Information of the Sultanate of Oman are useful: *Sultanate of Oman throughout 20 years, the promise and the fulfillment*, and *Oman, the modern state*, both without a date, and *Salṭanat ʿUmān wa-masīrat al-khayr, al-Minṭaḳa al-djanūbiyya*, Ẓafar 1986; D. Hawley, *Oman and its renaissance*, London 1977; Liesl Graz, *The Omanis, sentinels of the Gulf*, London and New York 1982, 121-4.

(G.R. SMITH)

SALAM (A.), a term of Islamic law. It is used to designate a particular contract classifiable as a contract of sale (*bayʿ* [*q.v.*]) and synonymous, in appropriate contexts, with the term *salaf*, nobably in ʿIrāḳī works of classical jurisprudence. Regarded as a category of transaction in its own right, *salam* has as its fundamental principle prepayment by a purchaser (*al-musallim*) for an object of sale (*al-musallam fīhi*, i.e.

merchandise constituting the subject-matter of the contract) to be delivered to him by the vendor (*al-musallam ilayhi*) on a date at the end of a specified period. In such a transaction, the consideration (i.e. the price, be it in cash or in kind) agreed upon at the contracting parties' meeting (*madjlis al-ʿaḳd*) for delivery of the merchandise is termed *raʾs al-māl*. Inasmuch as the latter was, as it still is, the normal Arabic term for "capital" in the financial sense of the word, it is not difficult to infer from it the essentially economic purpose that the *salam* was intended to serve, namely that of affording small traders the wherewithal to supply customers' needs and thereby enabling such traders to perform the same sort of basic function as that performed in modern developed economies by wholesalers in their business of supplying the needs of retailers and artisans.

Among features characteristic of a *salam* contract the most striking for those acquainted with the *Sharīʿa* are the unavailability of the subject-matter of the contract at the meeting of the parties, on the one hand, and the vendor's lack of possession of or title to it, on the other. What makes them so striking is that they seem to mark a fundamental departure from the *Sharīʿa*'s strict principles governing commercial transactions and expressly designed to exclude from the latter any possibility not only of *ribā* [*q.v.*] (i.e. unlawful gain or interest, in whatever form, on a capital loan or investment), but also—and very much more importantly in the context of *salam*—of *gharar* ("chance", i.e. risk, uncertainty, speculation). Be that as it may, the early mediaeval jurists, once conscious of the need to recognise the validity of a practice that was in effect an economic necessity meeting the legitimate needs of the public, deemed it both appropriate and expedient to accommodate *salam* within the ideal framework of the *Sharīʿa* law and found themselves able to invoke in support of it, *inter alia*, the authority of a Tradition attributed to the Prophet himself.

To incorporate the principle of *salam* in Islamic law was one thing; to implement it was another. On certain basic matters (e.g. that the price and object of a *salam* sale cannot both be currencies; that the objects of sale should be fungible (*mithlī*, i.e. replaceable by others answering to the same definition), weighable (*mawzūn, waznī*) or measurable (*makīl, kaylī*), etc.) the main Sunnī schools of law were broadly in agreement, but on many points of detail important differences of opinion took shape and prevailed in the doctrine of particular schools. And so it is that we find, for example, that in Ḥanafī law living animals are not held to be proper objects of a *salam* sale, whereas in Mālikī law the contrary is the case. Again, in Ḥanafī law the object of a *salam* sale must be in existence at the time of the contract and from the time the latter is concluded until the time it is delivered, while in Mālikī law the requirement is only that the object be available at the time when delivery falls due. Exceptional and peculiar to Shāfiʿī law is the surprising doctrine that *salam* can be an immediate transaction and not necessarily one providing for future delivery of the object of sale. Similarly exceptional and hardly less surprising is the Mālikī doctrine that the price for the object of sale need not be paid at the *madjlis al-ʿaḳd*, but may, by mutual understanding, be postponed for up to three days or, in certain circumstances, for even longer than that. And so on.

Since by its very nature a *salam* transaction denies the purchaser what is known as "option after inspection" (*khiyār al-ruʾya*) of the object of sale, a description of the latter is the only possible means of avoiding ignorance (*jahl*) of it and of safeguarding the *salam* contract against the intrusion of a material element of risk or uncertainty (*gharar*). According to Ibn Ḳudāma (541-620/1147-1223 [*q.v.*]), the well-known luminary of the Ḥanbalī school, knowledge of the subject-matter—designated *ʿilm* in his terminology—is essential to the validity of a *salam* contract and should be imparted by a description stating the genus and species of whatever is in question and declaring the condition of the latter, be it good or bad. According to the same jurist, both Abū Ḥanīfa and Mālik required the description to supply only such detail as was, in their view, sufficient to enable one to identify the object of sale, while Ibn Ḥanbal and al-Shāfiʿī required the detail to extend to such matters as colour, country of origin and other characteristics influencing price and use.

For obvious reasons, it is beyond the scope of this article to identify all the respects, or even all the most important respects, in which the doctrines of the four Sunnī schools of law coincide or diverge on the rules governing *salam* transactions. From what has been said hitherto it will be quite clear that important particulars of *salam* sale are matters on which the different schools do not always speak with one voice. Accordingly, in one's utilisation of sources identification of the schools to which data relate is a *sine qua non*.

Bibliography: N.A. Saleh, *Unlawful gain and legitimate profit in Islamic law*, Cambridge 1986 (esp. 71 ff.), a work in which the doctrine of the Ibāḍī school of law, peculiar to ʿUmān, is treated in addition to the doctrines of the four orthodox schools; A.L. Udovitch, *Partnership and profit in medieval Islam*, Princeton 1970, 72, 79; J.A. Wakin, *The function of documents in Islamic law*, Albany 1972, 193-200 (*Bāb al-salam* [in Arabic], Introd., 41-2). Particularly useful in some respects for Mālikī law is O. Pesle, *La vente dans la doctrine malékite*, Rabat 1940 (see esp. 175-96), which may be consulted along with D. Santillana, *Istituzioni di diritto musulmano malichita con riguardo anche al sistema sciafiita*, 2 vols., Rome 1925-38. For primary sources see the bibliographies of Saleh, Udovitch, Wakin and Santillana (Pesle, though citing his sources, offers no bibliography).

(J.D. Latham)

SALĀM (a.), verbal noun from *salima*, "to be safe, uninjured", used as substantive in the meaning of "safety, salvation", thence "peace" (in the sense of "quietness"), thence "salutation, greeting" (cf. Fr. *salut*); on the statements of the older Arab lexicographers, see *LʿA*[1], xv, 181-3, passim.

The word is of frequent occurrence in the Ḳurʾān, especially in the sūras which are attributed to the second and third Meccan periods. The oldest passage that contains *salām* is XCVII, 5, where it is said of the *Laylat al-Ḳadr*, "It is salvation until the coming of the dawn". *Salām* is also to be taken in this meaning in L, 34; XV, 46; XXI, 69; XI, 48. *Salām* means salvation in this world as well as in the next. In the latter meaning we find it used in the expression *Dār al-Salām* "the abode of salvation" for Paradise (X, 26; VI, 127). In the Medinan verse, V, 16, which is addressed to the *Ahl al-Kitāb*, we find the expression *subul al-salām*, the paths of salvation (cf. Isa. LIX, 8, *däräk shālōm*).

But *salām* is most frequently used in the Ḳurʾān as a form of salutation. Thus in LVI, 91 (first Meccan period), the people of the right hand are greeted by their companions in bliss with *salām laka* "Peace be upon thee" (according to al-Bayḍāwī; for other explanations see *LʿA*[1], xv, 184, 8 ff.; and allāh), *salām* (XXXVI, 58; XIV, 23; X, 10; XXXIII, 44) or *salām ʿalaikum* (XVI, 32; XXXIX, 73; XIII, 24) is the greeting which is given the blessed in Paradise or on entering Paradise (cf. also XXV, 75); *salāmᵃⁿ salāmᵃⁿ* in LVI, 26 (other reading *salāmᵘⁿ salāmᵘⁿ*; cf. XIX, 62) is presumably also intended as an auspicious exclamation (other interpretations in al-Bayḍāwī). Those on the Aʿrāf [*q.v.*] call to the dwellers in Paradise *salām ʿalaykum* (VII, 46). *Salām* is also the greeting of the guests of Ibrāhīm and his reply (LI, 25; XI, 69; cf. XV, 52). Ibrāhīm takes leave with *salām ʿalaika* (XIX, 48) from his father, who threatens him. In XX, 47, Mūsā in his address to Firʿawn is made to use the expression *al-salām ʿalā man ittabaʿa 'l-hudā* "peace be upon him who follows the right guidance". According to the first explanation in al-Bayḍāwī, *al-salām* here means the greeting of the angels and guardians of Paradise; but as these words are not at the beginning of the speech, an other interpretation prefers to consider it as an affirmative sentence and to take *salām* as "security from God's wrath and punishment" (cf. al-Bayḍāwī on the passage and *LʿA*[1], xv, 183, 7-8). *Salām ʿalaykum* "peace be upon you" is found in VI, 54, at the beginning of the message which the Prophet has to deliver to the believers and in XXVII, 59, a *salām* is uttered over God's chosen servants. As a benediction, *salām* is also used repeatedly in XXXVII, where at the end of the mention of each prophet a *salām* is uttered over him (verses 79, 109, 120, 130, 181; cf. also XIX, 15, 33). *Salām* may be used in an ironical sense in XLIII, 89, at parting from the unbelievers and *salām ʿalaykum* in XXVIII, 55 (other interpretations in al-Bayḍāwī). This might perhaps hold of *salāmᵃⁿ*, XXV, 63, also, with which the servants of the Merciful reply to the ignorant (*dj̲āhilūn*), but the commentators take it in the sense of *tasallumᵃⁿ* or *barāʾatᵃⁿ*. In LIX, 23 (Medinan) *al-salām* occurs as one of the names of God, which al-Bayḍāwī interprets as *maṣdar* used as *ṣifa* in the meaning of "the Faultless" (for other explanation, see *LʿA*[1], xv, 182, 7 ff., 20 ff.). *Al-salām* in the expressions *dār al-salām* and *subul al-salām* is therefore also interpreted as a name of God (cf. al-Bayḍāwī on VI, 127; X, 25; V, 16; *LʿA*[1], xv, 182, 2-3, and the notice at the end of this article). The word has even been taken to mean God in the formula *al-salām ʿalaykum* (Fak̲h̲r al-Dīn al-Rāzī, *Mafātīḥ al-g̲h̲ayb*, on VI, 54, Cairo 1278, III, 54, 21-2; *LʿA*[1], xv, 182, 8-9). It is improbable that the greeting is intended in *alḳā 'l-salāma* in IV, 94; another reading is *al-salama*, as in the similar expression in IV, 90-1; XVI, 28, 87.

The denominative verb *sallama* is first found in the Medinan sūras, namely, XXXIII, 56, where it is recommended to utter *ṣalāt* [*q.v.*] and *salām* over the Prophet, and in XXIV, 27, 61 (see below).

At quite an early period, the view became established that the *salām* greeting was an Islamic institution. This is, however, only correct in so far as the Ḳurʾān recommends the use of this greeting in a late Meccan passage and in two Medinan passages: in VI, 54, it is commanded to the Prophet: "If those come to you who believe in Our signs say: "Peace be upon you" (*salāmᵘⁿ ʿalaykum*). Your Lord hath laid down a law of mercy for himself"; and in XXIV, 27: "O ye believers, enter not into dwellings which are not your own before ye have asked leave and said *salām* (*wa-tusallimū*) on its inhabitants", etc.; similarly, XXIV, 61: "If ye enter dwellings, say *salām* upon one another (*fasallimū*)", etc. (cf. a similar prescription Matt. x, 12, Luke x, 5); iv, 86, where the more general expression for greeting (*ḥayyā*) is used, is also referred to the *salām* salutation. But Goldziher has pointed out (*ZDMG*, xlvi, 22-3) and quoted passages from poets in support of the view that *salām* was already in use as a greeting before Islam. The corresponding Hebrew and Aramaic expressions *s̲h̲ālōm lᵉkā, s̲h̲ᵉlām lāk̲ (lᵉk̲ōn), s̲h̲elāmā ʿalāk̲*, which go back to Old Testament usage (cf. Judges xix, 20, 2 Sam. xviii, 28, Dan. x, 19, 1 Chron. xii, 19), were also in use as greetings among the Jews and Christians (cf. Dalman, *Gramm. d. jüd.-palästin. Aramäisch*[2], Leipzig 1905, 244); according to *Talmūd Yᵉrus̲h̲almī, S̲h̲ᵉb̲īʿīt*, IV, 35b, *S̲h̲ālōm ʿalēk̲ām* was Israel's greeting. See also Pᵉs̲h̲ītta Matt. x, 12, xxvi, 49, Luke x, 5, xxiv, 36, John xx, 19, 21, 26, and Payne Smith, *Thes. Syriacus*, cols. 4189-90). A very great number of Nabataean inscriptions further show the use of *s̲h̲-l-m* to express good wishes in North-western Arabia and the Sinai Peninsula (*CIS*, ii, *Inscriptiones aramaeae*, i, no. 288 ff., twice repeated in nos. 244, 339, thrice repeated in no. 302) and the Arabic *s-l-m* frequently occurs in the Ṣafaitic inscriptions as a benedictive term. Cf. E. Littmann, *Zur Entzifferung der Ṣafā-Inschriften*, Leipzig 1901, 47, 52-3, 55, 56, 57, 59, 61, 64, 66, 67, 70; *Semitic inscriptions*, New York-London 1905, Safaïtic inscrs., nos. 5, 8, 12, 15, 69, 128, 134.

If the line *salāmaka rabbanā fī kulli fadj̲rⁱⁿ* quoted in *LʿA*[1], xv, 183, 5 from below, were genuine and really by Umayya b. Abi 'l-Ṣalt [*q.v.*], one might perhaps conclude from it that there was a benedictory use of the *salām* formula in the morning service in certain monotheistic circles of North Arabia. Presumably the usage, influenced by Christian and Jewish views, had given the word a special significance in the region of Aramaic culture. Lidzbarski's suggestion (in *ZS*, i, 85 ff.) that *salām* reproduces the idea expressed by σωτηρία need not be discussed here, but his explanation of *Islām* as the infinitive of a denominative verb *aslama* formed from *salām*-σωτηρία ("to enter into the state .... of *salām*"), cannot be reconciled with such expressions frequent in the Ḳurʾān as *aslama wadj̲hahu li 'llāh, aslama li-Rabb al-ʿālamīn*, etc.

Muḥammad must have placed a high religious value on the *salām* formula, as he considered it the greeting given by the angels to the blessed and used it as an auspicious salutation on the prophets who had preceded him. A *salām*, like that in the *tas̲h̲ahhud* (see below) or like the salutation of peace which closes the *ṣalāt* and has its parallel in the Jewish *tᵉphillā* (cf. E. Mittwoch, *Zur Entstehungsgeschichte des islam. Gebets u. Kultus*, in *AbhPrAkW*, phil.-hist. Kl. [1913], no. 2, p. 18), may have been from the first an essential feature of the ritual of divine service. According to a tradition (al-Buk̲h̲ārī, *al-Istiʾd̲h̲ān, bāb* 3, *al-Ad̲h̲ān, bāb* 148, 150), originally they uttered the *salām* at the close of the *ṣalāt* on God, on D̲j̲ibrīl, Mīk̲h̲āʾīl and other angels. With the remark that God is himself the *salām* (cf. Ḳurʾān, LIX, 23), the Prophet disapproved of this and laid down what should be said in the *tas̲h̲ahhud*; the *salām* utterance belongs to it in the form given below. On varying traditions regarding the *tas̲h̲ahhud*, see al-S̲h̲āfiʿī, *K. al-Umm*, Cairo 1321, i, 103 ff.; cf. also Goldziher, *Über die Eulogien*, etc. in *ZDMG*, l, 102.

In the ritual of the *ṣalāt* as legally prescribed, the benediction on God and the *salām* on the Prophet, on the worshipper and those present and on God's pious servants, precede the confession of faith in the *tas̲h̲ahhud* (*al-salāmu ʿalayka, ayyuhā 'l-nabiyyu, wa-raḥmatu 'llāhi wa-barakātuhu; al-salāmu ʿalaynā wa-ʿalā ʿibādi 'llāhi 'l-ṣāliḥīna*). Among the compulsory ceremonies of the *ṣalāt*, there is also at the end of it the *taslīmat al-ūlā*, the fuller form of which consists in the worshipper in a sitting position turning his head to right and left and saying each time *al-salāmu ʿalaykum wa-raḥmatu 'llāh*. See al-Bād̲j̲ūrī, *Ḥās̲h̲iya ʿalā s̲h̲arḥ Ibn*

Ḳāsim al-Ghazzī ʿalā matn Abī Shudjāʿ, Cairo 1321, i, 168, 170.

The preference of the Ḳurʾān for the *salām* formula and its liturgical use may have contributed considerably to the fact that it soon became considered an exclusively Muslim greeting (*taḥiyyat al-islām*). As already mentioned above, the Ḳurʾān prescribes the *salām* on the Prophet to follow the *taṣliya*. Tradition reports that the latter endeavoured to introduce it. When ʿUmayr b. Wahb was brought before him and gave him the pagan greeting (*anʿimū ṣabāḥan*), the Prophet said: "God has given us a better greeting than thine, namely *al-salām*, the greeting of the dwellers in Paradise (Ibn Hishām, 472, below, ff.; al-Ṭabarī, i, 1353, 10-11). Those around him are also said to have been eager to introduce this greeting. Al-Wāḳidī relates that ʿUrwa b. Masʿūd, who immediately after his conversion wanted to convert his own townsmen in Ṭāʾif to Islam, called the attention of Thaḳīf, who saluted in the heathen fashion, to the greeting of the dwellers in Paradise, *al-salām* (Ibn Saʿd, *al-Ṭabaḳāt*, v, 369; Sprenger, *Das Leben .... des Moḥammad*, iii, 482; Goldziher, *Muh. Stud.*, i, 264). According to Ibn Isḥāḳ, al-Mughīra b. Shuʿba instructed the deputation to Muḥammad from Thaḳīf how they were to salute the Prophet, but they would only use the greeting of the Djāhiliyya (Ibn Hishām, 916, 5 ff.; al-Ṭabarī, i, 1290, 9 ff.; Sprenger, *op. cit.*, iii, 485; Goldziher, *loc. cit.*). The Jews are said to have distorted this greeting with respect to Muḥammad to *al-sām ʿalayka* "death to you", whereupon the Prophet answered *wa-ʿalaykum* "and to you" (al-Bukhārī, *al-Istiʾdhān, bāb* 22; *al-Adab, bāb* 38; *LʿA*[1], xv, 206). According to Ibn Saʿd (iv/1, 163, 15), Abū Dharr was the first to greet the Prophet with the Muslim greeting. In the same author (iv/1, 82, 2) we find *salām ʿalaykum* at the beginning of a letter from Muʿāwiya to Abū Mūsā al-Ashʿarī.

The expressions which could be used were *salām* or *salām ʿalaykum (-ka)* or *al-salām ʿalaykum*. Umm Ayman is said to have used simply *(al-)salām* to the Prophet (Ibn Saʿd, viii, 163, 7-8, 9-10). In the Ḳurʾān, the use of *salām ʿalaykum* preponderates. Fakhr al-Dīn al-Rāzī endeavours to explain that the indefinite form is preferable and expresses the conception of perfect greeting (ii, 500, 35 ff., iii, 512, 11 ff.). Following him, al-Shāfiʿī is said to have preferred *salāmun ʿalayka* in the *tashahhud* (iii, 512, 35); but the Shāfiʿī school also allows the definite form here (al-Bādjūrī, i, 168; *LʿA*[1], xv, 182, 12-13). The formula *al-salām ʿalaykum* was, however, much used as a greeting. This undetermined form is expressly prescribed in the *taslīma* (Fakhr al-Dīn al-Rāzī, ii, 501, 5; al-Bādjūrī, I, 170; *LʿA*[1], xv, 182, 13 ff.). As a return greeting, *wa-ʿalaykum al-salām* became usual (for further details on this inversion see Fakhr al-Dīn al-Rāzī, ii, 500, 29 ff., iii, 512, 21 ff.). According to Ibn Saʿd (iv/1, 115, 19-20), ʿAbd Allāh b. ʿUmar replied with *salām ʿalaykum*.

According to some traditions, Muḥammad had described the expression *ʿalayka 'l-salām* as the salutation to the dead and insisted on being greeted with *al-salām ʿalayka* (al-Ṭabarī, iii, 2395; Madjd al-Dīn Ibn al-Athīr, *al-Nihāya fī gharīb al-ḥadīth wa'l-athar*, Cairo 1311, ii, 176 below). The first-named form of the greeting is actually found in elegiac verses (*op. cit.*, ii, 177; *LʿA*[1], xv, 182). But there are also traditions in which the Prophet greets the dead in the cemetery with an expression beginning with *(al-)salām* (al-Ṭabarī, iii, 2402, 10 ff.; Madjd al-Dīn Ibn al-Athīr and *LʿA*[1], *locc. cit.*). ʿAbd Allāh b. ʿUmar also on returning from a journey is said to have saluted the graves of the Prophet, of Abū Bakr and of his father with *al-salām ʿalayka* (Ibn Saʿd, iv/1, 115, 5 ff.).

The *salām* formula was very early extended by the addition of the words *wa-raḥmatu 'llāhi* or *wa-raḥmatu 'llāhi wa-barakātuhu*. The first extension became used in the *taslīma* and the second in the *tashahhud* (see above). Applicating the Ḳurʾānic commandment (IV, 86, "when ye are saluted with a salutation, salute the person with a better than his or at least return it") it is recommended (*sunna*) in the return greeting to add the wish of blessing and benediction or occasionally, when replying to a simple *salām*, only the former (cf. al-Bukhārī, *al-Istiʾdhān, bābs* 16, 18, 19). If anyone is saluted with the threefold formula, he must reply with the same (Fakhr al-Dīn al-Rāzī on sūra IV, 86, *op. cit.*, ii, 502, 14 ff.). According to Lane (*Manners and customs*[3], i, 229, note), the threefold formula was very common as a return greeting in Egypt; cf. also Nallino, *L'Arabo parlato in Egitto*[2], Milan 1913, 121. In Mecca, it is comparatively rarely used; the reply usual there is *weʿalēkum es-salām war-raḥma* (*we-raḥmatu 'llāh* or *wal-ikrām*); cf. Snouck Hurgronje, *Mekkanische Sprichwörter u. Redensarten*, The Hague 1886, 118. Landberg (*Études sur les dialectes de l'Arabie méridionale*, ii, 788, note) thought that the longer form recalls the priest's blessing in Num. vi, 24-6. The application of *ʿalaykum* to a single person is explained by saying that the plural suffix includes the two accompanying angels or the spirits attached to him (i.e. the person; Fakhr al-Dīn al-Rāzī, ii, 501, 19 ff., cf. iii, 513, 17 ff.).

At the conclusion of a letter, the expression *wa 'l-salāmu (ʿalayka, -kum)* is often used e.g. Ibn Saʿd, i/2, 27, 17, 27, 28, 2, 5, 23, 29, 13, 21. Al-Ḥarīrī (*Durrat al-ghawwās*, ed. Thorbecke, 108, 9 ff.) disapproves of the use here of the indefinite form (*salāmun*), which, according to the more correct use, should only be used at the beginning. *Wa 'l-salām* has occasionally the meaning of "and that is the end of it" (cf. Snouck Hurgronje, *op. cit.*, 92).

In keeping with Ḳurʾān, XX, 47, it became usual to use the form *al-salāmu ʿalā man ittabaʿa 'l-hudā* to non-Muslims when necessary (cf. Fakhr al-Dīn al-Rāzī, ii, 501, 26 ff., iv, 706, 19-20). It is found, for example, in letters ascribed to Muḥammad (al-Bukhārī, *al-Istiʾdhān, bāb* 24; Ibn Saʿd, i/2, 28, 10-11; cf. line 6 there at the beginning of the letter, *salāmun ʿalā man āmana*). Papyri of the year 91/710 bear early testimony to its use (*Papyri Schott-Reinhardt*, i, ed. C.H. Becker, Heidelberg 1906, i, 29, ii, 40-1, iii, 87-8, x, 11, xi, 7, xviii, 9). A letter from Muḥammad to the Jews of Maḳnā concludes, however, with *wa 'l-salām* (Ibn Saʿd, i/2, 28, 23); similarly a letter to the Christians in Ayla (*ibid.*, 29, 12-13). In *Ḥadīth*, also, a tendency is noticeable not to deny the *salām* greeting, at least as a reply, to unbelievers and the *Ahl al-Kitāb* (cf. al-Ṭabarī, *Tafsīr*[2], v, 111-12; Fakhr al-Dīn al-Rāzī, *loc. cit.*).

Salām means also a *ṣalawāt* litany, which is pronounced from the minarets every Friday about half an hour before the beginning of the midday service before the *adhān*. This part of the liturgy is repeated inside the mosque before the beginning of the regular ceremonies by several people with good voices standing on a *dikka* (Goldziher, *Über die Eulogien*, etc., in *ZDMG*, l, 103-4; cf. Lane, *op. cit.*, i, 117). The same name is given to the benedictions on the Prophet which are sung during the month of Ramaḍān about half an hour after midnight from the minarets (*ibid.*, ii, 264).

The auspicious formula *ʿalayhi 'l-salām*, which, according to the strictly orthodox opinion, like the *taṣliya*, should only follow the names of Prophets, but was more freely used in the earlier literature (cf. also al-Bu**kh**ārī, *al-Isti'dhān, bāb* 43: *Fāṭima ʿalayka 'l-salām*), was used by **Sh**īʿa without limitation of ʿAlī and his descendants also (Goldziher, in *ZDMG*, l, 121 ff.; Fa**kh**r al-Dīn al-Rāzī, iii, 511 ff.).

The Sunnīs of India make a magical use of the so-called seven *salāms* which refer to sūra XXXVI, 58; XXXVII, 79, 109, 120, 130; XXXIX, 73; XCVII, 5. In the morning of the festival of A**kh**ir-i Čahār-**sh**amba [see ṢAFAR], they write the seven *salāms* or have them written with saffron water, ink or rosewater on the leaf of a mango tree or a sacred fig tree, or of a plantain. They then wash off the writing in water and drink it in the hope that they may enjoy peace and happiness (**Dj**aʿfar **Sh**arīf-Herklots. *Islam in India or the Qānūn-i Islām*, new ed. W. Crooke, London 1921, 186-7).

On coins, *salām* (sometimes abbreviated to *s*) means "of full weight, complete" (cf. J.G. Stickel, *Das grossherz. Orient. Münzcabinet zu Jena (Handb. d. Morgenl. Münzkunde)*, Leipzig 1845, i, 43-4; O. Codrington, *A manual of Musulman numismatics*, London 1904, 10).

[Employed as a name of God, *al-Salām* is understood by the commentators as a *maṣdar* used metaphorically in the sense of *dhu 'l-salām, salām* being in this context an equivalent of *salāma* "the state of being preserved from ...". Whence there arise, fundamentally, two interpretations. God is *al-Salām* (1) inasmuch as He is preserved from all imperfection and infirmity (*dhu 'l-salāmat^i min kull naḳṣ^in wa-āfa*), and (2) inasmuch as created beings are preserved from all injustice on His part (*salima 'l-khalḳ min ẓulmihi*). Contrary to the commentary given by L. Gardet (in AL-ASMĀ' AL-ḤUSNĀ), the idea of "peace" is in no degree, here, taken into consideration. See D. Gimaret, *Les noms divins en Islam*, Paris 1988, 204-5].

Bibliography: In addition to that mentioned in the article: Ibn ʿAbd Rabbihi, *al-ʿIḳd al-farīd*, Būlāḳ 1293, i, 276-7; Lane, *op. cit.*, i, 298 ff.; Landberg, *Études sur les dialectes de l'Arabie méridionale*, Leiden 1905-13, ii, 776-81, 786-9; H. Ringgren, *Islam, 'aslama and muslim*, Horae Soederblomianae ii, Uppsala 1949.

(C. VAN ARENDONK-[D. GIMARET])

SALAMA B. DĪNĀR, Abū Ḥāzim al-Ma**kh**zūmī, called al-Aʿra**dj** "the Lame" (d. *ca.* 140/757), traditionist and judge in Medina, regarded as a proto-Ṣūfī mystic; he was of Persian origin. Various aphorisms (*ḥikam*) and elegant sayings of his are preserved in citations, and also his answers to questions put to him by the Umayyad caliph Sulaymān b. ʿAbd al-Malik [*q.v.*]; also, a collection of his *masā'il* [see AL-MASĀ'IL WA 'L-ADJWIBA] is extant in manuscript.

Bibliography: Ziriklī, *Aʿlām*, iii, 171-2; Sezgin, *GAS*, i, 634-5; R. Eisener, *Zwischen Faktum und Fiktion. Eine Studie zum Umayyadenkalifen Sulaimān b. ʿAbdalmalik und seinem Bild in den Quellen*, Wiesbaden 1987, 195-205. (C.E. BOSWORTH)

SALĀMA B. DJANDAL, a poet of pre-Islamic times, was a member of the clan al-Ḥāri**th**, which belonged to the large division of Saʿd b. Zayd Manāt of the tribe Tamīm. Ibn Sallām al-**Dj**umaḥī places him in the 7th class of poets (*Ṭabaḳāt al-shuʿarā'*, ed. Hell, Leiden 1916, 36). He is reckoned among the excellent poets of the *Djāhiliyya* [*q.v.*] of whom only a few poems are preserved (*al-muḳillūn*). According to two events mentioned in his verses, he must have flourished during the second half of the 6th century of our era. The *Naḳā'iḍ* of **Dj**arīr and al-Farazdaḳ [*q.vv.*] give two poems of Salāma, not included in his *dīwān*, where he celebrates the victory of **Dj**adūd, a battle, in which the clan of Minḳar, a division of Zayd Manāt, defeated the Banū **Sh**aybān of the tribe Bakr b. Wā'il. It must have taken place about the middle of the 6th century. In his longest poem (*Dīwān*, no. 3, v. 38), also included in the *Aṣmaʿiyyāt* (no. 42, v. 38), he refers to the end of the king al-Nuʿmān III [*q.v.*] of Ḥīra, who was trampled to death by elephants at the order of the Persian ruler **Kh**usraw Parwīz in 602, which provides a *terminus post quem* for Salāma's death. There is no evidence that he lived to the time of Islam, and none of his descendants appear to be named in the biographies of early Muslims.

Another reference in his *dīwān* has caused some confusion among scholars. There is a monothematic poem of four lines (no. 7) addressed to Ṣaʿṣaʿa b. Maḥmūd of the clan of Mar**th**ad, who had taken the poet's brother Aḥmar (sometimes mispelled Aḥmad) prisoner and released him without ransom on account of Salāma's intercession (cf. also al-**Dj**āḥiẓ, *al-Bayān wa 'l-tabyīn*, ed. ʿA.S. Hārūn, Cairo 1367/1948-50, iii, 318). A different report has it that al-Aḥmar had been taken prisoner in a raid led by ʿAmr b. Kul**th**ūm [*q.v.*] (*Dīwān ʿAmr*, introduction to poem no. 2, ed. F. Krenkow, in *Mashriḳ*, xx [1922], 591-611, cf. 592, and also Ibn Ḳutayba, *Shiʿr*, 147; *Aghānī*[1], ix, 183). Whether the two reports are mixed up, or whether Aḥmar b. **Dj**andal had been taken prisoner on two different occasions, cannot be established. If the latter is true, we have corroborating evidence for the life span of Salāma, since it makes him a contemporary of ʿAmr b. Kul**th**ūm.

Salāma's *dīwān* has come down to us in the recensions of al-Aṣmaʿī [*q.v.*] and of Abū ʿAmr al-**Sh**aybānī, the representatives of the Baṣran and the Kūfan schools respectively. The two recensions were united by Muḥammad b. al-Ḥasan al-Aḥwal (d. after 259/873), who pointed out occasional differences between the Baṣran and the Kūfan tradition. The text is preserved in four manuscripts. They form the basis of Fa**kh**r al-Dīn Ḳabāwa's edition (Aleppo 1387/1968), which supersedes the earlier editions of Cl. Huart (*JA*, 10e série, xv [1919], 71-105, with French translation) and L. Cheikho (Beirut 1920). The *dīwān* contains 8 poems, 136 verses in all. In addition, the editor collected 27 poems and fragments from other sources, amounting to 80 verses.

Salāma is reputed to have excelled in the description of horses (cf. Ibn Ḳutayba, *loc. cit.*), and, indeed, his most famous ode, included in the *Mufaḍḍaliyyāt* [*q.v.*] (no. XXII), contains a magnificent passage about the tribe's horses for battle (no. 1, vv. 5-15), in place of the conventional camel theme. The poem begins with a complaint of old age (vv. 1-3) and ends with tribal *fakhr*. There are two other polythematic odes in the *dīwān*, a tripartite form (no. 2) and a bipartite poem (no. 3), both ending with a combination of *fakhr* and *hidjā'* [*q.v.*], which is also the prevailing topic of Salāma's monothematic poems. His verses appear ancient in wording and imagery, and give the impression of authenticity. He refers to swords of Buṣrā and al-Madā'in, which are seldom mentioned in verses of later times, as swords were no longer obtained from there. That he mentions writing or even inkstands and parchment (no. 3, v. 2) is not at all strange as these things were more widely known than is generally admitted. The occurrence of the term *Allāh* (no. 1, v. 12) should not be taken as a sign of later interpolation, and Salāma's reference to *al-Raḥmān* (no. 3, v. 36) is hardly sufficient to prove that he was a Christian, as was assumed by L. Cheikho.

Bibliography: In addition to references in the article, see *The Mufaḍḍaliyyāt*, ed. C.J. Lyall, i, Arabic text, Oxford 1921 (no. XXII), ii, Translation and notes, *ibid.* 1918, iii, Indexes to the Arabic text, comp. by A.A. Bevan, London 1924 (GMS, N.S. III); *al-Aṣmaʿiyyāt*, ed. ʿA.S. Hārūn and A.M. Shākir, Cairo 1964 (no. 42); *The Naḳāʾiḍ of Djarīr and al-Farazdaḳ*, ed. A.A. Bevan, i-iii, Leiden 1905-12, i, 144 ff. See also Blachère, *HLA*, ii, 257; Sezgin, *GAS*, ii, 192. Verses of Salāma are cited in most books dealing with ancient Arabic poetry, e.g. in the *Lisān al-ʿArab* 40 times.

(F. Krenkow-[Renate Jacobi])

SALĀMA MŪSĀ, Egyptian journalist, encyclopaedist, socialist, political campaigner, enthusiastic moderniser and "westerniser". Born *ca.* 1887 to a well-to-do Coptic family near Zagazig, he died on 5 August 1958. He attended both Christian and Muslim *kuttābs*, a school of the Coptic Charitable Society, and then the "national" school. From there he went to the Tawfīḳiyya (where he taught briefly in 1919), and the Khedivial College in Cairo. As a youngster he read avidly the Arab dailies and reviews, that spread the new ideas from Europe and made accessible European literature; to *al-Muḳtaṭaf* he owed his scientific leanings and his simple, telegraphic style of writing that made his ideas accessible to a broad audience.

In 1907 he went to Paris. In Europe he was to develop his ideas about the emancipation of women; his book *al-Marʾa laysat luʿbat al-radjul* (Beirut 1956) voices his opinions on this subject. He went to London in 1908, joining Lincoln's Inn where he studied law, and following courses in Egyptology, geology, biology, and economics. There he became acquainted with the works of many of the authors (Darwin, Spencer, Shaw, H.G. Wells, Elliot Smith, Dostoyevsky, Tolstoy, Gorki, Sartre, Goethe, Nietzsche, Marx, Freud, Gandhi, etc.), who influenced him profoundly, discussed in *Hāʾulāʾi ʿallamūnī* (Cairo 1953). In Paris *L'Humanité* had introduced him to socialist ideas; in London he was to join the Fabian Society, where he met Shaw. From Shaw he derived many of his humanistic socialist ideas; he analyses his life and works in *Bernard Shaw* (Cairo 1957).

Throughout most of his life he wrote for the Egyptian press; his book *al-Ṣaḥāfa ... ḥirfa wa-risāla* (Cairo 1963) is on the profession of journalism. Returning to Egypt from Europe, he received his training on *al-Liwāʾ* newspaper. He was to collaborate on *al-Djāmiʿa, al-Muḳtaṭaf, al-Maḥrūsa, al-Akhbār, al-Balāgh, Djarīdat Miṣr, Madjallat al-Ḥadīth, al-Nidāʾ, al-Wafd al-Miṣrī, Akhbār al-Yawm, al-Djīl, al-Indhār* and many other journals. In 1914 he founded in Cairo the first Egyptian weekly, *al-Mustaḳbal*, dedicated to science and literature. From 1923 to 1929 he helped edit *al-Hilāl*. He wrote for its press: *Ashhar al-khuṭab wa-mashāhīr al-khuṭabāʾ* (Cairo 1924) an anthology of the most important European and Arab authors; *Ashhar ḳiṣaṣ al-ḥubb al-taʾrīkhiyya* (1925) love stories from history and from Arabic literature; *Aḥlām al-falāsifa* (1926) on the utopian ideas of philosophers from Plato onwards; *Ḥurriyyat al-fikr wa-abṭāluhā fi 'l-taʾrīkh* (1927) examining the struggle to maintain freedom of expression; *al-ʿAḳl al-bāṭin wa-maknūnāt al-nafs* (1927) a study on the theories of Freud and Jung, and *Taʾrīkh al-funūn wa-ashhar al-ṣuwar* (1927) partially dedicated to the development of art in Egypt. In 1929 he founded the monthly *al-Madjalla al-Djadīda* and the weekly *al-Miṣrī*; both were suppressed, but *al-Madjalla al-Djadīda* later reappeared. From 1940 to 1942 he collaborated on *al-Shuʾūn al-Idjtimāʿiyya*, the magazine of the Ministry for Social Affairs.

A pioneer in the creation of the Arab socialist movement, in 1920 he helped form the short-lived Egyptian Socialist Party. He was to acknowledge late in life that the ideas of Marx had had the most profound influence on him. He had published *al-Ishtirākiyya* (Cairo 1913), a short treatise on socialism (tr. in G. Haupt and M. Reberioux, *La Deuxième Internationale et l'Orient*, Paris 1967, 423-38, and in S.A. Hanna and G.H. Gardner, *Arab socialism*, Leiden 1969, 275-88). His *al-Dunyā baʿd thalāthīn ʿām* (1930) is on the prospects for socialism in Egypt. A collection of articles, *Mashāʿil al-ṭarīḳ li 'l-shabāb* (Cairo 1959) attempts to guide the young on the revolutionary road. His *Muḳaddimat al-subirmān* (Cairo 1910) on socialism, evolution, and eugenics, advocates the application of selective reproduction and sterilisation to produce a Superman. The second edition, *al-Yawm wa 'l-ghad* (Cairo 1927) discusses the ideas of Darwin, Nietzsche, and Shaw, and the emancipation of women. *Ḍabṭ al-tanāsul wa-manʿ al-ḥaml* (Cairo 1930), written with Dr Kāmil Labīb, returns to the necessity of improving the species and tackles birth control.

On his return to Egypt, he had publicised the theory of evolution; he discusses Darwin's *On the origin of the species* in his most popular work *Naẓariyyat al-taṭawwur wa-aṣl al-insān* (Cairo 1925), developed in *al-Insān ḳimmat al-taṭawwur* (Cairo 1961). He was to question the "commonly accepted mysteries" and turn to a belief in the "social value of religion." His book *Nushūʾ fikrat Allāh* (Cairo 1912) is a summary of the ideas of Grant Allen on *The evolution of the idea of God.*

Under the influence of Gandhi, he founded the league *al-Miṣrī li 'l-Miṣrī*, encouraging Egyptians to buy local products and to boycott foreign goods, arguing his case in *Djuyūbunā wa-djuyūb al-adjānib* (Cairo 1930). His *Ghāndī wa 'l-ḥaraka al-hindiyya* (Cairo 1934) describes the struggle of Gandhi against British imperialism. Mūsā's two principal foes in his writings were to be the British imperialists and Egyptian reactionaries; he was to wage a life-long battle in defence of democracy in Egypt. He was arrested and imprisoned on several occasions for alleged propaganda for a republican form of government and for writing on socialism and communism. Finding abhorrent the conduct of the palace and its supporters, he was amongst those intellectuals who welcomed the revolution of 1952. His *Ḥurriyyat al-ʿaḳl fī Miṣr* (Cairo 1945) deals with the lack of freedom of Egyptian intellectuals, and *Kitāb al-Thawrāt* (Beirut 1954) examines the French and Bolshevik Revolutions, and the two Egyptian revolutions of 1919 and 1952.

Altogether he wrote about 40 books, many of his writings first appearing in the periodical press. Amongst his collections of articles are *Mukhtārāt Salāma Mūsā* (Cairo 1926); *Fi 'l-ḥayāt wa 'l-adab* (Cairo 1930); *Ṭarīḳ al-madjd* (Cairo 1949); *Aḥādīth ilā 'l-shabāb* (Cairo 1957) and *Maḳālāt mamnūʿa* (Beirut 1959) a collection of censored and banned articles. In his *al-Balāgha al-ʿaṣriyya wa 'l-lugha al-ʿarabiyya* (Cairo 1945) he criticises traditional Arabic eloquence for being unable to reflect the ideas of his age; at one stage, he had advocated replacing the Arabic script by the Latin, since he felt that the Arabic characters obstructed scientific progress. On literature, his *al-Adab li 'l-shaʿb* (Cairo 1956) applies social realism to contemporary Egyptian and classical Arabic literature; whilst *al-Tadjdīd fi 'l-adab al-indjilīzī al-ḥadīth* (Cairo 1934) examines the development of modern English literary trends. He published several collections of stories: *Ḳiṣaṣ mukhtalifa* (Cairo 1930) a selection of stories, particularly from Russian literature; *Min adjl al-salām, ḳiṣaṣ sūfyātiyya* (Cairo 1956 with ʿAbd al-Munʿim Ṣubḥī); *Ruddū ilayya ḥayātī, madjmūʿa ḳiṣaṣiyya* (Cairo 1960); *Intiṣārāt insān* (Cairo 1960) and *Iftaḥū lahā 'l-bāb* (Cairo 1962). In *al-Djarīma wa 'l-ʿiḳāb* (Cairo 1912) he translated part of Dostoyevsky's *Crime and punishment*.

His writings on psychology were published in *al-Sīkūlūdjiyya fī ḥayātinā al-yawmiyya* (Cairo 1936); *al-Shakhṣiyya al-nādjiḥa* (Cairo 1942); *ʿAḳlī wa-ʿaḳluka* (Cairo 1947); *Muḥāwalāt sīkūlūdjiyya* (Cairo 1952) and *Dirāsāt sīkūlūdjiyya* (Beirut 1956). Amongst his varied studies, his book *Miṣr, Aṣl al-Ḥaḍāra* (Cairo 1934) is an analysis of Elliot Smith's ideas on pharaonic civilisation; *Fann al-ḥayāt* (Cairo 1929) is a description of love as a formative element in family and society; *Ḥayātuna baʿd al-khamsīn* (Cairo 1944) deals with life's problems after the age of 50; *al-Nahḍa al-Urubbiyya* (Cairo 1935) examines the renaissance in the west and its influence on Arab civilisation, whilst the unpublished *Muʿdjam al-afkār* is an analysis of movements of thought. *Al-Tathḳīf al-dhātī aw kayf nurabbī anfusanā* (Cairo 1946) is on his personal acculturation experience. His autobiography, *Tarbiyat Salāma Mūsā* (Cairo 1947, revised 1958), has been described by Jacques Berque as "one of the most moving books in modern Arabic literature" (a tr. was edited by L.O. Schuman, *The education of Salāma Mūsā*, Leiden 1961).

Bibliography: Giuseppe Contu, *Gli aspetti positivi e i limiti del laicismo in Salāmah Mūsā (1887-1958)*, Naples 1980; V. Egger, *A Fabian in Egypt: Salamah Musa and the rise of the professional classes in Egypt, 1909-39*, Lanham 1986; Ruzūḳ Fuʾād, *Salāma Mūsā faylasūf al-ṣaḥāfa*, Cairo 1962; Fatḥī Khalīl, *Salāma Mūsā wa-ʿaṣr al-ḳalaḳ*, Cairo 1965; Hinrī Riyāḍ, *Salāma Mūsā wa 'l-manhadj al-ishtirākī*, Beirut 1966; Maḥmūd al-Sharḳāwī, *Salāma Mūsā al-mufakkir wa 'l-insān*, Cairo 1956; Ghālī Shukrī, *Salāma Mūsā wa-azmat al-ḍamīr al-ʿarabī*, Cairo 1962; Kamel S. Abu Jaber, *Salāmah Mūsā: precursor of Arab Socialism*, in *MEJ*, xx, 1966, 196-206; A.D.H. Dessouki, *The views of Salama Musa on religion and secularism*, in *Islam and the Modern Age*, iv/3 (1973), 23-34; Sylvia G. Haim, *Salāma Mūsā, an appreciation of his autobiography*, in *WI*, N.S., ii (1953), 10-24; Sami A. Hanna and G.H. Gardner, *Salāma Mūsā 1887-1958, a pioneer of Arab Socialism*, in their *Arab socialism: a documentary survey*, Leiden 1969, 49-63; Ibrahim A. Ibrahim, *Salama Musa: an essay on culture alienation*, in *MES*, xv (1979), 346-57; M.S. Sfia, *Egypte: impact de l'idéologie socialiste sur l'intelligentsia arabe (Salāma Mūsā)*, in G. Haupt and M. Reberioux, *La Deuxième Internationale et l'Orient*, Paris 1967, 407-22.

(P.C. Sadgrove)

SALĀMĀN and **ABSĀL**, two characters who figure prominently in a series of pre-modern philosophical and mystical allegories written in Arabic and Persian. The characters are first mentioned by Ibn Sīnā [*q.v.*], in the ninth chapter of his *Kitāb al-Ishārāt wa 'l-tanbīhāt*, where he discusses the "Stages of the Gnostics" (*maḳāmāt al-ʿārifīn*). Here he states that:

> Gnostics have stages and degrees by which they are favoured over others while in their earthly life. It is as if their bodies were garments that they had removed and striped away (to move) toward the Realm of Sanctity (*ʿālam al-ḳuds*). They have things hidden within and manifest without that are denied by whomever would deny them but are deemed momentous by whomever has come to known them.
>
> We will tell you about these things. And when your ear has been struck by what it hears, and what you will hear has been narrated to you, it will be a story of Salāmān and Absāl.
>
> Know that Salāmān is a similitude coined for you and that Absāl is a similitude coined for your degree in gnosis (*ʿirfān*), if you be one of its folk. So decipher the symbolism (*al-ramz*), if you are able (iv, 48-51).

Ibn Sīnā also mentions the name of Absāl in his "Treatise on Destiny" (*Risāla fī 'l-ḳadar*) (Mehren, *Traités mystiques*, fasc. iii/5-6), but the story is not in the list of his compositions provided by Abū ʿUbayd al-Djūzdjānī [*q.v.*], the philosopher's companion, student, and biographer (despite al-Ṭūsī's assertion that it is), nor does it appear in any of the other traditional bibliographies of Ibn Sīnā's works (such as those of Ibn al-Ḳifṭī, Ibn Abī Uṣaybiʿa, or Ibn Khallikān [*q.vv.*]. No manuscript of the narrative has so far appeared.

In his commentary on *al-Ishārāt wa 'l-tanbīhāt*, Fakhr al-Dīn al-Rāzī [*q.v.*] suggests etymologies for the two names and states that there existed a story "among the Arabs" about the two characters, but he acknowledges that this version appears to have little connection with Ibn Sīnā's intent.

Our only source for the possible contents of the story is Naṣīr al-Dīn al-Ṭūsī's [*q.v.*] commentary on *al-Ishārāt wa 'l-tanbīhāt* (iv, 49-57). Al-Ṭūsī first recapitulates al-Rāzī's remarks. Then he summarises the contents of two versions of the story that he came across in the twenty years after he finished his commentary (for translations and full discussions of both versions, see Corbin, *Avicenna*, 204-41; cf. Heath, *Allegory*, 94-6. The allegorical decoding provided in the summaries below is al-Ṭūsī's).

The first version, which al-Ṭūsī believes "one of the common philosophers devised to fit the Shaykh's [i.e. Ibn Sīnā's] discussion", was purportedly of Greek origin and translated into Arabic by Ḥunayn b. Isḥāḳ [*q.v.*] (iv, 52). In this narrative, Salāmān is a young prince (the rational soul) whom his father (the active intellect) has engendered without recourse to a woman (matter) through the ingenuity of his minister (divine emanation). Salāmān is nursed by a young and beautiful woman, Absāl (the corporeal faculties), with whom he falls desperately in love. When his father, the king, disapproves of this attachment, Salāmān flees with Absāl to the lands of the far west (the material realm). Through his father's patient guidance, he is eventually freed of his ties to Absāl and assumes his rightful place on the throne. (A text of this version is included in *Tisʿ rasāʾil*, 112-19.)

Al-Ṭūsī ascribes the second version to Ibn Sīnā, and justifiably so since it contains a scene referred to by the philosopher in his "Treatise on Destiny" (mentioned above). In this rendition, Salāmān is a king (the rational soul) and Absāl is his younger brother (the theoretical faculty of the rational soul advanced to the level of the acquired intellect) who aids his older sibling while resisting the sexual advances of the latter's wife (the bodily faculties). After conquering the East and the West, Absāl is poisoned by his brother's wife. Learning this, Salāmān executes his wife and retires to solitary meditation of God.

The next major use of the characters apears in the *Treatise of Ḥayy b. Yaḳẓān*, written by the Andalusian philosopher Ibn Ṭufayl [*q.v.*]. Ibn Ṭufayl states in his introduction that he composed the narrative to clarify what Ibn Sīnā meant by the phrase "Oriental Philosophy" (*al-ḥikma al-mashriḳiyya*), and he refers to passages from the final chapters of *al-Ishārāt wa 'l-tanbīhāt*. Nevertheless, Ibn Ṭufayl's use of the characters is original, and his *Ḥayy b. Yaḳẓān* is a significant philosophical composition in its own right.

In this narrative, Salāmān and Absāl appear toward the end of the story, after the main character,

Ḥayy b. Yaḳẓān [*q.v.*], has perfected himself and achieved a state of union with the Divine. Absāl, who represents the inner dimension of religious spirituality, appears on Ḥayy's island seeking a place to engage in solitary spiritual contemplation. When the two meet, Absāl learns of Ḥayy's spiritual attainments and becomes his disciple. When Ḥayy discovers from Absāl of the existence of revealed religion among the latter's people, he decides to visit their island to inform them of the inner truths that their revelation contains. On the island, the two encounter Absāl's friend, Salāmān, who represents upright and sincere adherence to the external tenets and rituals of religion. Ḥayy finds that he cannot convey his spiritual and intellectual truths because the islanders are spiritually and mentally incapable of receiving them. So he and Absāl return to their island to pursue their pursuit of truth away from society.

The last major version of a story using the characters of Salāmān and Absāl occurs in a narrative of the same name by the Persian poet, D̲j̲āmī [*q.v.*], that is included as one of seven *mat̲h̲nawī*s in the poet's *Haft awrang*. D̲j̲āmī's version (translated into English by the 19th-century poet Edward Fitzgerald) follows fairly closely the plot line of the Greek story summarised above (see Arberry, *Fitzgerald's Salaman and Absal*, which supplies two versions by Fitzgerald as well as a literal English translation of D̲j̲āmī's Persian text). D̲j̲āmī explains the allegorical symbols of his story at its conclusion.

Bibliography: 1. Primary sources. Ibn Sīnā, *al-Is̲h̲ārāt wa 'l-tanbīhāt*, ed. Sulaymān Dunyā, 4 vols., Cairo 1960; idem, *Risāla fi 'l-ḳadar*, in A.F. Mehren (ed. and tr.), *Traités mystiques d'Abou ʿAli Hosain b. ʿAbdallâh b. Sînâ ou d'Avicenne*, Leiden 1889-99; idem, *Tisʿ rasāʾil fi 'l- ḥikma wa 'l-ṭabīʿiyyāt*, Istanbul 1881; Ibn Ṭufayl, *Risālat Ḥayy b. Yaḳẓān*, in Leon Gauthier (ed. and tr.), *Hayy ben Yaqdhân; roman philosophique d'Ibn Thofail*, [2]Beirut 1936, also in Aḥmad Amīn (ed.), *Ḥayy b. Yaḳẓān li-ibn Sīnā wa-ibn Ṭufayl wa 'l-Suhrawardī*, Cairo 1959; D̲j̲āmī, *Salāmān ū Absāl*, in *Haft awrang*, ed. Āḳā Murtaḍa and Mudarris Gīlānī, n.p. 1992.

2. Secondary sources. A.J. Arberry, *Fitzgerald's Salaman and Absal*, Cambridge 1956; H. Corbin, *Avicenne et le récit visionnaire*, 3 vols., Tehran and Paris 1952-4, Eng. tr. *Avicenna and the visionary recital*, New York 1969, repr. Princeton 1988; W.E. Goldman, *The life of Ibn Sīnā: a critical edition and annotated translation*, Albany 1974; L.E. Goodman, *Ibn Tufayl's Hayy ibn Yaqzân: a philosophical tale*, Los Angeles 1991; P. Heath, *Allegory and philosophy in Avicenna (Ibn Sînâ), with a translation of the Book of the Prophet Muḥammad's Ascent to Heaven*, Philadelphia 1992.

(P. Heath)

SALAMANCA [see S̲H̲ALAMANḲA].

SALAMIYYA, a town in central Syria in the district of Orontes (Nahr al-ʿĀṣī), about 25 miles south-east of Ḥamāt and 35 miles north-east of Ḥimṣ (for the town's exact situation, see Kiepert's map in M. von Oppenheim, *Vom Mittelmeer zum Persischen Golf*, Berlin 1899, i. 124 ff., and ii, 401; *National Geographic Atlas of the World*, 5th ed., Washington D.C. 1981, 178-9). Salamiyya lies in a fertile plain 1,500 feet above sea level, south of the D̲j̲abal al-Aʿlā and on the margin of the Syrian steppe. The older and more correct pronunciation of this town's name was Salamya (al-Iṣṭak̲h̲rī, 61; Ibn al-Faḳīh, 110), but the form Salamiyya is also found very early (al-Muḳaddasī, 190; Ibn K̲h̲urradād̲h̲bih, 76, 98) and is now the form almost universally in use (cf. also Yāḳūt, *Muʿd̲j̲am*, iii, 123; Littmann, *Semitic inscriptions*, 169 ff.). The *nisba* from the name is Salamī. The town seems to be the ancient Salamias or Salaminias, which flourished in the Christian period, but the references of the classical authors to this place are uncertain. Yāḳūt, *loc. cit.*, gives a popular etymology. The town, he says, was originally called *Salam-miʾa*, after the hundred surviving inhabitants of the destroyed town of al-Muʾtafika; the survivors then settled in Salamiyya and rebuilt it.

The situation of the town was important as an outpost of Syria, where main routes from the steppe (Palmyra) and ʿIrāḳ joined; but it was never of any great military importance. Salamiyya was conquered by the Arabs in the year 15/636, and became one of the towns of the *D̲j̲und* of Ḥimṣ; it was only after 906/1500 in the Mamlūk period that it was placed in the district of Ḥamāt for administrative purposes.

During the 2nd/8th century, soon after the victory of the ʿAbbāsids, the ʿAbbāsid Ṣāliḥ b. ʿAlī b. ʿAbd Allāh b. al-ʿAbbās, and later some of his descendants, settled down in Salamiyya. In 141/758, Ṣāliḥ b. ʿAlī had been appointed as the governor of southern and central Syria, and he paid some attention to reconstructing Salamiyya. The town is said to have been most indebted to Ṣāliḥ's son ʿAbd Allāh, who rebuilt it and developed the irrigation system of the locality and its environs (al-Yaʿḳūbī, *Buldān*, 324). This ʿAbd Allāh was held in high esteem by his cousins, the first two ʿAbbāsid caliphs. On his way to Jerusalem in 163/779-80, the caliph al-Mahdī stayed with ʿAbd Allāh in Salamiyya and admired his house (al-Ṭabarī, iii, 500, tr. H. Kennedy, *The History of al-Ṭabarī*, xxix, *Al-Manṣūr and al-Mahdī*, Albany 1990, 215). In this same year, ʿAbd Allāh, who had meanwhile married al-Mahdī's sister, was appointed as the governor of al-D̲j̲azīra. There are more scattered references to the fact that many ʿAbbāsid Hās̲h̲imids lived in Salamiyya from early ʿAbbāsid times (see, for instance, al-Nīsābūrī, *Istitār al-imām*, 115 ff., 123-5, tr. Ivanow in his *Ismaili tradition*, 160 ff., 171-3; Ibn Ḥazm, *D̲j̲amharat al-ansāb al-ʿArab*, ed. ʿAbd al-Salām M. Hārūn, Cairo 1391/1971, 20; Idrīs ʿImād al-Dīn, *ʿUyūn al-ak̲h̲bār*, iv, 365, 402).

Almost nothing has survived in Salamiyya from this early ʿAbbāsid period. There is the foundation inscription of a mosque on a stone (not *in situ*) at the entrance to the citadel. It is probable that this inscription is dated 150/767-8 and it belonged to a mosque founded by those ʿAbbāsids, which may have been destroyed later (about 290/903) by the Ḳarmaṭīs who invaded the town. Still another inscription stemming from an ʿAbbāsid has been found in the citadel; according to Littmann's plausible suggestion, it belongs with two other inscriptions to the period from 280/893-4 (or, for another view, see Hartmann, *Die arabischen Inschriften*, 55).

The fact that Salamiyya was the centre of an important branch of the Hās̲h̲imids and the isolated position of the town perhaps account for its important role in the early history of the Ismāʿīlī movement as the secret headquarters of the pre-Fāṭimid Ismāʿīlī *daʿwa*. According to the later Ismāʿīlīs, the early Ismāʿīlī *daʿwa* was organised and led by a number of hidden *imāms* (*al-aʾimma al-mastūrīn*), who were descendants of the S̲h̲īʿī *imām* D̲j̲aʿfar al-Ṣādiḳ. It was ʿAbd Allāh, a great-grandson of al-Ṣādiḳ and one of these hidden *imāms*, who, after living in different localities in K̲h̲ūzistān and ʿIrāḳ, fled to Syria and eventually settled down in Salamiyya at an unknown date around the beginning of the 3rd/9th century. At the time, Salamiyya was held by the ʿAbbāsid Muḥammad b. ʿAbd Allāh b. Ṣāliḥ, who had transformed the town into a flourishing commercial centre. The ᶜAlid ᶜAbd Allāh, the Ismāᶜīlī leader who then posed as an ordinary Hās͟himid and a merchant, was granted permission by the ᶜAbbāsid lord of the town to settle there; later, he built a sumptuous palace for himself in Salamiyya which evidently continued to be used by his descendants and successors as the central leaders of the Ismāᶜīlī *daᶜwa* (see al-Nīsābūrī, 116 ff., tr. Ivanow, 161 ff.; Idrīs ᶜImād al-Dīn, iv, 357-66). Salamiyya served as the headquarters of the Ismāᶜīlī movement until the year 289/902; it was from there that *dāᶜīs* were originally dispatched for propagating the Ismāᶜīlī teachings and initiating the *daᶜwa* in different regions. These activities were greatly intensified around the middle of the 3rd/9th century.

ᶜUbayd Allāh (ᶜAbd Allāh), the last of these hidden *imāms* and the future Fāṭimid caliph al-Mahdī, was born in Salamiyya in 259 or 260/873-4. In 286/899, not long after his accession to the central leadership of the movement, ᶜUbayd Allāh introduced some important changes into the doctrines propagated by the early Ismāᶜīlī *daᶜwa*. However, the new instructions issued from Salamiyya were not endorsed by certain regional *dāᶜīs*, notably Ḥamdān Ḳarmaṭ and his chief assistant ᶜAbdān, who led the *daᶜwa* in ᶜIrāḳ and adjacent areas. ᶜAbdān was dispatched on a fact-finding mission to Salamiyya. Having become convinced of ᶜUbayd Allāh's reform, Ḥamdān and ᶜAbdān broke away from the central leadership; the dissident view found supporters also in Baḥrayn and some eastern Ismāᶜīlī communities. The Ismāᶜīlī movement was now split into two rival factions, the dissident Ḳarmaṭīs and the loyal Fāṭimid Ismāᶜīlīs (see W. Madelung, *Das Imamat in der frühen ismailitischen Lehre*, in *Isl.*, xxxvii [1961], 65-86; F. Daftary, *A major schism in the early Ismāᶜīlī movement*, in *SI*, lxxvii [1993], 123-39). The *dāᶜī* Zikrawayh b. Mihrawayh, who had initially remained loyal to ᶜUbayd Allāh, soon manifested his own rebellious intentions and led the Ḳarmaṭī revolts of ᶜIrāḳ and Syria during 289-94/902-7 (H. Halm, *Die Söhne Zikrawaihs und das erste fatimidische Kalifat 290/903*, in *Die Welt des Orients*, x [1979], 30-53). ᶜUbayd Allāh had already left Salamiyya a year before the rebellious Ḳarmaṭīs, led by Zikrawayh's sons, entered it in 290/903. The Ḳarmaṭīs massacred the inhabitants of Salamiyya, also destroying ᶜUbayd Allāh's palace there. The success of the Ḳarmaṭīs in Syria was, however, short-lived. By 291/903, the Ḳarmaṭīs were severely defeated by an ᶜAbbāsid army near Salamiyya; and their leader in Syria, one of Zikrawayh's sons, was captured and taken before the ᶜAbbāsid caliph al-Muktafī, who had him executed. Meanwhile, ᶜUbayd Allāh had embarked on the fateful journey that took him to North Africa where he founded the Fāṭimid caliphate. It is not impossible that the quadrangular citadel in the centre of Salamiyya goes back to the Ismāᶜīlī period of the town; according to van Berchem, it belongs to an early period architecturally.

In the 4th/10th century, Salamiyya must have been in an area inhabited by Bedouins (Sayf al-Dawla's campaign; cf. Hartmann, in *ZDPV*, xxii [1899], 175, 176). At the end of the 5th/11th century, it was included in the possessions of the brigand K͟halaf b. Mulāᶜib, who acknowledged Fāṭimid suzerainty. There is evidence of this in an inscription in Kūfic characters, dated 481/1088, on the door beam of a mosque in Salamiyya. According to Ibn al-At͟hīr (x, 184), K͟halaf took Salamiyya in 476/1083-4; he was then already master of Ḥimṣ. But in 485/1092, he lost Ḥimṣ and the lands that went with it to the Sald͟jūḳ Tutus͟h, brother of Malik S͟hāh (Ibn al-Ḳalānisī, *D͟hayl taʾrīk͟h Dimas͟hk*, ed. H.F. Amedroz, Leiden 1908, 115, 120, 132, 149-50; Ibn Muyassar, *Ak͟hbār Miṣr*, ed. A.F. Sayyid, Cairo 1981, 63, 76). In the inscription, studied extensively by Rey, Hartmann, van Berchem and Littmann, K͟halaf says that he has erected this *mas͟hhad* on the tomb of the *ḳāʾid* Abu 'l-Ḥasan ᶜAlī b. D͟jarīr (or D͟jaᶜfar), whose servant (*ṣāniᶜ*) he calls himself. However, the Syrian Ismāᶜīlīs have traditionally regarded this tomb as that of their early *imām* ᶜAbd Allāh, one of the hidden *imāms* of the pre-Fāṭimid period, calling the mausoleum locally as the *maḳām al-imām*. H. Halm, who studied and reinterpreted the inscription in 1980, lends support to the local Syrian Ismāᶜīlī tradition by holding that the mausoleum was in all probability originally erected, about 400/1009, over the tomb of the *imām* ᶜAbd Allāh by the Kutāmī *ḳāʾid* ᶜAlī b. D͟jaᶜfar (b. Falāḥ), the Fāṭimid commander who seized Salamiyya for the Fāṭimids and whose name appears in the inscription, and that K͟halaf merely repaired the site, some four decades later (see Halm, *Les Fatimides à Salamya*, 144-7, with photographs of the site on 148-9).

During the Crusades, Salamiyya is never mentioned as a fortress but frequently as a meeting place for the Muslim armies. Politically it has always shared the fate of Ḥimṣ [*q.v.*]. Thus it passed to Riḍwān, son of Tutus͟h, in 496/11102-3. In 532/1137-8, the Atabeg Zankī b. Aḳ Sunḳur, who was then besieging Ḥimṣ, set out from Salamiyya on his campaign against the Greeks at S͟hayzar (Ibn al-At͟hīr, xi, 36 ff.), and in 570/1174-5 Ṣalāḥ al-Dīn obtained the town together with Ḥimṣ and Ḥamāt from the *amīr* Fak͟hr al-Dīn al-Zaᶜfarānī (*ibid.*, xi, 276). In 626/1229, we find the Ayyūbid al-Malik al-Kāmil I in Salamiyya as a staging-post for ᶜIrāḳ; the lord of Ḥamāt came there to submit to him. Two years later, al-Kāmil gave the town to Asad al-Dīn S͟hīrkūh, who rebuilt the fortress of S͟humaymis͟h north of it on one of the peaks of the D͟jabal al-Aᶜlā (*ibid.*, xii, 318, 329; van Berchem and Fatio, *Voyage en Syrie*, i, 171, 173) which had been destroyed by the earthquake of 552/1157 (Ibn al-ᶜAdīm, *Zubdat al-halab min taʾrīk͟h Ḥalab*, i, ed. S. Dahan, Damascus 1954, 306, tr. E. Blochet, *Histoire d'Alep*, Paris 1900, 21). In 698/1299, the Egyptian army was defeated at Salamiyya by the Mongols under G͟hāzān; the battle was followed by the brief Mongol occupation of the city of Damascus.

In the 8th/14th century, Salamiyya was part of the important frontier lands (called al-S͟harḳiyya) of the *mamlaka* of Damascus. Abu 'l-Fidāʾ, in whose territory as lord of Ḥamāt the town lay during the Mamlūk period, mentions an aqueduct between Salamiyya and Ḥamāt. In 726/1326, he went with his troops to clear out this channel (autobiography of Abu 'l-Fidāʾ in *RHC. Historiens Orientaux*, i, 168, 185; tr. P.M. Holt, *The memoirs of a Syrian Prince, Abu 'l-Fidāʾ, sultan of Ḥamāh*, Wiesbaden 1983, 18, 85). This aqueduct no longer exists. Perhaps it is the same as is mentioned by al-Dimas͟hḳī (207) as in existence between Ḥimṣ and Salamiyya and built by the ᶜAbbāsid ᶜAbd Allāh b. Ṣāliḥ. At this time Yāḳūt (*Muᶜd͟jam*, iii, 123) speaks of seven prayer-niches near Salamiyya below which some *tābiᶜūn* or Successors were buried; he also mentions the tomb of al-Nuᶜmān b. Bas͟hīr al-Anṣārī, the companion of the Prophet.

Under Ottoman rule, the town gradually ceased to be of importance. By the early decades of the 13th/19th century, Salamiyya was entirely deserted and lying in ruins, probably on account of the lack of adequate protection against the Bedouins (see C.L. Meryon's *Travels of Lady Hester Stanhope*, London 1846, ii, 93, 211-12, and L. de Laborde's *Voyage en*

Orient, Paris 1838, ii, 13, who visited Salamiyya in 1813 and 1827 respectively). A new phase in the history of Salamiyya began in the middle of the 13th/19th century. It was at that time that Ismāʿīl b. Muḥammad, the Ismāʿīlī *amīr* of Ḳadmūs who had succeeded in establishing his authority over a large section of the Ismāʿīlī community in Syria and who had been outlawed earlier for his rebellious activities, was permitted by the Ottoman authorities to settle permanently with his people in an area east of the Orontes river. The Ismāʿīlī settlers were also exempted from military conscription and taxation. These arrangements were evidently confirmed by a *fermān* of Sultan ʿAbd al-Medjīd, dated Shaʿbān 1265/July 1849. Ismāʿīl b. Muḥammad chose the ruins of Salamiyya as the site of his new Ismāʿīlī settlement. An increasing number of Ismāʿīlīs from the western mountains gradually joined the original settlers in Salamiyya, attracted by the prospect of receiving free land in a district where they would furthermore be neither taxed nor conscripted (for details, see N.N. Lewis, *The Ismaʿilis of Syria today*, in *Royal Central Asian Society Journal*, xxxiv [1952], 69 ff.; M. Ghālib, *The Ismailis of Syria*, Beirut 1970, 156 ff.).

By 1861, Salamiyya had become a large village with numerous dwellings in its restored fort (J.H. Skene, *Rambles in the deserts of Syria*, London 1864, 158). Soon the Ismāʿīlī settlers, whose numbers increased continuously by new arrivals, established villages around Salamiyya, expanding the cultivable land of the district and improving its irrigation. By 1878, Circassians also began to migrate to Salamiyya. However, the bulk of the land of Salamiyya and its villages remained in the hands of the Ismāʿīlīs. In time, the growth and prosperity of Salamiyya was officially recognised by the Ottoman authorities who, in 1884, created a special administrative district (*ḳaḍāʾ*) centred on Salamiyya within the *sandjaḳ* of Ḥamāt; a few years later, troops were stationed there, conscription was initiated, normal taxes were levied, and Salamiyya began to appear regularly in the annual *Sālnāme-yi Sūriye wilāyeti* of the Ottomans. By the end of the 13th/19th century, Salamiyya reportedly had more than 6,000 inhabitants, with a good irrigation system (V. Cuinet, *Syrie, Liban et Palestine*, Paris 1896, 436, 453 ff.). The last major migration of the Syrian Ismāʿīlīs to Salamiyya occurred in 1919; these settlers built their houses in a new quarter of the town known as the "quarter of the Ḳadmūsīs". In the present century, Salamiyya has become an important agricultural centre in Syria, where a variety of crops, including wheat and legumes, are cultivated.

In 1304/1887, the Ismāʿīlīs of Salamiyya, who, like the bulk of the Syrian Ismāʿīlīs, had hitherto belonged to the Muḥammad Shāhī branch of Nizārī Ismāʿīlism, transferred their allegiance to the Ḳāsim Shāhī line of Nizārī *imāms*, then represented by Agha Khān III. The latter organised the Ismāʿīlīs of Salamiyya and also built several schools and an agricultural institution there. With a population of 95,000 in 1993, the great majority of whom are Nizārī Ismāʿīlīs, Salamiyya now accounts for the largest concentration of Ismāʿīlīs in Syria as well as in the Near East. In recent years, the Ismāʿīlī community of Salamiyya has benefited from the communal and religious activities of Agha Khān IV, the 49th and present *imām* of the Ḳāsim Shāhī Nizārīs, whose father Prince ʿAlī Khān is buried in Salamiyya in a special mausoleum adjacent to the town's newly-constructed Ismāʿīlī centre (*djamāʿat-khāna*).

Bibliography (in addition to the works cited in the article): Aḥmad b. Ibrāhīm al-Nīsābūrī, *Istitār al-imām*, in *Akhbār al-Ḳarāmiṭa*, ed. S. Zakkār, ²Damascus 1982, 111-32; Muḥammad b. Muḥammad al-Yamānī, *Sīrat al-Ḥādjib Djaʿfar b. ʿAlī*, ed. W. Ivanow, in *Bull. of the Faculty of Arts, University of Egypt*, iv (1936), 107 ff.; Idrīs ʿImād al-Dīn b. al-Ḥasan, *ʿUyūn al-akhbār wa-funūn al-āthār*, iv, ed. M. Ghālib, Beirut 1973, 357-66; *RHC. Historiens Orientaux*, Paris 1872-1906, iii, 298 (Ibn Shaddād), 546 (Sibṭ Ibn al-Djawzī), 592 (Ibn al-ʿAdīm), v, 180 ff. (Abū Shāma); E. Sachau, *Reise in Syrien und Mesopotamien*, Leipzig 1883, 66; G. Le Strange, *Palestine under the Moslems*, London 1890, 510, 528; M. Sobernheim, *Meine Reise von Palmyra nach Selemiya*, in *ZDPV*, xxii (1899), 189-96; M. Hartmann, *Beiträge zur Kenntnis der syrischen Steppe*, in *ZDPV*, xxii (1899), 127-77, and xxiii (1901), 1-77, 97-158; M. van Berchem and E. Fatio, *Voyage en Syrie*, i, Cairo 1914, 167-71; W. Ivanow, *Ismaili tradition concerning the rise of the Fatimids*, London etc. 1942, index (also containing English tr. of al-Nīsābūrī's *Istitār al-imām*, 157-83, and al-Yamānī's *Sīrat al-Ḥādjib*, 184-223); M. Amīn, *Salamiyya fī khamsīn ḳarn*, Damascus n.d. [1986], 142-231; N.N. Lewis, *Nomads and settlers in Syria and Jordan, 1800-1980,* Cambridge 1987, 58-67, 219-22; F. Daftary, *The Ismāʿīlīs: their history and doctrines*, Cambridge 1990, index; H. Halm, *Das Reich des Mahdi*, Munich 1991, index. On the inscriptions, see E. Rey, *Rapport sur une mission scientifique accomplie en 1864-1865 dans le Nord de la Syrie*, in *Archives des Missions scientifiques et littéraires*, 2 série, iii, 345; M. Hartmann, *Die arabischen Inschriften in Salamja*, in *ZDPV*, xxiv (1901), 49-68; E. Littmann, *Semitic inscriptions*, New York 1905, 169-178; M. van Berchem, *Arabische Inschriften* (*Inschriften aus Syrien, Mesopotamien und Kleinasien, gesammelt von M. von Oppenheim*), i, Leipzig 1909, 32-4; H. Halm, *Les Fatimides à Salamya*, in *REI*, liv (1986), 133-49.

(J.H. Kramers-[F. Daftary])

SALAR, a Muslim and Turkic-speaking minority in Northwestern China.

They are otherwise called Sa-la in Chinese. Their total population in the P.R.C. is about 69,000 and the greater part of them live in the Sala Autonomous Prefecture of Hsün-hua, Ch'ing-hai province; the population here was *ca.* 49,000 in 1984. The Salar oral traditions unanimously tell that they emigrated from Samarḳand to Hsün-hua in 1370 under the reign of the first Ming Emperor. They are regarded to have originated from Salar (or Salor [see salur]) tribesmen of the Turkmen nation distributed in the Samarḳand region. The Ch'ing-hai Salars were firstly reported in Ch'ing source in the middle of the 18th century. The Salars are Muslims and some of them became adherents of the Ṣūfī order of the Djahriyya from the early 18th century. In 1781 conflicts broke out among the Salars, who had been divided into two sects, that of the New Teaching (Djahriyya) and that of the Old Teaching, but adherents of the New Sect were severely militarily repressed by the Ch'ing authorities. There were several rebellions of the Salar New Sect against the local authorities down to the late 19th century. The Salars at Hsün-hua consisted of eight *kung* (originally eleven *kung; kung* means village or community) with their base at Hsün-hua. They were engaged in farming, cattle-breeding, fishing, etc. In the Salar region, there were nine large, core mosques, each of which administered subordinate mosques. Religious leaders of Salar mosques, on the lines of *akhōn, imām, mullā, ḳāḍī* and *khaṭīb*, were known: festivals, such as the *ʿīd al-fiṭr, ḳurbān* and *barāt* were observed, and the Salars had tombs called *ḳubbas* (generally called *kumpei*). The Salars are now officially recognised as one of the 55 minority peoples of the P.R.C., and they coexist with the Han Chinese.

Bibliography: *Hsün-hua t'ing chih* ("The local gazetteer of the Hsün-hua Office") compiled in 1792; G.F. Andrew, *The crescent in Northwest China*, London 1921; N.N. Poppe, *Remarks on the Salar language*, in *Harvard Journal of Asiatic Studies*, xvi/3-4 (1953); E.R. Tenishev, *Salarskiy yazîk*, Mos 1962; E.R. Tenishev, *Salarskiy tekstî*, Mos 1964; J. Trippner, *Die Salaren, ihre Glaubensstreitigkeiten und ihr Aufstand 1781*, in *Central Asiatic Journal*, ix/4 (1964); *Sala tsu chien-shih* ("A short history of the Salars"), Sining 1982; T. Saguchi, *Shinkyô minzokushi kenkyû* ("Studies on history of minority peoples of Sinkiang"), Tokyo 1986. See also AL-ṢĪN.

(T. SAGUCHI)

SĀLĀR (P.), commander. From the older Pahlavi *sardār* there arose as early as the Sāsānid period the form *sālār* with the well-known change of *rd* to *l* and compensatory lengthening of the *a* (cf. *Grundr. d. Iran. Phil.*, i,[a] 267, 274). The synonymous word in modern Persian *sardār* is not a survival of the ancient *sardār*, but is a modern formation; indeed, the elements from which the ancient word was composed still exist in the modern language. The old Armenian took over the Pahlavi *sālār* in the form *sałar*; the form *sardār* which would give **sardar* in Armenian is not found in the latter language. A latter, probably modern Persian loan-word in Armenian is (*spa*) *salar* with *l* instead of *ł*. On this and on other late Armenian forms, cf. Hübschmann, *Arm. Gramm.*, i, 235, 239. In the first of these two references, the Pahlavi combinations of the word are also given. On the etymology, cf. also Horn, *Grundriss der neup. Etymologie*, 153; Hübschmann, *Persische Studien*, 72; Junker, *The Frahang i Pahlavīk*, Berlin 1912, 37, 79.

In the mediaeval Islamic Persian world and in those lands culturally affected by it, such as the central Arab lands of ʿIrāḳ and Syria, the Caucasus, Central Asia and Muslim India, *sālār* was essentially a military term, as e.g. in *sipah-sālār* "supreme army commander", the equivalent in Persian of the Arabic *amīr al-umarāʾ*, *ḥādjib al-ḥudjdjāb* or *al-ḥādjib al-kabīr* found amongst dynasties like the Sāmānids, Būyids, Ghaznawids and Great Saldjūḳs [see ISPAHSĀLĀR].

But *sālār* by itself was often used for the commander of a particular group, such as the commander of the Muslim *ghāzīs* or fighters for the faith centred on Lahore in the Ghaznawid period and organised for raiding into the Hindu *dār al-kufr* (see Bosworth, *The Ghaznavids*, 114). Certainly in the 5th/11th century, various of the towns and districts of Khurāsān seem to have had *sālār*s heading local forces organised either for defence or for *ghazw*. The *Sālār* of the district between Bādhghīs and Ḳuhistān called Būzgān was an active figure there in the events spanning the transition from Ghaznawid to Saldjūḳ rule in Khurāsān during the 1030s (see *ibid.*, 254, 261, 262-4), and some sources describe this Abu 'l-Ḳāsim ʿAbd al-Ṣamad al-Būzdjānī as becoming the Saldjūḳ Ṭoghrïl Beg's first vizier (see H. Bowen, *Notes on some early Seljuqid viziers*, in *BSOAS*, xx [1957], 105-7). Likewise, in Nīshāpūr at this time, a *sālār* of what was perhaps a local militia is mentioned, and this command may have been one of the functions of the town's *raʾīs* [see RAʾĪS. 2.] (see R.W. Bulliett, *The patricians of Nishapur, a study in medieval Islamic social history*, Cambridge, Mass. 1972, 68-9); he seems to have been regarded as a key figure in 429/1030 when it was a question of the establishing the authority of the dead sultan Maḥmūd of Ghazna's son Masʿūd in Nīshāpur rather than that of his brother Muḥammad (see Ibn Funduḳ, *Taʾrīkh-i Bayhaḳ*, ed. Bahmanyār, 267-8). There was a prominent family in Bayhaḳ, the Sālāriyān, the descendants of one *Sālār* Abu 'l-ʿAbbās al-Muḥsin al-Muṭṭawwiʿ, who had been head of the *ghāzīs* and had fought at Tarsus (*ibid.*, 124).

In administrative documents from mid-6th/12th century eastern Persia and Transoxania, *sālār*, together with such terms as *muḳaddam* and *sarhang*, appears as a rank for commanders just below the supreme commander (H. Horst, *Die Staatsverwaltung der Grosselǧūqen und Ḫōrazmšāhs (1038-1231)*, Wiesbaden 1964, 42, 47, 120, 160.

In general mediaeval Islamic usage, *sālār* is also found—as far west as Mamlūk Egypt and Syria—in such compounds as *ākhur-sālār* "head of the stables" and *khwān-sālār* "steward", given that these high royal household offices were usually allotted to high-ranking Turkish military commanders.

Bibliography: Given in the article.

(V.F. BÜCHNER-[C.E. BOSWORTH])

SĀLĀR DJANG (Sir), the title by which Mīr Turāb ʿAlī, a Sayyid of Persian descent and one of the greatest of modern Indian statesmen, was best known.

He was born at Ḥaydarābād, Deccan, on 2 January, 1829, and, his father having died not long after his birth, was educated by his uncle, Nawwāb Sirādj al-Mulk, Minister of the Ḥaydarābād State. He received an administrative appointment in 1848, at the age of 19, and on his uncle's death in 1853 succeeded him as Minister of the State. He was engaged in reforming the administration until 1857, the year of the Sepoy Mutiny, when the Niẓām, Nāṣir al-Dawla, died and was succeeded by his son Afḍal al-Dawla. The news of the seizure of Dihlī by the mutineers greatly excited the populace, and the British Residency was attacked by a turbulent mob, aided by some irregular troops, but throughout the darkest days of the rebellion Sālār Djang not only remained true to the British connection, but strengthened the hands of his master and suppressed disorder. The services of the State were recognised by the rendition of three of the districts assigned in 1853 on account of debts due to the Company, and by the cession of the territory of the rebellious Rādjā of Shorāpūr. In 1860 and again in 1867 plots to estrange the great Minister from his master and to ensure his dismissal were frustrated by two successive British Residents, and Sālār Djang remained in office. In 1868 an attempt was made to assassinate him but the assassin was arrested and executed, despite Sālār Djang's efforts to obtain a commutation of the sentence. On the death of Afḍal al-Dawla in 1869, Sālār Djang became one of the two co-regents of the State during the minority of his son and successor, Mīr Maḥbūb ʿAlī Khān, and on 5 January 1871, he was invested at Calcutta with the insignia of the G.C.S.I. In November 1875, he and other nobles represented the young Niẓām at Bombay on the occasion of the visit of the Prince of Wales to India, and in April 1876, he visited England and was presented to Queen Victoria. He received the honorary degree of D.C.L. from the University of Oxford and the Freedom of the City of London. In January 1883, he was engaged in making preparations for the contemplated visit of the Niẓām to Europe, but on 7 February, after entertaining Duke John of Mecklenburg-Schwerin, who was visiting Ḥaydarābād, on the Mīr ʿĀlam Lake, he was attacked by cholera and died on the following morning. Though always known by his first title, Sālār Djang, he bore the higher titles Shudjāʿ al-Dawla and Mukhtār al-Mulk.

Bibliography: Syed Hossain Bilgrami, *Memoir of*

Sir Sālār Jang, Shujā^c ud-Daula, Mukhtār ul-Mulk, G.C.S.I. Bombay 1883; Syed Hossain Bilgrami and C. Wilmott, *Historical and descriptive sketch of H.H. the Nizam's dominions*, Bombay 1883; see also ḤAYDARĀBĀD. b. (T.W. HAIG*)

ṢALĀT (A.), ritual prayer. Unlike other types of prayer—in particular the prayer of supplication [see DU^cĀ^ɔ], the remembrance of the Divine Names [see DHIKR] or Ṣūfī confraternities' litanies [see WIRD]—the *ṣalāt*, principal prayer of Islam, forms part of the *^cibādāt* or cultic obligations. The word clearly derives from the Syriac *ṣ^elōtā* "prayer" and had adopted its Arabic form before the Islamic period (see Jeffery, 198-9). The structure of this article will be as follows:

I. In the Ḳur^ɔān.
II. In *ḥadīth* and legal elaborations.
III. The five daily prayers.
IV. The other ritual prayers.
V. *Ṣalāt* and Islam.

I. *In the Ḳur^ɔān.*

A. General insistence on prayer. In the Sacred Book of Islam, *ṣalāt* stands out prominently in an atmosphere of invocation of God. It would be arbitrary to separate totally the "ritual prayer" from other forms of prayer. *Ṣalāt*, the whole of which expresses praise and adoration, thus becomes the echo of specific prayers in the Ḳur^ɔān (cf. III, 26; X, 10) and of the usual feelings which it inspires or reflects.

In the Ḳur^ɔānic universe in fact, there is no religion without prayer. This last is expressed by numerous roots and words which mark its different orientations: thus the prayer of supplication or invocation (*du^cā^ɔ*), the appeal for pardon (*istighfār*) and glorification (*tasbīḥ*). The quality of prayer and its acceptance by God are the object of precise considerations (XL, 50; XLI, 49-51; II, 186) and of careful advice (VII, 55-6; XXI, 90; XL, 60; cf. VI, 52). Particularly notable is the diversity of protagonists or subjects of prayer: outside Islam like the associators (VI, 108; VII, 32 and 35) or the Christian hermits (who are probably described in XXIV, 36-8); before Islam like the wife of Pharaoh (LXVI, 11), the Man of the Fish (=Jonah, XXI, 87), and the three great models represented by Abraham, Moses and Zachariah (e.g. XXVI, 83-9; XX, 25-35; XIX, 3-6); within Islam like Muḥammad and the other Muslims (e.g. III, 26-7; XVIII, 80-1; II, 286; XVII, 24); and after Islam, as it were, like those chosen to reside in the Gardens of Delight (X, 10). In short, before becoming the obligatory and codified activity which forms the object of this article, prayer is first of all, and always remains so in the Ḳur^ɔānic vision of the world, the fundamental fabric of religious behaviour.

It is necessary above all to avoid projecting indiscriminately upon the word *ṣalāt*, and upon the verb *ṣallā* which is constructed on the basis of this substantive, the technical sense of Muslim ritual prayer. In the shortest, and one of the most ancient sūras, the reading is *fa-ṣalli li-rabbika wa-nḥar*, "therefore make the prayer to your Lord and sacrifice [a victim]" (CVIII, 2); this "prayer" could not be the *ṣalāt*. Similarly, in IX, 99 (cf. 103), the *ṣalawāt al-rasūl* probably refer to the prayers of benediction pronounced by the Prophet on Bedouin bringing their offerings (cf. Paret, 210-11). In VIII, 35, *ṣalātuhum* denotes explicitly the prayer of unbelieving Meccans (cf. CVII, 4-7); while in VI, 162, *ṣalātī* represents the totality of the devotional activity of Muḥammad, his life of prayer. Other instances of the root *ṣ-l-w* may also have no connection with ritual prayer (e.g. XVII, 110; LXX, 34).

The fact remains, however, that the word *ṣalāt* most often denotes this ritual prayer, the forms and rhythms of which evolved gradually, but which became at a very early stage a constitutive and distinctive element of Islam.

B. Importance of ritual prayer. There exist 65 instances of *al-ṣalāt* in the singular with the definite article. These usages always seem to indicate a ritual prayer, this being a cultic act comprising certain prescribed gestures and words, which is considered the form of prayer most closely associated with the religion. Its importance is not determined only by the frequent occurrence of the word. The Ḳur^ɔān opens with the *Fātiḥa*, sūra I, and this is recited at every *rak^ca*. With its sober and full tenor, as with its wording in the first person plural, it is so well adapted to liturgical use that its composition for this very purpose can scarcely be doubted. Consequently, its location at the opening of the Ḳur^ɔān gives a particular emphasis to *ṣalāt*. The outstanding worth of the latter is again underlined in II, 3, and the remainder of the Ḳur^ɔānic text corroborates this status.

Furthermore, the Book places the origin of ritual prayer, under divine guidance, at the outset of humanity. All the prophets practised ritual prayer (cf. XIX, 58-9, and 55; XXI, 73). Abraham appealed to his Lord to grant to him and his descendents, the privilege of performing *ṣalāt* (XIV, 37, 40). The obligation of ritual prayer was intimated to Moses in a particularly solemn manner (X, 87; XX, 14), and to Jesus in a quite different atmosphere (XIX, 31). Thus ritual prayer belonged at all times to the correct and immutable religion which is professed as a *ḥanīf* [*q.v.*] (XXX, 30-1; XCVIII, 5). It is often said that the revealed Laws change with the Messengers of God, while the latter maintain the same proclamation of the Unique One (*tawḥīd*). This view of things needs to be extended. In the Ḳur^ɔān, ritual prayer is presented as the immediate and constant corollary of belief in God. Whatever variations may exist in the practical prescriptions, a *ṣalāt* forms part of Ḥanīfism.

C. *Ṣalāt* in the evolution of the Ḳur^ɔānic message. To the above-mentioned uses of the word in the singular with the definite article, there should be added two instances (both in XXIV, 58) of the singular in the genitive construction. Hence, in the technical sense of ritual prayer, there is a total of 67 uses in the singular without affix. None of them belong to the primaeval sūras, i.e. to the most ancient sūras of that which Blachère calls the first Meccan period (the verse LXXIII, 20 is, by general agreement, much later than the remainder of the sūra). It is possible that the word in question does not appear before the period which, on both sides of the Hidjra, extends approximately from 620 to 624. It is significant that there is a single example in the *ḥawāmīm* sūras (in XLII, 38, in the context of moral advice). On the other hand, II, IV, V, IX and XXIV, all of them Medinan and contemporary with or later than the changing of the *ḳibla*, contain 33 uses: half of the total in a text which covers no more than 20% of the length of the Ḳur^ɔān. In other words, in the five sūras mentioned above, *ṣalāt* is presented proportionally four times more than in the remainder of the Ḳur^ɔān. This is no accident. The sūras cited correspond to the establishment of Islam as an institutional religion. Ritual prayer is a fundamental element of this, which accounts for the frequency with which it is mentioned.

This analysis is corroborated by the close link between *ṣalāt* and *zakāt*, "purification" of riches through giving. These two practices are prescribed or approved of together at least 25 times: *wa-aḳīmū 'l-ṣalāt wa-ātū 'l-zakāt* (IV, 77, etc.). Now it is known that the notion of alms is also expressed in the Ḳurʾān by the word *ṣadaḳa* [*q.v.*] and by the verb *anfaḳa* (to give of one's goods), and that the concept underlying the three Arabic terms has experienced an evolution: first, free giving from person to person, then religious obligation in the context of Islam. Ultimately the *zakāt*, enjoined especially in the five sūras already mentioned, takes on the precise meaning of a communal tax. "Purification" is accomplished by contributing to the treasury of the community, and the distribution of these henceforward compulsory "alms" (*ṣadaḳāt*) is codified under eight headings in IX, 60. Mention of this obligatory tax alongside ritual prayer is further evidence of the communal importance and finality of the latter.

D. The times of *ṣalāt*. In sketching the general line of an evolution which ends in the establishment of prayer as a pillar for the religion of God and of His Messenger, a thorny problem has been left aside: which are, according to the Book of Islam, the hours and the times of official prayer? Was there in the lifetime of the Prophet a progressive organisation, the signs of which would be perceptible in the Ḳurʾān?

To answer this question, it is not enough to base conclusions on the verses where the word *ṣalāt* is mentioned. It is necessary to take into account all the passages which mention a communal prayer of the disciples of Muḥammad or present as a model his habits of prayer.

Muslim prayer is born from the personal prayer of Muḥammad. The most ancient Ḳurʾānic passages which give temporal indications are addressed to the Prophet. They all enjoin upon him nocturnal prayer (LXXIII, 2-7, etc.), and to this, one adds praise at the setting of the stars (LII, 48-9), another, invocation of the name of his Lord at the dawning and at the declining of the day (LXXVI, 25-6), the last, praise before the rising of the sun and before its setting (L, 39-40). No doubt from the same period is the reference to the dwellers in the Garden of Paradise who previously prayed on the earth, keeping vigil into the last hours of the night (*bi 'l-asḥār*: LI, 16-18).

With different words, the same rhythms, still at Mecca, are subsequently maintained (XX, 130; XVII, 78-80; XL, 55), but it is soon observed that a prayer group is formed around Muḥammad: "Enjoin *ṣalāt* upon your people" (XX, 132); "Stay with those who invoke their Lord" (XVIII, 28; cf. XXV, 64-5; XXXIX, 9).

In the years 620-4, the communal nature of prayer becomes manifest. The most ancient prescription first addressing the community of disciples seems to be VII, 204-6 (cf. XI, 112-4). In XXX, 17-18, the commandment given them is to pray to God evening and morning, then comes this phrase: "To Him be praise in the heavens and on the earth, at the declining of the day (*ʿashiyyan*) and when you are at midday (*wa-ḥīna tuẓhirūn*)". To give here to the word *ʿashiyy* a sense other than that which it habitually expresses in the Ḳurʾān (cf. XVII, 28 and XL, 55, parallels to XX, 130 or XLVIII, 9, etc.), would be arbitrary. On the other hand, the last section of the phrase does indeed seem to designate an additional time of prayer, the novelty of which is perceptible in II, 238: "Be steadfast in your prayers, in the median prayer as well (*wa 'l-ṣalāti 'l-wusṭā*)...".

The years following the changing of the *ḳibla* see the consolidation of the institutional nature of prayer. Then, as noted above, the link between ritual prayer and the communal tax becomes a great deal tighter (LXXIII, 20, etc.). In IV, 103, a degree of organisation emerges: "Ritual prayer is enjoined upon believers at fixed times". Finally, in XXIV, 58, on both sides of the middle of the day (cf. II, 238, quoted above), there are named incidentally "the prayer of the dawn (*fadjr*)" and the *ṣalāt al-ʿishāʾ*.

In the Ḳurʾān as a whole, the times of prayer are indicated with a richness of vocabulary which shows a practice still at the evolutionary stage. There are, it seems, three essential times (to which the median prayer is added somewhat later).

(a) At one of the "two extremities of the day" (XI, 114; cf. XX, 130), is the dawn prayer, *fadjr*, also called, with slight nuances, by a number of names: *bukra, ibkār, ghuduww* and *ghadāt*, as well as "before the rising of the sun" and "when you are in the morning".

(b) At the other extremity, is the decline of the day, *ʿashiyy*, in other words the second part of the afternoon, in particular its final phase, *aṣīl*, pl. *āṣāl*, to which apparently corresponds the *dulūk al-shams* of XVII, 78, as well as "before the setting of the sun" and "when you are in the evening".

(c) The nocturnal prayer is denoted by the verb *tahadjdjad* (*hapax* in XVII, 79) and by expressions such as *ānāʾ al-layl* or *zulaf min al-layl*. LXXIII, 20, recommends moderation in long vigils of prayer, and the explicit inauguration of the *ṣalāt al-ʿishāʾ* could be ascribed to the same purpose.

Alongside this daily division, prayer is subject to another temporal determination, this time in the weekly context. This is the Friday prayer, mentioned in a single passage of the Ḳurʾān: "O you who believe! When you are called to ritual prayer on the day of assembly, come quickly to the remembrance of God, leave your business" (LXII, 9; see DJUMʿA).

E. Conditions and characteristics of *ṣalāt*. A public call to prayer, expressed by the verb *nādā*, is mentioned twice (V, 58; LXII, 9). The necessity of ritual purification before prayer is indicated in a detailed fashion in IV, 43, and V, 6, which both authorise *tayammum*, this being the use of fine sand instead of water in the absence of the latter. Ritual prayer must be performed facing in a precise and constant direction. This direction is that of *al-masdjid al-ḥarām*, i.e. the Kaʿba of Mecca. This is stated three times, most emphatically, in II, 142-50. This outstanding passage, which can be dated with certainty in the year 2/624 (probably in the middle of the month of Shaʿbān, corresponding to mid-February, but possibly a month earlier, in Radjab), does not confine itself to instituting the *ḳibla*. It enjoins upon the believers the abandonment of a former *ḳibla*, which according to all extra-Ḳurʾānic evidence was the direction of Jerusalem (almost the opposite in fact, for Muslims then living in Medina). A problem remains: what was the *ḳibla* before the Hidjra? It was definitely the direction of Jerusalem, but: (1) the Prophet had probably approved it for the Anṣār of Yathrib two years before emigrating to there (cf. al-Ṭabarī, *Djāmiʿ*, ii, 4, 5, 12); but he did not adopt it himself until later, if the account of al-Barāʾ b. Maʿrūr is to be believed (cf. Ibn Hishām, 294; al-Ṭabarī, i, 1218-19); (2) the former practice of Muḥammad in the city of his birth remains uncertain. On these questions, see ḲIBLA.

Whatever the case may be, ritual prayer is animated in its entirety by two internal movements, glorification (*tasbīḥ*) and praise (cf. ḤAMDALA; and see XX, 130; XXXIII, 42; XL, 55; L, 39-40, etc.). Appeal for pardon is sometimes included here (XL, 55; cf. III, 17; VII, 204). These sentiments are inseparable from contrasting physical attitudes: standing upright and prostration (cf. II, 238; IV, 102; L, 39-40, etc.; in addition, for nocturnal prayer, XXV, 64; XXXIX, 9). The technical term *rakʿa* is absent from the Ḳurʾān, but bowing is often expressed by the corresponding verb, normally in association with prostration (V, 55; IX, 112; XLVIII, 29); however, it is not clear that these prostrations form part of *ṣalāt* (cf., in addition, II, 43; III, 43; XXII, 26 and 77). On the other hand, public reading of the Ḳurʾān is a manifest and vital element of it (VII, 204-6; XVII, 78; XVIII, 27-8; XXXIX, 45; XXXV, 29; LXXIII, 20, etc.).

II. *In* ḥadīth *and legal elaborations.*

The two principal Sunnī canonical collections of prophetic traditions both begin with *ḥadīth*s on the five pillars of Islam. After the affirmation of faith, they therefore deal with ritual prayer. Among the *ʿibādāt*, it is this which occupies by far the greatest amount of space in their work: 200 pages in the work of al-Bukhārī, and more than double this in Muslim's. This vast quantity of material is organised by both in a series of "books" (*kitāb*), which form three major blocks. First is the *sine qua non* condition of ritual prayer, this being legal purity (*ṭahāra*): to which correspond in al-Bukhārī's case books of ablution [see WUḌŪʾ], of general washing [see GHUSL], of menstruation [see ḤAYḌ], of washing with fine sand [see TAYAMMUM]. Then come traditions which determine general aspects and elements of *ṣalāt*. Finally, numerous books examine particular cases, such as the prayer of major festivals or that of funerals. This general organisation is not peculiar to the two *Ṣaḥīḥ*s but also belongs, with minor variations, to the other four canonical collections.

In the 3rd/9th century, when all these works were compiled, the time-table and conduct of prayers were fixed. Their detailed rules will be presented below in section III. They were liable to vary all the less in that judicial consideration of these fundamental matters had also, by this stage, been basically concluded. It was, in fact, the 2nd/8th century which saw the activity of the scholars who gave their names to the four great schools or *madhāhib* of Sunnī Islam. This article will seek neither to show the quite modest differences which divide them on the subject of *ṣalawāt* nor to determine their relationship to the traditions and to the traditionists. Considering from a broad perspective the ritualistic doctrine and practice which were then crystallised, our intention is merely to underline a number of principles which govern Muslim prayer and various aspects of its practice.

A. General principles of prayer.

1. *Perfected institutionalisation.* The *ṣalāt* of the traditions is entirely ritual, and linked to five times of the day. This divine determination is presented in two different manners. On the one hand, *ḥadīth*s related by Anas b. Mālik (sometimes quoting Abū Dharr, sometimes Mālik b. Ṣaʿṣaʿa) describe an ascension of the Prophet into the heavens, where he ultimately receives from God Himself, after some haggling, the prescription of five daily prayers for his community (al-Bukhārī, *Ṣalāt, bāb* 1 and *Manāḳib al-Anṣār, bāb* 42; Muslim, *Īmān*, nos. 259, 263, 264). On the other hand, Ibn Shihāb al-Zuhrī records a *ḥadīth* related by Abū Masʿūd al-Anṣārī according to which Gabriel descends five times to Muḥammad to induce him to pray, implicitly at the prescribed times (al-Bukhārī, *Mawāḳit, bāb* 1; Muslim, *Masādjid*, nos. 166-7).

2. *Obligatory nature.* The five prayers are obligatory every day for each Muslim man or woman who is past the age of puberty and of sound mind.

3. *The direction of prayer.* In all the ritual prayers, turning towards the Kaʿba is strictly obligatory; see ḲIBLA.

4. *Use of the Arabic language.* This is a very firm doctrine in the majority of the schools (see e.g. al-Suyūṭī, *al-Itḳān, nawʿ* 35, Beirut 1407/1987, i, 340-1). As regards the recitation of the *Fātiḥa* by a Muslim incapable of saying it in Arabic, the Ḥanafīs have, however, authorised the use of other languages. For discussions of this issue in Turkey and in Egypt in the 20th century, see ḲURʾĀN, i.

5. *The call to prayer.* Each of the five daily prayers is announced by the voice of the muezzin. This call to the Community (mentioned in the Ḳurʾān, as noted above) was established at Medina. Each prayer is preceded by two calls, separated by an interval of time; the first is the *adhān*, the second the *iḳāma* [*q.vv.*].

6. *The* rakʿa. This word denotes an invariable sequence of bodily positions and movements, accompanied by words, which belongs to the substance of *ṣalāt*. In every ritual prayer (with the exception of the prayer over the dead), the *rakʿa* is performed at least twice in succession. The practice of the *rakʿa* is described below, in section III, B.

7. *Importance of communal prayer.* Numerous traditions stress the excellence of the "prayer of the congregation" (*ṣalāt al-djamāʿa*). Two of them are particularly famous. On the one hand, "The prayer which a man performs in congregation is worth twenty-five of his prayers in his home or in the market-place" (al-Bukhārī, *Adhān, bābs* 30, 31, and *Ṣalāt, bāb* 87; Muslim, *Masādjid*, nos. 245-8, etc.). On the other, the Prophet contemplated personally burning down the houses of those who were not present at the prayer of the congregation (al-Bukhārī, *Adhān, bābs* 29, 34; Muslim, *Masādjid*, nos. 251-4, etc.). The call to ritual prayer demonstrates its communal nature. The latter is emphasised by the liturgical *Āmīn* added to the *Fātiḥa* (cf. al-Bukhārī, *Adhān, bābs* 111-13; Muslim, *Ṣalāt*, nos. 72-6), as by the invocation "To you be praise, our Lord!", said in response to the *imām*'s utterance "God hears him who praises Him" (see below, section III, B, third element of the *rakʿa*), and, furthermore, by the final salutations of the *imām* and of the other faithful. The obligation to participate in collective prayer is more strongly asserted by the Mālikīs (al-Malaṭāwī, 166-7) than by the Ḥanafīs (al-Ghāwidjī, 132 ff.). The participation of women is permitted, but not recommended. The favoured place for communal prayer is clearly the mosque: see MASDJID, i, C, 2.

8. *The* imām. For communal prayer to take place, two adults must be present, one of whom is the *imām* of the other. The *imām* is the *sine qua non* condition of congregational prayer. Numerous prophetic traditions determine his function. They are conveniently listed by Muslim, *Ṣalāt*, nos. 77-101, and by al-Bukhārī, *Ṣalāt, bābs* 43 ff. The *imām* must be male, of good reputation, educated. As a general rule, the faithful place themselves in ranks (*ṣufūf* [see ṢAFF]) behind the *imām*, perform the ritual gestures with him, and repeat his words. If there is only one man with the *imām*, he places himself to his right; if there are two or more, they place themselves behind him. Women always place themselves behind the men; if there is only one woman with the *imām*, she places herself behind him.

9. *The* djahr. In Ḳurʾān XVII, 110, the text reads "Do not raise your voice in your prayer, and do not pray in a whisper, but seek a way between the two." On the basis of a *khabar* of Ibn ʿAbbās, the commentators see in this a measure of caution in the face of Meccan unbelievers (cf. e.g. al-Rāzī, xxi, 70; al-

Ḳurṭubī, x, 343). But traditions show that Muḥammad, at Medina, said certain prayers in a loud voice (d̲j̲ahr) and others in a whisper (cf. al-Buk̲h̲ārī, Ad̲h̲ān, bābs 96, 97, 99, 100, 105, 108, etc.). From this it has been concluded that the Ḳurʾānic verse was calling, not for a happy medium, but for an alternation of the two styles. As a result, the imām is obliged to declaim in a loud voice the first two rakʿas of specific prayers, and in a whisper the other contingent rakʿas of these prayers and all the rakʿas of the other prayers (cf. al-Ghāwad̲j̲ī, 128-9; al-Malaṭāwī, 136-7).

10. The ṭumaʾnīna. Prayer must be performed soberly and calmly, with close attention to the rhythm as it unfolds. A tradition shows the Prophet making a worshipper who had neglected this principle start again three times (al-Buk̲h̲ārī, Ad̲h̲ān, bābs 95, 122; Muslim, Ṣalāt, no. 45). All the authors make this one of the fundamental requirements of ritual prayer (cf. Ibn ʿAbd al-Wahhāb, 31, 36; al-Ghāwid̲j̲ī, 127-8; al-Malaṭāwī, 135).

B. Various aspects. Anyone who has inadvertently omitted or misplaced one of the elements of the prayer and becomes aware of this before the end of the latter is obliged to perform or recast this element and furthermore, at the end of his prayer, to add immediately the "prayer of negligence" (ṣalāt al-sahw). This consists of performing two prostrations with their takbīr, then sitting for the tas̲h̲ahhud and the final salutation. This practice is blended with divergencies imposed by the different schools, and there are also elaborate subtleties according to the judicial qualification of the elements neglected, according to whether the negligence is or is not the act of an imām whose direction has been followed since the beginning or otherwise of the prayer, according to the certainty or simple doubt of the worshipper with regard to his own negligence, according also to faults which can include the performance of the "prayer of negligence" itself. See al-Ghāwid̲j̲ī, 236-41; al-Malaṭāwī, 159-63. It may be noted in passing that the worshipper can quite easily make a mistake over the number and the nature of the rakʿas which he has already performed especially if he adds supererogatory prayers at the beginning or at the end of a canonical prayer.

It should be stated that the issue of negligence is part of a corpus of traditional and judicial specifications. There is an abundance of minute regulations concerning the words and especially the gestures of prayer, the clothing and shoes to be worn for it, the behaviour to be followed, the place where it is to be performed and the ritual purity which is to be observed. Also worthy of note is the interesting notion of sutra [q.v.]. This word, which initially denotes a veil or a screen, is the technical term for any object placed by the worshipper some distance before him, in front of which no person should pass while the prayer is being performed.

The legislation regarding prayer is not devoid of flexibility. Traditions show Muḥammad as concerned to alleviate as far as possible the rigours of observance. Thus he shortened the prayer on one occasion, when a child began to cry in the congregation, appreciating the mother's distress (al-Buk̲h̲ārī, Ad̲h̲ān, bāb 65; Muslim, Ṣalāt, nos. 191, 192). Similarly, he was vehemently opposed to excessively long Ḳurʾānic readings during the ritual prayer and was concerned that people should not consider themselves obliged to imitate his own personal devotions (al-Buk̲h̲ārī, Ad̲h̲ān, bābs 60-4, 80-1; Muslim, Ṣalāt, nos. 182-90).

This flexibility is also in evidence on other occasions: cancellation of communal prayer when the weather is especially inclement, delay of the prayer of ẓuhr at times of excessive heat, and then the combination (d̲j̲amʿ) of the latter with the prayer of ʿaṣr, as also sometimes happens with the two prayers of mag̲h̲rib and of ʿis̲h̲āʾ. This amenity of combining the abovementioned prayers is especially accorded to one who is travelling in haste. Later jurisprudence (or indeed casuistry) did not omit to solve the particular difficulties (notably regarding orientation towards the ḳibla, and regarding the execution of the required gestures) encountered by the traveller (cf. below, section IV. F) and the invalid.

Having presented, in the first two sections of this article, the evolution and the fundamentals of ritual prayer in Islam, the next stage is to illustrate the long-established rules of ṣalāt.

III. The five daily prayers.

A. Distinctive characteristics of each. The five prayers differ from one another in terms of the vocal force with which they should be uttered, but most of all in terms of the time fixed for each and of its length.

1. The prayer of the morning (ṣubḥ) or of the dawn (fad̲j̲r) is of two rakʿas. Here the Fātiḥa and the Ḳurʾān are recited in a loud voice (d̲j̲ahr). Its time begins with "the true dawn" (al-fad̲j̲r al-ṣādiḳ), when faces can still not yet be recognised, and extends until the day-break as such, before the sun appears.

2. The prayer of midday (ẓuhr) is of four rakʿas. Here the Fātiḥa and the Ḳurʾān are recited in a whisper (isrār). Its time begins when the sun, passing the zenith, commences its decline. It normally continues until the time when the shadow of objects is equal to their height.

3. The prayer of ʿaṣr (middle and late afternoon) is of four rakʿas. Here the Fātiḥa and the Ḳurʾān are recited in a whisper. Its time begins when the shadow of objects is equal to their height, and it normally continues until the time when the light of the sun turns yellow; but this prayer may still be performed until the end of the day, before the setting of the sun.

4. The prayer of mag̲h̲rib (after the setting of the sun) is of three rakʿas. Here the Fātiḥa and the Ḳurʾān are recited in a loud voice. Its time begins when the sun has disappeared beneath the horizon, and normally continues until the disappearance of the twilight radiance or s̲h̲afaḳ [q.v.]. (Concerning the ancient Judaising deviation of Abu 'l-K̲h̲aṭṭāb, for whom the time of this prayer would begin only when the stars shine brightly, see Wasserstrom's article, in Bibl.).

5. The prayer of ʿis̲h̲āʾ (evening or beginning of the night), sometimes called ʿatama (black night), is of four rakʿas. Here the Fātiḥ and the Ḳurʾān are recited in a loud voice. Numerous traditions clearly fix the commencement of its time (e.g. al-Buk̲h̲ārī, Mawāḳīt, bāb 24, 1, repeated in Ad̲h̲ān, bāb 162, 1; al-Buk̲h̲ārī, ʿUmra, bāb 20, 1, parallel to D̲j̲ihād, bāb 136, 2, and to Muslim, Musāfirīn, no. 43; Muslim, Musāfirīn, no. 48): it is the disappearance of the s̲h̲afaḳ, that redness of the sky which follows the setting of the sun (cf. L ʿA, x, 180a; the opinion of Abū Ḥanīfa, who interpreted this s̲h̲afaḳ as the whiteness of the twilight coming after the redness of the sunset, seems to be isolated). It should be recalled that, in the Ḳurʾān, the word only occurs once, without connection with prayer and in an oath (LXXXIV, 16; cf. the commentaries of al-Ṭabarī, xxx, 119, and al-Rāzī, xxxi, 108-9). As for the symmetrically converse phenomenon in the circadian cycle, i.e. the column of zodiacal light called in Arabic al-fad̲j̲r al-kād̲h̲ib "the false dawn" (or d̲h̲anab al-sirḥān "the wolf's tail": cf. L ʿA, s.v. f-d̲j̲-r, at v, 45a),

the Muslims astronomers have made a detailed study of it which is of no relevance to this article. The normal time of the prayer of *ʿis͟hāʾ* extends until the end of the first third of the night.

For more details concerning the times of prayer, with references to *ḥadīt͟h*, see MĪḲĀT.

B. Conditions and development of prayer. The conditions (*s͟hurūṭ*) of prayer are nine in number according to Ibn ʿAbd al-Wahhāb (*al-Uṣūl*, 26-30): 1. Being a Muslim; 2. Mental health; 3. Discernment, i.e. the age of reason (seven years); 4. and 5. Ritual purity [see ṬAHĀRA and this article, above, section II]. This is attained on the one hand by *wuḍūʾ* or by *g͟husl*, which respectively annul the minor *ḥadat͟h* and the major *ḥadat͟h* (or *d̲j̲anāba*): this is the *ṭahāra ḥukmiyya*, "prescribed". On the other hand purity demands the elimination of any blemish (*k͟habat͟h*) from the body, the clothing and the place: this is the *ṭahāra ḥaḳīḳiyya*, "real". It is impossible to emphasise too much the considerable importance and the minute precision of the corresponding requirements; see also NAD̲J̲IS ("impure"); 6. Covering the pudenda in the sense intended by the law; 7. Being present at the time of the corresponding prayer; 8. Being turned in the direction of the *ḳibla*; 9. Formulating the intention (*niyya*) of performing the precise prayer which is about to be undertaken. These conditions are explicitly or implicitly common to all the judicial schools. On the other hand, the schools differ on a number of points regarding the bodily positions or the words or, indeed, the judicial nature of the obligation attached to such-and-such an element. Some of these details will be mentioned below. They do not affect the fundamental pattern of prayer, which is as follows.

The rite begins with sacralisation. First, the hands are raised above the shoulders, to the level of the ears, and the words *Allāhu akbar* "God is most great!" (cf. Ḳurʾān VI, 78) are said. This is the *takbīrat al-iḥrām*. The hands are then placed on the base of the chest, the right hand over the left: the position of *ḳabḍ* (cf. al-G͟hāwid̲j̲ī, 136 ff.). The Imāmīs and, classically, the Mālikīs, on the other hand, let the arms fall at this point: the position of *sadl* or *irsāl* (cf. al-Malaṭāwī, 137, 139-40; however, he considers as permitted the position of *ḳabḍ*, which is spreading in the Mag͟hrib under the influence of the Salafiyya [*q.v.*]).

The majority of Sunnīs add here an opening prayer (*duʿāʾ al-istiftāḥ*) as follows: *subḥānaka Allāhumma wa-bi-ḥamdika wa-tabāraka smuka wa-taʿālā d̲j̲adduka wa-lā ilāha g͟hayruka* "Glory to You, O God, and praise to You! Let Your name be blessed, exalted Your greatness! There is no other god but You!" (On other possible formulas, in particular the S͟hāfiʿī formula, see al-Ḳurṭubī, vii, 153-4; al-D̲j̲azāʾirī, 255-6).

And directly thereafter (except in the case of the Mālikīs), *aʿūd͟hu bi'l-Lāh min al-S͟hayṭān al-rad̲j̲īm* "I take refuge in God against the reprobate Demon".

Then begins the first *rakʿa*. This term ("an inclination") denotes an invariable series of attitudes and formulae which constitute an element to be repeated a set number of times in the course of a completed ritual prayer, which develops as follows:

1. Standing upright. Recitation of the Ḳurʾān (*ḳirāʾa*). Hands and arms are, as above, in the position of *ḳabḍ* or of *sadl* according to schools. First to be recited, with each *rakʿa*, is the *Fātiḥa*, to which the response *Āmīn* is added. Then, in the first two *rakʿas* only, another Ḳurʾānic passage is spoken. This is normally longer with the first *rakʿa* but shorter with the second. Brief sūras such as *al-Naṣr* (CX) or *al-Ik͟hlāṣ* (CXII) may be considered sufficient. The minimum requirement is three short verses or one long verse.

2. The worshipper says *Allāhu akbar*, then leans at a right-angle (*rukūʿ*), the hands placed on the knees, and says three times, *subḥāna rabbiya 'l-ʿaẓīm* "Glory to my Lord, the Great One".

3. The worshipper draws himself up (*iʿtidāl* or *rafʿ*), saying *samiʿa 'Llāhu li-man ḥamidahu* "God hears him who praises Him". Upright, he adds *Rabbanā, wa-laka 'l-ḥamd* "To You be praise, our Lord!" (cf. al-Buk͟hārī, *Ad͟hān, bāb* 82, and 128, 2; Muslim, *Ṣalāt*, nos. 28, 62, 77), or *Allāhumma, Rabbanā, laka 'l-ḥamd* "O God, our Lord, to You be praise!" (cf. al-Buk͟hārī, *Ad͟hān, bāb* 125; Muslim, *Ṣalāt*, nos. 86-9; al-G͟hāwid̲j̲ī, 145).

4. The worshipper prostrates himself (*sud̲j̲ūd*), saying *Allāhu akbar*, then says three times *Subḥāna rabbiya 'l-aʿlā* "Glory to my Lord, the Most High!" The body should then rest on the forehead (and the nose), the palms of both hands, both knees and both feet.

5. The worshipper raises his head to say *Allāhu akbar*, then he sits on his heels (*d̲j̲ulūs* or *ḳuʿūd*), knees on the ground, hands placed on the thighs. Then he says *Rabbi g͟hfir lī* "O my Lord, pardon me!"

6. The worshipper prostrates himself a second time, saying *Allāhu akbar*, then he says three times *Subḥāna rabbiya 'l-aʿlā* "Glory to my Lord, the Most High!" The Ḥanbalīs (cf. al-Mardāwī, 48) and the S͟hāfiʿīs return subsequently to a sitting position: this is the *d̲j̲alsat al-istirāḥa*, a practice which is now widespread among the Mālikīs.

He then stands upright for the second *rakʿa*, identical to the first.

At the end of this second *rakʿa*, instead of standing upright, the worshipper raises his head to say *Allāhu akbar*, then sits on his heels, knees on the ground, hands placed on the thighs. The *tas͟hahhud* "affirmation of faith", is then said, as follows: *al-taḥiyyāt li-Lāh, wa 'l-ṣalawāt wa 'l-ṭayyibāt. Al-salāmu ʿalayka, ayyuhā 'l-nabī, wa-raḥmatu Llāhi wa-barakātuh. Al-salāmu ʿalaynā wa-ʿalā ʿibādi Llāhi 'l-ṣāliḥīn. As͟hhadu an lā ilāha illā Llāhu waḥdahu lā s͟harīka lahu wa-as͟hhadu anna Muḥammadan ʿabduhu wa-rasūluhu* "To God be salutations, prayers and fine words. Peace be upon you, O Prophet, also the mercy and blessings of God. Peace be upon us and upon the good servants of God. I affirm that there is no god other than God, He alone, who has no partner; and I affirm that Muḥammad is His servant and His Messenger". At the beginning of this last phrase, the index finger of the right hand is raised to underline the declaration of Uniqueness. The *tas͟hahhud* above is the version given in al-Buk͟hārī, *Ad͟hān, bābs* 148, 150 (cf. Muslim, *Ṣalāt*, no. 55). The beginning of the formula differs slightly among the Mālikīs (cf. al-Malaṭāwī, 147).

After the *tas͟hahhud*, the worshipper stands up to say, as above, the third and the fourth *rakʿas*.

At the end of the latter, the *tas͟hahhud* is recited again, with the following addition: *Allāhumma ṣalli ʿalā Muḥammadin wa-ʿalā āli Muḥammadin kamā ṣallayta ʿalā Ibrāhīma wa-ʿalā āli Ibrāhīm, wa-bārik ʿalā Muḥammadin wa-ʿalā āli Muḥammadin kamā bārakta ʿalā Ibrāhīma wa-ʿalā āli Ibrāhīma fi 'l-ʿālamīn, innaka ḥamīdun mad̲j̲īd* "O God, bless Muḥammad and the family of Muḥammad as You blessed Abraham and the family of Abraham, and bless Muḥammad and the family of Muḥammad as You blessed Abraham and the family of Abraham in the worlds. You are worthy of praise and of glory!" This formula (called *al-ṣalawāt al-ibrāhīmiyya*) is inspired in part by Ḳurʾān, XXXIII, 56, and XI, 73, and is found in this form in al-Buk͟hārī, *Anbiyāʾ, bāb* 10, 5; Muslim, *Ṣalāt*, nos 65-6 (cf. also al-Malaṭāwī, 148-9; Ibn ʿAbd al-Wahhāb, 38-9; al-G͟hāwid̲j̲ī, 142).

Finally, still sitting, the worshipper turns to the right, saying *al-salāmu ʿalaykum wa-raḥmatu Llāhi wa-barakātuhu* "Peace be upon you, with the mercy and the blessings of God!" (only the first two Arabic words are strictly obligatory). Then he turns to the left, repeating these words. These two *taslīma*s terminate the prayer through the desacralisation (*taḥlīl*) of the one who has performed it. (In communal prayer, the *imām* makes only one salutation.)

The preceding pattern corresponds to the very frequent case of a prayer in four *rakʿa*s. If the prayer has only three *rakʿa*s, what would follow the fourth is done at the end of the third. If the prayer has only two *rakʿa*s, the second is followed immediately by the *tas̲h̲ahhud*, the "Abrahamic" prayer and the final salutation.

C. Actual practice. Having just described the performance of this ritual prayer, having earlier outlined the other rules regulating it, it would now be appropriate to examine how it is practised in reality. Certain countries, such as Egypt, are more observant in this regard than others, as is easily ascertained. But precise studies seem to be lacking on this subject. Such studies could, according to countries or regions, identify the practice of *ṣalāt* by men and women, individually or communally, for the daily prayers and for the Friday prayer, and enquire, naturally, into the contingent effects of urbanisation, of change of social class, of emigration to a country with a non-Muslim majority.

IV. *The other ritual prayers.*

These are, like the preceding, prayers codified by *fiḳh* and comprising the performance of a fixed number of *rakʿa*s. Numerous and varied, they are generally classified by the jurists according to their degree of obligation, which can vary according to the schools (*farḍ, wād̲j̲ib, sunna*). Principal aspects will be presented here in the following order: (1) The major community prayers which mark the week and the year (A and B); (2) The daily prayers which are not strictly obligatory, i.e. which do not form part of the *farāʾiḍ* (C, D, E); (3) Prayers which are performed in particular (F) or exceptional (G, H, I) circumstances; and (4) Finally, the prayer over a deceased person (J).

A. The Friday prayer (*ṣalāt al-d̲j̲umʿa*). The second Arabic word, which now denotes the above-named day of the week, initially signifies "meeting, assembly". It is in this sense that it is found (in the form *al-d̲j̲umuʿa*) in Ḳurʾān, LXII, 9. Before Islam, as is shown in D̲J̲UMʿA, the *yawm al-d̲j̲umuʿa* was nothing other than a market-day. It was usually known by another name, *yawm al-ʿarūba* or, without the article, *yawm ʿarūba* (see *LʿA*, s.v. *ʿ-r-b*, i, 593; al-Zamak̲h̲s̲h̲arī, *Kas̲h̲s̲h̲āf*, on LXII, 9, and al-Ḳurṭubī, xviii, 97: according to a *k̲h̲abar* of these two commentators, the first to have given this gathering the name of *d̲j̲umʿa*, was allegedly Kaʿb b. Luʾayy, an ancestor of Muḥammad, who lived some 150 years before him).

The Friday prayer is performed at the time of the midday prayer, which it replaces. It must take place in a mosque. It is only obligatory in substantial localities, and with the participation of a minimum number of men who are permanent residents, this number being (including the *imām*) four according to the Ḥanafīs, twelve according to the Mālikīs, and forty according to the S̲h̲āfiʿīs and the Ḥanbalīs. Women may participate, but it is not compulsory for them, and they are not included in the required number. (See B.A.B. Badrān, *al-ʿIbādāt al-islāmiyya. Muḳārana ʿalā 'l-mad̲h̲āhib al-arbaʿa*, Alexandria 1969, 95-6; al-G̲h̲āwid̲j̲ī, 160-5; al-Malaṭāwī, 184-5).

It is customary that the Muslim arriving at the mosque for this communal prayer first performs individually a prayer of two *rakʿa*s. After the call to prayer, the preacher, standing upright on the *minbar* [*q.v.*], delivers a double sermon [see K̲H̲UṬBA]. Both praise God and call for His blessings on the Prophet, before exhorting the believers. The two sermons are separated by a short pause, during which the orator sits. Subsequently, he normally leads personally an obligatory prayer of two *rakʿa*s, in a loud voice.

B. The prayer of the two feasts (*ṣalāt al-ʿīdayn*). See ʿĪD. The two feasts are that of the breaking of fast and that of sacrifices. The special prayer, in a very festive ambience, is of two *rakʿa*s, in a loud voice. Its time begins approximately half an hour after the rising of the sun, and concludes when it is at the middle of its course. There is neither *ad̲h̲ān* nor *iḳāma*. But numerous *takbīrāt* are added, their number and place varying slightly according to the judicial schools. At the first *rakʿa*, the sūra *al-Aʿlā* (LXXXVII) is usually read. The prayer is not preceded, but followed by a double *k̲h̲uṭba* performed like that of Friday and relating to the cultic duties of the feast being celebrated, as well as their religious significance. Although women are not obliged to do so, they are strongly advised to attend, even in a state of ritual impurity (in which case they are present for the prayer without performing it), in order to share in the communal joy and edification; cf. e.g. al-Buk̲h̲ārī, *ʿĪdayn*, *bāb*s 15, 21; Muslim, *ʿĪdayn*, nos. 10-12. In Jomier, 45-50, a detailed description is found of the prayer of the feast of sacrifices performed in Cairo in 1379/1960.

C. The *ṣalāt al-witr*. According to the Ḥanafīs, it is a duty (*wād̲j̲ib*) without being an obligation (*farḍ*) in the sense which they give to this word. But for the other schools, it is only a custom (*sunna*), albeit a particularly strong one (*muʾakkada*). The *ṣalāt al-witr* should be performed between the evening prayer and the dawn prayer (preferably towards the end of the night). For its history, see WITR. The term signifies "uneven" and denotes a special *rakʿa* which is performed in isolation or which is added to one or more pairs (*s̲h̲afʿ*) of *rakʿa*s. It is forbidden to perform other *rakʿa*s between this latter *rakʿa* and the canonical prayer of the dawn. The prayer of *witr* is generally of three *rakʿa*s; there are read, respectively, after the *Fātiḥa*, the sūras CXII to CXIV according to the Mālikī al-Malaṭāwī, 196, or LXXXVII (*al-Aʿlā*), CIX (*al-Kāfirūn*) and CXII (*al-Ik̲h̲lāṣ*) according to the Ḥanafī al-G̲h̲āwid̲j̲ī, 188. With the prayer of *witr* the question of *ḳunūt* is associated. In the article ḲUNŪT the various senses of this word in the Ḳurʾān and in tradition are set forth. The Mālikīs deny that there is a *ḳunūt* in the prayer of *witr* (al-Malaṭāwī, 196). The S̲h̲āfiʿīs use a formula transmitted by al-Tirmid̲h̲ī, the translation of which is to be found above, vol. V, 395. The Ḥanafīs (al-G̲h̲āwid̲j̲ī, 188-9) consider as a duty, after the performing of the third *rakʿa*, a *duʿāʾ al-ḳunūt* which begins with *Allāhumma, innā nastaʿīnuka wa-nastahdīka*. The translation is as follows: "O God! we ask for Your aid and Your guidance. We implore Your pardon and return to You. We believe in You, we submit ourselves to You, we praise You for all Your goodness. We are grateful for Your [favours] and not ungrateful, we reject and abandon those who are unfaithful to You. O God! it is You that we worship, to You that our prayers and our prostrations go towards You that we return with promptitude. We hope for Your mercy and fear Your anger: for Your severe punishment cannot fail to overtake the unbelievers. May the blessings and the peace of God be upon our master Muḥammad, and upon his Fami ly and his Companions!" This text, in a slightly shorter form, is found in Abū Dāwūd (*Marāsīl, bāb mā dj̲āʾa fī-man nāma ʿan al-ṣalāt*, 12-13), according to whom it was reportedly taught to Muḥammad by Dj̲ibrīl himself. As for the Imāmīs, on the contrary, for them the *ḳunūt* is a personal prayer of intercession (*duʿāʾ*), optional and meritorious, which is definitely said during the *witr*, but which is also said in each of the five daily prayers, while standing, between the Ḳurʾānic reading of the second *rakʿa* and the inclination which follows. This S̲h̲īʿī *ḳunūt* is of free content, but certain formulas are frequently used, in particular, the prayer mentioned in Ḳurʾān, II, 201.

D. The nocturnal prayer. See TAHADJ̲DJ̲UD and, for the prayers specific to the nights of Ramaḍān, TARĀWĪḤ.

E. Other supererogatory prayers (*nawāfil*). These are in particular groups of two or four *rakʿas*, the performance of which is recommended, according to the circumstances, before or after one or other of the five obligatory prayers (cf. al-G̲h̲āwidj̲ī, 204 ff.; al-Malaṭāwī, 157-8). But it is also possible, for example, to perform the prayer of the morning (*ṣalāt al-ḍuḥā*), of two *rakʿas* at least; its time begins approximately half an hour after the sunrise, and continues until midday (like the prayer of the two feasts).

F. Prayer on a journey (*ṣalāt al-musāfir*). The text reads in Ḳurʾān, IV, 101, "And when you are travelling through the land, it is no sin for you to shorten your prayer if you fear lest the unbelievers put you to the test; the unbelievers are for you a declared enemy" (cf. al-Rāzī, xi, 16-23; al-Ḳurṭubī, v, 351-62). This verse has been clarified, and its import extended to all journeys, by prophetic traditions, two in particular (Muslim, *Musāfirīn*, nos. 4, 8). The outcome of later elaborations is that the canonical prayers of *ẓuhr, ʿaṣr* and *ʿis̲h̲āʾ* are reduced to two *rakʿas* (instead of four) during every lawful journey of more than approximately 80 km/50 miles (sixteen parasangs for the Mālikīs and S̲h̲āfiʿīs, three days' walking for the Ḥanafīs). The journey is regarded as continuous unless it is broken by a halt of 15 days, according to the Ḥanafīs (al-G̲h̲āwidj̲ī, 27), or four full days according to the other schools (al-Ḳurṭubī, v, 357; al-Malaṭāwī, 179-80). The distance alone is taken into consideration, whatever the means of transport, and thus the duration of the effective displacement. Unlike the other schools, the Ḥanafīs regard the above-mentioned abridgement, not as something permitted but as a duty (*wādj̲ib*); as a result of this, in the case of error on the part of the believer in the course of the prayer, or if he performs it behind an *imām* who is not himself travelling, precise judicial consequences ensue. The prayers of *ṣubḥ* and of *mag̲h̲rib* remain unchanged.

G. The prayer of fear. See ṢALĀT AL-K̲H̲AWF.

H. The prayer appealing for rain (*ṣalāt al-istisḳāʾ*). This is a communal prayer, the time of which is the same as for the two feasts (above, B). But it takes place in an atmosphere of penitence and of supplication, in ordinary clothing and in the open air. Two *rakʿas* are performed. At the beginning of each, the *imām* appeals at length for the pardon of God. He then delivers a double *k̲h̲uṭba* (as in B above), exhorting the congregation to practise good deeds. At the end, facing the *ḳibla*, he turns his cloak inside out (a symbolic gesture, magical in origin), members of the congregation do the same, and he begs at length for the coming of rain. This ritual is based on the example of Muḥammad who, in his supplication, raised his hands high towards the sky (cf. the little "books" on *istisḳāʾ* which are located, in the two *Ṣaḥīḥs*, between the prayer of the two feasts and that of the eclipse. See also al-Malaṭāwī, 200-1; al-Ḳurṭubī, i, 418, xviii, 302, respectively on Ḳurʾān, II, 60 and LXXI, 10-11). On rogatory rites in pre-Islamic Arabia, see ISTISḲĀʾ.

I. The prayer of the eclipse (*ṣalāt al-kusūf*). It should first be noted that, in the language of *ḥadīt̲h̲*, the words *kusūf* and *k̲h̲usūf*, as well as the verbs of which they are the *maṣdars*, are employed interchangeably for the sun and for the moon. In the classical Arabic language, on the contrary, *kusūf* refers rather to the sun, while *k̲h̲usūf* is reserved for the moon (cf. *LʿA*, ix, 67a, 298). The fact remains that the two *Ṣaḥīḥs*, as well as al-Nasāʾī, devote a whole "book" to the *kusūf*. Here as elsewhere, the conduct of the Prophet has served as a model for the Community after him. In the case of eclipse of the sun or of the moon, a communal prayer of two *rakʿas* is held in the mosque. Its time is the same as that of the two feasts (see B, H). There is neither call to prayer nor *iḳāma* nor sermon. The Ḳurʾānic recitations are spoken in a whisper. The peculiarity of this prayer is that each *rakʿa* contains, after the inclination and the standing upright, which are very prolonged, a second long inclination and a second standing upright before the prostration (cf. al-Malaṭāwī, 200). See also K̲H̲USŪF.

J. The prayer over a dead person (*ṣalāt ʿalā 'l-mayyit*). It is also called *ṣalāt al-dj̲anāza* (or *dj̲ināza*). It is an obligation which is incumbent on the community (*farḍ kifāya*) and not on each individual concerned. Unlike the others, this prayer involves no performance of *rakʿa*. The *imām* stands upright facing the *ḳibla* (the body of the deceased being laid crosswise before him). The others line up in ranks behind him as for every ritual prayer. The *imām* says, in a loud voice, four *Allāhu akbars*. After the first, he gives praise to God; after the second, he says the "Abrahamic prayers" (see above, III. B, towards the end); after the third, he prays (*duʿāʾ*) for the deceased; after the fourth, he pronounces the final salutation (cf. *ibid.*). Several points need to be underlined. (1) The recitation of the *Fātiḥa* after the first *takbīra* is obligatory according to al-S̲h̲āfiʿī and Ibn Ḥanbal; it may optionally take the place of praise of God according to Ḥanafīs and Mālikīs (cf. al-Ḳurṭubī, viii, 222; al-G̲h̲āwidj̲ī, 176). (2) The *duʿāʾ* for the deceased, which is not said in a loud voice, does not have a fixed formula, but some fine traditional texts are to be found in al-Malaṭāwī, 212-13. They contain substantial variants when the deceased is a woman and in the case of a child. (3) The prayer *ʿalā 'l-mayyit* is performed only once, and normally in the presence of the corpse. However, this last condition is dispensed with, on the one hand when the body has disappeared in some natural disaster, such as a flood, or in battle, on the other hand when homage is rendered in several places to an eminent Muslim person who has recently died. (4) In reference to the Hypocrites of Medina [see AL-MUNĀFIḲŪN], it was enjoined upon Muḥammad, in Ḳurʾān, IX, 84, "Do not ever pray for one of them when he dies, and do not stand by his tomb; they have not believed in God and His Messenger, and they die in impiety". On this basis, and on that of diversely interpreted prophetic traditions, jurists have sought to determine which Muslims should be denied the ritual burial prayer. It may be recalled that the great judge of Rayy, ʿAbd al-Dj̲abbār, a Muʿtazilī but nevertheless a S̲h̲āfiʿī, refused to pray, in 385/995, over the mortal remains of the vizier Ibn ʿAbbād, on account of extortions which he had committed and for which he had shown no repentance. Al-Ḳurṭubī, viii, 221, asserts that the prayer should be performed over all

Muslims, even those guilty of serious sins, except for "heretics" and declared rebels (*ahl al-bida^c wa 'l-bug̲h̲āt*). Although suicide is denounced by Islam, the prayer should be performed over one who is guilty of this, according to al-G̲h̲āwid̲j̲ī, 180, and al-Malaṭāwī, 211, l. 8. For mortuary ablutions and the burial itself, see D̲J̲ANĀZA.

V. Ṣalāt *and Islam.*

A. The position of *ṣalāt* in relation to other religions. When Islam came into existence, and spread rapidly to the Near and Middle East, it came into contact there, besides traditional cults and gnostic sects, with four organised religions. Rabbinical Judaism, within a liturgical system which was essentially synagogical, already included three daily prayers which the believer is required to recite, even in isolation: at dawn (*s̲h̲aharit*), in the afternoon (*minḥāh*) and the evening (*arvit*). These *tefillōt* have a communal nature which is demonstrated by the use of the plural in their formulas. Syriac (or Byzantine) Christianity had structured monastic prayer in seven offices. The third religion, Manichaeism, although admittedly less actively manifest than the others, was far from being dead; it was to show itself unexpectedly active in the first two centuries of the caliphal empire. It is known that the Manichaean "hearers (*auditores*)" (as distinct from the "elect", to whom they were subordinate) were under an individual obligation to perform four prayers every day at fixed times (cf. Ibn al-Nadīm, *Fihrist*, ed. Tad̲j̲addud, 396-7, tr. Bayard Dodge, *The Fihrist of al-Nadim*, 790-1; al-S̲h̲ahrastānī, *al-Milal wa 'l-niḥal*, ed. Badrān, 629, tr. G. Monnot, *Livre des religions et des sectes*, i, 661). These ritual prayers were a sequence of prostrations, accompanied by praises to higher beings, and punctuated by return to the upright position. The formulas of adoration seem to have been impersonal, but with reference to Mani as "our Guide", in the plural (*hādīnā* in the text of the *Fihrist*). Mazdaeism, finally, imposed on each Zoroastrian the ritual of five daily prayers, to be said individually at prescribed times (cf. Mary Boyce, *Zoroastrians. Their religious beliefs and practices*, London 1979, 32-3; eadem, *Zoroastrianism*, Costa Mesa, Calif. 1992, 138-9; J. Duchesne-Guillemin, *La religion de l'Iran ancien*, Paris 1962, 76).

Five daily prayers: this is the rhythm of *ṣalāt*. It is known that Ignaz Goldziher saw here, not a simple coincidence but the result of a "Persian" influence (*Islamisme et parsisme*, in *RHR*, xliii [1901], 15, repr. in *Gesammelte Schriften*, Hildesheim 1970, iv, 246). It seems, indeed, inappropriate to attach too much importance to the number of prayers, the result of contingent evolution rather than of deliberate organisation. A comparison between religions would more usefully examine the integration of the cosmos in the prayer, or the converse, but such is not the subject of this article. Also very significant is the tonality of a rite, communal or otherwise. The value ascribed by *ḥadīt̲h̲* to prayer in assembly has been noted (cf. above, section II. A. 7), and there will be discussion below of the links woven between Muslims by their ritual prayer. However, the latter, it must alway be remembered, is fundamentally individual. Its obligation is personal. Almost all its formulas, excepting the *Fātiḥa*, are in the first person singular. The faithful, behind the *imām*, repeat the phrases which he himself has spoken in the singular and in his own name; he does not represent the congregation in any way but merely serves it as a model of correct practice. Without intermediary or intercession on the earth, the believer acts spiritually only on his own account (cf. Ḳur'ān, II, 48; VI, 164; etc.; R. Arnaldez, *L'Islam* Paris 1988, 22, 28). This general flavour was to be further accentuated by the Ṣūfīs. As far as ritual prayer is concerned, even when it is practised communally, the Muslim is alone before the One.

B. The place of *ṣalāt* in the Muslim religion. Ritual prayer is the heart of Islam. It is by means of it that the Muslim remains in permanent contact with the Ḳur'ān, from which it has been inseparable from the outset (cf. XVII, 78, etc.). Ḳur'ānic recitation is a fundamental element of all *ṣalāt*, as is prominently expressed by the recitation of the first sūra with each *rak^ca* (cf. above, section III. B. 1). It is also above all in ritual prayer that the worshipper adheres to and obeys the Muslim Law, since *ṣalāt*, which is the second pillar of Islam, includes the first, i.e. the profession of faith, explicitly contained and renewed in the call to prayer as in the *tas̲h̲ahhud*. Furthermore, the ritual prayer, of which the institutional link to *zakāt* has been observed above (cf. above, section I. C), is also intimately linked to the other two major cultic obligations, sc. fasting and the Pilgrimage. But even more than by virtue of this central situation among the *^cibādāt*, Muslim prayer owes its exceptional importance to the constant link which it establish between the faithful individual and the three supreme realities of his religious universe: the Community, the Prophet and God.

The link to the Community is first established by the marked preference for prayer performed communally (cf. above, section II. A. 7). It is remarkable that even in prayer spoken in isolation, modalities are retained which relate intrinsically to a congregational prayer: the *Āmīn* added to the *Fātiḥa* which is initially the response of the faithful to the recitation of the latter by the *imām*, and the final *taslīm*. The *Fātiḥa* itself is in the first person plural, as is a phrase of the *tas̲h̲ahhud*, "May peace be upon us and upon the good servants of God"; thus every *rak^ca* begins and concludes on a note of solidarity in the faith. But the communal nature of the prayer is expressed and realised to its ultimate extent in the mosque. "Place of prostration", zenith and epitome of the plastic and decorative arts, living museum of religious eloquence and chant, the mosque is furthermore a rich and complex institution [see MASD̲J̲ID]. Here are manifested vividly the unity and the diversity of Islam, of its tones, of its cultures. The mosque, in addition, is the setting for the great Friday prayer (cf. above, section IV. A). It is here that the local community finds and finds again its cohesion at all levels, by means of the assembly of believers, certainly, but also by virtue of the personality and the speech of the one who addresses them in the *k̲h̲uṭba*. In parallel, the Muslim community twice each year reaches a heightened awareness of its worldwide unity by the celebration of another ritual prayer, that of the two feasts (cf. above, section IV, B), both of which come at the conclusion of an intense collective process. The second, the "great feast", is in tune with the action of the pilgrims at Mecca and Minā. It is quite remarkable that, in regard to what is done there on 10 D̲h̲u 'l-Ḥid̲j̲d̲j̲a, a tradition explicitly underlines the pre-eminence of *ṣalāt* and of its *ḳibla* over ritual sacrifice (al-Buk̲h̲ārī, *Aḍāḥī*, *bāb* 12; Muslim, *Aḍāḥī*, no. 6). That which the Pilgrimage attains once per year, prayer accomplishes five times in a day. It turns the Muslim towards the centre of Islam; one can truly say that it makes the man a Muslim. Two traditions affirm this. "Between man and his association [with God], and unbelief, there is only the abandonment of ritual prayer" (Muslim, *Īmān*, no. 134); and "He who performs our ritual prayer, and turns towards our *ḳibla*, and eats animals slaughtered according to our manner, he is the Muslim" (al-Bukhārī, *Ṣalāt, bāb* 28). It is impossible to exaggerate the importance of the *ḳibla*. By turning from all quarters towards the symbolic place given by God to their Prophet, the Muslims converge, and their prayer thereby acquires, much more than by virtue of the contingent public performance of this individual rite, a communal nature. It is therefore not surprising that the simple words *ahl al-ḳibla*, meaning the people who maintain that prayer must be performed in the direction of the Kaʿba, have often been used to denote and define the members of the community (cf. Ibn Mādja, *Djanāʾiz*, 31, one of the earliest instances of this usage).

On the other hand, *ṣalāt* maintains incessantly the link between the Muslim and his Prophet. The latter is mentioned twice in the *tashahhud*, of which the second phrase is addressed directly to him. As for the prayers known as "Abrahamic" (cf. above, section III. B), they could be called Muḥammadan, since the name of Muḥammad occurs there four times, as often as that of Abraham, just before the *taslīm* of desacralisation. Thus each *ṣalāt*, like each second *rakʿa*, is concluded with veneration of the Messenger. But this is not all. It must not be forgotten that the entire content and the precise timing of the ritual prayer bear the mark of the Prophet. The Ḳurʾān, as has been seen, firmly lays down the principle of *ṣalāt* and its major characteristics. But almost all the details of its ritual, the temporal limits of its performance and the rules governing the abridgment or the combination of daily prayers as well as the performance of other ritual prayers, are based on the personal authority of the Prophet, in other words on the exemplary and inspired practice of the one of whom it is written, "In the Messenger of God, you surely have a fine model" (Ḳurʾān, XXXIII, 21; cf. al-Bukhārī, *Witr, bāb* 5; Muslim, *Musāfirīn*, no. 36). Invariably, even when no saying of Muḥammad is reported, the rule of the prayer is expressed in the words "I have seen the Prophet do thus" (al-Bukhārī, *Ṣalāt, bāb* 50; cf. *Adhān, bāb*s 95-6 etc.). In point of fact, *ṣalāt* is an imitation of Muḥammad.

However, the essence of *ṣalāt* is elsewhere. It is towards God that the Muslim turns his face (cf. Ḳurʾān, VI, 79). Hence the value of prayer. It may be asked for guidance in the making of a choice: cf. ISTIKHĀRA, and al-Ghāwidjī, 220-1 (who quotes al-Bukhārī, *Tahadjdjud, bāb* 25); the caliph al-Maʾmūn made this prayer before replying to a message of the basileus, as is related by al-Masʿūdī (*Murūdj*, vii, 5 = § 2779). Appeal may be made to it in the case of great need, in particular when recovery from an illness is sought. In any case, purification from one's sins is to be found in prayer; a well-known tradition likens prayer to a stream of water passing before the house of a man, who washes himself in it five times a day (al-Bukhārī, *Mawāḳīt, bāb* 6; Muslim, *Masādjid*, nos. 283-4). In a general manner, in charging with meaning all the gestural and verbal acts of prayer, the Muslims have merely developed the virtualities of its rite. For this purpose, they have contemplated numerous passages of the Ḳurʾān. "Say: My ritual prayer and my sacrificial offering, my life and my death, are for God, the Lord of the Worlds, who has no partner; this is the commandment which I have received, and I am the first of those who submit" (VI, 162-3); and "It is I who am God. There is no god other than Me. Therefore worship Me, and accomplish prayer in remembrance of Me" (XX, 14, addressed to Moses; cf. Isa. xliii. 11, and xlv. 5). The faithful of Islam were directed towards this spiritualisation by *ḥadīth*s such as the following, recounted by Abū Hurayra: "It is when he is in prostration that the man is closest to his Lord" (Muslim, *Ṣalāt*, no. 215). Another form of the same tradition, this time recounted by Ibn Masʿūd, is mentioned by al-Ṭabarsī/al-Tibrisī, *Madjmaʿ al-bayān*, in his commentary on a striking commandment of God to his Messenger, "Prostrate yourself and draw near!" (XCVI, 19). Mystics have specifically applied to ritual prayer the definition of *iḥsān* in the *ḥadīth* of Gabriel, "Good conduct is to worship God as if you saw Him: for you do not see Him, but He sees you" (al-Bukhārī, *Īmān, bāb* 37; Muslim, *Īmān*, no. 1). Al-Ghazālī devoted to ritual prayer the fourth volume of his interpretation of the *ʿibādāt* in the *Iḥyāʾ*. Here he insists on humility as the basis of a true prayer, and on the "presence of the heart" which must accompany it throughout. These are the same central perceptions as those shown by al-Rāzī in his commentary on Ḳurʾān, XXIX, 45: "Recite that which has been revealed to you of the Book and accomplish ritual prayer, for ritual prayer banishes lewdness and that which is denounced...". The author of the *Mafātīḥ al-ghayb* poses an analogy: "If a sweeper wore a garment of gold brocade, it would become impossible for him to concern himself with filth. Similarly, the man who performs prayer has put on the garment of religious fear (*taḳwā*), for he stands in the presence of God, the right hand placed over the left hand, in the attitude of one who looks upon a majestic king. The garment of religious fear is the finest of garments: it is more noble for the heart than is gold brocade for the body. Also, the man who wears it cannot concern himself at all with the filth of turpitude" (xxv, 72-3). This king, quite evidently, is the King of the Day of Judgment. This conviction gives meaning to the *ṣalāt* which numerous Muslims have sought to perform immediately before their death (cf. for example al-Masʿūdī, *Murūdj*, §§ 1774, 3361).

The Ṣūfīs were to do nothing in this context other than to develop, sometimes magnificently, the common spirituality of Islam. The central idea being always that of the presence, two lines emerge (cf. *djalāl* and *djamāl*): on the one hand, the presence of God makes it possible to speak to Him in confidence (*munādjāt*); on the other the presence before God as on the Day of Resurrection fills one with fear. During the *ṣalāt*, the worshipper leaves the world. It is a spiritual ascension comparable to the *miʿrādj* of the Prophet (Dāya, 168 = tr. Algar, 184; Schimmel, 218-19). Or further, according to a striking expression: "The key of the Garden is ritual prayer; and the key of ritual prayer is ritual purification" (Ibn Ḥanbal, iii, 340 [*sic*], towards the end). This prophetic tradition throws into sharp relief the two inseparable faces of *ṣalāt*, legal prescription and spiritual dimension.

Bibliography: 1. In Arabic or in Persian. Abū Dāwūd, *K. al-Marāsīl*, Cairo 1310/1893; Nadjm-i Rāzī (Dāya), *Mirṣād al-ʿibād*, iii, ch. 5 = ed. Riyāḥi, [3]Tehran 1366/1988, 167-9, tr. Hamid Algar, *The path of God's bondsmen*, New York 1982, 183-5; ʿAbd al-Raḥmān al-Djazāʾirī, *al-Fiḳh ʿalā 'l-madhāhib al-arbaʿa*, i, *Ḳism al-ʿibādāt*, Cairo 1358/1939; Wahbī Sulaymān al-Ghāwidjī, *al-Ṣalāt wa-aḥkāmuhā wifḳa madhhab ... Abī Ḥanīfa al-Nuʿmān*, [2]Beirut 1405/1985; al-Ghazālī, *Iḥyāʾ ʿulūm al-dīn*, 1st quarter, book iv, tr. E.E. Calverley, *Worship in Islam...*, Madras 1925, [2]Lahore 1977; Ibn ʿAbd al-Wahhāb, *Shurūṭ al-ṣalāt wa-wādjibātuhā wa-arkānuhā* (sequel to *al-Uṣūl al-thalātha*), Cairo n.d.; Ibn Ḥanbal, *Musnad*, Cairo 1313/1895, repr. Beirut

1398/1978; Ḳurṭubī, al-Ḏjāmiʿ li-aḥkām al-Ḳurʾān, 20 vols., ²Cairo 1372/1952, repr. Beirut 1407/1987 with 2 vols. of index; Lʿ*A* = Ibn Manẓūr, Lisān al-ʿArab, 15 vols., Būlāḳ 1300-8, repr. Beirut 1374-6/1955-6; Ḥasan Kāmil al-Malaṭāwī, Fiḳh al-ʿibādāt ʿalā madhab al-Imām Mālik, Cairo 1387/1968, ²1401/1981; ʿAlī b. Sulaymān al-Mardāwī (817-85/1414-80), al-Tanḳīḥ al-mushbiʿ fī tahrīr ahkām al-Muḳniʿ fī fiḳh Imām al-sunna Aḥmad b. Ḥanbal al-Shaybānī, al-Rawḍa, n.d.; Rāzī, al-Tafsīr al-kabīr, 32 vols., Cairo 1352/1933, repr. Tehran n.d.; Ṭabarī, Ḏjāmiʿ al-bayān, 30 vols., Cairo 1388-96/1968-76.

2. In European languages. A. d'Alverny, La prière selon le Coran. II. La prière rituelle, in Proche-Orient Chrétien, x (Jerusalem 1960), 303-17; A.K. Brohi, The spiritual dimension of prayer, in Islamic spirituality. Foundations, ed. S.H. Nasr, London 1987, 131-43; A. Jeffery, The foreign vocabulary of the Qurʾān, Baroda 1938, repr. Lahore 1977; S.D. Goitein, Studies in Islamic history and institutions, ch. iii: Prayer in Islam, Leiden 1966, 73-89; J. Jomier, Le pèlerinage musulman vu du Caire vers 1960, in MIDEO, ix (1967), 1-72; R. Paret, Der Koran. Kommentar und Konkordanz, Stuttgart 1971, ²1977; Annemarie Schimmel, Mystical dimensions of Islam, Chapel Hill 1975, 148-55; M.Z.A. Souidan, Prayer in Islam: hygienic, preventive and curative, Cairo 1976 (as an example of apologetic literature); St. M. Wasserstrom, The delay of Maghrib: a study in comparative polemics, in Logos Islamikos. Studia islamica in honorem Georgii Michaelis Wickens, ed. R.S. Savory and D.A. Agius, Toronto 1984, 269-86.   (G. MONNOT)

ṢALĀT AL-KHAWF (A.), "the prayer of fear". In a context of warfare "in the way of God", the text reads in Ḳurʾān, IV, 102: "When you are with the believers and you perform the prayer at their head, let a group of them pray with you, while they stand ready with their arms, and keep behind you during the prostration. Then let another group which has not yet prayed come to pray with you, while they stand guard, with weapons to hand. Those who refuse to believe would prefer that you lay aside your arms and your baggage, so that they may catch you unawares." This alternative ritual prayer has received its name from another passage of the Ḳurʾān: "If you fear [an attack, pray] on foot or on horseback" (II, 239). Notwithstanding the ellipses of syntax (which permit a different translation), the general sense of the first verse is clear: when a Muslim band is close to the enemy, one group will perform the ritual prayer while the other stands guard, then the roles are to be reversed.

The text of the Ḳurʾān is clarified by prophetic traditions. The canonical collections are of very varied scope with regard to this issue. Muslim has eight ḥadīths on the question, and Ibn Mādja only three, while al-Nasāʾī has compiled 27 of them. The general arrangement enunciated by the Ḳurʾān poses a series of technical questions. The traditions do not all convey the same answer.

The central question, which includes several gradations, is the following. Two prayer-groups are distinguished and separated by the Ḳurʾānic text; to these will be added their common imām who, it should be recalled, is obliged to perform the prayer in his own name. Thus there is a total of three praying units, singular or co-ordinated. The rules of prayer being as they are, for each of these units there are numerous judicial problems to be solved.

When is the takbīr of sacralisation pronounced? By all present together, with the imām, at the beginning of his prayer, even if one of the two groups then turns its back towards the ḳibla (Abū Dāwūd, no. 1240; al-

Nasāʾī, 141; cf. Muslim, no. 307). But according to others, the second group performs the takbīr at the beginning of its own prayer (Abū Dāwūd, no. 1239; cf. Muslim, no. 308).

How many rakʿas are performed by the imām, and how many by each of the two groups? The question is especially posed, historically, for the prayers of ẓuhr and of ʿaṣr, which normally have four rakʿas. There are three answers.

(a) The imām performs four rakʿas, successively guiding each of the groups as it performs two rakʿas: a tradition related by Ḏjābir (e.g. in Muslim, no. 311-12; Abū Dāwūd, no. 1248) and followed by Ḥasan al-Baṣrī according to al-Ḳurṭubī (v, 368) and al-Rāzī.

(b) The imām performs two rakʿas, successively guiding each of the groups as it performs only one rakʿa; a tradition related notably by Ibn ʿAbbās via Mudjāhid (e.g. al-Bukhārī, bāb 3; Abū Dāwūd, nos. 1246-7; cf. al-Tirmidhī, no. 567).

(c) The generally accepted solution: everybody performs two rakʿas. In other words, the number of rakʿas is the same for the prayer of fear as for the prayer on a journey (cf. ṢALĀT. IV. F; consequently, three rakʿas will be retained at the prayer of maghrib).

It being thus accepted that the imām performs the same number of rakʿas as each of the groups, the questions remain, how is the whole of the rite organised, and when does each of those praying perform the taslīm of desacralisation? The successive rakʿas will be designated by the following symbols: A = performed by group A only; B = performed by group B only; MA = performed by group A with Muḥammad (or at a later stage with the imām); MB = performed by group B with Muḥammad. Theoretically, a dozen or so solutions are possible. In fact, the canonical ḥadīths present three (appropriate references are given in each case):

MA, MB, B, A: tradition of Ibn ʿUmar via his son Sālim (al-Bukhārī, bāb 1; Muslim, no. 305; al-Nasāʾī, 139-40; al-Tirmidhī, no. 564), followed by certain Mālikī teachers (al-Ḳurṭubī, v, 366-7); Ibn Masʿūd (ibid.).

MA, B, MB, A: tradition of Ḏjabr b. ʿAbd Allāh (Muslim, no. 307; al-Nasāʾī, 143-4).

MA, A, MB, B: well-known tradition of Sahl b. Abī Ḥathma via Ṣāliḥ b. Khawwāt, which comprises two versions:

— Version transmitted by Yazīd b. Rūmān: Muḥammad performs the taslīm with group B at the very end (Muslim, no. 310; al-Nasāʾī, 139): this is the doctrine of al-Shāfiʿī and of Ibn Ḥanbal, according to al-Ḳurṭubī, v, 366.

— Version transmitted by al-Ḳāsim b. Muḥammad: Muḥammad performs the taslīm after the end of rakʿa "MB" (Abū Dāwūd, no. 1239; cf. Muslim, no. 309, and Ibn Mādja, no. 1259); this is the doctrine of Mālik (according to al-Ḳurṭubī) and of al-Malaṭāwī.

The community of traditionists and jurists acknowledge that these ḥadīths cannot be harmonised. They record various measures taken by Muḥammad in different circumstances, where the requirements of security were not always of the same urgency. Two examples are recalled with particular clarity. On the one hand, the encounter at Dhāt al-Riḳāʿ, in Nadjd, during the expedition against the Ghaṭafān, in 4/626 (cf. Ibn Hishām, i, 662; al-Ṭabarī, i, 1454-5; al-Masʿūdī, Murūdj, § 1489). The place is mentioned in the tradition of Sahl b. Abī Ḥathma, also for example in the tradition of Abū Hurayra (al-Nasāʾī, 141). The enemy was then located in the direction opposite to the ḳibla; while performing the prayer, the Muslims then turned their backs towards the adversary, putting themselves in the greatest danger. On the other hand, on an occasion when the Muslims, at ʿUsfān, confronted an enemy band commanded by Khālid b. al-Walīd, the enemy was located in the direction of the *ḳibla*, a much more advantageous situation (tradition of Abū ʿAyyāsh al-Zuraḳī, in Abū Dāwūd, no. 1236; al-Nasāʾī, 144-5).

The "prayer of fear" is specifically Muslim. However, the conflict between the duty, the desire or the need to pray on the one hand, and on the other the necessity of fighting, may be encountered in other religions. In the context, not of prayer admittedly, but of a pious work, this situation applied during the restoration of the walls of the Holy City, *ca.* 445 B.C.: "From that day forward half the men under me were engaged in the actual building, while the other half stood by holding their spears, shields and bows, and wearing coats of mail; and officers supervised all the people of Judah who were engaged on the wall" (*Neh.* iv, 16, tr. *NEB*).

Thus far, consideration has been given to the original arrangements applied to the prayer rite in order to permit its observance "in assembly" in proximity to the enemy, on the very solid basis of Ḳurʾān, IV, 102. But also quoted, at the outset, was another passage: "If you fear [an attack, pray] on foot or on horseback" (II, 239). In commenting on it, Fakhr al-Dīn correctly observes: "The prayer of fear is of two kinds. The first, when one is in a position of combat, and this is what is envisaged by this verse. The second, when one is not (yet) in a position of combat, is that which is mentioned in the sūrat al-Nisāʾ (IV)" (al-Rāzī, vi, 154). Once battle has been engaged or is imminent, in the presence of the enemy, there is a duty, according to Abū Hanifa, to delay the prayer until the situation is more favourable. But al-Shāfiʿī and Mālik firmly assert, on the contrary, that prayer should be observed at its proper time, during the battle itself, individually, even when mounted, with the understandable reduction to two *rakʿas* of the prayers which normally comprise four, and with two considerable relaxations of the ritual prescriptions. The first is, in case of necessity, abandonment of the *ḳibla*. The second is the replacement of bowings and prostrations by their *īmāʾ* (cf. the tradition related by Ibn ʿUmar, in al-Bukhārī, *bāb* 2 and Muslim, no. 306, and that related by al-Awzāʿī, in al-Bukhārī, *bāb* 4). This means that it is sufficient to signify the corresponding act by its outline. The body or the head is slightly inclined to symbolise and signify ritual bowing; a rather deeper inclination represents prostration. These relaxations of the rite are not isolated; on the contrary they are related to similar dispositions concerning the prayer of the traveller and that of the invalid. Thus Islamic law contains precedents which could be used to find solutions to other problems.

Bibliography: See the bibliography to ṢALĀT, and in particular Ḳurṭubī, iii, 223-6, v, 364-73; Malaṭāwī, 193-4; Rāzī, vi, 153-6, xi, 24-7. As for the four works of *sunan*, the "prayer of fear" is treated there as follows: Abū Dāwūd, ed. M.M. al-Dīn ʿAbd al-Ḥamīd, 4 vols., Cairo 1348/1930, ii, 11-18; Ibn Mādja, ed. M.F. ʿAbd al-Bāḳī, 2 vols., Cairo 1391/1972, i, 399-400; Nasāʾī, 10 vols., Cairo 1383/1964, iii, 136-46; Tirmidhī, ed. Aḥmad Muḥammad Shākir, 5 vols., Cairo 1356/1937, ii, 453-7.

(G. Monnot)

ṢALAWĀT [see TAṢLIYA].

al-**SALĀWĪ** [see AL-NĀṢIR AL-SALĀWĪ].

ṢALB (A.), "crucifixion". In Islamic doctrine and practice, it refers to a criminal punishment in which the body of the criminal, either living or dead, is affixed to or impaled on a beam or tree trunk and exposed for some days or longer.

Before Islam, many cultures, including the Persian and Roman ones, practised crucifixion as a punishment for traitors, rebels, robbers and criminal slaves (M. Hengle, *Crucifixion in the ancient world*, London 1977).

The Ḳurʾān refers to crucifixion in six places. The significant verse for legal practice is V, 33: "The recompense of those who make war on (*yuḥāribūn*) God and His messenger and sow corruption (*fasād*) in the earth shall but be that they shall be slain, or be crucified (*yuṣallabū*), or have their hands and feet cut off on opposite sides, or be banished from the earth...".

The standard *ḥadīth* collections report one case where Muḥammad practiced crucifixion (of persons who murdered a shepherd and stole camels). This account is, however, contradicted by many others describing a different punishment (cutting hands and feet and gouging eyes) (see al-Nasāʾī, *taḥrīm al-dam, bābs* 7-9). In another *ḥadīth*, the first crucifixion in Medina was by ʿUmar, of two slaves who killed their mistress (see Abū Dāwūd, *ṣalāt, bāb* 61).

Fiḳh [*q.v.*] applies the above verse chiefly to highway robbers, as *ḥadd* [*q.v.*; and see ḲATL]. The choice of crucifixion, instead of another of the four stated penalties, is governed by complex, contested rules. Most scholars require that a robber who both killed and took property be crucified, as a *ḥadd* penalty (see ḲATL); others, while requiring execution, do not demand crucifixion. For most scholars, offenders are to be beheaded before being crucified. Mālikīs, with most Ḥanafīs and most Twelver Shīʿīs, provide that the offender is crucified alive, but then killed by lance thrust. For the Ẓāhirīs, crucifixion itself must cause the death. Most scholars limit the period of crucifixion to three days (after which the body is to be washed, prayed over and buried).

Various minority views permit or prescribe crucifixion for crimes other than highway robbery, usually on authority of the same verse. These crimes include insults to the Prophet (*sabb al-nabī*) [see ḲATL], heresy (*zandaḳa*) [see MURTADD; ZINDĪḲ], sorcery [see SIḤR], and killing by stranglers (*khannāḳūn*) and assassins drugging their victims (*mubannidjūn*), such punishments sometimes represented as *ḥadd* and sometimes as *taʿzīr* [*q.v.*]. The quoted verse itself conceivably applies to anyone whose corrupting effect on society can be prevented only thereby (Ibn Taymiyya, *al-Siyāsa al-sharʿiyya*, Cairo 1322, 55). Al-Māwardī (apparently alone) permitted crucifixion while alive (but not necessarily to death) as a generally applicable form of *taʿzīr* (*al-Aḥkām al-sulṭāniyya*, Cairo 1966, 239; cf. al-Ramlī, *Nihāyat al-muḥtādj*, Cairo 1967, viii, 21).

Reports of actual crucifixions exist under most of these doctrinal headings. Exposure, often extremely prolonged, of headless bodies is common, especially for political or religious opponents [see e.g. ʿABD ALLĀH B. AL-ZUBAYR; ḤASANAK; IBN BAḲIYYA]. Crucifixion while alive also appears, such as for al-Ḥallādj [*q.v.*] and murderous slaves (H. Ritter, *Kreuzigung eines Knaben*, in *Oriens*, xxv [1976], 38-40, suggesting a frequency in the 7th/13th century of crucifixion to death).

In later Persian and Turkish usage, *ṣalb* meant "hanging". In the form of exposure after beheading, crucifixion is practised in Saudi Arabia today.

Bibliography: O. Spies, *Über die Kreuzigung im Islam*, in *Religion und Religionen: Festschrift für Gustav Mensching*, ed. R. Thomas, Bonn 1967, 143-56; L. Massignon, *La passion de Husayn Ibn Mansûr Hallâj*, repr. Paris 1975, i; J.L. Kraemer, *Apostates, rebels and brigands*, in *IOS*, x (1980), 34-73.

(F.E. Vogel)

SALDJŪḲIDS, a Turkish dynasty of mediaeval Islam which, at the peak of its power during the 5th-6th/11th-12th centuries, ruled over, either directly or through vassal princes, a wide area of Western Asia from Transoxania, Farghāna, the Semirečye and Khʷārazm in the east to Anatolia, Syria and the Ḥidjāz in the west. From the core of what became the Great Saldjūḳ empire, subordinate lines of the Saldjūḳ family maintained themselves in regions like Kirmān (till towards the end of the 6th/12th century), Syria (till the opening years of the 6th/12th century) and Rūm or Anatolia (till the beginning of the 8th/14th century) (see below, section III).

I. The historical significance of the Saldjūḳs
II. Origins and early history
III. The various branches of the Saldjūḳs
  1. The Great Saldjūḳs of Persia and ʿIrāḳ
  2. The Saldjūḳs of Western Persia and ʿIrāḳ
  3. The Saldjūḳs of Kirmān
  4. The Saldjūḳs of Syria
  5. The Saldjūḳs of Rūm
IV. Intellectual and religious history
  1. In Persia and ʿIrāḳ
  2. In Anatolia
V. Administrative, social and economic history
  1. In Persia and ʿIrāḳ
  2. In Anatolia
VI. Art and architecture
  1. In Persia
  2. In Anatolia
VII. Literature
  1. In Persia and ʿIrāḳ
  2. In Anatolia
VIII. Numismatics
  1. In Persia and ʿIrāḳ
  2. In Anatolia

I. The historical significance of the Saldjūḳs

The appearance of the Saldjūḳs undoubtedly marks a change in the course of the history of the central and eastern Islamic lands, but the nature and extent of this change, affecting a wide range of aspects of both material and religio-cultural life, are not easy to evaluate and have given rise to controversy (see below).

The Saldjūḳs arrived on the scene of the Islamic world only a few decades after the practical and moral authority of the ʿAbbāsid caliphs in Baghdād had reached its lowest ebb under the political and military tutelage of the Shīʿī Būyids [see buwayhids]. At the same time, many of the petty Arab principalities of ʿIrāḳ, al-Djazīra and northern Syria were also Shīʿī, but the most serious threat of all came from the constituting of the rival Ismāʿīlī Shīʿī caliphate in North Africa, Egypt and southern Syria of the Fāṭimids, still in a militant, expansionist stage and with a capital, Cairo, which was beginning to outstrip Baghdād in material and intellectual splendour alike.

The installation of the Turkish Saldjūḳs in Persia, ʿIrāk, al-Djazīra and northern Syria reversed this apparently unrelenting march of political Shīʿism, and it was to be another four centuries or so before Shīʿism would be able permanently to affect the religious complexion of large stretches of the northern tier of the Middle East, sc. Persia and eastern Anatolia (and, somewhat paradoxically, through the agency of further Turkish/Turkmen elements there, notably through the Ṣafawids and their Ḳizilbash followers). The Saldjūḳs were Sunnīs, and Ḥanafīs in *madhhab*, who wished to replace existing powers in Persia, including the Ghaznawids and the generally Shīʿī Daylamī dynasties of northern and western Persia (at the same time, by the removal of the latter relieving the ʿAbbāsids of a certain amount of pressure and constriction) without, however, giving up the fruits of military and political victory, which they now wished to enjoy themselves. This explains why, although al-Ḳāʾim welcomed Ṭoghrïl Beg's appearance at the outset, subsequent relations between the ʿAbbāsids and the Great Saldjūḳs were not always smooth. The caliphs soon found that they had little more freedom to manoeuvre than they had had under the Būyids. They only came into their own again during the middle years of the 6th/12th century, when they were able to show increased independence of mind and of freedom of action vis-à-vis the declining Saldjūḳs. This revival of the caliphate was to be transitory; both ʿAbbāsids and Saldjūḳs were shortly to be swept away by new, dynamic forces from the East, notably the Khʷārazmshāhs and above all the Mongols. Yet through the co-existence for something like 130 years of the two dynasties, the conditions were created for the development within Islam, even if dictated by practical necessity, of the concept of the caliph-imām as spiritual and moral leader and the sultan, in this case the Saldjūḳ one, as secular, executive leader of a large proportion of the Muslims (see further, khalīfa. (i) b; sulṭān; and below, section V. 1).

The irruption of the Saldjūḳs into the Islamic lands was only the beginning of a prolonged movement of peoples from Inner Asia into the Middle East, one which was to have long-term social and economic as well as political and constitutional effects. Whilst many of the Turkmen elements percolating into northern Persia all through the Saldjūḳ period passed on towards Anatolia, others became part of the increasing nomadic and transhumant population of Persia and the central Arab lands, and this process became accelerated in the time of the succeeding invaders mentioned above, sc. the Khʷārazmshāhs and Mongols, through the movements of Turco-Mongol peoples. There resulted a transformation of land utilisation, social organisation and ethnic composition in the territories affected, associated with new systems of land tenure such as the *iḳṭāʿ* and the later *soyurghal* [*q.vv.*] and with the pastoralisation of extensive areas of the northern tier of the Middle East, so that Turkish (and, to a much lesser extent, Mongol) tribesmen became integral parts of the population there, previously mainly Persian and Arab, bringing with them their languages. The use of these land grants to support professional soldiers, and the availability of reservoirs of tribal manpower, first of all in the Saldjūḳ period buttressed the authority of the sultans and their epigoni, the atabegs [see atabak]; but in the course of time it led to the political and military domination of Turkish dynasts or military leaders from Bengal to Algiers.

A further effect of the assumption of political leadership by the Great Saldjūḳs lay in the consolidation of Sunnī authority as the dominant ethos of rule in the central Islamic lands. Although barbarians at the outset (and the first Saldjūḳ sultans, at least in Persia and ʿIrāḳ, remained substantially unlettered), these Turks knew how to make the best use of the existing Persian and Arab administrative structures already in place, and the viziers and officials whom they employed, such as al-Kundurī, Niẓām al-Mulk and al-Ṭughrāʾī [*q.vv.*], shed as much lustre on their masters as had done the great viziers of the 4th/10th century on their Būyid employers. Culturally, the constituting of the Saldjūḳ empire marked a further step in the dethronement of Arabic from being the sole lingua franca of educated and polite society in the Middle East. Coming as they did through a Transoxania which was still substantially Iranian and into Persia proper, the Saldjūḳs—with no high-level Turkish cultural or literary heritage of their own—took over that of Persia, so that the Persian language became that of administration and culture in their lands of Persia and Anatolia. The Persian culture of the Rūm Saldjūḳs was particularly splendid, and it was only gradually that Turkish emerged there as a parallel language in the fields of government and *adab* [*q.v.*]; the Persian imprint on Ottoman civilisation was to remain strong until the 19th century.

The region of the Middle East where the coming of the Saldjūḳs was to have the most immediate and obvious impact, with enduring political, religious and cultural effects which are strongly visible today, was Anatolia. Here the Saldjūḳ sultanate of Rūm based on Ḳonya and other Turkish principalities in northern and eastern Anatolia took over the greater part of the former Byzantine and Armenian territories of Asia Minor. It is for this region that the geographical designation Turcia/Turchia, etc., first apparently appears specifically in Western European usage at the time of the Third Crusade of the Emperor Frederick Barbarossa (1187-92) (thus according to Cl. Cahen, *Pre-Ottoman Turkey. A general survey of the material and spiritual culture and history c. 1071-1330*, London 1968, 144-5).

The details of the Saldjūḳs' part in the gradual Turkification of Asia Minor will be considered below under section III. 5; see also ANADOLU. iii. i. But it should be noted that the consolidation of the Saldjūḳ sultanate of Rūm as the political, cultural, religious and geographical predecessor of the modern Turkish Republic, has been a salient point in the assessment of the general importance of the Saldjūḳs in Middle Eastern history by contemporary Turkish historians. Over some half-a-century, the role of the Saldjūḳs as the first Turkish, Islamic power to establish itself in the heartlands of the Islamic world (ignoring dynasties on the far peripheries like the G͟haznawids in Afg͟hānistān and India and the Ḳarak͟hānids in Transoxania) has been the starting-point for much analysis and speculation by these Turkish scholars. In part, this has been a reaction against 19th century European views, those formed in the light of the Greek and Balkan peoples' freeing themselves from what was viewed as Ottoman Turkish religious oppression and maladministration and in the light of the issues raised by the "Eastern Question", and expressed by such scholars as Ernest Renan. According to these views, the Turks, unlike the Semitic Arabs and the Indo-European or Aryan Persians, had contributed nothing to the fabric of Islamic civilisation since they came from the one region of the Old World, Inner Asia, from which no great religions or cultures have ever emerged. But it has also been a reaction against a long-established, inter-Islamic judgement, arising out of specific political conditions, sc. the four centuries' long domination by the Ottoman Turks of the heartlands of Arab-Islamic culture, the lands from Egypt to ʿIrāḳ. From this has arisen the contemptuous dismissal of the Turks as essentially unoriginal barbarians, deriving their culture from the Arabs and Persians, a nation of soldiers and administrators rather than one of creative achievers in the intellectual and cultural fields. The persistence of such views, still enshrined today in the school and university textbooks of the Arab world, reflect attitudes of ethnic disparagement (and enables the Turks to be cast as continuingly responsible for the ills and failures of Arab political systems and society since the break-up of the Ottoman empire). (See on these attitudes, B. Lewis, *The Mongols, the Turks and the Muslim polity*, in *Islam in history. Ideas, men and events in the Middle East*, London 1973, 179-98; U. Haarmann, *Ideology and history: the Arab image of the Turk through the centuries*, in *IJMES*, xx [1988], 175-96.)

It is not therefore surprising that 20th-century Turkish historians have combatted such attitudes and have seen the Saldjūḳ Turks as bringing new and valuable influences into the Islamic society which they found on entering it. According to such a view, elements of Turkish steppe culture were not completely overlaid but contributed to and enriched Islamic civilisation, which became a synthesis of Turkish plus existing Islamic elements: the principle of social mobility and democracy within the steppe tribal unit, the conception of world dominion which enabled the Turkish sultan to act as the executive counterpart of the caliph's universal religious and moral authority, the traces of the role in steppe life of Turkish holy men within later Turkish Ṣūfism, etc. Indeed, the Turks revitalised Islam. The going-back to the Saldjūḳs as Turkish heroes and as the founding fathers of the Muslim Turkish culture, actually goes back to the earlier part of the 20th century, to Ziyā Gök Alp and Kemāl Atatürk [*q.vv.*], figures who, in an age of Ottoman terminal decline or recent disappearance, tended to view the Ottoman interlude of Turkish history with ambivalent feelings: an empire tainted with cosmopolitanism and a semi-colony of the West. The Saldjūḳs who founded the Rūm sultanate, within almost the same geographical bounds as post-1922 Turkey, could thus be regarded as the precursors of the modern Republic. All sorts of other arguments have been brought into play here, such as the question whether the Turkish invasions of Anatolia from the later 5th/11th century onwards were unplanned plunder raids or part of a pre-planned grand strategy going back to the early decades of the century, a reasoning put forward by some Turkish nationalist historians (see further, below, section III. 1, 5).

These discussions have arisen out of the process, common enough in the recent history of central and eastern Europe as well as of Turkey, in which historical, linguistic and nationalist feelings are used as a formative impulse in, or as a justification for, the consolidation of a nation state, a process which has come into existence as a protest against, and in conflict with, the existing state pattern (see H. Kohn, *The idea of nationalism, a study in its origins and background*. New York 1961, 324-5, 329-31). As forming a fascinating case study, they have attracted the attention and the analyses of western orientalists, notably of Martin Strohmeier, *Seldschukische Geschichte und türkische Geschichtswissenschaft. Die Seldschuken im Urteil moderner Türkischer Historiker*, Berlin 1984, who surveys the whole topic in great detail, and of Gary Leiser in his useful *A history of the Seljuks. İbrahim Kafesoğlu's interpretation and the resulting controversy. Translated, edited and with an introduction* ..., Carbondale and Edwardsville, Ill. 1988, which makes available in an annotated English translation Kafesoğlu's lengthy *İA* article on the dynasty plus the views of other Turkish scholars involved in Saldjūḳ history, notably Osman Turan and Ahmed Ateş.

II. Origins and early history

The Saldjūḳs were in origin a family group or clan of the Og͟huz Turkish people. The Toḳuz Og͟huz or "nine tribes of the Og͟hūz" formed part of the early Gök Türk empire of the early 8th century, and as such are mentioned in that empire's royal annals, the Or-khon [*q.v.*] inscriptions. When that empire collapsed in 741, the Og̲h̲uz chief eventually acquired the military office of Yabg̲h̲u (a term which turns up later in the early history of the Saldjūḳs in Transoxania and K̲h̲urāsān, see below) of the right wing of the horde of the Western Turks. The Og̲h̲uz moved southwestwards through the Siberian steppes to the Aral Sea and the frontiers of Transoxania, and westwards to the Volga and South Russia. The Arab envoy to the king of the Bulg̲h̲ārs, Ibn Faḍlān [*q.v.*], found the Og̲h̲uz nomadising in the steppes between K̲h̲wārazm and the lower and middle Volga in the opening decades of the 4th/10th century; and with their appearance on the northern fringes of the Sāmānid amirate later in that century, they enter the full light of Islamic history [see G̲H̲UZZ].

(Following one of the conventional Western spellings, Saldjūḳ is used here in the *EI*. However, Barthold pointed out (*Turkestan*³, 257 n. 1; *Histoire des Turcs d'Asie centrale*, Paris 1945, 80) that the frequently-found spelling Seldjūḳ contravenes the rules of vowel harmony in Turkish languages and that Maḥmūd Kāshg̲h̲arī in his *Dīwān lughāt al-Turk* (ed. Kilisli Rifʿat Bey, i, 397, tr. Atalay, i, 428) spells the name with *kāf* and presumably front vowels, i.e. Seldjük or Selčük, with similar spellings in the *Kitāb-i Dede Ḳorḳut* and other texts. P. Pelliot, in his *Quelques noms turcs d'hommes et de peuples en -ar/-är, ur/ür,-ir/ir*, in *Oeuvres posthumes*, Paris 1949, ii, 176-7 n. 2, took a similar line: "si je donnerais une transcription scientifique, je parlerais des Säljük''. On the other hand, the spelling with *kāf* and implied back vowels is very old in the Arabic-script sources and in such Armenian renderings as *Salčʾuk*, pl. *Salčʾukhik*, of Kirakos of Gandja. Karl Menges suggested (in *JNES*, x [1951], 268 n. 2), an origin of the name in the verb *salmak* "attack, charge" (Clauson, *Etymological dictionary*, 824, has, however, for the root *sal-* the related but somewhat different meaning of "violently to move, agitate s. th.'') > *salčuk* "dashing, charging''. Many Western scholars have preferred to use some form of the name with back vowels, whilst commenting on the extremely fluid state of Turkish vowel harmony and orthography at this early period. See further C.E. Bosworth in *The Ghaznavids*, 299 n. 44, and the opening section of Kafesoğlu's *İA* art. *Selçuklular*, tr. Leiser, 21-2.)

Within the Og̲h̲uz people, the leading tribe was that of the Ḳïnïḳ, from whom their princes sprang, according to Kāshg̲h̲arī again (i, 56, tr. i, 55). The Saldjūḳ family or kin-group (it does not seem in origin to have been a much greater social group) came from the Ḳïnïḳ; later, when the Saldjūḳs had achieved power in Persia, attempts were made to give the family a glorious past, and T̲og̲h̲ril Beg's official Abu 'l-ʿAlāʾ Ibn Ḥassūl (d. 450/1058) linked them with the legendary Turkish king Afrāsiyāb. On somewhat more certain historical ground, during the 4th/10th century the Saldjūḳ leader (called Saldjūḳ b. Duḳaḳ b. Temür Yalïg̲h̲ "Iron bow'') seems to have held the office of Sü Bas̲h̲ï or military commander, at the side of the Yabg̲h̲u. Because of dissensions, the Saldjūḳs fled with their herds from the Yabg̲h̲u to Djand [*q.v.* in Suppl.] on the lower Syr Darya, and it was in this region that Saldjūḳ died and that his family and followers became Muslim; the hostility of these two branches of the Ḳïnïḳ was not resolved till 433/1041, when the Saldjūḳs, by then victorious in K̲h̲urāsān and K̲h̲wārazm, drove out from the latter province the Yabg̲h̲u ʿAlī's son and successor S̲h̲āh Malik (see Barthold, *Turkestan*, 177-8, 256-7; Bosworth, *op. cit.*, 210-19).

Now on the borders of K̲h̲wārazm and Transoxania, the Saldjūḳs and other Og̲h̲uz bands hired out their military services, to the Sāmānids [*q.v.*], by this time in increasing difficulties, to the latter's eventual supplanters north of the Oxus, the Ḳarak̲h̲ānids [see ILEK K̲H̲ĀNS] and to the local rulers in K̲h̲wārazm, moving into the steppe fringes of these regions and into the Ḳara Ḳum [*q.v.*] in what is now the Turkmenistan Republic. At the outset, the Saldjūḳs were led by the three sons of Saldjūḳ, Mūsā, Mīkāʾīl and Arslan Isrāʾīl [see ARSLAN B. SALDJŪḲ] (and possibly by a fourth one, Yūsuf) and, from the next generation, Mīkāʾīl's two sons T̲og̲h̲rïl Beg Muḥammad and Čag̲h̲rï Beg Dāwūd [*q.vv.*].

Bands of Og̲h̲uz were scattered after a defeat by Sultan Maḥmūd of G̲h̲azna [*q.v.*] in 428/1029 throughout K̲h̲urāsān and northern Persia (the so-called "ʿIrāḳī'' Turkmens), but whether a raid as far as Ād̲h̲arbāydjān and Armenia under Čag̲h̲rï Beg had taken place some ten years earlier is uncertain (though upheld as such by a nationalist-minded historian like Kafesoğlu as a kind of *praeparatio evangelica* for the Saldjūḳ incursions into Anatolia in the second half of the century). By 426/1035 the Saldjūḳs and their followers were asking Masʿūd b. Maḥmūd [*q.v.*] for a grant of Nasā, Farāwa and Sarak̲h̲s [*q.vv.*] and their pasture lands on the northern rim of K̲h̲urāsān. Over the next few years, they infiltrated K̲h̲urāsān and raided westwards into northern Persia, their lightly-armed and highly-mobile cavalrymen proving more than a match for the more heavily-armed but cumbersome G̲h̲aznawid army, so that with the defeat of Masʿūd at Dandānḳān [*q.v.* in Suppl.] in 431/1040, the Saldjūḳs were soon able to overrun K̲h̲urāsān and then to sweep into the remainder of Persia. We need not assume that the actual numbers of the Turkmens were very large, for the ways of life possible in the steppes meant that there were natural and environmental limitations on the numbers of the nomads. Yuri Bregel has implied, working from the 16,000 Og̲h̲uz mentioned by the G̲h̲aznawid historian Bayhaḳī as present on the battle field of Dandānḳān (*Taʾrīkh-i Masʿūdī*, ed. G̲h̲anī and Fayyāḍ, Tehran 1324/1945, 619), that we should probably assume, in this instance, a ratio of one fighting man to four other members of the family, yielding some 64,000 Turkmens moving into K̲h̲urāsān at this time (*Turko-Mongol influences in Central Asia*, in R.L. Canfield (ed.), *Turko-Persia in historical perspective*, Cambridge 1991, 58 and n. 10).

But various Kurdish and Daylamī dynasties of the Caspian regions and Djibāl were now attacked, although the process of overcoming the more powerful and long-established Būyids in Fārs and ʿIrāḳ was slower. It was not until 447/1055 that T̲og̲h̲rïl was first able to enter Bag̲h̲dād and depose the Būyid prince al-Malik al-Raḥīm K̲h̲usraw Fīrūz [*q.v.*], and the last Būyids to rule in southern Persia lost their power only a few years later. What had helped the Saldjūḳ chiefs to triumph, A.K.S. Lambton has suggested, were their obvious leadership qualities combined with a certain level of sophistication derived from a past in the steppes which had been not altogether unfamiliar with urban life in, for example, the towns on the lower Syr Darya; hence they were able to lead the Og̲h̲uz bands towards the formation of a higher political organism, the sultanate in Persia and ʿIrāḳ, than those Og̲h̲uz who stayed behind in the steppes between the Syr Darya and the lower Volga, what were later called the Ḳipčaḳ steppes (*Aspects of Saljūq-Ghuzz settlement in Persia*, in D.S. Richards (ed.), *Islamic civilisation 950-1150*, Oxford 1973, 111).

T̲og̲h̲rïl had already adopted something of the style

of an independent ruler during his first, temporary occupation of Nī<u>sh</u>āpūr [*q.v.*], the capital of <u>Kh</u>urāsān (429/1038), making the *<u>kh</u>uṭba* in his own name (though perhaps at the side of Sultan Masʿūd's name) and assuming the title of *al-Sulṭān al-Muʿaẓẓam* "Exalted Ruler", one which subsequently appears on his coins. He was now in touch with the ʿAbbāsid caliph in Bag<u>h</u>dād, the fount of legitimising authority for Sunnī rulers, and when he entered Bag<u>h</u>dād for a second time in 449/1058, al-Ḳāʾim [*q.v.*] bestowed on him *alḳāb* or honorific titles and robes of honour in the ʿAbbāsid colour of black. Ṭog<u>h</u>rïl was to exult in his role of deliverer of the caliph from the pressure of <u>Sh</u>īʿī powers like the Būyids, Mazyadids and Fāṭimids, and even aspired to take an ʿAbbāsid princess to wife, a proposal which her father fought off, however, for as long as possible (see below, 2). All this now gave Ṭog<u>h</u>rïl an authority quite different in nature from the limited authority which he had enjoyed under Turkish tribal custom as war leader and tribal chieftain, one which set the Sal<u>dj</u>ūḳs on the road to becoming rulers integrated within the Perso-Islamic monarchical tradition—a process which was never, however, fully completed (see below).

Ṭog<u>h</u>rïl had thus become supreme ruler over the former Būyid lands in western and southern Persia, in addition to the former <u>Gh</u>aznawid ones in the east, with the title of sultan and the position of head of the Saldjūḳ family, now starting on the process of becoming a ruling dynasty. His position crystallised the new division of authority, within the central and eastern lands of Sunnī Islam, between the ʿAbbāsid caliph-imām as spiritual and moral head and the Sal<u>dj</u>ūḳ sultan as secular ruler, and this dichotomy was to become a major feature of the Sal<u>dj</u>ūḳ period in Islamic history, although it was to be some considerable time before the writers on law and the state, constitutional theory would recognise the fait accompli. It could obviously not have been discernible to a writer like al-Māwardī (d. 450/1058 [*q.v.*]) in his *al-Aḥkām al-sulṭāniyya* (al-Māwardī had actually met Ṭog<u>h</u>rïl in the 1040s in a meeting near Rayy as the caliph's envoy, protesting against Turkmen depredations in Persia), and even when the process was perfectly apparent, e.g. to Abū Ḥāmid al-<u>Gh</u>azālī (d. 505/1111 [*q.v.*]), the latter was reluctant to spell out the full implications and resorted to what Carole Hillenbrand has called "pious dishonesty" or else to tortuous and casuistic argumentation (*Islamic orthodoxy or Realpolitik? Al-<u>Gh</u>azālī's views on government*, in *Iran, JBIPS*, xxxvi [1988], 86; see also Lambton, *Concepts of authority in Persia: eleventh to nineteenth centuries A.D.*, in *ibid.*, 97-8) in order to preserve the fiction of the caliph's supreme executive power over the *Dār al-Islām*. In fact, the direct authority of the caliphs within ʿIrāḳ and western Persia was to revive and expand considerably during the course of the 6th/12th century *pari passu* with the increased dynastic squabbling and diminished military effectiveness of the Great Sal<u>dj</u>ūḳ sultans (in addition to the articles KHALĪF and SULṬĀN, see for a good, concise account of these topics and events, T. Nagel, in U. Haarmann (ed.), *Geschichte der arabischen Welt*, Munich 1987, 146 ff.).

The sultans never conceived of themselves as despotic rulers over a monolithic empire, rulers in the Perso-Islamic tradition of the power state as it had developed, for instance, under the early <u>Gh</u>aznawids [*q.v.*]. They had risen to power as the successful military leaders of bands of their fellow-Og<u>h</u>uz tribesmen, and at the outset depended solely on these tribal elements. The position of the Sal<u>dj</u>ūḳ sultans was thus fundamentally different from their predecessors in the East, both from the Sāmānids, with their aristocratic Iranian background but a military dependence on professional, largely slave Turkish, troops, and from the <u>Gh</u>aznawids, themselves of slave origin and dependent on a purely professional, salaried standing army; likewise, their opponents in the West, the Būyids and Fāṭimids, had come to depend upon professional, multi-ethnic armies. The sultans did not prove to be wholly exempt from the pressures arising out of the ethos of power in the Middle East at this time; they endeavoured to increase their own authority and to some extent to marginalise the Turkmen tribal elements, yet these last remained strong within the empire, and on occasions, powerful enough to aspire, through their favoured candidates for the supreme office of sultan, to a controlling influence in the state.

In any case, the sultans, especially those of the 5th/11th century, could not divest themselves completely of their steppe origins, and we have no reason to think that they wished completely to do so. Ṭog<u>h</u>rïl, Čag<u>h</u>rï and Alp Arslan had grown up within the Og<u>h</u>uz tribe, and when they became Islamic territorial rulers they were nevertheless careful still to observe tribal law and custom when those did not clash with their new roles as sultans (but for an occasion when the new Islamic principles firmly overrode tribal custom, sc. in regard to the succession, see below, section III. 1). San<u>dj</u>ar, having within his <u>Kh</u>urāsānian dominions substantial groups of still unassimilated, tribally-organised Og<u>h</u>uz, was likewise conscious of his dual position. One later Turkish source states that, in accordance with ancient practice, he gave the right wing of his army to the Ḳayï and Bayat clans of the Og<u>h</u>uz and the left wing to the Bayïndir and Bičine (*Muntak<u>h</u>ab-i tawārī<u>kh</u>-i sal<u>dj</u>ūḳiyye*, quoted by İ.H. Uzunçarşılı, *Osmanlı devleti teşkilâtına medhal*, Istanbul 1941, 22-4). Several administrative documents from the period illustrate San<u>dj</u>ar's care to regulate his relations with his <u>Gh</u>uzz subjects; cf. Lambton, *The administration of Sanjar's empire as illustrated in the* ʿAtabat al-kataba, in *BSOAS*, xx (1957), 382, and eadem, *Aspects of Saljūq-Ghuzz settlement in Persia*, 109-11. During Malik <u>Sh</u>āh's reign, the great vizier of Alp Arslan and Malik <u>Sh</u>āh, Niẓām al-Mulk, commented in his *Siyāsat-nāma*, § 26, that the sultans had obligations towards their former backers, the Turkmens, hence should preserve some role for them in the state apparatus amidst the trends towards administrative and military centralisation and professionalism (see also Lambton, in *Camb. hist. of Iran*, v, 246-7).

The persistence of influences from the Og<u>h</u>uz tribal past is seen in the sultans' policy of allotting various provinces of the empire as appanages from Sal<u>dj</u>ūḳ male relatives who had a claim, by virtue of seniority or experience, to some share in the material advantages of power. Ṭog<u>h</u>rïl's brother Čag<u>h</u>rï had from the time of the Dandānḳān victory been left with control over the eastern territories: <u>Kh</u>urāsān; any lands north of the Oxus that he could conquer from the Ḳara<u>kh</u>ānids or from the Og<u>h</u>uz Yabg<u>h</u>u in <u>Kh</u>ʷārazm; and any further parts of Afg<u>h</u>ānistān that he could wrest from the <u>Gh</u>aznawids. (Exactly in what degree Čag<u>h</u>rï was considered by the Sal<u>dj</u>ūḳs' Turkmen followers as inferior in status to Ṭog<u>h</u>rïl, or whether he was inferior at all, is a question discussed by R.W. Bulliet in his article *Numismatic evidence for the relationship between Ṭughril Beg and Chaghrī Beg*, in D.K. Kouymjian (ed.), *Near Eastern numismatics iconography, epigraphy and history. Studies in honor of George C. Miles*, Beirut 1974, 289-96; his conclusion is that they were in fact equal, at least at the outset, and that this equality in status was recognised by symbols on their coins.) Čag̲h̲rī died in 452/1060, and his son Alp Arslan, already active latterly in the affairs of the East, took over power there; after Ṭog̲h̲rïl's death in 455/1063, he moved westwards and assumed supreme direction of the Sald̲j̲ūḳ empire; all subsequent rulers of the Great Sald̲j̲ūḳ line and the Sald̲j̲ūḳ rulers in ʿIrāḳ and western Persia sprang from Alp Arslan. A further brother of Ṭog̲h̲rïl's and Čag̲h̲rī's, Mūsā Bīg̲h̲ū or Payg̲h̲ū [see PAYG̲H̲Ū], was left to bring under his control as much as possible of Sīstān, at that time ruled by the Maliks of Nīmrūz of the Naṣrid line [see SĪSTĀN]. Čag̲h̲rī's eldest son Ḳāwurd [*q.v.*] was to expand southwards through Ḳuhistān to Kirmān, and in fact founded the largely autonomous Sald̲j̲ūḳ amirate in Kirmān which was to last for nearly a century and a half (see below, II, 4). Other members of the Sald̲j̲ūḳ family also received grants: Ibrāhīm Inal or Yinal (who may have been a cousin and half-brother on his mother's side to Ṭog̲h̲rïl but whose precise position within the family is not wholly clear, cf. V. Minorsky, *Äi̮nallu/Inallu*, in *RO*, xvii [1951-2], 5-6) received Ḳuhistān, and Ḳutlumus̲h̲ (or Ḳutamis̲h̲) b. Arslan Isrāʾīl received Gurgān and Ḳūmis, whilst the sons of Čag̲h̲rī, Yāḳūtī and Alp Arslan, accompanied Ṭog̲h̲rïl westwards at this time.

Over the following years, there was much discontent within the Sald̲j̲ūḳ family over the idea of father-son descent from Čag̲h̲rī to Alp Arslan and then to Malik S̲h̲āh. Already during Ṭog̲h̲rïl's lifetime, Ibrāhīm Inal and two of his nephews had rebelled unsuccessfully against Ṭog̲h̲rïl (451/1059). When Alp Arslan claimed the throne of the whole Sald̲j̲ūḳ dominions in 455/1063, his uncle Ḳutlumus̲h̲ revolted at Sāwa [*q.v.*] in the next year, voicing the old Turkish idea of the seniorate, the right of the eldest suitable male relative to have the supreme leadership; and when Malik S̲h̲āh succeeded to power in 465/1072, his uncle Ḳāwurd rebelled, but was executed at the prompting of Niẓām al-Mulk. As some compensation for the rejection of Ḳutlumus̲h̲'s claim, Alp Arslan deflected the latter's son Sulaymān, together with other Turkmen elements who were imbued with the spirit of plunder and *g̲h̲azw* and who were probably impatient of the increasingly centralised direction of the state, westwards into Anatolia, where new vistas of expansion opened up in the wake of the Sald̲j̲ūḳ victory over the Byzantines in 463/1071 of Malāzgird [*q.v.*]. In this way, there eventually came into being the Sald̲j̲ūḳ sultanate of Rūm based on Ḳonya (see below, section III. 5).

Bibliography: A good survey of both primary and secondary sources (to *ca.* 1960) is to be found in the *Bibl.* to Cl. Cahen's art. G̲H̲UZZ; especially to be noted is Cahen's further article *Le Malik-Nameh et l'histoire des origines seljukides*, in *Oriens*, ii (1949), 31-65, which brings together information from the lost *Malik-nāma* (which was probably written for the young prince Alp Arslan shortly after the death of his father Čag̲h̲rī Beg in 452/1060; see also Bosworth, *The Ghaznavids*, 219) preserved in Ṣadr al-Dīn al-Ḥusaynī, Ibn al-At̲h̲īr, Barhebraeus and Mīrk̲h̲ʷānd. Of additional and/or subsequent secondary sources, see R. Grousset, *L'empire des steppes*[4], 203 ff.; *İA*, arts. *Oğuzlar* (Faruk Sümer) and *Selçuklular* (Kafesoğlu); W. Barthold, *Four studies on the history of Central Asia. iii. A history of the Turkman people*, Leiden 1962, 99-102; C.E. Bosworth, in *Camb. hist. of Iran*, v, 15-23, 42 ff.; M.A. Köymen, *Büyük Selçuklu imparatorluğu tarihi.* i. *Kuruluş devri*, Ankara 1979; P.B. Golden, in *Camb. hist. of early Inner Asia*, Cambridge 1990, 361 ff.; art. TURKMENS. For chronology and genealogical tables, see Zambaur, *Manuel*, 143-4, 221-2; Bosworth, *The Islamic dynasties*, 115-18, 129-31; Leiser, *A history of the Seljuks*, 198-205.

III. The various branches of the Sald̲j̲ūḳs

The history of the Sald̲j̲ūḳ dynasty may now be followed through its component lines as listed above. Only salient events and major trends will be noted; for a detailed treatment of historical events, see the articles on individual sultans and princes and on the various provinces and regions ruled at times by the Sald̲j̲ūḳs.

1. The Great Sald̲j̲ūḳs of Persia and ʿIrāḳ (429-552/1038-1157)

The definitive capture of the former capital of G̲h̲aznawid K̲h̲urāsān, Nīs̲h̲āpūr, took place in 431/1040. Leaving affairs to his brother Čag̲h̲rī (see above, section II), Ṭog̲h̲rïl's main aim now was to expand westwards against the Daylamī and Kurdish princes of northern Persia, making Rayy his temporary capital and base for these operations. The securing of the rich lands of D̲j̲ibāl and the reduction of the Būyids were thus is objectives, with Ād̲h̲arbāyd̲j̲ān and the routes into the Caucasus, Armenia and Anatolia being left to the less-disciplined bands of Turkmens. The civil strife which broke out amongst the sons of the Būyid Abū Kālīd̲j̲ār [*q.v.*] after his death in 449/1048-9 facilitated Ṭog̲h̲rïl's intervention, especially when political chaos in Būyid Bag̲h̲dād seemed likely to lead to a degree of Fāṭimid control over the very capital of the ʿAbbāsids. In 447/1055 Ṭog̲h̲rïl assembled troops in D̲j̲ibāl and at Hamad̲h̲ān and marched on Bag̲h̲dād, ending there the feeble rule of the Būyid al-Malik al-Raḥim. Other Būyid princes survived only as Sald̲j̲ūḳ puppets in Fārs, and by 451/1060 all immediate threats to the ʿAbbāsids had been averted. Ṭog̲h̲rïl now exulted in his role of deliverer of the caliph. He received the honorific titles (*alḳāb* [see LAḲAB]) of *Rukn al-Dawla* and *Malik al-Mas̲h̲riḳ wa 'l-Mag̲h̲rib*, and was formally addressed as *Sulṭān* [*q.v.*] (a title for princes already in informal use, but now raised to the formal level and appearing as such e.g. on Ṭog̲h̲rïl's coins). He put pressure on al-Ḳāʾim to let him marry one of the ʿAbbāsid's daughters, so that the rapprochement between Sald̲j̲ūḳs and ʿAbbāsids, now the secular and spiritual leaders respectively of Sunnism in the central lands of the *Dār al-Islām*, begun by al-Ḳāʾim's marriage with a daughter of Čag̲h̲rī Beg some years before, could further be made closer (for a detailed analysis of this episode, and of Ṭog̲h̲rïl's probable motives, see G. Makdisi, *The marriage of Ṭug̲h̲ril Beg*, in *IJMES*, i [1970], 259-75).

Whilst Ṭog̲h̲rïl was occupied in the west, Čag̲h̲rī, from a base at Marw (which was to remain the Sald̲j̲ūḳ capital in the east up to and including Sand̲j̲ar's time), maintained control over K̲h̲ʷārazm against pressure from Ḳïpčaḳ nomads and a possible revival of Ḳarak̲h̲ānid ambitions their. He and his son Alp Arslan also kept up warfare against the G̲h̲aznawids, who, under Masʿūd's son Mawdūd [*q.v.*], were unreconciled to the loss of their Persian provinces; operations and counter-operations took place in northern Afg̲h̲ānistān during the 430s-440s/1040s-1050s until peace was finally made on the accession of the G̲h̲aznawid sultan Ibrāhīm b. Masʿūd in 451/1059, with a division of territories more or less dividing what is modern Afg̲h̲ānistān by a north-south line. It was during these years also that Čag̲h̲rī's son Ḳāwurd set up an amirate of his own in Kirmān (see below, 3), and Sald̲j̲ūḳ suzerainty was extended over the local maliks in the nearby province of Sīstān.

When the childless Ṭoghril died, Čaghrī's son Alp Arslan, who had been governing the province of Khurasān since his father's death, succeeded to the Saldjūḳ sultanate against the claims of another brother, Sulaymān. The great commanders of the Saldjūḳ army, and certainly Alp Arslan's vizier Niẓām al-Mulk, seem to have felt that the interests of the Saldjūḳ family and of their followers—and perhaps even the interests of the Saldjūḳ dominions, if such a sophisticated and prescient attitude may be attributed to their new ruling class—would best be served by a strong, unified rule; hence Alp Arslan became supreme sultan of all the Saldjūḳ lands. His ten years' reign (455-65/1063-73) and the twenty years' one of his son and successor Malik Shāh (465-85/1073-92) mark the zenith of the Great Saldjūḳ sultanate. Both rulers kept control over their far-flung territories by living lives of ceaseless journeying through the lands and campaigning on their borders. The threat of economic dislocation to the agricultural prosperity of Persia was alleviated by the deflection of the Turkmens and their herds westwards, against the Christian princes of the Caucasus and Anatolia and against the Fāṭimids and their allies in Syria, and Alp Arslan attached such importance to these projects that he fought in Georgia and Armenia personally in 456/1064 and 460/1068. Hence during their reigns, Persia and ʿIrāḳ enjoyed considerable agricultural and commercial prosperity.

Behind the two sultans stood the vizier Niẓām al-Mulk, whose influence was so marked and all-pervasive in the state that a later historian like Ibn al-Athīr calls his thirty years of office *al-dawla al-Niẓāmiyya*. Alp Arslan never himself visited Baghdād, but the Saldjūḳ presence was upheld there by a *shiḥna* or military governor, usually one of the Turkish commanders in the Saldjūḳ army of slave origin. During his reign, relations with the caliph were on the whole more cordial than they had been in Ṭoghril's time and were crowned in 464/1071-2 by the marriage of the sultan's daughter to al-Ḳāʾim's son and heir, the future caliph al-Muḳtadī [*q.v.*]. What gave Alp Arslan a great personal reputation as a Muslim hero was of course his campaign into Anatolia and defeat of the Byzantine emperor Romanus Diogenes at Malāzgird [*q.v.*] in 463/1071, although there are no indications that this was part of an official, systematic programme of aggressive expansionism in Asia Minor; Alp Arslan was probably content to nibble away at the eastern frontiers of Byzantium, and on this occasion confined himself to imposing tribute on Romanus and demanding the retrocession of some formerly Muslim border towns along the Byzantine-Muslim frontier (requirements which the deposition of the Emperor at Constantinople shortly afterwards rendered null and void).

Alp Arslan made Malik Shāh heir to the throne in 458/1066, and on this occasion, mindful of traditional obligations to his family, redistributed various governorships on the eastern fringes of the empire to princes of the Saldjūḳ family. The sultan was concerned to make firm the Saldjūḳ position on the far northeastern fringes of his empire, and several marriage alliances were made with the dominant Turkish power in Transoxania and eastern Turkestan, the Ḳarakhānids; but the granting out of these eastern march lands of the empire as appanages seems to indicate that the Great Saldjūḳs now regarded Persia and ʿIrāḳ as the real centre of gravity of their empire.

Malik Shāh continued and in some ways surpassed the achievements of his father, even though he was still only thirty-seven when he died. Niẓām al-Mulk remained the administrative mainstay of the sultanate, guiding the new, only eighteen-years old, monarch on his accession and hoping to mould him into the ideal of a Perso-Islamic despotic ruler, the image implicit in his treatise on statecraft, the *Siyāsat-nāma*. The vizier aimed at the creation of a centralised administration built around his *dīwān*, but the old Turkish ways and attitudes continued to be significant in regard to the sultan's conception of his own authority and his obligations to his own people, although these ways and attitudes are not always apparent from the exclusively Persian and Arabic sources. Senior members of the Saldjūḳ family were still very much conscious of what they regarded as their rights under steppe and tribal custom. Thus Ḳāwurd, Malik Shāh's uncle, a commander of great experience and *amīr* in Kirmān for a quarter of a century (see below, 3), took military action soon after Malik Shāh's accession in 465/1073 to enforce his claim to supreme power, as he saw it, since he was the senior member of the Saldjūḳ family, a claim grounded in the older, pre-Islamic ways, one which Malik Shāh nevertheless rejected on the grounds of the superiority of father-son descent in the transmission of power, the procedure which was now the norm in the new world of Perso-Islamic governmental tradition. It was the new, professional slave soldier element of Malik Shāh's army which secured for him the victory at Hamadhān over Ḳāwurd, rather than the Turkmen, tribal one, and the Turkmens established in those northern and eastern parts of Persia suitable for pastoral nomadism or transhumance probably now began to feel a certain alienation from what was going on in the sultans' main centres in the west at Hamadhān and Iṣfahān; these discontents were to well up in Khurāsān during the latter part of Sandjar's reign there (see below).

The new sultan was strong enough to exclude the ʿAbbāsid caliph from secular affairs in ʿIrāḳ, but day-to-day relations between the two powers were conducted through their respective viziers. The marriage alliance with the caliphate in 480/1087, when al-Muḳtadī married one of Malik Shāh's daughters, did not bring about the expected harmony, and shortly before he died Malik Shāh set about making Baghdād his winter capital and may even have toyed with the idea of deposing al-Muḳtadī and replacing him with his infant grandson, the offspring of the marriage just mentioned.

Externally, Malik Shāh inherited his father's concern about the northwestern territories, the regions of especial Turkmen concentration, Ādharbāydjān and Arrān, which he placed under his cousin Ismāʿīl b. Yāḳūtī b. Čaghrī's governorship, and he himself led campaigns against Georgia. But the policy of expansion into Anatolia by the sons of Qutlumush b. Arslan Isrāʾīl, Sulaymān and Manṣūr, who by 474/1081 were raiding as far as Iznik and the shores of the Sea of Marmara, was not an official one by the Saldjūḳ sultanate but the result of private enterprise by these cousins of the sultan, acting outside his own sphere of control, an enterprise which he did not necessarily regard with any great approval. Of more pressing importance to Malik Shāh was the upholding of Saldjūḳ authority in al-Djazīra and Syria against the local Arab amirates there, some of which were Shīʿī and therefore possibly pro-Fāṭimid in sentiment. From the Saldjūḳ bases in ʿIrāḳ and Syria (the latter province dominated after 471/1078 by Malik Shāh's brother Tutush, see below, 4), the sultan towards the end of his life secured the *khuṭba* for the ʿAbbāsids from the venal Sharīfs of Mecca and set about extending Saldjūḳ power down the west coast of Arabia into the Ḥidjāz and to Yemen and down the east coast into al-Aḥsā, projects permanently cut short by his death. At the other end of the empire, Malik Shāh had invaded Transoxania in 466/1073-4 in retaliation for a Ḳarakhānid attack on Ṭukhāristān prompted by Alp Arslan's death. He now in 482/1089 intervened militarily again in Transoxania in order to uphold Saldjūḳ overlordship, at a point when the Ḳarakhānid realm was internally troubled, and he even received the homage of the eastern Ḳarakhānid ruler of Kāshghar. With the Ghaznawids, however, the sultan had to treat on equal terms, arranging marriage links, although there seems to have been, certainly in the spheres of coinage and titulature, a perceptible Saldjūḳ cultural influence in Ghazna at this time.

Malik Shāh's death in 485/1092 marked the end of halcyon days for the Great Saldjūḳs. Instead of that sultan's firm rule, a situation immediately arose involving various young, untried princes and their ambitious mothers, with no wise and restraining hand in the state like that of Niẓām al-Mulk. An attempt by Malik Shāh's widow Terken Khātūn and the enemies of the recently-assassinated Niẓām al-Mulk to place Malik Shāh's four year-old son on the throne as Maḥmūd (I) failed. His older sons Berk-yaruḳ and Muḥammad Tapar, joined by their ambitious uncle Tutush until this latter was defeated and killed by Berk-yaruḳ's troops in 488/1095, now engaged in prolonged warfare with each other over the succession until Berk-yaruḳ died in 498/1105. Muḥammad brushed aside an attempt to raise Berk-yaruḳ's infant son to the throne as Malik Shāh (II), and from his base in Ādharbāydjān was able to succeed to the throne of the united Saldjūḳ dominions of western Persia and ʿIrāḳ, Khurāsān and the east having been placed by Berk-yaruḳ under the governorship of his young half-brother Aḥmad Sandjar (see below). Fortunately for the Saldjūḳs, distracted as they largely were by internal strife, the external frontiers of the empire held firm in these years, for the appearance of the Frankish Crusaders in the Syrian coastlands and the region of the upper Euphrates bend in 1098 and then the next year in Palestine was not felt as a major threat to the Saldjūḳ positions in central Syria and al-Djazīra. But the internecine warfare, affecting western Persia in particular, inevitably affected the personal authority of the contenders, who had to seek military support from the great slave commanders of the army and from the Turkmen begs and their personal followings. As a result, Turkmen principalities now began to take shape in provinces like Khūzistān, Diyār Bakr and al-Djazīra, headed by Turkish atabegs, nominally the tutors and guardians of young Saldjūḳ princes granted these provincial appanages according to the still-influential Turkish conception of a patrimonial share-out of offices and governorships. Not only did the central authority of the state decline in effectiveness, but continual warfare and the need for money to support the rival armies heralded a period of economic and social regression compared with the internal peace of previous reigns. The number of *iḳṭāʿ*s granted out during these years increased perceptibly, and the relaxation of central political control and general uncertainty and stress amongst the populace allowed a radical group of the Shīʿa like the Ismāʿīlīs or Assassins (see ISMĀʿĪLIYYA, and add to the *Bibl.* there, F. Daftary, *The Ismāʿīlīs, their history and doctrine*, Cambridge 1990) to strengthen their grip on various strongholds seized by them towards the end of Malik Shāh's reign in both Syria and Persia (see M.G.S. Hodgson, *The Order of Assassins. The struggle of the early Nizārī Ismāʿīlīs against the Islamic world*, The Hague 1955, 72-98; idem, in *Camb. hist. of Iran*, v, 424-51; Daftary, *op. cit.*, 324 ff.).

Muḥammad, undisputed sultan 498-511/1105-18, succeeded in re-asserting a good measure of control over the empire, with action against the Assassins in Djibāl and Daylam, and in 501/1108 he overthrew the Shīʿī Mazyadid *amīr* of Ḥilla in central ʿIrāḳ, Ṣadaḳa b. Manṣūr [see MAZYAD, BANŪ], thereby gaining the preponderance in ʿIrāḳ. Muḥammad was, indeed, the last Great Saldjūḳ sultan to rule the western parts of the empire with any degree of firmness, having left his brother Sandjar in Khurāsān as his viceroy, with the title of malik. When Muḥammad died, Sandjar was the senior member of the dynasty, and although it had been the practice over some eighty years for the supreme sultanate to be held by the Saldjūḳ who controlled western Persia and ʿIrāḳ, Sandjar's seniority gave him a special standing under Turkish tribal custom. He had first been appointed as governor of Khurāsān by Berk-yaruḳ, and Sandjar's coins minted up to 493/1100 acknowledge Berk-yaruḳ as his suzerain; but after that date, he had transferred his allegiance to Muḥammad (see N.M. Lowick, *Seljuq coins*, in *NC*, 7th ser., vol. x [1970], 244-6). He now assumed the role of supreme sultan, a move which the weaker, quarrelling sons of Muḥammad were unable to oppose, so that Sandjar's name was generally placed on their coins before their own; thus coins minted early in his reign by Maḥmūd (II) b. Muḥammad, sultan in western Persia and ʿIrāḳ (511-25/1118-31), attribute to Sandjar the title *al-Sulṭān al-Muʿaẓẓam* but simply give Maḥmūd's own name and patronymic.

Aḥmad Sandjar thus became ruler over northern Persia and Khurāsān, whilst his nephew Maḥmūd tried to maintain his authority in western Persia and ʿIrāḳ over his unruly brothers (see below, 2). Sandjar brought Maḥmūd, who was reluctant to acknowledge his uncle's supreme authority, to heel by defeating him in battle near Sāwa [*q.v.*] in 513/1119. Henceforth, Maḥmūd, and then his successors Ṭoghrïl (II) (526-9/1132-4) and Masʿūd (529-47/1134-52), remained clearly his vassals, with the title of sultans but in reality with the status of maliks; only latterly, during the period of Sandjar's preoccupation with affairs in Transoxania and Khʷārazm, did Masʿūd attain somewhat more freedom of action. Even so, the passage of time and the unprecedented length of Sandjar's rule in the east, first as malik and then as supreme sultan, in general strengthened Sandjar's moral authority within the dynasty.

Sandjar continued the policy of Berk-yaruḳ and Muḥammad by launching attacks on the Ismāʿīlīs of both Daylam and Ḳuhistān after the death in 518/1124 of Ḥasan-i Ṣabbāḥ, but without seriously affecting these sectarians' power in those localities. He also endeavoured, both as malik and then as sultan, to retain the Saldjūḳ overlordship established beyond the northeastern borders of the Saldjūḳ empire by his father Malik Shāh, who had made the Ḳarakhānids of Transoxania his tributaries. He placed Arslan Khān Muḥammad on the throne in Samarḳand in 495/1102 and confirmed the religious leadership in Bukhārā of the *ṣadr*s of the Āl-i Burhān [see ṢADR AL-ṢUDŪR], but at the end of Arslan Khān's long reign, Sandjar once more appeared at Samarḳand and placed a fresh nominee on the Ḳarakhānid throne. In neighbouring Khʷārazm, the Turkish Shāhs of the line of Anūshtigīn Gharčaʾī [see KHʷĀRAZM-SHĀHS] ruled also as

Sandjar's vassals; Ḳuṭb al-Dīn Muḥammad b. Anūshtigin always remained respectful towards the Saldjūḳ sultan, but his son Atsiz had his own ambitions and in 533/1138 rebelled openly against Sandjar's overlordship. The latter led expeditions against him on this and on subsequent occasions, but events were soon to prove that Saldjūḳ resources were overstretched in attempting to keep up any degree of military control beyond the Oxus. More lasting, however, was the assertion of Saldjūḳ suzerainty over, and the communication of a strong Saldjūḳ cultural influence within, the Ghaznawid sultanate in Afghānistān and northern India, when the sultan in 510/1117 placed his protégé Bahrām Shāh on the throne of Ghazna.

The catalyst for the ending of Saldjūḳ influence beyond the Oxus was the appearance within the Islamic lands there of a new power, the pagan Ḳara Khiṭay [*q.v.*] from northern China, who moved against Transoxania, provoking Sandjar to intervene as suzerain of the threatened Ḳarakhānids there. But in a fiercely-fought battle in the Ḳaṭwān steppes to the east of Samarḳand, the Muslim forces were routed by the Ḳara Khiṭay, and Sandjar and the Ḳarakhānid ruler Maḥmūd Khān had to flee southwards to Khurāsān (536/1141).

Sandjar's prestige was badly affected, and the remaining years of his reign were spent in trying to preserve his Khurāsānian possessions at a time when new, aggressive powers, in addition to the Ḳara Khiṭay (who soon showed that they had no ambitions south of the Oxus), were arising in the east, sc. the Khwārazm Shāhs and the Ghūrids [*q.v.*] from central Afghānistān. But it was stresses and discontents within Khurāsān which, despite Sandjar's attempts to stay attuned to Turkmen feeling there (see above, section II), brought his rule there to a dismal and painful end. The expense of warfare in these far eastern lands meant increased taxation demands on the population of Khurāsān, including on the bands there of nomadising Oghuz or Ghuzz. They became increasingly restive under Saldjūḳ financial oppression, until in 548/1153 they burst out into open revolt against the sultan. The province lapsed into chaos and violence, but most disastrously, Sandjar himself was captured by the Ghuzz and kept in close tutelage. He managed to escape only after a lengthy confinement, and shortly afterward died, at the age of seventy-one, in 552/1157. The leaderless commanders of the Saldjūḳ army in Khurāsān had offered the sultanate to the Ḳarakhānid Maḥmūd Khān, who was actually Sandjar's nephew. The then Saldjūḳ sultan in the west, Muḥammad (II) b. Maḥmūd, agreed to this, and it was clear that the *amīrs* of the Saldjūḳ army in Khurāsān regarded effective rule by the Saldjūḳ family there as finished, and in the ensuing years they were to divide out amongst themselves the power in Khurāsān. To contemporaries, it seemed like the end of an epoch, for Sandjar had ruled, as malik and sultan, for over sixty years.

2. The Saldjūḳs of Western Persia and ʿIrāḳ (511-90/1118-94)

The history of this line of sultans follows on from the reign of the last Great Saldjūḳ sultan in the west, Muḥammad b. Malik Shāh, but the unity and effectiveness of the sultanate here, briefly re-established by Muḥammad, could not be maintained. His sons and successors include several of mediocre capabilities, but some also of high calibre; yet the conditions in which they endeavoured to exercise their power were now very different from those of forceful rulers like Ṭoghrïl Beg, Alp Arslan and Malik Shāh. Following old Turkish practice of a patrimonial share-out of power, five of Muḥammad's sons contended for mastery in various parts of the realm over the next three or four decades: Maḥmūd, Masʿūd, Ṭoghrïl, Sulaymān Shāh and Saldjūḳ Shāh, all exerting some sort of authority for a while and all but the last actually ruling as sultans. With the succession permanently in dispute, a decisive voice was that of the Turkish atabegs, commanders who were originally attached as tutors to young Saldjūḳ princes sent out as provincial governors but who frequently arrogated to themselves political and military power in these governorships (see ATABAK, and. Lambton, *Continuity and change in medieval Persia*, London 1988, 229-33), and of those *amīrs* who had personal armies and could therefore lend their support to one or other of the contenders. Naturally, this support had its price: the interference of these *amīrs* in central government affairs and the increased alienation of state lands which had to be distributed as *iḳṭāʿ*s in payment to the military. The decay of the once mighty and united sultanate was lamented by contemporaries, and in Maḥmūd's reign, the secretary and historian Anūshirwān b. Khālid [*q.v.*] mourned the situation: "In Muḥammad's reign the kingdom was united and secure from all attacks; but when it passed to his son Maḥmūd, they split up that unity and destroyed its cohesion. They claimed a share with him in the power, and left him only a bare subsistence". He likewise asserts that, by the time of his death in 525/1131, Maḥmūd had got through the treasury of eighteen million dīnārs plus estates, jewels, clothing, etc., left by his father (al-Bundārī, 134-5, 155-6).

The general tendency during these years of civil strife between the sons of Muḥammad was for the sultan to exercise authority in ʿIrāḳ and southern Djibāl, but to have little beyond these regions; thus during Maḥmūd's reign (511-25/1118-31), Ṭoghrïl held northern Djibāl and the Caspian provinces and Maḥmūd was never able to dislodge him, whilst Masʿūd held Ādharbāydjān, Mawṣil and al-Djazīra. Even within ʿIrāḳ, Maḥmūd's position was challenged by local powers there like the Mazyadids and ambitious commanders like ʿImād al-Dīn Zangī (see on this last, H.A.R. Gibb, *Zengi and the fall of Edessa*, in *A history of the Crusades*, i, 449-62), so that the Saldjūḳ hold on ʿIrāḳ tended to be confined to the central part only. Anūshirwān b. Khālid, again, noted how Sandjar had appropriated all the northern Persian provinces as *iḳṭāʿ*s, how most of Fārs and Khūzistān was held by Maḥmūd's rival Saldjūḳ Shāh, and how the Mazyadid Dubays b. Ṣadaḳa held much of southern and central ʿIrāḳ, so that the sultan was left with only an exiguous amount of territory from which he could grant *iḳṭāʿ*s to his supporters, and had to resort to arbitrary confiscations (al-Bundārī, 134-5). The preoccupations of the Saldjūḳs within their own territories allowed the Christian Georgians, under the great David "the Restorer", to recover ground in eastern Transcaucasia [see AL-KURDJ]. A longer-term trend was that Saldjūḳ dissensions gave the ʿAbbāsids an opportunity to increase their military effectiveness and secular power during the course of the 6th/12th century, under the forceful rule of such figures as al-Mustarshid (512-29/1118-35 [*q.v.*]), al-Muḳtafī (530-55/1136-60 [*q.v.*]) and, above all, al-Nāṣir (575-622/1180-1225 [*q.v.*]). Their lengthy periods of rule contrasted with the frequent changes in the holders of power within the sultanate, and these caliphs were moreover served by capable viziers such as ʿAwn al-Dīn Ibn Hubayra and his son ʿIzz al-Dīn [see IBN HUBAYRA] dedicated to raising the effectiveness of the caliphate in the politics of the age. Accordingly, it became more and more difficult for the Saldjūḳs to maintain what they had come to regard as their rights in Baghdād, including the payment of tribute to them by the caliphs and the maintenance of a *shiḥna* within the city. The high points of Saldjūḳ authority at this time were reached in 529/1135, when Masᶜūd b. Muḥammad (529-47/1134-52) defeated the caliph al-Mustarshid outside Hamadhān, soon after which the caliph was mysteriously killed in the sultan's camp; and in 530/1136, when Masᶜūd deposed al-Mustarshid's successor al-Rāshid (529-30/1135-6 [*q.v.*])—who had assembled, but in the end unsuccessfully, a grand coalition of discontented Saldjūḳ princes and Turkish commanders against the sultan—and installed in his stead his uncle al-Muḳtafī. However, the new caliph soon began vigorously to assert his secular rights, to build up his army by purchasing Armenian and Greek slave soldiers and then to defy the sultan. When Masᶜūd died, al-Muḳtafī expelled from Baghdād the Saldjūḳ *shiḥna* and appropriated the sultan's palace and lands there; no representative of the Saldjūḳs were allowed in the capital again.

Ādharbāydjān, where Masᶜūd had maintained himself before achieving the sultanate, passed to the Saldjūḳ prince Dāwūd b. Maḥmūd, from where he made several attempts to secure the sultanate for himself; but by the end of Masᶜūd's reign, power in Ādharbāydjān was monopolised by two Turkish commanders, Eldigüz or Ildeniz [*q.v.*], atabeg of prince Arslan b. Ṭoghrïl (II), and Aḳ Sunḳur Aḥmadīlī [see AḤMADĪLĪS] of Marāgha. The line of Eldigüzids or Ildeñizids [*q.v.*] was to form a significant power in Arrān, most of Ādharbāydjān and parts of Djibāl until the early 7th/13th century: until the death of the last Saldjūḳ of Persia, Ṭoghrïl (III) b. Arslan (590/1194) as theoretical vassals of the Saldjūḳs, but thereafter as a fully-independent if short-lived dynasty. Likewise, Fārs was during Masᶜūd's reign dominated by the Turkish commander Boz Aba, who towards the end of his rule there supported the claims to the sultanate of two of the sons of Maḥmūd, Malik Shāh (III) (547-8/1152-3) and Muḥammad (II) 548-55/1153-60); after this, Fārs became the base for the atabeg dynasty there of the Salghurids [*q.v.*]. Mawṣil and al-Djazīra, a march province against the Frankish County of Edessa and various recalcitrant Turkmen potentates of Syria and southeastern Anatolia, was governed by a Saldjūḳ freedman Aḳ Ṣonḳur al-Bursuḳī [*q.v.*] until 519/1126, but he was the last ruler in this region who could really be described as a dependent of the Saldjūḳs, for the sultans' increasing difficulties were to allow Zangī after 521/1127 to achieve virtual independence there. Indicative of the growing real power of the Atabegs was the appearance of their names on Saldjūḳ coins minted from 511/1118 onwards, i.e. from the accession of Maḥmūd b. Muḥammad, whereas previously, only the names of the caliph and the sultan had been given on them (cf. Lowick, *Seljuq coins*, 246-50).

With Masᶜūd's death in 547/1152, the Saldjūḳ sultanate of the west entered its final phase of decline; Ibn al-Athīr writes that "with him, the fortunes of the Saldjūḳ family died; after him there was no banner to depend upon or to rally round". This juncture was also, as will be recalled from 1. above, the one when the senior member of the family, Sandjar, was becoming embroiled with the Ghuzz in Khurāsān, hence could give no help to his kinsmen in the west. Trends discernible during the previous three decades were now accentuated. The northwest of Persia remained dominated by the Eldigüzids and Aḥmadīlīs; Armenia and Diyār Bakr were disputed by the atabeg line of the Shāh Armanids of Akhlāṭ and the Ayyūbids [*q.vv.*]; Mawṣil and al-Djazīra were held by the Zangids; Turkmen governors controlled Khūzistān; and the Salghurids strengthened their grip on Fārs, one which was to endure well into Il-Khānid times. The caliph al-Muḳtafī was now the chief power in ᶜIrāḳ, and after 575/1180, al-Nāṣir b. al-Mustaḍīᵓ made himself a central figure in the politics and diplomacy of the central Islamic lands; but by now, the main threat to the ᶜAbbāsids came not from the Saldjūḳ sultans but from the vigorous and expanding Khʷārazm Shāhs.

Sultan Masᶜūd left no direct heir so that, as after his father Muḥammad's death, there ensued a series of succession disputes amongst the Saldjūḳ princes with claims to the throne, including his brother Sulaymān Shāh and various of his nephews, none of whom, with the exception of Muḥammad (II) b. Maḥmūd (548-54/1153-9), were of more than mediocre ability. They were all largely dependent on the support of the great Turkish commanders, who used Saldjūḳ claimants as shields for their own personal ambitions and who were often allied by marriage with the Saldjūḳ family; thus Arslan Shāh b. Ṭoghrïl (II) (556-71/1161-76) was the stepson of the atabeg Eldigüz, since the latter had married Ṭoghrïl's widow. The Saldjūḳ family still had a certain amount of *baraka* and prestige in its name, especially in the eyes of their Turkmen tribal followers. The Oghuz of Khurāsān treated the captive Sandjar in a contemptuous and humiliating fashion, but did not apparently ill-treat him, and when in 549/1154-5 the *amīrs* of the Saldjūḳ army in ᶜIrāḳ were trying to rally their forces against the caliph al-Muḳtafī, they brought out from his captivity in the citadel of Takrīt Arslan Shāh b. Ṭoghrïl (II), the future penultimate sultan of the dynasty, in order to inspirit the army and the Turkmens (al-Bundārī, 236-7). But such feelings now began to wear thin.

During his six years or so as sultan, Muḥammad (II) tried energetically to restore the Saldjūḳ position in ᶜIrāḳ, defeating his uncle and rival Sulaymān Shāh and besieging Baghdād (551-2/1157) before illness and death overtook him with his task inaccomplished. The Turkish commanders were at variance over the choice of a successor, for the prestige of the Saldjūk name still demanded a Saldjūḳ prince as nominal supreme ruler in western Persia. In 556/1161 Eldigüz's candidate Arslan b. Ṭoghrïl was installed in the capital Hamadhān, but the caliph al-Mustandjid [*q.v.*] refused to recognise him as sultan, fearing the constituting of a powerful Saldjūḳ-Eldigüzid state which would once again reduce caliphal power. Eldigüz and, after 570/1175, his sons Pahlawān Muḥammad and Ḳïzïl Arslan [*q.vv.*], secured the *khuṭba* for their protégé sultan Arslan in Khurāsān, now ruled by Turkish *amīrs*, and also in Mawṣil and al-Djazīra, by exerting pressure on the Zangids there; the Eldigüzids did indeed dominate the politics of northern Persia and beyond at this time, and were the most effective deterrent to the ambitions of the Khʷārazm Shāhs within Persia.

Arslan not surprisingly chafed under Eldigüzid tutelage. On Eldigüz's death he tried to break away from this, but himself died shortly afterwards, and Pahlawān Muḥammad now set up the last of the Saldjūḳ sultans of Persia, the child Ṭoghrïl (III) b. Arslan (571-90/1176-94). Ṭoghrïl was praised by contemporaries both for his learning and for his martial abilities. On reaching his maturity, Ṭoghrïl attempted, with aid from the Turkish commander in Rayy,

Ḳutlugh Inanč Muḥammad, to break away from Ḳïzïl Arslan ʿUthmān's grip, but failed and was seized and jailed by the latter, who then claimed the sultanate for himself before he died mysteriously a year later. Ṭoghrïl was released after two years' incarceration, gathered support in northern Persia and made himself master of Djibāl; but he was unable to prevail against the Khwārazm Shāh Tekish, and in a battle outside Rayy in 590/1194 was defeated and killed. Since the line of Ḳāwurd's descendants in Kirmān had ended only a few years before (see below, 3), this marked the end of the Saldjūḳ dynasty in Persia and ʿIrāḳ. The sources note that the dynasty began with a Ṭoghrïl and ended with a Ṭoghrïl. The dynasty's demise does not seem to have stirred up any feelings of regret or nostalgia; for almost four decades the sultans had been only one element, and that an increasingly enfeebled one, in the complex pattern of Persian politics on the eve of the twin catastrophes of Khwārazmian and then Mongol invasion.

Bibliography: The bibliography for a century and a half of the history of much of the central and eastern lands of Islam is immense. Detailed reference may be made to the bibls. to the articles on individual sultans, caliphs and atabegs. There are relevant sections in J. Sauvaget, *Introd. à l'histoire de l'Orient musulman*, 140 ff., in Cl. Cahen's English *refonte* and enlargement, *Jean Sauvaget's Introduction to the history of the Muslim East*, Berkeley and Los Angeles 1965, 151 ff., and Cahen's *Introd. à l'histoire du monde musulman médiéval VIIe-XVe siècle*, Paris 1982, 149-50. Kosuke Shimizu, *Bibliography on Seljuk studies*, Tokyo 1979, is based on a previous Turkish bibl. *The Index islamicus* of J.D. Pearson *et alii* has items on Saldjūḳ history in its sections on Turkey and Persia. Finally, there are extensive bibls. by Bosworth, in *Camb. hist. of Iran*, v, 683-9, and by Leiser, in *A history of the Seljuks*, 190-6; see also the bibl. given above in section I. Hence only some of the main sources specifically bearing on Saldjūḳ history will be noted here summarily.

1. Primary sources. Niẓām al-Mulk, *Siyāsat-nāma*; Ibn al-Djawzī, *Muntaẓam*; Ẓahīr al-Dīn Nīshāpūrī, *Saldjūḳ-nāma*; Sibṭ Ibn al-Djawzī, *Mirʾāt al-zamān*; Bundārī, *Zubdat al-nuṣra* (enshrines, via ʿImād al-Dīn al-Iṣfahānī, Anūshirwān b. Khālid's *Nafthat al-maṣdūr fī ṣudūr zamān al-futūr*; there is a continuation of Anūshirwān in the anonymous, so far unpublished, *Taʾrīkh al-Wuzarāʾ*, on which see K.A. Luther, in *Isl.*, xlv [1969], 117-28); Rāwandī, *Rāḥat al-ṣudūr*; Ṣadr al-Dīn al-Ḥusaynī, *Akhbār al-dawla al-saldjūḳiyya*; anon., *Mudjmal al-tawārīkh wa 'l-ḳiṣaṣ*; Ibn al-Athīr; Ibn Khallikān; Barhebraeus, *Chronography*; Muḥammad al-Yazdī, *al-ʿUrāḍa fi 'l-ḥikāya al-saldjūḳiyya*; Ibn al-Ṭiḳṭaḳā, *Fakhrī*; Ḥamd Allāh Mustawfī, *Taʾrīkh-i Guzīda*; Mīrkhwānd, *Rawḍat al-ṣafāʾ*. See on the sources of Saldjūḳ history in general, V.A. Hamdani, *A critical study of the sources for the history of the Saljūqs of ʿIrāq and Syria*, diss. Oxford University 1939, unpubl.; Cahen, *The historiography of the Seljuqid period*, in B. Lewis and P.M. Holt (eds.), *Historians of the Middle East*, London 1962, 59-78; K. Shimizu, *Bibliography on Saljuq studies*, Tokyo 1979.

2. Secondary sources. M.F. Sanaullah, *The decline of the Saljūqid empire*, Calcutta 1938; W. Barthold, *Histoire des Turcs d'Asie centrale*, Paris 1945, 79-93; M.A. Köymen, *Büyük Selçuklu imparatorluğu tarihi. II. İkinci imparatorluk devri*, Ankara 1954 (covers Sandjar's reign; the promised preceding volume on Sandjar as *malik* has never appeared); Cl. Cahen, *The Turkish invasion: the Selchükids*, in K.M. Setton and M.W. Baldwin, *A history of the Crusades*. i. *The first hundred years*, Philadelphia 1955, 135-76; ʿAbbās Iḳbāl, *Wizārat dar ʿahd-i salāṭīn-i buzurg-i Saldjūḳiyān*, Tehran 1338 *sh*./1959; C.E. Bosworth, *The political and dynastic history of the Iranian world (A.D. 1000-1217)*, in *Camb. hist. of Iran*, v, 1-202; Carla L. Klausner, *The Seljuk vezirate. A study of civil administration 1055-1194*, Cambridge, Mass. 1973; M.G.S. Hodgson, *The venture of Islam*. ii. *The expansion of Islam in the middle periods*, Chicago 1974, 42-61; G. Leiser (ed. and tr.), *A history of the Seljuks*; P.B. Golden, art. *Seljuq*, in *Dictionary of the Middle Ages*. For the chronological and genealogical connections of the Great Saldjūḳs and their branches in Kirmān and Syria, see C.E. Bosworth, *The new Islamic dynasties*, Edinburgh 1996, ch. X, no. 86.

3. The Saldjūḳs of Kirmān (440-582/1048-1186)

After his victory in Khurāsān, Ṭoghrïl Beg sent an expedition in 433/1041 to conquer the province of Kirmān, in southeastern Persia, from its Būyid ruler, ʿImād al-Dīn Abū Kālīdjār Marzubān [*q.v.*]. This was repulsed, but Saldjūḳ rule was imposed on Kirmān, and on the mountain peoples of the southern part of the province, the Ḳufṣ [*q.v.*] and Balūč [see BALŪČISTĀN. A.], by Ḳara Arslan Ḳāwurd in 440/1048. Eventually, this control was extended to the Arabian Sea coast in Makrān, and over the Gulf of Oman to ʿUmān, where a Saldjūḳ *shiḥna* was installed and suzerainty exerted over the local Arab rulers for nearly eighty years. The varied topography and climatic zones of Kirmān itself were congenial to Ḳāwurd's Ghuzz followers, who were able to practice there a transhumant way of life with their flocks, whilst the slave and other professional soldiers in his forces were granted *iḳṭāʿ*s from the agricultural lands there.

The detailed history of the Saldjūḳ amirate which now came into being can be followed in KIRMĀN. History, and only a few general points will be made here. The compact geographical boundaries of the amirate seem to have allowed a greater degree of administrative centralisation within it as compared with the lands of the wider Saldjūḳ sultanate in Persia and ʿIrāḳ. Muḥammad Shāh b. Malik Shāh of Kirmān (537-51/1142-56) had, according to the local historian Muḥammad b. Ibrāhīm, 29-30, a highly-developed espionage and intelligence system, both within Kirmān and outside, extending as far as Khurāsān and Iṣfahān. On the whole, and until the chaos of the last decade or so of the amirate's existence, Kirmān enjoyed a period of peace and prosperity. This was helped by the province's position on the trade routes which ran down from Khurāsān and Central Asia to the Gulf shores, carrying commerce which the *amīrs* themselves, since they drew a substantial income from transit taxes on merchants and from customs dues levied at ports like Tīz in Makrān (see below, section V. 1), encouraged considerably. Thus caravanserais were built and the roads protected against the brigandage of the Ḳufṣ and other lawless elements. During the long rule of Arslan Shāh (I) b. Kirmān Shāh (495-537/1101-42) and during that of Bahrām Shāh b. Ṭoghrïl Shāh (565-70/1170-5), foreign merchants, including Rūmīs and Indians, established trading colonies in the towns of Kirmān or Bardasīr (the *amīrs*' summer capital) and in Djīruft [*q.v.*] (the winter capital) (Afḍal al-Dīn Kirmānī, *ʿIḳd al-ʿulā*, Tehran 1311/1932-3, 70-1; Muḥammad b. Ibrāhīm, 25-6, 49). It was Arslan Shāh, one of the outstanding rulers of his family, who, according to Ibn al-Djawzī, in 533/1138-9 sought the mediation of Sultan Masʿūd b. Muḥammad in seeking the hand of the ʿAbbāsid caliph al-Mustarshid's widow; he had already cemented links with the main branch of the Saldjūḳs by marrying one of Muḥammad b. Malik Shāh's daughters. Indeed, relations with the supreme sultans in western Persia and ʿIrāḳ, and with Sandjar in the east, remained close; at the outset, Ḳāwurd's coins had acknowledged the authority of the ruler of the east, his father Čaghrī Beg, and in general, the Kirmān *amīrs* continued to express their subordination on their coins (see Lowick, *Seljuq coins*, 250-1, and Bulliet, *Numismatic evidence for the relationship between Ṭughril Beg and Chaghrī Beg*, 290-1).

For most of the amirate's existence, its rulers were content to enjoy their own province, but on certain occasions the *amīrs* endeavoured to extend their military power or their diplomatic activities beyond the boundaries of Kirmān. It was Ḳāwurd's army which in 454/1062 entered the neighbouring province of Fārs, defeated the Shabānkāraʾī Kurdish chief Faḍlūya there and ended the rule of the nominal rulers of Fārs, the Būyids; Fārs now became part of Ṭoghrïl Beg's sultanate, although Saldjūḳ control was not finally made firm until Faḍlūya was captured and killed in 461/1069. Ḳāwurd's own claim to the Great Saldjūḳ sultanate, as senior member of the family after Alp Arslan's death, and his resultant bid for power, have been mentioned above in 1. Arslan Shāh in 508/1114-15 invaded Fārs, then under the Turkish commander, on behalf of Muḥammad b. Malik Shāh, Čawuli Saḳāʾū, and also intervened at one point in a succession dispute at Yazd involving the vassal governor of the Saldjūḳs there, the Daylamī ʿAlāʾ al-Dawla Garshāsp [see KĀKŪYIDS].

Many of Kirmān's historic contacts were with the lands further east; in previous times Kirmān had formed part of such military empires as those of the Ṣaffārids (later 3rd/9th and early 4th/10th centuries) and of the Ghaznawids (early 5th/11th century). In the succession dispute of 510-12/1117-18 between the Ghaznawids Arslan Shāh and his brother Bahrām Shāh, the latter appealed to Arslan Shāh of Kirmān for help; but Arslan Shāh preferred to leave a situation which came more within Sandjar's sphere of interest (the dispute was in fact resolved by Sandjar's military support at Ghazna for Bahrām Shāh's candidature). At some date unspecified by Muḥammad b. Ibrāhīm, Ḳāwurd sent his son Amīrān Shāh with an army into Sīstān, although at this time Sīstān was attached, as a vassal state, to the Great Saldjūḳs controlling Khurāsān, to Ṭoghrïl's brother Mūsā Bīghū or Payghū and shortly afterwards to Čaghrī's son Yāḳūtī, and then in the next century, to Sandjar.

The events of the last years of the Saldjūḳ amirate in Kirmān were in many ways a replica of what had already happened in the Saldjūḳ lands of western Persia and Khurāsān. In a period of short-reigning *amīrs*, especially after 565/1170, the Saldjūḳ princes in Kirmān fell under the control of slave commander atabegs, such as Muʾayyid al-Dīn Rayḥān, the former atabeg of Ṭoghrïl Shāh b. Muḥammad (I) Shāh b. Arslan Shāh. The warfare which raged between the contenders for power devastated the countryside of Kirmān and imposed new financial burdens on its people. Added to this, from 575/1179-80 onwards, Kirmān was afflicted by fresh bands of Oghuz tribesmen deflected southwards from Khurāsān by the fighting there between the Khʷārazm Shāhs and the Ghūrids, and these bands brought further ruin to agriculture and trade, bringing about severe famine in towns like Bardasīr. Finally, in 582/1186, the Oghuz leader Malik Dīnār took over the province from the last Saldjūḳ *amīr*, Muḥammad (II) Shāh b. Bahrām Shāh, who fled and ultimately entered the service of the Ghūrids. This event came only eight years before the end also of the Saldjūḳ sultanate in Western Persia; only in Anatolia did the Saldjūḳs now remain as rulers.

Bibliography: In addition to the general primary sources for Saldjūḳ history listed in 2. above (Rāwandī, Bundārī, Ḥusaynī, Ibn al-Athīr, etc.), Kirmān is especially well served for this period by its quite abundant local histories, in particular, by Afḍal al-Dīn Kirmānī's *ʿIḳd al-ʿulā li 'l-mawḳif al-aʿlā* and his *Badāyiʿ al-zamān fī waḳāyiʿ Kirmān*, but also by what is in effect a special history of the Saldjūḳs of Kirmān, Muḥammad b. Ibrāhīm's *Taʾrīkh-Saldjūḳiyān-i Kirmān*. For full details, see the *Bibl.* to KIRMĀN.

Of secondary sources, see M.Th. Houtsma, *Zur Geschichte der Selǵuqen von Kermân*, in *ZDMG*, xxxix (1885), 362-410 (essentially a résumé of Houtsma's own edition of Muḥammad b. Ibrāhīm); Bosworth, in *Camb. hist. of Iran*, v, 58-60, 87-90, 117, 173-4; Erdoğan Merçil, *Kirman Selçukları*, Istanbul 1980.

4. The Saldjūḳs of Syria (471-511/1078-1117)

The Turkmen bands which had come westwards with the Saldjūḳ brothers went mainly towards Armenia, the Caucasus and Anatolia, but others of them infiltrated the regions of Diyār Bakr and the upper part of al-Djazīra. Already in the later part of Ṭoghrïl's reign, Turkmens had reached Malaṭya. In the 1060s they were harrying the countryside around Edessa (Urfa or al-Ruhā [*q.v.*]), and Alp Arslan during the course of his campaign against the Byzantines, attacked the city in spring 453/1071, and it may have accepted the nominal suzerainty of the Saldjūḳ sultan; over the next three decades, until the arrival of the Frankish Crusaders, Edessa was to be attacked by various Turkmen commanders, including the Saldjūḳ prince Tutush and the Artuḳid Suḳman of Ḥiṣn Kayfā and Mārdīn (see J.B. Segal, *Edessa 'The Blessed City'*, Oxford 1970, 220 ff.).

The Saldjūḳ sultans came to attach importance to Syria as the westwards extension of the position which they had established for themselves since Ṭoghrïl's time in Mawṣil and the southern parts of al-Djazīra, but most of all because it was a march province between themselves, the champions of Sunnī orthodoxy as they saw themselves, and their Shīʿī opponents and rivals, the Fāṭimids. Syria was a region of great fragmentation, politically, ethnically and confessionally, with a strong local strain of Shīʿism amongst the Muslim Arab tribes and principalities there; the First Crusade was shortly afterwards to take advantage of these political, tribal and sectarian divisions.

In the second half of the 5th/11th century, the Fāṭimids' hold on southern Syria and Palestine was progressively reduced, until by the time of appearance of the Franks, they held only some fortresses on the Palestinian and Lebanese coasts. This rolling-back of Fāṭimid control from inland Syria and Palestine was in part the work of various Turkmen commanders despatched there by the Great Saldjūḳs, and in part that of Turkmen begs and their flocks, allowed to infiltrate Syria and act on their own initiative. This latter was the case with the tribal beg Atsïz b. Uvak [*q.v.*] who first, in 463/1071, entered southern Syria and Palestine at the invitation of the Fāṭimid caliph al-Mustanṣir [*q.v.*], who hoped to use him as a counterforce against the rebellious Bedouin Arab tribesmen of the region. Atsïz tried to set up a Turkmen principality of his own there but, having fallen out with the Fāṭimids, whose army besieged him in Damascus, he had to appeal for aid to the Saldjūḳ sultan Malik Shāh. The latter in fact decided to allot central and southern Syria and Palestine as an appanage for his brother Tutush [*q.v.*]; once Tutush arrived in Syria, he lifted the siege of Damascus but executed his potential rival Atsïz (471/1078).

Tutush then began an amirate in Syria which lasted for seventeen years (471-88/1078-95). Northern Syria, with its strategically-placed centre of Aleppo, had been controlled by the Arab Mirdāsids [see MIRDĀS, BANŪ], latterly in full decline, and replaced after 472/1080 by the Saldjūḳs' vassal, the ʿUḳaylid Muslim b. Ḳuraysh [see ʿUKAYLIDS]. Disputes over possession of Aleppo between Tutush and the Saldjūḳ leader of raids into Rūm, Sulaymān b. Ḳutulmush (see below, 5), which ended in Sulaymān's defeat and death in battle in 479/1086, led to Malik Shāh's coming west from Iṣfahān personally with a large army in order to impose order in Syria. He occupied Aleppo and appointed various of his commanders as governors: Bozan in Edessa, Yaghï Siyan in Antioch, Aḳ Sonḳur in Aleppo and northern Syria, and the Turkmen beg Artuḳ in Jerusalem. Al-Djazīra and Syria were thus firmly brought within the supreme sultan's control, with Tutush's authority confined to central and southern Syria. All these local governors and Tutush were ordered to conduct operations against the coastal areas of the Levant, where petty rulers like Ibn ʿAmmār of Tripoli [see ʿAMMĀR, BANŪ] still enjoyed virtually undisturbed power.

The death of Malik Shāh in 485/1092 enabled Tutush to put forward his claim, as the most experienced of the surviving sons of Alp Arslan, to the supreme Saldjūḳ sultanate. He proclaimed himself sultan at Damascus, managed to kill Aḳ Sonḳur and Bozan, and extended his military power over all Syria and al-Djazīra, preparing to march eastwards into Persia against Malik Shāh's successor Berk-yaruḳ (see above, 1). But a majority of the great Turkish commanders—doubtless hoping to achieve a greater role in the state under the youthful Berk-yaruḳ than under the mature Tutush—eventually rallied to Berk-yaruḳ, and Tutush was defeated and killed near Rayy (Ṣafar 488/February 1095).

Berk-yaruḳ was never, however, able to exert his authority in the lands west of ʿIrāḳ, and Tutush's two sons Riḍwān and Duḳāḳ, encouraged by the latter's atabeg Ṭughtigin [*q.v.*], a former slave commander of Tutush's, succeeded to their father as maliks in Syria at Aleppo and Damascus respectively, refusing to recognise Berk-yaruḳ as sultan and making the *khuṭba* in Syria in their own names. The reigns of both of these princes largely coincided with the arrival in the Levant of the First Crusade, which injected a new element into the already complex political and dynastic rivalries in Syria.

Duḳāḳ (488-97/1095-1104) remained for all of his reign very much in the shadow of Ṭughtigin, who was not only his atabeg but also his stepfather, since Tutush had given Duḳāḳ's mother in marriage to Ṭughtigin. From the outset, Riḍwān (488-507/1095-1113 [*q.v.*]) was at odds with his brother and with Ṭughtigin, and in 489/1096 or the following year, the two sides clashed in battle near Ḳinnasrīn [*q.v.*], Riḍwān having secured troop reinforcements from the Fāṭimids. Duḳāḳ and Yaghï Siyan were decisively defeated, and had to agree to placing Riḍwān's name in the *khuṭbas* of Damascus and Antioch before their own. When the Crusaders besieged Yaghï Siyan in Antioch, Duḳāḳ and Ṭughtigin sent soldiers to reinforce an army sent by the supreme sultan Berk-yaruḳ, but failed to save the city (henceforth the centre of the Latin Principality of Antioch), and Riḍwān himself was soon afterwards defeated by the Franks. Duḳāḳ died in 497/1104, and Ṭughtigin simply replaced him at Damascus by Duḳāḳ's young brother Ertash or Begtash, until shortly afterwards Ṭughtigin dispensed with them and assumed both *de jure* and *de facto* power. With this, Saldjūḳ rule in Damascus ended.

Although there were local, temporary alliances amongst the Turkish and Arab princes of Syria and Palestine against the Crusaders, the irreconcilable division between Riḍwān and Ṭughtigin had allowed the Franks to continue their march southwards to Jerusalem and beyond. Damascus, a firmly Sunnī city and the bastion of orthodoxy in Syria, was, under the skilful rule of Ṭughtigin, able to withstand pressure from the Crusaders, and Ṭughtigin went on to found his own short-lived Turkish dynasty there, the Börids [see BŪRIDS]; before his death in 522/1128, he had in 509/1116 been reconciled to the Saldjūḳ sultan Maḥmūd b. Muḥammad and had been appointed governor for the Saldjūḳs over Syria.

After Duḳāḳ's death, the Aleppo branch of the Saldjūḳs of Syria had nevertheless another decade of life under Riḍwān. This last was in a more difficult position than his brother had been in Damascus. Aleppo was more exposed to Frankish attacks, both from the nearby County of Edessa and also from the Crusaders in the west Syrian Levantine coastlands. His willingness to use the Ismāʿīli or Assassin elements within Aleppo as his allies, in the often desperate situations in which he found himself, gave him a tainted reputation amongst the orthodox Muslims. Conscious of his weak position, he tried to avoid warfare if the risks were too high and, if necessary, to buy off the Crusader princes. He was perfectly prepared to ally with the Franks in the complex, petty rivalries of the north Syrian region, as in 501/1108, when he allied with Tancred of Edessa and Antioch against the lord of Mawṣil, the Saldjūḳ commander Čawuli Saḳāʾū and the latter's ally, the dispossessed Baldwin of Edessa; and when, later, Mawdūd of Mawṣil and Ṭughtigin organised an *djihād* against the Crusaders, Riḍwān sent only a small, token force.

Riḍwān died in 507/1113, and was succeeded briefly by his young sons Alp Arslan (507/1113) and Sulṭān Shāh (508-17/1114-23), the latter under the tutelage of the Artuḳids Il Ghāzī and then Nūr al-Dawla Balak, control of Aleppo falling after 517/1123 to Aḳ Ṣonḳor al-Bursuḳī. The Saldjūḳ sultans in western Persia and ʿIrāḳ thus no longer had any influence in Syrian affairs, and relations between ʿIrāḳ and Syria were henceforth to be the responsibility of autonomous, former Saldjūḳ commanders like Aḳ Sonḳur al-Bursuḳī and ʿImād al-Dīn Zangī. The long-term effect of direct Saldjūḳ interest in Syria, from the middle years of the 5th/11th century onwards for roughly half-a-century, had been to introduce the new element of Turkmen begs and their tribesmen, and in their followings, a number of Kurds also, into what had previously been a predominantly Semitic land; henceforth, the region became even more ethnically varied.

Bibliography: The main primary sources are Ibn al-Ḳalānisī; Ibn al-Furāt; Ibn ʿAsākir; Ibn al-Djawzī; Ibn al-ʿAdīm; Ibn al-Athīr. For a detailed survey of the Arabic sources, see Cahen, *La Syrie du nord à l'époque des Croisades et la principauté franque*, Paris 1940, introd. on the sources, 35-49.

Of secondary sources, see H.A.R. Gibb, *The Damascus chronicle of the Crusades ... from the Chronicle of Ibn al-Qalānisī*, London 1932, introd.; Cahen, *La Syrie du nord*, parts 1 and 2; idem, *The Turkish invasions: the Selchükids*; in *A history of the Crusades*, i; Kafesoğlu, *A history of the Seljuks*, tr. Leiser; Ali Sevim, *Suriye ve Filistin Selçukları tarihi*, Ankara 1983.

5. The Saldjūḳs of Rūm (*ca.* 483-707/*ca.* 1081-1307)

It is soon after Alp Arslan's victory at Malāzgird (see above, section III. 1) that we hear of the activities in Anatolia of the four sons of Ḳutalmïsh or Ḳutlumush b. Arslan Isrāʾīl, and the descendants of one of these sons, Sulaymān, were to found in central Anatolia the Saldjūḳ sultanate of Rūm based on Iconium or Konya [*q.v.*]. As noted above (*loc. cit.*), and *pace* the views of some modern Turkish nationalist historians, these activities seem to have been purely acts of individual enterprise, although later official historiography promoted by the Saldjūḳs of Rūm in the 7th/13th century asserted that the Great Saldjūḳ sultan Malik Shāh had, on his accession, personally bestowed the land of Rūm on his cousins, the sons of Ḳutalmïsh. In fact, these last seem earlier to have been under official Saldjūḳ surveillance, and only managed to escape to the safety of the fluid, governmentally uncontrolled Anatolian frontiers after Alp Arslan's death. Official disapproval continued under Malik Shāh, who had Manṣūr b. Ḳutalmïsh killed, and although Sulaymān escaped, he was later killed in battle, contending with his kinsman Tutush for control of Aleppo in 479/1086.

Meanwhile, Turkmen bands had been operating within Asia Minor, raiding as far as the shores of the Sea of Marmara and the Aegean, so that Sulaymān had reached Nicaea or Iznik in the far north-west of the land, and it is from this time that one may roughly date the beginnings of a Saldjūḳ principality in Anatolia. After Malik Shāh's death in 485/1092, Sulaymān's son Ḳïlïč Arslan I (485-500/1092-1107) managed to escape from captivity and was raised to the leadership of the Turkmens on northwestern Anatolia, only moving his capital to Konya after the Frankish armies of the First Crusade recaptured Nicaea in 1097. Malik Shāh had not had any definite plan for the overrunning of Anatolia. He did, however, regard himself as head of all the Turks, and wished to control the Turkmens, the most anarchically-inclined of his people, and in pursuit of this had been prepared to make an agreement with the Byzantine Emperor Alexis Comnenus, whose empire was being threatened by the Turkmens' depredations.

The infant Saldjūḳ principality in Konya was only one of several Turkmen *beylik*s which now took shape in central and eastern Anatolia, such as the Saltuḳids [see SALTUḲ OGHULLARÏ] in Erzerum, the Mengüdjekids [see MENGÜČEK] in Erzincan and other towns of the east, the Shāh Armanids [*q.v.*] of Sökmen's line in Akhlāṭ to the west of Lake Van and the Artuḳids [*q.v.*] in Diyārbakr. The most serious rival, because geographically closest to the Saldjūḳs, was the Dānishmendids [*q.v.*] of north-central Anatolia, who controlled the northerly route across the land via Sivas, Kayseri and Ankara, and who after 529/1134-5 enjoyed the title of *Malik* bestowed on them by the ʿAbbāsid caliph for their zeal in *ghazw* against the Byzantines.

When Ḳïlïč Arslan I was killed in battle, there was a temporary division of the Saldjūḳ lands. The appearance of the First Crusaders and a re-assertion of Byzantine power, plus the policy of containment of the Turkmens applied on their western frontier by the Great Saldjūḳ sultans in Persia and ʿIrāḳ, had meant that the various Turkish groups in Anatolia were confined to the interior of Asia Minor. There was some occasional cooperation between the Saldjūḳ of Rūm Rukn al-Dīn Masʿūd I b. Ḳïlïč Arslan I (510-51/1117-56) and the Dānishmendids against such foes as the Byzantines and the Armenians of Cilicia and Little Armenia, but after the death of the Dānishmendid Muhammad b. Gümüshtigin in 536/1142, the Saldjūḳs gradually secured the preponderance in central Anatolia. Masʿūd fought off only with difficulty a Byzantine attack on Konya led by Manuel I Comnenus (541/1147), being saved by the Emperor's receiving news of the appearance further west of the Second Crusade. Masʿūd's son ʿIzz al-Dīn Ḳïlïč Arslan II (551-*ca.* 581/1156-*ca.* 1185) secured revenge by inflicting a severe defeat on Manuel's army at the pass of Myriocephalon near Lake Eğridir in 572/1176, thereby preventing a further attack on the capital. Myriocephalon was as significant in its long-term effects as Malāzgird had been. The Frankish-Byzantine project for the recovery of Anatolia collapsed and Greek hopes of such a reconquest faded, a process to be sealed by the capture of Constantinople in 1204 by the Fourth Crusaders and the reduction of Byzantine control over Anatolia to the region around Nicaea and the principality of Trebizond. The Saldjūḳ sultanate of Rūm and the general Turkish presence were now an inassailable reality and could not be regarded in any way as temporary. In practice, as with Alp Arslan after Malāzgird, Ḳïlïč Arslan II's policy towards the Greeks was restrained and moderate, and he seems to have been content with the aim of uniting all the Turks of central and eastern Anatolia under his own rule rather than with dealing further direct blows at the Byzantine empire.

Neither the Muslim nor the Byzantine sources are very informative about the question of Saldjūḳ titulature and monarchical practices at this time. Greek writers had accorded the title of "sultan" to Sulaymān in the later 5th/11th century, but this can only have reflected an informal usage by Sulaymān's Turkmen followers, for neither the Great Saldjūḳ sultan not the ʿAbbāsid caliph can have bestowed it on him. Writers of the 6th/12th century seem to have described the rulers in Konya as *Malik*s more often than as sultans, but it is difficult to discern what the relationship between the two titles was at this time. From coins and inscriptions, and from some quasi-official documents, we know that Ḳïlïč Arslan II called himself "Sultan of the Arabs and the ʿAdjam", the latter term clearly implying the Turks rather than the Persians (as in traditional, earlier usage) and, latterly, "Sultan of the land of Rūm, and of the Armenians, Franks and Syria" (the Saldjūḳs referred to their land at this time, at least in informal usage, as Rūm, and themselves as the Saldjūḳs of Rūm; see RŪM. 2). The title of *Ghāzī*, employed by the Dānishmendids and the eastern Anatolian Turkmen princes, is absent amongst the Saldjūḳs. Like the Great Saldjūḳs of the 6th/12th century, young members of the Rūm Saldjūḳs had Atabegs at their sides, and these are still found—although little is known of them beyond their names—in the 7th/13th century; but the office never acquired in Rūm the importance, with its potentialities for seizure of *de facto* power in the state, which it did in the Saldjūḳ dominions further east.

A further consequence of the Myriocephalon victory was that it eventually opened up for the Saldjūḳs the way towards the Mediterranean shores and the ports of Antalya (seized by Kay Khusraw I in 601/1207) and Alanya (named ʿAlāʾiyya after the sultan ʿAlāʾ al-Dīn Kay Ḳubādh I, 616-34/1220-37). Also, towards the end of the 6th/12th century the Turkmen *amīr* of Tokat captured Samsun [see SĀMṢŪN], thus bringing Turkish arms to the Black Sea shores, and this was followed by the conquest of Sinope [see SINŪB] by ʿIzz al-Dīn Kay Kāwūs I (608-16/1211-20) from the Trebizond Comneni in 611/1214. Hence whereas the Turkish powers of Anatolia had been essentially landlocked and confined to the interior plateau, they now had access to the seas. For the Saldjūḳs, this was to mean exploitation of their position athwart the north-south trade routes of Anatolia and trade relations with the Venetians—enemies of the Byzantines—in Antalya, so that the sultanate benefited from Venetian trade with Alexandria. Commerce between the Black Sea ports and the great Crimean entrepôt of Sughdāḳ tended to be controlled by the Greek principality of Trebizond, but from 1225 to 1239, the date of the definitive conquest of South Russia and the Crimea by the Mongols of the Golden Horde [see BATU], Kay Ḳubādh I was able, through Kastamonu and the Black Sea ports, to establish his suzerainty in Sughdāḳ [*q.v.* and ḲIRĪM].

Towards the end of his life, in one of the periodic recrudescences of the old Turkish principle of patrimonial division, Ḳilič Arslan II divided his kingdom amongst his ten sons and some other male relatives, allotting various towns to each of them. Not surprisingly, a period of succession disputes and weakness ensued over the next two decades. In 1190 he Emperor Frederick Barbarossa and his Crusading army plundered Konya whilst Ḳilič Arslan took efuge in the citadel. But the crisis in the state was surmounted by the opening of the 7th/13th century, and he first forty years of this century were to mark the apogee of the sultanate under such rulers as Kay Kāwūs I and Kay Ḳubādh I. For half a century there was peace with Byzantium, the result of an agreement between Kay Kāwūs I and Theodore Lascaris, and the Saldjūḳs henceforth concentrated their military efforts on the eastern frontiers, in Cilicia, Syria, al-Djazīra, and against Trebizond. But these eastern fringes of Anatolia were now in fact becoming threatened by the expansionism of the Khʷārazm Shāhs [*q.v.*]. The Khʷārazmians first appeared in astern Anatolia in 623/1226, leading Kay Ḳubādh I o ally with the Ayyūbids of Syria and Diyārbakr, qually menaced. The Saldjūḳ sultan was now at the eight of his power, as undisputed master of most of Anatolia and suzerain of the surrounding smaller Christian Greek, Armenian and Georgian states; the nancial and artistic resources which he could command for building purposes and the splendour of his nanner of life are seen in the many palaces which he onstructed, such as the Ḳubādhābād palace on Lake eyşehir and the Kay Ḳubādhiyya one near Kayseri *q.vv.*], both only now being excavated properly.

The Mongols appeared in eastern Anatolia in 40/1242-3 at a time when the Ghiyāth al-Dīn Kay Khusraw II had only just with difficulty quelled the rolonged rebellion in eastern and northern Anatolia, hich had started in 638/1240, of a Turkish popular oly man, Baba Isḥāḳ, who claimed to be a prophetic essenger (*rasūl*) [see BĀBĀʾĪ, and below, section IV.]. Kay Khusraw II (634-44/1237-46) was distinctly ss capable than his predecessors, but he assembled n army which included, as well as his own troops, rmenians, Greeks and Franks; however, he was efeated by the Mongol commander Baydju at Köse agh [*q.v.*] in the region of Sivas (641/1243). Although the Mongols allowed the sultan to retain his throne in Konya, it was as a vassal of the Mongols liable to heavy tribute. There was subsequently dissent within the client Saldjūḳ state when the dead Kay Khusraw II's throne was disputed by the officials and commanders supporting his minor sons. Only in 659/1261 did Rukn al-Dīn Kay Kāwūs II establish a certain measure of power in Konya. But until his execution in 676/1277 by the Il Khānid Abaḳa after a Mongol defeat at the hands of the invading Mamlūk army of Baybars of Egypt and Syria, real power in the Saldjūḳ state was exercised by the *Parwāna* Muʿīn al-Dīn Sulaymān [*q.v.*], son of a former vizier of the Saldjūḳs, who worked closely with the Mongols and endeavoured to reduce tensions between incoming Turco-Mongol soldiers and the established Turkmen groups of Anatolia. His death marks the end of semi-independence for the sultans in Konya, for the Il Khānids now resorted to direct rule through their own alien Persian and Turco-Mongol official and commanders. The Saldjūḳ military forces were disbanded, to swell the ranks of malcontents and bandits throughout the Anatolian countryside.

Specifically Perso-Mongol institutions and practices were now introduced into Anatolia, in particular, fiscal ones (see below, section V. 2). Mongol taxation in Anatolia was undoubtedly heavy, but there was nevertheless little perceptible adverse effect on the general economic and commercial well-being of the area, with agricultural production and external trade remaining buoyant and with a continued endowment and construction of public and charitable buildings (see below, sections V. 2, and VI. 2).

The Il Khāns led various expeditions into Anatolia to quell local rulers such as the Ḳaramānids [see ḲARAMĀN-OGHULLARÏ] and Ashrafids [see ASHRAF-OGHULLARÏ] and other unrest, and to reassert Mongol financial demands, such as the expedition of Gaykhatu in 690-1/1291-2 which spread terror and devastation throughout southern Anatolia as far west as Menteshe [see MENTESHE-ELI] and the Aegean Sea coastlands. Various ambitious Turco-Mongol commanders within Anatolia also led revolts, contributing to a general atmosphere of disintegration and tyrannical rule. The *fainéant* Saldjūḳ sultan ʿAlāʾ al-Dīn Kay Ḳubādh III was executed by Ghazan Khān [*q.v.*] in 702/1303, and the sultanate disappeared, in obscure circumstances, in 707/1307. It was only after a period of control by the Il Khānids' commanders of the Čobanid family [see ČŪBĀNIDS] that Anatolia eventually emerged into the age of the *beyliks*, with a fragmentation of *ṭawāʾif* or petty principalities comparable to those in 5th/11th-century Muslim Spain.

Some descendants of the Rūm Saldjūḳs seem to have survived into later times. One Ḳilič Arslan b. Luṭfī b. Sawčī, possibly a Saldjūḳ, governed Alanya in the 1460s before the Ottoman annexation of 876/1471; and a later Ottoman historian, ʿĀlī, says that after the deposition of the last Saldjūḳ Ghiyāth al-Dīn Masʿūd III, Ghazan granted Sinope to a Saldjūḳ prince, Ghāzī Čelebi, who became active from there against the Greeks of Trebizond and the Genoese in the Black Sea.

Bibliography: 1. Sources. See the bibl. to the *EI*[1] art. SELDJŪḲS, brought up to date by that in Cl. Cahen, *Pre-Ottoman Turkey. A general survey of the material and spiritual culture and history c. 1071-1330*, London 1968, revised Fr. version, *La Turquie pré-Ottomane*, Istanbul 1988. Of special importance are the histories of the Anatolian authors Ibn Bībī, Aḳsarāyī's *Musāmarat al-akhbār* and the anonymous *Taʾrīkh-i āl-i Saldjūk*, plus the supplementary information from Arabic, other Persian, Greek, Armenian and Syriac sources. Still valuable is M.F. Köprülü's extended survey of sources in *Anadolu Selçukları tarihi'nin yerli kaynakları*, in *Belleten*, vii (1943), 379-522, now more easily accessible in an Eng. tr. and with valuable updating and further references by G. Leiser, *The Seljuks of Anatolia, their history and culture according to local Muslim sources*, Salt Lake City 1992.

2. Studies. Cahen, *op. cit.*; S. Vryonis, *The decline of medieval Hellenism in Asia Minor and the process of Islamization from the eleventh through the fifteenth century*, Berkeley, etc. 1971; Osman Turan, ch. *Anatolia in the period of the Seljuks and the Beyliks*, in *Camb. hist. Islam*, Cambridge 1970, i, 231-50; idem, *Selçuklar zamanında Türkiye. Siyâsi tarih Alp Arslan'dan Osman Gazi'ye 1071-1318*, Istanbul 1971; A.G.C. Savvides, *Byzantium in the Near East: its relations with the Seljuk sultanate of Rum in Asia Minor, the Armenians of Cilicia and the Mongols A.D. c. 1192-1237*, Thessalonike 1981; G. Leiser (tr. and ed.), *A history of the Seljuks. İbrahim Kafesoğlu's interpretation and the resultant controversy*, Carbondale and Edwardsville, Ill. 1988, 67-78. See also ANADOLU (iii) (i) on the course of the first Turkish conquests there, and the arts. on the individual sultans, KAY KĀWŪS I-II; KAY KHUSRAW I-III; KAY ḲUBĀDH I-III; ḲĪLĪDJ ARSLAN I-IV. For the chronology and genealogical connections of the Saldjūḳ sultans of Rūm, see C.E. Bosworth, *The new Islamic dynasties*, ch. XI, no. 102.

IV. Intellectual and religious history

1. In Persia and ʿIrāḳ

The territories of the Great Saldjūḳs and their successors here formed a mighty empire, of an extent not seen since the heyday of the ʿAbbāsid caliphate, that century between 750 and 850 A.D. As heads of this empire, the Saldjūḳ rulers in the second half of the 5th/11th century came to a working arrangement with the caliphs of their time which involved an affirmation of the caliph as the moral and spiritual head of the orthodox Sunnī community but which also incorporated the sultanate as the executive arm of the ideal Islamic government. The two were interconnected, for whilst the sultan derived, under the *sharīʿa*, his ruling authority from the caliph, the latter recognised that the sultanate provided the restraining and coercive power, Ibn Khaldūn's *wāziʿ*, which alone could bring about stability in civil government and thus enable the subjects to live the good Muslim life in the present world and to achieve salvation in the next. It was to be the task of al-Ghazālī, in particular—a man whose whole career was spent during the halcyon decades of Saldjūḳ power—to establish the theoretical bases for this relationship and partnership between caliph and sultan (see L. Binder, *Al-Ghazali's theory of Islamic government*, in *MW*, xlv [1955], 229-41).

The orthodox Sunnism which al-Ghazālī represented was thus the religious force behind the Saldjūḳ ideal of government. Now that the Shīʿī Būyids had been overthrown, Sunnism had behind it the full support of the Saldjūḳ ruling authority in the ʿIrāḳī and Persian lands, and it was at this time a vital, intellectually far-ranging force, uniting within itself many stimulating curents of thought. Thus although Muʿtazilism [see MUʿTAZILA] was in the end successfully challenged by what became the Ashʿarī and, later, the Māturīdī forms of *kalām* or dogmatic theology and argumentation, it still retained some strength amongst Sunnī scholars in Baghdād and in the eastern parts of the empire, notably Khurāsān, as also in Khʷārazm and Transoxania, as well as influencing some strains of Shīʿism. In addition to this, Sunnī orthodoxy was represented within the Saldjūḳ dominions by the traditionalist Ḥanbalism and, much more widely, by the two orthodox theological systems of the Ashʿarī and then the Māturīdī *kalām*, mentioned above, whose counterparts in the sphere of law or *fiḳh* tended to be the Shāfiʿī and Ḥanafī *madhhabs*, although the correspondence was not always an exact one, and the various *madhāhib* did not necessarily have ties to any particular theological school; George Makdisi has pointed out that Ashʿarism was not coterminous with Shāfiʿism and that there were Shāfiʿī opponents of the Ashʿarī *kalām*, though such opposition was obviously not so violent as e.g. amongst the Ḥanbalīs (see his *Ashʿarī and the Ashʿarites in Islamic religious history*, in *SI*, xvii [1962], 37-80, xviii [1963], 19-39; he also makes the general point here that the strength and importance of Ashʿarism in the historical development of Islamic theology has in any case been exaggerated). Shāfiʿism-Ashʿarism, which gave especial emphasis to tradition, *ḥadīth* [*q.v.*, and see ASHʿARIYYA], in the formation of law and theology, became implanted at Nīshāpūr in the early 5th/11th century through the efforts of certain famous *mutakallimūn* like Ibn Fūrak [*q.v.*], as part of a general eastwards expansion into Persia by Shāfiʿism in the 4th/10th century. Ḥanafism, with its greater emphasis on rationalism in the evolution of *fiḳh* [see ḤANAFIYYA] had early become dominant in Persia, spreading to Sāmānid Transoxania, and remaining entrenched in such northern Persian centres as Rayy. During the Saldjūḳ period it had the great advantage of support from the Turkish ruling establishment, above all, from such sultans as Ṭoghril Beg and Alp Arslan, who were especially fervent proponents of Ḥanafism. They pursued deliberate policies of appointing Ḥanafi *imāms*, *ḳāḍīs* and *khaṭībs* wherever possible within their dominions, and of curbing the Shāfiʿīs; it was not until after Alp Arslan's death that the Ashʿarī-Shāfiʿ vizier Niẓām al-Mulk was able cautiously to promote his own favoured party and to endeavour to redress the balance somewhat in favour of the Ashʿarīs and Shāfiʿīs (see for the effects of this policy in one place R.W. Bulliet, *The political-religious history of Nishapur in the eleventh century*, in D.S. Richards (ed.), *Islamic civilisation 950-1150*, Oxford 1973, 85-8). Ḥanbalism during the Saldjūḳ period was essentially centred on Baghdād and Damascus (the latter city, of course, only directly ruled by the Saldjūḳs for some forty years see above, section III. 4). It had been strengthened in the century preceding Ṭoghrïl Beg's appearance in the ʿAbbāsid capital through its rôle as the focus there for Sunnī opposition to the Būyids' pro-Shīʿ measures [see ḤANĀBILA]. After 447/1061 it had to compete there with other forms of Sunnism, such as the Shāfiʿism-Ashʿarism taught from the Baghdād *madrasa* or college founded by Niẓām al-Mulk in 459/1067 (see further on this, below), and with Muʿtazilism and Ṣūfī mysticism. But it produced one of the greatest theologico-political figures of Baghdād's history, Ibn ʿAḳīl (d. 513/1119 [*q.v.*]), and in the 6th/12th century Ḥanbalism enjoyed a resurgence in influence under the patronage of caliphal officials like ʿAwn al-Dīn Ibn Hubayra (d. 560/1165 [*q.v.*]) and the example of the Ṣūfī *shaykh* ʿAbd al-Ḳādir al-Djīlānī (d. 561/1146 [*q.v.*]; during this period, several Ḥanbalī *madrasas* were founded by influential patrons (see Makdisi, *Muslim institutions of learning in eleventh-century Baghdad*, in *BSOAS*, xxi [1961], 26-9). The deleterious effects of the sectarian social rivalries between Sunnī theological and legal schools, the Shīʿa and the Karrāmiyya, were visible in the social and religious turmoil in many of the town of the Saldjūḳ empire, from Baghdād to Harāt, mentioned below in section V.1, concerning the *ʿaṣabiyyāt* (see in general on Sunnism at this time, W. Madelung, *Religious trends in early Islamic Iran*, Albany 1988, 26-38).

The dominant forms of Sunnī *kalām* just described likewise triumphed in the end over the more speculative forms of Islamic thought, those of the *falāsifa* or philosophers [see FALĀSIFA; FAYLASŪF], with their Aristotelian or Neoplatonist forms of reasoning; al-Ghazālī's exposé in his autobiographical *al-Munḳidh min al-ḍalāl* of the insufficiency of philosophy to provide a sure foundation for man's salvation, and his polemic against its exponents, his *Tahāfut al-falāsifa*, were only two of several attempted refutations. Nevertheless, the succession of followers of the great Ibn Sīnā (d. 428/1037 [*q.v.*]) continued in the Persian lands during the Saldjūḳ period, and the scientist, philosopher and poet ʿUmar Khayyām (d. 526/1131 [*q.v.*]) regarded Ibn Sīnā as his master; it seems that ʿUmar entered the service of Malik Shāh after that sultan's expedition into Transoxania against the Ḳarakhānid Shams al-Mulk Naṣr in 466/1073-4 (see above, section III.1) and became one of his *nadīms* [*q.v.*] or intimates.

Above all, the overriding strength of Sunnism manifested itself in the religious-educational field, with the great impetus to the foundation and endowment of new *madrasas* and *masdjids*, mosque-colleges, under the patronage not only of the Saldjūḳ sultans but of numerous of their viziers, officials, of merchants, of city notables, etc. (see on this movement, below), a movement which affected not only the lands of Persia and ʿIrāḳ ruled over by the Saldjūḳs but also the more westerly ones of the Levant and Egypt, especially after the disappearance of the Shīʿī Fāṭimids from there.

Madrasas, mosque-colleges and associated teaching institutions like the *dār al-ʿilm* had existed in ʿIrāḳ and the Persian lands since at least the 4th/10th century, and the Būyids and such governors of theirs as Badr b. Ḥasanawayh [see ḤASANWAYH] had enthusiastically furthered and endowed their foundation. But their spread received an impetus under the Saldjūḳs through the patronage of great men like the Shāfiʿī-Ashʿarīs Niẓām al-Mulk and Malik Shāh's *mustawfī* or chief accountant Tādj al-Mulk Abu 'l-Ghanāʾim; the Ḥanafī *mustawfī* of Alp Arslan, Sharaf al-Mulk Abū Saʿd, who founded the shrine-college of Abū Ḥanīfa in Baghdād which seems to have been more important than the celebrated Niẓāmiyya there; and the Ḥanbalī viziers of the ʿAbbāsid caliphs, such as Niẓām al-Dīn Abū Naṣr Ibn Djahīr [see DJAHĪR, BANŪ], whose residence in the capital, subsequently turned into a *madrasa*, was presided over by the prominent scholar Ibn al-Djawzī [*q.v.*] (see Makdisi, *op. cit.*, 17 ff.). Best known is the network of Shāfiʿī-Ashʿarī colleges founded by Niẓām al-Mulk across the Saldjūḳ dominions (the later biographer of Shāfiʿī *ʿulamāʾ*, al-Subkī [*q.v.*], enumerates nine *Niẓāmiyyas*, of which five were in Khurāsān and the Caspian provinces, one in Djibāl and three in ʿIrāḳ); a novel feature here was that the vizier reserved for himself and his descendants administrative control of them. But the general religious and cultural significance of these institutions may have been disproportionately stressed in both the contemporary sources and in modern studies, for by the 6th/12th century the Niẓāmiyyas do not seem to have been particularly flourishing, and the descendants of the vizier had lost control of them. In Nīshāpūr, the *Niẓāmiyya* there was headed in the first half of that century by a pupil of al-Ghazālī's, but he was killed by the Oghuz in 548/1153-4, when several other *madrasas* and mosques were destroyed (see Bulliet, *The patricians of Nishapur. A study in medieval Islamic social history*, Cambridge, Mass. 1972, 73-5, 254-5, and, in general, MADRASA. I. 4 and NIẒĀM AL-MULK].

Much light is shown on the distribution of Shīʿism during the Saldjūḳ period by two Shīʿī works of the time, the *Kitāb al-Naḳd* of ʿAbd al-Djalīl Ḳazwīnī Rāzī (mid-6th/12th century) and the *Tabṣirat al-ʿawāmm* of Sayyid Murtaḍā Rāzī from the opening of the 7th/13th century. They confirm the impression of the historical and biographical sources that Khurāsān and Transoxania were strongholds of Sunnī orthodoxy, apart from communities of *sayyids* in places like Nīshāpūr, Ṭūs and Bayhaḳ, but that Shīʿism had some strong groups in northwestern Persia, with the Zaydīs in the Caspian provinces (where the *khuṭba* was still made in some places for the Zaydī *imām*), and the Djaʿfarīs or Twelvers influential in the urban centres of Djibāl like Rayy, Ḳazwīn, Ḳumm, Āwa and Kāshān, having their own *madrasas* and *ḳubbas* [*q.v.*] or tombs in some of these centres. The establishment of Ismāʿīlism in Daylam, the region of Iṣfāhan and Ḳuhistān has already been noted (above, section III, 1). The two great groups of the Sunnīs and Shīʿīs, although on occasion at odds with each other, and with the Shīʿa stimatised as *Rawāfiḍ* [see RĀFIḌA] in Sunnī works like Niẓām al-Mulk's *Siyāsat-nāma*, in practice mostly co-existed peacefully with each other, and Shīʿīs were represented quite significantly in the ranks of Saldjūḳ officialdom right up to the office of vizier; the common enemy of both was Ismāʿīlism (see A. Bausani, in *Camb. hist. of Iran*, v, 290-6; J. Calmard, *Le chiisme imamite en Iran à l'époque seldjoukide d'après le* Kitāb al-Naqd, in *Le monde iranien et l'Islam, sociétés et cultures*, i [Geneva-Paris, 1971], 43-67).

The Saldjūḳ period was further important for the development of Ṣūfism in provinces like Khurāsān, Transoxania and ʿIrāḳ, with a distinctive school of Ṣūfism now emerging in the Persian lands. This was particularly the case with Khurāsān, where Ṣūfism was henceforth to benefit much from official Saldjūḳ patronage, whereas, up to the opening of the 5th/11th century, *zuhd* or asceticism there had been mainly the province of the Karrāmiyya (on whom see below), with some adherents of the Malāmatiyya [*q.v.*] in the towns (see J. Chabbi, *Remarques sur le développement historique des mouvements ascétiques et mystiques au Khurasan*, in *SI*, xlvi [1977], 41-5, 55-9). In the early years of the Saldjūḳ period, the Sūfī *shaykh* and thaumaturge Abū Saʿīd b. Abi 'l-Khayr was still living (d. 440/1048-9 [*q.v.*]) and allegedly foretold the greatness of Ṭoghrïl and Čaghrï when they visited him at Mayhana [*q.v.*] (see F. Meier, *Abū Saʿīd-i Abū l-Ḫayr (357-440/967-1049), Wirklichkeit und Legende*, Leiden-Tehran-Liège 1976, 327-9). From the next generation or so were ʿAbd Allāh al-Anṣārī (d. 481/1089 [*q.v.*]) and Abu 'l-Ḳāsim al-Ḳushayrī (d. 465/1072) [*q.v.*]) who, together with Abū Ḥāmid al-Ghazālī (d. 505/1111 [*q.v.*]), did much to incorporate the moderate form of Ṣūfī mysticism into the fabric of Sunnī orthodoxy. A notable feature of Persian Ṣūfism at this time came to be its grouping around the *khānaḳāhs* [see KHĀNḲĀH] or dervish convents, and the influence of Khurāsānī *shaykhs* and their institutions spread westwards through the Saldjūḳ lands; thus Chabbi has noted that the founders of the *ribāṭs* [*q.v.*] or centres for devotion, study, preaching, etc., in Baghdād during the first half of the 5th/11th century were almost all Khurāsānīs (*La fonction du ribat à Bagdad du Ve siècle au début du VIIe siècle*, in *REI*, xlii

[1974], 107). The next century, the 6th/12th one, was notable for the formation of several of the major dervish orders (*ṭuruḳ* [see ṬARĪḲA]), including the Ḳādiriyya [*q.v.*], the Yasawiyya [see AḤMAD YASAWĪ], the Rifāᶜiyya, the Suhrawardiyya [*q.vv.*] and the Kubrawiyya [see KUBRĀ, NADJM AL-DĪN]. See further, J.S. Trimingham, *The Sufi orders in Islam*, Oxford 1971, 31-60; Bausani, in *Camb. hist. of Iran*, v, 296-302; Madelung, *op. cit.*, 49-53.

As just noted, the ascetic strain within Ṣūfism originally had had its counterpart in eastern Persia in the form of the ascetic but activist movement of the Karrāmiyya [*q.v.*], especially vociferous in Nīshāpūr and strong in the rural, mountainous, eastern fringes of the province, what is now western Afghānistān. In the early years of the 5th/11th century, the Karrāmiyya and their *khānaḳāh*s had enjoyed some patronage from the Ghaznawids; this favour disappeared with the advent of the Saldjūḳs and became an active disapproval on the part of the ruling authority, but the Karrāmiyya remained an assertive element in Nīshāpūr and elsewhere all through that same century (as their mention as participants in the *ᶜaṣabiyyāt* of the time shows); it was only during the course of the succeeding 6th/12th century that they were pushed eastwards into regions less accessible to Saldjūḳ control such as Gharčistān and Ghūr; thus the Karrāmī *madrasa* at Bayhaḳ, founded in the opening years of the 5th/11th century, had disappeared when the local historian Ibn Funduḳ wrote (sc. in 563/1168), although the Ḥanafī and Shāfiᶜī ones still survived (*Taʾrīkh-i Bayhaḳ*, ed. Aḥmad Bahmanyār, Tehran 1317/1938, 194, 220-1; and, in general on the Karrāmiyya, Madelung, *op. cit.*, 39-46).

Bibliography: Given in the article; see especially Bausani's ch. *Religion in the Saljuq period*, in *Camb. hist. Iran*, v, 283-302; and Madelung's *Religious trends in early Islamic Iran*, which in part covers the Saldjūḳ period, notably chs. 3-4, 6-7.

2. In Anatolia

The Turkmens who entered Anatolia no doubt brought with them vestiges of the pre-Islamic, Inner Asian shamanistic past (survivals of which were explored by Fuad Köprülü in various of his works, such as his *Influence du chamanisme turco-mongol sur les ordres mystiques musulmans*, Mems. de l'Institut de Turcologie de l'Université de Stamboul, N.S. 1, Istanbul 1929), but eventually became in considerable measure firm adherents of the near-universal Islamic *madhhab* for the Turks, the Ḥanafī one. But there seems to have been little original or creative theological and legal writing within Rūm until well into the 7th/13th century, and the Turks of Anatolia were content to take from the ample heritage of the flourishing and productive Ḥanafī scholarship of Khurāsān and Transoxiana, transmitted to the lands further west by those scholars who in the 7th/13th century moved westwards before the advancing Mongols, such as Yūsuf b. Abī Saᶜīd Aḥmad al-Sidjistānī, who composed at Sivas in 639/1241-2 his *Munyat al-muftī*, which became a popular law book throughout the central and eastern Islamic lands (cf. Brockelmann, I², 473, S I, 653). The concrete embodiments of the Islamic faith, in the form of mosques and *madrasa*s, were somewhat late in appearing in Anatolia. The earliest mosques appear in the dominions of the Saldjūḳs and of the Turkmen dynasties of the Dānishmendids, Mengüdjekids and Saltuḳids only after *ca.* 550/1155, whilst the earliest *madrasa* in Anatolia, known from its foundation inscription, was built at Kayseri in 589/1193; this institution had by that time been flourishing in the Arab-Persian lands further east for nearly two centuries. Only with the consolidation of the sultanate in the 7th/13th century do mosques and *madrasa*s become numerous in such towns as Konya, Kayseri and several other Anatolian ones, as also in Artukid Mārdīn [see MADRASA, III, at vol. V, 1145-6].

Mysticism soon enjoyed a particularly lively growth in Anatolia, not only drawing its strength from the Persian lands (see below) but also attracting such a figure as the great Arab mystic of Spanish Muslim origin, Ibn al-ᶜArabī (d. 638/1240 [*q.v.*]), who travelled to Malatya and as far as Sivas and Konya. He was followed by his disciple ᶜAfīf al-Dīn Sulaymān al-Tilimsānī (d. 690/1291 [*q.v.*]), who settled in Rūm for some time. Ibn al-ᶜArabī was to have a considerable influence in Anatolia through Ṣadr al-Dīn Ḳūnawī (d. 673/1274 [*q.v.*]), so that his works later became standard texts for study in the curricula of the Ottoman *madrasa*s. Contacts with North African pilgrims who returned home via Anatolia were sufficient for them to have a small mosque of their own in Konya. Yet it was the Persian spiritual and literary tradition which speedily became dominant, reflecting Persian influence in other spheres such as administration and court life (see below, section V. 2). The Saldjūḳ sultans themselves earlier adopted Persian epic names like Kay Kāwūs, Kay Khusraw and Kay Ḳubādh. The process was necessarily accentuated in the 7th/13th century when there arrived in Konya such distinguished refugees as Bahāʾ al-Dīn Muḥammad Walad (d. 628/1231) and his son Djalāl al-Dīn Rūmī (d. 672/1275 [*q.v.*]), from an ancient family in Balkh of preachers and mystics. Bahāʾ al-Dīn Walad was invited to his captal by the sultan Kay Ḳubādh I, but did not survive there for long. His son, on the other hand, spent the greater part of his adult life at Konya, and it was there that he composed his *Mathnawī* (see below, section VII. 2). The Saldjūḳ capital accordingly became the centre of the Mawlawī Ṣūfī order as developed by Mawlānā's son Sulṭān Walad (d. 712/1312 [*q.v.*]), with Rūmī's tomb as its spiritual power-house for centuries to come [see MAWLAWIYYA]. Another figure who came westwards to Rūm was Nadjm al-Dīn Rāzī Dāya (d. 654/156 [*q.v.*]), a former *murīd* of the Ṣūfī master Nadjm al-Dīn Kubrā [*q.v.*], eponymous founder of the Kubrawiyya order, who does not, however, seem to have found Anatolia congenial and who moved back to Tabrīz and Baghdād; even so, his *Mirṣād al-ᶜibād* (see below, section VII. 2) became very popular in Anatolia and was later translated into Turkish.

Such religious traditions and practices as those outlined above helped to consolidate what became the dominant, official Sunnism of Anatolia. But at a less exalted and articulate level were currents of beliefs which may well have gone back to the animistic past of the Turks, mentioned at the beginning of this section, especially amongst the Turkmens outside the towns, and there probably existed also ill-formed and emotionally-based pro-Shīᶜī feelings such as were to be undoubtedly discernible amongst the ᶜAlawī Turkmens of eastern Anatolia in the early Ottoman period. Only at times of particular political and social stress or upheaval did these somewhat inchoate trends of belief and thought come to the surface, assume tangible form and impinge on the wider political scene. Such was the case with the Bābāʾī movement, a religious one with social overtones, which disturbed much of Anatolia in the years just before the Mongol invasion there. Its leader, a popular, charismatic figure, Baba Isḥāḳ, defied the Saldjūḳ armies for some time, and his movement was never completely extinguished in the countryside. It seems to have included extremist, messianic S̲h̲īʿī elements which recrudesced, or merged, soon afterwards, in the Bektās̲h̲ī movement, a connection explicitly made by the 8th/14th-century Ṣūfī biographer Aflākī; Ḥādjdjī Bektās̲h̲ may have been a disciple of Baba Isḥāḳ [see BĀBĀʾī; BEKTĀS̲H̲IYYA].

Finally, a word should be said about the possible interaction of the great faiths in Anatolia, specifically between Islam and the Christian substratum there. It is hard to reach firm conclusions on such an elusive matter, but it seems that certain sultans, such as Kay Ḳubād̲h̲ I, were enlightened and tolerant rulers, conscious of the mixture of faiths and ethnoi over which they ruled. There were both Armenians and Greeks in the capital Konya, the latter with their monastery of St. Chariton and some Jews. Rūmī seems to have had harmonious relations with the local D̲h̲immīs, whilst remaining convinced of his own divine mission to convert them. Throughout Anatolia there was at the popular level an interchange, or double veneration, by Christians and Muslims at many holy sites (some no doubt with a continuity of mana going back to classical times), with the frequent equating of a saint of one faith with a saint of the other. The best-known of such equations is that of St. George with K̲h̲iḍr Ilyās [q.v.]; at Konya, Muslims revered St. Amphilochius in the guise of Aflāṭūn or Plato, whose tomb was considered to be located there; elsewhere, they identified Ṣarï Saltuḳ Dede [q.v.] with St. Nicholas and Ḥādjdjī Bektās̲h̲ at Ḳïrs̲h̲ehir with St. Charalambros.

Bibliography: F.W. Hasluck, Christianity and Islam under the sultans, Oxford 1929; Cahen, Pre-Ottoman Turkey, 248-61, 347-58; Vryonis, The decline of medieval Hellenism in Asia Minor; Köprülü, The Seljuks of Anatolia.

V. Administrative, social and economic history

1. In Persia and ʿIrāḳ

Such an empire as the Saldjūḳ one was not homogenous in social and ethnic composition, and, as noted above in section I, could not be ruled as a despotism, with a highly-centralised administration, like its predecessor in the eastern Persian lands, the G̲h̲aznawid empire. For, to take one prerequisite for centralised, authoritarian control over a far-flung empire, sc. an efficient internal espionage system and postal service network (barīd, later ulag̲h̲), the Saldjūḳ sultans deliberately eschewed this; Niẓām al-Mulk's lament that the Saldjūḳ sultans showed no interest in this system is well-known (Siyāsat-nāma, § 10), and Anūs̲h̲irwān b. K̲h̲ālid implies that Alp Arslan's abolition of the previously-existing barīd and k̲h̲abar system, on the basis of what he calls a "whim" (wahm) but which was more likely a deliberate choice, was a cause of the spread of Ismāʿīlism and of the terror in people's minds which exaggerated, ill-informed accounts of the Assassins' activities brought about (al-Bundārī, ed. Houtsma, 67).

In any case, the early sultans, with their Central Asian tribal origins, did not at first conceive of themselves as territorial monarchs but as leaders of nomadic hordes who happened to range with their flocks in search of pasture over a particularly large stretch of territory within the Dār al-Islām. But these ideas soon became modified as, already by the end of T̲og̲h̲rïl's reign and during that of Alp Arslan, the sultans settled down as rulers over a defined territory, even though the Saldjūḳs never, until the end of the dynasty, resided in one permanent, fixed capital. As rulers over an empire of vastly differing climatic and topographical zones, from the deserts and steppe lands of northern Syria and ʿIrāḳ to mountains and plateaux of Persia, they often moved between summer and winter capitals, echoing their nomadic past. Hence a fair number of the cities of their empire, including Nīs̲h̲āpūr, Rayy, Iṣfahān, Hamad̲h̲ān and Bag̲h̲dād itself, served at one time or another as centres for their power (see below). Normally, of course, the court and administrative departments of central government travelled with the sultans when they were on campaign or simply journeying across their lands.

Thus by Malik S̲h̲āh's reign, the sultan came to exercise a delimited territorial authority, although it was one exerted with different degrees of intensity. Right to the end of the Saldjūḳ empire, there were whole stretches of territory which were substantially left, usually on payment of some taxation, to their indigenous tribal peoples, such as those of Kurdistān and Luristān in D̲j̲ibāl and much of Fārs, and the Ḳufṣ and Balūč in Kirmān and Makrān, or to the Og̲h̲uz nomads in such areas as the Mūḳān steppes in Arrān [q.vv.] and the steppe lands of Gurgān and Dihistān [q.vv.] to the southeast of the Caspian Sea; and the sultans took care to maintain, as far as was possible with the demands of security and financial requirements, amicable links with such groups (see on the tribes during this period, A.K.S. Lambton, Aspects of Saljūq-Ghuzz settlement in Persia, in Richards (ed.), Islamic civilisation 950-1150, 121-4, and ĪLĀT. For the sultans' attitudes towards their fellow-Turkmens, see above, section II). Regarding the Kurds, Anūs̲h̲irwān b. K̲h̲ālid says that Muḥammad b. Malik S̲h̲āh carefully conciliated the S̲h̲abānkāra [q.v.], normally a turbulent element in Fārs and the scourge of the settled population, by attaching their chiefs to his service at court; when his successor Maḥmūd stopped this practice, the S̲h̲abānkāra reverted to their old plundering ways (al-Bundārī, 122), with deleterious effects on the economy of Fārs and the upper Persian Gulf region (see further, below). But in general, Lambton concluded (op. cit., 124-5), that the additional nomads who came into Persia with the Saldjūḳ invasions did not cause widespread dislocation but may even have contributed to the general prosperity of the lands in that they now supplied the cities and towns with milk and meat products and may have contributed to the stock of transport animals available for trading purposes.

On the fringes of the empire, local princes were often allowed to remain as feudatories. In the northwest, the S̲h̲addādids [q.v.] of Dwin and Gand̲j̲a and the Marwānids [q.v.] of Diyār Bakr were left in power until Malik S̲h̲āh's reign. In ʿIrāḳ, the ʿUḳaylids [q.v.] held Mawṣil till the end of the 5th/11th century, with minor branches persisting in Diyār Muḍar till the advent of the Zangids, whilst the Mazyadids [see MAZYAD, BANŪ] of Ḥilla in central ʿIrāḳ were particularly adept at playing off against each other the Saldjūḳ sultans and the ʿAbbāsid caliphs in order to preserve their own authority, a policy which was successful for over ninety years, until the middle years of the 6th/12th century. In the Caspian provinces, various petty princes were left alone, as were the survivors of the Kākūyid dynasty [q.v.] in central Persia. On the eastern fringes of the empire, the Maliks of Nīmrūz or Sīstān were left alone, and survived there long after the Saldjūḳs themselves had disappeared from history. Such dependents forwarded tribute and/or troops contingents to the sultans' armies when required; thus we read of the Kākūyid princes, the rulers of Sistan and the Bāwandids [q.v.] of Māzandarān participating in Sand̲j̲ar's wars. When the sultans were able to extend their authority by military force into lands outside the empire, as happened with the Ḳara<u>kh</u>ānids in Transoxania on various occasions, the <u>Gh</u>aznawids in eastern Af<u>gh</u>ānistān (see above, section III. 1) and the <u>Sh</u>īrwān<u>sh</u>āhs in eastern Caucasia (see al-Bundārī, 139-41), tribute would be exacted from those potentates, although this source of income was obviously sporadic.

Within the directly-administered areas of the empire, much land was, in the course of time, alienated by assignments of revenue on particular lands, *iḳṭā*ᶜs, a term which covered, however, a very wide variety of different types of grant (see Lambton, in *Camb. hist. of Iran*, v, 233-4; and IḲṬĀᶜ). The grants of the first Sal<u>dj</u>ūḳ sultans were mainly as appanages for other members of the family who had claims, under tribal concepts, of a share-out of the total assets of the ruling family or the chiefs; these were especially to be found in northern Persia, <u>Kh</u>urāsān and the upper Oxus lands (see above, sections II and III. 2). But grants were also made at an early date to the Turkish generals of the professional, standing army which Ṭo<u>gh</u>rïl in his later years, and then Alp Arslan and Malik <u>Sh</u>āh, were compelled to recruit after the danger of sole reliance on the O<u>gh</u>uz tribal bands had been demonstrated by the latter's part in the revolts of disgruntled Sal<u>dj</u>ūḳ princes, such as Ibrāhīm Inal and Ḳāwurd (see above, section I). Such earlier grants were delegations of the sultan's authority, and did not imply any hierarchy of vassalage or a bestowal of permanent territorial or financial rights. These last only crept in during the 6th/12th century, when the warring Sal<u>dj</u>ūḳ sultans and princes were desperate to acquire troops and had to alienate more and more lands to great commanders as the price of their military support. Eventually, the process was to lead to the formation of the autonomous atabeg principalities of northern and western Persia, of northern Syria and al-<u>D</u>jazīra and of eastern Anatolia (see above, section II), but, from the legal aspect, these principalities rested upon an act of usurpation and not one of delegation or vassalage. All these trends were to have long-term effects upon land utilisation, the social and economic status of the cultivators and the ethnic complexion of the regions in question. For a fuller consideration of the trends, see Lambton, *Landlord and peasant in Persia*, London 1953, ch. III; eadem, in *Camb. hist. of Iran*, v, 231 ff.; eadem, *Continuity and change in medieval Persia*, London 1988, 97-115; Bosworth, in *ibid.*, 82-4; and IḲṬĀᶜ.

The heart of the sultans' power lay in their own court entourage, the *dargāh*, whose smooth functioning was ensured by a series of influential officials such as the *wakīl-i dār* or intendant, the *ḥā<u>dj</u>ib*s or chamberlains, the *<u>dj</u>āma-dār* or master of the sultan's wardrobe, the *ā<u>kh</u>ur-sālār* or head of the royal stables, the *<u>kh</u>ʷān-sālār* or master of the royal kitchens; the latter's function were especially important for the dispensing of general hospitality in accordance with steppe traditions and of feasts (*<u>sh</u>ölen*) for the Sal<u>dj</u>ūḳs' tribal followers, the providing of which Niẓām al-Mulk (*Siyasat-nāma*, § 35) was keen to uphold (see Uzunçarsılı, *Osmanlı devletinin teşkilâtına medhal*, 33-41; Lambton, in *Camb. hist. of Iran*, v, 224-7, 238-90). These offices tended to be held by great Turkish commanders, either the ruler's slaves or his freedmen. The importance of the court entourage and its members within the state varied according to the ruling sultan's strength of character and his control over its factions and rivalries. The sultans' womenfolk might at times exercise an influence which could affect the direction or the running of the state, especially at the deaths of sultans and the not infrequent succession crises and disputes which ensued. The sultans normally proclaimed during their own lifetime one of their sons as heir (*walī al-ᶜahd*), but their wishes did not always prevail unchallenged, not only from discontented Sal<u>dj</u>ūḳ princes who thought they had claims to the throne (see above, sections II and III. 1) but also from the rulers' widows and other female relatives, pushing the claims of their own sons; this was notoriously the case when Malik <u>Sh</u>āh died, and his widow Terken <u>Kh</u>ātūn unsuccessfully proclaimed her own child Maḥmūd in Iṣfahān against Berk-yaruḳ (see on the role of the women at this time of troubles, Sanaullah, *op. cit.*, 8-17; and, in general, for courts and court life during the Sal<u>dj</u>ūḳ period, Bosworth, *EIr* art. *Courts and courtiers. iii. In the Islamic period to the Mongol conquest*).

The means by which this power of the sultans was exercised were, firstly, through the army and the coercive force which it could exert, and secondly, through the civil administration of the empire controlled by a series of *dīwān*s, both of which were, of course, interconnected through the overriding need for the provision of finance for them. By Malik <u>Sh</u>āh's time the army's main strength lay in its professional troops, in part supported by *iḳṭā*ᶜs but to a significant extent still paid directly in cash from the royal treasury (cf. Niẓām al-Mulk, *Siyāsat-nāma*, § 23). Its nucleus was the force of slave *<u>gh</u>ulām* and freedmen troops, a large proportion of whom, though not all, were Turks. Supplementing this were the free troops, and here, as with the slave core for an army, the Sal<u>dj</u>ūḳs were following in the steps of other Middle Eastern imperial powers like the Fāṭimids and <u>Gh</u>aznavids by recruiting from a wide array of races. Niẓām al-Mulk recommended the employment of Daylamīs, <u>Kh</u>urāsānīs, Georgians and <u>Sh</u>abānkāraʾī Kurds (*Siyāsat-nāma*, § 24). This army was normally stationed in the capital with the sultan himself; and according to Rāwandī, the number of cavalrymen was not allowed to fall below 46,000 (see M.F. Sanaullah, *The decline of the Saljūqid empire*, Calcutta 1938, 18-35; Uzunçarsılı, *op. cit.*, 56-61; Bosworth, in *Camb. hist. of Iran*, v, 80-1; Lambton, *Continuity and change in medieval Persia*, 4-14; <u>GH</u>ULĀM. ii; and ḤARB. v).

Complementing the court's role in the running of the state was the central administration, comprising essentially the *dīwān-i aᶜlā*, presided over by the sultan's chief executive officer, the vizier. The vizier, and the personnel of his bureaux, were normally representatives of the Perso-Islamic secretarial class. It is possible that, in the Sal<u>dj</u>ūḳ period, some of these had received an education and training in the *madrasas* (for which, see above, section IV. 1), although this point requires further research. The vizier headed a complex of *dīwān*s, his intermediary and link with the court being the *wakīl-i dār* (cf. al-Bundārī, 93-4). The *dīwān-i aᶜlā* was above all responsible for the provision of finance for the sultan and hence for the running of the empire, and had component *dīwān*s such as the chancery, for official and diplomatic correspondence (*in<u>sh</u>āʾ*); the finance bureau, for the collection of revenue and its allocation (*istīfāʾ*); the bureau for overseeing accounts and financial transactions (*i<u>sh</u>rāf*); and the department of the army (*ᶜarḍ*), responsible for the recruitment, payment and fighting calibre of the troops. The heads of these component bureaux were powerful officials in their own right, who not infrequently followed their own policies or had supporters at court who might be at odds with the vizier. Other high-ranking persons in the state, such as the sultans' consorts and the queen-mothers and Sal<u>dj</u>ūḳ princes allotted appanages in the provinces, might have their own households with miniature replicas of the central *dīwāns* (see Uzunçarsılı, *op. cit.*, 42-51; Lambton, in *Camb. hist. of Iran*, v, 257 ff.).

Nevertheless, the vizier was a very powerful figure throughout the Saldjūḳ period, with his position buttressed by the patronage which he exercised and the opportunities which he had for self-enrichment through confiscations, etc. He normally had his own *iḳṭā*ᶜs, and an outstanding figure like Niẓām al-Mulk built up around himself what was in effect a private army of *mamlūk*s and other retainers, the Niẓāmiyya [*q.v.*], who continued to play a significant role in politics well after their master's death.

Justice and equity of an "administrative" or "secular" kind was exercised through the sultan's own *maẓālim* [*q.v.*] jurisdiction, both personally and by delegation to special *maẓālim* courts. At the side of these, the local *ḳāḍī*s dispensed justice according to the *sharīᶜa*, and with the restatement of the relationship between caliph and sultan (see above), the judges, theoretically the deputies of the caliph and deriving their spiritual jurisdiction from him, were in practice appointed by the sultan and were salaried servants of the sultanate, as were the *khaṭīb*s [*q.v.*] or preachers of the Friday sermon and the *muḥtasib*s or market inspectors [see ḤISBA]. A chief judge of the empire, the *ḳāḍī-yi djumla-yi mamālīk*, is mentioned under Alp Arslan, with oversight of the religious law, of religious buildings and of *awḳāf* or pious trusts (which spread considerably within the Saldjūḳ empire as a result of benefactions from the great *amīr*s, the atabegs and the women in the ruling classes, see Lambton, *Continuity and change in medieval Persia*, 149-51), but the mass of judges were local officials in the towns of the empire and thus served as a link between the central government and the local urban communities (see eadem, in *Camb. hist. of Iran*, v, 269-72).

The cities and towns of Persia, ᶜIrāḳ, al-Djazīra and Syria seem in general to have flourished during the 5th/11th century, doubtless benefiting from the general internal peace in the years before Malik Shāh's death and having a resilience and continuity of tradition which enabled them to function and to prosper to a fair extent in the more troubled decades of the 6th/12th century, when the Crusaders and Ismāᶜīlīs destabilised Syria, when al-Djazīra and western Persia were affected by the warfare among rival Saldjūḳ princes and the atabegs, and when the ascendancy of anarchic Oghuz tribesmen in Khurāsān and Kirmān led to widespread looting and devastation there, a foretaste of the worse disasters which the arrival of the Mongols was to bring. Whether there was in the 6th/12th century a distinct decline in economic life, a deterioration of the status and richness of the town bourgeoisies, technological stagnation in construction and production methods, and even a decrease of population, as was asserted by E. Ashtor, requires further investigation (see his *A social and economic history of the Near East in the Middle Ages*, London 1976, 209-48). It is true that he adduces an array of natural disasters, including earthquakes and epidemics, from the chronicles of the Saldjūḳ period, and it may be true that the alienation of land as *iḳṭā*ᶜs, particularly after the weakening of the sultan's power from Berk-yaruḳ's accession onwards, reduced the amount of lands from which taxation could be directly collected and drove the rulers into an increased reliance on non-canonical taxes, *mukūs* [see MAKS]. Yet as a counter to this, one may note that the Saldjūḳ government, for its part, had an enduring interest in fostering, as far as possible, the economic well-being of the cities and towns, with their roles as centres of craft production and of long-distance trading, from which they derived so much of the taxation needed to run the empire. As Bulliet has observed, "given the desire on the part of the rulers to preserve the commercial, urban character of Islamic society, the cities were more important to the ruler than the ruler was to the cities" (*The patricians of Nishapur*, 61).

As in other regions and at other times of the premodern age, the cities and towns of the Saldjūḳ empire had no corporate or autonomous life of their own within the concept of divinely-dispensed authority in Islam. But the local historians of cities and towns like Nīshāpūr, Bayhaḳ, Harāt, Iṣfahān and Shīrāz certainly demonstrate the vitality of urban life at this time and the cohesiveness and common interests of their oligarchies, whether these comprised Ḥanafīs, Shāfiᶜīs or Ḥanbalīs (and also, in Khurāsān, Karrāmīs). This class of *ᶜulamā*ʾ, merchants and other notables largely monopolised such state offices as those of *ḳāḍī*, *khaṭīb*, etc. (see above). Above all, it was from their ranks that there came the *raʾīs* or mayor, the mouthpiece of the town notables vis-à-vis the provincial and central government; and, since the relations between the towns and the ruling authority were essentially financial, it was he who forwarded the taxation due from the town to the local *dīwān*. See, in general, RAʾĪS. 1. and 2.; Bosworth, *The Ghaznavids*, 171 ff.; Bulliet, *op. cit.*, 66-8. For the duties of a *raʾīs* in Māzandarān and Gurgān in the second quarter of the 12th century A.D., Lambton, *The administration of Sanjar's empire as illustrated in the* ᶜAtabat al-kataba, 383-7. For these institutions in Syria under Saldjūḳ rule, A. Havemann, *Riʾāsa und qaḍāʾ. Institutionen als Ausdruck wechselnde Kräfteverhältnisse in syrischen Städten vom 10. bis zum 12. Jahrhundert*, Freiburg-im Breisgau 1975, and idem, *The vizier and the raʾīs in Saljuq Syria: the struggle for urban self-representation*, in *IJMES*, xxi (1989), 233-42.

There were, of course, counterforces in the cities and towns and in their agricultural hinterlands working against this urban group solidarity in the face of external attackers or tyrannical government actions. The *ᶜaṣabiyyāt* or factional divisions noted by the geographer al-Muḳaddasī in the later 4th/10th century continued unabated throughout the Saldjūḳ period, breaking out into violence when the absence of external threat allowed such a luxury. The chroniclers and the local historians mention the perennial clashes between Sunnīs, above all, Ḥanbalīs, and Shīᶜī in Baghdād, and those between Ḥanafīs, Shāfiᶜīs and Karrāmīs, in varying combinations, in Nīshāpūr, Bayhaḳ, Harāt and other towns of Khurāsān. The Saldjūḳ sultans themselves, by their enthusiastic adoption of the Ḥanafī *madhhab* and by the efforts of their servants, from the ᶜAmīd al-Mulk al-Kundurī [*q.v.*] onwards, to further the cause of Ḥanafism (see above, section IV. 1), probably stimulated rather than stilled such passions, as various items of information in the sources suggest. In the course of Ḥanafī-Shāfiᶜī riots at Nīshāpūr during Sandjar's reign, seventy people from the former group were killed. In the reign of sultan Masᶜūd b. Muḥammad, a powerful group of the Turkish commanders, fiercely Ḥanafī, persecuted and expelled Shāfiᶜī *ᶜulamā*ʾ and other local notables adhering to Shāfiᶜism in Baghdād, Rayy and Iṣfahān, to the point that some of these last made politic conversions to Ḥanafism, whilst a purge of the Shāfiᶜīs at Iṣfahān in 542/1147-8 caused *fitna* there (al-Ḥusaynī, 125-6; al-Bundārī, 193-4, 220-1). Towards the end of Sandjar's reign and shortly afterwards, it was, according to Rāwandī, internal factional feuding, rather than the ravages of the O͟ghuz, which really consummated the ruin of the city (cited in Bulliet, *The political-religious history of Nishapur in the eleventh century*, 90-1). This last author has put forward the view that, earlier on, Niẓām al-Mulk was endeavouring to restore the balance in Nī͟shāpūr by favouring the less powerful S͟hāfiʿīs there against the dominant Ḥanafīs by his founding of *madrasas*, his Niẓāmiyyas, for which he personally retained the right of appointing the professors (*The patricians of Nishapur*, 72-4; and see above, section IV. 1); but not long after this, both of these *mad͟hhab*s were uniting in Nī͟shāpūr against the Karrāmiyya (see Ibn al-At͟hīr, ed. Beirut, x, 251, year 488/1095).

Another divisive element in certain cities and towns of the Sald͟jūḳ empire at this time was that of the *ʿayyār*s [*q.v.*] or mobsters. Bag͟hdād, the Syrian towns and those of K͟hurāsān suffered especially badly, but there is reason to believe that towns elsewhere had similar problems, conceivably evidence of some underlying social-political malaise in them such as the exclusion of sections of the urban populace from participation in higher municipal affairs; but this is conjecture. Outbreaks of *ʿayyār* violence were a matter of concern for the urban authorities, who alone could take steps to curb it; hence when, at Bayhaq, *ʿayyār*s took advantage of the relaxation of central authority in the state after Malik S͟hāh's death in 485/1092, one of the town's numerous and influential body of Sayyids organised, at his own expense, a police force of citizens and their slaves against unruly elements (Ibn Funduḳ, *Taʾrīk͟h-i Bayhaḳ*, ed. Bahmanyār, 274-5; cf. J. Aubin, *L'aristocratie urbain dans l'Iran seldjukide: l'exemple de Sabzavâr*, in *Mélanges René Crozet*, Poitiers 1966, 328).

As the secular counterparts of the caliphs, the Sunnī Sald͟jūḳ sultans had an obligation to further Islamic learning within their dominions. The role of them and their servants in the movement for founding *madrasas*, mosque- and shrine-colleges, etc., has been outlined above, in section IV. 1. The sultans of the first two or three generations were probably illiterate, and undoubtedly so in Persian and Arabic; it must be remembered that Malik S͟hāh was the first monarch not to grow up purely in the O͟ghuz tribal environment. Barthold (*Turkestan down to the Mongol invasion*[3], 308) thought that Sand͟jar remained illiterate all his life, but this requires further investigation. By the 6th/12th century, however, various of the sultans in western Persia and ʿIrāḳ are praised in the sources for their culture and education. Thus Anū͟shirwān b. K͟hālid, who is severely condemnatory about Maḥmūd b. Muḥammad's policies, nevertheless praises him for his fine Arabic scholarship, his knowledge of poetry and *adab*, history and *sīra*; and among the Sald͟jūḳ *amīr*s of Kirmān of this century, Arslan S͟hāh and Muḥammad S͟hāh encouraged scholarship by providing bursaries for students, pensions for the *fuḳahāʾ*, etc. (al-Bundārī, 156; Muḥammad b. Ibrāhīm, 25-6, 29).

Concerning the non-Muslim population of the empire, mentions of the *d͟himmī*s, Jews, Christians and Zoroastrians, become sparser in the Sald͟jūḳ period than for the preceding ones, e.g. the Būyid period. The Christians were still, however, strong in ʿIrāḳ and al-D͟jazīra and in such western Persian provinces as K͟hūzistān and Fārs and the city of Iṣfahān, and the ʿAbbāsids and the Sald͟jūḳ sultans in Bag͟hdād used the services extensively of Jews and Christians for the traditional pursuits of these last, such as administration and the practice of medicine. Despite mention still of a metropolitan for the Christians of Fārs in the early Sald͟jūḳ period, the western Persian communities of Christians and of Zoroastrians (the latter of whom were an important element in Būyid Fārs), seem to have fallen into decline, the prelude to the eventual disappearance of the Christians, at least, there. The Christians of ʿIrāḳ, on the other hand remained numerous and vigorous, and influential enough in public life to bring down on their heads sporadic Muslim persecution. Thus the caliph's vizier Abū S͟hud͟jāʿ al-Rūd͟hrāwarī [*q.v.*] in 484/1091 drastically enforced the discriminatory laws against *d͟himmī*s [see G͟HIYĀR], bringing about the conversion to Islam of the Christian head of the caliph's *dīwān al-inshāʾ*, Abū Saʿd Ibn al-Mawṣilāyā and of his nephew, the *ṣāḥib al-k͟habar* Abū Naṣr Hibat Allāh (al-Bundārī, 78; Ibn al-At͟hir, x, 186). In the east, the metropolitan of Marw was still the most important dignitary of the Nestorian Church in K͟hurāsān, and a bishop of Ṭūs is mentioned as late as 1279; Abū Saʿīd b. Abi 'l-K͟hayr of Mayhana (see above, section IV. 1) is said to have converted large numbers of Christians at Nī͟shāpūr around the time of the change from G͟haznawid to Sald͟jūḳ rule in the city (see Bosworth, *The Ghaznavids*, 200-2).

Jewish communities existed in most of the cities of Sald͟jūḳ Persia and ʿIrāḳ, often with a special quarter of their own, sometimes specifically called the *yahūdiyya*, and spiritually they were under the headship of the Rē͟sh Gālūthā. Special areas of concentration were the towns of Fārs and K͟hūzistān and in Iṣfahān, and towns like Ahwāz and S͟hu͟shtar had colonies of the Rād͟hānī merchants [see AL-RĀD͟HĀNIYYA]. The Spanish Jewish traveller during later Sald͟jūḳ times, Benjamin of Tudela (1179), mentions as Jewish centres in western Persia Susa, Ḥulwān, Hamad͟hān, Iṣfahān and S͟hīrāz, whilst in the east of Persia (which Benjamin did not visit), there were important communities in Marw, Harāt and Bal͟kh (this last having a *yahūdiyya* quarter and being known as a resort of Rād͟hānī merchants) which sent substantial financial contributions back to Mesopotamia (see W.J. Fischel, *The Jews of Central Asia (Khorasan) in mediaeval Hebrew and Islamic literature*, in *Historia Judaica*, New York, vii [1945], 35-42).

It is hard to find concrete information on trade and economic life within the Sald͟jūḳ empire. The rich geographical and travel literature in Arabic and then Persian of the 3rd-4th/9th-10th centuries dwindles almost to nothing during the Sald͟jūḳ period, and there is a general paucity of information in the historical sources. One region about which we know a certain amount is Kirmān and eastern Persia, from items mentioned by the local historians of Kirmān and noted above in section III. 3. They reveal the existence of an important trade route from the Persian Gulf and the Gulf of Oman shores northwards through Kirmān to Ḳuhistān and K͟hurāsān, a trade which had international ramifications, since Hindus and Greeks are mentioned as amongst the merchants at the trading suburb of Ḳumādīn (the Camadi of Marco Polo, through whose ruined site he passed in the later 7th/13th century, see Yule and Cordier, *The book of Ser Marco Polo*[3], London 1903, i, 97-9) outside D͟jīruft in Kirmān, where there were extensive warehouses for storing goods in transit (Muḥammad b. Ibrāhīm, 49). At the northern end of this trade route, Nī͟shāpūr was the great emporium of K͟hurāsān at this time, certainly up to the G͟huzz sackings of the second half of the 6th/12th century. It was probably the main centre in the Great Sald͟jūḳ state for the minting of the Sald͟jūḳs' gold coinage, judging by the number of extant dīnārs which were minted there (see further, below, section VIII. 1), and although information is regrettably lacking, it must have continued, as it did in Sāmānid and Ghaznawid times, to have commercial contacts with the Central Asian steppe lands and beyond.

The southern end of the route, running down to the Gulf of Oman and across it, connected the eastern Persian world with the Arabian one. Al-Muḳaddasī, 321, had noted that the name of Ḳā'in, in Ḳuhistān, had a great renown in ʿUmān; at the beginning of the Saldjūḳ period, the traveller Nāṣir-i Khusraw [*q.v.*] found that transactions at Faladj in central Arabia were done in the dīnārs of Nīshāpūr (*Safar-namā*, ed. Muḥammad Dabīr-Siyāḳī, Tehran 1335/1956, 106, tr. W.M. Thackston, *Nāṣer-e Khosraw's Book of Travels*, Albany 1986, 85). The Ḳufṣ or Kūfičī bandits who had been such a menace to commerce and to travellers along the edges of the central Great Desert of Persia in the Būyid period [see ḲUFṢ] seem to have been mastered by Ḳāwurd, who also took measures against another predatory people of the region, the Balūč; and Nāṣir-i Khusraw, again, found that the *amīr* of Ṭabas (al-Tamr) in the eastern part of the Great Desert, Abu 'l-Ḥasan Gīlakī, had established perfect security in a region formerly terrorised by the Ḳufṣ who must, in any case, have been pushed back southwards by the incoming bands of Oghuz (*op. cit.*, 124-5, tr. 99-100). Ḳāwurd further extended his power across the sea into ʿUmān, thereby controlling both sides of the lower Gulf (Muḥammad b. Ibrāhīm, 8-10; cf. above, section III. 3). This northwards-southwards-running trade route through eastern Persia was thus of prime importance all through the Saldjūḳ period as the link between the Indian Ocean shores and the Arabian peninsula with Khurāsān and Central Asia, and its significance continued to be recognised by the Khwārazm Shāh ʿAlā' al-Dīn Muḥammad [*q.v.*] when he annexed Kirmān in the early 7th/13th century and in 611/1214-15 proclaimed his authority over the ports of ʿUmān. Only did its importance decline during the Mongol and Il-Khānid periods in favour of a trade route further westwards and nearer the head of the Persian Gulf (see Aubin, *La ruine de Sîrâf et les routes du Golfe Persique*, in *Cahiers de civilisation médiévale*, ii/3 [1959], 300-1).

This last route, on the other hand, had been in eclipse during the Saldjūḳ period. The disappearance of firm Būyid control in Fārs allowed the Shabānkāra'ī Kurds to become a destructive force there as early as Alp Arslan's time, one which the governors deputed to govern the province for the Saldjūḳs, such as the atabeg Čawuli Saḳā'ū, did much to curb without, however, eliminating the problem completely, so that the prosperity of Fārs in Saldjūḳ times had many ups and downs. A further element of disruption within the Gulf was caused by the pirates of the island of Ḳays [*q.v.*]. Hence formerly flourishing ports of Fārs on the northern shore of the Gulf, such as Sīrāf [*q.v.*] and Nadjīram, which had had an international trade, as entrepôts for South and South-East Asian products destined for the central lands of the caliphate, fell into decline in the later 5th/11th century, despite efforts to revive their prosperity by the Saldjūḳ governor of Fārs, the atabeg Rukn al-Dawla Khumārtigin (Ibn al-Balkhī, *Fārs-nāma*, ed. Le Strange, 136-7, tr. idem, *Description of the province of Fars in Persia* ..., London 1912, 41-3, also in Sir Arnold Wilson, *The Persian Gulf*, London 1928, 94-6). What remained of the once great port of Sīrāf now had only a local commercial role to play, probably as a centre for pearl-fishing. The towns on or near the route going inland from the Gulf shores to western Persia were accordingly affected too, and Shīrāz during the Saldjūḳ period shrank from its peak of size and splendour as the Būyid *amīr* ʿAḍud al-Dawla's [*q.v.*] capital, and now had only a small area enclosed by a wall against the Shabānkāra and the Turkmens, with much of its former area ruinous; another fairly important town of Fārs, Kāzarūn, had suffered similarly (Ibn al-Balkhī, 132-4, 145-6, tr. 36-8, 55-6). It was only in the Il-Khānid and Muẓaffarid periods that Shīrāz revived completely (see Aubin, *op. cit.*, 297-9; SHĪRĀZ; SĪRĀF).

We have virtually no information about trade along the great, historic highway across Persia from ʿIrāḳ either via the more northerly Hamadhān route or the more southerly Iṣfahān one to Rayy and Khurāsān, although this must have continued to be a major commercial artery between the central Islamic lands and the northeastern fringes of the Islamic world, even after the comparative peace within the Saldjūḳ empire up to Malik Shāh's death had been brought to an end by fairly continuous fighting in Djibāl, Kurdistān and Luristān during the ensuing succession disputes. We do know, however, that the great cities along this route continued to thrive. Hamadhān [*q.v.*] was a lively trade centre with a prosperous agricultural hinterland, and in the later decades of the 6th/12th century served as the sultans' capital. Rayy [*q.v.*] was taken over by Ṭoghrïl Beg in 434/1042-3 from the Turkmen leader Ibrāhīm Inal when the former came westwards from Khurāsān, becoming his capital for a while, and the city flourished for the next half-century; fine dīnārs were minted there by Ṭoghrïl, Alp Arslan and Malik Shāh. After 485/1092, however, the internecine warfare had deleterious effects on the city's prosperity; from this date, the Saldjūḳ coins minted there become sparser and almost dry up, being of feeble quality, reflecting the degeneration of the coinage (see G.C. Miles, *The numismatic history of Rayy*, New York 1938, 196-217. The standard of the coinage is, of course, concrete evidence of the health or otherwise of the economy in general; for a consideration of the Great Saldjūḳs' coins, see below, section VIII. 1). It is Iṣfahān [*q.v.*] that we are best informed about. It finally passed into Ṭoghrïl's possession from the Kākūyids in 443/1051, and the sultan immediately put in hand measures for its revival after the preceeding years of warfare. Hence on his homeward journey in 444/1052, Nāṣir-i Khusraw found it in a highly flourishing state, wih busy markets, including a bazaar for the money-changers with 200 shops and fifty *khāns* in one street alone, whilst the caravan with which he travelled brought 300 assloads of goods (*Safar-nāma*, 123, tr. 98). Ṭoghrïl moved thither his capital from Rayy, and the city continued till the death of Muḥammad b. Malik Shāh to be a favoured centre for the sultans, directly administered by them and not granted out to one of their servants or commanders (Māfarrukhī, *K. Maḥāsin Iṣfahān*, ed. Sayyid Djalāl al-Dīn Ṭihrānī, Tehran 1312/1933, 101 ff.; and see, in general, on the cities of Persia at this time, Lambton, *Aspects of Saljūq-Ghuzz settlement in Persia*, 116-20).

One result of the general healthiness of the economies of the cities of Persia and of the countryside during the 5th/11th century at least seems to have been a buoyant revenue accrueing from the lands of the empire, comparing favourably both with the preceding Būyid period and certainly with the succeeding Mongol and Il-Khānid ones. We have no global figures stemming from the Saldjūḳ period itself, but the late Il-Khānid period writer Ḥamd Allāh

Mustawfī states, from a lost *Risāla-yi Malik Shāhī*, that the total revenue of the empire was in that sultan's time 215 million red gold dīnārs, the equivalent of rather more than 500 million of his own time but in fact a much higher figure than that during Il-Khānid times (cited in Lambton, *op. cit.*, 120-1).

Bibliography: Given in the article. There are no full-scale works devoted to Saldjūķ social and economic history, nor any chapters on them in *Camb. hist. of Iran*, v, but for administration, A.K.S. Lambton's magistral chapter *The internal structure of the Saljuq empire*, in *ibid.*, 203-82, provides a detailed account, to be supplemented now by Carla L. Klausner, *The Seljuk vezirate. A study of civil administration 1055-1194*, Cambridge, Mass. 1973, and Bulliet's *The patricians of Nishapur*. Also, Lambton's *Continuity and change in medieval Persia*, whilst covering a wider expanse of Persian history than just the Saldjūķ period, nevertheless contains much important material on Saldjūķ administration, land tenure and social conditions. The question of patronage, loyalty, clientship, etc. in the Saldjūķ empire has recently been examined by A. Jurado Aceituno, *La "ḫidma" selyuqí: la red de relaciones de dependencia mutua, la dinámica del poder y las formas de obtención de los beneficios*, diss. Universidad Autónoma de Madrid 1994, unpubl.

2. In Anatolia

The Saldjūķ administration in Anatolia was probably less developed and certainly less extensive in its sphere of operations than that of the Great Saldjūķs. The rulers depended on secretaries and officials from the Saldjūķ lands further east, essentially of Perso-Islamic culture, for any existing, pre-Saldjūķ Greek or Armenian officials would have been of little practical use, given their ignorance of Arabic and Persian and of the whole Islamic administrative tradition. Hence the administration, like the culture of the Rūm Saldjūķs, became strongly Persian in ethos. In the formative, earlier period, however, the possibility of extraneous influences from the earlier, Byzantine civilisation should be considered, and the question whether the Saldjūķs and, after them, the Ottomans, made use of Byzantine models or worked purely within the Perso-Islamic and/or native Turkish traditions, has been much discussed by scholars.

The sultan's chief executive was the vizier, but viziers never seem to have achieved the great power and influence in the state which several of those of the Great Saldjūķs enjoyed, at least before the mid-7th/13th century, when we then have the dominating figure of the *Parwāna* Muʿīn al-Dīn Sulaymān [*q.v.*] and other officials who had to act as intermediaries between the puppet sultans and their Mongol overlords. The chancery in Konya generally used Persian for correspondence, but Arabic was naturally of great importance e.g. for diplomatic relations with the Muslim powers of Syria, Egypt and ʿIrāķ; Ibn Bībī even mentions *nūṭār* = *notarioi*, who were presumably used for correspondence with Byzantine and other Christian powers and, possibly, for contacts with the indigenous Greek population of Anatolia. Also, Turkish must have been necessary for communicating with the increasing numbers of Turks amongst the Anatolian population, both in the towns and the countryside, and, in particular, with the army, whose payment was the responsibility of the central *dīwān* or one of its offshoots concerned with military affairs. When the Ķaramānid Shams al-Dīn Muḥammad captured Konya in 675/1277, he is said to have ordered that Turkish only should be used in the chancery there [see ĶARAMĀN-OGHULLARĪ, at vol. IV, 620a], but this innovation cannot have lasted very long.

The army, although arising out of the Turkmen bands which had raided across Anatolia from the outset, came to be a much more ethnically-varied force, not only because it contained Greeks and Armenians who had been captured and enslaved (although there is no sign of anything like the later Ottoman *dewshirme* [*q.v.*]), but also because companies of foreign troops, sometimes vaguely characterised as "Franks" (*firang*), were employed. The position is not clear regarding these, but they may have been mercenaries; for the 7th/13th century, Ibn Bībī speaks of hired troops (*djīra-khwār*), apparently including Khwārazmians, Armenians from Cilicia and Greeks from Trebizond.

Connected with the idea of continuity or discontinuity of institutions in Saldjūķ Anatolia, and the use of local peoples in the state apparatus, is the topic of the progress of Islamisation on the Anatolian plateau and attendant problems raised by it. Islamisation was clearly a gradual process, but exactly at what speed it progressed, and with what degree of violence and hardship for the indigenous peoples, are questions which have been discussed by historians. Undoubtedly, the Greeks and Armenians suffered from the uncontrolled raiding of barbaric Turkmens, often themselves only imperfectly Islamised, and they were exposed to the enslavement of their male children by the Muslim conquerors. The remaining churches and monasteries, cut off from their previous sources of benefactions and revenues, became impoverished. In general, there was some movement of the Christian population from the central plateau to the maritime fringes and to mountain areas, but of course, substantial Christian elements remained in the towns and countryside of central and inland Anatolia right up to the early 20th century and the exchange of Greek and Turkish populations in an age of sharpened nationalisms. Between these peoples and incoming Turkish groups some degree of intermarriage apparently took place, and contemporary Greek sources speak of a new generation of Anatolians of mixed ancestry, the *mixovarvaroi*, who could be found in the forces of some Turkish chiefs. Such intermarriage, added to the social and legal disadvantages of non-Muslims living under Islamic rule, must have favoured a degree of conversion and must have contributed to some decline in the numbers of Christians in Anatolia. Nevertheless, the situation of Christians under Turkish rule appears to have been more favourable than in the Arabo-Persian heartlands of the *Dār al-Islām*. The Saldjūķ sultans of Rūm retained something of the tolerance towards, or indifference to, other faiths which had characterised the Turks and Mongols in their Inner Asian homelands; they themselves married Greek and Georgian princesses; churches and monasteries remained in their dominions, and the Greek clergy found no difficulty in maintaining links with their Patriarchate in Constantinople. It must always be remembered, too, that the Turks were almost certainly still a minority within the lands they ruled, so that the Greco-Armenian presence within Anatolia remained a substantial one and may have favoured a some degree of religious syncretism with the local forms of Islam, a possibility explored by such scholars as F.W. Hasluck and Fuad Köprülü (see on this, above, section IV. 2).

Economic and commercial life within the core lands of the sultanate seems to have been flourishing, certainly by the early 7th/13th century. It was the frontier regions, where periodic fighting and raiding persisted, which suffered economic and social dislocation, whereas the sultans had an obvious interest in promoting the agricultural prosperity of their dominions. The taxes levied by the Sal̲dj̲ūḳ administration on the Christian populace may conceivably have been lighter than those of the retreating Byzantine fiscal system. With the virtual Mongol takeover of the Sal̲dj̲ūḳ sultanate in the later 7th/13th century, however, taxation on all classes must have increased perceptibly. Anatolia had to pay tribute to support the Mongol army and administration there, and there there were various taxes whose names are known but whose exact nature is unclear (e.g. *balīs̲h̲*, *ind̲j̲u* and *dalay*, although *ind̲j̲u* seems to denote domains in Rūm belonging to the Il K̲h̲ānid state). As part of the great vizier to the Mongols Ras̲h̲īd al-Dīn Ṭabīb's [*q.v.*] general financial re-ordering of the Il K̲h̲ānid empire in *ca.* 700/1300, an effort seems to have been made to recover *iḳṭā*ᶜs [*q.v.*] which had been transformed into *milk* [*q.v.*] or private property under the later Sal̲dj̲ūḳ sultans.

Despite these burdens, the lands of the sultanate continued in general to prosper. As noted above, during the first half of the 7th/13th century the sultans secured access to the Mediterranean and the Black Sea shores, and even made their presence felt as far away as the Crimea (see above, section III. 5). There was consequently a great fillip to internal trade and the transit trade across Anatolia, signalled by a perceptible building programme by the sultans, from Ḳïlïč Arslan II in the later 6th/12th century onwards, and by great men in the state, along the Anatolian caravan routes, seen in bridges, caravanserails, ᶜ*imāret*s and other facilities for travellers and merchants (see below, section VI. 2). The first tentative trade agreements were made with European powers like the Venetians, specifically in this case concerning access to Mediterranean trade through Antalya (610/1213 and 613/1216). At the same time, urban life within the sultanate revived by the later 6th/12th century from its depressed state under the later Byzantines, and many towns received new or strengthened walls, visible now in the walls of Alanya (those of Konya only having disappeared in recent times). Although the Sal̲dj̲ūḳ towns, almost all of them corresponding to their Byzantine and/or classical forerunners, had no more autonomy than the towns elsewhere in the Islamic world, they had a vigorous life, accentuated by the mélange of peoples and faiths within them. In the 7th/13th century we have mention of such groups of mixed parentage called *ikdīs̲h̲* "crossbreeds", and of the *ak̲h̲ī*s [*q.v.*], whose importance in almost all the towns of Anatolia was later to strike the Moroccan traveller Ibn Baṭṭūṭa.

Bibliography: See that for section III. 5 above, and especially Cahen, *Pre-Ottoman Turkey*, 143 ff., 314 ff., and Vryonis, *The decline of medieval Hellenism in Asia Minor*. For administrative organisation, see İ.H. Uzunçarşılı, *Osmanlı devleti teşkilâtina medhal*, Istanbul 1941, 64-107, and for military organisation, *ibid.*, 108-22, and A. Bombaci, *The army of the Saljuqs of Rūm*, in *AIUON*, xxxviii = N.S. xxviii (1978), 343-69. (C.E. Bosworth)

VI. Art and architecture

1. In Persia

This article will confine itself to the output of the Sal̲dj̲ūḳ period in Persia, for that was the centre of Sal̲dj̲ūḳ power; and while some Sal̲dj̲ūḳ rulers extended their authority far to the west, and even to the north-east at times, their hold on this territory was much more tenuous. Moreover, the visual arts in Syria and ᶜIrāḳ between *ca.* 1000 and *ca.* 1220 followed their own path, in which local traditions played a major role. For the art of the Sal̲dj̲ūḳs in Anatolia, see section 2. below.

The importance of Sal̲dj̲ūḳ art within the broader context of Islamic art as a whole lies in the way that it established the dominant position of Persia; one may compare the pivotal role of Italy in European art. It also determined the future development of art in the Persian world for centuries. In its own time its impact was felt, either through the agency of the Sal̲dj̲ūḳs themselves or through their successor states, from Syria to Northern India. The period 1000-1220 set benchmarks for all sorts of fields, from pottery and metalwork to the arts of the book and architecture. It is important to note that this time frame begins well before the Sal̲dj̲ūḳ period and ends well after it, a reminder that the chronology of artistic styles is often out of phase with that of political history. A by-product of this is that the overlap between Sal̲dj̲ūḳ art and that of the Būyids, G̲h̲aznawids, G̲h̲ūrids, Ḳarak̲h̲anids and K̲h̲ʷārazms̲h̲āhs—to name only some of the major stylistic groupings of the time—is such that these dynastic labels are often unhelpful if not downright misleading. The basic fact to bear in mind is the existence of an artistic *koiné* in the eastern Islamic world between 1000 and 1220. That *koiné*, moreover, was at its most vigorous in the years of Sal̲dj̲ūḳ decline and after the fall of the dynasty in 1194, and it owed much to the political unity imposed by the Sal̲dj̲ūḳs on eastern and western Persia. It is to this later period that the major technical advances of Sal̲dj̲ūḳ art can be attributed. The period from *ca.* 1150 (the pen case of 542/1148 in the Hermitage provides a convenient point of departure) saw an unprecedented expansion of figural decoration, whether in the form of narrative scenes (taken, for example, from the *S̲h̲āh-nāma* of Firdawsī), pictures of courtiers, animals, zodiacal themes, and images from the so-called "princely cycle" featuring hunting, banqueting, music-making and the like. Long benedictory inscriptions in Arabic now become the norm in the portable arts. Sculpture in stucco, ceramic and metal now takes on a new importance.

The sheer productivity of these centuries in the visual arts [see k̲h̲azaf and maᶜdin] represents, in comparison with the output of earlier centuries, a quantum leap forward. With this increased quantity—which is helped by a standardisation of shapes—comes an expansion in patronage, which now not only operates at court level but also has a new popular dimension, perhaps an expression of widespread urban wealth deriving from a buoyant economy. This art, then, reveals a cross-section of contemporary society and its tastes; luxury and utility Ḳurʾāns, large royal and small provincial mosques, expensive lustre or *mināʾī* [*q.v.*] pottery and coarse glazed ware reminiscent of folk art, elaborately inlaid metalwork and virtually plain cast pieces. One can identify numerous local schools, for example in architecture and ceramics. A natural by-product of this intensive activity was a wide range of technical and stylistic innovations. It must be remembered, however, that the picture is skewed, especially in the fields of pottery and metalwork, by the massive scale of illegal excavations in Persia over the past hundred years, for which there is no parallel in the rest of the Islamic world. In other countries most of the comparable material is still in the ground. And the paucity of detailed monographic studies of key objects and buildings means that much basic information is still either unavailable or inadequately contextualised.

Thus the originality of Sal̲dj̲ūḳ art is apt to be exaggerated. In many cases, the artists of the Saldjūḳ period (it is misleading to speak of "the Saldjūḳs" in this connection) consolidated, and indeed at times perfected, forms and ideas that had long been known. In architecture one may cite the 4-*īwān* plan, the dome chamber over the *miḥrāb* in the mosque, and the tomb tower; in Ḳurānic calligraphy, the apotheosis of the "New Style" of Kūfic, now integrated with lavish illumination; in metalwork, the technique of inlay using several metals; and in painting, the development of the frontispiece. Above all, there is surprisingly little for which a source right outside the Persian world can be posited. Although the Saldjūḳs themselves were Turks, it is hard to point to any specifically Turkish elements in the art of Persia and its eastern provinces in the period under review. This seems to point to the dominance of Persian artisans in the visual arts. Parenthetically, one may note that the picture in Anatolia, where people of Turkish extraction formed a larger proportion of the population, is distinctively different; there, references to pagan Turkish religious beliefs, funerary customs and royal ceremonial are frequently encountered (see section 2. below).

What of patronage? Only two pieces of Saldjūḳ pottery made for a person of high rank, one an *amīr*, the other a vizier, are known, and the situation is little better in the case of metalwork. The overwhelmingly rich and varied production in these fields ought presumably, therefore, to be attributed to patronage exercised at a lower level of society, such as merchants, members of the leaned class and professional people. Most of it was presumably made for the market, though this would not exclude its use by those of high rank. Architecture, involving as it did much larger sums of money, is a different story altogether. Inscriptions in mosques and mausolea mention the Saldjūḳ sultans themselves (e.g. Malik Shāh and Muḥammad), viziers (Niẓam al-Mulk, Tādj al-Mulk), Turkish chieftains (the towers of Kharraḳān), army commanders (Urmiya) and numerous *amīrs* (Marāgha, Mihmandust, Ḳazwīn and Abarḳūh).

Problems of provenance have bedevilled the study of the so-called "minor arts" in the Saldjūḳ period. These problems have been exacerbated by the fact that most of the known material has not been scientifically excavated and lacks inscriptions yielding solid information on provenance. Confusing and contradictory information on this topic proliferates. The very few securely provenanced pieces perforce act as a peg on which to hang all manner of other pieces, and their evidential value is simply not enough to justify this practice. It is now generally accepted (thanks to O. Watson) that virtually all lustre and *minā*ʾ*ī* wares—the most expensive ceramics of the period—were made in Kāshān (though the distinctive heavy red body of lustre tiles found in the Kirmān area suggests local production there), and this luxury ware was widely traded, to judge by the sherding carried out by A. Williamson and others. But conversely, many other slightly less luxurious but still fine wares cannot be securely associated with any one city or area, and they might therefore have been produced in several places independently (like the Sāmānid epigraphic ware of the 10th century, which was produced in both Samarḳand and Nīshāpūr, and apparently in Marw too). Similarly, the fact that the celebrated Bobrinski bucket and the Tiflis ewer both bear an inscription stating that they were made in Harāt indicates that fine inlaid metalwork was produced in that city, and the occurrence of craftsmen's *nisba*s indicating Khurāsānī cities—Harāt, Marw, Nīshāpūr—confirms the important role of this province in metalwork. But it is not enough to justify the wholesale attribution to Harāt of wares that merely share some of the features found on Harātī work. This is particularly unlikely for metalwork that is technically simpler than the inlaid pieces, since the demand for such simpler work must have been too widespread to be catered for by a single production centre. But exactly where these other Persian workshops were located must be determined by future research. The astonishing range of forms encountered in Saldjūḳ metalwork (including many derived from architectural forms) also points to numerous centres of production. It seems likely that some of the best craftsmen travelled widely to execute commissions, and that fine pieces (e.g. of Kāshān tilework) were shipped over long distances. There is evidence too of a division of labour in metalwork and lustreware that ensured a higher level of quality overall. But the key question remains; scholarship has not yet established whether the pockets of intense activity in a limited geographical area have a wider significance for pan-Persian production or whether they reflect a well-developed specialisation confined to a given area.

Laboratory examination has yet to be used in a systematic way on Saldjūḳ metalwork; the evidence that it would provide on alloys, for instance, could then be correlated with other factors—shape, technique, decoration—to create a more nuanced picture of the various known types. In the current state of knowledge it is safe to say that wares constructed from sheet metal were made of brass while most others were of quaternary alloy; true bronzes are uncommon.

The very few pieces of Saldjūḳ metalwork in silver point to a serious shortage of that metal which became more critical as the 11th century advanced. It was perhaps in part a result of the practice followed by the Viking traders travelling along the great Russian rivers, who hoarded the Islamic silver coins with which they were paid for slaves, furs and amber and who thus took the coins out of circulation. Indeed, the gradual cessation of the minting of silver coins in Persia and Anatolia in this period, and their replacement by copper dirhams, provides incontrovertible and, as it were, statistical evidence of this trend, anecdotal evidence of the survival or use of individual silver objects notwithstanding. Base metal had perforce to fill the gap, but its value was greatly enhanced by the practice of inlaying it with copper, silver, gold and a bituminous black substance, the whole giving an effect of polychrome splendour. Thus fine craftsmanship did duty for precious metal. This technique with its plethora of detail explains why such metalwork now bore elaborate figural scenes; even inscriptions took on human and animal form. These inlaid objects survive in large quantities, probably because their metal content (unlike that of silver and gold objects) was not sufficiently valuable to be worth melting down, whereas the intrinsic value of their top-quality craftsmanship was obvious.

In ceramics, the earliest dated underglaze-painted, lustre and *minā*ʾ*ī* wares are respectively placed by their inscriptions to the years 562/1166, 575/1179 and 582/1186, and therefore all postdate the death of the last Great Saldjūḳ ruler, Sandjar, in 552/1157. Conversely, in metalwork there are several pieces dated between 455/1063 and 542/1148—i.e., truly in the Saldjūḳ period. The frequency of dated ceramics (and many are signed) argues a higher status for fine pottery than had previously obtained. A new light body known as stone-paste or fritware was devised; it was made largely from ground quartz, with small quantities of ground glass and fine clay, presumably an attempt by Islamic potters to imitate the body of Chinese porcelain, though the necessary evidence of trade with China is missing. Such pieces were mostly moulded. Others belonged to categories known as silhouette or double-shell wares and in these, as in lakabi and other sgraffiato wares, much of the decoration was incised with a knife or a pointed object. Such incised wares continued a fashion well established before the Saldjūḳ period. Underglaze painting in blue and black was also popular, as was a type of translucent white ware, often pierced for greater effect. Many of the more expensive wares bear hurried cursive inscriptions in Persian love poetry of mostly indifferent quality, and praise the maker of the piece. Scientific analysis of pottery has successfully differentiated between the original ceramic and modern repairs to body and decoration alike, a crucial distinction since virtually no mediaeval pieces have remained intact.

A close connection existed between the most elaborate wares and book painting, including Ḳurʾānic illumination, as shown by figural types, narrative strips and numerous stylistic features, while many details of the shape and decoration of Saldjūḳ ceramics—handles, stepped feet, imitation chains, incising, gilding, fluting—derive from metalwork. Similarly, the ornamental sheen and decorative motifs of Saldjūḳ metalwork reveal close familiarity with manuscript illumination. All this points both to the interdependence of the arts in this period and to the existence of hierarchies within the visual arts.

The recent demonstration (Bloom, Blair and Wardwell, in *Ars Orientalis*, xxii [1992]) that the majority of textiles once thought to be Būyid or Saldjūḳ are in fact of modern manufacture has made it imperative to submit all so-called Saldjūḳ silks to scientific tests, and renders premature any art-historical enquiry into them.

It is not possible to say much about book painting in Saldjūḳ times, for the principal centre of production in this period was ʿIrāḳ, which was then under the control of the newly renascent caliphate [see TAṢWĪR]. Thus ʿIrāḳī painting, for all its stylistic affinities with Saldjūḳ art, cannot be brought into the present discussion. The most likely condidate to represent the largely vanished art of Saldjūḳ book painting is the verse romance *Warḳa wa Gulshāh*, written in Persian by the poet ʿAyyūḳī and signed by the painter ʿAbd al-Muʾmin al-Khūyī. This suggests a provenance in north-west Persia, but Anatolia is a distinct possibility too. The manuscript (in the Topkapı Sarayı library in Istanbul) has 70 brightly coloured illustrations in strip format against a plain coloured or patterned ground, with figural types of the kind familiar in *mināʾī* pottery, but with an unexpected additional feature: obtrusive animals which have been shown by Daneshvari to have iconographic significance, for example as symbolic and prophetic references to the action. A fragment of al-Ṣūfī's treatise *Fixed stars* in the Bodleian Library, Oxford (ms. Or. 133), undated and unprovenanced but probably of the 13th century, might be of Persian origin. But for all the paucity of the surviving material, the clear dependence of both fine ceramics and fine metalwork on manuscript painting and illumination shows clearly enough the high profile which the arts of the book enjoyed in the Saldjūḳ period. And book painting in Mesopotamia after the fall of the Saldjūḳ dynasty often has marked Persian features, a factor which suggests the existence of an earlier pan-Saldjūḳ school of painting in which distinctions between ʿIrāḳ and Persia were perhaps not very significant.

Several fine Saldjūḳ Ḳurʾāns have survived [see KHAṬṬ]. They include dated examples in Mashhad (466/1073), Tehran (485/1092 and 606-8/1209-11), Philadelphia (559/1164; produced in Hamadān) and London (582/1186), as well as examples which slightly pre-date the advent of the Saldjūḳs (London, 427/1036 and Dublin, 428/1037). There are also numerous undated but probably Saldjūḳ examples in Dublin, Paris, Istanbul, Tehran and London, to say nothing of parts of Ḳurʾāns or individual leaves in dozens of collections throughout the world. Saldjūḳ Ḳurʾāns are notable for their magnificent full-page or double-page frontispieces and colophon pages, often of pronounced geometric character, with script in panels taking a prime role. They are known both in *naskhī* and in "New Style", otherwise known as "East Persian", Kūfic. There is a substantial variation in scale—from small one-volume Ḳurʾāns measuring 12 by 10 cm to large ones of 41 by 28 cm and there are some in 30 or 60 parts, large and small, each part with its own frontispiece. The discrepancy in size and layout extends to the number of lines per page, which varies from 2 to 20, and to the scale, quantity and placing of illumination. The task of establishing dates and provenances for this ample material, and devising working categories for it, has only just begun.

In architecture even more than in other fields the dividing line, so far as style is concerned, between what is definably Saldjūḳ and what precedes that period is very hard to draw, though the Mongol invasion and the architectural vacuum that followed it means that there is a distinct break in continuity after *ca.* 1220. A few examples will make this clear. The characteristic minarets of Saldjūḳ type—lofty, cylindrical, set on a polygonal plinth and garnished with inscription bands and geometric brick patterning—are known from at least as early as the 1020s (Dāmghān, Simnān). Of the two standard types of Saldjūḳ mausoleum, the tomb tower perhaps reached its apogee in the Gunbad-i Ḳābūs, dated 397/1006-7 [*q.v.*], while the other type, the domed square, is already brought to a pitch of perfection in the so-called "Tomb of the Sāmānids" in Bukhārā, datable before 943. That building also exhibits a highly developed style of brick and terracotta ornament. Similarly, such standard features of Saldjūḳ architecture as the trilobed squinch and the *pīshṭāḳ* [*q.v.*] are already to be encountered in the 10th century (mausoleum of Arab-Ata, Tim). The same phenomenon can be detected in other art forms, for example in sgraffiato pottery or the continuity of ring and dot decoration from pre-Saldjūḳ to Saldjūḳ metalwork; and while the quantity and range of architectural tilework is indisputably a "Saldjūḳ" phenomenon, its roots in Islamic monuments lie as far back as Sāmarrā.

The distinctive Saldjūḳ contribution lies rather in the final establishment of several of the classical forms of Persia architecture and in the capacity of Saldjūḳ artists to draw out the utmost variety from these types. Mosques with one, two, three or four *īwāns* are known, and the 4-*īwān* plan receives its classic formulation in association with an open courtyard and a monumental domed chamber; a hierarchy of size distinguished major *īwāns* from minor ones [see MASDJID I.H]. The Friday Mosques of Zawāra, Ardistān and above all Iṣfahān, are outstanding examples of this trend. Saldjūḳ domed chambers are characterised by external simplicity, with a frank emphasis on the exterior zone of transition, now reduced to powerful contrasting geometric planes, while the interior is dominated by a highly elaborate transition zone (in the Iṣfahān area this made a leitmotif of the trilobed arch) whose depth, energy and rhythmical movement has as its foil the austere, low-relief articulation vouchsafed to the lower walls and to the inner dome itself. But other Saldjūḳ mosque types, such as the free-standing domed chamber or the arcaded hall, are also known.

In mausolea [see TURBĀ], the *pīshtāḳ* was developed from a simple salient porch to a great screen which conferred a grandiose façade on the building behind it (Ṭūs, Sarakhs). The originally simple formula of the domed square underwent other major changes too, notably in the development of a gallery zone (Sangbast), engaged corner columns (Takistān, Hamadān), and double dome (mausoleum of Sultan Sandjar, Marw). Lofty tomb towers proliferated across northern Persia, many of them built as secular memorials for *amīrs* and others of high rank, though some have *miḥrābs* and therefore served at least in part a religious purpose. Their form varied: some were square, cylindrical or flanged but most had 7, 8, 10 or 12 sides, with inner domes crowned by conical or polyhedral roofs. Their form was well suited to the development of brick ornament, for it ensured a constant change of plane and therefore much variety in the play of shadow. Here, too, some of the earliest uses of glazed tilework are to be found.

The impressive sequence of some 40 Saldjūḳ minarets [see MANĀRA. 1] comprises all manner of structural variations, including single or double staircases with or without a central column, flaring corbelled balconies, three-tier elevations, shafts articulated by flanges and engaged columns, and—an innovation destined to have a long history in Persian architecture—the double minaret flanking a portal, whether this was the entrance to a building or the *ḳibla īwān*. Thus the minaret came to have a symbolic rather than a strictly liturgical role. They also occur as free-standing monuments unrelated to other buildings, and in such cases seem to have functioned as land-locked lighthouses.

No Saldjūḳ palaces survive in good condition, though excavations have revealed the ground plan of the 4-*īwān* palace at Marw and the palatial kiosk of Ḳalʿa-yi Dukhtar in Ādharbaydjān still stands despite its ruined state. But the palaces of Tirmidh, Ghazna and Lashkar-i Bāzār, all yielding abundant decoration, belong to much the same cultural sphere even though they are linked to Sāmānid and Ghaznawid rulers respectively. The same situation applies in the case of the *madrasa*, a particularly serious deficiency given the unambiguous testimony of the literary sources that such buildings were erected throughout the Saldjūḳ empire [see MADRASA. III]. Controversial remains at Khargird, Ṭabas, Rayy, Samarḳand and near Sayot in Tadjkistan (Khʷadja Mashhad) permit no clear statement as to the form of the *madrasa* in Saldjūḳ times. The luxuriously embellished and largely ruined Shāh-i Mashhad of 571/1175-6 in Gharčistān, identified by its inscription as a *madrasa*, is a Ghūrid foundation, while the building at Zūzan, dated 615/1218-19 and also identified epigraphically as a *madrasa*, was erected by a governor of the Khʷārazm Shāhs. Taken together, their awesome scale and magnificence suggest that the *madrasas* of the Persian world in this period far outshone those from other Islamic territories.

Several caravansarais datable to the Saldjūḳ period are known; four of them—Ribāṭ-i Malik, Dāya Khātūn, Ribāṭ-i Māhī and Ribāṭ-i Sharaf—bear lavish decoration. Indeed, Ribāt-i Sharaf [*q.v.*; probably 508/1114-5, repaired 549/1154-5], with its huge double courtyard plan (repeated at Aḳče Ḳalʿa in Turkmenistan) is a museum of contemporary decorative techniques. This splendour, when linked to its location astride the main road from Marw to Nīshāpūr, makes it plausible that this building served as a royal stopover. Most Saldjūḳ caravansarais, however, are built for use rather than display, with rubble masonry, strong fortifications and minimal comfort. In many of these buildings the prescriptive power of the 4-*īwān* plan made itself felt.

Bibliography: (a) General. A.U. Pope and P. Ackerman (eds.), *Survey of Persian art* (contains chapters on most aspects of Saldjūḳ art, by a variety of authors); O. Grabar, *The visual arts, 1050-1350*, in J.A. Boyle (ed.), *Camb. hist. of Iran*, v, Cambridge 1968, 626-48; W. Watson (ed.), *The art of Iran and Anatolia from the 11th to the 13th century A.D. A colloquy held 25-28 June 1973. Colloquies on art & archaeology in Asia, No. 4*, London 1974 (see especially contributions by Allan, Baer, Fehérvári, Hillenbrand, Melikian-Chirvani, Schnyder and Siroux); L.I. Rempel' (ed.), *Khudozhestvennaya kul'tura Srednei Azii. IX-XIII veka*, Tashkent 1983; R. Ettinghausen and O. Grabar, *The art and architecture of Islam 650-1250*, Harmondsworth 1987; R. Hillenbrand (ed.), *The art of the Saljūqs in Iran and Anatolia. Proceedings of a symposium held in Edinburgh in 1982*, Costa Mesa 1994 (see esp. contributions by Allan, Blair, Esin, Finster, Hillenbrand, Melikian-Chirvani, O'Kane, Raby, Schmitz and Watson).

(b) Architecture. E. Diez, *Churasanische Baudenkmäler*, Berlin 1918; idem, *Persien. Islamische Baukunst in Churâsân*, Hagen i. W., Darmstadt and Gotha 1923; E. Cohn-Wiener, *Turan. Islamische Baukunst in Mittelasien*, Berlin 1930; A. Gabriel, *Le Masdjid-i Djumʿa d'Iṣfahān*, in *Ars Islamica*, ii (1935), 7-44; M.B. Smith, *Material for a corpus of early Iranian Islamic architecture*. I, in *Ars Islamica*, ii (1935), 153-71; II, in *ibid.*, iv (1937), 1-40; III, in *ibid.*, vi (1939), 1-10; idem, *The Manārs of Iṣfahān*, in *Āthār-é Īrān*, i (1936), 313-58; A. Godard, numerous articles in *ibid.*, i (1936), ii (1937), and iv (1939); J. Sauvaget, *Observations sur quelques mosquées seldjoukides*, in *AIEO Alger*, iv (1938), 81-120; B.P. Denike, *Arkhitekturni ornament Srednei Azii*, Moscow and Leningrad 1939; D.N. Wilber, *The development of mosaic faïence in Islamic architecture in Iran*, in *Ars Islamica*, vi (1939), 16-47; S.A. Dadashev, *Arkhitektura Azerbaidzhana, epokha Nizami*, Baku 1947; J. Sourdel-Thomine, *Deux minarets d'époque seljoukide en Afghanistan*, in *Syria*, xxx (1953), 108-36; A.M. Pribytkova, *Pamyatniki arkhitekturi XI veka v Turkmenii*, Moscow 1955; V.A. Nil'sen, *Monumentalnaya Bukharskogo oazisa*, Tashkent 1956; Godard, *Les anciennes mosquées de l'Iran*, in *Arts Asiatiques*, iii (1956), 48-63, 83-8; G.A. Pugačenkova, *Vydaiushčiesia pamyatniki arkhitekturi Uzbekistana*, Tashkent 1958; eadem, *Puti razvitiya arkhitekturi iuzhnogo Turkmenistana pori rabovladeniya i feodalizma*, in *Trudi Yuzhno Turkmenistanskoi Arkheologicheskoi Ekspeditsii*, vi, Moscow 1958; A. Maricq and G. Wiet, *Le Minaret de Djam* (Mémoires DAFA, 16), Paris 1959; L.S. Bretanitski, *Zodčestvo Azerbaidzhana XII-XV vv. i ego mesto v arkhitekture Perednego Vostoka*, Leningrad 1961; Pope, *Persian architecture*, London and New York 1965; D.B. Stronach and T. Cuyler Young, Jr., *Three octagonal Seljuq tomb towers from Iran*, in *Iran*, iv (1966), 1-20; Grabar, The earliest Islamic commemorative structures, notes and documents, in *Ars Orientalis*, vi (1966), 7-46; D. Hill and Grabar, *Islamic architecture and its decoration. A.D. 800-1500*, 2nd ed. London 1967; S.P. Scherr-Thoss, *Design and color in Islamic architecture. Turkey*,

Iran. Afghanistan, Washington, D.C. 1968; W. Kleiss, beginning with *Archaeologische Mitteilungen aus Iran*, N.F., ii (1969), over two dozen articles in that journal bearing on Sal̲dj̲ūḳ architecture; M.J. Casimir and B. Glatzer, *Šah-i Mašhad, a recently discovered Madrasah of the Ghurid period in Ğarğistan (Afghanistan)*, in *EW*, N.S., xxi (1971), 53-68; Sourdel-Thomine, *Le mausolée dit de Baba Hatim en Afghanistan*, in *REI*, xxxix (1971), 293-320; C. Adle and A.S. Melikian-Chirvani, *Les monuments du XIème siècle du Dâmqân*, in *St.Ir.*, i (1972), 229-97; Hillenbrand, *Saljūq monuments in Iran*. I, in *Oriental Art*, N.S., xviii (1972), 64-77; II, in *Iran*, x (1972), 45-56; III, in *Kunst des Orients*, x (1975), 45-79; IV, in *Oriental Art*, N.S., xxii (1976), 265-77; V, in *Iran*, xxv (1987), 55-76; E. Galdieri, *Isfahan. Masğid-i Ğumᶜa*, 3 vols., Rome 1972-84; Wilber, *Le Masğid-i Ğāmiᶜ de Qazwīn*, in *REI*, xli (1973), 199-229; A. Karrev, *Pamyatniki ark̲h̲itekturi Turkmenistana*, Leningrad 1974; Sourdel-Thomine, *Inscriptions sel̲dj̲oukides et salles à coupoles de Qazwīn en Iran*, in *REI*, xlii (1974), 3-43; Hillenbrand, *The tomb towers of Iran to 1550*, unpubl. D.-Phil. thesis, University of Oxford 1974; A. M. Hutt, *The development of the minaret in Iran under the Saljūqs*, unpubl. M.Phil. thesis, University of London 1974; Hillenbrand, *Saljūq dome chambers in northwest Iran*, in *Iran*, xiv (1976), 93-102; Hutt and L. Harrow, *Islamic architecture. Iran I*, London 1977; L. Kalus and J. Bergeret, *Analyse de décors épigraphiques et floraux à Qazwīn au début du VIème/XIIème siècle*, in *REI*, xlv/1 (1977), 89-130; D. Schlumberger and Sourdel-Thomine, *Lashkari Bazar. Une résidence royale ghaznévide et ghoride* (Mémoires DAFA, 18), Paris 1978; L. Ainy, *The Central Asian art of Avicenna epoch*, Dushanbe 1980; D. Brandenburg and K. Brusehoff, *Die Seldschuken. Baukunst des Islam in Persien und Turkmenien*, Graz 1980; Pugačenkova, *Pamyatniki iskusstva Sovetskogo soyuza. Srednyaya Aziya. spravočnik-putevoditel'*, Moscow 1983; S.S. Blair, *The octagonal pavilion at Natanz*, in *Muqarnas*, i (1983), 69-94; eadem, *The Madrasa at Zuzan. Islamic architecture in Eastern Iran on the eve of the Mongol invasions*, in *Muqarnas*, iii (1985), 75-91; A. Daneshvari, *Medieval tomb towers of Iran. An iconographical study*, Lexington 1986; M. Kervran, *Les structures funéraires et commémoratives en Iran et en Asie Centrale du 9ème au 12ème siècle*, unpubl. thèse d'Université de Paris-Sorbonne (Paris IV), 1987; Bretanitski, *K̲h̲udoz̲h̲estvennoe nasledie Perednego Vostoka epok̲h̲i feodalizma*, Moscow 1988; H. Laleh, *La structure fondamentale des arcs dans l'architecture sal̲dj̲ūkide de l'Irān*, unpubl. thèse de Doctorat d'Université de Paris-Sorbonne (Paris IV), 1989; Grabar, *The Great Mosque of Isfahan*, London 1990; Blair, *The monumental inscriptions from early Islamic Iran and Transoxiana*, Leiden 1992; Hillenbrand, *Islamic architecture. Form, function and meaning*, Edinburgh 1994.

(c) Other arts. O. von Falke, *Kunstgeschichte der Seidenweberei*, 2 vols., Berlin 1913; J.H. Schmidt, *Persische Seidenstoffe der Seldjukenzeit*, in *Ars Islamica*, ii (1935), 84-91; Ettinghausen, *A signed and dated Seljuq Qurᵓan*, in *Bull. of the American Institute for Persian Art and Archaeology*, iv (1935), 92-102; I. Stchoukine, *La peinture iranienne sous les derniers ᶜAbbasides et les Il-Khans*, Bruges 1936; Ettinghausen, *Evidence for the identification of Kashan pottery*, in *Ars Islamica*, iii (1936), 44-75; M. Bahrami, *Recherches sur les carreaux de revêtement dans la céramique persane du XIIIe au XVe siècle* (Paris 1937); L.T. Giuzal'ian, *Bronzov'ui kuvs̲h̲in 1182g.*, in *Pamyatniki epok̲h̲i Rustaveli*, Leningrad 1938, 227-36; R.B. Serjeant, *Materials for a history of Islamic textiles up to the Mongol conquest*, Beirut 1972; G.D. Guest, *Notes on the miniatures on a thirteenth-century beaker*, in *Ars Islamica*, x (1943), 148-52; M. Aga-Oghlu, *About a type of Islamic incense burner*, in *The Art Bulletin*, xxvii (1945), 28-45; Ettinghausen, *The Bobrinski "Kettle". Patron and style of an Islamic bronze*, in *Gazette des Beaux Arts*, 6e serie, xxiv (1943), 193-208; A. Lane, *Early Islamic pottery*, London 1947; M. Bahrami, *Gurgan faiences*, Cairo 1949; D.S. Rice, *The Wade Cup in the Cleveland Museum of Art*, Paris 1955; Ettinghausen, *The "Wade Cup" in the Cleveland Museum of Art, its origin and decorations*, in *Ars Orientalis*, ii (1957), 327-66; L.A. Mayer, *Islamic metalworkers and their works*, Geneva 1959; Ettinghausen, *Turkish elements on silver objects of the Seljuk period of Iran*, in *Communications of the First International Congress of Turkish Art, Ankara, 1959*, Ankara 1961, 128-33; M.S. Ipşiroğlu, *Saray-Alben. Diez'sche Klebebände aus den Berliner Sammlungen. Beschreibung und stilkritische Anmerkungen*, Wiesbaden 1964; Melikian-Chirvani, *Trois manuscrits de l'Iran seljoukide*, in *Arts Asiatiques*, xvi (1967), 3-51; Grabar, *Les arts mineurs de l'Orient musulman à partir du milieu du XIIe siècle*, in *Cahiers de civilisation médiévale*, xi (1968), 181-90; Giuzal'ian, *The bronze Qalamdan (pencase) 5452/1148 from the Hermitage Collection (1936-1965)*, in *Ars Orientalis*, vii (1968), 95-119; Ettinghausen, *Some comments on medieval Iranian art*, in *Artibus Asiae*, xxxi (1969), 276-300; idem, *The flowering of Seljuq art*, in *Metropolitan Museum Journal*, iii (1970), 113-31; Melikian-Chirvani, *Le roman de Varqè et Golšâh*, in *Arts Asiatiques*, xxii (special number), 1970, 1-262; Ipşiroğlu, *Das Bild im Islam. Ein Verbot und seine Folgen*, Vienna and Munich 1971; J.W. Allan, *Abu 'l-ᶜQāsim's treatise on ceramics*, in *Iran*, xi (1973), 111-20; G. Fehérvári, *Islamic pottery. A comprehensive study based on the Barlow Collection*, London 1973; Melikian-Chirvani, *Le bronze iranien*, Paris 1973; E. Atil, *Ceramics from the world of Islam*, Washington, D.C. 1975; O. Watson, *Persian lustre-painted pottery. The Rayy and Kashan styles*, in *Transactions of the Oriental Ceramic Society*, xl (1973-5), 1-19; Allan, *Incised wares of Iran and Anatolia in the 11th and 12th centuries*, in *Keramos*, lxiv (1974), 15-22; Melikian-Chirvani, *Les bronzes du Khorassân*, in *St.Ir.*, iii (1974), 29-50; II, in iv (1975), 51-71; III, in iv (1975), 187-205; IV, in v (1976), 203-12; V, in vi (1977), 185-210; VI, in viii (1979), 7-32; VII, in viii (1979), 223-43; Allan, *Silver: the key to bronze in early Islamic Iran*, in *Kunst des Orients*, xi (1976), 5-21; Fehérvári, *Islamic metalwork of the eighth to the fifteenth century in the Keir Collection*, London 1976; E.J. Grube, *Islamic pottery of the eighth to the fifteenth century*, London 1976; Allan, *Originally in bronze—a thirteenth century Persian school of metalworkers*, in *Iran*, xv (1977), 156-64; idem, *Persian metal technology 700-1300 A.D.*, Oxford 1979; M.S. Simpson, *Narrative structure of a medieval Iranian beaker*, in *Ars Orientalis*, xii (1981), 15-24; K. Otto-Dorn, *Das seldschukische Thronbild*, in *Persica*, x (1982), 149-203; Melikian-Chirvani, *Islamic metalwork from the Iranian world 8th to 18th centuries*, London 1982; idem, *Essais sur la sociologie de l'art islamique. I. Argenterie et féodalité dans l'Iran médiéval*, in C. Adle (ed.), *Art et société dans le monde Iranien*, Paris 1982, 143-75; E. Baer, *Metalwork in medieval Islamic art*, Albany 1982; Allan, *Islamic metalwork. The Nuhad Es-Sald Collection*, London 1982; Watson, *Persian lustre ware*, London 1985; A. Caiger-Smith, *Lustre pottery. Technique, tradition and innovation in Islam and the Western world*, London 1985; Melikian-Chirvani, *Silver in Islamic Iran: the evidence from literature and epigraphy*, in M. Vickers (ed.), *Pots and pans. A colloquium on precious metals and ceramics in the Muslim, Chinese and Graeco-Roman worlds* (Oxford Studies in Islamic Art, III), Oxford 1985, 89-106; Watson, *Pottery and metal shapes in Persia in the 12th and 13th centuries*, in *ibid.*, 205-12; Atil et alii, *Islamic metalwork in the Freer Gallery of Art*, Washington, D.C. 1985; Daneshvari, *Animal symbolism in Warqa wa Gulshah*, Oxford 1986; Baer, *Wider aspects of some Ghaznavid bronzes*, in *RSO*, lix (1987), 1-15; J.M. Rogers, *Ceramics*, in R.W. Ferrier (ed.), *The arts of Persia*, New Haven and London 1989, 255-62, 327-8 (esp. useful for material drawn from Russian publications); U. al-Khamis, *The origin of Iranian beak-spouted metal ewers. New considerations*, in *Persica*, xiv (1990-2), 37-65; S.S. Blair, J.M. Bloom and A.E. Wardwell, *Reevaluating the date of the "Buyid" silks by epigraphic and radiocarbon analysis*, in *Ars Orientalis*, xxii (1992), 1-41; D. James, *The master scribes. Qurʾans of the 10th to 14th centuries A.D.*, Oxford 1992; R. Ward, *Islamic metalwork*, London 1993; Grube, *Cobalt and lustre. The first centuries of Islamic pottery*, Oxford 1994; al-Khamis, *Early Islamic bronze and brass ewers from the 7th century to the mid-13th century A.D.*, unpubl. Ph.D. thesis, University of Edinburgh 1994.

(R. HILLENBRAND)

2. In Anatolia

N.B. Buildings and objects with dated inscriptions are indicated thus: *. TIEM = Türk ve Islam Eserleri Müzesi (Museum of Turkish and Islamic Art), Istanbul.

(a) *Architecture and its decoration*.

A general survey of the art and architecture of Anatolia in the Saldjūḳ period necessarily involves both the Sultanate of Konya (*ca.* 1118-1308) and its provincial capitals and the Turcoman amīrates which were subdued and more or less incorporated into it during the reigns of Kaykāwūs I and Kayḳubād I [*q.vv.*], among them the Dānishmendids, the Saltūḳids, the Mengüdjükids, and the Ayyūbid-Artuḳid confederation which Kayḳubād I defeated at the battle of Yassî Čimen (1230). These all had, however, their own traditions which were often locally persistent. This complicates a purely linear treatment of their art and architecture.

Building typology. The architecture of Saldjūḳ Anatolia is typologically very rich. Extant or recorded buildings include not only mosques, *madrasa*s and *khānḳāh*s but also hospitals (notably at Kayseri 602*/1205-6, Sivas 614*/1217-8 and Divriği 626*/1228-9) and tomb-towers and other mausolea (*türbe, kümbed*); and secular buildings—palaces, fortifications, dockyards, caravansarays, bridges, baths and even thermal establishments (*kaplîdja*), as at Ilgın, from which an inscription of 666/1267-8 in the name of the vizier Faḵhr al-Dīn ʿAlī (Ṣāḥib Ata) was recorded.

Mosques and complexes. A persistent plan for Great Mosques, possibly inherited from the Dānishmendids, is basilical, as at Sivas and Kayseri (both later 12th century), sometimes with a flat roof on wooden columns (cf. Otto-Dorn, 1959). The minarets of this early date are brick and tend to be exaggeratedly tall. Later 13th century minarets, such as the Burmalı Minare at Amasya (c. 640/1242-3) and the Ince Minare at Konya (?663/1264-5; Meinecke, 1976, ii, no. 78) in its original two-tiered form, also tend to height, though they are mostly in stone.

The evidence for complexes (*külliye*s [*q.v.*]), foundations including buildings of diverse functions, which in Ayyūbid Syria and Egypt had become standard by the early 13th century, is less good in Anatolia, largely because, with exceptions like the Great Mosque and Hospital at Divriği and the foundation of Huant (Khʷānd) Hatun at Kayseri (Shawwāl 635*/May-June 1238; cf. Akok, 1968), mosques, *madrasa*s and baths may have been adjacent but were not integrated structures, so that substantial parts could well have disappeared without damage to the rest. Funerary foundations, with the pyramidal or conical roof of a mausoleum clearly visible from the exterior, also appear to have been less common than in Ayyūbid Syria: among the exceptions are the Citadel Mosque at Konya (616-17/1219-21) replacing a mosque of Masʿūd I (d. 550/1155), which contains two mausolea with the tombs of the Sultans of Rūm (Kaykāwūs I is buried, however, in the hospital he founded at Sivas [614*/1217-8]); the hospital at Divriği (626*/1228-9) and the complex of Huant (Khʷānd) Hatun at Kayseri (Shawwāl 635*/May-June 1238). The mosque of the vizier Faḵhr al-Dīn ʿAlī (656*/1258; cf. Meinecke, 1976, ii, no. 79) was augmented by a *khānḳāh* (668*/1269-70; cf. Meinecke, 1976, ii, nos. 79 and 89) which on his death was partially transformed into a family mausoleum. Many other monuments contain provision for a mausoleum, even if they have no burials, but they are unmarked architecturally and may well have been afterthoughts.

Mausolea. The vast majority of mausolea are isolated tomb-towers. Despite marked local variation in decoration, their construction is basically standard, a pyramidal or conical drum with a pyramidal or conical roof on a raised square podium which houses the crypt. The interior often contains a *miḥrāb*, not necessarily because prayers were to be said there but to orient the burial. These *türbe*s or *kümbed*s derive from the brick tomb-towers of later-12th century Djibāl, as at Naḵhčiwān [*q.v.*] and Marāgha [*q.v.*], though they are virtually all of cut stone without any tilework. Many are anonymous but those which bear inscriptions are generally of *amīr*s or high-born ladies. In the cemeteries of Ahlat (Gabriel and Sauvaget, 1940; Karamağaralı, 1972) they occur alongside conventional inhumations with a cenotaph and head- and foot-stones. Another monumental tomb-type is the so-called Gömeç Hatun Türbe at Konya (late 13th century; cf. Meinecke, ii, no. 86), an open *īwān* built over a crypt and with traces of tile decoration on the façade. Such tombs remain quite common in the Kayseri area.

Fortifications. The building or restoration of fortifications by the Saldjūḳ sultans of Konya closely follows the unification of their territories, particularly in the reigns of Kaykāwūs I and Kayḳubād I as they subjugated the smaller Turcoman amirates and expanded into Byzantine territory. These include the walls of the city and Citadel of Konya (600*/1203-4 610*/1213-4 and 618/1221-2); Sinop (Rabīʿ I 612*/July 1215), Antalya (Djumādā I 617*/July 1220, 622*/1225-6, 626*/1228-9 and 642*/1244-5 and the Citadel of Kayseri (621*/1224-5). The walls and Citadel of Sivas were probably restored early in the reign of Kayḳubād I, and after his capture of Erzurum in 1230 its walls also were restored. The latest of his Turcoman rivals to build or restore their walls were the Mengüdjükids at Divriği (inscriptions of 634*/1236-7, 640*/1242-3, 650*/1252-3 and 652* 1254-5), long after they had accepted Saldjū suzerainty, and indeed when they had passed under Mongol overlordship. The most imposing structures were at Konya (Bombaci, 1969), but Sarre (1936; and cf. Laborde, 1836) pointed out that they were th walls not of the city but of Kayḳubād I's palace citadel, hence for show rather than defence. The mos

a. Divriği. Ulu Cami, north porch (all photographs courtesy Fondation Max van Berchem, Geneva).

b. Kayseri. Döner Kümbed.

a. Konya. Double-headed eagle from walls.

b. Erzurum. Çifte Minare Medrese, façade.

a. Van. Great Mosque, interior.

b. Konya. İnce Minare Medrese porch.

a. Sivas. Gök Medrese, porch.

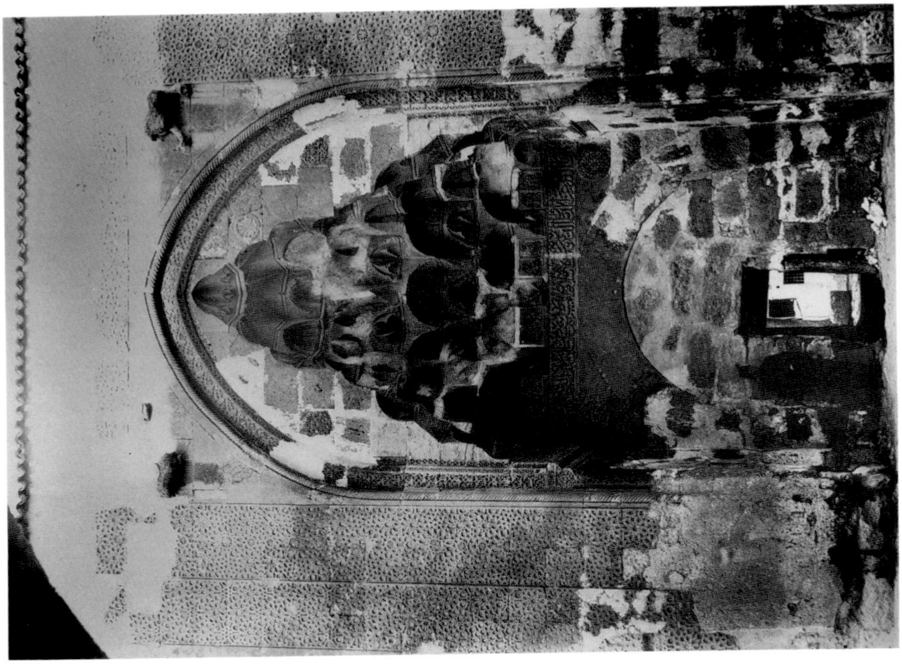

b. Sivas. Hospital of Kay Kāwūs I, porch.

a. Sivas. Çifte Minare Medrese, porch.

b. Konya. Köşk of Ḳilidj Arslan II.

Konya. Sahib Ata Mosque.

important fortifications are therefore those of Alanya/ʿAlāʾiyya [q.v.] (623-9*/1226-31; cf. Rice and Seton Lloyd, 1958) with a 5-bay naval dockyard (*tersāne*), unique among extant Islamic naval installations. This is attached by a curtain wall to the principal tower, the Kızıl Kule, which bears the signature of an engineer Abu 'l-ʿĀlī b. Abi 'l-Radjāʾ b. al-Kattānī al-Ḥalabī, whose name also appears on the walls of Sinop, refortified in 1215*.

Palaces. Of the pavilion (*köşk*) on the Citadel at Konya, a brick construction with mud-brick core, nothing survives, but a photograph of 1895 shows its upper floor corbelled out over a projecting rectangular tower of a line of inner walls and with an open arch showing the remains of a tile revetment on the exterior. This bore an inscription in the name of Ḳilidj Arslan, in Sarre's view (1936) of the fourth ruler of that name (655-63/1257-65 [q.v.]). Tile remains from the inner rooms include *mīnāʾī* tiles with human figures. Excavations are still continuing at the palace of Ḳubādābād [q.v.] on Lake Beyşehir and have so far revealed a complex plan, with a central four-*īwān* cour d'honneur, a mosque (633*/1235-6), baths, a quay and a small dockyard (*tersāne*), and a game reserve.

Khāns. One of the most striking features of Anatolian Saldjūḳ architecture is the chains of caravansarays roughly 25 km/16 miles, one day's march, apart [see KHĀN], linking the principal cities of the Sultanate of Rum, in particular Antalya, Eğridir and Konya; Konya and Afyon Karahisar; Konya and Denizli; Konya, Āḳ Sarāy and Kayseri; Kayseri and Sivas; Kayseri and Malatya; and Malatya, Sivas, Amasya and Sinop. No urban *khāns* of the Saldjūḳ period are preserved.

Though the earliest caravansarays date to the late 12th century, the capture of Antalya (1207) and the annexation of Sinop (1215) by Kaykāwūs I were essential preliminaries to developing them as chains. Their principal function was evidently to service the north-south overland trade of strategic exports such as timber and Ḳipčāḳ slaves from the Crimea to Antalya, whence they made their way by sea to the Ayyūbid states of Syria and Egypt, and to levy transit taxes on international trade. The peak period of foundations, 1230-45, follows hard upon the completion of the fortifications of Antalya. The Sultan Han near Āḳ Sarāy (Radjab 626*/June 1229) and the contemporary Sultan Han near Kayseri may well have been purposely built as halts for Kayḳubād I on his progresses from city to city, but these, like the smaller *khāns*, were also convenient for pilgrims on the *ḥadjdj* or for inter-urban trade, and in time of war could be used for garrisons or as refuges. Inexplicably, the east-west trade was much less favoured: despite the increasingly difficult terrain, the density of distribution east of Sivas very markedly decreases. This may explain why the Mkhargrdzeli governors of Ānī (Rogers, 1976) built their own chain of caravansarays to tap the trade along the Araxes.

The founders of these Anatolian caravansarays included the sultans and their ladies, viziers and *amīrs*. Their often well-preserved state suggests, moreover, that the specimen *wakfiyyas* of Saldjūḳ caravansarays published by Turan (1947-8) are typical and that most of them had *wakf* endowments. However, the Hekim Han near Malatya (615*/1218; Erdmann, 1961, i, no. 18) founded by an archdeacon and doctor, which bears inscriptions in Arabic, Syriac and Armenian, showing it to have been a family investment, is evidence that not all Saldjūḳ caravansarays need have been pious foundations.

With very few exceptions, for example the Evdir Han near Antalya (datable 1213-19; Erdmann, 1961, i, no. 55) which is built round an open courtyard, the nucleus of these caravansarays was a covered hall. This was the most appropriate to the Anatolian winter climate, though fireplaces and chimneys are generally absent. To the hall, as and when means permitted, a courtyard would be added, often much larger because it was cheaper to build and because the peak season of trade was the summer when shelter was less important. With the courtyard came elaborations. Sixteen out of the surviving courtyard and hall caravansarays include *masdjids* and some of them, like the Sultan Han near Kayseri, have a bath too. In the two Sultan Hans, *masdjids* take the form of richly decorated kiosks raised on a four-bay substructure. The Karatay Han (courtyard 638*/1240-1; Erdmann, 1961, i, no. 32) also includes a spring housed in a *türbe*-like building.

Many of these *khāns* are undecorated but practically all of them, though not built as fortresses, are fortress-like in their appearance, with stout buttresses and corner-towers. Many, however, have grand entrances, both to the courtyard and to the hall; although sometimes the hall porch is the richer, the decoration of the courtyard entrances is directly related to the elaborateness of the plan and the lavishness of the appurtenances. After the Sultan Hans, the richest decoration is that of the Karatay Han, the two porches of which (Erdmann, 1976, ii-ii, Plates 99-113) make use of ornamental bosses, elaborate *muḳarnas* [q.v.] systems and angular interlacing strapwork, with animal friezes on the courtyard side of the main entrance and high-relief waterspouts in the form of lions.

It is unclear how the considerable labour force employed at the peak building period of caravansarays (1230-45) was organised. The plans chosen must largely have depended on the terrain, so that variation is not necessarily significant; but the marked dissimilarities in buttresses and corner towers and the apparently random approach to the vaulting of halls and their lighting argue for an absence of centralised direction. The typology of decoration, which has little to do with, for example, tilework, is also difficult to reconstruct, not least because of the large proportion of undated buildings and because, as the work of Muḥammad b. Khawlān al-Dimashḳī on the Sultan Han near Āḳ Sarāy shows, a skilled decorator could vary his repertory to suit his employer. Neighbouring caravansarays tend to have somewhat similar decoration, which argues for the employment of local or provincial gangs of masons. Entrance-profiles were, however, probably largely standardised and analysis of these may well produce significant results.

Bridges. There has been no comprehensive survey of the bridges of Saldjūḳ Anatolia, but Taeschner (i, 182 ff., 236 ff.) observes that for the most part they lie on the major Roman roads and that, for example, most of the Saldjūḳ bridges in the neighbourhood of Sivas either incorporate or replace Roman structures (cf. Gabriel, 1934, 165-7). In the Saldjūḳ period, refortification and the construction of chains of caravansarays made bridge-building particularly important, not least because bridges offered another convenient way of levying transit taxes. Thus many, like the bridge over the Kızıl Irmak near Kayseri on the Kırşehir road (599*/1202-3) built by Rukn al-Din Sulaymān b. Ḳilidj Arslān II, are royal foundations.

Structure. With the striking exception of the Great Mosque and Hospital at Divriği (Tükel-Yavuz, 1978), the vaulting systems of which include types of domical vault, as well as groined and elaborately ribbed vaults closely paralleled in the chapter-houses, libraries and refectories of 12th-13th century Greater Armenian monasteries, as at Hagartsin (1248) and Sag͟hmossavank (1255) (cf. K͟hal'pak͟hčian 1953, 1971), most Anatolian Sald͟jūḳ architecture is structurally simple. Plans, moreover, are often stereotyped and much use is made of open courtyards with one, two or four *īwāns*: despite the harsh winter climate, only mosques are regularly covered.

Building materials. Brick occupies a minor place in the architecture of Sald͟jūḳ Anatolia (Bakırer, i-ii, 1981) and is most characteristic of immigrant or refugee craftsmen from D͟jibāl or Persia, for example, the work of Aḥmad b. Abī Bakr al-Marandī on the mausoleum of Kaykāwūs I in his Hospital at Sivas (4 S͟hawwāl 617*/2 December 1220). Though brick continues to be employed for domes, for example the Ince Minare and Büyük Karatay *madrasas* at Konya (latter 649*/1251-2), it generally gives way to stone and the only monument substantially of brick is the Great Mosque (Arık, 1969; Meinecke, 1976, ii, no. 96) at Malatya [*q.v.*]. The principal building material employed is volcanic tuff, carefully squared, with a rubble core. This was also widely used in 12th-13th century Greater Armenia, but though a few decorative features and, for example, the domed crossings of some of the larger caravansarays recall Armenian prototypes, the names of clearly Armenian craftsmen rarely occur and there are few or no obviously Armenian masons' marks. On the contrary, it is the influence of Western Georgia (Tao-Klargeti) which is apparent in the 13th century architecture of Erzurum; and where "Sald͟jūḳ" parallels with Armenian monuments are closest these are mostly of the late 13th or early 14th century (like the monastic church and its porch at Amag͟hu-Noravank) when, doubtless, Anatolian craftsmen, faced with the steady contraction of the building industry, were seeking employment elsewhere.

Despite the Anatolian builders' mastery of cut-stone masonry it is evident from Kayḳubād I's first restoration of the Citadel mosque at Konya (completed 617*/1220-1) that the sultans' taste ran to bichrome marble or marble veneer. This raised two problems: lack of available marble, which made the re-use of antique material or spolia inevitable; and a lack of craftsman able to work it. These had to be brought from Syria. The marble decoration of the Citadel mosque, notably a conspicuous angular knot in the spandrels of arches, is essentially that of contemporary Ayyūbid Aleppo, though the craftsman responsible, Muḥammad b. K͟hawlān (who also very probably executed the entrance porch of the Büyük Karatay *madrasa* at the same time), signs himself as al-Dimas͟hḳī, not al-Ḥalabī. Reminiscences of the Aleppo knot appear on later stone buildings at Konya, notably the Ince Minare *madrasa* (?663/1264-5; Meinecke, 1976, ii, no. 78), but Muḥammad b. K͟hawlān's earlier work cannot have been entirely to the sultans' taste, for when his signature recurs, on the Sultan Han near Āḳ Sarāy (Rad͟jab 626*/June 1229), the decoration and profiling are much closer to standard central Anatolian façade compositions. This rapid assimilation shows itself also on the grandest marble façade of all, the porch of the Gök Medrese, Sivas (670*/1271-2), signed by Kālūyān al-Ḳūnawī (the *nisba* doubtless referring to his specialisation in marble-work). Sarre (1936) and Bombaci (1969) also attribute the collection of marbles outside the Citadel gates of Konya (Laborde, 1836) to Kayḳubād I's own personal taste.

In addition to the marble re-used and re-carved in the above monuments, marble fragments were often incorporated unchanged. This is strikingly the case with the walls of the Zazadin Han (courtyard 634*/1236-7), which include a mass of fragments from Byzantine churches, including crosses. However, they could also be treated as part of the decoration, as on the façade of the mosque of Fak͟hr al-Dīn ʿAlī (Ṣāḥib Ata) at Konya, where to each side of the entrance a classical sarcophagus supports an ornamentally framed fountain and serves as a base for the whole composition.

Decoration. The different traditions of stone-carving, woodwork, stucco and tile-mosaic in Anatolian Sald͟jūḳ architecture (Öney, 1978) place its decoration among the richest in Islam. The contrast between this lavish decoration and the relatively simple structural forms implies, moreover, that craftsmen's inscriptions on buildings refer not to their architects but to their decorators, either masons or tile-mosaic specialists.

The decorative repertoire, which, strikingly, makes little use of monumental inscriptions, combines, in varying degrees, elements from the traditions of the Caucasus, Transcaucasia (Armenia and D͟jibāl), North Syria and the D͟jazīra: common elements include elaborately profiled entrance porches, and surface ornament of interlaces and foliate arabesques (in Ottoman Turkish appropriately termed *rūmī*) punctuated by carved friezes or high-relief sculpture which very often are figural (Otto-Dorn, 1978-9), including both the traditional Muslim court repertory and animals and monsters—dragons, sphinxes, harpies, gryphons and two-headed eagles, many of them shown as if they were heraldic, as on tiles and woodwork too. The only comparable repertory on carved stone is to be found in 12th-century material from G͟hazna [*q.v.*], though its treatment is stylistically unrelated.

In south-west and central Anatolia, at Konya, Kayseri, Niğde and Antalya and the caravansarays between them, these diverse traditions are homogeneously amalgamated, but further east one or other of them tends to be locally dominant. The tombstones of Ahlat and, for example, the dragon-compositions on the façade of the Çifte Minare *madrasa* at Erzurum, are barely islamicised versions of Armenian *k͟hačkars* (commemorative cross-stones). The façade of the Çifte Minare *madrasa* at Sivas (670*/1270-1; Rogers, 1974) and the west porch of the Great Mosque at Divriği (626*/1228-9 or later) are both indebted to the canon-tables of Greater or Cilician Armenian Gospel books. The north porch of the latter is heavily influenced *inter alia* by stucco *miḥrābs* recorded from D͟jibāl and the D͟jazīra: the building bears two signatures of an Ak͟hlāṭī craftsman, K͟hurrams͟hāh (or K͟hurs͟hāh) b. Mug͟hīt͟h, though neither its vaults nor its interior or its exterior decoration are at all reminiscent of Ahlat work (Karamağaralı, 1972; Rogers, 1988).

The influence of the Divriği mosque and hospital is also apparent, considerably moderated, on both the Çifte Minare *madrasa* and the Gök Medrese at Sivas (both 670*/1271-2). Its extravagance has evoked comparisons with the mid-13th century monuments of Konya signed by a craftsman K. l. w. k. b. ʿAbd Allāh (of obscure origins), whose name appears on the mosque of the vizier Fak͟hr al-Dīn ʿAlī (656*/1258), on the Ince Minare *madrasa* (?663/1264-5; Meinecke, 1976, ii, no. 78) and on a no longer extant mausoleum, the Nalıncı Baba Türbe (*ibid.*, no. 76): the latter two may also have been endowed by the vizier. However, their relation to the Divriği complex is not apparent and the very marked differences between the three Konya monuments testify rather to an inherent freakishly eclectic or "Baroque" tendency in Anatolian Saldjūḳ architectural decoration.

Possibly the most remarkable feature of Saldjūḳ monumental façades is the reproduction of entrance porches. A regrettably unpublished photogrammetric survey of the façades of the Çifte Minare *madrasa* at Erzurum (post-1230; Rogers, *Kunst des Orients*, 1974) and the Gök Medrese at Sivas (670*/1271-2) by Alpay Özdural of Middle East Technical University, Ankara, has demonstrated that the latter was copied to scale. Other copies (Ögel, 1966), smaller in size, include the Eşrefoğlu Camii at Beyşehir (699*/1299-1300) and the Hatuniye Medrese at Karaman (783*/1381-2) [see LĀRANDA. 2. Monuments]. The reasons for the popularity of this façade remain unknown and, apart from the Gök Medrese at Sivas which records, probably, the marble-worker involved, none bears a craftsman's name. Their repeated duplication points, anyway, to the employment of techniques described by Byzantine writers on architecture (Downey, 1948) but ill-attested elsewhere in mediaeval Islam.

Patronage. Although in the light of the foundation inscriptions extant, the overwhelming majority of Saldjūḳ buildings appears to have been the work of individual *amīrs* (Rogers, 1976), the sultans may well have been indirectly involved in giving grants of land (*tamlīk*) to found the *waḳf*s. Among individuals who were notably assiduous builders, the primacy is held by the vizier Fakhr al-Dīn ʿAlī (Ṣāḥib Ata), whose attested foundations include a *khān* at Ishaklı (647*/1249-50); the Taş Medrese and a *masdjid* at Āḳ Şehir (648*/1250-1), with a *khānḳāh* there (659*/1260-1); a mosque at Konya (656*/1258); the Sahabiye Medrese and a *sabīl* at Kayseri (665*-666*/1266-7 and 1267) (Akok, 1967); a thermal establishment and a *khān* at Ilgın (666/1267); the Gök Medrese at Sivas (670*/1271-2); a *khānḳāh* at Konya attached to his mosque there (668*/1269-70) and which was later transformed into a family mausoleum (682*/1283-4); and the Tahir or Zühre *masdjid* at Konya (*ca.* 1280). But another high official, the Pervāne Muʿīn al-Dīn Sulaymān [*q.v.*], was almost equally active in the Pontic provinces (Kaymaz, 1970, 187-8). At Sinop he built the Alaüddin Medrese (664*/1265-6, correcting *RCEA* 4505) and a mosque (667*/1268-9), a mosque at Merzifon (663*/1264-5) and the Durak Han near the confluence of the Gök Irmak and the Kızıl Irmak (664*/1265-6). There is also archival evidence that he founded a hospital at Tokat in 674/1275-6. Not surprisingly, Fakhr al-Dīn ʿAlī and Muʿīn al-Dīn Sulaymān were prominent among the high officials of the Anatolian Saldjūḳ sultans to profit from the decline of the central power and establish hereditary, if short-lived, local dynasties.

Tilework. Polychrome and terracotta tilework is widespread in Saldjūḳ Anatolia, though it only exceptionally occurs on the façades of buildings. The earliest uses of glazed-brick or cut faience mosaic in Saldjūḳ architecture (for example, Divriği, Kale Camii 576*/1180-1; Kayseri, Külük Camii, 607*/1210-11, or substantially later (cf. Meinecke, 1976, ii, no. 52); Sivas, Hospital of Kaykāwūs, 614*/1217-18) predate the Mongol invasion of Persia and show strong influence from Djibāl, both Marāgha and Marand, and from the Ildeñizid architecture of Nakhčiwān [*q.v.*; and see Jacobsthal, 1899]. The colours mostly used are turquoise and manganese-purple or -black, but by the 1240s, both cobalt blue and white occur. As the signature of the *bannā*ʾ Muḥammad b. Muḥammad b. ʿUthmān al-Ṭūsī on the tile-mosaic of the Sırçalı *madrasa* at Konya (640*/1242-3; Meinecke, 1976, i, 35-45; ii, no. 71) strongly suggests, innovation owed much to refugee craftsmen from Khurāsān or even Ghūrid Harāt. Al-Ṭūsī's workshop at Konya seems to have executed tile revetments from the Citadel Mosque, *ca.* 1235, up to the Büyük Karatay Medrese (649*/1251-2; Meinecke, 1976, ii, no. 75). This last houses by far the most elaborate decoration of any Anatolian Saldjūḳ monument, including large areas of cut faience mosaic and mosaics of relief-carved elements in turquoise and manganese-purple, as well as dadoes of hexagonal turquoise tiles with fired gilt decoration. The last elaborate tile mosaic decoration at Konya is in the funerary *khānḳāh*, dated 678*/1279-80 and restored in Muḥarram 682*/April 1283 (Meinecke, ii, no. 79 and 89), which the vizier Fakhr al-Dīn ʿAlī (Ṣāḥib Ata) added to his mosque (656*/1258). The revival of tile-mosaic in late 13th century Īl-Khānid Persia is very probably indebted to Anatolian craftsmen conscripted by Ghāzān Khan for the works he ordered at Tabrīz and elsewhere.

An even more characteristic feature of Anatolian Saldjūḳ architectural decoration is star and cross-tiles for the dadoes of palaces at Konya, Antalya, Ḳubādābād, Kayḳubādiyya and Diyarbekir [*q.vv.*], for the bath built at Kayseri by Huant (Khwānd) Hatun, the wife of Kayḳubād I in Shawwāl 635*/May-June 1238 and in the Roman theatre at Aspendos. The Ḳubādābād-Huant Hatun-Aspendos group is technically varied (Öney, 1974; 1978) including underglaze-painted, lustre-painted and sgraffiato tiles, with a rich repertory of human figures, animals, birds, Zodiac and planet figures and monsters, many of them, as on Saldjūḳ stonework, displayed in quasi- or pseudo-heraldic fashion: it has not been demonstrated that any of them were either personal or dynastic heraldic emblems (Rogers, 1977-8). Stylistically many of the tiles show closer similarities to underglaze-painted wares from Raḳḳa [*q.v.*] and other Euphrates potteries than to 13th century Kāshān tilework. But the lustre-painted tiles from Ḳubādābād and the tiles from Kayḳubādiyya are *sui generis* (cf. Aslanapa, 1965, Plates 5-8).

Stucco. The most elaborate uses of carved and moulded stucco in architectural decoration are the figural reliefs from the Saldjūḳ palaces. They include a fine frieze with a mounted dragon-slayer and a lion-slayer from Konya, TIEM 2831, and animal friezes and frames for windows, niches or wall-cupboards with phoenixes in the spandrels of their broken arches from Ḳubādābād, now in the Konya Musuem. In Sarre's view (1909, 22) the stone window hood in the TIEM (Kühnel, 1938, Pl. 7) was mistakenly attributed to Diyarbekir and is actually from Konya (or Ḳubādābād). Very similar fragments, now in the Historical Museum, Erevan, were discovered at Ānī [*q.v.*; cf. Marr, 1934], and phoenixes also decorate spandrels on the façades of the church of Tigran Honents (1215) there. This should, however, be seen in the context of the evident taste of the Mkhargrdzeli governors of the city for Anatolian Saldjūḳ decoration (Rogers, 1976).

In religious buildings, stucco was often used as a plain white ground for faience-mosaic inlay. The *miḥrāb* of the Ahi Şerefüddin or Arslanhane Camii at Ankara (*minbar* dated 688*/1289-90), however, brilliantly combines carved stucco inscriptions and pilasters with ceramic mosaic inlay, foreshadowing the elaborate carved stucco of early 14th century Īl-Khānid Persia.

(b) *The minor arts.*

Woodwork. Anatolia has always been rich in

wood, and the wood-carving of the Anatolian Sald̲j̲ūḳs, often in solid walnut, is among the finest in Islam. It was used not only for *minbar*s and other mosque furniture, doors and sets of window-shutters, but also for cenotaphs and folding Ḳurʾān-stands (*raḥle*) ingeniously carved from a single plank (Çulpan, 1968). Techniques included lattices of turned wood (*mas̲h̲rabiyya* [*q.v.*]) and tongue-and-groove panelling of polygons and stars set in a strapwork skeleton (*kündekārī*), as well as imitations of this worked on solid planks. On *minbars*, the names of scribes or calligraphers frequently appear alongside the craftsman's name: the latter describe themselves variously as *miʿmār*, as on the cenotaph of D̲j̲alāl al-Dīn Rūmī at Konya (5 D̲j̲umādā II 672*/17 December 1273; cf. Meinecke, 1976, ii, no. 84: the form of the original building is unknown), *bannāʾ*, and *nad̲j̲d̲j̲ār*. Although on the earliest of the known series of Anatolian Sald̲j̲ūḳ *minbars*, from the Great Mosque at Āḳ Sarāy, bearing the names of Masʿūd I and Ḳilid̲j̲ Arslān II and datable therefore pre-550/1155, a certain K̲h̲ʷād̲j̲a Nūs̲h̲tekīn al-D̲j̲amālī is named as *miʿmār al-masd̲j̲id wa 'l-minbar*, this must record not his workmanship but the official installation of the *minbar* which turned the *masd̲j̲id* into a Great Mosque.

Other important Sald̲j̲ūḳ wooden *minbar*s (Oral, 1962) include those from the Citadel mosque at Konya (Rad̲j̲ab 550*/September 1155); the Great Mosque at Siirt (611*/1214); the Great Mosque (Muḥarram 621*/January-February 1224 [Arık, 1969] and 638*/1240-1) at Malatya [*q.v.*]; and those from the Arslanhane Camii and the Kızıl Beg Camii at Ankara (689*/1290-1 and 699*/1299-1300, respectively) the work of a *nad̲j̲d̲j̲ār* who also built the *minbar* of the Great Mosque at Çorum. The finest of the series is the *minbar* of the Great Mosque at Divriği (638*/1240-1), the work of Aḥmad b. Ibrāhīm al-Tiflīsī and a scribe Muḥammad, with *mas̲h̲rabiyya* balustrades, grandly designed inscriptions and heavily undercut foliate arabesques. Wooden window-shutters and remains of a "Royal box" up in the rafters (Tükel-Yavuz, 1978), though in rather different styles, are equally sumptuous. The occurrence of *nisba*s among the woodworkers' names relating to Ak̲h̲lāṭ and Tiflīs/Tbilisi may or may not be significant. Even the Divriği *minbar* gives way, however, to the *raḥle* for the mausoleum-shrine of D̲j̲alāl al-Dīn Rūmī at Konya (678*/1279-80) (Konya Museum 352; Riefstahl, 1933) with rich carving on the outside and with painting inside of compositions of two-headed eagles and lions in scrolling arabesques under yellow varnish.

Ceramics and glass. Apart from finds of frit-ware at the Citadel in Konya (Akok, Alaüddin Köşkü, 1968), now in the Konya Museum, possibly made by craftsmen brought in from Raḳḳa or other Euphrates potteries, most Anatolian Sald̲j̲ūḳ pottery belongs to the large family of polychrome-stained sgraffiato wares manufactured in the Eastern Mediterranean from Cyprus to the Caucasus and Transcaucasia and the Black Sea. The Anatolian material is still undifferentiated and little, if anything, is known of where it was made; but, not surprisingly, figural decoration is conspicuous and close parallels to much of it have been excavated at Örenkale/Baylakan [see ÖRENKALE in Suppl.] in Ād̲h̲arbayd̲j̲ān (Yessen, 1959, Pls. I-XII). Heavy unglazed relief-wares, mostly crocks with lively animal-friezes, found at Ānī and other Eastern Anatolian sites (e.g. TIEM 1964) have also been found in quantity at Örenkale (Yessen, 1959, 192-205). Excavations at Ahlat, now in progress (cf. Karamağaralı, 1981), have also brought a wide range of kiln material to light and claims have been made that lustre-wares were made there.

The only recorded piece of fine glass from Sald̲j̲ūḳ Anatolia must have been a special commission. This is a gilt and enamelled dish found at Ḳubādābād, typically Syrian in manufacture, in the name of Kayk̲h̲usraw II (Otto-Dorn *et alii*, 1966; 1969-70).

Metalwork. Although Sald̲j̲ūḳ objects in precious metal with an Anatolian provenance are so far absent, the rich finds of silver and silver-gilt belt-trappings and drinking cups from 13th-14th century steppe-burials in South Russia, the Crimea and the northern Caucasus are evidence that Sald̲j̲ūḳ Anatolian silver- and goldsmith's-work was exported northwards (cf. Marshak and Kramarovsky, 1993), creating a tradition which was continued *in situ*, probably by Armenian goldsmiths and jewellers. Brass and steel were also worked, though many categories of object are represented by single specimens. South-eastern Anatolia and the D̲j̲azīra are particularly well represented. Significant numbers of mortars with cast and engraved decoration have come from Diyarbekir; and a group of cast candlesticks sparingly inlaid with silver have been attributed to Siirt (Allan, 1978). Two large 12th or 13th century drums engraved with human-headed Kufic and fine scrolls (TIEM 2832-3) were also discovered at Diyarbekir. And although the doors made by al-D̲j̲azarī (Hill, 1974, 191-5) for the palace of the Artuḳid ruler at Diyarbekir with cast brass plates inlaid with copper and silver and knockers of confronted dragons and knobs in the form of a lion's head have not survived, they were much imitated. Knockers of this type and brass plaques from the doors of the Ulu Cami, Cizre, bear the remains of an inscription in the name of Sand̲j̲ar S̲h̲āh, Atabak of D̲j̲azīrat Ibn ʿUmar [*q.v.*] in 1208 (*The Anatolian civilisations*, iii, 1983, D. 95). Dragon-knockers, in varying sizes and for other buildings include that in Berlin, Museum für Islamische Kunst I. 2242.

Other metalwork well represented from finds in Anatolia includes zoomorphic padlocks of well-known mediaeval Persian or Syrian type, brass/bronze mirrors and cast brass dirham ring-weights for steelyards. Types represented by single specimens are an open-work mosque-lamp from the Eşrefoğlu Camii at Beyşehir (Ankara, Etnografya Müzesi 7591) made in 699*/1299-1300 by a craftsman ʿAlī b. Muḥammad from Nuṣaybīn, evidently for the inauguration of the mosque; and an open-work cast brass set-square (Kocabaş, 1963), now in the Sadberk Hanım Museum in Istanbul. Evidence for fine steel-working, moreover, is a mirror inlaid in gold (Topkapı Saray Museum 2/1792; cf. Rice, 1961) with a rider trampling a dragon and with a procession of animals and monsters round the edge.

Manuscript illustration. Too few illustrated manuscripts have survived from mediaeval Anatolia to speak of school of painting there, and the two most important of those that do, the automaton book of al-D̲j̲azarī [*q.v.* in Suppl.], Topkapı Saray Library A. 3472 (S̲h̲aʿbān 602/April-May 1205), and the Dioscorides in the Shrine Library, Mas̲h̲had (Grube, 1959, 163-4), datable 542-72/1152-76, were executed for Artuḳid, not Sald̲j̲ūḳ patrons. The *Romance of Warḳa and Guls̲h̲āh*, Topkapı Saray Library H. 841, may well have been executed at Konya *ca.* 1240 (Ateş 1961; Melikian-Chirvani, 1970; Özergin, 1970), though by a painter of north-west Persian origin. A magical miscellany presented to Kayk̲h̲usraw III, Bibliothèque Nationale pers. 174 (Barrucand, 1990), dated variously Ramaḍān 670/April 1272 and mid-

Shawwāl 671/early May 1273, was, however, written partly at Āḳ Sarāy and partly at Kayseri. Many of its illustrations, of demons, angels and marvels, are of later date and the only original illustrations appear to be line-drawings of talismans.

Figural coinage. As with their neighbours, the Turcoman dynasties of northern Syria and the Djazīra, issues of figural types are common in the coinage of Saldjūḳ Anatolia. The prototypes are similarly varied (cf. Brown, 1974), Hellenistic, Roman and Byzantine, but other types bear Zodiac or planet figures, animals and monsters, some perhaps heraldic, and, in particular, the Lion and the Sun (*Shīr ū Khurshīd*). This device is most characteristic of the coinage of Kaykhusraw II, but the claim, following contemporary historians, that he adopted it at the behest of his Georgian wife, Rusudan (Gürcü Hatun), has not been proved. For a fuller discussion of these questions, see below, section VIII. 2.

Textiles. A silk with double-headed eagles and dragon-headed scrolls formerly in the church of St. Servatius, Siegburg (now Berlin, Kunstgewerbemuseum, 81.745) which has been attributed by Sarre to an Anatolian manufactory, and a medallion silk with addorsed lions in the Musée des Tissus, Lyons, bearing an inscription in the name of Kayḳubād b. Kaykhusraw, Kayḳubād I (or Kayḳubād III), is evidence for a silk industry in 13th century Anatolia. There is also copious literary evidence for the widespread manufacture of floor-coverings by nomads, perhaps, however, flat-weaves, not pile carpets. It is difficult to say what they looked like, but varied and undoubtedly ancient fragments from the Citadel Mosque at Konya, the Eşrefoğlu Camii at Beyşehir (Riefstahl, 1931) and the Great Mosque at Divriği are often accepted to be Saldjūḳ in date. Both relative and absolute chronologies are, however, lacking. No evidence, moreover, has been found that carpets were yet being exported to the northern Mediterranean countries.

Bibliography: Mahmut Akok, *Kayseri'de Hanud Hatun mimarî külliyesinin rölövesi*, in *Türk Arkeoloji Dergisi*, xvi/1 (1967), 5-44; idem, *Konya'da Alaüddin Köşkü. Selçuk sarayı ve köşkleri*, in *Türk Etnografya Dergisi*, xi (1968), 47-60; idem, *Kayseri'de Gevher Nesibe Sultan Darüşşifası ve Sahabiye Medresesi rölöve ve mimarisi*, in *Türk Arkeoloji Dergisi*, xvii/1 (1967) 133-84; idem, *Kayseri'de Tuzhisarı, Sultanhanı, Köşkmedrese ve Alaca mescit diye tanılan üç Selçuklu mimarî eserleri*, in *ibid.*, xvii/2 (1968), 5-41; idem, *Kayseri'de dört mezar anıtı*, in *Türk Etnografya Dergisi*, xii (1969), 17-53; *Konya'da Ince Minareli Medrese'nin rölöve ve mimarisi*, in *Türk Arkeoloji Dergisi*, xix/1 (1970), 5-36; J.W. Allan, *From Tabriz to Siirt, relocation of a 13th century metalworking school*, in *Iran*, xvi (1978), 182-3; *The Anatolian civilisations*, iii, Exhibition Catalogue, Istanbul 1983, 5-96 and nos. D 1-D 185; Oluş Arık, *Malatya Ulu Camiinin aslî plâni ve tarihi hakkında*, in *Vakıflar Dergisi*, viii (1969), 141-8; idem, *Bitlis yapılarında Selçuklu rönesansı*, Ankara 1971; Oktay Aslanapa, *Anadoluda Türk çini ve keramik sanatı*, Istanbul 1965; Ahmet Ateş, *Un vieux poème romanesque. Récit de Warkah et Gulshāh*, in *Ars Orientalis* iv (1961), 143-52; W. Bachmann, *Kirchen und Moscheen in Armenien und Kurdistan*, Leipzig 1913; Ömür Bakırer, *Selçuklu öncesi ve Selçuklu dönemi Anadolu mimarisinde tuğla kullanımı*, i-ii, Ankara, ODTÜ 1981; Marianne Barrucand, *The miniatures of the* Daqā'iq al-Ḥaqā'iq *(Bibliothèque Nationale Pers. 174). A testimony to the cultural diversity of medieval Anatolia*, in *Islamic Art*, iv (1990-1), 113-51; Mehmed. Behçet, *Sinop kitabeleri*, in *TTEM*, NS i/2 (1929), 35-45, i/4 (1930), 46 ff., i/5 (1931), 57-63; M. van Berchem and Halil Edhem, *CIA, iii. Asie Mineure*, i. *Sivas et Diwriği*, Cairo 1910; Abdürrahim Şerif Beygu, *Ahlat kitabeleri*, Istanbul 1932; idem, *Erzurum. Tarihi, anıtları, kitâbeleri*, Istanbul 1936; A. Bombaci, *Die Mauerinschriften von Konya*, in *Forschungen zur Kunst Asiens. In Memoriam Kurt Erdmann*, ed. O. Aslanapa and R. Naumann, Istanbul 1969, 67-73; Helen Mitchell Brown, *Some reflections on the figured coinage of the Artuqids and Zangids*, in *Near Eastern numismatics, iconography, epigraphy and history. Studies in honor of George C. Miles*, ed. D.K. Kouymjian, Beirut 1974, 353-8; Cevdet Çulpan, *Türk-Islâm tahta oymacılık sanatından. Rahleler*, Istanbul 1968; G. Downey, *Byzantine architects, their training and methods*, in *Byzantion*, xviii (1948), 99-118; Halil Edhem, *Anadolu Selçukluları devrinde mimarî ve tezyinî sanatlar*, in *Halil Edhem hatıra kitabı*, Ankara 1947, i, 279-97; *Enciclopedia Italiana*, arts. *Divriği, Diyarbekir, Erzurum*; K. and H. Erdmann, *Das anatolische Karavansaray des 13. Jahrhunderts*, i (2 vols.), Berlin 1961, ii-iii, Berlin 1976 (rev. by J.M. Rogers, in *BiOr*, xxxiv [1977], 395-400); K. Erdmann, *Ibn Bibi als kunsthistorische Quelle*, Istanbul 1963; idem, *Neue Arbeiten zur Türkischen Keramik*, in *Ars Orientalis*, v (1963), 121-219; Ülker Erginsoy, *Turkish metalwork*, in *The art and architecture of Turkey*, ed. Ekrem Akurgal, Fribourg 1980, 208-21; M. Ferit and M. Mesut [Koman], *Sahip Ata ile oğullarının hayatı ve eserleri*, Konya 1934; A. Gabriel, *Monuments turcs d'Anatolie*. i. *Kayseri, Niğde*, ii. *Amasya, Tokat, Sivas*, Paris 1931-4; idem and J. Sauvaget, *Voyages archéologiques dans la Turquie orientale*, i-ii, Paris 1940; Ismā'īl Ghālib, *Taḳwīm-i meskūkāt-i Seldjūḳiyye* (*Catalogue des monnaies seldjoukides*), Istanbul 1309/1891-2, [2]Ankara 1971; idem, *Catalogue des monnaies turcomanes du Musée Impérial Ottoman. Beni Ortok, Beni Zengui, Frou' Atabegyéh et Meliks Eyoubites de Meiyafarikin*, Constantinople 1894; E.H. Grube, *Materialien zur Dioskurides Arabicus*, in *Festschrift Ernst Kühnel*, Berlin 1959, 163-94; D.R. Hill, *The Book of Ingenious Mechanical Devices ... by Ibn al-Razzāz al-Jazarī*, Dordrecht-Boston 1974 (rev. by J.M. Rogers, in *BiOr*, xxxiii [1976], 358-63); H. Jacobsthal, *Mittelalterliche Backsteinbauten zu Nachtschewan im Araxesthale*, Berlin 1899; Beyhan Karamağaralı, *Ahlat mezartaşları*, Ankara 1972; eadem, *Ahlat'ta bulunan bir çini fırını*, in *Yıllık Araştırmalar Dergisi. iii. Ord. Prof. Suut Kemal Yetkin'in hatırasına*, Ankara 1981, 67-93; N. Kaymaz, *Pervâne Mu'inüddin Süleyman*, Ankara 1970; O.Kh. Khalpakhčian, *Arkhitektura armyanskikh trapeznykh*, in *Arkhitekturnoye Nasledstvo*, iii (1953), 130-47; idem, *Graždanskoye zodčestvo Armenii*, Moscow 1971; Hüseyin Kocabaş, *Une collection de cuivres seldjoukides*, in *Atti del secondo Congresso Internazionale di arte Turca, Venezia 1963*, Naples 1965, 123-8; E. Kühnel, *Die Sammlung türkischer und islamischer Kunst im Tschinili Köschk*, Berlin-Leipzig 1938; Aptullah Kuran, *Anadolu medreseleri*, i, Ankara 1969; H. de Laborde, *Voyage de l'Asie Mineure*, Paris 1836; N. Lowick, *The religious, the royal and the popular in the figural coinage of the Jazira*, in *The art of Syria and the Jazira 1100-1250*, ed. J. Raby, Oxford 1985, 159-74; H. Löytved, *Konya. Inschriften der seldschukischen Bauten*, Berlin 1907; N. Yu. Marr, *Ani. Knižnaya istoriya goroda i raskopki na meste gorodishča*, Moscow-Leningrad 1934; B.I. Marshak and M.G. Kramarovsky, *A silver bowl in the Walters Art Gallery, Baltimore*, in *Iran*, xxxi (1993), 119-26; M. Meinecke, *Fayencedekorationen seldschukischer Sakralbauten in Kleinasien*, i-ii, Tübingen 1976; A.S. Melikian Chirvani, *Le roman de Varqae et Golšāh*, in *Arts Asiatiques*, xxii (1970); Riḍwān Nāfīdh and Ismāʿīl Ḥaḳḳī [Uzunçarşılı], *Sīwās shehri*, Istanbul 1928; Semra Ögel, *Anadolu Selçuklularının taş tezyinatı*, Ankara 1966; Gönül Öney, *Kubadabad ceramics*, in *The art of Iran and Anatolia from the 11th to the 13th century AD*, ed. W. Watson, London 1974, 68-84; eadem, *Anadolu Selçuklu mimarisinde süsleme ve el sanatları*, Ankara 1978; eadem, *Architectural decoration and the minor arts*, in *The art and architecture of Turkey*, ed. Ekrem Akurgal, Fribourg 1980, 170-207; M. Zeki Oral, *Anadolu'da san'at değeri olan ahşap minberler, kitabeleri ve tarihçeleri*, in *Vakıflar Dergisi*, v (1962), 23-77; Kemal M. Özergin, *Selçuklu sanatçısı nakkaş Abdülmü'min el-Hoyî hakkında*, in *Belleten*, xxxiv (1970), 219-29; Katharina Otto-Dorn, *Türkische Keramik*, Ankara 1957; eadem, *Seldschukische Holzsäulenmoscheen in Kleinasien*, in *Festschrift Ernst Kühnel*, 59-88; eadem *et alii*, *Bericht über die Grabung in Kobadabad (Oktober, 1965)*, in *Archäologischer Anzeiger*, lxxxxi (1966), 170-83; *Bericht über die Grabung in Kobadabad (1966)*, in *ibid.*, lxxxiv (169-70), 438-596; eadem, *Figural stone reliefs on Seljuk sacred architecture in Anatolia*, in *Kunst des Orients*, xii/1-2 (1978-9), 103-49; D.S. Rice and Seton Lloyd, *Alanya (ʿAlāʾiyya)*, London 1958; Rice, *A Seljuq mirror*, in *Communications of the First International Congress of Turkish Art, Ankara, 1959*, Ankara 1961, 288-9; R.M. Riefstahl, *Primitive rugs of the "Konya" type in the mosque of Beyşehir*, in *Art Bulletin*, xiii (1931), 177-220; idem and P. Wittek, *Turkish architecture in South-West Anatolia*, Cambridge, Mass. 1931; idem, *A Seljuk Koran stand with painted lacquer decoration in the Museum of Konya*, in *Art Bulletin*, xv (1933), 361-73; J.M. Rogers, *Recent work on Seljuk Anatolia*, in *Kunst des Orients*, vi/2 (1970), 134-69; idem, *The date of the Çifte Minare Medrese at Erzurum*, in *ibid.*, viii/1-2 (1974), 77-119; idem, *Seljuk architectural decoration at Sivas*, in *The art of Iran and Anatolia from the 11th to the 13th century AD,* 13-27; idem, *The Mkhargrdzelis between East and West*, in *Bedi Kartlisa*, xxxiv (1976), 315-26; idem, *Royal inscriptions and royal caravansarays in Seljuk Anatolia,* in *Mémorial Gabriel*, ed. R.H. Ünal, Ankara 1977-8, 397-431; idem, *Calligraphy and common script. Epitaphs from two Muslim cemeteries, Aswan and Ahlat*, in *Content and context of visual arts in the Islamic world. In memoriam Richard Ettinghausen*, ed. Priscilla Soucek, New York 1988, 105-26; F. Sarre, *Reise in Kleinasien, Sommer 1895. Forschungen zur seldschukischen Kunst und Geographie des Landes*, Berlin 1896; idem, *Seldschukische Kleinkunst*, Berlin 1909; idem, *Der Kiosk von Konya,* Berlin 1936; Metin Sözen, *Anadolu medreseleri. i. Selçuklu ve Beylikler devri*, Istanbul 1970; Ahmet Temir, *Kırşehir emiri Caca Oğlu Nur el-Din'in 1272 tarihli arapça-moğolca vakfiyesi*, Ankara 1959; Ayşıl Tükel-Yavuz, *Documentation and comparative study of Alara Han,* in *Belleten*, xxxiii (1969), 461-91; eadem, *The geometric patterns of Anatolian Seljuk decorated vaults*, in *Fifth International Congress of Turkish art*, ed. G. Fehér, Budapest 1978, 863-79; eadem, *Divriği Ulu Camisi hünkâr mahfeli tonozu*, in *Divriği Ulu Camii ve Darüşşifası*, ed. Yılmaz Önge *et alii*, Ankara 1978, 137-54; O. Turan, *Selçuk devri vakfiyeleri. i. Şemseddin Altunapa vakfiyesi ve hayatı*, in *Belleten*, xi (1947), 197-236; idem, *Selçuk devri vakfiyeleri. ii. Mübarizüddin Ertokuş ve vakfiyesi*, in *Belleten*, xi (1947), 415-30; idem, *Selçuk devri vakfiyeleri. iii. Celâleddin Karatay vakıflar ve vakfiyeleri*, in *Belleten*, xii (1948), 17-171; Ismāʿīl Ḥaḳḳī Uzunčarshīlī-oghlu, *Tūḳād, Nīksār, Dhīle, Ṭorkhāl, Pazār, Amāsiya wilāyet ḳaḍā we nāḥiye merkezlerindeki kitābeler*, Istanbul 1345/1927; idem, *Afyon Karahisar, Sandıklı, Bolvadın, Çay, Ishaklı, Manisa, Birgi, Muğla, Milâs, Peçin, Denizli, Isparta, Atabey ve Eğirdirdeki kitabeler ve Sahip, Saruhan, Aydın, Menteşe, İnanç, Hamit oğulları hakkında malûmat*, Istanbul 1929; R.M. Ward, *Evidence for a school of painting at the Artuqid court,* in *The art of Syria and the Jazira 1100-1250*, 69-83; A.A. Yessen (ed.), *Trudy Azerbaydžanskoi (Oren-Kaliinskoi) Arkheologičeskoi Ekspeditsii. i. 1953-55 gg.*, Moscow-Leningrad 1959; Şerare Yetkin, *Anadolu'da Türk çini sanatının gelişmesi*, Istanbul 1972. (J.M. Rogers)

VII. Literature

1. In Persia and ʿIrāḳ

The Saldjūḳs were important patrons of Persian and, to a lesser extent, also of Arabic belles-lettres. In this article we shall begin by looking at the panegyric poetry directed towards them (it is here that the relationship between patron and client is most immediately obvious) before taking a briefer look at the narrative and didactic poetry and the literary prose that were composed under their patronage.

Generally speaking, the great majority of the *ḳaṣīdas* dedicated to the Saldjūḳ *amīrs* are in Persian, while the contemporary Arabic language poets more commonly direct their panegyrics to the *wazīrs* and other educated members of the bureaucracy; this contrasts with the situation under the Būyids, whose knowledge of Arabic and whose appreciation of Arabic poetry were evidently superior to those of the Saldjūḳ ruling family. The earliest major literary figure in the entourage of the Saldjūḳs was the bilingual writer ʿAlī b. al-Ḥasan al-Bākharzī (died 467/1075 [*q.v.*]). He was closely attached to Ṭoghrïl's minister al-Kundurī and is best known as the author of the *Dumyat al-ḳaṣr wa-ʿuṣrat ahl al-ʿaṣr*, an anthology of contemporary Arabic poets in the manner of and in continuation of al-Thaʿālibī's celebrated *Yatīmat al-dahr*. His Arabic *dīwān* is extant (see O. Rescher, in *RSO*, iv [1911-12], 726) but unpublished, though some of the poems are known from biographical sources. A few samples of his Persian verse, among them several *rubāʿiyyāt*, are quoted by ʿAwfī (*Lubāb*, i, 68-71).

Lāmiʿī Gurgānī [*q.v.*] is the author of an extant *dīwān* in Persian. He began his career as a panegyrist of the Ziyārid ruler of his native Gurgān, Anūshirwān b. Manūčihr, but then passed into the service of the Saldjūḳs. His *dīwān* contains poems in praise of al-Kundurī and Niẓām al-Mulk, as well as of the *amīr* Alp Arslan.

Azraḳī Harawī [*q.v.*] flourished under two Saldjūḳ princes (the ruler of Harāt Abu 'l-Fawāris Ṭoghānshāh b. Alp Arslan and his cousin Abu 'l-Muẓaffar Amīrānshāh), and has left a Persian *dīwān* consisting largely of poems in praise of these two men. Niẓāmī ʿArūḍī (*Čahār maḳāla*, ed. Ḳazwīnī, London-Leiden 1910, 43-4) singles out Ṭoghānshāh as a particularly generous patron of poetry and lists another half-dozen poets who served at his court, but all their works are now lost apart from stray verses.

During the early part of the reign of Malik Shāh, the young poet Muʿizzī Naysābūrī [*q.v.*] inherited from his father, Burhānī, the position of "prince of the poets" (*amīr al-shuʿarāʾ*); he was, in other words, the head of the bureaucratically organised hierarchy of professional panegyrists (or in any event of those who wrote in Persian) who congregated at the Saldjūḳ court. His extensive *dīwān* contains odes to the *amīrs* from Malik Shāh down to Sandjar, to their ministers and various other persons. He lived perhaps until the middle of the 6th/12th century.

Among the Arabic panegyrists of Niẓām al-Mulk we can mention Aḥmad b. ʿAbd al-Razzāḳ al-

Ṭanṭarānī, the author of an elaborate *ḳaṣīda tardjīʿiyya* in praise of the minister. Al-Ḥusayn b. ʿAlī al-Ṭughrāʾī al-Iṣbahānī (453-515/1061-1121 [*q.v.*]), was a secretary under Malik Shāh and his son Muḥammad I and then *wazīr* to the latter's son Masʿūd during his ill-fated rebellion against his brother Maḥmūd II. His Arabic *dīwān* contains odes to Muḥammad and Masʿūd, to Niẓām al-Mulk and his son Muʾayyad al-Mulk, and to other high-ranking officials. He has also left a number of books on alchemy. Ibrāhīm b. ʿUthmān al-Ghazzī (441-524/1049-1130 [*q.v.* in Suppl.]), whose *dīwān* still awaits publication, praised Malik Shāh and Sandjar, but especially the *wazīr* of the ruler of Kirmān, Mukarram b. al-ʿAlāʾ. The extensive *dīwān* of Aḥmad b. Muḥammad al-Arradjānī [*q.v.*] contains a few poems to Muḥammad b. Muḥammad b. Malik Shāh and his brother Maḥmūd, but the majority are dedicated to the *wazīrs* of the Saldjūḳs, especially to the sons of Niẓām al-Mulk.

During the long reign of Sandjar, a large number of Persian poets frequented his court; we can restrict ourselves to those whose *dīwāns* have actually survived. After the death of the already mentioned Muʿizzī, Sandjar's pre-eminent panegyrist appears to have been Awḥad al-Dīn Anwarī [*q.v.*]. According to Djuwaynī (ii, 8), he accompanied the *amīr* when, in 542/1147, the latter laid siege to the Khʷārazm Shāh Atsïz in Hazārasp and participated in the campaign by writing poems mocking the enemy, which Sandjar's archers shot into the besieged fortress. Atsïz retaliated by doing the same with verses of his court-poet and secretary, Rashīd al-Dīn Waṭwāṭ [*q.v.*] (who on other occasions also wrote poems in praise of Sandjar). Anwarī survived his master and went on to serve Sulaymān b. Muḥammad and others. Another poet whose services to Sandjar went beyond the purely literary was Adīb Ṣābir [*q.v.*] whom the Saldjūḳ ruler sent as a spy to the court of the just-mentioned Atsïz, where he was apprehended and executed.

The *dīwān* of ʿAbd al-Wāsiʿ Djabalī [see ʿABD AL-WĀSIʿ] consists largely of panegyrics to Sandjar and to various persons of his entourage, notably his son-in-law, the vassal ruler of Sīstān, the Naṣrid Malik of Nīmrūz Naṣr (II) b. Khalaf, but he also eulogised the Saldjūḳ ruler of Kirmān, Arslan (I) b. Kirmānshāh, and others.

Sayyid Ḥasan Ghaznawī [*q.v.*] began his poetic career as a panegyrist of the Ghaznavid Bahrāmshāh, but later attached himself to the more opulent Saldjūḳ court. He wrote poems for Sandjar, composed an elegy on the death of Masʿūd II and poems celebrating the coronation of Malikshāh III and of Sulaymān b. Muḥammad before finally attaching himself to the Ḳarakhānid Maḥmūd II.

The satirical poet Sūzanī Samarḳandī was attached to the court of the Ḳarakhānids, but on occasion also dedicated laudatory odes to Sandjar. ʿAmʿaḳ Bukhārī [*q.v.* in Suppl.] was, according to Niẓāmī ʿArūḍī (*op. cit.*, 46), the *amīr al-shuʿarāʾ* at the court of the Ḳarakhānid Khiḍr b. Ibrāhīm; his extant poems are mostly dedicated to Khiḍr and to his brother and predecessor Naṣr b. Ibrāhīm, but include also one poem to Naṣr's brother-in-law Sandjar, and Dawlatshāh (64-5) says that when Sandjar's daughter Māh-i Mulk Khātūn died (in 524/1130), the *amīr* commissioned the by then elderly ʿAmʿaḳ to write an elegy.

The Persian panegyrists of the Saldjūḳs of Western Persia after the time of Sandjar include Athīr Akhsīkatī, who praised Arslan b. Ṭoghrïl and others. ʿImādī Ghaznawī [*q.v.*], most of whose poems praise the Bāwandid prince Farāmarz b. Rustam, also sent a number of poems to the Saldjūḳ Ṭoghrïl II. Sharaf al-Dīn Shufurwa, besides serving the Atabegs of Ādharbāydjān, also dedicated poems to Arslan b. Ṭoghrïl and to Ṭoghrïl III. Another court poet of the Eldigüzids who on occasion composed odes to the Saldjūḳ *amīr* was Mudjīr al-Dīn Baylaḳānī.

The Saldjūḳs were the dedicatees of several important works of narrative and didactic poetry in Persian rhymed couplets. The romantic epic *Wīs u Rāmīn* of Fakhr al-Dīn Gurgānī [*q.v.*] contains a dedication to Ṭoghrïl I, to his minister Abū Naṣr b. Manṣūr and his governor in Iṣfahān, Abu 'l-Fatḥ b. Muḥammad, the poet's actual patron. Malik Shāh is the dedicatee of an anthology of verses from Firdawsī's *Shāh-nāma* compiled in 474/1081-2 by an otherwise unknown ʿAlī b. Aḥmad. Two long heroic epics in the style of Firdawsī's poem, the *Bahman-nāma* and the *Kūsh-nāma*, are the work of a single anonymous author, who dedicated them to Muḥammad b. Malik Shāh.

One important author of Arabic narrative poetry flourished in the same period, namely Ibn al-Habbāriyya [*q.v.*]. His versification of the book of *Kalīla wa-Dimna* under the title *Natāʾidj al-fitna fī naẓm Kalīla wa-Dimna* was dedicated to the minister Madjd al-Mulk. Later, he composed a collection of apparently original stories in verse with the title *al-Ṣādiḥ wa 'l-bāghim*. He ended his days as a poet at the court of the Saldjūḳ ruler of Kirmān, Īrānshāh.

The most important Persian narrative poet of the 6th/12th century, Niẓāmī [*q.v.*], had at least a tangential connection with the Saldjūḳs in so far as he dedicated the first of his romantic epics, *Khusraw u Shīrīn*, to the Atabeg of Ādharbāydjān Muḥammad Djahan-Pahlawān b. Eldigüz and included in it a eulogy on his patron's nominal master, Ṭoghrïl III. But all his other works are dedicated to local rulers of Transcaucasia and northern ʿIrāḳ.

The last major poet of the Saldjūḳs was Aḥmad b. Maḥmūd Ḳāniʿī, a native of Ṭūs who fled his homeland at the time of the Mongol invasion and made his way (via India, Aden, the Holy Cities and Baghdād) to Anatolia, where he served the Rūm Saldjūḳ Kay Ḳubād I and his successors Kay Khusraw II and Kay Kāwūs II, to whom he dedicated a Persian versification of (once again) *Kalīla wa-Dimna* in 658/1260. He is presumably identical with the *malik al-shuʿarāʾ amīr* Bahāʾ al-Dīn Ḳāniʿī of whom Aflākī (*Manāḳib al-ʿārifīn*, ed. Tahsin Yazıcı, Ankara 1959-61, 221, 322) says that he visited Mawlāna Djalāl al-Dīn Rūmī during his lifetime and, again (*ibid.*, 595), that he was among those who paid their respects at Rūmī's grave after he died in 672/1273. This produces at least an indirect link between the Saldjūḳs of Rūm and Rūmī, the most famous poet who lived in their domain.

The best-known work in Persian prose emanating from the Saldjūḳ courts is doubtless the *Siyāsat-nāma* (alias *Siyar al-mulūk*) of Malik Shāh's minister Niẓām al-Mulk. Apart from this, a number of major Persian historical works were dedicated to the Saldjūḳ rulers; these include the *Fārs-nāma* of Ibn al-Balkhī [*q.v.* in Suppl.] (dedicated to Muḥammad b. Malik Shāh), the Persian history of Anūshirwān b. Khālid [*q.v.*], who was *wazīr* to Maḥmūd II and Masʿūd (not extant, but its contents are known from the Arabic version by al-Bundarī), the *Saldjūḳ-nāma* of Ẓahīr al-Dīn Naysābūrī [see NĪSHĀPŪRĪ] and its continuation, the *Rāḥat al-ṣudūr* of Rāwandī [*q.v.*] (dedicated to the Rūm Saldjūḳ Kay Khusraw I). A survey of Saldjūḳ literature would hardly be complete without at least mentioning the celebrated astronomer and amateur poet in Arabic, ʿUmar Khayyām [*q.v.*], who flourished at the court of Malik S͟hāh, although his claim to a place in the history of Sald̲j̲ūḳ belles-lettres rests on the Persian *rubāʿiyyāt* and the *adab* composition *Nawrūz-nāma* that have been ascribed to him but are both of more than questionable authenticity.

Although the Sald̲j̲ūḳs were not the first Islamic dynasty to use Persian as the language of their court (the Sāmānids, Ziyārids and G̲h̲aznavids had done so before them), they were the first to do so in an empire which encompassed the greater part of the Persian-speaking world. This meant that the Persian of the Sald̲j̲ūḳ writers inevitably played a tremendous role in the standardisation of the classical Persian language and can indeed be said to represent classical Persian par excellence, as opposed to the pre-classical language of the previous period with its many local and dialect features. Similarly, the style of the Sald̲j̲ūḳ poets set the standard for later periods. Although the Sald̲j̲ūḳ *ḳaṣīda*, like that of the older K̲h̲urāsānian school of Persian poetry, stands very clearly under the influence of Arabic models, the nature of these models had shifted; while the K̲h̲urāsānian school had, on the whole, emulated the ancient Arabic poets of the *D̲j̲āhilī* and Umayyad periods, the Sald̲j̲ūḳ poets imitated the highly mannered style of the "modern" poets from the time of al-Mutanabbī onwards. It is this style which continued to dominate Persian literature until the dawn of the modern era.

Bibliography: For the individual Arabic and Persian authors discussed in this article, see the relevant entries in Brockelmann and Storey-de Blois respectively. For a detailed survey of the Arabic poets, see also ʿAlī D̲j̲awād al-Ṭāhir, *al-S̲h̲iʿr al-ʿarabī fi 'l-ʿIrāḳ wa-bilād al-ʿad̲j̲am fi 'l-ʿaṣr al-Sald̲j̲ūḳī*, Bag̲h̲dād 1958-61, 2nd ed., Beirut 1405/1985. (F.C. DE BLOIS)

2. In Anatolia

As noted above, in sections IV. 2 and V. 2, the high culture and the administration of the Sald̲j̲ūḳ Sultanate was essentially a Persian one, and it was in this language that works in such fields as historiography and, in part, mysticism, tended to be composed. Of contemporary historians, notable is Ibn Bībī's [*q.v.*] history of the Rūm Sald̲j̲ūḳs, *al-Awāmir al-ʿalāʾiyya*, completed in 680/181, covering the history of the preceding ninety years and existing in the original Persian full version and an epitome and in a later Turkish paraphrase. Other important sources on Rūm Sald̲j̲ūḳ history, such as Karīm al-Dīn Maḥmūd Aḳsarāyī's *Musāmarat al-ak̲h̲bār*, Ḳāḍī Aḥmad's *al-Walad al-s̲h̲afīḳ* and the anonymous *Taʾrīk̲h̲-i āl-i Sald̲j̲ūḳ*, actually stem from the 8th/14th century. But we know of the existence of other historical or para-historical works written during the 7th/13th century and now lost, such as the *S̲h̲āh-nāmas* extolling the deeds of the Rūm sultans by Aḥmad Ḳāniʿī and K̲h̲ʷād̲j̲a Dahhānī, the latter commissioned by ʿAlāʾ al-Dīn Kay Ḳubād̲h̲ (in Köprülü's view, Kay Ḳubād̲h̲ III, hence almost at the end of the family's life), producing 20,000 couplets on the dynasty's exploits.

Mystical theology and that branch of biographical literature devoted to the lives of Ṣūfī saints (the *manāḳib-nāmas*) flourished exceedingly in the strong mystical atmosphere and tradition of the age (see above, section IV. 2). The towering figure of Rūmī produced during his residence at Konya his poetic *dīwān* and his masterpiece, the *Mat̲h̲nawī*, and he was followed by his son Sulṭān Walad, proficient both in Persian and Turkish (see below). Nad̲j̲m al-Dīn Rāzī Dāya wrote his *Mirṣād al-ʿibād* in Sivas but dedicated it to Kay Ḳubād̲h̲ I and finally settled at Konya. Several *manāḳib-nāmas* were written about the famous saints of Sald̲j̲ūḳ Anatolia, those of the Mawlawīs attracting particular attention, although the outstanding and most informative work in this genre, the *Manāḳib al-ʿārifīn* of S̲h̲ams al-Dīn Aflākī [*q.v.*], dates from the first half of the 8th/14th century, hence after the demise of the Sald̲j̲ūḳs.

Arabic naturally retained supreme prestige as the language of dogmatic theology, law and science, and Anatolia became, in particular, a centre for the production, transmission and copying of Ḥanafī *fiḳh* texts. But Arabic was also a language used for mystical theology, as seen in the prolific works of Ibn al-ʿArabī, some of these being composed during his stays in Konya and other Anatolian towns during the early 7th/13th century (see above, IV. 2); thus his mystical poetic work the *Tard̲j̲umān al-as̲h̲wāḳ* was completed at Kayseri, and his disciple Ṣadr al-Dīn Ḳūnawī was the author of numerous works in Arabic, including commentaries on the Ḳurʾān, *Ḥadīt̲h̲* and the Ninety-Nine Most Beautiful Names of God, and works in the field of theoretical Ṣūfism.

All of these works emanated from learned or courtly circles in Rūm, but the day-to-day language of the Turkish masses, urban as well as rural, was of course Turkish. Although the Ḳaramānids' introduction of Turkish as the official language for the *dīwāns* in Konya (see above, section V. 2) was only a brief interlude, it served to demonstrate the fact that an adoption of Turkish for public purposes was now a practical possibility. However, the literary use of Turkish in the Sultanate was for long at the popular, folk-literature level. Little from this has survived. An anonymous *S̲h̲eyk̲h̲ Ṣanʿān ḳiṣṣaṣī* of unknown date was handed down by Güls̲h̲ehri (d. after 717/1317 [*q.v.*]), and a *Ṣalṣāl-nāme* in verse and prose by a poet S̲h̲eyyād ʿĪsā describes the caliph ʿAlī's struggle with the giant Ṣalṣāl. Such works reflected the contemporary spirit of *g̲h̲azw* evident also in the oldest-preserved work of the class of popular epics, the *Sald̲j̲ūḳ-nāme*, existing in both long and short versions, and the *Dānis̲h̲mend-nāme* on the heroic deeds of Dānis̲h̲mend G̲h̲āzī composed by Ibn al-ʿAlāʾ at the command of sultan Kay Kāwūs II.

But when it came to literature of a more elevated, artistic order, Turkish had an uphill fight to establish itself, and for long authors writing in it excused themselves for not using Persian or Arabic, Turkish being still regarded as the tongue of ignorant peasants or nomads, the *Atrāk-i bī-idrāk*. Rūmī included a few Turkish verses in his work, and from his long stay in the Sald̲j̲ūḳ capital must have been fully conversant with the language; but his son Sulṭān Walad can definitely be regarded as a significant Turkish author, for there are at least 367 Turkish verses scattered through this works, couched in a simple style and probably aimed at spreading Mawlawī ideas amongst the people. A contemporary of Rūmī's was the Ṣūfī poet Aḥmed Faḳīh of Konya, whose mystical *Čark̲h̲-nāme* was a forerunner of Mawlānā's work; though brief, it constitutes the first complete work in Anatolian Turkish. In addition to a *mat̲h̲nawī* on the Yūsuf and Zulayk̲h̲ā theme, Aḥmed Faḳīh's pupil S̲h̲eyyād Ḥamza left examples of secular, court poetry apparently written for the Turco-Mongol official classes of his time and milieu, whilst the K̲h̲ʷād̲j̲a Dahhānī mentioned above wrote both Persian and Turkish court poetry at the very end of the Sald̲j̲ūḳ period. Finally, it was at this time, and in the years immediately after the disappearance of the sultans, that the greatest poet in early Turkish, stemming from northwestern Anatolia, Yūnus Emre (*ca.* 648-720/*ca.* 1250-1320 [*q.v.*]) produced his moving Ṣūfī poetry. With this poet's later career, we enter the age of the *beyliks*, when the formation of several provincial capitals was to provide fresh opportunities for writers in Turkish.

Bibliography: For writers in Persian, see the standard histories of Persian literature e.g. Browne, *LHP*; Arberry, *Classical Persian literature*; Rypka, *History of Iranian literature*. For writers in Turkish, see *EI*[1] art. TURKS. B.III.a (Köprülü Zāde Mehmed Fu'ād); W. Björkman, in *PTF*, ii, 405-12. In general, see Cahen, *Pre-Ottoman Turkey*, 248-58; M.F. Köprülü, *The Seljuks of Anatolia*, tr. and ed. Leiser. (C.E. BOSWORTH)

VIII. Numismatics

1. In Persia and ʿIrāḳ

Coins were struck by all branches of the Saldjūḳ dynasty, but in widely varying quality and quantity. They were all Sunnī in character, acknowledging the spiritual leadership of the ʿAbbāsid caliphate, and inscribing the name of the reigning caliph in a place of honour where it proclaimed the ruler's support of orthodoxy. Despite their great domains, the Saldjūḳs never established an imperial coinage on the pattern of the Umayyads or early ʿAbbāsids, but were content to adapt themselves to coinage patterns previously established by the Buwayhids, Kākūyids or Kākawayhids and Ghaznawids [*q.vv.*]. Their coinage thus tends to be strongly regional in character, reflecting the general economic conditions in each of the major areas under their control. In order to facilitate trade, the alloy of regional coinages tended to be similar to the currencies of neighbouring states, such as the Fāṭimids in the west and the Ḳarakhānids and Ghaznawids in the east. The regional nature of the coinage was further emphasised by princes and governors who struck coins in their own name whenever they were permitted to, or when they felt their power was great enough to seize this privilege.

The origin of the complexity stemmed from the Saldjūḳ family's sudden coming to power fresh from lands beyond the frontiers of the *Dār al-Islām*. Their social organisation was that of central Asian nomads where tribal sense was strong but whose experience of oriental monarchy, imperial bureaucracy, or even coinage itself, was almost non-existent. The Saldjūḳs had very little time to adapt themselves to their sudden good fortune, and their history reveals that behind a façade of Islamic kingship lay a deeply ingrained lack of dynastic discipline, added to which their followers did not easily transform themselves into docile town-dwellers.

The nature of the Saldjūḳ state was fissiparous from the outset. After the battle of Dandānḳān [*q.v.* in Suppl.] in 431/1040, the Saldjūḳ conquests were divided amongst the family whose principal members all appear to have enjoyed the right of *sikka* [*q.v.*]; see above, II. and III. on the various branches of the family which evolved.

Most of the surviving Saldjūḳ coinage is struck in gold. There are a few fine silver dirhams, some billon coinage and a small number of copper *fulūs*. The gold dīnārs were not struck to a fixed weight standard, but the weight range of most lies between two and five gr. In the mints from Nīshāpur westwards, the flans were manufactured from virtually pure gold, as was the custom elsewhere in the Islamic world of the time. In the east, the Saldjūḳs followed the example of the mint of Ghazna by using base gold in the form of electrum for their dīnārs. The near-absence of silver coinage is one of the chief features of the monetary history of the Middle East between 450 and 570/1058-1175. As the minor coinage metal, silver does not appear to have been replaced by copper until the second quarter of the 6th/11th century, and no glass token currency was in circulation as it was in Fāṭimid Egypt. Thus while the nobility, army and great merchants were obviously paid and dealt in gold, it is far from clear how the daily economy was financed.

The family member who struck the most abundant coinage was Ṭoghrïl Beg, who had the good fortune to acquire the great mint towns of Nīshāpur in 432/1040-1, al-Rayy in 434/1042-3, Iṣfahān in 443/1051-2 and Baghdād (*Madīnat al-Salām*) in 447/1055. These mints, plus a considerable number of lesser ones, issued very large quantities of high-quality gold dīnārs in Ṭoghrïl's name until his death in 455/1063. Ḳara Arslan Ḳawurd also struck a plentiful coinage in Kirmān, principally from the mints of Bardasīr and Djīruft. The coinages of Čaghrï Beg, Mūsā Yabghu and Ibrāhīm Inal, however, are all very rare, reflecting either the poverty of eastern Khurāsān after the Saldjūḳ conquest or the nomads' inability to form a stable administrative system which could organise and sustain a sophisticated coinage.

Ṭoghrïl was succeeded by his nephew Alp Arslan in 455/1063 who, as governor of Harāt before his accession, struck coins on which he acknowledged his father Čaghrï as overlord. His coinage appears to have been somewhat less abundant than Ṭoghrïl's. Under Alp Arslan's son and successor Malik Shāh (465-85/1072-92), the plentiful coinage of dīnārs continued on the same pattern as before, although the use of electrum dīnārs apparently declined in the eastern mints, as it did with the contemporary Ghaznawids.

The succession struggles among Malik Shāh's sons were reflected in their complex coinages, but the decline in the quality and quantity of the coins themselves also reveals that the economy was gradually being ruined as a result of these conflicts. Nāsir al-Dīn Maḥmūd's coins are rare because of the confusions of his brief reign in Iṣfahān, 485-87/1092-4. After the death of his father, Rukn al-Dīn Berkyaruḳ first issued coinage at Rayy, and quickly established himself in power elsewhere because he was both older and more experienced than his brothers. After a turbulent reign, Berkyaruḳ was succeeded in 498/1105 by Ghiyāth al-Dīn Muḥammad. The last Great Saldjūḳ was Malik Shāh's youngest son, Muʿizz al-Dīn Sandjar, governor of Khurāsān from 490/1097, who was looked up to as the nominal head of the family until his death in 552/1157. There were also parallel lines of Saldjūḳ rulers in ʿIrāḳ Persia, Kirmān and Syria (see above, III.). The ruling members of these families normally acknowledged the overlordship of the Great Saldjūḳs on their coins.

The conspicuous decline in the quality of the currency during the 6th/12th century was due to structural problems within the Saldjūḳ state, which had no central bureaucracy that could impose uniform standards for the coinage and oversee its production. The ruler did not govern the cities in his realm directly, but through the agency of members of his family, their Atabegs [*q.v.*], *amīrs* of his army or locally powerful semi-independent governors, many of whom included their names on the coins they issued after those of the caliph and their principal overlords. The presence of these names makes the study of the later Saldjūḳ coinage particularly useful to the historian but their elucidation is greatly complicated by the fact that many of the pieces were so carelessly manufactured that their legends are often mis-struck, or the margins are missing from the flan. Thus it is often impossible to read the mint names and dates of striking. The coinage of the later Saldjūḳs leads on to that of their successors, such as the revived ʿAbbāsid caliphate in Baghdād, the Zangids in Mawṣil, the Artuḳids in Ḥiṣn Kayfā and Mārdīn, the Ildegizids in Ardabīl and the Salghūrids in Fārs.

Because the Saldjūḳs were champions of Sunnism, the legends on their coins reproduce the traditional ʿAbbāsid type, which had survived intact at Nīshāpur, the great mint for gold in Khurāsān under both the Sāmānids and the Ghaznawids. The religious legends, therefore, show little variation in their texts. The obverse field contained the first statement of the *kalima, lā ilāh illā Allāh waḥdahu lā sharīk lahu*. Around this were two marginal legends, the inner containing the mint and date formula and the outer inscribed with parts of vv. 4 and 5 of sūra XXX, *al-Rūm*. The reverse field contained the second statement of the *kalima*, *Muḥammad rasūl Allāh*, and the single marginal legend was an adaptation of v. 33 of sūra IX, *al-Ṭawba*.

Occasionally, the Saldjūḳs struck dīnārs which were intended to have talismanic qualities, such as an issue of Alp Arslan from Marw dated 461 which inscribed the ninety-nine beautiful names of God in the obverse and reverse fields. A more common practice was to engrave v. 255 of sūra II, *al-Baḳara*, the Throne Verse, in minute letters in the reverse field. This calligraphic *tour de force* is found on occasional issues from Iṣfahān, ʿAskar Mukram and Marw. On rare occasions, the engravers included their own names on their best works in tiny letters in the outer margins.

The secular legends outside the mint and date formula were limited to names and titles. The reigning caliph's name was usually placed below the *kalima* in the obverse field, sometimes, if space permitted, with his title *Amīr al-Muʾminīn*. On his own coinage in Madīnat al-Salām, the caliph was entitled *al-Imām*, and his heir's name also appeared vertically in either the obverse or reverse field. The rest of the space was devoted to the name and titles of the ruler who struck the coin and those of his secular overlords, if he was obliged to acknowledge any. In order of importance these were the *ism*, e.g. Ṭoghrïl Beg; *kunya,* Abū-Ṭālib; *laḳab* Muʿizz al-Dīn, Rukn al-Islām, ʿAḍud al-Dawla; and *ʿalāma* and *ʿunwan*, al-Amīr al-Adjall/Shāhanshāh, al-Sulṭān al-Aʿẓam or Muʿaẓẓam. Unlike the Sāmānids, Ghaznawids and Buwayhids, whose titulature was generally uniform in their various mints, having been based on titles and *laḳabs* actually conferred by the caliph, the Saldjūḳs were often inconsistent in their royal styles. This may have been a result of their decentralised mint system or because of their preference for the grand effect rather than strict accuracy. For example, until 438/1046-7, Ṭoghrïl was entitled *al-Amīr al-Adjall* on the coinage of Nīshāpūr, and *al-Amīr al-Sayyid* in Rayy. A look at any of the catalogues where Saldjūḳ coins appear will reveal many other examples of this practice. It is interesting to note that, in addition to their Turkish names, Ṭoghrïl and Alp Arslan were both given the Muslim *ism* of *Muḥammad*, which occasionally appears on their coinage. Ṭoghrïl was known as *Muḥammad b. Mīkāʾīl* on coins struck in Rayy and Hamadhān between 434 and 438. Alp Arslan was named *Muḥammad* on the coinage of Nīshāpur throughout his reign, but without the inclusion of his *nasab*, while the same mint called his son *Malik Shāh b. Muḥammad*. The later Great Saldjūḳs were commonly named as sons of Malik Shāh, but neither this nor any other Saldjūḳ *nasab* was ever used on coins struck at the caliph's mint in Baghdād. Lastly, the coins of Ṭoghrïl, Alp Arslan and Malik Shāh frequently placed the Saldjūḳ *tamgha*, the bow and arrow, above the obverse or reverse fields, or sometimes both. Other, more traditionally Islamic words were often inscribed in the same position, such as *li'llāh, naṣr, fatḥ, ʿadl* or isolated letters like *ẓ*, which was probably an abbreviation of *ẓafar*.

The coinage of Madīnat al-Salām occupies a special place in the history of the Saldjūḳ coinage because it throws some light on the relationship between the caliph and the ruler. Throughout Ṭoghrïl's rule, the caliph al-Ḳāʾim [*q.v.*] accorded him a full set of titles, *al-Sulṭān al-Muʿaẓẓam Shāhanshāh Rukn al-Dīn Ṭoghrïl Beg*, but in the brief period of uncertainty after Ṭoghrïl's death in 455/1063, the caliph seized the opportunity to strike coinage in his own name and that of his heir for the first time in nearly a century. Then on the coinage of 456 and 457 the ruler is described as *Shāhanshāh al-Aʿẓam ʿAḍud al-Dawla Abū Shudjāʿ Malik al-ʿArab wa 'l-ʿAdjam Alb Arslān*, while on the dīnārs of 461 and later he is simply styled *ʿAḍud al-Dawla Alb Arslān*. From then on it became the custom to name the Saldjūḳ ruler on the caliph's coinage with only one *laḳab*, possibly an epithet and his throne name. The caliph al-Muḳtadī [*q.v.*] termed the ruler *Djalāl al-Dawla Malik Shāh*. During the succession struggle after Malik Shāh's death in 485/1092, the caliph once again struck dīnārs in his own name. This was followed by an issue where the ruler was styled *Muʿizz al-Dawla al-Ḳāhira Berkyaruḳ*. In 489/1096 the caliph al-Mustaẓhir [*q.v.*], altered Berkyaruḳ's *laḳab* to *ʿAḍud al-Dawla*, while in 491/1098 and 493/1100 the caliph again struck dīnārs in his own name, under what circumstances is not clear. The caliph entitled his successor *Ghiyāth al-Dunyā wa 'l-Dīn Muḥammad*, and then when the state was divided after Muḥammad's death in 511/1118, the caliph al-Mustarshid [*q.v.*], named the senior ruler as *Muʿizz al-Dunyā wa 'l-Dīn Sandjar* and the ruler of ʿIrāḳ as *wa-walī ʿahdihi Mughīth al-Dunyā wa 'l-Dīn Maḥmūd*. Finally, the caliph al-Muḳtafī [*q.v.*], retained no more than the *laḳabs* of *Muʿizz al-Dunyā wa 'l-Dīn* and *Ghiyāth al-Dunyā wa 'l-Dīn*, until the inclusion of Saldjūḳ names on the caliph's coinage was dropped altogether after the death of Ghiyāth al-Dīn Masʿūd in 547/1152.

A much larger body of numismatic evidence needs to be assembled before a comprehensive and analytical study of the Saldjūḳ coinage can be made. This is particularly true of the post-Malik Shāh period, when the constantly changing political scene is chronicled by the frequent striking of coins in the names of two rulers, rebels and usurpers, local governors and Atabegs.

Bibliography: The most easily accessible works are S. Lane Poole, *Catalogue of oriental coins in the British Museum*, iii, London 1875-90; H. Lavoix, *Catalogue des monnaies musulmanes de la Bibliothèque Nationale*, iv, Paris 1887-96; İ. and C. Artuk, *Istanbul Arkeoloji Müzeleri teshirdeki Islâmi sikkeler kataloğu*, ii, Istanbul 1971; Ç. Alptekin, *Salçuklu paraları*, in *Salçuklu Araştırmaları Dergisi*, iii (1971); S. Album, *A checklist of popular Islamic coins*, Santa Rosa 1993; C.C. Miles, *The numismatic history of Rayy*, New York 1938, 196 ff. See also Sotheby's and Spink's catalogues 1982-93.

2. In Anatolia

The Rūm Saldjūḳ coinage is entirely separate in origin from that of their distant cousins the Great Saldjūḳs (see above, VIII. 1). Their earliest coin is a crudely executed copper *fals* struck by Rukn al-Dīn Masʿūd I b. Ḳïlïč Arslan (510-51/1116-56), which copies a contemporary Byzantine *folis* with a full-face imperial bust on the obverse, and the ruler's name on the reverse.

The earliest coinage of ʿIzz al-Dīn Ḳi̊li̊č Arslan II (551-88/1156-92) was similar to that of his father Masʿūd I. This was followed by the well-known design of a mounted lancer galloping to the right on the obverse, borrowed from Christian iconography where it portrayed St. George the warrior saint of Cappadocia. In 571/1175-6 Ḳi̊li̊č Arslan II introduced traditional Islamic gold dīnārs and silver dirhams to Anatolia, at the same time as the Zangids of Aleppo reintroduced silver coinage to Syria. There is a unique gold dinar of 573/1177-8, while the earliest silver is dated 571/1175-6. Both bear conventional legends, with the mint in the obverse margin and the caliph's name in the field, and the date in the reverse margin and the ruler's name in the field. They are known only from the mint of Konya.

The Rūm Saldjūḳ dirham was struck at the traditional Islamic weight standard of 2.90-3.00 grs of virtually pure silver, with the *kalima* and the caliph's name on the obverse, and the sultan's titles, name and patronymic on the reverse. The table which summarises the political information on the coinage shows that some rulers identified themselves with the spiritual leadership of the ʿAbbāsid caliphate by describing themselves as Helper, etc. of the Commander of the Faithful.

When Ḳi̊li̊č Arslan II abdicated in 588/1192 he divided his realm among his numerous sons and a daughter, and apparently granted them all the right of *sikka* [*q.v.*]. His youngest son, Ghiyāth al-Dīn Kay Khusraw I, who ruled in Konya, 588-93/1192-6, struck coins modelled on those of his father. The eldest son Rukn al-Dīn Sulaymān Shāh placed the mounted lancer on his copper coinage, and, exceptionally, on his rarely found silver and gold. Ḳuṭb al-Dīn Malik Shāh issued a rare but conventional dirham, Muʿizz al-Dīn Ḳaysar Shāh struck a lancer copper, Muḥyī al-Dīn Masʿūd struck coins in Ankara on which he was styled al-ʿAbd al-Daʿīf, and Mughīth al-Dīn ṬoghrῙl, ruling in Erzurum, issued a plentiful silver coinage.

After Sulaymān Shāh's death in 600/1203, the western Saldjūḳ realms were reunited under Ghiyāth al-Dīn Kay Khusraw I (second reign 601-7/1204-10). His silver coins are known from Konya, Kayseri and Malatya, and he was the last Saldjūḳ ruler to strike an abundant mounted lancer copper coinage. He was succeeded by ʿIzz al-Dīn Kay Kāwūs, 607-16/1210-19, and al-Manṣūr Kay Ḳubādh who ruled the appanage of Tokat during his brother's lifetime, and struck a beautiful mounted lancer coinage in silver and copper. The coinage of Kay Kāwūs I, purely Islamic in character, adopted the square in circle design favoured by the Ayyūbids on their silver coins of Damascus. It is known only from Konya and Sivas. Kay Kāwūs I was succeeded by his more famous brother ʿAlāʾ al-Dīn Kay Ḳubādh I, 616-34/1219-36. Under his rule, Rūm Saldjūḳ dirhams, struck in huge quantities in Sivas and Konya, with a small production from the mints of Kayseri, Erzincan and Erzurum, became an international trade coin throughout the Middle East. Copper is known only from Bilveren and Sivas. Other coins struck in the name of Kay Ḳubādh I were an undated silver dirham of Hetum I, King of Cilician Armenia, and a silver dirham from the mint of Dunaysir dated 625/1228, and a copper *fals* from Mārdīn dated 634/1236-7 struck by Artuḳ Arslan, the Artuḳid ruler of Mārdīn.

Kay Ḳubādh I's successor Ghiyāth al-Dīn Kay Khusraw II (634-44/1236-46), issued conventional epigraphic silver and a few gold coins in Sivas and Konya between 634/1236-7 and 638/1240-1, but from 638/1240-1 to 641/1243-4 he struck large quantities of the most famous Rūm Saldjūḳ coin bearing the device of the lion and sun and the caliph's name on the obverse. The auspicious sign of the sun in Leo was probably used to exemplify the ruler's power. On one rare issue of 640/1242-3 in gold and silver, the sun rests on the backs of two lions rampant with their tails interlaced.

The Mongol Il Khans exercised indirect rule rather than occupying Anatolia after their defeat of Kay Khusraw II at Köse Dagh at the end of 639/1242 (see above, section III. 5). Surprisingly, the Rūm Saldjūḳ coinage did not mention them as overlords until much later. However, the number of dirhams struck in 640 and 641 decreased, and the lion and sun type was abandoned in 641. Kay Khusraw II returned to a purely epigraphic style of coinage, and assumed the grandiloquent title *Ẓill Allāh fi 'l-ʿĀlam*, ''The Shadow of God in the World''. Before the Mongol victory, King Hetum of Armenia struck silver horseman dirhams bearing Kay Khusraw's name as overlord at the mint of Sis between 637 and 640; the Ayyūbid ruler of Aleppo, al-Malik al-Nāṣir Yūsuf II, struck silver dirhams dated 636 to 638; Artuḳ Arslan, the Artuḳid ruler of Mārdīn struck another dated 636 in Dunaysir, and a copper *fals* of Mārdīn dated 637, while Badr al-Dīn Luʾluʾ, the Luʾluʾid ruler of Mawṣil, issued gold dīnārs from 638 to 641.

On the gold and silver struck in Sivas and Konya, ʿIzz al-Dīn Kay Kāwūs II (644-7/1246-9) followed the square in circle design, and included the title *Ẓill Allāh fi 'l-ʿĀlam*. He introduced the Rūm Saldjūḳ practice of dating coins with *dīwānī* abbreviations of the Arabic names for the numbers, borrowed from accounting conventions, for the units and decades of the year. Al-Malik al-Kāmil Muḥammad II, the Ayyūbid ruler of Mayyāfāriḳīn and Āmid, also struck a few undated copper coins naming Kay Kāwūs II as overlord.

In 646 Rukn al-Dīn Ḳi̊li̊č Arslan IV challenged his brother Kay Kāwūs II, and demonstrated his sole power in Sivas by striking the last Saldjūḳ horseman coinage. Its artistic inspiration was Persian rather than Anatolian, replacing the warrior-saint of the Byzantines with an elaborately-dressed archer, drawing his bow on the back of a prancing horse. The Il Khān Hülegü's anger at the rivalry between Kay Kāwūs II and Ḳi̊li̊č Arslan IV caused him to establish a triumvirate among the three sons of Kay Khusraw II, and between 647 and 656 a conjoint coinage was issued in the names of ʿIzz al-Dīn Kay Kāwūs II, Rukn al-Dīn Ḳi̊li̊č Arslan IV and ʿAlāʾ al-Dīn Kay Ḳubādh II. Their silver is plentiful and a few gold coins are known, but there appears to be no copper. Most were struck in Sivas and Konya, but there were also minor mints in Kayseri, Malatya and Luʾluʾa. The latter, located in the Taurus mountains, appears to have been the Rūm Saldjūḳs' first mining mint. The one sign of disunity amongst the brothers on their coinage is a dirham of 652 struck in Kayseri which names only Ḳi̊li̊č Arslan IV and Kay Ḳubādh II.

When conjoint rule ended on the death of Kay Ḳubādh II, ʿIzz al-Dīn Kay Kāwūs II issued coins in his own name between 655 and 658/1257-60 at several western mints, the principal one being Konya and others in Ankara, Develü, Gümüşpazar and Luʾluʾa. After the fall of the Baghdād ʿAbbāsids in 656/1258 Kay Kāwūs continued to use the *kalima* and the caliph's name on his coins until 658/1260, when he replaced them with the laudation *al-ʿIzza li'llāh* ''Glory belongs to God!'' in the obverse field with the mint and date in the margin. In the east, Ḳi̊li̊č Arslan

Table. *Summary of names and titles found on the Rūm Saldjūķ coinage.*

Name	Laķab	Kunya	Regal style	Caliphal relationship	Laudation
Masʿūd (I)	[1]Rukn al-Dunyā wa 'l-Dīn	–	al-Sulṭān al-Muʿaẓẓam	–	–
Ķilič Arslan (II)	ʿIzz	–	al-Sulṭān al-Muʿaẓẓam	–	–
Kay Khusraw (I)	Ghiyāth	–	al-Sulṭān al-Muʿaẓẓam	–	–
Sulayman Shāh	Rukn	Abu 'l-Fatḥ	al-Malik al-Ķahir/ al-Sulṭān al-Ķāhir	Nāṣir Amīr al-Muʾminīn/ Burhān al-Muʾminīn	–
Malik Shāh	Ķuṭb	Abu 'l-Fatḥ	–	–	–
Ķayṣar Shāh	Muʿizz	–	al-Malik al-Muʾayyad	–	–
Masʿūd	Muḥyī	–	al-ʿAbd al-Ḍaʿīf	–	–
Ṭoghrīl	Mughīth	Abu 'l-Fatḥ	–		
Kay Khusraw (I) (2nd reign)	Ghiyāth	Abu 'l-Fatḥ	al-Sulṭān al-Muʿaẓẓam	–	al-Minna li'llāh
Kay Kāwūs (I)	ʿIzz	–	al-Sulṭān al-Ghālib	–	–

Kay Ķubā<u>dh</u> (I)	ʿAlāʾ	Abu 'l-Fatḥ	al-Malik al-Manṣūr/ al-Sulṭān al-Muʿaẓẓam/ al-Sulṭān al-Aʿẓam	Naṣr Amīr al-Muʾminīn/ - -	-
Kay <u>Kh</u>usraw (II)	<u>Gh</u>iyā<u>th</u>	Abu 'l-Fatḥ	al-Sulṭān al-Muʿaẓẓam/ al-Sulṭān al-Aʿẓam Ẓill Allāh fi 'l-ʿĀlam	Ķasīm Amīr al-Muʾminīn	
Kay Kāwūs (II) (1st reign)	ʿIzz	Abu 'l-Fatḥ	al-Sulṭān al-Aʿẓam Ẓill Allāh fi 'l-ʿĀlam	Ķasīm Amīr al-Muʾminīn	
Ķilič Arslan (IV)	Rukn	Abu 'l-Fatḥ	al-Sulṭān al-Aʿẓam	Ķasīm Amīr al-Muʾminīn	-
"Three Brothers" Kay Kāwūs (II)/ Ķilič Arslan (IV)/ Kay Ķubā<u>dh</u> (II)	ʿIzz/ Rukn/ ʿAlāʾ	-	al-Salāṭin al-ʿIẓām	-	-
Kay Kāwūs (II) (2nd reign)	ʿIzz	Abu 'l-Fatḥ	al-Sulṭān al-Aʿẓam	-	al-ʿIzza li'llāh
Ķilič Arslan (IV)	Rukn	Abu 'l-Fatḥ	al-Sulṭān al-Aʿẓam	Burhān Amīr al-Muʾminīn	al-ʿMinna li'llāh
Kay <u>Kh</u>usraw (III)	<u>Gh</u>iyā<u>th</u>	Abu 'l-Fatḥ	al-Sulṭān al-Aʿẓam	Burhān Amīr al-Muʾminīn	al-Mulk li'llāh
Masʿūd (II)	<u>Gh</u>iyā<u>th</u>	Abu 'l-Fatḥ	al-Sulṭān al-Aʿẓam Ẓill Allāh fi 'l-ʿĀlam	-	al-ʿUẓma li'llāh
Kay Ķubā<u>dh</u> (III)	ʿAlāʾ	Abu 'l-Fatḥ	al-Sulṭān al-Aʿẓam	-	al-Minna li'llāh

All *laķab*s include the phrase *al-Dunyā wa'l-Dīn*.

IV struck coins during his second period of rule (655-63/1257-64), still in the name of the caliph al-Mustaʿṣim until the year 662/1264, but in 663/1265 he issued dirhams in that of a fictive caliph *al-Imām al-Maʿṣūm Amīr al-Muʾminīn*, "the Immaculate Imām, Commander of the Faithful". Elsewhere he replaced the *kalima* and mention of the caliph with the laudation *al-Minna li'llāh*, "Grace be to God!". His principal mint was Sivas, but after the death of Kay Kāwūs II in 658 his coins were struck in Erzincan, ʿAlāʾiyya, Antalya, Bazar, Develü, Kayseri, Gümüşpazar, Luʾluʾa, Maʿdan Shehir, Maʿdan Sarus and Malatya. Ḳilič Arslan IV was succeeded by his son Ghiyāth al-Dīn Kay Khusraw III (663-81/1264-82), whose coinage from Erzincan, Erzurum, Antalya, Bazar, Sivas, Sarus, Sinop, Kastamunu, Konya, Kayseri, Gümüşpazar, Luʾluʾa and Maʿdan Shehir was distinguished by the laudation *al-Mulk li 'llāh*, "Sovereignty belongs to God!".

Kay Khusraw III was succeeded by his nephew ʿAlāʾ al-Dīn Kay Ḳubādh III b. Farāmurz in 681/1282, who lost the eastern territories to his cousin Ghiyāth al-Dīn Masʿūd II (first reign 681-97/1282-97). The coins of Masʿūd II, from Erzincan, Erzurum, Antalya, Sarı Kavak, Samsun, Sivas, Konya, Gümüşpazar, Ladik, Luʾluʾa, Maʿdan Bayburt, Maʿdan Shehir and Maʿdan Samasur, occasionally used the laudation *al-ʿUẓma li'llāh*, "Power belongs to God!".

The end of the Rūm Saldjūk coinage is obscure. Sovereignty alternated between Kay Ḳubādh III, Masʿūd II and his son Masʿūd III in the last decade of the seventh century and the first years of the eighth, but their crudely struck coins make it difficult to establish an accurate chronology based on numismatic evidence. Kay Ḳubādh III did occasionally place a lion passant or a lion and sun on his coins, some of which, struck in Erzincan, Sivas and Konya in 698, acknowledged the Il Khānid ruler Maḥmūd Ghazan as overlord. Other mints for Kay Ḳubādh III are Antalya, Sulaymān Shehir, Sarı Kavak, and perhaps Borlu.

During the last quarter of the seventh century, most coins were struck in silver, and gold became extremely rare. The internal coherence of the state had collapsed, and local governors often used the names of Masʿūd II and Kay Ḳubādh III to give validity to their own coinages. The coins of Kay Ḳubādh III largely disregarded the weight standard of the Islamic silver dirham, and their weight fell to 2.00-2.50 gr. Thus began the transition to the irregular, low weight Anatolian silver issued by the Beylik successors to the Rūm Saldjūḳs, first in the name of the Il Khānids, and later in their own names, which resulted in the introduction of the small silver *akče* as the unit of account in Anatolia by the second quarter of the 8th/14th century.

Bibliography: Rūm Saldjūḳ coinage has been extensively published, having been a particular favourite of Ottoman and modern Turkish numismatists. The Istanbul Mint Museum, the Yapı ve Kredi Kültür Merkezi, American Numismatic Society and Tübingen University have large collections of Rūm Saldjūḳ coins, as do the museums whose catalogues are listed below: İ. and C. Artuk, *Istanbul Arkeoloji Müzeleri teshirdeki islami sikkerler kataloğu*, Istanbul 1971; Ismāʿīl Ghālib Edhem, *Taḳwīm-i meskūkāt-i ʿothmāniyye*, Istanbul 1307/1889-90; G. Hennequin, *Catalogue des monnaies musulmanes de la Bibliothèque Nationale, iv, Asie pré-mongole. Les Salğuqs et leurs successeurs*, Paris 1985; S. Lane Poole, *Catalogue of oriental coins in the British Museum*, London 1875-90, iii; Aḥmed Tewḥīd, *Müze-yi Humāyūn meskūkāt-i islāmiyye ḳataloghları*, Istanbul 1321/1903-4. (R.E. Darley-Doran)

SALGHURIDS, a line of Atabegs which ruled in Fārs during the second half of the 6th/12th century and for much of the 7th/13th one (543-681/1148-1282).

They were of Türkmen origin, and Maḥmūd Kāshgharī considered them as a clan of the Oghuz tribe [see ghuzz], giving their particular *tamgha* (*Dīwān lughāt al-Turk*, Tkish. tr. Atalay, i, 56, iii, 141, 414); later sources such as Rashīd al-Dīn, Ḥamd Allāh Mustawfī's *Taʾrīkh-i Guzīda* and Abu 'l-Ghāzī's *Shadjara-yi Tarākima* were uncertain whether Salghur was a clan or the name of an eponymous ancestor of the Atabegs (cf. also W. Barthold, *A history of the Turkman people*, in *Four studies on the history of Central Asia*, iii, Leiden 1962, 119, who was sceptical about a connection of the Atabegs with the Salghur or Salur [*q.v.*] clan).

The Salghur clan played a role in the Turkmens' overrunning of Anatolia in the late 5th/11th century. Muẓaffar al-Dīn Sonḳur b. Mawdūd took advantage of the weakening power of the Great Saldjūḳ sultans and in 543/1148 established himself in Fārs after the death of the province's ruler Boz-aba (who may himself have been connected with the Salghur clan). After Sonḳur's death in 556/1161, he was succeeded by his brother Muẓaffar al-Dīn Zangī and then in 570/1175 by the latter's son Tekele or Degele, so that the hereditary rule of the Salghurids in Fārs became established, whilst at the same time they acknowledged, until 590/1194, the overlordship of the last Great Saldjūḳs. Tekele had eliminated his rival for power, Sonḳur's son Ḳuṭb al-Dīn Ṭoghrïl, in 577/1181-2, according to the *Niẓām al-tawārīkh* of al-Bayḍāwī (who was a contemporary in Fārs of the Salghurids of the 7th/13th century; his account is accordingly followed by Merçil, see *Bibl.*, and here), and he probably reigned until 594/1198, when his brother ʿIzz al-Dīn Saʿd (I) b. Zangī [*q.v.*] came to power. (It therefore seems probable that we should eliminate Ṭoghrïl from the list of Salghurids who actually ruled in Fārs, although he thus figures in much of the secondary literature, including in the *EI*[1] art., as being still alive and ruling in Fārs in the later 1190s and first years of the 13th century; there are significant differences in the information of the historians on the events of these years).

Saʿd, like his predecessors, campaigned against the local Shabānkāraʾī Kurdish bandits and intervened in the affairs of the neighbouring province of Kirmān [*q.v.*], and in 600/1203-4 captured Iṣfahān; but he came up against the growing power in Persia of the Khwārazm-Shāhs, was captured by ʿAlāʾ al-Dīn Muḥammad Shāh [*q.v.*] in 614/1217-18 and only released on payment of the tribute formerly paid to the Saldjūḳs and the cession of certain districts in Fārs as *iḳṭāʿ*s or land-grants for Khwārazmian commanders. The triumph of the Mongols released the Salghurids from this dependence on the Khwārazm-Shāhs but substituted another yoke. Saʿd's son Abū Bakr (succeeded on his father's death, more probably in 623/1226 than 628/1231) was the vassal of the Great Khān Ögedey and then of the Il-Khān Hülegü [*q.vv.*], and it was the former ruler who conferred on Abū Bakr the title of Ḳutlugh Khān in return for an annual tribute of 30,000 Ruknī dīnārs and the admission of a Mongol *shiḥna* to his principality.

The years after Abū Bakr's death in 658/1260 were filled with a succession of short-ruled Salghurid Atabegs: Muẓaffar al-Dīn Saʿd (II), ʿAḍud al-Dīn

Muḥammad, Muẓaffar al-Dīn Muḥammad Shāh, Muẓaffar al-Dīn Saldjūḳ Shāh, closing with Muẓaffar al-Dīn Ābish Khātūn, the daughter of Saᶜd (II), on whom Hülegü bestowed the Atabegate of Fārs. She reigned alone for a year (662-3/1263-4), at the end of which she married Mengü Temür, the eleventh son of Hülegü, who himself assumed *de facto* power in Fārs till his death in 681/1282, with Ābish Khātūn as only nominal Atabeg. The rule of the Salghurids, which had endured for over 130 years, came to an end at this point; Ābish Khātūn herself died in Mongol captivity at Tabrīz in 685/1286.

Fārs especially flourished in the 7th/13th century under the rule of the Salghurids, with a lively cultural and intellectual atmosphere in the capital Shīrāz [*q.v.*], where there lived at this time, *inter alios*, the Ḳāḍī al-Bayḍāwī, the scientist Ḳuṭb al-Dīn Shīrāzī and the historian Waṣṣāf [*q.vv.*]. The poet Saᶜdī [*q.v.*] was the panegyrist of the Atabegs, deriving his *takhalluṣ* from Abū Bakr b. Saᶜd (I); it was to this last that he dedicated his *Bustān* and to his son, the short-reigned Saᶜd (II), that he dedicated the *Gulistān* (cf. J. Rypka *et alii, History of Iranian literature*, Dordrecht 1968, 250). Coins were minted by most of the Atabegs up to and including Ābish Khātūn, with the exception possibly of the ephemeral rulers preceding her.

Genealogical table of the Salghurids

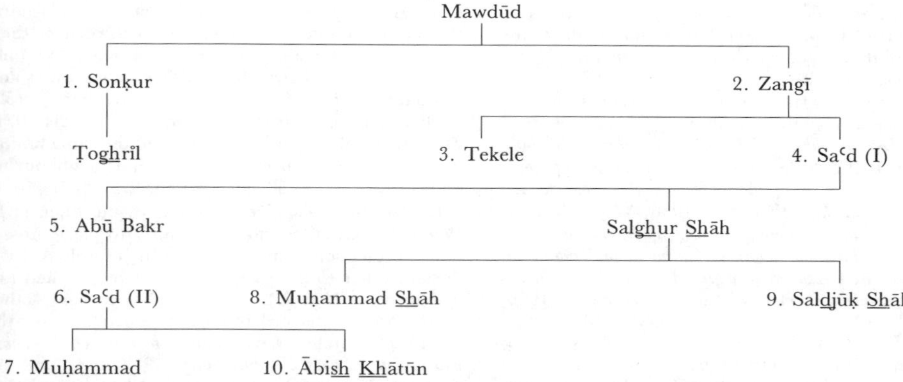

Bibliography: Zambaur, *Manuel*, 232; B. Spuler, *Die Mongolen in Iran*[1], Leipzig 1939, 144-5 and index; C.E. Bosworth, *The new Islamic dynasties*, Edinburgh 1996, ch. X, no. 98; Erdoğan Merçil, *Fars Atabegleri Salgurlar*, Ankara 1975, with a good survey of the primary sources (Afḍal al-Dīn Kirmānī; Nasawī; Ibn al-Athīr; Rashīd al-Dīn; Waṣṣāf; Aḥmad b. Zarkūb, *Shīrāz-nāma*; Mustawfī; etc.) at pp. XI-XIX.   (C.E. BOSWORTH)

SALḤĪN, also Silḥīn, the name of the royal palace of the Sabaean kings in their capital Mārib [*q.v.*]. The house of Salḥīn (*bytn slḥn*; e.g. *CIH* 373) is the building of ancient South Arabia which is most frequently mentioned in the Sabaic inscriptions of the first three centuries A.D. Its name is also attested in the forms Salḥēn and Σιλεῆ in the title of the Abyssinian king ᶜĒzānā in Ethiopic and Greek inscriptions of the fourth century A.D. from Aksum. Owing to the lack of excavations, the original site of the palace of Salḥīn in the area of the ancient town of Mārib has not yet been discovered.

Arab tradition enumerates Salḥīn in Mārib among the most famous castles of pre-Islamic Yemen, which are praised by the Arabs in their poems and proverbs (al-Hamdānī, *Ṣifa*, ed. Müller, 203, 11-15). Salḥīn is the foremost of the three castles of ancient Mārib (idem, *Iklīl*, viii, ed. M. al-Akwaᶜ al-Ḥiwālī, Damascus 1979, 99, 10), and it is supposed to have been the palace of Bilḳīs [*q.v.*] (*ibid.*, viii, 103, 2). It held the high rank of being the royal residence of the Ḥimyarite kings (Nashwān, *Shams*, 50, 9), and it was an important castle in the country of Yemen, which belonged to the *Tabābiᶜa* or Tubbaᶜs [*q.v.*], the kings of Yemen (Yāḳūt, *Muᶜḏjam*, iii, 115, 11). On the authority of Muḥammad b. Khālid, it is reported that the Sabaean kings lived in Mārib and in Ṣanᶜāʾ alternately, and whenever they resided in Mārib they stayed in Salḥīn (al-Hamdānī, *Iklīl*, viii, 106, 11-13).

It is said that the palace was built by order of Bilḳīs, the Queen of Sheba, the daughter of al-Hadhād, and that in it her throne stood, as mentioned in Ḳurʾān, XXVII, 23 (Nashwān, *Shams*, 50, 9-11); it is said as well that Solomon commanded the *djinn* to build the palace for Bilḳīs (al-Thaᶜlabī, *Ḳiṣaṣ al-anbiyāʾ*, Cairo 1889, 201). According to other traditions one of the *Tabābiᶜa* [see TUBBAᶜ] gave orders to construct Salḥīn (Yāḳūt, *Muᶜḏjam*, i, 535, 13), or else the demons built it for Dhū Bataᶜ, the king of Hamdān, when he arranged the marriage of Bilḳīs to Solomon (*ibid.*, iii, 115, 12), or when Dhū Bataᶜ himself married Bilḳīs at the behest of Solomon respectively (Ibn al-Athīr, i, 238, 1-2). People say that demons had written in a Ḥimyaritic inscription in Yemen: "We built Salḥīn, working on it continuously for seventy-seven years" (al-Ṭabarī, i, 585, 15-16; al-Hamdānī, *Iklīl*, viii, 104, 4-5). In other sources, the duration of the building of Salḥīn is supposed to have lasted seventy years (Yāḳūt, *Muᶜḏjam*, iii, 115, 18) or eighty years respectively (*ibid.*, i, 535, 13-14; *Tādj al-ᶜarūs*, s.v. Salḥīn). Al-Hamdānī, however, doubts whether the *djinn* could have written this for two reasons. In the first place, they say that the demons built Salḥīn in seventy-seven years, but between the visit of Bilḳīs to Solomon and his death there were at most seven years, and after Solomon's death the *djinn* refused to continue their work. In the second place, there is a saying of ᶜAlḳama b. Dhī Djadan, mentioning that human beings built Salḥīn and not the *djinn*, when he composed: "and will men built houses (henceforth) after Salḥīn (has been destroyed)?" (*Iklīl*, viii, 105, 3-9; for the variant of this verse, as it is rendered here, cf. Ibn Hishām, *Sīra*, 26, 12; al-Ṭabarī, i, 928, 13; Yāḳūt, iii, 115, 17; *Tādj al-ᶜarūs, loc. cit.*).

When the Abyssinians under their commander Aryāṭ conquered Yemen, they destroyed Salḥīn, Ghumdān [*q.v.*] and Baynūn [*q.v.*], castles which were without equals among men (Ibn Hi<u>sh</u>ām, *Sīra*, 26, 13-14; al-Ṭabarī, i, 928, 9-11); they were considered to be palaces of exceptional beauty and splendour, which people had never seen before (al-<u>Th</u>aʿlabī, *Ḳiṣaṣ*, 201). It seems that no remains of this castle were left in the Islamic period, since reportedly no traces of Salḥīn can be seen any more (Yāḳūt, iii, 115, 19).

From the no longer existent *dīwān* of the previously-mentioned ʿAlḳama, who was a descendant of the famous Ḥimyarite noble family <u>Dh</u>ū <u>D</u>jadan, belonging to the *ma<u>th</u>āmina* [*q.v.*], verses are quoted, in which the fate of Salḥīn is deplored, because the castle has been destroyed, so that now foxes bark in it, and because it has become deserted, it is as if it had never been inhabited (al-Hamdānī, *Iklīl*, viii, 103, 3-13). Yemenite nostalgia for times long passed is expressed by the verse "Inquire about Salḥīn and its days, the days when the kingdom belonged to Ḥimyar" (Na<u>sh</u>wān, *<u>Sh</u>ams*, 50, 12).

Bibliography (in addition to references given in the article): ʿAẓīmuddīn Aḥmad, *Die auf Südarabien bezüglichen Angaben Našwān's im Šams al-ʿulūm*, Leiden 1916; N.A. Faris, *The antiquities of South Arabia, being a translation of the eighth book of Al-Hamdānī's al-Iklīl*, Princeton 1938; W.W. Müller, *Ancient castles mentioned in the eighth volume of al-Hamdānī's Iklīl and evidence of them in pre-Islamic inscriptions*, in *Al-Hamdānī, a great Yemeni scholar. Studies on the occasion of his millennial anniversary*, Ṣanʿāʾ 1986, 139-57.

(W.W. MÜLLER)

AL-**ṢALĪB** (A.) pls. *ṣulub, ṣulbān*, a cross, and, particularly, the object of Christian veneration. The term is used for cross-shaped marks e.g. brands on camels and designs woven into cloth, and in legal contexts for the instrument of execution.

The Ḳurʾān refers in six places to the act of crucifying as a punishment. Four of these are set in ancient Egypt: in sūra XII, 41, Yūsuf predicts that one of the men jailed with him will be crucified and birds will eat from his head; in VII, 124, XX, 71, and XXVI, 49, Pharaoh vows to crucify the magicians who have disobeyed him by believing in Mūsā's God, with XX, 71, including the detail that he will use trunks of palm trees in doing this. In fact, according to Ibn ʿAbbās (al-Ṭabarī, *Tafsīr, ad* VII, 124), Pharaoh was the first to employ this means of execution.

The fifth occurrence, in V, 33, refers to crucifixion as the punishment for those who fight against God and the Prophet and spread evil in the land. This verse gave rise to the different views of legal experts concerning the execution of highway robbers: Mālik and Abū Ḥanīfa said they should be hung on a cross, tree or poles and torn apart with spears; while Ibn Ḥanbal said their bodies should be exposed on one of these after their execution [see ḤADD; ḲATL. ii; SALB; SARIḲA].

This verse is also the legal basis for the penalty against those guilty of heresy, *zandaḳa* [*q.v.*]; the crucifixion of al-Ḥusayn b. Manṣūr al-Hallā<u>d</u>j [*q.v.*] for his uninhibited ecstatic utterances is a well-documented example (L. Massignon, *La passion de Husayn Ibn Mansūr al-Hallāj*, nouvelle édition, Paris 1975, i, 496 ff., 655 ff.).

The sixth occurrence in IV, 157, the denial that the Jews crucified ʿĪsā [see ʿĪSĀ. xi], agrees well with the attitude implied in these verses, that execution is reserved for the disobedient and criminal. This denial occasioned a long tradition of Muslim exegetical elucidations (see N. Robinson, *Christ in Islam and Christianity*, London 1991, 127-41) and may have contributed towards the lack of interest in the atonement among Muslim polemical authors.

The rejection of the cross as the symbol of Christianity is attested in a number of *Ḥadīths*: on the last day, ʿĪsā will break the cross into pieces (al-Bu<u>kh</u>ārī, *Anbiyāʾ*, *bāb* 49, etc.; Ibn Ḥanbal, *Musnad*, ii, 240, 272, etc.); at the final judgement Christians, "the companions of the cross", will be condemned to hell on their confession that they worshipped ʿĪsā (al-Bu<u>kh</u>ārī, *Tawḥīd, bāb* 24); the cross is the sign of the Rūm [*q.v.*], the enemies of Islam (Ibn Ḥanbal, *Musnad*, iv, 91, v, 372, v, 409); the Prophet had objects bearing cross designs removed from his dwelling (al-Bu<u>kh</u>ārī, *Ṣalāt, bāb* 15; Ibn Ḥanbal, *Musnad*, vi, 52, 140, 237, etc., all reported on the authority of ʿĀʾi<u>sh</u>a). Restrictions were imposed upon public display of crosses from early times. According to Abū Yūsuf the Ḥanafī lawyer, Abū ʿUbayda Ibn al-<u>D</u>jarrāḥ [*q.v.*], acting on the advice of the caliph ʿUmar, permitted Christians in Syria to carry their crosses in procession on one day a year, but only outside towns and away from Muslim habitations and mosques (*Kitāb al-<u>Kh</u>arā<u>d</u>j*, Cairo 1397/1976-7, 152, tr. E. Fagnan, *Le livre de l'impôt foncier*, Paris 1921, 218-19); <u>Kh</u>ālid b. al-Walīd imposed the same limitation upon the Christians of Ḥīra and neighbouring towns (*ibid.*, 154, 158, tr. Fagnan, 222, 227).

Crosses in public places caused obvious offence. In Palestine, ʿUmar found it necessary to place crosses under protection, stipulating that in Jerusalem, Lydda and other towns they would not be violated (al-Ṭabarī, i, 2405 ff.). ʿAbd al-Malik and other Umayyad caliphs ordered their destruction on the outside of churches (see A. Fattal, *Le statut légal des non-Musulmans en pays d'Islam*, Beirut 1958, 183), and, on their imitations of Byzantine coins, had the symbol of the cross on the reverse subtly altered into a pillar by removing the bar (see W.E. Kaegi, *Byzantium and the early Islamic conquests*, Cambridge 1992, 223-7 and Pls. I-II at 207-8). The ʿAbbāsid caliph al-Mutawakkil forbade their display in processions (al-Ṭabarī, iii, 1390). Under later caliphs, Christians continued to exercise their restricted rights on feast days except when repression prevented them (Fattal, 207 ff.). It is not surprising that crosses were the immediate targets of religious riots in Muslim cities, or that at the time of the Crusades they were erected on mosques by invading Europeans and removed by Muslims. Curiously, the Fāṭimid caliph al-Ḥākim incorporated into his decrees against non-Muslims the requirement that Christians should wear crosses as distinctive signs [see AL-ḤĀKIM BI-AMR ALLĀH and its bibl.].

Many of these prohibitions against Christians were based on the precedent of the so-called "Covenant of ʿUmar", a formulation of the <u>*dh*</u>*immī* status which though of uncertain date reflects the attitudes of early centuries (Fattal, 60 ff. discusses views concerning its origin). According to the earliest version of this document, Christians agree not to display their crosses on streets and markets frequented by Muslims (al-Ṭurṭū<u>sh</u>ī, *Sirā<u>d</u>j al-mulūk*, Cairo 1289/1872, 135 ff.).

The cross and its significance does not feature prominently in Muslim polemical literature, which focusses rather on the two themes which challenged Muslim sensibilities, the Trinity and divinity of Jesus Christ, with no interest in doctrines of the atonement. In the early 3rd/9th century the Zaydī imām al-Ḳāsim b. Ibrāhīm al-Rassī explains the crucifixion briefly as a ransom to God (I. di Matteo, *Confutazione contro i Cristiani dello Zaydito al-Qāsim b. Ibrāhīm*, in *RSO*, ix [1922] 317) but does not discuss it further; while later in the same century, the independently-minded Muʿtazilī Abū ʿĪsā al-Warrāḳ [*q.v.*], whose refutation of Christianity is the most elaborate to survive from the early period, gives a concise description (D

Thomas, *Anti-Christian polemic in early Islam*, Cambridge 1992, 68-9, 72-7), but only mentions the crucifixion incidentally in the course of demonstrating the inadequacies of explanations of the Incarnation (see E. Platti (ed. and tr.), *Abū ʿĪsā al-Warrāq, Yaḥyā Ibn ʿAdī, de l'incarnation,* Louvain 1987 (CSCO, 490-1) e.g. §§ 63 ff.). Later polemicists follow Abū ʿĪsā's example and often refer to the crucifixion only in the course of questioning whether the divine character in Christ could suffer death (e.g. al-Nās̲h̲iʾ al-Akbar [*q.v.*], in J. van Ess, *Frühe muʿtazilitische Häresiographie*, Beirut 1971, 83-4; al-Bāḳillānī, *Kitāb al-Tamhīd*, ed. R. McCarthy, Beirut 1957, 97-8; Ibn Taymiyya, *al-D̲j̲awāb al-ṣaḥīḥ li-man baddala dīn al-Masīḥ*, Cairo 1905, iii, 42 ff.).

Two exceptions to this indifferent attitude are ʿAbd al-D̲j̲abbār b. Aḥmad and Ibn Ḥazm [*q.vv.*], who each attempt to show that the crucifixion need not have involved the person of ʿĪsā, and so could have happened in conformity with the understood teaching of sūra IV, 157-8. Ibn Ḥazm argues that the witnesses to the events of the crucifixion are not necessarily reliable (*K. al-Fiṣal fi 'l-milal wa 'l-ahwāʾ wa 'l-niḥal*, Cairo 1317, i, 58 ff.), while ʿAbd al-D̲j̲abbār employs a previously unknown account of the Passion, in which the individual crucified is not explicitly identified as Jesus, as the factual basis for his argument that ʿĪsā was not killed on the cross (*K. Tat̲h̲bīt dalāʾil al-nubuwwa*, ed. ʿA.-K. ʿUt̲h̲mān, Beirut 1966, 137 ff.; see S.M. Stern, *Quotations from apocryphal gospels in ʿAbd al-Jabbār*, in *Journal of Theological Studies*, N.S. xviii [1967], 34-57).

Attempts were made by Christians who wrote in Arabic to explain the significance of the crucifixion, but with little if any success (see M. Swanson, *The Cross of Christ in the earliest Arabic Melkite apologies*, in *Christian Arabic apologetics during the Abbasid period*, ed. J. Nielsen and K. Samir, Leiden 1994, 115-45, and the bibliography cited there). In more recent times, Christian teaching about the cross has received close attention from some Muslims, notably K. Hussein, *Ḳarya ẓālima*, Cairo 1954, tr. K. Cragg, *City of Wrong*, Amsterdam 1959 [see ʿĪsā. xv], and M.M. Ayoub, *Towards an Islamic Christology. II. the death of Jesus, reality or delusion*, in *MW*, lxx (1980), 91-121.

It was popularly thought among Muslims that the cross was actually worshipped by Christians; the caliph al-Mahdī suggests this in the course of his dialogue with the Nestorian patriarch Timothy I, which took place some time after 164/781 (see A. Mingana, *Timothy's apology for Christianity*, in *Woodbrooke Studies*, ii [1928], 39-40); the correspondence attributed to the caliph ʿUmar b. ʿAbd al-ʿAzīz and the emperor Leo III, though probably late 3rd/9th century, includes a discussion of it (see D. Sourdel, *Un pamphlet musulman anonyme d'époque ʿabbāside contre les Chrétiens*, in *REI*, xxxiv [1966], 29; see more fully, J.M. Gaudeul, *The correspondence between Leo and Umar: ʿUmar's letter re-discovered?*, in *Islamochristiana*, x [1984], 109-57); ʿAbd Allāh al-Hās̲h̲imī, the supposed opponent of ʿAbd al-Masīḥ al-Kindī [*q.v.*] mentions it among the practices he invites the Christian to renounce (*Risālat al-Kindī*, ed. A. Tien, London 1880, 1); it arises in the course of the reported debate between Christians and Muslims before al-Maʾmūn (see A. Guillaume, *A debate between Christian and Moslem doctors, Centenary Supplement to JRAS*, London 1924, 242; Swanson, *art. cit.*, 120-1, discusses dating).

Christians habitually defended the veneration of the cross (see A.-T. Khoury, *Apologétique byzantine contre l'Islam (VIIIe-XIIIe S.)*, Altenberge 1982, 121 ff.). And it is no surprise that the 3rd/9th century Christian apologist Abū Rāʾiṭa found it necessary to insist that the cross was not itself the object of worship but marked the direction of worship (see S. Griffith, *Ḥabīb ibn Ḫidmah Abū Rāʾiṭah, a Christian* mutakallim *of the first Abbāsid century*, in *Oriens Christianus*, lxiv [1980], 200), or that Arab lexicographers came to call the cross the *ḳibla* of the Christians.

Bibliography: A.S. Tritton, *The caliphs and their non-Muslim subjects*, Oxford 1930 (esp. ch. 7); H. Zayat, *La croix dans l'Islam*, Harissa 1935; C.E. Bosworth, *The concept of dhimma in early Islam*, in B. Braude and B. Lewis (eds.), *Christians and Jews in the Ottoman empire*, New York 1982, i, 37-51; S.H. Griffith, *Chapter ten of the* Scholion: *Theodore bar Kōnī's Apology for Christianity*, in *Orientalia Christiana Periodica*, xlvii [1981] 149-88; idem, *Theodore Abū Qurrah's Arabic tract on the Christian practice of venerating images*, in *JAOS*, cv [1985] 53-73; R.S. Humphreys, *Islamic history, a framework for inquiry*, London 1991, ch. 11.

(A.J. Wensinck-[D. Thomas])

SALĪḤ, an Arab tribe that the genealogists affiliate with the large tribal group, Ḳuḍāʿa [*q.v.*]. Around A.D. 400, it entered the Byzantine political orbit and became the dominant federate ally of Byzantium in the 5th century, its *foederati*.

It is practically certain that Salīḥ penetrated the Byzantine frontier from the region of Wādī Sirḥān. Ptolemy in his *Geography* speaks of a toponym, Ζαγμαΐς, in northern Arabia, identifiable with the Arabic Salīḥid name, Ḍud̲j̲ʿum/Ḍad̲j̲ʿum, and one of the affluents of Wādī Sirḥān is called Ḥidrid̲j̲/Ḥidrad̲j̲, also identifiable with another Salīḥid figure, al-Ḥidrid̲j̲ān. Precisely where in Byzantine Oriens/Bilād al-S̲h̲ām they settled as *foederati* is not known, but it was in the southern half of it, mainly in the *provincia* Arabia, and in the two Palestines, Secunda and Tertia.

Within federate tribal Salīḥ, the Ḍad̲j̲āʿima (pl. of Ḍad̲j̲ʿum) were the royal house. The eponym Ḍud̲j̲ʿum/Dad̲j̲ʿum is attested in the Greek source, Sozomen, as Ζόκομος, the tribal chief who converted to Christianity after a monk cured his wife of her sterility. Most of the historical figures among the Ḍad̲j̲āʿima/Zokomids, mentioned by the genealogists, are shadowy figures with the exception of two: Dāwūd and Ziyād, both with the same patronymic, Ibn al-Habūla. The first was the Salīḥid king whose name is associated with Dayr Dāwūd. Tradition says that his involvement in Christianity and the religious life weakened his warlike spirit and he was finally killed in the Gōlān in an encounter with a tribal coalition that formed against him. The second, Ziyād, is best known as the Salīḥid figure who fought the Kinda under the leadership of their king Ḥud̲j̲r, but was vanquished by them at the battle of Yawm al-Baradān (see below).

As the principal *foederati* of Byzantium in the 5th century, their main assignment was the protection of the Roman frontier facing the Arabian Peninsula from the raids of the pastoralists, the Saracens [*q.v.*] of the Greek and Latin sources. Legally, they were not Roman citizens but allies, whose relationship with Rome-Byzantium was governed by the *foedus*, the treaty. In return for their services as watchmen over the frontier, they were granted the privilege of settling on Roman territory and received the usual subsidies, either in money or in kind. Their chiefs were called phylarchs, and the term became technical in the Byzantine military system, meaning Arab chiefs in treaty relationship to Byzantium. In addition to protecting the Roman frontier, they took part in the two Persian Wars of the reign of Theodosius II, in 421-2 and 440-2, and possibly in the Vandal War of the Emperor Leo, who in 468 dispatched an expeditionary force against the Vandals of Africa. The Byzantines lost the battle of Cape Bon against the Vandals, and the Salīḥids probably lost heavily in that battle, which thus must have contributed to their eventual downfall in the Orient. Participation in the Persian and Vandal Wars relieves Salīḥid history of its marginality in fighting only the pastoralists of the Arabian Peninsula.

The conversion of their eponym, Ḍudj̲ᶜum/Zokomos, to Christianity set the tone of their involvement in religion, especially monastic Christianity. The one structure that is definitely associated with them is a monastery, Dayr Dāwūd, in present-day al-Turkumāniyya in northern Syria. It was built by the Salīḥid King Dāwūd, whose name, David, speaks for itself. He was nicknamed al-Lat̲h̲iḳ "the bedraggled" because he insisted on carrying water and mortar on his own back while building his monastery, as an act of piety.

More is known about their important contribution to poetry in Bilād al-S̲h̲ām in the 5th century. While Epinician odes were composed in Arabic for the victories of the Arab Queen Mavia over the Byzantine Emperor Valens, the poets of these victory odes have remained anonymous. But in the case of the Salīḥids, their court poet is known by name, ᶜAbd al-ᶜĀṣ, of the tribe of Iyād, who became the court poet of the Salīḥid king Dāwūd. The poet-laureateship of ᶜAbd al-ᶜĀṣ makes certain that the tradition of court poetry in Bilād al-S̲h̲ām started some hundred years before it was attested for the G̲h̲assānids, the Arab allies of Byzantium in the 6th century. Attractive is the fact that not only did Dāwūd have a court poet but also that he had a daughter, left anonymous in the sources who, too, was a poetess. Of her poetry, one solitary verse has survived in which she laments the death of her father Dāwūd at the hands of two tribesmen. The verse is redolent of contempt for the two "wolves" who killed the king of Salīḥ and the two regicides are not left anonymous: Ibn ᶜĀmir and Mas̲h̲dj̲aᶜa, from the tribes of Kalb and al-Namir respectively. The Yawm, the battle day, on which Dāwūd fell apparently occasioned the composition of some poetry, since a triplet has survived composed by one of the two regicides in which he prides himself and his tribe on their dispatch of Dāwūd, while the verse of his daughter, the Salīḥid princess, suggests that it was an answer to the triplet, perhaps belonging to a flyting poem.

Around A.D. 500, the star of the Salīḥids began to set, as more powerful tribal groups were approaching the Roman *limes*, Kinda and Ghassān [*q.vv.*]. They first vanquished the Salīḥids under the leadership of Ziyād b. al-Hābula at Yawm al-Baradān, but it was the latter that finally overturned them and superseded them as the dominant *foederati* of Byzantium in the 6th century, and thereby hangs a tale. The Salīḥid tax-collector, Sabīṭ, refused the sword of the G̲h̲assānid D̲j̲idh̲ᶜas pawn, whereupon the G̲h̲assānid unsheathed his sword and cut off Sabīṭ's head, a circumstance that gave rise to the saying "Take from D̲j̲idh̲ᶜ what D̲j̲idh̲ᶜ chooses to give you", *k̲h̲ud̲h̲ min D̲j̲idh̲ᶜⁱⁿ mā aᶜṭāka*.

Throughout this century, the Salīḥids lived in partial eclipse outshone by the G̲h̲assānids, who dominated the scene of Arab-Byzantine relations. But one of their phylarchs, who had the same name as the eponym, Ζώγυμος appears in 586 in the Byzantine army, fighting the Persians at the siege of Mārdīn, after the suspension of the G̲h̲assānid phylarchate for some five years in the eighties of the 6th century. The Salīḥids clearly remained federates of Byzantium, since they appear in the period of the conquest of Bilād al-S̲h̲ām, fighting the Muslim Arabs with other federate tribes at Dūmat al-D̲j̲andal and in Zīzāʾ in Trans-Jordan. After being worsted in the southern part of Oriens by the Muslim armies, they apparently moved to the north of Syria where ᶜAbu ᶜUbayda found them with the Tanūk̲h̲ in the *ḥād̲ir* (military encampment) of Ḳinnasrīn. When asked to accept Islam, they refused conversion and remained Christians.

Unlike the Tanūk̲h̲ and the G̲h̲assānids, these *foederati* of the 5th century did not prosper in Islamic times, presumably because they remained staunchly Christian and, so, isolated within the new Islamic order, with the exception of one Salīḥid, namely, Usāma b. Zayd. This scion of the old tribe served four Umayyad caliphs: al-Walīd and Sulaymān, who put him over the *k̲h̲arād̲j̲* of Egypt, and Yazīd b. ᶜAbd al-Malik and His̲h̲ām, whose *kātib* Usāma was.

In addition to political and social obscurity in the Muslim period, the Salīḥids were dispersed physically in various parts of the Fertile Crescent and in Egypt. They are represented in the 20th century best in Trans-Jordan, where traces of them have survived in a village called al-Salīḥī, which lies some 20 km/1[illegible] miles to the northwest of ᶜAmmān, in a spring called ᶜAyn al-Salīḥī, and in a valley called Wādī al-Salīḥī. And not far from these toponyms still live the al-Salīḥāt (Sleiḥat), almost certainly, because of the rarity of the name, the descendants of the ancient Salīḥids.

Bibliography: 1. Greek sources. Ptolemy, *Geography*, ed. C. Müller (Paris) I.pt.2. 1016; Sozomen, *Historia Ecclesiastica*, ed. J. Bidez, *GCS*, l, Berlin 1887, 299-300; Theophylact Simocatta, *Historiae* (Teubner), ed. C. de Boor and P. Wirth, Stuttgart 1972, 72-73.

2. Arabic sources. A. Manuscripts. His̲h̲ām b. al-Kalbī, *K. al-Nasab al-kabīr*, B.L., Add. 22376, fols. 21a, 80a, 91a, 91b; *K. Muk̲h̲taṣar al-d̲j̲amhara*, Yehuda Collection, Princeton, 2864; fols. 155b, 165a, 165b. B. Printed works. Muhammad b. Ḥabib, *al-Muḥabbar*, ed. I. Lichtenstädter, Ḥaydarābād 1942, 370-1; Ṭabarī, *Taʾrīk̲h̲*, ed. M. Ibrāhīm, iii, 378, 382; Balād̲h̲urī, *Futūḥ*, ed. Ṣ. Munad̲j̲d̲j̲id, Cairo 1956, i, 172; Masᶜūdī, *Tanbīh*, ed. A. al-Ṣāwī, Cairo 1938, 279; Yaᶜḳūbī, *Tāʾrīk̲h̲*, i, 204-7; Ibn al-At̲h̲īr, i, 506-11; Ibn Ḥazm, *D̲j̲amharat ansāb al-ᶜArab*, ed. ᶜA. Hārūn, Cairo 1962, 450; Ibn Durayd, *al-Is̲h̲tiḳāḳ*, ed. ᶜA. Hārūn, Cairo 1958, 545.

3. Modern literature. A. Musil, *Arabia Deserta*, New York 1927, 307; F.G. Peake, *History and tribes of Jordan*, Miami 1958, 166; Irfan Shahîd, *The last days of Salīḥ*, in *Arabica*, v (1958), 145-58; idem, *Byzantium and the Arabs in the fifth century*, Dumbarton Oaks, Washington, D.C. 1989, index *s.v.* Salīḥids.

(Irfān S̲h̲ahîd)

ṢĀLIḤ (A.), an adjective generally meaning "righteous", "virtuous", "incorrupt", used in the science of *ḥadīt̲h̲* [*q.v.*] criticism as a technical term indicating a transmitter who, although otherwise praised for his upright conduct, is known to have brought into circulation one or more traditions spuriously ascribed to the Prophet Muḥammad. It is the contents of such traditions, as well as their underlying meaning, that characterise their recognized inventor as *ṣāliḥ* rather than as *waḍḍāᶜ*, i.e. "forger", or *kad̲h̲d̲h̲āb*, "liar". Transmitters labelled *ṣāliḥ*, or its presumably slightly denigrating dimiutive *ṣuwayliḥ*, are those who are held responsible for certain traditions of an, on the whole, pleasing tenor, as long as they are harmless and do not give rise to confusion, *fitna* [*q.v.*], among the believers. Scores of *ṣāliḥ* transmitters are found in the lexicons of *ri*dj*āl* [*q.v.*] detailing the merits or demerits of *ḥadī*th transmitters. Not unfrequently they are at the same time accused of *ka*dh*ib*, i.e. "mendacity", for having fabricated traditions of a weightier substance, such as controversial ones dealing with *ḥalāl wa-ḥarām* [see SHARĪʿA] or others that are found ludicrous or otherwise objectionable, for example because of gross exaggeration. This accusation results in the qualifier *ka*dhdh*āb*.

In the *ri*dj*āl* dictionaries, numerous transmitters are assessed by means of strings of qualifications that seem at first glance mutually contradictory, such as the one attributed to ʿAbd al-Raḥmān b. Mahdī (d. 198/814) quoted in al-Khaṭīb al-Baghdādī's *Kifāya*, 22, - 6 f., where he describes someone's traditions as: ... *fīhi ḍuʿf wa-huwa ra*dj*ul ṣadūḳ fa-yaḳūlu ra*dj*ul ṣāliḥ al-ḥadī*th, or that of the *isnād* critic Yaʿḳūb b. Shayba (d. 262/876) depicting a transmitter as ... *ra*dj*ul ṣāliḥ ṣadūḳ* th*iḳa ḍaʿīf* dj*idd*an (cf. Ibn Ḥadjar, *Tah*dh*īb*, iii, 248). Examples of such strings of seemingly contradictory qualifications are legion and make it clear that *ṣāliḥ* and its near-equivalent *ṣadūḳ*, lit. "veracious", can be combined with *ḍuʿf* as well as th*iḳa*. This last-mentioned qualification, lit. "reliable person", is, like *ṣāliḥ* and *ṣadūḳ*, not to be taken at face value, for it is more often than not merely a non-committal term conveying, if anything, the ignorance of the user as to the true merits or demerits of the transmitter scrutinised. This can amply be substantiated in multi-volume th*iḳāt* collections, e.g. the *Kitāb al-*Th*iḳāt* of Ibn Ḥibbān al-Bustī (d. 354/965 [*q.v.*]), in which countless transmitters thus qualified are at the same time *ma*dj*hūl*, i.e. "anonymous".

Transmitters who are labelled *ṣāliḥ* are commonly described as overly pious through the observation of various, mostly supererogatory, ritual practices. Other, quasi-technical, terms for this class of transmitters are: *nāsik, ʿābid, zāhid*, and the like. Their godly behaviour, as well as the generally pleasing and edifying contents of the *ṣāliḥ* material transmitted by them, earns them the qualification *ṣāliḥ*. The contents of traditions deserving the label *ṣāliḥ*, rather than *mawḍūʿ*, "fabricated", "forged", can be summarised as falling under the headings of *tar*gh*īb wa-tarhīb*, "arousing desire and inspiring awe", *mawāʿiẓ*, "pious harangues", and *riḳāḳ* or *raḳāʾiḳ*, "subtle, elegant, ornate sayings". These tradition rubrics are replete with descriptions of the Day of Judgement, Heaven and Hell, the rewards or punishment therein, how to attain the one by performing salutary acts (*ṣāliḥāt*) and how, by eschewing crimes and sins, to avoid being cast into the other, as well as numerous traditions of a general nature, e.g. those listing human actions which are believed to be particularly pleasing to God, the so-called *faḍāʾil al-afʿāl* genre. Among this last genre all those traditions enumerating the rewards for people reciting a particular *sūra* of the Ḳurʾān are prominent. *Ṣāliḥ* traditions are moulded either in the form of prophetic dicta or implied in descriptions of the Prophet's alleged behaviour. Before the reputation of the early Islamic storyteller (*ḳāṣṣ* [*q.v.*]) worsened in the course of the second half of the 2nd/8th century, it was he who was often identified as purveyor of *ṣāliḥ* material. Although *ṣāliḥ* traditions can theoretically be found among those labelled *ṣaḥīḥ* [*q.v.*], the majority fall under the categories of *ḥasan* "fair" (a genuine euphemism for mostly poorly authenticated traditions) or *ḍaʿīf* "weak", traditions without any claim to reliability.

The acceptability of *ṣāliḥ* traditions from transmitters labelled *ṣāliḥ* varies with early *ḥadī*th experts. Mālik b. Anas (d. 179/795 [*q.v.*]) professed that he had no use for them (cf. al-Khaṭīb, *Kifāya*, 160) and, consequently, his *Muwaṭṭaʾ* is relatively free from them, but such collections as the *Musnad* of Aḥmad Ibn Ḥanbal (d. 241/856 [*q.v.*]) and also the Six Books are riddled with *ṣāliḥ* traditions, the latter especially in chapters entitled *zuhd, fitan, riḳāḳ, ṣifat al-*dj*anna, ṣifat al-nār, ādāb*, etc.

Throughout the centuries-long period of *ḥadī*th collecting, the gathering of *ṣāliḥ* traditions was widely encouraged, not, however, in order to distill from them juridical or doctrinal arguments (in Arabic, *li'l-iḥti*dj*ā*dj) but only for the sake of comparison or consideration (in Arabic, *li'l-iʿtibār*). This is the reason why Muslim tradition literature has preserved such masses of *ṣāliḥ* traditions. *Ṣāliḥ* traditions were even brought together in special collections, the one entitled *al-Tar*gh*īb wa 'l-tarhīb* by al-Mundhirī (d. 656/1258) being particularly popular (cf. Juynboll, *Muslim tradition*, 189-90).

To sum up, the statement attributed to the early Muslim *ḥadī*th expert Yaḥyā b. Saʿīd al-Ḳaṭṭān (d. 198/813) from Baṣra speaks volumes in the present context: "In nothing did we find *al-ṣāliḥūn* more mendacious (*ak*dh*ab*) than in (inventing) traditions" (cf. Muslim b. al-Ḥadjdjadj's introduction to his *Ṣaḥīḥ*, cited in *JSAI*, v [1984], 281). Furthermore, for Medina we have the assessment of the *faḳīh* Abu 'l-Zinād (d. 133/751) who is reported to have said (cf. al-Khaṭīb, *Kifāya*, 159): "In Medina I made the acquaintance of some hundred sh*ay*kh*s*, all of them th*iḳa*s, but their *ḥadī*th*s* should be well left alone." And the Kūfan Sufyān al-Thawrī (d. 161/778 [*q.v.*]) is recorded to have said (Ibn Radjab, 103), when confronted with the fact that, although wary, he did transmit traditions from Muḥammad b. al-Sāʾib al-Kalbī (d. 146/763 [see AL-KALBĪ, at IV, 495a]): "But I know his *ṣidḳ* from his *ka*dh*ib*!" Observations such as these three are indeed numerous in Muslim *ḥadī*th studies.

Bibliography: The most extensive early theoretical survey of different classes of *muḥaddi*th*ūn*, whose role in bringing spurious traditions into circulation was generally recognised, is that of Ibn Ḥibbān al-Bustī (d. 354/965), *Kitāb al-Ma*dj*rūḥīn*, Ḥaydarābād 1970, i, 48-74. Furthermore, Ibn Abī Ḥātim al-Rāzī, *Kitāb al-*Dj*arḥ wa 'l-taʿdīl*, Ḥaydarābād 1952, i/1, 37 f.; idem, *Taḳdimat al-maʿrifa li-kitāb al-*dj*arḥ wa 'l-taʿdīl*, Ḥaydarābād 1952, 10; al-Khaṭīb al-Baghdādī, *Kitāb al-kifāya fī ʿilm al-riwāya*, Ḥaydarābād 1357, 133-4, 158-61; Ibn Radjab, Sh*arḥ ʿilal al-Tirmi*dh*ī*, ed. Ṣubḥī Djāsir al-Ḥumayd, Baghdād 1396, 100-3, 113 ff.; Ibn al-Djawzī, *Kitāb al-Mawḍūʿāt*, ed. ʿAbd al-Raḥmān M. ʿUthmān, Cairo 1966-8, i, 39-42; Ibn al-Ṣalāḥ, *al-Muḳaddima* [*fī ʿilm al-ḥadī*th], ed. with *Maḥāsin al-iṣṭilāḥ* of Sirādj al-Dīn ʿUmar al-Bulḳīnī, by ʿĀʾisha ʿAbd al-Raḥmān Bint al-Shāṭiʾ, Cairo 1974, 104, 212-15; Nawawī, *Taḳrīb*, tr. W. Marçais (using the term "fraudes pieuses" for traditions of *ṣāliḥūn*) in *JA*, 9e séries, xvii (1901), 121-5; Djalāl al-Dīn al-Suyūṭī, *Tadrīb al-rāwī fī* sh*arḥ taḳrīb al-Nawawī*, ed. ʿAbd al-Wahhāb ʿAbd al-Laṭīf, Cairo 1966, i, 274-90. For the contemporary Muslim view, see e.g. Nūr al-Dīn ʿItr, *Manha*dj *al-naḳd fī ʿulūm al-ḥadī*th, Damascus 1972, 254, 284-5; idem, *Muʿ*dj*am al-muṣṭalaḥāt al-ḥadī*th*iyya*, Damascus 1977, 55; Ṣubḥī al-Ṣāliḥ, *ʿUlūm al-ḥadī*th *wa-muṣṭalaḥuhu*, Damascus 1959, 289-90. For a survey of *ṣāliḥ* against the background of other technical *ḥadīth* terms, see G.H.A. Juynboll, *Muslim tradition. Studies in chronology, provenance and authorship of early* ḥadīth, Cambridge 1983, 184-90. (G.H.A. JUYNBOLL)

ṢĀLIḤ, a prophet who, according to the Ḳurʾān, was sent to the people <u>Th</u>amūd [*q.v.*]. He is mentioned by name nine times in the Ḳurʾān, with the fullest versions of the story being told in VII, 73-9, XI, 61-8, XXVI, 141-59, and XXVII, 45-53; nineteen additional references to <u>Th</u>amūd by name, including extensive passages in LIV, 23-32 and XCI, 11-5, provide parallel accounts and specific details without mentioning the name Ṣāliḥ.

The story of Ṣāliḥ follows the standard Ḳurʾānic pattern of commission, mission, rejection and punishment (see ḲURʾĀN. 6.d; J. Wansbrough, *Quranic studies*, Oxford 1977, 21-5). Sent as a "sign" and a "warning", the prophet demanded that his people turn to him and pray to God alone, from whom they had received blessings. The people rejected Ṣāliḥ abruptly, calling him "bewitched" (*musaḥḥar*), a man like themselves, one whose claim to revelation was false; they would not give up the religion of their fathers and they doubted the idea of a day of judgement.

The focal point and distinctive element of the story of Ṣāliḥ comes in the account of the camel (*nāḳa*) sent as a "sign" (*āya*, VII, 73, XI, 64, XXVI, 154), "test" (*fitna*, LIV, 27) or "proof" (*mubṣira*, XVII, 59) by God. Ṣāliḥ told his people that the camel must be left alone to feed unharmed and drink unhindered. However, the people (or one person according to LIV, 29) hamstrung it and killed it. They then contemptuously asked Ṣāliḥ to bring about the punishment which he had threatened. He told them to stay in their houses for three days; then a storm broke out (LI, 44, LXIX, 5), perhaps an earthquake (VII, 78), and on the following morning they lay dead in their houses.

<u>Th</u>amūd, as a name of a historical people, is known from other sources, and thus the story of Ṣāliḥ is often thought to have a basis in history. The dwellings which the <u>Th</u>amūdic people had hewn out of the rocks according to the Ḳurʾān (VII, 74, XXVI, 149, LXXXIX, 9), the remains of which were still visible (XXIX, 38), are connected in folk-lore with the tombs at al-Ḥidjr [*q.v.*] = Madāʾin Ṣāliḥ, but this connection is unclear, these rock tombs are, in fact, essentially Nabataean [see NABAṬ], although the tomb inscription of Raḳā<u>sh</u>i bt. ʿAbd al-Manāt is written in Nabataean, with strong Arabic influence, and in Thamudic.

Muslim legend developed the story of Ṣāliḥ in its typical manner, providing stories of miraculous occurrences during his conception and birth, and his being called to prophethood at the age of forty. He was given a genealogy which traced him back to Noah through Shem, probably because of the frequent association of Noah and <u>Th</u>amūd in the Ḳurʾān (e.g. XIV, 9, "Has the story not reached you of those who were before you, the people of Noah, ʿĀd and <u>Th</u>amūd and those after them?"; also IX, 70, XXII, 42, XXV, 37-8, XL, 31, L, 12) who are linked thematically through the total destruction of their respective communities. Likewise, the period in which Ṣāliḥ lived was pictured as preceeding that of Abraham and coming after Hūd, because of the way the stories were structured sequentially in Ḳurʾān, VII, 65-84, for example. Muslims were aware that no Biblical prophet could be identified with Ṣāliḥ, but it was claimed that prophets such as Ṣāliḥ and Hūd were just as famous among the Arabs as were Abraham and his descendants.

The name itself Ṣāliḥ may well be a formation from the time of Muḥammad himself, from the root *ṣ-l-ḥ* with the connotation of "to be pious, upright". Its only appearance in pre-Islamic North Arabian may be in the form *Ṣ.l.ḥ* (vowelling unknown) twice attested in Safaitic [*q.v.*] inscriptions (F.V. Winnett and G. Lankester Harding, *Inscriptions from fifty Safaitic cairns*, Toronto 1978, nos. 2048, 2095; it is also found very occasionally in Sabaic and Ḥaḍramī), and it was clearly a very rare name, not attested in e.g. Nabataean, Palmyrene or Hatran. The story of the camel cannot be conclusively connected with any known past story either, although J.M. Rodwell, in his Ḳurʾān translation, suggested in it a possible reminiscence of the story of the milch-camel of al-Basūs [*q.v.*], the killing of which sparked off the famous pre-Islamic war in Arabia (*The Koran*, London 1909, 300-1).

Bibliography: Masʿūdī, *Murūd̲j̲*, iii, 83-90 = §§ 929-35; the *Tafsīr* tradition, esp. on sūra VII, 73-9; Ṭabarī, i, 244-52, Eng. tr. W.M. Brinner, *Prophets and patriarchs*, Albany 1987, 40-7; Kisāʾī, *Ḳiṣaṣ al-anbiyāʾ*, ed. J. Eisenberg, Leiden 1922, 110-17, Eng. tr. W.M. Thackston, *The tales of the prophets*, Boston 1978, 117-28; J. Halévy, *Le prophète Ṣāliḥ*, in *JA*, v (1905), 146-50; J. Horovitz, *Koranische Untersuchungen*, Berlin 1926, 94, 123; H. Speyer, *Die biblischen Erzählungen im Qoran*, Gräfenhainichen 1931, 118-19; A. van den Branden, *Histoire de Thamoud*, Beirut 1960; R. Bell, *A commentary on the Qurʾān*, 2 vols., Manchester 1991, i, 239-40.

(A. RIPPIN)

ṢĀLIḤ B. ʿABD AL-ḲUDDŪS b. ʿAbd Allāh b. ʿAbd al-Ḳuddūs al-Baṣrī, Abu 'l-Faḍl, a famous poet of the 2nd/8th century, and one of the first victims of the official inquisition inaugurated by the ʿAbbāsid Caliph al-Mahdī, died in 167/783. In this year Ba<u>sh</u><u>sh</u>ār b. Burd [*q.v.*] and Ṣāliḥ were accused of *zandaḳa* [*q.v.*] and executed.

References to Ṣāliḥ's poetry abound in the literature, but little concrete detail is known about his life. He was a *mawlā* of Asad or al-Azd. His father ʿAbd al-Ḳuddūs, son of a convert, probably of Persian origin, is supposed to have composed poems. He himself seems to have been a secretary to al-Manṣūr and a colleague of Ibn al-Muḳaffaʿ. Some traditions make him a *ḳāṣṣ* in Baṣra. He lived to become old, and according to one of his poems, he became blind.

His fame is due above all to the extensive use of gnomic expressions in his poems. He refers to an old book (Persian?) from which he borrowed his *ḥikam* or didactic sentences. A *Kitāb al-<u>Sh</u>ukūk* is attributed to him, perhaps to enhance the possibility that he was a sceptic. A study of his surviving poems shows that his title *ṣāḥib al-falsafa*—others call him *mutakallim*—is akin to truth, though no trace of *zandaḳa* or dualist thinking is visible in them. They leave no anti-Islamic impression, making his alleged death as a heretic suspicious. He considered poverty as worse than unbelief, and a life without external influence worthless. It is better to die, he says, than being a person for whose help no hope is harboured when something happens and for whose kindness and benefactions one has no hope. He was a moralist and publicised his ideas on religion through the medium of wise sayings, viewing religion as moral teaching, not as a rational or juristic system. Goldziher conjectured this as the reason behind Ṣāliḥ's inclusion among the *zindīḳs*.

Bibliography: Cheikho, in *Ma<u>sh</u>riḳ*, xxii (1924), 819 ff.; Goldziher, *Ṣāliḥ b. ʿAbd al-Ḳuddūs und das Zindīḳthum während der Regierung des Chaliphen al-Mahdī*, in *Transactions of the 9th Intern. Congr. of Orientalists*, London 1892, ii, 104-29; J. van Ess, *Die*

Hinrichtung des Ṣāliḥ b. ʿAbdalquddūs, in *Studien zur Geschichte und Kultur des Vorderen Orients. Festschrift für Bertold Spuler zum siebzigsten Geburtstag*, ed. H.R. Roemer und A. Noth, Leiden 1981, 53-66; idem, *Theologie und Gesellschaft im 2. und 3. Jahrhundert Hidschra. Eine Geschichte des religiösen Denkens im frühen Islam*, 6 vols., Berlin and New York 1991-, ii, 15-20; idem, *Theorie und Anekdote*, in *ZDMG*, cxxxv (1984), 22-30. Most of the surviving material on Ṣāliḥ has been collected and uncritically put together by ʿAbd Allāh Khaṭīb in *Ṣāliḥ b. ʿAbdalḳuddūs al-Baṣrī*, Baṣra 1967.

(Mohsen Zakeri)

ṢĀLIḤ b. **ʿALĪ** b. ʿAbd Allāh b. al-ʿAbbās, member of the ʿAbbāsid family (92-152/711-69) who played an important part in the success of the ʿAbbāsid revolution in Syria, assisting his brother ʿAbd Allāh in the assault on Damascus and, with Abū ʿAwn ʿAbd al-Malik b. Yazīd al-ʿAtakī leading the pursuit of the last Umayyad caliph, Marwān b. Muḥammad to Egypt.

He was appointed governor of Egypt on 1 Muḥarram, 133/9 August 750 and remained there for a year, establishing ʿAbbāsid power. On 1 Shaʿbān 1, 133/4 March 751 he was moved to Palestine and in the same year sent Saʿīd b. ʿAbd Allāh to lead the first *ṣāʾifa* [*q.v.*] or summer raid of ʿAbbāsid times against the Byzantines. After another short spell as governor of Egypt (5 Rabīʿ II 136/8 October/753 to 4 Ramaḍān 137/21 February 755), he spent the rest of his career in Syria and Palestine and on the Byzantine frontier. He seems to have enjoyed the confidence of his great-nephews, the caliphs al-Saffāḥ and al-Manṣūr, and, after the rebellion of his brother ʿAbd Allāh in 137/754, which he shrewdly refused to support, he was the senior ʿAbbāsid in Syria. He took over most of the Umayyad properties in the area, including the famed Dār al-Ṣabbāghīn at Ramla, at Aleppo and Salamiya, where his family were still living in al-Balādhurī's time. He played an important role in strengthening the defences of the Byzantine frontier with the rebuilding of Malaṭya, Marʿash and al-Maṣṣīṣa. He died in Syria in 152/769, but his sons al-Faḍl and ʿAbd al-Malik remained powerful in Syria until the end of al-Rashīd's reign.

Bibliography: Ṭabarī, iii; Yaʿḳūbī, *Taʾrīkh*; Kindī, *Kitāb al-Wulāt*, ed. Guest; Balādhurī, *Futūḥ*; Ibn al-ʿAdīm, *Zubdat al-Ḥalab*, ed. Dahhān, Damascus 1951; H. Kennedy, *The early ʿAbbasid Caliphate*, London 1981.

(A. Grohmann-[H. Kennedy])

ṢĀLIḤ b. **MIRDĀS** [see mirdās, banū].

ṢĀLIḤ b. **ṬARĪF**, a personage mentioned for the first time in the 4th/10th century in the text of Ibn Ḥawḳal, *Ṣurāt al-arḍ*, as having lived 200 years before and having been the alleged prophet of the Barghawāta, a Berber confederation of the Maṣmūda group, installed in the region of Tasmana, between Salé and Azemmour in Morocco.

Ṣāliḥ's father, Ṭarīf b. Shamaʿūn b. Yaʿḳūb b. Isḥāḳ, perhaps of Jewish origin, had been a companion of Maysara al-Matgharī, who had led a rising in 122/740 in northern Morocco at the time of the Khāridjite revolt; Ṭarīf was then recognised as the chief of the Tamasna tribe. His son Ṣāliḥ succeeded him *ca.* 131/748-9. According to the narrative of the "Great Prayer Leader", *ṣāḥib ṣalātihim*, Abū Ṣāliḥ Zammūr al-Barghawāṭī, sent as an ambassador to Cordova in 352/963, whom al-Bakrī (*Masālik*, mid-5th/11th century) mentions, Ṣāliḥ had taken part in the wars led by Maysara together with his father, and then is said to have taught his people a religious doctrine revealed to him and to have proclaimed himself a prophet. He is then said to have left for the East, instructing his son al-Yasaʿ/Ilyasaʿ, who succeeded in *ca.* 178/794-5, to keep this new religion secret. He himself would return in the time of his seventh successor. According to several sources, Ṣāliḥ allegedly lived, like his son also, as a good Muslim, and it was his grandson, Yūnus, who proclaimed that his grandfather was a prophet, Ṣāliḥ al-Muʾminīn, and to have proclaimed publicly the secret doctrine, with a Ḳurʾān in Berber. There are various obscurities regarding Ṣāliḥ b. Ṭarīf. Did he really leave for the East, or was it just Yūnus who took the road, as Ibn ʿIdhārī (*Bayān*, i) seems to assert, together with another tradition given by al-Bakrī? Yūnus allegedly invented, for his own purposes, by declaring himself a prophet, this new "Berber" religion suffused with Ṣufrī Khāridjism, by attributing it to his grandfather, who was supposed to have charged him with the task of revealing it; this latter explanation seems more plausible.

Bibliography: Ibn Ḥawḳal, tr. Kramers and Wiet; Bakrī, ed. and tr. de Slane; Ibn ʿIdhārī, *Bayān*, ed. Colin and Lévi-Provençal, Leiden 1948-51; M. Talbi, *Hérésie, acculturation et nationalisme des Berbères Bargawāta*, in *Actes du premier congrès d'études des cultures méditerranéennes d'influence arabo-berbère*, Algiers 1973, 217-33; Mbarek Redjala, *Les Barghwāta (origine de leur nom)*, in *ROMM*, n. 35 (1983), 115-25. See also the *Bibl.* to barghawāta.

(Chantal de La Veronne)

ṢĀLIḤ b. **YAḤYĀ** b. Ṣāliḥ b. Ḥusayn b. Khaḍir (d. 839/1436), *amīr* of the Druze family of the Banū Buḥtur whose family divided up, amongst brothers and cousins, the coastal region and mountain of the Shūf in present-day Lebanon, the area lying between Beirut and Sidon, with its chef-lieu as the little town of ʿAbay, from the 5th/11th century to the end of the 9th/15th one.

Ṣāliḥ b. Yaḥyā is above all known for having written a history of his family, published for the first time, from the B.N. unicum (fonds arabe 1670), in the journal *al-Machriq* (1898-9), and then issued in book form at Beirut by the Imprimerie Catholique in 1902 and 1928. A new edition, taking into account the critical remarks of J. Sauvaget (*BEO*, vii-viii [1937-8], 65-81) and respecting better the text's integralness, also preserving its dialectical style, has been published by F. Hours S.J. and Kamal Salibi as *Tārīḫ Bayrūt. Récits des anciens de la famille de Buḥtur b. ʿAlī, émir du Gharb de Beyrouth*, Beirut 1969 (Coll. Recherches, Dar el-Machreq).

Written in a distinctly unclassical language, it begins with topographical and historico-archaeological aspects of the town of Beirut, and then passes, for the greater part of the work, to the complete chronicle of members of the family, from the ancestor Buḥtur (6th/12th century) up to the author's own time, setting forth its subject in three chronological divisions (*ṭabaḳāt*), the third one revolving round Nāṣir al-Dīn al-Ḥusayn (d. 751/1350), the author's great-grandfather and most remarkable of the *amīrs* of the Gharb.

The work's considerable interest lies in the fact that it is one of the rare documents which allow us to penetrate within the daily life of a small rural fiefdom, administratively attached to Damascus in Ayyūbid and Mamlūk times. It gives, by means of personalised accounts and archival documents, a very lively idea of the life of the peoples living to the south of Beirut and their relations with *inter alios* the Mamlūk occupiers.

The Druze historian Ḥamza b. Aḥmad b. ʿUmar b.

Ṣāliḥ, called Ibn Asbāṭ al-Gharbī (d. 926/1520) made use of Ṣāliḥ b. Yaḥyā's text in his *Taʾrīkh*, and this was in turn made use of by the *amīr* Ḥaydar al-Shihābī (d. 1250/1835) in his *al-Ghurar al-ḥisān fī taʾrīkh ḥawādith al-zamān* (éd. Naʿīm Mughabghab, Cairo 1900).

Bibliography: Given in the article, to which should be added Brockelmann, II, 36 and II², 47, and Ziriklī, *Aʿlām*, ii, 276, iii, 198.

(L. POUZET)

AL-MALIK AL-**ṢĀLIḤ**, the regnal title of four Mamlūk sultans:

1. ʿImād al-Dīn Ismāʿīl, *regn.* 743-46/1342-45;
2. Ṣalāḥ al-Dīn Ṣāliḥ, *regn.* 752-55/1351-54;
3. Ṣalāḥ al-Dīn Ḥadjdjī, *regn.* 783-84/1381-82, 791-92/1389-90; and
4. Nāṣir al-Dīn Muḥammad b. al-Ẓāhir Ṭaṭar, *regn.* 824-5/1421-2.

1. AL-ṢĀLIḤ ʿIMĀD AL-DĪN ISMĀʿĪL, son of al-Nāṣir Muḥammad b. Ḳalāwūn [*q.v.*], was raised to the sultanate by his father's senior *amīrs* on 22 Muḥarram 743/28 June 1342 to succeed his brother al-Malik al-Nāṣir Aḥmad who had absconded, with all the royal treasures, to al-Karak. When, upon al-Nāṣir Muḥammad's death, none of the *amīrs* proved powerful enough to go it alone, they resorted to factional coalitions enabling two or more of them to rule jointly in the name of the Ḳalāwūnī sultan. Al-Ṣāliḥ Ismāʿīl's rule was upheld first by Arghūn al-ʿAlāʾī, his step-father, and Āḳsunḳur al-Salārī, who held the offices of *raʾs nawba* and *nāʾib al-salṭana* respectively. With Āḳsunḳur's subsequent elimination, Arghūn al-ʿAlāʾī held the reins of power while al-Ḥādjdj Āl Malik became *nāʾib al-salṭana*.

As the Ḳalāwūnī sultans' rule was nominal only, the *amīrs* never cut off, and even encouraged their connections with the harem which al-Nāṣir Muḥammad had left behind. Before long, the influence the harem exerted was enormous. During Ismāʿīl's reign e.g. the involvement in government affairs of harem women and servants increased to such extent that *iḳṭāʿāt* and land allowances could be obtained only through them. Owing to the influence of the chief eunuch, ʿAnbar al-Sakhartī, who had been Ismāʿīl's tutor, servants and eunuchs attained a status of such importance that they freely appropriated Mamlūk ways, while Al-Sakhartī surrounded himself with the ceremonial usually reserved for senior *amīrs*. Servants and eunuchs, moreover, were involved in an abortive attempt in 744/1343 of a group of *amīrs* to re-install Aḥmad in the sultanate. For all his piety and modesty, Ismāʿīl soon indulged himself in the pleasures of the harem and married Ittifāḳ, a slave-girl singer, lavishing on her expensive gifts from the royal treasures. Soon the sultan's household expenditures (*ḥawāʾidj-khāna*) exceeded his father's already extravagant practices. Even when in Muḥarram 745/May 1344 the sultanate was beset by a deep economic crisis (an annual budget deficit standing at 30 million *dirhams* with revenues at only 15 million *dirhams*), mere cosmetic measures were taken to diminish expenditure.

A particularly heavy burden on the treasury during Ismāʿīl's rule were the costly campaigns of the ruling *amīrs* against Aḥmad, still entrenched at al-Karak—after seven abortive campaigns they were forced to borrow money from merchants to finance a final attempt. Even then the city fell only when the Bedouin who had sided with Aḥmad deserted him for the reward of *iḳṭāʿāt* and lands. Aḥmad was subsequently executed (745/1344). Taking advantage of the government's obvious weakness, the Bedouin both in Egypt and Syria revolted. The rivalry between the Āl Muhannā and the Āl Faḍl over the leadership of the Bedouin in Syria on behalf of the government, *imrat al-ʿarab*, erupted into an open conflict. Other tribes in Syria, *al-ʿashīr*, soon took the law into their own hands. Internecine wars between the Bedouin tribes of Lower and Upper Egypt disrupted travel on the roads, damaged the irrigation system and prevented officials from levying taxes in their districts; expeditions despatched to subdue the Bedouin proved inadequate.

To this chaotic situation, the market reacted with increasing inflation and sharp monetary devaluation. Some relief came when in 745/1345 al-Ṣāliḥ Ismāʿīl granted the Venetians commercial privileges. Thereafter, Europeans were increasingly offered such commercial concessions as the revenues for the government from taxation on foreign trade offset the dwindling revenues from agriculture and local commerce. That commercial ties between the Mamlūk sultanate and Europe could be renewed stemmed from changes outside the sultanate. The Papal trade embargo against the sultanate which had been in force since the fall of Acre in 690/1291 was revoked because of pressure exerted by the European trading powers, who wanted to shift their trade back to the Levant after political changes hampered trade in the Black Sea region. After only a short reign, al-Ṣāliḥ Ismāʿīl died in Rabīʿ I 746/July 1345, from illness. Anxious to remain in power, Arghūn al-ʿAlāʾī, through a will Ismāʿīl had made under his guidance, guaranteed the succession of Shaʿbān [*q.v.*], Ismāʿīl's brother.

Bibliography: Maḳrīzī, *K. al-Sulūk*, i/3, Cairo 1939, 619-80; idem, *K. al-Muḳaffā*, ii, Beirut 1991, 66-9; Shams al-Dīn al-Shudjāʿī, *Taʾrīkh al-Malik al-Nāṣir Muḥammad*, i, Wiesbaden 1977, 230-77; Ibn Taghrī Birdī, *Nudjūm*, x, Cairo 1963, 78-98; idem, *Manhal*, ii, Cairo 1984, 425-27; R. Irwin, *The Middle East in the Middle Ages*, London 1986, 125-51; D. Ayalon, *The eunuchs in the Mamluk Sultanate*, in idem, *The Mamluk military society*, London 1979.

2. AL-ṢĀLIḤ ṢALĀḤ AL-DĪN ṢĀLIḤ (lived 738-61/1337-60) was the son of al-Nāṣir Muḥammad b. Ḳalāwūn [*q.v.*] by Ḳutlūmalik, the daughter of the *amīr* Tankiz al-Ḥusāmī, al-Nāṣir's *nāʾib* in Syria. Al-Ṣāliḥ was installed on the throne on 28 Djumādā II 752/2 August 1351 after the senior *amīrs* of his father's Mamlūk household who held power at the time had deposed his brother al-Nāṣir Ḥasan [*q.v.*]. Four days later, an open power struggle broke out between them and a triumvirate, of *Amīrs* Shaykhū (or Shaykhūn), Ṣarghatmush and Ṭāz, came out victorious. Wanting to avoid concentration of power in one hand, the three carefully separated control over the treasury from that over the army. Thus Shaykhū held the sultan's treasury (*al-khāṣṣ*) while Ṣarghatmush was responsible for the distribution of *iḳṭāʿ*s and the Mamlūks' promotion in the army. Suspicions, however, simmered and in Rabīʿ I 753/May-June 1352 Ṭāz accused Ṣarghatmush of attempting to restore al-Nāṣir Ḥasan. Later in Radjab/October, disgruntled erstwhile associates such as Baybughā Urūs, the *nāʾib* of Ḥamāt, his brother Mandjak al-Yūsufī and others, led an abortive coup in Syria. The rebels, together with Turkman and Bedouin tribes, looted Damascus and its suburbs before the Mamlūk army, nominally commanded by al-Ṣāliḥ Ṣāliḥ, defeated them. When Shaykhū and Ṣarghatmush learned that Ṭāz was plotting against them with al-Ṣāliḥ Ṣāliḥ, they did away with him, and on 2 Shawwāl 755/20 October 1354, deposed al-Ṣāliḥ Ṣāliḥ and restored al-Nāṣir Ḥasan to the throne.

With the ruling *amīrs* preoccupied with power

struggles, the Bedouin who had been under the patronage of al-Nāṣir Muḥammad and had accumulated power during his rule and after his death, took the law into their own hands. Internecine wars between the Āl Muhannā and Āl Faḍl over the *imrat al-ᶜarab* again rendered highways in Syria unsafe, compelling the government in 753/1352 to award the *imra* to both of them jointly. As in 752/1351, Upper Egypt was under the *de facto* control of Muḥammad b. Wāṣil al-Aḥdab, chief of the ᶜArak tribe. Attacks on the Bedouin throughout Egypt in 754/1353 ended a period of some fifteen years during which the country's resources had been consistently depleted by the destruction which the Bedouin wrought on commerce and agriculture and by the enormous government expenditure on efforts to contain them.

It was during al-Ṣāliḥ Ṣāliḥ's reign that the impact on the sultanate's economy of the Black Death, which had ravaged Egypt during 748-50/1347-9, became most obvious. The Mamlūk army was decimated, and *ḥalḳa* soldiers who had survived the epidemic were reduced to such miserable conditions that they resorted to leasing their *iḳṭāᶜāt* to civilians, which in turn led to the further decline of the army. Shortage in manpower caused large parts of the cultivated lands in Egypt to lie waste sharply reducing the treasury's revenues from agriculture. The state's deficit now reached such proportions that no one could be found willing to take responsibility for the treasury. Even the vizierate was an office no longer much desired. In order to reduce the deficit, the salaries of almost all officials in the sultan's household and governmental administration were cut down by half or two-thirds. The ruling *amīr*s further increased revenues by compelling the population to purchase products which the government owned or manufactured (*ṭarḥ*) or through the confiscation of property (*muṣādara* [*q.v.*]), notably of rich officials. In 755/1354 new attacks against Coptic scribes erupted throughout Egypt. Yielding to the rioting mob's demands, al-Ṣāliḥ Ṣāliḥ allowed them to destroy churches, while 25,000 *faddān*s of land belonging to the church as *awḳāf* were confiscated and redistributed mainly as *iḳṭāᶜāt* to Mamlūks. Under pressure from the *ᶜulamā*ᵓ and the masses, al-Ṣāliḥ Ṣāliḥ re-enacted the discriminating laws against the *dhimmī*s [*q.v.*] and decreed that no *dhimmī* could be employed anywhere in Egypt. With their church's source of revenues destroyed and the way for personal advancement blocked, the Copts reacted with massive waves of conversion to Islam, thereby hastening Egypt's religious transformation.

Bibliography: Maḳrīzī, *K. al-Sulūk*, ii/3, Cairo 1939, 843-930; Ibn Taghrī Birdī, *Nudjūm*, x, Cairo 1963, 254-87; idem, *Manhal*, vi, Cairo 1990, 330-3; Ibn Duḳmāḳ, *al-Djawhar al-thamīn*, Beirut 1985, 199-206; R. Irwin, *The Middle East in the Middle Ages*, London 1986, 125-51; D.P. Little, *Coptic conversion to Islam under the Bahri Mamluks*, in *BSOAS*, xxxix, 567-69.

3. AL-ṢĀLIḤ ṢALĀḤ AL-DĪN ḤĀDJDJĪ, son of al-Ashraf Shaᶜbān [*q.v.*] and great-grandson of al-Nāṣir Muḥammad b. Ḳalāwūn [*q.v.*], was placed on the throne at the age of ten, on 24 Ṣafar 783/21 May 1381, after the death of his brother, al-Manṣūr ᶜAlī. Since Rabīᶜ I 782/June 1380, the *amīr* Barḳūḳ al-ᶜUthmānī al-Yalbughāwī [*q.v.*] had become *atābak al-ᶜasākir* [*q.v.*], gaining the title of *amīr kabīr*, and was sultan in all but name. Barḳūḳ used his position to his advantage and bought large numbers of Mamlūks whom he lodged in Cairo's Citadel. Not having to rely on an alliance of *amīr*s, he freely bestowed amīrates upon his own Mamlūks and appointed trusted followers to key positions in government. Barḳūḳ's rule won such wide support that he became the first *amīr kabīr* to mint coins bearing his emblem, *rank* [*q.v.*], as sultans customarily did on their ascent to power. With his supremacy acknowledged, Barḳūḳ moved to bring Ḳalāwūnī rule to an end and, on 19 Ramaḍān 784/27 November 1382, deposed al-Ṣāliḥ Ḥādjdjī, a date conventionally considered as the beginning of the Circassian Mamlūk sultanate.

Symptoms of the decline of the Mamlūk economy, evident as early as the 1340s, were common during al-Ṣāliḥ Ḥādjdjī's brief reign. Decline in revenues pushed the government in 783-4/1381-2 to increase confiscation of office-holders' property and even of *awḳāf*. The outbreak of the plague in 783/1381 and a monetary crisis following Barḳūḳ's attempt to issue copper coins of heavy weight and rate to replace the silver *dirham* further worsened the economy.

Ḥādjdjī was briefly restored to the throne when in 6 Djumādā II 791/2 June 1389 Barḳūḳ's rivals, the *amīr*s Timurbughā al-Afḍalī, called Minṭāsh, and Yalbughā al-Nāṣirī, led a revolt against him and succeeded in temporarily exiling him from Egypt. According to one version, Ḥādjdjī was again put on the throne simply because he had been overthrown by Barḳūḳ. Ascending a second time, he took the regnal title of al-Malik al-Manṣūr (Ibn al-Furāt, ix, 94); but as with most Ḳalāwūnī princes, Ḥādjdjī was sultan in name only and his authority was severely restricted.

On 16 Shaᶜbān/10 August civil strife broke out between the two partners of the coalition behind Ḥādjdjī's rule. Minṭāsh came out the winner, and as *amīr kabīr* he became the real holder of power. Despite Minṭāsh's claim that with his struggle against Yalbughā he had, among other things, aimed at re-introducing independent sultanic rule, al-Manṣūr Ḥādjdjī was again put under harsh restrictions. His nominal reign came to an end when opposition to Minṭāsh's ruling faction lent its support to Barḳūḳ and thus enabled him to re-enter Cairo triumphantly on 14 Ṣafar 792/1 February 1390. Once again removed to confinement in the Citadel, al-Manṣūr Ḥādjdjī spent the last 22 years of his life in the harem. He died on 19 Shawwāl 814/4 February 1412.

Bibliography: Maḳrīzī, *K. al-Sulūk*, iii/2, Cairo 1939, 439-75, 620-703; Ibn Taghrī Birdī, *Nudjūm*, xi, Cairo 1963, 206-15, 309-81; idem, *Manhal*, v, Cairo 1988, 48-50; Ibn Ḥadjar al-ᶜAsḳalānī, *Inbā*ᵓ *al-ghumr bi-abnā*ᵓ *al-ᶜumr*, ii, Ḥaydarābād 1968, 45-92; Ibn al-Furāt, *Taᵓrīkh Ibn al-Furāt*, ix, Beirut 1936, 94-185.

4. AL-ṢĀLIḤ NĀṢIR AL-DĪN MUḤAMMAD B. AL-ẒĀHIR ṬAṬAR was the ten-year old son and ephemeral successor in 824/1421 of Sayf al-Dīn Ṭaṭar, but was himself replaced by al-Malik al-Ashraf Barsbay [*q.v.*] after a five-months' reign.

Bibliography: P.M. Holt, *The age of the Crusades. The Near East from the eleventh century to 1517*, London 1986, 184.

(AMALIA LEVANONI)

AL-MALIK AL-**ṢĀLIḤ ᶜIMĀD** AL-**DĪN** Ismāᶜīl b. al-Malik al-ᶜĀdil, an Ayyūbid prince, who was twice sultan of Damascus for short periods.

One of the many sons of al-ᶜĀdil Abū Bakr [*q.v.*], he was probably born just before *ca.* 600/1203-4, although no precise date has been recorded. His father assigned him Boṣrā and al-Sawād (the area east of Lake Tiberias) as an *iḳṭāᶜ*. He continued to hold these lands under his brother al-Muᶜaẓẓam ᶜĪsā [*q.v.*], although in 622/1225 he was brought to Damascus, temporarily under a cloud, because of his possible involvement in a plot by a local magnate, Ibn al-Kaᶜkī, to give him control of the city. After al-Muᶜaẓẓam's death in 624/1227 he maintained his position subject to al-Nāṣir Dāwūd [*q.v.*]. When Ismāʿīl's brothers al-Kāmil [*q.v.*] and al-Ashraf Mūsā, had jointly deprived al-Nāṣir of Damascus, Ismāʿīl was confirmed in his area of control in Radjab 626/May-June 1229. With other Ayyūbid princes, Ismāʿīl was in this same year sent by al-Kāmil to recover Ḥama for al-Muẓaffar Maḥmūd, and he commanded the *ʿaskar* of Damascus which gained Baalbek for al-Ashraf. Sibṭ Ibn al-Djawzī [see IBN AL-DJAWZĪ, ... SIBṬ] mentions Ismāʿīl as lieutenant of al-Ashraf Mūsa in Damascus in Ramaḍān 627/July-August 1231, and he took part in al-Kāmil's campaign against the Saldjūks of Rūm in 631/1233-4.

In Muḥarram 635/August 1237 he became ruler of Damascus after the death of al-Ashraf Mūsā, who had no sons and had designated Ismāʿīl as his successor. He also took over Baalbek, and was recognised as suzerain by al-Mudjāhid Shīrkūh of Ḥimṣ and by the ruler in Aleppo. In Djumāda II 635/February 1238 Ismāʿīl surrendered Damascus to the greater power of al-Kāmil, but was allowed to retain Baalbek and al-Biḳāʿ, Boṣrā and al-Sawād. However, al-Kāmil soon died (Radjab 635/March 1238), and in complicated circumstances Ismāʿīl seized Damascus in Ṣafar 637/September 1239 (for these and subsequent events, see AL-ṢĀLIḤ NADJM AL-DĪN AYYŪB). To attempt to maintain his position against al-Ṣāliḥ Ayyūb, now sultan of Egypt, Ismāʿīl sought many alliances, with Aleppo, with al-Nāṣir Dāwūd in Transjordan, with the Saldjūḳ sultan of Rūm (dirhams struck in 640/1242-3 name Kaykhusraw II as overlord), with elements of the Khʷārazmiyya, and with the Franks, to whom he was willing to surrender Jerusalem and other conquests of Ṣalāḥ al-Dīn such as Sidon and Beaufort, but not without arousing strong religious opposition. An attempted peace settlement with Ayyūb in 641/1243-4 (Damascus dirhams of this year name him as overlord) almost immediately broke down through lack of trust, probably justified.

The next year Ismāʿīl formed a Syrian coalition, including the Franks, which was defeated by the Egyptian army and Ayyūb's Khʷārazmian mercenaries between Gaza and Ascalon (Djumāda I 642/October 1244). Damascus was besieged and surrendered to Ayyūb's forces in Djumada I 643/October 1245. Later in 644/1246 Baalbek and Boṣrā were also taken from Ismāʿīl. He himself fled to Aleppo, whose ruler al-Nāṣir Yūsuf [*q.v.*] gave him protection and refused to hand him over to Ayyūb.

After the murder of al-Muʿaẓẓam Tūrānshāh [*q.v.*] and the tentative establishment of the Mamluk régime in Egypt, Ismāʿīl took part in the expedition which planned to restore Ayyūbid control there. Led by al-Nāṣir Yūsuf, the Syrian Ayyūbids were defeated at Kurāʿ in Dhu 'l-Ḳaʿda 648/February 1251. Ismāʿīl was one of many princes captured. After a short confinement in the Citadel at Cairo, on the eve of Sunday 27 Dhu 'l-Ḳaʿda/19 February he was taken out towards the Ḳarāfa Cemetery, strangled and buried unceremoniously.

Bibliography: For the primary sources, see the article AL-ṢĀLIḤ NADJM AL-DĪN AYYŪB. The fullest account of the period is in R.S. Humphreys, *From Saladin to the Mongols: the Ayyubids of Damascus, 1193-1260*, Albany 1977 (see the bibl. cited therein). For epigraphic references, see *RCEA*, xi, nos. 4054, 4155, 4186, 4197, 4246(?), 4247, and for the numismatic evidence, P. Balog, *The coinage of the Ayyubids*, London 1980, 242-8.

(D.S. RICHARDS)

AL-MALIK AL-**ṢĀLIḤ ISMĀʿĪL** B. BADR AL-DĪN LUʾLUʾ, Rukn al-Dīn, ephemeral ruler in Mawṣil [*q.v.*] after his father. Luʾluʾ [*q.v.*] had submitted to the Mongols, and Ismāʿīl, his eldest son, had journeyed to the Great Khān's ordo at Ḳaraḳorum in order to give his father's homage. When Luʾluʾ died in 657/1258, Ismāʿīl succeeded him, but now switched sides and opposed the Mongols. He joined forces with the Mamlūk Baybars [*q.v.*], but was killed, together with his young son, when the Mongols captured and sacked Mawṣil, so that the brief line of the Luʾluʾid Atabegs came to an end.

Bibliography: M. van Berchem, *Monuments et inscriptions de l'atabek Luʾluʾ de Mossoul*, in *Orientalische Studien ... Th. Nöldeke gewidmet*, Giessen 1906, i, 198, with the sources detailed in n. 3; R.S. Humphreys, *From Saladin to the Mongols, the Ayyubids of Damascus, 1193-1260*, Albany 1977, 468 nn. 55, 56. See also the *Bibl.* to LUʾLUʾ, BADR AL-DĪN.

(ED.)

AL-MALIK AL-**ṢĀLIḤ NADJM** AL-**DĪN AYYŪB** b. al-Kāmil Muḥammad, the last major sultan of the Ayyūbids [*q.v.*], born in Cairo in 603/1206-7 and died Shaʿbān 647/November 1249. Much of his life was spent in struggling for the paramount position which his father, al-Malik al-Kāmil [*q.v.*], had held, but he achieved it only at the end of his life and without re-establishing the dynasty's cohesion and cooperation. He was the creator of the Baḥriyya *mamlūk* corps which played a leading role in the formation of the succeeding régime.

As the eldest son, he was groomed for the succession and in Shaʿbān 625/August 1228 was proclaimed joint-sultan with the title al-Malik al-Ṣāliḥ and left as *nāʾib* in Egypt, with Fakhr al-Dīn b. Shaykh al-Shuyūkh as his adviser. He lost al-Kāmil's favour (aspirations to independence and the purchase of a 1000-strong *mamlūk* following are mentioned) and in 627/1229-30 he was sent to the Djazīra with no command or governorship, while his younger brother, al-ʿĀdil II [*q.v.*], replaced him as heir-apparent. In 630/1232-3 al-Kāmil gave him Ḥiṣn Kayfā and its dependencies. After lands lost to the Saldjūḳs of Rūm in 631-2/1233-5 were recovered early in 633/1236, Ayyūb was established as "independent sultan" in Āmid, Ḥarrān, Edessa, Nisibis, Khābūr, etc. As early as 634/1237 Ayyūb enrolled elements of the Khʷārazm-Shāh Djalāl al-Dīn's [*q.v.*] freebooting army and soon had experience of their unreliability and their mercenariness when in conflict with Badr al-Dīn Luʾluʾ [*q.v.*].

His opportunity to re-enter the mainstream of Ayyūbid politics occurred after the death of al-Kāmil (in Radjab 635/March 1238) when a cousin, al-Djawād Yūnus, conscious of the weakness of his position in Damascus, proposed an exchange of lands. Ayyūb arrived to take over Damascus in Djumāda II 636/January 1239, leaving his son, Tūrānshāh [*q.v.*], to rule in Ḥiṣn Kayfā. He planned an invasion of Egypt to unseat al-ʿĀdil II, whose counter moves were weakened by desertions of troops and plots in favour of Ayyūb. Al-Nāṣir Dāwūd [*q.v.*] proposed joint action with Ayyūb to win Egypt, but only if he himself were immediately given the former lands of his father al-Muʿaẓẓam ʿĪsā [*q.v.*], including Damascus. Unsuccessful in this, al-Nāṣir joined al-ʿĀdil in Egypt, again hoping to gain Damascus. Ayyūb moved to Nābulus (Shawwāl 636/May 1239) and there awaited the concentration of his Syrian allies. A peace settlement brokered by the caliph's envoys was all but agreed, when al-Ṣāliḥ Ismāʿīl [*q.v.*] and al-Mudjāhid Shīrkūh of Ḥimṣ, who had been treacherously delaying their assistance, descended on an undefended Damascus.

They entered the city on 26 Ṣafar 637/27 September 1239 and imprisoned Ayyūb's son, al-Mughīth ʿUmar. Deserted by most of his troops, Ayyūb was taken to al-Karak by al-Nāṣir Dāwūd, already dissatisfied with his alliance with al-ʿĀdil, and held there for six months (from Rabīʿ I to Ramaḍān 637/October 1239-April 1240). Although both al-ʿĀdil and Ismāʿīl demanded the person of Ayyūb, al-Nāṣir released him on the basis of promises that Ayyūb later claimed were forced, and they planned joint action. As both al-ʿĀdil and Ismāʿīl moved to crush Ayyūb between them, in Dhu 'l-Ḳaʿda 637/May-June 1240 al-ʿĀdil was deposed at Bilbays by his emirs who then invited Ayyūb to become sultan in Egypt.

Ayyūb entered the Cairo citadel on Sunday 25 Dhu 'l-Ḳaʿda 637/17 June 1240. Material for the internal affairs of Egypt in this period is exceedingly sparse and little is known about his government. For the next few years, he strengthened his position by purging the Egyptian army, increasing and promoting his own *mamlūk*s, and building a fortified residence for himself and the so-called Baḥriyya [*q.v.*] on the island of Rawḍa [*q.v.*] (work began Shaʿbān 638/February 1241).

A general Ayyūbid settlement, again at the expense of al-Nāṣir, was all but concluded in 641/1243. Ismāʿīl in Damascus recognised Ayyūb as suzerain (in Rabīʿ I/September), and was to release al-Mughīth ʿUmar. However, intercepted letters to Ayyūb's Khwārazmian allies and general lack of trust once more brought about a collapse. Al-Mughīth died in prison (Rabīʿ I 642/August 1244) and Ismāʿīl was suspected of his murder. Ayyūb was subsequently faced by an alliance of Syrian princes and Franks, the latter recruited by significant concessions of land. In response Ayyūb's troops, joined by the Khwārazmiyya, inflicted a major defeat on the Syrian coalition at the village of La Forbie or Farbiyā (Yāḳūt, iii, s.v.) between Ascalon and Gaza (12 Djumāda I 642/17 October 1244). Damascus was besieged, and surrendered in Djumāda I 643/October 1245. To Ayyūb's fury in Egypt, the terms made allowed Ismāʿīl his other possessions, but he then joined the Khwārazmiyya, who had changed sides, to attack Damascus. However, the power of the Khwārazmiyya was broken in Muḥarram 644/May 1246 by the armies of Aleppo and Ḥimṣ, part of a new grouping formed to curtail their depredations. Ayyūb's forces then took the rest of Ismāʿīl's lands, and Ayyūb himself, now at the peak of his power, came to Damascus in Dhu 'l-Ḳaʿda 644/March 1247 to organise his new possessions. Ismāʿīl had taken refuge with al-Nāṣir Yūsuf [*q.v.*] at Aleppo.

During 645-6/1247-9 there were gains from the Franks (Ascalon and Tiberias), arrests of former associates of Ismāʿīl, including the lord of Ṣalkhad ʿIzz al-Dīn Aybak, and anxieties about Aleppo's intentions. In 646/1248 al-Nāṣir Yūsuf took Ḥimṣ, but caliphal envoys, as ever worried by the Mongol threat, made a peace and both sides retired. Ayyūb's last success was to acquire al-Karak and the remnants of al-Nāṣir Dāwūd's principality in Djumāda II 647/September 1249.

In Muḥarram 647/April 1249 Ayyūb had returned to Egypt, carried in a litter as he was ill, and troubled by news of the crusade of Louis IX. After the early loss of Damietta (Ṣafar/June), a total collapse threatened to follow Ayyūb's death at the age of 49. This took place in camp at al-Manṣūra on the eve of Sunday, 14 Shaʿbān 647/21 November 1249. Shadjar al-Durr [*q.v.*] and the senior *amīr*s tried to conceal his death and managed affairs while summoning Tūrānshāh, for whom Ayyūb had written his political testament (see Cl. Cahen and I. Chabbouh, *Le testament d'al-Malik aṣ-Ṣāliḥ Ayyūb*, in *BÉt.Or.*, xxix, 97-114). The nature of Ayyūb's fatal complaint has been discussed by F. Klein-Franke (*What was the fatal disease of Al-Malik al-Ṣāliḥ ...*, in *Studies in Islamic history and civilization in honour of Professor David Ayalon*, ed. M. Sharon, Jerusalem 1986, 153-7).

Ibn Wāṣil [*q.v.*] gives a penetrating pen-portrait, stressing Ayyūb's mixture of forbidding authority and diffident and introspective solitariness. He was taciturn and clean-living. Unlike his father, he had no special taste for reading and scholarship. Even his hours of relaxation with his few special companions, in his *madjlis al-sharāb*, were sombre and undemonstrative.

Building was a passion. In addition to the residence on Rawḍa Island, he built palaces on the Nile bank at al-Lūḳ, the pavilions known as *Manāẓir al-Kabsh* (see M.G. Salmon, *Études sur la topographie du Caire*, in *MIFAO*, Cairo 1902, vii/2, 77-95), and the new town development, called after him al-Ṣāliḥiyya. Very important was the *madrasa* which he founded in Bayn al-Ḳaṣrayn for the four orthodox *madhāhib*. Site clearing started in Dhu 'l-Ḥidjdja 639/June 1242 and teaching began in 641/1243-4 (al-Maḳrīzī, *Khiṭaṭ*, ii, 374). His mausoleum near the *madrasa*, to which his corpse was transferred in Radjab 648/October 1250 (idem, *al-Sulūk*, i/2, 371), was restored in 1993 by the German Archaeological Institute in Cairo, which is now (1994) working on the surviving *īwān* of the *madrasa*.

Bibliography: The contemporary narrative sources are Ibn Wāṣil, *Mufarridj al-kurūb fī akhbār dawlat Banī Ayyūb*, ed. H.M. Rabie and S. ʿAshur, iv-v, Cairo 1972-7, and for post-645/1248, Paris, B.N. mss. 1702-3; Sibṭ Ibn al-Djawzī, *Mirʾāt al-zamān*, facs. ed. J.R. Jewett, Chicago 1907, and ed. Ḥaydarābād 1952, viii/2; Abū Shāma, *Dhayl ʿalā kitāb al-rawḍatayn*, ed. M. al-Kawthari, Cairo 1947. See also the standard later chronicles. The fullest account of this period is R.S. Humphreys, *From Saladin to the Mongols: the Ayyubids of Damascus, 1193-1260*, Albany 1977 (see the sources and bibl. cited therein). For epigraphic references, see *RCEA*, xi, nos. 4136, 4198, 4217-20 (*madrasa*), 4223, 4278, 4282, 4298-4301 (mausoleum), 4302-3, 4305, and for the numismatic evidence, P. Balog, *The coinage of the Ayyubids*, London 1980, 181-94. For the buildings of Ayyub, see K.A.C. Creswell, *The Muslim architecture of Egypt: II. Ayyubids and early Bahrite Mamluks, A.D. 1171-1326*, Oxford 1959, 84-7 (Rawḍa citadel and palace), 94-100 (*madrasa*), 100-3 (mausoleum). (D.S. RICHARDS)

AL-MALIK AL-**ṢĀLIḤ NŪR** AL-**DĪN** [see NŪR AL-DĪN MAḤMŪD B. ZANKĪ].

AL-MALIK AL-**ṢĀLIḤ SHAMS** AL-**DĪN** [see TŪRĀNSHĀH].

AL-**ṢĀLIḤIYYA**, the name of various places in the Middle East. These include:

1. A settlement of Diyār Muḍar in al-Djazīra, placed by Yāḳūt in the district of al-Ruhā [*q.v.*] or Edessa and said to have been laid out by the ʿAbbāsid governor of Syria ʿAbd al-Malik b. Ṣāliḥ. He also quotes a (now lost) history of Mawṣil by the Khālidiyyān[i] [*q.v.*] that the caliph al-Mahdī began the work of fortification there.

Bibliography: Yāḳūt, *Buldān*, ed. Beirut, iii, 389-90.

2. A settlement to the north of the old city of Damascus, on the slopes of Mount Ḳāsiyūn [*q.v.*]. Yāḳūt describes it as a large village with markets and

a Friday mosque, containing many saints' tombs and residences of holy men. Most of the inhabitants were immigrants from Jerusalem and were Ḥanbalī in *madhhab*. From the 6th/12th century, it became one of the strongholds of this school [see ḤANĀBILA, at III, 161]. It is now a well-to-do suburb of the modern conurbation of Damascus.

Bibliography: Yāḳūt, *Buldān*, ed. Beirut, iii, 390; Le Strange, *Palestine under the Moslems*, 529; Hachette World Guides, *The Middle East*, Paris 1966, 301. See also DIMASHḲ, at II, 283a.

(ED.)

ṢĀLIḤIYYA, a Ṣūfī *ṭarīḳa* [*q.v.*] from within the tradition established by the Moroccan Ṣūfī and teacher Aḥmad b. Idrīs (d. 1837 [*q.v.*]). The exact origin and, indeed, the reason for the name of the Ṣāliḥiyya is unclear. It appears to be an offshoot of the Rashīdiyya, the name given to *ṭarīḳa* founded by the Sudanese Ibrāhīm al-Rashīd al-Duwayḥī (d. 1874, [*q.v.* in Suppl.], a student of Ibn Idrīs. After his death in Mecca, Ibrāhīm al-Rashīd's *zāwiya* there was taken over by his nephew Shaykh b. Muḥammad b. Ṣāliḥ (d. 1919), who moved there from the Sudan. Sometime in about 1887, the Meccan-based branch became known as the Ṣāliḥiyya, while the Sudanese branch continued to be known as the Rashīdiyya. It is, in fact, very difficult to disentangle the various Ṣūfī traditions associated with the Rashīdiyya, Idrīsiyya, Ṣāliḥiyya and Dandarāwiyya [*q.v.* in Suppl.]. The Shaykh was succeeded as head of the order by his three sons in turn, al-Rashīd, Aḥmad and Ibrāhīm, the last of whom died in 1976.

The Ṣāliḥiyya was taken to Somalia and other regions of eastern Africa by pilgrims from the region who were initiated by the Shaykh or his sons in the Ḥidjāz. Communities (Somali, *jamaaᶜa*), dedicated to prayer and agriculture, were established throughout Somalia; by the 1930s, Cerulli estimated that there were 53 Ṣāliḥiyya *jamaaᶜas* there. These communities attracted ex-slaves or other marginal groups and opened up hitherto unutilised land.

The most famous Ṣāliḥiyya leader in Somalia, and his people's greatest poet, was Muḥammad b. ᶜAbd Allāh (Somali, Maḥammad ᶜAbdille) Ḥassān (1864-1920 [*q.v.*]), who was to lead the resistance to the Ethiopians, British and Italians for over two decades. Muḥammad was initiated by the Shaykh in Mecca in 1894. The following year he returned to Somalia and thereafter worked to spread the order, attacking the use of tobacco and the prevalence of saint-worship among his fellow countrymen. Four years later, in 1899, he began his *djihād* against imperialist encroachment.

Bibliography: E. Cerulli, *Somalia. Scritti vari editi ed inediti*, 3 vols., Rome 1957-64 (various articles); Said S. Samatar, *Oral poetry and Somali nationalism. The case of Sayyid Maḥammad ᶜAbdille Ḥasan*, Cambridge 1982. There is a brief manuscript *manāḳib* of Shaykh b. Muḥammad b. Ṣāliḥ in the I.M. Lewis Collection of Arabic materials from Somalia, the Library, London School of Economics and Political Science; R.S. O'Fahey, *Enigmatic saint. Aḥmad ibn Idrīs and the Idrīsī tradition*, London 1990; Ali Salih Karrar, *The Sufi brotherhoods in the Sudan*, London 1992.

(R.S. O'FAHEY)

AL-**ṢĀLIḤŪN** (A., pl. of *ṣāliḥ*) "the virtuous, upright ones", cited in the Ḳurʾān at VII, 168, XXI, 105 and LXXII, 11, and 30 other times as *ṣāliḥīn*.

The *ṣāliḥ* is associated by Ibn Taymiyya [*q.v.*] with the *ṣiddīḳs*, those asserting the truth, the *shahīds*, martyrs and the *abdāl*, substitutes, as all representing the *firḳa nādjiya*, the sect which alone will be saved out of the 73 into which, according to a *ḥadīth*, the *umma* or community will be divided (see H. Laoust, *La profession de foi de Ibn Baṭṭa*, Damascus 1958, 17 n.). This *ḥadīth* is to be set by the side of Ḳurʾān, LXXII, 11, "And that some of us are upright, and some of us not so; we have become [groups following] diverse ways".

Bibliography: Given in the article. (S. ORY)

SĀLIM (A.), intact, sound, i.e. free of damage or blemish, thus "well" as opposed to "ill," and therefore a synonym of *ṣaḥīḥ*. The word is used as a technical term in various fields: 1. Applied to money, *sālim* means unclipped coins of full weight, or a sum of money free from charges and deductions. 2. In grammar, it denotes two things: in *ṣarf* (morphology) a "sound" root, i.e., one in which none of the radicals is a "weak" letter (*ḥarf ᶜilla*, see ḤURŪF AL-HIDJĀʾ), nor a *hamza*, nor a geminate; in *naḥw* (syntax) a word with a "sound" ending, no matter whether the preceding radicals are weak or not. Thus the root *n-ṣ-r* is *sālim*, while the root *r-m-y* is not, both for the *ṣarfiyyūn* and the *naḥwiyyūn*; however, *b-y-ᶜ* is *sālim* only for the *naḥwiyyūn*, whereas *islanḳā* is *sālim* only for the *ṣarfiyyūn*, the latter because the root is *s-l-ḳ*, thus sound, and only the ending *-ā*, which is part of the pattern *ifᶜanlā* is "weak" (al-Sharīf al-Djurdjānī, *al-Taᶜrīfāt*, ed. ᶜAbd al-Raḥmān ᶜUmayra, Beirut 1408/1987, 154 [read *islanḳā* for *istalḳā*]).—The term *sālim* is also used to denote the "sound" plural (*al-djamᶜ al-sālim*) as opposed to the "broken" plural (*al-djamᶜ al-mukassar*) [see DJAMᶜ]. 3. In prosody, the term denotes a regular foot, which has not undergone any of the changes called *ziḥāfāt* or *ᶜilal* [see ᶜARŪḌ], or a line of poetry consisting of such feet. It is, therefore, particularly common in Persian prosody, where *ziḥāfāt* may not change from one line to the next as they do in Arabic. The lines will thus be *sālim* throughout the whole poem.

Bibliography: Tahānawī, *Kashshāf iṣṭilāḥāt al-funūn*, ed. A. Sprenger *et alii*, Calcutta 1862, i, 695-6; Khᵂārazmī, *Mafātīḥ al-ᶜulūm*, ed. G. van Vloten, Leiden 1895, 87 (prosody); L.P. Elwell-Sutton, *The Persian metres*, Cambridge 1976, index.

(W. BJÖRKMAN-[W.P. HEINRICHS])

SĀLIM, nom-de-plume (*makhlaṣ*) of Mirzā-zāde Meḥmed Emīn (1099-1156/1688-1743), an Ottoman author of a published biography of poets, a *dīwān*, several texts dealing with war, grammar and mysticism, a dictionary and an Ottoman translation of a Persian history, all of which are in manuscript form. Many of the details concerning his life are to be found in an autobiography included in his *tedhkire-yi shuᶜarāʾ* which is the work that qualifies him for inclusion in this encyclopaedia.

The seventh child of Shaykh al-Islām Mirzā Muṣṭafā Efendi, Sālim was born in Istanbul in Djumādā II 1099/June 1688. His father's professional pursuits became his own: he had a career in the *ᶜilmiyye* class in which the highest rank he reached was that of *ḳāḍī ᶜasker* of Rumeli. There is some disagreement on the date of his death. While all sources that mention it cite the month of Muḥarrem, some give the year as 1152/1739 and others as 1156/1743. The place where it occurred is also debated; it could have been either in Istanbul where he was buried near his father, or in Mafraḳ outside Damascus, (see Rāmiz, *Tedhkire-yi shuᶜarāʾ*, ms. Millet Kütüphanesi: Ali Emiri, Tarih, no. 762, fol. 135; Thüreyyā, iii, 3; Müstaḳīmzāde, 454).

In his autobiography (*Tedhkire-yi Sālim*, ms., B.L. Or. 7068, fols. 95a-97a; *ibid.*, ed. Aḥmed Djewdet, 337-44), Sālim provides rather detailed information about his own life, education and career up to the year

1133/1720. He began his studies when he was about seven years old with Yeñi-Bāgh̲čeli Čelebi Efendi who, later, handed him over to tutors whom he personally selected for his young charge. Sālim was also coached by his father in all the accepted studies of his time, but received special training in the *Ḥadīth̲* from a certain Muḥammad b. Salām al-Iskandarānī. Sālim continues to describe his climb up the ladder of the Ottoman learned hierarchy by informing his readers that under the aegis of Pas̲h̲maḳd̲j̲īzāde al-Seyyid ʿAlī Efendi he became *mülāzim* to Abū Saʿīd-zāde Feyḍullāh Efendi in 1104/1692. Two years later he was appointed *mudarris* at the *madrasa* of Siyāwus̲h̲ Pas̲h̲a in Eyyūb, and then served in the same capacity in other *madrasas* until, in the year 1125/1713, he reached the *Dār al-Ḥadīth̲* at the Süleymāniyye. Before the end of that year, he was given his first assignment as *ḳāḍī* of Salonika. He was back in Istanbul in 1126/1714 as *ḳāḍī* of G̲h̲alaṭa. Upon his dismissal from this post he was sent into exile. He and his father, who was then S̲h̲ayk̲h̲ al-Islām, spent the next few years in Trabzon. When they were pardoned, they took up residence in their sea-side home in Istanbul. In 1134/1721, Sālim completed his *tedhkire* and presented it to the Grand Vizier of the time, Dāmād Ibrāhīm Pas̲h̲a (?1073-1143/1662-1730) in the same year. He was, in fact, emulating a contemporary and rival biographer of poets, Ṣafāʾī (d. 1138/1725), who had done the same thing two years earlier and whose work Sālim evaluated rather negatively (Sālim, 429-30, 250, 262). Ibrāhīm Pas̲h̲a must have appreciated the *ted̲h̲kire* since he thanked its author by appointing him *ḳāḍī* of Istanbul the following year. A decade after, Sālim became *ḳāḍī ʿasker* of Anadolu and two years after that *ḳāḍī ʿasker* of Rumeli, but he never became S̲h̲ayk̲h̲ al-Islām like his father.

Mirzā-zāde Meḥmed Emīn's principal contribution to the Ottoman literary arts is his *Ted̲h̲kire-yi s̲h̲uʿarāʾ*, which contains details, as known to and described by the author, concerning the lives and works of over 400 Ottoman poets who were alive and active sometime between the years 1099/1688 and 1134/1722.

Sālim may be regarded as an innovator in the art of compiling biographies of poets: his type of biography does not seem to be intended to simply praise the poets. He appears to have been very much aware of the uninterrupted flow in the production of this literary genre that had been initiated in Ottoman society in the 10th/16th century. We must assume that he knew that he was operating within a well-established tradition, but this did not stop him from making adjustments in the way in which each poet and poem were treated. This is reflected in the very critical approach he adopted in his appraisal of both the poets and their poems. His attitude could be the result of the changed way of assessing literature that began to develop among some Ottomans in the early decades of the 11th/18th century with Nedīm's (d. 1143/1730 [*q.v.*]) successful efforts to relate his art more closely to local developments and everyday life. There was, at the same time, growing interest in European literatures that must have had some impact on the Ottoman litterateurs. In this respect, one may consider Sālim's *ted̲h̲kire* to be a valuable contribution, not only to the genre but also to Ottoman literature in general. His *ted̲h̲kire* is in two parts. The first is devoted to the usual eulogies which are in this case addressed to the reigning Sultan Aḥmed III (1115-43/1703-30), followed by Sultan Muṣṭafā I (1106-15/1695-1703) who preceded him, the Grand Vizier Dāmād Ibrāhīm Pas̲h̲a and the S̲h̲ayk̲h̲ al-Islām. Then follow the author's introductory remarks in which he reviews previous *ted̲h̲kire*s leading up to his own and then expresses his thoughts on the state of literature in his own day. The rest of the work is made up of the biographies of the poets. Each biography ends with samples of the poet's poems, some in their entirety, others in the form of a verse or two. The work finishes with a *temmet* ("It is completed") in which the author asks to be excused for his errors, but does not apologise for the tediously verbose and ornate style he uses. The *ted̲h̲kire* carries a date in the form of a chronogram which adds up to 1134/1722.

Bibliography: *Ted̲h̲kire-yi Sālim*, ed. Ahmed D̲j̲ewdet, Dār-i Saʿādet 1315; *Ted̲h̲kire-yi Sālim*, ms. B.L., Or. 7068; Süleymān Müstaḳīm-zāde, *Tuḥfe-yi k̲h̲aṭṭāṭīn*, Istanbul 1928, 454; Rāmiz, *Ted̲h̲kire-yi s̲h̲uʿarāʾ*, ms. Millet Kütüphanesi, Ali Emiri Efendi, no. 762. fol. 135; Meḥmed T̲h̲üreyyā, *Sid̲j̲ill-i ʿOt̲h̲mānī*, Istanbul 1313, iii, 3; Ṣafāʾī, *Ted̲h̲kiret ül-s̲h̲uʿarāʾ*, ms. Istanbul Universitesi Kütüphanesi, no. T. 3215; J. Stewart-Robinson, *The Ottoman biographies of poets*, in *JNES*, xxiv (1965), 57-74; Agâh Sırrı Levend, *Türk edebiyatı tarihi*, Ankara 1973, i, 251-352. (J. Stewart-Robinson)

SĀLIM b. MUḤAMMAD, ʿIzz al-Dīn Abu 'l-Nad̲j̲ā al-Sanhūrī al-Miṣrī, a Mālikī jurisconsult and *ḥadīth̲* expert. He came to head the Mālikī school of Cairo, whither he migrated from Sanhūr at the age of twenty-one (probably around 966/1558-9). He is particularly known for his mastery of *ḥadīth̲*, having dictated the "Six Books", and attracted numerous well-known scholars from Syria and the Hid̲j̲āz. He is said to have written several works. The best known of these are his commentary on the *Muk̲h̲taṣar* of al-K̲h̲alīl on *fiḳh* (extant) and, oddly, an epistle reportedly entitled *Faḍāʾil laylat al-niṣf min s̲h̲aʿbān* (Kaḥḥāla, iv, 204). He died on Tuesday, 3 D̲j̲umādā II 1015/7 October 1606, reportedly at around the age of seventy, which would place his birth date *ca.* 945/1538.

Bibliography: Brockelmann, in *EI*[1], s.v.; Muḥibbī, *K̲h̲ulāṣat al-at̲h̲ar*, ii, 204; Mak̲h̲lūf, *S̲h̲ad̲j̲arat al-nūr al-zakiyya*, Beirut 1349/1930, 289; Kaḥḥāla, *Muʿd̲j̲am al-muʾallifīn*, iv, 204; Hād̲j̲d̲j̲ī K̲h̲alīfa, *Kas̲h̲f*, Istanbul, ii, 1628; Aḥmad Bābā al-Timbuktī, *Nayl al-ibtihād̲j̲* (on the margin of Ibn Farḥūn), 157. (S.A. Jackson)

SALĪM, MUḤAMMAD ḲULĪ, an Indo-Persian poet of the 11th/17th century, died 1057/1647-8.

He originated from the S̲h̲āmlū tribe of the Turks and was a native of Tehran, but details regarding his life are scanty. In Persia he served under Mīrzā ʿAbd Allāh K̲h̲ān, governor of Lāhīd̲j̲ān [*q.v.*] in Gīlān. During this time he married and had a son. Among the eminent personalities to whom he addressed his poems in the beginning were the Ṣafawid rulers S̲h̲āh ʿAbbās I (r. 996-1038/1588-1629) and his successor S̲h̲āh Ṣafī I (r. 1038-52/1629-42). Perhaps his failure to find the desired patronage in his country led him to try his fortune in India. He set out by sea, reaching Gud̲j̲arāt around 1041/1631, coinciding with the early period of S̲h̲āh D̲j̲ahān's reign (1037-68/1628-59). It is likely that he sought access to the imperial court but was unsucessful; Wālih Dāg̲h̲istānī, author of the *Riyāḍ al-s̲h̲uʿarāʾ*, reports that the poet-laureate Kalīm [see kalīm, abū ṭālib], when asked by S̲h̲āh D̲j̲ahān to give his opinion about the poet, told the emperor that Salīm was poetically ill-provided since one of his *mat̲h̲nawī*s, which he said was written in praise of Kas̲h̲mīr, had been composed by him originally in praise of Gīlān and he had merely changed its title. This accusation supposedly prevented Salīm from winning royal patronage. Thereupon he attached himself to Mīr ʿAbd al-Salām Mas̲h̲hadī, called Islām K̲h̲ān, a prominent nobleman of the period, who successively held important government positions, ending as governor of the Deccan. Salīm stayed in his service until the latter's death on 14 S̲h̲awwāl 1057/12 November 1647. In the same year the poet also passed away, and his body was laid to rest in Kas̲h̲mīr.

In his character, Salīm has been described as a gross person indulging in improper jokes. He would display his wit indiscriminately without regard for the social status of the individual towards whom it was directed. On a certain occasion, while being entertained by the governor of Fārs, Imām Ḳulī K̲h̲ān (d. 1032/1622-3), the poet came out with an improvised couplet, displeasing to the host, who felt slighted by the allusion in it regarding his fatness.

Salīm's *dīwān* comprises poems representing *ḳaṣīda, g̲h̲azal, ḳiṭʿa, rubāʿī* and *mat̲h̲nawī*. Estimates vary regarding the total number of verses in the *dīwān*, but D̲h̲abīḥ Allāh Ṣafā places the total around 9,000 couplets. Salīm's poetry is praised by writers in general. Though he is accused of borrowing ideas from other poets—a practice in which he was certainly not alone—nevertheless it is accepted that his output contained many unique themes. Probably because he was not well educated in the formal sense of the term, his language sometimes bordered on the popular idiom. He was the author of several *mat̲h̲nawī*s, which occupy a special place in his collection. They include, in addition to his poem on Kas̲h̲mīr mentioned earlier, such pieces as *Ḳaḍā wa ḳadar* ("Fate and destiny"), *Dar taʿrīf-i asp* ("In praise of a horse"), *Dar taʿrīf-i bahār* ("In praise of spring"), *Dar taʿrif-i sarmā* ("In praise of winter"), *K̲h̲ar-i dallāl* ("The broker's donkey"), and *Dar s̲h̲ikāyat-i rūzgār* ("Complaint against the world"). In his *g̲h̲azal*s, Salīm displays an easy communication despite a tendency towards innovative and strange conceits. He is known for his expert use of similes and the figure of speech called *īhām* ("ambiguity").

Bibliography: *Kulliyyāt-i Salīm*, I.O. ms. 1558; *Dīwān-i Muḥammad Ḳulī Salīm*, ed. Raḥīm Riḍā, Tehran 1349/1970-1; *Mat̲h̲nawī ḳaḍā wa ḳadar*, ed. Sayyid Ḍiyāʾ al-Dīn Sad̲j̲d̲j̲ādī, in *Farhang-i Īrān-zamīn*, xxv (1983); Muḥammad Ṣāliḥ Kanbū, *S̲h̲āh D̲j̲ahān-nāma* (*ʿAmal-i Ṣāliḥ*), iii, ed. G̲h̲ulām Yazdānī and Waḥīd Ḳurays̲h̲ī, Lahore 1972; Muḥammad Ṭāhir Naṣrābādī, *Tad̲h̲kira-yi Naṣrābādī*, ed. Waḥīd Dastgardī, Tehran 1352/1973-4; Muḥammad Afḍal Sarkhus̲h̲, *Kalimāt al-s̲h̲uʿarāʾ* (*Tad̲h̲kira-yi Sarkhus̲h̲*), ed. Ṣādiḳ ʿAlī Dilāwarī, Lahore 1942; ʿAlī Ḳulī K̲h̲ān Wālih Dāg̲h̲istānī, *Riyāḍ al-s̲h̲uʿarāʾ*, B.L. ms. Add. 16,729; Mīr Ḥusayn Dūst Sanbhalī, *Tad̲h̲kira-yi Ḥusaynī*, Lakhnaw 1875; Sirād̲j̲ al-Dīn K̲h̲an Ārzū, *Mad̲j̲maʿ al-nafāʾis*, Bankipore ms., *Catalogue*, viii; G̲h̲ulām ʿAlī Āzād Bilgrāmī, *Sarw-i āzād*, Ḥaydarābād (Deccan) 1913; Luṭf ʿAlī Beg Ād̲h̲ar, *Ātis̲h̲kada*, i, ed. Ḥasan Sādāt Nāṣirī, Tehran 1336/1957-8; Laks̲h̲mī Narāyan S̲h̲afīḳ, *S̲h̲ām-i g̲h̲arībān*, ed. Akbar al-Dīn Ṣiddīḳī, Karachi 1977; Muḥammad Ḳudrat Allāh Gopāmawī, *Natāʾid̲j̲ al-afkār*, Bombay 1336/1957-8; Aḥmad ʿAlī K̲h̲ān Hās̲h̲imī Sandīlawī, *Mak̲h̲zan al-g̲h̲arāʾib*, ii, ed. Muḥammad Bāḳir, Lahore 1970; D̲h̲abīḥ Allāh Ṣafā, *Tārīk̲h̲-i adabiyyāt dar Īrān*, v/2, Tehran 1367/1988; Ḥusām al-Dīn Rās̲h̲idī, *Tad̲h̲kira-yi s̲h̲uʿarā-yi Kas̲h̲mīr*, i, Karachi 1967; Raḥīm Riḍā, Muḥammad Ḳulī Salīm Ṭihrānī, in *Mad̲j̲alla-yi Dānis̲h̲kada-yi Adabiyyāt u ʿUlūm-i Insānī*, Tehran, xv/2-3 (Nov. 1967-Feb. 1968); M.L. Rahman, *Persian literature in India during the time of Jahangir and Shah Jahan*, Baroda 1978; Aḥmad Gulčīn Maʿānī, *Kārwān-i Hind*, i, Mas̲h̲had 1369/1990.

(Munibur Rahman)

SALĪM b. K̲h̲alīl al-**NAḲḲĀS̲H̲**, Syrian Maronite journalist, historian, and pioneer of Arab theatre. Born 1850 in Beirut, he died in Alexandria on 25 November 1884. He studied Arabic, French and Italian. He worked on his uncle Nīḳūlā's *al-Misbāḥ* newspaper in Beirut and wrote for *al-Nad̲j̲āḥ* and *al-Zahra*. He was employed in the customs in Beirut in 1876. In the family tradition he became involved with the theatre with an adaptation, *Mayy wa-Hūrās* (Beirut 1875 written 1868), of Corneille's tragedy *Horace*, to which he had added poetry and songs. Seeking material support for a theatrical venture, he went to Egypt. The Khedive Ismāʿīl [*q.v.*] agreed to grant him use of a theatre, scenery, and costumes and financial support. Salīm began rehearsing his troupe in the summer of 1875, writing for it several plays in the literary language in prose and verse. Despite vehement criticism, he included women actresses in his troupe. They rehearsed his version of *ʿĀʾida* (Beirut 1875), to which he had added popular Arab airs. He performed his uncle Mārūn's [*q.v.*] *al-Bak̲h̲īl* and *Abu 'l-Ḥasan al-Mug̲h̲affal aw Hārūn al-Ras̲h̲īd*, and his own *Mayy wa-Hūrās* in Beirut. Though cholera initially prevented them from travelling, in 1876 he led the first Lebanese troupe to Egypt.

Joined by the Damascene Adīb Isḥāḳ [*q.v.*], the troupe, *al-Tiyātrū al-ʿArabī*, performed at the Zizinia theatre in Alexandria Mārūn's *Abu 'l-Ḥasan al-Mug̲h̲affal* and *al-Ḥasūd al-Salīṭ*, and Salīm's *Mayy wa-Hūrās, al-Kad̲h̲ūb* and *al-Ẓalūm*, in a season extending from December 1876 to February 1877. The répertoire is said to have also included *al-Bak̲h̲īl*, an adaptation of Racine's *Phèdre*, and his *Mithridate*, Meyerbeer's opera *L'Africaine, ʿĀʾida*, and *G̲h̲arāʾib al-Ṣudaf aw Salīm wa-Asmā* (in versions all attributed to Salīm), Racine's *Andromaque, al-Bārīsiyya al-ḥasnāʾ* (*La Belle Parisienne* by the Comtesse Dash), and *Charlemagne* (from the highly successful play of Henri de Bornier) (all adapted by Adīb), and *Zénobie* of l'abbé d'Aubignac. *Al-Kad̲h̲ūb* (Alexandria 1913) was an adaptation of Corneille's comedy *Le Menteur* made by Ḥabīb Musk and revised by Salīm. The tragicomedy *Ḥifẓ al-Wudād aw al-Ẓalūm* (Alexandria 1891), said to be a translation, is about intrigue and romance in an Arab court. Its performance later purportedly led to the expulsion of Yūsuf al-K̲h̲ayyāṭ's troupe in 1879, because the Khedive thought it alluded to him and his government disparagingly. *G̲h̲arāʾib al-Ṣudaf* (Alexandria n.d.) is a story of love and anti-colonial struggles in India. An anthology of Salīm's plays, *al-Masraḥ al-ʿArabī—dirāsāt wa-nuṣūṣ. 5. Salīm al-Naḳḳāsh*, ed. Muḥammad Yūsuf Nad̲j̲m, Beirut 1965, includes *ʿĀʾida, Mayy wa-Hūrās, al-Kad̲h̲ūb, G̲h̲arāʾib al-Ṣudaf* and *al-Ẓalūm*. Though audience response had been very supportive, and Salīm did his utmost to keep his company alive, he eventually ceded control to one of the actors, Yūsuf al-K̲h̲ayyāṭ (1877-95); some of its members were later to form the core of Sulaymān Ḳardāḥī's troupe (1882-1909).

It is claimed that it was D̲j̲amāl al-Dīn al-Afg̲h̲ānī [*q.v.*], who persuaded Salīm and Adīb to leave the theatre for the press; they had become members of his circle in Egypt. When the weekly *Miṣr*, founded in July 1877 in Cairo by Adīb, moved to Alexandria, Salīm helped edit it. The pair of them founded a daily *al-Tid̲j̲āra* in May 1878 in Alexandria; some of the best writers, al-Afg̲h̲ānī, Muḥammad ʿAbduh [*q.v.*], ʿAbd Allāh Nadīm [*q.v.*], Ibrāhīm al-Laḳḳānī and Amīn S̲h̲umayyil, were to write for it. Both papers, strongly nationalist, were suspended in November 1879 for their criticism of the government of Riyāḍ Pas̲h̲a and of foreign interference in Egyptian affairs. Salīm is said to have been a member of the radical nationalist *Miṣr al-Fatāt*/Jeune Egypte. After Adīb travelled to Paris, Salīm started publishing a daily *al-Maḥrūsa* and a weekly *al-ʿAṣr al-Djadīd* in Alexandria in January 1880; Salīm followed a more moderate line with these papers. When in 1881 Salīm was ill, ʿAbd Allāh Nadīm took over the running of both papers. With the return of Adīb and the reissue by him of *Miṣr* in December 1881, *al-ʿAṣr al-Djadīd* ceased to appear. *Al-Maḥrūsa*, opposing the nationalist policies of Colonel ʿUrābī, was suspended in June 1882 for its loyalty to the Khedive. After the riots of 11 June, Salīm was forced to flee; his press was destroyed. Salīm tried to restart *al-Maḥrūsa* in September 1882, but it was not till the beginning of 1884 that he got compensation for the destruction of his press, and *al-Maḥrūsa* reappeared as a weekly till his death.

The first three volumes of his lengthy *Miṣr li 'l-Miṣriyyīn aw ḥawādith al-fitna al-ʿUrābiyya*, Alexandria 1884-6, describing Egypt from the time of Muḥammad ʿAlī to Ismāʿīl, are said to have been printed, but then destroyed on government orders; volume iv covers Tawfīḳ's early reign; v, ʿUrābī; vi, the British occupation; and vii-ix, the ʿUrābist trials. *Riwāyat al-intiḳām aw al-hudjra al-sābiʿa* (Alexandria 1878) is a free translation by him and Adīb of the novel *Le dernier rendez-vouz* by the French writer Pierre Zaccone.

Bibliography: Y.A. Dāg̲h̲ir, *Maṣādir al-dirāsa al-adabiyya*, Beirut 1342-5, iii; A. Abul Naga, *Les sources françaises du théâtre égyptien (1870-1939)*, Algiers 1972, 16, 59-60, 68, 74, 109-12, 138, 157, 207; J. Khouéiri, *Théâtre arabe. Liban, 1847-1960*, Louvain 1984, 85-94; M.Y. Nadjm, *al-Masraḥiyya fi 'l-adab al-ʿarabī al-ḥadīth, 1847-1914*, Beirut 1967, 8, 38-40, 44-51, 54, 60, 70, 91, 94-103, 116, 176-177, 204-206, 446; Salīm's article, *Fawāʾid al-riwāyāt aw al-tiyātrāt*, in *al-Djinān*, v (1 August 1875), 517, 521-2, on his theatre and its mission; Salīm al-Bustānī, *al-Riwāyāt al-ʿarabiyya al-miṣriyya*, in *al-Djinān*, viii (1875), 442-4, and *al-Riwāyāt al-khidīwiyya al-tashkhīṣiyya*, in *ibid.*, xx (1875), 694-6; *Fādjiʿa waṭaniyya bi-wafāt Salīm al-Nakkāsh*, in *al-Muktaṭaf*, ix/4 (January 1885), 241; Ibrāhīm Ḥamāda, *Āyida bayn Firdī wa 'l-Nakkāsh*, in *al-Madjalla*, vi (1962), 67-72; Matti Moosa, *Naqqāsh and the rise of the native Arabic theatre in Syria*, in *JAL*, iii (1972), 106-17; Niḳūlā Yūsuf, *Salīm al-Nakkāsh, rāʾid al-ṣiḥāfa wa 'l-masraḥ*, in *al-Adīb*, xxv (1 October 1966), 2-6.

(P.C. Sadgrove)

al-SĀLIMĪ, Abū Muḥammad ʿAbd Allāh b. Ḥumayd b. Sullūm al-Sālimī, Nūr al-Dīn (*ca.* 1286-1332/*ca.* 1869-1914), generally known in the West as an ʿUmānī historian, but it was as *raʾīs al-nahḍa*, responsible for restoring the Imāmate in interior ʿUmān from 1913 to 1955, that his true role should be judged.

Born at al-Ḥawḳayn near al-Rustāḳ [*q.v.*], he went blind aged 12. His early studies were with the *ʿulamāʾ* of the region who had been active in securing the election of the only 19th-century Imām, ʿAzzān b. Ḳays (1868-71). But after the Sultanate was restored, with G̲h̲āfirī tribal support and British connivance, the centre of Ibāḍī resistance shifted from al-Rustāḳ, the stronghold of the Ḳays branch of the Āl Bū Saʿīd [*q.v.*], to the S̲h̲arḳiyya, and in about 1890 al-Sālimī moved to study with its leader, Ṣāliḥ b. ʿAlī al-Ḥārit̲h̲ī (1834-96) [*q.v.*], making a permanent home at al-Ḳābil. However, ʿĪsā b. Ṣāliḥ (1874-1946), who succeeded his father as *tamīma* of the S̲h̲arḳiyya Hināwīs, seems to have developed a personal antipathy to al-Sālimī and failed to support his attempts to reactivate the Imāmate after 1905. So he was forced into a somewhat cynical alliance with Ḥimyar b. Nāṣir al-Nabhānī (1874-1920), then consolidating his position as *tamīma* of the G̲h̲āfirī Banū Riyām confederation of the Djabal al-Ak̲h̲ḍar, to sponsor, as Imām, Sālim b. Rās̲h̲id (1301/1884-1920), a former pupil and one of the *s̲h̲ayk̲h̲s* of the Banū K̲h̲arūṣ, a tribe closely allied to the Banū Riyām but also with a long historical association with the Imāmate. Immediately after Sālim's *bayʿa* at Ḥimyar's capital Tanūf (12 Djumādā II 1331/20 May 1913), al-Sālimī returned to the S̲h̲arḳiyya with a delegation to espouse his cause there. After Izkī fell to the Imām, ʿĪsā reluctantly gave his allegiance, thus assuring the Imāmate of the loyalty of the main Hināwī tribes of central ʿUmān.

But al-Sālimī never saw the real success of his mission. To help finance the movement, he ordered the appropriation of all *waḳf* property that had been bequeathed for visiting graves and for reading the Ḳurʾān for the dead. This judgement led him into major dispute with his former teacher, Mādjid b. K̲h̲amīs al-ʿAbrī (*ca.* 1837-1927), who in ʿAzzān's time had also similarly opposed such dubious financial precedents, and so impassioned did the issue become that early in 1914 al-Sālimī went to see him at al-Ḥamrāʾ. On the way, he was killed when his donkey stumbled; he was buried at Tanūf.

It is against this background that the nature of his history of the Imāmate, *Tuḥfat al-aʿyān bi-sīrat ahl ʿUmān*, should be viewed. Finished *ca.* 1910, the story is continued down to the death in 1954 of the Imām Muḥammad b. ʿAbd Allāh al-K̲h̲alīlī by his son, Muḥammad (S̲h̲ayba), in the *Nahḍat al-aʿyān bi-ḥurriyyat ʿUmān* (Cairo n.d.); this contains a lengthy biography of his father which is the main source for this article. Amongst twenty-two works of his listed in it, attention should be drawn to such studies of major Ibāḍī scholarship as his edition of al-Rabīʿ b. Ḥabīb al-Farāhīdī's *ḥadīth* with a three-volume *S̲h̲arḥ*, and also to his close cooperation with the great Mzābi scholar and activist, Muḥammad b. Yūsuf Aṭfayyis̲h̲ (1236-1332/1820-1914). It was Muḥammad's son Abū Isḥāḳ Ibrāhīm Aṭfayyis̲h̲, who edited for publication the *Tuḥfa* (first ed. 2 vols., Cairo 1347 and 1350), as also another remarkable work of his, the *Djawhar al-niẓām fi ʿilmay 'l-adyān wa 'l-aḥkām*, a distillation in an *urdjūza* of guidelines and judgements written as a sort of aide-memoire for *ḳāḍīs*. His *Talḳīn al-ṣibyān* became the standard book of instruction for Ibāḍī children.

Bibliography: Given in the article.

(J.C. Wilkinson)

SĀLIMIYYA, the name of a mystical-theological school in Baṣra, based on the teachings of Muḥammad b. Aḥmad b. Sālim (d. 297/909) and his son Aḥmad b. Muḥammad b. Aḥmad b. Sālim (d. 356/967). In the sources, father and son are often confused. Both were pupils of the famous mystic Sahl b. ʿAbd Allāh al-Tustarī (d. 282/896 [*q.v.*]), Muḥammad b. Aḥmad for as long as 60 years; he therefore is to be considered as the main pupil of al-Tustarī.

While Muḥammad b. Aḥmad has a separate entry in the Ṣūfī lexica and handbooks (such as those by Abū Nuʿaym al-Iṣfahānī [*q.v.*], ʿAbd Allāh al-Anṣārī [see al-anṣārī al-harawī] and Abū ʿAbd al-Raḥmān al-Sulamī (d. 1021) [*q.v.*]), this is not the case for his son Aḥmad. The latter's most famous pupil was Abū Ṭālib al-Makkī (d. 386/996 [*q.v.*]), the author of the *Ḳūt al-ḳulūb*, the main model for the *Iḥyāʾ ʿulūm al-dīn* of Abū Ḥāmid al-G̲h̲azālī [*q.v.*]. Since no actual works of Muḥammad b. Sālim or of Aḥmad b. Sālim are known, even by title, the *Ḳūt al-ḳulūb* of al-Makkī must be considered as the main source for the doctrine of the Sālimiyya. The compilation of Sahl al-Tustarī's commentary on the Ḳurʾān does not stem from the Sālimiyya but from other pupils of al-Tustarī.

The existence of a tradition of the Sālimī school and doctrine in the 4th/10th century is attested by the Ṣūfī Ibn Khafīf al-Shīrāzī (d. 371/982 [*q.v.*]), whose work against it, the *al-Radd ʿalā Ibn Sālim* (i.e. Aḥmad b. Muḥammad), has not been preserved. The geographer al-Muḳaddasī [*q.v.*], who finished his description of the Islamic empire in 375/985, associated in Baṣra with adherents of the school. He relates that at that time they were Mālikīs, but that their founder had been a Ḥanafī, that they studied theology (*kalām*), for which they had their own books, and that their main concern was renunciation of the world (*zuhd*). None of the early sources mentions them explicitly as Ṣūfīs. Abū Naṣr al-Sarrādj (d. 378/989 [*q.v.*]), the author of the Ṣūfī handbook *al-Lumaʿ*, records a discussion with Aḥmad b. Sālim in Baṣra about mystical sayings of Abū Yazīd al-Bisṭāmī [*q.v.*], considered as heretical by Aḥmad. Aḥmad b. Sālim is also otherwise often mentioned in the *Lumaʿ*.

It was probably on account of Ibn Khafīf's lost work that a catalogue of alleged heretical views of the Sālimiyya came into being among the Ḥanbalīs. Reference to these views is first found in the works of Ibn al-Farrāʾ (d. 458/1066 [*q.v.*]); parts of them are repeated by later authors. There is no trace of such doctrines in the proper tradition of the Sālimiyya, i.e. in the *Ḳūt al-ḳulūb*. The catalogue deals with unfounded misrepresentations by opponents of the school, which should not be taken as authentic doctrines of the Sālimiyya. The real doctrine of the school is to be sought in al-Makkī's work, which is now being studied in a critical way. It shows a thoroughly orthodox and quite ascetic piety.

Bibliography: Makkī, *Ḳūt al-ḳulūb*, Cairo 1351/1932, 4 parts in 2 vols., tr. R. Gramlich, *Die Nahrung der Herzen. Abū Ṭālib al-Makkīs Qūt al-qulūb eingeleitet, übersetzt und kommentiert*, Stuttgart 1992 ff. (*Freiburger Islamstudien*, xvi, 1-4); Sarrādj, *al-Lumaʿ fi 'l-taṣawwuf*, ed. R. Nicholson, Leiden 1914, tr. R. Gramlich, *Schlaglichter über das Sufitum. Abū Naṣr as-Sarrāğs Kitāb al-lumaʿ eingeleitet, übersetzt und kommentiert*, Stuttgart 1990 (*Freiburger Islamstudien*, xiii), esp. 530-4; Sulamī, *Ṭabaḳāt al-ṣūfiyya*, Cairo 1389/1969, 414-17; Abū Nuʿaym al-Iṣfahānī, *Ḥilyat al-awliyāʾ*, Cairo 1351-7/1932-8, x, 378-9; Anṣārī, *Ṭabaḳāt al-ṣūfiyya*, Kābul 1340/1962, 257-8; ʿAbd al-Ḳāhir al-Baghdādī, *al-Farḳ bayna 'l-firaḳ*, Beirut 1393/1973, 247; Ibn al-Farrāʾ, *al-Muʿtamad fī uṣūl al-dīn*, Beirut 1974, 217-21; ʿAbd al-Ḳādir al-Djīlānī, *al-Ghunya li-ṭālibī ṭarīḳ al-ḥaḳḳ*, Cairo 1375/1956, i, 91-4; Goldziher, in *ZDMG*, lxi (1907), 73-80; Massignon, *Essai*², 294-300; G. Böwering, *The mystical vision of existence in classical Islam. The Qurʾanic hermeneutics of the Sufi Sahl at-Tustarī (d. 283/896)*, Berlin 1980, esp. 89-99; Gramlich, *Schlaglichter*, 18-19; idem, *Nahrung*, i, 15-16.

(L. Massignon-[B. Radtke])

SĀLIYĀNE (transliterated also sālyāne), a technical term in Ottoman administrative usage derived from the Persian *sāl* (year) meaning "yearly", "yearly allowance" or "stipend".

The term is applied especially to the yearly income allotted to some categories of provincial rulers and governors (16th-19th centuries). These were the members of the Girāy [*q.v.*] dynasty, some governors of maritime districts and other *sandjaḳ-begis* and *beglerbegis* whose income did not derive from *khāṣṣ* [*q.v.*] domains but consisted of a yearly allowance fixed at the time of their appointment. Their governments were termed as being "with *sāliyāne*" [see eyālet]. In those *sandjaḳ*s and *eyālet*s which were lying at great distances from the central seat of government, the *timār* [*q.v.*] régime was not instituted. All revenues there were controlled directly by the office of the *defterdār* [see daftardār] in the capital. The provincial treasuries in this case provided salaries in cash to the governors, the Janissary commanders and other military and administrative personnel, as well as the means for all local expenditure. The remainder of the revenue had to be transferred to the central treasury (see khazīne and irsāliyye]. In the 17th and 18th centuries there were nine *sāliyāne* provinces: Egypt [see miṣr], Baghdād [*q.v.*], Baṣra [*q.v.*], Ḥabesh [*q.v.*], Yemen [see yaman], al-Aḥsā [see al-ḥasā], the *odjaḳ*s of the West, Algiers [see djazāʾir-i gharb], Tunis (*Tūnus* [*q.v.*]) and Tripoli [see ṭarābulus-gharb]. In the province of Kefe [*q.v.*], Crete (Ottoman Girid [see iḳrīṭish]), *Djazāʾir-i Baḥr-i Safīd* [*q.v.*], in the *sandjaḳ*s of Chios [see saḳiz], Naxos [see naḳshe] and al-Mahdiyya (Tunisia) [*q.v.*], in the Cypriot *sandjaḳ*s of Kerynia (Ott. Girne), Paphos (Ott. Bāf) and Famagusta (Ott. Maghōsha [*q.v.*]), and Aleppo [see ḥalab], some governors had *sāliyāne* status. There all tax revenues went to the state treasury. The local *defterdār*s collected the taxes and paid the governor, the Janissaries and other regional officials their appointed yearly salaries and transferred any surplus to Istanbul. Such a surplus (*irsāliyye* [*q.v.*]) came regularly only from the provinces of Egypt, Baghdād and Baṣra. The bureaux of the *defterdār*'s office concerned were the *sāliyāne muḳāṭaʿasī ḳalemi* and the *taʾrīkhči ḳalemi* (see M. Sertoğlu, *Muhteva bakımından Başvekalet Arşivi*, Ankara 1955, 66).

Bibliography: A. Birken, *Die Provinzen des Osmanischen Reiches* (= Beihefte zum TAVO, Reihe B, Nr. 13), Wiesbaden 1976, 10-11; H. İnalcik, *The Ottoman empire. The classical age 1300-1600*, London 1973, 105; Muṣṭafā Nūrī Pasha, *Netāʾidj ül-wuḳūʿāt*, Istanbul 1327/1912, 4 vols., i, 127-32; C. Orhonlu, *Osmanlı imparatorluğu'nun güney siyaseti. Habeş eyaleti*, Istanbul 1974, 103, 106, 147, 224, 242; Pakalın, iii, 111-12; A. Tabakoğlu, *Gerileme dönemine girerken Osmanlı maliyesi*, Istanbul 1985, 46, 59-67, 111-13, 195-7 (statistical data for the 17th and 18th centuries).

(A.H. de Groot)

ṢALKHAD or Ṣarkhad, the Biblical Salka, already in Classical Antiquity one of the major settlements of the Auranitis or Ḥawrān [*q.v.*], the basalt region in southern Syria, now a small provincial town (population 1981: 6,476 inhabitants) on the southern flank of the Djabal al-Durūz, near the Jordanian border. In the Islamic era it was of prime importance as the southernmost advance post of Syria towards the desert lands of Arabia and on the junction of important trade routes, connecting the main north-south axis via Damascus with the road from the Mediterranean towards east to Baghdād and beyond. It was strongly fortified by a mighty castle, which formed a defensive line with the citadel of Buṣrā [see boṣrā], about 23 km/14 miles further west.

Today, its historic importance is only shown by the impressive ruins of the castle, built in solid black basalt masonry on the top of a steep volcanic eminence, and the isolated hexagonal Ayyūbid minaret in the city centre. Despite the poor state of preservation, the glorious past can be deduced in some detail from the chronicles or geographic manuals, and especially from a remarkable number of Arabic inscriptions re-used in recent constructions of the Druze population, who have resettled the completely abandoned ancient site since 1860. With the continuous removal in recent times of most of the traditional fabric, the excavation and clearing of the citadel has been undertaken by the Syrian Antiquities Organisation since 1991.

The history of Ṣalkhad, as a defensive bastion for Damascus, closely mirrors the fate of the Syrian capital, and its history has been similar to that of the neighbouring town of Buṣrā.

The Fāṭimid, Saldjūḳ, Būrid and Zangid periods. The citadel of Ṣalkhad was evidently founded or enlarged in 466/1073-4 by the chief of the Banū Kalb Bedouins, Ḥassān b. Mismār, as a base for attacks against Damascus, then belonging to the empire of the Fāṭimid caliph al-Mustanṣir. After the expulsion of the Fāṭimids from Syria in 468/1076 and the subsequent foundation of a new Saldjūḳ dynasty by Tādj al-Daula Tutush [see SALDJŪḲIDS. III. 4, and TUTUSH], the new master of Syria invested his sons Fallūs and Takīn as commanders at the castles at Ṣalkhad and Buṣrā. Shortly after, when power in 497/1104 passed to Ẓahīr al-Dīn Ṭughtakīn, the former *atābak* of the Saldjūḳ prince Duḳāḳ b. Tutush and founder of the Būrid dynasty [*q.v.*], he bestowed both cities on the general Gümüshtakīn al-Tādjī in 503/1110, who in turn bequeathed it to his *mamlūk* Altuntāsh (541-2/1146-7). Though the city of Buṣrā was improved greatly in this period, and consequently the same should be assumed for Ṣalkhad, not a single piece of building has been identified so far. This is also the case for the rule of Muʿīn al-Dīn Ūnūr, *atābak* of the last Būrid Mudjīr al-Dīn Abaḳ, who invested Mudjāhid al-Dīn Būzān al-Kurdī (542-55/1147-60) as commander of the citadel, to be succeeded briefly by his son Muḥammad (555/1160). The Zangid ruler Nūr al-Dīn Maḥmūd [*q.v.*], master of Damascus since 549/1154, bestowed Ṣalkhad and Buṣrā on Ṣadīḳ b. Djawlī (555-71/1160-76), followed eventually by a nephew. Again, as attested for Buṣrā, Ṣalkhad may also have further expanded, though the contemporary sources give no information.

The Ayyūbid period. Due to the continuous threat from the Crusaders, Ṣalkhad, like many of the Syrian cities and strongholds, attracted the attention of the Ayyūbid rulers. In 583/1187, the founder of the Ayyūbid dynasty, al-Malik al-Nāṣir Ṣalāḥ al-Dīn Yūsuf, when decisively defeating the Crusaders at the battle of Ḥaṭṭīn [*q.v.*], brought Ṣalkhad and Buṣrā into his possession. When dividing his empire among his family in 588/1186, both towns were bestowed on his son al-Malik al-Afḍal ʿAlī, the acting governor of the Damascus province since 582/1186. It seems that the citadel of Ṣalkhad, strengthened by additional fortifications before 589/1193 and in 591/1194-95, was deemed strategically more important than that of Buṣrā, where the rebuilding programme only started about a decade later in 599/1202-3. Consequently, when deposed as ruler of Damascus, al-Afḍal ʿAlī decided to take up his residence at Ṣalkhad in 592/1196, until five years later he bestowed Ṣalkhad on the *amīr* Zayn al-Dīn Ḳarādjā al-Ṣāliḥī, confirmed in this also by the current ruler of Damascus, al-ʿĀdil Abū Bakr, as is evident from the construction of an additional tower of the citadel in 601/1204-5 in the name of both personalities. In 604/1208 it was bequeathed to his son Nāṣir al-Dīn Yaʿḳūb, who held Ṣalkhad till 611/1214.

A peak of prosperity was reached under the Ayyūbid prince al-Muʿaẓẓam ʿĪsā, who invested his major-domo ʿIzz al-Dīn Aybak al-Muʿaẓẓamī with the fief of Ṣalkhad (611-44/1214-47), Aybak sponsored an extensive building programme: besides enlarging the citadel decisively (as attested by inscriptions), two caravanserails were constructed (in 611/1214-5 and 634/1236-7); the congregational mosque was extended by an additional aisle and by the singular hexagonal minaret (630/1233); and simultaneously also an ancient mosque repaired (630/1232-3). After the improvement of Ṣalkhad, Aybak turned his attention to other places of his fief, said to have included up to hundred villages. His activities ranged from the foundation of a caravanserail and a mosque at Sāla (632/1234-5), 17 km/10 miles further to the northeast, a castle (*ḳaṣr*) at the oasis of al-Azraḳ (634/1236-7), about 70 km/43 miles to the south (now in Jordan), the restoration of a caravanserail at Zurʿa/Ezraʿ (636/1238), *ca.* 60 km/37 miles to the northwest, the reactivation and extension of an open cistern at ʿInāḳ (636/1238-9 and 637/1239-40), 20 km/12 miles to the southeast, and the building of a mosque at al-ʿAyn (638/1240-1), 6 km/4 miles to the northwest. Except for the epigraphic texts, almost nothing has survived from these building enterprises. But the available data clearly testify to the systematic improvement of the region, evidently resulting in an increase of the rural population.

Following the deposition of Aybak al-Muʿaẓẓamī, the fief of Ṣalkhad henceforth was administered directly by members of the Ayyūbid family: al-Malik al-Ṣāliḥ Nadjm al-Dīn Ayyūb (644-7/1247-9), al-Muʿaẓẓam Tūrān Shāh (647-8/1249-50), al-ʿAzīz Muḥammad (648-58/1250-60), and al-Ẓāhir Ghāzī (658/1260). Despite a final extension of the citadel in 647/1249, the town had to suffer the military might of the victorious Mongol army in 658/1260.

The Mamlūk period. In the aftermath of the Mongol conquest, al-Ẓāhir Baybars [*q.v.*], who successfully expelled the Mongols from Syria and decisively reduced the Crusader dominions, systematically reorganised the Syrian provinces. The citadel of Ṣalkhad was immediately reactivated and soon extensively repaired and strengthened in 668/1270 and 669/1271 under the supervision of the *amīr* Balabān al-Afram, as testified by several inscriptions and a series of stone carvings with representations of the lion, the blazon [see RANK] of sultan Baybars, now dispersed throughout the region. Shortly thereafter, al-Manṣūr Ḳalāwūn in 679/1280-1 invested the *amīr* Sayf al-Dīn Basitī as governor of the city, and a certain ʿIzz al-Dīn as commander of the citadel, ordering the restoration of the fortification (inscription of 669/1271).

The later steady decline in Ṣalkhad's strategic importance, as also that of Buṣrā, is attested by its use as a place for disgraced Mamlūk officials. This first occurred when the former sultan al-ʿĀdil Kitbughā nominally acted as governor of Ṣalkhad after his forced resignation in 696/1297. This also occurred with the dismissed governor of Damascus, ʿIzz al-Dīn Aybak al-Ḥamawī, as well as for the powerful *amīrs* Aḳḳūsh al-Afram and Ḳarasunḳur al-Manṣūrī (both fleeing to the Mongol court in 711/1312), and finally also for Aḳḳūsh al-Ashrafī. Throughout this period, Ṣalkhad still flourished as regional centre, even maintaining a bath complex (*ḥammām*), registered in the inventory of the viceroy of Syria and governor of Damascus, Tankiz, compiled on the occasion of his dismissal in 740/1340.

Because of its heavily fortified citadel, Ṣalkhad retained some importance in the later Mamlūk period. In 824/1421 it served as retreat of the governor of Damascus Djaḳmaḳ al-Dawādār, after an unsuccessful revolt following the death of the sultan al-

Muʾayyad Shaykh. The latest historical datum marks the appointment in 842/1438-9 of the low-ranking official Khalīl al-Ẓāhirī (who was later in his career to compile the well-known manual of the Mamlūk state, see *Bibl.*) as commander of the citadel. In the wake of the Ottoman conquest of Syria (922/1516), resulting in a shift of importance to the northern provinces, Ṣalkhad was soon depopulated and deserted, only to be again resettled and rebuilt by Druze refugees immigrating from the Lebanon from the later 19th century onwards.

Bibliography: 1. Arabic texts. Ibn al-Athīr, ed. Beirut 1965, x, 668; xi, 20, 49-50, 54; xii, 97, 123, 141, 156, 160-1, 351, 489; Ibn Shaddād, *al-Aʿlāḳ al-khaṭīra*, ii/2, ed. Sāmī al-Dahān, Damascus 1956, 55-65; idem, *Tārīkh al-Malik al-Ẓāhir*, ed. Aḥmad Ḥuṭayṭ, Beirut 1983, 356; Abu 'l-Fidāʾ, *Taḳwīm*, 259; Maḳrīzī, *Sulūk*, ed. Muḥammad Muṣṭafā Ziyāda, i/1, Cairo 1934, 95, 111, 135, 146, 151, 168-9, 193, 216, 226; i/2, Cairo 1936, 309, 324, 326, 329, 368; i/3, Cairo 1939, 669, 683, 826, 883, 956; ii/1, Cairo 1941, 90, 110; ii/2, Cairo 1942, 379-80, 515; Khalīl al-Ẓāhirī, *Zubdat kashf al-mamālik*, ed. P. Ravaisse, Paris 1894, 46; ʿAbd al-Ḳādir al-Nuʿaymī, *al-Dāris fī tarīkh al-madāris*, ed. Djaʿfar al-Ḥasanī, 2 vols., Damascus 1948-51, i, 382-4, 386, 451-2, 551, 585; ii, 137, 258, 261, 271, 285. For the administrative manuals of Ibn Faḍl Allāh al-ʿUmarī, *Masālik al-abṣār*, and Ḳalḳashandī, *Ṣubḥ al-aʿshā*, see the translated excerpts by M. Gaudefroy-Demombynes, in *La Syrie à l'époque des Mamelouks*, Paris 1923, pp. cviii-x, 68, 178-9, 201.

2. Historical studies (to be consulted through the indices). (a) Fāṭimids. Th. Bianquis, *Damas et la Syrie sous la domination Fatimide (359-468/969-1076)*, 2 vols., Damascus 1986-9.—(b) Būrids and Zangids. Coşkun Alptekin, *Dimaşk atabegliği (Tog-Teginliler)*, Istanbul 1985; idem, *The reign of Zangi (521-541/1127-1146)*, Erzurum 1978; N. Elisséeff, *Nūr ad-Dīn: un grand prince musulman de Syrie au temps des croisades (511-569 H./1118-1174)*, 3 vols., Damascus 1967.—(c) Ayyūbids. R.S. Humphreys, *From Saladin to the Mongols: the Ayyubids of Damascus, 1193-1260*, Albany 1977.—(d) Mamluks. In the absence of an up-to-date monograph on the history of the Mamlūk period, reference may be made to related studies by I.M. Lapidus, *Muslim cities in the later Middle Ages*, Cambridge, Mass. 1967; M. Meinecke, *Die mamlukische Architektur in Ägypten und Syrien (648/1250 bis 923/1517)*, 2 vols., Glückstadt 1992.—(e) Late Ottomans. L. Schatkowski Schilcher, *The Hauran conflicts of the 1860s: a chapter in the rural history of modern Syria*, in *IJMES*, xiii (1981), 159-79.

3. Inscriptions. R. Dussaud and F. Macler, *Rapport sur une mission scientifique dans les regions desertique de la Syrie moyenne*, in *Nouvelles Archives des Missions scientifiques*, x (1902), 729-35 nos. 5-20; *RCEA*, vii (1936), no. 2704; ix (1937), nos. 3320, 3465, 3563, 3593-4; x (1939), nos. 3745, 3831, 3844, 3877; xi/1 (1941), nos. 4038, 4049-51, 4112; xi/2 (1942), nos. 4207, 4306-7, 4348-9; xii (1943), nos. 4403, 4611; xvi (1964), no. 6054; H. Gaube, *Arabische Inschriften in Syrien*, Beirut 1978, 136-7, nos. 246-50; S. Ory, *Cimetières et inscriptions du Ḥawrān et de Ğabal al-Durūz*, Paris 1989, 30-55, nos. 11-25.

4. Topography and monuments. J.G. Wetzstein, *Reisebericht über Hauran und die Trachonen*, Berlin 1860, 66-71; G. Le Strange, *Palestine under the Moslems*, London 1890, 529; M. von Oppenheim, *Vom Mittelmeer zum Persischen Golf*, i, Berlin 1899, 203-7; Gertrude Bell, *The desert and the sown*, London 1907, 82-100; R. Dussaud, *Topographie historique de la Syrie antique et médiévale*, Paris 1927, 348, 366; M. Meinecke, *Ṣalkhad, exemple de ville-forteresse islamique*, in J.-M. Dentzer and J. Dentzer-Feydy (eds.), *Le djebel al-ʿArab: histoire et patrimoine au Musée de Suweidāʾ*, Paris 1991, 93-100; idem, *The Great Mosques of the Ḥaurān*, in *Les Annales Archéologiques Arabes Syriennes*, xli (1994). (M. MEINECKE)

SALLĀM AL-TARDJUMĀN [see YĀDJŪDJ WA-MĀDJŪDJ].

SALLĀMA AL-ZARḲĀʾ (the "blue" Sallāma) was the star among the slave singing-girls (*ḳayna* [*q.v.*]) of Kūfa in the last years of the Umayyads and in the caliphate of al-Saffāḥ.

She belonged to the local "master of singing-girls" (*ṣāḥib ḳiyān; muḳayyin*) Ibn Rāmīn, a *mawlā* of the Marwānids, who ran an establishment offering the pleasures of musical entertainment and wine-drinking. His house was frequented mainly by the *ẓurafāʾ* (sing. *ẓarīf*) of Kūfa. Among them were the poets Ismāʿīl b. ʿAmmār and Muḥammad b. al-Ashʿath al-Zuhrī, who eulogised Sallāma in their verses, Muṭīʿ b. Iyās, Ḥammād ʿAdjrad, Ibn al-Muḳaffaʿ [*q.vv.*], and others. Sallāma had her own servants and acted like the lady of the house in receiving and entertaining the admirers of her art. She received most generous remunerations for her singing and lute-playing, not only from the above litterati and poets, but also from representatives of Kūfan society such as Rawḥ b. Ḥātim al-Muhallabī and Maʿn b. Zāʾida [*q.v.*]. Between Dhu 'l-Ḥidjdja 136 and Djumādā II 137/June-Nov. 754, Sallāma was acquired, for the amount of 80,000 *dirhams*, by Djaʿfar b. Sulaymān, a cousin of the caliphs al-Saffāḥ and al-Manṣūr, who later became governor of Medina (146-50/763-7, 161-6/778-83). Nothing is known about Sallāma's later life, except her honorific *kunya* Umm ʿUthmān. A former guest of her days at Ibn Rāmīn's who had dared to offer her a precious pearl from between his lips in exchange for a pearl-searching kiss from her was lashed to death by Djaʿfar b. Sulaymān.

Sallāma al-Zarḳāʾ is not to be confused (as in H.G. Farmer, *A history of Arabian Music*, London 1929, 122-4; ʿU.R. Kaḥḥāla, *Aʿlām al-nisāʾ*, ii, 226-8, and other sources) with her famous namesake Sallāmat al-Ḳass, and with the singing-girl al-Zarḳāʾ (*Aghānī*³, xv, 67; al-Suyūṭī, *al-Mustaẓraf min akhbār al-djawārī*, Beirut 1963, 67-8).

Bibliography: Ibn Ḳutayba, *ʿUyūn al-akhbār*, Cairo 1925-30, iv, 99-100; *Aghānī*³, xi, 364-8, *passim*, xv, 55-72, *passim*; al-Raḳīḳ al-Ḳayrawānī, *Ḳuṭb al-surūr*, Damascus 1969, 83-5; Abū ʿUbayd al-Bakrī, *Simṭ al-laʾālī*, Cairo 1935, 102; Nuwayrī, *Nihāyat al-arab*, Cairo 1923 ff., v, 75-8; Ibn Faḍl Allāh al-ʿUmarī, *Masālik al-abṣār*, facs. ed. Frankfurt 1988, x, 110-11; D. Sourdel, *La biographie d'Ibn al-Muqaffaʿ*, in *Arabica*, i (1954), 307 ff., esp. 311-12; K. al-Bustānī, *al-Nisāʾ al-ʿarabiyyāt*, Beirut 1964, 122-4. (E. NEUBAUER)

AL-**SALLĀMĪ**, ABŪ ʿALĪ AL-ḤUSAYN b. Aḥmad al-Bayhaḳī, historian of the Sāmānid period, who flourished in the middle decades of the 4th/10th century but whose exact dates of birth and death are unknown.

According to the local historian of Bayhaḳ, Ibn Funduḳ [see AL-BAYHAḲĪ, ẒAHĪR AL-DĪN ... B. FUNDUḲ] he was a pupil of the rather shadowy *nadīm* and *adīb* Ibrahīm b. Muḥammad al-Bayhaḳī [*q.v.*], author of the *K. al-Maḥāsin wa 'l-masāwī*, and according to al-Thaʿālibī, he was in the service of the Muḥtādjid *amīr* of Čaghāniyān [see MUḤTĀDJIDS], Abū Bakr Muḥammad and Abū ʿAlī Čaghānī, with whose fortunes in the Sāmānid state his own career was apparently link ed. Al-Sallāmī's fame arises from his history of the governors of Khurāsān, the *K. Wulāt Khurāsān*, which is now lost but which was used extensively (and independently of each other) by the Ghaznawid historian Gardīzī [*q.v.*] and then by Ibn al-Athīr for events in Khurāsān and Transoxania up to the death of Abū ʿAlī Čaghānī in 344/955 (this being the last event apparently taken from al-Sallāmī's work and common to the narratives of the two later historians). Al-Sallāmī's work was still known to, and cited by, the historian of the Mongols Djuwaynī [*q.v.*], but thereafter disappears from mention. There are also citations from other works of his in the sources; see Sezgin, *GAS*, i, 352.

Bibliography: W. Barthold, *Zur Geschichte der Ṣaffāriden*, in *Orientalische Studien ... Th. Nöldeke gewidmet*, Giessen 1906, i, 173-5; idem, *Turkestan*[3], p. xiii, 10-11; C.E. Bosworth, *The history of the Saffarids of Sistan and the Maliks of Nimruz (247/861 to 949/1542-3)*, Costa Mesa-New York 1994, 19-20.

(C.E. Bosworth)

SALLĀRIDS [see MUSĀFIRIDS].

SALM B. ʿAMR AL-**KHĀSIR**, early ʿAbbāsid poet (d. 186/802), born in Baṣra in a family of *mawālī*.

He was a pupil and *rāwī* of the poet Bashshār [*q.v.*], whose verse he is said to have plundered for motifs, and he befriended Abu 'l-ʿAtāhiya [*q.v.*] until they became estranged. When young, he moved to Baghdād and became a panegyrist of the caliphs al-Mahdī and al-Hādī, the Barmakids and other leading persons. He also excelled in elegies, which he sometimes seems to have prepared in advance. Notorious for his dissoluteness and libertinism (*mudjūn* [*q.v.*]) and even accused of heresy by later writers (probably unjustly), he is said to have become pious for a time but, relapsing, to have reverted to his former behaviour. This is one of the several explanations of his nickname "the Loser", among the other ones being the story that he sold a copy of the Ḳurʾān in exchange for a book of verse, or for a lute; or that he squandered a fortune inherited and earned with his poems (he is said to have left a large sum when he died). He is called a good poet with a natural talent (*maṭbūʿ mudjīd*), skilled in all poetic genres. He seems to have invented the ultra-short *radjaz* [*q.v.*] monometer (four syllables per line), employed in a poem praising al-Hādī. Ibn al-Muʿtazz, writing a century after his death, speaks of "his very numerous poems"; Ibn al-Nadīm mentions his poems as filling *ca.* 150 folios, but the *Dīwān*, still known in the 7th/13th century, is not preserved. Von Grunebaum was able to collect sixty fragments numbering 289 lines of verse, 278 being of unquestioned authenticity; a more recent collection was made by Nadjm. What remains of Salm's verse shows him to be a competent but not very original poet with an easy style.

Bibliography: G.E. von Grunebaum, *Three Arabic poets of the early Abbasid age*, in *Orientalia*, xvii (1948), 160-204, xix (1950), 53-80, xxii (1953), 262-83, repr. in his *Themes in mediaeval Arabic literature*, London 1981 (for Salm, see the second part and the beginning of the first); Muḥammad Yūsuf Nadjm, *Shuʿarāʾ ʿabbāsiyyūn*, Beirut 1959, 91-120. The Arabic sources are given in *GAS*, ii, 511-2, and see ix, 295; the chief ones being Ibn al-Muʿtazz, *Ṭabaḳāt al-shuʿarāʾ*, Cairo 1968, 99-106, *al-Aghānī*[3], xix, 260-87, *Taʾrīkh Baghdād*, ix, 136-40. A monograph is by Nāyif Maḥmūd Maʿrūf, *Salm al-Khāsir, shāʿir al-khulafāʾ wa 'l-umarāʾ fi 'l-ʿaṣr al-ʿabbāsī*, Beirut n.d. [1985?].

(G.J.H. van Gelder)

SALM B. **ZIYĀD** B. **ABĪHI**, Abū Ḥarb, Umayyad commander and governor, the third of the many sons of Abū Sufyān's bastard son Ziyād b. Abīhi [*q.v.*], d. 73/692.

The family of Ziyād already had a firm grip on the East in the later years of Muʿāwiya's caliphate, and when Yazīd I came to the throne, he appointed Salm as governor of Khurāsān (61/681), and the latter nominated another of his brothers, Yazid b. Ziyād, as his deputy in Sīstān. Salm proved himself a highly popular governor with the Arab troops in Khurāsān, largely on account of his military successes. He led raids across the Oxus against the Soghdian princes of Transoxania and to Samarḳand, and is said to have been the first Arab governor actually to winter across the river; he also raided Khwārazm. His lieutenants were, however, less successful in eastern Afghānistān against the Zunbīls, the local rulers of Zamīndāwar and Zābulistān [*q.vv.*], and the Kābul-Shāhs; his brothers Yazīd and Abū ʿUbayda were respectively killed and captured leading expeditions thither.

When Yazīd b. Muʿāwiya died, the Arab army in Khurāsān agreed with Salm to continue giving allegiance to him until the situation in the central lands of the caliphate should be clarified (63/683), but they soon renounced this allegiance; Salm was forced to return to Baṣra, and the East came to be dominated over the next years by the leader of the Ḳays party there [see ḲAYS and YAMAN], ʿAbd Allāh b. Khāzim al-Sulamī [*q.v.*], whom Salm had nominated as his successor over Khurāsān. In the prevailing uncertainty, Salm seems to have had the idea of giving allegiance to ʿAbd Allāh b. al-Zubayr [*q.v.*], but was arrested in Baṣra by the latter, who had just set himself up as anti-caliph in Arabia and the East. Salm was imprisoned at Mecca and mulcted of four million dirhams which he had gained from his two years' governorship. He subsequently contrived to escape when al-Ḥadjdjādj [*q.v.*] came to Mecca and the caliph ʿAbd al-Malik appointed him to the East once more, but he died at Baṣra in 73/692 before he could reach Khurāsān.

Bibliography: Balādhurī, *Ansāb*, ivB, 75-6; idem, *Futūḥ*, 397-8, 413-14; Ibn Ḳutayba, *Maʿārif*, ed. ʿUkkāsha, 348; Ṭabarī, i, 2706, ii, 391-5, 499-90; Wellhausen, *The Arab kingdom and its fall*, Calcutta 1927, 415-16; H. Lammens, *Le califat de Yazīd Ier*, in *MFOB*, vi (1913), 414; H.A.R. Gibb, *The Arab conquests in Central Asia*, London 1923, 21-2; Barthold, *Turkestan*[3]; C.E. Bosworth, *Sistan under the Arabs*, Rome 1968, 44-5, 48-9; M.A. Shaban, *The ʿAbbāsid Revolution*, Cambridge 1970, 39-42; G. Rotter, *Die Umayyaden und der zweite Bürgerkrieg (680-692)*, Wiesbaden 1982, 86-90, 92; Ziriklī, *Aʿlām*, iii, 167-8. (C.E. Bosworth)

SALMĀ [see ADJAʾ].

SALMĀN AL-**FĀRISĪ** [see Suppl.].

SALMĀN PĀK [see Suppl., *s.v.* SALMĀN AL-FĀRISĪ].

SALMĀN-I SĀWADJĪ, i.e. Djamāl al-Dīn Salmān b. Muḥammad-i Sāwadjī, Persian poet, panegyrist of the Djalāyirids [*q.v.*].

Salmān was born at the beginning of the 8th/14th century, probably in 709/1309 in Sāwa [*q.v.*]. His father held a post in the financial administration of the Ilkhānids [*q.v.*]. Among the first patrons of the young poet was the vizier Ghiyāth al-Dīn Muḥammad b. Rashīd al-Dīn Faḍl Allāh. It is likely that it was Dilshād Khātūn (d. before 753/1352), the widow of the Ilkhān Abū Saʿīd [*q.v.*], who encouraged Salmān to move to Baghdād and join the court of her new husband, Ḥasan-i Buzurg (d. 757/1356), founder of the

Djalāyirid dynasty. From 744/1343 on, Salmān was in the service of the Djalāyirids, and in time he was the teacher of Ḥasan-i Buzurg's son Uways (*r.* 757-76/1356-74). Most of Salmān's panegyrical *ḳaṣīdas* [*q.v.*] are in praise of the sultans Ḥasan and Uways and, notably, of Dilshād Khātūn. The service of the Djalāyirid house made Salmān a comparatively wealthy man, but frequent travel in the court's entourage seems to have damaged his health, for in a number of poems the poet complains of malaria, ailing feet and sore eyes and expresses his desire to lead a stationary and secluded life away from the court. In the last year of his life, under Uways's successor, Ḥusayn (*r.* 776-84/1374-82), Salmān fell from favour because of his apparent siding with Ḥusayn's rival Shāh Shudjāʿ. The most probable date of Salmān's death is Monday, 12 Ṣafar 778/30 June 1376.

Salmān's poetic work comprises about 21,000 *bayts*; it consists of his *dīwān* (*ḳaṣīdas*, *tarkībāt*, *tardjīʿāt*, *ḳiṭʿas* [*q.v.*], *ghazals* [*q.v.*], and *rubāʿīs* [*q.v.*]), a *Sāḳī-nāma*, a short *mathnawī* [*q.v.*], entitled *Firāḳ-nāma*, and a longer *mathnawī*, *Djamshīd u Khʷarshīd*, the latter being a romantic epic interspersed with lyrical *ghazals*. In his *ḳaṣīdas*, Salmān continues the tradition of the great classical masters such as Anwarī and Kamāl al-Dīn Ismāʿīl [*q.vv.*], and in his *ghazals* he is in some instances on a par with his contemporary Ḥāfiẓ [*q.v.*]. Like Ḥāfiẓ, Salmān was taken as a model by following generations of Persian and Turkish poets. His *mathnawī Djamshīd u Khʷarshīd* was adapted in an Anatolian Turkish version by Aḥmedī (d. 815/1412 [see AḤMADĪ]). At the moment, there is no truly critical edition of Salmān's *dīwān*, nor has his poetry so far been subjected to a critical study.

Bibliography: Browne, *LHP*, iii, 260-71; Dh. Ṣafā, *Tārīkh-i adabiyyāt dar Īrān*, iii/2, 1004-22; *Dīwān-i Salmān-i Sāwadjī*, ed. M. Mushfiḳ, Tehran 1336 *Sh.*/1957; *Kulliyyāt-i Salmān-i Sāwadjī*, ed. [M.] Āwistā, Tehran 1337 *Sh.*/1958; *Djamshīd u Khʷarshīd*, ed. J. Asmussen, Tehran 1348 *Sh.*/1969.

(M. GLÜNZ)

SALMĀNIYYA, the name applied to a sect of Shīʿī extremists (*ghulāt* [*q.v.*]) who paid special reverence to the *ṣaḥābī* Salmān al-Fārisī [*q.v.*] and are said to have regarded him as a prophet or even as a divine emanation superior to Muḥammad and ʿAlī b. Abī Ṭālib. The only two references to the sect originate from Rayy and its environs: the Salmāniyya are mentioned by the Ismāʿīlī author Abū Ḥātim al-Rāzī (d. 322/933-4) in his book *Kitāb al-Zīna* in the chapter on the Shīʿī sects (not yet printed; cf. Massignon, *Opera minora*, i, 475-6); in about 220/835 a certain ʿAlī b. al-ʿAbbās al-Kharādhīnī al-Rāzī (from the village of Kharādhīn near Rayy) is said to have written a refutation of the sect, entitled *K. al-Radd ʿalā 'l-Salmāniyya* (al-Nadjāshī, *Ridjāl*, lith. Bombay 1899, 180; ed. Muḥ. Djawād al-Nāʾīnī, Beirut 1988, ii, 78-9). The Salmāniyya were probably identical with the *aṣḥāb al-Sīn*, criticised by pseudo-Djābir al-Azdī, *K. al-Mādjid* (ms. Paris, B.N. ar. 5909); cf. Massignon, *op. cit.*, 477-8. As the sect is mentioned neither by Sunnī nor by Twelver Shīʿī heresiographers, it seems not to have played a major role and to have soon disappeared; hence the details of its doctrines are wrapped in obscurity.

Bibliography: L. Massignon, *Salmân Pâk et les prémices spirituelles de l'Islam iranien*, Soc. d'Et. Iraniennes, cahier vii, 1934, 47-52 (= *Opera minora*, Beirut 1963, i, 475-8).

(H. HALM)

SALMĀS, the name of a district, and of its mediaeval urban centre, in the western part of the Persian province of Ādharbāydjān. The district comprises a fertile plain near the northwestern corner of Lake Urmiya, bounded on the west by the Harāwīl mountain range with the pass of Khānasūr (2,408 m/7,900 feet) leading into Turkey, and on the south by the Kūh-i Awghān. The modern town of Salmās, Shābūr or Dīlmān (lat. 38° 13′ N., long. 44° 50′ E.), lies 48 km/30 miles to the south-south-west of Khōy [see KHOI] on the Zala Čay river. The region of Salmās has been inhabited since earliest known times, as shown by the remains there from the Urartian culture onwards. In classical Antiquity it came within the province of Persarmenia, and Constantine Porphyrogenitus mentions Salamas along with Chert (i.e. Khōy).

Salmās seems to have been conquered by Arab troops from Diyār Rabīʿa [*q.v.*], since al-Balādhurī states that the taxation of Salmās had long been transmitted to Mawṣil. In the 4th/10th century it came within the principality of the western branch of the Daylamī Musāfirids [*q.v.*] under Marzubān b. Muḥammad b. Musāfir. In 332/943-4 Marzubān fought off a Ḥamdānid raid on Salmās, and in 344/955-6 the Kurdish adventurer Daysam attacked it. Al-Iṣṭakhrī and Ibn Ḥawḳal describe Salmās as a small town of Ādharbāydjān, with a strong wall, in a fertile region. Al-Muḳaddasī describes it as a Kurdish town (these Kurds would be from the Hadhbānī tribe) and considered it as being administratively part of Armenia. In 456/1064 the inhabitants of Salmās joined the Saldjūḳ sultan Alp Arslan's expedition against the Byzantines, Armenians and Georgians. By Yāḳūt's time, however, the town was in ruins; yet in the mid-8th/14th century Ḥamd Allāh Mustawfī says that it was once more flourishing, with its wall, 8,000 paces in circumference, rebuilt in the time of the Il-Khān Ghazan by the vizier Khʷādja Tādj al-Dīn ʿAlī Shāh Tabrīzī; the revenues of Salmās (presumably the whole district) amounted to the substantial sum of 39,000 dīnārs (see Abū Dulaf, *Second Risāla*, ed. and tr. V. Minorsky, Cairo 1955, tr. 37, comm. 76; *Ḥudūd al-ʿālam*, tr. Minorsky, § 36.11, tr. 143; Le Strange, *Lands of the Eastern Caliphate*, 166; Schwarz, *Iran im Mittelalter*, 962, 1108-11). This mediaeval town of Salmās then gradually declined, and today must be marked by the village in the northwest of the Salmās district called in the early 20th century Kuhna Shahr ("old town") on the road from Albaḳ and Ḳaṭūr.

The modern chef-lieu of the district, in the 20th century known as Shāhpūr and before that as Dīlmān (which latter name seems to indicate a connection with the Daylamīs who at times controlled the region, e.g. the Musāfirids) lies in the centre of the plain (lat. 38° 13′ N., long. 44° 50′ E., alt. 1,430 m/4,690 ft.). In 1930 the town had some 8,000 inhabitants, almost all Shīʿī Muslims, but the surrounding villages included a good number with Christian populations, both Nestorian Assyrians and Catholic Chaldaeans, these last converted in the 18th century and having a bishop at Khosrawa; as early as 1281 there had been a Nestorian bishop of Salmās present at the consecration (*cheirotonia*) of the Patriarch Mar Yaballāhā in Baghdād (Assemani, ii, 456). It was in Urdī-Bihisht 1309/April-May 1930 that the town was largely destroyed by an earthquake, but rebuilt on Riḍā Shāh Pahlavī's orders. The region as a whole had suffered badly from the Russo-Turkish fighting in the First World War, and in the post-War period had occurred massacres of the Christian population by the Muslim Kurds; it was in 1918 that the Nestorian Patriarch Mār Shimʿūn Benjamin was murdered at Kuhna Shahr by the Kurdish bandit chief Ismāʿīl (Simko) b. ʿAlī Khān (see NASṬŪRIYYŪN and J.F. Coakley, *The*

Church of the East and the Church of England. A history of the Archbishop of Canterbury's Assyrian mission, Oxford 1992, 339-40). In *ca.* 1950 Shāhpūr and its rural environs had a population of 11,000, which had risen by 1991 to 60,570 (*Preliminary results of the 1991 census*, Statistical Centre of Iran, Population Division); administratively, it now falls within the *bakhsh* of the same name in the *shahrastān of* Khōy in the province (*ustān*) of Ādharbāydjān.

Worthy of note in the Salmās region is the Kurdish mountain fortress of Čahrīķ, on a rock in the gorge of the Zala Čay (illustr. in E.G. Browne (ed.), *Kitáb-i Nuqṭatu 'l-Káf*, Leiden 1910), where in 1264/1848 the Bāb, Sayyid ʿAlī Muḥammad Shīrāzī, was imprisoned by the governor there, Yaḥyā Khān, brother-in-law of Muḥammad Shāh Ķādjār [see BĀB].

The Salmās district is rich in antiquities from the Urartian period onwards, including an early Sāsānid bas-relief probably depicting Ardashīr I and his son Shāhpūr (I) receiving the homage of the defeated Armenians (see A. Gabriel, *Die Erforschung Persiens*, Vienna 1952, 169; Sylvia A. Matheson, *Persia: an archaeological guide*², London 1976, 88-9). At Kuhna Shahr is the brick tower from *ca* 700/1300-1 erected by Mīrī Khātūn, daughter of Arghun Āķā, governor of Khurāsān under the Il-Khānids Hülegü and Abaķa (C.F. Lehmann-Haupt, *Materialen zur ältesten Geschichte Armeniens*, in *Abh. GW Göttingen*, N.S., ix, 158-9; illustr. in idem, *Armenien einst und jetzt*, Berlin 1910, 320).

Bibliography (in addition to references given in the article): Ritter, *Erdkunde*, ix/2, 956-62; O. Blau, *Vom Urmiah-See nach dem Wan-See*, in *Petermanns Mitteilungen* (1863), 201-10; Razmara, *Farhang-i djughrāfiyā-yi Īrān-zamīn*, iv, 291-3.

(C.E. BOSWORTH)

SALOMON [see SULAYMĀN].

SALONIKA [see SELĀNĪK].

SALSABĪL (A.), the name of a fountain in paradise. It is mentioned only once in the Ķurʾān, in LXXVI, 18: the righteous who are in paradise in the hereafter "will be given there a cup to drink in which has been mixed ginger (*zandjabīl*), (from) a fountain therein named Salsabīl".

Exegetes approached the word from two directions: etymology linked to meaning, and grammar. The word was postulated to have been derived from *salla, salisa*, or *salsala* and all these roots were connected with the idea of being "easy to swallow" or "delightful in taste", attributes considered appropriate to liquids consumed in paradise. The presence of the letter *bāʾ* in the word was, according to some, simply to be understood as non-radical (*zāʾida*). More imaginative was the approach which saw the word composed of the imperative of the verb *saʾila* plus *sabīl*: "ask for a way!", according to Ibn Ķutayba, *Tafsīr gharīb al-Ķurʾān*, Cairo 1978, 4, some have said that the word suggests that the fountain is calling, "Ask me for a path to it (the fountain), O Muḥammad!" General opinion (including Ibn Ķutayba's) did not seem to favour this type of interpretation, however.

The grammatical issue, not unrelated to the suggestions regarding etymology and meaning, focused on the presence of the *tanwīn* at the end of the word (the absence of variant readings suggests that it was never read otherwise). If the word was a proper name, then, it was generally argued, it would normally not be fully declined, but rather should take a single *fatḥa* as a termination. If, however, it was understood as a description (*ṣifa*) of the water coming out of the fountain (as some of the meanings of the word suggested also), then a full declension with *tanwīn* was appropriate. Since the Ķurʾān said the fountain was "named" Salsabīl, this then led to a possible conclusion that the fountain had been named for its attribute (and that the verb "to name" here actually meant "to be described as": see al-Ṭabarī, *Djāmiʿ al-bayān*, Cairo 1905, xxix, 135). On the other hand, it was observed by most grammarians starting with al-Farrāʾ, *Maʿānī al-Ķurʾān*, Cairo 1972, iii, 217-18, that employing diptotes as triptotes was done in poetry and thus the presence of the phenomenon in the Ķurʾān was not problematic (and was also to be found in other passages, for example, LXVII, 4 and 15). Other grammarians, including al-Zadjdjādj, *Maʿānī al-Ķurʾān*, Beirut 1988, v, 261, simply observed that the *tanwīn* was required for the rhyme in the *sūra*.

In popular thought, Salsabīl was understood to be the name of the fountain and was sometimes taken as the name of one of the four rivers of paradise (see DJANNA, B. 1).

Bibliography: *Tafsīr* tradition on Ķurʾān, LXXVI, 18.

(A. RIPPIN)

AL-**SALṬ** or AL-SALT, a town in modern Jordan, approximately 28 km/17 miles west of ʿAmmān (30° 03′ N, 35° 42′ E.) at an elevation of about 840 m/2,755 feet. It is the seat of the governorate of the Balķāʾ [*q.v.*], and in 1993 its population was estimated at 60,740. It is situated in a rather mountainous, oak-covered area, with several springs that allow cultivation of the valley floors, notably with figs and pomegranates; Arab geographers and 19th-century European travellers mention the export of its grapes, raisins, wheat and lentils to Palestine.

The town was called Gadara during the Greco-Roman period, and the name al-Salṭ likely derives from the Roman administrative designation Regis Saltus, a crown domain within the province of Palaestina Prima that was probably granted by the Emperor Septimius Severus (A.D. 192-211). The tomb complex and adjacent reservoir and olive press discovered in 1978 on the outskirts of the city may have belonged to a family entrusted with this crown domain.

The first reference to the name al-Salṭ occurs in 512/1118, following the death of Baldwin I of Jerusalam, when his successor Baldwin II sent an envoy to the *atabeg* of Damascus Ẓahīr al-Dīn Ṭughtigin [see BŪRIDS] requesting an extension of the truce. Ṭughtigin responded positively on condition that the revenues from Djabal ʿAwf, Ḥannāna, al-Salṭ, al-Ghawr and al-Djawlān should be collected exclusively for the Muslims. Baldwin II refused this stipulation, and it seems that the earlier arrangement was terminated after Ṣalāḥ al-Dīn's victory at Ḥiṭṭīn in 583/1187, when the Muslims established their control over these lands, and in 588/1192 al-Salṭ was assigned to the sultan's brother and successor al-ʿĀdil. In 617/1220, al-ʿĀdil's son Sharaf al-Dīn ʿĪsā erected a citadel on a mountain known as Raʾs al-Amīr, in response to an attack on a caravan by a group from the Banū Raḥmān from the nearby village of Kafr Yahūda. This citadel later served as a place of banishment, as when in 637/1239 the family of al-Malik al-Ṣāliḥ, his treasury and his horses were sent there.

In 644/1246 some Khʷārazmian refugees settled at al-Salṭ, but were forced to flee to Karak when the town was attacked and burned by a certain Fakhr al-Dīn Ibn al-Shaykh. The Mongols reached al-Salṭ in 659/1260, where they were opposed by Badr al-Dīn Muḥammad al-Atābekī; he surrendered the town, but the Mongols retained him in authority there.

The Mamluk sultan al-Ẓāhir Baybars al-Bunduķdārī (d. 676/1277) repaired and expanded the citadel at al-Salṭ, and stationed troops there. He also renovated the town's mosque. Mamlūk period sources describe al-Salṭ as being prosperous and noted for its orchards. It came within the *wilāya* of al-Balḳā᾿, the sixth *wilāya* of the southern *ṣafḳa* of Damascus. The administrative status of al-Salṭ varied, but towards the end of the Mamlūk period it had eclipsed both Ḥiṣbān (Esbous) and ᶜAmmān. Its residents probably followed the Shāfiᶜī *madhhab*, for it is known that the town had a Shāfiᶜī *ḳāḍī*, and that the *amīr* Sayf al-Din Begtimur al-Ḥusāmī (d. 729/1328) founded a Shāfiᶜī *madrasa* there. A number of learned men with the name of al-Salṭī are listed in the biographical dictionaries of this time.

The Ottoman *tapu defters* provide significant information about al-Salṭ. In 954/1538 it was the seat of a *nāḥiya* comprising two *maḥallas*: Awāmla east of the citadel and Maḥallat Akrād west of the citadel; between them there were 168 households, ten bachelors, four imāms, ten Christians, and six soldiers who manned the citadel. An order by the sultan of 959/1551 states that al-Salṭ was in a ruinous state, which corroborates the population decline recorded in the *tapu defter* of 1005/1596. Both *defters* detail the sum of 12,000 *akčes* in dues that were collected from al-Salṭ as part of the allowances of the *mīr liwā* of ᶜAdjlūn. Christians paid the poll tax at the rate of 80 *akčes* per head. At the time, al-Salṭ was a market place for the district, while Ḥiṣbān is reported as having been derelict.

The citadel at al-Salṭ continued to be well maintained. In 1033/1623, Fakhr al-Dīn al-Maᶜnī II visited al-Salṭ and installed a garrison of fifty men there. It is claimed that the citadel was destroyed by Ibrāhīm Pasha [*q.v.*] during his presence in Syria between 1247/1831 and 1256/1840, and only ruins survive today, including trenches that give the neighbourhood the name of Khandaḳ.

Little data is available about al-Salṭ during the 17th, 18th, and early 19th centuries, but there is plentiful information from the second half of the 19th century in connection with the measures taken by the Ottomans to rejuvenate the region during the *Tanẓīmāt* period. Al-Salṭ's importance increased, but it remained administratively dependent upon either the Ḥawrān, Karak or Nābulus. Thus in 1313/1895, it was a seat of a *ḳaḍā᾿* within the *liwā* of Karak, that included its own *nāḥiya* and the *nāḥiyas* of ᶜAmmān, Djīza and Mādaba. *Sāl-nāmes* and other sources report about 300 villages belonging to this *ḳaḍā᾿*, but it is difficult to accept this figure unless derelict sites are included.

Al-Salṭ had a *ḳā᾿immaḳām*, Islamic and civil courts, and special courts for non-Muslims. In addition, it had departments for education, health, land registry, taxation, postal and telegraph services, and religious endowments. The various villages, quarters, tribes and Christian communities each had its own *mukhtār*. The town attracted people from the regions of Damascus, Ḥamā and Palestine, and particularly from Nābulus, and these new settlers were responsible for the flourishing of business and increased construction of houses, shops, baths, and other buildings; Christians, many from Palestine, also came to settle in the city, and were the pioneers in business; along with others, they came to dominate land ownership in the neighbouring villages. A number of missionary groups came to al-Salṭ, and it had several churches, among them Greek Orthodox, Roman Catholic, Greek Catholic and Protestant. A Chamber of Commerce was instituted in 1301/1884, and a Municipal Council in 1305/1888. The town enjoyed security, and through its military garrison maintained control over the region, especially the Abad, ᶜAdwān, and Banū Ṣakhr tribes. This security attracted the influx of capital, which is reflected in the town's Ottoman-style mansions, many of which survive today.

Al-Salṭ was ahead of the rest of the country in education because of the number of both state and missionary schools that were established there. The first secondary school in Jordan was established there in 1344/1925, and it accordingly had an important early role in building the modern state of Jordan.

Bibliography: 1. Primary sources. Le Strange, *Palestine under the Moslems*, 529-39; Aḥmad b. Muḥammad al-Khālidī al-Ṣafadi (d. 1034/1624), *Ta᾿rīkh al-Amīr Fakhr al-Dīn al-Maᶜnī*, ed. Asad Rustum and Fu᾿ād al-Bustānī, Beirut 1969; Dimashḳī, *Nukhbat al-dahr*, ed. Mehren, St. Petersburg 1866; Abu 'l-Fidā᾿, *Taḳwīm al-buldān*, ed. Reinaud and de Slane, Paris 1850; Ḳalḳashandī, *Ṣubḥ al-aᶜshā*, iv, xii, xiv, xviii-xix; Ibn Shaddād, *al-Aᶜlāḳ al-khaṭīra*, ed. Sāmī al-Dahhān; Ibn Faḍl Allāh al-ᶜUmarī, *Masālik al-abṣār*, ed. Ayman al-Sayyid, Cairo 1985; idem, *al-Taᶜrīf bi 'l-muṣṭala al-sharīf*, ed. Samīr al-Durūbī, ᶜAmmān 1992; Maḳrīzī, *Sulūk*, i/3, ii/3, iii/3; Ibn al-Athīr, x; Ibn Taghribirdī, *Nudjūm*, vi; Ibn Kathīr, *al-Bidāya wa 'l-nihāya*, Cairo 1939, xiii; *The detailed defter of liwā᾿ ᶜAjlūn (district of Ajlūn), Tapu defteri no. 970 Istanbul*, ed. Muhammad Adnan Bakhit and Noufan Raja Hmoud, ᶜAmmān 1989; eidem (eds.), *The detailed defter of liwa ᶜAjlūn (district of Ajlūn), Tapu defteri no. 185 Ankara 1005 A.H./1596 A.D.*, ᶜAmmān 1991.

2. 19th and early 20th-century travelers. G.R. Lees, *Life and adventure beyond Jordan*, London 1906, 102-5; J.G. Duncan, *Es-Salt*, in *Palestine Exploration Fund Quarterly Statement* (July 1928), 28-36; A. Goodrich-Freer, *In a Syrian saddle*, London 1905, 145-60; Baedeker, *Palestine and Syria*, Leipzig 1912, 136-8; L. Oliphant, *The land of Gilead*, London 1880, 199-202.

3. Studies. Djurdj Farīd Ṭāriḳ Dāwūd, *al-Salt wa-djiwāruhā, 1864-1921*, ᶜAmmān 1994; Yusūf Darwīsh Ghawānma, *Dirāsat fī ta᾿rīkh madīnat al-Salt*, in *Afkār*, xliii (1979), 90-9; Muḥammad ᶜAdnān al-Bakhīt, *Mamlakat al-Karak fī 'l-ᶜahd al-mamlūkī*, ᶜAmmān 1976; Saᶜd Muḥammad al-Mu᾿minī, *al-Ḳilāᶜ al-Islāmiyya fī 'l-Urdunn*, ᶜAmmān 1988; R. de Vaux, *Exploration de la région de Salt*, in *Revue Biblique*, xlvii (1938), 398-425.

(M.A. AL-BAKHIT)

SALṬANA (A.) "sovereignty, ruling power", from the verb *salṭana* "become ruler, exercise power", with *salāṭa* meaning "force" (*ḳahr*), thence by extension the holder of power. *Sulṭān* is found in the Ḳur᾿ān; see for a detailed discussion of the Islamic origins of the term and its later developments, SULṬĀN. The Arabic papyri from the first century of Islam have such expressions as *kharādj al-sulṭān* or *bayt māl al-sulṭān*, with the sense of "authority of the government, or of the governor, *wālī* or *ḥākim*". In the standard Arabic dictionaries (Ibn Durayd, *Djamhara*, iii, 27; Ibn Sīduh, *Mukhaṣṣaṣ*, iii, 133 ff.; Ibn Fāris, *Muᶜdjam maḳāyīs al-lugha*, iii, 95; *LᶜA*, iii, 2065-6; al-Fīrūzābādī, *Ḳāmūs*, ii, 365-6; *TᶜA*, v, 158-60; Buṭrus al-Bustānī, *Muḥīṭ al-muḥīṭ*, i, 680), *sulṭān* is invariably connected with the idea of constraint. In popular Arabic usage, *salīt* means "oil", in Yemen, "sesame oil", and *sulṭān* is thus connected with *salīt* because oil, it is asserted, serves to make things clear, just like political authority. Hence *amīrs* are described as *sulṭāns* because the latter term is the divine proof which is used to put the proof into practice.

The term was employed in the *fiḳh* works and in *adab* ones, whence the title of the first chapter of Ibn Ḳutayba's *ʿUyūn al-akhbār: kitāb al-sulṭān* (in which the author defines the role and attributes of the *sulṭān*). For the subsequent development in practice of *sulṭān* as a personal title, see SULṬĀN, in addition to which it should be noted that al-Ḳalḳashandī, speaking of the evolution of power in Egypt, states that, under the Fāṭimids, authority (*salṭana*) was acquired by the "vizierate of delegation" (*ṣārat salṭanatuhā wizārat al-tafwīḍ* (*Ṣubḥ*, ix, 403).

Salṭana is found in combination with many terms: *dār al-salṭana, dast al-salṭana, takht al-salṭana, sarīr al-salṭana, nimdjat al-salṭana* and *nāʾib al-salṭana*.

Bibliography: 1. Texts. ʿAbd al-Bāḳī, *al-Muʿdjam al-mufahras li-alfāẓ al-Ḳurʾān*, s.v.; Ibn Djamāʿa, *Taḥrīr al-aḥkām*, ed. and tr. H. Kofler, *Handbuch des islamischen Verwaltungsrechtes*, in *Islamica*, vi (1934), 349-414, vii (1935), 1-64; Ibn Ḳutayba, *ʿUyūn*, i, 1-15; Ḳalḳashandī, *Ṣubḥ*, v, 447-8, ix, 401-4; Maḳrīzī, *Khiṭaṭ*, i, 153.

2. Studies. C.H. Becker, *Barthold's Studien über Kalif und Sultan*, in *Isl.*, vi (1915-16), esp. 356 ff.; T.W. Arnold, *The caliphate*, London 1924, esp. 202 ff.; Barthold, *Turkestan down to the Mongol invasion*², 271; Ḥasan al-Bāshā, *al-Alḳāb al-islāmiyya*, Cairo 1955, 323-9; E. Tyan, *Institutions de droit public musulman. ii. Sultanat et califat*, Paris 1956, 7-79; Barthold, *Caliph and sulṭan*, tr. N.S. Doniach, in *IQ*, vii (1963), 117-35; G. Makdisi, *Les rapports entre calife et sultan à l'époque saljukide*, in *IJMES*, vi (1975), 228-36; A. Cheddadi, *Le jâh, une notion méconnue, le système de pouvoir chez Ibn Khaldun*, in *Annales ESC*, 35ᵉ année, no. 3-4 (1980), 534-50; A.K.S. Lambton, *State and government in mediaeval Islam*, Oxford 1981, 185-6; B. Lewis, *The political language of Islam*, Chicago and London 1988, 51-3; M. Talbi, *Les structures et les caractéristiques de l'Etat islamique traditionnel*, in *CT*, xxxvi, no. 143-4 = *Mélanges Bechir Tlili*, 231-56. See further the *bibl.* to SULṬĀN.

(MOUNIRA CHAPOUTOT-REMADI)

SALTUḲ OGHULLARÏ, a Türkmen dynasty that ruled a principality centred on Erzurum [*q.v.*] from *ca.* 465/1072 to 598/1202.

The information on this dynasty from all sources is rather sparse and somewhat confused. It was apparently founded by one Saltuḳ, who was among the Türkmen *beys* under Alp Arslan whom he sent to conquer Anatolia after the battle of Malāzgird [*q.v.*]. Ibn al-Athīr (d. 630/1233) says the founder was a certain Abu 'l-Ḳāsim, who may have been the same person. The Saltuḳ-oghullarï seem to have established the first Türkmen principality in Anatolia after Malāzgird. In addition to their capital at Erzurum, it included Bāybūrt, Shābīn Ḳarā Ḥiṣār, Terdjān, İspir, Oltu, Midjingerd, and sometimes Ḳars. In 496/1103, the ruler, with the title *malik*, was one ʿAlī, who was allied with the Saldjūḳ sultan Muḥammad Tapar in his struggle against Berk-yaruḳ. In 516/1123, the ʿAbbāsid caliph al-Mustarshid asked the Saltuḳ-oghullarï, among others, for military assistance against Dubays b. Ṣadaḳa, the Mazyadid ruler of Ḥilla [*q.v.*]. The next known Saltuḳid ruler was ʿAlī's brother, Ḍiyāʾ al-Dīn Ghāzī (d. 526/1131-2).

Meanwhile, taking advantage of the confusion caused by the Crusades and Saldjūḳ domestic strife, the Georgians began to attack eastern Anatolia. In 514/1120, David the Builder (1089-1125), assisted by the Ḳipčaḳs [*q.v.*], defeated a coalition of Turkish forces, which no doubt included the Saltuḳ-oghullarï, near Tiflīs (Tbilisi). A few years later, Ḍiyāʾ al-Dīn concluded a marriage alliance with the Artuḳids [*q.v.*]. He was succeeded by ʿAlī's son ʿIzz al-Dīn Saltuḳ (d. 563/1168). In 549/1154, the Georgians under Dimitri I (1125-55) defeated and captured ʿIzz al-Dīn near Ānī. He was ransomed by the Artuḳids and Suḳmān, the Shāh-i Arman [*q.v.*] at Akhlāṭ. The latter was married to one of his daughters. ʿIzz al-Dīn was among the coalition of Turkish forces that besieged the Georgians at Ānī in 556/1161, only to meet defeat again. Shortly thereafter, ʿIzz al-Dīn sent another daughter to marry Ḳilïdj Arslān II [*q.v.*], the Saldjūḳ sultan of Rūm. She was intercepted en route, however, by the Dānishmendid Yaghï-basan, who married her off to his nephew, the ruler of Ḳayṣariyya (Kayseri). This provoked a war between the Saldjūḳs and Dānishmendids. ʿIzz al-Dīn was succeeded by his son Nāṣir al-Dīn Muḥammad. Sometime during his reign, the Georgians attacked Erzurum for the first and last time.

It was presumably after this event that there occurred the curious incident in which Nāṣir al-Dīn's son Muẓaffar al-Dīn offered to convert to Christianity and marry the queen of Georgia, the famed Tʿamar (1184-1213). Muẓaffar al-Dīn went to Tiflīs with much pomp and expensive gifts, but the queen ultimately declined his offer. The subsequent fate of both Nāṣir al-Dīn and his son is unknown. Between at least 587/1191 and 597/1200-1, Nāṣir al-Dīn's sister Māmā Khātūn appeared as *malika* of Erzurum. She was allied with the Ayyūbid ruler of Mayyāfāriḳīn against the Shāh-i Arman. In 597/1200-1, she asked the Ayyūbid sultan al-Malik al-ʿĀdil in Cairo to arrange a husband for her. At that point, she seems to have been overthrown by Muẓaffar al-Dīn's brother Malik Shāh. These events probably disturbed the Saldjūḳ sultan of Rum, Sulaymān II, who was hostile to Ayyūbid ambitions in eastern Anatolia. Consequently, when he marched through Erzurum in 598/1202 on a campaign to Georgia, he imprisoned Malik-Shāh and annexed his territory, putting an end to the Saltuḳid dynasty. Under the Saltuḳ-oghullarï, Erzurum was a flourishing emporium and acquired a number of monumental buildings. Ḍiyāʾ al-Dīn built the Tepsi Minare and Kale Camii, and Nāṣir al-Dīn built or completed the Ulu Cami. Also noteworthy is the *türbe* of Māmā Khātūn in Terdjān.

Bibliography: O. Turan, *Doğu anadolu türk devletleri tarihi*, Istanbul 1973, repr. 1980, 1-21 (to be used with caution); F. Sümer, *Doğu anadolu'da türk beylikleri*, Ankara 1990, 17-45, which is a revised version of his article *Saltuklular* in *Selçuklu Araştırmaları Dergisi*, iii (1971), 391-434 (Sümer takes issue with Turan on many important points).

(G. LEISER)

SALTUḲIDS [see SALTUḲ OGHULLARÏ].

SALŪḲĪ, the name given by the Arabs to a member of the gazehound family, so-called because it pursues its quarry by sight and not by scent. The *salūḳī* stands about 25-6 ins. in height at the shoulder. The *salūḳī* has often been mistaken for the greyhound by travellers to the Middle East, but the ears are long and pendulous, while the greyhound's are short and pricked, and the greyhound is wider in the body and more heavily built. Whereas the greyhound is a sprinter, the *salūḳī* is possessed of great stamina.

Abundant evidence exists in Arabic literature that the *salūḳī* hunted oryx in the Djāhiliyya (see the *Muʿallaḳa* of Labīd (ll. 49-52); the *ḳaṣīda* of al-Nābigha (in C.J. Lyall (ed.), *A commentary on ten ancient Arabic poems*, Calcutta 1894, 154 ll. 13-18); and ʿAbda b. al-Ṭabīb (ll. 29-39) and Abū Dhuʾayb (ll. 36-48) both in the *Mufaḍḍaliyyāt*). The huntsman, armed with bow and arrows, would use a whole pack of *salūḳīs* and the latter would hunt down and exhaust the quarry which, when turned and fighting back with its long, straight horns, would be dispatched by the huntsman's bow, the huntsman being at this time unaffected by the strict prescriptions on the killing of prey which would come in Islamic times. Although such hunting is not mentioned in the extremely stereotyped pre-Islamic poetry, the hunting of the gazelle and the hare by *salūḳīs* must have taken place even before Islam.

The *salūḳī* has been a favourite hunter of the gazelle and the hare right through mediaeval times in the Middle East to the present day in Saudi Arabia and the Gulf. The former was hunted until fairly recent times by both *salūḳīs* and saker falcons (see Smith, *A new translation*, 254). The sakers would bind to the head of the gazelle to confuse and delay it, while the *salūḳīs* followed on and dragged the gazelle down for the huntsman to slaughter according to the prescriptions of Islam (see Allen and Smith, *Hunting techniques*, 114-15). The hare has always been, and continues to this day to be, coursed by the *salūḳī*. The latter will probably survive, despite the stronger interest now in birds of prey for hunting, because of the danger presented to the bird of prey when she tries to cope with the swift, jinking desert hare.

The origin of the word *salūḳī* is not easily arrived at. The word must have been used in pre-Islamic times, though its occurrence in the poetry of the period is rare (e.g. *Mufaḍḍaliyyāt*, 61, *banāt salūḳiyyayn* "the offspring of two *salūḳīs*"). The Arab geographers (listed in detail in Allen and Smith, *op. cit.*, 139, n. 25) suggest the name is the *nisba* of a place called Salūḳ in the Yemen near Taʿizz, or alternatively in the area of al-Lān to the west of the Caspian Sea, also called Salūḳ (*ibid.*, map 121). Viré in his article (*REI*, xli/2, 231-40) opts for the latter which he calls the "patrie d'origine de ces lévriers". There is no reason, either, why *salūḳī* should not be the *nisba* of one of the many Salūḳiyyas, towns founded by the ancient Seleucids and called after the dynasty. The most likely answer is that, for some reason, the Arabs regarded their prize hounds as being "Seleucid" (*salūḳī*), in some way connected with the dynasty which had controlled vast areas of the Middle East before Islam (see Smith, *The Arabian hound*, 457-64).

Bibliography: *al-Muʿallaḳāt al-ʿas͟hr*, ed. Aḥmad b. Amīn al-S͟hinḳīṭī, Cairo 1331; *Dīwān al-Mufaḍḍaliyyāt*, ed. C.J. Lyall, Beirut 1920; F. Viré, *A propos des chiens de chase* salūqī *et* zaġārī, in *REI*, xli/2 (1973), 231-40; M.J.S. Allen and G.R. Smith, *Some notes on hunting techniques and practices in the Arabian Peninsula*, in *Arabian Studies*, ii, 111 (photographs), 114-15, 120-8, 130-1; Smith, *The Arabian hound, the* salūqī *– further consideration of the word and other observations on the breed*, in *BSOAS*, xliii/3, 459-64; idem, *A new translation of certain passages of the hunting section of Usāma ibn Munqidh's* Iʿtibar, in *JSS*, xxvi/2 (1981), 235-57, *passim*; idem, *Hunting poetry* (ṭardiyyāt), in Julia Ashtiany *et alii* (eds.), *The Cambridge hist. of Arabic literature. ʿAbbasid belles-lettres*, Cambridge 1990, 167-85, esp. 169, 171, 178.

(G.R. Smith)

SALŪL, the name of two tribal groups in northern Arabia: a branch of K͟huzāʿa [*q.v.*] and a branch of the so-called Northern Arabian federation Ḳays ʿAylān [*q.v.*], more precisely, the Hawāzin [*q.v.*].

1. The lineage of the Salūl who were a branch of K͟huzāʿa was: Salūl b. Kaʿb b. ʿAmr b. Rabīʿa b. Ḥārit͟ha. The genealogists list, beside Salūl himself, the following descendants of his as eponyms of tribal groups (the term employed is *baṭn*): Ḳumayr b. Ḥabs͟hiya (variants: Ḥabs͟hiyya, Ḥabas͟hiyya, Ḥubs͟hiyya), Ḥulayl b. Ḥabs͟hiya, including the descendants of Abū G͟hubs͟hān, who were numerous and formed many tribal groups, Ḍāṭir b. Ḥabs͟hiya, Kulayb b. Ḥabs͟hiya, al-Ḥizmir (variants: al-Ḥirmiz, al-Ḥurmuz) b. Salūl, ʿAdī b. Salūl, Ḥabtar b. ʿAdī and Hanīʾa b. ʿAdī (see also Ibn Durayd, *al-Is͟htiḳāḳ*, ed. ʿAbd al-Salām Hārūn, Cairo 1378/1958, 468-73; cf. Caskel, *Ǧamharat an-nasab*, i, 198, 199; Ibn ʿAbd Rabbihi, *al-ʿIḳd al-farīd*, ed. Aḥmad Amīn *et alii*, Cairo 1384/1965; iii, 383; Hanīʾa's mother is said to have been the daughter of Salūl b. Ṣaʿṣaʿa (Ibn al-Kalbī, *Nasab Maʿadd wa 'l-Yaman al-kabīr*, ed. Nād͟jī Ḥasan, Beirut 1408/1988, ii, 446), which points to a link between the two tribal groups called Salūl).

There are two indications, both related to blood-revenge, that before Islam the Ḳumayr were the leading group among the Salūl, and possibly among the Kaʿb b. ʿAmr as a whole. First, one of the Ḳumayr, ʿAmr b. K͟hālid, vowed that he would not let the blood of a Kaʿbī go unavenged (*Nasab Maʿadd*, ii, 441). Second, when al-Walīd b. al-Mug͟hīra of the Ḳuras͟hī Banū Mak͟hzūm [*q.v.*] died of an injury caused by a K͟huzāʿī (who was either of the Ḳumayr or of the Hanīʾa), it was again a member of the Ḳumayr, Busr b. Sufyān, who intervened in the ensuing crisis. Busr guaranteed the payment of the blood-money agreed upon—a compromise was struck; K͟huzāʿa did not admit responsibility for al-Walīd's death. Busr even brought a son of his to Ḳurays͟h [*q.v.*] as hostage. But K͟hālid b. al-Walīd [*q.v.*], who was the son of the slain man, sent the boy back (*Nasab Maʿadd*, ii, 447; Ibn Ḥad͟jar, *Iṣāba*, ed. ʿAlī Muḥammad al-Bid͟jāwī, Cairo 1392/1972, i, 293; Muḥammad b. Ḥabīb, *al-Munammaḳ fī ak͟hbār Ḳurays͟h*, ed. K͟hūrs͟hīd Aḥmad Fāriḳ, Beirut 1405/1985, 191-9; Ibn His͟hām, *al-Sīra al-nabawiyya*, ed. al-Saḳḳā *et alii*, Beirut 1391/1971, ii, 52-4).

The crisis over al-Walīd's blood-money is illuminating with regard to Mecca's internal politics on the eve of Islam. One assumes that in the dispute, the Banū Hās͟him supported K͟huzāʿa: the Kaʿb b. ʿAmr of K͟huzāʿa, to whom the Salūl belonged, had an alliance with ʿAbd al-Muṭṭalib b. Hās͟him (Ibn Ḥabīb, *al-Munammaḳ*, 192-2). In this alliance, ʿAbd al-Muṭṭalib was the most important figure on the Ḳuras͟hī side. On the K͟huzāʿī side we find, among others, representatives of the following Salūl subdivisions: Ḳumayr, Ḍāṭir and Ḥabtar. As usual in tribal alliances, marriage links were agreed upon: ʿAbd al-Muṭṭalib married on that day the daughters of two of the K͟huzāʿī leaders who were party to the alliance, i.e. the representatives of Ḍāṭir and Ḥabtar. The former bore him the famous Abū Lahab [*q.v.*] (and see U. Rubin, *Abū Lahab and sūra cxi*, in *BSOAS*, xlii [1979], 16), while the latter bore him al-G͟haydāḳ (M.J. Kister, *On strangers and allies in Mecca*, in *JSAI*, xiii [1990], 140; M. Lecker, *The Banū Sulaym: a contribution to the study of early Islam*, Jerusalem 1989, 129). In other words, two of the Prophet's paternal uncles were born by Salūlī women (Ḥassān b. T͟hābit, *Dīwān*, ed. W. ʿArafat, London 1971, ii, 16-7; al-Balād͟hurī, *Ansāb al-as͟hrāf*, i, ed. Muḥammad Ḥamīdullāh, Cairo 1959, 71-2; art. K͟HUZĀʿA, at V, 78a-b; Kister, *op. cit.*, 151). The Mak͟hzūmī position in the dispute over al-Walīd's blood-money was supported by the *Aḥābīs͟h* [see ḤABAS͟H, ḤABAS͟HA, at the end] who at some stage were called upon by the Mak͟hzūm to intervene (Ibn Ḥabīb, *Munammaḳ*, 195-6).

The most important role played by the Salūl before Islam was the one associated with Mecca in general and the Kaʿba in particular. Their eponym Salūl is said to have been a custodian (*ḥādjib*) of the Kaʿba, and the same is said about his son Ḥabshiya b. Salūl and his grandson Ḥulayl b. Ḥabshiya, who was, according to some, the last Khuzāʿī custodian of the Kaʿba. According to others, the last custodian was Ḥulayl's son al-Muḥtarish, better known by his *kunya* Abū Ghubshān.

There are several versions concerning the transference of the authority over the Kaʿba, and over the affairs of Mecca in general, from Khuzāʿa to Ḳuraysh, more specifically to Ḳuṣayy b. Kilāb [*q.v.*] (and see KHUZĀʿA, at V, 77b-78a; Kister, *Mecca and the tribes of Arabia*, in *Studies in Islamic history and civilization in honour of David Ayalon*, ed. M. Sharon, Jerusalem and Leiden 1986, 50, repr. in idem, *Society and religion from Djāhiliyya to Islam*, Variorum Reprints, Aldershot 1990, no. II). For example, it is reported that Abū Ghubshān sold Ḳuṣayy his rights. The alleged sale is at the background of the popular saying "Incurring more loss than Abū Ghubshān's deal" (*akhsar min ṣafḳat Abī Ghubshān*; see KHUZĀʿA, at V, 78a). This version of the story was promulgated by people fanatically hostile to the so-called Southern tribes (*fa-yaqūlu 'l-mutaʿaṣṣibūna ʿalā 'l-Yamāniya inna Ḳuṣayy^an^ shtarā 'l-miftāḥ*, etc.; al-Wazīr al-Maghribī, *al-Īnās fī ʿilm al-ansāb*, ed. Ḥamad al-Djāsir, Riyāḍ 1400/1980, 114; obviously, the Khuzāʿa figure here as a Southern tribe). The Khuzāʿa could not remain indifferent to the way in which this crucial chapter of their pre-Islamic history was recorded: al-Wāḳidī concludes one of the variants of this version with a statement that it was denied by the elders of Khuzāʿa (*ḳāla 'l-Wāḳidī: wa-ḳad raʾaytu mashyakhata Khuzāʿa tunkiru hādhā*; al-Fāsī, *Shifāʾ al-gharām bi-akhbār al-balad al-ḥarām*, ed. ʿUmar ʿAbd al-Salām Tadmurī, Beirut 1405/1985, ii, 87). The Khuzāʿīs stated that Ḥulayl b. Ḥabshiya bequeathed to his son-in-law Ḳuṣayy the authority over the Kaʿba and Mecca. Their version is attested, for instance, in an autobiographical report going back to the Companion Khirāsh b. Umayya of the Salūl (*Shifāʾ al-gharām*, ii, 114). Ibn Isḥāḳ quotes the Khuzāʿī claim, adding that he did not hear this from non-Khuzāʿī sources, "and God knows best" (Ibn Hishām, *Sīra*, i, 124). The dispute over this matter no doubt dates back to the earliest stage of Islamic historiography and could even be pre-Islamic.

A prominent feature of the Salūl, and one concerning which there was continuity from the pre-Islamic period to at least the 2nd century A.H., was the *ḳiyāfa* [*q.v.*], i.e. the science of physiognomancy and the examination of traces on the ground. It was a Salūlī, Kurz b. ʿAlḳama, who allegedly tracked the Prophet and Abū Bakr when they left Mecca for the Hidjra. Upon viewing the Prophet's footprint, Kurz recognised it as being similar to that of Abraham, found at the *maḳām Ibrāhīm*; according to the science of *ḳiyāfa*, this similarity indicated that the Prophet descended from Abraham [see MAḲĀM IBRĀHĪM, at VI, esp. 105b]. Later, at the time of Muʿāwiya, Kurz reinstated the marks indicating the boundaries of the sacred territory of Mecca (*maʿālim al-ḥaram*, or *anṣāb al-ḥaram*; Ibn Saʿd, v, 338; Ibn Ḥadjar, *Iṣāba*, v, 583-4; Caskel, ii, 374). The continuity from pre-Islamic times is also reflected in Ibn al-Kalbī's remark that in his own time, Kurz's descendants were still trackers in Mecca (*Nasab Maʿadd*, ii, 444).

Since the Salūl, and the Banū Kaʿb b. ʿAmr in general, inhabited the vicinity of Mecca (the placenames ʿUsfān, al-Ẓahrān, Ḳudayd and Arāk are mentioned), their role in the struggle between the Prophet and Mecca was important. Indeed Muʿattib b. ʿAwf of the Salūl, more precisely of the Kulayb subdivision, participated in the Battle of Badr [*q.v.*], but this does not indicate the beginning of his tribe's involvement in the struggle: he was the client (*ḥalīf*) of the Makhzūm (Ibn Saʿd, iii/1, 189; al-Wāḳidī, *al-Maghāzī*, ed. J.M.B. Jones, London 1966, i, 155, 341; Ibn Hishām, *Sīra*, ii, 339), i.e. of one of the Prophet's Makhzūmī Companions, perhaps Abū Salama b. ʿAbd al-Asad.

Khirāsh b. Umayya of the Kulayb subdivision was also a client (*ḥalīf*) of the Makhzūm. He provides a valuable lead with regard to Salūl's role in the expedition of Muraysīʿ which took place more than a year, or, according to others, several months, before the expedition of Ḥudaybiya (cf. Jones, *The chronology of the maghāzī—a textual survey*, in *BSOAS*, xix [1957], 250-1, 254). The story of a small episode during the Muraysīʿ expedition reveals that Khirāsh was there, probably together with other Salūlīs. The party attacked by the Muslims at al-Muraysīʿ was of the Muṣṭaliḳ who were, like the Salūl themselves, a subdivision of the Khuzāʿa (see KHUZĀʿA, at V, 78b; on the territory of the Muṣṭaliḳ, cf. Lecker, *The Banū Sulaym*, 101n.). A member of the Muṣṭaliḳ, ʿĀmir b. Abī Ḍirār, who was the brother of their leader al-Ḥārith b. Abī Ḍirār, hit one of the Anṣār with an arrow (and probably killed him). Khirāsh threw himself on ʿĀmir in a display of Khuzāʿī solidarity so as to protect him from the Anṣār, who wanted to kill him (Ibn al-Athīr, *Usd al-ghāba*, Cairo 1280 A.H., ii, 108, quoting Ibn al-Kalbī; Ibn Ḥadjar, *Iṣāba*, ii, 269-70). This episode points to military co-operation between the Salūl and the Prophet some time before Ḥudaybiya. In other words, the Prophet was presumably playing one branch of Khuzāʿa against the other. In order to place this expedition in its correct historical context it has to be borne in mind that the Muṣṭaliḳ (and their brother clan Ḥayā) belonged to the *Aḥābīsh* (*Nasab Maʿadd*, ii, 455; Muḥammad b. Ḥabīb, *al-Muḥabbar*, ed. I. Lichtenstaedter, Ḥaydarābād 1361/1942, 246, 267; on the role of ʿAbd Manāf in this alliance see also idem, *Munammaḳ*, 230-1; for more sources see KHUZĀʿA, at V, 78a). This perfectly conforms to the statement that the Muṣṭaliḳ and the Ḥayā were the only groups of Khuzāʿa who did not have an alliance with the Prophet (Ḥassān b. Thābit, *Dīwān*, ii, 15-6).

From the expedition of Ḥudaybiya in 6/628 onwards (see AL-ḤUDAYBIYA; and Lecker, *The Ḥudaybiyya-treaty and the expedition against Khaybar*, in *JSAI*, v [1984], 1-11) the Salūl, or in any case many of them, were clearly on the Prophet's side. At Ḥudaybiya the above-mentioned Khirāsh b. Umayya was in the Prophet's camp. He was sent to Mecca as an envoy and was nearly killed by ʿIkrima b. Abī Djahl of the Makhzūm (al-Wāḳidī, ii, 600); then he participated in the expedition of Khaybar and in later expeditions, including the conquest of Mecca (Ibn Ḥadjar, *Iṣāba*, ii, 270; al-Wāḳidī, ii, 600, 843-5). But a more prominent role at Ḥudaybiya was played by the above-mentioned Busr b. Sufyān. Busr's status as a tribal leader meant that when he threw in his lot with the Prophet some time before Ḥudaybiya, he had the backing of a considerable force.

With regard to the conquest of Mecca by the Prophet in 8/630, it is reported that Busr, who was of the Ḳumayr subdivision, and Budayl b. Umm Aṣram of the Ḥabtar subdivision (whose grandmother was of the Ḳurashī Banū Hāshim) were sent to the Kaʿb in order to summon them to the expedition (Ibn al-

Athīr, *Usd*, i, 169; cf. Yāḳūt, s.v. *al-Watīr*; Abū ʿUbayd al-Bakrī, *Muʿdjam mā staʿdjam*, ed. Muṣṭafā al-Saḳḳā, Cairo 1364-71/1945-51, s.vv. *Fāthūr* and *al-Watīr*; al-ʿIṣāmī, *Simṭ al-nudjūm al-ʿawālī*, Cairo 1380, ii, 173-4). They were presumably sent to the Ḥabtar and Ḳumayr subdivisions, respectively. A large troop of the Kaʿb, divided into three tribal units, joined the Prophet at Ḳudayd, while other Kaʿbīs set out from Medina, where they had arrived some time before the expedition (see KHUZĀʿA, at V, 79a; Lecker, *The Banū Sulaym*, 143-4; al-Wāḳidī, ii, 800-1, 819, 896 [Ḥunayn], 990 [Tabūk]). However, not all of the Salūlīs were on the Prophet's side: while Busr b. Sufyān is said to have embraced Islam in 6/627-8 (i.e. before Ḥudaybiya) and to have spied for the Prophet in Mecca, the above-mentioned Kurz b. ʿAlḳama is said to have embraced Islam "on the day Mecca was conquered", i.e. he was not among the Salūlīs who helped the Prophet conquer Mecca.

Busr b. Sufyān is mentioned as the recipient, or one of the recipients, of a letter from the Prophet (see Ḥamīdullāh, *Madjmūʿat al-wathāʾiḳ al-siyāsiyya li'l-ʿahd al-nabawī wa'l-khilāfa al-rāshida*, [5]Beirut 1405/1985, 275-7; Ibn Ḥadjar, *Iṣāba*, i, 292; W.M. Watt, *Muhammad at Medina*, Oxford 1956, 355; cf. Lecker, *On the preservation of the letters of the Prophet Muḥammad*, forthcoming). In 9/630-1 the Prophet appointed Busr as a tax collector and sent him to his own tribal group, the Banū Kaʿb b. ʿAmr (see KHUZĀʿA, *loc. cit.*; Ibn Saʿd, ii/1, 115; cf. al-Wāḳidī, iii, 973-4).

In the Islamic period, some of the Kaʿb b. ʿAmr settled in Medina (Ibn Shabba, *Taʾrīkh al-Madīna al-munawwara*, ed. Fahīm Muḥammad Shaltūt, Mecca 1399/1979, i, 268; al-Samhūdī, *Wafāʾ al-wafā, ed.* ʿAbd al-Ḥamīd, Cairo 1374/1955, ii, 765). They included members of the Salūl: Ḳabīṣa b. Dhuʾayb, who was a high-ranking official in the court of the Umayyad caliph ʿAbd al-Malik b. Marwān [*q.v.*] (see e.g. al-Djahshiyārī, *al-Wuzarāʾ wa 'l-kuttāb*, ed. al-Saḳḳā *et al.*, Cairo 1401/1980, 34), was originally from Medina (Ibn ʿAsākir, *Taʾrīkh madīnat Dimashḳ*, facs. ed. ʿAmmān n.d., xiv, 392, l. 13; see also Caskel, ii, 454; his father, who died at the time of Muʿāwiya [*q.v.*], still inhabited Ḳudayd; Ibn Ḥadjar, *Iṣāba*, ii, 422). Ḳabīṣa was of the Ḳumayr subdivision. Another Salūlī whose descendants lived in Medina was Khirāsh b. Umayya of the Kulayb subdivision (*Nasab Maʿadd*, ii, 445; for a well in Mecca dug in the Islamic period by Khirāsh, or by another member of the Kaʿb, see al-Fākihī, *Akhbār Makka*, ed. ʿAbd al-Malik b. ʿAbd Allāh b. Duhaysh, Mecca 1407/1987, iv, 115, 116, 221; v, map no. 3; cf. the land near the Kaʿba granted by the Prophet to ʿUtba b. Farḳad al-Sulamī; Lecker, *The Banū Sulaym*, 132).

At the time of ʿUmar b. al-Khaṭṭāb, Ḳudayd and ʿUsfān north-west of Mecca were still at the heart of the territory of Khuzāʿa (cf. al-Balādhurī, *Futūḥ*, 452; KHUZĀʿA, at V, 79b), and this was probably true for the Salūl as well.

After the conquests, some of the Salūl settled in ʿIrāḳ (*Nasab Maʿadd*, ii, 445, where a member the Ḥizmir subdivision who was a *sharīf* in ʿIrāḳ and a government official is mentioned; *Khuzāʿat al-Ḥidjāz* and *Khuzāʿat al-ʿIrāḳ* are mentioned, with reference to the time of ʿAbd al-Malik, in al-Wazīr al-Maghribī, *Adab al-khawāṣṣ*, ed. al-Djāsir, Riyāḍ 1400/1980, 134). Others settled in Khurāsān: Mālik b. al-Haytham of the Ḳumayr was one of the *nuḳabāʾ* [see NAḲĪB] of the ʿAbbāsid *daʿwa*, and two of his sons were in charge of the *shurṭa* in the early ʿAbbāsid period (*Nasab Maʿadd*, ii, 442; Ibn Ḥazm, *Djamharat ansāb al-ʿarab*, ed. Hārūn, Cairo 1382/1962, 236; *Akhbār al-dawla al-ʿAbbāsiyya*, ed. ʿAbd al-ʿAzīz al-Dūrī and ʿAbd al-Djabbār al-Muṭṭalibī, Beirut 1971, 216; Sharon, *Black banners from the East*, Jerusalem 1983, 192; al-Ṭabarī, index; the prominent role played by Khuzāʿa and their *mawālī* in the *daʿwa* indicates that studying the history of this tribe after the conquests will further our understanding of the *daʿwa*; cf. Caskel, ii, 41). Mālik's brother, ʿAwf, was one of the *ḳuwwād* of the *daʿwa* and a mosque in Cairo (*miṣr*) was called after him (*Nasab Maʿadd*, ii, 442). The above-mentioned Kurz b. ʿAlḳama is said to have inhabited ʿAsḳalān (Ibn Ḥadjar, *Iṣāba*, v, 584). However, many Salūlīs probably never left Arabia: al-Ḳalḳashandī (d. 821/1418) reported that Barza near ʿUsfān was inhabited, among others, by the Salūl (see on this place, Lecker, *The Banū Sulaym*, xiii [map], 148).

2. The Salūl of the Hawāzin was either a man or a woman: Salūl was either the nickname of Murra, son of Ṣaʿṣaʿa b. Muʿāwiya b. Bakr b. Hawāzin; or the name of Murra's wife, a slave girl (*umm walad*) after whom her children were called (see e.g. Ibn al-Kalbī, *Nasab Maʿadd*, ii, 446; Aḥmad b. Muḥammad al-Ḳurṭubī, *al-Taʿrīf fi 'l-ansāb wa 'l-tanwīh li-dhawī 'l-aḥsāb*, ed. Saʿd ʿAbd al-Maḳṣūd Ẓalām, Cairo [1407/1986], 81; al-Baghdādī, *Khizānat al-adab*, ed. Hārūn, Cairo 1387-1406/1967-86, iv, 442; cf. Caskel, ii, 509); or the name of a daughter of Dhuhl b. Shaybān b. Thaʿlaba (i.e. the eponym of the Banū Dhuhl of the Bakr b. Wāʾil [*q.v.*]); she was married to Murra b. Ṣaʿṣaʿa b. Muʿāwiya b. Bakr b. Hawāzin and bore him all his sons, hence the Banū Murra were called after her Banū Salūl (Ibn al-Kalbī, *Djamharat al-nasab*, ed. Nādjī Ḥasan, Beirut 1407/1986, 379; Ibn Ḥazm, *Djamhara*, 271-2; cf. Caskel, i, 114, ii, 509). According to another version, only some of the Banū Murra were called Banū Salūl: Salūl bint Dhuhl b. Shaybān was the mother of the Banū Djandal b. Murra b. Ṣaʿṣaʿa (al-Ḥāzimī, *ʿUdjālat al-mubtadī wa-fuḍālat al-muntahī fī 'l-nasab*, ed. ʿAbd Allāh Kannūn, Cairo 1384/1965, 74; al-Wazīr al-Maghribī, *Īnās*, 186 n.). In other words, according to this version, the Banū Salūl were the descendants of Djandal b. Murra. The genealogists list the following as eponyms of tribal groups: Djandal b. Murra, ʿAmmāra b. Zābin, Ḥawza b. ʿAmr and Tamīma b. ʿAmr. The Salūl were not among the most prestigious tribes (al-Thaʿālibī, *Thimār al-ḳulūb fī 'l-muḍāf wa 'l-mansūb*, ed. Muḥammad Abu 'l-Faḍl Ibrāhīm, Cairo 1384/1965, 352; al-Dhahabī, *Siyar aʿlām al-nubalāʾ*, ed. Shuʿayb al-Arnāwūṭ *et al.*, Beirut 1401-9/1981-8, iv, 411; al-Djāḥiẓ, *al-Bayān wa 'l-tabyīn*, ed. Hārūn, Cairo 1395/1975, iv, 36).

The Salūl still inhabit their old territory south of Ṭāʾif, especially Wādī Bīsha (Ḥamad al-Djāsir, *al-Shāʿir ʿAbd Allāh b. Hammām al-Salūlī*, in *Madjallat al-ʿArab* [Riyāḍ], i [1386-7/1966-7], 37-43; C.J. Lyall, *The Dīwāns of ʿAbīd ibn al-Abraṣ and ʿĀmir ibn aṭ-Ṭufail*, Leiden and London 1913, 113-14; Yāḳūt, s.v. *Bīsha*).

Ḳarada b. Nufātha of the Salūl is said to have come to the Prophet in a delegation together with other Salūlīs. They embraced Islam and the Prophet declared him their leader (Ibn Ḥadjar, *Iṣāba*, v, 430-1; for another Salūlī, Nahīk b. Ḳuṣayy, said to have come to the Prophet, see *ibid.*, vi, 477). Abū Maryam Mālik b. Rabīʿa al-Salūlī reportedly gave the Prophet the pledge of allegiance at Ḥudaybiyya (*ibid.*, v, 724-5).

After the conquests, some of the Salūl settled in Kūfa (for Abū Maryam, see Ibn Saʿd, vi, 37; Ibn Mākūlā, *al-Ikmāl*, i, 227; see also Yāḳūt, s.v. *Djabbāna*; al-Balādhurī, *Futūḥ*, 285; ʿAbd Allāh b. Hammām al-Salūlī was in Kūfa at the time of Muʿāwiya;

see e.g. *Aghānī*[1], xiv, 120). Ibn al-Kalbī mentions several Salūlī supporters of ʿAlī b. Abī Ṭālib (see also Ibrāhīm b. Muḥammad al-Thaḳafī, *al-Ghārāt*, ed. Djalāl al-Dīn al-Muḥaddith, Tehran 1395/1975, index, s.v. ʿĀṣim b. Ḍamra and Hind b. ʿĀṣim; Ibn Ḥadjar, *Iṣāba*, ii, 13-4, s.v. Ḥubshī b. Djunāda). There were also Salūlīs in Mawṣil (cf. N. Abbott, *A new papyrus and a review of the administration of ʿUbaid Allāh b. al-Ḥabḥāb*, in *Arabic and Islamic Studies in Honor of Hamilton A.R. Gibb*, ed. G. Makdisi, Leiden 1965, 25; ʿUbayd Allāh was the ancestor of the Ḥabāḥiba who lived in Mawṣil, or of some of them; al-Azdī, *Taʾrīkh al-Mawṣil*, Cairo 1387/1967, 27). Other members of the Salūl settled in al-Andalus (Ibn Ḥazm, *Djamhara*, 272).

In the Islamic period, the Salūl, or some of them, were probably incorporated in the famous ʿĀmir b. Ṣaʿṣaʿa [*q.v.*], possibly as a result of conditions in the garrison cities. This development is reflected in the lineage of one of them, referred to as al-ʿĀmirī al-Salūlī, where ʿĀmir is inserted between Murra and Ṣaʿṣaʿa: ... Murra b. ʿĀmir b. Ṣaʿṣaʿa (Ibn Ḥadjar, *Iṣāba*, vi, 477, quoting Ibn al-Kalbī; Ibn al-Athīr, *Usd*, v, 44-5, s.v. Nahīk b. Ḳuṣayy ... b. Murra b. ʿĀmir b. Ṣaʿṣaʿa al-ʿĀmirī al-Salūlī).

Bibliography: Given in the article.

(M. Lecker)

SALUR, one of the Oghuz (Türkmen) tribes. They are first mentioned in Maḥmūd al-Kāshgharī's [*q.v.*] *Dīwān lughāt al-turk* (written 464/1072, tr. R. Dankoff and J. Kelly as *Compendium of the Turkic dialects*, Cambridge, Mass. 1982-5, i, 101) as one of the 22 branches of the Oghuz. They may, in fact, have been the chief branch of that confederation. In the 4th/10th century, the Oghuz were spread across a wide area from the Issïḳ-Kul west to the Caspian Sea (P. Golden, *The migrations of the Oğuz*, in *Archivum ottomanicum*, iv [1972], 45-84). According to Rashīd al-Dīn [*q.v.*], in his semi-legendary "*Oghuz-nāma*," i.e. the *Taʾrīkh-i Turkān wa Oghuz wa ḥikāyat-i djihangīrī-i ū* section of his *Djāmiʿ al-tawārīkh* (written *ca.* 710/1310), the name Salur, as derived from the verb *salmak*, meant "ready to attack, warrior." He adds that the Salur tribe traced its descent from Dagh Khān, one of the six sons of Oghuz Khān, and was among a subgroup of tribes known as the *üčok* (an analysis of this source is in F. Sümer, *Oğuzlar'a ait destanı mahiyetde eserler*, in *AÜDTCFD*, xvii [1959], 359-87; see also A.Z.V. Togan, *Oğuz destanı, Reşideddin oğuznamesi, tercüme ve tahlili*, Istanbul 1972, 51, 53-5, 138-42). In the Turkish epic *Dede Korkut* [*q.v.*], the earliest surviving version of which dates from 732/1332 but which appears to reflect certain events of the 4th-5th/10th-11th centuries, one Salur Kazan, who is the son-in-law and chief *bey* of Bayïndïr Khān, the king of the Oghuz, is the main protagonist. He struggles primarily against the Pečenegs (Sümer, *op. cit.*, 395-451).

By the 5th/11th century, most of the Oghuz had been converted, at least nominally, to Islam, and many of them had moved as far west as Khurāsān. Most of the Salur appear to have participated in this westward migration. They eventually travelled across northern Persia and through Ādharbāydjān, perhaps reaching eastern Anatolia in the late 5th/11th or early 6th/12th century as part of the general Saldjūḳ invasion. They are one of only six Oghuz tribes that can be identified in the Saldjūḳ realm before the Mongol invasion in the 7th/13th century (Cl. Cahen, *Pre-Ottoman Turkey*, London 1968, 35). After the founding of the Great Saldjūḳ Empire, some of the Salur established the Salghurid [*q.v.*] dynasty in Fārs (543-668/1148-1270) (M.F. Köprülü, *Osmanlı imparatorluğu'nun etnik menşei mes'eleleri*, in *Belleten*, vii [1943], 252, n. 1). Others moved into eastern, southern, and central Anatolia and were to be found around Amasya, Tokat, Sīwās, İsparta, Adana, and even Ṭarābulus (Tripoli) in Syria. They no doubt played an important military and political role in the Saldjūḳ sultanate of Rūm and may have been involved in the great uprising of the Türkmen known as the Bābāʾī [*q.v.*] revolt (638/1240). In the late 7th/13th century, one Salur Bey was a leader of "white-hatted" Türkmen who resisted the Mongols and their Saldjūḳ allies (O. Turan, *Selçuklular zamanında türkiye tarihi*, Istanbul 1984, 514-7).

The Salur were definitely an element in the rise of several *beyliks*. Some Salur served in the army of Bahrām Shāh (*ca.* 555-617/1160-1220) of the Mengüčekids [*q.v.*] of Erzindjān. They were with him when he joined a campaign against Georgia in 598/1202 led by the Saldjūḳ sultan of Rūm, Sulaymān II. In the view of Köprülü, the Ḳaramān-oghullarï [*q.v.*] were descended from the Ḳaramān branch of the Salur (his fundamental *Oghuz etnolozhisine dāʾir notlar*, in *TM*, i [1925], 193, n. 1). They also appeared in the *ulus* of Dhu 'l-Ḳadr [*q.v.*] around Elbistān (8th/14th century). The Salur who lived near Ṭarābulus migrated to the Čukur-Ova plain around Adana (7th/13th century) and became part of the *ulus* of the Ramaḍān-oghullarï [*q.v.*] (Sümer, *Çukur-Ova tarihine dair araştırmalar*, in *Tarih Araştırmaları Dergisi*, i [1963], 9, 23, 26-27, 29, 76; idem, *Osmanlı devrinde anadoluda yaşayan bazı üçoklu oğuz boylarına mensup teşekküller*, in *İstanbul Üniversitesi İktisat Fakültesi Mecmuasï*, xi [1952], 453-9, 486-92). The writer Fakhr al-Dīn Muḥammad b. Khʷādja Ḥasan al-Salghūrī al-Diwrīghī (b. 631/1236), who gained fame in both Turkish and Persian letters, was from this tribe (Turan, *Doğu anadolu türk devletleri tarihi*, Istanbul 1980, 69) as were the poet and statesman Ḳāḍī Burhān al-Dīn (d. *ca.* 800/1398 [*q.v.*]), who put an end to the government of Eretna [*q.v.*], and the poet Muṣṭafā b. Yūsuf (Ḳādī Ḍarīr) of Erzurum (d. second half of 8th/14th century) (Togan, *Umumi türk tarihine giriş*, Istanbul 1946, repr. 1981, 272). A Salur Khān also appears in the genealogy of Uzun Ḥasan (861-82/1457-78) of the Aḳ-Ḳoyunlu (J.E. Woods, *The Aqquyunlu*, Minneapolis 1976, 187). The Salur were still found around Sīwās and Adana in the early 10th/16th century, according to the Ottoman *defters* for those regions. In the former, they were called the Aḳ-Salur. By the first half of the 11th/17th century, the Salur were all settled and had lost their tribal organisation (Sümer, *Osmanlı devrinde ... teşekküller*, 453-9). There are many villages with the name Salur in Anatolia, even in western Anatolia, but it is difficult to determine when they were so named.

As for the Salur who remained in Khurāsān, mainly around Marw and Sarakhs, some migrated to China in the late 8th/14th century to become the present-day Salars [*q.v.*]. According to Abu 'l-Ghāzī Bahādur Khān's [*q.v.*] semi-legendary *Shadjara-i tarākima* (written 1070/1659), others migrated to Mangïshlaḳ or as far as ʿIrāḳ (Sümer, *Oğuzlar'a ait ... eserler*, 389-95, for analysis), perhaps in the 9th/15th century. Those who went to Mangïshlaḳ were led by the Ersarï [*q.v.* in Suppl.] who were at the head of the "outer Salur" in contrast to the "inner Salur", who included the Salur proper as well as the Tekke, Sarïḳ, and Yomut. These movements significantly reduced the number and power of the Salur in Khurāsān. Nevertheless, between 1525-35, the Salur of Khurāsān clashed with Ṣufyān Khān, the Özbeg ruler of Gurgāndj or Urgandj. They also joined other Türkmen in the struggle against the Shīʿī Ṣafawids. In 1597, they raided the area of Astarābād, but submitted the next year to Shāh ʿAbbās. This pacification was no doubt temporary. In 1843, the Salur and Tekke captured Marw and around 1838 they rose to support a revolt in Sarakhs led by a former governor of Khurāsān. The Persians crushed this revolt with great difficulty. The Salur subsequently lost their importance. Before the Russians began their occupation of Türkmenistan in 1869, the Salur lived primarily in the region between Sarakhs and the Murghāb River. In the early 20th century, they were still concentrated around Sarakhs and along the Harī Rūd River in Türkmenistan. In the 13th/19th century, travellers estimated their population to be anywhere between 2,000 and 20,000 families divided among three branches of the tribe: Yalawač, Ḳaramān, and Ana-Böleghi (Kiči-Agha). Since the coming of the Russians, they have maintained their identity under the leadership of the Tekke. They are now completely sedentary and have lost their tribal distinction.

Bibliography (in addition to works cited in the text): V.V. Barthold, *A history of the Turkmen people*, in vol. iii of *Four studies on the history of Central Asia*, Leiden 1962, 109 ff.; F. Sümer, *Oğuzlar (türkmenler): tarihleri-boy teşkilatı-destanları*, Ankara 1967, 138-41, 209-13, 327-35, 436-7; Cl. Cahen, *Les tribus turques d'Asie Occidentale pendant la période seljukide*, in *WZKM*, li (1948-52), 180-1; P. Golden, *An introduction to the history of the Turkic peoples*, Wiesbaden 1992, 205-8, 355, 400; *İA*, arts. *Salur* (Köprülü-Zāde Fuad-[İ. Kafesoğlu]) and *Türkmenler*, at 671 (M. Saray).

(G. LEISER)

SALWĀ (A.), a noun with a generic sense (*nomen unitatis, salwāt*, pl. *salāwā*, denotes first of all the quail (*Coturnix coturnix*), of the order of Galliformae, family of Phasianidae), from Latin *quaquila*, with the synonym *sumānā, sumānāt*, pl. *sumānayāt*. The two Semitic roots *s-l-w* and *s-m-n* evoke the idea of fatness; the same sense is found in the Hebrew *ślāw*, pl. *śalwīm*, and in the Syriac *salwai*.

It is under this name that the quail is mentioned in the Bible (Exod. xvi, 11-13; Num. xi, 31-2; Ps. lxxvii, 27; Ps. civ, 40; Wisdom of Solomon, xvi, 2) with regard to the exodus of the Israelites from Egypt to the Promised Land. Lacking provisions on their journey through the desert of Sin, between Elim and Sinai, they began to complain, and Moses had to call upon the Most High, who sent down to them a "rain" of quails and manna which covered the ground. In the following spring, weary of manna, they demanded more meat, and there came fresh clouds of quails from beyond the sea which came down upon their camp; there were so many that the Israelites were able to dry them, in the fashion of the Egyptians at that time, and thus live off them for over a month. These massive clouds of quails may be explained by the intense annual migrations and comings-and-goings of these birds who, like swallows and many other species, go to spend the winter, after nesting, in warm countries and then return for the summer to more temperate lands.

Having drawn this information from the Biblical texts, the Ḳurʾān evokes these occurrences in three places (II, 54/56; VII, 159/160; and XX, 79/82) without changing the terms of the story.

Some exegetes put forward the idea that *salwā* could possibly designate the grasshopper, the flying-fish, the grouse, the Casarka duck or the crane, etc., but such suggestions can be justified neither linguistically nor etologically, since most of these creatures are inedible and are unknown in the regions in question. It is on the other hand well-known that the quail is one of the most delicate game birds, much sought after by gourmets and assiduously hunted wherever it may pass by. Its nocturnal flights, sometimes in groups of hundreds, regularly reach the peripheries of the Mediterranean. Thus on the island of Capri, in September, the ground is covered by these birds arriving, to such an extent that, according to Tristram, the bishop, who drew a certain amount of revenue from them, bore the name "bishop of the quails".

In addition to the two names *salwā* and *sumānā*, the quail bears other appellations, in various regions and in the different local Arabic dialects. In the Near East there is *murayʿī, murʿat al-barr, summāna/simmāna, firr* and *firrī*, and in the Maghrib, *sammān, summīna, mallāḥa* and *darrādj*. An ancient belief held that the quail would be inevitably struck down by stormy weather, whence its name *ḳatīl al-raʿd* "the victim of thunder". In Berber, the names *tasemmant, tamryoust* and *tiberdfelt* are known for it. Corresponding to *salwā*, the Turkish name *bîldîrdjîn* is from the same root as the Persian *baldarčīn/bildirčīn/buldurčīn*, to which may be added local names like *badbada, būdana, gilča, karak, kardjafūk, karkarak, lārda, lārūda, waladj, wartadj, wartak, watak* and *wushm*.

As well as having succulent meat, the quail, according to al-Damīrī, has several specific qualities. Thus its head, buried in a dovecote, will make all parasites flee away, and, burnt and used to fumigate the wood, will free it from all woodworm. If a person whose eyes are affected by rheum carries one of its eyes on his person, he will be cured of his condition. Mixed with saffron, its gall is an excellent unguent for scurfy skin, and its dried and pounded-up dung placed on ulcers will make them disappear. Finally, in falconry, a sick goshawk can be cured by feeding to it quail's liver.

The partridge and quail have always been for hunters some of the most sought-after game birds. They were constantly the prey of falconry, from the wrist with the sparrow-hawk and merlin [see BAYZARA]. Other methods of capturing quail were and still are very varied. Since it constantly runs along the ground, only flying when forced and hemmed in, lurking in dense herbage and thickets, it is caught by means of a quail-call (*ṣaffāra*) which imitates the call of the male, reproduced in French by the onomatopoeic "paye-tes-dettes". In the Maghrib, hunters use their flowing burnouses as a net by spreading them over the bushes where quail rest when they arrive after their lengthy migration. They are, at that time, very vulnerable and the episodes related in the Bible set in the time of the exodus of the Israelites through the desert, are easily understandable. At the present time, shooting quail with pointer hounds reduces considerably the numbers of the species each year, but very recently, this has been modified by the commercial rearing of quails.

As well as being the main term for "quail", *salwā* is at the same time used for a land-hugging member of the Rallidae family (*tifliḳī*), the corncrake or land-rail (*Crex crex, Crex pratensis*), whose mode of life is quite similar to that of the quail, since it frequents similar habitats, keeping to the ground, hiding in thickets, long grass and crops, migrating more or less at the same times and towards the same latitudes; it is everywhere the "companion" of the quail and, moreover, its meat is enjoyed. For all these reasons and, being double the size of the quail, it has acquired the name in French of *roi de cailles*, likewise in German with *Wachtelkönig*, in Italian with *Re di quaglie* and in Spanish with *Guion de codornices* = "quails' guidon".

In the Maghrib, it is the "quails' mule" (*baghl al-sammān*) and the "slow, lazy one" (*abu 'l-rakhwa*) because of its clumsy flight, whilst in Berber it is the "quails' donkey" (*aryūl en-tsekkūrīn*). In al-Damīrī, it is mentioned under *ṣifrid*, being considered as very cowardly, whence the saying *adjban min ṣiffrid* "more cowardly that a corncrake". Finally, it is remarkable that al-Ḳazwīnī mentions neither the *salwā* nor the *ṣifrid*.

Bibliography (in alphabetical order): Allouse, *al-Ṭuyūr al-ʿIrāḳiyya/Birds of Iraq*, Baghdād 1960, ii, 7-10, 20-1; Aristotle, *History of animals*, Fr. tr. J. Tricot, Paris 1957, see table s.v. *ortux* and *krex*; A.E. Brehm, *Les oiseaux* (L'homme et les animaux), Fr. ed. Z. Gerbe, Paris 1878, 378-82, 695-98; F.O. Cave and J.D. Macdonald, *Birds of the Sudan*, London 1955, 10; Dr. Chenu, *Encyclopédie d'histoire naturelle*, Paris 1854, part iv, *Oiseaux*, 150; Damīrī, *Ḥayāt al-ḥayawān al-kubrā*, Cairo 1928-9, ii, 26; Djāḥiẓ, *Ḥayawān*, Cairo 1938-45, i, 213, 222, 11, 164, 111, 184, iv, 302, v, 246; H. Eisenstein, *Einführung in die arabische Zoographie*, Berlin 1990, index s.v. Wachtel; R.D. Etchecopar and F. Hüe, *Les oiseaux du Nord de l'Afrique*, Paris 1964, 174, 189 (with index of names by F. Vire); eidem, *Les oiseaux du Proche et Moyen Orient*, Paris 1970, 225, 245; M.L.Cl. Fillion, *Atlas de l'histoire naturelle de la Bible*, Lyons-Paris 1884, 70 no. 214; P. Geroudet, *La vie des oiseaux*, i, ²Paris 1947, 253-7, ii, ²Paris 1948, 229-32; E. Ghaleb, *al-Mawsūʿa fī ʿulūm al-ṭabīʿa/Dictionnaire des sciences de la nature*, Beirut 1965, s.vv. *salwā, sumānā, ṣifrid*; Ibn Manglī, *Uns al-malā*, tr. Viré, *De la chasse*, Paris 1984, 156 and n. 289; Islamic Republic of Iran, Dept. of the Environment, *Parrandigān-i Īrān/The birds of Iran*, ²Tehran 1983, 115, 126; Kushādjim, *K. al-Maṣāyid wa 'l-maṭārid*, Baghdād 1954, 285; A. al-Maʿlūf, *Muʿdjām al-ḥayawān/An Arabic zoological dictionary*, Cairo 1932, 173-4, 98-200; R. Meintertzhagen, *Birds of Egypt*, London 1930, s.vv. Quail, Corncrake; idem, *Birds of Arabia*, London 1954, 558, 567; U. Schapka, *Die persischen Vogelnamen*, diss. Univ. of Würzburg 1972, 22 no. 68, 28 no. 91, 130-1 nos. 438, 440; H.B. Tristram, *The natural history of the Bible*, London 1889, 231; F. Vigouroux, *Dict. de la Bible*, 2nd impr. Paris 1912, ii/1, 33-7; idem, *La Bible et le découvertes modernes*, Paris 1889, ii, 463-8; T. Wood, *Bible animals*, London 1884, 434. (F. Viré)

SĀM, a term originally referring to the Biblical personage, in modern times used also with linguistic reference.

1. The Biblical personage.

Here, Sām denotes in Arabic lore and tradition Shem, the son of Noah [see NŪḤ]. The Ḳurʾān does not mention any of the sons of Noah by name but alludes to them in VII, 64, X, 73, XI, 40, XXIII, 27 and XXVI, 119.

The Islamic tradition develops many details regarding Shem. His mother was ʿAmzūrah (cf. Jubilees, iv, 33) and he was born 98 years before the flood. He and his wife Ṣalīb were saved from the Deluge by entering the ark. They had four, five or six sons. After the incident of his father's accidental exposure of his genitals in which Shem (and Japheth [see YĀFITH]) covered them up while Ham [see ḤĀM] laughed, Shem was promised by Noah that God will shield Shem's descendants as Shem shielded Noah's private parts (al-Kisāʾī, *Ḳiṣaṣ al-anbiyāʾ*, ed. J. Eisenberg, Leiden 1922, 98-9; al-Ṭabarī, i, 212, Eng. tr. W. Brinner, *The history of al-Ṭabarī. Prophets and patriarchs*, Albany 1987, 11-2). Shem was then given "the middle of the earth" as his inheritance (cf. Ḳurʾān, XXXVII, 77), making him the ancestor of the Arabs and the Persians as well as the Byzantines according to some traditions (cf. Genesis, x, 21-31).

Reference to Shem is made on two other occasions in the Islamic tradition. According to al-Kisāʾī, the well into which Joseph [see YŪSUF] was thrown by his brothers was dug by Shem and had a sign on it which read, "This is the Well of Sorrows" (Kisāʾī, *Ḳiṣaṣ*, 159). More widespread is a story connected to Ḳurʾān, III, 49 (cf. V, 110) which concerns the ability of Jesus [see ʿĪSĀ] to raise the dead. Shem is frequently counted as one of the four persons revived by Jesus. Those who demanded this miracle of Jesus said, "Here is the tomb of Shem: raise him!", and Jesus complied. Shem's hair was white but he explained that it had only just turned that colour as a result of his fear that he was being raised for the final judgement. (Muḳātil b. Sulaymān, *Tafsīr*, Cairo 1979, i, 277; Abu 'l-Layth al-Samarḳandī, *Tafsīr*, Baghdād 1985, ii, 68-9; al-Kisāʾī, *Ḳiṣaṣ*, 307; al-Ḳurṭubī, *al-Djāmiʿ li-aḥkām al-Ḳurʾān*, Beirut 1967, iv, 94-5). The same story is told by al-Ṭabarī (i, 187; Eng. tr. F. Rosenthal, *The history of al-Ṭabarī. General introduction and From the creation to the flood*, Albany 1989, 357; al-Ṭabarī, *Djāmiʿ al-bayān*, Cairo 1905, xii, 22), concerning Ḳurʾān, XI, 39, with Ham as the character involved; the difference in identification is probably the result of an understanding that Ham would be the son properly afraid of the final judgement, rather than Shem.

Bibliography: Given in the article.

(A. Rippin)

2. With reference to the Semitic languages.

The relative adjective *sāmī* is used in modern Arabic as a rendition of "Semitic", "sémitique", etc., thus *al-lughāt al-sāmiyya* "the Semitic languages." Important for the introduction of this notion into the Arabic-speaking world was the Christian Arab novelist and historian Djirdjī Zaydān (1861-1914 [*q.v.*]) in his *al-Alfāẓ al-ʿarabiyya wa 'l-falsafa al-lughawiyya* (Beirut 1886, 3-5), where a classification of the Semitic languages is also offered. His source for these matters was his teacher at the American College of Beirut, Cornelis van Dijk (1818-95; see on him Kaḥḥāla viii, 142-3), to whom Zaydān's book is also dedicated. In his later work *Taʾrīkh al-lugha al-ʿarabiyya* (1st ed. Cairo 1904; ed. ʿIṣām Nūr al-Dīn, Beirut 1980, 37-8) he speaks of the various *al-lughāt al-sāmiyya*, but he also uses the singular *al-lugha al-sāmiyya* to denote the "mother" of all Semitic languages, as well as the noun *al-sāmiyyūn* for the people who spoke it. This usage seems to be well established at this time, as contemporary dictionaries of the Islamic languages show.

(a) *Precursors in the Islamic world.*

Some Muslim historians, starting with al-Masʿūdī (d. 345/956 [*q.v.*]), have a system of seven ancient nations (*umam*). They are defined first and foremost linguistically, but also in terms of once having been a single realm with an advanced state of civilisation. In al-Masʿūdī the Seven Nations include the Persians, the Chaldaeans, the Greeks (and other Europeans), the Libyans (i.e. Africans, including the ancient Egyptians), the Turks, the Indians, and the Chinese (*al-Tanbīh wa 'l-ishrāf*, ed. M.J. de Goeje, Leiden 1894, 77 ff.; cf. Tarif Khalidi, *Islamic historiography. The histories of Masʿūdī*, Albany 1975, 81-113). Al-Masʿūdī's "Chaldaeans" (*kaldāniyyūn*) consist of several smaller nations whose common kingdom, in the Fertile Crescent and the Arabian Peninsula, preceded that of the Persians and whose common language was Syriac. They included the Babylonians, Ninivites, Assyrians, Arameans (plus more recent descendants), the Hebrews, and the ancient Arabs. The author also comments on the close relationship between Arabic, Hebrew, and Syriac. I. Yu. Kračkovskii, therefore, did not hesitate to ascribe to al-Masᶜūdī the conception of a "Semitic" race (*Taʾrīkh al-adab al-djughrāfī*, Cairo 1963-5, 182-3; Khalidi, *op. cit.*, 93 and n. 2).

Notions about the relatedness of the several Semitic languages are, however, very sparse, as far as Muslim and Christian authors are concerned, although it stands to reason that, e.g., translators from Syriac into Arabic and specialists on the *materia medica*, who had to identify the names of drugs in various languages, would be aware of similarities. One of the few Arab grammarians who was interested in languages other than Arabic, Abū Ḥayyān al-Gharnāṭī (d. 745/1344 [*q.v.*]) wrote a work on the language of the Abyssinians (*ḥabash*), probably meaning Ethiopic, which has, however, not been preserved (Brockelmann, S II, 136). It is to the credit of the Jewish grammarians in the Islamic realm, who were steeped in all three languages, Hebrew, Aramaic and Arabic, that the foundation of Semitic studies—though not under that name—has to be placed. The first to propose explicit comparisons, mainly for exegetical purposes, was Yahūdā b. Ḳuraysh (*ca.* 900). For further names and literature, see JUDAEO-ARABIC, here at IV, 305.

(b) *The development of the notion "Semitic" in the West.*

The term "Semitic" for a family of related languages was coined by the historian, Biblical scholar, and influential Slavicist August Ludwig (von) Schlözer (1735-1809) who took his inspiration from the Biblical genealogy of *Genesis*, x (see *Repertorium für biblische und morgenländische Literatur*, viii [1781], 161; note, however, that Johann Christoph Adelung, *Mithridates*, i, 300, says, without reference, that Johann Gottfried Eichhorn (1752-1827) was the first to use this term). However, the fact that these languages were related had been recognised much earlier in the West (and in the East even before, see above). Guillaume Postel (Guilelmus Postellus) (1510-81), author of the first Western grammar of Classical Arabic (1538 or 1539), wrote comprehensive works on Hebrew, Syriac, Chaldaean, and Arabic, including speculations of a rather mystical nature about their common origin (cf. Fück, *Arabische Studien*, 39, 42-3). In the following two-and-a-half centuries, more than three dozen polyglot grammars, dictionaries, and chrestomathies were published, often covering all of the known Semitic languages (cf., e.g., the title of Bonifazio Finetti, *Trattato della lingua Ebraica e sue affine Rabbinica, Caldaica, Syra, Samaritana, Fenice e Punica, Arabica, Aethiopica ed Amharica*, Venice 1756) but not infrequently including also other Oriental languages, such as Armenian and Persian (bibliographies in Eichhorn, 403-4, 409-11, 484-5, and Adelung, 303-6). Important for comparative purposes were the four polyglot Bible editions. While all these collections were no doubt in tune with the polymathic *Zeitgeist* which produced collectanea, encyclopaedias, and other cumulative works in all and sundry fields, the relatedness of the Semitic languages and, in particular, the relationship between Hebrew and Arabic was more and more considered to be important for Biblical exegesis. Typical for this approach is the work of the Leyden Professor Albert Schultens (1686-1750), starting with his *Dissertatio theologico-philologica de utilitate linguae arabicae in interpretanda sacra lingua* (1706). Thanks to its indigenous lexicographers, Arabic had, of course, the richest attested vocabulary and was thus the language of choice in the endeavours of elucidating Biblical cruxes with recourse to cognates in related languages. However, it created a problem for the philologists in the 18th century, who still believed Hebrew to be the First Language, since Arabic with its case and mood inflection seemed to be rather more archaic. This dilemma was solved in 1788 by Johann Gottfried Hasse, who assumed, like others, that originally Arabic did not have the desinential inflections and that the latter were introduced into the language by Arab grammarians on the basis of Greek models (*sic*, see Gruntfest, in *Bibl.*).

Toward the end of the 18th century and ever-increasingly in the 19th century, Arabic and Semitic studies ceased to be *ancillae theologiae*. The great advances made in Indo-European comparative linguistics stimulated comparative Semitics. At the same time, the term "Semitic" was hypostasised to give birth to the term "Semites" which was used to designate not only the Proto-Semites, *Ursemiten*, before they broke up into the various Semitic peoples, but also the totality of the Semitic-speaking tribes and nations. With the growing interest in racial theories, a corollary of the rise of nationalism, the "Semites" became a race with a specific physical, but quite importantly also a mental make-up, most often contrasted with the Indo-European race. The first comparative grammar of the Semitic languages, Ernest Renan's (1833-92) *Histoire général et système comparé des langues sémitiques* (1853) was an embodiment of both tendencies. His negative characterising of the "Semites" (who have a knack for monotheism, but a lack of almost all other cultural achievements) was very influential, but did not go unchallenged. Suffice it to mention two works: Daniel (David) Chwolson, *Die semitischen Völker, Versuch einer Charakteristik* (Berlin 1872), and Theodor Nöldeke, *Zur Charakteristik der Semiten*, in *Orientalische Skizzen* (Berlin 1892). The more scholarly linguistic work was carried out by the founding fathers of modern Semitic studies: Franz Praetorius (1847-1927), Theodor Nöldeke (1836-1930), Ignazio Guidi (1844-1935) and William Wright (1830-89). Nöldeke and Wright produced comprehensive works on the Semitic languages (see *Bibl.*). The full harvest of all their work was brought in by Carl Brockelmann (1868-1956) in his monumental *Grundriss der vergleichenden Grammatik der semitischen Sprachen*, 2 vols., Berlin 1907-13. Though partly dated due to new discoveries and new methodologies, it has not yet been superseded.

Changes in the notion of "Semitic" in recent decades have to do with the clear recognition of the language family as being part of the larger Afroasiatic phylum. See below, section (c).

Bibliography: J.Ch. Adelung, *Mithridates oder allgemeine Sprachenkunde*. Erster Theil, Berlin 1806; J. Fück, *Die arabischen Studien in Europa*, Leipzig 1955; J.G. Eichhorn, *Geschichte der neuern Sprachenkunde*. Erste Abtheilung, Göttingen 1807; Y. Gruntfest, *From the history of Semitic linguistics in Europe: an early theory of redundancy of Arabic case-endings*, in K. Dévényi and T. Iványi (eds.), *Proceedings of the Colloquium on Arabic Grammar, Budapest, 1-7 September 1991 (= The Arabist, Budapest Studies in Arabic*, 3-4), Budapest 1991, 195-200; Th. Nöldeke, *Die Semitischen Sprachen*, ²Leipzig 1899 (written originally for the 9th ed. of the *Encyclopaedia Britannica*); W. Wright, *Lectures on the comparative grammar of the Semitic languages*, Cambridge 1890. See also ḤĀM.

(W.P. HEINRICHS)

(c) *The Semitic languages. An overview.*

The Semitic family of languages has a longer recorded history than any other linguistic group. The main languages and language groups of the family are reviewed below in the order of their first appearance. Thereafter, the genetic subgrouping of the family and the interrelationships of the various languages are considered.

The first attested Semitic languages are Akkadian and Eblaite, both of which were usually written on clay tablets in the cuneiform script originally developed for the writing of the non-Semitic Sumerian language in southern ʿIrāḳ. Mesopotamia Akkadian, the language of the Semitic Assyrians and Babylonians of Mesopotamia, is known from tens of thousands of documents in a wide variety of genres, such as myths and epics, letters, royal inscriptions, legal contracts, economic receipts, omens, and mathematical, medical and school texts. Akkadian begins to appear as early as the 26th century B.C., and the scattered documents of the earliest period are collectively referred to simply as Old Akkadian. From the beginning of the second millennium, two principal dialects are recorded: Assyrian, especially in texts from sites along or near the Tigris north of the Little Zāb; and Babylonian, in texts from sites along, near, and between the Euphrates and Tigris, mostly to the south of later Bag̲h̲dād. Scholars further sub-divide both of these dialects chronologically, at roughly 500-year intervals, into Old (2000-1500), Middle (1500-1000), and Neo-Assyrian and Babylonian (1000-600); Assyrian came to an end with the fall of the Assyrian empire near the end of the 7th century, whereas Babylonian continued to be written until the 1st century A.D. (Late Babylonian; the language had, however, probably ceased to be spoken and been replaced by Aramaic in most of the area long before). For much of the second millennium, Akkadian served as a lingua franca, and Akkadian texts from that period have been recovered from sites across most of the Near East, including Iran, Turkey, Syria, Lebanon, Israel, and Egypt. Eblaite is recorded on clay tablets dated to the 24th-23rd centuries B.C. found recently at the site of Tell Mardik̲h̲ in Syria (about 60 km/38 miles south of Aleppo); although the writing system is similar to that used for writing Akkadian, there are enough differences in spelling and sign usage that the language remains poorly understood; it appears, however, to be a close relative, or possibly even a dialect, of Akkadian.

Texts in Ugaritic, the language of the important ancient city of Ugarit (modern Ras Shamra near Latakia), date from the 14th-13th centuries B.C. Like Akkadian, Ugaritic was written on clay tablets in cuneiform, but whereas Akkadian cuneiform signs depict whole words (logograms) or syllables (i.e., comprise a syllabary), Ugaritic cuneiform is alphabetic, with one sign for each of the 27 consonants, plus three extras added at the end, two for *aleph* (*hamza*) with the vowels *i* and *u* (the original *aleph*, at the beginning of the alphabet, being used only for /ʾa/ and /ʾā/) and another to write certain words with /s/. The order of the Ugaritic alphabet, which is generally considered to be the original order, from which the Phoenician-Hebrew-Aramaic and, ultimately, the Arabic, are derived, is as follows: *ʾ b g ḫ d h w z ḥ ṭ y k ś l m ḏ n ẓ s ʿ p ṣ q r ṯ ġ t* (*ʾi ʾu s̀*). Some 1300 Ugaritic texts have been published thus far; most are administrative lists, but there are also many myths, rituals, omen texts, and letters.

The Canaanite group of languages, which includes Phoenician, Hebrew, and several poorly-attested dialects, begins to appear with the first identifiably Phoenician texts in about 1000 B.C., although short inscriptions that are less easily classified linguistically, in pictographic precursors to the Phoenician alphabet, are attested for perhaps five or six centuries before that date (in graffiti in Egyptian copper mines in the Sinai and in names on bronze arrowheads). Phoenician texts, especially royal inscriptions, are known from the ancient city-states of Byblos, Tyre and Sidon, as well as other sites. The Phoenician dialect of texts from the North African Tyrian colony of Carthage (Phoenician *qartḥadašt* "new-town"), and from Carthage's own colonies all around the Mediterranean, is referred to as Punic. The 22-letter Phoenician alphabet was borrowed and adapted for the writing of numerous other languages, including Hebrew, Aramaic (and thence for Arabic), and Greek (and thence for Etruscan and Latin). Hebrew is first attested archaeologically in inscriptions of the 10th century B.C., but it is likely that parts of the Hebrew Bible derive from a century or two earlier. Besides the biblical texts and numerous inscriptions from the biblical period, Hebrew was used for a vast literature in the centuries immediately thereafter, including texts such as the Dead Sea Scrolls (partly in Aramaic) and the Mishna, and in the Mediaeval period as well. Having died out as a spoken language, probably at some time around the turn of the era, Hebrew was revived in the last century and is thriving as the national language of modern Israel. Other Canaanite dialects, known only from a few inscriptions dating from the 9th to the 6th centuries B.C., include Moabite, Ammonite, and Edomite (all from sites in modern Jordan and southern Israel).

Aramaic is first attested in inscriptions found in Syria, Iraq, and Israel dating to the 9th and 8th centuries B.C. During the Persian empire, Aramaic served as an official language, a factor that helped both to standardise the language and to spread its common use: texts from this period are found as far afield as Elephantine in Egypt. The Aramaic of the biblical book of Ezra is also representative of this Imperial dialect. After the Achaemenid period the use of Aramaic continued to be very widespread, but dialectal differences became more and more apparent. The period of Middle Aramaic, from the 3rd century B.C. to the 2nd century A.D., comprises texts in the Ḥatran, Nabataean, Palmyrene and Old Syriac dialects, as well as the earliest Jewish Aramaic targums (translations) of the Bible and other writings. In Late Aramaic (from the 3rd century A.D.), dialectal distinctions become still more pronounced; in addition to Syriac, with its vast Christian literature, scholars generally recognise Late Eastern Aramaic, consisting of Babylonian Jewish Aramaic (the language of the Babylonian Talmud) and Mandaic, and Late Western Aramaic, consisting of three geographical/religious dialects: Galilean or Jewish Palestinian Aramaic (the language of the Palestinian Talmud and Midrashim), Samaritan Aramaic, and Judaean or Christian Palestinian Aramaic (Palestinian Syriac). Although largely displaced by the spread of Arabic, Aramaic has continued to be spoken until the present day, by Muslims and Christians in three small towns northeast of Damascus (Maʿlūlā [*q.v.*], D̲j̲ubbʿadīn, and Bak̲h̲ʿa), and by Jacobite Christians in a dialect cluster in southeastern Turkey (Ṭuroyo), by mostly Nestorian Christians and Jews in the Kurdistan area (Northeastern Neo-Aramaic or "Neo-Syriac"), and by the gnostic Mandaeans in western Iran (Neo-Mandaic); many speakers of Neo-Aramaic dialects have emigrated from the Middle East.

From the 6th century B.C. until the 5th century A.D., there are attested thousands of inscriptions in several dialects referred to collectively as Old (or, Epigraphic) South Arabian. As the name implies, most of these inscriptions have been discovered in the southern Arabian peninsula. The best-attested dialect is Sabaic; the others are Minaic, Qatabanian and Ḥaḍramitic. The texts are written in an alphabet whose letter shapes and order differ significantly from those of the Phoenician alphabet and its descendants and which served as the basis of the Ethiopian script. The alphabet preserves all of the consonants of Common Semitic, one more than does Arabic (an additional /s/. Although the Old South Arabian dialects share a number of linguistic features with Arabic, such as the use of broken plurals (and this to an even greater extent than classical Arabic), they also clearly have a number of important traits in common with the Ethiopian Semitic languages.

The closest linguistic relatives of classical Arabic are a group of inscriptional dialects subsumed under the term Old (or, Early) North Arabic, including Thamudic, Dedānite, Liḥyānite, Ḥasaean and Ṣafāʾitic, attested from about the 6th century B.C. to the 4th century A.D. Written in scripts derived from the Old South Arabian alphabet, these texts are found especially in central and northern Arabia as well as in southern Syria. It is out of the linguistic milieu of these and related dialects that classical Arabic emerged, although the written medium was no longer the Old South Arabian alphabet but rather a modified version of the Nabataean Aramaic script.

Ethiopian Semitic is first attested in inscriptions from the 4th century A.D. The earliest attested language is Geʿez, originally the language of Aksum, but ultimately the classical language of the Ethiopian Christian church, studied and promulgated as a literary language much like Arabic among Muslims and Latin in mediaeval Christian Europe. Early inscriptions were written in the Old South Arabian alphabet, the letters of which were later modified with the addition of diacritical marks for the vowels, so that a syllabary evolved. Closely related to classical Geʿez are two modern languages: Tigrinya, spoken by some three million people, mostly Christians, in Tigrai province of Eritrea; and Tigre, the language of some hundred thousand individuals, for the most part Muslims, of the northern hills, the plains, and the coastal areas of Eritrea. Geʿez, Tigrinya, and Tigre comprise northern Ethiopic. Southern Ethiopic consists of many modern languages and dialects, the most prominent among them being the following: Amharic (written since the 16th century), with over seven million speakers the second-most prominent modern Semitic language, after Arabic; Harari, the language of the Muslim city of Harar, unlike other Ethiopian Semitic languages usually written in Arabic script rather than the indigenous syllabary; and several varieties of Gurage, a linguistically and religiously mixed group of tribes that includes both Muslims and Christians.

Finally, there is a group of Semitic languages that has no written tradition, namely, the Modern South Arabian languages spoken by Muslims in eastern Yemen and western Oman. The most prominent of these is Mehri (including the dialects of Ḥarṣūsi and Baṭḥari); others are Djibbāli (also called Śheri or, improperly, Shkhawri), Hōbyōt, and Soḳoṭrī (on the island of Soḳoṭra [*q.v.*]). In sum, these languages probably have fewer than 100,000 speakers. Although proximity to Arabic (and the bilingualism of many of the speakers) has resulted in many Arabic loanwords and expressions in these languages, they are nevertheless quite distinct in their phonology and morphology.

The Semitic languages are generally held to constitute one branch of a larger linguistic entity now usually called Afroasiatic, although the earlier term Hamito-Semitic is still preferred by some scholars. Within Afroasiatic the language groups most closely related to Semitic are Egyptian and Berber. Classical Egyptian, attested from about 3300 B.C. until the 5th century A.D., was written in hieroglyphic, hieratic, and demotic scripts; it was continued in dialects of Coptic, which were written in a modified form of the Greek alphabet and probably spoken until the 15th century A.D. (and still in use as the liturgical language of the Coptic Christian church). The modern Berber languages, such as Tashelḥit, Tamazight, Kabyle and Tuareg, are spoken by Muslims; they exist as linguistic islands in a sea of Arabic across north Africa from Egypt to Mauritania [see BERBERS. V]. Other branches of the Afroasiatic phylum are the Cushitic languages of Ethiopia, Somalia and Kenya, such as Oromo, Somali, Sidamo, Agaw and Beja (the last perhaps a separate branch of Afroasiatic); the Omotic languages of western Ethiopia; and the very large group of Chadic languages of western Africa, the most prominent member of which is Hausa [*q.v.*].

The internal classification of the Semitic languages is much debated. It is generally agreed that there are two main branches, East Semitic and West Semitic. East Semitic comprises only Akkadian (and Eblaite), and differs from the rest of the family in that the primary form of the perfective verb is a prefix-conjugation, as in *taḳbir* "you (ms) buried"; *iṭrudū* (< **yaṭrudū*) "they (m) drove away" (cf. Arabic *lam taḳbir, lam yaṭrudū*). The imperfective form, corresponding to Arabic *yafʿalu*, has a bisyllabic base with a geminated medial radical: *taḳabbir* "you (will) bury", *iṭarradū* "they (will) drive away". There is a suffix conjugation corresponding formally to the Arabic perfect, but it is essentially a predicate adjective, as in *ḳabrāta* <**ḳabir-āta* "you (ms) are/were buried" (*ḳab*(*i*)*r* "buried"), *ṭardū* (< **ṭarid-ū*) "they (m) are/were driven away" (*ṭar*(*i*)*d* "driven away"), vs. Arabic *ḳabarta* "you buried" and *ṭaradū* "they drove away". It is the innovative development of the suffix-conjugation into an active perfective verb, and the concommitant relegation of the apocopate prefix-conjugation (*yafʿal*) to secondary usage, that set the rest of the languages (West Semitic) apart from Akkadian.

Among the West Semitic languages, it has been traditional to group Arabic, the Old and Modern South Arabian languages, and Ethiopian Semitic together as South Semitic, primarily on the basis of their common usage of pattern replacement for noun plurals. Some examples: Sabaic (Old South Arabian) *ḥrbt* "battle", pl. *ḥryb; ʿr* "mountain", pl. *ʾʿrr*; Mehri (Modern South Arabian) *bədēn* "body", pl. *bədawnət; śəlēṯ* "one-third", pl. *śəlwōṯ*; Geʿez (Ethiopian) *kalb* "dog", pl. *ʾakləbt, ʾaklāb*, or *kalabāt; kokab* "star", pl. *kawākəbt*. In contrast, the Canaanite and Aramaic dialects, as well as Ugaritic, in which external plurals are the norm (as in Hebrew *sûs* "horse", pl. *sûsîm*; Aramaic *yom* "day", pl. *yomin*), are grouped together as Northwest Semitic. Since, however, the Northwest Semitic languages exhibit vestiges of broken plurals (as in Hebrew *méleḵ* > **malk* "king", pl. *məlāḵîm* < **malakīm*), and since it is possible that the common use of broken plurals in Arabic, South Arabian, and Ethiopic reflects not a shared innovation (in a common intermediate ancestor) but a feature inherited from Common Semitic, some Semitists have more recently looked to the verbal system for evidence of the genetic classification of the languages. It is noted, for example, that Ethiopic and the Modern South Arabian languages share the bisyllabic base of the imperfective verb with Akkadian, as in Geᶜez *təkabbər* and Mehri *təḳawbər* "you (ms) will bury", whereas Arabic shares with the Northwest Semitic languages the loss of that form and the development of a new form in its place, as in Arabic *taḳbiru* (a form that is obscured in Hebrew and Aramaic by the loss of short final vowels; compare, however, Hebrew *yāḳûm* < **yaḳūmu* "he will arise" and *yāḳōm* < **yaḳum* "may he arise", *yaᶜale* < **yaᶜliyu* "he ascends" and *yaᶜal* < **yaᶜli(y)* "may he ascend"). By this criterion, one may classify Modern South Arabian and Ethiopic together as South Semitic and Arabic, Aramaic, and Canaanite together as Central Semitic. Thus it is the position of Arabic within the Semitic family that is least certain. (The position of the Old South Arabian languages in the more recent classification is also unclear; a recent study showing that the imperfective verb was probably not bisyllabic suggests that they belong in Central Semitic; see Nebes in *Bibl.*)

Bibliography: (1) General overviews of Semitic. G. Bergsträsser, *Einführung in die semitischen Sprachen*, Munich 1928, repr. Darmstadt 1972, Eng. tr. P.T. Daniels, *Introduction to the Semitic languages*, Winona Lake, Indiana 1983; J.H. Hospers, *A basic bibliography for the study of the Semitic languages*, 2 vols., Leiden 1973-4.—(2) Afroasiatic. C.T. Hodge (ed.), *Afroasiatic. A survey*, The Hague and Paris 1971; I.M. Diakonoff, *Afrasian languages*, Moscow 1988.—(3) On the position of Arabic within Semitic. W. Diem, *Die genealogische Stellung des Arabischen in den semitischen Sprachen. Ein ungelöstes Problem der Semitistik*, in W. Diem and S. Wild (eds.), *Studien aus Arabistik und Semitistik. Anton Spitaler zum siebzigsten Geburtstag*, Wiesbaden 1980, 65-85; K. Hecker, *Das Arabische im Rahmen der semitischen Sprachen*, in W. Fischer (ed.), *Grundriss der Arabischen Philologie*, Band 1, *Sprachwissenschaft*, Wiesbaden 1982, 6-16; R.M. Voigt, *The classification of Central Semitic*, in *JSS*, xxxii (1987), 1-21; A. Zaborski, *The position of Arabic within the Semitic dialect continuum*, in K. Dévényi and T. Iványi (eds.), *Proceedings of the Colloquium on Arabic Grammar, Budapest 1-7 September 1991 (= The Arabist. Budapest Studies in Arabic* 3-4), Budapest 1991, 365-75; N. Nebes, *Zur Form der Imperfektbasis des unvermehrten Grundstammes im Altsüdarabischen*, in W. Heinrichs and G. Schoeler (eds.), *Festschrift Ewald Wagner zum 65. Geburtstag*, Band 1, *Semitische Studien*, Beirut 1994, 59-81.

(J. Huehnergard)

SĀM, legendary ruler of Sīstān [*q.v.*] and vassal of the Kayānids, the epic kings of Īrān, was, according to al-Thaᶜālibī and Firdawsī, the son of Narīmān, the father of Zāl-Dastān and the grandfather of Rustam [*q.v.*]. This pedigree is the outcome of a long development spanning the entire history of the Iranian epic. In the Avesta, Sāma is the name of a clan to which Thrīta, "the third man who pressed the Haoma", belonged as well as his sons Urvākhshaya and Kərəsāspa (Yasna 9. 10). Kərəsāspa (Persian Karshāsp or Garshāsp), a formidable fighter against dragons and other evil powers, armed with a mace, is often described as *nairi.manah* ("of manly spirit"). The name of the clan became interchangeable with his personal name, while the epithet was interpreted as the name of his father (in Persian Narīmān, or Nīram). Traces of this stage can still be found in genealogies mentioned by Islamic writers (see e.g. al-Bīrūnī, *al-Āthār al-bāḳiya*, 104, "*wa-Karshāsp wa-huwa Sām b. Narīmān*..."; cf. Masᶜūdī, *Murūdj*, ed. Ch. Pellat, i, 273; "*Kursāf b. Narīmān*..."). However, in Sāsānid times, Karshāsp and Sām already began to be taken as the names of separate persons. Together with Thrīta or Athrat (Arabicised to Athraṭ) and Narīmān, they were fitted into a pedigree which is mentioned with many variations in Zoroastrian and Islamic sources (cf. Christensen, *Kayanides*, 130-1).

In the Pahlawi books, notably in *Bundahishn* and *Mēnōg ī khrad*, the original identity of Karshāsp and Sām is still evident. Like the former, Sām plays a part in eschatological events: he is said not to have died but to rest in a hidden place, guarded by 99,999 spirits (*fravāshīs*), until the day when he will be summoned to fight the demon Azhi Dahāka (in Persian Ḍaḥḥāk), who near the end of Time will escape from his captivity in the mountain Damāwand [*q.v.*]. Further analogies are the fights against several monsters attributed to Sām (Christensen, *op. cit.* 59-60, 101).

In the historical and epic sources of the Islamic period, Garshāsp and Sām (the form Sahm used by al-Ṭabarī is merely an orthographic error due to the ambiguity of the Pahlavi script) are usually kept apart, although they mostly belong to the same lineage, viz. the house of the vassal kings of Sīstān and Zābulistān who act as *djihān-pahlawān* ("chief champion") to the kings of Īrān. They are sometimes contemporaries, e.g. when they are named in the *Shāh-nāma* among the principal warriors of the army of Īrān (i, Farīdūn 692, 792). More often, however, Garshāsp is a remote ancestor of Sām's. According to the 6th/12th century chronicle *Mudjmal al-tawārīkh*, the career of Sām began during the reign of Farīdūn. After the death of his father Narīmān, he was sent out on expeditions to several parts of the world (cf. Spiegel, 248-50). In the *Shāh-nāma,* the story of his family completely fills the account of Manūčihr's reign. As the principal warrior of the realm, Sām replies to the speech delivered by this king at his accession to the throne (i, Manūčihr, 30 ff.), and restores order in the empire after the succession of the unjust king Nawdhar (i, Nawdhar, 22 ff.). On the whole, he is less prominent in Firdawsī's story than his son and grandson, being away most of the time on a campaign against the Gurgsārān (the "wolf-like people", living in a country by the same name) and rebellious warriors (*gurdān*) in Māzandarān. He becomes a full epic character only in the account of the birth of Zāl. Sām is portrayed as a proud nobleman who chooses to sacrifice his son rather than face the scorn of his peers when the child is born with grey hair. However, he equally shows the courage of repentance after he learns of the care bestowed on the abandoned child by the miraculous bird Sīmurgh [*q.v.*] (i, Manūčihr, 41 ff.). He supports his son in the matter of Zāl's courtship with Rūdāba, the daughter of the king of Kābul, in spite of his disapproval of a union with a descendant of Ḍaḥḥāk. An echo of the Avestan legend of Kərəsāspa can be heard in a letter written by Sām to the king of Īrān, relating his struggle with a dragon who had emerged from the river Kashaf (i, Manūčihr, 982 ff.). A parallel story, situated in Māzandarān, is told by Ibn Isfandiyār. Sām was still alive when Rustam was born (i, Manūčihr, 1514). His death, mentioned in the reign of king Nawdhar (i, Nawdhar, 127), incited the Tūranians to invade Īrān and Sīstān. The famous mace of Sām, with which he won the nickname *yak-zakhmī* ("with one stroke"), was inherited by Rustam.

In the *Garshāsp-nāma*, Asadī Ṭūsī [*q.v.*] tells about the birth of Sām as a descendant of Garshāsp, shortly before the latter's death, and the prediction of his future greatness. From a latter, but not precisely definable period, dates a *mathnawī* called *Sām-nāma*, which is preserved in redactions of varying lengths. The poem relates the adventures of Sām, son of Narīmān, in China, where he pretends to the hand of Parīdu<u>kh</u>t, the daughter of the king Fag<u>h</u>fūr. Actually, the poem is a forgery based almost entirely on the romance *Humāy wa Humāyūn* by <u>Kh</u>ʷād<u>j</u>ū [*q.v.*] Kamāl al-Dīn Kirmānī (689-753/1290-1352), for which not only the entire plot of the latter poem was copied but also its lines stolen. The anonymous plagiarist merely changed the names of the protagonists and added some episodes of a fairy-tale nature.

Bibliography: Bīrūnī, *al-Ā<u>th</u>ār al-bāḳiya* (*Chronologie orientalischer Völker*), ed. E. Sachau, Leipzig 1878; E.W. West, *Pahlavi texts*, i, Oxford 1880, 119, and iii, Oxford 1885, 63; F. Justi, *Iranisches Namenbuch*, Marburg 1895, 280-1; F. Wolff, *Avesta. Die heiligen Bücher der Parsen*, Strassburg 1910; Th. Nöldeke, *Das iranische Nationalepos*, Berlin 1920, 9-10, 45; A. Christensen, *Les Kayanides*, Copenhagen 1932, 129 ff.; Ibn Isfandiyār, *Taʾrī<u>kh</u>-i Ṭabaristān*, ed. ʿA. Iḳbāl, Tehran 1941, i, 89, tr. E.G. Browne, Leiden-London 1905, 41-2; Masʿūdī, *Murūd<u>j</u> al-<u>dh</u>ahab*, ed. Ch. Pellat, Beirut 1966; Asadī Ṭūsī, *Gar<u>sh</u>āsp-nāma*, ed. H. Yag<u>h</u>māʾī, Tehran 1354 <u>sh</u>./1975²; M. Mayrhofer, *Iranisches Personennamenbuch*, i, Vienna 1977, 74-5; Ehsan Yarshater, in *Camb. Hist. Iran*, iii/1, Cambridge 1983, 429-33; Firdawsī, *<u>Sh</u>āh-nāma*, ed. D<u>j</u>alāl <u>Kh</u>āliḳī Muṭlaḳ i, New York 1988; W.M. Brinner (tr.), *The History of al-Ṭabarī. iii. The Children of Israel*, Albany 1991, 115-16; D. Davis, *Epic and sedition*, Princeton 1993, 35-41.

On the *Sām-nāma*, see F. Spiegel, *Die Sage von Sâm und das Sâm-nâme*, in *ZDMG*, iii (1849), 245-61 (with a synopsis of the story); Ch. Rieu, *Catalogue of the Persian MSS. in the British Museum*, London 1881, ii, 543-4; H. Ethé, in *Deutsche Literaturzeitung*, 1881, no. 45, 1736; idem, in *GIrPh*, ii, 234-5; idem, *Catalogue of the Persian MSS. in the India Office Library*, London 1903, no. 1235; <u>Dh</u>abīh Allāh Ṣafā, *Ḥamāsasarāʾī dar Īrān*,³ Tehran 1352 <u>sh</u>./1973, 335-40.

(J.T.P. de Bruijn)

SĀM MĪRZĀ, Abū Naṣr, Persian poet and biographer of poets, with the poetical name *Sāmī* (923-74/1517-66), known for his *ta<u>dh</u>kira* of contemporary poets, the *Tuḥfa-yi Sāmī*. He was the third son of <u>Sh</u>āh Ismāʿīl I [*q.v.*].

1. Biography.

<u>Sh</u>āh Ismāʿīl (906-31/1501-24) and his eldest son and successor Ṭahmāsp I (931-84/1524-76) followed the practice of preparing the princes of the ruling family, already at an early age, for the direction of state affairs by appointing them to the post of governor under the guidance of an experienced *amīr* of the Ḳizil Ba<u>sh</u> (*lala*) (see Röhrborn, *Provinzen*, 38-9). Accordingly, Sām Mīrzā passed the greater part of his youth as nominal governor of <u>Kh</u>urāsān at Harāt [*q.v.*], first (927-36/1521-30) under Durmi<u>sh</u> <u>Kh</u>ān, later under Ḥusayn <u>Kh</u>ān, and then from 939-41/1533-5 under Ag<u>h</u>uzivar <u>Kh</u>ān, all three of them from the <u>Sh</u>amlu tribe.

Thus he was able on the one hand to experience the reverberation of a peak of Persian culture at the court of Ḥusayn Mīrzā Bayḳara (873-911/1469-1506), but on the other hand he became involved in the power struggle of the Ḳizil Ba<u>sh</u> through his *lalas*. It is even said that he was supported as a rival king against Ṭahmāsp by Ḥusayn <u>Kh</u>ān (Savory, *Studies*, no. V, 70). When Ḥusayn <u>Kh</u>ān was murdered soon afterwards (940/1534), Sām Mīrzā permitted himself to be seduced to insubordination. Without the king's permission he misused the Ḳizil Ba<u>sh</u>, put under his leadership for protecting Harat against the Özbegs, for a campaign against Ḳandahār, which failed miserably. It cost the life of his *lala* Ag<u>h</u>uzivar and of many other Ḳizil Ba<u>sh</u>, forced Sām Mīrzā to flee to Ṭabas by way of Sīstān, but above all attracted the lurking Özbegs into defenceless Harāt, where they exercised a reign of terror during fourteen months (*Tārī<u>kh</u>-i ʿĀlam-ārā*, 62-5). Ṭahmāsp had to take action in <u>Kh</u>urāsān himself in order to restore order in Harāt around 943/1537. On the way, he became reconciled with Sām Mīrzā, who already earlier had shown repentence (*Aḥsan al-tawārī<u>kh</u>*, 343, 357-8). But his political career had come to an end.

After then he lived in the shadow of the court, apparently as a presentable and worthy member of the royal family. He acted as such at the state reception of Sultan Ḥumāyūn in 951/1544, at which he excelled, like an ancient Persian knight, in the sportsman's-like *hunar numūdan* (*T.-i ʿĀlam-ārā*, 99). He had nothing to do with the devastating revolt of his elder brother Alḳās Mīrzā (953-5/1547-9 [*q.v.*]). He apparently lived for his literary studies, being occupied with his *Tuḥfa* at least since 957/1550. It was finished at the latest in 968/1560-1 (see Humāyūn-Farru<u>kh</u>, *Introd.* to the *Tuḥfa*, 17 ff.). In 969/1561-2 Sām Mīrzā fell into disgrace for a second time. He apparently came under suspicion of political intrigues, for he was interned with two sons of his brother Alḳās Mīrzā in the fortress of Ḳahḳaha, the place of confinement of political delinquents. He remained there until his death in an earthquake in 974/1566-7 (Tarbiyat, *Dāni<u>sh</u>mandan*, 173 *bis*; the date is confirmed by the chronogram *dawlat-ī Ṭahmāsp <u>sh</u>ud bāḳī*).

2. Literary work.

Sām Mīrzā has immortalised himself in literary history with his *Tuḥfa-yi Sāmī*, the summa of his involvement over many years with contemporary Persian poetry and its poets, contained in 714 short biographies of all those who had distinguished themselves in this field since <u>Sh</u>āh Ismāʿīl I's coming to power. However, the *curricula vitae* themselves are only dealt with in very rare cases. The biographies rather give information about a series of points, viz.: name – origin – working place – function – education – training – (human and artistic) qualifications – specialisation – works – career – eventually, end of life, and paradigmatic quotation of at least one verse. They are, however, rarely all dealt with; occasionally one or the other is missing. Not even the works or the favourite genres of poetry are noted down regularly, and a qualification is often also left out. Occasionally, a small scene illustrates a point and the author shows a preference for the piquant and the subtle. But two points are never missing, origin (scene of activity) and quotation of verses, the latter being often reduced to one single verse, which then is almost always the *maṭlaʿ* of a *<u>gh</u>azal* [*q.v.*]. This is not by accident, for the author considers poetry as the fruit of love (*Tuḥfa-yi Sāmī*, 2). In the separate chapters the place of origin often serves for an associative classification (cf. *Tuḥfa-yi Sāmī*, Introd., 19). For Sām Mīrzā does not think in a centralistic way but along lines of political integration; every place in the realm of the Ṣafawids counts, and the real image of Persian poetry emerges only from the totality of all the places where it is practised. In this context, still another point must be observed. It is remarkable how often the author mentions the occupation or profession of a poet or of his father. The more simple trades, such as those of a craftsman or a trader, attract his particular interest. He is apparently concerned with the spread and embedding of poetry in all social levels, from the craftsmen to the princess (cf. Humāyūn-Farrukh, *Tuḥfa-yi Sāmī*, Introd., 6-7).

The arrangement of the work seems to confirm this. It consists of seven chapters (*ṣaḥīfa*), in which the poets with a main occupation and those with an additional function are classified as follows. The first chapter is reserved for the princes of the period. It starts with Shāh Ismāʿīl and his descendants, but place is also devoted to the sworn enemies of the dynasty, even for the Özbeg ʿUbayd Allāh Khān, with whom the author was in hostile contact at Harāt itself. The second chapter deals with the most prominent *sādāt* and *ʿulamāʾ*, the offspring of the Prophet and the predecessors of the Shīʿī clergy. In the third chapter are found the viziers and other dignitaries of the class of scribes. The fourth chapter treats the great men who held court in one town or another and were occasionally active in poetry. Only in the fifth chapter are the real main figures, the poets, allowed to speak, the great among them in the first section, the less important, called "the rest", in the second one. The sixth chapter deals with Turkish-speaking poets who tried their hand at Persian verses too. The seventh and last chapter is devoted to the poetasters; it turns out to be particularly amusing and instructive (Humāyūn-Farrukh, Introd., 22-B).

Sām Mīrzā was prompted to compose his *Tuḥfa* by ʿAlī Shīr Nawāʾī's *Madjālis al-nafāʾis* [see MĪR ʿALĪ SHĪR NAWĀʾĪ], which he must have come to know at Harāt during the first period of his governorship. At that time his first *lala*, Durmīsh Khān, had the work translated into Persian (*Laṭāʾif-nāma*, 3). Not only the form of the selective and accentuated short biographies may have been inspired by this work, but also the motivation. Like his predecessor, Sām Mīrzā wants to save the many poets of his time from oblivion. However, the distinction from Nawāʾī is that Sām Mīrzā not only equals their delicacy of expression with that of the ancestors—as does Nawāʾī—but appreciates it even more highly (*Tuḥfa*, 3-4). While Nawāʾī exults in the idea according to which Khurāsān, with its capital Harāt, had reached the highest blossoming of Persian culture under its lord Ḥusayn Bayḳara, and concentrates his observation on the Khurāsānian poets, Sām Mīrzā's point is rather the overall picture of Ṣafawid poetry. Besides—and this also in contrast with Nawāʾī—, he only rarely mentions his relations with the subjects of his biographies, though he must have owed the great majority of his informations to personal relations (for the question of his sources, see M.I. Kazi, *Sam Mirza*, 86-7). Ultimately, the high value of his book lies in this point. Without it, we would not even know the names of many of the poets.

About the presentation itself it can be remarked that the length of a biography does not depend only on the number of the points treated and on the eventual inserted stories, or on the quotations of verses, but above all on the linguistic presentation. This goes from a concise, pragmatic turn of phrase to a highly-developed, manneristic one with rhyming prose and metaphorical expressions. Sām Mīrzā likes imaginative turns of phrase in particular when mentioning the end of life. He permits himself sporadically to be carried away by the name of a poet to a *metaphora continuata* in other accounts, as for instance in the case of Badr al-Dīn Hilālī [*q.v.*], who often visited the gifted prince at Harāt (*Tuḥfa*, no. 266). In general, a personal engagement with somebody, or also the latter's high standing incited him to a more intensive use of images.

Numerous statements of a literary-critical character are spread throughout the entire book; their critical clouds gather in the seventh *ṣaḥīfa*. In their totality, they point to the unusually trained and sharpened feeling of the author for stylistic nuances and quality. This is not only expressed in critical remarks on singular verses, which go as far as to suggest corrections (e.g. no. 429), but above all in the choice of the quotations of verses. Sām Mīrzā is less carried away by the refined, poetical play of ingenuity of the Tīmūrid period than by the art of subtly bending known motifs in order to give them a permanent garment in a *sahl-i mumtaniʿ* (inimitably beautiful elegance). In this respect, too, he distinguishes himself from Nawāʾī. Nothing might show this more clearly than the fact that the Tīmūrid high tightrope of exquisite poetical acrobatics of thoughts, the logogriph (*muʿammā*), is substantially less frequent in the *Tuḥfa* than it is in the *Madjālis*. Unfortunately, Sām Mīrzā's terminological palette does not correspond with the fullness and differentiation of his aesthetic formation. Qualifications like *matīn* (firm), *pur zūr* (powerful), *rangīn* (colourful), *āb-dār* (brilliant), *ba-čāshnī* (with good taste), *pur sūz u dard* (passionate), etc. might perhaps be better understood and described if all the verses thus estimated were gathered and those which are equally qualified were compared with one another. This would be all the more a desideratum since Sām Mīrzā, instead of a characterisation, often satisfies himself with a quotation of a verse and leaves it to the reader to formulate a judgement.

It is the more regrettable that Sām Mīrzā's *Dīwān*, of which Tarbiyat says that he once saw a manuscript with *ca.* 6,000 verses without any further indication, however, has not yet been published. Besides a *ghazal*, quoted by Tarbiyat (*Dānishmandān*, 173 *bis* f.) from an historical work (*Takmilat al-akhbār*), we possess only the quotations from his own work by the author himself at the end of the *Tuḥfa* (377-80), a *manḳabat ḳaṣīda* on ʿAlī with an introductory description of spring, a *rubāʿī* and four isolated verses (*maṭāliʿ*). The latter, in particular, correspond, in elegance and pointedness, to the ideal of the *sahl-i mumtaniʿ* to which Sām Mīrzā adhered, while the *ḳaṣīda* in its turn is completely free of any complexity of thoughts.

Bibliography: 1. Biography. (a) Sources. Not much specific material can be derived from the *tadhkiras*. More is found in the historical works of Khʷāndamīr; Ḥasan Beg Rumlu, *Aḥsan al-tawārīkh*, ed. Nawāʾī, Tehran 1357 *sh*; Iskandar Beg Munshī, *Tārīkh-i ʿālam-ārāyi ʿabbāsī*, i-ii, Tehran 1350 *sh*; *Takmilat al-akhbār* (to *Aḥsan al-tawārīkh*?), quoted by Tarbiyat, *Dānishmandān* 174 *bis*. (b) Studies. M.ʿA. Tarbiyat, *Dānishmandān i Ādharbāydjān*, Tehran 1314 *sh*, 176-174 *bis*; K. Röhrborn, *Provinzen und Zentralgewalt Persiens im 16. und 17. Jahrhundert*, Berlin 1966; Storey, i, 797-800; R.M. Savory, *Studies on the history of Safawid Iran*, Variorum Reprints, London 1987.

2. On the *Tuḥfa-yi Sami*. (a) Editions. W. Dastgirdī, Tehran 1314 *sh*; R. Humāyūn-Farrukh, Tehran n.d. (the best edition so far, used here); ed. of the 5th *ṣaḥīfa*, Iqbal Husayn, Patna 1934 (title: *The Tuhfa i Sami (Section V) of Sam Mirza Safawi*). (b) Studies. S. de Sacy, *Le présent sublime ou Histoire des poètes de Sam-mirza*, in *Notices et extraits*, iv, Paris 1798, 273-308; O. Frank, *Ueber die morgenländischen Handschriften der königlichen Hof- und Central-Bibliothek in München*, Munich 1814, 34-69; M.I. Kazi, *Sam Mirza and his "Tuḥfa-i-Sami"*, in *Indo-Iranica*, xiii/2 [1960], 69-89 (worth reading); Humāyūn-Farrukh,

Introd. to his edition. (c) Sources of Sām Mīrzā. To those mentioned by Kazi and Humāyūn-Farruk͟h should be added the ed. of the Persian tr. of Nawāʾī, *Madjālis al-nafāʾis*, the *Laṭāʾif-nāma* by Sulṭān Muḥammad-i Fak͟hrī-yi Harawī, made by ʿA.A. Ḥikmat, Tehran 1363 *s͟h*.   (B. REINERT)

SAMĀʾ (A.), literally "the upper part of anything, the sky, the heavens".

1. As a cosmological and theological term. According to Arabic lexicography (see Lane, s.v.), the word *samāʾ* is derived from the root *s-m-w* (= being or becoming high, elevated). As a noun, it may be used for anything that is "the higher or the highest" part of any physical or metaphysical reality, but it generally denotes the cosmological and theological entity which in English, with equal vagueness, is described as "heaven" or "sky". Fittingly, *samāʾ* is predominantly masculine, but it can be masculine or feminine; it is used as a singular or as a plural, as in the Ḳurʾān, II, 27, for the seven heavens; however, even then numerical plurality is not necessarily implied since the plural can be understood as a *pluralis amplitudinis* emphasising the overwhelming greatness of heaven. But *samāʾ* can also be expanded into the plural form *samāwāt*.

For the ancient Arabs, as also for the people of the surrounding countries, *samāʾ*, in the most common meaning of "heaven", was not primarily associated with the stars, but it was first the location for the "high-flying clouds". In poetical language it even appears to have been identified with the clouds, the providers of rain, or even rain itself. Thus the Arabs could think of themselves as the Banū māʾ al-samāʾ (= "The sons of the water of heaven"). Hence "heaven" from early on did not only represent a physical and cosmological entity but was linked to the ultimate hopes of mankind for a continued and happy existence on earth as it knew it. Physical highness in the cosmological world view corresponds to the metaphysical loftiness of spiritual aspiration, and the human mind may even be tempted by the identification of heaven with God Almighty. Considering the far-reaching spectrum of aspects which the term "heaven" displays before us, its dictionary meaning alone cannot sufficiently disclose the underlying cosmological and theological conceptions; and for the Arabic dictionary this resigned observation imposes itself especially also in view of the profound changes which these conceptions underwent in the course of Islam's dynamic cultural expansion, when the intellectual heritage of earlier cultures in the Middle East and in North Africa was adopted.

As the foreign vocabulary employed in the Ḳurʾān demonstrates (in our context the word *Firdaws* for the heavenly garden or Paradise may be explicitly mentioned), the exchange of ideas and theories about heaven and earth must have pre-dated the mission of the Prophet. But with the Ḳurʾānic texts a new beginning was made; above all, in place of particularistic and of merely local idolatry, the monotheistic sovereignty of God over the whole universe as the *Rabb al-ʿĀlamīn* (I, 2) became the centre of the new orientation. As in almost all other provinces of the human mind, the cosmological and theological views of heaven and earth proposed by the revealed book became the formative world model for Muslim culture up to our days. This world view no doubt has been modified in the minds of later generations along the lines of their expanding scientific horizons. But with the unceasing recitation of the Ḳurʾānic texts the physical as well as the spiritual notions of heaven and earth were constantly impressed on the minds of the faithful.

It started with the story of revelation itself, the prophetic call experienced in a cosmic vision that filled the whole space between heaven and earth: "This is naught but a revelation revealed, taught him by one terrible power, very strong; he stood poised, being on the higher horizon, then drew near and suspended hung, two bows'-length away, or nearer, then revealed to his servant that he revealed." (LIII, 5). "Higher horizon" is here the translation of *al-ufuḳ al-aʿlā*, which may be understood as a synonym of heaven joining the earth; hence a heaven that does not remain far removed from the world, the abode of mankind, but which approaches man in a divine communication. Such dividing lines between heaven(s) and earth(s) as the horizon may appear to be sharply drawn in the Arabic speech, but they are never absolutes. It is the bi-polar consequence of the Ḳurʾānic theology of creation that the division of heaven and earth is God's work, and thus also their ultimate union: "... the heavens and the earth were a mass all sewn up, and then then We unstitched them and of water fashioned every living thing." (XXI, 31).

Heaven, in the singular as well as in the plural, occurs over 300 times in the Ḳurʾān. But its description is surprisingly meagre; the communication neither of astronomical nor of apocryphal knowledge is intended, although heaven is also associated with the signs of the Zodiac (LXXXV, 1), the stars, the planets, and although the heavenly journey of the Prophet (XVII, 1) could have been the best occasion for a detailed description, as can be observed in later traditions. In most cases, however, heaven merely serves as reference point for God's greatness, which is above all beings in heaven and earth. Thus the central message is that God has created the heavens and the earths (LXV, 12: "It is God who created seven heavens, and of earths their like"), that He knows whatever exists in whatever form, and that all beings in heaven as well as on earth belong to Him—hence absolute monotheism expanded over the whole cosmos. The cosmological models which may have been alluded to in the revealed texts would then be mere figures of speech, in which the prophetic message of God's absolute rule found its adequate expression.

But the theological interpretation of creation did not extinguish human curiosity about the physical nature of the universe. The Ḳurʾānic texts about heaven and earth were not easily understood; they provided only a fragmentary view of the universe. As far as we can gather from the earliest sources preserved, Ḳurʾān readers with much curiosity, and some exposure to pre-Islamic literatures, soon offered explanations of the enigmatic and fragmentary texts on the cosmos. Similarly, the earliest commentators from whom we have at least some fragmentary explanations of Ḳurʾānic texts, often give brief answers to essentially physical questions about the heavens and whatever moves in them. Thus even such questions as the dynamic cause of the star movements in their spheres were discussed, and the answers came surprisingly close to what in later scholasticism was described as the theory of "impetus". But, in spite of such rare elements of primitive astrophysical teachings, heaven for the traditional scholar of Islam remained closely associated with rain, wind, ice, snow, and primarily with vegetation. It is a treasure or storage for such meteorological phenomena (LXIII, 7); it keeps them enclosed behind strong dams and safe doors.

Mud͟jāhid b. D͟jabr (d. 104/722) was one of those early commentators. In an unpublished cosmographical manuscript (Heidelberg Cod. Or. 317, fol. 100a-b), two remarkable diagrams of the various heavens and earths are preserved (which may, however, be only later additions), possibly illustrating his cosmological model of seven earths under a dome-like structure of seven heavens.

In several other sources, a systematic arrangement of these fourteen stages, neatly separated by an equal number of interspaces measuring 500 "years", underscores their physical nature, which otherwise might be too easily transposed into the psychological realm of types and archetypes, if not into that of ancient mythology. For the traditionalists no doubt delved deeply into the heritage of Near Eastern mythology. Thus the most mysterious arrangement of cosmic levels, and precisely for this reason certainly not a mere invention, starts with God's throne being supported by eight huge ibexes (*awʿāl*) of the cosmic dimension of 500 years; they stand on a sea as deep as the distance from earth to heaven; and only below these mysterious cosmic beings the seven heavens are spanned out, one below the other one. Finally, below all those heavens, and sometimes clearly separated from them by a celestial ocean, there follows a structure of seven earths. These are the main features of the traditional cosmology of Islam, which is further modified from one source to the other; the celestial ocean e.g. which is usually located in heavenly regions, may even be placed under the lowest earth. Common to all these models seems to be that the heavens are vaulted over the earths like a dome-structure, while the earths are arranged in horizontal levels, like a block with different storeys, as the above diagrams indicate. Heavens and earths cannot be clearly separated, as C. Houtman already noticed in his thorough investigation on *Der Himmel im Alten Testament* (see *Bibl.*). The theological or mythological roots become evident when we see that the seven earths in the older traditional texts are serving as the gradual stages of hell, in particular the store-houses of the various torture instruments: destructive winds, *d̲jinn*, brimstones of hell-fire, scorpions, vipers, and eventually the devils. This rather mythological structure—and that is its unexpected historical function—was in later texts apparently used to illustrate the geographical division of our globe.

Between the heavens and the earths, there is moreover not the clear-cut division that had been axiomatically postulated in pre-Islamic, Hellenistic philosophy, where the supra-lunar world was thought to remain eternally unchanged and having circular movements only. Even the heavens in traditional cosmology are described as being of material nature. Thus most commonly the lowest one is identified with the firmly-enclosed water of the celestial ocean, and the higher ones consist of different substances, such as white marble, iron, copper, silver, gold and ruby, while the space above them is filled with "deserts of light". The traditional authority Salmān al-Fārisī even had names for the seven heavens and associated precious stones and metals with them.

In this form, the cosmology of the seven heavens was especially developed by *The Book of Secrets of Enoch*, which may have originated within an Islamic milieu. In the estimation of R.H. Charles, this book is "the most elaborate account of the seven heavens that exists in any writing or in any language." When he interprets this account as an example of "growing ethical consciousness" within apocryphal literature (p. XXXIX), he gives us the decisive clue for a valid evaluation: not the teaching of any objective cosmological knowledge is intended, but man's ethical and religious concerns are to be extended to the highest and most remote reaches of creation.

Since this whole cosmological system of seven heavens and seven earths had entered such authoritative texts as the Ḳurʾān and *Ḥadīt̲h̲*, it could never henceforth be totally discarded. When the Hellenistic models of the cosmos had become known through numerous translations, a synthesis of the traditional and the translated cosmological notions was tried by some authors. As a result "the heavens" often were simply identified with "the spheres" (= *aflāk*) [see FALAK]. But there were important differences. Thus in the world-model of the traditional sources, all the stars were connected with the lowest heaven, while in the later models the fixed stars were invariably distinguished from the planets, for which at least one sphere each was reserved; or the sun, in traditional cosmology, was not linked to its sphere, but was said to pass through all heavens as it completed its (yearly?) course, and finally would reach the foundations of God's throne.

The brief and humble explanations of the Ḳurʾānic text by the early commentators were soon followed by penetrating speculations of the systematic theologians. The often enigmatic references to such cosmological and theological entities as heaven (or the heavens), the stars, meteorological phenomena, and the earth as being blessed by such heavenly gifts as light, clouds, winds and rain, stimulated their highly speculative minds and drove them to remarkable attempts at finding satisfactory answers to such questions as God's place in the universe: Did He really and physically reside in the heavens, or one particular heaven, or was He so far removed from all His creations that He could have no real relationship to His creatures? But if His transcendence was emphatically enunciated beyond all limits, how could this God still have revealed His will and His wisdom to the Prophet and all mankind, how could His creatures still hope to have access to Him and in prayer attract His attention when they were in need? Among the numerous cosmological theories discussed by the *mutakallimūn* and the free-minded intellectuals in the early Muslim community, we may concentrate on the thorny problem of God's physical presence in this universe. Was He sitting on His throne in highest heaven, or keeping infinitely above all heavens and all regions on and below earth, or was His presence in His creation so universal that no real distinction could be affirmed (cf. pantheistic monism)? Well before Aristotle's speculations about the "Unmoved Mover (or Movers)" became known in Arabic philosophical circles, the heretic thinker D̲j̲ahm b. Ṣafwān (executed in 129/746 [*q.v.*]) was accused by traditional scholars of having deviated from the explicit teachings of the Ḳurʾān by denying God's sitting on His throne. D̲j̲ahm and his followers were apparently especially eager to emphasise the infinity and ubiquity of the Eternal, without allowing His image to be tarnished by anthropomorphic conceptions. But the defenders of orthodoxy were concerned that such a rationalist commixture of the Creator with His creatures might eliminate all distinctions and obscure the personal presence of God Almighty in the universe; thus they insisted that the Ḳurʾānic texts should be understood literally, and the physical reality of the throne maintained.

Throne (*al-ʿars̲h̲*) and footstool (*al-kursī*) are closely connected with God's place in the universe, and they are essential conceptions for the "theology of the Ḳurʾān" (as far as there is one); God is emphatically called "the Lord of the Mighty Throne" (IX, 129), and this "Throne comprises the heavens and earth; the preserving of them oppresses Him not; He is the

All-High, the All-Glorious'' (II, 255). These texts, certainly in the circles of victorious traditional orthodoxy, were generally understood quite concretely, not merely as metaphorical assertions about God's universal rule. Throne and footstool were placed above the heavens and the earths, but they were, however, of the same concrete reality. Thus they can be measured together with them, and they are conceived as being in physical contact with each other and with the lower, physical parts of the world. As all reality was fashioned out of the four elements water, wind, light, and darkness, the throne was created out of God's own light; or it is said to have been made of a red hyacinth (Saʿīd al-Ṭāʾī), or again of a green emerald (Ḥammād). The footstool is said to be attached to God's throne, or to be standing in front of it. The curious fact that a certain creaking sound, which the Prophet was able to hear (see al-Ṭabarī, *Tafsīr*, on XXI, 21), is ascribed to it as elsewhere to heaven (*al-samāʾ*) indicates that it sometimes was identified with *al-samāʾ*, i.e. that it had an equal extension as heaven. But usually it is distinguished from the heavens, as the whole universe is described as a structure composed of a number of horizontal levels: uppermost, the throne—below it the footstool—then the seven heavens—and the seven earths, one on top of the other. Since the *kursī* is hollow and contains the whole world of heavens and earths in its cavity, the earthly observer—true to his daily experience—finds himself in a dome-like hemisphere. For the Muslim cosmologist and theologian, the Ḳurʾānic text (XXI, 34: ''It is He who created the night and the day, the sun and the moon, each swimming in a sky'') further emphasised the physical substance of the heavens and imposed on him a critical attitude that made it difficult for him to simply adopt the common Greek notions that the stars or their spheres are living beings, having souls, which are moving by their own will.

It may be said, then, that it was due to throne, footstool, the seven heavens and earths being mentioned in the Ḳurʾān that Muslim scholars of all disciplines continued to be attracted by the various branches of cosmology. When Greek science had been introduced into the Islamic world, throne and footstool were often identified with the ninth and eighth spheres respectively, exemplified in such an influential theological book as al-Īdjī's (d. 756/1356 [*q.v.*]) *Mawāḳif*. However, even an open-minded author like al-Ḳazwīnī (d. 682/1283 [*q.v.*]) was much more cautious, and explicitly opted for leaving it to God's knowledge whether this identification could be made (*ʿAdjāʾib al-makhlūḳāt*, i, 54). Similarly, the seven earths were identified with the Hellenistic scheme of seven climatic zones [see IḲLĪM], although this may have caused some problems since the traditional texts had handed over these earthly parts to the devils in hell and their torture instruments.

The early commentators and traditionists of Islam already adopted ideas and cosmological models from earlier cultures of the neighbouring countries. As this scientific heritage became richer through the numerous translations made between the 2nd and the 4th centuries A.H., the cosmological models were further developed along the lines of such authorities as Ptolemy, Hipparchus, etc. But the earlier theories were not simply forgotten or thrown away into the waste-paper baskets of history, as we might expect in accordance with the experiences of other cultures. Even an al-Bīrūnī [*q.v.*] remembered them; he naturally criticised them as outdated in his time, but the fact that he bothered about them at all demonstrates the influence—of whatever nature that may have been—which they still must have exerted on some of his contemporaries. Thus his discussion with Ibn Sīnā on the possibility of other worlds than ours may well be inspired by the traditional texts. The same may hold true for al-Bīrūnī's distinction between mathematical hypotheses, equally allowing a heliocentric as well as a geocentric universe, and an eventual decisive proof based on physical reasoning. Or the fact that Muslim scholars showed more extensive interests in the physical configuration of the universe than their Hellenistic masters (which is clearly evidenced not only by the use they made of Ptolemy's *Planetary hypotheses* but also by the numerous treatises with such titles as *Tarkīb al-aflāk*), was most likely the fruit of the Ḳurʾānic and traditional texts on the seven heavens. Similarly, Muslim authors showed a surprising critical spirit when the number of the spheres was discussed; some of them accepted the eight or nine spheres of Greek cosmology only under the condition that the highest were identified with the footstool and the throne respectively which the Ḳurʾān had added to the seven heavens.

Such foreign influences raised much suspicion and fear among the more traditionally-minded scholars. Hence a reaction set in against the almost completely Hellenised world view that had been spread in Muslim literature. Thus already two centuries after al-Bīrūnī, a scholar like Fakhr al-Dīn ar-Rāzī (d. 606/1209 [*q.v.*]), who proves to be widely read in all sorts of literatures available after the synthesis with the Hellenistic heritage had been achieved, still states categorically that all valid knowledge about the cosmos is to be reaped from the traditional, ''inspired'' sources of Islam and not from the scientific sources of ancient cultures (''there is no way to the knowledge of the heavens save through a traditional report'') (*Mafātīḥ al-ghayb*, vi, 149). In other words, the inner scientific value of the works inherited from pre-Islamic scholars was well known, but the knowledge derived from Islamic tradition still carried a functionality for the faithful which, outside the realm of faith, might not be understood.

But the heavens are not solely physical and astronomical entities, which for such speculative reasons as defining God's place in the universe were of interest also to the theologians; they have a special significance also for the simple worshipper and for the mystical experiences of the spiritually-elevated faithful. Thus when we examine such mystical writings as the *Futūḥāt al-Makkiyya* by Ibn ʿArabī (d. 638/1240 [*q.v.*]), one is surprised to find long passages, expounding esoteric teachings, which seem to follow the cosmological models of the seven heavens and the seven earths. But it soon becomes evident that the cosmological stages have hardly any other function than to serve as ''coordinate systems'' giving structure to the inner experiences and psychological states of the mystic.

Similarly, in sectarian circles, and principally in the literature of the Ismāʿīlī community, the symbolic significance of the seven heavens was stressed to the point that any physical or metaphysical reality which they had in the writings of the commentators, the *mutakallimūn* or the cosmologists, appears to have been suppressed. The fact that the various strata of interaction within an essentially political hierarchy were described in cosmological terms indicates, however, that the cosmology of the seven heavens had been widely accepted in Islamic literature as common language.

In both cases, mysticism as well as sectarian exchange, the decisive inspiration did not really come from the Ḳurʾānic world view of the seven heavens

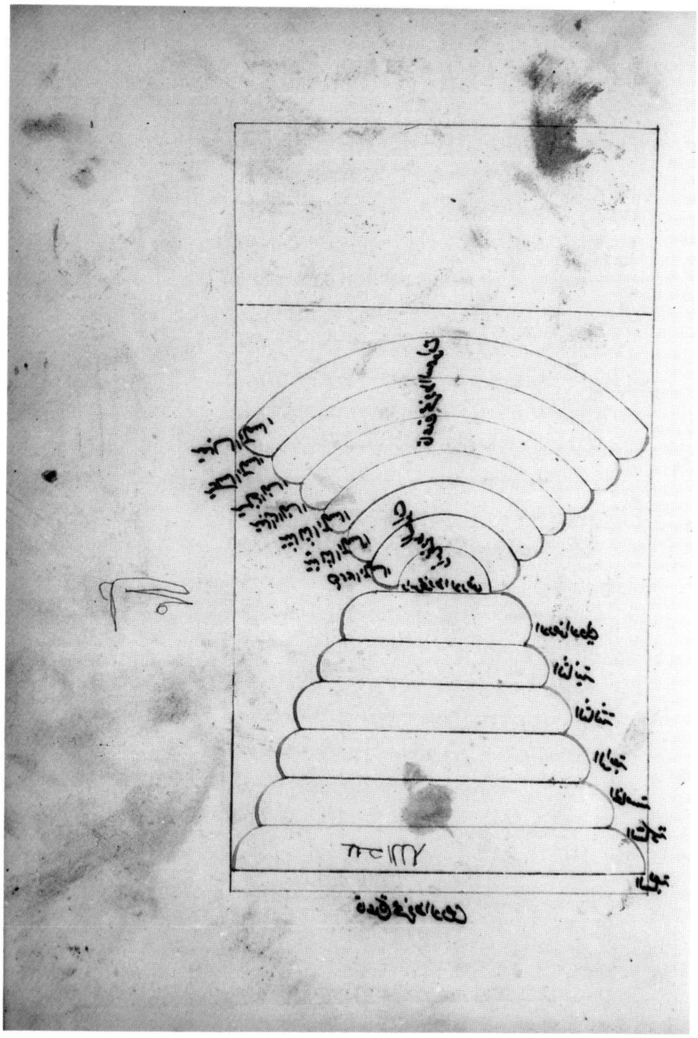

A simple representation of the seven heavens spanning the seven earths. For both zones the shape of a cone is assumed, but the opposition of the two is emphasized by the choice of curved lines for the heavens and horizontal ones for the earths.

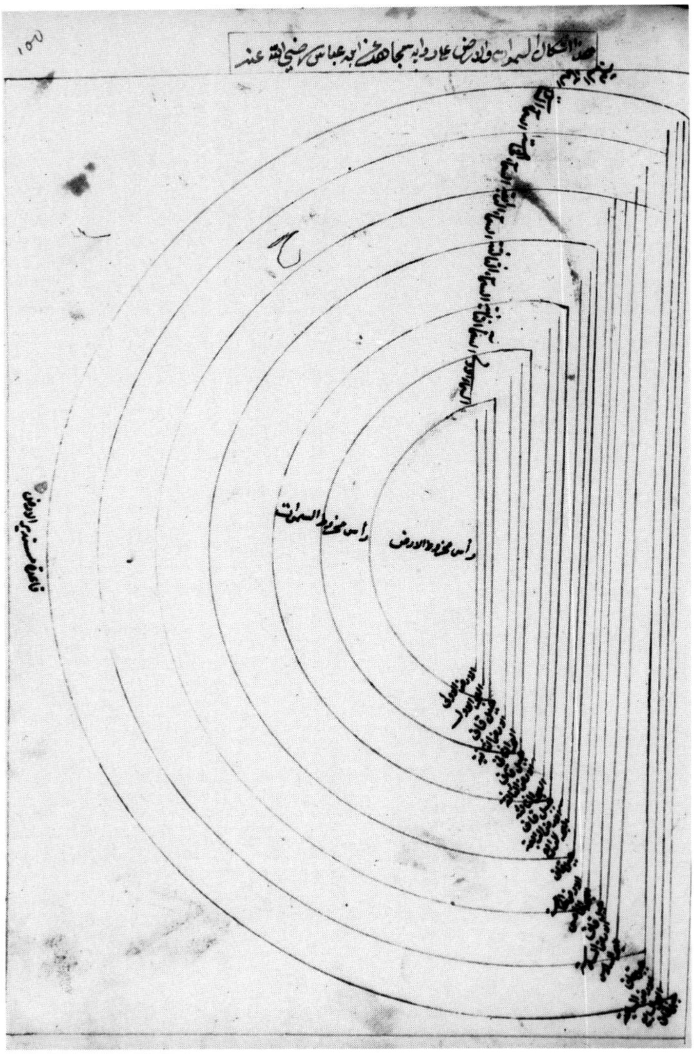

The cosmos described as a cone. Like a seven-fold dome, the seven heavens span the cone of the seven earths. The latter are part of a schematic "geography" based on a seven-fold division consisting of alternating earths, seas, and the Ḳāf mountains.

but rather from Neoplatonic teachings. A scheme was needed that would allow a graduated classification of spiritual descent from, and elevation to, the highest reality without a transgression beyond all frontiers to be feared. It is not surprising that both the spiritual and the political authorities turned to the cosmology of the seven heavens in search of this scheme; but the numerous ramifications of both these experiential and ideological traditions go far beyond the limits of the present discussion.

Bibliography: Note that most sources on the heavens and the earths in accordance with the traditional world view, even more so than those of the sciences inherited from the ancient authorities, are still unpublished manuscripts. 1. Manuscripts. Abu 'l-Shaykh, *K. al-ʿAẓama*, Istanbul, Köprülü ii, 138, 2, fols. 4a-118a; al-Ḳaramānī al-Āmidī, *R. fi 'l-hayʾa al-mabniyya ʿalā 'l-aḥādīth wa 'l-āthār*, Heidelberg, Cod. Heid. Or. 317; Ibn Abi 'l-Dunyā, *K. al-ʿAẓama*, Istanbul, Cârullâh 400, and Princeton, Garret C. 764; Ibn ʿArabī, *K. al-ʿAẓama*, Istanbul, Cârullâh 1080; Muḥāsibī, *K. al-ʿAẓama*, Istanbul, Cârullâh 1101; Sidjzī, *K. Tarkīb al-aflāk*, Istanbul, Lâleli 2707.

2. Printed works. M.M. Azmī, *Studies in early Ḥadīth literature (with a critical edition of some early texts)*, Beirut 1968; Battānī-C.A. Nallino (ed., tr. and comm.), *Opus astronomicum*, 3 vols., repr. Hildesheim-New York 1977; A. Bausani, *Cosmologia e religione nell' Islam*, in *Scientia*, cviii (1973), 723-67; Bīrūnī, tr. Jamil Ali, *K. Taḥdīd nihāyāt al-amākin li-taṣḥīḥ masāfāt al-masākin* (= *The determination of the coordinates of positions for the correction of distances between cities*), Beirut 1967; Cosmas Indicopleustès, ed. W. Wolska-Conus, *Topographie Chrétienne*, 3 vols., Paris 1968 ff.; Dimashkī, *Nukhbat al-dahr*, ed. Mehren; R. Eisler, *Weltenmantel und Himmelszelt*, Munich 1910; O. Eissfeldt, *Phönikische und griechische Kosmogonie*, in *Kleine Schriften*, iii, Tübingen 1963; Enoch, tr. R.H. Charles, *The Book of Enoch, or 1 Enoch*, Oxford 1912; R.M. Frank, *The Neoplatonism of Ǧahm Ibn Ṣafwân*, in *Le Muséon*, lxxix (1966), 395-424; G. Friedlander (tr.), *Pirkê de Rabbi Eliezer*, New York 1965; Eileen Gardiner, *Medieval visions of Heaven and Hell. A sourcebook*, New York-London 1993; Ghazālī, *al-Ḥikma fī makhlūkāt Allāh*, Cairo 1352/1934; A.M. Heinen (ed., tr. and comm.), *Islamic cosmology. A study of as-Suyūṭī's al-Hayʾa as-sanīya fī 'l-hayʾa as-sunnīya*, Beirut 1982; E. Honigmann, *Die sieben Klimata und die "poleis episêmoi"*, Heidelberg 1929; C. Houtman, *Der Himmel im Alten Testament. Israels Weltbild und Weltanschauung*, Leiden-New York-Köln 1993; Aḥmad M. al-Ḥūfī, *Maʿānī 'l-samāʾ wa 'l-arḍ fi 'l-Ḳurʾān*, Cairo 1987; Ibn Āyās, ed. L. Langlès, *Cosmographie composée ... par ... Mohhammed ben Ahmed ben Ayâs*, in *NE*, viii (1810); Ibn Ḳutayba, *Kitāb al-Anwāʾ*, Ḥaydarābād/Deccan 1375/1956; Ibn Rustah; Ibn al-Wardī, ed. ʿU. ʿAbd al-Rāziḳ, *Kharīdat al-ʿadjāʾib*, Cairo 1302-28/1884-1910; Ikhwān al-Ṣafāʾ, *Rasāʾil*, Bombay 1888, Cairo 1928, repr. Beirut 1957; Edith Jachimowicz, *Islamic cosmology*, in *Ancient cosmologies*, ed. Carmen Blacker and M. Loewe, London 1975, 143-71; P. Jensen, *Die Kosmologie der Babylonier*, Straßburg 1890, ²Berlin-New York 1974; E.S. Kennedy and B.L. van der Waerden, *The world-year of the Persians*, in *JAOS*, lxxxiii (1963), 315-27; Kennedy and M.H. Regier, *Prime meridians in medieval Islamic astronomy*, in *Vistae in astronomy*, xxviii (1985), 29-32; D.A. King, *Astronomical alignments in medieval Islamic religious architecture*, in *Annals of the New York Academy of Sciences* (1982), 303-12; idem, *The sacred direction in Islam. A study of the interaction of religion and science in the Middle Ages*, in *Interdisciplinary Science Reviews*, x/4 (1985), 315-28; W. Kirfel, *Die Kosmographie der Inder*, Bonn-Leipzig 1920; K. Kohl, *Über den Aufbau der Welt nach Ibn al-Haiṯam*, in *SBPMS Erl.*, liv-lv (1922-3), 140-79; Maria Kowalska, *Bericht über die Funktion der arabischen kosmographischen Literatur des Mittelalters*, in *Fol. Or.*, xi (1969), 175-80; P. Kunitzsch, *The Arabs and the stars*, Northampton 1986; Y.T. Langermann, *Ibn al Haytham's On the configuration of the World* (= *Al-Maqāla fi hayʾat al-ʿālam*), New York-London 1990; Maḳdisī, *K. al-Badʾ wa 'l-tarīkh*; Masʿūdī, *Murūdj*; idem, ed. ʿA.Al-Ṣāwī, *K. Akhbār al-zamān*, Beirut 1386/1966; P. Merlan, *Aristotle's unmoved movers*, in *Traditio*, iv (1946), 1-30; Middleton and W.E. Knowles, *A History of the theories of rain and other forms of precipitation*, London 1965; J.T. Milik (ed.), *The Books of Enoch*, Oxford 1976; M. Molé, *Culte, mythe et cosmologie dans l'Iran ancien*, Paris 1963; W.R. Morfill, *The Book of the Secrets of Enoch (translated from the Slavonic)*, Oxford 1896; M.K. Munitz, *Theories of the universe. From Babylonian myth to modern science*, New York 1957; C.A. Nallino, *ʿIlm al-falak* (= *Arabian astronomy. Its history during the medieval times*), Rome 1911; idem, *Sun, Moon, and Stars (Muhammadan)*, in *Encycl. of Religion and Ethics*, xii, 88-101; S.H. Nasr, *An introduction to Islamic cosmological doctrines*, Cambridge, Mass. 1964; idem, *Cosmographie en l'Islam pré-islamique et islamique; le problème de la continuité dans la civilisation iranienne*, in *Arabic and Islamic studies in honor of Hamilton A.R. Gibb*, ed. G. Makdisi, Leiden 1965, 507-25; idem and M. Mohaghegh (eds.), *Al-Biruni and Ibn Sina. al-Asʾila wa 'l-adjwiba* (= *Questions and answers*), Tehran 1973; F. Nau, *La Cosmographie au VIIe siècle chez les Syriens*, in *ROC*, xv (1910), 225-54; O. Neugebauer, *A history of ancient mathematical astronomy*, Berlin-Heidelberg-New York 1975; idem, *Notes on Ethiopic astronomy*, in *Orientalia*, xxxiii (1964), 49-71; idem, *Ethiopic astronomy and computus*, Vienna 1979; T. O'Shaughnessy, *God's throne and the biblical symbolism of the Qurʾān*, in *Numen*, xx (1973), 202-22; Ch. Pellat, *Dictons rimés, Anwāʾ et mansions lunaires chez les Arabes*, in *Arabica*, ii (1955), 17-41; W. Petri, *Ananija Shirakazi-ein armenischer Kosmograph des 7. Jahrhunderts*, in *ZDMG*, cxiv (1964), 269-88; D. Pingree, *The Thousands of Abū Maʿshar*, London 1968; idem, *Indian influence on early Sassanian and Arabic astronomy*, in *JOR*, xxxiii (1963-4), 1-8; C. Ptolemaeus, ed. J.L. Heiberg, *Claudii Ptolemaei opera quae exstant omnia*, I. *Syntaxis mathematica*, Leipzig 1898-1903 (= *Handbuch der Astronomie*. German tr. K. Manitius, corrected by O. Neugebauer, Leipzig 1963); II. *Opera astronomica minora*, Leipzig 1907; idem, ed. Sezgin, *Geography. Arabic translation (1465 A.D.)*, Repr. facs. ed. of the ms. Ayasofya 2610, Frankfurt a.M. 1987; H. Ritter, *L'Orthodoxie a-t-elle une part dans la décadence?*, in R. Brunschvig and G.E. von Grunebaum (eds.), *Classicisme et déclin culturel dans l'histoire de l'Islam*, Paris 1957, 167-83; S.M. Stern, *The earliest cosmological doctrines of Ismāʿīlism*, in his *Studies in early Ismāʿīlism*, Jerusalem-Leiden 1983, 3-29; B. Sticker, *Weltzeitalter und astronomische Perioden*, in *Saeculum*, iii (1953), 241-9; Carole Stott, *Celestial charts. Antique maps of the heavens*, New York 1991; Suhrāb, ed. H. von Mžik, *Das Kitāb ʿAdjāʾib al-akālīm as-sabʿa des Suhrāb; herausgegeben nach dem handschriflichen Unikum des Britischen Museums in London /Cod. 23379 ADD./*, Leipzig 1930; S. Toulmin, *The Astrophysics of Berossos the Chaldean*, in *Isis*, lviii

(1967), 65-76; Ṭūsī, ed. M. Sutūda, *ʿAdjāʾib al-makhlūḳāt*, Tehran 1966; B.L. van der Waerden, *Die Anfänge der Astronomie*, Groningen 1966; G. Vitestam, *K. ar-Radd ʿala 'l-djahmīya des Abū Saʿīd ʿUthmān b. Saʿīd ad-Dārimī*, Leiden 1960; E. Wiedemann, *Bemerkungen zur Astronomie und Kosmographie der Araber*, in *Aufsätze zur arabischen Wissenschaftsgeschichte*, i, 80-6; idem, *Anschauungen der Muslime über die Gestalt der Erde*, in *Archiv für Geschichte der Naturwissenschaften und der Technik*, i (1909), 310-19; idem, *Über die Dimensionen der Erde nach muslimischen Gelehrten*, in *ibid.*, iii (1912), 250-5; idem, *Über die Gestalt, Lage und Bewegung der Erde sowie philosophisch-astronomische Betrachtungen von Quṭb al- Dīn al-Schīrāzī*, in *ibid.*, 395-422; H.A. Wolfson, *The problem of the souls of the spheres from the Byzantine commentaries on Aristotle through the Arabs and St. Thomas to Kepler*, in *The Dumbarton Oaks Papers*, xvi (1962), 67-93; idem, *The plurality of immovable movers in Aristotle and Averroes*, in *Harvard Studies in Classical Philosophy*, lxiii (1958), 233-54. See also ʿILM AL-HAYʾA; ḲIBLA. ii; ḲUTB. (A. HEINEN)

2. As an astronomical term, see MAKKA. 4; MINṬAḲAT AL-BURŪDJ.

SAMĀʿ, verbal noun from the root *s-m-ʿ* (like *samʿ* and *simʿ*), signifying "hearing"; by extension, it often denotes "that which is heard", such as music, for example. The same applies to *istimāʿ* "listening" (Lane, *Lexicon*, 1427b, 1429b; *LʿA*, s.v.)

1. In music and mysticism.

The term is not found in the Ḳurʾān, but it exists in ancient Arabic, even in the sense of song or of musical performance (Lane, 1617b, s.v. *mus̲h̲ār*). In lexicology and in grammar, it signifies "that which is founded on authority", as opposed to *ḳiyāsī* "founded on analogy" (de Sacy, *Grammaire*, i, 347, and Lane, 1429b). In theology, it is opposed to *ʿaḳl*, "reason" (Goldziher, *Richtungen*, 136-7, 166). But it presents a specific sense in Ṣūfism, where it generally denote the hearing of music, the concert, and in its particular sense, the Ṣūfī tradition of spiritual concert, in a more or less ritualised form. *Samāʿ* is then considered to be the "nourishment of the soul", in other words, a devotional practice which, according to Ṣūfī authors, can induce intense emotional transports (*tawādjud*), states of grace (*aḥwāl*), of trance or of ecstasy (*wadj, wudjūd*) and even revelations. These manifestations are often accompanied by movements, physical agitation or dance which are of set form or otherwise, individual or collective, of which Persian miniatures have left numerous testimonies and of which certain forms are still in use.

The very sense of the term *samāʿ*, which has been widely discussed, suggests that it is actually *listening* which is spiritual, since music or poetry do not necessarily have a sacred nature. "Hearing", on the other hand, can be applied to any sound, natural, artificial or artistic, as well as to the "subtle" sounds of the hidden world or of the cosmos.

In its predominant sense, hearing is a synonym of "understanding", in other words, comprehension, acceptance and application of the Revelation, and the practice of *samāʿ*, beyond ecstacy or rapture, can be an unveiling of mysteries, a means of attaining higher knowledge (Rūzbihān, Gīsū Derāz).

Samāʿ does not seem to appear until the mid-3rd/9th century among the Ṣūfīs of Bag̲h̲dād, but while the association of music with ecstatic rites or practices is attested prior to Islam in the Religions of the Book (Molé), no solution has been found to the question of continuity between the latter and the Ṣūfī practice of *samāʿ*, in spite of numerous similarities. It could take the form of an extension of the hearing of the Ḳurʾān to that of religious *g̲h̲azal*s and *ḳaṣīda*s, or furthermore, of sacralisation of the secular concert and a sublimation of *ṭarab*, that new custom which spread very quickly to Iṣfahān, S̲h̲īrāz and in K̲h̲urāsān (Purdjawādī, 18). *Samāʿ* is thus initially an "oriental" phenomenon, promulgated in particular by the Persian disciples of Nūrī and of Djunayd. By the same token, all of the early authors dealing with *samāʿ* were Persians, with the exception of Abū Ṭālib Muḥammad al-Makkī (d. 386/996 [*q.v.*]). Subsequently, *samāʿ* spread to all areas, but found most favour in Persian, Turkish and Indian Islam. The first writings, composed a century after the inauguration of the custom of *samāʿ*, coincided with the first attacks on the part of traditionalists who sought to condemn music (such as Ibn Abi 'l-Dunyā (208-81/823-94 [*q.v.*]), the author of the *Dhamm al-malāhī*, cf. Robson), and constituted a reply to them. According to Purdjavādī (*ibid.*, 22), these writings may be arranged in three groups and periods:

(1) *4th/10th century*: ʿAbd al-Raḥmān al-Sulamī (d. 412/941 [*q.v.*]), whose *K. al-Samāʿ* is the first monograph devoted specifically to *samāʿ*; al-Makkī; al-Sarrādj (d. 378/988 [*q.v.*]); al-Kalābādhī (d. 380/990 [*q.v.*]); and Abū Manṣūr. They base their arguments on *ḥadīth*s and on the logia of the ancient mystics (Dhu 'l-Nūn al-Miṣrī), being concerned above all to defend *samāʿ* from its detractors.

(2) *5th/11th century*: al-Buk̲h̲ārī; Abu 'l-Ḳāsim al-Ḳus̲h̲ayrī (d. 466/1074 [*q.v.*]); al-G̲h̲azālī (d. 505/1111 [*q.v.*]). In these authors, too, the defensive aspect is featured, but the Ṣūfīs seem to rely on them more on account of their social and even political status.

(3) *7th-8th/13th-14th centuries*: Nadjm al-Dīn Kubrā [*q.v.*], Rūzbihān Baḳlī S̲h̲īrāzī (d. 606/1209); Aḥmad-i Djam; Nadjm al-Dīn Bag̲h̲dādī; ʿAbd al-Razzāḳ Kās̲h̲ānī; Aḥmad Ṭūsī (8th/14th century); etc. They take into account the social and ritual aspect and argue more rationally. After this period, *samāʿ* was included in its entirety among the customs of the mystics and was no longer the object of judicial debates. Writers confined themselves to extolling its qualities and its symbolic meanings, some going so far as to consider it an obligation for adepts (Aḥmad Ṭūsī, whose *Bawāriḳ* has been erroneously attributed to Aḥmad al-G̲h̲azālī (cf. Mojahed, 1980). After the 9th-10th/15th-16th centuries, the question of *samāʿ* seems to have been filed away or exhausted, and setting aside the orders which retained its practice and its theory (Mawlawīs, Čis̲h̲tīs), did not give rise to any more original literature (Gīsū Derāz).

The function of *samāʿ*, as well as its conditions of performance, have evolved in a sense which al-Hudjwīrī was the first to deplore, and which the aphorisms of the earliest Ṣūfīs (al-Ḥallādj, Dhu 'l-Nūn) had anticipated in their warnings. It became for some a form of delectation or a sensual pleasure, all the more so in that the rite now included dancing and was concluded with a meal. Furthermore, the proletariat indulged in profane *samāʿ*s, in other words concerts with a religious pretext (Pouzet), not to mention rites of trance inherited from paganism and superficially Islamised (berated by Ibn Taymiyya). In order to restrain the adepts and counter the criticisms of the jurists, the majority of authors established conditions (al-G̲h̲azālī) and rules of propriety (al-Nasafī), and distinguished between the types of concert (*samāʿ*) in terms of the nature of the hearing: some listen according to their ego (*samāʿ al-nafs*, or their nature, *ṭabʿ*), others according to the heart, others through the spirit. While for the first category, music (or *samāʿ*) is not to be permitted, as for the adepts, not all the *shaykhs* were unanimous as to the advantages which could be drawn from *samāʿ*. The contention was that *samāʿ* is dangerous for beginners and useless for the more advanced. Some maintained that it should be limited to the hearing of Ḳurʾānic psalmody (Ibn ʿArabī), others did not approve of it, but none explicitly discouraged it, with the exception of Aḥmad Sirhindī [*q.v.*].

It is remarkable that the conditions of admissibility of *samāʿ* have had practically no effect on the musical form itself, except that instruments with profane or dubious connotations are proscribed (al-Ghazālī). This is why certain instruments, such as the tambourine (*daff, bendir, mazhar*) and the *nāy* were more widespread, while certain orders were content with song. Similarly, romantic poems were adopted at a very early stage in Persia, on condition that they were to be interpreted by the adepts in a metaphorical sense—sometimes very subtle—relating to a spiritual object or to the person of the Prophet.

Faced with the diversity of attitudes, *samāʿ* has taken on extremely varied forms, especially in combining with or associating with collective *dhikr*, the ritualisation of an ecstatic technique, which probably appeared a few centuries later. At the present day, it is most often in the context of a ceremony of *dhikr* that *samāʿ* is performed, in the form of chant sometimes accompanied by instruments, whether in the course of one of the phases of the ritual, or in association with the metrical shape of the *dhikr*. Thus the distinction drawn by anthropologists between *samāʿ* and *dhikr*, on the basis of the participation of subjects, "set to music" in one case and "making music" in the other, is not applicable, all the more so in that even silent listening is generally accompanied by interior *dhikr* (*khafī*), as among the Mawlawīs, often being transformed into audible *dhikr* (*djahrī, djalī*). In its primary definition, *samāʿ* as hearing without acoustic participation of the adepts hardly survives except among the Mawlawīs, the Bektāshī-ʿAlawīs, the Indo-Pakistani Ḳawwālīs, and in the rites of marginal groups such as the Yazīdīs, the Ismāʿīlīs, the *māled* shamans of Balūčistān (types *damālī, ḳalandarī*). On the other hand, in many rituals (*ḥaḍra, ḥizb, dhikr*), it survives as the introductory part (Ḳādirīs of Kurdistān) or concluding part (Ṣūfī brotherhoods of the Maghrib). In all these cases, the hymns or the instrumental pieces constitute specific repertoires generally distinguished from the music of the secular environment by means of their rhythms, their structures and their texts. Faced with the diversity of musical techniques put into practice, it is difficult to identify in purely formal terms a notion of "music of *samāʿ*", except at the level of the force of expression, drawn from the *dhikr* as a form and as a mode of concentration. The difficulty in identifying a global specificity is due perhaps to the paradoxes underlined by certain *shaykhs* (al-Suhrawardī), according to which it is not *samāʿ* and dance which induce ecstasy, but ecstasy which arouses the dance, or furthermore, that *samāʿ* is only a revealing instrument and that it only supplies that which is brought to it by the hearer.

Bibliography: 1. Texts. Kalābādhī, *K. al-Taʿarruf*, tr. A.J. Arberry, *The doctrine of the Ṣūfīs*, Cambridge 1935; Hudjwīrī, *Kashf al-maḥdjūb*, tr. R.A. Nicholson, London 1911; al-Sarrādj al-Ṭūsī, *K. al-Lumaʿ*, ed. Nicholson, Leiden-London 1914; J. Robson (ed. and tr.), *Tracts on listening to music ... by Ibn Abî 'l-Dunyâ and ... Majd al-Dîn al-Ṭûsî al-Ghazzâlî*, London 1938; ʿAbd Allāh al-Anṣārī, *Ṭabaḳāt al-Ṣūfiyya*, Pers. tr. S. Mawlāʾī, Tehran 1362/1983; Rūzbihān Baḳlī Shīrāzī, *Risālat al-Ḳuds*, ed. Dj. Nūrbakhsh, Tehran 1351/1972; Ghazālī, *Iḥyāʾ*, tr. D.B. Macdonald, *Emotional religion in Islam as affected by music and singing ...*, in *JRAS* (1901), 195-252, 705-48 (1902), 1-28, 195-252; Ibn al-Djawzī, *Talbīs Iblīs*, tr. D.S. Margoliouth, *The devil's delusion*, in *IC*, ix-xxii (1935-48); Suhrawardī, *ʿAwārif al-maʿārif*, Persian tr. M. b. al-Kāshānī, Eng. tr. H. Wilberforce Clarke, 1891, repr. New York 1970, Ger. tr. and notes R. Gramlich, *Die Gaben der Erkenntnisse des ʿUmar as-Suhrawardī* (ʿAwārif al-maʿārif), Wiesbaden 1978; Ibn Taymiyya, *R. fī samāʿ wa 'l-raḳs wa 'l-ṣurākh*, in *Rasāʾil*, Cairo 1323/1905, 278-315, ed. tr. and comm. J. Michot; ʿIzz al-Dīn Ibn Ghānim al-Maḳdisī, *Ḥall al-rumūz wa-mafātīh al-kunūz*, Cairo 1317/1899; N. Purdjawādī, *Du risāla dar samāʿ*, in *Maʿārif*, v/3 (March 1989), 3-72; Aḥmad b. Muḥammad al-Ṭūsī, *al-Hadiyya al-saʿdiyya fī maʿānī 'l-wadjdiyya*, in *Mudjāhid* (1360/1981).

2. Studies. H. Ritter, *Der Reigen der tanzenden Derwische*, in *Zeitsch. Vergleich. Musikwissenschaft*, i (1933), 28-40; F. Meier, *Der Derwischtanz*, in *Asiatische Studien*, viii (1954), 107-36; Ritter, *Die Mewlanafeier in Konya*, in *Oriens*, xv (1962), 248 ff.; M. Molé, *La danse extatique en Islam*, in *Les dances sacrées*, Paris 1963, 145-280; S.Sh.Kh. Hussaini, *Bund samāʿ or closed audition*, in *IC*, xliv (1970), 177-85; A. Shiloah, *The theory of music in Arab writings* (*ca. 900 to 1900*), Répertoire international des sources musicales, Series B, Munich 1979; Hussaini, *Sayyid Muhammad al-Husayni Gîsûdirâz on Sufism*, Delhi 1983; L. Pouzet, *Prise de position autour du "samāʿ" en Orient musulman au VIIᵉ/XIIᵉ siècle*, in *SI*, lvii (1983), 193-234; R. Burckhardt Qureshi, *Qawwālī: sound, context and meaning in Indo-Muslim Ṣūfī music*, Cambridge, Mass. 1986; idem, *Listening to words through music: the Ṣūfī* samāʿ, in *Edebiyat*, ii (1988), 219-45; J. During, *Musique et extase. L'audition spirituelle dans la tradition soufie*, Paris 1988; idem, *Musique et mystique dans les traditions de l'Iran*, Paris 1989; idem, *L'autre oreille. Le pouvoir mystique de la musique au Moyen-orient*, in *Cahiers des Musiques Traditionelles*, iii (1990), 57-78; idem, *What is Sufi music?*, in *The legacy of mediaeval Persian Sufism*, ed. L. Lewisohn, New York 1992; Burckhardt Qureshi, *Localiser l'Islam. Le samāʿ à la cour royale des saints chishtī*, in *Cahiers des Musiques Traditionelles*, v (1992), 127-50; W. Feldman, *Musical genres and zikirs of the Sunni tariqats of Istanbul*, in R. Lifchez (ed.), *The dervish lodge*, Berkeley, etc. 187-202. (J. During)

2. As a term in education.

Here, *samāʿ* (pl. *samāʿāt*) means [certificate of] hearing, audition; authorisation, licence.

With the rise of the large *madrasas* [*q.v.*], founded by rulers who were important personalities such as Niẓām al-Mulk (d. 485/1092 [*q.v.*]) or Nūr al-Dīn Ibn Zangī (d. 569/1174 [*q.v.*]), habits, followed so far in instruction and teaching, especially those in *ḥadīth*, took on an official character. It was the period in which places of education and training spread towards remote villages and distant provinces. The principles developed and represented by al-Khaṭīb al-Baghdādī (d. 463/1071 [*q.v.*]), the great, critical systematiser of *ḥadīth* methodology, became dominant. The process accelerated when *ex officio* teaching posts and librarianships were established on a large scale, and scholarships were extended in view of the growing influx of students (*ṭullāb*). The result of this spreading praxis was that, beyond the purely idealistic point of view, the question was asked: Who, "under whom", "when" and "where", had assisted as auditor (*sāmiᶜ*) at a lecture on a certain work; who could show a certificate, an *idjāza* [*q.v.*] or, more exactly, an *idjāzat al-samāᶜ*, in short a *samāᶜ*. It is true that an author, or an adequately authorised *shaykh*, had always read his or another's work with his pupil (*ṭālib*), e.g. in a mosque, and had attested this for the latter with a corresponding *ḳirāʾa* note; but those who had joined the two without being involved and had only listened, had not been able to deduce for themselves any practical privilege from it. A new development grew up among jurists in the second half of the 4th/10th century, sc. of upgrading the auditor (*sāmiᶜ*) vis-à-vis the reader (*ḳāriʾ*). When teaching and learning were institutionalised in centres, a link-up was made with this provision.

Samāᶜāt can be shown to have existed generally from the 5th/11th century onwards. They reach their prime during the next two centuries, first in ᶜIrāḳ and then in Syria. After the Mongol storm, the centre of gravity shifted to Egypt. The *samāᶜāt* can be found at the end of manuscripts and/or on their title- and fly leaves and/or between parts and chapters. In these certificates, the composition of a *madjlis* is reflected, in the field of knowlege of tradition, including law, in the first place, and then in the fields of biographies and history, grammar and lexicography, *adab* in the widest sense of the word, but also of medicine, philosophy, etc.

The *samāᶜāt* of the lectures are quite variable in their outer form and organisation. The lectures are presided over by a *shaykh* (rarely a *shaykha*) as *musmiᶜ* (teacher); the reader (*ḳāriʾ*) sits before him, while a third person, the recorder (*kātib*), keeps the protocol, which, in small gatherings can also be kept by the *musmiᶜ* or the *ḳāriʾ*. In an ideal case, the three of them—including the *musmiᶜ*—are mentioned one after the other under their full names, titles, etc. in connection with the introductory formula *ḳaraʾa ᶜalayya*: the *shaykh* (with *isnād* [*q.v.*] if he is not the author himself) and the title of the work (equally with additions like autograph, *riwāya* [*q.v.*], owner, etc.); then the reader, and finally the recorder with a statement of the place (such as *madrasa, masdjid, dār, zāwiya, bayt, ribāṭ, dayr, khān*, etc.), date and duration of the lecture; a list of auditors (*sāmiᶜūn*) is also added: men, young males, women, young females, children (often with an exact indication of their age), and slaves accompanying higher-placed personalities. After an auditor's (*sāmiᶜ*) name in the list, there may be a remark that he was only present at certain parts (occasionally confirmed in his own hand in a gloss, but also in the work itself). At the end, the *musmiᶜ* usually confirms the entire note of *samāᶜ*, as he also may do in other places about the correctness of a statement. In more sizeable works, whose lecture (*ḳirāʾa*) extends over a longer period of time, the *musmiᶜ*, as well as the *ḳāriʾ* or the *kātib*, can be replaced by someone else. Not rarely a new *idjāza* is found after separate parts (*adjzāʾ*). The number of auditors amounts in general to between ten and twenty, but they may also be less or more, or even so many that the recorder, who may belong to the group of auditors (*kātib al-ṭabaḳa*, pl. *ṭibāḳ*), does not know all the names. He may be assisted by a *muthbit* (confirmer), taken from among the auditors, who confirms in a gloss certain places in the *idjāzat al-samāᶜ*, or from whose hand comes the list of auditors, etc. New *samāᶜāt* are often added in following or later sessions or are taken over in transcripts, etc. The *shaykh* may issue a note of *samāᶜ* for one single auditor personally, which is then introduced by the term *samiᶜa*. Already the great al-Samᶜānī (d. 562/1166 [*q.v.*]) made efforts to obtain and collect *samāᶜāt/masmūᶜāt* either by correspondence or through a third person. They played a role in purchases and estates. *Samāᶜāt* are inexhaustibly overflowing sources of a high documentary value for the spread of a work and its manuscripts, for the completion of the extensive biographical literature, for the busy relations of the learned centres between themselves, and for the history and archaeology of individual places.

Bibliography: Ṣ. al-Munadjdjid, *Idjāzat al-samāᶜ fī 'l-makhṭūṭāt al-ḳadīma*, in *RIMA*, i (1375/1955), 232-51; H. Ritter, *Authographs in Turkish libraries*, in *Oriens*, vi (1953), 63-90; G. Vajda, *Bibliography* [see IDJĀZA]; idem, *La transmission du savoir en Islam*, London 1983; P. MacKay, *Certificates of transmission on a manuscript of the* Maqāmāt *of Ḥarīrī*, Philadelphia 1971 (Trans. of the American Philosophical Society, lxi, 4); R. Sellheim, *Materialien zur arabischen Literaturgeschichte*, i-ii, Wiesbaden-Stuttgart 1976-87, *passim*; G. Makdisi, *The rise of colleges. Institutions of learning in Islam and the West*, Edinburgh 1981, *passim*; idem, *The rise of humanism in Classical Islam and the Christian West*, Edinburgh 1990, *passim*; G. Endress, in *Grundriss der arabischen Philologie*, Wiesbaden 1982-7, i, 278, 286-90, ii, 452; L.T. Librande, *The need to know: al-Ājurrī's* [d. 360/970] *Kitāb farḍ ṭalab al-ᶜilm*, in *BEO*, xlv (1993 [1994]), 89-159; S. Leder, *Dokumente zum Ḥadīt in Schrifttum und Unterricht aus Damaskus im 6./12. Jhdt.*, in *Oriens*, xxxiv (1994), 57-75. (R. SELLHEIM)

ṢAMAD [see ALLĀH; AL-ASMĀʾ AL-ḤUSNĀ].

SAMAK (A.), substantive with a generic sense (unit. *samaka*, pl. *asmāk, sumūk, simāk*), denoting fish in general, whether of fresh water or of the sea (P. *samak, māhī*, Tkish. *balık*, Tamahaḳḳ *emen*, pl. *imenān, asūlmei*, pl. *isūlmeien*). The term *samak*, which does not figure in the Ḳurʾān, is, in the work of Arab authors, often replaced by one of its two synonyms, *ḥūt* and *nūn* (pl. *nīnān, anwān*) from the Akkadian *nūnu*. However, *ḥūt* (pl. *aḥwāt, ḥītān*, in dialect, *ḥiyūta*) is applied primarily to very large fishes and to cetaceans.

1. Ichthyonomy.

It would be impossible here to list all the species which, in systematic ichthyology (*ismākiyya*), number more than a hundred thousand, and as in almost all other languages, Arabic ichthyonomy is abundant in its scale. Thus, for the Red Sea, the Arabian Gulf and the Indian Ocean, the orientalist G. Oman, of Naples, has assembled, in a recent and remarkable study (see *Bibl.*), close on eleven hundred names of fishes. For his part, Prof. A. Salonen, of Helsinki, has contributed about a thousand names drawn from Sumero-Akkadian (see *Bibl.*). The author of this article, for his part, has gathered, for the western Mediterranean basin (Egypt, Libya and the Maghrib), approximately twelve hundred terms. In this rich terminology, numerous appellations are formed from the nouns *samak* or *ḥūt* or *nūn* combined with a qualificative or a nominal complement. Within the range of the latter, this study will be limited to mentioning only those which evoke a Biblical or historical personage, authentic or legendary, in association with fishes or other aquatic creatures. First to be mentioned in this context is Jonah, Yūnus, known as *Ṣāḥib al-Ḥūt* "the man of the fish" (Ḳurʾān, XXXVII, 142; LXVIII, 48) and, with the same meaning, *Dhu 'l-Nūn* (Ḳurʾān, XXI, 87), who is said to have been swallowed by some kind of shark and not by a whale, the latter, with its filters, being capable of absorbing only plankton. Subsequently to be found are the *ḥūt Mūsā* or *samak Mūsā* "the fish of Moses", the *ḥūt Mūsā wa-Yūshaᶜ* "the fish of Moses and of

Joshua'' and the *ḥūt Sīdnā Sulaymān* ''the fish of our master Solomon''; these three names are given to the common sole (*Solea vulgaris*). The *sulṭān Ibrāhīm* ''the sultan Abraham'' is the name given to the red mullet (*Mullus barbatus*). The *Ibn Yaᶜḳūb* ''the son of Jacob'' is the common sargo (*Diplodus sargus*). The *samakat al-Iskandar* ''the fish of Alexander the Great'' is the hammer-head shark (*Sphyrna zygaena*). With the *ḥūt Sulaymān*, this is not a reference to the person but a phonetic adaptation of the Latin *salmo* for the common salmon (*Salmo salar*). Among the origins of the formation of Arabic names of fishes, the first to be noted are those which are drawn directly from Greco-Roman nomenclature, such as: *baramis*, the bream, from *Abramis brama; usbūr*, the sparid fish, from *Sparus; uṭrūṭ*, the trout, from *Trutta; bulbīs*, the barbel, from *Barbus; balamīda*, the pelamid, from *Pelamys*, also called *būnīt*, the bonito; *tūn, ṭūn, tunn*, the tunny fish, from *Thynnus; tunḳus*, the tench, from *Tinca; anḳalīs*, the eel, from *Anquilla; arrang, ranga, ranka*, the herring, from *Clupea harengus; rāya, radja*, the ray, from *Raia; surghūs*, the common sargo, from *Sargus vulgaris; sardīn*, the sardine, from *Clupea sardina; isfirnī, safarna, safarnāya*, the spet or barracuda, from *Sphyraena; isḳumrī*, the mackerel, from *Scomber; sillawr*, the sheat fish, from *Silurus; salmūn, ṣumūn*, the salmon, from *Salmo; ghādus*, the cod, from *Gadus; luṭṭ*, the burbot, from *Lota lota; lāṭis, lūṭis*, the Nile perch, from *Lates nilotica; lafūt*, the lophot, from *Lophotes; līmanda*, the dab, from *Limanda*. Numerous appellations are also encountered formed from the name of a terrestrial creature joined to the complement *-al-baḥr* ''of the sea'', such as: *sabuᶜ al-baḥr* ''beast of the sea'' for the sea wolf (*Anarhichas lupus*); *faras al-baḥr* ''horse of the sea'' for the bellows fish (*Centriscus*); *ḳunfudhat al-baḥr* ''hedgehog of the sea'' for the sea-urchin (*Diodon*). Similarly, many terms are composed of *abū* ''father of ...'' or *umm* ''mother of ...'', with the complement of a noun marking a characteristic of the fish concerned. The following are examples: *abū ḳarn* ''father of the horn'' for the unicorn fish (*Naseus unicornis*); *abū miṭraḳa* ''father of the hammer'' for the hammer-head shark (*Sphyrna zygaena*); *abū sayf* ''father of the sword'' for the swordfish (*Xiphias gladius*); *abū ṣundūḳ* ''father of the chest'' for the coffer fish (*Ostracion nasus*); *abū minḳar* ''father of the beak'' for the half-beak (*Hemiramphus*); *abū minshar* ''father of the saw'' for the sawfish (*Pristis pristis*); *abū dhaḳan* ''father of the beard'' for the goat fish or mullet (*Mullus barbatus*); *umm ḳarn* ''mother of the horn'' for the trigger fish (*Balistes*); *umm al-shabābīṭ* ''mother of the barbels'' for the barbel (*Barbus sharpeyi*). Some names derive from living foreign languages, and especially from Spanish, such as *anshūyah, andjūyah* (Spanish *anchoa*), the anchovy (*Engraulis boelema*); *arrang, ranga, ranka* (Spanish *arenque*), the herring (*Clupea harengus*); *bakūra* (Spanish *albacora*), the albacore (*Germo alalunga*); *durāda* (Spanish *dorado*), the goldfish (*Sparus aurata*). The influence of English, of French and of Italian should also not be disregarded. To the Persian *parastūg* ''swallow'' are related *barasūdj, barastūk, ṭarastudj* for the mullet (*Mullus*), and from the Turkish *alabalık* comes the name *alābālghā* for the trout. In a process contrary to these Arabic borrowings of foreign terms, systematic science has sometimes needed recourse to an Arabic term, which is then latinised, to specify a sub-species limited to a particular region. Thus *barda* = the pink sea-bream, is encountered again with *Chrysophrys berda; ḥaffāra* = the wrasse, with *Chrysophrys haffara*; *sarb* = the grey gilthead, with *Chrysophrys sarba*; *bashīr* = polypterus Bichir, with *Polypterus Bechir*; *buhār* = the diacope, with *Diacope bohar*; *bayaḍ, bayyāḍ* = a silurus of the Nile, with *Bagrus bajad*; *ḥarīd* = the parrot fish, with *Scarus harid*; *ḥalāwī* = the guitar fish, with *Rhinobatus halavi*; *durāb* = the chirocentrus, with *Chirocentrus dorab*; *dukmaḳ* = a silurus of the Nile, the Euphrates and the Niger, with *Bagrus docmac*; *ghubbān* = the green scarus, with *Scarus ghobban*; *safan* = the sephen skate, with *Raia sephen*; *saydjān* = the sidjan scarus, with *Scarus siganus*; *līmī* = umbra limi, with *Umbra limi*; *shalba* = a silurus of the Nile and the Niger, with *Schilbe mystus*; *ṭahmal* = a silurus, with *Pimelopterus tahmel*; *urfī* = the braize orphe, with *Pagrus orphus*; *bunnī al-Nīl* = the Nile barbel, with *Barbus bynni*; *lafūt* = the unicorn fish, with *Lophotes cepedianus*; *limma* = the limma ray, with *Raia lymma*; *abū ṣanṣūn* = the sansun kingfish, with *Caranx sansun*; *djiddāba* = the djeddaba kingfish, with *Caranx djeddaba*; *balam* = the anchovy, with *Engraulis boelema*.

2. Anatomy.

The anatomy of the fish is summarised in few words. The scales are called, according to the regions: *ḥarshaf, fiṣṣ, taflīs, ḳirāt, ḳishra, bashīr al-ḥūt* and *ashkāma* (Spanish: escamosa). For the gills and the bronchiae, organs of respiration, the only words found are: *khayshūm*, pl. *khayāshīm, khanshūsha, nakhshūsh* pl. *nakhāshīsh*. The cetaceans expel water by means of blow-holes or *naysam* pl. *nayāsim*. For the fins the terms are: *djanāḥ al-samak, ziᶜnifa, djāniḥa*. The eggs laid by the fishes (*ṭūmār*) constitute the spawn, *sarʾ al-samak, sirʾ, sarwa, ṣuᶜtur*, deposited in spawning-grounds or *masraʾ al-samak*, habitual sites peculiar to each species; it is there that the fry (*bulᶜūṭ*) develop.

3. Halieutics.

It is known that, since prehistoric times, fish has always provided one of the principal alimentary resources for riverside and coastal populations, especially of the Mediterranean, the Arabian Gulf and the Indian Ocean. It may thus be stated that fishing (*iṣṭiyād al-samak*) engendered both coastal and oceanic navigation, and this even before the long-range voyages of migration and of commercial traffic. First of all, it is important to distinguish between two very different types of fishing, sea fishing and fresh water fishing, the species of fish belonging to these two aquatic environments not being the same, although some migrate periodically from one to the other. The halieutic vocabulary for these two modes of fishing is quite abundant. In fishing on the high seas, associated with navigation, the principal instrument used is the large pouched net known as seine or drag-net (*djarf, djārūf, djarrāfa, ḳaṭṭāᶜa, baṭāna*) supported by floats of cork (*ᶜawwām, ḳurtīdj*) and terminating in a closed end (*khurṭūm*). It is towed by rowing boats and, when reckoned to be full, dragged to the shore. For tunny fishing, especially in Tunisia, the device used is a huge enclosure formed of meshed cloth with which the tunny bed is surrounded; this is the tuna net (*mazraba*). The catch is hoisted aboard the boats by means of gaffs and grapnels (*khaṣm al-ḳāḍī, muḳbulān, miḥdjān, ᶜaḳfā, ᶜuḳḳāfa*) or dispatched directly with harpoons (*khaṭūf, khaṭṭāf, ᶜaṭūf, kullāb, mudjīr, muᶜīn, mughīth, musahhil*). A third method of fishing at sea consists in stretching out a long cable which is held on the surface by floats and fitted, at regular intervals, with fish-hooks (*sannāra, ṣinnāra, shiṣṣ, mikhṭāf, mukhūṭāf*), baited and slightly submerged; this rope with fish-hooks is known as *balāngar, brungalī, shīrīnbak*. Finally, there is fishing by means of dragging a line fitted with gull-feathers; this is *dūzan bi 'l-rīsha* or *shalūsh*. The fishing-line, made from plaited horsehair, is called *sadjim, shalīf, būlīs*. The bait most often used is the talitrus, a small leaping crustacean, also known as the sand-flea (*Talitrus saltator*) or *kūkra*, in addition to the arenicol (*trīmūlīn*), a small beach worm (*Arenicola marina*).

Once ashore, the fisherman (*khannāḳ, ʿarakī*) delivers his catch to a fishmonger (*sammāk, ḥawwāt*) who maintains a shop (*khināḳa*) in the fish-market (*sūḳ al-khannāḳīn*).

Fishing in fresh water, practised in stagnant waters as well in the current of any watercourse and large river, employs diverse techniques. Where the depth allows, the fisherman enters the water directly, wherever he can find a foothold, thereby dispensing with the need for a boat. By this means he can deposit an eel-trap (*salla, radfūn, raḍfūn, wahhār*) with bait, which needs to be raised only once or twice daily. In the absence of such a trap, he contents himself with digging a channel in the water-bed (*ḳannūra*), in the place which he judges to be the best conduit for the aquatic fauna, and baits it copiously; eels, barbels, breams, carps and many others will soon arrive to feed there. When he sees his channel swarming with fish, he needs only a landing-net (*ghirāfa, ʿabb*) to draw out what he wants; eels are killed by means of a fish-gig (*bāla, fāla, ḥarba*). If the catch is particularly abundant, he may place some of the fish in buckets of water, transferring them, as a reserve, to a fish pond (*maḥḳān, djals, ikhādha, faḍla, birka*) prepared for this purpose. In the Maghrib and the Near East, a very popular and lucrative form of fishing, practised in fresh water as well as on the sea-shore, consists in the use of a stick fitted with the small bag-shaped net known as a cast net (*ṭarḥa, ṭarrāḥ, bayyāḥa*) with weights attached to its periphery in such a manner that it sinks to the bed of the water. The caster, who may stand up to waist-deep in the water, draws it slowly towards himself, thus imprisoning the creatures caught in it; everywhere, young fishermen are adept at this activity. Also to be mentioned, finally, is the virtually universal sport of angling with a fishing rod (*ḳaṣba, ḳannāra, ghawayyiṣ*) formed, usually, of numerous sections fastened together and terminating in a fine and very flexible tip (*dhabāb*) to the end of which the thread of the line is fastened, and this bears a floating bob, above the hook. The fishing rod is usually made of pieces of bamboo (*khayzurān*) or other types of wood; modern techniques use metallic or synthetic materials. This mode of fishing is of two types. The first consists in holding the cane motionless or laying it on the bank, watching for the movement of the float which shows that there has been a "nibble"; it is then necessary to "strike" at once. It is possible to fish with several rods simultaneously, and many amateur anglers come equipped with a bundle (*ṭunn*) of rods. The bait may be an earthworm (*dūda*) or a small fresh water crustacean, the water-beetle *Daphnia pulex* (*burghūth al-māʾ*) or a maggot (*duʿmūṣ*), or a crumb of bread or some boiled grain such as wheat or barley or hempseed (*shahdānidj, ḳunbuz*) or, finally, a small living fish, i.e. live bait. The second type of rod fishing, very popular with sporting anglers, is "casting" (*rimāya*). The line is wound on a reel (*dūlāb*) fixed to the base of the rod and instead of bait, a small metallic lure (*fitna, khadīʿa*) in the shape of an insect or a small fish is attached to the hook. This practice is not widely used in Arab countries, although it is very popular throughout Europe, and elsewhere.

4. Literature.

In the literary domain, there is scarcely any treatment of the subject on the part of the ancient Arab authors, the exception being Kushādjim who, in the 4th/10th century, devoted a chapter to fishing in his *Kitāb al-Maṣāyid* (see *Bibl.*). This chapter, brief though it is, is nevertheless valuable on account of the poetic extracts which it includes. Thus there are found there 12 verses by Ibn al-Rūmī (metre *kāmil*, rhyme *-aki*); two *urdjūza*s by Kushādjim himself, one of 28 hemistiches (rhyme *-āni*) and the other of 14 hemistiches (rhyme *-āʾ*); an *urdjūza* of 24 hemistiches (rhyme *-adi*) by al-Ṣanawbarī; and, finally, an *urdjūza* of 23 hemistiches (rhyme *-dā*) of Ibn al-Wazīr al-Ghassānī. It is not until the 8th/14th century that, with Ibn Manglī and his treatise on hunting, *Uns al-malā* (see *Bibl.*), more ample details are obtained regarding fishing with the net, with the harpoon, with chemicals (*dawāʾ*), with the eel-trap, with clay (*ṭīn*), and with the lantern (*fānūs*) and the pit (*ughwiyya*).

5. Licitness.

On account of the predominant place occupied by fish in the diet of Muslim populations, it has been the object of judicial dispositions based on Ḳurʾānic law, in particular the verse (V, 95) "You are permitted the game of the sea (*ṣayd al-baḥr*) and the food which is found there". Any fish of non-cartilaginous skeleton and devoid of blood may therefore be lawfully consumed, without a requirement for ritual slaughter. However, fish found dead may not be consumed. Also forbidden are: (1) fishes of cartilaginous skeleton, in other words the selachians or squalidae (*ḳirshiyyāt*) including the shark with its various species (*ḳirsh, awwāl, kawsadj, ḳanya, ḳayna, ṭufaylī, ḳuraysh, lakhm, kalb al-baḥr, bunbuk, liyāʾ, ḳaṣaf, abū minshar*), most of these names supplied by al-Damīrī; the hammer-head (*baḳra, miṭrāḳ al-baḥr, abū miṭraḳa, samakat al-Iskandar, naḍḍār*), the spotted dogfish (*gharrāʾ*) and the ray or skate, with its multiplicity of names (*raya, radja, warank, farank, yamāmat al-baḥr, shifnīn al-baḥr, tarsa, samak al-turs, daraḳa, samak al-limmā, ḥaṣīra, farsh, ḳubaʿ, ḥalwā, waṭwāṭa, maṣṣūn, maṣṣūla, abū mihmāz*; (2) the marine mammals or cetaceans (*ḥūtiyyāt*) including the whale (*wāla, bāla, ballīna, banīna, būlīna, ḥūt Yūnus*), the humpbacked whale (*ḳubaʿ, djamal al-baḥr*), the sperm-whale (*ʿanbar*), the porpoise (*khinzīr al-baḥr, bunbuk*), the dolphin (*dulfīn, danfīl, danfīr, darfīl, dukhas*), the narwhal (*karkaddan al-baḥr, ḥarīsh al-baḥr*), the finback (*hirkūl, manāra*), the orc or grampus (*urka, ḳattal*) and the white whale (*ḥafshrūsī, kalb al-baḥr*); (3) the amphibian mammals (*ḳawāzib, barmāʾiyyūn*) or pinnipeds (*ziʿnufiyyāt al-aḳdām*) including the seal (*shaykh al-baḥr, ʿidj al-baḥr, fuḳma, fuḳḳama, bū mnīr*), the monk seal (*al-shaykh al-yahūdī, abū marīna*), the walrus (*fīl al-baḥr, fazẓ*), the sea lion (*dubb al-baḥr, asad al-baḥr, baḳrat al-baḥr*) and the elephant seal (*fīl al-baḥr*); and (4) the sirenian mammals or "sea cows" (*khaylāniyyāt, banāt al-māʾ*) including the manatee (*kharūf al-baḥr, umm zubayba*) and the dugong (*aṭūm, maliṣa, nāḳa al-baḥr, zālikha, ḥanfāʾ*). As for *Rhytina stelleri*, the sea cow (*baḳarat al-baḥr*) of the Red Sea, it has been extinct for two centuries. All of these aquatic creatures have nevertheless always been hunted, either for their abundant stocks of fat, useful for many purposes and in particular for the making of soap and the fuelling of wicked lamps, or for their thick and very resistant hide, used in the manufacture of shields and, in particular, of protective shoes for the feet of camels required to traverse stony deserts.

6. As a source of diet.

Fish has been a staple source of nourishment for humanity from the outset. It is consumed in various forms. Firstly, it may be fried immediately after catching. On the other hand, it is the object of four principal modes of preservation. The first, much used in Egypt since the time of the Pharaohs, is dessication by exposure to the sun of large and small fish (*mushammaʿ, ṣaraṣ, bushūṭa, kūridj*) such as the stockfish (*bāḳālāw, bāḳālyū, baḳala, baḳlāwa*, from the Spanish *bacallao*). The next is salting and smoking (*tamlīḥ* and *tadkhīn*) for small fishes (*ṣayr*) such as the anchovy (*anshūwa, anshūyah, andjūyah, anshūba, shīḥa, shuṭūn, fasīkh, mulūḥa, maṭūṭ*) and the sand-smelt (*kushkush, balam, haff*); the same treatment is used for the salmon (*salāmūn, shalāmūn, ṣūmūn, ḥūt Sulaymān*). Also used is pickling or maceration with spices in brine (*salāmūra, sanamūra*). In Tunis this is the method used to preserve carp (*bunn*). Finally, there remains preservation in oil or vinegar and packing in metal containers; this applies to the sardine (*sardin, sarda, bisāriya, absāriya, ʿaram*), the cod, the mackerel and the herring. Delicacies such as caviar (*khibyāra*) and botargo (*baṭrakh*), are not widely consumed in Arab countries.

As for culinary preparations of fish, they are most varied and many are similar to those of Europe. Well-known, among others, is the fish stew (*munazzalat al-samak, mukbulā*) based on eel or carp. The ancient Arabic treatises on culinary art supply five recipes for fresh fish, five for salted, and three with the trigle or gurnard (*ṭirrīkh*) (see M. Rodinson, in *Bibl.*).

7. Fabulous marine creatures.

Arab authors naturalists and geographers, such as al-Ḳazwīnī, al-Damīrī and al-Djāḥiẓ, include in their descriptions of different seas the accounts of seafarers who encountered there enormous marine creatures, unidentifiable and very dangerous. Thus they mention the *fāṭūs* or *ḥūt al-ḥayḍ* which shatters the ships which it encounters, but which is put to flight when the sailors hang from the peripheral points of the vessel rags stained with menstrual blood (*ḥayḍ*). Also mentioned, in the Sea of China (*baḥr al-Ṣīn*), is a fish three hundred cubits in length which the inhabitants of the island of Wāḳwāḳ (Indonesian Archipelago) repel and banish by making the loudest possible noise, beating cauldrons and tomtoms. In the same sea lurks the *aṭam*, which has the head of a pig, is covered with a hairy fleece instead of scales, and shows female sexual organs; it is allegedly edible. In the Indian Ocean (*baḥr al-Hind*) there is a large fish nicknamed *kataba 'l-kitāb* "he has written the book", the juice of which produces an invisible ink legible only at night, and another large green fish with a serpent's head whose flesh, tasted only once, suppresses all appetite for several days.

8. Specific qualities.

These are numerous and for the most part beneficial. The flesh of the fish is of cold and humid texture. The best flesh is that of the sea fish, and more specifically, that of fishes with speckled back and delicate scales; but it causes thirst and may generate catarrh; it is appropriate for those with high temperatures and for young persons. It is necessary, however, to reject black or yellow fish, those of marshes which absorb mud, and in particular the bream (*abrāmīs*) and the grey mullet (*būrī*), which cause gastric disorders sometimes involving serious complications. On the other hand, Avicenna maintains that the flesh of the fish is, with honey, beneficial for the treatment of cataracts and for increasing visual acuity. According to al-Ḳazwīnī, this flesh is supposedly an aphrodisiac when consumed with fresh onions. An intoxicated person, exposed to the smell of fish, soon becomes sober and regains lucidity. The gall of fish in the form of eye-wash is a cure for watering eyes and, mixed with that of the marine turtle, it provides a golden phosphorescent ink.

9. Astronomy.

The substantives *samak* and *ḥūt* occur in astronomy for:

(1) The twelfth zodiacal constellation of *Pisces* (*burdj al-ḥūt*), with *al-samakatānⁱ* "the two fishes", the 24th star being called *al-ḥūt al-shimālī* "the northern fish". Also distinguished are the two stars *al-ḥūt al-sharḳī* "the eastern fish", and *al-ḥūt al-gharbī* "the western fish", near the ecliptic, under the Square of Pegasus.

(2) The 28th lunar house, with *baṭn al-ḥūt* "the belly of the fish" in the vicinity of Andromeda, i.e.: β (beta) *Andromedae*, mag. 2, 4 or "Merak" (*marāḳ al-marʾa 'l-musalsala*) "the lower belly of the woman enchained".

(3) The 6th boreal constellation of Andromeda, with its nickname of *al-marʾa al-musalsala wa 'l-samaka* "the woman enchained and the fish" (see above) on account of the "northern fish" which seems intent on biting Andromeda.

(4) The 14th austral constellation of the "southern fish" (*al-ḥūt al-djanūbī*), under the zodiacal *Aquarius*, with the star "Fomalhaut" (*fumm al-ḥūt*) "the mouth of the fish", i.e. α (alpha) *Piscis australis*, mag. 1,3.

Bibliography (in alphabetical order of authors): A. Benhamouda, *Les noms arabes des étoiles* (essay on identification), in *AIEO Alger*, ix (1951), 166-7, 191; Dr. Chenu, *Encyclopedie d'histoire naturelle* (vol. *Reptiles et poissons*), Paris 1874, 183-358; Damīrī, *K. Ḥayāt al-ḥayawān al-kubrā*, ed. Cairo 1937, under *ḥūt*, i, 267-73, *nūn*, ii, 371-4, *samak*, ii, 28-33; Djāḥiẓ, *K. al-Ḥayawān*, Cairo 1947, under *ḥūt*, *samak* and *passim*; Ibn Manglī, *Uns al-malā*, "*De la chasse*", tr. F. Viré, Paris 1984, 226-35; Ḳazwīnī, *ʿAdjāʾib al-makhlūkāt* (in margins of Damīrī, i, 66, ii, 87, 184-5, *passim*); Kushādjim, *K. al-Maṣāyid wa 'l-maṭārid*, ms. Istanbul, Fatih 4090 (*Bāb ṣayd al-baḥr*) fols. 153a-156b, ed. M.A. Talas, Baghdād 1954, 229-34 (same chapter, but incomplete); A. Malouf, *Muʿdjam al-ḥayawān, An Arabic zoological dictionary*, Cairo 1932, *passim*; G. Oman, *L'Ichtyonomie dans les pays arabes* (Red Sea, Indian Ocean, Arabian Gulf) (in Italian, English, French), publ. Instituto Universitario Orientale, Naples 1992; M. Rodinson, *Recherches sur les documents arabes relatifs à la cuisine*, in *REI* (1949), 103, 107 f., 119 f., 142; A. Salonen, *Die Fischerei im alten Mesopotamien nach sumerisch-akkadischen Quellen*, in *Annales Academiae Fennicae*, clxvi, Helsinki 1970; F. Terofal, *Les poissons d'eau douce*, éditions Solar (Guide vert poche), Paris 1987; idem, *Les poissons de mer*, Paris 1988; F. Vigouroux, *Dictionnaire de la Bible*, iv (under *Jourdain, Mer Morte, Nil, Palestine, Poisson*), v (under *Tiberiade, lac de*), Paris 1912. (F. Viré)

SAMAKATĀN [see AL-NUDJŪM].

SAMANDAL (var. *sanand, sandal, sabandal*, etc.), from Greek *salamandra* (in Arabic literature derived from Persian *sām* "fire" and *andarūn* "inside"), the salamander, which plays an important part in Arabic and Islamic folklore. According to an idea taken over from Greek literature (Aristotle, V, cap. 17), the animal passes through fire unharmed and even extinguishes it due to its coldness (al-Djāḥiẓ, *Ḥayawān*, v, 309, vi, 434; al-Damīrī, s.v.; al-Ḳazwīnī, *ʿAdjāʾib*, 442; Djābir b. Ḥayyān, *Das Buch der Gifte*, facs. ed. A. Siggel, 85a; in detail, al-Tawḥīdī, *Imtāʿ*, i, 182). Aristotle thought that the salamander proved that animal matter was unburnable. According to al-Ḳazwīnī and al-Damīrī, the salamander can cleanse its skin in the fire without burning, and many Arab authors agree that soft towels could be made of its fur, which can be cleaned with fire (in addition to the aforementioned works see al-Ibshīhī, *Mustaṭraf*, ii, 129). Ibn Khallikān claims to have seen such a piece himself (*Wafayāt*, no. 832; for a verse on the *samandal* by Yaʿḳūb b. Ṣābir al-Manḏanīḳī (b. 626/1288-9), see *ibid.* and in al-Damīrī, s.v. *ʿankabūt*).

In the Arabic sources there are, however, different

theories about the shape of the salamander. Many authors identify it as a bird (al-Djāḥiẓ, Ibn Khallikān, al-Ibshīhī; *Ḳāmūs* and *Tādj*, s.r.); only al-Damīrī, besides calling it a bird, describes it as a reddish-yellow coloured animal (*dābba*) with red eyes and a long tail. Al-Ḳazwīnī mentions it in the chapter on mice. According to the Arabic Physiologus, the salamander is a stone that extinguishes fire (Land, *Scholia*, 166, cap. 52; cf. *samandal* as a word for asbestos). Moreover, especially in the works of the Arab lexicographers, there are contaminations of the salamander with the phoenix (*Tahdhīb, Lisān, Tādj*), as well as with the bird that eats aconite (*bīsh*; *Ṣaḥāḥ*, s.r. *s-d-l*). The salamander is mostly thought to live in India (al-Damīrī) or in China (al-Ibshīhī).

In Arabic literature, one must distinguish the folkloristic statements on the salamander from the concrete descriptions—especially those from a medical point of view (Ibn al-Bayṭār, *Heil- und Nahrungsmittel*, tr. J. von Sontheimer, ii, 3; Ibn Sīnā, *Ḳānūn*, iii, 232; see also ᶜUmarī, *Masālik*, xx, 62; for its being mentioned in Greek literature, see Dioscorides, ii, cap. 67)—to be found under the lexeme *salāmand(a)rā*. There, the salamander is described more correctly as a sort of lizard or snake, its medical effects, including its poisonousness, are stressed, and the idea of its being unburnable is explicitly rejected.

Real varieties of salamanders (family *Salamandridae*, order *Urodela* of the amphibians) are not very common in the Orient. The fire salamander (*Salamandra salamandra*) which is black and has yellow or orange spots, is to be found in Asia Minor, Syria and North Africa. In Asia Minor we also find the Anatolian Salamander (*Mertensiella luschai*), the colour of which ranges from yellow to orange, with additional shiny black spots, and in the Caucasus there is the Caucasian salamander (*Mertensiella caucasica*), which is black with light spots. They both belong to a genus of varieties with slender bodies.

Bibliography: Arabic sources are given in the article. See also al-Ab Anastās al-Karmalī, *al-Samandal*, in *al-Mashriḳ*, vi (1903), 9-15; Amīn al-Maᶜlūf, *Muᶜdjam al-ḥayawān*, Cairo 1932, 213-15.

(H. Eisenstein)

SAMANDAR [see khazar].

al-**SAMᶜĀNĪ**, Abu 'l-Ḳāsim Aḥmad b. Manṣūr b. Muḥammad b. ᶜAbd al-Djabbār (487-23 Shawwāl 534/1094-11 June 1140), author of *Rawḥ al-arwāḥ fī sharḥ asmāᵓ al-malik al-fattāḥ* (ed. N. Māyil Harawī, Tehran 1368/1989), a long (600 pp.) Persian commentary on the divine names. His father Abu 'l-Muẓaffar Manṣūr (426-89/1035-96) wrote books in *tafsīr, ḥadīth, fiḳh*, and other subjects. Aḥmad studied with his eldest brother, Abū Bakr Muḥammad, the father of ᶜAbd al-Karīm al-Samᶜānī [*q.v.*], author of *al-Ansāb*, as well as several other teachers. In 529/1135 he travelled with ᶜAbd al-Karīm to Nīshāpūr to study *ḥadīth*. His nephew does not mention his writings but, in praising his virtues, speaks of his "elegant" (*malīḥ*) sermons and good poetry (*al-Ansāb*, ed. ᶜA. al-Bārūdī, iii, Beirut 1988, 299-301). His elegance is clear in *Rawḥ al-arwāḥ*, a work of extraordinary beauty that was certainly meant to be recited aloud. The prose ranks with that of contemporary classics such as Ghazālī's *Kīmiyā-yi saᶜādat*, but its main importance lies in its fresh interpretations of standard Islamic teachings on human salvation. Al-Samᶜānī pays little attention to the divine names themselves; instead, he uses each name as a starting point for a series of meditations on the relationship between human beings and God. The extraordinary emphasis on love prefigures the teachings of Rūmī and reflects the same spiritual ambience as Maybudī's Ḳurᵓān commentary *Kashf al-asrār wa-ᶜuddat al-abrār* (begun in 520/1126).

Bibliography: W.C. Chittick, *The myth of Adam's fall in Aḥmad Samᶜānī's* Rawḥ al-arwāḥ, in L. Lewisohn (ed.), *Classical Persian Sufism: from its origins to Rumi*, London 1993, 337-59.

(W.C. Chittick)

al-**SAMᶜĀNĪ**, Abū Saᶜd (incorrectly Saᶜīd) ᶜAbd al-Karīm b. Abī Bakr Muḥammad b. Abi 'l-Muẓaffar (al-)Manṣūr al-Tamīmī al-Marwazī al-Shafiᶜī, Tādj al-Islām (al-Dīn) Ḳiwām al-Dīn, also known as Ibn al-Samᶜānī (Samᶜān/Simᶜān, in the long, incomplete genealogy, being a branch of the tribe of Tamīm), important Arab biographer.

Born in Marw on Monday, 21 Shaᶜbān 506/10 February 1113, he died there on Monday, 1 Rabīᶜ I 562/26 December 1166. He was born into a learned family (for his father [466-510/1074-1116] see Ziriklī, vii, 112, and for his grandfather [426-89/1036-96] *ibid.*, vii, 303-4). His father, an authority in the fields of Shāfiᶜī law (al-Samᶜānī's grandfather having switched from the Ḥanafiyya to the Shāfiᶜiyya), Traditions, and homiletics, took him already as a two-year-old with him to the sessions on *ḥadīth*. A little later, in 509/1115, he travelled with him and his elder brother (*Taḥbīr*, i, 503-4) to Naysābūr, for additional instruction by the traditionists of that city. Returning to Marw and having a premonition of his imminent death, he entrusted his son to his two learned brothers. Under their guidance al-Samᶜānī received a comprehensive basic education in Ḳurᵓān, *fiḳh*, *ᶜarabiyya*, and *adab*. Not quite 20 years old, he embarked on the *ṭalab al-ᶜilm*, first, still under the tutelage of his two uncles, once more to Naysābūr for a special training in the *Ṣaḥīḥ* of Muslim [*q.v.*], then also to Ṭūs and other places. From his home town he visited the centres of learning of his time on three long journeys: 529-38/1135-43, 540-6/1145-51, and—together with his son ᶜAbd al-Raḥīm—549-52/1154-7. He went via Iṣfahān and Hamadān to Baghdād and its environs, to Mecca and Medina, to Damascus and Jerusalem (which at the time of his visit in 536/1141 had been in the hands of the Crusaders for 42 years), and, in the north and the east, to Khʷārazm, Samarḳand, Bukhārā, Balkh and Harāt. A number of these places with their important schools and academies he visited more than once (he also went on the Pilgrimage twice), even if that involved detours, constantly driven, as he was, by his desire for *ṭalab al-ᶜilm*.

This preoccupation of his informed not only his teaching in Marw and elsewhere but also his rich literary production which centred on the Prophetic Traditions and their transmission. With admirable orderliness and fastidiousness, he constantly strove to enlarge and correct his collected materials. Many of his more than 50 works most likely became casualties of the Mongol invasion. Marw was conquered in 618/1221. As late as 615/1218 Yāḳūt [*q.v.*] had participated in a *madjlis* of al-Samᶜānī's son ᶜAbd al-Raḥīm (537-617/1143-1220; al-Ṣafadī, xviii, 331) (see *Muᶜdjam*, i, 6); he had worked in the local libraries, *inter alia* those of the Samᶜānīs (*ibid.*, iv, 509) and had excerpted some of the great scholar's books, thus e.g. his biographical *magnum opus* on the Traditionists, namely:

(1) *al-Ansāb*. Arranged alphabetically according to *nisba* [*q.v.*], it contains 5,348 entries; each starts with an exact indication of the pronunciation of the *nisba*, gives the place, the person, or the group etc. to which the relative adjective refers, followed by the full name of the scholar in question with information on teachers and disciples (*isnād*), places and times of their ac-

tivities, and the date of death; as a rule, other personalities (including women) having the same *nisba* will be joined to the entry, so that the number of the scholars mentioned exceeds by twice or three times the amount of the number of entries, not counting the many additional persons that occur in a *vita* as teachers, colleagues, or disciples of the biographers. In not a few places al-Samᶜānī indicates the literature used by him; the small *Kitāb al-Ansāb* by Ibn al-Ḳaysarānī [*q.v.*], quoted by Yāḳūt, was likely also known to him. He finished the clean copy a few years before his death, but constantly added supplements. It was edited in facsimile by D.S. Margoliouth, Leiden-London 1912 (containing an introduction with a list of his works); edited by al-Muᶜallimī *et alii*, 13 vols., Ḥaydarābād/Deccan 1382-1402/1952-82 (with a detailed introd.); since 1976 reprints and new editions (in part) in Damascus and Beirut complete in 5 vols., ed. ᶜA.ᶜU. al-Bārūdī, Beirut 1988. Abridgements with supplements: the best-known is that of the historian ᶜIzz al-Dīn Ibn al-Athīr [*q.v.*], *al-Lubāb fī tahdhīb al-Ansāb*, 3 vols., Cairo 1357-69/1938-49 (repr. Beirut 1980); this was abbreviated and added to by al-Suyūṭī [*q.v.*], *Lubb al-Lubāb fī taḥrīr al-Ansāb*, ed. and annot. P.J. Veth, 2 vols., Leiden 1841-51 (repr. of vol. i, Baghdād [1963]).

(2) *al-Taḥbīr fi 'l-Muᶜdjam al-kabīr*, a work of more than 1,200 biographies of contemporary scholars, men and women, whom al-Samᶜānī had either encountered during his *ṭalab al-ḥadīth* at home and abroad, especially in Naysābūr and Iṣfahān, or with whom he had corresponded, or, finally, from whom he had received an *idjāza* [*q.v.*] through intermediaries. The biographies are brief but informative; they reflect diary entries. Al-Samᶜānī produced the clean copy in the year before his death, which may actually have overtaken him while doing this work; for the beginning and the end are missing in the ancient *unicum* Ẓāhiriyya, *ḥadīth* 529 (al-ᶜIshsh, 181). Ed. Munīra Nādjī Sālim, 2 vols., Baghdād 1395/1975; cf. eadem, in *al-Mawrid*, ii/4 (1973), 245-52 (reply to Muṭāᶜ al-Ṭarābīshī, in *MMLᶜA*, xlviii [1393/1973], 371-80); iii/3 (1974), 307-16; v/4 (1976), 29-58; eadem, *Tādj al-Islām Abū Saᶜd al-Samᶜānī wa-kitābuhu 'l-Taḥbīr fi 'l-Muᶜdjam al-kabīr*, Cairo (1976); for the question whether this work is the original of the *Taḥbīr* or rather a *Tahdhīb al-Taḥbīr*, see lastly Muṭāᶜ al-Ṭarābīshī, in *MMLᶜA*, lv (1400/1980), 149-63.

(3) *Muntakhab Muᶜdjam al-shuyūkh*, another biographical dictionary, covering al-Samᶜānī's teachers; unique copy of 647/1250 in Topkapı Sarayı, Ahmet III, 2953 (Karatay 6270; cf. Yāḳūt, *Irshād*, i, 253, 6); an edition has for a long time been announced by Munīra Nādjī Sālim and Nādjī Maᶜrūf. The work is possibly an excerpt from the unabridged version of no. 2.

(4) *Dhayl* to *Taʾrīkh Baghdād* of al-Khaṭīb al-Baghdādī [*q.v.*], known from quotations; excerpt: Leiden 1023 (de Goeje-Juynboll); for two other (?) excerpts see Munīra, *al-Taḥbīr*, i, 31; cf. Ibn al-Ṣābūnī, *Takmilat Ikmāl al-Ikmāl*, Baghdād 1377/1957, 241-2; M.ᶜA. Mudarris, *Rayḥānat al-adab*³, Tabrīz 1346/1967, i, 427. — As far as is presently known, the following biographical works have not been preserved, even in excerpts: *Wafayāt al-mutaʾakhkhirīn min al-ruwāt*, *Muᶜdjam al-shuyūkh* (a list of the teachers of his son), his early work, *Taʾrīkh Marw*, which Yāḳūt (*Muᶜdjam*, i, 751, 15) had read in the autograph, and his *Muᶜdjam al-buldān*; the last two are likely to have contained biographies of scholars, as well.

(5) *Adab al-imlāʾ wa 'l-istimlāʾ*, an important handbook on dictation as a method of transmission and instruction; the unique ms., Feyzullah 1557, was copied at Marw in 546/1152 (!). Ed. by Max Weisweiler, *Die Methode des Diktatkollegs*, Leiden 1952, with an extensive German summary of the contents; cf. idem, in *Oriens*, iv (1951), 27-57; A. Spitaler, in *OLZ*, xlix (1954), 529-36; new edition Beirut 1404/1984. Al-Samᶜānī mentions at the end that he has treated the topic exhaustively in his book *Ṭirāz al-dhahab fī adab al-ṭalab*. — On a ms. in Medina of his (6) *Adab al-ḳāḍī*, see O. Spies, in *ZDMG*, xc (1936), 115, on two additional ones in Cairo, Azhar, see Munīra, *al-Taḥbīr*, i, 31. — On a Cairene ms. of his (7) *Faḍāʾil al-Shaʾm*, see Brockelmann, S I, 565 no. 4 (no. 3, *al-Isfār ᶜan ḥukm al-asfār* [Mawṣil 34, 53,4] should be deleted because of faulty ascription [Mawṣil², v, 330]; on no. 7 "Gebete des Propheten", see E. Kohlberg, *A medieval Muslim scholar at work, Ibn Ṭāwūs and his library*, Leiden 1992, 100, no. 7: *al-Adᶜiya al-marwiyya min* (or *ᶜan*) *al-ḥadra al-nabawiyya*, and 157, no. 133: *Faḍāʾil al-ṣaḥāba*).

Bibliography: In addition to the works mentioned in the text, see Brockelmann, I², 401-2, S I, 564-5; H. Ritter, in *Isl.*, xvii (1928), 251; Barthold, *Turkestan*³, *passim*; F. Rosenthal, *A history of Muslim historiography*², Leiden 1968, *passim*; R. Sellheim, *Materialien zur arabischen Literaturgeschichte*, i-ii, Wiesbaden-Stuttgart 1976-87, *passim*; G. Makdisi, *The rise of humanism in Classical Islam and the Christian West*, Edinburgh 1990, *passim*; H. Halm, *Die Ausbreitung der šāfiᶜitischen Rechtsschule von den Anfängen bis zum 8./14. Jahrhundert*, Wiesbaden 1974, *passim*; Kh. al-Ziriklī, *al-Aᶜlām*, Beirut 1979, iv, 55; ᶜU.R. Kaḥḥāla, *Muᶜdjam al-muʾallifīn*, Damascus 1378/1958, vi, 4-5; idem, *al-Mustadrak ᶜalā Muᶜdjam al-muʾallifīn*, Beirut 1406/1985, 407; idem, *Muᶜdjam muṣannifī 'l-kutub al-ᶜarabiyya fi 'l-taʾrīkh wa 'l-tarādjim wa 'l-riḥalāt*, Beirut 1406/1986, 286; M.ᶜA. Mudarris, *Rayḥānat al-adab*², Tabrīz n.d. [*ca.* 1347/1968], iii, 75-6; Riyāḍ ᶜAbd al-Ḥamīd, *al-Tabādul al-thaḳāfī bayn bilād al-Shām wa-bilād Fāris*, Damascus 1409/1989, *passim*.

Main sources: Ibn ᶜAsākir, *Taʾrīkh Dimashḳ*, facs. ed., Medina 1407/1987, x, 433-4; Ibn al-Djawzī, *al-Muntaẓam*, x, 224-5; ᶜIzz al-Dīn Ibn al-Athīr, *al-Lubāb*, i, Cairo 1357/1938, 9-12; idem, *al-Kāmil*, Beirut 1385/1966, xi, 333; Ibn al-Dubaythī/al-Dhahabī, *al-Mukhtaṣar al-muḥtādj ilayh min [Dhayl] Taʾrīkh [Baghdād]*, Baghdād 1397/1977, iii, 67-8; Ibn al-Nadjdjār/Ibn al-Dimyāṭī, *al-Mustafād min Dhayl Taʾrīkh Baghdād*, Ḥaydarābād/Deccan 1399/1979, 172-3; Ibn Khallikān, s.v.; Dhahabī, *Tadhkirat al-ḥuffāẓ*, iv, 1316-9; idem, *al-ᶜIbar*, Kuwait 1963, iv, 178; idem, *Siyar aᶜlām al-nubalāʾ*, Beirut 1405/1985, xx, 456-65; Ṣafadī, *al-Wāfī*, xix, Wiesbaden-Beirut 1413/1993, 88-92; Yāfiᶜī, *Mirʾāt al-djanān*, Ḥaydarābād/Deccan 1338/1919, iii, 371-2; Subkī *Ṭabaḳāt al-Shāfiᶜiyya al-kubrā*, Cairo 1390/1970, vii, 180-5 (with a list of his works); Asnawī, *Ṭabaḳāt al-Shāfiᶜiyya*, Baghdād 1391/1971, ii, 55-6; Ibn Kathīr, *al-Bidāya wa 'l-nihāya*, xii, 175, 254; Ibn Ḳāḍī Shuhba, *Ṭabaḳāt al-Shāfiᶜiyya*, Ḥaydarābād/Deccan 1399/1979, ii, 11-3; Ibn Taghrībirdī, *al-Nudjūm al-zāhira*, Cairo 1353/1935, v, 375, 378; Ṭashköprüzāde, *Miftāḥ al-saᶜāda*, Cairo n.d. [*ca.* 1388/1968], i, 259-60; Ibn al-ᶜImād, *Shadharāt*, iv, 205-6; Ismāᶜīl Pasha, *Hadiyyat al-ᶜārifīn*, Istanbul 1951, i, 608-9.

(R. Sellheim)

SĀMĀNIDS, a Persian dynasty which ruled in Transoxania and then in Khurāsān also, at first as subordinate governors of the Ṭāhirids [*q.v.*] and then later autonomous, virtually independent rulers (204-395/819-1005).

Genealogical table of the Sāmānids

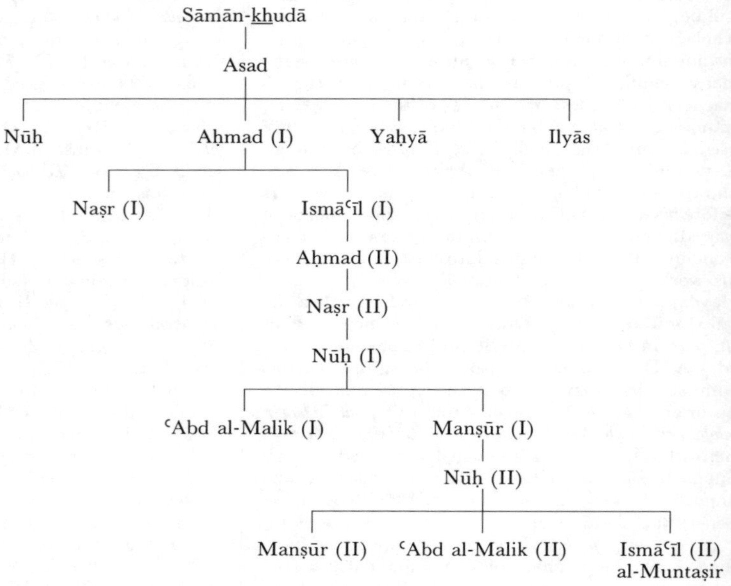

1. History, literary life and economic activity.

The early history of the Sāmānid family is obscure. They may have stemmed either from Soghdia or, perhaps more likely, from Ṭukhāristān south of the Oxus, probably from the petty landowners of the Balkh area. It was not possible to connect the Sāmānids with a noble Arab tribe, as the almost certainly originally Persian Ṭāhirids endeavoured to do, but the tradition later grew up of an aristocratic origin for the Sāmānids through descent from the Sāsānid warrior hero Bahrām Čūbīn [see BAHRĀM]; al-Bīrūnī, *al-Āthār al-bāḳiya*, ed. Sachau, 39, states that there was "universal agreement" over this claim (see C.E. Bosworth, *The heritage of rulership in early Islamic Iran and the search for dynastic connections with the past*, in *Iran, JBIPS*, xiv [1976], 58-9). All that we really know is that the *dihḳān* Sāmān-khudā apparently accepted Islam at the hands of the Umayyad governor of Khurāsān Asad b. ʿAbd Allāh al-Ḳasrī (i.e. at some point during 105-9/723-7 or 117-20/735-8), therefore naming his son after the Arab governor (see Bosworth, *Asad b. Sāmānḳodā*, in *EIr*).

However, nothing is heard of the family for several decades, until, at the ʿAbbāsid caliph al-Maʾmūn's behest, his governor in Khurāsān, Ghassān b. ʿAbbād, in *ca.* 204/819 rewarded the four sons of Asad b. Sāmān-khudā for their support to the ʿAbbāsids during the rebellion in Transoxania of Rāfiʿ b. al-Layth b. Sayyār [*q.v.*]. Nūḥ was given the governorship of Samarḳand; Aḥmad, Farghāna; Yaḥyā, Shāsh; and Ilyās, Harāt. This last branch of the Sāmānids south of the Oxus did not prosper, and Ibrāhīm b. Ilyās was in 253/867 defeated and captured by the Ṣaffārid invader of Bādhghīs, Yaʿḳūb b. al-Layth [see ṢAFFĀRIDS]. The ones in Transoxania, on the other hand, had a glorious future ahead of them. After Nūḥ died in 227/841-2, the governor of Khurāsān ʿAbd Allāh b. Ṭāhir [*q.v.*] appointed the remaining two brothers in Transoxania, Yaḥyā and Aḥmad, over Samarḳand and Soghdia. Very soon the line of Aḥmad (I) replaced that of Yaḥyā, and with the Ṣaffārid dispossession of the Ṭāhirids from Nīshāpūr in 259/873 and the lapse of Khurāsān into something like anarchy for the next two decades, Naṣr (I) b. Aḥmad b. Sāmān-khudā found himself in effect autonomous ruler in Transoxania, with his capital at Samarḳand. The caliph al-Muʿtamid formally invested him as governor of Transoxania in 261/875, and from the 250s onwards Naṣr began to mint dirhams of a mixed ʿAbbāsid-Sāmānid type, with the regular minting of dirhams and then of dīnārs beginning *ca.* 279/892 with the formal accession of Ismāʿīl b. Aḥmad; their father Aḥmad (I) had already issued his own copper *fulūs* at Samarḳand from 244/858 onwards (see G.C. Miles, in *Camb. hist. of Iran*, iv, 374).

However, fratricidal strife between Naṣr and Ismāʿīl, whom Naṣr had sent to subdue Bukhārā, ended in the military triumph of Ismāʿīl, although he left Naṣr as *de jure* ruler in Samarḳand till the latter's death there in 279/892. Ismāʿīl then assumed sole power, ruling over Transoxania and Farghāna from Bukhārā, whither the Sāmānid capital was now permanently transferred.

Abū Ibrāhīm Ismāʿīl (I) (279-95/892-907 [*q.v.*]) may be regarded as the real founder of the Sāmānid amirate, his power sealed by his victory over the Ṣaffārid ʿAmr b. al-Layth [*q.v.*] in 287/900, after which the caliph al-Muʿtaḍid appointed him governor of both Transoxania and Khurāsān. This was in practice the concession of independent rule there, given the distance of the Sāmānid lands from Baghdād and the shrinkage of the direct sphere of ʿAbbāsid political authority to ʿIrāḳ, Syria and western Persia, although the Sāmānids continued till the end to pay formal respect to the caliphs, placing them in the *khuṭba* of their territories and their names on their coins, and employing for themselves no higher title than that of *amīr*. One role which Ismāʿīl inherited as ruler of Transoxania was the defence of its northern frontiers against pressure from the nomads of Inner Asia, and in 280/893 he led an expedition into the steppes against the Ḳarluḳ [*q.v.*] Turks, capturing Ṭalas and bringing back a great booty of slaves and beasts.

Sāmānid suzerainty was asserted over various local rulers in the Syr Darya valley and on both sides of the upper Oxus, such as the princes of Us͟hrūsana [*q.v.*], the Abū Dāwūdids or Bānid̲j̲ūrids [*q.v.* in Suppl.] of Ṭuk͟hāristān and K͟huttal and the Muḥtād̲j̲ids [*q.v.*] of Čag͟hāniyān, and over the ancient kingdom of K͟hwārazm [*q.v.*]. In the west, he extended his authority over the Zaydī Imāms of the Caspian region, and in general, achieved a reputation as a capable and just ruler.

Ismāʿīl's son Abū Naṣr Aḥmad (II) (295-301/907-14) attempted to recover the Caspian provinces which had slipped from Sāmānid control, and sent two expeditions into Sīstān (298/911 and 299-300/912-13), where Ṣaffārid authority had fallen into disarray [see ṢAFFĀRIDS]. But he was murdered at Farabr by his Turkish slaves in D̲j̲umādā II 301/January 914, allegedly because of his excessive favour at court to the *ʿulamāʾ* and other members of the religious classes, thus earning for himself the posthumous title of *al-amīr al-s͟hahīd* "the martyred prince". The practice of awarding posthumous *laḳabs* had already begun with Aḥmad's father Ismāʿīl, who became known as *al-amīr al-māḍī* or *al-amīr al-ʿādil* "the late/just prince", and some of the subsequent *amīrs* further assumed regnal titles, such as Nūḥ (I) b. Naṣr's one of *al-malik al-muʾayyad*, appearing on his coins, and Nūḥ (II) b. Manṣūr's *al-malik al-manṣūr*, in addition to the titles given to them after their deaths (see Bosworth, *The titulature of the early Ghaznavids*, in *Oriens*, xv [1962], 214-15).

His eight-year old son Naṣr (II) [*q.v.*] succeeded for a reign of some 30 years (301-31/914-43). He faced prolonged internal opposition from his ambitious uncle and brothers, who at various times controlled Samarḳand and parts of K͟hurāsān and who stirred up in the cities popular elements which included the *ʿayyārs* and *g͟hāzīs*. Sāmānid armies penetrated as far westwards as Rayy in northern Persia, occupied in 314/926, when al-Muḳtadir formally granted its governorship to Naṣr. Sāmānid coins were issued from there till 920/932 and at various times thereafter (see Miles, *The numismatic history of Rayy*, New York 1938, 147 ff.), although control here was disputed with local Daylamī commanders and then with the Būyid Rukn al-Dawla [*q.v.*], who secured almost permanent control of the city after Naṣr's death. The later part of Naṣr's reign was noteworthy for the appearance in Transoxania of an extensive Ismāʿīlī S͟hīʿī *daʿwa*, with converts made up to the highest level at court before an orthodox Sunnī reaction and purge of these heretics set in; this episode was an exception to the normally firm upholding of Sunnī orthodoxy by the *amīrs* (cf. Barthold, *Turkestan*³, 242-4).

Naṣr's reign was in many ways the apogee of Sāmānid power and glory, aided to a significant extent by the services to the *amīrs* of capable viziers like Abū ʿAbd Allāh al-D̲j̲ayhānī and his son Abū ʿAlī Muḥammad [see AL-D̲J̲AYHĀNĪ in Suppl.] and Abu 'l-Faḍl Muḥammad al-Balʿamī [*q.v.*], who were celebrated as much for their own learning and patronage of scholars as for their statesmanship. Under these and other officials, the Sāmānid administration in Buk͟hārā reached a high level of specialisation and sophistication as the instrument of the *amīrs*' centralising policies. As with the administration of other provincial dynasties, the model was that of the caliphs in Bag͟hdād. The local historian of Buk͟hāra, Nars͟hak͟hī, describes ten *dīwāns*, beginning with those of the *wazīr*, the treasurer and the *ʿamīd al-mulk* or head of the chancery (see for these, Barthold, *op. cit.*, 229-32), and many of the bureaucratic techniques of these departments can be pieced together from the information given by the Sāmānid official Abū ʿAbd Allāh al-K͟hwārazmī [*q.v.*] in his encyclopaedia of the sciences, the *Mafātīḥ al-ʿulūm*, dedicated to the vizier Abu 'l-Ḥasan ʿUbayd Allāh al-ʿUtbī (see Bosworth, *Abū ʿAbdallāh al-Khwārazmī on the technical terms of the secretary's art*, in *JESHO*, xii [1969], 113-64). It was this efficient administrative system which brought in rich amounts of taxation from the agricultural oases of Soghdia, Farg͟hāna and K͟hurāsān, together with revenues from the slave traffic between Inner Asia and the Islamic lands further west (the *amīrs* levied customs duties at the Transoxanian frontier towns on imported Turkish slaves and at the Oxus crossings for their transit across the Sāmānid dominions), so that the 4th/10th century geographers and travellers like Ibn Ḥawḳal and al-Muḳaddasī could praise the Sāmānids for their mild rule and moderate taxation and could extol the cheapness of provisions and pleasantness of life in their lands.

The security of the realm rested, of course, on the powerful army which the Sāmānids maintained under the command of the Chief *Ḥād̲j̲ib*. The first troops of the Sāmānids must have been recruited from the free Iranians of Transoxania, long trained in the martial arts by their position on the northeastern frontiers of Islam facing the pagan steppes; but from at least the time of Ismāʿīl b. Aḥmad onwards, a Turkish slave guard around the *amīrs* comes into prominence, formed from Turks brought in from Inner Asia (see Barthold, *op. cit.*, 227-8; Bosworth, *An alleged embassy from the Emperor of China to the Amir Naṣr b. Aḥmad: a contribution to Sāmānid military history*, in M. Minovi and I. Afshar (eds.), *Yâd-nâme-ye îrânî-ye Minorsky*, Tehran 1969, 1-13; and G͟HULĀM. ii. Persia). This slave guard early made itself a force in the internal affairs of the state, with its own aims and interests. As noted above, Aḥmad (II) b. Ismāʿīl was killed by his *g͟hulāms*, and from the mid-4th/10th century onwards, the influence of the generals, and especially of the holders of the coveted post of Commander-in-Chief in K͟hurāsān, frequently resulted in the making and unmaking of Sāmānid princes, as the personal authority of the *amīrs* waned; symptomatic of the arrogance and independence of the Turkish generals was the fact that in 381/991 Abū ʿAlī Sīmd̲j̲ūrī appropriated all the state revenues in K͟hurāsān and assumed for himself the grandiose titles of *amīr al-umarāʾ, al-muʾayyad min al-samāʾ* "the supreme commander with heavenly backing" (see Bosworth, *The titulature of the early Ghaznavids*, 215).

After Naṣr's death, his son and successor Nūḥ (I) (331-43/943-54 [*q.v.*]) had to devote attention to the ambitions in K͟hurāsān of the powerful governor there, the Iranian noble Abū ʿAlī Čag͟hānī, endeavouring to replace him by the Turkish commander Ibrāhīm b. Sīmd̲j̲ūr and to maintain, in alliance with the Ziyārids [*q.v.*] of Gurgān and Ṭabaristān, the position in northern Persia against the Sāmānids' rivals, the Būyids. A disturbing portent for the remaining years of Sāmānid rule was a financial crisis in the state, caused by the cost of the wars in northern Persia and the expenses of the army in general. During the next reign, that of Abu 'l-Fawāris ʿAbd al-Malik (I) b. Nūḥ (343-50/954-61), the ascendancy of the Turkish slave commander Alptigin [*q.v.*] was notable, although when ʿAbd al-Malik died, he was unable to place on the throne his own candidate, the dead *amīr*'s young son Naṣr—who would have been a puppet in the hands of the military—and was forced to flee to G͟hazna, on the far eastern fringes of the Sāmānid lands. ᶜAbd al-Malik's brother Manṣūr (I) b. Nūḥ now ascended the throne (350-65/961-76 [*q.v.*]). His reign was in general peaceful, although fighting continued in northern Persia, on the whole favourably for the Sāmānids, and after Alptigin's death at G͟hazna (352/963), his Turkish successors in eastern Afg͟hānistān once more acknowledged the *amīr*'s overlordship.

The last twenty years or so of Sāmānid rule were ones of increased impotence of the *amīr*s in face of the ambitions of Turkish commanders like the Sīmd͟jūrīs, Tās͟h, Begtuzun and Fāʾiḳ K͟hāṣṣa, and deepening crisis in the state as its tax base shrank. Manṣūr (I)'s vizier, Abu 'l-Ḥusayn ᶜAbd Allāh al-ᶜUtbī, appointed in 367/977, did what he could to halt the decline and to stem the successes of the Būyids, who were poised to invade K͟hurāsān when the death of ᶜAḍud al-Dawla [*q.v.*] fortunately supervened in 372/983; but al-ᶜUtbī was murdered in 371/982 through the machinations of Abu 'l-Ḥasan Sīmd͟jūrī and Fāʾiḳ. Nūḥ (II) b. Manṣūr (365-87/976-97 [*q.v.*]) soon no longer had any authority in K͟hurāsān and was by the end of his reign reduced to controlling Soghdia only. He was forced to call in the assistance of Sebüktigin from G͟hazna against Fāʾiḳ and Abū ᶜAlī Sīmd͟jūrī after the latter had encouraged an invasion of the remaining Sāmānid lands from the north in 382/992 by the Turkish Ḳarak͟hānids under Bug͟hra K͟hān Hārūn [see ILEK K͟HĀNS]. Buk͟hārā and Samarḳand were temporarily occupied by the Turks, but although these were recovered by Nūḥ, the position got steadily worse.

A fresh Ḳarak͟hānid invasion took place in 386/996, and at this point, Sebüktigin and his son Maḥmūd [*q.v.*], who now controlled K͟hurāsān, came to an agreement with the Ḳarak͟hānid Ilig Naṣr b. ᶜAlī whereby Sebüktigin retained K͟hurāsān and the Ilig occupied the whole valley of the Syr Darya. Nūḥ died the next year, and the reign of the new *amīr*, his son Abu 'l-Ḥārit͟h Manṣūr (II) [*q.v.*] lasted only two years (387-9/997-9) before he was deposed by Fāʾiḳ and Begtuzun and replaced by his brother Abu 'l-Fawāris ᶜAbd al-Malik (II). Maḥmūd b. Sebüktigin by 398/999 secured for himself all the former Sāmānid lands south of the Oxus, and in this year the Ḳarak͟hānids under the Ilig Naṣr definitively took over Buk͟hārā without any serious resistance, thereby ending the dynasty's vestigial rule in Soghdia. A further brother of Manṣūr (II) and ᶜAbd al-Malik, Abū Ibrāhīm Ismāᶜīl (II) b. Nūḥ al-Muntaṣir [*q.v.*], attempted a revanche in the following years, but after some initial successes against the Ḳarak͟hānids was killed in 395/1005, the last hope of the Sāmānids.

The downfall of the Sāmānids meant that the north-eastern part of the Iranian world, first the Trans-Oxus provinces under the Ḳarak͟hānids and then, four decades later, the steppelands between the northern rim of the mountains of K͟hurāsān and the middle Oxus under the Sald͟jūḳs, passed for the first time into Turkish control. It was after this that the gradual process of the almost complete (save for the modern Tadjikistan) Turkicisation of these regions accelerated, a process which must however have begun already in Sāmānid times with the extensive influx of Turkish slave soldiers into the state apparatus and the peaceful settlement of sedentarised and Islamised Turks along the northern fringes of Transoxania. On the documentary evidence, the old Soghdian language disappeared towards the end of the Sāmānid period under pressure from New Persian, which was probably the day-to-day language of much of the Sāmānid bureaucracy's routine business (although it may be noted that the neo-Soghdian language Yag͟hnōbī has survived to this day in the valley of the Yag͟hnōb, an affluent of the upper Zarafs͟hān; see ĪRĀN. Languages, in Suppl.), and Turkish. There was, however, some counter-pressure against this trend from the *ᶜulamāʾ* and religious classes and from the higher bureaucracy, who were trained in the classical Arabic sciences, in favour of the use of Arabic as the language both of scholarship and of diplomacy. According to the 8th/14th century historian Ḥamd Allāh Mustawfī, the *amīr* Aḥmad (II) b. Ismāᶜīl changed the language of official business from Persian to Arabic, but the measure was unpopular and had to be rescinded. Thereafter, the two languages doubtless existed side-by-side in administrative usage. Of course, Arabic retained its primacy in the spheres of religion, learning and science. The achievements of the Sāmānid period in Arabic scholarship were very considerable, with Buk͟hārā and Samarḳand as centres for literary activity under the patronage of the *amīr*s themselves, as the plethora of poets and prose stylists appearing in the fourth *ḳism* of the K͟hurāsānian author Abū Manṣūr ᶜAbd al-Malik al-T͟haᶜālibī's [*q.v.*] literary anthology, the *Yatīmat al-dahr*, that on the Arabic littérateurs of K͟hurāsān, Transoxania and K͟hʷārazm, shows (see V. Danner, in *Camb. hist. Iran*, iv, 589-93).

But the 4th/10th century is notable for the florescence under the Sāmānids of a lively New Persian literature, one whose roots lay in the preceding century and whose poetic production came to a remarkable stage of maturity and expressiveness with such authors as Rūdakī, Daḳīḳī and Abu 'l-Ḥasan Kisāʾī of Marw [*q.vv.*]. This development of New Persian literature both in the Sāmānid dominions and at the other petty courts of the East does not necessarily imply promotion of this by the *amīr*s or princes as a conscious, proto-nationalist Persian policy (although the Sāmānid amīrs were undoubtedly interested in this, see below; one of the last rulers, Manṣūr (II) b. Nūḥ, is included by ᶜAwfī amongst the rulers who composed Persian poetry, examples of which he gives, see his *Lubāb al-albāb*, ed. Saᶜīd Nafīsī, Tehran 1335/1956, 23-4) but reflects rather the distance of K͟hurāsān, Transoxania and the upper Oxus principalities from the focus of Arab-Islamic life in the central lands of the caliphate, and also the vigorousness of Persian culture in the East, always strong at the local level. Certainly, it was the *dihḳān* class there which nurtured and cherished the old Persian epic traditions; this is especially clear in the case of the lord of Ṭūs, Abū Manṣūr Muḥammad b. ᶜAbd al-Razzāḳ, who in 346/957 commissioned the translation of Pahlavi texts of the national epic into New Persian, and these were utilised by Firdawsī [*q.v.*] for his *S͟hāh-nāma* and also, it seems, for the earlier, unfinished verse rendering (known from Firdawsī's incorporation of it within his own work) by Daḳīḳī (see V. Minorsky, *The older preface to the* Shāh-nāma, in *Studi in onore di Giorgio Levi della Vida*, Rome 1956, ii, 159-79; G. Lazard, *La langue des plus anciens monuments de la prose persane*, Paris 1963, 36-7). This New Persian literature of the Sāmānid period involved not only poetry but also prose, including prose versions of the national epic such as that of Abu 'l-Muʾayyad Balk͟hī, known from fragments (written in the reign of Nūḥ (II) b. Manṣūr); Persian translations and epitomes of al-Ṭabarī's *History* (made for Manṣūr (I) b. Nūḥ by his vizier Abū ᶜAlī Muḥammad Balᶜamī [*q.v.*]) and of his *Ḳurʾān commentary* (also done in this reign by a group of scholars); etc. (see Lazard, *op. cit.*, 38 ff.; idem, *Les premiers poètes persans (IXᵉ-Xᵉ siècles)*, Tehran-

1. Slip-painted dish, W:46.8 cm, H:6 cm. 52.11. Courtesy of the Freer Gallery of Art, Smithsonian Institution, Washington, D.C.

2. Slip-painted bowl, W:22.5 cm; H: 6.5 cm. Metropolitan Museum of Art Nishapur excavations, 1939. 40. 170.14. The Metropolitan Museum of Art, New York.

3. Cast bronze bottle, H:15 cm. Metropolitan Museum of Art Nishapur excavations, 1938. 39. 40. 48. The Metropolitan Museum of Art, New York.

4. Mausoleum of the Sāmānids, Bukhārā. Photograph: Yolande Crowe.

Paris 1342/1964; idem, in *Camb. hist. Iran*, iv, 606 ff.; J. Rypka *et alii, History of Iranian literature*, Dordrecht 1968, 139-71).

The economic strength of the Sāmānid state lay, as noted above, in the flourishing agriculture of the populous river valleys and oases of the region, and also in the craft industries of the towns and the commercial connections of the Sāmānid lands. These last lay at the southern end of trade routes coming from the Inner Asian steppes and, ultimately, from China, so that the Sāmānids could mediate the products of these distant lands to Bag͟hdād and other great centres of consumption in the central lands of the caliphate. Until the later 4th/10th century, when internal strife amongst the rival Turkish commanders and their strife with the *amīrs* set in, disorders completed by the Ḳarak͟hānid invasions, the Sāmānid lands generally enjoyed internal peace and freedom from external attack. Local industries and crafts could flourish, such as the *ṭirāz* [*q.v.*] workshops of Buk͟hārā, whose embroidered textiles were used, so Nars͟hak͟hī says, for payment of annual tribute to the caliphs (? in the earlier period of Ṭāhirid suzerainty over Transoxania), the famous paper production in Samarḳand, started by captured Chinese artisans [see KĀG͟HAD], arms and weapons from the metal industry of Farg͟hāna, etc. Various of the imports from the steppe and forest lands to the north, i.e. western Siberia and Russia, including furs, hides, honey, wax, cattle on the hoof, etc., exchanged for the textiles, leatherwork, grain and fruits of Transoxania, are listed by al-Muḳaddasī (tr. in Barthold, *Turkestan*, 235-6). Above all, Transoxania benefited from the trade in Turkish and Ṣaḳlabī [see ṢAḲĀLIBA] slaves, brought to the slave markets in frontier towns like Isfīd͟jāb and S͟hās͟h or captured in raids (see *ibid.*, 234-40).

As a result of this buoyant economic and commercial atmosphere, the revenues of the Sāmānid lands amounted to 45 million dirhams (within this, so Nars͟hak͟hī records, the land tax of Buk͟hārā and Karmīna yielded 1,168,566 dirhams). The *amīrs* themselves took over extensive estates from the Buk͟hār-k͟hudās as personal domains (*k͟hāṣṣa*), and groups like the *sayyids* of the ʿAlids and other *ʿulamāʾ* held much land in *waḳf*. The greatest item of expenditure was on the salaries of the army and the bureaucracy, which were, according to Niẓām al-Mulk (speaking of "former kings", i.e. the Sāmānids and G͟haznawids), paid in cash. However, there are signs of the beginning of the practice of granting out lands as assignments [see IḲṬĀʿ], already known in ʿIrāḳ and western Persia, so that revenues were subtracted from the central treasury; the Čag͟hānīs held extensive estates on the upper Oxus, and the Sīmd͟jūrīs in Ḳuhistān (cf. Barthold, *op. cit.*, 238-9). It seems that the old Persian *dihḳān* class began to decline in both K͟hurāsān and Transoxania during the Sāmānid period, parallel to increased centralisation in the state and a movement of population from the countryside to the towns; the factors at work here were doubtless complex, but it is true that we hear little of the *dihḳāns* as a landowning class in the ensuing Ḳarak͟hānid and Sald͟jūḳ periods, and the actual word *dihḳān* [*q.v.*] begins its semantic decline into the modern Persian meaning of "peasant" (cf. Frye, in *Camb. hist. of Iran*, iv, 152-3).

Consideration of the Sāmānid financial and economic situation is also bound up with that of their coinage. The *amīrs* were fortunate to control some of the best silver-producing veins in the eastern Islamic world, sc. in Badak͟hs͟hān and Farg͟hāna, and the sheer volume of coinage minted, and especially that in silver, is impressive. G.C. Miles enumerated no fewer than 47 mint places known to have issued coins in the name of the Sāmānids, not only—as one would expect—in Transoxania and K͟hurāsān—but as far afield as Sīstān, Fārs, D͟jibāl and the Caspian region, as the result of military campaigns there or of alliances with local potentates (see *Camb. hist. Iran*, iv, 374). A vast quantity of this coinage found its way outside the Islamic world into Siberia, northern Russia, Scandinavia and the Baltic shores, and even as far as the British Isles and Iceland, apparently as a result of trading operations which seem mysteriously to have been largely discontinued in the opening years of the 5th/11th century. The whole topic of this apparent one-way drain of Sāmānid silver northwards and westwards has been much discussed by both economic historians and numismatists, but remains substantially unexplained. Amongst the extensive literature here, see e.g. J. Duplessy, *La circulation des monnaies arabes en Europe occidentale du VIIIe au XIIIe siècle*, in *Revue Numismatique*, sér. 5, vol. xviii (1956), 101-63; T. Lewicki, *Le commerce des Sāmānides avec l'Europe orientale et centrale à la lumière des trésors de monnaies coufiques*, in D.K. Kouymjian (ed.), *Near Eastern numismatics, iconography, epigraphy and history. Studies in honor of George C. Miles*, Beirut 1974, 219-33; A.E. Lieber, *Did a 'silver crisis' in Central Asia affect the flow of Islamic coins into Scandinavia and eastern Europe?*, in *Commentationes de nummis saeculorum IX-XI in Suecia repertis*, N.S. 6. *Sigtuna papers*, Stockholm 1990, 207-12.

Bibliography (in addition to references given in the article):

1. Sources. Ṭabarī; Ḥamza Iṣfahānī; ʿUtbī; Gardīzī; Nars͟hak͟hī, tr. R.N. Frye, *The history of Bukhara*, Cambridge, Mass. 1954, with valuable notes; Ibn al-At͟hīr; D͟jūzd͟jānī; Mustawfī, *Guzīda*, Mīrk͟hʷānd, Fr. tr. Ch. Defrémery, *Histoire des Samanides*, Paris 1845.

2. Studies. Barthold, *Turkestan*³, 209-12, 214-15, 222-70; Spuler, *Iran*, 76-90, 107-11; Frye, ch. *The Samanids*, in *Camb. hist. Iran*, iv, 136-61; W.L. Treadwell, *The political history of the Sāmānid state*, D. Phil. diss. Oxford University 1991, unpubl.; Zambaur, *Manuel*, 202-3; Bosworth, *The Islamic new dynasties*, Edinburgh 1996, Ch. IX, no. 78. See also the arts. ISMĀʿĪL (I) B. AḤMAD; ISMĀʿĪL (II) B. NŪḤ AL-MUNTAṢIR; AL-MANṢŪR (I) and (II); NAṢR B. AḤMAD; NŪḤ (I) B. NAṢR; NŪḤ (II) B. MANṢŪR.

(C.E. BOSWORTH)

2. Art and architecture.

Although history and literature are fairly well documented, no clear picture exists of artistic achievements under the Sāmānids. The fertile oases under their rule are on the fringes of Inner Asia, a north-eastern *limes* for the Iranian world. The early caliphs wrested the eastern part of the area from Chinese suzerainty; over the centuries these lands have remained at the crossroad of trade routes and influences.

(a) *Applied arts. Ceramics.* They are the best testimony of Sāmānid craftsmanship, as in the finds of Afrāsiyāb/Samarḳand and Nīs͟hāpūr. Dating of the material is still not clear; the later rule of the Ḳarak͟hānids could be responsible for some of it. The pre-Islamic red body earthenware serves as support to white, black or russet slips and their décor under the new transparent lead glaze. When no slip is used, as in Nīs͟hāpūr, the body takes on a buff colour under the glaze. The decoration draws on five sources. First, the new but soon assimilated Arabic calligraphy painted in near black manganese. Second, the possible influence of late T'ang bichrome, copper green with iron brown or yellow, but not the earlier three-coloured décor; there are no shapes nor designs recalling Chinese originals. Third, strong echoes of textile designs ranging from stripes, triple dots, dotted circles and peacock-eyes to roundels containing birds, gazelles and palmettes. These designs start in pre-Islamic times and are still visible on local wall paintings and caves farther east. Strapwork patterns create original geometric overall decoration. Fourth, alien religions signal their survival by using their own symbols: in Nī<u>sh</u>āpūr, a few ceramics are painted with crosses; in Samarḳand it is the fish which is used, as in Egyptian lustreware. Communities of Nestorians and Syriacs still existed, as did also Manichaeans and Buddhists, the latter manifest in the overall pattern of a lotus base inside dishes. And fifth, paintings of figures, chiefly in Nī<u>sh</u>āpūr: hunters on horseback, seated rulers and dancers, all surrounded by fantastic animals and birds. Would they also be survivors of earlier times in a society becoming more and more Islamicised?

Thus dishes up to 45 cm wide, with a small or large cavetto, are usually covered in a white slip; they recall the new manufacturing of paper; this white ground acts as an ideal support for calligraphy. Ewers, bowls, often with a double recessed base, lamps, inkwells, even toys, all are coloured with a mixture of metal oxide and fine white clay; the mixture prevents the design from running under the transparent glaze. The use of a russet/iron colour points to the red of later Iznik pottery. When colour is required to run, no fine clay is added to the oxide. As for *sgraffito*, it appears to be an original means of decoration and is used as a visual counterpoint for the colour runs, usually green, yellow and purple in a dense patterning for large dishes and bowls. Unglazed wares consist of long-necked ewers, some with filtre, jars, gourds, cooking pots, oven shapes and moulds.

Glass. In the finds of Samarḳand, bottles are either freely blown or, when a pattern is required, mould-blown to produce a lattice or twisted pattern. The ewers are not unlike their ceramic counterparts; spoons and inkpots can be added to the list of shapes. Green and turquoise are the usual shades with the occasional blue or amber bottles, bowls, bangles and beads.

Metalwork. Since most metals were available in <u>Kh</u>urāsān and Transoxiana, the important metal industry of pre-Islamic times was carried over and adapted to the taste of the new rulers, although precise dating is still hazy. Early Arab governors of <u>Kh</u>urāsān sent gifts of silver and gold vessels to the caliph in Ba<u>gh</u>dād, as well as bowls and jugs of high-tin bronze. The latter, *safīdrūy*, with its appearance of silver, was a good substitute for precious metals. Cast objects of copper such as ewers, buckets and braziers, were of daily use. In archaeological finds, household objects like lamps, jugs, flat-bottom bottles, ewers, incense burners, some in the shape of a stupa, spoons and weights, were made of bronze. Bronze was also used for more personal items like rings, tweezers, mirrors and kohl sticks. Iron was used for sword, dagger and shovel blades, as well as for arrowheads.

Textiles. Already in Sāsānid times, local silk and cotton provided the yarn for goods appreciated well beyond the area. Early after the Islamic conquest, tributes of garments were sent to Ba<u>gh</u>dād from <u>Kh</u>urāsān. The *ṭirāz* [*q.v.*] factories of Nī<u>sh</u>āpūr and especially Marw produced very soft cotton fabrics as well as *ibrī<u>sh</u>im* and *ḳazz* silk. The only surviving silk from this period is the remarkable compound twill known as the shroud of Saint Josse [see ḤARĪR]. Its inscription reads *ʿizz wa-iḳbāl li ʾl ḳāʾid Abū Manṣūr Ba<u>kh</u>-takīn aṭāla ʾllāh baḳ[āʾahu]* ("Glory and prosperity to the Ḳāʾid Abū Manṣūr Ba<u>kh</u>-takīn, may God prolong his existence"). This was not to be the case, since he was put to death by ʿAbd al-Malik b. Nūḥ in 350/961.

Only through the eyes of contemporary historians can one appreciate the wealth of textiles produced in Sāmānid lands. The most popular and expensive could have been *zandanī<u>dj</u>ī* cloth exported as far as ʿIrāḳ and India. Niẓām al-Mulk noted that the Sāmānids dressed their newly-bought slaves in *zandanī<u>dj</u>ī*. Other villages near Bu<u>kh</u>ārā produced, in particular, cloaks, hats and prayer carpets. Of all the important towns with bazaars, Samarḳand was the best-known emporium of Transoxiana for its silver-coloured and red garments, brocades, *ḳazz* silk and Chinese silks. Near by, at the village of Wa<u>dh</u>ār, an expensive cloth of cotton woven on cotton, *wa<u>dh</u>ārī*, was made into a light resistant type of yellow overcoat, very popular in winter. From <u>Sh</u>ā<u>sh</u> came special capes with neck decoration, prayer carpets and cotton yarn.

Ivory. As dry climate does not lend itself to the preservation of ivory objects, only a few of these, such as chess pieces, have survived; in Samarḳand, spoons have been found with delicately carved handles.

(b) *Architecture*. The dearth of 4th/10th-century surviving monuments underlines the attitude of later Islamic rulers to the buildings of previous dynasties. Mud brick is still the basic building material in the area. Remains of impressive walls with an outward corrugated surface, visible in Marw, suggest the importance of main towns and the need to protect them, though in the capital Bu<u>kh</u>ārā, the Rīgistān, a large square, lay outside the pre-Islamic town, surrounded by ten *dīwāns* to the west of the well-fortified citadel. Stucco remains from palaces and affluent houses still have traces of painting. Large bazaars sheltered commerce and industry. Towards the end of the Sāmānid period, the town proper, unable to absorb the growing population, had become an unpleasant maze of filthy streets. Traces of early caravanserais survive along the trade routes and by the banks of the Oxus and the Jaxartes.

After the Muslim conquest, baked brick, seemingly a Mesopotamian tradition, was preferred to mud brick for mosques, tombs and important civic buildings. Yet in such buildings as the Nuh Gunbad ("nine domes") mosque in Bal<u>kh</u>, while the structural elements including the six massive columns (1.56 m in diameter) were of baked brick, the walls were still made of mud brick. The almost square structure (20 m^2), open on one side opposite the *ḳibla* wall, is entirely plastered and decorated with carved stucco. Spacious grid systems enclose palmettes, leaves, cones and buds not unlike those in Nī<u>sh</u>āpūr, Afrāsiyāb or Sayad near Du<u>sh</u>anbe, but in a more attractive manner than in the possibly contemporary mosque of Nāʾīn [*q.v.*] in Persia. In the Deggaron mosque of Hazāra near Bu<u>kh</u>ārā two series of three domes cover the building, the *ḳibla* domes being higher than the three others. Inside, the columns are less squat and the intrados of the arches broadly pleated; the domes sit on pendentives. The great mosque in <u>Kh</u>īwa echoes the other older tradition of an hypostile hall with wooden columns and carved capitals, four of which have early inscriptions. More wooden carvings have survived in the shape of a cusped-headed *miḥrāb* from Iskodar, in the Zaraf<u>sh</u>an valley, now in the Du<u>sh</u>anbe Museum, and a capital from the mosque in Obburdan, now in Ta<u>sh</u>kent.

A small number of single-domed tombs in baked brick illustrate the possible evolution of such constructions: the so-called tomb of the Sāmānids in Bu<u>kh</u>ārā, a domed square with four entrances, patterned brickwork and corner arches, and the ʿArab-Ata mausoleum in Tim, dated 367/977, with only one entrance emphasised by a complex design, with brickwork and corner arches in smoother patterns. If the inscription of the <u>Sh</u>īr Kabīr mausoleum at Ma<u>sh</u>had-i Miṣriyān in Dihistān allows for a late 4th/10th century dating, then part of its zone of transition with its four receeding arches could be later than its carved stucco *miḥrāb* and niche. Finally, with the restored Mīr Sayyid Bahrām mausoleum at Karmīna, between Samarḳand and Bu<u>kh</u>ārā, appears an early suggestion of a *pī<u>sh</u>tāḳ* [*q.v.*] or raised portal; it emphasises the doorway with a design of arches and frames. By the end of the period, baked brick with its new building possibilities, has asserted itself.

Bibliography: L. Ainy, *Iskusstvo srednei Azii epo<u>kh</u>i Avi<u>ts</u>enny* ("Arts of Central Asia in the time of Avicenna"), Du<u>sh</u>anbe 1980; J.W. Allan, *Nishapur. Metalwork of the early Islamic period*, New York 1982; S. Blair, *The monumental inscriptions from early Islamic Iran and Transoxiana*, Leiden 1992; M. Bulatov, *Mavzolei Samanidov-<u>zh</u>emču<u>zh</u>ina ar<u>kh</u>itektury Srednei Azii* ("The mausoleum of the Samanids, pearl of Central Asian architecture"), Tashkent 1963; Y. Crowe, *Slip-painted wares and Central Asia*, in *Trans. of the Oriental Ceramic Society*, l (1985-6), 58-67; B.P. Denike, *Quelques monuments de bois sculpté au Turkestan occidental*, in *Ars Islamica*, ii (1935), 69-83; L. Golombek, *The Abbasid mosque at Balkh*, in *Oriental Art*, xv (1969), 173-89; V.A. Kračkovska<u>ya</u>, *Evolyu<u>ts</u>i<u>ya</u> kufičeskogo pis'ma v Srednei Azii*, in *Epigrafika Vostoka*, iii (1949), 3-27; C.J. Lamm, *Glass from Iran in the National Museum, Stockholm*, Stockholm and London 1935; A.S. Melikian-Chirvani, *La plus ancienne mosquée de Balkh*, in *Arts Asiatiques*, xx (1969), 3-9; idem, *Islamic metalwork from the Iranian world, 8-18th centuries*, London 1982; *Oxus. 2000 Jahre Kunst am Oxusfluss in Mittelasien. Neue Funde aus der Sowjetrepublik Tadschikistan*, Exhibition Catalogue, Zurich 1989; A.M. Pribītkova, *Pamyatniki ar<u>kh</u>itektury Srednei Azii*, Moscow 1971; G.A. Pugačenkova, *Mavzolei Arab-ata*, in *Iskusstvo Zodči<u>kh</u> Uzbekistana*, ii, Tashkent 1963; eadem, *Iskusstvo Turkmenistana* ("Art of Turkmenistan"), Moscow 1967; R.B. Serjeant, *Islamic textiles*, Beirut 1972; *Terres secrètes de Samarcande: céramiques du VIIIe au XIIIe siècle*, Paris 1992, with bibl. in Russian; G. Ventrone, *Iscrizione insolite su ceramica samanide in collezioni italiane*, in *Gururājmañjarika. Studi in onore di Giuseppe Tucci*, i, Naples 1974, 221-232; L. Volov, *Plaited Kufic on Samanid epigraphic pottery*, in *Ars Orientalis*, vi (1966), 107-34; C.K. Wilkinson, *Nishapur pottery of the early Islamic period*, Metropolitan Museum of Art, New York 1973; idem, *Nishapur, some early Islamic buildings and their decoration*, New York 1987.

(YOLANDE CROWE)

SAMANNŪD, a town of the Delta in Egypt, in the <u>Gh</u>arbiyya province and on the western bank of the Nile (Dimyāṭ/Damietta branch), 8 km/5 miles east of the town of al-Maḥalla al-Kubrā [*q.v.*]. It is an old town, with the name in ancient Egyptian of Zab nutir, i.e. holy place. Greek documents call it Σεβεννυτος (Sebenytos), whence the Arabic name, and in Coptic it was known as Χεμνογτ (Djemnuti).

Samannūd had a very ancient Christian tradition. Athanasius I states that the town had a Melkite bishop in 352 and that the town's name often figures in the old martyrological literature. We know e.g. that the martyr St. Anub passed through Samannūd when coming from Atrib, where he had found the town's churches destroyed and a temple built in their place. In the 14th century, when the *Synaxarion* had already been put together, the body of Anub was at Samannūd, and there has always been a church in the town dedicated to St. Anub.

Arabic geographers like Ibn <u>Kh</u>urradā<u>dh</u>bih and al-Yaʿḳūbī mention the town in the 3rd/8th century, and in the 6th/12th century al-Idrīsī describes its lively commercial activity. From the Fāṭimid period, and after Badr al-<u>Dj</u>amalī's administrative reorganisation, an independent province called al-Samannūdiyya was set up.

In modern times, an administrative district was set up in 1826 called the *ḳism* of Samannūd, with its chef-lieu in the town, and after 1867 it was styled the *markaz* of Samannūd. In 1882 this last was, however, abolished and the district and its administration transferred to al-Maḥalla al-Kubrā. In 1928 it was re-established, and then, because of struggles between political parties, it was abolished three times in less than 7 years until it was definitively re-established in 1935, with the town of Samannūd as chef-lieu of the district.

Bibliography: John of Nikiu, tr. Zotenberg, 245, 366, 560; *Hist. des Patriarches*, in *Patrol. or.*, v, [460] 206, x, [547] 433; *Synaxaire*, in *Patrol. or.*, i, [76-7] 290-1; xvi, [973, 1050], 331, 408, xvii, [1218] 676; Abū <u>Sh</u>āma, *Rawḍatayn*, Cairo 1288, i, 269; Ḳalḳa<u>sh</u>andī, *Ṣubḥ al-aʿ<u>sh</u>ā*, Cairo 1331-8, iii, 327; Ibn Duḳmāḳ, ed. Cairo 1314, v, 77, 91; Maḳrīzī, *<u>Kh</u>iṭaṭ*, ed. Inst. Franç., iii, 223-4, iv, 101, ed. Būlāḳ, ii, 519; Ibn al-<u>Dj</u>īʿān, *al-Tuḥfa al-saniyya*, Cairo 1898, 60, 80; Carra de Vaux, *Abrégé des merveilles*, 217; G. Maspero, in *Jnal. des Savants* (1899), 79; ʿAlī Pa<u>sh</u>a Mubāraḳ, *<u>Kh</u>iṭaṭ <u>dj</u>adīda*, xii, 46-50, xvi, 65-6; Baedeker, *Egypt*; Guide Joanne, *Egypte*, 361, 366; J. Maspero, *Organis. milit. de l'Egypte byzantine*, 131, 139; *Hist. des Patr. d'Alexandrie*, 371-3; Caetani, *Chronogr. islamica*, 1707; bibl. given in J. Maspero and G. Wiet, *Matériaux p. servir à la géogr. de l'Egypte*, 29, 31-2, 106, 187-8; Ibn Mammātī, *Ḳawānīn al-dawāwīn*, ed. A.S. ʿAṭiyya, Cairo 1943, 576; Idrīsī, *Opus geographicum*, Naples-Rome 1970-84, 336-7, 340; Muḥammad Ramzī, *al-Ḳāmūs al-<u>dj</u>u<u>gh</u>rāfī li 'l-bilād al-miṣriyya*, Cairo 1955-68, ii/2, 69-76; R. Stewart, in *The Coptic encyclopedia*, New York 1989, vii, 2090.

(AYMAN F. SAYYID)

SAMARITANS [see AL-SĀMIRA].

SAMARḲAND, an ancient city of Transoxania, the Arabic Māʾ warāʾ al-Nahr [*q.v.*], situated on the southern bank of the Zarаf<u>sh</u>ān river or Nahr Ṣu<u>gh</u>d. In early Islamic times it was the first city of the region in extent and populousness, even when, as under the Sāmānids (3rd-4th/9th-10th centuries [*q.v.*]), Bu<u>kh</u>ārā [*q.v.*] was the administrative capital. Samarḳand's eminence arose from its position at the intersection of trade routes from India and Af<u>gh</u>ānistān via Bal<u>kh</u> and Tirmi<u>dh</u> [*q.vv.*] and from Persia via Marw [see MARW AL-<u>SH</u>ĀHI<u>DJ</u>ĀN] which then led northwards and eastwards into the Turkish steppes and along the Silk Road to eastern Turkistan and China; but above all it flourished because of the great fertility of the surrounding district of Soghdia or Ṣu<u>gh</u>d [*q.v.*], the highly-irrigated basin of the Zaraf<u>sh</u>ān which could support a dense agricultural population (see Barthold, *Turkestan down to the Mongol invasion*,[3] 83 ff.).

1. History.

The city—the second part of the name of which contains the Eastern Iranian word for "town", *kand*, frequent in Eastern Iranian place-names (cf.

Buddhist-Soghdian *knd-*, Christian Soghd. *kath, kanth*), while the first part has not yet been satisfactorily explained (cf. the attempts by Tomaschek, *Centralasiatische Studien*, i, *Sogdiana*, in *SB Ak. Wien*, lxxxvii [1887], 133 ff.)—is first found in the accounts of Alexander's campaigns in the east as Maracanda, Μαρακάνδα, whose site at Tepe Afrāsiyāb has yielded Hellenistic archaeological evidence (see P. Bernard, *Alexandre et l'Asie Centrale*, in *St.Ir.*, xix [1990], 29-32). Arrian (iii, 30) calls it βασίλεια τῆς Σογδιανῶν χώρας. Alexander occupied it several times during the fighting with Spitamenes and, according to Strabo (xi, ii, 4), razed it to the ground (while Arab legend makes him, as well as the Tubbaᶜ [*q.v.*] king Shamir Yurᶜish, founder of the city). Under the Diadochi—after the partition of 323 BC—as the capital of Sogdiana, it belonged to the satrapy of Bactria and was lost to the Seleucids with Bactria when Diodotos declared himself independent and the Graeco-Bactrian kingdom was founded during the reign of Antiochus II Theos; henceforth it was exposed to the attacks of the northern barbarians (cf. *PW*, xiv/2, art. *Marakanda*, cols. 1421-2). From this time up to the Muslim conquest it remained historically and economically separated from Persia, although cultural intercourse with Western lands continued. (On the settlement of Manichaeans in Samarkand, cf. J. Marquart, *Historische Glossen zu den alttürkischen Inschriften*, in *WZKM*, xii [1898], 163; the attempts made by E. West to refer Čīn and Čīnistān in the *Bundahishn* and *Bahmanyasht* to Samarkand are very unsatisfactory.) The only positive information is given by Chinese imperial historians and travellers (of which the former are unfortunately for the most part only available in obsolete translations). From the Han period the kingdom of K'ang-Kü is mentioned, whose chief territory, K'ang, is definitely identified in the T'ang Annals with Sa-mo-kian = Samarkand (cf. the passages in C. Ritter, *Erdkunde*, vii,² 657 ff.). According to the Annals of the Wei, compiled in 437 AD (cf. F. Hirth, in Marquart, *Die Chronologie der alttürkischen Inschriften*, Leipzig 1898, 65-6), the Čau-wu dynasty related to the Yüe-či (Kushan) had been reigning here since before the Christian era. Hiüen-tsang visited Sa-mo-kian in 630 AD and briefly describes it (St. Julien, *Mémoires sur les contrées Occidentales*, i, Paris 1857, 18-19; S. Beal, *Si-yu-ki, Buddhist Records*, i, 1884, 32-3, with valuable bibliographical note on p. 101).

The Muslim Arabs do not appear for certain in the affairs of Samarkand until the time of the governor of Khurāsān Kutayba b. Muslim [*q.v.*]; the alleged tomb at Afrāsiyāb of the *Shāh-i Zinda*, the Prophet Muhammad's cousin Kutham b. al-ᶜAbbās [*q.v.*], who was supposed to have been in Samarkand in 56/676 (cf. Barthold, *Turkestan*, 91-2), must have appeared later as part of a family cult inaugurated by the ᶜAbbāsids after they came to power in 132/750, possibly adapting a pre-Islamic cult on this site. The Iranian ruler of Samarkand at the time of Kutayba was Ṭarkhūn (probably a title rather than a personal name; for this very old title amongst the Turks of Inner Asia, possibly of Chinese origin, see R.N. Frye, *Ṭarxūn-Ṭürxün and Central Asian history*, in *HJAS*, xiv [1951], 110-11; C.E. Bosworth and Sir Gerard Clauson, *Al-Xwārazmī on the peoples of Central Asia*, in *JRAS* [1975], 11-12), called *malik Ṣughd* or *malik Samarkand* in the Arabic historical sources, and first mentioned in 85/704 in warfare with Kutayba at Bukhārā. In 91/710 Kutayba sent his brother ᶜAbd al-Raḥmān to Samarkand in order to collect tribute, which Ṭarkhūn paid; but the anti-Arab party in the city then deposed the latter, who was either killed or committed suicide. There replaced him another Soghdian prince, Ghūrak, who ruled in Samarkand for some 27 years until his death in 119/737 or 120/738, with an Arab garrison in his city. Gradually, the Arabs consolidated their position in Soghdia, but Ghūrak's policy towards them oscillated between conciliation and attempts to call in aid from the Chinese Emperors as nominal suzerains over Central Asia or from the Turks. In 102/721 the Türgesh appeared in Soghdia under their leader Kūr-ṣul or Köl-čur; and in 110/728 Ghūrak joined in a general rising of the Soghdians, with Turkish help, against the Arabs, so that the Arabs in Transoxania were temporarily reduced to their garrisons at Samarkand and at Dabūsiyya. Not till the late 730s, with the strong measures of the governor Naṣr b. Sayyār [*q.v.*], was Arab authority firmly established again (see Barthold, *Turkestan*, 184-93; H.A.R. Gibb, *The Arab conquests in Central Asia*, London 1923, 36, 42-8, 55, 60-1, 65 ff., 89-90).

Although Kutayba had built a mosque in Samarkand, the progress of Islamisation there, outside the Arab garrison, must have been slow. There were certainly adherents of many other faiths in the city at this time. In *ca.* 629 AD, the Chinese traveller Hiuen-tsang had found only two abandoned Buddhist monasteries there, and Buddhism had almost certainly disappeared a century or so later (Spuler, *Iran*, 218). But there was probably already a Nestorian Christian bishopric in Samarkand during the 6th century, and in the early 8th century, it was erected into a metropolitan see; at the beginning of the 9th/15th century, Clavijo (see below) still found many Christians in Samarkand, but the end of the community seems to have come within the reign of Ulugh Beg shortly afterwards, and nothing is thereafter heard of it (see B.R. Colless, *The Nestorian province of Samarqand*, in *Abr Nahrain*, xxiv [1986], 51-7). In the mid-4th/10th century, Ibn Ḥawkal described a Christian community (*ᶜumr*) with monastic cells, on the hill of Shāwdhār to the south of Samarkand, whose inhabitants included Christians from ᶜIrāk (Barthold, *Zur Geschichte des Christentums in Mittel-Asien bis zur mongolischen Eroberung*, Tübingen-Leipzig 1901, 22 ff., 30-1; Yule-Cordier, *Cathay and the way thither*, London 1915-16, i, 103-4, iii, 22-3; Ibn Ḥawkal, ed. Kramers, 498, tr. Kramers-Wiet, 477-8). Not long after this time, the *Ḥudūd al-ᶜālam*, tr. 113, § 25.13, comm. 352, mentions a convent of the Manichaeans at Samarkand (*khānagāh-i Mānawiyān*) with adherents called *nigūshāk* "auditores", doubtless the Manichaeans who had fled from ᶜIrāk in fear of persecution during the time of al-Muktadir.

In the early ᶜAbbāsid period, the Zarafshān valley was deeply affected during the caliphate of al-Mahdī (158-69/775-85) by the Neo-Mazdakite movement of the "wearers of white" led by al-Mukannaᶜ [*q.v.*], and the governor of Samarkand Djibrāʾīl b. Yaḥyā, helped to suppress the revolt in his area. Abū Muslim [*q.v.*] is said to have built the outer wall of the city (al-Ṭabarī, iii, 80, tr. J.A. Williams, Albany 1985, 203), and Hārūn al-Rashīd to have restored it after it had fallen into decay (al-Yaᶜkūbī, *Buldān*, 293, tr. Wiet, 110). The rebel against the central government Rāfiᶜ b. al-Layth [*q.v.*] began his outbreak in Samarkand in 190/806 by killing the governor there and seizing the city, holding it until he surrendered to al-Maʾmūn in 193/809 (al-Ṭabarī, iii, 707-8, tr. C.E. Bosworth, Albany 1989, 259-61). It is also from the early ᶜAbbāsid period that we have the first Islamic coins issued from Samarkand, beginning with issues of 142-4/759-62 (E. von Zambaur, *Die Münzprägungen des Islams, zeitlich und örtlich geordnet*, i, Wiesbaden 1968, 148-9).

At the command of al-Maʾmūn, the governor of

Khurāsān Ghassān b. ʿAbbād in *ca.* 204/819 allotted to the four sons of Asad b. Sāmān-Khudā various cities of Transoxania and eastern Khurāsān as governorships, and Nūḥ received Samarḳand. On his death in 227/842, the city eventually passed under the control of his brother Aḥmad (d. 250/864), whose copper *fulūs* were struck there from 244/858 onwards. With the collapse of Ṭāhirid authority in Khurāsān under Ṣaffārid attacks, Naṣr b. Aḥmad found himself virtually independent ruler of Transoxania with his capital at Samarḳand. However, his brother and eventual vanquisher Ismāʿīl, progenitor of all the future Sāmānid *amīrs*, made Bukhārā the Sāmānid capital, although Samarḳand remained over the following centuries the commercial centre of Transoxania.

It was, for a start, one of the principal markets for Turkish slaves brought from Inner Asia, and Ibn Ḥawḳal, 494, tr. 474, states that slaves trained at Samarḳand were the best of all from Transoxania. But one of its most famous products, exported all over the Islamic world, was paper, introduced thither by the Chinese artisans captured at the battle of Ṭalas in 133/751 (al-Thaʿālibī, *Laṭāʾif al-maʿārif*, ed. al-Abyārī and al-Ṣayrafī, 218, tr. Bosworth, *The Book of Curious and Entertaining Information*, Edinburgh 1968, 140; and see KĀGHAD). It was, moreover, a centre for scholarship. The great Ḥanafī theologian al-Māturīdī (d. *ca.* 333/944 [*q.v.*]) stemmed from the Māturīd quarter of Samarḳand, his tomb in the city being still shown in the 9th/15th century, and another Ḥanafī theologian and Ḳurʾān commentator was Abu 'l-Layth al-Samarḳandī (d. towards the end of the 4th/10th century [*q.v.*]). Unfortunately, the local history written in Arabic by the famous theologian Abū Ḥafṣ ʿUmar b. Muḥammad al-Nasafī (d. 537/1142-3 [*q.v.*]), the *Kitāb al-Ḳand fī maʿrifat ʿulamāʾ Samarḳand*, which dealt with the shrines and graves of local scholars and also with some of the city's historical events, has come down to us only in an abridgement of a Persian translation (see Storey, i, 371; Storey-Bregel, ii, 1112-15; Barthold, *Turkestan*, 15-16).

It is to the heyday of the Sāmānids, the 4th/10th century, that the descriptions of Samarḳand by the geographers al-Iṣṭakhrī, Ibn Ḥawḳal, al-Muḳaddasī and the author of the *Ḥudūd al-ʿālam* refer. They show that Samarḳand had the typical tripartite formation of Iranian towns: a citadel (*kuhandiz*, arabicised *ḳuhandiz* or translated *ḳalʿa*), the town proper (*shahristān, shāristān, madīna*) and suburbs (*rabaḍ*). The three parts are here given in their order from south to north. The citadel lay south of the town on an elevated site; it contained the administrative offices (*dār al-imāra*) and the prison (*ḥabs*). The town itself, of which the houses were built of clay and wood (cf. E. Herzfeld, in *Islam*, xi, 162, and E. Diez, *Persien*, i (*Kulturen der Erde*, xx, Hagen-Darmstadt 1923), 20), was also on a hill. A deep ditch (*khandaḳ*) had been dug around it to obtain the material for the surrounding earthen wall. The whole town was supplied with running water, which was brought from the south to the central square of the town called *Raʾs al-Ṭāḳ* by an aqueduct, a lead-covered artificial channel (or system of lead pipes?), running underground. It seems to have dated from the pre-Islamic period as its supervision, as is expressly stated, was in the hands of Zoroastrians, who were exempted from the poll-tax for this duty. This aqueduct made possible the irrigation of the extensive and luxurious gardens in the town. The town had four main gates; to the east, the *Bāb al-Ṣīn*, a memorial of the ancient connection with China due to the silk trade; to the north, the *Bāb Bukhārā*; to the west, the *Bāb al-Nawbahār*, which name, as in Bukhārā and Balkh, points to a (Buddhist) monastery; and to the south, the *Bāb al-Kabīr* or *Bāb Kishsh* (*bāb* stands for the Persian *darwāza*). The lower-lying suburbs adjoin the town, stretching towards the Zarafshān and surrounded by a wall with 8 gates. In them lay the majority of the bazaars, caravanserais and warehouses, which were rare in the city itself. The government offices of the Sāmānids and the Friday mosque were in the city itself. See al-Iṣṭakhrī, 316-23; Ibn Ḥawḳal, ed. Kramers, 491-501, tr. Kramers-Wiet, 472-9; al-Muḳaddasī, 278-9; *Ḥudūd al-ʿālam, loc. cit.*; al-Thaʿālibī, *Laṭāʾif al-maʿārif*, 217-19, tr. Bosworth, 140-1; Yāḳūt, *Buldān*, ed. Beirut, iii, 246-50; al-Ḳazwīnī, *Āthār al-bilād*, 395 ff.; Le Strange, *The lands of the eastern caliphate*, 460, 463-6.

Samarḳand was, together with Bukhārā, occupied by the incoming Ḳarakhānids in 382/992, and with the defeat of the last Sāmānid, Ismāʿīl b. Nūḥ al-Muntaṣir [*q.v.*], in 394/1004, passed definitively under Turkish control. In the second quarter of the 5th/11th century it became, under ʿAlī b. Hārūn Boghra Khān, called ʿAlītigin [*q.v.*], and then under the parallel line of the descendants of the Ilig Naṣr, the eventual capital of the western khānate of the Ḳarakhānids, covering Transoxania and western Farghāna [see ILEK KHĀNS]. With such rulers as Shams al-Mulk Naṣr b. Tamghač Khān Ibrāhīm, Samarḳand became in the later 5th/11th century a splendid cultural and artistic centre. The city also became a regular mint centre for the Ḳarakhānids. But after the battle of the Ḳaṭwān Steppe in 536/1141, when the Saldjūḳ sultan Sandjar [*q.v.*] and his vassal Maḥmūd b. Muḥammad Khān were decisively defeated by the pagan Ḳara Khiṭay [*q.v.*], Samarḳand and Bukhārā became the centre of a reduced Ḳarakhānid principality under Ḳara Khiṭay overlordship. It nevertheless continued to flourish commercially, and in *ca.* 1170 the Spanish Jewish traveller Benjamin of Tudela visited Samarḳand and allegedly found there 50,000 Jews (M.N. Adler, *The itinerary of Benjamin of Tudela*, London 1907, 59. The last Ḳarakhānid in Samarḳand, ʿUthmān Khān b. Ibrāhīm, was executed by the Khwārazm-Shāh ʿAlāʾ al-Dīn Muḥammad [*q.v.*] in 608/1212, and the city occupied by the Khwārazmians. But shortly afterwards, the Mongols of Čingiz Khān [*q.v.*] reached Transoxania, and after conquering Bukhārā in 616/1220, they arrived at Samarḳand, the concentration-point for the Khwārazm-Shāh's forces, in the spring of 617/1220. The city fell after a five days' siege (Rabīʿ I 617/May 1220, or possibly Muḥarram 617/March 1220). After it had been devastated, some of the citizens were allowed by the Mongols to return after payment of a ransom of 200,000 dīnārs (Djuwaynī-Boyle, i, 115-22; Barthold, *Turkestan*, 411-14).

For the next century-and-a-half, Samarḳand was only a shadow of its former self. The Taoist hermit Ch'ang-ch'un (travelled in Western Asia 1221-4) states that there were 100,000 families in the city before the Mongol sacking, but only a quarter of these remained in *Sie-mi-se-kan* after that (E. Bretschneider, *Mediaeval researches from eastern Asiatic sources*, London 1910, i, 76-9; on the form *Sie-mi-se-kan*, cf. the Latin travellers' *Semiscant* and Clavijo's *Cimesquinte*, Yule-Cordier, *Cathay and the way thither*, iii, 39). In the mid-8th/4th century, Ibn Baṭṭūṭa found the population much reduced, and the city ruinous and without a wall (*Riḥla*, iii, 51-2, tr. Gibb, iii, 567-8).

The revival of the town's prosperity began when Tīmūr [*q.v.*] after about 771/1369 became supreme in

Transoxania and chose Samarḳand as the capital of his continually-increasing kingdom, and began to adorn in with all splendour. In 808/1405 the Spanish envoy Ruy Gonzales de Clavijo visited it in its new glory (see the Spanish-Russian edition of his itinerary by I. Sreznevskiy in the *Sbornik otd. Russk. Yaz.*, xxviii [1881], 325 ff.; Eng. tr. Le Strange, *Narrative of the Spanish embassy ... 1403-1406*, London 1928). He gives Cimesquiente as the native name of the town, which he explains as *aldea gruesa* "large (lit. thick) village"; in this we have an echo of a Turkish corruption of the name of the town based on a popular etymology which connects it with *sämiz* "thick". The Bavarian soldier Johann Schiltberger seems also to have been in Samarḳand at this time (*Reisebuch*, Stuttgart 1885, 61, Eng. tr. J.B. Telfer, London 1879). Tīmūr's grandson Ulugh Beg (d. 853/1449 [*q.v.*]) embellished the city with his palace Čihil Sutūn and built his famous astronomical observatory there; on him, see W. Barthold, *Ulugh-Beg*, in *Four studies on the history of Central Asia*, ii, Leiden 1958. A very full description of the city in Tīmūr's day, which may be justly described as classical, is given by the memoirs of Bābur (*Bābur-nāma*, ed. Ilminski, 55 ff.; ed. Beveridge, 54b ff.; French tr. Pavet de Courteille, i, 96 ff.; Eng. tr. Beveridge, 74-86; Čaghatay (in translit.) and Persian ed. and tr. W.M. Thackston, Cambridge, Mass. 1993, 90 ff.), who captured Samarḳand for the first time in 903/1497 and held it for some months. In 906/1500 it was occupied by his rival, the Özbeg Shībānī Khān. After his death, Bābur, in alliance with the Shībānī Ṣafawid Ismāʿīl Shāh, succeeded in 916/1510 in once more victoriously invading Transoxania and occupying Samarḳand, but by the next year he found himself forced to withdraw completely to his Indian kingdom and leave the field to the Özbegs. Under the latter, Samarḳand was only the nominal capital and fell completely behind Bukhārā.

During the 18th century, Samarḳand fell into severe economic decline and in the middle years of that century was virtually uninhabited. However, when the extension of Russian Imperial power into Central Asia accelerated in the later 19th century, Samarḳand was occupied by Russian troops under General K.P. Kaufmann in November 1868 and a treaty of vassalage imposed on the *amīr* of Bukhārā, within whose territories Samarḳand had fallen. The city was now detached from Muẓaffar al-Dīn Khān's nominally independent khānate of Bukhārā and became part of the directly-ruled Russian Governorate-General of Turkestan. After 1871 a new Russian town sprang up to the west of the old city, with a station on the Trans-Caspia to Tashkent railway. The great anti-Russian rebellion of Turkestan in 1916, when the Tsarist government attempted to conscript the non-Russian local populations for labour service, began in the Samarḳand *oblast*. Under the Soviet régime, the *oblast* became one of those making up the Turkestan Autonomous SSR in 1918, and then in 1924, part of the Uzbek SSR, of which Samarḳand was at first the capital but replaced by Tashkent [*q.v.*] in 1930. Since 1990 it has come within the Uzbekistan Republic. The modern city (lat. 39° 40′ N., long. 66° 58′ E., altitude 710 m/2,330 feet), an important centre for the processing of foodstuffs and for industry, had in 1970 a population of 257,000 (see *BSE*², xxii, cols. 1571-7).

Bibliography (in addition to references given in the article): E. Schuyler, *Turkistan. Notes of a journey in Russian Turkistan, Khokand, Bukhara, and Kuldja*, London 1876, i, 225-67; F.H. Skrine and E.D. Ross, *The heart of Asia, a history of Russian Turkestan and the Central Asian khanates*..., London 1899, index; Yule-Cordier, *The Book of Ser Marco Polo*³, London 1922, i, 183-7; G.E. Wheeler, *The modern history of Soviet Central Asia*, London 1964, index.

(H.H. Schaeder-[C.E. Bosworth])

2. Architecture.

Archaeologists refer to the ruins of Samarḳand as Afrāsiyāb after the destruction of the town by Čingiz Khān [*q.v.*] in 617/1220. A museum on the site preserves fragments of stucco ornament and ceramics [see sāmānids. 2]. Thereafter, under Tīmūr and his successors, the earlier southern suburbs of the town became the new Samarḳand with its striking ceramic revetment and typical modular architecture. The shrine of Ḳutham b. al-ʿAbbās [*q.v.*] known as the *Shāh-i Zinda* "the living prince", had survived on the southern slopes of Afrāsiyāb. Recent excavations, particularly those directed by N.B. Nemtseva in 1962, have revealed the base of a 5th/11th-century minaret in the north-west corner of the shrine as well as an earlier mausoleum, the underground mosque and a semi-underground chamber, all reflected in the later renovations. The south-eastern corner of a *madrasa*, possibly a funerary construction, was excavated to the west and opposite the shrine, if a *waḳf* of the Ḳarakhānid Ibrāhīm b. Naṣr Tamghač Bughra Khān dated Radjab 458/June 1066, relates to it.

The *Shāh-i Zindā* ensemble. Cemeteries develop around shrines of holy men. Here mausolea are like scattered jewels with the shimmering of their blue-turquoise tile glazing enhanced with bichrome bands in white and black or turquoise. A series of tombs, with portal and domed room, lines an ancient north-south alley, while the shrine itself stands at its top northern end. Its lower section, off-centred to the east, overrides the old walls of Afrāsiyāb. The two main 9th/15th century *čahār ṭāḳ*s emphasise the entrance to the shrine (CT1) and the lower southern monumental entrance (CT2) to the whole alley; a subsidiary one (CT3), late 18th century, stands at the top of steps. Its southern face (CT1) carries remains of ten-pointed star vertical panels in tile mosaic which include hexagonal terra cotta elements around the stars.

1. The shrine, entered through delicately carved wooden doors (806/1403-4), consists of (a) a mausoleum/*gūr-khāna*, (b) a *ziyārāt-khāna* (735/1334-5), (c) a *masdjid* (15th century), (d) a minaret (11th century), (e) an ambulatory/*miyān-khāna*. The original mausoleum with its tiled *muḳarnas* and dome in blue and turquoise, was in (b). The *masdjid* stands over the older one, the *miḥrāb* inscription in tile mosaic, quotes surā II, 139.

2. At the southern end of the ensemble, the monumental entrance with *hazārbāf*, "a thousand weave" decoration, is dedicated to Ulugh Beg's son, ʿAbd al-Azīz (838/1434-5), and leads into the *čahār ṭāḳ* (CT2). On its west side, a doorway opens into a contemporary mosque. The east door leads into a later *madrasa* (1227/1812-13).

3. An excavated anonymous mausoleum, 7th/13th century.

4. The mausoleum of Khʷādja Aḥmad (1350s) remains the only surviving building to recall the older east-west road of the ensemble; it is "The work of Faḳr [b.] ʿAlī", and a variety of deep moulded glazed tiles enhance the portal: a band of calligraphy in white against a turquoise scroll, a frame of underglaze black painted star tiles with a turquoise glaze and a *girikh*, a "knot" decoration, in turquoise and unglazed terra cotta in the tympanum.

5. A mausoleum for an anonymous lady, earlier

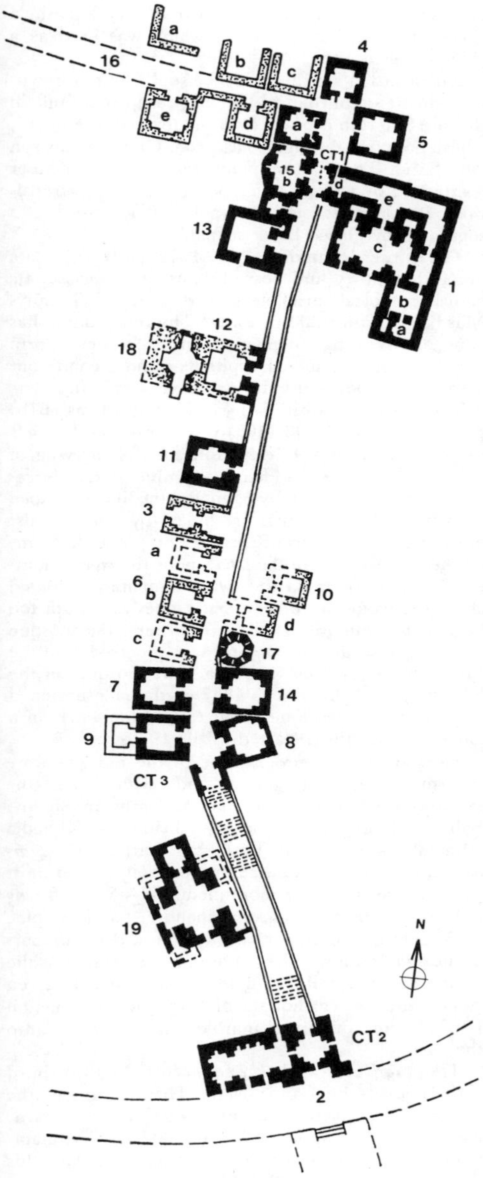

The Shāh-i Zinda, after Rogers.

known as ᶜArab Shāh, perhaps one of Tīmūr's first wives, Ḳutlūgh Āḳā (13 Ṣafar 762/12 December 1361). A restored plinth and two steps under the portal lead into the mausoleum. There are similar colour harmonies and moulded glazed tiles, inside and outside tiled *muḳarnas*, as in 4.

6. a.b.c.d. Excavated mausolea dating to the 1360s.

7. The mausoleum of Shād-i Mulk Āḳā (who died on 20 Djumādā II 773/29 December 1371) was built by her mother Turkān Āḳā (died 785/1383), Tīmūr's elder sister. The calligraphy of the portal in Arabic refers to the building and the daughter, the Persian below the *muḳarnas* praises the building. The Persian around the door frame mentions the "pearl" buried within. Three craftmen have left their signatures, with unclear *nisbas*: Birr al-Dīn, Shams al-Dīn and Zayn al-Dīn. Here is to be seen the best-preserved tile decoration of the ensemble. The restored portal over the entrance was originally higher. Eight frames arise from a plinth of three square ornate panels; they are hemmed in on either side by deeply carved turquoise engaged columns. Two of the frames are larger, with calligraphic and star patterns enclosed in a risen border. Underglazed painted tiles of irregular shapes, in delicate turquoise and white on blue, fill the spandrels with leafy lotuses around a raised roundel. These tiles are also used for the large frame inscription and around the four carved and glazed panels of the inner portal containing a lotus-filled *miḥrāb* and an upper roundel. The *muḳarnas* of the portal are echoed in those of the chamber, which measures about 42 m² and is all glazed with lotuses and leaves, small *girikh*s and *miḥrāb*s; large roundels almost fill the tiled wall panels, three aside. Eight black and white ribbed panels, each containing a "tear-drop" motif, meet at the apex of the inner dome in an eight-pointed star. A feeling of lightness emanates from the decoration despite its dense patterning.

8. Only the portal remains of the mausoleum of *Amīr* Ḥusayn/Tughlūḳ Tekīn, who died in 777/1376; he was one of Tīmūr's generals. The vault goes back to the 6th/12th century.

9. The Amīr-zāde mausoleum, 788/1386, stands east of an earlier crypt and on the south side of 7. In a similar manner, two frames filled with turquoise moulded rosettes and calligraphic *haft rang* [*q.v.*] tiles, are enclosed in risen borders, the lower part being two *haft rang* tile panels. The slightly recessed entrance is three-quarters framed by a band of square tiles with moulded square Kūfic (Muḥammad and ᶜAlī) based on minute lozenges of terra cotta, possibly gold originally, with a red dot or glazed in blue with turquoise and blue infill; above it, a tympanum of hexagonal star-filled tiles encompasses two central panels in *haft rang* tiles. A ribbed inner single shell dome over a plain chamber over 38 m² was plastered in the 19th century.

10. An excavated mausoleum, late 8th/14th century.

11. The mausoleum is the work of Ustād ᶜĀlim-i Nasafī in the 1380s, with turquoise glazed plugs in its south brick wall; there is no trace of the outer dome, only a 16-sided drum of *hazārbāf* panels in black and turquoise. The ceramic programme is a mixture of old and new techniques and designs. The vertical panels of the portal strapwork recall the design on the base of the Djām minaret [*q.v.*], sūra CIX, 1; CXII; and CXIV, 2-3. The panels and stars within also contain glazed moulded Kūfic inscriptions, mostly in white on a blue ground. Large floral *haft rang* tiles make up the inner panels and the corner engaged columns; yellow, pale green and light brown for red, now add to the general turquoise impression. A splendid turquoise *girikh* punctuates the border of the right outer wall. Rectangular panels filled with hexagonal tiles cover the walls of the shrine, and corner arches with *muḳarnas* lead to a dome covered in strapwork *girikh* filled with the same hexagonal tiles, all of which create a suffused turquoise vision.

12. The mausoleum known as that of Ulugh Sulṭān Begum, was built in the 1380s over part of the 5th/11th century *madrasa*. A roofless portal survives with *lādjward* (dark blue) tile panels, and framed and moulded turquoise glazed narrow *girikh* containing small *lādjward* tiles. A combination of calligraphic tiles in gold and white against a leafy scroll survives on the front. The red cinnabar, now visible, was originally hidden by the gold leaf décor. The use of dark blue

and gold, recalling Chinese textiles, appears here for the last time.

13. The mausoleum of "*Amīr* Burunduḳ", dated to the end of 8th/14th century, adjoins the Ṭūmān Āḳā complex to the south. Only the right side of the portal remains with its *hazārbāf* panel. Nine burials were found in the crypt, as well as some textiles.

14. "This is the tomb of the great and noble queen, Shīrīn Bika Āḳā, daughter of Ṭaraghay, 787[/1385-6]". Taraghay was the sister of Tīmūr. The mausoleum has the earliest double-shell dome with an outer bold *hazārbāf* pattern and remains of tile mosaic panels on the drum. The higher than usual portal, *ca.* 11 m, is decorated with a dense composition of calligraphic bands, arabesques and stylised flowers. Blue remains the dominant colour, with added turquoise and white, and a touch of light brown. The 36 m^2 mausoleum rises to a total height of about 18 m. The dado is tiled with hexagonal green tiles with gold cranes in flight inspired by contemporary Chinese textiles. The rest is painted plaster with elongated cartouches at the base of the sixteen-sided drum as in 19. The walls are divided into niche-shaped panels filled with vegetal or stylised leave patterns.

15. The mausoleum with two *hazārbāf* walls and a tiled double dome *ca.* 15 m high, is attributed to Ṭūmān Āḳā (808/1405-6); set next to the undated *masdjid/khānaḳāh* of Ṭūmān Āḳā, it contains the tomb of *Amīr* Abū Saᶜīd Mahdī b. Ḥaydār dated 733/1332-3 or 833/1429-30. Tile mosaics decorate the three entrances with blue and some black ground. In the north entrance to the mosque, the ten-pointed star pattern meshes with a blue *girikh*. This *girikh* is lined in white, a well-known device of carpet designers when a motif requires enhancing. Other colours are green, light brown, turquoise and plain terra cotta. Intricate plaster *muḳarnas* lead to the painted dome.

16. a.b.c.d.e. These excavated mausolea overlook the east-west road.

17. This octagonal mausoleum, with arch openings on all sides and crude *hazārbāf* décor, is dated to around 1440. It would have had a double dome. Remains of a plaster painted inscription can still be seen on the inside of the octagon (sūra II, 256).

18. A 9th/15th-century excavated burial vault is sited west of 12.

19. The two turquoise tiled double-domed buildings of the so-called Ḳāḍī-zāde Rūmī mausoleum, built in the 1420s, stand out from afar with their larger part rising to 23 m. *Hazārbāf* patterns animate both drums, with a *ḥadīth* inscription on the larger one. More patterning would have covered the south portal. Chambers were excavated to the west and east. The zone of transition and dome of the tomb chamber, almost 10 m^2, consist of elaborate plaster *muḳarnas*; the crypt contained remains of a female in her mid-thirties. This is the only building in the ensemble with a feeling of space, partly due to unpatterned plain walls or dados of unglazed hexagonal tiles framed by blue glazed strips.

The mosque of Ḥaḍrat Khiḍr. Its name recalls the saint-protector of travellers and master of the water of life, Khiḍr [*q.v.*]. On the south slope of Afrāsiyāb, this summer mosque, with its wooden columns, overlooks the site of the Iron Gate and the road to Tashkent. Built in the 19th century with two small minarets and a squat dome on foundations going back to Soghdian times, it was restored in 1915 by ᶜAbd al-Ḳādir Bakiev.

Little remains of the citadel in the western part of the town. It contained the usual administrative buildings, the treasury, the armoury, the Čihil Sutūn, the Gök Saray, and the palace with the Gök-Tash, a carved grey marble monolith which was used as a ceremonial throne.

Rūḥābād, "The abode of the soul", in mid-town. The shrine of Burhān al-Dīn Saghardjī was built in the late 8th/14th century over the tomb of the *shaykh*, whose body was brought back from China by his son Abū Saᶜīd. The massive plain square tomb chamber is crowned by a dome on an octagonal zone of transition. Its dado consists of unglazed octagonal tiles separated by glazed black strips.

The mausoleum of Saray Mulk Khānum is late 8th/14th century and possibly part of a *madrasa*. Its vanished portal briefly rivalled that of Tīmūr's Masdjid-i Djāmiᶜ 200 m away. The inner dome has gone; the semi-basement crypt in brick is cruciform like the main chamber. Despite its ruinous condition, a variety of tiles and paintings have survived.

The vast Masdjid-i Djāmiᶜ known as Bībī Khānum (801-8/1398-1405) was started on Tīmūr's return from India; 95 elephants for the carrying of quarried stones were added to an immense task force. Its *ṣaḥn* measures 87 m by 63 m and the four L-shaped halls, with 480 columns, are linked by four portals, one of which, the entrance *pīshṭāḳ* [*q.v.*], rises to 41 m. At the opposite end of the *ṣaḥn* stands the *miḥrāb* domed chamber; in India the two lateral minor domed chambers would have been extra gateways. Built too fast, with a minaret at all four corners, the mosque soon began to deteriorate and was superseded in the 11th/17th century by the Tilla Kārī mosque on the Rigistān (see below). The 1897 earthquake hastened the collapse of the domes, but restoration work on a long-term basis was started in the 1970s.

Parts of the tile programme of the mosque were determined by its large size and recall that of the slightly earlier gateway to the Aḳ Saray in Shahr-i Sabz and the contemporary shrine of Khʷādja Aḥmad Yasawī [*q.v.*] in Turkestan. Large-scale *hazārbāf* patterns, with a dominant of turquoise, cover most parts of the surviving monument; six-sided *haft rang* tiles still fill the space of some spandrels, and complex tile shapes including twelve-sided ones, decorate part of the *miḥrāb* dome. The restored portal as well as the plinth and dados of the main entrance are of carved stone. After the earthquake of 1875, the monumental Ḳurᵓān stand of carved marble was moved out into the *ṣaḥn*.

The *madrasa* and *khānaḳāh* of Muḥammad Sulṭān and the Gūr-i Mīr. The remains of the *madrasa* and *khānaḳāh*, on either side of a courtyard, were probably completed in 1401/803-4 by Muḥammad Sulṭān, Tīmūr's favourite grandson. After his death in Anatolia in 805/1403, Tīmūr had an octagonal mausoleum built for his remains, on the south side, known as the Gūr-i Mīr, "the World Master". Its turquoise melon-shaped double dome soars to a height of 37 m. A gigantic Kūfic inscription "God is eternal" runs round the drum. Tīmūr was buried here in 807/1405 as well as later Tīmūrids. Ulugh Beg added an eastern gallery to the mausoleum in 827/1424. Muḥammad b. Maḥmūd al-Bannāᵓ al-Iṣfahānī signed a concluding portal in 837/1434. An unfinished 11th/17th-century *īwān* still stands on the west side. The last standing minaret collapsed in 1903.

The inner room of the mausoleum, about 100 m^2, with its high cupola, has painted pendentives with gold leaf decoration; its dado, in onyx and further gaudy restoration in blue and gold, contrast with the dark nephrite of Tīmūr's cenotaph. The stone was brought by Ulugh Beg from Inner Asia in 828/1425 and is inscribed with Tīmūr's genealogy. This and other cenotaphs are surrounded by a delicately-carved marble railing. Six cenotaphs are echoed in the cruciform crypt by simpler tombstones similarly inscribed.

The *Rigistān*. In the 8th/14th and 9th/15th centuries, six main roads converged towards this sandy area, a crossroad of cultural and commercial life. When Ulugh Beg reshaped the square, he erected a *khānaḳāh*, a caravanserai and two mosques; only his *madrasa*, 56 m by 81 m, famous for its learned scholars, survives on the west side of the square with its *pīshṭāḳ* rising to 34.7 m. The mosque stands at the opposite end of its square courtyard with four corner domed halls; it is surrounded by a series of lesser *īwāns* each with two levels of cells. Only two of the four corner minarets have survived. Two inscriptions on the *pīshṭāḳ* and one on the portal of the mosque give dates between 820/1417 and 823/1421. Again, the *hazārbāf* decoration in turquoise and black covers the larger wall surfaces with details underlined in tile mosaics with or without unglazed geometric elements. The large patterns of the *pīshṭāḳ* vary from enhanced square Kūfic to bursting star motifs.

On the opposite side of the square, the master-builder ʿAbd al-Djabbār built the Shīr Dōr *madrasa* under Imām Ḳulī of the Djānids from 1028/1619 to 1045/1636. It is a feeble image of the Ulugh Beg *madrasa*, despite the lions in the spandrels of the entrance *pīshṭāḳ*, the melon-shaped domes and minarets on either side, and the lavish use of tile mosaics. The whole building, without a mosque, is slightly smaller than the Ulugh Beg *madrasa* although the imposing courtyard is bigger and allows two levels of blind arcades with rooms around it.

To its north-eastern side stands the hexagonal Čahār Su built with bricks from the Bībī Khānum mosque at the end of the 18th century under Murād Khān of Bukhārā. This bazaar crossroad was famous for its hatmakers.

A short distance to the north-west of it has been resited in the 1880s the grey marble platform of the Shībānīd dynasty with 31 inscribed tombstones.

Between the two *madrasas* of the Rigistān stands the Tilla-kārī "adorned with gold" *madrasa* (1056-70 1646-60). It is also a Djānid construction and combines the functions of a theological college and a *masdjid-i djāmiʿ*. The mosque on its west side replaced the crumbling Bībī Khānum. The recent and lavish restoration has included the rebuilding of a new turquoise dome over the *miḥrāb*.

The observatory of Ulugh Beg. ʿAbd al-Razzāḳ al-Samarḳandī records under the year 823/1420 the construction of the circular building 48 m wide, decorated with glazed bricks, and sited to the north-east of the town on the side of a rocky hill. Recent excavations have revealed at the centre of the inner hexagonal shape a deep stepped trench marked in degrees which was part of the gigantic sextant used for recording the movements of the planets and the stars. Contemporary texts mention shallow inner galleries on two floors above the ground floor service area, possibly painted with maps and charts if not decorative subjects. In the central area, and perpendicular to the wall of the sextant, stood a solar clock in the shape of a concave profile wall which would show up the shadow of the sextant.

The shrine of Čupan Ata stands on the same hill as the observatory but farther to the east. It is a rather coarsely-shaped mausoleum with a tombstone in a 16 m^2 chamber without a grave below. The very high drum has chamfered sides with monumental Kūfic inscriptions in tiles. It could have been a place of popular pilgrimage in the 9th/15th century.

The mausoleum of ʿIshrat khāna "The house of happiness" was built by Ḥabība Sulṭān Begum, wife of Sultan Abū Saʿīd, as a mausoleum for a daughter, and is dated by its *waḳf* to 869/1464. There are about 20 tombstones in the crypt. The double dome and high drum collapsed in 1903. The middle of the 28 m-long façade is dominated by a high *pīshṭāḳ* which opens into the 64 m^2 tomb chamber; on both sides of it and beyond its four corners, steps lead to the next floor and its various rooms. The western side of the ground floor contains a mosque. All ten types of vaulting are elaborate systems of arch nets with flat profiles. What survives of the *hazārbāf* decoration on the outer walls shows more restraint than earlier Tīmūrid architecture. A few *haft rang* stars and bands survive near the entrance. Inside, traces of blue and ochre painting of stylised vegetal motifs recall some of the painting in the mausoleum of Gawhar Shād in Harāt. No gold now remains visible. Polychrome glass from the windows was recovered in the excavations.

The ʿAbdī Dārūn "inside" ensemble was built in the 1440s to the south-east of the city near the ʿIshrat khāna. The mausoleum with its conical roof is set on foundations possibly going back to Sultan Sandjar; with its adjacent chambers, it stands behind the *khānaḳāh* by the north side of a large octagonal pool at the top of a long alleyway. On its eastern side was built a later wood-columned mosque as well as a *madrasa* south of it. The drum of the double-domed *khānakāh* has a bold Kūfic inscription; some tile mosaics survive within it. Muʿizz al-Dīn b. Muḥammad Yaʿḳūb b. ʿAbdī, a descendant of the caliph ʿUthmān, was supposedly a *ḳāḍī* in the Samarḳand of the 3rd/9th century.

The Aḳ Saray mausoleum. This now stands on its own to the south of the Gūr-i Mīr, an unfinished brick structure built in the 1470s, with plain walls and no outer dome. The portal rises to 19 m and leads into a cruciform dome chamber with a dado of polychrome tile mosaics with gold. Some painting with gilding survives in the vaulting. A headless skeleton was excavated in the crypt. Later Tīmūrids could have been buried in this building.

The Khʷādja Aḥrār ensemble. South of the town, the outdoor tomb of the powerful leader of the Naḳshbandiyya order Khʷādja ʿUbayd Allāh Aḥrār, known as Khʷādja Aḥrār [*q.v.* in Suppl.], who died in 896/1490, lies under a platform of grey and black marble which carries sixteen richly carved tombstones and is surrounded by a wall. A summer mosque looks over the square which lies to the west; on the north side stands the recently restored Nādir Dīwān Begi *madrasa* (1630-5), with its mosque probably built earlier. The decoration on the entrance portal with tiger and gazelle in spandrels, and the *pīshṭāḳ* in front of the domed *miḥrāb* chamber, vaguely echo Tīmūrid tile mosaics and calligraphic tiles.

The Namāz-gāh mosque stands in the north-western part of Samarḳand and was built by Nādir Dīwān Begi around 1040/1630. A *pīshṭāḳ* rises in front of a domed chamber between two groups of three blind arches. The baked brick surface shows no sign of surviving decoration.

Up to the building of the railway, there used to be on the left bank of the Zarafshān two large brick arches set at an angle to each other. One has since collapsed. They are said to have been part of a greater structure built under the Shībānīds to offset the current of the river during the spring high waters.

Although no gardens survive from the Tīmūrid

period or later, many are mentioned in contemporary texts and the *Bābur-nāma*. In his *Ẓafar-nāma*, Sharaf al-Dīn ʿAlī Yazdī describes the building of the Dilgushā garden in 799/1396, east of the town. The garden of "delights" was walled on four sides with a lofty tiled gateway in the middle of each side. Each corner contained a tiled pigeon tower; at the centre stood a domed pavilion. The main pathways were lined with poplars, and the grounds were divided into triangles and hexagons with borders of specific fruit trees: quince, apple, apricot, peach, pomegranate, pear, plum, pistachio and almond besides a variety of vines. Near-by was the Bagh-i Dulday "perfect" garden. Amongst a number of other gardens, to the west of the town stood the "new", the "paradise" and the "north" gardens; to the north could be found the "plan of the world" and the "four" gardens, the garden "of the square", and to the south, the "plane tree" garden. Most gardens had elaborate pavilions with rich tiling and wall paintings.

Bibliography: O.F. Akimushkin and A.A. Ivanov, *K čteniyu nadpisei s imenami masterov po mavzoleyakh Shakh-i Zinda*, in *Istoriya i kul'tura Narodov Sredney Azii*, ed. B.G. Gafurov and B.A. Litvinskii, Moscow 1976, 110-15; E. Blochet, *Les inscriptions de Samarkand*, in *Revue archéologique*, 3e série, no. 30 (1897), 67-77, 202-31; D. Brandenburg, *Samarkand*, Berlin 1972; M.S. Bulatov, *Geometričeskaya garmonizatsiya v arkhitekture Sredney Azii IX-XV vv*, Moscow 1978; E. Cohn-Wiener, *Turan*, Berlin 1930; L. Golombek and D. Wilber, *The Timurid architecture of Iran and Turan*, 2 vols., Princeton 1988, with comprehensive bibl.; U. Harb, *Ilkhanidische Stalaktitengewölbe. Beiträge zu Entwurf und Bautechnik*, in *Archäologische Mitteillungen aus Iran*, Ergänzungsband 4 (1978); D. Hill and O. Grabar, *Islamic architecture and its decoration*, London 1964; *Historical monuments of Islam in the U.S.S.R.*, Muslim Religious Board of Central Asia and Kazakhstan (title and text also in French and Russian), Tashkent n.d.; L. Kehren, *Brique émaillée du dôme de la grande mosquée de Samarkande*, in *JA*, cclv (1967), 185-93; E. Knobloch, *Beyond the Oxus*, London 1972; G. Michell (ed.), *Architecture of the Islamic world*, London 1978; V.V. Naumkin, *Samarcande, juste à temps. Les grandes archives photographiques*, Beirut 1992; N.B. Nemtseva, *Istoki kompozitsii i etapî formirovaniya an samblia Shakhi-Zinda*, in *Sovetskaya Arkheologiya*, i (1976), 94-106, tr. J.M. Rogers and Adil Yasin, *The origins and architectural development of the Shāh-i Zindeh*, in *Iran*, xv (1977), 51-73, with further bibl. in Russian; Rogers, *Central Asia historiography*, in *The dictionary of art*, forthcoming; G.A. Pugačenkova, *Ishrat-Khaneh and Ak-Saray. Two Timurid mausoleums in Samarkand*, in *Ars Orientalis*, v (1963), 177-89; eadem, *Arkhitektura observatorii Ulugbeka*, in *Iskusstvo Zodčikh Uzbekistana*, iv (Tashkent 1969), 107-31; S.E. Ratiya, *Mečet Bibi-Khanîm v Samarkande*, Moscow 1950; V.A. Shishkin, *Nadpisi v ansamble Shakhi-Zinda*, in *Zodčestvo Uzbekistana*, ii (1970), 7-71.

(Yolande Crowe)

al-**SAMARḲANDĪ** [see abu 'l-layth].

al-**SAMARḲANDĪ** [see djahm b. ṣafwān].

al-**SAMARḲANDĪ** [see niẓāmī ʿarūḍī].

al-**SAMARḲANDĪ, SHAMS** al-**DĪN**, Muḥammad b. Ashraf al-Ḥusaynī, an expert in both the ancient and Islamic sciences who composed important works on theology, logic, geometry and astronomy. He is most celebrated for his epistle on the art of disputation, *al-Risāla al-Samarḳandiyya fī ādāb al-baḥth* (in *Madjmūʿa mushtamila ʿalā al-ātī bayānuhū*, ed. Maḥmūd al-Imām al-Manṣūrī, Cairo 1353, 125-32), which was the most famous treatment of disputation and which became the subject of numerous commentaries (see Ḥādjdjī Khalīfa, *Kashf al-ẓunūn*, Istanbul 1951-3, i, 39). Unlike prior authors who had limited themselves exclusively to disputation in either theology or law under the rubric of *djadal, khilāf* or *munāẓara* [*q.v.*], al-Samarḳandī presented the first treatise applicable to any subject area—philosophy, law, theology—and thus the first attempt at a universal theory of disputation, referred to by his successors as simply the *ādāb al-baḥth*. The work is divided into three parts. The first gives definitions of technical terms such as *munāẓara, dalīl, amāra* and *naḳd*; the second states the procedure of debate (*tartīb al-baḥth*): who starts; what counts as a question; what objections are valid and when; how to determine the end of the debate (there is no judge), etc.; the final part gives examples of debates on questions (*masāʾil*) in theology, law, and philosophy. In his *Sharḥ al-muḳaddima al-burhāniyya* (i.e. of Burhān al-Dīn al-Nasafī, d. 687/1288 [*q.v.*]) (ms. Chester Beatty no 4396, at fol. 5b), which he completed according to I. Baghdatli in the year 690 (*Hadīyat al-ʿārifīn*, Istanbul 1951-3, ii, 106), and in which he implies that he studied with al-Nasafī, al-Samarḳandī mentions (at fol. 4a) that he treated the *ādāb al-baḥth* in his *Muʿtaḳadāt* (ʿĀrif Ḥikmat no. 206, Medina), *Ḳusṭās al-afkār fī taḥḳīḳ al-asrār* and *al-Anwār* (probably his *sharḥ* on the *Ḳusṭās*).

Manuscripts are the best source of information on his biography; Ḥādjdjī Khalīfa slipped in stating that al-Samarḳandī died around 600 A.H. (*Kashf*, i, 105). An important Istanbul manuscript apparently in the hand of his student (Laleli no. 2432, fol. 33b) states that he died 22 Shawwāl 702/9 June 1303. He wrote *shurūḥ* on several of his own works, including the *Ḳusṭās* (completed in 683) and his own *sharḥ* thereon (completed in 692 according to Istanbul, Fatih no. 3360), a standard work on Aristotelian logic, which contains, *inter alia*, a solution to the liar paradox (see L. Miller, *A brief history of the liar paradox in Islamic philosophy*, in *Of scholars, savants and their texts* (Munich 1989, 173-82), and a detailed discussion of the *ādāb al-baḥth*. Both his *al-Ṣaḥāʾif al-ilāhiyya* (completed in 680 according to Laleli no. 2432, fol. 33b), ed. Aḥ ʿAbd al-Raḥmān al-Sharīf, Kuwait 1985, and his *sharḥ* thereon, *al-Maʿārif fī al-ṣaḥāʾif*, were important theological works.

Other works include: *ʿAyn al-naẓar fī al-manṭiḳ fī ʿilm al-djadal*, a short treatment of the logic of juristic disputation concerned with, *inter alia*, implication (*talāzum*), (Cairo, Dār al-Kutub no. 197) (*manṭiḳ wa-ādāb al-baḥth*); cf. Ṣanʿāʾ, al-Maktaba al-Gharbiyya bi 'l-Djāmiʿ al-Kabīr, ms. s.v. *Ghayb al-naẓar*, obviously a misprint.

Ashkāl al-taʾsīs (ed. M. Suwaysī, Tunis 1984), a treatise on 35 fundamental postulates in the first book of Euclid's *Elements*. See H. Dilgan, *Demonstration du Ve postulate d'Euclide par Schams-ed-Din Samarqandi*, in *Rev. d'Histoire des Sciences*, xiii (1960), 191-6; A.I. Sabra, *Thabit ibn Qurra on Euclid's parallels postulate*, in *J. of the Warburg and Courtauld Inst.*, xxi (1968), 14 n. 19.

Al-Tadhkira fī 'l-hayʾa, a compendium on astronomy; *Aʿmāl-i taḳwīm-i kawākib-i thābita* (Leiden ms. no. 1196, 3 *pers.*), an astronomical chart for the year 1275-6; an anonymous commentary on Naṣīr al-Dīn al-Ṭūsī's *sharḥ* on Ptolemy's *Almagest* is also attributed to al-Samarḳandī (see Sezgin, vi, 94).

Al-R. al islāmiyya (Princeton, Yahuda no. 2367), an interpretation of the *shahāda*, is probably identical with Berlin ms. no. 2458, *Taḥḳīḳ kalimat al-shahāda* according to Mach; cf. *Bayān madhhab ahl al-sunna* and *R. fī kalimat al-tawḥīd* mentioned by Brockelmann.

Bibliography: Brockelmann, i, 468, S I, 840-1;

Sezgin, v, 99, 114-15, vi, 94; *Dict. of Scientific Biogr.*, xii, 91, iv, 155; H. Suter, *Die Mathematiker und Astronomen der Araber und ihre Werke*, Leipzig 1900, 157; R. Sellheim, *Arabische Handschriften. Materialen zur arabischen Literaturgeschichte*, Wiesbaden 1976, 162-3; R. Mach, *Catalogue of Arabic manuscripts (Yahuda Section) in the Garrett Collection, Princeton University Library*; L.B. Miller, *Islamic disputation theory. A study of the development of dialectic in Islam from the tenth through fourteenth centuries*, Ph.D. diss. Princeton 1984 unpubl., summarised in idem, *Disputatio(n)*. [*4*]. *Islamische Welt*, in *Lexikon des Mittelalters*, iii, Munich-Zurich 1986, 1119.

(L.B. Miller)

SĀMARRĀʾ, a town on the east bank of the middle Tigris in ʿIrāḳ, 125 km north of Bag͟hdād, of about 35 ha in 1924, and *ca.* 120 ha in the 1970s. Between 221/836 and 279/892 it was the capital of the ʿAbbāsid caliphs, and expanded to an occupied area of 57 km², one of the largest cities of ancient times, whose remains of collapsed pisé and brick walls are still largely visible.

The district was only lightly occupied in Antiquity. Apart from the Chalcolithic Samarran Culture excavated at the rich site of Tell al-Ṣuwwān, the city of *Sur-marrati*, refounded by Sennacherib in 690 BC, according to a stele in the Walters Art Gallery, Baltimore, may somewhat doubtfully be identified with a fortified site of Assyrian date at al-Ḥuways͟h opposite to modern Sāmarrāʾ. The ancient toponyms for Sāmarrāʾ are Gk. *Souma* (Ptolemy, V. c. 19; Zosimus, III, 30), Lat. *Sumere*, a fort mentioned during the retreat of the army of Julian the Apostate in A.D. 364 (Ammianus Marcellinus, XXV, 6, 8), and Syriac *S͟hūmaʿrā* (Hoffmann, *Auszüge*, 188; Michael the Syrian, iii, 88), described as a village.

The region experienced an upturn in its fortunes with the excavation of the Ḳāṭūl al-Kisrawī, the northern extension of the Nahrawān canal which drew water from the Tigris in the region of Sāmarrāʾ, attributed by Yāḳūt (*Muʿd͟jam*, s.v. *Ḳāṭūl*) to the Sāsānid king K͟husraw Anūs͟hirvān (A.D. 531-78). To celebrate this royal project, a commemorative tower (mod. Burd͟j al-Ḳāʾim) was built at the southern inlet (mod. Nahr al-Ḳāʾim) south of Sāmarrāʾ, and a palace with a walled hunting park at the northern inlet (mod. Nahr al-Raṣāṣī) near to al-Dawr. A supplementary canal, the Ḳāṭūl Abi ʾl-D͟jund, excavated by the ʿAbbāsid caliph Hārūn al-Ras͟hīd, was commemorated by a city in the form of a regular octagon (mod. Ḥuṣn al-Ḳādisiyya), called *al-Mubārak* and abandoned unfinished in 180/796. The plan is based upon that of the Round City of Bag͟hdād [*q.v.*].

Probably in 220/834-5, the caliph al-Muʿtaṣim [*q.v.*] left Bag͟hdād in search of a new capital. The sources all report that the reason was conflict between the caliph's regiment of Central Asian Turks and the population of Bag͟hdād. The caliph apparently sought a residence for the court, and a base for the ʿAbbāsid army, outside of Bag͟hdād, and was attracted by a region known for its hunting, but otherwise poor in natural resources.

The caliph's city was formally called Surra Man Raʾā ("he who sees it is delighted"). According to Yāḳūt (*Muʿd͟jam*, s.v. *Sāmarrā*), this original name was later shortened in popular usage to the present Sāmarrāʾ. It seems more probable, however, that Sāmarrāʾ is the Arabic version of the pre-Islamic toponym, and that Surra Man Raʾā, a verbal form of name unusual in Arabic which recalls earlier Akkadian and Sumerian practices, is a word-play invented at the caliph's court.

Surra Man Raʾā was laid out in 221/836 on the east bank of the Tigris around the pre-Islamic settlement, with the principal palace on the site of a monastery to the north. This palace complex, called in the sources *Dār al-K͟hilāfa, Dār al-K͟halīfa, Dār al-Sulṭān*, and *Dār Amīr al-Muʾminīn*, had two major sub-units, the *Dār al-ʿĀmma*, the public palace where the caliph sat in audience on Monday and Thursday, and *al-D͟jawsaḳ al-K͟hāḳānī*, the residence of the caliphs and their families, where four are buried. The site of the palace (125 ha), excavated by Viollet (1910), Herzfeld (1911-3), and recently by the Iraqi Directorate-General of Antiquities, has a square building, identifiable as the *Dār al-ʿĀmma*, opening onto a garden on the Tigris, with a court behind, two basins excavated in the conglomerate for summer occupation, a polo *maydān* [*q.v.*], and a second enclosed palace, probably *al-D͟jawsaḳ*.

It is not easy to reconstruct the plan of the original Surra Man Raʾā, because of later rebuilding. From the palace an avenue, later referred to by al-Yaʿḳūbī as *S͟hāriʿ Abī Aḥmad*, extended south 3.5 km to the markets, the mosque of al-Muʿtaṣim (both now under the modern town), and beyond. To the east of this avenue lay the cantonments of the Turk Waṣīf, to the west on the Tigris bank those of the Mag͟hāriba, a military unit apparently of Egyptian origin. The cantonment of K͟hāḳān ʿUrṭud͟j was placed north of al-D͟jawsaḳ, and may be identified with one of two quarters in this area. The two remaining military cantonments were located outside of Surra Man Raʾā, that of the Us͟hrūsaniyya, under al-Afs͟hīn K͟haydar b. Kāwūs al-Us͟hrūsanī [see al-afs͟hīn] at al-Maṭīra, the village 4 km south of modern Sāmarrāʾ (mod. al-D͟jubayriyya), and that of the Turks under As͟hnās 10 km north at Kark͟h Fayrūz (mod. S͟hayk͟h Walī). The area east of the city was walled as a hunting park (*al-Ḥayr*).

With the death of al-Muʿtaṣim in 227/842, came a point of decision: would Sāmarrāʾ be abandoned on the death of its founder, as many other princely sites, or would it become a more permanent ʿAbbāsid capital? Al-Wāt͟hiḳ (227-32/842-7 [*q.v.*]) chose to stay, and the population reacted by turning what was called a camp (*ʿAskar al-Muʿtaṣim*) into a real city. According to al-Yaʿḳūbī (*Buldān*, 264-5), al-Wāt͟hiḳ made some changes to the military disposition, but concentrated on the economic development of the city. He built a new palace called al-Hārūnī, which has been identified on the banks of the Tigris at al-Ḳuwayr, an unexcavated site partly flooded since the 1950s by the barrage at Sāmarrāʾ. Al-Hārūnī continued to be the residence of al-Mutawakkil, and was occupied during the 250s/860s by Turkish units.

The reign of al-Mutawakkil (232-47/847-61 [*q.v.*]) had a great effect on the appearance of the city, for he seems to have been a lover of architecture. In a list of his building projects which appears in several different versions, the new Congregational Mosque and up to 20 palaces are mentioned, totalling between 258 and 294 million dirhams. The new Congregational Mosque, with its spiral minaret, built between 235/849 and 237/851, formed part of an extension of the city to the east, extending into the old hunting park. Two new palaces with hunting parks were built in the south, at al-Iṣṭablāt, identified as al-ʿArūs, and al-Mus͟harraḥāt (not yet securely identified). A further palace, Balkuwārā, excavated by Herzfeld in 1911, was built on the Tigris bank south of al-Maṭīra, surrounded by a military cantonment for a new army corps under al-Mutawakkil's second son, al-Muʿtazz.

Three courses for horse-racing were built east of the

main city. Two have an out-and-back course 80 m wide and 10.42 km long with a spectators pavilion at the start, and the fourth a pattern of four circles around a central pavilion (5.3 km).

Under al-Mutawakkil, the city centre, which developed on the site of ʿAskar al-Muʿtaṣim, seems to have reached its greatest extent, and was described in its heyday by al-Yaʿḳūbī after the death of al-Mutawakkil (*Buldān*, 260-3). There were seven parallel avenues. The avenue adjacent to the Tigris, *Shāriʿ al-Khalīdj*, accommodated the quays for the river transport which was the principal means of supplying the city, and the cantonments of the Maghāriba. Although Herzfeld supposed that the alignment had disappeared, it now seems that the trace of the avenue lay inland from the river-bank, and still survives in part.

The principal avenue of al-Yaʿḳūbī, *al-Shāriʿ al-Aʿẓam* or *al-Sarīdja*, appears to be identical with the alignment of the ancient road from Baghdād to Mawṣil, following an irregular line from al-Maṭīra to beyond the *Dār al-Khilāfa*. Later called *Darb al-Sulṭān*, the alignment can be followed to the north to al-Dawr. Towards the southern end stood the tax registry, the *Dīwān al-Kharādj al-Aʿẓam*, probably outside the limits of the city in the time of al-Muʿtaṣim, and therefore possibly a replacement of an earlier building. To the northwest in succession lay the stables of the caliph, the slave market, the *madjlis* of the police, the great prison, and the main markets around the old congregational mosque of al-Muʿtaṣim. The avenue passed to the west of the *Dār al-Khilāfa*, and terminated with the residences of the great palace servants, which may have stood on the site of the earlier cantonments of Khāḳān ʿUrṭudj.

The second avenue, *Shāriʿ Abī Aḥmad*, was the original avenue of the time of al-Muʿtaṣim, narrowed from 60 to 10 metres, and ended at the south gate of the caliphal palace, called *Bāb al-Bustān* or *Bāb Aytākh*. Outside this gate stood the palace of al-ʿUmarī, and the residences of the leading Turks of Sāmarrāʾ: Aytākh, Barmash, Sīmā al-Dimashḳī, Bughā al-Kabīr, and Bughā al-Ṣaghīr.

The remaining avenues, *Shāriʿ al-Ḥayr al-Awwal, Shāriʿ Barghamish al-Turkī, Shāriʿ al-ʿAskar*, and *Shāriʿ al-Ḥayr al-Djadīd*, parallelled the *Shāriʿ Abī Aḥmad* to the east. These avenues were the quarters of military units: the Shākiriyya, the Turks, the Farāghina, the Khazar and the Khurāsānīs.

In 245/859 al-Mutawakkil began a new project to replace Surra Man Raʾā with a new caliphal city to the north of al-Karkh, called, according to its coinage, al-Mutawakkiliyya, although written sources call it al-Djaʿfariyya (al-Yaʿḳūbī) or al-Māḥūza (al-Ṭabarī, iii, 1438). A canal was dug from a point 62 km north to supply the new city, crossing by an aqueduct over the Ḳāṭūl, and running on both sides of the avenue, but the levelling was badly calculated, and little water flowed. The main palace, al-Djaʿfarī, is located at the inlet to the Ḳāṭūl al-Kisrawī, and is modelled on the Dār al-Khilāfa of Surra Man Raʾā. The city plan is organised around a central avenue leading south past the Abū Dulaf mosque to the cantonments of al-Karkh, thus similar to that of Surra Man Raʾā. The Sāsānid hunting park north of the Ḳāṭūl was reworked with a viewing platform at Tell al-Banāt close to modern al-Dawr. After the assassination of al-Mutawakkil in 247/861, the city was abandoned.

The reign of al-Mutawakkil was fundamental to the history of ʿAbbāsid Sāmarrāʾ. The expenditure on architecture, a high but not precisely calculable percentage of the state budget, stimulated the economic development of the city. But the drain on the treasury also played a role in the decade of troubles following al-Mutawakkil's death, which led to the making and unmaking of four caliphs, and military action in Sāmarrāʾ in three phases in 248/862-3, 251-2/865-6 and 256/870. Perhaps more significant was the isolation of the caliph with his army in Sāmarrāʾ, which left him exposed to forceful attempts by the soldiery to ameliorate their lot.

At any rate, during the decade after the accession of al-Muʿtamid in 256/870, the army was removed from Sāmarrāʾ by Abū Aḥmad al-Muwaffaḳ, although Sāmarrāʾ continued to be the official residence of the caliph until 279/892, when al-Muʿtaḍid reestablished Baghdād as capital. Al-Muʿtamid is not known to have revisited Sāmarrāʾ after 269/884, but he was buried there in 279/892. Between 274/887-8 and 281/894-5 there are several reports of looting the city, after which Sāmarrāʾ ceases to be mentioned frequently in the chronicles; one presumes therefore that a major depopulation occurred at this time.

Nevertheless, the area round the markets continued to be occupied, together with the outlying towns of al-Maṭīra and al-Karkh. Al-Muktafī attempted to resettle Sāmarrāʾ in 290/903, but found al-Djawsaḳ a ruin.

The two Shīʿī Imāms ʿAlī al-Hādī (d. 254/868) and al-Ḥasan al-ʿAskarī (d. 260/874) had a house on the Shāriʿ Abī Aḥmad, probably adjacent to the mosque of al-Muʿtaṣim, and were buried there. The Twelfth Imām disappeared nearby in a cleft commemorated by the Sardāb al-Mahdī in 260/874. The tomb was first developed in 333/944-5 by the Ḥamdānid Nāṣir al-Dawla, and subsequently by the Būyids. According to al-Shaykh Muḥammad al-Samāwī, *Washāʾidj al-sarrāʾ fī shaʾn Sāmarrāʾ*, a verse composition of the 13th/19th century on the history of the shrine, the double shrine continued to be rebuilt frequently, notably in 445/1053-4 by Arslān al-Basāsīrī and in 606/1209-10 by the caliph al-Nāṣir li-Dīn Allāh, whose work is commemorated by an inscription in the Sardāb. The present appearance of the shrine is to be attributed to work by the Persian Ḳādjār ruler Nāṣir al-Dīn Shāh in 1285/1868-9 and other more recent work.

From the 4th/10th century onwards, Sāmarrāʾ became a pilgrimage town. In the 6th/12th and 7th/13th centuries, the displacement to the east of the course of the Tigris south of Sāmarrāʾ led to the transfer of the Tigris road from Baghdād to Mawṣil to the west bank of the river, and a consequent loss of trade. Sāmarrāʾ was not apparently walled until 1834, when a wall was built out of ʿAbbāsid bricks, as a result of a charitable donation.

In the 1950s a barrage was constructed on the Tigris, in order to divert the spring flood waters down Wādī Tharthar and to end the disastrous periodic flooding of Baghdād. The lake formed behind the barrage drove the farming communities of the flood plain on to the steppe-land among the ʿAbbāsid ruins, and enlarged the town, which remains the market centre of its district.

Bibliography: Yaʿḳūbī, *Buldān*, 255-68, tr. Wiet, 44-63; E. Herzfeld, *Ausgrabungen von Samarra*. i. *Der Wandschmuck der Bauten von Samarra und seine Ornamentik*, Berlin 1923, iii. *Die Malereien von Samarra*, Berlin 1927, vi, *Geschichte der Stadt Samarra*, Hamburg 1948; K.A.C. Creswell, *Early Muslim architecture*, ii, Oxford 1940; Directorate-General of Antiquities, Iraq, *Ḥafriyyāt Sāmarrāʾ*, 1936-1939, 2 vols., Baghdād 1940; A. Sūsa, *Rayy Sāmarrāʾ fī ʿahd al-khilāfa al-ʿAbbāsiyya*, 2 vols., Baghdād 1948-9;

R.McC. Adams, *Land behind Baghdad*, Chicago 1965; J.M. Rogers, *Samarra, a study in medieval town-planning*, in A.H. Hourani and S.M. Stern (eds.), *The Islamic city*, Oxford 1970, 119-55; A. Northedge and R. Falkner, *The 1986 survey season at Samarra*, in *Iraq*, xlix (1987), 141-73; Northedge, *Karkh Fairuz at Samarra*, in *Mesopotamia*, xxii (1987), 251-64; idem, *The racecourses at Samarra*, in *BSOAS*, liii (1990), 31-56; idem, *The palace at Istabulat, Samarra*, in *Archéol. islamique*, iii (1992), 61-86; idem, *An interpretation of the Palace of the Caliph at Samarra* (*Dar al-Khilafa or Jawsaq al-Khaqani*), in *Ars Orientalis*, xxiii (1993), 143-71. (A. NORTHEDGE)

AL-**SAMĀWA** (A., "the elevated land").

1. Al-Samāwa was the name given, in the definition of al-Bakrī (*Muʿdjam mā staʿdjam*, Cairo 1364-71/1945-51, iii, 754, copied by Yāḳūt, *Buldān*, ed. Beirut, iii, 245), during mediaeval Islamic times to the desert and steppeland lying between al-Kūfa and Syria. Earlier geographers were more specific. Thus Ibn Ḥawḳal (ed. Kramers, 22, 34-5, tr. Kramers-Wiet, 21, 34, see also his map of the Arabian peninsula) defines it as the plain stretching from Dūmat al-Djandal [*q.v.*] in northwestern Arabia to ʿAyn al-Tamr [*q.v.*] in the desert on the fringes of the middle Euphrates and to the desert of Khusāf between al-Raḳḳa and Bālis [*q.vv.*], a region in general inhabited by the Banū Kalb and the Banū Fazāra [*q.vv.*]. The Samāwa was crossed by important caravan routes connecting ʿIrāḳ via Palmyra [see TADMUR] with Syria. In the early 4th/10th century, it was the locus of the Carmathian rising of Zikrawayh or Zakarūya [see ḲARMAṬĪ] which seriously affected ʿAbbāsid control over the Syrian districts to its west (see H. Halm, *Das Reich des Mahdi. Der Aufstieg der Fatimiden (875-973)*, Munich 1991, 68-9, 71, 170-1).

2. Al-Samāwa is also the name of a town in south-western ʿIrak (lat. 31°18′N., long 45°18′E.), on the lower Euphrates, appearing in history from the 11th/17th century onwards. It was attacked by the Wahhābiyya [*q.v.*] under ʿAbd Allāh b. Suʿūd b. Suʿūd in 1806, after he had sacked al-Nadjaf, and then again in 1808 it was plundered by Suʿūd b. Suʿūd (see A. Musil, *Northern Neǧd, a topographical itinerary*, New York 1928, 263-4). Since the later Ottoman period and then those of the British Mandate and independent ʿIrāḳ, al-Samāwa has been important as a crossing-place over the Euphrates for the Baghdād-Basra road and for the bridge carrying the metre-gauge railway connecting the two cities, hence it was one of the towns besieged by the rebels during the 1920 ʿIrāḳī revolt. During the Mandate and shortly afterwards, al-Samāwa came within the governorate (*liwāʾ*) of Dīwāniyya [*q.v.*], of which al-Samāwa was a component *ḳaḍāʾ*, but in contemporary ʿIrāḳ it is now the chef-lieu of the *liwāʾ* of al-Muthannā, with a population (1985 estimate) of 33,473.

Bibliography (in addition to references given in the article): A. Musil, *Verkehrswege über Samâwa zwischen al-ʿErâḳ und Syrien*, in *WZKM*, xxix (1915), 445-62; Naval Intelligence Division, Admiralty Handbooks, *Iraq and the Persian Gulf*, London 1944, index. (C.E. BOSWORTH)

AL-**SAMAWʾAL** B. **ʿĀDIYĀ**, Jewish-Arab poet, who lived in the middle of the 6th century A.D. His residence was in the famous castle of al-Ablaḳ (cf. Yāḳūt, s.v.) near Taymāʾ. His genealogy is uncertain. Though mostly called al-Samawʾal b. ʿĀdiyā (or ʿĀdiyāʾ) al-Yahūdī, other genealogies such as al-Samawʾal b. Gharīḍ b. ʿĀdiyā or al-Samawʾal b. Ḥiyyā b. ʿĀdiyā are also given. Some few poems attributed to a certain Saʿya (cf. Sezgin, *GAS*, ii, 250-1), who is said to have been al-Samawʾal's brother or, more probably, his grandson and to other members of his family are also handed down.

Even in the Middle Ages, only very few poems attributed to al-Samawʾal were known. His *Dīwān*, which was collected by Nifṭawayh [*q.v.*], contains only nine poems comprising 88 verses. From these poems again only two gained greater fame because they had been included in widely-known poetic anthologies even before Nifṭawayh's comparatively late compilation of the *Dīwān*. The first is a *fakhr* poem (no. 1 in the *Dīwān*), which Abū Tammām incorporated in his *Ḥamāsa* (no. 15) and on which Ṣafī al-Dīn al-Ḥillī (8th/14th century) composed a *takhmīs* (ed. Beirut 1962, 36-41). The poem, however, is attributed with good reason to other poets than al-Samawʾal as well. A second poem (no. 2 of the *Dīwān*) found its way into al-Aṣmaʿī's poetic anthology (*al-Aṣmaʿiyyāt*, no. 23) and parts of it are quoted in different other sources, among them Ibn Sallām al-Djumaḥī's *Ṭabaḳāt*. The poem contains reflections on birth, death and the Day of Judgment which may be, as Hirschberg proposed, references to Aggadic literature, thus, contrary to poem no. 1, pointing to the Jewish religion of its poet. The authenticity of the poem was defended by Hirschberg against Nöldeke's negative verdict. Levi Della Vida drew up the very probable hypothesis that the poem was in fact created by one of al-Samawʾal's descendants, who had already converted to Islam but still was acquainted with Jewish tradition.

Yet al-Samawʾal owes his fame less to his poetry than to a story, which gave rise to the saying "more loyal than al-Samawʾal". The story is told in different versions. According to Ibn Sallām, the poet and Kinda prince Imruʾ al-Ḳays [*q.v.*] had entrusted his arms to al-Samawʾal. As the Ghassānid phylarch al-Ḥārith b. Djabala [*q.v.*] heard about that, he set out against al-Samawʾal, who entrenched himself in his fortress. Al-Ḥārith, however, took hold of al-Samawʾal's son who happened to be outside the castle and threatened to kill him if al-Samawʾal would not deliver the deposited weapons. Yet al-Samawʾal prefered to witness his son to be killed by al-Ḥārith rather than to betray the trust commited to him. The story is referred to in a poem by al-Aʿshā [*q.v.*]. In discussing this poem, Caskel concluded that the reference to Imruʾ al-Ḳays in the story is a later invention. The poem no. 6 in al-Samawʾal's *Dīwān*, where the poet refers to his loyal keeping of "the coats of mail of the Kindī", is considered as spurious by Caskel.

In western scholarship, interest in al-Samawʾal concentrated on his Jewish religion, because one hoped that his poetry could throw some light on Jewish influence on early Islam. But since there is not a single poem of which al-Samawʾal's authorship has never been questioned, discussion have focused mainly on the problem of authenticity. These discussions were stirred up anew when a hitherto unknown poem, which contains numerous references to biblical history, was discovered in the Geniza. It became clear, however, that its poet was not al-Samawʾal b. ʿĀdiyā. Following a hint in one manuscript, some scholars have started to think that its author was an otherwise unknown poet bearing also the name al-Samawʾal, who is said to have been a member of the Jewish tribe of Ḳurayẓa [*q.v.*]. Kowalski attributed poem no. 7 in al-Samawʾal's *Dīwān*, of which he could convincingly show that it was the reply to a poem of Ḳays b. al-Khaṭīm [*q.v.*] by an anonymous Jewish poet in the time of the prophet Muḥammad, to this al-Samawʾal al-Ḳuraẓī. Yet it still remains rather unlikely that such a poet really existed. Whatever the case may be, al-Samawʾal's poems, though only partly or even not at all genuine in the narrow sense of the word, are still of interest to the history of Judaism in early Islamic times.

Bibliography: L. Cheikho, *Diwan d'as-Samaouʾal d'après la récension de Niftawaihi*, Beirut 1909, further ed. by M.Ḥ. Āl Yāsīn, Baghdād 1955; *al-Aṣmaʿiyyāt*, ed. Shākir and Hārūn, 82-6 (with comprehensive reference to further Arabic sources); Ibn Sallām, *Ṭabaḳāt*, ed. Shākir, i, 279-81; *Aghānī*³, vi, 322, 332-3, ix, 96-9, 119-20, xxii, 116-21; Ḥamza al-Iṣfahānī, *K. al-Amthāl*, ed. Ḳaṭāmish, ii, 415-16; Marzūḳī, *Sharḥ Dīwān al-Ḥamāsa*, i, 110-24; Th. Nöldeke, *Beiträge zur Kenntnis der Poesie der alten Araber*, Hanover 1864, 52-86; idem, *Samaual*, in *ZA*, xxvii (1912), 173-83; J.W. Hirschberg, *Der Dīwān des as-Samauʾal ibn ʿĀdijāʾ*, Cracow 1931 (with complete tr. of al-Samawʾal's poems); T. Kowalski, *A contribution to the problem of the authenticity of the Dīwān of as-Samauʾal*, in *ArO*, iii (1931), 156-61; G. Levi Della Vida, *A proposito di as-Samawʾal*, in *RSO*, xiii (1931), 53-72 (fundamental); W. Caskel, *Al-Aʿšà Nr. 25,6*, in *Studi orientalistici in onore di Giorgio Levi Della Vida*, Rome 1956, i, 132-40; Blachère, *HLA*, ii, 302; F. Sezgin, *GAS*, ii, 249-50 (full bibl.).

(TH. BAUER*)

SAMBAS, a town and river in the Province of Kalimantan Barat (West Kalimantan) in the Republic of Indonesia, lying just south of Sarawak at lat. 1° 20′ N. and long. 109° 15′ E. It is one of a number of Malay/Muslim-dominated estuarine settlements on the Borneo coast whose existence was based on trading relationships with non-Muslim native peoples in the interior and Chinese traders and miners. Local versions of the Islamisation of Borneo's West coast attribute the coming of Islam to Arabs from Palembang who were trading in the area from the mid-16th century.

At this time, Sambas was a tributary of the Peninsula Malay kingdom of Johor, but through a royal marriage in the 17th century came under the authority of Sukadana, another Bornean coastal settlement to the south. Descendants of Sultan Muḥammad Ṣafi al-Dīn, the first Muslim ruler of Sukadana, assumed power in Sambas and may have helped to spread Islam in the kingdom.

Sambas was not as influential as its more powerful neighbours Sukadana, Landak, Pontianak and Mempawa, and was prey to local wars and a haven for pirates. To bolster his authority, the Sultan of Sambas sent a mission to Batavia in 1818 requesting Dutch assistance, as a result of which the first Dutch Resident was installed. During the early 19th century there was an international dimension to local politics as the Dutch sought to extend their influence north of Sambas into Sarawak [*q.v.*], which they claimed was a tributary of Sambas, but to which Brunei also held claims. In 1841 when Malay chiefs rebelled against Brunei, James Brooke quelled the unrest and received the area as his from Brunei. The presence of the English "White Rajah" effectively stopped the northwards extension of Dutch authority on Borneo's West coast past Sambas. From 1846 the Dutch reorganised their Borneo possessions and in 1848 a new Dutch contract was made with Sultan Abū Bakr Tadj al-Dīn of Sambas, defining the boundaries of his kingdom.

During the 19th century, the organisation of Islam in Sambas was closely linked with the Sultan's court. There was an Imam and four Kiais, although after 1831 there were two Imams, Imam Tua and Imam Muda (Senior and Junior), probably an example of a dual appointment to resolve a local conflict. Later in the century, Kātib Djabr studied in Mecca with Shaykh Aḥmad b. Muḥammad Zayn (1856-1906) of Patani [*q.v.*], and later returned to Sambas to become Maharaja Imam.

The Imams of Sambas were in touch with events in the wider sphere, and in 1930 Shaykh Muḥammad Bashuni ʿImrān wrote to the editor of the Cairo reformist journal *al-Manār* [*q.v.*], to ask why Muslims were not as advanced as people in Europe, America and Japan.

Sambas shared in the reorganisation of Islam in Borneo carried out by the Netherlands East Indies government in 1937. This established *ḳāḍī* Courts and *ḳāḍī* Appeal Courts on the same lines as for Java and Madura. After 1945, in the independent Republic of Indonesia, the administration of Islam has been through the *Mahkamah Shariah*, under the Ministry of Religious Affairs.

Bibliography: E. Netscher, *Kronijk van Sambas en van Soekadana in het oorspronkelijk Maleisch*, in *TBG*, i/1 (1852); P.J. Veth, *Borneo's Westerafdeeling, geographische, statistisch, historisch, voorafgegaan schets des ganschen eilands*, 2 vols., Zaltbommel 1854-56; Jutta E. Bluhm, *A preliminary statement on the dialogue established between the reform magazine al Manar and the Malayo-Indonesian world*, in *Indonesia Circle*, xxxii (1983); M.B. Hooker, *Islamic law in South-East Asia*, Singapore 1984.

(VIRGINIA MATHESON HOOKER)

SAMBHAL [see MURĀDĀBĀD].

ṢAMGH, *ṣamagh* (A., pl. *ṣumūgh*) indicates gum resins, the desiccated latexes of several plants and the mixtures of natural resins (*rātīnadj*) with gum-like substances.

To the best-known gum resins belong: ammoniac (*wushshaḳ*), the product of the ammoniac gum tree; the so-called devil's dirt (*ḥiltīt*), the latex of the asafoetida (*andjudhān*) which, when exposed to the air, hardens into a dirty-yellow gum resin; wolfs' milk (*yattūʿ*), in several varieties of the class Euphorbia, with many sub-varieties; galbanum (*ḳinna*), the desiccated latex of *Ferula galbaniflua*, used as spice and medicine; myrrh (*murr*), from the bark of several varieties of thorny shrubs of *Commiphora abyssinica*; the often-described frankincense (*kundur* [see LUBĀN]) from various Boswellia varieties, indigenous in South Arabia and Somalia; sagapenum (*sakbīnadj*), the yellow, translucent resin from *Ferula Scowitziana* which causes irritation of the skin and whose smell resembles that of asafoetida; and camphor (*kāfūr*), the white, transparent mass of the camphor tree *Cinnamonum camphora* [see KĀFŪR], indigenous in East Asia. Most of the gum resins (28 in number) are enumerated and described by al-Nuwayrī, *Nihāya*, xi, 291-324; ʿUmar b. ʿAlī al-Ghassānī, *Muʿtamad*, ed. al-Saḳḳā, Beirut 1975, 287-92, has 20 gum resins; al-Bīrūnī, *Ṣaydana*, has 13 varieties (see the index of the Russian tr. by Karimov, Tashkent 1973); Ibn al-Bayṭār, *Djāmiʿ*, iii, 85,25 - 87,13 (= Leclerc, nos. 1407-16) has 9 varieties; other authors have less.

The word *ṣamgh* is usually used alone for *ṣamgh ʿarabī*, gum arabic, so called because it was exported from Arab ports and spread by the Arabs. It is the viscous secretion gained from the bark of the acacia tree (*al-ḳaraẓ*, in Morocco *al-ṭalḥ*), which represents several varieties of the acacia imported from Africa: *Acacia senegalensis*, from the steppe zones of West- and Central Africa to the right and left of Senegal, *Acacia abyssinica* and *Acacia nilotica*, from Africa and India, and many others.

In medicine, gum arabic is used as a palliative and

as an astringent for drying up putrescent ulcers. It helps the formation of new flesh in ulcers and stems the blood which flows from wounds; it also serves as cough medicine and for the preparation of collyria. The drug consists of roundish, colourless or yellowish pieces, up to a diameter of three cm, which fall easily into small pieces which shine like glass.

Bibliography: In addition to the works mentioned in the text, Rāzī, *Ḥāwī*, ed. Ḥaydarābād, xxi, 148-9 (no. 520); Ibn al-Djazzār, *Iʿtimād*, 65 (Publ. of the Inst. for the History of Arab Isl. Science), Frankfurt 1985; Ibn Samadjūn, *Djāmiʿ al-adwiya al-mufrada*, iii, 80-90 (Publ. Inst. Hist. Science), Frankfurt 1992; Ibn Hubal, *Mukhtārāt*, ed. Ḥaydarābād, ii, 164-5; Maimonides, *Sharḥ asmāʾ al-ʿuḳḳār*, ed. Meyerhof, Cairo 1940, nos. 124, 320, 321, 352, 380; Ibn al-Ḳuff, *ʿUmda*, ed. Ḥaydarābād, i, 247; Suwaydī, *Simāt*, ms. Paris ar. 3004, fol. 239a-b; F.A. Flückiger, *Pharmakognosie des Pflanzenreiches*, ^{3}Berlin 1891, 3-10; M.A.H. Ducros, *Essai sur le droguier populaire arabe du Caire*, Cairo 1930, see index, 154; G. Karsten, U. Weber and E. Stahl, *Lehrbuch der Pharmakognosie*, ^{9}Stuttgart 1962, 541, 581-5; H.A. Hoppe, *Drogenkunde*, ^{8}1975/77, i, 3-8, 1264-5.

(A. Dietrich)

al-**SAMHŪDĪ**, Nūr al-Dīn Abu 'l-Ḥasan ʿAlī b. ʿAfīf al-Dīn ʿAbd Allāh, al-Shāfiʿī, noted Egyptian scholar in history, theology, law, tradition, etc. (844-91/1440-1506).

He was born at Samhūd in Upper Egypt in Ṣafar 844/July 1440, the son of a *ḳāḍī*; in his genealogy, he claimed to be a Ḥasanid *sayyid*. His biography is given in detail by al-Sakhāwī, resumed in Ibn al-ʿImād and other subsequent biographical sources. He studied in Cairo from 853/1449 onwards under its celebrated scholars, and also received the Ṣūfī *khirḳa* or cloak. He made the Pilgrimage in 860/1456 and eventually settled in Medina, where he wrote a treatise urging the rebuilding and correct reconstruction of the Prophet's Mosque there. Whilst away in Mecca on the Lesser Pilgrimage or *ʿUmra* in Ramaḍān 886/November 1481, his valuable personal library was destroyed by a fire in the Prophet's Mosque in Medina. Returning to Cairo, he was honoured by the Mamlūk sultan Ḳāʾit Bāy [*q.v.*] and given a stipend. After visiting Jerusalem, he finally settled at Medina in late 890/1485, purchasing the house of the Companion Tamīm al-Dārī [*q.v.*] and acquiring the designation of *Shaykh al-Islām* there. He died on 18 Dhu 'l-Ḳaʿda 911/12 April 1506 and was buried in the Baḳīʿ al-Gharḳad [*q.v.*] cemetery.

Al-Samhūdī was a prolific author, and over twenty of his works are extant, some printed but most of them still in manuscript. Their subjects include *fiḳh*, genealogy, *ḥadīth*, *kalām*, the *manāsik* or ceremonies and practices of the Pilgrimage, various commentaries on legal and other works and a collection of *fatwās*. But his main fame stems from his histories of Medina, his adoptive home. He originally composed a history on an extended scale as *Iktifāʾ al-wafā bi-akhbār Dār al-Muṣṭafā* (thus in Ibn al-ʿImād; in Ḥādjdjī Khalīfa, vi, 450, *al-Wafā bi-mā yadjibu li-ḥaḍrat al-Muṣṭafā*), but this was destroyed in the Medina fire. However, he had made, at the request of a patron, a shorter version, the *Wafāʾ al-wafā*, completed in 886/1481, and fortunately, he had the manuscript of this abridgement with him in Mecca (printed Cairo 1326-7/1908-9, 2 vols., and ed. Muḥ. Muḥyī 'l-Dīn ʿAbd al-Ḥamīd, Cairo 1374/1955, repr. Beirut 1393/1973, 4 parts in 2 vols.). Finally, from this last in turn was made another epitome, the *Khulāṣat al-Wafā* (printed Būlāḳ 1285/1868-9, Cairo 1316/1898-9 and Mecca 1316/1898-9; two Persian translations of this also exist in manuscript, see Storey, i, 426-7). On all these works of al-Samhūdī, see Brockelmann, II^{2}, 223-4, S II, 223-4.

The *Wafāʾ al-wafā* is our principal source for the history and topography of the city, with details on its buildings, graves and shrines and on the various festivals and rituals. Al-Samhūdī quotes earlier authorities, including copious ones from what must have been one of the very first histories of Medina, that by the pupil of Mālik b. Anas, Ibn Zabāla al-Makhzūmī, completed in 199/814 (see Ḥādjdjī Khalīfa, i, 190 no. 228, ii, 44 no. 2302; Sezgin, *GAS*, i, 343-4; this book was known to al-Sakhāwī but has since disappeared).

Bibliography (in addition to references given in the article): 1. Sources. Sakhāwī, *Ḍawʾ*, v, 245-8; Ibn al-ʿImād, *Shadharāt*, viii, 50-1; ʿAbd al-Ḳādir al-ʿAydarūsī, *al-Nūr al-safir*, Baghdād 1353/1934-5, 58-60; Shawkānī, *al-Badr al-ṭāliʿ*, Cairo 1348/1929-30, i, 470-1; Ḥādjdjī Khalīfa, see Index at vii, 1190 (no. 7097).

2. Studies. F. Wüstenfeld, *Geschichte der Stadt Medina nach Samhudi*, Göttingen 1860 (= abbrev. tr. of the *Khulāṣat al-Wafā*); idem, *Die Geschichtsschreiber der Araber und ihre Werke*, Göttingen 1881-2, 507; Ziriklī, *Aʿlām*^{2}, v, 122-3; Kaḥḥāla, *Muʾallifīn*, vii, 129-30; Sarkīs, *Muʿdjam al-maṭbūʿāt*, i, cols. 1052-3; F. Rosenthal, *A history of Muslim historiography*^{2}, Leiden 1968, 476.

(C.E. Bosworth)

SĀMĪ, Shems ül-Dīn Frāsherī (Mod. Tkish. Şemseddin Sami Fraşeri), Ottoman Turkish author and lexicographer. He was born at Frāsher in Albania on 1 June 1850, of an old Muslim family whose ancestors had been granted this place as a fief by Sultan Meḥemmed II, and was educated in the Greek lycée at Yanina, at the same time receiving private instruction in Turkish, Persian and Arabic. He came to Istanbul in 1871 in order to take up journalism, and in 1874 was sent to Tripoli (North Africa) as the editor of *Wilāyet* newspaper. He returned to Istanbul 9 months later and founded the daily newspaper *Ṣabāḥ* in 1876. It was during these years also that he embarked on literary production, attaching himself to the new school of Ibrāhīm Shināsī and Nāmiḳ Kemāl [*q.vv.*], and producing a pioneer Turkish novel, *Taʿashshuḳ-i Ṭalʿat we Fitnet*, which criticised the marriage system then prevalent in Turkey. Moreover, in a famous article *Lisān-i Türki-yi ʿOthmānī*, published in *Ṣabāḥ*, he asserted the purist attitude that the language of the Ottoman empire was not the "Ottoman language" but the "Turkish language", and that the over-abundant Arabic and Persian words and phrases should be replaced by old Turkish ones which had fallen into disuse; he thus anticipated the language reform of the 20th century Turkish Republic.

Later, he became the editor of *Terdjümān-i Sharḳ* newspaper and the journals *ʿĀʾile* and *Hafta*. Meanwhile, he wrote a series of pamphlets for the *Djeyb Kütübkhānesi* series. In 1881 he was appointed as the secretary for the *Teftīsh-i ʿAskerī Ḳomisyonu*, or Army Inspection Commission, but, at the same time, began to publish his famous lexicographical works: *Ḳāmūs-i fransewī* (French-Turkish, 1882, and Turkish-French, 1885), the six-volume encyclopedia *Ḳāmūs al-aʿlām* and the *Ḳāmūs-i türkī* in two parts. In 1893 he was put under house arrest by ʿAbd ül-Ḥamīd II. He stayed in his home at Erenköy, Istanbul, and devoted the rest of his life to his works, from 1899 onwards being forbidden to receive guests; he died on 18 June 1904 in Istanbul.

Sāmī's greatest merit lies in the fields of lexicography and philology. As well as working on Turkish and Arabic, he also worked on producing an Albanian grammar, poems in this language and a book on the future of Albania. With his brother Naᶜīm Frās͟herī (1846-1900; see on him, F. Babinger, in *Isl.*, xi [1921], 99), he was among the leaders of the group which produced a Latin-based alphabet for Albanian in the 1880s. His best-known work is his Turkish dictionary, the *Ḳāmūs-i türkī*. In this work, the order of the words is alphabetical and the arrangement of the different meanings of the words is very clear. Sāmī represented a compromise between the different views prevailing in his time on the development of Turkish, and, despite his own far-reaching Turkish purism, his dictionary is a reflection of the educated Turkish of his time. Among his unpublished materials are an unfinished Arabic dictionary, comprehensive studies on the *Ḳutadgu bilig* and the Ork͟hon inscriptions, as well as works on Persian and Eastern Turki.

Bibliography: 1. Selected works. (a) Novel: *Taᶜas͟hs͟huḳ-i Ṭalᶜat we Fitnet*, 1872. (b) Plays: *Besā, yahud ᶜahd-i wefā*, 1875; *Sīdī Yahyā*, 1875; *Kāwe*, 1876. (c) Dictionaries: *Ḳāmūs-i Fransewī* (French-Turkish) 1882; *Ḳāmūs-i Fransewī* (Turkish-French) 1885; *Ḳāmūs al-aᶜlām*, 1888-98; *Ḳāmūs-i Türki*, 2 vols., 1899-1900. (d) Translations from the French: *Tārīk͟h-i müd͟jmel-i Fransa*, 1872; *Ik͟htiyār onbas͟hî*, 1873; *Galatée*, 1873; *S͟hayṭānîñ yādkārlarî*, 1878; *Sefīller*, 1879; *Robinson*, 1884. (e) Pamphlets: *Medeniyyet-i islāmiyye*, 1878; *Esāṭīr*, 1878; *Ḳadînlar*, 1878; *Gök*, 1878; *Yer*, 1878; *Insān*, 1878; *Emt͟hāl*, 1878; *Leṭāʾif*, 1882; *Yine insān*, 1885; *Lisān*, 1885; *Uṣūl-i tenkīd we tertīb*, 1885.

2. Studies. P. Horn, *Geschichte der türkischen Moderne*, Leipzig 1909; Agâh Sırrı Levend, *Şemseddin Sami*, Ankara 1969; Kenan Akyüz, in *PTF*, ii, 492-3, 499-500, 508-9, 574; *İA* art. *Şemseddin Sâmî* (Ömer Faruk Akün). (Çiğdem Balim)

al-**SĀMIRA** (more modern form, al-Samariyyūn), sing., al-Sāmirī (not to be confused with the Ḳurʾānic al-Sāmirī [*q.v.*]), denotes the Samaritans, that part of the people of Israel which does not identify itself with Judaism ("Judaism" being associated with that part of the people of Israel which survived the Babylonian Exile, hence with the destruction of the kingdom of Israel in the north of Palestine).

1. History of the community.

Historically, the Samaritans have been linked with Judaism since several centuries before the coming of Jesus Christ. They are nevertheless different, as also in the dating of the schism regarding the Holy Scriptures connected with the Karaites [*q.v.*], taking place around the appearance of Islam. The Samaritans only believe in the first five books of the Law (the Pentateuch, with variations, whilst the Karaites accept the written Law in its entirety (sc. virtually the Old Testament) but reject the oral one, i.e. the Talmud, what is understood in Judaism as the Mishnah and the Gemarah.

The Samaritan community is still in existence and active. At the beginning of the 20th century (1909) they were considered as almost extinct (in antiquity, they had numbered between one and two millions, and in mediaeval times had several communities, from Thessalonica to Damascus and Cairo), numbering only 173 (97 men and 76 women), but their numbers have now risen to 600. They live mainly at Nābulus [*q.v.*], at the foot of Mount Gerizim, which they set up in opposition to Jerusalem, and at Holon near Jaffa.

Leaving aside the historical notices, both traditional and modern, on their origins—which belong properly to the field of Biblical Studies—we shall turn to the position of the Samaritans at the appearance of Islam. Both the people and their laws, which were well-known in the Talmud (which observes that the Samaritans were more respectful of the Law than the Jews), as also in the Code of Justinian, are further known in the *fiḳh* treatises. Islam considered them as a People of the Book, and al-Māwardī, tr. Fagnan, *Les statuts gouvernementaux*, Algiers 1915, 302, states that "the poll-tax is also leviable on the Ṣabians and Samaritans, since their beliefs are basically identical with those of the Jews and Christians, even though they differ in practices". Arabic very soon replaced the Aramaic which the Samaritans had spoken and written—Hebrew being only a liturgical language since the beginning of the common era—at the time of the advent of Islam.

The Samaritans are important for the history of Islam, and their theories are probably at the root of the problem of *taḥrīf*. Whilst in the Rabbanite Jewish Pentateuch, accepted by the Christian churches, there is mention of the altar which God commanded to be built on Mount Ebal ("... and when you have passed over the Jordan, you shall set up these stones ... on Mount Ebal" (Deut. xxvii, 4) and not on Mount Gerizim, in the Samaritan Pentateuch this is the reverse. There are several reasons for accepting the Samaritan version; it suffices to read v. 12 and the description of Deut. xi, 29, or to think of the arid nature of Mount Ebal and the richness of Mount Gerizim.

According to Muslim historians, the Samaritans in general helped the incoming Arabs in their warfare in Palestine with the Byzantines during the early 7th century A.D. The Samaritans were known to the Arabs in the classical period as physicians, as shown by Ibn Abī Uṣaybiᶜa. Many writers, and especially travellers, such as al-Masᶜūdī, al-Idrīsī, Yāḳūt and al-Maḳrīzī, speak of them. Westerners, however, do not seem to have known about them at that time. The Crusader chronicles—unless, as is unlikely, some new source turns up—do not mention them. It was not until the 16th century that they were discovered by the West at the time of a melancholy attempt by a scholar who wrote to them in Samaritan characters telling them that they belonged to the ten lost tribes of Israel and, above all, leading the surviving Samaritans to believe that they stemmed from the communities traditionally said to have been deported by the Crusaders. The first Samaritan Pentateuch was brought into Europe by the Italian traveller Pietro della Valle, who went there in 1616.

But Judaism, including its European communities, knew them perfectly well, and Benjamin of Tudela went to see them in the second half of the 12th century. The Samaritans continued to have some of the institutions no longer existing in Judaism: the High Priest, the Priests and the Levites. In 1624 the last High Priest, a direct descendant of Phinehas b. Eliazar b. Aaron, died, and was replaced by another priestly family, the direct descendants of Itamar b. Aaron called Ha-Kohen Ha-Levi. In the course of time, this subtle distinction was abandoned, and the term Ha-Kohen Ha-Gadol was exclusively used. Another institution of a Biblical order which continued up to the 17th century (which may, however, have possibly stopped in the 16th century) was the use made of the ashes of the red heifer (cf. Ḳurʾān, II). The Samaritans did not use phylacteries, and their calendar was calculated each year by the Priests. It was a completely theocratic community in which there was never any distinction between Rabbi = teacher and Kohen = priest. These last lived under a régime of nazariate. Likewise, many practices were retained with regard to the field of impurity. Pietro della Valle observed the low wall inside which women remained at the time of their menstrual periods until they became ritually pure again. Comparison with the rules of the Falasha is interesting. The *Kitāb al-Kāfī*, the most extensive of their legal compendiums composed in Arabic in A.D. 1200, states (S. Noja, *Il Kitāb al-Kāfī dei Samaritani*, Naples 1970, 84): "When any of our community touches with his hand someone who is not of our religion and then sits down to food, he must rinse his hand, since anyone touching something with his hand after ablution invalidates that ablution". From this arose the Samaritans' revulsion from physical contact with those not of their community (cf. the Ḳurʾānic *lā misāsᵃ*) and, consequently, the ductus *n-ẓ-r (ibid.*, 34) concerning which Silvestre de Sacy noted: "suspecte d'infection (je lis *nāẓir* et je prend ce mot dans le sens de *nuẓira*, ex. *naẓra, deformitas, colorvitium*)". Another non-Samaritan piece of evidence from the 7th century mentions their custom current at that time of burning by fire any of their land over which a non-Samaritan had passed. This piece of evidence ends with the words *tanta illis est execratio utrisque*. Al-Shahrastānī was well aware of this when he wrote (tr. D. Gimaret and G. Monnot, *Le Livre des religions et des sectes*, Louvain 1986, 609), "they are more severe than the rest of the Jews in matters of ritual purity".

Nevertheless, much prudence is required in seeing, as has been done in the past, an imitation of Samaritan customs in many of the Islamic rules such as the positions in worship and the ritual formulae, since it may well be that the contrary is true: it was the Samaritans, with their great capacity for adaptation, who were inspired by the living practice of Islam.

Bibliography (in addition to references in the article): M.N. Adler, *The itinerary of Benjamin of Tudela*, New York 1907; A.D. Crown, *The Samaritans*, Tübingen 1989; idem and R. Pummer and A. Tal, *A companion to Samaritan studies*, Tübingen 1993.

2. Samaritan literature in Arabic.

When the Samaritans experienced the Islamic invasion, their language was Aramaic or, rather, one of the numerous forms of Aramaic with its own special characteristics. Above all, in phonology, their language was close to Palestinian Aramaic, with the disappearance of the laryngeals, a marked preference for prosthetic vowels, etc., whilst retaining some differences, such as the change *u* > *a* in closed, unstressed sylables. Their writing system was—and still is today—palaeo-Hebraic, i.e. the ancient system of writing, similar to Phoenician, which had been used all through Israel before the Babylonian Exile. On their return, the Jews, in order to distinguish themselves from the Samaritans, adopted the "square Hebrew", which has since then been permanently used by them all, including the Karaites; today, it is the writing system used in the State of Israel. After the time of the Arab conquest, the Samaritans began to speak Arabic without any break at all. In an unsystematic fashion, for writing down Arabic, they began to use the palaeo-Hebraic script equally with the Arabic script. A similar state of affairs is represented by the use or Karshūnī [*q.v.*] for writing Syriac.

The works written in Arabic (in the *Narbonne Chronicle*, there is quoted the first Samaritan who began to speak in Arabic), independent of writing system, cover all the aspects of their interests.

1. Translated works.

Translation of the Pentateuch. Several versions are involved. Five can be identified, given the fact that we still do not possess any critical edition. The Samaritans were interested above all in commentaries, and one can discern that they utilised versions of already-existing commentaries from Judaism and also—at a late date—from Arabic-speaking Christianity, naturally with adaptations.

Translations of various works. No work in this category can be considered as important.

2. Original works.

(a) *Chronicles*. At least seven of these exist. Some are short; others, like that of Abu 'l-Fatḥ, very lengthy.

The *Asāṭīr* ("stories"), very close to the Midrash.

The *Shalshala*, the "chain" of the high priests.

The *Tūlīda*, the "genealogy", also called "the Neubauer chronicle", from its editor.

The *Book of Joshua*. This book, completely in Arabic, has no connection with the relevant first historical book of the Old Testament. It is based on several sources, and was transcribed into Arabic by an anonymous author *ca.* A.D. 1300.

The "Adler-Seligsohn" chronicle, after the names of its editors.

The "Chronicle II" or "Macdonald-Cohen" one, after the names of its editors. Here it is the Arabic text which is the original, and not the Hebrew.

The *K. al-Taʾrīkh*, the Annals of Abu 'l-Fath, the longest and most complete. Dating from the 14th century, it has been brought up to the middle of the 19th century.

(b) *Commentaries on the Pentateuch*. These books, like the treatises on law, are considered by the Samaritans as their most important books, and were written originally in Arabic.

Various partial commentaries:

The *K. fī shurūḥ al-ʿashar kalimāt* "Commentary on the Decalogue" by Abu 'l-Ḥasan of Tyre.

al-Khuṭba al-djamīʿa or *Sharḥ azīnu*, on Deut. xxxii by the same author.

Commentary on Genesis (from i.2 to i.5) by Ṣadaḳa b. Munadjdjā b. Ṣadaḳa, called al-Ḥakīm.

The *Sharḥ al-Fātiḥa*, on the "*Fātiḥa*", i.e. on Deut. xxxii. 3-4, by Ibrāhīm al-Ḳabbāṣī, etc.

The most extensive and most popular is the commentary on the first four books of the Pentateuch written by Muslim b. Murdjān b. Ibrāhīm and his nephew Ibrāhīm b. Yaʿḳūb b. Murdjān in the last century.

(c) *Legal treatises*. These were also written in Arabic after the decline in the use of Aramaic. They include amongst others:

The *K. al-Kāfī* "The Sufficient", from A.D. 1042, by Yūsuf b. Salāma of ʿAskar, on "that which is sufficient for living according to the law of God"; in effect, a work of *fiḳh*.

K. Masāʾil al-khilāf "Book on questions of conflicting views", from A.D. 1106, by Munadjdjā b. Ṣadaḳa on the points of disagreement between the Samaritans, the Jews and the Karaites.

K. al-Tibakh "Book of the commandments", of A.D. 1030, by Abu 'l-Ḥasan of Tyre, involving polemics with the Jews.

K. al-Mīrāth "Book on inheritances", of A.D. 1170, by Abū Isḥāḳ Ibrāhīm, a physician at the court of Ṣalāḥ al-Dīn (Saladin), dealing with everything regarding successions.

K. al-Farāʾiḍ "Book on the division of inheritances", from the 14th century A.D. by Abu 'l-Faradj al-Kaththār.

K. al-ʿIrba "Book on nudity", by al-Muʿallim

Barakāt, on the basis of the teachings and *fatwās* of Abū Isḥāḳ Ibrāhīm.

(d) *Collections of* fatwās *for fixing the calendar:*

K. Ḥisāb al-sinīn "Book of the calculating of the years", of A.D. 1960, by Elazar ᶜAbd al-Muᶜīn b. Ṣadaḳa, which includes the information of previous astronomical works in order to determine the calendar for the year.

(e) *Works on grammar.*

K. al-Tawṭiʾa "The initiation", the first Samaritan Hebrew grammar, by Abū Isḥāḳ Ibrāhīm.

With the arrival *en masse* of Europeans in the Samaritan community in the 19th century and the development of a market for manuscripts, certain of these works, originally in Arabic, were translated and recopied into Hebrew in order to satisfy book-collectors and purchasers who did not know Arabic; the case of the work *Hilluk* is well-known. Translations have sometimes been taken for the originals by European scholars, naïve and excited, and encouraged by information from maleficent and unscrupulous dealers.

Today, still, Arabic is the sole spoken language, but one notes a certain revival of Hebrew, to the detriment of Aramaic, which remains truly a dead language.

Bibliography: E.N. Adler and M. Seligsohn, *Une nouvelle chronique samaritaine*, Paris 1903; I.R. Boid Mac Mhanainn, *The Samaritan Halachah*, in Crown, *The Samaritans*, Tübingen 1989, 624-49; idem, *Principles of Samaritan Halachah*, Leiden 1989; J.M. Cohen, *A Samaritan chronicle*, Leiden 1981; M. Gaster, *The chain of Samaritan High Priests*, in *JRAS* (1909), 393-420; Th.G.J. Juynboll, *Chronicon Samaritanum...Liber Josuae*, Leiden 1848; M.Ad. Neubauer, *Chronique samaritaine*, Paris 1873 (= *JA* [1869], ii, 385 ff.); S. Noja, *Il Kitāb al-Kāfī dei Samaritani*, Naples 1970; idem, *Abū al-Ḥasan al-Sūrī's discourses on the forbidden degrees of consanguinity in marriage in the Samaritan Kitab al-Tabbah*, in *Abr-Nahrain*, xi (1971), 110-15; J. Macdonald, *The Samaritan Chronicle No. II ... from Joshua to Nebuchadnezzar*, Berlin 1969; M. Pohl, *Kitāb al-Mīrāt, das Buch der Erbschaft der Samaritaners Abū Isḥāq Ibrāhīm*, Berlin 1974; S. Powels, *Der Kalender der Samaritaner anhand des Kitāb Ḥisāb as-sinīn*, Berlin 1977; H. Shehadeh, *The Arabic translation of the Samaritan Pentatheuch*, in Crown, *op. cit.*, 481-516; idem, *Some reflections on the Arabic translation of the Samaritan Pentatheuch*, in *Nordisk Judaistik*, xiv/1 (1933), 36-44; P. Stenhouse, *The Kitāb al-Tārīkh of Abu 'l-Fatḥ*, Sydney 1985; idem, *Samaritan Arabic*, in Crown, *op. cit.*, 585-623; E. Vilmar, *Abulfathi Annales Samaritani*, Gotha 1865; G. Wedel, *Halachic Literature*, in Crown, *op. cit.*, 468-80; P.R. Weis, *Abu 'l-Ḥasan al-Sūrī's discourse on the calendar in the Kitāb al-Tabbakh*, in *BJRL*, xxx/1 (1946); *The Samaritan News*, bi-weekly journal, first publ. Dec. 1969, in Hebrew. (S. Noja Noseda)

AL-**SĀMIRĪ** "the Samaritan", is the name in Ḳurʾān, XX, 85, 87 and 95 of the man who tempted the Israelites to the sin of the Golden Calf. The sin itself is mentioned twice in the Ḳurʾān. In the first narrative, VII, 148-57, the story is told of the sin of Israel and Aaron as in Exodus, xxxii, but with the elaboration that the calf cast out of metal was "lowing" (*khuwār*). The second version, XX, 83-98, presents al-Sāmirī as the tempter of Israel in the same situation. At al-Sāmirī's bidding, the Israelites cast their ornaments into the fire and he made out of them the lowing calf which was worshipped by the people although Aaron advised them not to do so. When challenged by Moses, al-Sāmirī justified himself by saying that he saw what the others did not see, the footsteps of the messenger (understood in Muslim tradition to be the tracks of the hooves of Gabriel's horse). Moses then announced his punishment to him: "So long as you live, you shall call out, 'Do not touch me' (*lā misāsᵃ*)" (XX, 97).

The Muslim tradition has had no doubt that al-Sāmirī was a Samaritan as known within the Jewish and Christian traditions. Al-Ṭabarī, *Djāmiᶜ al-bayān*, Cairo 1905, xvi, 152, and al-Zamakhsharī, *al-Kashshāf*, Beirut 1967, ii, 549, for example, understand al-Sāmirī to have been a prominent Israelite of the tribe of Sāmira whose name was Mūsā b. Ẓafar; his religion is understood to have differed from that of other Jews.

Scholars have extensively debated the question of how a Samaritan became involved with the Mosaic story of the golden calf. Bernard Heller in *al-Sāmirī* in *EI*[1] and *SEI* agreed with Goldziher (in his article *Lā Misāsa*) that al-Sāmirī was a representative of the Samaritans, a group which kept apart from non-Samaritans because of a special concern over purity. In a segregation of this kind—as in the Jewish laws regarding eating (Ḳurʾān, IV, 160)—Muḥammad saw a divine punishment. What did al-Sāmirī (= the Samaritans) have to atone for, such that he would be punished in this manner? For the sin of the golden calf. What was known as a ritual practice of the Samaritans—that contact with those outside their group created impurity—is put back into earlier times and explained as a punishment of al-Sāmirī for having incited the Israelites to make and worship the calf. But other theories have been put forth. Speyer suggested a reference to the story of Zimrī (and thus al-Sāmirī) ben Sālū from Num. xxv, 14, who was guilty of defying Moses in having relations with a Moabite woman. More recently, Schwartzbaum, developing a suggestion of Yehuda, has suggested that we have a tale in which the story of King Jeroboam's calves (one of which, according to Talmudic tradition, was able to talk, thus being parallel to the Ḳurʾānic idea of the golden calf "lowing") has merged with that of Moses and the golden calf. The conflation stemmed from Jeroboam's statement "Here are your gods, Israel, that brought you up from Egypt" (I Kings, xii, 28) in reference to his two golden calves, a statement which also appears in Exod., xxxii, 4, in the mouth of Aaron. Providing the link to al-Sāmirī is the point that Jeraboam's capital was in Shechem (I Kings, xii, 25), the Samaritan sacred centre. Schwartzbaum also sees remnants of the folkloric motif of the Wandering Jew in the story of al-Sāmirī who roams the world crying, "Do not touch me!" Regardless of how the story came about, the Ḳurʾān appears to present the earliest record of this midrashic development; aspects of it which are found in Jewish sources (e.g. in *Pirḳē de Rabbi Eliezer* and *Tanḥūma*) would seem to date from after the rise of Islam.

Bibliography: *Tafsīr* tradition on Ḳurʾān, XX, 83-98; I. Goldziher, *Lā Misāsa*, in *R. Afr.*, cclxviii (1908), 23-8; B. Speyer, *Die biblischen Erzählungen im Qoran*, Gräfenhainichen 1931, 329-33; A.S. Yahuda, *A contribution to Qurʾān and ḥadīth interpretation*, in S. Löwinger and J. Somogyi (eds.), *Ignace Goldziher memorial volume*, i, Budapest 1948, 286-90; H. Schwartzbaum, *Biblical and extra-biblical legends in Islamic folk-literature*, Beiträge zur Sprach- und Kulturgeschichte des Orients, Bd. 30, Walldorf-Hessen 1982, 14-7 and footnotes (which contain a complete bibliography of the topic).

(B. Heller-[A. Rippin])

AL-**ṢĀMIT**, "the Silent One", as opposed to *al-*

nāṭik "the Speaking One", a term used by several extremist S̲h̲īʿī sectarians (*g̲h̲ulāt*) to designate a messenger of God who does not reveal a new Law (*s̲h̲arīʿa*). The pair of terms is found in the notices concerning the doctrines of the Manṣūriyya and K̲h̲aṭṭābiyya [*q.vv.*] sects respectively (Saʿd b. ʿAbd Allāh al-Ḳummī, *K. al-Maḳālāt wa ʾl-firaḳ*, ed. Mas̲h̲kūr, 48, 51). According to the doctrine of the K̲h̲aṭṭābiyya, Muḥammad was the *nāṭik* and ʿAlī the *ṣāmit*; in the same sense the two terms are used in the earliest treatises of the Ismāʿīliyya [*q.v.*]; e.g. (Pseudo-) Dj̲aʿfar b. Manṣūr al-Yaman, *K. al-Kas̲h̲f*, ed. Strothmann, 77, 99-100, 103. Here, "the Silent Imām means that he is the master of the Inner Meaning (*ṣāḥib al-bāṭin*) who does not pronounce an outward revelation (*lā yanṭuḳu bi-s̲h̲arīʿatⁱⁿ zāhira*)" (*op. cit.*, 100). The term occurs in many early Ismāʿīlī writings (e.g. Dj̲aʿfar b. Manṣūr al-Yaman, *Asrār al-nuṭaḳāʾ*, ed. M. G̲h̲ālib, Beirut 1984, 248, 257, 263, quoted by W. Ivanow, *Ismaili tradition concerning the rise of the Fatimids*, Bombay 1942, 278, 293, 303; idem, *K. al-Fatarāt*, ms. Tübingen, pp. 110-11), but soon has been replaced by the terms *waṣī* (legatee) or *asās* (foundation): according to Abū Yaʿḳūb al-Sidj̲istānī (d. after 386/996), *It̲h̲bāt al-nubuwwāt*, ed. ʿĀrif Tāmir, Beirut 1966, 193, "Adam was the first *nāṭik* for the first cycle, whereas Seth was his silent *asās* (*asāsuhū al-ṣāmit*)." In later Ismāʿīlī writings, the term *ṣāmit* falls into disuse.

Bibliography: Given in the article.

(H. HALM)

SAMMĀ, the name of a Rādj̲pūt tribe in Sind. At the time of the Muslim advent into Sind (93/711-12) the Sammās were ostensibly already a well-formed tribe, with distinctive customs and with a recognised habitat, according to the much later *Čač-nāma*, which mentions the Sammā tribal leader as a Buddhist. The same source mentions the Sammās and their allied tribes, the Lāk̲h̲os and the Suhtas, as living in the territory from Lohāna (modern Sanghar, Ḥaydarābād District) down to the Arabian Sea coast.

The rival tribe of the Sumerās [*q.v.*] first find mention in the account of the G̲h̲aznawid Sultan Maḥmūd's return march from the Sōmnāth expedition (416/1026) [see SŪMANĀT]. Later, the Sumerās emerged as the dominant tribe in Sind, completely eclipsing the Sammās for over three centuries. But already towards the end of the reign of Muḥammad b. Tug̲h̲luḳ (d. 752/1351) the (Sammā) Dj̲āms were linking up with the rebels (Baranī, 523-5). The first half of the 8th/14th century witnessed a reversal of roles, with the Sammā chiefs emerging as strong, assertive leaders. The circumstances of this change are not fully known. Internecine warfare among the Sumerās, along with certain adverse changes in the course of the river Indus (see the *Taʾrīk̲h̲-i Ṭāhirī*, extracts in Elliot and Dowson, i, 271), and other unclear factors, may have sapped the energy of the Sumerās.

The final stage of the shift of power from the Sumerās to the Sammās is fairly well documented. It appears from the state documents of the Dihlī Sultanate that the Sumerās, in a desperate bid to retain the power that was slipping from their hands, sought the support and the protection of the Sultanate officials in Gudj̲arāt, Multān and lower Sind from the opening years of Fīrūz S̲h̲āh Tug̲h̲luḳ's reign (acc. 752/1351) onwards. These officials were keenly interested in keeping intact "the afflicted plant of the life of Hamīr Dodā Sumerā", the last Sumerā chief, for they needed Sumerā support against the rising Sammā tribe, who had already been giving much trouble to the Dihlī government by allying themselves with Mongol marauders, always active on the

borders, and with Sindhi malcontents (*Ins̲h̲āʾ-i Māhrū*, 100-3, 186-9). But Tug̲h̲luḳ efforts to give the Sumerā a new lease of life proved unavailing.

It is generally agreed that the Sammās were of Rādj̲pūt origin. They were closely related to the Dj̲aded̲j̲a Dj̲āms of Kāt̲h̲iāwāṛ, with whom they shared the title of *Dj̲ām*, one of uncertain derivation. The presence of Sindhi elements in their names also indicates their indigenous origin. There is little evidence about their conversion to Islām. The first Sammā chief is generally mentioned as Dj̲ām Fīrūz Unnar, who came to power in the early 1350s at T̲h̲aṭṭā [*q.v.*]. It is uncertain whether he was the same person who figures in Ibn Baṭṭūṭa's account as Wunar al-Sāmirī, a high official at Sīwistān under Sultan Muḥammad b. Tug̲h̲luḳ of Dihlī, who later rebelled and rose to chiefdom as Malik Fīrūz (iii, 105-7, tr. Gibb, iii, 599-600). Most Sindhi scholars are inclined to identify Ibn Baṭṭūṭa's "Wunar al-Sāmirī" with the Sammā chief who became the first ruler of the Sammā dynasty that ruled over Sind, with their capital at T̲h̲aṭṭā.

The chronology of the Sammā rulers as given in the *Taʾrīk̲h̲-i Sind* of Mīr Maʿṣūm Bhakkarī and in later chronicles which have followed him has been proved to be seriously at fault, as shown conclusively by Riazul Islam, *The rise of the Sammas in Sind* (see *Bibl.*), 1-24. The "tentative list" of the Sammā rulers and their chronology worked out by N.A. Baloch "is comparatively more authentic", see his article, in *Bibl.* For a more detailed and descriptive list, see Ḥusām al-Dīn Ras̲h̲idī's note in his edition of the *Maklī-nāma* (see *Bibl.*), 103-36.

It was during the joint reign of ʿAlāʾ al-Dīn Dj̲ām Dj̲ūnā and Ṣadr al-Dīn Bānhbīna that Tug̲h̲luḳid Dihlī Sultan Fīrūz S̲h̲āh led a long campaign against T̲h̲aṭṭā which began in the last months of 1365 and ended in 1367 with the intercession of the leading Suhrawardī saint of Sind, Sayyid Ḥusayn Dj̲alāl al-Dīn, called Mak̲h̲dūm-i Dj̲ahāniyan [see DJ̲ALĀL AL-DIN ... AL-BUK̲H̲ARĪ] (for details, see Riazul Islam, *op. cit.*). The two joint rulers made their submission to the sultan, and joined his return march to Dihlī. The sultan assigned the rule of Sind jointly to Dj̲ām ʿAlāʾ al-Dīn's son and to Tamāčī, son of Bānhbīna. Later, when Tamāčī showed signs of disaffection, he sent Dj̲ām ʿAlāʾ al-Dīn to take charge of the affairs at T̲h̲aṭṭā (ʿAfīf, 190-247). When the Tug̲h̲luḳ empire rapidly disintegrated after Fīrūz S̲h̲āh's death in 791/1388, the Sammās assumed complete independence.

The Sammā chiefs were rulers who provided Sind with a century and a half of prosperous and fairly peaceful dynastic rule. Their popularity is well reflected in folk tales and songs pertaining to the various rulers. The best ruler of the dynasty undoubtedly was Dj̲ām Niẓām al-Dīn (II) Ninda (866-914/1461-1508); his tomb is the most prominent monument at Maklī (near T̲h̲aṭṭā), the necropolis of mediaeval Sind (see Mīr ʿAlī S̲h̲īr Kāniʿ, *Maklī-nāma*, ed. Rās̲h̲idī, especially his Note at 88-103). The Dj̲ām was a great patron of art and culture, and enjoyed wide popularity at home and high prestige among the neighbouring kingdoms. The famous scholar Dj̲alāl al-Dīn Dawānī (d. 908/1502-3 [*q.v.*]) wanted to migrate from S̲h̲īrāz to settle in Sind under the patronage of the great Dj̲ām, but died before he could set out. However, two of his prominent disciples settled permanently at T̲h̲aṭṭā (Mīr Maʿṣūm, *Taʾrīk̲h̲-i Sind*, 74).

Sammā rule came to end with the arrival in Sind of the more powerful Arg̲h̲ūns, who had been displaced from Ḳandahār in Afg̲h̲ānistān by Bābur [*q.v.*] and their leader Shāh Beg Arghūn founded his own dynasty there after his victory over Fīrūz b. Ninda in 926/1520 [see ARGHŪN]. A branch of the Sammā tribe, known as the Djādedjā Sammās, ruled over Kāthiāwāŕ from the 7th/13th to the 9th/15th century, but never converted to Islam (see Baloch).

Bibliography: 1. Sources. ʿAlī Kūfī, *Čač-nāma* (or *Fatḥ-nāma*), ed. U.M. Daudpota, Ḥaydarābād, Deccan 1939, 39-40, 121-2, 218, 220-1; Ibn Baṭṭūṭa, see in article; Ḍiyāʾ al-Dīn Baranī, *Taʾrīkh-i Fīrūz-Shāhī*, ed. Sayyid Aḥmad Khān, Calcutta 1862, 523-4; ʿAyn al-Mulk Māhrū, *Inshāʾ*, ed. Sh. Abdur Rashid, Lahore 1963, 101-2, 186-8, 230-5; Djalāl al-Dīn Bukhārī, *Sirādj al-hidāya* or *Malfūẓāt*, ed. Qazi Sajjad Husain, New Delhi 1983, 360-1; idem, *Malfūẓāt*, incomplete part, ms. 1210, Royal Asiatic Soc. Calcutta, fols. 161a-172b; Shams Sirādj ʿAfīf, *T.-i Fīrūz-Shāhī*, ed. Wilayat Husain, Calcutta 1891, 190-247; Mīr Maʿṣūm Bhakkarī, *T.-i Sind*, ed. Daudpota, Poona 1938, 60-79; Sayyid Mīr ʿAlī Shīr Ḳāniʿ, *Maklī-nāma*, ed. Sayyid Ḥusām al-Dīn Rāshidī, Ḥaydarābād, Sind 1967, 88-189 (valuable for the editor's extensive notes, documentation, genealogies, photographs of monuments, copies of inscriptions, etc.); idem, *Tuḥfat al-kirām*, iii/1, ed. Rāshidī, Ḥaydarābād, Sind 1971, 99-110; Elliot and Dowson, *A history of India as told by its own historians*, i, London 1867.

2. Studies. Riazul Islam, *The rise of the Sammas in Sind*, in *IC*, xxii/4 (1948), 1-24; N.A. Baloch, *Chronology of the Samma rulers of Sind*, in *Procs. of the Pakistan Historical Records and Archives Commission*, Peshawar Session 1954, Karachi 1957, 23-9; U.M. Daudpota, *A dark period in the history of Sind*, in *ibid.*, 41-4; R.J. Najumdar *et alii* (eds.), *The history and culture of the Indian people. VI. The Delhi Sultanate*, Bombay 1960, 221-6; M. Habib and K.A. Nizami (eds.), *A comprehensive history of India. V. The Delhi Sultanat (A.D. 1206-1526)*, Delhi etc. 1970, 1118-34; Annemarie Schimmel, *Makli Hill*, Inst. of Central and West Asian Studies, Karachi 1983, 7-15; Riazul Islam, *Political ideas of Sayyid Husain Jalal ud-Din Bukhari Makhdum-i Jahaniyan*, in the press.

(RIAZUL ISLAM)

AL-**ṢAMMĀN**, in the vernacular pronounced as al-Ṣummān, a large tract of rugged, stony uplands in eastern Arabia, east of the sands of al-Dahnāʾ [*q.v.*]. Its south-eastern part is also called al-Ṣulb. Both *ṣammān* and *ṣulb* mean "hard, stony ground", while *ṣammān* has the additional connotation of "hard ground by the side of sands". In its narrow sense, limited to the north-western part, al-Ṣammān extends from al-Maʿḳalāʾ at its south-eastern extremity towards the gravel plain of al-Dibdiba in the north-east and Wādī al-Bāṭin at its north-western limit i.e. the area which lies between 45° 20′-47° E. and 28°-26° 45′ N. A broader definition of al-Ṣammān is the stretch of land between the road from al-Riyāḍ to al-Aḥsāʾ in the south to the road from al-Ḳaṣīm to al-Baṣra in the north. However, in today's usage al-Ṣammān is often understood as the entire area of hard ground running in parallel to al-Dahnāʾ from Wādī al-Bāṭin in the north towards a point at approximately 22° N., and to the east of al-Aflādj. The southern stretch, which is wedged between al-Dahnāʾ and the north-western sands of the Empty Quarter in the general area of the oasis of Yabrīn, is called Ṣammān Yabrīn. At about 22° N. the great gravel plain of Abū Baḥr protrudes southward from al-Ṣammān towards a point east of al-Sulayyil, where the sands of the Empty Quarter and the ʿUrūḳ al-Rumayla, the southern extension of al-Dahnāʾ, meet.

Philby writes that al-Ṣammān at many points consists of whitish sandy limestone overlying sandstone. Its uplands are intersected by many depressions where the rainwater collects in large pools (*khabārī*) and basins with spring wells (sing. *djaww*). Permanent water is found in numerous reservoirs in subterranean cavities (*duḥūl*). Following rains, al-Ṣammān turns into excellent grazing land, attracting Bedouins of the Muṭayr, al-ʿUdjmān, Banī Khālid, Ḳaḥṭān and Subayʿ tribes. From al-Aṣmaʿī is reported the saying, "Whoever grazes his herds during winter in al-Dahnāʾ, in spring in al-Ṣammān, and in late spring in al-Ḥimā, has completed [the cycle of] pasturing them [on the herbage that shoots up in the wake of rains]." Yāḳūt writes that in ancient times these pastures were the tribal land of the Banū Ḥanẓala. Al-Ṣammān and al-Ṣulb are mentioned by classical poets like al-Farazdaḳ, Djarīr, and especially Dhu 'l-Rumma, who also names many of their watering-places.

Bibliography: Ḥamad al-Djāsir, *al-Muʿdjam al-djughrāfī li 'l-bilād al-ʿArabiyya al-Suʿūdiyya al-Minṭaḳa al-Sharḳiyya*, iii, al-Riyāḍ 1981; Hamdānī, *Ṣifat Djazīrat al-ʿArab*; Muḥammad b. ʿAbd Allāh Ibn Bulayhid, *Ṣaḥīḥ al-akhbār ʿammā fī bilād al-ʿArab min al-āthār*, Cairo 1952; ʿAbd Allāh b. Muḥammad Ibn Khamīs, *al-Muʿdjam al-djughrāfī li 'l-Mamlaka al-ʿArabiyya al-Suʿūdiyya. Muʿdjam al-Yamāma*, al-Riyāḍ 1980; al-Ḥasan b. ʿAbd Allāh al-Iṣfahānī, *Bilād al-ʿArab*, al-Riyāḍ 1968; J.G. Lorimer, *Gazetteer of the Persian Gulf, ʿOmān, and Central Arabia*, Calcutta 1908-15; H.St.J.B. Philby, *The Empty Quarter*, New York 1933; Yāḳūt, *Muʿdjam al-buldān*, ed. Beirut, iii, 423; U. Thilo, *Die Ortsnamen in der altarabischen Poesie*, Wiesbaden 1958, 97-8.

(M. KURPERSHOEK)

SAMMŪR [see FANAK; FARW].

AL-**SAMN** (A.), butter, made from cows', goats' and ewes' milk, heated over the fire to extract its impurities, and hence called clarified butter (as distinct from *zubd* which is butter made from churned milk). Mediaeval dietetic texts state a preference for clarified butter made from cows' milk over goats' milk. Its medicinal benefits were as an antidote against poisons and snake bites, if ingested alone or mixed with honey, and as an ointment for the cure of boils and abscesses, including haemorrhoids. *Samn* was also used in the kitchen and, according to the anonymous *Kanz al-fawāʾid*, its use (at least in the urban milieu reflected by the culinary manuals) was almost exclusively limited to the preparation of egg dishes, such as omelettes, and sweet dishes made with flour; in the latter case, *samn* was often mixed with sesame oil (*shīradj*).

Bibliography: Ibn Ḥabīb, *al-Mukhtaṣar fī 'l-ṭibb (Compendio de medicina)*, ed. and Sp. tr. C. Álvarez de Morales and F. Girón Irueste, Madrid 1992; Ibn al-Ḳuff al-Karakī, *Djāmiʿ al-gharaḍ fī hifz al-siḥḥa wa-dafʿ al-maraḍ*, ed. S.K. Hamarneh, ʿAmmān 1989; *Kanz al-fawāʾid fī tanwīʿ al-mawāʾid*, ed. M. Marin and D. Waines, Beirut-Stuttgart 1993.

(J. RUSKA-[D. WAINES])

SAMORI TURE (1830-1900), the founder of an empire in West Africa during the 19th century.

A bloody tyrant and slave-merchant in colonial historiography, and a precursor of resistance for African nationalism, Samori never ranked as an emblematical figure for Islam in the sub-Saharan region. We now discern in him the figure of an imperial leader, with undoubtedly political and military qualities, whose resistance to the French and whose Islamic orientation arose more from the conjuncture of events than from a predetermined plan.

Samori arose from the Mandinka/Mandigo world, which had in particular given birth to the mediaeval empire of Mali [*q.v.*]. His political rise unfolded completely within the upper Niger valley and its right bank affluent the Milo (in modern Mali and Guinea). He was born into an aristocratic family, substantially de-Islamised, but incarnated through his actions the aspirations of a specialised social group, the Jula (Dioula) Muslims and traders, at that time stirred up by the indirect effects of the largely Fulani *dj̲ihāds* taking place in adjoining regions (1727, Futa Djalon, in modern Guinea; 1817, Masīna, in Mali; 1852, al-Ḥād̲j̲d̲j̲ ʿUmar, in the northern part of Guinea).

Samori's beginnings were those of the leader of a Mandingo band of troops. He first exercised his calling of arms, before 1860, in the service of various clans, notably that of his maternal relatives, the Kamara. In 1878, he personally took control of all Upper Niger, and in 1881 seized Kankan, the main Islamic city of the region.

The capture of Kankan brought into his circle numerous scholars. From now onwards, Samori was assisted by a secretary who wrote his correspondence in Arabic, but, above all, he installed in his immediate entourage, for eight years, Sidiki Sherifu Haidara, a *S̲h̲arīf* of Kankan and *s̲h̲ayk̲h̲* of the Ḳādiriyya, who became his master. At a time when he was still, at the age of 20, illiterate, Samori acquired in his shadow a taste for Arabic and for Ḳurʾānic recitation.

The people of Kankan were thus the agents of a grafting process of Islam. In 1884, at the end of Ramaḍān, he who was not yet anything more than a *kèlètigi* (war chief), and then a *faama* (political chief by right of conquest), assumed the title of *almami* (*al-imām*), borrowed from the neighbouring Fulani *dj̲ihāds*. In correspondence, he was after this time described as *amīr al-muʾminīn*. In December 1886, at the end of a period of study, he proclaimed himself *namutigi* ("master of tradition"), a dignity reserved for scholars of *ḥadīt̲h̲* and *fiḳh*, and led in person the Friday prayer. He also launched a forcible movement of Islamisation, imposing the *s̲h̲arīʿa* and the Islamic law of succession, nominating *ḳāḍīs* and making Ḳurʾānic teaching general by means of a network of paid schoolmasters (*karamoko*), forcing non-Muslims to convert. On this occasion he plunged into open conflict with Mandingo tradition and experienced the direct hostility of part of his family and his partisans. The excesses of this Islamic revolution, combined with defeats suffered at the hands of his main enemy in the region, the Senufo kingdom of Kenedugu (Sikasso), forced Samori to relax the system. This episode, which had hardly lasted four years, came to an end in 1889. There nevertheless remained of these attempts a strong Islamising tendency at the head of the empire, which at this time enjoyed its apogee with a population of about a million inhabitants and an area of not less than 200,000 km^2.

The threat from the French played an important role in this return to a more pragmatical attitude. The first clashes with the French, who were now reaching the river Niger (Bamako, 1 February 1883) and who marked out Samori as the enemy who was to be brought low. The history of relations between the French and Samori is one of a long series of treaties swiftly renounced (Kenyeba-Kura, 1886; Bisandugu, 1887; Nyako, 1889) and of frontal attacks which had various outcomes. Samori was forced to evacuate Upper Niger and to transfer his troops and faithful supporters further eastwards, to the north of the Ivory Coast, into lands populated by indifferent or hostile tribes. For several years, Samori's power reached a new peak. But, deprived of access to the ports of Freetown and Monrovia, which had allowed him to import rapid-firing arms, Samori was thrown back on to the defensive. He was abandoned by the Jula of Kong (in the north of the Ivory Coast), and destroyed their town (18 May 1897), whilst his son Sarankènyi-Mori massacred, against his orders, a French column near Bouna (20 August 1897). Deceived in his hopes of conciliating the British, menaced by the French who wished to avenge their dead, Samori had to relinquish territory in face of a combined offensive by the two colonial powers, mounted from the south. He tried at that point to get back, by a southerly movement, to the Upper Niger basin. It was there that he was captured by surprise, with leaves of the Ḳurʾān in his hand, by a reconnaissance party under Capt. Gouraud at Gelemu (western part of the Ivory Coast, 20 September 1898). Transferred to Saint-Louis in Senegal, and then deported with several of his supporters to Gabon, into a human and natural milieu totally different, he died there on 2 June 1900.

Bibliography: The bibl. of the Samorian movement is dominated by the monumental thesis of Yves Person, based on an extensive combing of the archives and far-reaching oral enquiries (861 informants, from 1955 to 1962). Without being basically challenged, Person's work may be criticised on certain points: the very concept of a "Jula revolution", which makes Samori the political expression of the trading minority, thereby underestimating in his approach the truly Mandingo warrior models—the essentially political vision of Samori's undertaking (erection of a sovereign power, defence of an identity), to the detriment of social aspects (notably, the extension of slavery as a result of the incessant warfare)—and a certain fascination for the author of the "genius" (a recurring term) of his hero.

Y. Person, *Samori. Une révolution Dyula*, 3 vols., Dakar 1968-75, pp. 2,377; *Cartes historiques de l'Afrique manding (fin du 19ème siècle). Samori. Une révolution Dyula*, Paris, Centre de Recherches Africaines 1940, 44 maps. See also Person, *Samori, construction et chute d'un empire*, in Ch.-A. Julien *et alii* (eds.), *Les Africains*, Paris 1977, i, 249-85 (résumé of the thesis), and *Samori and Islam*, in J.R. Willis (ed.), *Studies in West African Islamic history*, i, *The cultivators of Islam*, London 1979, 259-77.

Person has clearly shown the crushing weight of the "black legend" in French historiography, polemical and repetitive. Three works are worth mentioning: Commandant Peroz, *Au Soudan Français*, Paris 1889; Capitaine L.-G. Binger, *Du Niger au Golfe de Guinée*, Paris 1892, 2 vols.; Colonel Gallieni, *Deux campagnes au Soudan Français*, Paris 1891, which contains in particular the greater part of Peroz's report on his mission to Bisandugu, Samori's capital, in 1886. These three officers were direct participants in the events, and the first two had a long period of contact with Samori.

(J.-L. Triaud)

SAMOS [see sīsām].

SAMRŪ or Sumrū, Bēgam, the originally Muslim Indian wife of the European adventurer Walter Reinhardt Sombre or Samrū, who held the *pargana* [*q.v.*] of Sardhanā [*q.v.*] in northwestern India under the later Mug̲h̲al Emperor S̲h̲āh ʿAlam II [*q.v.*]. On Reinhardt's death in 1778, Bēgam Samrū kept up what was virtually a petty principality of Sardhanā, with an army which included some 300 European and half-breed mercenaries, and in 1792 married a French soldier of fortune Levassault. Toppled from control of Sardhanā in 1793 by a son of

Reinhardt's, Ẓafar-yāb Khān, in whose putsch Levassault died by his own hand, the Bēgam was nevertheless restored by the Irish adventurer George Thomas. After the British conquest of the Doʾāb [*q.v.*] in 1803, she tendered her loyalty to the British, who allowed her to retain her estates and to keep up a reduced army.

In 1781 she had been baptised a Roman Catholic, and at Sardhanā she built churches and schools, including a cathedral for a bishop appointed to the new see, and she also contributed to Hindu and Muslim charities; her foundations are still today an important centre for Christian activity in the Doʾāb. However, she was herself proficient in Persian and Urdu, and had a lively circle of poets in these two languages at her court, who included François Gottlieb Koine (var. Cohen!) "Farāsū", nephew by marriage of Ẓafar-yāb Khān, skilled also in Hindi poetry and described by Sprenger as "the one outstanding name in the annals of Anglo-Indian [Urdu] poetry". Her new palace in Sardhanā later became a Roman Catholic school; her Dihlī palace in the "Oriental Regency" style was used as a powder factory by the insurgents during the Sepoy Mutiny of 1857-8. After the death of this remarkable woman on 27 January 1836, her estates were resumed, but her large private fortune passed to the son of the marriage between Ẓafar-yāb's daughter and the Begam's Eurasian factor Dyce, David Ochterlony Dyce-Sombre, and on his death in London in 1851, her fortune mainly passed, after prolonged litigation, to his wife, daughter of Earl St. Vincent and subsequently Lady Forrester.

Bibliography: Capt. W. Francklin, *A military memoir of George Thomas*, Calcutta 1803, London 1805; H. Compton, *A particular account of the European military adventures of Hindustan*, London 1893, 400-10; H.G. Keene, *Hindustan under freelances 1770-1820*, London 1907, 76-83, 102-4, 192-6; C.E. Buckland, *Dictionary of Indian biography*, London 1908, s.v. *Samru Begam*; *Imperial gazetteer of India*², xxii, 105-7; P. Spear, *Twilight of the Mughuls, studies in late Mughul Delhi*, Cambridge 1951, 115, 149-50, 152, 211; Ram Babu Saksena, *European and Indo-European poets of Urdu and Persian*, repr. Lahore n.d. [*ca.* 1988], 88-96 (on Dyce-Sombre, "a scholar of Urdu and Persian and ... a poet"), 258-77 (on Ẓafar-yāb Khān and "Farāsū"); Brajendranath Banerji, *Begum Samru*, repr. Delhi 1989. A Persian *mathnawī* on the life of the Bēgam was completed in 1822, and is extant in a B.L. ms. Add. 25830 (Rieu, ii, 724a), with the Bēgam's own copy, reportedly with magnificent contemporary illustrations, in the Arabic and Persian Research Institute, Tonk, Rajasthan. See also SARDHANĀ.

(C.E. Bosworth and S. Digby)

ṢAMṢĀM al-DAWLA, Abū Kālīdjār Marzubān, Shams al-Milla (353-88/964-98), Buyid *amir* and eldest son of ʿAḍud al-Dawla [*q.v.*].

On his father's death in Shawwāl 372/March 983, Ṣamṣām al-Dawla succeeded to power as *amīr al-umarāʾ*, but his position was immediately disputed by another brother, Sharaf al-Dawla Shīrzīl, who seized Fārs and Khūzistān. From his base in ʿIrāḳ, Ṣamṣām al-Dawla had also to combat the Kurdish chief Bādh, ancestor of the Marwānid dynasty [see MARWĀNIDS] of Diyār Bakr, who had seized various towns in al-Djazīra and who even for a while held Mawṣil. Despite his repulse of Bādh's attack on Baghdād and the recovery of Mawṣil, Ṣamṣām al-Dawla had to allow him to retain Diyār Bakr and part of Ṭūr ʿAbdīn.

From 375/985-6 onwards, Ṣamṣām al-Dawla was again involved in disputes with Sharaf al-Dawla, but with a section of the Būyid army also espousing the cause of a further younger brother, Bahāʾ al-Dawla Fīrūz [*q.v.* in Suppl.], then only 15 years old. In the end, Ṣamṣām al-Dawla had to agree to place Sharaf al-Dawla first in the *khuṭba* of ʿIrāḳ, with himself retaining only the governorship of Baghdād; but Sharaf al-Dawla was able in 376/986-7 to seize Ṣamṣām al-Dawla at Shīrāz, partially blind him and imprison him at Sīrāf. He was freed in 379/989 after Sharaf al-Dawla's death, when Bahāʾ al-Dawla had succeeded to the office of supreme *amīr*. At the outset, Bahāʾ al-Dawla recognised Ṣamṣām al-Dawla as an equal ruler controlling Fārs, Kirmān and ʿUmān. Ṣamṣām al-Dawla now expanded into Khūzistān and seized Baṣra, with his troops led by the capable commander Abū ʿAlī al-Ḥasan b. Ustādh-Hurmuz, and he successfully resisted the claims of the sons of ʿIzz al-Dawla Bakhtiyār [*q.v.*], cousin of ʿAḍud al-Dawla. In the fighting with Bahāʾ al-Dawla which went on for some eight years, Ṣamṣām al-Dawla was gaining the upper hand when, in Dhu 'l-Ḥidjdja 388/November-December 998, he was murdered near Iṣfahān by one of the sons of ʿIzz al-Dawla, Nūr al-Dawla Abū Naṣr Shāh-Fīrūz; Bahāʾ al-Dawla had him buried in state within a mausoleum at Shīrāz.

Of Ṣamṣām al-Dawla's education and cultural background we know little, but his vizier ʿAbd Allāh Ibn Saʿdān [*q.v.* in Suppl.] (373-4/983-4) was famed for his circle of littérateurs and scholars in Baghdād, including Abū Ḥayyān al-Tawḥīdī [*q.v.*], and according to the *Ṣiwān al-ḥikma*, doubtfully ascribed to Abū Sulaymān al-Sidjistānī, the historian and philosopher Miskawayh [*q.v.*] served Ṣamṣām al-Dawla in Baghdād before going on to the court of Fakhr al-Dawla [*q.v.*] at Rayy.

Bibliography: 1. Sources. Miskawayh ends his history in 369/979-80, but much material can be found in Abū Shudjāʿ al-Rūdhrāwarī's *Dhayl* (in Amedroz and Margoliouth's *Eclipse of the ʿAbbasid caliphate*, iii, tr. vi), and this can be filled out with details from the general chroniclers such as Ibn al-Djawzī, Sibṭ Ibn al-Djawzī and Ibn al-Athīr.

2. Studies. See the historical narratives of events constructed by Mafizullah Kabir, in *The Buwaihid dynasty of Baghdad (334/946-447/1055)*, Calcutta 1964, and H. Busse, *Chalif und Grosskönig. Die Buyiden im Iraq (945-1055)*, Beirut-Wiesbaden 1969, indices; also J.L. Kraemer, *Humanism in the renaissance of Islam. The cultural revival during the Buyid age*, Leiden 1986, 37, 91, 191-6, 198-9.

(C.E. Bosworth)

ṢAMṢĀM al-DAWLA SHĀHNAWĀZ [see MAʾĀTHIR AL-UMARĀʾ].

ṢAMṢĀM al-SALṬANA, Nadjaf Ḳulī Khān, a Bakhtiyārī chief born about 1846. His father was Ḥusayn Ḳulī Khān, more commonly known as Īl-khānī, the first Bakhtiyārī leader to be formally designated *Īlkhān* of all the Bakhtiyārī by the imperial government in Tehran, and who was poisoned on the orders of prince Ẓill al-Sulṭān, the famous governor-general of Iṣfāhān, who feared his growing power. Ṣamṣām al-Salṭana was *Īlbeg* of the Bakhtiyārī in 1903-5 and later *Īlkhān*. He is remembered principally for the part he played as one of the leaders of the Bakhtiyārī intervention in the constitutional movement in Persia.

The Constitutional Revolution [see DUSTŪR. iv] gave the Bakhtiyārī khāns, particularly Ṣamṣām and his brother, Sardār-i Asʿad, the opportunity to transcend their traditional provincial roles and enter the national arena. Although Sardār-i Asʿad had been at least partially converted to the constitutionalist cause, Ṣamṣām appears to have been motivated largely by the desire to further his own personal and tribal interests.

During 1908 the Iṣfāhānī constitutionalists attempted to enlist wider support, including that of the Ba<u>kh</u>tiyārī, in their struggle against Iḳbāl al-Dawla, the new governor appointed by the reactionary Muḥammad ʿAlī <u>Sh</u>āh [*q.v.*]. In January 1909 Ṣamṣām, with a Ba<u>kh</u>tiyārī force, occupied Iṣfāhān and assumed the duties of governor. He asked the <u>Sh</u>āh to confirm him in this position but the <u>Sh</u>āh refused. Ṣamṣām convoked the provincial *an<u>dj</u>uman* and, on 3 May, telegraphed jointly with Sardār-i Asʿad to all the foreign legations warning of their intention to march on the capital to force on the Shah the restoration of the constitutional régime. On July 13 Tehran fell to the Ba<u>kh</u>tiyārī marching from the south and revolutionary forces led by Sipahdār-i Aʿẓam advancing from Ra<u>sh</u>t, and the <u>Sh</u>āh was deposed. Ṣamṣām was appointed governor of Iṣfāhān.

When, in the summer of 1911, the news of the return of the ex-<u>Sh</u>āh reached Tehran, Ṣamṣām entered the cabinet of Sipahdār as minister of war. The same day, 19 July, the Ma<u>dj</u>lis declared a state of siege and martial law, placing extraordinary powers in Ṣamṣām's hands. He advocated the Ma<u>dj</u>lis putting a price on the head of the ex-<u>Sh</u>āh and personally offered to assassinate him. On 26 July Ṣamṣām formed a new cabinet, becoming prime minister while retaining the post of minister of war. He mobilised his Ba<u>kh</u>tiyārī tribesmen to fight the forces of the ex-<u>Sh</u>āh but the arrival of the Ba<u>kh</u>tiyārī with their <u>kh</u>āns in Tehran and their exorbitant demands for money led to several resignation threats from Morgan Shuster, the American Treasurer-General. In August and September the Ba<u>kh</u>tiyārī, with the help of the Armenian revolutionary Yifrim <u>Kh</u>ān, defeated the supporters of Muḥammad ʿAlī. The hostility of Ṣamṣām and his cabinet to Shuster's efforts to reform Persia's finances came to a head when the latter attempted to collect taxes from prince ʿAlāʾ al-Dawla. On 2 November Russia protested at Shuster's confiscation of the property of prince *<u>Sh</u>uʿāʿ* al-Salṭana who, although having engaged in armed rebellion, was under Russian protection. Wu<u>th</u>ūḳ al-Dawla, minister of foreign affairs in Ṣamṣām's cabinet, apologised but Russia presented an ultimatum demanding the dismissal of Shuster. The Ma<u>dj</u>lis was inclined to resist but on 24 December Ṣamṣām and his cabinet, with the regent Nāṣir al-Mulk, forced its dissolution and accepted the Russian demands. Ṣamṣām remained prime minister until January 1913, when he resigned from the cabinet. In July 1913 Ba<u>kh</u>tiyārī domination suffered a further setback when the newly-formed government gendarmerie expelled all armed Ba<u>kh</u>tiyārī from Tehran.

In May 1918 Ṣamṣām again formed a government. As a repercussion of events in Russia, this cabinet, which had a nationalist character, abrogated all treaties with Russia and all concessions granted to Russians. This measure, which affected the interests of foreigners in general, accelerated the fall of Ṣamṣām's cabinet and its replacement by that of Wu<u>th</u>ūḳ al-Dawla, which signed the Anglo-Persian agreement of 9 August 1919. In the summer of 1921 Ṣamṣām was appointed governor-general of <u>Kh</u>urāsān to replace the military governor-general, Colonel Muḥammad Taḳī <u>Kh</u>ān Pasyān, but was prevented from taking up his post by Pasyān's resistance. Ṣamṣām died in 1930 while on a mission to mediate between the central government and rebellious Ba<u>kh</u>tiyārī tribes.

Bibliography: E.G. Browne, *The Persian revolution of 1905-1909*, Cambridge 1910, 266, 293, 298; W. Morgan Shuster, *The strangling of Persia*, London 1912, 36, 109-18, 158-62, 189; Yaḥyā Dawlatābādī, *Tārī<u>kh</u>-i muʿāṣir yā ḥayāt-i Yaḥyā*, Tehran 1328-1336/1949-1957, iii, 215-16; G.R. Garthwaite, *The Bakhtiyari Khans: tribal disunity in Iran 1880-1915*, diss. UCLA 1969, unpubl., 226-61.

(V. MINORSKY-[STEPHANIE CRONIN])

AL-**ṢAMṢĀMA**, the sword of the Arab warrior-poet ʿAmr b. Maʿdīkarib al-Zubaydī [*q.v.*], celebrated for the temper and cutting power of its blade. Like a number of the best Arab swords, its origin was traced back to Southern Arabia and a fabulous antiquity was ascribed to it. ʿAmr himself in a verse often quoted (*ʿIḳd*, ed. 1293, i, 46, ii, 70; Ibn Badrūn, 84; *Tā<u>dj</u> al-ʿarūs*, vi, 229) says that it had once belonged to Ibn <u>Dh</u>ī Ḳayfān "of the people of ʿĀd" (this member of an actual Ḥimyar clan (cf. M. Hartmann, *Die arabische Frage*, 331, 613) is identified with one of the last Ḥimyar kings of the family of <u>Dh</u>ū <u>Dj</u>adan; but very probably the poet only means to allude to the great age of his weapon).

The history and fortunes of al-Ṣamṣāma are rather involved; even in the poet's lifetime it came into the hands of a member of the Umayyad family, <u>Kh</u>ālid b. Saʿīd b. al-ʿĀṣ, the companion of the Prophet. The way in which he got possession of it is recorded with several variants by Ibn al-Kalbī (in al-Balā<u>dh</u>urī), Abū ʿUbayda (in the *A<u>gh</u>ānī*), al-Zuhrī (in Ibn Ḥubay<u>sh</u>; see *Bibl.*), and Sayf b. ʿUmar (in al-Ṭabarī). According to the last-named, <u>Kh</u>ālid won it in battle after routing ʿAmr b. Maʿdīkarib who was taking part in the revolt against Islam raised by the false prophet al-Aswad al-ʿAnsī [*q.v.*]; according to the three first, ʿAmr himself gave it to <u>Kh</u>ālid as a ransom for his sister (or wife) Rayḥāna, who was a prisoner of the Muslims. ʿAmr composed a poem on the occasion, of which several verses are frequently quoted in the Arab sources (Ibn Durayd, 49; *Lisān*, xv, 240, etc.). The tradition (al-Tibrīzī, in *Ḥamāsa*, ed. Freytag, 397, 12-15) which says that ʿAmr gave it to the caliph ʿUmar is quite denied by authority.

After the death of <u>Kh</u>ālid b. Saʿīd at the battle of Mar<u>dj</u> al-Ṣuffar during the conquest of Syria (14/635), al-Ṣamṣāma passed to his nephew Saʿīd b. al-ʿĀṣ b. Saʿīd b. al-Āṣ [*q.v.*], who lost it while defending the caliph ʿU<u>th</u>mān when the latter was besieged in his house at Medina (35/656). It was found by a Bedouin of the tribe of <u>Dj</u>uhayna, with whom it was discovered in the reign of Muʿāwiya. Restored to its former owner, it passed from one member to another of the family of the Banu 'l-ʿĀṣ until one of them, Ayyūb b. Abī Ayyūb, great-grandson of the son of Saʿīd, sold it to the caliph al-Mahdī (158-69/775-85) for about 80,000 dirhams. Henceforth, al-Ṣamṣāma was kept as a precious relic in the treasury of the ʿAbbāsids and its fame continued to increase; poets like Abu 'l-Hawl al-Ḥimyarī (al-<u>Dj</u>āḥiẓ, *Ḥayawān*, v, 30) and Salm al-<u>Kh</u>āsir sang its praises.

From different sources we learn of its existence in the caliphates of al-Hādī (169-70/785-6), Hārūn al-Ra<u>sh</u>īd (170-93/786-809), al-Wā<u>th</u>iḳ (227-32/842-7), and al-Mutawakkil (232-47/847-61), after which there is no longer any mention of it. The anecdotes recorded regarding the excellence of the famous sword during the period when it was in the hands of these caliphs have little chance of being authentic; a description which has a certain appearance of reality is the one given in al-Ṭabarī, iii, 1348, 4-8, in connection with the story of al-Wā<u>th</u>iḳ's using it to execute with his own hand in 231/845-6 Aḥmad b. Naṣr al-

Khuzāʿī, who was accused of having conspired against the caliph and of having maintained that the Ḳurʾān was not created, contrary to the view laid down by al-Maʾmūn: "It was a blade with a hilt at its end; three nails driven into it attached the blade to the hilt". It is apparent then that the famous al-Ṣamṣāma had nothing of value about it except its great age.

As to the name al-Ṣamṣāma, it is simply an epithet referring to the fine quality of the blade (the "cleaver") like muṣammim, which has the same significance. Ṣamṣāma is often used as a common noun, e.g. by al-Farazdaḳ (Naḳāʾiḍ, 385, 4) and by ʿAmr b. Maʿdīkarib himself (Ḥamāsa of al-Buḥturī, 83, ed. Cheikho, no. 237); Amālī of al-Ḳālī, iii, 154, 10), as well as by Muslim b. al-Walīd (ed. De Goeje, vi, 18) in a verse which Schwarzlose (see Bibl.) wrongly thought to refer to ʿAmr's sword, while the weapon given by Hārūn al-Rashīd to his general Yazīd b. Mazyad referred to in the verse is the sword of the Prophet, Dhu 'l-Faḳār [q.v.], as is evident from verse 25 of the same poem and the note by Ibn Khallikān (ed. Ihsān ʿAbbās, v, 329, tr. de Slane, 220).

Bibliography: Balādhurī, Futūḥ, 119-20; Ṭabarī, i, 1984, 1997; Aghānī, ed. Būlāḳ, xiv, 26-7, 2nd ed., 27; Ibn Badrūn, ed. Dozy, 84; ʿIḳd, ed. 1293, i, 66; Ibn Hudhayl al-Andalusī, La pârure des cavaliers et l'enseigne des preux, ed. L. Mercier, Paris 1922, 61-2; Ibn Sīduh, Mukhaṣṣaṣ, vi, 19, 28; Lisān, xv, 240; Tādj al-ʿarūs, viii, 370; Caetani, Annali dell' Islām, ii, 783, 787 (12 AH, §§ 65, 69; the latter gives the translation of an unpublished passage from the Kitāb al-Ghazawāt of Ibn Ḥubaysh, iii, 322 (14 AH, § 104 note), iv, 632 (21 AH, § 282); F. Schwarzlose, Die Waffen der alten Araber, Leipzig 1886, 36, 93-6, 129, 192-4.

(G. Levi Della Vida*)

ṢĀMSŪN (modern Turkish spelling, Samsun), a town of northern Asia Minor, in the classical Pontus. The Byzantine settlement, known as Amisus, attracted the attention of the Dānishmendids [q.v.]; as Sāmiya, it is mentioned in the historical epos known as the Dānishmend-nāme. The city passed into Turkish hands at the end of the 6th/12th century, but was temporarily retaken by the Byzantines; in 608-9/1212, Samsun formed part of the Comnene principality of Trebizond. When before 585/1189 Sultan Ḳi̊li̊dj Arslan divided up his state among his sons, the town fell to Rukn al-Dīn. A trade route linking the port with Amasya, Çorum and Ankara, and also with eastern Anatolia, apparently was of secondary importance. However, the town was linked by sea routes to Caffa (Kefe, Feodosiya) in the Crimea [see KEFE] and the northern coast of the Black Sea. Genoese sources record the presence of a Turkish kommerkiarios (customs collector) about 688/1289. In the 8th/14th century the area was controlled by the Djāndār Oghlu dynasty [see ISFENDIYĀR OGHLU], one of whose members, named Isfendiyār (b.) Bāyezīd, had a coin struck in Samsun, which unfortunately bears no date. From the Ottoman chronicler Neshrī we learn that in 795/1393 the Ottoman sultan Yi̊ldi̊ri̊m Bāyezīd I took over Kastamonu and Samsun, leaving a much reduced principality in the hands of Isfendiyār b. Bāyezīd. According to Hans Schiltberger, who was present in Anatolia at this time, Samsun was granted by Sultan Bāyezīd to the son of the former Bulgarian ruler Shishman, who had accepted Islam after the Ottoman conquest of Ti̊rnovo. Schiltberger also reports an invasion of land and water snakes in the countryside around Samsun; when the land snakes allegedly gained a "victory" over the water snakes, the court of Sultan Bāyezīd seems to have regarded this as a sign that the sultan, who already controlled the land, was also soon to dominate the seas.

In the 8th/14th century, Samsun had a resident Genoese population represented by a consul; after 701-2/1302 the latter was subordinate to the consul resident in Caffa, but, at least in principle, nominated by the authorities in Genoa. The Genoese lived in a separate settlement, a short distance away from the Muslim town, which the 9th/15th century chronicler ʿĀshiḳ-pasha-zāde calls Kāfir Samsun; he records that under Meḥemmed I (r. 805-24/1403-21), the Genoese abandoned their township after a fire, whereupon the inhabitants of the Muslim town, seeing their source of livelihood disappearing, voluntarily submitted to Ottoman domination. On the other hand, a Genoese citizen who had resided in Samsun for seven years claimed an indemnity for property losses suffered when the castle was burned by "the Turks" in 1422. In the following year, the sübashi̊ of Samsun also exercised authority over the Genoese settlement. By the middle of the century, Simisso, as Samsun was called by the Genoese, was no longer mentioned among the latter's colonies. The Genoese also occasionally had coins of low silver content struck in the town. At certain times, notaries were present to record the business transactions of their countrymen.

According to Genoese sources, millet, barley, beans and chickpeas were exported from Samsun to the territories north of the Black Sea. From the north, Samsun received hides and edible fats, in addition to slaves. Apparently the commerce of the town was much impeded by Tīmūr's campaign in Anatolia; a Greek merchant who visited Samsun at this time complained that nothing could be bought or sold there. The Spanish envoy to the court of Tīmūr, Ruy Gonzalez de Clavijo, also visited Samsun at approximately this time.

Ottoman documentation begins with a list of taxpayers from the reign of Bāyezīd II; 463 persons were recorded in this defter apart from the garrison. Samsun was located in the sandjak of Djānik. At this time a minute Frenkpazāri̊ quarter (6 taxpayers) housed the remaining Genoese merchants. The town (511 taxpayers in 984/1574) was heavily fortified, and in the 10th/16th century the hinterland was known for its onions, while a locally grown pear was pickled and sent to Istanbul. But the best-known local product undoubtedly was hemp, from which the ropes required by the Ottoman arsenal were manufactured. Certain lands were set aside for the growing of hemp (kendir khāṣṣlari̊) and the ḳāḍī of Samsun supervised delivery and payment to the growers. Pendjik [q.v.] accounts demonstrate that slaves from the northern coast of the Black Sea continued to be imported through Samsun.

In the early 11th/17th century the town seems to have lost a good deal of population; a register from the year 1052/1642-3 records only 58 taxpayers. However, Ewliyā Čelebi, who visited the Black Sea coast in 1050/1640, comments on the large number of notables (aʿyān) whom he encountered in Samsun; some of them were officers manning the fortress and others ʿulemā, although Samsun by this time had lost the medrese which it had possessed in the 10th/16th century. Ewliyā thought that the working population of Samsun consisted of seafaring men and hempworkers, who lived in tile-covered houses and struck him by their clean and tidy clothes; he specifically comments on the absence of very poor people (ʿawāmm). Thus it would appear that the depredations of the Cossacks, whose small, swift ships made the entire Black Sea coast unsafe during those years, inflicted severe but not lasting damage to the town. Ewliyā does, however, claim that Samsun was at one point occupied by the Cossacks and the fortifications seriously damaged; but by the time of his visit, the latter had been repaired.

The *Dj̲ihān-nümā*, a 11th/17th-century geographical text, contains some information on Samsun, which was probably put together not by the author Kātib Čelebi himself but by one of his collaborators. The geographer comments on the non-nucleated settlements of the Black Sea coast and the rustic character of the inhabitants. In his time, the castle of Samsun had fallen in ruins, but the town possessed one or more shop-lined streets, a mosque and a bath house. In actual fact, late 11th/17th century Samsun possessed at least four mosques: two of them went back to the Ilkh̲ānid period, the *mesdj̲id* of ʿĪsā Bābā dated from the 9th/15th century, while the Ḥadj̲dj̲ī Kh̲ātūn mosque had been founded in 1105-6/1694. Tournefort, who passed through Samsun in 1112-13/1701, did not observe any signs of commercial activity and paid no particular attention to the town. However, the Trabzon Armenian Minas Bîžîsh̲kiyan, whose travel notes date from 1232-5/1817-19, paints a somewhat different picture; he regarded Samsun as an important trade centre, with a substantial number of resident Armenians. This is all the more remarkable as Samsun had been burnt to the ground in 1221/1806, when a local governor was ousted by a rival of his who enjoyed central governement support. In 1244-5/1829 the town was still recovering from this disaster. The buildings of Samsun apparently made a pleasant impression on the Prussian general Helmuth von Moltke, who in 1253-4/1838 disembarked from a steamer and began his Anatolian travels in Samsun; but although he must have spent some time in the town and even made a map of it, he does not say anything specific about buildings or people. Henry Suter, who visited Samsun in the very same year, thought that the town had a population of 450 Turkish and 150 Greek families. This traveller commented on Samsun's well-stocked bazaars, but believed them to serve the transit trade rather than local consumption. In this period, the port did not possess a quay, and afforded only limited protection in case of storms. Yet Moltke observed that a considerable amount of trade was conducted through the port, and other European travellers of the time agreed with him. Many visitors were Persian and other merchants crossing the Black Sea on Austrian steamers in order to trade in Rumelia and central Europe. A.D. Mordtmann, who visited Samsun in 1266-7/1850, also made some acerbic comments on the lack of port facilities.

In an account of Asia Minor published in 1278-9/1862, Charles Texier adds a few details to this description. By the middle of the 13th/19th century, a governor had built a government house, into which antique columns and other finds from the ruins of the ancient city had been incorporated. The town by mid-century boasted a covered market, a kh̲ān, a public bath and four saints' graves. The quarters inhabited by Greeks and Armenians were located some distance away from the Muslim town; they both possessed a church and a school. Yet in terms of population, the town remained quite small; the Ottoman traveller Ferrukh̲ān Bey, who visited Samsun in 1263/1847 and to whom we owe a description of its physical layout, records 500 Turkish, 240 Greek, 60 Armenian and a few European households; he estimated total population at about 6,000. Cuinet records a much lower figure for 1276-7/1860, namely 3,000 persons. A disastrous fire in 1286/1869 constituted another setback. Yet in the 1890s Samsun's population had increased to 16,000. Referring to the period just before 1311/1894 Sh̲ems ül-Dīn Sāmī gives the more conservative figure of 11,000 persons; he regarded Samsun as the most active Black Sea port in Ottoman hands.

Early 14th/late 19th century growth was partly due to the spread of tobacco cultivation in the region, which was exported through Samsun; in addition, as Istanbul now depended increasingly on Anatolian grain, the grain trade grew in importance. In the aftermath of World War I, the area saw clashes between armed bands of Pontus Greek separatists and their Laz and Turkish opponents. Under the threat of British intervention, the Porte decided to send Muṣṭafā Kemāl, one of the most successful Ottoman generals of World War I, to restore order. He disembarked in Samsun on 19 May 1919, which became a Turkish national holiday after the proclamation of the Republic, and began to organise political resistance against the foreign occupation of Anatolia and eastern Thrace. However, Samsun was soon superseded as a centre of the Turkish nationalist forces.

During the Republican period, Samsun became the capital of a *wilāyet* and developed into a sizeable city (198,749 inhabitants in 1980). The railway reached Samsun in 1932; the port was modernised in 1960, and the Samsun Trade Fair, established in 1963, proved a boost to the local economy. However, agriculture, particularly tobacco cultivation, continues to be the economic mainstay of the province (involvement of 80.4% of the active population in 1975), which comprises extremely fertile areas such as the Çarşamba and Bafra plains, where two and even three harvests a year are possible. Though Samsun possesses large-scale factories producing copperware, artificial fertiliser and fodder, industry (4.9% of the active population in 1975) and services (6% of the active population in 1975) are of much less importance in the economy of the province. Small enterprises predominate; in 1980, only 20% of the active population consisted of wage and salary earners. From the 1950s onwards, mechanisation of agriculture has resulted in widespread emigration. This situation explains why, even in 1980, the percentage of persons able to read and write (61.7%) was lower than the average for Turkey as a whole. However, from 1981 onward, efforts have been made to bridge the gap, which include the establishment of a local university.

Bibliography: For older bibl., see J.H. Mordtmann's *EI*[1] art. and Besim Darkot, *İA* art. 1. Sources. ʿĀsh̲ık̲-pas̲h̲a-zāde, *Tewārīkh̲-i āl-i ʿOth̲mān*, Istanbul 1332/1913-14, 89-90, tr. more detailed than in this ed., R.F. Kreutel, *Vom Hirtenzelt zur Hohen Pforte*, Graz etc. 1959, 127-8; Ewliyā Čelebi, *Seyāḥat-nāme*, ii, Istanbul 1314/1896-7, 77-8; Kātib Čelebi, *Dj̲ihān-nümā*, Istanbul 1145/1732, 754-5.

2. Travellers. Ruy Gonzales de Clavijo, *Embassy to Tamerlane*, tr. Le Strange; Johannes Schiltberger, ed. and tr. U. Schlemmer, *Als Sklave im Osmanischen Reich und bei den Tataren 1394-1427*, Stuttgart 1983, 61-4; Ritter, *Erdkunde*, xviii/3. *Westasien-Kleinasien*, Berlin 1858, 796-806 (inc. notices of earlier travellers); Ferrukh̲ān Beg, *Bagh̲dād seyāḥat-nāmesi*, Istanbul 1284/1868; H. von Moltke, *Briefe über Zustände und Begebenheiten aus der Türkei*, Berlin 1876, 197-200; Ch. Texier, *Asie Mineure*, Paris 1862, 620; Van Lennep, *Travels in little-known parts of Asia Minor*, London 1870, i, 38-60; A.D. Mordtmann, ed. F. Babinger, *Anatolien. Skizzen und Reisebriefe aus Kleinasien*, Hanover 1925, 80-3.

3. Studies. Sāmī Bey Frās̲h̲erī, *Ḳāmūs al-aʿlām*,

iv, Istanbul 1311/1894, 2931-3; V. Cuinet, *La Turquie d'Asie*, Paris 1892-4, i, 102-6; anon., art. *Samsun*, in *Yurt Ansiklopedisi*, ix (major source of information, with extensive bibl.); Besim Darkot, *İA*, art. s.v. (fundamental, with bibl. of travellers' accounts); Cl. Cahen, *Pre-Ottoman Turkey*, London 1968, index; S. Vryonis, *The decline of medieval Hellenism*, Berkeley etc. 1971, 130, 161; *Tarih boyunca Samsun ve Samsun belediyesi*, Ankara 1977; *Bütün yönleriyle Samsun*, Ankara 1978; M. Balard, *La Romanie génoise (XIIe-début du XVe siècle)*, Rome 1978, i, 133-4, 360, 373, 339, ii, 668; Yaşar Yücel, *XII.-XV. yüzyıllar Kuzey-Bati Anadolu tarihi, Çobanoğulları Candaroğulları beylikleri*, Ankara 1980, 93, 148; Soraiya Faroqhi, *Towns and townsmen of Ottoman Anatolia*, Cambridge 1984, 90, 106-7, 130-1; Mehmed Saglam (ed.), *Birinci tarih boyunca Karadeniz Kongresi bildirileri*, Samsun 1988; Mehmed Öz, *Population, taxation and the regional economy in the district of Canik, according to Ottoman* Tahrir defters, *1455-1576*, Ph.D. diss., Cambridge Univ. 1990, unpubl.; Saglam (ed.), *İkinci tarih boyunca Karadeniz Kongresi bildirileri*, Samsun 1990. For a list of the *sālnāmes* of the *wilāyet* of Trabzon (late 19th-early 20th centuries), see Hasan Duman *Osmanlı yıllıkları (salnameler ve nevsaller)*, Istanbul 1982, 85-7.

(SURAIYA FAROQHI)

AL-**SAMT** (A.), azimuth or direction, a term in frequent use in Islamic astronomy. It is usually applied to the direction of a celestial object measured on the horizon, determined by the arc of the horizon between the east- or west-points and the foot of the vertical arc through the celestial object. The Arabic plural *al-sumūt* gave rise to the term azimuth and its equivalents in numerous European languages. But whilst in mediaeval astronomy the azimuth was usually measured from the east- or west-points, in modern astronomy it is measured clockwise from the north point.

The complementary arc measured from the meridian was called *inḥirāf*, and, for example, the term *munḥarifa* was applied to a vertical sundial inclined at a specific angle to the meridian [see MIZWALA]. The direction of Mecca, called *ḳibla* [*q.v.*], was usually measured from the meridian, and so it is the *inḥirāf* (for *inḥirāf al-ḳibla*) that is tabulated in mediaeval tables displaying the *ḳibla* for different geographical localities. Yet sometimes also *samt al-ḳibla* was used when the *ḳibla* is measured from the north point.

The expression *samt al-raʾs*, literally "direction of the head", was used to denote the point of the celestial sphere directly above the observer. This, through various modifications and distortions, produced zenith and its equivalents in European languages.

Muslim astronomers invariably included in their handbooks [see ZĪDJ] a chapter on the determination of the azimuth of the sun or any star from its altitude, realising that this is mathematically equivalent to the problem of determining the time from the altitude. Ibn Yūnus [*q.v.*] at the end of the 4th/10th century compiled a table of the solar azimuth for each 1° of solar altitude and each 1° of solar longitude, for the latitude of Cairo; there are about 10,000 entries in the book appropriately entitled *Kitāb al-Samt*. These tables formed part of a corpus of tables for astronomical time-keeping that was used in Cairo until the 13th19th century (see Pl. LXVI). Other tables of the same kind were later compiled for the latitudes of Damascus, Alexandria and Damietta. The universal tables of al-Khalīlī can be used to find the azimuth of the sun or any star from its altitude and declination and the local latitude (based on the complicated accurate formula) without any calculation beyond addition or subtraction and interpolation [see MĪḲĀT. ii].

Muslim astronomers also discussed the problem of determining the *inḥirāf* of the *ḳibla* by various techniques, and compiled tables displaying the *inḥirāf* as a function of the latitude and longitude difference from Mecca [see ḲIBLA. ii]. Of more immediate practical use were lists of coordinates and their *ḳibla* values. Such lists were often included on instruments, sometimes, for example, engraved on the mater of an astrolabe [see ASṬURLĀB]. From the 3rd/9th century onwards Muslim astrolabists marked the azimuth circles (*sammata*) on the plates of astrolabes. With such curves they could, for example, tell at a glance the altitude of the sun when it was in the *ḳibla*. That altitude was also tabulated for all solar longitudes for specific localities such as Cairo, Marāgha and Damascus, or represented graphically on the backs of various Ṣafawid astrolabes (see Pl. LXVII).

Various instruments were devised for demonstrating the azimuth of the *ḳibla* of different localities, usually in the form of charts or maps, mainly representing geographical reality (as defined by mediaeval coordinates) only crudely. In 1979, however, a device from Iṣfāhān *ca.* 1122/1710 became available for study. This is a map of the world centred on Mecca, so conceived that for any locality between Spain and China the direction and distance of Mecca are given correctly within the limits of mediaeval geographical coordinates (see Pl. LXVIII). The maker and engraver were—on the grounds of the distinctive calligraphy—most probably ʿAbd al-ʿAlī and his brother Muḥammad Bāḳir, who made for Shāh Ḥusayn in 1124/1712-13 the splendid astrolabe now in the British Museum. The grid serves both functions admirably for places between the Maghrib and Sind, but because the latitude curves are drawn as arcs of circles slight errors occur for localities in al-Andalus in the west and India and China in the east. This remarkable object escaped notice in the articles ḲIBLA. ii and MAKKA. iv. It is a mathematical device or a cartographic projection or a nomogram, depending on how one defines either expression, which enables the user to lay the non-uniform scale of a diametrical rule over a given locality and then simply read off the *ḳibla* on the outer scale and the distance to Mecca (in *farsakhs* [*q.v.*]) on the scale of the rule.

The positions of the *ca.* 150 localities are related to the coordinates in a set of geographical tables derived from a mysterious *Kitāb al-Aṭwāl wa 'l-ʿurūḍ li'l-Furs*, which seems to go back at least to the 5th/11th century, with certain positions modified from later *zīdjs* in the same tradition such as the *Zīdj-i Īlkhānī* of Naṣīr al-Dīn al-Ṭūsī [*q.v.*] and the *Zīdj-i Sulṭānī* of Ulugh Begh [*q.v.*].

Now the mathematics underlying the principle of the grid, which is not trivial, was known already in the 3rd/9th and 4th/10th centuries, and in fact the instrument reflects a genius and innovative spirit such as was typical of those centuries rather than the Ṣafawid period. Yet not a trace of a mention of such a device or such a Mecca-centred map has been found in Islamic literature. However, there is indeed evidence that such maps were available in previous centuries. In *al-Zīdj al-djadīd* of Ibn al-Shāṭir (*fl.* Damascus *ca.* 750/1350 [*q.v.*]) there is a geographical table with longitudes, latitudes and *ḳibla*-values for about 240 localities (ms. Oxford Seld. A30). The *ḳibla*-values, which are given to the nearest 10′, do not correspond to recomputation by any of the known exact or approximate methods used by the Muslim astronomers. The fact that they were read from a Mecca-centred

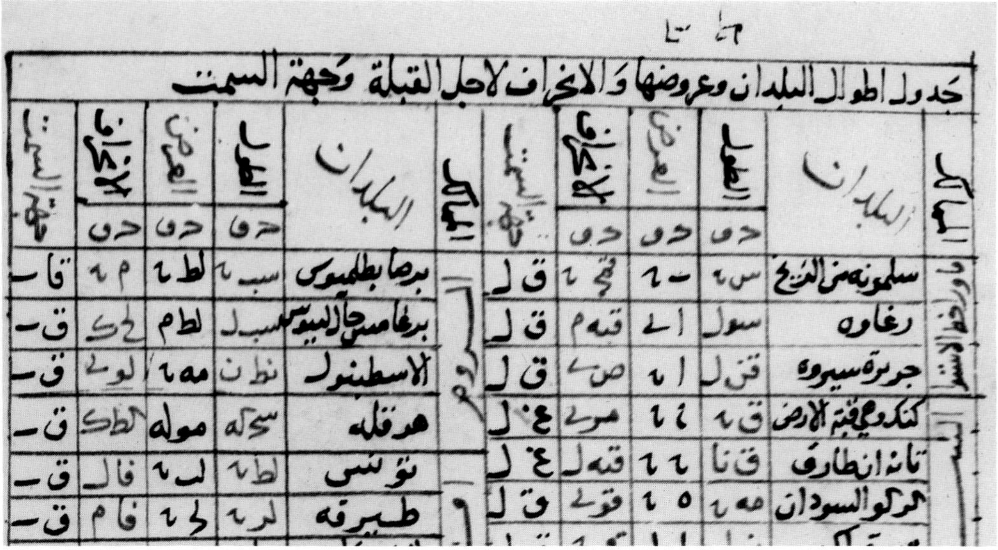

An extract from the geographical table in the Arabic recension of the *Zīdj-i Īlkhānī* by Shihāb al-Dīn al-Ḥalabī. The azimuths of the *ḳibla* are given to the nearest 10′ alongside the longitudes and latitudes of cities. Only in 1994 was it discovered that these *ḳibla*-values were read from a Mecca-centred world map. (From ms. Cairo Ṭalᶜat *mīḳāt* 226,1, courtesy of the Egyptian National Library).

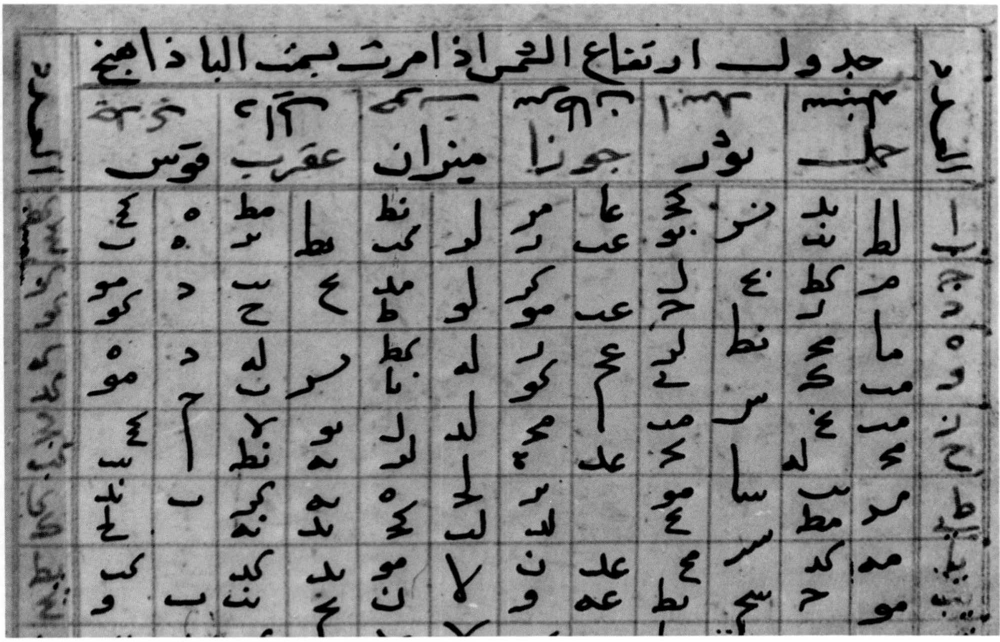

A table from mediaeval Cairo promising the altitude of the sun when it is in the direction of (the closed back of) the ventilator (*bādhahandj* [see BĀDGĪR]). Since the altitude at the winter solstice is zero, this means that the ventilators in Old Cairo were oriented with their openings facing perpendicular to the direction of winter sunrise (or about 27° E. of N.). This table led to the discovery that the entire medieval city is astronomically aligned (see further, *JAOS*, civ [1983], 97-133).

There are two sets of curves in the solar quadrant on the upper right of the back of this astrolabe by Muḥammad Muḳīm al-Yazdī (*ca.* 1060/1650). The set whose curves are not equally spaced enables the user to find, using the horizontal ecliptic scale, the altitude of the sun when it is in the *ḳibla* of various cities in ʿIrāḳ and Persia. For a given day of the year, one finds the solar longitude, moves along the corresponding circular are with the alidade up to the curve in question and reads off the solar altitude on the outer scale. One then observes the sun until it reaches that altitude, and then one is facing the *ḳibla*. The other set of curves, which are equally spaced, enables the user to determine, using the vertical ecliptic scale, the solar altitude at midday for a series of latitudes from 27° to 53° in 2°-steps. Private collection; photograph courtesy of the owner.

The *ḳibla*-dial from Iṣfahān, *ca*. 1120/1710, bearing a map of the world from which one can read the *ḳibla* and distance of Mecca for any locality in the Islamic world. Private collection, photograph by Margit Matthews, courtesy of the owner.

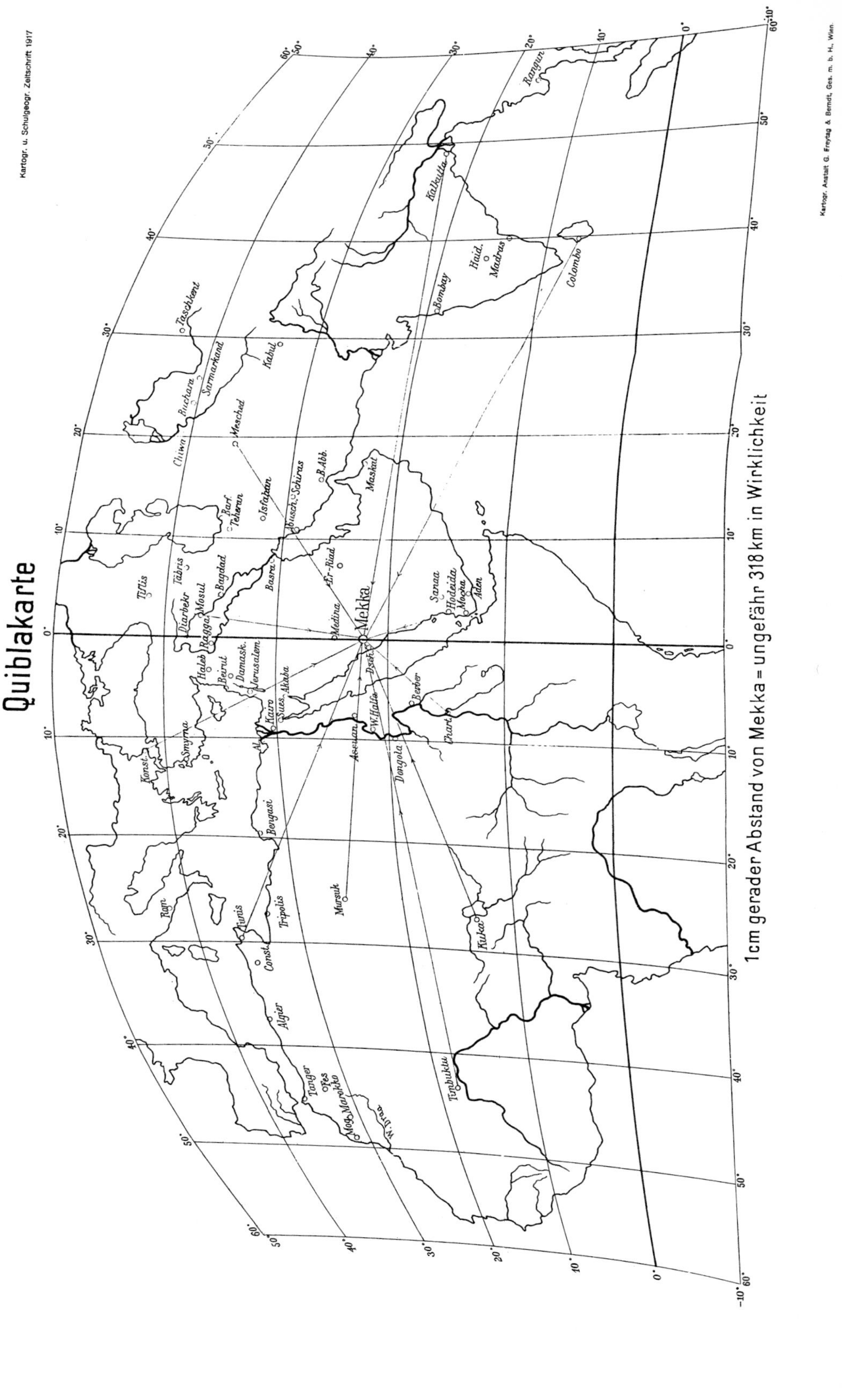
Quiblakarte
1cm gerader Abstand von Mekka = ungefähr 318 km in Wirklichkeit
Kartogr. u. Schulgeogr. Zeitschrift 1917
Kartogr. Anstalt G. Freytag & Berndt, Ges. m. b. H., Wien.
Mekka
Medina
Er-Riad
Basra
Bagdad
Mosul
Diarbekr
Täbris
Tiflis
Haleb
Beirut
Damask.
Jerusalem
Akaba
Sues
Kairo
Assuan
W.Halfa
Dongola
Berber
Chart.
Sanaa
Hodeida
Mocha
Aden
Maskat
B.Abb.
Schiras
Busch.
Isfahan
Teheran
Mesched
Buchara
Samarkand
Taschkent
Kabul
Bombay
Haid.
Madras
Colombo
Kalkutta
Rangun
Smyrna
Konst.
Bengasi
Tripolis
Tunis
Const.
Algier
Tanger
Fes
Marokko
Mog.
Mursuk
Kuka
Timbuktu
Rom

rectazimuthal map of the same kind as the Iṣfahān piece is confirmed by the ḳiblas for localities in the far west and the far east. But it was not Ibn al-S̲h̲āṭir who determined the ḳibla-values. A similar table with entries for about 245 localities is found in the Zīd̲j̲-i as̲h̲rafī of Sand̲j̲ar-i Kamālī, also known as Sayf-i Munad̲j̲d̲j̲im (fl. Yazd, ca. 710/1310) (ms. Paris B.N. supp. pers. 1488). Both tables stem from a common source, sc. al-Zīd̲j̲ al-Sand̲j̲arī of Abu 'l-Fatḥ al-K̲h̲āzinī (fl. in Marw ca. 515/1120 [q.v.]). In one of the three available mss. of this work (B.L. Or. 6669) there is a substantial fragment of the same table (one complete folio is missing). It appears that al-K̲h̲āzinī had access to a Mecca-centred map on which the ḳibla-values, estimated from the map, were indicated alongside the place names. He himself estimated the longitudes and latitudes and copied the ḳibla-values. Now the coordinates are essentially those of al-Bīrūnī [q.v.]. The fact that al-K̲h̲āzinī obtained his data from a map is proven by the occasional differences in the longitudes and latitudes, particularly in the minutes. If they can be clearly associated with scribal errors resulting from the nature of the abd̲j̲ad [q.v.] notation (thus, for example, when y-h (= yāʾ-hāʾ) for 10 + 5 = 15 is confused with n-h (= nūn-hāʾ) for 50 + 5 = 55), then we are dealing with transmission in manuscripts. But there are numerous modifications (for example, l-h (= lām-hāʾ) for 35 changing to m (= mīm) for 40) which result from misplacing localities on a map or misreading their positions. On the other hand, an Arabic recension of the Zīd̲j̲-i Īlk̲h̲ānī of al-Ṭūsī by the Syrian astronomer S̲h̲ihāb al-Dīn al-Ḥalabī (ms. Cairo Ṭalʿat mīḳāt 226, 1) contains a similar table which appears to have coordinates much closer to al-Bīrūnī's original values (the latter have not yet been critically edited).

It is abundantly clear that the basic idea behind a Mecca-centred map goes back at least as far as al-Bīrūnī. In his treatise on map-projections, Tasṭīḥ al-ṣuwar wa-tabṭīḥ al-kuwar, written ca. 395/1005, fairly early in his career, the great polymath describes eight different map-projections, one of which is "azimuth equidistant". The description is brief indeed, and it seems likely that al-Bīrūnī might have developed the theory and even presented a Mecca-centred map in another of the several treatises on mathematical geography that he wrote but that have not survived. There is, however, no mention of this projection in either his zīd̲j̲ entitled al-Ḳānūn al-Masʿūdī or his monumental book on the subject entitled Taḥdīd nihāyāt al-amākin.

The rediscovery of these Mecca-centred maps raises our understanding of Islamic mathematical geography to a new level. A rectazimuthal map was first used in Europe by the French scholar Guillaume Postell in the 16th century, and the underlying mathematical theory of such azimuth-distance projections centred on Mecca was first investigated by Carl Schoy ca. (see Pl. LXIX).

Bibliography: On the various etymologies, see C.A. Nallino, Etimologia araba e significato di ... "azimut"..., in RSO, viii (1919-21), 429, and P. Kunitzsch, Glossar der arabischen Fachausdrücke in der mittelalterlichen europäischen Astrolabliteratur, in Nachrichten der Akad. der Wiss. in Göttingen, phil.-hist. Klasse, Nr. 11 (1982), (printed separately, Göttingen 1983), 546-52 (92-9 of the separatum). On the determination of the azimuth from celestial altitudes, see C. Schoy, Das 20. Kapitel der großen Ḥākemitischen Tafeln des Ibn Jûnis. Über die Berechnung des Azimuths aus der Höhe und der Höhe aus dem Azimuth, in Annalen der Hydrographie und maritimen Meteorologie (Hamburg 1920), 97-112, repr. in idem,

Beiträge zur arabisch-islamischen Mathematik und Astronomie, 2 vols., Frankfurt am Main 1988, i, 215-29. On tables of solar azimuth and solar altitudes in specific latitudes, see idem, Gnomonik der Araber, Bd. I, Lieferung F, of E. von Bassermann-Jordan (ed.), Die Geschichte der Zeitmessung und der Uhren, Berlin and Leipzig 1923, repr. in idem, Beiträge, ii, 351-447, 42 (ii, 394, of the repr.), and D.A. King, Ibn Yūnus' Very useful tables for reckoning time by the sun, in Archive for History of Exact Science, x (1973), 342-94, repr. in idem, Islamic mathematical astronomy, London 1986, ²Aldershot 1993, no. IX, esp. 368. On ḳibla-tables, see idem, The earliest Islamic mathematical methods and tables for finding the direction of Mecca, in ZGAIW, iii (1986), 82-149, with corrections listed in ibid., iv (1987-8), 270, repr. in idem, Astronomy in the service of Islam, Aldershot 1993, no. XIV. On ḳibla-indicators, see idem and R.P. Lorch, Qibla charts, Qibla maps, and related instruments, ch. in J.B. Harley and D. Woodward (eds.), The history of cartography, ii/1, Cartography in the traditional Islamic and South Asian societies, Chicago and London 1992, 189-205, and eidem, Die Astrolabiensammlung des Germanischen Nationalmuseums, and Weltkarten zur Ermittlung der Richtung nach Mekka, in G. Bott (ed.), Focus Behaim-Globus, 2 vols., Nuremberg 1992, i, 167-71, ii, 686-91 (here the function of measuring distances is misinterpreted as being only approximate). On the astrolabe most probably by the same maker and engraver, see W.H. Morley, Description of a planispheric astrolabe constructed for Sháh Sultán Husain Safawí ..., London 1856, repr. as the introd. to R.T. Gunther, The astrolabes of the world, 2 vols., Oxford 1932, repr. in 1 vol., London 1976. On the Zīd̲j̲s of Ibn al-S̲h̲āṭir and Sandjar-i Kamālī, see E.S. Kennedy, A survey of Islamic astronomical tables, in Trans. of the American Philosophical Soc., N.S., xlvi/2 (1956), repr. n.d. [ca. 1989], 124 (no. 4), 125 (no. 11) and 162-4, respectively. On their geographical tables, see idem and Mary H. Kennedy, Geographical coordinates of localities from Islamic sources, Frankfurt am Main 1987, esp. pp. xvi (sub ASH), xxxi (sub SHA). On two of the many astrolabes from the four generations of al-Kirmānīs, see Gunther, Astrolabes of the world, i, 128-31 (nos. 15, 16, both misdated), and Sharon Gibbs and G. Saliba, Planispheric astrolabes in the National Museum of American History, Washington, D.C. 1984, 64-5 (no. 15). Bīrūnī's treatise on map projections is published as Aḥmad Saʿīdān, Kitāb Tasṭīḥ al-ṣuwar wa-tabṭīḥ al-kuwar li-Abī l-Rayḥān al-Bīrūnī al-mutawaffā sanat 440 H—Al-Bīrūnī on map projection (ms. Leiden 1068,9), in Dirāsāt (al-D̲j̲āmiʿa al-Urdunniyya), iv (1977), 7-22 (see esp. 21), with a new ed., tr. and comm. in J.L. Berggren, Al-Bīrūnī on plane maps of the sphere, in Jnal. for the History of Arabic Science, vi (1982), 47-169 (see esp. 67), and L. Richter-Bernburg, Al-Bīrūnī's Maqāla fi tasṭīḥ al-ṣuwar wa-tabṭīḥ al-kuwar. A translation of the preface with notes and commentary, in ibid., 113-122. On rectazimuthal cartographic grids, see Schoy, Azimutale und gegenazimutale Karten mit gleichabständigen parallelen Meridianen, in Annalen der Hydrographie und maritimen Meteorologie, xli (1913), 33-43; idem, Die gegenazimutale mittabstandstreue Karte in konstruktiver und theoretischer Behandlung, in ibid., 466-73; and idem, Die Mekka- oder Qiblakarte (Gegenazimutale mittabstandstreue Projektion mit Mekka als Kartenmitte), in Kartographische und schulgeographische Zeitschrift, vi (1917), 184-5, and 1 map, repr. in idem, Beiträge, i, 157-9, and Gnomonik der Araber, 43, 45 (ii, 395, 397 of the repr.). Earlier Western writings on rectazimuthal projections by cartographers, including Montucla, I. Craig and E. von Hammer, are mentioned by Schoy. (D.A. KING)

SAMUEL [see USHMŪʾĪL].

SAMŪM (A.), yielding Fr. simoun and Eng. simoom, a hot wind of the desert accompanied by whirlwinds of dust and sand, and set in motion by moving depressions which form within the trade winds or calm zones of the high, subtropical depressions. This wind is especially characteristic of the Sahara, in Egypt, in Arabia and in Mesopotamia. The word occurs in three passages of the Ḳurʾān, where it is, however, not especially applied to the wind. In sūra XV, 27, it is said that the *Dj̲ānn* were created from the fire of Samūm. In LII, 27, the punishment of the Samūm is mentioned; and according to I, 41, the "people of the left" were dwelling in *Samūm wa-Ḥamīm*.

The *Ḥadīt̲h̲* uses the word in the same sense; yet the meaning "hot wind" is here coming to the front. It is said that Hell takes breath two times a year: "its taking breath in summer is Samūm" (al-Tirmid̲h̲ī, *Dj̲ahannam, bāb* 9; cf. Ibn Mād̲j̲a, *Zuhd, bāb* 38). In al-Buk̲h̲ārī we find reference to the opinion that the hot air during the day is called *ḥarūr*, whereas it is called *samūm* at night (*Badʾ al-k̲h̲alḳ, bāb* 4).

In nearly every traveller's account the *samūm* is mentioned in the sense of the suffocating wind, often called simoom. From the innumerable references, a few may be picked out. C.M. Doughty mentions it in the neighbourhood of Madāʾin Ṣāliḥ as "a dry southern wind" against which the Bedouins "covered their faces up, to the eyes, with a lap of the kerchief". He again mentions it between Medina and Mecca and tells us that, according to the Bedouins, weak camels may be suffocated by it (*Travels in Arabia Deserta*, Cambridge 1888, i, 100, 188).

In Mecca, the north, north-east and east winds are called *samūm*. When it blows it makes the impression as if it came from a huge fire through the intermediacy of gigantic bellows (Snouck Hurgronje, *Mekkanische Sprichwörter und Redensarten*, no. 76). The season in which the sun enters the constellation of the Virgin (August) has an extremely bad reputation in Mecca, because in this time *ḥōm* and *wamd, samūm* and *azyab*, blow alternately (*loc. cit.*).

Concerning Egypt, Lane says (*Manners and customs*, Introduction): "Egypt is also subject particularly during spring and summer, to the hot wind called the "Samoom", which is still more oppressive than the khamáseen winds, but of much shorter duration, seldom lasting longer than a quarter of an hour or twenty minutes. It generally proceeds from the south-east, and carries with it clouds of dust and sands".

Concerning Ḳaṣr-i S̲h̲īrīn [*q.v.*], Ḥamd Allāh Mustawfī (*Nuzhat al-ḳulūb*, tr. Le Strange, 50) says: "Its climate is unwholesome, for in the hot season at most times the (hot) Simum blows".

Al-Masʿūdī, *Murūd̲j̲ al-d̲h̲ahab*, iii, 320-1 = § 1204 has a legendary report concerning the *d̲j̲ānn* which, according to the verse from the Ḳurʾān mentioned above, were created from the fire of the *samūm* (tr. R. Basset, *Mille et un contes, récits et légendes arabes*, Paris 1924, i, 57); see also A. Musil, *Reisen in Arabia Petraea*, Vienna 1907-8, iii, 3-4. In other parts of the Islamic world, other words are used for the *samūm*. In Europe, for instance, one finds the term sirocco.

The word is hardly used in North Africa, where the hot wind is called, after its direction of origin, and according to the various regions, *ḳeblī* or *s̲h̲arḳī*.

(A.J. WENSINCK*)